# *Federal*

# ENVIRONMENTAL LAWS

## 2004 EDITION

Amended through Pub.L. 108–209
of the Second Session of the
108th Congress (2003)

THOMSON
WEST

Mat #40220788

**ISBN** 0–314–11438–6



Cover photo courtesy of National Aeronautics and Space Administration.

# EXPLANATION

This pamphlet contains major Environmental Law statutes which have been enacted by Congress in an effort to address the problems of pollutants in the air, water, land, food, and drugs which provide us with living space and sustenance. This edition is current to Pub.L. 108–209 of the Second Session of the 108th Congress (2003). The laws bear not only the title and section classifications of the United States Code Annotated, identical to that of the United States Code, but also their Congressional Act and section designations. Historical and statutory notes and additional annotative material are available in the corresponding sections of the United States Code Annotated.

Westlaw supplements United States Code Annotated electronically and provides many useful materials for additional research. See the Westlaw guide following this explanation.

This convenient reference pamphlet, in form suitable for courtroom and office use, contains the text of the following:

Title 7

Agriculture, Sections 136 to 136y

Title 15

Commerce and Trade, Sections 791 to 798, 2601 to 2692, 2901 to 2908

Title 16

Conservation, Sections 528 to 531, 1361 to 1421h, 1451 to 1465, 1531 to 1544, 1600 to 1687, 2001 to 2009, 4701 to 4751, 6501 to 6591

Title 26

Internal Revenue Code, Sections 4611 to 4682, 9507 to 9509

Title 30

Mineral Lands and Mining, Sections 1201 to 1328

Title 33

Navigation and Navigable Waters, Sections 401 to 454, 1251 to 1387, 1401 to 1445, 1901 to 1915, 2601 to 2623, 2701 to 2761, 2801 to 2805, 3001 to 3076

Title 42

The Public Health and Welfare, Sections 300f to 300j–26, 2014, 2021 to 2021j, 2022, 2111, 2113, 2114, 4321 to 4370f, 4371 to 4375, 4901 to 4918, 6901 to 6992k, 7401 to 7671q, 8901 to 8912, 9601 to 9675, 10101 to 10270, 11001 to 11050, 13101 to 13109

Title 43

Public Lands, Sections 869 to 869–4, 1701 to 1785, 1801 to 1866

Title 46

Shipping, Sections 3703a, 12106

Title 46

Appendix, Shipping, Section 1274a

# EXPLANATION

Title 49

Transportation, Sections 47501 to 47510

See Table of Contents, page XI, for a description of the federal Acts included in this reference pamphlet.

THE PUBLISHER

May, 2004

# RELATED PRODUCTS FROM WEST

---

**FEDERAL PRACTICE**

**COURTROOM HANDBOOK ON FEDERAL EVIDENCE**
Steven Goode and Olin Guy Wellborn III

**FEDERAL CIVIL RULES HANDBOOK**
Steven Baicker–McKee, William Janssen and John B. Corr

**FEDERAL CRIMINAL RULES HANDBOOK**
Laurie L. Levenson

**MODERN SCIENTIFIC EVIDENCE**
David L. Faigman, David H. Kaye, Michael J. Saks and Joseph Sanders

**FEDERAL JURY PRACTICE AND INSTRUCTIONS**
Kevin F. O'Malley, Jay E. Grenig and William C. Lee
[*Also available in CD–ROM*]

**FEDERAL PRACTICE AND PROCEDURE**
Charles Alan Wright, Arthur R. Miller, Mary Kay Kane, Edward H. Cooper, Richard L. Marcus, Kenneth W. Graham, Victor James Gold, Richard D. Freer, Patrick J. Schiltz, Vikram David Amar, Joan E. Steinman, Nancy J. King, Susan R. Klein and Michael H. Graham
[*Also available in CD–ROM*]

**POLICE MISCONDUCT AND CIVIL RIGHTS—FEDERAL JURY PRACTICE AND INSTRUCTIONS**
Stephen Yagman
[*Includes Instructions on Disk*]

**WEST'S FEDERAL ADMINISTRATIVE PRACTICE**
Authored by Federal Practice Experts

**WEST'S FEDERAL FORMS**
Authored by Federal Practice Experts
[*Also available in CD–ROM*]

**FEDERAL COURT OF APPEALS MANUAL**
David G. Knibb

**FEDERAL PRACTICE AND PROCEDURE—FEDERAL PRACTICE DESKBOOK**
Charles Alan Wright and Mary Kay Kane

**HANDBOOK OF FEDERAL EVIDENCE**
Michael H. Graham

**TREATISE ON CONSTITUTIONAL LAW**
Ronald D. Rotunda and John E. Nowak

## RELATED PRODUCTS

**LITIGATING EMPLOYMENT DISCRIMINATION AND CIVIL RIGHTS CASES**
Harold S. Lewis, Jr. and Elizabeth J. Norman

**ADMINISTRATIVE LAW AND PRACTICE**
Charles H. Koch, Jr.

**FEDERAL RULES OF EVIDENCE WITH TRIAL OBJECTIONS**
Charles B. Gibbons

**BUSINESS AND COMMERCIAL LITIGATION IN FEDERAL COURTS**
Robert L. Haig, Editor–In–Chief

**NEWBERG ON CLASS ACTIONS, 3rd**
Herbert Newberg and Alba Conte

**HANDBOOK OF FEDERAL CIVIL DISCOVERY AND DISCLOSURE**
by Jay E. Grenig and Jeffrey S. Kinsler
*[Includes forms on Disk]*

**ANNOTATED MANUAL FOR COMPLEX LITIGATION**
David F. Herr

---

United States Code Annotated
West's Federal Practice Digest 4th
United States Code Congressional and Administrative News

---

**WEST'S CRIMINAL PRACTICE SERIES**

**Search and Seizure**
Wayne R. LaFave

**Substantive Criminal Law**
Wayne R. LaFave and Austin W. Scott, Jr.

**Criminal Law Defenses**
Paul H. Robinson

**Criminal Procedure**
Wayne R. LaFave and Jerold H. Israel

**Federal Sentencing Law and Practice**
Thomas W. Hutchison and David Yellen

**Federal Sentencing Guidelines Handbook**
Roger W. Haines, Jr. with Jennifer C. Woll and Frank O. Bowman III

---

CJS
West's Federal Case News
Federal Case News Weekly Pamphlet

**RELATED PRODUCTS**

Federal Civil Judicial Procedure and Rules
Federal Criminal Code and Rules
Federal Environmental Laws
Federal Immigration and Nationality Laws, Rules and Regulations
Federal Labor Laws
Federal Sentencing Guidelines Manual
Federal Social Security Laws, Selected Statutes and Regulations
Federal Intellectual Property Laws and Regulations
Federal Litigator Newsletter
Reference Manual on Scientific Evidence

**TAX PUBLICATIONS**

Federal Tax Regulations
Internal Revenue Code
Internal Revenue Acts

---

West Books, CD–ROM Libraries, Disk Products and Westlaw®
*The Ultimate Research System*

---

To order any of these Federal practice tools, call your
West Representative or **1–800–328–9352**.

**NEED RESEARCH HELP?**

You can get quality research results with free help—call the West Reference Attorneys when you have questions concerning WESTLAW or West Publications at 1–800–733–2889.

**NEED A NEW CASE TODAY?**

You can get copies of new court cases faxed to you today—office, courthouse or hotel, anywhere a fax machine is available. Call West*fax* at 1–800–562–2329.

**INTERNET ACCESS**

Contact the West Editorial Department directly with your questions and suggestions by e-mail at west.editor@thomson.com. Visit West's home page on the World Wide Web at http://west.thomson.com.

*

# WESTLAW ELECTRONIC RESEARCH GUIDE

## 1. Coordinating Legal Research With Westlaw

The Federal Environmental Laws Pamphlet provides federal statutory materials relating to environmental law. Westlaw contains a Federal Environmental Law database which provides additional resources. This guide is to assist in your effective use of Westlaw resources to supplement research using this publication.

## 2. Databases

A database is an aggregation of documents with one or more features in common. A database may contain statutes, court decisions, administrative materials, or commentaries. Every database has its own identifier. Database identifiers are used to identify the database to be searched. The Westlaw Directory is a comprehensive listing of databases, with information about each database and the types of documents each contains.

## 3. Updating Statutes

A Westlaw search may be used to ascertain whether a particular section of the United States Code dealing with the environment has been amended after this pamphlet was printed. After checking the coverage, sign on to the FENV–USC database and using the desired title number and section number, a query is entered in the following form:

CI(42 +3 7401)

This will retrieve section 7401 of Title 42 of the United States Code.

## 4. Retrieving Cases Citing a Statute

To find cases citing a particular statute, sign on to the FENV–CS database and using the desired title number and section number, a query is entered in the following form:

"15 U.S.C.* " +4 2601

This will retrieve cases citing section 2601 of Title 15 of the United States Code.

## 5. Key Number Search

Westlaw may be used to search any topic and key number in West's Key Number System. To retrieve cases with at least one headnote classified to the topic Health and Environment ⚷25.6, sign on to the FENV–CS database and enter

199K25.6

The topic name Health and Environment is replaced by its numerical equivalent 199 and the ⚷ by the letter k. A list of topics and their numerical equivalents is in the Westlaw reference manual and in the Westlaw directory.

## 6. Retrieving A Regulation In The Code of Federal Regulations

To find the text of a federal regulation, sign on to the FENV–CFR database. Using the desired citation, a query is entered in the following form:

CI(30 +3 717.17)

This will retrieve section 717.17 of Title 30 of the Code of Federal Regulations.

## 7. Retrieving a Federal Register Document

To find the text of a Federal Register document, sign on to the FENV–FR database. Using the desired citation, enter a query in the following form:

CI(52 +2 8225)

This will retrieve 52 FR 8225.

## 8. KeyCite®

Cases and other legal materials listed in KeyCite Scope can be researched through West's KeyCite service on Westlaw. Use KeyCite to check citations for form, parallel references, prior and later history, and comprehensive citator information, including citations to other decisions and secondary materials.

## 9. General Information

The information provided above illustrates some of the ways Westlaw can complement research using this pamphlet. However, this brief overview illustrates only some of the power of Westlaw. The full range of Westlaw search techniques is available to support your research from this series. Please consult the Westlaw manual for additional databases and information.

For more detailed information or assistance, contact your Westlaw Account Representative or call 1–800–Westlaw (1–800–937–8529).

# TABLE OF ACTS

Acid Precipitation Act of 1980 [APA § ____] (42 U.S.C.A. §§ 8901 to 8912)

Act to Prevent Pollution from Ships [APPS § ____] (33 U.S.C.A. §§ 1901 to 1915)

Asbestos Hazard Emergency Response Act of 1986 [see Toxic Substances Control Act §§ 201 to 214 (15 U.S.C.A. §§ 2641 to 2654)]

Atomic Energy Act of 1954 [AEA § ____] (42 U.S.C.A. §§ 2014, 2021, 2022, 2111, 2113, 2114)

Clean Air Act [CAA § ____] (42 U.S.C.A. §§ 7401 to 7671q)

Clean Vessel Act of 1992 [CVA § ____] (33 U.S.C.A. § 1322 note)

Clean Water Act [see Federal Water Pollution Control Act]

Coastal Zone Management Act of 1972 [CZMA § ____] (16 U.S.C.A. §§ 1451 to 1465)

Comprehensive Environmental Response, Compensation, and Liability Act of 1980 [CERCLA § ____] (42 U.S.C.A. §§ 9601 to 9675)

Edible Oil Regulatory Reform Act (33 U.S.C.A. § 2720)

Emergency Planning and Community Right–To–Know Act of 1986 [EPCRTKA § ____] (42 U.S.C.A. §§ 11001 to 11050)

Endangered Species Act of 1973 [ESA § ____] (16 U.S.C.A. §§ 1531 to 1544)

Energy Supply and Environmental Coordination Act of 1974 [ESECA § ____] (15 U.S.C.A. §§ 791 to 798)

Environmental Quality Improvement Act of 1970 [EQIA § ____] (42 U.S.C.A. §§ 4371 to 4375)

Federal Facility Compliance Act of 1992 [FFCA § ____] (42 U.S.C.A. § 6901 note)

Federal Insecticide, Fungicide, and Rodenticide Act [FIFRA § ____] (7 U.S.C.A. §§ 136 to 136y)

Federal Land Policy and Management Act of 1976 [FLPMA § ____] (43 U.S.C.A. §§ 1701 to 1785)

Federal Water Pollution Control Act [FWPCA § ____] (33 U.S.C.A. §§ 1251 to 1387)

Food Quality Protection Act of 1996 [FQPA § —] [see Federal Insecticide, Fungicide, and Rodenticide Act (7 U.S.C.A. §§ 136 to 136y)]

Forest and Rangeland Renewable Resources Planning Act of 1974 [FRRRPA § ____] (16 U.S.C.A. §§ 1600 to 1614)

Forest and Rangeland Renewable Resources Research Act of 1978 [FRRRRA § ____] (16 U.S.C.A. §§ 1641 to 1649)

Forest Ecosystems and Atmospheric Pollution Control Act of 1988 [see Forest and Rangeland Renewable Resources Research Act of 1978 § 3 (16 U.S.C.A. § 1642)]

Global Climate Protection Act of 1987 (15 U.S.C.A. § 2901 note)

Hazardous Substance Response Revenue Act of 1980 (see 26 U.S.C.A. §§ 4611, 4612, 4661, 4662)

Healthy Forest Restoration Act of 2003 (See 16 U.S.C.A. §§ 6501 to 6591)

Illinois Land Conservation Act of 1995 (16 U.S.C.A. § 1609 note)

Lead–Based Paint Exposure Reduction Act [LBPERA § ____] (15 U.S.C.A. §§ 2681 to 2692)

## TABLE OF ACTS

Lead Contamination Control Act of 1988 [see Public Health Service Act §§ 1461 to 1465 (42 U.S.C.A. §§ 300j–21 to 300j–26)]

Low–Level Radioactive Waste Policy Act [LLRWPA § ____] (42 U.S.C.A. §§ 2021b to 2021j)

Marine Mammal Protection Act of 1972 [MMPA § ____] (16 U.S.C.A. §§ 1361 to 1421h)

Marine Protection, Research, and Sanctuaries Act of 1972 [MPRSA § ____] (33 U.S.C.A. §§ 1401 to 1445)

Medical Waste Tracking Act of 1988 [see Solid Waste Disposal Act §§ 11001 to 11012 (42 U.S.C.A. 6992 to 6992 k)]

Merchant Marine Act of 1936 [MMA § 1104B] (46 U.S.C.A. App. § 1274a)

Mining and Mineral Resources Research Institute Act of 1984 [MMRRIA § ___] (30 U.S.C.A. §§ 1221 to 1230a)

Multiple–Use Sustained–Yield Act of 1960 [MUSYA § ____] (16 U.S.C.A. §§ 528 to 531)

National Climate Program Act [NCPA § ____] (15 U.S.C.A. §§ 2901 to 2908)

National Coastal Monitoring Act [NCMA § ____] (33 U.S.C.A. §§ 2801 to 2805)

National Contaminated Sediment Assessment and Management Act [NCSAMA § ____] (33 U.S.C.A. § 1271 and 33 U.S.C.A. § 1271 note)

National Environmental Policy Act of 1969 [NEPA § ____] (42 U.S.C.A. §§ 4321 to 4370f)

National Forest Management Act of 1976 [see Forest and Rangeland Renewable Resources Planning Act of 1974 §§ 2, 13 to 16 (16 U.S.C.A. §§ 1600, 1611 to 1614)]

National Invasive Species Act of 1996 [NISPA § —] [see Nonindigenous Aquatic Nuisance Prevention and Control Act of 1990 (16 U.S.C.A. §§ 4701 to 4751)]

National Ocean Pollution Planning Act of 1978 [NOPPA § —] (33 U.S.C.A. §§ 1701 to 1709)

Noise Control Act of 1972 [NCA § ____] (42 U.S.C.A. §§ 4901 to 4918)

Nonindigenous Aquatic Nuisance Prevention and Control Act of 1990 [NANPCA § ____] (16 U.S.C.A. §§ 4701 to 4751)

Nuclear Waste Policy Act of 1982 [NWPA § ____] (42 U.S.C.A. §§ 10101 to 10270)

Ocean Dumping Ban Act of 1988 [see Marine Protection, Research, and Sanctuaries Act of 1972 §§ 104B, 104C (33 U.S.C.A. §§ 1414b, 1414c)]

Oil Pollution Act of 1990 [OPA § ____] (33 U.S.C.A. §§ 2701 to 2761; 46 U.S.C.A. § 3703a)

Outer Continental Shelf Lands Act Amendments of 1978 [OCSLAA § ____] (43 U.S.C.A. §§ 1801 to 1866)

Outer Continental Shelf Operations Indemnification Clarification Act of 1988 [see Outer Continental Shelf Lands Act Amendments of 1978 (43 U.S.C.A. § 1801 note)]

Pollution Prevention Act of 1990 [PPA § ____] (42 U.S.C.A. §§ 13101 to 13109)

Public Health Service Act (Title XIV) [PHSA § ____] (42 U.S.C.A. §§ 300f to 300j–26)

Recreation and Public Purposes Act [RPPA §§ 1 to 6] (43 U.S.C.A. § 869 to 869–4)

Refuse Act of 1899 [see Rivers and Harbors Appropriations Acts—Selected Sections (33 U.S.C.A. § 407)]

Renewable Resources Extension Act of 1978 [RREA § ____] (16 U.S.C.A. §§ 1671 to 1676)

## TABLE OF ACTS



*

# TABLE OF CONTENTS



## THE CODE OF THE LAWS OF THE UNITED STATES OF AMERICA

### TITLE 7, AGRICULTURE



### TITLE 15, COMMERCE AND TRADE



### TITLE 16, CONSERVATION



### TITLE 26, INTERNAL REVENUE CODE



### TITLE 30, MINERAL LANDS AND MINING



### TITLE 33, NAVIGATION AND NAVIGABLE WATERS

# THE CODE OF THE LAWS OF THE UNITED STATES OF AMERICA

*

# THE CODE OF THE LAWS OF THE UNITED STATES OF AMERICA

# TITLE 7

# AGRICULTURE

## ENVIRONMENTAL PESTICIDE CONTROL

## FEDERAL INSECTICIDE, FUNGICIDE, AND RODENTICIDE ACT [FIFRA § ___]

**(7 U.S.C.A. §§ 136 to 136y)**

## CHAPTER 6—INSECTICIDES AND ENVIRONMENTAL PESTICIDE CONTROL

### SUBCHAPTER II—ENVIRONMENTAL PESTICIDE CONTROL



**Related Provisions**

*See, also, Toxic Substances Control, 15 U.S.C.A. § 2601 et seq., post.*

### SUBCHAPTER II—ENVIRONMENTAL PESTICIDE CONTROL

### § 136. Definitions

**[FIFRA § 2]**

For purposes of this subchapter—

**(a) Active ingredient**

The term "active ingredient" means—

(1) in the case of a pesticide other than a plant regulator, defoliant, desiccant, or nitrogen stabilizer an ingredient which will prevent, destroy, repel, or mitigate any pest;

(2) in the case of a plant regulator, an ingredient which, through physiological action, will accelerate or retard the rate of growth or rate of maturation or otherwise alter the behavior of ornamental or crop plants or the product thereof;

(3) in the case of a defoliant, an ingredient which will cause the leaves or foliage to drop from a plant;

(4) in the case of a desiccant, an ingredient which will artificially accelerate the dying of plant tissue; and

(5) in the case of a nitrogen stabilizer, an ingredient which will prevent or hinder the process of nitrification, denitrification, ammonia volatilization, or urease production through action affecting soil bacteria.

**(b) Administrator**

The term "Administrator" means the Administrator of the Environmental Protection Agency.

**(c) Adulterated**

The term "adulterated" applies to any pesticide if—

(1) its strength or purity falls below the professed standard of quality as expressed on its labeling under which it is sold;

(2) any substance has been substituted wholly or in part for the pesticide; or

(3) any valuable constituent of the pesticide has been wholly or in part abstracted.

**(d) Animal**

The term "animal" means all vertebrate and invertebrate species, including but not limited to man and other mammals, birds, fish, and shellfish.

**(e) Certified applicator, etc.**

**(1) Certified applicator**

The term "certified applicator" means any individual who is certified under section 136i of this title as authorized to use or supervise the use of any pesticide which is classified for restricted use. Any applicator who holds or applies registered pesticides, or uses dilutions of registered pesticides consistent with subsection (ee) of this section, only to provide a service of controlling pests without delivering any unapplied pesticide to any person so served is not deemed to be a seller or distributor of pesticides under this subchapter.

**(2) Private applicator**

The term "private applicator" means a certified applicator who uses or supervises the use of any pesticide which is classified for restricted use for purposes of producing any agricultural commodity on property owned or rented by the applicator or the applicator's employer or (if applied without compensation other than trading of personal services between producers of agricultural commodities) on the property of another person.

**(3) Commercial applicator**

The term "commercial applicator" means an applicator (whether or not the applicator is a private applicator with respect to some uses) who uses or supervises the use of any pesticide which is classified for restricted use for any purpose or on any property other than as provided by paragraph (2).

**(4) Under the direct supervision of a certified applicator**

Unless otherwise prescribed by its labeling, a pesticide shall be considered to be applied under the direct supervision of a certified applicator if it is applied by a competent person acting under the instructions and control of a certified applicator who is available if and when needed, even though such certified applicator is not physically present at the time and place the pesticide is applied.

**(f) Defoliant**

The term "defoliant" means any substance or mixture of substances intended for causing the leaves or foliage to drop from a plant, with or without causing abscission.

**(g) Desiccant**

The term "desiccant" means any substance or mixture of substances intended for artificially accelerating the drying of plant tissue.

**(h) Device**

The term "device" means any instrument or contrivance (other than a firearm) which is intended for trapping, destroying, repelling, or mitigating any pest or any other form of plant or animal life (other than man and other than bacteria, virus, or other microorganism on or in living man or other living animals); but not including equipment used for the application of pesticides when sold separately therefrom.

**(i) District court**

The term "district court" means a United States district court, the District Court of Guam, the District Court of the Virgin Islands, and the highest court of American Samoa.

**(j) Environment**

The term "environment" includes water, air, land, and all plants and man and other animals living therein, and the interrelationships which exist among these.

**(k) Fungus**

The term "fungus" means any non-chlorophyll-bearing thallophyte (that is, any non-chlorophyll-bearing plant of a lower order than mosses and liverworts), as for example, rust, smut, mildew, mold, yeast, and bacteria, except those on or in living man or other animals and those on or in processed food, beverages, or pharmaceuticals.

**(*l*) Imminent hazard**

The term "imminent hazard" means a situation which exists when the continued use of a pesticide during the time required for cancellation proceeding would be likely to result in unreasonable adverse effects on the environment or will involve unreasonable hazard to the survival of a species declared endangered or threatened by the Secretary pursuant to the Endangered Species Act of 1973 [16 U.S.C.A. § 1531 et seq.].

**(m) Inert ingredient**

The term "inert ingredient" means an ingredient which is not active.

**(n) Ingredient statement**

The term "ingredient statement" means a statement which contains—

(1) the name and percentage of each active ingredient, and the total percentage of all inert ingredients, in the pesticide; and

(2) if the pesticide contains arsenic in any form, a statement of the percentages of total and water soluble arsenic, calculated as elementary arsenic.

**(*o*) Insect**

The term "insect" means any of the numerous small invertebrate animals generally having the body more or less obviously segmented, for the most part belonging to the class insecta, comprising six-legged, usually winged forms, as for example, beetles, bugs, bees, flies, and to other allied classes of arthropods whose members are wingless and usually have more than six legs, as for example, spiders, mites, ticks, centipedes, and wood lice.

**(p) Label and labeling**

**(1) Label**

The term "label" means the written, printed, or graphic matter on, or attached to, the pesticide or device or any of its containers or wrappers.

**(2) Labeling**

The term "labeling" means all labels and all other written, printed, or graphic matter—

(A) accompanying the pesticide or device at any time; or

(B) to which reference is made on the label or in literature accompanying the pesticide or device, except to current official publications of the Environmental Protection Agency, the United States Departments of Agriculture and Interior, the Department of Health and Human Services, State experiment stations, State agricultural colleges, and other similar Federal or State institutions or agencies authorized by law to conduct research in the field of pesticides.

**(q) Misbranded**

(1) A pesticide is misbranded if—

(A) its labeling bears any statement, design, or graphic representation relative thereto or to its ingredients which is false or misleading in any particular;

(B) it is contained in a package or other container or wrapping which does not conform to the standards established by the Administrator pursuant to section 136w(c)(3) of this title;

(C) it is an imitation of, or is offered for sale under the name of, another pesticide;

(D) its label does not bear the registration number assigned under section 136e of this title to each establishment in which it was produced;

(E) any word, statement, or other information required by or under authority of this subchapter to appear on the label or labeling is not prominently placed thereon with such conspicuousness (as compared with other words, statements, designs, or graphic matter in the labeling) and in such terms as to render it likely to be read and understood by the ordinary individual under customary conditions of purchase and use;

(F) the labeling accompanying it does not contain directions for use which are necessary for effecting the purpose for which the product is intended and if complied with, together with any requirements imposed under section 136a(d) of this title, are adequate to protect health and the environment;

(G) the label does not contain a warning or caution statement which may be necessary and if complied with, together with any requirements imposed under section 136a(d) of this title, is adequate to protect health and the environment; or

(H) in the case of a pesticide not registered in accordance with section 136a of this title and intended for export, the label does not contain, in words prominently placed thereon with such conspicuousness (as compared with other words, statements, designs, or graphic matter in the labeling) as to render it likely to be noted by the ordinary individual under customary conditions of purchase and use, the following: "Not Registered for Use in the United States of America".

(2) A pesticide is misbranded if—

(A) the label does not bear an ingredient statement on that part of the immediate container (and on the outside container or wrapper of the retail package, if there be one, through which the ingredient statement on the immediate container cannot be clearly read) which is presented or displayed under customary conditions of purchase, except that a pesticide is not misbranded under this subparagraph if—

(i) the size or form of the immediate container, or the outside container or wrapper of the retail package, makes it impracticable to place the ingredient statement on the part which is presented or displayed under customary conditions of purchase; and

(ii) the ingredient statement appears prominently on another part of the immediate container, or outside container or wrapper, permitted by the Administrator;

(B) the labeling does not contain a statement of the use classification under which the product is registered;

(C) there is not affixed to its container, and to the outside container or wrapper of the retail package, if there be one, through which the required information on the immediate container cannot be clearly read, a label bearing—

(i) the name and address of the producer, registrant, or person for whom produced;

(ii) the name, brand, or trademark under which the pesticide is sold;

(iii) the net weight or measure of the content, except that the Administrator may permit reasonable variations; and

(iv) when required by regulation of the Administrator to effectuate the purposes of this subchapter, the registration number assigned to the pesticide under this subchapter, and the use classification; and

(D) the pesticide contains any substance or substances in quantities highly toxic to man, unless the label shall bear, in addition to any other matter required by this subchapter—

(i) the skull and crossbones;

(ii) the word "poison" prominently in red on a background of distinctly contrasting color; and

(iii) a statement of a practical treatment (first aid or otherwise) in case of poisoning by the pesticide.

**(r) Nematode**

The term "nematode" means invertebrate animals of the phylum nemathelminthes and class nematoda, that is, unsegmented round worms with elongated, fusiform, or saclike bodies covered with cuticle, and inhabiting soil, water, plants, or plant parts; may also be called nemas or eelworms.

**(s) Person**

The term "person" means any individual, partnership, association, corporation, or any organized group of persons whether incorporated or not.

**(t) Pest**

The term "pest" means (1) any insect, rodent, nematode, fungus, weed, or (2) any other form of terrestrial or aquatic plant or animal life or virus, bacteria, or other micro-organism (except viruses, bacteria, or other micro-organisms on or in living man or other living animals) which the Administrator declares to be a pest under section 136w(c)(1) of this title.

**(u) Pesticide**

The term "pesticide" means (1) any substance or mixture of substances intended for preventing, destroying, repelling, or mitigating any pest, (2) any substance or mixture of substances intended for use as a plant regulator, defoliant, or desiccant, and (3) any nitrogen stabilizer, except that the term "pesticide" shall not include any article that is a "new animal drug" within the meaning of section 321(w) of Title 21, that has been determined by the Secretary of Health and Human Services not to be a new animal drug by a regulation establishing conditions of use for the article, or that is an animal feed within the meaning of section 321(x) of Title 21 bearing or containing a new animal drug. The term "pesticide" does not include liquid chemical sterilant products (including any sterilant or subordinate disinfectant claims on such products) for use on a critical or semi-critical device, as defined in section 321 of Title 21. For purposes of the preceding sentence, the term "critical device" includes any device which is introduced directly into the human body, either into or in contact with the bloodstream or normally sterile areas of the body and the term "semi-critical device" includes any device which contacts intact mucous membranes but which does not ordinarily penetrate the blood barrier or otherwise enter normally sterile areas of the body.

**(v) Plant regulator**

The term "plant regulator" means any substance or mixture of substances intended, through physiological action, for accelerating or retarding the rate of growth or rate of maturation, or for otherwise altering the behavior of plants or the produce thereof, but shall not include substances to the extent that they are intended as plant nutrients, trace elements, nutritional chemicals, plant innoculants, and soil amendments. Also, the term "plant regulator" shall not be required to include any of such of those nutrient mixtures or soil amendments as are commonly known as vitamin-hormone horticultural products, intended for improvement, maintenance, survival, health, and propagation of plants, and as are not for pest destruction and are nontoxic, nonpoisonous in the undiluted packaged concentration.

**(w) Producer and produce**

The term "producer" means the person who manufactures, prepares, compounds, propagates, or processes any pesticide or device or active ingredient used in producing a pesticide. The term "produce" means to manufacture, prepare, compound, propagate, or process any pesticide or device or active ingredient used in producing a pesticide. The dilution by individuals of formulated pesticides for their own use and according to the directions on registered labels shall not of itself result in such individuals being included in the definition of "producer" for the purposes of this subchapter.

**(x) Protect health and the environment**

The terms "protect health and the environment" and "protection of health and the environment" mean protection against any unreasonable adverse effects on the environment.

**(y) Registrant**

The term "registrant" means a person who has registered any pesticide pursuant to the provisions of this subchapter.

**(z) Registration**

The term "registration" includes reregistration.

**(aa) State**

The term "State" means a State, the District of Columbia, the Commonwealth of Puerto Rico, the Virgin Islands, Guam, the Trust Territory of the Pacific Islands, and American Samoa.

**(bb) Unreasonable adverse effects on the environment**

The term "unreasonable adverse effects on the environment" means (1) any unreasonable risk to man or the environment, taking into account the economic, social, and environmental costs and benefits of the use of any pesticide, or (2) a human dietary risk from residues that result from a use of a pesticide in or on any food inconsistent with the standard under section 346a of Title 21. The Administrator shall consider the risks and benefits of public health pesticides separate from the risks and benefits of other pesticides. In weighing any regulatory action concerning a public health pesticide under this subchapter, the Administrator shall weigh any risks of the pesticide against the health risks such as the diseases transmitted by the vector to be controlled by the pesticide.

**(cc) Weed**

The term "weed" means any plant which grows where not wanted.

**(dd) Establishment**

The term "establishment" means any place where a pesticide or device or active ingredient used in producing a pesticide is produced, or held, for distribution or sale.

**(ee) To use any registered pesticide in a manner inconsistent with its labeling**

The term "to use any registered pesticide in a manner inconsistent with its labeling" means to use any registered pesticide in a manner not permitted by the labeling, except that the term shall not include (1) applying a pesticide at any dosage, concentration, or frequency less than that specified on the labeling unless the labeling specifically prohibits deviation from the specified dosage, concentration, or frequency, (2) applying a pesticide against any target pest not specified on the labeling if the application is to the crop, animal, or site specified on the labeling, unless the Administrator has required that the labeling specifically state that the pesticide may be used only for the pests specified on the labeling after the Administrator has determined that the use of the pesticide against other pests would cause an unreasonable adverse effect on the environment, (3) employing any method of application not prohibited by the labeling unless the labeling specifically states that the product may be applied only by the methods specified on the labeling, (4) mixing a pesticide or pesticides with a fertilizer when such mixture is not prohibited by the labeling, (5) any use of a pesticide in conformance with section 136c, 136p, or 136v of this title, or (6) any use of a pesticide in a manner that the Administrator determines to be consistent with the purposes of this subchapter. After March 31, 1979, the term shall not include the use of a pesticide for agricultural or forestry purposes at a dilution less than label dosage unless before or after that date the Administrator issues a regulation or advisory opinion consistent with the study provided for in section 27(b) of the Federal Pesticide Act of 1978, which regulation or advisory opinion specifically requires the use of definite amounts of dilution.

**(ff) Outstanding data requirement**

**(1) In general**

The term "outstanding data requirement" means a requirement for any study, information, or data that is necessary to make a determination under section 136a(c)(5) of this title and which study, information, or data—

**(A)** has not been submitted to the Administrator; or

**(B)** if submitted to the Administrator, the Administrator has determined must be resubmitted because it is not valid, complete, or adequate to make a determination under section 136a(c)(5) of this title and the regulations and guidelines issued under such section.

**(2) Factors**

In making a determination under paragraph (1)(B) respecting a study, the Administrator shall examine, at a minimum, relevant protocols, documentation of the conduct and analysis of the study, and the results of the study to determine whether the study and the results of the study fulfill the data requirement for which the study was submitted to the Administrator.

**(gg) To distribute or sell**

The term "to distribute or sell" means to distribute, sell, offer for sale, hold for distribution, hold for sale, hold for shipment, ship, deliver for shipment, release for shipment, or receive and (having so received) deliver or offer to deliver. The term does not include the holding or application of registered pesticides or use dilutions thereof by any applicator who provides a service of controlling pests without delivering any unapplied pesticide to any person so served.

**(hh) Nitrogen stabilizer**

The term "nitrogen stabilizer" means any substance or mixture of substances intended for preventing or hindering the process of nitrification, denitrification, ammonia volatilization, or urease production through action upon soil bacteria. Such term shall not include—

(1) dicyandiamide;

(2) ammonium thiosulfate; or

(3) any substance or mixture of substances.[1]—

(A) that was not registered pursuant to section 136a of this title prior to January 1, 1992; and

(B) that was in commercial agronomic use prior to January 1, 1992, with respect to which after January 1, 1992, the distributor or seller of the substance or mixture has made no specific claim of prevention or hindering of the process of nitrification, denitrification, ammonia volatilization[2] urease production regardless of the actual use or purpose for, or future use or purpose for, the substance or mixture.

Statements made in materials required to be submitted to any State legislative or regulatory authority, or required by such authority to be included in the labeling or other literature accompanying any such substance or mixture shall not be deemed a specific claim within the meaning of this subsection.

**(jj)[3] Maintenance applicator**

The term "maintenance applicator" means any individual who, in the principal course of such individual's employment, uses, or supervises the use of, a pesticide not classified for restricted use (other than a ready to use consumer products pesticide); for the purpose of providing structural pest control or lawn pest control including janitors, general maintenance personnel, sanitation personnel, and grounds maintenance personnel. The term "maintenance applicator" does not include private applicators as defined in section 136(e)(2) of this title; individuals who use antimicrobial pesticides, sanitizers or disinfectants; individuals employed by Federal, State, and local governments or any political subdivisions thereof, or individuals who use pesticides not classified for restricted use in or around their homes, boats, sod farms, nurseries, greenhouses, or other noncommercial property.

**(kk) Service technician**

The term "service technician" means any individual who uses or supervises the use of pesticides (other than a ready to use consumer products pesticide) for the purpose of providing structural pest control or lawn pest control on the property of another for a fee. The term "service technician" does not include individuals who use antimicrobial pesticides, sanitizers or disinfectants; or who otherwise apply ready to use consumer products pesticides.

**(ll) Minor use**

The term "minor use" means the use of a pesticide on an animal, on a commercial agricultural crop or site, or for the protection of public health where—

(1) the total United States acreage for the crop is less than 300,000 acres, as determined by the Secretary of Agriculture; or

(2) the Administrator, in consultation with the Secretary of Agriculture, determines that, based on information provided by an applicant for registration or a registrant, the use does not provide sufficient economic incentive to support the initial registration or continuing registration of a pesticide for such use and—

(A) there are insufficient efficacious alternative registered pesticides available for the use;

(B) the alternatives to the pesticide use pose greater risks to the environment or human health;

(C) the minor use pesticide plays or will play a significant part in managing pest resistance; or

(D) the minor use pesticide plays or will play a significant part in an integrated pest management program.

The status as a minor use under this subsection shall continue as long as the Administrator has not determined that, based on existing data, such use may cause an unreasonable adverse effect on the environment and the use otherwise qualifies for such status.

**(mm) Antimicrobial pesticide**

**(1) In general**

The term "antimicrobial pesticide" means a pesticide that—

(A) is intended to—

(i) disinfect, sanitize, reduce, or mitigate growth or development of microbiological organisms; or

(ii) protect inanimate objects, industrial processes or systems, surfaces, water, or other chemical substances from contamination, fouling, or deterioration caused by bacteria, viruses, fungi, protozoa, algae, or slime; and

(B) in the intended use is exempt from, or otherwise not subject to, a tolerance under section 346a of Title 21 or a food additive regulation under section 348 of Title 21.

**(2) Excluded products**

The term "antimicrobial pesticide" does not include—

(A) a wood preservative or antifouling paint product for which a claim of pesticidal activity other than or in addition to an activity described in paragraph (1) is made;

(B) an agricultural fungicide product; or

(C) an aquatic herbicide product.

**(3) Included products**

The term "antimicrobial pesticide" does include any other chemical sterilant product (other than liquid chemical sterilant products exempt under subsection (u) of this section), any other disinfectant product, any other industrial microbiocide product, and any other preservative product that is not excluded by paragraph (2).

**(nn) Public health pesticide**

The term "public health pesticide" means any minor use pesticide product registered for use and used predominantly in public health programs for vector control or for other recognized health protection uses, including the prevention or mitigation of viruses, bacteria, or other microorganisms (other than viruses, bacteria, or other microorganisms on or in living man or other living animal) that pose a threat to public health.

**(oo) Vector**

The term "vector" means any organism capable of transmitting the causative agent of human disease or capable of producing human discomfort or injury, including mosquitoes, flies, fleas, cockroaches, or other insects and ticks, mites, or rats.

(June 25, 1947, c. 125, § 2, as added Oct. 21, 1972, Pub.L. 92–516, § 2, 86 Stat. 975, and amended Dec. 28, 1973, Pub.L. 93–205, § 13(f), 87 Stat. 903; Nov. 28, 1975, Pub.L. 94–140, § 9, 89 Stat. 754; Sept. 30, 1978, Pub.L. 95–396, § 1, 92 Stat. 819; Oct. 25, 1988, Pub.L. 100–532, Title I, § 101, Title VI, § 601(a), Title VIII, § 801(a), 102 Stat. 2655, 2677, 2679; Dec. 13, 1991, Pub.L. 102–237, Title X, § 1006(a)(1), (2), (b)(3)(A), (B), 105 Stat. 1894, 1895; Aug. 3, 1996, Pub.L. 104–170, Title I, §§ 105(a), 120, Title II, §§ 210(a), 221, 230, Title III, § 304, 110 Stat. 1490, 1492, 1493, 1502, 1508, 1512.)

[1] So in original. Probably should not have a period.
[2] So in original. Probably should be followed by ", or".
[3] So in original. No subsec. (ii) has been enacted.

## HISTORICAL AND STATUTORY NOTES

**References in Text**

The Endangered Species Act of 1973, referred to in subsec. (*l*), is Pub.L. 93–205, Dec. 28, 1973, 87 Stat. 884, which is classified generally to chapter 35 (section 1531 et seq.) of Title 16, Conservation. For complete classification of this Act to the Code, see Short Title note set out under section 1531 of Title 16 and Tables.

Section 321 of title 21, referred to in subsec. (u), was amended and subsecs. (w) and (x) of section 321 no longer define "new animal drug" and "animal feed", but the terms are defined elsewhere in the section.

Section 27(b) of Federal Pesticide Act of 1978, referred to in subsec. (ee), is section 27(b) of Pub.L. 95–396, Sept. 30, 1978, 92 Stat. 841, which is set out as a note under section 136–4 of this title.

**Effective and Applicability Provisions**

2004 Acts

[Amendments made by Pub.L. 108–199, § 501, enacting the Pesticide Registration Improvement Act of 2003, to take effect 60 days after the date of enactment of this Act [Jan. 23, 2004], to take effect 60 days after Jan. 23, 2004, see Pub.L. 108–199, § 101(h), set out as a note under this section.]

1991 Acts

Amendments by Pub.L. 102–237 effective Dec. 13, 1991, see section 1101(a) of Pub.L. 102–237, set out as a note under section 1421 of this title.

1988 Acts

Section 901 of Pub.L. 100–532 provided that: "Except as otherwise provided in this Act, the amendments made by this Act [see Short Title of 1988 Amendments note set out under this section] shall take effect on the expiration of 60 days after the date of enactment of this Act [October 25, 1988]."

1973 Acts

Amendment by Pub.L. 93–205 effective Dec. 28, 1973, see section 16 of Pub.L. 93–205, set out as a note under section 1531 of Title 16, Conservation.

1975 Acts

Section 4 of Pub.L. 92–516, as amended Pub.L. 94–140, § 4, Nov. 28, 1975, 89 Stat. 752; Pub.L. 95–396, § 28, Sept. 30, 1978, 92 Stat. 842, provided that:

"(a) Except as otherwise provided in the Federal Insecticide, Fungicide, and Rodenticide Act [this subchapter], as amended by this Act and as otherwise provided by this section, the amendments made by this Act [see Short Title notes set out hereunder] shall take effect at the close of the date of the enactment of this Act [Oct. 21, 1972], provided if regulations are necessary for the implementation of any provision that becomes effective on the date of enactment, such regulations shall be promulgated and shall become effective within 90 days from the date of enactment of this Act.

"(b) The provisions of the Federal Insecticide, Fungicide, and Rodenticide Act [this subchapter] and the regulations thereunder as such existed prior to the enactment of this Act shall remain in effect until superseded by the amendments made by this Act and regulations thereunder.

"(c)(1) Two years after the enactment of this Act the Administrator shall have promulgated regulations providing for the registration and classification of pesticides under the provisions of this Act and thereafter shall register all new applications under such provisions.

"(2) Any requirements that a pesticide be registered for use only by a certified applicator shall not be effective until five years from the date of enactment of this Act.

"(3) A period of five years from date of enactment shall be provided for certification of applicators.

"(A) One year after the enactment of this Act the Administrator shall have prescribed the standards for the certification of applicators.

"(B) Each State desiring to certify applicators shall submit a State plan to the Administrator for the purpose provided by section 4(b).

"(C) As promptly as possible but in no event more than one year after submission of a State plan, the Administrator shall approve the State plan or disapprove it and indicate the reasons for disapproval. Consideration of plans resubmitted by States shall be expedited.

"(4) One year after the enactment of this Act the Administrator shall have promulgated and shall make effective regulations relating to the registration of establishments, permits for experimental use, and the keeping of books and records under the provisions of this Act.

"(d) No person shall be subject to any criminal or civil penalty imposed by the Federal Insecticide, Fungicide, and Rodenticide Act, as amended by this Act, for any act (or failure to act) occurring before the expiration of 60 days after the Administrator has published effective regulations in the Federal Register and taken such other action as may be necessary to permit compliance with the provisions under which the penalty is to be imposed.

"(e) For purposes of determining any criminal or civil penalty or liability to any third person in respect of any act or omission occurring before the expiration of the periods referred to in this section, the Federal Insecticide, Fungicide, and Rodenticide Act shall be treated as continuing in effect as if this Act had not been enacted."

**Short Title**

2004 Amendments

Pub.L. 108–199, Div. G, Title V, § 501(a), Jan. 23, 2004, 118 Stat. 419, provided that: "This section [enacting 7 U.S.C.A. § 136w–8, amending 7 U.S.C.A. §§ 136a, 136a–1, 136x, 136y, and enacting provisions set out as a note under 21 U.S.C.A. § 346a] may be cited as the 'Pesticide Registration Improvement Act of 2003'."

1996 Amendments

Pub.L. 104–170, § 1, Aug. 3, 1996, 110 Stat. 1489, provided that: "This Act [enacting sections 136i–2, 136r–1, 136w–5, 136w–6, and 136w–7 of this title, amending this section and sections 136a, 136a–1, 136d, 136q, 136s, 136w, 136w–3, 136x, and 136y of this title and sections 321, 331, 333, 342, and 346a of Title 21, Food and Drugs, and enacting provisions set out as notes under section 136i–2 of this title and sections 301 and 346a of Title 21] may be cited as the 'Food Quality Protection Act of 1996'."

[Another Food Quality Protection Act of 1996 was enacted by Pub.L. 104–170, Title IV, 110 Stat. 1513, see section 401(a) of Pub.L. 104–170, set out as a note under section 301 of Title 21.]

1988 Amendments

Section 1(a) of Pub.L. 100–532 provided that: "This Act [enacting section 136a–1 of this title, amending sections 136, 136a, 136b, 136c, 136d, 136f, 136g, 136h, 136i, 136j, 136k, 136*l*, 136m, 136n, 136*o*, 136p, 136q, 136s, 136v, 136w, 136w–1, 136w–2, and 136y of this title, and enacting provisions set out as notes under sections 136, 136m, and 136y of this title] may be cited as the 'Federal Insecticide, Fungicide, and Rodenticide Act Amendments of 1988'."

1978 Amendments

Section 29 of Pub.L. 95–396 provided that: "This Act [which enacted sections 136w–1 to 136w–4 of this title, amended sections 136 to 136f, 136h, 136j, 136*l*, 136*o*, 136q, 136r, 136u to 136w, 136x, and 136y of this title, enacted provisions set out as notes under sections 136a, 136*o*, and 136w–4 of this title, and amended provisions set out as a note under this section] may be cited as the 'Federal Pesticide Act of 1978'."

1972 Acts

Section 1 of Pub.L. 92–516 provided: "That this Act [which amended this subchapter generally, and enacted notes set out under this section, and amended sections 1261 and 1471 of Title 15, and sections 321 and 346a of Title 21] may be cited as the 'Federal Environmental Pesticide Control Act of 1972'."

Section 1(a) of Act June 25, 1947, c. 125, as added by Pub.L. 92–516, § 2, Oct. 21, 1972, 86 Stat. 973, provided that: "This Act [which enacted this subchapter] may be cited as the 'Federal Insecticide, Fungicide, and Rodenticide Act'."

**Prior Provisions**

A prior section 2 of Act June 25, 1947, was classfied to section 135 of this title prior to amendment of Act June 25, 1947 by Pub.L. 92–516.

**Federal Compliance with Pollution Control Standards**

For provisions relating to the responsibility of the head of each Executive agency for compliance with applicable pollution control standards, see Ex. Ord. No. 12088, Oct. 13, 1978, 43 F.R. 47707, as amended, set out as a note under section 4321 of Title 42, The Public Health and Welfare.

**Termination of Trust Territory of the Pacific Islands**

For termination of Trust Territory of the Pacific Island, see note set out preceding section 1681 of Title 48.

## § 136a. Registration of pesticides

### [FIFRA § 3]

**(a) Requirement of registration**

Except as provided by this subchapter, no person in any State may distribute or sell to any person any pesticide that is not registered under this subchapter. To the extent necessary to prevent unreasonable adverse effects on the environment, the Administrator may by regulation limit the distribution, sale, or use in any State of any pesticide that is not registered under this subchapter and that is not the subject of an experimental use permit under section 136c of this title or an emergency exemption under section 136p of this title.

**(b) Exemptions**

A pesticide which is not registered with the Administrator may be transferred if—

(1) the transfer is from one registered establishment to another registered establishment operated by the same producer solely for packaging at the second establishment or for use as a constituent part of another pesticide produced at the second establishment; or

(2) the transfer is pursuant to and in accordance with the requirements of an experimental use permit.

**(c) Procedure for registration**

**(1) Statement required**

Each applicant for registration of a pesticide shall file with the Administrator a statement which includes—

(A) the name and address of the applicant and of any other person whose name will appear on the labeling;

(B) the name of the pesticide;

(C) a complete copy of the labeling of the pesticide, a statement of all claims to be made for it, and any directions for its use;

(D) the complete formula of the pesticide;

(E) a request that the pesticide be classified for general use or for restricted use, or for both; and

(F) except as otherwise provided in paragraph (2)(D), if requested by the Administrator, a full description of the tests made and the results thereof upon which the claims are based, or alternatively a citation to data that appear in the public literature or that previously had been submitted to the Administrator and that the Administrator may consider in accordance with the following provisions:

(i) With respect to pesticides containing active ingredients that are initially registered under this subchapter after September 30, 1978, data submitted to support the application for the original registration of the pesticide, or an application for an amendment adding any new use to the registration and that pertains solely to such new use, shall not, without the written permission of the original data submitter, be considered by the Administrator to support an application by another person during a period of ten years following the date the Administrator first registers the pesticide, except that such permission shall not be required in the case of defensive data.

(ii) The period of exclusive data use provided under clause (i) shall be extended 1 additional year for each 3 minor uses registered after August 3, 1996, and within 7 years of the commencement of the exclusive use period, up to a total of 3 additional years for all minor uses registered by the Administrator if the Administrator, in consultation with the Secretary of Agriculture, determines that, based on information provided by an applicant for registration or a registrant, that—

(I) there are insufficient efficacious alternative registered pesticides available for the use;

(II) the alternatives to the minor use pesticide pose greater risks to the environment or human health;

(III) the minor use pesticide plays or will play a significant part in managing pest resistance; or

(IV) the minor use pesticide plays or will play a significant part in an integrated pest management program.

The registration of a pesticide for a minor use on a crop grouping established by the Administrator shall be considered for purposes of this clause 1 minor use for each representative crop for which data are provided in the crop grouping. Any additional exclusive use period under this clause shall be modified as appropriate or terminated if the registrant voluntarily cancels the product or deletes from the registration the minor uses which formed the basis for the extension of the additional exclusive use period or if the Administrator determines that the registrant is not actually marketing the product for such minor uses.

(iii) Except as otherwise provided in clause (i), with respect to data submitted after December 31, 1969, by an applicant or registrant to support an application for registration, experimental use permit, or amendment adding a new use to an existing registration, to support or maintain in effect an existing registration, or for reregistration, the Administrator may, without the permission of the original data submitter, consider any such item of data in support of an application by any other person (hereinafter in this subparagraph referred to as the "applicant") within the fifteen-year period following the date the data were originally submitted only if the applicant has made an offer to compensate the original data submitter and submitted such offer to the Administrator accompanied by evidence of delivery to the original data submitter of the offer. The terms and amount of compensation may be fixed by agreement between the original data submitter and the applicant, or, failing such agreement, binding arbitration under this subparagraph. If, at the end of ninety days after the date of delivery to the original data submitter of the offer to compensate, the original data submitter and the applicant have neither agreed on the amount and terms of compensation nor on a procedure for reaching an agreement on the amount and terms of compensation, either person may initiate binding arbitration proceedings by requesting the Federal Mediation and Conciliation Service to appoint an arbitrator from the roster of arbitrators maintained by such Service. The procedure and rules of the Service shall be applicable to the selection of such arbitrator and to such arbitration proceedings, and the findings and determination of the arbitrator shall be final and conclusive, and no official or court of the United States shall have power or jurisdiction to review any such findings and determination, except for fraud, misrepresentation, or other misconduct by one of the parties to the arbitration or the arbitrator where there is a verified complaint with supporting affidavits attesting to specific instances of such fraud, misrepresentation, or other misconduct. The parties to the arbitration shall share equally in the payment of the fee and expenses of the arbitrator. If the Administrator determines that an original data submitter has failed to participate in a procedure for reaching an agreement or in an arbitration proceeding as required by this subparagraph, or failed to comply with the terms of an agreement or arbitration decision concerning compensation under this subparagraph, the original data submitter shall forfeit the right to compensation for the use of the data in support of the application. Notwithstanding any other provision of this subchapter, if the Administrator determines that an applicant has failed to participate in a procedure for reaching an agreement or in an arbitration proceeding as required by this subparagraph, or failed to comply with the terms of an agreement or arbitration decision concerning compensation under this subparagraph, the Administrator shall deny the application or cancel the registration of the pesticide in support of which the data were used without further hearing. Before the Administrator takes action under either of the preceding two sentences, the Administrator shall furnish to the affected person, by certified mail, notice of intent to take action and allow fifteen days from the date of delivery of the notice for the affected person to respond. If a registration is denied or canceled under this subparagraph, the Administrator may make such order as the Administrator deems appropriate concerning the continued sale and use of existing stocks of such pesticide. Registration action by the Administrator shall not be delayed pending the fixing of compensation.

(iv) After expiration of any period of exclusive use and any period for which compensation is required for the use of an item of data under clauses (i), (ii), and (iii), the Administrator may consider such item of data in support of an application by any other applicant without the permission of the original data submitter and without an offer having been received to compensate the original data submitter for the use of such item of data.

(v) The period of exclusive use provided under clause (ii) shall not take effect until 1 year after August 3, 1996, except where an applicant or registrant is applying for the registration of a pesticide containing an active ingredient not previously registered.

(vi) With respect to data submitted after August 3, 1996, by an applicant or registrant to support an amendment adding a new use to an existing registration that does not retain any period of exclusive use, if such data relates solely to a minor use of a pesticide, such data shall not, without the written permission of the original data submitter, be considered by the Administrator to support an application for a minor use by another person during the period of 10 years following the date of submission of such data. The applicant or registrant at the time the new minor use is requested shall notify the Administrator that to the best of their knowledge the exclusive use period for the pesticide has expired and that the data pertaining solely to the minor use of a pesticide is eligible for the provisions of this paragraph. If the minor use registration which is supported by data submitted pursuant to this subsection is voluntarily canceled or if such data are subsequently used to support a nonminor use, the data shall no longer be subject to the exclusive use provisions of this clause but shall instead be considered by the Administrator in accordance with the provisions of clause (i), as appropriate.

(G) If the applicant is requesting that the registration or amendment to the registration of a pesticide be expedited, an explanation of the basis for the request must be submitted, in accordance with paragraph (10) of this subsection.

**(2) Data in support of registration**

**(A) In general**

The Administrator shall publish guidelines specifying the kinds of information which will be required to support the registration of a pesticide and shall revise such guidelines from time to time. If thereafter the Administrator requires any additional kind of information under subparagraph (B) of this paragraph, the Administrator shall permit sufficient time for applicants to obtain such additional information. The Administrator, in establishing standards for data requirements for the registration of pesticides with respect to minor uses, shall make such standards commensurate with the anticipated extent of use, pattern of use, the public health and agricultural need for such minor use, and the level and degree of potential beneficial or adverse effects on man and the environment. The Administrator shall not require a person to submit, in relation to a registration or reregistration of a pesticide for minor agricultural use under this subchapter, any field residue data from a geographic area where the pesticide will not be registered for such use. In the development of these standards, the Administrator shall consider the economic factors of potential national volume of use, extent of distribution, and the impact of the cost of meeting the requirements on the incentives for any potential registrant to undertake the development of the required data. Except as provided by section 136h of this title, within 30 days after the Administrator registers a pesticide under this subchapter the Administrator shall make available to the public the data called for in the registration statement together with such other scientific information as the Administrator deems relevant to the Administrator's decision.

**(B) Additional data**

**(i)** If the Administrator determines that additional data are required to maintain in effect an existing registration of a pesticide, the Administrator shall notify all existing registrants of the pesticide to which the determination relates and provide a list of such registrants to any interested person.

**(ii)** Each registrant of such pesticide shall provide evidence within ninety days after receipt of notification that it is taking appropriate steps to secure the additional data that are required. Two or more registrants may agree to develop jointly, or to share in the cost of developing, such data if they agree and advise the Administrator of their intent within ninety days after notification. Any registrant who agrees to share in the cost of producing the data shall be entitled to examine and rely upon such data in support of maintenance of such registration. The Administrator shall issue a notice of intent to suspend the registration of a pesticide in accordance with the procedures prescribed by clause (iv) if a registrant fails to comply with this clause.

**(iii)** If, at the end of sixty days after advising the Administrator of their agreement to develop jointly, or share in the cost of developing, data, the registrants have not further agreed on the terms of the data development arrangement or on a procedure for reaching such agreement, any of such registrants may initiate binding arbitration proceedings by requesting the Federal Mediation and Conciliation Service to appoint an arbitrator from the roster of arbitrators maintained by such Service. The procedure and rules of the Service shall be applicable to the selection of such arbitrator and to such arbitration proceedings, and the findings and determination of the arbitrator shall be final and conclusive, and no official or court of the United States shall have power or jurisdiction to review any such findings and determination, except for fraud, misrepresentation, or other misconduct by one of the parties to the arbitration or the arbitrator where there is a verified complaint with supporting affidavits attesting to specific instances of such fraud, misrepresentation, or other misconduct. All parties to the arbitration shall share equally in the payment of the fee and expenses of the arbitrator. The Administrator shall issue a notice of intent to suspend the registration of a pesticide in accordance with the procedures prescribed by clause (iv) if a registrant fails to comply with this clause.

**(iv)** Notwithstanding any other provision of this subchapter, if the Administrator determines that a registrant, within the time required by the Administrator, has failed to take appropriate steps to secure the data required under this subparagraph, to participate in a procedure for reaching agreement concerning a joint data development arrangement under this subparagraph or in an arbitration proceeding as required by this subparagraph, or to comply with the terms of an agreement or arbitration decision concerning a joint data development arrangement under this subparagraph, the Administrator may issue a notice of intent to suspend such registrant's registration of the pesticide for which additional data is required. The Administrator may include in the notice of intent to suspend such provisions as the Administrator deems appropriate concerning the continued sale and use of existing stocks of such pesticide. Any suspension proposed under this subparagraph shall become final and effective at the end of thirty days from receipt by the registrant of the notice of intent to suspend, unless during that time a request for hearing is made by a person adversely affected by the notice or the registrant has satisfied the Administrator that the registrant has complied fully with the requirements that served as a basis for the notice of intent to suspend. If a hearing is requested, a hearing shall be conducted under section 136d(d) of this title. The only matters for resolution at that hearing shall be whether the registrant has failed to take the action that served as the basis for the notice of intent to suspend the registration of the pesticide for which additional data is required, and whether the Administrator's determination with respect to the disposition of existing stocks is consistent with this subchapter. If a hearing is held, a decision after completion of such hearing shall be final. Notwithstanding any other provision of this subchapter, a hearing shall be held and a determination made within seventy-five days after receipt of a request for such hearing. Any registration suspended under this subparagraph shall be reinstated by the Administrator if the Administrator determines that the registrant has complied fully with the requirements that served as a basis for the suspension of the registration.

**(v)** Any data submitted under this subparagraph shall be subject to the provisions of paragraph (1)(D). Whenever such data are submitted jointly by two or more registrants, an agent shall be agreed on at the time of the joint submission to handle any subsequent data compensation matters for the joint submitters of such data.

**(vi)** Upon the request of a registrant the Administrator shall, in the case of a minor use, extend the deadline for the production of residue chemistry data under this subparagraph for data required solely to support that minor use until the final deadline for submission of data under section 136a–1 of this title for the other uses of the pesticide established as of August 3, 1996, if—

**(I)** the data to support other uses of the pesticide on a food are being provided;

**(II)** the registrant, in submitting a request for such an extension, provides a schedule, including interim dates to measure progress, to assure that the data production will be completed before the expiration of the extension period;

**(III)** the Administrator has determined that such extension will not significantly delay the Administrator's schedule for issuing a reregistration eligibility determination required under section 136a–1 of this title; and

**(IV)** the Administrator has determined that based on existing data, such extension would not significantly increase the risk of any unreasonable adverse effect on the environment. If the Administrator grants an extension under this clause, the Administrator shall monitor the development of the data and shall ensure that the registrant is meeting the schedule for the production of the data. If the Administrator determines that the registrant is not meeting or has not met the schedule for the production of such data, the Administrator may proceed in accordance with clause (iv) regarding the continued registration of the affected products with the minor use and shall inform the public of such action. Notwithstanding the provisions of this clause, the Administrator may take action to modify or revoke the extension under this clause if the Administrator determines that the extension for the minor use may cause an unreasonable adverse effect on the environment. In such circumstance, the Administrator shall provide, in writing to the registrant, a notice revoking the extension of time for submission of data. Such data shall instead be due in accordance with the date established by the Administrator for the submission of the data.

**(vii)** If the registrant does not commit to support a specific minor use of the pesticide, but is supporting and providing data in a timely and adequate fashion to support uses of the pesticide on a food, or if all uses of the pesticide are nonfood uses and the registrant does not commit to support a specific minor use of the pesticide but is supporting and providing data in a timely and adequate fashion to support other nonfood uses of the pesticide, the Administrator, at the written request of the registrant, shall not take any action pursuant to this clause in regard to such unsupported minor use until the final deadline established as of August 3, 1996, for the submission of data under section 136a–1 of this title for the supported uses identified pursuant to this clause unless the Administrator determines that the absence of the data is significant enough to cause human health or environmental concerns. On the basis of such determination, the Administrator may refuse the request for extension by the registrant. Upon receipt of the request from the registrant, the Administrator shall publish in the Federal Register a notice of the receipt of the request and the effective date upon which the uses not being supported will be voluntarily deleted from the registration pursuant to section 136d(f)(1) of this title. If the Administrator grants an extension under this clause, the Administrator shall monitor the development of the data for the uses being supported and shall ensure that the registrant is meeting the schedule for the production of such data. If the Administrator determines that the registrant is not meeting or has not met the schedule for the production of such data, the Administrator may proceed in accordance with clause (iv) of this subparagraph regarding the continued registration of the affected products with the minor and other uses and shall inform the public of such action in accordance with section 136d(f)(2) of this title. Notwithstanding the provisions of this clause, the Administrator may deny, modify, or revoke the temporary extension under this subparagraph if the Administrator determines that the continuation of the minor use may cause an unreasonable adverse effect on the environment. In the event of modification or revocation, the Administrator shall provide, in writing, to the registrant a notice revoking the temporary extension and establish a new effective date by which the minor use shall be deleted from the registration.

**(viii)(I)** If data required to support registration of a pesticide under subparagraph (A) is requested by a Federal or State regulatory authority, the Administrator shall, to the extent practicable, coordinate data requirements, test protocols, timetables, and standards of review and reduce burdens and redundancy caused to the registrant by multiple requirements on the registrant.

**(II)** The Administrator may enter into a cooperative agreement with a State to carry out subclause (I).

**(III)** Not later than 1 year after August 3, 1996, the Administrator shall develop a process to identify and assist in alleviating future disparities between Federal and State data requirements.

**(C) Simplified procedures**

Within nine months after September 30, 1978, the Administrator shall, by regulation, prescribe simplified procedures for the registration of pesticides, which shall include the provisions of subparagraph (D) of this paragraph.

**(D) Exemption**

No applicant for registration of a pesticide who proposes to purchase a registered pesticide from another producer in order to formulate such purchased pesticide into the pesticide that is the subject of the application shall be required to—

**(i)** submit or cite data pertaining to such purchased product; or

**(ii)** offer to pay reasonable compensation otherwise required by paragraph (1)(D) of this subsection for the use of any such data.

**(E) Minor use waiver**

In handling the registration of a pesticide for a minor use, the Administrator may waive otherwise applicable data requirements if the Administrator determines that the absence of such data will not prevent the Administrator from determining—

**(i)** the incremental risk presented by the minor use of the pesticide; and

**(ii)** that such risk, if any, would not be an unreasonable adverse effect on the environment.

**(3) Application**

**(A) In general**

The Administrator shall review the data after receipt of the application and shall, as expeditiously as possible, either register the pesticide in accordance with paragraph (5), or notify the applicant of the Administrator's determination that it does not comply with the provisions of the subchapter in accordance with paragraph (6).

**(B) Identical or substantially similar**

**(i)** The Administrator shall, as expeditiously as possible, review and act on any application received by the Administrator that—

**(I)** proposes the initial or amended registration of an end-use pesticide that, if registered as proposed, would be identical or substantially similar in composition and labeling to a currently-registered pesticide identified in the application, or that would differ in composition and labeling from such currently-registered pesticide only in ways that would not significantly increase the risk of unreasonable adverse effects on the environment; or

**(II)** proposes an amendment to the registration of a registered pesticide that does not require scientific review of data.

**(ii)** In expediting the review of an application for an action described in clause (i), the Administrator shall—

**(I)** within 45 days after receiving the application, notify the registrant whether or not the application is complete and, if the application is found to be incomplete, reject the application;

**(II)** within 90 days after receiving a complete application, notify the registrant if the application has been granted or denied; and

**(III)** if the application is denied, notify the registrant in writing of the specific reasons for the denial of the application.

**(C) Minor use registration**

**(i)** The Administrator shall, as expeditiously as possible, review and act on any complete application—

**(I)** that proposes the initial registration of a new pesticide active ingredient if the active ingredient is proposed to be registered solely for minor uses, or proposes a registration amendment solely for minor uses to an existing registration; or

(II) for a registration or a registration amendment that proposes significant minor uses.

(ii) For the purposes of clause (i)—

(I) the term "as expeditiously as possible" means that the Administrator shall, to the greatest extent practicable, complete a review and evaluation of all data, submitted with a complete application, within 12 months after the submission of the complete application, and the failure of the Administrator to complete such a review and evaluation under clause (i) shall not be subject to judicial review; and

(II) the term "significant minor uses" means 3 or more minor uses proposed for every non-minor use, a minor use that would, in the judgment of the Administrator, serve as a replacement for any use which has been canceled in the 5 years preceding the receipt of the application, or a minor use that in the opinion of the Administrator would avoid the reissuance of an emergency exemption under section 136p of this title for that minor use.

**(D) Adequate time for submission of minor use data**

If a registrant makes a request for a minor use waiver, regarding data required by the Administrator, pursuant to paragraph (2)(E), and if the Administrator denies in whole or in part such data waiver request, the registrant shall have a full-time period for providing such data. For purposes of this subparagraph, the term "full-time period" means the time period originally established by the Administrator for submission of such data, beginning with the date of receipt by the registrant of the Administrator's notice of denial.

**(4) Notice of application**

The Administrator shall publish in the Federal Register, promptly after receipt of the statement and other data required pursuant to paragraphs (1) and (2), a notice of each application for registration of any pesticide if it contains any new active ingredient or if it would entail a changed use pattern. The notice shall provide for a period of 30 days in which any Federal agency or any other interested person may comment.

**(5) Approval of registration**

The Administrator shall register a pesticide if the Administrator determines that, when considered with any restrictions imposed under subsection (d) of this section—

(A) its composition is such as to warrant the proposed claims for it;

(B) its labeling and other material required to be submitted comply with the requirements of this subchapter;

(C) it will perform its intended function without unreasonable adverse effects on the environment; and

(D) when used in accordance with widespread and commonly recognized practice it will not generally cause unreasonable adverse effects on the environment.

The Administrator shall not make any lack of essentiality a criterion for denying registration of any pesticide. Where two pesticides meet the requirements of this paragraph, one should not be registered in preference to the other. In considering an application for the registration of a pesticide, the Administrator may waive data requirements pertaining to efficacy, in which event the Administrator may register the pesticide without determining that the pesticide's composition is such as to warrant proposed claims of efficacy. If a pesticide is found to be efficacious by any State under section 136v(c) of this title, a presumption is established that the Administrator shall waive data requirements pertaining to efficacy for use of the pesticide in such State.

**(6) Denial of registration**

If the Administrator determines that the requirements of paragraph (5) for registration are not satisfied, the Administrator shall notify the applicant for registration of the Administrator's determination and of the Administrator's reasons (including the factual basis) therefor, and that, unless the applicant corrects the conditions and notifies the Administrator thereof during the 30-day period beginning with the day after the date on which the applicant receives the notice, the Administrator may refuse to register the pesticide. Whenever the Administrator refuses to register a pesticide, the Administrator shall notify the applicant of the Administrator's decision and of the Administrator's reasons (including the factual basis) therefor. The Administrator shall promptly publish in the Federal Register notice of such denial of registration and the reasons therefor. Upon such notification, the applicant for registration or other interested person with the concurrence of the applicant shall have the same remedies as provided for in section 136d of this title.

**(7) Registration under special circumstances**

Notwithstanding the provisions of paragraph (5)—

(A) The Administrator may conditionally register or amend the registration of a pesticide if the Administrator determines that (i) the pesticide and proposed use are identical or substantially similar to any currently registered pesticide and use thereof, or differ only in ways that would not significantly increase the risk of unreasonable adverse effects on the environment, and (ii) approving the registration or amendment in the manner proposed by the applicant would not significantly increase the risk of any unreasonable adverse effect on the environment. An applicant seeking conditional registration or amended registration under this subparagraph shall submit such data as would be required to obtain registration of a similar pesticide under paragraph (5). If the applicant is unable to submit an item of data because it has not yet been generated, the Administrator may register or amend the registration of the pesticide under such conditions as will require the submission of such data not later than the time such data are required to be submitted with respect to similar pesticides already registered under this subchapter.

(B) The Administrator may conditionally amend the registration of a pesticide to permit additional uses of such pesticide notwithstanding that data concerning the pesticide may be insufficient to support an unconditional amendment, if the Administrator determines that (i) the applicant has submitted satisfactory data pertaining to the proposed additional use, and (ii) amending the registration in the manner proposed by the applicant would not significantly increase the risk of any unreasonable adverse effect on the environment. Notwithstanding the foregoing provisions of this subparagraph, no registration of a pesticide may be amended to permit an additional use of such pesticide if the Administrator has issued a notice stating that such pesticide, or any ingredient thereof, meets or exceeds risk criteria associated in whole or in part with human dietary exposure enumerated in regulations issued under this subchapter, and during the pendency of any risk-benefit evaluation initiated by such notice, if (I) the additional use of such pesticide involves a major food or feed crop, or (II) the additional use of such pesticide involves a minor food or feed crop and the Administrator determines, with the concurrence of the Secretary of Agriculture, there is available an effective alternative pesticide that does not meet or exceed such risk criteria. An applicant seeking amended registration under this subparagraph shall submit such data as would be required to obtain registration of a similar pesticide under paragraph (5). If the applicant is unable to submit an item of data (other than data pertaining to the proposed additional use) because it has not yet been generated, the Administrator may amend the registration under such conditions as will require the submission of such data not later than the time such data are required to be submitted with respect to similar pesticides already registered under this subchapter.

(C) The Administrator may conditionally register a pesticide containing an active ingredient not contained in any currently registered pesticide for a period reasonably sufficient for the generation and submission of required data (which are lacking because a period reasonably sufficient for generation of the data has not elapsed since the Administrator first imposed the data requirement) on the condition that by the end of such period the Administrator receives such data and the data do not meet or exceed risk criteria enumerated in regulations issued under this subchapter, and on such other conditions as the Administrator may prescribe. A conditional registration under this subparagraph shall be granted only if the Administrator determines that use of the pesticide during such period will not cause any unreasonable adverse effect on the environment, and that use of the pesticide is in the public interest.

**(8) Interim administrative review**

Notwithstanding any other provision of this subchapter, the Administrator may not initiate a public interim administrative review process to develop a risk-benefit evaluation of the ingredients of a pesticide or any of its uses prior to initiating a formal action to cancel, suspend, or deny registration of such pesticide, required under this subchapter, unless such interim administrative process is based on a validated test or other significant evidence raising prudent concerns of unreasonable adverse risk to man or to the environment. Notice of the definition of the terms "validated test" and "other significant evidence" as used herein shall be published by the Administrator in the Federal Register.

**(9) Labeling**

**(A) Additional statements**

Subject to subparagraphs (B) and (C), it shall not be a violation of this subchapter for a registrant to modify the labeling of an antimicrobial pesticide product to include relevant information on product efficacy, product composition, container composition or design, or other characteristics that do not relate to any pesticidal claim or pesticidal activity.

**(B) Requirements**

Proposed labeling information under subparagraph (A) shall not be false or misleading, shall not conflict with or detract from any statement required by law or the Administrator as a condition of registration, and shall be substantiated on the request of the Administrator.

**(C) Notification and disapproval**

**(i) Notification**

A registration may be modified under subparagraph (A) if—

(I) the registrant notifies the Administrator in writing not later than 60 days prior to distribution or sale of a product bearing the modified labeling; and

(II) the Administrator does not disapprove of the modification under clause (ii).

**(ii) Disapproval**

Not later than 30 days after receipt of a notification under clause (i), the Administrator may disapprove the modification by sending the registrant notification in writing stating that the proposed language is not acceptable and stating the reasons why the Administrator finds the proposed modification unacceptable.

**(iii) Restriction on sale**

A registrant may not sell or distribute a product bearing a disapproved modification.

**(iv) Objection**

A registrant may file an objection in writing to a disapproval under clause (ii) not later than 30 days after receipt of notification of the disapproval.

**(v) Final action**

A decision by the Administrator following receipt and consideration of an objection filed under clause (iv) shall be considered a final agency action.

**(D) Use dilution**

The label or labeling required under this subchapter for an antimicrobial pesticide that is or may be diluted for use may have a different statement of caution or protective measures for use of the recommended diluted solution of the pesticide than for use of a concentrate of the pesticide if the Administrator determines that—

(i) adequate data have been submitted to support the statement proposed for the diluted solution uses; and

(ii) the label or labeling provides adequate protection for exposure to the diluted solution of the pesticide.

**(10) Expedited registration of pesticides**

(A) Not later than 1 year after August 3, 1996, the Administrator shall, utilizing public comment, develop procedures and guidelines, and expedite the review of an application for registration of a pesticide or an amendment to a registration that satisfies such guidelines.

(B) Any application for registration or an amendment, including biological and conventional pesticides, will be considered for expedited review under this paragraph. An application for registration or an amendment shall qualify for expedited review if use of the pesticide proposed by the application may reasonably be expected to accomplish 1 or more of the following:

(i) Reduce the risks of pesticides to human health.

(ii) Reduce the risks of pesticides to nontarget organisms.

(iii) Reduce the potential for contamination of groundwater, surface water, or other valued environmental resources.

(iv) Broaden the adoption of integrated pest management strategies, or make such strategies more available or more effective.

(C) The Administrator, not later than 30 days after receipt of an application for expedited review, shall notify the applicant whether the application is complete. If it is found to be incomplete, the Administrator may either reject the request for expedited review or ask the applicant for additional information to satisfy the guidelines developed under subparagraph (A).

**(d) Classification of pesticides**

**(1) Classification for general use, restricted use, or both**

(A) As a part of the registration of a pesticide the Administrator shall classify it as being for general use or for restricted use. If the Administrator determines that some of the uses for which the pesticide is registered should be for general use and that other uses for which it is registered should be for restricted use, the Administrator shall classify it for both general use and restricted use. Pesticide uses may be classified by regulation on the initial classification, and registered pesticides may be classified prior to reregistration. If some of the uses of the pesticide are classified for general use, and other uses are classified for restricted use, the directions relating to its general uses shall be clearly separated and distinguished from those directions relating to its restricted uses. The Administrator may require that its packaging and labeling for restricted uses shall be clearly distinguishable from its packaging and labeling for general uses.

(B) If the Administrator determines that the pesticide, when applied in accordance with its directions for use, warnings and cautions and for the uses for which it is registered, or for one or more of such uses, or in accordance with a widespread and commonly recognized practice, will not generally cause unreasonable adverse effects on the environment, the Administrator will classify the pesticide, or the particular use or uses of the pesticide to which the determination applies, for general use.

(C) If the Administrator determines that the pesticide, when applied in accordance with its directions for use, warnings and cautions and for the uses for which it is registered, or for one or more of such uses, or in accordance with a widespread and commonly recognized practice, may generally cause, without additional regulatory restrictions, unreasonable adverse effects on the environment, including injury to the applicator, the Administrator shall classify the pesticide, or the particular use or uses to which the determination applies, for restricted use:

(i) If the Administrator classifies a pesticide, or one or more uses of such pesticide, for restricted use because of a determination that the acute dermal or inhalation toxicity of the pesticide presents a hazard to the applicator or other persons, the pesticide shall be applied for any use to which the restricted classification applies only by or under the direct supervision of a certified applicator.

(ii) If the Administrator classifies a pesticide, or one or more uses of such pesticide, for restricted use because of a determination that its use without additional regulatory restriction may cause unreasonable adverse effects on the environment, the pesticide shall be applied for any use to which the determination applies only by or under the direct supervision of a certified applicator, or subject to such other restrictions as the Administrator may provide by regulation. Any such regulation shall be reviewable in the appropriate court of appeals upon petition of a person adversely affected filed within 60 days of the publication of the regulation in final form.

**(2) Change in classification**

If the Administrator determines that a change in the classification of any use of a pesticide from general use to restricted use is necessary to prevent unreasonable adverse effects on the environment, the Administrator shall notify the registrant of such pesticide of such determination at least forty-five days before making the change and shall publish the proposed change in the Federal Register. The registrant, or other interested person with the concurrence of the registrant, may seek relief from such determination under section 136d(b) of this title.

**(3) Change in classification from restricted use to general use**

The registrant of any pesticide with one or more uses classified for restricted use may petition the Administrator to change any such classification from restricted to general use. Such petition shall set out the basis for the registrant's position that restricted use classification is unnecessary because classification of the pesticide for general use would not cause unreasonable adverse effects on the environment. The Administrator, within sixty days after receiving such petition, shall notify the registrant whether the petition has been granted or denied. Any denial shall contain an explanation therefor and any such denial shall be subject to judicial review under section 136n of this title.

**(e) Products with same formulation and claims**

Products which have the same formulation, are manufactured by the same person, the labeling of which contains the same claims, and the labels of which bear a designation identifying the product as the same pesticide may be registered as a single pesticide; and additional names and labels shall be added to the registration by supplemental statements.

**(f) Miscellaneous**

**(1) Effect of change of labeling or formulation**

If the labeling or formulation for a pesticide is changed, the registration shall be amended to reflect such change if the Administrator determines that the change will not violate any provision of this subchapter.

**(2) Registration not a defense**

In no event shall registration of an article be construed as a defense for the commission of any offense under this subchapter. As long as no cancellation proceedings are in effect registration of a pesticide shall be prima facie evidence that the pesticide, its labeling and packaging comply with the registration provisions of the subchapter.

**(3) Authority to consult other federal agencies**

In connection with consideration of any registration or application for registration under this section, the Administrator may consult with any other Federal agency.

**(4) Mixtures of nitrogen stabilizers and fertilizer products**

Any mixture or other combination of—

(A) 1 or more nitrogen stabilizers registered under this subchapter; and

(B) 1 or more fertilizer products,

shall not be subject to the provisions of this section or sections 136a–1, 136c, 136e, 136m, and 136o(a)(2) of this title if the mixture or other combination is accompanied by the labeling required under this subchapter for the nitrogen stabilizer contained in the mixture or other combination, the mixture or combination is mixed or combined in accordance with such labeling, and the mixture or combination does not contain any active ingredient other than the nitrogen stabilizer.

**(g) Registration review**

**(1) General rule**

**(A) Periodic review**

The registrations of pesticides are to be periodically reviewed. The Administrator shall by regulation establish a procedure for accomplishing the periodic review of registrations. The goal of these regulations shall be a review of a pesticide's registration every 15 years. No registration shall be canceled as a result of the registration review process unless the Administrator follows the procedures and substantive requirements of section 136d of this title.

**(B) Limitation**

Nothing in this subsection shall prohibit the Administrator from undertaking any other review of a pesticide pursuant to this subchapter.

**(2) Data**

**(A) Submission required**

The Administrator shall use the authority in subsection (c)(2)(B) of this section to require the submission of data when such data are necessary for a registration review.

**(B) Data submission, compensation, and exemption**

For purposes of this subsection, the provisions of subsections (c)(1), (c)(2)(B), and (c)(2)(D) of this section shall be utilized for and be applicable to any data required for registration review.

**(h) Registration requirements for antimicrobial pesticides**

**(1) Evaluation of process**

To the maximum extent practicable consistent with the degrees of risk presented by an antimicrobial pesticide and the type of review appropriate to evaluate the risks, the Administrator shall identify and evaluate reforms to the antimicrobial registration process that would reduce review periods existing as of August 3, 1996, for antimicrobial pesticide product registration applications and applications for amended registration of antimicrobial pesticide products, including—

(A) new antimicrobial active ingredients;

(B) new antimicrobial end-use products;

(C) substantially similar or identical antimicrobial pesticides; and

(D) amendments to antimicrobial pesticide registrations.

**(2) Review time period reduction goal**

Each reform identified under paragraph (1) shall be designed to achieve the goal of reducing the review period following submission of a complete application, consistent with the degree of risk, to a period of not more than—

(A) 540 days for a new antimicrobial active ingredient pesticide registration;

(B) 270 days for a new antimicrobial use of a registered active ingredient;

(C) 120 days for any other new antimicrobial product;

(D) 90 days for a substantially similar or identical antimicrobial product;

(E) 90 days for an amendment to an antimicrobial registration that does not require scientific review of data; and

(F) 120 days for an amendment to an antimicrobial registration that requires scientific review of data and that is not otherwise described in this paragraph.

**(3) Implementation**

**(A) Proposed rulemaking**

**(i) Issuance**

Not later than 270 days after August 3, 1996, the Administrator shall publish in the Federal Register proposed regulations to accelerate and improve the review of antimicrobial pesticide products designed to implement, to the extent practicable, the goals set forth in paragraph (2).

**(ii) Requirements**

Proposed regulations issued under clause (i) shall—

(I) define the various classes of antimicrobial use patterns, including household, industrial, and institutional disinfectants and sanitizing pesticides, preservatives, water treatment, and pulp and paper mill additives, and other such products intended to disinfect, sanitize, reduce, or mitigate growth or development of microbiological organisms, or protect inanimate objects, industrial processes or systems, surfaces, water, or other chemical substances from contamination, fouling, or deterioration caused by bacteria, viruses, fungi, protozoa, algae, or slime;

**(II)** differentiate the types of review undertaken for antimicrobial pesticides;

**(III)** conform the degree and type of review to the risks and benefits presented by antimicrobial pesticides and the function of review under this subchapter, considering the use patterns of the product, toxicity, expected exposure, and product type;

**(IV)** ensure that the registration process is sufficient to maintain antimicrobial pesticide efficacy and that antimicrobial pesticide products continue to meet product performance standards and effectiveness levels for each type of label claim made; and

**(V)** implement effective and reliable deadlines for process management.

**(iii) Comments**

In developing the proposed regulations, the Administrator shall solicit the views from registrants and other affected parties to maximize the effectiveness of the rule development process.

**(B) Final regulations**

**(i) Issuance**

The Administrator shall issue final regulations not later than 240 days after the close of the comment period for the proposed regulations.

**(ii) Failure to meet goal**

If a goal described in paragraph (2) is not met by the final regulations, the Administrator shall identify the goal, explain why the goal was not attained, describe the element of the regulations included instead, and identify future steps to attain the goal.

**(iii) Requirements**

In issuing final regulations, the Administrator shall—

**(I)** consider the establishment of a certification process for regulatory actions involving risks that can be responsibly managed, consistent with the degree of risk, in the most cost-efficient manner;

**(II)** consider the establishment of a certification process by approved laboratories as an adjunct to the review process;

**(III)** use all appropriate and cost-effective review mechanisms, including—

**(aa)** expanded use of notification and non-notification procedures;

**(bb)** revised procedures for application review; and

**(cc)** allocation of appropriate resources to ensure streamlined management of antimicrobial pesticide registrations; and

**(IV)** clarify criteria for determination of the completeness of an application.

**(C) Expedited review**

This subsection does not affect the requirements or extend the deadlines or review periods contained in subsection (c)(3) of this section.

**(D) Alternative review periods**

If the final regulations to carry out this paragraph are not effective 630 days after August 3, 1996, until the final regulations become effective, the review period, beginning on the date of receipt by the Agency of a complete application, shall be—

**(i)** 2 years for a new antimicrobial active ingredient pesticide registration;

**(ii)** 1 year for a new antimicrobial use of a registered active ingredient;

**(iii)** 180 days for any other new antimicrobial product;

**(iv)** 90 days for a substantially similar or identical antimicrobial product;

**(v)** 90 days for an amendment to an antimicrobial registration that does not require scientific review of data; and

**(vi)** 120 days for an amendment to an antimicrobial registration that requires scientific review of data and that is not otherwise described in this subparagraph.

**(E) Wood preservatives**

An application for the registration, or for an amendment to the registration, of a wood preservative product for which a claim of pesticidal activity listed in section 136(mm) of this title is made (regardless of any other pesticidal claim that is made with respect to the product) shall be reviewed by the Administrator within the same period as that established under this paragraph for an antimicrobial pesticide product application, consistent with the degree of risk posed by the use of the wood preservative product, if the application requires the applicant to satisfy the same data requirements as are required to support an application for a wood preservative product that is an antimicrobial pesticide.

(F) Notification

(i) In general

Subject to clause (iii), the Administrator shall notify an applicant whether an application has been granted or denied not later than the final day of the appropriate review period under this paragraph, unless the applicant and the Administrator agree to a later date.

(ii) Final decision

If the Administrator fails to notify an applicant within the period of time required under clause (i), the failure shall be considered an agency action unlawfully withheld or unreasonably delayed for purposes of judicial review under chapter 7 of Title 5.

(iii) Exemption

This subparagraph does not apply to an application for an antimicrobial pesticide that is filed under subsection (c)(3)(B) of this section prior to 90 days after August 3, 1996.

(iv) Limitation

Notwithstanding clause (ii), the failure of the Administrator to notify an applicant for an amendment to a registration for an antimicrobial pesticide shall not be judicially reviewable in a Federal or State court if the amendment requires scientific review of data within—

(I) the time period specified in subparagraph (D)(vi), in the absence of a final regulation under subparagraph (B); or

(II) the time period specified in paragraph (2)(F), if adopted in a final regulation under subparagraph (B).

(4) Annual report

(A) Submission

Beginning on August 3, 1996, and ending on the date that the goals under paragraph (2) are achieved, the Administrator shall, not later than March 1 of each year, prepare and submit an annual report to the Committee on Agriculture of the House of Representatives and the Committee on Agriculture, Nutrition, and Forestry of the Senate.

(B) Requirements

A report submitted under subparagraph (A) shall include a description of—

(i) measures taken to reduce the backlog of pending registration applications;

(ii) progress toward achieving reforms under this subsection; and

(iii) recommendations to improve the activities of the Agency pertaining to antimicrobial registrations.

(June 25, 1947, c. 125, § 3, as added Oct. 21, 1972, Pub.L. 92–516, § 2, 86 Stat. 979, and amended Nov. 28, 1975, Pub.L. 94–140, § 12, 89 Stat. 755; Sept. 30, 1978, Pub.L. 95–396, §§ 2(a), 3–8, 92 Stat. 820, 824–827; Oct. 25, 1988, Pub.L. 100–532, Title I, §§ 102(b), 103, Title VI, § 601(b)(1), Title VIII, § 801(b), 102 Stat. 2667, 2677, 2680; Nov. 28, 1990, Pub.L. 101–624, Title XIV, § 1492, 104 Stat. 3628; Dec. 13, 1991, Pub.L. 102–237, Title X, § 1006(a)(3), (b)(1), (2), (c), 105 Stat. 1894 to 1896; Aug. 3, 1996, Pub.L. 104–170, Title I, §§ 105(b), 106(b), Title II, §§ 210(b), (c)(1), (d), (e), (f)(2), 222 to 224, 231, 250, 110 Stat. 1491, 1494 to 1497, 1499, 1503, 1504, 1508, 1510; Jan. 23, 2004, Pub.L. 108–199, Div. G, Title V, § 501(b), 118 Stat. 419.)

## HISTORICAL AND STATUTORY NOTES

**Codifications**

Section 1006(c) of Pub.L. 102–237 provided that the phrase sought to be struck out of subsec. (c)(2)(D) of this section by section 102(b)(2)(A) of Pub.L. 100–532 is to be deemed to be "an end–use product", rather than "an end use product", as such phrase appeared in section 102(b)(2)(A) of Pub.L. 100–532.

**Effective and Applicability Provisions**

2004 Acts

Pub.L. 108–199, Div. G, Title V, § 501(h), Jan. 23, 2004, 118 Stat. 434, provided that: "Except as otherwise provided in this section and the amendments made by this section, this section and the amendments made by this section [enacting 7 U.S.C.A. § 136w–8, amending this section and 7 U.S.C.A. §§ 136a–1, 136x, 136y, and enacting provisions set out as a note under 7 U.S.C.A. § 136] take effect on the date that is 60 days after the date of enactment of this Act [Jan. 23, 2004]."

1991 Acts

Amendments by Pub.L. 102–237 effective Dec. 13, 1991, see section 1101(a) of Pub.L. 102–237, set out as a note under section 1421 of this title.

1988 Acts

Amendment by Pub.L. 100–532 effective on expiration of 60 days after October 25, 1988, see section 901 of Pub.L. 100–532, set out as a note under section 136 of this title.

1978 Acts

Section 2(b) of Pub.L. 95–396 provided that: "The amendment to section 3(c)(1)(D) of the Federal Insecticide, Fungicide, and Rodenticide Act [subsec. (c)(1)(D) of this section] made by this section shall apply with respect to all applications for registration approved after the date of enactment of this Act [Sept. 30, 1978]."

1972 Acts

Section effective at the close of Oct. 21, 1972, except if regulations are necessary for the implementation of any provision that becomes effective on Oct. 21, 1972, and continuation in effect of the provisions of subchapter I of this chapter and regulations thereunder as in effect prior to Oct. 21, 1972, until superseded by provisions of Pub.L. 92–516 and regulations thereunder, see section 4 of Pub.L. 92–516, set out as a note under section 136 of this title.

**Severability of Provisions**

If any provision of Pub.L. 101–624 or the application thereof to any person or circumstance is held invalid, such invalidity not to affect other provisions or applications of Pub.L. 101–624 which can be given effect without regard to the invalid provision or application, see section 2519 of Pub.L. 101–624, set out as a note under section 1421 of this title.

**Prior Provisions**

A prior section 3 of act June 25, 1947, was classified to section 135a of this title prior to amendment of act June 25, 1947, by Pub. L. 92–516.

**Biological Pesticide Handling Study**

Section 1498 of Pub.L. 101–624 provided that:

"(a) **Study.**—Not later than September 30, 1992, the National Academy of Sciences shall conduct a study of the biological control programs and registration procedures utilized by the Food and Drug Administration, the Animal and Plant Health Inspection Service, and the Environmental Protection Agency.

"(b) **Development of procedures.**—Not later than 1 year after the completion of the study under subsection (a), the agencies and offices described in such subsection shall develop and implement a common process for reviewing and approving biological control applications that are submitted to such agencies and offices that shall be based on the study conducted under such subsection and the recommendation of the National Academy of Sciences, and other public comment."

**Pesticides Labeling Program; Education, Study and Report to Congress**

Pub.L. 100–478, Title I, § 1010, Oct. 7, 1988, 102 Stat. 2313, provided that:

"(a) **Education.** The Administrator of the Environmental Protection Agency in cooperation with the Secretary of Agriculture and the Secretary of the Interior, promptly upon enactment of this Act [which was approved Oct. 7, 1988], shall conduct a program to inform and educate fully persons engaged in agricultural food and fiber commodity production of any proposed pesticide labeling program or requirements that may be imposed by the Administrator in compliance with the Endangered Species Act (16 U.S.C. 1531 et seq.) [section 1531 et seq. of Title 16, Conservation]. The Administrator also shall provide the public with notice of, and opportunity for comment on, the elements of any such program and requirements based on compliance with the Endangered Species Act, including (but not limited to) an identification of any pesticides affected by the program; an explanation of the restriction or prohibition on the user or applicator of any such pesticide; an identification of those geographic areas affected by any pesticide restriction or prohibition; an identification of the effects of any restricted or prohibited pesticide on endangered or threatened species; and an identification of the endangered or threatened species along with a general description of the geographic areas in which such species are located wherein the application of a pesticide will be restricted, prohibited, or its use otherwise limited, unless the Secretary of the Interior determines that the disclosure of such information may create a substantial risk of harm to such species or its habitat.

"(b) **Study.** The Administrator of the Environmental Protection Agency, jointly with the Secretary of Agriculture and the Secretary of the Interior, shall conduct a study to identify reasonable and prudent means available to the Administrator to implement the endangered species pesticides labeling program which would comply with the Endangered Species Act of 1973, as amended, and which would allow persons to continue production of agricultural food and fiber commodities. Such study shall include investigation by the Administrator of the best available methods to develop maps and the best available alternatives to mapping as means of identifying those circumstances in which use of pesticides may be restricted; identification of alternatives to prohibitions on pesticide use, including, but not limited to, alternative pesticides and application methods and other agricultural practices which can be used in lieu of any pesticides whose use may be restricted by the labeling program; examination of methods to improve coordination among the Environmental Protection Agency, Department of Agriculture, and Department of the Interior in administration of the labeling program; and analysis of the means of implementing the endangered species pesticides labeling program or alternatives to such a program, if any, to promote the conservation of endangered or threatened species and to minimize the impacts to persons engaged in agricultural food and fiber commodity production and other affected pesticide users and applicators.

"(c) **Report.** The Administrator of the Environmental Protection Agency in cooperation with the Secretary of Agriculture and the Secretary of the Interior shall submit a report within one year of the date of enactment of this Act [Oct. 7, 1988], presenting the results of the study conducted pursuant to subsection (b) of this section to the Committee on Merchant Marine and Fisheries and the Committee on Agriculture of the United States House of Representatives, and the Committee on Environment and Public Works and the Committee on Agriculture, Nutrition, and Forestry of the United States Senate."

[Committee on Merchant Marine and Fisheries of House of Representatives abolished and any reference in any provision of law enacted before Jan. 4, 1995, to the Committee on Merchant Marine and Fisheries of the House of Representatives treated as referring to the Committee on Agriculture of the House of Representatives, in the case of a provision of law relating to inspection of seafood or seafood products, the Committee on National Security of the House of Representatives, in the case of a provision of law relating to interoceanic canals, the Merchant Marine Academy and State Maritime Academies, or national security aspects of merchant marine, the Committee on Resources of the House of Representatives, in the case of a provision of law relating to fisheries, wildlife, international fishing agreements marine affairs (including coastal zone management) except for measures relating to oil and other pollution of navigable waters, or oceanography, the Committee on Science of the House of Representatives, in the case of a provision of law relating to marine research, and the Committee on Transportation and Infrastructure of the House of Representatives, in the case of a provision of law relating to a matter other than a matter described above, see section 1(b)(3) of Pub.L. 104–14, set out as a note preceding section 21 of Title 2, The Congress.]

## § 136a–1. Reregistration of registered pesticides

**[FIFRA § 4]**

**(a) General rule**

The Administrator shall reregister, in accordance with this section, each registered pesticide containing any active ingredient contained in any pesticide first registered before November 1, 1984, except for any pesticide as to which the Administrator has determined, after November 1, 1984, and before the effective date of this section, that—

(1) there are no outstanding data requirements; and

(2) the requirements of section 136a(c)(5) of this title have been satisfied.

**(b) Reregistration phases**

Reregistrations of pesticides under this section shall be carried out in the following phases:

(1) The first phase shall include the listing under subsection (c) of this section of the active ingredients of the pesticides that will be reregistered.

(2) The second phase shall include the submission to the Administrator under subsection (d) of this section of notices by registrants respecting their intention to seek reregistration, identification by registrants of missing and inadequate data for such pesticides, and commitments by registrants to replace such missing or inadequate data within the applicable time period.

(3) The third phase shall include submission to the Administrator by registrants of the information required under subsection (e) of this section.

(4) The fourth phase shall include an independent, initial review by the Administrator under subsection (f) of this section of submissions under phases two and three, identification of outstanding data requirements, and the issuance, as necessary, of requests for additional data.

(5) The fifth phase shall include the review by the Administrator under subsection (g) of this section of data submitted for reregistration and appropriate regulatory action by the Administrator.

**(c) Phase one**

**(1) Priority for reregistration**

For purposes of the reregistration of the pesticides described in subsection (a) of this section, the Administrator shall list the active ingredients of pesticides and shall give priority to, among others, active ingredients (other than active ingredients for which registration standards have been issued before the effective date of this section) that—

(A) are in use on or in food or feed and may result in postharvest residues;

(B) may result in residues of potential toxicological concern in potable ground water, edible fish, or shellfish;

(C) have been determined by the Administrator before the effective date of this section to have significant outstanding data requirements; or

(D) are used on crops, including in greenhouses and nurseries, where worker exposure is most likely to occur.

**(2) Reregistration lists**

For purposes of reregistration under this section, the Administrator shall by order—

(A) not later than 70 days after the effective date of this section, list pesticide active ingredients for which registration standards have been issued before such effective date;

(B) not later than 4 months after such effective date, list the first 150 pesticide active ingredients, as determined under paragraph (1);

(C) not later than 7 months after such effective date, list the second 150 pesticide active ingredients, as determined under paragraph (1); and

(D) not later than 10 months after such effective date, list the remainder of the pesticide active ingredients, as determined under paragraph (1).

Each list shall be published in the Federal Register.

**(3) Judicial review**

The content of a list issued by the Administrator under paragraph (2) shall not be subject to judicial review.

**(4) Notice to registrants**

On the publication of a list of pesticide active ingredients under paragraph (2), the Administrator shall send by certified mail to the registrants of the pesticides containing such active ingredients a notice of the time by which the registrants are to notify the Administrator under subsection (d) of this section whether the registrants intend to seek or not to seek reregistration of such pesticides.

**(d) Phase two**

**(1) In general**

The registrant of a pesticide that contains an active ingredient listed under subparagraph (B), (C), or (D) of subsection (c)(2) of this section shall submit to the Administrator, within the time period prescribed by paragraph (4), the notice described in paragraph (2) and any information, commitment, or offer described in paragraph (3).

**(2) Notice of intent to seek or not to seek reregistration**

(A) The registrant of a pesticide containing an active ingredient listed under subparagraph (B),

(C), or (D) of subsection (c)(2) of this section shall notify the Administrator by certified mail whether the registrant intends to seek or does not intend to seek reregistration of the pesticide.

**(B)** If a registrant submits a notice under subparagraph (A) of an intention not to seek reregistration of a pesticide, the Administrator shall publish a notice in the Federal Register stating that such a notice has been submitted.

**(3) Missing or inadequate data**

Each registrant of a pesticide that contains an active ingredient listed under subparagraph (B), (C), or (D) of subsection (c)(2) of this section and for which the registrant submitted a notice under paragraph (2) of an intention to seek reregistration of such pesticide shall submit to the Administrator—

**(A)** in accordance with regulations issued by the Administrator under section 136a of this title, an identification of—

**(i)** all data that are required by regulation to support the registration of the pesticide with respect to such active ingredient;

**(ii)** data that were submitted by the registrant previously in support of the registration of the pesticide that are inadequate to meet such regulations; and

**(iii)** data identified under clause (i) that have not been submitted to the Administrator; and

**(B)** either—

**(i)** a commitment to replace the data identified under subparagraph (A)(ii) and submit the data identified under subparagraph (A)(iii) within the applicable time period prescribed by paragraph (4)(B); or

**(ii)** an offer to share in the cost to be incurred by a person who has made a commitment under clause (i) to replace or submit the data and an offer to submit to arbitration as described by section 136a(c)(2)(B) of this title with regard to such cost sharing.

For purposes of a submission by a registrant under subparagraph (A)(ii), data are inadequate if the data are derived from a study with respect to which the registrant is unable to make the certification prescribed by subsection (e)(1)(G) of this section that the registrant possesses or has access to the raw data used in or generated by such study. For purposes of a submission by a registrant under such subparagraph, data shall be considered to be inadequate if the data are derived from a study submitted before January 1, 1970, unless it is demonstrated to the satisfaction of the Administrator that such data should be considered to support the registration of the pesticide that is to be reregistered.

**(4) Time periods**

**(A)** A submission under paragraph (2) or (3) shall be made—

**(i)** in the case of a pesticide containing an active ingredient listed under subsection (c)(2)(B) of this section, not later than 3 months after the date of publication of the listing of such active ingredient;

**(ii)** in the case of a pesticide containing an active ingredient listed under subsection (c)(2)(C) of this section, not later than 3 months after the date of publication of the listing of such active ingredient; and

**(iii)** in the case of a pesticide containing an active ingredient listed under subsection (c)(2)(D) of this section, not later than 3 months after the date of publication of the listing of such active ingredient.

On application, the Administrator may extend a time period prescribed by this subparagraph if the Administrator determines that factors beyond the control of the registrant prevent the registrant from complying with such period.

**(B)** A registrant shall submit data in accordance with a commitment entered into under paragraph (3)(B) within a reasonable period of time, as determined by the Administrator, but not more than 48 months after the date the registrant submitted the commitment. The Administrator, on application of a registrant, may extend the period prescribed by the preceding sentence by no more than 2 years if extraordinary circumstances beyond the control of the registrant prevent the registrant from submitting data within such prescribed period. Upon application of a registrant, the Administrator shall, in the case of a minor use, extend the deadline for the production of residue chemistry data under this subparagraph for data required solely to support that minor use until the final deadline for submission of data under this section for the other uses of the pesticide established as of August 3, 1996, if—

**(i)** the data to support other uses of the pesticide on a food are being provided;

**(ii)** the registrant, in submitting a request for such an extension provides a schedule, including interim dates to measure progress, to assure that the data production will be completed before the expiration of the extension period;

**(iii)** the Administrator has determined that such extension will not significantly delay the Administrator's schedule for issuing a reregistration eligibility determination required under this section; and

**(iv)** the Administrator has determined that based on existing data, such extension would not significantly increase the risk of any unreasonable adverse effect on the environment. If the Administrator grants an extension under this subparagraph, the Administrator shall monitor the development of the data and shall ensure that the registrant is meeting the schedule for the production of the data. If the Administrator determines that the registrant is not meeting or has not met the schedule for the production of such data, the Administrator may proceed in accordance with clause (iv) of section 136a(c)(2)(B) of this title or other provisions of this section, as appropriate, regarding the continued registration of the affected products with the minor use and shall inform the public of such action. Notwithstanding the provisions of this subparagraph, the Administrator may take action to modify or revoke the extension under this subparagraph if the Administrator determines that the extension for the minor use may cause an unreasonable adverse effect on the environment. In such circumstance, the Administrator shall provide written notice to the registrant revoking the extension of time for submission of data. Such data shall instead be due in accordance with the date then established by the Administrator for submission of the data.

**(5) Cancellation and removal**

**(A)** If the registrant of a pesticide does not submit a notice under paragraph (2) or (3) within the time prescribed by paragraph (4)(A), the Administrator shall issue a notice of intent to cancel the registration of such registrant for such pesticide and shall publish the notice in the Federal Register and allow 60 days for the submission of comments on the notice. On expiration of such 60 days, the Administrator, by order and without a hearing, may cancel the registration or take such other action, including extension of applicable time periods, as may be necessary to enable reregistration of such pesticide by another person.

**(B)(i)** If—

**(I)** no registrant of a pesticide containing an active ingredient listed under subsection (c)(2) of this section notifies the Administrator under paragraph (2) that the registrant intends to seek reregistration of any pesticide containing that active ingredient;

**(II)** no such registrant complies with paragraph (3)(A); or

**(III)** no such registrant makes a commitment under paragraph (3)(B) to replace or submit all data described in clauses (ii) and (iii) of paragraph (3)(A);

the Administrator shall publish in the Federal Register a notice of intent to remove the active ingredient from the list established under subsection (c)(2) of this section and a notice of intent to cancel the registrations of all pesticides containing such active ingredient and shall provide 60 days for comment on such notice.

**(ii)** After the 60–day period has expired, the Administrator, by order, may cancel any such registration without hearing, except that the Administrator shall not cancel a registration under this subparagraph if—

**(I)** during the comment period a person acquires the rights of the registrant in that registration;

**(II)** during the comment period that person furnishes a notice of intent to reregister the pesticide in accordance with paragraph (2); and

**(III)** not later than 120 days after the publication of the notice under this subparagraph, that person has complied with paragraph (3) and the fee prescribed by subsection (i)(1) of this section has been paid.

**(6) Suspensions and penalties**

The Administrator shall issue a notice of intent to suspend the registration of a pesticide in accordance with the procedures prescribed by section 136a(c)(2)(B)(iv) of this title if the Administrator determines that (A) progress is insufficient to ensure the submission of the data required for such pesticide under a commitment made under paragraph (3)(B) within the time period prescribed by paragraph (4)(B) or (B) the registrant has not submitted such data to the Administrator within such time period. If the registrant does not commit to support a specific minor use of the pesticide, but is supporting and providing data in a timely and adequate fashion to support uses of the pesticide on a food, or if all uses of the pesticide are nonfood uses and the registrant does not commit to support a specific minor use of the pesticide but is supporting and providing data in a timely and adequate fashion to support other nonfood uses of the pesticide, the Administrator, at the written request of the registrant, shall not take any action pursuant to this paragraph in regard to such unsupported minor use until the final deadline established as of August 3, 1996, for the submission of data under this section for the supported uses identified pursuant to this paragraph unless the Administrator determines that the absence of the data is significant enough to cause human health or environmental concerns. On such a determination the Administrator may refuse the request for extension by the registrant. Upon receipt of the request from the registrant, the Administrator shall publish in the Federal Register a notice of the receipt of the request and the effective date upon which the uses not being supported will be voluntarily deleted from the registration pursuant to section 136d(f)(1) of this title. If the Administrator grants an extension under this paragraph, the Administrator shall monitor the development of the data for the uses being supported and shall ensure that the registrant is meeting the schedule for the production of such data. If the Administrator determines that the registrant is not meeting or has not met the schedule for the production of such data, the Administrator may proceed in accordance with section 136a(c)(2)(B)(iv) of this title regarding the continued registration of the affected products with the minor and other uses and shall inform the public of such action in accordance with section 136d(f)(2) of this title. Notwithstanding this subparagraph, the Administrator may deny, modify, or revoke the temporary extension under this paragraph if the Administrator determines that the continuation of the minor use may cause an unreasonable adverse effect on the environment. In the event of modification or revocation, the Administrator shall provide, in writing, to the registrant a notice revoking the temporary extension and establish a new effective date by which the minor use shall be deleted from the registration.

**(e) Phase three**

**(1) Information about studies**

Each registrant of a pesticide that contains an active ingredient listed under subparagraph (B), (C), or (D) of subsection (c)(2) of this section who has submitted a notice under subsection (d)(2) of this section of an intent to seek the reregistration of such pesticide shall submit, in accordance with the guidelines issued under paragraph (4), to the Administrator—

**(A)** a summary of each study concerning the active ingredient previously submitted by the registrant in support of the registration of a pesticide containing such active ingredient and considered by the registrant to be adequate to meet the requirements of section 136a of this title and the regulations issued under such section;

**(B)** a summary of each study concerning the active ingredient previously submitted by the registrant in support of the registration of a pesticide containing such active ingredient that may not comply with the requirements of section 136a of this title and the regulations issued under such section but which the registrant asserts should be deemed to comply with such requirements and regulations;

**(C)** a reformat of the data from each study summarized under subparagraph (A) or (B) by the registrant concerning chronic dosing, oncogenicity, reproductive effects, mutagenicity, neurotoxicity, teratogenicity, or residue chemistry of the active ingredient that were submitted to the Administrator before January 1, 1982;

**(D)** where data described in subparagraph (C) are not required for the active ingredient by regulations issued under section 136a of this title, a reformat of acute and subchronic dosing data submitted by the registrant to the Administrator before January 1, 1982, that the registrant considers to be adequate to meet the requirements of section 136a of this title and the regulations issued under such section;

**(E)** an identification of data that are required to be submitted to the Administrator under section 136d(a)(2) of this title indicating an adverse effect of the pesticide;

**(F)** an identification of any other information available that in the view of the registrant supports the registration;

**(G)** a certification that the registrant or the Administrator possesses or has access to the raw data used in or generated by the studies that the registrant summarized under subparagraph (A) or (B);

**(H)** either—

**(i)** a commitment to submit data to fill each outstanding data requirement identified by the registrant; or

**(ii)** an offer to share in the cost of developing such data to be incurred by a person who has made a commitment under clause (i) to submit such data, and an offer to submit to arbitration as described by section 136a(c)(2)(B) of this title with regard to such cost sharing; and

**(I)** evidence of compliance with section 136a(c)(1)(D)(ii) of this title and regulations issued thereunder with regard to previously submitted data as if the registrant were now seeking the original registration of the pesticide.

A registrant who submits a certification under subparagraph (G) that is false shall be considered to have violated this subchapter and shall be subject to the penalties prescribed by section 136*l* of this title.

**(2) Time periods**

**(A)** The information required by paragraph (1) shall be submitted to the Administrator—

**(i)** in the case of a pesticide containing an active ingredient listed under subsection (c)(2)(B) of this section, not later than 12 months after the date of publication of the listing of such active ingredient;

**(ii)** in the case of a pesticide containing an active ingredient listed under subsection (c)(2)(C) of this section, not later than 12 months after the date of publication of the listing of such active ingredient; and

**(iii)** in the case of a pesticide containing an active ingredient listed under subsection (c)(2)(D) of this section, not later than 12 months after the date of publication of the listing of such active ingredient.

**(B)** A registrant shall submit data in accordance with a commitment entered into under paragraph (1)(H) within a reasonable period of time, as determined by the Administrator, but not more than 48 months after the date the registrant submitted the commitment under such paragraph. The Administrator, on application of a registrant, may extend the period prescribed by the preceding sentence by no more than 2 years if extraordinary circumstances beyond the control of the registrant prevent the registrant from submitting data within such prescribed period. Upon application of a registrant, the Administrator shall, in the case of a minor use, extend the deadline for the production of residue chemistry data under this subparagraph for data required solely to support that minor use until the final deadline for submission of data under this section for the other uses of the pesticide established as of August 3, 1996, if—

**(i)** the data to support other uses of the pesticide on a food are being provided;

**(ii)** the registrant, in submitting a request for such an extension provides a schedule, including interim dates to measure progress, to assure that the data production will be completed before the expiration of the extension period;

**(iii)** the Administrator has determined that such extension will not significantly delay the Administrator's schedule for issuing a reregistration eligibility determination required under this section; and

**(iv)** the Administrator has determined that based on existing data, such extension would not significantly increase the risk of any unreasonable adverse effect on the environment. If the Administrator grants an extension under this subparagraph, the Administrator shall monitor the development of the data and shall ensure that the registrant is meeting the schedule for the production of the data. If the Administrator determines that the registrant is not meeting or has not met the schedule for the production of such data, the Administrator may proceed in accordance with clause (iv) of section 136a(c)(2)(B) of this title or other provisions of this section, as appropriate, regarding the continued registration of the affected products with the minor use and shall inform the public of such action. Notwithstanding the provisions of this subparagraph, the Administrator may take action to modify or revoke the extension under this subparagraph if the Administrator determines that the extension for the minor use may cause an unreasonable adverse effect on the environment. In such circumstance, the Administrator shall provide written notice to the registrant revoking the extension of time for submission of data. Such data shall instead be due in accordance with the date then established by the Administrator for submission of the data.

**(3) Cancellation**

**(A)** If the registrant of a pesticide fails to submit the information required by paragraph (1) within the time prescribed by paragraph (2), the Administrator, by order and without hearing, shall cancel the registration of such pesticide. If the registrant does not commit to support a specific minor use of the pesticide, but is supporting and providing data in a timely and adequate fashion to support uses of the pesticide on a food, or if all uses of the pesticide are nonfood uses and the registrant does not commit to support a specific minor use of the pesticide but is supporting and providing data in a timely and adequate fashion to support other nonfood uses of the pesticide, the Administrator, at the written request of the registrant, shall not take any action pursuant to this subparagraph in regard to such unsupported minor use until the final deadline established as of August 3, 1996, for the submission of data under this section for the supported uses identified pursuant to this subparagraph unless the Administrator determines that the absence of the data is significant enough to cause human health or environmental concerns. On the basis of such determination, the Administrator may refuse the request for extension by the registrant. Upon receipt of the request from the registrant, the Administrator shall publish in the Federal Register a notice of the receipt of the request and the effective date upon which the uses not being supported will be voluntarily deleted from the registration pursuant to section 136d(f)(1) of this title. If the Administrator grants an extension under this subparagraph, the Administrator shall monitor the development of the data for the uses being supported and shall ensure that the registrant is meeting the schedule for the production of such data. If the Administrator determines that the registrant is not meeting or has not met the schedule for the production of such data, the Administrator may proceed in accordance with section 136a(c)(2)(B)(iv) of this title regarding the continued registration of the affected products with the minor and other uses and shall inform the public of such action in accordance with section 136d(f)(2) of this title. Notwithstanding this subparagraph, the Administrator may deny, modify, or revoke the temporary extension under this subparagraph if the Administrator determines that the continuation of the minor use may cause an unreasonable adverse effect on the environment. In the event of modification or revocation, the Administrator shall provide, in writing, to the registrant a notice revoking the temporary extension and establish a new effective date by which the minor use shall be deleted from the registration.

(B)(i) If the registrant of a pesticide submits the information required by paragraph (1) within the time prescribed by paragraph (2) and such information does not conform to the guidelines for submissions established by the Administrator, the Administrator shall determine whether the registrant made a good faith attempt to conform its submission to such guidelines.

(ii) If the Administrator determines that the registrant made a good faith attempt to conform its submission to such guidelines, the Administrator shall provide the registrant a reasonable period of time to make any necessary changes or corrections.

(iii)(I) If the Administrator determines that the registrant did not make a good faith attempt to conform its submission to such guidelines, the Administrator may issue a notice of intent to cancel the registration. Such a notice shall be sent to the registrant by certified mail.

(II) The registration shall be canceled without a hearing or further notice at the end of 30 days after receipt by the registrant of the notice unless during that time a request for a hearing is made by the registrant.

(III) If a hearing is requested, a hearing shall be conducted under section 136d(d) of this title, except that the only matter for resolution at the hearing shall be whether the registrant made a good faith attempt to conform its submission to such guidelines. The hearing shall be held and a determination made within 75 days after receipt of a request for hearing.

**(4) Guidelines**

(A) Not later than 1 year after the effective date of this section, the Administrator, by order, shall issue guidelines to be followed by registrants in—

(i) summarizing studies;

(ii) reformatting studies;

(iii) identifying adverse information; and

(iv) identifying studies that have been submitted previously that may not meet the requirements of section 136a of this title or regulations issued under such section, under paragraph (1).

(B) Guidelines issued under subparagraph (A) shall not be subject to judicial review.

**(5) Monitoring**

The Administrator shall monitor the progress of registrants in acquiring and submitting the data required under paragraph (1).

**(f) Phase four**

**(1) Independent review and identification of outstanding data requirements**

(A) The Administrator shall review the submissions of all registrants of pesticides containing a particular active ingredient under subsections (d)(3) and (e)(1) of this section to determine if such submissions identified all the data that are missing or inadequate for such active ingredient. To assist the review of the Administrator under this subparagraph, the Administrator may require a registrant seeking reregistration to submit complete copies of studies summarized under subsection (e)(1) of this section.

(B) The Administrator shall independently identify and publish in the Federal Register the outstanding data requirements for each active ingredient that is listed under subparagraph (B), (C), or (D) of subsection (c)(2) of this section and that is contained in a pesticide to be reregistered under this section. The Administrator, at the same time, shall issue a notice under section 136a(c)(2)(B) of this title for the submission of the additional data that are required to meet such requirements.

**(2) Time periods**

(A) The Administrator shall take the action required by paragraph (1)—

(i) in the case of a pesticide containing an active ingredient listed under subsection (c)(2)(B) of this section, not later than 18 months after the date of the listing of such active ingredient;

(ii) in the case of a pesticide containing an active ingredient listed under subsection (c)(2)(C) of this section, not later than 24 months after the date of the listing of such active ingredient; and

(iii) in the case of a pesticide containing an active ingredient listed under subsection (c)(2)(D) of this section, not later than 33 months after the date of the listing of such active ingredient.

(B) If the Administrator issues a notice to a registrant under paragraph (1)(B) for the submission of additional data, the registrant shall submit such data within a reasonable period of time, as determined by the Administrator, but not to exceed 48 months after the issuance of such notice. The Administrator, on application of a registrant, may extend the period prescribed by the preceding sentence by no more than 2 years if extraordinary circumstances beyond the control of the registrant prevent the registrant from submitting data within such prescribed period. Upon application of a registrant, the Administrator shall, in the case of a minor use, extend the deadline for the production of residue chemistry data under this subparagraph for data required solely to support that minor use until the final deadline for submission of data under this section for the other uses of the pesticide established as of August 3, 1996, if—

(i) the data to support other uses of the pesticide on a food are being provided;

**(ii)** the registrant, in submitting a request for such an extension provides a schedule, including interim dates to measure progress, to assure that the data production will be completed before the expiration of the extension period;

**(iii)** the Administrator has determined that such extension will not significantly delay the Administrator's schedule for issuing a reregistration eligibility determination required under this section; and

**(iv)** the Administrator has determined that based on existing data, such extension would not significantly increase the risk of any unreasonable adverse effect on the environment. If the Administrator grants an extension under this subparagraph, the Administrator shall monitor the development of the data and shall ensure that the registrant is meeting the schedule for the production of the data. If the Administrator determines that the registrant is not meeting or has not met the schedule for the production of such data, the Administrator may proceed in accordance with clause (iv) of section 136a(c)(2)(B) of this title or other provisions of this section, as appropriate, regarding the continued registration of the affected products with the minor use and shall inform the public of such action. Notwithstanding the provisions of this subparagraph, the Administrator may take action to modify or revoke the extension under this subparagraph if the Administrator determines that the extension for the minor use may cause an unreasonable adverse effect on the environment. In such circumstance, the Administrator shall provide written notice to the registrant revoking the extension of time for submission of data. Such data shall instead be due in accordance with the date then established by the Administrator for submission of the data.

**(3) Suspensions and penalties**

The Administrator shall issue a notice of intent to suspend the registration of a pesticide in accordance with the procedures prescribed by section 136a(c)(2)(B)(iv) of this title if the Administrator determines that (A) tests necessary to fill an outstanding data requirement for such pesticide have not been initiated within 1 year after the issuance of a notice under paragraph (1)(B), or (B) progress is insufficient to ensure submission of the data referred to in clause (A) within the time period prescribed by paragraph (2)(B) or the required data have not been submitted to the Administrator within such time period. If the registrant does not commit to support a specific minor use of the pesticide, but is supporting and providing data in a timely and adequate fashion to support uses of the pesticide on a food, or if all uses of the pesticide are nonfood uses and the registrant does not commit to support a specific minor use of the pesticide but is supporting and providing data in a timely and adequate fashion to support other nonfood uses of the pesticide, the Administrator, at the written request of the registrant, shall not take any action pursuant to this paragraph in regard to such unsupported minor use until the final deadline established as of August 3, 1996, for the submission of data under this section for the supported uses identified pursuant to this paragraph unless the Administrator determines that the absence of the data is significant enough to cause human health or environmental concerns. On such a determination the Administrator may refuse the request for extension by the registrant. Upon receipt of the request from the registrant, the Administrator shall publish in the Federal Register a notice of the receipt of the request and the effective date upon which the uses not being supported will be voluntarily deleted from the registration pursuant to section 136d(f)(1) of this title. If the Administrator grants an extension under this paragraph, the Administrator shall monitor the development of the data for the uses being supported and shall ensure that the registrant is meeting the schedule for the production of such data. If the Administrator determines that the registrant is not meeting or has not met the schedule for the production of such data, the Administrator may proceed in accordance with section 136a(c)(2)(B)(iv) of this title regarding the continued registration of the affected products with the minor and other uses and shall inform the public of such action in accordance with section 136d(f)(2) of this title. Notwithstanding this subparagraph, the Administrator may deny, modify, or revoke the temporary extension under this paragraph if the Administrator determines that the continuation of the minor use may cause an unreasonable adverse effect on the environment. In the event of modification or revocation, the Administrator shall provide, in writing, to the registrant a notice revoking the temporary extension and establish a new effective date by which the minor use shall be deleted from the registration.

**(g) Phase five**

**(1) Data review**

The Administrator shall conduct a thorough examination of all data submitted under this section concerning an active ingredient listed under subsection (c)(2) of this section and of all other available data found by the Administrator to be relevant.

**(2) Reregistration and other actions**

**(A) In general**

The Administrator shall make a determination as to eligibility for reregistration—

(i) for all active ingredients subject to reregistration under this section for which tolerances or exemptions from tolerances are required under the Federal Food, Drug, and Cosmetic Act (21 U.S.C. 301 et seq.), not later than the last date for tolerance reassessment established under section 408(q)(1)(C) of that Act (21 U.S.C. 346a(q)(1)(C)); and

(ii) for all other active ingredients subject to reregistration under this section, not later than October 3, 2008.

**(B) Product-specific data**

**(i) In general**

Before reregistering a pesticide, the Administrator shall obtain any needed product-specific data regarding the pesticide by use of section 136a(c)(2)(B) of this title and shall review such data within 90 days after its submission.

**(ii) Timing**

**(I) In general**

Subject to subclause (II), the Administrator shall require that data under this subparagraph be submitted to the Administrator not later than 8 months after a determination of eligibility under subparagraph (A) has been made for each active ingredient of the pesticide, unless the Administrator determines that a longer period is required for the generation of the data.

**(II) Extraordinary circumstances**

In the case of extraordinary circumstances, the Administrator may provide such a longer period, of not more than 2 additional years, for submission of data to the Administrator under this subparagraph.

(C) After conducting the review required by paragraph (1) for each active ingredient of a pesticide and the review required by subparagraph (B) of this paragraph, the Administrator shall determine whether to reregister a pesticide by determining whether such pesticide meets the requirements of section 136a(c)(5) of this title. If the Administrator determines that a pesticide is eligible to be reregistered, the Administrator shall reregister such pesticide within 6 months after the submission of the data concerning such pesticide under subparagraph (B).

**(D) Determination to not reregister**

**(i) In general**

If after conducting a review under paragraph (1) or subparagraph (B) of this paragraph the Administrator determines that a pesticide should not be reregistered, the Administrator shall take appropriate regulatory action.

**(ii) Timing for regulatory action**

Regulatory action under clause (i) shall be completed as expeditiously as possible.

**(E)** As soon as the Administrator has sufficient information with respect to the dietary risk of a particular active ingredient, but in any event no later than the time the Administrator makes a determination under subparagraph (C) or (D) with respect to pesticides containing a particular active ingredient, the Administrator shall—

(i) reassess each associated tolerance and exemption from the requirement for a tolerance issued under section 408 of the Federal Food, Drug, and Cosmetic Act (21 U.S.C. 346a);

(ii) determine whether such tolerance or exemption meets the requirements of that Act [21 U.S.C.A. § 301 et seq.];

(iii) determine whether additional tolerances or exemptions should be issued;

(iv) publish in the Federal Register a notice setting forth the determinations made under this subparagraph; and

(v) commence promptly such proceedings under this subchapter and section 408 of the Federal Food, Drug, and Cosmetic Act [21 U.S.C.A. § 346a] as are warranted by such determinations.

**(h) Compensation of data submitter**

If data that are submitted by a registrant under subsection (d), (e), (f), or (g) of this section are used to support the application of another person under section 136a of this title, the registrant who submitted such data shall be entitled to compensation for the use of such data as prescribed by section 136a(c)(1)(D) of this title. In determining the amount of such compensation, the fees paid by the registrant under this section shall be taken into account.

**(i) Fees**

**(1) Initial fee for food or feed use pesticide active ingredients**

The registrants of pesticides that contain an active ingredient that is listed under subparagraph (B), (C), or (D) of subsection (c)(2) of this section and that is an active ingredient of any pesticide registered for a major food or feed use shall collectively pay a fee of $50,000 on submission of information under paragraphs (2) and (3) of subsection (d) of this section for such ingredient.

**(2) Final fee for food or feed use pesticide active ingredients**

**(A)** The registrants of pesticides that contain an active ingredient that is listed under subparagraph

(B), (C), or (D) of subsection (c)(2) of this section and that is an active ingredient of any pesticide registered for a major food or feed use shall collectively pay a fee of $100,000—

**(i)** on submission of information for such ingredient under subsection (e)(1) of this section if data are reformatted under subsection (e)(1)(C) of this section; or

**(ii)** on submission of data for such ingredient under subsection (e)(2)(B) of this section if data are not reformatted under subsection (e)(1)(C) of this section.

**(B)** The registrants of pesticides that contain an active ingredient that is listed under subsection (c)(2)(A) of this section and that is an active ingredient of any pesticide registered for a major food or feed use shall collectively pay a fee of $150,000 at such time as the Administrator shall prescribe.

**(3) Fees for other pesticide active ingredients**

**(A)** The registrants of pesticides that contain an active ingredient that is listed under subparagraph (B), (C), or (D) of subsection (c)(2) of this section and that is not an active ingredient of any pesticide registered for a major food or feed use shall collectively pay fees in amounts determined by the Administrator. Such fees may not be less than one-half of, nor greater than, the fees required by paragraphs (1) and (2). A registrant shall pay such fees at the times corresponding to the times fees prescribed by paragraphs (1) and (2) are to be paid.

**(B)** The registrants of pesticides that contain an active ingredient that is listed under subsection (c)(2)(A) of this section and that is not an active ingredient of any pesticide that is registered for a major food or feed use shall collectively pay a fee of not more than $100,000 and not less than $50,000 at such time as the Administrator shall prescribe.

**(4) Reduction or waiver of fees for minor use and other pesticides**

**(A)** An active ingredient that is contained only in pesticides that are registered solely for agricultural or nonagricultural minor uses, or a pesticide the value or volume of use of which is small, shall be exempt from the fees prescribed by paragraph (3).

**(B)** The Administrator shall exempt any public health pesticide from the payment of the fee prescribed under paragraph (3) if, in consultation with the Secretary of Health and Human Services, the Administrator determines, based on information supplied by the registrant, that the economic return to the registrant from sales of the pesticide does not support the registration or reregistration of the pesticide.

**(C)** An antimicrobial active ingredient, the production level of which does not exceed 1,000,000 pounds per year, shall be exempt from the fees prescribed by paragraph (3). For purposes of this subparagraph, the term "antimicrobial active ingredient" means any active ingredient that is contained only in pesticides that are not registered for any food or feed use and that are—

**(i)** sanitizers intended to reduce the number of living bacteria or viable virus particles on inanimate surface or in water or air;

**(ii)** bacteriostats intended to inhibit the growth of bacteria in the presence of moisture;

**(iii)** disinfectants intended to destroy or irreversibly inactivate bacteria, fungi, or viruses on surfaces or inanimate objects;

**(iv)** sterilizers intended to destroy viruses and all living bacteria, fungi, and their spores on inanimate surfaces; or

**(v)** fungicides or fungistats.

**(D)(i)** Notwithstanding any other provision of this subsection, in the case of a small business registrant of a pesticide, the registrant shall pay a fee for the reregistration of each active ingredient of the pesticide that does not exceed an amount determined in accordance with this subparagraph.

**(ii)** If during the 3–year period prior to reregistration the average annual gross revenue of the registrant from pesticides containing such active ingredient is—

**(I)** less than $5,000,000, the registrant shall pay 0.5 percent of such revenue;

**(II)** $5,000,000 or more but less than $10,000,000, the registrant shall pay 1 percent of such revenue; or

**(III)** $10,000,000 or more, the registrant shall pay 1.5 percent of such revenue, but not more than $150,000.

**(iii)** For the purpose of this subparagraph, a small business registrant is a corporation, partnership, or unincorporated business that—

**(I)** has 150 or fewer employees; and

**(II)** during the 3–year period prior to reregistration, had an average annual gross revenue from chemicals that did not exceed $40,000,000.

**(5) Maintenance fee**

**(A) In general**

Subject to other provisions of this paragraph, each registrant of a pesticide shall pay an annual fee by January 15 of each year for each registration, except that no fee shall be charged for more than 200 registrations held by any registrant.

**(B)** In the case of a pesticide that is registered for a minor agricultural use, the Administrator may reduce or waive the payment of the fee imposed under this paragraph if the Administrator determines that the fee would significantly reduce the availability of the pesticide for the use.

(C) **Total amount of fees**

The amount of each fee prescribed under subparagraph (A) shall be adjusted by the Administrator to a level that will result in the collection under this paragraph of, to the extent practicable, an aggregate amount of—

(i) for fiscal year 2004, $26,000,000;

(ii) for fiscal year 2005, $27,000,000;

(iii) for fiscal year 2006, $27,000,000;

(iv) for fiscal year 2007, $21,000,000; and

(v) for fiscal year 2008, $15,000,000.

(D) **Maximum amount of fees for registrants**

The maximum annual fee payable under this paragraph by—

(i) a registrant holding not more than 50 pesticide registrations shall be—

(I) for fiscal year 2004, $84,000;

(II) for each of fiscal years 2005 and 2006, $87,000;

(III) for fiscal year 2007, $68,000; and

(IV) for fiscal year 2008, $55,000; and

(ii) a registrant holding over 50 registrations shall be—

(I) for fiscal year 2004, $145,000;

(II) for each of fiscal years 2005 and 2006, $151,000;

(III) for fiscal year 2007, $117,000; and

(IV) for fiscal year 2008, $95,000.

(E) **Maximum amount of fees for small businesses**

(i) **In general**

For a small business, the maximum annual fee payable under this paragraph by—

(I) a registrant holding not more than 50 pesticide registrations shall be—

(aa) for fiscal year 2004, $59,000;

(bb) for each of fiscal years 2005 and 2006, $61,000;

(cc) for fiscal year 2007, $48,000; and

(dd) for fiscal year 2008, $38,500; and

(II) a registrant holding over 50 pesticide registrations shall be—

(aa) for fiscal year 2004, $102,000;

(bb) for each of fiscal years 2005 and 2006, $106,000;

(cc) for fiscal year 2007, $82,000; and

(dd) for fiscal year 2008, $66,500.

(ii) **Definition of small business**

(I) **In general—**

In clause (i), the term "small business" means a corporation, partnership, or unincorporated business that—

(aa) has 500 or fewer employees; and

(bb) during the 3-year period prior to the most recent maintenance fee billing cycle, had an average annual global gross revenue from pesticides that did not exceed $60,000,000.

(II) **Affiliates**

(aa) **In general**

In the case of a business entity with 1 or more affiliates, the gross revenue limit under subclause (I)(bb) shall apply to the gross revenue for the entity and all of the affiliates of the entity, including parents and subsidiaries, if applicable.

(bb) **Affiliated persons**

For the purpose of item (aa), persons are affiliates of each other if, directly or indirectly, either person controls or has the power to control the other person, or a third person controls or has the power to control both persons.

(cc) **Indicia of control**

For the purpose of item (aa), indicia of control include interlocking management or ownership, identity of interests among family members, shared facilities and equipment, and common use of employees.

(F) The Administrator shall exempt any public health pesticide from the payment of the fee prescribed under paragraph (3) if, in consultation with the Secretary of Health and Humans[1] Services, the Administrator determines, based on information supplied by the registrant, that the economic return to the registrant from sales of the pesticide does not support the registration or reregistration of the pesticide.

(G) If any fee prescribed by this paragraph with respect to the registration of a pesticide is not paid by a registrant by the time prescribed, the Administrator, by order and without hearing, may cancel the registration.

(H) The authority provided under this paragraph shall terminate on September 30, 2008.

(6) **Other fees**

Except as provided in section 136x of this title, during the period beginning on October 25, 1988, and ending on September 30, 2010, the Administrator may not levy any other fees for the registration of a pesticide under this subchapter except as provided in paragraphs (1) through (5).

**(7) Apportionment**

**(A)** If two or more registrants are required to pay any fee prescribed by paragraph (1), (2), or (3) with respect to a particular active ingredient, the fees for such active ingredient shall be apportioned among such registrants on the basis of the market share in United States sales of the active ingredient for the 3 calendar years preceding the date of payment of such fee, except that—

**(i)** small business registrants that produce the active ingredient shall pay fees in accordance with paragraph (4)(C); and

**(ii)** registrants who have no market share but who choose to reregister a pesticide containing such active ingredient shall pay the lesser of—

**(I)** 15 percent of the reregistration fee; or

**(II)** a proportionate amount of such fee based on the lowest percentage market share held by any registrant active in the marketplace.

In no event shall registrants who have no market share but who choose to reregister a pesticide containing such active ingredient collectively pay more than 25 percent of the total active ingredient reregistration fee.

**(B)** The Administrator, by order, may require any registrant to submit such reports as the Administrator determines to be necessary to allow the Administrator to determine and apportion fees under this subsection, to determine the registrant's eligibility for a reduction or waiver of a fee, to determine the volume usage for public health pesticides.

**(C)** If any such report is not submitted by a registrant after receiving notice of such report requirement, or if any fee prescribed by this subsection (other than paragraph (5)) for an active ingredient is not paid by a registrant to the Administrator by the time prescribed under this subsection, the Administrator, by order and without hearing, may cancel each registration held by such registrant of a pesticide containing the active ingredient with respect to which the fee is imposed. The Administrator shall reapportion the fee among the remaining registrants and notify the registrants that the registrants are required to pay to the Administrator any unpaid balance of the fee within 30 days after receipt of such notice.

**(j) Exemption of certain registrants**

The requirements of subsections (d), (e), (f), and (i) of this section (other than subsection (i)(5) of this section) regarding data concerning an active ingredient and fees for review of such data shall not apply to any person who is the registrant of a pesticide to the extent that, under section 136a(c)(2)(D) of this title, the person would not be required to submit or cite such data to obtain an initial registration of such pesticide.

**(k) Reregistration and expedited processing fund**

**(1) Establishment**

There shall be established in the Treasury of the United States a reregistration and expedited processing fund which shall be known as the Reregistration and Expedited Processing Fund.

**(2) Source and use**

**(A)** All moneys derived from fees collected by the Administrator under subsection (i) of this section shall be deposited in the fund and shall be available to the Administrator, without fiscal year limitation, specifically to offset the costs of reregistration and expedited processing of the applications specified in paragraph (3). Such moneys derived from fees may not be expended in any fiscal year to the extent such moneys derived from fees would exceed money appropriated for use by the Administrator and expended in such year for such costs of reregistration and expedited processing of such applications. The Administrator shall, prior to expending any such moneys derived from fees—

**(i)** effective October 1, 1997, adopt specific and cost accounting rules and procedures as approved by the General Accounting Office and the Inspector General of the Environmental Protection Agency to ensure that moneys derived from fees are allocated solely to the costs of reregistration and expedited processing of the applications specified in paragraph (3) in the same portion as appropriated funds;

**(ii)** prohibit the use of such moneys derived from fees to pay for any costs other than those necessary to achieve reregistration and expedited processing of the applications specified in paragraph (3); and

**(iii)** ensure that personnel and facility costs associated with the functions to be carried out under this paragraph do not exceed agency averages for comparable personnel and facility costs.

**(B)** The Administrator shall also—

**(i)** complete the review of unreviewed reregistration studies required to support the reregistration eligibility decisions scheduled for completion in accordance with subsection (*l*)(2) of this section; and

**(ii)** contract for such outside assistance as may be necessary for review of required studies, using a generally accepted competitive process for the selection of vendors of such assistance.

(3) **Review of inert ingredients; expedited processing of similar applications**

(A) The Administrator shall use for each of the fiscal years 2004 through 2006, approximately $3,300,000, and for each of fiscal years 2007 and 2008, between ⅛ and ⅐, of the maintenance fees collected in such fiscal year to obtain sufficient personnel and resources—

(i) to review and evaluate new inert ingredients; and

(ii) To ensure the expedited processing and review of any application that—

(I) proposes the initial or amended registration of an end-use pesticide that, if registered as proposed, would be identical or substantially similar in composition and labeling to a currently-registered pesticide identified in the application, or that would differ in composition and labeling from any such currently-registered pesticide only in ways that would not significantly increase the risk of unreasonable adverse effects on the environment;

(II) proposes an amendment to the registration of a registered pesticide that does not require scientific review of data; or

(III) proposes the initial or amended registration of an end use pesticide that, if registered as proposed, would be used for a public health pesticide.

(B) Any amounts made available under subparagraph (A) shall be used to obtain sufficient personnel and resources to carry out the activities described in such subparagraph that are in addition to the personnel and resources available to carry out such activities on October 25, 1988.

(C) So long as the Administrator has not met the time frames specified in clause (ii) of section 136a(c)(3)(B) of this title with respect to any application subject to section 136a(c)(3)(B) of this title that was received prior to August 3, 1996, the Administrator shall use the full amount of the fees specified in subparagraph (A) for the purposes specified therein. Once all applications subject to section 136a(c)(3)(B) of this title that were received prior to August 3, 1996, have been acted upon, no limitation shall be imposed by the preceding sentence of this subparagraph so long as the Administrator meets the time frames specified in clause (ii) of section 136a(c)(3)(B) of this title on 90 percent of affected applications in a fiscal year. Should the Administrator not meet such time frames in a fiscal year, the limitations imposed by the first sentence of this subparagraph shall apply until all overdue applications subject to section 136a(c)(3)(B) of this title have been acted upon.

(4) **Unused funds**

Money in the fund not currently needed to carry out this section shall be—

(A) maintained on hand or on deposit;

(B) invested in obligations of the United States or guaranteed thereby; or

(C) invested in obligations, participations, or other instruments that are lawful investments for fiduciary, trust, or public funds.

(5) **Accounting and performance**

The Administrator shall take all steps necessary to ensure that expenditures from fees authorized by subsection (i)(5)(C)(ii) of this section are used only to carry out the goals established under subsection (*l*) of this section. The Reregistration and Expedited Processing Fund shall be designated as an Environmental Protection Agency component for purposes of section 3515(c) of Title 31. The annual audit required under section 3521 of such title of the financial statements of activities under this subchapter under section 3515(b) of such title shall include an audit of the fees collected under subsection (i)(5)(C) of this section and disbursed, of the amount appropriated to match such fees, and of the Administrator's attainment of performance measures and goals established under subsection (*l*) of this section. Such an audit shall also include a review of the reasonableness of the overhead allocation and adequacy of disclosures of direct and indirect costs associated with carrying out the reregistration and expedited processing of the applications specified in paragraph (3), and the basis for and accuracy of all costs paid with moneys derived from such fees. The Inspector General shall conduct the annual audit and report the findings and recommendations of such audit to the Administrator and to the Committees on Agriculture of the House of Representatives and the Senate. The cost of such audit shall be paid for out of the fees collected under subsection (i)(5)(C) of this section.

(*l*) **Performance measures and goal**

The Administrator shall establish and publish annually in the Federal Register performance measures and goals. Such measures and goals shall include—

(1) the number of products reregistered, canceled, or amended, the status of reregistration, the number and type of data requests under section 136a(c)(2)(B) of this title issued to support product reregistration by active ingredient, the progress in reducing the number of unreviewed, required reregistration studies, the aggregate status of tolerances reassessed, and the number of applications for registration submitted under subsection (k)(3) of this section that were approved or disapproved;

(2) the future schedule for reregistrations, including the projection for such schedules that will be issued under subsection (g)(2)(A) and (B) of this section in the current fiscal year and the succeeding fiscal year; and

(3) the projected year of completion of the reregistrations under this section.

### (m) Judicial review

Any failure of the Administrator to take any action required by this section shall be subject to judicial review under the procedures prescribed by section 136n(b) of this title.

### (n) Authorization of funds to develop public health data

#### (1) "Secretary defined"

For the purposes of this section, "Secretary" means the Secretary of Health and Human Services, acting through the Public Health Service.

#### (2) Consultation

In the case of a pesticide registered for use in public health programs for vector control or for other uses the Administrator determines to be human health protection uses, the Administrator shall, upon timely request by the registrant or any other interested person, or on the Administrator's own initiative may, consult with the Secretary prior to taking final action to suspend registration under section 136a(c)(2)(B)(iv) of this title, or cancel a registration under section 136a–1, 136d(e), or 136d(f) of this title. In consultation with the Secretary, the Administrator shall prescribe the form and content of requests under this section.

#### (3) Benefits to support family

The Administrator, after consulting with the Secretary, shall make a determination whether the potential benefits of continued use of the pesticide for public health or health protection purposes are of such significance as to warrant a commitment by the Secretary to conduct or to arrange for the conduct of the studies required by the Administrator to support continued registration under section 136a of this title or reregistration under this section.

#### (4) Additional time

If the Administrator determines that such a commitment is warranted and in the public interest, the Administrator shall notify the Secretary and shall, to the extent necessary, amend a notice issued under section 136a(c)(2)(B) of this title to specify additional reasonable time periods for submission of the data.

#### (5) Arrangements

The Secretary shall make such arrangements for the conduct of required studies as the Secretary finds necessary and appropriate to permit submission of data in accordance with the time periods prescribed by the Administrator. Such arrangements may include Public Health Service intramural research activities, grants, contracts, or cooperative agreements with academic, public health, or other organizations qualified by experience and training to conduct such studies.

#### (6) Support

The Secretary may provide for support of the required studies using funds authorized to be appropriated under this section, the Public Health Service Act [42 U.S.C.A. § 201 et seq.], or other appropriate authorities. After a determination is made under subsection (d) of this section, the Secretary shall notify the Committees on Appropriations of the House of Representatives and the Senate of the sums required to conduct the necessary studies.

#### (7) Authorization of appropriations

There is authorized to be appropriated to carry out the purposes of this section $12,000,000 for fiscal year 1997, and such sums as may be necessary for succeeding fiscal years

(June 25, 1947, c. 125, § 4, formerly § 3A, as added and renumbered § 4, Oct. 25, 1988, Pub.L. 100–532, Title I, § 102(a), Title VIII, § 801(q)(2)(A), 102 Stat. 2655, 2683, and amended Nov. 28, 1990, Pub.L. 101–624, Title XIV, § 1493, 104 Stat. 3628; Dec. 13, 1991, Pub.L. 102–237, Title X, § 1006(a)(4), (e), (f), 105 Stat. 1895 to 1897; Aug. 3, 1996, Pub.L. 104–170, Title I, § 103, Title II, §§ 210(c)(2), (f)(1), 232, 237, Title V, § 501, 110 Stat. 1490, 1496, 1498, 1508, 1509, 1536; Pub.L. 107–73, Title III, Nov. 26, 2001, 115 Stat. 686; Feb. 20, 2003, Pub. L. 108–7, Div. K, Title III, 117 Stat. 513; Jan. 23, 2004, Pub.L. 108–199, Div. G, Title V, § 501(c), (d)(1), (e), 118 Stat. 419, 422 .)

[1] So in original. Probably should be "Human".

## HISTORICAL AND STATUTORY NOTES

### References in Text

The effective date of this section, referred to in subsec. (c), is 60 days after Oct. 25, 1988, see section 901 of Pub.L. 100–532, set out as a note under section 136 of this title.

Section 136a(c)(1)(D), referred to in subsecs. (e)(1)(I) and (h), was redesignated section 136a(c)(1)(F) of this title by Pub.L. 102–237, Title X, § 1006(a)(3)(b), Dec. 13, 1991, 105 Stat. 1894.

The Federal Food, Drug, and Cosmetic Act, referred to in subsec. (g)(2)(A) and (E), is Act June 25, 1938, c. 675, 52 Stat. 1040, as amended, which is classified generally to chapter 9 of Title 21, 21 U.S.C.A. § 301 et seq. For complete classification, see 21 U.S.C.A. § 301 and Tables.

The Public Health Service Act, referred to in subsec. (n)(6), is Act July 1, 1944, c. 373, 58 Stat. 682, as amended, which is classified generally to chapter 6A (section 201 et seq.) of Title 42, The Public Health and Welfare. For complete classification of this Act to the Code, see Short Title note set out under section 201 of Title 42 and Tables.

**Codifications**

Section 501(c)(2) of Pub.L. 108–199, which directed that "(7 U.S.C. 136(a)–1(i)(5)(C))" be amended, was executed to subsec. (i)(5)(C) of this section as the probable intent of Congress.

**Effective and Applicability Provisions**

2004 Acts

Amendments made by section 501 of Pub.L. 108–199 effective 60 days after Jan. 23, 2004, see Pub.L. 108–199, § 501(h), set out as a note under 7 U.S.C.A. § 136a.

1991 Acts

Amendments by Pub.L. 102–237 effective Dec. 13, 1991, see section 1101(a) of Pub.L. 102–237, set out as a note under section 1421 of this title.

1988 Acts

Section effective on expiration of 60 days after October 25, 1988, see section 901 of Pub.L. 100–532, set out as a note under section 136 of this title.

**Severability of Provisions**

If any provision of Pub.L. 101–624 or the application thereof to any person or circumstance is held invalid, such invalidity not to affect other provisions or applications of Pub.L. 101–624 which can be given effect without regard to the invalid provision or application, see section 2519 of Pub.L. 101–624, set out as a note under section 1421 of this title.

**Prior Provisions**

A prior section 4 of the Federal Insecticide, Fungicide, and Rodenticide Act was transferred by Pub.L. 100–532, Title VIII, § 801(q)(1)(A), (B), Oct. 25, 1988, 102 Stat. 2683, as follows:

1. Subsections (a), (b), and (c) were transferred to section 136i of this title and are set out as subsections (a), (b), and (c) thereof.

2. The section heading was deleted.

Another prior section 4 of Act June 25, 1947, was classified to section 135b of this title prior to amendment of Act June 25, 1947, by Pub.L. 92–516.

**Maximum Annual Fee Payable Adjustment**

Pub.L. 108–11, Title II, Apr. 16, 2003, 117 Stat. 603, provided that: "Within 30 days of enactment of this Act [within 30 days of Apr. 16, 2003], the Administrator of the Environmental Protection Agency shall adjust each 'maximum annual fee payable' pursuant to 7 U.S.C. 136a–1(i)(5)(D) and (E) [subsec. (i)(5)(D) and (E) of this section] in a manner such that maintenance fee collections made to reach the level authorized in division K of Public Law 108–7 [Pub.L. 108–7, Div. K, Feb. 20, 2003, 117 Stat. 474; see Tables for complete classification] shall be established in the same proportion as those maintenance fee collections authorized in Public Law 107–73 [Pub.L. 107–73, Nov. 26, 2001, 115 Stat. 651; see Tables for complete classification]."

## § 136b. Transferred

### [FIFRA former § 4]

### HISTORICAL AND STATUTORY NOTES

**Codifications**

Section, June 25, 1947, c. 125, § 4, as added Oct. 21, 1972, Pub.L. 92–516, § 2, 86 Stat. 983, and amended Nov. 28, 1975, Pub.L. 94–140, §§ 5, 11, 89 Stat. 753, 754; Sept. 30, 1978, Pub.L. 95–396, § 9, 92 Stat. 827; Oct. 25, 1988, Pub.L. 100–532, Title VIII, § 801(c), (q)(1)(B), 102 Stat. 2681, 2683, which related to use of restricted use pesticides and certification of applicators, was transferred to section 136i(a) to (c) of this title by Pub.L. 100–532, Title VIII, § 801(q)(1)(A), Oct. 25, 1988, 102 Stat. 2683.

## § 136c. Experimental use permits

### [FIFRA § 5]

**(a) Issuance**

Any person may apply to the Administrator for an experimental use permit for a pesticide. The Administrator shall review the application. After completion of the review, but not later than one hundred and twenty days after receipt of the application and all required supporting data, the Administrator shall either issue the permit or notify the applicant of the Administrator's determination not to issue the permit and the reasons therefor. The applicant may correct the application or request a waiver of the conditions for such permit within thirty days of receipt by the applicant of such notification. The Administrator may issue an experimental use permit only if the Administrator determines that the applicant needs such permit in order to accumulate information necessary to register a pesticide under section 136a of this title. An application for an experimental use permit may be filed at any time.

**(b) Temporary tolerance level**

If the Administrator determines that the use of a pesticide may reasonably be expected to result in any residue on or in food or feed, the Administrator may establish a temporary tolerance level for the residue of the pesticide before issuing the experimental use permit.

**(c) Use under permit**

Use of a pesticide under an experimental use permit shall be under the supervision of the Administrator, and shall be subject to such terms and conditions and be for such period of time as the Administrator may prescribe in the permit.

**(d) Studies**

When any experimental use permit is issued for a pesticide containing any chemical or combination of chemicals which has not been included in any previously registered pesticide, the Administrator may specify that studies be conducted to detect whether the use of the pesticide under the permit may cause unreasonable adverse effects on the environment. All results of such studies shall be reported to the Administrator before such pesticide may be registered under section 136a of this title.

**(e) Revocation**

The Administrator may revoke any experimental use permit, at any time, if the Administrator finds that its terms or conditions are being violated, or that its terms and conditions are inadequate to avoid unreasonable adverse effects on the environment.

**(f) State issuance of permits**

Notwithstanding the foregoing provisions of this section, the Administrator shall, under such terms and conditions as the Administrator may by regulations prescribe, authorize any State to issue an experimental use permit for a pesticide. All provisions of section 136i of this title relating to State plans shall apply with equal force to a State plan for the issuance of experimental use permits under this section.

**(g) Exemption for agricultural research agencies**

Notwithstanding the foregoing provisions of this section, the Administrator may issue an experimental use permit for a pesticide to any public or private agricultural research agency or educational institution which applies for such permit. Each permit shall not exceed more than a one-year period or such other specific time as the Administrator may prescribe. Such permit shall be issued under such terms and conditions restricting the use of the pesticide as the Administrator may require. Such pesticide may be used only by such research agency or educational institution for purposes of experimentation.

(June 25, 1947, c. 125, § 5, as added Oct. 21, 1972, Pub.L. 92–516, § 2, 86 Stat. 983, and amended Nov. 28, 1975, Pub.L. 94–140, § 10, 89 Stat. 754; Sept. 30, 1978, Pub.L. 95–396, § 10, 92 Stat. 828; Oct. 25, 1988, Pub.L. 100–532, Title VIII, § 801(d), (q)(1)(D), 102 Stat. 2681, 2683; Dec. 13, 1991, Pub.L. 102–237, Title X, § 1006(b)(1), 105 Stat. 1895.)

### HISTORICAL AND STATUTORY NOTES

**Effective and Applicability Provisions**

1991 Acts

Amendment by section 1006(b)(1) of Pub.L. 102–237 effective Dec. 13, 1991, see section 1101(a) of Pub.L. 102–237, set out as a note under section 1421 of this title.

1988 Acts

Amendment by Pub.L. 100–532 effective on expiration of 60 days after October 25, 1988, see section 901 of Pub.L. 100–532, set out as a note under section 136 of this title.

**1972 Acts**

Section effective at the close of Oct. 21, 1972, except if regulations are necessary for the implementation of any provision that becomes effective on Oct. 21, 1972, and continuation in effect of the provisions of subchapter I of this chapter and regulations thereunder as in effect prior to Oct. 21, 1972, until superseded by provisions of Pub.L. 92–516 and regulations thereunder, see section 4 of Pub.L. 92–516, set out as a note under section 136 of this title.

**Prior Provisions**

A prior section 5 of Act June 25, 1947, was classified to section 135c of this title prior to amendment of Act June 25, 1947, by Pub.L.92–516.

## § 136d. Administrative review; suspension

**[FIFRA § 6]**

**(a) Existing stocks and information**

**(1) Existing stocks**

The Administrator may permit the continued sale and use of existing stocks of a pesticide whose registration is suspended or canceled under this section, or section 136a or 136a–1 of this title, to such extent, under such conditions, and for such uses as the Administrator determines that such sale or use is not inconsistent with the purposes of this subchapter.

**(2) Information**

If at any time after the registration of a pesticide the registrant has additional factual information regarding unreasonable adverse effects on the environment of the pesticide, the registrant shall submit such information to the Administrator.

**(b) Cancellation and change in classification**

If it appears to the Administrator that a pesticide or its labeling or other material required to be submitted does not comply with the provisions of this subchapter or, when used in accordance with widespread and commonly recognized practice, generally causes unreasonable adverse effects on the environment, the Administrator may issue a notice of the Administrator's intent either—

(1) to cancel its registration or to change its classification together with the reasons (including the factual basis) for the Administrator's action, or

(2) to hold a hearing to determine whether or not its registration should be canceled or its classification changed.

Such notice shall be sent to the registrant and made public. In determining whether to issue any such notice, the Administrator shall include among those factors to be taken into account the impact of the action proposed in such notice on production and prices of agricultural commodities, retail food prices, and otherwise on the agricultural economy. At least 60 days prior to sending such notice to the registrant or making public such notice, whichever occurs first, the Administrator shall provide the Secretary of Agriculture with a copy of such notice and an analysis of such impact on the agricultural economy. If the Secretary comments in writing to the Administrator regarding the notice and analysis within 30 days after receiving them, the Administrator shall publish in the Federal Register (with the notice) the comments of the Secretary and the response of the Administrator with regard to the Secretary's comments. If the Secretary does not comment in writing to the Administrator regarding the notice and analysis within 30 days after receiving them, the Administrator may notify the registrant and make public the notice at any time after such 30-day period notwithstanding the foregoing 60-day time requirement. The time requirements imposed by the preceding 3 sentences may be waived or modified to the extent agreed upon by the Administrator and the Secretary. Notwithstanding any other provision of this subsection and section 136w(d) of this title, in the event that the Administrator determines that suspension of a pesticide registration is necessary to prevent an imminent hazard to human health, then upon such a finding the Administrator may waive the requirement of notice to and consultation with the Secretary of Agriculture pursuant to this subsection and of submission to the Scientific Advisory Panel pursuant to section 136w(d) of this title and proceed in accordance with subsection (c) of this section. When a public health use is affected, the Secretary of Health and Human Services should provide available benefits and use information, or an analysis thereof, in accordance with the procedures followed and subject to the same conditions as the Secretary of Agriculture in the case of agricultural pesticides. The proposed action shall become final and effective at the end of 30 days from receipt by the registrant, or publication, of a notice issued under paragraph (1), whichever occurs later, unless within that time either (i) the registrant makes the necessary corrections, if possible, or (ii) a request for a hearing is made by a person adversely affected by the notice. In the event a hearing is held pursuant to such a request or to the Administrator's determination under paragraph (2), a decision pertaining to registration or classification issued after completion of such hearing shall be final. In taking any final action under this subsection, the Administrator shall consider restricting a pesticide's use or uses as an alternative to cancellation and shall fully explain the reasons for these restrictions, and shall include among those factors to be taken into account the impact of such final action on production and prices of agricultural commodities, retail food prices, and otherwise on the agricultural economy, and the Administrator shall publish in the Federal Register an analysis of such impact.

**(c) Suspension**

**(1) Order**

If the Administrator determines that action is necessary to prevent an imminent hazard during the time required for cancellation or change in classification proceedings, the Administrator may, by order, suspend the registration of the pesticide immediately. Except as provided in paragraph (3), no order of suspension may be issued under this subsection unless the Administrator has issued, or at the same time issues, a notice of intention to cancel the registration or change the classification of the pesticide under subsection (b) of this section. Except as provided in paragraph (3), the Administrator shall notify the registrant prior to issuing any suspension order. Such notice shall include findings pertaining to the question of "imminent hazard". The registrant shall then have an opportunity, in accordance with the provisions of paragraph (2), for an expedited hearing before the Administrator on the question of whether an imminent hazard exists.

**(2) Expedite hearing**

If no request for a hearing is submitted to the Administrator within five days of the registrant's receipt of the notification provided for by paragraph (1), the suspension order may be issued and shall take effect and shall not be reviewable by a court. If a hearing is requested, it shall commence within five days of the receipt of the request for such hearing unless the registrant and the Administrator agree that it shall commence at a later time. The hearing shall be held in accordance with the provisions of subchapter II of chapter 5 of Title 5, except that the presiding officer need not be a certified administrative law judge. The presiding officer shall have ten days from the conclusion of the presentation of evidence to submit recommended findings and conclusions to the Administrator, who shall then have seven days to render a final order on the issue of suspension.

**(3) Emergency order**

Whenever the Administrator determines that an emergency exists that does not permit the Administrator to hold a hearing before suspending, the Administrator may issue a suspension order in advance of notification to the registrant. The Administrator may issue an emergency order under this paragraph before issuing a notice of intention to cancel the registration or change the classification of the pesticide under subsection (b) of this section and the Administrator shall proceed to issue the notice under subsection (b) of this section within 90 days of issuing an emergency order. If the Administrator does not issue a notice under subsection (b) of this section within 90 days of issuing an emergency order, the emergency order shall expire. In the case of an emergency order, paragraph (2) shall apply except that (A) the order of suspension shall be in effect pending the expeditious completion of the remedies provided by that paragraph and the issuance of a final order on suspension, and (B) no party other than the registrant and the Administrator shall participate except that any person adversely affected may file briefs within the time allotted by the Agency's rules. Any person so filing briefs shall be considered a party to such proceeding for the purposes of section 136n(b) of this title.

#### (4) Judicial review

A final order on the question of suspension following a hearing shall be reviewable in accordance with section 136n of this title, notwithstanding the fact that any related cancellation proceedings have not been completed. Any order of suspension entered prior to a hearing before the Administrator shall be subject to immediate review in an action by the registrant or other interested person with the concurrence of the registrant in an appropriate district court, solely to determine whether the order of suspension was arbitrary, capricious or an abuse of discretion, or whether the order was issued in accordance with the procedures established by law. The effect of any order of the court will be only to stay the effectiveness of the suspension order, pending the Administrator's final decision with respect to cancellation or change in classification. This action may be maintained simultaneously with any administrative review proceedings under this section. The commencement of proceedings under this paragraph shall not operate as a stay of order, unless ordered by the court.

### (d) Public hearings and scientific review

In the event a hearing is requested pursuant to subsection (b) of this section or determined upon by the Administrator pursuant to subsection (b) of this section, such hearing shall be held after due notice for the purpose of receiving evidence relevant and material to the issues raised by the objections filed by the applicant or other interested parties, or to the issues stated by the Administrator, if the hearing is called by the Administrator rather than by the filing of objections. Upon a showing of relevance and reasonable scope of evidence sought by any party to a public hearing, the Hearing Examiner shall issue a subpena to compel testimony or production of documents from any person. The Hearing Examiner shall be guided by the principles of the Federal Rules of Civil Procedure in making any order for the protection of the witness or the content of documents produced and shall order the payment of reasonable fees and expenses as a condition to requiring testimony of the witness. On contest, the subpena may be enforced by an appropriate United States district court in accordance with the principles stated herein. Upon the request of any party to a public hearing and when in the Hearing Examiner's judgment it is necessary or desirable, the Hearing Examiner shall at any time before the hearing record is closed refer to a Committee of the National Academy of Sciences the relevant questions of scientific fact involved in the public hearing. No member of any committee of the National Academy of Sciences established to carry out the functions of this section shall have a financial or other conflict of interest with respect to any matter considered by such committee. The Committee of the National Academy of Sciences shall report in writing to the Hearing Examiner within 60 days after such referral on these questions of scientific fact. The report shall be made public and shall be considered as part of the hearing record. The Administrator shall enter into appropriate arrangements with the National Academy of Sciences to assure an objective and competent scientific review of the questions presented to Committees of the Academy and to provide such other scientific advisory services as may be required by the Administrator for carrying out the purposes of this subchapter. As soon as practicable after completion of the hearing (including the report of the Academy) but not later than 90 days thereafter, the Administrator shall evaluate the data and reports before the Administrator and issue an order either revoking the Administrator's notice of intention issued pursuant to this section, or shall issue an order either canceling the registration, changing the classification, denying the registration, or requiring modification of the labeling or packaging of the article. Such order shall be based only on substantial evidence of record of such hearing and shall set forth detailed findings of fact upon which the order is based.

### (e) Conditional registration

**(1)** The Administrator shall issue a notice of intent to cancel a registration issued under section 136a(c)(7) of this title if (A) the Administrator, at any time during the period provided for satisfaction of any condition imposed, determines that the registrant has failed to initiate and pursue appropriate action toward fulfilling any condition imposed, or (B) at the end of the period provided for satisfaction of any condition imposed, that condition has not been met. The Administrator may permit the continued sale and use of existing stocks of a pesticide whose conditional registration has been canceled under this subsection to such extent, under such conditions, and for such uses as the Administrator may specify if the Administrator determines that such sale or use is not inconsistent with the purposes of this subchapter and will not have unreasonable adverse effects on the environment.

(2) A cancellation proposed under this subsection shall become final and effective at the end of thirty days from receipt by the registrant of the notice of intent to cancel unless during that time a request for hearing is made by a person adversely affected by the notice. If a hearing is requested, a hearing shall be conducted under subsection (d) of this section. The only matters for resolution at that hearing shall be whether the registrant has initiated and pursued appropriate action to comply with the condition or conditions within the time provided or whether the condition or conditions have been satisfied within the time provided, and whether the Administrator's determination with respect to the disposition of existing stocks is consistent with this subchapter. A decision after completion of such hearing shall be final. Notwithstanding any other provision of this section, a hearing shall be held and a determination made within seventy-five days after receipt of a request for such hearing.

**(f) General provisions**

**(1) Voluntary cancellation**

(A) A registrant may, at any time, request that a pesticide registration of the registrant be canceled or amended to terminate one or more pesticide uses.

(B) Before acting on a request under subparagraph (A), the Administrator shall publish in the Federal Register a notice of the receipt of the request and provide for a 30-day period in which the public may comment.

(C) In the case of a pesticide that is registered for a minor agricultural use, if the Administrator determines that the cancellation or termination of uses would adversely affect the availability of the pesticide for use, the Administrator—

(i) shall publish in the Federal Register a notice of the receipt of the request and make reasonable efforts to inform persons who so use the pesticide of the request; and

(ii) may not approve or reject the request until the termination of the 180-day period beginning on the date of publication of the notice in the Federal Register, except that the Administrator may waive the 180-day period upon the request of the registrant or if the Administrator determines that the continued use of the pesticide would pose an unreasonable adverse effect on the environment.

(D) Subject to paragraph (3)(B), after complying with this paragraph, the Administrator may approve or deny the request.

**(2) Publication of notice**

A notice of denial of registration, intent to cancel, suspension, or intent to suspend issued under this subchapter or a notice issued under subsection (c)(4) or (d)(5)(A) of section 136a–1 of this title shall be published in the Federal Register and shall be sent by certified mail, return receipt requested, to the registrant's or applicant's address of record on file with the Administrator. If the mailed notice is returned to the Administrator as undeliverable at that address, if delivery is refused, or if the Administrator otherwise is unable to accomplish delivery of the notice to the registrant or applicant after making reasonable efforts to do so, the notice shall be deemed to have been received by the registrant or applicant on the date the notice was published in the Federal Register.

**(3) Transfer of registration of pesticides registered for minor agricultural uses**

In the case of a pesticide that is registered for a minor agricultural use:

(A) During the 180–day period referred to in paragraph (1)(C)(ii), the registrant of the pesticide may notify the Administrator of an agreement between the registrant and a person or persons (including persons who so use the pesticide) to transfer the registration of the pesticide, in lieu of canceling or amending the registration to terminate the use.

(B) An application for transfer of registration, in conformance with any regulations the Administrator may adopt with respect to the transfer of the pesticide registrations, must be submitted to the Administrator within 30 days of the date of notification provided pursuant to subparagraph (A). If such an application is submitted, the Administrator shall approve the transfer and shall not approve the request for voluntary cancellation or amendment to terminate use unless the Administrator determines that the continued use of the pesticide would cause an unreasonable adverse effect on the environment.

(C) If the Administrator approves the transfer and the registrant transfers the registration of the pesticide, the Administrator shall not cancel or amend the registration to delete the use or rescind the transfer of the registration, during the 180-day period beginning on the date of the approval of the transfer unless the Administrator determines that the continued use of the pesticide would cause an unreasonable adverse effect on the environment.

(D) The new registrant of the pesticide shall assume the outstanding data and other requirements for the pesticide that are pending at the time of the transfer.

**(4) Utilization of data for voluntarily canceled pesticide**

When an application is filed with the Administrator for the registration of a pesticide for a minor use and another registrant subsequently voluntarily cancels its registration for an identical or substantially similar pesticide for an identical or substantially similar use, the Administrator shall process, review, and evaluate the pending application as if the voluntary cancellation had not yet taken place except that the Administrator shall not take such action if the Administrator determines that such minor use may cause an unreasonable adverse effect on the environment. In order to rely on this subsection, the applicant must certify that it agrees to satisfy any outstanding data requirements necessary to support the reregistration of the pesticide in accordance with the data submission schedule established by the Administrator.

**(g) Notice for stored pesticides with canceled or suspended registrations**

**(1) In general**

Any producer or exporter of pesticides, registrant of a pesticide, applicant for registration of a pesticide, applicant for or holder of an experimental use permit, commercial applicator, or any person who distributes or sells any pesticide, who possesses any pesticide which has had its registration canceled or suspended under this section shall notify the Administrator and appropriate State and local officials of—

(A) such possession,

(B) the quantity of such pesticide such person possesses, and

(C) the place at which such pesticide is stored.

**(2) Copies**

The Administrator shall transmit a copy of each notice submitted under this subsection to the regional office of the Environmental Protection Agency which has jurisdiction over the place of pesticide storage identified in the notice.

**(h) Judicial review**

Final orders of the Administrator under this section shall be subject to judicial review pursuant to section 136n of this title.

(June 25, 1947, c. 125, § 6, as added Oct. 21, 1972, Pub.L. 92–516, § 2, 86 Stat. 984, and amended Nov. 28, 1975, Pub.L. 94–140, § 1, 89 Stat. 751; Mar. 27, 1978, Pub.L. 95–251, § 2(a)(2), 92 Stat. 183, 184; Sept. 30, 1978, Pub.L. 95–396, §§ 11, 12, 92 Stat. 828; Nov. 8, 1984, Pub.L. 98–620, Title IV, § 402(4)(A), 98 Stat. 3357; Oct. 25, 1988, Pub.L. 100–532, Title II, § 201, Title IV, § 404, Title VIII, § 801(e), (q)(2)(B), 102 Stat. 2668, 2673, 2681, 2683; Nov. 28, 1990, Pub.L. 101–624, Title XIV, § 1494, 104 Stat. 3628; Dec. 13, 1991, Pub.L. 102–237, Title X, § 1006(a)(5), (b)(1), (2), (3)(C) to (E), 105 Stat. 1895, 1896; Aug. 3, 1996, Pub.L. 104–170, Title I, §§ 102, 106(a), Title II, §§ 210(g), (h), 233, 110 Stat. 1489, 1491, 1500, 1509.)

**HISTORICAL AND STATUTORY NOTES**

**Codifications**

"Subchapter II of chapter 5 of Title 5", referred to in subsec. (c)(2), was in the original "subchapter II of Title 5", and has been editorially changed as the probable intent of Congress.

**Effective and Applicability Provisions**

1988 Acts

Amendment by Pub.L. 100–532 effective on expiration of 60 days after October 25, 1988, see section 901 of Pub.L. 100–532, set out as a note under section 136 of this title.

1984 Acts

Amendment by Pub.L. 98–620 not to apply to cases pending on Nov. 8, 1984, see section 403 of Pub.L. 98–620, set out as a note under section 1657 of Title 28, Judiciary and Judicial Procedure.

1972 Acts

Section effective at the close of Oct. 21, 1972, except if regulations are necessary for the implementation of any provision that becomes effective on Oct. 21, 1972, and continuation in effect of the provisions of subchapter I of this chapter and regulations thereunder as in effect prior to Oct. 21, 1972, until superseded by provisions of Pub.L. 92–516 and regulations thereunder, see section 4 of Pub.L. 92–516, set out as a note under section 136 of this title.

**Change of Name**

In subsec. (d), "Administrative Law Judge" and "Administrative Law Judge's" were substituted for "Hearing Examiner" and "Hearing Examiner's", respectively, on authority of section 3 of Pub.L. 95–251, which provided that any reference in any law, regulation, or order to a hearing examiner appointed under section 3105 of Title 5, Government Organization and Employees, be deemed a reference to an administrative law judge.

**Severability of Provisions**

If any provision of Pub.L. 101–624 or the application thereof to any person or circumstance is held invalid, such invalidity not to affect other provisions or applications of Pub.L. 101–624 which can be given effect without regard to the invalid provision or application, see section 2519 of Pub.L. 101–624, set out as a note under section 1421 of this title.

**Prior Provisions**

A prior section 6 of Act June 25, 1947, was classified to section 135d of this title prior to amendment of Act June 25, 1947, by Pub.L. 92–516.

## § 136e. Registration of establishments

**[FIFRA § 7]**

**(a) Requirement**

No person shall produce any pesticide subject to this subchapter or active ingredient used in producing a pesticide subject to this subchapter in any State unless the establishment in which it is produced is registered with the Administrator. The application for registration of any establishment shall include the name and address of the establishment and of the producer who operates such establishment.

(b) **Registration**

Whenever the Administrator receives an application under subsection (a) of this section, the Administrator shall register the establishment and assign it an establishment number.

(c) **Information required**

(1) Any producer operating an establishment registered under this section shall inform the Administrator within 30 days after it is registered of the types and amounts of pesticides and, if applicable, active ingredients used in producing pesticides—

(A) which the producer is currently producing;

(B) which the producer has produced during the past year; and

(C) which the producer has sold or distributed during the past year.

The information required by this paragraph shall be kept current and submitted to the Administrator annually as required under such regulations as the Administrator may prescribe.

(2) Any such producer shall, upon the request of the Administrator for the purpose of issuing a stop sale order pursuant to section 136k of this title, inform the Administrator of the name and address of any recipient of any pesticide produced in any registered establishment which the producer operates.

(d) **Confidential records and information**

Any information submitted to the Administrator pursuant to subsection (c) of this section other than the names of the pesticides or active ingredients used in producing pesticides produced, sold, or distributed at an establishment shall be considered confidential and shall be subject to the provisions of section 136h of this title.

(June 25, 1947, c. 125, § 7, as added Oct. 21, 1972, Pub.L. 92–516, § 2, 86 Stat. 987, and amended Sept. 30, 1978, Pub.L. 95–396, § 13, 92 Stat. 829; Dec. 13, 1991, Pub.L. 102–237, Title X, § 1006(b)(1), (3)(F), (G), 105 Stat. 1895, 1896.)

### HISTORICAL AND STATUTORY NOTES

**Effective and Applicability Provisions**

1991 Acts

Amendments by Pub.L. 102–237 effective Dec. 13, 1991, see section 1101(a) of Pub.L. 102–237, set out as a note under section 1421 of this title.

1972 Acts

Section effective at the close of Oct. 21, 1972, except if regulations are necessary for the implementation of any provision that becomes effective on Oct. 21, 1972, and continuation in effect of the provisions of subchapter I of this chapter and regulations thereunder as in effect prior to Oct. 21, 1972, until superseded by provisions of Pub.L. 92–516 and regulations thereunder, see section 4 of Pub.L 92–516, set out as a note under section 136 of this title.

**Prior Provisions**

A prior section 7 of Act June 25, 1947, was classified to section 135e of this title prior to amendment of Act June 25, 1947, by Pub.L. 92–516.

## § 136f. Books and records

**[FIFRA § 8]**

(a) **Requirements**

The Administrator may prescribe regulations requiring producers, registrants, and applicants for registration to maintain such records with respect to their operations and the pesticides and devices produced as the Administrator determines are necessary for the effective enforcement of this subchapter and to make the records available for inspection and copying in the same manner as provided in subsection (b) of this section. No records required under this subsection shall extend to financial data, sales data other than shipment data, pricing data, personnel data, and research data (other than data relating to registered pesticides or to a pesticide for which an application for registration has been filed).

(b) **Inspection**

For the purposes of enforcing the provisions of this subchapter, any producer, distributor, carrier, dealer, or any other person who sells or offers for sale, delivers or offers for delivery any pesticide or device subject to this subchapter, shall, upon request of any officer or employee of the Environmental Protection Agency or of any State or political subdivision, duly designated by the Administrator, furnish or permit such person at all reasonable times to have access to, and to copy: (1) all records showing the delivery, movement, or holding of such pesticide or device, including the quantity, the date of shipment and receipt, and the name of the consignor and consignee; or (2) in the event of the inability of any person to produce records containing such information, all other records and information relating to such delivery, movement, or holding of the pesticide or device. Any inspection with respect to any records and information referred to in this subsection shall not extend to financial data, sales data other than shipment data, pricing data, personnel data; and research data (other than data relating to registered pesticides or to a pesticide for which an application for registration has been filed). Before undertaking an inspection under this subsection, the officer or employee must present to the owner, operator, or agent in charge of the establishment or other place where pesticides or devices are held for distribution or sale, appropriate credentials and a written statement as to the reason for the inspection, including a statement as to whether a violation of the law is suspected. If no violation is suspected, an alternate and sufficient reason shall be given in writing. Each such inspection shall be commenced and completed with reasonable promptness.

(June 25, 1947, c. 125, § 8, as added Oct. 21, 1972, Pub.L. 92–516, § 2, 86 Stat. 987, and amended Sept. 30, 1978, Pub.L. 95–396, § 14, 92 Stat. 829; Oct. 25, 1988, Pub.L. 100–532, Title III, § 301, 102 Stat. 2668; Dec. 13, 1991, Pub.L. 102–237, Title X, § 1006(b)(1), 105 Stat. 1895.)

### HISTORICAL AND STATUTORY NOTES

**Effective and Applicability Provisions**

1991 Acts

Amendment by section 1006(b)(1) of Pub.L. 102–237 effective Dec. 13, 1991, see section 1101(a) of Pub.L. 102–237, set out as a note under section 1421 of this title.

1988 Acts

Amendment by Pub.L. 100–532 effective on expiration of 60 days after October 25, 1988, see section 901 of Pub.L. 100–532, set out as a note under section 136 of this title.

1972 Acts

Section effective at the close of Oct. 21, 1972, except if regulations are necessary for the implementation of any provision that becomes effective on Oct. 21, 1972, and continuation in effect of the provisions of subchapter I of this chapter and regulations thereunder as in effect prior to Oct. 21, 1972, until superseded by provisions of Pub.L. 92–516 and regulations thereunder, see section 4 of Pub.L. 92–516, set out as a note under section 136 of this title.

**Prior Provisions**

A prior section 8 of Act June 25, 1947, was classified to section 135f of this title prior to amendment of Act June 25, 1947, by Pub.L. 92–516.

## § 136g. Inspection of establishments, etc.

### [FIFRA § 9]

**(a) In general**

(1) For purposes of enforcing the provisions of this subchapter, officers or employees of the Environmental Protection Agency or of any State duly designated by the Administrator are authorized to enter at reasonable times (A) any establishment or other place where pesticides or devices are held for distribution or sale for the purpose of inspecting and obtaining samples of any pesticides or devices, packaged, labeled, and released for shipment, and samples of any containers or labeling for such pesticides or devices, or (B) any place where there is being held any pesticide the registration of which has been suspended or canceled for the purpose of determining compliance with section 136q of this title.

(2) Before undertaking such inspection, the officers or employees must present to the owner, operator, or agent in charge of the establishment or other place where pesticides or devices are held for distribution or sale, appropriate credentials and a written statement as to the reason for the inspection, including a statement as to whether a violation of the law is suspected. If no violation is suspected, an alternate and sufficient reason shall be given in writing. Each such inspection shall be commenced and completed with reasonable promptness. If the officer or employee obtains any samples, prior to leaving the premises, the officer or employee shall give to the owner, operator, or agent in charge a receipt describing the samples obtained and, if requested, a portion of each such sample equal in volume or weight to the portion retained. If an analysis is made of such samples, a copy of the results of such analysis shall be furnished promptly to the owner, operator, or agent in charge.

**(b) Warrants**

For purposes of enforcing the provisions of this subchapter and upon a showing to an officer or court of competent jurisdiction that there is reason to believe that the provisions of this subchapter have been violated, officers or employees duly designated by the Administrator are empowered to obtain and to execute warrants authorizing—

(1) entry, inspection, and copying of records for purposes of this section or section 136f of this title;

(2) inspection and reproduction of all records showing the quantity, date of shipment, and the name of consignor and consignee of any pesticide or device found in the establishment which is adulterated, misbranded, not registered (in the case of a pesticide) or otherwise in violation of this subchapter and in the event of the inability of any person to produce records containing such information, all other records and information relating to such delivery, movement, or holding of the pesticide or device; and

(3) the seizure of any pesticide or device which is in violation of this subchapter.

**(c) Enforcement**

**(1) Certification of facts to Attorney General**

The examination of pesticides or devices shall be made in the Environmental Protection Agency or elsewhere as the Administrator may designate for the purpose of determining from such examinations whether they comply with the requirements of this subchapter. If it shall appear from any such examination that they fail to comply with the requirements of this subchapter, the Administrator shall cause notice to be given to the person against whom criminal or civil proceedings are contemplated. Any person so notified shall be given an opportunity to present the person's views, either orally or in writing, with regard to such contemplated proceedings, and if in the opinion of the Administrator it appears that the provisions of this subchapter have been violated by such person, then the Administrator shall certify the facts to the Attorney General, with a copy of the results of the analysis or the examination of such pesticide for the institution of a criminal proceeding pursuant to section 136*l*(b) of this title or a civil proceeding under section 136*l*(a) of this title, when the Administrator determines that such action will be sufficient to effectuate the purposes of this subchapter.

**(2) Notice not required**

The notice of contemplated proceedings and opportunity to present views set forth in this subsection are not prerequisites to the institution of any proceeding by the Attorney General.

**(3) Warning notices**

Nothing in this subchapter shall be construed as requiring the Administrator to institute proceedings for prosecution of minor violations of this subchapter whenever the Administrator believes that the public interest will be adequately served by a suitable written notice of warning.

(June 25, 1947, c. 125, § 9, as added Oct. 21, 1972, Pub.L. 92–516, § 2, 86 Stat. 1988, and amended Oct. 25, 1988, Pub.L. 100–532, Title III, § 302, 102 Stat. 2669; Dec. 13, 1991, Pub.L. 102–237, Title X, § 1006(b)(1), (3)(H), (I), 105 Stat. 1895, 1896.)

### HISTORICAL AND STATUTORY NOTES

**Effective and Applicability Provisions**

1991 Acts

Amendments by Pub.L. 102–237 effective Dec. 13, 1991, see section 1101(a) of Pub.L. 102–237, set out as a note under section 1421 of this title.

1988 Acts

Amendment by Pub.L. 100–532 effective on expiration of 60 days after October 25, 1988, see section 901 of Pub.L. 100–532, set out as a note under section 136 of this title.

1972 Acts

Section effective at the close of Oct. 21, 1972, except if regulations are necessary for the implementation of any provision that becomes effective on Oct. 21, 1972, and continuation in effect of the provisions of subchapter I of this chapter and regulations thereunder as in effect prior to Oct. 21, 1972, until superseded by provisions of Pub.L. 92–516 and regulations thereunder, see section 4 of Pub.L. 92–516, set out as a note under section 136 of this title.

**Prior Provisions**

A prior section 9 of Act June 25, 1947, was classified to section 135g of this title prior to amendment of Act June 25, 1947, by Pub.L. 92–516.

## § 136h. Protection of trade secrets and other information

**[FIFRA § 10]**

**(a) In general**

In submitting data required by this subchapter, the applicant may (1) clearly mark any portions thereof which in the applicant's opinion are trade secrets or commercial or financial information and (2) submit such market material separately from other material required to be submitted under this subchapter.

**(b) Disclosure**

Notwithstanding any other provision of this subchapter and subject to the limitations in subsections (d) and (e) of this section, the Administrator shall not make public information which in the Administrator's judgment contains or relates to trade secrets or commercial or financial information obtained from a person and privileged or confidential, except that, when necessary to carry out the provisions of this subchapter, information relating to formulas of products acquired by authorization of this subchapter may be revealed to any Federal agency consulted and may be revealed at a public hearing or in findings of fact issued by the Administrator.

**(c) Disputes**

If the Administrator proposes to release for inspection information which the applicant or registrant believes to be protected from disclosure under subsection (b) of this section, the Administrator shall notify the applicant or registrant, in writing, by certified mail. The Administrator shall not thereafter make available for inspection such data until thirty days after receipt of the notice by the applicant or registrant. During this period, the applicant or registrant may institute an action in an appropriate district court for a declaratory judgment as to whether such information is subject to protection under subsection (b) of this section.

**(d) Limitations**

(1) All information concerning the objectives, methodology, results, or significance of any test or experiment performed on or with a registered or previously registered pesticide or its separate ingredients, impurities, or degradation products, and any information concerning the effects of such pesticide on any organism or the behavior of such pesticide in the environment, including, but not limited to, data on safety to fish and wildlife, humans and other mammals, plants, animals, and soil, and studies on persistence, translocation and fate in the environment, and metabolism, shall be available for disclosure to the public. The use of such data for any registration purpose shall be governed by section 136a of this title. This paragraph does not authorize the disclosure of any information that—

(A) discloses manufacturing or quality control processes,

(B) discloses the details of any methods for testing, detecting, or measuring the quantity of any deliberately added inert ingredient of a pesticide, or

(C) discloses the identity or percentage quantity of any deliberately added inert ingredient of a pesticide,

unless the Administrator has first determined that disclosure is necessary to protect against an unreasonable risk of injury to health or the environment.

(2) Information concerning production, distribution, sale, or inventories of a pesticide that is otherwise entitled to confidential treatment under subsection (b) of this section may be publicly disclosed in connection with a public proceeding to determine whether a pesticide, or any ingredient of a pesticide, causes unreasonable adverse effects on health or the environment, if the Administrator determines that such disclosure is necessary in the public interest.

(3) If the Administrator proposes to disclose information described in clause (A), (B), or (C) of paragraph (1) or in paragraph (2) of this subsection, the Administrator shall notify by certified mail the submitter of such information of the intent to release such information. The Administrator may not release such information, without the submitter's consent, until thirty days after the submitter has been furnished such notice. Where the Administrator finds that disclosure of information described in clause (A), (B), or (C) of paragraph (1) of this subsection is necessary to avoid or lessen an imminent and substantial risk of injury to the public health, the Administrator may set such shorter period of notice (but not less than ten days) and such method of notice as the Administrator finds appropriate. During such period the data submitter may institute an action in an appropriate district court to enjoin or limit the proposed disclosure. The court may enjoin disclosure, or limit the disclosure or the parties to whom disclosure shall be made, to the extent that—

(A) in the case of information described in clause (A), (B), or (C) of paragraph (1) of this subsection, the proposed disclosure is not required to protect against an unreasonable risk of injury to health or the environment; or

(B) in the case of information described in paragraph (2) of this subsection, the public interest in availability of the information in the public proceeding does not outweigh the interests in preserving the confidentiality of the information.

### (e) Disclosure to contractors

Information otherwise protected from disclosure to the public under subsection (b) of this section may be disclosed to contractors with the United States and employees of such contractors if, in the opinion of the Administrator, such disclosure is necessary for the satisfactory performance by the contractor of a contract with the United States for the performance of work in connection with this subchapter and under such conditions as the Administrator may specify. The Administrator shall require as a condition to the disclosure of information under this subsection that the person receiving it take such security precautions respecting the information as the Administrator shall by regulation prescribe.

### (f) Penalty for disclosure by Federal employees

(1) Any officer or employee of the United States or former officer or employee of the United States who, by virtue of such employment or official position, has obtained possession of, or has access to, material the disclosure of which is prohibited by subsection (b) of this section, and who, knowing that disclosure of such material is prohibited by such subsection, willfully discloses the material in any manner to any person not entitled to receive it, shall be fined not more than $10,000 or imprisoned for not more than one year, or both. Section 1905 of Title 18 shall not apply with respect to the publishing, divulging, disclosure, or making known of, or making available, information reported or otherwise obtained under this subchapter. Nothing in this subchapter shall preempt any civil remedy under State or Federal law for wrongful disclosure of trade secrets.

(2) For the purposes of this section, any contractor with the United States who is furnished information as authorized by subsection (e) of this section, or any employee of any such contractor, shall be considered to be an employee of the United States.

### (g) Disclosure to foreign and multinational pesticide producers

(1) The Administrator shall not knowingly disclose information submitted by an applicant or registrant under this subchapter to any employee or agent of any business or other entity engaged in the production, sale, or distribution of pesticides in countries other than the United States or in addition to the United States or to any other person who intends to deliver such data to such foreign or multinational business or entity unless the applicant or registrant has consented to such disclosure. The Administrator shall require an affirmation from any person who intends to inspect data that such person does not seek access to the data for purposes of delivering it or offering it for sale to any such business or entity or its agents or employees and will not purposefully deliver or negligently cause the data to be delivered to such business or entity or its agents or employees. Notwithstanding any other provision of this subsection, the Administrator may disclose information to any person in connection with a public proceeding under law or regulation, subject to restrictions on the availability of information contained elsewhere in this subchapter, which information is relevant to a determination by the Administrator

with respect to whether a pesticide, or any ingredient of a pesticide, causes unreasonable adverse effects on health or the environment.

(2) The Administrator shall maintain records of the names of persons to whom data are disclosed under this subsection and the persons or organizations they represent and shall inform the applicant or registrant of the names and affiliations of such persons.

(3) Section 1001 of Title 18 shall apply to any affirmation made under paragraph (1) of this subsection.

(June 25, 1947, c. 125, § 10, as added Oct. 21, 1972, Pub.L. 92–516, § 2, 86 Stat. 989, and amended Sept. 30, 1978, Pub.L. 95–396, § 15, 92 Stat. 829; Nov. 8, 1984, Pub.L. 98–620, Title IV, § 402(4)(B), 98 Stat. 3357; Oct. 25, 1988, Pub.L. 100–532, Title VIII, § 801(f), 102 Stat. 2682; Dec. 13, 1991, Pub.L. 102–237, Title X, § 1006(b)(1), (2), (3)(J), 105 Stat. 1895, 1896.)

### HISTORICAL AND STATUTORY NOTES

**Effective and Applicability Provisions**

1991 Acts

Amendments by Pub.L. 102–237 effective Dec. 13, 1991, see section 1101(a) of Pub.L. 102–237, set out as a note under section 1421 of this title.

1988 Acts

Amendment by Pub.L. 100–532 effective 60 days after October 25, 1988, see section 901 of Pub.L. 100–532, set out as a note under section 136 of this title.

1984 Acts

Amendment by Pub.L. 98–620 not to apply to cases pending on Nov. 8, 1984, see section 403 of Pub.L. 98–620, set out as a note under section 1657 of Title 28, Judiciary and Judicial Procedure.

1972 Acts

Section effective at the close of Oct. 21, 1972, except if regulations are necessary for the implementation of any provision that becomes effective on Oct. 21, 1972, and continuation in effect of the provisions of subchapter I of this chapter and regulations thereunder as in effect prior to Oct. 21, 1972, until superseded by provisions of Pub.L. 92–516 and regulations thereunder, see section 4 of Pub.L. 92–516, set out as a note under section 136 of this title.

**Prior Provision**

A prior section 10 of Act June 25, 1947, was classified to section 135h of this title prior to amendment of Act June 25, 1947, by Pub.L. 92–516.

## § 136i. Use of restricted use pesticides; applicators

[FIFRA § 11]

### (a) Certification procedure

#### (1) Federal certification

In any State for which a State plan for applicator certification has not been approved by the Administrator, the Administrator, in consultation with the Governor of such State, shall conduct a program for the certification of applicators of pesticides. Such program shall conform to the requirements imposed upon the States under the provisions of subsection (a)(2) of this section and shall not require private applicators to take any examination to establish competency in the use of pesticides. Prior to the implementation of the program, the Administrator shall publish in the Federal Register for review and comment a summary of the Federal plan for applicator certification and shall make generally available within the State copies of the plan. The Administrator shall hold public hearings at one or more locations within the State if so requested by the Governor of such State during the thirty days following publication of the Federal Register notice inviting comment on the Federal plan. The hearings shall be held within thirty days following receipt of the request from the Governor. In any State in which the Administrator conducts a certification program, the Administrator may require any person engaging in the commercial application, sale, offering for sale, holding for sale, or distribution of any pesticide one or more uses of which have been classified for restricted use to maintain such records and submit such reports concerning the commercial application, sale, or distribution of such pesticide as the Administrator may by regulation prescribe. Subject to paragraph (2), the Administrator shall prescribe standards for the certification of applicators of pesticides. Such standards shall provide that to be certified, an individual must be determined to be competent with respect to the use and handling of the pesticides, or to the use and handling of the pesticide or class of pesticides covered by such individual's certification. The certification standard for a private applicator shall, under a State plan submitted for approval, be deemed fulfilled by the applicator completing a certification form. The Administrator shall further assure that such form contains adequate information and affirmations to carry out the intent of this subchapter, and may include in the form an affirmation that the private applicator has completed a training program approved by the Administrator so long as the program does not require the private applicator to take, pursuant to a requirement prescribed by the Administrator, any examination to establish competency in the use of the pesticide. The Administrator may require any pesticide dealer participating in a certification program to be licensed under a State licensing program approved by the Administrator.

#### (2) State certification

If any State, at any time, desires to certify applicators of pesticides, the Governor of such State shall submit a State plan for such purpose. The Administrator shall approve the plan submitted by any

State, or any modification thereof, if such plan in the Administrator's judgment—

(A) designates a State agency as the agency responsible for administering the plan throughout the State;

(B) contains satisfactory assurances that such agency has or will have the legal authority and qualified personnel necessary to carry out the plan;

(C) gives satisfactory assurances that the State will devote adequate funds to the administration of the plan;

(D) provides that the State agency will make such reports to the Administrator in such form and containing such information as the Administrator may from time to time require; and

(E) contains satisfactory assurances that State standards for the certification of applicators of pesticides conform with those standards prescribed by the Administrator under paragraph (1).

Any State certification program under this section shall be maintained in accordance with the State plan approved under this section.

**(b) State plans**

If the Administrator rejects a plan submitted under subsection (a)(2) of this section, the Administrator shall afford the State submitting the plan due notice and opportunity for hearing before so doing. If the Administrator approves a plan submitted under subsection (a)(2) of this section, then such State shall certify applicators of pesticides with respect to such State. Whenever the Administrator determines that a State is not administering the certification program in accordance with the plan approved under this section, the Administrator shall so notify the State and provide for a hearing at the request of the State, and, if appropriate corrective action is not taken within a reasonable time, not to exceed ninety days, the Administrator shall withdraw approval of such plan.

**(c) Instruction in integrated pest management techniques**

Standards prescribed by the Administrator for the certification of applicators of pesticides under subsection (a) of this section, and State plans submitted to the Administrator under subsection (a) of this section, shall include provisions for making instructional materials concerning integrated pest management techniques available to individuals at their request in accordance with the provisions of section 136u(c) of this title, but such plans may not require that any individual receive instruction concerning such techniques or to be shown to be competent with respect to the use of such techniques. The Administrator and States implementing such plans shall provide that all interested individuals are notified on the availability of such instructional materials.

**(d) In general**

No regulations prescribed by the Administrator for carrying out the provisions of this subchapter shall require any private applicator to maintain any records or file any reports or other documents.

**(e) Separate standards**

When establishing or approving standards for licensing or certification, the Administrator shall establish separate standards for commercial and private applicators.

(June 25, 1947, c. 125, § 11, formerly §§ 4 and 11, as added Oct. 21, 1972, Pub.L. 92–516, § 2, 86 Stat. 983, 989, and amended Nov. 28, 1975, Pub.L. 94–140, §§ 5, 11, 89 Stat. 753, 754; Sept. 30, 1978, Pub.L. 95–396, § 9, 92 Stat. 827; renumbered § 11 and amended Oct. 25, 1988, Pub.L. 100–532, Title VIII, § 801(c), (q)(1)(A) to (C), 102 Stat. 2681, 2683; Dec. 13, 1991, Pub.L. 102–237, Title X, § 1006(a)(6), (b)(1), (2), (3)(K), 105 Stat. 1895, 1896.)

### HISTORICAL AND STATUTORY NOTES

**Codifications**

Pub.L. 100–332, § 801(q)(1)(A), transferred subsecs. (a) to (c) of section 4 of Act June 25, 1947, which was classified to section 136b of this title, to subsecs. (a) to (c) of this section.

**Effective and Applicability Provisions**

1991 Acts

Amendments by Pub.L. 102–237 effective Dec. 13, 1991, see section 1101(a) of Pub.L. 102–237, set out as a note under section 1421 of this title.

1988 Acts

Amendment by Pub.L. 100–532 effective on expiration of 60 days after October 25, 1988, see section 901 of Pub.L. 100–532, set out as a note under section 136 of this title.

1972 Acts

Section effective at the close of Oct. 21, 1972, except if regulations are necessary for the implementation of any provision that becomes effective on Oct. 21, 1972, and continuation in effect of the provisions of subchapter I of this chapter and regulations thereunder as in effect prior to Oct. 21, 1972, until superseded by provisions of Pub.L. 92–516 and regulations thereunder, see section 4 of Pub.L. 92–516, set out as a note under section 136 of this title.

**Prior Provisions**

A prior section 11 of Act June 25, 1947, was classified to section 135i of this title prior to amendment of Act June 25, 1947, by Pub.L. 92–516.

## § 136i–1. Pesticide recordkeeping

**(a) Requirements**

(1) The Secretary of Agriculture, in consultation with the Administrator of the Environmental Protection Agency, shall require certified applicators of restricted use pesticides (of the type described under section 136a(d)(1)(C) of this title) to maintain records

comparable to records maintained by commercial applicators of pesticides in each State. If there is no State requirement for the maintenance of records, such applicator shall maintain records that contain the product name, amount, approximate date of application, and location of application of each such pesticide used for a 2–year period after such use.

(2) Within 30 days of a pesticide application, a commercial certified applicator shall provide a copy of records maintained under paragraph (1) to the person for whom such application was provided.

**(b) Access**

Records maintained under subsection (a) of this section shall be made available to any Federal or State agency that deals with pesticide use or any health or environmental issue related to the use of pesticides, on the request of such agency. Each such Federal agency shall conduct surveys and record the data from individual applicators to facilitate statistical analysis for environmental and agronomic purposes, but in no case may a government agency release data, including the location from which the data was derived, that would directly or indirectly reveal the identity of individual producers. In the case of Federal agencies, such access to records maintained under subsection (a) of this section shall be through the Secretary of Agriculture, or the Secretary's designee. State agency requests for access to records maintained under subsection (a) of this section shall be through the lead State agency so designated by the State.

**(c) Health care personnel**

When a health professional determines that pesticide information maintained under this section is necessary to provide medical treatment or first aid to an individual who may have been exposed to pesticides for which the information is maintained, upon request persons required to maintain records under subsection (a) of this section shall promptly provide record and available label information to that health professional. In the case of an emergency, such record information shall be provided immediately.

**(d) Penalty**

The Secretary of Agriculture shall be responsible for the enforcement of subsections (a), (b), and (c) of this section. A violation of such subsection shall—

(1) in the case of the first offense, be subject to a fine of not more than $500; and

(2) in the case of subsequent offenses, be subject to a fine of not less than $1,000 for each violation, except that the penalty shall be less than $1,000 if the Secretary determines that the person made a good faith effort to comply with such subsection.

**(e) Federal or State provisions**

The requirements of this section shall not affect provisions of other Federal or State laws.

**(f) Surveys and reports**

The Secretary of Agriculture and the Administrator of the Environmental Protection Agency, shall survey the records maintained under subsection (a) of this section to develop and maintain a data base that is sufficient to enable the Secretary and the Administrator to publish annual comprehensive reports concerning agricultural and nonagricultural pesticide use. The Secretary and Administrator shall enter into a memorandum of understanding to define their respective responsibilities under this subsection in order to avoid duplication of effort. Such reports shall be transmitted to Congress not later than April 1 of each year.

**(g) Regulations**

The Secretary of Agriculture and the Administrator of the Environmental Protection Agency shall promulgate regulations on their respective areas of responsibility implementing this section within 180 days after November 28, 1990.

(Pub.L. 101–624, Title XIV, § 1491, Nov. 28, 1990, 104 Stat. 3627; Dec. 13, 1991, Pub.L. 102–237, Title X, § 1006(d), 105 Stat. 1896.)

### HISTORICAL AND STATUTORY NOTES

**Codifications**

Section was enacted as part of the Food, Agriculture, Conservation and Trade Act of 1990, and not as part of the Federal Insecticide, Fungicide, and Rodenticide Act, which comprises this subchapter.

**Effective and Applicability Provisions**

1991 Acts

Amendment by Pub.L. 102–237 effective Dec. 13, 1991, see section 1101(a) of Pub.L. 102–237, set out as a note under section 1421 of this title.

**Severability of Provisions**

If any provision of Pub.L. 101–624 or the application thereof to any person or circumstance is held invalid, such invalidity not to affect other provisions or applications of Pub.L. 101–624 which can be given effect without regard to the invalid provision or application, see section 2519 of Pub.L. 101–624, set out as a note under section 1421 of this title.

## § 136i–2. Collection of pesticide use information

**(a) In general**

The Secretary of Agriculture shall collect data of statewide or regional significance on the use of pesticides to control pests and diseases of major crops and crops of dietary significance, including fruits and vegetables.

**(b) Collection**

The data shall be collected by surveys of farmers or from other sources offering statistically reliable data.

**(c) Coordination**

The Secretary of Agriculture shall, as appropriate, coordinate with the Administrator of the Environmental Protection Agency in the design of the surveys and make available to the Administrator the aggregate results of the surveys to assist the Administrator. (Pub.L. 104–170, Title III, § 302, Aug. 3, 1996, 110 Stat. 1512.)

**HISTORICAL AND STATUTORY NOTES**

**Codifications**

Section was enacted as part of the Food Quality Protection Act of 1996 and not as part of the Federal Insecticide, Fungicide, and Rodenticide Act of 1996, which comprises this subchapter.

**Pesticide Use Information Study**

Section 305 of Pub.L. 104–170 provided that:

"(a) The Secretary of Agriculture shall, in consultation with the Administrator of the Environmental Protection Agency, prepare a report to Congress evaluating the current status and potential improvements in Federal pesticide use information gathering activities. This report shall at least include—

"(1) an analysis of the quality and reliability of the information collected by the Department of Agriculture, the Environmental Protection Agency, and other Federal agencies regarding the agricultural use of pesticides; and

"(2) an analysis of options to increase the effectiveness of national pesticide use information collection, including an analysis of costs, burdens placed on agricultural producers and other pesticide users, and effectiveness in tracking risk reduction by those options.

"(b) The Secretary shall submit this report to Congress not later than 1 year following the date of enactment of this section [August 3, 1996]."

## § 136j. Unlawful acts

**[FIFRA § 12]**

**(a) In general**

(1) Except as provided by subsection (b) of this section, it shall be unlawful for any person in any State to distribute or sell to any person—

(A) any pesticide that is not registered under section 136a of this title or whose registration has been canceled or suspended, except to the extent that distribution or sale otherwise has been authorized by the Administrator under this subchapter;

(B) any registered pesticide if any claims made for it as a part of its distribution or sale substantially differ from any claims made for it as a part of the statement required in connection with its registration under section 136a of this title;

(C) any registered pesticide the composition of which differs at the time of its distribution or sale from its composition as described in the statement required in connection with its registration under section 136a of this title;

(D) any pesticide which has not been colored or discolored pursuant to the provisions of section 136w(c)(5) of this title;

(E) any pesticide which is adulterated or misbranded; or

(F) any device which is misbranded.

(2) It shall be unlawful for any person—

(A) to detach, alter, deface, or destroy, in whole or in part, any labeling required under this subchapter;

(B) to refuse to—

(i) prepare, maintain, or submit any records required by or under section 136c, 136e, 136f, 136i, or 136q of this title;

(ii) submit any reports required by or under section 136c, 136d, 136e, 136f, 136i, or 136q of this title; or

(iii) allow any entry, inspection, copying of records, or sampling authorized by this subchapter;

(C) to give a guaranty or undertaking provided for in subsection (b) of this section which is false in any particular, except that a person who receives and relies upon a guaranty authorized under subsection (b) of this section may give a guaranty to the same effect, which guaranty shall contain, in addition to the person's own name and address, the name and address of the person residing in the United States from whom the person received the guaranty or undertaking;

(D) to use for the person's own advantage or to reveal, other than to the Administrator, or officials or employees of the Environmental Protection Agency or other Federal executive agencies, or to the courts, or to physicians, pharmacists, and other qualified persons, needing such information for the performance of their duties, in accordance with such directions as the Administrator may prescribe, any information acquired by authority of this subchapter which is confidential under this subchapter;

(E) who is a registrant, wholesaler, dealer, retailer, or other distributor to advertise a product registered under this subchapter for restricted use without giving the classification of the product assigned to it under section 136a of this title;

(F) to distribute or sell, or to make available for use, or to use, any registered pesticide classified for restricted use for some or all purposes other than in accordance with section 136a(d) of this title and any regulations thereunder, except that it shall not be unlawful to sell, under regulations issued by the Administrator, a restricted use pesticide to a person who is not a certified applicator for application by a certified applicator;

**(G)** to use any registered pesticide in a manner inconsistent with its labeling;

**(H)** to use any pesticide which is under an experimental use permit contrary to the provisions of such permit;

**(I)** to violate any order issued under section 136k of this title;

**(J)** to violate any suspension order issued under section 136a(c)(2)(B), 136a–1, or 136d of this title;

**(K)** to violate any cancellation order issued under this subchapter or to fail to submit a notice in accordance with section 136d(g) of this title;

**(L)** who is a producer to violate any of the provisions of section 136e of this title;

**(M)** to knowingly falsify all or part of any application for registration, application for experimental use permit, any information submitted to the Administrator pursuant to section 136e of this title, any records required to be maintained pursuant to this subchapter, any report filed under this subchapter, or any information marked as confidential and submitted to the Administrator under any provision of this subchapter;

**(N)** who is a registrant, wholesaler, dealer, retailer, or other distributor to fail to file reports required by this subchapter;

**(O)** to add any substance to, or take any substance from, any pesticide in a manner that may defeat the purpose of this subchapter;

**(P)** to use any pesticide in tests on human beings unless such human beings (i) are fully informed of the nature and purposes of the test and of any physical and mental health consequences which are reasonably foreseeable therefrom, and (ii) freely volunteer to participate in the test;

**(Q)** to falsify all or part of any information relating to the testing of any pesticide (or any ingredient, metabolite, or degradation product thereof), including the nature of any protocol, procedure, substance, organism, or equipment used, observation made, or conclusion or opinion formed, submitted to the Administrator, or that the person knows will be furnished to the Administrator or will become a part of any records required to be maintained by this subchapter;

**(R)** to submit to the Administrator data known to be false in support of a registration; or

**(S)** to violate any regulation issued under section 136a(a) or 136q of this title.

**(b) Exemptions**

The penalties provided for a violation of paragraph (1) of subsection (a) of this section shall not apply to—

**(1)** any person who establishes a guaranty signed by, and containing the name and address of, the registrant or person residing in the United States from whom the person purchased or received in good faith the pesticide in the same unbroken package, to the effect that the pesticide was lawfully registered at the time of sale and delivery to the person, and that it complies with the other requirements of this subchapter, and in such case the guarantor shall be subject to the penalties which would otherwise attach to the person holding the guaranty under the provisions of this subchapter;

**(2)** any carrier while lawfully shipping, transporting, or delivering for shipment any pesticide or device, if such carrier upon request of any officer or employee duly designated by the Administrator shall permit such officer or employee to copy all of its records concerning such pesticide or device;

**(3)** any public official while engaged in the performance of the official duties of the public official;

**(4)** any person using or possessing any pesticide as provided by an experimental use permit in effect with respect to such pesticide and such use or possession; or

**(5)** any person who ships a substance or mixture of substances being put through tests in which the purpose is only to determine its value for pesticide purposes or to determine its toxicity or other properties and from which the user does not expect to receive any benefit in pest control from its use.

(June 25, 1947, c. 125, § 12, as added Oct. 21, 1972, Pub.L. 92–516, § 2, 86 Stat. 989, and amended Sept. 30, 1978, Pub.L. 95–396, § 16, 92 Stat. 832; Oct. 25, 1988, Pub.L. 100–532, Title VI, §§ 601(b)(2), 603, Title VIII, § 801(g), (q)(2)(B), 102 Stat. 2677, 2678, 2682, 2683; Dec. 13, 1991, Pub.L. 102–237, Title X, § 1006(a)(7), (b)(3)(L) to (O), 105 Stat. 1895, 1896.)

## HISTORICAL AND STATUTORY NOTES

**Effective and Applicability Provisions**

1991 Acts

Amendments by Pub.L. 102–237 effective Dec. 13, 1991, see section 1101(a) of Pub.L. 102–237, set out as a note under section 1421 of this title.

1988 Acts

Amendment by Pub.L. 100–532 effective on expiration of 60 days after October 25, 1988, see section 901 of Pub.L. 100–532, set out as a note under section 136 of this title.

1972 Acts

Section effective at the close of Oct. 21, 1972, except if regulations are necessary for the implementation of any provision that becomes effective on Oct. 21, 1972, and continuation in effect of the provisions of subchapter I of this chapter and regulations thereunder as in effect prior to Oct. 21, 1972, until superseded by provisions of Pub.L. 92–516 and regulations thereunder, see section 4 of Pub.L. 92–516, set out as a note under section 136 of this title.

**Prior Provisions**

A prior section 12 of Act June 25, 1947, was classified to section 135j of this title prior to amendment by Pub.L. 92–516.

## § 136k. Stop sale, use, removal, and seizure

[FIFRA § 13]

**(a) Stop sale, etc., orders**

Whenever any pesticide or device is found by the Administrator in any State and there is reason to believe on the basis of inspection or tests that such pesticide or device is in violation of any of the provisions of this subchapter, or that such pesticide or device has been or is intended to be distributed or sold in violation of any such provisions, or when the registration of the pesticide has been canceled by a final order or has been suspended, the Administrator may issue a written or printed "stop sale, use, or removal" order to any person who owns, controls, or has custody of such pesticide or device, and after receipt of such order no person shall sell, use, or remove the pesticide or device described in the order except in accordance with the provisions of the order.

**(b) Seizure**

Any pesticide or device that is being transported or, having been transported, remains unsold or in original unbroken packages, or that is sold or offered for sale in any State, or that is imported from a foreign country, shall be liable to be proceeded against in any district court in the district where it is found and seized for confiscation by a process in rem for condemnation if—

(1) in the case of a pesticide—

(A) it is adulterated or misbranded;

(B) it is not registered pursuant to the provisions of section 136a of this title;

(C) its labeling fails to bear the information required by this subchapter;

(D) it is not colored or discolored and such coloring or discoloring is required under this subchapter; or

(E) any of the claims made for it or any of the directions for its use differ in substance from the representations made in connection with its registration;

(2) in the case of a device, it is misbranded; or

(3) in the case of a pesticide or device, when used in accordance with the requirements imposed under this subchapter and as directed by the labeling, it nevertheless causes unreasonable adverse effects on the environment.

In the case of a plant regulator, defoliant, or desiccant, used in accordance with the label claims and recommendations, physical or physiological effects on plants or parts thereof shall not be deemed to be injury, when such effects are the purpose for which the plant regulator, defoliant, or desiccant was applied.

**(c) Disposition after condemnation**

If the pesticide or device is condemned it shall, after entry of the decree, be disposed of by destruction or sale as the court may direct and the proceeds, if sold, less the court costs, shall be paid into the Treasury of the United States, but the pesticide or device shall not be sold contrary to the provisions of this subchapter or the laws of the jurisdiction in which it is sold. On payment of the costs of the condemnation proceedings and the execution and delivery of a good and sufficient bond conditioned that the pesticide or device shall not be sold or otherwise disposed of contrary to the provisions of the subchapter or the laws of any jurisdiction in which sold, the court may direct that such pesticide or device be delivered to the owner thereof. The proceedings of such condemnation cases shall conform, as near as may be to the proceedings in admiralty, except that either party may demand trial by jury of any issue of fact joined in any case, and all such proceedings shall be at the suit of and in the name of the United States.

**(d) Court costs, etc.**—When a decree of condemnation is entered against the pesticide or device, court costs and fees, storage, and other proper expenses shall be awarded against the person, if any, intervening as claimant of the pesticide or device.

(June 25, 1947, c. 125, § 13, as added Oct. 21, 1972, Pub.L. 92–516, § 2, 86 Stat. 991, and amended Oct. 25, 1988, Pub.L. 100–532, Title VIII, § 801(h), 102 Stat. 2682.)

### HISTORICAL AND STATUTORY NOTES

**Effective and Applicability Provisions**

1988 Acts

Amendment by Pub.L. 100–532 effective on expiration of 60 days after October 25, 1988, see section 901 of Pub.L. 100–532, set out as a note under section 136 of this title.

1972 Acts

Section effective at the close of Oct. 21, 1972, except if regulations are necessary for the implementation of any provision that becomes effective on Oct. 21, 1972, and continuation in effect of the provisions of subchapter I of this chapter and regulations thereunder as in effect prior to Oct. 21, 1972, until superseded by provisions of Pub.L. 92–516 and regulations thereunder, see section 4 of Pub.L. 92–516, set out as a note under section 136 of this title.

**Prior Provision**

A prior section 13 of Act June 25, 1947, was classified to section 135k of this title prior to amendment of Act June 25, 1947, by Pub.L. 92–516.

## § 136*l*. Penalties

[FIFRA § 14]

### (a) Civil penalties

#### (1) In general

Any registrant, commercial applicator, wholesaler, dealer, retailer, or other distributor who violates any provision of this subchapter may be assessed a civil penalty by the Administrator of not more than $5,000 for each offense.

#### (2) Private applicator

Any private applicator or other person not included in paragraph (1) who violates any provision of this subchapter subsequent to receiving a written warning from the Administrator or following a citation for a prior violation, may be assessed a civil penalty by the Administrator of not more than $1,000 for each offense, except that any applicator not included under paragraph (1) of this subsection who holds or applies registered pesticides, or uses dilutions of registered pesticides, only to provide a service of controlling pests without delivering any unapplied pesticide to any person so served, and who violates any provision of this subchapter may be assessed a civil penalty by the Administrator of not more than $500 for the first offense nor more than $1,000 for each subsequent offense.

#### (3) Hearing

No civil penalty shall be assessed unless the person charged shall have been given notice and opportunity for a hearing on such charge in the county, parish, or incorporated city of the residence of the person charged.

#### (4) Determination of penalty

In determining the amount of the penalty, the Administrator shall consider the appropriateness of such penalty to the size of the business of the person charged, the effect on the person's ability to continue in business, and the gravity of the violation. Whenever the Administrator finds that the violation occurred despite the exercise of due care or did not cause significant harm to health or the environment, the Administrator may issue a warning in lieu of assessing a penalty.

#### (5) References to Attorney General

In case of inability to collect such civil penalty or failure of any person to pay all, or such portion of such civil penalty as the Administrator may determine, the Administrator shall refer the matter to the Attorney General, who shall recover such amount by action in the appropriate United States district court.

### (b) Criminal penalties

#### (1) In general

(A) Any registrant, applicant for a registration, or producer who knowingly violates any provision of this subchapter shall be fined not more than $50,000 or imprisoned for not more than 1 year, or both.

(B) Any commercial applicator of a restricted use pesticide, or any other person not described in subparagraph (A) who distributes or sells pesticides or devices, who knowingly violates any provision of this subchapter shall be fined not more than $25,000 or imprisoned for not more than 1 year, or both.

#### (2) Private applicator

Any private applicator or other person not included in paragraph (1) who knowingly violates any provision of this subchapter shall be guilty of a misdemeanor and shall on conviction be fined not more than $1,000, or imprisoned for not more than 30 days, or both.

#### (3) Disclosure of information

Any person, who, with intent to defraud, uses or reveals information relative to formulas of products acquired under the authority of section 136a of this title, shall be fined not more than $10,000, or imprisoned for not more than three years, or both.

#### (4) Acts of officers, agents, etc.

When construing and enforcing the provisions of this subchapter, the act, omission, or failure of any officer, agent, or other person acting for or employed by any person shall in every case be also deemed to be the act, omission, or failure of such person as well as that of the person employed.

(June 25, 1947, c. 125, § 14, as added Oct. 21, 1972, Pub.L. 92–516, § 2, 86 Stat. 992, and amended Sept. 30, 1978, Pub.L. 95–396, § 17, 92 Stat. 832; Oct. 25, 1988, Pub.L. 100–532, Title VI, § 604, 102 Stat. 2678; Dec. 13, 1991, Pub.L. 102–237, Title X, § 1006(a)(8), 105 Stat. 1895.)

### HISTORICAL AND STATUTORY NOTES

**Effective and Applicability Provisions**

1991 Acts

Amendments by section 1006(a)(8) of Pub.L. 102–237 effective Dec. 13, 1991, see section 1101(a) of Pub.L. 102–237, set out as a note under section 1421 of this title.

1988 Acts

Amendment by Pub.L. 100–532 effective on expiration of 60 days after October 25, 1988, see section 901 of Pub.L. 100–532, set out as a note under section 136 of this title.

1972 Acts

Section effective at the close of Oct. 21, 1972, except if regulations are necessary for the implementation of any provision that becomes effective on Oct. 21, 1972, and continuation in effect of the provisions of subchapter I of this chapter and regulations thereunder as in effect prior to Oct. 21, 1972, until superseded by provisions of Pub.L. 92–516 and regulations thereunder, see section 4 of Pub.L. 92–516, set out as a note under section 136 of this title.

## § 136m. Indemnities

**[FIFRA § 15]**

### (a) General indemnification

#### (1) In general

Except as otherwise provided in this section, if—

(A) the Administrator notifies a registrant under section 136d(c)(1) of this title that the Administrator intends to suspend a registration or that an emergency order of suspension of a registration under section 136d(c)(3) of this title has been issued;

(B) the registration in question is suspended under section 136d(c) of this title, and thereafter is canceled under section 136d(b), 136d(d), or 136d(f) of this title; and

(C) any person who owned any quantity of the pesticide immediately before the notice to the registrant under subparagraph (A) suffered losses by reason of suspension or cancellation of the registration;

the Administrator shall make an indemnity payment to the person.

#### (2) Exception

Paragraph (1) shall not apply if the Administrator finds that the person—

(A) had knowledge of facts that, in themselves, would have shown that the pesticide did not meet the requirements of section 136a(c)(5) of this title for registration; and

(B) continued thereafter to produce the pesticide without giving timely notice of such facts to the Administrator.

#### (3) Report

If the Administrator takes an action under paragraph (1) that requires the payment of indemnification, the Administrator shall report to the Committee on Agriculture of the House of Representatives, the Committee on Agriculture, Nutrition, and Forestry of the Senate, and the Committees on Appropriations of the House of Representatives and the Senate on—

(A) the action taken that requires the payment of indemnification;

(B) the reasons for taking the action;

(C) the estimated cost of the payment; and

(D) a request for the appropriation of funds for the payment.

#### (4) Appropriation

The Administrator may not make a payment of indemnification under paragraph (1) unless a specific line item appropriation of funds has been made in advance for the payment.

### (b) Indemnification of end users, dealers, and distributors

#### (1) End users

If—

(A) the Administrator notifies a registrant under section 136d(c)(1) of this title that the Administrator intends to suspend a registration or that an emergency order of suspension of a registration under section 136d(c)(3) of this title has been issued;

(B) the registration in question is suspended under section 136d(c) of this title, and thereafter is canceled under section 136d(b), 136d(d), or 136d(f) of this title; and

(C) any person who, immediately before the notice to the registrant under subparagraph (A), owned any quantity of the pesticide for purposes of applying or using the pesticide as an end user, rather than for purposes of distributing or selling it or further processing it for distribution or sale, suffered a loss by reason of the suspension or cancellation of the pesticide;

the person shall be entitled to an indemnity payment under this subsection for such quantity of the pesticide.

#### (2) Dealers and distributors

(A) Any registrant, wholesaler, dealer, or other distributor (hereinafter in this paragraph referred to as a "seller") of a registered pesticide who distributes or sells the pesticide directly to any person not described as an end user in paragraph (1)(C) shall, with respect to any quantity of the pesticide that such person cannot use or resell as a result of the suspension or cancellation of the pesticide, reimburse such person for the cost of first acquiring the pesticide from the seller (other than the cost of transportation, if any), unless the seller provided to the person at the time of distribution or sale a notice, in writing, that the pesticide is not subject to reimbursement by the seller.

(B) If—

(i) the Administrator notifies a registrant under section 136d(c)(1) of this title that the Administrator intends to suspend a registration or that an emergency order of suspension of a registration under section 136d(c)(3) of this title has been issued;

(ii) the registration in question is suspended under section 136d(c) of this title, and thereafter is canceled under section 136d(b), 136d(d), or 136d(f) of this title;

(iii) any person who, immediately before the notice to the registrant under clause (i)—

(I) had not been notified in writing by the seller, as provided under subparagraph (A), that any quantity of the pesticide owned by such person is not subject to reimbursement by the seller in the event of suspension or cancellation of the pesticide; and

(II) owned any quantity of the pesticide for purposes of—

(aa) distributing or selling it; or

(bb) further processing it for distribution or sale directly to an end user;

suffered a loss by reason of the suspension or cancellation of the pesticide; and

(iv) the Administrator determines on the basis of a claim of loss submitted to the Administrator by the person, that the seller—

(I) did not provide the notice specified in subparagraph (A) to such person; and

(II) is and will continue to be unable to provide reimbursement to such person, as provided under subparagraph (A), for the loss referred to in clause (iii), as a result of the insolvency or bankruptcy of the seller and the seller's resulting inability to provide such reimbursement;

the person shall be entitled to an indemnity payment under this subsection for such quantity of the pesticide.

(C) If an indemnity payment is made by the United States under this paragraph, the United States shall be subrogated to any right that would otherwise be held under this paragraph by a seller who is unable to make a reimbursement in accordance with this paragraph with regard to reimbursements that otherwise would have been made by the seller.

**(3) Source**

Any payment required to be made under paragraph (1) or (2) shall be made from the appropriation provided under section 1304 of Title 31.

**(4) Administrative settlement**

An administrative settlement of a claim for such indemnity may be made in accordance with the third paragraph of section 2414 of Title 28 and shall be regarded as if it were made under that section for purposes of section 1304 of Title 31.

**(c) Amount of payment**

**(1) In general**

The amount of an indemnity payment under subsection (a) or (b) of this section to any person shall be determined on the basis of the cost of the pesticide owned by the person (other than the cost of transportation, if any) immediately before the issuance of the notice to the registrant referred to in subsection (a)(1)(A), (b)(1)(A), or (b)(2)(B)(i) of this section, except that in no event shall an indemnity payment to any person exceed the fair market value of the pesticide owned by the person immediately before the issuance of the notice.

**(2) Special rule**

Notwithstanding any other provision of this subchapter, the Administrator may provide a reasonable time for use or other disposal of the pesticide. In determining the quantity of any pesticide for which indemnity shall be paid under this section, proper adjustment shall be made for any pesticide used or otherwise disposed of by the owner.

(June 25, 1947, c. 125, § 15, as added Oct. 21, 1972, Pub.L. 92–516, § 2, 86 Stat. 993, and amended Oct. 25, 1988, Pub.L. 100–532, Title V, § 501(a), 102 Stat. 2674.)

### HISTORICAL AND STATUTORY NOTES

**Effective and Applicability Provisions**

1988 Acts

Section 501(a) of Pub.L. 100–532 provided in part that amendment by Pub.L. 100–532 is effective 180 days after October 25, 1988.

1971 Acts

Section effective at the close of Oct. 21, 1972, except if regulations are necessary for the implementation of any provision that becomes effective on Oct. 21, 1972, and continuation in effect of the provisions of subchapter I of this chapter and regulations thereunder as in effect prior to Oct. 21, 1972, until superseded by provisions of Pub.L. 92–516 and regulations thereunder, see section 4 of Pub.L. 92–516, set out as a note under section 136 of this title.

**Interim Payments**

Section 501(b) of Pub.L. 100–532 provided that:

"(1) **Source.**—Any obligation of the Administrator to pay an indemnity arising under section 15 [this section], as it existed prior to the effective date of the amendment made by this section [see Effective Date note under section], shall be made from the appropriation provided under section 1304 of title 31, United States Code [section 1304 of Title 31, Money and Finance].

"(2) **Administrative settlement.**—An administrative settlement of a claim for such indemnity may be made in accordance with the third paragraph of section 2414 of title 28, United States Code [section 2414 of Title 28, Judiciary and Judicial Procedure], and shall be regarded as if it were made under that section for purposes of section 1304 of title 31, United States Code [section 1304 of Title 31]."

[Section 901 of Pub.L. 100–532 provided that this provision be effective 60 days after October 25, 1988].

## § 136n. Administrative procedure; judicial review

**[FIFRA § 16]**

**(a) District court review**

Except as otherwise provided in this subchapter, the refusal of the Administrator to cancel or suspend a registration or to change a classification not following a hearing and other final actions of the Administrator not committed to the discretion of the Administrator by law are judicially reviewable by the district courts of the United States.

**(b) Review by court of appeals**

In the case of actual controversy as to the validity of any order issued by the Administrator following a public hearing, any person who will be adversely affected by such order and who had been a party to the proceedings may obtain judicial review by filing in the United States court of appeals for the circuit wherein such person resides or has a place of business, within 60 days after the entry of such order, a petition praying that the order be set aside in whole or in part. A copy of the petition shall be forthwith transmitted by the clerk of the court to the Administrator or any officer designated by the Administrator for that purpose, and thereupon the Administrator shall file in the court the record of the proceedings on which the Administrator based the Administrator's order, as provided in section 2112 of Title 28. Upon the filing of such petition the court shall have exclusive jurisdiction to affirm or set aside the order complained of in whole or in part. The court shall consider all evidence of record. The order of the Administrator shall be sustained if it is supported by substantial evidence when considered on the record as a whole. The judgment of the court affirming or setting aside, in whole or in part, any order under this section shall be final, subject to review by the Supreme Court of the United States upon certiorari or certification as provided in section 1254 of Title 28. The commencement of proceedings under this section shall not, unless specifically ordered by the court to the contrary, operate as a stay of an order.

**(c) Jurisdiction of district courts**

The district courts of the United States are vested with jurisdiction specifically to enforce, and to prevent and restrain violations of, this subchapter.

**(d) Notice of judgments**

The Administrator shall, by publication in such manner as the Administrator may prescribe, give notice of all judgments entered in actions instituted under the authority of this subchapter.

(June 25, 1947, c. 125, § 16, as added Oct. 21, 1972, Pub.L. 92–516, § 2, 86 Stat. 994, and amended Nov. 8, 1984, Pub.L. 98–620, Title IV, § 402(4)(C), 98 Stat. 3357; Oct. 25, 1988, Pub.L. 100–532, Title VIII, § 801(i), 102 Stat. 2682; Dec. 13, 1991, Pub.L. 102–237, Title X, § 1006(b)(1), (2), (3)(P), 105 Stat. 1895, 1896.)

### HISTORICAL AND STATUTORY NOTES

**Effective and Applicability Provisions**

1991 Acts

Amendments by Pub.L. 102–237 effective Dec. 13, 1991, see section 1101(a) of Pub.L. 102–237, set out as a note under section 1421 of this title.

1988 Acts

Amendment by Pub.L. 100–532 effective on expiration of 60 days after October 25, 1988, see section 901 of Pub.L. 100–532, set out as a note under section 136 of this title.

1984 Acts

Amendment by Pub.L. 98–620 not to apply to cases pending on Nov. 8, 1984, see section 403 of Pub.L. 98–620, set out as a note under section 1657 of Title 28, Judiciary and Judicial Procedure.

1972 Acts

Section effective at the close of Oct. 21, 1972, except if regulations are necessary for the implementation of any provision that becomes effective on Oct. 21, 1972, and continuation in effect of the provisions of subchapter I of this chapter and regulations thereunder as in effect prior to Oct. 21, 1972, until superseded by provisions of Pub.L. 92–516 and regulations thereunder, see section 4 of Pub.L. 92–516, set out as a note under section 136 of this title.

## § 136*o*. Imports and exports

**[FIFRA § 17]**

**(a) Pesticides and devices intended for export**

Notwithstanding any other provision of this subchapter, no pesticide or device or active ingredient used in producing a pesticide intended solely for export to any foreign country shall be deemed in violation of this subchapter—

(1) when prepared or packed according to the specifications or directions of the foreign purchaser, except that producers of such pesticides and devices and active ingredients used in producing pesticides shall be subject to sections 136(p), (q)(1)(A), (C), (D), (E), (G), and (H), (q)(2)(A), (B), (C)(i) and (iii), and (D), 136e, and 136f of this title; and

(2) in the case of any pesticide other than a pesticide registered under section 136a or sold under section 136d(a)(1) of this title, if, prior to export, the foreign purchaser has signed a statement acknowledging that the purchaser understands that such pesticide is not registered for use in the United States and cannot be sold in the United States under this subchapter.

A copy of that statement shall be transmitted to an appropriate official of the government of the importing country.

**(b) Cancellation notices furnished to foreign governments**

Whenever a registration, or a cancellation or suspension of the registration of a pesticide becomes effective, or ceases to be effective, the Administrator shall transmit through the State Department notification thereof to the governments of other countries and to appropriate international agencies. Such notification shall, upon request, include all information related to the cancellation or suspension of the registration of the pesticide and information concerning other pesticides that are registered under section 136a of this title and that could be used in lieu of such pesticide.

**(c) Importation of pesticides and devices**

The Secretary of the Treasury shall notify the Administrator of the arrival of pesticides and devices and shall deliver to the Administrator, upon the Administrator's request, samples of pesticides or devices which are being imported into the United States, giving notice to the owner or consignee, who may appear before the Administrator and have the right to introduce testimony. If it appears from the examination of a sample that it is adulterated, or misbranded or otherwise violates the provisions set forth in this subchapter, or is otherwise injurious to health or the environment, the pesticide or device may be refused admission, and the Secretary of the Treasury shall refuse delivery to the consignee and shall cause the destruction of any pesticide or device refused delivery which shall not be exported by the consignee within 90 days from the date of notice of such refusal under such regulations as the Secretary of the Treasury may prescribe. The Secretary of the Treasury may deliver to the consignee such pesticide or device pending examination and decision in the matter on execution of bond for the amount of the full invoice value of such pesticide or device, together with the duty thereon, and on refusal to return such pesticide or device for any cause to the custody of the Secretary of the Treasury, when demanded, for the purpose of excluding them from the country, or for any other purpose, said consignee shall forfeit the full amount of said bond. All charges for storage, cartage, and labor on pesticides or devices which are refused admission or delivery shall be paid by the owner or consignee, and in default of such payment shall constitute a lien against any future importation made by such owner or consignee.

**(d) Cooperation in international efforts**

The Administrator shall, in cooperation with the Department of State and any other appropriate Federal agency, participate and cooperate in any international efforts to develop improved pesticide research and regulations.

**(e) Regulations**

The Secretary of the Treasury, in consultation with the Administrator, shall prescribe regulations for the enforcement of subsection (c) of this section.

(June 25, 1947, c. 125, § 17, as added Oct. 21, 1972, Pub.L. 92–516, § 2, 86 Stat. 995, and amended Sept. 30, 1978, Pub.L. 95–396, § 18(a), 92 Stat. 833; Oct. 25, 1988, Pub.L. 100–532, Title VIII, § 801(j), 102 Stat. 2682; Dec. 13, 1991, Pub.L. 102–237, Title X, § 1006(a)(9), (b)(2), 105 Stat. 1895.)

### HISTORICAL AND STATUTORY NOTES

**Effective and Applicability Provisions**

1991 Acts

Amendments by Pub.L. 102–237 effective Dec. 13, 1991, see section 1101(a) of Pub.L. 102–237, set out as a note under section 1421 of this title.

1988 Acts

Amendment by Pub.L. 100–532 effective on expiration of 60 days after October 25, 1988, see section 901 of Pub.L. 100–532, set out as a note under section 136 of this title.

1978 Acts

Section 18(b) of Pub.L. 95–396 provided that: "The amendment made by subsection (a)(1) of this section [amending subsec. (a) of this section] shall become effective one hundred and eighty days after the date of enactment of this Act [Sept. 30, 1978]."

1972 Acts

Section effective at the close of Oct. 21, 1972, except if regulations are necessary for the implementation of any provision that becomes effective on Oct. 21, 1972, and continuation in effect of the provisions of subchapter I of this chapter and regulations thereunder as in effect prior to Oct. 21, 1972, until superseded by provisions of Pub.L. 92–516 and regulations thereunder, see section 4 of Pub.L. 92–516, set out as a note under section 136 of this title.

## § 136p. Exemption of Federal and State agencies

**[FIFRA § 18]**

The Administrator may, at the Administrator's discretion, exempt any Federal or State agency from any provision of this subchapter if the Administrator determines that emergency conditions exist which require such exemption. The Administrator, in determining whether or not such emergency conditions exist, shall consult with the Secretary of Agriculture and the Governor of any State concerned if they request such determination.

(June 25, 1947, c. 125, § 18, as added Oct. 21, 1972, Pub.L. 92–516, § 2, 86 Stat. 995, and amended Nov. 28, 1975, Pub.L. 94–140, § 8, 89 Stat. 754; Oct. 25, 1988, Pub.L. 100–532, Title VIII, § 801(k), 102 Stat. 2682; Dec. 13, 1991, Pub.L. 102–237, Title X, § 1006(b)(1), (2), 105 Stat. 1895.)

### HISTORICAL AND STATUTORY NOTES

**Effective and Applicability Provisions**

1991 Acts

Amendments by Pub.L. 102–237 effective Dec. 13, 1991, see section 1101(a) of Pub.L. 102–237, set out as a note under section 1421 of this title.

1988 Acts

Amendment by Pub.L. 100–532 effective on expiration of 60 days after October 25, 1988, see section 901 of Pub.L. 100–532, set out as a note under section 136 of this title.

1972 Acts

Section effective at the close of Oct. 21, 1972, except if regulations are necessary for the implementation of any provision that becomes effective on Oct. 21, 1972, and continuation in effect of the provisions of subchapter I of this chapter and regulations thereunder as in effect prior to Oct. 21, 1972, until superseded by provisions of Pub.L. 92–516 and regulations thereunder, see section 4 of Pub.L. 92–516, set out as a note under section 136 of this title.

## § 136q. Storage, disposal, transportation, and recall

**[FIFRA § 19]**

### (a) Storage, disposal, and transportation

#### (1) Data requirements and registration of pesticides

The Administrator may require under section 136a or 136d of this title that—

(A) the registrant or applicant for registration of a pesticide submit or cite data or information regarding methods for the safe storage and disposal of excess quantities of the pesticide to support the registration or continued registration of a pesticide;

(B) the labeling of a pesticide contain requirements and procedures for the transportation, storage, and disposal of the pesticide, any container of the pesticide, any rinsate containing the pesticide, or any other material used to contain or collect excess or spilled quantities of the pesticide; and

(C) the registrant of a pesticide provide evidence of sufficient financial and other resources to carry out a recall plan under subsection (b) of this section, and provide for the disposition of the pesticide, in the event of suspension and cancellation of the pesticide.

#### (2) Pesticides

The Administrator may by regulation, or as part of an order issued under section 136d of this title or an amendment to such an order—

(A) issue requirements and procedures to be followed by any person who stores or transports a pesticide the registration of which has been suspended or canceled;

(B) issue requirements and procedures to be followed by any person who disposes of stocks of a pesticide the registration of which has been suspended; and

(C) issue requirements and procedures for the disposal of any pesticide the registration of which has been canceled.

#### (3) Containers, rinsates, and other materials

The Administrator may by regulation, or as part of an order issued under section 136d of this title or an amendment to such an order—

(A) issue requirements and procedures to be followed by any person who stores or transports any container of a pesticide the registration of which has been suspended or canceled, any rinsate containing the pesticide, or any other material used to contain or collect excess or spilled quantities of the pesticide;

(B) issue requirements and procedures to be followed by any person who disposes of stocks of any container of a pesticide the registration of which has been suspended, any rinsate containing the pesticide, or any other material used to contain or collect excess or spilled quantities of the pesticide; and

(C) issue requirements and procedures for the disposal of any container of a pesticide the registration of which has been canceled, any rinsate containing the pesticide, or any other material used to contain or collect excess or spilled quantities of the pesticide.

### (b) Recalls

#### (1) In general

If the registration of a pesticide has been suspended and canceled under section 136d of this title, and if the Administrator finds that recall of the pesticide is necessary to protect health or the environment, the Administrator shall order a recall of the pesticide in accordance with this subsection.

#### (2) Voluntary recall

If, after determining under paragraph (1) that a recall is necessary, the Administrator finds that voluntary recall by the registrant and others in the chain of distribution may be as safe and effective as a mandatory recall, the Administrator shall request the registrant of the pesticide to submit, within 60 days of the request, a plan for the voluntary recall of the pesticide. If such a plan is requested and submitted, the Administrator shall approve the plan and order the registrant to conduct the recall in accordance with the plan unless the Administrator determines, after an informal hearing, that the plan is inadequate to protect health or the environment.

#### (3) Mandatory recall

If, after determining under paragraph (1) that a recall is necessary, the Administrator does not request the submission of a plan under paragraph (2) or finds such a plan to be inadequate, the Administrator shall issue a regulation that prescribes a plan for the recall of the pesticide. A regulation issued under this paragraph may apply to any person who is or was a registrant, distributor, or seller of the pesticide, or any successor in interest to such a person.

#### (4) Recall procedure

A regulation issued under this subsection may require any person that is subject to the regulation to—

(A) arrange to make available one or more storage facilities to receive and store the pesticide to which the recall program applies, and inform the Administrator of the location of each such facility;

(B) accept and store at such a facility those existing stocks of such pesticide that are tendered by any other person who obtained the pesticide directly or indirectly from the person that is subject to such regulation;

(C) on the request of a person making such a tender, provide for proper transportation of the pesticide to a storage facility; and

(D) take such reasonable steps as the regulation may prescribe to inform persons who may be holders of the pesticide of the terms of the recall regulation and how those persons may tender the pesticide and arrange for transportation of the pesticide to a storage facility.

**(5) Contents of recall plan**

A recall plan established under this subsection shall include—

(A) the level in the distribution chain to which the recall is to extend, and a schedule for recall; and

(B) the means to be used to verify the effectiveness of the recall.

**(6) Requirements or procedures**

No requirement or procedure imposed in accordance with paragraph (2) of subsection (a) of this section may require the recall of existing stocks of the pesticide except as provided by this subsection.

**(c) Storage costs**

**(1) Submission of plan**

A registrant who wishes to become eligible for reimbursement of storage costs incurred as a result of a recall prescribed under subsection (b) of this section for a pesticide whose registration has been suspended and canceled shall, as soon as practicable after the suspension of the registration of the pesticide, submit to the Administrator a plan for the storage and disposal of the pesticide that meets criteria established by the Administrator by regulation.

**(2) Reimbursement**

Within a reasonable period of time after such storage costs are incurred and paid by the registrant, the Administrator shall reimburse the registrant, on request, for—

(A) none of the costs incurred by the registrant before the date of submission of the plan referred to in paragraph (1) to the Administrator;

(B) 100 percent of the costs incurred by the registrant after the date of submission of the plan to the Administrator or the date of cancellation of the registration of the pesticide, whichever is later, but before the approval of the plan by the Administrator;

(C) 50 percent of the costs incurred by the registrant during the 1-year period beginning on the date of the approval of the plan by the Administrator or the date of cancellation of the registration of the pesticide, whichever is later;

(D) none of the costs incurred by the registrant during the 3-year period beginning on the 366th day following approval of the plan by the Administrator or the date of cancellation of the registration of the pesticide, whichever is later; and

(E) 25 percent of the costs incurred by the registrant during the period beginning on the first day of the 5th year following the date of the approval of the plan by the Administrator or the date of cancellation of the registration of the pesticide, whichever is later, and ending on the date that a disposal permit for the pesticide is issued by a State or an alternative plan for disposal of the pesticide in accordance with applicable law has been developed.

**(d) Administration of storage, disposal, transportation, and recall programs**

**(1) Voluntary agreements**

Nothing in this section shall be construed as preventing or making unlawful any agreement between a seller and a buyer of any pesticide or other substance regarding the ultimate allocation of the costs of storage, transportation, or disposal of a pesticide.

**(2) Rule and regulation review**

Section 136w(a)(4) of this title shall not apply to any regulation issued under subsection (a)(2) or (b) of this section.

**(3) Limitations**

No registrant shall be responsible under this section for a pesticide the registration of which is held by another person. No distributor or seller shall be responsible under this section for a pesticide that the distributor or seller did not hold or sell.

**(4) Seizure and penalties**

If the Administrator finds that a person who is subject to a regulation or order under subsection (a)(2) or (b) of this section has failed substantially to comply with that regulation or order, the Administrator may take action under section 136k or 136l of this title or obtain injunctive relief under section 136n(c) of this title against such person or any successor in interest of any such person.

(e) **Container design**

(1) **Procedures**

(A) Not later than 3 years after the effective date of this subsection, the Administrator shall, in consultation with the heads of other interested Federal agencies, promulgate regulations for the design of pesticide containers that will promote the safe storage and disposal of pesticides.

(B) The regulations shall ensure, to the fullest extent practicable, that the containers—

(i) accommodate procedures used for the removal of pesticides from the containers and the rinsing of the containers;

(ii) facilitate the safe use of the containers, including elimination of splash and leakage of pesticides from the containers;

(iii) facilitate the safe disposal of the containers; and

(iv) facilitate the safe refill and reuse of the containers.

(2) **Compliance**

The Administrator shall require compliance with the regulations referred to in paragraph (1) not later than 5 years after the effective date of this subsection.

(f) **Pesticide residue removal**

(1) **Procedures**

(A) Not later than 3 years after the effective date of this subsection, the Administrator shall, in consultation with the heads of other interested Federal agencies, promulgate regulations prescribing procedures and standards for the removal of pesticides from containers prior to disposal.

(B) The regulations may—

(i) specify, for each major type of pesticide container, procedures and standards providing for, at a minimum, triple rinsing or the equivalent degree of pesticide removal;

(ii) specify procedures that can be implemented promptly and easily in various circumstances and conditions;

(iii) provide for reuse, whenever practicable, or disposal of rinse water and residue; and

(iv) be coordinated with requirements for the rinsing of containers imposed under the Solid Waste Disposal Act (42 U.S.C. 6901 et seq.).

(C) The Administrator may, at the discretion of the Administrator, exempt products intended solely for household use from the requirements of this subsection.

(2) **Compliance**

Effective beginning 5 years after the effective date of this subsection, a State may not exercise primary enforcement responsibility under section 136w–1 of this title, or certify an applicator under section 136i of this title, unless the Administrator determines that the State is carrying out an adequate program to ensure compliance with this subsection.

(3) **Solid Waste Disposal Act**

Nothing in this subsection shall affect the authorities or requirements concerning pesticide containers under the Solid Waste Disposal Act (42 U.S.C. 6901).

(g) **Pesticide container study**

(1) **Study**

(A) The Administrator shall conduct a study of options to encourage or require—

(i) the return, refill, and reuse of pesticide containers;

(ii) the development and use of pesticide formulations that facilitate the removal of pesticide residues from containers; and

(iii) the use of bulk storage facilities to reduce the number of pesticide containers requiring disposal.

(B) In conducting the study, the Administrator shall—

(i) consult with the heads of other interested Federal agencies, State agencies, industry groups, and environmental organizations; and

(ii) assess the feasibility, costs, and environmental benefits of encouraging or requiring various measures or actions.

(2) **Report**

Not later than 2 years after the effective date of this subsection, the Administrator shall submit to Congress a report describing the results of the study required under paragraph (1).

(h) **Relationship to Solid Waste Disposal Act**

(1) **In general**

Nothing in this section shall diminish the authorities or requirements of the Solid Waste Disposal Act (42 U.S.C. 6901 et seq.).

(2) **Antimicrobial products**

A household, industrial, or institutional antimicrobial product that is not subject to regulation under the Solid Waste Disposal Act (42 U.S.C. 6901 et seq.) shall not be subject to the provisions of subsections (a), (e), and (f) of this section, unless the Administrator determines that such product must be subject to such provisions to prevent an unreasonable adverse effect on the environment.

(June 25, 1947, c. 125, § 19, as added Oct. 21, 1972, Pub.L. 92–516, § 2, 86 Stat. 995, and amended Sept. 30, 1978, Pub.L. 95–396, § 19, 92 Stat. 833; Oct. 25, 1988, Pub.L. 100–532, Title IV, §§ 401–403, Title VIII, § 801(q)(1)(D), 102 Stat. 2669 to 2672, 2683; Aug. 3, 1996, Pub.L. 104–170, Title II, § 225, 110 Stat. 1507.)

HISTORICAL AND STATUTORY NOTES

**References in Text**

For effective date of this subsection, referred to in text, see section 901 of Pub.L. 100–532, set out as a note under section 136 of this title.

The Solid Waste Disposal Act, referred to in text, is Title II of Pub.L. 89–272, Oct. 20, 1965, 79 Stat. 997, as amended generally by Pub.L. 94–580, § 2, Oct. 21, 1976, 90 Stat. 2795, which is classified generally to chapter 82 (section 6901 et seq.) of Title 42. For complete classification of this Act to the Code, see Short Title of 1965 Acts note set out under section 6901 of Title 42, The Public Health and Welfare, and Tables.

**Effective and Applicability Provisions**

1988 Acts

Amendment by Pub.L. 100–532 effective on expiration of 60 days after October 25, 1988, see section 901 of Pub.L. 100–532, set out as a note under section 136 of this title.

1972 Acts

Section effective at the close of Oct. 21, 1972, except if regulations are necessary for the implementation of any provision that becomes effective on Oct. 21, 1972, and continuation in effect of the provisions of subchapter I of this chapter and regulations thereunder as in effect prior to Oct. 21, 1972, until superseded by provisions of Pub.L. 92–516 and regulations thereunder, see section 4 of Pub.L. 92–516, set out as a note under section 136 of this title.

## § 136r. Research and monitoring

[FIFRA § 20]

### (a) Research

The Administrator shall undertake research including research by grant or contract with other Federal agencies, universities, or others as may be necessary to carry out the purposes of this subchapter, and the Administrator shall conduct research into integrated pest management in coordination with the Secretary of Agriculture. The Administrator shall also take care to ensure that such research does not duplicate research being undertaken by any other Federal agency.

### (b) National monitoring plan

The Administrator shall formulate and periodically revise, in cooperation with other Federal, State, or local agencies, a national plan for monitoring pesticides.

### (c) Monitoring

The Administrator shall undertake such monitoring activities, including, but not limited to monitoring in air, soil, water, man, plants, and animals, as may be necessary for the implementation of this subchapter and of the national pesticide monitoring plan. The Administrator shall establish procedures for the monitoring of man and animals and their environment for incidential [1] pesticide exposure, including, but not limited to, the quantification of incidental human and environmental pesticide pollution and the secular trends thereof, and identification of the sources of contamination and their relationship to human and environmental effects. Such activities shall be carried out in cooperation with other Federal, State, and local agencies.

(June 25, 1947, c. 125, § 20, as added Oct. 21, 1972, Pub.L. 92–516, § 2, 86 Stat. 996, and amended Sept. 30, 1978, Pub.L. 95–396, § 20, 92 Stat. 834; Dec. 13, 1991, Pub.L. 102–237, Title X, § 1006(a)(10), (b)(1), 105 Stat. 1895.)

[1] So in original. Probably should read "incidental".

HISTORICAL AND STATUTORY NOTES

**Effective and Applicability Provisions**

1991 Acts

Amendments by section 1006(a)(10), (b)(1) of Pub.L. 102–237 effective Dec. 13, 1991, see section 1101(a) of Pub.L. 102–237, set out as a note under section 1421 of this title.

1972 Acts

Section effective at the close of Oct. 21, 1972, except if regulations are necessary for the implementation of any provision that becomes effective on Oct. 21, 1972, and continuation in effect of the provisions of subchapter I of this chapter and regulations thereunder as in effect prior to Oct. 21, 1972, until superseded by provisions of Pub.L. 92–516 and regulations thereunder, see section 4 of Pub.L. 92–516, set out as a note under section 136 of this title.

**Award of Grants**

Pub.L. 106–74, Title III, Oct. 20, 1999, 113 Stat. 1081, provided in part: "That notwithstanding 7 U.S.C. 136r [this section] and 15 U.S.C. 2609, beginning in fiscal year 2000 and thereafter, grants awarded under section 20 of the Federal Insecticide, Fungicide, and Rodenticide Act, as amended, [this section] and section 10 of the Toxic Substances Control Act, as amended, [15 U.S.C.A. § 2609] shall be available for research, development, monitoring, public education, training, demonstrations, and studies".

## § 136r–1. Integrated Pest Management

The Secretary of Agriculture, in cooperation with the Administrator, shall implement research, demonstration, and education programs to support adoption of Integrated Pest Management. Integrated Pest Management is a sustainable approach to managing pests by combining biological, cultural, physical, and chemical tools in a way that minimizes economic, health, and environmental risks. The Secretary of Agriculture and the Administrator shall make information on Integrated Pest Management widely available to pesticide users, including Federal agencies. Federal agencies shall use Integrated Pest Management techniques in carrying out pest management activities and shall promote Integrated Pest Management through procurement and regulatory policies, and other activities.

(Pub.L. 104–170, Title III, § 303, Aug. 3, 1996, 110 Stat. 1512.)

HISTORICAL AND STATUTORY NOTES

**Codifications**

Section was enacted as part of the Food Quality Protection Act of 1996 and not as part of the Federal Insecticide, Fungicide, and Rodenticide Act of 1996, which comprises this subchapter.

## § 136s. Solicitation of comments; notice of public hearings

[FIFRA § 21]

**(a) Secretary of Agriculture**

The Administrator, before publishing regulations under this subchapter, shall solicit the views of the Secretary of Agriculture in accordance with the procedure described in section 136w(a) of this title.

**(b) Secretary of Health and Human Services**

The Administrator, before publishing regulations under this subchapter for any public health pesticide, shall solicit the views of the Secretary of Health and Human Services in the same manner as the views of the Secretary of Agriculture are solicited under section 136w(a)(2) of this title.

**(c) Views**

In addition to any other authority relating to public hearings and solicitation of views, in connection with the suspension or cancellation of a pesticide registration or any other actions authorized under this subchapter, the Administrator may, at the Administrator's discretion, solicit the views of all interested persons, either orally or in writing, and seek such advice from scientists, farmers, farm organizations, and other qualified persons as the Administrator deems proper.

**(d) Notice**

In connection with all public hearings under this subchapter the Administrator shall publish timely notice of such hearings in the Federal Register.

(June 25, 1947, c. 125, § 21, as added Oct. 21, 1972, Pub.L. 92–516, § 2, 86 Stat. 996, and amended Nov. 28, 1975, Pub.L. 94–140, § 2(b), 89 Stat. 752; Oct. 25, 1988, Pub.L. 100–532, Title VIII, § 801(*l*), 102 Stat. 2682; Dec. 13, 1991, Pub.L. 102–237, Title X, § 1006(b)(1), (2), 105 Stat. 1895; Aug. 3, 1996, Pub.L. 104–170, Title II, § 234, 110 Stat. 1509.)

HISTORICAL AND STATUTORY NOTES

**Effective and Applicability Provisions**

1991 Acts

Amendments by Pub.L. 102–237 effective Dec. 13, 1991, see section 1101(a) of Pub.L. 102–237, set out as a note under section 1421 of this title.

1988 Acts

Amendment by Pub.L. 100–532 effective on expiration of 60 days after October 25, 1988, see section 901 of Pub.L. 100–532, set out as a note under section 136 of this title.

1972 Acts

Section effective at the close of Oct. 21, 1972, except if regulations are necessary for the implementation of any provision that becomes effective on Oct. 21, 1972, and continuation in effect of the provisions of subchapter I of this chapter and regulations thereunder as in effect prior to Oct. 21, 1972, until superseded by provisions of Pub.L. 92–516 and regulations thereunder, see section 4 of Pub.L. 92–516, set out as a note under section 136 of this title.

## § 136t. Delegation and cooperation

[FIFRA § 22]

**(a) Delegation.**

All authority vested in the Administrator by virtue of the provisions of this subchapter may with like force and effect be executed by such employees of the Environmental Protection Agency as the Administrator may designate for the purpose.

**(b) Cooperation.**

The Administrator shall cooperate with Department of Agriculture, any other Federal agency, and any appropriate agency of any State or any political subdivision thereof, in carrying out the provisions of this subchapter, and in securing uniformity of regulations.

(June 25, 1947, c. 125, § 22, as added Oct. 21, 1972, Pub.L. 92–516, § 2, 86 Stat. 996.)

HISTORICAL AND STATUTORY NOTES

**Effective and Applicability Provisions**

1972 Acts

Section effective at the close of Oct. 21, 1972, except if regulations are necessary for the implementation of any provision that becomes effective on Oct. 21, 1972, and continuation in effect of the provisions of subchapter I of this chapter and regulations thereunder as in effect prior to Oct. 21, 1972, until superseded by provisions of Pub.L. 92–516, and regulations thereunder, see section 4 of Pub.L. 92–516, set out as a note under section 136 of this title.

## § 136u. State cooperation, aid, and training

[FIFRA § 23]

**(a) Cooperative agreements.**

The Administrator may enter into cooperative agreements with States and Indian tribes—

(1) to delegate to any State or Indian tribe the authority to cooperate in the enforcement of this subchapter through the use of its personnel or facilities, to train personnel of the State or Indian tribe to cooperate in the enforcement of this subchapter, and to assist States and Indian tribes in implementing cooperative enforcement programs through grants-in-aid; and

(2) to assist States in developing and administering State programs, and Indian tribes that enter into cooperative agreements, to train and certify

applicators consistent with the standards the Administrator prescribes.

Effective with the fiscal year beginning October 1, 1978, there are authorized to be appropriated annually such funds as may be necessary for the Administrator to provide through cooperative agreements an amount equal to 50 percent of the anticipated cost to each State or Indian tribe, as agreed to under such cooperative agreements, of conducting training and certification programs during such fiscal year. If funds sufficient to pay 50 percent of the costs for any year are not appropriated, the share of each State and Indian tribe shall be reduced in a like proportion in allocating available funds.

**(b) Contracts for training.**

In addition, the Administrator may enter into contracts with Federal, State, or Indian tribal agencies for the purpose of encouraging the training of certified applicators.

**(c) Information and education.**

The Administrator shall, in cooperation with the Secretary of Agriculture, use the services of the cooperative State extension services to inform and educate pesticide users about accepted uses and other regulations made under this subchapter.

(June 25, 1947, c. 125, § 23, as added Oct. 21, 1972, Pub.L. 92–516, § 2, 86 Stat. 996, and amended Sept. 30, 1978, Pub.L. 95–396, § 21, 92 Stat. 834.)

### HISTORICAL AND STATUTORY NOTES

**State and Tribal Assistance Grants**

Pub.L. 105–276, Title III, Oct. 21, 1998, 112 Stat. 2499, provided in part: "That beginning in fiscal year 1999 and thereafter, pesticide program implementation grants under section 23(a)(1) of the Federal Insecticide, Fungicide and Rodenticide Act, as amended [subsec. (a)(1) of this section], shall be available for pesticide program development and implementation, including enforcement and compliance activities".

## § 136v. Authority of States

**[FIFRA § 24]**

**(a) In general**

A State may regulate the sale or use of any federally registered pesticide or device in the State, but only if and to the extent the regulation does not permit any sale or use prohibited by this subchapter.

**(b) Uniformity**

Such State shall not impose or continue in effect any requirements for labeling or packaging in addition to or different from those required under this subchapter.

**(c) Additional uses**

(1) A State may provide registration for additional uses of federally registered pesticides formulated for distribution and use within that State to meet special local needs in accord with the purposes of this subchapter and if registration for such use has not previously been denied, disapproved, or canceled by the Administrator. Such registration shall be deemed registration under section 136a of this title for all purposes of this subchapter, but shall authorize distribution and use only within such State.

(2) A registration issued by a State under this subsection shall not be effective for more than ninety days if disapproved by the Administrator within that period. Prior to disapproval, the Administrator shall, except as provided in paragraph (3) of this subsection, advise the State of the Administrator's intention to disapprove and the reasons therefor, and provide the State time to respond. The Administrator shall not prohibit or disapprove a registration issued by a State under this subsection (A) on the basis of lack of essentiality of a pesticide or (B) except as provided in paragraph (3) of this subsection, if its composition and use patterns are similar to those of a federally registered pesticide.

(3) In no instance may a State issue a registration for a food or feed use unless there exists a tolerance or exemption under the Federal Food, Drug, and Cosmetic Act [21 U.S.C.A. § 301 et seq.] that permits the residues of the pesticides on the food or feed. If the Administrator determines that a registration issued by a State is inconsistent with the Federal Food, Drug, and Cosmetic Act, or the use of, a pesticide under a registration issued by a State constitutes an imminent hazard, the Administrator may immediately disapprove the registration.

(4) If the Administrator finds, in accordance with standards set forth in regulations issued under section 136w of this title, that a State is not capable of exercising adequate controls to assure that State registration under this section will be in accord with the purposes of this subchapter or has failed to exercise adequate controls, the Administrator may suspend the authority of the State to register pesticides until such time as the Administrator is satisfied that the State can and will exercise adequate controls. Prior to any such suspension, the Administrator shall advise the State of the Administrator's intention to suspend and the reasons therefor and provide the State time to respond.

(June 25, 1947, c. 125, § 24, as added Oct. 21, 1972, Pub.L. 92–516, § 2, 86 Stat. 997, and amended Sept. 30, 1978, Pub.L. 95–396, § 22, 92 Stat. 835; Oct. 25, 1988, Pub.L. 100–532, Title VIII, § 801(m), 102 Stat. 2682.)

### HISTORICAL AND STATUTORY NOTES

**References in Text**

The Federal Food, Drug, and Cosmetic Act, referred to in subsec. (c)(3), is Act June 25, 1938, c. 675, 52 Stat. 1040, as amended, which is classified generally to chapter 9 (section 301 et seq.) of Title 21, Food and Drugs. For complete classification of this Act to the Code, see section 301 of Title 21 and Tables.

**Effective and Applicability Provisions**

1988 Acts

Amendment by Pub.L. 100–532 effective on expiration of 60 days after October 25, 1988, see section 901 of Pub.L. 100–532, set out as a note under section 136 of this title.

1972 Acts

Section effective at the close of Oct. 21, 1972, except if regulations are necessary for the implementation of any provision that becomes effective on Oct. 21, 1972, and continuation in effect of the provisions of subchapter I of this chapter and regulations thereunder as in effect prior to Oct. 21, 1972, until superseded by provisions of Pub.L. 92–516 and regulations thereunder, see section 4 of Pub.L. 92–516, set out as a note under section 136 of this title.

## § 136w. Authority of Administrator

**[FIFRA § 25]**

### (a) In general

#### (1) Regulations

The Administrator is authorized, in accordance with the procedure described in paragraph (2), to prescribe regulations to carry out the provisions of this subchapter. Such regulations shall take into account the difference in concept and usage between various classes of pesticides, including public health pesticides, and differences in environmental risk and the appropriate data for evaluating such risk between agricultural, nonagricultural, and public health pesticides.

#### (2) Procedure

##### (A) Proposed regulations

At least 60 days prior to signing any proposed regulation for publication in the Federal Register, the Administrator shall provide the Secretary of Agriculture with a copy of such regulation. If the Secretary comments in writing to the Administrator regarding any such regulation within 30 days after receiving it, the Administrator shall publish in the Federal Register (with the proposed regulation) the comments of the Secretary and the response of the Administrator with regard to the Secretary's comments. If the Secretary does not comment in writing to the Administrator regarding the regulation within 30 days after receiving it, the Administrator may sign such regulation for publication in the Federal Register any time after such 30–day period notwithstanding the foregoing 60–day time requirement.

##### (B) Final regulations

At least 30 days prior to signing any regulation in final form for publication in the Federal Register, the Administrator shall provide the Secretary of Agriculture with a copy of such regulation. If the Secretary comments in writing to the Administrator regarding any such final regulation within 15 days after receiving it, the Administrator shall publish in the Federal Register (with the final regulation) the comments of the Secretary, if requested by the Secretary, and the response of the Administrator concerning the Secretary's comments. If the Secretary does not comment in writing to the Administrator regarding the regulation within 15 days after receiving it, the Administrator may sign such regulation for publication in the Federal Register at any time after such 15–day period notwithstanding the foregoing 30–day time requirement. In taking any final action under this subsection, the Administrator shall include among those factors to be taken into account the effect of the regulation on production and prices of agricultural commodities, retail food prices, and otherwise on the agricultural economy, and the Administrator shall publish in the Federal Register an analysis of such effect.

##### (C) Time requirements

The time requirements imposed by subparagraphs (A) and (B) may be waived or modified to the extent agreed upon by the Administrator and the Secretary.

##### (D) Publication in the Federal Register

The Administrator shall, simultaneously with any notification to the Secretary of Agriculture under this paragraph prior to the issuance of any proposed or final regulation, publish such notification in the Federal Register.

#### (3) Congressional committees

At such time as the Administrator is required under paragraph (2) of this subsection to provide the Secretary of Agriculture with a copy of proposed regulations and a copy of the final form of regulations, the Administrator shall also furnish a copy of such regulations to the Committee on Agriculture of the House of Representatives and the Committee on Agriculture, Nutrition, and Forestry of the Senate.

#### (4) Congressional review of regulations

Simultaneously with the promulgation of any rule or regulation under this subchapter, the Administrator shall transmit a copy thereof to the Secretary of the Senate and the Clerk of the House of Representatives. The rule or regulation shall not become effective until the passage of 60 calendar days after the rule or regulation is so transmitted.

**(b) Exemption of pesticides**

The Administrator may exempt from the requirements of this subchapter by regulation any pesticide which the Administrator determines either (1) to be adequately regulated by another Federal agency, or (2) to be of a character which is unnecessary to be subject to this subchapter in order to carry out the purposes of this subchapter.

**(c) Other authority**

The Administrator, after notice and opportunity for hearing, is authorized—

(1) to declare a pest any form of plant or animal life (other than man and other than bacteria, virus, and other micro-organisms on or in living man or other living animals) which is injurious to health or the environment;

(2) to determine any pesticide which contains any substance or substances in quantities highly toxic to man;

(3) to establish standards (which shall be consistent with those established under the authority of the Poison Prevention Packaging Act (Public Law 91–601) [15 U.S.C.A. § 1471 et seq.]) with respect to the package, container, or wrapping in which a pesticide or device is enclosed for use or consumption, in order to protect children and adults from serious injury or illness resulting from accidental ingestion or contact with pesticides or devices regulated by this subchapter as well as to accomplish the other purposes of this subchapter;

(4) to specify those classes of devices which shall be subject to any provision of section 136(q)(1) or section 136e of this title upon the Administrator's determination that application of such provision is necessary to effectuate the purposes of this subchapter;

(5) to prescribe regulations requiring any pesticide to be colored or discolored if the Administrator determines that such requirement is feasible and is necessary for the protection of health and the environment; and

(6) to determine and establish suitable names to be used in the ingredient statement.

**(d) Scientific advisory panel**

**(1) In general**

The Administrator shall submit to an advisory panel for comment as to the impact on health and the environment of the action proposed in notices of intent issued under section 136d(b) of this title and of the proposed and final form of regulations issued under subsection (a) of this section within the same time periods as provided for the comments of the Secretary of Agriculture under such section 136d(b) and subsection (a) of this section. The time requirements for notices of intent and proposed and final forms of regulation may not be modified or waived unless in addition to meeting the requirements of section 136d(b) of this title or subsection (a) of this section, as applicable, the advisory panel has failed to comment on the proposed action within the prescribed time period or has agreed to the modification or waiver. The Administrator shall also solicit from the advisory panel comments, evaluations, and recommendations for operating guidelines to improve the effectiveness and quality of scientific analyses made by personnel of the Environmental Protection Agency that lead to decisions by the Administrator in carrying out the provisions of this subchapter. The comments, evaluations, and recommendations of the advisory panel submitted under this subsection and the response of the Administrator shall be published in the Federal Register in the same manner as provided for publication of the comments of the Secretary of Agriculture under such sections. The chairman of the advisory panel, after consultation with the Administrator, may create temporary subpanels on specific projects to assist the full advisory panel in expediting and preparing its evaluations, comments, and recommendations. The subpanels may be composed of scientists other than members of the advisory panel, as deemed necessary for the purpose of evaluating scientific studies relied upon by the Administrator with respect to proposed action. Such additional scientists shall be selected by the advisory panel. The panel referred to in this subsection shall consist of 7 members appointed by the Administrator from a list of 12 nominees, 6 nominated by the National Institutes of Health and 6 by the National Science Foundation, utilizing a system of staggered terms of appointment. Members of the panel shall be selected on the basis of their professional qualifications to assess the effects of the impact of pesticides on health and the environment. To the extent feasible to insure multidisciplinary representation, the panel membership shall include representation from the disciplines of toxicology, pathology, environmental biology, and related sciences. If a vacancy occurs on the panel due to expiration of a term, resignation, or any other reason, each replacement shall be selected by the Administrator from a group of 4 nominees, 2 submitted by each of the nominating entities named in this subsection. The Administrator may extend the term of a panel member until the new member is appointed to fill the vacancy. If a vacancy occurs due to resignation, or reason other than expiration of a term, the Administrator shall appoint a member to serve during the unexpired term utilizing the nomination process set forth in this subsection.

Should the list of nominees provided under this subsection be unsatisfactory, the Administrator may request an additional set of nominees from the nominating entities. The Administrator may require such information from the nominees to the advisory panel as the Administrator deems necessary, and the Administrator shall publish in the Federal Register the name, address, and professional affiliations of each nominee. Each member of the panel shall receive per diem compensation at a rate not in excess of that fixed for GS–18 of the General Schedule as may be determined by the Administrator, except that any such member who holds another office or position under the Federal Government the compensation for which exceeds such rate may elect to receive compensation at the rate provided for such other office or position in lieu of the compensation provided by this subsection. In order to assure the objectivity of the advisory panel, the Administrator shall promulgate regulations regarding conflicts of interest with respect to the members of the panel. The advisory panel established under this section shall be permanent. In performing the functions assigned by this subchapter, the panel shall consult and coordinate its activities with the Science Advisory Board established under the Environmental Research, Development, and Demonstration Authorization Act of 1978 [42 U.S.C.A. § 4365]. Whenever the Administrator exercises authority under section 136d(c) of this title to immediately suspend the registration of any pesticide to prevent an imminent hazard, the Administrator shall promptly submit to the advisory panel for comment, as to the impact on health and the environment, the action taken to suspend the registration of such pesticide.

**(2) Science Review Board**

There is established a Science Review Board to consist of 60 scientists who shall be available to the Scientific Advisory Panel to assist in reviews conducted by the Panel. Members of the Board shall be selected in the same manner as members of temporary subpanels created under paragraph (1). Members of the Board shall be compensated in the same manner as members of the Panel.

**(e) Peer review**

The Administrator shall, by written procedures, provide for peer review with respect to the design, protocols, and conduct of major scientific studies conducted under this subchapter by the Environmental Protection Agency or by any other Federal agency, any State or political subdivision thereof, or any institution or individual under grant, contract, or cooperative agreement from or with the Environmental Protection Agency. In such procedures, the Administrator shall also provide for peer review, using the advisory panel established under subsection (d) of this section or appropriate experts appointed by the Administrator from a current list of nominees maintained by such panel, with respect to the results of any such scientific studies relied upon by the Administrator with respect to actions the Administrator may take relating to the change in classification, suspension, or cancellation of a pesticide. Whenever the Administrator determines that circumstances do not permit the peer review of the results of any such scientific study prior to the Administrator's exercising authority under section 136d(c) of this title to immediately suspend the registration of any pesticide to prevent an imminent hazard, the Administrator shall promptly thereafter provide for the conduct of peer review as provided in this sentence. The evaluations and relevant documentation constituting the peer review that relate to the proposed scientific studies and the results of the completed scientific studies shall be included in the submission for comment forwarded by the Administrator to the advisory panel as provided in subsection (d) of this section. As used in this subsection, the term "peer review" shall mean an independent evaluation by scientific experts, either within or outside the Environmental Protection Agency, in the appropriate disciplines.

(June 25, 1947, c. 125, § 25, as added Oct. 21, 1972, Pub.L. 92–516, § 2, 86 Stat. 997, and amended Nov. 28, 1975, Pub.L. 94–140, §§ 2(a), 6, 7, 89 Stat. 751, 753; Sept. 30, 1978, Pub.L. 95–396, § 23, 92 Stat. 836; Dec. 17, 1980, Pub.L. 96–539, §§ 1, 2(a), 4, 94 Stat. 3194, 3195; Dec. 2, 1983, Pub.L. 98–201, § 1, 97 Stat. 1379; Nov. 8, 1984, Pub.L. 98–620, Title IV, § 402(4)(D), 98 Stat. 3357; June 27, 1988, Pub.L. 100–352, § 6(i), 102 Stat. 664; Oct. 25, 1988, Pub.L. 100–532, Title VI, §§ 602, 605, Title VIII, § 801(n), 102 Stat. 2678, 2679, 2683; Dec. 13, 1991, Pub.L. 102–237, Title X, § 1006(b)(1), (2), 105 Stat. 1895; Aug. 3, 1996, Pub.L. 104–170, Title I, § 104, Title II, § 235, 110 Stat. 1490, 1509.)

## HISTORICAL AND STATUTORY NOTES

**References in Text**

The Poison Prevention Packaging Act, referred to in subsec. (c)(3), is Pub.L. 91–601, Dec. 30, 1970, 84 Stat 1670, which is classified generally to chapter 39A (section 1471 et seq.) of Title 15, Commerce and Trade. For complete classification of this Act to the Code, see Short Title note set out under section 1471 of Title 15 and Tables.

Reference in subsec. (c)(4) to "section 136(q)(1)" was, in the original, a reference to "paragraph 2(q)(1)" and has been editorially translated as "section 136(q)(1)" as the probable intent of Congress.

GS–18 of the General Schedule, referred to in subsec. (d)(1), is classified to section 5332 of Title 5, Government Organization and Employees.

The Environmental Research, Development, and Demonstration Authorization Act of 1978, referred to in subsec. (d)(1), is Pub.L. 95–155, Nov. 8, 1977, 91 Stat. 1257, as amended. Provisions of the Act establishing the Science Advisory Board are classified to section 4365 of Title 42, The

Public Health and Welfare. For complete classification of this Act to the Code, see Tables.

**Effective and Applicability Provisions**

1991 Acts

Amendments by Pub.L. 102–237 effective Dec. 13, 1991, see section 1101(a) of Pub.L. 102–237, set out as a note under section 1421 of this title.

1988 Acts

Amendment by Pub.L. 100–532 effective on expiration of 60 days after October 25, 1988, see section 901 of Pub.L. 100–532, set out as a note under section 136 of this title.

Amendment by Pub.L. 100–352 effective ninety days after June 27, 1988, except that such amendment not apply to cases pending in the Supreme Court on such effective date or affect the right to review or the manner of reviewing the judgment or decree of a court which was entered before such effective date, see section 7 of Pub.L. 100–352, set out as a note under section 1254 of Title 28, Judiciary and Judicial Procedure.

1984 Acts

Amendment by Pub.L. 98–620 not to apply to cases pending on Nov. 8, 1984, see section 403 of Pub.L. 98–620, set out as a note under section 1657 of Title 28, Judiciary and Judicial Procedure.

1980 Acts

Section 2(b) of Pub.L. 96–539 provided that: "The provisions of this section [amending subsec. (e) of this section] shall become effective upon publication in the Federal Register of final procedures for peer review as provided in this section, but in no event shall such provisions become effective later than one year after the date of enactment of this Act [Dec. 17, 1980]."

1972 Acts

Section effective at the close of Oct. 21, 1972, except if regulations are necessary for the implementation of any provision that becomes effective on Oct. 21, 1972, and continuation in effect of the provisions of subchapter I of this chapter and regulations thereunder as in effect prior to Oct. 1, 1972, until superseded by provisions of Pub.L. 92–516 and regulations thereunder, see section 4 of Pub.L. 92–516, set out as a note under section 136 of this title.

**Transfer of Functions**

Any reference in any provision of law enacted before Jan. 4, 1995, to a function, duty, or authority of the Clerk of the House of Representatives treated as referring, with respect to that function, duty, or authority, to the officer of the House of Representatives exercising that function, duty, or authority, as determined by the Committee on House Oversight of the House of Representatives, see section 2(1) of Pub.L. 104–14, set out as a note preceding section 21 of Title 2, The Congress.

**FIFRA User Fees**

Pub.L. 101–508, Title I, § 1204(e), Nov. 5, 1990, 104 Stat. 1388–11, provided that: "Notwithstanding any provision of the Omnibus Budget Reconciliation Act of 1990, [for classification of Pub.L. 101–508, see Tables], nothing in this title [for classifications of Pub.L. 101–508, Title I, see Agricultural Reconciliation Act of 1990, set out as a Short Title note under section 1421 of this title and Tables], or the other provisions of this Act shall be construed to require or authorize the Administrator of the Environmental Protection Agency to assess or collect any fees of charges for services and activities authorized under the Federal Insecticide, Fungicide and Rodenticide Act (7 U.S.C. 136 et seq.) [this subchapter]."

**References to other Laws to GS–16,17, or 18 Pay Rates**

References in laws to the rates of pay for GS–16, 17, or 18, or to maximum rates of pay under the General Schedule, to be considered references to rates payable under specified sections of Title 5, Government Organization and Employees, see section 529 [title I, § 101(c)(1)] of Pub.L. 101–509, set out in a note under section 5376 of Title 5.

## § 136w–1. State primary enforcement responsibility

**[FIFRA § 26]**

**(a) In general**

For the purposes of this subchapter, a State shall have primary enforcement responsibility for pesticide use violations during any period for which the Administrator determines that such State—

(1) has adopted adequate pesticide use laws and regulations, except that the Administrator may not require a State to have pesticide use laws that are more stringent than this subchapter;

(2) has adopted and is implementing adequate procedures for the enforcement of such State laws and regulations; and

(3) will keep such records and make such reports showing compliance with paragraphs (1) and (2) of this subsection as the Administrator may require by regulation.

**(b) Special rules**

Notwithstanding the provisions of subsection (a) of this section, any State that enters into a cooperative agreement with the Administrator under section 136u of this title for the enforcement of pesticide use restrictions shall have the primary enforcement responsibility for pesticide use violations. Any State that has a plan approved by the Administrator in accordance with the requirements of section 136i of this title that the Administrator determines meets the criteria set out in subsection (a) of this section shall have the primary enforcement responsibility for pesticide use violations. The Administrator shall make such determinations with respect to State plans under section 136i of this title in effect on September 30, 1978, not later than six months after that date.

**(c) Administrator**

The Administrator shall have primary enforcement responsibility for those States that do not have primary enforcement responsibility under this subchapter. Notwithstanding the provisions of section 136(e)(1) of this title, during any period when the Administrator has such enforcement responsibility, section 136f(b) of this title shall apply to the books and records of commercial applicators and to any applicator who holds or applies pesticides, or uses dilutions of pesticides, only to provide a service of controlling pests without delivering any unapplied pesticide to any person so served, and section 136g(a) of this title shall apply to the establishment or other place where pesticides or devices are held for application by such persons with respect to pesticides or devices held for such application.

(June 25, 1947, c. 125, § 26, as added Sept. 30, 1978, Pub.L. 95–396, § 24(2), 92 Stat. 836, and amended Oct. 25, 1988, Pub.L. 100–532, Title VIII, § 801(*o*), (q)(1)(D), 102 Stat. 2683; Dec. 13, 1991, Pub.L. 102–237, Title X, § 1006(a)(11), 105 Stat. 1895.)

### HISTORICAL AND STATUTORY NOTES

**Effective and Applicability Provisions**

1991 Acts

Amendment by section 1006(a)(11) of Pub.L. 102–237 effective Dec. 13, 1991, see section 1101(a) of Pub.L. 102–237, set out as a note under section 1421 of this title.

1988 Acts

Amendment by Pub.L. 100–532 effective on expiration of 60 days after October 25, 1988, see section 901 of Pub.L. 100–532, set out as a note under section 136 of this title.

## § 136w–2. Failure by the State to assure enforcement of State pesticide use regulations

**[FIFRA § 27]**

### (a) Referral

Upon receipt of any complaint or other information alleging or indicating a significant violation of the pesticide use provisions of this subchapter, the Administrator shall refer the matter to the appropriate State officials for their investigation of the matter consistent with the requirements of this subchapter. If, within thirty days, the State has not commenced appropriate enforcement action, the Administrator may act upon the complaint or information to the extent authorized under this subchapter.

### (b) Notice

Whenever the Administrator determines that a State having primary enforcement responsibility for pesticide use violations is not carrying out (or cannot carry out due to the lack of adequate legal authority) such responsibility, the Administrator shall notify the State. Such notice shall specify those aspects of the administration of the State program that are determined to be inadequate. The State shall have ninety days after receipt of the notice to correct any deficiencies. If after that time the Administrator determines that the State program remains inadequate, the Administrator may rescind, in whole or in part, the State's primary enforcement responsibility for pesticide use violations.

### (c) Construction

Neither section 136w–1 of this title nor this section shall limit the authority of the Administrator to enforce this subchapter, where the Administrator determines that emergency conditions exist that require immediate action on the part of the Administrator and the State authority is unwilling or unable adequately to respond to the emergency.

(June 25, 1947, c. 125, § 27, as added Sept. 30, 1978, Pub.L. 95–396, § 24(2), 92 Stat. 837, and amended Oct. 25, 1988, Pub.L. 100–532, Title VIII, § 801(p), 102 Stat. 2683.)

### HISTORICAL AND STATUTORY NOTES

**Effective and Applicability Provisions**

1988 Acts

Amendment by Pub.L. 100–532 effective on expiration of 60 days after October 25, 1988, see section 901 of Pub.L. 100–532, set out as a note under section 136 of this title.

## § 136w–3. Identification of pests; cooperation with Department of Agriculture's program

**[FIFRA § 28]**

### (a) In general

The Administrator, in coordination with the Secretary of Agriculture, shall identify those pests that must be brought under control. The Administrator shall also coordinate and cooperate with the Secretary of Agriculture's research and implementation programs to develop and improve the safe use and effectiveness of chemical, biological, and alternative methods to combat and control pests that reduce the quality and economical production and distribution of agricultural products to domestic and foreign consumers.

### (b) Pest control availability

**(1) In general**

The administrator, in cooperation with the Secretary of Agriculture, shall identify—

(A) available methods of pest control by crop or animal;

(B) minor pest control problems, both in minor crops and minor or localized problems in major crops; and

(C) factors limiting the availability of specific pest control methods, such as resistance to control methods and regulatory actions limiting the availability of control methods.

**(2) Report**

The Secretary of Agriculture shall, not later than 180 days after November 28, 1990 and annually thereafter, prepare a report and send the report to the Administrator. The report shall—

(A) contain the information described in paragraph (1);

(B) identify the crucial pest control needs where a shortage of control methods is indicated by the information described in paragraph (1); and

(C) describe in detail research and extension efforts designed to address the needs identified in subparagraph (B).

**(c) Integrated pest management**

The Administrator, in cooperation with the Secretary of Agriculture, shall develop approaches to the control of pests based on integrated pest management that respond to the needs of producers, with a special emphasis on minor pests.

**(d) Public health pests**

The Administrator, in coordination with the Secretary of Agriculture and the Secretary of Health and Human Services, shall identify pests of significant public health importance and, in coordination with the Public Health Service, develop and implement programs to improve and facilitate the safe and necessary use of chemical, biological, and other methods to combat and control such pests of public health importance.

(June 25, 1947, c. 125, § 28, as added Sept. 30, 1978, Pub.L. 95–396, § 24(2), 92 Stat. 838, and amended Nov. 28, 1990, Pub.L. 101–624, Title XIV, § 1495, 104 Stat. 3629; Apr. 4, 1996, Pub.L. 104–127, Title VIII, § 862(b)(1), 110 Stat. 1174; Aug. 3, 1996, Pub.L. 104–170, Title II, § 236, 110 Stat. 1509.)

### HISTORICAL AND STATUTORY NOTES

**Severability of Provisions**

If any provision of Pub.L. 101–624 or the application thereof to any person or circumstance is held invalid, such invalidity not to affect other provisions or applications of Pub.L. 101–624 which can be given effect without regard to the invalid provision or application, see section 2519 of Pub.L. 101–624, set out as a note under section 1421 of this title.

## § 136w–4. Omitted

### HISTORICAL AND STATUTORY NOTES

**Codifications**

Section, Act June 25, 1947, c. 125, § 29, as added Sept. 30, 1978, Pub.L. 95–396, § 24(2), 92 Stat. 838, which required the Administrator of the Environmental Protection Agency to submit an annual report to Congress relating to filing of applications for conditional registration under 7 U.S.C.A. § 136a(c)(7)(B), (C), terminated, effective May 15, 2000, pursuant to Pub.L. 104–66, § 3003, as amended, set out as a note under 31 U.S.C.A. § 1113. See, also, page 164 of House Document No. 103–7.

## § 136w–5. Minimum requirements for training of maintenance applicators and service technicians

**[FIFRA § 30]**

Each State may establish minimum requirements for training of maintenance applicators and service technicians. Such training may include instruction in the safe and effective handling and use of pesticides in accordance with the Environmental Protection Agency approved labeling, and instruction in integrated pest management techniques. The authority of the Administrator with respect to minimum requirements for training of maintenance applicators and service technicians shall be limited to ensuring that each State understands the provisions of this section.

(June 25, 1947, c. 125, § 30, as added Aug. 3, 1996, Pub.L. 104–170, Title I, § 121(2), 110 Stat. 1492.)

### HISTORICAL AND STATUTORY NOTES

**Prior Provisions**

A prior section 30 of Act June 25, 1947, c. 125, was renumbered section 33 and is classified to section 136x of this title.

## § 136w–6. Environmental Protection Agency minor use program

**[FIFRA § 31]**

**(a) Establishment and functions**

The Administrator shall assure coordination of minor use issues through the establishment of a minor use program within the Office of Pesticide Programs. Such office shall be responsible for coordinating the development of minor use programs and policies and consulting with growers regarding minor use issues and registrations and amendments which are submitted to the Environmental Protection Agency.

**(b) Public report**

The Office of Pesticide Programs shall prepare a public report concerning the progress made on the registration of minor uses, including implementation of the exclusive use as an incentive for registering new minor uses, within 3 years of the passage of the Food Quality Protection Act of 1996.

(June 25, 1947, c. 125, § 31, as added Aug. 3, 1996, Pub.L. 104–170, Title II, § 210(i), 110 Stat. 1500.)

### HISTORICAL AND STATUTORY NOTES

**Reference in Text**

The passage of the Food Quality Protection Act of 1996, referred to in subsec.(b), probably means the date of enactment of Pub.L. 104–170, which was approved Aug. 3,1996.

**Prior Provision**

A prior section 31 of Act June 25, 1947, c. 125, was renumbered section 34 and is classified to section 136*l* of this title.

## § 136w–7. Department of Agriculture minor use program

**[FIFRA § 32]**

**(a) In general**

The Secretary of Agriculture (hereinafter in this section referred to as the "Secretary") shall assure the coordination of the responsibilities of the Department of Agriculture related to minor uses of pesticides, including—

(1) carrying out the Inter-Regional Project Number 4 (IR–4) as described in section 450i(e) of this title and the national pesticide resistance monitoring program established under section 1651 of the Food, Agriculture, Conservation, and Trade Act of 1990 (7 U.S.C. 5882);

(2) supporting integrated pest management research;

(3) consulting with growers to develop data for minor uses; and

(4) providing assistance for minor use registrations, tolerances, and reregistrations with the Environmental Protection Agency.

**(b) Minor use pesticide data and revolving fund**

**(1) Minor use pesticide data**

**(A) Grant authority**

The Secretary, in consultation with the Administrator, shall establish a program to make grants for the development of data to support minor use pesticide registrations and reregistrations. The amount of any such grant shall not exceed ½ of the cost of the project for which the grant is made.

**(B) Applicants**

Any person who wants to develop data to support minor use pesticide registrations and reregistrations may apply for a grant under subparagraph (A). Priority shall be given to an applicant for such a grant who does not directly receive funds from the sale of pesticides registered for minor uses.

**(C) Data ownership**

Any data that is developed under a grant under subparagraph (A) shall be jointly owned by the Department of Agriculture and the person who received the grant. Such a person shall enter into an agreement with the Secretary under which such person shall share any fee paid to such person under section 136a(c)(1)(F) of this title.

**(2) Minor Use Pesticide Data Revolving Fund**

**(A) Establishment**

There is established in the Treasury of the United States a revolving fund to be known as the Minor Use Pesticide Data Revolving Fund. The Fund shall be available without fiscal year limitation to carry out the authorized purposes of this subsection.

**(B) Contents of the Fund**

There shall be deposited in the Fund—

(i) such amounts as may be appropriated to support the purposes of this subsection; and

(ii) fees collected by the Secretary for any data developed under a grant under paragraph (1)(A).

**(C) Authorizations of appropriations**

There are authorized to be appropriated for each fiscal year to carry out the purposes of this subsection $10,000,000 to remain available until expended.

(June 25, 1947, c. 125, § 32, as added Aug. 3, 1996, Pub.L. 104–170, Title II, § 210(j), 110 Stat. 1501.)

**HISTORICAL AND STATUTORY NOTES**

**References in Text**

Section 1651 of the Food, Agriculture, Conservation, and Trade Act of 1990, referred to in subsec. (a)(1), was classified to section 5882 of this title prior to repeal by Pub.L. 104–127, Title VIII, § 862(a), Apr. 4, 1996, 110 Stat. 1174.

## § 136w–8. Pesticide registration service fees

**[FIFRA § 33]**

**(a) Definition of costs**

In this section, the term "costs", when used with respect to review and decisionmaking pertaining to an application for which registration service fees are paid under this section, means—

(1) costs to the extent that—

(A) officers and employees provide direct support for the review and decisionmaking for covered pesticide applications, associated tolerances, and corresponding risk and benefits information and analyses;

(B) persons and organizations under contract with the Administrator engage in the review of the applications, and corresponding risk and benefits information and assessments; and

(C) advisory committees and other accredited persons or organizations, on the request of the Administrator, engage in the peer review of risk or benefits information associated with covered pesticide applications;

(2) costs of management of information, and the acquisition, maintenance, and repair of computer and telecommunication resources (including software), used to support review of pesticide applications, associated tolerances, and corresponding risk and benefits information and analyses; and

(3) costs of collecting registration service fees under subsections (b) and (c) of this section and reporting, auditing, and accounting under this section.

**(b) Fees**

**(1) In general**

Effective beginning on the effective date of the Pesticide Registration Improvement Act of 2003, the Administrator shall assess and collect covered pesticide registration service fees in accordance with this section.

**(2) Covered pesticide registration applications**

**(A) In general**

An application for the registration of a pesticide covered by this subchapter that is received by the Administrator on or after the effective date of the Pesticide Registration Improvement Act of 2003 shall be subject to a registration service fee under this section.

**(B) Existing applications**

**(i) In general**

Subject to clause (ii), an application for the registration of a pesticide that was submitted to the Administrator before the effective date of the Pesticide Registration Improvement Act of 2003 and is pending on that effective date shall be subject to a service fee under this section if the application is for the registration of a new active ingredient that is not listed in the Registration Division 2003 Work Plan of the Office of Pesticide Programs of the Environmental Protection Agency.

**(ii) Tolerance or exemption fees**

The amount of any fee otherwise payable for an application described in clause (i) under this section shall be reduced by the amount of any fees paid to support the related petition for a pesticide tolerance or exemption under the Federal Food, Drug, and Cosmetic Act (21 U.S.C. 301 et seq.).

**(C) Documentation**

An application subject to a registration service fee under this section shall be submitted with documentation certifying—

(i) payment of the registration service fee; or

(ii) a request for a waiver from or reduction of the registration service fee.

**(3) Schedule of covered applications and registration service fees**

**(A) In general**

Not later than 30 days after the effective date of the Pesticide Registration Improvement Act of 2003, the Administrator shall publish in the Federal Register a schedule of covered pesticide registration applications and corresponding registration service fees.

**(B) Report**

Subject to paragraph (6), the schedule shall be the same as the applicable schedule appearing in the Congressional Record on pages S11631 through S11633, dated September 17, 2003.

**(4) Pending pesticide registration applications**

**(A) In general**

An applicant that submitted a registration application to the Administrator before the effective date of the Pesticide Registration Improvement Act of 2003, but that is not required to pay a registration service fee under paragraph (2)(B), may, on a voluntary basis, pay a registration service fee in accordance with paragraph (2)(B).

**(B) Voluntary fee**

The Administrator may not compel payment of a registration service fee for an application described in subparagraph (A).

**(C) Documentation**

An application for which a voluntary registration service fee is paid under this paragraph shall be submitted with documentation certifying—

(i) payment of the registration service fee; or

(ii) a request for a waiver from or reduction of the registration service fee.

**(5) Resubmission of pesticide registration applications**

If a pesticide registration application is submitted by a person that paid the fee for the application under paragraph (2), is determined by the Administrator to be complete, and is not approved or is withdrawn (without a waiver or refund), the submission of the same pesticide registration application by the same person (or a licensee, assignee, or successor of the person) shall not be subject to a fee under paragraph (2).

**(6) Fee adjustment**

Effective for a covered pesticide registration application received on or after October 1, 2005, the Administrator shall—

**(A)** increase by 5 percent the service fee payable for the application under paragraph (3); and

**(B)** publish in the Federal Register the revised registration service fee schedule.

**(7) Waivers and reductions**

**(A) In general**

An applicant for a covered pesticide registration may request the Administrator to waive or reduce the amount of a registration service fee payable under this section under the circumstances described in subparagraphs (D) through (G).

**(B) Documentation**

**(i) In general**

A request for a waiver from or reduction of the registration service fee shall be accompanied by appropriate documentation demonstrating the basis for the waiver or reduction.

**(ii) Certification**

The applicant shall provide to the Administrator a written certification, signed by a responsible officer, that the documentation submitted to support the waiver or reduction request is accurate.

**(iii) Inaccurate documentation**

An application shall be subject to the applicable registration service fee payable under paragraph (3) if, at any time, the Administrator determines that—

**(I)** the documentation supporting the waiver or reduction request is not accurate; or

**(II)** based on the documentation or any other information, the waiver or reduction should not have been granted or should not be granted.

**(C) Determination to grant or deny request**

As soon as practicable, but not later than 60 days, after the date on which the Administrator receives a request for a waiver or reduction of a registration service fee under this paragraph, the Administrator shall—

**(i)** determine whether to grant or deny the request; and

**(ii)** notify the applicant of the determination.

**(D) Minor uses**

**(i) In general**

The Administrator may waive or reduce a registration service fee for an application for minor uses for a pesticide.

**(ii) Supporting documentation**

An applicant requesting a waiver under this subparagraph shall provide supporting documentation that demonstrates, to the satisfaction of the Administrator, that anticipated revenues from the uses that are the subject of the application would be insufficient to justify imposition of the full application fee.

**(E) IR–4 waiver**

The Administrator shall waive the registration service fee for an application if the Administrator determines that—

**(i)** the application is solely associated with a tolerance petition submitted in connection with the Inter–Regional Project Number 4 (IR–4) as described in section 2 of Public Law 89–106 (7 U.S.C. 450i(e)); and

**(ii)** the waiver is in the public interest.

**(F) Small businesses**

**(i) In general**

The Administrator shall waive 50 percent of the registration service fees payable by an entity for a covered pesticide registration application under this section if the entity is a small business (as defined in section 136a–1(i)(5)(E)(ii) of this title) at the time of application.

**(ii) Waiver of fees**

The Administrator shall waive all of the registration service fees payable by an entity under this section if the entity—

**(I)** is a small business (as defined in section 136a–1(i)(5)(E)(ii) of this title) at the time of application; and

**(II)** has average annual global gross revenues described in section 136a–1(i)(5)(E)(ii)(I)(bb) of this title that does not exceed $10,000,000, at the time of application.

**(iii) Formation for waiver**

The Administrator shall not grant a waiver under this subparagraph if the Administrator determines that the entity submitting the application has been formed or manipulated primarily for the purpose of qualifying for the waiver.

**(iv) Documentation**

An entity requesting a waiver under this subparagraph shall provide to the Administrator—

(I) documentation demonstrating that the entity is a small business (as defined in section 136a–1(i)(5)(E)(ii) of this title) at the time of application; and

(II) if the entity is requesting a waiver of all registration service fees payable under this section, documentation demonstrating that the entity has an average annual global gross revenues described in section 136a–1(i)(5)(E)(ii)(I)(bb of this title) that does not exceed $10,000,000, at the time of application.

**(G) Federal and State agency exemptions**

An agency of the Federal Government or a State government shall be exempt from covered registration service fees under this section.

**(8) Refunds**

**(A) Early withdrawals**

If, during the first 60 days after the beginning of the applicable decision time review period under subsection (f)(3) of this section, a covered pesticide registration application is withdrawn by the applicant, the Administrator shall refund all but 10 percent of the total registration service fee payable under paragraph (3) for the application.

**(B) Withdrawals after the first 60 days of decision review time period**

**(i) In general**

If a covered pesticide registration application is withdrawn after the first 60 days of the applicable decision time review period, the Administrator shall determine what portion, if any, of the total registration service fee payable under paragraph (3) for the application may be refunded based on the proportion of the work completed at the time of withdrawal.

**(ii) Timing**

The Administrator shall—

(I) make the determination described in clause (i) not later than 90 days after the date the application is withdrawn; and

(II) provide any refund as soon as practicable after the determination.

**(C) Discretionary refunds**

**(i) In general**

In the case of a pesticide registration application that has been filed with the Administrator and has not been withdrawn by the applicant, but for which the Administrator has not yet made a final determination, the Administrator may refund a portion of a covered registration service fee if the Administrator determines that the refund is justified.

**(ii) Basis**

The Administrator may provide a refund for an application under this subparagraph—

(I) on the basis that, in reviewing the application, the Administrator has considered data submitted in support of another pesticide registration application; or

(II) on the basis that the Administrator completed portions of the review of the application before the effective date of this section.

**(D) Credited fees**

In determining whether to grant a refund under this paragraph, the Administrator shall take into account any portion of the registration service fees credited under paragraph (2) or (4).

**(c) Pesticide registration fund**

**(1) Establishment**

There is established in the Treasury of the United States a Pesticide Registration Fund to be used in carrying out this section (referred to in this section as the "Fund"), consisting of—

(A) such amounts as are deposited in the Fund under paragraph (2);

(B) any interest earned on investment of amounts in the Fund under paragraph (4); and

(C) any proceeds from the sale or redemption of investments held in the Fund.

**(2) Deposits in fund**

Subject to paragraph (4), the Administrator shall deposit fees collected under this section in the Fund.

**(3) Expenditures from fund**

**(A) In general**

Subject to subparagraphs (B) and (C) and paragraph (4), the Administrator may make expenditures from the Fund—

(i) to cover the costs associated with the review and decisionmaking pertaining to all applications for which registration service fees have been paid under this section; and

**(ii)** to otherwise carry out this section.

**(B) Worker protection**

For each of fiscal years 2004 through 2008, the Administrator shall use approximately 1/17 of the amount in the Fund (but not more than $1,000,000, and not less than $750,000, for any fiscal year) to enhance current scientific and regulatory activities related to worker protection.

**(C) New inert ingredients**

For each of fiscal years 2004 and 2005, the Administrator shall use approximately 1/34 of the amount in the Fund (but not to exceed $500,000 for any fiscal year) for the review and evaluation of new inert ingredients.

**(4) Collections and appropriations acts**

The fees authorized by this section and amounts deposited in the Fund—

**(A)** shall be collected and made available for obligation only to the extent provided in advance in appropriations Acts; and

**(B)** shall be available without fiscal year limitation.

**(5) Unused funds**

Amounts in the Fund not currently needed to carry out this section shall be—

**(A)** maintained readily available or on deposit;

**(B)** invested in obligations of the United States or guaranteed by the United States; or

**(C)** invested in obligations, participations, or other instruments that are lawful investments for fiduciary, trust, or public funds.

**(d) Assessment of fees**

**(1) Definition of covered functions**

In this subsection, the term "covered functions" means functions of the Office of Pesticide Programs of the Environmental Protection Agency, as identified in key programs and projects of the final operating plan for the Environmental Protection Agency submitted as part of the budget process for fiscal year 2002, regardless of any subsequent transfer of 1 or more of the functions to another office or agency or the subsequent transfer of a new function to the Office of Pesticide Programs.

**(2) Minimum amount of appropriations**

For fiscal years 2004, 2005, and 2006 only, registration service fees may not be assessed for a fiscal year under this section unless the amount of appropriations for salaries, contracts, and expenses for the functions (as in existence in fiscal year 2002) of the Office of Pesticide Programs of the Environmental Protection Agency for the fiscal year (excluding the amount of any fees appropriated for the fiscal year) are equal to or greater than the amount of appropriations for covered functions for fiscal year 2002 (excluding the amount of any fees appropriated for the fiscal year).

**(3) Use of fees**

Registration service fees authorized by this section shall be available, in the aggregate, only to defray increases in the costs associated with the review and decisionmaking for the review of pesticide registration applications and associated tolerances (including increases in the number of full-time equivalent positions in the Environmental Protection Agency engaged in those activities) over the costs for fiscal year 2002, excluding costs paid from fees appropriated for the fiscal year.

**(4) Compliance**

The requirements of paragraph (2) shall have been considered to have been met for any fiscal year if the amount of appropriations for salaries, contracts, and expenses for the functions (as in existence in fiscal year 2002) of the Office of Pesticide Programs of the Environmental Protection Agency for the fiscal year (excluding the amount of any fees appropriated for the fiscal year) is not more than 3 percent below the amount of appropriations for covered functions for fiscal year 2002 (excluding the amount of any fees appropriated for the fiscal year).

**(5) Subsequent authority**

If the Administrator does not assess registration service fees under subsection (b) of this section during any portion of a fiscal year as the result of paragraph (2) and is subsequently permitted to assess the fees under subsection (b) of this section during the fiscal year, the Administrator shall assess and collect the fees, without any modification in rate, at any time during the fiscal year, notwithstanding any provisions of subsection (b) of this section relating to the date fees are to be paid.

**(e) Reforms to reduce decision time review periods**

To the maximum extent practicable consistent with the degrees of risk presented by pesticides and the type of review appropriate to evaluate risks, the Administrator shall identify and evaluate reforms to the pesticide registration process under this subchapter with the goal of reducing decision review periods in effect on the effective date of the Pesticide Registration Improvement Act of 2003 for pesticide registration actions for covered pesticide registration applications (including reduced risk applications).

**(f) Decision time review periods**

**(1) In general**

Not later than 30 days after the effective date of the Pesticide Registration Improvement Act of 2003, the Administrator shall publish in the Federal Register a schedule of decision review periods for covered pesticide registration actions and corresponding registration service fees under this subchapter.

**(2) Report**

The schedule shall be the same as the applicable schedule appearing in the Congressional Record on pages S11631 through S11633, dated September 17, 2003.

**(3) Applications subject to decision time review periods**

The decision time review periods specified in paragraph (1) shall apply to—

(A) covered pesticide registration applications subject to registration service fees under subsection (b)(2) of this section;

(B) covered pesticide registration applications for which an applicant has voluntarily paid registration service fees under subsection (b)(4) of this section; and

(C) covered pesticide registration applications listed in the Registration Division 2003 Work Plan of the Office of Pesticide Programs of the Environmental Protection Agency.

**(4) Start of decision time review period**

**(A) In general**

Except as provided in subparagraphs (C), (D), and (E), in the case of a pesticide registration application accompanied by the registration service fee required under this section, the decision time review period begins 21 days after the date on which the Administrator receives the covered pesticide registration application.

**(B) Completeness of application**

In conducting an initial screening of an application, the Administrator shall determine—

(i) whether—

(I) the applicable registration service fee has been paid; or

(II) the application contains a waiver or refund request; and

(ii) whether the application—

(I) contains all necessary forms, data, draft labeling, and, documentation certifying payment of any registration service fee required under this section; or

(II) establishes a basis for any requested waiver or reduction.

**(C) Applications with waiver or reduction requests**

**(i) In general**

In the case of an application submitted with a request for a waiver or reduction of registration service fees under subsection (b)(7) of this section, the decision time review period shall be determined in accordance with this subparagraph.

**(ii) Request granted with no additional fees required**

If the Administrator grants the waiver or reduction request and no additional fee is required, the decision time review period begins on the earlier of—

(I) the date on which the Administrator grants the request; or

(II) the date that is 60 days after the date of receipt of the application.

**(iii) Request granted with additional fees required**

If the Administrator grants the waiver or reduction request, in whole or in part, but an additional registration service fee is required, the decision time review period begins on the date on which the Administrator receives certification of payment of the applicable registration service fee.

**(iv) Request denied**

If the Administrator denies the waiver or reduction request, the decision time review period begins on the date on which the Administrator receives certification of payment of the applicable registration service fee.

**(D) Pending applications**

**(i) In general**

The start of the decision time review period for applications described in clause (ii) shall be the date on which the Administrator receives certification of payment of the applicable registration service fee.

**(ii) Applications**

Clause (i) applies to—

(I) covered pesticide registration applications for which voluntary fees have been paid under subsection (b)(4)of this section; and

(II) covered pesticide registration applications received on or after the effective date of the Pesticide Registration Improvement Act of 2003 but submitted without the applicable registration service fee required under this section due to the inability of the Administrator to assess fees under subsection (d)(1) of this section.

**(E) 2003 work plan**

In the case of a covered pesticide registration application listed in the Registration Division 2003 Work Plan of the Office of Pesticide Programs of the Environmental Protection Agency, the decision time review period begins on the date that is 30 days after the effective date of the Pesticide Registration Improvement Act of 2003.

**(5) Extension of decision time review period**

The Administrator and the applicant may mutually agree in writing to extend a decision time review period under this subsection.

**(g) Judicial review**

**(1) In general**

Any applicant adversely affected by the failure of the Administrator to make a determination on the application of the applicant for registration of a new active ingredient or new use for which a registration service fee is paid under this section may obtain judicial review of the failure solely under this section.

**(2) Scope**

**(A) In general**

In an action brought under this subsection, the only issue on review is whether the Administrator failed to make a determination on the application specified in paragraph (1) by the end of the applicable decision time review period required under subsection (f) of this section for the application.

**(B) Other actions**

No other action authorized or required under this section shall be judicially reviewable by a Federal or State court.

**(3) Timing**

**(A) In general**

A person may not obtain judicial review of the failure of the Administrator to make a determination on the application specified in paragraph (1) before the expiration of the 2–year period that begins on the date on which the decision time review period for the application ends.

**(B) Meeting with administrator**

To be eligible to seek judicial review under this subsection, a person seeking the review shall first request in writing, at least 120 days before filing the complaint for judicial review, a decision review meeting with the Administrator.

**(4) Remedies**

The Administrator may not be required or permitted to refund any portion of a registration service fee paid in response to a complaint that the Administrator has failed to make a determination on the covered pesticide registration application specified in paragraph (1) by the end of the applicable decision review period.

**(h) Accounting**

The Administrator shall—

(1) provide an annual accounting of the registration service fees paid to the Administrator and disbursed from the Fund, by providing financial statements in accordance with—

(A) the Chief Financial Officers Act of 1990 (Public Law 101–576; 104 Stat. 2838) and amendments made by that Act; and

(B) the Government Management Reform Act of 1994 (Public Law 103–356; 108 Stat. 3410) and amendments made by that Act;

(2) provide an accounting describing expenditures from the Fund authorized under subsection (c) of this section; and

(3) provide an annual accounting describing collections and expenditures authorized under subsection (d) of this section.

**(i) Auditing**

**(1) Financial statements of agencies**

For the purpose of section 3515(c) of Title 31, the Fund shall be considered a component of an executive agency.

**(2) Components**

The annual audit required under sections 3515(b) and 3521 of that title of the financial statements of activities under this section shall include an analysis of—

(A) the fees collected under subsection (b) of this section and disbursed;

(B) compliance with subsection (f) of this section;

(C) the amount appropriated to meet the requirements of subsection (d)(1) of this section; and

(D) the reasonableness of the allocation of the overhead allocation of costs associated with the review and decisionmaking pertaining to applications under this section.

(3) **Inspector general**

The Inspector General of the Environmental Protection Agency shall—

(A) conduct the annual audit required under this subsection; and

(B) report the findings and recommendations of the audit to the Administrator and to the appropriate committees of Congress.

(j) **Personnel levels**

All full-time equivalent positions supported by fees authorized and collected under this section shall not be counted against the agency-wide personnel level goals of the Environmental Protection Agency.

(k) **Reports**

(1) **In general**

Not later than March 1, 2005, and each March 1 thereafter through March 1, 2009, the Administrator shall publish an annual report describing actions taken under this section.

(2) **Contents**

The report shall include—

(A) a review of the progress made in carrying out each requirement of subsections (e) and (f) of this section, including—

(i) the number of applications reviewed, including the decision times for each application specified in subsection (f) of this section;

(ii) the number of actions pending in each category of actions described in subsection (f)(3) of this section, as well as the number of inert ingredients;

(iii) to the extent determined appropriate by the Administrator and consistent with the authorities of the Administrator and limitations on delegation of functions by the Administrator, recommendations for—

(I) expanding the use of self-certification in all appropriate areas of the registration process;

(II) providing for accreditation of outside reviewers and the use of outside reviewers to conduct the review of major portions of applications; and

(III) reviewing the scope of use of the notification process to cover broader categories of registration actions; and

(iv) **the use of performance-based contracts, other contracts, and procurement to ensure that—**

(I) the goals of this subchapter for the timely review of applications for registration are met; and

(II) the registration program is administered in the most productive and cost effective manner practicable;

(B) a description of the staffing and resources relating to the costs associated with the review and decisionmaking pertaining to applications; and

(C) a review of the progress in meeting the timeline requirements of section 136a–1(g) of this title.

(3) **Method**

The Administrator shall publish a report required by this subsection by such method as the Administrator determines to be the most effective for efficiently disseminating the report, including publication of the report on the Internet site of the Environmental Protection Agency.

(*l*) **Savings clause**

Nothing in this section affects any other duties, obligations, or authorities established by any other section of this subchapter, including the right to judicial review of duties, obligations, or authorities established by any other section of this subchapter.

(m) **Termination of effectiveness**

(1) **In general**

Except as provided in paragraph (2), the authority provided by this section terminates on September 30, 2008.

(2) **Phase out**

(A) **Fiscal year 2009**

During fiscal year 2009, the requirement to pay and collect registration service fees applies, except that the level of registration service fees payable under this section shall be reduced 40 percent below the level in effect on September 30, 2008.

(B) **Fiscal year 2010**

During fiscal year 2010, the requirement to pay and collect registration service fees applies, except that the level of registration service fees payable under this section shall be reduced 70 percent below the level in effect on September 30, 2008.

(C) **September 30, 2010**

Effective September 30, 2010, the requirement to pay and collect registration service fees terminates.

(D) **Decision review periods**

(i) **Pending applications**

In the case of an application received under this section before September 30, 2008, the application shall be reviewed in accordance with subsection (f) of this section.

(ii) **New applications**

In the case of an application received under this section on or after September 30, 2008, subsection (f) of this section shall not apply to the application.

(June 25, 1947, c. 125, § 33, as added Jan. 23, 2004, Pub.L. 108–199, Div. G, Title V, § 501(f)(2), 117 Stat. 422)

### HISTORICAL AND STATUTORY NOTES

**References in Text**

The effective date of the Pesticide Registration Improvement Act of 2003, referred to in text, is the effective date of Pub.L. 108–199, Div. G, Title V, § 501, Jan. 23, 2004, 118 Stat. 419, which is 60 days after Jan. 23, 2004, see Pub.L. 108–199, Div. G, Title V, § 501(h), set out as a note under 7 U.S.C.A. § 136a.

This subchapter, referred to in text, originally read "this Act", meaning the Federal Insecticide, Fungicide, and Rodenticide Act, Act June 25, 1947, c. 125, as amended generally by Pub.L. 92–516, Oct. 21, 1972, 86 Stat. 973, which is classified principally to this subchapter. For complete classification, see Short Title note set out under 7 U.S.C.A. § 136 and Tables.

The effective date of this section, referred to in subsec. (b)(8)(C)((ii)(II), is the effective date of Pub.L. 108–199, Div. G, Title V, § 501, Jan. 23, 2004, 118 Stat. 419, which is 60 days after Jan. 23, 2004, see Pub.L. 108–199, Div. G, Title V, § 501(h), set out as a note under 7 U.S.C.A. § 136a.

The Federal Food, Drug, and Cosmetic Act, referred to in subsec. (b)(2)(B)(ii), is Act June 25, 1938, c. 675, 52 Stat. 1040, as amended, which is principally classified to chapter 9 of Title 21, 21 U.S.C.A. § 301 et seq. For complete classification, see Short Title set out at 21 U.S.C.A. § 301 and Tables.

The Chief Financial Officers Act of 1990, referred to in subsec. (h)(1)(A), is Pub.L. 101–576, Nov. 15, 1990, 104 Stat. 2838. For complete classification, see Short Title note set out under 31 U.S.C.A. § 501 and Tables.

The Government Management Reform Act of 1994, referred to in subsec. (h)(1)(B), is Pub.L. 103–356, Oct. 13, 1994, 108 Stat. 3410. For complete classification, see Short Title note set out under 31 U.S.C.A. § 3301 and Tables.

**Effective and Applicability Provisions**

2004 Acts

Section effective 60 days after Jan. 23, 2004, see Pub.L. 108–199, Div. G, Title V, § 501(h), set out as a note under 7 U.S.C.A. § 136a.

**Prior Provisions**

A prior section 33 of the Federal Insecticide, Fungicide, and Rodenticide Act, Act June 25, 1947, c. 125, 61 Stat. 163, relating to the Department of Agriculture minor use program, was redesignated as section 34 of that Act by Pub.L. 108–199, Jan. 23, 2004, 118 Stat. 42, and is classified to 7 U.S.C.A. § 136x.

## § 136x. Severability

**[FIFRA § 34]**

If any provision of this subchapter or the application thereof to any person or circumstance is held invalid, the invalidity shall not affect other provisions or applications of this subchapter which can be given effect without regard to the invalid provision or application, and to this end the provisions of this subchapter are severable.

(June 25, 1947, c. 125, § 34, formerly § 26, as added Oct. 21, 1972, Pub.L. 92–516, § 2, 86 Stat. 998; renumbered § 30, Sept. 30, 1978, Pub.L. 95–396, § 24(1), 92 Stat. 836; renumbered § 33, Aug. 3, 1996, Pub.L. 104–170, Title I, § 121(1), 110 Stat. 1492; renumbered § 34, Jan. 23, 2004, Pub.L. 108–199, Div. G, Title V, § 501(f)(1), 118 Stat. 422.)

### HISTORICAL AND STATUTORY NOTES

**Effective and Applicability Provisions**

2004 Acts

Amendments made by Pub.L. 108–199, § 501, redesignating section 33 of the Federal Insecticide, Fungicide, and Rodenticide Act [this section] as section 34 of that Act, to take effect 60 days after Jan. 23, 2004, see Pub.L. 108–199, § 501(h), set out as a note under 7 U.S.C.A. § 136a.

1972 Acts

Section effective at the close of Oct. 21, 1972, except if regulations are necessary for the implementation of any provision that becomes effective on Oct. 21, 1972, and continuation in effect of the provisions of subchapter I of this chapter and regulations thereunder as in effect prior to Oct. 21, 1972, until superseded by provisions of Pub.L. 92–516 and regulations thereunder, see section 4 of Pub.L. 92–516, set out as a note under section 136 of this title.

**Prior Provisions**

A prior section 34 of the Federal Insecticide, Fungicide, and Rodenticide Act, Act June 25, 1947, c. 125, 61 Stat. 163, as amended, relating to authorization of appropriations, was redesignated as section 35 of that Act by Pub.L. 108–199, Jan. 23, 2004, 118 Stat. 422, and is classified to 7 U.S.C.A. § 136y.

## § 136y. Authorization of appropriations

**[FIFRA § 35]**

There is authorized to be appropriated to carry out this subchapter (other than section 136u(a) of this title)—

(1) $83,000,000 for fiscal year 1989, of which not more than $13,735,500 shall be available for research under this subchapter;

(2) $95,000,000 for fiscal year 1990, of which not more than $14,343,600 shall be available for research under this subchapter; and

(3) $95,000,000 for fiscal year 1991, of which not more than $14,978,200 shall be available for research under this subchapter.

(June 25, 1947, c. 125, § 35, formerly § 27, as added Oct. 21, 1972, Pub.L. 92–516, § 2, 86 Stat. 998, and amended July 2, 1975, Pub.L. 94–51, 89 Stat. 257; Oct. 10, 1975, Pub.L. 94–109, 89 Stat. 571; Nov. 28, 1975, Pub.L. 94–140, § 3, 89 Stat. 752; renumbered § 31 and amended Sept. 30, 1978, Pub.L. 95–396, §§ 24(1), 25, 92 Stat. 836, 838; Dec. 17, 1980, Pub.L. 96–539, § 3, 94 Stat. 3195; Dec. 2, 1983, Pub.L. 98–201, § 2, 97 Stat. 1380; Dec. 23, 1985, Pub.L. 99–198, Title XVII, § 1768, 99 Stat. 1656; Oct. 25, 1988, Pub.L. 100–532, Title VII, § 701, 102 Stat. 2679; renumbered § 34, Aug. 3, 1996, Pub.L. 104–170, Title I, § 121(1), 110 Stat. 1492; renumbered § 35, Jan. 23, 2004, Pub.L. 108–199, Div. G, Title V, § 501(f)(1), 118 Stat. 422.)

## HISTORICAL AND STATUTORY NOTES

**Codifications**

Another section 1768(a) to (f) of Pub.L. 99–198 enacted sections 154a and 159 and amended sections 151, 154, and 157 of Title 21, Food and Drugs.

**Effective and Applicability Provisions**

2004 Acts

Amendments made by Pub.L. 108–199, § 501(f)(1), redesignating section 34 of the Federal Insecticide, Fungicide, and Rodenticide Act [this section] as section 35 of that Act, to take effect 60 days after Jan. 23, 2004, see Pub.L. 108–199, § 501(h), set out as a note under 7 U.S.C.A. § 136a.

1988 Acts

Section 701 of Pub.L. 100–532 provided in part that amendment by Pub.L. 100–532 be effective Oct. 1, 1988.

1972 Acts

Section effective at the close of Oct. 21, 1972, except if regulations are necessary for the implementation of any provision that becomes effective on Oct. 21, 1972, and continuation in effect of the provisions of subchapter I of this chapter and regulations thereunder as in effect prior to Oct. 21, 1972, until superseded by provisions of Pub.L. 92–516 and regulations thereunder, see section 4 of Pub.L. 92–516, set out as a note under section 136 of this title.

*

# TITLE 15
# COMMERCE AND TRADE

# ENERGY SUPPLY AND ENVIRONMENTAL COORDINATION

## ENERGY SUPPLY AND ENVIRONMENTAL COORDINATION ACT OF 1974 [ESECA § ——]

**(15 U.S.C.A. §§ 791 to 798)**

## CHAPTER 16C—ENERGY SUPPLY AND ENVIRONMENTAL COORDINATION



### § 791. Congressional declaration of purpose

**[ESECA § 1(b)]**

The purposes of this chapter are (1) to provide for a means to assist in meeting the essential needs of the United States for fuels, in a manner which is consistent, to the fullest extent practicable, with existing national commitments to protect and improve the environment, and (2) to provide requirements for reports respecting energy resources.

(Pub.L. 93–319, § 1(b), June 22, 1974, 88 Stat. 246.)

#### HISTORICAL AND STATUTORY NOTES

**References in Text**

This chapter, referred to in text, was in the original "this Act", meaning Pub.L. 93–319 which, in addition to enacting this chapter and provision set out as a note under this section, enacted sections 1857c–10 and 1857f–6f of Title 42, The Public Health and Welfare, and amended sections 1857b–1, 1957c–5, 1857c–8, 1857c–9, 1857d–1, 1857f–1, 1857f–6e, 1857f–7, 1857h–5, and 1857l of Title 42. For complete classification of this Act to the Code, see Tables.

**Short Title**

Section 1(a) of Pub.L. 93–319 provided that Pub.L. 93–319 [which enacted this chapter and §§ 1857c–10 and 1857f–6f of Title 42, The Public Health and Welfare, and amended §§ 1857b–1, 1857c–5, 1857c–8, 1857c–9, 1857d–1, 1857f–1, 1857f–6e, 1857f–7, 1857h–5, and 1857l of Title 42] may be cited as the "Energy Supply and Environmental Coordination Act of 1974".

### § 792. Coal conversion and allocation

**[ESECA § 2]**

**(a) Powerplant and fuel burning installations**

The Federal Energy Administrator—

(1) shall, by order, prohibit any powerplant, and

(2) may, by order, prohibit any major fuel burning installation, other than a powerplant,

from burning natural gas or petroleum products as its primary energy source, if the requirements of subsection (b) of this section are met and if (A) the Federal Energy Administrator determines such powerplant or installation on June 22, 1974, had, or thereafter acquires or is designed with, the capability and necessary plant equipment to burn coal, or (B) such powerplant or installation is required to meet a design or construction requirement under subsection (c) of this section.

**(b) Prerequisites to issuance or effectiveness of orders prohibiting use of natural gas or petroleum products as primary energy source**

The requirements referred to in subsection (a) of this section are as follows:

(1) An order under subsection (a) of this section may not be issued with respect to a powerplant or installation unless the Federal Energy Administrator finds (A) that the burning of coal by such plant or installation, in lieu of petroleum products or natural gas, is practicable and consistent with the purposes of this chapter, (B) that coal and coal transportation facilities will be available during the period the order is in effect, and (C) in the case of a powerplant, that the prohibition under subsection (a) of this section will not impair the reliability of service in the area served by such plant. Such an order shall be rescinded or modified to the extent the Federal Energy Administrator determines that

any requirement described in subparagraph (A), (B), or (C) of this paragraph is no longer met; and such an order may at any time be modified if the Federal Energy Administrator determines that such order, as modified, complies with the requirements of this section.

**(2)(A)** Before issuing an order under subsection (a) of this section which is applicable to a powerplant or installation for a period ending on or before June 30, 1975, the Federal Energy Administrator (i) shall give notice to the public and afford interested persons an opportunity for written presentations of data, views, and arguments, (ii) shall consult with the Administrator of the Environmental Protection Agency, and (iii) shall take into account the likelihood that the powerplant or installation will be permitted to burn coal after June 30, 1975.

**(B)** An order described in subparagraph (A) of this paragraph shall not become effective until the date which the Administrator of the Environmental Protection Agency certifies pursuant to section 1857c–10(d)(1)(A) of Title 42 is the earliest date that such plant or installation will be able to comply with the air pollution requirements which will be applicable to it. Such order shall not be effective for any period certified by the Administrator of the Environmental Protection Agency pursuant to section 1857c–10(d)(3)(B) of Title 42.

**(3)(A)** Before issuing an order under subsection (a) of this section which is applicable to a powerplant or installation after June 30, 1975 (or modifying an order to which paragraph (2) applies, so as to apply such order to a powerplant or installation after such date), the Federal Energy Administrator shall give notice to the public and afford interested persons an opportunity for oral and written presentations of data, views, and arguments.

**(B)** An order (or modification thereof) described in subparagraph (A) of this paragraph shall not become effective until (i) the Administrator of the Environmental Protection Agency notifies the Federal Energy Administrator under section 1857c–10(d)(1)(B) of Title 42 that such plant or installation will be able on and after July 1, 1975, to burn coal and to comply with all applicable air pollution requirements without a compliance date extension under section 1857c–10(c) of Title 42, or (ii) if such notification is not given, the date which the Administrator of the Environmental Protection Agency certifies pursuant to section 1857c–10(d)(1)(B) of Title 42 is the earliest date that such plant or installation will be able to comply with all applicable requirements of such 1857c–10 of Title 42. Such order (or modification) shall not be effective during any period certified by the Administrator of the Environmental Protection Agency under section 1857c–10(d)(3)(B) of Title 42.

**(c) Construction and design of powerplants or other major fuel burning installations**

The Federal Energy Administrator may require that any powerplant or other major fuel burning installation in the early planning process (other than a combustion gas turbine or combined cycle unit) be designed and constructed so as to be capable of using coal as its primary energy source. No powerplant or other major fuel burning installation may be required under this subsection to be so designed and constructed, if the Administrator determines that (1) in the case of a powerplant to do so is likely to result in an impairment of reliability or adequacy of service, or (2) an adequate and reliable supply of coal is not expected to be available. In considering whether to impose a design and construction requirement under this subsection, the Federal Energy Administrator shall consider the existence and effects of any contractual commitment for the construction of such facilities and the capability of the owner to recover any capital investment made as a result of any requirement imposed under this subsection.

**(d) Allocation of coal**

The Federal Energy Administrator may, by rule or order, allocate coal (1) to any powerplant or major fuel-burning installation to which an order under subsection (a) of this section has been issued, or (2) to any other person to the extent necessary to carry out the purposes of this chapter.

**(e) Definitions**

For purposes of this section:

(1) The term "powerplant" means a fossil-fuel fired electric generating unit which produces electric power for purposes of sale or exchange.

(2) The term "coal" includes coal derivatives.

**(f) Expiration of authority; effective dates**

(1) Authority to issue orders or rules under subsections (a) through (d) of this section shall expire at midnight, December 31, 1978. Such a rule or order may take effect at any time before January 1, 1985.

(2) Authority to amend, repeal, rescind, modify, or enforce such rules or orders shall expire at midnight, December 31, 1984; but the expiration of such authority shall not affect any administrative or judicial proceeding which relates to any act or omission which occurred prior to January 1, 1985.

(Pub.L. 93–319, § 2, June 22, 1974, 88 Stat. 246; Pub.L. 94–163, Title I, § 101, Dec. 22, 1975, 89 Stat. 875; Pub.L. 95–70, § 7, July 21, 1977, 91 Stat. 277.)

HISTORICAL AND STATUTORY NOTES

**References in Text**

This chapter, referred to in subsecs. (b)(1) and (d), was in the original "this Act", meaning Pub.L. 93–319. For complete classification of this Act to the Code, see Short Title note set out under section 791 of this title and Tables.

Section 1857c–10 of Title 42, referred to in subsec. (b)(2)(B), (3)(B), was in the original a reference to section 119 of the Clean Air Act, and was repealed by Pub.L. 95–95, § 112(b), which provided in part that references in this section to section 1857c–10 shall be construed to refer to section 7413(d) of Title 42 and to paragraph (5) thereof in particular. Subsequently, section 7413 of Title 42 was amended generally by Pub.L. 101–549, Title VII, § 701, Nov. 15, 1990, 104 Stat. 2672, and, as so amended, subsec. (d) no longer relates to final compliance orders. See section 7413(a) of Title 42 for provisions relating generally to compliance orders. For further details, see Compliance Orders note set out under this section.

**Transfer of Functions**

Federal Energy Administration terminated and functions vested by law in Administrator thereof transferred to Secretary of Energy (unless otherwise specifically provided) by sections 715(a) and 7293 of Title 42, The Public Health and Welfare.

**Compliance Orders**

Pub.L. 95–95, Title I, § 112(b), Aug. 7, 1977, 91 Stat. 709, repealed section 119 of the Clean Air Act, which was classified to section 1857c–10 of Title 42, The Public Health and Welfare, and related to the Administrator's authority to deal with the energy shortage. Section 112(b) of Pub.L. 95–95 provided that:

"(1) Section 119 of such Act [section 1857c–10 of Title 42, The Public Health and Welfare] is hereby repealed. All references to such section 119 [section 1857c–10 of Title 42] or subsections thereof in section 2 of the Energy Supply and Environmental Coordination Act of 1974 (Public Law 93–319) [this section] or any amendment thereto, or any subsequent enactment which supersedes such Act [Pub.L. 93–319, June 22, 1974, 88 Stat. 246], shall be construed to refer to section 113(d) of the Clean Air Act [section 7413(d) of Title 42] and to paragraph (5) thereof in particular. Any certification or notification required to be given by the Administrator of the Environmental Protection Agency under section 2 of the Energy Supply and Environmental Coordination Act of 1974 [this section] or any amendment thereto, or any subsequent enactment which supersedes such Act, shall be given only when the Governor of the State in which is located the source to which the proposed order under section 113(d) (5) of the Clean Air Act [section 7413(d) (5) of Title 42] is to be issued gives his prior written concurrence.

"(2) In the case of any major stationary source to which any requirement is applicable under section 113(d) (5) (B) of the Clean Air Act [section 7413(d) (5) (B) of Title 42] and for which certification is required under section 2 of the Energy Supply and Environmental Coordination Act of 1974 [this section] or any amendment thereto, or any subsequent enactment which supersedes such Act [Pub.L. 93–319], the Administrator of the Environmental Protection Agency shall certify the date which he determines is the earliest date that such source will be able to comply with all such requirements. In the case of any plant or installation which the Administrator of the Environmental Protection Agency determines (after consultation with the State) will not be subject to an order under section 113(d) of the Clean Air Act [section 7413(d) of Title 42] and for which certification is required under section 2 of the Energy Supply and Environmental Coordination Act of 1974 [this section] or any amendment thereto, or any subsequent enactment which supersedes such Act [Pub.L. 93–319], the Administrator of the Environmental Protection Agency shall certify the date which he determines is the earliest date that such plant or installation will be able to burn coal in compliance with all applicable emission limitations under the implementation plan.

"(3) Any certification required under section 2 of the Energy Supply and Environmental Coordination Act of 1974 [this section] or any amendment thereto, or any subsequent enactment which supersedes such Act [Pub.L. 93–319], or under this subsection may be provided in an order under section 113(d) of the Clean Air Act [section 7413(d) of Title 42]."

## § 793. Protection of public health and environment

**[ESECA § 7]**

### (a) Distribution of low sulfur fuel

Any allocation program provided for in section 792 of this title or in the Emergency Petroleum Allocation Act of 1973 [15 U.S.C.A. § 751 et seq.], shall, to the maximum extent practicable, include measures to assure that available low sulfur fuel will be distributed on a priority basis to those areas of the United States designated by the Administrator of the Environmental Protection Agency as requiring low sulfur fuel to avoid or minimize adverse impact on public health.

### (b) Study of chronic effects of sulfur oxide emissions among exposed populations

In order to determine the health effects of emissions of sulfur oxides to the air resulting from any conversions to burning coal to which section 119 of the Clean Air Act [42 U.S.C.A. § 1857c–10] applies, the Department of Health and Human Services shall, through the National Institute of Environmental Health Sciences and in cooperation with the Environmental Protection Agency, conduct a study of chronic effects among exposed populations. The sum of $3,500,000 is authorized to be appropriated for such a study. In order to assure that long-term studies can be conducted without interruption, such sums as are appropriated shall be available until expended.

### (c) Major Federal actions significantly affecting the quality of the human environment

(1) No action taken under the Clean Air Act [42 U.S.C.A. § 7401 et seq.] shall be deemed a major Federal action significantly affecting the quality of the human environment within the meaning of the Nation-

al Environmental Policy Act of 1969 [42 U.S.C.A. § 4321 et seq.].

(2) No action under section 792 of this title for a period of one year after initiation of such action shall be deemed a major Federal action significantly affecting the quality of the human environment within the meaning of the National Environmental Policy Act of 1969 [42 U.S.C.A. § 4321 et seq.]. However, before any action under section 792 of this title that has a significant impact on the environment is taken, if practicable, or in any event within sixty days after such action is taken, an environmental evaluation with analysis equivalent to that required under section 102(2)(C) of the National Environmental Policy Act [42 U.S.C.A. § 4332(2)(C) ], to the greatest extent practicable within this time constraint, shall be prepared and circulated to appropriate Federal, State, and local government agencies and to the public for a thirty-day comment period after which a public hearing shall be held upon request to review outstanding environmental issues. Such an evaluation shall not be required where the action in question has been preceded by compliance with the National Environmental Policy Act by the appropriate Federal agency. Any action taken under section 792 of this title which will be in effect for more than a one-year period or any action to extend an action taken under section 792 of this title to a total period of more than one year shall be subject to the full provisions of the National Environmental Policy Act, notwithstanding any other provision of this chapter.

**(d) Importation of hydroelectric energy**

In order to expedite the prompt construction of facilities for the importation of hydroelectric energy thereby helping to reduce the shortage of petroleum products in the United States, the Federal Power Commission is hereby authorized and directed to issue a Presidential permit pursuant to Executive Order 10485 of September 3, 1953, for the construction, operation, maintenance, and connection of facilities for the transmission of electric energy at the borders of the United States without preparing an environmental impact statement pursuant to section 102 of the National Environmental Policy Act of 1969 [42 U.S.C.A. § 4332] for facilities for the transmission of electric energy between Canada and the United States in the vicinity of Fort Covington, New York.

(Pub.L. 93–319, § 7, June 22, 1974, 88 Stat. 259; Pub.L. 96–88, Title V, § 509(b), Oct. 17, 1979, 93 Stat. 695.)

### HISTORICAL AND STATUTORY NOTES

**References in Text**

The Emergency Petroleum Allocation Act of 1973, referred to in subsec. (a), is Pub.L. 93–159, Nov. 27, 1973, 87 Stat. 628, as amended, which was classified generally to chapter 16A (§ 751 et seq.) of this title, was omitted from the Code pursuant to section 760g of this title, which provided for the expiration of the President's authority under that chapter on Sept. 30, 1981.

Section 119 of the Clean Air Act [42 U.S.C.A. § 1857c–10], referred to in subsec. (b), was repealed by Pub.L. 95–95, § 112(b)(1), Aug. 7, 1977, 91 Stat. 709, which is set out as a Compliance Orders note under section 792 of this title. A new section 119 of the Clean Air Act was added by Pub.L. 95–95, § 117(b), and is classified to section 7419 of Title 42, The Public Health and Welfare.

The Clean Air Act, referred to in subsec. (c), is act July 14, 1955, ch. 360, 69 Stat. 322, as amended, which is classified generally to chapter 85 (§ 7401 et seq.) of Title 42. For complete classification of this Act of the Code, see Short Title note set out under section 7401 of Title 42 and Tables.

The National Environmental Policy Act of 1969, referred to in subsec. (c), is Pub.L. 91–190, Jan. 1, 1970, 83 Stat. 852, as amended, which is classified generally to chapter 55 (§ 4321 et seq.) of Title 42. For complete classification of this Act to the Code, see Short Title note set out under section 4321 of Title 42 and Tables.

This chapter, referred to in subsec. (c)(2), was in the original "this Act", meaning Pub.L. 93–319. For complete classification of this Act to the Code, see Short Title note set out under section 791 of this title and Tables.

Executive Order 10485 of September 3, 1953, referred to in subsec. (d) is Ex.Ord. No. 10485, Sept. 3, 1953, 18 F.R. 5397, and is set out as a note under section 717b of this title.

**Change of Name**

"Department of Health and Human Services" substituted for "Department of Health, Education, and Welfare" in subsec. (b), pursuant to section 509(b) of Pub.L. 96–88, which is classified to section 3508(b) of Title 20, Education.

**Transfer of Functions**

Federal Power Commission terminated and functions, personnel, property, funds, etc., transferred to Secretary of Energy (except for certain functions transferred to Federal Energy Regulatory Commission) by sections 7151(b), 7171(a), 7172(a)(1), 7291, and 7293 of Title 42, The Public Health and Welfare.

## § 794. Energy conservation study

[ESECA § 8]

**(a) Study of conservation methods**

The Federal Energy Administrator shall conduct a study on potential methods of energy conservation and, not later than six months after June 22, 1974, shall submit to Congress a report on the results of such study. The study shall include, but not be limited to, the following:

(1) the energy conservation potential of restricting exports of fuels or energy-intensive products, or goods, including an analysis of balance-of-payments and foreign relations implications of any such restrictions;

(2) alternative requirements, incentives, or disincentives for increasing industrial recycling and resource recovery in order to reduce energy demand,

including the economic costs and fuel consumption tradeoff which may be associated with such recycling and resource recovery in lieu of transportation and use of virgin materials; and

(3) means for incentives or disincentives to increase efficiency of industrial use of energy.

**(b) Emergency mass transportation assistance plan**

Within ninety days of June 22, 1974, the Secretary of Transportation, after consultation with the Federal Energy Administrator, shall submit to the Congress for appropriate action an "Emergency Mass Transportation Assistance Plan" for the purpose of conserving energy by expanding and improving public mass transportation systems and encouraging increased ridership as alternatives to automobile travel.

**(c) Recommendations in plan**

Such plan shall include, but shall not be limited to—

(1) recommendations for emergency temporary grants to assist States and local public bodies and agencies thereof in the payment of operating expenses incurred in connection with the provision of expanded mass transportation service in urban areas;

(2) recommendations for additional emergency assistance for the purchase of buses and rolling stock for fixed rail, including the feasibility of accelerating the timetable for such assistance under section 142(a)(2) of Title 23 for the purpose of providing additional capacity for and encouraging increased use of public mass transportation systems;

(3) recommendations for a program of demonstration projects to determine the feasibility of fare-free and low-fare urban mass transportation systems, including reduced rates for elderly and handicapped persons during nonpeak hours of transportation;

(4) recommendations for additional emergency assistance for the construction of fringe and transportation corridor parking facilities to serve bus and other mass transportation passengers;

(5) recommendations on the feasibility of providing tax incentives for persons who use public mass transportation systems.

(Pub.L. 93–319, § 8, June 22, 1974, 88 Stat. 260.)

### HISTORICAL AND STATUTORY NOTES

**Transfer of Functions**

Federal Energy Administration terminated and functions vested by law in Administrator thereof transferred to Secretary of Energy (unless otherwise specifically provided) by sections 7151(a) and 7293 of Title 42, The Public Health and Welfare.

## § 795. Report to Congress by January 31, 1975

[ESECA § 9]

The Administrator of the Environmental Protection Agency shall report to Congress not later than January 31, 1975, on the implementation of sections 3 through 7 of the Energy Supply and Environmental Coordination Act of 1974.

(Pub.L. 93–319, § 9, June 22, 1974, 88 Stat. 261.)

### HISTORICAL AND STATUTORY NOTES

**References in Text**

Sections 3 through 7 of the Energy Supply and Environmental Coordination Act of 1974, referred to in text, are §§ 3 through 7 of Pub.L. 93–319, June 22, 1974, 88 Stat. 248–260, which sections enacted § 793 of this title and § 1857c–10 of Title 42, The Public Health and Welfare, and amended §§ 1857c–5, 1857c–8, 1857c–9, 1857d–1, 1857f–1, and 1857h–5 of Title 42. Section 1857c–10 of Title 42 was repealed by Pub.L. 95–95, § 112(b)(1). On enactment of Pub.L. 95–95, sections 1857c–5, 1857c–8, 1857c–9, 1857d–1, 1857f–1, and 1857h–5 were reclassified to sections 7410, 7413, 7414, 7416, 7521, and 7607, respectively of Title 42.

## § 796. Reporting of energy information

[ESECA § 11]

**(a) Authority of Federal Energy Administrator to request, acquire, and collect energy information; rules and regulations**

For the purpose of assuring that the Federal Energy Administrator, the Congress, the States, and the public have access to and are able to obtain reliable energy information, the Federal Energy Administrator shall request, acquire, and collect such energy information as he determines to be necessary to assist in the formulation of energy policy or to carry out the purposes of this chapter or the Emergency Petroleum Allocation Act of 1973 [15 U.S.C.A. § 751 et. seq.]. The Federal Energy Administrator shall promptly promulgate rules pursuant to subsection (b)(1)(A) of this section requiring reports of such information to be submitted to the Federal Energy Administrator at least every ninety calendar days.

**(b) Powers of Federal Energy Administrator in obtaining energy information; verification of accuracy; compliance orders**

(1) In order to obtain energy information for the purpose of carrying out the provisions of subsection (a) of this section, the Federal Energy Administrator is authorized—

(A) to require, by rule, any person who is engaged in the production, processing, refining, transportation by pipeline, or distribution (at other than the retail level) of energy resources to submit reports;

(B) to sign and issue subpenas for the attendance and testimony of witnesses and the production of books, records, papers, and other documents;

(C) to require any person, by general or special order, to submit answers in writing to interrogatories, requests for reports or for other information; and such answers or other submissions shall be made within such reasonable period, and under oath or otherwise, as the Federal Energy Administrator may determine; and

(D) to administer oaths.

(2) For the purpose of verifying the accuracy of any energy information requested, acquired, or collected by the Federal Energy Administrator, the Federal Energy Administrator, or any officer or employer[1] duly designated by him, upon presenting appropriate credentials and a written notice from the Federal Energy Administrator to the owner, operator, or agent in charge, may—

(A) enter, at reasonable times, any business premise or facility; and

(B) inspect, at reasonable times and in a reasonable manner, any such premise or facility, inventory and sample any stock of energy resources therein, and examine and copy books, records, papers, or other documents, relating to any such energy information.

(3) Any United States district court within the jurisdiction of which any inquiry is carried on may, upon petition by the Attorney General at the request of the Federal Energy Administrator, in the case of refusal to obey a subpena or order of the Federal Energy Administrator issued under this section, issue an order requiring compliance therewith; and any failure to obey the order of the court may be punished by the court as a contempt thereof.

**(c) Development of initial report; quarterly reports; accounting practices**

(1) The Federal Energy Administrator shall exercise the authorities granted to him under subsection (b)(1)(A) of this section to develop, within thirty days after June 22, 1974, as full and accurate a measure as is reasonably practicable of—

(A) domestic reserves and production;

(B) imports; and

(C) inventories;

of crude oil, residual fuel oil, refined petroleum products, natural gas, and coal.

(2) For each calendar quarter beginning with the first complete calendar quarter following June 22, 1974, the Federal Energy Administrator shall develop and publish a report containing the following energy information:

(A) Imports of crude oil, residual fuel oil, refined petroleum products (by product), natural gas, and coal, identifying (with respect to each such oil, product, gas, or coal) country of origin, arrival point, quantity received, and the geographic distribution within the United States.

(B) Domestic reserves and production of crude oil, natural gas, and coal.

(C) Refinery activities, showing for each refinery within the United States (i) the amounts of crude oil run by such refinery, (ii) amounts of crude oil allocated to such refinery pursuant to regulations and orders of the Federal Energy Administrator, his delegate pursuant to the Emergency Petroleum Allocation Act of 1973 [15 U.S.C.A. § 751 et seq.], or any other person authorized by law to issue regulations and orders with respect to the allocation of crude oil, (iii) percentage of refinery capacity utilized, and (iv) amounts of products refined from such crude oil.

(D) Report of inventories, on a national, regional, and State-by-State basis—

(i) of various refined petroleum products, related refiners, refineries, suppliers to refiners, share of market, and allocation fractions;

(ii) of various refined petroleum products, previous quarter deliveries and anticipated three-month available supplies;

(iii) of anticipated monthly supply of refined petroleum products, amount of set-aside for assignment by the State, anticipated State requirements, excess or shortfall of supply, and allocation fraction of base year; and

(iv) of LPG by State and owner: quantities stored, and existing capacities, and previous priorities on types, inventories of suppliers, and changes in supplier inventories.

(3) In order to carry out his responsibilities under subsection (a) of this section, the Federal Energy Administrator shall require, pursuant to subsection (b)(1)(A) of this section, that persons engaged, in whole or in part, in the production of crude oil or natural gas—

(A) keep energy information in accordance with the accounting practices developed pursuant to section 503 of the Energy Policy and Conservation Act [42 U.S.C.A. § 6383], and

(B) submit reports with respect to energy information kept in accordance with such practices.

The Administrator shall file quarterly reports with the President and the Congress compiled from accounts kept in accordance with such section 503 and submitted to the Administrator in accordance with this paragraph. Such reports shall present energy information in the categories specified in subsection (c) of such section 503 to the extent that such information may be compiled from such accounts. Such energy information shall be collected and such quarterly reports made for each calendar quarter which begins 6 months after the date on which the accounting practices developed pursuant to such section 503 are made effective.

**(d) Confidential information**

Upon a showing satisfactory to the Federal Energy Administrator by any person that any energy information obtained under this section from such person would, if made public, divulge methods or processes entitled to protection as trade secrets or other proprietary information of such person, such information, or portion thereof, shall be confidential in accordance with the provisions of section 1905 of Title 18; except that such information, or part thereof, shall not be deemed confidential for purposes of disclosure, upon request, to (1) any delegate of the Federal Energy Administrator for the purpose of carrying out this chapter and the Emergency Petroleum Allocation Act of 1973 [15 U.S.C.A. § 751 et seq.], (2) the Attorney General, the Secretary of the Interior, the Federal Trade Commission, the Federal Power Commission, or the General Accounting Office, when necessary to carry out those agencies' duties and responsibilities under this and other statutes, and (3) the Congress, or any committee of Congress upon request of the Chairman.

**(e) Definitions**

As used in this section:

(1) The term "energy information" includes (A) all information in whatever form on (i) fuel reserves, exploration, extraction, and energy resources (including petrochemical feedstocks) wherever located; (ii) production, distribution, and consumption of energy and fuels wherever carried on; and (B) matters relating to energy and fuels, such as corporate structure and proprietary relationships, costs, prices, capital investment, and assets, and other matters directly related thereto, wherever they exist.

(2) The term "person" means any natural person, corporation, partnership, association, consortium, or any entity organized for a common business purpose, wherever situated, domiciled, or doing business, who directly or through other persons subject to their control does business in any part of the United States.

(3) The term "United States" when used in the geographical sense means the States, the District of Columbia, Puerto Rico, and the territories and possessions of the United States.

**(f) Availability of energy information**

Information obtained by the Administration under authority of this chapter shall be available to the public in accordance with the provisions of section 552 of Title 5.

**(g) Independent nature of authority to gather energy information**

The authority contained in this section is in addition to, independent of, not limited by, and not in limitation of, any other authority of the Federal Energy Administrator.

(Pub.L. 93–319, § 11, June 22, 1974, 88 Stat. 262; Pub.L. 94–163, Title V, §§ 505(a), 506, Dec. 22, 1975, 89 Stat. 960; Pub.L. 95–620, Title VII, § 762(d), Nov. 9, 1978, 92 Stat. 3346.)

[1] So in original. Probably should read "employee".

## HISTORICAL AND STATUTORY NOTES

**References in Text**

This chapter, referred to in subsec. (a), was in the original "this Act", meaning Pub.L. 93–319. For complete classification of this Act to the Code, see Short Title note set out under section 791 of this title and Tables.

The Emergency Petroleum Allocation Act of 1973, referred to in subsecs. (a), (c)(2)(C), and (d), is Pub.L. 93–159, Nov. 27, 1974, 87 Stat. 628, which was classified generally to chapter 16A (§ 751 et seq.) of this title and which was omitted from the Code pursuant to section 760g of this title, which provided for the expiration of the President's authority under that chapter on Sept. 30, 1981.

**Effective and Applicability Provisions**

1978 Acts

Amendment by Pub.L. 95–620 effective 180 days after Nov. 9, 1978, see section 901 of Pub.L. 95–620, set out as an Effective Date note under section 8301 of Title 42, The Public Health and Welfare.

1975 Acts

Section 505(b) of Pub.L. 94–163 provided that: "The amendment made by subsection (a) to section 11(c) of the Energy Supply and Environmental Coordination Act of 1974 [enacting subsec. (c)(3) of this section] shall take effect on the first day of the first accounting quarter to which such practices apply."

**Transfer of Functions**

Federal Energy Administration terminated and functions vested by law in Administrator thereof transferred to Secretary of Energy (unless otherwise specifically provided) by sections 7151(a) and 7293 of Title 42, The Public Health and Welfare.

Federal Power Commission terminated and functions, personnel, property, funds, etc., transferred to Secretary of Energy (except for certain functions transferred to Federal Energy Regulatory Commission) by sections 7151(b), 7171(a), 7172(a)(1), 7291, and 7293 of Title 42.

## § 797. Enforcement

**[ESECA § 12]**

**(a) Violations**

It shall be unlawful for any person to violate any provision of section 792 of this title (relating to coal conversion and allocation) or section 796 of this title (relating to energy information) or to violate any rule, regulation, or order issued pursuant to any such provision.

**(b) Penalties; injunctions; declaratory judgments**

(1) Whoever violates any provision of subsection (a) of this section shall be subject to a civil penalty of not more than $2,500 for each violation.

(2) Whoever willfully violates any provision of subsection (a) of this section shall be fined not more than $5,000 for each violation.

(3) It shall be unlawful for any person to offer for sale or distribute in commerce any coal in violation of an order or regulation issued pursuant to section 792(d) of this title. Any person who knowingly and willfully violates this paragraph after having been subjected to a civil penalty for a prior violation of the same provision of any order or regulation issued pursuant to section 792(d) of this title shall be fined not more than $50,000, or imprisoned not more than six months, or both.

(4) Whenever it appears to the Federal Energy Administrator or any person authorized by the Federal Energy Administrator to exercise authority under section 792 of this title or section 796 of this title that any individual or organization has engaged, is engaged, or is about to engage in acts or practices constituting a violation of subsection (a) of this section the Federal Energy Administrator or such person may request the Attorney General to bring a civil action to enjoin such acts or practices, and upon a proper showing, a temporary restraining order or a preliminary or permanent injunction shall be granted without bond. In such action, the court may also issue mandatory injunctions commanding any person to comply with any provision, the violation of which is prohibited by subsection (a) of this section.

(5) Any person suffering legal wrong because of any act or practice arising out of any violation of subsection (a) of this section may bring a civil action for appropriate relief, including an action for a declaratory judgment or writ of injunction. United States district courts shall have jurisdiction of actions under this paragraph without regard to the amount in controversy. Nothing in this paragraph shall authorize any person to recover damages.

(Pub.L. 93–319, § 12, June 22, 1974, 88 Stat. 264.)

### HISTORICAL AND STATUTORY NOTES

**Transfer of Functions**

Federal Energy Administration terminated and functions vested by law in Administrator thereof transferred to Secretary of Energy (unless otherwise specifically provided) by sections 7151(a) and 7293 of Title 42, The Public Health and Welfare.

## § 798. Definitions

**[ESECA § 14]**

**(a)** For purposes of this chapter and the Clean Air Act [42 U.S.C.A. § 7401 et seq.] the term "Federal Energy Administrator" means the Administrator of the Federal Energy Administration established by Federal Energy Administration Act of 1974 [15 U.S.C.A. § 761 et seq.]; except that until such Administrator takes office and after such Administration ceases to exist, such term means any officer of the United States designated as Federal Energy Administrator by the President for purposes of this chapter and section 119 of the Clean Air Act [42 U.S.C.A. § 1857c–10].

**(b)** For purposes of this chapter, the term "petroleum product" means crude oil, residual fuel oil, or any refined petroleum product (as defined in section 752(5) of this title).

(Pub.L. 93–319, § 14, June 22, 1974, 88 Stat. 265.)

### HISTORICAL AND STATUTORY NOTES

**References in Text**

This chapter, referred to in subsecs. (a) and (b), was in the original "this Act", meaning Pub.L. 93–319. For complete classification of this Act to the Code, see Short Title note set out under section 791 of this title and Tables.

The Clean Air Act, referred to in subsec. (a), is act July 14, 1955, ch. 360, 69 Stat. 322, as amended, which is classified generally to chapter 85 (§ 7401 et seq.) of Title 42, The Public Health and Welfare. For complete classification of this Act to the Code, see Short Title note set out under section 7401 of Title 42 and Tables.

Section 119 of the Clean Air Act [42 U.S.C.A. § 1857c–10], referred to in subsec. (a), was repealed by Pub.L. 95–95, § 112(b)(1), Aug. 7, 1977, 91 Stat. 709, which is set out as a Compliance Orders note under section 792 of this title. A new section 119 of the Clean Air Act was added by Pub.L. 95–95, § 117(b), and is classified to section 7419 of Title 42.

The Federal Energy Administration Act of 1974, referred to in subsec. (a), is Pub.L. 93–275, May 7, 1974, 88 Stat. 96, which is classified to § 761 et seq. of this title. For complete classification of this Act to the Code, see Short Title note set out under section 761 of this title and Tables.

Section 752 of this title, referred to in subsec. (b), was omitted from the Code pursuant to section 760g of this title, which provided for the expiration of the President's authority under that section on Sept. 30, 1981.

**Transfer of Functions**

Federal Energy Administration terminated and functions vested by law in Administrator thereof transferred to Secretary of Energy (unless otherwise specifically provided) by sections 7151(a) and 7293 of Title 42, The Public Health and Welfare.

# TOXIC SUBSTANCES CONTROL

## TOXIC SUBSTANCES CONTROL ACT [TSCA § ____]

**(15 U.S.C.A. §§ 2601 to 2692)**

## CHAPTER 53—TOXIC SUBSTANCES CONTROL



**Related Provisions**

*See, also, Environmental Pesticide Control, 7 U.S.C.A. § 136 et seq., ante.*

### SUBCHAPTER I—CONTROL OF TOXIC SUBSTANCES

### § 2601. Findings, policy, and intent

**[TSCA § 2]**

**(a) Findings**

The Congress finds that—

(1) human beings and the environment are being exposed each year to a large number of chemical substances and mixtures;

(2) among the many chemical substances and mixtures which are constantly being developed and produced, there are some whose manufacture, processing, distribution in commerce, use, or disposal may present an unreasonable risk of injury to health or the environment; and

(3) the effective regulation of interstate commerce in such chemical substances and mixtures also necessitates the regulation of intrastate commerce in such chemical substances and mixtures.

**(b) Policy**

It is the policy of the United States that—

(1) adequate data should be developed with respect to the effect of chemical substances and mixtures on health and the environment and that the development of such data should be the responsibility of those who manufacture and those who process such chemical substances and mixtures;

(2) adequate authority should exist to regulate chemical substances and mixtures which present an unreasonable risk of injury to health or the environment, and to take action with respect to chemical substances and mixtures which are imminent hazards; and

(3) authority over chemical substances and mixtures should be exercised in such a manner as not to impede unduly or create unnecessary economic barriers to technological innovation while fulfilling the primary purpose of this chapter to assure that such innovation and commerce in such chemical substances and mixtures do not present an unreasonable risk of injury to health or the environment.

**(c) Intent of Congress**

It is the intent of Congress that the Administrator shall carry out this chapter in a reasonable and prudent manner, and that the Administrator shall consider the environmental, economic, and social impact of any action the Administrator takes or proposes to take under this chapter.

(Pub.L. 94–469, Title I, § 2, Oct. 11, 1976, 90 Stat. 2003; renumbered Title I, Pub.L. 99–519, § 3(c)(1), Oct. 22, 1986, 100 Stat. 2989.)

### HISTORICAL AND STATUTORY NOTES

**Effective and Applicability Provisions**

1976 Acts

Section 31 of Title I of Pub.L. 94–469; remanded Title I, Pub.L. 99–519, § 3(c), Oct. 22, 1986, 100 Stat. 2989, provided that: "Except as provided in section 4(f) [section 2603(f) of this title], this Act [enacting this chapter] shall take effect on January 1, 1977."

**Short Title**

1992 Amendments

Pub.L. 102–550, Title X, § 1021(c), Oct. 28, 1992, 106 Stat. 3924, provided that: "This subtitle [subtitle B (§ 1021) of Title X of Pub.L. 102–550, enacting sections 2681 to 2692 of this title and amending sections 2606, 2610, 2612, 2615, 2616, 2618, and 2619 of this title] may be cited as the 'Lead-Based Paint Exposure Reduction Act'."

1986 Amendments

Section 1 of Pub.L. 99–519 provided that: "This Act [enacting sections 2641 to 2654 of this title, and section 4022 of Title 20, Education, amending sections 2614, 2618, and 2619 of this title and sections 4014 and 4021 of Title 20, and enacting provisions set out as a note under section 4014 of Title 20] may be cited as the 'Asbestos Hazard Emergency Response Act of 1986'."

1976 Acts

Section 1 of Pub.L. 94–469 provided that: "This Act [enacting this chapter and provisions set out as notes under this section] may be cited as the 'Toxic Substances Control Act'."

**Federal Compliance with Pollution Control Standards**

For provisions relating to the responsibility of the head of each Executive agency for compliance with applicable pollution control standards, see Ex. Ord. No. 12088, Oct. 13, 1978, 43 F.R. 47707, set out as a note under section 4321 of Title 42, The Public Health and Welfare.

## § 2602. Definitions

**[TSCA § 3]**

As used in this chapter:

(1) the[1] term "Administrator" means the Administrator of the Environmental Protection Agency.

(2)(A) Except as provided in subparagraph (B), the term "chemical substance" means any organic or inorganic substance of a particular molecular identity, including—

(i) any combination of such substances occurring in whole or in part as a result of a chemical reaction or occurring in nature and

(ii) any element or uncombined radical.

(B) Such term does not include—

(i) any mixture,

(ii) any pesticide (as defined in the Federal Insecticide, Fungicide, and Rodenticide Act) [7 U.S.C.A. § 136 et seq.] when manufactured, processed, or distributed in commerce for use as a pesticide,

(iii) tobacco or any tobacco product,

(iv) any source material, special nuclear material, or byproduct material (as such terms are defined in the Atomic Energy Act of 1954 [42 U.S.C.A. § 2011 et seq.] and regulations issued under such Act),

(v) any article the sale of which is subject to the tax imposed by section 4181 of the Internal Revenue Code of 1986 [26 U.S.C.A. 4181] (determined without regard to any exemptions from such tax provided by section 4182 or 4221 or any other provision of such code), and

**(vi)** any food, food additive, drug, cosmetic, or device (as such terms are defined in section 201 of the Federal Food, Drug, and Cosmetic Act (21 U.S.C.A. 321]) when manufactured, processed, or distributed in commerce for use as a food, food additive, drug, cosmetic, or device.

The term "food" as used in clause (vi) of this subparagraph includes poultry and poultry products (as defined in sections 4(e) and 4(f) of the Poultry Products Inspection Act [21 U.S.C. 453(e) and (f) ] ), meat and meat food products (as defined in section 1(j) of the Federal Meat Inspection Act [21 U.S.C. 601(j) ] ), and eggs and egg products (as defined in section 4 of the Egg Products Inspection Act [21 U.S.C. 1033] ).

**(3)** The term "commerce" means trade, traffic, transportation, or other commerce (A) between a place in a State and any place outside of such State, or (B) which affects trade, traffic, transportation, or commerce described in clause (A).

**(4)** The terms "distribute in commerce" and "distribution in commerce" when used to describe an action taken with respect to a chemical substance or mixture or article containing a substance or mixture mean to sell, or the sale of, the substance, mixture, or article in commerce; to introduce or deliver for introduction into commerce, or the introduction or delivery for introduction into commerce of, the substance, mixture, or article; or to hold, or the holding of, the substance, mixture, or article after its introduction into commerce.

**(5)** The term "environment" includes water, air, and land and the interrelationship which exists among and between water, air, and land and all living things.

**(6)** The term "health and safety study" means any study of any effect of a chemical substance or mixture on health or the environment or on both, including underlying data and epidemiological studies, studies of occupational exposure to a chemical substance or mixture, toxicological, clinical, and ecological studies of a chemical substance or mixture, and any test performed pursuant to this chapter.

**(7)** The term "manufacture" means to import into the customs territory of the United States (as defined in general note 2 of the Harmonized Tariff Schedule of the United States), produce, or manufacture.

**(8)** The term "mixture" means any combination of two or more chemical substances if the combination does not occur in nature and is not, in whole or in part, the result of a chemical reaction; except that such term does include any combination which occurs, in whole or in part, as a result of a chemical reaction if none of the chemical substances comprising the combination is a new chemical substance and if the combination could have been manufactured for commercial purposes without a chemical reaction at the time the chemical substances comprising the combination were combined.

**(9)** The term "new chemical substance" means any chemical substance which is not included in the chemical substance list compiled and published under section 2607(b) of this title.

**(10)** The term "process" means the preparation of a chemical substance or mixture, after its manufacture, for distribution in commerce—

**(A)** in the same form or physical state as, or in a different form or physical state from, that in which it was received by the person so preparing such substance or mixture, or

**(B)** as part of an article containing the chemical substance or mixture.

**(11)** The term "processor" means any person who processes a chemical substance or mixture.

**(12)** The term "standards for the development of test data" means a prescription of—

**(A)** the—

**(i)** health and environmental effects, and

**(ii)** information relating to toxicity, persistence, and other characteristics which affect health and the environment,

for which test data for a chemical substance or mixture are to be developed and any analysis that is to be performed on such data, and

**(B)** to the extent necessary to assure that data respecting such effects and characteristics are reliable and adequate—

**(i)** the manner in which such data are to be developed,

**(ii)** the specification of any test protocol or methodology to be employed in the development of such data, and

**(iii)** such other requirements as are necessary to provide such assurance.

**(13)** The term "State" means any State of the United States, the District of Columbia, the Commonwealth of Puerto Rico, the Virgin Islands, Guam, the Canal Zone, American Samoa, the Northern Mariana Islands, or any other territory or possession of the United States.

**(14)** The term "United States", when used in the geographic sense, means all of the States.

(Pub.L. 94–469, Title I, § 3, Oct. 11, 1976, 90 Stat. 2004; Pub.L. 99–514, § 2, Oct. 22, 1986, 100 Stat. 2095; renumbered Title I, Pub.L. 99–519, § 3(c)(1), Oct. 22, 1986, 100 Stat. 2989, and amended Pub.L. 100–418, Title I, § 1214(e)(1), Aug. 23, 1988, 102 Stat. 1156.)

1 So in original. Probably should be capitalized.

HISTORICAL AND STATUTORY NOTES

**References in Text**

The Federal Insecticide, Fungicide, and Rodenticide Act, referred to in par. (2)(B)(ii), is Act June 25, 1947, c. 125, as amended generally by Pub.L. 92–516, Oct. 21, 1972, 86 Stat. 973, which is classified generally to subchapter II (§ 136 et seq.) of chapter 6 of Title 7, Agriculture. For complete classification of this Act to the Code, see Short Title note set out under section 136 of Title 7 and Tables.

The Atomic Energy Act of 1954, referred to in par. (2)(B)(iv), is Act Aug. 30, 1954, c. 1073, 68 Stat. 919, as amended, which is classified generally to chapter 23 (§ 2011 et seq.) of Title 42, The Public Health and Welfare. For complete classification of this Act to the Code, see Short Title note set out under section 2011 of Title 42 and Tables.

The Harmonized Tariff Schedule of the United States, referred to in par. (7), is not set out in the Code. See Publication of Harmonized Tariff Schedule note set out under section 1202 of Title 19, Customs Duties.

For definition of Canal Zone, Governor of the Canal Zone, and Panama Canal Company, referred to in par. (13), see section 3602(b) of Title 22, Foreign Relations and Intercourse.

**Effective and Applicability Provisions**

1988 Acts

Amendment by Pub.L. 100–418 effective Jan. 1, 1989, and applicable with respect to articles entered on or after such date, see section 1217(b)(1) of Pub.L. 100–418, set out as an Effective Date note under section 3001 of Title 19, Customs Duties.

## § 2603. Testing of chemical substances and mixtures

[TSCA § 4]

**(a) Testing requirements**

If the Administrator finds that—

**(1)(A)(i)** the manufacture, distribution in commerce, processing, use, or disposal of a chemical substance or mixture, or that any combination of such activities, may present an unreasonable risk of injury to health or the environment,

**(ii)** there are insufficient data and experience upon which the effects of such manufacture, distribution in commerce, processing, use, or disposal of such substance or mixture or of any combination of such activities on health or the environment can reasonably be determined or predicted, and

**(iii)** testing of such substance or mixture with respect to such effects is necessary to develop such data; or

**(B)(i)** a chemical substance or mixture is or will be produced in substantial quantities, and (I) it enters or may reasonably be anticipated to enter the environment in substantial quantities or (II) there is or may be significant or substantial human exposure to such substance or mixture,

**(ii)** there are insufficient data and experience upon which the effects of the manufacture, distribution in commerce, processing, use, or disposal of such substance or mixture or of any combination of such activities on health or the environment can reasonably be determined or predicted, and

**(iii)** testing of such substance or mixture with respect to such effects is necessary to develop such data; and

**(2)** in the case of a mixture, the effects which the mixture's manufacture, distribution in commerce, processing, use, or disposal or any combination of such activities may have on health or the environment may not be reasonably and more efficiently determined or predicted by testing the chemical substances which comprise the mixture;

the Administrator shall by rule require that testing be conducted on such substance or mixture to develop data with respect to the health and environmental effects for which there is an insufficiency of data and experience and which are relevant to a determination that the manufacture, distribution in commerce, processing, use, or disposal of such substance or mixture, or that any combination of such activities, does or does not present an unreasonable risk of injury to health or the environment.

**(b) Testing requirement rule**

(1) A rule under subsection (a) of this section shall include—

**(A)** identification of the chemical substance or mixture for which testing is required under the rule,

**(B)** standards for the development of test data for such substance or mixture, and

**(C)** with respect to chemical substances which are not new chemical substances and to mixtures, a specification of the period (which period may not be of unreasonable duration) within which the persons required to conduct the testing shall submit to the Administrator data developed in accordance with the standards referred to in subparagraph (B).

In determining the standards and period to be included, pursuant to subparagraphs (B) and (C), in a rule under subsection (a) of this section, the Administrator's considerations shall include the relative costs of the various test protocols and methodologies which may be required under the rule and the reasonably foreseeable availability of the facilities and personnel needed to perform the testing required under the rule. Any such rule may require the submission to the Administrator of preliminary data during the period prescribed under subparagraph (C).

**(2)(A)** The health and environmental effects for which standards for the development of test data may be prescribed include carcinogenesis, mutagenesis, teratogenesis, behavioral disorders, cumulative or synergistic effects, and any other effect which may present an unreasonable risk of injury to health or the environment. The characteristics of chemical substances and mixtures for which such standards may be prescribed include persistence, acute toxicity, subacute toxicity, chronic toxicity, and any other characteristic which may present such a risk. The methodologies that may be prescribed in such standards include epidemiologic studies, serial or hierarchical tests, in vitro tests, and whole animal tests, except that before prescribing epidemiologic studies of employees, the Administrator shall consult with the Director of the National Institute for Occupational Safety and Health.

**(B)** From time to time, but not less than once each 12 months, the Administrator shall review the adequacy of the standards for development of data prescribed in rules under subsection (a) of this section and shall, if necessary, institute proceedings to make appropriate revisions of such standards.

**(3)(A)** A rule under subsection (a) of this section respecting a chemical substance or mixture shall require the persons described in subparagraph (B) to conduct tests and submit data to the Administrator on such substance or mixture, except that the Administrator may permit two or more of such persons to designate one such person or a qualified third party to conduct such tests and submit such data on behalf of the persons making the designation.

**(B)** The following persons shall be required to conduct tests and submit data on a chemical substance or mixture subject to a rule under subsection (a) of this section:

**(i)** Each person who manufactures or intends to manufacture such substance or mixture if the Administrator makes a finding described in subsection (a)(1)(A)(ii) or (a)(1)(B)(ii) of this section with respect to the manufacture of such substance or mixture.

**(ii)** Each person who processes or intends to process such substance or mixture if the Administrator makes a finding described in subsection (a)(1)(A)(ii) or (a)(1)(B)(ii) of this section with respect to the processing of such substance or mixture.

**(iii)** Each person who manufactures or processes or intends to manufacture or process such substance or mixture if the Administrator makes a finding described in subsection (a)(1)(A)(ii) or (a)(1)(B)(ii) of this section with respect to the distribution in commerce, use, or disposal of such substance or mixture.

**(4)** Any rule under subsection (a) of this section requiring the testing of and submission of data for a particular chemical substance or mixture shall expire at the end of the reimbursement period (as defined in subsection (c)(3)(B) of this section) which is applicable to test data for such substance or mixture unless the Administrator repeals the rule before such date; and a rule under subsection (a) of this section requiring the testing of and submission of data for a category of chemical substances or mixtures shall expire with respect to a chemical substance or mixture included in the category at the end of the reimbursement period (as so defined) which is applicable to test data for such substance or mixture unless the Administrator before such date repeals the application of the rule to such substance or mixture or repeals the rule.

**(5)** Rules issued under subsection (a) of this section (and any substantive amendment thereto or repeal thereof) shall be promulgated pursuant to section 553 of Title 5 except that (A) the Administrator shall give interested persons an opportunity for the oral presentation of data, views, or arguments, in addition to an opportunity to make written submissions; (B) a transcript shall be made of any oral presentation; and (C) the Administrator shall make and publish with the rule the findings described in paragraph (1)(A) or (1)(B) of subsection (a) of this section and, in the case of a rule respecting a mixture, the finding described in paragraph (2) of such subsection.

**(c) Exemption**

**(1)** Any person required by a rule under subsection (a) of this section to conduct tests and submit data on a chemical substance or mixture may apply to the Administrator (in such form and manner as the Administrator shall prescribe) for an exemption from such requirement.

**(2)** If, upon receipt of an application under paragraph (1), the Administrator determines that—

**(A)** the chemical substance or mixture with respect to which such application was submitted is equivalent to a chemical substance or mixture for which data has been submitted to the Administrator in accordance with a rule under subsection (a) of this section or for which data is being developed pursuant to such a rule, and

**(B)** submission of data by the applicant on such substance or mixture would be duplicative of data which has been submitted to the Administrator in accordance with such rule or which is being developed pursuant to such rule,

the Administrator shall exempt, in accordance with paragraph (3) or (4), the applicant from conducting tests and submitting data on such substance or mixture under the rule with respect to which such application was submitted.

**(3)(A)** If the exemption under paragraph (2) of any person from the requirement to conduct tests and submit test data on a chemical substance or mixture is granted on the basis of the existence of previously submitted test data and if such exemption is granted during the reimbursement period for such test data (as prescribed by subparagraph (B)), then (unless such person and the persons referred to in clauses (i) and (ii) agree on the amount and method of reimbursement) the Administrator shall order the person granted the exemption to provide fair and equitable reimbursement (in an amount determined under rules of the Administrator)—

**(i)** to the person who previously submitted such test data, for a portion of the costs incurred by such person in complying with the requirement to submit such data, and

**(ii)** to any other person who has been required under this subparagraph to contribute with respect to such costs, for a portion of the amount such person was required to contribute.

In promulgating rules for the determination of fair and equitable reimbursement to the persons described in clauses (i) and (ii) for costs incurred with respect to a chemical substance or mixture, the Administrator shall, after consultation with the Attorney General and the Federal Trade Commission, consider all relevant factors, including the effect on the competitive position of the person required to provide reimbursement in relation to the person to be reimbursed and the share of the market for such substance or mixture of the person required to provide reimbursement in relation to the share of such market of the persons to be reimbursed. An order under this subparagraph shall, for purposes of judicial review, be considered final agency action.

**(B)** For purposes of subparagraph (A), the reimbursement period for any test data for a chemical substance or mixture is a period—

**(i)** beginning on the date such data is submitted in accordance with a rule promulgated under subsection (a) of this section, and

**(ii)** ending—

**(I)** five years after the date referred to in clause (i), or

**(II)** at the expiration of a period which begins on the date referred to in clause (i) and which is equal to the period which the Administrator determines was necessary to develop such data,

whichever is later.

**(4)(A)** If the exemption under paragraph (2) of any person from the requirement to conduct tests and submit test data on a chemical substance or mixture is granted on the basis of the fact that test data is being developed by one or more persons pursuant to a rule promulgated under subsection (a) of this section, then (unless such person and the persons referred to in clauses (i) and (ii) agree on the amount and method of reimbursement) the Administrator shall order the person granted the exemption to provide fair and equitable reimbursement (in an amount determined under rules of the Administrator)—

**(i)** to each such person who is developing such test data, for a portion of the costs incurred by each such person in complying with such rule, and

**(ii)** to any other person who has been required under this subparagraph to contribute with respect to the costs of complying with such rule, for a portion of the amount such person was required to contribute.

In promulgating rules for the determination of fair and equitable reimbursement to the persons described in clauses (i) and (ii) for costs incurred with respect to a chemical substance or mixture, the Administrator shall, after consultation with the Attorney General and the Federal Trade Commission, consider the factors described in the second sentence of paragraph (3)(A). An order under this subparagraph shall, for purposes of judicial review, be considered final agency action.

**(B)** If any exemption is granted under paragraph (2) on the basis of the fact that one or more persons are developing test data pursuant to a rule promulgated under subsection (a) of this section and if after such exemption is granted the Administrator determines that no such person has complied with such rule, the Administrator shall (i) after providing written notice to the person who holds such exemption and an opportunity for a hearing, by order terminate such exemption, and (ii) notify in writing such person of the requirements of the rule with respect to which such exemption was granted.

### (d) Notice

Upon the receipt of any test data pursuant to a rule under subsection (a) of this section, the Administrator shall publish a notice of the receipt of such data in the Federal Register within 15 days of its receipt. Subject to section 2613 of this title, each such notice shall (1) identify the chemical substance or mixture for which data have been received; (2) list the uses or intended uses of such substance or mixture and the information required by the applicable standards for the development of test data; and (3) describe the nature of the test data developed. Except as otherwise provided in section 2613 of this title, such data shall be made available by the Administrator for examination by any person.

### (e) Priority list

**(1)(A)** There is established a committee to make recommendations to the Administrator respecting the chemical substances and mixtures to which the Administrator should give priority consideration for the promulgation of a rule under subsection (a) of this section. In making such a recommendation with respect to any chemical substance or mixture, the committee shall consider all relevant factors, including—

(i) the quantities in which the substance or mixture is or will be manufactured,

(ii) the quantities in which the substance or mixture enters or will enter the environment,

(iii) the number of individuals who are or will be exposed to the substance or mixture in their places of employment and the duration of such exposure,

(iv) the extent to which human beings are or will be exposed to the substance or mixture,

(v) the extent to which the substance or mixture is closely related to a chemical substance or mixture which is known to present an unreasonable risk of injury to health or the environment,

(vi) the existence of data concerning the effects of the substance or mixture on health or the environment,

(vii) the extent to which testing of the substance or mixture may result in the development of data upon which the effects of the substance or mixture on health or the environment can reasonably be determined or predicted, and

(viii) the reasonably foreseeable availability of facilities and personnel for performing testing on the substance or mixture.

The recommendations of the committee shall be in the form of a list of chemical substances and mixtures which shall be set forth, either by individual substance or mixture or by groups of substances or mixtures, in the order in which the committee determines the Administrator should take action under subsection (a) of this section with respect to the substances and mixtures. In establishing such list, the committee shall give priority attention to those chemical substances and mixtures which are known to cause or contribute to or which are suspected of causing or contributing to cancer, gene mutations, or birth defects. The committee shall designate chemical substances and mixtures on the list with respect to which the committee determines the Administrator should, within 12 months of the date on which such substances and mixtures are first designated, initiate a proceeding under subsection (a) of this section. The total number of chemical substances and mixtures on the list which are designated under the preceding sentence may not, at any time, exceed 50.

(B) As soon as practicable but not later than nine months after January 1, 1977, the committee shall publish in the Federal Register and transmit to the Administrator the list and designations required by subparagraph (A) together with the reasons for the committee's inclusion of each chemical substance or mixture on the list. At least every six months after the date of the transmission to the Administrator of the list pursuant to the preceeding[1] sentence, the committee shall make such revisions in the list as it determines to be necessary and shall transmit them to the Administrator together with the committee's reasons for the revisions. Upon receipt of any such revision, the Administrator shall publish in the Federal Register the list with such revision, the reasons for such revision, and the designations made under subparagraph (A). The Administrator shall provide reasonable opportunity to any interested person to file with the Administrator written comments on the committee's list, any revision of such list by the committee, and designations made by the committee, and shall make such comments available to the public. Within the 12-month period beginning on the date of the first inclusion on the list of a chemical substance or mixture designated by the committee under subparagraph (A) the Administrator shall with respect to such chemical substance or mixture either initiate a rulemaking proceeding under subsection (a) of this section or if such a proceeding is not initiated within such period, publish in the Federal Register the Administrator's reason for not initiating such a proceeding.

(2)(A) The committee established by paragraph (1)(A) shall consist of eight members as follows:

(i) One member appointed by the Administrator from the Environmental Protection Agency.

(ii) One member appointed by the Secretary of Labor from officers or employees of the Department of Labor engaged in the Secretary's activities under the Occupational Safety and Health Act of 1970 [29 U.S.C.A. § 651 et seq.].

(iii) One member appointed by the Chairman of the Council on Environmental Quality from the Council or its officers or employees.

(iv) One member appointed by the Director of the National Institute for Occupational Safety and Health from officers or employees of the Institute.

(v) One member appointed by the Director of the National Institute of Environmental Health Sciences from officers or employees of the Institute.

(vi) One member appointed by the Director of the National Cancer Institute from officers or employees of the Institute.

(vii) One member appointed by the Director of the National Science Foundation from officers or employees of the Foundation.

(viii) One member appointed by the Secretary of Commerce from officers or employees of the Department of Commerce.

(B)(i) An appointed member may designate an individual to serve on the committee on the member's behalf. Such a designation may be made only with the approval of the applicable appointing authority and only if the individual is from the entity from which the member was appointed.

**(ii)** No individual may serve as a member of the committee for more than four years in the aggregate. If any member of the committee leaves the entity from which the member was appointed, such member may not continue as a member of the committee, and the member's position shall be considered to be vacant. A vacancy in the committee shall be filled in the same manner in which the original appointment was made.

**(iii)** Initial appointments to the committee shall be made not later than the 60th day after January 1, 1977. Not later than the 90th day after such date the members of the committee shall hold a meeting for the selection of a chairperson from among their number.

**(C)(i)** No member of the committee, or designee of such member, shall accept employment or compensation from any person subject to any requirement of this chapter or of any rule promulgated or order issued thereunder, for a period of at least 12 months after termination of service on the committee.

**(ii)** No person, while serving as a member of the committee, or designee of such member, may own any stocks or bonds, or have any pecuniary interest, of substantial value in any person engaged in the manufacture, processing, or distribution in commerce of any chemical substance or mixture subject to any requirement of this chapter or of any rule promulgated or order issued thereunder.

**(iii)** The Administrator, acting through attorneys of the Environmental Protection Agency, or the Attorney General may bring an action in the appropriate district court of the United States to restrain any violation of this subparagraph.

**(D)** The Administrator shall provide the committee such administrative support services as may be necessary to enable the committee to carry out its function under this subsection.

**(f) Required actions**

Upon the receipt of—

(1) any test data required to be submitted under this chapter, or

(2) any other information available to the Administrator,

which indicates to the Administrator that there may be a reasonable basis to conclude that a chemical substance or mixture presents or will present a significant risk of serious or widespread harm to human beings from cancer, gene mutations, or birth defects, the Administrator shall, within the 180-day period beginning on the date of the receipt of such data or information, initiate appropriate action under section 2604, 2605, or 2606 of this title to prevent or reduce to a sufficient extent such risk or publish in the Federal Register a finding that such risk is not unreasonable. For good cause shown the Administrator may extend such period for an additional period of not more than 90 days. The Administrator shall publish in the Federal Register notice of any such extension and the reasons therefor. A finding by the Administrator that a risk is not unreasonable shall be considered agency action for purposes of judicial review under chapter 7 of Title 5. This subsection shall not take effect until two years after January 1, 1977.

**(g) Petition for standards for the development of test data**

A person intending to manufacture or process a chemical substance for which notice is required under section 2604(a) of this title and who is not required under a rule under subsection (a) of this section to conduct tests and submit data on such substance may petition the Administrator to prescribe standards for the development of test data for such substance. The Administrator shall by order either grant or deny any such petition within 60 days of its receipt. If the petition is granted, the Administrator shall prescribe such standards for such substance within 75 days of the date the petition is granted. If the petition is denied, the Administrator shall publish, subject to section 2613 of this title, in the Federal Register the reasons for such denial.

(Pub.L. 94–469, Title I, § 4, Oct. 11, 1976, 90 Stat. 2006; renumbered Title I, Pub.L. 99–519, § 3(c)(1), Oct. 22, 1986, 100 Stat. 2989.)

[1] So in original. Probably should be "preceding".

### HISTORICAL AND STATUTORY NOTES

**References in Text**

The Occupational Safety and Health Act of 1970, referred to in text, is Pub.L. 91–596, Dec. 29, 1970, 84 Stat. 1590, as amended, which is classified principally to chapter 15 (§ 651 et seq.) of Title 29, Labor. For complete classification of this Act to the Code, see Short Title note set out under section 651 of Title 29 and Tables.

**Effective and Applicability Provisions**

1976 Acts

Section effective Jan. 1, 1977, except as provided in subsec. (f) of this section, see section 31 of Pub.L. 94–469, set out as a note under section 2601 of this title.

## § 2604. Manufacturing and processing notices

**[TSCA § 5]**

**(a) In general**

(1) Except as provided in subsection (h) of this section, no person may—

**(A)** manufacture a new chemical substance on or after the 30th day after the date on which the

Administrator first publishes the list required by section 2607(b) of this title, or

**(B)** manufacture or process any chemical substance for a use which the Administrator has determined, in accordance with paragraph (2), is a significant new use,

unless such person submits to the Administrator, at least 90 days before such manufacture or processing, a notice, in accordance with subsection (d) of this section, of such person's intention to manufacture or process such substance and such person complies with any applicable requirement of subsection (b) of this section.

**(2)** A determination by the Administrator that a use of a chemical substance is a significant new use with respect to which notification is required under paragraph (1) shall be made by a rule promulgated after a consideration of all relevant factors, including—

**(A)** the projected volume of manufacturing and processing of a chemical substance,

**(B)** the extent to which a use changes the type or form of exposure of human beings or the environment to a chemical substance,

**(C)** the extent to which a use increases the magnitude and duration of exposure of human beings or the environment to a chemical substance, and

**(D)** the reasonably anticipated manner and methods of manufacturing, processing, distribution in commerce, and disposal of a chemical substance.

**(b) Submission of test data**

**(1)(A)** If (i) a person is required by subsection (a)(1) of this section to submit a notice to the Administrator before beginning the manufacture or processing of a chemical substance, and (ii) such person is required to submit test data for such substance pursuant to a rule promulgated under section 2603 of this title before the submission of such notice, such person shall submit to the Administrator such data in accordance with such rule at the time notice is submitted in accordance with subsection (a)(1) of this section.

**(B)** If—

**(i)** a person is required by subsection (a)(1) of this section to submit a notice to the Administrator, and

**(ii)** such person has been granted an exemption under section 2603(c) of this title from the requirements of a rule promulgated under section 2603 of this title before the submission of such notice,

such person may not, before the expiration of the 90 day period which begins on the date of the submission in accordance with such rule of the test data the submission or development of which was the basis for the exemption, manufacture such substance if such person is subject to subsection (a)(1)(A) of this section or manufacture or process such substance for a significant new use if the person is subject to subsection (a)(1)(B) of this section.

**(2)(A)** If a person—

**(i)** is required by subsection (a)(1) of this section to submit a notice to the Administrator before beginning the manufacture or processing of a chemical substance listed under paragraph (4), and

**(ii)** is not required by a rule promulgated under section 2603 of this title before the submission of such notice to submit test data for such substance,

such person shall submit to the Administrator data prescribed by subparagraph (B) at the time notice is submitted in accordance with subsection (a)(1) of this section.

**(B)** Data submitted pursuant to subparagraph (A) shall be data which the person submitting the data believes show that—

**(i)** in the case of a substance with respect to which notice is required under subsection (a)(1)(A) of this section, the manufacture, processing, distribution in commerce, use, and disposal of the chemical substance or any combination of such activties will not present an unreasonable risk of injury to health or the environment, or

**(ii)** in the case of a chemical substance with respect to which notice is required under subsection (a)(1)(B) of this section, the intended significant new use of the chemical substance will not present an unreasonable risk of injury to health or the environment.

**(3)** Data submitted under paragraph (1) or (2) shall be made available, subject to section 2613 of this title, for examination by interested persons.

**(4)(A)(i)** The Administrator may, by rule, compile and keep current a list of chemical substances with respect to which the Administrator finds that the manufacture, processing, distribution in commerce, use, or disposal, or any combination of such activities, presents or may present an unreasonable risk of injury to health or the environment.

**(ii)** In making a finding under clause (i) that the manufacture, processing, distribution in commerce, use, or disposal of a chemical substance or any combination of such activities presents or may present an unreasonable risk of injury to health or the environment, the Administrator shall consider all relevant factors, including—

**(I)** the effects of the chemical substance on health and the magnitude of human exposure to such substance; and

(II) the effects of the chemical substance on the environment and the magnitude of environmental exposure to such substance.

(B) The Administrator shall, in prescribing a rule under subparagraph (A) which lists any chemical substance, identify those uses, if any, which the Administrator determines, by rule under subsection (a)(2) of this section, would constitute a significant new use of such substance.

(C) Any rule under subparagraph (A), and any substantive amendment or repeal of such a rule, shall be promulgated pursuant to the procedures specified in section 553 of Title 5, except that (i) the Administrator shall give interested persons an opportunity for the oral presentation of data, views, or arguments, in addition to an opportunity to make written submissions, (ii) a transcript shall be kept of any oral presentation, and (iii) the Administrator shall make and publish with the rule the finding described in subparagraph (A).

**(c) Extension of notice period**

The Administrator may for good cause extend for additional periods (not to exceed in the aggregate 90 days) the period, prescribed by subsection (a) or (b) of this section before which the manufacturing or processing of a chemical substance subject to such subsection may begin. Subject to section 2613 of this title, such an extension and the reasons therefor shall be published in the Federal Register and shall constitute a final agency action subject to judicial review.

**(d) Content of notice; publications in the Federal Register**

(1) The notice required by subsection (a) of this section shall include—

(A) insofar as known to the person submitting the notice or insofar as reasonably ascertainable, the information described in subparagraphs (A), (B), (C), (D), (F), and (G) of section 2607(a)(2) of this title, and

(B) in such form and manner as the Administrator may prescribe, any test data in the possession or control of the person giving such notice which are related to the effect of any manufacture, processing, distribution in commerce, use, or disposal of such substance or any article containing such substance, or of any combination of such activities, on health or the environment, and

(C) a description of any other data concerning the environmental and health effects of such substance, insofar as known to the person making the notice or insofar as reasonably ascertainable.

Such a notice shall be made available, subject to section 2613 of this title, for examination by interested persons.

(2) Subject to section 2613 of this title, not later than five days (excluding Saturdays, Sundays and legal holidays) after the date of the receipt of a notice under subsection (a) of this section or of data under subsection (b) of this section, the Administrator shall publish in the Federal Register a notice which—

(A) identifies the chemical substance for which notice or data has been received;

(B) lists the uses or intended uses of such substance; and

(C) in the case of the receipt of data under subsection (b) of this section, describes the nature of the tests performed on such substance and any data which was developed pursuant to subsection (b) of this section or a rule under section 2603 of this title.

A notice under this paragraph respecting a chemical substance shall identify the chemical substance by generic class unless the Administrator determines that more specific identification is required in the public interest.

(3) At the beginning of each month the Administrator shall publish a list in the Federal Register of (A) each chemical substance for which notice has been received under subsection (a) of this section and for which the notification period prescribed by subsection (a), (b), or (c) of this section has not expired, and (B) each chemical substance for which such notification period has expired since the last publication in the Federal Register of such list.

**(e) Regulation pending development of information**

(1)(A) If the Administrator determines that—

(i) the information available to the Administrator is insufficient to permit a reasoned evaluation of the health and environmental effects of a chemical substance with respect to which notice is required by subsection (a) of this section; and

(ii)(I) in the absence of sufficient information to permit the Administrator to make such an evaluation, the manufacture, processing, distribution in commerce, use, or disposal of such substance, or any combination of such activities, may present an unreasonable risk of injury to health or the environment, or

(II) such substance is or will be produced in substantial quantities, and such substance either enters or may reasonably be anticipated to enter the environment in substantial quantities or there is or may be significant or substantial human exposure to the substance,

the Administrator may issue a proposed order, to take effect on the expiration of the notification period applicable to the manufacturing or processing of such substance under subsection (a), (b), or (c) of this section, to prohibit or limit the manufacture, processing, distribution in commerce, use, or disposal of such substance or to prohibit or limit any combination of such activities.

**(B)** A proposed order may not be issued under subparagraph (A) respecting a chemical substance (i) later than 45 days before the expiration of the notification period applicable to the manufacture or processing of such substance under subsection (a), (b), or (c) of this section, and (ii) unless the Administrator has, on or before the issuance of the proposed order, notified, in writing, each manufacturer or processor, as the case may be, of such substance of the determination which underlies such order.

**(C)** If a manufacturer or processor of a chemical substance to be subject to a proposed order issued under subparagraph (A) files with the Administrator (within the 30-day period beginning on the date such manufacturer or processor received the notice required by subparagraph (B)(ii) ) objections specifying with particularity the provisions of the order deemed objectionable and stating the grounds therefor, the proposed order shall not take effect.

**(2)(A)(i)** Except as provided in clause (ii), if with respect to a chemical substance with respect to which notice is required by subsection (a) of this section, the Administrator makes the determination described in paragraph (1)(A) and if—

**(I)** the Administrator does not issue a proposed order under paragraph (1) respecting such substance, or

**(II)** the Administrator issues such an order respecting such substance but such order does not take effect because objections were filed under paragraph (1)(C) with respect to it,

the Administrator, through attorneys of the Environmental Protection Agency, shall apply to the United States District Court for the District of Columbia or the United States district court for the judicial district in which the manufacturer or processor, as the case may be, of such substance is found, resides, or transacts business for an injunction to prohibit or limit the manufacture, processing, distribution in commerce, use, or disposal of such substance (or to prohibit or limit any combination of such activities).

**(ii)** If the Administrator issues a proposed order under paragraph (1)(A) respecting a chemical substance but such order does not take effect because objections have been filed under paragraph (1)(C) with respect to it, the Administrator is not required to apply for an injunction under clause (i) respecting such substance if the Administrator determines, on the basis of such objections, that the determinations under paragraph (1)(A) may not be made.

**(B)** A district court of the United States which receives an application under subparagraph (A)(i) for an injunction respecting a chemical substance shall issue such injunction if the court finds that—

**(i)** the information available to the Administrator is insufficient to permit a reasoned evaluation of the health and environmental effects of a chemical substance with respect to which notice is required by subsection (a) of this section; and

**(ii)(I)** in the absence of sufficient information to permit the Administrator to make such an evaluation, the manufacture, processing, distribution in commerce, use, or disposal of such substance, or any combination of such activities, may present an unreasonable risk of injury to health or the environment, or

**(II)** such substance is or will be produced in substantial quantities, and such substance either enters or may reasonably be anticipated to enter the environment in substantial quantities or there is or may be significant or substantial human exposure to the substance.

**(C)** Pending the completion of a proceeding for the issuance of an injunction under subparagraph (B) respecting a chemical substance, the court may, upon application of the Administrator made through attorneys of the Environmental Protection Agency, issue a temporary restraining order or a preliminary injunction to prohibit the manufacture, processing, distribution in commerce, use, or disposal of such a substance (or any combination of such activities) if the court finds that the notification period applicable under subsection (a), (b), or (c) of this section to the manufacturing or processing of such substance may expire before such proceeding can be completed.

**(D)** After the submission to the Administrator of test data sufficient to evaluate the health and environmental effects of a chemical substance subject to an injunction issued under subparagraph (B) and the evaluation of such data by the Administrator, the district court of the United States which issued such injunction shall, upon petition dissolve the injunction unless the Administrator has initiated a proceeding for the issuance of a rule under section 2605(a) of this title respecting the substance. If such a proceeding has been initiated, such court shall continue the injunction in effect until the effective date of the rule promulgated in such proceeding or, if such proceeding is terminated without the promulgation of a rule, upon the termination of the proceeding, whichever occurs first.

**(f) Protection against unreasonable risks**

**(1)** If the Administrator finds that there is a reasonable basis to conclude that the manufacture, processing, distribution in commerce, use, or disposal of a chemical substance with respect to which notice is required by subsection (a) of this section, or that any combination of such activities, presents or will present an unreasonable risk of injury to health or environment before a rule promulgated under section 2605 of this title can protect against such risk, the Administrator shall, before the expiration of the notification period applicable under subsection (a), (b), or (c) of this section to the manufacturing or processing of such substance, take the action authorized by paragraph (2) or (3) to the extent necessary to protect against such risk.

(2) The Administrator may issue a proposed rule under section 2605(a) of this title to apply to a chemical substance with respect to which a finding was made under paragraph (1)—

**(A)** a requirement limiting the amount of such substance which may be manufactured, processed, or distributed in commerce,

**(B)** a requirement described in paragraph (2), (3), (4), (5), (6), or (7) of section 2605(a) of this title, or

**(C)** any combination of the requirements referred to in subparagraph (B).

Such a proposed rule shall be effective upon its publication in the Federal Register. Section 2605(d)(2)(B) of this title shall apply with respect to such rule.

(3)(A) The Administrator may—

**(i)** issue a proposed order to prohibit the manufacture, processing, or distribution in commerce of a substance with respect to which a finding was made under paragraph (1), or

**(ii)** apply, through attorneys of the Environmental Protection Agency, to the United States District Court for the District of Columbia or the United States district court for the judicial district in which the manufacturer, or processor, as the case may be, of such substance, is found, resides, or transacts business for an injunction to prohibit the manufacture, processing, or distribution in commerce of such substance.

A proposed order issued under clause (i) respecting a chemical substance shall take effect on the expiration of the notification period applicable under subsection (a), (b), or (c) of this section to the manufacture or processing of such substance.

**(B)** If the district court of the United States to which an application has been made under subparagraph (A)(ii) finds that there is a reasonable basis to conclude that the manufacture, processing, distribution in commerce, use, or disposal of the chemical substance with respect to which such application was made, or that any combination of such activities, presents or will present an unreasonable risk of injury to health or the environment before a rule promulgated under section 2605 of this title can protect against such risk, the court shall issue an injunction to prohibit the manufacture, processing, or distribution in commerce of such substance or to prohibit any combination of such activities.

**(C)** The provisions of subparagraphs (B) and (C) of subsection (e)(1) of this section shall apply with respect to an order issued under clause (i) of subparagraph (A); and the provisions of subparagraph (C) of subsection (e)(2) of this section shall apply with respect to an injunction issued under subparagraph (B).

**(D)** If the Administrator issues an order pursuant to subparagraph (A)(i) respecting a chemical substance and objections are filed in accordance with subsection (e)(1)(C) of this section, the Administrator shall seek an injunction under subparagraph (A)(ii) respecting such substance unless the Administrator determines, on the basis of such objections, that such substance does not or will not present an unreasonable risk of injury to health or the environment.

**(g) Statement of reasons for not taking action**

If the Administrator has not initiated any action under this section or section 2605 or 2606 of this title to prohibit or limit the manufacture, processing, distribution in commerce, use, or disposal of a chemical substance, with respect to which notification or data is required by subsection (a)(1)(B) or (b) of this section, before the expiration of the notification period applicable to the manufacturing or processing of such substance, the Administrator shall publish a statement of the Administrator's reasons for not initiating such action. Such a statement shall be published in the Federal Register before the expiration of such period. Publication of such statement in accordance with the preceding sentence is not a prerequisite to the manufacturing or processing of the substance with respect to which the statement is to be published.

**(h) Exemptions**

(1) The Administrator may, upon application, exempt any person from any requirement of subsection (a) or (b) of this section to permit such person to manufacture or process a chemical substance for test marketing purposes—

**(A)** upon a showing by such person satisfactory to the Administrator that the manufacture, processing, distribution in commerce, use, and disposal of such substance, and that any combination of such activities, for such purposes will not present any unreasonable risk of injury to health or the environment, and

**(B)** under such restrictions as the Administrator considers appropriate.

(2)(A) The Administrator may, upon application, exempt any person from the requirement of subsection (b)(2) of this section to submit data for a chemical substance. If, upon receipt of an application under the preceding sentence, the Administrator determines that—

(i) the chemical substance with respect to which such application was submitted is equivalent to a chemical substance for which data has been submitted to the Administrator as required by subsection (b)(2) of this section, and

(ii) submission of data by the applicant on such substance would be duplicative of data which has been submitted to the Administrator in accordance with such subsection,

the Administrator shall exempt the applicant from the requirement to submit such data on such substance. No exemption which is granted under this subparagraph with respect to the submission of data for a chemical substance may take effect before the beginning of the reimbursement period applicable to such data.

(B) If the Administrator exempts any person, under subparagraph (A), from submitting data required under subsection (b)(2) of this section for a chemical substance because of the existence of previously submitted data and if such exemption is granted during the reimbursement period for such data, then (unless such person and the persons referred to in clauses (i) and (ii) agree on the amount and method of reimbursement) the Administrator shall order the person granted the exemption to provide fair and equitable reimbursement (in an amount determined under rules of the Administrator)—

(i) to the person who previously submitted the data on which the exemption was based, for a portion of the costs incurred by such person in complying with the requirement under subsection (b)(2) of this section to submit such data, and

(ii) to any other person who has been required under this subparagraph to contribute with respect to such costs, for a portion of the amount such person was required to contribute.

In promulgating rules for the determination of fair and equitable reimbursement to the persons described in clauses (i) and (ii) for costs incurred with respect to a chemical substance, the Administrator shall, after consultation with the Attorney General and the Federal Trade Commission, consider all relevant factors, including the effect on the competitive position of the person required to provide reimbursement in relation to the persons to be reimbursed and the share of the market for such substance of the person required to provide reimbursement in relation to the share of such market of the persons to be reimbursed. For purposes of judicial review, an order under this subparagraph shall be considered final agency action.

(C) For purposes of this paragraph, the reimbursement period for any previously submitted data for a chemical substance is a period—

(i) beginning on the date of the termination of the prohibition, imposed under this section, on the manufacture or processing of such substance by the person who submitted such data to the Administrator, and

(ii) ending—

(I) five years after the date referred to in clause (i), or

(II) at the expiration of a period which begins on the date referred to in clause (i) and is equal to the period which the Administrator determines was necessary to develop such data,

whichever is later.

(3) The requirements of subsections (a) and (b) of this section do not apply with respect to the manufacturing or processing of any chemical substance which is manufactured or processed, or proposed to be manufactured or processed, only in small quantities (as defined by the Administrator by rule) solely for purposes of—

(A) scientific experimentation or analysis, or

(B) chemical research on, or analysis of such substance or another substance, including such research or analysis for the development of a product,

if all persons engaged in such experimentation, research, or analysis for a manufacturer or processor are notified (in such form and manner as the Administrator may prescribe) of any risk to health which the manufacturer, processor, or the Administrator has reason to believe may be associated with such chemical substance.

(4) The Administrator may, upon application and by rule, exempt the manufacturer of any new chemical substance from all or part of the requirements of this section if the Administrator determines that the manufacture, processing, distribution in commerce, use, or disposal of such chemical substance, or that any combination of such activities, will not present an unreasonable risk of injury to health or the environment. A rule promulgated under this paragraph (and any substantive amendment to, or repeal of, such a rule) shall be promulgated in accordance with paragraphs (2) and (3) of section 2605(c) of this title.

(5) The Administrator may, upon application, make the requirements of subsections (a) and (b) of this section inapplicable with respect to the manufacturing or processing of any chemical substance (A) which exists temporarily as a result of a chemical reaction in the manufacturing or processing of a mixture or another chemical substance, and (B) to which there is no, and will not be, human or environmental exposure.

(6) Immediately upon receipt of an application under paragraph (1) or (5) the Administrator shall publish in the Federal Register notice of the receipt of such application. The Administrator shall give interested persons an opportunity to comment upon any such application and shall, within 45 days of its receipt, either approve or deny the application. The Administrator shall publish in the Federal Register notice of the approval or denial of such an application.

**(i) "Manufacture" and "process" defined**

For purposes of this section, the terms "manufacture" and "process" mean manufacturing or processing for commercial purposes.

(Pub.L. 94–469, Title I, § 5, Oct. 11, 1976, 90 Stat. 2012; renumbered Title I, Pub.L. 99–519, § 3(c)(1), Oct. 22, 1986, 100 Stat. 2989.)

## § 2605. Regulation of hazardous chemical substances and mixtures

**[TSCA § 6]**

**(a) Scope of regulation**

If the Administrator finds that there is a reasonable basis to conclude that the manufacture, processing, distribution in commerce, use, or disposal of a chemical substance or mixture, or that any combination of such activities, presents or will present an unreasonable risk of injury to health or the environment, the Administrator shall by rule apply one or more of the following requirements to such substance or mixture to the extent necessary to protect adequately against such risk using the least burdensome requirements:

(1) A requirement (A) prohibiting the manufacturing, processing, or distribution in commerce of such substance or mixture, or (B) limiting the amount of such substance or mixture which may be manufactured, processed, or distributed in commerce.

(2) A requirement—

(A) prohibiting the manufacture, processing, or distribution in commerce of such substance or mixture for (i) a particular use or (ii) a particular use in a concentration in excess of a level specified by the Administrator in the rule imposing the requirement, or

(B) limiting the amount of such substance or mixture which may be manufactured, processed, or distributed in commerce for (i) a particular use or (ii) a particular use in a concentration in excess of a level specified by the Administrator in the rule imposing the requirement.

(3) A requirement that such substance or mixture or any article containing such substance or mixture be marked with or accompanied by clear and adequate warnings and instructions with respect to its use, distribution in commerce, or disposal or with respect to any combination of such activities. The form and content of such warnings and instructions shall be prescribed by the Administrator.

(4) A requirement that manufacturers and processors of such substance or mixture make and retain records of the processes used to manufacture or process such substance or mixture and monitor or conduct tests which are reasonable and necessary to assure compliance with the requirements of any rule applicable under this subsection.

(5) A requirement prohibiting or otherwise regulating any manner or method of commercial use of such substance or mixture.

(6)(A) A requirement prohibiting or otherwise regulating any manner or method of disposal of such substance or mixture, or of any article containing such substance or mixture, by its manufacturer or processor or by any other person who uses, or disposes of, it for commercial purposes.

(B) A requirement under subparagraph (A) may not require any person to take any action which would be in violation of any law or requirement of, or in effect for, a State or political subdivision, and shall require each person subject to it to notify each State and political subdivision in which a required disposal may occur of such disposal.

(7) A requirement directing manufacturers or processors of such substance or mixture (A) to give notice of such unreasonable risk of injury to distributors in commerce of such substance or mixture and, to the extent reasonably ascertainable, to other persons in possession of such substance or mixture or exposed to such substance or mixture, (B) to give public notice of such risk of injury, and (C) to replace or repurchase such substance or mixture as elected by the person to which the requirement is directed.

Any requirement (or combination of requirements) imposed under this subsection may be limited in application to specified geographic areas.

**(b) Quality control**

If the Administrator has a reasonable basis to conclude that a particular manufacturer or processor is manufacturing or processing a chemical substance or mixture in a manner which unintentionally causes the chemical substance or mixture to present or which will cause it to present an unreasonable risk of injury to health or the environment—

(1) the Administrator may by order require such manufacturer or processor to submit a description of the relevant quality control procedures followed in the manufacturing or processing of such chemical substance or mixture; and

(2) if the Administrator determines—

(A) that such quality control procedures are inadequate to prevent the chemical substance or mixture from presenting such risk of injury, the Administrator may order the manufacturer or processor to revise such quality control procedures to the extent necessary to remedy such inadequacy; or

(B) that the use of such quality control procedures has resulted in the distribution in commerce of chemical substances or mixtures which present an unreasonable risk of injury to health or the environment, the Administrator may order the manufacturer or processor to (i) give notice of such risk to processors or distributors in commerce of any such substance or mixture, or to both, and, to the extent reasonably ascertainable, to any other person in possession of or exposed to any such substance, (ii) to give public notice of such risk, and (iii) to provide such replacement or repurchase of any such substance or mixture as is necessary to adequately protect health or the environment.

A determination under subparagraph (A) or (B) of paragraph (2) shall be made on the record after opportunity for hearing in accordance with section 554 of Title 5. Any manufacturer or processor subject to a requirement to replace or repurchase a chemical substance or mixture may elect either to replace or repurchase the substance or mixture and shall take either such action in the manner prescribed by the Administrator.

**(c) Promulgation of subsection (a) rules**

**(1)** In promulgating any rule under subsection (a) of this section with respect to a chemical substance or mixture, the Administrator shall consider and publish a statement with respect to—

**(A)** the effects of such substance or mixture on health and the magnitude of the exposure of human beings to such substance or mixture,

**(B)** the effects of such substance or mixture on the environment and the magnitude of the exposure of the environment to such substance or mixture,

**(C)** the benefits of such substance or mixture for various uses and the availability of substitutes for such uses, and

**(D)** the reasonably ascertainable economic consequences of the rule, after consideration of the effect on the national economy, small business, technological innovation, the environment, and public health.

If the Administrator determines that a risk of injury to health or the environment could be eliminated or reduced to a sufficient extent by actions taken under another Federal law (or laws) administered in whole or in part by the Administrator, the Administrator may not promulgate a rule under subsection (a) of this section to protect against such risk of injury unless the Administrator finds, in the Administrator's discretion, that it is in the public interest to protect against such risk under this chapter. In making such a finding the Administrator shall consider (i) all relevant aspects of the risk, as determined by the Administrator in the Administrator's discretion, (ii) a comparison of the estimated costs of complying with actions taken under this chapter and under such law (or laws), and (iii) the relative efficiency of actions under this chapter and under such law (or laws) to protect against such risk of injury.

**(2)** When prescribing a rule under subsection (a) the Administrator shall proceed in accordance with section 553 of Title 5 (without regard to any reference in such section to sections 556 and 557 of such title), and shall also (A) publish a notice of proposed rulemaking stating with particularity the reason for the proposed rule; (B) allow interested persons to submit written data, views, and arguments, and make all such submissions publicly available; (C) provide an opportunity for an informal hearing in accordance with paragraph (3); (D) promulgate, if appropriate, a final rule based on the matter in the rulemaking record (as defined in section 2618(a) of this title), and (E) make and publish with the rule the finding described in subsection (a) of this section.

**(3)** Informal hearings required by paragraph (2)(C) shall be conducted by the Administrator in accordance with the following requirements:

**(A)** Subject to subparagraph (B), an interested person is entitled—

**(i)** to present such person's position orally or by documentary submissions (or both), and

**(ii)** if the Administrator determines that there are disputed issues of material fact it is necessary to resolve, to present such rebuttal submissions and to conduct (or have conducted under subparagraph (B)(ii) ) such cross-examination of persons as the Administrator determines (I) to be appropriate, and (II) to be required for a full and true disclosure with respect to such issues.

**(B)** The Administrator may prescribe such rules and make such rulings concerning procedures in such hearings to avoid unnecessary costs or delay. Such rules or rulings may include (i) the imposition of reasonable time limits on each interested person's oral presentations, and (ii) requirements that any cross-examination to which a person may be entitled under subparagraph (A) be conducted by the Administrator on behalf of that person in such manner as the Administrator determines (I) to be appropriate, and (II) to be required for a full and true disclosure with respect to disputed issues of material fact.

**(C)(i)** Except as provided in clause (ii), if a group of persons each of whom under subparagraphs (A) and (B) would be entitled to conduct (or have conducted) cross-examination and who are determined by the Administrator to have the same or similar interests in the proceeding cannot agree upon a single representative of such interests for purposes of cross-examination, the Administrator may make rules and rulings (I) limiting the representation of such interest for such purposes, and (II) governing the manner in which such cross-examination shall be limited.

**(ii)** When any person who is a member of a group with respect to which the Administrator has made a determination under clause (i) is unable to agree upon group representation with the other members of the group, then such person shall not be denied under the authority of clause (i) the opportunity to conduct (or have conducted) cross-examination as to issues affecting the person's particular interests if (I) the person satisfies the Administrator that the person has made a reasonable and good faith effort to reach agreement upon group representation with the other members of the group and (II) the Administrator determines that there are substantial and relevant issues which are not adequately presented by the group representative.

**(D)** A verbatim transcript shall be taken of any oral presentation made, and cross-examination conducted in any informal hearing under this subsection. Such transcript shall be available to the public.

**(4)(A)** The Administrator may, pursuant to rules prescribed by the Administrator, provide compensation for reasonable attorneys' fees, expert witness fees, and other costs of participating in a rulemaking proceeding for the promulgation of a rule under subsection (a) of this section to any person—

**(i)** who represents an interest which would substantially contribute to a fair determination of the issues to be resolved in the proceeding, and

**(ii)** if—

**(I)** the economic interest of such person is small in comparison to the costs of effective participation in the proceeding by such person, or

**(II)** such person demonstrates to the satisfaction of the Administrator that such person does not have sufficient resources adequately to participate in the proceeding without compensation under this subparagraph.

In determining for purposes of clause (i) if an interest will substantially contribute to a fair determination of the issues to be resolved in a proceeding, the Administrator shall take into account the number and complexity of such issues and the extent to which representation of such interest will contribute to widespread public participation in the proceeding and representation of a fair balance of interests for the resolution of such issues.

**(B)** In determining whether compensation should be provided to a person under subparagraph (A) and the amount of such compensation, the Administrator shall take into account the financial burden which will be incurred by such person in participating in the rulemaking proceeding. The Administrator shall take such action as may be necessary to ensure that the aggregate amount of compensation paid under this paragraph in any fiscal year to all persons who, in rulemaking proceedings in which they receive compensation, are persons who either—

**(i)** would be regulated by the proposed rule, or

**(ii)** represent persons who would be so regulated,

may not exceed 25 per centum of the aggregate amount paid as compensation under this paragraph to all persons in such fiscal year.

**(5)** Paragraph (1), (2), (3), and (4) of this subsection apply to the promulgation of a rule repealing, or making a substantive amendment to, a rule promulgated under subsection (a) of this section.

**(d) Effective date**

**(1)** The Administrator shall specify in any rule under subsection (a) of this section the date on which it shall take effect, which date shall be as soon as feasible.

**(2)(A)** The Administrator may declare a proposed rule under subsection (a) of this section to be effective upon its publication in the Federal Register and until the effective date of final action taken, in accordance with subparagraph (B), respecting such rule if—

**(i)** the Administrator determines that—

**(I)** the manufacture, processing, distribution in commerce, use, or disposal of the chemical substance or mixture subject to such proposed rule or any combination of such activities is likely to result in an unreasonable risk of serious or widespread injury to health or the environment before such effective date; and

**(II)** making such proposed rule so effective is necessary to protect the public interest; and

**(ii)** in the case of a proposed rule to prohibit the manufacture, processing, or distribution of a chemical substance or mixture because of the risk determined under clause (i)(I), a court has in an action under section 2606 of this title granted relief with respect to such risk associated with such substance or mixture.

Such a proposed rule which is made so effective shall not, for purposes of judicial review, be considered final agency action.

**(B)** If the Administrator makes a proposed rule effective upon its publication in the Federal Register, the Administrator shall, as expeditiously as possible, give interested persons prompt notice of such action, provide reasonable opportunity, in accordance with paragraphs (2) and (3) of subsection (c) of this section, for a hearing on such rule, and either promulgate such rule (as proposed or with modifications) or revoke it; and if such a hearing is requested, the Administrator shall commence the hearing within five days from the date such request is made unless the Administrator and the person making the request agree upon a later date for the hearing to begin, and after the hearing is concluded the Administrator shall, within ten days of the conclusion of the hearing, either promulgate such rule (as proposed or with modifications) or revoke it.

**(e) Polychlorinated biphenyls**

**(1)** Within six months after January 1, 1977, the Administrator shall promulgate rules to—

**(A)** prescribe methods for the disposal of polychlorinated biphenyls, and

**(B)** require polychlorinated biphenyls to be marked with clear and adequate warnings, and instructions with respect to their processing, distribution in commerce, use, or disposal or with respect to any combination of such activities.

Requirements prescribed by rules under this paragraph shall be consistent with the requirements of paragraphs (2) and (3).

**(2)(A)** Except as provided under subparagraph (B), effective one year after January 1, 1977, no person may manufacture, process, or distribute in commerce or use any polychlorinated biphenyl in any manner other than in a totally enclosed manner.

**(B)** The Administrator may by rule authorize the manufacture, processing, distribution in commerce or use (or any combination of such activities) of any polychlorinated biphenyl in a manner other than in a totally enclosed manner if the Administrator finds that such manufacture, processing, distribution in commerce, or use (or combination of such activities) will not present an unreasonable risk of injury to health or the environment.

**(C)** For the purposes of this paragraph, the term "totally enclosed manner" means any manner which will ensure that any exposure of human beings or the environment to a polychlorinated biphenyl will be insignificant as determined by the Administrator by rule.

**(3)(A)** Except as provided in subparagraphs (B) and (C)—

**(i)** no person may manufacture any polychlorinated biphenyl after two years after January 1, 1977, and

**(ii)** no person may process or distribute in commerce any polychlorinated biphenyl after two and one-half years after such date.

**(B)** Any person may petition the Administrator for an exemption from the requirements of subparagraph (A), and the Administrator may grant by rule such an exemption if the Administrator finds that—

**(i)** an unreasonable risk of injury to health or environment would not result, and

**(ii)** good faith efforts have been made to develop a chemical substance which does not present an unreasonable risk of injury to health or the environment and which may be substituted for such polychlorinated biphenyl.

An exemption granted under this subparagraph shall be subject to such terms and conditions as the Administrator may prescribe and shall be in effect for such period (but not more than one year from the date it is granted) as the Administrator may prescribe.

**(C)** Subparagraph (A) shall not apply to the distribution in commerce of any polychlorinated biphenyl if such polychlorinated biphenyl was sold for purposes other than resale before two and one half years after October 11, 1976.

**(4)** Any rule under paragraph (1), (2)(B), or (3)(B) shall be promulgated in accordance with paragraphs (2), (3), and (4) of subsection (c) of this section.

**(5)** This subsection does not limit the authority of the Administrator, under any other provision of this chapter or any other Federal law, to take action respecting any polychlorinated biphenyl.

(Pub.L. 94–469, Title I, § 6, Oct. 11, 1976, 90 Stat. 2020; renumbered Title I, Pub.L. 99–519, § 3(c)(1), Oct. 22, 1986, 100 Stat. 2989.)

## § 2606. Imminent hazards

**[TSCA § 7]**

**(a) Actions authorized and required**

**(1)** The Administrator may commence a civil action in an appropriate district court of the United States—

**(A)** for seizure of an imminently hazardous chemical substance or mixture or any article containing such a substance or mixture,

**(B)** for relief (as authorized by subsection (b) of this section) against any person who manufactures, processes, distributes in commerce, or uses, or disposes of, an imminently hazardous chemical substance or mixture or any article containing such a substance or mixture, or

**(C)** for both such seizure and relief.

A civil action may be commenced under this paragraph notwithstanding the existence of a rule under section 2603 of this title, 2604 of this title, 2605 of this title, or subchapter IV of this chapter or an order under section 2604 of this title or subchapter IV of this chapter, and notwithstanding the pendency of any administrative or judicial proceeding under any provision of this chapter.

(2) If the Administrator has not made a rule under section 2605(a) of this title immediately effective (as authorized by section 2605(d)(2)(A)(i) of this title) with respect to an imminently hazardous chemical substance or mixture, the Administrator shall commence in a district court of the United States with respect to such substance or mixture or article containing such substance or mixture a civil action described in subparagraph (A), (B), or (C) of paragraph (1).

**(b) Relief authorized**

(1) The district court of the United States in which an action under subsection (a) of this section is brought shall have jurisdiction to grant such temporary or permanent relief as may be necessary to protect health or the environment from the unreasonable risk associated with the chemical substance, mixture, or article involved in such action.

(2) In the case of an action under subsection (a) of this section brought against a person who manufactures, processes, or distributes in commerce a chemical substance or mixture or an article containing a chemical substance or mixture, the relief authorized by paragraph (1) may include the issuance of a mandatory order requiring (A) in the case of purchasers of such substance, mixture, or article known to the defendant, notification to such purchasers of the risk associated with it; (B) public notice of such risk; (C) recall; (D) the replacement or repurchase of such substance, mixture, or article; or (E) any combination of the actions described in the preceding clauses.

(3) In the case of an action under subsection (a) of this section against a chemical substance, mixture, or article, such substance, mixture, or article may be proceeded against by process of libel for its seizure and condemnation. Proceedings in such an action shall conform as nearly as possible to proceedings in rem in admiralty.

**(c) Venue and consolidation**

(1)(A) An action under subsection (a) of this section against a person who manufactures, processes, or distributes a chemical substance or mixture or an article containing a chemical substance or mixture may be brought in the United States District Court for the District of Columbia, or for any judicial district in which any of the defendants is found, resides, or transacts business; and process in such an action may be served on a defendant in any other district in which such defendant resides or may be found. An action under subsection (a) of this section against a chemical substance, mixture, or article may be brought in any United States district court within the jurisdiction of which the substance, mixture, or article is found.

(B) In determining the judicial district in which an action may be brought under subsection (a) of this section in instances in which such action may be brought in more than one judicial district, the Administrator shall take into account the convenience of the parties.

(C) Subpeonas [1] requiring attendance of witnesses in an action brought under subsection (a) of this section may be served in any judicial district.

(2) Whenever proceedings under subsection (a) of this section involving identical chemical substances, mixtures, or articles are pending in courts in two or more judicial districts, they shall be consolidated for trial by order of any such court upon application reasonably made by any party in interest, upon notice to all parties in interest.

**(d) Action under section 2605**

Where appropriate, concurrently with the filing of an action under subsection (a) of this section or as soon thereafter as may be practicable, the Administrator shall initiate a proceeding for the promulgation of a rule under section 2605(a) of this title.

**(e) Representation**

Notwithstanding any other provision of law, in any action under subsection (a) of this section, the Administrator may direct attorneys of the Environmental Protection Agency to appear and represent the Administrator in such an action.

**(f) "Imminently hazardous chemical substance or mixture" defined**

For the purposes of subsection (a) of this section, the term "imminently hazardous chemical substance or mixture" means a chemical substance or mixture which presents an imminent and unreasonable risk of serious or widespread injury to health or the environment. Such a risk to health or the environment shall be considered imminent if it is shown that the manufacture, processing, distribution in commerce, use, or disposal of the chemical substance or mixture, or that any combination of such activities, is likely to result in such injury to health or the environment before a final rule under section 2605 of this title can protect against such risk.

(Pub.L. 94–469, Title I, § 7, Oct. 11, 1976, 90 Stat. 2026; renumbered Title I, Pub.L. 99–519, § 3(c)(1), Oct. 22, 1986, 100 Stat. 2989, and amended Pub.L. 102–550, Title X, § 1021(b)(1), Oct. 28, 1992, 106 Stat. 3923.)

[1] So in original. Probably should be "subpoenas".

## § 2607. Reporting and retention of information

[TSCA § 8]

### (a) Reports

(1) The Administrator shall promulgate rules under which—

(A) each person (other than a small manufacturer or processor) who manufactures or processes or proposes to manufacture or process a chemical substance (other than a chemical substance described in subparagraph (B)(ii) ) shall maintain such records, and shall submit to the Administrator such reports, as the Administrator may reasonably require, and

(B) each person (other than a small manufacturer or processor) who manufactures or processes or proposes to manufacture or process—

(i) a mixture, or

(ii) a chemical substance in small quantities (as defined by the Administrator by rule) solely for purposes of scientific experimentation or analysis or chemical research on, or analysis of, such substance or another substance, including any such research or analysis for the development of a product,

shall maintain records and submit to the Administrator reports but only to the extent the Administrator determines the maintenance of records or submission of reports, or both, is necessary for the effective enforcement of this chapter.

The Administrator may not require in a rule promulgated under this paragraph the maintenance of records or the submission of reports with respect to changes in the proportions of the components of a mixture unless the Administrator finds that the maintenance of such records or the submission of such reports, or both, is necessary for the effective enforcement of this chapter. For purposes of the compilation of the list of chemical substances required under subsection (b) of this section, the Administrator shall promulgate rules pursuant to this subsection not later than 180 days after January 1, 1977.

(2) The Administrator may require under paragraph (1) maintenance of records and reporting with respect to the following insofar as known to the person making the report or insofar as reasonably ascertainable:

(A) The common or trade name, the chemical identity, and the molecular structure of each chemical substance or mixture for which such a report is required.

(B) The categories or proposed categories of use of each such substance or mixture.

(C) The total amount of each such substance and mixture manufactured or processed, reasonable estimates of the total amount to be manufactured or processed, the amount manufactured or processed for each of its categories of use, and reasonable estimates of the amount to be manufactured or processed for each of its categories of use or proposed categories of use.

(D) A description of the byproducts resulting from the manufacture, processing, use, or disposal of each such substance or mixture.

(E) All existing data concerning the environmental and health effects of such substance or mixture.

(F) The number of individuals exposed, and reasonable estimates of the number who will be exposed, to such substance or mixture in their places of employment and the duration of such exposure.

(G) In the initial report under paragraph (1) on such substance or mixture, the manner or method of its disposal, and in any subsequent report on such substance or mixture, any change in such manner or method.

To the extent feasible, the Administrator shall not require under paragraph (1), any reporting which is unnecessary or duplicative.

(3)(A)(i) The Administrator may by rule require a small manufacturer or processor of a chemical substance to submit to the Administrator such information respecting the chemical substance as the Administrator may require for publication of the first list of chemical substances required by subsection (b) of this section.

(ii) The Administrator may by rule require a small manufacturer or processor of a chemical substance or mixture—

(I) subject to a rule proposed or promulgated under section 2603, 2604(b)(4), or 2605 of this title, or an order in effect under section 2604(e) of this title, or

(II) with respect to which relief has been granted pursuant to a civil action brought under section 2604 or 2606 of this title,

to maintain such records on such substance or mixture, and to submit to the Administrator such reports on such substance or mixture, as the Administrator may reasonably require. A rule under this clause requiring reporting may require reporting with respect to the matters referred to in paragraph (2).

(B) The Administrator, after consultation with the Administrator of the Small Business Administration, shall by rule prescribe standards for determining the manufacturers and processors which qualify as small manufacturers and processors for purposes of this paragraph and paragraph (1).

**(b) Inventory**

(1) The Administrator shall compile, keep current, and publish a list of each chemical substance which is manufactured or processed in the United States. Such list shall at least include each chemical substance which any person reports, under section 2604 of this title or subsection (a) of this section, is manufactured or processed in the United States. Such list may not include any chemical substance which was not manufactured or processed in the United States within three years before the effective date of the rules promulgated pursuant to the last sentence of subsection (a)(1) of this section. In the case of a chemical substance for which a notice is submitted in accordance with section 2604 of this title, such chemical substance shall be included in such list as of the earliest date (as determined by the Administrator) on which such substance was manufactured or processed in the United States. The Administrator shall first publish such a list not later than 315 days after January 1, 1977. The Administrator shall not include in such list any chemical substance which is manufactured or processed only in small quantities (as defined by the Administrator by rule) solely for purposes of scientific experimentation or analysis or chemical research on, or analysis of, such substance or another substance, including such research or analysis for the development of a product.

(2) To the extent consistent with the purposes of this chapter, the Administrator may, in lieu of listing, pursuant to paragraph (1), a chemical substance individually, list a category of chemical substances in which such substance is included.

**(c) Records**

Any person who manufactures, processes, or distributes in commerce any chemical substance or mixture shall maintain records of significant adverse reactions to health or the environment, as determined by the Administrator by rule, alleged to have been caused by the substance or mixture. Records of such adverse reactions to the health of employees shall be retained for a period of 30 years from the date such reactions were first reported to or known by the person maintaining such records. Any other record of such adverse reactions shall be retained for a period of five years from the date the information contained in the record was first reported to or known by the person maintaining the record. Records required to be maintained under this subsection shall include records of consumer allegations of personal injury or harm to health, reports of occupational disease or injury, and reports or complaints of injury to the environment submitted to the manufacturer, processor, or distributor in commerce from any source. Upon request of any duly designated representative of the Administrator, each person who is required to maintain records under this subsection shall permit the inspection of such records and shall submit copies of such records.

**(d) Health and safety studies**

The Administrator shall promulgate rules under which the Administrator shall require any person who manufactures, processes, or distributes in commerce or who proposes to manufacture, process, or distribute in commerce any chemical substance or mixture (or with respect to paragraph (2), any person who has possession of a study) to submit to the Administrator—

(1) lists of health and safety studies (A) conducted or initiated by or for such person with respect to such substance or mixture at any time, (B) known to such person, or (C) reasonably ascertainable by such person, except that the Administrator may exclude certain types or categories of studies from the requirements of this subsection if the Administrator finds that submission of lists of such studies are unnecessary to carry out the purposes of this chapter; and

(2) copies of any study contained on a list submitted pursuant to paragraph (1) or otherwise known by such person.

**(e) Notice to Administrator of substantial risks**

Any person who manufactures, processes, or distributes in commerce a chemical substance or mixture and who obtains information which reasonably supports the conclusion that such substance or mixture presents a substantial risk of injury to health or the environment shall immediately inform the Administrator of such information unless such person has actual knowledge that the Administrator has been adequately informed of such information.

**(f) "Manufacture" and "process" defined**

For purposes of this section, the terms "manufacture" and "process" mean manufacture or process for commercial purposes.

(Pub.L. 94–469, Title I, § 8, Oct. 11, 1976, 90 Stat. 2027; renumbered Title I, Pub.L. 99–519, § 3(c)(1), Oct. 22, 1986, 100 Stat. 2989.)

## HISTORICAL AND STATUTORY NOTES

**Asbestos Information**

Pub.L. 100–577, Oct. 31, 1988, 102 Stat. 2901, provided that:

**"Section 1. Short title.**

"This Act may be cited as the 'Asbestos Information Act of 1988'.

**"Sec. 2. Submission of information by manufacturers.**

"Within 90 days after the date of the enactment of this Act [Oct. 31, 1988], any person who manufactured or processed, before the date of the enactment of this Act, asbestos or asbestos-containing material that was prepared for sale for use as surfacing material, thermal system insulation, or miscellaneous material in buildings (or whose corporate predecessor manufactured or processed such asbestos or material) shall submit to the Administrator of the Environmental Protection Agency the years of manufacture, the types or classes of product, and, to the extent available, other identifying characteristics reasonably necessary to identify or distinguish the asbestos or asbestos-containing material. Such person also may submit to the Administrator protocols for samples of asbestos and asbestos-containing material.

**"Sec. 3. Publication of information.**

"Within 30 days after the date of the enactment of this Act [Oct. 31, 1988], the Administrator shall publish a notice in the Federal Register that explains how, when, and where the information specified in section 2 is to be submitted. The Administrator shall receive and organize the information submitted under section 2 and, within 180 days after the date of the enactment of this Act, shall publish the information. In carrying out this section, the Administrator may not—

"(1) review the information submitted under section 2 for accuracy, or

"(2) analyze such information to determine whether it is reasonably necessary to identify or distinguish the particular asbestos or asbestos-containing material.

**"Sec. 4. Definitions.**

"In this Act:

"(1) The term 'asbestos' means—

"(A) chrysotile, amosite, or crocidolite, or

"(B) in fibrous form, tremolite, anthophyllite, or actinolite.

"(2) The term 'asbestos-containing material' means any material containing more than one percent asbestos by weight.

"(3) The term 'identifying characteristics' means a description of asbestos or asbestos-containing material, including—

"(A) the mineral or chemical constituents (or both) of the asbestos or material by weight or volume (or both),

"(B) the types or classes of the product in which the asbestos or material is contained,

"(C) the designs, patterns, or textures of the product in which the asbestos or material is contained, and

"(D) the means by which the product in which the asbestos or material is contained may be distinguishable from other products containing asbestos or asbestos-containing material.

"(4) The term 'miscellaneous material' means building material on structural components, structural members, or fixtures, such as floor and ceiling tiles. The term does not include surfacing material or thermal system insulation.

"(5) The term 'protocol' means any procedure for taking, handling, and preserving samples of asbestos and asbestos-containing material and for testing and analyzing such samples for the purpose of determining the person who manufactured or processed for sale such samples and the identifying characteristics of such samples.

"(6) The term 'surfacing material' means material in a building that is sprayed on surfaces, troweled on surfaces, or otherwise applied to surfaces for acoustical, fireproofing, or other purposes, such as acoustical plaster on ceilings and fireproofing material on structural members.

"(7) The term 'thermal system insulation' means material in a building applied to pipes, fittings, boilers, breeching, tanks, ducts, or other structural components to prevent heat loss or gain or water condensation, or for other purposes."

## § 2608. Relationship to other Federal laws

**[TSCA § 9]**

### (a) Laws not administered by the Administrator

(1) If the Administrator has reasonable basis to conclude that the manufacture, processing, distribution in commerce, use, or disposal of a chemical substance or mixture, or that any combination of such activities, presents or will present an unreasonable risk of injury to health or the environment and determines, in the Administrator's discretion, that such risk may be prevented or reduced to a sufficient extent by action taken under a Federal law not administered by the Administrator, the Administrator shall submit to the agency which administers such law a report which describes such risk and includes in such description a specification of the activity or combination of activities which the Administrator has reason to believe so presents such risk. Such report shall also request such agency—

(A)(i) to determine if the risk described in such report may be prevented or reduced to a sufficient extent by action taken under such law, and

(ii) if the agency determines that such risk may be so prevented or reduced, to issue an order declaring whether or not the activity or combination of activities specified in the description of such risk presents such risk; and

(B) to respond to the Administrator with respect to the matters described in subparagraph (A).

Any report of the Administrator shall include a detailed statement of the information on which it is based and shall be published in the Federal Register. The agency receiving a request under such a report shall make the requested determination, issue the requested order, and make the requested response within such time as the Administrator specifies in the request, but such time specified may not be less than 90 days from the date the request was made. The response of an agency shall be accompanied by a detailed statement of the findings and conclusions of the agency and shall be published in the Federal Register.

(2) If the Administrator makes a report under paragraph (1) with respect to a chemical substance or mixture and the agency to which such report was made either—

(A) issues an order declaring that the activity or combination of activities specified in the description of the risk described in the report does not present the risk described in the report, or

(B) initiates, within 90 days of the publication in the Federal Register of the response of the agency under paragraph (1), action under the law (or laws) administered by such agency to protect against such risk associated with such activity or combination of activities,

the Administrator may not take any action under section 2605 or 2606 of this title with respect to such risk.

(3) If the Administrator has initiated action under section 2605 or 2606 of this title with respect to a risk associated with a chemical substance or mixture which was the subject of a report made to an agency under paragraph (1), such agency shall before taking action under the law (or laws) administered by it to protect against such risk consult with the Administrator for the purpose of avoiding duplication of Federal action against such risk.

**(b) Laws administered by the Administrator**

The Administrator shall coordinate actions taken under this chapter with actions taken under other Federal laws administered in whole or in part by the Administrator. If the Administrator determines that a risk to health or the environment associated with a chemical substance or mixture could be eliminated or reduced to a sufficient extent by actions taken under the authorities contained in such other Federal laws, the Administrator shall use such authorities to protect against such risk unless the Administrator determines, in the Administrator's discretion, that it is in the public interest to protect against such risk by actions taken under this chapter. This subsection shall not be construed to relieve the Administrator of any requirement imposed on the Administrator by such other Federal laws.

**(c) Occupational safety and health**

In exercising any authority under this chapter, the Administrator shall not, for purposes of section 653(b)(1) of Title 29, be deemed to be exercising statutory authority to prescribe or enforce standards or regulations affecting occupational safety and health.

**(d) Coordination**

In administering this chapter, the Administrator shall consult and coordinate with the Secretary of Health and Human Services and the heads of any other appropriate Federal executive department or agency, any relevant independent regulatory agency, and any other appropriate instrumentality of the Federal Government for the purpose of achieving the maximum enforcement of this chapter while imposing the least burdens of duplicative requirements on those subject to the chapter and for other purposes. The Administrator shall, in the report required by section 2629 of this title, report annually to the Congress on actions taken to coordinate with such other Federal departments, agencies, or instrumentalities, and on actions taken to coordinate the authority under this chapter with the authority granted under other Acts referred to in subsection (b) of this section.

(Pub.L. 94–469, Title I, § 9, Oct. 11, 1976, 90 Stat. 2030; Pub.L. 96–88, Title V, § 509(b), Oct. 17, 1979, 93 Stat. 695; renumbered Title I, Pub.L. 99–519, § 3(c)(1), Oct. 22, 1986, 100 Stat. 2989.)

### HISTORICAL AND STATUTORY NOTES

**Change of Name**

"Secretary of Health and Human Services" was substituted for "Secretary of Health, Education, and Welfare" in subsec. (d), pursuant to section 509(b) of Pub.L. 96–88 which is classified to section 3508 of Title 20, Education.

**Termination of Reporting Requirements**

For termination, effective May 15, 2000, of provisions in subsec. (d) of this section relating to reporting certain coordinating actions annually to Congress in the report required by 15 U.S.C.A. § 2629, see Pub.L. 104–66, § 3003, as amended, set out as a note under 31 U.S.C.A. § 1113, and page 90 of House Document No. 103–7.

## § 2609. Research, development, collection, dissemination, and utilization of data

**[TSCA § 10]**

**(a) Authority**

The Administrator shall, in consultation and cooperation with the Secretary of Health and Human Services and with other heads of appropriate departments and agencies, conduct such research, development, and monitoring as is necessary to carry out the purposes of this chapter. The Administrator may enter into contracts and may make grants for research, development, and monitoring under this subsection. Contracts may be entered into under this subsection without regard to section 3324(a) and (b) of Title 31 and section 5 of Title 41.

**(b) Data systems**

(1) The Administrator shall establish, administer, and be responsible for the continuing activities of an interagency committee which shall design, establish, and coordinate an efficient and effective system, within the Environmental Protection Agency, for the collection, dissemination to other Federal departments and agencies, and use of data submitted to the Administrator under this chapter.

(2)(A) The Administrator shall, in consultation and cooperation with the Secretary of Health and Human Services and other heads of appropriate departments and agencies design, establish, and coordinate an efficient and effective system for the retrieval of toxicological and other scientific data which could be useful to the Administrator in carrying out the purposes of this chapter. Systematized retrieval shall be developed for use by all Federal and other departments and agencies with responsibilities in the area of regulation or study of chemical substances and mixtures and their effect on health or the environment.

**(B)** The Administrator, in consultation and cooperation with the Secretary of Health and Human Services, may make grants and enter into contracts for the development of a data retrieval system described in subparagraph (A). Contracts may be entered into under this subparagraph without regard to section 3324(a) and (b) of Title 31 and section 5 of Title 41.

**(c) Screening techniques**

The Administrator shall coordinate, with the Assistant Secretary for Health of the Department of Health and Human Services, research undertaken by the Administrator and directed toward the development of rapid, reliable, and economical screening techniques for carcinogenic, mutagenic, teratogenic, and ecological effects of chemical substances and mixtures.

**(d) Monitoring**

The Administrator shall, in consultation and cooperation with the Secretary of Health and Human Services, establish and be responsible for research aimed at the development, in cooperation with local, State, and Federal agencies, of monitoring techniques and instruments which may be used in the detection of toxic chemical substances and mixtures and which are reliable, economical, and capable of being implemented under a wide variety of conditions.

**(e) Basic research**

The Administrator shall, in consultation and cooperation with the Secretary of Health and Human Services, establish research programs to develop the fundamental scientific basis of the screening and monitoring techniques described in subsections (c) and (d) of this section, the bounds of the reliability of such techniques, and the opportunities for their improvement.

**(f) Training**

The Administrator shall establish and promote programs and workshops to train or facilitate the training of Federal laboratory and technical personnel in existing or newly developed screening and monitoring techniques.

**(g) Exchange of research and development results**

The Administrator shall, in consultation with the Secretary of Health and Human Services and other heads of appropriate departments and agencies, establish and coordinate a system for exchange among Federal, State, and local authorities of research and development results respecting toxic chemical substances and mixtures, including a system to facilitate and promote the development of standard data format and analysis and consistent testing procedures.

(Pub.L. 94–469, Title I, § 10, Oct. 11, 1976, 90 Stat. 2031; Pub.L. 96–88, Title V, § 509(b), Oct. 17, 1979, 93 Stat. 695; renumbered Title I, Pub.L. 99–519, § 3(c)(1), Oct. 22, 1986, 100 Stat. 2989.)

### HISTORICAL AND STATUTORY NOTES

**Codifications**

In subsecs. (a) and (b)(2)(B), "section 3324(a) and (b) of Title 31" was substituted for references to section 3648 of the Revised Statutes (31 U.S.C. 529) on authority of Pub.L. 97–258, § 4(b), Sept. 13, 1982, 96 Stat. 1067, the first section of which enacted Title 31, Money and Finance.

**Change of Name**

"Secretary of Health and Human Services" was substituted for "Secretary of Health, Education, and Welfare" in subsecs. (a), (b), (d), (e), and (g), and "Department of Health and Human Services" was substituted for "Department of Health, Education, and Welfare" in subsec. (c), pursuant to section 509(b) of Pub.L. 96–88, which is classified to section 3508(b) of Title 20, Education.

**Availability of Grants**

Grants awarded under this section are available for research, development, monitoring, public education, training, demonstrations, and studies, beginning in fiscal year 2000 and thereafter, see provisions of Pub.L. 106–74, Title III, set out as a note under 7 U.S.C.A. § 136r.

## § 2610. Inspections and subpoenas

**[TSCA § 11]**

**(a) In general**

For purposes of administering this chapter, the Administrator, and any duly designated representative of the Administrator, may inspect any establishment, facility, or other premises in which chemical substances, mixtures, or products subject to subchapter IV of this chapter are manufactured, processed, stored, or held before or after their distribution in commerce and any conveyance being used to transport chemical substances, mixtures, such products, or such articles in connection with distribution in commerce. Such an inspection may only be made upon the presentation of appropriate credentials and of a written notice to the owner, operator, or agent in charge of the premises or conveyance to be inspected. A separate notice shall be given for each such inspection, but a notice shall not be required for each entry made during the period covered by the inspection. Each such inspection shall be commenced and completed with reasonable promptness and shall be conducted at reasonable times, within reasonable limits, and in a reasonable manner.

**(b) Scope**

(1) Except as provided in paragraph (2), an inspection conducted under subsection (a) of this section shall extend to all things within the premises or conveyance inspected (including records, files, papers, processes, controls, and facilities) bearing on whether the requirements of this chapter applicable to the chemical substances, mixtures, or products subject to subchapter IV of this chapter within such premises or conveyance have been complied with.

(2) No inspection under subsection (a) of this section shall extend to—

(A) financial data,

(B) sales data (other than shipment data),

(C) pricing data,

(D) personnel data, or

(E) research data (other than data required by this chapter or under a rule promulgated thereunder),

unless the nature and extent of such data are described with reasonable specificity in the written notice required by subsection (a) of this section for such inspection.

**(c) Subpoenas**

In carrying out this chapter, the Administrator may by subpoena require the attendance and testimony of witnesses and the production of reports, papers, documents, answers to questions, and other information that the Administrator deems necessary. Witnesses shall be paid the same fees and mileage that are paid witnesses in the courts of the United States. In the event of contumacy, failure, or refusal of any person to obey any such subpoena, any district court of the United States in which venue is proper shall have jurisdiction to order any such person to comply with such subpoena. Any failure to obey such an order of the court is punishable by the court as a contempt thereof.

(Pub.L. 94–469, Title I, § 11, Oct. 11, 1976, 90 Stat. 2032; renumbered Title I, Pub.L. 99–519, § 3(c)(1), Oct. 22, 1986, 100 Stat. 2989, and amended Pub.L. 102–550, Title X, § 1021(b)(2), (3), Oct. 28, 1992, 106 Stat. 3923.)

## § 2611. Exports

[TSCA § 12]

**(a) In general**

(1) Except as provided in paragraph (2) and subsection (b) of this section, this chapter (other than section 2607 of this title) shall not apply to any chemical substance, mixture, or to an article containing a chemical substance or mixture, if—

(A) it can be shown that such substance, mixture, or article is being manufactured, processed, or distributed in commerce for export from the United States, unless such substance, mixture, or article was, in fact, manufactured, processed, or distributed in commerce, for use in the United States, and

(B) such substance, mixture, or article (when distributed in commerce), or any container in which it is enclosed (when so distributed), bears a stamp or label stating that such substance, mixture, or article is intended for export.

(2) Paragraph (1) shall not apply to any chemical substance, mixture, or article if the Administrator finds that the substance, mixture, or article will present an unreasonable risk of injury to health within the United States or to the environment of the United States. The Administrator may require, under section 2603 of this title, testing of any chemical substance or mixture exempted from this chapter by paragraph (1) for the purpose of determining whether or not such substance or mixture presents an unreasonable risk of injury to health within the United States or to the environment of the United States.

**(b) Notice**

(1) If any person exports or intends to export to a foreign country a chemical substance or mixture for which the submission of data is required under section 2603 or 2604(b) of this title, such person shall notify the Administrator of such exportation or intent to export and the Administrator shall furnish to the government of such country notice of the availability of the data submitted to the Administrator under such section for such substance or mixture.

(2) If any person exports or intends to export to a foreign country a chemical substance or mixture for which an order has been issued under section 2604 of this title or a rule has been proposed or promulgated under section 2604 or 2605 of this title, or with respect to which an action is pending, or relief has been granted under section 2604 or 2606 of this title, such person shall notify the Administrator of such exportation or intent to export and the Administrator shall furnish to the government of such country notice of such rule, order, action, or relief.

(Pub.L. 94–469, Title I, § 12, Oct. 11, 1976, 90 Stat. 2033; renumbered Title I, Pub.L. 99–519, § 3(c)(1), Oct. 22, 1986, 100 Stat. 2989.)

## § 2612. Entry into customs territory of the United States

[TSCA § 13]

**(a) In general**

(1) The Secretary of the Treasury shall refuse entry into the customs territory of the United States (as defined in general note 2 of the Harmonized Tariff Schedule of the United States) of any chemical substance, mixture, or article containing a chemical substance or mixture offered for such entry if—

(A) it fails to comply with any rule in effect under this chapter, or

(B) it is offered for entry in violation of section 2604 of this title, 2605 of this title, or subchapter IV of this chapter, a rule or order under section 2604 of this title, 2605 of this title, or subchapter IV of this chapter, or an order issued in a civil action brought under section 2604 of this title, 2606 of this title or subchapter IV of this chapter.

(2) If a chemical substance, mixture, or article is refused entry under paragraph (1), the Secretary of the Treasury shall notify the consignee of such entry refusal, shall not release it to the consignee, and shall cause its disposal or storage (under such rules as the Secretary of the Treasury may prescribe) if it has not been exported by the consignee within 90 days from the date of receipt of notice of such refusal, except that the Secretary of the Treasury may, pending a review by the Administrator of the entry refusal, release to the consignee such substance, mixture, or article on execution of bond for the amount of the full invoice of such substance, mixture, or article (as such value is set forth in the customs entry), together with the duty thereon. On failure to return such substance, mixture, or article for any cause to the custody of the Secretary of the Treasury when demanded, such consignee shall be liable to the United States for liquidated damages equal to the full amount of such bond. All charges for storage, cartage, and labor on and for disposal of substances, mixtures, or articles which are refused entry or release under this section shall be paid by the owner or consignee, and in default of such payment shall constitute a lien against any future entry made by such owner or consignee.

**(b) Rules**

The Secretary of the Treasury, after consultation with the Administrator, shall issue rules for the administration of subsection (a) of this section.

(Pub.L. 94–469, Title I, § 13, Oct. 11, 1976, 90 Stat. 2034; renumbered Title I, Pub.L. 99–519, § 3(c)(1), Oct. 22, 1986, 100 Stat. 2989, and amended Pub.L. 100–418, Title I, § 1214(e)(2), Aug. 23, 1988, 102 Stat. 1156; Pub.L. 102–550, Title X, § 1021(b)(4), Oct. 28, 1992, 106 Stat. 3923.)

### HISTORICAL AND STATUTORY NOTES

**References in Text**

The Harmonized Tariff Schedule of the United States, referred to in subsec. (a), is not set out in the Code. See Publication of Harmonized Tariff Schedules note set out under section 1202 of Title 19, Customs Duties.

**Effective and Applicability Provisions**

1988 Acts

Amendment by Pub.L. 100–418 effective Jan. 1, 1989, and applicable with respect to articles entered on or after such date, see section 1217(b)(1) of Pub.L. 100–418, set out as an Effective Date note under section 3001 of Title 19, Customs Duties.

## § 2613. Disclosure of data

**[TSCA § 14]**

**(a) In general**

Except as provided by subsection (b) of this section, any information reported to, or otherwise obtained by, the Administrator (or any representative of the Administrator) under this chapter, which is exempt from disclosure pursuant to subsection (a) of section 552 of Title 5 by reason of subsection (b)(4) of such section, shall, notwithstanding the provisions of any other section of this chapter, not be disclosed by the Administrator or by any officer or employee of the United States, except that such information—

(1) shall be disclosed to any officer or employee of the United States—

(A) in connection with the official duties of such officer or employee under any law for the protection of health or the environment, or

(B) for specific law enforcement purposes;

(2) shall be disclosed to contractors with the United States and employees of such contractors if in the opinion of the Administrator such disclosure is necessary for the satisfactory performance by the contractor of a contract with the United States entered into on or after October 11, 1976, for the performance of work in connection with this chapter and under such conditions as the Administrator may specify;

(3) shall be disclosed if the Administrator determines it necessary to protect health or the environment against an unreasonable risk of injury to health or the environment; or

(4) may be disclosed when relevant in any proceeding under this chapter, except that disclosure in such a proceeding shall be made in such manner as to preserve confidentiality to the extent practicable without impairing the proceeding.

In any proceeding under section 552(a) of Title 5 to obtain information the disclosure of which has been denied because of the provisions of this subsection, the Administrator may not rely on section 552(b)(3) of such title to sustain the Administrator's action.

**(b) Data from health and safety studies**

(1) Subsection (a) does not prohibit the disclosure of—

(A) any health and safety study which is submitted under this chapter with respect to—

(i) any chemical substance or mixture which, on the date on which such study is to be disclosed has been offered for commercial distribution, or

(ii) any chemical substance or mixture for which testing is required under section 2603 of this title or for which notification is required under section 2604 of this title, and

(B) any data reported to, or otherwise obtained by, the Administrator from a health and safety study which relates to a chemical substance or mixture described in clause (i) or (ii) of subparagraph (A).

This paragraph does not authorize the release of any data which discloses processes used in the manufacturing or processing of a chemical substance or mixture or, in the case of a mixture, the release of data disclosing the portion of the mixture comprised by any of the chemical substances in the mixture.

(2) If a request is made to the Administrator under subsection (a) of section 552 of Title 5 for information which is described in the first sentence of paragraph (1) and which is not information described in the second sentence of such paragraph, the Administrator may not deny such request on the basis of subsection (b)(4) of such section.

**(c) Designation and release of confidential data**

(1) In submitting data under this chapter, a manufacturer, processor, or distributor in commerce may (A) designate the data which such person believes is entitled to confidential treatment under subsection (a) of this section, and (B) submit such designated data separately from other data submitted under this chapter. A designation under this paragraph shall be made in writing and in such manner as the Administrator may prescribe.

(2)(A) Except as provided by subparagraph (B), if the Administrator proposes to release for inspection data which has been designated under paragraph (1)(A), the Administrator shall notify, in writing and by certified mail, the manufacturer, processor, or distributor in commerce who submitted such data of the intent to release such data. If the release of such data is to be made pursuant to a request made under section 552(a) of Title 5, such notice shall be given immediately upon approval of such request by the Administrator. The Administrator may not release such data until the expiration of 30 days after the manufacturer, processor, or distributor in commerce submitting such data has received the notice required by this subparagraph.

(B)(i) Subparagraph (A) shall not apply to the release of information under paragraph (1), (2), (3), or (4) of subsection (a) of this section, except that the Administrator may not release data under paragraph (3) of subsection (a) of this section unless the Administrator has notified each manufacturer, processor, and distributor in commerce who submitted such data of such release. Such notice shall be made in writing by certified mail at least 15 days before the release of such data, except that if the Administrator determines that the release of such data is necessary to protect against an imminent, unreasonable risk of injury to health or the environment, such notice may be made by such means as the Administrator determines will provide notice at least 24 hours before such release is made.

(ii) Subparagraph (A) shall not apply to the release of information described in subsection (b)(1) of this section other than information described in the second sentence of such subsection.

**(d) Criminal penalty for wrongful disclosure**

(1) Any officer or employee of the United States or former officer or employee of the United States, who by virtue of such employment or official position has obtained possession of, or has access to, material the disclosure of which is prohibited by subsection (a) of this section, and who knowing that disclosure of such material is prohibited by such subsection, willfully discloses the material in any manner to any person not entitled to receive it, shall be guilty of a misdemeanor and fined not more than $5,000 or imprisoned for not more than one year, or both. Section 1905 of Title 18 does not apply with respect to the publishing, divulging, disclosure, or making known of, or making available, information reported or otherwise obtained under this chapter.

(2) For the purposes of paragraph (1), any contractor with the United States who is furnished information as authorized by subsection (a)(2) of this section, and any employee of any such contractor, shall be considered to be an employee of the United States.

**(e) Access by Congress**

Notwithstanding any limitation contained in this section or any other provision of law, all information reported to or otherwise obtained by the Administrator (or any representative of the Administrator) under this chapter shall be made available, upon written request of any duly authorized committee of the Congress, to such committee.

(Pub.L. 94–469, Title I, § 14, Oct. 11, 1976, 90 Stat. 2034; renumbered Title I, Pub.L. 99–519, § 3(c)(1), Oct. 22, 1986, 100 Stat. 2989.)

## § 2614. Prohibited acts

**[TSCA § 15]**

It shall be unlawful for any person to—

(1) fail or refuse to comply with (A) any rule promulgated or order issued under section 2603 of this title, (B) any requirement prescribed by section 2604 or 2605 of this title, (C) any rule promulgated or order issued under section 2604 or 2605 of this title, or (D) any requirement of subchapter II of

this chapter or any rule promulgated or order issued under subchapter II of this chapter;

(2) use for commercial purposes a chemical substance or mixture which such person knew or had reason to know was manufactured, processed, or distributed in commerce in violation of section 2604 or 2605 of this title, a rule or order under section 2604 or 2605 of this title, or an order issued in action brought under section 2604 or 2606 of this title;

(3) fail or refuse to (A) establish or maintain records, (B) submit reports, notices, or other information, or (C) permit access to or copying of records, as required by this chapter or a rule thereunder; or

(4) fail or refuse to permit entry or inspection as required by section 2610 of this title.

(Pub.L. 94–469, Title I, § 15, Oct. 11, 1976, 90 Stat. 2036; renumbered Title I and amended Pub.L. 99–519, § 3(b)(1), (c)(1), Oct. 22, 1986, 100 Stat. 2988, 2989.)

## § 2615. Penalties

**[TSCA § 16]**

**(a) Civil**

(1) Any person who violates a provision of section 2614 or 2689 of this title shall be liable to the United States for a civil penalty in an amount not to exceed $25,000 for each such violation. Each day such a violation continues shall, for purposes of this subsection, constitute a separate violation of section 2614 or 2689 of this title.

(2)(A) A civil penalty for a violation of section 2614 or 2689 of this title shall be assessed by the Administrator by an order made on the record after opportunity (provided in accordance with this subparagraph) for a hearing in accordance with section 554 of Title 5. Before issuing such an order, the Administrator shall give written notice to the person to be assessed a civil penalty under such order of the Administrator's proposal to issue such order and provide such person an opportunity to request, within 15 days of the date the notice is received by such person, such a hearing on the order.

(B) In determining the amount of a civil penalty, the Administrator shall take into account the nature, circumstances, extent, and gravity of the violation or violations and, with respect to the violator, ability to pay, effect on ability to continue to do business, any history of prior such violations, the degree of culpability, and such other matters as justice may require.

(C) The Administrator may compromise, modify, or remit, with or without conditions, any civil penalty which may be imposed under this subsection. The amount of such penalty, when finally determined, or the amount agreed upon in compromise, may be deducted from any sums owing by the United States to the person charged.

(3) Any person who requested in accordance with paragraph (2)(A) a hearing respecting the assessment of a civil penalty and who is aggrieved by an order assessing a civil penalty may file a petition for judicial review of such order with the United States Court of Appeals for the District of Columbia Circuit or for any other circuit in which such person resides or transacts business. Such a petition may only be filed within the 30-day period beginning on the date the order making such assessment was issued.

(4) If any person fails to pay an assessment of a civil penalty—

(A) after the order making the assessment has become a final order and if such person does not file a petition for judicial review of the order in accordance with paragraph (3), or

(B) after a court in an action brought under paragraph (3) has entered a final judgment in favor of the Administrator,

the Attorney General shall recover the amount assessed (plus interest at currently prevailing rates from the date of the expiration of the 30-day period referred to in paragraph (3) or the date of such final judgment, as the case may be) in an action brought in any appropriate district court of the United States. In such an action, the validity, amount, and appropriateness of such penalty shall not be subject to review.

**(b) Criminal**

Any person who knowingly or willfully violates any provision of section 2614 or 2689 of this title, shall, in addition to or in lieu of any civil penalty which may be imposed under subsection (a) of this section for such violation, be subject, upon conviction, to a fine of not more than $25,000 for each day of violation, or to imprisonment for not more than one year, or both.

(Pub.L. 94–469, Title I, § 16, Oct. 11, 1976, 90 Stat. 2037; renumbered Title I, Pub.L. 99–519, § 3(c)(1), Oct. 22, 1986, 100 Stat. 2989, and amended Pub.L. 102–550, Title X, § 1021(b)(5), Oct. 28, 1992, 106 Stat. 3923.)

## § 2616. Specific enforcement and seizure

**[TSCA § 17]**

**(a) Specific enforcement**

(1) The district courts of the United States shall have jurisdiction over civil actions to—

(A) restrain any violation of section 2614 or 2689 of this title,

(B) restrain any person from taking any action prohibited by section 2604 of this title, 2605 of this title, or subchapter IV of this subchapter, or by a rule or order under section 2604 of this title, 2605 of this title, or subchapter IV of this chapter,

(C) compel the taking of any action required by or under this chapter, or

(D) direct any manufacturer or processor of a chemical substance, mixture, or product subject to subchapter IV of this subchapter manufactured or processed in violation of section 2604 of this title, 2605 of this title, or subchapter IV of this chapter, or a rule or order under section 2604 of this title, 2605 of this title, or subchapter IV of this chapter, and distributed in commerce, (i) to give notice of such fact to distributors in commerce of such substance, mixture, or product and, to the extent reasonably ascertainable, to other persons in possession of such substance, mixture, or product or exposed to such substance, mixture, or product, (ii) to give public notice of such risk of injury, and (iii) to either replace or repurchase such substance, mixture, or product, whichever the person to which the requirement is directed elects.

(2) A civil action described in paragraph (1) may be brought—

(A) in the case of a civil action described in subparagraph (A) of such paragraph, in the United States district court for the judicial district wherein any act, omission, or transaction constituting a violation of section 2614 of this title occurred or wherein the defendant is found or transacts business, or

(B) in the case of any other civil action described in such paragraph, in the United States district court for the judicial district wherein the defendant is found or transacts business.

In any such civil action process may be served on a defendant in any judicial district in which a defendant resides or may be found. Subpoenas requiring attendance of witnesses in any such action may be served in any judicial district.

**(b) Seizure**

Any chemical substance, mixture, or product subject to subchapter IV of this chapter which was manufactured, processed, or distributed in commerce in violation of this chapter or any rule promulgated or order issued under this chapter or any article containing such a substance or mixture shall be liable to be proceeded against, by process of libel, for the seizure and condemnation of such substance, mixture, product, or article, in any district court of the United States within the jurisdiction of which such substance, mixture, product, or article is found. Such proceedings shall conform as nearly as possible to proceedings in rem in admiralty.

(Pub.L. 94–469, Title I, § 17, Oct. 11, 1976, 90 Stat. 2037; renumbered Title I, Pub.L. 99–519, § 3(c)(1), Oct. 22, 1986, 100 Stat. 2989, and amended Pub.L. 102–550, Title X, § 1021(b)(6), (7), Oct. 28, 1992, 106 Stat. 3923.)

### HISTORICAL AND STATUTORY NOTES

**Federal Rules of Civil Procedure**

Admiralty and maritime rules of practice (which included libel procedures) were superseded, and civil and admiralty procedures in United States district courts were unified, effective July 1, 1966, see rule 1 and Supplemental Rules for Certain Admiralty and Maritime Claims, Title 28, Appendix, Judiciary and Judicial Procedure.

## § 2617. Preemption

[TSCA § 18]

**(a) Effect on State law**

(1) Except as provided in paragraph (2), nothing in this chapter shall affect the authority of any State or political subdivision of a State to establish or continue in effect regulation of any chemical substance, mixture, or article containing a chemical substance or mixture.

(2) Except as provided in subsection (b) of this section—

(A) if the Administrator requires by a rule promulgated under section 2603 of this title the testing of a chemical substance or mixture, no State or political subdivision may, after the effective date of such rule, establish or continue in effect a requirement for the testing of such substance or mixture for purposes similar to those for which testing is required under such rule; and

(B) if the Administrator prescribes a rule or order under section 2604 or 2605 of this title (other than a rule imposing a requirement described in subsection (a)(6) of section 2605 of this title) which is applicable to a chemical substance or mixture, and which is designed to protect against a risk of injury to health or the environment associated with such substance or mixture, no State or political subdivision of a State may, after the effective date of such requirement, establish or continue in effect, any requirement which is applicable to such substance or mixture, or an article containing such substance or mixture, and which is designed to protect against such risk unless such requirement (i) is identical to the requirement prescribed by the Administrator, (ii) is adopted under the authority of the Clean Air Act [42 U.S.C.A. § 7401 et seq.] or any other Federal law, or (iii) prohibits the use of such substance or mixture in such State or political subdivision (other than its use in the manufacture or processing of other substances or mixtures).

**(b) Exemption**

Upon application of a State or political subdivision of a State the Administrator may by rule exempt from subsection (a)(2) of this section, under such conditions as may be prescribed in such rule, a requirement of such State or political subdivision designed to protect against a risk of injury to health or the environment associated with a chemical substance, mixture, or article containing a chemical substance or mixture if—

(1) compliance with the requirement would not cause the manufacturing, processing, distribution in commerce, or use of the substance, mixture, or article to be in violation of the applicable requirement under this chapter described in subsection (a)(2) of this section, and

(2) the State or political subdivision requirement (A) provides a significantly higher degree of protection from such risk than the requirement under this chapter described in subsection (a)(2) of this section and (B) does not, through difficulties in marketing, distribution, or other factors, unduly burden interstate commerce.

(Pub.L. 94–469, Title I, § 18, Oct. 11, 1976, 90 Stat. 2038; renumbered Title I, Pub.L. 99–519, § 3(c)(1), Oct. 22, 1986, 100 Stat. 2989.)

### HISTORICAL AND STATUTORY NOTES

**References in Text**

The Clean Air Act, referred to in subsec. (a)(2)(B), is Act July 14, 1955, c. 360, 69 Stat. 322, as amended, classified generally to chapter 85 (§ 7401 et seq.) of Title 42, the Public Health and Welfare. For complete classification of this Act to the Code, see Short Title note set out under section 7401 of Title 42 and Tables.

## § 2618. Judicial review

[TSCA § 19]

**(a) In general**

(1)(A) Not later than 60 days after the date of the promulgation of a rule under section 2603(a), 2604(a)(2), 2604(b)(4), 2605(a), 2605(e), or 2607 of this title, or under subchapter II or IV of this chapter, any person may file a petition for judicial review of such rule with the United States Court of Appeals for the District of Columbia Circuit or for the circuit in which such person resides or in which such person's principal place of business is located. Courts of appeals of the United States shall have exclusive jurisdiction of any action to obtain judicial review (other than in an enforcement proceeding) of such a rule if any district court of the United States would have had jurisdiction of such action but for this subparagraph.

(B) Courts of appeals of the United States shall have exclusive jurisdiction of any action to obtain judicial review (other than in an enforcement proceeding) of an order issued under subparagraph (A) or (B) of section 2605(b)(1) of this title if any district court of the United States would have had jurisdiction of such action but for this subparagraph.

(2) Copies of any petition filed under paragraph (1)(A) shall be transmitted forthwith to the Administrator and to the Attorney General by the clerk of the court with which such petition was filed. The provisions of section 2112 of Title 28 shall apply to the filing of the rulemaking record of proceedings on which the Administrator based the rule being reviewed under this section and to the transfer of proceedings between United States courts of appeals.

(3) For purposes of this section, the term "rulemaking record" means—

(A) the rule being reviewed under this section;

(B) in the case of a rule under section 2603(a) of this title, the finding required by such section, in the case of a rule under section 2604(b)(4) of this title, the finding required by such section, in the case of a rule under section 2605(a) of this title the finding required by section 2604(f) or 2605(a) of this title, as the case may be, in the case of a rule under section 2605(a) of this title, the statement required by section 2605(c)(1) of this title, and in the case of a rule under section 2605(e) of this title, the findings required by paragraph (2)(B) or (3)(B) of such section, as the case may be [1] and in the case of a rule under subchapter IV of this chapter, the finding required for the issuance of such a rule;

(C) any transcript required to be made of oral presentations made in proceedings for the promulgation of such rule;

(D) any written submission of interested parties respecting the promulgation of such rule; and

(E) any other information which the Administrator considers to be relevant to such rule and which the Administrator identified, on or before the date of the promulgation of such rule, in a notice published in the Federal Register.

**(b) Additional submissions and presentations; modifications**

If in an action under this section to review a rule the petitioner or the Administrator applies to the court for leave to make additional oral submissions or written presentations respecting such rule and shows to the satisfaction of the court that such submissions and presentations would be material and that there were reasonable grounds for the submissions and failure to make such submissions and presentations in the proceeding before the Administrator, the court may order the Administrator to provide additional opportunity to make such submissions and presentations. The Administrator may modify or set aside the rule being reviewed or make a new rule by reason of the additional submissions and presentations and shall file such modified or new rule with the return of such submissions and presentations. The court shall thereafter review such new or modified rule.

**(c) Standard of review**

(1)(A) Upon the filing of a petition under subsection (a)(1) of this section for judicial review of a rule, the court shall have jurisdiction (i) to grant appropriate relief, including interim relief, as provided in chapter 7 of Title 5 and (ii) except as otherwise provided in subparagraph (B), to review such rule in accordance with chapter 7 of Title 5.

**(B)** Section 706 of Title 5 shall apply to review of a rule under this section, except that—

**(i)** in the case of review of a rule under section 2603(a), 2604(b)(4), 2605(a), or 2605(e) of this title, the standard for review prescribed by paragraph (2)(E) of such section 706 shall not apply and the court shall hold unlawful and set aside such rule if the court finds that the rule is not supported by substantial evidence in the rulemaking record (as defined in subsection (a)(3) of this section) taken as a whole;

**(ii)** in the case of review of a rule under section 2605(a) of this title, the court shall hold unlawful and set aside such rule if it finds that—

**(I)** a determination by the Administrator under section 2605(c)(3) of this title that the petitioner seeking review of such rule is not entitled to conduct (or have conducted) cross-examination or to present rebuttal submissions, or

**(II)** a rule of, or ruling by, the Administrator under section 2605(c)(3) of this title limiting such petitioner's cross-examination or oral presentations,

has precluded disclosure of disputed material facts which was necessary to a fair determination by the Administrator of the rulemaking proceeding taken as a whole; and section 706(2)(D) shall not apply with respect to a determination, rule, or ruling referred to in subclause (I) or (II); and

**(iii)** the court may not review the contents and adequacy of—

**(I)** any statement required to be made pursuant to section 2605(c)(1) of this title, or

**(II)** any statement of basis and purpose required by section 553(c) of Title 5, to be incorporated in the rule

except as part of a review of the rulemaking record taken as a whole.

The term "evidence" as used in clause (i) means any matter in the rulemaking record.

**(C)** A determination, rule, or ruling of the Administrator described in subparagraph (B)(ii) may be reviewed only in an action under this section and only in accordance with such subparagraph.

**(2)** The judgment of the court affirming or setting aside, in whole or in part, any rule reviewed in accordance with this section shall be final, subject to review by the Supreme Court of the United States upon certiorari or certification, as provided in section 1254 of Title 28.

**(d) Fees and costs**

The decision of the court in an action commenced under subsection (a) of this section, or of the Supreme Court of the United States on review of such a decision, may include an award of costs of suit and reasonable fees for attorneys and expert witnesses if the court determines that such an award is appropriate.

**(e) Other remedies**

The remedies as provided in this section shall be in addition to and not in lieu of any other remedies provided by law.

(Pub.L. 94–469, Title I, § 19, Oct. 11, 1976, 90 Stat. 2039; renumbered Title I and amended Pub.L. 99–519, § 3(b)(2), (c)(1), Oct. 22, 1986, 100 Stat. 2989; Pub.L. 102–550, Title X, § 1021(b)(8), Oct. 28, 1992, 106 Stat. 3923.)

[1] So in original. Probably should be followed by a comma.

## § 2619. Citizens' civil actions

**[TSCA § 20]**

**(a) In general**

Except as provided in subsection (b) of this section, any person may commence a civil action—

**(1)** against any person (including (A) the United States, and (B) any other governmental instrumentality or agency to the extent permitted by the eleventh amendment to the Constitution) who is alleged to be in violation of this chapter or any rule promulgated under section 2603, 2604, or 2605 of this title, or subchapter II or IV of this chapter, or order issued under section 2604 of this title or subchapter II or IV of this chapter to restrain such violation, or

**(2)** against the Administrator to compel the Administrator to perform any act or duty under this chapter which is not discretionary.

Any civil action under paragraph (1) shall be brought in the United States district court for the district in which the alleged violation occurred or in which the defendant resides or in which the defendant's principal place of business is located. Any action brought under paragraph (2) shall be brought in the United States District Court for the District of Columbia, or the United States district court for the judicial district in which the plaintiff is domiciled. The district courts of the United States shall have jurisdiction over suits brought under this section, without regard to the amount in controversy or the citizenship of the parties. In any civil action under this subsection process may be served on a defendant in any judicial district in which the defendant resides or may be found and subpoenas for witnesses may be served in any judicial district.

**(b) Limitation**

No civil action may be commenced—

(1) under subsection (a)(1) of this section to restrain a violation of this chapter or rule or order under this chapter—

(A) before the expiration of 60 days after the plaintiff has given notice of such violation (i) to the Administrator, and (ii) to the person who is alleged to have committed such violation, or

(B) if the Administrator has commenced and is diligently prosecuting a proceeding for the issuance of an order under section 2615(a)(2) of this title to require compliance with this chapter or with such rule or order or if the Attorney General has commenced and is diligently prosecuting a civil action in a court of the United States to require compliance with this chapter or with such rule or order, but if such proceeding or civil action is commenced after the giving of notice, any person giving such notice may intervene as a matter of right in such proceeding or action; or

(2) under subsection (a)(2) of this section before the expiration of 60 days after the plaintiff has given notice to the Administrator of the alleged failure of the Administrator to perform an act or duty which is the basis for such action or, in the case of an action under such subsection for the failure of the Administrator to file an action under section 2606 of this title, before the expiration of ten days after such notification.

Notice under this subsection shall be given in such manner as the Administrator shall prescribe by rule.

**(c) General**

(1) In any action under this section, the Administrator, if not a party, may intervene as a matter of right.

(2) The court, in issuing any final order in any action brought pursuant to subsection (a) of this section, may award costs of suit and reasonable fees for attorneys and expert witnesses if the court determines that such an award is appropriate. Any court, in issuing its decision in an action brought to review such an order, may award costs of suit and reasonable fees for attorneys if the court determines that such an award is appropriate.

(3) Nothing in this section shall restrict any right which any person (or class of persons) may have under any statute or common law to seek enforcement of this chapter or any rule or order under this chapter or to seek any other relief.

**(d) Consolidation**

When two or more civil actions brought under subsection (a) of this section involving the same defendant and the same issues or violations are pending in two or more judicial districts, such pending actions, upon application of such defendants to such actions which is made to a court in which any such action is brought, may, if such court in its discretion so decides, be consolidated for trial by order (issued after giving all parties reasonable notice and opportunity to be heard) of such court and tried in—

(1) any district which is selected by such defendant and in which one of such actions is pending,

(2) a district which is agreed upon by stipulation between all the parties to such actions and in which one of such actions is pending, or

(3) a district which is selected by the court and in which one of such actions is pending.

The court issuing such an order shall give prompt notification of the order to the other courts in which the civil actions consolidated under the order are pending.

(Pub.L. 94–469, Title I, § 20, Oct. 11, 1976, 90 Stat. 2041; renumbered Title I and amended Pub.L. 99–519, § 3(b)(3), (c)(1), Oct. 22, 1986, 100 Stat. 2989; Pub.L. 102–550, Title X, § 1021(b)(9), Oct. 28, 1992, 106 Stat. 3923.)

## § 2620. Citizens' petitions

**[TSCA § 21]**

**(a) In general**

Any person may petition the Administrator to initiate a proceeding for the issuance, amendment, or repeal of a rule under section 2603, 2605, or 2607 of this title or an order under section 2604(e) or 2605(b)(2) of this title.

**(b) Procedures**

(1) Such petition shall be filed in the principal office of the Administrator and shall set forth the facts which it is claimed establish that it is necessary to issue, amend, or repeal a rule under section 2603, 2605, or 2607 of this title or an order under section 2604(e), 2605(b)(1)(A), or 2605(b)(1)(B) of this title.

(2) The Administrator may hold a public hearing or may conduct such investigation or proceeding as the Administrator deems appropriate in order to determine whether or not such petition should be granted.

(3) Within 90 days after filing of a petition described in paragraph (1), the Administrator shall either grant or deny the petition. If the Administrator grants such petition, the Administrator shall promptly commence an appropriate proceeding in accordance with section 2603, 2604, 2605, or 2607 of this title. If the Administrator denies such petition, the Administrator shall publish in the Federal Register the Administrator's reasons for such denial.

(4)(A) If the Administrator denies a petition filed under this section (or if the Administrator fails to grant or deny such petition within the 90-day period) the petitioner may commence a civil action in a district court of the United States to compel the Administrator to initiate a rulemaking proceeding as requested in the petition. Any such action shall be filed within 60 days after the Administrator's denial of the petition or, if the Administrator fails to grant or deny the petition within 90 days after filing the petition, within 60 days after the expiration of the 90-day period.

**(B)** In an action under subparagraph (A) respecting a petition to initiate a proceeding to issue a rule under section 2603, 2605, or 2607 of this title or an order under section 2604(e) or 2605(b)(2) of this title, the petitioner shall be provided an opportunity to have such petition considered by the court in a de novo proceeding. If the petitioner demonstrates to the satisfaction of the court by a preponderance of the evidence that—

**(i)** in the case of a petition to initiate a proceeding for the issuance of a rule under section 2603 of this title or an order under section 2604(e) of this title—

**(I)** information available to the Administrator is insufficient to permit a reasoned evaluation of the health and environmental effects of the chemical substance to be subject to such rule or order; and

**(II)** in the absence of such information, the substance may present an unreasonable risk to health or the environment, or the substance is or will be produced in substantial quantities and it enters or may reasonably be anticipated to enter the environment in substantial quantities or there is or may be significant or substantial human exposure to it; or

**(ii)** in the case of a petition to initiate a proceeding for the issuance of a rule under section 2605 or 2607 of this title or an order under section 2605(b)(2) of this title, there is a reasonable basis to conclude that the issuance of such a rule or order is necessary to protect health or the environment against an unreasonable risk of injury to health or the environment.[1]

the court shall order the Administrator to initiate the action requested by the petitioner. If the court finds that the extent of the risk to health or the environment alleged by the petitioner is less than the extent of risks to health or the environment with respect to which the Administrator is taking action under this chapter and there are insufficient resources available to the Administrator to take the action requested by the petitioner, the court may permit the Administrator to defer initiating the action requested by the petitioner until such time as the court prescribes.

**(C)** The court in issuing any final order in any action brought pursuant to subparagraph (A) may award costs of suit and reasonable fees for attorneys and expert witnesses if the court determines that such an award is appropriate. Any court, in issuing its decision in an action brought to review such an order, may award costs of suit and reasonable fees for attorneys if the court determines that such an award is appropriate.

**(5)** The remedies under this section shall be in addition to, and not in lieu of, other remedies provided by law.

(Pub.L. 94–469, Title I, § 21, Oct. 11, 1976, 90 Stat. 2042; renumbered Title I, Pub.L. 99–519, § 3(c)(1), Oct. 22, 1986, 100 Stat. 2989.)

[1] So in original. The period should probably be a semicolon.

## § 2621. National defense waiver

[TSCA § 22]

The Administrator shall waive compliance with any provision of this chapter upon a request and determination by the President that the requested waiver is necessary in the interest of national defense. The Administrator shall maintain a written record of the basis upon which such waiver was granted and make such record available for in camera examination when relevant in a judicial proceeding under this chapter. Upon the issuance of such a waiver, the Administrator shall publish in the Federal Register a notice that the waiver was granted for national defense purposes, unless, upon the request of the President, the Administrator determines to omit such publication because the publication itself would be contrary to the interests of national defense, in which event the Administrator shall submit notice thereof to the Armed Services Committees of the Senate and the House of Representatives.

(Pub.L. 94–469, Title I, § 22, Oct. 11, 1976, 90 Stat. 2044; renumbered Title I, Pub.L. 99–519, § 3(c)(1), Oct. 22, 1986, 100 Stat. 2989.)

### HISTORICAL AND STATUTORY NOTES

**Change of Name**

Committee on Armed Services of the House of Representatives changed to the Committee on National Security of the House of Representatives, see section 1(a)(1) of Pub.L. 104–14, set out as a note preceding section 21 of Title 2, The Congress.

## § 2622. Employee protection

[TSCA § 23]

**(a) In general**

No employer may discharge any employee or otherwise discriminate against any employee with respect to the employee's compensation, terms, conditions, or privileges of employment because the employee (or any person acting pursuant to a request of the employee) has—

(1) commenced, caused to be commenced, or is about to commence or cause to be commenced a proceeding under this chapter;

(2) testified or is about to testify in any such proceeding; or

(3) assisted or participated or is about to assist or participate in any manner in such a proceeding or in any other action to carry out the purposes of this chapter.

**(b) Remedy**

(1) Any employee who believes that the employee has been discharged or otherwise discriminated against by any person in violation of subsection (a) of this section may, within 30 days after such alleged violation occurs, file (or have any person file on the employee's behalf) a complaint with the Secretary of Labor (hereinafter in this section referred to as the "Secretary") alleging such discharge or discrimination. Upon receipt of such a complaint, the Secretary shall notify the person named in the complaint of the filing of the complaint.

(2)(A) Upon receipt of a complaint filed under paragraph (1), the Secretary shall conduct an investigation of the violation alleged in the complaint. Within 30 days of the receipt of such complaint, the Secretary shall complete such investigation and shall notify in writing the complainant (and any person acting on behalf of the complainant) and the person alleged to have committed such violation of the results of the investigation conducted pursuant to this paragraph. Within ninety days of the receipt of such complaint the Secretary shall, unless the proceeding on the complaint is terminated by the Secretary on the basis of a settlement entered into by the Secretary and the person alleged to have committed such violation, issue an order either providing the relief prescribed by subparagraph (B) or denying the complaint. An order of the Secretary shall be made on the record after notice and opportunity for agency hearing. The Secretary may not enter into a settlement terminating a proceeding on a complaint without the participation and consent of the complainant.

(B) If in response to a complaint filed under paragraph (1) the Secretary determines that a violation of subsection (a) of this section has occurred, the Secretary shall order (i) the person who committed such violation to take affirmative action to abate the violation, (ii) such person to reinstate the complainant to the complainant's former position together with the compensation (including back pay), terms, conditions, and privileges of the complainant's employment, (iii) compensatory damages, and (iv) where appropriate, exemplary damages. If such an order issued, the Secretary, at the request of the complainant, shall assess against the person against whom the order is issued a sum equal to the aggregate amount of all costs and expenses (including attorney's fees) reasonably incurred, as determined by the Secretary, by the complainant for, or in connection with, the bringing of the complaint upon which the order was issued.

**(c) Review**

(1) Any employee or employer adversely affected or aggrieved by an order issued under subsection (b) of this section may obtain review of the order in the United States Court of Appeals for the circuit in which the violation, with respect to which the order was issued, allegedly occurred. The petition for review must be filed within sixty days from the issuance of the Secretary's order. Review shall conform to chapter 7 of Title 5.

(2) An order of the Secretary, with respect to which review could have been obtained under paragraph (1), shall not be subject to judicial review in any criminal or other civil proceeding.

**(d) Enforcement**

Whenever a person has failed to comply with an order issued under subsection (b)(2) of this section, the Secretary shall file a civil action in the United States district court for the district in which the violation was found to occur to enforce such order. In actions brought under this subsection, the district courts shall have jurisdiction to grant all appropriate relief, including injunctive relief and compensatory and exemplary damages.

**(e) Exclusion**

Subsection (a) of this section shall not apply with respect to any employee who, acting without direction from the employee's employer (or any agent of the employer), deliberately causes a violation of any requirement of this chapter.

(Pub.L. 94–469, Title I, § 23, Oct. 11, 1976, 90 Stat. 2044; Pub.L. 98–620, Title IV, § 402(19), Nov. 8, 1984, 98 Stat. 3358; renumbered Title I, Pub.L. 99–519, § 3(c)(1), Oct. 22, 1986, 100 Stat. 2989.)

### HISTORICAL AND STATUTORY NOTES

**Effective and Applicability Provisions**

1984 Acts

Amendment by Pub.L. 98–620 not applicable to cases pending on Nov. 8, 1984, see section 403 of Pub.L. 98–620, set out as an Effective Date note under section 1657 of Title 28, Judiciary and Judicial Procedure.

## § 2623. Employment effects

[TSCA § 24]

**(a) In general**

The Administrator shall evaluate on a continuing basis the potential effects on employment (including reductions in employment or loss of employment from threatened plant closures) of—

(1) the issuance of a rule or order under section 2603, 2604, or 2605 of this title, or

(2) a requirement of section 2604 or 2605 of this title.

**(b) Investigations**

(1) Any employee (or any representative of an employee) may request the Administrator to make an investigation of—

(A) a discharge or layoff or threatened discharge or layoff of the employee, or

(B) adverse or threatened adverse effects on the employee's employment,

allegedly resulting from a rule or order under section 2603, 2604, or 2605 of this title or a requirement of section 2604 or 2605 of this title. Any such request shall be made in writing, shall set forth with reasonable particularity the grounds for the request, and shall be signed by the employee, or representative of such employee, making the request.

(2)(A) Upon receipt of a request made in accordance with paragraph (1) the Administrator shall (i) conduct the investigation requested, and (ii) if requested by any interested person, hold public hearings on any matter involved in the investigation unless the Administrator, by order issued within 45 days of the date such hearings are requested, denies the request for the hearings because the Administrator determines there are no reasonable grounds for holding such hearings. If the Administrator makes such a determination, the Administrator shall notify in writing the person requesting the hearing of the determination and the reasons therefor and shall publish the determination and the reasons therefor in the Federal Register.

(B) If public hearings are to be held on any matter involved in an investigation conducted under this subsection—

(i) at least five days' notice shall be provided the person making the request for the investigation and any person identified in such request,

(ii) such hearings shall be held in accordance with section 2605(c)(3) of this title, and

(iii) each employee who made or for whom was made a request for such hearings and the employer of such employee shall be required to present information respecting the applicable matter referred to in paragraph (1)(A) or (1)(B) together with the basis for such information.

(3) Upon completion of an investigation under paragraph (2), the Administrator shall make findings of fact, shall make such recommendations as the Administrator deems appropriate, and shall make available to the public such findings and recommendations.

(4) This section shall not be construed to require the Administrator to amend or repeal any rule or order in effect under this chapter.

(Pub.L. 94–469, Title I, § 24, Oct. 11, 1976, 90 Stat. 2045; renumbered Title I, Pub.L. 99–519, § 3(c)(1), Oct. 22, 1986, 100 Stat. 2989.)

## § 2624. Studies

[TSCA § 25]

**(a) Indemnification study**

The Administrator shall conduct a study of all Federal laws administered by the Administrator for the purpose of determining whether and under what conditions, if any, indemnification should be accorded any person as a result of any action taken by the Administrator under any such law. The study shall—

(1) include an estimate of the probable cost of any indemnification programs which may be recommended;

(2) include an examination of all viable means of financing the cost of any recommended indemnification; and

(3) be completed and submitted to Congress within two years from the effective date of enactment of this chapter.

The General Accounting Office shall review the adequacy of the study submitted to Congress pursuant to paragraph (3) and shall report the results of its review to the Congress within six months of the date such study is submitted to Congress.

**(b) Classification, storage, and retrieval study**

The Council on Environmental Quality, in consultation with the Administrator, the Secretary of Health and Human Services, the Secretary of Commerce, and the heads of other appropriate Federal departments or agencies, shall coordinate a study of the feasibility of establishing (1) a standard classification system for chemical substances and related substances, and (2) a standard means for storing and for obtaining rapid access to information respecting such substances. A report on such study shall be completed and submitted to Congress not later than 18 months after the effective date of enactment of this chapter.

(Pub.L. 94–469, Title I, § 25, Oct. 11, 1976, 90 Stat. 2046; Pub.L. 96–88, Title V, § 509(b), Oct. 17, 1979, 93 Stat. 695; renumbered Title I, Pub.L. 99–519, § 3(c)(1), Oct. 22, 1986, 100 Stat. 2989.)

### HISTORICAL AND STATUTORY NOTES

**References in Text**

The "effective date of enactment of this chapter", referred to in subsecs. (a)(3) and (b), probably means January 1, 1977, the effective date of the chapter prescribed by section 31 of Pub.L. 94–469, which is set out as a note under section 2601 of this title, rather than October 11, 1976, the date of enactment.

**Change of Name**

"Secretary of Health and Human Services" was substituted for "Secretary of Health, Education, and Welfare" in subsec. (b), pursuant to § 509 of Pub.L. 96–88 which is classified to § 3508(b) of Title 20, Education.

## § 2625. Administration

[TSCA § 26]

### (a) Cooperation of Federal agencies

Upon request by the Administrator, each Federal department and agency is authorized—

(1) to make its services, personnel, and facilities available (with or without reimbursement) to the Administrator to assist the Administrator in the administration of this chapter; and

(2) to furnish to the Administrator such information, data, estimates, and statistics, and to allow the Administrator access to all information in its possession as the Administrator may reasonably determine to be necessary for the administration of this chapter.

### (b) Fees

(1) The Administrator may, by rule, require the payment of a reasonable fee from any person required to submit data under section 2603 or 2604 of this title to defray the cost of administering this chapter. Such rules shall not provide for any fee in excess of $2,500 or, in the case of a small business concern, any fee in excess of $100. In setting a fee under this paragraph, the Administrator shall take into account the ability to pay of the person required to submit the data and the cost to the Administrator of reviewing such data. Such rules may provide for sharing such a fee in any case in which the expenses of testing are shared under section 2603 or 2604 of this title.

(2) The Administrator, after consultation with the Administrator of the Small Business Administration, shall by rule prescribe standards for determining the persons which qualify as small business concerns for purposes of paragraph (1).

### (c) Action with respect to categories

(1) Any action authorized or required to be taken by the Administrator under any provision of this chapter with respect to a chemical substance or mixture may be taken by the Administrator in accordance with that provision with respect to a category of chemical substances or mixtures. Whenever the Administrator takes action under a provision of this chapter with respect to a category of chemical substances or mixtures, any reference in this chapter to a chemical substance or mixture (insofar as it relates to such action) shall be deemed to be a reference to each chemical substance or mixture in such category.

(2) For purposes of paragraph (1):

(A) The term "category of chemical substances" means a group of chemical substances the members of which are similar in molecular structure, in physical, chemical, or biological properties, in use, or in mode of entrance into the human body or into the environment, or the members of which are in some other way suitable for classification as such for purposes of this chapter, except that such term does not mean a group of chemical substances which are grouped together solely on the basis of their being new chemical substances.

(B) The term "category of mixtures" means a group of mixtures the members of which are similar in molecular structure, in physical, chemical, or biological properties, in use, or in the mode of entrance into the human body or into the environment, or the members of which are in some other way suitable for classification as such for purposes of this chapter.

### (d) Assistance office

The Administrator shall establish in the Environmental Protection Agency an identifiable office to provide technical and other nonfinancial assistance to manufacturers and processors of chemical substances and mixtures respecting the requirements of this chapter applicable to such manufacturers and processors, the policy of the Agency respecting the application of such requirements to such manufacturers and processors, and the means and methods by which such manufacturers and processors may comply with such requirements.

### (e) Financial disclosures

(1) Except as provided under paragraph (3), each officer or employee of the Environmental Protection Agency and the Department of Health and Human Services who—

(A) performs any function or duty under this chapter, and

(B) has any known financial interest (i) in any person subject to this chapter or any rule or order in effect under this chapter, or (ii) in any person who applies for or receives any grant or contract under this chapter,

shall, on February 1, 1978, and on February 1 of each year thereafter, file with the Administrator or the Secretary of Health and Human Services (hereinafter in this subsection referred to as the "Secretary"), as appropriate, a written statement concerning all such interests held by such officer or employee during the preceding calendar year. Such statement shall be made available to the public.

(2) The Administrator and the Secretary shall—

(A) act within 90 days of January 1, 1977—

(i) to define the term "known financial interests" for purposes of paragraph (1), and

(ii) to establish the methods by which the requirement to file written statements specified in paragraph (1) will be monitored and enforced, including appropriate provisions for review by the Administrator and the Secretary of such statements; and

(B) report to the Congress on June 1, 1978, and on June 1 of each year thereafter with respect to such statements and the actions taken in regard thereto during the preceding calendar year.

(3) The Administrator may by rule identify specific positions with the Environmental Protection Agency, and the Secretary may by rule identify specific positions with the Department of Health and Human Services, which are of a nonregulatory or nonpolicy-making nature, and the Administrator and the Secretary may by rule provide that officers or employees occupying such positions shall be exempt from the requirements of paragraph (1).

(4) This subsection does not supersede any requirement of chapter 11 of Title 18.

(5) Any officer or employee who is subject to, and knowingly violates, this subsection or any rule issued thereunder, shall be fined not more than $2,500 or imprisoned not more than one year, or both.

**(f) Statement of basis and purpose**

Any final order issued under this chapter shall be accompanied by a statement of its basis and purpose. The contents and adequacy of any such statement shall not be subject to judicial review in any respect.

**(g) Assistant Administrator**

(1) The President, by and with the advice and consent of the Senate, shall appoint an Assistant Administrator for Toxic Substances of the Environmental Protection Agency. Such Assistant Administrator shall be a qualified individual who is, by reason of background and experience, especially qualified to direct a program concerning the effects of chemicals on human health and the environment. Such Assistant Administrator shall be responsible for (A) the collection of data, (B) the preparation of studies, (C) the making of recommendations to the Administrator for regulatory and other actions to carry out the purposes and to facilitate the administration of this chapter, and (D) such other functions as the Administrator may assign or delegate.

(2) The Assistant Administrator to be appointed under paragraph (1) shall be in addition to the Assistant Administrators of the Environmental Protection Agency authorized by section 1(d) of Reorganization Plan No. 3 of 1970.

(Pub.L. 94–469, Title I, § 26, Oct. 11, 1976, 90 Stat. 2046; Pub.L. 96–88, Title V, § 509(b), Oct. 17, 1979, 93 Stat. 695; Pub.L. 98–80, § 2(c)(2)(A), Aug. 23, 1983, 97 Stat. 485; renumbered Title I, Pub.L. 99–519, § 3(c)(1), Oct. 22, 1986, 100 Stat. 2989.)

### HISTORICAL AND STATUTORY NOTES

**References in Text**

Reorganization Plan No. 3 of 1970, referred to in text, is set out in the Appendix to Title 5, Government Organization and Employees.

**Change of Name**

"Department of Health and Human Services" was substituted for "Department of Health, Education, and Welfare" in subsec. (e)(1) and (3), and "Secretary of Health and Human Services" was substituted for "Secretary of Health, Education, and Welfare" in subsec. (e)(1), pursuant to § 509(b) of Pub.L. 96–88 which is classified to § 3508(b) of Title 20, Education.

**Termination of Reporting Requirements**

For termination, effective May 15, 2000, of provisions in subsec. (e)(2)(B) of this section relating to annual report to Congress, see Pub.L. 104–66, § 3003, as amended, set out as a note under 31 U.S.C.A. § 1113, and pages 93 and 164 of House Document No. 103–7.

## § 2626. Development and evaluation of test methods

**[TSCA § 27]**

**(a) In general**

The Secretary of Health and Human Services, in consultation with the Administrator and acting through the Assistant Secretary for Health, may conduct, and make grants to public and nonprofit private entities and enter into contracts with public and private entities for, projects for the development and evaluation of inexpensive and efficient methods (1) for determining and evaluating the health and environmental effects of chemical substances and mixtures, and their toxicity, persistence, and other characteristics which affect health and the environment, and (2) which may be used for the development of test data to meet the requirements of rules promulgated under section 2603 of this title. The Administrator shall consider such methods in prescribing under section 2603 of this title standards for the development of test data.

**(b) Approval by Secretary**

No grant may be made or contract entered into under subsection (a) of this section unless an application therefor has been submitted to and approved by the Secretary. Such an application shall be submitted in such form and manner and contain such information as the Secretary may require. The Secretary may apply such conditions to grants and contracts under subsection (a) of this section as the Secretary determines are necessary to carry out the purposes of such subsection. Contracts may be entered into under such subsection without regard to section 3324(a) and (b) of Title 31 and section 5 of Title 41.

(Pub.L. 94–469, Title I, § 27, Oct. 11, 1976, 90 Stat. 2049; Pub.L. 96–88, Title V, § 509(b), Oct. 17, 1979, 93 Stat. 695; renumbered Title I, Pub.L. 99–519, § 3(c)(1), Oct. 22, 1986, 100 Stat. 2989, and amended Pub.L. 104–66, Title I, § 1061(a), Dec. 21, 1995, 109 Stat. 719.)

#### HISTORICAL AND STATUTORY NOTES

**Codifications**

In subsec. (b), "section 3324(a) and (b) of Title 31" was substituted for reference to section 3648 of the Revised Statutes (31 U.S.C. 529) on authority of Pub.L. 97–258, § 4(b), Sept. 13, 1982, 96 Stat. 1067, the first section of which enacted Title 31, Money and Finance.

**Change of Name**

"Secretary of Health and Human Services" was substituted for "Secretary of Health, Education, and Welfare" in subsec. (a), pursuant to § 509(b) of Pub.L. 96–88 which is classified to § 3508(b) of Title 20, Education.

## § 2627. State programs

[TSCA § 28]

**(a) In general**

For the purpose of complementing (but not reducing) the authority of, or actions taken by, the Administrator under this chapter, the Administrator may make grants to States for the establishment and operation of programs to prevent or eliminate unreasonable risks within the States to health or the environment which are associated with a chemical substance or mixture and with respect to which the Administrator is unable or is not likely to take action under this chapter for their prevention or elimination. The amount of a grant under this subsection shall be determined by the Administrator, except that no grant for any State program may exceed 75 per centum of the establishment and operation costs (as determined by the Administrator) of such program during the period for which the grant is made.

**(b) Approval by Administrator**

(1) No grant may be made under subsection (a) of this section unless an application therefor is submitted to and approved by the Administrator. Such an application shall be submitted in such form and manner as the Administrator may require and shall—

(A) set forth the need of the applicant for a grant under subsection (a) of this section,

(B) identify the agency or agencies of the State which shall establish or operate, or both, the program for which the application is submitted,

(C) describe the actions proposed to be taken under such program,

(D) contain or be supported by assurances satisfactory to the Administrator that such program shall, to the extent feasible, be integrated with other programs of the applicant for environmental and public health protection,

(E) provide for the making of such reports and evaluations as the Administrator may require, and

(F) contain such other information as the Administrator may prescribe.

(2) The Administrator may approve an application submitted in accordance with paragraph (1) only if the applicant has established to the satisfaction of the Administrator a priority need, as determined under rules of the Administrator, for the grant for which the application has been submitted. Such rules shall take into consideration the seriousness of the health effects in a State which are associated with chemical substances or mixtures, including cancer, birth defects, and gene mutations, the extent of the exposure in a State of human beings and the environment to chemical substances and mixtures, and the extent to which chemical substances and mixtures are manufactured, processed, used, and disposed of in a State.

**(c) Annual reports**

Not later than six months after the end of each of the fiscal years 1979, 1980, and 1981, the Administrator shall submit to the Congress a report respecting the programs assisted by grants under subsection (a) of this section in the preceding fiscal year and the extent to which the Administrator has disseminated information respecting such programs.

**(d) Authorization**

For the purpose of making grants under subsection (a) of this section, there are authorized to be appropriated $1,500,000 for each of the fiscal years 1982 and 1983. Sums appropriated under this subsection shall remain available until expended.

(Pub.L. 94–469, Title I, § 28, Oct. 11, 1976, 90 Stat. 2049; Pub.L. 97–129, § 1(a), Dec. 29, 1981, 95 Stat. 1686; renumbered Title I, Pub.L. 99–519, § 3(c)(1), Oct. 22, 1986, 100 Stat. 2989.)

## § 2628. Authorization of appropriations

[TSCA § 29]

There are authorized to be appropriated to the Administrator for purposes of carrying out this chapter (other than sections 2626 and 2627 of this title and subsections (a) and (c) through (g) of section 2609 of this title) $58,646,000 for the fiscal year 1982 and $62,000,000 for the fiscal year 1983. No part of the funds appropriated under this section may be used to construct any research laboratories.

(Pub.L. 94–469, Title I, § 29, Oct. 11, 1976, 90 Stat. 2050; Pub.L. 97–129, § 1(b), Dec. 29, 1981, 95 Stat. 1686; renumbered Title I, Pub.L. 99–519, § 3(c)(1), Oct. 22, 1986, 100 Stat. 2989.)

## § 2629. Annual report

[TSCA § 30]

The Administrator shall prepare and submit to the President and the Congress on or before January 1, 1978, and on or before January 1 of each succeeding year a comprehensive report on the administration of this chapter during the preceding fiscal year. Such reports shall include—

(1) a list of the testing required under section 2603 of this title during the year for which the report is made and an estimate of the costs incurred during such year by the persons required to perform such tests;

(2) the number of notices received during such year under section 2604 of this title, the number of such notices received during such year under such section for chemical substances subject to a rule, and a summary of any action taken during such year under section 2604(g) of this title;

(3) a list of rules issued during such year under section 2605 of this title;

(4) a list, with a brief statement of the issues, of completed or pending judicial actions under this chapter and administrative actions under section 2615 of this title during such year;

(5) a summary of major problems encountered in the administration of this chapter; and

(6) such recommendations for additional legislation as the Administrator deems necessary to carry out the purposes of this chapter.

(Pub.L. 94–469, Title I, § 30, Oct. 11, 1976, 90 Stat. 2050; renumbered Title I, Pub.L. 99–519, § 3(c)(1), Oct. 22, 1986, 100 Stat. 2989.)

### HISTORICAL AND STATUTORY NOTES

**Termination of Reporting Requirements**

For termination, effective May 15, 2000, of provisions in this section relating to submitting annual report to Congress, see Pub.L. 104–66, § 3003, as amended, set out as a note under 31 U.S.C.A. § 1113, and page 163 of House Document No. 103–7.

# SUBCHAPTER II—ASBESTOS HAZARD EMERGENCY RESPONSE

## § 2641. Congressional findings and purpose

[TSCA § 201]

**(a) Findings**

The Congress finds the following:

(1) The Environmental Protection Agency's rule on local educational agency inspection for, and notification of, the presence of friable asbestos-containing material in school buildings includes neither standards for the proper identification of asbestos-containing material and appropriate response actions with respect to friable asbestos-containing material, nor a requirement that response actions with respect to friable asbestos-containing material be carried out in a safe and complete manner once actions are found to be necessary. As a result of the lack of regulatory guidance from the Environmental Protection Agency, some schools have not undertaken response action while many others have undertaken expensive projects without knowing if their action is necessary, adequate, or safe. Thus, the danger of exposure to asbestos continues to exist in schools, and some exposure actually may have increased due to the lack of Federal standards and improper response action.

(2) There is no uniform program for accrediting persons involved in asbestos identification and abatement, nor are local educational agencies required to use accredited contractors for asbestos work.

(3) The guidance provided by the Environmental Protection Agency in its "Guidance for Controlling Asbestos–Containing Material in Buildings" is insufficient in detail to ensure adequate responses. Such guidance is intended to be used only until the regulations required by this subchapter become effective.

(4) Because there are no Federal standards whatsoever regulating daily exposure to asbestos in other public and commercial buildings, persons in addition to those comprising the Nation's school population may be exposed daily to asbestos.

**(b) Purpose**

The purpose of this subchapter is—

(1) to provide for the establishment of Federal regulations which require inspection for asbestos-containing material and implementation of appropriate response actions with respect to asbestos-containing material in the Nation's schools in a safe and complete manner;

(2) to mandate safe and complete periodic reinspection of school buildings following response actions, where appropriate; and

(3) to require the Administrator to conduct a study to find out the extent of the danger to human health posed by asbestos in public and commercial

buildings and the means to respond to any such danger.

(Pub.L. 94–469, Title II, § 201, as added Pub.L. 99–519, § 2, Oct. 22, 1986, 100 Stat. 2970.)

## § 2642. Definitions

[TSCA § 202]

For purposes of this subchapter—

**(1) Accredited asbestos contractor**

The term "accredited asbestos contractor" means a person accredited pursuant to the provisions of section 2646 of this title.

**(2) Administrator**

The term "Administrator" means the Administrator of the Environmental Protection Agency.

**(3) Asbestos**

The term "asbestos" means asbestiform varieties of—

(A) chrysotile (serpentine),
(B) crocidolite (riebeckite),
(C) amosite (cummingtonite-grunerite),
(D) anthophyllite,
(E) tremolite, or
(F) actinolite.

**(4) Asbestos-containing material**

The term "asbestos-containing material" means any material which contains more than 1 percent asbestos by weight.

**(5) EPA guidance document**

The term "Guidance for Controlling Asbestos-Containing Material in Buildings", means the Environmental Protection Agency document with such title as in effect on March 31, 1986.

**(6) Friable asbestos-containing material**

The term "friable asbestos-containing material" means any asbestos-containing material applied on ceilings, walls, structural members, piping, duct work, or any other part of a building which when dry may be crumbled, pulverized, or reduced to powder by hand pressure. The term includes non-friable asbestos-containing material after such previously non-friable material becomes damaged to the extent that when dry it may be crumbled, pulverized, or reduced to powder by hand pressure.

**(7) Local educational agency**

The term "local educational agency" means—

(A) any local educational agency as defined in section 7801 of Title 20,

(B) the owner of any private, nonprofit elementary or secondary school building, and

(C) the governing authority of any school operated under the defense dependents' education system provided for under the Defense Dependents' Education Act of 1978 (20 U.S.C. 921 et seq.).

**(8) Most current guidance document**

The term "most current guidance document" means the Environmental Protection Agency's "Guidance for Controlling Asbestos-Containing Material in Buildings" as modified by the Environmental Protection Agency after March 31, 1986.

**(9) Non-profit elementary or secondary school**

The term "non-profit elementary or secondary school" means any elementary or secondary school (as defined in section 7801 of Title 20) owned and operated by one or more nonprofit corporations or associations no part of the net earnings of which inures, or may lawfully inure, to the benefit of any private shareholder or individual.

**(10) Public and commercial building**

The term "public and commercial building" means any building which is not a school building, except that the term does not include any residential apartment building of fewer than 10 units.

**(11) Response action**

The term "response action" means methods that protect human health and the environment from asbestos-containing material. Such methods include methods described in chapters 3 and 5 of the Environmental Protection Agency's "Guidance for Controlling Asbestos-Containing Materials in Buildings".

**(12) School**

The term "school" means any elementary or secondary school as defined in section 7801 of Title 20.

**(13) School building**

The term "school building" means—

(A) any structure suitable for use as a classroom, including a school facility such as a laboratory, library, school eating facility, or facility used for the preparation of food,

(B) any gymnasium or other facility which is specially designed for athletic or recreational activities for an academic course in physical education,

(C) any other facility used for the instruction of students or for the administration of educational or research programs, and

(D) any maintenance, storage, or utility facility, including any hallway, essential to the operation of any facility described in subparagraphs (A), (B), or (C).

**(14) State**

The term "State" means a State, the District of Columbia, the Commonwealth of Puerto Rico, Guam, American Samoa, the Northern Marianas, the Trust Territory of the Pacific Islands, and the Virgin Islands.

(Pub.L. 94–469, Title II, § 202, as added Pub.L. 99–519, § 2, Oct. 22, 1986, 100 Stat. 2971, and amended Pub.L. 103–382, Title III, § 391(c)(1) to (3), Oct. 20, 1994, 108 Stat. 4022; Pub.L. 107–110, Title X, § 1076(f)(1), Jan. 8, 2002, 105 Stat. 2091.)

### HISTORICAL AND STATUTORY NOTES

**References in Text**

The Defense Dependent's Education Act of 1978, referred to in par. (7)(C), is Title XIV of Pub.L. 95–561, Nov. 1, 1978, 92 Stat. 2365, as amended, which is classified principally to chapter 25A (§ 921 et seq.) of Title 20, Education. For complete classification of this Act to the Code, see Short Title note set out under section 921 of Title 20 and Tables.

**Effective and Applicability Provisions**

2002 Acts

Except as otherwise provided, amendments by Pub.L. 107–110 effective Jan. 8, 2002, see Pub.L. 107–110, § 5, set out as a note under 20 U.S.C.A. § 6301.

**Termination of Trust Territory of the Pacific Islands**

For termination of Trust Territory of the Pacific Islands, see note set out preceding section 1681 of Title 48, Territories and Insular Possessions.

## § 2643. EPA regulations

[TSCA § 203]

**(a) In general**

Within 360 days after October 22, 1986, the Administrator shall promulgate regulations as described in subsections (b) through (i) of this section. With respect to regulations described in subsections (b), (c), (d), (e), (f), (g), and (i) of this section, the Administrator shall issue an advanced notice of proposed rulemaking within 60 days after October 22, 1986, and shall propose regulations within 180 days after October 22, 1986. Any regulation promulgated under this section must protect human health and the environment.

**(b) Inspection**

The Administrator shall promulgate regulations which prescribe procedures, including the use of personnel accredited under section 2646(b) or (c) of this title and laboratories accredited under section 2646(d) of this title, for determining whether asbestos-containing material is present in a school building under the authority of a local educational agency. The regulations shall provide for the exclusion of any school building, or portion of a school building, if (1) an inspection of such school building (or portion) was completed before the effective date of the regulations, and (2) the inspection meets the procedures and other requirements of the regulations under this subchapter or of the "Guidance for Controlling Asbestos-Containing Materials in Buildings" (unless the Administrator determines that an inspection in accordance with the guidance document is inadequate). The regulations shall require inspection of any school building (or portion of a school building) that is not excluded by the preceding sentence.

**(c) Circumstances requiring response actions**

(1) The Administrator shall promulgate regulations which define the appropriate response action in a school building under the authority of a local educational agency in at least the following circumstances:

**(A) Damage**

Circumstances in which friable asbestos-containing material or its covering is damaged, deteriorated, or delaminated.

**(B) Significant damage**

Circumstances in which friable asbestos-containing material or its covering is significantly damaged, deteriorated, or delaminated.

**(C) Potential damage**

Circumstances in which—

(i) friable asbestos-containing material is in an area regularly used by building occupants, including maintenance personnel, in the course of their normal activities, and

(ii) there is a reasonable likelihood that the material or its covering will become damaged, deteriorated, or delaminated.

**(D) Potential significant damage**

Circumstances in which—

(i) friable asbestos-containing material is in an area regularly used by building occupants, including maintenance personnel, in the course of their normal activities, and

(ii) there is a reasonable likelihood that the material or its covering will become significantly damaged, deteriorated, or delaminated.

(2) In promulgating such regulations, the Administrator shall consider and assess the value of various technologies intended to improve the decisionmaking process regarding response actions and the quality of any work that is deemed necessary, including air monitoring and chemical encapsulants.

**(d) Response actions**

**(1) In general**

The Administrator shall promulgate regulations describing a response action in a school building under the authority of a local educational agency, using the least burdensome methods which protect human health and the environment. In determining the least burdensome methods, the Administrator shall take into account local circumstances, including occupancy and use patterns within the school building and short- and long-term costs.

**(2) Response action for damaged asbestos**

In the case of a response action for the circumstances described in subsection (c)(1)(A) of this section, methods for responding shall include methods identified in chapters 3 and 5 of the "Guidance for Controlling Asbestos-Containing Material in Buildings".

**(3) Response action for significantly damaged asbestos**

In the case of a response action for the circumstances described in subsection (c)(1)(B) of this section, methods for responding shall include methods identified in chapter 5 of the "Guidance for Controlling Asbestos-Containing Material in Buildings".

**(4) Response action for potentially damaged asbestos**

In the case of a response action for the circumstances described in subsection (c)(1)(C) of this section, methods for responding shall include methods identified in chapters 3 and 5 of the "Guidance for Controlling Asbestos-Containing Material in Buildings", unless preventive measures will eliminate the reasonable likelihood that the asbestos-containing material will become damaged, deteriorated, or delaminated.

**(5) Response action for potentially significantly damaged asbestos**

In the case of a response action for the circumstances described in subsection (c)(1)(D) of this section, methods for responding shall include methods identified in chapter 5 of the "Guidance for Controlling Asbestos-Containing Material in Buildings", unless preventive measures will eliminate the reasonable likelihood that the asbestos-containing material will become significantly damaged, deteriorated, or delaminated.

**(6) "Preventive measures" defined**

For purposes of this section, the term "preventive measures" means actions which eliminate the reasonable likelihood of asbestos-containing material becoming damaged, deteriorated, or delaminated, or significantly damaged [1] deteriorated, or delaminated (as the case may be) or which protect human health and the environment.

**(7) EPA information or advisory**

The Administrator shall, not later than 30 days after November 28, 1990, publish and distribute to all local education agencies and State Governors information or an advisory to—

(A) facilitate public understanding of the comparative risks associated with in-place management of asbestos-containing building materials and removals;

(B) promote the least burdensome response actions necessary to protect human health, safety, and the environment; and

(C) describe the circumstances in which asbestos removal is necessary to protect human health.

Such information or advisory shall be based on the best available scientific evidence and shall be revised, republished, and redistributed as appropriate, to reflect new scientific findings.

**(e) Implementation**

The Administrator shall promulgate regulations requiring the implementation of response actions in school buildings under the authority of a local educational agency and, where appropriate, for the determination of when a response action is completed. Such regulations shall include standards for the education and protection of both workers and building occupants for the following phases of activity:

(1) Inspection.

(2) Response Action.[2]

(3) Post-response action, including any periodic reinspection of asbestos-containing material and long-term surveillance activity.

**(f) Operations and maintenance**

The Administrator shall promulgate regulations to require implementation of an operations and maintenance and repair program as described in chapter 3 of the "Guidance for Controlling Asbestos-Containing Materials in Buildings" for all friable asbestos-containing material in a school building under the authority of a local educational agency.

**(g) Periodic surveillance**

The Administrator shall promulgate regulations to require the following:

(1) An identification of the location of friable and non-friable asbestos in a school building under the authority of a local educational agency.

(2) Provisions for surveillance and periodic reinspection of such friable and non-friable asbestos.

(3) Provisions for education of school employees, including school service and maintenance personnel, about the location of and safety procedures with respect to such friable and non-friable asbestos.

**(h) Transportation and disposal**

The Administrator shall promulgate regulations which prescribe standards for transportation and disposal of asbestos-containing waste material to protect human health and the environment. Such regulations shall include such provisions related to the manner in which transportation vehicles are loaded and unloaded as will assure the physical integrity of containers of asbestos-containing waste material.

**(i) Management plans**

**(1) In general**

The Administrator shall promulgate regulations which require each local educational agency to develop an asbestos management plan for school buildings under its authority, to begin implementation of such plan within 990 days after October 22, 1986, and to complete implementation of such plan in a timely fashion. The regulations shall require that each plan include the following elements, wherever relevant to the school building:

**(A)** An inspection statement describing inspection and response action activities carried out before October 22, 1986.

**(B)** A description of the results of the inspection conducted pursuant to regulations under subsection (b) of this section, including a description of the specific areas inspected.

**(C)** A detailed description of measures to be taken to respond to any friable asbestos-containing material pursuant to the regulations promulgated under subsections (c), (d), and (e) of this section, including the location or locations at which a response action will be taken, the method or methods of response action to be used, and a schedule for beginning and completing response actions.

**(D)** A detailed description of any asbestos-containing material which remains in the school building once response actions are undertaken pursuant to the regulations promulgated under subsections (c), (d), and (e) of this section.

**(E)** A plan for periodic reinspection and long-term surveillance activities developed pursuant to regulations promulgated under subsection (g) of this section, and a plan for operations and maintenance activities developed pursuant to regulations promulgated under subsection (f) of this section.

**(F)** With respect to the person or persons who inspected for asbestos-containing material and who will design or carry out response actions with respect to the friable asbestos-containing material, one of the following statements:

**(i)** If the State has adopted a contractor accreditation plan under section 2646(b) of this title, a statement that the person (or persons) is accredited under such plan.

**(ii)** A statement that the local educational agency used (or will use) persons who have been accredited by another State which has adopted a contractor accreditation plan under section 2646(b) of this title or is accredited pursuant to an Administrator-approved course under section 2646(c) of this title.

**(G)** A list of the laboratories that analyzed any bulk samples of asbestos-containing material found in the school building or air samples taken to detect asbestos in the school building and a statement that each laboratory has been accredited pursuant to the accreditation program under section 2646(d) of this title.

**(H)** With respect to each consultant who contributed to the management plan, the name of the consultant and one of the following statements:

**(i)** If the State has adopted a contractor accreditation plan under section 2646(b) of this title, a statement that the consultant is accredited under such plan.

**(ii)** A statement that the contractor is accredited by another State which has adopted a contractor accreditation plan under section 2646(b) of this title or is accredited pursuant to an Administrator-approved course under section 2646(c) of this title.

**(I)** An evaluation of resources needed to successfully complete response actions and carry out reinspection, surveillance, and operation and maintenance activities.

**(2) Statement by contractor**

A local educational agency may require each management plan to contain a statement signed by an accredited asbestos contractor that such contractor has prepared or assisted in the preparation of such plan, or has reviewed such plan, and that such plan is in compliance with the applicable regulations and standards promulgated or adopted pursuant to this section and other applicable provisions of law. Such a statement may not be signed by a contractor who, in addition to preparing or assisting in preparing the management plan, also implements (or will implement) the management plan.

**(3) Warning labels**

**(A)** The regulations shall require that each local educational agency which has inspected for and discovered any asbestos-containing material with respect to a school building shall attach a warning label to any asbestos-containing material still in routine maintenance areas (such as boiler rooms) of the school building, including—

**(i)** friable asbestos-containing material which was responded to by a means other than removal, and

**(ii)** asbestos-containing material for which no response action was carried out.

**(B)** The warning label shall read, in print which is readily visible because of large size or bright color, as follows: **"CAUTION: ASBESTOS. HAZARDOUS. DO NOT DISTURB WITHOUT PROPER TRAINING AND EQUIPMENT."**

**(4) Plan may be submitted in stages**

A local educational agency may submit a management plan in stages, with each submission of the agency covering only a portion of the school buildings under the agency's authority, if the agency determines that such action would expedite the identification and abatement of hazardous asbestos-containing material in the school buildings under the authority of the agency.

**(5) Public availability**

A copy of the management plan developed under the regulations shall be available in the administrative offices of the local educational agency for inspection by the public, including teachers, other school personnel, and parents. The local educational agency shall notify parent, teacher, and employee organizations of the availability of such plan.

**(6) Submission to State Governor**

Each plan developed under this subsection shall be submitted to the State Governor under section 2645 of this title.

**(j) Changes in regulations**

Changes may be made in the regulations promulgated under this section only by rule in accordance with section 553 of Title 5. Any such change must protect human health and the environment.

**(k) Changes in guidance document**

Any change made in the "Guidance for Controlling Asbestos-Containing Material in Buildings" shall be made only by rule in accordance with section 553 of Title 5, unless a regulation described in this section dealing with the same subject matter is in effect. Any such change must protect human health and the environment.

**(*l*) Treatment of Department of Defense schools**

**(1) Secretary to act in lieu of Governor**

In the administration of this subchapter, any function, duty, or other responsibility imposed on a Governor of a State shall be carried out by the Secretary of Defense with respect to any school operated under the defense dependents' education system provided for under the Defense Dependents' Education Act of 1978 (20 U.S.C. 921 et seq.).

**(2) Regulations**

The Secretary of Defense, in cooperation with the Administrator, shall, to the extent feasible and consistent with the national security, take such action as may be necessary to provide for the identification, inspection, and management (including abatement) of asbestos in any building used by the Department of Defense as an overseas school for dependents of members of the Armed Forces. Such identification, inspection, and management (including abatement) shall, subject to the preceding sentence, be carried out in a manner comparable to the manner in which a local educational agency is required to carry out such activities with respect to a school building under this subchapter.

**(m) Waiver**

The Administrator, upon request by a Governor and after notice and comment and opportunity for a public hearing in the affected State, may waive some or all of the requirements of this section and section 2644 of this title with respect to such State if it has established and is implementing a program of asbestos inspection and management that contains requirements that are at least as stringent as the requirements of this section and section 2644 of this title.

(Pub.L. 94–469, Title II, § 203, as added Pub.L. 99–519, § 2, Oct. 22, 1986, 100 Stat. 2972, and amended Pub.L. 101–637, § 13, Nov. 28, 1990, 104 Stat. 4593.)

[1] So in original. Probably should be followed by a comma.

[2] So in original. Probably should not be capitalized.

HISTORICAL AND STATUTORY NOTES

**References in Text**

The Defense Dependents' Education Act of 1978, referred to in subsec. (*l*)(1), is Title XIV of Pub.L. 95–561, Nov. 1, 1978, 92 Stat. 2365, as amended, which is classified principally to chapter 25A (§ 921 et seq.) of Title 20, Education. For complete classification of this Act to the Code, see Short Title note set out under section 921 of Title 20 and Tables.

## § 2644. Requirements if EPA fails to promulgate regulations

[TSCA § 204]

**(a) In general**

**(1) Failure to promulgate**

If the Administrator fails to promulgate within the prescribed period—

**(A)** regulations described in section 2643(b) of this title (relating to inspection);

**(B)** regulations described in section 2643(c), (d), (e), (f), (g), and (i) of this title (relating to responding to asbestos); or

**(C)** regulations described in section 2643(h) of this title (relating to transportation and disposal);

each local educational agency shall carry out the requirements described in this section in subsection (b); subsections (c), (d), and (e); or subsection (f); respectively, in accordance with the Environmental Protection Agency's most current guidance document.

**(2) Stay by court**

If the Administrator has promulgated regulations described in paragraph (1)(A), (B), or (C) within the prescribed period, but the effective date of such regulations has been stayed by a court for a period of more than 30 days, a local educational agency shall carry out the pertinent requirements described in this subsection in accordance with the Environmental Protection Agency's most current guidance document.

**(3) Effective period**

The requirements of this section shall be in effect until such time as the Administrator promulgates the pertinent regulations or until the stay is lifted (as the case may be).

**(b) Inspection**

(1) Except as provided in paragraph (2), the local educational agency, within 540 days after October 22, 1986, shall conduct an inspection for asbestos-containing material, using personnel accredited under section 2646(b) or (c) of this title and laboratories accredited under section 2646(d) of this title, in each school building under its authority.

(2) The local educational agency may exclude from the inspection requirement in paragraph (1) any school building, or portion of a school building, if (A) an inspection of such school building (or portion) was completed before the date on which this section goes into effect, and (B) the inspection meets the inspection requirements of this section.

**(c) Operation and maintenance**

The local educational agency shall, within 720 days after October 22, 1986, develop and begin implementation of an operation and maintenance plan with respect to friable asbestos-containing material in a school building under its authority. Such plan shall provide for the education of school service and maintenance personnel about safety procedures with respect to asbestos-containing material, including friable asbestos-containing material.

**(d) Management plan**

**(1) In general**

The local educational agency shall—

(A) develop a management plan for responding to asbestos-containing material in each school building under its authority and submit such plan to the Governor under section 2645 of this title within 810 days after October 22, 1986,

(B) begin implementation of such plan within 990 days after October 22, 1986, and

(C) complete implementation of such plan in a timely fashion.

**(2) Plan requirements**

The management plan shall—

(A) include the elements listed in section 2643(i)(1) of this title, including an inspection statement as described in paragraph (3) of this section,[1]

(B) provide for the attachment of warning labels as described in section 2643(i)(3) of this title,

(C) be prepared in accordance with the most current guidance document,

(D) meet the standard described in paragraph (4) for actions described in that paragraph, and

(E) be submitted to the State Governor under section 2645 of this title.

**(3) Inspection statement**

The local educational agency shall complete an inspection statement, covering activities carried out before October 22, 1986, which meets the following requirements:

(A) The statement shall include the following information:

(i) The dates of inspection.

(ii) The name, address, and qualifications of each inspector.

(iii) A description of the specific areas inspected.

(iv) A list of the laboratories that analyzed any bulk samples of asbestos-containing material or air samples of asbestos found in any school building and a statement describing the qualifications of each laboratory.

(v) The results of the inspection.

(B) The statement shall state whether any actions were taken with respect to any asbestos-containing material found to be present, including a specific reference to whether any actions were taken in the boiler room of the building. If any such action was taken, the following items of information shall be included in the statement:

(i) The location or locations at which the action was taken.

(ii) A description of the method of action.

(iii) The qualifications of the persons who conducted the action.

**(4) Standard**

The ambient interior concentration of asbestos after the completion of actions described in the most current guidance document, other than the type of action described in sections 2643(f) of this title and subsection (c) of this section, shall not exceed the ambient exterior concentration, discounting any contribution from any local stationary source. Either a scanning electron microscope or a transmission electron microscope shall be used to determine the ambient interior concentration. In the absence of reliable measurements, the ambient exterior concentration shall be deemed to be—

(A) less than 0.003 fibers per cubic centimeter if a scanning electron microscope is used, and

(B) less than 0.005 fibers per cubic centimeter if a transmission electron microscope is used.

**(5) Public availability**

A copy of the management plan shall be available in the administrative offices of the local educational agency for inspection by the public, including teachers, other school personnel, and parents. The local educational agency shall notify parent, teacher, and employee organizations of the availability of such plan.

**(e) Building occupant protection**

The local educational agency shall provide for the protection of building occupants during each phase of activity described in this section.

**(f) Transportation and disposal**

The local educational agency shall provide for the transportation and disposal of asbestos in accordance with the most recent version of the Environmental Protection Agency's "Asbestos Waste Management Guidance" (or any successor to such document).

(Pub.L. 94–469, Title II, § 204, as added Pub.L. 99–519, § 2, Oct. 22, 1986, 100 Stat. 2977.)

1 So in original. Probably should be "subsection,".

## § 2645. Submission to State Governor

**[TSCA § 205]**

**(a) Submission**

Within 720 days after October 22, 1986 (or within 810 days if there are no regulations under section 2643(i) of this title), a local educational agency shall submit a management plan developed pursuant to regulations promulgated under section 2643(i) of this title (or under section 2644(d) of this title if there are no regulations) to the Governor of the State in which the local educational agency is located.

**(b) Governor requirements**

Within 360 days after October 22, 1986, the Governor of each State—

(1) shall notify local educational agencies in the State of where to submit their management plans under this section, and

(2) may establish administrative procedures for reviewing management plans submitted under this section.

If the Governor establishes procedures under paragraph (2), the Governor shall designate to carry out the reviews those State officials who are responsible for implementing environmental protection or other public health programs, or with authority over asbestos programs, in the State.

**(c) Management plan review**

**(1) Review of plan**

The Governor may disapprove a management plan within 90 days after the date of receipt of the plan if the plan—

(A) does not conform with the regulations under section 2643(i) of this title (or with section 2644(d) of this title if there are no regulations),

(B) does not assure that contractors who are accredited pursuant to this subchapter will be used to carry out the plan, or

(C) does not contain a response action schedule which is reasonable and timely, taking into account circumstances relevant to the speed at which the friable asbestos-containing material in the school buildings under the local educational agency's authority should be responded to, including human exposure to the asbestos while the friable asbestos-containing material remains in the school building, and the ability of the local educational agency to continue to provide educational services to the community.

**(2) Revision of plan**

If the State Governor disapproves a plan, the State Governor shall explain in writing to the local educational agency the reasons why the plan was disapproved and the changes that need to be made in the plan. Within 30 days after the date on which notice is received of disapproval of its plan, the local educational agency shall revise the plan to conform with the State Governor's suggested changes. The Governor may extend the 30-day period for not more than 90 days.

**(d) Deferral of submission**

**(1) Request for deferral**

A local educational agency may request a deferral, to May 9, 1989, of the deadline under subsection (a) of this section. Upon approval of such a request, the deadline under subsection (a) of this section is deferred until May 9, 1989, for the local educational agency which submitted the request. Such a request may cover one or more schools under the authority of the agency and shall include a list of all the schools covered by the request. A local educational agency shall file any such request with the State Governor by October 12, 1988, and shall include with the request either of the following statements:

(A) A statement—

(i) that the State in which the agency is located has requested from the Administrator, before June 1, 1988, a waiver under section 2643(m) of this title; and

(ii) that gives assurance that the local educational agency has carried out the notification and, in the case of a public school, public meeting required by paragraph (2).

(B) A statement, the accuracy of which is sworn to by a responsible official of the agency (by notarization or other means of certification), that includes the following with respect to each school for which a deferral is sought in the request:

(i) A statement that, in spite of the fact that the local educational agency has made a good faith effort to meet the deadline for submission of a management plan under subsection (a) of this section, the agency will not be able to meet the deadline. The statement shall include a brief explanation of the reasons why the deadline cannot be met.

(ii) A statement giving assurance that the local educational agency has made available for inspection by the public, at each school for which a deferral is sought in the request, at least one of the following documents:

(I) A solicitation by the local educational agency to contract with an accredited asbestos contractor for inspection or management plan development.

(II) A letter attesting to the enrollment of school district personnel in an Environmental Protection Agency-accredited training course for inspection and management plan development.

(III) Documentation showing that an analysis of suspected asbestos-containing material from the school is pending at an accredited laboratory.

(IV) Documentation showing that an inspection or management plan has been completed in at least one other school under the local educational agency's authority.

(iii) A statement giving assurance that the local educational agency has carried out the notification and, in the case of a public school, public meeting required by paragraph (2).

(iv) A proposed schedule outlining all significant activities leading up to submission of a management plan by May 9, 1989, including inspection of the school (if not completed at the time of the request) with a deadline of no later than December 22, 1988, for entering into a signed contract with an accredited asbestos contractor for inspection (unless such inspections are to be performed by school personnel), laboratory analysis of material from the school suspected of containing asbestos, and development of the management plan.

**(2) Notification and public meeting**

Before filing a deferral request under paragraph (1), a local educational agency shall notify affected parent, teacher, and employee organizations of its intent to file such a request. In the case of a deferral request for a public school, the local educational agency shall discuss the request at a public meeting of the school board with jurisdiction over the school, and affected parent, teacher, and employee organizations shall be notified in advance of the time and place of such meeting.

**(3) Response by Governor**

(A) Not later than 30 days after the date on which a Governor receives a deferral request under paragraph (1) from a local educational agency, the Governor shall respond to the local educational agency in writing by acknowledging whether the request is complete or incomplete. If the request is incomplete, the Governor shall identify in the response the items that are missing from the request.

(B) A local educational agency may correct any deficiencies in an incomplete deferral request and refile the request with the Governor. In any case in which the local educational agency decides to refile the request, the agency shall refile the request, and the Governor shall respond to such refiled request in the manner described in subparagraph (A), no later than 15 days after the local educational agency has received a response from the Governor under subparagraph (A).

(C) Approval of a deferral request under this subsection occurs only upon the receipt by a local educational agency of a written acknowledgment from the Governor that the agency's deferral request is complete.

**(4) Submission and review of plan**

A local educational agency whose deferral request is approved shall submit a management plan to the Governor not later than May 9, 1989. Such management plan shall include a copy of the deferral request and the statement accompanying such request. Such management plan shall be reviewed in accordance with subsection (c) of this section, except that the Governor may extend the 30–day period for revision of the plan under subsection (c)(2) of this section for only an additional 30 days (for a total of 60 days).

**(5) Implementation of plan**

The approval of a deferral request from a local educational agency shall not be considered to be a waiver or exemption from the requirement under section 2643(i) of this title for the local educational agency to begin implementation of its management plan by July 9, 1989.

**(6) EPA notice**

**(A)** Not later than 15 days after July 18, 1988, the Administrator shall publish in the Federal Register the following:

**(i)** A notice describing the opportunity to file a request for deferral under this subsection.

**(ii)** A list of the State offices (including officials (if available) in each State as designated under subsection (b) of this section) with which deferral requests should be filed.

**(B)** As soon as practicable, but in no event later than 30 days, after July 18, 1988, the Administrator shall mail a notice describing the opportunity to file a request for deferral under this subsection to each local educational agency and to each State office in the list published under subparagraph (A).

**(e) Status reports**

(1) Not later than December 31, 1988, the Governor of each State shall submit to the Administrator a written statement on the status of management plan submissions and deferral requests by local educational agencies in the State. The statement shall be made available to local educational agencies in the State and shall contain the following:

**(A)** A list containing each local educational agency that submitted a management plan by October 12, 1988.

**(B)** A list containing each local educational agency whose deferral request was approved.

**(C)** A list containing each local educational agency that failed to submit a management plan by October 12, 1988, and whose deferral request was disapproved.

**(D)** A list containing each local educational agency that failed to submit a management plan by October 12, 1988, and did not submit a deferral request.

(2) Not later than December 31, 1989, the Governor of each State shall submit to the Administrator an updated version of the written statement submitted under paragraph (1). The statement shall be made available to local educational agencies in the State and shall contain the following:

**(A)** A list containing each local educational agency whose management plan was submitted and not disapproved as of October 9, 1989.

**(B)** A list containing each local educational agency whose management plan was submitted and disapproved, and which remains disapproved, as of October 9, 1989.

**(C)** A list containing each local educational agency that submitted a management plan after May 9, 1989, and before October 10, 1989.

**(D)** A list containing each local educational agency that failed to submit a management plan as of October 9, 1989.

(Pub.L. 94–469, Title II, § 205, as added Pub.L. 99–519, § 2, Oct. 22, 1986, 100 Stat. 2979, and amended Pub.L. 100–368, §§ 1(a), 2, July 18, 1988, 102 Stat. 829, 831.)

## § 2646. Contractor and laboratory accreditation

**[TSCA § 206]**

**(a) Contractor accreditation**

A person may not—

**(1)** inspect for asbestos-containing material in a school building under the authority of a local educational agency or in a public or commercial building,

**(2)** prepare a management plan for such a school, or

**(3)** design or conduct response actions, other than the type of action described in sections 2643(f) and 2644(c) of this title, with respect to friable asbestos-containing material in such a school or in a public or commercial building,

unless such person is accredited by a State under subsection (b) of this section or is accredited pursuant to an Administrator-approved course under subsection (c) of this section.

**(b) Accreditation by State**

**(1) Model plan**

**(A) Persons to be accredited**

Within 180 days after October 22, 1986, the Administrator, in consultation with affected organizations, shall develop a model contractor accreditation plan for States to give accreditation to persons in the following categories:

**(i)** Persons who inspect for asbestos-containing material in school buildings under the authority of a local educational agency or in public or commercial buildings.

**(ii)** Persons who prepare management plans for such schools.

**(iii)** Persons who design or carry out response actions, other than the type of action described in sections 2643(f) and 2644(c) of this title, with respect to friable asbestos-containing material in such schools or in public or commercial buildings.

(B) Plan requirements

The plan shall include a requirement that any person in a category listed in paragraph (1) achieve a passing grade on an examination and participate in continuing education to stay informed about current asbestos inspection and response action technology. The examination shall demonstrate the knowledge of the person in areas that the Administrator prescribes as necessary and appropriate in each of the categories. Such examinations may include requirements for knowledge in the following areas:

(i) Recognition of asbestos-containing material and its physical characteristics.

(ii) Health hazards of asbestos and the relationship between asbestos exposure and disease.

(iii) Assessing the risk of asbestos exposure through a knowledge of percentage weight of asbestos-containing material, friability, age, deterioration, location and accessibility of materials, and advantages and disadvantages of dry and wet response action methods.

(iv) Respirators and their use, care, selection, degree of protection afforded, fitting, testing, and maintenance and cleaning procedures.

(v) Appropriate work practices and control methods, including the use of high efficiency particle absolute vacuums, the use of amended water, and principles of negative air pressure equipment use and procedures.

(vi) Preparing a work area for response action work, including isolating work areas to prevent bystander or public exposure to asbestos, decontamination procedures, and procedures for dismantling work areas after completion of work.

(vii) Establishing emergency procedures to respond to sudden releases.

(viii) Air monitoring requirements and procedures.

(ix) Medical surveillance program requirements.

(x) Proper asbestos waste transportation and disposal procedures.

(xi) Housekeeping and personal hygiene practices, including the necessity of showers, and procedures to prevent asbestos exposure to an employee's family.

(2) State adoption of plan

Each State shall adopt a contractor accreditation plan at least as stringent as the model plan developed by the Administrator under paragraph (1), within 180 days after the commencement of the first regular session of the legislature of such State which is convened following the date on which the Administrator completes development of the model plan. In the case of a school operated under the defense dependents' education system provided for under the Defense Dependents' Education Act of 1978 (20 U.S.C. 921 et seq.), the Secretary of Defense shall adopt a contractor accreditation plan at least as stringent as that model.

(c) Accreditation by Administrator-approved course

(1) Course approval

Within 180 days after October 22, 1986, the Administrator shall ensure that any Environmental Protection Agency-approved asbestos training course is consistent with the model plan (including testing requirements) developed under subsection (b) of this section. A contractor may be accredited by taking and passing such a course.

(2) Treatment of persons with previous EPA asbestos training

A person who—

(A) completed an Environmental Protection Agency-approved asbestos training course before October 22, 1986, and

(B) passed (or passes) an asbestos test either before or after October 22, 1986,

may be accredited under paragraph (1) if the Administrator determines that the course and test are equivalent to the requirements of the model plan developed under subsection (b) of this section. If the Administrator so determines, the person shall be considered accredited for the purposes of this subchapter until a date that is one year after the date on which the State in which such person is employed establishes an accreditation program pursuant to subsection (b) of this section.

(3) Lists of courses

The Administrator, in consultation with affected organizations, shall publish (and revise as necessary)—

(A) a list of asbestos courses and tests in effect before October 22, 1986, which qualify for equivalency treatment under paragraph (2), and

(B) a list of asbestos courses and tests which the Administrator determines under paragraph (1) are consistent with the model plan and which will qualify a contractor for accreditation under such paragraph.

(d) Laboratory accreditation

(1) The Administrator shall provide for the development of an accreditation program for laboratories by the National Institute of Standards and Technology

in accordance with paragraph (2). The Administrator shall transfer such funds as are necessary to the National Institute of Standards and Technology to carry out such program.

(2) The National Institute of Standards and Technology, upon request by the Administrator, shall, in consultation with affected organizations—

(A) within 360 days after October 22, 1986, develop an accreditation program for laboratories which conduct qualitative and semi-quantitative analyses of bulk samples of asbestos-containing material, and

(B) within 720 days after October 22, 1986, develop an accreditation program for laboratories which conduct analyses of air samples of asbestos from school buildings under the authority of a local educational agency.

(3) A laboratory which plans to carry out any such analysis shall comply with the requirements of the accreditation program.

**(e) Financial assistance contingent on use of accredited persons**

(1) A school which is an applicant for financial assistance under section 505 of the Asbestos School Hazard Abatement Act of 1984 [20 U.S.C.A. § 4014] is not eligible for such assistance unless the school, in carrying out the requirements of this subchapter—

(A) uses a person (or persons)—

(i) who is accredited by a State which has adopted an accreditation plan based on the model plan developed under subsection (b) of this section, or

(ii) who is accredited pursuant to an Administrator-approved course under subsection (c) of this section, and

(B) uses a laboratory (or laboratories) which is accredited under the program developed under subsection (d) of this section.

(2) This subsection shall apply to any financial assistance provided under the Asbestos School Hazard Abatement Act of 1984 [20 U.S.C.A. § 4011 et seq.] for activities performed after the following dates:

(A) In the case of activities performed by persons, after the date which is one year after October 22, 1986.

(B) In the case of activities performed by laboratories, after the date which is 180 days after the date on which a laboratory accreditation program is completed under subsection (d) of this section.

**(f) List of EPA-approved courses**

Not later than August 31, 1988, and every three months thereafter until August 31, 1991, the Administrator shall publish in the Federal Register a list of all Environmental Protection Agency-approved asbestos training courses for persons to achieve accreditation in each category described in subsection (b)(1)(A) of this section and for laboratories to achieve accreditation. The Administrator may continue publishing such a list after August 31, 1991, at such times as the Administrator considers it useful. The list shall include the name and address of each approved trainer and, to the extent available, a list of all the geographic sites where training courses will take place. The Administrator shall provide a copy of the list to each State official on the list published by the Administrator under section 2645(d)(6) of this title and to each regional office of the Environmental Protection Agency.

(Pub.L. 94–469, Title II, § 206, as added Pub.L. 99–519, § 2, Oct. 22, 1986, 100 Stat. 2980, and amended Pub.L. 100–368, § 3, July 18, 1988, 102 Stat. 832; Pub.L. 100–418, Title V, § 5115(c), Aug. 23, 1988, 102 Stat. 1433; Pub.L. 101–637, § 15(a)(1), (2), Nov. 28, 1990, 104 Stat. 4596.)

## HISTORICAL AND STATUTORY NOTES

**References in Text**

The Defense Dependents' Education Act of 1978, referred to in subsec. (b)(2), is Title XIV of Pub.L. 95–561, Nov. 1, 1978, 92 Stat. 2365, as amended, which is classified principally to chapter 25A (§ 921 et seq.) of Title 20, Education. For complete classification of this Act to the Code, see Short Title note set out under section 921 of Title 20 and Tables.

The Asbestos School Hazard Abatement Act of 1984, referred to in subsec. (e)(2), is Title V of Pub.L. 98–377, Aug. 11, 1984, 98 Stat. 1287, as amended, which is classified generally to subchapter V (§ 4011 et seq.) of chapter 52 of Title 20. For complete classification of this Act to the Code, see Short Title note set out under section 4011 of Title 20 and Tables.

**Effective and Applicability Provisions**

1990 Acts

Section 15(c) of Pub.L. 101–637 provided that: "This section [amending this section and section 2647 of this title and enacting provisions set out as notes under this section] shall take effect upon the expiration of the 12-month period following the date of the enactment of this Act [Nov. 28, 1990]. The Administrator may extend the effective date for a period not to exceed one year if the Administrator determines that accredited asbestos contractors are needed to perform school-site abatement required under the Asbestos Hazard Emergency Response Act [of 1986] (15 U.S.C. 2641) and such an extension is necessary to ensure effective implementation of section 203 of the Toxic Substances Control Act [15 U.S.C.A. § 2643]."

**Revision of Model Contractor Accreditation Program**

Section 15(a)(3) of Pub.L. 101–637 provided that: "Not later than one year after the date of the enactment of this Act [Nov. 28, 1990], the Administrator of the Environmental Protection Agency shall revise the model contractor accreditation plan promulgated under section 206(b)(1) of the Toxic Substances Control Act (15 U.S.C. 2646(b)(1)) to increase the minimum number of hours of training, including additional hours of hands-on health and safety training, required for asbestos abatement workers and to make such other changes as may be necessary to implement the amendments made by paragraphs (1) and (2) [amending this section]."

**EPA Administrator Not Exercising "Statutory Authority" Under OSHA Law in Exercising Authority Under this Chapter**

Section 15(b) of Pub.L. 101–637 provided that: "In exercising any authority under the Toxic Substances Control Act [15 U.S.C.A. § 2601 et seq.] in connection with the amendment made by subsection (a) of this section [amending this section and section 2647 of this title], the Administrator of the Environmental Protection Agency shall not, for purposes of section 4(b)(1) of the Occupational Safety and Health Act of 1970 (29 U.S.C. 653(b)(1)), be considered to be exercising statutory authority to prescribe or enforce standards or regulations affecting occupational safety and health."

## § 2647. Enforcement

[TSCA § 207]

### (a) Penalties

Any local educational agency—

(1) which fails to conduct an inspection pursuant to regulations under section 2643(b) of this title or under section 2644(b) of this title,

(2) which knowingly submits false information to the Governor regarding any inspection pursuant to regulations under section 2643(i) of this title or knowingly includes false information in any inspection statement under section 2644(d)(3) of this title,

(3) which fails to develop a management plan pursuant to regulations under section 2643(i) of this title or under section 2644(d) of this title,

(4) which carries out any activity prohibited by section 2655 of this title, or

(5) which knowingly submits false information to the Governor regarding a deferral request under section 2645(d) of this title.[1]

is liable for a civil penalty of not more than $5,000 for each day during which the violation continues. Any civil penalty under this subsection shall be assessed and collected in the same manner, and subject to the same provisions, as in the case of civil penalties assessed and collected under section 2615 of this title. For purposes of this subsection, a "violation" means a failure to comply with respect to a single school building. The court shall order that any civil penalty collected under this subsection be used by the local educational agency for purposes of complying with this subchapter. Any portion of a civil penalty remaining unspent after compliance by a local educational agency is completed shall be deposited into the Asbestos Trust Fund established by section 4022 of Title 20.

### (b) Relationship to subchapter I of this chapter

A local educational agency is not liable for any civil penalty under subchapter I of this chapter for failing or refusing to comply with any rule promulgated or order issued under this subchapter.

### (c) Enforcement considerations

(1) In determining the amount of a civil penalty to be assessed under subsection (a) of this section against a local educational agency, the Administrator shall consider—

(A) the significance of the violation;

(B) the culpability of the violator, including any history of previous violations under this chapter;

(C) the ability of the violator to pay the penalty; and

(D) the ability of the violator to continue to provide educational services to the community.

(2) Any action ordered by a court in fashioning relief under section 2619 of this title shall be consistent with regulations promulgated under section 2643 of this title (or with the requirements of section 2644 of this title if there are no regulations).

### (d) Citizen complaints

Any person may file a complaint with the Administrator or with the Governor of the State in which the school building is located with respect to asbestos-containing material in a school building. If the Administrator or Governor receives a complaint under this subsection containing allegations which provide a reasonable basis to believe that a violation of this chapter has occurred, the Administrator or Governor shall investigate and respond (including taking enforcement action where appropriate) to the complaint within a reasonable period of time.

### (e) Citizen petitions

(1) Any person may petition the Administrator to initiate a proceeding for the issuance, amendment, or repeal of a regulation or order under this subchapter.

(2) Such petition shall be filed in the principal office of the Administrator and shall set forth the facts which it is claimed establish that it is necessary to issue, amend, or repeal a regulation or order under this subchapter.

(3) The Administrator may hold a public hearing or may conduct such investigation or proceeding as the Administrator deems appropriate in order to determine whether or not such petition should be granted.

(4) Within 90 days after filing of a petition described in paragraph (1), the Administrator shall either grant or deny the petition. If the Administrator grants such petition, the Administrator shall promptly commence an appropriate proceeding in accordance with this subchapter. If the Administrator denies such petition, the Administrator shall publish in the Federal Register the Administrator's reasons for such

denial. The granting or denial of a petition under this subsection shall not affect any deadline or other requirement of this subchapter.

**(f) Citizen civil actions with respect to EPA regulations**

(1) Any person may commence a civil action without prior notice against the Administrator to compel the Administrator to meet the deadlines in section 2643 of this title for issuing advanced notices of proposed rulemaking, proposing regulations, and promulgating regulations. Any such action shall be brought in the district court of the United States for the District of Columbia.

(2) In any action brought under paragraph (1) in which the court finds the Administrator to be in violation of any deadline in section 2643 of this title, the court shall set forth a schedule for promulgating the regulations required by section 2643 of this title and shall order the Administrator to comply with such schedule. The court may extend any deadline (which has not already occurred) in section 2644(b), (c), or (d) of this title for a period of not more than 6 months, if the court-ordered schedule will result in final promulgation of the pertinent regulations within the extended period. Such deadline extensions may not be granted by the court beginning 720 days after October 22, 1986.

(3) Section 2619 of this title shall apply to civil actions described in this subsection, except to the extent inconsistent with this subsection.

**(g) Failure to attain accreditation; penalty**

Any contractor who—

(1) inspects for asbestos-containing material in a school, public or commercial building;

(2) designs or conducts response actions with respect to friable asbestos-containing material in a school, public or commercial building; or

(3) employs individuals to conduct response actions with respect to friable asbestos-containing material in a school, public or commercial building;

and who fails to obtain the accreditation under section 2646 of this title, or in the case of employees to require or provide for the accreditation required, is liable for a civil penalty of not more than $5,000 for each day during which the violation continues, unless such contractor is a direct employee of the Federal Government.

(Pub.L. 94–469, Title II, § 207, as added Pub.L. 99–519, § 2, Oct. 22, 1986, 100 Stat. 2983, and amended Pub.L. 100–368, § 5, July 18, 1988, 102 Stat. 833; Pub.L. 101–637, § 15(a)(4), Nov. 28, 1990, 104 Stat. 4596.)

[1] So in original. The period probably should be a comma.

**HISTORICAL AND STATUTORY NOTES**

**Effective and Applicability Provisions**

1990 Acts

Amendment by Pub.L. 101–637 effective upon expiration of 12–month period following Nov. 28, 1990, with provisions for extension, see section 15(c) of Pub.L. 101–637, set out as a note under section 2646 of this title.

**EPA Administrator Not Exercising "Statutory Authority" Under OSHA Law in Exercising Authority Under this Chapter**

In exercising any authority under this chapter in connection with amendment made by Pub.L. 101–637, Administrator of Environmental Protection Agency not, for purposes of section 653(b)(1) of Title 29, Labor, to be considered to be exercising statutory authority to prescribe or enforce standards or regulations affecting occupational safety and health, see section 15(b) of Pub.L. 101–637, set out as a note under section 2646 of this title.

## § 2648. Emergency authority

[TSCA § 208]

**(a) Emergency action**

**(1) Authority**

Whenever—

(A) the presence of airborne asbestos or the condition of friable asbestos-containing material in a school building governed by a local educational agency poses an imminent and substantial endangerment to human health or the environment, and

(B) the local educational agency is not taking sufficient action (as determined by the Administrator or the Governor) to respond to the airborne asbestos or friable asbestos-containing material,

the Administrator or the Governor of a State is authorized to act to protect human health or the environment.

**(2) Limitations on Governor's action**

The Governor of a State shall notify the Administrator within a reasonable period of time before the Governor plans to take an emergency action under this subsection. After such notification, if the Administrator takes an emergency action with respect to the same hazard, the Governor may not carry out (or continue to carry out, if the action has been started) the emergency action.

**(3) Notification**

The following notification shall be provided before an emergency action is taken under this subsection:

(A) In the case of a Governor taking the action, the Governor shall notify the local educational agency concerned.

(B) In the case of the Administrator taking the action, the Administrator shall notify both the local educational agency concerned and the Governor of the State in which such agency is located.

**(4) Cost recovery**

The Administrator or the Governor of a State may seek reimbursement for all costs of an emergency action taken under this subsection in the United States District Court for the District of Columbia or for the district in which the emergency action occurred. In any action seeking reimbursement from a local educational agency, the action shall be brought in the United States District Court for the district in which the local educational agency is located.

**(b) Injunctive relief**

Upon receipt of evidence that the presence of airborne asbestos or the condition of friable asbestos-containing material in a school building governed by a local educational agency poses an imminent and substantial endangerment to human health or the environment—

(1) the Administrator may request the Attorney General to bring suit, or

(2) the Governor of a State may bring suit,

to secure such relief as may be necessary to respond to the hazard. The district court of the United States in the district in which the response will be carried out shall have jurisdiction to grant such relief, including injunctive relief.

(Pub.L. 94–469, Title II, § 208, as added Pub.L. 99–519, § 2, Oct. 22, 1986, 100 Stat. 2985.)

## § 2649. State and Federal law

**[TSCA § 209]**

**(a) No preemption**

Nothing in this subchapter shall be construed, interpreted, or applied to preempt, displace, or supplant any other State or Federal law, whether statutory or common.

**(b) Cost and damage awards**

Nothing in this subchapter or any standard, regulation, or requirement promulgated pursuant to this subchapter shall be construed or interpreted to preclude any court from awarding costs and damages associated with the abatement, including the removal, of asbestos-containing material, or a portion of such costs, at any time prior to the actual date on which such material is removed.

**(c) State may establish more requirements**

Nothing in this subchapter shall be construed or interpreted as preempting a State from establishing any additional liability or more stringent requirements with respect to asbestos in school buildings within such State.

**(d) No Federal cause of action**

Nothing in this subchapter creates a cause of action or in any other way increases or diminishes the liability of any person under any other law.

**(e) Intent of Congress**

It is not the intent of Congress that this subchapter or rules, regulations, or orders issued pursuant to this subchapter be interpreted as influencing, in either the plaintiff's or defendant's favor, the disposition of any civil action for damages relating to asbestos. This subsection does not affect the authority of any court to make a determination in an adjudicatory proceeding under applicable State law with respect to the admission into evidence or any other use of this subchapter or rules, regulations, or orders issued pursuant to this subchapter.

(Pub.L. 94–469, Title II, § 209, as added Pub.L. 99–519, § 2, Oct. 22, 1986, 100 Stat. 2986.)

## § 2650. Asbestos contractors and local educational agencies

**[TSCA § 210]**

**(a) Study**

**(1) General requirement**

The Administrator shall conduct a study on the availability of liability insurance and other forms of assurance against financial loss which are available to local educational agencies and asbestos contractors with respect to actions required under this subchapter. Such study shall examine the following:

(A) The extent to which liability insurance and other forms of assurance against financial loss are available to local educational agencies and asbestos contractors.

(B) The extent to which the cost of insurance or other forms of assurance against financial loss has increased and the extent to which coverage has become less complete.

(C) The extent to which any limitation in the availability of insurance or other forms of assurance against financial loss is the result of factors other than standards of liability in applicable law.

(D) The extent to which the existence of the regulations required by subsections (c) and (d) of section 2643 of this title and the accreditation of contractors under section 2646 of this title has affected the availability or cost of insurance or other forms of assurance against financial loss.

(E) The extent to which any limitation on the availability of insurance or other forms of assurance against financial loss is inhibiting inspections for asbestos-containing material or the development or implementation of management plans under this subchapter.

(F) Identification of any other impediments to the timely completion of inspections or the development and implementation of management plans under this subchapter.

**(2) Interim report**

Not later than April 1, 1988, the Administrator shall submit to the Congress an interim report on the progress of the study required by this subsection, along with preliminary findings based on information collected to that date.

**(3) Final report**

Not later than October 1, 1990, the Administrator shall submit to the Congress a final report on the study required by this subsection, including final findings based on the information collected.

**(b) State action**

On the basis of the interim report or the final report of the study required by subsection (a) of this section, a State may enact or amend State law to establish or modify a standard of liability for local educational agencies or asbestos contractors with respect to actions required under this subchapter.

(Pub.L. 94–469, Title II, § 210, as added Pub.L. 99–519, § 2, Oct. 22, 1986, 100 Stat. 2986.)

## § 2651. Public protection

**[TSCA § 211]**

**(a) Public protection**

No State or local educational agency may discriminate against a person in any way, including firing a person who is an employee, because the person provided information relating to a potential violation of this subchapter to any other person, including a State or the Federal Government.

**(b) Labor Department review**

Any public or private employee or representative of employees who believes he or she has been fired or otherwise discriminated against in violation of subsection (a) of this section may within 90 days after the alleged violation occurs apply to the Secretary of Labor for a review of the firing or alleged discrimination. The review shall be conducted in accordance with section 660(c) of Title 29.

(Pub.L. 94–469, Title II, § 211, as added Pub.L. 99–519, § 2, Oct. 22, 1986, 100 Stat. 2987.)

## § 2652. Asbestos Ombudsman

**[TSCA § 212]**

**(a) Appointment**

The Administrator shall appoint an Asbestos Ombudsman, who shall carry out the duties described in subsection (b) of this section.

**(b) Duties**

The duties of the Asbestos Ombudsman are—

(1) to receive complaints, grievances, and requests for information submitted by any person with respect to any aspect of this subchapter,

(2) to render assistance with respect to the complaints, grievances, and requests received, and

(3) to make such recommendations to the Administrator as the Ombudsman considers appropriate.

(Pub.L. 94–469, Title II, § 212, as added Pub.L. 99–519, § 2, Oct. 22, 1986, 100 Stat. 2987.)

## § 2653. EPA study of asbestos-containing material in public buildings

**[TSCA § 213]**

Within 360 days after October 22, 1986, the Administrator shall conduct and submit to the Congress the results of a study which shall—

(1) assess the extent to which asbestos-containing materials are present in public and commercial buildings;

(2) assess the condition of asbestos-containing material in commercial buildings and the likelihood that persons occupying such buildings, including service and maintenance personnel, are, or may be, exposed to asbestos fibers;

(3) consider and report on whether public and commercial buildings should be subject to the same inspection and response action requirements that apply to school buildings;

(4) assess whether existing Federal regulations adequately protect the general public, particularly abatement personnel, from exposure to asbestos during renovation and demolition of such buildings; and

(5) include recommendations that explicitly address whether there is a need to establish standards for, and regulate asbestos exposure in, public and commercial buildings.

(Pub.L. 94–469, Title II, § 213, as added Pub.L. 99–519, § 2, Oct. 22, 1986, 100 Stat. 2987.)

## § 2654. Transitional rules

**[TSCA § 214]**

Any regulation of the Environmental Protection Agency under subchapter I of this chapter which is inconsistent with this subchapter shall not be in effect after October 22, 1986. Any advanced notice of proposed rulemaking, any proposed rule, and any regulation of the Environmental Protection Agency in effect before October 22, 1986, which is consistent with the regulations required under section 2643 of this title shall remain in effect and may be used to meet the requirements of section 2643 of this title, except that any such regulation shall be enforced under this chapter.

(Pub.L. 94–469, Title II, § 214, as added Pub.L. 99–519, § 2, Oct. 22, 1986, 100 Stat. 2988.)

## § 2655. Worker protection

**[TSCA § 215]**

### (a) Prohibition on certain activities

Until the local educational agency with authority over a school has submitted a management plan (for the school) which the State Governor has not disapproved as of the end of the period for review and revision of the plan under section 2645 of this title, the local educational agency may not do either of the following in the school:

(1) Perform, or direct an employee to perform, renovations or removal of building materials, except emergency repairs, in the school, unless—

(A) the school is carrying out work under a grant awarded under section 4014 of Title 20; or

(B) an inspection that complies with the requirements of regulations promulgated under section 2643 of this title has been carried out in the school and the agency complies with the following sections of title 40 of the Code of Federal Regulations:

(i) Paragraphs (g), (h), and (i) of section 763.90 (response actions).

(ii) Appendix D to subpart E of part 763 (transport and disposal of asbestos waste).

(2) Perform, or direct an employee to perform, operations and maintenance activities in the school, unless the agency complies with the following sections of title 40 of the Code of Federal Regulations:

(A) Section 763.91 (operations and maintenance), including appendix B to subpart E of part 763.

(B) Paragraph (a)(2) of section 763.92 (training and periodic surveillance).

### (b) Employee training and equipment

Any school employee who is directed to conduct emergency repairs involving any building material containing asbestos or suspected of containing asbestos, or to conduct operations and maintenance activities, in a school—

(1) shall be provided the proper training to safely conduct such work in order to prevent potential exposure to asbestos; and

(2) shall be provided the proper equipment and allowed to follow work practices that are necessary to safely conduct such work in order to prevent potential exposure to asbestos.

### (c) "Emergency repair" defined

For purposes of this section, the term "emergency repair" means a repair in a school building that was not planned and was in response to a sudden, unexpected event that threatens either—

(1) the health or safety of building occupants; or

(2) the structural integrity of the building.

(Pub.L. 94–469, Title II, § 215, as added Pub.L. 100–368, § 4(a), July 18, 1988, 102 Stat. 832.)

#### HISTORICAL AND STATUTORY NOTES

**Effective and Applicability Provisions**

1988 Acts

Section 4(c) of Pub.L. 100–368 provided that: "Section 215 of the Toxic Substances Control Act [this section], as added by subsection (a), shall take effect on October 12, 1988."

## § 2656. Training grants

**[TSCA § 216]**

### (a) Grants

The Administrator is authorized to award grants under this section to nonprofit organizations that demonstrate experience in implementing and operating health and safety asbestos training and education programs for workers who are or will be engaged in asbestos-related activities (including State and local governments, colleges and universities, joint labor-management trust funds, and nonprofit government employee organizations) to establish and, or, operate asbestos training programs on a not-for-profit basis. Applications for grants under this subsection shall be submitted in such form and manner, and contain such information, as the Administrator prescribes.

### (b) Authorization

Of such sums as are authorized to be appropriated pursuant to section 4021(a) of Title 20 for the fiscal years 1991, 1992, 1993, 1994, and 1995, not more than $5,000,000 are authorized to be appropriated to carry out this section in each such fiscal year.

(Pub.L. 94–469, Title II, § 216, as added Pub.L. 101–637, § 16(a)(1), Nov. 28, 1990, 104 Stat. 4597.)

#### HISTORICAL AND STATUTORY NOTES

**Effective and Applicability Provisions**

1990 Acts

Section 16(b) of Pub.L. 101–637 provided that: "Section 216 of the Toxic Substances Control Act [this section], as added by subsection (a), shall take effect on the date of the enactment of this Act [Nov. 28, 1990]."

## SUBCHAPTER III—INDOOR RADON ABATEMENT

## § 2661. National goal

### [TSCA § 301]

The national long-term goal of the United States with respect to radon levels in buildings is that the air within buildings in the United States should be as free of radon as the ambient air outside of buildings. (Pub.L. 94–469, Title III, § 301, as added Pub.L. 100–551, § 1(a), Oct. 28, 1988, 102 Stat. 2755.)

### HISTORICAL AND STATUTORY NOTES

**Report on Recommended Policy for Dealing with Radon in Assisted Housing**

Pub. L. 100–628, Title X, § 1091, Nov. 7, 1988, 102 Stat. 3283, provided that:

"(a) **Purposes.**—The purposes of this section are—

"(1) to require the Department of Housing and Urban Development to develop an effective departmental policy for dealing with radon contamination that utilizes any Environmental Protection Agency guidelines and standards to ensure that occupants of housing covered by this section are not exposed to hazardous levels of radon; and

"(2) to require the Department of Housing and Urban Development to assist the Environmental Protection Agency in reducing radon contamination.

"(b) **Program.**—

"(1) **Applicability.**—The housing covered by this section is—

"(A) multifamily housing owned by the Department of Housing and Urban Development;

"(B) public housing and Indian housing assisted under the United States Housing Act of 1937 [42 U.S.C.A. § 1437 et seq.];

"(C) housing receiving project-based assistance under section 8 of the United States Housing Act of 1937 [42 U.S.C.A. § 1437f];

"(D) housing assisted under section 236 of the National Housing Act [12 U.S.C.A. § 1715 z-1]; and

"(E) housing assisted under section 221(d)(3) of the National Housing Act [12 U.S.C.A. § 1715l(d)(3)].

"(2) **In general.**—The Secretary of Housing and Urban Development shall develop and recommend to the Congress a policy for dealing with radon contamination that specifies programs for education, research, testing, and mitigation of radon hazards in housing covered by this section.

"(3) **Standards.**—In developing the policy, the Secretary shall utilize any guidelines, information, or standards established by the Environmental Protection Agency for—

"(A) testing residential and nonresidential structures for radon;

"(B) identifying elevated radon levels;

"(C) identifying when remedial actions should be taken; and

"(D) identifying geographical areas that are likely to have elevated levels of radon.

"(4) **Coordination.**—In developing the policy, the Secretary shall coordinate the efforts of the Department of Housing and Urban Development with the Environmental Protection Agency, and other appropriate Federal agencies, and shall consult with State and local governments, the housing industry, consumer groups, health organizations, appropriate professional organizations, and other appropriate experts.

"(5) **Report.**—The Secretary shall submit a report to the Congress within 1 year after the date of the enactment of this Act [Nov. 7, 1988] that describes the Secretary's recommended policy for dealing with radon contamination and the Secretary's reasons for recommending such policy. The report shall include an estimate of the housing covered by this section that is likely to have hazardous levels of radon.

"(c) **Cooperation with Environmental Protection Agency.**—Within 6 months after the date of the enactment of this Act [Nov. 7, 1988], the Secretary and the Administrator of the Environmental Protection Agency shall enter into a memorandum of understanding describing the Secretary's plan to assist the Administrator in carrying out the Environmental Protection Agency's authority to assess the extent of radon contamination in the United States and assist in the development of measures to avoid and reduce radon contamination.

"(d) **Definitions.**—For purposes of this section:

"(1) **Administrator.**—The term 'Administrator' means the Administrator of the Environmental Protection Agency.

"(2) **Secretary.**—The term 'Secretary' means the Secretary of Housing and Urban Development.

"(e) **Authorization.**—Funds available for housing covered by this section shall be available to carry out this section with respect to such housing."

## § 2662. Definitions

### [TSCA § 302]

For purposes of this subchapter:

(1) The term "local educational agency" means—

(A) any local educational agency as defined in section 7801 of Title 20;

(B) the owner of any nonprofit elementary or secondary school building; and

(C) the governing authority of any school operated pursuant to section 241 of Title 20, as in effect before enactment of the Improving America's Schools Act of 1994, or successor authority, relating to impact aid for children who reside on Federal property.

(2) The term "nonprofit elementary or secondary school" has the meaning given such term by section 2642(8) [1] of this title,

(3) The term "radon" means the radioactive gaseous element and its short-lived decay products produced by the disintegration of the element radium occurring in air, water, soil, or other media.

(4) The term "school building" has the meaning given such term by section 2642(13) of this title.

(Pub.L. 94–469, Title III, § 302, as added Pub.L. 100–551, § 1(a), Oct. 28, 1988, 102 Stat. 2755, and amended Pub.L. 103–382, Title III, §§ 391(c)(4), 392(b)(2), Oct. 20, 1994, 108 Stat. 4022, 4026; Pub.L. 107–110, Title X, § 1076(f)(2), Jan. 8, 2002, 115 Stat. 2091.)

[1] So in original. Probably should be "2642(9)".

### HISTORICAL AND STATUTORY NOTES

**References in Text**

Section 241 of Title 20, as in effect before enactment of the Improving America's Schools Act of 1994, referred to in par. (1)(C), means section 241 of Title 20, Education, prior to its repeal by Pub.L. 103–382 Title III, § 331(b), Oct. 20, 1994, 108 Stat. 3965.

**Effective and Applicability Provisions**

2002 Acts

Except as otherwise provided, amendments by Pub.L. 107–110 effective Jan. 8, 2002, see Pub.L. 107–110, § 5, set out as a note under 20 U.S.C.A. § 6301.

## § 2663. EPA citizen's guide

[TSCA § 303]

**(a) Publication**

In order to make continuous progress toward the long-term goal established in section 2661 of this title, the Administrator of the Environmental Protection Agency shall, not later than June 1, 1989, publish and make available to the public an updated version of its document titled "A Citizen's Guide to Radon". The Administrator shall revise and republish the guide as necessary thereafter.

**(b) Information included**

**(1) Action levels**

The updated citizen's guide published as provided in subsection (a) of this section shall include a description of a series of action levels indicating the health risk associated with different levels of radon exposure.

**(2) Other information**

The updated citizen's guide shall also include information with respect to each of the following:

(A) The increased health risk associated with the exposure of potentially sensitive populations to different levels of radon.

(B) The increased health risk associated with the exposure to radon of persons engaged in potentially risk-increasing behavior.

(C) The cost and technological feasibility of reducing radon concentrations within existing and new buildings.

(D) The relationship between short-term and long-term testing techniques and the relationship between (i) measurements based on both such techniques, and (ii) the actions [1] levels set forth as provided in paragraph (1).

(E) Outdoor radon levels around the country.

(Pub.L. 94–469, Title III, § 303, as added Pub.L. 100–551, § 1(a), Oct. 28, 1988, 102 Stat. 2755.)

[1] So in original. Probably should be "action".

## § 2664. Model construction standards and techniques

[TSCA § 304]

The Administrator of the Environmental Protection Agency shall develop model construction standards and techniques for controlling radon levels within new buildings. To the maximum extent possible, these standards and techniques should be developed with the assistance of organizations involved in establishing national building construction standards and techniques. The Administrator shall make a draft of the document containing the model standards and techniques available for public review and comment. The model standards and techniques shall provide for geographic differences in construction types and materials, geology, weather, and other variables that may affect radon levels in new buildings. The Administrator shall make final model standards and techniques available to the public by June 1, 1990. The Administrator shall work to ensure that organizations responsible for developing national model building codes, and authorities which regulate building construction within States or political subdivisions within States, adopt the Agency's model standards and techniques.

(Pub.L. 94–469, Title III, § 304, as added Pub.L. 100–551, § 1(a), Oct. 28, 1988, 102 Stat. 2756.)

## § 2665. Technical assistance to States for radon programs

[TSCA § 305]

**(a) Required activities**

The Administrator (or another Federal department or agency designated by the Administrator) shall develop and implement activities designed to assist State radon programs. These activities may include, but are not limited to, the following:

(1) Establishment of a clearinghouse of radon related information, including mitigation studies, public information materials, surveys of radon levels, and other relevant information.

(2) Operation of a voluntary proficiency program for rating the effectiveness of radon measurement devices and methods, the effectiveness of radon mitigation devices and methods, and the effectiveness of private firms and individuals offering radon-related architecture, design, engineering, measurement, and mitigation services. The proficiency pro-

gram under this subparagraph shall be in operation within one year after October 28, 1988.

(3) Design and implementation of training seminars for State and local officials and private and professional firms dealing with radon and addressing topics such as monitoring, analysis, mitigation, health effects, public information, and program design.

(4) Publication of public information materials concerning radon health risks and methods of radon mitigation.

(5) Operation of cooperative projects between the Environmental Protection Agency's Radon Action Program and the State's radon program. Such projects shall include the Home Evaluation Program, in which the Environmental Protection Agency evaluates homes and States demonstrate mitigation methods in these homes. To the maximum extent practicable, consistent with the objectives of the evaluation and demonstration, homes of low-income persons should be selected for evaluation and demonstration.

(6) Demonstration of radon mitigation methods in various types of structures and in various geographic settings and publication of findings. In the case of demonstration of such methods in homes, the Administrator should select homes of low-income persons, to the maximum extent practicable and consistent with the objectives of the demonstration.

(7) Establishment of a national data base with data organized by State concerning the location and amounts of radon.

(8) Development and demonstration of methods of radon measurement and mitigation that take into account unique characteristics, if any, of nonresidential buildings housing child care facilities.

**(b) Discretionary assistance**

Upon request of a State, the Administrator (or another Federal department or agency designated by the Administrator) may provide technical assistance to such State in development or implementation of programs addressing radon. Such assistance may include, but is not limited to, the following:

(1) Design and implementation of surveys of the location and occurrence of radon within a State.

(2) Design and implementation of public information and education programs.

(3) Design and implementation of State programs to control radon in existing or new structures.

(4) Assessment of mitigation alternatives in unusual or unconventional structures.

(5) Design and implementation of methods for radon measurement and mitigation for nonresidential buildings housing child care facilities.

**(c) Information provided to professional organizations**

The Administrator, or another Federal department or agency designated by the Administrator, shall provide appropriate information concerning technology and methods of radon assessment and mitigation to professional organizations representing private firms involved in building design, engineering, and construction.

**(d) Proficiency rating program and training seminar**

**(1) Authorization**

There is authorized to be appropriated not more than $1,500,000 for the purposes of initially establishing the proficiency rating program under subsection (a)(2) of this section and the training seminars under subsection (a)(3) of this section.

**(2) Charge imposed**

To cover the operating costs of such proficiency rating program and training seminars, the Administrator shall impose on persons applying for a proficiency rating and on private and professional firms participating in training seminars such charges as may be necessary to defray the costs of the program or seminars. No such charge may be imposed on any State or local government.

**(3) Special account**

Funds derived from the charges imposed under paragraph (2) of this subsection shall be deposited in a special account in the Treasury. Amounts in the special account are authorized to be appropriated only for purposes of administering such proficiency rating program or training seminars or for reimbursement of funds appropriated to the Administrator to initially establish such program or seminars.

**(4) Reimbursement of general fund**

During the first three years of the program and seminars, the Administrator shall make every effort, consistent with the goals and successful operation of the program and seminars, to set charges imposed under paragraph (2) of this subsection so that an amount in excess of operation costs is collected. Such excess amount shall be used to reimburse the General Fund of the Treasury for the full amount appropriated to initially establish the program and seminars.

**(5) Research**

The Administrator shall, in conjunction with other Federal agencies, conduct research to develop, test, and evaluate radon and radon progeny measurement methods and protocols. The purpose of such research shall be to assess the ability of those methods and protocols to accurately assess exposure to radon progeny. Such research shall include—

**(A)** conducting comparisons among radon and radon progeny measurement techniques;

**(B)** developing measurement protocols for different building types under varying operating conditions; and

**(C)** comparing the exposures estimated by stationary monitors and protocols to those measured by personal monitors, and issue guidance documents that—

**(i)** provide information on the results of research conducted under this paragraph; and

**(ii)** describe model State radon measurement and mitigation programs.

**(6) Mandatory proficiency testing program study**

**(A)** The Administrator shall conduct a study to determine the feasibility of establishing a mandatory proficiency testing program that would require that—

**(i)** any product offered for sale, or device used in connection with a service offered to the public, for the measurement of radon meets minimum performance criteria; and

**(ii)** any operator of a device, or person employing a technique, used in connection with a service offered to the public for the measurement of radon meets a minimum level of proficiency.

**(B)** The study shall also address procedures for—

**(i)** ordering the recall of any product sold for the measurement of radon which does not meet minimum performance criteria;

**(ii)** ordering the discontinuance of any service offered to the public for the measurement of radon which does not meet minimum performance criteria; and

**(iii)** establishing adequate quality assurance requirements for each company offering radon measurement services to the public to follow. The study shall identify enforcement mechanisms necessary to the success of the program. The Administrator shall report the findings of the study with recommendations to Congress by March 1, 1991.

**(7) User fee**

In addition to any charge imposed pursuant to paragraph (2) of this subsection, the Administrator shall collect user fees from persons seeking certification under the radon proficiency program in an amount equal to $1,500,000 to cover the Environmental Protection Agency's cost of conducting research pursuant to paragraph (5) for each of the fiscal years 1991, 1992, 1993, 1994, and 1995. Such funds shall be deposited in the account established pursuant to paragraph (3).

**(e) Authorization**

**(1)** There is authorized to be appropriated for the purposes of carrying out sections 2663, 2664, and 2665 of this title an amount not to exceed $3,000,000 for each of fiscal years 1989, 1990, and 1991.

**(2)** No amount appropriated under this subsection may be used by the Environmental Protection Agency to administer the grant program under section 2666 of this title.

**(3)** No amount appropriated under this subsection may be used to cover the costs of the proficiency rating program under subsection (a)(2) of this section.

(Pub.L. 94–469, Title III, § 305, as added Pub.L. 100–551, § 1(a), Oct. 28, 1988, 102 Stat. 2756, and amended Pub.L. 101–508, Title X, § 10202, Nov. 5, 1990, 104 Stat. 1388–393; Pub.L. 104–66, Title II, § 2021(*l*), Dec. 21, 1995, 109 Stat. 728.)

### HISTORICAL AND STATUTORY NOTES

**References in Text**

Section 403(c) of the Superfund Amendments and Reauthorization Act of 1986, referred to in subsec. (d), is section 403(c) of Pub.L. 99–499, which is set out as a note under section 7401 of Title 42, The Public Health and Welfare.

## § 2666. Grant assistance to States for radon programs

**[TSCA § 306]**

**(a) In general**

For each fiscal year, upon application of the Governor of a State, the Administrator may make a grant, subject to such terms and conditions as the Administrator considers appropriate, under this section to the State for the purpose of assisting the State in the development and implementation of programs for the assessment and mitigation of radon.

**(b) Application**

An application for a grant under this section in any fiscal year shall contain such information as the Administrator shall require, including each of the following:

**(1)** A description of the seriousness and extent of radon exposure in the State.

**(2)** An identification of the State agency which has the primary responsibility for radon programs and which will receive the grant, a description of the roles and responsibilities of the lead State agency and any other State agencies involved in radon programs, and description of the roles and responsibilities of any municipal, district, or areawide organization involved in radon programs.

(3) A description of the activities and programs related to radon which the State proposes in such year.

(4) A budget specifying Federal and State funding of each element of activity of the grant application.

(5) A 3-year plan which outlines long range program goals and objectives, tasks necessary to achieve them, and resource requirements for the entire 3-year period, including anticipated State funding levels and desired Federal funding levels. This clause shall apply only for the initial year in which a grant application is made.

**(c) Eligible activities**

Activities eligible for grant assistance under this section are the following:

(1) Survey of radon levels, including special surveys of geographic areas or classes of buildings (such as, among others, public buildings, school buildings, high-risk residential construction types).

(2) Development of public information and educational materials concerning radon assessment, mitigation, and control programs.

(3) Implementation of programs to control radon in existing and new structures.

(4) Purchase by the State of radon measurement equipment or devices.

(5) Purchase and maintenance of analytical equipment connected to radon measurement and analysis, including costs of calibration of such equipment.

(6) Payment of costs of Environmental Protection Agency-approved training programs related to radon for permanent State or local employees.

(7) Payment of general overhead and program administration costs.

(8) Development of a data storage and management system for information concerning radon occurrence, levels, and programs.

(9) Payment of costs of demonstration of radon mitigation methods and technologies as approved by the Administrator, including State participation in the Environmental Protection Agency Home Evaluation Program.

(10) A toll-free radon hotline to provide information and technical assistance.

**(d) Preference to certain States**

Beginning in fiscal year 1991, the Administrator shall give a preference for grant assistance under this section to States that have made reasonable efforts to ensure the adoption, by the authorities which regulate building construction within that State or political subdivisions within States, of the model construction standards and techniques for new buildings developed under section 2664 of this title.

**(e) Priority activities and projects**

The Administrator shall support eligible activities contained in State applications with the full amount of available funds. In the event that State applications for funds exceed the total funds available in a fiscal year, the Administrator shall give priority to activities or projects proposed by States based on each of the following criteria:

(1) The seriousness and extent of the radon contamination problem to be addressed.

(2) The potential for the activity or project to bring about reduction in radon levels.

(3) The potential for development of innovative radon assessment techniques, mitigation measures as approved by the Administrator, or program management approaches which may be of use to other States.

(4) Any other uniform criteria that the Administrator deems necessary to promote the goals of the grant program and that the Administrator provides to States before the application process.

**(f) Federal share**

The Federal share of the cost of radon program activities implemented with Federal assistance under this section in any fiscal year shall not exceed 75 percent of the costs incurred by the State in implementing such program in the first year of a grant to such State, 60 percent in the second year, and 50 percent in the third year. Federal assistance shall be made on the condition that the non-Federal share is provided from non-Federal funds.

**(g) Assistance to local governments**

States may, at the Governor's discretion, use funds from grants under this section to assist local governments in implementation of activities eligible for assistance under paragraphs (2), (3), and (6) of subsection (c) of this section.

**(h) Information**

(1) The Administrator may request such information, data, and reports developed by the State as he considers necessary to make the determination of continuing eligibility under this section.

(2) Any State receiving funds under this section shall provide to the Administrator all radon-related information generated in its activities, including the results of radon surveys, mitigation demonstration projects, and risk communication studies.

(3) Any State receiving funds under this section shall maintain, and make available to the public, a list of firms and individuals within the State that have received a passing rating under the Environmental Protection Agency proficiency rating program referred to in section 2665(a)(2) of this title. The list shall also include the address and phone number of such firms and individuals, together with the proficiency rating received by each. The Administrator shall make such list available to the public at appropriate locations in each State which does not receive funds under this section unless the State assumes such responsibility.

**(i) Limitations**

(1) No grant may be made under this section in any fiscal year to a State which in the preceding fiscal year received a grant under this section unless the Administrator determines that such State satisfactorily implemented the activities funded by the grant in such preceding fiscal year.

(2) The costs of implementing paragraphs (4) and (9) of subsection (c) of this section shall not in the aggregate exceed 50 percent of the amount of any grant awarded under this section to a State in a fiscal year. In implementing such paragraphs, a State should make every effort, consistent with the goals and successful operation of the State radon program, to give a preference to low-income persons.

(3) The costs of general overhead and program administration under subsection (c)(7) of this section shall not exceed 25 percent of the amount of any grant awarded under this section to a State in a fiscal year.

(4) A State may use funds received under this section for financial assistance to persons only to the extent such assistance is related to demonstration projects or the purchase and analysis of radon measurement devices.

**(j) Authorization**

(1) There is authorized to be appropriated for grant assistance under this section an amount not to exceed $10,000,000 for each of fiscal years 1989, 1990, and 1991.

(2) There is authorized to be appropriated for the purpose of administering the grant program under this section such sums as may be necessary for each of such fiscal years.

(3) Notwithstanding any other provision of this section, not more than 10 percent of the amount appropriated to carry out this section may be used to make grants to any one State.

(4) Funds not obligated to States in the fiscal year for which funds are appropriated under this section shall remain available for obligation during the next fiscal year.

(5) No amount appropriated under this subsection may be used to cover the costs of the proficiency rating program under section 2665(a)(2) of this title.

(Pub.L. 94–469, Title III, § 306, as added Pub.L. 100–551, § 1(a), Oct. 28, 1988, 102 Stat. 2758.)

## § 2667. Radon in schools

**[TSCA § 307]**

**(a) Study of radon in schools**

**(1) Authority**

The Administrator shall conduct a study for the purpose of determining the extent of radon contamination in the Nation's school buildings.

**(2) List of high probability areas**

In carrying out such study, the Administrator shall identify and compile a list of areas within the United States which the Administrator determines have a high probability of including schools which have elevated levels of radon.

**(3) Basis of list**

In compiling such list, the Administrator shall make such determinations on the basis of, among other things, each of the following:

(A) Geological data.

(B) Data on high radon levels in homes and other structures nearby any such school.

(C) Physical characteristics of the school buildings.

**(4) Survey**

In conducting such study the Administrator shall design a survey which when completed allows Congress to characterize the extent of radon contamination in schools in each State. The survey shall include testing from a representative sample of schools in each high-risk area identified in paragraph (1) and shall include additional testing, to the extent resources are available for such testing. The survey also shall include any reliable testing data supplied by States, schools, or other parties.

**(5) Assistance**

(A) The Administrator shall make available to the appropriate agency of each State, as designated by the Governor of such State, a list of high risk areas within each State, including a delineation of such areas and any other data available to the Administrator for schools in that State. To assist such agencies, the Administrator also shall provide guidance and data detailing the risks associated with high radon levels, technical guidance and related information concerning testing for radon within schools, and methods of reducing radon levels.

(B) In addition to the assistance authorized by subparagraph (A), the Administrator is authorized to make available to the appropriate agency of each State, as designated by the Governor of such State, devices suitable for use by such agencies in conducting tests for radon within the schools under the jurisdiction of any such State agency. The Administrator is authorized to make available to such agencies the use of laboratories of the Environmental Protection Agency, or to recommend laboratories, to evaluate any such devices for the presence of radon levels.

**(6) Diagnostic and remedial efforts**

The Administrator is authorized to select, from high-risk areas identified in paragraph (2), school buildings for purposes of enabling the Administrator to undertake diagnostic and remedial efforts to reduce the levels of radon in such school buildings. Such diagnostic and remedial efforts shall be carried out with a view to developing technology and expertise for the purpose of making such technology and expertise available to any local educational agency and the several States.

**(7) Status report**

On or before October 1, 1989, the Administrator shall submit to the Congress a status report with respect to action taken by the Administrator in conducting the study required by this section, including the results of the Administrator's diagnostic and remedial work. On or before October 1, 1989, the Administrator shall submit a final report setting forth the results of the study conducted pursuant to this section, including the results of the Administrator's diagnostic and remedial work, and the recommendations of the Administrator.

**(b) Authorization**

For the purpose of carrying out the provisions of paragraph (6) of subsection (a) of this section, there are authorized to be appropriated such sums, not to exceed $500,000, as may be necessary. For the purpose of carrying out the provisions of this section other than such paragraph (6), there are authorized to be appropriated such sums, not to exceed $1,000,000, as may be necessary.

(Pub.L. 94–469, Title III, § 307, as added Pub.L. 100–551, § 1(a), Oct. 28, 1988, 102 Stat. 2761.)

## § 2668. Regional radon training centers

[TSCA § 308]

**(a) Funding program**

Upon application of colleges, universities, institutions of higher learning, or consortia of such institutions, the Administrator may make a grant or cooperative agreement, subject to such terms and conditions as the Administrator considers appropriate, under this section to the applicant for the purpose of establishing and operating a regional radon training center.

**(b) Purpose of centers**

The purpose of a regional radon training center is to develop information and provide training to Federal and State officials, professional and private firms, and the public regarding the health risks posed by radon and demonstrated methods of radon measurement and mitigation.

**(c) Applications**

Any colleges, universities, institutions of higher learning or consortia of such institutions may submit an application for funding under this section. Such applications shall be submitted to the Administrator in such form and containing such information as the Administrator may require.

**(d) Selection criteria**

The Administrator shall support at least 3 eligible applications with the full amount of available funds. The Administrator shall select recipients of funding under this section to ensure that funds are equitably allocated among regions of the United States, and on the basis of each of the following criteria:

(1) The extent to which the applicant's program will promote the purpose described in subsection (b) of this section.

(2) The demonstrated expertise of the applicant regarding radon measurement and mitigation methods and other radon-related issues.

(3) The demonstrated expertise of the applicant in radon training and in activities relating to information development and dissemination.

(4) The seriousness of the radon problem in the region.

(5) The geographical coverage of the proposed center.

(6) Any other uniform criteria that the Administrator deems necessary to promote the purpose described in subsection (b) of this section and that the Administrator provides to potential applicants prior to the application process.

**(e) Termination of funding**

No funding may be given under this section in any fiscal year to an applicant which in the preceding fiscal year received funding under this section unless the Administrator determines that the recipient satisfactorily implemented the activities that were funded in the preceding year.

**(f) Authorization**

There is authorized to be appropriated to carry out the program under this section not to exceed $1,000,000 for each of fiscal years 1989, 1990, and 1991.

(Pub.L. 94–469, Title III, § 308, as added Pub.L. 100–551, § 1(a), Oct. 28, 1988, 102 Stat. 2762.)

## § 2669. Study of radon in Federal buildings

**[TSCA § 309]**

### (a) Study requirement

The head of each Federal department or agency that owns a Federal building shall conduct a study for the purpose of determining the extent of radon contamination in such buildings. Such study shall include, in the case of a Federal building using a nonpublic water source (such as a well or other groundwater), radon contamination of the water.

### (b) High-risk Federal buildings

(1) The Administrator shall identify and compile a list of areas within the United States which the Administrator, in consultation with Federal departments and agencies, determines have a high probability of including Federal buildings which have elevated levels of radon.

(2) In compiling such list, the Administrator shall make such determinations on the basis of, among other things, the following:

(A) Geological data.

(B) Data on high radon levels in homes and other structures near any such Federal building.

(C) Physical characteristics of the Federal buildings.

### (c) Study designs

Studies required under subsection (a) of this section shall be based on design criteria specified by the Administrator. The head of each Federal department or agency conducting such a study shall submit, not later than July 1, 1989, a study design to the Administrator for approval. The study design shall follow the most recent Environmental Protection Agency guidance documents, including "A Citizen's Guide to Radon"; the "Interim Protocol for Screening and Follow Up: Radon and Radon Decay Products Measurements"; the "Interim Indoor Radon & Radon Decay Product Measurement Protocol"; and any other recent guidance documents. The study design shall include testing data from a representative sample of Federal buildings in each high-risk area identified in subsection (b) of this section. The study design also shall include additional testing data to the extent resources are available, including any reliable data supplied by Federal agencies, States, or other parties.

### (d) Information on risks and testing

(1) The Administrator shall provide to the departments or agencies conducting studies under subsection (a) of this section the following:

(A) Guidance and data detailing the risks associated with high radon levels.

(B) Technical guidance and related information concerning testing for radon within Federal buildings and water supplies.

(C) Technical guidance and related information concerning methods for reducing radon levels.

(2) In addition to the assistance required by paragraph (1), the Administrator is authorized to make available, on a cost reimbursable basis, to the departments or agencies conducting studies under subsection (a) of this section devices suitable for use by such departments or agencies in conducting tests for radon within Federal buildings. For the purpose of assisting such departments or agencies in evaluating any such devices for the presence of radon levels, the Administrator is authorized to recommend laboratories or to make available to such departments or agencies, on a cost reimbursable basis, the use of laboratories of the Environmental Protection Agency.

### (e) Study deadline

Not later than June 1, 1990, the head of each Federal department or agency conducting a study under subsection (a) of this section shall complete the study and provide the study to the Administrator.

### (f) Report to Congress

Not later than October 1, 1990, the Administrator shall submit a report to the Congress describing the results of the studies conducted pursuant to subsection (a) of this section.

(Pub.L. 94–469, Title III, § 309, as added Pub.L. 100–551, § 1(a), Oct. 28, 1988, 102 Stat. 2763.)

## § 2670. Regulations

**[TSCA § 310]**

The Administrator is authorized to issue such regulations as may be necessary to carry out the provisions of this subchapter.

(Pub.L. 94–469, Title III, § 310, as added Pub.L. 100–551, § 1(a), Oct. 28, 1988, 102 Stat. 2764.)

## § 2671. Additional authorizations

**[TSCA § 311]**

Amounts authorized to be appropriated in this subchapter for purposes of carrying out the provisions of this subchapter are in addition to amounts authorized to be appropriated under other provisions of law for radon-related activities.

(Pub.L. 94–469, Title III, § 311, as added Pub.L. 100–551, § 1(a), Oct. 28, 1988, 102 Stat. 2764.)

## SUBCHAPTER IV—LEAD EXPOSURE REDUCTION

### § 2681. Definitions

[TSCA § 401]

For the purposes of this subchapter:

**(1) Abatement**

The term "abatement" means any set of measures designed to permanently eliminate lead-based paint hazards in accordance with standards established by the Administrator under this subchapter. Such term includes—

(A) the removal of lead-based paint and lead-contaminated dust, the permanent containment or encapsulation of lead-based paint, the replacement of lead-painted surfaces or fixtures, and the removal or covering of lead-contaminated soil; and

(B) all preparation, cleanup, disposal, and postabatement clearance testing activities associated with such measures.

**(2) Accessible surface**

The term "accessible surface" means an interior or exterior surface painted with lead-based paint that is accessible for a young child to mouth or chew.

**(3) Deteriorated paint**

The term "deteriorated paint" means any interior or exterior paint that is peeling, chipping, chalking or cracking or any paint located on an interior or exterior surface or fixture that is damaged or deteriorated.

**(4) Evaluation**

The term "evaluation" means risk assessment, inspection, or risk assessment and inspection.

**(5) Friction surface**

The term "friction surface" means an interior or exterior surface that is subject to abrasion or friction, including certain window, floor, and stair surfaces.

**(6) Impact surface**

The term "impact surface" means an interior or exterior surface that is subject to damage by repeated impacts, for example, certain parts of door frames.

**(7) Inspection**

The term "inspection" means (A) a surface-by-surface investigation to determine the presence of lead-based paint, as provided in section 4822(c) of Title 42, and (B) the provision of a report explaining the results of the investigation.

**(8) Interim controls**

The term "interim controls" means a set of measures designed to reduce temporarily human exposure or likely exposure to lead-based paint hazards, including specialized cleaning, repairs, maintenance, painting, temporary containment, ongoing monitoring of lead-based paint hazards or potential hazards, and the establishment and operation of management and resident education programs.

**(9) Lead-based paint**

The term "lead-based paint" means paint or other surface coatings that contain lead in excess of 1.0 milligrams per centimeter squared or 0.5 percent by weight or (A) in the case of paint or other surface coatings on target housing, such lower level as may be established by the Secretary of Housing and Urban Development, as defined in section 4822(c) of Title 42, or (B) in the case of any other paint or surface coatings, such other level as may be established by the Administrator.

**(10) Lead-based paint hazard**

The term "lead-based paint hazard" means any condition that causes exposure to lead from lead-contaminated dust, lead-contaminated soil, lead-contaminated paint that is deteriorated or present in accessible surfaces, friction surfaces, or impact surfaces that would result in adverse human health effects as established by the Administrator under this subchapter.

**(11) Lead-contaminated dust**

The term "lead-contaminated dust" means surface dust in residential dwellings that contains an area or mass concentration of lead in excess of levels determined by the Administrator under this subchapter to pose a threat of adverse health effects in pregnant women or young children.

**(12) Lead-contaminated soil**

The term "lead-contaminated soil" means bare soil on residential real property that contains lead at or in excess of the levels determined to be hazardous to human health by the Administrator under this subchapter.

**(13) Reduction**

The term "reduction" means measures designed to reduce or eliminate human exposure to lead-based paint hazards through methods including interim controls and abatement.

**(14) Residential dwelling**

The term "residential dwelling" means—

(A) a single-family dwelling, including attached structures such as porches and stoops; or

(B) a single-family dwelling unit in a structure that contains more than 1 separate residential dwelling unit, and in which each such unit is used or occupied, or intended to be used or occupied, in whole or in part, as the home or residence of 1 or more persons.

**(15) Residential real property**

The term "residential real property" means real property on which there is situated 1 or more residential dwellings used or occupied, or intended to be used or occupied, in whole or in part, as the home or residence of 1 or more persons.

**(16) Risk assessment**

The term "risk assessment" means an on-site investigation to determine and report the existence, nature, severity and location of lead-based paint hazards in residential dwellings, including—

(A) information gathering regarding the age and history of the housing and occupancy by children under age 6;

(B) visual inspection;

(C) limited wipe sampling or other environmental sampling techniques;

(D) other activity as may be appropriate; and

(E) provision of a report explaining the results of the investigation.

**(17) Target housing**

The term "target housing" means any housing constructed prior to 1978, except housing for the elderly or persons with disabilities (unless any child who is less than 6 years of age resides or is expected to reside in such housing for the elderly or persons with disabilities) or any 0–bedroom dwelling. In the case of jurisdictions which banned the sale or use of lead-based paint prior to 1978, the Secretary of Housing and Urban Development, at the Secretary's discretion, may designate an earlier date.

(Pub.L. 94–469, Title IV, § 401, as added Pub.L. 102–550, Title X, § 1021(a), Oct. 28, 1992, 106 Stat. 3912.)

## § 2682. Lead-based paint activities training and certification

**[TSCA § 402]**

**(a) Regulations**

**(1) In general**

Not later than 18 months after October 28, 1992, the Administrator shall, in consultation with the Secretary of Labor, the Secretary of Housing and Urban Development, and the Secretary of Health and Human Services (acting through the Director of the National Institute for Occupational Safety and Health), promulgate final regulations governing lead-based paint activities to ensure that individuals engaged in such activities are properly trained; that training programs are accredited; and that contractors engaged in such activities are certified. Such regulations shall contain standards for performing lead-based paint activities, taking into account reliability, effectiveness, and safety. Such regulations shall require that all risk assessment, inspection, and abatement activities performed in target housing shall be performed by certified contractors, as such term is defined in section 4851b of Title 42. The provisions of this section shall supersede the provisions set forth under the heading "Lead Abatement Training and Certification" and under the heading "Training Grants" in title III of the Act entitled "An Act making appropriations for the Departments of Veterans Affairs and Housing and Urban Development, and for sundry independent agencies, commissions, corporations, and offices for the fiscal year ending September 30, 1992, and for other purposes", Public Law 102–139 [105 Stat. 765, 42 U.S.C.A. 4822 note], and upon October 28, 1992, the provisions set forth in such public law under such headings shall cease to have any force and effect.

**(2) Accreditation of training programs**

Final regulations promulgated under paragraph (1) shall contain specific requirements for the accreditation of lead-based paint activities training programs for workers, supervisors, inspectors and planners, and other individuals involved in lead-based paint activities, including, but not limited to, each of the following:

(A) Minimum requirements for the accreditation of training providers.

(B) Minimum training curriculum requirements.

(C) Minimum training hour requirements.

(D) Minimum hands-on training requirements.

(E) Minimum trainee competency and proficiency requirements.

(F) Minimum requirements for training program quality control.

**(3) Accreditation and certification fees**

The Administrator (or the State in the case of an authorized State program) shall impose a fee on—

(A) persons operating training programs accredited under this subchapter; and

(B) lead-based paint activities contractors certified in accordance with paragraph (1).

The fees shall be established at such level as is necessary to cover the costs of administering and enforcing the standards and regulations under this section which are applicable to such programs and contractors. The fee shall not be imposed on any State, local government, or nonprofit training program. The Administrator (or the State in the case of an authorized State program) may waive the fee for lead-based paint activities contractors under subparagraph (A) for the purpose of training their own employees.

**(b) Lead-based paint activities**

For purposes of this subchapter, the term "lead-based paint activities" means—

(1) in the case of target housing, risk assessment, inspection, and abatement; and

(2) in the case of any public building constructed before 1978, commercial building, bridge, or other structure or superstructure, identification of lead-based paint and materials containing lead-based paint, deleading, removal of lead from bridges, and demolition.

For purposes of paragraph (2), the term "deleading" means activities conducted by a person who offers to eliminate lead-based paint or lead-based paint hazards or to plan such activities.

**(c) Renovation and remodeling**

**(1) Guidelines**

In order to reduce the risk of exposure to lead in connection with renovation and remodeling of target housing, public buildings constructed before 1978, and commercial buildings, the Administrator shall, within 18 months after October 28, 1992, promulgate guidelines for the conduct of such renovation and remodeling activities which may create a risk of exposure to dangerous levels of lead. The Administrator shall disseminate such guidelines to persons engaged in such renovation and remodeling through hardware and paint stores, employee organizations, trade groups, State and local agencies, and through other appropriate means.

**(2) Study of certification**

The Administrator shall conduct a study of the extent to which persons engaged in various types of renovation and remodeling activities in target housing, public buildings constructed before 1978, and commercial buildings are exposed to lead in the conduct of such activities or disturb lead and create a lead-based paint hazard on a regular or occasional basis. The Administrator shall complete such study and publish the results thereof within 30 months after October 28, 1992.

**(3) Certification determination**

Within 4 years after October 28, 1992, the Administrator shall revise the regulations under subsection (a) of this section to apply the regulations to renovation or remodeling activities in target housing, public buildings constructed before 1978, and commercial buildings that create lead-based paint hazards. In determining which contractors are engaged in such activities, the Administrator shall utilize the results of the study under paragraph (2) and consult with the representatives of labor organizations, lead-based paint activities contractors, persons engaged in remodeling and renovation, experts in lead health effects, and others. If the Administrator determines that any category of contractors engaged in renovation or remodeling does not require certification, the Administrator shall publish an explanation of the basis for that determination.

(Pub.L. 94–469, Title IV, § 402, as added Pub.L. 102–550, Title X, § 1021(a), Oct. 28, 1992, 106 Stat. 3914.)

## § 2683. Identification of dangerous levels of lead

**[TSCA § 403]**

Within 18 months after October 28, 1992, the Administrator shall promulgate regulations which shall identify, for purposes of this subchapter and the Residential Lead–Based Paint Hazard Reduction Act of 1992 [42 U.S.C.A. § 4851 et seq.], lead-based paint hazards, lead-contaminated dust, and lead-contaminated soil.

(Pub.L. 94–469, Title IV, § 403, as added Pub.L. 102–550, Title X, § 1021(a), Oct. 28, 1992, 106 Stat. 3916.)

### HISTORICAL AND STATUTORY NOTES

**References in Text**

The Residential Lead-Based Paint Hazard Reduction Act of 1992, referred to in text, is Title X of Pub.L. 102–550, Oct. 28, 1992, 106 Stat. 3897, which is classified principally to chapter 63A (§ 4851 et seq.) of Title 42, The Public Health and Welfare. For complete classification of this Act to the Code, see Short Title note set out under section 4851 of Title 42 and Tables.

## § 2684. Authorized State programs

**[TSCA § 404]**

**(a) Approval**

Any State which seeks to administer and enforce the standards, regulations, or other requirements established under section 2682 or 2686 of this title, or both, may, after notice and opportunity for public hearing, develop and submit to the Administrator an application, in such form as the Administrator shall require, for authorization of such a State program. Any such State may also certify to the Administrator at the time of submitting such program that the State program meets the requirements of paragraphs (1) and (2) of subsection (b) of this section. Upon submission of such certification, the State program shall be deemed to be authorized under this section, and shall apply in such State in lieu of the corresponding Federal program under section 2682 or 2686 of this title, or both, as the case may be, until such time as the Administrator disapproves the program or withdraws the authorization.

**(b) Approval or disapproval**

Within 180 days following submission of an application under subsection (a) of this section, the Administrator shall approve or disapprove the application. The Administrator may approve the application only if, after notice and after opportunity for public hearing, the Administrator finds that—

(1) the State program is at least as protective of human health and the environment as the Federal program under section 2682 or 2686 of this title, or both, as the case may be, and

(2) such State program provides adequate enforcement.

Upon authorization of a State program under this section, it shall be unlawful for any person to violate or fail or refuse to comply with any requirement of such program.

**(c) Withdrawal of authorization**

If a State is not administering and enforcing a program authorized under this section in compliance with standards, regulations, and other requirements of this subchapter, the Administrator shall so notify the State and, if corrective action is not completed within a reasonable time, not to exceed 180 days, the Administrator shall withdraw authorization of such program and establish a Federal program pursuant to this subchapter.

**(d) Model State program**

Within 18 months after October 28, 1992, the Administrator shall promulgate a model State program which may be adopted by any State which seeks to administer and enforce a State program under this subchapter. Such model program shall, to the extent practicable, encourage States to utilize existing State and local certification and accreditation programs and procedures. Such program shall encourage reciprocity among the States with respect to the certification under section 2682 of this title.

**(e) Other State requirements**

Nothing in this subchapter shall be construed to prohibit any State or political subdivision thereof from imposing any requirements which are more stringent than those imposed by this subchapter.

**(f) State and local certification**

The regulations under this subchapter shall, to the extent appropriate, encourage States to seek program authorization and to use existing State and local certification and accreditation procedures, except that a State or local government shall not require more than 1 certification under this section for any lead-based paint activities contractor to carry out lead-based paint activities in the State or political subdivision thereof.

**(g) Grants to States**

The Administrator is authorized to make grants to States to develop and carry out authorized State programs under this section. The grants shall be subject to such terms and conditions as the Administrator may establish to further the purposes of this subchapter.

**(h) Enforcement by Administrator**

If a State does not have a State program authorized under this section and in effect by the date which is 2 years after promulgation of the regulations under section 2682 or 2686 of this title, the Administrator shall, by such date, establish a Federal program for section 2682 or 2686 of this title (as the case may be) for such State and administer and enforce such program in such State.

(Pub.L. 94–469, Title IV, § 404, as added Pub.L. 102–550, Title X, § 1021(a), Oct. 28, 1992, 106 Stat. 3916.)

## § 2685. Lead abatement and measurement

[TSCA § 405]

**(a) Program to promote lead exposure abatement**

The Administrator, in cooperation with other appropriate Federal departments and agencies, shall conduct a comprehensive program to promote safe, effective, and affordable monitoring, detection, and abatement of lead-based paint and other lead exposure hazards.

**(b) Standards for environmental sampling laboratories**

(1) The Administrator shall establish protocols, criteria, and minimum performance standards for laboratory analysis of lead in paint films, soil, and dust. Within 2 years after October 28, 1992, the Administrator, in consultation with the Secretary of Health and Human Services, shall establish a program to certify laboratories as qualified to test substances for lead content unless the Administrator determines, by the date specified in this paragraph, that effective voluntary accreditation programs are in place and operating on a nationwide basis at the time of such determination. To be certified under such program, a laboratory shall, at a minimum, demonstrate an ability to test substances accurately for lead content.

(2) Not later than 24 months after October 28, 1992, and annually thereafter, the Administrator shall publish and make available to the public a list of

certified or accredited environmental sampling laboratories.

(3) If the Administrator determines under paragraph (1) that effective voluntary accreditation programs are in place for environmental sampling laboratories, the Administrator shall review the performance and effectiveness of such programs within 3 years after such determination. If, upon such review, the Administrator determines that the voluntary accreditation programs are not effective in assuring the quality and consistency of laboratory analyses, the Administrator shall, not more than 12 months thereafter, establish a certification program that meets the requirements of paragraph (1).

**(c) Exposure studies**

(1) The Secretary of Health and Human Services (hereafter in this subsection referred to as the "Secretary"), acting through the Director of the Centers for Disease Control,[1] (CDC), and the Director of the National Institute of Environmental Health Sciences, shall jointly conduct a study of the sources of lead exposure in children who have elevated blood lead levels (or other indicators of elevated lead body burden), as defined by the Director of the Centers for Disease Control.

(2) The Secretary, in consultation with the Director of the National Institute for Occupational Safety and Health, shall conduct a comprehensive study of means to reduce hazardous occupational lead abatement exposures. This study shall include, at a minimum, each of the following—

(A) Surveillance and intervention capability in the States to identify and prevent hazardous exposures to lead abatement workers.

(B) Demonstration of lead abatement control methods and devices and work practices to identify and prevent hazardous lead exposures in the workplace.

(C) Evaluation, in consultation with the National Institute of Environmental Health Sciences, of health effects of low and high levels of occupational lead exposures on reproductive, neurological, renal, and cardiovascular health.

(D) Identification of high risk occupational settings to which prevention activities and resources should be targeted.

(E) A study assessing the potential exposures and risks from lead to janitorial and custodial workers.

(3) The studies described in paragraphs (1) and (2) shall, as appropriate, examine the relative contributions to elevated lead body burden from each of the following:

(A) Drinking water.

(B) Food.

(C) Lead-based paint and dust from lead-based paint.

(D) Exterior sources such as ambient air and lead in soil.

(E) Occupational exposures, and other exposures that the Secretary determines to be appropriate.

(4) Not later than 30 months after October 28, 1992, the Secretary shall submit a report to the Congress concerning the studies described in paragraphs (1) and (2).

**(d) Public education**

(1) The Administrator, in conjunction with the Secretary of Health and Human Services, acting through the Director of the Agency for Toxic Substances and Disease Registry, and in conjunction with the Secretary of Housing and Urban Development, shall sponsor public education and outreach activities to increase public awareness of—

(A) the scope and severity of lead poisoning from household sources;

(B) potential exposure to sources of lead in schools and childhood day care centers;

(C) the implications of exposures for men and women, particularly those of childbearing age;

(D) the need for careful, quality, abatement and management actions;

(E) the need for universal screening of children;

(F) other components of a lead poisoning prevention program;

(G) the health consequences of lead exposure resulting from lead-based paint hazards;

(H) risk assessment and inspection methods for lead-based paint hazards; and

(I) measures to reduce the risk of lead exposure from lead-based paint.

(2) The activities described in paragraph (1) shall be designed to provide educational services and information to—

(A) health professionals;

(B) the general public, with emphasis on parents of young children;

(C) homeowners, landlords, and tenants;

(D) consumers of home improvement products;

(E) the residential real estate industry; and

(F) the home renovation industry.

(3) In implementing the activities described in paragraph (1), the Administrator shall assure coordination with the President's Commission on Environ-

mental Quality's education and awareness campaign on lead poisoning.

(4) The Administrator, in consultation with the Chairman of the Consumer Product Safety Commission, shall develop information to be distributed by retailers of home improvement products to provide consumers with practical information related to the hazards of renovation and remodeling where lead-based paint may be present.

**(e) Technical assistance**

**(1) Clearinghouse**

Not later than 6 months after October 28, 1992, the Administrator shall establish, in consultation with the Secretary of Housing and Urban Development and the Director of the Centers for Disease Control, a National Clearinghouse on Childhood Lead Poisoning (hereinafter in this section referred to as "Clearinghouse"). The Clearinghouse shall—

(A) collect, evaluate, and disseminate current information on the assessment and reduction of lead-based paint hazards, adverse health effects, sources of exposure, detection and risk assessment methods, environmental hazards abatement, and clean-up standards;

(B) maintain a rapid-alert system to inform certified lead-based paint activities contractors of significant developments in research related to lead-based paint hazards; and

(C) perform any other duty that the Administrator determines necessary to achieve the purposes of this chapter.

**(2) Hotline**

Not later than 6 months after October 28, 1992, the Administrator, in cooperation with other Federal agencies and with State and local governments, shall establish a single lead-based paint hazard hotline to provide the public with answers to questions about lead poisoning prevention and referrals to the Clearinghouse for technical information.

**(f) Products for lead-based paint activities**

Not later than 30 months after October 28, 1992, the President shall, after notice and opportunity for comment, establish by rule appropriate criteria, testing protocols, and performance characteristics as are necessary to ensure, to the greatest extent possible and consistent with the purposes and policy of this subchapter, that lead-based paint hazard evaluation and reduction products introduced into commerce after a period specified in the rule are effective for the intended use described by the manufacturer. The rule shall identify the types or classes of products that are subject to such rule. The President, in implementation of the rule, shall, to the maximum extent possible, utilize independent testing laboratories, as appropriate, and consult with such entities and others in developing the rules. The President may delegate the authorities under this subsection to the Environmental Protection Agency or the Secretary of Commerce or such other appropriate agency.

(Pub.L. 94–469, Title IV, § 405, as added Pub.L. 102–550, Title X, § 1021(a), Oct. 28, 1992, 106 Stat. 3917.)

1 So in original. The comma probably should not appear.

## § 2686. Lead hazard information pamphlet [TSCA § 406]

**(a) Lead hazard information pamphlet**

Not later than 2 years after October 28, 1992, after notice and opportunity for comment, the Administrator of the Environmental Protection Agency, in consultation with the Secretary of Housing and Urban Development and with the Secretary of Health and Human Services, shall publish, and from time to time revise, a lead hazard information pamphlet to be used in connection with this subchapter and section 4852d of Title 42. The pamphlet shall—

(1) contain information regarding the health risks associated with exposure to lead;

(2) provide information on the presence of lead-based paint hazards in federally assisted, federally owned, and target housing;

(3) describe the risks of lead exposure for children under 6 years of age, pregnant women, women of childbearing age, persons involved in home renovation, and others residing in a dwelling with lead-based paint hazards;

(4) describe the risks of renovation in a dwelling with lead-based paint hazards;

(5) provide information on approved methods for evaluating and reducing lead-based paint hazards and their effectiveness in identifying, reducing, eliminating, or preventing exposure to lead-based paint hazards;

(6) advise persons how to obtain a list of contractors certified pursuant to this subchapter in lead-based paint hazard evaluation and reduction in the area in which the pamphlet is to be used;

(7) state that a risk assessment or inspection for lead-based paint is recommended prior to the purchase, lease, or renovation of target housing;

(8) state that certain State and local laws impose additional requirements related to lead-based paint in housing and provide a listing of Federal, State, and local agencies in each State, including address and telephone number, that can provide information about applicable laws and available governmental and private assistance and financing; and

(9) provide such other information about environmental hazards associated with residential real property as the Administrator deems appropriate.

**(b) Renovation of target housing**

Within 2 years after October 28, 1992, the Administrator shall promulgate regulations under this subsection to require each person who performs for compensation a renovation of target housing to provide a lead hazard information pamphlet to the owner and occupant of such housing prior to commencing the renovation.

(Pub.L. 94–469, Title IV, § 406, as added Pub.L. 102–550, Title X, § 1021(a), Oct. 28, 1992, 106 Stat. 3920.)

## § 2687. Regulations

**[TSCA § 407]**

The regulations of the Administrator under this subchapter shall include such recordkeeping and reporting requirements as may be necessary to insure the effective implementation of this subchapter. The regulations may be amended from time to time as necessary.

(Pub.L. 94–469, Title IV, § 407, as added Pub.L. 102–550, Title X, § 1021(a), Oct. 28, 1992, 106 Stat. 3921.)

## § 2688. Control of lead-based paint hazards at Federal facilities

**[TSCA § 408]**

Each department, agency, and instrumentality of executive, legislative, and judicial branches of the Federal Government (1) having jurisdiction over any property or facility, or (2) engaged in any activity resulting, or which may result, in a lead-based paint hazard, and each officer, agent, or employee thereof, shall be subject to, and comply with, all Federal, State, interstate, and local requirements, both substantive and procedural (including any requirement for certification, licensing, recordkeeping, or reporting or any provisions for injunctive relief and such sanctions as may be imposed by a court to enforce such relief) respecting lead-based paint, lead-based paint activities, and lead-based paint hazards in the same manner, and to the same extent as any nongovernmental entity is subject to such requirements, including the payment of reasonable service charges. The Federal, State, interstate, and local substantive and procedural requirements referred to in this subsection include, but are not limited to, all administrative orders and all civil and administrative penalties and fines regardless of whether such penalties or fines are punitive or coercive in nature, or whether imposed for isolated, intermittent or continuing violations. The United States hereby expressly waives any immunity otherwise applicable to the United States with respect to any such substantive or procedural requirement (including, but not limited to, any injunctive relief, administrative order, or civil or administrative penalty or fine referred to in the preceding sentence, or reasonable service charge). The reasonable service charges referred to in this section include, but are not limited to, fees or charges assessed for certification and licensing, as well as any other nondiscriminatory charges that are assessed in connection with a Federal, State, interstate, or local lead-based paint, lead-based paint activities, or lead-based paint hazard activities program. No agent, employee, or officer of the United States shall be personally liable for any civil penalty under any Federal, State, interstate, or local law relating to lead-based paint, lead-based paint activities, or lead-based paint hazards with respect to any act or omission within the scope of his official duties.

(Pub.L. 94–469, Title IV, § 408, as added Pub.L. 102–550, Title X, § 1021(a), Oct. 28, 1992, 106 Stat. 3921.)

## § 2689. Prohibited acts

**[TSCA § 409]**

It shall be unlawful for any person to fail or refuse to comply with a provision of this subchapter or with any rule or order issued under this subchapter.

(Pub.L. 94–469, Title IV, § 409, as added Pub.L. 102–550, Title X, § 1021(a), Oct. 28, 1992, 106 Stat. 3921.)

## § 2690. Relationship to other Federal law

**[TSCA § 410]**

Nothing in this subchapter shall affect the authority of other appropriate Federal agencies to establish or enforce any requirements which are at least as stringent as those established pursuant to this subchapter.

(Pub.L. 94–469, Title IV, § 410, as added Pub.L. 102–550, Title X, § 1021(a), Oct. 28, 1992, 106 Stat. 3921.)

## § 2691. General provisions relating to administrative proceedings

**[TSCA § 411]**

**(a) Applicability**

This section applies to the promulgation or revision of any regulation issued under this subchapter.

**(b) Rulemaking docket**

Not later than the date of proposal of any action to which this section applies, the Administrator shall establish a rulemaking docket for such action (hereinafter in this subsection referred to as a "rule"). Whenever a rule applies only within a particular State, a second (identical) docket shall be established in the appropriate regional office of the Environmental Protection Agency.

**(c) Inspection and copying**

(1) The rulemaking docket required under subsection (b) of this section shall be open for inspection by the public at reasonable times specified in the notice of proposed rulemaking. Any person may copy docu-

ments contained in the docket. The Administrator shall provide copying facilities which may be used at the expense of the person seeking copies, but the Administrator may waive or reduce such expenses in such instances as the public interest requires. Any person may request copies by mail if the person pays the expenses, including personnel costs to do the copying.

(2)(A) Promptly upon receipt by the agency, all written comments and documentary information on the proposed rule received from any person for inclusion in the docket during the comment period shall be placed in the docket. The transcript of public hearings, if any, on the proposed rule shall also be included in the docket promptly upon receipt from the person who transcribed such hearings. All documents which become available after the proposed rule has been published and which the Administrator determines are of central relevance to the rulemaking shall be placed in the docket as soon as possible after their availability.

(B) The drafts of proposed rules submitted by the Administrator to the Office of Management and Budget for any interagency review process prior to proposal of any such rule, all documents accompanying such drafts, and all written comments thereon by other agencies and all written responses to such written comments by the Administrator shall be placed in the docket no later than the date of proposal of the rule. The drafts of the final rule submitted for such review process prior to promulgation and all such written comments thereon, all documents accompanying such drafts, and written responses thereto shall be placed in the docket no later than the date of promulgation.

**(d) Explanation**

(1) The promulgated rule shall be accompanied by an explanation of the reasons for any major changes in the promulgated rule from the proposed rule.

(2) The promulgated rule shall also be accompanied by a response to each of the significant comments, criticisms, and new data submitted in written or oral presentations during the comment period.

(3) The promulgated rule may not be based (in part or whole) on any information or data which has not been placed in the docket as of the date of such promulgation.

**(e) Judicial review**

The material referred to in subsection (c)(2)(B) of this section shall not be included in the record for judicial review.

**(f) Effective date**

The requirements of this section shall take effect with respect to any rule the proposal of which occurs after 90 days after October 28, 1992.

(Pub.L. 94–469, Title IV, § 411, as added Pub.L. 102–550, Title X, § 1021(a), Oct. 28, 1992, 106 Stat. 3922.)

## § 2692. Authorization of appropriations

**[TSCA § 412]**

There are authorized to be appropriated to carry out the purposes of this subchapter such sums as may be necessary.

(Pub.L. 94–469, Title IV, § 412, as added Pub.L. 102–550, Title X, § 1021(a), Oct. 28, 1992, 106 Stat. 3923.)

# NATIONAL CLIMATE PROGRAM

## NATIONAL CLIMATE PROGRAM ACT [NCPA § ______]

**(15 U.S.C.A. §§ 2901 to 2908)**

## CHAPTER 56—NATIONAL CLIMATE PROGRAM



### § 2901. Findings

[NCPA § 2]

The Congress finds and declares the following:

(1) Weather and climate change affect food production, energy use, land use, water resources and other factors vital to national security and human welfare.

(2) An ability to anticipate natural and man-induced changes in climate would contribute to the soundness of policy decisions in the public and private sectors.

(3) Significant improvements in the ability to forecast climate on an intermediate and long-term basis are possible.

(4) Information regarding climate is not being fully disseminated or used, and Federal efforts have given insufficient attention to assessing and applying this information.

(5) Climate fluctuation and change occur on a global basis, and deficiencies exist in the system for monitoring global climate changes. International cooperation for the purpose of sharing the benefits and costs of a global effort to understand climate is essential.

(6) The United States lacks a well-defined and coordinated program in climate-related research, monitoring, assessment of effects, and information utilization.

(Pub.L. 95–367, § 2, Sept. 17, 1978, 92 Stat. 601.)

#### HISTORICAL AND STATUTORY NOTES

**Short Title**

Section 1 of Pub.L. 95–367 provided: "That this Act [enacting this chapter, amending section 25 of former Title 31, Money and Finance, and enacting provisions set out as a note under section 25 of former Title 31] may be cited as the 'National Climate Program Act'."

**Global Climate Protection**

Pub.L. 100–204, Title XI, §§ 1101 to 1106, Dec. 22, 1987, 101 Stat. 1407, as amended Pub.L. 103–199, Title VI, § 603(1), Dec. 17, 1993, 107 Stat. 2327, provided that:

"**Sec. 1101. Short Title.**

"This title [this note] may be cited as the 'Global Climate Protection Act of 1987'.

"**Sec. 1102. Findings.**

"The Congress finds as follows:

"(1) There exists evidence that manmade pollution—the release of carbon dioxide, chlorofluorocarbons, methane, and other trace gases into the atmosphere—may be producing a long-term and substantial increase in the average temperature on Earth, a phenomenon known as global warming through the greenhouse effect.

"(2) By early in the next century, an increase in Earth temperature could—

"(A) so alter global weather patterns as to have an effect on existing agricultural production and on the habitability of large portions of the Earth; and

"(B) cause thermal expansion of the oceans and partial melting of the polar ice caps and glaciers, resulting in rising sea levels.

"(3) Important research into the problem of climate change is now being conducted by various United States Government and international agencies, and the continuation and intensification of those efforts will be crucial to the development of an effective United States response.

"(4) While the consequences of the greenhouse effect may not be fully manifest until the next century, ongoing pollution and deforestation may be contributing now to an irreversible process. Necessary actions must be identified and implemented in time to protect the climate.

"(5) The global nature of this problem will require vigorous efforts to achieve international cooperation aimed at minimizing and responding to adverse climate change; such international cooperation will be greatly enhanced by United States leadership. A key step in international cooperation will be the meeting of the Governing Council of the United Nations Environment Program, scheduled for June 1989, which will seek to determine a direction for worldwide efforts to control global climate change.

"(6) Effective United States leadership in the international arena will depend upon a coordinated national policy.

"**Sec. 1103. Mandate for action on the global climate.**

"**(a) Goals of United States Policy.**—United States policy should seek to—

"(1) increase worldwide understanding of the greenhouse effect and its environmental and health consequences;

"(2) foster cooperation among nations to develop more extensive and coordinated scientific research efforts with respect to the greenhouse effect;

"(3) identify technologies and activities to limit mankind's adverse effect on the global climate by—

"(A) slowing the rate of increase of concentrations of greenhouse gases in the atmosphere in the near term; and

"(B) stabilizing or reducing atmospheric concentrations of greenhouse gases over the long term; and

"(4) work toward multilateral agreements.

"**(b) Formulation of United States Policy.**—The President, through the Environmental Protection Agency, shall be responsible for developing and proposing to Congress a coordinated national policy on global climate change. Such policy formulation shall consider research findings of the Committee on Earth Sciences of the Federal Coordinating Council on Science and Engineering Technology, the National Academy of Sciences, the National Oceanic and Atmospheric Administration, the National Science Foundation, the National Aeronautic and Space Administration, the Department of Energy, the Environmental Protection Agency, and other organizations engaged in the conduct of scientific research.

"**(c) Coordination of United States Policy in the International Arena.**—The Secretary of State shall be responsible to coordinate those aspects of United States policy requiring action through the channels of multilateral diplomacy, including the United Nations Environment Program and other international organizations. In the formulation of these elements of United States policy, the Secretary of State shall, under the direction of the President, work jointly with the Administrator of the Environmental Protection Agency and other United States agencies concerned with environmental protection, consistent with applicable Federal law.

"**Sec. 1104. Report to Congress.**

"Not later than 24 months after the date of enactment of this Act [Dec. 22, 1987], the Secretary of State and the Administrator of the Environmental Protection Agency shall jointly submit to all committees of jurisdiction in the Congress a report which shall include—

"(1) a summary analysis of current international scientific understanding of the greenhouse effect, including its environmental and health consequences;

"(2) an assessment of United States efforts to gain international cooperation in limiting global climate change; and

"(3) a description of the strategy by which the United States intends to seek further international cooperation to limit global climate change.

"**Sec. 1105. International Year of Global Climate Protection.**

"In order to focus international attention and concern on the problem of global warming, and to foster further work on multilateral treaties aimed at protecting the global climate, the Secretary of State shall undertake all necessary steps to promote, within the United Nations system, the early designation of an International Year of Global Climate Protection.

"**Sec. 1106. Climate Protection and United States Relations with the Independent States of the Former Soviet Union.**

"In recognition of the respective leadership roles of the United States and the independent states of the former Soviet Union in the international arena, and of the extent to which they are producers of atmospheric pollutants, the Congress urges that the President accord the problem of climate protection a high priority on the agenda of United States relations with the independent states."

## § 2902. Purpose

[NCPA § 3]

It is the purpose of the Congress in this chapter to establish a national climate program that will assist the Nation and the world to understand and respond to natural and man-induced climate processes and their implications.

(Pub.L. 95–367, § 3, Sept. 17, 1978, 92 Stat. 601.)

## § 2903. Definitions

[NCPA § 4]

As used in this chapter, unless the context otherwise requires:

(1) The term "Board" means the Climate Program Policy Board.

(2) The term "Office" means the National Climate Program Office.

(3) The term "Program" means the National Climate Program.

(4) The term "Secretary" means the Secretary of Commerce.

(Pub.L. 95–367, § 4, Sept. 17, 1978, 92 Stat. 601; Pub.L. 99–272, Title VI, § 6084(a), Apr. 7, 1986, 100 Stat. 136.)

## § 2904. National Climate Program

[NCPA § 5]

### (a) Establishment

The President shall establish a National Climate Program in accordance with the provisions, findings and purposes of this chapter.

### (b) Duties

The President shall—

(1) promulgate the 5-year plans described in subsection (d)(9) of this section;

(2) define the roles in the Program of Federal officers, departments, and agencies, including the Departments of Agriculture, Commerce, Defense, Energy, Interior, State, and Transportation; the Environmental Protection Agency; the National Aeronautics and Space Administration; the Council on Environmental Quality; the National Science

Foundation; and the Office of Science and Technology Policy; and

(3) provide for Program coordination.

**(c) National Climate Program Office**

(1) The Secretary shall establish within the Department of Commerce a National Climate Program Office not later than 30 days after September 17, 1978.

(2) The Office shall—

(A) serve as the lead entity responsible for administering the program;

(B) be headed by a Director who shall represent the Climate Program Policy Board and shall be spokesperson for the program;

(C) serve as the staff for the Board and its supporting committees and working groups;

(D) review each agency budget request transmitted under subsection (g)(1) of this section and submit an analysis of the requests to the Board for its review;

(E) be responsible for coordinating interagency participation in international climate-related activities; and

(F) work with the National Academy of Sciences and other private, academic, State, and local groups in preparing and implementing the 5-year plan (described in subsection (d)(9) of this section) and the program.

The analysis described in subparagraph (D) shall include an analysis of how each agency's budget request relates to the priorities and goals of the program established pursuant to this chapter.

(3) The Secretary may provide, through the Office, financial assistance, in the form of contracts or grants or cooperative agreements, for climate-related activities which are needed to meet the goals and priorities of the program set forth in the 5-year plan pursuant to subsection (d)(9) of this section, if such goals and priorities are not being adequately addressed by any Federal department, agency, or instrumentality.

(4) Each Federal officer, employee, department and agency involved in the Program shall cooperate with the Secretary in carrying out the provisions of this chapter.

**(d) Program elements**

The Program shall include, but not be limited to, the following elements:

(1) assessments of the effect of climate on the natural environment, agricultural production, energy supply and demand, land and water resources, transportation, human health and national security. Such assessments shall be conducted to the maximum extent possible by those Federal agencies having national programs in food, fiber, raw materials, energy, transportation, land and water management, and other such responsibilities, in accordance with existing laws and regulations. Where appropriate such assessments may include recommendations for action;

(2) basic and applied research to improve the understanding of climate processes, natural and man induced, and the social, economic, and political implications of climate change;

(3) methods for improving climate forecasts on a monthly, seasonal, yearly, and longer basis;

(4) global data collection, and monitoring and analysis activities to provide reliable, useful and readily available information on a continuing basis;

(5) systems for the management and active dissemination of climatological data, information and assessments, including mechanisms for consultation with current and potential users;

(6) measures for increasing international cooperation in climate research, monitoring, analysis and data dissemination;

(7) mechanisms for intergovernmental climate-related studies and services including participation by universities, the private sector and others concerned with applied research and advisory services. Such mechanisms may provide, among others, for the following State and regional services and functions: (A) studies relating to and analyses of climatic effects on agricultural production, water resources, energy needs, and other critical sectors of the economy; (B) atmospheric data collection and monitoring on a statewide and regional basis; (C) advice to regional, State, and local government agencies regarding climate-related issues; (D) information to users within the State regarding climate and climatic effects; and (E) information to the Secretary regarding the needs of persons within the States for climate-related services, information, and data. The Secretary may make annual grants to any State or group of States, which grants shall be made available to public or private educational institutions, to State agencies, and to other persons or institutions qualified to conduct climate-related studies or provide climate-related services;

(8) experimental climate forecast centers, which shall (A) be responsible for making and routinely updating experimental climate forecasts of a monthly, seasonal, annual, and longer nature, based on a variety of experimental techniques; (B) establish procedures to have forecasts reviewed and their accuracy evaluated; and (C) protect against premature reliance on such experimental forecasts; and

(9) a preliminary 5-year plan, to be submitted to the Congress for review and comment, not later than 180 days after September 17, 1978, and a final

5-year plan to be submitted to the Congress not later than 1 year after September 17, 1978, that shall be revised and extended at least once every four years. Each plan shall establish the goals and priorities for the Program, including the intergovernmental program described in paragraph (7), over the subsequent 5-year period, and shall contain details regarding (A) the role of Federal agencies in the programs, (B) Federal funding required to enable the Program to achieve such goals, and (C) Program accomplishments that must be achieved to ensure that Program goals are met within the time frame established by the plan.

**(e) Climate Program Policy Board**

(1) The Secretary shall establish and maintain an interagency Climate Program Policy Board, consisting of representatives of the Federal agencies specified in subsection (b)(2) of this section and any other agency which the Secretary determines should participate in the Program.

(2) The Board shall—

(A) be responsible for coordinated planning and progress review for the Program;

(B) review all agency and department budget requests related to climate transmitted under subsection (g)(1) of this section and submit a report to the Office of Management and Budget concerning such budget requests;

(C) establish and maintain such interagency groups as the Board determines to be necessary to carry out its activities; and

(D) consult with and seek the advice of users and producers of climate data, information, and services to guide the Board's efforts, keeping the Director and the Congress advised of such contacts.

(3) The Board biennially shall select a Chair from among its members. A Board member who is a representative of an agency may not serve as Chair of the Board for a term if an individual who represented that same agency on the Board served as the Board's Chair for the previous term.

**(f) Cooperation**

(1) The Program shall be conducted so as to encourage cooperation with, and participation in the Program by, other organizations or agencies involved in related activities. For this purpose the Secretary shall cooperate and participate with other Federal agencies, and foreign, international, and domestic organizations and agencies involved in international or domestic climate-related programs.

(2) The Secretary and the Secretary of State shall cooperate with the Office in (A) providing representation at climate-related international meetings and conferences in which the United States participates, and (B) coordinating the activities of the Program with the climate programs of other nations and international agencies and organizations, including the World Meteorological Organization, the International Council of Scientific Unions, the United Nations Environmental Program, the United Nations Educational, Scientific, and Cultural Organization, the World Health Organization, and Food and Agriculture Organization.

**(g) Budgeting**

Each Federal agency and department participating in the Program, shall prepare and submit to the Office of Management and Budget, on or before the date of submission of departmental requests for appropriations to the Office of Management and Budget, an annual request for appropriations for the Program for the subsequent fiscal year and shall transmit a copy of such request to the National Climate Program Office. The Office of Management and Budget shall review the request for appropriations as an integrated, coherent, multiagency request.

(Pub.L. 95–367, § 5(a) to (g)(1), Sept. 17, 1978, 92 Stat. 601 to 603; Pub.L. 99–272, Title VI, § 6084(b) to (f), Apr. 7, 1986, 100 Stat. 136, 137.)

### HISTORICAL AND STATUTORY NOTES

**Codifications**

Subsec. (g) of this section in the original was par. (1) of section 5(g) of Pub.L. 95–367 and has been set out without such par. (1) designation for purposes of codification. Par. (2) of such section amended section 25 of Title 31, Money and Finance, and enacted provisions formerly set out as a note under section 25 of Title 31. Section 25 of Title 31 was repealed by Pub.L. 97–258, § 4(b), Sept. 13, 1982, 96 Stat. 1067.

**Termination of Reporting Requirements**

Section 3003(a)(1) of Pub.L. 104–66, relating to termination of reporting requirements, set out as a note under 31 U.S.C.A. § 1113, not applicable to any report required to be submitted under subsec. (d)(9) of this section, see section 1(11) of Pub.L. 107–74, set out as a note under 31 U.S.C.A. § 1113.

For termination, effective May 15, 2000, of provisions of law requiring submittal to Congress of any annual, semiannual, or other regular periodic report listed in House Document No. 103–7 (in which the quadrennially revised and extended 5-year plan under subsec. (d)(9) of this section is listed on page 53), see section 3003 of Pub.L. 104–66, as amended, set out as a note under 31 U.S.C.A. § 1113.

## § 2905. Repealed. Pub.L. 99–272, Title VI, § 6084(g), Apr. 7, 1986, 100 Stat. 137

### HISTORICAL AND STATUTORY NOTES

Section, Pub.L. 95–367, § 6, Sept. 17, 1978, 92 Stat. 603, related to the establishment and requirements of intergovernmental climate programs.

## § 2906. Annual report

[NCPA § 7]

The Secretary shall prepare and submit to the President and the authorizing committees of the Congress, not later than March 31 of each year, a report on the activities conducted pursuant to this chapter during the preceding fiscal year, including—

**(a)** a summary of the achievements of the Program during the previous fiscal year;

**(b)** an analysis of the progress made toward achieving the goals and objectives of the Program;

**(c)** a copy of the 5-year plan and any changes made in such plan;

**(d)** a summary of the multiagency budget request for the Program of section 2904(g) of this title; and

**(e)** any recommendations for additional legislation which may be required to assist in achieving the purposes of this chapter.

(Pub.L. 95–367, § 7, Sept. 17, 1978, 92 Stat. 604; Pub.L. 97–375, Title II, § 202(b), Dec. 21, 1982, 96 Stat. 1822.)

### HISTORICAL AND STATUTORY NOTES

**Termination of Reporting Requirements**

Section 3003(a)(1) of Pub.L. 104–66, relating to termination of reporting requirements, set out as a note under 31 U.S.C.A. § 1113, not applicable to any report required to be submitted under this section, see section 1(12) of Pub.L. 107–74, set out as a note under 31 U.S.C.A. § 1113.

For termination, effective May 15, 2000, of provisions in this section relating to submitting annual report to Congress, see section 3003 of Pub.L. 104–66, as amended, set out as a note under 31 U.S.C.A. § 1113, and page 53 of House Document No. 103–7.

## § 2907. Contract and grant authority; records and audits

[NCPA § 8]

**(a)** Functions vested in any Federal officer or agency by this chapter or under the Program may be exercised through the facilities and personnel of the agency involved or, to the extent provided or approved in advance in appropriation Acts, by other persons or entities under contracts or grant arrangements entered into by such officer or agency.

**(b)(1)** Each person or entity to which Federal funds are made available under a contract or grant arrangement as authorized by this chapter shall keep such records as the Director of the Office shall prescribe, including records which fully disclose the amount and disposition by such person or entity of such funds, the total cost of the activities for which such funds were so made available, the amount of that portion of such cost supplied from other sources, and such other records as will facilitate an effective audit.

**(2)** The Director of the Office and the Comptroller General of the United States, or any of their duly authorized representatives, shall, until the expiration of 3 years after the completion of the activities (referred to in paragraph (1)) of any person or entity pursuant to any contract or grant arrangement referred to in subsection (a) of this section, have access for the purpose of audit and examination to any books, documents, papers, and records of such person or entity which, in the judgment of the Director or the Comptroller General, may be related or pertinent to such contract or grant arrangement.

(Pub.L. 95–367, § 8, Sept. 17, 1978, 92 Stat. 604.)

## § 2908. Authorization of appropriations

[NCPA § 9]

In addition to any other funds otherwise authorized to be appropriated for the purpose of conducting climate-related programs, there are authorized to be appropriated to the Secretary, for the purpose of carrying out the provisions of this chapter, not to exceed $50,000,000 for the fiscal year ending September 30, 1979, not to exceed $65,000,000 for the fiscal year ending September 30, 1980, and not to exceed $25,500,000 for the fiscal year ending September 30, 1981, of which amount not less than $2,653,000 shall be made directly available to the National Climate Program Office in the form of a budget item separate from the activities of the National Oceanic and Atmospheric Administration.

(Pub.L. 95–367, § 9, Sept. 17, 1978, 92 Stat. 605; Pub.L. 96–547, § 1, Dec. 18, 1980, 94 Stat. 3217.)

*

# TITLE 16
# CONSERVATION

## RENEWABLE SURFACE RESOURCES OF NATIONAL FORESTS

## MULTIPLE–USE SUSTAINED–YIELD ACT OF 1960 [MUSYA § ____]

**(16 U.S.C.A. §§ 528 to 531)**

## CHAPTER 2—NATIONAL FORESTS



### § 528. Development and administration of renewable surface resources for multiple use and sustained yield of products and services; Congressional declaration of policy and purpose

[MUSYA § 1]

It is the policy of the Congress that the national forests are established and shall be administered for outdoor recreation, range, timber, watershed, and wildlife and fish purposes. The purposes of sections 528 to 531 of this title are declared to be supplemental to, but not in derogation of, the purposes for which the national forests were established as set forth in section 475 of this title. Nothing herein shall be construed as affecting the jurisdiction or responsibilities of the several States with respect to wildlife and fish on the national forests. Nothing herein shall be construed so as to affect the use or administration of the mineral resources of national forest lands or to affect the use or administration of Federal lands not within national forests.

(Pub.L. 86–517, § 1, June 12, 1960, 74 Stat. 215.)

#### HISTORICAL AND STATUTORY NOTES

**Short Title**

1960 Acts

Pub.L. 86–517, § 5, as added Pub.L. 94–588, § 19, Oct. 22, 1976, 90 Stat. 2962, provided that: "This Act [enacting sections 528 to 531 of this title] may be cited as the 'Multiple-Use Sustained-Yield Act of 1960'."

**Pilot Program of Charges and Fees for Harvest of Forest Botanical Products**

Pub.L. 106–113, Div. B, § 1000(a)(3) [Title III, § 339], Nov. 29, 1999, 113 Stat. 1535, 1501A–199, as amended Pub.L. 108–108, Title III, § 335, Nov. 10, 2003, 117 Stat. 1312, provided that:

"(a) **Definition of forest botanical product.**—For purposes of this section, the term 'forest botanical product' means any naturally occurring mushrooms, fungi, flowers, seeds, roots, bark, leaves, and other vegetation (or portion thereof) that grow on National Forest System lands. The term does not include trees, except as provided in regulations issued under this section by the Secretary of Agriculture.

"(b) **Recovery of fair market value for products.**—The Secretary of Agriculture shall develop and implement a pilot program to charge and collect fees under subsection (c) [of this note] for forest botanical products harvested on National Forest System lands. The Secretary shall establish appraisal methods and bidding procedures to determine the fair market value of forest botanical products harvested under the pilot program.

"(c) **Fees.**—

"(1) **Imposition and collection.**—Under the pilot program, the Secretary of Agriculture shall charge and collect from a person who harvests forest botanical products on National Forest System lands a fee in an amount established by the Secretary to recover at least a portion of the fair market value of the harvested forest botanical products and a portion of the costs incurred by the Department of Agriculture associated with granting, modifying, or monitoring the authorization for harvest of the forest botanical products, including the costs of any environmental or other analysis.

"(2) **Security.**—The Secretary may require a person assessed a fee under this subsection to provide security to ensure that the Secretary receives the fees imposed under this subsection from the person.

"(d) **Sustainable harvest levels for forest botanical products.**—The Secretary of Agriculture shall conduct appropriate analyses to determine whether and how the harvest of forest botanical products on National Forest System lands can be conducted on a sustainable basis. The Secretary may not permit under the pilot program the harvest of forest botanical products at levels in excess of sustainable harvest levels, as defined pursuant to the Multiple–Use Sustained–Yield Act of 1960 (16 U.S.C. 528 et seq.). The Secretary shall establish procedures and timeframes to monitor and revise the harvest levels established for forest botanical products.

"(e) **Waiver authority.**—

"(1) **Personal use.**—The Secretary of Agriculture shall establish a personal use harvest level for each forest botanical product, and the harvest of a forest botanical product below that level by a person for personal use shall not be subject to a fee under subsection (c) [of this note].

"(2) **Other exceptions.**—The Secretary may also waive the application of subsection (b) or (c) [of this note] pursuant to such regulations as the Secretary may prescribe.

"(f) **Deposit and use of funds.**—

"(1) **Deposit.**—Funds collected under the pilot program in accordance with subsection (c) [of this note] shall be deposited into a special account in the Treasury of the United States.

"(2) **Funds available.**—Funds deposited into the special account in accordance with paragraph (1) shall be available for expenditure by the Secretary of Agriculture under paragraph (3) without further appropriation, and shall remain available for expenditure until the date specified in subsection (h)(2) [of this note].

"(3) **Authorized uses.**—The funds made available under paragraph (2) shall be expended at units of the National Forest System in proportion to the fees collected at that unit under subsection (c) [of this note] to pay for the costs of conducting inventories of forest botanical products, determining sustainable levels of harvest, monitoring and assessing the impacts of harvest levels and methods, conducting restoration activities, including any necessary vegetation, and covering costs of the Department of Agriculture described in subsection (c)(1) [of this note].

"(4) **Treatment of fees.**—Funds collected under subsection (c) [of this note] shall not be taken into account for the purposes of the following laws:

"(A) The sixth paragraph under the heading 'FOREST SERVICE' in the Act of May 23, 1908 (16 U.S.C. 500) and section 13 of the Act of March 1, 1911 (commonly known as the Weeks Act; 16 U.S.C. 500).

"(B) The fourteenth paragraph under the heading 'FOREST SERVICE' in the Act of March 4, 1913 (16 U.S.C. 501).

"(C) Section 33 of the Bankhead–Jones Farm Tenant Act (7 U.S.C. 1012).

"(D) The Act of August 8, 1937, and the Act of May 24, 1939 (43 U.S.C. 1181a et seq.) [43 U.S.C.A. §§ 1181a et seq., 1181f–1 et seq.].

"(E) Section 6 of the Act of June 14, 1926 (commonly known as the Recreation and Public Purposes Act; 43 U.S.C. 869–4).

"(F) Chapter 69 of title 31, United States Code [31 U.S.C.A. § 6901 et seq.].

"(G) Section 401 of the Act of June 15, 1935 (16 U.S.C. 715s).

"(H) Section 4 of the Land and Water Conservation Fund Act of 1965 (16 U.S.C. 460*l*–6a).

"(I) Any other provision of law relating to revenue allocation.

"(g) **Reporting requirements.**—As soon as practicable after the end of each fiscal year in which the Secretary of Agriculture collects fees under subsection (c) [of this note] or expends funds from the special account under subsection (f) [of this note], the Secretary shall submit to the Congress a report summarizing the activities of the Secretary under the pilot program, including the funds generated under subsection (c) [of this note], the expenses incurred to carry out the pilot program, and the expenditures made from the special account during that fiscal year.

"(h) **Duration of pilot program.**—

"(1) **Collection of fees.**—The Secretary of Agriculture may collect fees under the authority of subsection (c) [of this note] until September 30, 2009.

"(2) **Use of special account.**—The Secretary may make expenditures from the special account under subsection (f) [of this note] until September 30 of the fiscal year following the last fiscal year specified in paragraph (1). After that date, amounts remaining in the special account shall be transferred to the general fund of the Treasury."

[Pub.L. 108–108, § 335(3), purporting to amend subsec. (d)(1) of this note, was executed to subsec. (e)(1) of this note as the probable intent of Congress.]

## § 529. Authorization of development and administration; consideration to relative values of resources; areas of wilderness

**[MUSYA § 2]**

The Secretary of Agriculture is authorized and directed to develop and administer the renewable surface resources of the national forests for multiple use and sustained yield of the several products and services obtained therefrom. In the administration of the national forests due consideration shall be given to the relative values of the various resources in particular areas. The establishment and maintenance of areas of wilderness are consistent with the purposes and provisions of sections 528 to 531 of this title.

(Pub.L. 86–517, § 2, June 12, 1960, 74 Stat. 215.)

### HISTORICAL AND STATUTORY NOTES

**Transfer of Functions**

Enforcement functions of Secretary or other official in Department of Agriculture, insofar as they involve lands and programs under jurisdiction of that Department, related to compliance with the provisions of sections 528 to 531 of this title with respect to pre-construction, construction, and initial operation of transportation system for Canadian and Alaskan natural gas were transferred to the Federal Inspector, Office of Federal Inspector for the Alaska Natural Gas Transportation System, until the first anniversary of date of initial operation of the Alaska Natural Gas Transportation System, see Reorg. Plan No. 1 of 1979, §§ 102(f), 203(a), 44 F.R. 33663, 33666, 93 Stat. 1373, 1376, eff. July 1, 1979, set out in Appendix 1 to Title 5, Government Organization and Employees.

## § 530. Cooperation for purposes of development and administration with State and local governmental agencies and others

**[MUSYA § 3]**

In the effectuation of sections 528 to 531 of this title the Secretary of Agriculture is authorized to cooperate with interested State and local governmental agencies and others in the development and management of the national forests.

(Pub.L. 86–517, § 3, June 12, 1960, 74 Stat. 215.)

### HISTORICAL AND STATUTORY NOTES

**Transfer of Functions**

Enforcement functions of Secretary or other official in Department of Agriculture, insofar as they involve lands and programs under jurisdiction of that Department, related to compliance with the provisions of sections 528 to 531 of this title with respect to pre-construction, construction, and initial operation of transportation system for Canadian and Alaskan natural gas were transferred to the Federal Inspector, Office of Federal Inspector for the Alaska Natural Gas Transportation System, until the first anniversary of date of initial operation of the Alaska Natural Gas Transportation System, see Reorg. Plan No. 1 of 1979, §§ 102(f), 203(a), 44 F.R. 33663, 33666, 93 Stat. 1373, 1376, eff. July 1, 1979, set out in Appendix 1 to Title 5, Government Organization and Employees.

## § 531. Definitions

**[MUSYA § 4]**

As used in sections 528 to 531 of this title the following terms shall have the following meanings:

**(a)** "Multiple use" means: The management of all the various renewable surface resources of the national forests so that they are utilized in the combination that will best meet the needs of the American people; making the most judicious use of the land for some or all of these resources or related services over areas large enough to provide sufficient latitude for periodic adjustments in use to conform to changing needs and conditions; that some land will be used for less than all of the resources; and harmonious and coordinated management of the various resources, each with the other, without impairment of the productivity of the land, with consideration being given to the relative values of the various resources, and not necessarily the combination of uses that will give the greatest dollar return or the greatest unit output.

**(b)** "Sustained yield of the several products and services" means the achievement and maintenance in perpetuity of a high-level annual or regular periodic output of the various renewable resources of the national forests without impairment of the productivity of the land.

(Pub.L. 86–517, § 4, June 12, 1960, 74 Stat. 215.)

# MARINE MAMMAL PROTECTION

## MARINE MAMMAL PROTECTION ACT OF 1972 [MMPA § ____]

**(16 U.S.C.A. §§ 1361, 1362, 1371 to 1389, 1401 to 1407, 1411 to 1418, 1421 to 1421h)**

## CHAPTER 31—MARINE MAMMAL PROTECTION



### SUBCHAPTER I—GENERALLY

### § 1361. Congressional findings and declaration of policy

**[MMPA § 2]**

The Congress finds that—

(1) certain species and population stocks of marine mammals are, or may be, in danger of extinction or depletion as a result of man's activities;

(2) such species and population stocks should not be permitted to diminish beyond the point at which they cease to be a significant functioning element in the ecosystem of which they are a part, and, consistent with this major objective, they should not be permitted to diminish below their optimum sustainable population. Further measures should be immediately taken to replenish any species or population stock which has already diminished below that population. In particular, efforts should be made to protect essential habitats, including the rookeries, mating grounds, and areas of similar significance

for each species of marine mammal from the adverse effect of man's actions;

(3) there is inadequate knowledge of the ecology and population dynamics of such marine mammals and of the factors which bear upon their ability to reproduce themselves successfully;

(4) negotiations should be undertaken immediately to encourage the development of international arrangements for research on, and conservation of, all marine mammals;

(5) marine mammals and marine mammal products either—

(A) move in interstate commerce, or

(B) affect the balance of marine ecosystems in a manner which is important to other animals and animal products which move in interstate commerce,

and that the protection and conservation of marine mammals and their habitats is therefore necessary to insure the continuing availability of those products which move in interstate commerce; and

(6) marine mammals have proven themselves to be resources of great international significance, esthetic and recreational as well as economic, and it is the sense of the Congress that they should be protected and encouraged to develop to the greatest extent feasible commensurate with sound policies of resource management and that the primary objective of their management should be to maintain the health and stability of the marine ecosystem. Whenever consistent with this primary objective, it should be the goal to obtain an optimum sustainable population keeping in mind the carrying capacity of the habitat.

(Pub.L. 92–522, § 2, Oct. 21, 1972, 86 Stat. 1027; Pub.L. 97–58, § 1(b)(1), Oct. 9, 1981, 95 Stat. 979; Pub.L. 103–238, § 3, Apr. 30, 1994, 108 Stat. 532.)

## HISTORICAL AND STATUTORY NOTES

**Effective and Applicability Provisions**

1972 Acts

Section 4 of Pub.L. 92–522 provided that: "The provisions of this Act [enacting this chapter] shall take effect upon the expiration of the sixty-day period following the date of its enactment [Oct. 21, 1972]."

**Short Title**

2000 Amendments

Pub.L. 106–555, § 1, Dec. 21, 2000, 114 Stat. 2765, provided that: "This Act [enacting section 1421f–1 of this title and provisions set out as notes under sections 917a, 1361, 1433, 1851, 1855, 5101, and 5107 of this title, and amending sections 1362, 1421f–1, 1421g, 1421h, 1433, 1434, 5101 to 5103, 5106, 5107a, 5107b, 5108, and 5156 of this title] may be cited as the 'Striped Bass Conservation, Atlantic Coastal Fisheries Management, and Marine Mammal Rescue Assistance Act of 2000'."

Pub.L. 106–555, Title II, § 201, Dec. 21, 2000, 114 Stat. 2767, provided that: "This title [enacting section 1421f–1 of this title, amending sections 1362, 1421g, 1421h, 1433, and 1434 of this title, enacting provisions set out as notes under sections 917a, 1361, and 1433 of this title, and amending provisions set out as a note under section 1855 of this title] may be cited as the 'Marine Mammal Rescue Assistance Act of 2000'."

1997 Amendments

Pub.L. 105–42, § 1(a), Aug. 15, 1997, 111 Stat. 1122, provided that: "This Act [which enacted sections 962, 1412, 1413, 1414a, 1415 and 1416 of this title, repealed former sections 1412 to 1416 and 1418 of this title, amended sections 952, 953, 1362, 1371, 1374, 1378, 1380, 1385, 1411 and 1417 of this title and the heading of subchapter IV of this chapter, and enacted provisions set out as notes in this section and section 1362 of this title] may be cited as the 'International Dolphin Conservation Program Act'."

1994 Amendments

Section 1 of Pub.L. 103–238 provided that: "This Act [enacting sections 1386, 1387, 1388, and 1389 of this title, amending this section and sections 1362, 1371, 1372, 1374, 1375, 1379, 1380, 1382, 1383, 1383a, 1383b, 1384, 1407, 1421, 1421a, 1421b, 1421c, 1421d, 1421e, 1421f, 1421g, 1421h, and 4107 of this title, repealing former sections 1384 and 1407 of this title, and enacting provisions set out as notes under this section and sections 1362, 1374, 1538, and 1539 of this title] may be cited as the 'Marine Mammal Protection Act Amendments of 1994'."

1992 Amendments

Pub.L. 102–587, Title III, § 3001, Nov. 4, 1992, 106 Stat. 5059, provided that: "This title [enacting subchapter V of this chapter, amending sections 1362, 1372, 1379, and 1382 of this title and section 183c of the Appendix to Title 46, Shipping, and enacting provisions set out as notes under sections 1421 and 1421a of this title of this title] may be cited as the 'Marine Mammal Health and Stranding Response Act'."

Pub.L. 102–523, § 1, Oct. 26, 1992, 106 Stat. 3425, provided that: "This Act [enacting subchapter IV of this chapter, and amending sections 952, 953, 973r and 1362 of this title] may be cited as the 'International Dolphin Conservation Act of 1992'."

1988 Amendments

Pub.L. 100–711, § 1, Nov. 2, 1988, 102 Stat. 4755, provided: "That this Act [enacting sections 1383a and 1383b of this title, amending sections 1166, 1371, 1372, 1374, 1378, 1379, 1380, 1384, 1402, and 1407 of this title and section 1978 of Title 22, Foreign Relations and Intercourse, and enacting provisions set out as notes under this section and section 1384 of this title] may be cited as the 'Marine Mammal Protection Act Amendments of 1988'."

1972 Acts

Section 1 of Pub.L. 92–522 provided in part that: "This Act [enacting this chapter] may be cited as the 'Marine Mammal Protection Act of 1972'."

**Relationship of Marine Mammal Protection Act Amendments of 1994 to Other Law**

Section 2(b) of Pub.L. 103–238 provided that: "Except as otherwise expressly provided, nothing in this Act [see Short Title of 1994 Amendments note set out under this section] is intended to amend, repeal, or otherwise affect any other provision of law."

**Indian Treaty Rights; Alaska Native Subsistence**

Section 14 of Pub.L. 103–238 provided that:

"Nothing in this Act [see Short Title note set out under this section] including any amendments to the Marine Mammal Protection Act of 1972 [this chapter] made by this Act—

"(1) alters or is intended to alter any treaty between the United States and one or more Indian tribes; or

"(2) affects or otherwise modifies the provisions of section 101(b) of the Marine Mammal Protection Act of 1972 (16 U.S.C. 1371(b) [section 1371(b) of this title]), except as specifically provided in the amendment made by section 4(b) of this Act [amending 1371(b) of this title]."

**Implementing Regulations for Marine Mammal Protection Act Amendments of 1994**

Section 15(b) of Pub.L 103–238 provided that: "Except as provided otherwise in this Act or the amendments to the Marine Mammal Protection Act of 1972 (16 U.S.C. 1361 et seq.) [this chapter] made by this Act [see Short Title note set out under this section] the Secretary of Commerce or the Secretary of the Interior, as appropriate, shall, after notice and opportunity for public comment, promulgate regulations to implement this Act and the amendments made by this Act by January 1, 1995."

**Purposes and Findings of 1997 Amendments**

Pub.L. 105–42, § 2, provided that:

"**(a) Purposes.**—The purposes of this Act [the International Dolphin Conservation Program Act; for classification, see Tables] are—

"(1) to give effect to the Declaration of Panama, signed October 4, 1995, by the Governments of Belize, Colombia, Costa Rica, Ecuador, France, Honduras, Mexico, Panama, Spain, the United States of America, Vanuatu, and Venezuela, including the establishment of the International Dolphin Conservation Program, relating to the protection of dolphins and other species, and the conservation and management of tuna in the eastern tropical Pacific Ocean;

"(2) to recognize that nations fishing for tuna in the eastern tropical Pacific Ocean have achieved significant reductions in dolphin mortality associated with that fishery; and

"(3) to eliminate the ban on imports of tuna from those nations that are in compliance with the International Dolphin Conservation Program.

"**(b) Findings.**—The Congress finds that—

"(1) the nations that fish for tuna in the eastern tropical Pacific Ocean have achieved significant reductions in dolphin mortality associated with the purse seine fishery from hundreds of thousands annually to fewer than 5,000 annually;

"(2) the provisions of the Marine Mammal Protection Act of 1972 that impose a ban on imports from nations that fish for tuna in the eastern tropical Pacific Ocean have served as an incentive to reduce dolphin mortalities;

"(3) tuna canners and processors of the United States have led the canning and processing industry in promoting a dolphin-safe tuna market; and

"(4) 12 signatory nations to the Declaration of Panama, including the United States, agreed under that Declaration to require that the total annual dolphin mortality in the purse seine fishery for yellowfin tuna in the eastern tropical Pacific Ocean not exceed 5,000 animals, with the objective of progressively reducing dolphin mortality to a level approaching zero through the setting of annual limits and with the goal of eliminating dolphin mortality."

**Study on Effects of Dolphin Feeding**

Pub.L. 102–567, Title III, § 306, Oct. 29, 1992, 106 Stat. 4284, provided that:

"**(a) Study.**—The Secretary of Commerce shall conduct a study in the eastern Gulf of Mexico on the effects of feeding of noncaptive dolphins by human beings. The study conducted pursuant to this section shall be designed to detect any behavior or diet modification resulting from this feeding and to identify the effects, if any, of these modifications on the health and well-being of the dolphins.

"**(b) External review.**—In design and conduct of the study required under subsection (a), the Secretary shall consult with the National Academy of Sciences and the Marine Mammal Commission.

"**(c) Report.**—Within 18 months after the date of the enactment of this Act [Oct. 29, 1992], the Secretary shall submit to the Committee on Merchant Marine and Fisheries of the House of Representatives and the Committee on Commerce, Science, and Transportation of the Senate a report on the results of the study conducted pursuant to subsection (a)."

[Committee on Merchant Marine and Fisheries of House of Representatives abolished and any reference in any provision of law enacted before Jan. 4, 1995, to the Committee on Merchant Marine and Fisheries of the House of Representatives treated as referring to the Committee on Agriculture of the House of Representatives, in the case of a provision of law relating to inspection of seafood or seafood products, the Committee on National Security of the House of Representatives, in the case of a provision of law relating to interoceanic canals, the Merchant Marine Academy and State Maritime Academies, or national security aspects of merchant marine, the Committee on Resources of the House of Representatives, in the case of a provision of law relating to fisheries, wildlife, international fishing agreements marine affairs (including coastal zone management) except for measures relating to oil and other pollution of navigable waters, or oceanography, the Committee on Science of the House of Representatives, in the case of a provision of law relating to marine research, and the Committee on Transportation and Infrastructure of the House of Representatives, in the case of a provision of law relating to a matter other than a matter described above, see section 1(b)(3) of Pub.L. 104–14, set out as a note preceding section 21 of Title 2, The Congress.]

**Study on Mortality of Atlantic Dolphin**

Pub.L. 100–711, § 7, Nov. 23, 1988, 102 Stat. 4771, provided that:

"**(a)** The Secretary of Commerce shall conduct a study regarding the east coast epidemic during 1987 and 1988 which has caused substantial mortality within the North Atlantic coastal population of Atlantic bottle-nosed dolphin. The study shall examine—

"(1) the cause or causes of the epidemic;

"(2) the effect of the epidemic on coastal and offshore populations of Atlantic bottle-nosed dolphin;

"(3) the extent to which pollution may have contributed to the epidemic;

"(4) whether other species and populations of marine mammals were affected by those factors which contributed to the epidemic; and

"(5) any other matters pertaining to the causes and effects of the epidemic.

"(b) On or before January 1, 1989, the Secretary shall submit to the Committee on Commerce, Science, and Transportation of the Senate and the Committee on Merchant Marine and Fisheries of the House of Representatives a plan for conducting the study required in subsection (a)."

[Committee on Merchant Marine and Fisheries of House of Representatives abolished and any reference in any provision of law enacted before Jan. 4, 1995, to the Committee on Merchant Marine and Fisheries of the House of Representatives treated as referring to the Committee on Agriculture of the House of Representatives, in the case of a provision of law relating to inspection of seafood or seafood products, the Committee on National Security of the House of Representatives, in the case of a provision of law relating to interoceanic canals, the Merchant Marine Academy and State Maritime Academies, or national security aspects of merchant marine, the Committee on Resources of the House of Representatives, in the case of a provision of law relating to fisheries, wildlife, international fishing agreements marine affairs (including coastal zone management) except for measures relating to oil and other pollution of navigable waters, or oceanography, the Committee on Science of the House of Representatives, in the case of a provision of law relating to marine research, and the Committee on Transportation and Infrastructure of the House of Representatives, in the case of a provision of law relating to a matter other than a matter described above, see section 1(b)(3) of Pub.L. 104–14, set out as a note preceding section 21 of Title 2, The Congress.]

**International Discussion to Advance Understanding of Cetacean Life**

Pub.L. 95–426, Title VI, § 602, Oct. 7, 1978, 92 Stat. 985, provided that:

"It is the sense of the Congress that the President should convey to all countries having an interest in cetacean sea life the serious concern of the Congress regarding the continuing destruction of these marine mammals (highlighted by the recent slaughter of dolphins in the Sea of Japan by Japanese fishermen) and should encourage such countries—

"(1) to join in international discussions with other such countries in order to advance general understanding of cetacean life and thereby facilitate an effective use of the living marine resources of the world which does not jeopardize the natural balance of the aquatic environment;

"(2) to participate in an exchange of information with the National Marine Fisheries Service of the United States Department of Commerce, including cooperation in studies of—

"(A) the impact of cetaceans on ecologically related human foodstuffs, and

"(B) alternative methods of dealing with cetacean problems as they occur;

"(3) to cooperate in establishing an international cetacean commission to advance understanding of cetacean life and to insure the effective conservation and protection of cetaceans on a global scale; and

"(4) to adopt comprehensive marine mammal protection legislation."

## § 1362. Definitions

**[MMPA § 3]**

For the purposes of this chapter—

(1) The term "depletion" or "depleted" means any case in which—

(A) the Secretary, after consultation with the Marine Mammal Commission and the Committee of Scientific Advisors on Marine Mammals established under subchapter III of this chapter, determines that a species or population stock is below its optimum sustainable population;

(B) a State, to which authority for the conservation and management of a species or population stock is transferred under section 1379 of this title, determines that such species or stock is below its optimum sustainable population; or

(C) a species or population stock is listed as an endangered species or a threatened species under the Endangered Species Act of 1973 [16 U.S.C.A. § 1531 et seq.].

(2) The terms "conservation" and "management" mean the collection and application of biological information for the purposes of increasing and maintaining the number of animals within species and populations of marine mammals at their optimum sustainable population. Such terms include the entire scope of activities that constitute a modern scientific resource program, including, but not limited to, research, census, law enforcement, and habitat acquisition and improvement. Also included within these terms, when and where appropriate, is the periodic or total protection of species or populations as well as regulated taking.

(3) The term "district court of the United States" includes the District Court of Guam, District Court of the Virgin Islands, District Court of Puerto Rico, District Court of the Canal Zone, and, in the case of American Samoa and the Trust Territory of the Pacific Islands, the District Court of the United States for the District of Hawaii.

(4) The term "humane" in the context of the taking of a marine mammal means that method of taking which involves the least possible degree of pain and suffering practicable to the mammal involved.

(5) The term "intermediary nation" means a nation that exports yellowfin tuna or yellowfin tuna products to the United States and that imports yellowfin tuna or yellowfin tuna products that are subject to a direct

ban on importation into the United States pursuant to section 1371(a)(2)(B) of this title.

**(6)** The term "marine mammal" means any mammal which (A) is morphologically adapted to the marine environment (including sea otters and members of the orders Sirenia, Pinnipedia and Cetacea), or (B) primarily inhabits the marine environment (such as the polar bear); and, for the purposes of this chapter, includes any part of any such marine mammal, including its raw, dressed, or dyed fur or skin.

**(7)** The term "marine mammal product" means any item of merchandise which consists, or is composed in whole or in part, of any marine mammal.

**(8)** The term "moratorium" means a complete cessation of the taking of marine mammals and a complete ban on the importation into the United States of marine mammals and marine mammal products, except as provided in this chapter.

**(9)** The term "optimum sustainable population" means, with respect to any population stock, the number of animals which will result in the maximum productivity of the population or the species, keeping in mind the carrying capacity of the habitat and the health of the ecosystem of which they form a constituent element.

**(10)** The term "person" includes (A) any private person or entity, and (B) any officer, employee, agent, department, or instrumentality of the Federal Government, of any State or political subdivision thereof, or of any foreign government.

**(11)** The term "population stock" or "stock" means a group of marine mammals of the same species or smaller taxa in a common spatial arrangement, that interbreed when mature.

**(12)(A)** Except as provided in subparagraph (B), the term "Secretary" means—

**(i)** the Secretary of the department in which the National Oceanic and Atmospheric Administration is operating, as to all responsibility, authority, funding, and duties under this chapter with respect to members of the order Cetacea and members, other than walruses, of the order Pinnipedia, and

**(ii)** the Secretary of the Interior as to all responsibility, authority, funding, and duties under this chapter with respect to all other marine mammals covered by this chapter.

**(B)** in [1] section 1387 of this title and subchapter V of this chapter (other than section 1421f–1 of this title) the term "Secretary" means the Secretary of Commerce.

**(13)** The term "take" means to harass, hunt, capture, or kill, or attempt to harass, hunt, capture, or kill any marine mammal.

**(14)** The term "United States" includes the several States, the District of Columbia, the Commonwealth of Puerto Rico, the Virgin Islands of the United States, American Samoa, Guam, and Northern Mariana Islands.

**(15)** The term "waters under the jurisdiction of the United States" means—

**(A)** the territorial sea of the United States;

**(B)** the waters included within a zone, contiguous to the territorial sea of the United States, of which the inner boundary is a line coterminous with the seaward boundary of each coastal State, and the other boundary is a line drawn in such a manner that each point on it is 200 nautical miles from the baseline from which the territorial sea is measured; and

**(C)** the areas referred to as eastern special areas in Article 3(1) of the Agreement between the United States of America and the Union of Soviet Socialist Republics on the Maritime Boundary, signed June 1, 1990; in particular, those areas east of the maritime boundary, as defined in that Agreement, that lie within 200 nautical miles of the baselines from which the breadth of the territorial sea of Russia is measured but beyond 200 nautical miles of the baselines from which the breadth of the territorial sea of the United States is measured, except that this subparagraph shall not apply before the date on which the Agreement between the United States and the Union of Soviet Socialist Republics on the Maritime Boundary, signed June 1, 1990, enters into force for the United States.

**(16)** The term "fishery" means—

**(A)** one or more stocks of fish which can be treated as a unit for purposes of conservation and management and which are identified on the basis of geographical, scientific, technical, recreational, and economic characteristics; and

**(B)** any fishing for such stocks.

**(17)** The term "competent regional organization"—

**(A)** for the tuna fishery in the eastern tropical Pacific Ocean, means the Inter–American Tropical Tuna Commission; and

**(B)** in any other case, means an organization consisting of those nations participating in a tuna fishery, the purpose of which is the conservation and management of that fishery and the management of issues relating to that fishery.

**(18)(A)** The term "harassment" means any act of pursuit, torment, or annoyance which—

**(i)** has the potential to injure a marine mammal or marine mammal stock in the wild; or

**(ii)** has the potential to disturb a marine mammal or marine mammal stock in the wild by causing disruption of behavioral patterns, including, but not limited to, migration, breathing, nursing, breeding, feeding, or sheltering.

(B) In the case of a military readiness activity (as defined in section 315(f) of Public Law 107–314; 16 U.S.C. 703 note) or a scientific research activity conducted by or on behalf of the Federal Government consistent with section 1374(c)(3) of this title, the term "harassment" means—

(i) any act that injures or has the significant potential to injure a marine mammal or marine mammal stock in the wild; or

(ii) any act that disturbs or is likely to disturb a marine mammal or marine mammal stock in the wild by causing disruption of natural behavioral patterns, including, but not limited to, migration, surfacing, nursing, breeding, feeding, or sheltering, to a point where such behavioral patterns are abandoned or significantly altered.

(C) The term "Level A harassment" means harassment described in subparagraph (A)(i) or, in the case of a military readiness activity or scientific research activity described in subparagraph (B), harassment described in subparagraph (B)(i).

(D) The term "Level B harassment" means harassment described in subparagraph (A)(ii) or, in the case of a military readiness activity or scientific research activity described in subparagraph (B), harassment described in subparagraph (B)(ii).

(19) The term "strategic stock" means a marine mammal stock—

(A) for which the level of direct human-caused mortality exceeds the potential biological removal level;

(B) which, based on the best available scientific information, is declining and is likely to be listed as a threatened species under the Endangered Species Act of 1973 [16 U.S.C.A. § 1531 et seq.] within the foreseeable future; or

(C) which is listed as a threatened species or endangered species under the Endangered Species Act of 1973 (16 U.S.C. 1531 et seq.), or is designated as depleted under this chapter.

(20) The term "potential biological removal level" means the maximum number of animals, not including natural mortalities, that may be removed from a marine mammal stock while allowing that stock to reach or maintain its optimum sustainable population. The potential biological removal level is the product of the following factors:

(A) The minimum population estimate of the stock.

(B) One-half the maximum theoretical or estimated net productivity rate of the stock at a small population size.

(C) A recovery factor of between 0.1 and 1.0.

(21) The term "Regional Fishery Management Council" means a Regional Fishery Management Council established under section 1852 of this title.

(22) The term "bona fide research" means scientific research on marine mammals, the results of which—

(A) likely would be accepted for publication in a referred scientific journal;

(B) are likely to contribute to the basic knowledge of marine mammal biology or ecology; or

(C) are likely to identify, evaluate, or resolve conservation problems.

(23) The term "Alaska Native organization" means a group designated by law or formally chartered which represents or consists of Indians, Aleuts, or Eskimos residing in Alaska.

(24) The term "take reduction plan" means a plan developed under section 1387 of this title.

(25) The term "take reduction team" means a team established under section 1387 of this title.

(26) The term "net productivity rate" means the annual per capita rate of increase in a stock resulting from additions due to reproduction, less losses due to mortality.

(27) The term "minimum population estimate" means an estimate of the number of animals in a stock that—

(A) is based on the best available scientific information on abundance, incorporating the precision and variability associated with such information; and

(B) provides reasonable assurance that the stock size is equal to or greater than the estimate.

(28) The term "International Dolphin Conservation Program" means the international program established by the agreement signed in LaJolla, California, in June, 1992, as formalized, modified, and enhanced in accordance with the Declaration of Panama.

(29) The term "Declaration of Panama" means the declaration signed in Panama City, Republic of Panama, on October 4, 1995.

(Pub.L. 92–522, § 3, Oct. 21, 1972, 86 Stat. 1028; Pub.L. 93–205, § 13(e)(1), Dec. 28, 1973, 87 Stat. 903; Pub.L. 94–265, Title IV, § 404(a), Apr. 13, 1976, 90 Stat. 360; Pub.L. 97–58, § 1(a), (b)(2), Oct. 9, 1981, 95 Stat. 979; Pub.L. 102–251, Title III, § 304, Mar. 9, 1992, 106 Stat. 65; Pub.L. 102–523, § 2(c), Oct. 26, 1992, 106 Stat. 3432; Pub.L. 102–582, Title IV, § 401(a), Nov. 2, 1992, 106 Stat. 4909; Pub.L. 102–587, Title III, § 3004(b), Nov. 4, 1992, 106 Stat. 5067; Pub.L. 103–238, §§ 12, 16(a), 24(a)(2), Apr. 30, 1994, 108 Stat. 557, 559, 565; Pub.L. 104–208, Div. A, Title I, § 101(a) [Title II, § 211(b)], Sept. 30, 1996, 110 Stat. 3009–41; Pub.L. 104–297, Title IV, § 405(b)(2), (3), Oct. 11, 1996, 110 Stat. 3621; Pub.L. 105–42, § 3, Aug. 15, 1997, 111 Stat. 1123; Pub.L. 106–555, Title II, § 202(b), Dec. 21, 2000, 114 Stat. 2768; Pub.L. 108–136, Div. A, Title III, § 319(a), Nov. 24, 2003, 117 Stat. 1433.)

[1] So in original. Probably should be capitalized.

## HISTORICAL AND STATUTORY NOTES

### References in Text

The Endangered Species Act of 1973, referred to in pars. (1)(C) and (19)(B), (C), is Pub.L. 93–205, Dec. 28, 1973, 87 Stat. 884, as amended, which is classified principally to chapter 35 (section 1531 et seq.) of this title. For complete classification of this Act to the Code, see Short Title note set out under section 1531 of this title and Tables.

For definition of Canal Zone, referred to in par. (3), see section 3602(b) of Title 22, Foreign Relations and Intercourse.

Section 315(f) of Public Law 107–314, referred to in subsec. (18)(B), is Pub.L. 107–314, Div. A, Title III, § 315(f), Dec. 2, 2002, 116 Stat. 2509, which is set out as a note under 16 U.S.C.A. § 703.

### Codifications

"Subchapter III of this chapter", referred to in par. (1)(A), in the original read "Title II of this Act", which has been codified as subchapter III of this chapter in view of the codification of sections 1361 and 1362 as subchapter I and of sections 1371 to 1384 as subchapter II.

In par. (12)(B), subchapter V of this chapter was in the original "title IV", meaning title IV of Pub.L. 92–522, originally added as "title III" of Pub.L. 92–522 by section 3303(a) of Pub.L. 102–587 and redesignated "title IV" of Pub.L. 92–522 by section 24(b)(1) of Pub.L. 103–238, which is codified to subchapter V of this chapter. Another title III of Pub.L. 92–522 was added by section 2(a) of Pub.L. 102–523 and enacted subchapter IV of this chapter.

### Effective and Applicability Provisions

1997 Acts

Section 8 of Pub.L. 105–42 provided that:

"**(a) Amendments to take effect when IDCP in force.**—Sections 3 through 7 of this Act [amending sections 952, 953, 1362, 1371, 1374, 1378, 1380, 1385, 1411 and 1417 of this title, amending the heading of subchapter IV of this chapter, enacting sections 962, 1412, 1413, 1414a, 1415, and 1416 of this title and repealing former sections 1412 to 1416 and 1418 of this title] (except for section 304 of the Marine Mammal Protection Act of 1972 as added by section 6 of this Act [section 1414a of this title]) shall become effective upon—

"(1) certification by the Secretary of Commerce that—

"(A) sufficient funding is available to complete the first year of the study required under section 304(a) of the Marine Mammal Protection Act of 1972 [section 1414a(a) of this title], as so added; and

"(B) the study has commenced; and

"(2) certification by the Secretary of State to Congress that a binding resolution of the Inter-American Tropical Tuna Commission or other legally binding instrument establishing the International Dolphin Conservation Program [IDCP] has been adopted and is in force.

"**(b) Special effective date.**—Notwithstanding subsection (a), the Secretary of Commerce may issue regulations under—

"(1) subsection (f)(2) of the Dolphin Protection Consumer Information Act (16 U.S.C. 1385(f)(2)), as added by section 5(b) of this Act;

(2) section 303(a) of the Marine Mammal Protection Act of 1972 (16 U.S.C. 1413(a)), as added by section 6(c) of this Act,

at any time after the date of enactment of this Act [Aug. 15, 1997]."

[The Secretary of Commerce made the certification referred to in section 8(a)(1) of Pub.L. 105–42, set out above, on July 27, 1998, and the Secretary of State made the certification referred to in section 8(a)(2) of Pub.L 105–42 on March 3, 1999.]

1996 Acts

Amendment by Pub.L. 104–208, Div. A, Title I, § 101(a) [Title II, § 211(b)], Sept. 30, 1996, 110 Stat. 3009–41, effective 15 days after Oct. 11, 1996, see Pub.L. 104–208, Div. A, Title I, § 101(a) [Title II, § 211(b)], Sept. 30, 1996, 110 Stat. 3009–41, set out as a note under section 1801 of this title.

1994 Acts

Section 24(e) of Pub.L. 103–238 provided that: "The amendments made by subsection (a) [construing prior amendment to par. (11) of this section as amendment to par. (12) of this section] shall be effective as if enacted as part of section 3004 of the Marine Mammal Health and Stranding Response Act (106 Stat. 5067) [section 3004 of Pub.L. 102–587, which was approved Nov. 4, 1992]."

1992 Acts

Amendment to par. (15) by Pub.L. 102–251 to take effect on the date on which the Agreement between the United States and the Union of Soviet Socialist Republics on the Maritime Boundary, signed June 1, 1990, enters into force for the United States, with the authority to prescribe implementing regulations effective on Mar. 9, 1992, but with no such regulation to be effective until the date on which the Agreement enters into force for the United States, see section 308 of Pub.L. 102–251, set out as a note under section 773 of this title.

1976 Acts

Section 404(b) of Pub.L. 94–265, which provided that the amendment to this section by section 404(a) of Pub.L. 94–265 took effect Mar. 1, 1977, was omitted in the general revision of section 404 by Pub.L. 104–297, Title II, § 205, Oct. 11, 1996, 110 Stat. 3609.

1973 Acts

Amendment by Pub.L. 93–205 effective Dec. 28, 1973, see section 16 of Pub.L. 93–205, set out as an Effective Date note under section 1531 of this title.

Section effective upon expiration of sixty-day period following Oct. 21, 1972, see section 4 of Pub.L. 92–522, set out as an Effective Date note under section 1361 of this title.

### Repeals

Section 404(a) of Pub.L. 94–265, set out in the credit to this section, was omitted in the general revision of section 404 by Pub.L. 104–297, Title II, § 205, Oct. 11, 1996, 110 Stat. 3609.

Pub.L. 102–251, Title III, § 304, Mar. 9, 1992, 106 Stat. 65, set out in the credit to this section, was repealed by Pub.L. 104–297, Title IV, § 405(b)(2), Oct. 11, 1996, 110 Stat. 3621.

### Termination of Advisory Committees

Advisory committees in existence on Jan. 5, 1973, to terminate not later than the expiration of the two-year period following Jan. 5, 1973, unless, in the case of a committee established by the President or an officer of the Federal Government, such committee is renewed by appropriate action prior to the expiration of such two-year period, or in the case of a committee established by the Congress, its duration is otherwise provided by law, see section 14 of Pub.L. 92–463, Oct. 6, 1972, 86 Stat. 776, set out in Appendix 2 to Title 5, Government Organization and Employees.

**Construction of Amendment**

Section 24(a)(1) of Pub.L. 103–238 provided that:

"(1) **Execution of prior amendments.**—The amendments set forth in section 3004(b) of the Marine Mammal Health and Stranding Response Act (106 Stat. 5067) [amending par. (11) of this section]—

"(A) are deemed to have been made by that section to section 3(12) of the Marine Mammal Protection Act of 1972 (16 U.S.C. 1362(12) [par. (12) of this section]); and

"(B) shall not be considered to have been made by that section to section 3(11) of that Act (16 U.S.C. 1362(11) [par. (11) of this section])."

## SUBCHAPTER II—CONSERVATION AND PROTECTION OF MARINE MAMMALS

### HISTORICAL AND STATUTORY NOTES

**Codifications**

"Subchapter II" in the original read "Title I" but has been codified as subchapter II in view of the codification of sections 1361 and 1362 as subchapter I.

## § 1371. Moratorium on taking and importing marine mammals and marine mammal products

**[MMPA § 101]**

**(a) Imposition; exceptions**

There shall be a moratorium on the taking and importation of marine mammals and marine mammal products, commencing on the effective date of this chapter, during which time no permit may be issued for the taking of any marine mammal and no marine mammal or marine mammal product may be imported into the United States except in the following cases:

(1) Consistent with the provisions of section 1374 of this title, permits may be issued by the Secretary for taking, and importation for purposes of scientific research, public display, photography for educational or commercial purposes, or enhancing the survival or recovery of a species or stock, or for importation of polar bear parts (other than internal organs) taken in sport hunts in Canada. Such permits, except permits issued under section 1374(c)(5) of this title, may be issued if the taking or importation proposed to be made is first reviewed by the Marine Mammal Commission and the Committee of Scientific Advisors on Marine Mammals established under subchapter III of this chapter. The Commission and Committee shall recommend any proposed taking or importation, other than importation under section 1374(c)(5) of this title, which is consistent with the purposes and policies of section 1361 of this title. If the Secretary issues such a permit for importation, the Secretary shall issue to the importer concerned a certificate to that effect in such form as the Secretary of the Treasury prescribes, and such importation may be made upon presentation of the certificate to the customs officer concerned.

(2) Marine mammals may be taken incidentally in the course of commercial fishing operations and permits may be issued therefor under section 1374 of this title subject to regulations prescribed by the Secretary in accordance with section 1373 of this title, or in lieu of such permits, authorizations may be granted therefor under section 1387 of this title, subject to regulations prescribed under that section by the Secretary without regard to section 1373 of this title. Such authorizations may be granted under subchapter IV of this chapter with respect to purse seine fishing for yellowfin tuna in the eastern tropical Pacific Ocean, subject to regulations prescribed under that subchapter by the Secretary without regard to section 1373 of this title. In any event it shall be the immediate goal that the incidental kill or incidental serious injury of marine mammals permitted in the course of commercial fishing operations be reduced to insignificant levels approaching a zero mortality and serious injury rate. The Secretary of the Treasury shall ban the importation of commercial fish or products from fish which have been caught with commercial fishing technology which results in the incidental kill or incidental serious injury of ocean mammals in excess of United States standards. For purposes of applying the preceding sentence, the Secretary—

(A) shall insist on reasonable proof from the government of any nation from which fish or fish products will be exported to the United States of the effects on ocean mammals of the commercial fishing technology in use for such fish or fish products exported from such nation to the United States;

(B) in the case of yellowfin tuna harvested with purse seine nets in the eastern tropical Pacific Ocean, and products therefrom, to be exported to the United States, shall require that the government of the exporting nation provide documentary evidence that—

(i)(I) the tuna or products therefrom were not banned from importation under this paragraph before the effective date of section 4 of the International Dolphin Conservation Program Act; or

(II) the tuna or products therefrom were harvested after the effective date of section 4 of the International Dolphin Conservation Program Act by vessels of a nation which participates in the International Dolphin Conservation Program, and such harvesting nation is either a member of the Inter–American Tropical Tuna Commission or has initiated (and within 6 months thereafter completed) all steps required of applicant nations, in accordance with article V, paragraph 3 of the Convention establishing the Inter–American Tropical Tuna Commission, to become a member of that organization;

**(ii)** such nation is meeting the obligations of the International Dolphin Conservation Program and the obligations of membership in the Inter–American Tropical Tuna Commission, including all financial obligations; and

**(iii)** the total dolphin mortality limits, and per-stock per-year dolphin mortality limits permitted for that nation's vessels under the International Dolphin Conservation Program do not exceed the limits determined for 1997, or for any year thereafter, consistent with the objective of progressively reducing dolphin mortality to a level approaching zero through the setting of annual limits and the goal of eliminating dolphin mortality, and requirements of the International Dolphin Conservation Program;

**(C)** shall not accept such documentary evidence if—

**(i)** the government of the harvesting nation does not provide directly or authorize the Inter–American Tropical Tuna Commission to release complete and accurate information to the Secretary in a timely manner—

**(I)** to allow determination of compliance with the International Dolphin Conservation Program; and

**(II)** for the purposes of tracking and verifying compliance with the minimum requirements established by the Secretary in regulations promulgated under section 1385(f) of this title; or

**(ii)** after taking into consideration such information, findings of the Inter–American Tropical Tuna Commission, and any other relevant information, including information that a nation is consistently failing to take enforcement actions on violations which diminish the effectiveness of the International Dolphin Conservation Program, the Secretary, in consultation with the Secretary of State, finds that the harvesting nation is not in compliance with the International Dolphin Conservation Program.

**(D)** shall require the government of any intermediary nation to certify and provide reasonable proof to the Secretary that it has not imported, within the preceding six months, any yellowfin tuna or yellowfin tuna products that are subject to a direct ban on importation to the United States under subparagraph (B);

**(E)** shall, six months after importation of yellowfin tuna or tuna products has been banned under this section, certify such fact to the President, which certification shall be deemed to be a certification for the purposes of section 1978(a) of Title 22 for as long as such ban is in effect; and

**(F)(i)** except as provided in clause (ii), in the case of fish or products containing fish harvested by a nation whose fishing vessels engage in high seas driftnet fishing, shall require that the government of the exporting nation provide documentary evidence that the fish or fish product was not harvested with a large-scale driftnet in the South Pacific Ocean after July 1, 1991, or in any other water of the high seas after January 1, 1993, and

**(ii)** in the case of tuna or a product containing tuna harvested by a nation whose fishing vessels engage in high seas driftnet fishing, shall require that the government of the exporting nation provide documentary evidence that the tuna or tuna product was not harvested with a large-scale driftnet anywhere on the high seas after July 1, 1991.

For purposes of subparagraph (F), the term "driftnet" has the meaning given such term in section 4003 of the Driftnet Impact Monitoring, Assessment, and Control Act of 1987 (16 U.S.C. 1822 note), except that, until January 1, 1994, the term "driftnet" does not include the use in the northeast Atlantic Ocean of gillnets with a total length not to exceed five kilometers if the use is in accordance with regulations adopted by the European Community pursuant to the October 28, 1991, decision by the Council of Fisheries Ministers of the Community.

**(3)(A)** The Secretary, on the basis of the best scientific evidence available and in consultation with the Marine Mammal Commission, is authorized and directed, from time to time, having due regard to the distribution, abundance, breeding habits, and times and lines of migratory movements of such marine mammals, to determine when, to what extent, if at all, and by what means, it is compatible with this chapter to waive the requirements of this section so as to allow taking, or importing of any marine mammal, or any marine mammal product, and to adopt suitable regulations, issue permits, and make determinations in accordance with sections 1372, 1373, 1374, and 1381 of this title permitting and governing such taking and importing, in accordance with such determinations: *Provided, however,* That the Secretary, in making such determinations, must be assured that the taking of such marine mammal is in accord with sound principles of resource protection and conservation as provided in the purposes and policies of this chapter: *Provided further, however,* That no marine mammal or no marine mammal product may be imported into the United States unless the Secretary certifies that the program for taking marine mammals in the country of origin is consistent with the provisions and policies of this chapter. Products of nations not so certified may not be imported into the United States for any purpose, including processing for exportation.

**(B)** Except for scientific research purposes, photography for educational or commercial purposes, or enhancing the survival or recovery of a species or stock as provided for in paragraph (1) of this subsection, or as provided for under paragraph (5) of this subsection, during the moratorium no permit may be issued for the taking of any marine mammal which has been designated by the Secretary as depleted, and no importation may be made of any such mammal.

**(4)(A)** Except as provided in subparagraphs (B) and (C), the provisions of this chapter shall not apply to the use of measures—

**(i)** by the owner of fishing gear or catch, or an employee or agent of such owner, to deter a marine mammal from damaging the gear or catch;

**(ii)** by the owner of other private property, or an agent, bailee, or employee of such owner, to deter a marine mammal from damaging private property;

**(iii)** by any person, to deter a marine mammal from endangering personal safety; or

**(iv)** by a government employee, to deter a marine mammal from damaging public property,

so long as such measures do not result in the death or serious injury of a marine mammal.

**(B)** The Secretary shall, through consultation with appropriate experts, and after notice and opportunity for public comment, publish in the Federal Register a list of guidelines for use in safely deterring marine mammals. In the case of marine mammals listed as endangered species or threatened species under the Endangered Species Act of 1973 [16 U.S.C.A. § 1531 et seq.], the Secretary shall recommend specific measures which may be used to nonlethally deter marine mammals. Actions to deter marine mammals consistent with such guidelines or specific measures shall not be a violation of this chapter.

**(C)** If the Secretary determines, using the best scientific information available, that certain forms of deterrence have a significant adverse effect on marine mammals, the Secretary may prohibit such deterrent methods, after notice and opportunity for public comment, through regulation under this chapter.

**(D)** The authority to deter marine mammals pursuant to subparagraph (A) applies to all marine mammals, including all stocks designated as depleted under this chapter.

**(5)(A)(i)** Upon request therefor by citizens of the United States who engage in a specified activity (other than commercial fishing) within a specified geographical region, the Secretary shall allow, during periods of not more than five consecutive years each, the incidental, but not intentional, taking by citizens while engaging in that activity within that region of small numbers of marine mammals of a species or population stock if the Secretary, after notice (in the Federal Register and in newspapers of general circulation, and through appropriate electronic media, in the coastal areas that may be affected by such activity) and opportunity for public comment—

**(I)** finds that the total of such taking during each five-year (or less) period concerned will have a negligible impact on such species or stock and will not have an unmitigable adverse impact on the availability of such species or stock for taking for subsistence uses pursuant to subsection (b) of this section or section 1379(f) of this title or, in the case of a cooperative agreement under both this chapter and the Whaling Convention Act of 1949 [16 U.S.C.A. § 916 et seq.], pursuant to section 1382(c) of this title; and

**(II)** prescribes regulations setting forth—

**(aa)** permissible methods of taking pursuant to such activity, and other means of effecting the least practicable adverse impact on such species or stock and its habitat, paying particular attention to rookeries, mating grounds, and areas of similar significance, and on the availability of such species or stock for subsistence uses; and

**(bb)** requirements pertaining to the monitoring and reporting of such taking.

**(ii)** For a military readiness activity (as defined in section 315(f) of Public Law 107–314; 16 U.S.C. 703 note), a determination of "least practicable adverse impact on such species or stock" under clause (i)(II)(aa) shall include consideration of personnel safety, practicality of implementation, and impact on the effectiveness of the military readiness activity. Before making the required determination, the Secretary shall consult with the Department of Defense regarding personnel safety, practicality of implementation, and impact on the effectiveness of the military readiness activity.

**(iii)** Notwithstanding clause (i), for any authorization affecting a military readiness activity (as defined in section 315(f) of Public Law 107–314; 16 U.S.C. 703 note), the Secretary shall publish the notice required by such clause only in the Federal Register.

**(B)** The Secretary shall withdraw, or suspend for a time certain (either on an individual or class basis, as appropriate) the permission to take marine mammals under subparagraph (A) pursuant to a specified activity within a specified geographical region if the Secretary finds, after notice and opportunity for public comment (as required under subparagraph (A) unless subparagraph (C) (i) applies), that—

**(i)** the regulations prescribed under subparagraph (A) regarding methods of taking, monitoring, or reporting are not being substantially complied with by a person engaging in such activity; or

**(ii)** the taking allowed under subparagraph (A) pursuant to one or more activities within one or more regions is having, or may have, more than a negligible impact on the species or stock concerned.

**(C)(i)** The requirement for notice and opportunity for public comment in subparagraph (B) shall not apply in the case of a suspension of permission to take if the Secretary determines that an emergency exists which poses a significant risk to the well-being of the species or stock concerned.

**(ii)** Sections 1373 and 1374 of this title shall not apply to the taking of marine mammals under the authority of this paragraph.

**(D)(i)** Upon request therefor by citizens of the United States who engage in a specified activity (other than commercial fishing) within a specific geographic region, the Secretary shall authorize, for periods of not more than 1 year, subject to such conditions as the Secretary may specify, the incidental, but not intentional, taking by harassment of small numbers of marine mammals of a species or population stock by such citizens while engaging in that activity within that region if the Secretary finds that such harassment during each period concerned—

**(I)** will have a negligible impact on such species or stock, and

**(II)** will not have an unmitigable adverse impact on the availability of such species or stock for taking for subsistence uses pursuant to subsection (b) of this section, or section 1379(f) of this title or pursuant to a cooperative agreement under section 1388 of this title.

**(ii)** The authorization for such activity shall prescribe, where applicable—

**(I)** permissible methods of taking by harassment pursuant to such activity, and other means of effecting the least practicable impact on such species or stock and its habitat, paying particular attention to rookeries, mating grounds, and areas of similar significance, and on the availability of such species or stock for taking for subsistence uses pursuant to subsection (b) of this section or section 1379(f) of this title or pursuant to a cooperative agreement under section 1388 of this title,

**(II)** the measures that the Secretary determines are necessary to ensure no unmitigable adverse impact on the availability of the species or stock for taking for subsistence uses pursuant to subsection (b) of this section or section 1379(f) of this title or pursuant to a cooperative agreement under section 1388 of this title, and

**(III)** requirements pertaining to the monitoring and reporting of such taking by harassment, including requirements for the independent peer review of proposed monitoring plans or other research proposals where the proposed activity may affect the availability of a species or stock for taking for subsistence uses pursuant to subsection (b) of this section or section 1379(f) of this title or pursuant to a cooperative agreement under section 1388 of this title.

**(iii)** The Secretary shall publish a proposed authorization not later than 45 days after receiving an application under this subparagraph and request public comment through notice in the Federal Register, newspapers of general circulation, and appropriate electronic media and to all locally affected communities for a period of 30 days after publication. Not later than 45 days after the close of the public comment period, if the Secretary makes the findings set forth in clause (i), the Secretary shall issue an authorization with appropriate conditions to meet the requirements of clause (ii).

**(iv)** The Secretary shall modify, suspend, or revoke an authorization if the Secretary finds that the provisions of clauses (i) or (ii) are not being met.

**(v)** A person conducting an activity for which an authorization has been granted under this subparagraph shall not be subject to the penalties of this chapter for taking by harassment that occurs in compliance with such authorization.

**(vi)** For a military readiness activity (as defined in section 315(f) of Public Law 107–314; 16 U.S.C. 703 note), a determination of "least practicable adverse impact on such species or stock" under clause (i)(I) shall include consideration of personnel safety, practicality of implementation, and impact on the effectiveness of the military readiness activity. Before making the required determination, the Secretary shall consult with the Department of Defense regarding personnel safety, practicality of implementation, and impact on the effectiveness of the military readiness activity.

**(vii)** Notwithstanding clause (iii), for any authorization affecting a military readiness activity (as defined in section 315(f) of Public Law 107–314; 16 U.S.C. 703 note), the Secretary shall publish the notice required by such clause only in the Federal Register.

**(E)(i)** During any period of up to 3 consecutive years, the Secretary shall allow the incidental, but not the intentional, taking by persons using vessels of the United States or vessels which have valid fishing permits issued by the Secretary in accordance with section 1824(b) of this title, while engaging in commercial fishing operations, or marine mammals from a species or stock designated as depleted because of its listing as an endangered species or threatened species under the Endangered Species Act of 1973 (16 U.S.C. 1531 et seq.) if the Secretary, after notice and opportunity for public comment, determines that—

**(I)** the incidental mortality and serious injury from commercial fisheries will have a negligible impact on such species or stock;

**(II)** a recovery plan has been developed or is being developed for such species or stock pursuant to the Endangered Species Act of 1973; and

**(III)** where required under section 1387 of this title, a monitoring program is established under subsection (d) of such section, vessels engaged in such fisheries are registered in accordance with such section, and a take reduction plan has been developed or is being developed for such species or stock.

**(ii)** Upon a determination by the Secretary that the requirements of clause (i) have been met, the Secretary shall publish in the Federal Register a list of those fisheries for which such determination was made, and, for vessels required to register under section 1387 of this title, shall issue an appropriate permit for each authorization granted under such section to vessels to which this paragraph applies. Vessels engaged in a fishery included in the notice published by the Secretary under this clause which are not required to register under section 1387 of this title shall not be subject to the penalties of this chapter for the incidental taking of marine mammals to which this paragraph applies, so long as the owner or master of such vessel reports any incidental mortality or injury of such marine mammals to the Secretary in accordance with section 1387 of this title.

**(iii)** If, during the course of the commercial fishing season, the Secretary determines that the level of incidental mortality or serious injury from commercial fisheries for which a determination was made under clause (i) has resulted or is likely to result in an impact that is more than negligible on the endangered or threatened species or stock, the Secretary shall use the emergency authority granted under section 1387 of this title to protect such species or stock, and may modify any permit granted under this paragraph as necessary.

**(iv)** The Secretary may suspend for a time certain or revoke a permit granted under this subparagraph only if the Secretary determines that the conditions or limitations set forth in such permit are not being complied with. The Secretary may amend or modify, after notice and opportunity for public comment, the list of fisheries published under clause (ii) whenever the Secretary determines there has been a significant change in the information or conditions used to determine such list.

**(v)** Sections 1373 and 1374 of this title shall not apply to the taking of marine mammals under the authority of this subparagraph.

**(vi)** This subparagraph shall not govern the incidental taking of California sea otters and shall not be deemed to amend or repeal the Act of November 7, 1986 (Public Law 99–625; 100 Stat. 3500).

**(F)** Notwithstanding the provisions of this subsection, any authorization affecting a military readiness activity (as defined in section 315(f) of Public Law 107–314; 16 U.S.C. 703 note) shall not be subject to the following requirements:

**(i)** In subparagraph (A), "within a specified geographical region" and "within that region of small numbers".

**(ii)** In subparagraph (B), "within a specified geographical region" and "within one or more regions".

**(iii)** In subparagraph (D), "within a specific geographic region", "of small numbers", and "within that region".

**(6)(A)** A marine mammal product may be imported into the United States if the product—

**(i)** was legally possessed and exported by any citizen of the United States in conjunction with travel outside the United States, provided that the product is imported into the United States by the same person upon the termination of travel;

**(ii)** was acquired outside of the United States as part of a cultural exchange by an Indian, Aleut, or Eskimo residing in Alaska; or

**(iii)** is owned by a Native inhabitant of Russia, Canada, or Greenland and is imported for noncommercial purposes in conjunction with travel within the United States or as part of a cultural exchange with an Indian, Aleut, or Eskimo residing in Alaska.

**(B)** For the purposes of this paragraph, the term—

**(i)** "Native inhabitant of Russia, Canada, or Greenland" means a person residing in Russia, Canada, or Greenland who is related by blood, is a member of the same clan or ethnological grouping, or shares a common heritage with an Indian, Aleut, or Eskimo residing in Alaska; and

(ii) "cultural exchange" means the sharing or exchange of ideas, information, gifts, clothing, or handicrafts between an Indian, Aleut, or Eskimo residing in Alaska and a Native inhabitant of Russia, Canada, or Greenland, including rendering of raw marine mammal parts as part of such exchange into clothing or handicrafts through carving, painting, sewing, or decorating.

**(b) Exemptions for Alaskan natives**

Except as provided in section 1379 of this title, the provisions of this chapter shall not apply with respect to the taking of any marine mammal by any Indian, Aleut, or Eskimo who resides in Alaska and who dwells on the coast of the North Pacific Ocean or the Arctic Ocean if such taking—

(1) is for subsistence purposes; or

(2) is done for purposes of creating and selling authentic native articles of handicrafts and clothing: *Provided,* That only authentic native articles of handicrafts and clothing may be sold in interstate commerce: *And provided further,* That any edible portion of marine mammals may be sold in native villages and towns in Alaska or for native consumption. For the purposes of this subsection, the term "authentic native articles of handicrafts and clothing" means items composed wholly or in some significant respect of natural materials, and which are produced, decorated, or fashioned in the exercise of traditional native handicrafts without the use of pantographs, multiple carvers, or other mass copying devices. Traditional native handicrafts include, but are not limited to weaving, carving, stitching, sewing, lacing, beading, drawing, and painting; and

(3) in each case, is not accomplished in a wasteful manner.

Notwithstanding the preceding provisions of this subsection, when, under this chapter, the Secretary determines any species or stock of marine mammal subject to taking by Indians, Aleuts, or Eskimos to be depleted, he may prescribe regulations upon the taking of such marine mammals by any Indian, Aleut, or Eskimo described in this subsection. Such regulations may be established with reference to species or stocks, geographical description of the area included, the season for taking, or any other factors related to the reason for establishing such regulations and consistent with the purposes of this chapter. Such regulations shall be prescribed after notice and hearing required by section 1373 of this title and shall be removed as soon as the Secretary determines that the need for their imposition has disappeared. In promulgating any regulation or making any assessment pursuant to a hearing or proceeding under this subsection or section 1386(b)(2) of this title, or in making any determination of depletion under this subsection or finding regarding unmitigable adverse impacts under subsection (a)(5) of this section that affects stocks or persons to which this subsection applies, the Secretary shall be responsible for demonstrating that such regulation, assessment, determination, or finding is supported by substantial evidence on the basis of the record as a whole. The preceding sentence shall only be applicable in an action brought by one or more Alaska Native organizations representing persons to which this subsection applies.

**(c) Taking in defense of self or others**

It shall not be a violation of this chapter to take a marine mammal if such taking is imminently necessary in self-defense or to save the life of a person in immediate danger, and such taking is reported to the Secretary within 48 hours. The Secretary may seize and dispose of any carcass.

**(d) Good Samaritan exemption**

It shall not be a violation of this chapter to take a marine mammal if—

(1) such taking is imminently necessary to avoid serious injury, additional injury, or death to a marine mammal entangled in fishing gear or debris;

(2) reasonable care is taken to ensure the safe release of the marine mammal, taking into consideration the equipment, expertise, and conditions at hand;

(3) reasonable care is exercised to prevent any further injury to the marine mammal; and

(4) such taking is reported to the Secretary within 48 hours.

**(e) Chapter not to apply to incidental takings by United States citizens employed on foreign vessels outside the United States EEZ**

The provisions of this chapter shall not apply to a citizen of the United States who incidentally takes any marine mammal during fishing operations outside the United States exclusive economic zone (as defined in section 1802 of this title) when employed on a foreign fishing vessel of a harvesting nation which is in compliance with the International Dolphin Conservation Program.

**(f) Exemption of actions necessary for national defense**

(1) The Secretary of Defense, after conferring with the Secretary of Commerce, the Secretary of the Interior, or both, as appropriate, may exempt any action or category of actions undertaken by the Department of Defense or its components from compliance with any requirement of this chapter, if the

Secretary determines that it is necessary for national defense.

(2) An exemption granted under this subsection—

**(A)** subject to subparagraph (B), shall be effective for a period specified by the Secretary of Defense; and

**(B)** shall not be effective for more than 2 years.

(3)(A) The Secretary of Defense may issue additional exemptions under this subsection for the same action or category of actions, after—

**(i)** conferring with the Secretary of Commerce, the Secretary of the Interior, or both as appropriate; and

**(ii)** making a new determination that the additional exemption is necessary for national defense.

**(B)** Each additional exemption under this paragraph shall be effective for a period specified by the Secretary of Defense, of not more than 2 years.

(4) Not later than 30 days after issuing an exemption under paragraph (1) or an additional exemption under paragraph (3), the Secretary of Defense shall submit to the Committee on Armed Services of the House of Representatives and the Committee on Armed Services of the Senate notice describing the exemption and the reasons therefor. The notice may be provided in classified form if the Secretary of Defense determines that use of the classified form is necessary for reasons of national security.

(Pub.L. 92–522, Title I, § 101, Oct. 21, 1972, 86 Stat. 1029; Pub.L. 93–205, § 13(e)(2), Dec. 28, 1973, 87 Stat. 903; Pub.L. 97–58, § 2, Oct. 9, 1981, 95 Stat. 979; Pub.L. 98–364, Title I, § 101, July 17, 1984, 98 Stat. 440; Pub.L. 99–659, Title IV, § 411(a), Nov. 14, 1986, 100 Stat. 3741; Pub.L. 100–711, §§ 4(a), 5(c), (e)(1), Nov. 23, 1988, 102 Stat. 4765, 4766, 4769, 4771; Pub.L. 101–627, § 901(g), Nov. 28, 1990, 104 Stat. 4467; Pub.L. 102–582, Title I, § 103, Title IV, § 401(b), Nov. 2, 1992, 106 Stat. 4903, 4909; Pub.L. 103–238, § 4, Apr. 30, 1994, 108 Stat. 532; Pub.L. 104–208, Div. A, Title I, § 101(a) [Title II, § 211(b)], Sept. 30, 1996, 110 Stat. 3009–41; Pub.L. 105–18, Title II, § 2003, June 12, 1997, 111 Stat. 174; Pub.L. 105–42, § 4(a) to (c), Aug. 15, 1997, 111 Stat. 1123, 1124; Pub.L. 108–136, Div. A, Title III, § 319(b), (c), Nov. 24, 2003, 117 Stat. 1434.)

## HISTORICAL AND STATUTORY NOTES

### References in Text

The effective date of this chapter, referred to in subsec. (a), means the effective date of Pub.L. 92–522. See section 4 of Pub.L. 92–522, set out as an Effective Date note under section 1361 of this title.

The Driftnet Impact Monitoring, Assessment, and Control Act of 1987, including section 4003 of such Act, referred to in subsec. (a)(2), enacted as Pub.L. 100–220, Title IV, Dec. 29, 1987, 101 Stat. 1447, is set out as a note under section 1822 of this title.

The Endangered Species Act of 1973, referred to in subsec. (a)(4)(B), (5)(E)(i), is Pub.L. 93–205, Dec. 28, 1973, 87 Stat. 884, as amended, which is classified principally to chapter 35 (section 1531 et seq.) of this title. For complete classification of this Act to the Code, see Short Title note set out under section 1531 of this title and Tables.

The Whaling Convention Act of 1949, referred to in subsec. (a)(5)(A)(i), is Act Aug. 9, 1950, c. 653, 64 Stat. 421, as amended, which is classified generally to subchapter II (section 916 et seq.) of chapter 14 of this title. For complete classification of this Act to the Code, see Short Title note set out under section 916 of this title and Tables.

Section 315(f) of Public Law 107–314, referred to in subsec. (a)(5), is Pub.L. 107–314, Div. A, Title III, § 315(f), Dec. 2, 2002, 116 Stat. 2509, which is set out as a note under 16 U.S.C.A. § 703.

The Act of November 7, 1986, referred to in subsec. (a)(5)(E)(vi), is Pub.L. 99–625, 100 Stat. 3500, which amended section 718b of this title, enacted provisions set out as a note under section 1536 of this title and amended provisions set out in the note table under section 668dd of this title.

"This chapter", referred to in subsec. (e), originally read "this Act", meaning the Marine Mammal Protection Act of 1972, which is principally classified to this chapter. For complete classification, see Tables.

This Chapter, referred to in subsec. (f)(1), originally read "this Act," meaning The Marine Mammal Protection Act of 1972, Pub.L. 95–522, Oct. 21, 1972, 86 Stat. 1027, as amended, which is classified to 16 U.S.C.A. § 1361 et seq.

### Codifications

The amendment to subsec. (a)(2), indicated by the direction in Pub.L. 105–42, § 5(c) to strike section 901(g) of the Dolphin Protection Consumer Information Act, Pub.L. 101–627, which amended subsec. (a)(2) by, inter alia, adding subpar. (E), was not executed to the text as probable intent of Congress in light of amendments to subsec. (a)(2) by Pub.L. 105–42, § 4(a) to (c).

"Subchapter III of this chapter", referred to in subsec. (a)(1), in the original "title II of this Act" but has been codified as subchapter III in view of the codification of sections 1361 and 1362 as subchapter I and of sections 1371 to 1384 as subchapter II.

### Effective and Applicability Provisions

1997 Acts

For effective date of amendment to this section by Pub.L. 105–42, see section 8 of Pub.L. 105–42, set out as a note under section 1362 of this title.

1996 Acts

Amendment by Pub.L. 104–208, Div. A, Title I, § 101(a) [Title II, § 211(b)], Sept. 30, 1996, 110 Stat. 3009–41, effective 15 days after Oct. 11, 1996, see Pub.L. 104–208, Div. A, Title I, § 101(a) [Title II, § 211(b)], Sept. 30, 1996, 110 Stat. 3009–41, set out as a note under section 1801 of this title.

1973 Acts

Amendment by Pub.L. 93–205 effective Dec. 28, 1973, see section 16 of Pub.L. 93–205 set out as an Effective Date note under section 1531 of this title.

1972 Acts

Section effective upon expiration of sixty-day period following Oct. 21, 1972, see section 4 of Pub.L. 92–522, set out as an Effective Date note under section 1361 of this title.

**Termination of Advisory Committees**

Advisory committees in existence on Jan. 5, 1973, to terminate not later than the expiration of the two-year period following Jan. 5, 1973, unless, in the case of a committee established by the President or an officer of the Federal Government, such committee is renewed by appropriate action prior to the expiration of such two-year period, or in the case of a committee established by the Congress, its duration is otherwise provided by law, see section 14 of Pub.L. 92–463, Oct. 6, 1972, 86 Stat. 776, set out in Appendix 2 to Title 5, Government Organization and Employees.

## § 1372. Prohibitions

**[MMPA § 102]**

**(a) Taking**

Except as provided in sections 1371, 1373, 1374, 1379, 1381, 1383, and 1383a, and 1387 of this title and subchapter V of this chapter, it is unlawful—

(1) for any person subject to the jurisdiction of the United States or any vessel or other conveyance subject to the jurisdiction of the United States to take any marine mammal on the high seas;

(2) except as expressly provided for by an international treaty, convention, or agreement to which the United States is a party and which was entered into before the effective date of this subchapter or by any statute implementing any such treaty, convention, or agreement—

(A) for any person or vessel or other conveyance to take any marine mammal in waters or on lands under the jurisdiction of the United States; or

(B) for any person to use any port, harbor, or other place under the jurisdiction of the United States to take or import marine mammals or marine mammal products; and

(3) for any person, with respect to any marine mammal taken in violation of this subchapter, to possess that mammal or any product from that mammal;

(4) for any person to transport, purchase, sell, export, or offer to purchase, sell, or export any marine mammal or marine mammal product—

(A) that is taken in violation of this chapter; or

(B) for any purpose other than public display, scientific research, or enhancing the survival of a species or stock as provided for under subsection 1374(c) of this title; and

(5) for any person to use, in a commercial fishery, any means or methods of fishing in contravention of any regulations or limitations, issued by the Secretary for that fishery to achieve the purposes of this chapter.

**(b) Importation of pregnant or nursing mammals; depleted species or stock; inhumane taking**

Except pursuant to a permit for scientific research, or for enhancing the survival or recovery of a species or stock, issued under section 1374(c) of this title, it is unlawful to import into the United States any marine mammal if such mammal was—

(1) pregnant at the time of taking;

(2) nursing at the time of taking, or less than eight months old, whichever occurs later;

(3) taken from a species or population stock which the Secretary has, by regulation published in the Federal Register, designated as a depleted species or stock; or

(4) taken in a manner deemed inhumane by the Secretary.

Notwithstanding the provisions of paragraphs (1) and (2), the Secretary may issue a permit for the importation of a marine mammal, if the Secretary determines that such importation is necessary for the protection or welfare of the animal.

**(c) Importation of illegally taken mammals**

It is unlawful to import into the United States any of the following:

(1) Any marine mammal which was—

(A) taken in violation of this subchapter; or

(B) taken in another country in violation of the law of that country.

(2) Any marine mammal product if—

(A) the importation into the United States of the marine mammal from which such product is made is unlawful under paragraph (1) of this subsection; or

(B) the sale in commerce of such product in the country of origin of the product is illegal;

(3) Any fish, whether fresh, frozen, or otherwise prepared, if such fish was caught in a manner which the Secretary has proscribed for persons subject to the jurisdiction of the United States, whether or not any marine mammals were in fact taken incident to the catching of the fish.

**(d) Nonapplicability of prohibitions**

Subsections (b) and (c) of this section shall not apply—

(1) in the case of marine mammals or marine mammal products, as the case may be, to which subsection (b)(3) of this section applies, to such items imported into the United States before the date on which the Secretary publishes notice in the Federal Register of his proposed rulemaking with respect to the designation of the species or stock concerned as depleted; or

(2) in the case of marine mammals or marine mammal products to which subsection (c)(1)(B) or (c)(2)(B) of this section applies, to articles imported

into the United States before the effective date of the foreign law making the taking or sale, as the case may be, of such marine mammals or marine mammal products unlawful.

**(e) Retroactive effect**

This chapter shall not apply with respect to any marine mammal taken before the effective date of this chapter, or to any marine mammal product consisting of, or composed in whole or in part of, any marine mammal taken before such date.

**(f) Commercial taking of whales**

It is unlawful for any person or vessel or other conveyance to take any species of whale incident to commercial whaling in waters subject to the jurisdiction of the United States.

(Pub.L. 92–522, Title I, § 102, Oct. 21, 1972, 86 Stat. 1032; Pub.L. 93–205, § 13(e)(3), Dec. 28, 1973, 87 Stat. 903; Pub.L. 95–136, § 4, Oct. 18, 1977, 91 Stat. 1167; Pub.L. 97–58, § 3(a), Oct. 9, 1981, 95 Stat. 981; Pub.L. 100–711, §§ 2(b), 5(b), (e)(2), Nov. 23, 1988, 102 Stat. 4763, 4769, 4771; Pub.L. 102–587, Title III, § 3004(a)(1), Nov. 4, 1992, 106 Stat. 5067; Pub.L. 103–238, §§ 5(a), 13(c), 24(c)(9), Apr. 30, 1994, 108 Stat. 536, 558, 566.)

### HISTORICAL AND STATUTORY NOTES

**References in Text**

The effective date of this subchapter, referred to in subsec. (a)(2), means the effective date of Title I of Pub.L. 92–522. See section 4 of Pub.L. 92–522, set out as an Effective Date note under section 1361 of this title.

The effective date of this chapter referred to in subsec. (e), means the effective date of Pub.L. 92–522. See section 4 of Pub.L. 92–522, set out as an Effective Date note under section 1361 of this title.

**Codifications**

In subsec. (a), subchapter V of this chapter was in the original "title IV", meaning title IV of Pub.L. 92–522, originally added as "title III" of Pub.L. 92–522 by section 3303(a) of Pub.L. 102–587, and redesignated "title IV" of Pub.L. 92–522 by section 24(b)(1) of Pub.L. 103–238, which is codified to subchapter V of this chapter. Another title III of Pub.L. 92–522 was added by section 2(a) of Pub.L. 102–523 and enacted subchapter IV of this chapter.

**Effective and Applicability Provisions**

1973 Acts

Amendment by Pub.L. 93–205 effective Dec. 28, 1973, see section 16 of Pub.L. 93–205, set out as an Effective Date note under section 1531 of this title.

1972 Acts

Section effective upon expiration of sixty-day period following Oct. 21, 1972, see section 4 of Pub.L. 92–522, set out as an Effective Date note under section 1361 of this title.

## § 1373. Regulations on taking of marine mammals

**[MMPA § 103]**

**(a) Necessity and appropriateness**

The Secretary, on the basis of the best scientific evidence available and in consultation with the Marine Mammal Commission, shall prescribe such regulations with respect to the taking and importing of animals from each species of marine mammal (including regulations on the taking and importing of individuals within population stocks) as he deems necessary and appropriate to insure that such taking will not be to the disadvantage of those species and population stocks and will be consistent with the purposes and policies set forth in section 1361 of this title.

**(b) Factors considered in prescribing regulations**

In prescribing such regulations, the Secretary shall give full consideration to all factors which may affect the extent to which such animals may be taken or imported, including but not limited to the effect of such regulations on—

(1) existing and future levels of marine mammal species and population stocks;

(2) existing international treaty and agreement obligations of the United States;

(3) the marine ecosystem and related environmental considerations;

(4) the conservation, development, and utilization of fishery resources; and

(5) the economic and technological feasibility of implementation.

**(c) Allowable restrictions**

The regulations prescribed under subsection (a) of this section for any species or population stock of marine mammal may include, but are not limited to, restrictions with respect to—

(1) the number of animals which may be taken or imported in any calendar year pursuant to permits issued under section 1374 of this title;

(2) the age, size, or sex (or any combination of the foregoing) of animals which may be taken or imported, whether or not a quota prescribed under paragraph (1) of this subsection applies with respect to such animals;

(3) the season or other period of time within which animals may be taken or imported;

(4) the manner and locations in which animals may be taken or imported; and

(5) fishing techniques which have been found to cause undue fatalities to any species of marine mammal in a fishery.

**(d) Procedure**

Regulations prescribed to carry out this section with respect to any species or stock of marine mammals must be made on the record after opportunity for an agency hearing on both the Secretary's determination to waive the moratorium pursuant to section

1371(a)(3)(A) of this title and on such regulations, except that, in addition to any other requirements imposed by law with respect to agency rulemaking, the Secretary shall publish and make available to the public either before or concurrent with the publication of notice in the Federal Register of his intention to prescribe regulations under this section—

(1) a statement of the estimated existing levels of the species and population stocks of the marine mammal concerned;

(2) a statement of the expected impact of the proposed regulations on the optimum sustainable population of such species or population stock;

(3) a statement describing the evidence before the Secretary upon which he proposes to base such regulations; and

(4) any studies made by or for the Secretary or any recommendations made by or for the Secretary or the Marine Mammal Commission which relate to the establishment of such regulations.

### (e) Periodic review

Any regulation prescribed pursuant to this section shall be periodically reviewed, and may be modified from time to time in such manner as the Secretary deems consistent with and necessary to carry out the purposes of this chapter.

### (f) Report to Congress

Within six months after the effective date of this chapter and every twelve months thereafter, the Secretary shall report to the public through publication in the Federal Register and to the Congress on the current status of all marine mammal species and population stocks subject to the provisions of this chapter. His report shall describe those actions taken and those measures believed necessary, including where appropriate, the issuance of permits pursuant to this subchapter to assure the well-being of such marine mammals.

(Pub.L. 92–522, Title I, § 103, Oct. 21, 1972, 86 Stat. 1033.)

## HISTORICAL AND STATUTORY NOTES

**References in Text**

The effective date of this chapter, referred to in subsec. (f), means the effective date of Pub.L. 92–522. See section 4 of Pub.L. 92–522, set out as an Effective Date note under section 1361 of this title.

**Effective and Applicability Provisions**

Section effective upon expiration of sixty-day period following Oct. 21, 1972, see section 4 of Pub.L. 92–522, set out as an Effective Date note under section 1361 of this title.

**Marine Mammal Populations Report**

Pub.L. 101–627, Title XI, § 1101, Nov. 28, 1990, 104 Stat. 4468, provided that:

"The Secretary of Commerce, in consultation with the Secretary of the Interior, shall provide to the Committee on Commerce, Science, and Transportation of the Senate and the Committee on Merchant Marine and Fisheries of the House of Representatives within 12 months after the date of enactment of this Act [Nov. 28, 1990] a report—

"(1) assessing population sizes and trends of harbor seals, sea otters, California sea lions, and northern sea lions off the coast of the State of Washington, which assessment shall include the historic, present, and projected population sizes and the overall health of current populations of such marine mammals;

"(2) assessing the effectiveness of sections 101(a)(3)(A) and 109(h) of the Marine Mammal Protection Act of 1972 (16 U.S.C. 1371(a)(3)(A) and 1379(h)) [sections 1371(a)(3)(A) and 1379(h) of this title] with particular emphasis on the management of the lower Columbia River and Puget Sound marine mammal populations, which assessment shall describe how the agencies are interpreting and implementing such sections, how often such sections have been invoked, and whether such sections have been effective in the management of marine mammal populations and in responding to the problems which such sections were intended to address; and

"(3) specifying long range management plans for the species of marine mammals listed in paragraph (1)."

[Committee on Merchant Marine and Fisheries of House of Representatives abolished and any reference in any provision of law enacted before Jan. 4, 1995, to the Committee on Merchant Marine and Fisheries of the House of Representatives treated as referring to the Committee on Agriculture of the House of Representatives, in the case of a provision of law relating to inspection of seafood or seafood products, the Committee on National Security of the House of Representatives, in the case of a provision of law relating to interoceanic canals, the Merchant Marine Academy and State Maritime Academies, or national security aspects of merchant marine, the Committee on Resources of the House of Representatives, in the case of a provision of law relating to fisheries, wildlife, international fishing agreements marine affairs (including coastal zone management) except for measures relating to oil and other pollution of navigable waters, or oceanography, the Committee on Science of the House of Representatives, in the case of a provision of law relating to marine research, and the Committee on Transportation and Infrastructure of the House of Representatives, in the case of a provision of law relating to a matter other than a matter described above, see section 1(b)(3) of Pub.L. 104–14, set out as a note preceding section 21 of Title 2, The Congress.]

## § 1374. Permits

### [MMPA § 104]

### (a) Issuance

The Secretary may issue permits which authorize the taking or importation of any marine mammal. Permits for the incidental taking of marine mammals in the course of commercial fishing operations may only be issued as specifically provided for in sections [1] 1371(a)(5) or 1416 of this title, or subsection (h) of this section.

**(b) Requisite provisions**

Any permit issued under this section shall—

(1) be consistent with any applicable regulation established by the Secretary under section 1373 of this title, and

(2) specify—

(A) the number and kind of animals which are authorized to be taken or imported,

(B) the location and manner (which manner must be determined by the Secretary to be humane) in which they may be taken, or from which they may be imported,

(C) the period during which the permit is valid, and

(D) any other terms or conditions which the Secretary deems appropriate.

In any case in which an application for a permit cites as a reason for the proposed taking the overpopulation of a particular species or population stock, the Secretary shall first consider whether or not it would be more desirable to transplant a number of animals (but not to exceed the number requested for taking in the application) of that species or stock to a location not then inhabited by such species or stock but previously inhabited by such species or stock.

**(c) Importation for scientific research, public display, or enhancing survival or recovery of species or stock**

(1) Any permit issued by the Secretary which authorizes the taking or importation of a marine mammal for purposes of scientific research, public display, or enhancing the survival or recovery of a species or stock shall specify, in addition to the conditions required by subsection (b) of this section, the methods of capture, supervision, care, and transportation which must be observed pursuant to such taking or importation. Any person authorized to take or import a marine mammal for purposes of scientific research, public display, or enhancing the survival or recovery of a species or stock shall furnish to the Secretary a report on all activities carried out by him pursuant to that authority.

(2)(A) A permit may be issued to take or import a marine mammal for the purpose of public display only to a person which the Secretary determines—

(i) offers a program for education or conservation purposes that is based on professionally recognized standards of the public display community;

(ii) is registered or holds a license issued under 7 U.S.C. 2131 et seq.; and

(iii) maintains facilities for the public display of marine mammals that are open to the public on a regularly scheduled basis and that access to such facilities is not limited or restricted other than by charging of an admission fee.

(B) A permit under this paragraph shall grant to the person to which it is issued the right, without obtaining any additional permit or authorization under this chapter, to—

(i) take, import, purchase, offer to purchase, possess, or transport the marine mammal that is the subject of the permit; and

(ii) sell, export, or otherwise transfer possession of the marine mammal, or offer to sell, export, or otherwise transfer possession of the marine mammal—

(I) for the purpose of public display, to a person that meets the requirements of clauses (i), (ii), and (iii) of subparagraph (A);

(II) for the purpose of scientific research, to a person that meets the requirements of paragraph (3); or

(III) for the purpose of enhancing the survival or recovery of a species or stock, to a person that meets the requirements of paragraph (4).

(C) A person to which a marine mammal is sold or exported or to which possession of a marine mammal is otherwise transferred under the authority of subparagraph (B) shall have the rights and responsibilities described in subparagraph (B) with respect to the marine mammal without obtaining any additional permit or authorization under this chapter. Such responsibilities shall be limited to—

(i) for the purpose of public display, the responsibility to meet the requirements of clauses (i), (ii), and (iii) of subparagraph (A),

(ii) for the purpose of scientific research, the responsibility to meet the requirements of paragraph (3), and

(iii) for the purpose of enhancing the survival or recovery of a species or stock, the responsibility to meet the requirements of paragraph (4).

(D) If the Secretary—

(i) finds in concurrence with the Secretary of Agriculture, that a person that holds a permit under this paragraph for a marine mammal, or a person exercising rights under subparagraph (C), no longer meets the requirements of subparagraph (A)(ii) and is not reasonably likely to meet those requirements in the near future, or

(ii) finds that a person that holds a permit under this paragraph for a marine mammal, or a person exercising rights under subparagraph (C), no longer meets the requirements of subparagraph (A)(i) or (iii) and is not reasonably likely to meet those requirements in the near future, the Secretary may revoke the permit in accordance with subsection (e) of this section, seize the marine mammal, or cooperate with other persons authorized to hold marine mammals under this chapter for disposition of the marine mammal. The Secretary may recover from the person expenses incurred by the Secretary for that seizure.

**(E)** No marine mammal held pursuant to a permit issued under subparagraph (A), or by a person exercising rights under subparagraph (C), may be sold, purchased, exported, or transported unless the Secretary is notified of such action no later than 15 days before such action, and such action is for purposes of public display, scientific research, or enhancing the survival or recovery of a species or stock. The Secretary may only require the notification to include the information required for the inventory established under paragraph (10).

**(3)(A)** The Secretary may issue a permit under this paragraph for scientific research purposes to an applicant which submits with its permit application information indicating that the taking is required to further a bona fide scientific purpose. The Secretary may issue a permit under this paragraph before the end of the public review and comment period required under subsection (d)(2) of this section if delaying issuance of the permit could result in injury to a species, stock, or individual, or in loss of unique research opportunities.

**(B)** No permit issued for purposes of scientific research shall authorize the lethal taking of a marine mammal unless the applicant demonstrates that a nonlethal method of conducting the research is not feasible. The Secretary shall not issue a permit for research which involves the lethal taking of a marine mammal from a species or stock that is depleted, unless the Secretary determines that the results of such research will directly benefit that species or stock, or that such research fulfills a critically important research need.

**(C)** Not later than 120 days after April 30, 1994, the Secretary shall issue a general authorization and implementing regulations allowing bona fide scientific research that may result only in taking by Level B harassment of a marine mammal. Such authorization shall apply to persons which submit, by 60 days before commencement of such research, a letter of intent via certified mail to the Secretary containing the following:

**(i)** The species or stocks of marine mammals which may be harassed.

**(ii)** The geographic location of the research.

**(iii)** The period of time over which the research will be conducted.

**(iv)** The purpose of the research, including a description of how the definition of bona fide research as established under this chapter would apply.

**(v)** Methods to be used to conduct the research.

Not later than 30 days after receipt of a letter of intent to conduct scientific research under the general authorization, the Secretary shall issue a letter to the applicant confirming that the general authorization applies, or, if the proposed research is likely to result in the taking (including Level A harassment) of a marine mammal, shall notify the applicant that subparagraph (A) applies.

**(4)(A)** A permit may be issued for enhancing the survival or recovery of a species or stock only with respect to a species or stock for which the Secretary, after consultation with the Marine Mammal Commission and after notice and opportunity for public comment, has first determined that—

**(i)** taking or importation is likely to contribute significantly to maintaining or increasing distribution or numbers necessary to ensure the survival or recovery of the species or stock; and

**(ii)** taking or importation is consistent (I) with any conservation plan adopted by the Secretary under section 1383b(b) of this title or any recovery plan developed under section 1533(f) of this title for the species or stock, or (II) if there is no conservation or recovery plan in place, with the Secretary's evaluation of the actions required to enhance the survival or recovery of the species or stock in light of the factors that would be addressed in a conservation plan or a recovery plan.

**(B)** A permit issued in accordance with this paragraph may allow the captive maintenance of a marine mammal from a depleted species or stock only if the Secretary—

**(i)** determines that captive maintenance is likely to contribute to the survival or recovery of the species or stock by maintaining a viable gene pool, increasing productivity, providing biological information, or establishing animal reserves;

**(ii)** determines that the expected benefit to the affected species or stock outweighs the expected benefit of alternatives which do not require removal of animals from the wild; and

**(iii)** requires that the marine mammal or its progeny be returned to the natural habitat of the species or stock as soon as feasible, consistent with the objectives of any applicable conservation plan or recovery plan, or of any evaluation by the Secretary under subparagraph (A).

The Secretary may allow the public display of such a marine mammal only if the Secretary determines that such display is incidental to the authorized maintenance and will not interfere with the attainment of the survival or recovery objectives.

**(5)(A)** The Secretary may issue a permit for the importation of polar bear parts (other than internal organs) taken in sport hunts in Canada to an applicant which submits with its permit application proof that the polar bear was legally harvested in Canada by the applicant. Such a permit shall be issued if the Secretary, in consultation with the Marine Mammal Commission and after notice and opportunity for public comment, finds that—

**(i)** Canada has a monitored and enforced sport hunting program consistent with the purposes of the Agreement on the Conservation of Polar Bears;

**(ii)** Canada has a sport hunting program based on scientifically sound quotas ensuring the maintenance of the affected population stock at a sustainable level;

**(iii)** the export and subsequent import are consistent with the provisions of the Convention on International Trade in Endangered Species of Wild Fauna and Flora and other international agreements and conventions; and

**(iv)** the export and subsequent import are not likely to contribute to illegal trade in bear parts.

**(B)** The Secretary shall establish and charge a reasonable fee for permits issued under this paragraph. All fees collected under this paragraph shall be available to the Secretary until expended for use in developing and implementing cooperative research and management programs for the conservation of polar bears in Alaska and Russia pursuant to section 1383(d) of this title.

**(C)(i)** The Secretary shall undertake a scientific review of the impact of permits issued under this paragraph on the polar bear population stocks in Canada within 2 years after April 30, 1994. The Secretary shall provide an opportunity for public comment during the course of such review, and shall include a response to such public comment in the final report on such review.

**(ii)** The Secretary shall not issue permits under this paragraph after September 30, 1996, if the Secretary determines, based on the scientific review, that the issuance of permits under this paragraph is having a significant adverse impact on the polar bear population stocks in Canada. The Secretary may review such determination annually thereafter, in light of the best scientific information available, and shall complete the review not later than January 31 in any year a review is undertaken. The Secretary may issue permits under this paragraph whenever the Secretary determines, on the basis of such annual review, that the issuance of permits under this paragraph is not having a significant adverse impact on the polar bear population stocks in Canada.

**(D)** The Secretary of the Interior shall, expeditiously after the expiration of the applicable 30 day period under subsection (d)(2) of this section, issue a permit for the importation of polar bear parts (other than internal organs) from polar bears taken in sport hunts in Canada before February 18, 1997, to each applicant who submits, with the permit application, proof that the polar bear was legally harvested in Canada by the applicant. The Secretary shall issue such permits without regard to the provisions of subparagraphs (A) and (C)(ii) of this paragraph, subsection (d)(3) of this section, and sections 1371 and 1372 of this title. This subparagraph shall not apply to polar bear parts that were imported before June 12, 1997.

**(6)** A permit may be issued for photography for educational or commercial purposes involving marine mammals in the wild only to an applicant which submits with its permit application information indicating that the taking will be limited to Level B harassment, and the manner in which the products of such activities will be made available to the public.

**(7)** Upon request by a person for a permit under paragraph (2), (3), or (4) for a marine mammal which is in the possession of any person authorized to possess it under this chapter and which is determined under guidance under section 1421a(a) of this title not to be releasable to the wild, the Secretary shall issue the permit to the person requesting the permit if that person—

**(A)** meets the requirements of clauses (i), (ii), and (iii) of paragraph (2)(A), in the case of a request for a permit under paragraph (2);

**(B)** meets the requirements of paragraph (3), in the case of a request for a permit under that paragraph; or

**(C)** meets the requirements of paragraph (4), in the case of a request for a permit under that paragraph.

**(8)(A)** No additional permit or authorization shall be required to possess, sell, purchase, transport, export, or offer to sell or purchase the progeny of marine mammals taken or imported under this subsection, if such possession, sale, purchase, transport, export, or offer to sell or purchase is—

**(i)** for the purpose of public display, and by or to, respectively, a person which meets the requirements of clauses (i), (ii), and (iii) of paragraph (2)(A);

**(ii)** for the purpose of scientific research, and by or to, respectively, a person which meets the requirements of paragraph (3); or

**(iii)** for the purpose of enhancing the survival or recovery of a species or stock, and by or to, respectively, a person which meets the requirements of paragraph (4).

**(B)(i)** A person which has a permit under paragraph (2), or a person exercising rights under paragraph (2)(C), which has possession of a marine mammal that gives birth to progeny shall—

**(I)** notify the Secretary of the birth of such progeny within 30 days after the date of birth; and

**(II)** notify the Secretary of the sale, purchase, or transport of such progeny no later than 15 days before such action.

**(ii)** The Secretary may only require notification under clause (i) to include the information required for the inventory established under paragraph (10).

**(C)** Any progeny of a marine mammal born in captivity before April 30, 1994, and held in captivity for the purpose of public display shall be treated as though born after April 30, 1994.

**(9)** No marine mammal may be exported for the purpose of public display, scientific research, or enhancing the survival or recovery of a species or stock unless the receiving facility meets standards that are comparable to the requirements that a person must meet to receive a permit under this subsection for that purpose.

**(10)** The Secretary shall establish and maintain an inventory of all marine mammals possessed pursuant to permits issued under paragraph (2)(A), by persons exercising rights under paragraph (2)(C), and all progeny of such marine mammals. The inventory shall contain, for each marine mammal, only the following information which shall be provided by a person holding a marine mammal under this chapter:

**(A)** The name of the marine mammal or other identification.

**(B)** The sex of the marine mammal.

**(C)** The estimated or actual birth date of the marine mammal.

**(D)** The date of acquisition or disposition of the marine mammal by the permit holder.

**(E)** The source from whom the marine mammal was acquired including the location of the take from the wild, if applicable.

**(F)** If the marine mammal is transferred, the name of the recipient.

**(G)** A notation if the animal was acquired as the result of a stranding.

**(H)** The date of death of the marine mammal and the cause of death when determined.

**(d) Application procedures; notice; hearing; review**

**(1)** The Secretary shall prescribe such procedures as are necessary to carry out this section, including the form and manner in which application for permits may be made.

**(2)** The Secretary shall publish notice in the Federal Register of each application made for a permit under this section. Such notice shall invite the submission from interested parties, within thirty days after the date of the notice, of written data or views, with respect to the taking or importation proposed in such application.

**(3)** The applicant for any permit under this section must demonstrate to the Secretary that the taking or importation of any marine mammal under such permit will be consistent with the purposes of this chapter and the applicable regulations established under section 1373 of this title.

**(4)** If within thirty days after the date of publication of notice pursuant to paragraph (2) of this subsection with respect to any application for a permit any interested party or parties request a hearing in connection therewith, the Secretary may, within sixty days following such date of publication, afford to such party or parties an opportunity for such a hearing.

**(5)** As soon as practicable (but not later than thirty days) after the close of the hearing or, if no hearing is held, after the last day on which data, or views, may be submitted pursuant to paragraph (2) of this subsection, the Secretary shall (A) issue a permit containing such terms and conditions as he deems appropriate, or (B) shall deny issuance of a permit. Notice of the decision of the Secretary to issue or to deny any permit under this paragraph must be published in the Federal Register within ten days after the date of issuance or denial.

**(6)** Any applicant for a permit, or any party opposed to such permit, may obtain judicial review of the terms and conditions of any permit issued by the Secretary under this section or of his refusal to issue such a permit. Such review, which shall be pursuant to chapter 7 of Title 5, may be initiated by filing a petition for review in the United States district court for the district wherein the applicant for a permit resides, or has his principal place of business, or in the United States District Court for the District of Columbia, within sixty days after the date on which such permit is issued or denied.

**(e) Modification, suspension, and revocation**

**(1)** The Secretary may modify, suspend, or revoke in whole or part any permit issued by him under this section—

**(A)** in order to make any such permit consistent with any change made after the date of issuance of such permit with respect to any applicable regulation prescribed under section 1373 of this title,

(B) in any case in which a violation of the terms and conditions of the permit is found, or

(C) if, in the case of a permit under subsection (c)(5) of this section authorizing importation of polar bear parts, the Secretary, in consultation with the appropriate authority in Canada, determines that the sustainability of Canada's polar bear population stocks are being adversely affected or that sport hunting may be having a detrimental effect on maintaining polar bear population stocks throughout their range.

(2) Whenever the Secretary shall propose any modification, suspension, or revocation of a permit under this subsection, the permittee shall be afforded opportunity, after due notice, for a hearing by the Secretary with respect to such proposed modification, suspension, or revocation. Such proposed action by the Secretary shall not take effect until a decision is issued by him after such hearing. Any action taken by the Secretary after such a hearing is subject to judicial review on the same basis as is any action taken by him with respect to a permit application under paragraph (5) of subsection (d) of this section.

(3) Notice of the modification, suspension, or revocation of any permit by the Secretary shall be published in the Federal Register within ten days from the date of the Secretary's decision.

### (f) Possession of permit by issuee or his agent

Any permit issued under this section must be in the possession of the person to whom it is issued (or an agent of such person) during—

(1) the time of the authorized or taking importation;

(2) the period of any transit of such person or agent which is incident to such taking or importation; and

(3) any other time while any marine mammal taken or imported under such permit is in the possession of such person or agent.

A duplicate copy of the issued permit must be physically attached to the container, package, enclosure, or other means of containment, in which the marine mammal is placed for purposes of storage, transit, supervision, or care.

### (g) Fees

The Secretary shall establish and charge a reasonable fee for permits issued under this section.

### (h) General permits

(1) Consistent with the regulations prescribed pursuant to section 1373 of this title and to the requirements of section 1371 of this title, the Secretary may issue an annual permit to a United States purse seine fishing vessel for the taking of such marine mammals, and shall issue regulations to cover the use of any such annual permits.

(2) Such annual permits for the incidental taking of marine mammals in the course of commercial purse seine fishing for yellowfin tuna in the eastern tropical Pacific Ocean shall be governed by section 1416 of this title, subject to the regulations issued pursuant to section 1413 of this title.

(Pub.L. 92–522, Title I, § 104, Oct. 21, 1972, 86 Stat. 1034; Pub.L. 98–364, Title I, § 102, July 17, 1984, 98 Stat. 440; Pub.L. 100–711, §§ 4(d), 5(d), Nov. 23, 1988, 102 Stat. 4767, 4769; Pub.L. 103–238, § 5(b), Apr. 30, 1994, 108 Stat. 537; Pub.L. 105–18, Title II, § 5004, June 12, 1997, 111 Stat. 187; Pub.L. 105–42, § 4(d), Aug. 15, 1997, 111 Stat. 1125; Pub.L. 105–277, Div. A, § 101(e) [Title I], Oct. 21, 1998, 112 Stat. 2681–238; Pub.L. 106–31, Title V, § 5004(1), May 21, 1999, 113 Stat. 110; Pub.L. 108–108, Title I, § 149, Nov. 10, 2003, 117 Stat. 1281.)

[1] So in original. Probably should be "section".

## HISTORICAL AND STATUTORY NOTES

### Codifications

Amendment by Pub.L. 108–108, Title I, § 149, directing amendment of "section 104 (16 U.S.C. 1374)", was executed to section 104 of the Marine Mammal Protection Act of 1972, Pub.L. 92–522, Oct. 21, 1972, 86 Stat. 1034, which enacted this section, as the probable intent of Congress.

Amendment by section 101(e) [Title I] of Div. A of Pub.L. 105–277, directing substitution of "available to the Secretary until expended for use" for "available to the Secretary for use" in the second sentence, was executed to the second sentence of subsec. (c)(5)(B) of this section, as the probable intent of Congress, notwithstanding directory language reference to subsec. "(c)(50)(B)". Subsequently, Pub.L. 106–31, Title V, § 5004(1), May 21, 1999, 113 Stat. 110 amended the directory language of Pub.L. 105–277, Div. A, § 101(e) [Title I], substituting "section 104(c)(5)(B) of the Marine Mammal Protection Act of 1972 (16 U.S.C. 1361–1407)" for "section 104(c)(50)(B) of the Marine Mammal Protection Act (16 U.S.C. 1361–1407)".

### Effective and Applicability Provisions

1999 Acts

Amendment of this section by Pub.L. 106–31 effective as if included in Pub.L. 105–277 on the date of its enactment, see section 5004(4) of Pub.L. 106–31, set out as a note under section 544b of this title.

1997 Acts

For effective date of amendment to this section by Pub.L. 105–42, see section 8 of Pub.L. 105–42, set out as a note under section 1362 of this title.

1994 Acts

Section effective upon expiration of sixty-day period following Oct. 21, 1972, see section 4 of Pub.L. 92–522, set out as an Effective Date note under section 1361 of this title.

### Abolition of House Committee on Merchant Marine and Fisheries

Committee on Merchant Marine and Fisheries of House of Representatives abolished and any reference in any provision of law enacted before Jan. 4, 1995, to the Committee on

Merchant Marine and Fisheries of the House of Representatives treated as referring to the Committee on Agriculture of the House of Representatives, in the case of a provision of law relating to inspection of seafood or seafood products, the Committee on National Security of the House of Representatives, in the case of a provision of law relating to interoceanic canals, the Merchant Marine Academy and State Maritime Academies, or national security aspects of merchant marine, the Committee on Resources of the House of Representatives, in the case of a provision of law relating to fisheries, wildlife, international fishing agreements marine affairs (including coastal zone management) except for measures relating to oil and other pollution of navigable waters, or oceanography, the Committee on Science of the House of Representatives, in the case of a provision of law relating to marine research, and the Committee on Transportation and Infrastructure of the House of Representatives, in the case of a provision of law relating to a matter other than a matter described above, see section 1(b)(3) of Pub.L. 104–14, set out as a note preceding section 21 of Title 2, The Congress.

**Modification of Permits Existing Prior to April 30, 1994**

Section 5(c) of Pub.L. 103–238 provided that: "Any permit issued under section 104(c)(2) of the Marine Mammal Protection Act of 1972 (16 U.S.C. 1374(c)(2)) [subsec. (c)(2) of this section] before the date of the enactment of this Act [Apr. 30, 1994] is hereby modified to be consistent with that section as amended by this Act."

## § 1375. Penalties

[MMPA § 105]

**(a)(1)** Any person who violates any provision of this subchapter or of any permit or regulation issued thereunder, except as provided in section 1387 of this title, may be assessed a civil penalty by the Secretary of not more than $10,000 for each such violation. No penalty shall be assessed unless such person is given notice and opportunity for a hearing with respect to such violation. Each unlawful taking or importation shall be a separate offense. Any such civil penalty may be remitted or mitigated by the Secretary for good cause shown. Upon any failure to pay a penalty assessed under this subsection, the Secretary may request the Attorney General to institute a civil action in a district court of the United States for any district in which such person is found, resides, or transacts business to collect the penalty and such court shall have jurisdiction to hear and decide any such action.

(2) In any case involving an alleged unlawful importation of a marine mammal or marine mammal product, if such importation is made by an individual for his own personal or family use (which does not include importation as an accommodation to others or for sale or other commercial use), the Secretary may, in lieu of instituting a proceeding under paragraph (1), allow the individual to abandon the mammal or product, under procedures to be prescribed by the Secretary, to the enforcement officer at the port of entry.

**(b)** Any person who knowingly violates any provision of this subchapter or of any permit or regulation issued thereunder (except as provided in section 1387 of this title) shall, upon conviction, be fined not more than $20,000 for each such violation, or imprisoned for not more than one year, or both.

(Pub.L. 92–522, Title I, § 105, Oct. 21, 1972, 86 Stat. 1036; Pub.L. 97–58, § 3(b), Oct. 9, 1981, 95 Stat. 982; Pub.L. 103–238, § 13(a), (b), Apr. 30, 1994, 108 Stat. 558.)

### HISTORICAL AND STATUTORY NOTES

**Effective and Applicability Provisions**

1972 Acts

Section effective upon expiration of sixty-day period following Oct. 21, 1972, see section 4 of Pub.L. 92–522, set out as an Effective Date note under section 1361 of this title.

## § 1375a. Disposition of fines

On or after November 29, 1999, all fines collected by the United States Fish and Wildlife Service for violations of the Marine Mammal Protection Act (16 U.S.C. 1362–1407) [16 U.S.C.A. §§ 1362 to 1407] and implementing regulations shall be available to the Secretary, without further appropriation, to be used for the expenses of the United States Fish and Wildlife Service in administering activities for the protection and recovery of manatees, polar bears, sea otters, and walruses, and shall remain available until expended.

(Pub.L. 106–113, Div. B, § 1000(a)(3) [Title I], Nov. 29, 1999, 113 Stat. 1535, 1501A–139).

### HISTORICAL AND STATUTORY NOTES

**Codifications**

Section was not enacted as part of the Marine Mammal Protection Act of 1972, which comprises this chapter.

## § 1376. Seizure and forfeiture of cargo

[MMPA § 106]

**(a) Application of consistent provisions**

Any vessel or other conveyance subject to the jurisdiction of the United States that is employed in any manner in the unlawful taking of any marine mammal shall have its entire cargo or the monetary value thereof subject to seizure and forfeiture. All provisions of law relating to the seizure, judicial forfeiture, and condemnation of cargo for violation of the customs laws, the disposition of such cargo, and the proceeds from the sale thereof, and the remission or mitigation of any such forfeiture, shall apply with respect to the cargo of any vessel or other conveyance seized in connection with the unlawful taking of a marine mammal insofar as such provisions of law are applicable and not inconsistent with the provisions of this subchapter.

**(b) Penalties**

Any vessel subject to the jurisdiction of the United States that is employed in any manner in the unlawful taking of any marine mammal shall be liable for a civil penalty of not more than $25,000. Such penalty shall be assessed by the district court of the United States having jurisdiction over the vessel. Clearance of a vessel against which a penalty has been assessed, from a port of the United States, may be withheld until such penalty is paid, or until a bond or otherwise satisfactory surety is posted. Such penalty shall constitute a maritime lien on such vessel which may be recovered by action in rem in the district court of the United States having jurisdiction over the vessel.

**(c) Reward for information leading to conviction**

Upon the recommendation of the Secretary, the Secretary of the Treasury is authorized to pay an amount equal to one-half of the fine incurred but not to exceed $2,500 to any person who furnishes information which leads to a conviction for a violation of this subchapter. Any officer or employee of the United States or of any State or local government who furnishes information or renders service in the performance of his official duties shall not be eligible for payment under this section.

(Pub.L. 92–522, Title I, § 106, Oct. 21, 1972, 86 Stat. 1036.)

### HISTORICAL AND STATUTORY NOTES

**Effective and Applicability Provisions**

1972 Acts

Section effective upon expiration of sixty-day period following Oct. 21, 1972, see section 4 of Pub.L. 92–522, set out as an Effective Date note under section 1361 of this title.

## § 1377. Enforcement

### [MMPA § 107]

**(a) Utilization of personnel**

Except as otherwise provided in this subchapter, the Secretary shall enforce the provisions of this subchapter. The Secretary may utilize, by agreement, the personnel, services, and facilities of any other Federal agency for purposes of enforcing this subchapter.

**(b) State officers and employees**

The Secretary may also designate officers and employees of any State or of any possession of the United States to enforce the provisions of this subchapter. When so designated, such officers and employees are authorized to function as Federal law enforcement agents for these purposes, but they shall not be held and considered as employees of the United States for the purposes of any laws administered by the Director of the Office of Personnel Management.

**(c) Warrants and other process for enforcement**

The judges of the district courts of the United States and the United States magistrates may, within their respective jurisdictions, upon proper oath or affirmation showing probably cause, issue such warrants or other process, including warrants or other process issued in admiralty proceedings in United States district courts, as may be required for enforcement of this subchapter and any regulations issued thereunder.

**(d) Execution of process; arrest; search; seizure**

Any person authorized by the Secretary to enforce this subchapter may execute any warrant or process issued by any officer or court of competent jurisdiction for the enforcement of this subchapter. Such person so authorized may, in addition to any other authority conferred by law—

(1) with or without warrant or other process, arrest any person committing in his presence or view a violation of this subchapter or the regulations issued thereunder;

(2) with a warrant or other process, or without a warrant if he has reasonable cause to believe that a vessel or other conveyance subject to the jurisdiction of the United States or any person on board is in violation of any provision of this subchapter or the regulations issued thereunder, search such vessel or conveyance and arrest such person;

(3) seize the cargo of any vessel or other conveyance subject to the jurisdiction of the United States used or employed contrary to the provisions of this subchapter or the regulations issued hereunder or which reasonably appears to have been so used or employed; and

(4) seize, whenever and wherever found, all marine mammals and marine mammal products taken or retained in violation of this subchapter or the regulations issued thereunder and shall dispose of them in accordance with regulations prescribed by the Secretary.

**(e) Disposition of seized cargo**

(1) Whenever any cargo or marine mammal or marine mammal product is seized pursuant to this section, the Secretary shall expedite any proceedings commenced under section 1375(a) or (b) of this title. All marine mammals or marine mammal products or other cargo so seized shall be held by any person authorized by the Secretary pending disposition of such proceedings. The owner or consignee of any such marine mammal or marine mammal product or other cargo so seized shall, as soon as practicable following such seizure, be notified of that fact in accordance with regulations established by the Secretary.

(2) The Secretary may, with respect to any proceeding under section 1375(a) or (b) of this title, in lieu

of holding any marine mammal or marine mammal product or other cargo, permit the person concerned to post bond or other surety satisfactory to the Secretary pending the disposition of such proceeding.

(3)(A) Upon the assessment of a penalty pursuant to section 1375(a) of this title, all marine mammals and marine mammal products or other cargo seized in connection therewith may be proceeded against in any court of competent jurisdiction and forfeited to the Secretary for disposition by him in such manner as he deems appropriate.

(B) Upon conviction for violation of section 1375(b) of this title, all marine mammals and marine mammal products seized in connection therewith shall be forfeited to the Secretary for disposition by him in such manner as he deems appropriate. Any other property or item so seized may, at the discretion of the court, be forfeited to the United States or otherwise disposed of.

(4) If with respect to any marine mammal or marine mammal product or other cargo so seized—

(A) a civil penalty is assessed under section 1375(a) of this title and no judicial action is commenced to obtain the forfeiture of such mammal or product within thirty days after such assessment, such marine mammal or marine mammal product or other cargo shall be immediately returned to the owner or the consignee; or

(B) no conviction results from an alleged violation of section 1375(b) of this title, such marine mammal or marine mammal product or other cargo shall immediately be returned to the owner or consignee if the Secretary does not, with[1] thirty days after the final disposition of the case involving such alleged violation, commence proceedings for the assessment of a civil penalty under section 1375(a) of this title.

(Pub.L. 92–522, Title I, § 107, Oct. 21, 1972, 86 Stat. 1037; 1978 Reorg.Plan No. 2, § 102, eff. Jan. 1, 1979, 43 F.R. 36037, 92 Stat. 3783.)

[1] So in original. Probably should be "within".

### HISTORICAL AND STATUTORY NOTES

**Effective and Applicability Provisions**

1972 Acts

Section effective upon expiration of sixty-day period following Oct. 21, 1972, see section 4 of Pub.L. 92–522, set out as an Effective Date note under section 1361 of this title.

**Change of Name**

United States magistrate appointed under section 631 of Title 28, Judiciary and Judicial Procedure, to be known as United States magistrate judge after Dec. 1, 1990, with any reference to United States magistrate or magistrate in Title 28, in any other Federal statute, etc., deemed a reference to United States magistrate judge appointed under section 631 of Title 28, see section 321 of Pub.L. 101–650, set out as a note under section 631 of Title 28.

**Transfer of Functions**

"Director of the Office of Personnel Management" was substituted for "Civil Service Commission" in subsec. (b) pursuant to Reorg. Plan No. 2 of 1978, § 102, 43 F.R. 36037, 92 Stat. 3783, set out under section 1101 of Title 5, Government Organization and Employees, which transferred all functions vested by statute in the United States Civil Service Commission to the Director of the Office of Personnel Management (except as otherwise specified), effective Jan. 1, 1979, as provided by section 1–102 of Ex. Ord. No. 12107, Dec. 28, 1978, 44 F.R. 1055, set out under section 1101 of Title 5.

## § 1378. International program

### [MMPA § 108]

**(a) Duties of Secretary**

The Secretary, through the Secretary of State, shall—

(1) initiate negotiations as soon as possible for the development of bilateral or multilateral agreements with other nations for the protection and conservation of all marine mammals covered by this chapter;

(2) initiate—

(A) negotiations as soon as possible with all foreign governments which are engaged in, or which have persons or companies engaged in, commercial fishing operations which are found by the Secretary to be unduly harmful to any species or population stock of marine mammal, for the purpose of entering into bilateral and multilateral treaties with such countries to protect marine mammals, with the Secretary of State to prepare a draft agenda relating to this matter for discussion at appropriate international meetings and forums;

(B) discussions with foreign governments whose vessels harvest yellowfin tuna with purse seines in the eastern tropical Pacific Ocean, for the purpose of concluding, through the Inter-American Tropical Tuna Commission or such other bilateral or multilateral institutions as may be appropriate, international arrangements for the conservation of marine mammals taken incidentally in the course of harvesting such tuna, which should include provisions for (i) cooperative research into alternative methods of locating and catching yellowfin tuna which do not involve the taking of marine mammals, (ii) cooperative research on the status of affected marine mammal population stocks, (iii) reliable monitoring of the number, rate, and species of marine mammals taken by vessels of harvesting nations, (iv) limitations on incidental take levels based upon the best scientific information available, and (v) the use of the best marine mammal safety techniques and equipment that are economically and technologically practicable to reduce the incidental kill and serious injury of marine mammals to insignificant levels approaching a zero mortality and serious injury rate;

(C) negotiations to revise the Convention for the Establishment of an Inter-American Tropical Tuna Commission (1 U.S.T. 230; TIAS 2044) which will incorporate—

(i) the conservation and management provisions agreed to by the nations which have signed the Declaration of Panama and in the Straddling Fish Stocks and Highly Migratory Fish Stocks Agreement, as opened for signature on December 4, 1995; and

(ii) a revised schedule of annual contributions to the expenses of the Inter-American Tropical Tuna Commission that is equitable to participating nations; and

(D) discussions with those countries participating, or likely to participate, in the International Dolphin Conservation Program, for the purpose of identifying sources of funds needed for research and other measures promoting effective protection of dolphins, other marine species, and the marine ecosystem;

(3) encourage such other agreements to promote the purposes of this chapter with other nations for the protection of specific ocean and land regions which are of special significance to the health and stability of marine mammals;

(4) initiate the amendment of any existing international treaty for the protection and conservation of any species of marine mammal to which the United States is a party in order to make such treaty consistent with the purposes and policies of this chapter;

(5) seek the convening of an international ministerial meeting on marine mammals before July 1, 1973, for the purposes of (A) the negotiation of a binding international convention for the protection and conservation of all marine mammals, and (B) the implementation of paragraph (3) of this section; and

(6) provide to the Congress by not later than one year after October 21, 1972, a full report on the results of his efforts under this section.

**(b) Consultations and studies concerning North Pacific fur seals**

(1) In addition to the foregoing, the Secretary shall—

(A) in consultation with the Marine Mammal Commission established by section 1401 of this title, undertake a study of the North Pacific fur seals to determine whether herds of such seals subject to the jurisdiction of the United States are presently at their optimum sustainable population and what population trends are evident; and

(B) in consultation with the Secretary of State, promptly undertake a comprehensive study of the provisions of this chapter, as they relate to North Pacific fur seals, and the provisions of the North Pacific Fur Seal Convention signed on February 9, 1957, as extended (hereafter referred to in this subsection as the "Convention"), to determine what modifications, if any, should be made to the provisions of the Convention, or of this chapter, or both, to make the Convention and this chapter consistent with each other.

The Secretary shall complete the studies required under this paragraph not later than one year after October 21, 1972, and shall immediately provide copies thereof to Congress.

(2) If the Secretary finds—

(A) as a result of the study required under paragraph (1)(A) of this subsection, that the North Pacific fur seal herds are below their optimum sustainable population and are not trending upward toward such level, or have reached their optimum sustainable population but are commencing a downward trend, and believes the herds to be in danger of depletion; or

(B) as a result of the study required under paragraph (1)(B) of this subsection, that modifications of the Convention are desirable to make it and this chapter consistent;

he shall, through the Secretary of State, immediately initiate negotiations to modify the Convention so as to (i) reduce or halt the taking of seals to the extent required to assure that such herds attain and remain at their optimum sustainable population, or (ii) make the Convention and this chapter consistent; or both, as the case may be. If negotiations to so modify the Convention are unsuccessful, the Secretary shall, through the Secretary of State, take such steps as may be necessary to continue the existing Convention beyond its present termination date so as to continue to protect and conserve the North Pacific fur seals and to prevent a return to pelagic sealing.

**(c) Description of annual results of discussions; proposals for further action**

The Secretary shall include a description of the annual results of discussions initiated and conducted pursuant to subsection (a)(2)(B) of this section, as well as any proposals for further action to achieve the purposes of that subsection, in the report required under section 1373(f) of this title.

(Pub.L. 92–522, Title I, § 108, Oct. 21, 1972, 86 Stat. 1038; Pub.L. 100–711, § 4(b), (c), Nov. 23, 1988, 102 Stat. 4766, 4767; Pub.L. 105–42, § 4(e), Aug. 15, 1997, 111 Stat. 1125.)

HISTORICAL AND STATUTORY NOTES

**Effective and Applicability Provisions**

1997 Acts

For effective date of amendment to this section by Pub.L. 105–42, see section 8 of Pub.L. 105–42, set out as a note under section 1362 of this title.

1972 Acts

Section effective upon expiration of sixty-day period following Oct. 21, 1972, see section 4 of Pub.L. 92–522, set out as an Effective Date note under section 1361 of this title.

## § 1379. Transfer of management authority [MMPA § 109]

**(a) State enforcement of State laws or regulations prohibited without transfer to State of management authority by Secretary**

No State may enforce, or attempt to enforce, any State law or regulation relating to the taking of any species (which term for purposes of this section includes any population stock) of marine mammal within the State unless the Secretary has transferred authority for the conservation and management of that species (hereinafter referred to in this section as "management authority") to the State under subsection (b) (1) of this section.

**(b) Findings prerequisite to transfer of authority; State program; implementation**

(1) Subject to paragraph (2) and subsection (f) of this section, the Secretary shall transfer management authority for a species of marine mammal to a State if the Secretary finds, after notice and opportunity for public comment, that the State has developed and will implement a program for the conservation and management of the species that—

(A) is consistent with the purposes, policies, and goals of this chapter and with international treaty obligations;

(B) requires that all taking of the species be humane;

(C) does not permit the taking of the species unless and until—

(i) the State has determined, under a process consistent with the standards set forth in subsection (c) of this section—

(I) that the species is at its optimum sustainable population (hereinafter in this section referred to as "OSP"), and

(II) the maximum number of animals of that species that may be taken without reducing the species below its OSP, and

(ii) the determination required under clause (i) is final and implemented under State law, and, if a cooperative allocation agreement for the species is required under subsection (d) (1) of this section, such an agreement is implemented;

(D) does not permit the taking of a number of animals of the species that exceeds the maximum number determined pursuant to subparagraph (C) (i) (II), and, in the case of taking for subsistence uses (as defined in subsection (f) (2) of this section), does not permit the taking of a number of animals that would be inconsistent with the maintenance of the species at its OSP;

(E) does not permit the taking of the species for scientific research, public display, or enhancing the survival or recovery of a species or stock, except for taking for such purposes that is undertaken by, or on behalf of, the State;

(F) provides procedures for acquiring data, and evaluating such data and other new evidence, relating to the OSP of the species, and the maximum take that would maintain the species at that level, and, if required on the basis of such evaluation, for amending determinations under subparagraph (C) (i);

(G) provides procedures for the resolution of differences between the State and the Secretary that might arise during the development of a cooperative allocation agreement under subsection (d) (1) of this section; and

(H) provides for the submission of an annual report to the Secretary regarding the administration of the program during the reporting period.

(2) During the period between the transfer of management authority for a species to a State under paragraph (1) and the time at which the implementation requirements under paragraph (1)(C)(ii) are complied with—

(A) the State program shall not apply with respect to the taking of the species within the State for any purpose, or under any condition, provided for under section 1371 of this title; and

(B) the Secretary shall continue to regulate, under this title, all takings of the species within the State.

(3) After the determination required under paragraph (1)(C)(i) regarding a species is final and implemented under State law and after a cooperative allocation agreement described in subsection (d)(1) of this section, if required, is implemented for such species—

(A) such determination shall be treated, for purposes of applying this subchapter beyond the territory of the State, as a determination made in accordance with section 1373 of this title and as an applicable waiver under section 1371(a) (3) of this title;

(B) the Secretary shall regulate, without regard to this section other than the allocations specified under such an agreement, the taking of the species—

(i) incidentally in the course of commercial fishing operations (whether provided for under section 1371(a) (2) or (4) of this title), or in the course of other specified activities provided for under section 1371(a) (5) of this title, in the zone described in section 1362(14) (B) of this title, and

(ii) for scientific research, public display, or enhancing the survival or recovery of a species or stock (other than by, or on behalf of, the State), except that any taking authorized under a permit issued pursuant to section 1371(a)(1) of this title after October 9, 1981 allowing the removal of live animals from habitat within the State shall not be effective if the State agency disapproves, on or before the date of issuance of the permit, such taking as being inconsistent with the State program; and

(C) section 1371(b) of this title shall not apply.

**(c) Standards with which State process must comply**

The State process required under subsection (b) (1) (C) of this section must comply with the following standards:

(1) The State agency with management authority for the species (hereinafter in this section referred to as the "State agency") must make an initial determination regarding the factors described in clause (i) of that subsection. The State agency must identify, and make available to the public under reasonable circumstances, the documentation supporting such initial determination. Unless request for a hearing under paragraph (2) regarding the initial determination is timely made, the initial determination shall be treated as final under State law.

(2) The State agency shall provide opportunity, at the request of any interested party, for a hearing with respect to the initial determination made by it under paragraph (1) at which interested parties may—

(A) present oral and written evidence in support of or against such determination; and

(B) cross-examine persons presenting evidence at the hearing.

The State agency must give public notice of the hearing and make available to the public within a reasonable time before commencing the hearing a list of the witnesses for the State and a general description of the documentation and other evidence that will be relied upon by such witnesses.

(3) The State agency, solely on the basis of the record developed at a hearing held pursuant to paragraph (2), must make a decision regarding its initial determination under paragraph (1) and shall include with the record a statement of the findings and conclusions, and the reason or basis therefor, on all material issues.

(4) Opportunity for judicial review of the decision made by the State agency on the record under paragraph (3), under scope of review equivalent to that provided for in section 706(2) (A) through (E) of Title 5, must be available under State law. The Secretary may not initiate judicial review of any such decision.

**(d) Cooperative allocation agreements**

(1) If the range of a species with respect to which a determination under paragraph (1) (C) (i) of subsection (b) of this section is made extends beyond the territorial waters of the State, the State agency and the Secretary (who shall first coordinate with the Marine Mammal Commission and the appropriate Regional Fishery Management Council established under section 1852 of this title) shall enter into a cooperative allocation agreement providing procedures for allocating, on a timely basis, such of the number of animals, as determined under paragraph (1) (C) (i) (II) of subsection (b) of this section, as may be appropriate with priority of allocation being given firstly to taking for subsistence uses in the case of the State of Alaska, and secondly to taking for purposes provided for under section 1371(a) of this title within the zone described in section 1362(14) (B) of this title.

(2) If the State agency requests the Secretary to regulate the taking of a species to which paragraph (1) applies within the zone described in section 1362(14) (B) of this title for subsistence uses or for hunting, or both, in a manner consistent with the regulation by the State agency of such taking within the State, the Secretary shall adopt, and enforce within such zone, such of the State agency's regulatory provisions as the Secretary considers to be consistent with his administration of section 1371(a) of this title within such zone. The Secretary shall adopt such provisions through the issuance of regulations under section 553 of Title 5, and with respect to such issuance the Regulatory Flexibility Act [5 U.S.C.A. § 601 et seq.], the Paperwork Reduction Act, Executive Order Numbered 12291, dated February 17, 1981, and the thirty-day notice requirement in subsection (d) of such section 553 shall not apply. For purposes of sections 1375, 1376, and 1377 of this title, such regulations shall be treated as having been issued under this subchapter.

**(e) Revocation of transfer of management authority**

(1) Subject to paragraph (2), the Secretary shall revoke, after opportunity for a hearing, any transfer of management authority made to a State under subsection (b) (1) of this section if the Secretary finds that the State program for the conservation and management of the species concerned is not being implemented, or is being implemented in a manner inconsistent

with the provisions of this section or the provisions of the program. The Secretary shall also establish a procedure for the voluntary return by a State to the Secretary of species management authority that was previously transferred to the State under subsection (b)(1) of this section.

(2)(A) The Secretary may not revoke a transfer of management authority under paragraph (1) unless—

(i) the Secretary provides to the State a written notice of intent to revoke together with a statement, in detail, of those actions, or failures to act, on which such intent is based; and

(ii) during the ninety-day period after the date of the notice of intent to revoke—

(I) the Secretary provides opportunity for consultation between him and the State concerning such State actions or failures to act and the remedial measures that should be taken by the State, and

(II) the State does not take such remedial measures as are necessary, in the judgment of the Secretary, to bring its conservation and management program, or the administration or enforcement of the program, into compliance with the provisions of this section.

(B) When a revocation by the Secretary of a transfer of management authority to a State becomes final, or the State voluntarily returns management authority to the Secretary, the Secretary shall regulate the taking, and provide for the conservation and management, of the species within the State in accordance with the provisions of this chapter (and in the case of Alaskan Natives, section 1371(b) of this title and subsection (i) of this section shall apply upon such revocation or return of management authority).

**(f) Transfer of management authority to State of Alaska**

(1) The Secretary may not transfer management authority to the State of Alaska under subsection (b)(1) of this section for any species of marine mammal unless—

(A) the State has adopted and will implement a statute and regulations that insure that the taking of the species for subsistence uses—

(i) is accomplished in a nonwasteful manner,

(ii) will be the priority consumptive use of the species, and

(iii) if required to be restricted, such restriction will be based upon—

(I) the customary and direct dependence upon the species as the mainstay of livelihood,

(II) local residency, and

(III) the availability of alternative resources; and

(B) the State has adopted a statute or regulation that requires that any consumptive use of marine mammal species, other than for subsistence uses, will be authorized during a regulatory year only if the appropriate agency first makes findings, based on an administrative record before it, that—

(i) such use will have no significant adverse impact upon subsistence uses of the species, and

(ii) the regulation of such use, including, but not limited to, licensing of marine mammal hunting guides and the assignment of guiding areas, will, to the maximum extent practicable, provide economic opportunities for the residents of the rural coastal villages of Alaska who engage in subsistence uses of that species.

(2) For purposes of paragraph (1), the term "subsistence uses" means the customary and traditional uses by rural Alaska residents of marine mammals for direct personal or family consumption as food, shelter, fuel, clothing, tools, or transportation; for the making and selling of handicraft articles out of nonedible byproducts of marine mammals taken for personal or family consumption; and for barter, or sharing for personal or family consumption. As used in this paragraph—

(A) The term "family" means all persons related by blood, marriage, or adoption, or any person living within a household on a permanent basis.

(B) The term "barter" means the exchange of marine mammals or their parts, taken for subsistence uses—

(i) for other wildlife or fish or their parts, or

(ii) for other food or for nonedible items other than money if the exchange is of a limited and noncommercial nature.

**(g) Environmental impact statement not required**

Neither the transfer of management authority to a State under subsection (b)(1) of this section, nor the revocation or voluntary return of such authority under subsection (e) of this section, shall be deemed to be an action for which an environmental impact statement is required under section 4332 of Title 42.

**(h) Taking of marine mammals as part of official duties**

(1) Nothing in this subchapter or subchapter V of this chapter shall prevent a Federal, State, or local government official or employee or a person designated under section 1382(c) of this title from taking, in the course of his or her duties as an official, employee, or designee, a marine mammal in a humane manner (including euthanasia) if such taking is for—

(A) the protection or welfare of the mammal,

(B) the protection of the public health and welfare, or

(C) the nonlethal removal of nuisance animals.

(2) Nothing in this subchapter shall prevent the Secretary or a person designated under section 1382(c) of this title from importing a marine mammal into the United States if such importation is necessary to render medical treatment that is not otherwise available.

(3) In any case in which it is feasible to return to its natural habitat a marine mammal taken or imported under circumstances described in this subsection, steps to achieve that result shall be taken.

**(i) Regulations covering taking of marine mammals by Alaskan natives**

The Secretary may (after providing notice thereof in the Federal Register and in newspapers of general circulation, and through appropriate electronic media, in the affected area and providing opportunity for a hearing thereon in such area) prescribe regulations requiring the marking, tagging, and reporting of animals taken pursuant to section 1371(b) of this title.

**(j) Grants to develop or administer State conservation and management programs**

The Secretary may make grants to States to assist them—

(1) in developing programs, to be submitted for approval under subsection (b) of this section, for the conservation and management of species of marine mammals; and

(2) in administering such programs if management authority for such species is transferred to the State under such subsection.

Grants made under this subsection may not exceed 50 per centum of the costs of developing a State program before Secretarial approval, or of administering the program thereafter.

**(k) Delegation of administration and enforcement to States**

The Secretary is authorized and directed to enter into cooperative arrangements with the appropriate officials of any State for the delegation to such State of the administration and enforcement of this subchapter: *Provided*, That any such arrangement shall contain such provisions as the Secretary deems appropriate to insure that the purposes and policies of this chapter will be carried out.

**(*l*) Authorization of appropriations**

(1) There are authorized to be appropriated to the Department of the Interior, for the purposes of carrying out this section, not to exceed $400,000 for each of the fiscal years ending September 30, 1979, September 30, 1980, and September 30, 1981.

(2) There are authorized to be appropriated to the Department of Commerce, for the purposes of carrying out this section, not to exceed $225,000 for each of the fiscal years ending September 30, 1979, September 30, 1980, and September 30, 1981.

(Pub.L. 92–522, Title I, § 109, Oct. 21, 1972, 86 Stat. 1040; Pub.L. 95–316, § 1, July 10, 1978, 92 Stat. 380; Pub.L. 97–58, § 4(a), Oct. 9, 1981, 95 Stat. 982; Pub.L. 100–711, § 5(a), (e)(3), Nov. 23, 1988, 102 Stat. 4769, 4771; Pub.L. 102–587, Title III, § 3004(a)(2), Nov. 4, 1992, 106 Stat. 5067; Pub.L. 103–238, § 24(c)(10), Apr. 30, 1994, 108 Stat. 566.)

## HISTORICAL AND STATUTORY NOTES

**References in Text**

Section 1362(14) of this title, referred to in subsecs. (b)(3)(B)(i) and (d), was redesignated 16 U.S.C.A. § 1362(15) by Pub.L. 102–582, Title IV, § 401(a), Nov. 2, 1992, 106 Stat. 4909.

The Regulatory Flexibility Act, referred to in subsec. (d)(2), is Pub.L. 96–354, Sept. 19, 1980, 94 Stat. 1164, which is classified generally to chapter 6 (section 601 et seq.) of Title 5, Government Organization and Employees. For complete classification of this Act to the Code, see Short Title note set out under section 601 of Title 5 and Tables.

The Paperwork Reduction Act, referred to in subsec. (d)(2), probably means the Paperwork Reduction Act of 1980, Pub.L. 96–511, Dec. 11, 1980, 94 Stat. 2812, as amended, which was classified principally to chapter 35 of Title 44, 44 U.S.C.A. § 3501 et seq., prior to the general amendment of that chapter by the Paperwork Reduction Act of 1995, Pub.L. 104–13, § 2, May 22, 1995, 109 Stat. 163. For complete classification, see Short Title of 1980 Amendments note set out under 44 U.S.C.A. § 101 and Tables.

Executive Order Numbered 12291, dated February 17, 1981, referred to in subsec. (d)(2), is set out as a note under section 601 of Title 5, Government Organization and Employees.

**Codifications**

In subsec. (h)(1), subchapter V of this chapter was in the original "title IV", meaning title IV of Pub.L. 92–522, originally added as "title III" of Pub.L. 92–522 by section 3303(a) of Pub.L. 102–587, and redesignated "title IV" of Pub.L. 92–522 by section 24(b)(1) of Pub.L. 103–238, which is codified to subchapter V of this chapter. Another title III of Pub.L. 92–522 was added by section 2(a) of Pub.L. 102–523 and enacted subchapter IV of this chapter.

**Effective and Applicability Provisions**

1972 Acts

Section effective upon expiration of sixty-day period following Oct. 21, 1972, see section 4 of Pub.L. 92–522, set out as an Effective Date note under section 1361 of this title.

**Cooperative Agreements Under Endangered Species Act**

Section 4(b) of Pub.L. 97–58 provided that: "Nothing in the amendments made by subsection (a) [amending this section] shall be construed as affecting in any manner, or to any extent, any cooperative agreement entered into by a State under section 6(c) of the Endangered Species Act of 1973 (16 U.S.C. 1535(c) ) [section 1535(c) of this title] before, on, or after the date of the enactment of this Act [Oct. 9, 1981]."

## § 1380. Marine mammal research grants

[MMPA § 110]

### (a) Authorization; research concerning yellowfin tuna; annual report

The Secretary is authorized to make grants, or to provide financial assistance in such other form as he deems appropriate, to any Federal or State agency, public or private institution, or other person for the purpose of assisting such agency, institution, or person to undertake research in subjects which are relevant to the protection and conservation of marine mammals. In carrying out this subsection, the Secretary shall undertake a program of, and shall provide financial assistance for, research into new methods of locating and catching yellowfin tuna without the incidental taking of marine mammals. The Secretary shall include a description of the annual results of research carried out under this section in the report required under section 1373(f) of this title.

### (b) Terms and conditions

Any grant or other financial assistance provided by the Secretary pursuant to this section shall be subject to such terms and conditions as the Secretary deems necessary to protect the interests of the United States and shall be made after review by the Marine Mammal Commission.

### (c) Gulf of Maine ecosystem protection

(1) No later than 1 year after April 30, 1994, the Secretary of Commerce shall convene a regional workshop for the Gulf of Maine to assess human-caused factors affecting the health and stability of that marine ecosystem, of which marine mammals are a part. The workshop shall be conducted in consultation with the Marine Mammal Commission, the adjacent coastal States, individuals with expertise in marine mammal biology and ecology, representatives from environmental organizations, the fishing industry, and other appropriate persons. The goal of the workshop shall be to identify such factors, and to recommend a program of research and management to restore or maintain that marine ecosystem and its key components that—

(A) protects and encourages marine mammals to develop to the greatest extent feasible commensurate with sound policies of resource management;

(B) has as the primary management objective the maintenance of the health and stability of the marine ecosystems;

(C) ensures the fullest possible range of management options for future generations; and

(D) permits nonwasteful, environmentally sound development of renewable and nonrenewable resources.

(2) On or before December 31, 1995, the Secretary of Commerce shall submit to the Committee on Merchant Marine and Fisheries of the House of Representatives and the Committee on Commerce, Science and Transportation of the Senate a report containing the results of the workshop under this subsection, proposed regulatory or research actions, and recommended legislative action.

### (d) Bering Sea ecosystem protection

(1) The Secretary of Commerce, in consultation with the Secretary of the Interior, the Marine Mammal Commission, the State of Alaska, and Alaska Native organizations, shall, not later than 180 days after April 30, 1994, undertake a scientific research program to monitor the health and stability of the Bering Sea marine ecosystem and to resolve uncertainties concerning the causes of population declines of marine mammals, sea birds, and other living resources of that marine ecosystem. The program shall address the research recommendations developed by previous workshops on Bering Sea living marine resources, and shall include research on subsistence uses of such resources and ways to provide for the continued opportunity for such uses.

(2) To the maximum extent practicable, the research program undertaken pursuant to paragraph (1) shall be conducted in Alaska. The Secretary of Commerce shall utilize, where appropriate, traditional local knowledge and may contract with a qualified Alaska Native organization to conduct such research.

(3) The Secretary of Commerce, the Secretary of the Interior, and the Commission shall address the status and findings of the research program in their annual reports to Congress required by sections 1373(f) and 1404 of this title.

(Pub.L. 92–522, Title I, § 110, Oct. 21, 1972, 86 Stat. 1041; Pub.L. 95–136, § 1, Oct. 18, 1977, 91 Stat. 1167; Pub.L. 95–316, § 2, July 10, 1978, 92 Stat. 380; Pub.L. 97–58, § 5, Oct. 9, 1981, 95 Stat. 986; Pub.L. 100–711, § 4(e), Nov. 23, 1988, 102 Stat. 4768; Pub.L. 103–238, § 20, Apr. 30, 1994, 108 Stat. 560; Pub.L 105–42, § 4(f), Aug. 15, 1997, 111 Stat. 1125.)

### HISTORICAL AND STATUTORY NOTES

**References in Text**

Provisions of section 1373(f) of this title, requiring annual reports to Congress, referred to in subsec. (d)(3), terminated, effective May 15, 2000. See Termination of Reporting Requirements note set out under 16 U.S.C.A. § 1373.

Section 1404 of this title, referred to in subsec. (d)(3), was omitted from the Code.

**Effective and Applicability Provisions**

1997 Acts

For effective date of amendment to this section by Pub.L. 105–42, see section 8 of Pub.L. 105–42, set out as a note under section 1362 of this title.

1972 Acts

Section effective upon expiration of sixty-day period following Oct. 21, 1972, see section 4 of Pub.L. 92–522, set out as an Effective Date note under section 1361 of this title.

**Abolition of House Committee on Merchant Marine and Fisheries**

Committee on Merchant Marine and Fisheries of House of Representatives abolished and any reference in any provision of law enacted before Jan. 4, 1995, to the Committee on Merchant Marine and Fisheries of the House of Representatives treated as referring to the Committee on Agriculture of the House of Representatives, in the case of a provision of law relating to inspection of seafood or seafood products, the Committee on National Security of the House of Representatives, in the case of a provision of law relating to interoceanic canals, the Merchant Marine Academy and State Maritime Academies, or national security aspects of merchant marine, the Committee on Resources of the House of Representatives, in the case of a provision of law relating to fisheries, wildlife, international fishing agreements marine affairs (including coastal zone management) except for measures relating to oil and other pollution of navigable waters, or oceanography, the Committee on Science of the House of Representatives, in the case of a provision of law relating to marine research, and the Committee on Transportation and Infrastructure of the House of Representatives, in the case of a provision of law relating to a matter other than a matter described above, see section 1(b)(3) of Pub.L. 104–14, set out as a note preceding section 21 of Title 2, The Congress.

## § 1381. Commercial fisheries gear development [MMPA § 111]

### (a) Research and development program; report to Congress; authorization of appropriations

The Secretary of the department in which the National Oceanic and Atmospheric Administration is operating (hereafter referred to in this section as the "Secretary") is hereby authorized and directed to immediately undertake a program of research and development for the purpose of devising improved fishing methods and gear so as to reduce to the maximum extent practicable the incidental taking of marine mammals in connection with commercial fishing. At the end of the full twenty-four calendar month period following October 21, 1972, the Secretary shall deliver his report in writing to the Congress with respect to the results of such research and development. For the purposes of this section, there is hereby authorized to be appropriated the sum of $1,000,000 for the fiscal year ending June 30, 1973, and the same amount for the next fiscal year. Funds appropriated for this section shall remain available until expended.

### (b) Reduction of level of taking of marine mammals incidental to commercial fishing operations

The Secretary, after consultation with the Marine Mammal Commission, is authorized and directed to issue, as soon as practicable, such regulations, covering the twenty-four-month period referred to in section 1371(a)(2) of this title, as he deems necessary or advisable, to reduce to the lowest practicable level the taking of marine mammals incidental to commercial fishing operations. Such regulations shall be adopted pursuant to section 553 of Title 5. In issuing such regulations, the Secretary shall take into account the results of any scientific research under subsection (a) of this section and, in each case, shall provide a reasonable time not exceeding four months for the persons affected to implement such regulations.

### (c) Reduction of level of taking of marine mammals in tuna fishery

Additionally, the Secretary and Secretary of State are directed to commence negotiations within the Inter-American Tropical Tuna Commission in order to effect essential compliance with the regulatory provisions of this chapter so as to reduce to the maximum extent feasible the incidental taking of marine mammals by vessels involved in the tuna fishery. The Secretary and Secretary of State are further directed to request the Director of Investigations of the Inter-American Tropical Tuna Commission to make recommendations to all member nations of the Commission as soon as is practicable as to the utilization of methods and gear devised under subsection (a) of this section.

### (d) Research and observation

Furthermore, after timely notice and during the period of research provided in this section, duly authorized agents of the Secretary are hereby empowered to board and to accompany any commercial fishing vessel documented under the laws of the United States, there being space available, on a regular fishing trip for the purpose of conducting research or observing operations in regard to the development of improved fishing methods and gear as authorized by this section. Such research and observation shall be carried out in such manner as to minimize interference with fishing operations. The Secretary shall provide for the cost of quartering and maintaining such agents. No master, operator, or owner of such a vessel shall impair or in any way interfere with the research or observation being carried out by agents of the Secretary pursuant to this section.

(Pub.L. 92–522, Title I, § 111, Oct. 21, 1972, 86 Stat. 1041.)

HISTORICAL AND STATUTORY NOTES

**Effective and Applicability Provisions**

1972 Acts

Section effective upon expiration of sixty-day period following Oct. 21, 1972, see section 4 of Pub.L. 92–522, set out as an Effective Date note under section 1361 of this title.

## § 1382. Regulations and administration

[MMPA § 112]

### (a) Consultation with Federal agencies

The Secretary, in consultation with any other Federal agency to the extent that such agency may be affected, shall prescribe such regulations as are necessary and appropriate to carry out the purposes of this subchapter.

### (b) Cooperation by Federal agencies

Each Federal agency is authorized and directed to cooperate with the Secretary, in such manner as may be mutually agreeable, in carrying out the purposes of this subchapter.

### (c) Contracts, leases, and cooperative agreements

The Secretary may enter into such contracts, leases, cooperative agreements, or other transactions as may be necessary to carry out the purposes of this subchapter or subchapter V of this chapter and on such terms as he deems appropriate with any Federal or State agency, public or private institution, or other person.

### (d) Annual review; suspension of program

The Secretary shall review annually the operation of each program in which the United States participates involving the taking of marine mammals on land. If at any time the Secretary finds that any such program cannot be administered on lands owned by the United States or in which the United States has an interest in a manner consistent with the purposes of [1] policies of this chapter, he shall suspend the operation of that program and shall include in the annual report to the public and the Congress required under section 1373(f) of this title his reasons for such suspension, together with recommendations for such legislation as he deems necessary and appropriate to resolve the problem.

### (e) Measures to alleviate impacts on strategic stocks

If the Secretary determines, based on a stock assessment under section 1386 of this title or other significant new information obtained under this chapter, that impacts on rookeries, mating grounds, or other areas of similar ecological significance to marine mammals may be causing the decline or impeding the recovery of a strategic stock, the Secretary may develop and implement conservation or management measures to alleviate those impacts. Such measures shall be developed and implemented after consultation with the Marine Mammal Commission and the appropriate Federal agencies and after notice and opportunity for public comment.

(Pub.L. 92–522, Title I, § 112, Oct. 21, 1972, 86 Stat. 1042; Pub.L. 96–470, Title II, § 201(e), Oct. 19, 1980, 94 Stat. 2241; Pub.L. 102–587, Title III, § 3004(a)(3), Nov. 4, 1992, 106 Stat. 5067; Pub.L. 103–238, §§ 7(a), 24(c)(11), Apr. 30, 1994, 108 Stat. 542, 566.)

[1] So in original. Probably should be "or".

HISTORICAL AND STATUTORY NOTES

**Codifications**

In subsec. (c), subchapter V of this chapter was in the original "title IV", meaning title IV of Pub.L. 92–522, originally added as "title III" of Pub.L. 92–522 by section 3303(a) of Pub.L. 102–587, and redesignated "title IV" of Pub.L. 92–522 by section 24(b)(1) of Pub.L. 103–238, which is codified to subchapter V of this chapter. Another title III of Pub.L. 92–522 was added by section 2(a) of Pub.L. 102–523 and enacted subchapter IV of this chapter.

**Effective and Applicability Provisions**

1972 Acts

Section effective upon expiration of sixty-day period following Oct. 21, 1972, see section 4 of Pub.L. 92–522, set out as an Effective Date note under section 1361 of this title.

## § 1383. Application to other treaties and conventions

[MMPA § 113]

### (a) Generally; findings; waiver of penalties

The provisions of this subchapter shall be deemed to be in addition to and not in contravention of the provisions of any existing international treaty, convention, or agreement, or any statute implementing the same, which may otherwise apply to the taking of marine mammals. Upon a finding by the Secretary that the provisions of any international treaty, convention, or agreement, or any statute implementing the same has been made applicable to persons subject to the provisions of this subchapter in order to effect essential compliance with the regulatory provisions of this chapter so as to reduce to the lowest practicable level the taking of marine mammals incidental to commercial fishing operations, section 1375 of this title may not apply to such persons.

### (b) Review of effectiveness of Agreement on the Conservation of Polar Bears

Not later than 1 year after April 30, 1994, the Secretary of the Interior shall, in consultation with the contracting parties, initiate a review of the effectiveness of the Agreement on the Conservation of Polar Bears, as provided for in Article IX of the Agreement, and establish a process by which future reviews shall be conducted.

**(c) Review of implementation of Agreement on the Conservation of Polar Bears; report**

The Secretary of the Interior, in consultation with the Secretary of State and the Marine Mammal Commission, shall review the effectiveness of United States implementation of the Agreement on the Conservation of Polar Bears, particularly with respect to the habitat protection mandates contained in Article II. The Secretary shall report the results of this review to the Committee on Merchant Marine and Fisheries of the House of Representatives and the Committee on Commerce, Science, and Transportation of the Senate not later than April 1, 1995.

**(d) Consultation regarding conservation of polar bears in Russia and Alaska; report**

Not later than 6 months after April 30, 1994, the Secretary of the Interior, acting through the Secretary of State and in consultation with the Marine Mammal Commission and the State of Alaska, shall consult with the appropriate officials of the Russian Federation on the development and implementation of enhanced cooperative research and management programs for the conservation of polar bears in Alaska and Russia. The Secretary shall report the results of this consultation and provide periodic progress reports on the research and management programs to the Committee on Merchant Marine and Fisheries of the House of Representatives and the Committee on Commerce, Science and Transportation of the Senate.

(Pub.L. 92–522, Title I, § 113(a), Oct. 21, 1972, 86 Stat. 1042; Pub.L. 103–238, § 7(b), Apr. 30, 1994, 108 Stat. 542.)

### HISTORICAL AND STATUTORY NOTES

**Codifications**

Section consists of subsec. (a) of section 113 of Pub.L. 92–522, which was designated as subsec. (a) for a second time by section 7(b)(1) of Pub.L. 103–238, and subsecs. (b) to (d) of Pub.L. 92–522, as added by section 7(b)(2) of Pub.L. 103–238. Another subsec. (b) of section 113 of Pub.L. 92–522 amended section 659 of this title.

**Effective and Applicability Provisions**

1972 Acts

Section effective upon expiration of sixty-day period following Oct. 21, 1972, see section 4 of Pub.L. 92–522, set out as an Effective Date note under section 1361 of this title.

**Abolition of House Committee on Merchant Marine and Fisheries**

Committee on Merchant Marine and Fisheries of House of Representatives abolished and any reference in any provision of law enacted before Jan. 4, 1995, to the Committee on Merchant Marine and Fisheries of the House of Representatives treated as referring to the Committee on Agriculture of the House of Representatives, in the case of a provision of law relating to inspection of seafood or seafood products, the Committee on National Security of the House of Representatives, in the case of a provision of law relating to interoceanic canals, the Merchant Marine Academy and State Maritime Academies, or national security aspects of merchant marine, the Committee on Resources of the House of Representatives, in the case of a provision of law relating to fisheries, wildlife, international fishing agreements marine affairs (including coastal zone management) except for measures relating to oil and other pollution of navigable waters, or oceanography, the Committee on Science of the House of Representatives, in the case of a provision of law relating to marine research, and the Committee on Transportation and Infrastructure of the House of Representatives, in the case of a provision of law relating to a matter other than a matter described above, see section 1(b)(3) of Pub.L. 104–14, set out as a note preceding section 21 of Title 2, The Congress.

## § 1383a. Interim exemption for commercial fisheries

**[MMPA § 114]**

**(a) Effective and termination dates of preemptive provisions; law governing incidental taking of marine mammals in course of commercial yellowfin tuna fishing**

(1) During the period beginning on November 23, 1988, and until superseded by regulations prescribed under section 1387 of this title, or until September 1, 1995, whichever is earlier, except as provided in paragraph (2), the provisions of this section, rather than sections 1371, 1373, and 1374 of this title, shall govern the incidental taking of marine mammals in the course of commercial fishing operations by persons using vessels of the United States and vessels which have valid fishing permits issued by the Secretary in accordance with section 1824(b) of this title. In any event it shall be the immediate goal that the incidental kill or serious injury of marine mammals permitted in the course of commercial fishing operations be reduced to insignificant levels approaching a zero mortality and serious injury rate.

(2) The provisions of this section other than subsection (e)(6)(A) of this section shall not govern the incidental taking of marine mammals in the course of commercial yellowfin tuna fishing subject to section 1374(h)(2) of this title.

**(b) Proposed and final list of fisheries taking marine mammals; publication in Federal Register; grant of exemption; conditions; suspension of grant of exemption; administration of exemption provisions; fees**

(1) The Secretary shall, after consultation with the Marine Mammal Commission—

(A) publish in the Federal Register, for public comment, not later than sixty days after November 23, 1988, a proposed list of those fisheries, along with a statement of the marine mammals and the approximate number of vessels or persons involved in each such fishery, that have—

(i) frequent incidental taking of marine mammals;

(ii) occasional incidental taking of marine mammals; or

(iii) a remote likelihood of or no known incidental taking of marine mammals;

(B) publish in the Federal Register not later than one hundred and twenty days after November 23, 1988, a final list of the fisheries and other information required by paragraph (A), together with a summary of the provisions of this section and information sufficient to advise vessel owners on how to obtain an exemption and otherwise comply with the requirements of this section; and

(C) at least once each year thereafter, and at such other times as the Secretary considers appropriate, reexamine, based on information gathered from the program established under subsections (c), (d), (e), and (f) of this section, and other relevant sources and after notice and opportunity for public comment, the classification of fisheries and other determinations required under subparagraph (A) and publish in the Federal Register any necessary changes.

(2)(A) An exemption shall be granted by the Secretary in accordance with this section for a vessel engaged in a fishery identified under paragraph (1)(A)(i) or (ii), upon receipt by the Secretary of a completed registration form providing the name of the vessel owner, the name and description of the vessel, the fisheries in which it will be engaged, and such other information as the Secretary considers necessary. A decal or other physical evidence that the exemption is current and valid shall be issued by the Secretary at the time an exemption is granted, and so long as the exemption remains current and valid, shall be reissued annually thereafter.

(B) No exemption may be granted under this section to the owner of a vessel unless such vessel—

(i) is a vessel of the United States; or

(ii) has a valid fishing permit issued by the Secretary in accordance with section 1824(b) of this title.

(C) Notwithstanding any other provision of this subchapter, exemptions granted under this section shall authorize the incidental taking of marine mammals, other than California sea otters, from any species or stock, including a population stock designated as depleted, but shall not authorize the intentional lethal taking of any Steller sea lion, any cetacean, or any marine mammals from a population stock designated as depleted.

(3)(A) Beginning two hundred and forty days after November 23, 1988, each owner of a vessel engaged in any fishery identified under paragraph (1)(A)(i) or (ii) shall, in order to engage lawfully in that fishery—

(i) have registered with the Secretary in order to obtain for each such vessel owned an exemption for the purpose of incidentally taking marine mammals in accordance with this section;

(ii) ensure that a decal or such other physical evidence of a current and valid exemption as the Secretary may require is displayed on or is in the possession of the master of each such vessel; and

(iii) report as required by subsection (c) of this section.

(B) Any owner of a vessel receiving an exemption under this section for any fishery identified under paragraph (1)(A)(i) shall, as a condition of that exemption, take on board a natural resource observer if requested to do so by the Secretary.

(C) An owner of a vessel engaged in a fishery identified under paragraph (1)(A)(i) or (ii) who—

(i) fails to obtain from the Secretary an exemption under this section;

(ii) fails to maintain a current and valid exemption; or

(iii) fails to ensure that a decal or other physical evidence of such exemption issued by the Secretary is displayed on or is in possession of the master of the vessel,

and the master of any such vessel engaged in such fishery, shall be deemed to have violated this subchapter, and shall be subject to the penalties of this subchapter except in the case of unknowing violations before January 1, 1990.

(D) If the owner of a vessel has obtained and maintains a current and valid exemption from the Secretary under this section and meets the requirements set forth in this section, the owner of such vessel, and the master and crew members of the vessel, shall not be subject to the penalties set forth in this subchapter for the incidental taking of marine mammals while such vessel is engaged in a fishery to which the exemption applies.

(E) Each owner of a vessel engaged in any fishery not identified in paragraph (1)(A)(i) or (ii), and the master and crew members of such a vessel, shall not be subject to the penalties set forth in this subchapter for the incidental taking of marine mammals if such owner reports to the Secretary, in such form and manner as the Secretary may require, instances of lethal incidental taking in the course of that fishery.

(4) The Secretary shall suspend or revoke an exemption granted under this section and shall not issue a decal or other physical evidence of the exemption for any vessel until the owner of such vessel complies with the reporting requirements under subsection (c) of

this section and such requirements to take on board a natural resource observer under paragraph (3)(B) as are applicable to such vessel.

(5)(A) The Secretary shall develop, in consultation with the appropriate States, Regional Fishery Management Councils, and other interested parties, the means by which the granting and administration of exemptions under this section shall be integrated and coordinated, to the maximum extent practicable, with existing fishery licenses, registrations, and related programs.

(B) The Secretary shall utilize newspapers of general circulation, fishery trade associations, electronic media, and other means of advising commercial fishermen of the provisions of this section and the means by which they can comply with its requirements.

(C) The Secretary is authorized to charge a fee for the granting of an exemption under this subsection. The level of fees charged under this subparagraph shall not exceed the administrative costs incurred in granting an exemption. Fees collected under this subparagraph shall be available to the Under Secretary of Commerce for Oceans and Atmosphere for expenses incurred in the granting and administration of exemptions under this section.

**(c) Compilation of information by vessel owners; contents**

The owner of each vessel holding an exemption granted under subsection (b) of this section shall regularly compile information which shall be used in a report to be submitted to the Secretary at the close of the fishing season or annually, as the Secretary may prescribe. Such report shall be submitted in such form as the Secretary may require and shall include the following:

(1) the type of fishery engaged in by the owner's vessel;

(2) the date and approximate time of any incidental taking of a marine mammal, together with the area in which the incidental taking occurred, the fishing gear used at the time of the incidental taking, and the species of fish involved; and

(3) for each incidental taking, the number and species of marine mammals involved, whether the marine mammals were deterred from gear or catch, incidentally injured, incidentally killed, or lethally removed to protect gear, catch, or human life.

If there was no incidental taking of marine mammals during the reporting period, a report stating that fact shall be filed with the Secretary.

**(d) Program for enhancement and verification of information received from vessel owners; confidentiality of information**

(1) The Secretary shall establish a program to enhance the quality of and verify information received from reports submitted by owners of vessels who have been granted an exemption under subsection (b) of this section. The program shall include, but not be limited to—

(A) education efforts regarding the information that must be submitted;

(B) interviews with fishermen; and

(C) other such information gathering and verification activities that will enable the Secretary to determine reliably the nature, type, and extent of the incidental taking of marine mammals that occurs in a fishery.

Except to the extent authorized by the provisions of subsection (e) of this section, the program shall not include placement of observers aboard exempted vessels.

(2) Information obtained under this subsection shall be subject to the confidentiality provisions of subsection (j) of this section.

**(e) Observers on board exempted vessels; confidentiality of information; authorization of appropriations**

(1) For each fishery identified under subsection (b)(1)(A)(i) of this section, the Secretary shall, after consultation with the appropriate Regional Fishery Management Councils, other Federal and State agencies, and other interested parties, and subject to paragraph (6), place observers on board exempted vessels so as to monitor not less than 20 percent nor more than 35 percent of the fishing operations by vessels in the fishery to obtain statistically reliable information on the species and number of marine mammals incidentally taken in the fishery. If the Secretary determines that fewer than 20 percent of the fishing operations by vessels in the fishery will be monitored during the course of the fishing season, the Secretary shall implement the alternative observation program described in subsection (f) of this section to the extent necessary to supplement the observer program described in this subsection.

(2) When determining the distribution of observers among fisheries and between vessels in a particular fishery, the Secretary shall be guided by the following standards:

(A) the requirement to obtain the best scientific information available;

(B) the requirement that assignment of observers is fair and equitable among fisheries and among vessels in a fishery;

(C) consistent with paragraph (1), the requirement that no individual person or vessel, or group of persons or vessels, be subject to excessive or overly burdensome observer coverage; and

(D) where practicable, the need to minimize costs and avoid duplication.

(3) If the Secretary finds that, for reasons beyond his or her control, the Secretary cannot assign observers to all the fisheries identified under subsection (b)(1)(A)(i) of this section at the level of observer coverage set forth in paragraph (1), the Secretary shall allocate available observers among such fisheries, consistent with paragraph (2), according to the following priority:

(A) those fisheries that incidentally take marine mammals from any population stock designated as depleted;

(B) those fisheries that incidentally take marine mammals from population stocks that the Secretary believes are declining;

(C) those fisheries other than those described in subparagraphs (A) and (B) in which the greatest incidental take of marine mammals occur; and

(D) any other fishery identified under subsection (b)(1)(A)(i) of this section.

The Secretary may, with the consent of the vessel owner, station an observer on board a vessel engaged in a fishery not identified under subsection (b)(1)(A)(i) of this section.

(4) Information gathered by observers shall be subject to the provisions of subsection (j) of this section. Consistent with the requirements of paragraph (1), the Secretary shall, if requested by the Appropriate [1] Regional Fishery Management Council, or in the case of a State fishery, the State, require observers to collect additional information, including but not limited to the quantities, species, and physical condition of target and non-target fishery resources and, if requested by the Secretary of the Interior, seabirds.

(5) Notwithstanding the provisions of paragraph (4), the Secretary may decline to require observers to collect information described in such paragraph, if the Secretary finds in writing, following public notice and opportunity for comment, that such information will not contribute to the protection of marine mammals or the understanding of the marine ecosystem, including fishery resources and seabirds.

(6) The Secretary shall not be required to place an observer on a vessel in a fishery if the Secretary finds that—

(A) in a situation where harvesting vessels are delivering fish to a processing vessel and the catch is not taken on board the harvesting vessel, statistically reliable information can be obtained from an observer on board the processing vessel to which the fish are delivered;

(B) the facilities of a vessel for the quartering of an observer, or for carrying out observer functions, are so inadequate or unsafe that the health or safety of the observer or the safe operation of the vessel would be jeopardized; or

(C) for reasons beyond the control of the Secretary, an observer is not available.

(7)(A) An observer on a vessel (or the observer's personal representative) under the requirements of this section or section 1374 of this title that is ill, disabled, injured, or killed from service as an observer on that vessel may not bring a civil action under any law of the United States for that illness, disability, injury, or death against the vessel or vessel owner, except that a civil action may be brought against the vessel owner for the owner's willful misconduct.

(B) This paragraph does not apply if the observer is engaged by the owner, master, or individual in charge of a vessel to perform any duties in service to the vessel.

(8) There are authorized to be appropriated to the Department of Commerce for the purposes of carrying out this subsection not to exceed $2,700,000 for fiscal year 1989 and not to exceed $8,000,000 for each of the fiscal years 1990, 1991, 1992, and 1993.

**(f) Alternative observation program**

(1) The Secretary shall establish an alternative observation program to provide statistically reliable information on the species and number of marine mammals incidentally taken in those fisheries identified pursuant to subsection (b)(1)(A)(i) of this section for which the required level of observer coverage has not been met or for any other fisheries about which such reliable information is not otherwise available. The alternative program shall include, but not be limited to, direct observation of fishing activities from vessels, airplanes, or points on shore.

(2) Individuals engaged in the alternative observation program shall collect scientific information on the fisheries subject to observation, consistent with the requirements of paragraph (1) and subsection (e)(4) and (5) of this section. All information collected shall be subject to the provisions of subsection (j) of this section.

**(g) Review of information and evaluation of effects of incidental taking on population stocks of marine mammals; promulgation of emergency regulations to mitigate immediate and significant adverse impacts; action to mitigate non-immediate impacts**

(1) The Secretary shall review information regarding the incidental taking of marine mammals and evaluate the effects of such incidental taking on the affected population stocks of marine mammals.

(2) If the Secretary finds, based on the information received from the programs established under subsections (c), (d), (e), and (f) of this section, that the incidental taking of marine mammals in a fishery is having an immediate and significant adverse impact on a marine mammal population stock or, in the case of Steller sea lions and North Pacific fur seals, that more than 1,350 and 50, respectively, will be incidentally killed during a calendar year, the Secretary shall consult with appropriate Regional Fishery Management Councils and State fishery managers and prescribe emergency regulations to prevent to the maximum extent practicable any further taking. Any emergency regulations prescribed under this paragraph—

(A) shall, to the maximum extent practicable, avoid interfering with existing State or regional fishery management plans;

(B) shall be published in the Federal Register together with the reasons therefor;

(C) shall remain in effect for not more than one hundred and eighty days or until the end of the fishing season, whichever is earlier; and

(D) may be terminated by the Secretary at an earlier date by publication in the Federal Register of a notice of termination if the Secretary determines the reasons for the emergency regulations no longer exist.

In prescribing emergency regulations under this paragraph, the Secretary shall take into account the economics of the fishery concerned and the availability of existing technology to prevent or minimize incidental taking of marine mammals.

(3) If the Secretary finds, based on information received from the programs established under subsections (c), (d), (e), and (f) of this section, that incidental taking of marine mammals in a fishery is not having an immediate and significant adverse impact on a marine mammal population stock but that it will likely have a significant adverse impact over a period of time longer than one year, the Secretary shall request the appropriate Regional Fishery Management Council or State to initiate, recommend, or take such action within its authority as it considers necessary to mitigate the adverse impacts, including adjustments to requirements on fishing times or areas or the imposition of restrictions on the use of vessels or gear.

(4) The Secretary shall impose appropriate conditions and restrictions on an exemption granted under subsection (b) of this section if—

(A) a Regional Fishery Management Council or State does not act in a reasonable period of time on a request made by the Secretary under paragraph (3); or

(B) if the Secretary determines after notice and opportunity for public comment that the purposes of this section would be better served by such action.

**(h) Information and management system for processing and analyzing reports and information; accessibility to public**

The Secretary shall design and implement an information management system capable of processing and analyzing reports received from the programs established under subsections (c), (d), (e), and (f) of this section, and other relevant sources, including Federal and State enforcement authorities, marine mammal stranding networks, and the marine mammal researchers. The information shall be made accessible to the public on a continuing basis, but in any case no later than six months after it is received, subject to the provisions of subsection (j) of this section.

**(i) Utilization of services of State and Federal agencies and private entities**

When carrying out the Secretary's responsibilities under subsections (b), (d), (e), (f), and (h) of this section, the Secretary shall, to the maximum extent practicable, utilize the services and programs of State agencies, Federal agencies (including programs established by Regional Fishery Management Councils), marine fisheries commissions, universities, and private entities, on a reimbursable basis or otherwise. The Secretary is authorized to enter into contracts and agreements to carry out his or her responsibilities and shall establish appropriate guidelines to ensure that other programs used or contracted for will meet the same standards as a program established by the Secretary. A person contracting with the Secretary to provide observer services under subsection (e) of this section must provide evidence of financial responsibility in an amount and form prescribed by the Secretary to compensate employees (or their survivors) adequately for any illness, disability, injury, or death from service on a vessel.

**(j) Confidentiality of information; exceptions**

(1) Any information collected under subsection (c), (d), (e), (f), or (h) of this section shall be confidential and shall not be disclosed except—

(A) to Federal employees whose duties require access to such information;

(B) to State employees pursuant to an agreement with the Secretary that prevents public disclosure of the identity or business of any person;

(C) when required by court order; or

(D) in the case of scientific information involving fisheries, to employees of Regional Fishery Management Councils who are responsible for fishery management plan development and monitoring.

(2) The Secretary shall prescribe such procedures as may be necessary to preserve such confidentiality, except that the Secretary shall release or make public any such information in aggregate, summary, or other form which does not directly or indirectly disclose the identity or business of any person.

**(k) Regulations**

The Secretary, in consultation with any other Federal agency to the extent that such agency may be affected, shall prescribe such regulations as necessary and appropriate to carry out the purposes of this section.

**(*l*) Suggested regime governing incidental taking of marine mammals following termination of interim exemptions**

(1) The Chairman of the Marine Mammal Commission shall, after consultation with interested parties and not later than February 1, 1990, transmit to the Secretary and make available to the public recommended guidelines to govern the incidental taking of marine mammals in the course of commercial fishing operations, other than those subject to section 1374(h)(2) of this title, after October 1, 1993. Such guidelines shall be developed by the Commission and its Committee of Scientific Advisers on Marine Mammals and shall—

(A) be designed to provide a scientific rationale and basis for determining how many marine mammals may be incidentally taken under a regime to be adopted to govern such taking after October 1, 1993;

(B) be based on sound principles of wildlife management, and be consistent with and in furtherance of the purposes and policies set forth in this chapter; and

(C) to the maximum extent practicable, include as factors to be considered and utilized in determining permissible levels of such taking—

(i) the status and trends of the affected marine mammal population stocks;

(ii) the abundance and annual net recruitment of such stocks;

(iii) the level of confidence in the knowledge of the affected stocks; and

(iv) the extent to which incidental taking will likely cause or contribute to their decline or prevent their recovery to optimum sustainable population levels.

(2) The Secretary shall advise the Chairman of the Commission in writing if the Secretary determines that any additional information or explanation of the Chairman's recommendations is needed, and the Chairman shall respond in writing to any such request by the Secretary.

(3) On or before February 1, 1991, the Secretary, after consultation with the Marine Mammal Commission, Regional Fishery Management Councils, and other interested governmental and nongovernmental organizations, shall publish in the Federal Register, for public comment, the suggested regime that the Secretary considers should, if authorized by enactment of any additional legislation, govern incidental taking of marine mammals, other than those subject to section 1374(h)(2) of this title, after October 1, 1993. The suggested regime shall include—

(A) the scientific guidelines to be used in determining permissible levels of incidental taking;

(B) a description of the arrangements for consultation and cooperation with other Federal agencies, the appropriate Regional Fishery Management Councils and States, the commercial fishing industry, and conservation organizations; and

(C) a summary of such regulations and legislation as would be necessary to implement the suggested regime.

(4) On or before January 1, 1992, the Secretary, after consultation with the Marine Mammal Commission, and consideration of public comment, shall transmit to the Committee on Commerce, Science, and Transportation of the Senate and the Committee on Merchant Marine and Fisheries of the House of Representatives recommendations pertaining to the incidental taking of marine mammals, other than those subject to section 1374(h)(2) of this title, after October 1, 1993. The recommendations shall include—

(A) the suggested regime developed under paragraph (3) of this subsection as modified after comment and consultations;

(B) a proposed schedule for implementing the suggested regime; and

(C) such recommendations for additional legislation as the Secretary considers necessary or desirable to implement the suggested regime.

**(m) Consultation with Secretary of the Interior**

The Secretary shall consult with the Secretary of the Interior prior to taking actions or making determinations under this section that affect or relate to species or population stocks of marine mammals for which the Secretary of the Interior is responsible under this subchapter.

**(n) Owner of fixed commercial fishing gear deemed owner of vessel engaged in fishery in which gear deployed**

For the purposes of this section, the owner of fixed or other commercial fishing gear that is deployed with or without the use of a vessel shall be deemed to be an owner of a vessel engaged in the fishery in which that gear is deployed.

**(*o*) Definitions**

As used in this section—

**(1)** the term "fishery" has the same meaning as it does in section 1802(8) of this title.

**(2)** the term "Secretary" means the Secretary of Commerce.

**(3)** the term "vessel engaged in a fishery" means a fishing vessel as defined in section 2101(11a) of Title 46 or a fish processing vessel as defined in section 2101(11b) of that title, which is engaged in fishery.

**(4)** the term "vessel of the United States" has the same meaning as it does in section 1802(27) of this title.

(Pub.L. 92–522, Title I, § 114, as added Pub.L. 100–711, § 2(a)(2), Nov. 23, 1988, 102 Stat. 4755, and amended Pub.L. 103–86, Sept. 30, 1993, 107 Stat. 930; Pub.L. 103–228, Mar. 31, 1994, 108 Stat. 281; Pub.L. 103–238, § 15(a), Apr. 30, 1994, 108 Stat. 559; Pub.L. 104–43, Title IV, § 404(a)(1), Nov. 3, 1995, 109 Stat. 390; Pub.L. 104–208, Div. A, Title I, § 101(a) [Title II, § 211(b)], Sept. 30, 1996, 110 Stat. 3009–41.)

1 So in original. Probably should not be capitalized.

### HISTORICAL AND STATUTORY NOTES

**References in Text**

Section 1802 of this title, referred to in subsec. (*o*)(1), (4), was subsequently amended and pars. (8) and (27) no longer define the terms "fishery" and "vessel of the United States". Those terms are defined in pars. (13) and (43) of 16 U.S.C.A. § 1802.

**Effective and Applicability Provisions**

1996 Acts

Amendment by Pub.L. 104–208, Div. A, Title I, § 101(a) [Title II, § 211(b)], Sept. 30, 1996, 110 Stat. 3009–41, effective 15 days after Oct. 11, 1996, see Pub.L. 104–208, Div. A, Title I, § 101(a) [Title II, § 211(b)], Sept. 30, 1996, 110 Stat. 3009–41, set out as a note under section 1801 of this title.

1995 Acts

Section 404(a)(2) of Pub.L. 104–43 provided that: "The amendment made by paragraph (1) [amending subsec. (a)(1)] shall be effective on and after April 30, 1994."

**Abolition of House Committee on Merchant Marine and Fisheries**

Committee on Merchant Marine and Fisheries of House of Representatives abolished and any reference in any provision of law enacted before Jan. 4, 1995, to the Committee on Merchant Marine and Fisheries of the House of Representatives treated as referring to the Committee on Agriculture of the House of Representatives, in the case of a provision of law relating to inspection of seafood or seafood products, the Committee on National Security of the House of Representatives, in the case of a provision of law relating to interoceanic canals, the Merchant Marine Academy and State Maritime Academies, or national security aspects of merchant marine, the Committee on Resources of the House of Representatives, in the case of a provision of law relating to fisheries, wildlife, international fishing agreements marine affairs (including coastal zone management) except for measures relating to oil and other pollution of navigable waters, or oceanography, the Committee on Science of the House of Representatives, in the case of a provision of law relating to marine research, and the Committee on Transportation and Infrastructure of the House of Representatives, in the case of a provision of law relating to a matter other than a matter described above, see section 1(b)(3) of Pub.L. 104–14, set out as a note preceding section 21 of Title 2, The Congress.

## § 1383b. Status review; conservation plans [MMPA § 115]

**(a) Determinations by rule; notice and hearing; findings; final rule on status of species or stock involved**

**(1)** In any action by the Secretary to determine if a species or stock should be designated as depleted, or should no longer be designated as depleted, regardless of whether such action is taken on the initiative of the Secretary or in response to a petition for a status review, the Secretary shall only make such a determination by issuance of a rule, after notice and opportunity for public comment and after a call for information in accordance with paragraph (2).

**(2)** The Secretary shall make any determination described in paragraph (1) solely on the basis of the best scientific information available. Prior to the issuance of a proposed rule concerning any such determination, the Secretary shall publish in the Federal Register a call to assist the Secretary in obtaining scientific information from individuals and organizations concerned with the conservation of marine mammals, from persons in any industry which might be affected by the determination, and from academic institutions. In addition, the Secretary shall utilize, to the extent the Secretary determines to be feasible, informal working groups of interested parties and other methods to gather the necessary information.

**(3)(A)** If the Secretary receives a petition for a status review as described in paragraph (1), the Secretary shall publish a notice in the Federal Register that such a petition has been received and is available for public review.

**(B)** Within sixty days after receipt of the petition, the Secretary shall publish a finding in the Federal Register as to whether the petition presents substantial information indicating that the petitioned action may be warranted.

**(C)** If the Secretary makes a positive finding under subparagraph (B), the Secretary shall include in the Federal Register notice, a finding that—

**(i)** a review of the status of the species or stock will be commenced promptly; or

**(ii)** a prompt review of the petition is precluded by other pending status determination petitions and that expeditious progress is being made to process pending status determination petitions under this subchapter.

In no case after making a finding under this subparagraph shall the Secretary delay commencing a review of the status of a species or stock for more than one hundred and twenty days after receipt of the petition.

**(D)** No later than two hundred and ten days after the receipt of the petition, the Secretary shall publish in the Federal Register a proposed rule as to the status of the species or stock, along with the reasons underlying the proposed status determination. Persons shall have at least sixty days to submit comments on such a proposed rule.

**(E)** Not later than ninety days after the close of the comment period on a proposed rule issued under subparagraph (D), the Secretary shall issue a final rule on the status of the species or stock involved, along with the reasons for the status determination. If the Secretary finds with respect to such a proposed rule that there is substantial disagreement regarding the sufficiency or accuracy of the available information relevant to a status determination, the Secretary may delay the issuance of a final rule for a period of not more than six months for purposes of soliciting additional information.

**(F)** Notwithstanding subparagraphs (D) and (E) of this paragraph and section 553 of Title 5, the Secretary may issue a final rule as to the status of a species or stock any time sixty or more days after a positive finding under subparagraph (B) if the Secretary determines there is substantial information available to warrant such final status determination and further delay would pose a significant risk to the well-being of any species or stock. Along with the final rule, the Secretary shall publish in the Federal Register detailed reasons for the expedited determination.

**(b) Conservation plans; preparation and implementation**

(1) The Secretary shall prepare conservation plans—

**(A)** By [1] December 31, 1989, for North Pacific fur seals;

**(B)** by December 31, 1990, for Steller sea lions; and

**(C)** as soon as possible, for any species or stock designated as depleted under this subchapter, except that a conservation plan need not be prepared if the Secretary determines that it will not promote the conservation of the species or stock.

(2) Each plan shall have the purpose of conserving and restoring the species or stock to its optimum sustainable population. The Secretary shall model such plans on recovery plans required under section 1533(f) of this title.

(3) The Secretary shall act expeditiously to implement each conservation plan prepared under paragraph (1). Each year, the Secretary shall specify in the annual report prepared under section 1373(f) of this title what measures have been taken to prepare and implement such plans.

(4) If the Secretary determines that a take reduction plan is necessary to reduce the incidental taking of marine mammals in the course of commercial fishing operations from a strategic stock, or for species or stocks which interact with a commercial fishery for which the Secretary has made a determination under section 1387(f)(1) of this title, any conservation plan prepared under this subsection for such species or stock shall incorporate the take reduction plan required under section 1387 of this title for such species or stock.

(Pub.L. 92–522, Title I, § 115, as added Pub.L. 100–711, § 3, Nov. 23, 1988, 102 Stat. 4763, and amended Pub.L. 103–238, § 8, Apr. 30, 1994, 108 Stat. 543.)

[1] So in original. Probably should not be capitalized.

## § 1384. Authorization of appropriations [MMPA § 116]

**(a) Department of Commerce**

(1) There are authorized to be appropriated to the Department of Commerce, for purposes of carrying out its functions and responsibilities under this subchapter (other than sections 1386 and 1387 of this title) and subchapter V of this chapter, $12,138,000 for fiscal year 1994, $12,623,000 for fiscal year 1995, $13,128,000 for fiscal year 1996, $13,653,000 for fiscal year 1997, $14,200,000 for fiscal year 1998, and $14,768,000 for fiscal year 1999.

(2) There are authorized to be appropriated to the Department of Commerce, for purposes of carrying out sections 1386 and 1387 of this title, $20,000,000 for each of the fiscal years 1994 through 1999.

**(b) Department of the Interior**

There are authorized to be appropriated to the Department of the Interior, for purposes of carrying out its functions and responsibilities under this subchapter, $8,000,000 for fiscal year 1994, $8,600,000 for fiscal year 1995, $9,000,000 for fiscal year 1996, $9,400,000 for fiscal year 1997, $9,900,000 for fiscal year 1998, and $10,296,000 for fiscal year 1999.

(Pub.L. 92–522, Title I, § 116, formerly § 114, Oct. 21, 1972, 86 Stat. 1043; Pub.L. 95–136, § 2, Oct. 18, 1977, 91 Stat. 1167; Pub.L. 95–316, § 3, July 10, 1978, 92 Stat. 380; renumbered § 116, Pub.L. 100–711, § 2(a)(1), Nov. 23, 1988, 102 Stat. 4755; Pub.L. 103–238, § 9(a), Apr. 30, 1994, 108 Stat. 543.)

### HISTORICAL AND STATUTORY NOTES

**Prior Provisions**

A prior section 1384, Pub.L. 97–58, § 7(a), (b), Oct. 9, 1981, 95 Stat. 987; Pub.L. 98–364,Title I, § 104(1), (2), July 17, 1984, 98 Stat. 442; Pub.L. 100–711, § 6(1), (2), Nov. 23, 1988, 102 Stat. 4771, which authorized appropriations for the Depts. of Commerce and Interior, to carry out such functions and responsibilities as they might have been given under this subchapter, for fiscal years 1982 through 1993, was repealed by Pub.L. 103–238, § 9(c), Apr. 30, 1994, 108 Stat. 543.

## § 1385. Dolphin protection

**(a) Short title**

This section may be cited as the "Dolphin Protection Consumer Information Act".

**(b) Findings**

The Congress finds that—

(1) dolphins and other marine mammals are frequently killed in the course of tuna fishing operations in the eastern tropical Pacific Ocean and high seas driftnet fishing in other parts of the world;

(2) it is the policy of the United States to support a worldwide ban on high seas driftnet fishing, in part because of the harmful effects that such driftnets have on marine mammals, including dolphins; and

(3) consumers would like to know if the tuna they purchase is falsely labeled as to the effect of the harvesting of the tuna on dolphins.

**(c) Definitions**

For purposes of this section—

(1) the terms "driftnet" and "driftnet fishing" have the meanings given those terms in section 4003 of the Driftnet Impact Monitoring, Assessment, and Control Act of 1987 (16 U.S.C. 1822 note);

(2) the term "eastern tropical Pacific Ocean" means the area of the Pacific Ocean bounded by 40 degrees north latitude, 40 degrees south latitude, 160 degrees west longitude, and the western coastlines of North, Central, and South America;

(3) the term "label" means a display of written, printed, or graphic matter on or affixed to the immediate container of any article;

(4) the term "Secretary" means the Secretary of Commerce; and

(5) the term "tuna product" means a food item which contains tuna and which has been processed for retail sale, except perishable sandwiches, salads, or other products with a shelf life of less than 3 days.

**(d) Labeling standard**

(1) It is a violation of section 45 of Title 15 for any producer, importer, exporter, distributor, or seller of any tuna product that is exported from or offered for sale in the United States to include on the label of that product the term "dolphin safe" or any other term or symbol that falsely claims or suggests that the tuna contained in the product were harvested using a method of fishing that is not harmful to dolphins if the product contains tuna harvested—

(A) on the high seas by a vessel engaged in driftnet fishing;

(B) outside the eastern tropical Pacific Ocean by a vessel using purse seine nets—

(i) in a fishery in which the Secretary has determined that a regular and significant association occurs between dolphins and tuna (similar to the association between dolphins and tuna in the eastern tropical Pacific Ocean), unless such product is accompanied by a written statement, executed by the captain of the vessel and an observer participating in a national or international program acceptable to the Secretary, certifying that no purse seine net was intentionally deployed on or used to encircle dolphins during the particular voyage on which the tuna were caught and no dolphins were killed or seriously injured in the sets in which the tuna were caught; or

(ii) in any other fishery (other than a fishery described in subparagraph (D)) unless the product is accompanied by a written statement executed by the captain of the vessel certifying that no purse seine net was intentionally deployed on or used to encircle dolphins during the particular voyage on which the tuna was harvested;

(C) in the eastern tropical Pacific Ocean by a vessel using a purse seine net unless the tuna meet the requirements for being considered dolphin safe under paragraph (2); or

(D) by a vessel in a fishery other than one described in subparagraph (A), (B), or (C) that is identified by the Secretary as having a regular and significant mortality or serious injury of dolphins, unless such product is accompanied by a written statement executed by the captain of the vessel and an observer participating in a national or international program acceptable to the Secretary that no dolphins were killed or seriously injured in the sets or other gear deployments in which the tuna were caught, provided that the Secretary determines that such an observer statement is necessary.

(2) For purposes of paragraph (1)(C), a tuna product that contains tuna harvested in the eastern tropical Pacific Ocean by a vessel using purse seine nets is dolphin safe if—

(A) the vessel is of a type and size that the Secretary has determined, consistent with the

International Dolphin Conservation Program, is not capable of deploying its purse seine nets on or to encircle dolphins; or

(B)(i) the product is accompanied by a written statement executed by the captain providing the certification required under subsection (h) of this section;

(ii) the product is accompanied by a written statement executed by—

(I) the Secretary or the Secretary's designee;

(II) a representative of the Inter-American Tropical Tuna Commission; or

(III) an authorized representative of a participating nation whose national program meets the requirements of the International Dolphin Conservation Program,

which states that there was an observer approved by the International Dolphin Conservation Program on board the vessel during the entire trip and that such observer provided the certification required under subsection (h) of this section; and

(iii) the statements referred to in clauses (i) and (ii) are endorsed in writing by each exporter, importer, and processor of the product; and

(C) the written statements and endorsements referred to in subparagraph (B) comply with regulations promulgated by the Secretary which provide for the verification of tuna products as dolphin safe.

(3)(A) The Secretary of Commerce shall develop an official mark that may be used to label tuna products as dolphin safe in accordance with this Act.[1]

(B) A tuna product that bears the dolphin safe mark developed under subparagraph (A) shall not bear any other label or mark that refers to dolphins, porpoises, or marine mammals.

(C) It is a violation of section 45 of Title 15 to label a tuna product with any label or mark that refers to dolphins, porpoises, or marine mammals other than the mark developed under subparagraph (A) unless—

(i) no dolphins were killed or seriously injured in the sets or other gear deployments in which the tuna were caught;

(ii) the label is supported by a tracking and verification program which is comparable in effectiveness to the program established under subsection (f) of this section; and

(iii) the label complies with all applicable labeling, marketing, and advertising laws and regulations of the Federal Trade Commission, including any guidelines for environmental labeling.

(D) If the Secretary determines that the use of a label referred to in subparagraph (C) is substantially undermining the conservation goals of the International Dolphin Conservation Program, the Secretary shall report that determination to the United States Senate Committee on Commerce, Science, and Transportation and the United States House of Representatives Committees on Resources and on Commerce, along with recommendations to correct such problems.

(E) It is a violation of section 45 of Title 15 willingly and knowingly to use a label referred to in subparagraph (C) in a campaign or effort to mislead or deceive consumers about the level of protection afforded dolphins under the International Dolphin Conservation Program.

### (e) Enforcement

Any person who knowingly and willfully makes a statement or endorsement described in subsection (d)(2)(B) of this section that is false is liable for a civil penalty of not to exceed $100,000 assessed in an action brought in any appropriate district court of the United States on behalf of the Secretary.

### (f) Regulations

The Secretary, in consultation with the Secretary of the Treasury, shall issue regulations to implement this Act,[1] including regulations to establish a domestic tracking and verification program that provides for the effective tracking of tuna labeled under subsection (d) of this section. In the development of these regulations, the Secretary shall establish appropriate procedures for ensuring the confidentiality of proprietary information the submission of which is voluntary or mandatory. The regulations shall address each of the following items:

(1) The use of weight calculation for purposes of tracking tuna caught, landed, processed, and exported.

(2) Additional measures to enhance current observer coverage, including the establishment of criteria for training, and for improving monitoring and reporting capabilities and procedures.

(3) The designation of well location, procedures for sealing holds, procedures for monitoring and certifying both above and below deck, or through equally effective methods, the tracking and verification of tuna labeled under subsection (d) of this section.

(4) The reporting, receipt, and database storage of radio and facsimile transmittals from fishing vessels containing information related to the tracking and verification of tuna, and the definition of set.

(5) The shore-based verification and tracking throughout the fishing, transshipment, and canning process by means of Inter-American Tropical Tuna Commission trip records or otherwise.

(6) The use of periodic audits and spot checks for caught, landed, and processed tuna products labeled in accordance with subsection (d) of this section.

(7) The provision of timely access to data required under this subsection by the Secretary from harvesting nations to undertake the actions required in paragraph (6) of this paragraph.[2]

The Secretary may make such adjustments as may be appropriate to the regulations promulgated under this subsection to implement an international tracking and verification program that meets or exceeds the minimum requirements established by the Secretary under this subsection.

**(g) Secretarial findings**

(1) Between March 1, 1999, and March 31, 1999, the Secretary shall, on the basis of the research conducted before March 1, 1999, under section 1414a(a) of this title, information obtained under the International Dolphin Conservation Program, and any other relevant information, make an initial finding regarding whether the intentional deployment on or encirclement of dolphins with purse seine nets is having a significant adverse impact on any depleted dolphin stock in the eastern tropical Pacific Ocean. The initial finding shall be published immediately in the Federal Register and shall become effective upon a subsequent date determined by the Secretary.

(2) Between July 1, 2001, and December 31, 2002, the Secretary shall, on the basis of the completed study conducted under section 1414a(a) of this title, information obtained under the International Dolphin Conservation Program, and any other relevant information, make a finding regarding whether the intentional deployment on or encirclement of dolphins with purse seine nets is having a significant adverse impact on any depleted dolphin stock in the eastern tropical Pacific Ocean. The finding shall be published immediately in the Federal Register and shall become effective upon a subsequent date determined by the Secretary.

**(h) Certification by captain and observer**

(1) Unless otherwise required by paragraph (2), the certification by the captain under subsection (d)(2)(B)(i) of this section and the certification provided by the observer as specified in subsection (d)(2)(B)(ii) of this section shall be that no dolphins were killed or seriously injured during the sets in which the tuna were caught.

(2) The certification by the captain under subsection (d)(2)(B)(i) of this section and the certification provided by the observer as specified under subsection (d)(2)(B)(ii) of this section shall be that no tuna were caught on the trip in which such tuna were harvested using a purse seine net intentionally deployed on or to encircle dolphins, and that no dolphins were killed or seriously injured during the sets in which the tuna were caught, if the tuna were caught on a trip commencing—

(A) before the effective date of the initial finding by the Secretary under subsection (g)(1) of this section;

(B) after the effective date of such initial finding and before the effective date of the finding of the Secretary under subsection (g)(2) of this section, where the initial finding is that the intentional deployment on or encirclement of dolphins is having a significant adverse impact on any depleted dolphin stock; or

(C) after the effective date of the finding under subsection (g)(2) of this section, where such finding is that the intentional deployment on or encirclement of dolphins is having a significant adverse impact on any such depleted stock.

(Pub.L. 101–627, Title IX, § 901(a) to (f), (h), (i), Nov. 28, 1990, 104 Stat. 4465; Pub.L. 105–42, § 5, Aug. 15, 1997, 111 Stat. 1125.)

[1] So in original. Probably should be "this section".

[2] So in original. Probably should be "this subsection".

## HISTORICAL AND STATUTORY NOTES

**References in Text**

The Driftnet Impact Monitoring, Assessment, and Control Act of 1987, including section 4003 of such Act, referred to in subsec. (c)(1), is Pub.L. 100–220, Title IV, Dec. 29, 1987, 101 Stat. 1447, which is set out as a note under section 1822 of this title.

**Codifications**

Section was enacted by the Dolphin Protection Consumer Information Act, not as part of the Marine Mammal Protection Act of 1972, which comprises this chapter.

Former subsec. (g) of this section enacted section 1371 (a)(2)(E) of this title including concluding sentence.

**Effective and Applicability Provisions**

1997 Acts

For effective date of amendments to this section by Pub.L. 105–42, see section 8 of Pub.L. 105–42, set out as a note under section 1362 of this title.

## § 1386. Stock assessments

**[MMPA § 117]**

**(a) In general**

Not later than August 1, 1994, the Secretary shall, in consultation with the appropriate regional scientific review group established under subsection (d) of this section, prepare a draft stock assessment for each marine mammal stock which occurs in waters under the jurisdiction of the United States. Each draft stock assessment, based on the best scientific information available, shall—

(1) describe the geographic range of the affected stock, including any seasonal or temporal variation in such range;

(2) provide for such stock the minimum population estimate, current and maximum net productivity rates, and current population trend, including a description of the information upon which these are based;

(3) estimate the annual human-caused mortality and serious injury of the stock by source and, for a strategic stock, other factors that may be causing a decline or impeding recovery of the stock, including effects on marine mammal habitat and prey;

(4) describe commercial fisheries that interact with the stock, including—

(A) the approximate number of vessels actively participating in each such fishery;

(B) the estimated level of incidental mortality and serious injury of the stock by each such fishery on an annual basis;

(C) seasonal or area differences in such incidental mortality or serious injury; and

(D) the rate, based on the appropriate standard unit of fishing effort, of such incidental mortality and serious injury, and an analysis stating whether such level is insignificant and is approaching a zero mortality and serious injury rate;

(5) categorize the status of the stock as one that either—

(A) has a level of human-caused mortality and serious injury that is not likely to cause the stock to be reduced below its optimum sustainable population; or

(B) is a strategic stock, with a description of the reasons therefor; and

(6) estimate the potential biological removal level for the stock, describing the information used to calculate it, including the recovery factor.

**(b) Public comment**

(1) The Secretary shall publish in the Federal Register a notice of the availability of a draft stock assessment or any revision thereof and provide an opportunity for public review and comment during a period of 90 days. Such notice shall include a summary of the assessment and a list of the sources of information or published reports upon which the assessment is based.

(2) Subsequent to the notice of availability required under paragraph (1), if requested by a person to which section 1371(b) of this title applies, the Secretary shall conduct a proceeding on the record prior to publishing a final stock assessment or any revision thereof for any stock subject to taking under section 1371(b) of this title.

(3) After consideration of the best scientific information available, the advice of the appropriate regional scientific review group established under subsection (d) of this section, and the comments of the general public, the Secretary shall publish in the Federal Register a notice of availability and a summary of the final stock assessment or any revision thereof, not later than 90 days after—

(A) the close of the public comment period on a draft stock assessment or revision thereof; or

(B) final action on an agency proceeding pursuant to paragraph (2).

**(c) Review and revision**

(1) The Secretary shall review stock assessments in accordance with this subsection—

(A) at least annually for stocks which are specified as strategic stocks;

(B) at least annually for stocks for which significant new information is available; and

(C) at least once every 3 years for all other stocks.

(2) If the review under paragraph (1) indicates that the status of the stock has changed or can be more accurately determined, the Secretary shall revise the stock assessment in accordance with subsection (b) of this section.

**(d) Regional scientific review groups**

(1) Not later than 60 days after April 30, 1994, the Secretary of Commerce shall, in consultation with the Secretary of the Interior (with respect to marine mammals under that Secretary's jurisdiction), the Marine Mammal Commission, the Governors of affected adjacent coastal States, regional fishery and wildlife management authorities, Alaska Native organizations and Indian tribes, and environmental and fishery groups, establish three independent regional scientific review groups representing Alaska, the Pacific Coast (including Hawaii), and the Atlantic Coast (including the Gulf of Mexico), consisting of individuals with expertise in marine mammal biology and ecology, population dynamics and modeling, commercial fishing technology and practices, and stocks taken under section 1371(b) of this title. The Secretary of Commerce shall, to the maximum extent practicable, attempt to achieve a balanced representation of viewpoints among the individuals on each regional scientific review group. The regional scientific review groups shall advise the Secretary on—

(A) population estimates and the population status and trends of such stocks;

(B) uncertainties and research needed regarding stock separation, abundance, or trends, and factors affecting the distribution, size, or productivity of the stock;

(C) uncertainties and research needed regarding the species, number, ages, gender, and reproductive status of marine mammals;

(D) research needed to identify modifications in fishing gear and practices likely to reduce the incidental mortality and serious injury of marine mammals in commercial fishing operations;

(E) the actual, expected, or potential impacts of habitat destruction, including marine pollution and natural environmental change, on specific marine mammal species or stocks, and for strategic stocks, appropriate conservation or management measures to alleviate any such impacts; and

(F) any other issue which the Secretary or the groups consider appropriate.

(2) The scientific review groups established under this subsection shall not be subject to the Federal Advisory Committee Act (5 App. U.S.C.).

(3) Members of the scientific review groups shall serve without compensation, but may be reimbursed by the Secretary, upon request, for reasonable travel costs and expenses incurred in performing their obligations.

(4) The Secretary may appoint or reappoint individuals to the regional scientific review groups under paragraph (1) as needed.

**(e) Effect on section 1371(b) of this title**

This section shall not affect or otherwise modify the provisions of section 1371(b) of this title.

(Pub.L. 92–522, Title I, § 117, as added Pub.L. 103–238, § 10, Apr. 30, 1994, 108 Stat. 544.)

**HISTORICAL AND STATUTORY NOTES**

**References in Text**

The Federal Advisory Committee Act, referred to in subsec. (d)(2), is Pub.L. 92–463, Oct. 6, 1972, 86 Stat. 770, as amended, which is set out in Appendix 2 to Title 5, Government Organization and Employees.

## § 1387. Taking of marine mammals incidental to commercial fishing operations

**[MMPA § 118]**

**(a) In general**

(1) Effective on April 30, 1994, and except as provided in section 1383a of this title and in paragraphs (2), (3), and (4) of this subsection, the provisions of this section shall govern the incidental taking of marine mammals in the course of commercial fishing operations by persons using vessels of the United States or vessels which have valid fishing permits issued by the Secretary in accordance with section 1824(b) of this title. In any event it shall be the immediate goal that the incidental mortality or serious injury of marine mammals occurring in the course of commercial fishing operations be reduced to insignificant levels approaching a zero mortality and serious injury rate within 7 years after April 30, 1994.

(2) In the case of the incidental taking of marine mammals from species or stocks designated under this chapter as depleted on the basis of their listing as threatened species or endangered species under the Endangered Species Act of 1973 (16 U.S.C. 1531 et seq.), both this section and section 1371(a)(5)(E) of this chapter shall apply.

(3) Sections[1] 1374(h) of this title and subchapter IV of this chapter, and not this section, shall govern the taking of marine mammals in the course of commercial purse seine fishing for yellowfin tuna in the eastern tropical Pacific Ocean.

(4) This section shall not govern the incidental taking of California sea otters and shall not be deemed to amend or repeal the Act of November 7, 1986 (Public Law 99–625; 100 Stat. 3500).

(5) Except as provided in section 1371(c) of this title, the intentional lethal take of any marine mammal in the course of commercial fishing operations is prohibited.

(6) Sections 1373 and 1374 of this title shall not apply to the incidental taking of marine mammals under the authority of this section.

**(b) Zero mortality rate goal**

(1) Commercial fisheries shall reduce incidental mortality and serious injury of marine mammals to insignificant levels approaching a zero mortality and serious injury rate within 7 years after April 30, 1994.

(2) Fisheries which maintain insignificant serious injury and mortality levels approaching a zero rate shall not be required to further reduce their mortality and serious injury rates.

(3) Three years after April 30, 1994, the Secretary shall review the progress of all commercial fisheries, by fishery, toward reducing incidental mortality and serious injury to insignificant levels approaching a zero rate. The Secretary shall submit to the Committee on Commerce, Science, and Transportation of the Senate and the Committee on Merchant Marine and Fisheries of the House of Representatives a report setting forth the results of such review within 1 year after commencement of the review. The Secretary shall note any commercial fishery for which additional information is required to accurately assess the level of incidental mortality and serious injury of marine mammals in the fishery.

(4) If the Secretary determines after review under paragraph (3) that the rate of incidental mortality and serious injury of marine mammals in a commercial fishery is not consistent with paragraph (1), then the

Secretary shall take appropriate action under subsection (f) of this section.

**(c) Registration and authorization**

(1) The Secretary shall, within 90 days after April 30, 1994—

(A) publish in the Federal Register for public comment, for a period of not less than 90 days, any necessary changes to the Secretary's list of commercial fisheries published under section 1383a(b)(1) of this title and which is in existence on March 31, 1994 (along with an explanation of such changes and a statement describing the marine mammal stocks interacting with, and the approximate number of vessels or persons actively involved in, each such fishery), with respect to commercial fisheries that have—

(i) frequent incidental mortality and serious injury of marine mammals;

(ii) occasional incidental mortality and serious injury of marine mammals; or

(iii) a remote likelihood of or no known incidental mortality or serious injury of marine mammals;

(B) after the close of the period for such public comment, publish in the Federal Register a revised list of commercial fisheries and an update of information required by subparagraph (A), together with a summary of the provisions of this section and information sufficient to advise vessel owners on how to obtain an authorization and otherwise comply with the requirements of this section; and

(C) at least once each year thereafter, and at such other times as the Secretary considers appropriate, reexamine, based on information gathered under this chapter and other relevant sources and after notice and opportunity for public comment, the classification of commercial fisheries and other determinations required under subparagraph (A) and publish in the Federal Register any necessary changes.

(2)(A) An authorization shall be granted by the Secretary in accordance with this section for a vessel engaged in a commercial fishery listed under paragraph (1)(A) (i) or (ii), upon receipt by the Secretary of a completed registration form providing the name of the vessel owner and operator, the name and description of the vessel, the fisheries in which it will be engaged, the approximate time, duration, and location of such fishery operations, and the general type and nature of use of the fishing gear and techniques used. Such information shall be in a readily usable format that can be efficiently entered into and utilized by an automated or computerized data processing system. A decal or other physical evidence that the authorization is current and valid shall be issued by the Secretary at the time an authorization is granted, and so long as the authorization remains current and valid, shall be reissued annually thereafter.

(B) No authorization may be granted under this section to the owner of a vessel unless such vessel—

(i) is a vessel of the United States; or

(ii) has a valid fishing permit issued by the Secretary in accordance with section 1824(b) of this title.

(C) Except as provided in subsection (a) of this section, an authorization granted under this section shall allow the incidental taking of all species and stocks of marine mammals to which this chapter applies.

(3)(A) An owner of a vessel engaged in any fishery listed under paragraph (1)(A) (i) or (ii) shall, in order to engage in the lawful incidental taking of marine mammals in a commercial fishery—

(i) have registered as required under paragraph (2) with the Secretary in order to obtain for each such vessel owned and used in the fishery an authorization for the purpose of incidentally taking marine mammals in accordance with this section, except that owners of vessels holding valid certificates of exemption under section 1383a of this title are deemed to have registered for purposes of this subsection for the period during which such exemption is valid;

(ii) ensure that a decal or such other physical evidence of a current and valid authorization as the Secretary may require is displayed on or is in the possession of the master of each such vessel;

(iii) report as required by subsection (e) of this section; and

(iv) comply with any applicable take reduction plan and emergency regulations issued under this section.

(B) Any owner of a vessel receiving an authorization under this section for any fishery listed under paragraph (1)(A)(i) or (ii) shall, as a condition of that authorization, take on board an observer if requested to do so by the Secretary.

(C) An owner of a vessel engaged in a fishery listed under paragraph (1)(A)(i) or (ii) who—

(i) fails to obtain from the Secretary an authorization for such vessel under this section;

(ii) fails to maintain a current and valid authorization for such vessel; or

(iii) fails to ensure that a decal or other physical evidence of such authorization issued by the Secretary is displayed on or is in possession of the master of the vessel,

and the master of any such vessel engaged in such fishery, shall be deemed to have violated this subchapter, and for violations of clauses (i) and (ii) shall be subject to the penalties of this subchapter, and for violations of clause (iii) shall be subject to a fine of not more than $100 for each offense.

(D) If the owner of a vessel has obtained and maintains a current and valid authorization from the Secretary under this section and meets the requirements set forth in this section, including compliance with any regulations to implement a take reduction plan under this section, the owner of such vessel, and the master and crew members of the vessel, shall not be subject to the penalties set forth in this subchapter for the incidental taking of marine mammals while such vessel is engaged in a fishery to which the authorization applies.

(E) Each owner of a vessel engaged in any fishery not listed under paragraph (1)(A)(i) or (ii), and the master and crew members of such a vessel, shall not be subject to the penalties set forth in this subchapter for the incidental taking of marine mammals if such owner reports to the Secretary, in the form and manner required under subsection (e) of this section, instances of incidental mortality or injury of marine mammals in the course of that fishery.

(4)(A) The Secretary shall suspend or revoke an authorization granted under this section and shall not issue a decal or other physical evidence of the authorization for any vessel until the owner of such vessel complies with the reporting requirements under subsection (e) of this section and such requirements to take on board an observer under paragraph (3)(B) as are applicable to such vessel. Previous failure to comply with the requirements of section 1383a of this title shall not bar authorization under this section for an owner who complies with the requirements of this section.

(B) The Secretary may suspend or revoke an authorization granted under this subsection, and may not issue a decal or other physical evidence of the authorization for any vessel which fails to comply with a take reduction plan or emergency regulations issued under this section.

(C) The owner and master of a vessel which fails to comply with a take reduction plan shall be subject to the penalties of sections 1375 and 1377 of this title, and may be subject to section 1376 of this title.

(5)(A) The Secretary shall develop, in consultation with the appropriate States, affected Regional Fishery Management Councils, and other interested persons, the means by which the granting and administration of authorizations under this section shall be integrated and coordinated, to the maximum extent practicable, with existing fishery licenses, registrations, and related programs.

(B) The Secretary shall utilize newspapers of general circulation, fishery trade associations, electronic media, and other means of advising commercial fishermen of the provisions of this section and the means by which they can comply with its requirements.

(C) The Secretary is authorized to charge a fee for the granting of an authorization under this section. The level of fees charged under this subparagraph shall not exceed the administrative costs incurred in granting an authorization. Fees collected under this subparagraph shall be available to the Under Secretary of Commerce for Oceans and Atmosphere for expenses incurred in the granting and administration of authorizations under this section.

**(d) Monitoring of incidental takes**

(1) The Secretary shall establish a program to monitor incidental mortality and serious injury of marine mammals during the course of commercial fishing operations. The purposes of the monitoring program shall be to—

(A) obtain statistically reliable estimates of incidental mortality and serious injury;

(B) determine the reliability of reports of incidental mortality and serious injury under subsection (e) of this section; and

(C) identify changes in fishing methods or technology that may increase or decrease incidental mortality and serious injury.

(2) Pursuant to paragraph (1), the Secretary may place observers on board vessels as necessary, subject to the provisions of this section. Observers may, among other tasks—

(A) record incidental mortality and injury, or by catch of other nontarget species;

(B) record numbers of marine mammals sighted; and

(C) perform other scientific investigations.

(3) In determining the distribution of observers among commercial fisheries and vessels within a fishery, the Secretary shall be guided by the following standards:

(A) The requirement to obtain statistically reliable information.

(B) The requirement that assignment of observers is fair and equitable among fisheries and among vessels in a fishery.

(C) The requirement that no individual person or vessel, or group of persons or vessels, be subject to excessive or overly burdensome observer coverage.

(D) To the extent practicable, the need to minimize costs and avoid duplication.

(4) To the extent practicable, the Secretary shall allocate observers among commercial fisheries in accordance with the following priority:

(A) The highest priority for allocation shall be for commercial fisheries that have incidental mortality or serious injury of marine mammals from stocks listed as endangered species or threatened species under the Endangered Species Act of 1973 (16 U.S.C. 1531 et seq.).

(B) The second highest priority for allocation shall be for commercial fisheries that have incidental mortality and serious injury of marine mammals from strategic stocks.

(C) The third highest priority for allocation shall be for commercial fisheries that have incidental mortality or serious injury of marine mammals from stocks for which the level of incidental mortality and serious injury is uncertain.

(5) The Secretary may establish an alternative observer program to provide statistically reliable information on the species and number of marine mammals incidentally taken in the course of commercial fishing operations. The alternative observer program may include direct observation of fishing activities from vessels, airplanes, or points on shore.

(6) The Secretary is not required to place an observer on a vessel in a fishery if the Secretary finds that—

(A) in a situation in which harvesting vessels are delivering fish to a processing vessel, and the catch is not taken on board the harvesting vessel, statistically reliable information can be obtained from an observer on board the processing vessel to which the fish are delivered;

(B) the facilities on a vessel for quartering of an observer, or for carrying out observer functions, are so inadequate or unsafe that the health or safety of the observer or the safe operation of the vessel would be jeopardized; or

(C) for reasons beyond the control of the Secretary, an observer is not available.

(7) The Secretary may, with the consent of the vessel owner, station an observer on board a vessel engaged in a fishery not listed under subsection (c)(1)(A)(i) or (ii) of this section.

(8) Any proprietary information collected under this subsection shall be confidential and shall not be disclosed except—

(A) to Federal employees whose duties require access to such information;

(B) to State or tribal employees pursuant to an agreement with the Secretary that prevents public disclosure of the identity or business of any person;

(C) when required by court order; or

(D) in the case of scientific information involving fisheries, to employees of Regional Fishery Management Councils who are responsible for fishery management plan development and monitoring.

(9) The Secretary shall prescribe such procedures as may be necessary to preserve such confidentiality, except that the Secretary shall release or make public upon request any such information in aggregate, summary, or other form which does not directly or indirectly disclose the identity or business of any person.

**(e) Reporting requirement**

The owner or operator of a commercial fishing vessel subject to this chapter shall report all incidental mortality and injury of marine mammals in the course of commercial fishing operations to the Secretary by mail or other means acceptable to the Secretary within 48 hours after the end of each fishing trip on a standard postage-paid form to be developed by the Secretary under this section. Such form shall be capable of being readily entered into and usable by an automated or computerized data processing system and shall require the vessel owner or operator to provide the following:

(1) The vessel name, and Federal, State, or tribal registration numbers of the registered vessel.

(2) The name and address of the vessel owner or operator.

(3) The name and description of the fishery.

(4) The species of each marine mammal incidentally killed or injured, and the date, time, and approximate geographic location of such occurrence.

**(f) Take reduction plans**

(1) The Secretary shall develop and implement a take reduction plan designed to assist in the recovery or prevent the depletion of each strategic stock which interacts with a commercial fishery listed under subsection (c)(1)(A)(i) or (ii) of this section, and may develop and implement such a plan for any other marine mammal stocks which interact with a commercial fishery listed under subsection (c)(1)(A)(i) of this section which the Secretary determines, after notice and opportunity for public comment, has a high level of mortality and serious injury across a number of such marine mammal stocks.

(2) The immediate goal of a take reduction plan for a strategic stock shall be to reduce, within 6 months of its implementation, the incidental mortality or serious injury of marine mammals incidentally taken in the course of commercial fishing operations to levels less than the potential biological removal level established for that stock under section 1386 of this title. The long-term goal of the plan shall be to reduce, within 5 years of its implementation, the incidental mortality or serious injury of marine mammals incidentally taken in the course of commercial fishing operations to insignificant levels approaching a zero mortality and

serious injury rate, taking into account the economics of the fishery, the availability of existing technology, and existing State or regional fishery management plans.

(3) If there is insufficient funding available to develop and implement a take reduction plan for all such stocks that interact with commercial fisheries listed under subsection (c)(1)(A)(i) or (ii) of this section, the Secretary shall give highest priority to the development and implementation of take reduction plans for species or stocks whose level of incidental mortality and serious injury exceeds the potential biological removal level, those that have a small population size, and those which are declining most rapidly.

(4) Each take reduction plan shall include—

**(A)** a review of the information in the final stock assessment published under section 1386(b) of this title and any substantial new information;

**(B)** an estimate of the total number and, if possible, age and gender, of animals from the stock that are being incidentally lethally taken or seriously injured each year during the course of commercial fishing operations, by fishery;

**(C)** recommended regulatory or voluntary measures for the reduction of incidental mortality and serious injury;

**(D)** recommended dates for achieving the specific objectives of the plan.

(5)(A) For any stock in which incidental mortality and serious injury from commercial fisheries exceeds the potential biological removal level established under section 1386 of this title, the plan shall include measures the Secretary expects will reduce, within 6 months of the plan's implementation, such mortality and serious injury to a level below the potential biological removal level.

**(B)** For any stock in which human-caused mortality and serious injury exceeds the potential biological removal level, other than a stock to which subparagraph (A) applies, the plan shall include measures the Secretary expects will reduce, to the maximum extent practicable within 6 months of the plan's implementation, the incidental mortality and serious injury by such commercial fisheries from that stock. For purposes of this subparagraph, the term "maximum extent practicable" means to the lowest level that is feasible for such fisheries within the 6–month period.

(6)(A) At the earliest possible time (not later than 30 days) after the Secretary issues a final stock assessment under section 1386(b) of this title for a strategic stock, the Secretary shall, and for stocks that interact with a fishery listed under subsection (c)(1)(A)(i) of this section for which the Secretary has made a determination under paragraph (1), the Secretary may—

**(i)** establish a take reduction team for such stock and appoint the members of such team in accordance with subparagraph (C); and

**(ii)** publish in the Federal Register a notice of the team's establishment, the names of the team's appointed members, the full geographic range of such stock, and a list of all commercial fisheries that cause incidental mortality and serious injury of marine mammals from such stock.

**(B)** The Secretary may request a take reduction team to address a stock that extends over one or more regions or fisheries, or multiple stocks within a region or fishery, if the Secretary determines that doing so would facilitate the development and implementation of plans required under this subsection.

**(C)** Members of take reduction teams shall have expertise regarding the conservation or biology of the marine mammal species which the take reduction plan will address, or the fishing practices which result in the incidental mortality and serious injury of such species. Members shall include representatives of Federal agencies, each coastal State which has fisheries which interact with the species or stock, appropriate Regional Fishery Management Councils, interstate fisheries commissions, academic and scientific organizations, environmental groups, all commercial and recreational fisheries groups and gear types which incidentally take the species or stock, Alaska Native organizations or Indian tribal organizations, and others as the Secretary deems appropriate. Take reduction teams shall, to the maximum extent practicable, consist of an equitable balance among representatives of resource user interests and nonuser interests.

**(D)** Take reduction teams shall not be subject to the Federal Advisory Committee Act [5 U.S.C.A. App. 3, § 1 et seq.]. Meetings of take reduction teams shall be open to the public, and prior notice of meetings shall be made public in a timely fashion.

**(E)** Members of take reduction teams shall serve without compensation, but may be reimbursed by the Secretary, upon request, for reasonable travel costs and expenses incurred in performing their duties as members of the team.

(7) Where the human-caused mortality and serious injury from a strategic stock is estimated to be equal to or greater than the potential biological removal level established under section 1386 of this title for such stock and such stock interacts with a fishery listed under subsection (c)(1)(A)(i) or (ii) of this section, the following procedures shall apply in the development of the take reduction plan for the stock:

**(A)(i)** Not later than 6 months after the date of establishment of a take reduction team for the stock, the team shall submit a draft take reduction plan for such stock to the Secretary, consistent with the other provisions of this section.

(ii) Such draft take reduction plan shall be developed by consensus. In the event consensus cannot be reached, the team shall advise the Secretary in writing on the range of possibilities considered by the team, and the views of both the majority and minority.

(B)(i) The Secretary shall take the draft take reduction plan into consideration and, not later than 60 days after the submission of the draft plan by the team, the Secretary shall publish in the Federal Register the plan proposed by the team, any changes proposed by the Secretary with an explanation of the reasons therefor, and proposed regulations to implement such plan, for public review and comment during a period of not to exceed 90 days.

(ii) In the event that the take reduction team does not submit a draft plan to the Secretary within 6 months, the Secretary shall, not later than 8 months after the establishment of the team, publish in the Federal Register a proposed take reduction plan and implementing regulations, for public review and comment during a period of not to exceed 90 days.

(C) Not later than 60 days after the close of the comment period required under subparagraph (B), the Secretary shall issue a final take reduction plan and implementing regulations, consistent with the other provisions of this section.

(D) The Secretary shall, during a period of 30 days after publication of a final take reduction plan, utilize newspapers of general circulation, fishery trade associations, electronic media, and other means of advising commercial fishermen of the requirements of the plan and how to comply with them.

(E) The Secretary and the take reduction team shall meet every 6 months, or at such other intervals as the Secretary determines are necessary, to monitor the implementation of the final take reduction plan until such time that the Secretary determines that the objectives of such plan have been met.

(F) The Secretary shall amend the take reduction plan and implementing regulations as necessary to meet the requirements of this section, in accordance with the procedures in this section for the issuance of such plans and regulations.

(8) Where the human-caused mortality and serious injury from a strategic stock is estimated to be less than the potential biological removal level established under section 1386 of this title for such stock and such stock interacts with a fishery listed under subsection (c)(1)(A)(i) or (ii) of this section, or for any marine mammal stocks which interact with a commercial fishery listed under subsection (c)(1)(A)(i) of this section for which the Secretary has made a determination under paragraph (1), the following procedures shall apply in the development of the take reduction plan for such stock:

(A)(i) Not later than 11 months after the date of establishment of a take reduction team for the stock, the team shall submit a draft take reduction plan for the stock to the Secretary, consistent with the other provisions of this section.

(ii) Such draft take reduction plan shall be developed by consensus. In the event consensus cannot be reached, the team shall advise the Secretary in writing on the range of possibilities considered by the team, and the views of both the majority and minority.

(B)(i) The Secretary shall take the draft take reduction plan into consideration and, not later than 60 days after the submission of the draft plan by the team, the Secretary shall publish in the Federal Register the plan proposed by the team, any changes proposed by the Secretary with an explanation of the reasons therefor, and proposed regulations to implement such plan, for public review and comment during a period of not to exceed 90 days.

(ii) In the event that the take reduction team does not submit a draft plan to the Secretary within 11 months, the Secretary shall, not later than 13 months after the establishment of the team, publish in the Federal Register a proposed take reduction plan and implementing regulations, for public review and comment during a period of not to exceed 90 days.

(C) Not later than 60 days after the close of the comment period required under subparagraph (B), the Secretary shall issue a final take reduction plan and implementing regulations, consistent with the other provisions of this section.

(D) The Secretary shall, during a period of 30 days after publication of a final take reduction plan, utilize newspapers of general circulation, fishery trade associations, electronic media, and other means of advising commercial fishermen of the requirements of the plan and how to comply with them.

(E) The Secretary and the take reduction team shall meet on an annual basis, or at such other intervals as the Secretary determines are necessary, to monitor the implementation of the final take reduction plan until such time that the Secretary determines that the objectives of such plan have been met.

(F) The Secretary shall amend the take reduction plan and implementing regulations as necessary to meet the requirements of this section, in accordance with the procedures in this section for the issuance of such plans and regulations.

(9) In implementing a take reduction plan developed pursuant to this subsection, the Secretary may, where necessary to implement a take reduction plan to protect or restore a marine mammal stock or species covered by such plan, promulgate regulations which include, but are not limited to, measures to—

(A) establish fishery-specific limits on incidental mortality and serious injury of marine mammals in commercial fisheries or restrict commercial fisheries by time or area;

(B) require the use of alternative commercial fishing gear or techniques and new technologies, encourage the development of such gear or technology, or convene expert skippers' panels;

(C) educate commercial fishermen, through workshops and other means, on the importance of reducing the incidental mortality and serious injury of marine mammals in affected commercial fisheries; and

(D) monitor, in accordance with subsection (d) of this section, the effectiveness of measures taken to reduce the level of incidental mortality and serious injury of marine mammals in the course of commercial fishing operations.

(10)(A) Notwithstanding paragraph (6), in the case of any stock to which paragraph (1) applies for which a final stock assessment has not been published under section 1386(b)(3) of this title by April 1, 1995, due to a proceeding under section 1386(b)(2) of this title, or any Federal court review of such proceeding, the Secretary shall establish a take reduction team under paragraph (6) for such stock as if a final stock assessment had been published.

(B) The draft stock assessment published for such stock under section 1386(b)(1) of this title shall be deemed the final stock assessment for purposes of preparing and implementing a take reduction plan for such stock under this section.

(C) Upon publication of a final stock assessment for such stock under section 1386(b)(3) of this title the Secretary shall immediately reconvene the take reduction team for such stock for the purpose of amending the take reduction plan, and any regulations issued to implement such plan, if necessary, to reflect the final stock assessment or court action. Such amendments shall be made in accordance with paragraph (7)(F) or (8)(F), as appropriate.

(D) A draft stock assessment may only be used as the basis for a take reduction plan under this paragraph for a period of not to exceed two years, or until a final stock assessment is published, whichever is earlier. If, at the end of the two-year period, a final stock assessment has not been published, the Secretary shall categorize such stock under section 1386(a)(5)(A) of this title and shall revoke any regulations to implement a take reduction plan for such stock.

(E) Subparagraph (D) shall not apply for any period beyond two years during which a final stock assessment for such stock has not been published due to review of a proceeding on such stock assessment by a Federal court. Immediately upon final action by such court, the Secretary shall proceed under subparagraph (C).

(11) Take reduction plans developed under this section for a species or stock listed as a threatened species or endangered species under the Endangered Species Act of 1973 (16 U.S.C. 1531 et seq.) shall be consistent with any recovery plan developed for such species or stock under section 4 of such Act [16 U.S.C.A. § 1533].

**(g) Emergency regulations**

(1) If the Secretary finds that the incidental mortality and serious injury of marine mammals from commercial fisheries is having, or is likely to have, an immediate and significant adverse impact on a stock or species, the Secretary shall take actions as follows:

(A) In the case of a stock or species for which a take reduction plan is in effect, the Secretary shall—

(i) prescribe emergency regulations that, consistent with such plan to the maximum extent practicable, reduce incidental mortality and serious injury in that fishery; and

(ii) approve and implement, on an expedited basis, any amendments to such plan that are recommended by the take reduction team to address such adverse impact.

(B) In the case of a stock or species for which a take reduction plan is being developed, the Secretary shall—

(i) prescribe emergency regulations to reduce such incidental mortality and serious injury in that fishery; and

(ii) approve and implement, on an expedited basis, such plan, which shall provide methods to address such adverse impact if still necessary.

(C) In the case of a stock or species for which a take reduction plan does not exist and is not being developed, or in the case of a commercial fishery listed under subsection (c)(1)(A)(iii) of this section which the Secretary believes may be contributing to such adverse impact, the Secretary shall—

(i) prescribe emergency regulations to reduce such incidental mortality and serious injury in that fishery, to the extent necessary to mitigate such adverse impact;

(ii) immediately review the stock assessment for such stock or species and the classification of such commercial fishery under this section to determine if a take reduction team should be established; and

**(iii)** may, where necessary to address such adverse impact on a species or stock listed as a threatened species or endangered species under the Endangered Species Act of 1973 (16 U.S.C. 1531 et seq.), place observers on vessels in a commercial fishery listed under subsection (c)(1)(A)(iii) of this section, if the Secretary has reason to believe such vessels may be causing the incidental mortality and serious injury to marine mammals from such stock.

(2) Prior to taking action under paragraph (1)(A), (B), or (C), the Secretary shall consult with the Marine Mammal Commission, all appropriate Regional Fishery Management Councils, State fishery managers, and the appropriate take reduction team (if established).

(3) Emergency regulations prescribed under this subsection—

**(A)** shall be published in the Federal Register, together with an explanation thereof;

**(B)** shall remain in effect for not more than 180 days or until the end of the applicable commercial fishing season, whichever is earlier; and

**(C)** may be terminated by the Secretary at an earlier date by publication in the Federal Register of a notice of termination, if the Secretary determines that the reasons for emergency regulations no longer exist.

(4) If the Secretary finds that incidental mortality and serious injury of marine mammals in a commercial fishery is continuing to have an immediate and significant adverse impact on a stock or species, the Secretary may extend the emergency regulations for an additional period of not more than 90 days or until reasons for the emergency no longer exist, whichever is earlier.

### (h) Penalties

Except as provided in subsection (c) of this section, any person who violates this section shall be subject to the provisions of sections 1375 and 1377 of this title, and may be subject to section 1376 of this title as the Secretary shall establish by regulations.

### (i) Assistance

The Secretary shall provide assistance to Regional Fishery Management Councils, States, interstate fishery commissions, and Indian tribal organizations in meeting the goal of reducing incidental mortality and serious injury to insignificant levels approaching a zero mortality and serious injury rate.

### (j) Contributions

For purposes of carrying out this section, the Secretary may accept, solicit, receive, hold, administer, and use gifts, devises, and bequests.

### (k) Consultation with Secretary of the Interior

The Secretary shall consult with the Secretary of the Interior prior to taking actions or making determinations under this section that affect or relate to species or population stocks of marine mammals for which the Secretary of the Interior is responsible under this subchapter.

### (*l*) Definitions

As used in this section and section 1371(a)(5)(E) of this title, each of the terms "fishery" and "vessel of the United States" has the same meaning it does in section 1802 of this title.

(Pub.L. 92–522, Title I, § 118, as added Pub.L. 103–238, § 11, Apr. 30, 1994, 108 Stat. 546, and amended Pub.L. 104–208, Div. A, Title I, § 101(a) [Title II, § 211(b)], Sept. 30, 1996, 110 Stat. 3009–41.)

[1] So in original. Probably should be "Section".

## HISTORICAL AND STATUTORY NOTES

### References in Text

The Endangered Species Act of 1973, referred to in subsecs. (a)(2), (d)(4)(A), (f)(11), and (g)(1)(C)(iii), is Pub.L. 93–205, Dec. 28, 1973, 87 Stat. 884, as amended, which is classified principally to chapter 35 (section 1531 et seq.) of this title. For complete classification of this Act to the Code, see Short Title note set out under section 1531 of this title and Tables.

The Act of November 7, 1986, referred to in subsec. (a)(4), is Pub.L. 99–625, 100 Stat. 3500, which amended section 718b of this title, enacted provisions set out as a note under section 1536 of this title and amended provisions set out in the note table under section 668dd of this title.

The Federal Advisory Committee Act, referred to in subsec. (f)(6)(D), is Pub.L. 92–463, Oct. 6, 1972, 86 Stat. 770, as amended, which is set out in Appendix 2 to Title 5, Government Organization and Employees.

### Effective and Applicability Provisions

1996 Acts

Amendment by Pub.L. 104–208, Div. A, Title I, § 101(a) [Title II, § 211(b)], Sept. 30, 1996, 110 Stat. 3009–41, effective 15 days after Oct. 11, 1996, see Pub.L. 104–208, Div. A, Title I, § 101(a) [Title II, § 211(b)], Sept. 30, 1996, 110 Stat. 3009–41, set out as a note under section 1801 of this title.

### Abolition of House Committee on Merchant Marine and Fisheries

Committee on Merchant Marine and Fisheries of House of Representatives abolished and any reference in any provision of law enacted before Jan. 4, 1995, to the Committee on Merchant Marine and Fisheries of the House of Representatives treated as referring to the Committee on Agriculture of the House of Representatives, in the case of a provision of law relating to inspection of seafood or seafood products, the Committee on National Security of the House of Representatives, in the case of a provision of law relating to interoceanic canals, the Merchant Marine Academy and State Maritime Academies, or national security aspects of merchant marine, the Committee on Resources of the House of Representatives, in the case of a provision of law relating to fisheries, wildlife, international fishing agreements marine affairs (including coastal zone management) except for measures relating to oil and other pollution of navigable waters, or oceanography, the Committee on Science of the House of Representatives, in the case of a provision of law relating to marine research, and the Committee on Transportation and Infrastructure of the House of Representatives, in the case of a provision of law relating to a matter other than a matter described above, see section 1(b)(3) of Pub.L. 104–14, set out as a note preceding section 21 of Title 2, The Congress.

## § 1388. Marine mammal cooperative agreements in Alaska

**[MMPA § 119]**

### (a) In general

The Secretary may enter into cooperative agreements with Alaska Native organizations to conserve marine mammals and provide co-management of subsistence use by Alaska Natives.

### (b) Grants

Agreements entered into under this section may include grants to Alaska Native organizations for, among other purposes—

(1) collecting and analyzing data on marine mammal populations;

(2) monitoring the harvest of marine mammals for subsistence use;

(3) participating in marine mammal research conducted by the Federal Government, States, academic institutions, and private organizations; and

(4) developing marine mammal co-management structures with Federal and State agencies.

### (c) Effect of jurisdiction

Nothing in this section is intended or shall be construed—

(1) as authorizing any expansion or change in the respective jurisdiction of Federal, State, or tribal governments over fish and wildlife resources; or

(2) as altering in any respect the existing political or legal status of Alaska Natives, or the governmental or jurisdictional status of Alaska Native communities or Alaska Native entities.

### (d) Authorization of appropriations

There are authorized to be appropriated for the purposes of carrying out this section—

(1) $1,500,000 to the Secretary of Commerce for each of the fiscal years 1994, 1995, 1996, 1997, 1998, and 1999; and

(2) $1,000,000 to the Secretary of the Interior for each of the fiscal years 1994, 1995, 1996, 1997, 1998, and 1999.

The amounts authorized to be appropriated under this subsection are in addition to the amounts authorized to be appropriated under section 1384 of this title.

(Pub.L. 92–522, Title I, § 119, as added Pub.L. 103–238, § 19, Apr. 30, 1994, 108 Stat. 559.)

## § 1389. Pacific Coast Task Force; Gulf of Maine

**[MMPA § 120]**

### (a) Pinniped removal authority

Notwithstanding any other provision of this subchapter, the Secretary may permit the intentional lethal taking of pinnipeds in accordance with this section.

### (b) Application

(1) A State may apply to the Secretary to authorize the intentional lethal taking of individually identifiable pinnipeds which are having a significant negative impact on the decline or recovery of salmonid fishery stocks which—

(A) have been listed as threatened species or endangered species under the Endangered Species Act of 1973 (16 U.S.C. 1531 et seq.);

(B) the Secretary finds are approaching threatened species or endangered species status (as those terms are defined in that Act); or

(C) migrate through the Ballard Locks at Seattle, Washington.

(2) Any such application shall include a means of identifying the individual pinniped or pinnipeds, and shall include a detailed description of the problem interaction and expected benefits of the taking.

### (c) Actions in response to application

(1) Within 15 days of receiving an application, the Secretary shall determine whether the application has produced sufficient evidence to warrant establishing a Pinniped-Fishery Interaction Task Force to address the situation described in the application. If the Secretary determines sufficient evidence has been provided, the Secretary shall establish a Pinniped-Fishery Interaction Task Force and publish a notice in the Federal Register requesting public comment on the application.

(2) A Pinniped-Fishery Interaction Task Force established under paragraph (1) shall consist of designated employees of the Department of Commerce, scientists who are knowledgeable about the pinniped interaction that the application addresses, representatives of affected conservation and fishing community organizations, Indian Treaty tribes, the States, and

such other organizations as the Secretary deems appropriate.

(3) Within 60 days after establishment, and after reviewing public comments in response to the Federal Register notice under paragraph (1), the Pinniped-Fishery Interaction Task Force shall—

(A) recommend to the Secretary whether to approve or deny the proposed intentional lethal taking of the pinniped or pinnipeds, including along with the recommendation a description of the specific pinniped individual or individuals, the proposed location, time, and method of such taking, criteria for evaluating the success of the action, and the duration of the intentional lethal taking authority; and

(B) suggest nonlethal alternatives, if available and practicable, including a recommended course of action.

(4) Within 30 days after receipt of recommendations from the Pinniped-Fishery Interaction Task Force, the Secretary shall either approve or deny the application. If such application is approved, the Secretary shall immediately take steps to implement the intentional lethal taking, which shall be performed by Federal or State agencies, or qualified individuals under contract to such agencies.

(5) After implementation of an approved application, the Pinniped-Fishery Interaction Task Force shall evaluate the effectiveness of the permitted intentional lethal taking or alternative actions implemented. If implementation was ineffective in eliminating the problem interaction, the Task Force shall recommend additional actions. If the implementation was effective, the Task Force shall so advise the Secretary, and the Secretary shall disband the Task Force.

**(d) Considerations**

In considering whether an application should be approved or denied, the Pinniped-Fishery Interaction Task Force and the Secretary shall consider—

(1) population trends, feeding habits, the location of the pinniped interaction, how and when the interaction occurs, and how many individual pinnipeds are involved;

(2) past efforts to nonlethally deter such pinnipeds, and whether the applicant has demonstrated that no feasible and prudent alternatives exist and that the applicant has taken all reasonable nonlethal steps without success;

(3) the extent to which such pinnipeds are causing undue injury or impact to, or imbalance with, other species in the ecosystem, including fish populations; and

(4) the extent to which such pinnipeds are exhibiting behavior that presents an ongoing threat to public safety.

**(e) Limitation**

The Secretary shall not approve the intentional lethal taking of any pinniped from a species or stock that is—

(1) listed as a threatened species or endangered species under the Endangered Species Act of 1973 (16 U.S.C. 1531 et seq.);

(2) depleted under this chapter; or

(3) a strategic stock.

**(f) California sea lions and Pacific harbor seals; investigation and report**

(1) The Secretary shall engage in a scientific investigation to determine whether California sea lions and Pacific harbor seals—

(A) are having a significant negative impact on the recovery of salmonid fishery stocks which have been listed as endangered species or threatened species under the Endangered Species Act of 1973 (16 U.S.C. 1531 et seq.), or which the Secretary finds are approaching such endangered species or threatened species status; or

(B) are having broader impacts on the coastal ecosystems of Washington, Oregon, and California.

The Secretary shall conclude this investigation and prepare a report on its results no later than October 1, 1995.

(2) Upon completion of the scientific investigation required under paragraph (1), the Secretary shall enter into discussions with the Pacific States Marine Fisheries Commission, on behalf of the States of Washington, Oregon, and California, for the purpose of addressing any issues or problems identified as a result of the scientific investigation, and to develop recommendations to address such issues or problems. Any recommendations resulting from such discussions shall be submitted, along with the report, to the Committee on Merchant Marine and Fisheries of the House of Representatives and the Committee on Commerce, Science, and Transportation of the Senate.

(3) The Secretary shall make the report and the recommendations submitted under paragraph (2) available to the public for review and comment for a period of 90 days.

(4) There are authorized to be appropriated to the Secretary such sums as are necessary to carry out the provisions of this subsection.

(5) The amounts appropriated under section 4107(c) of this title and allocated to the Pacific States Marine Fisheries Commission may be used by the Commission to participate in discussions with the Secretary under paragraph (2).

**(g) Regionwide pinniped-fishery interaction study**

(1) The Secretary may conduct a study, of not less than three high predation areas in anadromous fish migration corridors within the Northwest Region of the National Marine Fisheries Service, on the interaction between fish and pinnipeds. In conducting the study, the Secretary shall consult with other State and Federal agencies with expertise in pinniped-fishery interaction. The study shall evaluate—

(A) fish behavior in the presence of predators generally;

(B) holding times and passage rates of anadromous fish stocks in areas where such fish are vulnerable to predation;

(C) whether additional facilities exist, or could be reasonably developed, that could improve escapement for anadromous fish; and

(D) other issues the Secretary considers relevant.

(2) Subject to the availability of appropriations, the Secretary may, not later than 18 months after the commencement of the study under this subsection, transmit a report on the results of the study to the Committee on Commerce, Science, and Transportation of the Senate and the Committee on Merchant Marine and Fisheries of the House of Representatives.

(3) The study conducted under this subsection may not be used by the Secretary as a reason for delaying or deferring a determination or consideration under subsection (c) or (d) of this section.

**(h) Gulf of Maine Task Force**

The Secretary shall establish a Pinniped-Fishery Interaction Task Force to advise the Secretary on issues or problems regarding pinnipeds interacting in a dangerous or damaging manner with aquaculture resources in the Gulf of Maine. No later than 2 years from April 30, 1994, the Secretary shall after notice and opportunity for public comment submit to the Committee on Merchant Marine and Fisheries of the House of Representatives and the Committee on Commerce, Science, and Transportation of the Senate a report containing recommended available alternatives to mitigate such interactions.

**(i) Requirements applicable to task forces**

(1) Any task force established under this section—

(A) shall to the maximum extent practicable, consist of an equitable balance among representatives of resource user interests and nonuser interests; and

(B) shall not be subject to the Federal Advisory Committee Act (5 App. U.S.C.).

(2) Meetings of any task force established under this section shall be open to the public, and prior notice of those meetings shall be given to the public by the task force in a timely fashion.

**(j) Gulf of Maine harbor porpoise**

(1) Nothing in section 1386 of this title shall prevent the Secretary from publishing a stock assessment for Gulf of Maine harbor porpoise in an expedited fashion.

(2) In developing and implementing a take reduction plan under section 1387 of this title for Gulf of Maine harbor porpoise, the Secretary shall consider all actions already taken to reduce incidental mortality and serious injury of such stock, and may, based on the recommendations of the take reduction team for such stock, modify the time period required for compliance with section 1387(f)(5)(A) of this title, but in no case may such modification extend the date of compliance beyond April 1, 1997.

(Pub.L. 92–522, Title I, § 120, as added Pub.L. 103–238, § 23, Apr. 30, 1994, 108 Stat. 562.)

## HISTORICAL AND STATUTORY NOTES

**References in Text**

The Endangered Species Act of 1973, and that Act, referred to in subsecs. (b)(1)(A), (B), (e)(1), and (f)(1)(A), is Pub.L. 93–205, Dec. 28, 1973, 87 Stat. 884, as amended, which is classified principally to chapter 35 (section 1531 et seq.) of this title. For complete classification of this Act to the Code, see Short Title note set out under section 1531 of this title and Tables.

The Federal Advisory Committee Act, referred to in subsec. (i)(1)(B), is Pub.L. 92–463, Oct. 6, 1972, 86 Stat. 770, as amended, which is set out in Appendix 2 to Title 5, Government Organization and Employees.

**Abolition of House Committee on Merchant Marine and Fisheries**

Committee on Merchant Marine and Fisheries of House of Representatives abolished and any reference in any provision of law enacted before Jan. 4, 1995, to the Committee on Merchant Marine and Fisheries of the House of Representatives treated as referring to the Committee on Agriculture of the House of Representatives, in the case of a provision of law relating to inspection of seafood or seafood products, the Committee on National Security of the House of Representatives, in the case of a provision of law relating to interoceanic canals, the Merchant Marine Academy and State Maritime Academies, or national security aspects of merchant marine, the Committee on Resources of the House of Representatives, in the case of a provision of law relating to fisheries, wildlife, international fishing agreements marine affairs (including coastal zone management) except for measures relating to oil and other pollution of navigable waters, or oceanography, the Committee on Science of the House of Representatives, in the case of a provision of law relating to marine research, and the Committee on Transportation and Infrastructure of the House of Representatives, in the case of a provision of law relating to a matter other than a matter described above, see section 1(b)(3) of Pub.L. 104–14, set out as a note preceding section 21 of Title 2, The Congress.

## SUBCHAPTER III—MARINE MAMMAL COMMISSION

### HISTORICAL AND STATUTORY NOTES

**Codifications**

"Subchapter III" in the original read "Title II" but has been codified as subchapter III in view of the codification of sections 1361 and 1362 as subchapter I and of sections 1371 to 1384 as subchapter II.

## § 1401. Establishment

**[MMPA § 201]**

**(a) Designation**

There is hereby established the Marine Mammal Commission (hereafter referred to in this subchapter as the "Commission").

**(b) Membership and term of office**

(1) Effective September 1, 1982, the Commission shall be composed of three members who shall be appointed by the President, by and with the advice and consent of the Senate. The President shall make his selection from a list of individuals knowledgeable in the fields of marine ecology and resource management, and who are not in a position to profit from the taking of marine mammals. Such list shall be submitted to him by the Chairman of the Council on Environmental Quality and unanimously agreed to by that Chairman, the Secretary of the Smithsonian Institution, the Director of the National Science Foundation and the Chairman of the National Academy of Sciences. No member of the Commission may, during his period of service on the Commission, hold any other position as an officer or employee of the United States except as a retired officer or retired civilian employee of the United States.

(2) The term of office for each member shall be three years; except that of the members initially appointed to the Commission, the term of one member shall be for one year, the term of one member shall be for two years, and the term of one member shall be for three years. No member is eligible for reappointment; except that any member appointed to fill a vacancy occurring before the expiration of the term for which his predecessor was appointed (A) shall be appointed for the remainder of such term, and (B) is eligible for reappointment for one full term. A member may serve after the expiration of his term until his successor has taken office.

**(c) Chairman**

The President shall designate a Chairman of the Commission (hereafter referred to in this subchapter as the "Chairman") from among its members.

**(d) Compensation; reimbursement for travel expenses**

Members of the Commission shall each be compensated at a rate equal to the daily equivalent of the rate for GS–18 of the General Schedule under section 5332 of Title 5 for each day such member is engaged in the actual performance of duties vested in the Commission. Each member shall be reimbursed for travel expenses, including per diem in lieu of subsistence, as authorized by section 5703 of Title 5, for persons in Government service employed intermittently.

**(e) Executive Director**

The Commission shall have an Executive Director, who shall be appointed (without regard to the provisions of Title 5 governing appointments in the competitive service) by the Chairman with the approval of the Commission and shall be paid at a rate not in excess of the rate for GS–18 of the General Schedule under section 5332 of Title 5. The Executive Director shall have such duties as the Chairman may assign.

(Pub.L. 92–522, Title II, § 201, Oct. 21, 1972, 86 Stat. 1043; Pub.L. 97–389, Title II, § 202, Dec. 29, 1982, 96 Stat. 1951; Pub.L. 98–364, Title I, § 103(a), July 17, 1984, 98 Stat. 441.)

### HISTORICAL AND STATUTORY NOTES

**References in Text**

The provisions of Title 5 governing appointments in the competitive service, referred to in subsec. (e), are classified to section 3301 et seq. of Title 5.

**Effective and Applicability Provisions**

1972 Acts

Section effective upon expiration of sixty-day period following Oct. 21, 1972, see section 4 of Pub.L. 92–522, set out as an Effective Date note under section 1361 of this title.

## § 1402. Duties of Commission

**[MMPA § 202]**

**(a) Reports and recommendations**

The Commission shall—

(1) undertake a review and study of the activities of the United States pursuant to existing laws and international conventions relating to marine mammals, including, but not limited to, the International Convention for the Regulation of Whaling, the Whaling Convention Act of 1949 [16 U.S.C.A. § 916 et seq.], the Interim Convention on the Conservation of North Pacific Fur Seals, and the Fur Seal Act of 1966 [16 U.S.C.A. § 1151 et seq.];

(2) conduct a continuing review of the condition of the stocks of marine mammals, of methods for their protection and conservation, of humane means of taking marine mammals, of research programs conducted or proposed to be conducted under the authority of this chapter, and of all applications for permits for scientific research, public display, or enhancing the survival or recovery of a species or stock;

(3) undertake or cause to be undertaken such other studies as it deems necessary or desirable in connection with its assigned duties as to the protection and conservation of marine mammals;

(4) recommend to the Secretary and to other Federal officials such steps as it deems necessary or desirable for the protection and conservation of marine mammals;

(5) recommend to the Secretary of State appropriate policies regarding existing international arrangements for the protection and conservation of marine mammals, and suggest appropriate international arrangements for the protection and conservation of marine mammals;

(6) recommend to the Secretary such revisions of the endangered species list and threatened species list published pursuant to section 1533(c)(1) of this title, as may be appropriate with regard to marine mammals; and

(7) recommend to the Secretary, other appropriate Federal officials, and Congress such additional measures as it deems necessary or desirable to further the policies of this chapter, including provisions for the protection of the Indians, Eskimos, and Aleuts whose livelihood may be adversely affected by actions taken pursuant to this chapter.

**(b) Consultation with Secretary; reports to Secretary before publication**

The Commission shall consult with the Secretary at such intervals as it or he may deem desirable, and shall provide each annual report required under section 1404 of this title, before submission to Congress, to the Secretary for comment.

**(c) Availability of reports for public inspection**

The reports and recommendations which the Commission makes shall be matters of public record and shall be available to the public at all reasonable times. All other activities of the Commission shall be matters of public record and available to the public in accordance with the provisions of section 552 of Title 5.

**(d) Recommendations; explanation for non-adoption**

Any recommendations made by the Commission to the Secretary and other Federal officials shall be responded to by those individuals within one hundred and twenty days after receipt thereof. Any recommendations which are not followed or adopted shall be referred to the Commission together with a detailed explanation of the reasons why those recommendations were not followed or adopted.

(Pub.L. 92–522, Title II, § 202, Oct. 21, 1972, 86 Stat. 1044; Pub.L. 93–205, § 13(e)(4), Dec. 28, 1973, 87 Stat. 903; Pub.L. 97–58, § 6(1), Oct. 9, 1981, 95 Stat. 987; Pub.L. 100–711, § 5(e)(4), Nov. 23, 1988, 102 Stat. 4771.)

### HISTORICAL AND STATUTORY NOTES

**References in Text**

The Whaling Convention Act of 1949, referred to in subsec. (a)(1), is Act Aug. 9, 1950, c. 653, 64 Stat. 421, as amended, which is classified generally to subchapter II (section 916 et seq.) of chapter 14 of this title. For complete classification of this Act to the Code, see Short Title note set out under section 916 of this title and Tables.

The Fur Seal Act of 1966 referred to in subsec. (a)(1), is Pub.L. 89–702, Nov. 2, 1966, 80 Stat. 1091, as amended, which is classified generally to chapter 24 (section 1151 et seq.) of this title. For complete classification of this Act to the Code, see Short Title note set out under section 1151 of this title and Tables.

Section 1404 of this Title, referred to in subsec. (b), was omitted from the Code.

**Effective and Applicability Provisions**

1973 Acts

Amendment by Pub.L. 93–205 effective Dec. 28, 1973, see section 16 of Pub.L. 93–205, set out as an Effective Date note under section 1531 of this title.

1972 Acts

Section effective upon expiration of sixty-day period following Oct. 21, 1972, see section 4 of Pub.L. 92–522, set out as an Effective Date note under section 1361 of this title.

## § 1403. Committee of Scientific Advisors on Marine Mammals

**[MMPA § 203]**

**(a) Establishment; membership**

The Commission shall establish, within ninety days after its establishment, a Committee of Scientific Advisors on Marine Mammals (hereafter referred to in this subchapter as the "Committee"). Such Committee shall consist of nine scientists knowledgeable in marine ecology and marine mammal affairs appointed by the Chairman after consultation with the Chairman of the Council on Environmental Quality, the Secretary of the Smithsonian Institution, the Director of the National Science Foundation, and the Chairman of the National Academy of Sciences.

**(b) Compensation; reimbursement for travel expenses**

Except for United States Government employees, members of the Committee shall each be compensated at a rate equal to the daily equivalent of the rate for GS–18 of the General Schedule under section 5332 of Title 5, for each day such member is engaged in the actual performance of duties vested in the Committee. Each member shall be reimbursed for travel expenses, including per diem in lieu of subsistence, as authorized by section 5703 of Title 5 for persons in Government service employed intermittently.

**(c) Consultation with Commission on studies and recommendations; explanation for nonadoption**

The Commission shall consult with the Committee on all studies and recommendations which it may propose to make or has made, on research programs conducted or proposed to be conducted under the authority of this chapter, and on all applications for permits for scientific research. Any recommendations made by the Committee or any of its members which are not adopted by the Commission shall be transmitted by the Commission to the appropriate Federal agency and to the appropriate committees of Congress with a detailed explanation of the Commission's reasons for not accepting such recommendations.

(Pub.L. 92–522, Title II, § 203, Oct. 21, 1972, 86 Stat. 1044.)

### HISTORICAL AND STATUTORY NOTES

**Effective and Applicability Provisions**

1972 Acts

Section effective upon expiration of sixty-day period following Oct. 21, 1972, see section 4 of Pub.L. 92–522, set out as an Effective Date note under section 1361 of this title.

**Termination of Advisory Committees**

Advisory Committees in existence on January 5, 1973, to terminate not later than the expiration of the two-year period following January 5, 1973, unless, in the case of a committee established by the President or an officer of the Federal Government, such committee is renewed by appropriate action prior to the expiration of such two-year period, or in the case of a committee established by the Congress, its duration is otherwise provided for by law, see section 14 of Pub.L. 92–463, Oct. 6, 1972, 86 Stat. 776, set out in Appendix 2 to Title 5, Government Organization and Employees.

## § 1404. Omitted

### HISTORICAL AND STATUTORY NOTES

**Codifications**

Section, Pub.L. 92–522, Title II, § 204, Oct. 21, 1972, 86 Stat. 1045, which required the Marine Mammal Commission to transmit to Congress, annually by January 31, a report including a description of activities and accomplishments of the Commission during the preceding year, all findings and recommendations made pursuant to section 1402 of this title, and any responses to such recommendations, was terminated, effective May 15, 2000, pursuant to Pub.L. 104–66, Title III, § 3003, Dec. 21, 1995, 109 Stat. 734, as amended, which is set out as a note under section 1113 of Title 31. See, also, House Document No. 103–7, page 176.

## § 1405. Coordination with other Federal agencies

[MMPA § 205]

The Commission shall have access to all studies and data compiled by Federal agencies regarding marine mammals. With the consent of the appropriate Secretary or Agency head, the Commission may also utilize the facilities or services of any Federal agency and shall take every feasible step to avoid duplication of research and to carry out the purposes of this chapter.

(Pub.L. 92–522, Title II, § 205, Oct. 21, 1972, 86 Stat. 1045.)

### HISTORICAL AND STATUTORY NOTES

**Effective and Applicability Provisions**

1972 Acts

Section effective upon expiration of sixty-day period following Oct. 21, 1972, see section 4 of Pub.L. 92–522, set out as an Effective Date note under section 1361 of this title.

## § 1406. Administration

[MMPA § 206]

The Commission, in carrying out its responsibilities under this subchapter, may—

(1) employ and fix the compensation of such personnel;

(2) acquire, furnish, and equip such office space;

(3) enter into such contracts or agreements with, or provide such grants to, other organizations, both public and private;

(4) procure the services of such experts or consultants or an organization thereof as is authorized under section 3109 of Title 5 (but at rates for individuals not to exceed $100 per diem); and

(5) incur such necessary expenses and exercise such other powers, as are consistent with and reasonably required to perform its functions under this subchapter; except that no fewer than 11 employees must be employed under paragraph (1) at any time. Financial and administrative services (including those related to budgeting, accounting, financial reporting, personnel, and procurement) shall be provided the Commission by the General Services Administration, for which payment shall be made in advance, or by reimbursement from funds of the Commission in such amounts as may be agreed upon by the Chairman and the Administrator of General Services.

(Pub.L. 92–522, Title II, § 206, Oct. 21, 1972, 86 Stat. 1045; Pub.L. 97–58, § 6(2), Oct. 9, 1981, 95 Stat. 987; Pub.L. 98–364, Title I, § 103(b), July 17, 1984, 98 Stat. 442.)

### HISTORICAL AND STATUTORY NOTES

**Effective and Applicability Provisions**

1972 Acts

Section effective upon expiration of sixty-day period following Oct. 21, 1972, see section 4 of Pub.L. 92–522, set out as an Effective Date note under section 1361 of this title.

## § 1407. Authorization of appropriations

[MMPA § 207]

There are authorized to be appropriated to the Marine Mammal Commission, for purposes of carrying out this subchapter, $1,500,000 for fiscal year 1994, $1,550,000 for fiscal year 1995, $1,600,000 for fiscal year 1996, $1,650,000 for fiscal year 1997, $1,700,000 for fiscal year 1998, and $1,750,000 for fiscal year 1999.

(Pub.L. 92–522, Title II, § 207, Oct. 21, 1972, 86 Stat. 1046; Pub.L. 95–136, § 3, Oct. 18, 1977, 91 Stat. 1167; Pub.L. 95–316, § 4, July 10, 1978, 92 Stat. 381; Pub.L. 103–238, § 9(b), Apr. 30, 1994, 108 Stat. 543.)

### HISTORICAL AND STATUTORY NOTES

**Prior Provisions**

A prior section 1407, Pub.L. 97–58, § 7(c), Oct. 9, 1981, 95 Stat. 987; Pub.L. 98–364, Title I, § 104(3), July 17, 1984, 98 Stat. 442; Pub.L. 100–711, § 6(3), Nov. 23, 1988, 102 Stat. 4771, which authorized appropriations to carry out this subchapter for fiscal years 1982 through 1993, was repealed by Pub.L. 103–238, § 9(c), Apr. 30, 1994, 108 Stat. 543.

## SUBCHAPTER IV—INTERNATIONAL DOLPHIN CONSERVATION PROGRAM

### HISTORICAL AND STATUTORY NOTES

**Codifications**

"Subchapter IV" in the original read "Title III" but has been codified as subchapter IV in view of the codification of sections 1361 and 1362 as subchapter I, section 1371 et seq. as subchapter II, and section 1401 et seq. as subchapter III.

## § 1411. Findings and policy

**[MMPA § 301]**

**(a) Findings**

The Congress finds the following:

(1) The yellowfin tuna fishery of the eastern tropical Pacific Ocean has resulted in the deaths of millions of dolphins.

(2) Significant awareness and increased concern for the health and safety of dolphin populations has encouraged a change in fishing methods worldwide.

(3) United States tuna fishing vessels have led the world in the development of fishing methods to reduce dolphin mortalities in the eastern tropical Pacific Ocean and United States tuna processing companies have voluntarily promoted the marketing of tuna that is dolphin safe.

(4) Nations harvesting yellowfin tuna in the eastern tropical Pacific Ocean have demonstrated their willingness to participate in appropriate multilateral agreements to reduce dolphin mortality progressively to a level approaching zero through the setting of annual limits, with the goal of eliminating dolphin mortality in that fishery. Recognition of the International Dolphin Conservation Program will assure that the existing trend of reduced dolphin mortality continues; that individual stocks of dolphins are adequately protected; and that the goal of eliminating all dolphin mortality continues to be a priority.

**(b) Policy**

It is the policy of the United States to—

(1) eliminate the marine mammal mortality resulting from the intentional encirclement of dolphins and other marine mammals in tuna purse seine fisheries;

(2) support the International Dolphin Conservation Program and efforts within the Program to reduce, with the goal of eliminating, the mortality referred to in paragraph (1);

(3) ensure that the market of the United States does not act as an incentive to the harvest of tuna caught with driftnets or caught by purse seine vessels in the eastern tropical Pacific Ocean not operating in compliance with the International Dolphin Conservation Program;

(4) secure appropriate multilateral agreements to ensure that United States tuna fishing vessels shall have continued access to productive tuna fishing grounds in the South Pacific Ocean and elsewhere; and

(5) encourage observer coverage on purse seine vessels fishing for tuna outside of the eastern tropical Pacific Ocean in a fishery in which the Secretary has determined that a regular and significant association occurs between marine mammals and tuna, and in which tuna is harvested through the use of purse seine nets deployed on or to encircle marine mammals.

(Pub.L. 92–522, Title III, § 301, as added Pub.L. 102–523, § 2(a), Oct. 26, 1992, 106 Stat. 3425; Pub.L. 105–42, § 6(b), Aug. 15, 1997, 111 Stat. 1129.)

### HISTORICAL AND STATUTORY NOTES

**Effective and Applicability Provisions**

1997 Acts

For effective date of amendment to this section by Pub.L. 105–42, see section 8 of Pub.L. 105–42, set out as a note under section 1362 of this title.

## § 1412. International Dolphin Conservation Program

**[MMPA § 302]**

The Secretary of State, in consultation with the Secretary, shall seek to secure a binding international agreement to establish an International Dolphin Conservation Program that requires—

(1) that the total annual dolphin mortality in the purse seine fishery for yellowfin tuna in the eastern tropical Pacific Ocean shall not exceed 5,000 animals with a commitment and objective to progressively

reduce dolphin mortality to a level approaching zero through the setting of annual limits;

(2) the establishment of a per-stock per-year dolphin mortality limit, to be in effect through calendar year 2000, at a level between 0.2 percent and 0.1 percent of the minimum population estimate, as calculated, revised, or approved by the Secretary;

(3) the establishment of a per-stock per-year dolphin mortality limit, beginning with the calendar year 2001, at a level less than or equal to 0.1 percent of the minimum population estimate as calculated, revised, or approved by the Secretary;

(4) that if a dolphin mortality limit is exceeded under—

(A) paragraph (1), all sets on dolphins shall cease for the applicable fishing year; and

(B) paragraph (2) or (3), all sets on the stocks covered under paragraph (2) or (3) and any mixed schools that contain any of those stocks shall cease for the applicable fishing year;

(5) a scientific review and assessment to be conducted in calendar year 1998 to—

(A) assess progress in meeting the objectives set for calendar year 2000 under paragraph (2); and

(B) as appropriate, consider recommendations for meeting these objectives;

(6) a scientific review and assessment to be conducted in calendar year 2000—

(A) to review the stocks covered under paragraph (3); and

(B) as appropriate to consider recommendations to further the objectives set under that paragraph;

(7) the establishment of a per vessel maximum annual dolphin mortality limit consistent with the established per-year mortality limits, as determined under paragraphs (1) through (3); and

(8) the provision of a system of incentives to vessel captains to continue to reduce dolphin mortality, with the goal of eliminating dolphin mortality.

(Pub.L. 92–522, Title III, § 302, as added Pub.L. 105–42, § 6(c), Aug. 15, 1997, 111 Stat. 1130.)

### HISTORICAL AND STATUTORY NOTES

**Effective and Applicability Provisions**

1997 Acts

For effective date of enactment of this section by Pub.L. 105–42, see section 8 of Pub.L. 105–42, set out as a note under section 1362 of this title.

**Prior Provisions**

A prior section 1412, Pub.L. 92–522, title III, § 302, as added by Pub.L. 102–523, § 2(a), Oct. 26, 1992, 106 Stat. 3426, related to international agreements to establish global moratorium to prohibit certain tuna harvesting practices prior to repeal by Pub.L. 105–42, § 6(c), Aug. 15, 1997, 111 Stat. 1130.

## § 1413. Regulatory authority of the Secretary [MMPA § 303]

**(a) Regulations**

(1) The Secretary shall issue regulations, and revise those regulations as may be appropriate, to implement the International Dolphin Conservation Program.

(2)(A) The Secretary shall issue regulations to authorize and govern the taking of marine mammals in the eastern tropical Pacific Ocean, including any species of marine mammal designated as depleted under this chapter but not listed as endangered or threatened under the Endangered Species Act (16 U.S.C. 1531 et seq.), by vessels of the United States participating in the International Dolphin Conservation Program.

(B) Regulations issued under this section shall include provisions—

(i) requiring observers on each vessel;

(ii) requiring use of the backdown procedure or other procedures equally or more effective in avoiding mortality of, or serious injury to, marine mammals in fishing operations;

(iii) prohibiting intentional sets on stocks and schools in accordance with the International Dolphin Conservation Program;

(iv) requiring the use of special equipment, including dolphin safety panels in nets, monitoring devices as identified by the International Dolphin Conservation Program to detect unsafe fishing conditions that may cause high incidental dolphin mortality before nets are deployed by a tuna vessel, operable rafts, speedboats with towing bridles, floodlights in operable condition, and diving masks and snorkels;

(v) ensuring that the backdown procedure during sets of purse seine net on marine mammals is completed and rolling of the net to sack up has begun no later than 30 minutes before sundown;

(vi) banning the use of explosive devices in all purse seine operations;

(vii) establishing per vessel maximum annual dolphin mortality limits, total dolphin mortality limits and per-stock per-year mortality limits in accordance with the International Dolphin Conservation Program;

(viii) preventing the making of intentional sets on dolphins after reaching either the vessel maximum annual dolphin mortality limits, total dolphin mortality limits, or per-stock per-year mortality limits;

(ix) preventing the fishing on dolphins by a vessel without an assigned vessel dolphin mortality limit;

(x) allowing for the authorization and conduct of experimental fishing operations, under such terms and conditions as the Secretary may prescribe, for the purpose of testing proposed improvements in fishing techniques and equipment that may reduce or eliminate dolphin mortality or serious injury do not require the encirclement of dolphins in the course of commercial yellowfin tuna fishing;

(xi) authorizing fishing within the area covered by the International Dolphin Conservation Program by vessels of the United States without the use of special equipment or nets if the vessel takes an observer and does not intentionally deploy nets on, or encircle, dolphins, under such terms and conditions as the Secretary may prescribe; and

(xii) containing such other restrictions and requirements as the Secretary determines are necessary to implement the International Dolphin Conservation Program with respect to vessels of the United States.

(C) Adjustments to requirements.—The Secretary may make such adjustments as may be appropriate to requirements of subparagraph (B) that pertain to fishing gear, vessel equipment, and fishing practices to the extent the adjustments are consistent with the International Dolphin Conservation Program.

**(b) Consultation**

In developing any regulation under this section, the Secretary shall consult with the Secretary of State, the Marine Mammal Commission, and the United States Commissioners to the Inter-American Tropical Tuna Commission appointed under section 952 of this title.

**(c) Emergency regulations**

(1) If the Secretary determines, on the basis of the best scientific information available (including research conducted under section 1414a of this title and information obtained under the International Dolphin Conservation Program) that the incidental mortality and serious injury of marine mammals authorized under this subchapter is having, or is likely to have, a significant adverse impact on a marine mammal stock or species, the Secretary shall—

(A) notify the Inter-American Tropical Tuna Commission of his or her determination, along with recommendations to the Commission as to actions necessary to reduce incidental mortality and serious injury and mitigate such adverse impact; and

(B) prescribe emergency regulations to reduce incidental mortality and serious injury and mitigate such adverse impact.

(2) Before taking action under subparagraph (A) or (B) of paragraph (1), the Secretary shall consult with the Secretary of State, the Marine Mammal Commission, and the United States Commissioners to the Inter-American Tropical Tuna Commission.

(3) Emergency regulations prescribed under this subsection—

(A) shall be published in the Federal Register, together with an explanation thereof;

(B) shall remain in effect for the duration of the applicable fishing year; and

(C) may be terminated by the Secretary at an earlier date by publication in the Federal Register of a notice of termination if the Secretary determines that the reasons for the emergency action no longer exist.

(4) If the Secretary finds that the incidental mortality and serious injury of marine mammals in the yellowfin tuna fishery in the eastern tropical Pacific Ocean is continuing to have a significant adverse impact on a stock or species, the Secretary may extend the emergency regulations for such additional periods as may be necessary.

(5) Within 120 days after the Secretary notifies the United States Commissioners to the Inter-American Tropical Tuna Commission of the Secretary's determination under paragraph (1)(A), the United States Commissioners shall call for a special meeting of the Commission to address the actions necessary to reduce incidental mortality and serious injury and mitigate the adverse impact which resulted in the determination. The Commissioners shall report the results of the special meeting in writing to the Secretary and to the Secretary of State. In their report, the Commissioners shall—

(A) include a description of the actions taken by the harvesting nations or under the International Dolphin Conservation Program to reduce the incidental mortality and serious injury and measures to mitigate the adverse impact on the marine mammal species or stock;

(B) indicate whether, in their judgment, the actions taken address the problem adequately; and

(C) if they indicate that the actions taken do not address the problem adequately, include recommendations of such additional action to be taken as may be necessary.

(Pub.L. 92–522, Title III, § 303, as added Pub.L. 105–42, § 6(c), Aug. 15, 1997, 111 Stat. 1131.)

## HISTORICAL AND STATUTORY NOTES

**References in Text**

The Endangered Species Act, referred to in subsec. (a)(2)(A), is the Endangered Species Act of 1973. Pub.L.

93–205, Dec. 28, 1973, 87 Stat. 884, as amended, which is classified generally to chapter 35 (§ 1531 et seq.) of this title.

**Effective and Applicability Provisions**

1997 Acts

For effective date of enactment of this section by Pub.L. 105–42, see section 8 of Pub.L. 105–42, set out as a note under section 1362 of this title.

**Prior Provisions**

A prior section 1413, Pub.L. 92–522, title III, § 303, as added by Pub.L. 102–523, § 2(a), Oct. 26, 1992, 106 Stat. 3426, related to research programs prior to repeal by Pub.L. 105–42, § 6(c), Aug. 15, 1997, 111 Stat. 1130.

## § 1414. Repealed. Pub.L. 105–42, § 6(c), Aug. 15, 1997, 111 Stat. 1130

**[MMPA § 304]**

**HISTORICAL AND STATUTORY NOTES**

Section, Pub.L. 92–522, Title III, § 304, as added Pub.L. 102–523, § 2(a), Oct. 26, 1992, 106 Stat. 3428, related to reviews, reports and recommendations.

A prior section 304 of Pub. L. 92–522 was renumbered section 404 and is classified to 16 U.S.C.A. § 1421c.

**Effective and Applicability Provisions**

1997 Acts

For effective date of repeal of this section, see section 8 of Pub.L. 105–42 set out as a note under section 1362 of this title.

## § 1414a. Research

**[MMPA § 304]**

**(a) Required research**

**(1) In general**

The Secretary shall, in consultation with the Marine Mammal Commission and the Inter–American Tropical Tuna Commission, conduct a study of the effect of intentional encirclement (including chase) on dolphins and dolphin stocks incidentally taken in the course of purse seine fishing for yellowfin tuna in the eastern tropical Pacific Ocean. The study, which shall commence on October 1, 1997, shall consist of abundance surveys as described in paragraph (2) and stress studies as described in paragraph (3), and shall address the question of whether such encirclement is having a significant adverse impact on any depleted dolphin stock in the eastern tropical Pacific Ocean.

**(2) Population abundance surveys**

The abundance surveys under this subsection shall survey the abundance of such depleted stocks and shall be conducted during each of the calendar years 1998, 1999, and 2000.

**(3) Stress studies**

The stress studies under this subsection shall include—

(A) a review of relevant stress-related research and a 3–year series of necropsy samples from dolphins obtained by commercial vessels;

(B) a 1-year review of relevant historical demographic and biological data related to dolphins and dolphin stocks referred to in paragraph (1); and

(C) an experiment involving the repeated chasing and capturing of dolphins by means of intentional encirclement.

**(4) Report**

No later than 90 days after publishing the finding under subsection (g)(2) of section 1385 of this title, the Secretary shall complete and submit a report containing the results of the research described in this subsection to the United States Senate Committee on Commerce, Science, and Transportation and the United States House of Representatives Committees on Resources and on Commerce, and to the Inter–American Tropical Tuna Commission.

**(b) Other research**

**(1) In general**

In addition to conducting the research described in subsection (a) of this section, the Secretary shall, in consultation with the Marine Mammal Commission and in cooperation with the nations participating in the International Dolphin Conservation Program and the Inter–American Tropical Tuna Commission, undertake or support appropriate scientific research to further the goals of the International Dolphin Conservation Program.

**(2) Specific areas of research**

Research carried out under paragraph (1) may include—

(A) projects to devise cost-effective fishing methods and gear so as to reduce, with the goal of eliminating, the incidental mortality and serious injury of marine mammals in connection with commercial purse seine fishing in the eastern tropical Pacific Ocean;

(B) projects to develop cost-effective methods of fishing for mature yellowfin tuna without setting nets on dolphins or other marine mammals;

(C) projects to carry out stock assessments for those marine mammal species and marine mammal stocks taken in the purse seine fishery for yellowfin tuna in the eastern tropical Pacific Ocean, including species or stocks not within waters under the jurisdiction of the United States; and

(D) projects to determine the extent to which the incidental take of nontarget species, including juvenile tuna, occurs in the course of purse seine fishing for yellowfin tuna in the eastern tropical Pacific Ocean, the geographic location of the incidental take, and the impact of that incidental take on tuna stocks and nontarget species.

**(c) Authorization of appropriations**

(1) There are authorized to be appropriated to the Secretary the following amounts, to be used by the Secretary to carry out the research described in subsection (a) of this section:

(A) $4,000,000 for fiscal year 1998.

(B) $3,000,000 for fiscal year 1999.

(C) $4,000,000 for fiscal year 2000.

(D) $1,000,000 for fiscal year 2001.

(2) In addition to the amount authorized to be appropriated under paragraph (1), there are authorized to be appropriated to the Secretary for carrying out this section $3,000,000 for each of the fiscal years 1998, 1999, 2000, and 2001.

(Pub.L. 92–522, Title III, § 304, as added Pub.L. 105–42, § 6(c), Aug. 15, 1997, 111 Stat. 1133.)

### HISTORICAL AND STATUTORY NOTES

**Effective and Applicability Provisions**

1997 Acts

This section was excepted from the effective date provision of section 8 of Pub.L. 105–42, which is set out as a note under section 1362 of this title, and which otherwise makes its provisions effective upon certification by the Secretary of Commerce that sufficient funding is available to complete the first year of the study of the effect of intentional encirclement on dolphins, as required by subsec. (a) of this section, and that the study has commenced, and certification by the Secretary of State to Congress that a binding resolution of the Inter–American Tropical Tuna Commission or other legally binding instrument establishing the International Dolphin Conservation Program has been adopted and is in force, see section 8 of Pub.L. 105–42, set out as a note under section 1362 of this title.

**Prior Provisions**

A prior section 304 of the Marine Mammal Protection Act of 1972, Pub.L. 92–522, Title III, § 304, as added Pub.L. 102–523, § 2(a), Oct. 26, 1992, 106 Stat. 3428, dealing with reviews, reports, and recommendations by the Secretary, was codified as section 1414 of this title and was repealed by Pub.L. 105–42, §§ 6(c), 8, Aug. 15, 1997, 111 Stat. 1130.

## § 1415. Reports by the Secretary

**[MMPA § 305]**

Notwithstanding section 1373(f) of this title, the Secretary shall submit annual reports to the Congress which include—

(1) results of research conducted pursuant to section 1414a of this title;

(2) a description of the status and trends of stocks of tuna;

(3) a description of the efforts to assess, avoid, reduce, and minimize the bycatch of juvenile yellowfin tuna and bycatch of nontarget species;

(4) a description of the activities of the International Dolphin Conservation Program and of the efforts of the United States in support of the Program's goals and objectives, including the protection of dolphin stocks in the eastern tropical Pacific Ocean, and an assessment of the effectiveness of the Program;

(5) actions taken by the Secretary under section 1371(a)(2)(B) of this title and section 1371(d) of this title;

(6) copies of any relevant resolutions and decisions of the Inter–American Tropical Tuna Commission, and any regulations promulgated by the Secretary under this subchapter; and

(7) any other information deemed relevant by the Secretary.

(Pub.L. 92–522, Title III, § 305, as added Pub.L. 105–42, § 6(c), Aug. 15, 1997, 111 Stat. 1134.)

### HISTORICAL AND STATUTORY NOTES

**Effective and Applicability Provisions**

1997 Acts

For effective date of enactment of this section by Pub.L. 105–42, see section 8 of Pub.L. 105–42, set out as a note under section 1362 of this title.

**Prior Provisions**

A prior section 1415, Pub.L. 92–522, Title III, § 305, as added Pub.L. 102–523, § 2(a), Oct. 26, 1992, 106 Stat. 3428, related to international commitments, prior to repeal by Pub.L. 105–42, § 6(c), Aug. 15, 1997, 111 Stat. 1130.

## § 1416. Permits

**[MMPA § 306]**

**(a) In general**

(1) Consistent with the regulations issued pursuant to section 1413 of this title, the Secretary shall issue a permit to a vessel of the United States authorizing participation in the International Dolphin Conservation Program and may require a permit for the person actually in charge of and controlling the fishing operation of the vessel. The Secretary shall prescribe such procedures as are necessary to carry out this subsection, including requiring the submission of—

(A) the name and official number or other identification of each fishing vessel for which a permit is sought, together with the name and address of the owner thereof; and

(B) the tonnage, hold capacity, speed, processing equipment, and type and quantity of gear, including an inventory of special equipment required under section 1413 of this title, with respect to each vessel.

(2) The Secretary is authorized to charge a fee for granting an authorization and issuing a permit under this section. The level of fees charged under this paragraph may not exceed the administrative cost incurred in granting an authorization and issuing a permit. Fees collected under this paragraph shall be available to the Under Secretary of Commerce for Oceans and Atmosphere for expenses incurred in granting authorizations and issuing permits under this section.

(3) After the effective date of the International Dolphin Conservation Program Act, no vessel of the United States shall operate in the yellowfin tuna fishery in the eastern tropical Pacific Ocean without a valid permit issued under this section.

**(b) Permit sanctions**

(1) In any case in which—

(A) a vessel for which a permit has been issued under this section has been used in the commission of an act prohibited under section 1417 of this title;

(B) the owner or operator of any such vessel or any other person who has applied for or been issued a permit under this section has acted in violation of section 1417 of this title; or

(C) any civil penalty or criminal fine imposed on a vessel, owner or operator of a vessel, or other person who has applied for or been issued a permit under this section has not been paid or is overdue, the Secretary may—

(i) revoke any permit with respect to such vessel, with or without prejudice to the issuance of subsequent permits;

(ii) suspend such permit for a period of time considered by the Secretary to be appropriate;

(iii) deny such permit; or

(iv) impose additional conditions or restrictions on any permit issued to, or applied for by, any such vessel or person under this section.

(2) In imposing a sanction under this subsection, the Secretary shall take into account—

(A) the nature, circumstances, extent, and gravity of the prohibited acts for which the sanction is imposed; and

(B) with respect to the violator, the degree of culpability, any history of prior offenses, and other such matters as justice requires.

(3) Transfer of ownership of a vessel, by sale or otherwise, shall not extinguish any permit sanction that is in effect or is pending at the time of transfer of ownership. Before executing the transfer of ownership of a vessel, by sale or otherwise, the owner shall disclose in writing to the prospective transferee the existence of any permit sanction that will be in effect or pending with respect to the vessel at the time of transfer.

(4) In the case of any permit that is suspended for the failure to pay a civil penalty or criminal fine, the Secretary shall reinstate the permit upon payment of the penalty or fine and interest thereon at the prevailing rate.

(5) No sanctions shall be imposed under this section unless there has been a prior opportunity for a hearing on the facts underlying the violation for which the sanction is imposed, either in conjunction with a civil penalty proceeding under this subchapter or otherwise.

(Pub.L. 92–522, Title III, § 306, as added Pub.L. 105–42, § 6(c), Aug. 15, 1997, 111 Stat. 1135.)

### HISTORICAL AND STATUTORY NOTES

**References in Text**

For the effective date of the International Dolphin Conservation Program Act [Pub.L. 105–42], referred to in subsec. (a)(3), see section 8 of Pub.L. 105–42, set out as a note under section 1362 of this title.

**Effective and Applicability Provisions**

1997 Acts

For effective date of enactment of this section by Pub.L. 105–42, see section 8 of Pub.L. 105–42, set out as a note under section 1362 of this title.

**Prior Provisions**

A prior section 1416, Pub.L. 92–522, Title III, § 306, as added Pub.L. 102–523, § 2(a), Oct. 26, 1992, 106 Stat. 3430, related to permits for taking dolphins, prior to repeal by Pub.L. 105–42, § 6(c), Aug. 15, 1997, 111 Stat. 1130.

## § 1417. Prohibitions

**[MMPA § 307]**

**(a) In general**

It is unlawful—

(1) for any person to sell, purchase, offer for sale, transport, or ship, in the United States, any tuna or tuna product unless the tuna or tuna product is either dolphin safe or has been harvested in compliance with the International Dolphin Conservation Program by a country that is a member of the Inter–American Tropical Tuna Commission or has initiated and within 6 months thereafter completed all steps required of applicant nations in accordance with Article V, paragraph 3 of the Convention establishing the Inter–American Tropical Tuna Commission, to become a member of that organization;

(2) except as provided for in subsection[1] 1371(d) of this title, for any person or vessel subject to the jurisdiction of the United States intentionally to set a purse seine net on or to encircle any marine mammal in the course of tuna fishing operations in

the eastern tropical Pacific Ocean except in accordance with this subchapter and regulations issued pursuant to this subchapter; and

(3) for any person to import any yellowfin tuna or yellowfin tuna product or any other fish or fish product in violation of a ban on importation imposed under section 1371(a)(2) of this title;

(4) for any person to violate any regulation promulgated under this subchapter;

(5) for any person to refuse to permit any duly authorized officer to board a vessel subject to that person's control for purposes of conducting any search or inspection in connection with the enforcement of this subchapter; and

(6) for any person to assault, resist, oppose, impede, intimidate, or interfere with any such authorized officer in the conduct of any search or inspection described in paragraph (5).

**(b) Penalties**

**(1) Civil penalty**

A person that knowingly and willfully violates subsection (a)(1), (2), (3), (4), or (5) of this section shall be subject to a civil penalty under section 1375(a) of this title.

**(2) Criminal penalty**

A person that knowingly and willfully violates subsection (a)(5) or (a)(6) of this section shall be subject to a criminal penalty under section 1375(b) of this title.

**(c) Civil forfeitures**

Any vessel (including its fishing gear, appurtenances, stores, and cargo) used, and any fish (or its fair market value) taken or retained, in any manner, in connection with or as a result of the commission of any act prohibited by this section shall be subject to forfeiture to the United States in the manner provided in section 1860 of this title.

(Pub.L. 92–522, Title III, § 307, as added Pub.L. 102–523, § 2(a), Oct. 26, 1992, 106 Stat. 3431, and amended Pub.L. 104–208, Div. A, Title I, § 101(a) [Title II, § 211(b)], Sept. 30, 1996, 110 Stat. 3009–41; Pub.L.105–42, § 6(d), Aug. 15, 1997, 111 Stat. 1136.)

1 So in original. Probably should be "section".

### HISTORICAL AND STATUTORY NOTES

**Effective and Applicability Provisions**

1997 Acts

For effective date of amendment of this section by Pub.L. 105–42, see section 8 of Pub.L. 105–42, set out as a note under section 1362 of this title.

1996 Acts

Amendment by Pub.L. 104–208, Div. A, Title I, § 101(a) [Title II, § 211(b)], Sept. 30, 1996, 110 Stat. 3009–41, effective 15 days after Oct. 11, 1996, see Pub.L. 104–208, Div. A, Title I, § 101(a) [Title II, § 211(b)], Sept. 30, 1996, 110 Stat. 3009–41, set out as a note under section 1801 of this title.

## § 1418. Repealed. Pub.L. 105–42, § 6(e), Aug. 15, 1997, 111 Stat. 1137

**[MMPA § 308]**

### HISTORICAL AND STATUTORY NOTES

Section, Pub.L. 92–522, Title III, § 308, as added Pub.L. 102–523, § 2(a), Oct. 26, 1992, 106 Stat. 3432, related to authorization of appropriations.

**Effective Date of Repeal**

For effective date of repeal of this section by Pub.L. 105–42, see section 8 of Pub.L. 105–42, set out as a note under section 1362 of this title.

# SUBCHAPTER V—MARINE MAMMAL HEALTH AND STRANDING RESPONSE

### HISTORICAL AND STATUTORY NOTES

**Codifications**

"Subchapter V", comprised of "Title III" of Pub.L. 92–522, as added by Pub.L. 102–587, Title III, § 3003(a), Nov. 4, 1992, 106 Stat. 5060, and redesignated as "Title IV" of Pub.L. 92–522 by Pub.L. 103–238, § 24(b)(1), Apr. 30, 1994, 108 Stat. 566, has been codified as subchapter V in view of the codification of section 1361 and 1362 as subchapter I, section 1371 et seq. as subchapter II, and section 1401 et seq. as subchapter III. Another "Title III" of Pub.L. 92–522, as added by Pub.L. 102–523, § 2(a), Oct. 26, 1992, 106 Stat. 3425, is classified to subchapter IV (section 1411 et seq.) of this title.

## § 1421. Establishment of Program

**[MMPA § 401]**

**(a) Establishment**

The Secretary shall, in consultation with the Secretary of the Interior, the Marine Mammal Commission, and individuals with knowledge and experience in marine science, marine mammal science, marine mammal veterinary and husbandry practices, and marine conservation, including stranding network participants, establish a program to be known as the "Marine Mammal Health and Stranding Response Program".

**(b) Purposes**

The purposes of the Program shall be to—

(1) facilitate the collection and dissemination of reference data on the health of marine mammals and health trends of marine mammal populations in the wild;

(2) correlate the health of marine mammals and marine mammal populations, in the wild, with available data on physical, chemical, and biological environmental parameters; and

(3) coordinate effective responses to unusual mortality events by establishing a process in the Department of Commerce in accordance with section 1421c of this title.

(Pub.L. 92–522, Title IV, § 401, formerly Title III, § 301, as added Pub.L. 102–587, Title III, § 3003(a), Nov. 4, 1992, 106 Stat. 5060; renumbered § 401 and amended Pub.L. 103–238, § 24(b), (c)(1), Apr. 30, 1994, 108 Stat. 565, 566.)

### HISTORICAL AND STATUTORY NOTES

**Short Title**

1992 Acts

For short title of this subchapter as the Marine Mammal Health and Stranding Response Act, see section 3001 of Pub.L. 102–587, set out as a note under section 1361 of this title.

**Congressional Statement of Findings**

Section 3002 of Pub.L. 102–587 provided that:

"The Congress finds the following:

"(1) Current stranding network participants have performed an undeniably valuable and ceaseless job of responding to marine mammal strandings over the last 15 years.

"(2) Insufficient understanding of the connection between marine mammal health and the physical, chemical, and biological parameters of their environment prevents an adequate understanding of the causes of marine mammal unusual mortality events.

"(3) An accurate assessment of marine mammal health, health trends in marine mammal populations in the wild, and causes of marine mammal unusual mortality events cannot be made without adequate reference data on marine mammals and the environment in which they live.

"(4) A systematic assessment of the sources, presence, levels, and effects of potentially harmful contaminants on marine mammals would provide a better understanding of some of the causes of marine mammal unusual mortality events and may serve as an indicator of the general health of our coastal and marine environments.

"(5) Responses to marine mammal unusual mortality events are often uncoordinated, due to the lack of sufficient contingency planning.

"(6) Standardized methods for the reporting of dying, dead, or otherwise incapacitated marine mammals in the wild would greatly assist in the determination of the causes of marine mammal unusual mortality events and enhance general knowledge of marine mammal species.

"(7) A formal system for collection, preparation, and archiving of, and providing access to, marine mammal tissues will enhance efforts to investigate the health of marine mammals and health trends of marine mammal populations, and to develop reference data.

"(8) Information on marine mammals, including results of analyses of marine mammal tissues, should be broadly available to the scientific community, including stranding network participants, through a marine mammal data base."

## § 1421a. Determination; data collection and dissemination

**[MMPA § 402]**

**(a) Determination for release**

The Secretary shall, in consultation with the Secretary of the Interior, the Marine Mammal Commission, and individuals with knowledge and experience in marine science, marine mammal science, marine mammal veterinary and husbandry practices, and marine conservation, including stranding network participants, develop objective criteria, after an opportunity for public review and comment, to provide guidance for determining at what point a rehabilitated marine mammal is releasable to the wild.

**(b) Collection**

The Secretary shall, in consultation with the Secretary of the Interior, collect and update, periodically, existing information on—

(1) procedures and practices for—

(A) rescuing and rehabilitating stranded marine mammals, including criteria used by stranding network participants, on a species-by-species basis, for determining at what point a marine mammal undergoing rescue and rehabilitation is returnable to the wild; and

(B) collecting, preserving, labeling, and transporting marine mammal tissues for physical, chemical, and biological analyses;

(2) appropriate scientific literature on marine mammal health, disease, and rehabilitation;

(3) strandings, which the Secretary shall compile and analyze, by region, to monitor species, numbers, conditions, and causes of illnesses and deaths of stranded marine mammals; and

(4) other life history and reference level data, including marine mammal tissue analyses, that would allow comparison of the causes of illness and deaths in stranded marine mammals with physical, chemical, and biological environmental parameters.

**(c) Availability**

The Secretary shall make information collected under this section available to stranding network participants and other qualified scientists.

(Pub.L. 92–522, Title IV, § 402, formerly Title III, § 302, as added Pub.L. 102–587, Title III, § 3003(a), Nov. 4, 1992, 106 Stat. 5061, and renumbered § 402, Pub.L. 103–238, § 24(b), Apr. 30, 1994, 108 Stat. 565.)

### HISTORICAL AND STATUTORY NOTES

**Objective Criteria For Determination of Release; Collection and Availability of Information; Contingency Plan For Responding to Unusual Mortality Event**

Section 3003(b) of Pub.L. 102–587 provided that:

"The Secretary of Commerce shall—

"(1) in accordance with section 302(a) and (b) of the Marine Mammal Protection Act of 1972, as amended by this Act [subsecs. (a) and (b) of this section], and not later than 24 months after the date of enactment of this Act [Nov. 4, 1992]—

"(A) develop and implement objective criteria to determine at what point a marine mammal undergoing rehabilitation is returnable to the wild; and

"(B) collect and make available information on marine mammal health and health trends; and

"(2) in accordance with section 304(b) of the Marine Mammal Protection Act of 1972, as amended by this Act [section 1421c(b) of this title], issue a detailed contingency plan for responding to any unusual mortality event—

"(A) in proposed form by not later than 18 months after the date of enactment of this Act [Nov. 4, 1992]; and

"(B) in final form by not later than 24 months after the date of enactment of this Act [Nov. 4, 1992]."

## § 1421b. Stranding response agreements

### [MMPA § 403]

**(a) In general**

The Secretary may enter into an agreement under section 1382(c) of this title with any person to take marine mammals under section 1379(h)(1) of this title in response to a stranding.

**(b) Required provision**

An agreement authorized by subsection (a) of this section shall—

(1) specify each person who is authorized to perform activities under the agreement; and

(2) specify any terms and conditions under which a person so specified may delegate that authority to another person.

**(c) Review**

The Secretary shall periodically review agreements under section 1382(c) of this title that are entered into pursuant to this subchapter, for performance adequacy and effectiveness.

(Pub.L. 92–522, Title IV, § 403, formerly Title III, § 303, as added Pub.L. 102–587, Title III, § 3003(a), Nov. 4, 1992, 106 Stat. 5061, and renumbered § 403, Pub.L. 103–238, § 24(b), Apr. 30, 1994, 108 Stat. 565.)

## § 1421c. Unusual mortality event response

### [MMPA § 404]

**(a) Response**

**(1) Working group**

(A) The Secretary, acting through the Office, shall establish, in consultation with the Secretary of the Interior, a marine mammal unusual mortality event working group, consisting of individuals with knowledge and experience in marine science, marine mammal science, marine mammal veterinary and husbandry practices, marine conservation, and medical science, to provide guidance to the Secretary and the Secretary of the Interior for—

(i) determining whether an unusual mortality event is occurring;

(ii) determining, after an unusual mortality event has begun, if response actions with respect to that event are no longer necessary; and

(iii) developing the contingency plan in accordance with subsection (b) of this section, to assist the Secretary in responding to unusual mortality events.

(B) The Federal Advisory Committee Act (5 App.U.S.C.) shall not apply to the marine mammal unusual mortality event working group established under this paragraph.

**(2) Response timing**

The Secretary, in consultation with the Secretary of the Interior, shall to the extent necessary and practicable—

(A) within 24 hours after receiving notification from a stranding network participant that an unusual mortality event might be occurring, contact as many members as is possible of the unusual mortality event working group for guidance; and

(B) within 48 hours after receiving such notification—

(i) make a determination as to whether an unusual mortality event is occurring;

(ii) inform the stranding network participant of that determination; and

(iii) if the Secretary has determined an unusual mortality event is occurring, designate an Onsite Coordinator for the event, in accordance with subsection (c) of this section.

**(b) Contingency plan**

**(1) In general**

The Secretary shall, in consultation with the Secretary of the Interior and the unusual mortality event working group, and after an opportunity for public review and comment, issue a detailed contingency plan for responding to any unusual mortality event.

**(2) Contents**

The contingency plan required under this subsection shall include—

(A) a list of persons, including stranding network participants, at a regional, State, and local level, who can assist the Secretary in implementing a coordinated and effective response to an unusual mortality event;

(B) the types of marine mammal tissues and analyses necessary to assist in diagnosing causes of unusual mortality events;

(C) training, mobilization, and utilization procedures for available personnel, facilities, and other resources necessary to conduct a rapid and effective response to unusual mortality events; and

(D) such requirements as are necessary to—

(i) minimize death of marine mammals in the wild and provide appropriate care of marine mammals during an unusual mortality event;

(ii) assist in identifying the cause or causes of an unusual mortality event;

(iii) determinc the effects of an unusual mortality event on the size estimates of the affected populations of marine mammals; and

(iv) identify any roles played in an unusual mortality event by physical, chemical, and biological factors, including contaminants.

**(c) Onsite coordinators**

**(1) Designation**

(A) The Secretary shall, in consultation with the Secretary of the Interior, designate one or more Onsite Coordinators for an unusual mortality event, who shall make immediate recommendations to the stranding network participants on how to proceed with response activities.

(B) An Onsite Coordinator so designated shall be one or more appropriate Regional Directors of the National Marine Fisheries Service or the United States Fish and Wildlife Service, or their designees.

(C) If, because of the wide geographic distribution, multiple species of marine mammals involved, or magnitude of an unusual mortality event, more than one Onsite Coordinator is designated, the Secretary shall, in consultation with the Secretary of the Interior, designate which of the Onsite Coordinators shall have primary responsibility with respect to the event.

**(2) Functions**

(A) An Onsite Coordinator designated under this subsection shall coordinate and direct the activities of all persons responding to an unusual mortality event in accordance with the contingency plan issued under subsection (b) of this section, except that—

(i) with respect to any matter that is not covered by the contingency plan, an Onsite Coordinator shall use his or her best professional judgment; and

(ii) the contingency plan may be temporarily modified by an Onsite Coordinator, consulting as expeditiously as possible with the Secretary, the Secretary of the Interior, and the unusual mortality event working group.

(B) An Onsite Coordinator may delegate to any qualified person authority to act as an Onsite Coordinator under this subchapter.

(Pub.L. 92–522, Title IV, § 404, formerly Title III, § 304, as added Pub.L. 102–587, Title III, § 3003(a), Nov. 4, 1992, 106 Stat. 5062, and renumbered § 404, Pub.L. 103–238, § 24(b), Apr. 30, 1994, 108 Stat. 565.)

### HISTORICAL AND STATUTORY NOTES

**References in Text**

The Federal Advisory Committee Act, referred to in subsec. (a)(1)(B), is Pub.L. 92–463, Oct. 6, 1972, 86 Stat. 770, as amended, which is set out in Appendix 2 to Title 5, Government Organization and Employees.

## § 1421d. Unusual mortality event activity funding

**[MMPA § 405]**

**(a) Establishment of Fund**

There is established in the Treasury an interest bearing fund to be known as the "Marine Mammal Unusual Mortality Event Fund", which shall consist of amounts deposited into the Fund under subsection (c) of this section.

**(b) Uses**

**(1) In general**

Amounts in the Fund—

(A) shall be available only for use by the Secretary, in consultation with the Secretary of the Interior—

(i) to compensate persons for special costs incurred in acting in accordance with the contingency plan issued under section 1421c(b) of this title or under the direction of an Onsite Coordinator for an unusual mortality event;

(ii) for reimbursing any stranding network participant for costs incurred in preparing and transporting tissues collected with respect to an unusual mortality event for the Tissue Bank; and

(iii) for care and maintenance of marine mammal seized under section 1374(c)(2)(D) of this title; and

(B) shall remain available until expended.

**(2) Pending claims**

If sufficient amounts are not available in the Fund to satisfy any authorized pending claim, such claim shall remain pending until such time as sufficient amounts are available. All authorized pending claims shall be satisfied in the order received.

**(c) Deposits into Fund**

There shall be deposited into the Fund—

"(1) in accordance with section 302(a) and (b) of the Marine Mammal Protection Act of 1972, as amended by this Act [subsecs. (a) and (b) of this section], and not later than 24 months after the date of enactment of this Act [Nov. 4, 1992]—

"(A) develop and implement objective criteria to determine at what point a marine mammal undergoing rehabilitation is returnable to the wild; and

"(B) collect and make available information on marine mammal health and health trends; and

"(2) in accordance with section 304(b) of the Marine Mammal Protection Act of 1972, as amended by this Act [section 1421c(b) of this title], issue a detailed contingency plan for responding to any unusual mortality event—

"(A) in proposed form by not later than 18 months after the date of enactment of this Act [Nov. 4, 1992]; and

"(B) in final form by not later than 24 months after the date of enactment of this Act [Nov. 4, 1992]."

## § 1421b. Stranding response agreements

### [MMPA § 403]

**(a) In general**

The Secretary may enter into an agreement under section 1382(c) of this title with any person to take marine mammals under section 1379(h)(1) of this title in response to a stranding.

**(b) Required provision**

An agreement authorized by subsection (a) of this section shall—

(1) specify each person who is authorized to perform activities under the agreement; and

(2) specify any terms and conditions under which a person so specified may delegate that authority to another person.

**(c) Review**

The Secretary shall periodically review agreements under section 1382(c) of this title that are entered into pursuant to this subchapter, for performance adequacy and effectiveness.

(Pub.L. 92–522, Title IV, § 403, formerly Title III, § 303, as added Pub.L. 102–587, Title III, § 3003(a), Nov. 4, 1992, 106 Stat. 5061, and renumbered § 403, Pub.L. 103–238, § 24(b), Apr. 30, 1994, 108 Stat. 565.)

## § 1421c. Unusual mortality event response

### [MMPA § 404]

**(a) Response**

**(1) Working group**

**(A)** The Secretary, acting through the Office, shall establish, in consultation with the Secretary of the Interior, a marine mammal unusual mortality event working group, consisting of individuals with knowledge and experience in marine science, marine mammal science, marine mammal veterinary and husbandry practices, marine conservation, and medical science, to provide guidance to the Secretary and the Secretary of the Interior for—

**(i)** determining whether an unusual mortality event is occurring;

**(ii)** determining, after an unusual mortality event has begun, if response actions with respect to that event are no longer necessary; and

**(iii)** developing the contingency plan in accordance with subsection (b) of this section, to assist the Secretary in responding to unusual mortality events.

**(B)** The Federal Advisory Committee Act (5 App.U.S.C.) shall not apply to the marine mammal unusual mortality event working group established under this paragraph.

**(2) Response timing**

The Secretary, in consultation with the Secretary of the Interior, shall to the extent necessary and practicable—

**(A)** within 24 hours after receiving notification from a stranding network participant that an unusual mortality event might be occurring, contact as many members as is possible of the unusual mortality event working group for guidance; and

**(B)** within 48 hours after receiving such notification—

**(i)** make a determination as to whether an unusual mortality event is occurring;

**(ii)** inform the stranding network participant of that determination; and

**(iii)** if the Secretary has determined an unusual mortality event is occurring, designate an Onsite Coordinator for the event, in accordance with subsection (c) of this section.

**(b) Contingency plan**

**(1) In general**

The Secretary shall, in consultation with the Secretary of the Interior and the unusual mortality event working group, and after an opportunity for public review and comment, issue a detailed contingency plan for responding to any unusual mortality event.

**(2) Contents**

The contingency plan required under this subsection shall include—

**(A)** a list of persons, including stranding network participants, at a regional, State, and local level, who can assist the Secretary in implementing a coordinated and effective response to an unusual mortality event;

(B) the types of marine mammal tissues and analyses necessary to assist in diagnosing causes of unusual mortality events;

(C) training, mobilization, and utilization procedures for available personnel, facilities, and other resources necessary to conduct a rapid and effective response to unusual mortality events; and

(D) such requirements as are necessary to—

(i) minimize death of marine mammals in the wild and provide appropriate care of marine mammals during an unusual mortality event;

(ii) assist in identifying the cause or causes of an unusual mortality event;

(iii) determine the effects of an unusual mortality event on the size estimates of the affected populations of marine mammals; and

(iv) identify any roles played in an unusual mortality event by physical, chemical, and biological factors, including contaminants.

**(c) Onsite coordinators**

**(1) Designation**

(A) The Secretary shall, in consultation with the Secretary of the Interior, designate one or more Onsite Coordinators for an unusual mortality event, who shall make immediate recommendations to the stranding network participants on how to proceed with response activities.

(B) An Onsite Coordinator so designated shall be one or more appropriate Regional Directors of the National Marine Fisheries Service or the United States Fish and Wildlife Service, or their designees.

(C) If, because of the wide geographic distribution, multiple species of marine mammals involved, or magnitude of an unusual mortality event, more than one Onsite Coordinator is designated, the Secretary shall, in consultation with the Secretary of the Interior, designate which of the Onsite Coordinators shall have primary responsibility with respect to the event.

**(2) Functions**

(A) An Onsite Coordinator designated under this subsection shall coordinate and direct the activities of all persons responding to an unusual mortality event in accordance with the contingency plan issued under subsection (b) of this section, except that—

(i) with respect to any matter that is not covered by the contingency plan, an Onsite Coordinator shall use his or her best professional judgment; and

(ii) the contingency plan may be temporarily modified by an Onsite Coordinator, consulting as expeditiously as possible with the Secretary, the Secretary of the Interior, and the unusual mortality event working group.

(B) An Onsite Coordinator may delegate to any qualified person authority to act as an Onsite Coordinator under this subchapter.

(Pub.L. 92–522, Title IV, § 404, formerly Title III, § 304, as added Pub.L. 102–587, Title III, § 3003(a), Nov. 4, 1992, 106 Stat. 5062, and renumbered § 404, Pub.L. 103–238, § 24(b), Apr. 30, 1994, 108 Stat. 565.)

### HISTORICAL AND STATUTORY NOTES

**References in Text**

The Federal Advisory Committee Act, referred to in subsec. (a)(1)(B), is Pub.L. 92–463, Oct. 6, 1972, 86 Stat. 770, as amended, which is set out in Appendix 2 to Title 5, Government Organization and Employees.

## § 1421d. Unusual mortality event activity funding

**[MMPA § 405]**

**(a) Establishment of Fund**

There is established in the Treasury an interest bearing fund to be known as the "Marine Mammal Unusual Mortality Event Fund", which shall consist of amounts deposited into the Fund under subsection (c) of this section.

**(b) Uses**

**(1) In general**

Amounts in the Fund—

(A) shall be available only for use by the Secretary, in consultation with the Secretary of the Interior—

(i) to compensate persons for special costs incurred in acting in accordance with the contingency plan issued under section 1421c(b) of this title or under the direction of an Onsite Coordinator for an unusual mortality event;

(ii) for reimbursing any stranding network participant for costs incurred in preparing and transporting tissues collected with respect to an unusual mortality event for the Tissue Bank; and

(iii) for care and maintenance of marine mammal seized under section 1374(c)(2)(D) of this title; and

(B) shall remain available until expended.

**(2) Pending claims**

If sufficient amounts are not available in the Fund to satisfy any authorized pending claim, such claim shall remain pending until such time as sufficient amounts are available. All authorized pending claims shall be satisfied in the order received.

**(c) Deposits into Fund**

There shall be deposited into the Fund—

(1) amounts appropriated to the Fund;

(2) other amounts appropriated to the Secretary for use with respect to unusual mortality events; and

(3) amounts received by the United States in the form of gifts, devises, and bequests under subsection (d) of this section.

**(d) Acceptance of donations**

For purposes of carrying out this subchapter and section 1374(c)(2)(D) of this title, the Secretary may accept, solicit, and use the services of volunteers, and may accept, solicit, receive, hold, administer, and use gifts, devises, and bequests.

(Pub.L. 92–522, Title IV, § 405, formerly Title III, § 305, as added Pub.L. 102–587, Title III, § 3003(a), Nov. 4, 1992, 106 Stat. 5064; renumbered § 405, and amended Pub.L. 103–238, §§ 6, 16(b), 24(b), (c)(2), Apr. 30, 1994, 108 Stat. 542, 559, 565, 566.)

## § 1421e. Liability

[MMPA § 406]

**(a) In general**

A person who is authorized to respond to a stranding pursuant to an agreement entered into under section 1382(c) of this title is deemed to be an employee of the government for purposes of chapter 171 of Title 28, with respect to actions of the person that are—

(1) in accordance with the agreement; and

(2) in the case of an unusual mortality event, in accordance with—

(A) the contingency plan issued under section 1421c(b) of this title;

(B) the instructions of an Onsite Coordinator designated under section 1421c(c) of this title; or

(C) the best professional judgment of an Onsite Coordinator, in the case of any matter that is not covered by the contingency plan.

**(b) Limitation**

Subsection (a) of this section does not apply to actions of a person described in that subsection that are grossly negligent or that constitute willful misconduct.

(Pub.L. 92–522, Title IV, § 406, formerly Title III, § 306, as added Pub.L. 102–587, Title III, § 3003(a), Nov. 4, 1992, 106 Stat. 5064; renumbered § 406, and amended Pub.L. 103–238, § 24(b), (c)(3), (4), Apr. 30, 1994, 108 Stat. 565, 566.)

## § 1421f. National Marine Mammal Tissue Bank and tissue analysis

[MMPA § 407]

**(a) Tissue Bank**

**(1) In general**

The Secretary shall make provision for the storage, preparation, examination, and archiving of marine mammal tissues. Tissues archived pursuant to this subsection shall be known as the "National Marine Mammal Tissue Bank".

**(2) Guidance for marine mammal tissue collection, preparation, and archiving**

The Secretary shall, in consultation with individuals with knowledge and expertise in marine science, marine mammal science, marine mammal veterinary and husbandry practices, and marine conservation, issue guidance, after an opportunity for public review and comment, for marine mammal tissue collection, preparation, archiving, and quality control procedures, regarding—

(A) appropriate and uniform methods and standards for those activities to provide confidence in marine mammal tissue samples used for research; and

(B) documentation of procedures used for collecting, preparing, and archiving those samples.

**(3) Source of tissue**

In addition to tissues taken during marine mammal unusual mortality events, the Tissue Bank shall incorporate tissue samples taken from other sources in the wild, including—

(A) samples from marine mammals taken incidental to commercial fishing operations;

(B) samples from marine mammals taken for subsistence purposes;

(C) biopsy samples; and

(D) any other samples properly collected.

**(b) Tissue analysis**

The Secretary shall, in consultation with the Marine Mammal Commission, the Secretary of the Interior, and individuals with knowledge and experience in marine science, marine mammal science, marine mammal veterinary and husbandry practices, and marine conservation, issue guidance, after an opportunity for public review and comment, for analyzing tissue samples (by use of the most effective and advanced diagnostic technologies and tools practicable) as a means to monitor and measure overall health trends in representative species or populations of marine mammals, including—

(1) the levels of, and if possible, the effects of, potentially harmful contaminants; and

(2) the frequency of, and if possible, the causes and effects of abnormal lesions or anomalies.

**(c) Data base**

(1) **In general**

The Secretary shall maintain a central data base which provides an effective means for tracking and accessing data on marine mammals, including relevant data on marine mammal tissues collected for and maintained in the Tissue Bank.

(2) **Contents**

The data base established under this subsection shall include—

(A) reference data on the health of marine mammals and populations of marine mammals; and

(B) data on species of marine mammals that are subject to unusual mortality events.

(d) **Access**

The Secretary shall, in consultation with the Secretary of the Interior, establish criteria, after an opportunity for public review and comment, for access to—

(1) marine mammal tissues in the Tissue Bank;

(2) analyses conducted pursuant to subsection (b) of this section; and

(3) marine mammal data in the data base maintained under subsection (c) of this section;

which provide for appropriate uses of the tissues, analyses, and data by qualified scientists, including stranding network participants.

(Pub.L. 92–522, Title IV, § 407, formerly Title III, § 307, as added Pub.L. 102–587, Title III, § 3003(a), Nov. 4, 1992, 106 Stat. 5065, and renumbered § 407, Pub.L. 103–238, § 24(b), Apr. 30, 1994, 108 Stat. 565.)

## § 1421f–1. John H. Prescott Marine Mammal Rescue Assistance Grant Program

(a) **In general**

(1) Subject to the availability of appropriations, the Secretary shall conduct a grant program to be known as the John H. Prescott Marine Mammal Rescue Assistance Grant Program, to provide grants to eligible stranding network participants for the recovery or treatment of marine mammals, the collection of data from living or dead stranded marine mammals for scientific research regarding marine mammal health, and facility operation costs that are directly related to those purposes.

(2)(A) The Secretary shall ensure that, to the greatest extent practicable, funds provided as grants under this subsection are distributed equitably among the stranding regions designated as of December 21, 2000, and in making such grants shall give preference to those facilities that have established records for rescuing or rehabilitating sick and stranded marine mammals in each of the respective regions, or subregions.

(B) In determining priorities among such regions, the Secretary may consider—

(i) any episodic stranding or any mortality event other than an event described in section 1421h(6) of this title, that occurred in any region in the preceding year;

(ii) data regarding average annual strandings and mortality events per region; and

(iii) the size of the marine mammal populations inhabiting a geographic area within such a region.

(b) **Application**

To receive a grant under this section, a stranding network participant shall submit an application in such form and manner as the Secretary may prescribe.

(c) **Consultation**

The Secretary shall consult with the Marine Mammal Commission, a representative from each of the designated stranding regions, and other individuals who represent public and private organizations that are actively involved in rescue, rehabilitation, release, scientific research, marine conservation, and forensic science regarding stranded marine mammals, regarding the development of criteria for the implementation of the grant program and the awarding of grants under the program.

(d) **Limitation**

The amount of a grant under this section shall not exceed $100,000.

(e) **Matching requirement**

(1) **In general**

The non-Federal share of the costs of an activity conducted with a grant under this section shall be 25 percent of such costs.

(2) **In-kind contributions**

The Secretary may apply to the non-Federal share of an activity conducted with a grant under this section the amount of funds, and the fair market value of property and services, provided by non-Federal sources and used for the activity.

(f) **Administrative expenses**

Of amounts available each fiscal year to carry out this section, the Secretary may expend not more than 6 percent or $80,000, whichever is greater, to pay the administrative expenses necessary to carry out this section.

(g) **Definitions**

In this section:

**(1) Designated stranding region**

The term "designated stranding region" means a geographic region designated by the Secretary for purposes of administration of this subchapter.

**(2) Secretary**

The term "Secretary" has the meaning given that term in section 1362(12)(A) or this title.

**(h) Authorization of appropriations**

There are authorized to be appropriated to carry out this section $5,000,000 for each of fiscal years 2001 through 2003, to remain available until expended, of which—

(1) $4,000,000 may be available to the Secretary of Commerce; and

(2) $1,000,000 may be available to the Secretary of the Interior.

(Pub.L. 95–522, Title IV, § 408, as added Pub.L. 106–555, Title II, § 202(a)(2), Dec. 21, 2000, 114 Stat. 2767.)

## § 1421g. Authorization of appropriations

**[MMPA § 408]**

There is authorized to be appropriated—

(1) to the Secretary for carrying out this subchapter (other than sections 1421d and 1421f of this title) $250,000 for each of fiscal years 1993 and 1994;

(2) to the Secretary for carrying out section 1421f of this title, $250,000 for each of fiscal years 1993 and 1994; and

(3) to the Fund, $500,000 for fiscal year 1993.

(Pub.L. 92–522, Title IV, § 409, formerly Title III, § 308, as added Pub.L. 102–587, Title III, § 3003(a), Nov. 4, 1992, 106 Stat. 5066; renumbered § 408 and amended Pub.L. 103–238, § 24(b), (c)(5), (6), Apr. 30, 1994, 108 Stat. 565, 566; renumbered § 409, Pub.L. 106–555, Title II, § 202(a)(1), Dec. 21, 2000, 114 Stat. 2767.)

## § 1421h. Definitions

**[MMPA § 409]**

In this subchapter, the following definitions apply:

(1) The term "Fund" means the Marine Mammal Unusual Mortality Event Fund established by section 1421d(a) of this title.

(2) The term "Office" means the Office of Protected Resources, in the National Marine Fisheries Service.

(3) The term "stranding" means an event in the wild in which—

(A) a marine mammal is dead and is—

(i) on a beach or shore of the United States; or

(ii) in waters under the jurisdiction of the United States (including any navigable waters); or

(B) a marine mammal is alive and is—

(i) on a beach or shore of the United States and unable to return to the water;

(ii) on a beach or shore of the United States and, although able to return to the water, is in need of apparent medical attention; or

(iii) in the waters under the jurisdiction of the United States (including any navigable waters), but is unable to return to its natural habitat under its own power or without assistance.

(4) The term "stranding network participant" means a person who is authorized by an agreement under section 1382(c) of this title to take marine mammals as described in section 1379(h)(1) of this title in response to a stranding.

(5) The term "Tissue Bank" means the National Marine Tissue Bank provided for under section 1421f(a) of this title.

(6) The term "unusual mortality event" means a stranding that—

(A) is unexpected;

(B) involves a significant die-off of any marine mammal population; and

(C) demands immediate response.

(Pub.L. 92–522, Title IV, § 410, formerly Title III, § 309, as added Pub.L. 102–587, Title III, § 3003(a), Nov. 4, 1992, 106 Stat. 5066; renumbered § 409 and amended Pub.L. 103–238, § 24(b), (c)(7), (8), Apr. 30, 1994, 108 Stat. 565, 566; renumbered § 410, Pub.L. 106–555, Title II, § 202(a)(1), Dec. 21, 2000, 114 Stat. 2767.)

# COASTAL ZONE MANAGEMENT

## COASTAL ZONE MANAGEMENT ACT OF 1972 [CZMA § _____]

**(16 U.S.C.A. §§ 1451 to 1465)**

## CHAPTER 33—COASTAL ZONE MANAGEMENT



**Related Provisions**

*See, also, Federal Land Policy and Management, 43 U.S.C.A. § 1701 et seq., post and Outer Continental Shelf Resource Management, 43 U.S.C.A. § 1801 et seq., post.*

## § 1451. Congressional findings

**[CZMA § 302]**

The Congress finds that—

**(a)** There is a national interest in the effective management, beneficial use, protection, and development of the coastal zone.

**(b)** The coastal zone is rich in a variety of natural, commercial, recreational, ecological, industrial, and esthetic resources of immediate and potential value to the present and future well-being of the Nation.

**(c)** The increasing and competing demands upon the lands and waters of our coastal zone occasioned by population growth and economic development, including requirements for industry, commerce, residential development, recreation, extraction of mineral resources and fossil fuels, transportation and navigation, waste disposal, and harvesting of fish, shellfish, and other living marine resources, have resulted in the loss of living marine resources, wildlife, nutrient-rich areas, permanent and adverse changes to ecological systems, decreasing open space for public use, and shoreline erosion.

**(d)** The habitat areas of the coastal zone, and the fish, shellfish, other living marine resources, and wildlife therein, are ecologically fragile and consequently extremely vulnerable to destruction by man's alterations.

**(e)** Important ecological, cultural, historic, and esthetic values in the coastal zone which are essential to the well-being of all citizens are being irretrievably damaged or lost.

**(f)** New and expanding demands for food, energy, minerals, defense needs, recreation, waste disposal, transportation, and industrial activities in the Great Lakes, territorial sea, exclusive economic zone, and Outer Continental Shelf are placing stress on these areas and are creating the need for resolution of serious conflicts among important and competing uses and values in coastal and ocean waters; [1]

**(g)** Special natural and scenic characteristics are being damaged by ill-planned development that threatens these values.

**(h)** In light of competing demands and the urgent need to protect and to give high priority to natural systems in the coastal zone, present state and local institutional arrangements for planning and regulating land and water uses in such areas are inadequate.

**(i)** The key to more effective protection and use of the land and water resources of the coastal zone is to encourage the states to exercise their full authority over the lands and waters in the coastal zone by assisting the states, in cooperation with Federal and local governments and other vitally affected interests, in developing land and water use programs for the coastal zone, including unified policies, criteria, standards, methods, and processes for dealing with land and water use decisions of more than local significance.

(j) The national objective of attaining a greater degree of energy self-sufficiency would be advanced by providing Federal financial assistance to meet state and local needs resulting from new or expanded energy activity in or affecting the coastal zone.

(k) Land uses in the coastal zone, and the uses of adjacent lands which drain into the coastal zone, may significantly affect the quality of coastal waters and habitats, and efforts to control coastal water pollution from land use activities must be improved.

(*l*) Because global warming may result in a substantial sea level rise with serious adverse effects in the coastal zone, coastal states must anticipate and plan for such an occurrence.

(m) Because of their proximity to and reliance upon the ocean and its resources, the coastal states have substantial and significant interests in the protection, management, and development of the resources of the exclusive economic zone that can only be served by the active participation of coastal states in all Federal programs affecting such resources and, wherever appropriate, by the development of state ocean resource plans as part of their federally approved coastal zone management programs.

(Pub.L. 89–454, Title III, § 302, as added Pub.L. 92–583, Oct. 27, 1972, 86 Stat. 1280, and amended Pub.L. 94–370, § 2, July 26, 1976, 90 Stat. 1013; Pub.L. 96–464, § 2, Oct. 17, 1980, 94 Stat. 2060; Pub.L. 101–508, Title VI, § 6203(a), Nov. 5, 1990, 104 Stat. 1388–300.)

1 So in original. Probably should be a period.

## HISTORICAL AND STATUTORY NOTES

### Short Title

1996 Amendments

Pub.L. 104–150, § 1, June 3, 1996, 110 Stat. 1380, provided that: "This Act [enacting section 1465 of this title, amending sections 1454, 1455a, 1456a, 1456b, 1461, and 1464 of this title, and enacting provisions set out as a note under section 1454 of this title] may be cited as the 'Coastal Zone Protection Act of 1996'."

1990 Amendments

Section 6201 of Pub.L. 101–508 provided that: "This subtitle [enacting sections 1455b, 1456c and 1460 of this title, amending this section and sections 1452, 1453, 1454, 1455, 1455a, 1456, 1456a, 1456b, 1458, 1461 and 1464 of this title, and enacting provisions set out as notes under this section and section 1455 of this title] may be cited as the 'Coastal Zone Act Reauthorization Amendments of 1990'."

1986 Amendments

Pub.L. 99–272, Title VI, § 6041, Apr. 7, 1986, 100 Stat. 124, provided that: "This subtitle [amending sections 1455, 1455a, 1456a, 1458, 1461, and 1464 of this title, repealing sections 1456c and 1460 of this title and repealing provisions set out as a note under this section] may be cited as the 'Coastal Zone Management Reauthorization Act of 1985'."

1980 Amendments

Section 1 of Pub.L. 96–464 provided: "That this Act [enacting sections 1455a and 1463a of this title, amending sections 1451, 1452, 1453, 1455, 1456a, 1456b, 1458, 1461, 1462, and 1464 of this title, and enacting provisions set out as notes under sections 1455, 1458, and 1463a of this title] may be cited as the 'Coastal Zone Management Improvement Act of 1980'."

1976 Amendments

Section 1 of Pub.L. 94–370 provided: "That this Act [which enacted section 1511a of Title 15, Commerce and Trade, and sections 1456a to 1456c of this title, amended section 5316 of Title 5, Government Organization and Employees, and sections 1451, 1453 to 1456, and 1457 to 1464 of this title, and enacted provisions set out as notes under section 1511a of Title 15 and section 1462 of this title] may be cited as the 'Coastal Zone Management Act Amendments of 1976'."

1972 Amendments

Section 301 of Pub.L. 89–454, as added by Pub.L. 92–583, provided that: "This title [enacting this chapter] may be cited as the 'Coastal Zone Management Act of 1972'."

### Harmful Algal Blooms and Hypoxia Research and Control

Pub.L. 105–383, Title VI, Nov. 13, 1998, 112 Stat. 3447, provided that:

**"Sec. 601. Short Title.**

"This title [Title VI of Pub.L. 105–383, Nov. 13, 1998, 112 Stat. 3447, enacting provisions set out as notes under this section] may be cited as the 'Harmful Algal Bloom and Hypoxia Research and Control Act of 1998'.

**"Sec. 602. Findings.**

"The Congress finds that—

"(1) the recent outbreak of the harmful microbe *Pfiesteria piscicida* in the coastal waters of the United States is one example of potentially harmful algal blooms composed of naturally occurring species that reproduce explosively and that are increasing in frequency and intensity in the Nation's coastal waters;

"(2) other recent occurrences of harmful algal blooms include red tides in the Gulf of Mexico and the Southeast; brown tides in New York and Texas; ciguatera fish poisoning in Hawaii, Florida, Puerto Rico, and the United States Virgin Islands; and shellfish poisonings in the Gulf of Maine, the Pacific Northwest, and the Gulf of Alaska;

"(3) in certain cases, harmful algal blooms have resulted in fish kills, the deaths of numerous endangered West Indian manatees, beach and shellfish bed closures, threats to public health and safety, and concern among the public about the safety of seafood;

"(4) according to some scientists, the factors causing or contributing to harmful algal blooms may include excessive nutrients in coastal waters, other forms of pollution, the transfer of harmful species through ship ballast water, and ocean currents;

"(5) harmful algal blooms may have been responsible for an estimated $1,000,000,000 in economic losses during the past decade;

"(6) harmful algal blooms and blooms of non-toxic algal species may lead to other damaging marine conditions such as hypoxia (reduced oxygen concentrations), which are harmful or fatal to fish, shellfish, and benthic organisms;

"(7) according to the National Oceanic and Atmospheric Administration in the Department of Commerce, 53 percent of United States estuaries experience hypoxia for at least part of the year and a 7,000 square mile area in the Gulf of Mexico off Louisiana and Texas suffers from hypoxia;

"(8) according to some scientists, a factor believed to cause hypoxia is excessive nutrient loading into coastal waters;

"(9) there is a need to identify more workable and effective actions to reduce nutrient loadings to coastal waters;

"(10) the National Oceanic and Atmospheric Administration, through its ongoing research, education, grant, and coastal resource management programs, possesses a full range of capabilities necessary to support a near and long-term comprehensive effort to prevent, reduce, and control harmful algal blooms and hypoxia;

"(11) funding for the research and related programs of the National Oceanic and Atmospheric Administration will aid in improving the Nation's understanding and capabilities for addressing the human and environmental costs associated with harmful algal blooms and hypoxia; and

"(12) other Federal agencies such as the Environmental Protection Agency, the Department of Agriculture, and the National Science Foundation, along with the States, Indian tribes, and local governments, conduct important work related to the prevention, reduction, and control of harmful algal blooms and hypoxia.

**"Sec. 603. Assessments.**

**"(a) Establishment of Inter-Agency Task Force.**—The President, through the Committee on Environment and Natural Resources of the National Science and Technology Council, shall establish an Inter-Agency Task Force on Harmful Algal Blooms and Hypoxia (hereinafter referred to as the 'Task Force"). The Task Force shall consist of the following representatives from—

"(1) the Department of Commerce (who shall serve as Chairman of the Task Force);

"(2) the Environmental Protection Agency;

"(3) the Department of Agriculture;

"(4) the Department of the Interior;

"(5) the Department of the Navy;

"(6) the Department of Health and Human Services;

"(7) the National Science Foundation;

"(8) the National Aeronautics and Space Administration;

"(9) the Food and Drug Administration;

"(10) the Office of Science and Technology Policy;

"(11) the Council on Environmental Quality; and

"(12) such other Federal agencies as the President considers appropriate.

**"(b) Assessment of harmful algal blooms**—

"(1) Not later than 12 months after the date of enactment of this title [Nov. 13, 1998], the Task Force, in cooperation with the coastal States, Indian tribes, and local governments, industry (including agricultural organizations), academic institutions, and non-governmental organizations with expertise in coastal zone management, shall complete and submit to the Congress an assessment which examines the ecological and economic consequences of harmful algal blooms, alternatives for reducing, mitigating, and controlling harmful algal blooms, and the social and economic costs and benefits of such alternatives.

"(2) The assessment shall—

"(A) identify alternatives for preventing unnecessary duplication of effort among Federal agencies and departments with respect to harmful algal blooms; and

"(B) provide for Federal cooperation and coordination with and assistance to the coastal States, Indian tribes, and local governments in the prevention, reduction, management, mitigation, and control of harmful algal blooms and their environmental and public health impacts.

**"(c) Assessment of hypoxia.**—

"(1) Not later than 12 months after the date of enactment of this title [Nov. 13, 1998], the Task Force, in cooperation with the States, Indian tribes, local governments, industry, agricultural, academic institutions, and non-governmental organizations with expertise in watershed and coastal zone management, shall complete and submit to the Congress an assessment which examines the ecological and economic consequences of hypoxia in United States coastal waters, alternatives for reducing, mitigating, and controlling hypoxia, and the social and economic costs and benefits of such alternatives.

"(2) The assessment shall—

"(A) establish needs, priorities, and guidelines for a peer-reviewed, inter-agency research program on the causes, characteristics, and impacts of hypoxia;

"(B) identify alternatives for preventing unnecessary duplication of effort among Federal agencies and departments with respect to hypoxia; and

"(C) provide for Federal cooperation and coordination with and assistance to the States, Indian tribes, and local governments in the prevention, reduction, management, mitigation, and control of hypoxia and its environmental impacts.

[So in original. No subsec. (d) was enacted.]

**"(e) Disestablishment of Task Force.**—The President may disestablish the Task Force after submission of the plan in section 604(d) [probably should read "604(b)" of this note].

**"Sec. 604. Northern Gulf of Mexico Hypoxia.**

**"(a) Assessment report.**—Not later than May 30, 1999, the Task Force shall complete and submit to Congress and the President an integrated assessment of hypoxia in the northern Gulf of Mexico that examines: the distribution, dynamics, and causes; ecological and economic consequences; sources and loads of nutrients transported by the Mississippi River to the Gulf of Mexico; effects of reducing nutrient loads; methods for reducing nutrient loads; and the social and economic costs and benefits of such methods.

**"(b) Submission of a plan.**—No later than March 30, 2000, the President, in conjunction with the chief executive officers of the States, shall develop and submit to Congress a plan, based on the integrated assessment submitted under subsection (a), for reducing, mitigating, and controlling hypoxia in the northern Gulf of Mexico. In developing such plan, the President shall consult with State, Indian tribe, and local governments, academic, agricultural, industry, and environmental groups and representatives. Such plan shall include incentive-based partnership approaches. The plan shall also include the social and economic costs and benefits of the measures for reducing, mitigating, and controlling hypoxia. At least 90 days before the President submits such plan to the Congress, a summary of the proposed plan shall be published in the Federal Register for a public comment period of not less than 60 days.

**"Sec. 605. Authorization of Appropriations.**

"There are authorized to be appropriated to the Secretary of Commerce for research, education, and monitoring activities related to the prevention, reduction, and control of harmful algal blooms and hypoxia, $15,000,000 for fiscal year 1999, $18,250,000 for fiscal year 2000, and $19,000,000 for fiscal year 2001, to remain available until expended. The Secretary shall consult with the States on a regular basis regarding the development and implementation of the activities authorized under this section. Of such amounts for each fiscal year—

"(1) $1,500,000 for fiscal year 1999, $1,500,000 for fiscal year 2000, and $2,000,000 for fiscal year 2001 may be used to enable the National Oceanic and Atmospheric Administration to carry out research and assessment activities, including procurement of necessary research equipment, at research laboratories of the National Ocean Service and the National Marine Fisheries Service;

"(2) $4,000,000 for fiscal year 1999, $5,500,000 for fiscal year 2000, and $5,500,000 for fiscal year 2001 may be used to carry out the Ecology and Oceanography of Harmful Algal Blooms (ECOHAB) project under the Coastal Ocean Program established under section 201(c) of Public Law 102–567 [Pub.L. 102–567, Oct. 29, 1992, 106 Stat. 4280, which was not classified to the Code];

"(3) $1,000,000 for fiscal year 1999, $2,000,000 for fiscal year 2000, and $2,000,000 for fiscal year 2001 may be used by the National Ocean Service of the National Oceanic and Atmospheric Administration to carry out a peer-reviewed research project on management measures that can be taken to prevent, reduce, control, and mitigate harmful algal blooms;

"(4) $5,500,000 for each of the fiscal years 1999, 2000, and 2001 may be used to carry out Federal and State annual monitoring and analysis activities for harmful algal blooms administered by the National Ocean Service of the National Oceanic and Atmospheric Administration; and

"(5) $3,000,000 for fiscal year 1999, $3,750,000 for fiscal year 2000, and $4,000,000 for fiscal year 2001 may be used for activities related to research and monitoring on hypoxia by the National Ocean Service and the Office of Oceanic and Atmospheric Research of the National Oceanic and Atmospheric Administration.

**"Sec. 606. Protection of States' Rights.**

"**(a)** Nothing in this title shall be interpreted to adversely affect existing State regulatory or enforcement power which has been granted to any State through the Clean Water Act [Act June 30, 1948, c. 758, 62 Stat. 1155; which is classified generally to 33 U.S.C.A. § 1251 et seq.] or Coastal Zone Management Act of 1972 [Pub.L. 92–583, Oct. 27, 1972, 86 Stat. 1280, which is classified generally to 16 U.S.C.A. § 1451 et seq.].

"**(b)** Nothing in this title shall be interpreted to expand the regulatory or enforcement power of the Federal Government which has been delegated to any State through the Clean Water Act or Coastal Zone Management Act of 1972."

**Findings and Purposes of the Coastal Zone Act Reauthorization Amendments of 1990**

Section 6202 of Pub.L. 101–508 provided that:

"**(a) Findings.**—Congress finds and declares the following:

"(1) Our oceans, coastal waters, and estuaries constitute a unique resource. The condition of the water quality in and around the coastal areas is significantly declining. Growing human pressures on the coastal ecosystem will continue to degrade this resource until adequate actions and policies are implemented.

"(2) Almost one-half of our total population now lives in coastal areas. By 2010, the coastal population will have grown from 80,000,000 in 1960 to 127,000,000 people, an increase of approximately 60 percent, and population density in coastal counties will be among the highest in the Nation.

"(3) Marine resources contribute to the Nation's economic stability. Commercial and recreational fishery activities support an industry with an estimated value of $12,000,000,000 a year.

"(4) Wetlands play a vital role in sustaining the coastal economy and environment. Wetlands support and nourish fishery and marine resources. They also protect the Nation's shores from storm and wave damage. Coastal wetlands contribute an estimated $5,000,000,000 to the production of fish and shellfish in the United States coastal waters. Yet, 50 percent of the Nation's coastal wetlands have been destroyed, and more are likely to decline in the near future.

"(5) Nonpoint source pollution is increasingly recognized as a significant factor in coastal water degradation. In urban areas, storm water and combined sewer overflow are linked to major coastal problems, and in rural areas, run-off from Agricultural activities may add to coastal pollution.

"(6) Coastal planning and development control measures are essential to protect coastal water quality, which is subject to continued ongoing stresses. Currently, not enough is being done to manage and protect our coastal resources.

"(7) Global warming results from the accumulation of man-made gases, released into the atmosphere from such activities as the burning of fossil fuels, deforestation, and the production of chlorofluorocarbons, which trap solar heat in the atmosphere and raise temperatures worldwide. Global warming could result in significant global sea level rise by 2050 resulting from ocean expansion, the melting of snow and ice, and the gradual melting of the polar ice cap. Sea level rise will result in the loss of natural resources such as beaches, dunes, estuaries, and wetlands, and will contribute to the salinization of drinking water supplies. Sea level rise will also result in damage to properties, infrastructures, and public works. There is a growing need to plan for sea level rise.

"(8) There is a clear link between coastal water quality and land use activities along the shore. State management programs under the Coastal Zone Management Act of 1972 (16 U.S.C. 1451 et seq.) [this chapter] are among the best tools for protecting coastal resources and must play a larger role, particularly in improving coastal zone water quality.

"(9) All coastal States should have coastal zone management programs in place that conform to the Coastal Zone Management Act of 1972, as amended by this Act [this chapter].

"**(b) Purpose.**—It is the purpose of Congress in this subtitle [subtitle C (sections 6201–6217) of title VI of Pub.L. 101–508, see Short Title of 1990 amendment note under this section] to enhance the effectiveness of the Coastal Zone Management Act of 1972 [this chapter] by increasing our understanding of the coastal environment and expanding the ability of State coastal zone management programs to address coastal environmental problems."

**Establishment of Positions and Fixing of Compensation by Secretary of Commerce; Appointments**

Section 15(c) of Pub.L. 94–370, July 26, 1976, 90 Stat. 1013, which related to establishment and compensation of four new positions without regard to the provisions of chapter 51 of Title 5, was repealed by Pub.L. 99–272, Title VI, § 6045(3), Apr. 7, 1986, 100 Stat. 127.

## § 1452. Congressional declaration of policy

**[CZMA § 303]**

The Congress finds and declares that it is the national policy—

(1) to preserve, protect, develop, and where possible, to restore or enhance, the resources of the Nation's coastal zone for this and succeeding generations;

(2) to encourage and assist the states to exercise effectively their responsibilities in the coastal zone through the development and implementation of management programs to achieve wise use of the land and water resources of the coastal zone, giving full consideration to ecological, cultural, historic, and esthetic values as well as the needs for compatible economic development, which programs should at least provide for—

(A) the protection of natural resources, including wetlands, floodplains, estuaries, beaches, dunes, barrier islands, coral reefs, and fish and wildlife and their habitat, within the coastal zone,

(B) the management of coastal development to minimize the loss of life and property caused by improper development in flood-prone, storm surge, geological hazard, and erosion-prone areas and in areas likely to be affected by or vulnerable to sea level rise, land subsidence, and saltwater intrusion, and by the destruction of natural protective features such as beaches, dunes, wetlands, and barrier islands,

(C) the management of coastal development to improve, safeguard, and restore the quality of coastal waters, and to protect natural resources and existing uses of those waters,

(D) priority consideration being given to coastal-dependent uses and orderly processes for siting major facilities related to national defense, energy, fisheries development, recreation, ports and transportation, and the location, to the maximum extent practicable, of new commercial and industrial developments in or adjacent to areas where such development already exists,

(E) public access to the coasts for recreation purposes,

(F) assistance in the redevelopment of deteriorating urban waterfronts and ports, and sensitive preservation and restoration of historic, cultural, and esthetic coastal features,

(G) the coordination and simplification of procedures in order to ensure expedited governmental decisionmaking for the management of coastal resources,

(H) continued consultation and coordination with, and the giving of adequate consideration to the views of, affected Federal agencies,

(I) the giving of timely and effective notification of, and opportunities for public and local government participation in, coastal management decisionmaking,

(J) assistance to support comprehensive planning, conservation, and management for living marine resources, including planning for the siting of pollution control and aquaculture facilities within the coastal zone, and improved coordination between State and Federal coastal zone management agencies and State and wildlife agencies, and

(K) the study and development, in any case in which the Secretary considers it to be appropriate, of plans for addressing the adverse effects upon the coastal zone of land subsidence and of sea level rise; and

(3) to encourage the preparation of special area management plans which provide for increased specificity in protecting significant natural resources, reasonable coastal-dependent economic growth, improved protection of life and property in hazardous areas, including those areas likely to be affected by land subsidence, sea level rise, or fluctuating water levels of the Great Lakes, and improved predictability in governmental decisionmaking;

(4) to encourage the participation and cooperation of the public, state and local governments, and interstate and other regional agencies, as well as of the Federal agencies having programs affecting the coastal zone, in carrying out the purposes of this chapter;

(5) to encourage coordination and cooperation with and among the appropriate Federal, State, and local agencies, and international organizations where appropriate, in collection, analysis, synthesis, and dissemination of coastal management information, research results, and technical assistance, to support State and Federal regulation of land use

practices affecting the coastal and ocean resources of the United States; and

(6) to respond to changing circumstances affecting the coastal environment and coastal resource management by encouraging States to consider such issues as ocean uses potentially affecting the coastal zone.

(Pub.L. 89–454, Title III, § 303, as added Pub.L. 92–583, Oct. 27, 1972, 86 Stat. 1281, and amended Pub.L. 96–464, § 3, Oct. 17, 1980, 94 Stat. 2060; Pub.L. 101–508, Title VI, § 6203(b), Nov. 5, 1990, 104 Stat. 1388–301; Pub.L. 102–587, Title II, § 2205(b)(2), Nov. 4, 1992, 106 Stat. 5050.)

## § 1453. Definitions

**[CZMA § 304]**

For purposes of this chapter—

(1) The term "coastal zone" means the coastal waters (including the lands therein and thereunder) and the adjacent shorelands (including the waters therein and thereunder), strongly influenced by each other and in proximity to the shorelines of the several coastal states, and includes islands, transitional and intertidal areas, salt marshes, wetlands, and beaches. The zone extends, in Great Lakes waters, to the international boundary between the United States and Canada and, in other areas, seaward to the outer limit of State title and ownership under the Submerged Lands Act (43 U.S.C. 1301 et seq.), the Act of March 2, 1917, (48 U.S.C. 749) [48 U.S.C.A. § 731 et seq.], the Covenant to Establish a Commonwealth of the Northern Mariana Islands in Political Union with the United States of America, as approved by the Act of March 24, 1976 (48 U.S.C. 1801 et seq.), or section 1 of the Act of November 20, 1963 (48 U.S.C. 1705), as applicable. The zone extends inland from the shorelines only to the extent necessary to control shorelands, the uses of which have a direct and significant impact on the coastal waters, and to control those geographical areas which are likely to be affected by or vulnerable to sea level rise. Excluded from the coastal zone are lands the use of which is by law subject solely to the discretion of or which is held in trust by the Federal Government, its officers or agents.

(2) The term "coastal resource of national significance" means any coastal wetland, beach, dune, barrier island, reef, estuary, or fish and wildlife habitat, if any such area is determined by a coastal state to be of substantial biological or natural storm protective value.

(3) The term "coastal waters" means (A) in the Great Lakes area, the waters within the territorial jurisdiction of the United States consisting of the Great Lakes, their connecting waters, harbors, roadsteads, and estuary-type areas such as bays, shallows, and marshes and (B) in other areas, those waters, adjacent to the shorelines, which contain a measurable quantity or percentage of sea water, including, but not limited to, sounds, bays, lagoons, bayous, ponds, and estuaries.

(4) The term "coastal state" means a state of the United States in, or bordering on, the Atlantic, Pacific, or Arctic Ocean, the Gulf of Mexico, Long Island Sound, or one or more of the Great Lakes. For the purposes of this chapter, the term also includes Puerto Rico, the Virgin Islands, Guam, the Commonwealth of the Northern Mariana Islands, and the Trust Territories of the Pacific Islands, and American Samoa.

(5) The term "coastal energy activity" means any of the following activities if, and to the extent that (A) the conduct, support, or facilitation of such activity requires and involves the siting, construction, expansion, or operation of any equipment or facility; and (B) any technical requirement exists which, in the determination of the Secretary, necessitates that the siting, construction, expansion, or operation of such equipment or facility be carried out in, or in close proximity to, the coastal zone of any coastal state;

(i) Any outer Continental Shelf energy activity.

(ii) Any transportation, conversion, treatment, transfer, or storage of liquefied natural gas.

(iii) Any transportation, transfer, or storage of oil, natural gas, or coal (including, but not limited to, by means of any deepwater port, as defined in section 1502(10) of Title 33).

For purposes of this paragraph, the siting, construction, expansion, or operation of any equipment or facility shall be "in close proximity to" the coastal zone of any coastal state if such siting, construction, expansion, or operation has, or is likely to have, a significant effect on such coastal zone.

(6) The term "energy facilities" means any equipment or facility which is or will be used primarily—

(A) in the exploration for, or the development, production, conversion, storage, transfer, processing, or transportation of, any energy resource; or

(B) for the manufacture, production, or assembly of equipment, machinery, products, or devices which are involved in any activity described in subparagraph (A).

The term includes, but is not limited to (i) electric generating plants; (ii) petroleum refineries and associated facilities; (iii) gasification plants; (iv) facilities used for the transportation, conversion, treatment, transfer, or storage of liquefied natural gas; (v) uranium enrichment or nuclear fuel processing facilities; (vi) oil and gas facilities, including platforms, assembly plants, storage depots, tank farms, crew and supply bases, and refining complexes; (vii) facilities including deepwater ports, for the transfer of petroleum; (viii) pipelines and transmission facilities; and (ix) terminals which are associated with any of the foregoing.

**(6a)** The term "enforceable policy" means State policies which are legally binding through constitutional provisions, laws, regulations, land use plans, ordinances, or judicial or administrative decisions, by which a State exerts control over private and public land and water uses and natural resources in the coastal zone.

**(7)** The term "estuary" means that part of a river or stream or other body of water having unimpaired connection with the open sea, where the sea water is measurably diluted with fresh water derived from land drainage. The term includes estuary-type areas of the Great Lakes.

**(8)** The term "estuarine sanctuary" means a research area which may include any part or all of an estuary and any island, transitional area, and upland in, adjoining, or adjacent to such estuary, and which constitutes to the extent feasible a natural unit, set aside to provide scientists and students the opportunity to examine over a period of time the ecological relationships within the area.

**(9)** The term "Fund" means the Coastal Zone Management Fund established under section 1456a(b) of this title.

**(10)** The term "land use" means activities which are conducted in, or on the shorelands within, the coastal zone, subject to the requirements outlined in section 1456(g) of this title.

**(11)** The term "local government" means any political subdivision of, or any special entity created by, any coastal state which (in whole or part) is located in, or has authority over, such state's coastal zone and which (A) has authority to levy taxes, or to establish and collect user fees, or (B) provides any public facility or public service which is financed in whole or part by taxes or user fees. The term includes, but is not limited to, any school district, fire district, transportation authority, and any other special purpose district or authority.

**(12)** The term "management program" includes, but is not limited to, a comprehensive statement in words, maps, illustrations, or other media of communication, prepared and adopted by the state in accordance with the provisions of this chapter, setting forth objectives, policies, and standards to guide public and private uses of lands and waters in the coastal zone.

**(13)** The term "outer Continental Shelf energy activity" means any exploration for, or any development or production of, oil or natural gas from the outer Continental Shelf (as defined in section 1331(a) of Title 43) or the siting, construction, expansion, or operation of any new or expanded energy facilities directly required by such exploration, development, or production.

**(14)** The term "person" means any individual; any corporation, partnership, association, or other entity organized or existing under the laws of any state; the Federal Government; any state, regional, or local government; or any entity of any such Federal, state, regional, or local government.

**(15)** The term "public facilities and public services" means facilities or services which are financed, in whole or in part, by any state or political subdivision thereof, including, but not limited to, highways and secondary roads, parking, mass transit, docks, navigation aids, fire and police protection, water supply, waste collection and treatment (including drainage), schools and education, and hospitals and health care. Such term may also include any other facility or service so financed which the Secretary finds will support increased population.

**(16)** The term "Secretary" means the Secretary of Commerce.

**(17)** The term "special area management plan" means a comprehensive plan providing for natural resource protection and reasonable coastal-dependent economic growth containing a detailed and comprehensive statement of policies; standards and criteria to guide public and private uses of lands and waters; and mechanisms for timely implementation in specific geographic areas within the coastal zone.

**(18)** The term "water use" means a use, activity, or project conducted in or on waters within the coastal zone.

(Pub.L. 89–454, Title III, § 304, as added Pub.L. 92–583, Oct. 27, 1972, 86 Stat. 1281, and amended Pub.L. 94–370, § 3, July 26, 1976, 90 Stat. 1013; Pub.L. 96–464, § 4, Oct. 17, 1980, 94 Stat. 2061; Pub.L. 101–508, Title VI, § 6204, Nov. 5, 1990, 104 Stat. 1388–302; Pub.L. 102–587, Title II, § 2205(b)(3)–(7), Nov. 4, 1992, 106 Stat. 5050, 5051.)

## HISTORICAL AND STATUTORY NOTES

**References in Text**

The Submerged Lands Act, referred to in par. (1), is Act May 22, 1953, c. 65, 67 Stat. 29, as amended, which is classified generally to subchapters I and II (sections 1301 et seq., 1311 et seq.) of chapter 29 of Title 43, Public Lands. For complete classification of this Act to the Code, see Short Title note set out under section 1301 of Title 43 and Tables.

The Act of March 2, 1917, referred to in par. (1) is Act Mar. 2, 1917, c. 145, 39 Stat. 961, as amended, known as the Puerto Rican Federal Relations Act and also popularly known as the Jones Act, which is classified principally to chapter 4 (section 731 et seq.) of Title 48, Territories and Insular Possessions. Section 8 of this Act is classified to section 749 of Title 48. For complete classification of this Act to the Code, see Short Title note set out under section 731 of Title 48 and Tables.

The Act of March 24, 1976, referred to in par. (1), is Pub.L. 94–241, Mar. 24, 1976, 90 Stat. 263, as amended, which is classified as a note entitled "Covenant to Establish Commonwealth of Northern Mariana Islands in Political Union with the United States of America" under section 1681 of Title 48, Territories and Insular Possessions.

Section 1 of the Act of November 20, 1963, referred to in par. (1), is section 1 of Pub.L. 88–183, Nov. 20, 1963, 77 Stat. 338, which was formerly classified to section 1701 of Title 48, Possessions and Insular Territories. Such section, which related to the authority of the Secretary of the Interior to transfer tidelands, submerged lands, and filled lands to the governments of Guam, Virgin Islands and American Samoa, was repealed by Pub.L. 93–435, § 5, Oct. 5, 1974, 88 Stat. 1212. Similar provisions were enacted by section 1 of Pub.L. 93–435, Oct. 5, 1974, 88 Stat. 1210, as amended, and are classified to section 1705 of Title 48.

Section 1502 of Title 33, referred to in par. (5)(iii), was subsequently amended, and the definition of "deepwater port" was transferred to 33 U.S.C.A. § 1502(9).

**Codifications**

Amendment of par. (1) by section 6204(a) of Pub.L. 101–508 was executed to the second sentence of par. (1), notwithstanding directory language reciting that it be executed to the third sentence, as the probable intent of Congress.

## § 1454. Submittal of state program for approval

**[CZMA § 305]**

Any coastal state which has completed the development of its management program shall submit such program to the Secretary for review and approval pursuant to section 1455 of this title.

(Pub.L. 89–454, Title III, § 305, as added Pub.L. 92–583, Oct. 27, 1972, 86 Stat. 1282, and amended Pub.L. 93–612, § 1(1), Jan. 2, 1975, 88 Stat. 1974; Pub.L. 94–370, § 4, July 26, 1976, 90 Stat. 1015; Pub.L. 101–508, Title VI, § 6205, Nov. 5, 1990, 104 Stat. 1388–302; Pub.L. 102–587, Title II, § 2205(b)(1)(A), Nov. 4, 1992, 106 Stat. 5050; Pub.L. 104–150, § 2(a), (b)(1), June 3, 1996, 110 Stat. 1380.)

### HISTORICAL AND STATUTORY NOTES

**Effective and Applicability Provisions**

1996 Acts

Section 2(b)(3) of Pub.L. 104–150 provided that: "This subsection [amending this section and section 1456a of this title] shall take effect on October 1, 1999."

## § 1455. Administrative grants

**[CZMA § 306]**

**(a) Authorization; matching funds**

The Secretary may make grants to any coastal state for the purpose of administering that state's management program, if the state matches any such grant according to the following ratios of Federal-to-State contributions for the applicable fiscal year:

(1) For those States for which programs were approved prior to November 5, 1990, 1 to 1 for any fiscal year.

(2) For programs approved after November 5, 1990, 4 to 1 for the first fiscal year, 2.3 to 1 for the second fiscal year, 1.5 to 1 for the third fiscal year, and 1 to 1 for each fiscal year thereafter.

**(b) Grants to coastal states; requirements**

The Secretary may make a grant to a coastal state under subsection (a) of this section only if the Secretary finds that the management program of the coastal state meets all applicable requirements of this chapter and has been approved in accordance with subsection (d) of this section.

**(c) Allocation of grants to coastal states**

Grants under this section shall be allocated to coastal states with approved programs based on rules and regulations promulgated by the Secretary which shall take into account the extent and nature of the shoreline and area covered by the program, population of the area, and other relevant factors. The Secretary shall establish, after consulting with the coastal states, maximum and minimum grants for any fiscal year to promote equity between coastal states and effective coastal management.

**(d) Mandatory adoption of State management program for coastal zone**

Before approving a management program submitted by a coastal state, the Secretary shall find the following:

(1) The State has developed and adopted a management program for its coastal zone in accordance with rules and regulations promulgated by the Secretary, after notice, and with the opportunity of full participation by relevant Federal agencies, State agencies, local governments, regional organizations, port authorities, and other interested parties and individuals, public and private, which is adequate to carry out the purposes of this chapter and is consistent with the policy declared in section 1452 of this title.

(2) The management program includes each of the following required program elements:

(A) An identification of the boundaries of the coastal zone subject to the management program.

(B) A definition of what shall constitute permissible land uses and water uses within the coastal zone which have a direct and significant impact on the coastal waters.

(C) An inventory and designation of areas of particular concern within the coastal zone.

(D) An identification of the means by which the State proposes to exert control over the land uses and water uses referred to in subparagraph

(B), including a list of relevant State constitutional provisions, laws, regulations, and judicial decisions.

(E) Broad guidelines on priorities of uses in particular areas, including specifically those uses of lowest priority.

(F) A description of the organizational structure proposed to implement such management program, including the responsibilities and interrelationships of local, areawide, State, regional, and interstate agencies in the management process.

(G) A definition of the term "beach" and a planning process for the protection of, and access to, public beaches and other public coastal areas of environmental, recreational, historical, esthetic, ecological, or cultural value.

(H) A planning process for energy facilities likely to be located in, or which may significantly affect, the coastal zone, including a process for anticipating the management of the impacts resulting from such facilities.

(I) A planning process for assessing the effects of, and studying and evaluating ways to control, or lessen the impact of, shoreline erosion, and to restore areas adversely affected by such erosion.

(3) The State has—

(A) coordinated its program with local, areawide, and interstate plans applicable to areas within the coastal zone—

(i) existing on January 1 of the year in which the State's management program is submitted to the Secretary; and

(ii) which have been developed by a local government, an areawide agency, a regional agency, or an interstate agency; and

(B) established an effective mechanism for continuing consultation and coordination between the management agency designated pursuant to paragraph (6) and with local governments, interstate agencies, regional agencies, and areawide agencies within the coastal zone to assure the full participation of those local governments and agencies in carrying out the purposes of this chapter; except that the Secretary shall not find any mechanism to be effective for purposes of this subparagraph unless it requires that—

(i) the management agency, before implementing any management program decision which would conflict with any local zoning ordinance, decision, or other action, shall send a notice of the management program decision to any local government whose zoning authority is affected;

(ii) within the 30-day period commencing on the date of receipt of that notice, the local government may submit to the management agency written comments on the management program decision, and any recommendation for alternatives; and

(iii) the management agency, if any comments are submitted to it within the 30-day period by any local government—

(I) shall consider the comments;

(II) may, in its discretion, hold a public hearing on the comments; and

(III) may not take any action within the 30-day period to implement the management program decision.

(4) The State has held public hearings in the development of the management program.

(5) The management program and any changes thereto have been reviewed and approved by the Governor of the State.

(6) The Governor of the State has designated a single State agency to receive and administer grants for implementing the management program.

(7) The State is organized to implement the management program.

(8) The management program provides for adequate consideration of the national interest involved in planning for, and managing the coastal zone, including the siting of facilities such as energy facilities which are of greater than local significance. In the case of energy facilities, the Secretary shall find that the State has given consideration to any applicable national or interstate energy plan or program.

(9) The management program includes procedures whereby specific areas may be designated for the purpose of preserving or restoring them for their conservation, recreational, ecological, historical, or esthetic values.

(10) The State, acting through its chosen agency or agencies (including local governments, areawide agencies, regional agencies, or interstate agencies) has authority for the management of the coastal zone in accordance with the management program. Such authority shall include power—

(A) to administer land use and water use regulations to control development [1] to ensure compliance with the management program, and to resolve conflicts among competing uses; and

(B) to acquire fee simple and less than fee simple interests in land, waters, and other property through condemnation or other means when necessary to achieve conformance with the management program.

(11) The management program provides for any one or a combination of the following general techniques for control of land uses and water uses within the coastal zone:

(A) State establishment of criteria and standards for local implementation, subject to administrative review and enforcement.

(B) Direct State land and water use planning and regulation.

(C) State administrative review for consistency with the management program of all development plans, projects, or land and water use regulations, including exceptions and variances thereto, proposed by any State or local authority or private developer, with power to approve or disapprove after public notice and an opportunity for hearings.

(12) The management program contains a method of assuring that local land use and water use regulations within the coastal zone do not unreasonably restrict or exclude land uses and water uses of regional benefit.

(13) The management program provides for—

(A) the inventory and designation of areas that contain one or more coastal resources of national significance; and

(B) specific and enforceable standards to protect such resources.

(14) The management program provides for public participation in permitting processes, consistency determinations, and other similar decisions.

(15) The management program provides a mechanism to ensure that all State agencies will adhere to the program.

(16) The management program contains enforceable policies and mechanisms to implement the applicable requirements of the Coastal Nonpoint Pollution Control Program of the State required by section 1455b of this title.

**(e) Amendment or modification of State management program for coastal zone**

A coastal state may amend or modify a management program which it has submitted and which has been approved by the Secretary under this section, subject to the following conditions:

(1) The State shall promptly notify the Secretary of any proposed amendment, modification, or other program change and submit it for the Secretary's approval. The Secretary may suspend all or part of any grant made under this section pending State submission of the proposed amendments, modification, or other program change.

(2) Within 30 days after the date the Secretary receives any proposed amendment, the Secretary shall notify the State whether the Secretary approves or disapproves the amendment, or whether the Secretary finds it is necessary to extend the review of the proposed amendment for a period not to exceed 120 days after the date the Secretary received the proposed amendment. The Secretary may extend this period only as necessary to meet the requirements of the National Environmental Policy Act of 1969 (42 U.S.C. 4321 et seq.). If the Secretary does not notify the coastal state that the Secretary approves or disapproves the amendment within that period, then the amendment shall be conclusively presumed as approved.

(3)(A) Except as provided in subparagraph (B), a coastal state may not implement any amendment, modification, or other change as part of its approved management program unless the amendment, modification, or other change is approved by the Secretary under this subsection.

(B) The Secretary, after determining on a preliminary basis, that an amendment, modification, or other change which has been submitted for approval under this subsection is likely to meet the program approval standards in this section, may permit the State to expend funds awarded under this section to begin implementing the proposed amendment, modification, or change. This preliminary approval shall not extend for more than 6 months and may not be renewed. A proposed amendment, modification, or change which has been given preliminary approval and is not finally approved under this paragraph shall not be considered an enforceable policy for purposes of section 1456 of this title.

(Pub.L. 89–454, Title III, § 306, as added Pub.L. 92–583, Oct. 27, 1972, 86 Stat. 1283, and amended Pub.L. 93–612, § 1(2), Jan. 2, 1975, 88 Stat. 1974; Pub.L. 94–370, § 5, July 26, 1976, 90 Stat. 1017; Pub.L. 96–464, § 5(a), Oct. 17, 1980, 94 Stat. 2062; Pub.L. 99–272, Title VI, § 6043(b)(1), (c), Apr. 7, 1986, 100 Stat. 124, 125; Pub.L. 101–508, Title VI, § 6206(a), Nov. 5, 1990, 104 Stat. 1388–303; Pub.L. 102–587, Title II, § 2205(b)(1)(A), (B), (8), Nov. 4, 1992, 106 Stat. 5050, 5051.)

1 So in original. Probably should be followed by a comma.

## HISTORICAL AND STATUTORY NOTES

**References in Text**

The National Environmental Policy Act of 1969, referred to in subsec. (e)(2), is Pub.L. 91–190, Jan. 1, 1970, 83 Stat. 852, as amended, which is classified generally to chapter 55 (section 4321 et seq.) of Title 42, The Public Health and Welfare. For complete classification of this Act to the Code, see Short Title note set out under section 4321 of Title 42 and Tables.

**Effective and Applicability Provisions**

1980 Acts

Section 5(b) of Pub.L. 96–464 provided that: "The amendments made by subsection (a)(1) and (2) of this section [amending subsecs. (a) and (b) of this section] apply with respect to grants made after September 30, 1980, under section 306 of the Coastal Zone Management Act of 1972 [this section] and, within two hundred and seventy days after such date, the Secretary of Commerce shall issue regulations relating to the administration of subsection (a) of such section 306 (as so amended by such subsection (a) (1) ) [subsec. (a) of this section]."

**Additional Program Requirements**

Section 6206(b) of Pub.L. 101–508 provided that:

"Each State which submits a management program for approval under section 306 of the Coastal Zone Management Act of 1972 [this section], as amended by this subtitle (including a State which submitted a program before the date of enactment of this Act [Nov. 5, 1990] ), shall demonstrate to the Secretary—

"(1) that the program complies with section 306(d)(14) and (15) of that Act [subsec. (d)(14) and (15) of this section] by not later than 3 years after the date of the enactment of this Act [Nov. 5, 1990]; and

"(2) that the program complies with section 306(d)(16) of that Act [subsec. (d)(16) of this section], by not later than 30 months after the date of publication of final guidance under section 6217(g) of this Act [section 1455b(g) of this title]."

## § 1455a. Coastal resource improvement program

### [CZMA § 306A]

**(a) Definitions**

For purposes of this section—

(1) The term "eligible coastal state" means a coastal state that for any fiscal year for which a grant is applied for under this section—

(A) has a management program approved under section 1455 of this title; and

(B) in the judgment of the Secretary, is making satisfactory progress in activities designed to result in significant improvement in achieving the coastal management objectives specified in section 1452(2)(A) through (K) of this title.

(2) The term "urban waterfront and port" means any developed area that is densely populated and is being used for, or has been used for, urban residential recreational, commercial, shipping or industrial purposes.

**(b) Resource management improvement grants**

The Secretary may make grants to any eligible coastal state to assist that state in meeting one or more of the following objectives:

(1) The preservation or restoration of specific areas of the state that (A) are designated under the management program procedures required by section 1455(d)(9) of this title because of their conservation recreational, ecological, or esthetic values, or (B) contain one or more coastal resources of national significance, or for the purpose of restoring and enhancing shellfish production by the purchase and distribution of clutch material on publicly owned reef tracts.

(2) The redevelopment of deteriorating and underutilized urban waterfronts and ports that are designated in the state's management program pursuant to section 1455(d)(2)(C) of this title as areas of particular concern.

(3) The provision of access to public beaches and other public coastal areas and to coastal waters in accordance with the planning process required under section 1455(d)(2)(G) of this title.

(4) The development of a coordinated process among State agencies to regulate and issue permits for aquaculture facilities in the coastal zone.

**(c) Uses, terms and conditions of grants**

(1) Each grant made by the Secretary under this section shall be subject to such terms and conditions as may be appropriate to ensure that the grant is used for purposes consistent with this section.

(2) Grants made under this section may be used for—

(A) the acquisition of fee simple and other interests in land;

(B) low-cost construction projects determined by the Secretary to be consistent with the purposes of this section, including but not limited to, paths, walkways, fences, parks, and the rehabilitation of historic buildings and structures; except that not more than 50 per centum of any grant made under this section may be used for such construction projects;

(C) in the case of grants made for objectives described in subsection (b) (2) of this section—

(i) the rehabilitation or acquisition of piers to provide increased public use, including compatible commercial activity,

(ii) the establishment of shoreline stabilization measures including the installation or rehabilitation of bulkheads for the purpose of public safety or increasing public access and use, and

(iii) the removal or replacement of pilings where such action will provide increased recreational use of urban waterfront areas,

but activities provided for under this paragraph shall not be treated as construction projects subject to the limitations in paragraph (B);

(D) engineering designs, specifications, and other appropriate reports; and

(E) educational, interpretive, and management costs and such other related costs as the Secretary determines to be consistent with the purposes of this section.

**(d) State matching contributions; ratio; maximum amount of grants**

(1) The Secretary may make grants to any coastal state for the purpose of carrying out the project or purpose for which such grants are awarded, if the state matches any such grant according to the follow-

ing ratios of Federal to state contributions for the applicable fiscal year: 4 to 1 for fiscal year 1986; 2.3 to 1 for fiscal year 1987; 1.5 to 1 for fiscal year 1988; and 1 to 1 for each fiscal year after fiscal year 1988.

(2) Grants provided under this section may be used to pay a coastal state's share of costs required under any other Federal program that is consistent with the purposes of this section.

(3) The total amount of grants made under this section to any eligible coastal state for any fiscal year may not exceed an amount equal to 10 per centum of the total amount appropriated to carry out this section for such fiscal year.

**(e) Allocation of grants to local governments and other agencies**

With the approval of the Secretary, an eligible coastal state may allocate to a local government, an areawide agency designated under section 3334 of Title 42, a regional agency, or an interstate agency, a portion of any grant made under this section for the purpose of carrying out this section; except that such an allocation shall not relieve that state of the responsibility for ensuring that any funds so allocated are applied in furtherance of the state's approved management program.

**(f) Other technical and financial assistance**

In addition to providing grants under this section, the Secretary shall assist eligible coastal states and their local governments in identifying and obtaining other sources of available Federal technical and financial assistance regarding the objectives of this section.

(Pub.L. 89–454, Title III, § 306A, as added Pub.L. 96–464, § 6, Oct. 17, 1980, 94 Stat. 2062, and amended Pub.L. 99–272, Title VI, § 6043(b)(2), Apr. 7, 1986, 100 Stat. 124; Pub.L. 101–508, Title VI, §§ 6207, 6216(a), Nov. 5, 1990, 104 Stat. 1388–307, 1388–314; Pub.L. 102–587, Title II, § 2205(b)(9) to (12), Nov. 4, 1992, 106 Stat. 5051; Pub.L. 104–150, § 7(1), June 3, 1996, 110 Stat. 1381.)

### HISTORICAL AND STATUTORY NOTES

**Codifications**

Section 6216a of Pub.L. 101–508 directed the amendment of section 306a(b)(1) of the Coastal Zone Management Act of 1972. There is no such section of such Act. Section 306A(b)(1) of such Act is classified to subsec. (b)(1) of this section, and such amendment was executed to such subsec. as the probable intent of Congress.

## § 1455b. Protecting coastal waters

**(a) In general**

**(1) Program development**

Not later than 30 months after the date of the publication of final guidance under subsection (g) of this section, each State for which a management program has been approved pursuant to section 306 of the Coastal Zone Management Act of 1972 [16 U.S.C.A. § 1455] shall prepare and submit to the Secretary and the Administrator a Coastal Nonpoint Pollution Control Program for approval pursuant to this section. The purpose of the program shall be to develop and implement management measures for nonpoint source pollution to restore and protect coastal waters, working in close conjunction with other State and local authorities.

**(2) Program coordination**

A State program under this section shall be coordinated closely with State and local water quality plans and programs developed pursuant to sections 1288, 1313, 1329, and 1330 of Title 33 and with State plans developed pursuant to the Coastal Zone Management Act of 1972 , as amended by this Act [16 U.S.C.A. § 1451 et seq.]. The program shall serve as an update and expansion of the State nonpoint source management program developed under section 1329 of Title 33, as the program under that section relates to land and water uses affecting coastal waters.

**(b) Program contents**

Each State program under this section shall provide for the implementation, at a minimum, of management measures in conformity with the guidance published under subsection (g) of this section, to protect coastal waters generally, and shall also contain the following:

**(1) Identifying land uses**

The identification of, and a continuing process for identifying, land uses which, individually or cumulatively, may cause or contribute significantly to a degradation of—

(A) those coastal waters where there is a failure to attain or maintain applicable water quality standards or protect designated uses, as determined by the State pursuant to its water quality planning processes; or

(B) those coastal waters that are threatened by reasonably foreseeable increases in pollution loadings from new or expanding sources.

**(2) Identifying critical coastal areas**

The identification of, and a continuing process for identifying, critical coastal areas adjacent to coastal waters referred to in paragraph (1)(A) and (B), within which any new land uses or substantial expansion of existing land uses shall be subject to management measures in addition to those provided for in subsection (g) of this section.

**(3) Management measures**

The implementation and continuing revision from time to time of additional management measures applicable to the land uses and areas identified pursuant to paragraphs (1) and (2) that are necessary to achieve and maintain applicable water quality standards under section 1313 of Title 33 and protect designated uses.

**(4) Technical assistance**

The provision of technical and other assistance to local governments and the public for implementing the measures referred to in paragraph (3), which may include assistance in developing ordinances and regulations, technical guidance, and modeling to predict and assess the effectiveness of such measures, training, financial incentives, demonstration projects, and other innovations to protect coastal water quality and designated uses.

**(5) Public participation**

Opportunities for public participation in all aspects of the program, including the use of public notices and opportunities for comment, nomination procedures, public hearings, technical and financial assistance, public education, and other means.

**(6) Administrative coordination**

The establishment of mechanisms to improve coordination among State agencies and between State and local officials responsible for land use programs and permitting, water quality permitting and enforcement, habitat protection, and public health and safety, through the use of joint project review, memoranda of agreement, or other mechanisms.

**(7) State coastal zone boundary modification**

A proposal to modify the boundaries of the State coastal zone as the coastal management agency of the State determines is necessary to implement the recommendations made pursuant to subsection (e) of this section. If the coastal management agency does not have the authority to modify such boundaries, the program shall include recommendations for such modifications to the appropriate State authority.

**(c) Program submission, approval, and implementation**

**(1) Review and approval**

Within 6 months after the date of submission by a State of a program pursuant to this section, the Secretary and the Administrator shall jointly review the program. The program shall be approved if—

(A) the Secretary determines that the portions of the program under the authority of the Secretary meet the requirements of this section and the Administrator concurs with that determination; and

(B) the Administrator determines that the portions of the program under the authority of the Administrator meet the requirements of this section and the Secretary concurs with that determination.

**(2) Implementation of approved program**

If the program of a State is approved in accordance with paragraph (1), the State shall implement the program, including the management measures included in the program pursuant to subsection (b) of this section, through—

(A) changes to the State plan for control of nonpoint source pollution approved under section 1329 of Title 33; and

(B) changes to the State coastal zone management program developed under section 306 of the Coastal Zone Management Act of 1972, as amended by this Act [16 U.S.C.A. § 1455].

**(3) Withholding coastal management assistance**

If the Secretary finds that a coastal State has failed to submit an approvable program as required by this section, the Secretary shall withhold for each fiscal year until such a program is submitted a portion of grants otherwise available to the State for the fiscal year under section 306 of the Coastal Zone Management Act of 1972 [16 U.S.C.A. § 1455], as follows:

(A) 10 percent for fiscal year 1996.

(B) 15 percent for fiscal year 1997.

(C) 20 percent for fiscal year 1998.

(D) 30 percent for fiscal year 1999 and each fiscal year thereafter.

The Secretary shall make amounts withheld under this paragraph available to coastal States having programs approved under this section.

**(4) Withholding water pollution control assistance**

If the Administrator finds that a coastal State has failed to submit an approvable program as required by this section, the Administrator shall withhold from grants available to the State under section 1329 of Title 33, for each fiscal year until such a program is submitted, an amount equal to a percentage of the grants awarded to the State for the preceding fiscal year under that section, as follows:

(A) For fiscal year 1996, 10 percent of the amount awarded for fiscal year 1995.

(B) For fiscal year 1997, 15 percent of the amount awarded for fiscal year 1996.

(C) For fiscal year 1998, 20 percent of the amount awarded for fiscal year 1997.

(D) For fiscal year 1999 and each fiscal year thereafter, 30 percent of the amount awarded for fiscal year 1998 or other preceding fiscal year.

The Administrator shall make amounts withheld under this paragraph available to States having programs approved pursuant to this subsection.

**(d) Technical assistance**

The Secretary and the Administrator shall provide technical assistance to coastal States and local governments in developing and implementing programs under this section. Such assistance shall include—

(1) methods for assessing water quality impacts associated with coastal land uses;

(2) methods for assessing the cumulative water quality effects of coastal development;

(3) maintaining and from time to time revising an inventory of model ordinances, and providing other assistance to coastal States and local governments in identifying, developing, and implementing pollution control measures; and

(4) methods to predict and assess the effects of coastal land use management measures on coastal water quality and designated uses.

**(e) Inland coastal zone boundaries**

**(1) Review**

The Secretary, in consultation with the Administrator of the Environmental Protection Agency, shall, within 18 months after November 5, 1990, review the inland coastal zone boundary of each coastal State program which has been approved or is proposed for approval under section 306 of the Coastal Zone Management Act of 1972 [16 U.S.C.A. § 1455], and evaluate whether the State's coastal zone boundary extends inland to the extent necessary to control the land and water uses that have a significant impact on coastal waters of the State.

**(2) Recommendation**

If the Secretary, in consultation with the Administrator, finds that modifications to the inland boundaries of a State's coastal zone are necessary for that State to more effectively manage land and water uses to protect coastal waters, the Secretary, in consultation with the Administrator, shall recommend appropriate modifications in writing to the affected State.

**(f) Financial assistance**

**(1) In general**

Upon request of a State having a program approved under section 306 of the Coastal Zone Management Act of 1972 [16 U.S.C.A. § 1455], the Secretary, in consultation with the Administrator, may provide grants to the State for use for developing a State program under this section.

**(2) Amount**

The total amount of grants to a State under this subsection shall not exceed 50 percent of the total cost to the State of developing a program under this section.

**(3) State share**

The State share of the cost of an activity carried out with a grant under this subsection shall be paid from amounts from non-Federal sources.

**(4) Allocation**

Amounts available for grants under this subsection shall be allocated among States in accordance with regulations issued pursuant to section 306(c) of the Coastal Zone Management Act of 1972 [16 U.S.C.A. § 1455(c) ], except that the Secretary may use not more than 25 percent of amounts available for such grants to assist States which the Secretary, in consultation with the Administrator, determines are making exemplary progress in preparing a State program under this section or have extreme needs with respect to coastal water quality.

**(g) Guidance for coastal nonpoint source pollution control**

**(1) In general**

The Administrator, in consultation with the Secretary and the Director of the United States Fish and Wildlife Service and other Federal agencies, shall publish (and periodically revise thereafter) guidance for specifying management measures for sources of nonpoint pollution in coastal waters.

**(2) Content**

Guidance under this subsection shall include, at a minimum—

(A) a description of a range of methods, measures, or practices, including structural and nonstructural controls and operation and maintenance procedures, that constitute each measure;

(B) a description of the categories and subcategories of activities and locations for which each measure may be suitable;

(C) an identification of the individual pollutants or categories or classes of pollutants that may be controlled by the measures and the water quality effects of the measures;

(D) quantitative estimates of the pollution reduction effects and costs of the measures;

(E) a description of the factors which should be taken into account in adapting the measures to specific sites or locations; and

(F) any necessary monitoring techniques to accompany the measures to assess over time the success of the measures in reducing pollution loads and improving water quality.

**(3) Publication**

The Administrator, in consultation with the Secretary, shall publish—

(A) proposed guidance pursuant to this subsection not later than 6 months after November 5, 1990; and

(B) final guidance pursuant to this subsection not later than 18 months after November 5, 1990.

(4) **Notice and comment**

The Administrator shall provide to coastal States and other interested persons an opportunity to provide written comments on proposed guidance under this subsection.

(5) **Management measures**

For purposes of this subsection, the term "management measures" means economically achievable measures for the control of the addition of pollutants from existing and new categories and classes of nonpoint sources of pollution, which reflect the greatest degree of pollutant reduction achievable through the application of the best available nonpoint pollution control practices, technologies, processes, siting criteria, operating methods, or other alternatives.

**(h) Authorization of appropriations**

(1) **Administrator**

There is authorized to be appropriated to the Administrator for use for carrying out this section not more than $1,000,000 for each of fiscal years 1992, 1993, and 1994.

(2) **Secretary**

(A) Of amounts appropriated to the Secretary for a fiscal year under section 318(a)(4) of the Coastal Zone Management Act of 1972, as amended by this Act, not more than $1,000,000 shall be available for use by the Secretary for carrying out this section for that fiscal year, other than for providing in the form of grants under subsection (f) of this section.

(B) There is authorized to be appropriated to the Secretary for use for providing in the form of grants under subsection (f) of this section not more than—

(i) $6,000,000 for fiscal year 1992;
(ii) $12,000,000 for fiscal year 1993;
(iii) $12,000,000 for fiscal year 1994; and
(iv) $12,000,000 for fiscal year 1995.

**(i) Definitions**

In this section—

(1) the term "Administrator" means the Administrator of the Environmental Protection Agency;

(2) the term "coastal state" has the meaning given the term "coastal State" under section 304 of the Coastal Zone Management Act of 1972 (16 U.S.C. 1453) [16 U.S.C.A. § 1453];

(3) each of the terms "coastal waters" and "coastal zone" has the meaning that term has in the Coastal Zone Management Act of 1972 [16 U.S.C.A. § 1451 et seq.];

(4) the term "coastal management agency" means a State agency designated pursuant to section 306(d)(6) of the Coastal Zone Management Act of 1972 [16 U.S.C.A. § 1455(d)(6) ];

(5) the term "land use" includes a use of waters adjacent to coastal waters; and

(6) the term "Secretary" means the Secretary of Commerce.

(Pub.L. 101–508, Title VI, § 6217, Nov. 5, 1990, 104 Stat. 1388–314; Pub.L. 102–587, Title II, § 2205(b)(24), Nov. 4, 1992, 106 Stat. 5052.)

## HISTORICAL AND STATUTORY NOTES

**References in Text**

The Coastal Zone Management Act of 1972, referred to in subsecs. (a)(2) and (i)(3), is Pub.L. 89–454, Title III (section 301 et seq.), as added Pub.L. 92–583, Oct. 27, 1972, 86 Stat. 1280, as amended, which is classified generally to this chapter.

Section 306 of the Coastal Zone Management Act of 1972, referred to in subsecs. (a)(1), (c)(2)(B), (3), (e)(1) and (f)(1), is section 306 of this same Act, which is classified to section 1455 of this title.

Section 306(c) of the Coastal Zone Management Act of 1972, referred to in subsec. (f)(4), is section 1455(c) of this same Act, which is classified to section 1455(c) of this title.

Section 304 of the Coastal Management Act of 1972, referred to in subsec. (i)(2), is section 304 of this same Act, which is classified to section 1453 of this title.

Section 306(d)(6) of the Coastal Zone Management Act of 1972, referred to in subsec. (i)(4), is section 306(d)(6) of this same Act, which is classified to section 1455(d)(6) of this title.

Section 318(a)(4) of the Coastal Zone Management Act of 1972, referred to in subsec. (h)(2), is section 318(a)(4) of this same Act, which is classified to section 1464(a)(4) of this title.

Section 318(a)(4) of the Coastal Zone Management Act of 1972, referred to in subsec. (h)(2)(A), which is section 318(a)(4) of this same Act and which was classified to section 1464(a)(4) of this title, was amended generally by Pub.L. 104–150, § 4(1), June 3, 1996, 110 Stat. 1381, and, as so amended, does not contain a par. (4).

As amended by this Act, referred to in subsecs. (a)(2), (c)(2)(B) and (h)(2), is a reference to the amendment of the Coastal Zone Management Act of 1972 by Pub.L. 101–508, Title VI, Subtitle C (section 6201 et seq.), Nov. 5, 1990, 104 Stat. 1388–299, known as the Coastal Zone Act Reauthorization Amendments of 1990, which is classified generally to this chapter.

For complete classification of these Acts to the Code, see Short Title notes set out under section 1451 of this title and Tables.

**Codifications**

Section was enacted as part of the Coastal Zone Act Reauthorization Amendments of 1990, and not as part of the Coastal Zone Management Act of 1972, which comprises this chapter.

## § 1456. Coordination and cooperation

[CZMA § 307]

### (a) Federal agencies

In carrying out his functions and responsibilities under this chapter, the Secretary shall consult with, cooperate with, and, to the maximum extent practicable, coordinate his activities with other interested Federal agencies.

### (b) Adequate consideration of views of Federal agencies

The Secretary shall not approve the management program submitted by a state pursuant to section 1455 of this title unless the views of Federal agencies principally affected by such program have been adequately considered.

### (c) Consistency of Federal activities with State management programs; Presidential exemption; certification

(1)(A) Each Federal agency activity within or outside the coastal zone that affects any land or water use or natural resource of the coastal zone shall be carried out in a manner which is consistent to the maximum extent practicable with the enforceable policies of approved State management programs. A Federal agency activity shall be subject to this paragraph unless it is subject to paragraph (2) or (3).

(B) After any final judgment, decree, or order of any Federal court that is appealable under section 1291 or 1292 of Title 28, or under any other applicable provision of Federal law, that a specific Federal agency activity is not in compliance with subparagraph (A), and certification by the Secretary that mediation under subsection (h) of this section is not likely to result in such compliance, the President may, upon written request from the Secretary, exempt from compliance those elements of the Federal agency activity that are found by the Federal court to be inconsistent with an approved State program, if the President determines that the activity is in the paramount interest of the United States. No such exemption shall be granted on the basis of a lack of appropriations unless the President has specifically requested such appropriations as part of the budgetary process, and the Congress has failed to make available the requested appropriations.

(C) Each Federal agency carrying out an activity subject to paragraph (1) shall provide a consistency determination to the relevant State agency designated under section 1455(d)(6) of this title at the earliest practicable time, but in no case later than 90 days before final approval of the Federal activity unless both the Federal agency and the State agency agree to a different schedule.

(2) Any Federal agency which shall undertake any development project in the coastal zone of a state shall insure that the project is, to the maximum extent practicable, consistent with the enforceable policies of approved State management programs.

(3)(A) After final approval by the Secretary of a state's management program, any applicant for a required Federal license or permit to conduct an activity, in or outside of the coastal zone, affecting any land or water use or natural resource of the coastal zone of that state shall provide in the application to the licensing or permitting agency a certification that the proposed activity complies with the enforceable policies of the state's approved program and that such activity will be conducted in a manner consistent with the program. At the same time, the applicant shall furnish to the state or its designated agency a copy of the certification, with all necessary information and data. Each coastal state shall establish procedures for public notice in the case of all such certifications and, to the extent it deems appropriate, procedures for public hearings in connection therewith. At the earliest practicable time, the state or its designated agency shall notify the Federal agency concerned that the state concurs with or objects to the applicant's certification. If the state or its designated agency fails to furnish the required notification within six months after receipt of its copy of the applicant's certification, the state's concurrence with the certification shall be conclusively presumed. No license or permit shall be granted by the Federal agency until the state or its designated agency has concurred with the applicant's certification or until, by the state's failure to act, the concurrence is conclusively presumed, unless the Secretary, on his own initiative or upon appeal by the applicant, finds, after providing a reasonable opportunity for detailed comments from the Federal agency involved and from the state, that the activity is consistent with the objectives of this chapter or is otherwise necessary in the interest of national security.

(B) After the management program of any coastal state has been approved by the Secretary under section 1455 of this title, any person who submits to the Secretary of the Interior any plan for the exploration or development of, or production from, any area which has been leased under the Outer Continental Shelf Lands Act (43 U.S.C. 1331 et seq.) and regulations under such Act shall, with respect to any exploration, development, or production described in such plan and affecting any land or water use or natural resource of the coastal zone of such state, attach to such plan a certification that each activity which is described in detail in such plan complies with the enforceable policies of such state's approved management program and will be carried out in a manner consistent with such program. No Federal official or agency shall grant such person any license or permit for any activity described in detail in such plan until such state or its designated agency receives a copy of such certification and plan, together with any other necessary data and information, and until—

(i) such state or its designated agency, in accordance with the procedures required to be established by such state pursuant to subparagraph (A), concurs with such person's certification and notifies the Secretary and the Secretary of the Interior of such concurrence;

(ii) concurrence by such state with such certification is conclusively presumed as provided for in subparagraph (A), except if such state fails to concur with or object to such certification within three months after receipt of its copy of such certification and supporting information, such state shall provide the Secretary, the appropriate federal agency, and such person with a written statement describing the status of review and the basis for further delay in issuing a final decision, and if such statement is not so provided, concurrence by such state with such certification shall be conclusively presumed; or

(iii) the Secretary finds, pursuant to subparagraph (A), that each activity which is described in detail in such plan is consistent with the objectives of this chapter or is otherwise necessary in the interest of national security.

If a state concurs or is conclusively presumed to concur, or if the Secretary makes such a finding, the provisions of subparagraph (A) are not applicable with respect to such person, such state, and any Federal license or permit which is required to conduct any activity affecting land uses or water uses in the coastal zone of such state which is described in detail in the plan to which such concurrence or finding applies. If such state objects to such certification and if the Secretary fails to make a finding under clause (iii) with respect to such certification, or if such person fails substantially to comply with such plan as submitted, such person shall submit an amendment to such plan, or a new plan, to the Secretary of the Interior. With respect to any amendment or new plan submitted to the Secretary of the Interior pursuant to the preceding sentence, the applicable time period for purposes of concurrence by conclusive presumption under subparagraph (A) is 3 months.

**(d) Application of local governments for Federal assistance; relationship of activities with approved management programs**

State and local governments submitting applications for Federal assistance under other Federal programs, in or outside of the coastal zone, affecting any land or water use of natural resource of the coastal zone shall indicate the views of the appropriate state or local agency as to the relationship of such activities to the approved management program for the coastal zone. Such applications shall be submitted and coordinated in accordance with the provisions of section 6506 of Title 31. Federal agencies shall not approve proposed projects that are inconsistent with the enforceable policies of a coastal state's management program, except upon a finding by the Secretary that such project is consistent with the purposes of this chapter or necessary in the interest of national security.

**(e) Construction with other laws**

Nothing in this chapter shall be construed—

(1) to diminish either Federal or state jurisdiction, responsibility, or rights in the field of planning, development, or control of water resources, submerged lands, or navigable waters; nor to displace, supersede, limit, or modify any interstate compact or the jurisdiction or responsibility of any legally established joint or common agency of two or more states or of two or more states and the Federal Government; nor to limit the authority of Congress to authorize and fund projects;

(2) as superseding, modifying, or repealing existing laws applicable to the various Federal agencies; nor to affect the jurisdiction, powers, or prerogatives of the International Joint Commission, United States and Canada, the Permanent Engineering Board, and the United States operating entity or entities established pursuant to the Columbia River Basin Treaty, signed at Washington, January 17, 1961, or the International Boundary and Water Commission, United States and Mexico.

**(f) Construction with existing requirements of water and air pollution programs**

Notwithstanding any other provision of this chapter, nothing in this chapter shall in any way affect any requirement (1) established by the Federal Water Pollution Control Act, as amended [33 U.S.C.A. § 1251 et seq.], or the Clean Air Act, as amended [42 U.S.C.A. § 7401 et seq.], or (2) established by the Federal Government or by any state or local government pursuant to such Acts. Such requirements shall be incorporated in any program developed pursuant to this chapter and shall be the water pollution control and air pollution control requirements applicable to such program.

**(g) Concurrence with programs which affect inland areas**

When any state's coastal zone management program, submitted for approval or proposed for modification pursuant to section 1455 of this title, includes requirements as to shorelands which also would be subject to any Federally supported national land use program which may be hereafter enacted, the Secretary, prior to approving such program, shall obtain the concurrence of the Secretary of the Interior, or such other Federal official as may be designated to administer the national land use program, with respect to that portion of the coastal zone management program affecting such inland areas.

**(h) Mediation of disagreements**

In case of serious disagreement between any Federal agency and a coastal state—

(1) in the development or the initial implementation of a management program under section 1454 of this title; or

(2) in the administration of a management program approved under section 1455 of this title;

the Secretary, with the cooperation of the Executive Office of the President, shall seek to mediate the differences involved in such disagreement. The process of such mediation shall, with respect to any disagreement described in paragraph (2), include public hearings which shall be conducted in the local area concerned.

**(i) Application fee for appeals**

(1) With respect to appeals under subsections (c)(3) and (d) of this section which are submitted after November 5, 1990, the Secretary shall collect an application fee of not less than $200 for minor appeals and not less than $500 for major appeals, unless the Secretary, upon consideration of an applicant's request for a fee waiver, determines that the applicant is unable to pay the fee.

(2)(A) The Secretary shall collect such other fees as are necessary to recover the full costs of administering and processing such appeals under subsection (c) of this section.

(B) If the Secretary waives the application fee under paragraph (1) for an applicant, the Secretary shall waive all other fees under this subsection for the applicant.

(3) Fees collected under this subsection shall be deposited into the Coastal Zone Management Fund established under section 1456a of this title.

(Pub.L. 89–454, Title III, § 307, as added Pub.L. 92–583, Oct. 27, 1972, 86 Stat. 1285 and amended Pub.L. 94–370, § 6, July 26, 1976, 90 Stat. 1018; Pub.L. 95–372, Title V, § 504, Sept. 18, 1978, 92 Stat. 693; Pub.L. 101–508, Title VI, § 6208, Nov. 5, 1990, 104 Stat. 1388–307; Pub.L. 102–587, Title II, § 2205(b)(13), (14), Nov. 4, 1992, 106 Stat. 5051.)

### HISTORICAL AND STATUTORY NOTES

**References in Text**

The Outer Continental Shelf Lands Act, referred to in subsec. (c)(3)(B), is Act Aug. 7, 1953, c. 345, 67 Stat. 462, as amended, which is classified generally to subchapter III (section 1331 et seq.) of chapter 29 of Title 43, Public Lands. For complete classification of this Act to the Code, see Short Title note set out under section 1331 of Title 43 and Tables.

The Federal Water Pollution Control Act, referred to in subsec. (f), is Act June 30, 1948, c. 758, as amended generally by Pub.L. 92–500, § 2, Oct. 18, 1972, 86 Stat. 816, which is classified generally to chapter 26 (section 1251 et seq.) of Title 33, Navigation and Navigable Waters. For complete classification of this Act to the Code, see Short Title note set out under section 1251 of Title 33 and Tables.

The Clean Air Act, referred to in subsec. (f), is Act July 14, 1955, c. 360, as amended generally by Pub.L. 88–206, Dec. 17, 1963, 77 Stat. 392, and later by Pub.L. 95–95, Aug. 7, 1977, 91 Stat. 685. The Clean Air Act was originally classified to chapter 15B (section 1857 et seq.) of Title 42, The Public Health and Welfare. On enactment of Pub.L. 95–95, the Act was reclassified to chapter 85 (section 7401 et seq.) of Title 42. For complete classification of this Act to the Code, see Short Title note set out under section 7401 of Title 42 and Tables.

**Codifications**

Amendment of subsec. (c)(3)(B) by Pub.L. 101–508, Title VI, § 6208(b)(3), was executed following "with", notwithstanding directory language which recited that it be executed following "complies", as the probable intent of Congress.

In subsec. (d), "section 6506 of Title 31" was substituted for "Title IV of the Intergovernmental Coordination [Cooperation] Act of 1968 [42 U.S.C.A. § 4231 et seq.]" on authority of Pub.L. 97–258, § 4(b), Sept. 13, 1982, 96 Stat. 1067, the first section of which enacted Title 31, Money and Finance.

## § 1456a. Coastal Zone Management Fund [CZMA § 308]

(a)(1) The obligations of any coastal state or unit of general purpose local government to repay loans made pursuant to this section as in effect before November 5, 1990, and any repayment schedule established pursuant to this chapter as in effect before November 5, 1990, are not altered by any provision of this chapter. Such loans shall be repaid under authority of this subsection and the Secretary may issue regulations governing such repayment. If the Secretary finds that any coastal state or unit of local government is unable to meet its obligations pursuant to this subsection because the actual increases in employment and related population resulting from coastal energy activity and the facilities associated with such activity do not provide adequate revenues to enable such State or unit to meet such obligations in accordance with the appropriate repayment schedule, the Secretary shall, after review of the information submitted by such State or unit, take any of the following actions:

(A) Modify the terms and conditions of such loan.

(B) Refinance the loan.

(C) Recommend to the Congress that legislation be enacted to forgive the loan.

(2) Loan repayments made pursuant to this subsection shall be retained by the Secretary as offsetting collections, and shall be deposited into the Coastal

Zone Management Fund established under subsection (b) of this section.

**(b)(1)** The Secretary shall establish and maintain a fund, to be known as the "Coastal Zone Management Fund", which shall consist of amounts retained and deposited into the Fund under subsection (a) of this section and fees deposited into the Fund under section 1456(i)(3) of this title.

**(2)** Subject to amounts provided in appropriation Acts, amounts in the Fund shall be available to the Secretary for use for the following:

**(A)** Expenses incident to the administration of this chapter, in an amount not to exceed for each of fiscal years 1997, 1998, and 1999 the higher of—

**(i)** $4,000,000; or

**(ii)** 8 percent of the total amount appropriated under this chapter for the fiscal year.

**(B)** After use under subparagraph (A)—

**(i)** projects to address management issues which are regional in scope, including interstate projects;

**(ii)** demonstration projects which have high potential for improving coastal zone management, especially at the local level;

**(iii)** emergency grants to State coastal zone management agencies to address unforeseen or disaster-related circumstances;

**(iv)** appropriate awards recognizing excellence in coastal zone management as provided in section 1460 of this title; and

**(v)** to provide financial support to coastal states for use for investigating and applying the public trust doctrine to implement State management programs approved under section 1455 of this title.

**(vi)** Redesignated (v)

**(3)** Omitted

(Pub.L. 89–454, Title III, § 308, as added Pub.L. 94–370, § 7, July 26, 1976, 90 Stat. 1019, and amended Pub.L. 95–372, Title V, §§ 501, 503(a) to (d), Sept. 18, 1978, 92 Stat. 690, 692, 693; Pub.L. 96–464, § 7, Oct. 17, 1980, 94 Stat. 2064; Pub.L. 99–272, Title VI, § 6047, Apr. 7, 1986, 100 Stat. 128; Pub.L. 101–508, Title VI, § 6209, Nov. 5, 1990, 104 Stat. 1388–308; Pub.L. 102–587, Title II, § 2205(b)(1)(A), (B), (15) to (18), Nov. 4, 1992, 106 Stat. 5050, 5052; Pub.L. 104–150, §§ 2(b)(2), 5, June 3, 1996, 110 Stat. 1380, 1381.)

### HISTORICAL AND STATUTORY NOTES

**Codifications**

Section 2(b)(2) of Pub.L. 104–150 directed the amendment of section 308(b)(2)(B) of the Coastal Zone Management Act of 1972 (16 U.S.C. 1457(b)(2)(B)). Section 308 of such Act is section 308 of Pub.L. 89–454, Title III, as added Pub.L. 94–370, § 7, July 26, 1976, 90 Stat. 1019, as amended, which is classified to section 1456a of this title [this section]. Such amendment was executed to this section as the probable intent of Congress.

Section 1460 of this title, referred to in subsec. (b)(2)(B)(iv), was in the original section 314. Translation was made to section 1460 of this title as the probable intent of Congress.

Subsec. (b)(3) of this section, which required the Secretary to transmit to Congress, annually on December 1, a report on the Fund, including the balance of the Fund and an itemization of deposits and disbursements during the preceding fiscal year, was terminated effective May 15, 2000, pursuant to Pub.L. 104–66, Title III, § 3003, Dec. 21, 1995, 109 Stat. 734, as amended, which is set out as a note under section 1113 of Title 31. See, also, House Document No. 103–7, page 143.

**Extension of Loan Making Authority Under Subsection (d)(1); Amount of Loan**

Pub.L. 99–626, § 6, Nov. 7, 1986, 100 Stat. 3506, provided that: "The authority of the Secretary of Commerce to make loans under paragraph (1) of subsection (d) of section 308 of the Coastal Zone Management Act of 1972 (Public Law 92–583, 16 U.S.C. 1451, et seq.) as amended [subsec. (d)(1) of this section], shall extend to September 30, 1987, for loans made to eligible States or units pursuant to and in accord with agreements entered into between the Secretary and any State prior to September 30, 1986, that provided for a total sum of loans to be made to that State or its units, but such loan authority shall be limited to $7,000,000."

1996 Acts

## § 1456b. Coastal zone enhancement grants

**[CZMA § 309]**

### (a) "Coastal zone enhancement objective" defined

For purposes of this section, the term "coastal zone enhancement objective" means any of the following objectives:

(1) Protection, restoration, or enhancement of the existing coastal wetlands base, or creation of new coastal wetlands.

(2) Preventing or significantly reducing threats to life and destruction of property by eliminating development and redevelopment in high-hazard areas, managing development in other hazard areas, and anticipating and managing the effects of potential sea level rise and Great Lakes level rise.

(3) Attaining increased opportunities for public access, taking into account current and future public access needs, to coastal areas of recreational, historical, aesthetic, ecological, or cultural value.

(4) Reducing marine debris entering the Nation's coastal and ocean environment by managing uses and activities that contribute to the entry of such debris.

(5) Development and adoption of procedures to assess, consider, and control cumulative and secondary impacts of coastal growth and development, including the collective effect on various individual uses or activities on coastal resources, such as coastal wetlands and fishery resources.

(6) Preparing and implementing special area management plans for important coastal areas.

(7) Planning for the use of ocean resources.

(8) Adoption of procedures and enforceable policies to help facilitate the siting of energy facilities and Government facilities and energy-related activities and Government activities which may be of greater than local significance.

(9) Adoption of procedures and policies to evaluate and facilitate the siting of public and private aquaculture facilities in the coastal zone, which will enable States to formulate, administer, and implement strategic plans for marine aquaculture.

**(b) Limits on grants**

(1) Subject to the limitations and goals established in this section, the Secretary may make grants to coastal states to provide funding for development and submission for Federal approval of program changes that support attainment of one or more coastal zone enhancement objectives.

(2)(A) In addition to any amounts provided under section 1455 of this title, and subject to the availability of appropriations, the Secretary may make grants under this subsection to States for implementing program changes approved by the Secretary in accordance with section 1455(e) of this title.

(B) Grants under this paragraph to implement a program change may not be made in any fiscal year after the second fiscal year that begins after the approval of that change by the Secretary.

**(c) Evaluation of State proposals by Secretary**

The Secretary shall evaluate and rank State proposals for funding under this section, and make funding awards based on those proposals, taking into account the criteria established by the Secretary under subsection (d) of this section. The Secretary shall ensure that funding decisions under this section take into consideration the fiscal and technical needs of proposing States and the overall merit of each proposal in terms of benefits to the public.

**(d) Promulgation of regulations by Secretary**

Within 12 months following November 5, 1990, and consistent with the notice and participation requirements established in section 1463 of this title, the Secretary shall promulgate regulations concerning coastal zone enhancement grants that establish—

(1) specific and detailed criteria that must be addressed by a coastal state (including the State's priority needs for improvement as identified by the Secretary after careful consultation with the State) as part of the State's development and implementation of coastal zone enhancement objectives;

(2) administrative or procedural rules or requirements as necessary to facilitate the development and implementation of such objectives by coastal states; and

(3) other funding award criteria as are necessary or appropriate to ensure that evaluations of proposals, and decisions to award funding, under this section are based on objective standards applied fairly and equitably to those proposals.

**(e) No State contribution required**

A State shall not be required to contribute any portion of the cost of any proposal for which funding is awarded under this section.

**(f) Funding**

Beginning in fiscal year 1991, not less than 10 percent and not more than 20 percent of the amounts appropriated to implement sections 1455 and 1455a of this title shall be retained by the Secretary for use in implementing this section, up to a maximum of $10,000,000 annually.

**(g) Eligibility; suspension of State for noncompliance**

If the Secretary finds that the State is not undertaking the actions committed to under the terms of the grant, the Secretary shall suspend the State's eligibility for further funding under this section for at least one year.

(Pub.L. 89–454, Title III, § 309, as added Pub.L. 94–370, § 8, July 26, 1976, 90 Stat. 1028, and amended Pub.L. 96–464, § 8, Oct. 17, 1980, 94 Stat. 2064; Pub.L. 101–508, Title VI, § 6210, Nov. 5, 1990, 104 Stat. 1388–309; Pub.L. 102–587, Title II, § 2205(b)(1)(B), Nov. 4, 1992, 106 Stat. 5050; Pub.L. 104–150, §§ 3, 7(2), June 3, 1996, 110 Stat. 1380, 1382.)

### HISTORICAL AND STATUTORY NOTES

**Codifications**

Section 6210 of Pub.L. 101–508 directed the amendment of section 309 of the Coastal Zone Management Act of 1972 (16 U.S.C. 1452b). Section 309 of such Act is this section, and such amendment was executed to this section as the probable intent of Congress.

## § 1456c. Technical assistance

**[CZMA § 310]**

(a) The Secretary shall conduct a program of technical assistance and management-oriented research necessary to support the development and implementation of State coastal management program amendments under section 1456b of this title, and appropriate to the furtherance of international cooperative efforts and technical assistance in coastal zone management. Each department, agency, and instrumentality of the executive branch of the Federal Government may assist the Secretary, on a reimbursable basis or otherwise, in carrying out the purposes of this section, including the furnishing of information to the extent permitted by law, the transfer of personnel with their consent and without prejudice to their position and rating, and the performance of any research, study, and technical assistance which does not interfere with the performance of the primary duties of such department, agency, or instrumentality. The Secretary may enter into contracts or other arrangements with any qualified person for the purposes of carrying out this subsection.

(b)(1) The Secretary shall provide for the coordination of technical assistance, studies, and research activities under this section with any other such activities that are conducted by or subject to the authority of the Secretary.

(2) The Secretary shall make the results of research and studies conducted pursuant to this section available to coastal states in the form of technical assistance publications, workshops, or other means appropriate.

(3) The Secretary shall consult with coastal states on a regular basis regarding the development and implementation of the program established by this section.

(Pub.L. 89–454, Title III, § 310, as added Pub.L. 101–508, Title VI, § 6211, Nov. 5, 1990, 104 Stat. 1388–311.)

### HISTORICAL AND STATUTORY NOTES

**Prior Provisions**

A prior section 1456c, Pub.L. 89–454, Title III, § 310, as added Pub.L. 94–370, § 9, July 26, 1976, 90 Stat. 1029, which related to research and technical assistance for coastal zone management, was repealed by Pub.L. 99–272, Title VI, § 6045(1), Apr. 7, 1986, 100 Stat. 127.

## § 1456d. Coastal and Estuarine Land Conservation Program

The Secretary shall establish a Coastal and Estuarine Land Conservation Program, for the purpose of protecting important coastal and estuarine areas that have significant conservation, recreation, ecological, historical, or aesthetic values, or that are threatened by conversion from their natural or recreational state to other uses: *Provided further,* That by September 30, 2002, the Secretary shall issue guidelines for this program delineating the criteria for grant awards: *Provided further,* That the Secretary shall distribute these funds in consultation with the States' Coastal Zone Managers' or Governors' designated representatives based on demonstrated need and ability to successfully leverage funds, and shall give priority to lands which can be effectively managed and protected and which have significant ecological value: *Provided further,* That grants funded under this program shall require a 100 percent match from other sources.

(Pub.L. 107–77, Title II, Nov. 28, 2001, 115 Stat. 776.)

### HISTORICAL AND STATUTORY NOTES

**Codifications**

This section was enacted as part of the Department of Commerce and Related Agencies Appropriations Act, 2002, and also as part of the Departments of Commerce, Justice and State, the Judiciary, and Related Agencies Appropriations Act, 2002, and not as part of the Coastal Zone Management Act of 1972 which comprises this chapter.

**National Oceanic and Atmospheric Administration, Procurement, Acquisition and Construction**

Pub.L. 108–7, Div. B, Title II, Feb. 20, 2003, 117 Stat. 75, provided in part: "That the Secretary shall establish a Coastal and Estuarine Land Conservation Program, for the purpose of protecting important coastal and estuarine areas that have significant conservation, recreation, ecological, historical, or aesthetic values, or that are threatened by conversion from their natural or recreational state to other uses."

Similar provisions were contained in the following Appropriations Acts:

Pub.L. 107–77, Title II, Nov. 28, 2001, 115 Stat. 776.

## § 1457. Public hearings

**[CZMA § 311]**

All public hearings required under this chapter must be announced at least thirty days prior to the hearing date. At the time of the announcement, all agency materials pertinent to the hearings, including documents, studies, and other data, must be made available to the public for review and study. As similar materials are subsequently developed, they shall be made available to the public as they become available to the agency.

(Pub.L. 89–454, Title III, § 311, formerly, § 308, as added Pub.L. 92–583, Oct. 27, 1972, 86 Stat. 1287, and renumbered Pub.L. 94–370, § 7, July 26, 1976, 90 Stat. 1019.)

## § 1458. Review of performance

**[CZMA § 312]**

### (a) Evaluation of adherence with terms of grants

The Secretary shall conduct a continuing review of the performance of coastal states with respect to coastal management. Each review shall include a written evaluation with an assessment and detailed findings concerning the extent to which the state has implemented and enforced the program approved by the Secretary, addressed the coastal management needs identified in section 1452(2)(A) through (K) of this title, and adhered to the terms of any grant, loan, or cooperative agreement funded under this chapter.

### (b) Public participation; notice of meetings; reports

In evaluating a coastal state's performance, the Secretary shall conduct the evaluation in an open and public manner, and provide full opportunity for public participation, including holding public meetings in the

State being evaluated and providing opportunities for the submission of written and oral comments by the public. The Secretary shall provide the public with at least 45 days' notice of such public meetings by placing a notice in the Federal Register, by publication of timely notices in newspapers of general circulation within the State being evaluated, and by communications with persons and organizations known to be interested in the evaluation. Each evaluation shall be prepared in report form and shall include written responses to the written comments received during the evaluation process. The final report of the evaluation shall be completed within 120 days after the last public meeting held in the State being evaluated. Copies of the evaluation shall be immediately provided to all persons and organizations participating in the evaluation process.

**(c) Suspension of financial assistance for noncompliance; notification of Governor; length of suspension**

(1) The Secretary may suspend payment of any portion of financial assistance extended to any coastal state under this chapter, and may withdraw any unexpended portion of such assistance, if the Secretary determines that the coastal state is failing to adhere to (A) the management program or a State plan developed to manage a national estuarine reserve established under section 1461 of this title, or a portion of the program or plan approved by the Secretary, or (B) the terms of any grant or cooperative agreement funded under this chapter.

(2) Financial assistance may not be suspended under paragraph (1) unless the Secretary provides the Governor of the coastal state with—

(A) written specifications and a schedule for the actions that should be taken by the State in order that such suspension of financial assistance may be withdrawn; and

(B) written specifications stating how those funds from the suspended financial assistance shall be expended by the coastal state to take the actions referred to in subparagraph (A).

(3) The suspension of financial assistance may not last for less than 6 months or more than 36 months after the date of suspension.

**(d) Withdrawal of approval of program**

The Secretary shall withdraw approval of the management program of any coastal state and shall withdraw financial assistance available to that State under this chapter as well as any unexpended portion of such assistance, if the Secretary determines that the coastal state has failed to take the actions referred to in subsection (c)(2)(A) of this section.

**(e) Notice and hearing**

Management program approval and financial assistance may not be withdrawn under subsection (d) of this section, unless the Secretary gives the coastal state notice of the proposed withdrawal and an opportunity for a public hearing on the proposed action. Upon the withdrawal of management program approval under this subsection (d) of this section, the Secretary shall provide the coastal state with written specifications of the actions that should be taken, or not engaged in, by the state in order that such withdrawal may be canceled by the Secretary.

(Pub.L. 89–454, Title III, § 312, formerly § 309, as added Pub.L. 92–583, Oct. 27, 1972, 86 Stat. 1287, renumbered and amended Pub.L. 94–370, §§ 7, 10, July 26, 1976, 90 Stat. 1019, 1029; Pub.L. 96–464, § 9(a), Oct. 17, 1980, 94 Stat. 2065; Pub.L. 99–272, Title VI, § 6043(a), Apr. 7, 1986, 100 Stat. 124; Pub.L. 101–508, Title VI, §§ 6212, 6216(b), Nov. 5, 1990, 104 Stat. 1388–311, 1388–314; Pub.L. 102–587, Title II, § 2205(b)(1)(A), (C), Nov. 4, 1992, 106 Stat. 5050.)

### HISTORICAL AND STATUTORY NOTES

**Issuance of Regulations**

Section 9(b) of Pub.L. 96–464 provided that: "Within two hundred and seventy days after the date of the enactment of this Act [Oct. 17, 1980], the Secretary of Commerce shall issue such regulations as may be necessary or appropriate to administer section 312 of the Coastal Zone Management Act of 1972 (as amended by subsection (a) of this section) [this section]."

## § 1459. Records and audit

**[CZMA § 313]**

**(a) Maintenance of records by recipients of grants or financial assistance**

Each recipient of a grant under this chapter or of financial assistance under section 1456a of this title, as in effect before November 5, 1990, shall keep such records as the Secretary shall prescribe, including records which fully disclose the amount and disposition of the funds received under the grant and of the proceeds of such assistance, the total cost of the project or undertaking supplied by other sources, and such other records as will facilitate an effective audit.

**(b) Access by Secretary and Comptroller General to records, books, etc., of recipients of grants or financial assistance for audit and examination**

The Secretary and the Comptroller General of the United States, or any of their duly authorized representatives, shall—

(1) after any grant is made under this chapter or any financial assistance is provided under section 1456a of this title, as in effect before November 5, 1990; and

(2) until the expiration of 3 years after—

(A) completion of the project, program, or other undertaking for which such grant was made or used, or

(B) repayment of the loan or guaranteed indebtedness for which such financial assistance was provided,

have access for purposes of audit and examination to any record, book, document, and paper which belongs to or is used or controlled by, any recipient of the grant funds or any person who entered into any transaction relating to such financial assistance and which is pertinent for purposes of determining if the grant funds or the proceeds of such financial assistance are being, or were, used in accordance with the provisions of this chapter.

(Pub.L. 89–454, Title III, § 313, formerly § 310, as added Pub.L. 92–583, Oct. 27, 1972, 86 Stat. 1287, renumbered and amended Pub.L. 94–370, §§ 7, 11, July 26, 1976, 90 Stat. 1019, 1030; Pub.L. 102–587, Title II, § 2205(b)(19), Nov. 4, 1992, 106 Stat. 5052.)

### HISTORICAL AND STATUTORY NOTES

**Codifications**

Another section 313 of Pub.L. 89–454, Title III, as added Pub.L. 101–508, Title VI, § 6213, Nov. 5, 1990, 104 Stat. 1388–312, is classified to section 1460 of this title.

## § 1460. Walter B. Jones excellence in coastal zone management awards

**[CZMA § 314]**

**(a) Establishment**

The Secretary shall, using sums in the Coastal Zone Management Fund established under section 1456a of this title and other amounts available to carry out this chapter (other than amounts appropriated to carry out sections 1454, 1455, 1455a, 1456b, 1456c, and 1461 of this title), implement a program to promote excellence in coastal zone management by identifying and acknowledging outstanding accomplishments in the field.

**(b) Annual selection of recipients**

The Secretary shall select annually—

(1) one individual, other than an employee or officer of the Federal Government, whose contribution to the field of coastal zone management has been the most significant;

(2) 5 local governments which have made the most progress in developing and implementing the coastal zone management principles embodied in this chapter; and

(3) up to 10 graduate students whose academic study promises to contribute materially to development of new or improved approaches to coastal zone management.

**(c) Solicitation of nominations for local government recipients**

In making selections under subsection (b)(2) of this section the Secretary shall solicit nominations from the coastal states, and shall consult with experts in local government planning and land use.

**(d) Solicitation of nominations for graduate student recipients**

In making selections under subsection (b)(3) of this section the Secretary shall solicit nominations from coastal states and the National Sea Grant College Program.

**(e) Funding; types of awards**

Using sums in the Coastal Zone Management Fund established under section 1456a of this title and other amounts available to carry out this chapter (other than amounts appropriated to carry out sections 1454, 1455, 1455a, 1456b, 1456c, and 1461 of this title), the Secretary shall establish and execute appropriate awards, to be known as the "Walter B. Jones Awards," including—

(1) cash awards in an amount not to exceed $5,000 each;

(2) research grants; and

(3) public ceremonies to acknowledge such awards.

(Pub.L. 89–454, Title III, § 314, formerly § 313, as added Pub.L. 101–508, Title VI, § 6213, Nov. 5, 1990, 104 Stat. 1388–312, renumbered § 314 and amended Pub.L 102–587, Title II, § 2205(b)(20), Nov. 4, 1992, 106 Stat. 5052.)

### HISTORICAL AND STATUTORY NOTES

**Prior Provisions**

A prior section 1460, Pub.L. 89–454, Title III, § 314, formerly § 311, as added Pub.L. 92–583, Oct. 27, 1972, 86 Stat. 1287, and renumbered Pub.L. 94–370, § 7, July 26, 1976, 90 Stat. 1019, which related to the establishment of the Coastal Zone Management Advisory Committee, was repealed by Pub.L. 99–272, Title VI, § 6045(2), Apr. 7, 1986, 100 Stat. 127.

## § 1461. National Estuarine Research Reserve System

**[CZMA § 315]**

**(a) Establishment of System**

There is established the National Estuarine Research Reserve System (hereinafter referred to in this section as the "System") that consists of—

(1) each estuarine sanctuary designated under this section as in effect before April 7, 1986; and

(2) each estuarine area designated as a national estuarine reserve under subsection (b) of this section.

Each estuarine sanctuary referred to in paragraph (1) is hereby designated as a national estuarine reserve.

**(b) Designation of national estuarine reserves**

After April 7, 1986, the Secretary may designate an estuarine area as a national estuarine reserve if—

(1) the Governor of the coastal state in which the area is located nominates the area for that designation; and

(2) the Secretary finds that—

(A) the area is a representative estuarine ecosystem that is suitable for long-term research and contributes to the biogeographical and typological balance of the System;

(B) the law of the coastal state provides long-term protection for reserve resources to ensure a stable environment for research;

(C) designation of the area as a reserve will serve to enhance public awareness and understanding of estuarine areas, and provide suitable opportunities for public education and interpretation; and

(D) the coastal state in which the area is located has complied with the requirements of any regulations issued by the Secretary to implement this section.

**(c) Estuarine research guidelines**

The Secretary shall develop guidelines for the conduct of research within the System that shall include—

(1) a mechanism for identifying, and establishing priorities among, the coastal management issues that should be addressed through coordinated research within the System;

(2) the establishment of common research principles and objectives to guide the development of research programs within the System;

(3) the identification of uniform research methodologies which will ensure comparability of data, the broadest application of research results, and the maximum use of the System for research purposes;

(4) the establishment of performance standards upon which the effectiveness of the research efforts and the value of reserves within the System in addressing the coastal management issues identified in paragraph (1) may be measured; and

(5) the consideration of additional sources of funds for estuarine research than the funds authorized under this chapter, and strategies for encouraging the use of such funds within the System, with particular emphasis on mechanisms established under subsection (d) of this section.

In developing the guidelines under this section, the Secretary shall consult with prominent members of the estuarine research community.

**(d) Promotion and coordination of estuarine research**

The Secretary shall take such action as is necessary to promote and coordinate the use of the System for research purposes including—

(1) requiring that the National Oceanic and Atmospheric Administration, in conducting or supporting estuarine research, give priority consideration to research that uses the System; and

(2) consulting with other Federal and State agencies to promote use of one or more reserves within the System by such agencies when conducting estuarine research.

**(e) Financial assistance**

(1) The Secretary may, in accordance with such rules and regulations as the Secretary shall promulgate, make grants—

(A) to a coastal state—

(i) for purposes of acquiring such lands and waters, and any property interests therein, as are necessary to ensure the appropriate long-term management of an area as a national estuarine reserve,

(ii) for purposes of operating or managing a national estuarine reserve and constructing appropriate reserve facilities, or

(iii) for purposes of conducting educational or interpretive activities; and

(B) to any coastal state or public or private person for purposes of supporting research and monitoring within a national estuarine reserve that are consistent with the research guidelines developed under subsection (c) of this section.

(2) Financial assistance provided under paragraph (1) shall be subject to such terms and conditions as the Secretary considers necessary or appropriate to protect the interests of the United States, including requiring coastal states to execute suitable title documents setting forth the property interest or interests of the United States in any lands and waters acquired in whole or part with such financial assistance.

(3)(A) The amount of the financial assistance provided under paragraph (1)(A)(i) with respect to the acquisition of lands and waters, or interests therein, for any one national estuarine reserve may not exceed an amount equal to 50 percent of the costs of the lands, waters, and interests therein or $5,000,000, whichever amount is less.

(B) The amount of the financial assistance provided under paragraph (1)(A)(ii) and (iii) and paragraph (1)(B) may not exceed 70 percent of the costs incurred to achieve the purposes described in those paragraphs with respect to a reserve; except that the amount of the financial assistance provided under paragraph

(1)(A)(iii) may be up to 100 percent of any costs for activities that benefit the entire System.

(C) Notwithstanding subparagraphs (A) and (B), financial assistance under this subsection provided from amounts recovered as a result of damage to natural resources located in the coastal zone may be used to pay 100 percent of the costs of activities carried out with the assistance.

**(f) Evaluation of System performance**

(1) The Secretary shall periodically evaluate the operation and management of each national estuarine reserve, including education and interpretive activities, and the research being conducted within the reserve.

(2) If evaluation under paragraph (1) reveals that the operation and management of the reserve is deficient, or that the research being conducted within the reserve is not consistent with the research guidelines developed under subsection (c) of this section, the Secretary may suspend the eligibility of that reserve for financial assistance under subsection (e) of this section until the deficiency or inconsistency is remedied.

(3) The Secretary may withdraw the designation of an estuarine area as a national estuarine reserve if evaluation under paragraph (1) reveals that—

(A) the basis for any one or more of the findings made under subsection (b)(2) of this section regarding that area no longer exists; or

(B) a substantial portion of the research conducted within the area, over a period of years, has not been consistent with the research guidelines developed under subsection (c) of this section.

**(g) Report**

The Secretary shall include in the report required under section 1462 of this title information regarding—

(1) new designations of national estuarine reserves;

(2) any expansion of existing national estuarine reserves;

(3) the status of the research program being conducted within the System; and

(4) a summary of the evaluations made under subsection (f) of this section.

(Pub.L. 89–454, Title III, § 315, formerly § 312, as added Pub.L. 92–583, Oct. 27, 1972, 86 Stat. 1288, renumbered and amended Pub.L. 94–370, §§ 7, 12, July 26, 1976, 90 Stat. 1019, 1030; Pub.L. 96–464, § 11, Oct. 17, 1980, 94 Stat. 2067; Pub.L. 99–272, Title VI, § 6044, Apr. 7, 1986, 100 Stat. 125; Pub.L. 101–508, Title VI, § 6214, Nov. 5, 1990, 104 Stat. 1388–313; Pub.L. 102–587, Title II, § 2205(b)(1)(A), (B), (21), (22), Nov. 4, 1992, 106 Stat. 5050, 5052; Pub.L. 104–150, § 6, June 3, 1996, 110 Stat. 1381.)

## § 1462. Coastal zone management reports

**[CZMA § 316]**

**(a) Biennial reports**

The Secretary shall consult with the Congress on a regular basis concerning the administration of this chapter and shall prepare and submit to the President for transmittal to the Congress a report summarizing the administration of this chapter during each period of two consecutive fiscal years. Each report, which shall be transmitted to the Congress not later than April 1 of the year following the close of the biennial period to which it pertains, shall include, but not be restricted to (1) an identification of the state programs approved pursuant to this chapter during the preceding Federal fiscal year and a description of those programs; (2) a listing of the states participating in the provisions of this chapter and a description of the status of each state's programs and its accomplishments during the preceding Federal fiscal year; (3) an itemization of the allocation of funds to the various coastal states and a breakdown of the major projects and areas on which these funds were expended; (4) an identification of any state programs which have been reviewed and disapproved, and a statement of the reasons for such action; (5) a summary of evaluation findings prepared in accordance with subsection (a) of section 1458 of this title, and a description of any sanctions imposed under subsections (c) and (d) of section 1458 of this title; (6) a listing of all activities and projects which, pursuant to the provisions of subsection (c) or subsection (d) of section 1456 of this title, are not consistent with an applicable approved state management program; (7) a summary of the regulations issued by the Secretary or in effect during the preceding Federal fiscal year; (8) a summary of a coordinated national strategy and program for the Nation's coastal zone including identification and discussion of Federal, regional, state, and local responsibilities and functions therein; (9) a summary of outstanding problems arising in the administration of this chapter in order of priority; (10) a description of the economic, environmental, and social consequences of energy activity affecting the coastal zone and an evaluation of the effectiveness of financial assistance under section 1456a of this title in dealing with such consequences; (11) a description and evaluation of applicable interstate and regional planning and coordination mechanisms developed by the coastal states; (12) a summary and evaluation of the research, studies, and training conducted in support of coastal zone management; and (13) such other information as may be appropriate.

**(b) Recommendations for legislation**

The report required by subsection (a) of this section shall contain such recommendations for additional legislation as the Secretary deems necessary to achieve the objectives of this chapter and enhance its effective operation.

**(c) Review of other Federal programs; report to Congress**

(1) The Secretary shall conduct a systematic review of Federal programs, other than this chapter, that affect coastal resources for purposes of identifying conflicts between the objectives and administration of such programs and the purposes and policies of this chapter. Not later than 1 year after October 17, 1980, the Secretary shall notify each Federal agency having appropriate jurisdiction of any conflict between its program and the purposes and policies of this chapter identified as a result of such review.

(2) The Secretary shall promptly submit a report to the Congress consisting of the information required under paragraph (1) of this subsection. Such report shall include recommendations for changes necessary to resolve existing conflicts among Federal laws and programs that affect the uses of coastal resources.

(Pub.L. 89–454, Title III, § 316, formerly § 313, as added Pub.L. 92–583, Oct. 27, 1972, 86 Stat. 1288, renumbered and amended Pub.L. 94–370, §§ 7, 13, July 26, 1976, 90 Stat. 1019, 1030; Pub.L. 96–464, § 10, Oct. 17, 1980, 94 Stat. 2066; Pub.L. 102–587, Title II, § 2205(b)(23), Nov. 4, 1992, 106 Stat. 5052.)

**HISTORICAL AND STATUTORY NOTES**

**Shellfish Sanitation**

Section 16 of Pub.L. 94–370 provided that:

"(a) The Secretary of Commerce shall—

"(1) undertake a comprehensive review of all aspects of the molluscan shellfish industry, including, but not limited to, the harvesting, processing, and transportation of such shellfish; and

"(2) evaluate the impact of Federal law concerning water quality on the molluscan shellfish industry.

The Secretary of Commerce shall, not later than April 30, 1977, submit a report to the Congress of the findings, comments, and recommendations (if any) which result from such review and evaluation.

"(b) The Secretary of Health, Education, and Welfare [now Health and Human Services] shall not promulgate final regulations concerning the national shellfish safety program before June 30, 1977. At least 60 days prior to the promulgation of any such regulations, the Secretary of Health, Education, and Welfare, in consultation with the Secretary of Commerce, shall publish an analysis (1) of the economic impact of such regulations on the domestic shellfish industry, and (2) the cost of such national shellfish safety program relative to the benefits that it is expected to achieve."

## § 1463. Rules and regulations

**[CZMA § 317]**

The Secretary shall develop and promulgate, pursuant to section 553 of Title 5, after notice and opportunity for full participation by relevant Federal agencies, state agencies, local governments, regional organizations, port authorities, and other interested parties, both public and private, such rules and regulations as may be necessary to carry out the provisions of this chapter.

(Pub.L. 89–454, Title III, § 317, formerly § 314, as added Pub.L. 92–583, Oct. 27, 1972, 86 Stat. 1288, and renumbered Pub.L. 94–370, § 7, July 26, 1976, 90 Stat. 1019.)

## § 1463a. Omitted

**HISTORICAL AND STATUTORY NOTES**

**Codifications**

Section, Pub.L. 96–464, § 12(a) to (g), Oct. 17, 1980, 94 Stat. 2067; Pub.L. 98–620, Title IV, § 402(20), Nov. 8, 1984, 98 Stat. 3358, which set forth procedures and definitions applicable to Congressional disapproval for final rules, was omitted pursuant to section 12(h) of Pub.L. 96–464 providing that this section shall cease to have any force or effect after Sept. 30, 1985.

## § 1463b. National Coastal Resources Research and Development Institute

**(a) Establishment by Secretary; administration**

The Secretary of Commerce shall provide for the establishment of a National Coastal Resources Research and Development Institute (hereinafter in this section referred to as the "Institute") to be administered by the Oregon State Marine Science Center.

**(b) Purposes of Institute**

The Institute shall conduct research and carry out educational and demonstration projects designed to promote the efficient and responsible development of ocean and coastal resources, including arctic resources. Such projects shall be based on biological, geological, genetic, economic and other scientific research applicable to the purposes of this section and shall include studies on the economic diversification and environmental protection of the Nation's coastal areas.

**(c) Determination of Institute policies**

(1) The policies of the Institute shall be determined by a Board of Governors composed of—

(A) two representatives appointed by the Governor of Oregon;

(B) one representative appointed by the Governor of Alaska;

(C) one representative appointed by the Governor of Washington;

(D) one representative appointed by the Governor of California; and

(E) one representative appointed by the Governor of Hawaii.

(2) Such policies shall include the selection, on a nationally competitive basis, of the research, projects, and studies to be supported by the Institute in accordance with the purposes of this section.

**(d) Establishment of Advisory Council; functions and composition**

(1) The Board of Governors shall establish an Advisory Council composed of specialists in ocean and coastal resources from the academic community.

(2) To the maximum extent practicable, the Advisory Council shall be composed of such specialists from every coastal region of the Nation.

(3) The Advisory Council shall provide such advice to the Board of Governors as such Board shall request, including recommendations regarding the support of research, projects, and studies in accordance with the purposes of this section.

**(e) Administration of Institute**

The Institute shall be administered by a Director who shall be appointed by the Chancellor of the Oregon Board of Higher Education in consultation with the Board of Governors.

**(f) Evaluation of Institute by Secretary**

The Secretary of Commerce shall conduct an ongoing evaluation of the activities of the Institute to ensure that funds received by the Institute under this section are used in a manner consistent with the provisions of this section.

**(g) Report to Secretary**

The Institute shall report to the Secretary of Commerce on its activities within 2 years after July 17, 1984.

**(h) Access to Institute books, records, and documents**

The Comptroller General of the United States, and any of his duly authorized representatives, shall have access, for the purpose of audit and examination, to any books, documents, papers and records of the Institute that are pertinent to the funds received under this section.

**(i) Status of Institute employees**

Employees of the Institute shall not, by reason of such employment, be considered to be employees of the Federal Government for any purpose.

**(j) Authorization of appropriations**

For the purposes of this section, there are authorized to be appropriated in each fiscal year $5,000,000, commencing with fiscal year 1985.

(Pub.L. 98–364, Title II, § 201, July 17, 1984, 98 Stat. 443.)

### HISTORICAL AND STATUTORY NOTES

**Codifications**

This section was not enacted as part of the Coastal Zone Management Act of 1972, which comprises this chapter.

## § 1464. Authorization of appropriations

**[CZMA § 318]**

**(a) Sums appropriated to Secretary**

There are authorized to be appropriated to the Secretary, to remain available until expended—

(1) for grants under sections 1455, 1455a, and 1456b of this title—

(A) $47,600,000 for fiscal year 1997;

(B) $49,000,000 for fiscal year 1998; and

(C) $50,500,000 for fiscal year 1999; and

(2) for grants under section 1461 of this title—

(A) $4,400,000 for fiscal year 1997;

(B) $4,500,000 for fiscal year 1998; and

(C) $4,600,000 for fiscal year 1999.

**(b) Limitations**

Federal funds received from other sources shall not be used to pay a coastal state's share of costs under section 1455 or 1456b of this title.

**(c) Reversion to Secretary of unobligated State funds; availability of funds**

The amount of any grant, or portion of a grant, made to a State under any section of this chapter which is not obligated by such State during the fiscal year, or during the second fiscal year after the fiscal year, for which it was first authorized to be obligated by such State shall revert to the Secretary. The Secretary shall add such reverted amount to those funds available for grants under the section for such reverted amount was originally made available.

(Pub.L. 89–454, Title III, § 318, formerly § 315, as added Pub.L. 92–583, Oct. 27, 1972, 86 Stat. 1289, amended Pub.L. 93–612, § 1(3), Jan. 2, 1975, 88 Stat. 1974, renumbered and amended Pub.L. 94–370, §§ 7, 14, July 26, 1976, 90 Stat. 1019, 1031; amended Pub.L. 95–372, Title V, §§ 502, 503(e), (f), Sept. 18, 1978, 92 Stat. 692, 693; Pub.L. 96–464, § 13, Oct. 17, 1980, 94 Stat. 2070; Pub.L. 99–272, Title VI, § 6046, Apr. 7, 1986, 100 Stat. 127; Pub.L. 99–626, § 7, Nov. 7, 1986, 100 Stat. 3506; Pub.L. 101–508, Title VI, § 6215, Nov. 5, 1990, 104 Stat. 1388–313; Pub.L. 104–150, § 4, June 3, 1996, 110 Stat. 1381.)

### HISTORICAL AND STATUTORY NOTES

**Codifications**

Amendment to this section by section 6046 of Pub.L. 99–272, which directed that this section be amended by revising par. (1), striking former par. (2), renumbering former pars. (3) to (6) as (2) to (5), respectively, and revising pars. (3) to (5), as so renumbered, has been executed to pars.

(1) to (6) of subsec. (a) of this section as the probable intent of Congress.

## § 1465. Appeals to the Secretary

[CZMA § 319]

### (a) Notice

The Secretary shall publish in the Federal Register a notice indicating when the decision record has been closed on any appeal to the Secretary taken from a consistency determination under section 1456(c) or (d) of this title. No later than 90 days after the date of publication of this notice, the Secretary shall—

(1) issue a final decision in the appeal; or

(2) publish a notice in the Federal Register detailing why a decision cannot be issued within the 90–day period.

### (b) Deadline

In the case where the Secretary publishes a notice under subsection (a)(2) of this section, the Secretary shall issue a decision in any appeal filed under section 1456 of this title no later than 45 days after the date of the publication of the notice.

### (c) Application

This section applies to appeals initiated by the Secretary and appeals filed by an applicant.

(Pub.L. 89–454, Title III, § 319, as added Pub.L. 104–150, § 8, June 3, 1996, 110 Stat. 1382.)

# ENDANGERED SPECIES

## ENDANGERED SPECIES ACT OF 1973 [ESA § ____]

**(16 U.S.C.A. §§ 1531 to 1544)**

## CHAPTER 35—ENDANGERED SPECIES



### § 1531. Congressional findings and declaration of purposes and policy

[ESA § 2]

**(a) Findings**

The Congress finds and declares that—

**(1)** various species of fish, wildlife, and plants in the United States have been rendered extinct as a consequence of economic growth and development untempered by adequate concern and conservation;

**(2)** other species of fish, wildlife, and plants have been so depleted in numbers that they are in danger of or threatened with extinction;

**(3)** these species of fish, wildlife, and plants are of esthetic, ecological, educational, historical, recreational, and scientific value to the Nation and its people;

**(4)** the United States has pledged itself as a sovereign state in the international community to conserve to the extent practicable the various species of fish or wildlife and plants facing extinction, pursuant to—

**(A)** migratory bird treaties with Canada and Mexico;

**(B)** the Migratory and Endangered Bird Treaty with Japan;

**(C)** the Convention on Nature Protection and Wildlife Preservation in the Western Hemisphere;

**(D)** the International Convention for the Northwest Atlantic Fisheries;

**(E)** the International Convention for the High Seas Fisheries of the North Pacific Ocean;

**(F)** the Convention on International Trade in Endangered Species of Wild Fauna and Flora; and

**(G)** other international agreements; and

**(5)** encouraging the States and other interested parties, through Federal financial assistance and a system of incentives, to develop and maintain conservation programs which meet national and international standards is a key to meeting the Nation's international commitments and to better safeguarding, for the benefit of all citizens, the Nation's heritage in fish, wildlife, and plants.

**(b) Purposes**

The purposes of this chapter are to provide a means whereby the ecosystems upon which endangered species and threatened species depend may be conserved, to provide a program for the conservation of such endangered species and threatened species, and to take such steps as may be appropriate to achieve the purposes of the treaties and conventions set forth in subsection (a) of this section.

**(c) Policy**

**(1)** It is further declared to be the policy of Congress that all Federal departments and agencies shall seek to conserve endangered species and threatened species and shall utilize their authorities in furtherance of the purposes of this chapter.

**(2)** It is further declared to be the policy of Congress that Federal agencies shall cooperate with State and local agencies to resolve water resource issues in concert with conservation of endangered species.

(Pub.L. 93–205, § 2, Dec. 28, 1973, 87 Stat. 884; Pub.L. 96–159, § 1, Dec. 28, 1979, 93 Stat. 1225; Pub.L. 97–304, § 9(a), Oct. 13, 1982, 96 Stat. 1426; Pub.L. 100–478, Title I, § 1013(a), Oct. 7, 1988, 102 Stat. 2315.)

### HISTORICAL AND STATUTORY NOTES

**References in Text**

This chapter, referred to in subsecs. (b) and (c)(1), in the original read "this Act", meaning the Endangered Species Act of 1973, Pub.L. 93–205, Dec. 28, 1973, 81 Stat. 884, as amended, which is classified principally to this chapter. For complete classification, see Short Title note set out below and Tables.

**Effective and Applicability Provisions**

1973 Acts

Section 16 of Pub.L. 93–205 provided that: "This Act [enacting this chapter, amending sections 460k–1, 460*l*–9, 668dd, 715i, 715s, 1362, 1371, 1372, and 1402 of this title and section 136 of Title 7, Agriculture, repealing sections 668aa to 668cc–6 of this title, and enacting provisions set out as notes under this section] shall take effect on the date of its enactment [Dec. 28, 1973]."

**Short Title**

1982 Amendments

Section 1 of Pub.L. 97–304 provided: "That this Act [amending sections 1531, 1532, 1533, 1535, 1536, 1537a, 1538, 1539, 1540, and 1542 of this title and enacting provisions set out as notes under sections 1533, 1537a, and 1539 of this title] may be cited as the 'Endangered Species Act Amendments of 1982'."

1978 Amendments

Pub.L. 95–632, § 1, Nov. 10, 1978, 92 Stat. 3751, provided: "That this Act [amending sections 1532 to 1536, 1538 to 1540, and 1542 of this title] may be cited as the 'Endangered Species Act Amendments of 1978'."

1973 Acts

Section 1 of Pub.L. 93–205 provided: "That this Act [enacting this chapter, amending sections 460k–1, 460*l*–9, 668dd, 715i, 715s, 1362, 1371, 1372 and 1402 of this title and section 136 of Title 7, Agriculture, repealing sections 668aa to 668cc–6 of this title, and enacting provisions set out as notes under this section] may be cited as the 'Endangered Species Act of 1973'."

**Relationship to Endangered Species Act of 1973**

Pub.L. 102–251, Title III, § 305, Mar. 9, 1992, 106 Stat. 66, as amended Pub.L. 104–208, Div. A, Title I, § 101(a) [Title II, § 211(b)], Sept. 30, 1996, 110 Stat. 3009–41, provided that: "The special areas defined in section 3(24) of the Magnuson-Stevens Fishery Conservation and Management Act (16 U.S.C. 1802(24)) [section 1802(24) of this title] shall be considered places that are subject to the jurisdiction of the United States for the purposes of the Endangered Species Act of 1973 (16 U.S.C. 1531 et seq.) [this chapter]."

[Amendment by Pub.L. 104–208, Div. A, Title I, § 101(a) [Title II, § 211(b)], Sept. 30, 1996, 110 Stat. 3009–41, effective 15 days after Oct. 11, 1996, see Pub.L. 104–208, Div. A, Title I, § 101(a) [Title II, § 211(b)], Sept. 30, 1996, 110 Stat. 3009–41, set out as a note under section 1801 of this title.]

[Section 305 of Pub.L. 102–251 effective on the date on which the Agreement between the United States and the Union of Soviet Socialist Republics on the Maritime Boundary, signed June 1, 1990, enters into force for the United States, with authority to prescribe implementing regulations effective Mar. 9, 1992, but with no such regulation to be effective until the date on which the Agreement enters into force for the United States, see section 308 of Pub.L. 102–251, set out as a note under section 773 of this title.]

## § 1532. Definitions

**[ESA § 3]**

For the purposes of this chapter—

(1) The term "alternative courses of action" means all alternatives and thus is not limited to original project objectives and agency jurisdiction.

(2) The term "commercial activity" means all activities of industry and trade, including, but not limited to, the buying or selling of commodities and activities conducted for the purpose of facilitating such buying and selling: *Provided, however*, That it does not include exhibition of commodities by museums or similar cultural or historical organizations.

(3) The terms "conserve", "conserving", and "conservation" mean to use and the use of all methods and procedures which are necessary to bring any endangered species or threatened species to the point at which the measures provided pursuant to this chapter are no longer necessary. Such methods and procedures include, but are not limited to, all activities associated with scientific resources management such as research, census, law enforcement, habitat acquisition and maintenance, propagation, live trapping, and transplantation, and, in the extraordinary case where population pressures within a given ecosystem cannot be otherwise relieved, may include regulated taking.

(4) The term "Convention" means the Convention on International Trade in Endangered Species of Wild Fauna and Flora, signed on March 3, 1973, and the appendices thereto.

(5)(A) The term "critical habitat" for a threatened or endangered species means—

(i) the specific areas within the geographical area occupied by the species, at the time it is listed in accordance with the provisions of section 1533 of this title, on which are found those physical or biological features (I) essential to the conservation of the species and (II) which may require special management considerations or protection; and

(ii) specific areas outside the geographical area occupied by the species at the time it is listed in accordance with the provisions of section 1533 of this title, upon a determination by the Secretary that such areas are essential for the conservation of the species.

(B) Critical habitat may be established for those species now listed as threatened or endangered species for which no critical habitat has heretofore been established as set forth in subparagraph (A) of this paragraph.

(C) Except in those circumstances determined by the Secretary, critical habitat shall not include the entire geographical area which can be occupied by the threatened or endangered species.

(6) The term "endangered species" means any species which is in danger of extinction throughout all or a significant portion of its range other than a species of the Class Insecta determined by the Secretary to constitute a pest whose protection under the provisions of this chapter would present an overwhelming and overriding risk to man.

(7) The term "Federal agency" means any department, agency, or instrumentality of the United States.

(8) The term "fish or wildlife" means any member of the animal kingdom, including without limitation any mammal, fish, bird (including any migratory, nonmigratory, or endangered bird for which protection is also afforded by treaty or other international agreement), amphibian, reptile, mollusk, crustacean, arthropod or other invertebrate, and includes any part, product, egg, or offspring thereof, or the dead body or parts thereof.

(9) The term "foreign commerce" includes, among other things, any transaction—

(A) between persons within one foreign country;

(B) between persons in two or more foreign countries;

(C) between a person within the United States and a person in a foreign country; or

(D) between persons within the United States, where the fish and wildlife in question are moving in any country or countries outside the United States.

(10) The term "import" means to land on, bring into, or introduce into, or attempt to land on, bring into, or introduce into, any place subject to the jurisdiction of the United States, whether or not such landing, bringing, or introduction constitutes an importation within the meaning of the customs laws of the United States.

(11) Repealed. Pub.L. 97–304, § 4(b), Oct. 13, 1982, 96 Stat. 1420.

(12) The term "permit or license applicant" means, when used with respect to an action of a Federal agency for which exemption is sought under section 1536 of this title, any person whose application to such agency for a permit or license has been denied primarily because of the application of section 1536(a) of this title to such agency action.

(13) The term "person" means an individual, corporation, partnership, trust, association, or any other private entity; or any officer, employee, agent, department, or instrumentality of the Federal Government, of any State, municipality, or political subdivision of a State, or of any foreign government; any State, municipality, or political subdivision of a State; or any other entity subject to the jurisdiction of the United States.

(14) The term "plant" means any member of the plant kingdom, including seeds, roots and other parts thereof.

(15) The term "Secretary" means, except as otherwise herein provided, the Secretary of the Interior or the Secretary of Commerce as program responsibilities are vested pursuant to the provisions of Reorganization Plan Numbered 4 of 1970; except that with respect to the enforcement of the provisions of this chapter and the Convention which pertain to the importation or exportation of terrestrial plants, the term also means the Secretary of Agriculture.

(16) The term "species" includes any subspecies of fish or wildlife or plants, and any distinct population segment of any species of vertebrate fish or wildlife which interbreeds when mature.

(17) The term "State" means any of the several States, the District of Columbia, the Commonwealth of Puerto Rico, American Samoa, the Virgin Islands, Guam, and the Trust Territory of the Pacific Islands.

(18) The term "State agency" means any State agency, department, board, commission, or other governmental entity which is responsible for the management and conservation of fish, plant, or wildlife resources within a State.

(19) The term "take" means to harass, harm, pursue, hunt, shoot, wound, kill, trap, capture, or collect, or to attempt to engage in any such conduct.

(20) The term "threatened species" means any species which is likely to become an endangered species within the foreseeable future throughout all or a significant portion of its range.

(21) The term "United States", when used in a geographical context, includes all States.

(Pub.L. 93–205, § 3, Dec. 28, 1973, 87 Stat. 885; Pub.L. 94–359, § 5, July 12, 1976, 90 Stat. 913; Pub.L. 95–632, § 2, Nov. 10, 1978, 92 Stat. 3751; Pub.L. 96–159, § 2, Dec. 28, 1979, 93 Stat. 1225; Pub.L. 97–304, § 4(b), Oct. 13, 1982, 96 Stat. 1420; Pub.L. 100–478, Title I, § 1001, Oct. 7, 1988, 102 Stat. 2306.)

## HISTORICAL AND STATUTORY NOTES

### References in Text

This chapter, referred to in text, in the original read "this Act", meaning the Endangered Species Act of 1973, which is classified principally to this chapter. For complete classification, see Short Title note set out under section 1531 of this title and Tables.

The customs laws of the United States, referred to in par. (10), are classified generally to Title 19.

Reorganization Plan No. 4 of 1970, referred to in par. (15), is Reorg. Plan No. 4 of 1970, eff. Oct. 3, 1970, 35 F.R. 15627, 84 Stat. 2090, which is set out in the Appendix to Title 5, Government Organization and Employees.

**Effective and Applicability Provisions**

1973 Acts

Section effective Dec. 28, 1973, see section 16 of Pub.L. 93–205, set out as an Effective Date note under section 1531 of this title.

## § 1533. Determination of endangered species and threatened species

**[ESA § 4]**

### (a) Generally

(1) The Secretary shall by regulation promulgated in accordance with subsection (b) of this section determine whether any species is an endangered species or a threatened species because of any of the following factors:

(A) the present or threatened destruction, modification, or curtailment of its habitat or range;

(B) overutilization for commercial, recreational, scientific, or educational purposes;

(C) disease or predation;

(D) the inadequacy of existing regulatory mechanisms; or

(E) other natural or manmade factors affecting its continued existence.

(2) With respect to any species over which program responsibilities have been vested in the Secretary of Commerce pursuant to Reorganization Plan Numbered 4 of 1970—

(A) in any case in which the Secretary of Commerce determines that such species should—

(i) be listed as an endangered species or a threatened species, or

(ii) be changed in status from a threatened species to an endangered species,

he shall so inform the Secretary of the Interior, who shall list such species in accordance with this section;

(B) in any case in which the Secretary of Commerce determines that such species should—

(i) be removed from any list published pursuant to subsection (c) of this section, or

(ii) be changed in status from an endangered species to a threatened species,

he shall recommend such action to the Secretary of the Interior, and the Secretary of the Interior, if he concurs in the recommendation, shall implement such action; and

(C) the Secretary of the Interior may not list or remove from any list any such species, and may not change the status of any such species which are listed, without a prior favorable determination made pursuant to this section by the Secretary of Commerce.

(3)(A) The Secretary, by regulation promulgated in accordance with subsection (b) of this section and to the maximum extent prudent and determinable—

(i) shall, concurrently with making a determination under paragraph (1) that a species is an endangered species or a threatened species, designate any habitat of such species which is then considered to be critical habitat; and

(ii) may, from time-to-time thereafter as appropriate, revise such designation.

(B)(i) The Secretary shall not designate as critical habitat any lands or other geographical areas owned or controlled by the Department of Defense, or designated for its use, that are subject to an integrated natural resources management plan prepared under section 670a of this title, if the Secretary determines in writing that such plan provides a benefit to the species for which critical habitat is proposed for designation.

(ii) Nothing in this paragraph affects the requirement to consult under section 1536(a)(2) of this title with respect to an agency action (as that term is defined in that section).

(iii) Nothing in this paragraph affects the obligation of the Department of Defense to comply with section 1538 of this title, including the prohibition preventing extinction and taking of endangered species and threatened species.

### (b) Basis for determinations

(1)(A) The Secretary shall make determinations required by subsection (a)(1) of this section solely on the basis of the best scientific and commercial data available to him after conducting a review of the status of the species and after taking into account those efforts, if any, being made by any State or foreign nation, or any political subdivision of a State or foreign nation, to protect such species, whether by predator control, protection of habitat and food supply, or other conservation practices, within any area under its jurisdiction, or on the high seas.

(B) In carrying out this section, the Secretary shall give consideration to species which have been—

(i) designated as requiring protection from unrestricted commerce by any foreign nation, or pursuant to any international agreement; or

(ii) identified as in danger of extinction, or likely to become so within the foreseeable future, by any State agency or by any agency of a foreign nation that is responsible for the conservation of fish or wildlife or plants.

(2) The Secretary shall designate critical habitat, and make revisions thereto, under subsection (a) (3) of this section on the basis of the best scientific data available and after taking into consideration the economic impact, the impact on national security, and any other relevant impact, of specifying any particular area as critical habitat. The Secretary may exclude any area from critical habitat if he determines that the benefits of such exclusion outweigh the benefits of specifying such area as part of the critical habitat, unless he determines, based on the best scientific and commercial data available, that the failure to designate such area as critical habitat will result in the extinction of the species concerned.

(3)(A) To the maximum extent practicable, within 90 days after receiving the petition of an interested person under section 553(e) of Title 5, to add a species to, or to remove a species from, either of the lists published under subsection (c) of this section, the Secretary shall make a finding as to whether the petition presents substantial scientific or commercial information indicating that the petitioned action may be warranted. If such a petition is found to present such information, the Secretary shall promptly commence a review of the status of the species concerned. The Secretary shall promptly publish each finding made under this subparagraph in the Federal Register.

(B) Within 12 months after receiving a petition that is found under subparagraph (A) to present substantial information indicating that the petitioned action may be warranted, the Secretary shall make one of the following findings:

(i) The petitioned action is not warranted, in which case the Secretary shall promptly publish such finding in the Federal Register.

(ii) The petitioned action is warranted, in which case the Secretary shall promptly publish in the Federal Register a general notice and the complete text of a proposed regulation to implement such action in accordance with paragraph (5).

(iii) The petitioned action is warranted, but that—

(I) the immediate proposal and timely promulgation of a final regulation implementing the petitioned action in accordance with paragraphs (5) and (6) is precluded by pending proposals to determine whether any species is an endangered species or a threatened species, and

(II) expeditious progress is being made to add qualified species to either of the lists published under subsection (c) of this section and to remove from such lists species for which the protections of this chapter are no longer necessary,

in which case the Secretary shall promptly publish such finding in the Federal Register, together with a description and evaluation of the reasons and data on which the finding is based.

(C)(i) A petition with respect to which a finding is made under subparagraph (B)(iii) shall be treated as a petition that is resubmitted to the Secretary under subparagraph (A) on the date of such finding and that presents substantial scientific or commercial information that the petitioned action may be warranted.

(ii) Any negative finding described in subparagraph (A) and any finding described in subparagraph (B) (i) or (iii) shall be subject to judicial review.

(iii) The Secretary shall implement a system to monitor effectively the status of all species with respect to which a finding is made under subparagraph (B)(iii) and shall make prompt use of the authority under paragraph 7[1] to prevent a significant risk to the well being of any such species.

(D)(i) To the maximum extent practicable, within 90 days after receiving the petition of an interested person under section 553(e) of Title 5, to revise a critical habitat designation, the Secretary shall make a finding as to whether the petition presents substantial scientific information indicating that the revision may be warranted. The Secretary shall promptly publish such finding in the Federal Register.

(ii) Within 12 months after receiving a petition that is found under clause (i) to present substantial information indicating that the requested revision may be warranted, the Secretary shall determine how he intends to proceed with the requested revision, and shall promptly publish notice of such intention in the Federal Register.

(4) Except as provided in paragraphs (5) and (6) of this subsection, the provisions of section 553 of Title 5 (relating to rulemaking procedures), shall apply to any regulation promulgated to carry out the purposes of this chapter.

(5) With respect to any regulation proposed by the Secretary to implement a determination, designation, or revision referred to in subsection (a) (1) or (3) of this section, the Secretary shall—

(A) not less than 90 days before the effective date of the regulation—

(i) publish a general notice and the complete text of the proposed regulation in the Federal Register, and

(ii) give actual notice of the proposed regulation (including the complete text of the regulation) to the State agency in each State in which the species is believed to occur, and to each county or equivalent jurisdiction in which the species is believed to occur, and invite the comment of such agency, and each such jurisdiction, thereon;

**(B)** insofar as practical, and in cooperation with the Secretary of State, give notice of the proposed regulation to each foreign nation in which the species is believed to occur or whose citizens harvest the species on the high seas, and invite the comment of such nation thereon;

**(C)** give notice of the proposed regulation to such professional scientific organizations as he deems appropriate;

**(D)** publish a summary of the proposed regulation in a newspaper of general circulation in each area of the United States in which the species is believed to occur; and

**(E)** promptly hold one public hearing on the proposed regulation if any person files a request for such a hearing within 45 days after the date of publication of general notice.

**(6) (A)** Within the one-year period beginning on the date on which general notice is published in accordance with paragraph (5) (A) (i) regarding a proposed regulation, the Secretary shall publish in the Federal Register—

**(i)** if a determination as to whether a species is an endangered species or a threatened species, or a revision of critical habitat, is involved, either—

**(I)** a final regulation to implement such determination,

**(II)** a final regulation to implement such revision or a finding that such revision should not be made,

**(III)** notice that such one-year period is being extended under subparagraph (B) (i), or

**(IV)** notice that the proposed regulation is being withdrawn under subparagraph (B) (ii), together with the finding on which such withdrawal is based; or

**(ii)** subject to subparagraph (C), if a designation of critical habitat is involved, either—

**(I)** a final regulation to implement such designation, or

**(II)** notice that such one-year period is being extended under such subparagraph.

**(B)(i)** If the Secretary finds with respect to a proposed regulation referred to in subparagraph (A) (i) that there is substantial disagreement regarding the sufficiency or accuracy of the available data relevant to the determination or revision concerned, the Secretary may extend the one-year period specified in subparagraph (A) for not more than six months for purposes of soliciting additional data.

**(ii)** If a proposed regulation referred to in subparagraph (A) (i) is not promulgated as a final regulation within such one-year period (or longer period if extension under clause (i) applies) because the Secretary finds that there is not sufficient evidence to justify the action proposed by the regulation, the Secretary shall immediately withdraw the regulation. The finding on which a withdrawal is based shall be subject to judicial review. The Secretary may not propose a regulation that has previously been withdrawn under this clause unless he determines that sufficient new information is available to warrant such proposal.

**(iii)** If the one-year period specified in subparagraph (A) is extended under clause (i) with respect to a proposed regulation, then before the close of such extended period the Secretary shall publish in the Federal Register either a final regulation to implement the determination or revision concerned, a finding that the revision should not be made, or a notice of withdrawal of the regulation under clause (ii), together with the finding on which the withdrawal is based.

**(C)** A final regulation designating critical habitat of an endangered species or a threatened species shall be published concurrently with the final regulation implementing the determination that such species is endangered or threatened, unless the Secretary deems that—

**(i)** it is essential to the conservation of such species that the regulation implementing such determination be promptly published; or

**(ii)** critical habitat of such species is not then determinable, in which case the Secretary, with respect to the proposed regulation to designate such habitat, may extend the one-year period specified in subparagraph (A) by not more than one additional year, but not later than the close of such additional year the Secretary must publish a final regulation, based on such data as may be available at that time, designating, to the maximum extent prudent, such habitat.

**(7)** Neither paragraph (4), (5), or (6) of this subsection nor section 553 of Title 5 shall apply to any regulation issued by the Secretary in regard to any emergency posing a significant risk to the well-being of any species of fish or wildlife or plants, but only if—

**(A)** at the time of publication of the regulation in the Federal Register the Secretary publishes therein detailed reasons why such regulation is necessary; and

**(B)** in the case such regulation applies to resident species of fish or wildlife, or plants, the Secretary gives actual notice of such regulation to the State agency in each State in which such species is believed to occur.

Such regulation shall, at the discretion of the Secretary, take effect immediately upon the publication of the regulation in the Federal Register. Any regulation promulgated under the authority of this paragraph shall cease to have force and effect at the close of the 240-day period following the date of publication unless, during such 240-day period, the rulemaking procedures which would apply to such regulation without regard to this paragraph are complied with. If at any time after issuing an emergency regulation the Secretary determines, on the basis of the best appropriate data available to him, that substantial evidence does not exist to warrant such regulation, he shall withdraw it.

(8) The publication in the Federal Register of any proposed or final regulation which is necessary or appropriate to carry out the purposes of this chapter shall include a summary by the Secretary of the data on which such regulation is based and shall show the relationship of such data to such regulation; and if such regulation designates or revises critical habitat, such summary shall, to the maximum extent practicable, also include a brief description and evaluation of those activities (whether public or private) which, in the opinion of the Secretary, if undertaken may adversely modify such habitat, or may be affected by such designation.

**(c) Lists**

(1) The Secretary of the Interior shall publish in the Federal Register a list of all species determined by him or the Secretary of Commerce to be endangered species and a list of all species determined by him or the Secretary of Commerce to be threatened species. Each list shall refer to the species contained therein by scientific and common name or names, if any, specify with respect to each such species over what portion of its range it is endangered or threatened, and specify any critical habitat within such range. The Secretary shall from time to time revise each list published under the authority of this subsection to reflect recent determinations, designations, and revisions made in accordance with subsections (a) and (b) of this section.

(2) The Secretary shall—

(A) conduct, at least once every five years, a review of all species included in a list which is published pursuant to paragraph (1) and which is in effect at the time of such review; and

(B) determine on the basis of such review whether any such species should—

(i) be removed from such list;

(ii) be changed in status from an endangered species to a threatened species; or

(iii) be changed in status from a threatened species to an endangered species.

Each determination under subparagraph (B) shall be made in accordance with the provisions of subsections (a) and (b) of this section.

**(d) Protective regulations**

Whenever any species is listed as a threatened species pursuant to subsection (c) of this section, the Secretary shall issue such regulations as he deems necessary and advisable to provide for the conservation of such species. The Secretary may by regulation prohibit with respect to any threatened species any act prohibited under section 1538(a)(1) of this title, in the case of fish or wildlife, or section 1538(a)(2) of this title, in the case of plants, with respect to endangered species; except that with respect to the taking of resident species of fish or wildlife, such regulations shall apply in any State which has entered into a cooperative agreement pursuant to section 1535(c) of this title only to the extent that such regulations have also been adopted by such State.

**(e) Similarity of appearance cases**

The Secretary may, by regulation of commerce or taking, and to the extent he deems advisable, treat any species as an endangered species or threatened species even though it is not listed pursuant to this section if he finds that—

(A) such species so closely resembles in appearance, at the point in question, a species which has been listed pursuant to such section that enforcement personnel would have substantial difficulty in attempting to differentiate between the listed and unlisted species;

(B) the effect of this substantial difficulty is an additional threat to an endangered or threatened species; and

(C) such treatment of an unlisted species will substantially facilitate the enforcement and further the policy of this chapter.

**(f) Recovery plans**

(1) The Secretary shall develop and implement plans (hereinafter in this subsection referred to as "recovery plans") for the conservation and survival of endangered species and threatened species listed pursuant to this section, unless he finds that such a plan will not promote the conservation of the species. The Secretary, in developing and implementing recovery plans, shall, to the maximum extent practicable—

(A) give priority to those endangered species or threatened species, without regard to taxonomic classification, that are most likely to benefit from such plans, particularly those species that are, or may be, in conflict with construction or other development projects or other forms of economic activity;

(B) incorporate in each plan—

(i) a description of such site-specific management actions as may be necessary to achieve the plan's goal for the conservation and survival of the species;

(ii) objective, measurable criteria which, when met, would result in a determination, in accordance with the provisions of this section, that the species be removed from the list; and

(iii) estimates of the time required and the cost to carry out those measures needed to achieve the plan's goal and to achieve intermediate steps toward that goal.

(2) The Secretary, in developing and implementing recovery plans, may procure the services of appropriate public and private agencies and institutions, and other qualified persons. Recovery teams appointed pursuant to this subsection shall not be subject to the Federal Advisory Committee Act.

(3) The Secretary shall report every two years to the Committee on Environment and Public Works of the Senate and the Committee on Merchant Marine and Fisheries of the House of Representatives on the status of efforts to develop and implement recovery plans for all species listed pursuant to this section and on the status of all species for which such plans have been developed.

(4) The Secretary shall, prior to final approval of a new or revised recovery plan, provide public notice and an opportunity for public review and comment on such plan. The Secretary shall consider all information presented during the public comment period prior to approval of the plan.

(5) Each Federal agency shall, prior to implementation of a new or revised recovery plan, consider all information presented during the public comment period under paragraph (4).

**(g) Monitoring**

(1) The Secretary shall implement a system in cooperation with the States to monitor effectively for not less than five years the status of all species which have recovered to the point at which the measures provided pursuant to this chapter are no longer necessary and which, in accordance with the provisions of this section, have been removed from either of the lists published under subsection (c) of this section.

(2) The Secretary shall make prompt use of the authority under paragraph 7 [1] of subsection (b) of this section to prevent a significant risk to the well being of any such recovered species.

**(h) Agency guidelines; publication in Federal Register; scope; proposals and amendments: notice and opportunity for comments**

The Secretary shall establish, and publish in the Federal Register, agency guidelines to insure that the purposes of this section are achieved efficiently and effectively. Such guidelines shall include, but are not limited to—

(1) procedures for recording the receipt and the disposition of petitions submitted under subsection (b)(3) of this section;

(2) criteria for making the findings required under such subsection with respect to petitions;

(3) a ranking system to assist in the identification of species that should receive priority review under subsection (a)(1) of this section; and

(4) a system for developing and implementing, on a priority basis, recovery plans under subsection (f) of this section.

The Secretary shall provide to the public notice of, and opportunity to submit written comments on, any guideline (including any amendment thereto) proposed to be established under this subsection.

**(i) Submission to State agency of justification for regulations inconsistent with State agency's comments or petition**

If, in the case of any regulation proposed by the Secretary under the authority of this section, a State agency to which notice thereof was given in accordance with subsection (b)(5)(A)(ii) of this section files comments disagreeing with all or part of the proposed regulation, and the Secretary issues a final regulation which is in conflict with such comments, or if the Secretary fails to adopt a regulation pursuant to an action petitioned by a State agency under subsection (b)(3) of this section, the Secretary shall submit to the State agency a written justification for his failure to adopt regulations consistent with the agency's comments or petition.

(Pub.L. 93–205, § 4, Dec. 28, 1973, 87 Stat. 886; Pub.L. 94–359, § 1, July 12, 1976, 90 Stat. 911; Pub.L. 95–632, §§ 11, 13, Nov. 10, 1978, 92 Stat. 3764, 3766; Pub.L. 96–159, § 3, Dec. 28, 1979, 93 Stat. 1225; Pub.L. 97–304, § 2(a), Oct. 13, 1982, 96 Stat. 1411; Pub.L. 100–478, Title I, §§ 1002 to 1004, Oct. 7, 1988, 102 Stat. 2306; Pub.L. 108–136, Div. A, Title III, § 318, Nov. 24, 2003, 117 Stat. 1433.)

[1] So in original. Probably should be "paragraph (7)".

## HISTORICAL AND STATUTORY NOTES

**References in Text**

Reorganization Plan No. 4 of 1970, referred to in subsec. (a)(2),is Reorg. Plan No. 4 of 1970, eff. Oct. 3, 1970, 35 F.R. 15627, 84 Stat. 2090, which is set out in the Appendix to Title 5, Government Organization and Employees.

This chapter, referred to in subsecs. (b)(3)(B)(iii)(II), (4), (8), (e)(C) and (g)(1), in the original read "this Act", meaning the Endangered Species Act of 1973, which is classified principally to this chapter. For complete classification, see Short Title note set out under section 1531 of this title and Tables.

The Federal Advisory Committee Act, referred to in subsec. (f)(2), is set out in Appendix 2 to Title 5, Government Organization and Employees.

**Effective and Applicability Provisions**

1982 Acts

Section 2(b) of Pub.L. 97–304 provided that:

"(1) Any petition filed under section 4(c)(2) of the Endangered Species Act of 1973 [subsec. (c)(2) of this section] (as in effect on the day before the date of the enactment of this Act) [Oct. 13, 1982] and any regulation proposed under section 4(f) of such Act of 1973 [subsec. (f) of this section] (as in effect on such day) that is pending on such date of enactment [Oct. 13, 1982] shall be treated as having been filed or proposed on such date of enactment [Oct. 13, 1982] under section 4(b) of such Act of 1973 [subsec. (b) of this section] (as amended by subsection (a)); and the procedural requirements specified in such section 4(b) [subsec. (b) of this section] (as so amended) regarding such petition or proposed regulation shall be deemed to be complied with to the extent that like requirements under such section 4 [this section] (as in effect before the date of the enactment of this Act) [Oct. 13, 1982] were complied with before such date of enactment [Oct. 13, 1982].

"(2) Any regulation proposed after, or pending on, the date of the enactment of this Act [Oct. 13, 1982] to designate critical habitat for a species that was determined before such date of enactment [Oct. 13, 1982] to be endangered or threatened shall be subject to the procedures set forth in section 4 of such Act of 1973 [this section] (as amended by subsection (a)) for regulations proposing revisions to critical habitat instead of those for regulations proposing the designation of critical habitat.

"(3) Any list of endangered species or threatened species (as in effect under section 4(c) of such Act of 1973 [subsec. (c) of this section] on the day before the date of the enactment of this Act) [Oct. 13, 1982] shall remain in effect unless and until determinations regarding species and designations and revisions of critical habitats that require changes to such list are made in accordance with subsection (b)(5) of such Act of 1973 [subsec. (b)(5) of this section] (as added by subsection (a)).

"(4) Section 4(a)(3)(A) of such Act of 1973 [subsec. (a)(3)(A) of this section] (as added by subsection (a)) shall not apply with respect to any species which was listed as an endangered species or a threatened species before November 10, 1978."

1973 Acts

Section effective Dec. 28, 1973, see section 16 of Pub.L. 93–205, set out as an Effective Date note under section 1531 of this title.

**Abolition of House Committee on Merchant Marine and Fisheries**

Committee on Merchant Marine and Fisheries of House of Representatives abolished and any reference in any provision of law enacted before Jan. 4, 1995, to the Committee on Merchant Marine and Fisheries of the House of Representatives treated as referring to the Committee on Agriculture of the House of Representatives, in the case of a provision of law relating to inspection of seafood or seafood products, the Committee on National Security of the House of Representatives, in the case of a provision of law relating to interoceanic canals, the Merchant Marine Academy and State Maritime Academies, or national security aspects of merchant marine, the Committee on Resources of the House of Representatives, in the case of a provision of law relating to fisheries, wildlife, international fishing agreements marine affairs (including coastal zone management) except for measures relating to oil and other pollution of navigable waters, or oceanography, the Committee on Science of the House of Representatives, in the case of a provision of law relating to marine research, and the Committee on Transportation and Infrastructure of the House of Representatives, in the case of a provision of law relating to a matter other than a matter described above, see section 1(b)(3) of Pub.L. 104–14, set out as a note preceding section 21 of Title 2, The Congress.

## § 1534. Land acquisition

**[ESA § 5]**

### (a) Implementation of conservation program; authorization of Secretary and Secretary of Agriculture

The Secretary, and the Secretary of Agriculture with respect to the National Forest System, shall establish and implement a program to conserve fish, wildlife, and plants, including those which are listed as endangered species or threatened species pursuant to section 1533 of this title. To carry out such a program, the appropriate Secretary—

(1) shall utilize the land acquisition and other authority under the Fish and Wildlife Act of 1956, as amended [16 U.S.C.A. § 742a et seq.], the Fish and Wildlife Coordination Act, as amended [16 U.S.C.A. § 661 et seq.], and the Migratory Bird Conservation Act [16 U.S.C.A. § 715 et seq.], as appropriate; and

(2) is authorized to acquire by purchase, donation, or otherwise, lands, waters, or interest therein, and such authority shall be in addition to any other land acquisition authority vested in him.

### (b) Availability of funds for acquisition of lands, waters, etc.

Funds made available pursuant to the Land and Water Conservation Fund Act of 1965, as amended [16 U.S.C.A. § 460*l*–4 et seq.], may be used for the purpose of acquiring lands, waters, or interests therein under subsection (a) of this section.

(Pub.L. 93–205, § 5, Dec. 28, 1973, 87 Stat. 889; Pub.L. 95–632, § 12, Nov. 10, 1978, 92 Stat. 3766.)

### HISTORICAL AND STATUTORY NOTES

**References in Text**

The Fish and Wildlife Act of 1956, as amended, referred to in subsec. (a)(1), is classified generally to sections 742a to 742d and 742e to 742j–2 of this title. For complete classification, see Short Title note set out under section 742a of this title and Tables.

The Fish and Wildlife Coordination Act, as amended, referred to in subsec. (a)(1), is classified generally to sections

661 to 666c of this title. For complete classification, see Short Title note set out under section 661 of this title and Tables volume.

The Migratory Bird Conservation Act, referred to in subsec. (a)(1), is classified generally to subchapter III of chapter 7 of this title (16 U.S.C.A. § 715 et seq.). For complete classification, see section 715 of this title and Tables volume.

The Land and Water Conservation Fund Act of 1965, as amended, referred to in subsec. (b), is classified to section 460*l*–4 et seq. of this title. For complete classification, see Short Title note set out under section 460*l*–4 of this title and Tables volume.

**Effective and Applicability Provisions**

1973 Acts

Section effective Dec. 28, 1973, see section 16 of Pub.L. 93–205, set out as an Effective Date note under section 1531 of this title.

## § 1535. Cooperation with States [ESA § 6]

**(a) Generally**

In carrying out the program authorized by this chapter, the Secretary shall cooperate to the maximum extent practicable with the States. Such cooperation shall include consultation with the States concerned before acquiring any land or water, or interest therein, for the purpose of conserving any endangered species or threatened species.

**(b) Management agreements**

The Secretary may enter into agreements with any State for the administration and management of any area established for the conservation of endangered species or threatened species. Any revenues derived from the administration of such areas under these agreements shall be subject to the provisions of section 715s of this title.

**(c) Cooperative agreements**

(1) In furtherance of the purposes of this chapter, the Secretary is authorized to enter into a cooperative agreement in accordance with this section with any State which establishes and maintains an adequate and active program for the conservation of endangered species and threatened species. Within one hundred and twenty days after the Secretary receives a certified copy of such a proposed State program, he shall make a determination whether such program is in accordance with this chapter. Unless he determines, pursuant to this paragraph, that the State program is not in accordance with this chapter, he shall enter into a cooperative agreement with the State for the purpose of assisting in implementation of the State program. In order for a State program to be deemed an adequate and active program for the conservation of endangered species and threatened species, the Secretary must find, and annually thereafter reconfirm such finding, that under the State program—

(A) authority resides in the State agency to conserve resident species of fish or wildlife determined by the State agency or the Secretary to be endangered or threatened;

(B) the State agency has established acceptable conservation programs, consistent with the purposes and policies of this chapter, for all resident species of fish or wildlife in the State which are deemed by the Secretary to be endangered or threatened, and has furnished a copy of such plan and program together with all pertinent details, information, and data requested to the Secretary;

(C) the State agency is authorized to conduct investigations to determine the status and requirements for survival of resident species of fish and wildlife;

(D) the State agency is authorized to establish programs, including the acquisition of land or aquatic habitat or interests therein, for the conservation of resident endangered or threatened species of fish or wildlife; and

(E) provision is made for public participation in designating resident species of fish or wildlife as endangered or threatened; or

that under the State program—

(i) the requirements set forth in subparagraphs (C), (D), and (E) of this paragraph are complied with, and

(ii) plans are included under which immediate attention will be given to those resident species of fish and wildlife which are determined by the Secretary or the State agency to be endangered or threatened and which the Secretary and the State agency agree are most urgently in need of conservation programs; except that a cooperative agreement entered into with a State whose program is deemed adequate and active pursuant to clause (i) and this clause shall not affect the applicability of prohibitions set forth in or authorized pursuant to section 1533(d) of this title or section 1538(a) (1) of this title with respect to the taking of any resident endangered or threatened species.

(2) In furtherance of the purposes of this chapter, the Secretary is authorized to enter into a cooperative agreement in accordance with this section with any State which establishes and maintains an adequate and active program for the conservation of endangered species and threatened species of plants. Within one hundred and twenty days after the Secretary receives a certified copy of such a proposed State program, he shall make a determination whether such program is in accordance with this chapter. Unless he determines, pursuant to this paragraph, that the

State program is not in accordance with this chapter, he shall enter into a cooperative agreement with the State for the purpose of assisting in implementation of the State program. In order for a State program to be deemed an adequate and active program for the conservation of endangered species of plants and threatened species of plants, the Secretary must find, and annually thereafter reconfirm such finding, that under the State program—

**(A)** authority resides in the State agency to conserve resident species of plants determined by the State agency or the Secretary to be endangered or threatened;

**(B)** the State agency has established acceptable conservation programs, consistent with the purposes and policies of this chapter, for all resident species of plants in the State which are deemed by the Secretary to be endangered or threatened, and has furnished a copy of such plan and program together with all pertinent details, information, and data requested to the Secretary;

**(C)** the State agency is authorized to conduct investigations to determine the status and requirements for survival of resident species of plants; and

**(D)** provision is made for public participation in designating resident species of plants as endangered or threatened; or

that under the State program—

**(i)** the requirements set forth in subparagraphs (C) and (D) of this paragraph are complied with, and

**(ii)** plans are included under which immediate attention will be given to those resident species of plants which are determined by the Secretary or the State agency to be endangered or threatened and which the Secretary and the State agency agree are most urgently in need of conservation programs; except that a cooperative agreement entered into with a State whose program is deemed adequate and active pursuant to clause (i) and this clause shall not affect the applicability of prohibitions set forth in or authorized pursuant to section 1533(d) or section 1538(a)(1) of this title with respect to the taking of any resident endangered or threatened species.

**(d) Allocation of funds**

**(1)** The Secretary is authorized to provide financial assistance to any State, through its respective State agency, which has entered into a cooperative agreement pursuant to subsection (c) of this section to assist in development of programs for the conservation of endangered and threatened species or to assist in monitoring the status of candidate species pursuant to subparagraph (C) of section 1533(b)(3) of this title and recovered species pursuant to section 1533(g) of this title. The Secretary shall allocate each annual appropriation made in accordance with the provisions of subsection (i) of this section to such States based on consideration of—

**(A)** the international commitments of the United States to protect endangered species or threatened species;

**(B)** the readiness of a State to proceed with a conservation program consistent with the objectives and purposes of this chapter;

**(C)** the number of endangered species and threatened species within a State;

**(D)** the potential for restoring endangered species and threatened species within a State;

**(E)** the relative urgency to initiate a program to restore and protect an endangered species or threatened species in terms of survival of the species;

**(F)** the importance of monitoring the status of candidate species within a State to prevent a significant risk to the well being of any such species; and

**(G)** the importance of monitoring the status of recovered species within a State to assure that such species do not return to the point at which the measures provided pursuant to this chapter are again necessary.

So much of the annual appropriation made in accordance with provisions of subsection (i) of this section allocated for obligation to any State for any fiscal year as remains unobligated at the close thereof is authorized to be made available to that State until the close of the succeeding fiscal year. Any amount allocated to any State which is unobligated at the end of the period during which it is available for expenditure is authorized to be made available for expenditure by the Secretary in conducting programs under this section.

**(2)** Such cooperative agreements shall provide for (A) the actions to be taken by the Secretary and the States; (B) the benefits that are expected to be derived in connection with the conservation of endangered or threatened species; (C) the estimated cost of these actions; and (D) the share of such costs to be borne by the Federal Government and by the States; except that—

**(i)** the Federal share of such program costs shall not exceed 75 percent of the estimated program cost stated in the agreement; and

**(ii)** the Federal share may be increased to 90 percent whenever two or more States having a common interest in one or more endangered or threatened species, the conservation of which may be enhanced by cooperation of such States, enter jointly into an agreement with the Secretary.

The Secretary may, in his discretion, and under such rules and regulations as he may prescribe, advance funds to the State for financing the United States pro rata share agreed upon in the cooperative agreement. For the purposes of this section, the non-Federal share may, in the discretion of the Secretary, be in the form of money or real property, the value of which will be determined by the Secretary, whose decision shall be final.

**(e) Review of State programs**

Any action taken by the Secretary under this section shall be subject to his periodic review at no greater than annual intervals.

**(f) Conflicts between Federal and State laws**

Any State law or regulation which applies with respect to the importation or exportation of, or interstate or foreign commerce in, endangered species or threatened species is void to the extent that it may effectively (1) permit what is prohibited by this chapter or by any regulation which implements this chapter, or (2) prohibit what is authorized pursuant to an exemption or permit provided for in this chapter or in any regulation which implements this chapter. This chapter shall not otherwise be construed to void any State law or regulation which is intended to conserve migratory, resident, or introduced fish or wildlife, or to permit or prohibit sale of such fish or wildlife. Any State law or regulation respecting the taking of an endangered species or threatened species may be more restrictive than the exemptions or permits provided for in this chapter or in any regulation which implements this chapter but not less restrictive than the prohibitions so defined.

**(g) Transition**

(1) For purposes of this subsection, the term "establishment period" means, with respect to any State, the period beginning on December 28, 1973 and ending on whichever of the following dates first occurs: (A) the date of the close of the 120-day period following the adjournment of the first regular session of the legislature of such State which commences after December 28, 1973, or (B) the date of the close of the 15-month period following December 28, 1973.

(2) The prohibitions set forth in or authorized pursuant to sections 1533(d) and 1538(a)(1)(B) of this title shall not apply with respect to the taking of any resident endangered species or threatened species (other than species listed in Appendix I to the Convention or otherwise specifically covered by any other treaty or Federal law) within any State—

**(A)** which is then a party to a cooperative agreement with the Secretary pursuant to subsection (c) of this section (except to the extent that the taking of any such species is contrary to the law of such State); or

**(B)** except for any time within the establishment period when—

**(i)** the Secretary applies such prohibition to such species at the request of the State, or

**(ii)** the Secretary applies such prohibition after he finds, and publishes his finding, that an emergency exists posing a significant risk to the well-being of such species and that the prohibition must be applied to protect such species. The Secretary's finding and publication may be made without regard to the public hearing or comment provisions of section 553 of Title 5 or any other provision of this chapter; but such prohibition shall expire 90 days after the date of its imposition unless the Secretary further extends such prohibition by publishing notice and a statement of justification of such extension.

**(h) Regulations**

The Secretary is authorized to promulgate such regulations as may be appropriate to carry out the provisions of this section relating to financial assistance to States.

**(i) Appropriations**

(1) To carry out the provisions of this section for fiscal years after September 30, 1988, there shall be deposited into a special fund known as the cooperative endangered species conservation fund, to be administered by the Secretary, an amount equal to 5 percent of the combined amounts covered each fiscal year into the Federal aid to wildlife restoration fund under section 669b of this title, and paid, transferred, or otherwise credited each fiscal year to the Sport Fishing Restoration Account established under 1016 of the Act of July 18, 1984.

(2) Amounts deposited into the special fund are authorized to be appropriated annually and allocated in accordance with subsection (d) of this section.

(Pub.L. 93–205, § 6, Dec. 28, 1973, 87 Stat. 889; Pub.L. 95–212, Dec. 19, 1977, 91 Stat. 1493; Pub.L. 95–632, § 10, Nov. 10, 1978, 92 Stat. 3762; Pub.L. 96–246, May 23, 1980, 94 Stat. 348; Pub.L. 97–304, §§ 3, 8(b), Oct. 13, 1982, 96 Stat. 1416, 1426; Pub.L. 100–478, Title I, § 1005, Oct. 7, 1988, 102 Stat. 2307.)

## HISTORICAL AND STATUTORY NOTES

**References in Text**

This chapter, referred to in subsecs. (a), (c), (d)(1)(B), (G), (f), and (g)(2)(B)(ii), in the original read "this Act", meaning the Endangered Species Act of 1973, which is classified principally to this chapter. For complete classification, see Short Title note set out under section 1531 of this title and Tables.

Section 1016 of the Act of July 18, 1984, referred to in subsec. (i), probably means Pub.L. 98–369, Div. A, Title X,

§ 1016, July 18, 1984, 98 Stat. 1019, which enacted section 9504 of Title 26, Internal Revenue Code, amended section 9503 of Title 26, repealed section 13107 of Title 46, Shipping, and enacted provisions set out as a note under section 9504 of Title 26.

**Effective and Applicability Provisions**

1973 Acts

Section effective Dec. 28, 1973, see section 16 of Pub.L. 93–205, set out as an Effective Date note under section 1531 of this title.

**Cooperative Agreements With States Unaffected by 1981 Amendment of Marine Mammal Protection Act**

Nothing in the amendment of section 109 of the Marine Mammal Protection Act of 1972 [section 1379 of this title] by section 4(a) of Pub.L. 97–58 to be construed as affecting in any manner, or to any extent, any cooperative agreement entered into by a State under subsec. (c) of this section before, on, or after Oct. 9, 1981, see section 4(b) of Pub.L. 97–58, set out as a note under section 1379 of this title.

## § 1536. Interagency cooperation

[ESA § 7]

### (a) Federal agency actions and consultations

(1) The Secretary shall review other programs administered by him and utilize such programs in furtherance of the purposes of this chapter. All other Federal agencies shall, in consultation with and with the assistance of the Secretary, utilize their authorities in furtherance of the purposes of this chapter by carrying out programs for the conservation of endangered species and threatened species listed pursuant to section 1533 of this title.

(2) Each Federal agency shall, in consultation with and with the assistance of the Secretary, insure that any action authorized, funded, or carried out by such agency (hereinafter in this section referred to as an "agency action") is not likely to jeopardize the continued existence of any endangered species or threatened species or result in the destruction or adverse modification of habitat of such species which is determined by the Secretary, after consultation as appropriate with affected States, to be critical, unless such agency has been granted an exemption for such action by the Committee pursuant to subsection (h) of this section. In fulfilling the requirements of this paragraph each agency shall use the best scientific and commercial data available.

(3) Subject to such guidelines as the Secretary may establish, a Federal agency shall consult with the Secretary on any prospective agency action at the request of, and in cooperation with, the prospective permit or license applicant if the applicant has reason to believe that an endangered species or a threatened species may be present in the area affected by his project and that implementation of such action will likely affect such species.

(4) Each Federal agency shall confer with the Secretary on any agency action which is likely to jeopardize the continued existence of any species proposed to be listed under section 1533 of this title or result in the destruction or adverse modification of critical habitat proposed to be designated for such species. This paragraph does not require a limitation on the commitment of resources as described in subsection (d) of this section.

### (b) Opinion of Secretary

(1)(A) Consultation under subsection (a) (2) of this section with respect to any agency action shall be concluded within the 90-day period beginning on the date on which initiated or, subject to subparagraph (B), within such other period of time as is mutually agreeable to the Secretary and the Federal agency.

(B) In the case of an agency action involving a permit or license applicant, the Secretary and the Federal agency may not mutually agree to conclude consultation within a period exceeding 90 days unless the Secretary, before the close of the 90th day referred to in subparagraph (A)—

(i) if the consultation period proposed to be agreed to will end before the 150th day after the date on which consultation was initiated, submits to the applicant a written statement setting forth—

(I) the reasons why a longer period is required,

(II) the information that is required to complete the consultation, and

(III) the estimated date on which consultation will be completed; or

(ii) if the consultation period proposed to be agreed to will end 150 or more days after the date on which consultation was initiated, obtains the consent of the applicant to such period.

The Secretary and the Federal agency may mutually agree to extend a consultation period established under the preceding sentence if the Secretary, before the close of such period, obtains the consent of the applicant to the extension.

(2) Consultation under subsection (a) (3) of this section shall be concluded within such period as is agreeable to the Secretary, the Federal agency, and the applicant concerned.

(3)(A) Promptly after conclusion of consultation under paragraph (2) or (3) of subsection (a) of this section, the Secretary shall provide to the Federal agency and the applicant, if any, a written statement setting forth the Secretary's opinion, and a summary of the information on which the opinion is based, detailing how the agency action affects the species or its critical habitat. If jeopardy or adverse modification is found, the Secretary shall suggest those reasonable and prudent alternatives which he believes would not violate subsection (a) (2) of this section and can be taken by the Federal agency or applicant in implementing the agency action.

**(B)** Consultation under subsection (a) (3) of this section, and an opinion issued by the Secretary incident to such consultation, regarding an agency action shall be treated respectively as a consultation under subsection (a) (2) of this section, and as an opinion issued after consultation under such subsection, regarding that action if the Secretary reviews the action before it is commenced by the Federal agency and finds, and notifies such agency, that no significant changes have been made with respect to the action and that no significant change has occurred regarding the information used during the initial consultation.

**(4)** If after consultation under subsection (a)(2) of this section, the Secretary concludes that—

**(A)** the agency action will not violate such subsection, or offers reasonable and prudent alternatives which the Secretary believes would not violate such subsection;

**(B)** the taking of an endangered species or a threatened species incidental to the agency action will not violate such subsection; and

**(C)** if an endangered species or threatened species of a marine mammal is involved, the taking is authorized pursuant to section 1371(a)(5) of this title;

the Secretary shall provide the Federal agency and the applicant concerned, if any, with a written statement that—

**(i)** specifies the impact of such incidental taking on the species,

**(ii)** specifies those reasonable and prudent measures that the Secretary considers necessary or appropriate to minimize such impact,

**(iii)** in the case of marine mammals, specifies those measures that are necessary to comply with section 1371(a)(5) of this title with regard to such taking, and

**(iv)** sets forth the terms and conditions (including, but not limited to, reporting requirements) that must be complied with by the Federal agency or applicant (if any), or both, to implement the measures specified under clauses (ii) and (iii).

**(c) Biological assessment**

**(1)** To facilitate compliance with the requirements of subsection (a) (2) of this section, each Federal agency shall, with respect to any agency action of such agency for which no contract for construction has been entered into and for which no construction has begun on November 10, 1978, request of the Secretary information whether any species which is listed or proposed to be listed may be present in the area of such proposed action. If the Secretary advises, based on the best scientific and commercial data available, that such species may be present, such agency shall conduct a biological assessment for the purpose of identifying any endangered species or threatened species which is likely to be affected by such action. Such assessment shall be completed within 180 days after the date on which initiated (or within such other period as is mutually agreed to by the Secretary and such agency, except that if a permit or license applicant is involved, the 180-day period may not be extended unless such agency provides the applicant, before the close of such period, with a written statement setting forth the estimated length of the proposed extension and the reasons therefor) and, before any contract for construction is entered into and before construction is begun with respect to such action. Such assessment may be undertaken as part of a Federal agency's compliance with the requirements of section 102 of the National Environmental Policy Act of 1969 (42 U.S.C. 4332).

**(2)** Any person who may wish to apply for an exemption under subsection (g) of this section for that action may conduct a biological assessment to identify any endangered species or threatened species which is likely to be affected by such action. Any such biological assessment must, however, be conducted in cooperation with the Secretary and under the supervision of the appropriate Federal agency.

**(d) Limitation on commitment of resources**

After initiation of consultation required under subsection (a) (2) of this section, the Federal agency and the permit or license applicant shall not make any irreversible or irretrievable commitment of resources with respect to the agency action which has the effect of foreclosing the formulation or implementation of any reasonable and prudent alternative measures which would not violate subsection (a) (2) of this section.

**(e) Endangered Species Committee**

**(1)** There is established a committee to be known as the Endangered Species Committee (hereinafter in this section referred to as the "Committee").

**(2)** The Committee shall review any application submitted to it pursuant to this section and determine in accordance with subsection (h) of this section whether or not to grant an exemption from the requirements of subsection (a) (2) of this section for the action set forth in such application.

**(3)** The Committee shall be composed of seven members as follows:

**(A)** The Secretary of Agriculture.

**(B)** The Secretary of the Army.

(C) The Chairman of the Council of Economic Advisors.

(D) The Administrator of the Environmental Protection Agency.

(E) The Secretary of the Interior.

(F) The Administrator of the National Oceanic and Atmospheric Administration.

(G) The President, after consideration of any recommendations received pursuant to subsection (g) (2) (B) of this section shall appoint one individual from each affected State, as determined by the Secretary, to be a member of the Committee for the consideration of the application for exemption for an agency action with respect to which such recommendations are made, not later than 30 days after an application is submitted pursuant to this section.

(4)(A) Members of the Committee shall receive no additional pay on account of their service on the Committee.

(B) While away from their homes or regular places of business in the performance of services for the Committee, members of the Committee shall be allowed travel expenses, including per diem in lieu of subsistence, in the same manner as persons employed intermittently in the Government service are allowed expenses under section 5703 of Title 5.

(5)(A) Five members of the Committee or their representatives shall constitute a quorum for the transaction of any function of the Committee, except that, in no case shall any representative be considered in determining the existence of a quorum for the transaction of any function of the Committee if that function involves a vote by the Committee on any matter before the Committee.

(B) The Secretary of the Interior shall be the Chairman of the Committee.

(C) The Committee shall meet at the call of the Chairman or five of its members.

(D) All meetings and records of the Committee shall be open to the public.

(6) Upon request of the Committee, the head of any Federal agency is authorized to detail, on a nonreimbursable basis, any of the personnel of such agency to the Committee to assist it in carrying out its duties under this section.

(7)(A) The Committee may for the purpose of carrying out its duties under this section hold such hearings, sit and act at such times and places, take such testimony, and receive such evidence, as the Committee deems advisable.

(B) When so authorized by the Committee, any member or agent of the Committee may take any action which the Committee is authorized to take by this paragraph.

(C) Subject to the Privacy Act [5 U.S.C.A. § 552a], the Committee may secure directly from any Federal agency information necessary to enable it to carry out its duties under this section. Upon request of the Chairman of the Committee, the head of such Federal agency shall furnish such information to the Committee.

(D) The Committee may use the United States mails in the same manner and upon the same conditions as a Federal agency.

(E) The Administrator of General Services shall provide to the Committee on a reimbursable basis such administrative support services as the Committee may request.

(8) In carrying out its duties under this section, the Committee may promulgate and amend such rules, regulations, and procedures, and issue and amend such orders as it deems necessary.

(9) For the purpose of obtaining information necessary for the consideration of an application for an exemption under this section the Committee may issue subpenas for the attendance and testimony of witnesses and the production of relevant papers, books, and documents.

(10) In no case shall any representative, including a representative of a member designated pursuant to paragraph (3) (G) of this subsection, be eligible to cast a vote on behalf of any member.

**(f) Promulgation of regulations; form and contents of exemption application**

Not later than 90 days after November 10, 1978, the Secretary shall promulgate regulations which set forth the form and manner in which applications for exemption shall be submitted to the Secretary and the information to be contained in such applications. Such regulations shall require that information submitted in an application by the head of any Federal agency with respect to any agency action include, but not be limited to—

(1) a description of the consultation process carried out pursuant to subsection (a) (2) of this section between the head of the Federal agency and the Secretary; and

(2) a statement describing why such action cannot be altered or modified to conform with the requirements of subsection (a) (2) of this section.

**(g) Application for exemption; report to Committee**

(1) A Federal agency, the Governor of the State in which an agency action will occur, if any, or a permit or license applicant may apply to the Secretary for an exemption for an agency action of such agency if, after consultation under subsection (a) (2) of this section, the Secretary's opinion under subsection (b) of this

section indicates that the agency action would violate subsection (a) (2) of this section. An application for an exemption shall be considered initially by the Secretary in the manner provided for in this subsection, and shall be considered by the Committee for a final determination under subsection (h) of this section after a report is made pursuant to paragraph (5). The applicant for an exemption shall be referred to as the "exemption applicant" in this section.

**(2)(A)** An exemption applicant shall submit a written application to the Secretary, in a form prescribed under subsection (f) of this section, not later than 90 days after the completion of the consultation process; except that, in the case of any agency action involving a permit or license applicant, such application shall be submitted not later than 90 days after the date on which the Federal agency concerned takes final agency action with respect to the issuance of the permit or license. For purposes of the preceding sentence, the term "final agency action" means (i) a disposition by an agency with respect to the issuance of a permit or license that is subject to administrative review, whether or not such disposition is subject to judicial review; or (ii) if administrative review is sought with respect to such disposition, the decision resulting after such review. Such application shall set forth the reasons why the exemption applicant considers that the agency action meets the requirements for an exemption under this subsection.

**(B)** Upon receipt of an application for exemption for an agency action under paragraph (1), the Secretary shall promptly (i) notify the Governor of each affected State, if any, as determined by the Secretary, and request the Governors so notified to recommend individuals to be appointed to the Endangered Species Committee for consideration of such application; and (ii) publish notice of receipt of the application in the Federal Register, including a summary of the information contained in the application and a description of the agency action with respect to which the application for exemption has been filed.

**(3)** The Secretary shall within 20 days after the receipt of an application for exemption, or within such other period of time as is mutually agreeable to the exemption applicant and the Secretary—

**(A)** determine that the Federal agency concerned and the exemption applicant have—

**(i)** carried out the consultation responsibilities described in subsection (a) of this section in good faith and made a reasonable and responsible effort to develop and fairly consider modifications or reasonable and prudent alternatives to the proposed agency action which would not violate subsection (a) (2) of this section;

**(ii)** conducted any biological assessment required by subsection (c) of this section; and

**(iii)** to the extent determinable within the time provided herein, refrained from making any irreversible or irretrievable commitment of resources prohibited by subsection (d) of this section; or

**(B)** deny the application for exemption because the Federal agency concerned or the exemption applicant have not met the requirements set forth in subparagraph (A) (i), (ii), and (iii).

The denial of an application under subparagraph (B) shall be considered final agency action for purposes of chapter 7 of Title 5.

**(4)** If the Secretary determines that the Federal agency concerned and the exemption applicant have met the requirements set forth in paragraph (3) (A) (i), (ii), and (iii) he shall, in consultation with the Members of the Committee, hold a hearing on the application for exemption in accordance with sections 554, 555, and 556 (other than subsection (b) (1) and (2) thereof) of Title 5 and prepare the report to be submitted pursuant to paragraph (5).

**(5)** Within 140 days after making the determinations under paragraph (3) or within such other period of time as is mutually agreeable to the exemption applicant and the Secretary, the Secretary shall submit to the Committee a report discussing—

**(A)** the availability of reasonable and prudent alternatives to the agency action, and the nature and extent of the benefits of the agency action and of alternative courses of action consistent with conserving the species or the critical habitat;

**(B)** a summary of the evidence concerning whether or not the agency action is in the public interest and is of national or regional significance;

**(C)** appropriate reasonable mitigation and enhancement measures which should be considered by the Committee; and

**(D)** whether the Federal agency concerned and the exemption applicant refrained from making any irreversible or irretrievable commitment of resources prohibited by subsection (d) of this section.

**(6)** To the extent practicable within the time required for action under subsection (g) of this section, and except to the extent inconsistent with the requirements of this section, the consideration of any application for an exemption under this section and the conduct of any hearing under this subsection shall be in accordance with sections 554, 555, and 556 (other than subsection (b) (3) of section 556) of Title 5.

**(7)** Upon request of the Secretary, the head of any Federal agency is authorized to detail, on a nonreimbursable basis, any of the personnel of such agency to the Secretary to assist him in carrying out his duties under this section.

(8) All meetings and records resulting from activities pursuant to this subsection shall be open to the public.

**(h) Grant of exemption**

(1) The Committee shall make a final determination whether or not to grant an exemption within 30 days after receiving the report of the Secretary pursuant to subsection (g) (5) of this section. The Committee shall grant an exemption from the requirements of subsection (a) (2) of this section for an agency action if, by a vote of not less than five of its members voting in person—

(A) it determines on the record, based on the report of the Secretary, the record of the hearing held under subsection (g) (4) of this section and on such other testimony or evidence as it may receive, that—

(i) there are no reasonable and prudent alternatives to the agency action;

(ii) the benefits of such action clearly outweigh the benefits of alternative courses of action consistent with conserving the species or its critical habitat, and such action is in the public interest;

(iii) the action is of regional or national significance; and

(iv) neither the Federal agency concerned nor the exemption applicant made any irreversible or irretrievable commitment of resources prohibited by subsection (d) of this section; and

(B) it establishes such reasonable mitigation and enhancement measures, including, but not limited to, live propagation, transplantation, and habitat acquisition and improvement, as are necessary and appropriate to minimize the adverse effects of the agency action upon the endangered species, threatened species, or critical habitat concerned.

Any final determination by the Committee under this subsection shall be considered final agency action for purposes of chapter 7 of Title 5.

(2)(A) Except as provided in subparagraph (B), an exemption for an agency action granted under paragraph (1) shall constitute a permanent exemption with respect to all endangered or threatened species for the purposes of completing such agency action—

(i) regardless whether the species was identified in the biological assessment; and

(ii) only if a biological assessment has been conducted under subsection (c) of this section with respect to such agency action.

(B) An exemption shall be permanent under subparagraph (A) unless—

(i) the Secretary finds, based on the best scientific and commercial data available, that such exemption would result in the extinction of a species that was not the subject of consultation under subsection (a) (2) of this section or was not identified in any biological assessment conducted under subsection (c) of this section, and

(ii) the Committee determines within 60 days after the date of the Secretary's finding that the exemption should not be permanent.

If the Secretary makes a finding described in clause (i), the Committee shall meet with respect to the matter within 30 days after the date of the finding.

**(i) Review by Secretary of State; violation of international treaty or other international obligation of United States**

Notwithstanding any other provision of this chapter, the Committee shall be prohibited from considering for exemption any application made to it, if the Secretary of State, after a review of the proposed agency action and its potential implications, and after hearing, certifies, in writing, to the Committee within 60 days of any application made under this section that the granting of any such exemption and the carrying out of such action would be in violation of an international treaty obligation or other international obligation of the United States. The Secretary of State shall, at the time of such certification, publish a copy thereof in the Federal Register.

**(j) Exemption for national security reasons**

Notwithstanding any other provision of this chapter, the Committee shall grant an exemption for any agency action if the Secretary of Defense finds that such exemption is necessary for reasons of national security.

**(k) Exemption decision not considered major Federal action; environmental impact statement**

An exemption decision by the Committee under this section shall not be a major Federal action for purposes of the National Environmental Policy Act of 1969 [42 U.S.C.A. § 4321 et seq.]: *Provided*, That an environmental impact statement which discusses the impacts upon endangered species or threatened species or their critical habitats shall have been previously prepared with respect to any agency action exempted by such order.

**(*l*) Committee order granting exemption; cost of mitigation and enhancement measures; report by applicant to Council on Environmental Quality**

(1) If the Committee determines under subsection (h) of this section that an exemption should be granted with respect to any agency action, the Committee shall issue an order granting the exemption and specifying the mitigation and enhancement measures established pursuant to subsection (h) of this section which

shall be carried out and paid for by the exemption applicant in implementing the agency action. All necessary mitigation and enhancement measures shall be authorized prior to the implementing of the agency action and funded concurrently with all other project features.

(2) The applicant receiving such exemption shall include the costs of such mitigation and enhancement measures within the overall costs of continuing the proposed action. Notwithstanding the preceding sentence the costs of such measures shall not be treated as project costs for the purpose of computing benefit-cost or other ratios for the proposed action. Any applicant may request the Secretary to carry out such mitigation and enhancement measures. The costs incurred by the Secretary in carrying out any such measures shall be paid by the applicant receiving the exemption. No later than one year after the granting of an exemption, the exemption applicant shall submit to the Council on Environmental Quality a report describing its compliance with the mitigation and enhancement measures prescribed by this section. Such a report shall be submitted annually until all such mitigation and enhancement measures have been completed. Notice of the public availability of such reports shall be published in the Federal Register by the Council on Environmental Quality.

**(m) Notice requirement for citizen suits not applicable**

The 60-day notice requirement of section 1540(g) of this title shall not apply with respect to review of any final determination of the Committee under subsection (h) of this section granting an exemption from the requirements of subsection (a) (2) of this section.

**(n) Judicial review**

Any person, as defined by section 1532(13) of this title, may obtain judicial review, under chapter 7 of Title 5, of any decision of the Endangered Species Committee under subsection (h) of this section in the United States Court of Appeals for (1) any circuit wherein the agency action concerned will be, or is being, carried out, or (2) in any case in which the agency action will be, or is being, carried out outside of any circuit, the District of Columbia, by filing in such court within 90 days after the date of issuance of the decision, a written petition for review. A copy of such petition shall be transmitted by the clerk of the court to the Committee and the Committee shall file in the court the record in the proceeding, as provided in section 2112, of Title 28. Attorneys designated by the Endangered Species Committee may appear for, and represent the Committee in any action for review under this subsection.

**(*o*) Exemption as providing exception on taking of endangered species**

Notwithstanding sections 1533(d) and 1538(a)(1)(B) and (C) of this title, sections 1371 and 1372 of this title, or any regulation promulgated to implement any such section—

(1) any action for which an exemption is granted under subsection (h) of this section shall not be considered to be a taking of any endangered species or threatened species with respect to any activity which is necessary to carry out such action; and

(2) any taking that is in compliance with the terms and conditions specified in a written statement provided under subsection (b)(4)(iv) of this section shall not be considered to be a prohibited taking of the species concerned.

**(p) Exemptions in Presidentially declared disaster areas**

In any area which has been declared by the President to be a major disaster area under the Disaster Relief and Emergency Assistance Act [42 U.S.C.A. § 5121 et seq.], the President is authorized to make the determinations required by subsections (g) and (h) of this section for any project for the repair or replacement of a public facility substantially as it existed prior to the disaster under section 405 or 406 of the Disaster Relief and Emergency Assistance Act [42 U.S.C.A. §§ 5171 or 5172], and which the President determines (1) is necessary to prevent the recurrence of such a natural disaster and to reduce the potential loss of human life, and (2) to involve an emergency situation which does not allow the ordinary procedures of this section to be followed. Notwithstanding any other provision of this section, the Committee shall accept the determinations of the President under this subsection.

(Pub.L. 93–205, § 7, Dec. 28, 1973, 87 Stat. 892; Pub.L. 95–632, § 3, Nov. 10, 1978, 92 Stat. 3752; Pub.L. 96–159, § 4, Dec. 28, 1979, 93 Stat. 1226; Pub.L. 97–304, §§ 4(a), 8(b), Oct. 13, 1982, 96 Stat. 1417, 1426; Pub.L. 99–659, Title IV, § 411(b), (c), Nov. 14, 1986, 100 Stat. 3742; Pub.L. 100–707, Title I, § 109(g), Nov. 23, 1988, 102 Stat. 4709.)

## HISTORICAL AND STATUTORY NOTES

**References in Text**

This chapter, referred to in subsecs. (a)(1) and (j), in the original read "this Act", meaning the Endangered Species Act of 1973, which is classified principally to this chapter. For complete classification, see Short Title note set out under section 1531 of this title and Tables.

The Privacy Act, referred to in subsec. (e)(7)(C), is enacted section 552a of Title 5, Government Organization and Employees, and provisions set out as notes under section 552a of Title 5. For complete classification, see Short Title note set out under section 552a of Title 5 and Tables volume.

The National Environmental Policy Act of 1969, referred to in subsec. (k), is classified generally to chapter 55 of Title 42 (42 U.S.C.A. § 4321 et seq.). Section 102 of the National Environmental Policy Act of 1969, referred to in subsec. (c)(1), is classified to section 4332 of Title 42. For complete classification, see Short Title note set out under section 4321 of Title 42 and Tables.

The Disaster Relief and Emergency Assistance Act, redesignated "The Robert T. Stafford Disaster Relief and Emergency Assistance Act" by Pub.L. 93–288, § 1, as amended by 100–707, § 102(a), referred to in subsec. (p), is classified principally to chapter 68 of Title 42, (42 U.S.C.A. § 5121 et seq.). Sections 405 and 406 of the Disaster and Emergency Assistance Act are classified to sections 5171 and 5172 of Title 42. For complete classification, see Short Title note set out under section 5121 of Title 42 and Tables.

**Effective and Applicability Provisions**

1973 Acts

Section effective Dec. 28, 1973, see section 16 of Pub.L. 93–205, set out as an Effective Date note under section 1531 of this title.

**Deferral of Agency Action**

Pub.L. 105–18, Title II, § 3003, June 12, 1997, 111 Stat. 176, provided that:

" **(a) Consultation and conferencing.**—As provided by regulations issued under the Endangered Species Act (16 U.S.C. 1531 et seq.) [this chapter] for emergency situations, formal consultation or conferencing under section 7(a)(2) or section 7(a)(4) of the Act [subsec.(a)(2) or (a)(4) of this section] for any action authorized, funded or carried out by any Federal agency to repair a Federal or non-Federal flood control project, facility or structure may be deferred by the Federal agency authorizing, funding or carrying out the action, if the agency determines that the repair is needed to respond to an emergency causing an imminent threat to human lives and property in 1996 or 1997. Formal consultation or conferencing shall be deferred until the imminent threat to human lives and property has been abated. For purposes of this section, the term repair shall include preventive and remedial measures to restore the project, facility or structure to remove an imminent threat to human lives and property.

"**(b) Reasonable and prudent measures.**—Any reasonable and prudent measures specified under section 7 of the Endangered Species Act (16 U.S.C. 1536)[this section] to minimize the impact of an action taken under this section shall be related both in nature and extent to the effect of the action taken to repair the flood control project, facility or structure."

**Translocation of California Sea Otters**

Pub.L. 99–625, § 1, Nov. 7, 1986, 100 Stat. 3500, provided that:

"**(a) Definitions.**—For purposes of this section—

"(1) The term 'Act' means the Endangered Species Act of 1973 (16 U.S.C. 1531 et seq.) [this chapter].

"(2) The term 'agency action' has the meaning given that term in section 7(a)(2) of the Act [subsec. (a)(2) of this section].

"(3) The term 'experimental population' means the population of sea otters provided for under a plan developed under subsection (b).

"(4) The phrase 'parent population' means the population of sea otters existing in California on the date on which proposed regulations setting forth a proposed plan under subsection (b) are issued.

"(5) The phrase 'prospective action' refers to any prospective agency action that—

"(A) may affect either the experimental population or the parent population; and

"(B) has evolved to the point where meaningful consultation under section 7(a)(2) or (3) of the Act [subsec. (a)(2) or (3) of this section] can take place.

"(6) The term 'Secretary' means the Secretary of the Interior.

"(7) The term 'Service' means the United States Fish and Wildlife Service.

"**(b) Plan specifications.**—The Secretary may develop and implement, in accordance with this section, a plan for the relocation and management of a population of California sea otters from the existing range of the parent population to another location. The plan, which must be developed by regulation and administered by the Service in cooperation with the appropriate State agency, shall include the following:

"(1) The number, age, and sex of sea otters proposed to be relocated.

"(2) The manner in which the sea otters will be captured, translocated, released, monitored, and protected.

"(3) The specification of a zone (hereinafter referred to as the 'translocation zone') to which the experimental population will be relocated. The zone must have appropriate characteristics for furthering the conservation of the species.

"(4) The specification of a zone (hereinafter referred to as the 'management zone') that—

"(A) surrounds the translocation zone; and

"(B) does not include the existing range of the parent population or adjacent range where expansion is necessary for the recovery of the species.

The purpose of the management zone is to (i) facilitate the management of sea otters and the containment of the experimental population within the translocation zone, and (ii) to prevent, to the maximum extent feasible, conflict with other fishery resources within the management zone by the experimental population. Any sea otter found within the management zone shall be treated as a member of the experimental population. The Service shall use all feasible non-lethal means and measures to capture any sea otter found within the management zone and return it to either the translocation zone or to the range of the parent population.

"(5) Measures, including an adequate funding mechanism, to isolate and contain the experimental population.

"(6) A description of the relationship of the implementation of the plan to the status of the species under the Act [this chapter] and to determinations of the Secretary under section 7 of the Act [this section].

"**(c) Status of members of the experimental population.**—(1) Any member of the experimental population shall be treated while within the translocation zone as a threatened species for purposes of the Act [this chapter], except that—

"(A) section 7 of the Act [this section] shall only apply to agency actions that—

"(i) are undertaken within the translocation zone,

"(ii) are not defense-related agency actions, and

"(iii) are initiated after the date of the enactment of this section; and

"(B) with respect to defense-related actions within the translocation zone, members of the experimental population shall be treated as members of a species that is proposed to be listed under section 4 of the Act [16 U.S.C.A. § 1533].

For purposes of this paragraph, the term 'defense-related agency action' means an agency action proposed to be carried out directly by a military department.

"(2) For purposes of section 7 of the Act [this section], any member of the experimental population shall be treated while within the management zone as a member of a species that is proposed to be listed under section 4 of the Act [16 U.S.C.A. § 1533]. Section 9 of the Act [16 U.S.C.A. § 1538] applies to members of the experimental population; except that any incidental taking of such a member during the course of an otherwise lawful activity within the management zone, may not be treated as a violation of the Act [this chapter] or the Marine Mammal Protection Act of 1972 [16 U.S.C.A. § 1361 et seq.].

"**(d) Implementation of plan.**—The Secretary shall implement the plan developed under subsection (b)—

"(1) after the Secretary provides an opinion under section 7(b) of the Act [subsec. (b) of this section] regarding each prospective action for which consultation was initiated by a Federal agency or requested by a prospective permit or license applicant before April 1, 1986; or

"(2) if no consultation under section 7(a)(2) or (3) [subsec. (a)(2) or (3) of this section] regarding any prospective action is initiated or requested by April 1, 1986, at any time after that date.

"**(e) Consultation and effect of opinion.**—A Federal agency shall promptly consult with the Secretary, under section 7(a)(3) of the Act [subsec. (a)(3) of this section], at the request of, and in cooperation with, any permit or license applicant regarding any prospective action. The time limitations applicable to consultations under section 7(a)(2) of the Act [subsec. (a)(2) of this section] apply to consultations under the preceding sentence. In applying section 7(b)(3)(B) [subsec. (b)(3)(B) of this section] with respect to an opinion on a prospective action that is provided after consultation under section 7(a)(3), that opinion shall be treated as the opinion issued after consultation under section 7(a)(2) unless the Secretary finds, after notice and opportunity for comment in accordance with section 553 of title 5, United States Code [5 U.S.C.A. § 553], that a significant change has been made with respect to the action or that a significant change has occurred regarding the information used during the initial consultation. The interested party may petition the Secretary to make a finding under the preceding sentence. The Secretary may implement any reasonable and prudent alternatives specified in any opinion referred to in this subsection through appropriate agreements with any such Federal agency, prospective permit or license applicant, or other interested party.

"**(f) Construction.**—For purposes of implementing the plan, no act by the Service, an authorized State agency, or an authorized agent of the Service or such an agency with respect to a sea otter that is necessary to effect the relocation or management of any sea otter under the plan may be treated as a violation of any provision of the Act [this chapter] or the Marine Mammal Protection Act of 1972 (16 U.S.C. 1361 et seq.) [16 U.S.C.A. § 1361 et seq.]."

## § 1537. International cooperation

**[ESA § 8]**

### (a) Financial assistance

As a demonstration of the commitment of the United States to the worldwide protection of endangered species and threatened species, the President may, subject to the provisions of section 1306 of Title 31, use foreign currencies accruing to the United States Government under the Agricultural Trade Development and Assistance Act of 1954 [7 U.S.C.A. § 1691 et seq.] or any other law to provide to any foreign country (with its consent) assistance in the development and management of programs in that country which the Secretary determines to be necessary or useful for the conservation of any endangered species or threatened species listed by the Secretary pursuant to section 1533 of this title. The President shall provide assistance (which includes, but is not limited to, the acquisition, by lease or otherwise, of lands, waters, or interests therein) to foreign countries under this section under such terms and conditions as he deems appropriate. Whenever foreign currencies are available for the provision of assistance under this section, such currencies shall be used in preference to funds appropriated under the authority of section 1542 of this title.

### (b) Encouragement of foreign programs

In order to carry out further the provisions of this chapter, the Secretary, through the Secretary of State, shall encourage—

(1) foreign countries to provide for the conservation of fish or wildlife and plants including endangered species and threatened species listed pursuant to section 1533 of this title;

(2) the entering into of bilateral or multilateral agreements with foreign countries to provide for such conservation; and

(3) foreign persons who directly or indirectly take fish or wildlife or plants in foreign countries or on the high seas for importation into the United States for commercial or other purposes to develop and carry out with such assistance as he may provide, conservation practices designed to enhance such fish or wildlife or plants and their habitat.

### (c) Personnel

After consultation with the Secretary of State, the Secretary may—

(1) assign or otherwise make available any officer or employee of his department for the purpose of cooperating with foreign countries and international organizations in developing personnel resources and

programs which promote the conservation of fish or wildlife or plants; and

(2) conduct or provide financial assistance for the educational training of foreign personnel, in this country or abroad, in fish, wildlife, or plant management, research and law enforcement and to render professional assistance abroad in such matters.

### (d) Investigations

After consultation with the Secretary of State and the Secretary of the Treasury, as appropriate, the Secretary may conduct or cause to be conducted such law enforcement investigations and research abroad as he deems necessary to carry out the purposes of this chapter.

(Pub.L. 93–205, § 8, Dec. 28, 1973, 87 Stat. 892; Pub.L. 96–159, § 5, Dec. 28, 1979, 93 Stat. 1228.)

## HISTORICAL AND STATUTORY NOTES

**References in Text**

The Agricultural Trade Development and Assistance Act of 1954, referred to in subsec. (a), is Act July 10, 1954, c. 469, 68 Stat. 454, as amended, which is classified generally to chapter 41 (section 1691 et seq.) of Title 7, Agriculture. For complete classification of this Act to the Code, see Short Title note set out under section 1691 of Title 7 and Tables.

This chapter, referred to in subsecs. (b) and (d), in the original read "this Act", meaning the Endangered Species Act of 1973, which is classified principally to this chapter. For complete classification, see Short Title note set out under section 1531 of this title and Tables.

**Codifications**

In subsec. (a), "section 1306 of Title 31" was substituted for "section 1415 of the Supplemental Appropriation Act, 1953 (31 U.S.C. 724)" on authority of Pub.L. 97–258, § 4(b), Sept. 13, 1982, 96 Stat. 1067, the first section of which enacted Title 31.

**Effective and Applicability Provisions**

1973 Acts

Section effective Dec. 28, 1973, see section 16 of Pub.L. 93–205, set out as an Effective Date note under section 1531 of this title.

**Conservation of Sea Turtles; Importation of Shrimp**

Pub.L. 101–162, Title VI, § 609, Nov. 21, 1989, 103 Stat. 1037, provided that:

"(a) The Secretary of State, in consultation with the Secretary of Commerce, shall, with respect to those species of sea turtles the conservation of which is the subject of regulations promulgated by the Secretary of Commerce on June 29, 1987—

"(1) initiate negotiations as soon as possible for the development of bilateral or multilateral agreements with other nations for the protection and conservation of such species of sea turtles;

"(2) initiate negotiations as soon as possible with all foreign governments which are engaged in, or which have persons or companies engaged in, commercial fishing operations which, as determined by the Secretary of Commerce, may affect adversely such species of sea turtles, for the purpose of entering into bilateral and multilateral treaties with such countries to protect such species of sea turtles;

"(3) encourage such other agreements to promote the purposes of this section with other nations for the protection of specific ocean and land regions which are of special significance to the health and stability of such species of sea turtles;

"(4) initiate the amendment of any existing international treaty for the protection and conservation of such species of sea turtles to which the United States is a party in order to make such treaty consistent with the purposes and policies of this section; and

"(5) provide to the Congress by not later than one year after the date of enactment of this section [Nov. 21, 1989]

"(A) a list of each nation which conducts commercial shrimp fishing operations within the geographic range of distribution of such sea turtles;

"(B) a list of each nation which conducts commercial shrimp fishing operations which may affect adversely such species of sea turtles; and

"(C) a full report on—

"(i) the results of his efforts under this section; and

"(ii) the status of measures taken by each nation listed pursuant to paragraph (A) or (B) to protect and conserve such sea turtles.

"(b)(1) **In general.**—The importation of shrimp or products from shrimp which have been harvested with commercial fishing technology which may affect adversely such species of sea turtles shall be prohibited not later than May 1, 1991, except as provided in paragraph (2).

"(2) **Certification procedure.**—The ban on importation of shrimp or products from shrimp pursuant to paragraph (1) shall not apply if the President shall determine and certify to the Congress not later than May 1, 1991, and annually thereafter that—

"(A) the government of the harvesting nation has provided documentary evidence of the adoption of a regulatory program governing the incidental taking of such sea turtles in the course of such harvesting that is comparable to that of the United States; and

"(B) the average rate of that incidental taking by the vessels of the harvesting nation is comparable to the average rate of incidental taking of sea turtles by United States vessels in the course of such harvesting; or

"(C) the particular fishing environment of the harvesting nation does not pose a threat of the incidental taking of such sea turtles in the course of such harvesting."

## § 1537a. Convention implementation

[ESA § 8A]

### (a) Management Authority and Scientific Authority

The Secretary of the Interior (hereinafter in this section referred to as the "Secretary") is designated as the Management Authority and the Scientific Authority for purposes of the Convention and the respective functions of each such Authority shall be carried out through the United States Fish and Wildlife Service.

**(b) Management Authority functions**

The Secretary shall do all things necessary and appropriate to carry out the functions of the Management Authority under the Convention.

**(c) Scientific Authority functions; determinations**

(1) The Secretary shall do all things necessary and appropriate to carry out the functions of the Scientific Authority under the Convention.

(2) The Secretary shall base the determinations and advice given by him under Article IV of the Convention with respect to wildlife upon the best available biological information derived from professionally accepted wildlife management practices; but is not required to make, or require any State to make, estimates of population size in making such determinations or giving such advice.

**(d) Reservations by the United States under Convention**

If the United States votes against including any species in Appendix I or II of the Convention and does not enter a reservation pursuant to paragraph (3) of Article XV of the Convention with respect to that species, the Secretary of State, before the 90th day after the last day on which such a reservation could be entered, shall submit to the Committee on Merchant Marine and Fisheries of the House of Representatives, and to the Committee on the Environment and Public Works of the Senate, a written report setting forth the reasons why such a reservation was not entered.

**(e) Wildlife Preservation in Western Hemisphere**

(1) The Secretary of the Interior (hereinafter in this subsection referred to as the "Secretary"), in cooperation with the Secretary of State, shall act on behalf of, and represent, the United States in all regards as required by the Convention on Nature Protection and Wildlife Preservation in the Western Hemisphere (56 Stat. 1354, T.S. 982, hereinafter in this subsection referred to as the "Western Convention"). In the discharge of these responsibilities, the Secretary and the Secretary of State shall consult with the Secretary of Agriculture, the Secretary of Commerce, and the heads of other agencies with respect to matters relating to or affecting their areas of responsibility.

(2) The Secretary and the Secretary of State shall, in cooperation with the contracting parties to the Western Convention and, to the extent feasible and appropriate, with the participation of State agencies, take such steps as are necessary to implement the Western Convention. Such steps shall include, but not be limited to—

(A) cooperation with contracting parties and international organizations for the purpose of developing personnel resources and programs that will facilitate implementation of the Western Convention;

(B) identification of those species of birds that migrate between the United States and other contracting parties, and the habitats upon which those species depend, and the implementation of cooperative measures to ensure that such species will not become endangered or threatened; and

(C) identification of measures that are necessary and appropriate to implement those provisions of the Western Convention which address the protection of wild plants.

(3) No later than September 30, 1985, the Secretary and the Secretary of State shall submit a report to Congress describing those steps taken in accordance with the requirements of this subsection and identifying the principal remaining actions yet necessary for comprehensive and effective implementation of the Western Convention.

(4) The provisions of this subsection shall not be construed as affecting the authority, jurisdiction, or responsibility of the several States to manage, control, or regulate resident fish or wildlife under State law or regulations.

(Pub.L. 93–205, § 8A, as added Pub.L. 96–159, § 6(a)(1), Dec. 28, 1979, 93 Stat. 1228, and amended Pub.L. 97–304, § 5, Oct. 13, 1982, 96 Stat. 1421.)

## HISTORICAL AND STATUTORY NOTES

**Effective and Applicability Provisions**

1982 Acts

Section 5(b) of Pub.L. 97–304 provided that: "The amendment made by paragraph (1) of subsection (a) [enacting subsec. (c)(2) of this section] shall take effect January 1, 1981."

**Abolition of House Committee on Merchant Marine and Fisheries**

Committee on Merchant Marine and Fisheries of House of Representatives abolished and any reference in any provision of law enacted before Jan. 4, 1995, to the Committee on Merchant Marine and Fisheries of the House of Representatives treated as referring to the Committee on Agriculture of the House of Representatives, in the case of a provision of law relating to inspection of seafood or seafood products, the Committee on National Security of the House of Representatives, in the case of a provision of law relating to interoceanic canals, the Merchant Marine Academy and State Maritime Academies, or national security aspects of merchant marine, the Committee on Resources of the House of Representatives, in the case of a provision of law relating to fisheries, wildlife, international fishing agreements marine affairs (including coastal zone management) except for measures relating to oil and other pollution of navigable waters, or oceanography, the Committee on Science of the House of Representatives, in the case of a provision of law relating to marine research, and the Committee on Transportation and Infrastructure of the House of Representatives, in the case of a provision of law relating to a matter other than a matter described above, see section 1(b)(3) of Pub.L. 104–14, set out as a note preceding section 21 of Title 2, The Congress.

**Endangered Species Scientific Authority; Interim Performance of Functions of Commission**

Section 6(b) of Pub.L. 96–159, provided that until such time as the Chairman, Members, and Executive Secretary of the International Convention Advisory Commission are appointed, but not later than 90 days after Dec. 28, 1979, the functions of the Commission be carried out by the Endangered Species Scientific Authority as established by Ex. Ord. No. 11911, formerly set out as a note under section 1537 of this title, with staff and administrative support being provided by the Secretary of the Interior as set forth in that Executive order.

## § 1538. Prohibited acts

**[ESA § 9]**

### (a) Generally

(1) Except as provided in sections 1535(g)(2) and 1539 of this title, with respect to any endangered species of fish or wildlife listed pursuant to section 1533 of this title it is unlawful for any person subject to the jurisdiction of the United States to—

(A) import any such species into, or export any such species from the United States;

(B) take any such species within the United States or the territorial sea of the United States;

(C) take any such species upon the high seas;

(D) possess, sell, deliver, carry, transport, or ship, by any means whatsoever, any such species taken in violation of subparagraphs (B) and (C);

(E) deliver, receive, carry, transport, or ship in interstate or foreign commerce, by any means whatsoever and in the course of a commercial activity, any such species;

(F) sell or offer for sale in interstate or foreign commerce any such species; or

(G) violate any regulation pertaining to such species or to any threatened species of fish or wildlife listed pursuant to section 1533 of this title and promulgated by the Secretary pursuant to authority provided by this chapter.

(2) Except as provided in sections 1535(g)(2) and 1539 of this title, with respect to any endangered species of plants listed pursuant to section 1533 of this title, it is unlawful for any person subject to the jurisdiction of the United States to—

(A) import any such species into, or export any such species from, the United States;

(B) remove and reduce to possession any such species from areas under Federal jurisdiction; maliciously damage or destroy any such species on any such area; or remove, cut, dig up, or damage or destroy any such species on any other area in knowing violation of any law or regulation of any State or in the course of any violation of a State criminal trespass law;

(C) deliver, receive, carry, transport, or ship in interstate or foreign commerce, by any means whatsoever and in the course of a commercial activity, any such species;

(D) sell or offer for sale in interstate or foreign commerce any such species; or

(E) violate any regulation pertaining to such species or to any threatened species of plants listed pursuant to section 1533 of this title and promulgated by the Secretary pursuant to authority provided by this chapter.

### (b) Species held in captivity or controlled environment

(1) The provisions of subsections (a)(1)(A) and (a)(1)(G) of this section shall not apply to any fish or wildlife which was held in captivity or in a controlled environment on (A) December 28, 1973, or (B) the date of the publication in the Federal Register of a final regulation adding such fish or wildlife species to any list published pursuant to subsection (c) of section 1533 of this title: *Provided*, That such holding and any subsequent holding or use of the fish or wildlife was not in the course of a commercial activity. With respect to any act prohibited by subsections (a)(1)(A) and (a)(1)(G) of this section which occurs after a period of 180 days from (i) December 28, 1973, or (ii) the date of publication in the Federal Register of a final regulation adding such fish or wildlife species to any list published pursuant to subsection (c) of section 1533 of this title, there shall be a rebuttable presumption that the fish or wildlife involved in such act is not entitled to the exemption contained in this subsection.

(2)(A) The provisions of subsection (a)(1) of this section shall not apply to—

(i) any raptor legally held in captivity or in a controlled environment on November 10, 1978; or

(ii) any progeny of any raptor described in clause (i);

until such time as any such raptor or progeny is intentionally returned to a wild state.

(B) Any person holding any raptor or progeny described in subparagraph (A) must be able to demonstrate that the raptor or progeny does, in fact, qualify under the provisions of this paragraph, and shall maintain and submit to the Secretary, on request, such inventories, documentation, and records as the Secretary may by regulation require as being reasonably appropriate to carry out the purposes of this paragraph. Such requirements shall not unnecessarily duplicate the requirements of other rules and regulations promulgated by the Secretary.

**(c) Violation of Convention**

(1) It is unlawful for any person subject to the jurisdiction of the United States to engage in any trade in any specimens contrary to the provisions of the Convention, or to possess any specimens traded contrary to the provisions of the Convention, including the definitions of terms in article I thereof.

(2) Any importation into the United States of fish or wildlife shall, if—

(A) such fish or wildlife is not an endangered species listed pursuant to section 1533 of this title but is listed in Appendix II to the Convention,

(B) the taking and exportation of such fish or wildlife is not contrary to the provisions of the Convention and all other applicable requirements of the Convention have been satisfied,

(C) the applicable requirements of subsections (d), (e), and (f) of this section have been satisfied, and

(D) such importation is not made in the course of a commercial activity,

be presumed to be an importation not in violation of any provision of this chapter or any regulation issued pursuant to this chapter.

**(d) Imports and exports**

**(1) In general**

It is unlawful for any person, without first having obtained permission from the Secretary, to engage in business—

(A) as an importer or exporter of fish or wildlife (other than shellfish and fishery products which (i) are not listed pursuant to section 1533 of this title as endangered species or threatened species, and (ii) are imported for purposes of human or animal consumption or taken in waters under the jurisdiction of the United States or on the high seas for recreational purposes) or plants; or

(B) as an importer or exporter of any amount of raw or worked African elephant ivory.

**(2) Requirements**

Any person required to obtain permission under paragraph (1) of this subsection shall—

(A) keep such records as will fully and correctly disclose each importation or exportation of fish, wildlife, plants, or African elephant ivory made by him and the subsequent disposition made by him with respect to such fish, wildlife, plants, or ivory;

(B) at all reasonable times upon notice by a duly authorized representative of the Secretary, afford such representative access to his place of business, an opportunity to examine his inventory of imported fish, wildlife, plants, or African elephant ivory and the records required to be kept under subparagraph (A) of this paragraph, and to copy such records; and

(C) file such reports as the Secretary may require.

**(3) Regulations**

The Secretary shall prescribe such regulations as are necessary and appropriate to carry out the purposes of this subsection.

**(4) Restriction on consideration of value or amount of African elephant ivory imported or exported**

In granting permission under this subsection for importation or exportation of African elephant ivory, the Secretary shall not vary the requirements for obtaining such permission on the basis of the value or amount of ivory imported or exported under such permission.

**(e) Reports**

It is unlawful for any person importing or exporting fish or wildlife (other than shellfish and fishery products which (1) are not listed pursuant to section 1533 of this title as endangered or threatened species, and (2) are imported for purposes of human or animal consumption or taken in waters under the jurisdiction of the United States or on the high seas for recreational purposes) or plants to fail to file any declaration or report as the Secretary deems necessary to facilitate enforcement of this chapter or to meet the obligations of the Convention.

**(f) Designation of ports**

(1) It is unlawful for any person subject to the jurisdiction of the United States to import into or export from the United States any fish or wildlife (other than shellfish and fishery products which (A) are not listed pursuant to section 1533 of this title as endangered species or threatened species, and (B) are imported for purposes of human or animal consumption or taken in waters under the jurisdiction of the United States or on the high seas for recreational purposes) or plants, except at a port or ports designated by the Secretary of the Interior. For the purpose of facilitating enforcement of this chapter and reducing the costs thereof, the Secretary of the Interior, with approval of the Secretary of the Treasury and after notice and opportunity for public hearing, may, by regulation, designate ports and change such designations. The Secretary of the Interior, under such terms and conditions as he may prescribe, may permit

the importation or exportation at nondesignated ports in the interest of the health or safety of the fish or wildlife or plants, or for other reasons if, in his discretion, he deems it appropriate and consistent with the purpose of this subsection.

(2) Any port designated by the Secretary of the Interior under the authority of section 668cc–4(d) of this title, shall, if such designation is in effect on December 27, 1973, be deemed to be a port designated by the Secretary under paragraph (1) of this subsection until such time as the Secretary otherwise provides.

**(g) Violations**

It is unlawful for any person subject to the jurisdiction of the United States to attempt to commit, solicit another to commit, or cause to be committed, any offense defined in this section.

(Pub.L. 93–205, § 9, Dec. 28, 1973, 87 Stat. 893; Pub.L. 95–632, § 4, Nov. 10, 1978, 92 Stat. 3760; Pub.L. 97–304, § 9(b), Oct. 13, 1982, 96 Stat. 1426; Pub.L. 100–478, Title I, § 1006, Title II, § 2301, Oct. 7, 1988, 102 Stat. 2308, 2321; Pub.L. 100–653, Title IX, § 905, Nov. 14, 1988, 102 Stat. 3835.)

### HISTORICAL AND STATUTORY NOTES

**References in Text**

This chapter, referred to in subsec. (a)(1)(G), (2)(E), (c)(2), (e), and (f)(1), in the original read "this Act", meaning the Endangered Species Act of 1973, which is classified principally to this chapter. For complete classification, see Short Title note set out under section 1531 of this title and Tables.

Section 668cc–4(d) of this title, referred to in subsec. (f)(2), was repealed by Pub.L. 93–205, § 14, Dec. 28, 1973, 87 Stat. 903.

**Effective and Applicability Provisions**

1973 Acts

Section effective Dec. 28, 1973, see section 16 of Pub.L. 93–205, set out as an Effective Date note under section 1531 of this title.

**Human Activities Within Proximity of Whales**

Pub.L. 103–238, § 17, Apr. 30, 1994, 108 Stat. 559, provided that:

"**(a) Lawful approaches.**—In waters of the United States surrounding the State of Hawaii, it is lawful for a person subject to the jurisdiction of the United States to approach, by any means other than an aircraft, no closer than 100 yards to a humpback whale, regardless of whether the approach is made in waters designated under section 222.31 of title 50, Code of Federal Regulations, as cow/calf waters.

"**(b) Termination of legal effect of certain regulations.**—Subsection (b) of section 222.31 of title 50, Code of Federal Regulations, shall cease to be in force and effect."

## § 1539. Exceptions

[ESA § 10]

**(a) Permits**

(1) The Secretary may permit, under such terms and conditions as he shall prescribe—

**(A)** any act otherwise prohibited by section 1538 of this title for scientific purposes or to enhance the propagation or survival of the affected species, including, but not limited to, acts necessary for the establishment and maintenance of experimental populations pursuant to subsection (j) of this section; or

**(B)** any taking otherwise prohibited by section 1538(a)(1)(B) of this title if such taking is incidental to, and not the purpose of, the carrying out of an otherwise lawful activity.

(2)**(A)** No permit may be issued by the Secretary authorizing any taking referred to in paragraph (1)(B) unless the applicant therefor submits to the Secretary a conservation plan that specifies—

**(i)** the impact which will likely result from such taking;

**(ii)** what steps the applicant will take to minimize and mitigate such impacts, and the funding that will be available to implement such steps;

**(iii)** what alternative actions to such taking the applicant considered and the reasons why such alternatives are not being utilized; and

**(iv)** such other measures that the Secretary may require as being necessary or appropriate for purposes of the plan.

**(B)** If the Secretary finds, after opportunity for public comment, with respect to a permit application and the related conservation plan that—

**(i)** the taking will be incidental;

**(ii)** the applicant will, to the maximum extent practicable, minimize and mitigate the impacts of such taking;

**(iii)** the applicant will ensure that adequate funding for the plan will be provided;

**(iv)** the taking will not appreciably reduce the likelihood of the survival and recovery of the species in the wild; and

**(v)** the measures, if any, required under subparagraph (A)(iv) will be met;

and he has received such other assurances as he may require that the plan will be implemented, the Secretary shall issue the permit. The permit shall contain such terms and conditions as the Secretary deems necessary or appropriate to carry out the purposes of this paragraph, including, but not limited to, such reporting requirements as the Secretary deems necessary for determining whether such terms and conditions are being complied with.

**(C)** The Secretary shall revoke a permit issued under this paragraph if he finds that the permittee is not complying with the terms and conditions of the permit.

**(b) Hardship exemptions**

(1) If any person enters into a contract with respect to a species of fish or wildlife or plant before the date of the publication in the Federal Register of notice of consideration of that species as an endangered species and the subsequent listing of that species as an endangered species pursuant to section 1533 of this title will cause undue economic hardship to such person under the contract, the Secretary, in order to minimize such hardship, may exempt such person from the application of section 1538(a) of this title to the extent the Secretary deems appropriate if such person applies to him for such exemption and includes with such application such information as the Secretary may require to prove such hardship; except that (A) no such exemption shall be for a duration of more than one year from the date of publication in the Federal Register of notice of consideration of the species concerned, or shall apply to a quantity of fish or wildlife or plants in excess of that specified by the Secretary; (B) the one-year period for those species of fish or wildlife listed by the Secretary as endangered prior to December 28, 1973 shall expire in accordance with the terms of section 668cc–3 of this title; and (C) no such exemption may be granted for the importation or exportation of a specimen listed in Appendix I of the Convention which is to be used in a commercial activity.

(2) As used in this subsection, the term "undue economic hardship" shall include, but not be limited to:

(A) substantial economic loss resulting from inability caused by this chapter to perform contracts with respect to species of fish and wildlife entered into prior to the date of publication in the Federal Register of a notice of consideration of such species as an endangered species;

(B) substantial economic loss to persons who, for the year prior to the notice of consideration of such species as an endangered species, derived a substantial portion of their income from the lawful taking of any listed species, which taking would be made unlawful under this chapter; or

(C) curtailment of subsistence taking made unlawful under this chapter by persons (i) not reasonably able to secure other sources of subsistence; and (ii) dependent to a substantial extent upon hunting and fishing for subsistence; and (iii) who must engage in such curtailed taking for subsistence purposes.

(3) The Secretary may make further requirements for a showing of undue economic hardship as he deems fit. Exceptions granted under this section may be limited by the Secretary in his discretion as to time, area, or other factor of applicability.

**(c) Notice and review**

The Secretary shall publish notice in the Federal Register of each application for an exemption or permit which is made under this section. Each notice shall invite the submission from interested parties, within thirty days after the date of the notice, of written data, views, or arguments with respect to the application; except that such thirty-day period may be waived by the Secretary in an emergency situation where the health or life of an endangered animal is threatened and no reasonable alternative is available to the applicant, but notice of any such waiver shall be published by the Secretary in the Federal Register within ten days following the issuance of the exemption or permit. Information received by the Secretary as a part of any application shall be available to the public as a matter of public record at every stage of the proceeding.

**(d) Permit and exemption policy**

The Secretary may grant exceptions under subsections (a)(1)(A) and (b) of this section only if he finds and publishes his finding in the Federal Register that (1) such exceptions were applied for in good faith, (2) if granted and exercised will not operate to the disadvantage of such endangered species, and (3) will be consistent with the purposes and policy set forth in section 1531 of this title.

**(e) Alaska natives**

(1) Except as provided in paragraph (4) of this subsection the provisions of this chapter shall not apply with respect to the taking of any endangered species or threatened species, or the importation of any such species taken pursuant to this section, by—

(A) any Indian, Aleut, or Eskimo who is an Alaskan Native who resides in Alaska; or

(B) any non-native permanent resident of an Alaskan native village;

if such taking is primarily for subsistence purposes. Non-edible byproducts of species taken pursuant to this section may be sold in interstate commerce when made into authentic native articles of handicrafts and clothing; except that the provisions of this subsection shall not apply to any non-native resident of an Alaskan native village found by the Secretary to be not primarily dependent upon the taking of fish and wildlife for consumption or for the creation and sale of authentic native articles of handicrafts and clothing.

(2) Any taking under this subsection may not be accomplished in a wasteful manner.

(3) As used in this subsection—

(i) The term "subsistence" includes selling any edible portion of fish or wildlife in native villages and towns in Alaska for native consumption within native villages or towns; and

(ii) The term "authentic native articles of handicrafts and clothing" means items composed wholly or in some significant respect of natural materials, and which are produced, decorated, or fashioned in the exercise of traditional native handicrafts without the use of pantographs, multiple carvers, or other mass copying devices. Traditional native handicrafts include, but are not limited to, weaving, carving, stitching, sewing, lacing, beading, drawing, and painting.

(4) Notwithstanding the provisions of paragraph (1) of this subsection, whenever the Secretary determines that any species of fish or wildlife which is subject to taking under the provisions of this subsection is an endangered species or threatened species, and that such taking materially and negatively affects the threatened or endangered species, he may prescribe regulations upon the taking of such species by any such Indian, Aleut, Eskimo, or non-Native Alaskan resident of an Alaskan native village. Such regulations may be established with reference to species, geographical description of the area included, the season for taking, or any other factors related to the reason for establishing such regulations and consistent with the policy of this chapter. Such regulations shall be prescribed after a notice and hearings in the affected judicial districts of Alaska and as otherwise required by section 1373 of this title, and shall be removed as soon as the Secretary determines that the need for their impositions has disappeared.

**(f) Pre-Act endangered species parts exemption; application and certification; regulation; validity of sales contract; separability; renewal of exemption; expiration of renewal certification**

(1) As used in this subsection—

(A) The term "pre-Act endangered species part" means—

(i) any sperm whale oil, including derivatives thereof, which was lawfully held within the United States on December 28, 1973, in the course of a commercial activity; or

(ii) any finished scrimshaw product, if such product or the raw material for such product was lawfully held within the United States on December 28, 1973, in the course of a commercial activity.

(B) The term "scrimshaw product" means any art form which involves the substantial etching or engraving of designs upon, or the substantial carving of figures, patterns, or designs from, any bone or tooth of any marine mammal of the order Cetacea. For purposes of this subsection, polishing or the adding of minor superficial markings does not constitute substantial etching, engraving, or carving.

(2) The Secretary, pursuant to the provisions of this subsection, may exempt, if such exemption is not in violation of the Convention, any pre-Act endangered species part from one or more of the following prohibitions:

(A) The prohibition on exportation from the United States set forth in section 1538(a)(1)(A) of this title.

(B) Any prohibition set forth in section 1538(a)(1)(E) or (F) of this title.

(3) Any person seeking an exemption described in paragraph (2) of this subsection shall make application therefor to the Secretary in such form and manner as he shall prescribe, but no such application may be considered by the Secretary unless the application—

(A) is received by the Secretary before the close of the one-year period beginning on the date on which regulations promulgated by the Secretary to carry out this subsection first take effect;

(B) contains a complete and detailed inventory of all pre-Act endangered species parts for which the applicant seeks exemption;

(C) is accompanied by such documentation as the Secretary may require to prove that any endangered species part or product claimed by the applicant to be a pre-Act endangered species part is in fact such a part; and

(D) contains such other information as the Secretary deems necessary and appropriate to carry out the purposes of this subsection.

(4) If the Secretary approves any application for exemption made under this subsection, he shall issue to the applicant a certificate of exemption which shall specify—

(A) any prohibition in section 1538(a) of this title which is exempted;

(B) the pre-Act endangered species parts to which the exemption applies;

(C) the period of time during which the exemption is in effect, but no exemption made under this subsection shall have force and effect after the close of the three-year period beginning on the date of issuance of the certificate unless such exemption is renewed under paragraph (8); and

(D) any term or condition prescribed pursuant to paragraph (5)(A) or (B), or both, which the Secretary deems necessary or appropriate.

(5) The Secretary shall prescribe such regulations as he deems necessary and appropriate to carry out

the purposes of this subsection. Such regulations may set forth—

(A) terms and conditions which may be imposed on applicants for exemptions under this subsection (including, but not limited to, requirements that applicants register inventories, keep complete sales records, permit duly authorized agents of the Secretary to inspect such inventories and records, and periodically file appropriate reports with the Secretary); and

(B) terms and conditions which may be imposed on any subsequent purchaser of any pre-Act endangered species part covered by an exemption granted under this subsection;

to insure that any such part so exempted is adequately accounted for and not disposed of contrary to the provisions of this chapter. No regulation prescribed by the Secretary to carry out the purposes of this subsection shall be subject to section 1533(f)(2)(A)(i) of this title.

(6)(A) Any contract for the sale of pre-Act endangered species parts which is entered into by the Administrator of General Services prior to the effective date of this subsection and pursuant to the notice published in the Federal Register on January 9, 1973, shall not be rendered invalid by virtue of the fact that fulfillment of such contract may be prohibited under section 1538(a)(1)(F) of this title.

(B) In the event that this paragraph is held invalid, the validity of the remainder of this chapter, including the remainder of this subsection, shall not be affected.

(7) Nothing in this subsection shall be construed to—

(A) exonerate any person from any act committed in violation of paragraphs (1)(A), (1)(E), or (1)(F) of section 1538(a) of this title prior to July 12, 1976; or

(B) immunize any person from prosecution for any such act.

(8)(A)(i) [1] Any valid certificate of exemption which was renewed after October 13, 1982, and was in effect on March 31, 1988, shall be deemed to be renewed for a six-month period beginning on October 7, 1988. Any person holding such a certificate may apply to the Secretary for one additional renewal of such certificate for a period not to exceed 5 years beginning on October 7, 1988.

(B) If the Secretary approves any application for renewal of an exemption under this paragraph, he shall issue to the applicant a certificate of renewal of such exemption which shall provide that all terms, conditions, prohibitions, and other regulations made applicable by the previous certificate shall remain in effect during the period of the renewal.

(C) No exemption or renewal of such exemption made under this subsection shall have force and effect after the expiration date of the certificate of renewal of such exemption issued under this paragraph.

(D) No person may, after January 31, 1984, sell or offer for sale in interstate or foreign commerce, any pre-Act finished scrimshaw product unless such person holds a valid certificate of exemption issued by the Secretary under this subsection, and unless such product or the raw material for such product was held by such person on October 13, 1982.

**(g) Burden of proof**

In connection with any action alleging a violation of section 1538 of this title, any person claiming the benefit of any exemption or permit under this chapter shall have the burden of proving that the exemption or permit is applicable, has been granted, and was valid and in force at the time of the alleged violation.

**(h) Certain antique articles; importation; port designation; application for return of articles**

(1) Sections 1533(d) and 1538(a) and (c) of this title do not apply to any article which—

(A) is not less than 100 years of age;

(B) is composed in whole or in part of any endangered species or threatened species listed under section 1533 of this title;

(C) has not been repaired or modified with any part of any such species on or after December 28, 1973; and

(D) is entered at a port designated under paragraph (3).

(2) Any person who wishes to import an article under the exception provided by this subsection shall submit to the customs officer concerned at the time of entry of the article such documentation as the Secretary of the Treasury, after consultation with the Secretary of the Interior, shall by regulation require as being necessary to establish that the article meets the requirements set forth in paragraph (1)(A), (B), and (C).

(3) The Secretary of the Treasury, after consultation with the Secretary of the Interior, shall designate one port within each customs region at which articles described in paragraph (1)(A), (B), and (C) must be entered into the customs territory of the United States.

(4) Any person who imported, after December 27, 1973, and on or before November 10, 1978, any article described in paragraph (1) which—

(A) was not repaired or modified after the date of importation with any part of any endangered species or threatened species listed under section 1533 of this title;

**(B)** was forfeited to the United States before November 10, 1978, or is subject to forfeiture to the United States on such date of enactment, pursuant to the assessment of a civil penalty under section 1540 of this title; and

**(C)** is in the custody of the United States on November 10, 1978;

may, before the close of the one-year period beginning on November 10, 1978, make application to the Secretary for return of the article. Application shall be made in such form and manner, and contain such documentation, as the Secretary prescribes. If on the basis of any such application which is timely filed, the Secretary is satisfied that the requirements of this paragraph are met with respect to the article concerned, the Secretary shall return the article to the applicant and the importation of such article shall, on and after the date of return, be deemed to be a lawful importation under this chapter.

**(i) Noncommercial transshipments**

Any importation into the United States of fish or wildlife shall, if—

**(1)** such fish or wildlife was lawfully taken and exported from the country of origin and country of reexport, if any;

**(2)** such fish or wildlife is in transit or transshipment through any place subject to the jurisdiction of the United States en route to a country where such fish or wildlife may be lawfully imported and received;

**(3)** the exporter or owner of such fish or wildlife gave explicit instructions not to ship such fish or wildlife through any place subject to the jurisdiction of the United States, or did all that could have reasonably been done to prevent transshipment, and the circumstances leading to the transshipment were beyond the exporter's or owner's control;

**(4)** the applicable requirements of the Convention have been satisfied; and

**(5)** such importation is not made in the course of a commercial activity,

be an importation not in violation of any provision of this chapter or any regulation issued pursuant to this chapter while such fish or wildlife remains in the control of the United States Customs Service.

**(j) Experimental populations**

**(1)** For purposes of this subsection, the term "experimental population" means any population (including any offspring arising solely therefrom) authorized by the Secretary for release under paragraph (2), but only when, and at such times as, the population is wholly separate geographically from nonexperimental populations of the same species.

**(2)(A)** The Secretary may authorize the release (and the related transportation) of any population (including eggs, propagules, or individuals) of an endangered species or a threatened species outside the current range of such species if the Secretary determines that such release will further the conservation of such species.

**(B)** Before authorizing the release of any population under subparagraph (A), the Secretary shall by regulation identify the population and determine, on the basis of the best available information, whether or not such population is essential to the continued existence of an endangered species or a threatened species.

**(C)** For the purposes of this chapter, each member of an experimental population shall be treated as a threatened species; except that—

**(i)** solely for purposes of section 1536 of this title (other than subsection (a)(1) thereof), an experimental population determined under subparagraph (B) to be not essential to the continued existence of a species shall be treated, except when it occurs in an area within the National Wildlife Refuge System or the National Park System, as a species proposed to be listed under section 1533 of this title; and

**(ii)** critical habitat shall not be designated under this chapter for any experimental population determined under subparagraph (B) to be not essential to the continued existence of a species.

**(3)** The Secretary, with respect to populations of endangered species or threatened species that the Secretary authorized, before October 13, 1982, for release in geographical areas separate from the other populations of such species, shall determine by regulation which of such populations are an experimental population for the purposes of this subsection and whether or not each is essential to the continued existence of an endangered species or a threatened species.

(Pub.L. 93–205, § 10, Dec. 28, 1973, 87 Stat. 896; Pub.L. 94–359, §§ 2, 3, July 12, 1976, 90 Stat. 911, 912; Pub.L. 95–632, § 5, Nov. 10, 1978, 92 Stat. 3760; Pub.L. 96–159, § 7, Dec. 28, 1979, 93 Stat. 1230; Pub.L. 97–304, § 6(1) to (3), (4)(A), (5), (6), Oct. 13, 1982, 96 Stat. 1422 to 1424; Pub.L. 100–478, Title I, §§ 1011, 1013(b), (c), Oct. 7, 1988, 102 Stat. 2314, 2315.)

[1] So in original. No cl. (ii) has been enacted.

## HISTORICAL AND STATUTORY NOTES

**References in Text**

Section 668cc–3 of this title, referred to in subsec. (b), was repealed by Pub.L. 93–205, § 14, Dec. 28, 1973, 87 Stat. 903.

This chapter, referred to in subsecs. (b)(2), (e)(1), (4), (f)(5), (6)(B), (g), (h)(4), (i), (j)(2)(C)(ii), in the original read "this Act", meaning the Endangered Species Act of 1973, which is classified principally to this chapter. For complete classification, see Short Title note set out under section 1531 of this title and Tables.

Pre-Act, referred to in subsec. (f), means the period prior to the effective date of the Endangered Species Act of 1973, Dec. 28, 1973. See section 16 of Pub.L. 93–205, set out as an Effective Date note under section 1531 of this title.

Subsec. (f) of section 1533 of this title, referred to in subsec. (f)(5), which related to promulgation of regulations by the Secretary was struck out, and subsec. (g) of section 1533 of this title was redesignated as subsec. (f), by Pub.L. 97–304, § 2(a)(4)(B), (C), Oct. 13, 1982, 96 Stat. 1415. For provisions related to promulgation of regulations, see subsecs. (b) and (h) of section 1533 of this title.

Effective date of this subsection, referred to in subsec. (f)(6)(A), probably means the date of enactment of subsec. (f) by section 2 of Pub.L. 94–359, July 12, 1976.

**Effective and Applicability Provisions**

1982 Acts

Section 6(4)(B) of Pub.L. 97–304 provided that: "The amendment made by subparagraph (A) [amending subsec. (h)(1) of this section] shall take effect of January 1, 1981."

1973 Acts

Section effective Dec. 28, 1973, see section 16 of Pub.L. 93–205, set out as an Effective Date note under section 1531 of this title.

**Scrimshaw Exemptions**

Pub.L. 103–238, § 18, Apr. 30, 1994, 108 Stat. 559, provided that: "Notwithstanding any other provision of law, any valid certificate of exemption renewed by the Secretary (or deemed to be renewed) under section 10(f)(8) of the Endangered Species Act of 1973 (16 U.S.C. 1539(f)(8) [subsec. (f)(8) of this section]) for any person holding such a certificate with respect to the possession of pre-Act finished scrimshaw products or raw material for such products shall remain valid for a period not to exceed 5 years beginning on the date of enactment of this Act [Apr. 30, 1994]."

## § 1540. Penalties and enforcement

[ESA § 11]

### (a) Civil penalties

(1) Any person who knowingly violates, and any person engaged in business as an importer or exporter of fish, wildlife, or plants who violates, any provision of this chapter, or any provision of any permit or certificate issued hereunder, or of any regulation issued in order to implement subsection (a)(1)(A), (B), (C), (D), (E), or (F), (a)(2)(A), (B), (C), or (D), (c), (d) (other than regulation relating to recordkeeping or filing of reports), (f) or (g) of section 1538 of this title, may be assessed a civil penalty by the Secretary of not more than $25,000 for each violation. Any person who knowingly violates, and any person engaged in business as an importer or exporter of fish, wildlife, or plants who violates, any provision of any other regulation issued under this chapter may be assessed a civil penalty by the Secretary of not more than $12,000 for each such violation. Any person who otherwise violates any provision of this chapter, or any regulation, permit, or certificate issued hereunder, may be assessed a civil penalty by the Secretary of not more than $500 for each such violation. No penalty may be assessed under this subsection unless such person is given notice and opportunity for a hearing with respect to such violation. Each violation shall be a separate offense. Any such civil penalty may be remitted or mitigated by the Secretary. Upon any failure to pay a penalty assessed under this subsection, the Secretary may request the Attorney General to institute a civil action in a district court of the United States for any district in which such person is found, resides, or transacts business to collect the penalty and such court shall have jurisdiction to hear and decide any such action. The court shall hear such action on the record made before the Secretary and shall sustain his action if it is supported by substantial evidence on the record considered as a whole.

(2) Hearings held during proceedings for the assessment of civil penalties authorized by paragraph (1) of this subsection shall be conducted in accordance with section 554 of Title 5. The Secretary may issue subpenas for the attendance and testimony of witnesses and the production of relevant papers, books, and documents, and administer oaths. Witnesses summoned shall be paid the same fees and mileage that are paid to witnesses in the courts of the United States. In case of contumacy or refusal to obey a subpena served upon any person pursuant to this paragraph, the district court of the United States for any district in which such person is found or resides or transacts business, upon application by the United States and after notice to such person, shall have jurisdiction to issue an order requiring such person to appear and give testimony before the Secretary or to appear and produce documents before the Secretary, or both, and any failure to obey such order of the court may be punished by such court as a contempt thereof.

(3) Notwithstanding any other provision of this chapter, no civil penalty shall be imposed if it can be shown by a preponderance of the evidence that the defendant committed an act based on a good faith belief that he was acting to protect himself or herself, a member of his or her family, or any other individual from bodily harm, from any endangered or threatened species.

### (b) Criminal violations

(1) Any person who knowingly violates any provision of this chapter, of any permit or certificate issued hereunder, or of any regulation issued in order to implement subsection (a)(1)(A), (B), (C), (D), (E), or (F); (a)(2)(A), (B), (C), or (D), (c), (d) (other than a regulation relating to recordkeeping, or filing of reports), (f), or (g) of section 1538 of this title shall, upon

conviction, be fined not more than $50,000 or imprisoned for not more than one year, or both. Any person who knowingly violates any provision of any other regulation issued under this chapter shall, upon conviction, be fined not more than $25,000 or imprisoned for not more than six months, or both.

(2) The head of any Federal agency which has issued a lease, license, permit, or other agreement authorizing a person to import or export fish, wildlife, or plants, or to operate a quarantine station for imported wildlife, or authorizing the use of Federal lands, including grazing of domestic livestock, to any person who is convicted of a criminal violation of this chapter or any regulation, permit, or certificate issued hereunder may immediately modify, suspend, or revoke each lease, license, permit or other agreement. The Secretary shall also suspend for a period of up to one year, or cancel, any Federal hunting or fishing permits or stamps issued to any person who is convicted of a criminal violation of any provision of this chapter or any regulation, permit, or certificate issued hereunder. The United States shall not be liable for the payments of any compensation, reimbursement, or damages in connection with the modification, suspension, or revocation of any leases, licenses, permits, stamps, or other agreements pursuant to this section.

(3) Notwithstanding any other provision of this chapter, it shall be a defense to prosecution under this subsection if the defendant committed the offense based on a good faith belief that he was acting to protect himself or herself, a member of his or her family, or any other individual, from bodily harm from any endangered or threatened species.

**(c) District court jurisdiction**

The several district courts of the United States, including the courts enumerated in section 460 of Title 28, shall have jurisdiction over any actions arising under this chapter. For the purpose of this chapter, American Samoa shall be included within the judicial district of the District Court of the United States for the District of Hawaii.

**(d) Rewards and incidental expenses**

The Secretary or the Secretary of the Treasury shall pay, from sums received as penalties, fines, or forfeitures of property for any violation of this chapter or any regulation issued hereunder (1) a reward to any person who furnishes information which leads to an arrest, a criminal conviction, civil penalty assessment, or forfeiture of property for any violation of this chapter or any regulation issued hereunder, and (2) the reasonable and necessary costs incurred by any person in providing temporary care for any fish, wildlife, or plant pending the disposition of any civil or criminal proceeding alleging a violation of this chapter with respect to that fish, wildlife, or plant. The amount of the reward, if any, is to be designated by the Secretary or the Secretary of the Treasury, as appropriate. Any officer or employee of the United States or any State or local government who furnishes information or renders service in the performance of his official duties is ineligible for payment under this subsection. Whenever the balance of sums received under this section and section 3375(d) of this title, as penalties or fines, or from forfeitures of property, exceed $500,000, the Secretary of the Treasury shall deposit an amount equal to such excess balance in the cooperative endangered species conservation fund established under section 1535(i) of this title.

**(e) Enforcement**

(1) The provisions of this chapter and any regulations or permits issued pursuant thereto shall be enforced by the Secretary, the Secretary of the Treasury, or the Secretary of the Department in which the Coast Guard is operating, or all such Secretaries. Each such Secretary may utilize by agreement, with or without reimbursement, the personnel, services, and facilities of any other Federal agency or any State agency for purposes of enforcing this chapter.

(2) The judges of the district courts of the United States and the United States magistrate judges may, within their respective jurisdictions, upon proper oath or affirmation showing probable cause, issue such warrants or other process as may be required for enforcement of this chapter and any regulation issued thereunder.

(3) Any person authorized by the Secretary, the Secretary of the Treasury, or the Secretary of the Department in which the Coast Guard is operating, to enforce this chapter may detain for inspection and inspect any package, crate, or other container, including its contents, and all accompanying documents, upon importation or exportation. Such person may make arrests without a warrant for any violation of this chapter if he has reasonable grounds to believe that the person to be arrested is committing the violation in his presence or view, and may execute and serve any arrest warrant, search warrant, or other warrant or civil or criminal process issued by any officer or court of competent jurisdiction for enforcement of this chapter. Such person so authorized may search and seize, with or without a warrant, as authorized by law. Any fish, wildlife, property, or item so seized shall be held by any person authorized by the Secretary, the Secretary of the Treasury, or the Secretary of the Department in which the Coast Guard is operating pending disposition of civil or criminal proceedings, or the institution of an action in rem for forfeiture of such fish, wildlife, property, or item pursuant to paragraph (4) of this subsection; except that the Secretary may, in lieu of holding such fish, wildlife, property, or item, permit the owner or con-

signee to post a bond or other surety satisfactory to the Secretary, but upon forfeiture of any such property to the United States, or the abandonment or waiver of any claim to any such property, it shall be disposed of (other than by sale to the general public) by the Secretary in such a manner, consistent with the purposes of this chapter, as the Secretary shall by regulation prescribe.

**(4)(A)** All fish or wildlife or plants taken, possessed, sold, purchased, offered for sale or purchase, transported, delivered, received, carried, shipped, exported, or imported contrary to the provisions of this chapter, any regulation made pursuant thereto, or any permit or certificate issued hereunder shall be subject to forfeiture to the United States.

**(B)** All guns, traps, nets, and other equipment, vessels, vehicles, aircraft, and other means of transportation used to aid the taking, possessing, selling, purchasing, offering for sale or purchase, transporting, delivering, receiving, carrying, shipping, exporting, or importing of any fish or wildlife or plants in violation of this chapter, any regulation made pursuant thereto, or any permit or certificate issued thereunder shall be subject to forfeiture to the United States upon conviction of a criminal violation pursuant to subsection (b)(1) of this section.

**(5)** All provisions of law relating to the seizure, forfeiture, and condemnation of a vessel for violation of the customs laws, the disposition of such vessel or the proceeds from the sale thereof, and the remission or mitigation of such forfeiture, shall apply to the seizures and forfeitures incurred, or alleged to have been incurred, under the provisions of this chapter, insofar as such provisions of law are applicable and not inconsistent with the provisions of this chapter; except that all powers, rights, and duties conferred or imposed by the customs laws upon any officer or employee of the Treasury Department shall, for the purposes of this chapter, be exercised or performed by the Secretary or by such persons as he may designate.

**(6)** The Attorney General of the United States may seek to enjoin any person who is alleged to be in violation of any provision of this chapter or regulation issued under authority thereof.

### (f) Regulations

The Secretary, the Secretary of the Treasury, and the Secretary of the Department in which the Coast Guard is operating, are authorized to promulgate such regulations as may be appropriate to enforce this chapter, and charge reasonable fees for expenses to the Government connected with permits or certificates authorized by this chapter including processing applications and reasonable inspections, and with the transfer, board, handling, or storage of fish or wildlife or plants and evidentiary items seized and forfeited under this chapter. All such fees collected pursuant to this subsection shall be deposited in the Treasury to the credit of the appropriation which is current and chargeable for the cost of furnishing the services. Appropriated funds may be expended pending reimbursement from parties in interest.

### (g) Citizen suits

**(1)** Except as provided in paragraph (2) of this subsection any person may commence a civil suit on his own behalf—

**(A)** to enjoin any person, including the United States and any other governmental instrumentality or agency (to the extent permitted by the eleventh amendment to the Constitution), who is alleged to be in violation of any provision of this chapter or regulation issued under the authority thereof; or

**(B)** to compel the Secretary to apply, pursuant to section 1535(g)(2)(B)(ii) of this title, the prohibitions set forth in or authorized pursuant to section 1533(d) or 1538(a)(1)(B) of this title with respect to the taking of any resident endangered species or threatened species within any State; or

**(C)** against the Secretary where there is alleged a failure of the Secretary to perform any act or duty under section 1533 of this title which is not discretionary with the Secretary.

The district courts shall have jurisdiction, without regard to the amount in controversy or the citizenship of the parties, to enforce any such provision or regulation, or to order the Secretary to perform such act or duty, as the case may be. In any civil suit commenced under subparagraph (B) the district court shall compel the Secretary to apply the prohibition sought if the court finds that the allegation that an emergency exists is supported by substantial evidence.

**(2)(A)** No action may be commenced under subparagraph (1)(A) of this section—

**(i)** prior to sixty days after written notice of the violation has been given to the Secretary, and to any alleged violator of any such provision or regulation;

**(ii)** if the Secretary has commenced action to impose a penalty pursuant to subsection (a) of this section; or

**(iii)** if the United States has commenced and is diligently prosecuting a criminal action in a court of the United States or a State to redress a violation of any such provision or regulation.

**(B)** No action may be commenced under subparagraph (1)(B) of this section—

**(i)** prior to sixty days after written notice has been given to the Secretary setting forth the reasons why an emergency is thought to exist with respect to an endangered species or a threatened species in the State concerned; or

(ii) if the Secretary has commenced and is diligently prosecuting action under section 1535(g)(2)(B)(ii) of this title to determine whether any such emergency exists.

(C) No action may be commenced under subparagraph (1)(C) of this section prior to sixty days after written notice has been given to the Secretary; except that such action may be brought immediately after such notification in the case of an action under this section respecting an emergency posing a significant risk to the well-being of any species of fish or wildlife or plants.

(3)(A) Any suit under this subsection may be brought in the judicial district in which the violation occurs.

(B) In any such suit under this subsection in which the United States is not a party, the Attorney General, at the request of the Secretary, may intervene on behalf of the United States as a matter of right.

(4) The court, in issuing any final order in any suit brought pursuant to paragraph (1) of this subsection, may award costs of litigation (including reasonable attorney and expert witness fees) to any party, whenever the court determines such award is appropriate.

(5) The injunctive relief provided by this subsection shall not restrict any right which any person (or class of persons) may have under any statute or common law to seek enforcement of any standard or limitation or to seek any other relief (including relief against the Secretary or a State agency).

**(h) Coordination with other laws**

The Secretary of Agriculture and the Secretary shall provide for appropriate coordination of the administration of this chapter with the administration of the animal quarantine laws (as defined in section 136a(f) of Title 21) and section 306 of the Tariff Act of 1930 (19 U.S.C. 1306). Nothing in this chapter or any amendment made by this Act shall be construed as superseding or limiting in any manner the functions of the Secretary of Agriculture under any other law relating to prohibited or restricted importations or possession of animals and other articles and no proceeding or determination under this chapter shall preclude any proceeding or be considered determinative of any issue of fact or law in any proceeding under any Act administered by the Secretary of Agriculture. Nothing in this chapter shall be construed as superseding or limiting in any manner the functions and responsibilities of the Secretary of the Treasury under the Tariff Act of 1930 [19 U.S.C.A. § 1202 et seq.], including, without limitation, section 527 of that Act (19 U.S.C. 1527), relating to the importation of wildlife taken, killed, possessed, or exported to the United States in violation of the laws or regulations of a foreign country.

(Pub.L. 93–205, § 11, Dec. 28, 1973, 87 Stat. 897; Pub.L. 94–359, § 4, July 12, 1976, 90 Stat. 913; Pub.L. 95–632, §§ 6 to 8, Nov. 10, 1978, 92 Stat. 3761, 3762; Pub.L. 97–79, § 9(e), Nov. 16, 1981, 95 Stat. 1079; Pub.L. 97–304, §§ 7, 9(c), Oct. 13, 1982, 96 Stat. 1425, 1427; Pub.L. 98–327, § 4, June 25, 1984, 98 Stat. 271; Pub.L. 100–478, Title I, § 1007, Oct. 7, 1988, 102 Stat. 2309; Pub.L. 101–650, Title III, § 321, Dec. 1, 1990, 104 Stat. 5117; Pub.L. 107–171, Title X, § 10418(b)(3), May 13, 2002, 116 Stat. 508.)

## HISTORICAL AND STATUTORY NOTES

**References in Text**

This chapter, referred to in subsecs. (a)(1), (a)(3), (b) to (f), (g)(1)(A), and (h), in the original read "this Act", meaning the Endangered Species Act of 1973, which is classified principally to this chapter. For complete classification, see Short Title note set out under section 1531 of this title and Tables.

The customs laws, referred to in subsec. (e)(5), are classified generally to Title 19.

The amendments "made by this Act", referred to in subsec. (h), refer to the amendments made by Pub.L. 93–205, which amended sections 460k–1, 460*l*–9, 668dd, 715i, 715s, 1362, 1371, 1372 and 1402 of this title and section 136 of Title 7, and repealed sections 668aa to 668cc–6 of this title.

The Tariff Act of 1930, referred to in subsec. (h), is classified generally to chapter 4 of Title 19 (19 U.S.C.A. § 1202 et seq.). For complete classification, see section 1654 of Title 19 and Tables.

**Effective and Applicability Provisions**

1981 Acts

Section 9(f) of Pub.L. 97–79 provided that: "The amendment specified in subsection 9(e) of this Act [amending subsec. (d) of this section] shall take effect beginning in fiscal year 1983."

1973 Acts

Section effective Dec. 28, 1973, see section 16 of Pub.L. 93–205, set out as an Effective Date note under section 1531 of this title.

**Change of Name**

United States magistrate appointed under section 631 of Title 28, Judiciary and Judicial Procedure, to be known as United States magistrate judge after Dec. 1, 1990, with any reference to United States magistrate or magistrate in Title 28, in any other Federal statute, etc., deemed a reference to United States magistrate judge appointed under section 631 of Title 28, see section 321 of Pub.L. 101–650, set out as a note under section 631 of Title 28.

## § 1541. Endangered plants

**[ESA § 12]**

The Secretary of the Smithsonian Institution, in conjunction with other affected agencies, is authorized and directed to review (1) species of plants which are now or may become endangered or threatened and (2) methods of adequately conserving such species, and to report to Congress, within one year after December

28, 1973, the results of such review including recommendations for new legislation or the amendment of existing legislation.

(Pub.L. 93–205, § 12, Dec. 28, 1973, 87 Stat. 901.)

### HISTORICAL AND STATUTORY NOTES

**Effective and Applicability Provisions**

1973 Acts

Section effective Dec. 28, 1973, see section 16 of Pub.L. 93–205, set out as an Effective Date note under section 1531 of this title.

## § 1542. Authorization of appropriations

[ESA § 15]

**(a) In general**

Except as provided in subsections (b), (c), and (d) of this section, there are authorized to be appropriated—

(1) not to exceed $35,000,000 for fiscal year 1988, $36,500,000 for fiscal year 1989, $38,000,000 for fiscal year 1990, $39,500,000 for fiscal year 1991, and $41,500,000 for fiscal year 1992 to enable the Department of the Interior to carry out such functions and responsibilities as it may have been given under this chapter;

(2) not to exceed $5,750,000 for fiscal year 1988, $6,250,000 for each of fiscal years 1989 and 1990, and $6,750,000 for each of fiscal years 1991 and 1992 to enable the Department of Commerce to carry out such functions and responsibilities as it may have been given under this chapter; and

(3) not to exceed $2,200,000 for fiscal year 1988, $2,400,000 for each of fiscal years 1989 and 1990, and $2,600,000 for each of fiscal years 1991 and 1992, to enable the Department of Agriculture to carry out its functions and responsibilities with respect to the enforcement of this chapter and the Convention which pertain to the importation or exportation of plants.

**(b) Exemptions**

There are authorized to be appropriated to the Secretary to assist him and the Endangered Species Committee in carrying out their functions under sections [1] 1536(e), (g), and (h) of this title not to exceed $600,000 for each of fiscal years 1988, 1989, 1990, 1991, and 1992.

**(c) Convention implementation**

There are authorized to be appropriated to the Department of the Interior for purposes of carrying out section 1537a(e) of this title not to exceed $400,000 for each of fiscal years 1988, 1989, and 1990, and $500,000 for each of fiscal years 1991 and 1992, and such sums shall remain available until expended.

(Pub.L. 93–205, § 15, Dec. 28, 1973, 87 Stat. 903; Pub.L. 94–325, June 30, 1976, 90 Stat. 724; Pub.L. 95–632, § 9, Nov. 10, 1978, 92 Stat. 3762; Pub.L. 96–159, § 8, Dec. 28, 1979, 93 Stat. 1230; Pub.L. 97–304, § 8(a), Oct. 13, 1982, 96 Stat. 1425; Pub.L. 100–478, Title I, § 1009, Oct. 7, 1988, 102 Stat. 2312.)

[1] So in original. Probably should be "section".

### HISTORICAL AND STATUTORY NOTES

**References in Text**

This chapter, referred to in subsec. (a) in the original read "this Act", meaning the Endangered Species Act of 1973, which is classified principally to this chapter. For complete classification, see Short Title note set out under section 1531 of this title and Tables.

**Effective and Applicability Provisions**

1973 Acts

Section effective Dec. 28, 1973, see section 16 of Pub.L. 93–205, set out as an Effective Date note under section 1531 of this title.

## § 1543. Construction with Marine Mammal Protection Act of 1972

[ESA § 17]

Except as otherwise provided in this chapter, no provision of this chapter shall take precedence over any more restrictive conflicting provision of the Marine Mammal Protection Act of 1972 [16 U.S.C.A. § 1361 et seq.].

(Pub.L. 93–205, § 17, Dec. 28, 1973, 87 Stat. 903.)

### HISTORICAL AND STATUTORY NOTES

**References in Text**

This chapter, referred to in text, in the original read "this Act", meaning the Endangered Species Act of 1973, which is classified principally to this chapter. For complete classification, see Short Title note set out under section 1531 of this title and Tables.

The Marine Mammal Protection Act of 1972, referred to in text, is classified generally to chapter 31 of this title ( 16 U.S.C.A. § 1361 et seq.). For complete classification, see Short Title note set out under section 1361 of this title and Tables.

**Effective and Applicability Provisions**

1973 Acts

Section effective Dec. 28, 1973, see section 16 of Pub.L. 93–205, set out as an Effective Date note under section 1531 of this title.

## § 1544. Annual cost analysis by Fish and Wildlife Service

[ESA § 18]

Notwithstanding section 3003 of Public Law 104–66 (31 U.S.C. 1113 note; 109 Stat. 734), on or before January 15, 1990, and each January 15 thereafter, the Secretary of the Interior, acting through the Fish and Wildlife Service, shall submit to the Congress an annual report covering the preceding fiscal year which shall contain—

(1) an accounting on a species by species basis of all reasonably identifiable Federal expenditures made primarily for the conservation of endangered or threatened species pursuant to this chapter; and

(2) an accounting on a species by species basis of all reasonably identifiable expenditures made primarily for the conservation of endangered or threatened species pursuant to this chapter by States receiving grants under section 1535 of this title.

(Pub.L. 93–205, § 18, as added Pub.L. 100–478, Title I, § 1012, Oct. 7, 1988, 102 Stat. 2314; Pub.L. 106–201, § 1(a), May 18, 2000, 114 Stat. 307.)

### HISTORICAL AND STATUTORY NOTES

**References in Text**

Public Law 104–66, referred to in text, is the Federal Reports Elimination and Sunset Act of 1995. See tables for complete classification.

This chapter, referred to in pars. (1), (2), in the original read "this Act", meaning the Endangered Species Act of 1973, which is classified principally to this chapter. For complete classification, see Short Title note set out under section 1531 of this title and Tables.

**Effective and Applicability Provisions**

2000 Acts

Pub.L. 106–201, § 1(b), May 18, 2000, 114 Stat. 307, provided that:

"The amendment made by this section [amending this section] takes effect on the earlier of—

"(1) the date of enactment of this Act [May 18, 2000]; or

"(2) December 19, 1999."

## §§ 1545 to 1599. Reserved for future legislation

# FOREST AND RANGELAND RESOURCES

## CHAPTER 36—FOREST AND RANGELAND RENEWABLE RESOURCES PLANNING



# FOREST AND RANGELAND RENEWABLE RESOURCES PLANNING ACT OF 1974 [FRRRPA § ____]

**(16 U.S.C.A. §§ 1600 to 1614)**

## SUBCHAPTER I—PLANNING

### § 1600. Congressional findings [FRRRPA § 2]

The Congress finds that—

(1) the management of the Nation's renewable resources is highly complex and the uses, demand for, and supply of the various resources are subject to change over time;

(2) the public interest is served by the Forest Service, Department of Agriculture, in cooperation with other agencies, assessing the Nation's renewable resources, and developing and preparing a na-

tional renewable resource program, which is periodically reviewed and updated;

(3) to serve the national interest, the renewable resource program must be based on a comprehensive assessment of present and anticipated uses, demand for, and supply of renewable resources from the Nation's public and private forests and rangelands, through analysis of environmental and economic impacts, coordination of multiple use and sustained yield opportunities as provided in the Multiple-Use Sustained-Yield Act of 1960 (74 Stat. 215; 16 U.S.C. 528–531), and public participation in the development of the program;

(4) the new knowledge derived from coordinated public and private research programs will promote a sound technical and ecological base for effective management, use, and protection of the Nation's renewable resources;

(5) inasmuch as the majority of the Nation's forests and rangeland is under private, State, and local governmental management and the Nation's major capacity to produce goods and services is based on these nonfederally managed renewable resources, the Federal Government should be a catalyst to encourage and assist these owners in the efficient long-term use and improvement of these lands and their renewable resources consistent with the principles of sustained yield and multiple use;

(6) the Forest Service, by virtue of its statutory authority for management of the National Forest System, research and cooperative programs, and its role as an agency in the Department of Agriculture, has both a responsibility and an opportunity to be a leader in assuring that the Nation maintains a natural resource conservation posture that will meet the requirements of our people in perpetuity; and

(7) recycled timber product materials are as much a part of our renewable forest resources as are the trees from which they originally came, and in order to extend our timber and timber fiber resources and reduce pressures for timber production from Federal lands, the Forest Service should expand its research in the use of recycled and waste timber product materials, develop techniques for the substitution of these secondary materials for primary materials, and promote and encourage the use of recycled timber product materials.

(Pub.L. 93–378, § 2, as added Pub.L. 94–588, § 2, Oct. 22, 1976, 90 Stat. 2949.)

### HISTORICAL AND STATUTORY NOTES

**References in Text**

The Multiple-Use Sustained-Yield Act of 1960, referred to in par. (3), is Pub.L. 86–517, June 12, 1960, 74 Stat. 215, which is classified to section 528 to 531 of this title. For complete classification of this Act to the Code, see Short Title note set out under section 528 of this title and Tables.

**Short Title**

1988 Amendments

Pub.L. 100–521, § 1, Oct. 24, 1988, 102 Stat. 2601, provided that: "This Act [amending section 1642 of this title and enacting provisions set out as a note under section 1642 of this title] may be cited as the 'Forest Ecosystems and Atmospheric Pollution Research Act of 1988'."

1987 Amendments

Pub.L. 100–231, § 1, Jan. 5, 1988, 101 Stat. 1565, provided: "This Act [amending sections 1674 and 1675 of this title and provisions set out as a note under section 1671 of this title] may be cited as the 'Renewable Resources Extension Act Amendments of 1987'."

1980 Amendments

Pub.L. 96–554, § 1, Dec. 19, 1980, 94 Stat. 3257, provided: "That this Act [enacting subchapter IV of this chapter and provision set out as a note under section 1681 of this title] may be cited as the 'Wood Residue Utilization Act of 1980'."

1978 Amendments

Pub.L. 95–307, § 1, June 30, 1978, 92 Stat. 353, provided: "That this Act [enacting subchapter II of this chapter, repealing sections 581 to 581i of this title, and enacting provisions set out as a note under sections 1641 of this title] may be cited as the 'Forest and Rangeland Renewable Resources Research Act of 1978'."

Pub.L. 95–306, § 1, June 30, 1978, 92 Stat. 349, provided: "That this Act [enacting subchapter III of this chapter and provisions set out as a note under section 1671 of this title] may be cited as the 'Renewable Resources Extension Act of 1978'."

1976 Amendments

Section 1 of Pub.L. 94–588 provided: "That this Act [enacting this section and sections 472a, 576b, 1611, 1612, 1613, and 1614 of this title, amending sections 500, 515, 516, 518, 1602, 1604, 1606, 1608, 1609, and 1610 of this title, repealing sections 476, 513, 513 note, and 514 of this title, and enacting provisions set out as notes under this section and sections 476, 528, and 594–2 of this title] may be cited as the 'National Forest Management Act of 1976'."

1974 Acts

Section 1 of Pub.L. 93–378 provided: "That this Act [which enacted this subchapter and amended section 581h of this title] may be cited as the 'Forest and Rangeland Renewable Resources Planning Act of 1974'."

**Separability of Provisions**

Section 21 of Pub.L. 94–588 provided that: "If any provision of this Act [see Short Title of 1976 Amendment note set out above] or the application thereof to any person or circumstances is held invalid, the validity of the remainder of the Act and of the application of such provision to other persons and circumstances shall not be affected thereby."

## § 1601. Renewable Resource Assessment

**[FRRRPA § 3(a)]**

**(a) Preparation by Secretary of Agriculture; time of preparation, updating and contents**

In recognition of the vital importance of America's renewable resources of the forest, range, and other associated lands to the Nation's social and economic well-being, and of the necessity for a long term perspective in planning and undertaking related national renewable resource programs administered by the Forest Service, the Secretary of Agriculture shall prepare a Renewable Resource Assessment (hereinafter called the "Assessment"). The Assessment shall be prepared not later than December 31, 1975, and shall be updated during 1979 and each tenth year thereafter, and shall include but not be limited to—

(1) an analysis of present and anticipated uses, demand for, and supply of the renewable resources, with consideration of the international resource situation, and an emphasis of pertinent supply and demand and price relationship trends;

(2) an inventory, based on information developed by the Forest Service and other Federal agencies, of present and potential renewable resources, and an evaluation of opportunities for improving their yield of tangible and intangible goods and services, together with estimates of investment costs and direct and indirect returns to the Federal Government;

(3) a description of Forest Service programs and responsibilities in research, cooperative programs and management of the National Forest System, their interrelationships, and the relationship of these programs and responsibilities to public and private activities;

(4) a discussion of important policy considerations, laws, regulations, and other factors expected to influence and affect significantly the use, ownership, and management of forest, range, and other associated lands; and [1]

(5) an analysis of the potential effects of global climate change on the condition of renewable resources on the forests and rangelands of the United States; and

(6) an analysis of the rural and urban forestry opportunities to mitigate the buildup of atmospheric carbon dioxide and reduce the risk of global climate change,[2]

### (b) Omitted

### (c) Contents of Assessments

The Secretary shall report in the 1979 and subsequent Assessments on:

(1) the additional fiber potential in the National Forest System including, but not restricted to, forest mortality, growth, salvage potential, potential increased forest products sales, economic constraints, alternate markets, contract considerations, and other multiple use considerations;

(2) the potential for increased utilization of forest and wood product wastes in the National Forest System and on other lands, and of urban wood wastes and wood product recycling, including recommendations to the Congress for actions which would lead to increased utilization of material now being wasted both in the forests and in manufactured products; and

(3) the milling and other wood fiber product fabrication facilities and their location in the United States, noting the public and private forested areas that supply such facilities, assessing the degree of utilization into product form of harvested trees by such facilities, and setting forth the technology appropriate to the facilities to improve utilization either individually or in aggregate units of harvested trees and to reduce wasted wood fibers. The Secretary shall set forth a program to encourage the adoption by these facilities of these technologies for improving wood fiber utilization.

### (d) [3] Public involvement; consultation with governmental departments and agencies

In developing the reports required under subsection (c) of this section, the Secretary shall provide opportunity for public involvement and shall consult with other interested governmental departments and agencies.

### (d) [3] Congressional policy of multiple use sustained yield management; examination and certification of lands; estimate of appropriations necessary for reforestation and other treatment; budget requirements; authorization of appropriations

(1) It is the policy of the Congress that all forested lands in the National Forest System shall be maintained in appropriate forest cover with species of trees, degree of stocking, rate of growth, and conditions of stand designed to secure the maximum benefits of multiple use sustained yield management in accordance with land management plans. Accordingly, the Secretary is directed to identify and report to the Congress annually at the time of submission of the President's budget together with the annual report provided for under section 1606(c) of this title, beginning with submission of the President's budget for fiscal year 1978, the amount and location by forests and States and by productivity class, where practicable, of all lands in the National Forest System where objectives of land management plans indicate the need to reforest areas that have been cut-over or otherwise denuded or deforested, and all lands with stands of trees that are not growing at their best potential rate of growth. All national forest lands treated from year to year shall be examined after the first and third growing seasons and certified by the Secretary in the report provided for under this subsection as to stock-

ing rate, growth rate in relation to potential and other pertinent measures. Any lands not certified as satisfactory shall be returned to the backlog and scheduled for prompt treatment. The level and types of treatment shall be those which secure the most effective mix of multiple use benefits.

(2) Notwithstanding the provisions of section 1607 of this title, the Secretary shall annually for eight years following October 22, 1976, transmit to the Congress in the manner provided in this subsection an estimate of the sums necessary to be appropriated, in addition to the funds available from other sources, to replant and otherwise treat an acreage equal to the acreage to be cut over that year, plus a sufficient portion of the backlog of lands found to be in need of treatment to eliminate the backlog within the eight-year period. After such eight-year period, the Secretary shall transmit annually to the Congress an estimate of the sums necessary to replant and otherwise treat all lands being cut over and maintain planned timber production on all other forested lands in the National Forest System so as to prevent the development of a backlog of needed work larger than the needed work at the beginning of the fiscal year. The Secretary's estimate of sums necessary, in addition to the sums available under other authorities, for accomplishment of the reforestation and other treatment of National Forest System lands under this section shall be provided annually for inclusion in the President's budget and shall also be transmitted to the Speaker of the House and the President of the Senate together with the annual report provided for under section 1606(c) of this title at the time of submission of the President's budget to the Congress beginning with the budget for fiscal year 1978. The sums estimated as necessary for reforestation and other treatment shall include moneys needed to secure seed, grow seedlings, prepare sites, plant trees, thin, remove deleterious growth and underbrush, build fence to exclude livestock and adverse wildlife from regeneration areas and otherwise establish and improve growing forests to secure planned production of trees and other multiple use values.

(3) Effective for the fiscal year beginning October 1, 1977, and each fiscal year thereafter, there is hereby authorized to be appropriated for the purpose of reforesting and treating lands in the National Forest System $200,000,000 annually to meet requirements of this subsection (d). All sums appropriated for the purposes of this subsection shall be available until expended.

### (e) Report on herbicides and pesticides

The Secretary shall submit an annual report to the Congress on the amounts, types, and uses of herbicides and pesticides used in the National Forest System, including the beneficial or adverse effects of such uses.

(Pub.L. 93–378, § 3, formerly § 2, Aug. 17, 1974, 88 Stat. 476; renumbered § 3 and amended Pub.L. 94–588, §§ 2 to 4, Oct. 22, 1976, 90 Stat. 2949, 2950; Pub.L. 101–624, Title XXIV, § 2408(a), Nov. 28, 1990, 104 Stat. 4061.)

[1] So in original. The word "and" probably should not appear.

[2] So in original. The comma should probably be a period.

[3] So in original. Two subsecs. (d) have been enacted.

## HISTORICAL AND STATUTORY NOTES

**Codifications**

Subsec. (b) of this section, omitted from this codification, amended section 581h of this title.

**Transfer of Functions**

The enforcement functions of the Secretary of Agriculture or other appropriate officer or entity in the Department of Agriculture, insofar as they involve lands and programs under the jurisdiction of that Department, related to compliance with system activities requiring coordination and approval under general authorities of this chapter as they relate to pre-construction, construction, and initial operation of an approved transportation system for the transport of Canadian natural gas and Alaskan natural gas as such terms are defined in the Alaskan Natural Gas Transportation Act of 1976, section 719 et seq. of Title 15, Commerce and Trade, were transferred to the Federal Inspector for the Alaska Natural Gas Transportation System, effective July 1, 1979, until the first anniversary of the date of initial operation of the Alaska Natural Gas Transportation System, pursuant to sections 102(f) and 203(a) of 1979 Reorg. Plan No. 1, June 12, 1979, 44 F.R. 33665, 33666, 93 Stat. 1373, set out in Appendix 1 to Title 5.

**Severability of Provisions**

If any provision of Pub.L. 101–624 or the application thereof to any person or circumstance is held invalid, such invalidity not to affect other provisions or applications of Pub.L. 101–624 which can be given effect without regard to the invalid provision or application, see section 2519 of Pub.L. 101–624, set out as a note under section 1421 of Title 7, Agriculture.

**Termination of Reporting Requirements**

For termination, effective May 15, 2000, of provisions in subsecs. (d)(1) and (e) of this section relating to submitting annual reports to Congress, see section 3003 of Pub.L. 104–66, as amended, set out as a note under 31 U.S.C.A. § 1113 and pages 45 and 47 of House Document No. 103–7.

**Presidential Commission on State and Private Forests**

Pub.L. 101–624, Title XII, § 1245, Nov. 28, 1990, 104 Stat. 3548, as amended Pub.L. 102–237, Title X, § 1018(b), Dec. 13, 1991, 105 Stat. 1905, provided that:

"**(a) Establishment.**—The President shall establish a Commission on State and Private Forests (hereafter in this section referred to as the 'Commission') which shall assess the status of the State and private forest lands of the United States, the problems affecting these lands, and the potential contribution of these lands to the renewable natural resource needs of the United States associated with their improved management and protection.

"(b) **Composition.**—The Commission shall be composed of 25 members to be appointed by the President, including Federal, State, and local officials, timber industry representatives, nonindustrial private forest landowners, conservationists, and community leaders. No more than five members shall be appointed from any one State. Not fewer than 20 members shall be appointed by the President from nominations submitted by the following Members of Congress:

"(1) The chairman of the Committee on Agriculture of the House of Representatives.

"(2) The ranking minority member of the Committee on Agriculture of the House of Representatives.

"(3) The chairman of the Committee on Agriculture, Nutrition, and Forestry of the Senate.

"(4) The ranking minority member of the Committee on Agriculture, Nutrition, and Forestry of the Senate.

"(c) **Vacancy.**—A vacancy on the Commission shall be filled by appointment by the President in the manner provided in subsection (b).

"(d) **Chairperson.**—The Commission shall elect a chairperson from among the members of the Commission by a majority vote.

"(e) **Meetings.**—The Commission shall meet at the call of the chairperson or a majority of the members of the Commission.

"(f) **Duties.**—

"(1) **Study.**—The Commission shall conduct a study that shall include—

"(A) an assessment using existing inventories of the current status of the State and private forest lands of the United States, including—

"(i) ownership status and past and future trends;

"(ii) the production of timber and nontimber resources from such lands; and

"(iii) landowner attitudes toward the protection and management of these lands;

"(B) a review of the problems affecting the State and private forest lands of the United States, including—

"(i) resource losses to insects, disease, fire, and damaging weather;

"(ii) inadequate reforestation;

"(iii) fragmentation and conversion of the forest land base; and

"(iv) management options;

"(C) constraints on, and opportunities for, providing multiresource outputs from forest lands;

"(D) administrative and legislative recommendations for addressing the problems and capitalizing on the potential of these lands for contributing to the renewable natural resource needs of the United States.

"(2) **Findings and recommendations.**—On the basis of its study, the Commission shall make findings and develop recommendations for consideration by the President with respect to the future demands placed on State and private forests in meeting both commodity and noncommodity needs of the United States in anticipation of impending changes in the management of the national forests, especially with regard to timber harvest. This assessment should focus on the role of State and private forest lands and help to identify means of improving their contribution to meeting the timber and nontimber needs of the United States.

"(3) **Report.**—The Commission shall submit to the President, not later than December 1, 1992, a report containing its findings and recommendations. The President shall submit the report to the Committee on Agriculture of the House of Representatives and the Committee on Agriculture, Nutrition, and Forestry of the Senate, and the report is authorized to be printed as a House Document.

"(g) **Operations in general**—

"(1) **Agency cooperation.**—The heads of executive agencies, the General Accounting Office, the Office of Technology Assessment, and the Congressional Budget Office shall cooperate with the Commission.

"(2) **Compensation.**—Members of the Commission shall serve without compensation for work on the Commission. While away from their homes or regular places of business in the performance of duties of the Commission, members of the Commission shall be allowed travel expenses, including per diem in lieu of subsistence, as authorized by law for persons serving intermittently in the Government service under section 5703 of title 5 of the United States Code. [Section 5703 of Title 5, Government Organization and Employees].

"(3) **Director.**—To the extent there are sufficient funds available to the Commission and subject to such rules as may be adopted by the Commission, the Commission, without regard to the provisions of title 5 of the United States Code [Title 5] governing appointments in the competitive service and without regard to the provisions of chapter 51 and subchapter III of chapter 53 of such title [chapter 51 and subchapter III of chapter 53 of Title V] relating to the classification and General Schedule pay rates, may—

"(A) appoint and fix the compensation of a director; and

"(B) appoint and fix the compensation of such additional personnel as the Commission determines necessary to assist it to carry out its duties and functions.

"(4) **Staff and services.**—On the request of the Commission, the heads of executive agencies, the Comptroller General, and the Director of the Office of Technology Assessment may furnish the Commission with such office, personnel or support services as the head of the agency, or office, and the chairperson of the Commission agree are necessary to assist the Commission to carry out its duties and functions. The Commission shall not be required to pay, or reimburse, any agency for office, personnel or support services provided by this subsection.

"(5) **Exemptions.**—

"(A) **FACA.**—The Commission shall be exempt from sections 7(d), 10(e), 10(f), and 14 of the Federal Advisory Committee Act (5 U.S.C. App. 2, 1 et seq. [sections 7(d), 10(e), 10(f), and 14 of Appendix 2 of Title 5].

"(B) **Title 5.**—The Commission shall be exempt from the requirements of sections 4301 through 4305 of title 5 of the United States Code [sections 4301 through 4305 of Title 5].

"(h) **Authorization of appropriations and spending authority.**—

"(1) **Authorization of appropriations.**—There is authorized to be appropriated such sums as are necessary to implement this section.

"(2) **Spending authority.**—Any spending authority (as defined in section 401 of the Congressional Budget Act of 1974 [section 651 of Title 2, The Congress]) provided in this title [Title XII of Pub.L. 101–624, Nov. 28, 1990, 104 Stat. 3521, for distribution of which see Short Title note set out under section 2101 of this title and Tables] shall be effective for any fiscal year only to such extent or in such amounts as are provided in appropriation Acts.

"(i) **Termination.**—The Presidential Commission on State and Private Forests shall cease to exist 90 days following the submission of its report to the President."

[Amendment by Pub.L. 102–237 effective Dec. 13, 1991, see section 1101(a) of Pub.L. 102–237, set out as a note under section 1421 of Title 7, Agriculture.]

## § 1602. Renewable Resource Program; preparation by Secretary of Agriculture and transmittal to President; purpose and development of program; time of preparation, updating and contents

[FRRRPA § 4]

In order to provide for periodic review of programs for management and administration of the National Forest System, for research, for cooperative State and private Forest Service programs, and for conduct of other Forest Service activities in relation to the findings of the Assessment, the Secretary of Agriculture, utilizing information available to the Forest Service and other agencies within the Department of Agriculture, including data prepared pursuant to section 1010a of Title 7, shall prepare and transmit to the President a recommended Renewable Resource Program (hereinafter called the "Program"). The Program transmitted to the President may include alternatives, and shall provide in appropriate detail for protection, management, and development of the National Forest System, including forest development roads and trails; for cooperative Forest Service programs; and for research. The Program shall be developed in accordance with principles set forth in the Multiple-Use Sustained-Yield Act of June 12, 1960 (74 Stat. 215; 16 U.S.C. 528–531), and the National Environmental Policy Act of 1969 (83 Stat. 852) [42 U.S.C.A. § 4321 et seq.]. The Program shall be prepared not later than December 31, 1975, to cover the four-year period beginning October 1, 1976, and at least each of the four fiscal decades next following such period, and shall be updated no later than during the first half of the fiscal year ending September 30, 1980, and the first half of each fifth fiscal year thereafter to cover at least each of the four fiscal decades beginning next after such updating. The Program shall include, but not be limited to—

(1) an inventory of specific needs and opportunities for both public and private program investments. The inventory shall differentiate between activities which are of a capital nature and those which are of an operational nature;

(2) specific identification of Program outputs, results anticipated, and benefits associated with investments in such a manner that the anticipated costs can be directly compared with the total related benefits and direct and indirect returns to the Federal Government;

(3) a discussion of priorities for accomplishment of inventoried Program opportunities, with specified costs, outputs, results, and benefits;

(4) a detailed study of personnel requirements as needed to implement and monitor existing and ongoing programs; and

(5) Program recommendations which—

(A) evaluate objectives for the major Forest Service programs in order that multiple-use and sustained-yield relationships among and within the renewable resources can be determined;

(B) explain the opportunities for owners of forests and rangeland to participate in programs to improve and enhance the condition of the land and the renewable resource products therefrom;

(C) recognize the fundamental need to protect and, where appropriate, improve the quality of soil, water, and air resources;

(D) state national goals that recognize the interrelationships between and interdependence within the renewable resources;

(E) evaluate the impact of the export and import of raw logs upon domestic timber supplies and prices; and

(F) account for the effects of global climate change on forest and rangeland conditions, including potential effects on the geographic ranges of species, and on forest and rangeland products.

(Pub.L. 93–378, § 4, formerly § 3, Aug. 17, 1974, 88 Stat. 477, renumbered and amended Pub.L. 94–588, §§ 2, 5, Oct. 22, 1976, 90 Stat. 2949, 2951; amended Pub.L. 101–624, Title XXIV, § 2408(b), Nov. 28, 1990, 104 Stat. 4061.)

### HISTORICAL AND STATUTORY NOTES

**References in Text**

The Multiple-Use Sustained-Yield Act of 1960, referred to in text, is classified to sections 528 to 531 of this title. For complete classification, see Short Title note set out under section 528 of this title and Tables.

The National Environmental Policy Act of 1969, referred to in text, is classified generally to chapter 55 of Title 42 (42 U.S.C.A. § 4321 et seq.). For complete classification, see Short Title note set out under section 4321 of Title 42 and Tables.

**Transfer of Functions**

For transfer of certain enforcement functions of Secretary or other official in Department of Agriculture under this subchapter to Federal Inspector, Office of Federal Inspector for the Alaska Natural Gas Transportation System, see Transfer of Functions note set out under section 1601 of this title.

**Severability of Provisions**

If any provision of Pub.L. 101–624 or the application thereof to any person or circumstance is held invalid, such invalidity not to affect other provisions or applications of Pub.L. 101–624 which can be given effect without regard to the invalid provision or application, see section 2519 of Pub.L. 101–624, set out as a note under section 1421 of Title 7, Agriculture.

## § 1603. National Forest System resource inventories; development, maintenance, and updating by Secretary of Agriculture as part of Assessment

**[FRRRPA § 5]**

As a part of the Assessment, the Secretary of Agriculture shall develop and maintain on a continuing basis a comprehensive and appropriately detailed inventory of all National Forest System lands and renewable resources. This inventory shall be kept current so as to reflect changes in conditions and identify new and emerging resources and values.

(Pub.L. 93–378, § 5, formerly § 4, Aug. 17, 1974, 88 Stat. 477, renumbered Pub.L. 94–588, § 2, Oct. 22, 1976, 90 Stat. 2949.)

## § 1604. National Forest System land and resource management plans

**[FRRRPA § 6]**

**(a) Development, maintenance, and revision by Secretary of Agriculture as part of program; coordination**

As a part of the Program provided for by section 1602 of this title, the Secretary of Agriculture shall develop, maintain, and, as appropriate, revise land and resource management plans for units of the National Forest System, coordinated with the land and resource management planning processes of State and local governments and other Federal agencies.

**(b) Criteria**

In the development and maintenance of land management plans for use on units of the National Forest System, the Secretary shall use a systematic interdisciplinary approach to achieve integrated consideration of physical, biological, economic, and other sciences.

**(c) Incorporation of standards and guidelines by Secretary; time of completion; progress reports; existing management plans**

The Secretary shall begin to incorporate the standards and guidelines required by this section in plans for units of the National Forest System as soon as practicable after October 22, 1976, and shall attempt to complete such incorporation for all such units by no later than September 30, 1985. The Secretary shall report to the Congress on the progress of such incorporation in the annual report required by section 1606(c) of this title. Until such time as a unit of the National Forest System is managed under plans developed in accordance with this subchapter, the management of such unit may continue under existing land and resource management plans.

**(d) Public participation in management plans; availability of plans; public meetings**

The Secretary shall provide for public participation in the development, review, and revision of land management plans including, but not limited to, making the plans or revisions available to the public at convenient locations in the vicinity of the affected unit for a period of at least three months before final adoption, during which period the Secretary shall publicize and hold public meetings or comparable processes at locations that foster public participation in the review of such plans or revisions.

**(e) Required assurances**

In developing, maintaining, and revising plans for units of the National Forest System pursuant to this section, the Secretary shall assure that such plans—

(1) provide for multiple use and sustained yield of the products and services obtained therefrom in accordance with the Multiple-Use Sustained-Yield Act of 1960 [16 U.S.C.A. §§ 528–531], and, in particular, include coordination of outdoor recreation, range, timber, watershed, wildlife and fish, and wilderness; and

(2) determine forest management systems, harvesting levels, and procedures in the light of all of the uses set forth in subsection (c)(1) of this section, the definition of the terms "multiple use" and "sustained yield" as provided in the Multiple-Use Sustained-Yield Act of 1960, and the availability of lands and their suitability for resource management.

**(f) Required provisions**

Plans developed in accordance with this section shall—

(1) form one integrated plan for each unit of the National Forest System, incorporating in one document or one set of documents, available to the public at convenient locations, all of the features required by this section;

(2) be embodied in appropriate written material, including maps and other descriptive documents, reflecting proposed and possible actions, including

the planned timber sale program and the proportion of probable methods of timber harvest within the unit necessary to fulfill the plan;

(3) be prepared by an interdisciplinary team. Each team shall prepare its plan based on inventories of the applicable resources of the forest;

(4) be amended in any manner whatsoever after final adoption after public notice, and, if such amendment would result in a significant change in such plan, in accordance with the provisions of subsections (e) and (f) of this section and public involvement comparable to that required by subsection (d) of this section; and

(5) be revised (A) from time to time when the Secretary finds conditions in a unit have significantly changed, but at least every fifteen years, and (B) in accordance with the provisions of subsections (e) and (f) of this section and public involvement comparable to that required by subsection (d) of this section.

**(g) Promulgation of regulations for development and revision of plans; environmental considerations; resource management guidelines; guidelines for land management plans**

As soon as practicable, but not later than two years after October 22, 1976, the Secretary shall in accordance with the procedures set forth in section 553 of Title 5, promulgate regulations, under the principles of the Multiple-Use Sustained-Yield Act of 1960 [16 U.S.C.A. §§ 528 to 531], that set out the process for the development and revision of the land management plans, and the guidelines and standards prescribed by this subsection. The regulations shall include, but not be limited to—

(1) specifying procedures to insure that land management plans are prepared in accordance with the National Environmental Policy Act of 1969 [42 U.S.C.A. § 4321 et seq.], including, but not limited to, direction on when and for what plans an environmental impact statement required under section 102(2)(C) of that Act [42 U.S.C.A. § 4332(2)(C)] shall be prepared;

(2) specifying guidelines which—

(A) require the identification of the suitability of lands for resource management;

(B) provide for obtaining inventory data on the various renewable resources, and soil and water, including pertinent maps, graphic material, and explanatory aids; and

(C) provide for methods to identify special conditions or situations involving hazards to the various resources and their relationship to alternative activities;

(3) specifying guidelines for land management plans developed to achieve the goals of the Program which—

(A) insure consideration of the economic and environmental aspects of various systems of renewable resource management, including the related systems of silviculture and protection of forest resources, to provide for outdoor recreation (including wilderness), range, timber, watershed, wildlife, and fish;

(B) provide for diversity of plant and animal communities based on the suitability and capability of the specific land area in order to meet overall multiple-use objectives, and within the multiple-use objectives of a land management plan adopted pursuant to this section, provide, where appropriate, to the degree practicable, for steps to be taken to preserve the diversity of tree species similar to that existing in the region controlled by the plan;

(C) insure research on and (based on continuous monitoring and assessment in the field) evaluation of the effects of each management system to the end that it will not produce substantial and permanent impairment of the productivity of the land;

(D) permit increases in harvest levels based on intensified management practices, such as reforestation, thinning, and tree improvement if (i) such practices justify increasing the harvests in accordance with the Multiple-Use Sustained-Yield Act of 1960, and (ii) such harvest levels are decreased at the end of each planning period if such practices cannot be successfully implemented or funds are not received to permit such practices to continue substantially as planned;

(E) insure that timber will be harvested from National Forest System lands only where—

(i) soil, slope, or other watershed conditions will not be irreversibly damaged;

(ii) there is assurance that such lands can be adequately restocked within five years after harvest;

(iii) protection is provided for streams, streambanks, shorelines, lakes, wetlands, and other bodies of water from detrimental changes in water temperatures, blockages of water courses, and deposits of sediment, where harvests are likely to seriously and adversely affect water conditions or fish habitat; and

(iv) the harvesting system to be used is not selected primarily because it will give the greatest dollar return or the greatest unit output of timber; and

(F) insure that clearcutting, seed tree cutting, shelterwood cutting, and other cuts designed to regenerate an evenaged stand of timber will be used as a cutting method on National Forest System lands only where—

(i) for clearcutting, it is determined to be the optimum method, and for other such cuts it is determined to be appropriate, to meet the objectives and requirements of the relevant land management plan;

(ii) the interdisciplinary review as determined by the Secretary has been completed and the potential environmental, biological, esthetic, engineering, and economic impacts on each advertised sale area have been assessed, as well as the consistency of the sale with the multiple use of the general area;

(iii) cut blocks, patches, or strips are shaped and blended to the extent practicable with the natural terrain;

(iv) there are established according to geographic areas, forest types, or other suitable classifications the maximum size limits for areas to be cut in one harvest operation, including provision to exceed the established limits after appropriate public notice and review by the responsible Forest Service officer one level above the Forest Service officer who normally would approve the harvest proposal: *Provided*, That such limits shall not apply to the size of areas harvested as a result of natural catastrophic conditions such as fire, insect and disease attack, or windstorm; and

(v) such cuts are carried out in a manner consistent with the protection of soil, watershed, fish, wildlife, recreation, and esthetic resources, and the regeneration of the timber resource.

**(h) Scientific committee to aid in promulgation of regulations; termination; revision committees; clerical and technical assistance; compensation of committee members**

(1) In carrying out the purposes of subsection (g) of this section, the Secretary of Agriculture shall appoint a committee of scientists who are not officers or employees of the Forest Service. The committee shall provide scientific and technical advice and counsel on proposed guidelines and procedures to assure that an effective interdisciplinary approach is proposed and adopted. The committee shall terminate upon promulgation of the regulations, but the Secretary may, from time to time, appoint similar committees when considering revisions of the regulations. The views of the committees shall be included in the public information supplied when the regulations are proposed for adoption.

(2) Clerical and technical assistance, as may be necessary to discharge the duties of the committee, shall be provided from the personnel of the Department of Agriculture.

(3) While attending meetings of the committee, the members shall be entitled to receive compensation at a rate of $100 per diem, including traveltime, and while away from their homes or regular places of business they may be allowed travel expenses, including per diem in lieu of subsistence, as authorized by section 5703 of Title 5, for persons in the Government service employed intermittently.

**(i) Consistency of resource plans, permits, contracts, and other instruments with land management plans; revision**

Resource plans and permits, contracts, and other instruments for the use and occupancy of National Forest System lands shall be consistent with the land management plans. Those resource plans and permits, contracts, and other such instruments currently in existence shall be revised as soon as practicable to be made consistent with such plans. When land management plans are revised, resource plans and permits, contracts, and other instruments, when necessary, shall be revised as soon as practicable. Any revision in present or future permits, contracts, and other instruments made pursuant to this section shall be subject to valid existing rights.

**(j) Effective date of land management plans and revisions**

Land management plans and revisions shall become effective thirty days after completion of public participation and publication of notification by the Secretary as required under subsection (d) of this section.

**(k) Development of land management plans**

In developing land management plans pursuant to this subchapter, the Secretary shall identify lands within the management area which are not suited for timber production, considering physical, economic, and other pertinent factors to the extent feasible, as determined by the Secretary, and shall assure that, except for salvage sales or sales necessitated to protect other multiple-use values, no timber harvesting shall occur on such lands for a period of 10 years. Lands once identified as unsuitable for timber production shall continue to be treated for reforestation purposes, particularly with regard to the protection of other multiple-use values. The Secretary shall review his decision to classify these lands as not suited for timber production at least every 10 years and shall return these lands to timber production whenever he determines that conditions have changed so that they have become suitable for timber production.

**(*l*) Program evaluation; process for estimating long-term costs and benefits; summary of data included in annual report**

The Secretary shall—

(1) formulate and implement, as soon as practicable, a process for estimating long-terms [1] costs and benefits to support the program evaluation requirements of this subchapter. This process shall include requirements to provide information on a representative sample basis of estimated expenditures associated with the reforestation, timber stand improvement, and sale of timber from the National Forest System, and shall provide a comparison of these expenditures to the return to the Government resulting from the sale of timber; and

(2) include a summary of data and findings resulting from these estimates as a part of the annual report required pursuant to section 1606(c) of this title, including an identification on a representative sample basis of those advertised timber sales made below the estimated expenditures for such timber as determined by the above cost process; and [2]

**(m) Establishment of standards to ensure culmination of mean annual increment of growth; silvicultural practices; salvage harvesting; exceptions**

The Secretary shall establish—

(1) standards to insure that, prior to harvest, stands of trees throughout the National Forest System shall generally have reached the culmination of mean annual increment of growth (calculated on the basis of cubic measurement or other methods of calculation at the discretion of the Secretary): *Provided*, That these standards shall not preclude the use of sound silvicultural practices, such as thinning or other stand improvement measures: *Provided further*, That these standards shall not preclude the Secretary from salvage or sanitation harvesting of timber stands which are substantially damaged by fire, windthrow or other catastrophe, or which are in imminent danger from insect or disease attack; and

(2) exceptions to these standards for the harvest of particular species of trees in management units after consideration has been given to the multiple uses of the forest including, but not limited to, recreation, wildlife habitat, and range and after completion of public participation processes utilizing the procedures of subsection (d) of this section.

(Pub.L. 93–378, § 6, formerly § 5, Aug. 17, 1974, 88 Stat. 477; renumbered § 6 and amended Pub.L. 94–588, §§ 2, 6, 12(a), Oct. 22, 1976, 90 Stat. 2949, 2952, 2958.)

[1] So in original. Probably should be "long-term".

[2] So in original. The "; and" probably should be a period.

## HISTORICAL AND STATUTORY NOTES

**References in Text**

The Multiple-Use Sustained-Yield Act of 1960, referred to in subsecs. (e) and (g), is classified to sections 528 to 531 of this title. For complete classification, see Short Title note set out under section 528 of this title and Tables.

The National Environmental Policy Act of 1969, referred to in subsec. (g)(1), is classified generally to chapter 55 of Title 42 (42 U.S.C.A. § 4321 et seq.). For complete classification, see Short Title note set out under section 4321 of Title 42 and Tables.

**Transfer of Functions**

For transfer of certain enforcement functions of Secretary or other official in Department of Agriculture under this subchapter to Federal Inspector, Office of Federal Inspector for the Alaska Natural Gas Transportation System, see Transfer of Functions note set out under section 1601 of this title.

**Revision of Forest Plans**

Pub.L. 108–108, Title III, § 320, Nov. 10, 2003, 117 Stat. 1306, provided that: "Prior to October 1, 2004, the Secretary of Agriculture shall not be considered to be in violation of subparagraph 6(f)(5)(A) of the Forest and Rangeland Renewable Resources Planning Act of 1974 (16 U.S.C. 1604(f)(5)(A) [subsec. (f)(5)(A) of this section]) solely because more than 15 years have passed without revision of the plan for a unit of the National Forest System. Nothing in this section exempts the Secretary from any other requirement of the Forest and Rangeland Renewable Resources Planning Act (16 U.S.C. 1600 et seq.) [Pub.L. 93–378, Aug. 17, 1974, 88 Stat. 476] or any other law: *Provided*, That if the Secretary is not acting expeditiously and in good faith, within the funding available, to revise a plan for a unit of the National Forest System, this section [this note] shall be void with respect to such plan and a court of proper jurisdiction may order completion of the plan on an accelerated basis."

Similar provisions were contained in the following prior Appropriations Acts:

Pub.L. 108–7, Div. F, Title III, § 320, Feb. 20, 2003, 117 Stat. 274.

Pub.L. 107–63, Title III, § 327, Nov. 5, 2001, 115 Stat. 470.

**Forest Land and Resource Management Plans of Forest Service and Bureau of Land Management**

Pub.L. 101–121, Title III, § 312, Oct. 23, 1989, 103 Stat. 743, provided that: "The Forest Service and Bureau of Land Management are to continue to complete as expeditiously as possible development of their respective Forest Land and Resource Management Plans to meet all applicable statutory requirements. Notwithstanding the date in section 6(c) of the NFMA (16 U.S.C. 1600) [subsec. (c) of this section], the Forest Service, and the Bureau of Land Management under separate authority, may continue the management of lands within their jurisdiction under existing land and resource management plans pending the completion of new plans. Nothing shall limit judicial review of particular activities on these lands: *Provided, however*, That there shall be no challenges to any existing plan on the sole basis that the plan in its entirety is outdated, or in the case of the Bureau of Land Management, solely on the basis that the plan does not incorporate information available subsequent to the completion of the existing plan: *Provided further*, That any and all particular activities to be carried out under existing plans may nevertheless be challenged."

Similar provisions were contained in the following prior Appropriations Acts:

Pub.L. 100–446, Title III, § 314, Sept. 27, 1988, 102 Stat. 1825.

Pub.L. 100–202, § 101(g)[Title III, § 314], Dec. 22, 1987, 101 Stat. 1329–254.

Pub.L. 99–591, Title I, § 101(h)[Title II, § 201], Oct. 30, 1986, 100 Stat. 3341–268.

Pub.L. 99–500, Title I, § 101(h)[Title II, § 201], Oct. 18, 1986, 100 Stat. 1783–268.

**Expeditious Completion of Management Plans; Continuation of Present Plans Pending Development of New Plans; Judicial Review**

Pub.L. 99–500, Title I, § 101(h) [Title II, § 201], Oct. 18, 1986, 100 Stat.1783–268, provided in part that: "The Forest Service is to continue to complete as expeditiously as possible development of land and resource management plans to meet the requirements of the National Forest Management Act of 1976 (NFMA) [Pub.L. 94–588, Oct. 22, 1976, 90 Stat. 2949]. Notwithstanding the date in section 6(c) of the NFMA (16 U.S.C. 1600) [probably means section 6(c) of Pub.L. 93–378 which is classified to subsec. (c) of this section], the Forest Service may continue the management of units of the National Forest System under existing land and resource management plans pending the completion of plans developed in accordance with the Act [this chapter]. Nothing shall limit judicial review of particular activities on management units of the National Forest System: *Provided, however,* That there shall be no challenges to any existing plan on the sole basis that the plan in its entirety is outdated: *Provided further,* That any and all particular activities to be carried out under existing plans may nevertheless be challenged."

[An identical provision is contained in Pub.L. 99–591, Title I, § 101(h) [Title II, § 201], Oct. 30, 1986, 100 Stat. 3341–268.]

## § 1605. Protection, use and management of renewable resources on non-Federal lands; utilization of Assessment, surveys and Program by Secretary of Agriculture to assist States, etc.

**[FRRRPA § 7]**

The Secretary of Agriculture may utilize the Assessment, resource surveys, and Program prepared pursuant to this subchapter to assist States and other organizations in proposing the planning for the protection, use, and management of renewable resources on non-Federal land.

(Pub.L. 93–378, § 7, formerly § 6, Aug. 17, 1974, 88 Stat. 478, renumbered Pub.L. 94–588, § 2, Oct. 22, 1976, 90 Stat. 2949.)

## § 1606. Budget requests by President for Forest Service activities

**[FRRRPA § 8]**

**(a) Transmittal to Speaker of House and President of Senate of Assessment, Program and Statement of Policy used in framing requests; time for transmittal; implementation by President of programs established under Statement of Policy unless Statement subsequently disapproved by Congress; time for disapproval**

On the date Congress first convenes in 1976 and thereafter following each updating of the Assessment and the Program, the President shall transmit to the Speaker of the House of Representatives and the President of the Senate, when Congress convenes, the Assessment as set forth in section 1601 of this title and the Program as set forth in section 1602 of this title, together with a detailed Statement of Policy intended to be used in framing budget requests by that Administration for Forest Service activities for the five- or ten-year program period beginning during the term of such Congress for such further action deemed appropriate by the Congress. Following the transmission of such Assessment, Program, and Statement of Policy, the President shall, subject to other actions of the Congress, carry out programs already established by law in accordance with such Statement of Policy or any subsequent amendment or modification thereof approved by the Congress, unless, before the end of the first period of ninety calendar days of continuous session of Congress after the date on which the President of the Senate and the Speaker of the House are recipients of the transmission of such Assessment, Program, and Statement of Policy, either House adopts a resolution reported by the appropriate committee of jurisdiction disapproving the Statement of Policy. For the purpose of this subsection, the continuity of a session shall be deemed to be broken only by an adjournment sine die, and the days on which either House is not in session because of an adjournment of more than three days to a day certain shall be excluded in the computation of the ninety-day period. Notwithstanding any other provision of this subchapter, Congress may revise or modify the Statement of Policy transmitted by the President, and the revised or modified Statement of Policy shall be used in framing budget requests.

**(b) Contents of requests to show extent of compliance of projected programs and policies with policies approved by Congress; requests not conforming to approved policies; expenditure of appropriations**

Commencing with the fiscal budget for the year ending September 30, 1977, requests presented by the President to the Congress governing Forest Service activities shall express in qualitative and quantitative terms the extent to which the programs and policies projected under the budget meet the policies approved by the Congress in accordance with subsection (a) of this section. In any case in which such budget so presented recommends a course which fails to meet the policies so established, the President shall specifically set forth the reason or reasons for requesting the Congress to approve the lesser programs or policies presented. Amounts appropriated to carry out the policies approved in accordance with subsection (a) of this section shall be expended in accordance with the Congressional Budget and Impoundment Control Act of 1974.

**(c) Annual evaluation report to Congress of Program components; time of submission; status of major research programs; application of findings; status, etc., of cooperative forestry assistance programs and activities**

For the purpose of providing information that will aid Congress in its oversight responsibilities and improve the accountability of agency expenditures and activities, the Secretary of Agriculture shall prepare an annual report which evaluates the component elements of the Program required to be prepared by section 1602 of this title which shall be furnished to the Congress at the time of submission of the annual fiscal budget commencing with the third fiscal year after August 17, 1974. With regard to the research component of the program, the report shall include, but not be limited to, a description of the status of major research programs, significant findings, and how these findings will be applied in National Forest System management and in cooperative State and private Forest Service programs. With regard to the cooperative forestry assistance part of the Program, the report shall include, but not be limited to, a description of the status, accomplishments, needs, and work backlogs for the programs and activities conducted under the Cooperative Forestry Assistance Act of 1978 [16 U.S.C.A. § 2101 et seq.].

**(d) Required contents of annual evaluation report**

These annual evaluation reports shall set forth progress in implementing the Program required to be prepared by section 1602 of this title, together with accomplishments of the Program as they relate to the objectives of the Assessment. Objectives should be set forth in qualitative and quantitative terms and accomplishments should be reported accordingly. The report shall contain appropriate measurements of pertinent costs and benefits. The evaluation shall assess the balance between economic factors and environmental quality factors. Program benefits shall include, but not be limited to, environmental quality factors such as esthetics, public access, wildlife habitat, recreational and wilderness use, and economic factors such as the excess of cost savings over the value of foregone benefits and the rate of return on renewable resources.

**(e) Additional required contents of annual evaluation report**

The reports shall indicate plans for implementing corrective action and recommendations for new legislation where warranted.

**(f) Form of annual evaluation report**

The reports shall be structured for Congress in concise summary form with necessary detailed data in appendices.

(Pub.L. 93–378, § 8, formerly § 7, Aug. 17, 1974, 88 Stat. 478; renumbered § 8 and amended Pub.L. 94–588, §§ 2, 7, 12(b), Oct. 22, 1976, 90 Stat. 2949, 2956, 2958; Pub.L. 95–313, § 15, formerly § 12, July 1, 1978, 92 Stat. 374; renumbered § 15, Pub.L. 101–624, Title XII, § 1215(1), Nov. 28, 1990, 104 Stat. 3525.)

## HISTORICAL AND STATUTORY NOTES

**References in Text**

Congressional Budget and Impoundment Control Act of 1974, referred to in subsec. (b), is Pub.L. 93–344, July 12, 1974, 88 Stat. 297, as amended. For complete classification, see Short Title note set out under section 621 of Title 2 and Tables.

The Cooperative Forestry Assistance Act of 1978, referred to in subsec. (c), is classified principally to chapter 41 of this title (16 U.S.C.A. § 2101 et seq.). For complete classification, see Short Title note set out under section 2101 of this title and Tables.

**Effective and Applicability Provisions**

1978 Acts

Amendment by Pub.L. 95–313 effective Oct. 1, 1978, see section 17 of Pub.L. 95–313, set out as a note under section 2101 of this title.

**Statement of Policy**

Pub.L. 96–514, Title III, § 310, Dec. 12, 1980, 94 Stat. 2984, provided that:

"The Statement of Policy transmitted by the President to the Speaker of the House of Representatives and the President of the Senate on June 19, 1980, as required under section 8 of the Forest and Rangeland Renewable Resources Planning Act of 1974 [this section], is revised and modified to read as follows:

**"STATEMENT OF POLICY**

**"BASIC PRINCIPLES**

"It is the policy of the United States—

"(1) forests and rangeland, in all ownerships, should be managed to maximize their net social and economic contributions to the Nation's well being, in an environmentally sound manner.

"(2) the Nation's forested land, except such public land that is determined by law or policy to be maintained in its existing or natural state, should be managed at levels that realize its capabilities to satisfy the Nation's need for food, fiber, energy, water, soil stability, wildlife and fish, recreation, and esthetic values.

"(3) the productivity of suitable forested land, in all ownerships, should be maintained and enhanced to minimize the inflationary impacts of wood product prices on the domestic economy and permit a net export of forest products by the year 2030.

"(4) in order to achieve this goal, it is recognized that in the major timber growing regions most of the commercial timber lands will have to be brought to and maintained, where possible, at 90 percent of their potential level of growth, consistent with the provisions of the National Forest Management Act of 1976 on Federal lands, so that all resources are utilized in the combination that will best meet the needs of the American people.

"(5) forest and rangeland protection programs should be improved to more adequately protect forest and rangeland resources from fire, erosion, insects, disease, and the introduction or spread of noxious weeds, insects, and animals.

"(6) the Federal agencies carrying out the policies contained in this Statement will cooperate and coordinate their efforts to accomplish the goals contained in this Statement and will consult, coordinate, and cooperate with the planning efforts of the States.

"(7) in carrying out the Assessment and the Program under the Forest and Rangeland Renewable Resources Planning Act of 1974 [this subchapter] and the Appraisal and the Program under the Soil and Water Resources Conservation Act of 1977 [section 2001 et seq. of this title], the Secretary of Agriculture shall assure that resource and economic information and evaluation data will be continually improved so that the best possible information is always available for use by Federal agencies and the public.

"RANGE LAND DATA BASE AND ITS IMPROVEMENT

"The data on and understanding of the cover and condition of range lands is less refined than the data on and understanding of commercial forest land. Range lands have significant value in the production of water and protection of watersheds; the production of fish and wildlife food and habitat; recreation; and the production of livestock forage. An adequate data base on the cover and condition of range lands should be developed by the year 1990. Currently, cattle production from these lands is annually estimated at 213 million animal unit months of livestock forage. These lands should be maintained and enhanced, including their water and other resource values, so that they can annually provide 310 million animal units months of forage by the year 2030, along with other benefits.

"GENERAL ACCEPTANCE OF HIGH BOUND PROGRAM

"Congress generally accepts the 'high-bound' program described on pages 7 through 18 of the 1980 Report to Congress on the Nation's Renewable Resources prepared by the Secretary of Agriculture. However, Congress finds that the 'high-bound' program may not be sufficient to accomplish the goals contained in this statement, particularly in the areas of range and watershed resources, State and private forest cooperation and timber management.

"STATE AND PRIVATE LANDS

"States and owners of private forest and rangelands will be encouraged, consistent with their individual objectives, to manage their land in support of this Statement of Policy. The State and private forestry and range programs of the Forest Service will be essential to the furtherance of this Statement of Policy.

"FUNDING THE GOALS

"In order to accomplish the policy goals contained in this statement by the year 2030, the Federal Government should adequately fund programs of research (including cooperative research), extension, cooperative forestry assistance and protection, and improved management of the forest and rangelands. The Secretary of Agriculture shall continue his efforts to evaluate the cost-effectiveness of the renewable resource programs."

**Statement of Purposes of Amendment by Cooperative Forestry Assistance Act of 1978**

Section 12 of Pub.L. 95–313 provided in part that the amendment of subsec. (c) of this section by Pub.L. 95–313 is to insure that Congress has adequate information to implement its oversight responsibilities and to provide accountability for expenditures and activities under the Cooperative Forestry Assistance Act of 1978. See Short Title note set out under section 2101 of this title for distribution of the Cooperative Forestry Assistance Act of 1978 in the Code.

## § 1606a. Reforestation Trust Fund

**(a) Establishment; source of funds**

There is established in the Treasury of the United States a trust fund, to be known as the Reforestation Trust Fund (hereinafter in this section referred to as the "Trust Fund"), consisting of such amounts as are transferred to the Trust Fund under subsection (b) (1) of this section and any interest earned on investment of amounts in the Trust Fund under subsection (c) (2) of this section.

**(b) Transfer of certain tariff receipts to Trust Fund; fiscal year limitation; quarterly transfers; adjustment of estimates**

(1) Subject to the limitation in paragraph (2), the Secretary of the Treasury shall transfer to the Trust Fund an amount equal to the sum of the tariffs received in the Treasury after January 1, 1989, under headings 4401 through 4412 and subheadings 4418.50.00, 4418.90.20, 4420.10.00, 4420.90.80, 4421.90.10 through 4421.90.20, and 4421.90.70 of chapter 44, subheadings 6808.00.00 and 6809.11.00 of chapter 68 and subheading 9614.10.00 of chapter 96 of the Harmonized Tariff Schedule of the United States.

(2) The Secretary shall not transfer more than $30,000,000 to the Trust Fund for any fiscal year.

(3) The amounts required to be transferred to the Trust Fund under paragraph (1) shall be transferred at least quarterly from the general fund of the Treasury to the Trust Fund on the basis of estimates made by the Secretary of the Treasury. Proper adjustment shall be made in the amounts subsequently transferred to the extent prior estimates were in excess of or less than the amounts required to be transferred.

**(c) Report to Congress; printing as House and Senate document; investments; sale and redemption of obligations; credits for Trust Fund**

(1) It shall be the duty of the Secretary of the Treasury to hold the Trust Fund, and (after consultation with the Secretary of Agriculture) to report to the Congress each year on the financial condition and the results of the operations of the Trust Fund during the preceding fiscal year and on its expected condition and operations during the next fiscal year. Such report shall be printed as both a House and Senate document of the session of the Congress to which the report is made.

(2)(A) It shall be the duty of the Secretary of the Treasury to invest such portion of the Trust Fund as is not, in his judgment, required to meet current withdrawals. Such investments may be made only in interest-bearing obligations of the United States or in obligations guaranteed as to both principal and interest by the United States. For such purpose, such obligations may be acquired (i) on original issue at the issue price, or (ii) by purchase of outstanding obligations at the market price. The purposes for which obligations of the United States may be issued under chapter 31 of Title 31 are hereby extended to authorize the issuance at par of special obligations exclusively to the Trust Fund. Such special obligations shall bear interest at a rate equal to the average rate of interest, computed as to the end of the calendar month next preceding the date of such issue, borne by all marketable interest-bearing obligations of the United States then forming a part of the Public Debt; except that where such average rate is not a multiple of one-eighth of 1 percent, the rate of interest of such special obligations shall be the multiple of one-eighth of 1 percent next lower than such average rate. Such special obligations shall be issued only if the Secretary of the Treasury determines that the purchase of other interest-bearing obligations of the United States, or of obligations guaranteed as to both principal and interest by the United States on original issue or at the market price, is not in the public interest.

(B) Any obligation acquired by the Trust Fund (except special obligations issued exclusively to the Trust Fund) may be sold by the Secretary of the Treasury at the market price, and such special obligations may be redeemed at par plus accrued interest.

(C) The interest on, and the proceeds from the sale or redemption of, any obligations held in the Trust Fund shall be credited to and form a part of the Trust Fund.

**(d) Obligations from Trust Fund**

The Secretary of Agriculture is on and after December 19, 1985, authorized to obligate such sums as are available in the Trust Fund (including any amounts not obligated in previous fiscal years) for—

(1) reforestation and timber stand improvement as specified in section 1601(d) of this title and other forest stand improvement activities to enhance forest health and reduce hazardous fuel loads of forest stands in the National Forest System; and

(2) properly allocable administrative costs of the Federal Government for the activities specified above.

(Pub.L. 96–451, Title III, § 303, Oct. 14, 1980, 94 Stat. 1991; Pub.L. 97–424, Title IV, § 422, Jan. 6, 1983, 96 Stat. 2164; Pub.L. 99–190, § 101(d) [Title II, § 201], Dec. 19, 1985, 99 Stat. 1245; Pub.L. 100–418, Title I, § 1214(r), Aug. 23, 1988, 102 Stat. 1160; Pub.L. 105–83, Title III, § 322, Nov. 14, 1997, 111 Stat. 1596.)

### HISTORICAL AND STATUTORY NOTES

**Codifications**

Section was not enacted as part of the Forest and Rangeland Renewable Resources Planning Act of 1974, which comprises this subchapter.

In subsec. (c)(2)(A), "chapter 31 of Title 31" was substituted for "the Second Liberty Bond Act, as amended" on authority of Pub.L. 97–258, § 4(b), Sept. 13, 1982, 96 Stat. 1067, the first section of which enacted Title 31, Money and Finance.

**Effective and Applicability Provisions**

1988 Acts

Amendment by Pub.L. 100–418, effective Jan. 1, 1989, and applicable with respect to articles entered on or after such date, see section 1217(b)(1) of Pub.L. 100–418, set out as a note under section 3001 of Title 19, Customs Duties.

## § 1607. National Forest System renewable resources; development and administration by Secretary of Agriculture in accordance with multiple use and sustained yield concepts for products and services; target year for operational posture of resources; budget requests

**[FRRRPA § 9]**

The Secretary of Agriculture shall take such action as will assure that the development and administration of the renewable resources of the National Forest System are in full accord with the concepts for multiple use and sustained yield of products and services as set forth in the Multiple-Use Sustained-Yield Act of 1960 [16 U.S.C.A. §§ 528–531]. To further these concepts, the Congress hereby sets the year 2000 as the target year when the renewable resources of the National Forest System shall be in an operating posture whereby all backlogs of needed treatment for their restoration shall be reduced to a current basis and the major portion of planned intensive multiple-use sustained-yield management procedures shall be installed and operating on an environmentally-sound basis. The annual budget shall contain requests for funds for an orderly program to eliminate such backlogs: *Provided*, That when the Secretary finds that (1) the backlog of areas that will benefit by such treatment has been eliminated, (2) the cost of treating the remainder of such area exceeds the economic and environmental benefits to be secured from their treatment, or (3) the total supplies of the renewable resources of the United States are adequate to meet the future needs of the American people, the budget request for these elements of restoration may be adjusted accordingly.

(Pub.L. 93–378, § 9, formerly § 8, Aug. 17, 1974, 88 Stat. 479, renumbered Pub.L. 94–588, § 2, Oct. 22, 1976, 90 Stat. 2949.)

### HISTORICAL AND STATUTORY NOTES

**References in Text**

The Multiple-Use Sustained-Yield Act of 1960, referred to in text, is classified to sections 528 to 531 of this title. For complete classification, see Short Title note set out under section 528 of this title and Tables.

**Transfer of Functions**

For transfer of certain enforcement functions of Secretary or other official in Department of Agriculture under this subchapter to Federal Inspector, Office of Federal Inspector for the Alaska Natural Gas Transportation System, see Transfer of Functions note set out under section 1601 of this title.

## § 1608. National Forest Transportation System [FRRRPA § 10]

### (a) Congressional declaration of policy; time for development; method of financing; financing of forest development roads

The Congress declares that the installation of a proper system of transportation to service the National Forest System, as is provided for in sections 532 to 538 of this title, shall be carried forward in time to meet anticipated needs on an economical and environmentally sound basis, and the method chosen for financing the construction and maintenance of the transportation system should be such as to enhance local, regional, and national benefits: *Provided*, That limitations on the level of obligations for construction of forest roads by timber purchasers shall be established in annual appropriation Acts.

### (b) Construction of temporary roadways in connection with timber contracts, and other permits or leases

Unless the necessity for a permanent road is set forth in the forest development road system plan, any road constructed on land of the National Forest System in connection with a timber contract or other permit or lease shall be designed with the goal of reestablishing vegetative cover on the roadway and areas where the vegetative cover has been disturbed by the construction of the road, within ten years after the termination of the contract, permit, or lease either through artificial or natural means. Such action shall be taken unless it is later determined that the road is needed for use as a part of the National Forest Transportation System.

### (c) Standards of roadway construction

Roads constructed on National Forest System lands shall be designed to standards appropriate for the intended uses, considering safety, cost of transportation, and impacts on land and resources.

(Pub.L. 93–378, § 10, formerly § 9, Aug. 17, 1974, 88 Stat. 479, renumbered and amended Pub.L. 94–588, §§ 2, 8, Oct. 22, 1976, 90 Stat. 2949, 2956; Pub.L. 97–100, Title II, § 201, Dec. 23, 1981, 95 Stat. 1405.)

### HISTORICAL AND STATUTORY NOTES

**Transfer of Functions**

For transfer of certain enforcement functions of Secretary or other official in Department of Agriculture under this subchapter to Federal Inspector, Office of Federal Inspector for the Alaska Natural Gas Transportation System, see Transfer of Functions note set out under section 1601 of this title.

**County Payment Mitigation.—Transportation System Moratorium.**

Pub.L. 105–174, § 3006, May 1, 1998, 112 Stat. 85, provided that:

"(a)(1) This section provides compensation for loss of revenues that would have been provided to counties if no road moratorium, as described in subsection (a)(2) [of this note], were implemented or no substitute sales offered as described in subsection (b)(1) [of this note]. This section does not endorse or prohibit the road building moratorium nor does it affect the applicability of existing law to any moratorium.

"(2) The Chief of the Forest Service, Department of Agriculture, in his sole discretion, may offer any timber sales that were scheduled October 1, 1997, or thereafter, to be offered in fiscal year 1998 or fiscal year 1999 even if such sales would have been delayed or halted as a result of any moratorium (resulting from the Federal Register proposal of January 28, 1998, pages 4351–4354) [63 FR 4351] on construction of roads in roadless areas within the National Forest System adopted as policy or by regulation that would otherwise be applicable to such sales.

"(3) Any sales offered pursuant to subsection (a)(2) shall.—

"(A) comply with all applicable laws and regulations and be consistent with applicable land and resource management plans, except any regulations or plan amendments which establish or implement the moratorium referred to in subsection (a)(2); and

"(B) be subject to administrative appeals pursuant to part 215 of title 36 of the Code of Federal Regulations [36 CFR 215] and to judicial review.

"(b)(1) For any previously scheduled sales that are not offered pursuant to subsection (a)(2) [of this note], the Chief may, to the extent practicable, offer substitute sales within the same State in fiscal year 1998 or fiscal year 1999. Such substitute sales shall be subject to the requirements of subsection (a)(3) [of this note].

"(2)(A) The Chief shall pay as soon as practicable after fiscal year 1998 and fiscal year 1999 to any State in which sales previously scheduled to be offered that are referred to in, but not offered pursuant to, subsection (a)(2) [of this note] would have occurred, 25 percent of any anticipated receipts from such sales that—

"(i) were scheduled from fiscal year 1998 or fiscal year 1999 sales in the absence of any moratorium referred to in subsection (a)(2) [of this note]; and

"(ii) are not offset by revenues received in such fiscal years from substitute projects authorized pursuant to subsection (b)(1) [of this note].

"(B) After reporting the amount of funds required to make any payments required by subsection (b)(2)(A) [of this note], and the source from which such funds are to be derived, to the Committees on Appropriations of the House of Representatives and the Senate, the Chief shall make any payments required by subsection (b)(2)(A) [of this note] from any funds available to the Forest Service in fiscal year 1998 or fiscal year 1999, subject to approval of the Committees on Appropriations of the House of Representatives and the Senate, that are not specifically earmarked for another purpose by the applicable appropriation Act or a committee or conference report thereon.

"(C) Any State which receives payments required by subsection (b)(2)(A) [of this note] shall expend such funds only in the manner, and for the purposes, prescribed in section 500 of title 16, United States Code.

"(c)(1) During the term of the moratorium referred to in subsection (a)(2) [of this note], the Chief shall prepare and submit to the Committees on Appropriations of the House of Representatives and the Senate a report on each of the following—

"(A) a study of whether standards and guidelines in existing land and resource management plans compel or encourage entry into roadless areas within the National Forest System for the purpose of constructing roads or undertaking any other ground-disturbing activities;

"(B) an inventory of all roads within the National Forest System and the uses which they serve, in a format that will inform and facilitate the development of a long-term Forest Service transportation policy; and

"(C) a comprehensive and detailed analysis of the economic and social effects of the moratorium referred to in subsection (a)(2) [of this note] on county, State, and regional levels."

## § 1609. National Forest System

### [FRRRPA § 11]

### (a) Congressional declaration of constituent elements and purposes; lands etc., included within; return of lands to public domain

Congress declares that the National Forest System consists of units of federally owned forest, range, and related lands throughout the United States and its territories, united into a nationally significant system dedicated to the long-term benefit for present and future generations, and that it is the purpose of this section to include all such areas into one integral system. The "National Forest System" shall include all national forest lands reserved or withdrawn from the public domain of the United States, all national forest lands acquired through purchase, exchange, donation, or other means, the national grasslands and land utilization projects administered under title III of the Bankhead-Jones Farm Tenant Act [7 U.S.C.A. § 1010 et seq.], and other lands, waters, or interests therein which are administered by the Forest Service or are designated for administration through the Forest Service as a part of the system. Notwithstanding the provisions of section 473 of this title, no land now or hereafter reserved or withdrawn from the public domain as national forests pursuant to section 471 of this title, or any act supplementary to and amendatory thereof, shall be returned to the public domain except by an act of Congress.

### (b) Location of Forest Service offices

The on-the-ground field offices, field supervisory offices, and regional offices of the Forest Service shall be so situated as to provide the optimum level of convenient, useful services to the public, giving priority to the maintenance and location of facilities in rural areas and towns near the national forest and Forest Service program locations in accordance with the standards in section 2204b–1(b) of Title 7.

(Pub.L. 93–378, § 11, formerly § 10, Aug. 17, 1974, 88 Stat. 480, renumbered and amended Pub.L. 94–588, §§ 2, 9, Oct. 22, 1976, 90 Stat. 2949, 2957.)

### HISTORICAL AND STATUTORY NOTES

**References in Text**

The Bankhead-Jones Farm Tenant Act, referred to in subsec. (a), is Act July 22, 1937, c. 517, 50 Stat. 522, as amended. Title III of the Bankhead-Jones Farm Tenant Act is classified generally to subchapter III of chapter 33 of Title 7 (7 U.S.C.A. § 1010 et seq.). For complete classification, see Short Title note set out under section 1000 of Title 7 and Tables.

Section 471 of this title, referred to in subsec. (a), was repealed by Pub.L. 94–579, Title VII, § 704(a), Oct. 21, 1976, 90 Stat. 2792.

**Transfer of Functions**

For transfer of certain enforcement functions of Secretary or other official in Department of Agriculture under this subchapter to Federal Inspector, Office of Federal Inspector for the Alaska Natural Gas Transportation System, see Transfer of Functions note set out under section 1601 of this title.

**Land Conveyances Involving Joliet Army Ammunition Plant, Illinois**

Pub.L. 104–106, Div. B, Title XXIX, Feb. 10, 1996, 110 Stat. 594, as amended Pub.L. 106–65, Div. B, Title XXVIII,

§ 2842, Oct. 5, 1999, 113 Stat. 863, provided for the conversion of the Joliet Army Ammunition Plant to the Midewin National Tallgrass Prairie, Illinois, and the conveyance of certain real property at the Arsenal for a national cemetery, a Will County, Illinois, landfill for waste generated in the county to be closed and capped after 23 years of operation, and industrial parks to replace all or a part of lost economic activity, with provisions prohibiting construction of title to restrict or lessen the degree of cleanup required to be carried out under environmental laws, and provisions authorizing retention of real property used for environmental cleanup by the Secretary of the Army until the transfer occurs.

## § 1610. Implementation of provisions by Secretary of Agriculture; utilization of information and data of other organizations; avoidance of duplication of planning, etc.; "renewable resources" defined

[FRRRPA § 12]

In carrying out this subchapter, the Secretary of Agriculture shall utilize information and data available from other Federal, State, and private organizations and shall avoid duplication and overlap of resource assessment and program planning efforts of other Federal agencies. The term "renewable resources" shall be construed to involve those matters within the scope of responsibilities and authorities of the Forest Service on August 17, 1974 and on the date of enactment of any legislation amendatory or supplementary thereto.

(Pub.L. 93–378, § 12, formerly § 11, Aug. 17, 1974, 88 Stat. 480, renumbered and amended Pub.L. 94–588, §§ 2, 10, Oct. 22, 1976, 90 Stat. 2949, 2957.)

### HISTORICAL AND STATUTORY NOTES

**Transfer of Functions**

For transfer of certain enforcement functions of Secretary or other official in Department of Agriculture under this subchapter to Federal Inspector, Office of Federal Inspector for the Alaska Natural Gas Transportation System, see Transfer of Functions note set out under section 1601 of this title.

## § 1611. Timber

[FRRRPA § 13]

### (a) Limitations on removal; variations in allowable sale quantity; public participation

The Secretary of Agriculture shall limit the sale of timber from each national forest to a quantity equal to or less than a quantity which can be removed from such forest annually in perpetuity on a sustained-yield basis: *Provided*, That, in order to meet overall multiple-use objectives, the Secretary may establish an allowable sale quantity for any decade which departs from the projected long-term average sale quantity that would otherwise be established: *Provided further*, That any such planned departure must be consistent with the multiple-use management objectives of the land management plan. Plans for variations in the allowable sale quantity must be made with public participation as required by section 1604(d) of this title. In addition, within any decade, the Secretary may sell a quantity in excess of the annual allowable sale quantity established pursuant to this section in the case of any national forest so long as the average sale quantities of timber from such national forest over the decade covered by the plan do not exceed such quantity limitation. In those cases where a forest has less than two hundred thousand acres of commercial forest land, the Secretary may use two or more forests for purposes of determining the sustained yield.

### (b) Salvage harvesting

Nothing in subsection (a) of this section shall prohibit the Secretary from salvage or sanitation harvesting of timber stands which are substantially damaged by fire, windthrow, or other catastrophe, or which are in imminent danger from insect or disease attack. The Secretary may either substitute such timber for timber that would otherwise be sold under the plan or, if not feasible, sell such timber over and above the plan volume.

(Pub.L. 93–378, § 13, as added Pub.L. 94–588, § 11, Oct. 22, 1976, 90 Stat. 2957.)

### HISTORICAL AND STATUTORY NOTES

**Transfer of Functions**

For transfer of certain enforcement functions of Secretary or other official in Department of Agriculture under this subchapter to Federal Inspector, Office of Federal Inspector for the Alaska Natural Gas Transportation System, see Transfer of Functions note set out under section 1601 of this title.

**Emergency Salvage Timber Sale Program**

Pub.L. 104–19, Title II, § 2001, July 27, 1995, 109 Stat. 240, as amended Pub.L. 104–134, Title I, § 101(c)[Title III, § 316], Apr. 26, 1996, 110 Stat. 1321–202; renumbered Title I Pub.L. 104–140, § 1(a), May 2, 1996, 110 Stat. 1327, provided that:

"(a) **Definitions.**—For purposes of this section:

"(1) The term 'appropriate committees of Congress' means the Committee on Resources, the Committee on Agriculture, and the Committee on Appropriations of the House of Representatives and the Committee on Energy and Natural Resources, the Committee on Agriculture, Nutrition, and Forestry, and the Committee on Appropriations of the Senate.

"(2) The term 'emergency period' means the period beginning on the date of the enactment of this section [July 27, 1995] and ending on December 31, 1996.

"(3) The term 'salvage timber sale' means a timber sale for which an important reason for entry includes the removal of disease- or insect-infested trees, dead, damaged, or down trees, or trees affected by fire or imminently susceptible to fire or insect attack. Such term also includes the removal of associated trees or trees lacking the characteristics of a healthy and viable ecosystem for the purpose of ecosystem improvement or rehabilitation, except that any such sale must include an identifiable salvage component of trees described in the first sentence.

"(4) The term 'Secretary concerned' means—

"(A) the Secretary of Agriculture, with respect to lands within the National Forest System; and

"(B) the Secretary of the Interior, with respect to Federal lands under the jurisdiction of the Bureau of Land Management.

"(b) **Completion of salvage timber sales.**—

"(1) **Salvage timber sales.**—Using the expedited procedures provided in subsection (c), the Secretary concerned shall prepare, advertise, offer, and award contracts during the emergency period for salvage timber sales from Federal lands described in subsection (a)(4). During the emergency period, the Secretary concerned is to achieve, to the maximum extent feasible, a salvage timber sale volume level above the programmed level to reduce the backlogged volume of salvage timber. The preparation, advertisement, offering, and awarding of such contracts shall be performed utilizing subsection (c) and notwithstanding any other provision of law, including a law under the authority of which any judicial order may be outstanding on or after the date of the enactment of this Act [July 27, 1995].

"(2) **Use of salvage sale funds.**—To conduct salvage timber sales under this subsection, the Secretary concerned may use salvage sale funds otherwise available to the Secretary concerned.

"(3) **Sales in preparation.**—Any salvage timber sale in preparation on the date of the enactment of this Act [July 27, 1995] shall be subject to the provisions of this section.

"(c) **Expedited procedures for emergency salvage timber sales.**—

"(1) **Sale documentation.**—

"(A) **Preparation.**—For each salvage timber sale conducted under subsection (b), the Secretary concerned shall prepare a document that combines an environmental assessment under section 102(2) of the National Environmental Policy Act of 1969 (42 U.S.C. 4332(2)) [section 4332(2) of Title 42, The Public Health and Welfare] (including regulations implementing such section) and a biological evaluation under section 7(a)(2) of the Endangered Species Act of 1973 (16 U.S.C. 1536(a)(2)) [section 1536(a)(2) of this title] and other applicable Federal law and implementing regulations. A document embodying decisions relating to salvage timber sales proposed under authority of this section shall, at the sole discretion of the Secretary concerned and to the extent the Secretary concerned considers appropriate and feasible, consider the environmental effects of the salvage timber sale and the effect, if any, on threatened or endangered species, and to the extent the Secretary concerned, at his sole discretion, considers appropriate and feasible, be consistent with any standards and guidelines from the management plans applicable to the National Forest or Bureau of Land Management District on which the salvage timber sale occurs.

"(B) **Use of existing materials.**—In lieu of preparing a new document under this paragraph, the Secretary concerned may use a document prepared pursuant to the National Environmental Policy Act of 1969 (42 U.S.C. 4321 et seq.) [section 4321 et seq. of Title 42] before the date of the enactment of this Act [July 27, 1995], a biological evaluation written before such date, or information collected for such a document or evaluation if the document, evaluation, or information applies to the Federal lands covered by the proposed sale.

"(C) **Scope and content.**—The scope and content of the documentation and information prepared, considered, and relied on under this paragraph is at the sole discretion of the Secretary concerned.

"(2) **Reporting requirements.**—Not later than August 30, 1995, the Secretary concerned shall submit a report to the appropriate committees of Congress on the implementation of this section. The report shall be updated and resubmitted to the appropriate committees of Congress every six months thereafter until the completion of all salvage timber sales conducted under subsection (b). Each report shall contain the following:

"(A) The volume of salvage timber sales sold and harvested, as of the date of the report, for each National Forest and each district of the Bureau of Land Management.

"(B) The available salvage volume contained in each National Forest and each district of the Bureau of Land Management.

"(C) A plan and schedule for an enhanced salvage timber sale program for fiscal years 1995, 1996, and 1997 using the authority provided by this section for salvage timber sales.

"(D) A description of any needed resources and personnel, including personnel reassignments, required to conduct an enhanced salvage timber sale program through fiscal year 1997.

"(E) A statement of the intentions of the Secretary concerned with respect to the salvage timber sale volume levels specified in the joint explanatory statement of managers accompanying the conference report on H.R. 1158, House Report 104-124.

"(3) **Advancement of sales authorized.**—The Secretary concerned may begin salvage timber sales under subsection (b) intended for a subsequent fiscal year before the start of such fiscal year if the Secretary concerned determines that performance of such salvage timber sales will not interfere with salvage timber sales intended for a preceding fiscal year.

"(4) **Decisions.**—The Secretary concerned shall design and select the specific salvage timber sales to be offered under subsection (b) on the basis of the analysis contained in the document or documents prepared pursuant to paragraph (1) to achieve, to the maximum extent feasible, a salvage timber sale volume level above the program level.

"(5) **Sale preparation.**—

"(A) **Use of available authorities.**—The Secretary concerned shall make use of all available authority, including the employment of private contractors and the use of expedited fire contracting procedures, to prepare and advertise salvage timber sales under subsection (b).

"(B) **Exemptions.**—The preparation, solicitation, and award of salvage timber sales under subsection (b) shall be exempt from—

"(i) the requirements of the Competition in Contracting Act (41 U.S.C. 253 et seq.) [probably means the Competition in Contracting Act of 1984, Pub.L. 98–369, Div. B, Title VIII, July 18, 1984, 98 Stat. 1175, for classifications to which see Short Title note under section 251 of Title 41, Public Contracts, and Tables] and the implementing regulations in the Federal Acquisition Regulation issued pursuant to section 25(c) of the Office of Federal Procurement Policy Act (41 U.S.C. 421(c)) [section 421(c) of Title 41] and any departmental acquisition regulations; and

"(ii) the notice and publication requirements in section 18 of such Act (41 U.S.C. 416) [section 416 of Title 41] and 8(e) of the Small Business Act (15 U.S.C. 637(e)) [section 637(e) of Title 15, Commerce and Trade] and the implementing regulations in the Federal Acquisition Regulations and any departmental acquisition regulations.

"(C) **Incentive payment recipients; report.**—The provisions of section 3(d)(1) of the Federal Workforce Restructuring Act of 1994 (Public Law 103–226; 5 U.S.C. 5597 note) [set out as a note under section 5597 of Title 5, Government Organization and Employees] shall not apply to any former employee of the Secretary concerned who received a voluntary separation incentive payment authorized by such Act [Pub.L. 103–226, Mar. 30, 1994, 108 Stat. 111, for classifications to which see Short Title note under section 2101 of Title 5 and Tables] and accepts employment pursuant to this paragraph. The Director of the Office of Personnel Management and the Secretary concerned shall provide a summary report to the appropriate committees of Congress, the Committee on Government Reform and Oversight of the House of Representatives, and the Committee on Governmental Affairs of the Senate regarding the number of incentive payment recipients who were rehired, their terms of reemployment, their job classifications, and an explanation, in the judgment of the agencies involved of how such reemployment without repayment of the incentive payments received is consistent with the original waiver provisions of such Act. This report shall not be conducted in a manner that would delay the rehiring of any former employees under this paragraph, or affect the normal confidentiality of Federal employees.

"(6) **Cost considerations.**—Salvage timber sales undertaken pursuant to this section shall not be precluded because the costs of such activities are likely to exceed the revenues derived from such activities.

"(7) **Effect of salvage sales.**—The Secretary concerned shall not substitute salvage timber sales conducted under subsection (b) for planned non-salvage timber sales.

"(8) **Reforestation of salvage timber sale parcels.**—The Secretary concerned shall plan and implement reforestation of each parcel of land harvested under a salvage timber sale conducted under subsection (b) as expeditiously as possible after completion of the harvest on the parcel, but in no case later than any applicable restocking period required by law or regulation.

"(9) **Effect on judicial decisions.**—The Secretary concerned may conduct salvage timber sales under subsection (b) notwithstanding any decision, restraining order, or injunction issued by a United States court before the date of the enactment of this section [July 27, 1995].

"(d) **Direction to complete timber sales on lands covered by option 9.**—Notwithstanding any other law (including a law under the authority of which any judicial order may be outstanding on or after the date of enactment of this Act [July 27, 1995]), the Secretary concerned shall expeditiously prepare, offer, and award timber sale contracts on Federal lands described in the 'Record of Decision for Amendments to Forest Service and Bureau of Land Management Planning Documents Within the Range of the Northern Spotted Owl', signed by the Secretary of the Interior and the Secretary of Agriculture on April 13, 1994. The Secretary concerned may conduct timber sales under this subsection notwithstanding any decision, restraining order, or injunction issued by a United States court before the date of the enactment of this section. The issuance of any regulation pursuant to section 4(d) of the Endangered Species Act of 1973 (16 U.S.C. 1533(d)) [section 1533(d) of this title] to ease or reduce restrictions on non-Federal lands within the range of the northern spotted owl shall be deemed to satisfy the requirements of section 102(2)(C) of the National Environmental Policy Act of 1969 (42 U.S.C. 4332(2)(C)) [section 4332(2)(C) of Title 42], given the analysis included in the Final Supplemental Impact Statement on the Management of the Habitat for Late Successional and Old Growth Forest Related Species Within the Range of the Northern Spotted Owl, prepared by the Secretary of Agriculture and the Secretary of the Interior in 1994, which is, or may be, incorporated by reference in the administrative record of any such regulation. The issuance of any such regulation pursuant to section 4(d) of the Endangered Species Act of 1973 (16 U.S.C. 1533(d)) shall not require the preparation of an environmental impact statement under section 102(2)(C) of the National Environmental Policy Act of 1969 (42 U.S.C. 4332(2)(C)).

"(e) **Administrative review.**—Salvage timber sales conducted under subsection (b), timber sales conducted under subsection (d), and any decision of the Secretary concerned in connection with such sales, shall not be subject to administrative review.

"(f) **Judicial review.**—

"(1) **Place and time of filing.**—A salvage timber sale to be conducted under subsection (b), and a timber sale to be conducted under subsection (d), shall be subject to judicial review only in the United States district court for the district in which the affected Federal lands are located. Any challenge to such sale must be filed in such district court within 15 days after the date of initial advertisement of the challenged sale. The Secretary concerned may not agree to, and a court may not grant, a waiver of the requirements of this paragraph.

"(2) **Effect of filing on agency action.**—For 45 days after the date of the filing of a challenge to a salvage timber sale to be conducted under subsection (b) or a timber sale to be conducted under subsection (d), the Secretary concerned shall take no action to award the challenged sale.

"(3) **Prohibition on restraining orders, preliminary injunctions, and relief pending review.**—No restraining order, preliminary injunction, or injunction pending appeal shall be issued by any court of the United States with respect to any decision to prepare, advertise, offer, award, or operate a salvage timber sale pursuant to subsection (b) or any decision to prepare, advertise, offer, award, or operate a timber sale pursuant to subsection (d). Section 705 of title 5, United States Code, shall not apply to any challenge to such a sale.

"(4) **Standard of review.**—The courts shall have authority to enjoin permanently, order modification of, or void an individual salvage timber sale if it is determined by a review of the record that the decision to prepare, advertise, offer, award, or operate such sale was arbitrary and capricious or otherwise not in accordance with applicable law (other than those laws specified in subsection (i)).

"(5) **Time for decision.**—Civil actions filed under this subsection shall be assigned for hearing at the earliest possible date. The court shall render its final decision relative to any challenge within 45 days from the date such challenge is brought, unless the court determines that a longer period of time is required to satisfy the requirement of the United States Constitution. In order to reach a decision within 45 days, the district court may assign all or part of any such case or cases to one or more Special Masters, for prompt review and recommendations to the court.

"(6) **Procedures.**—Notwithstanding any other provision of law, the court may set rules governing the procedures of any proceeding brought under this subsection which set page limits on briefs and time limits on filing briefs and motions and other actions which are shorter than the limits specified in the Federal rules of civil or appellate procedure.

"(7) **Appeal.**—Any appeal from the final decision of a district court in an action brought pursuant to this subsection shall be filed not later than 30 days after the date of decision.

"(g) **Exclusion of certain Federal lands.**—

"(1) **Exclusion.**—The Secretary concerned may not select, authorize, or undertake any salvage timber sale under subsection (b) with respect to lands described in paragraph (2).

"(2) **Description of excluded lands.**—The lands referred to in paragraph (1) are as follows:

"(A) Any area on Federal lands included in the National Wilderness Preservation System.

"(B) Any roadless area on Federal lands designated by Congress for wilderness study in Colorado or Montana.

"(C) Any roadless area on Federal lands recommended by the Forest Service or Bureau of Land Management for wilderness designation in its most recent land management plan in effect as of the date of the enactment of this Act [July 27, 1995].

"(D) Any area on Federal lands on which timber harvesting for any purpose is prohibited by statute.

"(h) **Rulemaking.**—The Secretary concerned is not required to issue formal rules under section 553 of title 5, United States Code, to implement this section or carry out the authorities provided by this section.

"(i) **Effect on other laws.**—The documents and procedures required by this section for the preparation, advertisement, offering, awarding, and operation of any salvage timber sale subject to subsection (b) and any timber sale under subsection (d) shall be deemed to satisfy the requirements of the following applicable Federal laws (and regulations implementing such laws):

"(1) The Forest and Rangeland Renewable Resources Planning Act of 1974 (16 U.S.C. 1600 et seq.) [section 1600 et seq. of this title].

"(2) The Federal Land Policy and Management Act of 1976 (43 U.S.C. 1701 et seq.) [section 1701 et seq. of Title 43, Public Lands].

"(3) The National Environmental Policy Act of 1969 (42 U.S.C. 4321 et seq.) [section 4321 et seq. of Title 42].

"(4) The Endangered Species Act of 1973 (16 U.S.C. 1531 et seq.) [section 1531 et seq. of this title].

"(5) The National Forest Management Act of 1976 (16 U.S.C. 472a et seq.) [Pub.L. 94–588, Oct. 22, 1976, 90 Stat. 2949, for classifications to which see Short Title note under section 1600 of this Title and Tables].

"(6) The Multiple-Use Sustained-Yield Act of 1960 (16 U.S.C. 528 et seq.) [section 528 et seq. of this title].

"(7) Any compact, executive agreement, convention, treaty, and international agreement, and implementing legislation related thereto.

"(8) All other applicable Federal environmental and natural resource laws.

"(j) **Expiration date.**—The authority provided by subsections (b) and (d) shall expire on December 31, 1996. The terms and conditions of this section shall continue in effect with respect to salvage timber sale contracts offered under subsection (b) and timber sale contracts offered under subsection (d) until the completion of performance of the contracts.

"(k) **Award and release of previously offered and unawarded timber sale contracts.**—

"(1) **Award and release required.**—Notwithstanding any other provision of law, within 45 days after the date of the enactment of this Act [July 27, 1995], the Secretary concerned shall act to award, release, and permit to be completed in fiscal years 1995 and 1996, with no change in originally advertised terms, volumes, and bid prices, all timber sale contracts offered or awarded before that date in any unit of the National Forest System or district of the Bureau of Land Management subject to section 318 of Public Law 101–121 (103 Stat. 745) [not classified to the Code]. The return of the bid bond of the high bidder shall not alter the responsibility of the Secretary concerned to comply with this paragraph.

"(2) **Threatened or endangered bird species.**—No sale unit shall be released or completed under this subsection if any threatened or endangered bird species is known to be nesting within the acreage that is the subject of the sale unit.

"(3) **Alternative offer in case of delay.**—If for any reason a sale cannot be released and completed under the terms of this subsection within 45 days after the date of the enactment of this Act [July 27, 1995], the Secretary concerned shall provide the purchaser an equal volume of timber, of like kind and value, which shall be subject to the terms of the original contract and shall not count against current allowable sale quantities.

"(*l*) **Effect on plans, policies, and activities.**—Compliance with this section shall not require or permit any administrative action, including revisions, amendment, consultation, supplementation, or other action, in or for any land management plan, standard, guideline, policy, regional guide, or multiforest plan because of implementation or impacts, site-specific or cumulative, of activities authorized or required by this section, except that any such administrative action with respect to salvage timber sales is permitted to the extent necessary, at the sole discretion of the Secretary concerned, to meet the salvage timber sale goal specified in subsection (b)(1) of this section or to reflect the effects of the salvage program. The Secretary concerned shall not rely on salvage timber sales as the basis for administrative action limiting other multiple use activities nor be required to offer a particular salvage timber sale. No project decision shall be required to be halted or delayed by such documents or guidance, implementation, or impacts."

**Timber Sales Pipeline Restoration Funds**

Pub.L. 104–134, Title I, § 101(c)[Title III, § 327], Apr. 26, 1996, 110 Stat. 1321–206; renumbered Title I Pub.L. 104–140, § 1(a), May 2, 1996, 110 Stat. 1327, provided that:

"**(a)** The Secretary of Agriculture and the Secretary of the Interior shall each establish a Timber Sales Pipeline Restoration Fund (hereinafter 'Agriculture Fund' and 'Interior Fund' or 'Funds'). Any revenues received from sales released under section 2001(k) of the fiscal year 1995 Supplemental Appropriations for Disaster Assistance and Rescissions Act [probably means section 2001(k) of Pub.L. 104–19, set out as a note under this section], minus the funds necessary to make payments to States or local governments under other law concerning the distribution of revenues derived from the affected lands, which are in excess of $37,500,000 (hereinafter 'excess revenues') shall be deposited into the Funds. The distribution of excess revenues between the Agriculture Fund and Interior Fund shall be calculated by multiplying the total of excess revenues times a fraction with a denominator of the total revenues received from all sales released under such section 2001(k) and numerators of the total revenues received from such sales on lands within the National Forest System and the total revenues received from such sales on lands administered by the Bureau of Land Management, respectively: *Provided*, That revenues or portions thereof from sales released under such section 2001(k), minus the amounts necessary for State and local government payments and other necessary deposits, may be deposited into the Funds immediately upon receipt thereof and subsequently redistributed between the Funds or paid into the United States Treasury as miscellaneous receipts as may be required when the calculation of excess revenues is made.

"**(b)(1)** From the funds deposited into the Agriculture Fund and into the Interior Fund pursuant to subsection (a)—

"**(A)** seventy-five percent shall be available, without fiscal year limitation or further appropriation, for preparation of timber sales, other than salvage sales as defined in section 2001(a)(3) of the fiscal year 1995 Supplemental Appropriations for Disaster Assistance and Rescissions Act [probably means section 2001(a)(3) of Pub.L. 104–19, set out as a note under this section], which—

"**(i)** are situated on lands within the National Forest System and lands administered by the Bureau of Land Management, respectively; and

"**(ii)** are in addition to timber sales for which funds are otherwise available in this Act [probably means Pub.L. 104–134, Title I, § 101(c), Apr. 26, 1996, 104 Stat. 1321–156; renumbered Title I Pub.L. 104–140, § 1(a), May 2, 1996, 104 Stat. 1327, known as the Department of the Interior and Related Agencies Appropriations Act, 1996, see Tables for classification] or other appropriations Acts; and

"**(B)** twenty-five percent shall be available, without fiscal year limitation or further appropriation, to expend on the backlog of recreation projects on lands within the National Forest System and lands administered by the Bureau of Land Management, respectively.

"**(2)** Expenditures under this subsection for preparation of timber sales may include expenditures for Forest Service activities within the forest land management budget line item and associated timber roads, and Bureau of Land Management activities within the Oregon and California grant lands account and the forestry management area account, as determined by the Secretary concerned.

"**(c)** Revenues received from any timber sale prepared under subsection (b) or under this subsection, minus the amounts necessary for State and local government payments and other necessary deposits, shall be deposited into the Fund from which funds were expended on such sale. Such deposited revenues shall be available for preparation of additional timber sales and completion of additional recreation projects in accordance with the requirements set forth in subsection (b).

"**(d)** The Secretary concerned shall terminate all payments into the Agriculture Fund or the Interior Fund, and pay any unobligated funds in the affected Fund into the United States Treasury as miscellaneous receipts, whenever the Secretary concerned makes a finding, published in the Federal Register, that sales sufficient to achieve the total allowable sales quantity of the National Forest System for the Forest Service or the allowable sales level for the Oregon and California grant lands for the Bureau of Land Management, respectively, have been prepared.

"**(e)** Any timber sales prepared and recreation projects completed under this section shall comply with all applicable environmental and natural resource laws and regulations.

"**(f)** The Secretary concerned shall report annually to the Committees on Appropriations of the United States Senate and the House of Representatives on expenditures made from the Fund for timber sales and recreation projects, revenues received into the Fund from timber sales, and timber sale preparation and recreation project work undertaken during the previous year and projected for the next year under the Fund. Such information shall be provided for each Forest Service region and Bureau of Land Management State office.

"**(g)** The authority of this section shall terminate upon the termination of both Funds in accordance with the provisions of subsection (d)."

## § 1612. Public participation

**[FRRRPA § 14]**

### (a) Adequate notice and opportunity to comment

In exercising his authorities under this subchapter and other laws applicable to the Forest Service, the Secretary, by regulation, shall establish procedures, including public hearings where appropriate, to give the Federal, State, and local governments and the public adequate notice and an opportunity to comment upon the formulation of standards, criteria, and guidelines applicable to Forest Service programs.

**(b) Advisory boards**

In providing for public participation in the planning for and management of the National Forest System, the Secretary, pursuant to the Federal Advisory Committee Act (86 Stat. 770) and other applicable law, shall establish and consult such advisory boards as he deems necessary to secure full information and advice on the execution of his responsibilities. The membership of such boards shall be representative of a cross section of groups interested in the planning for and management of the National Forest System and the various types of use and enjoyment of the lands thereof.

(Pub.L. 93–378, § 14, as added Pub.L. 94–588, § 11, Oct. 22, 1976, 90 Stat. 2958.)

## HISTORICAL AND STATUTORY NOTES

**References in Text**

The Federal Advisory Committee Act, referred to in text, is set out in Appendix 2 to Title 5.

**Transfer of Functions**

For transfer of certain enforcement functions of Secretary or other official in Department of Agriculture under this subchapter to Federal Inspector, Office of Federal Inspector for the Alaska Natural Gas Transportation System, see Transfer of Functions note set out under section 1601 of this title.

**Forest Service Decision Making and Appeals Reform**

Pub.L. 102–381, Title III, § 322, Oct. 5, 1992, 106 Stat. 1419, provided that:

"**(a) In general.**—In accordance with this section, the Secretary of Agriculture, acting through the Chief of the Forest Service, shall establish a notice and comment process for proposed actions of the Forest Service concerning projects and activities implementing land and resource management plans developed under the Forest and Rangeland Renewable Resources Planning Act of 1974 (16 U.S.C. 1601 et seq.) and shall modify the procedure for appeals of decisions concerning such projects.

"**(b) Notice and comment.**—

"**(1) Notice.**—Prior to proposing an action referred to in subsection (a), the Secretary shall give notice of the proposed action, and the availability of the action for public comment by—

"(A) promptly mailing notice about the proposed action to any person who has requested it in writing, and to persons who are known to have participated in the decisionmaking process; and,

"(B)(i) in the case of an action taken by the Chief of the Forest Service, publishing notice of action in the Federal Register; or

"(ii) in the case of any other action referred to in subsection (a), publishing notice of the action in a newspaper of general circulation that has previously been identified in the Federal Register as the newspaper in which notice under this paragraph may be published.

"**(2) Comment.**—The Secretary shall accept comments on the proposed action within 30 days after publication of the notice in accordance with paragraph (1).

"**(c) Right to appeal.**—Not later than 45 days after the date of issuance of a decision of the Forest Service concerning actions referred to in subsection (a), a person who was involved in the public comment process under subsection (b) through submission of written or oral comments or by otherwise notifying the Forest Service of their interest in the proposed action may file an appeal.

"**(d) Disposition of an appeal.**—

"**(1) Informal disposition.**—

"**(A) In general.**—Subject to subparagraph (B), a designated employee of the Forest Service shall offer to meet with each individual who files an appeal in accordance with subsection (c) and attempt to dispose of the appeal.

"**(B) Time and location of the meeting.**—Each meeting in accordance with subparagraph (A) shall take place—

"(i) not later than 15 days after the closing date for filing an appeal; and

"(ii) at a location designated by the Chief of the Forest Service that is in the vicinity of the lands affected by the decision.

"**(2) Formal review.**—If the appeal is not disposed of in accordance with paragraph (1), an appeals review officer designated by the Chief of the Forest Service shall review the appeal and recommend in writing, to the official responsible for deciding the appeal, the appropriate disposition of the appeal. The official responsible for deciding the appeal shall then decide the appeal. The appeals review officer shall be a line officer at least at the level of the agency official who made the initial decision on the project or activity that is under appeal, who has not participated in the initial decision and will not be responsible for implementation of the initial decision after the appeal is decided.

"**(3) Time for disposition.**—Disposition of appeals under this subsection shall be completed not later than 30 days after the closing date for filing of an appeal, provided that the Forest Service may extend the closing date by an additional 15 days.

"(4) If the Secretary fails to decide the appeal within the 45-day period, the decision on which the appeal is based shall be deemed to be a final agency action for the purpose of chapter 7 of title 5, United States Code [5 U.S.C.A. § 701 et seq.].

"**(e) Stay.**—Unless the Chief of the Forest Service determines that an emergency situation exists with respect to a decision of the Forest Service, implementation of the decision shall be stayed during the period beginning on the date of the decision—

"(1) for 45 days, if an appeal is not filed, or

"(2) for an additional 15 days after the date of the disposition of an appeal under this section, if the agency action is deemed final under subsection (d)(4)."

## § 1613. Promulgation of regulations

[FRRRPA § 15]

The Secretary of Agriculture shall prescribe such regulations as he determines necessary and desirable to carry out the provisions of this subchapter.

(Pub.L. 93–378, § 15, as added Pub.L. 94–588, § 11, Oct. 22, 1976, 90 Stat. 2958.)

### HISTORICAL AND STATUTORY NOTES

**Transfer of Functions**

For transfer of certain enforcement functions of Secretary or other official in Department of Agriculture under this subchapter to Federal Inspector, Office of Federal Inspector for the Alaska Natural Gas Transportation System, see Transfer of Functions note set out under section 1601 of this title.

## § 1614. Severability

[FRRRPA § 16]

If any provision of this subchapter or the application thereof to any person or circumstances is held invalid, the validity of the remainder of this subchapter and of the application of such provision to other persons and circumstances shall not be affected thereby.

(Pub.L. 93–378, § 16, as added Pub.L. 94–588, § 11, Oct. 22, 1976, 90 Stat. 2958.)

# FOREST AND RANGELAND RENEWABLE RESOURCES RESEARCH ACT OF 1978 [FRRRRA § ____]

**(16 U.S.C.A. §§ 1641 to 1650)**

## SUBCHAPTER II—RESEARCH

## § 1641. Findings and purpose

[FRRRRA § 2]

**(a) Findings**

Congress finds the following:

(1) Forests and rangeland, and the resources of forests and rangeland, are of strategic economic and ecological importance to the United States, and the Federal Government has an important and substantial role in ensuring the continued health, productivity, and sustainability of the forests and rangeland of the United States.

(2) Over 75 percent of the productive commercial forest land in the United States is privately owned, with some 60 percent owned by small nonindustrial private owners. These 10,000,000 nonindustrial private owners are critical to providing both commodity and noncommodity values to the citizens of the United States.

(3) The National Forest System manages only 17 percent of the commercial timberland of the United States, with over half of the standing softwoods inventory located on that land. Dramatic changes in Federal agency policy during the early 1990's have significantly curtailed the management of this vast timber resource, causing abrupt shifts in the supply of timber from public to private ownership. As a result of these shifts in supply, some 60 percent of total wood production in the United States is now coming from private forest land in the southern United States.

(4) At the same time that pressures are building for the removal of even more land from commercial production, the Federal Government is significantly reducing its commitment to productivity-related research regarding forests and rangeland, which is critically needed by the private sector for the sustained management of remaining available timber and forage resources for the benefit of all species.

(5) Uncertainty over the availability of the United States timber supply, increasing regulatory burdens, and the lack of Federal Government support for research is causing domestic wood and paper producers to move outside the United States to find reliable sources of wood supplies, which in turn results in a worsening of the United States trade balance, the loss of employment and infrastructure investments, and an increased risk of infestations of exotic pests and diseases from imported wood products.

(6) Wood and paper producers in the United States are being challenged not only by shifts in Federal Government policy, but also by international competition from tropical countries where growth rates of trees far exceed those in the United States. Wood production per acre will need to quadruple from 1996 levels for the United States forestry sector to remain internationally competitive on an ever decreasing forest land base.

(7) Better and more frequent forest inventorying and analysis is necessary to identify productivity-related forestry research needs and to provide forest managers with the current data necessary to make timely and effective management decisions.

**(b) Relationship to other law**

This subchapter shall be deemed to complement the policies and direction set forth in the Forest and Rangeland Renewable Resources Planning Act of 1974 [16 U.S.C.A. § 1600 et seq.].

**(c) Purpose**

It is the purpose of this subchapter to authorize the Secretary to expand research activities to encompass international forestry and natural resource issues on a global scale.

(Pub.L. 95–307, § 2, June 30, 1978, 92 Stat. 353; Pub.L. 101–513, Title VI, § 611(a)(1), formerly § 607(a)(1), Nov. 5, 1990, 104 Stat. 2072; renumbered § 611(a)(1), Pub.L. 102–574, § 2(a)(1), Oct. 29, 1992, 106 Stat. 4593; Pub.L. 105–185, Title II, § 253(a), June 23, 1998, 112 Stat. 558.)

### HISTORICAL AND STATUTORY NOTES

**References in Text**

The Forest and Rangeland Renewable Resources Planning Act of 1974, referred to in subsec. (b), is classified principally to subchapter I of this chapter (16 U.S.C.A. § 1600 et seq.). For complete classification, see Short Title note set out under section 1600 of this title and Tables.

This subchapter, referred to in subsec. (c), in the original read "this Act", meaning the Forest and Rangeland Renewable Resources Research Act of 1978, which enacted this subchapter, repealed sections 581 to 581i of this title, and enacted provisions set out as a note under section 1641 of this title. For complete classification, see Short Title note set out under section 1600 of this title and Tables.

**Effective and Applicability Provisions**

1990 Acts

Section 9 of Pub.L. 95–307 which provided that Pub.L. 95–307 (enacting this subchapter, repealing sections 581 to 581i of this title, and enacting provisions set out as a note under section 1600 of this title) is effective Oct. 1, 1978, was amended generally by Pub.L. 101–624 and is classified to section 1648 of this title.

**Short Title**

1978 Acts

For Short Title of Pub.L. 95–307, June 30, 1978, 92 Stat. 353, as the Forest and Rangeland Renewable Resources Research Act of 1978, see short title note set out under section 1600 of this title.

## § 1642. Investigations, experiments, tests, and other activities

**[FRRRRA § 3]**

**(a) Authorization; scope and purposes of activities**

The Secretary is authorized to conduct, support, and cooperate in investigations, experiments, tests, and other activities the Secretary deems necessary to obtain, analyze, develop, demonstrate, and disseminate scientific information about protecting, managing, and utilizing forest and rangeland renewable resources in rural, suburban, and urban areas. The activities conducted, supported, or cooperated in by the Secretary under this subchapter shall include, but not be limited to, the five major areas of renewable resource research identified in paragraphs (1) through (5) of this subsection.

(1) Renewable resource management research shall include, as appropriate, research activities related to managing, reproducing, planting, and growing vegetation on forests and rangelands for timber, forage, water, fish and wildlife, aesthetics, recreation, wilderness, energy production, activities related to energy conservation, and other purposes, including activities for encouraging improved reforestation of forest lands from which timber has been harvested; determining the role of forest and rangeland management in the productive use of forests and rangelands, in diversified agriculture, and in mining, transportation, and other industries; and developing alternatives for the management of forests and rangelands that will make possible the most effective use of their multiple products and services.

(2) Renewable resource environmental research shall include, as appropriate, research activities related to understanding and managing surface and subsurface water flow, preventing and controlling erosion, and restoring damaged or disturbed soils on forest and rangeland watersheds; maintaining and improving wildlife and fish habitats; managing vegetation to reduce air and water pollution, provide amenities, and for other purposes; and understanding, predicting, and modifying weather, climatic, and other environmental conditions that affect the protection and management of forests and rangelands.

(3) Renewable resource protection research shall include, as appropriate, research activities related to protecting vegetation and other forest and rangeland resources, including threatened and endangered flora and fauna, as well as wood and wood products in storage or use, from fires, insects, diseases, noxious plants, animals, air pollutants, and other agents through biological, chemical, and mechanical control methods and systems; and protecting people, natural resources, and property from fires in rural areas.

(4) Renewable resource utilization research shall include, as appropriate, research activities related to harvesting, transporting, processing, marketing, distributing, and utilizing wood and other materials derived from forest and rangeland renewable resources; recycling and fully utilizing wood fiber; producing and conserving energy; and testing forest products, including necessary fieldwork associated therewith.

(5) Renewable resource assessment research shall include, as appropriate, research activities re-

lated to developing and applying scientific knowledge and technology in support of the survey and analysis of forest and rangeland renewable resources described in subsection (b) of this section.

**(b) Development of periodic Renewable Resource Assessment through survey and analysis of conditions; implementation; authorization of appropriations**

(1) To ensure the availability of adequate data and scientific information for development of the periodic Renewable Resource Assessment provided for in section 1601 of this title, the Secretary of Agriculture shall make and keep current a comprehensive survey and analysis of the present and prospective conditions of and requirements for renewable resources of the forests and rangelands of the United States and of the supplies of such renewable resources, including a determination of the present and potential productivity of the land, and of such other facts as may be necessary and useful in the determination of ways and means needed to balance the demand for and supply of these renewable resources, benefits, and uses in meeting the needs of the people of the United States. The Secretary shall conduct the survey and analysis under such plans as the Secretary may determine to be fair and equitable, and cooperate with appropriate officials of each State and, either through them or directly, with private or other entities.

(2) In implementing this subsection, the Secretary is authorized to develop and implement improved methods of survey and analysis of forest inventory information, for which purposes there are hereby authorized to be appropriated annually $10,000,000.

**(c) Program of research and study relative to health and productivity of domestic forest ecosystems; advisory committee; reports**

(1) The Secretary, acting through the United States Forest Service, shall establish not later than 180 days after October 24, 1988, a 10–year program (hereinafter in this subsection referred to as the "Program") to—

(A) increase the frequency of forest inventories in matters that relate to atmospheric pollution and conduct such surveys as are necessary to monitor long-term trends in the health and productivity of domestic forest ecosystems;

(B) determine the scope of the decline in the health and productivity of domestic forest ecosystems;

(C) accelerate and expand existing research efforts (including basic forest ecosystem research) to evaluate the effects of atmospheric pollutants on forest ecosystems and their role in the decline in domestic forest health and productivity;

(D) study the relationship between atmospheric pollution and other climatological, chemical, physical, and biological factors that may affect the health and productivity of domestic forest ecosystems;

(E) develop recommendations for solving or mitigating problems related to the effects of atmospheric pollution on the health and productivity of domestic forest ecosystems;

(F) foster cooperation among Federal, State, and private researchers and encourage the exchange of scientific information on the effects of atmospheric pollutants on forest ecosystems among the United States, Canada, European nations, and other nations;

(G) support the long-term funding of research programs and related efforts to determine the causes of declines in the health and productivity of domestic forest ecosystems and the effects of atmospheric pollutants on the health and productivity of domestic forest ecosystems; and

(H) enlarge the Eastern Hardwood Cooperative by devoting additional resources to field analysis of the response of hardwood species to atmospheric pollution, and other factors that may affect the health and productivity of these ecosystems.

(2) The Secretary shall establish a committee to advise the Secretary in developing and carrying out the Program, which shall be composed of scientists with training and experience in various disciplines, including atmospheric, ecological, and biological sciences. Such scientists shall be selected from among individuals who are actively performing research for Federal or State agencies or for private industries, institutions, or organizations.

(3) The Secretary shall coordinate the Program with existing research efforts of Federal and State agencies and private industries, institutions, or organizations.

(4) The Secretary shall submit to the President and to Congress the following reports:

(A) Not less than 30 days before establishing the Program, the Secretary shall submit an initial program report—

(i) discussing existing information about declining health and productivity of forest ecosystems on public and private lands in North America and Europe;

(ii) outlining the findings and status of all current research and monitoring efforts in North America and Europe on the causes and effects of atmospheric pollution on the health and productivity of forest ecosystems;

(iii) describing the Program; and

(iv) estimating the cost of implementing the Program for each fiscal year of its duration.

(B) Not later than January 15, 1990, and January 15 of each year thereafter, during which the Program is in operation following the year in which the initial program report is submitted, the Secretary shall submit an annual report—

(i) updating information about declining health and productivity of forest ecosystems on public and private lands in North America and Europe;

(ii) updating the findings and status of all current research and monitoring efforts in North America and Europe on the causes and effects of atmospheric pollution on the health and productivity of forest ecosystems, including efforts conducted under the Program;

(iii) recommending additional research and monitoring efforts to be undertaken under the Program to determine the effects of atmospheric pollution on the health and productivity of domestic forest ecosystems; and

(iv) recommending methods for solving or mitigating problems stemming from the effects of atmospheric pollution on the health and productivity of domestic forest ecosystems.

(C) Not later than 10 years after the date on which the initial program report is submitted, the Secretary shall submit a final report—

(i) reviewing existing information about declining health and productivity of forest ecosystems on public and private lands in North America and Europe;

(ii) reviewing the nature and findings of all research and monitoring efforts conducted under the Program and any other relevant research and monitoring efforts related to the effects of atmospheric pollution on forest ecosystem; and

(iii) making final recommendations for solving or mitigating problems stemming from the effects of atmospheric pollution on the health and productivity of domestic forest ecosystems.

## (d) High priority forestry and rangeland research and education

### (1) In general

The Secretary may conduct, support, and cooperate in forestry and rangeland research and education that is of the highest priority to the United States and to users of public and private forest land and rangeland in the United States.

### (2) Priorities

The research and education priorities include the following:

(A) The biology of forest organisms and rangeland organisms.

(B) Functional characteristics and cost-effective management of forest and rangeland ecosystems.

(C) Interactions between humans and forests and rangeland.

(D) Wood and forage as a raw material.

(E) International trade, competition, and cooperation.

### (3) Northeastern States research cooperative

At the request of the Governor of the State of Maine, New Hampshire, New York, or Vermont, the Secretary may cooperate with the northeastern States of New Hampshire, New York, Maine, and Vermont, land-grant colleges and universities of those States, natural resources and forestry schools of those States, other Federal agencies, and other interested persons in those States to coordinate and improve ecological and economic research relating to agricultural research, extension, and education, including—

(A) research on ecosystem health, forest management, product development, economics, and related fields;

(B) research to assist those States and landowners in those States to achieve sustainable forest management;

(C) technology transfer to the wood products industry of technologies that promote efficient processing, pollution prevention, and energy conservation;

(D) dissemination of existing and new information to landowners, public and private resource managers, State forest citizen advisory committees, and the general public through professional associations, publications, and other information clearinghouse activities; and

(E) analysis of strategies for the protection of areas of outstanding ecological significance or high biological diversity, and strategies for the provision of important recreational opportunities and traditional uses, including strategies for areas identified through State land conservation planning processes.

## (e) Forest inventory and analysis

### (1) Program required

In compliance with other applicable provisions of law, the Secretary shall establish a program to inventory and analyze, in a timely manner, public and private forests and their resources in the United States.

### (2) Annual state inventory

#### (A) In general

Not later than the end of each full fiscal year beginning after June 23, 1998, the Secretary shall prepare for each State, in cooperation with the State forester for the State, an inventory of forests and their resources in the State.

**(B) Sample plots**

For purposes of preparing the inventory for a State, the Secretary shall measure annually 20 percent of all sample plots that are included in the inventory program for that State.

**(C) Compilation of inventory**

On completion of the inventory for a year, the Secretary shall make available to the public a compilation of all data collected for that year from measurements of sample plots as well as any analysis made of the samples.

**(3) 5-year reports**

Not more often than every 5 full fiscal years after June 23, 1998, the Secretary shall prepare, publish, and make available to the public a report, prepared in cooperation with State foresters, that—

(A) contains a description of each State inventory of forests and their resources, incorporating all sample plot measurements conducted during the 5 years covered by the report;

(B) displays and analyzes on a nationwide basis the results of the annual reports required by paragraph (2), and

(C) contains an analysis of forest health conditions and trends over the previous 2 decades, with an emphasis on such conditions and trends during the period subsequent to the immediately preceding report under this paragraph.

**(4) National standards and definitions**

To ensure uniform and consistent data collection for all forest land that is publicly or privately owned and for each State, the Secretary shall develop, in consultation with State foresters and Federal land management agencies not under the jurisdiction of the Secretary, and publish national standards and definitions to be applied in inventorying and analyzing forests and their resources under this subsection. The standards shall include a core set of variables to be measured on all sample plots under paragraph (2) and a standard set of tables to be included in the reports under paragraph (3).

**(5) Protection for private property rights**

The Secretary shall obtain authorization from property owners prior to collecting data from sample plots located on private property pursuant to paragraphs (2) and (3).

**(6) Strategic plan**

Not later than 180 days after June 23, 1998, the Secretary shall prepare and submit to Congress a strategic plan to implement and carry out this subsection, including the annual updates required by paragraph (2) and the reports required by paragraph (3), that shall describe in detail—

(A) the financial resources required to implement and carry out this subsection, including the identification of any resources required in excess of the amounts provided for forest inventorying and analysis in recent appropriations Acts;

(B) the personnel necessary to implement and carry out this subsection, including any personnel in addition to personnel currently performing inventorying and analysis functions;

(C) the organization and procedures necessary to implement and carry out this subsection, including proposed coordination with Federal land management agencies and State foresters;

(D) the schedules for annual sample plot measurements in each State inventory required by paragraph (2) within the first 5-year interval after June 23, 1998;

(E) the core set of variables to be measured in each sample plot under paragraph (2) and the standard set of tables to be used in each State and national report under paragraph (3); and

(F) the process for employing, in coordination with the Secretary of Energy and the Administrator of the National Aeronautics and Space Administration, remote sensing, global positioning systems, and other advanced technologies to carry out this subsection, and the subsequent use of the technologies.

(Pub.L. 95–307, § 3, June 30, 1978, 92 Stat. 353; Pub.L. 96–294, Title II, § 254, June 30, 1980, 94 Stat. 707; Pub.L. 100–521, § 3, Oct. 24, 1988, 102 Stat. 2601; Pub.L. 101–624, Title XII, § 1241(a), Nov. 28, 1990, 104 Stat. 3544; Pub.L. 105–185, Title II, § 253(b), (c), June 23, 1998, 112 Stat. 559; Pub.L. 105–277, Div. A, § 101(a) [Title VII, § 753(a)], Oct. 21, 1998, 112 Stat. 2681–32.)

## HISTORICAL AND STATUTORY NOTES

**References in Text**

This subchapter, referred to in subsec. (a), in the original read "this Act", meaning the Forest and Rangeland Renewable Resources Research Act of 1978, which enacted this subchapter, repealed sections 581 to 581i of this title, and enacted provisions set out as a note under section 1641 of this title. For complete classification, see Short Title note set out under section 1600 of this title and Tables.

**Effective and Applicability Provisions**

1998 Acts

Amendment of this section by Pub.L. 105–277, § 101(a) [Title VII, § 753] effective on the date of enactment of the Agricultural Research, Extension, and Education Reform Act of 1998 [June 23, 1998], see Pub.L. 105–277, § 101(a) [Title VII, § 753(f)] set out as a note under section 343 of Title 7.

**Severability of Provisions**

If any provision of Pub.L. 101–624 or the application thereof to any person or circumstance is held invalid, such invalidity not to affect other provisions or applications of

Pub.L. 101–624 which can be given effect without regard to the invalid provision or application, see section 2519 of Pub.L. 101–624, set out as a note under section 1421 of Title 7, Agriculture.

**Semiarid Agroforestry Research Center**

Section 1243 of Pub.L. 101–624 provided that:

"(a) **Semiarid Agroforestry Research, Development, and Demonstration Center.**—The Secretary of Agriculture shall establish at the Forestry Sciences Laboratory of the United States Forest Service, in Lincoln, Nebraska, a Semiarid Agroforestry Research, Development, and Demonstration Center (hereafter referred to in this section as the 'Center') and appoint a Director to manage and coordinate the program established at the Center under subsection (b).

"(b) **Program.**—The Secretary shall establish a program at the Center and seek the participation of Federal or State governmental entities, land-grant colleges or universities, State agricultural experiment stations, State and private foresters, the National Arbor Day Foundation, and other nonprofit foundations in such program to conduct or assist research, investigations, studies, and surveys to—

"(1) develop sustainable agroforestry systems on semiarid lands that minimize topsoil loss and water contamination and stabilize or enhance crop productivity;

"(2) adapt, demonstrate, document, and model the effectiveness of agroforestry systems under different farming systems and soil or climate conditions;

"(3) develop dual use agroforestry systems compatible with paragraphs (1) and (2) which would provide high-value forestry products for commercial sale from semiarid land;

"(4) develop and improve the drought and pest resistance characteristics of trees for conservation forestry and agroforestry applications in semiarid regions, including the introduction and breeding of trees suited for the Great Plains region of the United States;

"(5) develop technology transfer programs that increase farmer and public acceptance of sustainable agroforestry systems;

"(6) develop improved windbreak and shelterbelt technologies for drought preparedness, soil and water conservation, environmental quality, and biological diversity on semiarid lands;

"(7) develop technical and economic concepts for sustainable agroforestry on semiarid lands, including the conduct of economic analyses of the costs and benefits of agroforestry systems and the development of models to predict the economic benefits under soil or climate conditions;

"(8) provide international leadership in the development and exchange of agroforestry practices on semiarid lands worldwide;

"(9) support research on the effects of agroforestry systems on semiarid lands in mitigating nonpoint source water pollution;

"(10) support research on the design, establishment, and maintenance of tree and shrub plantings to regulate the deposition of snow along roadways; and

"(11) conduct sociological, demographic, and economic studies as needed to develop strategies for increasing the use of forestry conservation and agroforestry practices.

"(c) **Information collection and dissemination.**—The Secretary shall establish at the Center a program, to be known as the National Clearinghouse on Agroforestry Conservation and Promotion to—

"(1) collect, analyze, and disseminate information on agroforestry conservation technologies and practices; and

"(2) promote the use of such information by landowners and those organizations associated with forestry and tree promotion.

"(d) **Authorization of Appropriations.**—There are authorized to be appropriated $5,000,000 annually to carry out this section."

**Southern Forest Regeneration Program**

Section 1242 of Pub.L. 101–624 provided that:

"(a) **Establishment.**—The Secretary of Agriculture shall make a grant to a State for the establishment, within such State, of a center, to be known as the "Southern Forest Regeneration Center" (hereafter referred to in this section as the "Center"), to study forest regeneration problems and forest productivity in the southern region of the United States.

"(b) **Duties of Center.**—The Center shall study forest regeneration problems and forest productivity in the southern region of the United States, including—

"(1) nursery management concerns that will lead to improved seedling quality;

"(2) forest management practices that account for environmental stresses; and

"(3) the development of low-cost forest regeneration methods that provide options for wood products, species diversity, wildlife habitat, and production of clean air and water.

"(c) **Establishment of other Programs.**—The Secretary of Agriculture may establish other programs in other regions of the United States, or a comprehensive National program, to carry out the purposes of this section as the Secretary determines appropriate.

"(d) **Authorization of Appropriations.**—There are authorized to be appropriated such sums as may be necessary to carry out this section."

**Forest Ecosystems and Atmospheric Pollution Research; Congressional Statement of Findings**

Section 2 of Pub.L. 100–521 provided that: "Congress finds that—

"(1) the health and productivity of forests in certain regions of the United States are declining;

"(2) there is a special concern about the decline of certain hardwood species, particularly sugar maples and oaks, in the eastern United States and the effects of atmospheric pollutants on the health and productivity of these forests;

"(3) declines in the productivity of certain commercially important Southern pine species have been measured;

"(4) existing research indicates that atmospheric pollution, including ozone, acidic deposition, and heavy metals, may contribute to this decline;

"(5) there is an urgent need to expand and better coordinate existing Federal, State, and private research, including research by private industry, to determine the cause of changes in the health and productivity of domestic forest ecosystems and to monitor and evaluate the effects of atmospheric pollutants on such ecosystems; and

"(6) such research and monitoring should not impede efforts to control atmospheric pollutants."

## § 1643. Implementation of provisions

**[FRRRRA § 4(a)–(c)]**

### (a) Establishment and maintenance of research facilities; acquisition, expenditures, etc., for property

In implementing this subchapter, the Secretary is authorized to establish and maintain a system of experiment stations, research laboratories, experimental areas, and other forest and rangeland research facilities. The Secretary is authorized, with donated or appropriated funds, to acquire by lease, donation, purchase, exchange, or otherwise, land or interests in land within the United States needed to implement this subchapter, to make necessary expenditures to examine, appraise, and survey such property, and to do all things incident to perfecting title thereto in the United States.

### (b) Acceptance, holding, and administration of gifts, donations, and bequests; use and investment of gifts, proceeds, etc.; funding requirements

In implementing this subchapter, the Secretary is authorized to accept, hold, and administer gifts, donations, and bequests of money, real property, or personal property from any source not otherwise prohibited by law and to use such gifts, donations, and bequests to (1) establish or operate any forest and rangeland research facility within the United States, or (2) perform any forest and rangeland renewable resource research activity authorized by this subchapter. Such gifts, donations, and bequests, or the proceeds thereof, and money appropriated for these purposes shall be deposited in the Treasury in a special fund. At the request of the Secretary, the Secretary of the Treasury may invest or reinvest any money in the fund that in the opinion of the Secretary is not needed for current operations. Such investments shall be in public debt securities with maturities suitable for the needs of the fund and bearing interest at prevailing market rates. There are hereby authorized to be expended from such fund such amounts as may be specified in annual appropriation Acts, which shall remain available until expended.

### (c) Cooperation with international, Federal, State, and other governmental agencies, public and private agencies, etc.; funding requirements for contributions from cooperators

In implementing this subchapter, the Secretary may cooperate with international, Federal, State, and other governmental agencies, with public or private agencies, institutions, universities, and organizations, and with businesses and individuals in the United States and in other countries. The Secretary may receive money and other contributions from cooperators under such conditions as the Secretary may prescribe. Any money contributions received under this subsection shall be credited to the applicable appropriation or fund to be used for the same purposes and shall remain available until expended as the Secretary may direct for use in conducting research activities authorized by this subchapter and in making refunds to contributors.

(Pub.L. 95–307, § 4(a)–(c), June 30, 1978, 92 Stat. 354; Pub.L. 101–513, Title VI, § 611(a)(2), formerly § 607(a)(2), Nov. 5, 1990, 104 Stat. 2072, renumbered § 611(a)(2), Pub.L. 102–574, § 2(a)(1), Oct. 29, 1992, 106 Stat. 4593.)

#### HISTORICAL AND STATUTORY NOTES

**References in Text**

This subchapter, referred to in text, in the original read "this Act", meaning the Forest and Rangeland Renewable Resources Research Act of 1978, which enacted this subchapter, repealed sections 581 to 581i of this title, and enacted provisions set out as a note under section 1641 of this title. For complete classification, see Short Title note set out under section 1600 of this title and Tables.

## § 1644. Forestry and rangeland competitive research grants

**[FRRRRA § 5]**

### (a) Competitive grant authority

In addition to any grants made under other laws, the Secretary is authorized to make competitive grants that will further research activities authorized by this subchapter to Federal, State, and other governmental agencies, public or private agencies, institutions, universities, and organizations, and businesses and individuals in the United States. In making these grants, the Secretary shall emphasize basic and applied research activities that are important to achieving the purposes of this subchapter, and shall obtain, through review by qualified scientists and other methods, participation in research activities by scientists throughout the United States who have expertise in matters related to forest and rangeland renewable resources. Grants under this section shall be made at the discretion of the Secretary under whatever conditions the Secretary may prescribe, after publicly soliciting research proposals, allowing sufficient time for submission of the proposals, and considering qualitative, quantitative, financial, administrative, and other factors that the Secretary deems important in judging, comparing, and accepting the proposals. The Secretary may reject any or all proposals received under this section if the Secretary determines that it is in the public interest to do so.

**(b) Emphasis on certain high priority forestry research**

The Secretary may use up to 5 percent of the amounts made available for research under section 1642 of this title to make competitive grants regarding forestry research in the high priority research areas identified under section 1642(d) of this title.

**(c) Emphasis on certain high priority rangeland research**

The Secretary may use up to 5 percent of the amounts made available for research under section 1642 of this title to make competitive grants regarding rangeland research in the high priority research areas identified under section 1642(d) of this title.

**(d) Priorities**

In making grants under subsections (b) and (c) of this section, the Secretary shall give priority to research proposals under which—

(1) the proposed research will be collaborative research organized through a center of scientific excellence;

(2) the applicant agrees to provide matching funds (in the form of direct funding or in-kind support) in an amount equal to not less than 50 percent of the grant amount; and

(3) the proposed research will be conducted as part of an existing private and public partnership or cooperative research effort and involves several interested research partners.

(Pub.L. 95–307, § 5, June 30, 1978, 92 Stat. 355; Pub.L. 105–185, Title II, § 253(d), June 23, 1998, 112 Stat. 561.)

### HISTORICAL AND STATUTORY NOTES

**References in Text**

This subchapter, referred to in text, in the original read "this Act", meaning the Forest and Rangeland Renewable Resources Research Act of 1978, which enacted this subchapter, repealed sections 581 to 581i of this title, and enacted provisions set out as a note under section 1641 of this title. For complete classification, see Short Title note set out under section 1600 of this title and Tables.

## § 1645. General provisions

**[FRRRRA § 6]**

**(a) Availability of funds to cooperators and grantees**

The Secretary may make funds available to cooperators and grantees under this subchapter without regard to the provisions of section 3324(a) and (b) of Title 31, which prohibits advances of public money.

**(b) Coordination of cooperative aid and grants with other aid and grant authorities**

To avoid duplication, the Secretary shall coordinate cooperative aid and grants under this subchapter with cooperative aid and grants the Secretary makes under any other authority.

**(c) Dissemination of knowledge and technology developed from research activities; cooperation with specified entities**

The Secretary shall use the authorities and means available to the Secretary to disseminate the knowledge and technology developed from research activities conducted under or supported by this subchapter. In meeting this responsibility, the Secretary shall cooperate, as the Secretary deems appropriate, with the entities identified in subsection (d)(3) of this section and with others.

**(d) Additional implementative authorities**

In implementing this subchapter, the Secretary, as the Secretary deems appropriate and practical, shall—

(1) use, and encourage cooperators and grantees to use, the best available scientific skills from a variety of disciplines within and outside the fields of agriculture and forestry;

(2) seek, and encourage cooperators and grantees to seek, a proper mixture of short-term and long-term research and a proper mixture of basic and applied research;

(3) avoid unnecessary duplication and coordinate activities under this section among agencies of the Department of Agriculture and with other affected Federal departments and agencies, State agricultural experiment stations, State extension services, State foresters or equivalent State officials, forestry schools, and private research organizations; and

(4) encourage the development, employment, retention, and exchange of qualified scientists and other specialists through postgraduate, postdoctoral, and other training, national and international exchange of scientists, and other incentives and programs to improve the quality of forest and rangeland renewable resources research.

**(e) Construction of statutory provisions**

This subchapter shall be construed as supplementing all other laws relating to the Department of Agriculture and shall not be construed as limiting or repealing any existing law or authority of the Secretary except as specifically cited in this subchapter.

**(f) Definitions**

For the purposes of this subchapter, the terms "United States" and "State" shall include each of the several States, the District of Columbia, the Commonwealth of Puerto Rico, the Virgin Islands of the United States, the Commonwealth of the Northern Mariana Islands, the Trust Territory of the Pacific

Islands, and the territories and possessions of the United States.

(Pub.L. 95–307, § 6, June 30, 1978, 92 Stat. 355.)

### HISTORICAL AND STATUTORY NOTES

**References in Text**

This subchapter, referred to in text, in the original read "this Act", meaning the Forest and Rangeland Renewable Resources Research Act of 1978, which enacted this subchapter, repealed sections 581 to 581i of this title, and enacted provisions set out as a note under section 1641 of this title. For complete classification, see Short Title note set out under section 1600 of this title and Tables.

**Codifications**

In subsec. (a), "section 3324(a) and (b) of Title 31" was substituted for "section 3648 of the Revised Statutes (31 U.S.C. 529)" on authority of Pub.L. 97–258, § 4(b), Sept. 13, 1982, 96 Stat. 1067, the first section of which enacted Title 31, Money and Finance.

## § 1646. Authorization of appropriations

**[FRRRRA § 7]**

There are hereby authorized to be appropriated annually such sums as may be needed to implement this subchapter. Funds appropriated under this subchapter shall remain available until expended.

(Pub.L. 95–307, § 7, June 30, 1978, 92 Stat. 356.)

### HISTORICAL AND STATUTORY NOTES

**References in Text**

This subchapter, referred to in text, in the original read "this Act", meaning the Forest and Rangeland Renewable Resources Research Act of 1978, which enacted this subchapter, repealed sections 581 to 581i of this title, and enacted provisions set out as a note under section 1641 of this title. For complete classification, see Short Title note set out under section 1600 of this title and Tables.

## § 1647. Other Federal programs

**[FRRRRA § 8]**

**(a) Repeal of statutory authorities relating to investigation, experiments, and tests in reforestation and forest products**

The Act of May 22, 1928, known as the McSweeney-McNary Act (45 Stat. 699–702, as amended; 16 U.S.C. 581, 581a, 581b–581i), is hereby repealed.

**(b) Force and effect of cooperative and other agreements under repealed statutory authorities relating to investigation, etc., in reforestation and forest products**

Contracts and cooperative and other agreements under the McSweeney-McNary Act shall remain in effect until revoked or amended by their own terms or under other provisions of law.

**(c) Issuance of rules and regulations for implementation of provisions and coordination with agricultural research, extension, and teaching provisions**

The Secretary is authorized to issue such rules and regulations as the Secretary deems necessary to implement the provisions of this subchapter and to coordinate this subchapter with title XIV of the Food and Agriculture Act of 1977 [7 U.S.C.A. § 3101 et seq.].

**(d) Availability of funds appropriated under repealed statutory authorities relating to investigation, etc., in reforestation and forest products**

Funds appropriated under the authority of the McSweeney-McNary Act shall be available for expenditure for the programs authorized under this subchapter.

(Pub.L. 95–307, § 8, June 30, 1978, 92 Stat. 356.)

### HISTORICAL AND STATUTORY NOTES

**References in Text**

This subchapter, referred to in text, in the original read "this Act", meaning the Forest and Rangeland Renewable Resources Research Act of 1978, which enacted this subchapter, repealed sections 581 to 581i of this title, and enacted provisions set out as a note under section 1641 of this title. For complete classification, see Short Title note set out under section 1600 of this title and Tables.

The Food and Agriculture Act of 1977, referred to in subsec. (c), is Pub.L. 95–113, Sept. 29, 1977, 91 Stat. 913, as amended. Title XIV of the Food and Agriculture Act of 1977, known as the "National Agricultural Research, Extension, and Teaching Policy Act of 1977", is classified principally to chapter 64 of Title 7 (7 U.S.C.A. § 3101 et seq.). For complete classification of this title to the Code, see Short Title note set out under section 3101 of Title 7 and Tables.

## § 1648. Recycling research

**[FRRRRA § 9]**

**(a) Findings**

Congress finds that—

(1) the United States is amassing vast amounts of solid wastes, which is presenting an increasing problem for municipalities in locating suitable disposal sites;

(2) a large proportion of these wastes consists of paper and other wood wastes;

(3) less than one-third of these paper and wood wastes are recycled;

(4) additional recycling would result in reduced solid waste landfill disposal and would contribute to a reduced rate of removal of standing timber from forest lands; and

(5) additional research is needed to develop technological advances to address barriers to increased

recycling of paper and wood wastes and utilization of products consisting of recycled materials.

**(b) Recycling research program**

The Secretary is authorized to conduct, support, and cooperate in an expanded wood fiber recycling research program, including the acquisition of necessary equipment. The Secretary shall seek to ensure that the program includes the cooperation and support of private industry and that program goals include the application of such research to industry and consumer needs.

**(c) Authorization of appropriations**

In addition to any other funds made available to implement section 1642 of this title, for the 5-year period beginning on October 1, 1990, there are authorized to be appropriated annually $10,000,000 to implement this section.

(Pub.L. 95–307, § 9, as added Pub.L. 101–624, Title XII, § 1241(b), Nov. 28, 1990, 104 Stat. 3544.)

**HISTORICAL AND STATUTORY NOTES**

**Codifications**

Section 1241(b) of Pub.L. 101–624 directed that section 9 of the Forest and Rangeland Renewable Research Act of 1978 is amended. Section 9 of such Act is set out as a note under section 1641 of this title. The directory language of section 1241(b) of Pub.L. 101–624 was interpreted to mean the addition of another section 9 to such Act, set out as this section, as the probable intent of Congress.

**Severability of Provisions**

If any provision of Pub.L. 101–624 or the application thereof to any person or circumstance is held invalid, such invalidity not to affect other provisions or applications of Pub.L. 101–624 which can be given effect without regard to the invalid provision or application, see section 2519 of Pub.L. 101–624, set out as a note under section 1421 of Title 7, Agriculture.

**Prior Provisions**

A prior section 9 of Pub.L. 95–307, June 30, 1978, 92 Stat. 357, which provided the effective date for Pub.L. 95–307, was set out as a note under section 1641 of this title prior to general amendment by Pub.L. 101–624.

## § 1649. Forestry Student Grant Program [FRRRRA § 10]

**(a) Establishment**

The Secretary shall establish a program, to be known as the "Forestry Student Grant Program" (hereafter referred to in this section as the "Program"), to provide assistance to expand the professional education of forestry, natural resources, and environmental scientists.

**(b) Student grants**

Under the Program the Secretary shall provide assistance for the establishment of a competitive grant fellowship program to assist graduate, and undergraduate minority and female, students attending institutions having programs in forestry and natural resources.

**(c) Eligibility**

The Secretary shall ensure that students concentrating in the following studies shall be eligible for assistance under subsection (b) of this section:

(1) Forestry.

(2) Biology and forest organisms.

(3) Ecosystem function and management.

(4) Human-forest interaction.

(5) International trade, competition, and cooperation.

(6) Wood as a raw material.

(7) Economics and policy.

**(d) Authorization of appropriations**

There are authorized to be appropriated such sums as may be necessary to carry out this section.

(Pub.L. 95–307, § 10, as added Pub.L. 101–624, Title XII, § 1252, Nov. 28, 1990, 104 Stat. 3553.)

**HISTORICAL AND STATUTORY NOTES**

**Severability of Provisions**

If any provision of Pub.L. 101–624 or the application thereof to any person or circumstance is held invalid, such invalidity not to affect other provisions or applications of Pub.L. 101–624 which can be given effect without regard to the invalid provision or application, see section 2519 of Pub.L. 101–624, set out as a note under section 1421 of Title 7, Agriculture.

## § 1650. Hardwood technology transfer and applied research

**(a) Authority of Secretary**

The Secretary of Agriculture (hereinafter the "Secretary") is hereby and hereafter authorized to conduct technology transfer and development, training, dissemination of information and applied research in the management, processing and utilization of the hardwood forest resource. This authority is in addition to any other authorities which may be available to the Secretary including, but not limited to, the Cooperative Forestry Assistance Act of 1978, as amended (16 U.S.C. 2101 et seq.), and the Forest and Rangeland Renewable Resources Act of 1978, as amended (16 U.S.C. 1600–1614).[1]

**(b) Grants, contracts, and cooperative agreements, gifts and donations**

In carrying out this authority, the Secretary may enter into grants, contracts, and cooperative agreements with public and private agencies, organizations, corporations, institutions and individuals. The Secretary may accept gifts and donations pursuant to section 2269 of Title 7 including gifts and donations from a donor that conducts business with any agency of the Department of Agriculture or is regulated by the Secretary of Agriculture.

**(c) Use of assets of Wood Education and Resource Center; establishment of Institute of Hardwood Technology Transfer and Applied Research**

The Secretary is hereby and hereafter authorized to operate and utilize the assets of the Wood Education and Resource Center (previously named the Robert C. Byrd Hardwood Technology Center in West Virginia) as part of a newly formed "Institute of Hardwood Technology Transfer and Applied Research" (hereinafter the "Institute"). The Institute, in addition to the Wood Education and Resource Center, will consist of a Director, technology transfer specialists from State and Private Forestry, the Forestry Sciences Laboratory in Princeton, West Virginia, and any other organizational unit of the Department of Agriculture as the Secretary deems appropriate. The overall management of the Institute will be the responsibility of the Forest Service, State and Private Forestry.

**(d) Generation of revenue; deposit into Hardwood Technology Transfer and Applied Research Fund**

The Secretary is hereby and hereafter authorized to generate revenue using the authorities provided herein. Any revenue received as part of the operation of the Institute shall be deposited into a special fund in the Treasury of the United States, known as the "Hardwood Technology Transfer and Applied Research Fund", which shall be available to the Secretary until expended, without further appropriation, in furtherance of the purposes of this section, including upkeep, management, and operation of the Institute and the payment of salaries and expenses.

**(e) Authorization of appropriations**

There are hereby and hereafter authorized to be appropriated such sums as necessary to carry out the provisions of this section.

(Pub.L. 106–113, Div. B, § 1000(a)(3) [Title III, § 332], Nov. 29, 1999, 113 Stat. 1535, 1501A–197.)

[1] So in original.

## HISTORICAL AND STATUTORY NOTES

### Codifications

Section was enacted as part of the Department of the Interior and Related Agencies Appropriations Act, 2000, and not as part of the Forest and Rangeland Renewable Resources Research Act of 1978 which comprises this subchapter.

### Temporary Authority to Conduct Hardwood Technology Transfer and Applied Research

Pub.L. 105–277, Div. A, § 101(e) [Title III, § 343], Oct. 21, 1998, 112 Stat. 2681–297, provided that:

"(a) The Secretary of Agriculture (hereinafter the 'Secretary') is hereby authorized to conduct technology transfer and development, training, dissemination of information and applied research in the management, processing and utilization of the hardwood forest resource. This authority is in addition to any other authorities which may be available to the Secretary including, but not limited to, the Cooperative Forestry Assistance Act of 1978, as amended (16 U.S.C. 2101 et. seq.), and the Forest and Rangeland Renewable Resources Act of 1978, as amended (16 U.S.C. 1600–1614).

"(b) In carrying out this authority, the Secretary may enter into grants, contracts, and cooperative agreements with public and private agencies, organizations, corporations, institutions and individuals. The Secretary may accept gifts and donations pursuant to the Act of October 10, 1978 (7 U.S.C. 2269) including gifts and donations from a donor that conducts business with any agency of the Department of Agriculture or is regulated by the Secretary of Agriculture.

"(c) The Secretary is authorized, on such terms and conditions as the Secretary may prescribe, to assume all rights, title, and interest, including all outstanding assets, of the Robert C. Byrd Hardwood Technology Center, Inc. (herein after the 'Center'), a nonprofit corporation existing under the laws of the State of West Virginia: *Provided*, That the Board of Directors of the Center requests such an action and dissolves the corporation consistent with the Articles of Incorporation and the laws of the State of West Virginia.

"(d) The Secretary is authorized to operate and utilize the assets of the Center as part of a newly formed 'Institute of Hardwood Technology Transfer and Applied Research' (hereinafter the 'Institute'). The Institute, in addition to the Center, will consist of a Director, technology transfer specialists from State and Private Forestry, the Forestry Sciences Laboratory in Princeton, West Virginia, and any other organizational unit of the Department of Agriculture as the Secretary deems appropriate. The overall management of the Institute will be the responsibility of the USDA Forest Service, State and Private Forestry.

"(e) The Secretary is authorized to generate revenue using the authorities provided herein. Any revenue received as part of the operation of the Institute shall be deposited into a special fund in the Treasury of the United States, known as the 'Hardwood Technology Transfer and Applied Research Fund', which shall be available to the Secretary until expended, without further appropriation, in furtherance of the purposes of this section, including upkeep, management, and operation of the Institute and the payment of salaries and expenses.

"(f) There are hereby authorized to be appropriated such sums as necessary to carry out the provisions of this section [this note]."

# RENEWABLE RESOURCES EXTENSION ACT OF 1978 [RREA § ____]

(16 U.S.C.A. §§ 1671 to 1676)

## SUBCHAPTER III—EXTENSION PROGRAMS

### § 1671. Congressional statement of findings

[RREA § 2]

Congress finds that—

(1) the extension program of the Department of Agriculture and the extension activities of each State provide useful and productive educational programs for private forest and range landowners and processors and consumptive and nonconsumptive users of forest and rangeland renewable resources, and these educational programs complement research and assistance programs conducted by the Department of Agriculture;

(2) to meet national goals, it is essential that all forest and rangeland renewable resources (hereinafter in this subchapter referred to as "renewable resources"), including fish and wildlife, forage, outdoor recreation opportunities, timber, and water, be fully considered in designing educational programs for landowners, processors, and users;

(3) more efficient utilization and marketing of renewable resources extend available supplies of such resources, provide products to consumers at prices less than they would otherwise be, and promote reasonable returns on the investments of landowners, processors, and users;

(4) trees and forests in urban areas improve the esthetic quality, reduce noise, filter impurities from the air and add oxygen to it, save energy by moderating temperature extremes, control wind and water erosion, and provide habitat for wildlife; and

(5) trees and shrubs used as shelterbelts protect farm lands from wind and water erosion, promote moisture accumulation in the soil, and provide habitat for wildlife.

(Pub.L. 95–306, § 2, June 30, 1978, 92 Stat. 349.)

#### HISTORICAL AND STATUTORY NOTES

**Effective and Applicability Provisions**

1978 Acts

Section 8 of Pub.L. 95–306, as amended Pub.L. 100–231, § 2(2), Jan. 5, 1988, 101 Stat. 1565; Pub.L. 107–171, Title VIII, § 8101(b)(2), May 13, 2002, 116 Stat. 475, provided that: "The provisions of this Act [enacting this subchapter and provisions set out as a note under section 1600 of this title] shall be effective for the period beginning October 1, 1978, and ending September 30, 2007."

**Short Title**

1978 Acts

For Short Title of Renewable Resources Extension Act of 1978, see short title note set out under section 1600 of this title.

### § 1672. General program authorization

[RREA § 3]

**(a) Types of programs; preconditions and cooperation with State program directors, etc.**

The Secretary of Agriculture (hereinafter in this subchapter referred to as the "Secretary"), under conditions the Secretary may prescribe and in cooperation with the State directors of cooperative extension service programs and eligible colleges and universities, shall—

(1) provide educational programs that enable individuals to recognize, analyze, and resolve problems dealing with renewable resources, including forest- and range-based outdoor recreation opportunities, trees and forests in urban areas, and trees and shrubs in shelterbelts;

(2) use educational programs to disseminate the results of research on renewable resources;

(3) conduct educational programs that transfer the best available technology to those involved in the management and protection of forests and rangelands and the processing and use of their associated renewable resources;

(4) develop and implement educational programs that give special attention to the educational needs of small, private nonindustrial forest landowners;

(5) develop and implement educational programs in range and fish and wildlife management;

(6) assist in providing continuing education programs for professionally trained individuals in fish and wildlife, forest, range, and watershed management and related fields;

(7) help forest and range landowners in securing technical and financial assistance to bring appropriate expertise to bear on their problems;

(8) help identify areas of needed research regarding renewable resources;

(9) in cooperation with State foresters or equivalent State officials, promote public understanding of the energy conservation, economic, social, environmental, and psychological values of trees and open space in urban and community area environments and expand knowledge of the ecological relationships and benefits of trees and related resources in urban and community environments; and

(10) conduct a comprehensive natural resource and environmental education program for landowners and managers, public officials, and the public, with particular emphasis on youth.

**(b) "Eligible colleges and universities" defined**

As used in this subchapter, the term "eligible colleges and universities" means colleges and universities eligible to be supported and maintained, in whole or in part, with funds made available under the provisions of the Act of July 2, 1862 (12 Stat. 503–505, as amended; 7 U.S.C. 301–305, 307, 308), and the Act of August 30, 1890 (26 Stat. 417–419, as amended; 7 U.S.C. 321–326, 328), including Tuskegee Institute, and colleges and universities eligible for assistance under the Act of October 10, 1962 (76 Stat. 806–807, as amended; 16 U.S.C. 582a, 582a–1–582a–7).

**(c) Use of appropriate educational methods required; scope of methods**

In implementing this section, all appropriate educational methods may be used, including, but not limited to, meetings, short courses, workshops, tours, demonstrations, publications, news releases, and radio and television programs.

(Pub.L. 95–306, § 3, June 30, 1978, 92 Stat. 349, Pub.L. 101–624, Title XII, §§ 1219(b)(1), 1251(b), Nov. 28, 1990, 104 Stat. 3538, 3552; Pub.L. 102–237, Title X, § 1018(d), Dec. 13, 1991, 105 Stat. 1905.)

### HISTORICAL AND STATUTORY NOTES

**References in Text**

The Act of July 2, 1862 (12 Stat. 503–505, as amended; 7 U.S.C. 301–305, 307, 308), referred to in subsec. (b), is popularly known as the Morrill Act and also as the First Morrill Act, which is classified generally to subchapter I of chapter 13 of Title 7 (7 U.S.C.A. § 301 et seq.). For complete classification, see Short Title note set out under section 301 of Title 7 and Tables.

The Act of August 30, 1890 (26 Stat. 417–419, as amended; 7 U.S.C. 321–326, 328), referred to in subsec. (b), is popularly known as the Agricultural College Act of 1890 and also as the Second Morrill Act, which is classified generally to subchapter II of chapter 13 of Title 7 (7 U.S.C.A. § 321 et seq.). For complete classification, see Short Title note set out under section 321 of Title 7 and Tables.

The Act of October 10, 1962 (76 Stat. 806–807, as amended), referred to in subsec. (b), is the McIntire-Stennis Act of 1962, which is classified principally to subchapter III of chapter 3 of this title (16 U.S.C.A. § 582a et seq.). For complete classification, see Short Title note set out under section 582a of this title and Tables.

**Effective and Applicability Provisions**

1991 Acts

Amendments by Pub.L. 102–237 effective Dec. 13, 1991, see section 1101(a) of Pub.L. 102–237, set out as a note under section 1421 of Title 7, Agriculture.

**Severability of Provisions**

If any provision of Pub.L. 101–624 or the application thereof to any person or circumstance is held invalid, such invalidity not to affect other provisions or applications of Pub.L. 101–624 which can be given effect without regard to the invalid provision or application, see section 2519 of Pub.L. 101–624, set out as a note under section 1421 of Title 7, Agriculture.

## § 1673. State programs

[RREA § 4]

**(a) Development by State program director, etc., of comprehensive and coordinated program by mutual agreement; consultations; review procedure**

The State director of cooperative extension programs (hereinafter in this subchapter referred to as the "State director") and the administrative heads of extension for eligible colleges and universities in each State shall jointly develop, by mutual agreement, a single comprehensive and coordinated renewable resources extension program in which the role of each eligible college and university is well-defined. In meeting this responsibility, the State director and the administrative heads of extension for eligible colleges and universities shall consult and seek agreement with the administrative technical representatives and the forestry representatives provided for by the Secretary in implementation of the Act of October 10, 1962 (76 Stat. 806–807, as amended; 16 U.S.C. 582a, 582a–1–582a–7), in the State. Each State's renewable resources extension program shall be submitted to the Secretary annually. The National Agricultural Research, Extension, Education, and Economics Advisory Board established under section 3123 of Title 7 shall review and make recommendations to the Secretary pertaining to programs conducted under this subchapter.

**(b) Encouragement by State director, etc., of cooperation between county and State extension staffs and appropriate Federal and State agencies and organizations**

The State director and the administrative heads of extension for eligible colleges and universities in each State shall encourage close cooperation between extension staffs at the county and State levels, and State and Federal research organizations dealing with renewable resources, State and Federal agencies that manage forests and rangelands and their associated renewable resources, State and Federal agencies that have responsibilities associated with the processing or use of renewable resources, and other agencies or organizations the State director and administrative heads of extension deem appropriate.

**(c) Administration and coordination of program by State director; exception**

Each State renewable resources extension program shall be administered and coordinated by the State director, except that, in States having colleges eligible to receive funds under the Act of August 30, 1890 (26 Stat. 417–419, as amended; 7 U.S.C. 321–326, 328), including Tuskegee Institute, the State renewable resources extension program shall be administered by the State director and the administrative head or heads of extension for the college or colleges eligible to receive such funds.

**(d) Appointment and use of advisory committees by State director, etc.; composition of advisory committees**

In meeting the provisions of this section, each State director and administrative heads of extension for eligible colleges and universities shall appoint and use one or more advisory committees comprised of forest and range landowners, professionally trained individuals in fish and wildlife, forest, range, and watershed management, and related fields, as appropriate, and other suitable persons.

**(e) "State" defined**

For the purposes of this subchapter, the term "State" means any one of the fifty States, the Commonwealth of Puerto Rico, Guam, the District of Columbia, and the Virgin Islands of the United States.

(Pub.L. 95–306, § 4, June 30, 1978, 92 Stat. 350; Pub.L. 104–127, Title VIII, § 802(b)(3), Apr. 4, 1996, 110 Stat. 1159.)

### HISTORICAL AND STATUTORY NOTES

**References in Text**

The Act of October 10, 1962 (76 Stat. 806–807, as amended), referred to in subsec. (a), is the McIntire-Stennis Act of 1962, which is classified generally to subchapter III of chapter 3 of this title (16 U.S.C.A. § 582a et seq.). For complete classification, see Short Title note set out under section 582a of this title and Tables.

The Act of August 30, 1890 (26 Stat. 417–419, as amended; 7 U.S.C. 321–326, 328), referred to in subsec. (c), is popularly known as the Agricultural College Act of 1890 and also as the Second Morrill Act, which is classified principally to subchapter II of chapter 13 of Title 7 (7 U.S.C.A. § 321 et seq.). For complete classification, see Short Title note set out under section 321 of Title 7 and Tables.

## § 1674. Renewable Resources Extension Program plan

**[RREA § 5]**

**(a) Preparation and submission to Congress; purposes; contents**

The Secretary shall prepare a five-year plan for implementing this subchapter, which is to be called the "Renewable Resources Extension Program" and shall submit such plan to the Committee on Agriculture of the House of Representatives and the Committee on Agriculture, Nutrition, and Forestry of the Senate no later than the last day of the first half of the fiscal year ending September 30, 1980, and the last day of the first half of each fifth fiscal year thereafter. The Renewable Resources Extension Program shall provide national emphasis and direction as well as guidance to State directors and administrative heads of extension for eligible colleges and universities in the development of their respective State renewable resources extension programs, which are to be appropriate in terms of the conditions, needs, and opportunities in each State. The Renewable Resources Extension Program shall contain, but not be limited to, brief outlines of general extension programs for fish and wildlife management (for both game and nongame species), range management, timber management (including brief outlines of general extension programs for timber utilization, timber harvesting, timber marketing, wood utilization, and wood products marketing), and watershed management (giving special attention to water quality protection), as well as brief outlines of general extension programs for recognition and enhancement of forest- and range-based outdoor recreation opportunities, for urban and community forestry activities, and for planting and management of trees and shrubs in shelterbelts, and give special attention to water quality protection and natural resource and environmental education for landowners and managers, public officials, and the public.

**(b) Considerations governing preparation**

In preparing the Renewable Resources Extension Program, the Secretary shall take into account the respective capabilities of private forests and rangelands for yielding renewable resources and the relative needs for such resources identified in the periodic Renewable Resource Assessment provided for in section 1601 of this title and the periodic appraisal of land and water resources provided for in section 2004 of this title.

**(c) Omitted**

**(d) Review of activities and evaluation of progress**

To assist Congress and the public in evaluating the Renewable Resources Extension Program, the program shall include a review of activities undertaken in response to the preceding five-year plan and an evaluation of the progress made toward accomplishing the goals and objectives set forth in such preceding plan. Such review and evaluation shall be displayed in the program, for the Nation as a whole, and for each State.

(Pub.L. 95–306, § 5, June 30, 1978, 92 Stat. 351; Pub.L. 100–231, § 3, Jan. 5, 1988, 101 Stat. 1565; Pub.L. 101–624, Title XII, §§ 1219(b)(2), 1251(c), Nov. 28, 1990, 104 Stat. 3539, 3553.)

HISTORICAL AND STATUTORY NOTES

**Codifications**

Subsec. (c) of this section, which required the Secretary to furnish Congress with an annual report on the Renewable Resources Extension Program at the time of submission of each annual fiscal budget, terminated, effective May 15, 2000, pursuant to Pub.L. 104–66, Title III, § 3003, Dec. 21, 1995, 109 Stat. 734, as amended, set out as a note under 31 U.S.C.A. § 1113. See, also, House Document No. 103–7, page 45.

**Severability of Provisions**

If any provision of Pub.L. 101–624 or the application thereof to any person or circumstance is held invalid, such invalidity not to affect other provisions or applications of Pub.L. 101–624 which can be given effect without regard to the invalid provision or application, see section 2519 of Pub.L. 101–624, set out as a note under section 1421 of Title 7, Agriculture.

## § 1674a. Expanded programs

[RREA § 5A]

**(a) In general**

The Secretary, acting through the Extension Service and the State cooperative extension services, and in consultation with State foresters or equivalent State officials, school boards, and universities, shall expand forestry and natural resources education programs conducted under this subchapter for private forest owners and managers, public officials, youth, and the general public, and shall include guidelines for the transfer of technology.

**(b) Activities**

**(1) In general**

In expanding the programs conducted under this subchapter, the Secretary shall ensure that activities are undertaken to promote policies and practices that enhance the health, vitality, productivity, economic value, and environmental attributes of the forest lands of the United States.

**(2) Types**

The activities referred to in paragraph (1) shall include—

(A) demonstrating and teaching landowners and forest managers the concepts of multiple-use and sustainable natural resource management;

(B) conducting comprehensive environmental education programs that assist citizens to participate in environmentally positive activities such as tree planting, recycling, erosion prevention, and waste management; and

(C) educational programs and materials that will improve the capacity of schools, local governments and resource agencies to deliver forestry and natural resources information to young people, environmentally concerned citizens, and action groups.

(Pub.L. 95–306, § 5A, as added Pub.L. 101–624, Title XII, § 1251(a), Nov. 28, 1990, 104 Stat. 3552.)

HISTORICAL AND STATUTORY NOTES

**Severability of Provisions**

If any provision of Pub.L. 101–624 or the application thereof to any person or circumstance is held invalid, such invalidity not to affect other provisions or applications of Pub.L. 101–624 which can be given effect without regard to the invalid provision or application, see section 2519 of Pub.L. 101–624, set out as a note under section 1421 of Title 7, Agriculture.

## § 1674b. Sustainable forestry outreach initiative

[RREA § 5B]

The Secretary shall establish a program, to be known as the "Sustainable Forestry Outreach Initiative", to educate landowners concerning the following:

(1) The value and benefits of practicing sustainable forestry.

(2) The importance of professional forestry advice in achieving sustainable forestry objectives.

(3) The variety of public and private sector resources available to assist the landowners in planning for and practicing sustainable forestry.

(Pub.L. 95–306, § 5B, as added Pub.L. 107–171, Title VIII, § 8101(a), May 13, 2002, 116 Stat. 474.)

## § 1675. Authorization of appropriations; criteria for eligibility of States for funds

[RREA § 6]

There is authorized to be appropriated to carry out this subchapter $30,000,000 for each of fiscal years 2002 through 2007. Generally, States shall be eligible for funds appropriated under this subchapter according to the respective capabilities of their private forests and rangelands for yielding renewable resources and relative needs for such resources identified in the periodic Renewable Resource Assessment provided for in section 1601 of this title and the periodic appraisal of land and water resources provided for in section 2004 of this title.

(Pub.L. 95–306, § 6, June 30, 1978, 92 Stat. 352; Pub.L. 100–231, § 2(1), Jan. 5, 1988, 101 Stat. 1565; Pub.L. 105–185, Title III, § 301(h), June 23, 1998, 112 Stat. 563; Pub.L. 107–171, Title VIII, § 8101(b)(1), May 13, 2002, 116 Stat. 474.)

HISTORICAL AND STATUTORY NOTES

**References in Text**

This subchapter, referred to in text, originally read "this Act", meaning the Renewable Resources Extension Act of 1978, or RREA, Pub.L. 95–306, June 30, 1978, 92 Stat. 349, which is principally classified to this subchapter. For complete classification, see short title note set out under 16 U.S.C.A. § 1600 and Tables.

### § 1676. Issuance of rules and regulations for implementation of provisions and coordination with agricultural, research, extension, and teaching provisions

[RREA § 7]

The Secretary is authorized to issue such rules and regulations as the Secretary deems necessary to implement the provisions of this subchapter and to coordinate this subchapter with title XIV of the Food and Agriculture Act of 1977 [7 U.S.C.A. § 3101 et seq.].

(Pub.L. 95–306, § 7, June 30, 1978, 92 Stat. 352.)

#### HISTORICAL AND STATUTORY NOTES

**References in Text**

The Food and Agriculture Act of 1977, referred to in text, is Pub.L. 95–113, Sept. 29, 1977, 91 Stat. 913, as amended. Title XIV of the Food and Agriculture Act of 1977, known as the "National Agricultural Research, Extension, and Teaching Policy Act of 1977", is classified principally to chapter 64 of Title 7 (7 U.S.C.A. § 3101 et seq.). For complete classification, see Short Title note set out under section 3101 of Title 7 and Tables.

# WOOD RESIDUE UTILIZATION ACT OF 1980 [WRUA § _____]

**(16 U.S.C.A. §§ 1681 to 1687)**

## SUBCHAPTER IV—WOOD RESIDUE UTILIZATION

### § 1681. Congressional statement of purpose

[WRUA § 2]

The purpose of this subchapter is to develop, demonstrate, and make available information on feasible methods that have potential for commercial application to increase and improve utilization, in residential, commercial, and industrial or powerplant applications, of wood residues resulting from timber harvesting and forest protection and management activities occurring on public and private forest lands, and from the manufacture of forest products, including woodpulp.

(Pub.L. 96–554, § 2, Dec. 19, 1980, 94 Stat. 3257.)

#### HISTORICAL AND STATUTORY NOTES

**Effective and Applicability Provisions**

1980 Acts

Section 9 of Pub.L. 96–554 provided that: "This Act [enacting this subchapter and provision set out as a note under section 1600 of this title] shall become effective October 1, 1981."

**Short Title**

1980 Acts

For Short Title of Pub.L. 96–554, Dec. 19, 1980, 94 Stat. 3257, as the Wood Residue Utilization Act of 1980, see short title note set out under section 1600 of this title.

### § 1682. Pilot projects and demonstrations

[WRUA § 3]

**(a) Establishment, implementation**

The Secretary may establish pilot projects and demonstrations to carry out the purposes of this subchapter. The pilot projects and demonstrations established under this section (1) may be operated by the Secretary; or (2) may be carried out through contracts or agreements with owners of private forest lands or other persons, or in conjunction with projects, contracts, or agreements entered into under any other authority which the Secretary may possess: *Provided*, That nothing contained in this subchapter shall abrogate or modify provisions of existing contracts or agreements, including contracts or agreements for the sale of national forest timber, except to the extent such changes are mutually agreed to by the parties to such contracts or agreements.

**(b) Scope; residue removal credits**

Pilot projects and demonstrations carried out under this section may include, but are not limited to (1) establishment and operation of utilization demonstration areas; (2) establishment and operation of fuel wood concentration and distribution centers; and (3) construction of access roads needed to facilitate wood residue utilization: *Provided*, That residue removal credits may be utilized by the Secretary only as provided in section 1683 of this title.

(Pub.L. 96–554, § 3, Dec. 19, 1980, 94 Stat. 3257.)

### § 1683. Pilot projects; requirements; residue removal credits as compensation; implementation guidelines

[WRUA § 4]

The Secretary may carry out pilot wood residue utilization projects under which purchasers of National Forest System timber under contracts awarded prior to October 1, 1986, may, except as otherwise provided in this section, be required to remove wood residues not purchased by them to points of prospective use in return for compensation in the form of "residue removal credits." Such projects may be carried out where the Secretary identifies situations in which pilot wood residue utilization projects on the National Forest System can provide important information on various methods and approaches to increasing the utilization, in residential, commercial, and industrial or powerplant applications, of wood residues and where such information cannot reasonably be obtained unless the pilot projects are done in conjunction with normal National Forest timber sale activities. The residue removal credits shall be applied against the amount payable for the timber purchased and shall represent the anticipated cost of removal of wood residues. The following guidelines shall apply to projects carried out under this section:

(1) Except in cases where wood residue removal is determined to be necessary for fire prevention, site preparation for regeneration, wildlife habitat improvement, or other land management purposes, the Secretary may not provide for removal of wood residues in instances where the anticipated cost of removal would exceed the anticipated value.

(2) The residue removal credits authorized by this section shall not exceed the amount payable by the purchaser for timber after the application of all other designated charges and credits.

(3) The Secretary may sell the wood residues removed to points of prospective use for not less than their appraised value.

(4) Pilot projects, demonstrations, and other programs established pursuant to this subchapter shall be carried out in a manner which does not result in an adverse effect on the furnishing of timber, free of charge, under any other provision of law.

(5) Wood residues shall be collected from a site so as to avoid soil depletion or erosion giving full consideration to the protection of wildlife habitat.

(6) For the purposes of section 500 of this title, (A) any residue removal credit applied under this section shall be considered as "money received" or "moneys received", respectively, and (B) the "money received" or "moneys received", respectively, from the sales of wood residues removed to points of prospective use shall be the proceeds of the sales less the sum of any residue removal credit applied with respect to such residues plus any costs incurred by the Forest Service in processing and storing such residues.

(Pub.L. 96–554, § 4, Dec. 19, 1980, 94 Stat. 3257.)

## § 1684. Annual reports

[WRUA § 5]

The Secretary shall make annual reports to the Congress on the programs authorized by this subchapter. These reports shall be submitted with the reports required under section 1606(c) of this title.

(Pub.L. 96–554, § 5, Dec. 19, 1980, 94 Stat. 3258.)

## § 1685. Regulations

[WRUA § 6]

The Secretary shall issue such regulations as the Secretary deems necessary to implement the provisions of this subchapter.

(Pub.L. 96–554, § 6, Dec. 19, 1980, 94 Stat. 3258.)

## § 1686. Definitions

[WRUA § 7]

For purposes of this subchapter, the term:

(1) "Anticipated cost of removal" means the projected cost of removal of wood residues from timber sales areas to points of prospective use, as determined by the Secretary at the time of advertisement of the timber sales contract in accordance with appropriate appraisal and sale procedures.

(2) "Anticipated value" means the projected value of wood residues as fuel or other merchantable wood products, as determined by the Secretary at the time of advertisement of the timber sales contract in accordance with appropriate appraisal and sale procedures.

(3) "Points of prospective use" means the locations where the wood residues are sold or otherwise put to use, as determined by the Secretary in accordance with appropriate appraisal and sale procedures.

(4) "Person" means an individual, partnership, joint-stock company, corporation, association, trust, estate, or any other legal entity, or any agency of Federal or State government or of a political subdivision of a State.

(5) "Secretary" means the Secretary of Agriculture.

(6) "Wood residues" includes, but is not limited to, logging slash, down timber material, woody plants, and standing live or dead trees which do not meet utilization standards because of size, species, merchantable volume, or economic selection criteria and which, in the case of live trees, are surplus to growing stock needs.

(Pub.L. 96–554, § 7, Dec. 19, 1980, 94 Stat. 3258.)

## § 1687. Authorization of appropriations

[WRUA § 8]

There is hereby authorized to be appropriated not to exceed $25,000,000 for each of the fiscal years 1982, 1983, 1984, 1985, and 1986 to carry out the pilot projects and demonstrations authorized by section

1682 of this title, the residue removal credits authorized by section 1683 of this title, and the other provisions of this subchapter: *Provided*, That not to exceed $2,500,000 of such amount may be appropriated for administrative expenses to carry out this subchapter for the period beginning October 1, 1981, and ending September 30, 1986. Such sums shall be in addition to those provided under other provisions of law and shall remain available until expended.

(Pub.L. 96–554, § 8, Dec. 19, 1980, 94 Stat. 3259.)

# SOIL AND WATER RESOURCES

## SOIL AND WATER RESOURCES CONSERVATION ACT OF 1977 [SWRCA § ___]

(16 U.S.C.A. §§ 2001 to 2009)

## CHAPTER 40—SOIL AND WATER RESOURCES CONSERVATION



### § 2001. Congressional findings

[SWRCA § 2]

The Congress finds that:

(1) There is a growing demand on the soil, water, and related resources of the Nation to meet present and future needs.

(2) The Congress, in its concern for sustained use of the resource base,[1] of the United States, has ensured that the Department of Agriculture possesses information, technical expertise, and a delivery system for providing assistance to land users with respect to conservation and use of soils; plants; woodlands; watershed protection and flood prevention; the conservation, development, utilization, and disposal of water; animal husbandry; fish and wildlife management; recreation; community development; and related resource uses.

(3) Resource appraisal is basic to effective soil and water conservation. Since individual and governmental decisions concerning soil and water resources often transcend administrative boundaries and affect other programs and decisions, a coordinated appraisal and program framework are essential.

(Pub.L. 95–192, § 2, Nov. 18, 1977, 91 Stat. 1407; Pub.L. 103–354, Title II, § 246(f)(2)(A), Oct. 13, 1994, 108 Stat. 3225.)

1 So in original. The comma probably should be deleted.

#### HISTORICAL AND STATUTORY NOTES

**Short Title**

1977 Acts

Section 1 of Pub.L. 95–192 provided: "That this Act [enacting this chapter] may be cited as the 'Soil and Water Resources Conservation Act of 1977'."

### § 2002. Definitions

[SWRCA § 3]

As used in this chapter:

(1) The term "Secretary" means the Secretary of Agriculture.

(2) The term "soil, water, and related resources" means those resources which come within the scope of the programs administered and participated in by the Secretary of Agriculture.

(3) The term "soil and water conservation program" means a set of guidelines for attaining the purposes of this chapter.

(Pub.L. 95–192, § 3, Nov. 18, 1977, 91 Stat. 1407; Pub.L. 103–354, Title II, § 246(f)(2)(B), Oct. 13, 1994, 108 Stat. 3225.)

#### HISTORICAL AND STATUTORY NOTES

**Transfer of Functions**

The enforcement functions of the Secretary of Agriculture or other appropriate officer or entity in the Department of Agriculture, insofar as they involve lands and programs under the jurisdiction of that Department, related to compliance with system activities requiring coordination and approval under general authorities of this chapter as they relate to preconstruction, construction, and initial operation of an approved transportation system for the transport of Canadian natural gas and Alaskan natural gas as such terms are defined in the Alaskan Natural Gas Transportation Act of 1976, section 719 et seq. of Title 15, Commerce and Trade, were transferred to the Federal Inspector for the Alaska Natural Gas Transportation System, effective July 1, 1979, until the first anniversary of the date of initial operation of the Alaska Natural Gas Transportation System, pursuant to sections 102(f) and 203(a) of 1979 Reorg. Plan No. 1, June 12, 1979, 44 F.R. 33665, 33666, 93 Stat. 1373, set out in the Appendix 1 to Title 5, Government Organization and Employees.

## § 2003. Congressional policy and declaration of purpose

[SWRCA § 4]

### (a) Responsiveness to long-term needs

In order to further the conservation of soil, water, and related resources, it is declared to be the policy of the United States and purpose of this chapter that the conduct of programs administered by the Secretary of Agriculture for the conservation of such resources shall be responsive to the long-term needs of the Nation, as determined under the provisions of this chapter.

### (b) Full utilization of cooperative arrangements with State agencies

Recognizing that the arrangements under which the Federal Government cooperates with State soil and water conservation agencies and other appropriate State natural resource agencies such as those concerned with forestry and fish and wildlife and, through conservation districts, with other local units of government and land users, have effectively aided in the protection and improvement of the Nation's basic resources, including the restoration and maintenance of resources damaged by improper use, it is declared to be the policy of the United States that these arrangements and similar cooperative arrangements should be utilized to the fullest extent practicable to achieve the purpose of this chapter consistent with the roles and responsibilities of the non-Federal agencies, landowners and land users.

### (c) Attainment of policies and purposes

The Secretary shall promote the attainment of the policies and purposes expressed in this chapter by—

(1) appraising on a continuing basis the soil, water, and related resources of the Nation;

(2) developing and updating periodically a program for furthering the conservation, protection, and enhancement of the soil, water, and related resources of the Nation consistent with the roles and program responsibilities of other Federal agencies and State and local governments; and

(3) providing to Congress and the public, through reports, the information developed pursuant to paragraphs (1) and (2) of this subsection, and by providing Congress with an annual evaluation report as provided in section 2006 of this title.

(Pub.L. 95–192, § 4, Nov. 18, 1977, 91 Stat. 1407.)

### HISTORICAL AND STATUTORY NOTES

**Transfer of Functions**

For transfer of certain enforcement functions of Secretary or other official in Department of Agriculture under this chapter to Federal Inspector, Office of Federal Inspector for the Alaska Natural Gas Transportation System, see Transfer of Functions note set out under section 2002 of this title.

## § 2004. Continuing appraisal of soil, water, and related resources

[SWRCA § 5]

### (a) Data

In recognition of the importance of and need for obtaining and maintaining information on the current status of soil, water, and related resources, the Secretary is authorized and directed to carry out a continuing appraisal of the soil, water, and related resources of the Nation. The appraisal shall include, but not be limited to—

(1) data on the quality and quantity of soil, water, and related resources, including fish and wildlife habitats;

(2) data on the capability and limitations of those resources for meeting current and projected demands on the resource base;

(3) data on the changes that have occurred in the status and condition of those resources resulting from various past uses, including the impact of farming technologies, techniques, and practices;

(4) data on current Federal and State laws, policies, programs, rights, regulations, ownerships, and their trends and other considerations relating to the use, development, and conservation of soil, water, and related resources;

(5) data on the costs and benefits of alternative soil and water conservation practices; and

(6) data on alternative irrigation techniques regarding their costs, benefits, and impact on soil and water conservation, crop production, and environmental factors.

### (b) Collection of data

The appraisal shall utilize data collected under this chapter and pertinent data and information collected by the Department of Agriculture and other Federal, State, and local agencies and organizations. The Secretary shall establish an integrated system capable of using combinations of resource data to determine the quality and capabilities for alternative uses of the resource base and to identify areas of local, State, and National concerns and related roles pertaining to soil and water conservation, resource use and development, and environmental improvement.

### (c) Public participation

The appraisal shall be made in cooperation with conservation districts, State soil and water conservation agencies, and other appropriate citizen groups, and local and State agencies under such procedures as the Secretary may prescribe to insure public participation.

**(d) Completion dates**

The Secretary shall conduct four comprehensive appraisals under this section, to be completed by December 31, 1979, December 31, 1986, December 31, 1995, and December 31, 2005, respectively. The Secretary may make such additional interim appraisals as the Secretary considers appropriate.

(Pub.L. 95–192, § 5, Nov. 18, 1977, 91 Stat. 1408; Pub.L. 99–198, Title XII, § 1252(a), Dec. 23, 1985, 99 Stat. 1516.)

### HISTORICAL AND STATUTORY NOTES

**Transfer of Functions**

For transfer of certain enforcement functions of Secretary or other official in Department of Agriculture under this chapter to Federal Inspector, Office of Federal Inspector for the Alaska Natural Gas Transportation System, see Transfer of Functions note set out under section 2002 of this title.

## § 2005. Soil and water conservation program

[SWRCA § 6]

**(a) Program development**

The Secretary is hereby authorized and directed to develop in cooperation with and participation by the public through conservation districts, State and national organizations and agencies, and other appropriate means, a national soil and water conservation program (hereinafter called the "program") to be used as a guide in carrying out the activities of the Secretary which assist landowners and land users, at their request, in furthering soil and water conservation on the private and non-Federal lands of the Nation. The program shall set forth direction for future soil and water conservation efforts of the United States Department of Agriculture based on the current soil, water, and related resource appraisal developed in accordance with section 2004 of this title, taking into consideration both the long- and short-term needs of the Nation, the landowners, and the land users, and the roles and responsibilities of Federal, State, and local governments in such conservation efforts. The program shall also include but not be limited to—

(1) analysis of the Nation's soil, water, and related resource problems;

(2) analysis of existing Federal, State, and local government authorities and adjustments needed;

(3) an evaluation of the effectiveness of the soil and water conservation ongoing programs and the overall progress being achieved by Federal, State, and local programs and the landowners and land users in meeting the soil and water conservation objectives of this chapter;

(4) identification and evaluation of alternative methods for the conservation, protection, environmental improvement, and enhancement of soil and water resources, in the context of alternative time frames, and a recommendation of the preferred alternatives and the extent to which they are being implemented;

(5) investigation and analysis of the practicability, desirability, and feasibility of collecting organic waste materials, including manure, crop and food wastes, industrial organic waste, municipal sewage sludge, logging and wood-manufacturing residues, and any other organic refuse, composting, or similarly treating such materials, transporting and placing such materials onto the land to improve soil tilth and fertility. The analysis shall include the projected cost of such collection, transportation, and placement in accordance with sound locally approved soil and water conservation practices;

(6) analysis of the Federal and non-Federal inputs required to implement the program;

(7) analysis of costs and benefits of alternative soil and water conservation practices; and

(8) investigation and analysis of alternative irrigation techniques regarding their costs, benefits, and impact on soil and water conservation, crop production, and environmental factors.

**(b) Completion dates**

The initial program shall be completed not later than December 31, 1979, and program updates shall be completed by December 31, 1987, December 31, 1997, and December 31, 2007, respectively.

(Pub.L. 95–192, § 6, Nov. 18, 1977, 91 Stat. 1409; Pub.L. 99–198, Title XII, § 1252(b), Dec. 23, 1985, 99 Stat. 1516; Pub.L. 103–354, Title II, § 246(f)(2)(C), Oct. 13, 1994, 108 Stat. 3225.)

### HISTORICAL AND STATUTORY NOTES

**Transfer of Functions**

For transfer of certain enforcement functions of Secretary or other official in Department of Agriculture under this chapter to Federal Inspector, Office of Federal Inspector for the Alaska Natural Gas Transportation System, see Transfer of Functions note set out under section 2002 of this title.

## § 2005a. Repealed. Pub.L. 104–127, Title III, § 336(e), Apr. 4, 1996, 110 Stat. 1007

### HISTORICAL AND STATUTORY NOTES

Section, Pub.L. 99–198, Title XII, § 1251, Dec. 23, 1985, 99 Stat. 1516, related to technical assistance for water resources.

## § 2005b. Repealed. Pub.L. 107–171, Title II, § 2502(b), May 13, 2002, 116 Stat. 267

### HISTORICAL AND STATUTORY NOTES

Section, Pub.L. 104–127, Title III, § 386, Apr. 4, 1996, 110 Stat. 1017, related to conservation of private grazing land. See now 16 U.S.C.A. § 3839bb.

## § 2006. Reports to Congress

[SWRCA § 7]

**(a) Appraisal, program, and detailed statement of policy when Congress convenes**

(1) At the time Congress convenes in 1980, 1987, 1996, and 2006, the President shall transmit to the Speaker of the House of Representatives and the President of the Senate the appraisal developed under section 2004 of this title and completed prior to the end of the previous year.

(2) At the time Congress convenes in 1980, 1988, 1998, and 2008, the President shall transmit to the Speaker of the House of Representatives and the President of the Senate the initial program or updated program developed under section 2005 of this title and completed prior to the end of the previous year, together with a detailed statement of policy regarding soil and water conservation activities of the United States Department of Agriculture.

**(b) Annual report accompanying budget covering program effectiveness**

The Secretary, during budget preparation for fiscal year 1982 and annually thereafter during the period this chapter is in effect, shall prepare and transmit to the Congress, through the President, a report to accompany the budget which evaluates the program's effectiveness in attaining the purposes of this chapter. The report, prepared in concise summary form with appropriate detailed appendices, shall contain pertinent data from the current resource appraisal required to be prepared by section 2004 of this title, shall set forth the progress in implementing the program required to be developed by section 2005 of this title, and shall contain appropriate measurements of pertinent costs and benefits. The evaluation shall assess the balance between economic factors and environmental quality factors. The report shall also indicate plans for implementing action and recommendations for new legislation where warranted.

(Pub.L. 95–192, § 7, Nov. 18, 1977, 91 Stat. 1410; Pub.L. 99–198, Title XII, § 1252(c), Dec. 23, 1985, 99 Stat. 1516.)

## § 2007. Authorization of appropriations

[SWRCA § 8]

There are authorized to be appropriated such funds as may be necessary to carry out the purposes of this chapter.

(Pub.L. 95–192, § 8, Nov. 18, 1977, 91 Stat. 1411.)

## § 2008. Utilization of available information and data

[SWRCA § 9]

In the implementation of this chapter, the Secretary shall utilize information and data available from other Federal, State, and local governments, and private organizations and he shall coordinate his actions with the resource appraisal and planning efforts of other Federal agencies and avoid unnecessary duplication and overlap of planning and program efforts.

(Pub.L. 95–192, § 9, Nov. 18, 1977, 91 Stat. 1411.)

### HISTORICAL AND STATUTORY NOTES

**Transfer of Functions**

For transfer of certain enforcement functions of Secretary or other official in Department of Agriculture under this chapter to Federal Inspector, Office of Federal Inspector for the Alaska Natural Gas Transportation System, see Transfer of Functions note set out under section 2002 of this title.

## § 2009. Termination of program

[SWRCA § 10]

The provisions of this chapter shall terminate on December 31, 2008.

(Pub.L. 95–192, § 10, Nov. 18, 1977, 91 Stat. 1411; Pub.L. 99–198, Title XII, § 1252(d), Dec. 23, 1985, 99 Stat. 1517.)

# AQUATIC NUISANCE PREVENTION AND CONTROL

## NONINDIGENOUS AQUATIC NUISANCE PREVENTION AND CONTROL ACT OF 1990 [NANPCA § ___]

**(16 U.S.C.A. §§ 4701 to 4751)**

## CHAPTER 67—AQUATIC NUISANCE PREVENTION AND CONTROL

SUBCHAPTER I—GENERAL PROVISIONS



## SUBCHAPTER I—GENERAL PROVISIONS

### § 4701. Findings and purposes

**[NANPCA § 1002]**

**(a) Findings**

The Congress finds that—

(1) the discharge of untreated water in the ballast tanks of vessels and through other means results in unintentional introductions of nonindigenous species to fresh, brackish, and saltwater environments;

(2) when environmental conditions are favorable, nonindigenous species become established, may compete with or prey upon native species of plants, fish, and wildlife, may carry diseases or parasites that affect native species, and may disrupt the aquatic environment and economy of affected near-shore areas;

(3) the zebra mussel was unintentionally introduced into the Great Lakes and has infested—

(A) waters south of the Great Lakes, into a good portion of the Mississippi River drainage;

(B) waters west of the Great Lakes, into the Arkansas River in Oklahoma; and

(C) waters east of the Great Lakes, into the Hudson River and Lake Champlain;

(4) the potential economic disruption to communities affected by the zebra mussel due to its colonization of water pipes, boat hulls and other hard surfaces has been estimated at $5,000,000,000 by the year 2000, and the potential disruption to the diversity and abundance of native fish and other species by the zebra mussel and ruffe, round goby, and other nonindigenous species could be severe;

(5) the zebra mussel was discovered on Lake Champlain during 1993 and the opportunity exists to act quickly to establish zebra mussel controls before Lake Champlain is further infested and management costs escalate;

(6) in 1992, the zebra mussel was discovered at the northernmost reaches of the Chesapeake Bay watershed;

(7) the zebra mussel poses an imminent risk of invasion in the main waters of the Chesapeake Bay;

(8) since the Chesapeake Bay is the largest recipient of foreign ballast water on the East Coast, there is a risk of further invasions of other nonindigenous species;

(9) the zebra mussel is only one example of thousands of nonindigenous species that have become

established in waters of the United States and may be causing economic and ecological degradation with respect to the natural resources of waters of the United States;

**(10)** since their introduction in the early 1980's in ballast water discharges, ruffe—

**(A)** have caused severe declines in populations of other species of fish in Duluth Harbor (in Minnesota and Wisconsin);

**(B)** have spread to Lake Huron; and

**(C)** are likely to spread quickly to most other waters in North America if action is not taken promptly to control their spread;

**(11)** examples of nonindigenous species that, as of October 26, 1996, infest coastal waters of the United States and that have the potential for causing adverse economic and ecological effects include—

**(A)** the mitten crab (Eriocher sinensis) that has become established on the Pacific Coast;

**(B)** the green crab (Carcinus maenas) that has become established in the coastal waters of the Atlantic Ocean;

**(C)** the brown mussel (Perna perna) that has become established along the Gulf of Mexico; and

**(D)** certain shellfish pathogens;

**(12)** many aquatic nuisance vegetation species, such as Eurasian watermilfoil, hydrilla, water hyacinth, and water chestnut, have been introduced to waters of the United States from other parts of the world causing or having a potential to cause adverse environmental, ecological, and economic effects;

**(13)** if preventive management measures are not taken nationwide to prevent and control unintentionally introduced nonindigenous aquatic species in a timely manner, further introductions and infestations of species that are as destructive as, or more destructive than, the zebra mussel or the ruffe infestations may occur;

**(14)** once introduced into waters of the United States, aquatic nuisance species are unintentionally transported and introduced into inland lakes and rivers by recreational boaters, commercial barge traffic, and a variety of other pathways; and

**(15)** resolving the problems associated with aquatic nuisance species will require the participation and cooperation of the Federal Government and State governments, and investment in the development of prevention technologies.

**(b) Purposes**

The purposes of this chapter are—

**(1)** to prevent unintentional introduction and dispersal of nonindigenous species into waters of the United States through ballast water management and other requirements;

**(2)** to coordinate federally conducted, funded or authorized research, prevention [1] control, information dissemination and other activities regarding the zebra mussel and other aquatic nuisance species;

**(3)** to develop and carry out environmentally sound control methods to prevent, monitor and control unintentional introductions of nonindigenous species from pathways other than ballast water exchange;

**(4)** to understand and minimize economic and ecological impacts of nonindigenous aquatic nuisance species that become established, including the zebra mussel; and

**(5)** to establish a program of research and technology development and assistance to States in the management and removal of zebra mussels.

(Pub.L. 101–646, Title I, § 1002, Nov. 29, 1990, 104 Stat. 4761; Pub.L. 104–182, Title III, § 308(a), Aug. 6, 1996, 110 Stat. 1689; Pub.L. 104–332, § 2(a)(1), (h)(1), Oct. 26, 1996, 110 Stat. 4073, 4091.)

[1] So in original. Probably should be "prevention, control".

## HISTORICAL AND STATUTORY NOTES

**References in Text**

This chapter, referred to in subsec. (b), read in the original, this Act, meaning the Nonindigenous Aquatic Nuisance Prevention and Control Act of 1990, which enacted this chapter. For complete classification, see Short Title note under this section and Tables.

**Effective and Applicability Provisions**

1996 Acts

Amendment by Pub.L. 104–182 effective Aug. 6, 1996, except as otherwise specifically provided, see section 2(b) of Pub.L. 104–182, set out as a note under section 300f of Title 42, The Public Health and Welfare.

**Short Title**

1996 Amendments

Section 1(a) of Pub.L. 104–332 provided that: "This Act [enacting sections 4713 and 4714 of this title, amending this chapter, chapter 15B (§ 941 et seq.) of this title, section 491g of this title, section 42 of Title 18, Crimes and Criminal Procedure, and section 2761 of Title 33, Navigation and Navigable Waters, enacting provisions set out as a note under this section, and amending provisions set out as notes of this section, section 941 of this Title, and section 2701 of Title 33] may be cited as the 'National Invasive Species Act of 1996'."

1990 Acts

Section 1001 of Pub.L. 101–646, as amended Pub.L. 104–332, § 2(h)(1), Oct. 26, 1996, 110 Stat. 4091, provided that: "This title [enacting this chapter] may be cited as the 'Nonindigenous Aquatic Nuisance Prevention and Control Act of 1990'."

**Statutory Construction of National Invasive Species Act of 1996**

Section 3 of Pub.L. 104–332 provided that: "Nothing in this Act or the amendments made by this Act [Pub.L.

104–332, Oct. 26, 1996, 110 Stat. 4073, for classification of which to the Code, see Short Title of 1996 Amendments note set out under this section and Tables] is intended to affect the authorities and responsibilities of the Great Lakes Fishery Commission established under article II of the Convention on Great Lakes Fisheries between the United States of America and Canada, signed at Washington on September 10, 1954 (hereafter in this section referred to as the 'Convention' [such 'Convention' is not classified to the Code, but referred to in section 931 of this title]), including the authorities and responsibilities of the Great Lakes Fishery Commission—

"(1) for developing and implementing a comprehensive program for eradicating or minimizing populations of sea lamprey in the Great Lakes watershed; and

"(2) carrying out the duties of the Commission specified in the Convention (including any amendment thereto) and the Great Lakes Fishery Act of 1956 [Act June 4, 1956, c. 358, 70 Stat. 242, as amended] (16 U.S.C. 931 et seq.)."

**Report on Establishment of Program**

Pub.L. 102–567, Title II, § 203(b), Oct. 29, 1992, 106 Stat. 4281, provided that: "Not later than one year after the date of the enactment of this Act [Oct. 29, 1992], the Secretary of Commerce shall submit a report to the Congress on progress toward establishing a nonindigenous aquatic nuisance prevention and control program within the National Oceanic and Atmospheric Administration and projected funding for such a program for the following five fiscal years."

## § 4702. Definitions

**[NANPCA § 1003]**

As used in this chapter, the term—

(1) "aquatic nuisance species" means a nonindigenous species that threatens the diversity or abundance of native species or the ecological stability of infested waters, or commercial, agricultural, aquacultural or recreational activities dependent on such waters;

(2) "Assistant Secretary" means the Assistant Secretary of the Army (Civil Works);

(3) "ballast water" means any water and associated sediments used to manipulate the trim and stability of a vessel;

(4) "Director" means the Director of the United States Fish and Wildlife Service;

(5) "exclusive economic zone" means the Exclusive Economic Zone of the United States established by Proclamation Number 5030, dated March 10, 1983, and the equivalent zone of Canada;

(6) "environmentally sound" methods, efforts, actions or programs means methods, efforts, actions or programs to prevent introductions or control infestations of aquatic nuisance species that minimize adverse impacts to the structure and function of an ecosystem and adverse effects on non-target organisms and ecosystems and emphasize integrated pest management techniques and nonchemical measures;

(7) "Great Lakes" means Lake Ontario, Lake Erie, Lake Huron (including Lake St. Clair), Lake Michigan, Lake Superior, and the connecting channels (Saint Mary's River, Saint Clair River, Detroit River, Niagara River, and Saint Lawrence River to the Canandian[1] Border), and includes all other bodies of water within the drainage basin of such lakes and connecting channels.

(8) "Great Lakes region" means the 8 States that border on the Great Lakes;

(9) "Indian tribe" means any Indian tribe, band, nation, or other organized group or community, including any Alaska Native village or regional corporation (as defined in or established pursuant to the Alaska Native Claims Settlement Act (43 U.S.C. 1601 et seq.)) that is recognized as eligible for the special programs and services provided by the United States to Indians because of their status as Indians;

(10) "interstate organization" means an entity—

(A) established by—

(i) an interstate compact that is approved by Congress;

(ii) a Federal statute; or

(iii) a treaty or other international agreement with respect to which the United States is a party; and

(B)(i) that represents 2 or more—

(I) States or political subdivisions thereof; or

(II) Indian tribes; or

(ii) that represents—

(I) 1 or more States or political subdivisions thereof; and

(II) 1 or more Indian tribes; or

(iii) that represents the Federal Government and 1 or more foreign governments; and

(C) has jurisdiction over, serves as forum for coordinating, or otherwise has a role or responsibility for the management of, any land or other natural resource;

(11) "nonindigenous species" means any species or other viable biological material that enters an ecosystem beyond its historic range, including any such organism transferred from one country into another;

(12) "Secretary" means the Secretary of the department in which the Coast Guard is operating;

(13) "Task Force" means the Aquatic Nuisance Species Task Force established under section 4721 of this title;

(14) "territorial sea" means the belt of the sea measured from the baseline of the United States

determined in accordance with international law, as set forth in Presidential Proclamation Number 5928, dated December 27, 1988;

(15) "Under Secretary" means the Under Secretary of Commerce for Oceans and Atmosphere;

(16) "waters of the United States" means the navigable waters and the territorial sea of the United States; and

(17) "unintentional introduction" means an introduction of nonindigenous species that occurs as the result of activities other than the purposeful or intentional introduction of the species involved, such as the transport of nonindigenous species in ballast or in water used to transport fish, mollusks or crustaceans for aquaculture or other purposes.

(Pub.L. 101–646, Title I, § 1003, Nov. 29, 1990, 104 Stat. 4762; Pub.L. 102–580, Title III, § 302(b)(2), Oct. 31, 1992, 106 Stat. 4839; Pub.L. 104–332, § 2(a)(2), (h)(1), (3), Oct. 26, 1996, 110 Stat. 4075, 4091.)

[1] So in original. Probably should be "Canadian".

### HISTORICAL AND STATUTORY NOTES

**References in Text**

This chapter, referred to in text, read in the original, this Act, meaning the Nonindigenous Aquatic Nuisance Prevention and Control Act of 1990, which enacted this chapter. For complete classification, see Short Title note under section 4701 of this title and Tables.

The Alaska Native Claims Settlement Act, referred to in par. (9), is classified principally to chapter 33 of Title 43 (43 U.S.C.A. § 1601 et seq.). For complete classification, see Short Title note set out under section 1601 of Title 43 and Tables.

**Change of Name**

Any reference in any provision of law enacted before Jan. 4, 1995, to the Committee on Public Works and Transportation of the House of Representatives treated as referring to the Committee on Transportation and Infrastructure of the House of Representatives, see section 1(a)(9) of Pub.L. 104–14, set out as a note preceding section 21 of Title 2, The Congress.

**Abolition of House Committee on Merchant Marine and Fisheries**

Committee on Merchant Marine and Fisheries of House of Representatives abolished and any reference in any provision of law enacted before Jan. 4, 1995, to the Committee on Merchant Marine and Fisheries of the House of Representatives treated as referring to the Committee on Agriculture of the House of Representatives, in the case of a provision of law relating to inspection of seafood or seafood products, the Committee on National Security of the House of Representatives, in the case of a provision of law relating to interoceanic canals, the Merchant Marine Academy and State Maritime Academies, or national security aspects of merchant marine, the Committee on Resources of the House of Representatives, in the case of a provision of law relating to fisheries, wildlife, international fishing agreements marine affairs (including coastal zone management) except for measures relating to oil and other pollution of navigable waters, or oceanography, the Committee on Science of the House of Representatives, in the case of a provision of law relating to marine research, and the Committee on Transportation and Infrastructure of the House of Representatives, in the case of a provision of law relating to a matter other than a matter described above, see section 1(b)(3) of Pub.L. 104–14, set out as a note preceding section 21 of Title 2, The Congress.

## SUBCHAPTER II—PREVENTION OF UNINTENTIONAL INTRODUCTIONS OF NONINDIGENOUS AQUATIC SPECIES

## § 4711. Aquatic nuisance species in waters of United States

**[NANPCA § 1101]**

**(a) Great Lakes guidelines**

**(1) In general**

Not later than 6 months after November 29, 1990, the Secretary shall issue voluntary guidelines to prevent the introduction and spread of aquatic nuisance species into the Great Lakes through the exchange of ballast water of vessels prior to entering those waters.

**(2) Content of guidelines**

The guidelines issued under this subsection shall—

(A) ensure to the maximum extent practicable that ballast water containing aquatic nuisance species is not discharged into the Great Lakes;

(B) protect the safety of—

(i) each vessel; and

(ii) the crew and passengers of each vessel;

(C) take into consideration different vessel operating conditions; and

(D) be based on the best scientific information available.

**(b) Regulations**

**(1) In general**

Not later than 2 years after November 29, 1990, the Secretary, in consultation with the Task Force, shall issue regulations to prevent the introduction and spread of aquatic nuisance species into the Great Lakes through the ballast water of vessels.

**(2) Content of regulations**

The regulations issued under this subsection shall—

(A) apply to all vessels equipped with ballast water tanks that enter a United States port on the Great Lakes after operating on the waters beyond the exclusive economic zone;

(B) require a vessel to—

(i) carry out exchange of ballast water on the waters beyond the exclusive economic zone prior to entry into any port within the Great Lakes;

(ii) carry out an exchange of ballast water in other waters where the exchange does not pose a threat of infestation or spread of aquatic nuisance species in the Great Lakes and other waters of the United States, as recommended by the Task Force under section 4712(a)(1) of this title; or

(iii) use environmentally sound alternative ballast water management methods if the Secretary determines that such alternative methods are as effective as ballast water exchange in preventing and controlling infestations of aquatic nuisance species;

(C) not affect or supersede any requirements or prohibitions pertaining to the discharge of ballast water into waters of the United States under the Federal Water Pollution Control Act (33 U.S.C. 1251 et seq.);

(D) provide for sampling procedures to monitor compliance with the requirements of the regulations;

(E) prohibit the operation of a vessel in the Great Lakes if the master of the vessel has not certified to the Secretary or the Secretary's designee by not later than the departure of that vessel from the first lock in the St. Lawrence Seaway that the vessel has complied with the requirements of the regulations;

(F) protect the safety of—

(i) each vessel; and

(ii) the crew and passengers of each vessel;

(G) take into consideration different operating conditions; and

(H) be based on the best scientific information available.

**(3) Additional regulations**

In addition to promulgating regulations under paragraph (1), the Secretary, in consultation with the Task Force, shall, not later than November 4, 1994, issue regulations to prevent the introduction and spread of aquatic nuisance species into the Great Lakes through ballast water carried on vessels that enter a United States port on the Hudson River north of the George Washington Bridge.

**(4) Education and technical assistance programs**

The Secretary may carry out education and technical assistance programs and other measures to promote compliance with the regulations issued under this subsection.

**(c) Voluntary national guidelines**

**(1) In general**

Not later than 1 year after October 26, 1996, and after providing notice and an opportunity for public comment, the Secretary shall issue voluntary guidelines to prevent the introduction and spread of nonindigenous species in waters of the United States by ballast water operations and other operations of vessels equipped with ballast water tanks.

**(2) Content of guidelines**

The voluntary guidelines issued under this subsection shall—

(A) ensure to the maximum extent practicable that aquatic nuisance species are not discharged into waters of the United States from vessels;

(B) apply to all vessels equipped with ballast water tanks that operate in waters of the United States;

(C) protect the safety of—

(i) each vessel; and

(ii) the crew and passengers of each vessel;

(D) direct a vessel that is carrying ballast water into waters of the United States after operating beyond the exclusive economic zone to—

(i) carry out the exchange of ballast water of the vessel in waters beyond the exclusive economic zone;

(ii) exchange the ballast water of the vessel in other waters where the exchange does not pose a threat of infestation or spread of nonindigenous species in waters of the United States, as recommended by the Task Force under section 4712(a)(1) of this title; or

(iii) use environmentally sound alternative ballast water management methods, including modification of the vessel ballast water tanks and intake systems, if the Secretary determines that such alternative methods are at least as effective as ballast water exchange in preventing and controlling infestations of aquatic nuisance species;

(E) direct vessels to carry out management practices that the Secretary determines to be necessary to reduce the probability of unintentional nonindigenous species transfer resulting from—

(i) ship operations other than ballast water discharge; and

(ii) ballasting practices of vessels that enter waters of the United States with no ballast water on board;

(F) provide for the keeping of records that shall be submitted to the Secretary, as prescribed by the guidelines, and that shall be maintained on board each vessel and made available for inspection, upon request of the Secretary and in a manner consistent with subsection (i) of this section, in order to enable the Secretary to determine compliance with the guidelines, including—

(i) with respect to each ballast water exchange referred to in clause (ii), reporting on the precise location and thoroughness of the exchange; and

(ii) any other information that the Secretary considers necessary to assess the rate of effective compliance with the guidelines;

(G) provide for sampling procedures to monitor compliance with the guidelines;

(H) take into consideration—

(i) vessel types;

(ii) variations in the characteristics of point of origin and receiving water bodies;

(iii) variations in the ecological conditions of waters and coastal areas of the United States; and

(iv) different operating conditions;

(I) be based on the best scientific information available;

(J) not affect or supersede any requirements or prohibitions pertaining to the discharge of ballast water into waters of the United States under the Federal Water Pollution Control Act (33 U.S.C. 1251 et seq.); and

(K) provide an exemption from ballast water exchange requirements to passenger vessels with operating ballast water systems that are equipped with treatment systems designed to kill aquatic organisms in ballast water, unless the Secretary determines that such treatment systems are less effective than ballast water exchange at reducing the risk of transfers of invasive species in the ballast water of passenger vessels; and

(L) not apply to crude oil tankers engaged in the coastwise trade.

**(3) Education and technical assistance programs**

Not later than 1 year after October 26, 1996, the Secretary shall carry out education and technical assistance programs and other measures to encourage compliance with the guidelines issued under this subsection.

**(d) Report to Congress**

Not sooner than 24 months after the date of issuance of guidelines pursuant to subsection (c) of this section and not later than 30 months after such date, and after consultation with interested and affected persons, the Secretary shall prepare and submit to Congress a report containing the information required pursuant to paragraphs (1) and (2) of subsection (e) of this section.

**(e) Periodic review and revision**

**(1) In general**

Not later than 3 years after the date of issuance of guidelines pursuant to subsection (c) of this section, and not less frequently than every 3 years thereafter, the Secretary shall, in accordance with criteria developed by the Task Force under paragraph (3)—

(A) assess the compliance by vessels with the voluntary guidelines issued under subsection (c) of this section and the regulations promulgated under this chapter;

(B) establish the rate of compliance that is based on the assessment under subparagraph (A);

(C) assess the effectiveness of the voluntary guidelines and regulations referred to in subparagraph (A) in reducing the introduction and spread of aquatic nuisance species by vessels; and

(D) as necessary, on the basis of the best scientific information available—

(i) revise the guidelines and regulations referred to in subparagraph (A);

(ii) promulgate additional regulations pursuant to subsection (f)(1) of this section; or

(iii) carry out each of clauses (i) and (ii).

**(2) Special review and revision**

Not later than 90 days after the Task Force makes a request to the Secretary for a special review and revision for coastal and inland waterways designated by the Task Force, the Secretary shall—

(A) conduct a special review of guidelines and regulations applicable to those waterways in accordance with the review procedures under paragraph (1); and

(B) as necessary, in the same manner as provided under paragraph (1)(D)—

(i) revise those guidelines;

(ii) promulgate additional regulations pursuant to subsection (f)(1) of this section; or

(iii) carry out each of clauses (i) and (ii).

**(3) Criteria for effectiveness**

Not later than 18 months after October 26, 1996, the Task Force shall submit to the Secretary criteria for determining the adequacy and effectiveness of the voluntary guidelines issued under subsection (c) of this section.

**(f) Authority of Secretary**

**(1) General regulations**

If, on the basis of a periodic review conducted under subsection (e)(1) of this section or a special review conducted under subsection (e)(2) of this section, the Secretary determines that—

(A) the rate of effective compliance (as determined by the Secretary) with the guidelines issued pursuant to subsection (c) of this section is inadequate; or

(B) the reporting by vessels pursuant to those guidelines is not adequate for the Secretary to assess the compliance with those guidelines and provide a rate of compliance of vessels, including the assessment of the rate of compliance of vessels under subsection (e)(2) of this section,

the Secretary shall promptly promulgate regulations that meet the requirements of paragraph (2).

**(2) Requirements for regulations**

The regulations promulgated by the Secretary under paragraph (1)—

(A) shall—

(i) not be promulgated sooner than 180 days following the issuance of the report to Congress submitted pursuant to subsection (d) of this section;

(ii) make mandatory the requirements included in the voluntary guidelines issued under subsection (c) of this section; and

(iii) provide for the enforcement of the regulations; and

(B) may be regional in scope.

**(3) International regulations**

The Secretary shall revise regulations promulgated under this subsection to the extent required to make such regulations consistent with the treatment of a particular matter in any international agreement, agreed to by the United States, governing management of the transfer of nonindigenous aquatic species by vessel.

**(g) Sanctions**

**(1) Civil penalties**

Any person who violates a regulation promulgated under subsection (b) or (f) of this section shall be liable for a civil penalty in an amount not to exceed $25,000. Each day of a continuing violation constitutes a separate violation. A vessel operated in violation of the regulations is liable in rem for any civil penalty assessed under this subsection for that violation.

**(2) Criminal penalties**

Any person who knowingly violates the regulations promulgated under subsection (b) or (f) of this section is guilty of a class C felony.

**(3) Revocation of clearance**

Upon request of the Secretary, the Secretary of the Treasury shall withhold or revoke the clearance of a vessel required by section 91 of the Appendix to Title 46, if the owner or operator of that vessel is in violation of the regulations issued under subsection (b) or (f) of this section.

**(4) Exception to sanctions**

This subsection does not apply to a failure to exchange ballast water if—

(A) the master of a vessel, acting in good faith, decides that the exchange of ballast water will threaten the safety or stability of the vessel, its crew, or its passengers; and

(B) the recordkeeping and reporting requirements of this chapter are complied with.

**(h) Coordination with other agencies**

In carrying out the programs under this section, the Secretary is encouraged to use, to the maximum extent practicable, the expertise, facilities, members, or personnel of established agencies and organizations that have routine contact with vessels, including the Animal and Plant Health Inspection Service of the Department of Agriculture, the National Cargo Bureau, port administrations, and ship pilots' associations.

**(i) Consultation with Canada, Mexico, and other foreign governments**

In developing the guidelines issued and regulations promulgated under this section, the Secretary is encouraged to consult with the Government of Canada, the Government of Mexico, and any other government of a foreign country that the Secretary, in consultation with the Task Force, determines to be necessary to develop and implement an effective international program for preventing the unintentional introduction and spread of nonindigenous species.

**(j) International cooperation**

The Secretary, in cooperation with the International Maritime Organization of the United Nations and the Commission on Environmental Cooperation established pursuant to the North American Free Trade Agreement, is encouraged to enter into negotiations with the governments of foreign countries to develop and implement an effective international program for preventing the unintentional introduction and spread of nonindigenous species.

**(k) Safety exemption**

**(1) Master discretion**

The master of a vessel is not required to conduct a ballast water exchange if the master decides that the exchange would threaten the safety or stability of the vessel, its crew, or its passengers because of adverse weather, vessel architectural design, equipment failure, or any other extraordinary conditions.

**(2) Other requirements**

**(A) In general**

Except as provided in subparagraph (B), a vessel that does not exchange ballast water on the high seas under paragraph (1) shall not be restricted from discharging ballast water in any harbor.

**(B) Great Lakes**

Subparagraph (A) shall not apply in a case in which a vessel is subject to the regulations issued by the Secretary under subsection (b) of this section.

**(3) Crude oil tanker ballast facility study**

**(A)** Within 60 days of October 26, 1996, the Secretary of the department in which the Coast Guard is operating, in consultation with the Under Secretary of Commerce for Oceans and Atmosphere, affected shoreside ballast water facility operators, affected crude oil tanker operators, and interested parties, shall initiate a study of the effectiveness of existing shoreside ballast water facilities used by crude oil tankers in the coastwise trade off Alaska in preventing the introduction of nonindigenous aquatic species into the waters off Alaska, as well as the cost and feasibility of modifying such facilities to improve such effectiveness.

**(B)** The study required under subparagraph (A) shall be submitted to the Congress by no later than October 1, 1997.

**(*l*) Non-discrimination**

The Secretary shall ensure that vessels registered outside of the United States do not receive more favorable treatment than vessels registered in the United States when the Secretary performs studies, reviews compliance, determines effectiveness, establishes requirements, or performs any other responsibilities under this chapter.

(Pub.L. 101–646, Title I, § 1101, Nov. 29, 1990, 104 Stat. 4763; Pub.L. 102–580, Title III, § 302(b)(1), Oct. 31, 1992, 106 Stat. 4839; Pub.L. 102–587, Title IV, § 4002, Nov. 4, 1992, 106 Stat. 5068; Pub.L. 104–332, § 2(b)(2), (h)(1), Oct. 26, 1996, 110 Stat. 4075, 4091.)

### HISTORICAL AND STATUTORY NOTES

**References in Text**

This chapter, referred to in text, read in the original, this Act, meaning the Nonindigenous Aquatic Nuisance Prevention and Control Act of 1990, which enacted this chapter. For complete classification, see Short Title note under section 4701 of this title and Tables.

The Federal Water Pollution Control Act, referred to in subsecs. (b)(2)(C) and (c)(2)(J), as completely revised by Pub.L. 92–500, § 2, Oct. 18, 1972, 86 Stat. 816, is classified principally to chapter 26 of Title 33 (33 U.S.C.A. § 1251 et seq.). For complete classification, see Short Title note set out under section 1251 of Title 33 and Tables.

October 26, 1996, referred to in subsec. (k)(3), was in the original "the date of enactment of this Act", which was translated as meaning the date of enactment of Pub.L. 104–332, which amended this section generally, to reflect the probable intent of Congress.

## § 4712. National ballast water management information

**[NANPCA § 1102]**

**(a) Studies on introduction of aquatic nuisance species by vessels**

**(1) Ballast exchange study**

The Task Force, in cooperation with the Secretary, shall conduct a study—

**(A)** to assess the environmental effects of ballast water exchange on the diversity and abundance of native species in receiving estuarine, marine, and fresh waters of the United States; and

**(B)** to identify areas within the waters of the United States and the exclusive economic zone, if any, where the exchange of ballast water does not pose a threat of infestation or spread of aquatic nuisance species in the Great Lakes and other waters of the United States.

**(2) Biological study**

The Task Force, in cooperation with the Secretary, shall conduct a study to determine whether aquatic nuisance species threaten the ecological characteristics and economic uses of Lake Champlain and other waters of the United States other than the Great Lakes.

**(3) Shipping study**

The Secretary shall conduct a study to determine the need for controls on vessels entering waters of the United States, other than the Great Lakes, to minimize the risk of unintentional introduction and dispersal of aquatic nuisance species in those waters. The study shall include an examination of—

**(A)** the degree to which shipping may be a major pathway of transmission of aquatic nuisance species in those waters;

**(B)** possible alternatives for controlling introduction of those species through shipping; and

**(C)** the feasibility of implementing regional versus national control measures.

**(b) Ecological and ballast water discharge surveys**

**(1) Ecological surveys**

**(A) In general**

The Task Force, in cooperation with the Secretary, shall conduct ecological surveys of the Chesapeake Bay, San Francisco Bay, and Honolulu Harbor and, as necessary, of other estuaries of national significance and other waters that the Task Force determines—

**(i)** to be highly susceptible to invasion by aquatic nuisance species resulting from ballast water operations and other operations of vessels; and

(ii) to require further study.

**(B) Requirements for surveys**

In conducting the surveys under this paragraph, the Task Force shall, with respect to each such survey—

(i) examine the attributes and patterns of invasions of aquatic nuisance species; and

(ii) provide an estimate of the effectiveness of ballast water management and other vessel management guidelines issued and regulations promulgated under this subchapter in abating invasions of aquatic nuisance species in the waters that are the subject of the survey.

**(2) Ballast water discharge surveys**

**(A) In general**

The Secretary, in cooperation with the Task Force, shall conduct surveys of ballast water discharge rates and practices in the waters referred to in paragraph (1)(A) on the basis of the criteria under clauses (i) and (ii) of such paragraph.

**(B) Requirements for surveys**

In conducting the surveys under this paragraph, the Secretary shall—

(i) examine the rate of, and trends in, ballast water discharge in the waters that are the subject of the survey; and

(ii) assess the effectiveness of voluntary guidelines issued, and regulations promulgated, under this subchapter in altering ballast water discharge practices to reduce the probability of accidental introductions of aquatic nuisance species.

**(3) Columbia River**

The Secretary, in cooperation with the Task Force and academic institutions in each of the States affected, shall conduct an ecological and ballast water discharge survey of the Columbia River system consistent with the requirements of paragraphs (1) and (2).

**(c) Reports**

**(1) Ballast exchange**

Not later than 18 months after November 29, 1990, and prior to the effective date of the regulations issued under section 4711(b) of this title, the Task Force shall submit a report to the Congress that presents the results of the study required under subsection (a)(1) of this section and makes recommendations with respect to such regulations.

**(2) Biological and shipping studies**

Not later than 18 months after November 29, 1990, the Secretary and the Task Force shall each submit to the Congress a report on the results of their respective studies under paragraphs (2) and (3) of subsection (a) of this section.

**(d) Negotiations**

The Secretary, working through the International Maritime Organization, is encouraged to enter into negotiations with the governments of foreign countries concerning the planning and implementation of measures aimed at the prevention and control of unintentional introductions of aquatic nuisance species in coastal waters.

**(e) Regional research grants**

Out of amounts appropriated to carry out this subsection for a fiscal year, the Under Secretary may—

(1) make available not to exceed $750,000 to fund research on aquatic nuisance species prevention and control in the Chesapeake Bay through grants, to be competitively awarded and subject to peer review, to universities and research institutions;

(2) make available not to exceed $500,000 to fund research on aquatic nuisance species prevention and control in the Gulf of Mexico through grants, to be competitively awarded and subject to peer review, to universities and research institutions;

(3) make available not to exceed $500,000 to fund research on aquatic nuisance species prevention and control for the Pacific Coast through grants, to be competitively awarded and subject to peer review, to universities and research institutions;

(4) make available not to exceed $500,000 to fund research on aquatic nuisance species prevention and control for the Atlantic Coast through grants, to be competitively awarded and subject to peer review, to universities and research institutions; and

(5) make available not to exceed $750,000 to fund research on aquatic nuisance species prevention and control in the San Francisco Bay-Delta Estuary through grants, to be competitively awarded and subject to peer review, to universities and research institutions.

**(f) National ballast information clearinghouse**

**(1) In general**

The Secretary shall develop and maintain, in consultation and cooperation with the Task Force and the Smithsonian Institution (acting through the Smithsonian Environmental Research Center), a clearinghouse of national data concerning—

(A) ballasting practices;

(B) compliance with the guidelines issued pursuant to section 4711(c) of this title; and

(C) any other information obtained by the Task Force under subsection (b) of this section.

**(2) Report**

In consultation and cooperation with the Task Force and the Smithsonian Institution (acting through the Smithsonian Environmental Research Center), the Secretary shall prepare and submit to the Task Force and the Congress, on a biennial basis, a report that synthesizes and analyzes the data referred to in paragraph (1) relating to—

(A) ballast water delivery and management; and

(B) invasions of aquatic nuisance species resulting from ballast water.

(Pub.L. 101–646, Title I, § 1102, Nov. 29, 1990, 104 Stat. 4764; Pub.L. 104–332, § 2(c), (g), (h)(1), Oct. 26, 1996, 110 Stat. 4081, 4091; Pub.L. 105–362, Title XV, § 1502(d), Nov. 10 1998, 112 Stat. 3295.)

## § 4713. Armed Services ballast water programs [NANPCA § 1103]

**(a) Department of Defense vessels**

Subject to operational conditions, the Secretary of Defense, in consultation with the Secretary, the Task Force, and the International Maritime Organization, shall implement a ballast water management program for seagoing vessels of the Department of Defense to minimize the risk of introduction of nonindigenous species from releases of ballast water.

**(b) Coast Guard vessels**

Subject to operational conditions, the Secretary, in consultation with the Task Force and the International Maritime Organization, shall implement a ballast water management program for seagoing vessels of the Coast Guard to minimize the risk of introduction of nonindigenous species from releases of ballast water.

(Pub.L. 101–646, Title I, § 1103, as added Pub.L. 104–332, § 2(d), Oct. 26, 1996, 110 Stat. 4083.)

## § 4714. Ballast water management demonstration program [NANPCA § 1104]

**(a) "Technologies and practices" defined**

For purposes of this section, the term "technologies and practices" means those technologies and practices that—

(1) may be retrofitted—

(A) on existing vessels or incorporated in new vessel designs; and

(B) on existing land-based ballast water treatment facilities;

(2) may be designed into new water treatment facilities;

(3) are operationally practical;

(4) are safe for a vessel and crew;

(5) are environmentally sound;

(6) are cost-effective;

(7) a vessel operator is capable of monitoring; and

(8) are effective against a broad range of aquatic nuisance species.

**(b) Demonstration program**

**(1) In general**

During the 18–month period beginning on the date that funds are made available by appropriations pursuant to section 4741(e) of this title, the Secretary of the Interior and the Secretary of Commerce, with the concurrence of and in cooperation with the Secretary, shall conduct a ballast water management demonstration program to demonstrate technologies and practices to prevent aquatic nonindigenous species from being introduced into and spread through ballast water in the Great Lakes and other waters of the United States.

**(2) Location**

The installation and construction of the technologies and practices used in the demonstration program conducted under this subsection shall be performed in the United States.

**(3) Vessel selection**

In demonstrating technologies and practices on vessels under this subsection, the Secretary of the Interior and the Secretary of Commerce, shall—

(A) use only vessels that—

(i) are approved by the Secretary;

(ii) have ballast water systems conducive to testing aboard-vessel or land-based technologies and practices applicable to a significant number of merchant vessels; and

(iii) are—

(I) publicly or privately owned; and

(II) in active use for trade or other cargo shipment purposes during the demonstration;

(B) select vessels for participation in the program by giving priority consideration—

(i) first, to vessels documented under chapter 121 of Title 46;

(ii) second, to vessels that are a majority owned by citizens of the United States, as determined by the Secretary; and

(iii) third, to any other vessels that regularly call on ports in the United States; and

(C) seek to use a variety of vessel types, including vessels that—

(i) call on ports in the United States and on the Great Lakes; and

(ii) are operated along major coasts of the United States and inland waterways, including the San Francisco Bay and Chesapeake Bay.

**(4) Selection of technologies and practices**

In selecting technologies and practices for demonstration under this subsection, the Secretary of the Interior and the Secretary of Commerce shall give priority consideration to technologies and practices identified as promising by the National Research Council Marine Board of the National Academy of Sciences in its report on ships' ballast water operations issued in July 1996.

**(5) Report**

Not later than 3 years after October 26, 1996, the Secretary of the Interior and the Secretary of Commerce shall prepare and submit a report to the Congress on the demonstration program conducted pursuant to this section. The report shall include findings and recommendations of the Secretary of the Interior and the Secretary of Commerce concerning technologies and practices.

**(c) Authorities; consultation and cooperation with International Maritime Organization and Task Force**

**(1) Authorities**

In conducting the demonstration program under subsection (b) of this section, the Secretary of the Interior may—

(A) enter into cooperative agreements with appropriate officials of other agencies of the Federal Government, agencies of States and political subdivisions thereof, and private entities;

(B) accept funds, facilities, equipment, or personnel from other Federal agencies; and

(C) accept donations of property and services.

**(2) Consultation and cooperation**

The Secretary of the Interior shall consult and cooperate with the International Maritime Organization and the Task Force in carrying out this section.

(Pub.L. 101–646, Title I, § 1104, as added Pub.L. 104–332, § 2(d), Oct. 26, 1996, 110 Stat. 4083.)

## SUBCHAPTER III—PREVENTION AND CONTROL OF AQUATIC NUISANCE SPECIES DISPERSAL

## § 4721. Establishment of Task Force

[NANPCA § 1201]

**(a) Task Force**

There is hereby established an "Aquatic Nuisance Species Task Force".

**(b) Membership**

Membership of the Task Force shall consist of—

(1) the Director;

(2) the Under Secretary;

(3) the Administrator of the Environmental Protection Agency;

(4) the Commandant of the United States Coast Guard;

(5) the Assistant Secretary;

(6) the Secretary of Agriculture; and

(7) the head of any other Federal agency that the chairpersons designated under subsection (d) of this section deem appropriate.

**(c) Ex officio members**

The chairpersons designated under subsection (d) of this section shall invite representatives of the Great Lakes Commission, the Lake Champlain Basin Program, the Chesapeake Bay Program, the San Francisco Bay-Delta Estuary Program, and State agencies and other governmental entities to participate as ex officio members of the Task Force.

**(d) Chairpersons**

The Director and the Under Secretary shall serve as co-chairpersons of the Task Force and shall be jointly responsible, and are authorized to undertake such activities as may be necessary, for carrying out this subchapter in consultation and cooperation with the other members of the Task Force.

**(e) Memorandum of understanding**

Within six months of November 29, 1990, the Director and the Under Secretary shall develop a memorandum of understanding that describes the role of each in jointly carrying out this subchapter.

**(f) Coordination**

Each Task Force member shall coordinate any action to carry out this subchapter with any such action by other members of the Task Force, and regional, State and local entities.

(Pub.L. 101–646, Title I, § 1201, Nov. 29, 1990, 104 Stat. 4765; Pub.L. 104–182, Title III, § 308(b), Aug. 6, 1996, 110 Stat. 1689; Pub.L. 104–332, § 2(e)(2), (h)(1), Oct. 26, 1996, 110 Stat. 4085, 4091.)

### HISTORICAL AND STATUTORY NOTES

**Effective and Applicability Provisions**

1996 Acts

Amendment by Pub.L. 104–182 effective Aug. 6, 1996, except as otherwise specifically provided, see section 2(b) of Pub.L. 104–182, set out as a note under section 300f of Title 42, The Public Health and Welfare.

## § 4722. Aquatic nuisance species program

[NANPCA § 1202]

### (a) In general

The Task Force shall develop and implement a program for waters of the United States to prevent introduction and dispersal of aquatic nuisance species; to monitor, control and study such species; and to disseminate related information.

### (b) Content

The program developed under subsection (a) of this section shall—

(1) identify the goals, priorities, and approaches for aquatic nuisance species prevention, monitoring, control, education and research to be conducted or funded by the Federal Government;

(2) describe the specific prevention, monitoring, control, education and research activities to be conducted by each Task Force member;

(3) coordinate aquatic nuisance species programs and activities of Task Force members and affected State agencies;

(4) describe the role of each Task Force member in implementing the elements of the program as set forth in this subchapter;

(5) include recommendations for funding to implement elements of the program; and

(6) develop a demonstration program of prevention, monitoring, control, education and research for the zebra mussel, to be implemented in the Great Lakes and any other waters infested, or likely to become infested in the near future, by the zebra mussel.

### (c) Prevention

#### (1) In general

The Task Force shall establish and implement measures, within the program developed under subsection (a) of this section, to minimize the risk of introduction of aquatic nuisance species to waters of the United States, including—

(A) identification of pathways by which aquatic organisms are introduced to waters of the United States;

(B) assessment of the risk that an aquatic organism carried by an identified pathway may become an aquatic nuisance species; and

(C) evaluation of whether measures to prevent introductions of aquatic nuisance species are effective and environmentally sound.

#### (2) Implementation

Whenever the Task Force determines that there is a substantial risk of unintentional introduction of an aquatic nuisance species by an identified pathway and that the adverse consequences of such an introduction are likely to be substantial, the Task Force shall, acting through the appropriate Federal agency, and after an opportunity for public comment, carry out cooperative, environmentally sound efforts with regional, State and local entities to minimize the risk of such an introduction.

### (d) Monitoring

The Task Force shall establish and implement monitoring measures, within the program developed under subsection (a) of this section, to—

(1) detect unintentional introductions of aquatic nuisance species;

(2) determine the dispersal of aquatic nuisance species after introduction; and

(3) provide for the early detection and prevention of infestations of aquatic nuisance species in unaffected drainage basins.

### (e) Control

#### (1) In general

The Task Force may develop cooperative efforts, within the program established under subsection (a) of this section, to control established aquatic nuisance species to minimize the risk of harm to the environment and the public health and welfare. For purposes of this chapter, control efforts include eradication of infestations, reductions of populations, development of means of adapting human activities and public facilities to accommodate infestations, and prevention of the spread of aquatic nuisance species from infested areas. Such control efforts shall be developed in consultation with affected Federal agencies, States, Indian Tribes, local governments, interjurisdictional organizations, and other appropriate entities. Control actions authorized by this section shall be based on the best available scientific information and shall be conducted in an environmentally sound manner.

#### (2) Decisions

The Task Force or any other affected agency or entity may recommend that the Task Force initiate a control effort. In determining whether a control program is warranted, the Task Force shall evaluate the need for control (including the projected consequences of no control and less than full control); the technical and biological feasibility and cost-effectiveness of alternative control strategies and actions; whether the benefits of control, including costs avoided, exceed the costs of the program; the risk of harm to non-target organisms and ecosystems, public health and welfare; and such other considerations the Task Force determines appropriate. The Task Force shall also determine the nature and extent of control of target aquatic nuisance species that is feasible and desirable.

(3) **Programs**

If the Task Force determines in accordance with paragraph (2) that control of an aquatic nuisance species is warranted, the Task Force shall develop a proposed control program to achieve the target level of control. A notice summarizing the proposed action and soliciting comments shall be published in the Federal Register, in major newspapers in the region affected, and in principal trade publications of the industries affected. Within 180 days of proposing a control program, and after consultation with affected governmental and other appropriate entities and taking into consideration other comments received, the Task Force shall complete development of the proposed control program.

**(f) Research**

**(1) Priorities**

The Task Force shall, within the program developed under subsection (a) of this section, conduct research concerning—

(A) the environmental and economic risks and impacts associated with the introduction of aquatic nuisance species into the waters of the United States;

(B) the principal pathways by which aquatic nuisance species are introduced and dispersed;

(C) possible methods for the prevention, monitoring and control of aquatic nuisance species; and

(D) the assessment of the effectiveness of prevention, monitoring and control methods.

**(2) Protocol**

Within 90 days of November 29, 1990, the Task Force shall establish and follow a protocol to ensure that research activities carried out under this subchapter do not result in the introduction of aquatic nuisance species to waters of the United States.

**(3) Grants for research**

The Task Force shall allocate funds authorized under this chapter for competitive research grants to study all aspects of aquatic nuisance species, which shall be administered through the National Sea Grant College Program and the Cooperative Fishery and Wildlife Research Units. Grants shall be conditioned to ensure that any recipient of funds follows the protocol established under paragraph (2) of this subsection.

**(g) Technical assistance**

The Task Force shall, within the program developed under subsection (a) of this section, provide technical assistance to State and local governments and persons to minimize the environmental, public health, and safety risks associated with aquatic nuisance species, including an early warning system for advance notice of possible infestations and appropriate responses.

**(h) Education**

The Task Force shall, with the program developed under subsection (a) of this section, establish and implement educational programs through Sea Grant Marine Advisory Services and any other available resources that it determines to be appropriate to inform the general public, State governments, governments of political subdivisions of States, and industrial and recreational users of aquatic resources in connection with matters concerning the identification of aquatic nuisance species, and control methods for such species, including the prevention of the further distribution of such species.

**(i) Zebra mussel demonstration program**

**(1) Zebra mussel**

**(A) In general**

The Task Force shall, within the program developed under subsection (a) of this section, undertake a program of prevention, monitoring, control, education and research for the zebra mussel to be implemented in the Great Lakes and any other waters of the United States infested or likely to become infested by the zebra mussel, including—

(i) research and development concerning the species life history, environmental tolerances and impacts on fisheries and other ecosystem components, and the efficacy of control mechanisms and means of avoiding or minimizing impacts;

(ii) tracking the dispersal of the species and establishment of an early warning system to alert likely areas of future infestations;

(iii) development of control plans in coordination with regional, State and local entities; and

(iv) provision of technical assistance to regional, State and local entities to carry out this section.

**(B) Public facility research and development**

The Assistant Secretary, in consultation with the Task Force, shall develop a program of research, technology development, and demonstration for the environmentally sound control of zebra mussels in and around public facilities. The Assistant Secretary shall collect and make available, through publications and other appropriate means, information pertaining to such control methods.

**(C) Voluntary guidelines**

Not later than 1 year after October 26, 1996, the Task Force shall develop and submit to the Secretary voluntary guidelines for controlling the spread of the zebra mussel and, if appropriate, other aquatic nuisance species through recreational activities, including boating and fishing. Not later than 4 months after the date of such submission, and after providing notice and an opportunity for public comment, the Secretary shall issue voluntary guidelines that are based on the guidelines developed by the Task Force under this subparagraph.

**(2) Dispersal containment analysis**

**(A) Research**

The Administrator of the Environmental Protection Agency, in cooperation with the National Science Foundation and the Task Force, shall provide research grants on a competitive basis for projects that—

(i) identify environmentally sound methods for controlling the dispersal of aquatic nuisance species, such as the zebra mussel; and

(ii) adhere to research protocols developed pursuant to subsection (f)(2) of this section.

**(B) Authorization of appropriations**

There are authorized to be appropriated to the Environmental Protection Agency to carry out this paragraph, $500,000.

**(3) Dispersal barrier demonstration**

**(A) In general**

The Assistant Secretary, in consultation with the Task Force, shall investigate and identify environmentally sound methods for preventing and reducing the dispersal of aquatic nuisance species between the Great Lakes-Saint Lawrence drainage and the Mississippi River drainage through the Chicago River Ship and Sanitary Canal, including any of those methods that could be incorporated into the operation or construction of the lock system of the Chicago River Ship and Sanitary Canal.

**(B) Report**

Not later than 18 months after October 26, 1996, the Assistant Secretary shall issue a report to the Congress that includes recommendations concerning—

(i) which of the methods that are identified under the study conducted under this paragraph are most promising with respect to preventing and reducing the dispersal of aquatic nuisance species; and

(ii) ways to incorporate those methods into ongoing operations of the United States Army Corps of Engineers that are conducted at the Chicago River Ship and Sanitary Canal.

**(C) Authorization of appropriations**

There are authorized to be appropriated to the Department of the Army, to carry out this paragraph, $750,000.

**(4) Contributions**

To the extent allowable by law, in carrying out the studies under paragraphs (2) and (3), the Administrator of the Environmental Protection Agency and the Secretary of the Army may enter into an agreement with an interested party under which that party provides in kind or monetary contributions for the study.

**(5) Technical assistance**

The Great Lakes Environmental Research Laboratory of the National Oceanic and Atmospheric Administration shall provide technical assistance to appropriate entities to assist in the research conducted pursuant to this subsection.

**(j) Implementation**

**(1) Regulations**

The Director, the Secretary, and the Under Secretary may issue such rules and regulations as may be necessary to implement this section.

**(2) Participation of others**

The Task Force shall provide opportunities for affected Federal agencies which are not part of the Task Force, State and local government agencies, and regional and other entities with the necessary expertise to participate in control programs. If these other agencies or entities have sufficient authority or jurisdiction and expertise and where this will be more efficient or effective, responsibility for implementing all or a portion of a control program may be delegated to such agencies or entities.

**(k) Reports**

(1) Not later than 12 months after November 29, 1990, the Task Force shall submit a report describing the program developed under subsection (a) of this section, including the research protocol required under subsection (f)(2) of this section, to the Congress.

(2) On an annual basis after the submission of the report under paragraph (1), the Task Force shall submit a report to the Congress detailing progress in carrying out this section.

(Pub.L. 101–646, Title I, § 1202, Nov. 29, 1990, 104 Stat. 4766; Pub.L. 104–332, § 2(e)(3), (4), (g), (h)(1), Oct. 26, 1996, 110 Stat. 4085, 4087, 4091.)

HISTORICAL AND STATUTORY NOTES

**References in Text**

This chapter, referred to in subsecs. (e)(1) and (f)(3), read in the original, this Act, meaning the Nonindigenous Aquatic Nuisance Prevention and Control Act of 1990, which enacted this chapter. For complete classification, see Short Title note under section 4701 of this title and Tables.

## § 4723. Regional coordination

[NANPCA § 1203]

**(a) Great Lakes panel**

**(1) In general**

Not later than 30 days following November 29, 1990, the Task Force shall request that the Great Lakes Commission (established under Article IV of the Great Lakes Compact to which the Congress granted consent in the Act of July 24, 1968, P.L. 90–419) convene a panel of Great Lakes region representatives from Federal, State and local agencies and from private environmental and commercial interests to—

(A) identify priorities for the Great Lakes region with respect to aquatic nuisance species;

(B) make recommendations to the Task Force regarding programs to carry out section 4722(i) of this title;

(C) assist the Task Force in coordinating Federal aquatic nuisance species program activities in the Great Lakes region;

(D) coordinate, where possible, aquatic nuisance species program activities in the Great Lakes region that are not conducted pursuant to this chapter;

(E) provide advice to public and private individuals and entities concerning methods of controlling aquatic nuisance species; and

(F) submit annually a report to the Task Force describing activities within the Great Lakes region related to aquatic nuisance species prevention, research,[1] control.

**(2) Consultation**

The Task Force shall request that the Great Lakes Fishery Commission provide information to the panel convened under this subsection on technical and policy matters related to the international fishery resources of the Great Lakes.

**(3) Canadian participation**

The panel convened under this subsection is encourage [2] to invite representatives from the Federal, provincial or territorial governments of Canada to participate as observers.

**(b) Western regional panel**

Not later than 30 days after October 26, 1996, the Task Force shall request a Western regional panel, comprised of Western region representatives from Federal, State, and local agencies and from private environmental and commercial interests, to—

(1) identify priorities for the Western region with respect to aquatic nuisance species;

(2) make recommendations to the Task Force regarding an education, monitoring (including inspection), prevention, and control program to prevent the spread of the zebra mussel west of the 100th Meridian pursuant to section 4722(i) of this title;

(3) coordinate, where possible, other aquatic nuisance species program activities in the Western region that are not conducted pursuant to this chapter;

(4) develop an emergency response strategy for Federal, State, and local entities for stemming new invasions of aquatic nuisance species in the region;

(5) provide advice to public and private individuals and entities concerning methods of preventing and controlling aquatic nuisance species infestations; and

(6) submit annually a report to the Task Force describing activities within the Western region related to aquatic nuisance species prevention, research, and control.

**(c) Additional regional panels**

The Task Force shall—

(1) encourage the development and use of regional panels and other similar entities in regions in addition to the Great Lakes and Western regions (including providing financial assistance for the development and use of such entities) to carry out, with respect to those regions, activities that are similar to the activities described in subsections (a) and (b) of this section; and

(2) cooperate with regional panels and similar entities that carry out the activities described in paragraph (1).

(Pub.L. 101–646, Title I, § 1203, Nov. 29, 1990, 104 Stat. 4769; Pub.L. 104–332, § 2(e)(5), (h)(1), Oct. 26, 1996, 110 Stat. 4087, 4091.)

[1] So in original. Probably should be followed by "and".

[2] So in original. Probably should be "encouraged".

HISTORICAL AND STATUTORY NOTES

**References in Text**

Article IV of the Great Lakes Compact to which the Congress granted consent in the Act of July 24, 1968, P.L. 90–419, referred to in subsec. (a)(1), is not classified to the Code.

This chapter, referred to in subsecs. (a)(1)(D) and (b)(3), read in the original, this Act, meaning the Nonindigenous Aquatic Nuisance Prevention and Control Act of 1990, which enacted this chapter. For complete classification, see Short Title note under section 4701 of this title and Tables.

## § 4724. State aquatic nuisance species management plans

[NANPCA § 1204]

### (a) State or interstate invasive species management plans

#### (1) In general

After providing notice and opportunity for public comment, the Governor of each State may prepare and submit, or the Governors of the States and the governments of the Indian tribes involved in an interstate organization, may jointly prepare and submit—

(A) a comprehensive management plan to the Task Force for approval which identifies those areas or activities within the State or within the interstate region involved, other than those related to public facilities, for which technical, enforcement, or financial assistance (or any combination thereof) is needed to eliminate or reduce the environmental, public health, and safety risks associated with aquatic nuisance species, particularly the zebra mussel; and

(B) a public facility management plan to the Assistant Secretary for approval which is limited solely to identifying those public facilities within the State or within the interstate region involved for which technical and financial assistance is needed to reduce infestations of zebra mussels.

#### (2) Content

Each plan shall, to the extent possible, identify the management practices and measures that will be undertaken to reduce infestations of aquatic nuisance species. Each plan shall—

(A) identify and describe State and local programs for environmentally sound prevention and control of the target aquatic nuisance species;

(B) identify Federal activities that may be needed for environmentally sound prevention and control of aquatic nuisance species and a description of the manner in which those activities should be coordinated with State and local government activities;

(C) identify any authority that the State (or any State or Indian tribe involved in the interstate organization) does not have at the time of the development of the plan that may be necessary for the State (or any State or Indian tribe involved in the interstate organization) to protect public health, property, and the environment from harm by aquatic nuisance species; and

(D) a schedule of implementing the plan, including a schedule of annual objectives, and enabling legislation.

#### (3) Consultation

(A) In developing and implementing a management plan, the State or interstate organization should, to the maximum extent practicable, involve local governments and regional entities, Indian tribes, and public and private organizations that have expertise in the control of aquatic nuisance species.

(B) Upon the request of a State or the appropriate official of an interstate organization, the Task Force or the Assistant Secretary, as appropriate under paragraph (1), may provide technical assistance in developing and implementing a management plan.

#### (4) Plan approval

Within 90 days after the submission of a management plan, the Task Force or the Assistant Secretary in consultation with the Task Force, as appropriate under paragraph (1), shall review the proposed plan and approve it if it meets the requirements of this subsection or return the plan to the Governor or the interstate organization with recommended modifications.

### (b) Grant program

#### (1) State grants

The Director may, at the recommendation of the Task Force, make grants to States with management plans approved under subsection (a) of this section for the implementation of those plans.

#### (2) Application

An application for a grant under this subsection shall include an identification and description of the best management practices and measures which the State proposes to utilize in implementing an approved management plan with any Federal assistance to be provided under the grant.

#### (3) Federal share

(A) The Federal share of the cost of each comprehensive management plan implemented with Federal assistance under this section in any fiscal year shall not exceed 75 percent of the cost incurred by the State in implementing such management program and the non–Federal share of such costs shall be provided from non–Federal sources.

(B) The Federal share of the cost of each public facility management plan implemented with Federal assistance under this section in any fiscal year shall not exceed 50 percent of the cost incurred by the State in implementing such management program and the non–Federal share of such costs shall be provided from non–Federal sources.

(4) **Adminisrative [1] costs**

For the purposes of this section, administrative costs for activities and programs carried out with a grant in any fiscal year shall not exceed 5 percent of the amount of the grant in that year.

(5) **In-kind contributions**

In addition to cash outlays and payments, in-kind contributions of property or personnel services by non-Federal interests for activities under this section may be used for the non-Federal share of the cost of those activities.

(c) **Enforcement assistance**

Upon request of a State or Indian tribe, the Director or the Under Secretary, to the extent allowable by law and in a manner consistent with section 141 of Title 14, may provide assistance to a State or Indian tribe in enforcing an approved State or interstate invasive species management plan.

(Pub.L. 101–646, Title I, § 1204, Nov. 29, 1990, 104 Stat. 4770; Pub.L. 104–332, § 2(e)(6), (h)(1), Oct. 26, 1996, 110 Stat. 4089, 4091.)

[1] So in original. Probably should be "Administrative".

## § 4725. Relationship to other laws

[NANPCA § 1205]

All actions taken by Federal agencies in implementing the provisions of section 4722 of this title shall be consistent with all applicable Federal, State, and local environmental laws. Nothing in this chapter shall affect the authority of any State or political subdivision thereof to adopt or enforce control measures for aquatic nuisance species, or diminish or affect the jurisdiction of any State over species of fish and wildlife. Compliance with the control and eradication measures of any State or political subdivision thereof regarding aquatic nuisance species shall not relieve any person of the obligation to comply with the provisions of this subchapter.

(Pub.L. 101–646, Title I, § 1205, Nov. 29, 1990, 104 Stat. 4771; Pub.L. 104–332, § 2(h)(1), Oct. 26, 1996, 110 Stat. 4091.)

## § 4726. International cooperation

[NANPCA § 1206]

(a) **Advice**

The Task Force shall provide timely advice to the Secretary of State concerning aquatic nuisance species that infest waters shared with other countries.

(b) **Negotiations**

The Secretary of State, in consultation with the Task Force, is encouraged to initiate negotiations with the governments of foreign countries concerning the planning and implementation of prevention, monitoring, research, education, and control programs related to aquatic nuisance species infesting shared water resources.

(Pub.L. 101–646, Title I, § 1206, Nov. 29, 1990, 104 Stat. 4771; Pub.L. 104–332, § 2(h)(1), Oct. 26, 1996, 110 Stat. 4091.)

## § 4727. Intentional introductions policy review

[NANPCA § 1207]

Within one year of November 29, 1990, the Task Force shall, in consultation with State fish and wildlife agencies, other regional, State and local entities, potentially affected industries and other interested parties, identify and evaluate approaches for reducing the risk of adverse consequences associated with intentional introduction of aquatic organisms and submit a report of their findings, conclusions and recommendations to the Congress.

(Pub.L. 101–646, Title I, § 1207, Nov. 29, 1990, 104 Stat. 4771; Pub.L. 104–332, § 2(g), (h)(1), Oct. 26, 1996, 110 Stat. 4091.)

## § 4728. Brown tree snake control program

[NANPCA § 1209]

The Task Force shall, within the program developed under subsection (a),[1] undertake a comprehensive, environmentally sound program in coordination with regional, territorial, State and local entities to control the brown tree snake (Boiga irregularis) in Guam and other areas where the species is established outside of its historic range.

(Pub.L. 101–646, Title I, § 1209, Nov. 29, 1990, 104 Stat. 4772; Pub.L. 104–332, § 2(h)(1), Oct. 26, 1996, 110 Stat. 4091.)

[1] So in original. Probably should be "subsection (a) of section 4722 of this title".

### HISTORICAL AND STATUTORY NOTES

**Codification**

No subsection (a) has been enacted.

# SUBCHAPTER IV—AUTHORIZATIONS OF APPROPRIATION

## § 4741. Authorization of appropriations

[NANPCA § 1301]

(a) **Prevention of unintentional introductions**

There are authorized to be appropriated to develop and implement the provisions of subchapter II of this chapter—

(1) $500,000 until the end of fiscal year 1992 to the Secretary to carry out sections 4711 and 4712(a)(3) of this title;

(2) $2,000,000 until the end of fiscal year 1992 to the Director and Under Secretary to carry out the

studies under sections 4712(a)(1) and 4712(a)(2[1] of this title;

(3) to the Secretary to carry out section 4711 of this title—

(A) $2,000,000 for each of fiscal years 1997 and 1998; and

(B) $3,000,000 for each of fiscal years 1999 through 2002;

(4) for each of fiscal years 1997 through 2002, to carry out paragraphs (1) and (2) of section 4712(b) of this title—

(A) $1,000,000 to the Department of the Interior, to be used by the Director; and

(B) $1,000,000 to the Secretary; and

(5) for each of fiscal years 1997 through 2002—

(A) $3,000,000, which shall be made available from funds otherwise authorized to be appropriated if such funds are so authorized, to the Under Secretary to carry out section 4712(e) of this title; and

(B) $500,000 to the Secretary to carry out section 4712(f) of this title.

**(b) Task Force and aquatic nuisance species program**

There are authorized to be appropriated for each of fiscal years 1997 through 2002 to develop and implement the provisions of subchapter III of this chapter—

(1) $6,000,000 to the Department of the Interior, to be used by the Director to carry out sections 4722 and 4728 of this title;

(2) $1,000,000 to the Department of Commerce, to be used by the Under Secretary to carry out section 4722 of this title;

(3) $1,625,000, which shall be made available from funds otherwise authorized to be appropriated if such funds are so authorized, to fund aquatic nuisance species prevention and control research under section 4722(i) of this title at the Great Lakes Environmental Research Laboratory of the National Oceanic and Atmospheric Administration, of which $500,000 shall be made available for grants, to be competitively awarded and subject to peer review, for research relating to Lake Champlain;

(4) $5,000,000 for competitive grants for university research on aquatic nuisance species under section 4722(f)(3) of this title as follows:

(A) $2,800,000, which shall be made available from funds otherwise authorized to be appropriated if such funds are so authorized, to fund grants under section 1124 of Title 33;

(B) $1,200,000 to fund grants to colleges for the benefit of agriculture and the mechanic arts referred to in section 322 of Title 7; and

(C) $1,000,000 to fund grants through the Cooperative Fisheries and Wildlife Research Unit Program of the United States Fish and Wildlife Service;

(5) $3,000,000 to the Department of the Army, to be used by the Assistant Secretary to carry out section 4722(i)(1)(B) of this title; and

(6) $300,000 to the Department of the Interior, to be used by the Director to fund regional panels and similar entities under section 4723 of this title, of which $100,000 shall be used to fund activities of the Great Lakes Commission.

(7) Repealed. Pub.L. 104–332, § 2(f)(2)(B), Oct. 26, 1996, 110 Stat. 4090

**(c) Grants for State management programs**

There are authorized to be appropriated for each of fiscal years 1997 through 2002 $4,000,000 to the Department of the Interior, to be used by the Director for making grants under section 4724 of this title, of which $1,500,000 shall be used by the Director, in consultation with the Assistant Secretary, for management of aquatic nuisance vegetation species.

**(d) Intentional introductions policy review**

There are authorized to be appropriated for fiscal year 1991, $500,000 to the Director and the Under Secretary to conduct the intentional introduction policy review under section 4727 of this title.

**(e) Ballast water management demonstration program**

There are authorized to be appropriated $2,500,000 to carry out section 4714 of this title.

**(f) Research**

There are authorized to be appropriated to the Director $1,000,000 to carry out research on the prevention, monitoring, and control of aquatic nuisance species in Narragansett Bay, Rhode Island. The funds shall be made available for use by the Department of Environmental Management of the State of Rhode Island.

(Pub.L. 101–646, Title I, § 1301, Nov. 29, 1990, 104 Stat. 4772; Pub.L. 102–186, § 4(b)(2), Dec. 4, 1991, 105 Stat. 1283; Pub.L. 104–332, § 2(f), (h)(1), Oct. 26, 1996, 110 Stat. 4090, 4091.)

[1] So in original. Probably should be followed by a closing parenthesis.

## SUBCHAPTER V—COOPERATIVE ENVIRONMENTAL ANALYSES

### § 4751. Environmental impact analyses [NANPCA § 1401]

The Secretary of State, in consultation with the Council on Environmental Quality, is encouraged to enter into negotiations with the governments of Canada and Mexico to provide for reciprocal cooperative environmental impact analysis of major Federal actions which have significant transboundary effects on the quality of the human environment in the United States, Canada, and Mexico.

(Pub.L. 101–646, Title I, § 1401, Nov. 29, 1990, 104 Stat. 4773; Pub.L. 104–332, § 2(h)(1), Oct. 26, 1996, 110 Stat. 4091.)

# HEALTHY FOREST RESTORATION

## HEALTHY FORESTS RESTORATION ACT OF 2003

**(16 U.S.C.A. §§ 6501 to 6591)**

## CHAPTER 84—HEALTHY FOREST RESTORATION



### § 6501. Purposes

The purposes of this chapter are—

(1) to reduce wildfire risk to communities, municipal water supplies, and other at-risk Federal land through a collaborative process of planning, prioritizing, and implementing hazardous fuel reduction projects;

(2) to authorize grant programs to improve the commercial value of forest biomass (that otherwise contributes to the risk of catastrophic fire or insect or disease infestation) for producing electric energy, useful heat, transportation fuel, and petroleum-based product substitutes, and for other commercial purposes;

(3) to enhance efforts to protect watersheds and address threats to forest and rangeland health, including catastrophic wildfire, across the landscape;

(4) to promote systematic gathering of information to address the impact of insect and disease infestations and other damaging agents on forest and rangeland health;

(5) to improve the capacity to detect insect and disease infestations at an early stage, particularly with respect to hardwood forests; and

(6) to protect, restore, and enhance forest ecosystem components—

(A) to promote the recovery of threatened and endangered species;

(B) to improve biological diversity; and

(C) to enhance productivity and carbon sequestration.

(Pub.L. 108–148, § 2, Dec. 3, 2003, 117 Stat. 1888.)

#### HISTORICAL AND STATUTORY NOTES

**References in Text**

This chapter, referred to in text, originally read "this Act", meaning the Healthy Forests Restoration Act of 2003, Pub.L. 108–148, Dec. 3, 2003, 117 Stat. 1887, which enacted this chapter.

**Short Title**

2003 Amendments

Pub.L. 108–148, § 1(a), Dec. 3, 2003, 117 Stat. 1887, provided that: "This Act [enacting this chapter and 16 U.S.C.A. § 2103b and amending provisions set out as notes under 7 U.S.C.A. § 8101] may be cited as the 'Healthy Forests Restoration Act of 2003'."

### § 6502. Definitions

In this chapter:

**(1) Federal land**

The term "Federal land" means—

(A) land of the National Forest System (as defined in section 1609(a) of this title) administered by the Secretary of Agriculture, acting through the Chief of the Forest Service; and

(B) public lands (as defined in section 1702 of Title 43), the surface of which is administered by the Secretary of the Interior, acting through the Director of the Bureau of Land Management.

**(2) Indian tribe**

The term "Indian tribe" has the meaning given the term in section 450b of Title 25.

(Pub.L. 108–148, § 3, Dec. 3, 2003, 117 Stat. 1888.)

HISTORICAL AND STATUTORY NOTES

**References in Text**

This chapter, referred to in text, originally read "this Act", meaning the Healthy Forests Restoration Act of 2003, Pub.L. 108–148, Dec. 3, 2003, 117 Stat. 1887, which enacted this chapter.

## SUBCHAPTER I—HAZARDOUS FUEL REDUCTION ON FEDERAL LAND

### § 6511. Definitions

In this subchapter:

**(1) At-risk community**

The term "at-risk community" means an area—

(A) that is comprised of—

(i) an interface community as defined in the notice entitled "Wildland Urban Interface Communities Within the Vicinity of Federal Lands That Are at High Risk From Wildfire" issued by the Secretary of Agriculture and the Secretary of the Interior in accordance with title IV of the Department of the Interior and Related Agencies Appropriations Act, 2001 (114 Stat. 1009) (66 Fed. Reg. 753, January 4, 2001); or

(ii) a group of homes and other structures with basic infrastructure and services (such as utilities and collectively maintained transportation routes) within or adjacent to Federal land;

(B) in which conditions are conducive to a large-scale wildland fire disturbance event; and

(C) for which a significant threat to human life or property exists as a result of a wildland fire disturbance event.

**(2) Authorized hazardous fuel reduction project**

The term "authorized hazardous fuel reduction project" means the measures and methods described in the definition of "appropriate tools" contained in the glossary of the Implementation Plan, on Federal land described in section 6512(a) of this title and conducted under sections 6513 and 6514 of this title.

**(3) Community wildfire protection plan**

The term "community wildfire protection plan" means a plan for an at-risk community that—

(A) is developed within the context of the collaborative agreements and the guidance established by the Wildland Fire Leadership Council and agreed to by the applicable local government, local fire department, and State agency responsible for forest management, in consultation with interested parties and the Federal land management agencies managing land in the vicinity of the at-risk community;

(B) identifies and prioritizes areas for hazardous fuel reduction treatments and recommends the types and methods of treatment on Federal and non-Federal land that will protect 1 or more at-risk communities and essential infrastructure; and

(C) recommends measures to reduce structural ignitability throughout the at-risk community.

**(4) Condition class 2**

The term "condition class 2", with respect to an area of Federal land, means the condition class description developed by the Forest Service Rocky Mountain Research Station in the general technical report entitled "Development of Coarse-Scale Spatial Data for Wildland Fire and Fuel Management" (RMRS-87), dated April 2000 (including any subsequent revision to the report), under which—

(A) fire regimes on the land have been moderately altered from historical ranges;

(B) there exists a moderate risk of losing key ecosystem components from fire;

(C) fire frequencies have increased or decreased from historical frequencies by 1 or more return intervals, resulting in moderate changes to—

(i) the size, frequency, intensity, or severity of fires; or

(ii) landscape patterns; and

(D) vegetation attributes have been moderately altered from the historical range of the attributes.

**(5) Condition class 3**

The term "condition class 3", with respect to an area of Federal land, means the condition class description developed by the Rocky Mountain Research Station in the general technical report referred to in paragraph (4) (including any subsequent revision to the report), under which—

(A) fire regimes on land have been significantly altered from historical ranges;

(B) there exists a high risk of losing key ecosystem components from fire;

(C) fire frequencies have departed from historical frequencies by multiple return intervals, resulting in dramatic changes to—

(i) the size, frequency, intensity, or severity of fires; or

(ii) landscape patterns; and

(D) vegetation attributes have been significantly altered from the historical range of the attributes.

**(6) Day**

The term "day" means—

(A) a calendar day; or

(B) if a deadline imposed by this subchapter would expire on a nonbusiness day, the end of the next business day.

**(7) Decision document**

The term "decision document" means—

(A) a decision notice (as that term is used in the Forest Service Handbook);

(B) a decision record (as that term is used in the Bureau of Land Management Handbook); and

(C) a record of decision (as that term is used in applicable regulations of the Council on Environmental Quality).

**(8) Fire regime I**

The term "fire regime I" means an area—

(A) in which historically there have been low-severity fires with a frequency of 0 through 35 years; and

(B) that is located primarily in low elevation forests of pine, oak, or pinyon juniper.

**(9) Fire regime II**

The term "fire regime II" means an area—

(A) in which historically there are stand replacement severity fires with a frequency of 0 through 35 years; and

**(B) That is located primarily in low- to mid-elevation rangeland, grassland, or shrubland.**

**(10) Fire regime III**

The term "fire regime III" means an area—

(A) in which historically there are mixed severity fires with a frequency of 35 through 100 years; and

(B) that is located primarily in forests of mixed conifer, dry Douglas fir, or wet Ponderosa pine.

**(11) Implementation Plan**

The term "Implementation Plan" means the Implementation Plan for the Comprehensive Strategy for a Collaborative Approach for Reducing Wildland Fire Risks to Communities and the Environment, dated May 2002, developed pursuant to the conference report to accompany the Department of the Interior and Related Agencies Appropriations Act, 2001 (House Report No. 106–64) (and subsequent revisions).

**(12) Municipal water supply system**

The term "municipal water supply system" means the reservoirs, canals, ditches, flumes, laterals, pipes, pipelines, and other surface facilities and systems constructed or installed for the collection, impoundment, storage, transportation, or distribution of drinking water.

**(13) Resource management plan**

The term "resource management plan" means—

(A) a land and resource management plan prepared for 1 or more units of land of the National Forest System described in section 6502(1)(A) of this title under section 1604 of this title; or

(B) a land use plan prepared for 1 or more units of the public land described in section 6502(1)(A) of this title under section 1712 of Title 43.

**(14) Secretary**

The term "Secretary" means—

(A) the Secretary of Agriculture, with respect to land of the National Forest System described in section 6502(1)(A) of this title; and

(B) the Secretary of the Interior, with respect to public lands described in section 6502(1)(B) of this title.

**(15) Threatened and endangered species habitat**

The term "threatened and endangered species habitat" means Federal land identified in—

(A) a determination that a species is an endangered species or a threatened species under the Endangered Species Act of 1973 (16 U.S.C. 1531 et seq.);

(B) a designation of critical habitat of the species under that Act; or

(C) a recovery plan prepared for the species under that Act.

**(16) Wildland-urban interface**

The term "wildland-urban interface" means—

(A) an area within or adjacent to an at-risk community that is identified in recommendations to the Secretary in a community wildfire protection plan; or

(B) in the case of any area for which a community wildfire protection plan is not in effect—

(i) an area extending ½-mile from the boundary of an at-risk community;

(ii) an area within 1½ miles of the boundary of an at-risk community, including any land that—

(I) has a sustained steep slope that creates the potential for wildfire behavior endangering the at-risk community;

(II) has a geographic feature that aids in creating an effective fire break, such as a road or ridge top; or

(III) is in condition class 3, as documented by the Secretary in the project-specific environmental analysis; and

(iii) an area that is adjacent to an evacuation route for an at-risk community that the Secretary determines, in cooperation with the at-risk community, requires hazardous fuel reduction to provide safer evacuation from the at-risk community.

(Pub.L. 108–148, Title I, § 101, Dec. 3, 2003, 117 Stat. 1889.)

#### HISTORICAL AND STATUTORY NOTES

**References in Text**

This subchapter, referred to in text, originally read "this title", meaning Title I of the Healthy Forests Restoration Act of 2003, Pub.L. 108–148, Title I, § 101 et seq., Dec. 3, 2003, 117 Stat. 1889, which enacted this subchapter.

Title IV of the Department of the Interior and Related Agencies Appropriations Act, 2001, referred to in par. (1)(A)(i), is Pub.L. 106–291, Title IV, Oct. 11, 2000, 114 Stat. 1009, which is not classified to the Code.

The Department of the Interior and Related Agencies Appropriations Act, 2001, referred to in par. (11), is Pub.L. 106–291, Oct. 11, 2000, 114 Stat. 922; see Tables for complete classification.

The Endangered Species Act of 1973, referred to in par. (15)(A), is Pub.L. 93–205, Dec. 28, 1973, 87 Stat. 884, also known as ESA, which is classified principally to chapter 35 of this title, 16 U.S.C.A. § 1531 et seq; see Tables for complete classification.

## § 6512. Authorized hazardous fuel reduction projects

### (a) Authorized projects

As soon as practicable after December 3, 2003, the Secretary shall implement authorized hazardous fuel reduction projects, consistent with the Implementation Plan, on—

(1) Federal land in wildland-urban interface areas;

(2) condition class 3 Federal land, in such proximity to a municipal water supply system or a stream feeding such a system within a municipal watershed that a significant risk exists that a fire disturbance event would have adverse effects on the water quality of the municipal water supply or the maintenance of the system, including a risk to water quality posed by erosion following such a fire disturbance event;

(3) condition class 2 Federal land located within fire regime I, fire regime II, or fire regime III, in such proximity to a municipal water supply system or a stream feeding such a system within a municipal watershed that a significant risk exists that a fire disturbance event would have adverse effects on the water quality of the municipal water supply or the maintenance of the system, including a risk to water quality posed by erosion following such a fire disturbance event;

(4) Federal land on which windthrow or blowdown, ice storm damage, the existence of an epidemic of disease or insects, or the presence of such an epidemic on immediately adjacent land and the imminent risk it will spread, poses a significant threat to an ecosystem component, or forest or rangeland resource, on the Federal land or adjacent non-Federal land; and

(5) Federal land not covered by paragraphs (1) through (4) that contains threatened and endangered species habitat, if—

(A) natural fire regimes on that land are identified as being important for, or wildfire is identified as a threat to, an endangered species, a threatened species, or habitat of an endangered species or threatened species in a species recovery plan prepared under section 1533 of this title, or a notice published in the Federal Register determining a species to be an endangered species or a threatened species or designating critical habitat;

(B) the authorized hazardous fuel reduction project will provide enhanced protection from catastrophic wildfire for the endangered species, threatened species, or habitat of the endangered species or threatened species; and

(C) the Secretary complies with any applicable guidelines specified in any management or recovery plan described in subparagraph (A).

### (b) Relation to agency plans

An authorized hazardous fuel reduction project shall be conducted consistent with the resource management plan and other relevant administrative policies or decisions applicable to the Federal land covered by the project.

### (c) Acreage limitation

Not more than a total of 20,000,000 acres of Federal land may be treated under authorized hazardous fuel reduction projects.

### (d) Exclusion of certain Federal land

The Secretary may not conduct an authorized hazardous fuel reduction project that would occur on—

(1) a component of the National Wilderness Preservation System;

(2) Federal land on which the removal of vegetation is prohibited or restricted by Act of Congress or Presidential proclamation (including the applicable implementation plan); or

(3) a Wilderness Study Area.

**(e) Old growth stands**

**(1) Definitions**

In this subsection and subsection (f) of this section:

**(A) Applicable period**

The term "applicable period" means—

(i) the 2–year period beginning on December 3, 2003; or

(ii) in the case of a resource management plan that the Secretary is in the process of revising as of December 3, 2003.

**(B) Covered project**

The term "covered project" means an authorized hazardous fuel reduction project carried out on land described in paragraph (1), (2), (3), or (5) of subsection (a) of this section.

**(C) Management direction**

The term "management direction" means definitions, designations, standards, guidelines, goals, or objectives established for an old growth stand under a resource management plan developed in accordance with applicable law, including section 1604(g)(3)(B) of this title.

**(D) Old growth stand**

The term "old growth stand" has the meaning given the term under management direction used pursuant to paragraphs (3) and (4), based on the structure and composition characteristic of the forest type, and in accordance with applicable law, including section 1604(g)(3)(B) of this title.

**(2) Project requirements**

In carrying out a covered project, the Secretary shall fully maintain, or contribute toward the restoration of, the structure and composition of old growth stands according to the pre-fire suppression old growth conditions characteristic of the forest type, taking into account the contribution of the stand to landscape fire adaptation and watershed health, and retaining the large trees contributing to old growth structure.

**(3) Newer management direction**

**(A) In general**

If the management direction for an old growth stand was established on or after December 15, 1993, the Secretary shall meet the requirements of paragraph (2) in carrying out a covered project by implementing the management direction.

**(B) Amendments or revisions**

Any amendment or revision to management direction for which final administrative approval is granted after December 3, 2003 shall be consistent with paragraph (2) for the purpose of carrying out covered projects.

**(4) Older management direction**

**(A) In general**

If the management direction for an old growth stand was established before December 15, 1993, the Secretary shall meet the requirements of paragraph (2) in carrying out a covered project during the applicable period by implementing the management direction.

**(B) Review required**

Subject to subparagraph (C), during the applicable period for management direction referred to in subparagraph (A), the Secretary shall—

(i) review the management direction for affected covered projects, taking into account any relevant scientific information made available since the adoption of the management direction; and

(ii) amend the management direction for affected covered projects to be consistent with paragraph (2), if necessary to reflect relevant scientific information the Secretary did not consider in formulating the management direction.

**(C) Review not completed**

If the Secretary does not complete the review of the management direction in accordance with subparagraph (B) before the end of the applicable period, the Secretary shall not carry out any portion of affected covered projects in stands that are identified as old growth stands (based on substantial supporting evidence) by any person during scoping, within the period—

(i) beginning at the close of the applicable period for the management direction governing the affected covered projects; and

(ii) ending on the earlier of—

(I) the date the Secretary completes the action required by subparagraph (B) for the management direction applicable to the affected covered projects; or

(II) the date on which the acreage limitation specified in subsection (c) of this section (as that limitation may be adjusted by a subsequent Act of Congress) is reached.

**(5) Limitation to covered projects**

Nothing in this subsection requires the Secretary to revise or otherwise amend a resource management plan to make the project requirements of paragraph (2) apply to an activity other than a covered project.

**(f) Large tree retention**

**(1) In general**

Except in old growth stands where the management direction is consistent with subsection (e)(2) of this section, the Secretary shall carry out a covered project in a manner that—

(A) focuses largely on small diameter trees, thinning, strategic fuel breaks, and prescribed fire to modify fire behavior, as measured by the projected reduction of uncharacteristically severe wildfire effects for the forest type (such as adverse soil impacts, tree mortality or other impacts); and

(B) maximizes the retention of large trees, as appropriate for the forest type, to the extent that the trees promote fire-resilient stands.

**(2) Wildfire risk**

Nothing in this subsection prevents achievement of the purposes described in section 6501(1) of this title.

**(g) Monitoring and assessing forest and rangeland health**

**(1) In general**

For each Forest Service administrative region and each Bureau of Land Management State Office, the Secretary shall—

(A) monitor the results of a representative sample of the projects authorized under this subchapter for each management unit; and

(B) not later than 5 years after December 3, 2003, and each 5 years thereafter, issue a report that includes—

(i) an evaluation of the progress towards project goals; and

(ii) recommendations for modifications to the projects and management treatments.

**(2) Consistency of projects with recommendations**

An authorized hazardous fuel reduction project approved following the issuance of a monitoring report shall, to the maximum extent practicable, be consistent with any applicable recommendations in the report.

**(3) Similar vegetation types**

The results of a monitoring report shall be made available for use (if appropriate) in an authorized hazardous fuels reduction project conducted in a similar vegetation type on land under the jurisdiction of the Secretary.

**(4) Monitoring and assessments**

Monitoring and assessment shall include a description of the changes in condition class, using the Fire Regime Condition Class Guidebook or successor guidance, specifically comparing end results to—

(A) pretreatment conditions;

(B) historical fire regimes; and

(C) any applicable watershed or landscape goals or objectives in the resource management plan or other relevant direction.

**(5) Multiparty monitoring**

**(A) In general**

In an area where significant interest is expressed in multiparty monitoring, the Secretary shall establish a multiparty monitoring, evaluation, and accountability process in order to assess the positive or negative ecological and social effects of authorized hazardous fuel reduction projects and projects conducted pursuant to section 6554 of this title.

**(B) Diverse stakeholders**

The Secretary shall include diverse stakeholders (including interested citizens and Indian tribes) in the process required under subparagraph (A).

**(C) Funding**

Funds to carry out this paragraph may be derived from operations funds for projects described in subparagraph (A).

**(6) Collection of monitoring data**

The Secretary may collect monitoring data by entering into cooperative agreements or contracts with, or providing grants to, small or micro-businesses, cooperatives, nonprofit organizations, Youth Conservation Corps work crews, or related State, local, and other non-Federal conservation corps.

**(7) Tracking**

For each administrative unit, the Secretary shall track acres burned, by the degree of severity, by large wildfires (as defined by the Secretary).

**(8) Monitoring and maintenance of treated areas**

The Secretary shall, to the maximum extent practicable, develop a process for monitoring the need for maintenance of treated areas, over time, in order to preserve the forest health benefits achieved.

(Pub.L. 108–148, Title I, § 102, Dec. 3, 2003, 117 Stat. 1892.)

HISTORICAL AND STATUTORY NOTES

**References in Text**

This subchapter, referred to in subsec. (g)(1)(A), originally read "this title", meaning Title I of the Healthy Forests Restoration Act of 2003, Pub.L. 108–148, Title I, § 101 et seq., Dec. 3, 2003, 117 Stat. 1889, which enacted this subchapter.

## § 6513. Prioritization

**(a) In general**

In accordance with the Implementation Plan, the Secretary shall develop an annual program of work for Federal land that gives priority to authorized hazardous fuel reduction projects that provide for the protection of at-risk communities or watersheds or that implement community wildfire protection plans.

**(b) Collaboration**

**(1) In general**

The Secretary shall consider recommendations under subsection (a) of this section that are made by at-risk communities that have developed community wildfire protection plans.

**(2) Exemption**

The Federal Advisory Committee Act (5 U.S.C. App.) shall not apply to the planning process and recommendations concerning community wildfire protection plans.

**(c) Administration**

**(1) In general**

Federal agency involvement in developing a community wildfire protection plan, or a recommendation made in a community wildfire protection plan, shall not be considered a Federal agency action under the National Environmental Policy Act of 1969 (42 U.S.C. 4321 et seq.).

**(2) Compliance**

In implementing authorized hazardous fuel reduction projects on Federal land, the Secretary shall, in accordance with section 6514 of this title, comply with the National Environmental Policy Act of 1969 (42 U.S.C. 4321 et seq.).

**(d) Funding allocation**

**(1) Federal land**

**(A) In general**

Subject to subparagraph (B), the Secretary shall use not less than 50 percent of the funds allocated for authorized hazardous fuel reduction projects in the wildland-urban interface.

**(B) Applicability and allocation**

The funding allocation in subparagraph (A) shall apply at the national level. The Secretary may allocate the proportion of funds differently than is required under subparagraph (A) within individual management units as appropriate, in particular to conduct authorized hazardous fuel reduction projects on land described in section 6512(a)(4) of this title.

**(C) Wildland-urban interface**

In the case of an authorized hazardous fuel reduction project for which a decision notice is issued during the 1-year period beginning on December 3, 2003, the Secretary shall use existing definitions of the term "wildland-urban interface" rather than the definition of that term provided under section 6511 of this title.

**(2) Non-Federal land**

**(A) In general**

In providing financial assistance under any provision of law for hazardous fuel reduction projects on non-Federal land, the Secretary shall consider recommendations made by at-risk communities that have developed community wildfire protection plans.

**(B) Priority**

In allocating funding under this paragraph, the Secretary should, to the maximum extent practicable, give priority to communities that have adopted a community wildfire protection plan or have taken proactive measures to encourage willing property owners to reduce fire risk on private property.

(Pub.L. 108–148, Title I, § 103, Dec. 3, 2003, 117 Stat. 1896.)

HISTORICAL AND STATUTORY NOTES

**References in Text**

The National Environmental Policy Act of 1969, referred to in subsec. (c)(1) and (2), is Pub.L. 91–190, Jan. 1, 1970, 83 Stat. 852, also known as NEPA, which enacted chapter 55 of Title 42, 42 U.S.C.A. § 4321 et seq.

## § 6514. Environmental analysis

**(a) Authorized hazardous fuel reduction projects**

Except as otherwise provided in this subchapter, the Secretary shall conduct authorized hazardous fuel reduction projects in accordance with—

(1) the National Environmental Policy Act of 1969 (42 U.S.C. 4331 et seq.); and

(2) other applicable laws.

**(b) Environmental assessment or environmental impact statement**

The Secretary shall prepare an environmental assessment or an environmental impact statement pursuant to section 102(2) of the National Environmental Policy Act of 1969 (42 U.S.C. 4332(2)) for each authorized hazardous fuel reduction project.

**(c) Consideration of alternatives**

**(1) In general**

Except as provided in subsection (d) of this section, in the environmental assessment or environmental impact statement prepared under subsection (b) of this section, the Secretary shall study, develop, and describe—

**(A)** the proposed agency action;

**(B)** the alternative of no action; and

**(C)** an additional action alternative, if the additional alternative—

**(i)** is proposed during scoping or the collaborative process under subsection (f) of this section; and

**(ii)** meets the purpose and need of the project, in accordance with regulations promulgated by the Council on Environmental Quality.

**(2) Multiple additional alternatives**

If more than 1 additional alternative is proposed under paragraph (1)(C), the Secretary shall—

**(A)** select which additional alternative to consider, which is a choice that is in the sole discretion of the Secretary; and

**(B)** provide a written record describing the reasons for the selection.

**(d) Alternative analysis process for projects in wildland-urban interface**

**(1) Proposed agency action and 1 action alternative**

For an authorized hazardous fuel reduction project that is proposed to be conducted in the wildland-urban interface, the Secretary is not required to study, develop, or describe more than the proposed agency action and 1 action alternative in the environmental assessment or environmental impact statement prepared pursuant to section 102(2) of the National Environmental Policy Act of 1969 (42 U.S.C. 4332(2)).

**(2) Proposed agency action**

Notwithstanding paragraph (1), but subject to paragraph (3), if an authorized hazardous fuel reduction project proposed to be conducted in the wildland-urban interface is located no further than 1½ miles from the boundary of an at-risk community, the Secretary is not required to study, develop, or describe any alternative to the proposed agency action in the environmental assessment or environmental impact statement prepared pursuant to section 102(2) of the National Environmental Policy Act of 1969 (42 U.S.C. 4332(2)).

**(3) Proposed agency action and community wildfire protection plan alternative**

In the case of an authorized hazardous fuel reduction project described in paragraph (2), if the at-risk community has adopted a community wildfire protection plan and the proposed agency action does not implement the recommendations in the plan regarding the general location and basic method of treatments, the Secretary shall evaluate the recommendations in the plan as an alternative to the proposed agency action in the environmental assessment or environmental impact statement prepared pursuant to section 102(2) of the National Environmental Policy Act of 1969 (42 U.S.C. 4332(2)).

**(e) Public notice and meeting**

**(1) Public notice**

The Secretary shall provide notice of each authorized hazardous fuel reduction project in accordance with applicable regulations and administrative guidelines.

**(2) Public meeting**

During the preparation stage of each authorized hazardous fuel reduction project, the Secretary shall—

**(A)** conduct a public meeting at an appropriate location proximate to the administrative unit of the Federal land on which the authorized hazardous fuel reduction project will be conducted; and

**(B)** provide advance notice of the location, date, and time of the meeting.

**(f) Public collaboration**

In order to encourage meaningful public participation during preparation of authorized hazardous fuel reduction projects, the Secretary shall facilitate collaboration among State and local governments and Indian tribes, and participation of interested persons, during the preparation of each authorized fuel reduction project in a manner consistent with the Implementation Plan.

**(g) Environmental analysis and public comment**

In accordance with section 102(2) of the National Environmental Policy Act of 1969 (42 U.S.C. 4332(2)) and the applicable regulations and administrative guidelines, the Secretary shall provide an opportunity for public comment during the preparation of any environmental assessment or environmental impact statement for an authorized hazardous fuel reduction project.

**(h) Decision document**

The Secretary shall sign a decision document for authorized hazardous fuel reduction projects and provide notice of the final agency actions.

(Pub.L. 108–148, Title I, § 104, Dec. 3, 2003, 117 Stat. 1897.)

HISTORICAL AND STATUTORY NOTES

**References in Text**

This subchapter, referred to in subsec. (a), originally read "this title", meaning Title I of the Healthy Forests Restoration Act of 2003, Pub.L. 108–148, Title I, § 101 et seq., Dec. 3, 2003, 117 Stat. 1889, which enacted this subchapter.

The National Environmental Policy Act of 1969, referred to in subsec. (a)(1), is Pub.L. 91–190, Jan. 1, 1970, 83 Stat. 852, also known as NEPA, which enacted chapter 55 of Title 42, 42 U.S.C.A. § 4321et seq.

Section 102(2) of the National Environmental Policy Act of 1969, referred to in subsecs. (b), (d)(1) to (3), and (g), is Pub.L. 91–190, Title I, § 102(2), Jan. 1, 1970, 83 Stat. 853, which is classified to 42 U.S.C.A. § 4332(2).

## § 6515. Special administrative review process

**(a) Interim final regulations**

**(1) In general**

Not later than 30 days after December 3, 2003, the Secretary of Agriculture shall promulgate interim final regulations to establish a predecisional administrative review process for the period described in paragraph (2) that will serve as the sole means by which a person can seek administrative review regarding an authorized hazardous fuel reduction project on Forest Service land.

**(2) Period**

The predecisional administrative review process required under paragraph (1) shall occur during the period—

(A) beginning after the completion of the environmental assessment or environmental impact statement; and

(B) ending not later than the date of the issuance of the final decision approving the project.

**(3) Eligibility**

To be eligible to participate in the administrative review process for an authorized hazardous fuel reduction project under paragraph (1), a person shall submit to the Secretary, during scoping or the public comment period for the draft environmental analysis for the project, specific written comments that relate to the proposed action.

**(4) Effective date**

The interim final regulations promulgated under paragraph (1) shall take effect on the date of promulgation of the regulations.

**(b) Final regulations**

The Secretary shall promulgate final regulations to establish the process described in subsection (a)(1) of this section after the interim final regulations have been published and reasonable time has been provided for public comment.

**(c) Administrative review**

**(1) In general**

A person may bring a civil action challenging an authorized hazardous fuel reduction project in a Federal district court only if the person has challenged the authorized hazardous fuel reduction project by exhausting—

(A) the administrative review process established by the Secretary of Agriculture under this section; or

(B) the administrative hearings and appeals procedures established by the Department of the Interior.

**(2) Issues**

An issue may be considered in the judicial review of an action under section 6516 of this title only if the issue was raised in an administrative review process described in paragraph (1).

**(3) Exception**

**(A) In general**

An exception to the requirement of exhausting the administrative review process before seeking judicial review shall be available if a Federal court finds that the futility or inadequacy exception applies to a specific plaintiff or claim.

**(B) Information**

If an agency fails or is unable to make information timely available during the administrative review process, a court should evaluate whether the administrative review process was inadequate for claims or issues to which the information is material.

(Pub.L. 108–148, Title I, § 105, Dec. 3, 2003, 117 Stat. 1899.)

HISTORICAL AND STATUTORY NOTES

**References in Text**

This subchapter, referred to in subsecs. (a) and (c)(1), originally read "this title", meaning Title I of the Healthy Forests Restoration Act of 2003, Pub.L. 108–148, Title I, § 101 et seq., Dec. 3, 2003, 117 Stat. 1889, which enacted this subchapter.

## § 6516. Judicial review in United States district courts

**(a) Venue**

Notwithstanding section 1391 of Title 28, or other applicable law, an authorized hazardous fuels reduction project conducted under this subchapter shall be subject to judicial review only in the United States district court for a district in which the Federal land to be treated under the authorized hazardous fuels reduction project is located.

**(b) Expeditious completion of judicial review**

In the judicial review of an action challenging an authorized hazardous fuel reduction project under subsection (a) of this section, Congress encourages a court of competent jurisdiction to expedite, to the maximum extent practicable, the proceedings in the action with the goal of rendering a final determination on jurisdiction, and (if jurisdiction exists) a final determination on the merits, as soon as practicable after the date on which a complaint or appeal is filed to initiate the action.

**(c) Injunctions**

**(1) In general**

Subject to paragraph (2), the length of any preliminary injunctive relief and stays pending appeal covering an authorized hazardous fuel reduction project carried out under this subchapter shall not exceed 60 days.

**(2) Renewal**

**(A) In general**

A court of competent jurisdiction may issue 1 or more renewals of any preliminary injunction, or stay pending appeal, granted under paragraph (1).

**(B) Updates**

In each renewal of an injunction in an action, the parties to the action shall present the court with updated information on the status of the authorized hazardous fuel reduction project.

**(3) Balancing of short- and long-term effects**

As part of its weighing the equities while considering any request for an injunction that applies to an agency action under an authorized hazardous fuel reduction project, the court reviewing the project shall balance the impact to the ecosystem likely affected by the project of—

(A) The short- and long-term effects of undertaking the agency action; against

(B) The short- and long-term effects of not undertaking the agency action.

(Pub.L. 108–148, Title I, § 106, Dec. 3, 2003, 117 Stat. 1900.)

**HISTORICAL AND STATUTORY NOTES**

**References in Text**

This subchapter, referred to in text, originally read "this title", meaning Title I of the Healthy Forests Restoration Act of 2003, Pub.L. 108–148, Title I, § 101 et seq., Dec. 3, 2003, 117 Stat. 1889, which enacted this subchapter.

The National Environmental Policy Act of 1969, referred to in subsec. (a), is Pub.L. 91–190, Jan. 1, 1970, 83 Stat. 852, also known as NEPA, which enacted chapter 55 of Title 42, 42 U.S.C.A. § 4321et seq.

## § 6517. Effect of subchapter

**(a) Other authority**

Nothing in this subchapter affects, or otherwise biases, the use by the Secretary of other statutory or administrative authority (including categorical exclusions adopted to implement the National Environmental Policy Act of 1969 (42 U.S.C. 4321 et seq.)) to conduct a hazardous fuel reduction project on Federal land (including Federal land identified in section 6512(d) of this title) that is not conducted using the process authorized by section 6514 of this title.

**(b) National Forest System**

For projects and activities of the National Forest System other than authorized hazardous fuel reduction projects, nothing in this subchapter affects, or otherwise biases, the notice, comment, and appeal procedures for projects and activities of the National Forest System contained in part 215 of title 36, Code of Federal Regulations, or the consideration or disposition of any legal action brought with respect to the procedures.

(Pub.L. 108–148, Title I, § 107, Dec. 3, 2003, 117 Stat. 1900.)

**HISTORICAL AND STATUTORY NOTES**

**References in Text**

This subchapter, referred to in text, originally read "this title", meaning Title I of the Healthy Forests Restoration Act of 2003, Pub.L. 108–148, Title I, § 101 et seq., Dec. 3, 2003, 117 Stat. 1889, which enacted this subchapter.

## § 6518. Authorization of appropriations

There is authorized to be appropriated $760,000,000 for each fiscal year to carry out—

(1) activities authorized by this subchapter; and

(2) other hazardous fuel reduction activities of the Secretary, including making grants to States, local governments, Indian tribes, and other eligible recipients for activities authorized by law.

(Pub.L. 108–148, Title I, § 108, Dec. 3, 2003, 117 Stat. 1901.)

**HISTORICAL AND STATUTORY NOTES**

**References in Text**

This subchapter, referred to in par. (1), originally read "this title", meaning Title I of the Healthy Forests Restoration Act of 2003, Pub.L. 108–148, Title I, § 101 et seq., Dec. 3, 2003, 117 Stat. 1889, which enacted this subchapter.

# SUBCHAPTER II—BIOMASS

## § 6531. Biomass commercial utilization grant program

**(a) In general**

In addition to any other authority of the Secretary of Agriculture to make grants to a person that owns or operates a facility that uses biomass as a raw material to produce electric energy, sensible heat, transportation fuel, or substitutes for petroleum-based products, the Secretary may make grants to a person that owns or operates a facility that uses biomass for wood-based products or other commercial purposes to offset the costs incurred to purchase biomass.

**(b) Authorization of appropriations**

There is authorized to be appropriated to carry out this section $5,000,000 for each of fiscal years 2004 through 2008.

(Pub.L. 108–148, Title II, § 203, Dec. 3, 2003, 117 Stat. 1902.)

## SUBCHAPTER III—WATERSHED FORESTRY ASSISTANCE

## § 6541. Findings and purposes

**(a) Findings**

Congress finds that—

(1) there has been a dramatic shift in public attitudes and perceptions about forest management, particularly in the understanding and practice of sustainable forest management;

(2) it is commonly recognized that the proper stewardship of forest land is essential to sustaining and restoring the health of watersheds;

(3) forests can provide essential ecological services in filtering pollutants, buffering important rivers and estuaries, and minimizing flooding, which makes forest restoration worthy of special focus; and

(4) strengthened education, technical assistance, and financial assistance for nonindustrial private forest landowners and communities, relating to the protection of watershed health, is needed to realize the expectations of the general public.

**(b) Purposes**

The purposes of this subchapter are—

(1) to improve landowner and public understanding of the connection between forest management and watershed health;

(2) to encourage landowners to maintain tree cover on property and to use tree plantings and vegetative treatments as creative solutions to watershed problems associated with varying land uses;

(3) to enhance and complement forest management and buffer use for watersheds, with an emphasis on community watersheds;

(4) to establish new partnerships and collaborative watershed approaches to forest management, stewardship, and conservation;

(5) to provide technical and financial assistance to States to deliver a coordinated program that enhances State forestry best-management practices programs, and conserves and improves forested land and potentially forested land, through technical, financial, and educational assistance to qualifying individuals and entities; and

(6) to maximize the proper management and conservation of wetland forests and to assist in the restoration of those forests.

(Pub.L. 108–148, Title III, § 301, Dec. 3, 2003, 117 Stat. 1902.)

### HISTORICAL AND STATUTORY NOTES

**References in Text**

This subchapter, referred to in subsec. (b), originally read "this title", meaning Title III of the Healthy Forests Restoration Act of 2003, Pub.L. 108–148, Title III, § 301 et seq., Dec. 3, 2003, 117 Stat. 1902, which enacted this subchapter.

## § 6542. Tribal watershed forestry assistance

**(a) In general**

The Secretary of Agriculture (referred to in this section as the "Secretary"), acting through the Chief of the Forest Service, shall provide technical, financial, and related assistance to Indian tribes for the purpose of expanding tribal stewardship capacities and activities through tribal forestry best-management practices and other means at the tribal level to address watershed issues on land under the jurisdiction of or administered by the Indian tribes.

**(b) Technical assistance to protect water quality**

**(1) In general**

The Secretary, in cooperation with Indian tribes, shall develop a program to provide technical assistance to protect water quality, as described in paragraph (2).

**(2) Purpose of program**

The program under this subsection shall be designed—

(A) to build and strengthen watershed partnerships that focus on forested landscapes at the State, regional, tribal, and local levels;

(B) to provide tribal forestry best-management practices and water quality technical assistance directly to Indian tribes;

(C) to provide technical guidance to tribal land managers and policy makers for water quality protection through forest management;

(D) to complement tribal efforts to protect water quality and provide enhanced opportunities for consultation and cooperation among Federal agencies and tribal entities charged with responsibility for water and watershed management; and

(E) to provide enhanced forest resource data and support for improved implementation and monitoring of tribal forestry best-management practices.

**(c) Watershed forestry program**

**(1) In general**

The Secretary shall establish a watershed forestry program in cooperation with Indian tribes.

**(2) Programs and projects**

Funds or other support provided under the program shall be made available for tribal forestry best-management practices programs and watershed forestry projects.

**(3) Annual awards**

The Secretary shall annually make awards to Indian tribes to carry out this subsection.

**(4) Project elements and objectives**

A watershed forestry project shall accomplish critical forest stewardship, watershed protection, and restoration needs within land under the jurisdiction of or administered by an Indian tribe by demonstrating the value of trees and forests to watershed health and condition through—

(A) the use of trees as solutions to water quality problems;

(B) application of and dissemination of monitoring information on forestry best-management practices relating to watershed forestry;

(C) watershed–scale forest management activities and conservation planning;

(D) the restoration of wetland and stream-side forests and the establishment of riparian vegetative buffers; and

(E) tribal–based planning, involvement, and action through State, tribal, local, and nonprofit partnerships.

**(5) Prioritization**

An Indian tribe that participates in the program under this subsection shall prioritize watersheds in land under the jurisdiction of or administered by the Indian tribe to target watershed forestry projects funded under this subsection.

**(6) Watershed forester**

The Secretary may provide to Indian tribes under this section financial and technical assistance to establish a position of tribal forester to lead tribal programs and coordinate small watershed-level projects.

**(d) Distribution**

The Secretary shall devote—

(1) at least 75 percent of the funds made available for a fiscal year under subsection (e) of this section to the program under subsection (c) of this section; and

(2) the remainder of the funds to deliver technical assistance, education, and planning in the field to Indian tribes.

**(e) Authorization of appropriations**

There is authorized to be appropriated to carry out this section $2,500,000 for each of fiscal years 2004 through 2008.

(Pub.L. 108–148, Title III, § 303, Dec. 3, 2003, 117 Stat. 1905.)

## SUBCHAPTER IV—INSECT INFESTATIONS AND RELATED DISEASES

### § 6551. Findings and purpose

**(a) Findings**

Congress finds that—

(1) high levels of tree mortality resulting from insect infestation (including the interaction between insects and diseases) may result in—

(A) increased fire risk;

(B) loss of old trees and old growth;

(C) loss of threatened and endangered species;

(D) loss of species diversity;

(E) degraded watershed conditions;

(F) increased potential for damage from other agents of disturbance, including exotic, invasive species; and

(G) decreased timber values;

(2)(A) forest–damaging insects destroy hundreds of thousands of acres of trees each year;

(B) in the West, more than 21,000,000 acres are at high risk of forest-damaging insect infestation, and in the South, more than 57,000,000 acres are at risk across all land ownerships; and

(C) severe drought conditions in many areas of the South and West will increase the risk of forest-damaging insect infestations;

(3) the hemlock woolly adelgid is—

(A) destroying streamside forests throughout the mid-Atlantic and Appalachian regions;

(B) threatening water quality and sensitive aquatic species; and

(C) posing a potential threat to valuable commercial timber land in northern New England;

(4)(A) the emerald ash borer is a nonnative, invasive pest that has quickly become a major threat to hardwood forests because an emerald ash borer infestation is almost always fatal to affected trees; and

(B) the emerald ash borer pest threatens to destroy more than 692,000,000 ash trees in forests in Michigan and Ohio alone, and between 5 and 10 percent of urban street trees in the Upper Midwest;

**(5)(A)** epidemic populations of Southern pine beetles are ravaging forests in Alabama, Arkansas, Florida, Georgia, Kentucky, Mississippi, North Carolina, South Carolina, Tennessee, and Virginia; and

**(B)** in 2001, Florida and Kentucky experienced 146 percent and 111 percent increases, respectively, in Southern pine beetle populations;

**(6)** those epidemic outbreaks of Southern pine beetles have forced private landowners to harvest dead and dying trees, in rural areas and increasingly urbanized settings;

**(7)** according to the Forest Service, recent outbreaks of the red oak borer in Arkansas and Missouri have been unprecedented, with more than 1,000,000 acres infested at population levels never seen before;

**(8)** much of the damage from the red oak borer has taken place in national forests, and the Federal response has been inadequate to protect forest ecosystems and other ecological and economic resources;

**(9)(A)** previous silvicultural assessments, while useful and informative, have been limited in scale and scope of application; and

**(B)** there have not been sufficient resources available to adequately test a full array of individual and combined applied silvicultural assessments;

**(10)** only through the full funding, development, and assessment of potential applied silvicultural assessments over specific time frames across an array of environmental and climatic conditions can the most innovative and cost effective management applications be determined that will help reduce the susceptibility of forest ecosystems to attack by forest pests;

**(11)(A)** often, there are significant interactions between insects and diseases;

**(B)** many diseases (such as white pine blister rust, beech bark disease, and many other diseases) can weaken trees and forest stands and predispose trees and forest stands to insect attack; and

**(C)** certain diseases are spread using insects as vectors (including Dutch elm disease and pine pitch canker); and

**(12)** funding and implementation of an initiative to combat forest pest infestations and associated diseases should not come at the expense of supporting other programs and initiatives of the Secretary.

**(b) Purposes**

The purposes of this subchapter are—

**(1)** to require the Secretary to develop an accelerated basic and applied assessment program to combat infestations by forest-damaging insects and associated diseases;

**(2)** to enlist the assistance of colleges and universities (including forestry schools, land grant colleges and universities, and 1890 Institutions), State agencies, and private landowners to carry out the program; and

**(3)** to carry out applied silvicultural assessments.

(Pub.L. 108–148, Title IV, § 401, Dec. 3, 2003, 117 Stat. 1907.)

### HISTORICAL AND STATUTORY NOTES

**References in Text**

This subchapter, referred to in subsec. (b), originally read "this title", meaning Title IV of the Healthy Forests Restoration Act of 2003, Pub.L. 108–148, Title IV, § 401 et seq., Dec. 3, 2003, 117 Stat. 1907, which enacted this subchapter.

## § 6552. Definitions

In this subchapter:

**(1) Applied silvicultural assessment**

**(A) In general**

The term "applied silvicultural assessment" means any vegetative or other treatment carried out for information gathering and research purposes.

**(B) Inclusions**

The term "applied silvicultural assessment" includes timber harvesting, thinning, prescribed burning, pruning, and any combination of those activities.

**(2) 1890 Institution**

**(A) In general**

The term "1890 Institution" means a college or university that is eligible to receive funds under the Act of August 30, 1890 (7 U.S.C. 321 et seq.).

**(B) Inclusion**

The term "1890 Institution" includes Tuskegee University.

**(3) Forest-damaging insect**

The term "forest-damaging insect" means—

**(A)** a Southern pine beetle;
**(B)** a mountain pine beetle;
**(C)** a spruce bark beetle;
**(D)** a gypsy moth;
**(E)** a hemlock woolly adelgid;
**(F)** an emerald ash borer;
**(G)** a red oak borer;
**(H)** a white oak borer; and
**(I)** such other insects as may be identified by the Secretary.

(4) **Secretary**

The term "Secretary" means—

(A) the Secretary of Agriculture, acting through the Forest Service, with respect to National Forest System land; and

(B) the Secretary of the Interior, acting through appropriate offices of the United States Geological Survey, with respect to federally owned land administered by the Secretary of the Interior.

(Pub.L. 108–148, Title IV, § 402, Dec. 3, 2003, 117 Stat. 1908.)

### HISTORICAL AND STATUTORY NOTES

**References in Text**

This subchapter, referred to in text, originally read "this title", meaning Title IV of the Healthy Forests Restoration Act of 2003, Pub.L. 108 148, Title IV, § 401 et seq., Dec. 3, 2003, 117 Stat. 1907, which enacted this subchapter.

Act of August 30, 1890, referred to in par. (2)(A), is Act Aug. 30, 1890, c. 841, 26 Stat. 417, as amended, known as the Agricultural College Act of 1890 and also as the Second Morrill Act, which is classified principally to subchapter II of chapter 13 of Title 7, 7 U.S.C.A. § 321 et seq. For complete classification , see Short Title note set out under 7 U.S.C.A. § 321 and Tables.

## § 6553. Accelerated information gathering regarding forest-damaging insects

**(a) Information gathering**

The Secretary, acting through the Forest Service and United States Geological Survey, as appropriate, shall establish an accelerated program—

(1) to plan, conduct, and promote comprehensive and systematic information gathering on forest-damaging insects and associated diseases, including an evaluation of—

(A) infestation prevention and suppression methods;

(B) effects of infestations and associated disease interactions on forest ecosystems;

(C) restoration of forest ecosystem efforts;

(D) utilization options regarding infested trees; and

(E) models to predict the occurrence, distribution, and impact of outbreaks of forest-damaging insects and associated diseases;

(2) to assist land managers in the development of treatments and strategies to improve forest health and reduce the susceptibility of forest ecosystems to severe infestations of forest-damaging insects and associated diseases on Federal land and State and private land; and

(3) to disseminate the results of the information gathering, treatments, and strategies.

**(b) Cooperation and assistance**

The Secretary shall—

(1) establish and carry out the program in cooperation with—

(A) scientists from colleges and universities (including forestry schools, land grant colleges and universities, and 1890 Institutions);

(B) Federal, State, and local agencies; and

(C) private and industrial landowners; and

(2) designate such colleges and universities to assist in carrying out the program.

(Pub.L. 108–148, Title IV, § 403, Dec. 3, 2003, 117 Stat. 1909.)

## § 6554. Applied silvicultural assessments

**(a) Assessment efforts**

For information gathering and research purposes, the Secretary may conduct applied silvicultural assessments on Federal land that the Secretary determines is at risk of infestation by, or is infested with, forest-damaging insects.

**(b) Limitations**

**(1) Exclusion of certain areas**

Subsection (a) of this section does not apply to—

(A) a component of the National Wilderness Preservation System;

(B) any Federal land on which, by Act of Congress or Presidential proclamation, the removal of vegetation is restricted or prohibited;

(C) a congressionally-designated wilderness study area; or

(D) an area in which activities under subsection (a) of this section would be inconsistent with the applicable land and resource management plan.

**(2) Certain treatment prohibited**

Nothing in subsection (a) of this section authorizes the application of insecticides in municipal watersheds or associated riparian areas.

**(3) Peer review**

**(A) In general**

Before being carried out, each applied silvicultural assessment under this subchapter shall be peer reviewed by scientific experts selected by the Secretary, which shall include non-Federal experts.

**(B) Existing peer review processes**

The Secretary may use existing peer review processes to the extent the processes comply with subparagraph (A).

**(c) Public notice and comment**

**(1) Public notice**

The Secretary shall provide notice of each applied silvicultural assessment proposed to be carried out under this section.

**(2) Public comment**

The Secretary shall provide an opportunity for public comment before carrying out an applied silviculture assessment under this section.

**(d) Categorical exclusion**

**(1) In general**

Applied silvicultural assessment and research treatments carried out under this section on not more than 1,000 acres for an assessment or treatment may be categorically excluded from documentation in an environmental impact statement and environmental assessment under the National Environmental Policy Act of 1969 (42 U.S.C. 4321 et seq.).

**(2) Administration**

Applied silvicultural assessments and research treatments categorically excluded under paragraph (1)—

**(A)** shall not be carried out in an area that is adjacent to another area that is categorically excluded under paragraph (1) that is being treated with similar methods; and

**(B)** shall be subject to the extraordinary circumstances procedures established by the Secretary pursuant to section 1508.4 of title 40, Code of Federal Regulations.

**(3) Maximum categorical exclusion**

The total number of acres categorically excluded under paragraph (1) shall not exceed 250,000 acres.

**(4) No additional findings required**

In accordance with paragraph (1), the Secretary shall not be required to make any findings as to whether an applied silvicultural assessment project, either individually or cumulatively, has a significant effect on the environment.

(Pub.L. 108–148, Title IV, § 404, Dec. 3, 2003, 117 Stat. 1910.)

### HISTORICAL AND STATUTORY NOTES

**References in Text**

This subchapter, referred to in subsec. (b)(3)(A), originally read "this title", meaning Title IV of the Healthy Forests Restoration Act of 2003, Pub.L. 108–148, Title IV, § 401 et seq., Dec. 3, 2003, 117 Stat. 1907, which enacted this subchapter.

The National Environmental Policy Act of 1969, referred to in subsec. (d)(1), is Pub.L. 91–190, Jan. 1, 1970, 83 Stat. 852, also known as NEPA, which enacted chapter 55 of Title 42, 42 U.S.C.A. § 4321 et seq.

## § 6555. Relation to other laws

The authority provided to each Secretary under this subchapter is supplemental to, and not in lieu of, any authority provided to the Secretaries under any other law.

(Pub.L. 108–148, Title IV, § 405, Dec. 3, 2003, 117 Stat. 1911.)

### HISTORICAL AND STATUTORY NOTES

**References in Text**

This subchapter, referred to in text, originally read "this title", meaning Title IV of the Healthy Forests Restoration Act of 2003, Pub.L. 108–148, Title IV, § 401 et seq., Dec. 3, 2003, 117 Stat. 1907, which enacted this subchapter.

## § 6556. Authorization of appropriations

There are authorized to be appropriated such sums as are necessary to carry out this subchapter for each of fiscal years 2004 through 2008.

(Pub.L. 108–148, Title IV, § 406, Dec. 3, 2003, 117 Stat. 1911.)

### HISTORICAL AND STATUTORY NOTES

**References in Text**

This subchapter, referred to in text, originally read "this title", meaning Title IV of the Healthy Forests Restoration Act of 2003, Pub.L. 108–148, Title IV, § 401 et seq., Dec. 3, 2003, 117 Stat. 1907, which enacted this subchapter.

# SUBCHAPTER V—HEALTHY FORESTS RESERVE PROGRAM

## § 6571. Establishment of healthy forests reserve program

**(a) Establishment**

The Secretary of Agriculture shall establish the healthy forests reserve program for the purpose of restoring and enhancing forest ecosystems—

(1) to promote the recovery of threatened and endangered species;

(2) to improve biodiversity; and

(3) to enhance carbon sequestration.

**(b) Coordination**

The Secretary of Agriculture shall carry out the healthy forests reserve program in coordination with the Secretary of the Interior and the Secretary of Commerce.

(Pub.L. 108–148, Title V, § 501, Dec. 3, 2003, 117 Stat. 1911.)

## § 6572. Eligibility and enrollment of lands in program

**(a) In general**

The Secretary of Agriculture, in coordination with the Secretary of the Interior and the Secretary of Commerce, shall describe and define forest ecosystems that are eligible for enrollment in the healthy forests reserve program.

**(b) Eligibility**

To be eligible for enrollment in the healthy forests reserve program, land shall be—

(1) private land the enrollment of which will restore, enhance, or otherwise measurably increase the likelihood of recovery of a species listed as endangered or threatened under section 1533 of this title; and

(2) private land the enrollment of which will restore, enhance, or otherwise measurably improve the well-being of species that—

(A) are not listed as endangered or threatened under section 1533 of this title; but

(B) are candidates for such listing, State-listed species, or special concern species.

**(c) Other considerations**

In enrolling land that satisfies the criteria under subsection (b) of this section, the Secretary of Agriculture shall give additional consideration to land the enrollment of which will—

(1) improve biological diversity; and

(2) increase carbon sequestration.

**(d) Enrollment by willing owners**

The Secretary of Agriculture shall enroll land in the healthy forests reserve program only with the consent of the owner of the land.

**(e) Maximum enrollment**

The total number of acres enrolled in the healthy forests reserve program shall not exceed 2,000,000 acres.

**(f) Methods of enrollment**

**(1) In general**

Land may be enrolled in the healthy forests reserve program in accordance with—

(A) a 10–year cost-share agreement;

(B) a 30–year easement; or

(C) an easement of not more than 99 years.

**(2) Proportion**

The extent to which each enrollment method is used shall be based on the approximate proportion of owner interest expressed in that method in comparison to the other methods.

**(g) Enrollment priority**

**(1) Species**

The Secretary of Agriculture shall give priority to the enrollment of land that provides the greatest conservation benefit to—

(A) primarily, species listed as endangered or threatened under 1533 of this title; and

(B) secondarily, species that—

(i) are not listed as endangered or threatened under section 1533 of this title; but

(ii) are candidates for such listing, State-listed species, or special concern species.

**(2) Cost-effectiveness**

The Secretary of Agriculture shall also consider the cost-effectiveness of each agreement or easement, and associated restoration plans, so as to maximize the environmental benefits per dollar expended.

(Pub.L. 108–148, Title V, § 502, Dec. 3, 2003, 117 Stat. 1911.)

## § 6573. Restoration plans

**(a) In general**

Land enrolled in the healthy forests reserve program shall be subject to a restoration plan, to be developed jointly by the landowner and the Secretary of Agriculture, in coordination with the Secretary of Interior.

**(b) Practices**

The restoration plan shall require such restoration practices as are necessary to restore and enhance habitat for—

(1) species listed as endangered or threatened under section 1533 of this title; and

(2) animal or plant species before the species reach threatened or endangered status, such as candidate, State-listed species, and special concern species.

(Pub.L. 108–148, Title V, § 503, Dec. 3, 2003, 117 Stat. 1912.)

## § 6574. Financial assistance

**(a) Easements of not more than 99 years**

In the case of land enrolled in the healthy forests reserve program using an easement of not more than 99 years described in section 6572(f)(1)(C) of this title, the Secretary of Agriculture shall pay the owner of the land an amount equal to not less than 75 percent, nor more than 100 percent, of (as determined by the Secretary)—

(1) the fair market value of the enrolled land during the period the land is subject to the easement, less the fair market value of the land encumbered by the easement; and

(2) the actual costs of the approved conservation practices or the average cost of approved practices carried out on the land during the period in which the land is subject to the easement.

**(b) Thirty-year easement**

In the case of land enrolled in the healthy forests reserve program using a 30–year easement, the Secretary of Agriculture shall pay the owner of the land an amount equal to not more than (as determined by the Secretary)—

(1) 75 percent of the fair market value of the land, less the fair market value of the land encumbered by the easement; and

(2) 75 percent of the actual costs of the approved conservation practices or 75 percent of the average cost of approved practices.

**(c) Ten-year agreement**

In the case of land enrolled in the healthy forests reserve program using a 10–year cost-share agreement, the Secretary of Agriculture shall pay the owner of the land an amount equal to not more than (as determined by the Secretary)—

(1) fifty percent of the actual costs of the approved conservation practices; or

(2) fifty percent of the average cost of approved practices.

**(d) Acceptance of contributions**

The Secretary of Agriculture may accept and use contributions of non-Federal funds to make payments under this section.

(Pub.L. 108–148, Title V, § 504, Dec. 3, 2003, 117 Stat. 1913.)

## § 6575. Technical assistance

**(a) In general**

The Secretary of Agriculture shall provide landowners with technical assistance to assist the owners in complying with the terms of plans (as included in agreements or easements) under the healthy forests reserve program.

**(b) Technical service providers**

The Secretary of Agriculture may request the services of, and enter into cooperative agreements with, individuals or entities certified as technical service providers under section 3842 of this title, to assist the Secretary in providing technical assistance necessary to develop and implement the healthy forests reserve program.

(Pub.L. 108–148, Title V, § 505, Dec. 3, 2003, 117 Stat. 1913.)

## § 6576. Protections and measures

**(a) Protections**

In the case of a landowner that enrolls land in the program and whose conservation activities result in a net conservation benefit for listed, candidate, or other species, the Secretary of Agriculture shall make available to the landowner safe harbor or similar assurances and protection under—

(1) section 1536(b)(4) of this title; or

(2) section 1539(a)(1) of this title.

**(b) Measures**

If protection under subsection (a) of this section requires the taking of measures that are in addition to the measures covered by the applicable restoration plan agreed to under section 6573 of this title, the cost of the additional measures, as well as the cost of any permit, shall be considered part of the restoration plan for purposes of financial assistance under section 6504 of this title.

(Pub.L. 108–148, Title V, § 506, Dec. 3, 2003, 117 Stat. 1914.)

## § 6577. Involvement by other agencies and organizations

In carrying out this subchapter, the Secretary of Agriculture may consult with—

(1) nonindustrial private forest landowners;

(2) other Federal agencies;

(3) State fish and wildlife agencies;

(4) State forestry agencies;

(5) State environmental quality agencies;

(6) other State conservation agencies; and

(7) nonprofit conservation organizations.

(Pub.L. 108–148, Title V, § 507, Dec. 3, 2003, 117 Stat. 1914.)

### HISTORICAL AND STATUTORY NOTES

**References in Text**

This subchapter, referred to in text, originally read "this title", meaning Title V of the Healthy Forests Restoration Act of 2003, Pub.L. 108–148, Title V, § 501 et seq., Dec. 3, 2003, 117 Stat. 1911, which enacted this subchapter.

## § 6578. Authorization of appropriations

There are authorized to be appropriated to carry out this subchapter—

(1) $25,000,000 for fiscal year 2004; and

(2) such sums as are necessary for each of fiscal years 2005 through 2008.

(Pub.L. 108–148, Title V, § 508, Dec. 3, 2003, 117 Stat. 1914.)

### HISTORICAL AND STATUTORY NOTES

**References in Text**

This subchapter, referred to in text, originally read "this title", meaning Title V of the Healthy Forests Restoration Act of 2003, Pub.L. 108–148, Title V, § 501 et seq., Dec. 3, 2003, 117 Stat. 1911, which enacted this subchapter.

# SUBCHAPTER VI—MISCELLANEOUS

## § 6591. Forest stands inventory and monitoring program to improve detection of and response to environmental threats

**(a) In general**

The Secretary of Agriculture shall carry out a comprehensive program to inventory, monitor, characterize, assess, and identify forest stands (with emphasis on hardwood forest stands) and potential forest stands—

(1) in units of the National Forest System (other than those units created from the public domain); and

(2) on private forest land, with the consent of the owner of the land.

**(b) Issues to be addressed**

In carrying out the program, the Secretary shall address issues including—

(1) early detection, identification, and assessment of environmental threats (including insect, disease, invasive species, fire, and weather-related risks and other episodic events);

(2) loss or degradation of forests;

(3) degradation of the quality forest stands caused by inadequate forest regeneration practices;

(4) quantification of carbon uptake rates; and

(5) management practices that focus on preventing further forest degradation.

**(c) Early warning system**

In carrying out the program, the Secretary shall develop a comprehensive early warning system for potential catastrophic environmental threats to forests to increase the likelihood that forest managers will be able to—

(1) isolate and treat a threat before the threat gets out of control; and

(2) prevent epidemics, such as the American chestnut blight in the first half of the twentieth century, that could be environmentally and economically devastating to forests.

**(d) Authorization of appropriations**

There is authorized to be appropriated to carry out this section $5,000,000 for each of fiscal years 2004 through 2008.

(Pub.L. 108–148, Title VI, § 601, Dec. 3, 2003, 117 Stat. 1914.)

*

# TITLE 26
# INTERNAL REVENUE CODE
## ENVIRONMENTAL TAXES

(26 U.S.C.A. §§ 4611 to 4682)

## CHAPTER 38—ENVIRONMENTAL TAXES



### HISTORICAL AND STATUTORY NOTES

**Prior Provisions**

A prior chapter 38, consisting of sections 4521–4603 and relating to import taxes, was repealed by Pub.L. 87–456, Title III, § 302(d), May 24, 1962, 76 Stat.77, and Pub.L. 94–455, Title XIX, § 1904(a)(15), Oct. 4, 1976, 90 Stat. 1814.

Repeal of sections 4521, 4531, 4532, 4541, 4542, 4551 to 4553, 4561, 4562, 4571, 4572, 4581, 4582, 4601 to 4603 effective with respect to articles entered, or withdrawn from warehouse, for consumption on or after Aug. 31, 1963, see § 501(a) of Pub.L. 87–456, set out as a note preceding § 1202 of Title 19, Customs Duties.

Repeal of sections 4591 to 4597 effective the first day of the first month which begins more than 90 days after Oct. 4, 1976, see § 1904(d) of Pub.L. 94–455, set out as a note under § 4041 of this title.

Section 4521, Act Aug. 16, 1954, c. 736, 68A Stat. 539, imposed a tax on petroleum products imported into the United States. See Revised Tariff Schedules set out in § 1202 of Title 19, Customs Duties.

Section 4531, Act Aug. 16, 1954, c. 736, 68A Stat. 540, imposed a tax on coal imported into the United States.

Section 4532, Act Aug. 16, 1954, c. 736, 68A Stat. 540, provided a tax exemption on coal where exports exceeded imports.

Section 4541, Act Aug. 16, 1954, c. 736, 68A Stat. 541, imposed a tax on copper imported into the United States.

Section 4542, Act Aug. 16, 1954, c. 736, 68A Stat. 541, provided for exemptions to tax imposed under section 4541.

Section 4551, Act Aug. 16, 1954, c. 736, 68A Stat. 542, imposed a tax on lumber imported into the United States.

Section 4552, Act Aug. 16, 1954, c. 736, 68A Stat. 542, provided definitions relating to section 4551.

Section 4553, Act Aug. 16, 1954, c. 736, 68A Stat. 542, provided for exemptions to tax imposed under section 4551.

Section 4561, Act Aug. 16, 1954, c. 736, 68A Stat. 543, imposed a tax on animal oils imported into the United States.

Section 4562, Act Aug. 16, 1954, c. 736, 68A Stat. 543, provided for tax exemptions for United States vessels.

Section 4571, Act Aug. 16, 1954, c. 736, 68A Stat. 543, 544, imposed a tax on seeds and seed oil imported into the United States.

Section 4572, Act Aug. 16, 1954, c. 736, 68A Stat. 543, 544, provided for tax exemptions for certain uses of rapeseed oil.

Section 4581, Act Aug. 16, 1954, c. 736, 68A Stat. 544, imposed a tax on imports of any article, merchandise, or combination (except oils specified in section 4511), 10 percent or more of the quantity by weight of which consists of, or is derived directly or indirectly from, one or more of the products specified in sections 4561 and 4571, or of the oils, fatty acids, or salts specified in section 4511.

Section 4582, Act Aug. 16, 1954, c. 736, 68A Stat. 544, provided for exemptions to tax imposed under section 4581.

Section 4591, Act Aug. 16, 1954, c. 736, 68A Stat. 545, related to the imposition of a tax on all oleomargarine imported from foreign countries.

Section 4592, Act Aug. 16, 1954, c. 736, 68A Stat. 545, related to definitions of oleomargarine, manufacturer, wholesale dealer, and retail sales.

Section 4593, Act Aug. 16, 1954, c. 736, 68A Stat. 546, related to exemptions to the tax imposed by former § 4591.

Section 4594, Act Aug. 16, 1954, c. 736, 68A Stat. 546, related to packing requirements for manufacturers of oleomargarine.

Section 4595, Act Aug. 16, 1954, c. 736, 68A Stat. 546, related to wholesale and retail selling requirements for oleomargarine.

Section 4596, Act Aug. 16, 1954, c. 736, 68A Stat. 547, related to the filing of bonds by manufacturers of oleomargarine.

Section 4597, Act Aug. 16, 1954, c. 736, 68A Stat. 547, related to books and returns of wholesale dealers and manufacturers.

Section 4601, Acts Aug. 16, 1954, c. 736, 68A Stat. 548; Sept. 2, 1958, Pub.L. 85–859, Title I, § 119(b)(4), 72 Stat. 1286, related to applicability of certain tariff provisions.

Section 4602, Act Aug. 16, 1954, c. 736, 68A Stat. 548, related to contravention of trade agreements by certain taxes.

Section 4603, Act Aug. 16, 1954, c. 736, 68A Stat. 548, provided for cross references.

SUBCHAPTER A—TAX ON PETROLEUM



## § 4611. Imposition of tax

**(a) General Rule.**—There is hereby imposed a tax at the rate specified in subsection (c) on—

(1) crude oil received at a United States refinery, and

(2) petroleum products entered into the United States for consumption, use, or warehousing.

**(b) Tax on certain uses and exportation.—**

**(1) In general.**—If—

(A) any domestic crude oil is used in or exported from the United States, and

(B) before such use or exportation, no tax was imposed on such crude oil under subsection (a),

then a tax at the rate specified in subsection (c) is hereby imposed on such crude oil.

**(2) Exception for use on premises where produced.**—Paragraph (1) shall not apply to any use of crude oil for extracting oil or natural gas on the premises where such crude oil was produced.

**(c) Rate of tax.—**

**(1) In general.**—The rate of the taxes imposed by this section is the sum of—

(A) the Hazardous Substance Superfund financing rate, and

(B) the Oil Spill Liability Trust Fund financing rate.—

**(2) Rates.**—For purposes of paragraph (1)—

(A) the Hazardous Substance Superfund financing rate is 9.7 cents a barrel, and

(B) the Oil Spill Liability Trust Fund financing rate is 5 cents a barrel.

**(d) Persons liable for tax.—**

**(1) Crude oil received at refinery.**—The tax imposed by subsection (a)(1) shall be paid by the operator of the United States refinery.

**(2) Imported petroleum product.**—The tax imposed by subsection (a)(2) shall be paid by the person entering the product for consumption, use, or warehousing.

**(3) Tax on certain uses or exports.**—The tax imposed by subsection (b) shall be paid by the person using or exporting the crude oil, as the case may be.

**(e) Application of Hazardous Substance Superfund financing rate.—**

**(1) In general.**—Except as provided in paragraphs (2) and (3), the Hazardous Substance Superfund financing rate under this section shall apply after December 31, 1986, and before January 1, 1996.

**(2) No tax if unobligated balance in Fund exceeds $3,500,000,000.**—If on December 31, 1993, or December 31, 1994—

(A) the unobligated balance in the Hazardous Substance Superfund exceeds $3,500,000,000, and

(B) the Secretary, after consultation with the Administrator of the Environmental Protection Agency, determines that the unobligated balance in the Hazardous Substance Superfund will exceed $3,500,000,000 on December 31 of 1994 or 1995, respectively, if no tax is imposed under section 59A, this section, and sections 4661 and 4671,

then no tax shall be imposed under this section (to the extent attributable to the Hazardous Substance Superfund financing rate) during 1994 or 1995, as the case may be.

**(3) No tax if amounts collected exceed $11,970,000,000.—**

**(A) Estimates by Secretary.**—The Secretary as of the close of each calendar quarter (and at such other times as the Secretary determines appropriate) shall make an estimate of the amount of taxes which will be collected under section 59A, this section (to the extent attributable to the Hazardous Substance Superfund financing rate), and sections 4661 and 4671 and credited to the Hazardous Substance Superfund during the period beginning January 1, 1987, and ending December 31, 1995.

**(B) Termination if $11,970,000,000 credited before January 1, 1996.**—If the Secretary estimates under subparagraph (A) that more than $11,970,000,000 will be credited to the Fund before January 1, 1996, the Hazardous Substance Superfund financing rate under this section shall not apply after the date on which (as estimated by the Secretary) $11,970,000,000 will be so credited to the Fund.

**(f) Application of Oil Spill Liability Trust Fund financing rate.—**

**(1) In general.**—Except as provided in paragraph (2), the Oil Spill Liability Trust Fund financing rate under subsection (c) shall apply after December 31, 1989, and before January 1, 1995.

**(2) No tax if unobligated balance in Fund exceeds $1,000,000,000.**—The Oil Spill Liability Trust Fund financing rate shall not apply during any calendar quarter if the Secretary estimates that as of the close of the preceding calendar quarter the unobligated balance in the Oil Spill Liability Trust Fund exceeds $1,000,000,000.

(Added Pub.L. 96–510, Title II, § 211(a), Dec. 11, 1980, 94 Stat. 2797, and amended Pub.L. 99–499, Title V, §§ 511(a), 512(a), (b), Oct. 17, 1986, 100 Stat. 1760, 1761; Pub.L. 99–509, Title VIII, § 8032(a), (c)(1), (2), Oct. 21, 1986, 100 Stat. 1957, 1958; Pub.L. 100–647, Title VI, § 6108, Nov. 10, 1988, 102 Stat. 3712; Pub.L. 101–221, § 8(a), Dec. 12, 1989, 103 Stat. 1891; Pub.L. 101–239, Title VII, § 7505(a), (b), Dec. 19, 1989, 103 Stat. 2363; Pub.L. 101–508, Title XI, § 11231(a)(1)(B), (2), (b), Nov. 5, 1990, 104 Stat. 1388–445.)

### HISTORICAL AND STATUTORY NOTES

**Codifications**

Amendments by Pub.L. 99–509, Title VIII, § 8031(a), (b), and (d)(1), Oct. 21, 1986, 100 Stat. 1955, to subsecs. (a) to (e) were not executed to text pursuant to Pub.L. 99–509, Title VIII, § 8031(e)(2) which provided that the amendments made by section 8031 shall not take effect if the Superfund Amendments and Reauthorization Act of 1986 is enacted. The Superfund Amendments and Reauthorization Act of 1986 was enacted as Pub.L. 99–499, approved Oct. 17, 1986.

**Effective and Applicability Provisions**

1989 Acts

Section 8(b) of Pub.L. 101–221 provided that: "The amendment made by subsection (a) [amending subsec. (c)(2)(A) of this section] shall take effect on the date of enactment of this Act [Dec. 12, 1989]."

1986 Acts

Pub.L. 101–239, Title VII, § 7505(d)(1), Dec. 19, 1989, 103 Stat. 2363, provided that: "For purposes of sections 8032(d) [set out as an Effective Date of 1986 Amendment note under this section] and 8033(c) [enacting provisions set out as notes under section 9509 of this title] of the Omnibus Budget Reconciliation Act of 1986, the commencement date is January 1, 1990."

Section 8032(d) of Pub.L. 99–509 provided that:

"**(1) In general.**—Except as provided in paragraph (2), the amendments made by this section [amending this section and sections 4612, 4661, 4671, and 9507 of this title] shall take effect on the commencement date (as defined in section 4611(f)(2) of the Internal Revenue Code of 1954, as added by this section). [Subsec. (f)(2) of this section].

"**(2) Coordination with superfund reauthorization.**—The amendments made by this section shall take effect only if the Superfund Amendments and Reauthorization Act of 1986 is enacted. [Pub.L. 99–499, Oct. 17, 1986, 100 Stat. 1613]."

Section 511(c) of Pub.L. 99–499 provided that: "The amendments made by this section [amending subsec. (d) of this section and repealing section 9653 of Title 42, The Public Health and Welfare] shall take effect on January 1, 1987."

Section 512(d) of Pub.L. 99–499 provided that: "The amendments made by this section [enacting a new subsec. (c) and amending subsecs. (a)–(e) of this section and section 4612(d) of this title] shall take effect on January 1, 1987."

1980 Acts

Section 211(c) of Pub.L. 96–510 provided that: "The amendments made by this section [enacting subchapters A and B of this chapter] shall take effect on April 1, 1981."

**Short Title**

1980 Acts

For short title of Title II of Pub.L. 96–510 as the "Hazardous Substance Response Revenue Act of 1980", see note set out under section 1 of this title.

## § 4612. Definitions and special rules

**(a) Definitions.**—For purposes of this subchapter—

**(1) Crude oil.**—The term "crude oil" includes crude oil condensates and natural gasoline.

**(2) Domestic crude oil.**—The term "domestic crude oil" means any crude oil produced from a well located in the United States.

**(3) Petroleum product.**—The term "petroleum product" includes crude oil.

**(4) United States.**—

**(A) In general.**—The term "United States" means the 50 States, the District of Columbia, the Commonwealth of Puerto Rico, any possession of the United States, the Commonwealth of the Northern Mariana Islands, and the Trust Territory of the Pacific Islands.

**(B) United States includes continental shelf areas.**—The principles of section 638 shall apply for purposes of the term "United States".

**(C) United States includes foreign trade zones.**—The term "United States" includes any foreign trade zone of the United States.

**(5) United States refinery.**—The term "United States refinery" means any facility in the United States at which crude oil is refined.

**(6) Refineries which produce natural gasoline.**—In the case of any United States refinery which produces natural gasoline from natural gas, the gasoline so produced shall be treated as received at such refinery at the time so produced.

**(7) Premises.**—The term "premises" has the same meaning as when used for purposes of determining gross income from the property under section 613.

**(8) Barrel.**—The term "barrel" means 42 United States gallons.

**(9) Fractional part of barrel.**—In the case of a fraction of a barrel, the tax imposed by section 4611 shall be the same fraction of the amount of such tax imposed on a whole barrel.

**(b) Only 1 tax imposed with respect to any product.**—No tax shall be imposed by section 4611 with respect to any petroleum product if the person who would be liable for such tax establishes that a prior tax imposed by such section has been imposed with respect to such product.

**(c) Credit where crude oil returned to pipeline.**—Under regulations prescribed by the Secretary, if an operator of a United States refinery—

(1) removes crude oil from a pipeline, and

(2) returns a portion of such crude oil into a stream of other crude oil in the same pipeline,

there shall be allowed as a credit against the tax imposed by section 4611 to such operator an amount equal to the product of the rate of tax imposed by section 4611 on the crude oil so removed by such operator and the number of barrels of crude oil returned by such operator to such pipeline. Any crude oil so returned shall be treated for purposes of this subchapter as crude oil on which no tax has been imposed by section 4611.

**(d) Credit against portion of tax attributable to oil spill rate.**—There shall be allowed as a credit against so much of the tax imposed by section 4611 as is attributable to the Oil Spill Liability Trust Fund financing rate for any period an amount equal to the excess of—

(1) the sum of—

(A) the aggregate amounts paid by the taxpayer before January 1, 1987, into the Deepwater Port Liability Trust Fund and the Offshore Oil Pollution Compensation Fund, and

(B) the interest accrued on such amounts before such date, over

(2) the amount of such payments taken into account under this subsection for all prior periods.

The preceding sentence shall also apply to amounts paid by the taxpayer into the Trans–Alaska Pipeline Liability Fund to the extent of amounts transferred from such Fund into the Oil Spill Liability Trust Fund. For purposes of this subsection, all taxpayers which would be members of the same affiliated group (as defined in section 1504(a)) if section 1504(a)(2) were applied by substituting "100 percent" for "80 percent" shall be treated as 1 taxpayer.

**(e) Income tax credit for unused payments into Trans–Alaska Pipeline Liability Fund.**—

**(1) In general.**—For purposes of section 38, the current year business credit shall include the credit determined under this subsection.

**(2) Determination of credit.**—

**(A) In general.**—The credit determined under this subsection for any taxable year is an amount equal to the aggregate credit which would be allowed to the taxpayer under subsection (d) for amounts paid into the Trans–Alaska Pipeline Liability Fund had the Oil Spill Liability Trust Fund financing rate not ceased to apply.

**(B) Limitation.**—

**(i) In general.**—The amount of the credit determined under this subsection for any taxable year with respect to any taxpayer shall not exceed the excess of—

**(I)** the amount determined under clause (ii), over

**(II)** the aggregate amount of the credit determined under this subsection for prior taxable years with respect to such taxpayer.

**(ii) Overall limitation.**—The amount determined under this clause with respect to any taxpayer is the excess of—

**(I)** the aggregate amount of credit which would have been allowed under subsection (d) to the taxpayer for periods before the termination date specified in section 4611(f)(1), if amounts in the Trans–Alaska Pipeline Liability Fund which are actually transferred into the Oil Spill Liability Fund were transferred on January 1, 1990, and the Oil Spill Liability Trust Fund financing rate did not terminate before such termination date, over

**(II)** the aggregate amount of the credit allowed under subsection (d) to the taxpayer.

**(3) Cost of income tax credit borne by Trust Fund.**—

**(A) In general.**—The Secretary shall from time to time transfer from the Oil Spill Liability Trust Fund to the general fund of the Treasury amounts equal to the credits allowed by reason of this subsection.

**(B) Trust Fund balance may not be reduced below $1,000,000,000.**—Transfers may be made under subparagraph (A) only to the extent that the unobligated balance of the Oil Spill Liability Trust Fund exceeds $1,000,000,000. If any transfer is not made by reason of the preceding sentence, such transfer shall be made as soon as permitted under such sentence.

**(4) No carryback.**—No portion of the unused business credit for any taxable year which is attributable to the credit determined under this subsection may be carried to a taxable year beginning on or before the date of the enactment of this paragraph.

**(f) Disposition of revenues from Puerto Rico and the Virgin Islands.**—The provisions of subsections (a)(3) and (b)(3) of section 7652 shall not apply to any tax imposed by section 4611.

(Added Pub.L. 96–510, Title II, § 211(a), Dec. 11, 1980, 94 Stat. 2798, and amended Pub.L. 99–499, Title V, § 512(c), Oct. 17, 1986, 100 Stat. 1761; Pub.L. 99–509, Title VIII, § 8032(b), Oct. 21, 1986, 100 Stat. 1957; Pub.L. 101–239, Title VII, § 7505(c), Dec. 19, 1989, 103 Stat. 2363; Pub.L. 101–380, Title IX, § 9002, Aug. 18, 1990, 104 Stat. 574; Pub.L. 102–486, Title XIX, § 1922(a), Oct. 24, 1992, 106 Stat. 3028.)

## HISTORICAL AND STATUTORY NOTES

**References in Text**

The date of the enactment of this paragraph, referred to in subsec. (e)(4), is the date of the enactment of Pub.L. 102–486, which enacted subsec. (e) and which was approved Oct. 24, 1992.

**Codifications**

Amendments by Pub.L. 99–509, Title VIII, § 8031(c), Oct. 21, 1986, 100 Stat. 1955, to subsecs. (c) and (d) were not executed to text pursuant to Pub.L. 99–509, Title VIII, § 8031(e)(2) which provided that the amendments made by section 8031 shall not take effect if the Superfund Amendments and Reauthorization Act of 1986 is enacted. The Superfund Amendments and Reauthorization Act of 1986 was enacted as Pub.L. 99–499, approved Oct. 17, 1986.

**Effective and Applicability Provisions**

1992 Acts

Section 1922(b) of Pub.L. 102–486 provided that: "The amendments made by this section [enacting subsec. (e) and redesigning former subsec. (e) as (f)] shall apply to taxable years beginning after the date of the enactment of this Act [Oct. 24, 1992]."

1986 Acts

Amendment by Pub.L. 99–509, effective on the commencement date as defined in section 4611(f)(2), set out as a note under section 4611 of this title, and effective only if the Superfund Amendments and Reauthorization Act of 1980 is enacted (The Superfund Amendments and Reauthorization Act of 1986 was enacted as Pub.L. 99–499, Oct. 17, 1986, 100 Stat. 1613), see section 8032(d) of Pub.L. 99–509, set out as a note under section 4611 of this title.

Amendment by Pub.L. 99–499 effective Jan. 1, 1987, see section 512(d) of Pub.L. 99–499, set out as a note under section 4611 of this title.

1980 Acts

Section effective April 1, 1981, see section 211(c) of Pub.L. 96–510, set out as a note under section 4611 of this title.

## SUBCHAPTER B—TAX ON CERTAIN CHEMICALS



## § 4661. Imposition of tax

**(a) General rule.**—There is hereby imposed a tax on any taxable chemical sold by the manufacturer, producer, or importer thereof.

**(b) Amount of tax.**—The amount of the tax imposed by subsection (a) shall be determined in accordance with the following table:

| In the case of: | The tax is the following amount per ton |
|---|---|
| Acetylene | $4.87 |
| Benzene | 4.87 |
| Butane | 4.87 |
| Butylene | 4.87 |
| Butadiene | 4.87 |
| Ethylene | 4.87 |
| Methane | 3.44 |
| Naphthalene | 4.87 |
| Propylene | 4.87 |
| Toluene | 4.87 |
| Xylene | 4.87 |
| Ammonia | 2.64 |
| Antimony | 4.45 |
| Antimony trioxide | 3.75 |
| Arsenic | 4.45 |
| Arsenic trioxide | 3.41 |
| Barium sulfide | 2.30 |
| Bromine | 4.45 |
| Cadmium | 4.45 |
| Chlorine | 2.70 |
| Chromium | 4.45 |
| Chromite | 1.52 |
| Potassium dichromate | 1.69 |
| Sodium dichromate | 1.87 |
| Cobalt | 4.45 |
| Cupric sulfate | 1.87 |
| Cupric oxide | 3.59 |
| Cuprous oxide | 3.97 |
| Hydrochloric acid | 0.29 |
| Hydrogen fluoride | 4.23 |
| Lead oxide | 4.14 |
| Mercury | 4.45 |
| Nickel | 4.45 |
| Phosphorus | 4.45 |
| Stannous chloride | 2.85 |
| Stannic chloride | 2.12 |
| Zinc chloride | 2.22 |
| Zinc sulfate | 1.90 |
| Potassium hydroxide | 0.22 |
| Sodium hydroxide | 0.28 |
| Sulfuric acid | 0.26 |
| Nitric acid | 0.24 |

For periods before 1992, the item relating to xylene in the preceding table shall be applied by substituting "10.13" for "4.87".

**(c) Termination.**—No tax shall be imposed under this section during any period during which the Hazardous Substance Superfund financing rate under section 4611 does not apply.

(Added Pub.L. 96–510, Title II, § 211(a), Dec. 11, 1980, 94 Stat. 2798, and amended Pub.L. 99–499, Title V, § 513(a), Oct. 17, 1986, 100 Stat. 1761; Pub.L. 99–509, Title VIII, § 8032(c)(3), Oct. 21, 1986, 100 Stat. 1958.)

## HISTORICAL AND STATUTORY NOTES

**Codifications**

Amendment by Pub.L. 99–509, Title VIII, § 8031(d)(2), Oct. 21, 1986, 100 Stat. 1956, to subsec. (c) was not executed to text pursuant to Pub.L. 99–509, Title VIII, § 8031(e)(2) which provided that the amendments made by section 8031 shall not take effect if the Superfund Amendments and Reauthorization Act of 1986 is enacted. The Superfund Amendments and Reauthorization Act of 1986 was enacted as Pub.L. 99–499, approved Oct. 17, 1986.

**Effective and Applicability Provisions**

1986 Acts

Amendment by Pub.L. 99–509, effective on the commencement date as defined in section 4611(f)(2), set out as a note under section 4611 of this title, and effective only if the Superfund Amendments and Reauthorization Act of 1986 is enacted (The Superfund Amendments and Reauthorization Act of 1986 was enacted as Pub.L. 99–499, Oct. 17, 1986, 100 Stat. 1613), see section 8032(d) of Pub.L. 99–509, set out as a note under section 4611 of this title.

Section 513(h) of Pub.L. 99–499 provided that:

**"(1) In general.**—Except as otherwise provided in this subsection [subsec. (h) of section 513 amending subsec. (b) of this section and section 4662 of this title] the amendments made by this section [amending subsec. (b) of this section and section 4662 of this title] shall take effect on January 1, 1987.

**"(2) Repeal of tax on xylene for periods before October 1, 1985.—**

**"(A) Refund of tax previously imposed.—**

**"(i) In general.**—In the case of any tax imposed by section 4661 of the Internal Revenue Code of 1954 [of this title] on the sale or use of xylene before October 1, 1985, such tax (including interest, additions to tax, and additional amounts) shall not be assessed, and if assessed, the assessment shall be abated, and if collected shall be credited or refunded (with interest) as an overpayment.

**"(ii) condition to allowance.**—Clause (i) shall not apply to a sale of xylene unless the person who (but for clause (i)) would be liable for the tax imposed by section 4661 on such sale meets requirements similar to the requirements of paragraph (1) of section 6416(a) of such Code [section 6416(a) of this title]. For purposes of the preceding sentence, subparagraph (A) of section 6416(a)(1) of such Code [section 6416(a)(1) of this title] shall be applied without regard to the material preceding 'has not collected'.

**"(B) Waiver of statute of limitations.**—If on the date of the enactment of this Act [Oct. 17, 1986] (or at any time within 1 year after such date of enactment) refund or credit of any overpayment of tax resulting from the application of subparagraph (A) is barred by any law or rule of law, refund or credit of such overpayment shall, nevertheless, be made or allowed if claim therefor is filed before the date 1 year after the date of the enactment of this Act [Oct. 17, 1986].

**"(C) Xylene to include isomers.**—For purposes of this paragraph, the term 'xylene' shall include any isomer of xylene whether or not separated.

**"(3) Inventory exchanges.—**

**"(A) In general.**—except as otherwise provided in this paragraph, the amendment made by subsection (f) [amending subsec. (c) of section 4662 of this title] shall apply as if included in the amendments made by section 211 of the Hazardous Substance Response Revenue Act of 1980 [which enacted this chapter].

**"(B) Recipient must agree to treatment as manufacturer.**—In the case of any inventory exchange before January 1, 1987, the amendment made by subsection (f) [amending subsec. (c) of section 4662 of this title] shall apply only if the person receiving the chemical from the manufacturer, producer, or importer in the exchange agrees to be treated as the manufacturer, producer, or importer of such chemical for purposes of subchapter B of chapter 38 of the Internal Revenue Code of 1954 [subchapter B of Chap. 38 of this title].

**"(C) Exception where manufacturer paid tax.**—In the case of any inventory exchange before January 1, 1987, the amendment made by subsection (f) shall not apply if the manufacturer, producer, or importer treated such exchange as a sale for purposes of section 4661 of such Code [section 4661 of this title] and paid the tax imposed by such section.

**"(D) Registration requirements.**—Section 4662(c)(2)(B) of such Code [section 4662(c)(2)(B) of this title] (as added by subsection (f) [amending subsec. (c) of section 4662 of this title]) shall apply to exchanges made after December 31, 1986.

**"(4) Exports of taxable substances.**—Subclause (II) of section 4662(e)(2)(A)(ii) of such Code [subclause (II) of section 4662(e)(2)(A) of this title] (as added by this section) shall not apply to the export of any taxable substance (as defined in section 4672(a) of such Code) [section 4672(a) of this title] before January 1, 1989.

**"(5) Sales of intermediate hydrocarbon streams.—**

**"(A) In general.**—Except as otherwise provided in this paragraph, the amendment made by subsection (g) [amending subsec. (b)(10) of section 4662 of this title] shall apply as if included in the amendments made by section 211 of the Hazardous Substances Response Revenue Act of 1980 [which enacted this chapter].

**"(B) Purchaser must agree to treatment as manufacturer.**—In the case of any sale before January 1, 1987, of any intermediate hydrocarbon stream, the amendment made by subsection (g) [amending subsec. (b)(10) of section 4662 of this title] shall apply only if the purchaser agrees to be treated as the manufacturer, producer, or importer for purposes of subchapter B of chapter 38 of such Code [subchapter B of chapter 38 of this title].

**"(C) Exception where manufacturer paid tax.**—In the case of any sale before January 1, 1987, of any intermediate hydrocarbon stream, the amendment made by subsection (g) [amending subsec. (b)(10) of section 4662 of this title] shall not apply if the manufacturer, producer, or importer of such stream paid the tax imposed by section 4661 [of this title] with respect to such sale on all taxable chemicals contained in such stream.

**"(D) Registration requirements.**—Section 4662(b)(10)(C) of such Code (as added by subsection (g) [amending subsec. (b)(10) of section 4662 of this title]) shall apply to exchanges made after December 31, 1986."

1980 Acts

Section effective April 1, 1981, see section 211(c) of Pub.L. 96–510, set out as a note under section 4611 of this title.

## § 4662. Definitions and special rules

**(a) Definitions.**—For purposes of this subchapter—

**(1) Taxable chemical.**—Except as provided in subsection (b), the term "taxable chemical" means any substance—

**(A)** which is listed in the table under section 4661(b), and

**(B)** which is manufactured or produced in the United States or entered into the United States for consumption, use, or warehousing.

**(2) United States.**—The term "United States" has the meaning given such term by section 4612(a)(4).

**(3) Importer.**—The term "importer" means the person entering the taxable chemical for consumption, use, or warehousing.

**(4) Ton.**—The term "ton" means 2,000 pounds. In the case of any taxable chemical which is a gas, the term "ton" means the amount of such gas in cubic feet which is the equivalent of 2,000 pounds on a molecular weight basis.

**(5) Fractional part of ton.**—In the case of a fraction of a ton, the tax imposed by section 4661 shall be the same fraction of the amount of such tax imposed on a whole ton.

**(b) Exceptions; other special rules.**—For purposes of this subchapter—

**(1) Methane or butane used as a fuel.**—Under regulations prescribed by the Secretary, methane or butane shall be treated as a taxable chemical only if it is used otherwise than as a fuel or in the manufacture or production of any motor fuel, diesel fuel, aviation fuel, or jet fuel (and, for purposes of section 4661(a), the person so using it shall be treated as the manufacturer thereof).

**(2) Substances used in the production of fertilizer.**—

**(A) In general.**—In the case of nitric acid, sulfuric acid, ammonia, or methane used to produce ammonia which is a qualified fertilizer substance, no tax shall be imposed under section 4661(a).

**(B) Qualified fertilizer substance.**—For purposes of this section, the term "qualified fertilizer substance" means any substance—

**(i)** used in a qualified fertilizer use by the manufacturer, producer, or importer,

**(ii)** sold for use by any purchaser in a qualified fertilizer use, or

**(iii)** sold for resale by any purchaser for use, or resale for ultimate use, in a qualified fertilizer use.

**(C) Qualified fertilizer use.**—The term "qualified fertilizer use" means any use in the manufacture or production of fertilizer or for direct application as a fertilizer.

**(D) Taxation of nonqualified sale or use.**—For purposes of section 4661(a), if no tax was imposed by such section on the sale or use of any chemical by reason of subparagraph (A), the first person who sells or uses such chemical other than in a sale or use described in subparagraph (A) shall be treated as the manufacturer of such chemical.

**(3) Sulfuric acid produced as a byproduct of air pollution control.**—In the case of sulfuric acid produced solely as a byproduct of and on the same site as air pollution control equipment, no tax shall be imposed under section 4661.

**(4) Substances derived from coal.**—For purposes of this subchapter, the term "taxable chemical" shall not include any substance to the extent derived from coal.

**(5) Substances used in the production of motor fuel, etc.**—

**(A) In general.**—In the case of any chemical described in subparagraph (D) which is a qualified fuel substance, no tax shall be imposed under section 4661(a).

**(B) Qualified fuel substance.**—For purposes of this section, the term "qualified fuel substance" means any substance—

**(i)** used in a qualified fuel use by the manufacturer, producer, or importer,

**(ii)** sold for use by any purchaser in a qualified fuel use, or

**(iii)** sold for resale by any purchaser for use, or resale for ultimate use, in a qualified fuel use.

**(C) Qualified fuel use.**—For purposes of this subsection, the term "qualified fuel use" means—

**(i)** any use in the manufacture or production of any motor fuel, diesel fuel, aviation fuel, or jet fuel, or

**(ii)** any use as such a fuel.

**(D) Chemicals to which paragraph applies.**—For purposes of this subsection, the chemicals described in this subparagraph are acetylene, benzene, butylene, butadiene, ethylene, naphthalene, propylene, toluene, and xylene.

**(E) Taxation of nonqualified sale or use.**—For purposes of section 4661(a), if no tax was imposed by such section on the sale or use of any chemical by reason of subparagraph (A), the first person who sells or uses such chemical other than in a sale or use described in subparagraph (A) shall be treated as the manufacturer of such chemical.

**(6) Substance having transitory presence during refining process, etc.**—

(A) **In general.**—No tax shall be imposed under section 4661(a) on any taxable chemical described in subparagraph (B) by reason of the transitory presence of such chemical during any process of smelting, refining, or otherwise extracting any substance not subject to tax under section 4661(a).

(B) **Chemicals to which subparagraph (A) applies.**—The chemicals described in this subparagraph are—

(i) barium sulfide, cupric sulfate, cupric oxide, cuprous oxide, lead oxide, zinc chloride, and zinc sulfate, and

(ii) any solution or mixture containing any chemical described in clause (i).

(C) **Removal treated as use.**—Nothing in subparagraph (A) shall be construed to apply to any chemical which is removed from or ceases to be part of any smelting, refining, or other extraction process.

(7) **Special rule for xylene.**—Except in the case of any substance imported into the United States or exported from the United States, the term "xylene" does not include any separated isomer of xylene.

(8) **Recycled chromium, cobalt, and nickel.**—

(A) **In general.**—No tax shall be imposed under section 4661(a) on any chromium, cobalt, or nickel which is diverted or recovered in the United States from any solid waste as part of a recycling process (and not as part of the original manufacturing or production process).

(B) **Exemption not to apply while corrective action uncompleted.**—Subparagraph (A) shall not apply during any period that required corrective action by the taxpayer at the unit at which the recycling occurs is uncompleted.

(C) **Required corrective action.**—For purposes of subparagraph (B), required corrective action shall be treated as uncompleted during the period—

(i) beginning on the date that the corrective action is required by the Administrator or an authorized State pursuant to—

(I) a final permit under section 3005 of the Solid Waste Disposal Act or a final order under section 3004 or 3008 of such Act, or

(II) a final order under section 106 of the Comprehensive Environmental Response, Compensation, and Liability Act of 1980, and

(ii) ending on the date the Administrator or such State (as the case may be) certifies to the Secretary that such corrective action has been completed.

(D) **Special rule for groundwater treatment.**—In the case of corrective action requiring groundwater treatment, such action shall be treated as completed as of the close of the 10-year period beginning on the date such action is required if such treatment complies with the permit or order applicable under subparagraph (C)(i) throughout such period. The preceding sentence shall cease to apply beginning on the date such treatment ceases to comply with such permit or order.

(E) **Solid waste.**—For purposes of this paragraph, the term "solid waste" has the meaning given such term by section 1004 of the Solid Waste Disposal Act, except that such term shall not include any byproduct, coproduct, or other waste from any process of smelting, refining, or otherwise extracting any metal.

(9) **Substances used in the production of animal feed.**—

(A) **In general.**—In the case of—

(i) nitric acid,

(ii) sulfuric acid,

(iii) ammonia, or

(iv) methane used to produce ammonia,

which is a qualified animal feed substance, no tax shall be imposed under section 4661(a).

(B) **Qualified animal feed substance.**—For purposes of this section, the term "qualified animal feed substance" means any substance—

(i) used in a qualified animal feed use by the manufacturer, producer, or importer,

(ii) sold for use by any purchaser in a qualified animal feed use, or

(iii) sold for resale by any purchaser for use, or resale for ultimate use, in a qualified animal feed use.

(C) **Qualified animal feed use.**—The term "qualified animal feed use" means any use in the manufacture or production of animal feed or animal feed supplements, or of ingredients used in animal feed or animal feed supplements.

(D) **Taxation of nonqualified sale or use.**—For purposes of section 4661(a), if no tax was imposed by such section on the sale or use of any chemical by reason of subparagraph (A), the 1st person who sells or uses such chemical other than in a sale or use described in subparagraph (A) shall be treated as the manufacturer of such chemical.

(10) **Hydrocarbon streams containing mixtures of organic taxable chemicals.**—

(A) **In general.**—No tax shall be imposed under section 4661(a) on any organic taxable chemical while such chemical is part of an intermediate hydrocarbon stream containing one or more organic taxable chemicals.

(B) **Removal, etc., treated as use.**—For purposes of this part, if any organic taxable chemical on which no tax was imposed by reason of subparagraph (A) is isolated, extracted, or otherwise removed from, or ceases to be part of, an intermediate hydrocarbon stream—

(i) such isolation, extraction, removal, or cessation shall be treated as use by the person causing such event, and

(ii) such person shall be treated as the manufacturer of such chemical.

**(C) Registration requirement.**—Subparagraph (A) shall not apply to any sale of any intermediate hydrocarbon stream unless the registration requirements of clauses (i) and (ii) of subsection (c)(2)(B) are satisfied.

**(D) Organic taxable chemical.**—For purposes of this paragraph, the term "organic taxable chemical" means any taxable chemical which is an organic substance.

**(c) Use and certain exchanges by manufacturer, etc.**—

**(1) Use treated as sale.**—Except as provided in subsections (b) and (e), if any person manufactures, produces, or imports any taxable chemical and uses such chemical, then such person shall be liable for tax under section 4661 in the same manner as if such chemical were sold by such person.

**(2) Special rules for inventory exchanges.**

**(A) In general.**—Except as provided in this paragraph, in any case in which a manufacturer, producer, or importer of a taxable chemical exchanges such chemical as part of an inventory exchange with another person—

(i) such exchange shall not be treated as a sale, and

(ii) such other person shall, for purposes of section 4661, be treated as the manufacturer, producer, or importer of such chemical.

**(B) Registration requirement.**—Subparagraph (A) shall not apply to any inventory exchange unless—

(i) both parties are registered with the Secretary as manufacturers, producers, or importers of taxable chemicals, and

(ii) the person receiving the taxable chemical has, at such time as the Secretary may prescribe, notified the manufacturer, producer, or importer of such person's registration number and the internal revenue district in which such person is registered.

**(C) Inventory exchange.**—For purposes of this paragraph, the term "inventory exchange" means any exchange in which 2 persons exchange property which is, in the hands of each person, property described in section 1221(a)(1).

**(d) Refund or credit for certain uses.**—

**(1) In general.**—Under regulations prescribed by the Secretary, if—

**(A)** a tax under section 4661 was paid with respect to any taxable chemical, and

**(B)** such chemical was used by any person in the manufacture or production of any other substance which is a taxable chemical,

then an amount equal to the tax so paid shall be allowed as a credit or refund (without interest) to such person in the same manner as if it were an overpayment of tax imposed by such section. In any case to which this paragraph applies, the amount of any such credit or refund shall not exceed the amount of tax imposed by such section on the other substance manufactured or produced (or which would have been imposed by such section on such other substance but for subsection (b) or (e) of this section).

**(2) Use as fertilizer.**—Under regulations prescribed by the Secretary, if—

**(A)** a tax under section 4661 was paid with respect to nitric acid, sulfuric acid, ammonia, or methane used to make ammonia without regard to subsection (b)(2), and

**(B)** any person uses such substance as a qualified fertilizer substance,

then an amount equal to the excess of the tax so paid over the tax determined with regard to subsection (b)(2) shall be allowed as a credit or refund (without interest) to such person in the same manner as if it were an overpayment of tax imposed by this section.

**(3) Use as qualified fuel.**—Under regulations prescribed by the Secretary, if—

**(A)** a tax under section 4661 was paid with respect to any chemical described in subparagraph (D) of subsection (b)(5) without regard to subsection (b)(5), and

**(B)** any person uses such chemical as a qualified fuel substance,

then an amount equal to the excess of the tax so paid over the tax determined with regard to subsection (b)(5) shall be allowed as a credit or refund (without interest) to such person in the same manner as if it were an overpayment of tax imposed by this section.

**(4) Use in the production of animal feed.** Under regulations prescribed by the Secretary, if—

**(A)** a tax under section 4661 was paid with respect to nitric acid, sulfuric acid, ammonia, or methane used to produce ammonia, without regard to subsection (b)(9), and

**(B)** any person uses such substance as a qualified animal feed substance,

then an amount equal to the excess of the tax so paid over the tax determined with regard to subsection (b)(9) shall be allowed as a credit or refund (without interest) to such person in the same manner as if it were an overpayment of tax imposed by this section.

**(e) Exemption for exports of taxable chemicals.—**

**(1) Tax-free sales.—**

**(A) In general.**—No tax shall be imposed under section 4661 on the sale by the manufacturer or producer of any taxable chemical for export, or for resale by the purchaser to a second purchaser for export.

**(B) Proof of export required.**—Rules similar to the rules of section 4221(b) shall apply for purposes of subparagraph (A).

**(2) Credit or refund where tax paid.—**

**(A) In general.**—Except as provided in subparagraph (B), if—

**(i)** tax under section 4661 was paid with respect to any taxable chemical, and

**(ii)(I)** such chemical was exported by any person, or

**(II)** such chemical was used as a material in the manufacture or production of a substance which was exported by any person and which, at the time of export, was a taxable substance (as defined in section 4672(a)),

credit or refund (without interest) of such tax shall be allowed or made to the person who paid such tax.

**(B) Condition to allowance.**—No credit or refund shall be allowed or made under subparagraph (A) unless the person who paid the tax establishes that he—

**(i)** has repaid or agreed to repay the amount of the tax to the person who exported the taxable chemical or taxable substance (as so defined), or

**(ii)** has obtained the written consent of such exporter to the allowance of the credit or the making of the refund.

**(3) Refunds directly to exporter.**—The Secretary shall provide, in regulations, the circumstances under which a credit or refund (without interest) of the tax under section 4661 shall be allowed or made to the person who exported the taxable chemical or taxable substance, where—

**(A)** the person who paid the tax waives his claim to the amount of such credit or refund, and

**(B)** the person exporting the taxable chemical or taxable substance provides such information as the Secretary may require in such regulations.

**(4) Regulations.**—The Secretary shall prescribe such regulations as may be necessary to carry out the purposes of this subsection.

**(f) Disposition of revenues from Puerto Rico and the Virgin Islands.**—The provisions of subsections (a)(3) and (b)(3) of section 7652 shall not apply to any tax imposed by section 4661.

(Added Pub.L. 96–510, Title II, § 211(a), Dec. 11, 1980, 94 Stat. 2799, and amended Pub.L. 98–369, Div. A, Title X, § 1019(a) to (c), July 18, 1984, 98 Stat. 1022 to 1024; Pub.L. 99–499, Title V, § 513(b) to (g), Oct. 17, 1986, 100 Stat. 1762 to 1765; Pub.L. 100–647, Title II, § 2001(a), Nov. 10, 1988, 102 Stat. 3593, 3594; Pub.L. 106–170, Title V, § 532(c)(2)(U), Dec. 17, 1999, 113 Stat. 1931.)

## HISTORICAL AND STATUTORY NOTES

### References in Text

Sections 3005, 3004 and 3008 of the Solid Waste Disposal Act, referred to in subsec. (b)(8)(C)(i)(I), and section 1004 of that Act, referred to in subsec. (b)(8)(E), are classified, respectively, to sections 6925, 6924, 6928, and 6903 of Title 42, The Public Health and Welfare.

Section 106 of the Comprehensive Environmental Response, Compensation, and Liability Act of 1980, referred to in subsec. (b)(8)(C)(i)(II), is classified to section 9606 of Title 42.

### Effective and Applicability Provisions

1999 Acts

Amendment by section 532(c)(2)(U) of Pub.L. 106–170 shall apply to any instrument held, acquired, or entered into, any transaction entered into, and supplies held or acquired on or after Dec. 17, 1999, see section 532(d) of Pub.L. 106–170, set out as a note under section 170 of this title.

1988 Acts

Amendment by Pub.L. 100–647 effective as if included in the provision of the Superfund Revenue Act of 1986 [Pub.L. 99–499, Oct. 17, 1986, 100 Stat. 1613] to which it relates, see section 2001(e) of Pub.L. 100–647, set out as a note under section 56 of this title."

1986 Acts

Amendment by Pub.L. 99–499 effective Jan. 1, 1987, except as otherwise provided, see section 513(h) of Pub.L. 99–499, set out as a note under section 4661 of this title.

1984 Acts

Section 1019(d) of Pub.L. 98–369 provided that:

"**(1) In general.**—The amendments made by this section [amending subsecs. (b) to (d) of this section] shall take effect as if included in the amendments made by section 211(a) of the Hazardous Substance Response Revenue Act of 1980 [Pub.L. 96–510, which enacted this section].

"**(2) Waiver of limitation.**—If refund or credit of any overpayment of tax resulting from the application of the amendments made by this section is prevented at any time before the date which for one year after the date of the enactment of this Act [July 18, 1984] by the operation of any law or rule of law (including res judicata), refund or credit of such overpayment (to the extent attributable to the application of such amendments) may, nevertheless, be made or allowed if claim therefor is filed on or before the date which for one year after the date of the enactment of this Act [July 18, 1984]."

1980 Acts

Section effective April 1, 1981, see section 211(c) of Pub.L. 96–510, set out as a note under section 4611 of this title.

## SUBCHAPTER C—TAX ON CERTAIN IMPORTED SUBSTANCES



### HISTORICAL AND STATUTORY NOTES

**Codifications**

A former subchapter C relating to tax on hazardous wastes, consisting of sections 4681 and 4682, was repealed by Pub.L. 99–499, Title V, § 514(a)(1), Oct. 17, 1986, 100 Stat. 1767.

## § 4671. Imposition of tax

**(a) General rule.**—There is hereby imposed a tax on any taxable substance sold or used by the importer thereof.

**(b) Amount of tax.**—

**(1) In general.**—Except as provided in paragraph (2), the amount of the tax imposed by subsection (a) with respect to any taxable substance shall be the amount of the tax which would have been imposed by section 4661 on the taxable chemicals used as materials in the manufacture or production of such substance if such taxable chemicals had been sold in the United States for use in the manufacture or production of such taxable substance.

**(2) Rate where importer does not furnish information to Secretary.**—If the importer does not furnish to the Secretary (at such time and in such manner as the Secretary shall prescribe) sufficient information to determine under paragraph (1) the amount of the tax imposed by subsection (a) on any taxable substance, the amount of the tax imposed on such taxable substance shall be 5 percent of the appraised value of such substance as of the time such substance was entered into the United States for consumption, use, or warehousing.

**(3) Authority to prescribe rate in lieu of paragraph (2) rate.**—The Secretary may prescribe for each taxable substance a tax which, if prescribed, shall apply in lieu of the tax specified in paragraph (2) with respect to such substance. The tax prescribed by the Secretary shall be equal to the amount of tax which would be imposed by subsection (a) with respect to the taxable substance if such substance were produced using the predominant method of production of such substance.

**(c) Exemptions for substances taxed under sections 4611 and 4661.**—No tax shall be imposed by this section on the sale or use of any substance if tax is imposed on such sale or use under section 4611 or 4661.

**(d) Tax-free sales, etc. for substances used as certain fuels or in the production of fertilizer or animal feed.**—Rules similar to the following rules shall apply for purposes of applying this section with respect to taxable substances used or sold for use as described in such rules:

(1) Paragraphs (2), (5), and (9) of section 4662(b) (relating to tax-free sales of chemicals used as fuel or in the production of fertilizer or animal feed).

(2) Paragraphs (2), (3), and (4) of section 4662(d) (relating to refund or credit of tax on certain chemicals used as fuel or in the production of fertilizer or animal feed).

**(e) Termination.**—No tax shall be imposed under this section during any period during which the Hazardous Substance Superfund financing rate under section 4611 does not apply.

(Added Pub.L. 99–499, Title V, § 515(a), Oct. 17, 1986, 100 Stat. 1767, and amended Pub.L. 99–509, Title VIII, § 8032(c)(3), Oct. 21, 1986, 100 Stat. 1958.)

### HISTORICAL AND STATUTORY NOTES

**Effective and Applicability Provisions**

1986 Acts

Amendment by Pub.L. 99–509, effective on the commencement date as defined in section 4611(f)(2) of this title, set out as a note under section 4611 of this title, and effective only if the Superfund Amendments and Reauthorization Act of 1986 is enacted (The Superfund Amendments and Reauthorization Act of 1986 was enacted as Pub.L. 99–499, Oct. 17, 1986, 100 Stat. 1613), see section 8032(d) of Pub.L. 99–509, set out as a note under section 4611 of this title.

Section 515(c) of Pub.L. 99–499 provided that: "The amendments made by this section [enacting this section, section 4672 of this title and provisions set out as notes under this section] shall take effect on January 1, 1989."

**Study and Report**

Section 515(d) of Pub.L. 99–499, provided that:

"**(1) In general.**—The Secretary of the Treasury or his delegate shall conduct a study of issues relating to the implementation of—

"(A) the tax imposed by the section 4671 of the Internal Revenue Code of 1986 (as added by this section) [this section], and

"(B) the credit for exports of taxable substances under section 4661(e)(2)(A)(ii)(II) of such Code [section 4662(e)(2)(A)(ii)(II) of this title]."

In conducting such study, the Secretary of the Treasury or his delegate shall consult with the Environmental Protection Agency and the International Trade Commission.

"**(2) Report.**—The report of the study under paragraph (1) shall be submitted not later than January 1, 1988, to the Committee on Ways and Means of the House of Representatives and the Committee on Finance of the Senate."

## § 4672. Definitions and special rules

**(a) Taxable substance.**—For purposes of this subchapter—

(1) **In general.**—The term "taxable substance" means any substance which, at the time of sale or use by the importer, is listed as a taxable substance by the Secretary for purposes of this subchapter.

(2) **Determination of substances on list.**—A substance shall be listed under paragraph (1) if—

(A) the substance is contained in the list under paragraph (3), or

(B) the Secretary determines, in consultation with the Administrator of the Environmental Protection Agency and the Commissioner of Customs, that taxable chemicals constitute more than 50 percent of the weight (or more than 50 percent of the value) of the materials used to produce such substance (determined on the basis of the predominant method of production).

If an importer or exporter of any substance requests that the Secretary determine whether such substance be listed as a taxable substance under paragraph (1) or be removed from such listing, the Secretary shall make such determination within 180 days after the date the request was filed.

(3) **Initial list of taxable substances.**—

Cumene
Styrene
Ammonium nitrate
Nickel oxide
Isopropyl alcohol
Ethylene glycol
Vinyl chloride
Polyethylene resins, total
Polybutadiene
Styrene-butadiene, latex
Styrene-butadiene, snpf
Synthetic rubber, not containing fillers
Urea
Ferronickel
Ferrochromium nov 3 pct
Ferrochrome ov 3 pct. carbon
Unwrought nickel
Nickel waste and scrap
Wrought nickel rods and wire
Nickel powders
Phenolic resins
Polyvinylchloride resins
Polystyrene resins and copolymers
Ethyl alcohol for nonbeverage use
Ethylbenzene
Methylene chloride
Polypropylene
Propylene glycol
Formaldehyde
Acetone
Acrylonitrile
Methanol
Propylene oxide
Ethylene oxide
Cyclohexane
Isophthalic acid
Maleic anhydride
Ethyl methyl ketone
Chloroform
Carbon tetrachloride
Chromic acid
Hydrogen peroxide
Polystyrene homopolymer resins
Melamine
Acrylic and methacrylic acid resins
Vinyl resins
Vinyl resins, NSPF.

(4) **Modifications to list.**—The Secretary shall add to the list under paragraph (3) substances which meet either the weight or value tests of paragraph (2)(B) and may remove from such list only substances which meet neither of such tests.

(b) **Other definitions.**—For purposes of this subchapter—

(1) **Importer.**—The term "importer" means the person entering the taxable substance for consumption, use, or warehousing.

(2) **Taxable chemicals; United States.**—The terms "taxable chemical" and "United States" have the respective meanings given such terms by section 4662(a).

(c) **Disposition of revenues from Puerto Rico and the Virgin Islands.**—The provisions of subsections (a)(3) and (b)(3) of section 7652 shall not apply to any tax imposed by section 4671.

(Added Pub.L. 99–499, Title V, § 515(a), Oct. 17, 1986, 100 Stat. 1768, and amended Pub.L. 100–647, Title II, § 2001(b), Nov. 10, 1988, 102 Stat. 3594.)

### HISTORICAL AND STATUTORY NOTES

**Effective and Applicability Provisions**

1988 Acts

Amendment by Pub.L. 100–647 effective, except as otherwise provided, as if included in the provision of Pub.L. 99–499 to which it relates, see section 2001(e) of Pub.L. 100–647, set out as a note under section 56 of this title.

1986 Acts

Section effective Jan. 1, 1989, see section 515(c) of Pub.L. 99–499, set out as a note under section 4671 of this title.

## SUBCHAPTER D—OZONE-DEPLETING CHEMICALS, ETC.



## § 4681. Imposition of tax

(a) **General rule.**—There is hereby imposed a tax on—

(1) any ozone-depleting chemical sold or used by the manufacturer, producer, or importer thereof, and

(2) any imported taxable product sold or used by the importer thereof.

(b) **Amount of tax.—**

(1) **Ozone-depleting chemicals.—**

(A) **In general.**—The amount of the tax imposed by subsection (a) on each pound of ozone-depleting chemical shall be an amount equal to—

(i) the base tax amount, multiplied by

(ii) the ozone-depletion factor for such chemical.

(B) **Base tax amount.**—The base tax amount for purposes of subparagraph (A) with respect to any sale or use during any calendar year after 1995 shall be $5.35 increased by 45 cents for each year after 1995.

(2) **Imported taxable product.—**

(A) **In general.**—The amount of the tax imposed by subsection (a) on any imported taxable product shall be the amount of tax which would have been imposed by subsection (a) on the ozone-depleting chemicals used as materials in the manufacture or production of such product if such ozone-depleting chemicals had been sold in the United States on the date of the sale of such imported taxable product.

(B) **Certain rules to apply.**—Rules similar to the rules of paragraphs (2) and (3) of section 4671(b) shall apply.

(Added Pub.L. 101–239, Title VII, § 7506(a), Dec. 19, 1989, 103 Stat. 2364, and amended Pub.L. 101–508, Title XI, § 11203(c), Nov. 5, 1990, 104 Stat. 1388–422; Pub.L. 102–486, Title XIX, § 1931(a), Oct. 24, 1992, 106 Stat. 3029; Pub.L. 105–34, Title XIV, § 1432(c)(1), Aug. 5, 1997, 111 Stat. 1050.)

## HISTORICAL AND STATUTORY NOTES

### Effective and Applicability Provisions

1992 Acts

Section 1931(d) of Pub.L. 102–486 provided that: "The amendments made by this section [amending subsec. (b)(1)(B) of this section and subsecs. (g)(2)(B) and (h)(2)(C) of section 4682 of this title] shall apply to taxable chemicals sold or used on or after January 1, 1993."

1990 Acts

Section 11203(e) of Pub.L. 101–508 provided that: "The amendments made by this section [amending this section and section 4682 of this title, and enacting provisions set out as a note under section 4682 of this title] shall take effect on January 1, 1991".

1989 Acts

Section 7506(c) of Pub.L. 101–239 provided that:

"(1) **In general.**—The amendments made by this section [enacting this section and section 4682 of this title] shall take effect on January 1, 1990.

"(2) **No deposits required before April 1, 1990.**—No deposit of any tax imposed by subchapter D of chapter 38 of the Internal Revenue Code of 1986, as added by this section [this subchapter], shall be required to be made before April 1, 1990.

"(3) **Notification of changes in international agreements.**—The Secretary of the Treasury or his delegate shall notify the Committee on Ways and Means of the House of Representatives and the Committee on Finance of the Senate of changes in the Montreal Protocol and of other international agreements to which the United States is a signatory relating to ozone-depleting chemicals."

### Prior Provisions

A prior section 4681, added Pub.L. 96–510, Title II, § 231(a), Dec. 11, 1980, 94 Stat. 2804, which imposed a tax on receipt of hazardous waste, was set out in subchapter C of this chapter prior to the repeal of that section by Pub.L. 99–499, Title V, § 514(a)(1), Oct. 17, 1986, 100 Stat. 1767.

## § 4682. Definitions and special rules

(a) **Ozone-depleting chemical.**—For purposes of this subchapter—

(1) **In general.**—The term "ozone-depleting chemical" means any substance—

(A) which, at the time of the sale or use by the manufacturer, producer, or importer, is listed as an ozone-depleting chemical in the table contained in paragraph (2), and

(B) which is manufactured or produced in the United States or entered into the United States for consumption, use, or warehousing.

(2) **Ozone-depleting chemicals.—**

| Common name: | Chemical nomenclature: |
|---|---|
| CFC–11 | trichlorofluoromethane |
| CFC–12 | dichlorodifluoromethane |
| CFC–113 | trichlorotrifluoroethane |
| CFC–114 | 1,2–dichloro–1,1,2,2,–tetra-fluoroethane |
| CFC–115 | chloropentafluoroethane |
| Halon–1211 | bromochlorodifluoromethane |
| Halon–1301 | bromotrifluoromethane |
| Halon–2402 | dibromotetrafluoroethane. |
| Carbon tetrachloride | tetrachloromethane |
| Methyl chloroform | 1,1,1-trichloroethane |
| CFC–13 | CF3C1 |
| CFC–111 | C2FC15 |
| CFC–112 | C2F2C14 |
| CFC–211 | C3FC17 |
| CFC–212 | C3F2C16 |
| CFC–213 | C3F3C15 |
| CFC–214 | C3F4C14 |
| CFC–215 | C3F5C13 |
| CFC–216 | C3F6C12 |
| CFC–217 | C3F7C1. |

(b) **Ozone-depletion factor.**—For purposes of this subchapter, the term "ozone-depletion factor" means, with respect to an ozone-depleting chemical, the factor assigned to such chemical under the following table:

| Ozone-depleting chemical: | Ozone-depletion factor: |
|---|---|
| CFC–11 | 1.0 |
| CFC–12 | 1.0 |
| CFC–113 | 0.8 |

| Ozone-depleting chemical: | Ozone-depletion factor: |
|---|---|
| CFC–114 | 1.0 |
| CFC–115 | 0.6 |
| Halon–1211 | 3.0 |
| Halon–1301 | 10.0 |
| Halon–2402 | 6.0 |
| Carbon tetrachloride | 1.1 |
| Methyl chloroform | 0.1 |
| CFC–13 | 1.0 |
| CFC–111 | 1.0 |
| CFC–112 | 1.0 |
| CFC–211 | 1.0 |
| CFC–212 | 1.0 |
| CFC–213 | 1.0 |
| CFC–214 | 1.0 |
| CFC–215 | 1.0 |
| CFC–216 | 1.0 |
| CFC–217 | 1.0. |

**(c) Imported taxable product.**—For purposes of this subchapter—

**(1) In general.**—The term "imported taxable product" means any product (other than an ozone-depleting chemical) entered into the United States for consumption, use, or warehousing if any ozone-depleting chemical was used as material in the manufacture or production of such product.

**(2) De minimis exception.**—The term "imported taxable product" shall not include any product specified in regulations prescribed by the Secretary as using a de minimis amount of ozone-depleting chemicals as materials in the manufacture or production thereof. The preceding sentence shall not apply to any product in which any ozone-depleting chemical (other than methyl chloroform) is used for purposes of refrigeration or air conditioning, creating an aerosol or foam, or manufacturing electronic components.

**(d) Exceptions.**—

**(1) Recycling.**—No tax shall be imposed by section 4681 on any ozone-depleting chemical which is diverted or recovered in the United States as part of a recycling process (and not as part of the original manufacturing or production process), or on any recycled Halon–1301 or recycled Halon–2402 imported from any country which is a signatory to the Montreal Protocol on Substances that Deplete the Ozone Layer.

**(2) Use in further manufacture.**—

**(A) In general.**—No tax shall be imposed by section 4681—

**(i)** on the use of any ozone-depleting chemical in the manufacture or production of any other chemical if the ozone-depleting chemical is entirely consumed in such use,

**(ii)** on the sale by the manufacturer, producer, or importer of any ozone-depleting chemical—

**(I)** for a use by the purchaser which meets the requirements of clause (i), or

**(II)** for resale by the purchaser to a second purchaser for a use by the second purchaser which meets the requirements of clause (i).

Clause (ii) shall apply only if the manufacturer, producer, and importer, and the 1st and 2d purchasers (if any), meet such registration requirements as may be prescribed by the Secretary.

**(B) Credit or refund.**—Under regulations prescribed by the Secretary, if—

**(i)** a tax under this subchapter was paid with respect to any ozone-depleting chemical, and

**(ii)** such chemical was used (and entirely consumed) by any person in the manufacture or production of any other chemical,

then an amount equal to the tax so paid shall be allowed as a credit or refund (without interest) to such person in the same manner as if it were an overpayment of tax imposed by section 4681.

**(3) Exports.**—

**(A) In general.**—Except as provided in subparagraph (B), rules similar to the rules of section 4662(e) (other than section 4662(e)(2)(A)(ii)(II)) shall apply for purposes of this subchapter.

**(B) Limit on benefit.**—

**(i) In general.**—The aggregate tax benefit allowable under subparagraph (A) with respect to ozone-depleting chemicals manufactured, produced, or imported by any person during a calendar year shall not exceed the sum of—

**(I)** the amount equal to the 1986 export percentage of the aggregate tax which would (but for this subsection and subsection (g)) be imposed by this subchapter with respect to the maximum quantity of ozone-depleting chemicals permitted to be manufactured or produced by such person during such calendar year under regulations prescribed by the Environmental Protection Agency (other than chemicals with respect to which subclause (II) applies),

**(II)** the aggregate tax which would (but for this subsection and subsection (g)) be imposed by this subchapter with respect to any additional production allowance granted to such person with respect to ozone-depleting chemicals manufactured or produced by such person during such calendar year by the Environmental Protection Agency under 40 CFR Part 82 (as in effect on September 14, 1989), and

(III) the aggregate tax which was imposed by this subchapter with respect to ozone-depleting chemicals imported by such person during the calendar year.

(ii) **1986 export percentage.**—A person's 1986 export percentage is the percentage equal to the ozone-depletion factor adjusted pounds of ozone-depleting chemicals manufactured or produced by such person during 1986 which were exported during 1986, divided by the ozone-depletion factor adjusted pounds of all ozone-depleting chemicals manufactured or produced by such person during 1986. The percentage determined under the preceding sentence shall be computed by taking into account the sum of such person's direct 1986 exports (as determined by the Environmental Protection Agency) and such person's indirect 1986 exports (as allocated to such person by such Agency in determining such person's consumption and production rights for ozone-depleting chemicals).

**(C) Separate application of limit for newly listed chemicals.—**

(i) **In general.**—Subparagraph (B) shall be applied separately with respect to newly listed chemicals and other chemicals.

(ii) **Application to newly listed chemicals.**—In applying subparagraph (B) to newly listed chemicals—

(I) subparagraph (B) shall be applied by substituting "1989" for "1986" each place it appears, and

(II) clause (i)(II) thereof shall be applied by substituting for the regulations referred to therein any regulations (whether or not prescribed by the Secretary) which the Secretary determines are comparable to the regulations referred to in such clause with respect to newly listed chemicals.

(iii) **Newly listed chemical.**—For purposes of this subparagraph, the term "newly listed chemical" means any substance which appears in the table contained in subsection (a)(2) below Halon–2402.

**(e) Other definitions.**—For purposes of this subchapter—

**(1) Importer.**—The term "importer" means the person entering the article for consumption, use, or warehousing.

**(2) United States.**—The term "United States" has the meaning given such term by section 4612(a)(4).

**(f) Special rules.—**

**(1) Fractional parts of a pound.**—In the case of a fraction of a pound, the tax imposed by this subchapter shall be the same fraction of the amount of such tax imposed on a whole pound.

**(2) Disposition of revenues from Puerto Rico and the Virgin Islands.**—The provisions of subsections (a)(3) and (b)(3) of section 7652 shall not apply to any tax imposed by this subchapter.

**(g) Chemicals used as propellants in metered-dose inhalers.—**

**(1) Exemption from tax.—**

**(A) In general.**—No tax shall be imposed by section 4681 on—

(i) any use of any substance as a propellant in metered-dose inhalers, or

(ii) any qualified sale by the manufacturer, producer, or importer of any substance.

**(B) Qualified sale.**—For purposes of subparagraph (A), the term "qualified sale" means any sale by the manufacturer, producer, or importer of any substance—

(i) for use by the purchaser as a propellant in metered dose inhalers, or

(ii) for resale by the purchaser to a 2d purchaser for such use by the 2d purchaser.

The preceding sentence shall apply only if the manufacturer, producer, and importer, and the 1st and 2d purchasers (if any) meet such registration requirements as may be prescribed by the Secretary.

**(2) Overpayments.**—If any substance on which tax was paid under this subchapter is used by any person as a propellant in metered-dose inhalers, credit or refund without interest shall be allowed to such person in an amount equal to the tax so paid. Amounts payable under the preceding sentence with respect to uses during the taxable year shall be treated as described in section 34(a) for such year unless claim thereof has been timely filed under this paragraph.

**(h) Imposition of floor stocks taxes.—**

**(1) January 1, 1990, tax.**—On any ozone-depleting chemical which on January 1, 1990, is held by any person (other than the manufacturer, producer, or importer thereof) for sale or for use in further manufacture, there is hereby imposed a floor stocks tax in an amount equal to the tax which would be imposed by section 4681 on such chemical if the sale of such chemical by the manufacturer, producer, or importer thereof had occurred during 1990.

**(2) Other tax-increase dates.—**

**(A) In general.**—If, on any tax-increase date, any ozone-depleting chemical is held by any person (other than the manufacturer, producer, or importer thereof) for sale or for use in further manufacture, there is hereby imposed a floor stocks tax.

(B) **Amount of tax.**—The amount of the tax imposed by subparagraph (A) shall be the excess (if any) of—

(i) the tax which would be imposed under section 4681 on such substance if the sale of such chemical by the manufacturer, producer, or importer thereof had occurred on the tax-increase date, over

(ii) the prior tax (if any) imposed by this subchapter on such substance.

(C) **Tax-increase date.**—For purposes of this paragraph, the term "tax-increase date" means January 1 of any calendar year after 1991.

(3) **Due date.**—The taxes imposed by this subsection on January 1 of any calendar year shall be paid on or before June 30 of such year.

(4) **Application of other laws.**—All other provisions of law, including penalties, applicable with respect to the taxes imposed by section 4681 shall apply to the floor stocks taxes imposed by this subsection.

(Added Pub.L. 101–239, Title VII, § 7506(a), Dec. 19, 1989, 103 Stat. 2365, and amended Pub.L. 101–508, Title XI, §§ 11203(a), (b), (d), 11701(g), Nov. 5, 1990, 104 Stat. 1388–421, 1388–422, 1388–508; Pub.L. 102–486, Title XIX, §§ 1931(b), (c), 1932(a) to (c), Oct. 24, 1992, 106 Stat. 3029 to 3031; Pub.L. 104–188, Title I, § 1803(a)(1), (b), Aug. 20, 1996, 110 Stat. 1892, 1893; Pub.L. 105–34, Title IX, § 903(a), Title XIV, § 1432(c)(2), Aug. 5, 1997, 111 Stat. 873, 1051.)

## HISTORICAL AND STATUTORY NOTES

### Effective and Applicability Provisions

1997 Acts

Section 903(b) of Pub.L. 105–34 provided that: "The amendment made by subsection (a) [amending subsec. (d)(1) of this section] shall take effect on the date of the enactment of this Act [Aug. 5, 1997]."

1996 Acts

Section 1803(c) of Pub.L. 104–188 provided that:

"(1) **Recycled halon.**—

"(A) **In general.**—Except as provided in subparagraph (B), the amendment made by subsection (a)(1) [amending subsec. (d)(1) of this section] shall take effect on January 1, 1997.

"(B) **Halon–1211.**—In the case of Halon–1211, the amendment made by subsection (a)(1) [amending subsec. (d)(1) of this section] shall take effect on January 1, 1998.

"(2) **Metered-dose inhalers.**—The amendment made by subsection (b) [amending subsec. (g)(4) of this section] shall take effect on the 7th day after the date of the enactment of this Act [Aug. 20, 1996]."

1992 Acts

Section 1932(d) of Pub.L. 102–486 provided that: "The amendments made by this section [enacting subsec. (g)(4) and (5) and amending subsec. (g)(2)(A)] shall apply to sales and uses on or after January 1, 1993."

Amendment by Pub.L. 102–486, applicable to taxable chemicals sold or used on or after January 1, 1993, see section 1931(d) of Pub.L. 102–486 set out as a note under section 4681 of this title

1990 Acts

Amendment by section 11701 of Pub.L. 101–508 effective as if included in the provision of the Revenue Reconciliation Act of 1989 [Title VII of Pub.L. 101–239] to which such amendment relates, see section 11701(n) of Pub.L. 101–508, set out as a note under section 42 of this title.

Amendment by section 11203(a), (b), and (d) of Pub.L. 101–508 effective Jan. 1, 1991, see section 11203(e) of Pub.L. 101–508, set out as a note under section 4681 of this title.

1989 Acts

Section to take effect on Jan. 1, 1990, but with no deposit of any tax imposed by this subchapter required to be made before Apr. 1, 1990, see section 7506(c)(1), (2) of Pub.L. 101–239, set out as a note under section 4681 of this title.

### Prior Provisions

A prior section 4682, added Pub.L. 96–510, Title II, § 231(a), Dec. 11, 1980, 94 Stat. 2804, which contained definitions and special rules related to tax imposed under section 4681 of this title, was set out in subchapter C of this chapter prior to the repeal of that section by Pub.L. 99–499, Title V, § 514(a)(1), Oct. 17, 1986, 100 Stat. 1767.

### Certification System

Section 1803(a)(2) of Pub.L. 104–188 provided that: "The Secretary of the Treasury, after consultation with the Administrator of the Environmental Protection Agency, shall develop a certification system to ensure compliance with the recycling requirement for imported halon under section 4682(d)(1) of the Internal Revenue Code of 1986, as amended by paragraph (1) [subsec. (d)(1) of this section, as amended by section 1803(a)(1) of Pub.L. 104–188]."

### Notification of Changes in International Agreements

For provisions requiring the Secretary of the Treasury or his delegate to notify the Committee on Ways and Means of the House of Representatives and the Committee on Finance of the Senate of changes in the Montreal Protocol and of other international agreements to which the United States is a signatory relating to ozone-depleting chemicals, see section 7506(c)(3) of Pub.L. 101–239, set out as part of an Effective Date of 1989 Amendment note under section 4681 of this title.

### Deposits for 1st Quarter of 1991

Section 11203(f) of Pub.L. 101–508 provided that: "No deposit of any tax imposed by subchapter D of chapter 38 of the Internal Revenue Code of 1986 [26 U.S.C.A. §§ 4681, 4682] on any substance treated as an ozone-depleting chemical by reason of the amendment made by subsection (a)(1) [amending table set forth in subsec. (a)(2) of this section] shall be required to be made before April 1, 1991."

# TRUST FUNDS

**(26 U.S.C.A. §§ 9507 to 9509)**

## CHAPTER 98—TRUST FUND CODE

**Subchapter**



### SUBCHAPTER A—ESTABLISHMENT OF TRUST FUNDS

**Sec.**



#### HISTORICAL AND STATUTORY NOTES

**Codifications**

The amendment by section 8033(b) of Pub.L. 99–509, which provided for adding item 9507 to the table of sections for subchapter A, did not take effect pursuant to section 8033(c)(2)(C) of Pub.L. 99–509 and the enactment of the Superfund Amendments and Reauthorization Act of 1986 (Pub.L. 99–499).

### § 9507. Hazardous Substance Superfund

**(a) Creation of trust fund.**—There is established in the Treasury of the United States a trust fund to be known as the "Hazardous Substance Superfund" (hereinafter in this section referred to as the "Superfund"), consisting of such amounts as may be—

(1) appropriated to the Superfund as provided in this section,

(2) appropriated to the Superfund pursuant to section 517(b) of the Superfund Revenue Act of 1986, or

(3) credited to the Superfund as provided in section 9602(b).

**(b) Transfers to Superfund.**—There are hereby appropriated to the Superfund amounts equivalent to—

(1) the taxes received in the Treasury under section 59A, 4611, 4661, or 4671 (relating to environmental taxes),

(2) amounts recovered on behalf of the Superfund under the Comprehensive Environmental Response, Compensation, and Liability Act of 1980 (hereinafter in this section referred to as "CERCLA"),

(3) all moneys recovered or collected under section 311(b)(6)(B) of the Clean Water Act,

(4) penalties assessed under title I of CERCLA, and

(5) punitive damages under section 107(c)(3) of CERCLA.

In the case of the tax imposed by section 4611, paragraph (1) shall apply only to so much of such tax as is attributable to the Hazardous Substance Superfund financing rate under section 4611(c).

**(c) Expenditures from Superfund.—**

**(1) In general.**—Amounts in the Superfund shall be available, as provided in appropriation Acts, only for purposes of making expenditures—

**(A)** to carry out the purposes of—

(i) paragraphs (1), (2), (5), and (6) of section 111(a) of CERCLA as in effect on the date of the enactment of the Superfund Amendments and Reauthorization Act of 1986,

(ii) section 111(c) of CERCLA (as so in effect), other than paragraphs (1) and (2) thereof, and

(iii) section 111(m) of CERCLA (as so in effect), or

**(B)** hereafter authorized by a law which does not authorize the expenditure out of the Superfund for a general purpose not covered by subparagraph (A) (as so in effect).

**(2) Exception for certain transfers, etc., of hazardous substances.**—No amount in the Superfund or derived from the Superfund shall be available or used for the transfer or disposal of hazardous waste carried out pursuant to a cooperative agreement between the Administrator of the Environmental Protection Agency and a State if the following conditions apply—

**(A)** the transfer or disposal, if made on December 13, 1985, would not comply with a State or local requirement,

**(B)** the transfer is to a facility for which a final permit under section 3005(a) of the Solid Waste Disposal Act was issued after January 1, 1983, and before November 1, 1984, and

**(C)** the transfer is from a facility identified as the McColl Site in Fullerton, California.

**(d) Authority to borrow.—**

**(1) In general.**—There are authorized to be appropriated to the Superfund, as repayable advances, such sums as may be necessary to carry out the purposes of the Superfund.

**(2) Limitation on aggregate advances.**—The maximum aggregate amount of repayable advances to the Superfund which is outstanding at any one time shall not exceed an amount equal to the amount which the Secretary estimates will be equal to the sum of the amounts appropriated to the Superfund under subsection (b)(1) during the following 24 months.

**(3) Repayment of advances.**—

**(A) In general.**—Advances made to the Superfund shall be repaid, and interest on such advances shall be paid, to the general fund of the Treasury when the Secretary determines that moneys are available for such purposes in the Superfund.

**(B) Final repayment.**—No advance shall be made to the Superfund after December 31, 1995, and all advances to such Fund shall be repaid on or before such date.

**(C) Rate of interest.**—Interest on advances made to the Superfund shall be at a rate determined by the Secretary of the Treasury (as of the close of the calendar month preceding the month in which the advance is made) to be equal to the current average market yield on outstanding marketable obligations of the United States with remaining periods to maturity comparable to the anticipated period during which the advance will be outstanding and shall be compounded annually.

**(e) Liability of United States limited to amount in trust fund.**—

**(1) General rule.**—Any claim filed against the Superfund may be paid only out of the Superfund.

**(2) Coordination with other provisions.**—Nothing in CERCLA or the Superfund Amendments and Reauthorization Act of 1986 (or in any amendment made by either of such Acts) shall authorize the payment by the United States Government of any amount with respect to any such claim out of any source other than the Superfund.

**(3) Order in which unpaid claims are to be paid.**—If at any time the Superfund has insufficient funds to pay all of the claims payable out of the Superfund at such time, such claims shall, to the extent permitted under paragraph (1), be paid in full in the order in which they were finally determined.

(Added Pub.L. 99–499, Title V, § 517(a), Oct. 17, 1986, 100 Stat. 1772, and amended Pub.L. 99–509, Title VIII, § 8032(c)(4), Oct. 21, 1986, 100 Stat. 1959; Pub.L. 101–508, Title XI, § 11231(c), Nov. 5, 1990, 104 Stat. 1388–445.)

## HISTORICAL AND STATUTORY NOTES

### References in Text

Section 517(b) of the Superfund Revenue Act of 1986, referred to in subsec. (a)(2), is section 517(b) of Pub.L. 99–499, which is set out as a note under this section.

The Comprehensive Environmental Response, Compensation, and Liability Act of 1980 and CERCLA, referred to in subsecs. (b)(2), (e)(2) is Pub.L. 96–510, Dec. 11, 1980, 94 Stat. 2767, as amended, which is classified principally to chapter 103 (section 9601 et seq.) of Title 42, The Public Health and Welfare.

Title I of that Act, referred to in subsec. (b)(4), is classified generally to subchapter I (section 9601 et seq.) of chapter 103 of Title 42. For complete classification of that Act to the Code, see Short Title note set out under section 9601 of Title 42 and Tables volume.

Section 311(b)(6)(B) of the Clean Water Act, referred to in subsec. (b)(3), is classified to section 1321(b)(6)(B) of Title 33, Navigation and Navigable Waters.

Section 107(c)(3) of CERCLA, referred to in subsec. (b)(5), is classified to section 9607(c)(3) of Title 42.

Pars. (1), (2), (5), and (6) of section 111(a) of CERCLA, referred to in subsec. (c)(1)(A)(i), are classified to section 9611(a)(1), (2), (5) and (6) of Title 42.

Sections 111(c) and 111(m) of CERCLA, referred to in subsec. (c)(1)(A)(ii) and (c)(1)(A)(iii), respectively, are classified to section 9611(c), (m) of Title 42.

The date of the enactment of the Superfund Amendments and Reauthorization Act of 1986, referred to in subsec. (c)(1)(A)(i), is the date of the enactment of Pub.L. 99–499, which was approved Oct. 17, 1986.

Section 3005(a) of the Solid Waste Disposal Act, referred to in subsec. (c)(2)(B), is classified to section 6925(a) of Title 42, The Public Health and Welfare.

The Superfund Amendments and Reauthorization Act of 1986, referred to in subsec. (e)(2), is Pub.L. 99–499, Oct. 17, 1986, 100 Stat. 1613. For complete classification of this Act to the Code, see Short Title of 1986 Amendment note set out under section 9601 of Title 42 and Tables volume.

### Effective and Applicability Provisions

1986 Acts

Amendment by Pub.L. 99–509 effective on the commencement date as defined in section 4611(f)(2) of this title, set out as a note under section 4611 of this title, and effective only if the Superfund Amendments and Reauthorization Act of 1986 is enacted (The Superfund Amendments and Reauthorization Act of 1986 was enacted as Pub.L. 99–499, Oct. 17, 1986, 100 Stat. 1613), see section 8032(d) of Pub.L. 99–509, set out as a note under section 4611 of this title.

Section 517(e) of Pub.L. 99–499 provided:

"**(1) In general.**—The amendments made by this section [enacting this section, amending section 9601(11) of this title, repealing sections 9631 to 9633 of Title 42, The Public Health and Welfare, and enacting provisions set out as notes under this section] shall take effect on January 1, 1987.

"**(2) Superfund treated as continuation of old trust fund.**—The Hazardous Substance Superfund established by the amendments made by this section shall be treated for all purposes of law as a continuation of the Hazardous Substance Response Trust Fund established by section 221 of the Hazardous Substance Response Revenue Act of 1980 [former section 9631 of Title 42, The Public Health and Welfare]. Any reference in any law to the Hazardous Substance Response Trust Fund established by such section 221 shall be deemed to include (wherever appropriate) a reference to the Hazardous Substance Superfund established by the amendments made by this section."

**Prior Provisions**

A prior section 9507 was renumbered 9509.

**Authorization of Appropriation**

Section 517(b) of Pub.L. 99–499 as amended Pub.L. 101–508, Title XI, § 11231(d), Nov. 5, 1990, 104 Stat. 1388–445, provided that: "There is authorized to be appropriated, out of any money in the Treasury not otherwise appropriated, to the Hazardous Substance Superfund for fiscal year—

"(1) 1987, $250,000,000,

"(2) 1988, $250,000,000,

"(3) 1989, $250,000,000,

"(4) 1990, $250,000,000,

"(5) 1991, $250,000,000, and

"(6) 1992, $250,000,000,

"(7) 1993, $250,000,000,

"(8) 1994, $250,000,000, and

"(9) 1995, $250,000,000,

plus for each fiscal year an amount equal to so much of the aggregate amount authorized to be appropriated under this subsection (and paragraph (2) of section 221(b) of the Hazardous Substance Response Act of 1980 [former section 9631(b) of Title 42, The Public Health and Welfare], as in effect before its repeal) as has not been appropriated before the beginning of the fiscal year involved."

[Section 11231(d) of Pub.L. 101–508 directed that section 517(b) of Pub.L. 99–599 be amended by striking out "and" at the end of par. (4), "by striking the period at the end of paragraph (5) and inserting ', and',", and by adding at the end thereof pars. (6) through (9) (with par. (9) ending in a period); section 517(b)(5) of Pub.L. 99–499, as originally enacted, ended with a comma; Pub.L. 104–188, Title I, § 1704(t)(44), Aug. 20, 1996, 110 Stat. 1889, provided that section 11231(d) of Pub.L. 101–508 was to be applied as if "comma" appeared instead of "period" (in the directory language relating to the amendment to par. (5)) and as if the par. (9) proposed to be added ended with a comma (instead of a period); amendment by section 11231(d) of Pub.L. 101–508, as modified by section 1704(t)(44) of Pub.L. 104–188, was executed by striking out "and" at the end of par. (4), by substituting ", and" for the comma at the end of par. (5), and by adding pars. (6) through (9), with par. (9) ending in a comma, as the probable intent of Congress.]

## § 9508. Leaking Underground Storage Tank Trust Fund

**(a) Creation of Trust Fund.**—There is established in the Treasury of the United States a trust fund to be known as the "Leaking Underground Storage Tank Trust Fund", consisting of such amounts as may be appropriated or credited to such Trust Fund as provided in this section or section 9602(b).

**(b) Transfers to Trust Fund.**—There are hereby appropriated to the Leaking Underground Storage Tank Trust Fund amounts equivalent to—

(1) taxes received in the Treasury under section 4041(d) (relating to additional taxes on motor fuels),

(2) taxes received in the Treasury under section 4081 (relating to tax on gasoline, diesel fuel, and kerosene) to the extent attributable to the Leaking Underground Storage Tank Trust Fund financing rate under such section,

(3) taxes received in the Treasury under section 4091 (relating to tax on aviation fuel) to the extent attributable to the Leaking Underground Storage Tank Trust Fund financing rate under such section,

(4) taxes received in the Treasury under section 4042 (relating to tax on fuel used in commercial transportation on inland waterways) to the extent attributable to the Leaking Underground Storage Tank Trust Fund financing rate under such section, and

(5) amounts received in the Treasury and collected under section 9003(h)(6) of the Solid Waste Disposal Act.

For purposes of this subsection, there shall not be taken into account the taxes imposed by sections 4041 and 4081 on diesel fuel sold for use or used as fuel in a diesel-powered boat.

**(c) Expenditures.**—

**(1) In general.**—Except as provided in paragraph (2), amounts in the Leaking Underground Storage Tank Trust Fund shall be available, as provided in appropriation Acts, only for purposes of making expenditures to carry out section 9003(h) of the Solid Waste Disposal Act as in effect on the date of the enactment of the Superfund Amendments and Reauthorization Act of 1986.

**(2) Transfers from Trust Fund for certain repayments and credits.**—

**(A) In general.**—The Secretary shall pay from time to time from the Leaking Underground Storage Tank Trust Fund into the general fund of the Treasury amounts equivalent to—

(i) amounts paid under—

(I) section 6420 (relating to amounts paid in respect of gasoline used on farms),

(II) section 6421 (relating to amounts paid in respect of gasoline used for certain nonhighway purposes or by local transit systems), and

(III) section 6427 (relating to fuels not used for taxable purposes), and

(ii) credits allowed under section 34,

with respect to the taxes imposed by section 4041(d) or by sections 4081 and 4091 (to the extent attributable to the Leaking Underground Storage Tank Trust Fund financing rate under such sections).

(B) **Transfers based on estimates.**—Transfers under subparagraph (A) shall be made on the basis of estimates by the Secretary, and proper adjustments shall be made in amounts subsequently transferred to the extent prior estimates were in excess of or less than the amounts required to be transferred.

**(d) Liability of the United States limited to amount in Trust Fund.**—

(1) **General rule.**—Any claim filed against the Leaking Underground Storage Tank Trust Fund may be paid only out of such Trust Fund.

(2) **Coordination with other provisions.**—Nothing in the Comprehensive Environmental Response, Compensation, and Liability Act of 1980 or the Superfund Amendments and Reauthorization Act of 1986 (or in any amendment made by either of such Acts) shall authorize the payment by the United States Government of any amount with respect to any such claim out of any source other than the Leaking Underground Storage Tank Trust Fund.

(3) **Order in which unpaid claims are to be paid.**—If at any time the Leaking Underground Storage Tank Trust Fund has insufficient funds to pay all of the claims out of such Trust Fund at such time, such claims shall, to the extent permitted under paragraph (1), be paid in full in the order in which they were finally determined.

(Added Pub.L. 99–499, Title V, § 522(a), Oct. 17, 1986, 100 Stat. 1780, and amended Pub.L. 100–203, Title X, § 10502(d)(16), (17), Dec. 22, 1987, 101 Stat. 1330–445; Pub.L. 101–239, Title VII, § 7822(b)(7), Dec. 19, 1989, 103 Stat. 2425; Pub.L. 103–66, Title XIII, §§ 13163(c), 13242(d)(42), Aug. 10, 1993, 107 Stat. 454, 528; Pub.L. 105–34, Title X, § 1032(e)(13), Aug. 5, 1997, 111 Stat. 935.)

### HISTORICAL AND STATUTORY NOTES

**References in Text**

Section 9003(h) of the Solid Waste Disposal Act, referred to in subsecs. (b)(5), (c)(1), is classified to section 6991b(h) of Title 42, The Public Health and Welfare. Par. (6) thereof is classified to par. (6) of section 6991b(h) of Title 42.

The date of the enactment of the Superfund Amendments and Reauthorization Act of 1986, referred to in subsec. (c)(1), is the date of the enactment of Pub.L. 99–499, which was approved Oct. 17, 1986.

The Comprehensive Environmental Response, Compensation, and Liability Act of 1980, referred to in subsec. (d)(2), is Pub.L. 96–510, Dec. 11, 1980, 94 Stat. 2767, as amended, which is classified principally to chapter 103 (section 9601 et seq.) of Title 42. For complete classification of this Act to the Code, see Short Title note set out under section 9601 of Title 42 and Tables volume.

The Superfund Amendments and Reauthorization Act of 1986, referred to in subsec. (d)(2), is Pub.L. 99–499, Oct. 17, 1986, 100 Stat. 1613. For complete classification of this Act to the Code, see Short Title of 1986 Amendment note set out under section 9601 of Title 42 and Tables volume.

**Codifications**

Amendment by Pub.L. 103–66, § 13242(d)(42)(C), which directed the substitution of "4081" for "4091"in the last sentence of subsec. (b) could not be executed to text since the last sentence of subsec. (b) contains no reference to "4091".

**Effective and Applicability Provisions**

1997 Acts

Amendment to subsec. (b)(2) of this section by section 1032(e)(13) of Pub.L. 105–34, effective July 1, 1998, see section 1032(f) of Pub.L. 105–34 set out as a note under section 4041 of this title.

1993 Acts

Amendment by section 13163(c) of Pub.L. 103–66 effective Jan. 1, 1994, see section 13163(d) of Pub.L. 103–66, set out as a note under section 4041 of this title.

Amendment by section 13242(d)(42) of Pub.L. 103–66 effective Jan. 1, 1994, see section 13242(e) of Pub.L. 103–66, set out as a note under section 4041 of this title.

1989 Acts

Amendment by Pub.L. 101–239 to take effect as if included in the provisions of Pub.L. 100–203, Title X, to which such amendment relates, see section 7823 of Pub.L. 101–239, set out as a note under section 26 of this title.

1987 Acts

Amendment by section 10502(d)(16) of Pub.L. 100–203 applicable to sales after Mar. 31, 1988, see section 10502(e) of Pub.L. 100–203, set out as a note under section 40 of this title.

Amendment by section 10502(d)(17) of Pub.L. 100–203 treated as if included in the amendments made by section 521 of Pub.L. 99–499, except that reference to section 4091 of this title in subsec. (c)(2)(A) of this section not applicable to sales before Apr. 1, 1988, see section 2001(d)(1)(A) of Pub.L. 100–647, set out as a note under section 4041 of this title.

1986 Acts

Section 522(c) of Pub.L. 99–499 provided: "The amendments made by this section [enacting this section] shall take effect on January 1, 1987."

## § 9509. Oil Spill Liability Trust Fund

**(a) Creation of Trust Fund.**—There is established in the Treasury of the United States a trust fund to be known as the "Oil Spill Liability Trust Fund", consisting of such amounts as may be appropriated or credited to such Trust Fund as provided in this section or section 9602(b).

**(b) Transfers to Trust Fund.**—There are hereby appropriated to the Oil Spill Liability Trust Fund amounts equivalent to—

(1) taxes received in the Treasury under section 4611 (relating to environmental tax on petroleum) to the extent attributable to the Oil Spill Liability Trust Fund financing rate under section 4611(c),

(2) amounts recovered under the Oil Pollution Act of 1990 for damages to natural resources which are required to be deposited in the Fund under section 1006(f) of such Act,

(3) amounts recovered by such Trust Fund under section 1015 of such Act,

(4) amounts required to be transferred by such Act from the revolving fund established under section 311(k) of the Federal Water Pollution Control Act,

(5) amounts required to be transferred by the Oil Pollution Act of 1990 from the Deepwater Port Liability Fund established under section 18(f) of the Deepwater Port Act of 1974,

(6) amounts required to be transferred by the Oil Pollution Act of 1990 from the Offshore Oil Pollution Compensation Fund established under section 302 of the Outer Continental Shelf Lands Act Amendments of 1978,

(7) amounts required to be transferred by the Oil Pollution Act of 1990 from the Trans-Alaska Pipeline Liability Fund established under section 204 of the Trans-Alaska Pipeline Authorization Act, and

(8) any penalty paid pursuant to section 311 of the Federal Water Pollution Control Act, section 309(c) of such Act (as a result of violations of such section 311), the Deepwater Port Act of 1974, or section 207 of the Trans-Alaska Pipeline Authorization Act.

**(c) Expenditures.—**

**(1) Expenditure purposes.**—Amounts in the Oil Spill Liability Trust Fund shall be available, as provided in appropriation Acts or section 6002(b) of the Oil Pollution Act of 1990, only for purposes of making expenditures—

(A) for the payment of removal costs and other costs, expenses, claims, and damages referred to in section 1012 of such Act,

(B) to carry out sections 5 and 7 of the Intervention on the High Seas Act relating to oil pollution or the substantial threat of oil pollution,

(C) for the payment of liabilities incurred by the revolving fund established by section 311(k) of the Federal Water Pollution Control Act,

(D) to carry out subsections (b), (c), (d), (j), and (*l*) of section 311 of the Federal Water Pollution Control Act with respect to prevention, removal, and enforcement related to oil discharges (as defined in such section),

(E) for the payment of liabilities incurred by the Deepwater Port Liability Fund, and

(F) for the payment of liabilities incurred by the Offshore Oil Pollution Compensation Fund.

**(2) Limitations on expenditures.—**

**(A) $1,000,000,000 per incident, etc.**—The maximum amount which may be paid from the Oil Spill Liability Trust Fund with respect to—

(i) any single incident shall not exceed $1,000,000,000, and

(ii) natural resource damage assessments and claims in connection with any single incident shall not exceed $500,000,000.

**(B) $30,000,000 minimum balance.**—Except in the case of payments of removal costs, a payment may be made from such Trust Fund only if the amount in such Trust Fund after such payment will not be less than $30,000,000.

**(d) Authority to borrow.—**

**(1) In general.**—There are authorized to be appropriated to the Oil Spill Liability Trust Fund, as repayable advances, such sums as may be necessary to carry out the purposes of such Trust Fund.

**(2) Limitation on amount outstanding.**—The maximum aggregate amount of repayable advances to the Oil Spill Liability Trust Fund which is outstanding at any one time shall not exceed $1,000,000,000.

**(3) Repayment of advances.—**

**(A) In general.**—Advances made to the Oil Spill Liability Trust Fund shall be repaid, and interest on such advances shall be paid, to the general fund of the Treasury when the Secretary determines that moneys are available for such purposes in such Fund.

**(B) Final repayment.**—No advance shall be made to the Oil Spill Liability Trust Fund after December 31, 1994, and all advances to such Fund shall be repaid on or before such date.

**(C) Rate of interest.**—Interest on advances made pursuant to this subsection shall be—

(i) at a rate determined by the Secretary of the Treasury (as of the close of the calendar month preceding the month in which the advance is made) to be equal to the current average market yield on outstanding marketable obligations of the United States with remaining periods to maturity comparable to the anticipated period during which the advance will be outstanding, and

(ii) compounded annually.

**(e) Liability of the United States limited to amount in Trust Fund.—**

**(1) General rule.**—Any claim filed against the Oil Spill Liability Trust Fund may be paid only out of such Trust Fund.

**(2) Coordination with other provisions.**—Nothing in the Oil Pollution Act of 1990 (or in any amendment made by such Act) shall authorize the payment by the United States Government of any amount with respect to any such claim out of any source other than the Oil Spill Liability Trust Fund.

**(3) Order in which unpaid claims are to be paid.**—If at any time the Oil Spill Liability Trust Fund has insufficient funds (or is unable by reason of subsection (c)(2)) to pay all of the claims out of such Trust Fund at such time, such claims shall, to the extent permitted under paragraph (1) and such subsection, be paid in full in the order in which they were finally determined.

**(f) References to Oil Pollution Act of 1990.**—Any reference in this section to the Oil Pollution Act of 1990 or any other Act referred to in a subparagraph of subsection (c)(1) shall be treated as a reference to such Act as in effect on the date of the enactment of this subsection.

(Added Pub.L. 99–509, Title VIII, § 8033(a), Oct. 21, 1986, 100 Stat. 1959, § 9507, and renumbered § 9509, Pub.L. 99–509, Title VIII, § 8033(c)(2)(B), Oct. 21, 1986, 100 Stat. 1962; Pub.L. 100–647, Title I, § 1018(u)(20), Nov. 10, 1988, 102 Stat. 3591, as amended Pub.L. 101–239, Title VII, § 7811(m)(3), Dec. 19, 1989, 103 Stat. 2412; Pub.L. 101–239, Title VII, § 7505(d)(2), Dec. 19, 1989, 103 Stat. 2364; Pub.L. 101–380, Title IX, § 9001, Aug. 18, 1990, 104 Stat. 573.)

## HISTORICAL AND STATUTORY NOTES

### References in Text

The Oil Pollution Act of 1990, referred to in text, is Pub.L. 101–380, Aug. 18, 1990, 104 Stat. 484, which is classified principally to chapter 40 (§ 2701 et seq.) of Title 33, Navigation and Navigable Waters. For complete classification of the Act to the Code see Short Title note under section 2701 of Title 33 and Tables.

Section 1006(f) of the Oil Pollution Act of 1990, referred to in subsec. (b)(2), is classified to section 2706(f) of Title 33.

Section 1015 of the Oil Pollution Act of 1990, referred to in subsec. (b)(3), is classified to section 2715 of Title 33.

Section 311(k) of the Federal Water Pollution Control Act, referred to in subsec. (b)(4), was classified to section 1321(k) of Title 33 prior to its repeal by the Oil Pollution Act of 1990 [Pub.L. 101–380].

Section 18(f) of the Deepwater Port Act of 1974, referred to in subsec. (b)(5), was classified to section 1517(f) of Title 33 prior to its repeal by the Oil Pollution Act of 1990 [Pub.L. 101–380].

Section 302 of the Outer Continental Shelf Lands Act Amendments of 1978, referred to in subsec. (b)(6), was classified to section 1812 of Title 43, Public Lands, prior to its repeal by the Oil Pollution Act of 1990 [Pub.L. 101–380].

Section 204 of the Trans–Alaska Pipeline Authorization Act, referred to in subsec. (b)(7), is classified to section 1653 of Title 43.

Section 311 of the Federal Water Pollution Control Act, referred to in subsec. (b)(8), is classified to section 1321 of Title 33.

Section 309(c) of the Federal Water Pollution Control Act, referred to in subsec. (b)(8), is classified to section 1319(c) of Title 33.

The Deepwater Port Act of 1974, referred to in subsec. (b)(8), is Pub.L. 93–627, Jan. 3, 1975, 88 Stat. 2126, as amended, which is classified generally to chapter 29 (§ 1501 et seq.) of Title 33. For complete classification of this Act to the Code, see Short Title note set out under section 1501 of Title 33 and Tables.

Section 207 of the Trans–Alaska Pipeline Authorization Act, referred to in subsec. (b)(8), is classified to section 1656 of Title 43

Section 6002(b) of the Oil Pollution Act of 1990, referred to in the provisions of subsec. (c)(1), is classified to section 2752(b) of Title 33.

Section 1012 of the Oil Pollution Act of 1990, referred to in subsec. (c)(1)(A), is classified to section 2712 of Title 33.

Sections 5 and 7 of the Intervention on the High Seas Act, referred to in subsec. (c)(1)(B), are classified, respectively, to sections 1474 and 1476 of Title 33.

Section 311(k) of the Federal Water Pollution Control Act, referred to in subsec. (c)(1)(C), was classified to section 1321(k) of Title 33 prior to its repeal by the Oil Pollution Act of 1990 [Pub.L. 101–380].

Section 311 of the Federal Water Pollution Control Act, referred to in subsec. (c)(1)(D), is classified to section 1321 of Title 33.

The date of enactment of this subsection, referred to in subsec. (f), probably means the date of enactment of Pub.L. 101–380, which was approved Aug. 18, 1990.

### Codifications

Amendment by Pub.L. 101–239, § 7811(m)(3), corrected directory language of section 1018(u)(20) of Pub.L. 100–647 to reflect renumbering of former section 9507 of this title as 9509 by section 8033(c)(2)(B) of Pub.L. 99–509. See 1988 and 1989 Amendment notes set out under this section.

### Effective and Applicability Provisions

1989 Acts

Amendment by part I of subtitle H of Title VII (§§ 7811 to 7816) of Pub.L. 101–239 to take effect as if included in the provisions of Pub.L. 100–647 to which such amendment relates, see section 7817 of Pub.L. 101–239, set out as a note under section 1 of this title.

1988 Acts

Amendment by Pub.L. 100–647 effective as if included in the provisions of Pub.L. 99–514 to which such amendment relates, except that no addition to tax shall be made under section 6654 or 6655 of this title for any period before Apr. 16, 1989 (Mar. 16, 1989 in the case of a taxpayer subject to section 6655 of this title) with respect to any underpayment to the extent such underpayment was created or increased by any provision of Titles I or II of Pub.L. 100–647, see section 1019 of Pub.L. 100–647, set out as a note under section 1 of this title.

1986 Acts

For provision that for purposes of section 8033(c) of Pub.L. 99–509, which enacted provisions set out as notes under this section and renumbered this section, the commencement date is Jan. 1, 1990, see section 7505(d)(1) of Pub.L. 101–239, Title VII, Dec. 19, 1989, 103 Stat. 2363, set out as a note under section 4611 of this title.

Section 8033(c)(1) of Pub.L. 99–509 provided that: "The amendments made by this section [enacting this section] shall take effect on the commencement date (as defined in section 4611 of the Internal Revenue Code of 1954 [now 1986], as amended by this part) [section 4611 of this title]."

**Termination of Oil Spill Liability Trust Fund Annual Report**

Pub.L. 107–295, Title III, § 322(a), Nov. 25, 2002, 116 Stat. 2103, provided that: "The report regarding the Oil Spill Liability Trust Fund required by the Conference Report (House Report 101–892) [101st Cong., 2nd session, Oct. 16, 1990] accompanying the Department of Transportation and Related Agencies Appropriations Act, 1991 [Pub.L. 101–516, Nov. 5, 1990, 104 Stat. 2155; see Tables for classification], as that requirement was amended by section 1122 of the Federal Reports Elimination and Sunset Act of 1995 (Public Law 104–66) [Pub.L. 104–66, Title I, § 1122(a), Dec. 21, 1995, 109 Stat. 724, set out as a note under this section], shall no longer be submitted to the Congress."

**Quarterly Reports to Congress on Oil Spill Liability Trust Fund**

Pub.L. 104–66, Title I, § 1122(a), Dec. 21, 1995, 109 Stat. 724, provided: "The quarterly report regarding the Oil Spill Liability Trust Fund required to be submitted to the House and Senate Committees on Appropriations under House Report 101–892 [101st Cong., 2d Session, Oct. 16, 1990], accompanying the appropriations for the Coast Guard in the Department of Transportation and Related Agencies Appropriations Act, 1991 [Pub.L. 101–516, Nov. 5, 1990, 104 Stat. 2155], shall be submitted not later than 30 days after the end of the fiscal year in which this Act is enacted and annually thereafter."

[House Report 101–892, 101st Cong., 2d Session, Oct. 16, 1990, directed the Coast Guard to submit quarterly reports to the House and Senate Committees on Appropriations detailing and summarizing all transfers to and expenditures from the Oil Spill Liability Trust Fund, with each report to account for each transfer to and expenditure from the Fund as authorized by section 9509 of the Internal Revenue Code of 1986 [this section] and sections 5003 and 5004 of Pub.L. 101–380 [sections 2733 and 2734 of Title 33, Navigation and Navigable Waters] and to show also the amount collectible under section 9509(b)(2), (3), and (8) of the Internal Revenue Code of 1986 [this section]. The House Report also directed that the reports of the Coast Guard to Congress indicate those authorized expenditures that are subject to limitations and further required that the Coast Guard confer with the Committees as to the format for the reports.]

**Deepwater Port Liability Fund**

Section 2003(b) of Pub.L. 101–380 provided that: "Any amounts remaining in the Deepwater Port Liability Fund established under section 18(f) of the Deepwater Port Act of 1974 (33 U.S.C. 1517(f)) [subsec. (f) of former section 1517 of Title 33] shall be deposited in the Oil Spill Liability Trust Fund established under section 9509 of the Internal Revenue Code of 1986 (26 U.S.C. 9509) [this section]. The Oil Spill Liability Trust Fund shall assume all liability incurred by the Deepwater Port Liability Fund."

**Offshore Oil Pollution Compensation Fund**

Section 2004 of Pub.L. 101–380 provided that: "Title III of the Outer Continental Shelf Lands Act Amendments of 1978 (43 U.S.C. 1811–1824) is repealed. Any amounts remaining in the Offshore Oil Pollution Compensation Fund established under section 302 of that title (43 U.S.C. 1812) shall be deposited in the Oil Spill Liability Trust Fund established under section 9509 of the Internal Revenue Code of 1986 (26 U.S.C. 9509) [this section]. The Oil Spill Liability Trust Fund shall assume all liability incurred by the Offshore Oil Pollution Compensation Fund."

**Deposit of Certain Penalties into Oil Spill Liability Trust Fund.**

Section 4304 of Pub.L. 101–380 provided that: "Penalties paid pursuant to section 311 of the Federal Water Pollution Control Act [section 1321 of Title 33, Navigation and Navigable Waters], section 309(c) of that Act [section 1319(c) of Title 33], as a result of violations of section 311 of that Act, and the Deepwater Port Act of 1974 [section 1501 et seq. of Title 33], shall be deposited in the Oil Spill Liability Trust Fund created under section 9509 of the Internal Revenue Code of 1986 (26 U.S.C. 9509) [this section]."

**Coordination with Superfund Reauthorization**

Section 8033(c)(2) of Pub.L. 99–509 provided that: "If the Superfund Amendments and Reauthorization Act of 1986 [Pub.L. 99–499] is enacted—

"**(A)** subsection (a) of this section [enacting section 9507 of this title] shall be applied by substituting 'section 9508' for 'section 9506',

"**(B)** section 9507 of the Internal Revenue Code of 1954 [now 1986], as added by this section [section 9507 of this title], is hereby redesignated as section 9509 of such Code [this section], and

"**(C)** in lieu of the amendment made by subsection (b), the table of sections for subchapter A of chapter 98 of such Code is amended by adding after the item relating to section 9508 the following new item:

"Sec. 9509. Oil Spill Liability Trust Fund."

*

# TITLE 30

# MINERAL LANDS AND MINING

## SURFACE MINING CONTROL AND RECLAMATION

### CHAPTER 25—SURFACE MINING CONTROL AND RECLAMATION

**Related Provisions**

*See, also, Solid Waste Disposal, 42 U.S.C.A. § 6901 et seq., post; and Uranium Mill Tailings Radiation Control, 42 U.S.C.A. § 7901 et seq., post.*

# SURFACE MINING CONTROL AND RECLAMATION ACT OF 1977 [SMCRA § ——]

**(30 U.S.C.A. §§ 1201, 1202, 1211)**

## SUBCHAPTER I—STATEMENT OF FINDINGS AND POLICY

### § 1201. Congressional findings [SMCRA § 101]

The Congress finds and declares that—

**(a)** extraction of coal and other minerals from the earth can be accomplished by various methods of mining, including surface mining;

**(b)** coal mining operations presently contribute significantly to the Nation's energy requirements; surface coal mining constitutes one method of extraction of the resource; the overwhelming percentage of the Nation's coal reserves can only be extracted by underground mining methods, and it is, therefore, essential to the national interest to insure the existence of an expanding and economically healthy underground coal mining industry;

**(c)** many surface mining operations result in disturbances of surface areas that burden and adversely affect commerce and the public welfare by destroying or diminishing the utility of land for commercial, industrial, residential, recreational, agricultural, and forestry purposes, by causing erosion and landslides, by contributing to floods, by polluting the water, by destroying fish and wildlife habitats, by impairing natural beauty, by damaging the property of citizens, by creating hazards dangerous to life and property by degrading the quality of life in local communities, and by counteracting governmental programs and efforts to conserve soil, water, and other natural resources;

**(d)** the expansion of coal mining to meet the Nation's energy needs makes even more urgent the establishment of appropriate standards to minimize damage to the environment and to productivity of the soil and to protect the health and safety of the public.[1]

**(e)** surface mining and reclamation technology are now developed so that effective and reasonable regulation of surface coal mining operations by the States and by the Federal Government in accordance with the requirements of this chapter is an appropriate and necessary means to minimize so far as practicable the adverse social, economic, and environmental effects of such mining operations;

**(f)** because of the diversity in terrain, climate, biologic, chemical, and other physical conditions in areas subject to mining operations, the primary governmental responsibility for developing, authorizing, issuing, and enforcing regulations for surface mining and reclamation operations subject to this chapter should rest with the States;

**(g)** surface mining and reclamation standards are essential in order to insure that competition in interstate commerce among sellers of coal produced in different States will not be used to undermine the ability of the several States to improve and maintain adequate standards on coal mining operations within their borders;

**(h)** there are a substantial number of acres of land throughout major regions of the United States disturbed by surface and underground coal on which little or no reclamation was conducted, and the impacts from these unreclaimed lands impose social and economic costs on residents in nearby and adjoining areas as well as continuing to impair environmental quality;

**(i)** while there is a need to regulate surface mining operations for minerals other than coal, more data and analyses are needed to serve as a basis for effective and reasonable regulation of such operations;

**(j)** surface and underground coal mining operations affect interstate commerce, contribute to the economic well-being, security, and general welfare of the Nation and should be conducted in an environmentally sound manner; and

**(k)** the cooperative effort established by this chapter is necessary to prevent or mitigate adverse environmental effects of present and future surface coal mining operations.

(Pub.L. 95–87, Title I, § 101, Aug. 3, 1977, 91 Stat. 447.)

[1] So in original. The period probably should be a semicolon.

## HISTORICAL AND STATUTORY NOTES

**References in Text**

This chapter, referred to in subsecs. (e), (f), and (k), was in the original "this Act", meaning Pub.L. 95–87, Aug. 3, 1977, 91 Stat. 445, as amended, which enacted this chapter and amended section 1114 of Title 18, Crimes and Criminal Procedure. For complete classification of this Act to the Code, see Short Title note set out below and Tables.

**Short Title**

1990 Amendments

Pub.L. 101–508, Title VI, Subtitle A, § 6001, Nov. 5, 1990, 104 Stat. 1388–289, provided that: "This subtitle [enacting section 1240a of this title, amending sections 1231, 1232, 1233, 1234, 1235, 1236, 1237, 1239, 1257 and 1302 of this title, and enacting provisions set out as a note under section 1231 of this title] may be cited as the 'Abandoned Mine Reclamation Act of 1990'."

Pub.L. 101–498, § 1, Nov. 2, 1990, 104 Stat. 1207, provided that: "This Act [enacting section 1230a of this title] may be cited as the 'Strategic and Critical Minerals Act of 1990'."

1988 Amendments

Pub.L. 100–483, § 13, Oct. 12, 1988, 102 Stat. 2341, provided that: "This Act [amending sections 1221(a)(1), (a)(2)(A), (b), 1222(a), 1224(a), 1226(d), 1229(a)(7), (e), and 1230(b) of this title; and enacting note provisions set out under this section and section 1229 of this title] may be cited as the 'Mining and Mineral Resources Research Institute Amendments of 1988'."

1977 Amendments

Section 1 of Pub.L. 95–87 provided: "That this Act [which enacted this chapter and amended section 1114 of Title 18] may be cited as the 'Surface Mining Control and Reclamation Act of 1977'."

Pub.L. 98–409, § 11, as added Pub.L. 100–483, § 12, Oct. 12, 1988, 102 Stat. 2341, and amended Pub.L. 104–312, § 1(b), Oct. 19, 1996, 110 Stat. 3819, provided that: "This Act [enacting subchapter III of this chapter] may be cited as the 'Mining and Mineral Resources Institutes Act'."

## § 1202. Statement of purpose

**[SMCRA § 102]**

It is the purpose of this chapter to—

**(a)** establish a nationwide program to protect society and the environment from the adverse effects of surface coal mining operations;

**(b)** assure that the rights of surface landowners and other persons with a legal interest in the land or appurtenances thereto are fully protected from such operations;

**(c)** assure that surface mining operations are not conducted where reclamation as required by this chapter is not feasible;

**(d)** assure that surface coal mining operations are so conducted as to protect the environment;

**(e)** assure that adequate procedures are undertaken to reclaim surface areas as contemporaneously as possible with the surface coal mining operations;

**(f)** assure that the coal supply essential to the Nation's energy requirements, and to its economic and social well-being is provided and strike a balance between protection of the environment and agricultural productivity and the Nation's need for coal as an essential source of energy;

**(g)** assist the States in developing and implementing a program to achieve the purposes of this chapter;

**(h)** promote the reclamation of mined areas left without adequate reclamation prior to August 3, 1977, and which continue, in their unreclaimed condition, to substantially degrade the quality of the environment, prevent or damage the beneficial use of land or water resources, or endanger the health or safety of the public;

(i) assure that appropriate procedures are provided for the public participation in the development, revision, and enforcement of regulations, standards, reclamation plans, or programs established by the Secretary or any State under this chapter;

(j) provide a means for development of the data and analyses necessary to establish effective and reasonable regulation of surface mining operations for other minerals;

(k) encourage the full utilization of coal resources through the development and application of underground extraction technologies;

(*l*) stimulate, sponsor, provide for and/or supplement present programs for the conduct of research investigations, experiments, and demonstrations, in the exploration, extraction, processing, development, and production of minerals and the training of mineral engineers and scientists in the field of mining, minerals resources, and technology, and the establishment of an appropriate research and training center in various States; and

(m) wherever necessary, exercise the full reach of Federal constitutional powers to insure the protection of the public interest through effective control of surface coal mining operations.

(Pub.L. 95–87, Title I, § 102, Aug. 3, 1977, 91 Stat. 448.)

### HISTORICAL AND STATUTORY NOTES

**References in Text**

This chapter, referred to in the introductory text and pars. (c), (g), and (i), was in the original "this Act", meaning Pub.L. 95–87, Aug. 3, 1977, 91 Stat. 445, as amended, which enacted this chapter and amended section 1114 of Title 18, Crimes and Criminal Procedure. For complete classification of this Act to the Code, see Short Title note set out under section 1201 of this title and Tables.

## SUBCHAPTER II—OFFICE OF SURFACE MINING RECLAMATION AND ENFORCEMENT

## § 1211. Office of Surface Mining Reclamation and Enforcement

**[SMCRA § 201]**

**(a) Establishment**

There is established in the Department of the Interior, the Office of Surface Mining Reclamation and Enforcement (hereinafter referred to as the "Office").

**(b) Appointment, compensation, duties, etc., of Director; employees**

The Office shall have a Director who shall be appointed by the President, by and with the advice and consent of the Senate, and shall be compensated at the rate provided for level V of the Executive Schedule under section 5315 [1] of Title 5, and such other employees as may be required. Pursuant to section 5108 of Title 5, and after consultation with the Secretary, the Director of the Office of Personnel Management shall determine the necessary number of positions in general schedule employees in grade 16, 17, and 18 to perform functions of this subchapter and shall allocate such positions to the Secretary. The Director shall have the responsibilities provided under subsection (c) of this section and those duties and responsibilities relating to the functions of the Office which the Secretary may assign, consistent with this chapter. Employees of the Office shall be recruited on the basis of their professional competence and capacity to administer the provisions of this chapter. The Office may use, on a reimbursable basis when appropriate, employees of the Department and other Federal agencies to administer the provisions of this chapter, providing that no legal authority, program, or function in any Federal agency which has as its purpose promoting the development or use of coal or other mineral resources or regulating the health and safety of miners under provisions of the Federal Coal Mine Health and Safety Act of 1969 (83 Stat. 742) [30 U.S.C.A. § 801 et seq.], shall be transferred to the Office.

**(c) Duties of Secretary**

The Secretary, acting through the Office, shall—

(1) administer the programs for controlling surface coal mining operations which are required by this chapter; review and approve or disapprove State programs for controlling surface coal mining operations and reclaiming abandoned mined lands; make those investigations and inspections necessary to insure compliance with this chapter; conduct hearings, administer oaths, issue subpenas, and compel the attendance of witnesses and production of written or printed material as provided for in this chapter; issue cease-and-desist orders; review and vacate or modify or approve orders and decisions; and order the suspension, revocation, or withholding of any permit for failure to comply with any of the provisions of this chapter or any rules and regulations adopted pursuant thereto;

(2) publish and promulgate such rules and regulations as may be necessary to carry out the purposes and provisions of this chapter;

(3) administer the State grant-in-aid program for the development of State programs for surface and mining and reclamation operations provided for in subchapter V of this chapter;

(4) administer the program for the purchase and reclamation of abandoned and unreclaimed mined areas pursuant to subchapter IV of this chapter;

(5) administer the surface mining and reclamation research and demonstration project authority provided for in this chapter;

(6) consult with other agencies of the Federal Government having expertise in the control and reclamation of surface mining operations and assist States, local governments, and other eligible agencies in the coordination of such programs;

(7) maintain a continuing study of surface mining and reclamation operations in the United States;

(8) develop and maintain an Information and Data Center on Surface Coal Mining, Reclamation, and Surface Impacts of Underground Mining, which will make such data available to the public and the Federal, regional, State, and local agencies conducting or concerned with land use planning and agencies concerned with surface and underground mining and reclamation operations;

(9) assist the States in the development of State programs for surface coal mining and reclamation operations which meet the requirements of this chapter, and at the same time, reflect local requirements and local environmental and agricultural conditions;

(10) assist the States in developing objective scientific criteria and appropriate procedures and institutions for determining those areas of a State to be designated unsuitable for all or certain types of surface coal mining pursuant to section 1272 of this title;

(11) monitor all Federal and State research programs dealing with coal extraction and use and recommend to Congress the research and demonstration projects and necessary changes in public policy which are designated to (A) improve feasibility of underground coal mining, and (B) improve surface mining and reclamation techniques directed at eliminating adverse environmental and social impacts;

(12) cooperate with other Federal agencies and State regulatory authorities to minimize duplication of inspections, enforcement, and administration of this chapter; and

(13) perform such other duties as may be provided by law and relate to the purposes of this chapter.

**(d) Restriction on use of Federal coal mine health and safety inspectors**

The Director shall not use either permanently or temporarily any person charged with responsibility of inspecting coal mines under the Federal Coal Mine Health and Safety Act of 1969 [30 U.S.C.A. § 801 et seq.], unless he finds and publishes such finding in the Federal Register, that such activities would not interfere with such inspections under the 1969 Act.

**(e) Repealed. Pub.L. 96–511, § 4(b), Dec. 11, 1980, 94 Stat. 2826**

**(f) Conflict of interest; penalties; rules and regulations; report to Congress**

No employee of the Office or any other Federal employee performing any function or duty under this chapter shall have a direct or indirect financial interest in underground or surface coal mining operations. Whoever knowingly violates the provisions of the above sentence shall, upon conviction, be punished by a fine of not more than $2,500, or by imprisonment for not more than one year, or both. The Director shall (1) within sixty days after August 3, 1977, publish regulations, in accordance with section 553 of Title 5, to establish the methods by which the provisions of this subsection will be monitored and enforced, including appropriate provisions for the filing by such employees and the review of statements and supplements thereto concerning their financial interests which may be affected by this subsection, and (2) report to the Congress as part of the annual report (section 1296 of this title) on the actions taken and not taken during the preceding calendar year under this subsection.

**(g) Petition for issuance, amendment, or repeal of rule; filing; hearing or investigation; notice of denial**

(1) After the Secretary has adopted the regulations required by section 1251 of this title, any person may petition the Director to initiate a proceeding for the issuance, amendment, or repeal of a rule under this chapter.

(2) Such petitions shall be filed in the principal office of the Director and shall set forth the facts which it is claimed established that it is necessary to issue, amend, or repeal a rule under this chapter.

(3) The Director may hold a public hearing or may conduct such investigation or proceeding as the Director deems appropriate in order to determine whether or not such petition should be granted.

(4) Within ninety days after filing of a petition described in paragraph (1), the Director shall either grant or deny the petition. If the Director grants such petition, the Director shall promptly commence an appropriate proceeding in accordance with the provisions of this chapter. If the Director denies such petition, the Director shall so notify the petitioner in writing setting forth the reasons for such denial.

(Pub.L. 95–87, Title II, § 201, Aug. 3, 1977, 91 Stat. 449; Pub.L. 95–240, Title I, § 100, Mar. 7, 1978, 92 Stat. 109; 1978 Reorg. Plan No. 2, § 102, eff. Jan. 1, 1979, 43 F.R. 36037, 92 Stat. 3783; Pub.L. 96–511, § 4(b), Dec. 11, 1980, 94 Stat. 2826.)

[1] So in original. Probably should be "section 5316".

HISTORICAL AND STATUTORY NOTES

**References in Text**

This chapter, referred to in text, was in the original "this Act", meaning Pub.L. 95–87, Aug. 3, 1977, 91 Stat. 445, as amended, which enacted this chapter and amended section 1114 of Title 18, Crimes and Criminal Procedure. For complete classification of this Act to the Code, see Short Title note set out under section 1201 of this title and Tables.

The general schedule, referred to in subsec. (b), is set out under section 5332 of Title 5, Government Organization and Employees.

The Federal Coal Mine Health and Safety Act of 1969, referred to in subsecs. (b) and (d), is Pub.L. 91–173, Dec. 30, 1969, 83 Stat. 742, as amended, which was redesignated the Federal Mine Safety and Health Act of 1977 by Pub.L. 95–164, Title I, § 101, Nov. 9, 1977, 91 Stat. 1290, and is classified principally to chapter 22 (section 801 et seq.) of this title. For complete classification of this Act to the Code, see Short Title note set out under section 801 of this title and Tables.

**Effective and Applicability Provisions**

1980 Acts

Amendment by Pub.L. 96–511 effective on Apr. 1, 1981, see section 5 of Pub.L. 96–511, set out as a note under section 3501 of Title 44, Public Printing and Documents.

**Transfer of Functions**

"The Director of the Office of Personnel Management" was substituted for "a majority of members of the Civil Service Commission" in subsec. (b) pursuant to Reorg. Plan No. 2 of 1978, § 102, 43 F.R. 36037, 92 Stat. 3783, set out under section 1101 of Title 5, Government Organization and Employees, which transferred all functions vested by statute in the United States Civil Service Commission to the Director of the Office of Personnel Management (except as otherwise specified), effective Jan. 1, 1979, as provided by section 1–102 of Ex. Ord. No. 12107, Dec. 28, 1978, 44 F.R. 1055, set out under section 1101 of Title 5.

**Travel and Per Diem Expenses of State and Tribal Personnel Attending Sponsored Training**

Pub.L. 108–108, Title I, Nov. 10, 2003, 117 Stat. 1256, provided in part that: "Appropriations for the Office of Surface Mining Reclamation and Enforcement may provide for the travel and per diem expenses of State and tribal personnel attending Office of Surface Mining Reclamation and Enforcement sponsored training."

Similar provisions were contained in the following prior Appropriations Acts:

Pub.L. 108–7, Div. F, Title I, Feb. 20, 2003, 117 Stat. 230.

Pub.L. 107–63, Title I, Nov. 5, 2001, 115 Stat. 429.

Pub.L. 106–291, Title I, Oct. 11, 2000, 114 Stat. 933.

Pub.L. 106–113, Div. B, § 1000(a)(3) [Title I], Nov. 29, 1999, 113 Stat. 1535, 1501A–147.

Pub.L. 105–277, Div. A, § 101(e) [Title I], Oct. 21, 1998, 112 Stat. 2681–244.

Pub.L. 105–83, Title I, Nov. 14, 1997, 111 Stat. 1553.

Pub.L. 104–208, Div. A, Title I, § 101(d) [Title I], Sept. 30, 1996, 110 Stat. 3009–191.

Pub.L. 104–134, Title I, § 101(c) [Title I], Apr. 26, 1996, 110 Stat. 1321–168; renumbered Title I Pub.L. 104–140, § 1(a), May 26, 1996, 110 Stat. 1327.

Pub.L. 103–332, Title I, Sept. 30, 1994, 108 Stat. 2510.

Pub.L. 103–138, Title I, Nov. 11, 1993, 107 Stat. 1389.

Pub.L. 102–381, Title I, Oct. 5, 1992, 106 Stat. 1387.

Pub.L. 102–154, Title I, Nov. 13, 1991, 105 Stat. 1002.

Pub.L. 101–512, Title I, Nov. 5, 1990, 104 Stat. 1927.

Pub.L. 101–121, Title I, Oct. 23, 1989, 103 Stat. 712.

Pub.L. 100–446, Title I, Sept. 27, 1988, 102 Stat. 1793.

# MINING AND MINERAL RESOURCES RESEARCH INSTITUTE ACT OF 1984 [MMRRIA § ______]

**(30 U.S.C.A. §§ 1221 to 1230a)**

## SUBCHAPTER III—STATE MINING AND MINERAL RESOURCES RESEARCH INSTITUTES

HISTORICAL AND STATUTORY NOTES

**Codification**

Subchapter was not enacted as part of the Surface Mining Control and Reclamation Act of 1977 which comprises this chapter.

### § 1221. Authorization of State allotments to institutes

**[MMRRIA § 1]**

**(a)(1)** There are authorized to be appropriated to the Secretary of the Interior (hereafter in this subchapter referred to as the "Secretary") funds adequate to provide for each participating State $400,000 for each of the fiscal years ending September 30, 1990, through September 30, 1994, to assist the States in carrying on the work of a competent and qualified mining and mineral resources research institute or center (hereafter in this subchapter referred to as the "institute") at one public college or university in the State which meets the eligibility criteria established in section 1230 of this title.

**(2)(A)** Funds appropriated under this section shall be made available for grants to be matched on a basis of no less than 2 non-Federal dollars for each Federal dollar.

(B) If there is more than one such eligible college or university in a State, funds appropriated under this subchapter shall, in the absence of a designation to the contrary by act of the legislature of the State, be granted to one such college or university designated by the Governor of the State.

(C) Where a State does not have a public college or university eligible under section 1230 of this title, the Committee on Mining and Mineral Resources Research established in section 1229 of this title (hereafter in this subchapter referred to as the "Committee") may allocate the State's allotment to one private college or university which it determines to be eligible under such section.

(b) It shall be the duty of each institute to plan and conduct, or arrange for a component or components of the college or university with which it is affiliated to conduct research, investigations, demonstrations, and experiments of either, or both, a basic or practical nature in relation to mining and mineral resources, and to provide for the training of mineral engineers and scientists through such research, investigations, demonstrations, and experiments. The subject of such research, investigation, demonstration, experiment, and training may include exploration; extraction; processing; development; production of fuel and nonfuel mineral resources; mining and mineral technology; supply and demand for minerals; conservation and best use of available supplies of minerals; the economic, legal, social, engineering, recreational, biological, geographic, ecological, and other aspects of mining, mineral resources, and mineral reclamation. Such research, investigation, demonstration, experiment and training shall consider the interrelationship with the natural environment, the varying conditions and needs of the respective States, and mining and mineral resources research projects being conducted by agencies of the Federal and State Governments and other institutes.

(Pub. L. 98–409, § 1, Aug. 29, 1984, 98 Stat. 1536; Pub.L. 100–483, §§ 2–4, Oct. 12, 1988, 102 Stat. 2339.)

## HISTORICAL AND STATUTORY NOTES

**Codifications**

Section was not enacted as part of the Surface Mining Control and Reclamation Act of 1977 which comprises this chapter.

**Prior Provisions**

A prior section 1221, Pub.L. 95–87, Title III, § 301, Aug. 3, 1977, 91 Stat. 451, contained provisions similar to this section covering fiscal years 1978 through 1984.

**Short Title**

For popular name of Pub.L. 98–409, which is classified to this subchapter, as the "Mining and Mineral Resources Research Institute Act of 1984", see section 11 of Pub.L. 98–409, set out as a note under section 1201 of this title.

## § 1222. Research funds to institutes

[MMRRIA § 2]

**(a) Authorization of appropriations**

There is authorized to be appropriated to the Secretary not more than $15,000,000 for each of the fiscal years ending September 30, 1990, through September 30, 1994, which shall remain available until expended. Such funds when appropriated shall be made available to an institute or to institutes participating in a generic mineral technology center to meet the necessary expenses for purposes of—

(1) specific mineral research and demonstration projects of broad application, which could not otherwise be undertaken, including the expenses of planning and coordinating regional mining and mineral resources research projects by two or more institutes; and

(2) research into any aspects of mining and mineral resources problems related to the mission of the Department of the Interior, which are deemed by the Committee to be desirable and are not otherwise being studied.

There is authorized to be appropriated to the Secretary not more than $1,800,000 for each of the fiscal years after fiscal year 1996 to be made available by the Secretary to an institute or institutes experienced in investigating the continental shelf regions of the United States, the deep seabed and near shore environments of islands, and the Arctic and cold water regions as a source for nonfuel minerals. Such funds are to be used by the institute or institutes to assist in developing domestic technological capabilities required for the location of, and the efficient and environmentally sound recovery of, minerals (other than oil and gas) from the Nation's shallow and deep seabed.

**(b) Application for funds; contents**

Each application for funds under subsection (a) of this section shall state, among other things, the nature of the project to be undertaken; the period during which it will be pursued; the qualifications of the personnel who will direct and conduct it; the estimated costs; the importance of the project to the Nation, region, or State concerned; its relation to other known research projects theretofore pursued or being pursued; the extent to which the proposed project will provide opportunity for the training of mining and mineral engineers and scientists; and the extent of participation by nongovernmental sources in the project.

**(c) Research facilities; selection of institutes; designation of funds for scholarships and fellowships**

The Committee shall review all such funding applications and recommend to the Secretary the use of the institutes, insofar as practicable, to perform special research. Recommendations shall be made without regard to the race, religion, or sex of the personnel who will conduct and direct the research, and on the basis of the facilities available in relation to the particular needs of the research project; special geographic, geologic, or climatic conditions within the immediate vicinity of the institute; any other special requirements of the research project; and the extent to which such project will provide an opportunity for training individuals as mineral engineers and scientists. The Committee shall recommend to the Secretary the designation and utilization of such portions of the funds authorized to be appropriated by this section as it deems appropriate for the purpose of providing scholarships, graduate fellowships, and postdoctoral fellowships.

**(d) Requirements for receipt of funds**

No funds shall be made available under subsection (a) of this section except for a project approved by the Secretary and all funds shall be made available upon the basis of merit of the project, the need for the knowledge which it is expected to produce when completed, and the opportunity it provides for the training of individuals as mineral engineers and scientists.

**(e) Restriction on application of funds**

No funds made available under this section shall be applied to the acquisition by purchase or lease of any land or interests therein, or the rental, purchase, construction, preservation, or repair of any building.

(Pub.L. 98–409, § 2, Aug. 29, 1984, 98 Stat. 1537; Pub.L. 100–483, § 5, Oct. 12, 1988, 102 Stat. 2339; Pub.L. 104–312, § 1(a), Oct. 19, 1996, 110 Stat. 3819.)

### HISTORICAL AND STATUTORY NOTES

**Codifications**

Section was not enacted as part of the Surface Mining Control and Reclamation Act of 1977 which comprises this chapter.

**Prior Provisions**

A prior section 1222, Pub.L. 95–87, Title III, § 302, Aug. 3, 1977, 91 Stat. 452, contained provisions similar to this section covering fiscal years 1978 through 1984.

## § 1223. Funding criteria

**[MMRRIA § 3]**

(a) Funds available to institutes under sections 1221 and 1222 of this title shall be paid at such times and in such amounts during each fiscal year as determined by the Secretary, and upon vouchers approved by him. Each institute shall—

(1) set forth its plan to provide for the training of individuals as mineral engineers and scientists under a curriculum appropriate to the field of mineral resources and mineral engineering and related fields;

(2) set forth policies and procedures which assure that Federal funds made available under this subchapter for any fiscal year will supplement and, to the extent practicable, increase the level of funds that would, in the absence of such Federal funds, be made available for purposes of this subchapter, and in no case supplant such funds; and

(3) have an officer appointed by its governing authority who shall receive and account for all funds paid under the provisions of this subchapter and shall make an annual report to the Secretary on or before the first day of September of each year, on work accomplished and the status of projects underway, together with a detailed statement of the amounts received under any provisions of this subchapter during the preceding fiscal year, and of its disbursements on schedules prescribed by the Secretary.

If any of the funds received by the authorized receiving officer of any institute under the provisions of this subchapter shall by any action or contingency be found by the Secretary to have been improperly diminished, lost, or misapplied, such funds shall be replaced by the State concerned and until so replaced no subsequent appropriation shall be allotted or paid to any institute of such State.

(b) The institutes are authorized and encouraged to plan and conduct programs under this subchapter in cooperation with each other and with such other agencies and individuals as may contribute to the solution of the mining and mineral resources problems involved. Moneys appropriated pursuant to this subchapter shall be available for paying the necessary expenses of planning, coordinating, and conducting such cooperative research.

(Pub.L. 98–409, § 3, Aug. 29, 1984, 98 Stat. 1538.)

### HISTORICAL AND STATUTORY NOTES

**Codifications**

Section was not enacted as part of the Surface Mining Control and Reclamation Act of 1977 which comprises this chapter.

**Prior Provisions**

A prior section 1223, Pub.L. 95–87, Title III, § 303, Aug. 3, 1977, 91 Stat. 453, contained provisions similar to this section covering fiscal years 1978 through 1984.

## § 1224. Duties of Secretary

**[MMRRIA § 4]**

**(a) Consulting with other agencies; prescribing rules and regulations; furnishing advice and assistance; coordinating research**

The Secretary, acting through the Director of the United States Bureau of Mines, shall administer this subchapter and, after full consultation with other interested Federal agencies, shall prescribe such rules and regulations as may be necessary to carry out its provisions. The Secretary shall furnish such advice and assistance as will best promote the purposes of this subchapter, shall participate in coordinating research initiated under this subchapter by the institutes, shall indicate to them such lines of inquiry that seem most important, and shall encourage and assist in the establishment and maintenance of cooperation by and between the institutes and between them and other research organizations, the United States Department of the Interior, and other Federal establishments.

**(b) Annual ascertainment of compliance**

On or before the first day of July in each year beginning after August 29, 1984, the Secretary shall ascertain whether the requirements of section 1223(a) of this title have been met as to each institute and State.

**(c) Omitted**

(Pub.L. 98–409, § 4, Aug. 29, 1984, 98 Stat. 1538; Pub.L. 100–483, § 6, Oct. 12, 1988, 102 Stat. 2340; Pub.L. 102–285, § 10(b), May 18, 1992, 106 Stat. 172.)

### HISTORICAL AND STATUTORY NOTES

**Codifications**

Section was not enacted as part of the Surface Mining Control and Reclamation Act of 1977 which comprises this chapter.

Subsec. (c) of this section, which required the Secretary to submit annual reports to Congress on the receipts, expenditures, and work of the institutes in all states under the provisions of this subchapter, was terminated, effective May 15, 2000, pursuant to Pub.L. 104–66, Title III, § 3003, Dec. 21, 1995, 109 Stat. 734, as amended, which is set out as a note under 31 U.S.C.A. § 1113. See, also, House Document No. 103–7, page 109.

**Change of Name**

Pub.L. 102–285, § 10(b), May 18, 1992, 106 Stat. 172, provided that, on and after May 18, 1992, the Bureau of Mines is redesignated and shall thereafter be known as the United States Bureau of Mines. See note under section 1 of Title 30, Mineral Lands and Mining.

**Prior Provisions**

A prior section 1224, Pub.L. 95–87, Title III, § 304, Aug. 3, 1977, 91 Stat. 454, contained provisions similar to this section covering fiscal years 1978 through 1984.

## § 1225. Effect on colleges and universities

**[MMRRIA § 5]**

Nothing in this subchapter shall be construed to impair or modify the legal relationship existing between any of the colleges or universities under whose direction an institute is established and the government of the State in which it is located, and nothing in this subchapter shall in any way be construed to authorize Federal control or direction of education at any college or university.

(Pub.L. 98–409, § 5, Aug. 29, 1984, 98 Stat. 1539.)

### HISTORICAL AND STATUTORY NOTES

**Codifications**

Section was not enacted as part of the Surface Mining Control and Reclamation Act of 1977 which comprises this chapter.

**Prior Provisions**

A prior section 1225, Pub.L. 95–87, Title III, § 305, Aug. 3, 1977, 91 Stat. 454, contained provisions similar to this section covering fiscal years 1978 through 1984.

## § 1226. Research

**[MMRRIA § 6]**

**(a) Coordination with existing programs; availability of information to public**

The Secretary shall obtain the continuing advice and cooperation of all agencies of the Federal Government concerned with mining and mineral resources, of State and local governments, and of private institutions and individuals to assure that the programs authorized by this subchapter will supplement and not be redundant with respect to established mining and minerals research programs, and to stimulate research in otherwise neglected areas, and to contribute to a comprehensive nationwide program of mining and minerals research, with due regard for the protection and conservation of the environment. The Secretary shall make generally available information and reports on projects completed, in progress, or planned under the provisions of this subchapter, in addition to any direct publication of information by the institutes themselves.

**(b) Effect on Federal agencies**

Nothing in this subchapter is intended to give or shall be construed as giving the Secretary any authority over mining and mineral resources research conducted by any agency of the Federal Government, or as repealing or diminishing existing authorities or responsibilities of any agency of the Federal Government to plan and conduct, contract for, or assist in research in its area of responsibility and concern with regard to mining and mineral resources.

**(c) Availability of results to public**

No research, demonstration, or experiment shall be carried out under this subchapter by an institute financed by grants under this subchapter, unless all uses, products, processes, patents, and other developments resulting therefrom, with such exception or limitation, if any, as the Secretary may find necessary in the public interest, are made available promptly to the general public. Patentable inventions shall be governed by the provisions of Public Law 96–517. Nothing contained in this section shall deprive the owner of any background patent relating to any such activities of any rights which that owner may have under that patent.

**(d) Authorization of appropriations**

(1) There is authorized to be appropriated to the Secretary $450,000 for each of the fiscal years ending September 30, 1990, through September 30, 1994, to administer this subchapter. No funds may be withheld by the Secretary for administrative expenses from those authorized to be appropriated by sections 1221 and 1222 of this title.

(2) There are authorized to be appropriated to the Secretary such sums as are necessary for the printing and publishing of the results of activities carried out by institutes and generic mineral technology centers under this subchapter, but such appropriations shall not exceed $550,000 in any single fiscal year.

(Pub.L. 98–409, § 6, Aug. 29, 1984, 98 Stat. 1539; Pub.L. 100–483, § 7, Oct. 12, 1988, 102 Stat. 2340.)

### HISTORICAL AND STATUTORY NOTES

**References in Text**

Public Law 96–517, referred to in subsec. (c), is Pub.L. 96–517, Dec. 12, 1980, 94 Stat. 3015. Section 6(a) of Pub.L. 96–517, relating to patent rights in inventions made with Federal assistance, is classified to chapter 18 (section 200 et seq.) of Title 35, Patents. For complete classification of this Act to the Code, see Tables.

**Codifications**

Section was not enacted as part of the Surface Mining Control and Reclamation Act of 1977 which comprises this chapter.

**Prior Provisions**

A prior section 1226, Pub.L. 95–87, Title III, § 306, Aug. 3, 1977, 91 Stat. 454, contained provisions similar to this section covering fiscal years 1978 through 1984.

## § 1227. Center for cataloging

**[MMRRIA § 7]**

The Secretary shall establish a center for cataloging current and projected scientific research in all fields of mining and mineral resources. Each Federal agency doing mining and mineral resources research shall cooperate by providing the cataloging center with information on work underway or scheduled by it. The cataloging center shall classify and maintain for public use a catalog of mining and mineral resources research and investigation projects in progress or scheduled by all Federal agencies and by such non-Federal agencies of government, colleges, universities, private institutions, firms, and individuals as may make such information available.

(Pub.L. 98–409, § 7, Aug. 29, 1984, 98 Stat. 1540.)

### HISTORICAL AND STATUTORY NOTES

**Codifications**

Section was not enacted as part of the Surface Mining Control and Reclamation Act of 1977 which comprises this chapter.

**Prior Provisions**

A prior section 1227, Pub.L. 95–87, Title III, § 307, Aug. 3, 1977, 91 Stat. 455, contained provisions similar to this section covering fiscal years 1978 through 1984.

## § 1228. Interagency cooperation

**[MMRRIA § 8]**

The President shall, by such means as he deems appropriate, clarify agency responsibility for Federal mining and mineral resources research and provide for interagency coordination of such research, including the research authorized by this subchapter. Such coordination shall include—

(1) continuing review of the adequacy of the Government-wide program in mining and mineral resources research;

(2) identification and elimination of duplication and overlap between agency programs;

(3) identification of technical needs in various mining and mineral resources research categories;

(4) recommendations with respect to allocation of technical effort among Federal agencies;

(5) review of technical manpower needs, and findings concerning management policies to improve the quality of the Government-wide research effort; and

(6) actions to facilitate interagency communication at management levels.

(Pub.L. 98–409, § 8, Aug. 29, 1984, 98 Stat. 1540.)

### HISTORICAL AND STATUTORY NOTES

**Codifications**

Section was not enacted as part of the Surface Mining Control and Reclamation Act of 1977 which comprises this chapter.

**Prior Provisions**

A prior section 1228, Pub.L. 95–87, Title III, § 308, Aug. 3, 1977, 91 Stat. 455, contained provisions similar to this section covering fiscal years 1978 through 1984.

## § 1229. Committee on Mining and Mineral Resources Research

**[MMRRIA § 9]**

**(a) Appointment; composition**

The Secretary shall appoint a Committee on Mining and Mineral Resources Research composed of—

(1) the Assistant Secretary of the Interior responsible for minerals and mining research, or his delegate;

(2) the Director, United States Bureau of Mines, or his delegate;

(3) the Director, United States Geological Survey, or his delegate;

(4) the Director of the National Science Foundation, or his delegate;

(5) the President, National Academy of Sciences, or his delegate;

(6) the President, National Academy of Engineering, or his delegate; and

(7) not more than 7 other persons who are knowledgeable in the fields of mining and mineral resources research, including two university administrators involved in the conduct of programs authorized by this subchapter, 3 representatives from the mining industry, a working miner, and a representative from the conservation community. In making these 7 appointments, the Secretary shall consult with interested groups.

**(b) Consultation and recommendations**

The Committee shall consult with, and make recommendations to, the Secretary on all matters relating to mining and mineral resources research and the determinations that are required to be made under this subchapter. The Secretary shall consult with, and consider recommendations of, such Committee in such matters.

**(c) Compensation, travel, subsistence and related expenses**

Committee members, other than officers or employees of Federal, State, or local governments, shall be, for each day (including traveltime) during which they are performing Committee business, paid at a rate fixed by the Secretary but not[1] excess of the daily equivalent of the maximum rate of pay for grade GS–18 of the General Schedule under section 5332 of Title 5, and shall be fully reimbursed for travel, subsistence, and related expenses.

**(d) Chairmanship of Committee**

The Committee shall be jointly chaired by the Assistant Secretary of the Interior responsible for minerals and mining and a person to be elected by the Committee from among the members referred to in paragraphs (5), (6), and (7) of subsection (a) of this section.

**(e) National plan for research**

The Committee shall develop a national plan for research in mining and mineral resources, considering ongoing efforts in the universities, the Federal Government, and the private sector, and shall formulate and recommend a program to implement the plan utilizing resources provided for under this subchapter. The Committee shall submit such plan to the Secretary, the President, and the Congress on or before March 1, 1986, and shall submit an annual update of such plan by January 15 of each calendar year.

**(f) Application of Federal Advisory Committee Act**

Section 10 of the Federal Advisory Committee Act (5 U.S.C. App.) shall not apply to the Committee. (Pub.L. 98–409, § 9, Aug. 29, 1984, 98 Stat. 1540; Pub.L. 100–483, §§ 8, 9, Oct. 12, 1988, 102 Stat. 2340; Pub.L. 102–285, § 10(b), May 18, 1992, 106 Stat. 172.)

[1] So in original. Probably should be followed by "in".

## HISTORICAL AND STATUTORY NOTES

**References in Text**

The Federal Advisory Committee Act, referred to in subsec. (f), is Pub.L. 92–463, Oct. 6, 1972, 86 Stat. 770, as amended, which is set out in the Appendix to Title 5, Government Organization and Employees.

**Codifications**

Section was not enacted as part of the Surface Mining Control and Reclamation Act of 1977 which comprises this chapter.

**Change of Name**

Pub.L. 102–285, § 10(b), May 18, 1992, 106 Stat. 172, provided that, on and after May 18, 1992, the Bureau of Mines is redesignated and shall thereafter be known as the United States Bureau of Mines. See note under section 1 of Title 30, Mineral Lands and Mining.

**Prior Provisions**

A prior section 1229, Pub.L. 95–87, Title III, § 309, Aug. 3, 1977, 91 Stat. 455, contained provisions similar to this section covering fiscal years 1978 through 1984.

**Reports to Congressional Committees**

Section 11 of Pub.L. 100–483 provided that:

"(a) **Report on Programs.**—The Committee on Mining and Mineral Resources Research established under section 9 of the Mining and Mineral Resources Research Institute Act of 1984 (30 U.S.C. 1229) [this section] shall submit a report by January 15, 1992, to the Committee on Interior and Insular Affairs [now Committee on Natural Resources] of the United States House of Representatives and the Committee on Energy and Natural Resources of the United States Senate on the programs established under that Act [this subchapter]. Such report may be submitted in conjunction with the annual plan update required by section 9(e) of such Act (30 U.S.C. 1229(e)) [subsec. (e) of this section] and shall include, but not necessarily be limited to, each of the following:

"(1) A review of the activities of the institutes and generic mineral technology centers established under the

Mining and Mineral Resources Research Institute Act of 1984 [this subchapter].

"(2) A review of each institute's eligibility pursuant to section 10 of the Mining and Mineral Resources Research Institute Act of 1984 (30 U.S.C. 1230) [section 1230 of this title].

"(3) A review of each generic mineral technology center's eligibility. In conducting such review the committee shall consider the following criteria:

"(A) Relevance and effectiveness of the research conducted.

"(B) Need for further research in the generic area.

"(4) Recommendations on establishing a mechanism by which new generic mineral technology centers can be established and existing centers can be phased-out or consolidated upon the completion of their mission.

"(b) **Report on Proposal for Center.**—The committee shall submit a proposal to establish a Generic Mineral Technology Center on Strategic and Critical Minerals to the Committee on Interior and Insular Affairs [now Committee on Natural Resources] of the United States House of Representatives and the Committee on Energy and Natural Resources of the United States Senate by January 15, 1990."

[Any reference in any provision of law enacted before Jan. 4, 1995, to the Committee on Natural Resources of the House of Representatives treated as referring to the Committee on Resources of the House of Representatives, see section 1(a)(8) of Pub.L. 104–14, set out as a note preceding section 21 of Title 2, The Congress.]

## § 1230. Eligibility criteria

[MMRRIA § 10]

(a) The Committee shall determine the eligibility of a college or university to participate as a mining and mineral resources research institute under this subchapter using criteria which include—

(1) the presence of a substantial program of graduate instruction and research in mining or mineral extraction or closely related fields which has a demonstrated history of achievement;

(2) evidence of institutional commitment for the purposes of this subchapter;

(3) evidence that such institution has or can obtain significant industrial cooperation in activities within the scope of this subchapter; and

(4) the presence of an engineering program in mining or minerals extraction that is accredited by the Accreditation Board for Engineering and Technology, or evidence of equivalent institutional capability as determined by the Committee.

(b)(1) Notwithstanding the provisions of subsection (a) of this section, those colleges or universities which, on October 12, 1988, have a mining or mineral resources research institute program which has been found to be eligible pursuant to this subchapter shall continue to be eligible subject to review at least once during the period authorized by the Mining and Mineral Resources Research Institute Amendments of 1988, under the provisions of subsection (a) of this section. The results of such review shall be submitted by January 15, 1992, pursuant to section 11(a)(2) of the Mining and Mineral Resources Research Institute Amendments of 1988.

(2) Generic mineral technology centers established by the Secretary under this subchapter are to be composed of institutes eligible pursuant to subsection (a) of this section. Existing generic mineral technology centers shall continue to be eligible under this subchapter subject to at least one review prior to January 15, 1992, pursuant to section 11(a)(3) of the Mining and Mineral Resources Research Institute Amendments of 1988.

(Pub.L. 98–409, § 10, Aug. 29, 1984, 98 Stat. 1541; Pub.L. 100–483, § 10, Oct. 12, 1988, 102 Stat. 2340.)

### HISTORICAL AND STATUTORY NOTES

**References in Text**

The Mining and Mineral Resources Research Institute Amendments of 1988, referred to in subsec. (b)(1), is Pub.L. 100–483, Oct. 12, 1988, 102 Stat. 2341, which amended this subchapter. Section 11(a)(2), (3) of such Amendments of 1988, referred to in subsec. (b)(1), (2), is set out as a note under section 1229 of this title. For complete classification of this Act to the Code, see Short Title of 1988 Amendment note under section 1201 of this title and Tables.

**Codifications**

Section was not enacted as part of the Surface Mining Control and Reclamation Act of 1977 which comprises this chapter.

## § 1230a. Strategic Resources Generic Mineral Technology Center

[MMRRIA § 12]

**(a) Establishment**

The Secretary of[1] Interior is authorized and directed to establish a Strategic Resources Mineral Technology Center (hereinafter referred to as the "center") for the purpose of improving existing, and developing new, technologies that will decrease the dependence of the United States on supplies of strategic and critical minerals.

**(b) Functions**

The center shall—

(1) provide for studies and technology development in the areas of mineral extraction and refining processes, product substitution and conservation of mineral resources through recycling and advanced processing and fabrication methods;

(2) identify new deposits of strategic and critical mineral resources; and

(3) facilitate the transfer of information, studies, and technologies developed by the center to the private sector.

**(c) Criteria**

The Secretary shall establish the center referred to in subsection (a) of this section at a university that—

(1) does not currently host a generic mineral technology center;

(2) has established advanced degree programs in geology and geological engineering, and metallurgical and mining engineering;

(3) has expertise in materials and advanced processing research; and

(4) is located west of the 100th meridian.

**(d) Authorization of appropriations**

There is authorized to be appropriated such sums as may be necessary to carry out this section.

(Pub.L. 98–409, § 12, as added Pub.L. 101–498, § 2, Nov. 2, 1990, 104 Stat. 1207.)

[1] So in original. Probably should be "of the".

# SURFACE MINING CONTROL AND RECLAMATION ACT OF 1977 [SMCRA § ______]

**(30 U.S.C.A. §§ 1231 to 1243, 1251 to 1279, 1281, 1291 to 1309b, 1311 to 1316, 1321 to 1328)**

## SUBCHAPTER IV—ABANDONED MINE RECLAMATIONS

### § 1231. Abandoned Mine Reclamation Fund [SMCRA § 401]

**(a) Establishment; administration; State funds**

There is created on the books of the Treasury of the United States a trust fund to be known as the Abandoned Mine Reclamation Fund (hereinafter referred to as the "fund") which shall be administered by the Secretary of the Interior. State abandoned mine reclamation funds (State funds) generated by grants from this subchapter shall be established by each State pursuant to an approved State program.

**(b) Sources of deposits to fund**

The fund shall consist of amounts deposited in the fund, from time to time derived from—

(1) the reclamation fees levied under section 1232 of this title;

(2) any user charge imposed on or for land reclaimed pursuant to this subchapter, after expenditures for maintenance have been deducted;

(3) donations by persons, corporations, associations, and foundations for the purposes of this subchapter;

(4) recovered moneys as provided for in this subchapter; and

(5) interest credited to the fund under subsection (e) of this section.

**(c) Use of moneys**

Moneys in the fund may be used for the following purposes:

(1) reclamation and restoration of land and water resources adversely affected by past coal mining, including but not limited to reclamation and restoration of abandoned surface mine areas, abandoned coal processing areas, and abandoned coal refuse disposal areas; sealing and filling abandoned deep mine entries and voids; planting of land adversely affected by past coal mining to prevent erosion and sedimentation; prevention, abatement, treatment, and control of water pollution created by coal mine drainage including restoration of stream beds, and construction and operation of water treatment plants; prevention, abatement, and control of burning coal refuse disposal areas and burning coal in situ; prevention, abatement, and control of coal mine subsidence; and establishment of self-sustaining, individual State administered programs to insure private property against damages caused by land subsidence resulting from underground coal mining in those States which have reclamation plans approved in accordance with section 1253 of this title: *Provided*, That funds used for this purpose shall not exceed $3,000,000 of the funds made available to any State under section 1232(g)(1) of this title;

(2) for transfer on an annual basis to the Secretary of Agriculture for use under section 1236 of this title;

(3) acquisition and filling of voids and sealing of tunnels, shafts, and entryways under section 1239 of this title;

(4) acquisition of land as provided for in this subchapter;

(5) enforcement and collection of the reclamation fee provided for in section 1232 of this title;

(6) studies, research, and demonstration projects by the Department of the Interior to such extent or in such amounts as are provided in appropriation Acts with public and private organizations conducted in accordance with section 3501 of the Omnibus Budget Reconciliation Act of 1986, conducted for the purposes of this subchapter;

(7) restoration, reclamation, abatement, control, or prevention of adverse effects of coal mining which constitutes an emergency as provided for in this subchapter;

(8) grants to the States to accomplish the purposes of this subchapter;

(9) administrative expenses of the United States and each State to accomplish the purposes of this subchapter;

(10) for use under section 1240a of this title;

(11) for the purpose of section 1257(c) of this title, except that not more than $10,000,000 shall annually be available for such purpose;

(12) for the purpose described in section 1232(h) of this title; and

(13) all other necessary expenses to accomplish the purposes of this subchapter.

**(d) Moneys available upon appropriation; no fiscal year limitation**

Moneys from the fund shall be available for the purposes of this subchapter, only when appropriated therefor, and such appropriations shall be made without fiscal year limitations.

**(e) Interest**

The Secretary of the Interior shall notify the Secretary of the Treasury as to what portion of the fund is not, in his judgment, required to meet current withdrawals. The Secretary of the Treasury shall invest such portion of the fund in public debt securities with maturities suitable for the needs of such fund and bearing interest at rates determined by the Secretary of the Treasury, taking into consideration current market yields on outstanding marketable obligations of the United States of comparable maturities. The income on such investments shall be credited to, and form a part of, the fund.

(Pub.L. 95–87, Title IV, § 401, Aug. 3, 1977, 91 Stat. 456; Pub.L. 98–473, Title I, § 101(c), Oct. 12, 1984, 98 Stat. 1875; Pub.L. 101–508, Title VI, § 6002, Nov. 5, 1990, 104 Stat. 1388–289; Pub.L. 102–486, Title XIX, § 19143(b)(3)(A), Title XXV, § 2504(c)(1), Oct. 24, 1992, 106 Stat. 3056, 3105.)

## HISTORICAL AND STATUTORY NOTES

**References in Text**

Section 3501 of the Omnibus Budget Reconciliation Act of 1986, referred to in subsec. (c)(6), is section 3501 of Pub.L. 99–509, Title III, Oct. 21, 1986, 100 Stat. 1891, which is classified as a note under this section.

**Effective and Applicability Provisions**

1990 Acts

Section 6014 of Pub.L. 101–508 provided that: "The amendments made by this subtitle [enacting section 1240a of this title, amending this section and sections 1232 to 1237, 1239, 1257 and 1302 of this title, and enacting provisions set out as notes under this section] shall take effect at the beginning of the first fiscal year immediately following the fiscal year in which this subtitle is enacted [Pub.L. 101–508 was approved on Nov. 5, 1990; the next fiscal year began on Oct. 1, 1991]."

**Savings Provisions**

Section 6013 of Pub.L. 101–508 provided that: "Nothing in this subtitle [Subtitle A (section 6001 et seq.) of Pub.L. 101–508, Title VI, Nov. 5, 1990, 104 Stat. 1388–289, for distribution of which, see Short Title of 1990 Amendment note set out under section 1201 of title and Tables] shall be construed to affect the certifications made by the State of Wyoming, the State of Montana, and the State of Louisiana to the Secretary of the Interior prior to the date of enactment of this subtitle [Nov. 5, 1990] that such State has completed the reclamation of eligible abandoned coal mine lands."

**Abandoned Mine Reclamation Fund; Donations for Projects Under the Appalachian Clean Streams Initiative and Under the Western Mine Lands Restoration Partnership Initiative**

Pub.L. 105–277, § 101(e) [Title I], Oct. 21, 1998, 112 Stat. 2681–245, provided in part that: "[H]ereafter, donations received to support projects under the Appalachian Clean Streams Initiative and under the Western Mine Lands Restoration Partnerships Initiative, pursuant to 30 U.S.C. 1231 [this section], shall be credited to this account and remain available until expended without further appropriation for projects sponsored under these initiatives, directly through agreements with other Federal agencies, or through grants to States, and funding to local governments, or tax exempt private entities."

**Abandoned Mine Reclamation Research and Development**

Pub.L. 99–509, Title III, § 3501, Oct. 21, 1986, 100 Stat. 1891, provided that: "After the enactment of this Act [Oct. 21, 1986], the research and demonstration authorities of the Department of the Interior under the provisions of section 401(c)(6) of the Surface Mining Control and Reclamation Act of 1977 (Public Law 95–87) [subsec. (c)(6) of this section] shall be transferred to, and carried out by, the Director of the Bureau of Mines. Research and demonstration projects under such provision shall be selected by a panel appointed by the Director of the Bureau of Mines to be comprised of 9 persons, including 4 representatives of State abandoned mine reclamation programs, 4 representatives of the Bureau of Mines, and one representative of the Office of Surface Mining Reclamation and Enforcement."

[Pub.L. 102–285, § 10(b), May 18, 1992, 106 Stat. 172, provided that, on and after May 18, 1992, the Bureau of Mines is redesignated and shall thereafter be known as the United States Bureau of Mines. See note under section 1 of Title 30, Mineral Lands and Mining.]

## § 1232. Reclamation fee

[SMCRA § 402]

### (a) Payment; rate

All operators of coal mining operations subject to the provisions of this chapter shall pay to the Secretary of the Interior, for deposit in the fund, a reclamation fee of 35 cents per ton of coal produced by surface coal mining and 15 cents per ton of coal produced by underground mining or 10 per centum of the value of the coal at the mine, as determined by the Secretary, whichever is less, except that the reclamation fee for lignite coal shall be at a rate of 2 per centum of the value of the coal at the mine, or 10 cents per ton, whichever is less.

### (b) Due date

Such fee shall be paid no later than thirty days after the end of each calendar quarter beginning with the first calendar quarter occurring after August 3, 1977, and ending September 30, 2004, after which time the fee shall be established at a rate to continue to provide for the deposit referred to in subsection (h) of this section.

### (c) Submission of statement

Together with such reclamation fee, all operators of coal mine operations shall submit a statement of the amount of coal produced during the calendar quarter, the method of coal removal and the type of coal, the accuracy of which shall be sworn to by the operator and notarized. Such statement shall include an identification of the permittee of the surface coal mining operation, any operator in addition to the permittee, the owner of the coal, the preparation plant, tripple,[1] or loading point for the coal, and the person purchasing the coal from the operator. The report shall also specify the number of the permit required under section 1256 of this title and the mine safety and health identification number. Each quarterly report shall contain a notification of any changes in the information required by this subsection since the date of the preceding quarterly report. The information contained in the quarterly reports under this subsection shall be maintained by the Secretary in a computerized database.

### (d) Penalty

(1) Any person, corporate officer, agent or director, on behalf of a coal mine operator, who knowingly makes any false statement, representation or certification, or knowingly fails to make any statement, representation or certification required in this section shall, upon conviction, be punished by a fine of not more than $10,000, or by imprisonment for not more than one year, or both.

(2) The Secretary shall conduct such audits of coal production and the payment of fees under this subchapter as may be necessary to ensure full compliance with the provisions of this subchapter. For purposes of performing such audits the Secretary (or any duly designated officer, employee, or representative of the Secretary) shall, at all reasonable times, upon request, have access to, and may copy, all books, papers, and other documents of any person subject to the provisions of this subchapter. The Secretary may at any time conduct audits of any surface coal mining and reclamation operation, including without limitation, tipples and preparation plants, as may be necessary in the judgment of the Secretary to ensure full and complete payment of the fees under this subchapter.

### (e) Civil action to recover fee

Any portion of the reclamation fee not properly or promptly paid pursuant to this section shall be recoverable, with statutory interest, from coal mine operators, in any court of competent jurisdiction in any action at law to compel payment of debts.

### (f) Cooperation from other agencies

All Federal and State agencies shall fully cooperate with the Secretary of the Interior in the enforcement of this section. Whenever the Secretary believes that any person has not paid the full amount of the fee payable under subsection (a) of this section the Secretary shall notify the Federal agency responsible for ensuring compliance with the provisions of section 4121 of Title 26.

### (g) Allocation of funds

(1) Except as provided in subsection (h) of this section, moneys deposited into the fund shall be allocated by the Secretary to accomplish the purposes of this subchapter as follows:

(A) 50 percent of the reclamation fees collected annually in any State (other than fees collected with respect to Indian lands) shall be allocated annually by the Secretary to the State, subject to such State having each of the following:

(i) An approved abandoned mine reclamation program pursuant to section 1235 of this title.

(ii) Lands and waters which are eligible pursuant to section 1234 of this title (in the case of a State not certified under section 1240a(a) of this title) or pursuant to section 1240a(b) of this title (in the case of a State certified under section 1240a(a) of this title).

(B) 50 percent of the reclamation fees collected annually with respect to Indian lands shall be allocated annually by the Secretary to the Indian tribe having jurisdiction over such lands, subject to such tribe having each of the following:

(i) an [2] approved abandoned mine reclamation program pursuant to section 1235 of this title.

(ii) Lands and waters which are eligible pursuant to section 1234 of this title (in the case of an Indian tribe not certified under section 1240a(a) of this title) or pursuant to section 1240a(b) of this title (in the case of a tribe certified under section 1240a(a) of this title).

(C) The funds allocated by the Secretary under this paragraph to States and Indian tribes shall only be used for annual reclamation project construction and program administration grants.

(D) To the extent not expended within 3 years after the date of any grant award under this paragraph, such grant shall be available for expenditure by the Secretary in any area under paragraph (2), (3), (4), or (5).

(2) 20 percent of the amounts available in the fund in any fiscal year which are not allocated under paragraph (1) in that fiscal year (including that interest accruing as provided in section 1231(e) of this title and including funds available for reallocation pursuant to paragraph (1)(D)), shall be allocated to the Secretary only for the purpose of making the annual transfer to the Secretary of Agriculture under section 1231(c)(2) of this title.

(3) Amounts available in the fund which are not allocated to States and Indian tribes under paragraph (1) or allocated under paragraphs (2) and (5) are authorized to be expended by the Secretary for any of the following:

(A) For the purpose of section 1257(c) of this title, either directly or through grants to the States, subject to the limitation contained in section 1231(c)(11) of this title.

(B) For the purpose of section 1240 of this title (relating to emergencies).

(C) For the purpose of meeting the objectives of the fund set forth in section 1233(a) of this title for eligible lands and waters pursuant to section 1234 of this title in States and on Indian lands where the State or Indian tribe does not have an approved abandoned mine reclamation program pursuant to section 1235 of this title.

(D) For the administration of this subchapter by the Secretary.

(4)(A) Amounts available in the fund which are not allocated under paragraphs (1), (2), and (5) or expended under paragraph (3) in any fiscal year are authorized to be expended by the Secretary under this paragraph for the reclamation or drainage abatement of lands and waters within unreclaimed sites which are mined for coal or which were affected by such mining, wastebanks, coal processing or other coal mining processes and left in an inadequate reclamation status.

(B) Funds made available under this paragraph may be used for reclamation or drainage abatement at a site referred to in subparagraph (A) if the Secretary makes either of the following findings:

(i) A finding that the surface coal mining operation occurred during the period beginning on August 4, 1977, and ending on or before the date on which the Secretary approved a State program pursuant to section 1253 of this title for a State in which the site is located, and that any funds for reclamation or abatement which are available pursuant to a bond or other form of financial guarantee or from any other source are not sufficient to provide for adequate reclamation or abatement at the site.

(ii) A finding that the surface coal mining operation occurred during the period beginning on August 4, 1977, and ending on or before November 5, 1990, and that the surety of such mining operator became insolvent during such period, and as of November 5, 1990, funds immediately available from proceedings relating to such insolvency, or from any financial guarantee or other source are not sufficient to provide for adequate reclamation or abatement at the site.

(C) In determining which sites to reclaim pursuant to this paragraph, the Secretary shall follow the priorities stated in paragraphs (1) and (2) of section 1233(a) of this title. The Secretary shall ensure that priority is given to those sites which are in the immediate vicinity of a residential area or which have an adverse economic impact upon a local community.

(D) Amounts collected from the assessment of civil penalties under section 1268 of this title are authorized to be appropriated to carry out this paragraph.

(E) Any State may expend grants made available under paragraphs (1) and (5) for reclamation and abatement of any site referred to in subparagraph (A) if the State, with the concurrence of the Secretary, makes either of the findings referred to in clause (i) or (ii) of subparagraph (B) and if the State determines that the reclamation priority of the site is the same or more urgent than the reclamation priority for eligible lands and waters pursuant to section 1234 of this title under the priorities stated in paragraphs (1) and (2) of section 1233(a) of this title.

(F) For the purposes of the certification referred to in section 1240a(a) of this title, sites referred to in subparagraph (A) of this paragraph shall be considered as having the same priorities as those stated in section 1233(a) of this title for eligible lands and waters pursuant to section 1234 of this title. All sites referred to in subparagraph (A) of this paragraph within any State shall be reclaimed prior to such State making the certification referred to in section 1240a(a) of this title.

(5) The Secretary shall allocate 40 percent of the amount in the fund after making the allocation referred to in paragraph (1) for making additional annual grants to States and Indian tribes which are not certified under section 1240a(a) of this title to supplement grants received by such States and Indian tribes pursuant to paragraph (1)(C) until the priorities stated in paragraphs (1) and (2) of section 1233(a) of this title have been achieved by such State or Indian tribe. The allocation of such funds for the purpose of making such expenditures shall be through a formula based on the amount of coal historically produced in the State or from the Indian lands concerned prior to August 3, 1977. Funds allocated or expended by the Secretary under paragraphs (2), (3), or (4) of this subsection for any State or Indian tribe shall not be deducted against any allocation of funds to the State or Indian tribe under paragraph (1) or under this paragraph.

(6) Any State may receive and retain, without regard to the 3–year limitation referred to in paragraph (1)(D), up to 10 percent of the total of the grants made annually to such State under paragraphs (1) and (5) if such amounts are deposited into either—

(A) a special trust fund established under State law pursuant to which such amounts (together with all interest earned on such amounts) are expended by the State solely to achieve the priorities stated in section 1233(a) of this title after September 30, 1995, or

(B) an acid mine drainage abatement and treatment fund established under State law as provided in paragraph (7).

(7)(A) Any State may establish under State law an acid mine drainage abatement and treatment fund from which amounts (together with all interest earned on such amounts) are expended by the State to implement, in consultation with the Soil Conservation Service, acid mine drainage abatement and treatment plans approved by the Secretary. Such plans shall provide for the comprehensive abatement of the causes and treatment of the effects of acid mine drainage within qualified hydrologic units affected by coal mining practices.

(B) The plan shall include, but shall not be limited to, each of the following:

(i) An identification of the qualified hydrologic unit.

(ii) The extent to which acid mine drainage is affecting the water quality and biological resources within the hydrologic unit.

(iii) An identification of the sources of acid mine drainage within the hydrologic unit.

(iv) An identification of individual projects and the measures proposed to be undertaken to abate and treat the causes or effects of acid mine drainage within the hydrologic unit.

(v) The cost of undertaking the proposed abatement and treatment measures.

(vi) An identification of existing and proposed sources of funding for such measures.

(vii) An analysis of the cost-effectiveness and environmental benefits of abatement and treatment measures.

(C) The Secretary may approve any plan under this paragraph only after determining that such plan meets the requirements of this paragraph. In conducting an analysis of the items referred to in clauses (iv), (v), and (vii) the Director of the Office of Surface Mining shall obtain the comments of the Director of the United States Bureau of Mines. In approving plans under this paragraph, the Secretary shall give a priority to those plans which will be implemented in coordination with measures undertaken by the Secretary of Agriculture under section 1236 of this title.

(D) For purposes of this paragraph, the term "qualified hydrologic unit" means a hydrologic unit—

(i) in which the water quality has been significantly affected by acid mine drainage from coal mining practices in a manner which adversely impacts biological resources; and

(ii) which contains lands and waters which are—

(I) eligible pursuant to section 1234 of this title and include any of the priorities stated in paragraph (1), (2), or (3) of section 1233(a) of this title; and

(II) proposed to be the subject of the expenditures by the State (from amounts available from the forfeiture of bonds required under section 1259 of this title or from other State sources) to mitigate acid mine drainage.

(8) Of the funds available for expenditure under this subsection in any fiscal year, the Secretary shall allocate annually not less than $2,000,000 for expenditure in each State, and for each Indian tribe, having an approved abandoned mine reclamation program pursuant to section 1235 of this title and eligible lands and waters pursuant to section 1234 of this title so long as an allocation of funds to such State or such tribe is necessary to achieve the priorities stated in paragraphs (1) and (2) of section 1233(a) of this title.

**(h) Transfer of funds to Combined Fund**

(1) In the case of any fiscal year beginning on or after October 1, 1995, with respect to which fees are required to be paid under this section, the Secretary shall, as of the beginning of such fiscal year and

before any allocation under subsection (g) of this section, make the transfer provided in paragraph (2).

(2) The Secretary shall transfer from the fund to the United Mine Workers of America Combined Benefit Fund established under section 9702 of Title 26 for any fiscal year an amount equal to the sum of—

(A) the amount of the interest which the Secretary estimates will be earned and paid to the Fund during the fiscal year, plus

(B) the amount by which the amount described in subparagraph (A) is less than $70,000,000.

(3)(A) The aggregate amount which may be transferred under paragraph (2) for any fiscal year shall not exceed the amount of expenditures which the trustees of the Combined Fund estimate will be debited against the unassigned beneficiaries premium account under section 9704(e) of Title 26 for the fiscal year of the Combined Fund in which the transfer is made.

(B) The aggregate amount which may be transferred under paragraph (2)(B) for all fiscal years shall not exceed an amount equivalent to all interest earned and paid to the fund after September 30, 1992, and before October 1, 1995.

(4) If, for any fiscal year, the amount transferred is more or less than the amount required to be transferred, the Secretary shall appropriately adjust the amount transferred for the next fiscal year.

(Pub.L. 95–87, Title IV, § 402, Aug. 3, 1977, 91 Stat. 457; Pub.L. 100–34, Title I, § 101, May 7, 1987, 101 Stat. 300; Pub.L. 101–508, Title VI, §§ 6003, 6004, Nov. 5, 1990, 104 Stat. 1388–290, 1388–291; Pub.L. 102–285, § 10(b), May 18, 1992, 106 Stat. 172; Pub.L. 102–486, Title XIX, § 19143(b)(1), (2), (3)(B), Title XXV, § 2515, Oct. 24, 1992, 106 Stat. 3056, 3113.)

[1] So in original. Probably should be "tipple,".

[2] So in original. Probably should be capitalized.

## HISTORICAL AND STATUTORY NOTES

**References in Text**

This chapter, referred to in subsec. (a), was in the original "this Act", meaning Pub.L. 95–87, Aug. 3, 1977, 91 Stat. 445, as amended, which enacted this chapter and amended section 1114 of Title 18, Crimes and Criminal Procedure. For complete classification of this Act to the Code, see Short Title note set out under section 1201 of this title and Tables.

**Effective and Applicability Provisions**

1990 Acts

Amendment by Pub.L. 101–508 effective Oct. 1, 1991, see section 6014 of Pub.L. 101–508, set out as a note under section 1231 of this title.

**Change of Name**

Pub.L. 102–285, § 10(b), May 18, 1992, 106 Stat. 172, provided that, on and after May 18, 1992, the Bureau of Mines is redesignated and shall thereafter be known as the United States Bureau of Mines. See note under section 1 of Title 30, Mineral Lands and Mining.

**Savings Provisions**

Nothing in Subtitle A (section 6001 et seq.) of Title VI of Pub.L. 101–508, shall be construed to affect the certifications made by the States of Wyoming, Montana, and Louisiana to the Secretary of the Interior prior to Nov. 5, 1990, that each such State has completed the reclamation of eligible abandoned coal mine lands, see section 6013 of Pub.L. 101–508, set out as a note under section 1231 of this title.

## § 1233. Objectives of fund

[SMCRA § 403]

**(a) Priorities**

Expenditure of moneys from the fund on lands and water eligible pursuant to section 1234 of this title for the purposes of this subchapter, except as provided for under section 1240a of this title, shall reflect the following priorities in the order stated:

(1) the protection of public health, safety, general welfare, and property from extreme danger of adverse effects of coal mining practices;

(2) the protection of public health, safety, and general welfare from adverse effects of coal mining practices;

(3) the restoration of land and water resources and the environment previously degraded by adverse effects of coal mining practices including measures for the conservation and development of soil, water (excluding channelization), woodland, fish and wildlife, recreation resources, and agricultural productivity.[1]

(4) the protection, repair, replacement, construction, or enhancement of public facilities such as utilities, roads, recreation, and conservation facilities adversely affected by coal mining practices;

(5) the development of publicly owned land adversely affected by coal mining practices including land acquired as provided in this subchapter for recreation and historic purposes, conservation, and reclamation purposes and open space benefits.

(6) Redesignated (5).

**(b) Utilities and other facilities**

(1) Any State or Indian tribe not certified under section 1240a(a) of this title may expend up to 30 percent of the funds allocated to such State or Indian tribe in any year through the grants made available under paragraphs (1) and (5) of section 1232(g) of this title for the purpose of protecting, repairing, replacing, constructing, or enhancing facilities relating to water supply, including water distribution facilities and treatment plants, to replace water supplies adversely affected by coal mining practices.

(2) If the adverse effect on water supplies referred to in this subsection occurred both prior to and after August 3, 1977, or as the case may be, the dates (and under the criteria) set forth under section 1232(g)(4)(B) of this title, section 1234 of this title shall not be construed to prohibit a State or Indian tribe referred to in paragraph (1) from using funds referred to in such paragraph for the purposes of this subsection if the State or Indian tribe determines that such adverse effects occurred predominantly prior to August 3, 1977, or as the case may be, the dates (and under the criteria) set forth under section 1232(g)(4)(B) of this title.

**(c) Inventory**

For the purposes of assisting in the planning and evaluation of reclamation projects pursuant to section 1235 of this title, and assisting in making the certification referred to in section 1240a(a) of this title, the Secretary shall maintain an inventory of eligible lands and waters pursuant to section 1234 of this title which meet the priorities stated in paragraphs (1) and (2) of subsection (a) of this section. Under standardized procedures established by the Secretary, States and Indian tribes with approved abandoned mine reclamation programs pursuant to section 1235 of this title may offer amendments to update the inventory as it applies to eligible lands and waters under the jurisdiction of such States or tribes. The Secretary shall provide such States and tribes with the financial and technical assistance necessary for the purpose of making inventory amendments. The Secretary shall compile and maintain an inventory for States and Indian lands in the case when a State or Indian tribe does not have an approved abandoned mine reclamation program pursuant to section 1235 of this title. On a regular basis, but not less than annually, the projects completed under this subchapter shall be so noted on the inventory under standardized procedures established by the Secretary.

(Pub.L. 95–87, Title IV, § 403, Aug. 3, 1977, 91 Stat. 458; Pub.L. 101–508, Title VI, § 6005, Nov. 5, 1990, 104 Stat. 1388–294; Pub.L. 102–486, Title XXV, § 2504(c)(2), (e), Oct. 24, 1992, 106 Stat. 3105, 3106.)

1 So in original. The period probably should be a semicolon.

### HISTORICAL AND STATUTORY NOTES

**Effective and Applicability Provisions**

1990 Acts

Amendment by Pub.L. 101–508 effective Oct. 1, 1991, see section 6014 of Pub.L. 101–508, set out as a note under section 1231 of this title.

**Savings Provisions**

Nothing in Subtitle A (section 6001 et seq.) of Title VI of Pub.L. 101–508, shall be construed to affect the certifications made by the States of Wyoming, Montana, and Louisiana to the Secretary of the Interior prior to Nov. 5, 1990, that each such State has completed the reclamation of eligible abandoned coal mine lands, see section 6013 of Pub.L. 101–508, set out as a note under section 1231 of this title.

## § 1234. Eligible lands and water

**[SMCRA § 404]**

Lands and water eligible for reclamation or drainage abatement expenditures under this subchapter are those which were mined for coal or which were affected by such mining, wastebanks, coal processing, or other coal mining processes, except as provided for under section 1240a of this title, and abandoned or left in an inadequate reclamation status prior to August 3, 1977, and for which there is no continuing reclamation responsibility under State or other Federal laws. For other provisions relating to lands and waters eligible for such expenditures, see section 1232(g)(4) of this title, section 1233(b)(1) of this title, and section 1239 of this title. Surface coal mining operations on lands eligible for remining shall not affect the eligibility of such lands for reclamation and restoration under this subchapter after the release of the bond or deposit for any such operation as provided under section 1269 of this title. In the event the bond or deposit for a surface coal mining operation on lands eligible for remining is forfeited, funds available under this subchapter may be used if the amount of such bond or deposit is not sufficient to provide for adequate reclamation or abatement, except that if conditions warrant the Secretary shall immediately exercise his authority under section 1240 of this title.

(Pub.L. 95–87, Title IV, § 404, Aug. 3, 1977, 91 Stat. 459; Pub.L. 101–508, Title VI, § 6006, Nov. 5, 1990, 104 Stat. 1388–295; Pub.L. 102–486, Title XXV, § 2503(d), Oct. 24, 1992, 106 Stat. 3103.)

### HISTORICAL AND STATUTORY NOTES

**Legislative History**

1977 Acts

House Report No. 95–218 and House Conference Report No. 95–493, see 1977 U.S. Code Cong. and Adm. News, p. 593.

1990 Acts

House Report No. 101–881, House Conference Report No. 101–964, and Statement by President, see 1990 U.S. Code Cong. and Adm. News, p. 2017.

1992 Acts

House Report No. 102–474(Parts I–IX), House Conference Report No. 102–1018, and Statement by President, see 1992 U.S. Code Cong. and Adm. News, p. 1953.

**Effective and Applicability Provisions**

1990 Acts

Amendment by Pub.L. 101–508 effective Oct. 1, 1991, see section 6014 of Pub.L. 101–508, set out as a note under section 1231 of this title.

**Savings Provisions**

Nothing in Subtitle A (section 6001 et seq.) of Title VI of Pub.L. 101–508, shall be construed to affect the certifications made by the States of Wyoming, Montana, and Louisiana to the Secretary of the Interior prior to Nov. 5, 1990, that each such State has completed the reclamation of eligible abandoned coal mine lands, see section 6013 of Pub.L. 101–508, set out as a note under section 1231 of this title.

## § 1235. State reclamation program [SMCRA § 405]

### (a) Promulgation of regulations

Not later than the end of the one hundred and eighty-day period immediately following August 3, 1977, the Secretary shall promulgate and publish in the Federal Register regulations covering implementation of an abandoned mine reclamation program incorporating the provisions of this subchapter and establishing procedures and requirements for preparation, submission, and approval of State programs consisting of the plan and annual submissions of projects.

### (b) Submission of State Reclamation Plan and annual projects

Each State having within its borders coal mined lands eligible for reclamation under this subchapter, may submit to the Secretary a State Reclamation Plan and annual projects to carry out the purposes of this subchapter.

### (c) Restriction

The Secretary shall not approve, fund, or continue to fund a State abandoned mine reclamation program unless that State has an approved State regulatory program pursuant to section 1253 of this title.

### (d) Approval of State program; withdrawal

If the Secretary determines that a State has developed and submitted a program for reclamation of abandoned mines and has the ability and necessary State legislation to implement the provisions of this subchapter, sections 1232 and 1240 of this title excepted, the Secretary shall approve such State program and shall grant to the State exclusive responsibility and authority to implement the provisions of the approved program: *Provided,* That the Secretary shall withdraw such approval and authorization if he determines upon the basis of information provided under this section that the State program is not in compliance with the procedures, guidelines, and requirements established under subsection (a) of this section.

### (e) Contents of State Reclamation Plan

Each State Reclamation Plan shall generally identify the areas to be reclaimed, the purposes for which the reclamation is proposed, the relationship of the lands to be reclaimed and the proposed reclamation to surrounding areas, the specific criteria for ranking and identifying projects to be funded, and the legal authority and programmatic capability to perform such work in conformance with the provisions of this subchapter.

### (f) Annual application for support; contents

On an annual basis, each State having an approved State Reclamation Plan may submit to the Secretary an application for the support of the State program and implementation of specific reclamation projects. Such annual requests shall include such information as may be requested by the Secretary including:

(1) a general description of each proposed project;

(2) a priority evaluation of each proposed project;

(3) a statement of the estimated benefits in such terms as: number of acres restored, miles of stream improved, acres of surface lands protected from subsidence, population protected from subsidence, air pollution, hazards of mine and coal refuse disposal area fires;

(4) an estimate of the cost for each proposed project;

(5) in the case of proposed research and demonstration projects, a description of the specific techniques to be evaluated or objective to be attained;

(6) an identification of lands or interest therein to be acquired and the estimated cost; and

(7) in each year after the first in which a plan is filed under this subchapter, an inventory of each project funded under the previous year's grant: which inventory shall include details of financial expenditures on such project together with a brief description of each such project, including project locations, landowner's name, acreage, type of reclamation performed.

### (g) Costs

The costs for each proposed project under this section shall include: actual construction costs, actual operation and maintenance costs of permanent facilities, planning and engineering costs, construction inspection costs, and other necessary administrative expenses.

### (h) Grant of funds

Upon approval of State Reclamation Plan by the Secretary and of the surface mine regulatory program pursuant to section 1253 of this title, the Secretary shall grant, on an annual basis, funds to be expended in such State pursuant to section 1232(g) of this title and which are necessary to implement the State reclamation program as approved by the Secretary.

**(i) Program monitorship**

The Secretary, through his designated agents, will monitor the progress and quality of the program. The States shall not be required at the start of any project to submit complete copies of plans and specifications.

**(j) Annual report to Secretary**

The Secretary shall require annual and other reports as may be necessary to be submitted by each State administering the approved State reclamation program with funds provided under this subchapter. Such reports shall include that information which the Secretary deems necessary to fulfill his responsibilities under this subchapter.

**(k) Eligible lands of Indian tribes**

Indian tribes having within their jurisdiction eligible lands pursuant to section 1234 of this title or from which coal is produced, shall be considered as a "State" for the purposes of this subchapter except for purposes of subsection (c) of this section with respect to the Navajo, Hopi and Crow Indian Tribes.

**(*l*) State liability**

No State shall be liable under any provision of Federal law for any costs or damages as a result of action taken or omitted in the course of carrying out a State abandoned mine reclamation plan approved under this section. This subsection shall not preclude liability for cost or damages as a result of gross negligence or intentional misconduct by the State. For purposes of the preceding sentence, reckless, willful, or wanton misconduct shall constitute gross negligence.

(Pub.L. 95–87, Title IV, § 405, Aug. 3, 1977, 91 Stat. 459; Pub.L. 100–71, Title I, July 11, 1987, 101 Stat. 416; Pub.L. 101–508, Title VI, §§ 6007, 6012(d)(1), (2), Nov. 5, 1990, 104 Stat. 1388–295, 1388–298.)

## HISTORICAL AND STATUTORY NOTES

**Effective and Applicability Provisions**

1990 Acts

Amendment by Pub.L. 101–508 effective Oct. 1, 1991, see section 6014 of Pub.L. 101–508, set out as a note under section 1231 of this title.

**Savings Provisions**

Nothing in Subtitle A (section 6001 et seq.) of Title VI of Pub.L. 101–508, shall be construed to affect the certifications made by the States of Wyoming, Montana, and Louisiana to the Secretary of the Interior prior to Nov. 5, 1990, that each such State has completed the reclamation of eligible abandoned coal mine lands, see section 6013 of Pub.L. 101–508, set out as a note under section 1231 of this title.

**Grant of Funds to States Under Surface Mining Control and Reclamation Act**

Pub.L. 97–377, Title I, § 150, Dec. 21, 1982, 96 Stat. 1918, provided that: "Within 60 days of receipt of a complete abandoned mine reclamation fund grant application from any eligible State under the provisions of the Surface Mining Control and Reclamation Act (91 Stat. 460) the Secretary of Interior shall grant to such State any and all funds available for such purposes in the applicable appropriations Act."

## § 1236. Reclamation of rural lands

**[SMCRA § 406]**

**(a) Agreements with landowners for conservation treatment**

In order to provide for the control and prevention of erosion and sediment damages from unreclaimed mined lands, and to promote the conservation and development of soil and water resources of unreclaimed mined lands and lands affected by mining, the Secretary of Agriculture is authorized to enter into agreements of not more than ten years with landowners (including owners of water rights), residents, and tenants, and individually or collectively, determined by him to have control for the period of the agreement of lands in question therein, providing for land stabilization, erosion, and sediment control, and reclamation through conservation treatment, including measures for the conservation and development of soil, water (excluding stream channelization), woodland, wildlife, and recreation resources, and agricultural productivity of such lands. Such agreements shall be made by the Secretary with the owners, including owners of water rights, residents, or tenants (collectively or individually) of the lands in question.

**(b) Conservation and development plans**

The landowner, including the owner of water rights, resident, or tenant shall furnish to the Secretary of Agriculture a conservation and development plan setting forth the proposed land uses and conservation treatment which shall be mutually agreed by the Secretary of Agriculture and the landowner, including owner of water rights, resident, or tenant to be needed on the lands for which the plan was prepared. In those instances where it is determined that the water rights or water supply of a tenant, landowner, including owner of water rights, resident, or tenant have been adversely affected by a surface or underground coal mine operation which has removed or disturbed a stratum so as to significantly affect the hydrologic balance, such plan may include proposed measures to enhance water quality or quantity by means of joint action with other affected landowners, including owner of water rights, residents, or tenants in consultation with appropriate State and Federal agencies.

**(c) Agreement to effect plan**

Such plan shall be incorporated in an agreement under which the landowner, including owner of water rights, resident, or tenant shall agree with the Secretary of Agriculture to effect the land uses and conservation treatment provided for in such plan on the lands described in the agreement in accordance with the terms and conditions thereof.

**(d) Financial and other assistance; determination by Secretary**

In return for such agreement by the landowner, including owner of water rights, resident, or tenant, the Secretary of Agriculture is authorized to furnish financial and other assistance to such landowner, including owner of water rights, resident, or tenant, in such amounts and subject to such conditions as the Secretary of Agriculture determines are appropriate in the public interest for carrying out the land use and conservation treatment set forth in the agreement. Grants made under this section, depending on the income-producing potential of the land after reclaiming, shall provide up to 80 per centum of the cost of carrying out such land uses and conservation treatment on not more than one hundred and twenty acres of land occupied by such owner, including water rights owners, resident, or tenant, or on not more than one hundred and twenty acres of land which has been purchased jointly by such landowners, including water rights owners, residents, or tenants, under an agreement for the enhancement of water quality or quantity or on land which has been acquired by an appropriate State or local agency for the purpose of implementing such agreement; except the Secretary may reduce the matching cost share where he determines that (1) the main benefits to be derived from the project are related to improving offsite water quality, offsite esthetic values, or other offsite benefits, and (2) the matching share requirement would place a burden on the landowner which would probably prevent him from participating in the program: *Provided, however*, That the Secretary of Agriculture may allow for land use and conservation treatment on such lands occupied by any such owner in excess of such one hundred and twenty acre limitation up to three hundred and twenty acres, but in such event the amount of the grant to such landowner to carry out such reclamation on such lands shall be reduced proportionately. Notwithstanding any other provision of this section with regard to acreage limitations, the Secretary of Agriculture may carry out reclamation treatment projects to control erosion and improve water quality on all lands within a hydrologic unit, consisting of not more than 25,000 acres, if the Secretary determines that treatment of such lands as a hydrologic unit will achieve greater reduction in the adverse effects of past surface mining practices than would be achieved if reclamation was done on individual parcels of land.

**(e) Termination of agreements**

The Secretary of Agriculture may terminate any agreement with a landowner including water rights owners, operator, or occupier by mutual agreement if the Secretary of Agriculture determines that such termination would be in the public interest, and may agree to such modification of agreements previously entered into hereunder as he deems desirable to carry out the purposes of this section or to facilitate the practical administration of the program authorized herein.

**(f) Preservation and surrender of history and allotments**

Notwithstanding any other provision of law, the Secretary of Agriculture, to the extent he deems it desirable to carry out the purposes of this section, may provide in any agreement hereinunder for (1) preservation for a period not to exceed the period covered by the agreement and an equal period thereafter of the cropland, crop acreage, and allotment history applicable to land covered by the agreement for the purpose of any Federal program under which such history is used as a basis for an allotment or other limitation on the production of such crop; or (2) surrender of any such history and allotments.

**(g) Rules and regulations**

The Secretary of Agriculture shall be authorized to issue such rules and regulations as he determines are necessary to carry out the provisions of this section.

**(h) Utilization of Soil Conservation Service**

In carrying out the provisions of this section, the Secretary of Agriculture shall utilize the services of the Soil Conservation Service.

**(i) Repealed. Pub.L. 101–508, Title VI, § 6012(c), Nov. 5, 1990, 104 Stat. 1388–298**

(Pub.L. 95–87, Title IV, § 406, Aug. 3, 1977, 91 Stat. 460; Pub.L. 97–98, Title XV, § 1551, Dec. 22, 1981, 95 Stat. 1344; Pub.L. 101–508, Title VI, §§ 6008, 6012(c), (d)(3), Nov. 5, 1990, 104 Stat. 1388–295, 1388–298.)

### HISTORICAL AND STATUTORY NOTES

**Effective and Applicability Provisions**

1990 Acts

Amendment by Pub.L. 101–508 effective Oct. 1, 1991, see section 6014 of Pub.L. 101–508, set out as a note under section 1231 of this title.

**Savings Provisions**

Nothing in Subtitle A (section 6001 et seq.) of Title VI of Pub.L. 101–508, shall be construed to affect the certifications made by the States of Wyoming, Montana, and Louisiana to the Secretary of the Interior prior to Nov. 5, 1990, that each such State has completed the reclamation of eligible abandoned coal mine lands, see section 6013 of Pub.L. 101–508, set out as a note under section 1231 of this title.

## § 1237. Acquisition and reclamation of land adversely affected by past coal mining practices

**[SMCRA § 407]**

### (a) Findings of fact; notice; right of entry

If the Secretary or the State pursuant to an approved State program, makes a finding of fact that—

(1) land or water resources have been adversely affected by past coal mining practices; and

(2) the adverse effects are at a stage where, in the public interest, action to restore, reclaim, abate, control, or prevent should be taken; and

(3) the owners of the land or water resources where entry must be made to restore, reclaim, abate, control, or prevent the adverse effects of past coal mining practices are not known, or readily available; or

(4) the owners will not give permission for the United States, the States, political subdivisions, their agents, employees, or contractors to enter upon such property to restore, reclaim, abate, control, or prevent the adverse effects of past coal mining practices;

then, upon giving notice by mail to the owners if known or if not known by posting notice upon the premises and advertising once in a newspaper of general circulation in the municipality in which the land lies, the Secretary, his agents, employees, or contractors, or the State pursuant to an approved State program, shall have the right to enter upon the property adversely affected by past coal mining practices and any other property to have access to such property to do all things necessary or expedient to restore, reclaim, abate, control, or prevent the adverse effects. Such entry shall be construed as an exercise of the police power for the protection of public health, safety, and general welfare and shall not be construed as an act of condemnation of property nor of trespass thereon. The moneys expended for such work and the benefits accruing to any such premises so entered upon shall be chargeable against such land and shall mitigate or offset any claim in or any action brought by any owner of any interest in such premises for any alleged damages by virtue of such entry: *Provided, however*, That this provision is not intended to create new rights of action or eliminate existing immunities.

### (b) Studies or exploratory work

The Secretary, his agents, employees, or contractors or the State pursuant to an approved State program, shall have the right to enter upon any property for the purpose of conducting studies or exploratory work to determine the existence of adverse effects of past coal mining practices and to determine the feasibility of restoration, reclamation, abatement, control, or prevention of such adverse effects. Such entry shall be construed as an exercise of the police power for the protection of public health, safety, and general welfare and shall not be construed as an act of condemnation of property nor trespass thereon.

### (c) Requirements for acquisition of affected land

The Secretary or the State pursuant to an approved State program, may acquire any land, by purchase, donation, or condemnation, which is adversely affected by past coal mining practices if the Secretary determines that acquisition of such land is necessary to successful reclamation and that—

(1) the acquired land, after restoration, reclamation, abatement, control, or prevention of the adverse effects of past coal mining practices, will serve recreation and historic purposes, conservation and reclamation purposes or provide open space benefits; and

(2) permanent facilities such as a treatment plant or a relocated stream channel will be constructed on the land for the restoration, reclamation, abatement, control, or prevention of the adverse effects of past coal mining practices; or

(3) acquisition of coal refuse disposal sites and all coal refuse thereon will serve the purposes of this subchapter or that public ownership is desirable to meet emergency situations and prevent recurrences of the adverse effects of past coal mining practices.

### (d) Title to affected land; value

Title to all lands acquired pursuant to this section shall be in the name of the United States or, if acquired by a State pursuant to an approved program, title shall be in the name of the State. The price paid for land acquired under this section shall reflect the market value of the land as adversely affected by past coal mining practices.

### (e) State participation; grants

States are encouraged as part of their approved State programs, to reclaim abandoned and unreclaimed mined lands within their boundaries and, if necessary, to acquire or to transfer such lands to the Secretary or the appropriate State regulatory authority under appropriate Federal regulations. The Secretary is authorized to make grants on a matching basis to States in such amounts as he deems appropriate for the purpose of carrying out the provisions of this subchapter but in no event shall any grant exceed 90 per centum of the cost of acquisition of the lands for which the grant is made. When a State has made any such land available to the Federal Government under this subchapter, such State shall have a preference right to purchase such lands after reclamation at fair market value less the State portion of the original acquisition price. Notwithstanding the provisions of paragraph (1) of subsection (c) of this section, reclaimed land may be sold to the State or local government in which it is located at a price less than fair market value, which in no case shall be less than the cost to the United States of the purchase and reclamation of the land, as negotiated by the Secretary, to be used for a valid public purpose. If any land sold to a State or local government under this paragraph is not used for a valid public purpose as specified by the Secretary in the terms of the sales agreement then all right, title, and interest in such land shall revert to the United States. Money received from such sale shall be deposited in the fund.

**(f) Rules and regulations**

The Secretary, in formulating regulations for making grants to the States to acquire land pursuant to this section, shall specify that acquired land meet the criteria provided for in subsections (c) and (d) of this section. The Secretary may provide by regulation that money derived from the lease, rental, or user charges of such acquired land and facilities thereon will be deposited in the fund.

**(g) Public sale; notice and hearing**

(1) Where land acquired pursuant to this section is deemed to be suitable for industrial, commercial, residential, or recreational development, the Secretary may sell or authorize the States to sell such land by public sale under a system of competitive bidding, at not less than fair market value and under such other regulations promulgated to insure that such lands are put to proper use consistent with local and State land use plans, if any, as determined by the Secretary.

(2) The Secretary or the State pursuant to an approved State program, when requested after appropriate public notice shall hold a public hearing, with the appropriate notice, in the county or counties or the appropriate subdivisions of the State in which lands acquired pursuant to this section are located. The hearings shall be held at a time which shall afford local citizens and governments the maximum opportunity to participate in the decision concerning the use or disposition of the lands after restoration, reclamation, abatement, control, or prevention of the adverse effects of past coal mining practices.

**(h) Construction or rehabilitation of housing for disabled, displaced, or dislocated persons; grants**

In addition to the authority to acquire land under subsection (d) of this section the Secretary is authorized to use money in the fund to acquire land by purchase, donation, or condemnation, and to reclaim and transfer acquired land to any State or to a political subdivision thereof, or to any person, firm, association, or corporation, if he determines that such is an integral and necessary element of an economically feasible plan for the project to construct or rehabilitate housing for persons disabled as the result of employment in the mines or work incidental thereto, persons displaced by acquisition of land pursuant to this section, or persons dislocated as the result of adverse effects of coal mining practices which constitute an emergency as provided in section 1240 of this title or persons dislocated as the result of natural disasters or catastrophic failures from any cause. Such activities shall be accomplished under such terms and conditions as the Secretary shall require, which may include transfers of land with or without monetary consideration: *Provided*, That, to the extent that the consideration is below the fair market value of the land transferred, no portion of the difference between the fair market value and the consideration shall accrue as a profit to such persons, firm, association, or corporation. No part of the funds provided under this subchapter may be used to pay the actual construction costs of housing. The Secretary may carry out the purposes of this subsection directly or he may make grants and commitments for grants, and may advance money under such terms and conditions as he may require to any State, or any department, agency, or instrumentality of a State, or any public body or nonprofit organization designated by a State.

(Pub.L. 95–87, Title IV, § 407, Aug. 3, 1977, 91 Stat. 462; Pub.L. 101–508, Title VI, § 6012(d)(4)–(7), Nov. 5, 1990, 104 Stat. 1388–298.)

## HISTORICAL AND STATUTORY NOTES

**Legislative History**

1977 Acts

House Report No. 95–218 and House Conference Report No. 95–493, see 1977 U.S. Code Cong. and Adm. News, p. 593.

1990 Acts

House Report No. 101–881, House Conference Report No. 101–964, and Statement by President, see 1990 U.S. Code Cong. and Adm. News, p. 2017.

**Effective and Applicability Provisions**

1990 Acts

Amendment by Pub.L. 101–508 effective Oct. 1, 1991, see section 6014 of Pub.L. 101–508, set out as a note under section 1231 of this title.

**Savings Provisions**

Nothing in Subtitle A (section 6001 et seq.) of Title VI of Pub.L. 101–508, shall be construed to affect the certifications made by the States of Wyoming, Montana, and Louisiana to the Secretary of the Interior prior to Nov. 5, 1990, that each such State has completed the reclamation of eligible abandoned coal mine lands, see section 6013 of Pub.L. 101–508, set out as a note under section 1231 of this title.

## § 1238. Liens

[SMCRA § 408]

### (a) Filing of statement and appraisal

Within six months after the completion of projects to restore, reclaim, abate, control, or prevent adverse effects of past coal mining practices on privately owned land, the Secretary or the State, pursuant to an approved State program, shall itemize the moneys so expended and may file a statement thereof in the office of the county in which the land lies which has the responsibility under local law for the recording of judgments against land, together with a notarized appraisal by an independent appraiser of the value of the land before the restoration, reclamation, abatement, control, or prevention of adverse effects of past coal mining practices if the moneys so expended shall result in a significant increase in property value. Such statement shall constitute a lien upon the said land. The lien shall not exceed the amount determined by the appraisal to be the increase in the market value of the land as a result of the restoration, reclamation, abatement, control, or prevention of the adverse effects of past coal mining practices. No lien shall be filed against the property of any person, in accordance with this subsection, who owned the surface prior to May 2, 1977, and who neither consented to nor participated in nor exercised control over the mining operation which necessitated the reclamation performed hereunder.

### (b) Petition

The landowner may proceed as provided by local law to petition within sixty days of the filing of the lien, to determine the increase in the market value of the land as a result of the restoration, reclamation, abatement, control, or prevention of the adverse effects of past coal mining practices. The amount reported to be the increase in value of the premises shall constitute the amount of the lien and shall be recorded with the statement herein provided. Any party aggrieved by the decision may appeal as provided by local law.

### (c) Recordation

The lien provided in this section shall be entered in the county office in which the land lies and which has responsibility under local law for the recording of judgments against land. Such statement shall constitute a lien upon the said land as of the date of the expenditure of the moneys and shall have priority as a lien second only to the lien of real estate taxes imposed upon said land.

(Pub.L. 95–87, Title IV, § 408, Aug. 3, 1977, 91 Stat. 465.)

## § 1239. Filling voids and sealing tunnels

[SMCRA § 409]

### (a) Congressional declaration of hazardous conditions

The Congress declares that voids, and open and abandoned tunnels, shafts, and entryways resulting from any previous mining operation, constitute a hazard to the public health or safety and that surface impacts of any underground or surface mining operation may degrade the environment. The Secretary, at the request of the Governor of any State, or the the[1] governing body of an Indian tribe, is authorized to fill such voids, seal such abandoned tunnels, shafts, and entryways, and reclaim surface impacts of underground or surface mines which the Secretary determines could endanger life and property, constitute a hazard to the public health and safety, or degrade the environment. State regulatory authorities are authorized to carry out such work pursuant to an approved abandoned mine reclamation program.

### (b) Limitation on funds

Funds available for use in carrying out the purpose of this section shall be limited to those funds which must be allocated to the respective States or Indian tribes under the provisions of paragraphs (1) and (5) of section 1232(g) of this title.

### (c) Limitation on expenditures

(1) The Secretary may make expenditures and carry out the purposes of this section in such States where requests are made by the Governor or governing body of an Indian tribe for those reclamation projects which meet the priorities stated in section 1233(a)(1) of this title, except that for the purposes of this section the reference to coal in section 1233(a)(1) of this title shall not apply.

(2) The provisions of section 1234 of this title shall apply to this section, with the exception that such mined lands need not have been mined for coal.

(3) The Secretary shall not make any expenditures for the purposes of this section in those States which have made the certification referred to in section 1240a(a) of this title.

### (d) Disposal of mine wastes

In those instances where mine waste piles are being reworked for conservation purposes, the incremental costs of disposing of the wastes from such operations by filling voids and sealing tunnels may be eligible for funding providing that the disposal of these wastes meets the purposes of this section.

### (e) Land acquisition

The Secretary may acquire by purchase, donation, easement, or otherwise such interest in land as he determines necessary to carry out the provisions of this section.

(Pub.L. 95–87, Title IV, § 409, Aug. 3, 1977, 91 Stat. 465; Pub.L. 101–508, Title VI, § 6009, Nov. 5, 1990, 104 Stat. 1388–296.)

[1] So in original.

HISTORICAL AND STATUTORY NOTES

**Effective and Applicability Provisions**

1990 Amendments

Amendment by Pub.L. 101–508 effective Oct. 1, 1991, see section 6014 of Pub.L. 101–508, set out as note under section 1231 of this title.

**Savings Provisions**

Nothing in Subtitle A (section 6001 et seq.) of Title VI of Pub.L. 101–508, shall be construed to affect the certifications made by the States of Wyoming, Montana, and Louisiana to the Secretary of the Interior prior to Nov. 5, 1990, that each such State has completed the reclamation of eligible abandoned coal mine lands, see section 6013 of Pub.L. 101–508, set out as a note under section 1231 of this title.

## § 1240. Emergency powers

**[SMCRA § 410]**

(a) The Secretary is authorized to expend moneys from the fund for the emergency restoration, reclamation, abatement, control, or prevention of adverse effects of coal mining practices, on eligible lands, if the Secretary makes a finding of fact that—

(1) an emergency exists constituting a danger to the public health, safety, or general welfare; and

(2) no other person or agency will act expeditiously to restore, reclaim, abate, control, or prevent the adverse effects of coal mining practices.

(b) The Secretary, his agents, employees, and contractors shall have the right to enter upon any land where the emergency exists and any other land to have access to the land where the emergency exists to restore, reclaim, abate, control, or prevent the adverse effects of coal mining practices and to do all things necessary or expedient to protect the public health, safety, or general welfare. Such entry shall be construed as an exercise of the police power and shall not be construed as an act of condemnation of property nor of trespass thereof. The moneys expended for such work and the benefits accruing to any such premises so entered upon shall be chargeable against such land and shall mitigate or offset any claim in or any action brought by any owner of any interest in such premises for any alleged damages by virtue of such entry: *Provided, however*, That this provision is not intended to create new rights of action or eliminate existing immunities.

(Pub.L. 95–87, Title IV, § 410, Aug. 3, 1977, 91 Stat. 466.)

## § 1240a. Certification

**[SMCRA § 411]**

**(a) Certification of completion of coal reclamation**

The Governor of a State, or the head of a governing body of an Indian tribe, with an approved abandoned mine reclamation program under section 1235 of this title may certify to the Secretary that all of the priorities stated in section 1233(a) of this title for eligible lands and waters pursuant to section 1234 of this title have been achieved. The Secretary, after notice in the Federal Register and opportunity for public comment, shall concur with such certification if the Secretary determines that such certification is correct.

**(b) Eligible lands, waters, and facilities**

If the Secretary has concurred in a State or tribal certification under subsection (a) of this section, for purposes of determining the eligibility of lands and waters for annual grants under section 1232(g)(1) of this title, section 1234 of this title shall not apply, and eligible lands, waters, and facilities shall be those—

(1) which were mined or processed for minerals or which were affected by such mining or processing, and abandoned or left in an inadequate reclamation status prior to August 3, 1977; and

(2) for which there is no continuing reclamation responsibility under State or other Federal laws. In determining the eligibility under this subsection of Federal lands, waters, and facilities under the jurisdiction of the Forest Service or Bureau of Land Management, in lieu of the August 3, 1977, date referred to in paragraph (1) the applicable date shall be August 28, 1974, and November 26, 1980, respectively.

**(c) Priorities**

Expenditures of moneys for lands, waters, and facilities referred to in subsection (b) of this section shall reflect the following objectives and priorities in the order stated (in lieu of the priorities set forth in section 1233 of this title):

(1) The protection of public health, safety, general welfare, and property from extreme danger of adverse effects of mineral mining and processing practices.

(2) The protection of public health, safety, and general welfare from adverse effects of mineral mining and processing practices.

(3) The restoration of land and water resources and the environment previously degraded by the adverse effects of mineral mining and processing practices.

**(d) Specific sites and areas not eligible**

Sites and areas designated for remedial action pursuant to the Uranium Mill Tailings Radiation Control Act of 1978 (42 U.S.C. 7901 and following) or which have been listed for remedial action pursuant to the Comprehensive Environmental Response Compensation and Liability Act of 1980 (42 U.S.C. 9601 and following) shall not be eligible for expenditures from the Fund under this section.

**(e) Utilities and other facilities**

Reclamation projects involving the protection, repair, replacement, construction, or enhancement of utilities, such as those relating to water supply, roads, and such other facilities serving the public adversely affected by mineral mining and processing practices, and the construction of public facilities in communities impacted by coal or other mineral mining and processing practices, shall be deemed part of the objectives set forth, and undertaken as they relate to, the priorities stated in subsection (c) of this section.

**(f) Public facilities related to coal or minerals industry**

Notwithstanding subsection (e) of this section, where the Secretary has concurred in the certification referenced in subsection (a) of this section and where the Governor of a State or the head of a governing body of an Indian tribe determines there is a need for activities or construction of specific public facilities related to the coal or minerals industry in States impacted by coal or minerals development and the Secretary concurs in such need, then the State or Indian tribe, as the case may be, may use annual grants made available under section 1232(g)(1) of this title to carry out such activities or construction.

**(g) Application of other provisions**

The provisions of sections 1237 and 1238 of this title shall apply to subsections (a) through (e) of this section, except that for purposes of this section the references to coal in sections 1237 and 1238 of this title shall not apply.

(Pub.L. 95–87, Title IV, § 411, as added Pub.L. 101–508, Title VI, § 6010(2), Nov. 5, 1990, 104 Stat. 1388–296.)

### HISTORICAL AND STATUTORY NOTES

**References in Text**

The Uranium Mill Tailings Radiation Control Act of 1978, referred to in subsec. (d), is Pub.L. 95–604, Nov. 8, 1978, 92 Stat. 3021, as amended, which is classified principally to chapter 88 (section 7901 et seq.) of Title 42, The Public Health and Welfare. For complete classification of this Act to the Code, see Short Title note set out under section 7901 of Title 42 and Tables.

The Comprehensive Environmental Response Compensation and Liability Act of 1980, referred to in subsec. (d), is Pub.L. 96–510, Dec. 11, 1980, 94 Stat. 2767, as amended, which is classified principally to chapter 103 (sections 9601 et seq.) of Title 42, The Public Health and Welfare. For complete classification of this Act to the Code, see Short Title note set out under section 9601 of Title 42 and Tables.

**Codifications**

Another section 411 of Pub.L. 95–87 is classified to section 1241 of this title. Such section is redesignated section 412 of Pub.L. 95–87, eff. Oct. 1, 1991, pursuant to sections 6010(1) and 6014 of Pub.L. 101–508. Such section remains classified to section 1241 of this title after such redesignation on Oct. 1, 1991.

**Effective and Applicability Provisions**

1990 Acts

Section effective Oct. 1, 1991, see section 6014 of Pub.L. 101–508, set out as a note under section 1231 of this title.

**Savings Provisions**

Nothing in Subtitle A (section 6001 et seq.) of Title VI of Pub.L. 101–508, shall be construed to affect the certifications made by the States of Wyoming, Montana, and Louisiana to the Secretary of the Interior prior to Nov. 5, 1990, that each such State has completed the reclamation of eligible abandoned coal mine lands, see section 6013 of Pub.L. 101–508, set out as note under section 1231 of this title.

## § 1241. Omitted

### HISTORICAL AND STATUTORY NOTES

**Codifications**

Section, Pub.L. 95–87, Title IV, § 412, formerly § 411, Aug. 3, 1977, 91 Stat. 466, renumbered Pub.L.101–508, Title VI, § 6010(1), Nov. 5, 1990, 104 Stat. 1388–296, which required the Secretary of the Interior or the State pursuant to an approved State program to annually submit to Congress reports on operations under the fund together with recommendations for future use of the fund, terminated, effective May 15, 2000, pursuant to Pub.L. 104–66, § 3003, as amended, which is set out as a note under 31 U.S.C.A. § 1113. See, also, page 109 of House Document No. 103–7.

## § 1242. Powers of Secretary or State

[SMCRA § 413]

**(a) Engage in work, promulgate rules and regulations, etc., to implement and administer this subchapter**

The Secretary or the State pursuant to an approved State program, shall have the power and authority, if not granted it otherwise, to engage in any work and to do all things necessary or expedient, including promulgation of rules and regulations, to implement and administer the provisions of this subchapter.

**(b) Engage in cooperative projects**

The Secretary or the State pursuant to an approved State program, shall have the power and authority to engage in cooperative projects under this subchapter with any other agency of the United States of America, any State and their governmental agencies.

(c) **Request for action to restrain interference with regard to this subchapter**

The Secretary or the State pursuant to an approved State program, may request the Attorney General, who is hereby authorized to initiate, in addition to any other remedies provided for in this subchapter, in any court of competent jurisdiction, an action in equity for an injunction to restrain any interference with the exercise of the right to enter or to conduct any work provided in this subchapter.

(d) **Construct and operate plants for control and treatment of water pollution resulting from mine drainage**

The Secretary or the State pursuant to an approved State program, shall have the power and authority to construct and operate a plant or plants for the control and treatment of water pollution resulting from mine drainage. The extent of this control and treatment may be dependent upon the ultimate use of the water: *Provided*, That the above provisions of this paragraph shall not be deemed in any way to repeal or supersede any portion of the Federal Water Pollution Control Act (33 U.S.C.A. 1151, et seq. as amended) [33 U.S.C.A. § 1251 et seq.] and no control or treatment under this subsection shall in any way be less than that required under the Federal Water Pollution Control Act. The construction of a plant or plants may include major interceptors and other facilities appurtenant to the plant.

(e) **Transfer funds**

The Secretary may transfer funds to other appropriate Federal agencies, in order to carry out the reclamation activities authorized by this subchapter.

(Pub.L. 95–87, Title IV, § 413, formerly § 412, Aug. 3, 1977, 91 Stat. 466, renumbered Pub.L. 101–508, Title VI, § 6010(1), Nov. 5, 1990, 104 Stat. 1388–296.)

### HISTORICAL AND STATUTORY NOTES

**References in Text**

The Federal Water Pollution Control Act (33 U.S.C.A. 1151, et seq. as amended), referred to in subsec. (d), is Act June 30, 1948, c. 758, 62 Stat. 1155, formerly classified to chapter 23 (section 1151 et seq.) of Title 33, Navigation and Navigable Waters, which was completely revised by Pub.L. 92–500, § 2, Oct. 18, 1972, 86 Stat. 816, and is now classified generally to chapter 26 (section 1251 et seq.) of Title 33. For complete classification of this Act to the Code, see Short Title note set out under section 1251 of Title 33 and Tables.

## § 1243. Interagency cooperation

**[SMCRA § 414]**

All departments, boards, commissioners, and agencies of the United States of America shall cooperate with the Secretary by providing technical expertise, personnel, equipment, materials, and supplies to implement and administer the provisions of this subchapter.

(Pub.L. 95–87, Title IV, § 414, formerly § 413, Aug. 3, 1977, 91 Stat. 467, renumbered Pub.L. 101–508, Title VI, § 6010(1), Nov. 5, 1990, 104 Stat. 1388–296.)

# SUBCHAPTER V—CONTROL OF THE ENVIRONMENTAL IMPACTS OF SURFACE COAL MINING

## § 1251. Environmental protection standards

**[SMCRA § 501]**

**(a)** Not later than the end of the ninety-day period immediately following August 3, 1977, the Secretary shall promulgate and publish in the Federal Register regulations covering an interim regulatory procedure for surface coal mining and reclamation operations setting mining and reclamation performance standards based on and incorporating the provisions set out in section 1252(c) of this title. The issuance of the interim regulations shall be deemed not to be a major Federal action within the meaning of section 4332(2)(c) of Title 42. Such regulations, which shall be concise and written in plain, understandable language shall not be promulgated and published by the Secretary until he has—

**(A)** published proposed regulations in the Federal Register and afforded interested persons and State and local governments a period of not less than thirty days after such publication to submit written comments thereon;

**(B)** obtained the written concurrence of the Administrator of the Environmental Protection Agency with respect to those regulations promulgated under this section which relate to air or water quality standards promulgated under the authority of the Federal Water Pollution Control Act, as amended [33 U.S.C.A. § 1251 et seq.]; and the Clean Air Act, as amended [42 U.S.C.A. § 7401 et seq.]; and

**(C)** held at least one public hearing on the proposed regulations.

The date, time, and place of any hearing held on the proposed regulations shall be set out in the publication of the proposed regulations. The Secretary shall consider all comments and relevant data presented at such hearing before final promulgation and publication of the regulations.

**(b)** Not later than one year after August 3, 1977, the Secretary shall promulgate and publish in the Federal Register regulations covering a permanent regulatory procedure for surface coal mining and reclamation operations performance standards based on and conforming to the provisions of this subchapter and establishing procedures and requirements for preparation, submission, and approval of State programs; and development and implementation of Federal programs under the subchapter. The Secretary shall promulgate these regulations, which shall be concise and written in plain, understandable language in accordance with the procedures in subsection (a) of this section.

(Pub.L. 95–87, Title V, § 501, Aug. 3, 1977, 91 Stat. 467.)

### HISTORICAL AND STATUTORY NOTES

**References in Text**

The Federal Water Pollution Control Act, as amended, referred to in subsec. (a)(B), is Act June 30, 1948, c. 758, 62 Stat. 1155, formerly classified to chapter 23 (section 1151 et seq.) of Title 33, Navigation and Navigable Waters, which was completely revised by Pub.L. 92–500, § 2, Oct. 18, 1972, 86 Stat. 816, and is classified generally to chapter 26 (section 1251 et seq.) of Title 33. For complete classification of this Act to the Code, see Short Title note set out under section 1251 of Title 33 and Tables.

The Clean Air Act, as amended, referred to in subsec. (a)(B), is Act July 14, 1955, c. 360, as amended generally by Pub.L. 88–206, Dec. 17, 1963, 77 Stat. 392, and later by Pub.L. 95–95, Aug. 7, 1977, 91 Stat. 685. The Clean Air Act was originally classified to chapter 15B (section 1857 et seq.) of Title 42, The Public Health and Welfare. On enactment of Pub.L. 95–95, the Act was reclassified to chapter 85 (section 7401 et seq.) of Title 42. For complete classification of this Act to the Code, see Short Title note set out under section 7401 of Title 42 and Tables volume.

## § 1251a. Abandoned coal refuse sites

(1) Notwithstanding any other provision of the Surface Mining Control and Reclamation Act of 1977 [30 U.S.C.A. § 1201 et seq.] to the contrary, the Secretary of the Interior shall, within one year after October 24, 1992, publish proposed regulations in the Federal Register, and after opportunity for public comment publish final regulations, establishing environmental protection performance and reclamation standards, and separate permit systems applicable to operations for the on-site reprocessing of abandoned coal refuse and operations for the removal of abandoned coal refuse on lands that would otherwise be eligible for expenditure under section 404 and section 402(g)(4) of the Surface Mining Control and Reclamation Act of 1977 [30 U.S.C.A. §§ 1234 and 1232(g)(4)].

(2) The standards and permit systems referred to in paragraph (1) shall distinguish between those operations which reprocess abandoned coal refuse on-site, and those operations which completely remove abandoned coal refuse from a site for the direct use of such coal refuse, or for the reprocessing of such coal refuse, at another location. Such standards and permit systems shall be premised on the distinct differences between operations for the on-site reprocessing, and operations for the removal, of abandoned coal refuse and other types of surface coal mining operations.

(3) The Secretary of the Interior may devise a different standard than any of those set forth in section 515 and section 516 of the Surface Mining Control and Reclamation Act of 1977 [30 U.S.C.A. §§ 1265 and 1266], and devise a separate permit system, if he determines, on a standard-by-standard basis, that a different standard may facilitate the on-site reprocessing, or the removal, of abandoned coal refuse in a manner that would provide the same level of environmental protection as under section 515 and section 516.

(4) Not later than 30 days prior to the publication of the proposed regulations referred to in this section, the Secretary shall submit a report to the Committee on Interior and Insular Affairs of the United States House of Representatives, and the Committee on Energy and Natural Resources of the United States Senate containing a detailed description of any environmental protection performance and reclamation standards, and separate permit systems, devised pursuant to this section.

(Pub.L. 102–486, Title XXV, § 2503(e), Oct. 24, 1992, 106 Stat. 3103.)

### HISTORICAL AND STATUTORY NOTES

**References in Text**

The Surface Mining Control and Reclamation Act of 1977, referred to in paragraphs (1) and (3), is Pub.L. 95–87, Aug. 3, 1977, 91 Stat. 445, as amended, which is classified generally to this chapter. For complete classification of this Act to the Code, see Short Title note set out under section 1201 of this title and Tables.

**Codifications**

Section was not enacted as part of the Surface Mining Control and Reclamation Act of 1977 which comprises this chapter.

**Change of Name**

Committee on Interior and Insular Affairs of the House of Representatives changed to Committee on Natural Resources of the House of Representatives on Jan. 5, 1993, by House Resolution No. 5, One Hundred Third Congress.

Any reference in any provision of law enacted before Jan. 4, 1995, to the Committee on Natural Resources of the House of Representatives treated as referring to the Committee on Resources of the House of Representatives, see section 1(a)(8) of Pub.L. 104–14, set out as a note preceding section 21 of Title 2, The Congress.

## § 1252. Initial regulatory procedures

**[SMCRA § 502]**

**(a) State regulation**

No person shall open or develop any new or previously mined or abandoned site for surface coal mining operations on lands on which such operations are regulated by a State unless such person has obtained a permit from the State's regulatory authority.

**(b) Interim standards**

All surface coal mining operations on lands on which such operations are regulated by a State which commence operations pursuant to a permit issued on or after six months from August 3, 1977, shall comply, and such permits shall contain terms requiring compliance with, the provisions set out in subsection (c) of this section. Prior to final disapproval of a State program or prior to promulgation of a Federal program or a Federal lands program pursuant to this chapter, a State may issue such permits.

**(c) Full compliance with environmental protection performance standards**

On and after nine months from August 3, 1977, all surface coal mining operations on lands on which such operations are regulated by a State shall comply with the provisions of subsections (b)(2), (b)(3), (b)(5), (b)(10), (b)(13), (b)(15), (b)(19), and (d) of section 1265 of this title or, where a surface coal mining operation will remove an entire coal seam or seams running through the upper fraction of a mountain, ridge, or hill by removing all of the overburden and creating a level plateau or a gently rolling contour with no highwalls remaining, such operation shall comply with the requirements of section 1265(c)(4) and (5) of this title without regard to the requirements of section 1265(b)(3) or (d)(2) and (3) of this title, with respect to lands from which overburden and the coal seam being mined have not been removed: *Provided, however*, That surface coal mining operations in operation pursuant to a permit issued by a State before August 3, 1977, issued to a person as defined in section 1291(19) of this title in existence prior to May 2, 1977 and operated by a person whose total annual production of coal from surface and underground coal mining operations does not exceed one hundred thousand tons shall not be subject to the provisions of this subsection except with reference to the provision of section 1265(d)(1) of this title until January 1, 1979.

**(d) Permit application**

Not later than two months following the approval of a State program pursuant to section 1253 of this title or the implementation of a Federal program pursuant to section 1254 of this title, regardless of litigation contesting that approval or implementation, all operators of surface coal mines in expectation of operating such mines after the expiration of eight months from the approval of a State program or the implementation of a Federal program, shall file an application for a permit with the regulatory authority. Such application shall cover those lands to be mined after the expiration of eight months from the approval of a State program or the implementation of a Federal program. The regulatory authority shall process such applications and grant or deny a permit within eight months after the date of approval of the State program or the implementation of the Federal program, unless specially enjoined by a court of competent jurisdiction, but in no case later than forty-two months from August 3, 1977.

**(e) Federal enforcement program**

Within six months after August 3, 1977, the Secretary shall implement a Federal enforcement program which shall remain in effect in each State as surface coal mining operations are required to comply with the provisions of this chapter, until the State program has been approved pursuant to this chapter or until a Federal program has been implemented pursuant to this chapter. The enforcement program shall—

(1) include inspections of surface coal mine sites which may be made (but at least one inspection for every site every six months), without advance notice to the mine operator and for the purpose of ascertaining compliance with the standards of subsections (b) and (c) above. The Secretary shall order any necessary enforcement action to be implemented pursuant to the Federal enforcement provision of this subchapter to correct violations identified at the inspections;

(2) provide that upon receipt of inspection reports indicating that any surface coal mining operation has been found in violation of subsections (b) and (c) above, during not less than two consecutive State inspections or upon receipt by the Secretary of information which would give rise to reasonable belief that such standards are being violated by any surface coal mining operation, the Secretary shall order the immediate inspection of such operation by Federal inspectors and the necessary enforcement actions, if any, to be implemented pursuant to the Federal enforcement provisions of this subchapter. When the Federal inspection results from information provided to the Secretary by any person, the Secretary shall notify such person when the Federal inspection is proposed to be carried out and such person shall be allowed to accompany the inspector during the inspection;

(3) provide that the State regulatory agency file with the Secretary and with a designated Federal office centrally located in the county or area in which the inspected surface coal mine is located copies of inspection reports made;

(4) provide that moneys authorized by section 1302 of this title shall be available to the Secretary prior to the approval of a State program pursuant to this chapter to reimburse the State for conducting those inspections in which the standards of this chapter are enforced and for the administration of this section.[1]

(5) for purposes of this section, the term "Federal inspector" means personnel of the Office of Surface Mining Reclamation and Enforcement and such

additional personnel of the United States Geological Survey, Bureau of Land Management, or of the Mining Enforcement and Safety Administration so designated by the Secretary, or such other personnel of the Forest Service, Soil Conservation Service, or the Agricultural Stabilization and Conservation Service as arranged by appropriate agreement with the Secretary on a reimbursable or other basis;[2]

**(f) Interim period**

Following the final disapproval of a State program, and prior to promulgation of a Federal program or a Federal lands program pursuant to this chapter, including judicial review of such a program, existing surface coal mining operations may continue surface mining operations pursuant to the provisions of this section. During such period no new permits shall be issued by the State whose program has been disapproved. Permits which lapse during such period may continue in full force and effect until promulgation of a Federal program or a Federal lands program.

(Pub.L. 95–87, Title V, § 502, Aug. 3, 1977, 91 Stat. 468.)

[1] So in original. The period probably should be a semicolon.

[2] So in original. The semicolon probably should be a period.

**HISTORICAL AND STATUTORY NOTES**

**References in Text**

This chapter, referred to in the introductory text of subsec. (e) and in subsecs. (e)(4) and (f), was in the original "this Act", meaning Pub.L. 95–87, Aug. 3, 1977, 91 Stat. 445, as amended, which enacted this chapter and amended section 1114 of Title 18, Crimes and Criminal Procedure. For complete classification of this Act to the Code, see Short Title note set out under section 1201 of this title and Tables.

## § 1253. State programs

**[SMCRA § 503]**

**(a) Regulation of surface coal mining and reclamation operations; submittal to Secretary; time limit; demonstration of effectiveness**

Each State in which there are or may be conducted surface coal mining operations on non-Federal lands, and which wishes to assume exclusive jurisdiction over the regulation of surface coal mining and reclamation operations, except as provided in sections 1271 and 1273 of this title and subchapter IV of this chapter, shall submit to the Secretary, by the end of the eighteenth-month period beginning on August 3, 1977, a State program which demonstrates that such State has the capability of carrying out the provisions of this chapter and meeting its purposes through—

(1) a State law which provides for the regulation of surface coal mining and reclamation operations in accordance with the requirements of this chapter;

(2) a State law which provides sanctions for violations of State laws, regulations, or conditions of permits concerning surface coal mining and reclamation operations, which sanctions shall meet the minimum requirements of this chapter, including civil and criminal actions, forfeiture of bonds, suspensions, revocations, and withholding of permits, and the issuance of cease-and-desist orders by the State regulatory authority or its inspectors;

(3) a State regulatory authority with sufficient administrative and technical personnel, and sufficient funding to enable the State to regulate surface coal mining and reclamation operations in accordance with the requirements of this chapter;

(4) a State law which provides for the effective implementations, maintenance, and enforcement of a permit system, meeting the requirements of this subchapter for the regulations of surface coal mining and reclamation operations for coal on lands within the State;

(5) establishment of a process for the designation of areas as unsuitable for surface coal mining in accordance with section 1272 of this title provided that the designation of Federal lands unsuitable for mining shall be performed exclusively by the Secretary after consultation with the State; and [1]

(6) establishment for the purposes of avoiding duplication, of a process for coordinating the review and issuance of permits for surface coal mining and reclamation operations with any other Federal or State permit process applicable to the proposed operations; and

(7) rules and regulations consistent with regulations issued by the Secretary pursuant to this chapter.

**(b) Approval of program**

The Secretary shall not approve any State program submitted under this section until he has—

(1) solicited and publicly disclosed the views of the Administrator of the Environmental Protection Agency, the Secretary of Agriculture, and the heads of other Federal agencies concerned with or having special expertise pertinent to the proposed State program;

(2) obtained the written concurrence of the Administrator of the Environmental Protection Agency with respect to those aspects of a State program which relate to air or water quality standards promulgated under the authority of the Federal Water Pollution Control Act, as amended [33 U.S.C.A. § 1251 et seq.], and the Clean Air Act, as amended [42 U.S.C.A. § 7401 et seq.];

(3) held at least one public hearing on the State program within the State; and

(4) found that the State has the legal authority and qualified personnel necessary for the enforcement of the environmental protection standards.

The Secretary shall approve or disapprove a State program, in whole or in part, within six full calendar months after the date such State program was submitted to him.

**(c) Notice of disapproval**

If the Secretary disapproves any proposed State program in whole or in part, he shall notify the State in writing of his decision and set forth in detail the reasons therefor. The State shall have sixty days in which to resubmit a revised State program or portion thereof. The Secretary shall approve or disapprove the resubmitted State program or portion thereof within sixty days from the date of resubmission.

**(d) Inability of State to take action**

For the purposes of this section and section 1254 of this title, the inability of a State to take any action the purpose of which is to prepare, submit or enforce a State program, or any portion thereof, because the action is enjoined by the issuance of an injunction by any court of competent jurisdiction shall not result in a loss of eligibility for financial assistance under subchapters IV and VII of this chapter or in the imposition of a Federal program. Regulation of the surface coal mining and reclamation operations covered or to be covered by the State program subject to the injunction shall be conducted by the State pursuant to section 1252 of this title, until such time as the injunction terminates or for one year, whichever is shorter, at which time the requirements of this section and section 1254 of this title shall again be fully applicable.

(Pub.L. 95–87, Title V, § 503, Aug. 3, 1977, 91 Stat. 470.)

[1] So in original.

**HISTORICAL AND STATUTORY NOTES**

**References in Text**

This chapter, referred to in subsec. (a), was in the original "this Act", meaning Pub.L. 95–87, Aug. 3, 1977, 91 Stat. 445, as amended, which enacted this chapter and amended section 1114 of Title 18, Crimes and Criminal Procedure. For complete classification of this Act to the Code, see Short Title note set out under section 1201 of this title and Tables volume.

The Federal Water Pollution Control Act, as amended, referred to in subsec. (b)(2), is Act June 30, 1948, c. 758, 62 Stat. 1155, formerly classified to chapter 23 (section 1151 et seq.) of Title 33, Navigation and Navigable Waters, which was completely revised by Pub.L. 92–500, § 2, Oct. 18, 1972, 86 Stat. 816, and is classified generally to chapter 26 (section 1251 et seq.) of Title 33. For complete classification of this Act to the Code, see Short Title note set out under section 1251 of Title 33 and Tables volume.

The Clean Air Act, as amended, referred to in subsec. (b)(2), is Act July 14, 1955, c. 360, as amended generally by Pub.L. 88–206, Dec. 17, 1963, 77 Stat. 392, and later by Pub.L. 95–95, Aug. 7, 1977, 91 Stat. 685. The Clean Air Act was originally classified to chapter 15B (section 1857 et seq.) of Title 42, The Public Health and Welfare. On enactment of Pub.L. 95–95, the Act was reclassified to chapter 85 (section 7401 et seq.) of Title 42. For complete classification of this Act to the Code, see Short Title note set out under section 7401 of Title 42 and Tables volume.

## § 1254. Federal programs

**[SMCRA § 504]**

**(a) Promulgation and implementation by Secretary for State**

The Secretary shall prepare and, subject to the provisions of this section, promulgate and implement a Federal program for a State no later than thirty-four months after August 3, 1977, if such State—

(1) fails to submit a State program covering surface coal mining and reclamation operations by the end of the eighteen-month period beginning on August 3, 1977;

(2) fails to resubmit an acceptable State program within sixty days of disapproval of a proposed State program: *Provided,* That the Secretary shall not implement a Federal program prior to the expiration of the initial period allowed for submission of a State program as provided for in clause (1) of this subsection; or

(3) fails to implement, enforce, or maintain its approved State program as provided for in this chapter.

If State compliance with clause (1) of this subsection requires an act of the State legislature, the Secretary may extend the period of submission of a State program up to an additional six months. Promulgation and implementation of a Federal program vests the Secretary with exclusive jurisdiction for the regulation and control of surface coal mining and reclamation operations taking place on lands within any State not in compliance with this chapter. After promulgation and implementation of a Federal program the Secretary shall be the regulatory authority. If a Federal program is implemented for a State, section 1272(a), (c), and (d) of this title shall not apply for a period of one year following the date of such implementation. In promulgating and implementing a Federal program for a particular State the Secretary shall take into consideration the nature of that State's terrain, climate, biological, chemical, and other relevant physical conditions.

**(b) Federal enforcement of State program**

In the event that a State has a State program for surface coal mining, and is not enforcing any part of such program, the Secretary may provide for the Federal enforcement, under the provisions of section 1271 of this title, of that part of the State program not being enforced by such State.

**(c) Notice and hearing**

Prior to promulgation and implementation of any proposed Federal program, the Secretary shall give adequate public notice and hold a public hearing in the affected State.

**(d) Review of permits**

Permits issued pursuant to a previously approved State program shall be valid but reviewable under a Federal program. Immediately following promulgation of a Federal program, the Secretary shall undertake to review such permits to determine that the requirements of this chapter are not violated. If the Secretary determines any permit to have been granted contrary to the requirements of this chapter, he shall so advise the permittee and provide him an opportunity for hearing and a reasonable opportunity for submission of a new application and reasonable time, within a time limit prescribed in regulations promulgated pursuant to section 1251(b) of this title, to conform ongoing surface mining and reclamation operations to the requirements of the Federal program.

**(e) Submission of State program after implementation of Federal program**

A State which has failed to obtain the approval of a State program prior to implementation of a Federal program may submit a State program at any time after such implementation. Upon the submission of such a program, the Secretary shall follow the procedures set forth in section 1253(b) of this title and shall approve or disapprove the State program within six months after its submittal. Approval of a State program shall be based on the determination that the State has the capability of carrying out the provisions of this chapter and meeting its purposes through the criteria set forth in section 1253(a)(1) through (6) of this title. Until a State program is approved as provided under this section, the Federal program shall remain in effect and all actions taken by the Secretary pursuant to such Federal program, including the terms and conditions of any permit issued thereunder shall remain in effect.

**(f) Validity of Federal program permits under superseding State program**

Permits issued pursuant to the Federal program shall be valid under any superseding State program: *Provided,* That the Federal permittee shall have the right to apply for a State permit to supersede his Federal permit. The State regulatory authority may review such permits to determine that the requirements of this chapter and the approved State program are not violated. Should the State program contain additional requirements not contained in the Federal program, the permittee will be provided opportunity for hearing and a reasonable time, within a time limit prescribed in regulations promulgated pursuant to section 1251 of this title, to conform ongoing surface mining and reclamation operations to the additional State requirements.

**(g) Preemption of State statutes or regulations**

Whenever a Federal program is promulgated for a State pursuant to this chapter, any statutes or regulations of such State which are in effect to regulate surface mining and reclamation operations subject to this chapter shall, insofar as they interfere with the achievement of the purposes and the requirements of this chapter and the Federal program, be preempted and superseded by the Federal program. The Secretary shall set forth any State law or regulation which is preempted and superseded by the Federal program.

**(h) Coordination of issuance and review of Federal program permits with any other Federal or State permit process**

Any Federal program shall include a process for coordinating the review and issuance of permits for surface mining and reclamation operations with any other Federal or State permit process applicable to the proposed operation.

(Pub.L. 95–87, Title V, § 504, Aug. 3, 1977, 91 Stat. 471.)

### HISTORICAL AND STATUTORY NOTES

**References in Text**

This chapter, referred to in subsecs. (a), (d), (e), (f), and (g), was in the original "this Act", meaning Pub.L. 95–87, Aug. 3, 1977, 91 Stat. 445, as amended, which enacted this chapter and amended section 1114 of Title 18, Crimes and Criminal Procedure. For complete classification of this Act to the Code, see Short Title note set out under section 1201 of this title and Tables.

## § 1255. State laws

**[SMCRA § 505]**

**(a)** No State law or regulation in effect on August 3, 1977, or which may become effective thereafter, shall be superseded by any provision of this chapter or any regulation issued pursuant thereto, except insofar as such State law or regulation is inconsistent with the provisions of this chapter.

**(b)** Any provision of any State law or regulation in effect upon August 3, 1977, or which may become effective thereafter, which provides for more stringent land use and environmental controls and regulations of surface coal mining and reclamation operation than do the provisions of this chapter or any regulation issued pursuant thereto shall not be construed to be inconsistent with this chapter. The Secretary shall set forth any State law or regulation which is construed to be inconsistent with this chapter. Any provision of any State law or regulation in effect on August 3, 1977, or which may become effective thereafter, which provides for the control and regulation of surface mining and reclamation operations for which no provision is contained in this chapter shall not be construed to be inconsistent with this chapter.

(Pub.L. 95–87, Title V, § 505, Aug. 3, 1977, 91 Stat. 473.)

### HISTORICAL AND STATUTORY NOTES

**References in Text**

This chapter, referred to in text, was in the original "this Act", meaning Pub.L. 95–87, Aug. 3, 1977, 91 Stat. 455, as amended, which enacted this chapter and amended section 1114 of Title 18, Crimes and Criminal Procedure. For complete classification of this Act to the Code, see Short Title note set out under section 1201 of this title and Tables.

**Legislative History**

1977 Acts

House Report No. 95–218 and House Conference Report No. 95–493, see 1977 U.S. Code Cong. and Adm. News, p. 593.

## § 1256. Permits

### [SMCRA § 506]

#### (a) Persons engaged in surface coal mining within State; time limit; exception

No later than eight months from the date on which a State program is approved by the Secretary, pursuant to section 1253 of this title, or no later than eight months from the date on which the Secretary has promulgated a Federal program for a State not having a State program pursuant to section 1254 of this title, no person shall engage in or carry out on lands within a State any surface coal mining operations unless such person has first obtained a permit issued by such State pursuant to an approved State program or by the Secretary pursuant to a Federal program; except a person conducting surface coal mining operations under a permit from the State regulatory authority, issued in accordance with the provisions of section 1252 of this title, may conduct such operations beyond such period if an application for a permit has been filed in accordance with the provisions of this chapter, but the initial administrative decision has not been rendered.

#### (b) Term

All permits issued pursuant to the requirements of this chapter shall be issued for a term not to exceed five years: *Provided*, That if the applicant demonstrates that a specified longer term is reasonably needed to allow the applicant to obtain necessary financing for equipment and the opening of the operation and if the application is full and complete for such specified longer term, the regulatory authority may grant a permit for such longer term. A successor in interest to a permittee who applies for a new permit within thirty days of succeeding to such interest and who is able to obtain the bond coverage of the original permittee may continue surface coal mining and reclamation operations according to the approved mining and reclamation plan of the original permittee until such successor's application is granted or denied.

#### (c) Termination

A permit shall terminate if the permittee has not commenced the surface coal mining operations covered by such permit within three years of the issuance of the permit: *Provided*, That the regulatory authority may grant reasonable extensions of time upon a showing that such extensions are necessary by reason of litigation precluding such commencement or threatening substantial economic loss to the permittee, or by reason of conditions beyond the control and without the fault or negligence of the permittee: *Provided further*, That in the case of a coal lease issued under the Federal Mineral Leasing Act, as amended [30 U.S.C.A. § 181 et seq.], extensions of time may not extend beyond the period allowed for diligent development in accordance with section 7 of that Act [30 U.S.C.A. § 207]: *Provided further*, That with respect to coal to be mined for use in a synthetic fuel facility or specific major electric generating facility, the permittee shall be deemed to have commenced surface mining operations at such time as the construction of the synthetic fuel or generating facility is initiated.

#### (d) Renewal

(1) Any valid permit issued pursuant to this chapter shall carry with it the right of successive renewal upon expiration with respect to areas within the boundaries of the existing permit. The holders of the permit may apply for renewal and such renewal shall be issued (provided that on application for renewal the burden shall be on the opponents of renewal), subsequent to fulfillment of the public notice requirements of sections 1263 and 1264 of this title unless it is established that and written findings by the regulatory authority are made that—

(A) the terms and conditions of the existing permit are not being satisfactorily met;

(B) the present surface coal mining and reclamation operation is not in compliance with the environmental protection standards of this chapter and the approved State plan or Federal program pursuant to this chapter; or

(C) the renewal requested substantially jeopardizes the operator's continuing responsibility on existing permit areas;

(D) the operator has not provided evidence that the performance bond in effect for said operation will continue in full force and effect for any renewal requested in such application as well as any additional bond the regulatory authority might require pursuant to section 1259 of this title; or

(E) any additional revised or updated information required by the regulatory authority has not been provided. Prior to the approval of any renewal of permit the regulatory authority shall provide notice to the appropriate public authorities.

(2) If an application for renewal of a valid permit includes a proposal to extend the mining operation beyond the boundaries authorized in the existing permit, the portion of the application for renewal of a valid permit which addresses any new land areas shall be subject to the full standards applicable to new applications under this chapter: *Provided, however,* That if the surface coal mining operations authorized by a permit issued pursuant to this chapter were not subject to the standards contained in section 1260(b)(5)(A) and (B) of this title by reason of complying with the proviso of section 1260(b)(5) of this title, then the portion of the application for renewal of the permit which addresses any new land areas previously identified in the reclamation plan submitted pursuant to section 1258 of this title shall not be subject to the standards contained in section 1260(b)(5)(A) and (B) of this title.

(3) Any permit renewal shall be for a term not to exceed the period of the original permit established by this chapter. Application for permit renewal shall be made at least one hundred and twenty days prior to the expiration of the valid permit.

(Pub.L. 95–87, Title V, § 506, Aug. 3, 1977, 91 Stat. 473.)

### HISTORICAL AND STATUTORY NOTES

**References in Text**

This chapter, referred to in subsecs. (a), (b), and (d), was in the original "this Act", meaning Pub.L. 95–87, Aug. 3, 1977, 91 Stat. 445, as amended, which enacted this chapter and amended section 1114 of Title 18, Crimes and Criminal Procedure. For complete classification of this Act to the Code, see Short Title note set out under section 1201 of this title and Tables.

## § 1257. Application requirements

### [SMCRA § 507]

**(a) Fee**

Each application for a surface coal mining and reclamation permit pursuant to an approved State program or a Federal program under the provisions of this chapter shall be accompanied by a fee as determined by the regulatory authority. Such fee may be less than but shall not exceed the actual or anticipated cost of reviewing, administering, and enforcing such permit issued pursuant to a State or Federal program. The regulatory authority may develop procedures so as to enable the cost of the fee to be paid over the term of the permit.

**(b) Submittal; contents**

The permit application shall be submitted in a manner satisfactory to the regulatory authority and shall contain, among other things—

(1) the names and addresses of (A) the permit applicant; (B) every legal owner of record of the property (surface and mineral), to be mined; (C) the holders of record of any leasehold interest in the property; (D) any purchaser of record of the property under a real estate contract; and (E) the operator if he is a person different from the applicant; and (F) if any of these are business entities other than a single proprietor, the names and addresses of the principals, officers, and resident agent;

(2) the names and addresses of the owners of record of all surface and subsurface areas adjacent to any part of the permit area;

(3) a statement of any current or previous surface coal mining permits in the United States held by the applicant and the permit identification and each pending application;

(4) if the applicant is a partnership, corporation, association, or other business entity, the following where applicable: the names and addresses of every officer, partner, director, or person performing a function similar to a director, of the applicant, together with the name and address of any person owning, of record 10 per centum or more of any class of voting stock of the applicant and a list of all names under which the applicant, partner, or principal shareholder previously operated a surface mining operation within the United States within the five-year period preceding the date of submission of the application;

(5) a statement of whether the applicant, any subsidiary, affiliate, or persons controlled by or under common control with the applicant, has ever held a Federal or State mining permit which in the five-year period prior to the date of submission of the application has been suspended or revoked or has had a mining bond or similar security deposited in lieu of bond forfeited [1] and, if so, a brief explanation of the facts involved;

(6) a copy of the applicant's advertisement to be published in a newspaper of general circulation in the locality of the proposed site at least once a week for four successive weeks, and which includes the ownership, a description of the exact location and boundaries of the proposed site sufficient so that the proposed operation is readily locatable by local residents, and the location of where the application is available for public inspection;

(7) a description of the type and method of coal mining operation that exists or is proposed, the engineering techniques proposed or used, and the equipment used or proposed to be used;

(8) the anticipated or actual starting and termination dates of each phase of the mining operation and number of acres of land to be affected;

(9) the applicant shall file with the regulatory authority on an accurate map or plan, to an appropriate scale, clearly showing the land to be affected as of the date of the application, the area of land within the permit area upon which the applicant has the legal right to enter and commence surface mining operations and shall provide to the regulatory authority a statement of those documents upon which the applicant bases his legal right to enter and commence surface mining operations on the area affected, and whether that right is the subject of pending court litigation: *Provided*, That nothing in this chapter shall be construed as vesting in the regulatory authority the jurisdiction to adjudicate property title disputes.[2]

(10) the name of the watershed and location of the surface stream or tributary into which surface and pit drainage will be discharged;

(11) a determination of the probable hydrologic consequences of the mining and reclamation operations, both on and off the mine site, with respect to the hydrologic regime, quantity and quality of water in surface and ground water systems including the dissolved and suspended solids under seasonal flow conditions and the collection of sufficient data for the mine site and surrounding areas so that an assessment can be made by the regulatory authority of the probable cumulative impacts of all anticipated mining in the area upon the hydrology of the area and particularly upon water availability: *Provided, however*, That this determination shall not be required until such time as hydrologic information on the general area prior to mining is made available from an appropriate Federal or State agency: *Provided further*, That the permit shall not be approved until such information is available and is incorporated into the application;

(12) when requested by the regulatory authority, the climatological factors that are peculiar to the locality of the land to be affected, including the average seasonal precipitation, the average direction and velocity of prevailing winds, and the seasonal temperature ranges;

(13) accurate maps to an appropriate scale clearly showing (A) the land to be affected as of the date of application and (B) all types of information set forth on topographical maps of the United States Geological Survey of a scale of 1:24,000 or 1:25,000 or larger, including all manmade features and significant known archeological sites existing on the date of application. Such a map or plan shall among other things specified by the regulatory authority show all boundaries of the land to be affected, the boundary lines and names of present owners of record of all surface areas abutting the permit area, and the location of all buildings within one thousand feet of the permit area;

(14) cross-section maps or plans of the land to be affected including the actual area to be mined, prepared by or under the direction of and certified by a qualified registered professional engineer, or professional geologist with assistance from experts in related fields such as land surveying and landscape architecture, showing pertinent elevation and location of test borings or core samplings and depicting the following information: the nature and depth of the various strata of overburden; the location of subsurface water, if encountered, and its quality; the nature and thickness of any coal or rider seam above the coal seam to be mined; the nature of the stratum immediately beneath the coal seam to be mined; all mineral crop lines and the strike and dip of the coal to be mined, within the area of land to be affected; existing or previous surface mining limits; the location and extent of known workings of any underground mines, including mine openings to the surface; the location of aquifers; the estimated elevation of the water table; the location of spoil, waste, or refuse areas and topsoil preservation areas; the location of all impoundments for waste or erosion control; any settling or water treatment facility; constructed or natural drainways and the location of any discharges to any surface body of water on the area of land to be affected or adjacent thereto; and profiles at appropriate cross sections of the anticipated final surface configuration that will be achieved pursuant to the operator's proposed reclamation plan;

(15) a statement of the result of test borings or core samplings from the permit area, including logs of the drill holes; the thickness of the coal seam found, an analysis of the chemical properties of such coal; the sulfur content of any coal seam; chemical analysis of potentially acid or toxic forming sections of the overburden; and chemical analysis of the stratum lying immediately underneath the coal to be mined except that the provisions of this paragraph (15) may be waived by the regulatory authority with respect to the specific application by a written determination that such requirements are unnecessary;

(16) for those lands in the permit application which a reconnaissance inspection suggests may be prime farm lands, a soil survey shall be made or obtained according to standards established by the Secretary of Agriculture in order to confirm the exact location of such prime farm lands, if any; and

(17) information pertaining to coal seams, test borings, core samplings, or soil samples as required

by this section shall be made available to any person with an interest which is or may be adversely affected: *Provided*, That information which pertains only to the analysis of the chemical and physical properties of the coal (excepting information regarding such mineral or elemental content which is potentially toxic in the environment) shall be kept confidential and not made a matter of public record.

**(c) Assistance to small coal operators**

(1) If the regulatory authority finds that the probable total annual production at all locations of a coal surface mining operator will not exceed 300,000 tons, the cost of the following activities, which shall be performed by a qualified public or private laboratory or such other public or private qualified entity designated by the regulatory authority, shall be assumed by the regulatory authority upon the written request of the operator in connection with a permit application:

(A) The determination of probable hydrologic consequences required by subsection (b)(11) of this section, including the engineering analyses and designs necessary for the determination.

(B) The development of cross-section maps and plans required by subsection (b)(14) of this section.

(C) The geologic drilling and statement of results of test borings and core samplings required by subsection (b)(15) of this section.

(D) The collection of archaeological information required by subsection (b)(13) of this section and any other archaeological and historical information required by the regulatory authority, and the preparation of plans necessitated thereby.

(E) Pre-blast surveys required by section 1265(b)(15)(E) of this title.

(F) The collection of site-specific resource information and production of protection and enhancement plans for fish and wildlife habitats and other environmental values required by the regulatory authority under this chapter.

(2) The Secretary shall provide or assume the cost of training coal operators that meet the qualifications stated in paragraph (1) concerning the preparation of permit applications and compliance with the regulatory program, and shall ensure that qualified coal operators are aware of the assistance available under this subsection.

**(d) Reclamation plan**

Each applicant for a permit shall be required to submit to the regulatory authority as part of the permit application a reclamation plan which shall meet the requirements of this chapter.

**(e) Public inspection**

Each applicant for a surface coal mining and reclamation permit shall file a copy of his application for public inspection with the recorder at the courthouse of the county or an appropriate public office approved by the regulatory authority where the mining is proposed to occur, except for that information pertaining to the coal seam itself.

**(f) Insurance certificate**

Each applicant for a permit shall be required to submit to the regulatory authority as part of the permit application a certificate issued by an insurance company authorized to do business in the United States certifying that the applicant has a public liability insurance policy in force for the surface mining and reclamation operations for which such permit is sought, or evidence that the applicant has satisfied other State or Federal self-insurance requirements. Such policy shall provide for personal injury and property damage protection in an amount adequate to compensate any persons damaged as a result of surface coal mining and reclamation operations including use of explosives and entitled to compensation under the applicable provisions of State law. Such policy shall be maintained in full force and effect during the terms of the permit or any renewal, including the length of all reclamation operations.

**(g) Blasting plan**

Each applicant for a surface coal mining and reclamation permit shall submit to the regulatory authority as part of the permit application a blasting plan which shall outline the procedures and standards by which the operator will meet the provisions of section 1265(b)(15) of this title.

**(h) Reimbursement of costs**

A coal operator that has received assistance pursuant to subsection (c)(1) or (2) of this section shall reimburse the regulatory authority for the cost of the services rendered if the program administrator finds that the operator's actual and attributed annual production of coal for all locations exceeds 300,000 tons during the 12 months immediately following the date on which the operator is issued the surface coal mining and reclamation permit.

(Pub.L. 95–87, Title V, § 507, Aug. 3, 1977, 91 Stat. 474; Pub.L. 101–508, Title VI, § 6011, Nov. 5, 1990, 104 Stat. 1388–297; Pub.L. 102–486, Title XXV, § 2513, Oct. 24, 1992, 106 Stat. 3112.)

[1] So in original. Probably should be "forfeited".

[2] So in original. The period probably should be a semicolon.

## HISTORICAL AND STATUTORY NOTES

**References in Text**

This chapter, referred to in subsecs. (a), (b)(9), and (d), was in the original "this Act", meaning Pub.L. 95–87, Aug. 3, 1977, 91 Stat. 445, as amended, which enacted this chapter and amended section 1114 of Title 18, Crimes and Criminal Procedure. For complete classification of this Act to the Code, see Short Title note set out under section 1201 of this title and Tables.

This chapter, referred to in subsec. (c)(1)(F), was in the original "this Act", meaning Pub.L. 95–87, Aug. 3, 1977, 91 Stat. 445, as amended, which enacted this chapter and amended section 1114 of Title 18, Crimes and Criminal Procedure. For complete classification of this Act to the Code, see Short Title note set out under section 1201 of this title and Tables.

**Effective and Applicability Provisions**

1990 Acts

Amendment by Pub.L. 101–508 effective Oct. 1, 1991, see section 6014 of Pub.L. 101–508, set out as a note under section 1231 of this title.

**Savings Provisions**

Nothing in Subtitle A (section 6001 et seq.) of Title VI of Pub.L. 101–508, shall be construed to affect the certifications made by the States of Wyoming, Montana, and Louisiana to the Secretary of the Interior prior to Nov. 5, 1990, that each such State has completed the reclamation of eligible abandoned coal mine lands, see section 6013 of Pub.L. 101–508, set out as a note under section 1231 of this title.

**Preparation of Cross-Sections, Maps, and Plans by or Under Direction of Qualified Registered Professional Engineers, Geologists, or Land Surveyors**

Pub.L. 98–146, Title I, § 115, Nov. 4, 1983, 97 Stat. 938, provided that: "Notwithstanding section 507(b)(14) of the Surface Mining Control and Reclamation Act of 1977 (Public Law 95–87) [subsec. (b)(14) of this section], cross-sections, maps or plans of land to be affected by an application for a surface mining and reclamation permit shall be prepared by or under the direction of a qualified registered professional engineer or geologist, or qualified registered professional land surveyor in any State which authorizes land surveyors to prepare and certify such maps or plans."

## § 1258. Reclamation plan requirements

### [SMCRA § 508]

(a) Each reclamation plan submitted as part of a permit application pursuant to any approved State program or a Federal program under the provisions of this chapter shall include, in the degree of detail necessary to demonstrate that reclamation required by the State or Federal program can be accomplished, a statement of:

(1) the identification of the lands subject to surface coal mining operations over the estimated life of those operations and the size, sequence, and timing of the subareas for which it is anticipated that individual permits for mining will be sought;

(2) the condition of the land to be covered by the permit prior to any mining including:

(A) the uses existing at the time of the application, and if the land has a history of previous mining, the uses which preceded any mining; and

(B) the capability of the land prior to any mining to support a variety of uses giving consideration to soil and foundation characteristics, topography, and vegetative cover, and, if applicable, a soil survey prepared pursuant to section 1257(b)(16) of this title; and

(C) the productivity of the land prior to mining, including appropriate classification as prime farm lands, as well as the average yield of food, fiber, forage, or wood products from such lands obtained under high levels of management;

(3) the use which is proposed to be made of the land following reclamation, including a discussion of the utility and capacity of the reclaimed land to support a variety of alternative uses and the relationship of such use to existing land use policies and plans, and the comments of any owner of the surface, State and local governments or agencies thereof which would have to initiate, implement, approve or authorize the proposed use of the land following reclamation;

(4) a detailed description of how the proposed postmining land use is to be achieved and the necessary support activities which may be needed to achieve the proposed land use;

(5) the engineering techniques proposed to be used in mining and reclamation and a description of the major equipment; a plan for the control of surface water drainage and of water accumulation; a plan, where appropriate, for backfilling, soil stabilization, and compacting, grading, and appropriate revegetation; a plan for soil reconstruction, replacement, and stabilization, pursuant to the performance standards in section 1265(b)(7)(A), (B), (C), and (D) of this title, for those food, forage, and forest lands identified in section 1265(b)(7) of this title; an estimate of the cost per acre of the reclamation, including a statement as to how the permittee plans to comply with each of the requirements set out in section 1265 of this title;

(6) the consideration which has been given to maximize the utilization and conservation of the solid fuel resource being recovered so that reaffecting the land in the future can be minimized;

(7) a detailed estimated timetable for the accomplishment of each major step in the reclamation plan;

(8) the consideration which has been given to making the surface mining and reclamation operations consistent with surface owner plans, and applicable State and local land use plans and programs;

(9) the steps to be taken to comply with applicable air and water quality laws and regulations and any applicable health and safety standards;

(10) the consideration which has been given to developing the reclamation plan in a manner consistent with local physical environmental, and climatological conditions;

(11) all lands, interests in lands, or options on such interests held by the applicant or pending bids on interests in lands by the applicant, which lands are contiguous to the area to be covered by the permit;

(12) the results of test boring which the applicant has made at the area to be covered by the permit, or other equivalent information and data in a form satisfactory to the regulatory authority, including the location of subsurface water, and an analysis of the chemical properties including acid forming properties of the mineral and overburden: *Provided*, That information which pertains only to the analysis of the chemical and physical properties of the coal (excepting information regarding such mineral or elemental contents which is potentially toxic in the environment) shall be kept confidential and not made a matter of public record;

(13) a detailed description of the measures to be taken during the mining and reclamation process to assure the protection of:

(A) the quality of surface and ground water systems, both on- and off-site, from adverse effects of the mining and reclamation process;

(B) the rights of present users to such water; and

(C) the quantity of surface and ground water systems, both on- and off-site, from adverse effects of the mining and reclamation process or to provide alternative sources of water where such protection of quantity cannot be assured;

(14) such other requirements as the regulatory authority shall prescribe by regulations.

(b) Any information required by this section which is not on public file pursuant to State law shall be held in confidence by the regulatory authority.

(Pub.L. 95–87, Title V, § 508, Aug. 3, 1977, 91 Stat. 478.)

### HISTORICAL AND STATUTORY NOTES

**References in Text**

This chapter, referred to in subsec. (a), was in the original "this Act", meaning Pub.L. 95–87, Aug. 3, 1977, 91 Stat. 445, as amended, which enacted this chapter and amended section 1114 of Title 18, Crimes and Criminal Procedure. For complete classification of this Act to the Code, see Short Title note set out under section 1201 of this title and Tables.

## § 1259. Performance bonds

### [SMCRA § 509]

**(a) Filing with regulatory authority; scope; number and amount**

After a surface coal mining and reclamation permit application has been approved but before such a permit is issued, the applicant shall file with the regulatory authority, on a form prescribed and furnished by the regulatory authority, a bond for performance payable, as appropriate, to the United States or to the State, and conditional upon faithful performance of all the requirements of this chapter and the permit. The bond shall cover that area of land within the permit area upon which the operator will initiate and conduct surface coal mining and reclamation operations within the initial term of the permit. As succeeding increments of surface coal mining and reclamation operations are to be initiated and conducted within the permit area, the permittee shall file with the regulatory authority an additional bond or bonds to cover such increments in accordance with this section. The amount of the bond required for each bonded area shall depend upon the reclamation requirements of the approved permit; shall reflect the probable difficulty of reclamation giving consideration to such factors as topography, geology of the site, hydrology, and revegetation potential, and shall be determined by the regulatory authority. The amount of the bond shall be sufficient to assure the completion of the reclamation plan if the work had to be performed by the regulatory authority in the event of forfeiture and in no case shall the bond for the entire area under one permit be less than $10,000.

**(b) Liability period; execution**

Liability under the bond shall be for the duration of the surface coal mining and reclamation operation and for a period coincident with operator's responsibility for revegetation requirements in section 1265 of this title. The bond shall be executed by the operator and a corporate surety licensed to do business in the State where such operation is located, except that the operator may elect to deposit cash, negotiable bonds of the United States Government or such State, or negotiable certificates of deposit of any bank organized or transacting business in the United States. The cash deposit or market value of such securities shall be equal to or greater than the amount of the bond required for the bonded area.

**(c) Bond of applicant without separate surety; alternate system**

The regulatory authority may accept the bond of the applicant itself without separate surety when the applicant demonstrates to the satisfaction of the regulatory authority the existence of a suitable agent to receive service of process and a history of financial solvency and continuous operation sufficient for authorization to self-insure or bond such amount or in lieu of the establishment of a bonding program, as set forth in this section, the Secretary may approve as part of a State or Federal program an alternative system that will achieve the objectives and purposes of the bonding program pursuant to this section.

**(d) Deposit of cash or securities**

Cash or securities so deposited shall be deposited upon the same terms as the terms upon which surety bonds may be deposited. Such securities shall be security for the repayment of such negotiable certificate of deposit.

**(e) Adjustments**

The amount of the bond or deposit required and the terms of each acceptance of the applicant's bond shall be adjusted by the regulatory authority from time to time as affected land acreages are increased or decreased or where the cost of future reclamation changes.

(Pub.L. 95–87, Title V, § 509, Aug. 3, 1977, 91 Stat. 479.)

**HISTORICAL AND STATUTORY NOTES**

**References in Text**

This chapter, referred to in subsec. (a), was in the original "this Act", meaning Pub.L. 95–87, Aug. 3, 1977, 91 Stat. 445, as amended, which enacted this chapter and amended section 1114 of Title 18, Crimes and Criminal Procedure. For complete classification of this Act to the Code, see Short Title note set out under section 1201 of this title and Tables.

## § 1260. Permit approval or denial

**[SMCRA § 510]**

**(a) Basis for decision; notification of applicant and local government officials; burden of proof**

Upon the basis of a complete mining application and reclamation plan or a revision or renewal thereof, as required by this chapter and pursuant to an approved State program or Federal program under the provisions of this chapter, including public notification and an opportunity for a public hearing as required by section 1263 of this title, the regulatory authority shall grant, require modification of, or deny the application for a permit in a reasonable time set by the regulatory authority and notify the applicant in writing. The applicant for a permit, or revision of a permit, shall have the burden of establishing that his application is in compliance with all the requirements of the applicable State or Federal program. Within ten days after the granting of a permit, the regulatory authority shall notify the local governmental officials in the local political subdivision in which the area of land to be affected is located that a permit has been issued and shall describe the location of the land.

**(b) Requirements for approval**

No permit or revision application shall be approved unless the application affirmatively demonstrates and the regulatory authority finds in writing on the basis of the information set forth in the application or from information otherwise available which will be documented in the approval, and made available to the applicant, that—

(1) the permit application is accurate and complete and that all the requirements of this chapter and the State or Federal program have been complied with;

(2) the applicant has demonstrated that reclamation as required by this chapter and the State or Federal program can be accomplished under the reclamation plan contained in the permit application;

(3) the assessment of the probable cumulative impact of all anticipated mining in the area on the hydrologic balance specified in section 1257(b) of this title has been made by the regulatory authority and the proposed operation thereof has been designed to prevent material damage to hydrologic balance outside permit area;

(4) the area proposed to be mined is not included within an area designated unsuitable for surface coal mining pursuant to section 1272 of this title or is not within an area under study for such designation in an administrative proceeding commenced pursuant to section 1272(a)(4)(D) or section 1272(c) of this title (unless in such an area as to which an administrative proceeding has commenced pursuant to section 1272(a)(4)(D) of this title, the operator making the permit application demonstrates that, prior to January 1, 1977, he has made substantial legal and financial commitments in relation to the operation for which he is applying for a permit);

(5) the proposed surface coal mining operation, if located west of the one hundredth meridian west longitude, would—

(A) not interrupt, discontinue, or preclude farming on alluvial valley floors that are irrigated or naturally subirrigated, but, excluding undeveloped range lands which are not significant to farming on said alluvial valley floors and those lands as to which the regulatory authority finds that if the farming that will be interrupted, discontinued, or precluded is of such small acreage as to be of negligible impact on the farm's agricultural production, or

(B) not materially damage the quantity or quality of water in surface or underground water systems that supply these valley floors in (A) of subsection (b)(5) of this section:

*Provided,* That this paragraph (5) shall not affect those surface coal mining operations which in the year preceding August 3, 1977, (I) produced coal in commercial quantities, and were located within or adjacent to alluvial valley floors or (II) had obtained specific permit approval by the State regulatory authority to conduct surface coal mining operations within said alluvial valley floors.

With respect to such surface mining operations which would have been within the purview of the foregoing proviso but for the fact that no coal was so produced in commercial quantities and no such specific permit approval was so received, the Secretary, if he determines that substantial financial and legal commitments were made by an operator prior to January 1, 1977, in connection with any such operation, is authorized, in accordance with such regulations as the Secretary may prescribe, to enter into an agreement with that operator pursuant to which the Secretary may, notwithstanding any other provision of law, lease other Federal coal deposits to such operator in exchange for the relinquishment by such operator of his Federal lease covering coal deposits involving such mining operations, or pursuant to section 1716 of Title 43, convey to the fee holder of any such coal deposits involving such mining operations the fee title to other available Federal coal deposits in exchange for the fee title to such deposits so involving such mining operations. It is the policy of the Congress that the Secretary shall develop and carry out a coal exchange program to acquire private fee coal precluded from being mined by the restrictions of this paragraph (5) in exchange for Federal coal which is not so precluded. Such exchanges shall be made under section 1716 of Title 43;

**(6)** in cases where the private mineral estate has been severed from the private surface estate, the applicant has submitted to the regulatory authority—

**(A)** the written consent of the surface owner to the extraction of coal by surface mining methods; or

**(B)** a conveyance that expressly grants or reserves the right to extract the coal by surface mining methods; or

**(C)** if the conveyance does not expressly grant the right to extract coal by surface mining methods, the surface-subsurface legal relationship shall be determined in accordance with State law: *Provided*, That nothing in this chapter shall be construed to authorize the regulatory authority to adjudicate property rights disputes.

**(c) Schedule of violations**

The applicant shall file with his permit application a schedule listing any and all notices of violations of this chapter and any law, rule, or regulation of the United States, or of any department or agency in the United States pertaining to air or water environmental protection incurred by the applicant in connection with any surface coal mining operation during the three-year period prior to the date of application. The schedule shall also indicate the final resolution of any such notice of violation. Where the schedule or other information available to the regulatory authority indicates that any surface coal mining operation owned or controlled by the applicant is currently in violation of this chapter or such other laws referred to[1] this subsection, the permit shall not be issued until the applicant submits proof that such violation has been corrected or is in the process of being corrected to the satisfaction of the regulatory authority, department, or agency which has jurisdiction over such violation and no permit shall be issued to an applicant after a finding by the regulatory authority, after opportunity for hearing, that the applicant, or the operator specified in the application, controls or has controlled mining operations with a demonstrated pattern of willful violations of this chapter of such nature and duration with such resulting irreparable damage to the environment as to indicate an intent not to comply with the provisions of this chapter.

**(d) Prime farmland mining permit**

**(1)** In addition to finding the application in compliance with subsection (b) of this section, if the area proposed to be mined contains prime farmland pursuant to section 1257(b)(16) of this title, the regulatory authority shall, after consultation with the Secretary of Agriculture, and pursuant to regulations issued hereunder by the Secretary of[2] Interior with the concurrence of the Secretary of Agriculture, grant a permit to mine on prime farmland if the regulatory authority finds in writing that the operator has the technological capability to restore such mined area, within a reasonable time, to equivalent or higher levels of yield as non-mined prime farmland in the surrounding area under equivalent levels of management and can meet the soil reconstruction standards in section 1265(b)(7) of this title. Except for compliance with subsection (b) of this section, the requirements of this paragraph (1) shall apply to all permits issued after August 3, 1977.

**(2)** Nothing in this subsection shall apply to any permit issued prior to August 3, 1977, or to any revisions or renewals thereof, or to any existing surface mining operations for which a permit was issued prior to August 3, 1977.

**(e) Modification of prohibition**

After October 24, 1992, the prohibition of subsection (c) of this section shall not apply to a permit application due to any violation resulting from an unanticipated event or condition at a surface coal mining operation on lands eligible for remining under a permit held by the person making such application. As used in this subsection, the term "violation" has the same meaning as such term has under subsection (c) of this section. The authority of this subsection and section 1265(b)(20)(B) of this title shall terminate on September 30, 2004.

(Pub.L. 95–87, Title V, § 510, Aug. 3, 1977, 91 Stat. 480; Pub.L. 102–486, Title XXV, § 2503(a), Oct. 24, 1992, 106 Stat. 3102.)

[1] So in original. Probably should be followed by "in".

[2] So in original. Probably should be "of the".

### HISTORICAL AND STATUTORY NOTES

**References in Text**

This chapter, referred to in subsecs. (a), (b), and (c), was in the original "this Act", meaning Pub.L. 95–87, Aug. 3, 1977, 91 Stat. 445, as amended, which enacted this chapter and amended section 1114 of Title 18, Crimes and Criminal Procedure. For complete classification of this Act to the Code, see Short Title note set out under section 1201 of this title and Tables.

## § 1261. Revision of permits

[SMCRA § 511]

### (a) Application and revised reclamation plan; requirements; extensions to area covered

(1) During the term of the permit the permittee may submit an application for a revision of the permit, together with a revised reclamation plan, to the regulatory authority.

(2) An application for a revision of a permit shall not be approved unless the regulatory authority finds that reclamation as required by this chapter and the State or Federal program can be accomplished under the revised reclamation plan. The revision shall be approved or disapproved within a period of time established by the State or Federal program. The regulatory authority shall establish guidelines for a determination of the scale or extent of a revision request for which all permit application information requirements and procedures, including notice and hearings, shall apply: *Provided*, That any revisions which propose significant alterations in the reclamation plan shall, at a minimum, be subject to notice and hearing requirements.

(3) Any extensions to the area covered by the permit except incidental boundary revisions must be made by application for another permit.

### (b) Transfer, assignment, or sale of rights under permit

No transfer, assignment, or sale of the rights granted under any permit issued pursuant to this chapter shall be made without the written approval of the regulatory authority.

### (c) Review of outstanding permits

The regulatory authority shall within a time limit prescribed in regulations promulgated by the regulatory authority, review outstanding permits and may require reasonable revision or modification of the permit provisions during the term of such permit: *Provided*, That such revision or modification shall be based upon a written finding and subject to notice and hearing requirements established by the State or Federal program.

(Pub.L. 95–87, Title V, § 511, Aug. 3, 1977, 91 Stat. 483.)

### HISTORICAL AND STATUTORY NOTES

**References in Text**

This chapter, referred to in subsecs. (a)(2), and (b), was in the original "this Act", meaning Pub.L. 95–87, Aug. 3, 1977, 91 Stat. 445, as amended, which enacted this chapter and amended section 1114 of Title 18, Crimes and Criminal Procedure. For complete classification of this Act to the Code, see Short Title note set out under section 1201 of this title and Tables.

## § 1262. Coal exploration permits

[SMCRA § 512]

### (a) Regulations; contents

Each State or Federal program shall include a requirement that coal exploration operations which substantially disturb the natural land surface be conducted in accordance with exploration regulations issued by the regulatory authority. Such regulations shall include, at a minimum (1) the requirement that prior to conducting any exploration under this section, any person must file with the regulatory authority notice of intention to explore and such notice shall include a description of the exploration area and the period of supposed exploration and (2) provisions for reclamation in accordance with the performance standards in section 1265 of this title of all lands disturbed in exploration, including excavations, roads, drill holes, and the removal of necessary facilities and equipment.

### (b) Confidential information

Information submitted to the regulatory authority pursuant to this subsection as confidential concerning trade secrets or privileged commercial or financial information which relates to the competitive rights of the person or entity intended to explore the described area shall not be available for public examination.

### (c) Penalties

Any person who conducts any coal exploration activities which substantially disturb the natural land surface in violation of this section or regulations issued pursuant thereto shall be subject to the provisions of section 1268 of this title.

### (d) Limitation on removal of coal

No operator shall remove more than two hundred and fifty tons of coal pursuant to an exploration permit without the specific written approval of the regulatory authority.

**(e) Law governing exploration of Federal lands**

Coal exploration on Federal lands shall be governed by section 4 of the Federal Coal Leasing Amendments Act of 1975 (90 Stat. 1085).

(Pub.L. 95–87, Title V, § 512, Aug. 3, 1977, 91 Stat. 483.)

### HISTORICAL AND STATUTORY NOTES

**References in Text**

Section 4 of the Federal Coal Leasing Amendments Act of 1975 (90 Stat. 1085), referred to in subsec. (e), is section 4 of Pub.L. 94–377, Aug. 4, 1976, 90 Stat. 1085, redesignated the Federal Coal Leasing Amendments Act of 1976, which amended section 201(b) of this title.

## § 1263. Public notice and public hearings

[SMCRA § 513]

**(a) Submittal of advertisement to regulatory authority; notification of local governmental bodies**

At the time of submission of an application for a surface coal mining and reclamation permit, or revision of an existing permit, pursuant to the provisions of this chapter or an approved State program, the applicant shall submit to the regulatory authority a copy of his advertisement of the ownership, precise location, and boundaries of the land to be affected. At the time of submission such advertisement shall be placed by the applicant in a local newspaper of general circulation in the locality of the proposed surface mine at least once a week for four consecutive weeks. The regulatory authority shall notify various local governmental bodies, planning agencies, and sewage and water treatment authorities, of[1] water companies in the locality in which the proposed surface mining will take place, notifying them of the operator's intention to surface mine a particularly described tract of land and indicating the application's permit number and where a copy of the proposed mining and reclamation plan may be inspected. These local bodies, agencies, authorities, or companies may submit written comments within a reasonable period established by the regulatory authority on the mining applications with respect to the effect of the proposed operation on the environment which are within their area of responsibility. Such comments shall immediately be transmitted to the applicant by the regulatory authority and shall be made available to the public at the same locations as are the mining applications.

**(b) Objections to permit applications; informal conference; record**

Any person having an interest which is or may be adversely affected or the officer or head of any Federal, State, or local governmental agency or authority shall have the right to file written objections to the proposed initial or revised application for a permit for surface coal mining and reclamation operation with the regulatory authority within thirty days after the last publication of the above notice. Such objections shall immediately be transmitted to the applicant by the regulatory authority and shall be made available to the public. If written objections are filed and an informal conference requested, the regulatory authority shall then hold an informal conference in the locality of the proposed mining, if requested within a reasonable time of the receipt of such objections or request. The date, time and location of such informal conference shall be advertised by the regulatory authority in a newspaper of general circulation in the locality at least two weeks prior to the scheduled conference date. The regulatory authority may arrange with the applicant upon request by any party to the administrative proceeding access to the proposed mining area for the purpose of gathering information relevant to the proceeding. An electronic or stenographic record shall be made of the conference proceeding, unless waived by all parties. Such record shall be maintained and shall be accessible to the parties until final release of the applicant's performance bond. In the event all parties requesting the informal conference stipulate agreement prior to the requested informal conference and withdraw their request, such informal conference need not be held.

**(c) Prior Federal coal lease hearing as evidence**

Where the lands included in an application for a permit are the subject of a Federal coal lease in connection with which hearings were held and determinations were made under section 201(a)(3)(A), (B) and (C) of this title, such hearings shall be deemed as to the matters covered to satisfy the requirements of this section and section 1264 of this title and such determinations shall be deemed to be a part of the record and conclusive for purposes of sections 1260, 1264 of this title and this section.

(Pub.L. 95–87, Title V, § 513, Aug. 3, 1977, 91 Stat. 484.)

[1] So in original. Probably should be "or".

### HISTORICAL AND STATUTORY NOTES

**References in Text**

This chapter, referred to in subsec. (a), was in the original "this Act", meaning Pub.L. 95–87, Aug. 3, 1977, 91 Stat. 445, as amended, which enacted this chapter and amended section 1114 of Title 18, Crimes and Criminal Procedure. For complete classification of this Act to the Code, see Short Title note set out under section 1201 of this title and Tables.

## § 1264. Decisions of regulatory authority and appeals

[SMCRA § 514]

**(a) Issuance of findings within 60 days after informal conference**

If an informal conference has been held pursuant to section 1263(b) of this title, the regulatory authority shall issue and furnish the applicant for a permit and persons who are parties to the administrative proceedings with the written finding of the regulatory authority, granting or denying the permit in whole or in part and stating the reasons therefor, within the sixty days of said hearings.

**(b) Decision without informal conference; notification within a reasonable time**

If there has been no informal conference held pursuant to section 1263(b) of this title, the regulatory authority shall notify the applicant for a permit within a reasonable time as determined by the regulatory authority and set forth in regulations, taking into account the time needed for proper investigation of the site, the complexity of the permit application, and whether or not written objection to the application has been filed, whether the application has been approved or disapproved in whole or part.

**(c) Request for rehearing on reasons for final determination; time; issuance of decision**

If the application is approved, the permit shall be issued. If the application is disapproved, specific reasons therefor must be set forth in the notification. Within thirty days after the applicant is notified of the final decision of the regulatory authority on the permit application, the applicant or any person with an interest which is or may be adversely affected may request a hearing on the reasons for the final determination. The regulatory authority shall hold a hearing within thirty days of such request and provide notification to all interested parties at the time that the applicant is so notified. If the Secretary is the regulatory authority the hearing shall be of record and governed by section 554 of Title 5. Where the regulatory authority is the State, such hearing shall be of record, adjudicatory in nature and no person who presided at a conference under section 1263(b) of this title shall either preside at the hearing or participate in this decision thereon or in any administrative appeal therefrom. Within thirty days after the hearing the regulatory authority shall issue and furnish the applicant, and all persons who participated in the hearing, with the written decision of the regulatory authority granting or denying the permit in whole or in part and stating the reasons therefor.

**(d) Temporary relief**

Where a hearing is requested pursuant to subsection (c) of this section, the Secretary, where the Secretary is the regulatory authority, or the State hearing authority may, under such conditions as it may prescribe, grant such temporary relief as it deems appropriate pending final determination of the proceedings if—

(1) all parties to the proceedings have been notified and given an opportunity to be heard on a request for temporary relief;

(2) the person requesting such relief shows that there is a substantial likelihood that he will prevail on the merits of the final determination of the proceeding; and

(3) such relief will not adversely affect the public health or safety or cause significant imminent environmental harm to land, air, or water resources.

**(e) Power of regulatory authority with respect to rehearing**

For the purpose of such hearing, the regulatory authority may administer oaths, subpoena witnesses, or written or printed materials, compel attendance of the witness, or production of the materials, and take evidence including but not limited to site inspections of the land to be affected and other surface coal mining operations carried on by the applicant in the general vicinity of the proposed operation. A verbatim record of each public hearing required by this chapter shall be made, and a transcript made available on the motion of any party or by order of the regulatory authority.

**(f) Right to appeal in accordance with section 1276 of this title**

Any applicant or any person with an interest which is or may be adversely affected who has participated in the administrative proceedings as an objector, and who is aggrieved by the decision of the regulatory authority, or if the regulatory authority fails to act within the time limits specified in this chapter shall have the right to appeal in accordance with section 1276 of this title.

(Pub.L. 95–87, Title V, § 514, Aug. 3, 1977, 91 Stat. 485.)

### HISTORICAL AND STATUTORY NOTES

**References in Text**

This chapter, referred to in subsecs. (e), and (f), was in the original "this Act", meaning Pub.L. 95–87, Aug. 3, 1977, 91 Stat. 445, as amended, which enacted this chapter and amended section 1114 of Title 18, Crimes and Criminal Procedure. For complete classification of this Act to the Code, see Short Title note set out under section 1201 of this title and Tables.

## § 1265. Environmental protection performance standards

[SMCRA § 515]

**(a) Permit requirement**

Any permit issued under any approved State or Federal program pursuant to this chapter to conduct surface coal mining operations shall require that such surface coal mining operations will meet all applicable performance standards of this chapter, and such other requirements as the regulatory authority shall promulgate.

**(b) General standards**

General performance standards shall be applicable to all surface coal mining and reclamation operations and shall require the operation as a minimum to—

(1) conduct surface coal mining operations so as to maximize the utilization and conservation of the solid fuel resource being recovered so that reaffecting the land in the future through surface coal mining can be minimized;

(2) restore the land affected to a condition capable of supporting the uses which it was capable of supporting prior to any mining, or higher or better uses of which there is reasonable likelihood, so long as such use or uses do not present any actual or probable hazard to public health or safety or pose any actual or probable threat of water diminution or pollution, and the permit applicants' declared proposed land use following reclamation is not deemed to be impractical or unreasonable, inconsistent with applicable land use policies and plans, involves unreasonable delay in implementation, or is violative of Federal, State, or local law;

(3) except as provided in subsection (c) of this section with respect to all surface coal mining operations backfill, compact (where advisable to insure stability or to prevent leaching of toxic materials), and grade in order to restore the approximate original contour of the land with all highwalls, spoil piles, and depressions eliminated (unless small depressions are needed in order to retain moisture to assist revegetation or as otherwise authorized pursuant to this chapter): *Provided, however,* That in surface coal mining which is carried out at the same location over a substantial period of time where the operation transects the coal deposit, and the thickness of the coal deposits relative to the volume of the overburden is large and where the operator demonstrates that the overburden and other spoil and waste materials at a particular point in the permit area or otherwise available from the entire permit area is insufficient, giving due consideration to volumetric expansion, to restore the approximate original contour, the operator, at a minimum, shall backfill, grade, and compact (where advisable) using all available overburden and other spoil and waste materials to attain the lowest practicable grade but not more than the angle of repose, to provide adequate drainage and to cover all acid-forming and other toxic materials, in order to achieve an ecologically sound land use compatible with the surrounding region: *And provided further,* That in surface coal mining where the volume of overburden is large relative to the thickness of the coal deposit and where the operator demonstrates that due to volumetric expansion the amount of overburden and other spoil and waste materials removed in the course of the mining operation is more than sufficient to restore the approximate original contour, the operator shall after restoring the approximate contour, backfill, grade, and compact (where advisable) the excess overburden and other spoil and waste materials to attain the lowest grade but not more than the angle of repose, and to cover all acid-forming and other toxic materials, in order to achieve an ecologically sound land use compatible with the surrounding region and that such overburden or spoil shall be shaped and graded in such a way as to prevent slides, erosion, and water pollution and is revegetated in accordance with the requirements of this chapter;

(4) stabilize and protect all surface areas including spoil piles affected by the surface coal mining and reclamation operation to effectively control erosion and attendant air and water pollution;

(5) remove the topsoil from the land in a separate layer, replace it on the backfill area, or if not utilized immediately, segregate it in a separate pile from other spoil and when the topsoil is not replaced on a backfill area within a time short enough to avoid deterioration of the topsoil, maintain a successful cover by quick growing plant or other means thereafter so that the topsoil is preserved from wind and water erosion, remains free of any contamination by other acid or toxic material, and is in a usable condition for sustaining vegetation when restored during reclamation, except if topsoil is of insufficient quantity or of poor quality for sustaining vegetation, or if other strata can be shown to be more suitable for vegetation requirements, then the operator shall remove, segregate, and preserve in a like manner such other strata which is best able to support vegetation;

(6) restore the topsoil or the best available subsoil which is best able to support vegetation;

(7) for all prime farm lands as identified in section 1257(b)(16) of this title to be mined and reclaimed, specifications for soil removal, storage, replacement, and reconstruction shall be established by the Secretary of Agriculture, and the operator shall, as a minimum, be required to—

(A) segregate the A horizon of the natural soil, except where it can be shown that other available soil materials will create a final soil having a greater productive capacity; and if not utilized immediately, stockpile this material separately from other spoil, and provide needed protection from wind and water erosion or contamination by other acid or toxic material;

(B) segregate the B horizon of the natural soil, or underlying C horizons or other strata, or a combination of such horizons or other strata that are shown to be both texturally and chemically suitable for plant growth and that can be shown to be equally or more favorable for plant growth than the B horizon, in sufficient quantities to create in the regraded final soil a root zone of comparable depth and quality to that which existed in the natural soil; and if not utilized immediately, stockpile this material separately from other spoil, and provide needed protection from wind and water erosion or contamination by other acid or toxic material;

**(C)** replace and regrade the root zone material described in (B) above with proper compaction and uniform depth over the regraded spoil material; and

**(D)** redistribute and grade in a uniform manner the surface soil horizon described in subparagraph (A);

**(8)** create, if authorized in the approved mining and reclamation plan and permit, permanent impoundments of water on mining sites as part of reclamation activities only when it is adequately demonstrated that—

**(A)** the size of the impoundment is adequate for its intended purposes;

**(B)** the impoundment dam construction will be so designed as to achieve necessary stability with an adequate margin of safety compatible with that of structures constructed under Public Law 83–566 (16 U.S.C. 1006);

**(C)** the quality of impounded water will be suitable on a permanent basis for its intended use and that discharges from the impoundment will not degrade the water quality below water quality standards established pursuant to applicable Federal and State law in the receiving stream;

**(D)** the level of water will be reasonably stable;

**(E)** final grading will provide adequate safety and access for proposed water users; and

**(F)** such water impoundments will not result in the diminution of the quality or quantity of water utilized by adjacent or surrounding landowners for agricultural, industrial[1] recreational, or domestic uses;

**(9)** conducting[2] any augering operation associated with surface mining in a manner to maximize recoverability of mineral reserves remaining after the operation and reclamation are complete; and seal all auger holes with an impervious and noncombustible material in order to prevent drainage except where the regulatory authority determines that the resulting impoundment of water in such auger holes may create a hazard to the environment or the public health or safety: *Provided*, That the permitting authority may prohibit augering if necessary to maximize the utilization, recoverability or conservation of the solid fuel resources or to protect against adverse water quality impacts;

**(10)** minimize the disturbances to the prevailing hydrologic balance at the mine-site and in associated offsite areas and to the quality and quantity of water in surface and ground water systems both during and after surface coal mining operations and during reclamation by—

**(A)** avoiding acid or other toxic mine drainage by such measures as, but not limited to—

**(i)** preventing or removing water from contact with toxic producing deposits;

**(ii)** treating drainage to reduce toxic content which adversely affects downstream water upon being released to water courses;

**(iii)** casing, sealing, or otherwise managing boreholes, shafts, and wells and keep[3] acid or other toxic drainage from entering ground and surface waters;

**(B)(i)** conducting surface coal mining operations so as to prevent, to the extent possible using the best technology currently available, additional contributions of suspended solids to streamflow, or runoff outside the permit area, but in no event shall contributions be in excess of requirements set by applicable State or Federal law;

**(ii)** constructing any siltation structures pursuant to subparagraph (B)(i) of this subsection prior to commencement of surface coal mining operations, such structures to be certified by a qualified registered engineer or a qualified registered professional land surveyor in any State which authorizes land surveyors to prepare and certify such maps or plans to be constructed as designed and as approved in the reclamation plan;

**(C)** cleaning out and removing temporary or large settling ponds or other siltation structures from drainways after disturbed areas are revegetated and stabilized; and depositing the silt and debris at a site and in a manner approved by the regulatory authority;

**(D)** restoring recharge capacity of the mined area to approximate premining conditions;

**(E)** avoiding channel deepening or enlargement in operations requiring the discharge of water from mines;

**(F)** preserving throughout the mining and reclamation process the essential hydrologic functions of alluvial valley floors in the arid and semiarid areas of the country; and

**(G)** such other actions as the regulatory authority may prescribe;

**(11)** with respect to surface disposal of mine wastes, tailings, coal processing wastes, and other wastes in areas other than the mine working or excavations, stabilize all waste piles in designated areas through construction in compacted layers including the use of incombustible and impervious materials if necessary and assure the final contour of the waste pile will be compatible with natural surroundings and that the site can and will be stabilized and revegetated according to the provisions of this chapter;

**(12)** refrain from surface coal mining within five hundred feet from active and abandoned underground mines in order to prevent breakthroughs and to protect health or safety of miners: *Provided*, That the regulatory authority shall permit an operator to mine near, through or partially through an abandoned underground mine or closer to an active underground mine if (A) the nature, timing, and sequencing of the approximate coincidence of specific surface mine activities with specific underground mine activities are jointly approved by the regulatory authorities concerned with surface mine regulation and the health and safety of underground miners, and (B) such operations will result in improved resource recovery, abatement of water pollution, or elimination of hazards to the health and safety of the public;

**(13)** design, locate, construct, operate, maintain, enlarge, modify, and remove or abandon, in accordance with the standards and criteria developed pursuant to subsection (f) of this section, all existing and new coal mine waste piles consisting of mine wastes, tailings, coal processing wastes, or other liquid and solid wastes, and used either temporarily or permanently as dams or embankments;

**(14)** insure that all debris, acid-forming materials, toxic materials, or materials constituting a fire hazard are treated or buried and compacted or otherwise disposed of in a manner designed to prevent contamination of ground or surface waters and that contingency plans are developed to prevent sustained combustion;

**(15)** insure that explosives are used only in accordance with existing State and Federal law and the regulations promulgated by the regulatory authority, which shall include provisions to—

**(A)** provide adequate advance written notice to local governments and residents who might be affected by the use of such explosives by publication of the planned blasting schedule in a newspaper of general circulation in the locality and by mailing a copy of the proposed blasting schedule to every resident living within one-half mile of the proposed blasting site and by providing daily notice to resident/occupiers in such areas prior to any blasting;

**(B)** maintain for a period of at least three years and make available for public inspection upon request a log detailing the location of the blasts, the pattern and depth of the drill holes, the amount of explosives used per hole, and the order and length of delay in the blasts;

**(C)** limit the type of explosives and detonating equipment, the size, the timing and frequency of blasts based upon the physical conditions of the site so as to prevent (i) injury to persons, (ii) damage to public and private property outside the permit area, (iii) adverse impacts on any underground mine, and (iv) change in the course, channel, or availability of ground or surface water outside the permit area;

**(D)** require that all blasting operations be conducted by trained and competent persons as certified by the regulatory authority;

**(E)** provide that upon the request of a resident or owner of a man-made dwelling or structure within one-half mile of any portion of the permitted area the applicant or permittee shall conduct a pre-blasting survey of such structures and submit the survey to the regulatory authority and a copy to the resident or owner making the request. The area of the survey shall be decided by the regulatory authority and shall include such provisions as the Secretary shall promulgate.

**(16)** insure that all reclamation efforts proceed in an environmentally sound manner and as contemporaneously as practicable with the surface coal mining operations: *Provided, however*, That where the applicant proposes to combine surface mining operations with underground mining operations to assure maximum practical recovery of the mineral resources, the regulatory authority may grant a variance for specific areas within the reclamation plan from the requirement that reclamation efforts proceed as contemporaneously as practicable to permit underground mining operations prior to reclamation:

**(A)** if the regulatory authority finds in writing that:

**(i)** the applicant has presented, as part of the permit application, specific, feasible plans for the proposed underground mining operations;

**(ii)** the proposed underground mining operations are necessary or desirable to assure maximum practical recovery of the mineral resource and will avoid multiple disturbance of the surface;

**(iii)** the applicant has satisfactorily demonstrated that the plan for the underground mining operations conforms to requirements for underground mining in the jurisdiction and that permits necessary for the underground mining operations have been issued by the appropriate authority;

**(iv)** the areas proposed for the variance have been shown by the applicant to be necessary for the implementing of the proposed underground mining operations;

(v) no substantial adverse environmental damage, either on-site or off-site, will result from the delay in completion of reclamation as required by this chapter;

(vi) provisions for the off-site storage of spoil will comply with paragraph (22);

(B) if the Secretary has promulgated specific regulations to govern the granting of such variances in accordance with the provisions of this subsection and section 1251 of this title, and has imposed such additional requirements as he deems necessary;

(C) if variances granted under the provisions of this subsection are to be reviewed by the regulatory authority not more than three years from the date of issuance of the permit; and

(D) if liability under the bond filed by the applicant with the regulatory authority pursuant to section 1259(b) of this title shall be for the duration of the underground mining operations and until the requirements of this subsection and section 1269 of this title have been fully complied with.[4]

(17) insure that the construction, maintenance, and postmining conditions of access roads into and across the site of operations will control or prevent erosion and siltation, pollution of water, damage to fish or wildlife or their habitat, or public or private property;

(18) refrain from the construction of roads or other access ways up a stream bed or drainage channel or in such proximity to such channel so as to seriously alter the normal flow of water;

(19) establish on the regraded areas, and all other lands affected, a diverse, effective, and permanent vegetative cover of the same seasonal variety native to the area of land to be affected and capable of self-regeneration and plant succession at least equal in extent of cover to the natural vegetation of the area; except, that introduced species may be used in the revegetation process where desirable and necessary to achieve the approved postmining land use plan;

(20)(A) assume the responsibility for successful revegetation, as required by paragraph (19) above, for a period of five full years after the last year of augmented seeding, fertilizing, irrigation, or other work in order to assure compliance with paragraph (19) above, except in those areas or regions of the country where the annual average precipitation is twenty-six inches or less, then the operator's assumption of responsibility and liability will extend for a period of ten full years after the last year of augmented seeding, fertilizing, irrigation, or other work: *Provided*, That when the regulatory authority approves a long-term intensive agricultural postmining land use, the applicable five- or ten-year period of responsibility for revegetation shall commence at the date of initial planting for such long-term intensive agricultural postmining land use: *Provided further*, That when the regulatory authority issues a written finding approving a long-term, intensive, agricultural postmining land use as part of the mining and reclamation plan, the authority may grant exception to the provisions of paragraph (19) above;

(B) on lands eligible for remining assume the responsibility for successful revegetation for a period of two full years after the last year of augmented seeding, fertilizing, irrigation, or other work in order to assure compliance with the applicable standards, except in those areas or regions of the country where the annual average precipitation is twenty-six inches or less, then the operator's assumption of responsibility and liability will be extended for a period of five full years after the last year of augmented seeding, fertilizing, irrigation, or other work in order to assure compliance with the applicable standards.

(21) protect offsite areas from slides or damage occurring during the surface coal mining and reclamation operations, and not deposit spoil material or locate any part of the operations or waste accumulations outside the permit area;

(22) place all excess spoil material resulting from coal surface mining and reclamation activities in such a manner that—

(A) spoil is transported and placed in a controlled manner in position for concurrent compaction and in such a way to assure mass stability and to prevent mass movement;

(B) the areas of disposal are within the bonded permit areas and all organic matter shall be removed immediately prior to spoil placement;

(C) appropriate surface and internal drainage systems and diversion ditches are used so as to prevent spoil erosion and movement;

(D) the disposal area does not contain springs, natural water courses or wet weather seeps unless lateral drains are constructed from the wet areas to the main underdrains in such a manner that filtration of the water into the spoil pile will be prevented;

(E) if placed on a slope, the spoil is placed upon the most moderate slope among those upon which, in the judgment of the regulatory authority, the spoil could be placed in compliance with all the requirements of this chapter, and shall be placed, where possible, upon, or above, a natural terrace, bench, or berm, if such placement provides additional stability and prevents mass movement;

(F) where the toe of the spoil rests on a downslope, a rock toe buttress, of sufficient size to prevent mass movement, is constructed;

(G) the final configuration is compatible with the natural drainage pattern and surroundings and suitable for intended uses;

(H) design of the spoil disposal area is certified by a qualified registered professional engineer in conformance with professional standards; and

(I) all other provisions of this chapter are met.[4]

(23) meet such other criteria as are necessary to achieve reclamation in accordance with the purposes of this chapter, taking into consideration the physical, climatological, and other characteristics of the site; and [5]

(24) to the extent possible using the best technology currently available, minimize disturbances and adverse impacts of the operation on fish, wildlife, and related environmental values, and achieve enhancement of such resources where practicable;

(25) provide for an undisturbed natural barrier beginning at the elevation of the lowest coal seam to be mined and extending from the outslope for such distance as the regulatory authority shall determine shall be retained in place as a barrier to slides and erosion.

**(c) Procedures; exception to original contour restoration requirements**

(1) Each State program may and each Federal program shall include procedures pursuant to which the regulatory authority may permit surface mining operations for the purposes set forth in paragraph (3) of this subsection.

(2) Where an applicant meets the requirements of paragraphs (3) and (4) of this subsection a permit without regard to the requirement to restore to approximate original contour set forth in subsection (b)(3) or (d)(2) and (3) of this section may be granted for the surface mining of coal where the mining operation will remove an entire coal seam or seams running through the upper fraction of a mountain, ridge, or hill (except as provided in subsection (c)(4)(A) hereof) by removing all of the overburden and creating a level plateau or a gently rolling contour with no highwalls remaining, and capable of supporting postmining uses in accord with the requirements of this subsection.

(3) In cases where an industrial, commercial, agricultural, residential or public facility (including recreational facilities) use is proposed or [6] the postmining use of the affected land, the regulatory authority may grant a permit for a surface mining operation of the nature described in subsection (c)(2) of this section where—

(A) after consultation with the appropriate land use planning agencies, if any, the proposed postmining land use is deemed to constitute an equal or better economic or public use of the affected land, as compared with premining use;

(B) the applicant presents specific plans for the proposed postmining land use and appropriate assurances that such use will be—

(i) compatible with adjacent land uses;

(ii) obtainable according to data regarding expected need and market;

(iii) assured of investment in necessary public facilities;

(iv) supported by commitments from public agencies where appropriate;

(v) practicable with respect to private financial capability for completion of the proposed use;

(vi) planned pursuant to a schedule attached to the reclamation plan so as to integrate the mining operation and reclamation with the postmining land use; and

(vii) designed by a registered engineer in conformance with professional standards established to assure the stability, drainage, and configuration necessary for the intended use of the site;

(C) the proposed use would be consistent with adjacent land uses, and existing State and local land use plans and programs;

(D) the regulatory authority provides the governing body of the unit of general-purpose government in which the land is located and any State or Federal agency which the regulatory agency, in its discretion, determines to have an interest in the proposed use, an opportunity of not more than sixty days to review and comment on the proposed use;

(E) all other requirements of this chapter will be met.

(4) In granting any permit pursuant to this subsection the regulatory authority shall require that—

(A) the toe of the lowest coal seam and the overburden associated with it are retained in place as a barrier to slides and erosion;

(B) the reclaimed area is stable;

(C) the resulting plateau or rolling contour drains inward from the outslopes except at specified points;

(D) no damage will be done to natural watercourses;

(E) spoil will be placed on the mountaintop bench as is necessary to achieve the planned postmining land use: *Provided*, That all excess spoil material not retained on the mountaintop shall be placed in accordance with the provisions of subsection (b)(22) of this section;

(F) insure stability of the spoil retained on the mountaintop and meet the other requirements of this chapter;[7]

(5) The regulatory authority shall promulgate specific regulations to govern the granting of permits in accord with the provisions of this subsection, and may impose such additional requirements as he deems to be necessary.

(6) All permits granted under the provisions of this subsection shall be reviewed not more than three years from the date of issuance of the permit, unless the applicant affirmatively demonstrates that the proposed development is proceeding in accordance with the terms of the approved schedule and reclamation plan.

**(d) Steep-slope surface coal mining standards**

The following performance standards shall be applicable to steep-slope surface coal mining and shall be in addition to those general performance standards required by this section: *Provided, however,* That the provisions of this subsection (d) shall not apply to those situations in which an operator is mining on flat or gently rolling terrain, on which an occasional steep slope is encountered through which the mining operation is to proceed, leaving a plain or predominantly flat area or where an operator is in compliance with provisions of subsection (c) hereof:

(1) Insure that when performing surface coal mining on steep slopes, no debris, abandoned or disabled equipment, spoil material, or waste mineral matter be placed on the downslope below the bench or mining cut: *Provided,* That spoil material in excess of that required for the reconstruction of the approximate original contour under the provisions of subsection (b)(3) or (d)(2) of this section shall be permanently stored pursuant to subsection (b)(22) of this section.

(2) Complete backfilling with spoil material shall be required to cover completely the highwall and return the site to the appropriate original contour, which material will maintain stability following mining and reclamation.

(3) The operator may not disturb land above the top of the highwall unless the regulatory authority finds that such disturbance will facilitate compliance with the environmental protection standards of this section: *Provided, however,* That the land disturbed above the highwall shall be limited to that amount necessary to facilitate said compliance.

(4) For the purposes of this subsection (d), the term "steep slope" is any slope above twenty degrees or such lesser slope as may be defined by the regulatory authority after consideration of soil, climate, and other characteristics of a region or State.

**(e) Variances to original contour restoration requirements**

(1) Each State program may and each Federal program shall include procedures pursuant to which the regulatory authority may permit variances for the purposes set forth in paragraph (3) of this subsection, provided that the watershed control of the area is improved; and further provided complete backfilling with spoil material shall be required to cover completely the highwall which material will maintain stability following mining and reclamation.

(2) Where an applicant meets the requirements of paragraphs (3) and (4) of this subsection a variance from the requirement to restore to approximate original contour set forth in subsection (d)(2) of this section may be granted for the surface mining of coal where the owner of the surface knowingly requests in writing, as a part of the permit application that such a variance be granted so as to render the land, after reclamation, suitable for an industrial, commercial, residential, or public use (including recreational facilities) in accord with the further provisions of (3) and (4) of this subsection.

(3)(A) After consultation with the appropriate land use planning agencies, if any, the potential use of the affected land is deemed to constitute an equal or better economic or public use;

(B) is designed and certified by a qualified registered professional engineer in conformance with professional standards established to assure the stability, drainage, and configuration necessary for the intended use of the site; and

(C) after approval of the appropriate state environmental agencies, the watershed of the affected land is deemed to be improved.

(4) In granting a variance pursuant to this subsection the regulatory authority shall require that only such amount of spoil will be placed off the mine bench as is necessary to achieve the planned postmining land use, insure stability of the spoil retained on the bench, meet all other requirements of this chapter, and all spoil placement off the mine bench must comply with subsection (b)(22) of this section.

(5) The regulatory authority shall promulgate specific regulations to govern the granting of variances in accord with the provisions of this subsection, and may impose such additional requirements as he deems to be necessary.

(6) All exceptions granted under the provisions of this subsection shall be reviewed not more than three years from the date of issuance of the permit, unless the permittee affirmatively demonstrates that the proposed development is proceeding in accordance with the terms of the reclamation plan.

**(f) Standards and criteria for coal mine waste piles**

The Secretary, with the written concurrence of the Chief of Engineers, shall establish within one hundred and thirty-five days from August 3, 1977, standards and criteria regulating the design, location, construction, operation, maintenance, enlargement, modification, removal, and abandonment of new and existing coal mine waste piles referred to in subsection (b)(13) of this section and section 1266(b)(5) of this title. Such standards and criteria shall conform to the standards and criteria used by the Chief of Engineers to insure that flood control structures are safe and effectively perform their intended function. In addition to engineering and other technical specifications the standards and criteria developed pursuant to this subsection must include provisions for: review and approval of plans and specifications prior to construction, enlargement, modification, removal, or abandonment; performance of periodic inspections during construction; issuance of certificates of approval upon completion of construction; performance of periodic safety inspections; and issuance of notices for required remedial or maintenance work.

(Pub.L. 95–87, Title V, § 515, Aug. 3, 1977, 91 Stat. 486; Pub.L. 99–500, Title I, § 101(h) [Title I, § 123], Oct. 18, 1986, 100 Stat. 3341–267; Pub.L. 99–591, Title I, § 101(h) [Title I, § 123], Oct. 30, 1986, 100 Stat. 3341–267; Pub.L. 102–486, Title XXV, § 2503(b), Oct. 24, 1992, 106 Stat. 3102.)

1 So in original. Probably should be followed by a comma.

2 So in original. Probably should be "conduct".

3 So in original. Probably should be "keeping".

4 So in original. The period probably should be a semicolon.

5 So in original. The word "and" probably should appear at end of par. (24).

6 So in original. Probably should be "for".

7 So in original. The semicolon probably should be a period.

## HISTORICAL AND STATUTORY NOTES

**References in Text**

This chapter, referred to in subsecs. (a), (b), and (c), was in the original "this Act", meaning Pub. 95–87, Aug. 3, 1977, 91 Stat. 445, as amended, which enacted this chapter and amended section 1114 of Title 18, Crimes and Criminal Procedure. For complete classification of this Act to the Code, see Short Title note set out under section 1201 of this title and Tables.

Public Law 83–566, referred to in subsec. (b)(8)(B), is Act Aug. 4, 1954, c. 656, 68 Stat. 666, as amended, known as the Watershed Protection and Flood Prevention Act, which is classified generally to chapter 18 (section 1001 et seq.) of Title 16, Conservation. For complete classification of this Act to the Code, see Short Title note set out under section 1001 of Title 16 and Tables volume.

## § 1266. Surface effects of underground coal mining operations

### [SMCRA § 516]

**(a) Rules and regulations**

The Secretary shall promulgate rules and regulations directed toward the surface effects of underground coal mining operations, embodying the following requirements and in accordance with the procedures established under section 1251 of this title: *Provided, however*, That in adopting any rules and regulations the Secretary shall consider the distinct difference between surface coal mining and underground coal mining. Such rules and regulations shall not conflict with nor supersede any provision of the Federal Coal Mine Health and Safety Act of 1969 [30 U.S.C.A. § 801 et seq.] nor any regulation issued pursuant thereto, and shall not be promulgated until the Secretary has obtained the written concurrence of the head of the department which administers such Act.

**(b) Permit requirements**

Each permit issued under any approved State or Federal program pursuant to this chapter and relating to underground coal mining shall require the operator to—

(1) adopt measures consistent with known technology in order to prevent subsidence causing material damage to the extent technologically and economically feasible, maximize mine stability, and maintain the value and reasonably foreseeable use of such surface lands, except in those instances where the mining technology used requires planned subsidence in a predictable and controlled manner: *Provided*, That nothing in this subsection shall be construed to prohibit the standard method of room and pillar mining;

(2) seal all portals, entryways, drifts, shafts, or other openings between the surface and underground mine working when no longer needed for the conduct of the mining operations;

(3) fill or seal exploratory holes no longer necessary for mining, maximizing to the extent technologically and economically feasible return of mine and processing waste, tailings, and any other waste incident to the mining operation, to the mine workings or excavations;

(4) with respect to surface disposal of mine wastes, tailings, coal processing wastes, and other wastes in areas other than the mine workings or excavations, stabilize all waste piles created by the permittee from current operations through construction in compacted layers including the use of incombustible and impervious materials if necessary and assure that the leachate will not degrade below water quality standards established pursuant to applicable Federal and State law surface or ground waters and that the final contour of the waste accumulation will be compatible with natural surroundings and that the site is stabilized and revegetated according to the provisions of this section;

(5) design, locate, construct, operate, maintain, enlarge, modify, and remove, or abandon, in accordance with the standards and criteria developed pursuant to section 1265(f) of this title, all existing and new coal mine waste piles consisting of mine wastes, tailings, coal processing wastes, or other liquid and solid wastes and used either temporarily or permanently as dams or embankments;

(6) establish on regraded areas and all other lands affected, a diverse and permanent vegetative cover capable of self-regeneration and plant succession and at least equal in extent of cover to the natural vegetation of the area;

(7) protect offsite areas from damages which may result from such mining operations;

(8) eliminate fire hazards and otherwise eliminate conditions which constitute a hazard to health and safety of the public;

(9) minimize the disturbances of the prevailing hydrologic balance at the minesite and in associated offsite areas and to the quantity of water in surface ground water systems both during and after coal mining operations and during reclamation by—

(A) avoiding acid or other toxic mine drainage by such measures as, but not limited to—

(i) preventing or removing water from contact with toxic producing deposits;

(ii) treating drainage to reduce toxic content which adversely affects downstream water upon being released to water courses;

(iii) casing, sealing, or otherwise managing boreholes, shafts, and wells to keep acid or other toxic drainage from entering ground and surface waters; and

(B) conducting surface coal mining operations so as to prevent, to the extent possible using the best technology currently available, additional contributions of suspended solids to streamflow or runoff outside the permit area (but in no event shall such contributions be in excess of requirements set by applicable State or Federal law), and avoiding channel deepening or enlargement in operations requiring the discharge of water from mines;

(10) with respect to other surface impacts not specified in this subsection including the construction of new roads or the improvement or use of existing roads to gain access to the site of such activities and for haulage, repair areas, storage areas, processing areas, shipping areas, and other areas upon which are sited structures, facilities, or other property or materials on the surface, resulting from or incident to such activities, operate in accordance with the standards established under section 1265 of this title for such effects which result from surface coal mining operations: *Provided*, That the Secretary shall make such modifications in the requirements imposed by this paragraph as are necessary to accommodate the distinct difference between surface and underground coal mining;

(11) to the extent possible using the best technology currently available, minimize disturbances and adverse impacts of the operation on fish, wildlife, and related environmental values, and achieve enhancement of such resources where practicable;

(12) locate openings for all new drift mines working acid-producing or iron-producing coal seams in such a manner as to prevent a gravity discharge of water from the mine.

**(c) Suspension of underground coal mining operations in urbanized areas**

In order to protect the stability of the land, the regulatory authority shall suspend underground coal mining under urbanized areas, cities, towns, and communities and adjacent to industrial or commercial buildings, major impoundments, or permanent streams if he finds imminent danger to inhabitants of the urbanized areas, cities, towns, and communities.

**(d) Applicability of this subchapter to surface operations and surface impacts incident to underground coal mining operations**

The provisions of this subchapter relating to State and Federal programs, permits, bonds, inspections and enforcement, public review, and administrative and judicial review shall be applicable to surface operations and surface impacts incident to an underground coal mine with such modifications to the permit application requirements, permit approval or denial procedures, and bond requirements as are necessary to accommodate the distinct difference between surface and underground coal mining. The Secretary shall promulgate such modifications in accordance with the rulemaking procedure established in section 1251 of this title.

(Pub.L. 95–87, Title V, § 516, Aug. 3, 1977, 91 Stat. 495.)

## HISTORICAL AND STATUTORY NOTES

**References in Text**

The Federal Coal Mine Health and Safety Act of 1969, referred to in subsec. (a), is Pub.L. 91–173, Dec. 30, 1969, 83 Stat. 742, as amended, which was redesignated the Federal Mine Safety and Health Act of 1977 by Pub.L. 95–164, Title I, § 101, Nov. 9, 1977, 91 Stat. 1290, and is classified principally to chapter 22 (section 801 et seq.) of this title. For complete classification of this Act to the Code, see Short Title note set out under section 801 of this title and Tables.

This chapter, referred to in subsec. (b), was in the original, "this Act", meaning Pub.L. 95–87, Aug. 3, 1977, 91 Stat. 445, as amended, which enacted this chapter and amended section 1114 of Title 18, Crimes and Criminal Procedure. For complete classification of this Act to the Code, see Short Title note set out under section 1201 of this title and Tables volume.

## § 1267. Inspections and monitoring

[SMCRA § 517]

### (a) Inspections of surface coal mining and reclamation operations

The Secretary shall cause to be made such inspections of any surface coal mining and reclamation operations as are necessary to evaluate the administration of approved State programs, or to develop or enforce any Federal program, and for such purposes authorized representatives of the Secretary shall have a right of entry to, upon, or through any surface coal mining and reclamation operations.

### (b) Records and reports; monitoring systems; evaluation of results

For the purpose of developing or assisting in the development, administration, and enforcement of any approved State or Federal program under this chapter or in the administration and enforcement of any permit under this chapter, or of determining whether any person is in violation of any requirement of any such State or Federal program or any other requirement of this chapter—

(1) the regulatory authority shall require any permittee to (A) establish and maintain appropriate records, (B) make monthly reports to the regulatory authority, (C) install, use, and maintain any necessary monitoring equipment or methods, (D) evaluate results in accordance with such methods, at such locations, intervals, and in such manner as a regulatory authority shall prescribe, and (E) provide such other information relative to surface coal mining and reclamation operations as the regulatory authority deems reasonable and necessary;

(2) for those surface coal mining and reclamation operations which remove or disturb strata that serve as aquifers which significantly insure the hydrologic balance of water use either on or off the mining site, the regulatory authority shall specify those—

(A) monitoring sites to record the quantity and quality of surface drainage above and below the minesite as well as in the potential zone of influence;

(B) monitoring sites to record level, amount, and samples of ground water and aquifers potentially affected by the mining and also directly below the lowermost (deepest) coal seam to be mined;

(C) records of well logs and borehole data to be maintained; and

(D) monitoring sites to record precipitation.

The monitoring data collection and analysis required by this section shall be conducted according to standards and procedures set forth by the regulatory authority in order to assure their reliability and validity; and

(3) the authorized representatives of the regulatory authority, without advance notice and upon presentation of appropriate credentials (A) shall have the right of entry to, upon, or through any surface coal mining and reclamation operations or any premises in which any records required to be maintained under paragraph (1) of this subsection are located; and (B) may at reasonable times, and without delay, have access to and copy any records, inspect any monitoring equipment or method of operation required under this chapter.

### (c) Inspection intervals

The inspections by the regulatory authority shall (1) occur on an irregular basis averaging not less than one partial inspection per month and one complete inspection per calendar quarter for the surface coal mining and reclamation operation covered by each permit; (2) occur without prior notice to the permittee or his agents or employees except for necessary onsite meetings with the permittee; and (3) include the filing of inspection reports adequate to enforce the requirements of and to carry out the terms and purposes of this chapter.

### (d) Maintenance of sign

Each permittee shall conspicuously maintain at the entrances to the surface coal mining and reclamation operations a clearly visible sign which sets forth the name, business address, and phone number of the permittee and the permit number of the surface coal mining and reclamation operations.

### (e) Violations

Each inspector, upon detection of each violation of any requirement of any State or Federal program or of this chapter, shall forthwith inform the operator in writing, and shall report in writing any such violation to the regulatory authority.

### (f) Availability of information to public

Copies of any records, reports, inspection materials, or information obtained under this subchapter by the regulatory authority shall be made immediately available to the public at central and sufficient locations in the county, multicounty, and State area of mining so that they are conveniently available to residents in the areas of mining.

### (g) Conflict of interest; penalty; publication of regulations; report to Congress

No employee of the State regulatory authority performing any function or duty under this chapter shall have a direct or indirect financial interest in any underground or surface coal mining operation. Whoever knowingly violates the provisions of this subsection shall, upon conviction, be punished by a fine of not more than $2,500, or by imprisonment of not more than one year, or by both. The Secretary shall (1) within sixty days after August 3, 1977, publish in the Federal Register, in accordance with section 553 of Title 5, regulations to establish methods by which the provisions of this subsection will be monitored and enforced by the Secretary and such State regulatory authority, including appropriate provisions for the filing by such employees and the review of statements and supplements thereto concerning any financial interest which may be affected by this subsection, and (2) report to the Congress as part of the Annual Report (section 1296 of this title) on actions taken and not taken during the preceding year under this subsection.

**(h) Review; procedures for inspections**

(1) Any person who is or may be adversely affected by a surface mining operation may notify the Secretary or any representative of the Secretary responsible for conducting the inspection, in writing, of any violation of this chapter which he has reason to believe exists at the surface mining site. The Secretary shall, by regulation, establish procedures for informal review of any refusal by a representative of the Secretary to issue a citation with respect to any such alleged violation. The Secretary shall furnish such persons requesting the review a written statement of the reasons for the Secretary's final disposition of the case.

(2) The Secretary shall also, by regulation, establish procedures to insure that adequate and complete inspections are made. Any such person may notify the Secretary of any failure to make such inspections, after which the Secretary shall determine whether adequate and complete inspections have been made. The Secretary shall furnish such persons a written statement of the reasons for the Secretary's determination that adequate and complete inspections have or have not been conducted.

(Pub.L. 95–87, Title V, § 517, Aug. 3, 1977, 91 Stat. 498.)

### HISTORICAL AND STATUTORY NOTES

**References in Text**

This chapter, referred to in subsecs. (b), (c), (e), (g), and (h)(1), was in the original "this Act", meaning Pub.L. 95–87, Aug. 3, 1977, 91 Stat. 445, as amended, which enacted this chapter and amended section 1114 of Title 18, Crimes and Criminal Procedure. For complete classification of this Act to the Code, see Short Title note set out under section 1201 of this title and Tables.

## § 1268. Penalties

**[SMCRA § 518]**

**(a) Civil penalties for violations of permit conditions and provisions of this subchapter**

In the enforcement of a Federal program or Federal lands program, or during Federal enforcement pursuant to section 1252 of this title or during Federal enforcement of a State program pursuant to section 1271 of this title, any permittee who violates any permit condition or who violates any other provision of this subchapter, may be assessed a civil penalty by the Secretary, except that if such violation leads to the issuance of a cessation order under section 1271 of this title, the civil penalty shall be assessed. Such penalty shall not exceed $5,000 for each violation. Each day of continuing violation may be deemed a separate violation for purposes of penalty assessments. In determining the amount of the penalty, consideration shall be given to the permittee's history of previous violations at the particular surface coal mining operation; the seriousness of the violation, including any irreparable harm to the environment and any hazard to the health or safety of the public; whether the permittee was negligent; and the demonstrated good faith of the permittee charged in attempting to achieve rapid compliance after notification of the violation.

**(b) Hearing**

A civil penalty shall be assessed by the Secretary only after the person charged with a violation described under subsection (a) of this section has been given an opportunity for a public hearing. Where such a public hearing has been held, the Secretary shall make findings of fact, and he shall issue a written decision as to the occurrence of the violation and the amount of the penalty which is warranted, incorporating, when appropriate, an order therein requiring that the penalty be paid. When appropriate, the Secretary shall consolidate such hearings with other proceedings under section 1271 of this title. Any hearing under this section shall be of record and shall be subject to section 554 of Title 5. Where the person charged with such a violation fails to avail himself of the opportunity for a public hearing, a civil penalty shall be assessed by the Secretary after the Secretary has determined that a violation did occur, and the amount of the penalty which is warranted, and has issued an order requiring that the penalty be paid.

**(c) Notice of violation; action required of violator; waiver of legal rights**

Upon the issuance of a notice or order charging that a violation of this chapter has occurred, the Secretary shall inform the operator within thirty days of the proposed amount of said penalty. The person charged with the penalty shall then have thirty days to pay the proposed penalty in full or, if the person wishes to contest either the amount of the penalty or the fact of the violation, forward the proposed amount to the Secretary for placement in an escrow account. If through administrative or judicial review of the proposed penalty, it is determined that no violation occurred, or that the amount of the penalty should be reduced, the Secretary shall within thirty days remit the appropriate amount to the person, with interest at the rate of 6 percent, or at the prevailing Department of the Treasury rate, whichever is greater. Failure to forward the money to the Secretary within thirty days shall result in a waiver of all legal rights to contest the violation or the amount of the penalty.

**(d) Civil action to recover civil penalties**

Civil penalties owed under this chapter, may be recovered in a civil action brought by the Attorney General at the request of the Secretary in any appropriate district court of the United States.

**(e) Willful violations**

Any person who willfully and knowingly violates a condition of a permit issued pursuant to a Federal program, a Federal lands program or Federal enforcement pursuant to section 1252 of this title or during Federal enforcement of a State program pursuant to section 1271 of this title or fails or refuses to comply with any order issued under section 1271 or section 1276 of this title, or any order incorporated in a final decision issued by the Secretary under this chapter, except an order incorporated in a decision issued under subsection (b) of this section or section 1294 of this title, shall, upon conviction, be punished by a fine of not more than $10,000, or by imprisonment for not more than one year or both.

**(f) Corporate violations**

Whenever a corporate permittee violates a condition of a permit issued pursuant to a Federal program, a Federal lands program or Federal enforcement pursuant to section 1252 of this title or Federal enforcement of a State program pursuant to section 1271 of this title or fails or refuses to comply with any order issued under section 1271 of this title, or any order incorporated in a final decision issued by the Secretary under this chapter except an order incorporated in a decision issued under subsection (b) of this section or section 1293 of this title, any director, officer, or agent of such corporation who willfully and knowingly authorized, ordered, or carried out such violation, failure, or refusal shall be subject to the same civil penalties, fines, and imprisonment that may be imposed upon a person under subsections (a) and (e) of this section.

**(g) False statements, representations, or certifications**

Whoever knowingly makes any false statement, representation, or certification, or knowingly fails to make any statement, representation, or certification in any application, record, report, plant, or other document filed or required to be maintained pursuant to a Federal program or a Federal lands program or any order of decision issued by the Secretary under this chapter, shall, upon conviction, be punished by a fine of not more than $10,000, or by imprisonment for not more than one year or both.

**(h) Failure to correct violation**

Any operator who fails to correct a violation for which a citation has been issued under section 1271(a) of this title within the period permitted for its correction (which period shall not end until the entry of a final order by the Secretary, in the case of any review proceedings under section 1275 of this title initiated by the operator wherein the Secretary orders, after an expedited hearing, the suspension of the abatement requirements of the citation after determining that the operator will suffer irreparable loss or damage from the application of those requirements, or until the entry of an order of the court, in the case of any review proceedings under section 1276 of this title initiated by the operator wherein the court orders the suspension of the abatement requirements of the citation), shall be assessed a civil penalty of not less than $750 for each day during which such failure or violation continues.

**(i) Effect on additional enforcement right or procedure available under State law**

As a condition of approval of any State program submitted pursuant to section 1253 of this title, the civil and criminal penalty provisions thereof shall, at a minimum, incorporate penalties no less stringent than those set forth in this section, and shall contain the same or similar procedural requirements relating thereto. Nothing herein shall be construed so as to eliminate any additional enforcement right or procedures which are available under State law to a State regulatory authority but which are not specifically enumerated herein.

(Pub.L. 95–87, Title V, § 518, Aug. 3, 1977, 91 Stat. 499.)

### HISTORICAL AND STATUTORY NOTES

**References in Text**

This chapter, referred to in subsecs. (c) to (g), was in the original "this Act", meaning Pub.L. 95–87, Aug. 3, 1977, 91 Stat. 445, as amended, which enacted this chapter and amended section 1114 of Title 18, Crimes and Criminal Procedure. For complete classification of this Act to the Code, see Short Title note set out under section 1201 of this title and Tables.

## § 1269. Release of performance bonds or deposits

**[SMCRA § 519]**

**(a) Filing of request; submittal of copy of advertisement; notification by letter of intent to seek release**

The permittee may file a request with the regulatory authority for the release of all or part of a performance bond or deposit. Within thirty days after any application for bond or deposit release has been filed with the regulatory authority, the operator shall submit a copy of an advertisement placed at least once a week for four successive weeks in a newspaper of general circulation in the locality of the surface coal mining operation. Such advertisement shall be considered part of any bond release application and shall contain a notification of the precise location of the land affected, the number of acres, the permit and the date approved, the amount of the bond filed and the portion sought to be released, and the type and appropriate dates of reclamation work performed, and a description of the results achieved as they relate to the operator's approved reclamation plan. In addition, as part of any bond release application, the applicant shall submit copies of letters which he has sent to adjoining property owners, local governmental bodies, planning agencies, and sewage and water treatment authorities, or water companies in the locality in which the surface coal mining and reclamation activities took place, notifying them of his intention to seek release from the bond.

**(b) Inspection and evaluation; notification of decision**

Upon receipt of the notification and request, the regulatory authority shall within thirty days conduct an inspection and evaluation of the reclamation work involved. Such evaluation shall consider, among other things, the degree of difficulty to complete any remaining reclamation, whether pollution of surface and subsurface water is occurring, the probability of continuance of future occurrence of such pollution, and the estimated cost of abating such pollution. The regulatory authority shall notify the permittee in writing of its decision to release or not to release all or part of the performance bond or deposit within sixty days from the filing of the request, if no public hearing is held pursuant to subsection (f) of this section, and if there has been a public hearing held pursuant to subsection (f) of this section, within thirty days thereafter.

**(c) Requirements for release**

The regulatory authority may release in whole or in part said bond or deposit if the authority is satisfied the reclamation covered by the bond or deposit or portion thereof has been accomplished as required by this chapter according to the following schedule:

(1) When the operator completes the backfilling, regrading, and drainage control of a bonded area in accordance with his approved reclamation plan, the release of 60 per centum of the bond or collateral for the applicable permit area.

(2) After revegetation has been established on the regraded mined lands in accordance with the approved reclamation plan. When determining the amount of bond to be released after successful revegetation has been established, the regulatory authority shall retain that amount of bond for the revegetated area which would be sufficient for a third party to cover the cost of reestablishing revegetation and for the period specified for operator responsibility in section 1265 of this title of reestablishing revegetation. No part of the bond or deposit shall be released under this paragraph so long as the lands to which the release would be applicable are contributing suspended solids to streamflow or runoff outside the permit area in excess of the requirements set by section 1265(b)(10) of this title or until soil productivity for prime farm lands has returned to equivalent levels of yield as nonmined land of the same soil type in the surrounding area under equivalent management practices as determined from the soil survey performed pursuant to section 1257(b)(16) of this title. Where a silt dam is to be retained as a permanent impoundment pursuant to section 1265(b)(8) of this title, the portion of bond may be released under this paragraph so long as provisions for sound future maintenance by the operator or the landowner have been made with the regulatory authority.

(3) When the operator has completed successfully all surface coal mining and reclamation activities, the release of the remaining portion of the bond, but not before the expiration of the period specified for operator responsibility in section 1265 of this title: *Provided, however,* That no bond shall be fully released until all reclamation requirements of this chapter are fully met.

**(d) Notice of disapproval**

If the regulatory authority disapproves the application for release of the bond or portion thereof, the authority shall notify the permittee, in writing, stating the reasons for disapproval and recommending corrective actions necessary to secure said release and allowing opportunity for a public hearing.

**(e) Notice to municipality**

When any application for total or partial bond release is filed with the regulatory authority, the regulatory authority shall notify the municipality in which a surface coal mining operation is located by certified mail at least thirty days prior to the release of all or a portion of the bond.

**(f) Objections to release; hearing**

Any person with a valid legal interest which might be adversely affected by release of the bond or the responsible officer or head of any Federal, State, or local governmental agency which has jurisdiction by law or special expertise with respect to any environmental, social, or economic impact involved in the operation, or is authorized to develop and enforce environmental standards with respect to such operations shall have the right to file written objections to the proposed release from bond to the regulatory authority within thirty days after the last publication of the above notice. If written objections are filed, and a hearing requested, the regulatory authority shall inform all the interested parties, of the time and place of the hearing, and hold a public hearing in the locality of the surface coal mining operation proposed for bond release within thirty days of the request for such hearing. The date, time, and location of such public hearings shall be advertised by the regulatory authority in a newspaper of general circulation in the locality for two consecutive weeks, and shall hold a public hearing in the locality of the surface coal mining operation proposed for bond release or at the State capital at the option of the objector, within thirty days of the request for such hearing.

**(g) Informal conference**

Without prejudice to the rights of the objectors, the applicant, or the responsibilities of the regulatory authority pursuant to this section, the regulatory authority may establish an informal conference as provided in section 1263 of this title to resolve such written objections.

**(h) Power of regulatory authority with respect to informal conference**

For the purpose of such hearing the regulatory authority shall have the authority and is hereby empowered to administer oaths, subpena witnesses, or written or printed materials, compel the attendance of witnesses, or production of the materials, and take evidence including but not limited to inspections of the land affected and other surface coal mining operations carried on by the applicant in the general vicinity. A verbatim record of each public hearing required by this chapter shall be made, and a transcript made available on the motion of any party or by order of the regulatory authority.

(Pub.L. 95–87, Title V, § 519, Aug. 3, 1977, 91 Stat. 501.)

### HISTORICAL AND STATUTORY NOTES

**References in Text**

This chapter, referred to in subsecs. (c) and (h), was in the original "this Act", meaning Pub.L. 95–87, Aug. 3, 1977, 91 Stat. 445, as amended, which enacted this chapter and amended section 1114 of Title 18, Crimes and Criminal Procedure. For complete classification of this Act to the Code, see Short Title note set out under section 1201 of this title and Tables.

## § 1270. Citizens suits

**[SMCRA § 520]**

**(a) Civil action to compel compliance with this chapter**

Except as provided in subsection (b) of this section, any person having an interest which is or may be adversely affected may commence a civil action on his own behalf to compel compliance with this chapter—

(1) against the United States or any other governmental instrumentality or agency to the extent permitted by the eleventh amendment to the Constitution which is alleged to be in violation of the provisions of this chapter or of any rule, regulation, order or permit issued pursuant thereto, or against any other person who is alleged to be in violation of any rule, regulation, order or permit issued pursuant to this subchapter; or

(2) against the Secretary or the appropriate State regulatory authority to the extent permitted by the eleventh amendment to the Constitution where there is alleged a failure of the Secretary or the appropriate State regulatory authority to perform any act or duty under this chapter which is not discretionary with the Secretary or with the appropriate State regulatory authority.

The district courts shall have jurisdiction, without regard to the amount in controversy or the citizenship of the parties.

**(b) Limitation on bringing of action**

No action may be commenced—

(1) under subsection (a)(1) of this section—

(A) prior to sixty days after the plaintiff has given notice in writing of the violation (i) to the Secretary, (ii) to the State in which the violation occurs, and (iii) to any alleged violator; or

(B) if the Secretary or the State has commenced and is diligently prosecuting a civil action in a court of the United States or a State to require compliance with the provisions of this chapter, or any rule, regulation, order, or permit issued pursuant to this chapter, but in any such action in a court of the United States any person may intervene as a matter of right; or

(2) under subsection (a)(2) of this section prior to sixty days after the plaintiff has given notice in writing of such action to the Secretary, in such manner as the Secretary shall by regulation prescribe, or to the appropriate State regulatory authority, except that such action may be brought immediately after such notification in the case where the violation or order complained of constitutes an imminent threat to the health or safety of the plaintiff or would immediately affect a legal interest of the plaintiff.

(c) **Venue; intervention**

(1) Any action respecting a violation of this chapter or the regulations thereunder may be brought only in the judicial district in which the surface coal mining operation complained of is located.

(2) In such action under this section, the Secretary, or the State regulatory authority, if not a party, may intervene as a matter of right.

(d) **Costs; filing of bonds**

The court, in issuing any final order in any action brought pursuant to subsection (a) of this section, may award costs of litigation (including attorney and expert witness fees) to any party, whenever the court determines such award is appropriate. The court may, if a temporary restraining order or preliminary injunction is sought require the filing of a bond or equivalent security in accordance with the Federal Rules of Civil Procedure.

(e) **Effect on other enforcement methods**

Nothing in this section shall restrict any right which any person (or class of persons) may have under any statute or common law to seek enforcement of any of the provisions of this chapter and the regulations thereunder, or to seek any other relief (including relief against the Secretary or the appropriate State regulatory authority).

(f) **Action for damages**

Any person who is injured in his person or property through the violation by any operator of any rule, regulation, order, or permit issued pursuant to this chapter may bring an action for damages (including reasonable attorney and expert witness fees) only in the judicial district in which the surface coal mining operation complained of is located. Nothing in this subsection shall affect the rights established by or limits imposed under State Workmen's Compensation laws.

(Pub.L. 95–87, Title V, § 520, Aug. 3, 1977, 91 Stat. 503.)

### HISTORICAL AND STATUTORY NOTES

**References in Text**

This chapter, referred to in subsecs. (a) to (c), (e), and (f), was in the original "this Act", meaning Pub.L. 95–87, Aug. 3, 1977, 91 Stat. 445, as amended, which enacted this chapter and amended section 1114 of Title 18, Crimes and Criminal Procedure. For complete classification of this Act to the Code, see Short Title note set out under section 1201 of this title and Tables.

The Federal Rules of Civil Procedure, referred to in subsec. (d), are set out in the Appendix to Title 28, Judiciary and Judicial Procedure.

## § 1271. Enforcement

[SMCRA § 521]

(a) **Notice of violation; Federal inspection; waiver of notification period; cessation order; affirmative obligation on operator; suspension or revocation of permits; contents of notices and orders**

(1) Whenever, on the basis of any information available to him, including receipt of information from any person, the Secretary has reason to believe that any person is in violation of any requirement of this chapter or any permit condition required by this chapter, the Secretary shall notify the State regulatory authority, if one exists, in the State in which such violation exists. If no such State authority exists or the State regulatory authority fails within ten days after notification to take appropriate action to cause said violation to be corrected or to show good cause for such failure and transmit notification of its action to the Secretary, the Secretary shall immediately order Federal inspection of the surface coal mining operation at which the alleged violation is occurring unless the information available to the Secretary is a result of a previous Federal inspection of such surface coal mining operation. The ten-day notification period shall be waived when the person informing the Secretary provides adequate proof that an imminent danger of significant environmental harm exists and that the State has failed to take appropriate action. When the Federal inspection results from information provided to the Secretary by any person, the Secretary shall notify such person when the Federal inspection is proposed to be carried out and such person shall be allowed to accompany the inspector during the inspection.

(2) When, on the basis of any Federal inspection, the Secretary or his authorized representative determines that any condition or practices exist, or that any permittee is in violation of any requirement of this chapter or any permit condition required by this chapter, which condition, practice, or violation also creates an imminent danger to the health or safety of the public, or is causing, or can reasonably be expected to cause significant, imminent environmental harm to land, air, or water resources, the Secretary or his authorized representative shall immediately order a cessation of surface coal mining and reclamation operations or the portion thereof relevant to the condition, practice, or violation. Such cessation order shall remain in effect until the Secretary or his authorized representative determines that the condition, practice, or violation has been abated, or until modified, vacated, or terminated by the Secretary or his authorized representative pursuant to paragraph (5) of this subsection. Where the Secretary finds that the ordered cessation of surface coal mining and reclamation oper-

ations, or any portion thereof, will not completely abate the imminent danger to health or safety of the public or the significant imminent environmental harm to land, air, or water resources, the Secretary shall, in addition to the cessation order, impose affirmative obligations on the operator requiring him to take whatever steps the Secretary deems necessary to abate the imminent danger or the significant environmental harm.

(3) When, on the basis of a Federal inspection which is carried out during the enforcement of a Federal program or a Federal lands program, Federal inspection pursuant to section 1252, or section 1254(b) of this title, or during Federal enforcement of a State program in accordance with subsection (b) of this section, the Secretary or his authorized representative determines that any permittee is in violation of any requirement of this chapter or any permit condition required by this chapter; but such violation does not create an imminent danger to the health or safety of the public, or cannot be reasonably expected to cause significant, imminent environmental harm to land, air, or water resources, the Secretary or authorized representative shall issue a notice to the permittee or his agent fixing a reasonable time but not more than ninety days for the abatement of the violation and providing opportunity for public hearing.

If, upon expiration of the period of time as originally fixed or subsequently extended, for good cause shown and upon the written finding of the Secretary or his authorized representative, the Secretary or his authorized representative finds that the violation has not been abated, he shall immediately order a cessation of surface coal mining and reclamation operations or the portion thereof relevant to the violation. Such cessation order shall remain in effect until the Secretary or his authorized representative determines that the violation has been abated, or until modified, vacated, or terminated by the Secretary or his authorized representative pursuant to paragraph (5) of this subsection. In the order of cessation issued by the Secretary under this subsection, the Secretary shall determine the steps necessary to abate the violation in the most expeditious manner possible, and shall include the necessary measures in the order.

(4) When, on the basis of a Federal inspection which is carried out during the enforcement of a Federal program or a Federal lands program, Federal inspection pursuant to section 1252 or section 1254 of this title or during Federal enforcement of a State program in accordance with subsection (b) of this section, the Secretary or his authorized representative determines that a pattern of violations of any requirements of this chapter or any permit conditions required by this chapter exists or has existed, and if the Secretary or his authorized representative also find that such violations are caused by the unwarranted failure of the permittee to comply with any requirements of this chapter or any permit conditions, or that such violations are willfully caused by the permittee, the Secretary or his authorized representative shall forthwith issue an order to the permittee to show cause as to why the permit should not be suspended or revoked and shall provide opportunity for a public hearing. If a hearing is requested the Secretary shall inform all interested parties of the time and place of the hearing. Upon the permittee's failure to show cause as to why the permit should not be suspended or revoked, the Secretary or his authorized representative shall forthwith suspend or revoke the permit.

(5) Notices and orders issued pursuant to this section shall set forth with reasonable specificity the nature of the violation and the remedial action required, the period of time established for abatement, and a reasonable description of the portion of the surface coal mining and reclamation operation to which the notice or order applies. Each notice or order issued under this section shall be given promptly to the permittee or his agent by the Secretary or his authorized representative who issues such notice or order, and all such notices and orders shall be in writing and shall be signed by such authorized representatives. Any notice or order issued pursuant to this section may be modified, vacated, or terminated by the Secretary or his authorized representative. A copy of any such order or notice shall be sent to the State regulatory authority in the State in which the violation occurs: *Provided,* That any notice or order issued pursuant to this section which requires cessation of mining by the operator shall expire within thirty days of actual notice to the operator unless a public hearing is held at the site or within such reasonable proximity to the site that any viewings of the site can be conducted during the course of public hearing.

**(b) Inadequate State enforcement; notice and hearing**

Whenever on the basis of information available to him, the Secretary has reason to believe that violations of all or any part of an approved State program result from a failure of the State to enforce such State program or any part thereof effectively, he shall after public notice and notice to the State, hold a hearing thereon in the State within thirty days of such notice. If as a result of said hearing the Secretary finds that there are violations and such violations result from a failure of the State to enforce all or any part of the State program effectively, and if he further finds that the State has not adequately demonstrated its capability and intent to enforce such State program, he shall give public notice of such finding. During the period beginning with such public notice and ending when such State satisfies the Secretary that it will enforce this chapter, the Secretary shall enforce, in the manner provided by this chapter, any permit condition required under this chapter, shall issue new or revised permits in accordance with requirements of this chapter, and may issue such notices and orders as are necessary for compliance therewith: *Provided*, That in the case of a State permittee who has met his obligations under such permit and who did not willfully secure the issuance of such permit through fraud or collusion, the Secretary shall give the permittee a reasonable time to conform ongoing surface mining and reclamation to the requirements of this chapter before suspending or revoking the State permit.

**(c) Civil action for relief**

The Secretary may request the Attorney General to institute a civil action for relief, including a permanent or temporary injunction, restraining order, or any other appropriate order in the district court of the United States for the district in which the surface coal mining and reclamation operation is located or in which the permittee thereof has his principal office, whenever such permittee or his agent (A) violates or fails or refuses to comply with any order or decision issued by the Secretary under this chapter, or (B) interferes with, hinders, or delays the Secretary or his authorized representatives in carrying out the provisions of this chapter, or (C) refuses to admit such authorized representative to the mine, or (D) refuses to permit inspection of the mine by such authorized representative, or (E) refuses to furnish any information or report requested by the Secretary in furtherance of the provisions of this chapter, or (F) refuses to permit access to, and copying of, such records as the Secretary determines necessary in carrying out the provisions of this chapter. Such court shall have jurisdiction to provide such relief as may be appropriate. Temporary restraining orders shall be issued in accordance with rule 65 of the Federal Rules of Civil Procedure, as amended. Any relief granted by the court to enforce an order under clause (A) of this section shall continue in effect until the completion or final termination of all proceedings for review of such order under this subchapter, unless, prior thereto, the district court granting such relief sets it aside or modifies it.

**(d) Sanctions; effect on additional enforcement rights under State law**

As a condition of approval of any State program submitted pursuant to section 1253 of this title, the enforcement provisions thereof shall, at a minimum, incorporate sanctions no less stringent than those set forth in this section, and shall contain the same or similar procedural requirements relating thereto. Nothing herein shall be construed so as to eliminate any additional enforcement rights or procedures which are available under State law to a State regulatory authority but which are not specifically enumerated herein.

(Pub.L. 95–87, Title V, § 521, Aug. 3, 1977, 91 Stat. 504.)

### HISTORICAL AND STATUTORY NOTES

**References in Text**

This chapter, referred to in subsecs. (a) to (c), was in the original "this Act", Meaning Pub.L. 95–87, Aug. 3, 1977, 91 Stat. 445, as amended, which enacted this chapter and amended section 1114 of Title 18, Crimes and Criminal Procedure. For complete classification of this Act to the Code, see Short title note set out under section 1201 of this title and Tables.

Rule 65 of the Federal Rules of Civil Procedure, referred to in subsec. (c), is set out in the Appendix to Title 28, Judiciary and Judicial Procedure.

## § 1272. Designating areas unsuitable for surface coal mining

**[SMCRA § 522]**

**(a) Establishment of State planning process; standards; State process requirements; integration with present and future land use planning and regulation processes; savings provisions**

(1) To be eligible to assume primary regulatory authority pursuant to section 1253 of this title, each State shall establish a planning process enabling objective decisions based upon competent and scientifically sound data and information as to which, if any, land areas of a State are unsuitable for all or certain types of surface coal mining operations pursuant to the standards set forth in paragraphs (2) and (3) of this subsection but such designation shall not prevent the mineral exploration pursuant to the chapter of any area so designated.

(2) Upon petition pursuant to subsection (c) of this section, the State regulatory authority shall designate an area as unsuitable for all or certain types of surface coal mining operations if the State regulatory authority determines that reclamation pursuant to the requirements of this chapter is not technologically and economically feasible.

(3) Upon petition pursuant to subsection (c) of this section, a surface area may be designated unsuitable for certain types of surface coal mining operations if such operations will—

(A) be incompatible with existing State or local land use plans or programs; or

(B) affect fragile or historic lands in which such operations could result in significant damage to important historic, cultural, scientific, and esthetic values and natural systems; or

(C) affect renewable resource lands in which such operations could result in a substantial loss or reduction of long-range productivity of water supply or of food or fiber products, and such lands to include aquifers and aquifer recharge areas; or

(D) affect natural hazard lands in which such operations could substantially endanger life and property, such lands to include areas subject to frequent flooding and areas of unstable geology.

(4) To comply with this section, a State must demonstrate it has developed or is developing a process which includes—

(A) a State agency responsible for surface coal mining lands review;

(B) a data base and an inventory system which will permit proper evaluation of the capacity of different land areas of the State to support and permit reclamation of surface coal mining operations;

(C) a method or methods for implementing land use planning decisions concerning surface coal mining operations; and

(D) proper notice, opportunities for public participation, including a public hearing prior to making any designation or redesignation, pursuant to this section.

(5) Determinations of the unsuitability of land for surface coal mining, as provided for in this section, shall be integrated as closely as possible with present and future land use planning and regulation processes at the Federal, State, and local levels.

(6) The requirements of this section shall not apply to lands on which surface coal mining operations are being conducted on August 3, 1977, or under a permit issued pursuant to this chapter, or where substantial legal and financial commitments in such operation were in existence prior to January 4, 1977.

**(b) Review of Federal lands**

The Secretary shall conduct a review of the Federal lands to determine, pursuant to the standards set forth in paragraphs (2) and (3) of subsection (a) of this section, whether there are areas on Federal lands which are unsuitable for all or certain types of surface coal mining operations: *Provided, however,* That the Secretary may permit surface coal mining on Federal lands prior to the completion of this review. When the Secretary determines an area on Federal lands to be unsuitable for all or certain types of surface coal mining operations, he shall withdraw such area or condition any mineral leasing or mineral entries in a manner so as to limit surface coal mining operations on such area. Where a Federal program has been implemented in a State pursuant to section 1254 of this title, the Secretary shall implement a process for designation of areas unsuitable for surface coal mining for non-Federal lands within such State and such process shall incorporate the standards and procedures of this section. Prior to designating Federal lands unsuitable for such mining, the Secretary shall consult with the appropriate State and local agencies.

**(c) Petition; intervention; decision**

Any person having an interest which is or may be adversely affected shall have the right to petition the regulatory authority to have an area designated as unsuitable for surface coal mining operations, or to have such a designation terminated. Such a petition shall contain allegations of facts with supporting evidence which would tend to establish the allegations. Within ten months after receipt of the petition the regulatory authority shall hold a public hearing in the locality of the affected area, after appropriate notice and publication of the date, time, and location of such hearing. After a person having an interest which is or may be adversely affected has filed a petition and before the hearing, as required by this subsection, any person may intervene by filing allegations of facts with supporting evidence which would tend to establish the allegations. Within sixty days after such hearing, the regulatory authority shall issue and furnish to the petitioner and any other party to the hearing, a written decision regarding the petition, and the reasons therefore.[1] In the event that all the petitioners stipulate agreement prior to the requested hearing, and withdraw their request, such hearing need not be held.

**(d) Statement**

Prior to designating any land areas as unsuitable for surface coal mining operations, the regulatory authority shall prepare a detailed statement on (i) the potential coal resources of the area, (ii) the demand for coal resources, and (iii) the impact of such designation on the environment, the economy, and the supply of coal.

**(e) Prohibition on certain Federal public and private surface coal mining operations**

After August 3, 1977, and subject to valid existing rights no surface coal mining operations except those which exist on August 3, 1977, shall be permitted—

(1) on any lands within the boundaries of units of the National Park System, the National Wildlife Refuge Systems, the National System of Trails, the National Wilderness Preservation System, the Wild and Scenic Rivers System, including study rivers designated under section 1276(a) of Title 16 and National Recreation Areas designated by Act of Congress;

(2) on any Federal lands within the boundaries of any national forest: *Provided, however,* That surface coal mining operations may be permitted on such lands if the Secretary finds that there are no significant recreational, timber, economic, or other

values which may be incompatible with such surface mining operations and—

(A) surface operations and impacts are incident to an underground coal mine; or

(B) where the Secretary of Agriculture determines, with respect to lands which do not have significant forest cover within those national forests west of the 100th meridian, that surface mining is in compliance with the Multiple-Use Sustained-Yield Act of 1960 [16 U.S.C.A. §§ 528–531], the Federal Coal Leasing Amendments Act of 1975, the National Forest Management Act of 1976, and the provisions of this chapter: *And provided further*, That no surface coal mining operations may be permitted within the boundaries of the Custer National Forest;

(3) which will adversely affect any publicly owned park or places included in the National Register of Historic Sites unless approved jointly by the regulatory authority and the Federal, State, or local agency with jurisdiction over the park or the historic site;

(4) within one hundred feet of the outside right-of-way line of any public road, except where mine access roads or haulage roads join such right-of-way line and except that the regulatory authority may permit such roads to be relocated or the area affected to lie within one hundred feet of such road, if after public notice and opportunity for public hearing in the locality a written finding is made that the interests of the public and the landowners affected thereby will be protected; or

(5) within three hundred feet from any occupied dwelling, unless waived by the owner thereof, nor within three hundred feet of any public building, school, church, community, or institutional building, public park, or within one hundred feet of a cemetery.

(Pub.L. 95–87, Title V, § 522, Aug. 3, 1977, 91 Stat. 507.)

1 So in original. Probably should be "therefor".

## HISTORICAL AND STATUTORY NOTES

**References in Text**

The chapter and this chapter, referred to in subsecs. (a)(1), (a)(2), (a)(6), and (e)(2)(B), were in the original "the Act" and "this Act", respectively, meaning Pub.L. 95–87, Aug. 3, 1977, 91 Stat. 445, as amended, which enacted this chapter and amended section 1114 of Title 18, Crimes and Criminal Procedure. For complete classification of this Act to the Code, see Short Title note set out under section 1201 of this title and Tables.

The Multiple-Use Sustained-Yield Act of 1960, referred to in subsec. (e)(2)(B), is Pub.L. 86–517, June 12, 1960, 74 Stat. 215, as amended, which is classified to sections 528 to 531 of Title 16, Conservation. For complete classification of this Act to the Code, see Short Title note set out under section 528 of Title 16 and Tables volume.

The Federal Coal Leasing Amendments Act of 1975, referred to in subsec. (e)(2)(B), is Pub.L. 94–377, Aug. 4, 1976, 90 Stat. 1083, which was redesignated the Federal Coal Leasing Amendments Act of 1976 by Pub.L. 95–554, § 8, Oct. 30, 1978, 92 Stat. 2075, and which enacted sections 202a, 208–1, and 208–2 of this title, amended sections 184, 191, 201, 203, 207, 209, and 352 of this title, repealed sections 201–1 and 204 of this title, and enacted provisions set out as notes under sections 181, 184, 201, 201–1, 203, and 204 of this title. For complete classification of this Act to the Code, see Short Title of 1976 Amendment note set out under section 181 of this title and Tables volume.

The National Forest Management Act of 1976, referred to in subsec. (e)(2)(B), is Pub.L. 94–588, Oct. 22, 1976, 90 Stat. 2949, as amended, which enacted sections 472a, 521b, 1600, and 1611 to 1614 of Title 16, Conservation, amended sections 500, 515, 516, 518, 576b, 581h, and 1601 to 1610 of Title 16, repealed sections 476, 513, and 514 of Title 16, enacted provisions set out as notes under sections 476, 513, 528, 594–2, and 1600 of Title 16. For complete classification of this Act to the Code, see Short Title of 1976 Amendment note set out under section 1600 of Title 16 and Tables volume.

# § 1273. Federal lands

[SMCRA § 523]

**(a) Promulgation and implementation of Federal lands program**

No later than one year after August 3, 1977, the Secretary shall promulgate and implement a Federal lands program which shall be applicable to all surface coal mining and reclamation operations taking place pursuant to any Federal law on any Federal lands: *Provided*, That except as provided in section 1300 of this title the provisions of this chapter shall not be applicable to Indian lands. The Federal lands program shall, at a minimum, incorporate all of the requirements of this chapter and shall take into consideration the diverse physical, climatological, and other unique characteristics of the Federal lands in question. Where Federal lands in a State with an approved State program are involved, the Federal lands program shall, at a minimum, include the requirements of the approved State program: *Provided*, That the Secretary shall retain his duties under sections 201(a), (2)(B) [1] and 201(a)(3) of this title, and shall continue to be responsible for designation of Federal lands as unsuitable for mining in accordance with section 1272(b) of this title.

**(b) Incorporation of requirements into any lease, permit, or contract issued by Secretary which may involve surface coal mining and reclamation operations**

The requirements of this chapter and the Federal lands program or an approved State program for State regulation of surface coal mining on Federal lands under subsection (c) of this section, whichever is applicable, shall be incorporated by reference or otherwise in any Federal mineral lease, permit, or contract issued by the Secretary which may involve surface coal mining and reclamation operations. Incorporation of such requirements shall not, however, limit in any way the authority of the Secretary to subsequently issue new regulations, revise the Federal lands program to deal with changing conditions or changed technology, and to require any surface mining and reclamation operations to conform with the requirements of this chapter and the regulations issued pursuant to this chapter.

**(c) State cooperative agreements**

Any State with an approved State program may elect to enter into a cooperative agreement with the Secretary to provide for State regulation of surface coal mining and reclamation operations on Federal lands within the State, provided the Secretary determines in writing that such State has the necessary personnel and funding to fully implement such a cooperative agreement in accordance with the provision of this chapter. States with cooperative agreements existing on August 3, 1977, may elect to continue regulation on Federal lands within the State, prior to approval by the Secretary of their State program, or imposition of a Federal program, provided that such existing cooperative agreement is modified to fully comply with the initial regulatory procedures set forth in section 1252 of this title. Nothing in this subsection shall be construed as authorizing the Secretary to delegate to the States his duty to approve mining plans on Federal lands, to designate certain Federal lands as unsuitable for surface coal mining pursuant to section 1272 of this title, or to regulate other activities taking place on Federal lands.

**(d) Development of program to assure no unreasonable denial to any class of coal purchasers**

The Secretary shall develop a program to assure that with respect to the granting of permits, leases, or contracts for coal owned by the United States, that no class of purchasers of the mined coal shall be unreasonably denied purchase thereof.

(Pub.L. 95–87, Title V, § 523, Aug. 3, 1977, 91 Stat. 510.)

1 So in original. Probably should be "201(a)(2)(B)".

### HISTORICAL AND STATUTORY NOTES

**References in Text**

This chapter, referred to in subsecs. (a) to (c), was in the original "this Act", meaning Pub.L. 95–87, Aug. 3, 1977, 91 Stat. 445, as amended, which enacted this chapter and amended section 1114 of Title 18, Crimes and Criminal Procedure. For complete classification of this Act to the Code, see Short Title note set out under section 1201 of this title and Tables.

## § 1274. Public agencies, public utilities, and public corporations

**[SMCRA § 524]**

Any agency, unit, or instrumentality of Federal, State, or local government, including any publicly owned utility or publicly owned corporation of Federal, State, or local government, which proposes to engage in surface coal mining operations which are subject to the requirements of this chapter shall comply with the provisions of this subchapter.

(Pub.L. 95–87, Title V, § 524, Aug. 3, 1977, 91 Stat. 511.)

### HISTORICAL AND STATUTORY NOTES

**References in Text**

This chapter, referred to in text, was in the original "this Act", meaning Pub.L. 95–87, Aug. 3, 1977, 91 Stat. 445, as amended, which enacted this chapter and amended section 1114 of Title 18, Crimes and Criminal Procedure. For complete classification of this Act to the Code, see Short Title note set out under section 1201 of this title and Tables.

## § 1275. Review by Secretary

**[SMCRA § 525]**

**(a) Application for review of order or notice; investigation; hearing; notice**

(1) A permittee issued a notice or order by the Secretary pursuant to the provisions of paragraphs (2) and (3) of subsection (a) of section 1271 of this title, or pursuant to a Federal program or the Federal lands program or any person having an interest which is or may be adversely affected by such notice or order or by any modification, vacation, or termination of such notice or order, may apply to the Secretary for review of the notice or order within thirty days of receipt thereof or within thirty days of its modification, vacation, or termination. Upon receipt of such application, the Secretary shall cause such investigation to be made as he deems appropriate. Such investigation shall provide an opportunity for a public hearing, at the request of the applicant or the person having an interest which is or may be adversely affected, to enable the applicant or such person to present information relating to the issuance and continuance of such notice or order or the modification, vacation, or termination thereof. The filing of an application for review under this subsection shall not operate as a stay of any order or notice.

(2) The permittee and other interested persons shall be given written notice of the time and place of the hearing at least five days prior thereto. Any such hearing shall be of record and shall be subject to section 554 of Title 5.

**(b) Findings of fact; issuance of decision**

Upon receiving the report of such investigation, the Secretary shall make findings of fact, and shall issue a written decision, incorporating therein an order vacating, affirming, modifying, or terminating the notice or order, or the modification, vacation, or termination of such notice or order complained of and incorporate his findings therein. Where the application for review concerns an order for cessation of surface coal mining and reclamation operations issued pursuant to the provisions of paragraph (2) or (3) of subsection (a) of section 1271 of this title, the Secretary shall issue the written decision within thirty days of the receipt of the application for review, unless temporary relief has been granted by the Secretary pursuant to subsection (c) of this section or by the court pursuant to subsection (c) of section 1276 of this title.

**(c) Temporary relief; issuance of order or decision granting or denying relief**

Pending completion of the investigation and hearing required by this section, the applicant may file with the Secretary a written request that the Secretary grant temporary relief from any notice or order issued under section 1271 of this title, a Federal program or the Federal lands program together with a detailed statement giving reasons for granting such relief. The Secretary shall issue an order or decision granting or denying such relief expeditiously: *Provided*, That where the applicant requests relief from an order for cessation of coal mining and reclamation operations issued pursuant to paragraph (2) or (3) of subsection (a) of section 1271 of this title, the order or decision on such a request shall be issued within five days of its receipt. The Secretary may grant such relief, under such conditions as he may prescribe, if—

(1) a hearing has been held in the locality of the permit area on the request for temporary relief in which all parties were given an opportunity to be heard;

(2) the applicant shows that there is substantial likelihood that the findings of the Secretary will be favorable to him; and

(3) such relief will not adversely affect the health or safety of the public or cause significant, imminent environmental harm to land, air, or water resources.

**(d) Notice and hearing with respect to section 1271 order to show cause**

Following the issuance of an order to show cause as to why a permit should not be suspended or revoked pursuant to section 1271 of this title, the Secretary shall hold a public hearing after giving written notice of the time, place, and date thereof. Any such hearing shall be of record and shall be subject to section 554 of Title 5. Within sixty days following the public hearing, the Secretary shall issue and furnish to the permittee and all other parties to the hearing a written decision, and the reasons therefor, concerning suspension or revocation of the permit. If the Secretary revokes the permit, the permittee shall immediately cease surface coal mining operations on the permit area and shall complete reclamation within a period specified by the Secretary, or the Secretary shall declare as forfeited the performance bonds for the operation.

**(e) Costs**

Whenever an order is issued under this section, or as a result of any administrative proceeding under this chapter, at the request of any person, a sum equal to the aggregate amount of all costs and expenses (including attorney fees) as determined by the Secretary to have been reasonably incurred by such person for or in connection with his participation in such proceedings, including any judicial review of agency actions, may be assessed against either party as the court, resulting from judicial review or the Secretary, resulting from administrative proceedings, deems proper.

(Pub.L. 95–87, Title V, § 525, Aug. 3, 1977, 91 Stat. 511.)

### HISTORICAL AND STATUTORY NOTES

**References in Text**

This chapter, referred to in subsec. (e), was in the original "this Act", meaning Pub.L. 95–87, Aug. 3, 1977, 91 Stat. 445, as amended, which enacted this chapter and amended section 1114 of Title 18, Crimes and Criminal Procedure. For complete classification of this Act to the Code, see Short Title note set out under section 1201 of this title and Tables.

## § 1276. Judicial review

**[SMCRA § 526]**

**(a) Review by United States District Court; venue; filing of petition; time**

(1) Any action of the Secretary to approve or disapprove a State program or to prepare or promulgate a Federal program pursuant to this chapter shall be subject to judicial review by the United States District Court for the District which includes the capital of the State whose program is at issue. Any action by the Secretary promulgating national rules or regulations including standards pursuant to sections 1251, 1265, 1266, and 1273 of this title shall be subject to judicial review in the United States District Court for the District of Columbia Circuit. Any other action constituting rulemaking by the Secretary shall be subject to judicial review only by the United States District Court for the District in which the surface coal mining operation is located. Any action subject to judicial review under this subsection shall be affirmed unless the court concludes that such action is arbitrary, capricious, or otherwise inconsistent with law. A petition for review of any action subject to judicial review under this subsection shall be filed in the appropriate Court within sixty days from the date of such action, or after such date if the petition is based solely on grounds arising after the sixtieth day. Any such

petition may be made by any person who participated in the administrative proceedings and who is aggrieved by the action of the Secretary.

(2) Any order or decision issued by the Secretary in a civil penalty proceeding or any other proceeding required to be conducted pursuant to section 554 of Title 5 shall be subject to judicial review on or before 30 days from the date of such order or decision in accordance with subsection (b) of this section in the United States District Court for the district in which the surface coal mining operation is located. In the case of a proceeding to review an order or decision issued by the Secretary under the penalty section of this chapter, the court shall have jurisdiction to enter an order requiring payment of any civil penalty assessment enforced by its judgment. This availability of review established in this subsection shall not be construed to limit the operations of rights established in section 1270 of this title.

**(b) Evidence; conclusiveness of findings; orders**

The court shall hear such petition or complaint solely on the record made before the Secretary. Except as provided in subsection (a) of this section, the findings of the Secretary if supported by substantial evidence on the record considered as a whole, shall be conclusive. The court may affirm, vacate, or modify any order or decision or may remand the proceedings to the Secretary for such further action as it may direct.

**(c) Temporary relief; prerequisites**

In the case of a proceeding to review any order or decision issued by the Secretary under this chapter, including an order or decision issued pursuant to subsection (c) or (d) of section 1275 of this title pertaining to any order issued under paragraph (2), (3), or (4) of subsection (a) of section 1271 of this title for cessation of coal mining and reclamation operations, the court may, under such conditions as it may prescribe, grant such temporary relief as it deems appropriate pending final determination of the proceedings if—

(1) all parties to the proceedings have been notified and given an opportunity to be heard on a request for temporary relief;

(2) the person requesting such relief shows that there is a substantial likelihood that he will prevail on the merits of the final determination of the proceeding; and

(3) such relief will not adversely affect the public health or safety or cause significant imminent environmental harm to land, air, or water resources.

**(d) Stay of action, order, or decision of Secretary**

The commencement of a proceeding under this section shall not, unless specifically ordered by the court, operate as a stay of the action, order, or decision of the Secretary.

**(e) Action of State regulatory authority**

Action of the State regulatory authority pursuant to an approved State program shall be subject to judicial review by a court of competent jurisdiction in accordance with State law, but the availability of such review shall not be construed to limit the operation of the rights established in section 1270 of this title except as provided therein.

(Pub.L. 95–87, Title V, § 526, Aug. 3, 1977, 91 Stat. 512.)

### HISTORICAL AND STATUTORY NOTES

**References in Text**

This chapter, referred to in subsecs. (a) and (c), was in the original "this Act", meaning Pub.L. 95–87, Aug. 3, 1977, 91 Stat. 445, as amended, which enacted this chapter and amended section 1114 of Title 18, Crimes and Criminal Procedure. For complete classification of this Act to the Code, see Short Title note set out under section 1201 of this title and Tables.

## § 1277. Special bituminous coal mines

**[SMCRA § 527]**

**(a) Issuance of separate regulations; criteria**

The regulatory authority is authorized to issue separate regulations for those special bituminous coal surface mines located west of the 100th meridian west longitude which meet the following criteria:

(1) the excavation of the specific mine pit takes place on the same relatively limited site for an extended period of time;

(2) the excavation of the specific mine pit follows a coal seam having an inclination of fifteen degrees or more from the horizontal, and continues in the same area proceeding downward with lateral expansion of the pit necessary to maintain stability or as necessary to accommodate the orderly expansion of the total mining operation;

(3) the excavation of the specific mine pit involves the mining of more than one coal seam and mining has been initiated on the deepest coal seam contemplated to be mined in the current operation;

(4) the amount of material removed is large in proportion to the surface area disturbed;

(5) there is no practicable alternative method of mining the coal involved;

(6) there is no practicable method to reclaim the land in the manner required by this chapter; and

(7) the specific mine pit has been actually producing coal since January 1, 1972, in such manner as to meet the criteria set forth in this section, and, because of past duration of mining, is substantially

committed to a mode of operation which warrants exceptions to some provisions of this subchapter.

**(b) New bituminous coal surface mines**

Such separate regulations shall also contain a distinct part to cover and pertain to new bituminous coal surface mines which may be developed after August 3, 1977, on lands immediately adjacent to lands upon which are located special bituminous mines existing on January 1, 1972. Such new mines shall meet the criteria of subsection (a) of this section except for paragraphs (3) and (7), and all requirements of State law, notwithstanding in whole or part the regulations issued pursuant to subsection (c) of this section. In the event of an amendment or revision to the State's regulatory program, regulations, or decisions made thereunder governing such mines, the Secretary shall issue such additional regulations as necessary to meet the purposes of this chapter.

**(c) Scope of alternative regulations**

Such alternative regulations may pertain only to the standards governing onsite handling of spoils, elimination of depressions capable of collecting water, creation of impoundments, and regrading to the approximate original contour and shall specify that remaining highwalls are stable. All other performance standards in this subchapter shall apply to such mines.

(Pub.L. 95–87, Title V, § 527, Aug. 3, 1977, 91 Stat. 513.)

### HISTORICAL AND STATUTORY NOTES

**References in Text**

This chapter, referred to in subsecs. (a)(6) and (b), was in the original "this Act", meaning Pub.L. 95–87, Aug. 3, 1977, 91 Stat. 445, as amended, which enacted this chapter and amended section 1114 of Title 18, Crimes and Criminal Procedure. For complete classification of this Act to the Code, see Short Title note set out under section 1201 of this title and Tables.

## § 1278. Surface mining operations not subject to this chapter

**[SMCRA § 528]**

The provisions of this chapter shall not apply to any of the following activities:

(1) the extraction of coal by a landowner for his own noncommercial use from land owned or leased by him; and

(2) the extraction of coal as an incidental part of Federal, State or local government-financed highway or other construction under regulations established by the regulatory authority.

(3) Redesignated (2).

(Pub.L. 95–87, Title V, § 528, Aug. 3, 1977, 91 Stat. 514; Pub.L. 100–34, Title II, § 201(a), May 7, 1987, 101 Stat. 300.)

### HISTORICAL AND STATUTORY NOTES

**References in Text**

This chapter, referred to in text, was in the original "this Act", meaning Pub.L. 95–87, Aug. 3, 1977, 91 Stat. 445, as amended, which enacted this chapter and amended section 1114 of Title 18, Crimes and Criminal Procedure. For complete classification of this Act to the Code, see Short Title note set out under section 1201 of this title and Tables.

**Effective and Applicability Provisions**

1987 Acts

Section 201(b) to (e) of Pub.L. 100–34 provided that:

"**(b) Effective date for new operations.**—The amendments made by this section [amending pars. (1) to (3) of this section] shall take effect on the date 30 days after the enactment of this Act [May 7, 1987] with respect to each operator commencing surface coal mining operations on or after such date.

"**(c) Effective date for existing operations.**—The amendments made by this section [amending pars. (1) to (3) of this section] shall take effect on the date 6 months after the enactment of this Act [May 7, 1987] with respect to each operator commencing surface coal mining operations pursuant to an authorization under State law before the date 30 days after the enactment of this Act [May 7, 1987]. Nothing in this Act [probably means section, which amended pars. (1) to (3) of this section and enacted this note] shall preclude reclamation activities pursuant to State law or regulations at the site of any surface coal mine which was exempt from the Surface Mining Control and Reclamation Act of 1977 [this chapter] under section 528(2) of that Act [par. (2) of this section], as in effect before the enactment of this Act [May 7, 1987].

"**(d) Effect on State law.**—To the extent that any provision of a State law, or of a State regulation, adopted pursuant to the exception under section 528(2) of the Surface Mining Control and Reclamation Act of 1977 [par. (2) of this section] as in effect before the enactment of this Act [May 7, 1987], is inconsistent with the amendments made by this section [amending pars. (1) to (3) of this section], such provision shall be of no further force and effect after the effective date of such amendments.

"**(e) Definition.**—For purposes of this section, the term 'surface coal mining operations' has the meaning provided by section 701(28) of the Surface Mining Control and Reclamation Act of 1977 [section 1291(28) of this title]."

## § 1279. Anthracite coal mines

**[SMCRA § 529]**

**(a)** The Secretary is authorized to and shall issue separate regulations according to time schedules established in this chapter for anthracite coal surface mines, if such mines are regulated by environmental protection standards of the State in which they are located. Such alternative regulations shall adopt, in each instance, the environmental protection provisions of the State regulatory program in existence on August 3, 1977, in lieu of sections 1265 and 1266 of this title. Provisions of sections 1259 and 1269 of this title are applicable except for specified bond limits and period of revegetation responsibility. All other provisions of this chapter apply and the regulation issued by the Secretary of Interior for each State anthracite regulatory program shall so reflect: *Provided, however*, That upon amendment of a State's regulatory program for anthracite mining or regulations thereunder in force in lieu of the above-cited sections of this chapter, the Secretary shall issue such additional regulations as necessary to meet the purposes of this chapter.

**(b)** Omitted.

(Pub.L. 95–87, Title V, § 529, Aug. 3, 1977, 91 Stat. 514.)

### HISTORICAL AND STATUTORY NOTES

**References in Text**

This chapter, referred to in text, was in the original "this Act", meaning Pub.L. 95–87, Aug. 3, 1977, 91 Stat. 445, as amended, which enacted this chapter and amended section 1114 of Title 18, Crimes and Criminal Procedure. For complete classification of this Act to the Code, see Short Title note set out under section 1201 of this title and Tables.

**Codifications**

Subsec. (b) of this section, which required the Secretary of the Interior to submit biennial reports to Congress on the effectiveness of State anthracite regulatory programs operating in conjunction with this chapter with respect to protecting the environment, was terminated, effective May 15, 2000, pursuant to Pub.L. 104–66, Title III, § 3003, Dec. 21, 1995, 109 Stat. 734, as amended, which is set out as a note under 31 U.S.C.A. § 1113. See, also, House Document No. 103–7, page 109.

## SUBCHAPTER VI—DESIGNATION OF LANDS UNSUITABLE FOR NONCOAL MINING

## § 1281. Designation procedures

**[SMCRA § 601]**

**(a) Review of Federal land areas for unsuitability for noncoal mining**

With respect to Federal lands within any State, the Secretary of Interior may, and if so requested by the Governor of such State shall, review any area within such lands to assess whether it may be unsuitable for mining operations for minerals or materials other than coal, pursuant to the criteria and procedures of this section.

**(b) Criteria considered in determining designations**

An area of Federal land may be designated under this section as unsuitable for mining operations if (1) such area consists of Federal land of a predominantly urban or suburban character, used primarily for residential or related purposes, the mineral estate of which remains in the public domain, or (2) such area consists of Federal land where mining operations would have an adverse impact on lands used primarily for residential or related purposes.

**(c) Petition for exclusion; contents; hearing; temporary land withdrawal**

Any person having an interest which is or may be adversely affected shall have the right to petition the Secretary to seek exclusion of an area from mining operations pursuant to this section or the redesignation of an area or part thereof as suitable for such operations. Such petition shall contain allegations of fact with supporting evidence which would tend to substantiate the allegations. The petitioner shall be granted a hearing within a reasonable time and finding with reasons therefor upon the matter of their petition. In any instance where a Governor requests the Secretary to review an area, or where the Secretary finds the national interest so requires, the Secretary may temporarily withdraw the area to be reviewed from mineral entry or leasing pending such review: *Provided, however*, That such temporary withdrawal be ended as promptly as practicable and in no event shall exceed two years.

**(d) Limitation on designations; rights preservation; regulations**

In no event is a land area to be designated unsuitable for mining operations under this section on which mining operations are being conducted prior to the holding of a hearing on such petition in accordance with subsection (c) of this section. Valid existing rights shall be preserved and not affected by such designation. Designation of an area as unsuitable for mining operations under this section shall not prevent subsequent mineral exploration of such area, except that such exploration shall require the prior written consent of the holder of the surface estate, which consent shall be filed with the Secretary. The Secretary may promulgate, with respect to any designated area, regulations to minimize any adverse effects of such exploration.

**(e) Statement**

Prior to any designation pursuant to this section, the Secretary shall prepare a detailed statement on (i) the potential mineral resources of the area, (ii) the demand for such mineral resources, and (iii) the impact of such designation or the absence of such designation on the environment, economy, and the supply of such mineral resources.

**(f) Area withdrawal**

When the Secretary designates an area of Federal lands as unsuitable for all or certain types of mining operations for minerals and materials other than coal pursuant to this section he may withdraw such area from mineral entry or leasing, or condition such entry or leasing so as to limit such mining operations in accordance with his determination, if the Secretary also determines, based on his analysis pursuant to subsection (e) of this section, that the benefits resulting from such designation would be greater than the benefits to the regional or national economy which could result from mineral development of such area.

**(g) Right to appeal**

Any party with a valid legal interest who has appeared in the proceedings in connection with the Secretary's determination pursuant to this section and who is aggrieved by the Secretary's decision (or by his failure to act within a reasonable time) shall have the right of appeal for review by the United States district court for the district in which the pertinent area is located.

(Pub.L. 95–87, Title VI, § 601, Aug. 3, 1977, 91 Stat. 515.)

## SUBCHAPTER VII—ADMINISTRATIVE AND MISCELLANEOUS PROVISIONS

### § 1291. Definitions

**[SMCRA § 701]**

For the purposes of this chapter—

(1) "alluvial valley floors" means the unconsolidated stream laid deposits holding streams where water availability is sufficient for subirrigation or flood irrigation agricultural activities but does not include upland areas which are generally overlain by a thin veneer of colluvial deposits composed chiefly of debris from sheet erosion, deposits by unconcentrated runoff or slope wash, together with talus, other mass movement accumulation and windblown deposits;

(2) "approximate original contour" means that surface configuration achieved by backfilling and grading of the mined area so that the reclaimed area, including any terracing or access roads, closely resembles the general surface configuration of the land prior to mining and blends into and complements the drainage pattern of the surrounding terrain, with all highwalls and spoil piles eliminated; water impoundments may be permitted where the regulatory authority determines that they are in compliance with section 1265(b)(8) of this title;

(3) "commerce" means trade, traffic, commerce, transportation, transmission, or communication among the several States, or between a State and any other place outside thereof, or between points in the same State which directly or indirectly affect interstate commerce;

(4) "Federal lands" means any land, including mineral interests, owned by the United States without regard to how the United States acquired ownership of the land and without regard to the agency having responsibility for management thereof, except Indian lands: *Provided*, That for the purposes of this chapter lands or mineral interests east of the one hundredth meridian west longitude owned by the United States and entrusted to or managed by the Tennessee Valley Authority shall not be subject to sections 1304 (Surface Owner Protection) and 1305 (Federal Lessee Protection) of this title.[1]

(5) "Federal lands program" means a program established by the Secretary pursuant to section 1273 of this title to regulate surface coal mining and reclamation operations on Federal lands;

(6) "Federal program" means a program established by the Secretary pursuant to section 1254 of this title to regulate surface coal mining and reclamation operations on lands within a State in accordance with the requirements of this chapter;

(7) "fund" means the Abandoned Mine Reclamation Fund established pursuant to section 1231 of this title;

(8) "imminent danger to the health and safety of the public" means the existence of any condition or practice, or any violation of a permit or other requirement of this chapter in a surface coal mining and reclamation operation, which condition, practice, or violation could reasonably be expected to cause substantial physical harm to persons outside the permit area before such condition, practice, or violation can be abated. A reasonable expectation of death or serious injury before abatement exists if a rational person, subjected to the same conditions or practices giving rise to the peril, would not expose himself or herself to the danger during the time necessary for abatement;

(9) "Indian lands" means all lands, including mineral interests, within the exterior boundaries of any Federal Indian reservation, notwithstanding the issuance of any patent, and including rights-of-way, and all lands including mineral interests held in trust for or supervised by an Indian tribe;

(10) "Indian tribe" means any Indian tribe, band, group, or community having a governing body recognized by the Secretary;

(11) "lands within any State" or "lands within such State" means all lands within a State other than Federal lands and Indian lands;

(12) "Office" means the Office of Surface Mining Reclamation and Enforcement established pursuant to subchapter II of this chapter;

(13) "operator" means any person, partnership, or corporation engaged in coal mining who removes or intends to remove more than two hundred and fifty tons of coal from the earth by coal mining within twelve consecutive calendar months in any one location;

(14) "other minerals" means clay, stone, sand, gravel, metalliferous and nonmetalliferous ores, and any other solid material or substances of commercial value excavated in solid form from natural deposits on or in the earth, exclusive of coal and those minerals which occur naturally in liquid or gaseous form;

(15) "permit" means a permit to conduct surface coal mining and reclamation operations issued by the State regulatory authority pursuant to a State program or by the Secretary pursuant to a Federal program;

(16) "permit applicant" or "applicant" means a person applying for a permit;

(17) "permit area" means the area of land indicated on the approved map submitted by the operator with his application, which area of land shall be covered by the operator's bond as required by section 1259 of this title and shall be readily identifiable by appropriate markers on the site;

(18) "permittee" means a person holding a permit;

(19) "person" means an individual, partnership, association, society, joint stock company, firm, company, corporation, or other business organization;

(20) the term "prime farmland" shall have the same meaning as that previously prescribed by the Secretary of Agriculture on the basis of such factors as moisture availability, temperature regime, chemical balance, permeability, surface layer composition, susceptibility to flooding, and erosion characteristics, and which historically have been used for intensive agricultural purposes, and as published in the Federal Register.[1]

(21) "reclamation plan" means a plan submitted by an applicant for a permit under a State program or Federal program which sets forth a plan for reclamation of the proposed surface coal mining operations pursuant to section 1258 of this title;

(22) "regulatory authority" means the State regulatory authority where the State is administering this chapter under an approved State program or the Secretary where the Secretary is administering this chapter under a Federal program;

(23) "Secretary" means the Secretary of the Interior, except where otherwise described;

(24) "State" means a State of the United States, the District of Columbia, the Commonwealth of Puerto Rico, the Virgin Islands, American Samoa, and Guam;

(25) "State program" means a program established by a State pursuant to section 1253 of this title to regulate surface coal mining and reclamation operations, on lands within such State in accord with the requirements of this chapter and regulations issued by the Secretary pursuant to this chapter;

(26) "State regulatory authority" means the department or agency in each State which has primary responsibility at the State level for administering this chapter;

(27) "surface coal mining and reclamation operations" means surface mining operations and all activities necessary and incident to the reclamation of such operations after August 3, 1977;

(28) "surface coal mining operations" means—

(A) activities conducted on the surface of lands in connection with a surface coal mine or subject to the requirements of section 1266 of this title surface operations and surface impacts incident to an underground coal mine, the products of which enter commerce or the operations of which directly or indirectly affect interstate commerce. Such activities include excavation for the purpose of obtaining coal including such common methods as contour, strip, auger, mountaintop removal, box cut, open pit, and area mining, the uses of explosives and blasting, and in situ distillation or retorting, leaching or other chemical or physical processing, and the cleaning, concentrating, or other processing or preparation, loading of coal for interstate commerce at or near the mine site: *Provided, however*, That such activities do not include the extraction of coal incidental to the extraction of other minerals where coal does not exceed 16⅔ per centum of the tonnage of minerals removed for purposes of commercial use or sale or coal explorations subject to section 1262 of this title; and

(B) the areas upon which such activities occur or where such activities disturb the natural land surface. Such areas shall also include any adjacent land the use of which is incidental to any such activities, all lands affected by the construction of new roads or the improvement or use of existing roads to gain access to the site of such activities and for haulage, and excavations, workings, impoundments, dams, ventilation shafts, entryways, refuse banks, dumps, stockpiles, overburden piles, spoil banks, culm banks, tailings, holes or depressions, repair areas, storage areas, processing areas, shipping areas and other areas upon which are sited structures, facilities, or other property or materials on the surface, resulting from or incident to such activities; and [2]

(29) "unwarranted failure to comply" means the failure of a permittee to prevent the occurrence of any violation of his permit or any requirement of this chapter due to indifference, lack of diligence, or lack of reasonable care, or the failure to abate any violation of such permit or the chapter due to

indifference, lack of diligence, or lack of reasonable care;

(30) "lignite coal" means consolidated lignitic coal having less than 8,300 British thermal units per pound, moist and mineral matter free;

(31) the term "coal laboratory", as used in subchapter VIII of this chapter, means a university coal research laboratory established and operated pursuant to a designation made under section 1311 of this title;

(32) the term "institution of higher education" as used in subchapters VIII and IX of this chapter, means any such institution as defined by section 1001 of Title 20;

(33) the term "unanticipated event or condition" as used in section 1260(e) of this title means an event or condition encountered in a remining operation that was not contemplated by the applicable surface coal mining and reclamation permit; and

(34) the term "lands eligible for remining" means those lands that would otherwise be eligible for expenditures under section 1234 of this title or under section 1232(g)(4) of this title.

(Pub.L. 95–87, Title VII, § 701, Aug. 3, 1977, 91 Stat. 516; Pub.L. 102–486, Title XXV, § 2503(c), Oct. 24, 1992, 106 Stat. 3103; Pub.L. 105–244, Title I, § 102(a)(10), Oct. 7, 1998, 112 Stat. 1620.)

[1] So in original. The period probably should be a semicolon.

[2] So in original. The word "and" probably should not appear.

### HISTORICAL AND STATUTORY NOTES

**References in Text**

This chapter, referred to in text, was in the original "this Act", meaning Pub.L. 95–87, Aug. 3, 1977, 91 Stat. 445, as amended, which enacted this chapter and amended section 1114 of Title 18, Crimes and Criminal Procedure. For complete classification of this Act to the Code, see Short Title note set out under section 1201 of this title and Tables.

**Effective and Applicability Provisions**

1998 Acts

Amendment by Pub.L. 105–244 effective Oct. 1, 1998, except as otherwise provided, see section 3 of Pub.L. 105–244, set out as a note under section 1001 of Title 20.

## § 1292. Other Federal laws

[SMCRA § 702]

### (a) Construction of chapter as superseding, amending, modifying, or repealing certain laws

Nothing in this chapter shall be construed as superseding, amending, modifying, or repealing the Mining and Minerals Policy Act of 1970 (30 U.S.C. 21a), the National Environmental Policy Act of 1969 (42 U.S.C. 4321–47), or any of the following Acts or with any rule or regulation promulgated thereunder, including, but not limited to—

(1) The Federal Metal and Nonmetallic Mine Safety Act (30 U.S.C. 721–740).

(2) The Federal Coal Mine Health and Safety Act of 1969 (83 Stat. 742) [30 U.S.C.A. § 801 et seq.].

(3) The Federal Water Pollution Control Act (79 Stat. 903), as amended [33 U.S.C.A. § 1251 et seq.], the State laws enacted pursuant thereto, or other Federal laws relating to preservation of water quality.

(4) The Clean Air Act, as amended [42 U.S.C.A. § 7401 et seq.].

(5) The Solid Waste Disposal Act [42 U.S.C.A. § 6901 et seq.].

(6) The Refuse Act of 1899 (33 U.S.C. 407).

(7) The Fish and Wildlife Coordination Act of 1934 (16 U.S.C. 661–666c).

(8) The Mineral Leasing Act of 1920, as amended (30 U.S.C. 181 et seq.).

### (b) Effect on authority of Secretary or heads of other Federal agencies

Nothing in this chapter shall affect in any way the authority of the Secretary or the heads of other Federal agencies under other provisions of law to include in any lease, license, permit, contract, or other instrument such conditions as may be appropriate to regulate surface coal mining and reclamation operations on land under their jurisdiction.

### (c) Cooperation

To the greatest extent practicable each Federal agency shall cooperate with the Secretary and the States in carrying out the provisions of this chapter.

### (d) Major Federal action

Approval of the State programs, pursuant to section 1253(b) of this title, promulgation of Federal programs, pursuant to section 1254 of this title, and implementation of the Federal lands programs, pursuant to section 1273 of this title, shall not constitute a major action within the meaning of section 102(2)(C) of the National Environmental Policy Act of 1969 (42 U.S.C. 4332). Adoption of regulations under section 1251(b) of this title shall constitute a major action within the meaning of section 102(2)(C) of the National Environmental Policy Act of 1969 (42 U.S.C. 4332).

(Pub.L. 95–87, Title VII, § 702, Aug. 3, 1977, 91 Stat. 519.)

### HISTORICAL AND STATUTORY NOTES

**References in Text**

This chapter, referred to in subsecs. (a) to (c), was in the original "this Act", meaning Pub.L. 95–87, Aug. 3, 1977, 91 Stat. 445, as amended, which enacted this chapter and amended section 1114 of Title 18, Crimes and Criminal Procedure. For complete classification of this Act to the

Code, see Short Title note set out under section 1201 of this title and Tables.

The Mining and Minerals Policy Act of 1970 (30 U.S.C. 21a), referred to in subsec. (a), is Pub.L. 91–631, Dec. 31, 1970, 84 Stat. 1876, which enacted section 21a of this title and provisions set out as a note under section 21a of this title. For complete classification of this Act to the Code, see Short Title note set out under section 21a of this title and Tables volume.

The National Environmental Policy Act of 1969 (42 U.S.C. 4321–47), referred to in subsec. (a), is Pub.L. 91–190, Jan. 1, 1970, 83 Stat. 852, as amended, which is classified generally to chapter 55 (section 4321 et seq.) of Title 42, The Public Health and Welfare. For complete classification of this Act to the Code, see Short Title note set out under section 4321 of Title 42 and Tables volume.

The Federal Metal and Nonmetallic Mine Safety Act (30 U.S.C. 721–740), referred to in subsec. (a)(1), is Pub.L. 89–577, Sept. 16, 1966, 80 Stat. 772, which was classified generally to chapter 21 (section 721 et seq.) of this title and was repealed by Pub.L. 95–164, Title III, § 306(a), Nov. 9, 1977, 91 Stat. 1322.

The Federal Coal Mine Health and Safety Act of 1969 (83 Stat. 742), referred to in subsec. (a)(2), is Pub.L. 91–173, Dec. 30, 1969, 83 Stat. 742, as amended, which was redesignated the Federal Mine Safety and Health Act of 1977 by Pub.L. 95–164, Title I, § 101, Nov. 9, 1977, 91 Stat. 1290, and is classified principally to chapter 22 (section 801 et seq.) of this title. For complete classification of this Act to the Code, see Short Title note set out under section 801 of this title and Tables volume.

The Federal Water Pollution Control Act (79 Stat. 903), as amended, referred to in subsec. (a)(3), is Act June 30, 1948, c. 758, 62 Stat. 1155, as amended, formerly classified to chapter 23 (section 1151 et seq.) of Title 33, Navigation and Navigable Waters, which was completely revised by Pub.L. 92–500, § 2, Oct. 18, 1972, 86 Stat. 816, and is now classified generally to chapter 26 (section 1251 et seq.) of Title 33. For complete classification of this Act to the Code, see Short Title note set out under section 1251 of Title 33 and Tables volume.

The Clean Air Act, as amended, referred to in subsec. (a)(4), is Act July 14, 1955, c. 360, as amended generally by Pub.L. 88–206, Dec. 17, 1963, 77 Stat. 392, and later by Pub.L. 95–95, Aug. 7, 1977, 91 Stat. 685. The Clean Air Act was originally classified to chapter 15B (section 1857 et seq.) of Title 42, The Public Health and Welfare. On enactment of Pub.L. 95–95, the Act was reclassified to chapter 85 (section 7401 et seq.) of Title 42. For complete classification of this Act to the Code, see Short Title note set out under section 7401 of Title 42 and Tables volume.

The Solid Waste Disposal Act, referred to in subsec. (a)(5), is Title II of Pub.L. 89–272, Oct. 20, 1965, 79 Stat. 997, as amended generally by Pub.L. 94–580, § 2, Oct. 21, 1976, 90 Stat. 2795, which is classified generally to chapter 82 (section 6901 et seq.) of Title 42. For complete classification of this Act to the Code, see Short Title note set out under section 6901 of Title 42 and Tables volume.

The Refuse Act of 1899 (33 U.S.C. 407), referred to in subsec. (a)(6), probably means Act Mar. 3, 1899, c. 425, § 13, 30 Stat. 1152, which enacted section 407 of Title 33, Navigation and Navigable Waters.

The Fish and Wildlife Coordination Act of 1934 (16 U.S.C. 661–666c), referred to in subsec. (a)(7), is Act Mar. 10, 1934, c. 55, 48 Stat. 401, as amended, which is classified generally to sections 661 to 666c of Title 16, Conservation. For complete classification of this Act to the Code, see Short Title note set out under section 661 of Title 16 and Tables volume.

The Mineral Leasing Act of 1920, as amended (30 U.S.C. 181 et seq.), referred to in subsec. (a)(8), is Act Feb. 25, 1920, c. 85, 41 Stat. 437, as amended, which is classified principally to chapter 3A (section 181 et seq.) of this title. For complete classification of this Act to the Code, see Short Title note set out under section 181 of this title and Tables volume.

## § 1293. Employee protection

### [SMCRA § 703]

### (a) Retaliatory practices prohibited

No person shall discharge, or in any other way discriminate against, or cause to be fired or discriminated against, any employee or any authorized representative of employees by reason of the fact that such employee or representative has filed, instituted, or caused to be filed or instituted any proceeding under this chapter, or has testified or is about to testify in any proceeding resulting from the administration or enforcement of the provisions of this chapter.

### (b) Review by Secretary; investigation; notice; hearing; findings of fact; judicial review

Any employee or a representative of employees who believes that he has been fired or otherwise discriminated against by any person in violation of subsection (a) of this section may, within thirty days after such alleged violation occurs, apply to the Secretary for a review of such firing or alleged discrimination. A copy of the application shall be sent to the person or operator who will be the respondent. Upon receipt of such application, the Secretary shall cause such investigation to be made as he deems appropriate. Such investigation shall provide an opportunity for a public hearing at the request of any party to such review to enable the parties to present information relating to the alleged violation. The parties shall be given written notice of the time and place of the hearing at least five days prior to the hearing. Any such hearing shall be of record and shall be subject to section 554 of Title 5. Upon receiving the report of such investigation the Secretary shall make findings of fact. If he finds that a violation did occur, he shall issue a decision incorporating therein his findings and an order requiring the party committing the violation to take such affirmative action to abate the violation as the Secretary deems appropriate, including, but not limited to, the rehiring or reinstatement of the employee or representative of employees to his former position with compensation. If he finds that there was no violation, he will issue a finding. Orders issued by the Secretary under this subsection shall be subject to judicial review in the same manner as orders and decisions of the Secretary are subject to judicial review under this chapter.

**(c) Costs**

Whenever an order is issued under this section to abate any violation, at the request of the applicant a sum equal to the aggregate amount of all costs and expenses (including attorneys' fees) to have been reasonably incurred by the applicant for, or in connection with, the institution and prosecution of such proceedings, shall be assessed against the persons committing the violation.

(Pub.L. 95–87, Title VII, § 703, Aug. 3, 1977, 91 Stat. 520.)

#### HISTORICAL AND STATUTORY NOTES

**References in Text**

This chapter, referred to in subsecs. (a) and (b), was in the original "this Act", meaning Pub.L. 95–87, Aug. 3, 1977, 91 Stat. 445, as amended, which enacted this chapter and amended section 1114 of Title 18, Crimes and Criminal Procedure. For complete classification of this Act to the Code, see Short Title note set out under section 1201 of this title and Tables.

## § 1294. Penalty

**[SMCRA § 704]**

Any person who shall, except as permitted by law, willfully resist, prevent, impede, or interfere with the Secretary or any of his agents in the performance of duties pursuant to this chapter shall be punished by a fine of not more than $5,000 or by imprisonment for not more than one year, or both.

(Pub.L. 95–87, Title VII, § 704, Aug. 3, 1977, 91 Stat. 520.)

#### HISTORICAL AND STATUTORY NOTES

**References in Text**

This chapter, referred to in text, was in the original "this Act", meaning Pub.L. 95–87, Aug. 3, 1977, 91 Stat. 445, as amended, which enacted this chapter and amended section 1114 of Title 18, Crimes and Criminal Procedure. For complete classification of this Act to the Code, see Short Title note set out under section 1201 of this title and Tables.

**Codifications**

Section 704 of Pub.L. 95–87 also amended section 1114 of Title 18, Crimes and Criminal Procedure.

## § 1295. Grants to States

**[SMCRA § 705]**

**(a) Assisting any State in development, administration, and enforcement of State programs under this chapter**

The Secretary is authorized to make annual grants to any State for the purpose of assisting such State in developing, administering, and enforcing State programs under this chapter. Except as provided in subsection (c) of this section, such grants shall not exceed 80 per centum of the total costs incurred during the first year, 60 per centum of total costs incurred during the second year, and 50 per centum of the total costs incurred during each year thereafter.

**(b) Assisting any State in development, administration, and enforcement of its State programs**

The Secretary is authorized to cooperate with and provide assistance to any State for the purpose of assisting it in the development, administration, and enforcement of its State programs. Such cooperation and assistance shall include—

(1) technical assistance and training including provision of necessary curricular and instruction materials, in the development, administration, and enforcement of the State programs; and

(2) assistance in preparing and maintaining a continuing inventory of information on surface coal mining and reclamation operations for each State for the purposes of evaluating the effectiveness of the State programs. Such assistance shall include all Federal departments and agencies making available data relevant to surface coal mining and reclamation operations and to the development, administration, and enforcement of State programs concerning such operations.

**(c) Increases in annual grants**

If, in accordance with section 1273(d) of this title, a State elects to regulate surface coal mining and reclamation operations on Federal lands, the Secretary may increase the amount of the annual grants under subsection (a) of this section by an amount which he determines is approximately equal to the amount the Federal Government would have expended for such regulation if the State had not made such election.

(Pub.L. 95–87, Title VII, § 705, Aug. 3, 1977, 91 Stat. 520.)

#### HISTORICAL AND STATUTORY NOTES

**References in Text**

This chapter, referred to in subsec. (a), was in the original "this Act", meaning Pub.L. 95–87, Aug. 3, 1977, 91 Stat. 445, as amended, which enacted this chapter and amended section 1114 of Title 18, Crimes and Criminal Procedure. For complete classification of this Act to the Code, see Short Title note set out under section 1201 of this title and Tables.

## § 1296. Annual report to President and Congress

**[SMCRA § 706]**

The Secretary shall submit annually to the President and the Congress a report concerning activities conducted by him, the Federal Government, and the States pursuant to this chapter. Among other matters, the Secretary shall include in such report recommendations for additional administrative or legislative action as he deems necessary and desirable to accomplish the purposes of this chapter.

(Pub.L. 95–87, Title VII, § 706, Aug. 3, 1977, 91 Stat. 521.)

### HISTORICAL AND STATUTORY NOTES

**References in Text**

This chapter, referred to in text, was in the original "this Act", meaning Pub.L. 95–87, Aug. 3, 1977, 91 Stat. 445, as amended, which enacted this chapter and amended section 1114 of Title 18, Crimes and Criminal Procedure. For complete classification of this Act to the Code, see Short Title note set out under section 1201 of this title and Tables.

## § 1297. Separability

### [SMCRA § 707]

If any provision of this chapter or the applicability thereof to any person or circumstances is held invalid, the remainder of this chapter and the application of such provision to other persons or circumstances shall not be affected thereby.

(Pub.L. 95–87, Title VII, § 707, Aug. 3, 1977, 91 Stat. 521.)

### HISTORICAL AND STATUTORY NOTES

**References in Text**

This chapter, referred to in text, was in the original "this Act", meaning Pub.L. 95–87, Aug. 3, 1977, 91 Stat. 445, as amended, which enacted this chapter and amended section 1114 of Title 18, Crimes and Criminal Procedure. For complete classification of this Act to the Code, see Short Title note set out under section 1201 of this title and Tables.

## § 1298. Alaskan surface coal mine study

### [SMCRA § 708]

**(a) Contract with National Academy of Sciences–National Academy of Engineering**

The Secretary is directed to contract to such extent or in such amounts as are provided in advance in appropriation Acts with the National Academy of Sciences–National Academy of Engineering for an indepth study of surface coal mining conditions in the State of Alaska in order to determine which, if any, of the provisions of this chapter should be modified with respect to surface coal mining operations in Alaska.

**(b) Report to President and Congress**

The Secretary shall report on the findings of the study to the President and Congress no later than two years after August 3, 1977.

**(c) Draft of legislation**

The Secretary shall include in his report a draft of legislation to implement any changes recommended to this chapter.

**(d) Modification of applicability of environmental protection provisions of this chapter to surface coal mining operations in Alaska; publication in Federal Register; hearing**

Until one year after the Secretary has made this report to the President and Congress, or three years after August 3, 1977, whichever comes first, the Secretary is authorized to modify the applicability of any environmental protection provision of this chapter, or any regulation issued pursuant thereto, to any surface coal mining operation in Alaska from which coal has been mined during the year preceding August 3, 1977, if he determines that it is necessary to insure the continued operation of such surface coal mining operation. The Secretary may exercise this authority only after he has (1) published notice of proposed modification in the Federal Register and in a newspaper of general circulation in the area of Alaska in which the affected surface coal mining operation is located, and (2) held a public hearing on the proposed modification in Alaska.

**(e) Interim regulations**

In order to allow new mines in Alaska to continue orderly development, the Secretary is authorized to issue interim regulations pursuant to section 1251(b) of this title including those modifications to the environmental standards as required based on the special physical, hydrological and climatic conditions in Alaska but with the purpose of protecting the environment to an extent equivalent to those standards for the other coal regions.

**(f) Authorization of appropriations**

There is authorized to be appropriated for the purpose of this section $250,000: *Provided*, That no new budget authority is authorized to be appropriated for fiscal year 1977.

(Pub.L. 95–87, Title VII, § 708, Aug. 3, 1977, 91 Stat. 521.)

### HISTORICAL AND STATUTORY NOTES

**References in Text**

This chapter, referred to in subsecs. (a), (c), and (d), was in the original "this Act", meaning Pub.L. 95–87, Aug. 3, 1977, 91 Stat. 445, as amended, which enacted this chapter and amended section 1114 of Title 18, Crimes and Criminal Procedure. For complete classification of this Act to the Code, see Short Title note set out under section 1201 of this title and Tables.

## § 1299. Study of reclamation standards for surface mining of other minerals

### [SMCRA § 709]

**(a) Contract with National Academy of Sciences-National Academy of Engineering; requirements**

The Chairman of the Council on Environmental Quality is directed to contract to such extent or in such amounts as are provided in appropriation Acts with the National Academy of Sciences–National Academy of Engineering, other Government agencies or private groups as appropriate, for an in-depth study of current and developing technology for surface and open pit mining and reclamation for minerals other than coal designed to assist in the establishment of effective and reasonable regulation of surface and open pit mining and reclamation for minerals other than coal. The study shall—

(1) assess the degree to which the requirements of this chapter can be met by such technology and the costs involved;

(2) identify areas where the requirements of this chapter cannot be met by current and developing technology;

(3) in those instances describe requirements most comparable to those of this chapter which could be met, the costs involved, and the differences in reclamation results between these requirements and those of this chapter; and

(4) discuss alternative regulatory mechanisms designed to insure the achievement of the most beneficial postmining land use for areas affected by surface and open pit mining.

**(b) Submittal of study with legislative recommendation to President and Congress**

The study together with specific legislative recommendations shall be submitted to the President and the Congress no later than eighteen months after August 3, 1977: *Provided*, That, with respect to surface or open pit mining for sand and gravel the study shall be submitted no later than twelve months after August 3, 1977: *Provided further*, That with respect to mining for oil shale and tar sands that a preliminary report shall be submitted no later than twelve months after August 3, 1977.

**(c) Authorization of appropriations**

There are authorized to be appropriated for the purpose of this section $500,000: *Provided*, That no new budget authority is authorized to be appropriated for fiscal year 1977.

(Pub.L. 95–87, Title VII, § 709, Aug. 3, 1977, 91 Stat. 522.)

### HISTORICAL AND STATUTORY NOTES

**References in Text**

This chapter, referred to in subsec. (a), was in the original "this Act", meaning Pub.L. 95–87, Aug. 3, 1977, 91 Stat. 445, as amended, which enacted this chapter and amended section 1114 of Title 18, Crimes and Criminal Procedure. For complete classification of this Act to the Code, see Short title note set out under section 1201 of this title and Tables.

## § 1300. Indian lands

[SMCRA § 710]

**(a) Study of regulation of surface mining; consultation with tribe; proposed legislation**

The Secretary is directed to study the question of the regulation of surface mining on Indian lands which will achieve the purpose of this chapter and recognize the special jurisdictional status of these lands. In carrying out this study the Secretary shall consult with Indian tribes. The study report shall include proposed legislation designed to allow Indian tribes to elect to assume full regulatory authority over the administration and enforcement of regulation of surface mining of coal on Indian lands.

**(b) Submittal of study to Congress**

The study report required by subsection (a) of this section together with drafts of proposed legislation and the view of each Indian tribe which would be affected shall be submitted to the Congress as soon as possible but not later than January 1, 1978.

**(c) Compliance with interim environmental protection standards of this chapter**

On and after one hundred and thirty-five days from August 3, 1977, all surface coal mining operations on Indian lands shall comply with requirements at least as stringent as those imposed by subsections (b)(2), (b)(3), (b)(5), (b)(10), (b)(13), (b)(19), and (d) of section 1265 of this title and the Secretary shall incorporate the requirements of such provisions in all existing and new leases issued for coal on Indian lands.

**(d) Compliance with permanent environmental protection standards of this chapter**

On and after thirty months from August 3, 1977, all surface coal mining operations on Indian lands shall comply with requirements at least as stringent as those imposed by sections 1257, 1258, 1259, 1260, 1265, 1266, 1267, and 1269 of this title and the Secretary shall incorporate the requirements of such provisions in all existing and new leases issued for coal on Indian lands.

**(e) Inclusion and enforcement of terms and conditions of leases**

With respect to leases issued after August 3, 1977, the Secretary shall include and enforce terms and conditions in addition to those required by subsections (c) and (d) of this section as may be requested by the Indian tribe in such leases.

**(f) Approval of changes in terms and conditions of leases**

Any change required by subsection (c) or (d) of this section in the terms and conditions of any coal lease on Indian lands existing on August 3, 1977, shall require the approval of the Secretary.

**(g) Participation of tribes**

The Secretary shall provide for adequate participation by the various Indian tribes affected in the study authorized in this section and not more than $700,000 of the funds authorized in section 1302(a) of this title shall be reserved for this purpose.

**(h) Jurisdictional status**

The Secretary shall analyze and make recommendations regarding the jurisdictional status of Indian Lands [1] outside the exterior boundaries of Indian reservations: *Provided*, That nothing in this chapter shall change the existing jurisdictional status of Indian Lands [1].

**(i) Grants**

The Secretary shall make grants to the Navajo, Hopi, Northern Cheyenne, and Crow tribes to assist such tribes in developing regulations and programs for regulating surface coal mining and reclamation operations on Indian lands, except that nothing in this subsection may be construed as providing such tribes with the authorities set forth under section 1253 of this title. Grants made under this subsection shall be used to establish an office of surface mining regulation for each such tribe. Each such office shall—

(1) develop tribal regulations and program policies with respect to surface mining;

(2) assist the Office of Surface Mining Reclamation and Enforcement established by section 1211 of this title in the inspection and enforcement of surface mining activities on Indian lands, including, but not limited to, permitting, mine plan review, and bond release; and

(3) sponsor employment training and education in the area of mining and mineral resources.

(Pub.L. 95–87, Title VII, § 710, Aug. 3, 1977, 91 Stat. 523; Pub.L. 102–486, Title XXV, § 2514, Oct. 24, 1992, 106 Stat. 3112.)

1 So in original. Probably should be "lands".

### HISTORICAL AND STATUTORY NOTES

**References in Text**

This chapter, referred to in subsecs. (a) and (h), was in the original "this Act", meaning Pub.L. 95–87, Aug. 3, 1977, 91 Stat. 445, as amended, which enacted this chapter and amended section 1114 of Title 18, Crimes and Criminal Procedure. For complete classification of this Act to the Code, see Short Title note set out under section 1201 of this title and Tables.

## § 1301. Environmental practices

**[SMCRA § 711]**

In order to encourage advances in mining and reclamation practices or to allow post-mining land use for industrial, commercial, residential, or public use (including recreational facilities), the regulatory authority with approval by the Secretary may authorize departures in individual cases on an experimental basis from the environmental protection performance standards promulgated under sections 1265 and 1266 of this title. Such departures may be authorized if (i) the experimental practices are potentially more or at least as environmentally protective, during and after mining operations, as those required by promulgated standards; (ii) the mining operations approved for particular land-use or other purposes are not larger or more numerous than necessary to determine the effectiveness and economic feasibility of the experimental practices; and (iii) the experimental practices do not reduce the protection afforded public health and safety below that provided by promulgated standards.

(Pub.L. 95–87, Title VII, § 711, Aug. 3, 1977, 91 Stat. 523.)

## § 1302. Authorization of appropriations

**[SMCRA § 712]**

There is authorized to be appropriated to the Secretary for the purposes of this chapter the following sums; and all such funds appropriated shall remain available until expended:

**(a)** For the implementation and funding of sections 1252, 1273, and 1300 of this title, there are authorized to be appropriated to the Secretary of the Interior the sum of $10,000,000 for the fiscal year ending September 30, 1978, $25,000,000 for each of the two succeeding fiscal years, and in such fiscal years such additional amounts as may be necessary for increases in salary, pay, retirement, other employee benefits authorized by law, and other nondiscretionary costs.

**(b)** For the implementation and funding of section 1257(c) of this title, see the provisions of section 1231(c)(11) of this title.

**(c)** For the implementation and funding of section 1295 of this title and for the administrative and other purposes of this chapter, except as otherwise provided for in this chapter, authorization is provided for the sum of $20,000,000 for the fiscal year ending September 30, 1978, and $30,000,000 for each of the two succeeding fiscal years and such funds that are required thereafter.

**(d)** In order that the implementation of the requirements of this chapter may be initiated in a timely and orderly manner, the Secretary is authorized, subject to the approval of the appropriation Committees of the House and of the Senate, to utilize not to exceed $2,000,000 of the appropriations otherwise available to him for the fiscal year ending September 30, 1977, for the administration and other purposes of the chapter.

(Pub.L. 95–87, Title VII, § 712, Aug. 3, 1977, 91 Stat. 524; Pub.L. 95–343, § 1, Aug. 11, 1978, 92 Stat. 473; Pub.L. 101–508, Title VI, § 6012(b), Nov. 5, 1990, 104 Stat. 1388–298.)

HISTORICAL AND STATUTORY NOTES

**References in Text**

This chapter, referred to in text, was in the original "this Act", meaning Pub.L. 95–87, Aug. 3, 1977, 91 Stat. 445, as amended, which enacted this chapter and amended section 1114 of Title 18, Crimes and Criminal Procedure. For complete classification of this Act to the Code, see Short Title note set out under section 1201 of this title and Tables.

**Effective and Applicability Provisions**

1990 Acts

Amendment by Pub.L. 101–508 effective Oct. 1, 1991, see section 6014 of Pub.L. 101–508, set out as a note under section 1231 of this title.

**Savings Provisions**

Nothing in Subtitle A (section 6001 et seq.) of Title VI of Pub.L. 101–508, shall be construed to affect the certifications made by the States of Wyoming, Montana, and Louisiana to the Secretary of the Interior prior to Nov. 5, 1990, that each such State has completed the reclamation of eligible abandoned coal mine lands, see section 6013 of Pub.L. 101–508, set out as a note under section 1231 of this title.

**Crediting Additional Amount From Performance Bond Forfeitures**

Pub.L. 105–277, Div. A, § 101(e) [Title I], Oct. 21, 1998, 112 Stat. 2681–244, provided in part that: "Notwithstanding 31 U.S.C. 3302, an additional amount shall be credited to this account, to remain available until expended, from performance bond forfeitures in fiscal year 1999 and thereafter."

**Cost-based Fees for Products of the Mine Map Repository; Collection and Credit to Program Account**

Pub.L. 105–277, Div. A, § 101(e) [Title I], Oct. 21, 1998, 112 Stat. 2681–244, provided in part that: "Beginning in fiscal year 1999 and thereafter, cost-based fees for the products of the Mine Map Repository shall be established (and revised as needed) in Federal Register Notices, and shall be collected and credited to this account, to be available until expended for the costs of administering this program."

## § 1303. Coordination of regulatory and inspection activities

[SMCRA § 713]

(a) The President shall, to the extent appropriate, and in keeping with the particular enforcement requirements of each Act referred to herein, insure the coordination of regulatory and inspection activities among the departments, agencies, and instrumentalities to which such activities are assigned by this chapter, by the Clean Air Act [42 U.S.C.A. § 7401 et seq.], by the Water Pollution Control Act [33 U.S.C.A. § 1251 et seq.], by the Department of Energy Organization Act [42 U.S.C.A. § 7101 et seq.], and by existing or subsequently enacted Federal mine safety and health laws, except that no such coordination shall be required with respect to mine safety and health inspections, advance notice of which is or may be prohibited by existing or subsequently enacted Federal mine safety and health laws.

(b) The President may execute the coordination required by this section by means of an Executive order, or by any other mechanism he determines to be appropriate.

(Pub.L. 95–87, Title VII, § 713, Aug. 3, 1977, 91 Stat. 524.)

HISTORICAL AND STATUTORY NOTES

**References in Text**

This chapter, referred to in subsec. (a), was in the original "this Act", meaning Pub.L. 95–87, Aug. 3, 1977, 91 Stat. 445, as amended, which enacted this chapter and amended section 1114 of Title 18, Crimes and Criminal Procedure. For complete classification of this Act to the Code, see Short Title note set out under section 1201 of this title and Tables.

The Clean Air Act, referred to in subsec. (a), is Act July 14, 1955, c. 360, as amended generally by Pub.L. 88–206, Dec. 17, 1963, 77 Stat. 392, and later by Pub.L. 95–95, Aug. 7, 1977, 91 Stat. 685. The Clean Air Act was originally classified to chapter 15B (section 1857 et seq.) of Title 42, The Public Health and Welfare. On enactment of Pub.L. 95–95, the Act was reclassified to chapter 85 (section 7401 et seq.) of Title 42. For complete classification of this Act to the Code, see Short Title note set out under section 7401 of Title 42 and Tables volume.

The Water Pollution Control Act, referred to in subsec. (a), probably means Act June 30, 1948, c. 758, 62 Stat. 1155, known as the Federal Water Pollution Control Act, formerly classified to chapter 23 (section 1151 et seq.) of Title 33, Navigation and Navigable Waters, which was completely revised by Pub.L. 92–500, § 2, Oct. 18, 1972, 86 Stat. 816, and is classified generally to chapter 26 (section 1251 et seq.) of Title 33. For complete classification of this Act to the Code, see Short Title note set out under section 1251 of Title 33 and Tables volume.

The Department of Energy Organization Act, referred to in subsec. (a), is Pub.L. 95–91, Aug. 4, 1977, 91 Stat. 565, as amended, which is classified principally to chapter 84 (section 7101 et seq.) of Title 42, The Public Health and Welfare. For complete classification of this Act to the Code, see Short Title note set out under section 7101 of Title 42 and Tables volume.

## § 1304. Surface owner protection

[SMCRA § 714]

**(a) Applicability**

The provisions of this section shall apply where coal owned by the United States under land the surface rights to which are owned by a surface owner as defined in this section is to be mined by methods other than underground mining techniques.

**(b) Lease of coal deposits governed by section 201 of this title**

Any coal deposits subject to this section shall be offered for lease pursuant to section 201(a) of this title.

**(c) Consent to lease by surface owner**

The Secretary shall not enter into any lease of Federal coal deposits until the surface owner has given written consent to enter and commence surface mining operations and the Secretary has obtained evidence of such consent. Valid written consent given by any surface owner prior to August 3, 1977, shall be deemed sufficient for the purposes of complying with this section.

**(d) Preferences**

In order to minimize disturbance to surface owners from surface coal mining of Federal coal deposits and to assist in the preparation of comprehensive land-use plans required by section 201(a) of this title, the Secretary shall consult with any surface owner whose land is proposed to be included in a leasing tract and shall ask the surface owner to state his preference for or against the offering of the deposit under his land for lease. The Secretary shall, in his discretion but to the maximum extent practicable, refrain from leasing coal deposits for development by methods other than underground mining techniques in those areas where a significant number of surface owners have stated a preference against the offering of the deposits for lease.

**(e) "Surface owner" defined**

For the purpose of this section the term "surface owner" means the natural person or persons (or corporation, the majority stock of which is held by a person or persons who meet the other requirements of this section) who—

(1) hold legal or equitable title to the land surface;

(2) have their principal place of residence on the land; or personally conduct farming or ranching operations upon a farm or ranch unit to be affected by surface coal mining operations; or receive directly a significant portion of their income, if any, from such farming or ranching operations; and

(3) have met the conditions of paragraphs (1) and (2) for a period of at least three years prior to the granting of the consent.

In computing the three-year period the Secretary may include periods during which title was owned by a relative of such person by blood or marriage during which period such relative would have met the requirements of this subsection.

**(f) Exception**

This section shall not apply to Indian lands.

**(g) Effect on property rights of United States or any other landowner**

Nothing in this section shall be construed as increasing or diminishing any property rights by the United States or by any other landowner.

(Pub.L. 95–87, Title VII, § 714, Aug. 3, 1977, 91 Stat. 524.)

## § 1305. Federal lessee protection

**[SMCRA § 715]**

In those instances where the coal proposed to be mined by surface coal mining operations is owned by the Federal Government and the surface is subject to a lease or a permit issued by the Federal Government, the application for a permit shall include either:

(1) the written consent of the permittee or lessee of the surface lands involved to enter and commence surface coal mining operations on such land, or in lieu thereof;

(2) evidence of the execution of a bond or undertaking to the United States or the State, whichever is applicable, for the use and benefit of the permittee or lessee of the surface lands involved to secure payment of any damages to the surface estate which the operations will cause to the crops, or to the tangible improvements of the permittee or lessee of the surface lands as may be determined by the parties involved, or as determined and fixed in an action brought against the operator or upon the bond in a court of competent jurisdiction. This bond is in addition to the performance bond required for reclamation under this chapter.

(Pub.L. 95–87, Title VII, § 715, Aug. 3, 1977, 91 Stat. 525.)

### HISTORICAL AND STATUTORY NOTES

**References in Text**

This chapter, referred to in text, was in the original "this Act", meaning Pub.L. 95–87, Aug. 3, 1977, 91 Stat. 445, as amended, which enacted this chapter and amended section 1114 of Title 18, Crimes and Criminal Procedure. For complete classification of this Act to the Code, see Short Title note set out under section 1201 of this title and Tables.

## § 1306. Effect on rights of owner of coal in Alaska to conduct surface mining operations

**[SMCRA § 716]**

Nothing in this chapter shall be construed as increasing or diminishing the rights of any owner of coal in Alaska to conduct or authorize surface coal mining operations for coal which has been or is hereafter conveyed out of Federal ownership to the State of Alaska or pursuant to the Alaska Native Claims Settlement Act [43 U.S.C.A. § 1601 et seq.]: *Provided*, That such surface coal mining operations meet the requirements of this chapter.

(Pub.L. 95–87, Title VII, § 716, Aug. 3, 1977, 91 Stat. 526.)

HISTORICAL AND STATUTORY NOTES

**References in Text**

This chapter, referred to in text, was in the original "this Act", meaning Pub.L. 95–87, Aug. 3, 1977, 91 Stat. 445, as amended, which enacted this chapter and amended section 1114 of Title 18, Crimes and Criminal Procedure. For complete classification of this Act to the Code, see Short Title note set out under section 1201 of this title and Tables.

The Alaska Native Claims Settlement Act, referred to in text, is Pub.L. 92–203, Dec. 18, 1971, 85 Stat. 688, as amended, which is classified generally to chapter 33 (section 1601 et seq.) of Title 43, Public Lands. For complete classification of this Act to the Code, see Short Title note set out under section 1601 of Title 43 and Tables volume.

## § 1307. Water rights and replacement

[SMCRA § 717]

(a) Nothing in this chapter shall be construed as affecting in any way the right of any person to enforce or protect, under applicable law, his interest in water resources affected by a surface coal mining operation.

(b) The operator of a surface coal mine shall replace the water supply of an owner of interest in real property who obtains all or part of his supply of water for domestic, agricultural, industrial, or other legitimate use from an underground or surface source where such supply has been affected by contamination, diminution, or interruption proximately resulting from such surface coal mine operation.

(Pub.L. 95–87, Title VII, § 717, Aug. 3, 1977, 91 Stat. 526.)

HISTORICAL AND STATUTORY NOTES

**References in Text**

This chapter, referred to in subsec. (a), was in the original "this Act", meaning Pub.L. 95–87, Aug. 3, 1977, 91 Stat. 445, as amended, which enacted this chapter and amended section 1114 of Title 18, Crimes and Criminal Procedure. For complete classification of this Act to the Code, see Short Title note set out under section 1201 of this title and Tables.

## § 1308. Advance appropriations

[SMCRA § 718]

Notwithstanding any other provision of this chapter, no authority to make payments under this chapter shall be effective except to such extent or in such amounts as are provided in advance in appropriation Acts.

(Pub.L. 95–87, Title VII, § 718, Aug. 3, 1977, 91 Stat. 526.)

HISTORICAL AND STATUTORY NOTES

**References in Text**

This chapter, referred to in text, was in the original "this Act", meaning Pub.L. 95–87, Aug. 3, 1977, 91 Stat. 445, as amended, which enacted this chapter and amended section 1114 of Title 18, Crimes and Criminal Procedure. For complete classification of this Act to the Code, see Short Title note set out under section 1201 of this title and Tables.

## § 1309. Certification and training of blasters

[SMCRA § 719]

In accordance with this chapter, the Secretary of the Interior (or the approved State regulatory authority as provided for in section 1253 of this title) shall promulgate regulations requiring the training, examination, and certification of persons engaging in or directly responsible for blasting or use of explosives in surface coal mining operations.

(Pub.L. 95–87, Title VII, § 719, Aug. 3, 1977, 91 Stat. 526.)

HISTORICAL AND STATUTORY NOTES

**References in Text**

This chapter, referred to in text, was in the original "this Act", meaning Pub.L. 95–87, Aug. 3, 1977, 91 Stat. 445, as amended, which enacted this chapter and amended section 1114 of Title 18, Crimes and Criminal Procedure. For complete classification of this Act to the Code, see Short Title note set out under section 1201 of this title and Tables.

## § 1309a. Subsidence

[SMCRA § 720]

**(a) Requirements**

Underground coal mining operations conducted after October 24, 1992, shall comply with each of the following requirements:

(1) Promptly repair, or compensate for, material damage resulting from subsidence caused to any occupied residential dwelling and structures related thereto, or non-commercial building due to underground coal mining operations. Repair of damage shall include rehabilitation, restoration, or replacement of the damaged occupied residential dwelling and structures related thereto, or non-commercial building. Compensation shall be provided to the owner of the damaged occupied residential dwelling and structures related thereto or non-commercial building and shall be in the full amount of the diminution in value resulting from the subsidence. Compensation may be accomplished by the purchase, prior to mining, of a noncancellable premium-prepaid insurance policy.

(2) Promptly replace any drinking, domestic, or residential water supply from a well or spring in existence prior to the application for a surface coal mining and reclamation permit, which has been affected by contamination, diminution, or interruption resulting from underground coal mining operations.

Nothing in this section shall be construed to prohibit or interrupt underground coal mining operations.

**(b) Regulations**

Within one year after October 24, 1992, the Secretary shall, after providing notice and opportunity for public comment, promulgate final regulations to implement subsection (a) of this section.

(Pub.L. 95–87, Title VII, § 720, as added Pub.L. 102–486, Title XXV, § 2504(a)(1), Oct. 24, 1992, 106 Stat. 3104.)

### HISTORICAL AND STATUTORY NOTES

**Review of Existing Requirements and Report to Congress**

Section 2504(a)(2) of Pub.L. 102–486 provided that:

"**(A)** The Secretary of the Interior shall review existing requirements related to underground coal mine subsidence and natural gas and petroleum pipeline safety. Such review shall consider the following with respect to subsidence: notification; mitigation; coordination; requirements of the Natural Gas Pipeline Safety Act and the Hazardous Liquid Pipeline Safety Act [section 1671 et seq. and section 2001 et seq. of Appendix to Title 49, Transportation]; and the status of Federal, State and local laws, as well as common law, with respect to prevention or mitigation of damage from subsidence.

"**(B)** The review shall also include a survey of the status of Federal, State, and local laws, as well as common law, with respect to the responsibilities of the relevant parties for costs resulting from damage due to subsidence or from mitigation efforts undertaken to prevent damage from subsidence.

"**(C)** In conducting the review, the Secretary of the Interior shall consult with the Secretary of Transportation, the Attorney General of the United States, appropriate officials of relevant States, and owners and representatives of natural gas and petroleum pipeline companies and coal companies.

"**(D)** The Secretary of the Interior shall submit a report detailing the results of the review to the Committee on Energy and Natural Resources of the United States Senate and the Committee on Interior and Insular Affairs [now Committee on Natural Resources] of the United States House of Representatives within 18 months of enactment of this Act [Oct. 24, 1992]. Where appropriate, the Secretary of the Interior shall commence a rulemaking to address any deficiencies in existing law determined in the review under subparagraph (A) regarding notification, coordination and mitigation."

[Any reference in any provision of law enacted before Jan. 4, 1995, to the Committee on Natural Resources of the House of Representatives treated as referring to the Committee on Resources of the House of Representatives, see section 1(a)(8) of Pub.L. 104–14, set out as a note preceding section 21 of Title 2, The Congress.]

## § 1309b. Research

**[SMCRA § 721]**

The Office of Surface Mining Reclamation and Enforcement is authorized to conduct studies, research and demonstration projects relating to the implementation of, and compliance with, subchapter V of this chapter, and provide technical assistance to states[1] for that purpose. Prior to approving any such studies, research or demonstration projects the Director, Office of Surface Mining Reclamation and Enforcement, shall first consult with the Director, Bureau of Mines, and obtain a determination from such Director that the Bureau of Mines is not already conducting like or similar studies, research or demonstration projects. Studies, research and demonstration projects for the purposes of subchapter IV of this chapter shall only be conducted in accordance with section 1231(c)(6) of this title.

(Pub.L. 95–87, Title VII, § 721, as added Pub.L. 102–486, Title XXV, § 2504(c)(3), Oct. 24, 1992, 106 Stat. 3105.)

[1] So in original. Probably should be capitalized.

# SUBCHAPTER VIII—UNIVERSITY COAL RESEARCH LABORATORIES

## § 1311. Establishment of university coal research laboratories

**[SMCRA § 801]**

**(a) Designation by Secretary of Energy**

The Secretary of Energy, after consultation with the National Academy of Engineering, shall designate thirteen institutions of higher education at which university coal research laboratories will be established and operated. Ten such designations shall be made as provided in subsection (e) of this section and the remaining three shall be made in fiscal year 1980.

**(b) Criteria**

In making designations under this section, the Secretary of Energy shall consider the following criteria:

**(1)** Those ten institutions of higher education designated as provided in subsection (e) of this section shall be located in a State with abundant coal reserves.

**(2)** The institution of higher education shall have experience in coal research, expertise in several areas of coal research, and potential or currently active, outstanding programs in coal research.

**(3)** The institution of higher education has the capacity to establish and operate the coal laboratories to be assisted under this subchapter.

**(c) Location of coal laboratories**

Not more than one coal laboratory established pursuant to this subchapter shall be located in a single State and at least one coal laboratory shall be established within each of the major coal provinces recognized by the United States Bureau of Mines, including Alaska.

**(d) Period for submission of applications for designation; contents**

The Secretary of Energy shall establish a period, not in excess of ninety days after August 3, 1977, for the submission of applications for designation under this section. Any institution of higher education desiring to be designated under this subchapter shall submit an application to the Secretary of Energy in such form, at such time, and containing or accompanied by such information as the Secretary of Energy may reasonably require. Each application shall—

(1) describe the facilities to be established for coal energy resources and conversion research and research on related environmental problems including facilities for interdisciplinary academic research projects by the combined efforts of specialists such as mining engineers, mineral engineers, geochemists, mineralogists, mineral economists, fuel scientists, combustion engineers, mineral preparation engineers, coal petrographers, geologists, chemical engineers, civil engineers, mechanical engineers, and ecologists;

(2) set forth a program for the establishment of a test laboratory for coal characterization which, in addition, may be used as a site for the exchange of coal research activities by representatives of private industry engaged in coal research and characterization;

(3) set forth a program for providing research and development activities for students engaged in advanced study in any discipline which is related to the development of adequate energy supplies in the United States. The research laboratory shall be associated with an ongoing educational and research program on extraction and utilization of coal.

**(e) Time limit**

The Secretary of Energy shall designate the ten institutions of higher education under this section not later than ninety days after the date on which such applications are to be submitted.

(Pub.L. 95–87, Title VIII, § 801, Aug. 3, 1977, 91 Stat. 526; Pub.L. 95–617, Title VI, § 604(a), (c), Nov. 9, 1978, 92 Stat. 3166, 3167; Pub.L. 102–285, § 10(b), May 18, 1992, 106 Stat. 172.)

**HISTORICAL AND STATUTORY NOTES**

**Change of Name**

Pub.L. 102–285, § 10(b), May 18, 1992, 106 Stat. 172, provided that, on and after May 18, 1992, the Bureau of Mines is redesignated and shall thereafter be known as the United States Bureau of Mines. See note under section 1 of Title 30, Mineral Lands and Mining.

## § 1312. Financial assistance

**[SMCRA § 802]**

(a) The Secretary of Energy is authorized to make grants to any institution of higher education designated under section 1311 of this title to pay the Federal share of the cost of establishing (including the construction of such facilities as may be necessary) and maintaining a coal laboratory.

(b) Each institution of higher education designated pursuant to section 1311 of this title shall submit an application to the Secretary of Energy. Each such application shall—

(1) set forth the program to be conducted at the coal laboratory which includes the purposes set forth in section 1311(d) of this title;

(2) provide assurances that the university will pay from non-Federal sources the remaining costs of carrying out the program set forth;

(3) provide such fiscal control and fund accounting procedures as may be necessary to assure the proper disbursement of and accounting for Federal funds received under this subchapter;

(4) provide for making an annual report which shall include a description of the activities conducted at the coal laboratory and an evaluation of the success of such activities, and such other necessary reports in such form and containing such information as the Secretary of Energy may require, and for keeping such records and affording such access thereto as may be necessary to assure the correctness and verification of such reports; and

(5) set forth such policies and procedures as will insure that Federal funds made available under this section for any fiscal year will be so used as to supplement and, to the extent practical, increase the level of funds that would, in the absence of such Federal funds, be made available for the purposes of the activities described in subsections (d)(1), (2), and (3) of section 1311 of this title, and in no case supplant such funds.

(Pub.L. 95–87, Title VIII, § 802, Aug. 3, 1977, 91 Stat. 527; Pub.L. 95–617, Title VI, § 604(c), Nov. 9, 1978, 92 Stat. 3167.)

## § 1313. Limitation on payments

**[SMCRA § 803]**

(a) No institutions of higher education may receive more than $4,000,000 for the construction of its coal research laboratory, including initially installed fixed equipment, nor may it receive more than $1,500,000 for initially installed movable equipment, nor may it receive more than $500,000 for new program startup expenses.

(b) No institution of higher education may receive more than $1,500,000 per year from the Federal Government for operating expenses.

(Pub.L. 95–87, Title VIII, § 803, Aug. 3, 1977, 91 Stat. 528.)

## § 1314. Payments; Federal share of operating expenses

**[SMCRA § 804]**

(a) From the amounts appropriated pursuant to section 1316 of this title, the Secretary of Energy shall pay to each institution of higher education having an application approved under this subchapter an amount equal to the Federal share of the cost of carrying out that application. Such payments may be in installments, by way of reimbursement, or by way of advance with necessary adjustments on account of underpayments or overpayments.

(b) The Federal share of operating expenses for any fiscal year shall not exceed 50 per centum of the cost of the operation of a coal research laboratory.
(Pub.L. 95–87, Title VIII, § 804, Aug. 3, 1977, 91 Stat. 528; Pub.L. 95–617, Title VI, § 604(c), Nov. 9, 1978, 92 Stat. 3167.)

## § 1315. Advisory Council on Coal Research [SMCRA § 805]

**(a) Establishment; members**

There is established an Advisory Council on Coal Research which shall be composed of—

(1) the Secretary of Energy, who shall be Chairman;

(2) the Director of the United States Bureau of Mines of the Department of the Interior;

(3) the President of the National Academy of Sciences;

(4) the President of the National Academy of Engineering;

(5) the Director of the United States Geological Survey; and

(6) six members appointed by the Secretary of Energy from among individuals who, by virtue of experience or training, are knowledgeable in the field of coal research and mining, and who are representatives of institutions of higher education, industrial users of coal and coal-derived fuels, the coal industry, mine workers, nonindustrial consumer groups, and institutions concerned with the preservation of the environment.

**(b) Furnishing advice to Secretary of Energy**

The Advisory Council shall advise the Secretary of Energy with respect to the general administration of this subchapter, and furnish such additional advice as he may request.

**(c) Annual report to President; transmittal to Congress**

The Advisory Council shall make an annual report of its findings and recommendations (including recommendations for changes in the provisions of this subchapter) to the President not later than December 31 of each calendar year. The President shall transmit each such report to the Congress.

**(d) Compensation and travel expenses**

(1) Members of the Council who are not regular officers or employees of the United States Government shall, while serving on business of the Council, be entitled to receive compensation at rates fixed by the Secretary of Energy but not exceeding the daily rate prescribed for GS–18 of the General Schedule under section 5332 of Title 5 and while so serving away from their homes or regular places of business, they may be allowed travel expenses, including per diem in lieu of subsistence, as authorized by section 5703 of Title 5 for persons in the Government service employed intermittently.

(2) Members of the Council who are officers or employees of the Government shall be reimbursed for travel, subsistence, and other necessary expenses incurred by them in carrying out their duties on the Council.

**(e) Alternate members**

Whenever a member of the Council appointed under clauses (1) through (5) is unable to attend a meeting, that member shall appoint an appropriate alternate to represent him for that meeting.
(Pub.L. 95–87, Title VIII, § 805, Aug. 3, 1977, 91 Stat. 528; Pub.L. 95–617, Title VI, § 604(c), Nov. 9, 1978, 92 Stat. 3167; Pub.L. 102–285, § 10(b), May 18, 1992, 106 Stat. 172.)

### HISTORICAL AND STATUTORY NOTES

**Change of Name**

Pub.L. 102–285, § 10(b), May 18, 1992, 106 Stat. 172, provided that, on and after May 18, 1992, the Bureau of Mines is redesignated and shall thereafter be known as the United States Bureau of Mines. See note under section 1 of Title 30, Mineral Lands and Mining.

**Termination of Advisory Committees**

Advisory committees established after Jan. 5, 1973, to terminate not later than the expiration of the two-year period beginning on the date of their establishment, unless, in the case of a committee established by the President or an officer of the Federal Government, such committee is renewed by appropriate action prior to the expiration of such two-year period, or in the case of a committee established by the Congress, its duration is otherwise provided for by law. See section 14 of Pub.L. 92–463, Oct. 6, 1972, 86 Stat. 776, set out in Appendix 2 to Title 5, Government Organization and Employees.

## § 1316. Authorization of appropriations [SMCRA § 806]

(a) For the ten institutions referred to in the last sentence of section 1311(a) of this title, there are authorized to be appropriated not to exceed $30,000,000 for the fiscal year ending September 30, 1979 (including the cost of construction, equipment, and startup expenses), and not to exceed $7,500,000 for the fiscal year 1980 and for each fiscal year thereafter through the fiscal year ending before October 1, 1984, to carry out the provisions of this subchapter.

(b) For the three remaining institutions referred to in the last sentence of section 1311(a) of this title, there are authorized to be appropriated not to exceed $6,500,000 for the fiscal year 1980 (including the cost of construction, equipment, and startup expenses), and not to exceed $2,000,000 for each fiscal year after fiscal year 1980 ending before October 1, 1984, to carry out the provisions of this subchapter.

(Pub.L. 95–87, Title VIII, § 806, Aug. 3, 1977, 91 Stat. 529; Pub.L. 95–617, Title VI, § 604(b), Nov. 9, 1978, 92 Stat. 3166.)

## SUBCHAPTER IX—ENERGY RESOURCE GRADUATE FELLOWSHIPS

### § 1321. Fellowship awards

**[SMCRA § 901]**

**(a) Graduate study and research in areas of applied science and engineering relating to production, conservation, and utilization of fuels and energy**

The Secretary of Energy is authorized to award under the provisions of this subchapter not to exceed one thousand fellowships for the fiscal year ending September 30, 1979, and each of the five succeeding fiscal years. Fellowships shall be awarded under the provisions of this subchapter for graduate study and research in those areas of applied science and engineering that are related to the production, conservation, and utilization of fuels and energy. Fellowships shall be awarded to students in programs leading to master's degrees. Such fellowships may be awarded for graduate study and research at any institution of higher education, library, archive, or any other research center approved by the Secretary of Energy after consultation with the Secretary of Education.

**(b) Term**

Such fellowships shall be awarded for such periods as the Secretary of Energy may determine, but not to exceed two years.

**(c) Replacement awards**

In addition to the number of fellowships authorized to be awarded by subsection (a) of this section, the Secretary of Energy is authorized to award fellowships equal to the number previously awarded during any fiscal year under this subchapter but vacated prior to the end of the period for which they were awarded; except that each fellowship awarded under this subsection shall be for such period of graduate work or research, not in excess of the remainder of the period for which the fellowship which it replaces was awarded as the Secretary of Energy may determine.

(Pub.L. 95–87, Title IX, § 901, Aug. 3, 1977, 91 Stat. 529; Pub.L. 95–91, Title III, § 301(a), Title VII, §§ 703, 707, Aug. 4, 1977, 91 Stat. 577, 606, 607; Pub.L. 96–88, Title III, § 301(a)(1), Title V, § 507, Oct. 17, 1979, 93 Stat. 677, 692.)

#### HISTORICAL AND STATUTORY NOTES

**Transfer of Functions**

"Secretary of Energy" was substituted for "Administrator ERDA" and "Administrator", meaning the Administrator of the Energy Research and Development Administration, in text pursuant to sections 301(a), 703, and 707 of Pub.L. 95–91, which are classified to sections 7151(a), 7293, 7297 of Title 42, The Public Health and Welfare, and which terminated the Energy Research and Development Administration and transferred its functions and the functions of the Administrator thereof (with certain exceptions) to the Secretary of Energy.

"Secretary of Education" was substituted for "Commissioner of Education" in subsec. (a), pursuant to sections 301(a)(1) and 507 of Pub.L. 96–88, which are classified to sections 3441(a)(1) and 3507 of Title 20, Education, and which transferred all functions of the Commissioner of Education to the Secretary of Education.

### § 1322. Fellowship recipients

**[SMCRA § 902]**

Recipients of fellowships under this subchapter shall be—

**(a)** persons who have been accepted by an institution of higher education for graduate study leading to an advanced degree or for a professional degree, and

**(b)** persons who plan a career in the field of energy resources, production, or utilization.

(Pub.L. 95–87, Title IX, § 902, Aug. 3, 1977, 91 Stat. 530.)

### § 1323. Distribution of fellowships

**[SMCRA § 903]**

In awarding fellowships under the provisions of this subchapter, the Secretary of Energy shall endeavor to provide equitable distribution of such fellowships throughout the Nation, except that the Secretary of Energy shall give special attention to institutions of higher education, libraries, archives, or other research centers which have a demonstrated capacity to offer courses of study or research in the field of energy resources and conservation and conversion and related disciplines. In carrying out his responsibilities under this section, the Secretary of Energy shall take into consideration the projected need for highly trained engineers and scientists in the field of energy sources.

(Pub.L. 95–87, Title IX, § 903, Aug. 3, 1977, 91 Stat. 530; Pub.L. 95–91, Title III, § 301(a), Title VII, §§ 703, 707, Aug. 4, 1977, 91 Stat. 577, 606, 607.)

#### HISTORICAL AND STATUTORY NOTES

**Transfer of Functions**

"Secretary of Energy" was substituted for "Administrator", meaning the Administrator of the Energy Research and Development Administration, in text pursuant to sections 301(a), 703, and 707 of Pub.L. 95–91, which are classified to sections 7151(a), 7293, 7297 of Title 42, The Public Health and Welfare, and which terminated the Energy Research and Development Administration and transferred its functions and the functions of the Administrator thereof (with certain exceptions) to the Secretary of Energy.

## § 1324. Stipends and allowances

[SMCRA § 904]

**(a)** Each person awarded a fellowship under this subchapter shall receive a stipend of not more than $10,000 for each academic year of study. An additional amount of $500 for each such calendar year of study shall be paid to such person on account of each of his dependents.

**(b)** In addition to the amount paid to such person pursuant to subsection (a) of this section there shall be paid to the institution of higher education at which each such person is pursuing his course of study, 100 per centum of the amount paid to such person less the amount paid on account of such person's dependents, to such person less any amount charged such person for tuition.

(Pub.L. 95–87, Title IX, § 904, Aug. 3, 1977, 91 Stat. 530.)

## § 1325. Limitation on fellowships

[SMCRA § 905]

No fellowship shall be awarded under this subchapter for study at a school or department of divinity. For the purpose of this section, the term "school or department of divinity" means an institution or department or branch of an institution, whose program is specifically for the education of students to prepare them to become ministers of religion or to enter upon some other religious vocation or to prepare them to teach theological subjects.

(Pub.L. 95–87, Title IX, § 905, Aug. 3, 1977, 91 Stat. 530.)

## § 1326. Fellowship conditions

[SMCRA § 906]

**(a)** A person awarded a fellowship under the provisions of this subchapter shall continue to receive the payments provided in section 1324(a) of this title only during such periods as the Secretary of Energy finds that he is maintaining satisfactory proficiency in, and devoting essentially full time to, study or research in the field in which such fellowship was awarded, in an institution of higher education, and is not engaging in gainful employment other than part-time employment in teaching, research, or similar activities, approved by the Secretary of Energy.

**(b)** The Secretary of Energy shall require reports containing such information in such forms and to be filed at such times as he determines necessary from each person awarded a fellowship under the provisions of this subchapter. Such reports shall be accompanied by a certificate from an appropriate official at the institution of higher education, library, archive, or other research center approved by the Secretary of Energy, stating that such person is making satisfactory progress in, and is devoting essentially full time to the research for which the fellowship was awarded.

(Pub.L. 95–87, Title IX, § 906, Aug. 3, 1977, 91 Stat. 530; Pub.L. 95–91, Title III, § 301(a), Title VII, §§ 703, 707, Aug. 4, 1977, 91 Stat. 577, 606, 607.)

### HISTORICAL AND STATUTORY NOTES

**Transfer of Functions**

"Secretary of Energy" was substituted for "Administrator", meaning the Administrator of the Energy Research and Development Administration, in text pursuant to sections 301(a), 703, and 707 of Pub.L. 95–91, which are classified to sections 7151(a), 7293, 7297 of Title 42, The Public Health and Welfare, and which terminated the Energy Research and Development Administration and transferred its functions and the functions of the Administrator thereof (with certain exceptions) to the Secretary of Energy.

## § 1327. Authorization of appropriations

[SMCRA § 907]

There are authorized to be appropriated $11,000,000 for the fiscal year ending September 30, 1979, and for each of the five succeeding fiscal years. For payments for the initial awarding of fellowships awarded under this subchapter, there are authorized to be appropriated for the fiscal year ending September 30, 1979, and for each of the five succeeding fiscal years, such sums as may be necessary in order that fellowships already awarded might be completed.

(Pub.L. 95–87, Title IX, § 907, Aug. 3, 1977, 91 Stat. 531.)

## § 1328. Research, development projects, etc., relating to alternative coal mining technologies

[SMCRA § 908]

**(a) Authority of Secretary of the Interior to conduct, promote, etc.**

The Secretary of the Interior is authorized to conduct and promote the coordination and acceleration of, research, studies, surveys, experiments, demonstration projects, and training relating to—

(1) the development and application of coal mining technologies which provide alternatives to surface disturbance and which maximize the recovery of available coal resources, including the improvement of present underground mining methods, methods for the return of underground mining wastes to the mine void, methods for the underground mining of thick coal seams and very deep seams; and

(2) safety and health in the application of such technologies, methods, and means.

**(b) Contracts and grants**

In conducting the activities authorized by this section, the Secretary of the Interior may enter into contracts with and make grants to qualified institutions, agencies, organizations, and persons.

**(c) Authorization of appropriations**

There are authorized to be appropriated to the Secretary of the Interior, to carry out the purposes of this section, $35,000,000 for each fiscal year beginning with the fiscal year 1979, and for each year thereafter for the next four years.

**(d) Publication in Federal Register; report to Congress**

At least sixty days before any funds are obligated for any research studies, surveys, experiments or demonstration projects to be conducted or financed under this chapter in any fiscal year, the Secretary of the Interior in consultation with the heads of other Federal agencies having the authority to conduct or finance such projects, shall determine and publish such determinations in the Federal Register that such projects are not being conducted or financed by any other Federal agency. On December 31 of each calendar year, the Secretary shall report to the Congress on the research studies, surveys, experiments or demonstration projects, conducted or financed under this chapter, including, but not limited to, a statement of the nature and purpose of each project, the Federal cost thereof, the identity and affiliation of the persons engaged in such projects, the expected completion date of the projects and the relationship of the projects to other such projects of a similar nature.

**(e) Availability of information to public**

Subject to the patent provisions of section 306(d) of this Act, all information and data resulting from any research studies, surveys, experiments, or demonstration projects conducted or financed under this chapter shall be promptly made available to the public.

(Pub.L. 95–87, Title IX, § 908, Aug. 3, 1977, 91 Stat. 531; Pub.L. 95–91, Title III, § 301(a), Title VII, §§ 703, 707, Aug. 4, 1977, 91 Stat. 577, 606, 607; Pub.L. 97–257, Title I, § 100, Sept. 10, 1982, 96 Stat. 841.)

## HISTORICAL AND STATUTORY NOTES

**References in Text**

This chapter, referred to in subsecs. (d) and (e), was in the original "this Act", meaning Pub.L. 95–87, Aug. 3, 1977, 91 Stat. 445, as amended, which enacted this chapter and amended section 1114 of Title 18, Crimes and Criminal Procedure. For complete classification of this Act to the Code, see Short Title note set out under section 1201 of this title and Tables.

Section 306(d) of this Act, referred to in subsec. (e), was classified to section 1226(d) of this title and was omitted from the Code pursuant to the replacement of subchapter III (section 1221 et seq.) of this chapter by Pub.L. 98–409. See section 1226(c) of this title.

**Transfer of Functions**

"Secretary of the Interior" was substituted for "Secretary of Energy" in subsecs. (a) to (d) pursuant to section 100 of Pub.L. 97–257, which is set out as a note under section 7152 of Title 42, The Public Health and Welfare, and which transferred to, and vested in, the Secretary of the Interior all functions vested in, or delegated to, the Secretary of Energy and the Department of Energy under this section.

Previously, "Secretary of Energy" was substituted for "Administrator", meaning the Administrator of the Energy Research and Development Administration, in subsecs. (a) to (d) pursuant to sections 301(a), 703, and 707 of Pub.L. 95–91, which are classified to sections 7151(a), 7293, 7297 of Title 42, and which terminated the Energy Research and Development Administration and transferred its functions and the functions of the Administrator thereof (with certain exceptions) to the Secretary of Energy.

# TITLE 33

# NAVIGATION AND NAVIGABLE WATERS

## PROTECTION OF NAVIGABLE WATERS AND OF HARBOR AND RIVER IMPROVEMENTS GENERALLY

**(33 U.S.C.A. §§ 401 to 430, 441 to 454)**

## CHAPTER 9—PROTECTION OF NAVIGABLE WATERS AND OF HARBOR AND RIVER IMPROVEMENTS GENERALLY

SUBCHAPTER I—IN GENERAL

## SUBCHAPTER I—IN GENERAL

### § 401. Construction of bridges, causeways, dams or dikes generally; exemptions

It shall not be lawful to construct or commence the construction of any bridge, causeway, dam, or dike over or in any port, roadstead, haven, harbor, canal, navigable river, or other navigable water of the United States until the consent of Congress to the building of such structures shall have been obtained and until the plans for (1) the bridge or causeway shall have been submitted to and approved by the Secretary of Transportation, or (2) the dam or dike shall have been submitted to and approved by the Chief of Engineers and Secretary of the Army. However, such structures may be built under authority of the legislature of a State across rivers and other waterways the navigable portions of which lie wholly within the limits of a single State, provided the location and plans thereof are submitted to and approved by the Secretary of Transportation or by the Chief of Engineers and Secretary of the Army before construction is commenced. When plans for any bridge or other structure have been approved by the Secretary of Transportation or by the Chief of Engineers and Secretary of the Army, it shall not be lawful to deviate from such plans either before or after completion of the structure unless modification of said plans has previously been submitted to and received the approval of the Secretary of Transportation or the Chief of Engineers and the Secretary of the Army. The approval required by this section of the location and plans or any modification of plans of any bridge or causeway does not apply to any bridge or causeway over waters that are not subject to the ebb and flow of the tide and that are not used and are not susceptible to use in their natural condition or by reasonable improvement as a means to transport interstate or foreign commerce.

(Mar. 3, 1899, c. 425, § 9, 30 Stat. 1151; Oct. 15, 1982, Pub.L. 97–322, Title I, § 107(b), 96 Stat. 1582; Jan. 12, 1983, Pub.L. 97–449, § 2(f), 96 Stat. 2440.)

#### HISTORICAL AND STATUTORY NOTES

**Codifications**

Section was part of the Rivers and Harbors Appropriation Act of 1899, and together with section 403 of this title superseded Act Sept. 19, 1890, c. 907, § 7, 26 Stat. 454, as amended by Act July 13, 1892, c. 158, § 3, 27 Stat. 88, which prohibited the erection of obstructions to navigation, and prohibited the erection of bridges over navigable waters under State legislation before the approval of the plans by the Secretary of War, and prohibited the alteration of channels unless authorized by that Secretary.

**Transfer of Functions**

Enforcement functions of Secretary or other official in Department of Transportation related to compliance with permits for bridges across navigable waters issued under this section with respect to pre-construction, construction, and initial operation of transportation system for Canadian and Alaskan natural gas were transferred to the Federal Inspector, Office of Federal Inspector for the Alaska Natural Gas Transportation System, until the first anniversary of date of initial operation of the Alaska Natural Gas Transportation System, see Reorg. Plan No. 1 of 1979, §§ 102(c), 203(a), 44 F.R. 33663, 33666, 93 Stat. 1373, 1376, effective July 1, 1979, set out in Appendix 1 to Title 5, Government Organization and Employees.

All functions, powers, and duties of the Secretary of the Army [formerly War] and other offices and officers of the Department of the Army [formerly War] under this section to the extent that they relate generally to the location and clearances of bridges and causeways in the navigable waters of the United States were transferred to and vested in the Secretary of Transportation by Pub.L. 89–670, § 6(g)(6)(A),

Oct. 15, 1966, 80 Stat. 941. Pub.L. 97–449 amended this section to reflect the transfer made by section 6(g)(6)(A) of Pub.L. 89–670, and repealed section 6(g)(6)(A).

**Short Title**

2002 Acts

Pub.L. 107–310, § 1(a), Dec. 2, 2002, 116 Stat. 2450, provided that: "This Act [enacting 33 U.S.C.A. § 467g–1, amending 33 U.S.C.A. § 467, § 467e, § 467f, § 467g, § 467h and § 467j, redesignating the credits for 33 U.S.C.A. § 467h to § 467j, and enacting provisions set out as a note under 33 U.S.C.A. § 467] may be cited as the 'Dam Safety and Security Act of 2002'."

## § 402. Construction of bridges, etc., over Illinois and Mississippi Canal

The provisions of section 401 of this title are made applicable alike to the completed and uncompleted portions of the Illinois and Mississippi Canal. Whenever the Secretary of the Army shall approve plans for a bridge to be built across said canal he may, in his discretion, and subject to such terms and conditions as in his judgment are equitable, expedient, and just to the public, grant to the person or corporation building and owning such bridge a right of way across the lands of the United States on either side of and adjacent to the said canal; also the privilege of occupying so much of said lands as may be necessary for the piers, abutments, and other portions of the bridge structure and approaches.

(June 13, 1902, c. 1079, § 10, 32 Stat. 374.)

### HISTORICAL AND STATUTORY NOTES

**Codifications**

Section was part of the River and Harbor Appropriation Act of 1902.

**Change of Name**

The Department of War was designated the Department of the Army and the title of the Secretary of War was changed to Secretary of the Army by section 205(a) of Act July 26, 1947, c. 343, Title II, 61 Stat. 501. Section 205(a) of Act July 26, 1947, was repealed by section 53 of Act Aug. 10, 1956, c. 1041, 70A Stat. 641. Section 1 of Act Aug. 10, 1956, enacted "Title 10, Armed Forces", which in sections 3010 to 3013 continued the Military Department of the Army under the administrative supervision of a Secretary of the Army.

**Transfer of Functions**

All functions, powers, and duties of the Secretary of the Army and other offices and officers of the Department of the Army under section 401 of this title to the extent that they relate generally to the location and clearances of bridges and causeways in the navigable waters of the United States were transferred to and vested in the Secretary of Transportation by Pub.L. 89–670, § 6(g)(6)(A), Oct. 15, 1966, 80 Stat. 941. Pub.L. 97–449 amended section 401 of this title to reflect the transfer made by section 6(g)(6)(A) of Pub.L. 89–670, and repealed section 6(g)(6)(A).

## § 403. Obstruction of navigable waters generally; wharves; piers, etc.; excavations and filling in

The creation of any obstruction not affirmatively authorized by Congress, to the navigable capacity of any of the waters of the United States is prohibited; and it shall not be lawful to build or commence the building of any wharf, pier, dolphin, boom, weir, breakwater, bulkhead, jetty, or other structures in any port, roadstead, haven, harbor, canal, navigable river, or other water of the United States, outside established harbor lines, or where no harbor lines have been established, except on plans recommended by the Chief of Engineers and authorized by the Secretary of the Army; and it shall not be lawful to excavate or fill, or in any manner to alter or modify the course, location, condition, or capacity of, any port, roadstead, haven, harbor, canal, lake, harbor or refuge, or inclosure within the limits of any breakwater, or of the channel of any navigable water of the United States, unless the work has been recommended by the Chief of Engineers and authorized by the Secretary of the Army prior to beginning the same.

(Mar. 3, 1899, c. 425, § 10, 30 Stat. 1151.)

### HISTORICAL AND STATUTORY NOTES

**Codifications**

Section was part of the Rivers and Harbors Appropriation Act of 1899.

**Change of Name**

The Department of War was designated the Department of the Army and the title of the Secretary of War was changed to Secretary of the Army by section 205(a) of Act July 26, 1947, c. 343, Title II, 61 Stat. 501. Section 205(a) of Act July 26, 1947, was repealed by section 53 of Act Aug. 10, 1956, c. 1041, 70A Stat. 641. Section 1 of Act Aug. 10, 1956, enacted "Title 10, Armed Forces", which in sections 3010 to 3013 continued the Military Department of the Army under the administrative supervision of a Secretary of the Army.

**Transfer of Functions**

Enforcement functions of Secretary of the Army, Chief of Engineers, or other official in Corps of Engineers of the United States Army related to compliance with permits for structures in navigable waters issued under this section with respect to pre-construction, construction, and initial operation of transportation system for Canadian and Alaskan natural gas were transferred to the Federal Inspector, Office of Federal Inspector for the Alaska Natural Gas Transportation System, until the first anniversary of date of initial operation of the Alaska Natural Gas Transportation System, see Reorg. Plan No. 1 of 1979, §§ 102(b), 203(a), 44 F.R. 33663, 33666, 93 Stat. 1373, 1376, effective July 1, 1979, set out in Appendix 1 to Title 5, Government Organization and Employees.

All functions, powers, and duties of the Secretary of the Army and other offices and officers of the Department of the Army under section 401 of this title to the extent that they relate generally to the location and clearances of bridges and causeways in the navigable waters of the United States were transferred to and vested in the Secretary of Transportation by Pub.L. 89–670, § 6(g)(6)(A), Oct. 15, 1966, 80 Stat. 941. Pub.L. 97–449 amended section 401 of this title to reflect the transfer made by section 6(g)(6)(A) of Pub.L. 89–670, and repealed section 6(g)(6)(A).

**Prior Provisions**

Act Sept. 19, 1890, c. 907, § 10, 26 Stat. 454, was probably omitted from the Code as superseded by this section but it was held by the Circuit Court of Appeals in Wishkah Boom Co., Wash.1905, 136 F. 42, 68 C.C.A. 592 (appeal dismissed [1906] 26 S.Ct. 765, 202 U.S. 613, 50 L.Ed. 1171), that it was not superseded so far as it related to the continuance of obstructions. It provided that:

"The creation of any obstruction, not affirmatively authorized by law, to the navigable capacity of any waters, in respect of which the United States has jurisdiction, is hereby prohibited. The continuance of any such obstruction, except bridges, piers, docks, and wharves, and similar structures erected for business purposes, whether heretofore or hereafter created, shall constitute an offense and each week's continuance of any such obstruction shall be deemed a separate offense. Every person and every corporation which shall be guilty of creating or continuing any such unlawful obstruction in this act mentioned, or who shall violate the provisions of the last four preceding sections of this act, shall be deemed guilty of a misdemeanor, and on conviction thereof shall be punished by a fine not exceeding five thousand dollars, or by imprisonment (in the case of a natural person) not exceeding one year, or by both such punishments, in the discretion of the court, the creating or continuing of any unlawful obstruction in this act mentioned may be prevented and such obstruction may be caused to be removed by the injunction of any circuit court [district court] exercising jurisdiction in any district in which such obstruction may be threatened or may exist; and proper proceedings in equity to this end may be instituted under the direction of the Attorney-General of the United States."

This section and section 9 of Act Mar. 3, 1899 (section 401 of this title) superseded provisions of Act Sept. 19, 1890, c. 907, § 7, 26 Stat. 454, as amended by Act July 13, 1892, c. 158, § 3, 27 Stat. 110, which prohibited the erection of obstructions to navigation, and prohibited the erection of bridges over navigable waters under State legislation before the approval of the plans by the Secretary of War, and prohibited the alteration of channels unless authorized by said Secretary.

## § 403a. Omitted

### HISTORICAL AND STATUTORY NOTES

**Codifications**

Section, Acts Sept. 19, 1890, c. 907, § 10, 26 Stat. 454; Mar. 3, 1911, c. 231, § 291, 36 Stat. 1167, related to obstruction of navigable waters. See Prior Provisions note set out under section 403 of this title.

## § 403b. Lighting at docks and boat launching facilities

Whenever the Secretary considers a permit application for a dock or a boat launching facility under section 403 of this title, the Secretary shall consider the needs of such facility for lighting from sunset to sunrise to make such facility's presence known within a reasonable distance.

(Pub.L. 99–662, Title IX, § 946, Nov. 17, 1986, 100 Stat. 4200.)

### HISTORICAL AND STATUTORY NOTES

**"Secretary" Defined**

Secretary means the Secretary of the Army, see section 2 of Pub.L. 100–676, set out as a note under 33 U.S.C.A. § 2201.

## § 404. Establishment of harbor lines; conditions to grants for extension of piers, etc.

Where it is made manifest to the Secretary of the Army that the establishment of harbor lines is essential to the preservation and protection of harbors he may, and is, authorized to cause such lines to be established, beyond which no piers, wharves, bulkheads, or other works shall be extended or deposits made, except under such regulations as may be prescribed from time to time by him: *Provided*, That, whenever the Secretary of the Army grants to any person or persons permission to extend piers, wharves, bulkheads, or other works, or to make deposits in any tidal harbor or river of the United States beyond any harbor lines established under authority of the United States, he shall cause to be ascertained the amount of tidewater displaced by any such structure or by any such deposits, and he shall, if he deem it necessary, require the parties to whom the permission is given to make compensation for such displacement either by excavating in some part of the harbor, including tidewater channels between high and low water mark, to such an extent as to create a basin for as much tidewater as may be displaced by such structure or by such deposits, or in any other mode that may be satisfactory to him.

(Mar. 3, 1899, c. 425, § 11, 30 Stat. 1151.)

### HISTORICAL AND STATUTORY NOTES

**Codifications**

Section was part of the Rivers and Harbors Appropriation Act of 1899.

**Change of Name**

The Department of War was designated the Department of the Army and the title of the Secretary of War was changed to Secretary of the Army by section 205(a) of Act July 26, 1947, c. 343, Title II, 61 Stat. 501. Section 205(a) of Act July 26, 1947, was repealed by section 53 of Act Aug. 10, 1956, c. 1041, 70A Stat. 641. Section 1 of Act Aug. 10, 1956, enacted "Title 10, Armed Forces", which in sections 3010 to 3013 continued the Military Department of the Army under the administrative supervision of a Secretary of the Army.

**Transfer of Functions**

All functions, powers, and duties of the Secretary of the Army and other offices and officers of the Department of the Army under section 401 of this title to the extent that they relate generally to the location and clearances of bridges and causeways in the navigable waters of the United States were transferred to and vested in the Secretary of Transportation by Pub.L. 89–670, § 6(g)(6)(A), Oct. 15, 1966, 80 Stat. 941. Pub.L. 97–449 amended section 401 of this title to reflect the transfer made by section 6(g)(6)(A) of Pub.L. 89–670, and repealed section 6(g)(6)(A).

**Prior Provisions**

This section and section 406 of this title superseded Act Aug. 11, 1888, c. 860, § 12, 25 Stat. 425, as amended by Act Sept. 19, 1890, c. 907, § 12, 26 Stat. 455, which authorized the establishment of harbor lines, and prescribed a penalty for a violation of the section, or any rule made in pursuance of it.

Section also superseded Act Aug. 18, 1894, c. 299, § 9, 28 Stat. 364, which contained provisions for compensation for tide water displaced similar to the proviso in this section.

Act Aug. 5, 1886, c. 929, § 2, 24 Stat. 329, which was probably omitted from the Code as superseded by this section, provided that: "In places where harbor-lines have not been established, and where deposits of débris of mines or stamp works can be made without injury to navigation, within lines to be established by the Secretary of War, said officer may, and is hereby authorized to, cause such lines to be established; and within such lines such deposits may be made, under regulations to be from time to time prescribed by him."

## § 405. Establishment and modification of harbor lines on Potomac and Anacostia Rivers

The provisions of section 404 of this title are made applicable to the Potomac and Anacostia Rivers, and after July 25, 1912, harbor lines in the District of Columbia, or elsewhere on said rivers, shall be established or modified as therein provided.

(July 25, 1912, c. 253, § 1, 37 Stat. 206.)

### HISTORICAL AND STATUTORY NOTES

**Codifications**

Section is part of section 1 of the Rivers and Harbors Appropriation Act of 1912.

## § 406. Penalty for wrongful construction of bridges, piers, etc.; removal of structures

Every person and every corporation that shall violate any of the provisions of sections 401, 403, and 404 of this title or any rule or regulation made by the Secretary of the Army in pursuance of the provisions of section 404 of this title shall be deemed guilty of a misdemeanor, and on conviction thereof shall be punished by a fine not exceeding $2,500 nor less than $500, or by imprisonment (in the case of a natural person) not exceeding one year, or by both such punishments, in the discretion of the court. And further, the removal of any structures or parts of structures erected in violation of the provisions of the said sections may be enforced by the injunction of any district court exercising jurisdiction in any district in which such structures may exist, and proper proceedings to this end may be instituted under the direction of the Attorney General of the United States.

(Mar. 3, 1899, c. 425, § 12, 30 Stat. 1151; Feb. 20, 1900, c. 23, § 2, 31 Stat. 32; Mar. 3, 1911, c. 231, § 291, 36 Stat. 1167.)

### HISTORICAL AND STATUTORY NOTES

**Codifications**

Section is from Act Mar. 3, 1899, popularly known as the Rivers and Harbors Appropriation Act of 1899.

**Change of Name**

The Department of War was designated the Department of the Army and the title of the Secretary of War was changed to Secretary of the Army by section 205(a) of Act July 26, 1947, c. 343, Title II, 61 Stat. 501. Section 205(a) of Act July 26, 1947, was repealed by section 53 of Act Aug. 10, 1956, c. 1041, 70A Stat. 641. Section 1 of Act Aug. 10, 1956, enacted "Title 10, Armed Forces", which in sections 3010 to 3013 continued the Military Department of the Army under the administrative supervision of a Secretary of the Army.

**Transfer of Functions**

All functions, powers, and duties of the Secretary of the Army and other offices and officers of the Department of the Army under section 401 of this title to the extent that they relate generally to the location and clearances of bridges and causeways in the navigable waters of the United States were transferred to and vested in the Secretary of Transportation by Pub.L. 89–670, § 6(g)(6)(A), Oct. 15, 1966, 80 Stat. 941, which created the Department of Transportation. Pub.L. 97–449 amended section 401 of this title to reflect the transfer made by section 6(g)(6)(A) of Pub.L. 89–670, and repealed section 6(g)(6)(A).

## § 407. Deposit of refuse in navigable waters generally

It shall not be lawful to throw, discharge, or deposit, or cause, suffer, or procure to be thrown, discharged, or deposited either from or out of any ship, barge, or other floating craft of any kind, or from the shore, wharf, manufacturing establishment, or mill of any kind, any refuse matter of any kind or description whatever other than that flowing from streets and sewers and passing therefrom in a liquid state, into any navigable water of the United States, or into any tributary of any navigable water from which the same shall float or be washed into such navigable water; and it shall not be lawful to deposit, or cause, suffer, or procure to be deposited material of any kind in any place on the bank of any navigable water, or on the bank of any tributary of any navigable water, where the same shall be liable to be washed into such navigable water, either by ordinary or high tides, or by storms or floods, or otherwise, whereby navigation shall or may be impeded or obstructed: *Provided*, That nothing herein contained shall extend to, apply to, or prohibit the operations in connection with the improvement of navigable waters or construction of public works, considered necessary and proper by the

United States officers supervising such improvement or public work: *And provided further,* That the Secretary of the Army, whenever in the judgment of the Chief of Engineers anchorage and navigation will not be injured thereby, may permit the deposit of any material above mentioned in navigable waters, within limits to be defined and under conditions to be prescribed by him, provided application is made to him prior to depositing such material; and whenever any permit is so granted the conditions thereof shall be strictly complied with, and any violation thereof shall be unlawful.

(Mar. 3, 1899, c. 425, § 13, 30 Stat. 1152.)

### HISTORICAL AND STATUTORY NOTES

**Codifications**

Section was enacted as part of the Rivers and Harbors Appropriation Act of 1899, Act Mar. 3, 1899, c. 425, 30 Stat. 1121.

**Change of Name**

The Department of War was designated the Department of the Army and the title of the Secretary of War was changed to Secretary of the Army by section 205(a) of Act July 26, 1947, c. 343, Title II, 61 Stat. 501. Section 205(a) of Act July 26, 1947, was repealed by section 53 of Act Aug. 10, 1956, c. 1041, 70A Stat. 641. Section 1 of Act Aug. 10, 1956, enacted "Title 10, Armed Forces", which in sections 3010 to 3013 continued the military Department of the Army under the administrative supervision of a Secretary of the Army.

**Transfer of Functions**

All functions, powers, and duties of the Secretary of the Army and other offices and officers of the Department of the Army under section 401 of this title to the extent that they relate generally to the location and clearances of bridges and causeways in the navigable waters of the United States were transferred to and vested in the Secretary of Transportation by Pub.L. 89–670, § 6(g)(6)(A), Oct. 15, 1966, 80 Stat. 941, which created the Department of Transportation. Pub.L. 97–449 amended section 401 of this title to reflect the transfer made by section 6(g)(6)(A) of Pub.L. 89–670, and repealed section 6(g)(6)(A).

**Prior Provisions**

This section and sections 408, 411, and 412 of this title, superseded Act Aug. 18, 1894, c. 299, §§ 6, 7, 8, 28 Stat. 363, which prohibited the depositing of refuse in navigable waters for the improvement of which money had been appropriated, and the injury to sea walls and other works built by the Government, and prescribed penalties for violations, including penalties against masters, etc., and vessels.

Section also superseded Act Sept. 19, 1890, c. 907, § 6, 26 Stat. 453, which prohibited obstructing navigation by deposits of refuse, etc., in navigable waters.

**Short Title**

1899 Acts

This section is popularly known as the Refuse Act of 1899.

**Termination of Discharge Permit Program**

No permits for discharges into navigable waters to be issued under this section after Oct. 18, 1972, and the discharge permit program to be carried out instead under section 1342 of this title, with applications under this section pending on Oct. 18, 1972, to be deemed applications for permits under section 1342, see section 1342 of this title.

## § 407a. Deposit of debris of mines and stamp works

In places where harbor-lines have not been established, and where deposits of debris of mines or stamp works can be made without injury to navigation, within lines to be established by the Secretary of the Army, said officer may, and is authorized to, cause such lines to be established; and within such lines such deposits may be made, under regulations to be from time to time prescribed by him.

(Aug. 5, 1886, c. 929, § 2, 24 Stat. 329.)

### HISTORICAL AND STATUTORY NOTES

**Change of Name**

The Department of War was designated the Department of the Army and the title of the Secretary of War was changed to Secretary of the Army by section 205(a) of Act July 26, 1947, c. 343, Title II, 61 Stat. 501. Section 205(a) of Act July 26, 1947, was repealed by section 53 of Act Aug. 10, 1956, c. 1041, 70A Stat. 641. Section 1 of Act Aug. 10, 1956, enacted "Title 10, Armed Forces", which in sections 3010 to 3013 continued the Military Department of the Army under the administrative supervision of a Secretary of the Army.

**Transfer of Functions**

All functions, powers, and duties of the Secretary of the Army and other offices and officers of the Department of the Army under section 401 of this title to the extent that they relate generally to the location and clearances of bridges and causeways in the navigable waters of the United States were transferred to and vested in the Secretary of Transportation by Pub.L. 89–670, § 6(g)(6)(A), Oct. 15, 1966, 80 Stat. 941, which created the Department of Transportation. Pub.L. 97–449 amended section 401 of this title to reflect the transfer made by section 6(g)(6)(A) of Pub.L. 89–670, and repealed section 6(g)(6)(A).

## § 408. Taking possession of, use of, or injury to harbor or river improvements

It shall not be lawful for any person or persons to take possession of or make use of for any purpose, or build upon, alter, deface, destroy, move, injure, obstruct by fastening vessels thereto or otherwise, or in any manner whatever impair the usefulness of any sea wall, bulkhead, jetty, dike, levee, wharf, pier, or other work built by the United States, or any piece of plant, floating or otherwise, used in the construction of such work under the control of the United States, in whole or in part, for the preservation and improvement of any of its navigable waters or to prevent floods, or as boundary marks, tide gauges, surveying stations, buoys, or other established marks, nor remove for ballast or other purposes any stone or other material composing such works: *Provided,* That the Secretary of the Army may, on the recommendation of the Chief of Engineers, grant permission for the temporary occupation or use of any of the aforementioned public works when in his judgment such occupation or use will not be injurious to the public interest: *Provided further,* That the Secretary may, on the recommendation of the Chief of Engineers, grant permission for the alteration or permanent occupation or use of any of the aforementioned public works when in the judgment of the Secretary such occupation or use will not be injurious to the public interest and will not impair the usefulness of such work.

(Mar. 3, 1899, c. 425, § 14, 30 Stat. 1152; Aug. 15, 1985, Pub.L. 99–88, Title I, § 100, 99 Stat. 315.)

### HISTORICAL AND STATUTORY NOTES

**Codifications**

Section was enacted as part of the Rivers and Harbors Appropriation Act of 1899, Act Mar. 3, 1899, c. 425, 30 Stat. 1121.

**Change of Name**

The Department of War was designated the Department of the Army and the title of the Secretary of War was changed to Secretary of the Army by section 205(a) of Act July 26, 1947, c. 343, Title II, 61 Stat. 501. Section 205(a) of Act July 26, 1947, was repealed by section 53 of Act Aug. 10, 1956, c. 1041, 70A Stat. 641. Section 1 of Act Aug. 10, 1956, enacted "Title 10, Armed Forces" which in sections 3010 to 3013 continued the Department of the Army under the administrative supervision of a Secretary of the Army.

**Transfer of Functions**

All functions, powers, and duties of the Secretary of the Army and other offices and officers of the Department of the Army under section 401 of this title to the extent that they relate generally to the location and clearances of bridges and causeways in the navigable waters of the United States were transferred to and vested in the Secretary of Transportation by Pub.L. 89–670, § 6(g)(6)(A), Oct. 15, 1966, 80 Stat. 941, which created the Department of Transportation. Pub.L. 97–449 amended section 401 of this title to reflect the transfer made by section 6(g)(6)(A) of Pub.L. 89–670, and repealed section 6(g)(6)(A).

**Prior Provisions**

Section superseded Act Sept. 19, 1890, c. 907, § 9, 26 Stat. 426, which prohibited persons taking possession of or using or injuring government works in navigable waters.

Act Aug. 14, 1876, c. 267, § 3, 19 Stat. 139, penalizing persons injuring any pier breakwater, or other work of the United States for the improvement of rivers or harbors or navigation, was probably omitted from the Code as superseded by this section.

## § 409. Obstruction of navigable waters by vessels; floating timber; marking and removal of sunken vessels

It shall not be lawful to tie up or anchor vessels or other craft in navigable channels in such a manner as to prevent or obstruct the passage of other vessels or craft; or to sink, or permit or cause to be sunk, vessels or other craft in navigable channels; or to float loose timber and logs, or to float what is known as "sack rafts of timber and logs" in streams or channels actually navigated by steamboats in such manner as to obstruct, impede, or endanger navigation. And whenever a vessel, raft or other craft is wrecked and sunk in a navigable channel, it shall be the duty of the owner, lessee, or operator of such sunken craft to immediately mark it with a buoy or beacon during the day and a lighted lantern at night, and to maintain such marks until the sunken craft is removed or abandoned, and the neglect or failure of the said owner, lessee, or operator so to do shall be unlawful; and it shall be the duty of the owner, lessee, or operator of such sunken craft to commence the immediate removal of the same, and prosecute such removal diligently, and failure to do so shall be considered as an abandonment of such craft, and subject the same to removal by the United States as provided for in sections 411 to 416, 418, and 502 of this title.

(Mar. 3, 1899, c. 425, § 15, 30 Stat. 1152; Nov. 17, 1986, Pub.L. 99–662, Title IX, § 939(a), 100 Stat. 4199.)

### HISTORICAL AND STATUTORY NOTES

**Codifications**

Section was enacted as part of the Rivers and Harbors Appropriation Act of 1899, Act Mar. 3, 1899, c. 425, 30 Stat. 1121.

## § 410. Exception as to floating loose timber, sack rafts, etc.; violation of regulations; penalty

The prohibition contained in section 409 of this title against floating loose timber and logs, or sack rafts, so called, of timber and logs in streams or channels actually navigated by steamboats, shall not apply to any navigable river or waterway of the United States or any part thereof whereon the floating of loose timber and logs and sack rafts of timber and logs is the principal method of navigation. But such method of navigation on such river or waterway or part thereof shall be subject to the rules and regulations prescribed by the Secretary of the Army as provided in this section.

The Secretary of the Army shall have power, and he is authorized and directed to prescribe rules and regulations, which he may at any time modify, to govern and regulate the floating of loose timber and logs, and sack rafts, (so called) of timber and logs and other methods of navigation on the streams and waterways, or any thereof, of the character, as to navigation, heretofore in this section described. The said rules and regulations shall be so framed as to equitably adjust conflicting interests between the different methods or forms of navigation; and the said rules and regulations shall be published at least once in such newspaper or newspapers of general circulation as in the opinion of the Secretary of the Army shall be best adapted to give notice of said rules and regulations to persons affected thereby and locally interested therein. And all modifications of said rules and regulations shall be similarly published. And such rules and regulations when so prescribed and published as to any such stream or waterway shall have the force of law, and any violation thereof shall be a misdemeanor, and every person convicted of such violation shall be punished by a fine of not exceeding $2,500 nor less than $500, or by imprisonment (in case of a natural person) for not less than thirty days nor more than one year, or by both such fine and imprisonment, in the discretion of the court: *Provided,* That the proper action to enforce the provisions of this section may be commenced before any magistrate judge, judge, or court of the United States, and such magistrate judge, judge, or court shall proceed in respect thereto as authorized by law in the case of crimes or misdemeanors committed against the United States.

The right to alter, amend, or repeal this section at any time is reserved.

(May 9, 1900, c. 387, §§ 1–3, 31 Stat. 172; July 26, 1947, c. 343, Title II, § 205(a), 61 Stat. 501; Oct. 17, 1968, Pub.L. 90–578, Title IV, § 402(b)(2), 82 Stat. 1118; Dec. 1, 1990, Pub.L. 101–650, Title III, § 321, 104 Stat. 5117.)

### HISTORICAL AND STATUTORY NOTES

**Change of Name**

The Department of War was designated the Department of the Army and the title of the Secretary of War was changed to Secretary of the Army by section 205(a) of Act July 26, 1947, c. 343, Title II, 61 Stat. 501. Section 205(a) of Act July 26, 1947, was repealed by section 53 of Act Aug. 10, 1956, c. 1041, 70A Stat. 641. Section 1 of Act Aug. 10, 1956, enacted "Title 10, Armed Forces" which in sections 3010 to 3013 continued the Department of the Army under the administrative supervision of a Secretary of the Army.

"Magistrate judge" substituted in text for "magistrate" pursuant to section 321 of Pub.L. 101–650, set out as a note under 28 U.S.C.A. § 631. Previously, "magistrate" was substituted for "commissioner" pursuant to Pub.L. 90–578. See chapter 43 of Title 28 [28 U.S.C.A. § 631 et seq.].

**Transfer of Functions**

All functions, powers, and duties of the Secretary of the Army and other offices and officers of the Department of the Army under section 401 of this title to the extent that they relate generally to the location and clearances of bridges and causeways in the navigable waters of the United States were transferred to and vested in the Secretary of Transportation by Pub.L. 89–670, § 6(g)(6)(A), Oct. 15, 1966, 80 Stat. 941, which created the Department of Transportation. Pub.L. 97–449 amended section 401 of this title to reflect the transfer made by section 6(g)(6)(A) of Pub.L. 89–670, and repealed section 6(g)(6)(A).

## § 411. Penalty for wrongful deposit of refuse; use of or injury to harbor improvements, and obstruction of navigable waters generally

Every person and every corporation that shall violate, or that shall knowingly aid, abet, authorize, or instigate a violation of the provisions of sections 407, 408, 409, 414, and 415 of this title shall be guilty of a misdemeanor, and on conviction thereof shall be punished by a fine of up to $25,000 per day, or by imprisonment (in the case of a natural person) for not less than thirty days nor more than one year, or by both such fine and imprisonment, in the discretion of the court, one-half of said fine to be paid to the person or persons giving information which shall lead to conviction.

(Mar. 3, 1899, c. 425, § 16, 30 Stat. 1153; Oct. 12, 1996, Pub.L. 104–303, Title II, § 218(a), 110 Stat. 3696.)

### HISTORICAL AND STATUTORY NOTES

**Codifications**

Section is part of section 16 of Act Mar. 3, 1899. The balance of such section, relating to liability of masters, pilots, and so forth and of vessels engaged in violations, is set out as section 412 of this title.

## § 412. Liability of masters, pilots, etc., and of vessels engaged in violations

Any and every master, pilot, and engineer, or person or persons acting in such capacity, respectively, on board of any boat or vessel who shall knowingly engage in towing any scow, boat, or vessel loaded with any material specified in section 407 of this title to any point or place of deposit or discharge in any harbor or navigable water, elsewhere than within the limits defined and permitted by the Secretary of the Army, or who shall willfully injure or destroy any work of the United States contemplated in section 408 of this title, or who shall willfully obstruct the channel of any waterway in the manner contemplated in section 409 of this title, shall be deemed guilty of a violation of this Act, and shall upon conviction be punished as provided in section 411 of this title, and shall also have his license revoked or suspended for a term to be fixed by the judge before whom tried and convicted. And any boat, vessel, scow, raft, or other craft used or employed in violating any of the provisions of sections 407, 408, 409, 414, and 415 of this title shall be liable for the pecuniary penalties specified in section 411 of this title, and in addition thereto for the amount of the damages done by said boat, vessel, scow, raft, or other craft, which latter sum shall be placed to the credit of the appropriation for the improvement of the harbor or waterway in which the damage occurred, and said boat, vessel, scow, raft, or other craft may be proceeded against summarily by way of libel in any district court of the United States having jurisdiction thereof. (Mar. 3, 1899, c. 425, § 16, 30 Stat. 1153; Oct. 12, 1996, Pub.L. 104–303, Title II, § 218(a)(1), 110 Stat. 3696.)

### HISTORICAL AND STATUTORY NOTES

**References in Text**

This Act, referred to in text, is Act Mar. 3, 1899, c. 425, 30 Stat. 1148, as amended, popularly known as the Rivers and Harbors Appropriation Act of 1899, which enacted sections 401, 403, 404, 406, 407, 408, 409, 411 to 416, 418, 502, 549, and 687 of this title, and amended section 686 of this title. For complete classification of this Act to the Code, see Tables.

**Codifications**

Section is part of section 16 of Act Mar. 3, 1899. The balance of such section, relating to penalties for the wrongful deposit of refuse, is set out as section 411 of this title.

**Change of Name**

The Department of War was designated the Department of the Army and the title of the Secretary of War was changed to Secretary of the Army by section 205(a) of Act July 26, 1947, c. 343, Title II, 61 Stat. 501. Section 205(a) of Act July 26, 1947, was repealed by section 53 of Act Aug. 10, 1956, c. 1041, 70A Stat. 641. Section 1 of Act Aug. 10, 1956, enacted "Title 10, Armed Forces" which in sections 3010 to 3013 continued the Department of the Army under the administrative supervision of a Secretary of the Army.

**Transfer of Functions**

All functions, powers, and duties of the Secretary of the Army and other offices and officers of the Department of the Army under section 401 of this title to the extent that they relate generally to the location and clearances of bridges and causeways in the navigable waters of the United States were transferred to and vested in the Secretary of Transportation by Pub.L. 89–670, § 6(g)(6)(A), Oct. 15, 1966, 80 Stat. 941, which created the Department of Transportation. Pub.L. 97–449 amended section 401 of this title to reflect the transfer made by section 6(g)(6)(A) of Pub.L. 89–670, and repealed section 6(g)(6)(A).

## § 413. Duty of United States attorneys and other Federal officers in enforcement of provisions; arrest of offenders

The Department of Justice shall conduct the legal proceedings necessary to enforce the provisions of sections 401, 403, 404, 406, 407, 408, 409, 411, and 412 of this title; and it shall be the duty of United States attorneys to vigorously prosecute all offenders against the same whenever requested to do so by the Secretary of the Army or by any of the officials hereinafter designated, and it shall furthermore be the duty of said United States attorneys to report to the Attorney General of the United States the action taken by him against offenders so reported, and a transcript of such reports shall be transmitted to the Secretary of the Army by the Attorney General; and for the better enforcement of the said provisions and to facilitate the detection and bringing to punishment of such offenders, the officers and agents of the United States in charge of river and harbor improvements, and the assistant engineers and inspectors employed under them by authority of the Secretary of the Army, and the United States collectors of customs and other revenue officers shall have power and authority to swear out process, and to arrest and take into custody, with or without process, any person or persons who may commit any of the acts or offenses prohibited by the said sections, or who may violate any of the provisions of the same: *Provided,* That no person shall be arrested without process for any offense not committed in the presence of some one of the aforesaid officials: *And provided further,* That whenever any arrest is made under such sections, the person so arrested shall be brought forthwith before a magistrate judge, judge, or court of the United States for examination of the offenses alleged against him; and such magistrate judge, judge, or court shall proceed in respect thereto as authorized by law in case of crimes against the United States.

(Mar. 3, 1899, c. 425, § 17, 30 Stat. 1153; July 26, 1947, c. 343, Title II, § 205(a), 61 Stat. 501; June 25, 1948, c. 646, § 1, 62 Stat. 909; Oct. 17, 1968, Pub.L. 90–578, Title IV, § 402(b)(2), 82 Stat. 1118; Dec. 1, 1990, Pub.L. 101–650, Title III, § 321, 104 Stat 5117.)

### HISTORICAL AND STATUTORY NOTES

**Codifications**

Section was enacted as part of the Rivers and Harbors Appropriation Act of 1899, Act Mar. 3, 1899, c. 425, 30 Stat. 1121.

**Change of Name**

Act June 25, 1948, eff. Sept. 1, 1948, substituted "United States attorneys" for "district attorneys of the United States" and "district attorneys". See section 541 of Title 28, Judiciary and Judicial Procedure, and Historical and Revision note set out thereunder.

The Department of War was designated the Department of the Army and the title of the Secretary of War was changed to Secretary of the Army by section 205(a) of Act July 26, 1947, c. 343, Title II, 61 Stat. 501. Section 205(a) of Act July 26, 1947, was repealed by section 53 of Act Aug. 10, 1956, c. 1041, 70A Stat. 641. Section 1 of Act Aug. 10, 1956, enacted "Title 10, Armed Forces" which in sections 3010 to 3013 continued the Department of the Army under the administrative supervision of a Secretary of the Army.

"Magistrate judge" substituted in text for "magistrate" pursuant to section 321 of Pub.L. 101–650, set out as a note under 28 U.S.C.A. § 631. Previously, "magistrate" was substituted for "commissioner" pursuant to Pub.L. 90–578. See chapter 43 of Title 28 [28 U.S.C.A. § 631 et seq.].

**Transfer of Functions**

All functions, powers, and duties of the Secretary of the Army and other offices and officers of the Department of the Army under section 401 of this title to the extent that they relate generally to the location and clearances of bridges and causeways in the navigable waters of the United States were transferred to and vested in the Secretary of Transportation by Pub.L. 89–670, § 6(g)(6)(A), Oct. 15, 1966, 80 Stat. 941, which created the Department of Transportation. Pub.L. 97–449 amended section 401 of this title to reflect the transfer made by section 6(g)(6)(A) of Pub.L. 89–670, and repealed section 6(g)(6)(A).

All offices of collector of customs, comptroller of customs, surveyor of customs, and appraiser of merchandise in the Bureau of Customs of the Department of the Treasury to which appointments were required to be made by the President with the advice and consent of the Senate were ordered abolished with such offices to be terminated not later than Dec. 31, 1966, by Reorg. Plan No. 1 of 1965, eff. May 25, 1965, 30 F.R. 7035, 79 Stat. 1317, set out in Appendix 1 to Title 5, Government Organization and Employees. All functions of the offices eliminated were already vested in the Secretary of the Treasury by Reorg. Plan No. 26 of 1950, eff. July 31, 1950, 15 F.R. 4935, 64 Stat. 1280, set out in Appendix 1 to Title 5.

**Prior Provisions**

Act Sept. 19, 1890, c. 907, § 11, 26 Stat. 455, was probably omitted from the Code as superseded by this section, or as rendered obsolete by Act Mar. 3, 1899, different sections of which superseded provisions of the Act of 1890, the enforcement of which was provided for by section 11. It read as follows: "It shall be the duty of officers and agents having the supervision, on the part of the United States, of the works in progress for the preservation and improvement of said navigable waters, and, in their absence, of the United States collectors of customs and other revenue officers to enforce the provisions of this act by giving information to the district attorney of the United States for the district in which any violation of any provision of this act shall have been committed: *Provided*, That the provisions of this act shall not apply to Torch Lake, Houghton County, Michigan."

## § 414. Removal by Secretary of the Army of sunken water craft generally; liability of owner, lessee, or operator

(a) Whenever the navigation of any river, lake, harbor, sound, bay, canal, or other navigable waters of the United States shall be obstructed or endangered by any sunken vessel, boat, water craft, raft, or other similar obstruction, and such obstruction has existed for a longer period than thirty days, or whenever the abandonment of such obstruction can be legally established in a less space of time, the sunken vessel, boat, water craft, raft, or other obstruction shall be subject to be broken up, removed, sold, or otherwise disposed of by the Secretary of the Army at his discretion, without liability for any damage to the owners of the same: *Provided*, That in his discretion, the Secretary of the Army may cause reasonable notice of such obstruction of not less than thirty days, unless the legal abandonment of the obstruction can be established in a less time, to be given by publication, addressed "To whom it may concern," in a newspaper published nearest to the locality of the obstruction, requiring the removal thereof: *And provided also*, That the Secretary of the Army may, in his discretion, at or after the time of giving such notice, cause sealed proposals to be solicited by public advertisement, giving reasonable notice of not less than ten days, for the removal of such obstruction as soon as possible after the expiration of the above specified thirty days' notice, in case it has not in the meantime been so removed, these proposals and contracts, at his discretion, to be conditioned that such vessel, boat, water craft, raft, or other obstruction, and all cargo and property contained therein, shall become the property of the contractor, and the contract shall be awarded to the bidder making the proposition most advantageous to the United States: *Provided*, That such bidder shall give satisfactory security to execute the work: *Provided further*, That any money received from the sale of any such wreck, or from any contractor for the removal of wrecks, under this paragraph shall be covered into the Treasury of the United States.

(b) The owner, lessee, or operator of such vessel, boat, watercraft, raft, or other obstruction as described in this section shall be liable to the United States for the cost of removal or destruction and disposal as described which exceeds the costs recovered under subsection (a) of this section. Any amount recovered from the owner, lessee, or operator of such vessel pursuant to this subsection to recover costs in excess of the proceeds from the sale or disposition of such vessel shall be deposited in the general fund of the Treasury of the United States.

(Mar. 3, 1899, c. 425, § 19, 30 Stat. 1154; Nov. 17, 1986, Pub.L. 99–662, Title IX, § 939(b), 100 Stat. 4199.)

### HISTORICAL AND STATUTORY NOTES

**Codifications**

Section was enacted as part of the Rivers and Harbors Appropriation Act of 1899, Act Mar. 3, 1899, c. 425, 30 Stat. 1121.

**Change of Name**

The Department of War was designated the Department of the Army and the title of the Secretary of War was changed to Secretary of the Army by section 205(a) of Act July 26, 1947, c. 343, Title II, 61 Stat. 501. Section 205(a) of Act July 26, 1947, was repealed by section 53 of Act Aug. 10, 1956, c. 1041, 70A Stat. 641. Section 1 of Act Aug. 10, 1956, enacted "Title 10, Armed Forces" which in sections 3010 to 3013 continued the Department of the Army under the administrative supervision of a Secretary of the Army.

**Transfer of Functions**

All functions, powers and duties of the Secretary of the Army and other offices and officers of the Department of the Army under section 401 of this title to the extent that they relate generally to the location and clearances of bridges and causeways in the navigable waters of the United States were transferred to and vested in the Secretary of Transportation by Pub.L. 89–670, § 6(g)(6)(A), Oct. 15, 1966, 80 Stat. 941, which created the Department of Transportation, Pub.L. 97–449 amended section 401 of this title to reflect the transfer made by section 6(g)(6)(A) of Pub.L. 89–670, and repealed section 6(g)(6)(A).

For transfer of certain functions insofar as they pertain to the Air Force, and to the extent that they were not previously transferred to the Secretary of the Air Force and Department of the Air Force from the Secretary of the Army and Department of the Army, see Secretary of Defense Transfer Order No. 40 [App. A(57) ], July 22, 1949.

**Prior Provisions**

Section superseded Act June 14, 1880, c. 211, § 4, 21 Stat. 197, and Act Aug. 2, 1882, c. 375, 22 Stat. 208, which required the Secretary of War to give notice to the persons interested in wrecks obstructing navigation of the purpose of the Secretary to remove the same unless such parties should do so, and authorized the Secretary to remove the same on the failure of the parties interested to do so, and to sell the same to the highest bidder, and also authorized the Secretary to dispose of any sunken vessel or cargo before removal.

Section also superseded Act Sept. 19, 1890, c. 907, § 8, 26 Stat. 454, which authorized the Secretary of War to remove wrecks remaining for more than two months.

## § 415. Summary removal of water craft obstructing navigation; liability of owner, lessee, or operator

### (a) Removal authority

Under emergency, in the case of any vessel, boat, water craft, or raft, or other similar obstruction, sinking or grounding, or being unnecessarily delayed in any Government canal or lock, or in any navigable waters mentioned in section 414 of this title, in such manner as to stop, seriously interfere with, or specially endanger navigation, in the opinion of the Secretary of the Army, or any agent of the United States to whom the Secretary may delegate proper authority, the Secretary of the Army or any such agent shall have the right to take immediate possession of such boat, vessel, or other water craft, or raft, so far as to remove or to destroy it and to clear immediately the canal, lock, or navigable waters aforesaid of the obstruction thereby caused, using his best judgment to prevent any unnecessary injury; and no one shall interfere with or prevent such removal or destruction: *Provided,* That the officer or agent charged with the removal or destruction of an obstruction under this section may in his discretion give notice in writing to the owners of any such obstruction requiring them to remove it: *And provided further,* That the actual expense, including administrative expenses, of removing any such obstruction as aforesaid shall be a charge against such craft and cargo; and if the owners thereof fail or refuse to reimburse the United States for such expense within thirty days after notification, then the officer or agent aforesaid may sell the craft or cargo, or any part thereof that may not have been destroyed in removal, and the proceeds of such sale shall be covered into the Treasury of the United States.

### (b) Removal requirement

Not later than 24 hours after the Secretary of the Department in which the Coast Guard is operating issues an order to stop or delay navigation in any navigable waters of the United States because of conditions related to the sinking or grounding of a vessel, the owner or operator of the vessel, with the approval of the Secretary of the Army, shall begin removal of the vessel using the most expeditious removal method available or, if appropriate, secure the vessel pending removal to allow navigation to resume. If the owner or operator fails to begin removal or to secure the vessel pending removal or fails to complete removal on an expedited basis, the Secretary of the Army shall remove or destroy the vessel using the summary removal procedures under subsection (a) of this section.

### (c) Liability of owner, lessee, or operator

The owner, lessee, or operator of such vessel, boat, watercraft, raft, or other obstruction as described in this section shall be liable to the United States for the actual cost, including administrative costs, of removal or destruction and disposal as described which exceeds the costs recovered under subsection (a) of this section. Any amount recovered from the owner, lessee, or operator of such vessel pursuant to this subsection to recover costs in excess of the proceeds from the sale or disposition of such vessel shall be deposited in the general fund of the Treasury of the United States.

(Mar. 3, 1899, c. 425, § 20, 30 Stat. 1154; Nov. 17, 1986, Pub.L. 99–662, Title IX, § 939(b), 100 Stat. 4199; Oct. 12, 1996, Pub.L. 104–303, Title II, § 218(b), 110 Stat. 3696.)

### HISTORICAL AND STATUTORY NOTES

**Codifications**

Section contains part of section 20 of Act Mar. 3, 1899. Another portion of that section appropriating money necessary to execute its provisions is classified to section 416 of this title.

Section 20 of Act Mar. 3, 1899 also contained a repealing clause with a proviso saving pending actions and rights of actions. It was amended by Act Feb. 20, 1900, c. 23, § 3, 31 Stat. 32, and again amended by Act June 13, 1902, c. 1079, § 12, 32 Stat. 375, by adding another proviso which is classified to section 418 of this title.

**Change of Name**

The Department of War was designated the Department of the Army and the title of the Secretary of War was changed to Secretary of the Army by section 205(a) of Act July 26, 1947, c. 343, Title II, 61 Stat. 501. Section 205(a) of Act July 26, 1947, was repealed by section 53 of Act Aug. 10, 1956, c. 1041, 70A Stat. 641. Section 1 of Act Aug. 10, 1956, enacted "Title 10, Armed Forces" which in sections 3010 to 3013 continued the Department of the Army under the administrative supervision of a Secretary of the Army.

**Transfer of Functions**

All functions, powers, and duties of the Secretary of the Army and other offices and officers of the Department of the Army under section 401 of this title to the extent that they relate generally to the location and clearances of bridges and causeways in the navigable waters of the United States were transferred to and vested in the Secretary of Transportation by Pub.L. 89–670, § 6(g)(6)(A), Oct. 15, 1966, 80 Stat. 941, which created the Department of Transportation. Pub.L. 97–449 amended section 401 of this title to reflect the transfer made by section 6(g)(6)(A) of Pub.L. 89–670, and repealed section 6(g)(6)(A).

For transfer of certain functions insofar as they pertain to the Air Force, and to the extent that they were not previously transferred to the Secretary of the Air Force and Department of the Air Force from the Secretary of the Army and Department of the Army, see Secretary of Defense Transfer Order No. 40 [App. A(57) ], July 22, 1949.

## § 416. Appropriations for removal of sunken water craft

Such sum of money as may be necessary to execute sections 414 and 415 of this title is hereby appropriated out of any money in the Treasury not otherwise appropriated, to be paid out on the requisition of the Secretary of the Army.

(Mar. 3, 1899, c. 425, § 20, 30 Stat. 1155; July 26, 1947, c. 343, Title II, § 205(a), 61 Stat. 501.)

### HISTORICAL AND STATUTORY NOTES

**Codifications**

Section contains a portion of section 20 of Act Mar. 3, 1899. See Codification note set out under section 415 of this title.

**Change of Name**

The Department of War was designated the Department of the Army and the title of the Secretary of War was changed to Secretary of the Army by section 205(a) of Act July 26, 1947, c. 343, Title II, 61 Stat. 501. Section 205(a) of Act July 26, 1947, was repealed by section 53 of Act Aug. 10, 1956, c. 1041, 70A Stat. 641. Section 1 of Act Aug. 10, 1956, enacted "Title 10, Armed Forces", which in sections 3010 to 3013 continued the Military Department of the Army under the administrative supervision of a Secretary of the Army.

**Appropriations**

Section 2 of Act June 26, 1934, c. 756, 48 Stat. 1225, which was classified to section 725a of former Title 31, Money and Finance, repealed the permanent appropriation under the title "Removing sunken vessels or craft obstructing or endangering navigation (8x888)" effective July 1, 1935, and provided that such portions of any acts as make permanent appropriations to be expended under such account are amended so as to authorize, in lieu thereof, annual appropriations from the general fund of the Treasury in identical terms and in such amounts as now provided by the laws providing such permanent appropriations.

## § 417. Expenses of investigations by Department of the Army

Expenses incurred by the Engineer Department of the Department of the Army in all investigations, inspections, hearings, reports, service of notice, or other action incidental to examination of plans or sites of bridges or other structures built or proposed to be built in or over navigable waters, or to examinations into alleged violations of laws for the protection and preservation of navigable waters, or to the establishment or marking of harbor lines, shall be payable from any funds which may be available for the improvement, maintenance, operation, or care of the waterways or harbors affected, or if such funds are not available in sums judged by the Chief of Engineers to be adequate, then from any funds available for examinations, surveys, and contingencies of rivers and harbors.

(Mar. 3, 1905, c. 1482, § 6, 33 Stat. 1148; July 26, 1947, c. 343, Title II, § 205(a), 61 Stat. 501.)

### HISTORICAL AND STATUTORY NOTES

**Change of Name**

The Department of War was designated the Department of the Army and the title of the Secretary of War was changed to Secretary of the Army by section 205(a) of Act July 26, 1947, c. 343, Title II, 61 Stat. 501. Section 205(a) of Act July 26, 1947, was repealed by section 53 of Act Aug. 10, 1956, c. 1041, 70A Stat. 641. Section 1 of Act Aug. 10, 1956, enacted "Title 10, Armed Forces", which in sections 3010 to 3013 continued the Military Department of the Army under the administrative supervision of a Secretary of the Army.

**Transfer of Functions**

All functions, powers, and duties of the Secretary of the Army and other offices and officers of the Department of the Army under section 401 of this title to the extent that they relate generally to the location and clearances of bridges and causeways in the navigable waters of the United States were transferred to and vested in the Secretary of Transportation by Pub.L. 89–670, § 6(g)(6)(A), Oct. 15, 1966, 80 Stat. 941, which created the Department of Transportation. Pub.L. 97–449 amended section 401 of this title to reflect the transfer made by section 6(g)(6)(A) of Pub.L. 89–670, and repealed section 6(g)(6)(A).

## § 418. Provisions for protection of New York Harbor unaffected

Nothing contained in sections 401, 403, 404, 406, 407, 408, 409, 411 to 416, and 502 of this title shall be construed as repealing, modifying, or in any manner affecting the provisions of subchapter III of this chapter.

(Mar. 3, 1899, c. 425, § 20, 30 Stat. 1154; Feb. 20, 1900, c. 23, § 3, 31 Stat. 32; June 13, 1902, c. 1079, § 12, 32 Stat. 375.)

### HISTORICAL AND STATUTORY NOTES

**References in Text**

Subchapter III (section 441 et seq.) of this chapter, referred to in text, was in the original a reference to the Act of June 29, 1888, as amended by section 3 of the River and Harbor Act of August 18, 1894.

**Codifications**

Section contains part of section 20 of Act Mar. 3, 1899. See Codification note set out under section 415 of this title.

## § 419. Regulation by Secretary governing transportation and dumping of dredgings, refuse, etc., into navigable waters; oyster lands; appropriations

The Secretary of the Army is authorized and empowered to prescribe regulations to govern the transportation and dumping into any navigable water, or waters adjacent thereto, of dredgings, earth, garbage, and other refuse materials of every kind or description, whenever in his judgment such regulations are required in the interest of navigation. Such regulations shall be posted in conspicuous and appropriate places for the information of the public; and every person or corporation which shall violate the said regulations, or any of them, shall be deemed guilty of a misdemeanor and shall be subject to the penalties prescribed in sections 411 and 412 of this title, for violation of the provisions of section 407 of this title: *Provided,* That any regulations made in pursuance hereof may be enforced as provided in section 413 of this title, the provisions whereof are made applicable to the said regulations: *Provided further,* That this section shall not apply to any waters within the jurisdictional boundaries of any State which are now or may hereafter be used for the cultivation of oysters under the laws of such State, except navigable channels which have been or may hereafter be improved by the United States, or to be designated as navigable channels by competent authority, and in making such improvements of channels, the material dredged shall not be deposited upon any ground in use in accordance with the laws of such State for the cultivation of oysters, except in compliance with said laws: *And provided further,* That any expense necessary in executing this section may be paid from funds available for the improvement of the harbor or waterway, for which regulations may be prescribed, and in case no such funds are available the said expense may be paid from appropriations made by Congress for examinations, surveys, and contingencies of rivers and harbors.

(Mar. 3, 1905, c. 1482, § 4, 33 Stat. 1147.)

### HISTORICAL AND STATUTORY NOTES

**Change of Name**

The Department of War was designated the Department of the Army and the title of the Secretary of War was changed to Secretary of the Army by section 205(a) of Act July 26, 1947, c. 343, Title II, 61 Stat. 501. Section 205(a) of Act July 26, 1947, was repealed by section 53 of Act Aug. 10, 1956, c. 1041, 70A Stat. 641. Section 1 of Act Aug. 10, 1956, enacted "Title 10, Armed Forces" which in sections 3010 to 3013 continued the Department of the Army under the administrative supervision of a Secretary of the Army.

**Transfer of Functions**

All functions, powers, and duties of the Secretary of the Army and other offices and officers of the Department of the Army under section 401 of this title to the extent that they relate generally to the location and clearances of bridges and causeways in the navigable waters of the United States were transferred to and vested in the Secretary of Transportation by Pub.L. 89–670, § 6(g)(6)(A), Oct. 15, 1966, 80 Stat. 941, which created the Department of Transportation. Pub.L. 97–449 amended section 401 of this title to reflect the transfer made by section 6(g)(6)(A) of Pub.L. 89–670, and repealed section 6(g)(6)(A).

## § 419a. Management practices to extend capacity and useful life of dredged material disposal areas

The Secretary of the Army, acting through the Chief of Engineers, shall utilize and encourage the utilization of such management practices as he determines appropriate to extend the capacity and useful life of dredged material disposal areas such that the need for new dredged material disposal areas is kept to a minimum. Management practices authorized by this section shall include, but not be limited to, the construction of dikes, consolidation and dewatering of dredged material, and construction of drainage and outflow facilities.

(Pub.L. 94–587, § 148, Oct. 22, 1976, 90 Stat. 2931.)

## § 420. Piers and cribs on Mississippi and St. Croix Rivers

The owners of sawmills on the Mississippi River and the Saint Croix River in the States of Wisconsin and Minnesota are authorized and empowered under the direction of the Secretary of the Army, to construct piers or cribs in front of their mill property on the banks of the river, for the protection of their mills and rafts against damage by floods and ice: *Provided, however,* That the piers or cribs so constructed shall not interfere with or obstruct the navigation of the river. And in case any pier or crib constructed under authority of this section shall at any time, and for any cause, be found to obstruct the navigation of the river, the Government expressly reserves the right to remove or direct the removal of it, at the cost and expense of the owners thereof.

(R.S. § 5254; May 1, 1882, c. 112, 22 Stat. 52.)

### HISTORICAL AND STATUTORY NOTES

**Codifications**

R.S. § 5254 derived from Act Mar. 3, 1873, c. 278, 17 Stat. 606.

**Change of Name**

The Department of War was designated the Department of the Army and the title of the Secretary of War was changed to Secretary of the Army by section 205(a) of Act July 26, 1947, c. 343, Title II, 61 Stat. 501. Section 205(a) of Act July 26, 1947, was repealed by section 53 of Act Aug. 10, 1956, c. 1041, 70A Stat. 641. Section 1 of Act Aug. 10, 1956, enacted

"Title 10, Armed Forces" which in sections 3010 to 3013 continued the Department of the Army under the administrative supervision of a Secretary of the Army.

**Transfer of Functions**

All functions, powers, and duties of the Secretary of the Army and other offices and officers of the Department of the Army under section 401 of this title to the extent that they relate generally to the location and clearances of bridges and causeways in the navigable waters of the United States were transferred to and vested in the Secretary of Transportation by Pub.L. 89–670, § 6(g)(6)(A), Oct. 15, 1966, 80 Stat. 941, which created the Department of Transportation. Pub.L. 97–449 amended section 401 of this title to reflect the transfer made by section 6(g)(6)(A) of Pub.L. 89–670, and repealed section 6(g)(6)(A).

## § 421. Deposit of refuse, etc., in Lake Michigan near Chicago

It shall not be lawful to throw, discharge, dump, or deposit, or cause, suffer, or procure, to be thrown, discharged, dumped, or deposited, any refuse matter of any kind or description whatever other than that flowing from streets and sewers and passing therefrom in a liquid state into Lake Michigan, at any point opposite or in front of the county of Cook, in the State of Illinois, or the county of Lake in the State of Indiana, within eight miles from the shore of said lake, unless said material shall be placed inside of a breakwater so arranged as not to permit the escape of such refuse material into the body of the lake and cause contamination thereof; and no officer of the Government shall dump or cause or authorize to be dumped any material contrary to the provisions of this section: *Provided, however,* That the provisions of this section shall not apply to work in connection with the construction, repair, and protection of breakwaters and other structures built in aid of navigation, or for the purpose of obtaining water supply. Any person violating any provision of this section shall be guilty of a misdemeanor, and on conviction thereof shall be fined for each offense not exceeding $1,000.

(June 23, 1910, c. 359, 36 Stat. 593.)

### HISTORICAL AND STATUTORY NOTES

**Codifications**

Section is from Act June 23, 1910, popularly known as the Rivers and Harbors Act of 1910.

## § 422. Modification and extension of harbor lines at Chicago

The Secretary of the Army is authorized, in his discretion, to modify and extend harbor lines in front of the city of Chicago in such manner as to permit park extension work which may be desired by the municipal authorities, including the changing and widening of the southern entrance to the Chicago Harbor.

(Aug. 26, 1912, c. 408, § 5, 37 Stat. 626.)

### HISTORICAL AND STATUTORY NOTES

**Codifications**

Section is from Act Aug. 26, 1912, popularly known as the Deficiency Appropriation Act for 1912.

**Change of Name**

The Department of War was designated the Department of the Army and the title of the Secretary of War was changed to Secretary of the Army by section 205(a) of Act July 26, 1947, c. 343, Title II, 61 Stat. 501. Section 205(a) of Act July 26, 1947, was repealed by section 53 of Act Aug. 10, 1956, c. 1041, 70A Stat. 641. Section 1 of Act Aug. 10, 1956, enacted "Title 10, Armed Forces" which in sections 3010 to 3013 continued the Department of the Army under the administrative supervision of a Secretary of the Army.

**Transfer of Functions**

All functions, powers, and duties of the Secretary of the Army and other offices and officers of the Department of the Army under section 401 of this title to the extent that they relate generally to the location and clearances of bridges and causeways in the navigable waters of the United States were transferred to and vested in the Secretary of Transportation by Pub.L. 89–670, § 6(g)(6)(A), Oct. 15, 1966, 80 Stat. 941, which created the Department of Transportation. Pub.L. 97–449 amended section 401 of this title to reflect the transfer made by section 6(g)(6)(A) of Pub.L. 89–670, and repealed section 6(g)(6)(A).

## § 423. Establishment of pierhead and bulkhead lines in Wilmington Harbor, California

The Secretary of the Army is authorized to fix and establish pierhead and bulkhead lines, either or both, in the inner harbor of San Pedro, otherwise known as Wilmington Harbor, California, beyond which no piers, wharves, bulkheads, or other works shall be extended or deposits made except under such regulations as shall be prescribed from time to time by the Secretary of the Army.

(Mar. 26, 1908, No. 14, 35 Stat. 569.)

### HISTORICAL AND STATUTORY NOTES

**Change of Name**

The Department of War was designated the Department of the Army and the title of the Secretary of War was changed to Secretary of the Army by section 205(a) of Act July 26, 1947, c. 343, Title II, 61 Stat. 501. Section 205(a) of Act July 26, 1947, was repealed by section 53 of Act Aug. 10, 1956, c. 1041, 70A Stat. 641. Section 1 of Act Aug. 10, 1956, enacted "Title 10, Armed Forces" which in sections 3010 to 3013 continued the Department of the Army under the administrative supervision of a Secretary of the Army.

**Transfer of Functions**

All functions, powers, and duties of the Secretary of the Army and other offices and officers of the Department of the Army under section 401 of this title to the extent that they relate generally to the location and clearances of bridges and causeways in the navigable waters of the United States were transferred to and vested in the Secretary of Transportation by Pub.L. 89–670, § 6(g)(6)(A), Oct. 15, 1966, 80 Stat. 941, which created the Department of Transportation. Pub.L. 97–449 amended section 401 of this title to reflect the transfer made by section 6(g)(6)(A) of Pub.L. 89–670, and repealed section 6(g)(6)(A).

## § 424. Establishment of pierhead or bulkhead lines in Newport Harbor, California

The Secretary of the Army is authorized and directed to fix and establish pierhead and bulkhead lines, either or both, at Newport Harbor, California, in accordance with plan dated United States Engineer Office, Los Angeles, California, March 25, 1913, and entitled "Newport Bay, California", showing harbor lines, beyond which no piers, wharfs, bulkheads, or other works shall be extended or deposit made, except under such regulations as shall be prescribed from time to time by the Secretary of the Army.

(July 27, 1916, c. 260, § 3, 39 Stat. 411.)

### HISTORICAL AND STATUTORY NOTES

**Codifications**

Section is from Act July 27, 1916, popularly known as the Rivers and Harbors Appropriation Act of 1916.

**Change of Name**

The Department of War was designated the Department of the Army and the title of the Secretary of War was changed to Secretary of the Army by section 205(a) of Act July 26, 1947, c. 343, Title II, 61 Stat. 501. Section 205(a) of Act July 26, 1947, was repealed by section 53 of Act Aug. 10, 1956, c. 1041, 70A Stat. 641. Section 1 of Act Aug. 10, 1956, enacted "Title 10, Armed Forces", which in sections 3010 to 3013 continued the Department of the Army under the administrative supervision of a Secretary of the Army.

**Transfer of Functions**

All functions, powers, and duties of the Secretary of the Army and other offices and officers of the Department of the Army under section 401 of this title to the extent that they relate generally to the location and clearances of bridges and causeways in the navigable waters of the United States were transferred to and vested in the Secretary of Transportation by Pub.L. 89–670, § 6(g)(6)(A), Oct. 15, 1966, 80 Stat. 941, which created the Department of Transportation. Pub.L. 97–449 amended section 401 of this title to reflect the transfer made by section 6(g)(6)(A) of Pub.L. 89–670, and repealed section 6(g)(6)(A).

## § 424a. Modification of harbor lines in Newport Harbor, California

The Secretary of the Army is authorized to modify from time to time, the harbor lines at Newport Harbor, California, established in pursuance of section 424 of this title: *Provided,* That in his opinion such modification will not injuriously affect the interests of navigation.

(Mar. 3, 1925, c. 467, § 10, 43 Stat. 1197.)

### HISTORICAL AND STATUTORY NOTES

**Change of Name**

The Department of War was designated the Department of the Army and the title of the Secretary of War was changed to Secretary of the Army by section 205(a) of Act July 26, 1947, c. 343, Title II, 61 Stat. 501. Section 205(a) of Act July 26, 1947, was repealed by section 53 of Act Aug. 10, 1956, c. 1041, 70A Stat. 641. Section 1 of Act Aug. 10, 1956, enacted "Title 10, Armed Forces" which in sections 3010 to 3013 continued the Department of the Army under the administrative supervision of a Secretary of the Army.

**Transfer of Functions**

All functions, powers, and duties of the Secretary of the Army and other offices and officers of the Department of the Army under section 401 of this title to the extent that they relate generally to the location and clearances of bridges and causeways in the navigable waters of the United States were transferred to and vested in the Secretary of Transportation by Pub.L. 89–670, § 6(g)(6)(A), Oct. 15, 1966, 80 Stat. 941, which created the Department of Transportation. Pub.L. 97–449 amended section 401 of this title to reflect the transfer made by section 6(g)(6)(A) of Pub.L. 89–670, and repealed section 6(g)(6)(A).

## § 425. Omitted

### HISTORICAL AND STATUTORY NOTES

**Codifications**

Section, Act June 7, 1924, c. 316, § 9, 43 Stat. 606, directed Secretary of War to investigate depositing of polluting substances into navigable streams and report the results to Congress not later than two years from June 7, 1924.

## § 426. Investigations concerning erosion of shores of coastal and lake waters

The Chief of Engineers of the United States Army, under the direction of the Secretary of the Army, is authorized and directed to cause investigations and studies to be made in cooperation with the appropriate agencies of the various States on the Atlantic, Pacific, and gulf coasts and on the Great Lakes, and of the States of Alaska and Hawaii, the Commonwealth of Puerto Rico, and the possessions of the United States, with a view to devising effective means of preventing erosion of the shores of coastal and lake waters by waves and currents; and any expenses incident and necessary thereto may be paid from funds appropriated for General Investigations, Civil Functions, Department of the Army: *Provided,* That the Department of the Army may release to the appropriate cooperating agencies information obtained by these investigations and studies prior to the formal transmission of reports to Congress: *Provided further,* That no money shall be expended under authority of this section in any State which does not provide for cooperation with the agents of the United States and contribute to the project such funds or services as the Secretary of the Army may deem appropriate and require; that there shall be organized under the Chief of Engineers,

United States Army, a Board of seven members, of whom four shall be officers of the Corps of Engineers and three shall be civilian engineers selected by the Chief of Engineers with regard to their special fitness in the field of beach erosion and shore protection. The Board will furnish such technical assistance as may be directed by the Chief of Engineers in the conduct of such studies as may be undertaken and will review the reports of the investigations made. In the consideration of such studies as may be referred to the Board by the Chief of Engineers, the Board shall, when it considers it necessary and with the sanction of the Chief of Engineers, make, as a board or through its members, personal examination of localities under investigation: *Provided further*, That the civilian members of the Board may be paid at rates not to exceed $100 a day for each day of attendance at Board meetings, not to exceed thirty days per annum, in addition to the traveling and other necessary expenses connected with their duties on the Board in accordance with the provisions of section 5703 of Title 5.

(July 3, 1930, c. 847, § 2, 46 Stat. 945; July 14, 1960, Pub.L. 86–645, Title I, § 103, 74 Stat. 484.)

## HISTORICAL AND STATUTORY NOTES

**References in Text**

The Board, referred to in text, means the Beach Erosion Board, which was abolished by Pub.L. 88–172, § 1, Nov. 7, 1963, 77 Stat. 304. See note set out below.

**Codifications**

"Section 5703 of Title 5" was substituted for "section 5 of the Administrative Expenses Act of 1946, as amended (5 U.S.C. 73b–2)", on authority of Pub.L. 89–554, § 7(b), Sept. 6, 1966, 80 Stat. 631, the first section of which enacted Title 5, Government Organization and Employees.

**Great Lakes Levels Study**

Pub.L. 99–662, Title VII, § 706, Nov. 17, 1986, 100 Stat. 4158, provided that:

"(a) The Secretary, in cooperation with the National Oceanic and Atmospheric Administration, the Federal Emergency Management Agency, the International Joint Commission, and other appropriate Federal, State, and local agencies and the private sector, is authorized to conduct a study of shoreline protection and beach erosion control policy and related projects of the Secretary, in view of the current situation and long-term expected increases in the levels of the Great Lakes. Such study shall include, but is not limited to—

"(1) a study to determine the magnitude and extent of current and expected future shoreline erosion on the Great Lakes and connecting channels occurring as a result of high water levels. The study shall examine the impacts of the long-term cold weather cycle on lake levels and shoreline damage. The study shall also examine the relationship of shoreline damage to the regulation of outflows from Lake Superior and Lake Erie in accordance with approved regulation plans of the International Joint Commission;

"(2) an economic and hydrologic analysis to determine whether changes in the inflows and outflows of the existing structures may be desirable to reduce shoreline damages, and whether further regulation of the outflow of Lake Erie may be warranted to achieve better regulation of the water levels of the Great Lakes;

"(3) a summary of the legal and institutional impacts of rising lake levels on riparian lands; and

"(4) recommendations for new or additional criteria for Federal participation in shoreline protection projects along the Great Lakes and connecting channels.

"(b) Within three years after the date of enactment of this Act [Nov. 17, 1986], the Secretary shall transmit the studies prepared pursuant to subsection (a) of this section, together with supporting documentation and the recommendations of the Secretary, to the Committee on Environment and Public Works of the Senate and Committee on Public Works and Transportation of the House of Representatives.

"(c) For the purposes of this section, there is authorized to be appropriated to the Secretary for the fiscal year ending September 30, 1987, or thereafter, the sum of $3,000,000, such sum to remain available until expended."

[Any reference in any provision of law enacted before Jan. 4, 1995, to the Committee on Public Works and Transportation of the House of Representatives treated as referring to the Committee on Transportation and Infrastructure of the House of Representatives, see section 1(a)(9) of Pub.L. 104–14, set out as a note preceding section 21 of Title 2, The Congress.]

**Study of Rising Oceans**

Pub.L. 99–662, Title VII, § 731, Nov. 17, 1986, 100 Stat. 4165, provided that:

"(a) The Congress finds that increasing scientific evidence indicates the level of the oceans will rise significantly over the next seventy-five years.

"(b) The Secretary, in cooperation with the National Oceanic and Atmospheric Administration, the Federal Emergency Management Agency, and other appropriate Federal, State, and local agencies and the private sector, is authorized to conduct a study of shoreline protection and beach erosion control policy and related projects of the Secretary, in view of the prospect for long-term increases in the levels of the ocean. Such study shall include, but is not limited to—

"(1) an assessment of the probability and the extent of coastal flooding and erosion;

"(2) an appraisal of various strategies for managing relocation, disinvestment, and reinvestment in coastal communities exposed to coastal flooding and erosion;

"(3) a summary of the legal and institutional impact of rising sea level on riparian lands; and

"(4) recommendations for new or additional criteria for Federal participation in shoreline protection projects.

"(c) Within three years after the date of enactment of this Act [Nov. 17, 1986], the Secretary shall transmit the study prepared pursuant to subsection (b) of this section, together with supporting documentation and the recommendations of the Secretary, to the Committee on Environment and Public Works of the Senate and the Committee on Public Works and Transportation of the House of Representatives.

"(d) There is authorized to be appropriated $3,000,000 for fiscal years beginning after September 30, 1986, to carry out this section, such sum to remain available until expended."

[Any reference in any provision of law enacted before Jan. 4, 1995, to the Committee on Public Works and Transportation of the House of Representatives treated as referring to the Committee on Transportation and Infrastructure of the House of Representatives, see section 1(a)(9) of Pub.L. 104–14, set out as a note preceding section 21 of Title 2, The Congress.]

**Abolition of Beach Erosion Board**

Pub.L. 88–172, § 1, Nov. 7, 1963, 77 Stat. 304, provided in part: "That the Board established by section 2 of the River and Harbor Act approved July 3, 1930, as amended (33 U.S.C. 426), referred to as the Beach Erosion Board, is hereby abolished." For the transfer of functions of the Beach Erosion Board to the Coastal Engineering Research Center and the Board of Engineers for Rivers and Harbors, see sections 426–1 and 426–3 of this title.

**Application of Existing Law to Surveys Relating to Shore Protection**

Pub.L. 87–874, § 103(b), Oct. 23, 1962, 76 Stat. 1179, provided that: "All provisions of existing law relating to surveys of rivers and harbors shall apply to surveys relating to shore protection and section 2 of the River and Harbor Act approved July 3, 1930, as amended (33 U.S.C. 426), is modified to the extent inconsistent herewith."

## § 426–1. Coastal Engineering Research Center; establishment; powers and functions

There shall be established under the Chief of Engineers, United States Army, a Coastal Engineering Research Center which, except as hereinafter provided in section 426–3 of this title, shall be vested with all the functions of the Beach Erosion Board, including the authority to make general investigations as provided in section 426a of this title, and such additional functions as the Chief of Engineers may assign.

(Pub.L. 88–172, § 1, Nov. 7, 1963, 77 Stat. 304.)

### HISTORICAL AND STATUTORY NOTES

**Codifications**

Section was enacted as part of section 1 of Pub.L. 88–172. The remainder of said section 1, abolishing the Beach Erosion Board, is classified as a note under section 426 of this title.

**Abolition of Beach Erosion Board**

Section 1 of Pub.L. 88–172 provided in part for the abolition of the Beach Erosion Board, and is set out as a note under section 426 of this title. For the transfer of certain functions of said Board to the Board of Engineers for Rivers and Harbors, see section 426–3 of this title.

## § 426–2. Board on Coastal Engineering Research

The functions of the Coastal Engineering Research Center established by section 426–1 of this title, shall be conducted with the guidance and advice of a Board on Coastal Engineering Research, constituted by the Chief of Engineers in the same manner as the present Beach Erosion Board.

(Pub.L. 88–172, § 2, Nov. 7, 1963, 77 Stat. 305.)

### HISTORICAL AND STATUTORY NOTES

**Compensation of Board**

Pub.L. 91–611, Title I, § 105, Dec. 31, 1970, 84 Stat. 1819, provided that: "The civilian members of the Board on Coastal Engineering Research authorized by the Act of November 7, 1963 (33 U.S.C. 426–2) may be paid at rates not to exceed the daily equivalent of the rate for GS–18 for each day of attendance at Board meetings, not to exceed thirty days per year, in addition to the traveling and other necessary expenses connected with their duties on the Board in accordance with the provisions of 5 U.S.C. 5703(b), (d), and 5707."

**Abolition of Beach Erosion Board**

Section 1 of Pub.L. 88–172 provided in part for the abolition of the Beach Erosion Board, and is set out as a note under section 426 of this title. For transfer of functions of the Board to the Coastal Engineering Research Center and the Board of Engineers for Rivers and Harbors, see sections 426–1 and 426–3 of this title.

## § 426–3. Transfer of functions of Beach Erosion Board

All functions of the Beach Erosion Board pertaining to review of reports of investigations made concerning erosion of the shores of coastal and lake waters, and the protection of such shores, are hereby transferred to the Board established by section 541 of this title, referred to as the Board of Engineers for Rivers and Harbors.

(Pub.L. 88–172, § 3, Nov. 7, 1963, 77 Stat. 305.)

### HISTORICAL AND STATUTORY NOTES

**Termination of Board of Engineers for Rivers and Harbors and Reassignment of Duties and Responsibilities**

For termination of Board of Engineers for Rivers and Harbors 180 days after Oct. 31, 1992, and reassignment of duties and responsibilities by Secretary of Army, see section 223 of Pub.L. 102–580, set out as a note under 33 U.S.C.A. § 541.

**Abolition of Beach Erosion Board**

All functions of the Beach Erosion Board pertaining to review of reports of investigations made concerning erosion of the shores of coastal and lake waters, and the protection of such shores, are hereby transferred to the Board established by section 541 of this title, referred to as the Board of Engineers for Rivers and Harbors.

## § 426a. Additional investigations concerning erosion of shores of coastal and lake waters; payment of costs; "shores" defined

In addition to participating in cooperative investigations and studies with agencies of the various States as authorized in section 426 of this title, it shall be the duty of the Chief of Engineers, through the Coastal Engineering Research Center, to make general investigations with a view to preventing erosion of the shores of the United States by waves and currents and determining the most suitable methods for the protection, restoration, and development of beaches; and to publish from time to time such useful data and information concerning the erosion and protection of beaches and shore lines as the Center may deem to be of value to the people of the United States. The cost of the general investigations authorized by sections 426a to 426d of this title shall be borne wholly by the United States. As used in said sections, the word "shores" includes the shore lines of the Atlantic and Pacific Oceans, the Gulf of Mexico, the Great Lakes, Lake Champlain, and estuaries and bays directly connected therewith.

(July 31, 1945, c. 334, § 1, 59 Stat. 508; Nov. 7, 1963, Pub.L. 88–172, § 1, 77 Stat. 304.)

### HISTORICAL AND STATUTORY NOTES

**Codifications**

Coastal Engineering Research Center has been substituted for Beach Erosion Board pursuant to Pub.L. 88–172, § 1, providing in part for the abolition of the Beach Erosion Board, which is set out as a note under section 426 of this title. For transfer of investigatory functions of the Beach Erosion Board to the Coastal Engineering Research Center, see section 426–1 of this title.

## § 426b. Applicability of existing laws; projects referred to Board of Engineers for Rivers and Harbors

All provisions of existing law relating to examinations and surveys and to works of improvement of rivers and harbors shall apply, insofar as practicable, to examinations and surveys and to works of improvement relating to shore protection; except that all projects having to do with shore protection shall be referred for consideration and recommendation to the Board of Engineers for Rivers and Harbors.

(July 31, 1945, c. 334, § 2, 59 Stat. 508; Nov. 7, 1963, Pub.L. 88–172, § 1, 77 Stat. 304.)

### HISTORICAL AND STATUTORY NOTES

**Codifications**

Provision for the referral of projects having to do with shore protection for consideration and recommendation to the Beach Erosion Board have been omitted as obsolete in view of the abolition of the Beach Erosion Board and the transfer of its review function to the Board of Engineers for Rivers and Harbors by Pub.L. 88–172, § 1. See section 426–3 of this title.

**Termination of Board of Engineers for Rivers and Harbors and Reassignment of Duties and Responsibilities**

For termination of Board of Engineers for Rivers and Harbors 180 days after Oct. 31, 1992, and reassignment of duties and responsibilities by Secretary of Army, see section 223 of Pub.L. 102–580, set out as a note under 33 U.S.C.A. § 541.

## § 426c. Report by Coastal Engineering Research Center

The Coastal Engineering Research Center, in making its report on any cooperative investigation and studies under the provisions of section 426 of this title, relating to shore protection work shall, in addition to any other matters upon which it may be required to report, state its opinion as to (a) the advisability of adopting the project; (b) what public interest, if any, is involved in the proposed improvement; and (c) what share of the expense, if any, should be borne by the United States.

(July 31, 1945, c. 334, § 3, 59 Stat. 508; Nov. 7, 1963, Pub.L. 88–172, § 1, 77 Stat. 304.)

### HISTORICAL AND STATUTORY NOTES

**Codifications**

Coastal Engineering Research Center has been substituted for Beach Erosion Board pursuant to Pub.L. 88–172, § 1, providing in part for the abolition of the Beach Erosion Board, which is set out as a note under section 426 of this title. For transfer of investigatory functions of the Beach Erosion Board to the Coastal Engineering Research Center see section 426–1 of this title.

## § 426d. Payment of expenses

Any expenses incident and necessary in the undertaking of the general investigations authorized by sections 426a to 426d of this title may be paid from funds appropriated prior to or after July 31, 1945, for examinations, surveys, and contingencies for rivers and harbors.

(July 31, 1945, c. 334, § 4, 59 Stat. 508.)

## § 426e. Federal aid in protection of shores

**(a) Declaration of policy**

With the purpose of preventing damage to the shores and beaches of the United States, its Territories and possessions and promoting and encouraging the healthful recreation of the people, it is declared to be the policy of the United States, subject to sections 426e to 426h–1 of this title, to promote shore protection projects and related research that encourage the protection, restoration, and enhancement of sandy beaches, including beach restoration and periodic beach nourishment, on a comprehensive and coordinated basis by the Federal Government, States, localities, and private enterprises. In carrying out this policy, preference shall be given to areas in which there has been a Federal investment of funds and areas with respect to which the need for prevention or mitigation of damage to shores and beaches is attributable to Federal navigation projects or other Federal activities.

**(b) Federal contribution; maximum amount; exceptions**

The Federal contribution in the case of any project referred to in subsection (a) of this section shall not exceed one-half of the cost of the project, and the remainder shall be paid by the State, municipality, or other political subdivision in which the project is located, except that (1) the costs allocated to the restoration and protection of Federal property shall be borne fully by the Federal Government, (2) Federal participation in the cost of a project for restoration and protection of State, county, and other publicly owned shore parks and conservation areas may be, in the discretion of the Chief of Engineers, not more than 70 per centum of the total cost exclusive of land costs, when such areas: Include a zone which excludes permanent human habitation; include but are not limited to recreational beaches; satisfy adequate criteria for conservation and development of the natural resources of the environment; extend landward a sufficient distance to include, where appropriate, protective dunes, bluffs, or other natural features which serve to protect the uplands from damage; and provide essentially full park facilities for appropriate public use, all of which shall meet with the approval of the Chief of Engineers, and (3) Federal participation in the cost of a project providing hurricane protection may be, in the discretion of the Secretary[1] not more than 70 per centum of the total cost exclusive of land costs.

**(c) Periodic beach nourishment; "construction" defined**

When in the opinion of the Chief of Engineers the most suitable and economical remedial measures would be provided by periodic beach nourishment, the term "construction" may be construed for the purposes of sections 426e to 426h–1 of this title to include the deposit of sand fill at suitable intervals of time to furnish sand supply to project shores for a length of time specified by the Chief of Engineers.

**(d) Shores other than public**

Shores other than public will be eligible for Federal assistance if there is benefit such as that arising from public use or from the protection of nearby public property or if the benefits to those shores are incidental to the project, and the Federal contribution to the project shall be adjusted in accordance with the degree of such benefits.

**(e) Authorization of projects**

**(1) In general**

No Federal contributions shall be made with respect to a project under sections 426e to 426h–1 of this title unless the plan therefor shall have been specifically adopted and authorized by Congress after investigation and study by the Coastal Engineering Research Center under the provisions of section 426 of this title as amended and supplemented, or, in the case of a small project under section 426g or 426h of this title, unless the plan therefor has been approved by the Chief of Engineers.

**(2) Studies**

**(A) In general**

The Secretary shall—

**(i)** recommend to Congress studies concerning shore protection projects that meet the criteria established under sections 426e to 426h–1 of this title (including subparagraph (B)(iii)) and other applicable law;

**(ii)** conduct such studies as Congress requires under applicable laws; and

**(iii)** report the results of the studies to the Committee on Environment and Public Works of the Senate and the Committee on Transportation and Infrastructure of the House of Representatives.

**(B) Recommendations for shore protection projects**

**(i) In general**

The Secretary shall recommend to Congress the authorization or reauthorization of shore protection projects based on the studies conducted under subparagraph (A).

**(ii) Considerations**

In making recommendations, the Secretary shall consider the economic and ecological benefits of the shore protection project.

**(C) Coordination of projects**

In conducting studies and making recommendations for a shore protection project under this paragraph, the Secretary shall—

**(i)** determine whether there is any other project being carried out by the Secretary or the head of another Federal agency that may be complementary to the shore protection project; and

**(ii)** if there is such a complementary project, describe the efforts that will be made to coordinate the projects.

**(3) Shore protection projects**

**(A) In general**

The Secretary shall construct, or cause to be constructed, any shore protection project authorized by Congress, or separable element of such a project, for which funds have been appropriated by Congress.

**(B) Agreements**

**(i) Requirement**

After authorization by Congress, and before commencement of construction, of a shore protection project or separable element, the Secretary shall enter into a written agreement with a non-Federal interest with respect to the project or separable element.

**(ii) Terms**

The agreement shall—

**(I)** specify the life of the project; and

**(II)** ensure that the Federal Government and the non-Federal interest will cooperate in carrying out the project or separable element.

**(C) Coordination of projects**

In constructing a shore protection project or separable element under this paragraph, the Secretary shall, to the extent practicable, coordinate the project or element with any complementary project identified under paragraph (2)(C).

(Aug. 13, 1946, c. 960, § 1, 60 Stat. 1056; July 28, 1956, c. 768, 70 Stat. 702; Oct. 23, 1962, Pub.L. 87–874, Title I, § 103(a)(1)–(3), 76 Stat. 1178; Nov. 7, 1963, Pub.L. 88–172, § 1, 77 Stat. 304; Dec. 31, 1970, Pub.L. 91–611, Title II, § 208, 84 Stat. 1829; Oct. 12, 1996, Pub.L. 104–303, Title II, § 227(a), (b), (e)(2)(A), (B), 110 Stat. 3698, 3703.)

1 So in original. Probably should be followed by a comma.

## HISTORICAL AND STATUTORY NOTES

**Codifications**

Coastal Engineering Research Center, referred to in subsec. (e), has been substituted for Beach Erosion Board pursuant to Pub.L. 88–172, § 1, providing in part for the abolition of the Beach Erosion Board and for transfer of functions of the Beach Erosion Board to the Coastal Engineering Research Center. See section 426–1 of this title.

**Beach Recreation**

Pub.L. 106–541, Title II, § 220, Dec. 11, 2000, 114 Stat. 2596, provided that: "Not later than 1 year after the date of enactment of this Act [Dec. 11, 2000], the Secretary shall develop and implement procedures to ensure that all of the benefits of a beach restoration project, including those benefits attributable to recreation, hurricane and storm damage reduction, and environmental protection and restoration, are displayed in reports for such projects."

**Shore Management Program**

Pub.L. 106–53, Title II, § 213, Aug. 17, 1999, 113 Stat. 291, provided that:

"(a) **Review.**—The Secretary shall review the implementation of the Corps of Engineers shore management program, with particular attention to—

"(1) inconsistencies in implementation among the divisions and districts of the Corps of Engineers; and

"(2) complaints by or potential inequities regarding property owners in the Savannah District, including an accounting of the number and disposition of complaints in the Savannah District during the 5-year period preceding the date of enactment of this Act [Aug. 17, 1999].

"(b) **Report.**—As expeditiously as practicable, but not later than 1 year after the date of enactment of this Act [Aug. 17, 1999], the Secretary shall submit to the Committee on Transportation and Infrastructure of the House of Representatives and the Committee on Environment and Public Works of the Senate a report describing the results of the review under subsection (a)."

**Report on Shores of the United States**

Pub.L. 106–53, Title II, § 215(c), Aug. 17, 1999, 113 Stat. 293, provided that:

"(1) **In general.**—Not later than 3 years after the date of enactment of this Act [Aug. 17, 1999], the Secretary shall report to Congress on the state of the shores of the United States.

"(2) **Contents.**—The report shall include—

"(A) a description of—

"(i) the extent of, and economic and environmental effects caused by, erosion and accretion along the shores of the United States; and

"(ii) the causes of such erosion and accretion;

"(B) a description of resources committed by Federal, State, and local governments to restore and renourish shores;

"(C) a description of the systematic movement of sand along the shores of the United States; and

"(D) recommendations regarding—

"(i) appropriate levels of Federal and non-Federal participation in shore protection; and

"(ii) use of a systems approach to sand management.

"(3) **Use of specific location data.**—In developing the report, the Secretary shall use data from specific locations on the coasts of the Atlantic Ocean, Pacific Ocean, Great Lakes, and Gulf of Mexico."

**Report to Congress on Shoreline Protection Programs**

Pub.L. 101–640, Title III, § 309, Nov. 28, 1990, 104 Stat. 4638, provided that: "Not later than 1 year after the date of the enactment of this Act [Nov. 28, 1990], the Secretary shall transmit to Congress a report on the advisability of not participating in the planning, implementation, or maintenance of any beach stabilization or renourishment project involving Federal funds unless the State in which the proposed project will be located has established or committed to establish a beach front management program that includes—

"(1) restrictions on new development seaward of an erosion setback line (based on preproject beach size) of at least 30 times the annual erosion rate;

"(2) restrictions on construction of new structural stabilization projects, such as seawalls and groins, and their reconstruction if damaged by 50 percent or more;

"(3) provisions for the relocation of structures in erosion-prone areas;

"(4) provisions to assure public access to beaches stabilized or renourished with Federal funds after January 1, 1991; and

"(5) such other provisions as the Secretary may prescribe by regulation to prevent hazardous or environmentally damaging shoreline development."

## § 426f. Reimbursements

### (a) In general

The Secretary is authorized to reimburse non-Federal interests for work done by them, after initiation of the survey studies which form the basis for the project or separable element of the project, on authorized projects or separable elements which individually do not exceed $1,000,000 in total cost: *Provided,* That the work which may have been done on the projects or separable elements is approved by the Chief of Engineers as being in accordance with the authorized projects or separable elements: *Provided further,* That such reimbursement shall be subject to appropriations applicable thereto or funds available therefor and shall not take precedence over other pending projects or separable elements of higher priority for improvements.

### (b) Agreements

#### (1) Requirement

After authorization of reimbursement by the Secretary under this section, and before commencement of construction, of a shore protection project, the Secretary shall enter into a written agreement with the non-Federal interest with respect to the project or separable element.

#### (2) Terms

The agreement shall—

(A) specify the life of the project; and

(B) ensure that the Federal Government and the non-Federal interest will cooperate in carrying out the project or separable element.

(Aug. 13, 1946, c. 960, § 2, 60 Stat. 1056; July 28, 1956, c. 768, 70 Stat. 703; Oct. 23, 1962, Pub.L. 87–874, Title I, § 103(a)(4), 76 Stat. 1178; Oct. 12, 1996, Pub.L. 104–303, Title II, § 227(c)(1), 110 Stat. 3699.)

### HISTORICAL AND STATUTORY NOTES

**Change of Name**

The Department of War was designated the Department of the Army and the title of the Secretary of War was changed to Secretary of the Army by section 205(a) of Act July 26, 1947, c. 343, Title II, 61 Stat. 501. Section 205(a) of Act July 26, 1947, was repealed by section 53 of Act Aug. 10, 1956, c. 1041, 70A Stat. 641. Section 1 of Act Aug. 10, 1956, enacted "Title 10, Armed Forces" which in sections 3010 to 3013 continued the Department of the Army under the administrative supervision of a Secretary of the Army.

**Transfer of Functions**

All functions, powers, and duties of the Secretary of the Army and other offices and officers of the Department of the Army under section 401 of this title to the extent that they relate generally to the location and clearances of bridges and causeways in the navigable waters of the United States were transferred to and vested in the Secretary of Transportation by Pub.L. 89–670, § 6(g)(6)(A), Oct. 15, 1966, 80 Stat. 941, which created the Department of Transportation. Pub.L. 97–449 amended section 401 of this title to reflect the transfer made by section 6(g)(6)(A) of Pub.L. 89–670, and repealed section 6(g)(6)(A).

## § 426g. Authorization of small projects not specifically authorized; expenditures; local cooperation; work to be complete; exceptions

The Secretary is authorized to undertake construction of small shore and beach restoration and protection projects not specifically authorized by Congress, which otherwise comply with section 426e of this title, when he finds that such work is advisable, and he is further authorized to allot from any appropriations hereafter made for civil works, not to exceed $30,000,000 for any one fiscal year for the Federal share of the costs of construction of such projects: *Provided,* That not more than $3,000,000 shall be allotted for this purpose for any single project and the total amount allotted shall be sufficient to complete the Federal participation in the project under this section including periodic nourishment as provided for under section 426e(c) of this title: *Provided further,* That the provisions of local cooperation specified in section 426e of this title shall apply: *And provided further,* That the work shall be complete in itself and shall not commit the United States to any additional improvement to insure its successful operation, except for participation in periodic beach nourishment in accordance with section 426e(c) of this title, and as may result from the normal procedure applying to projects authorized after submission of survey reports.

(Aug. 13, 1946, c. 960, § 3, 60 Stat. 1056; July 28, 1956, c. 768, 70 Stat. 703; Oct. 23, 1962, Pub.L. 87–874, Title I, § 103(a)(4), 76 Stat. 1178; Oct. 27, 1965, Pub.L. 89–298, Title III, § 310(b), 79 Stat. 1095; Dec. 31, 1970, Pub.L. 91–611, Title I, § 112(b), 84 Stat. 1821; Nov. 17, 1986, Pub.L. 99–662, Title IX, § 915(e), 100 Stat. 4191; Oct. 12, 1996, Pub.L. 104–303, Title II, § 227(e)(2)(C), 110 Stat. 3703; Aug. 17, 1999, Pub.L. 106–53, Title II, § 226, 113 Stat. 298.)

### HISTORICAL AND STATUTORY NOTES

**Effective and Applicability Provisions**

1986 Acts

Section 915(i) of Pub.L. 99–662 provided that: "The amendments made by this section [enacting section 2290 of this title and amending sections 426g, 426i, 577, 603a, 701g, 701r, and 701s of this title] shall not apply to any project under contract for construction on the date of enactment of this Act [Nov. 17, 1986]."

1970 Acts

Section 915(i) of Pub. L. 99-662 provided that: "The amendments made by this section [amending this section and sections 426i, 577, 603a, 701g, 701r, and 701s of this title] shall not apply to any project under contract for construction on the date of enactment of this Act [Nov. 17, 1986]."

**Change of Name**

The Department of War was designated the Department of the Army and the title of the Secretary of War was changed to Secretary of the Army by section 205(a) of Act July 26, 1947, c. 343, Title II, 61 Stat. 501. Section 205(a) of Act July 26, 1947, was repealed by section 53 of Act Aug. 10, 1956, c. 1041, 70A Stat. 641. Section 1 of Aug. 10, 1956, enacted "Title 10, Armed Forces" which in sections 3010 to 3013 continued the Department of the Army under the administrative supervision of a Secretary of the Army.

**Transfer of Functions**

All functions, powers, and duties of the Secretary of the Army and other offices and officers of the Department of the Army under section 401 of this title to the extent that they relate generally to the location and clearances of bridges and causeways in the navigable waters of the United States were transferred to and vested in the Secretary of Transportation by Pub.L. 89–670, § 6(g)(6)(A), Oct. 15, 1966, 80 Stat. 941, which created the Department of Transportation. Pub.L. 97–449 amended section 401 of this title to reflect the transfer made by section 6(g)(6)(A) of Pub.L. 89–670, and repealed section 6(g)(6)(A).

**Projects Under Contract for Construction on December 31, 1970**

Section 112(c) of Pub.L. 91–611 provided that: "The amendments made by this section [to this section and section 577(a), (b) of this title] shall not apply to any project under contract for construction on the date of enactment of this Act [Dec. 31, 1970]."

## § 426g–1. State and regional plans

The Secretary may—

(1) cooperate with any State in the preparation of a comprehensive State or regional plan for the conservation of coastal resources located within the boundaries of the State;

(2) encourage State participation in the implementation of the plan; and

(3) submit to Congress reports and recommendations with respect to appropriate Federal participation in carrying out the plan.

(Aug. 13, 1946, c. 960, § 4, as added Oct. 12, 1996, Pub.L. 104–303, Title II, § 227(d)(2), 110 Stat. 3700.)

### HISTORICAL AND STATUTORY NOTES

**Prior Provisions**

A prior section 4 of Act Aug. 13, 1946, was renumbered section 5 of that Act, and was classified to section 426h of this title prior to repeal by Pub.L. 104–303.

## § 426h. National shoreline erosion control development and demonstration program

**(a) Establishment of erosion control program**

The Secretary shall establish and conduct a national shoreline erosion control development and demonstration program for a period of 6 years beginning on the date that funds are made available to carry out this section.

**(b) Requirements**

**(1) In general**

The erosion control program shall include provisions for—

(A) projects consisting of planning, designing, and constructing prototype engineered and vegetative shoreline erosion control devices and methods during the first 3 years of the erosion control program;

(B) adequate monitoring of the prototypes throughout the duration of the erosion control program;

(C) detailed engineering and environmental reports on the results of each demonstration project carried out under the erosion control program; and

(D) technology transfers to private property owners and State and local entities.

**(2) Emphasis**

The projects carried out under the erosion control program shall emphasize, to the extent practicable—

(A) the development and demonstration of innovative technologies;

(B) efficient designs to prevent erosion at a shoreline site, taking into account the life-cycle cost of the design, including cleanup, maintenance, and amortization;

(C) natural designs, including the use of vegetation or temporary structures that minimize permanent structural alterations;

(D) the avoidance of negative impacts to adjacent shorefront communities;

(E) in areas with substantial residential or commercial interests adjacent to the shoreline, designs that do not impair the aesthetic appeal of the interests;

(F) the potential for long-term protection afforded by the technology; and

(G) recommendations developed from evaluations of the original 1974 program established under the Shoreline Erosion Control Demonstration Act of 1974 (42 U.S.C. 1962d–5 note; 88 Stat. 26), including—

(i) adequate consideration of the subgrade;

(ii) proper filtration;

(iii) durable components;

(iv) adequate connection between units; and

(v) consideration of additional relevant information.

(3) Sites

(A) In general

Each project under the erosion control program shall be carried out at a privately owned site with substantial public access, or a publicly owned site, on open coast or on tidal waters.

(B) Selection

The Secretary shall develop criteria for the selection of sites for the projects, including—

(i) a variety of geographical and climatic conditions;

(ii) the size of the population that is dependent on the beaches for recreation, protection of homes, or commercial interests;

(iii) the rate of erosion;

(iv) significant natural resources or habitats and environmentally sensitive areas; and

(v) significant threatened historic structures or landmarks.

(C) Areas

Projects under the erosion control program shall be carried out at not fewer than—

(i) 2 sites on each of the shorelines of the Atlantic and Pacific coasts, including the city of Miami Beach, Florida;

(ii) 2 sites on the shoreline of the Great Lakes; and

(iii) 1 site on the shoreline of the Gulf of Mexico.

(4) Determination of feasibility

Implementation of a project under this section is contingent upon a determination by the Secretary that such project is feasible.

(c) Consultation

(1) Parties

The Secretary shall carry out the erosion control program in consultation with—

(A) the Secretary of Agriculture, particularly with respect to vegetative means of preventing and controlling shoreline erosion;

(B) Federal, State, and local agencies;

(C) private organizations;

(D) the Coastal Engineering Research Center established under section 426–1 of this title; and

(E) university research facilities.

(2) Agreements

The consultation described in paragraph (1) may include entering into agreements with other Federal, State, or local agencies or private organizations to carry out functions described in subsection (b)(1) of this section when appropriate.

(d) Report

Not later than 60 days after the conclusion of the erosion control program, the Secretary shall prepare and submit an erosion control program final report to the Committee on Environment and Public Works of the Senate and the Committee on Transportation and Infrastructure of the House of Representatives. The report shall include a comprehensive evaluation of the erosion control program and recommendations regarding the continuation of the erosion control program.

(e) Funding

(1) Responsibility

The cost of and responsibility for operation and maintenance (excluding monitoring) of a demonstration project under the erosion control program shall be borne by non-Federal interests on completion of construction of the demonstration project.

(2) Authorization of appropriations

There is authorized to be appropriated $21,000,000 to carry out this section.

(Aug. 13, 1946, c. 960, § 5, as added Oct. 12, 1996, Pub.L. 104–303, Title II, § 227(e)(1), 110 Stat. 3700, and amended Pub.L. 106–53, Title V, § 581, Aug. 17, 1999, 113 Stat. 375.)

HISTORICAL AND STATUTORY NOTES

**References in Text**

The Shoreline Erosion Control Demonstration Act of 1974, referred to in subsec. (b)(2)(G), is Pub.L. 93–251, Title I, § 54, Mar. 7, 1974, 88 Stat. 26, which is set out as a note under section 1962d–5 of Title 42, The Public Health and Welfare.

**Prior Provisions**

A prior section, Act Aug. 13, 1946, c. 960, § 5, formerly § 4, 60 Stat. 1057; July 28, 1956, c. 768, 70 Stat. 703, renumbered § 5, Oct. 12, 1996, Pub.L. 104–303, Title II, § 227(d)(1), 110 Stat. 3700, which defined the word "shores" as used in sections 426e to 426h of this title to include all the shorelines of the Atlantic and Pacific Oceans, the Gulf of Mexico, the Great Lakes, and lakes, estuaries, and bays directly connected therewith, was repealed by Pub.L. 104–303, Title II, § 227(e)(1), Oct. 12, 1996, 110 Stat. 3700.

## § 426h–1. Definitions

In sections 426e to 426h–1 of this title, the following definitions apply:

(1) Erosion control program

The term "erosion control program" means the national shoreline erosion control development and demonstration program established under this section.

(2) Secretary

The term "Secretary" means the Secretary of the Army.

**(3) Separable element**

The term "separable element" has the meaning provided by section 2213(f) of this title.

**(4) Shore**

The term "shore" includes each shoreline of the Atlantic and Pacific Oceans, the Gulf of Mexico, the Great Lakes, and lakes, estuaries, and bays directly connected therewith.

**(5) Shore protection project**

The term "shore protection project" includes a project for beach nourishment, including the replacement of sand.

(Aug. 13, 1946, c. 960, § 6, as added Oct. 12, 1996, Pub.L. 104–303, Title II, § 227(e)(1), 110 Stat. 3702.)

## § 426i. Shore damage prevention or mitigation

**(a) In general**

The Secretary of the Army is authorized to investigate, study, plan, and implement structural and nonstructural measures for the prevention or mitigation of shore damages attributable to Federal navigation works and shore damage attributable to the Atlantic Intracoastal Waterway and the Gulf Intracoastal Waterway, if a non-Federal public body agrees to operate and maintain such measures, and, in the case of interests in real property acquired in conjunction with nonstructural measures, to operate and maintain the property for public purposes in accordance with regulations prescribed by the Secretary.

**(b) Cost sharing**

The costs of implementing measures under this section shall be cost-shared in the same proportion as the cost-sharing provisions applicable to the project causing the shore damage.

**(c) Requirement for specific authorization**

No such project shall be initiated without specific authorization by Congress if the Federal first cost exceeds $5,000,000.

**(d) Coordination**

The Secretary shall—

(1) coordinate the implementation of the measures under this section with other Federal and non-Federal shore protection projects in the same geographic area; and

(2) to the extent practicable, combine mitigation projects with other shore protection projects in the same area into a comprehensive regional project.

(Pub.L. 90–483, Title I, § 111, Aug. 13, 1968, 82 Stat. 735; Pub.L. 99–662, Title IX, §§ 915(f), 940, Nov. 17, 1986, 100 Stat. 4191, 4199; Pub.L. 106–53, § 214, Aug. 17, 1999, 113 Stat. 291.)

### HISTORICAL AND STATUTORY NOTES

**Effective and Applicability Provisions**

1986 Acts

Amendment of this section by section 915 of Pub.L. 99–662 not to apply to any project under contract for construction on Nov. 17, 1986, see section 915(i) of Pub.L. 99–662, set out as a note under section 426g of this title.

## § 426i–1. Construction of shoreline protection projects by non-Federal interests

**(a) Authority**

Non-Federal interests are authorized to undertake shoreline protection projects on the coastline of the United States, subject to obtaining any permits required pursuant to Federal and State laws in advance of actual construction.

**(b) Studies and engineering**

**(1) By non-Federal interests**

A non-Federal interest may prepare, for review and approval by the Secretary, the necessary studies and engineering for any construction to be undertaken under subsection (a) of this section.

**(2) By Secretary**

Upon request of an appropriate non-Federal interest, the Secretary may undertake all necessary studies and engineering for any construction to be undertaken under subsection (a) of this section and provide technical assistance in obtaining all necessary permits for such construction if the non-Federal interest contracts with the Secretary to furnish the United States funds for the studies and engineering during the period that the studies and engineering will be conducted.

**(c) Completion of studies**

The Secretary is authorized to complete and transmit to the appropriate non-Federal interests any study for shoreline protection which was initiated before October 31, 1992, or, upon the request of such non-Federal interest, to terminate the study and transmit the partially completed study to the non-Federal interest for completion. Studies subject to this subsection shall be completed without regard to the requirements of subsection (b) of this section.

**(d) Authority to carry out improvement**

**(1) In general**

Any non-Federal interest which has received from the Secretary pursuant to subsection (b) or (c) of this section a favorable recommendation to carry out a shoreline protection project or separable element thereof, based on the results of completed studies and engineering for the project or element, may carry out the project or element if a final environmental impact statement has been filed for the project or element.

**(2) Permits**

Any plan of improvement proposed to be implemented in accordance with this subsection shall be deemed to satisfy the requirements for obtaining the appropriate permits required under the Secretary's authority and such permits shall be granted subject to the non-Federal interest's acceptance of the terms and conditions of such permits if the Secretary determines that the applicable regulatory criteria and procedures have been satisfied.

**(3) Monitoring**

The Secretary shall monitor any project for which permits are granted under this subsection in order to ensure that such project is constructed (and, in those cases where such activities will not be the responsibility of the Secretary, operated and maintained) in accordance with the terms and conditions of such permits.

**(e) Reimbursement**

**(1) General rule**

Subject to the enactment of appropriation Acts, the Secretary is authorized to reimburse any non-Federal interest an amount equal to the estimate of the Federal share, without interest, of the cost of any authorized shoreline protection project, or separable element thereof, constructed under this section—

(A) if, after authorization and before initiation of construction of the project or separable element, the Secretary approves the plans for construction of such project by such non-Federal interest and enters into a written agreement with the non-Federal interest with respect to the project or separable element (including the terms of cooperation); and

(B) if the Secretary finds, after a review of studies and engineering prepared pursuant to this section, that construction of the project or separable element is economically justified and environmentally acceptable.

**(2) Matters to be considered in reviewing plans**

In reviewing plans under this subsection, the Secretary shall consider budgetary and programmatic priorities and other factors that the Secretary deems appropriate.

**(3) Monitoring**

The Secretary shall regularly monitor and audit any project for shore protection constructed under this section by a non-Federal interest in order to ensure that such construction is in compliance with the plans approved by the Secretary and that the costs are reasonable.

**(4) Limitation on reimbursements**

No reimbursement shall be made under this section unless and until the Secretary has certified that the work for which reimbursement is requested has been performed in accordance with applicable permits or approved plans.

(Pub.L. 102–580, Title II, § 206, Oct. 31, 1992, 106 Stat. 4828; Pub.L. 104–303, Title II, § 227(c)(2), Oct. 12, 1996, 110 Stat. 3700.)

**"Secretary" Defined**

Secretary means the Secretary of the Army, see section 2 of Pub.L. 100–676, set out as a note under 33 U.S.C.A. § 2201.

## § 426i–2. National coastal data bank

**(1) Establishment of data bank**

Not later than 2 years after August 17, 1999, the Secretary shall establish a national coastal data bank containing data on the geophysical and climatological characteristics of the shores of the United States.

**(2) Content**

To the extent practicable, the national coastal data bank shall include data regarding current and predicted shore positions, information on federally authorized shore protection projects, and data on the movement of sand along the shores of the United States, including impediments to such movement caused by natural and manmade features.

**(3) Access**

The national coastal data bank shall be made readily accessible to the public.

(Pub.L. 106–53, Title II, § 215(d), Aug. 17, 1999, 113 Stat. 293.)

### HISTORICAL AND STATUTORY NOTES

**"Secretary" Defined**

Secretary means the Secretary of the Army, see section 2 of Pub.L. 100–676, set out as a note under 33 U.S.C.A. § 2201.

## § 426j. Placement on State beaches of sand dredged in constructing and maintaining navigation inlets and channels adjacent to such beaches

The Secretary of the Army, acting through the Chief of Engineers, is authorized upon request of the State, to place on the beaches of such State beach-quality sand which has been dredged in constructing and maintaining navigation inlets and channels adjacent to such beaches, if the Secretary deems such action to be in the public interest and upon payment by such State of 35 percent of the increased cost thereof above the cost required for alternative methods of disposing of such sand. At the request of the State, the Secretary may enter into an agreement with a political subdivision of the State to place sand on the beaches of the political subdivision of the State under the same terms and conditions required in the first sentence of this section; except that the political subdivision shall be responsible for providing any payments required under such sentence in lieu of the State. In carrying out this section, the Secretary shall give consideration to the schedule of the State, or the schedule of the responsible political subdivision of the requesting State, for providing its share of funds for placing such sand on the beaches of the State or the political subdivision and shall, to the maximum extent practicable, accommodate such schedule.

(Pub.L. 94–587, § 145, Oct. 22, 1976, 90 Stat. 2931; Pub.L. 99–662, Title IX, § 933, Nov. 17, 1986, 100 Stat. 4197; Pub.L. 100–676, § 35, Nov. 17, 1988, 102 Stat. 4031; Pub.L. 102–580, Title II, § 207, Oct. 31, 1992, 106 Stat. 4829; Pub.L. 106–53, Title II, § 217(a), Aug. 17, 1999, 113 Stat. 294.)

### HISTORICAL AND STATUTORY NOTES

**Great Lakes Basin**

Pub.L. 106–53, Title II, § 217(b), Aug. 17, 1999, 113 Stat. 294, provided that: "The Secretary shall work with the State of Ohio, other Great Lakes States, and political subdivisions of the States to fully implement and maximize beneficial reuse of dredged material as provided under section 145 of the Water Resources Development Act of 1976 (33 U.S.C. 426j)."

## § 426k. Five year demonstration program to temporarily increase diversion of water from Lake Michigan at Chicago, Illinois

**(a) Authorization of Secretary of the Army; purpose; amounts of increase; incremental accomplishment; effects on Illinois Waterway; responsibilities for development, implementation, and supervision**

In order to alleviate water damage on the shoreline of Lake Michigan and others of the Great Lakes during periods of abnormally high water levels in the Great Lakes, and to improve the water quality of the Illinois Waterway, the Secretary of the Army, acting through the Chief of Engineers, is authorized to carry out a five-year demonstration program to temporarily increase the diversion of water from Lake Michigan at Chicago, Illinois, for the purpose of testing the practicability of increasing the average annual diversion from the present limit of three thousand two hundred cubic feet per second to ten thousand cubic feet per second. The demonstration program will increase the controllable diversion by various amounts calculated to raise the average annual diversion above three thousand two hundred cubic feet per second up to ten thousand cubic feet per second. The increase in diversion rate will be accomplished incrementally and will take into consideration the effects of such increase on the Illinois Waterway. The program will be developed by the Chief of Engineers in cooperation with the State of Illinois and the Metropolitan Sanitary District of Greater Chicago. The program will be implemented by the State of Illinois and the Metropolitan Sanitary District of Greater Chicago under the supervision of the Chief of Engineers.

**(b) Establishment of monthly controllable diversion rates; average annual level of Lake Michigan and total diversion for succeeding accounting year**

During the demonstration program a controllable diversion rate will be established for each month calculated to establish an annual average diversion from three thousand two hundred cubic feet per second to not more than ten thousand cubic feet per second. When the level of Lake Michigan is below its average level, the total diversion for the succeeding accounting year shall not exceed three thousand two hundred cubic feet per second on an annual basis. The average level of Lake Michigan will be based upon the average monthly level for the period from 1900 to 1975.

**(c) River stages approaching bankfull conditions on Illinois Waterway or Mississippi River or further increased diversion adversely affecting St. Lawrence Seaway water levels: limitation on diversion**

When river stages approach or are predicted to approach bankfull conditions at the established flood warning stations on the Illinois Waterway or the Mississippi River, or when further increased diversion of water from Lake Michigan would adversely affect water levels necessary for navigational requirements of the Saint Lawrence Seaway in its entirety throughout the Saint Lawrence River and Great Lakes–Saint Lawrence Seaway, water shall not be diverted directly from Lake Michigan at the Wilmette, O'Brien, or Chicago River control structures other than as necessary for navigational requirements.

**(d) Additional study and demonstration program: determination of effects on Great Lakes levels and Illinois Waterway water quality and susceptibility to additional flooding and investigation of other adverse or beneficial impacts; report and recommendations to Congress**

The Chief of Engineers shall conduct a study and a demonstration program to determine the effects of the increased diversion on the levels of the Great Lakes, on the water quality of the Illinois Waterway, and on the susceptibility of the Illinois Waterway to additional flooding. The study and demonstration program will also investigate any adverse or beneficial impacts which result from this section. The Chief of Engineers, at the end of five years after October 22, 1976, will submit to the Congress the results of this study and demonstration program including recommendations whether to continue this authority or to change the criteria stated in subsection (b) of this section.

**(e) "Controllable diversion" defined**

For purposes of this section, controllable diversion is defined as that diversion at Wilmette, O'Brien, and Chicago River control structures which is not attributable to leakage or which is not necessary for navigational requirements.

(Pub.L. 94–587, § 166, Oct. 22, 1976, 90 Stat. 2934.)

## § 426*l*. Protection of Lake Ontario

**(a) Plan for shoreline protection and beach erosion control; report to Congress**

The Secretary of the Army, acting through the Chief of Engineers, is directed to develop a plan for shoreline protection and beach erosion control along Lake Ontario, and report on such plan to the Congress as soon as practicable. Such report shall include recommendations on measures of protection and proposals for equitable cost sharing, together with recommendations for regulating the level of Lake Ontario to assure maximum protection of the natural environment and to hold shoreline damage to a minimum.

**(b) Minimization of damage and erosion to Lake Ontario shoreline**

Until the Congress receives and acts upon the report required under subsection (a) of this section, all Federal agencies having responsibilities affecting the level of Lake Ontario shall, consistent with existing authority, make every effort to discharge such responsibilities in a manner so as to minimize damage and erosion to the shoreline of Lake Ontario.

**(c) Authorization of appropriations**

There is authorized to be appropriated to carry out this section $2,000,000.

**(d) Short title**

This section may be cited as the "Lake Ontario Protection Act of 1976."

(Pub.L. 94–587, § 180, Oct. 22, 1976, 90 Stat. 2939.)

## § 426m. Collection and removal of drift and debris from publicly maintained commercial boat harbors and adjacent land and water areas

**(a) Congressional findings**

The Congress finds that drift and debris on or in publicly maintained commercial boat harbors and the land and water areas immediately adjacent thereto threaten navigational safety, public health, recreation, and the harborfront environment.

**(b) Responsibility of Secretary of the Army for development of projects; project undertakings exempt from specific Congressional approval**

(1) The Secretary of the Army, acting through the Chief of Engineers, shall be responsible for developing projects for the collection and removal of drift and debris from publicly maintained commercial boat harbors and from land and water areas immediately adjacent thereto.

(2) The Secretary of the Army, acting through the Chief of Engineers, is authorized to undertake projects developed under paragraph (1) of this subsection without specific congressional approval when the total Federal cost for the project is less than $400,000.

**(c) Federal share of costs; responsibility of non-Federal interests in future project development to recover cost or repair sources**

The Federal share of the cost of any project developed pursuant to subsection (b) of this section shall be two-thirds of the cost of the project. The remainder of such costs shall be paid by the State, municipality, or other political subdivision in which the project is to be located, except that any costs associated with the collections and removal of drift and debris from federally owned lands shall be borne by the Federal Government. Non-Federal interests in future project development under subsection (b) of this section shall be required to recover the full cost of drift or debris removal from any identified owner of piers or other potential sources of drift or debris, or to repair such sources so that they no longer create a potential source of drift or debris.

**(d) Responsibility for providing lands, easements, and right-of-way necessary for projects; agreement to maintain projects and hold United States free from damages; regulation of project area following project completion; technical advice**

Any State, municipality, or other political subdivision where any project developed pursuant to subsection (b) of this section is located shall provide all lands, easements, and right-of-way necessary for the project, including suitable access and disposal areas, and shall agree to maintain such projects and hold and save the United States free from any damages which may result from the non-Federal sponsor's performance of, or failure to perform, any of its required responsibilities of cooperation for the project. Non-Fededal [1] interest shall agree to regulate any project area following project completion so that such area will not become a future source of drift and debris. The Chief of Engineers shall provide technical advice to non-Federal interests on the implementation of this subsection.

**(e) Definitions**

For the purposes of this section—

(1) the term "drift" includes any buoyant material that, when floating in the navigable waters of the United States, may cause damage to a commercial or recreational vessel; and

(2) the term "debris" includes any abandoned or dilapidated structure or any sunken vessel or other object that can reasonably be expected to collapse or otherwise enter the navigable waters of the United States as drift within a reasonable period.

**(f) Authorization of appropriations**

There is authorized to be appropriated to carry out this section such sums as may be necessary for fiscal years beginning after September 30, 1986.

(Pub.L. 94–587, § 202, Oct. 22, 1976, 90 Stat. 2945; Pub.L. 99–662, Title XI, § 1129(a), Nov. 17, 1986, 100 Stat. 4246.)

1 So in original. Probably should be "Non-Federal".

## § 426n. Technical assistance to States and local governments; cost sharing

**(a) Upon request of the Governor of a State, or the appropriate official of local government, the Secretary is authorized to provide designs, plans, and specifications, and such other technical assistance as he deems advisable to such State or local government for its use in carrying out—**

(1) projects for removing accumulated snags and other debris, and clearing and straightening channels in navigable streams and tributaries thereof; and

(2) projects for renovating navigable streams and tributaries thereof by means of predominantly nonstructural methods judged by the Secretary to be cost effective, for the purpose of improved drainage, water quality, and habitat diversity.

**(b) The non-Federal share of the cost of any designs, plans, specifications or technical assistance provided under subsection (a) of this section shall be 50 percent.**

(Pub.L. 99–662, Title IX, § 942, Nov. 17, 1986, 100 Stat. 4199.)

### HISTORICAL AND STATUTORY NOTES

**"Secretary" Defined**

Secretary means the Secretary of the Army, see section 2 of Pub.L. 100–676, set out as a note under 33 U.S.C.A. § 2201.

## § 426*o*. Great Lakes material disposal

In planning and implementing any navigation project (including maintenance thereof) on the Great Lakes and adjacent waters, the Secretary shall consult and cooperate with concerned States in selecting disposal areas for dredged material which is suitable for beach nourishment.

(Pub.L. 99–662, Title XI, § 1154, Nov. 17, 1986, 100 Stat. 4256.)

### HISTORICAL AND STATUTORY NOTES

**"Secretary" Defined**

Secretary means the Secretary of the Army, see section 2 of Pub.L. 100–676, set out as a note under 33 U.S.C.A. § 2201.

## § 426*o*–1. Great Lakes dredging levels adjustment

**(a) Definition of Great Lake**

In this section, the term "Great Lake" means Lake Superior, Lake Michigan, Lake Huron (including Lake St. Clair), Lake Erie, and Lake Ontario (including the St. Lawrence River to the 45th parallel of latitude).

**(b) Dredging levels**

In operating and maintaining Federal channels and harbors of, and the connecting channels between, the Great Lakes, the Secretary shall conduct such dredging as is necessary to ensure minimal operation depths consistent with the original authorized depths of the channels and harbors when water levels in the Great Lakes are, or are forecast to be, below the International Great Lakes Datum of 1985.

(Pub.L. 106–541, Title III, § 343, Dec. 11, 2000, 114 Stat. 2613.)

### HISTORICAL AND STATUTORY NOTES

**"Secretary" Defined**

Secretary means the Secretary of the Army, see section 2 of Pub.L. 100–676, set out as a note under 33 U.S.C.A. § 2201.

## § 426p. Corps of Engineers

**(a) Technical and other assistance**

The Secretary of the Army may —

(1) provide emergency assistance to prevent or reduce damage attributable to high water levels in the Great Lakes, including provision of sandbags, sheeting, and stones and other armoring devices (taking account of flooding and erosion of other property which may be caused by such activity) but not including construction of permanent structures;

(2) provide technical assistance to individuals and local governments with respect to measures to prevent or reduce such damage; and

(3) compile and disseminate information on—

(A) water levels of the Great Lakes,

(B) techniques for prevention or reduction of such damage, and

(C) emergency relief available to persons who suffer economic injury attributable to high water levels in the Great Lakes.

**(b) Issuance of permits**

**(1) Consideration of flooding and erosion**

In issuing a permit under—

(A) section 403 of this title; or

(B) section 1344 of this title;

for any activity carried out with assistance under this title, the Secretary of the Army shall take account of flooding and erosion of other property which may be caused by such activity.

**(2) Bank stabilization**

**(A) General rule**

In issuing permits under sections 403 and 1344 of this title for a project involving dredging of any portion of the Great Lakes, the Secretary of the Army shall, if feasible, encourage for bank stabilization purposes the disposal of nonhazardous compatible sand from such project on shorelines affected by erosion.

**(B) Consultation**

In carrying out subparagraph (A), the Secretary of the Army shall consult affected State and local governments.

(Pub.L. 100–707, Title II, § 203, Nov. 23, 1988, 102 Stat. 4712.)

### HISTORICAL AND STATUTORY NOTES

**References in Text**

Reference to "this title" in subsec. (b)(1), is to Title II of Pub. L. 100–707, Nov. 23, 1988, 102 Stat. 4711, known as the "Great Lakes Planning Assistance Act of 1988". For classification of this Act to the Code, see Short Title note below.

**Short Title**

1988 Acts

Section 201 of Pub. L. 100–707 provided that: "This title [amending sections 3501–3503 of Title 16, Conservation; enacting provisions set out as notes under sections 3501 and 3505 of Title 16; and enacting this section and provisions set out as notes under this section] may be cited as the 'Great Lakes Planning Assistance Act of 1988'."

**Great Lakes Damage Assistance and Prevention; Damage Assistance Program**

Section 202 of Pub. L. 100–707 provided that:

"**(a) In general.**—The Director is authorized to provide assistance to Great Lakes States in the establishment of State programs to reduce and prevent damage attributable to high water levels in the Great Lakes.

"**(b) Grants.**—Upon application by a Great Lakes State within 1 year after the date of enactment of this Act, the Director may make a one-time grant to the State of not more than $250,000 for use by the State for—

"(1) preparation of plans for mitigation, warning, emergency operations, and emergency assistance;

"(2) coordination of available State and Federal assistance;

"(3) development and implementation of nonstructural measures to reduce or prevent damage attributable to high water levels in the Great Lakes, including establishment of setback requirements and other conditions on construction and reconstruction of public and private facilities, mapping of flooding zones, and technical assistance; and

"(4) assisting local governments in developing and implementing plans for nonstructural reduction and prevention of damages attributable to high water levels in the Great Lakes.

"**(c) Technical assistance.**—The Director may provide technical assistance to Great Lakes States for carrying out any activity carried out with assistance under this section.

"**(d) State matching.**—A State which receives a grant under this section shall match the grant with an amount of funds from non-Federal sources equal to 25 percent of the amount of the grant.

"**(e) Authorization.**—There are authorized to be appropriated for making grants under this section not more than $2,000,000 for fiscal years beginning after September 30, 1988."

**Great Lakes Damage Assistance and Prevention; Definitions**

Section 205 of Pub. L. 100–707 provided that:

"For purposes of this title—

"**(1) Director.**—The term 'Director' means the Director of the Federal Emergency Management Agency.

"**(2) High water levels.**—The term 'high water levels' means water levels above the long-term average of water levels from 1900.

"**(3) Local government.**—The term 'local government' means a county, city, village, town, district, or other political subdivision of a Great Lakes State and an Indian tribe or authorized tribal organization.

"**(4) Great Lakes State.**—The term 'Great Lakes State' means Minnesota, Wisconsin, Illinois, Ohio, Michigan, Indiana, Pennsylvania, and New York."

## §§ 427 to 430. Repealed. July 31, 1945, c. 334, § 5, 59 Stat. 508

### HISTORICAL AND STATUTORY NOTES

Section 427, Act June 26, 1936, c. 849, § 1, 49 Stat. 1982, related to the improvement and protection of beaches and the definition of a beach.

Section 428, Act June 26, 1936, c. 849, § 2, 49 Stat. 1982, related to investigations by the Beach Erosion Board and the duties of the Board. See section 426–1 of this title.

Section 429, Act June 26, 1936, c. 849, § 3, 49 Stat. 1983, related to investigative reports by the Beach Erosion Board. See section 426–1 of this title.

Section 430, Act June 26, 1936, c. 849, § 4, 49 Stat. 1983, related to the payment of expenses incident to investigations by the Board. See section 426–1 of this title.

## SUBCHAPTER III—NEW YORK HARBOR, HARBOR OF HAMPTON ROADS, AND HARBOR OF BALTIMORE

### § 441. Deposit of refuse prohibited; penalty

The placing, discharging, or depositing, by any process or in any manner, of refuse, dirt, ashes, cinders, mud, sand, dredgings, sludge, acid, or any other matter of any kind, other than that flowing from streets, sewers, and passing therefrom in a liquid state, in the waters of any harbor subject to this subchapter, within the limits which shall be prescribed by the supervisor of the harbor, is strictly forbidden, and every such act is made a misdemeanor, and every person engaged in or who shall aid, abet, authorize, or instigate a violation of this section, shall, upon conviction, be punishable by fine or imprisonment, or both, such fine to be not less than $250 nor more than $2,500, and the imprisonment to be not less than thirty days nor more than one year, either or both united, as the judge before whom conviction is obtained shall decide, one-half of said fine to be paid to the person or persons giving information which shall lead to conviction of this misdemeanor.

(June 29, 1888, c. 496, § 1, 25 Stat. 209; Aug. 28, 1958, Pub.L. 85–802, § 1(1), 72 Stat. 970.)

#### HISTORICAL AND STATUTORY NOTES

**Effective and Applicability Provisions**

1958 Acts

Section 2 of Pub.L. 85–802 provided that: "This Act [amending this section and sections 442, 446, 447, 449, 451, and 451a of this title, and adding section 451b of this title] shall take effect on the sixtieth day after the date of its enactment [Aug. 28, 1958]."

**Prior Provisions**

Section 1 of Act June 29, 1888 superseded Act Aug. 5, 1886, c. 929, § 3, 24 Stat. 329, which provided as follows:

"**Sec. 3.** It shall not be lawful to cast, throw, empty, or unlade, or cause, suffer, or procure to be cast, thrown, emptied, or unladen, either from or out of any ship, vessel, lighter, barge, boat, or other craft, or from the shore, pier, wharf, or mills of any kind whatever, any ballast, stone, slate, gravel, earth, slack, rubbish, wreck, filth, slabs, edgings, sawdust, slag or cinders or other refuse or mill-waste of any kind, into New York Harbor: Provided, That nothing herein contained shall extend, or be construed to extend, to the casting out, unlading, or throwing out of any ship or vessel, lighter, barge, boat, or other craft, any stones, rocks, bricks, lime, or other materials used, or to be used, in or toward the building, repairing, or keeping in repair any quay, pier, wharf, weir, bridge, building, or other work lawfully erected or to be erected on the banks or sides of said harbor, or to the casting out, unloading or depositing of any material excavated for the improvement of navigable waters, into such places and in such manner as may be deemed by the United States officer supervising the improvement of said harbor most judicious and practicable and for the best interests of such improvement."

### § 442. Liability of officers of towing vessel

Any and every master and engineer, or person or persons acting in such capacity, respectively, on board of any boat or vessel, who shall knowingly engage in towing any scow, boat, or vessel loaded with any such prohibited matter to any point or place of deposit, or discharge in the waters of any harbor subject to this subchapter, or to any point or place elsewhere than within the limits defined and permitted by the supervisor of the harbor, shall be deemed guilty of a violation of section 441 of this title, and shall, upon conviction, be punishable as provided for offenses in violation of section 441 of this title, and shall also have his license revoked or suspended for a term to be fixed by the judge before whom tried and convicted.

(June 29, 1888, c. 496, § 2, 25 Stat. 209; Aug. 28, 1958, Pub.L. 85–802, § 1(2), 72 Stat. 970.)

#### HISTORICAL AND STATUTORY NOTES

**Effective and Applicability Provisions**

1958 Acts

Amendment by Pub.L. 85–802 effective sixtieth day after Aug. 28, 1958, see section 2 of Pub.L. 85–802, set out as a note under section 441 of this title.

### § 443. Permit for dumping; penalty for taking or towing boat or scow without permit

In all cases of receiving on board of any scows or boats such forbidden matter or substance as described in section 441 of this title, the owner or master, or person acting in such capacity on board of such scows or boats, before proceeding to take or tow the same to the place of deposit, shall apply for and obtain from the supervisor of the harbor appointed, as provided in section 451 of this title, a permit defining the precise limits within which the discharge of such scows or boats may be made; and it shall not be lawful for the owner or master, or person acting in such capacity, of any tug or towboat to tow or move any scow or boat so loaded with such forbidden matter until such permit shall have been obtained; and every person violating the foregoing provisions of this section shall be deemed guilty of a misdemeanor, and on conviction thereof shall be punished by a fine of not more than $1,000 nor less than $500, and in addition thereto the master of any tug or towboat so offending shall have his license revoked or suspended for a term to be fixed by the judge before whom tried and convicted.

(June 29, 1888, c. 496, § 3, 25 Stat. 209; Aug. 18, 1894, c. 299, § 3, 28 Stat. 360; May 28, 1908, c. 212, § 8, 35 Stat. 426.)

#### HISTORICAL AND STATUTORY NOTES

**Codifications**

Section was enacted as part of section 3 of Act June 29, 1888. Said section 3 of Act June 29, 1888 enacted sections 443 to 448 of this title.

Section 3 of Act June 29, 1888, as originally enacted, provided as follows:

"In all cases of receiving on board of any scows or boats such forbidden matter or substance as herein described, it shall be the duty of the owner or master, or person acting in such capacity, on board of such scows or boats, before proceeding to take or tow the same to the place of deposit, to apply for and obtain from the supervisor of the harbor appointed hereunder a permit defining the precise limits within which the discharge of such scows or boats may be made; and any deviation from such dumping or discharging place specified in such permit shall be a misdemeanor within the meaning of this act; and the master and engineer, or person or persons acting in such capacity, on board of any towboat towing such scows or boats, shall be equally guilty of such offense with the master or person acting in the capacity of master of the scow, and be liable to equal punishment."

Section 3 was amended by Act Aug. 18, 1894 to read as follows:

"In all cases of receiving on board of any scows or boats such forbidden matter or substance as herein described, the owner or master, or person acting in such capacity on board of such scows or boats, before proceeding to take or tow the same to the place of deposit, shall apply for and obtain from the supervisor of the harbor appointed hereunder a permit defining the precise limits within which the discharge of such scows or boats may be made; and it shall not be lawful for the owner or master, or person acting in such capacity, of any tug or towboat to tow or move any scow or boat so loaded with such forbidden matter until such permit shall have been obtained; and every person violating the foregoing provisions of this section shall be deemed guilty of a misdemeanor, and on conviction thereof shall be punished by a fine of not more than one thousand nor less than five hundred dollars, and in addition thereto the master of any tug or towboat so offending shall have his license revoked, or suspended for a term to be fixed by the judge before whom tried and convicted. And any deviation from such dumping or discharging place specified in such permit shall be a misdemeanor, and the owner and master, or person acting in the capacity of master, of any scows or boats dumping or discharging such forbidden matter in any place other than that specified in such permit shall be liable to punishment therefor as provided in section one of the said Act of June twenty-ninth, eighteen hundred and eighty-eight [section 441 of this title]; and the owner and master, or person acting in the capacity of master, of any tug or towboat towing such scows or boats shall be liable to equal punishment with the owner and master, or person acting in the capacity of master, of the scows or boats; and further, every scowman or other employee on board of both scows and towboats shall be deemed to have knowledge of the place of dumping specified in such permit, and the owners and masters, or persons acting in the capacity of masters, shall be liable to punishment, as aforesaid, for any unlawful dumping, within the meaning of this Act or of the said Act of June twenty-ninth, eighteen hundred and eighty-eight, which may be caused by the negligence or ignorance of such scowman or other employee; and, further, neither defect in machinery nor avoidable accidents to scows or towboats, nor unfavorable weather, nor improper handling or moving of scows or boats of any kind whatsoever, shall operate to release the owners and masters and employees of scows and towboats from the penalties hereinbefore mentioned. Every scow or boat engaged in the transportation of dredgings, earth, sand, mud, cellar dirt, garbage, or other offensive material of any description shall have its name or number and owner's name painted in letters and numbers at least fourteen inches long on both sides of the scow or boat; these names and numbers shall be kept distinctly legible at all times, and no scow or boat not so marked shall be used to transport or dump any such material. The supervisor of the harbor of New York, designated as provided in section five of the said Act of June twenty-ninth, eighteen hundred and eighty-eight [section 451 of this title], is authorized and directed to appoint inspectors and deputy inspectors, and, for the purpose of enforcing the provisions of this Act and of the Act aforesaid, and of detecting and bringing to punishment offenders against the same, the said supervisor of the harbor, and the inspectors and deputy inspectors so appointed by him, shall have power and authority: First. To arrest and take into custody, with or without process, any person or persons who may commit any of the acts or offenses prohibited by this section and by the Act of June twenty-ninth, eighteen hundred and eighty-eight, aforesaid, or who may violate any of the provisions of the same: Provided, That no person shall be arrested without process for any offense not committed in the presence of the supervisor or his inspectors or deputy inspectors, or either of them: And provided further, That whenever any such arrest is made the person or persons so arrested shall be brought forthwith before a commissioner, judge, or court of the United States for examination of the offenses alleged against him; and such commissioner, judge, or court shall proceed in respect thereto as authorized by law in case of crimes against the United States. Second. To go on board of any scow or towboat engaged in unlawful dumping of prohibited material, or in moving the same without a permit as required in this section of this Act, and to seize and hold said boats until they are discharged by action of the commissioner, judge, or court of the United States before whom the offending persons are brought. Third. To arrest and take into custody any witness or witnesses to such unlawful dumping of prohibited material, the said witnesses to be released under proper bonds. Fourth. To go on board of any towboat having in tow scows or boats loaded with such prohibited material, and accompany the same to the place of dumping whenever such action appears to be necessary to secure compliance with the requirements of this Act and of the Act aforesaid. Fifth. To enter gas and oil works and all other manufacturing works for the purpose of discovering the disposition made of sludge, acid, or other injurious material, whenever there is good reason to believe that such sludge, acid, or other injurious material is allowed to run into the tidal waters of the harbor in violation of section one of the aforesaid Act of June twenty-ninth, eighteen hundred and eighty-eight [section 441 of this title]. Every person who, directly or indirectly, gives any sum of money or other bribe, present, or reward or makes any offer of the same to any inspector, deputy inspector, or other employee of the office of the supervisor of the harbor with intent to influence such inspector, deputy inspector, or other employee to permit or overlook any violation of the provisions of this section or of the said Act of June twenty-ninth, eighteen hundred and eighty-eight, shall, on conviction thereof, be fined not less than five hundred dollars nor more than one thousand dollars, and be imprisoned not less than six months nor more than one year. Every permit issued in accordance with the provisions of this section of this Act which may not be taken up by an inspector or deputy inspector shall be returned within forty-eight hours after issuance to the office of the supervisor of the harbor; such permit shall bear an indorsement by the master of the towboat, or the person acting in such capacity, stating whether the permit has been used, and if so the time and place of dumping. Any person violating the provisions of this section shall be liable to a fine of not more than five hundred dollars nor less than one hundred dollars."

Section 3 was further amended by Act May 28, 1908, c. 212, § 8, to read as set forth in this section and sections 444 to 448 of this title.

## § 444. Dumping at other place than designated dumping grounds; penalty; person liable; excuses for deviation

Any deviation from such dumping or discharging place specified in such permit shall be a misdemeanor, and the owner and master, or person acting in the capacity of master, of any scows or boats dumping or discharging such forbidden matter in any place other than that specified in such permit shall be liable to punishment therefor as provided in section 441 of this title; and the owner and master, or person acting in the capacity of master, of any tug or towboat towing such scows or boats shall be liable to equal punishment with the owner and master, or person acting in the capacity of master, of the scows or boats; and, further, every scowman or other employee on board of both scows and towboats shall be deemed to have knowledge of the place of dumping specified in such permit, and the owners and masters, or persons acting in the capacity of masters, shall be liable to punishment, as aforesaid, for any unlawful dumping, within the meaning of this Act and this subchapter, which may be caused by the negligence or ignorance of such scowman or other employee; and, further, neither defect in machinery nor avoidable accidents to scows or towboats, nor unfavorable weather, nor improper handling or moving of scows or boats of any kind whatsoever shall operate to release the owners and master and employees of scows and towboats from the penalties mentioned in section 441 of this title.

(June 29, 1888, c. 496, § 3, 25 Stat. 209; Aug. 18, 1894, c. 299, § 3, 28 Stat. 360; May 28, 1908, c. 212, § 8, 35 Stat. 426.)

### HISTORICAL AND STATUTORY NOTES

**References in Text**

This Act, referred to in text, is Act Aug. 18, 1894, c. 299, 28 Stat. 356, as amended, which enacted sections 1, 31, and 452 of this title and amended sections 443 to 448 and 499 of this title. For complete classification of this Act to the Code, see Tables.

**Codifications**

Section was enacted as part of section 3 of Act June 29, 1888. Said section 3 of Act June 29, 1888 enacted sections 443 to 448 of this title. See Codification note set out under section 443 of this title.

## § 445. Equipment and marking of boats or scows

Every scow or boat engaged in the transportation of dredgings, earth, sand, mud, cellar dirt, garbage, or other offensive material of any description shall have its name or number and owner's name painted in letters and numbers at least fourteen inches long on both sides of the scow or boat; these names and numbers shall be kept distinctly legible at all times, and no scow or boat not so marked shall be used to transport or dump any such material. Each such scow or boat shall be equipped at all times with a life line or rope extending at least the length of and three feet above the deck thereof, such rope to be attached to the coaming thereof, also with a life preserver and a life buoy for each person on board thereof, also with anchor to weigh not less than two hundred and seventy-five pounds, and at least one hundred feet of cable attached thereto; a list of the names of all men employed on any such scow or boat shall be kept by the owner or master thereof and the said list shall be open to the inspection of all parties. Failure to comply with any of the foregoing provisions shall render the owner of such scow or boat liable upon conviction thereof to a penalty of not more than $500: *Provided,* That the requirements in regard to life line or rope contained in this section shall not apply to any scow or boat the deck outside the coaming or rail of which shall not exceed one foot in width: *And provided further,* That on any such scow or boat its name or number and owner's name painted in letters and numbers, at least fourteen inches long on both ends of such scow or boat, shall be a compliance with the provisions of this section in regard to name, number, and owner's name.

(June 29, 1888, c. 496, § 3, 25 Stat. 209; Aug. 18, 1894, c. 299, § 3, 28 Stat. 360; May 28, 1908, c. 212, § 8, 35 Stat. 426; Feb. 16, 1909, c. 132, 35 Stat. 623.)

### HISTORICAL AND STATUTORY NOTES

**Codifications**

Section was enacted as part of section 3 of Act June 29, 1888. Said section 3 of Act June 29, 1888 enacted sections 443 to 448 of this title. See Codification note set out under section 443 of this title.

Provisos are from Act Feb. 16, 1909.

## § 446. Inspectors; appointment, powers, and duties

Each supervisor of a harbor is authorized and directed to appoint inspectors and deputy inspectors, and for the purposes of enforcing this subchapter and the Act of August 18, 1894, entitled "An Act making appropriations for the construction, repair, and preservation of certain public works on rivers and harbors, and for other purposes" (28 Stat. 338), and of detecting and bringing to punishment offenders against the same, the said supervisor of the harbor, and the inspectors and deputy inspectors so appointed by him, shall have power and authority.

First. To arrest and take into custody, with or without process, any person or persons who may commit any of the acts or offenses prohibited by this subchapter, or who may violate any of the provisions of the same: *Provided,* That no person shall be arrested without process for any offense not committed in the presence of the supervisor or his inspectors or deputy inspectors, or either of them: *And provided further,* That whenever any such arrest is made the person or persons so arrested shall be brought forthwith before a magistrate judge, judge, or court of the United States for examination of the offenses alleged against him; and such magistrate judge, judge, or court shall proceed in respect thereto as authorized by law in case of crimes against the United States.

Second. To go on board of any scow or towboat engaged in unlawful dumping of prohibited material, or in moving the same without a permit, as required in sections 443 to 448 of this title, or otherwise violating sections 443 to 448 of this title, and to seize and hold said boats until they are discharged by action of the magistrate judge, judge, or court of the United States before whom the offending persons are brought.

Third. To arrest and take into custody any witness or witnesses to such unlawful dumping of prohibited material, the said witnesses to be released under proper bonds.

Fourth. To go on board of any towboat having in tow scows or boats loaded with such prohibited material, and accompany the same to the place of dumping, whenever such action appears to be necessary to secure compliance with the requirements of this subchapter and of the Act aforesaid.

Fifth. To enter gas and oil works and all other manufacturing works for the purpose of discovering the disposition made of sludge, acid, or other injurious material, whenever there is good reason to believe that such sludge, acid, or other injurious material is allowed to run into tidal waters of the harbor in violation of section 441 of this title.

(June 29, 1888, c. 496, § 3, 25 Stat. 209; Aug. 18, 1894, c. 299, § 3, 28 Stat. 360; May 28, 1908, c. 212, § 8, 35 Stat. 426; Aug. 28, 1958, Pub.L. 85–802, § 1(3), 72 Stat. 970; Oct. 17, 1968, Pub.L. 90–578, Title IV, § 402(b)(2), 82 Stat. 1118; Dec. 1, 1990, Pub.L. 101–650, Title III, § 321, 104 Stat. 5117.)

### HISTORICAL AND STATUTORY NOTES

#### References in Text

The Act of August 18, 1894, referred to in provision preceding First paragraph, and Act aforesaid, referred to in Fourth paragraph, mean Act Aug. 18, 1894, c. 299, 28 Stat. 356, as amended, which enacted sections 1, 31, and 452 of this title and amended sections 443 to 448 and 499 of this title. For complete classification of this Act to the Code, see Tables.

Sections 443 to 448 of this title, referred to in the Second paragraph, read in the original "this section of this Act" meaning section 3 of Act June 29, 1888, which enacted sections 443 to 448 of this title. The provision of section 3 relating to issuance of permits is classified to section 443 of this title.

#### Codifications

Section was enacted as part of section 3 of Act June 29, 1888. Said section 3 of Act June 29, 1888 enacted sections 443 to 448 of this title. See Codification note set out under section 443 of this title.

#### Effective and Applicability Provisions

1958 Acts

Amendment by Pub.L. 85–802 effective sixtieth day after Aug. 28, 1958, see section 2 of Pub.L. 85–802, set out as a note under section 441 of this title.

#### Change of Name

"Magistrate judge" substituted in text for "magistrate" pursuant to section 321 of Pub.L. 101–650, set out as a note under 28 U.S.C.A. § 631. Previously, "magistrate" was substituted for "commissioner" pursuant to Pub.L. 90–578. See chapter 43 of Title 28 [28 U.S.C.A. § 631 et seq.].

## § 447. Bribery of inspector; penalty

Every person who, directly or indirectly, gives any sum of money or other bribe, present, or reward, or makes any offer of the same to any inspector, deputy inspector, or other employee of the office of any supervisor of a harbor with intent to influence such inspector, deputy inspector, or other employee to permit or overlook any violation of the provisions of this subchapter, shall, on conviction thereof, be fined not less than $500 nor more than $1,000, and be imprisoned not less than six months nor more than one year.

(June 29, 1888, c. 496, § 3, 25 Stat. 209; Aug. 18, 1894, c. 299, § 3, 28 Stat. 360; May 28, 1908, c. 212, § 8, 35 Stat. 426; Aug. 28, 1958, Pub.L. 85–802, § 1(4), 72 Stat. 970.)

### HISTORICAL AND STATUTORY NOTES

#### Codifications

Section was enacted as part of section 3 of Act June 29, 1888. Said section 3 of Act June 29, 1888 enacted sections 443 to 448 of this title. See Codification note set out under section 443 of this title.

#### Effective and Applicability Provisions

1958 Acts

Amendment by Pub.L. 85–802 effective sixtieth day after Aug. 28, 1958, see section 2 of Pub.L. 85–802, set out as a note under section 441 of this title.

## § 448. Return of permit; penalty for failure to return

Every permit issued in accordance with the provisions of sections 443 to 448 of this title, which may not be taken up by an inspector or deputy inspector, shall be returned within four days after issuance to the office of the supervisor of the harbor; such permit shall bear an indorsement by the master of the towboat, or the person acting in such capacity, stating whether the permit has been used, and, if so, the time and place of dumping. Any person violating the provisions of this section shall be liable to a fine of not more than $500 nor less than $100.

(June 29, 1888, c. 496, § 3, 25 Stat. 209; Aug. 18, 1894, c. 299, § 3, 28 Stat. 360; May 28, 1908, c. 212, § 8, 35 Stat. 428.)

### HISTORICAL AND STATUTORY NOTES

**References in Text**

Sections 443 to 448 of this title, referred to in text, were in the original "this section of this Act", meaning section 3 of Act June 29, 1888, which enacted sections 443 to 448 of this title. The provision of section 3 relating to issuance of permits is classified to section 443 of this title.

**Codifications**

Section was enacted as part of section 3 of Act June 29, 1888. Said section 3 of Act June 29, 1888 enacted sections 443 to 448 of this title. See Codification note set out under section 443 of this title.

## § 449. Disposition of dredged matter; persons liable; penalty

All mud, dirt, sand, dredgings, and material of every kind and description whatever taken, dredged, or excavated from any slip, basin, or shoal in any harbor subject to this subchapter, and placed on any boat, scow, or vessel for the purpose of being taken or towed upon the waters of that harbor to a place of deposit, shall be deposited and discharged at such place or within such limits as shall be defined and specified by the supervisor of the harbor, as in sections 443 to 448 of this title prescribed, and not otherwise. Every person, firm, or corporation being the owner of any slip, basin, or shoal, from which such mud, dirt, sand, dredgings, and material shall be taken, dredged, or excavated, and every person, firm, or corporation in any manner engaged in the work of dredging or excavating any such slip, basin, or shoal, or of removing such mud, dirt, sand, or dredgings therefrom, shall severally be responsible for the deposit and discharge of all such mud, dirt, sand, or dredgings at such place or within such limits so defined and prescribed by said supervisor of the harbor; and for every violation of the provisions of this section the person offending shall be guilty of an offense, and shall be punished by a fine equal to the sum of $5 for every cubic yard of mud, dirt, sand, dredgings, or material not deposited or discharged as required by this section.

(June 29, 1888, c. 496, § 4, 25 Stat. 210; Aug. 28, 1958, Pub.L. 85–802, § 1(5), 72 Stat. 970.)

### HISTORICAL AND STATUTORY NOTES

**References in Text**

Sections 443 to 448 of this title, referred to in text, were in the original "the third section of this Act", meaning section 3 of Act June 29, 1888, which enacted sections 443 to 448 of this title. The provision of section 3 relating to specification of the limits within which to discharge is classified to section 443 of this title.

**Codifications**

Section was enacted as part of section 4 of Act June 29, 1888, which enacted sections 449 and 450 of this title.

**Effective and Applicability Provisions**

1958 Acts

Amendment by Pub.L. 85–802 effective sixtieth day after Aug. 28, 1958, see section 2 of Pub.L. 85–802, set out as a note under section 441 of this title.

## § 450. Liability of vessel

Any boat or vessel used or employed in violating any provision of this subchapter, shall be liable to the pecuniary penalties imposed thereby, and may be proceeded against, summarily by way of libel in any district court of the United States having jurisdiction thereof.

(June 29, 1888, c. 496, § 4, 25 Stat. 210.)

### HISTORICAL AND STATUTORY NOTES

**Codifications**

Section was enacted as part of section 4 of Act June 29, 1888, which enacted sections 449 and 450 of this title.

## § 451. Supervisor of harbor; appointment and duties

An officer of the Corps of Engineers shall, for each harbor subject to this subchapter, be designated by the Secretary of the Army as supervisor of the harbor, to act under the direction of the Chief of Engineers in enforcing the provisions of this subchapter, and in detecting offenders against the same. Each such officer shall have personal charge and supervision under the Chief of Engineers, and shall direct the patrol boats and other means to detect and bring to punishment offenders against the provisions of this subchapter.

(June 29, 1888, c. 496, § 5, 25 Stat. 210; June 29, 1949, c. 278, 63 Stat. 300; July 12, 1952, c. 707, 66 Stat. 596; Aug. 28, 1958, Pub.L. 85–802, § 1(6), 72 Stat. 970.)

### HISTORICAL AND STATUTORY NOTES

**Effective and Applicability Provisions**

1958 Acts

Amendment by Pub.L. 85–802 effective sixtieth day after Aug. 28, 1958, see section 2 of Pub.L. 85–802, set out as a note under section 441 of this title.

**Change of Name**

The Department of War was designated the Department of the Army and the title of the Secretary of War was changed to Secretary of the Army by section 205(a) of Act July 26, 1947, c. 343, Title II, 61 Stat. 501. Section 205(a) of Act July 26, 1947, was repealed by section 53 of Act Aug. 10, 1956, c. 1041, 70A Stat. 641. Section 1 of Act Aug. 10, 1956, enacted

"Title 10, Armed Forces" which in sections 3010 to 3013 continued the Department of the Army under the administrative supervision of a Secretary of the Army.

## § 451a. Harbors subject to this subchapter

The following harbors shall be subject to this subchapter:

(1) The harbor of New York.

(2) The harbor of Hampton Roads.

(3) The harbor of Baltimore.

(June 29, 1888, c. 496, § 6, 25 Stat. 210; Aug. 28, 1958, Pub.L. 85–802, § 1(7), 72 Stat. 970.)

### HISTORICAL AND STATUTORY NOTES

**Effective and Applicability Provisions**

1958 Acts

Amendment by Pub.L. 85–802 effective sixtieth day after Aug. 28, 1958, see section 2 of Pub.L. 85–802, set out as a note under section 441 of this title.

## § 451b. Waters included within subchapter

For the purposes of this subchapter—

(1) The term "harbor of New York" means the tidal waters of the harbor of New York, its adjacent and tributary waters, and those of Long Island Sound.

(2) The term "harbor of Hampton Roads" means the tidal waters of the harbors of Norfolk, Portsmouth, Newport News, Hampton Roads, and their adjacent and tributary waters, so much of the Chesapeake Bay and its tributaries as lies within the State of Virginia, and so much of the Atlantic Ocean and its tributaries as lies within the jurisdiction of the United States within or to the east of the State of Virginia.

(3) The term "harbor of Baltimore" means the tidal waters of the harbor of Baltimore and its adjacent and tributary waters, and so much of Chesapeake Bay and its tributaries as lies within the State of Maryland.

(June 29, 1888, c. 496, § 7, as added Aug. 28, 1958, Pub.L. 85–802, § 1(8), 72 Stat. 970.)

### HISTORICAL AND STATUTORY NOTES

**Effective and Applicability Provisions**

1958 Acts

Section effective sixtieth day after Aug. 28, 1958, see section 2 of Pub.L. 85–802, set out as an Effective Date of 1958 Amendment note under section 441 of this title.

## § 452. Taking shellfish or otherwise interfering with navigation in New York Harbor channels; penalty; arrest and procedure

It shall be unlawful for any person or persons to engage in fishing or dredging for shellfish in any of the channels leading to and from the harbor of New York, or to interfere in any way with the safe navigation of those channels by ocean steamships and ships of deep draft.

Any person or persons violating the foregoing provisions of this section shall be deemed guilty of a misdemeanor, and on conviction thereof shall be punished by fine or imprisonment, or both, such fine to be not more than $250 nor less than $50, and the imprisonment to be not more than six months nor less than thirty days, either or both united, as the judge before whom conviction is obtained shall decide.

It shall be the duty of the United States supervisor of the harbor to enforce this section, and the deputy inspectors of the said supervisor shall have authority to arrest and take into custody, with or without process, any person or persons, who may commit any of the acts or offenses prohibited by this section: *Provided,* That no person shall be arrested without process for any offense not committed in the presence of the supervisor or his inspector or deputy inspectors, or either of them: *And provided further,* That whenever any such arrest is made the person or persons so arrested shall be brought forthwith before a magistrate judge, judge, or court of the United States for examination of the offenses alleged against him; and such magistrate judge, judge or court shall proceed in respect thereto as authorized by law in case of crimes against the United States.

(Aug. 18, 1894, c. 299, § 2, 28 Stat. 360; Oct. 17, 1968, Pub.L. 90–578, Title IV, § 402(b)(2), 82 Stat. 1118; Dec. 1, 1990, Pub.L. 101–650, Title III, § 321, 104 Stat. 5117.)

### HISTORICAL AND STATUTORY NOTES

**Codifications**

Section was not enacted as part of Act June 29, 1888, c. 496, 25 Stat. 209, which comprises this subchapter.

**Change of Name**

"Magistrate judge" substituted in text for "magistrate" pursuant to section 321 of Pub.L. 101–650, set out as a note under 28 U.S.C.A. § 631. Previously, "magistrate" was substituted for "commissioner" pursuant to Pub.L. 90–578. See chapter 43 of Title 28 [28 U.S.C.A. § 631 et seq.].

## § 453. Regulations for navigation of Ambrose Channel; exclusion of tows and sailing vessels

The Secretary of the Army is authorized to make such rules and regulations for the navigation of Ambrose Channel as he may deem necessary or expedient to insure its safe use in all kinds of weather, night and day, for all vessels under control and running under their own power, and to this end he may, in his discretion, forbid its use to tows of every description and to sailing vessels.

(Mar. 4, 1913, c. 144, § 1, 37 Stat. 803.)

HISTORICAL AND STATUTORY NOTES

**Codifications**

Section was not enacted as part of Act June 29, 1888, c. 496, 25 Stat. 209, which comprises this subchapter.

**Change of Name**

The Department of War was designated the Department of the Army and the title of the Secretary of War was changed to Secretary of the Army by section 205(a) of Act July 26, 1947, c. 343, Title II, 61 Stat. 501. Section 205(a) of Act July 26, 1947, was repealed by section 53 of Act Aug. 10, 1956, c. 1041, 70A Stat. 641. Section 1 of Act Aug. 10, 1956, enacted "Title 10, Armed Forces" which in sections 3010 to 3013 continued the Department of the Army under the administrative supervision of a Secretary of the Army.

## § 454. Consent of Congress to obstruction of waters by New York City

The consent of Congress is given to the city of New York, in the State of New York, to obstruct navigation of any river or other waterway which does not form a connecting link between other navigable waters of the United States, and lying wholly within the limits of said city, by closing all or any portion of the same or by building structures in or over the same when the said city shall be lawfully authorized to do so by the State of New York: *Provided, however,* That any such obstruction shall be unlawful unless the location and plans for the proposed work or works before the commencement thereof shall have been filed with and approved by the Secretary of the Army and Chief of Engineers; and when the plans for any such obstruction have been approved by the Chief of Engineers and by the Secretary of the Army it shall not be lawful to deviate from such plans either before or after the completion of such obstruction, unless the modification of such plans has previously been submitted to and received the approval of the Chief of Engineers and the Secretary of the Army: *And provided further,* That the city of New York shall be liable for any damage that may be inflicted upon private property by reason of any of the provisions of this section.

The right to alter, amend, or repeal this section is expressly reserved, and the United States shall incur no liability for the alteration, amendment, or repeal thereof to the city of New York, or to the owner or owners, or any other persons interested in any obstruction which shall have been constructed under its provisions.

(June 25, 1910, c. 436, §§ 1, 2, 36 Stat. 866, 867.)

HISTORICAL AND STATUTORY NOTES

**Codifications**

Section was not enacted as part of Act June 29, 1888, c. 496, 25 Stat. 209, which comprises this subchapter.

**Change of Name**

The Department of War was designated the Department of the Army and the title of the Secretary of War was changed to Secretary of the Army by section 205(a) of Act July 26, 1947, c. 343, Title II, 61 Stat. 501. Section 205(a) of Act July 26, 1947, was repealed by section 53 of Act Aug. 10, 1956, c. 1041, 70A Stat. 641. Section 1 of Act Aug. 10, 1956, enacted "Title 10, Armed Forces" which in sections 3010 to 3013 continued the Department of the Army under the administrative supervision of a Secretary of the Army.

**Transfer of Functions**

All functions, powers, and duties of the Secretary of the Army and other offices and officers of the Department of the Army under section 401 of this title to the extent that they relate generally to the location and clearances of bridges and causeways in the navigable waters of the United States were transferred to and vested in the Secretary of Transportation by Pub.L. 89–670, § 6(g)(6)(A), Oct. 15, 1966, 80 Stat. 941. Pub.L. 97–449 amended section 401 of this title to reflect the transfer made by section 6(g)(6)(A) of Pub.L. 89–670, and repealed section 6(g)(6)(A).

# WATER POLLUTION PREVENTION AND CONTROL

## FEDERAL WATER POLLUTION CONTROL ACT [FWPCA § ______]

**(33 U.S.C.A. §§ 1251 to 1387)**

## CHAPTER 26—WATER POLLUTION PREVENTION AND CONTROL

### SUBCHAPTER I—RESEARCH AND RELATED PROGRAMS



### SUBCHAPTER II—GRANTS FOR CONSTRUCTION OF TREATMENT WORKS



Sec.

### SUBCHAPTER II—GRANTS FOR CONSTRUCTION OF TREATMENT WORKS—Cont'd



### SUBCHAPTER III—STANDARDS AND ENFORCEMENT

**Related Provisions**

*See, also, Safety of Public Water Systems, 42 U.S.C.A. § 300f et seq., post; Water Resources Research, 42 U.S.C.A. § 10301 et seq., post.*

## SUBCHAPTER I—RESEARCH AND RELATED PROGRAMS

### § 1251. Congressional declaration of goals and policy

**[FWPCA § 101]**

**(a) Restoration and maintenance of chemical, physical and biological integrity of Nation's waters; national goals for achievement of objective**

The objective of this chapter is to restore and maintain the chemical, physical, and biological integrity of the Nation's waters. In order to achieve this objective it is hereby declared that, consistent with the provisions of this chapter—

(1) it is the national goal that the discharge of pollutants into the navigable waters be eliminated by 1985;

(2) it is the national goal that wherever attainable, an interim goal of water quality which provides for the protection and propagation of fish, shellfish, and wildlife and provides for recreation in and on the water be achieved by July 1, 1983;

(3) it is the national policy that the discharge of toxic pollutants in toxic amounts be prohibited;

(4) it is the national policy that Federal financial assistance be provided to construct publicly owned waste treatment works;

(5) it is the national policy that areawide waste treatment management planning processes be developed and implemented to assure adequate control of sources of pollutants in each State;

(6) it is the national policy that a major research and demonstration effort be made to develop technology necessary to eliminate the discharge of pollutants into the navigable waters, waters of the contiguous zone, and the oceans; and

(7) it is the national policy that programs for the control of nonpoint sources of pollution be developed and implemented in an expeditious manner so as to enable the goals of this chapter to be met through the control of both point and nonpoint sources of pollution.

**(b) Congressional recognition, preservation, and protection of primary responsibilities and rights of States**

It is the policy of the Congress to recognize, preserve, and protect the primary responsibilities and rights of States to prevent, reduce, and eliminate pollution, to plan the development and use (including restoration, preservation, and enhancement) of land and water resources, and to consult with the Administrator in the exercise of his authority under this chapter. It is the policy of Congress that the States manage the construction grant program under this chapter and implement the permit programs under sections 1342 and 1344 of this title. It is further the policy of the Congress to support and aid research relating to the prevention, reduction, and elimination of pollution, and to provide Federal technical services and financial aid to State and interstate agencies and municipalities in connection with the prevention, reduction, and elimination of pollution.

**(c) Congressional policy toward Presidential activities with foreign countries**

It is further the policy of Congress that the President, acting through the Secretary of State and such national and international organizations as he determines appropriate, shall take such action as may be necessary to insure that to the fullest extent possible all foreign countries shall take meaningful action for the prevention, reduction, and elimination of pollution in their waters and in international waters and for the achievement of goals regarding the elimination of discharge of pollutants and the improvement of water quality to at least the same extent as the United States does under its laws.

**(d) Administrator of Environmental Protection Agency to administer chapter**

Except as otherwise expressly provided in this chapter, the Administrator of the Environmental Protection Agency (hereinafter in this chapter called "Administrator") shall administer this chapter.

**(e) Public participation in development, revision, and enforcement of any regulation, etc.**

Public participation in the development, revision, and enforcement of any regulation, standard, effluent limitation, plan, or program established by the Administrator or any State under this chapter shall be provided for, encouraged, and assisted by the Administrator and the States. The Administrator, in cooperation with the States, shall develop and publish regulations specifying minimum guidelines for public participation in such processes.

**(f) Procedures utilized for implementing chapter**

It is the national policy that to the maximum extent possible the procedures utilized for implementing this chapter shall encourage the drastic minimization of paperwork and interagency decision procedures, and the best use of available manpower and funds, so as to prevent needless duplication and unnecessary delays at all levels of government.

**(g) Authority of States over water**

It is the policy of Congress that the authority of each State to allocate quantities of water within its jurisdiction shall not be superseded, abrogated or otherwise impaired by this chapter. It is the further policy of Congress that nothing in this chapter shall be construed to supersede or abrogate rights to quantities of water which have been established by any State. Federal agencies shall co-operate with State and local agencies to develop comprehensive solutions to prevent, reduce and eliminate pollution in concert with programs for managing water resources.

(June 30, 1948, c. 758, Title I, § 101, as added Oct. 18, 1972, Pub.L. 92–500, § 2, 86 Stat. 816, and amended Dec. 27, 1977, Pub.L. 95–217, §§ 5(a), 26(b), 91 Stat. 1567, 1575; Feb. 4, 1987, Pub.L. 100–4, Title III, § 316(b), 101 Stat. 60.)

## HISTORICAL AND STATUTORY NOTES

**Codifications**

The Federal Water Pollution Control Act, comprising this chapter, was originally enacted by Act June 30, 1948, c. 758, 62 Stat. 1155, and amended by Acts July 17, 1952, c. 927, 66 Stat. 755; July 9, 1956, c. 518, 70 Stat. 498; June 25, 1959, Pub.L. 86–70, 73 Stat. 141; July 12, 1960, Pub.L. 86–624, 74 Stat. 411; July 20, 1961, Pub.L. 87–88, 75 Stat. 204; Oct. 2, 1965, Pub.L. 89–234, 79 Stat. 903; Nov. 3, 1966, Pub.L. 89–753, 80 Stat. 1246; Apr. 3, 1970, Pub.L. 91–224, 84 Stat. 91; Dec. 31, 1970, Pub.L. 91–611, 84 Stat. 1818; July 9, 1971, Pub.L. 92–50, 85 Stat. 124; Oct. 13, 1971, Pub.L. 92–137, 85 Stat. 379; Mar. 1, 1972, Pub.L. 92–240, 86 Stat. 47, and was formerly classified first to section 466 et seq. of this title and later to section 1151 et seq. of this title. The Act is shown herein, however, as having been added by Pub.L. 92–500 without reference to such intervening amendments because of the extensive amendment, reorganization, and expansion of the Act's provisions by Pub.L. 92–500.

**Savings Provisions**

Section 4 of Pub.L. 92–500 provided that:

"**(a)** No suit, action, or other proceeding lawfully commenced by or against the Administrator or any other officer or employee of the United States in his official capacity or in relation to the discharge of his official duties under the Federal Water Pollution Control Act as in effect immediately prior to the date of enactment of this Act [Oct. 18, 1972] shall abate by reason of the taking effect of the amendment made by section 2 of this Act [which enacted this chapter]. The court may, on its own motion or that of any party made at any time within twelve months after such taking effect, allow the same to be maintained by or against the Administrator or such officer or employee.

"**(b)** All rules, regulations, orders, determinations, contracts, certifications, authorizations, delegations or other actions duly issued, made, or taken by or pursuant to the Federal Water Pollution Control Act as in effect immediately prior to the date of enactment of this Act [Oct. 18, 1972], and pertaining to any functions, powers, requirements, and duties under the Federal Water Pollution Control Act as in effect immediately prior to the date of enactment of this Act [Oct. 18, 1972], shall continue in full force and effect after the date of enactment of this Act [Oct. 18, 1972] until modified or rescinded in accordance with the Federal Water Pollution Control Act as amended by this Act [this chapter].

"**(c)** The Federal Water Pollution Control Act as in effect immediately prior to the date of enactment of this Act [Oct. 18, 1972] shall remain applicable to all grants made from funds authorized for the fiscal year ending June 30, 1972, and prior fiscal years, including any increases in the monetary amount of any such grant which may be paid from authorizations for fiscal years beginning after June 30, 1972, except as specifically otherwise provided in section 202 of the Federal Water Pollution Control Act as amended by this Act [section 1282 of this title] and in subsection (c) of section 3 of this Act."

**Severability of Provisions**

Section 512 of Act June 30, 1948, c. 758, Title V, as added Oct. 18, 1972, Pub.L. 92–500, § 2, 86 Stat. 894, provided that: "If any provision of this Act [this chapter], or the application of any provision of this Act [this chapter] to any person or circumstance, is held invalid, the application of such provision to other persons or circumstances, and the remainder of this Act [this chapter], shall not be affected thereby."

**Short Title**

2002 Amendments

Pub.L. 107–303, § 1(a), Nov. 27, 2002, 116 Stat. 2355, provided that: "This Act [enacting 33 U.S.C.A. § 1271a, amending 33 U.S.C.A. §§ 1254, 1266, 1268, 1270, 1285, 1290, 1324, 1329, 1330 and 1375, enacting provisions set out as notes under this section, 31 U.S.C.A. § 1113 and 33 U.S.C.A. § 1254, and repealing provisions set out as a note under 20 U.S.C.A. § 50] may be cited as the 'Great Lakes and Lake Champlain Act of 2002'."

Pub.L. 107–303, Title I, § 101, Nov. 27, 2002, 116 Stat. 2355, provided that: "This Title [enacting 33 U.S.C.A. § 1271a, and amending 33 U.S.C.A. § 1268] may be cited as the 'Great Lakes Legacy Act of 2002'."

Pub.L. 107–303, Title II, § 201, Nov. 27, 2002, 116 Stat. 2358, provided that: "This Title [amending 33 U.S.C.A. § 1270] may be cited as the 'Daniel Patrick Moynihan Lake Champlain Basin Program Act of 2002'."

2000 Amendments

Pub.L. 106–457, Title VI, § 601, Nov. 7, 2000, 114 Stat. 1975, provided that: "This title [enacting section 1300 of this title] may be cited as the 'Alternative Water Sources Act of 2000'."

Pub.L. 106–457, Title V, § 501, Nov. 7, 2000, 114 Stat. 1973, provided that: "This title [enacting section 1273 of this title] may be cited as the 'Lake Pontchartrain Basin Restoration Act of 2000'."

Pub.L. 106–457, Title IV, § 401, Nov. 7, 2000, 114 Stat. 1973, provided that: "This title [amending section 1269 of this title] may be cited as the 'Long Island Sound Restoration Act'."

Pub.L. 106–457, Title II, § 201, Nov. 7, 2000, 114 Stat. 1967, provided that: "This title [amending section 1267 of this title and enacting provisions set out as a note under section 1267 of this title] may be cited as the 'Chesapeake Bay Restoration Act of 2000'."

Pub.L. 106–284, § 1, Oct. 10, 2000, 114 Stat. 870, provided that: "This Act [enacting sections 1346 and 1375a of this title and amending sections 1254, 1313, 1314, 1362, and 1377 of this title] may be cited as the 'Beaches Environmental Assessment and Coastal Health Act of 2000'."

1994 Amendments

Pub.L. 103–431, § 1, Oct. 31, 1994, 108 Stat. 4396, provided that: "This Act [amending section 1311 of this title] may be cited as the 'Ocean Pollution Reduction Act'."

1990 Amendments

Pub.L. 101–596, § 1, Nov. 16, 1990, 104 Stat. 3000, provided that: "This Act [enacting sections 1269 and 1270 and amending sections 1268 and 1324 of this title, and enacting note provisions under this section and section 1270 of this title] may be cited as the 'Great Lakes Critical Programs Act of 1990'."

Pub.L. 101–596, Title II, § 201, Nov. 16, 1990, 104 Stat. 3004, provided that: "This part [enacting section 1269 and amending section 1416 of this title] may be cited as the 'Long Island Sound Improvement Act of 1990'."

Pub.L. 101–596, Title III, § 301, Nov. 16, 1990, 104 Stat. 3006, provided that: "This title [enacting section 1270 and amending section 1324(d)(2) of this title and enacting note provision under section 1270 of this title] may be cited as the 'Lake Champlain Special Designation Act of 1990'."

1988 Amendments

Pub.L. 100–653, Title X, § 1001, Nov. 14, 1988, 102 Stat. 3835, provided that: "This title [amending section 1330(a)(2)(B) of this title and enacting provisions set out as notes under section 1330 of this title] may be cited as the 'Massachusetts Bay Protection Act of 1988'."

1987 Amendments

Section 1(a) of Pub.L. 100–4 provided that: "This Act [enacting sections 1254a, 1267, 1268, 1281b, 1329, 1330, 1377, 1381, 1382, 1383, 1384, 1385, 1386, 1387, and 1414a of this title, amending sections 1251, 1254, 1256, 1262, 1281, 1282, 1283, 1284, 1285, 1287, 1288, 1291, 1311, 1312, 1313, 1314, 1317, 1318, 1319, 1321, 1322, 1324, 1342, 1344, 1345, 1361, 1362, 1365, 1369, 1375, and 1376 of this title, and enacting provisions set out as notes under sections 1251, 1284, 1311, 1317, 1319, 1330, 1342, 1345, 1362, 1375, and 1414a of this title and section 1962d–20 of Title 42, The Public Health and Welfare] may be cited as the 'Water Quality Act of 1987'."

1981 Amendments

Pub.L. 97–117, § 1, Dec. 29, 1981, 95 Stat. 1623, provided that: "This Act [enacting sections 1298, 1299, and 1313a of this title, amending sections 1281 to 1285, 1287, 1291, 1292, 1296, 1311, and 1314 of this title, and enacting provisions set out as notes under sections 1311 and 1375 of this title] may be cited as the 'Municipal Wastewater Treatment Construction Grant Amendments of 1981'."

1977 Amendments

Section 1 of Pub.L. 95–217 provided: "That this Act [enacting sections 1281a, 1294 to 1296, and 1297 of this title, amending sections 1251, 1252, 1254 to 1256, 1259, 1262, 1263, 1281, 1282 to 1288, 1291, 1292, 1311, 1314, 1315, 1317 to 1319, 1321 to 1324, 1328, 1341, 1342, 1344, 1345, 1362, 1364, 1375, and 1376 of this title, enacting provisions set out as notes under sections 1251, 1284, 1286, 1314, 1321, 1342, 1344, and 1376 of this title, and amending a provision set out as a note under this section] may be cited as the 'Clean Water Act of 1977'."

1972 Acts

Section 519, formerly section 518, of Act June 30, 1948, c. 758, Title V, as added Oct. 18, 1972, Pub.L. 92–500, § 2, 86 Stat. 896, amended Dec. 27, 1977, Pub.L. 95–217, § 2, 91 Stat. 1566, and renumbered Feb. 4, 1987, Pub.L. 100–4, Title V, § 506, 101 Stat. 76, provided that: "This Act [enacting this chapter] may be cited as the 'Federal Water Pollution Control Act' (commonly referred to as the Clean Water Act)."

Section 1 of Pub.L. 92–500 provided: "That this Act [enacting this chapter, amending section 24 of Title 12, Banks and Banking, sections 633 and 636 of Title 15, Commerce and Trade, and section 711 of former Title 31, Money and Finance, and enacting provisions set out as notes under this section and sections 1281 and 1361 of this title] may be cited as the 'Federal Water Pollution Control Act Amendments of 1972'."

**Standards**

For provisions relating to the responsibility of the head of each Executive agency for compliance with applicable pollution control standards, see Ex. Ord. No. 12088, Oct. 13, 1978, 43 F.R. 47707, set out as a note under section 4321 of Title 42, The Public Health and Welfare.

**Seafood Processing Study; Submittal of Results to Congress Not Later Than January 1, 1979**

Pub.L. 95–217, § 74, Dec. 27, 1977, 91 Stat. 1609, provided that the Administrator of the Environmental Protection Agency conduct a study to examine the geographical, hydrological, and biological characteristics of marine waters to determine the effects of seafood processes which dispose of untreated natural wastes into such waters and to include in this study an examination of technologies which may be used in such processes to facilitate the use of the nutrients in these wastes or to reduce the discharge of such wastes into the marine environment and to submit the result of this study to Congress not later than Jan. 1, 1979.

**Oversight Study**

Section 5 of Pub.L. 92–500 authorized the Comptroller General of the United States to conduct a study and review of the research, pilot, and demonstration programs related to prevention and control of water pollution conducted, supported, or assisted by any Federal agency pursuant to any federal law or regulation and assess conflicts between these programs and their coordination and efficacy, and to report to Congress thereon by Oct. 1, 1973.

**International Trade Study**

Section 6 of Pub.L. 92–500 provided that:

"(a) The Secretary of Commerce, in cooperation with other interested Federal agencies and with representatives of industry and the public, shall undertake immediately an investigation and study to determine—

"(1) the extent to which pollution abatement and control programs will be imposed on, or voluntarily undertaken by, United States manufacturers in the near future and the probable short- and long-range effects of the costs of such programs (computed to the greatest extent practicable on an industry-by-industry basis) on (A) the production costs of such domestic manufacturers, and (B) the market prices of the goods produced by them;

"(2) the probable extent to which pollution abatement and control programs will be implemented in foreign industrial nations in the near future and the extent to which the production costs (computed to the greatest extent practicable on an industry-by-industry basis) of foreign manufacturers will be affected by the costs of such programs;

"(3) the probable competitive advantage which any article manufactured in a foreign nation will likely have in relation to a comparable article made in the United States if that foreign nation—

"(A) does not require its manufacturers to implement pollution abatement and control programs,

"(B) requires a lesser degree of pollution abatement and control in its programs, or

"(C) in any way reimburses or otherwise subsidizes its manufacturers for the costs of such program;

"(4) alternative means by which any competitive advantage accruing to the products of any foreign nation as a result of any factor described in paragraph (3) may be (A) accurately and quickly determined, and (B) equalized, for example, by the imposition of a surcharge or duty, on a foreign product in an amount necessary to compensate for such advantage; and

"(5) the impact, if any, which the imposition of a compensating tariff of other equalizing measure may have in encouraging foreign nations to implement pollution and abatement control programs.

"(b) The Secretary shall make an initial report to the President and Congress within six months after the date of enactment of this section [Oct. 18, 1972] of the results of the study and investigation carried out pursuant to this section and shall make additional reports thereafter at such times as he deems appropriate taking into account the development of relevant data, but not less than once every twelve months."

**International Agreements**

Section 7 of Pub.L. 92–500 provided that: "The President shall undertake to enter into international agreement to apply uniform standards of performance for the control of the discharge and emission of pollutants from new sources, uniform controls over the discharge and emission of toxic pollutants, and uniform controls over the discharge of pollutants into the ocean. For this purpose the President shall negotiate multilateral treaties, conventions, resolutions, or other agreements, and formulate, present, or support proposals at the United Nations and other appropriate international forums."

**National Policies and Goal Study**

Section 10 of Pub.L. 92–500 authorized the President to make a full and complete investigation and study of all national policies and goals established by law to determine what the relationship should be between these policies and goals, taking into account the resources of the Nation, and to report the results of his investigation and study together with his recommendations to Congress not later than two years after Oct. 18, 1972.

**Efficiency Study**

Section 11 of Pub.L. 92–500 authorized the President, by utilization of the General Accounting Office, to conduct a full and complete investigation and study of ways and means of most effectively using all of the various resources, facilities, and personnel of the Federal Government in order to most efficiently carry out the provisions of this chapter and to report the results of his investigation and study together with his recommendations to Congress not later than two hundred and seventy days after Oct. 18, 1972.

**Sex Discrimination**

Section 13 of Pub.L. 92–500 provided that: "No person in the United States shall on the ground of sex be excluded from participation in, be denied the benefits of, or be subjected to discrimination under any program or activity receiving Federal Assistance under this Act [see Short Title note above], the Federal Water Pollution Control Act [this chapter], or the Environmental Financing Act [set out as a note under section 1281 of this title]. This section shall be enforced through agency provisions and rules similar to those already established, with respect to racial and other discrimination, under title VI of the Civil Rights Act of 1964 [section 2000d et seq. of Title 42, The Public Health and Welfare]. However, this remedy is not exclusive and will not prejudice or cut off any other legal remedies available to a discriminatee."

**Prevention, Control, and Abatement of Environmental Pollution at Federal Facilities**

Ex. Ord. No. 12088, Oct. 13, 1978, 43 F.R. 47707, set out as a note under section 4321 of Title 42, The Public Health and Welfare, provides for the prevention, control, and abatement of environmental pollution at federal facilities.

**National Shellfish Indicator Program**

Pub.L. 102–567, Title III, § 308, Oct. 29, 1992, 106 Stat. 4286, as amended Pub.L. 105–362, Title II, § 201(b), Nov. 10, 1998, 112 Stat. 3282, provided that:

"(a) **Establishment of a research program.**—The Secretary of Commerce, in cooperation with the Secretary of Health and Human Services and the Administrator of the Environmental Protection Agency, shall establish and administer a 5–year national shellfish research program (hereafter in this section referred to as the 'Program') for the purpose of improving existing classification systems for shellfish growing waters using the latest technological advancements in microbiology and epidemiological methods. Within 12 months after the date of enactment of this Act [Oct. 29, 1992], the Secretary of Commerce, in cooperation with the advisory committee established under subsection (b) and the Consortium, shall develop a comprehensive 5–year plan for the Program which shall at a minimum provide for—

"(1) an environmental assessment of commercial shellfish growing areas in the United States, including an evaluation of the relationships between indicators of fecal contamination and human enteric pathogens;

"(2) the evaluation of such relationships with respect to potential health hazards associated with human consumption of shellfish;

"(3) a comparison of the current microbiological methods used for evaluating indicator bacteria and human enteric pathogens in shellfish and shellfish growing waters with new technological methods designed for this purpose;

"(4) the evaluation of current and projected systems for human sewage treatment in eliminating viruses and other human enteric pathogens which accumulate in shellfish;

"(5) the design of epidemiological studies to relate microbiological data, sanitary survey data, and human shellfish consumption data to actual hazards to health associated with such consumption; and

"(6) recommendations for revising Federal shellfish standards and improving the capabilities of Federal and State agencies to effectively manage shellfish and ensure the safety of shellfish intended for human consumption.

"(b) **Advisory committee.**—(1) For the purpose of providing oversight of the Program on a continuing basis, an advisory committee (hereafter in this section referred to as the 'Committee') shall be established under a memorandum of understanding between the Interstate Shellfish Sanitation Conference and the National Marine Fisheries Service.

"(2) The Committee shall—

"(A) identify priorities for achieving the purpose of the Program;

"(B) review and recommend approval or disapproval of Program work plans and plans of operation;

"(C) review and comment on all subcontracts and grants to be awarded under the Program;

"(D) receive and review progress reports from the Consortium and program subcontractors and grantees; and

"(E) provide such other advice on the Program as is appropriate.

"(3) The Committee shall consist of at least ten members and shall include—

"(A) three members representing agencies having authority under State law to regulate the shellfish industry, of whom one shall represent each of the Atlantic, Pacific, and Gulf of Mexico shellfish growing regions;

"(B) three members representing persons engaged in the shellfish industry in the Atlantic, Pacific, and Gulf of Mexico shellfish growing regions (who shall be appointed from among at least six recommendations by the industry members of the Interstate Shellfish Sanitation Conference Executive Board), of whom one shall represent the shellfish industry in each region;

"(C) three members, of whom one shall represent each of the following Federal agencies: the National Oceanic and Atmospheric Administration, the Environmental Protection Agency, and the Food and Drug Administration; and

"(D) one member representing the Shellfish Institute of North America.

"(4) The Chairman of the Committee shall be selected from among the Committee members described in paragraph (3)(A).

"(5) The Committee shall establish and maintain a subcommittee of scientific experts to provide advice, assistance, and information relevant to research funded under the Program, except that no individual who is awarded, or whose application is being considered for, a grant or subcontract under the Program may serve on such subcommittee. The membership of the subcommittee shall, to the extent practicable, be regionally balanced with experts who have scientific knowledge concerning each of the Atlantic, Pacific, and Gulf of Mexico shellfish growing regions. Scientists from the National Academy of Sciences and appropriate Federal agencies (including the National Oceanic and Atmospheric Administration, Food and Drug Administration, Centers for Disease Control, National Institutes of Health, Environmental Protection Agency, and National Science Foundation) shall be considered for membership on the subcommittee.

"(6) Members of the Committee and its scientific subcommittee established under this subsection shall not be paid for serving on the Committee or subcommittee, but shall receive travel expenses as authorized by section 5703 of title 5, United States Code [section 5703 of Title 5, Government Organization and Employees].

"(c) **Contract with consortium.**—Within 30 days after the date of enactment of this Act [Oct. 29, 1992], the Secretary of Commerce shall seek to enter into a cooperative agreement or contract with the Consortium under which the Consortium will—

"(1) be the academic administrative organization and fiscal agent for the Program;

"(2) award and administer such grants and subcontracts as are approved by the Committee under subsection (b);

"(3) develop and implement a scientific peer review process for evaluating grant and subcontractor applications prior to review by the Committee;

"(4) in cooperation with the Secretary of Commerce and the Committee, procure the services of a scientific project director;

"(5) develop and submit budgets, progress reports, work plans, and plans of operation for the Program to the Secretary of Commerce and the Committee; and

"(6) make available to the Committee such staff, information, and assistance as the Committee may reasonably require to carry out its activities.

"**(d) Authorization of appropriations.**—(1) Of the sums authorized under section 4(a) of the National Oceanic and Atmospheric Administration Marine Fisheries Program Authorization Act (Public Law 98–210; 97 Stat. 1409) [section 4(a) of Pub.L. 98–210, Dec. 6, 1983, 97 Stat. 1409, which is not classified to the Code], there are authorized to be appropriated to the Secretary of Commerce $5,200,000 for each of the fiscal years 1993 through 1997 for carrying out the Program. Of the amounts appropriated pursuant to this authorization, not more than 5 percent of such appropriation may be used for administrative purposes by the National Oceanic and Atmospheric Administration. The remaining 95 percent of such appropriation shall be used to meet the administrative and scientific objectives of the Program.

"(2) The Interstate Shellfish Sanitation Conference shall not administer appropriations authorized under this section, but may be reimbursed from such appropriations for its expenses in arranging for travel, meetings, workshops, or conferences necessary to carry out the Program.

"**(e) Definitions.**—As used in this section, the term—

"(1) 'Consortium' means the Louisiana Universities Marine Consortium; and

"(2) 'shellfish' means any species of oyster, clam, or mussel that is harvested for human consumption."

**Definition of "Administrator"**

Section 1(d) of Pub.L. 100–4 provided that: "For purposes of this Act [see Short Title of 1987 Amendment note set out above], the term 'Administrator' means the Administrator of the Environmental Protection Agency."

**Limitation on Payments**

Section 2 of Pub.L. 100–4 provided that: "No payments may be made under this Act [see Short Title of 1987 Amendment note set out above] except to the extent provided in advance in appropriation Acts."

**Contiguous Zone of United States**

For extension of contiguous zone of United States, see Proc. No. 7219, set out as a note under 43 U.S.C.A. § 1331.

## § 1252. Comprehensive programs for water pollution control

### [FWPCA § 102]

**(a) Preparation and development**

The Administrator shall, after careful investigation, and in cooperation with other Federal agencies, State water pollution control agencies, interstate agencies, and the municipalities and industries involved, prepare or develop comprehensive programs for preventing, reducing, or eliminating the pollution of the navigable waters and ground waters and improving the sanitary condition of surface and underground waters. In the development of such comprehensive programs due regard shall be given to the improvements which are necessary to conserve such waters for the protection and propagation of fish and aquatic life and wildlife, recreational purposes, and the withdrawal of such waters for public water supply, agricultural, industrial, and other purposes. For the purpose of this section, the Administrator is authorized to make joint investigations with any such agencies of the condition of any waters in any State or States, and of the discharges of any sewage, industrial wastes, or substance which may adversely affect such waters.

**(b) Planning for reservoirs; storage for regulation of streamflow**

(1) In the survey or planning of any reservoir by the Corps of Engineers, Bureau of Reclamation, or other Federal agency, consideration shall be given to inclusion of storage for regulation of streamflow, except that any such storage and water releases shall not be provided as a substitute for adequate treatment or other methods of controlling waste at the source.

(2) The need for and the value of storage for regulation of streamflow (other than for water quality) including but not limited to navigation, salt water intrusion, recreation, esthetics, and fish and wildlife, shall be determined by the Corps of Engineers, Bureau of Reclamation, or other Federal agencies.

(3) The need for, the value of, and the impact of, storage for water quality control shall be determined by the Administrator, and his views on these matters shall be set forth in any report or presentation to Congress proposing authorization or construction of any reservoir including such storage.

(4) The value of such storage shall be taken into account in determining the economic value of the entire project of which it is a part, and costs shall be allocated to the purpose of regulation of streamflow in a manner which will insure that all project purposes, share equitably in the benefit of multiple-purpose construction.

(5) Costs of regulation of streamflow features incorporated in any Federal reservoir or other impoundment under the provisions of this chapter shall be determined and the beneficiaries identified and if the benefits are widespread or national in scope, the costs of such features shall be nonreimbursable.

(6) No license granted by the Federal Energy Regulatory Commission for a hydroelectric power project shall include storage for regulation of streamflow for the purpose of water quality control unless the Administrator shall recommend its inclusion and such reser-

voir storage capacity shall not exceed such proportion of the total storage required for the water quality control plan as the drainage area of such reservoir bears to the drainage area of the river basin or basins involved in such water quality control plan.

**(c) Basins; grants to State agencies**

(1) The Administrator shall, at the request of the Governor of a State, or a majority of the Governors when more than one State is involved, make a grant to pay not to exceed 50 per centum of the administrative expenses of a planning agency for a period not to exceed three years, which period shall begin after October 18, 1972, if such agency provides for adequate representation of appropriate State, interstate, local, or (when appropriate) international interests in the basin or portion thereof involved and is capable of developing an effective, comprehensive water quality control plan for a basin or portion thereof.

(2) Each planning agency receiving a grant under this subsection shall develop a comprehensive pollution control plan for the basin or portion thereof which—

(A) is consistent with any applicable water quality standards, effluent and other limitations, and thermal discharge regulations established pursuant to current law within the basin;

(B) recommends such treatment works as will provide the most effective and economical means of collection, storage, treatment, and elimination of pollutants and recommends means to encourage both municipal and industrial use of such works;

(C) recommends maintenance and improvement of water quality within the basin or portion thereof and recommends methods of adequately financing those facilities as may be necessary to implement the plan; and

(D) as appropriate, is developed in cooperation with, and is consistent with any comprehensive plan prepared by the Water Resources Council, any areawide waste management plans developed pursuant to section 1288 of this title, and any State plan developed pursuant to section 1313(e) of this title.

(3) For the purposes of this subsection the term "basin" includes, but is not limited to, rivers and their tributaries, streams, coastal waters, sounds, estuaries, bays, lakes, and portions thereof as well as the lands drained thereby.

(June 30, 1948, c. 758, Title I, § 102, as added Oct. 18, 1972, Pub.L. 92–500, § 2, 86 Stat. 817, and amended Aug. 4, 1977, Pub.L. 95–91, Title IV, § 402(a)(1)(A), 91 Stat. 583; Dec. 27, 1977, Pub.L. 95–217, § 5(b), 91 Stat. 1567; Dec. 21, 1995, Pub.L. 104–66, Title II, § 2021(a), 109 Stat. 726.)

**HISTORICAL AND STATUTORY NOTES**

**Transfer of Functions**

"Federal Energy Regulatory Commission" was substituted for "Federal Power Commission" in subsec. (b)(6) on authority of Pub.L. 95–91, Title IV, § 402(a)(1)(A), Aug. 4, 1977, 91 Stat. 583, which is classified to section 7172(a)(1)(A) of Title 42, The Public Health and Welfare.

**Environmental Dredging**

Pub.L. 101–640, Title III, § 312, Nov. 28, 1990, 104 Stat. 4639, which was formerly set out as a note under this section, is now set out as section 1272 of this title.

## § 1252a. Reservoir projects, water storage; modification; storage for other than for water quality, opinion of Federal agency, committee resolutions of approval; provisions inapplicable to projects with certain prescribed water quality benefits in relation to total project benefits

**[FWPCA § 102A]**

In the case of any reservoir project authorized for construction by the Corps of Engineers, Bureau of Reclamation, or other Federal agency when the Administrator of the Environmental Protection Agency determines pursuant to section 1252(b) of this title that any storage in such project for regulation of streamflow for water quality is not needed, or is needed in a different amount, such project may be modified accordingly by the head of the appropriate agency, and any storage no longer required for water quality may be utilized for other authorized purposes of the project when, in the opinion of the head of such agency, such use is justified. Any such modification of a project where the benefits attributable to water quality are 15 per centum or more but not greater than 25 per centum of the total project benefits shall take effect only upon the adoption of resolutions approving such modification by the appropriate committees of the Senate and House of Representatives. The provisions of the section shall not apply to any project where the benefits attributable to water quality exceed 25 per centum of the total project benefits.

(Pub.L. 93–251, Title I, § 65, Mar. 7, 1974, 88 Stat. 30.)

**HISTORICAL AND STATUTORY NOTES**

**Codifications**

Section was not enacted as part of the Federal Water Pollution Control Act which comprises this chapter.

## § 1253. Interstate cooperation and uniform laws

**[FWPCA § 103]**

**(a)** The Administrator shall encourage cooperative activities by the States for the prevention, reduction, and elimination of pollution, encourage the enactment of improved and, so far as practicable, uniform State laws relating to the prevention, reduction, and elimination of pollution; and encourage compacts between States for the prevention and control of pollution.

**(b)** The consent of the Congress is hereby given to two or more States to negotiate and enter into agreements or compacts, not in conflict with any law or treaty of the United States, for (1) cooperative effort and mutual assistance for the prevention and control of pollution and the enforcement of their respective laws relating thereto, and (2) the establishment of such agencies, joint or otherwise, as they may deem desirable for making effective such agreements and compacts. No such agreement or compact shall be binding or obligatory upon any State a party thereto unless and until it has been approved by the Congress.

(June 30, 1948, c. 758, Title I, § 103, as added Oct. 18, 1972, Pub.L. 92–500, § 2, 86 Stat. 818.)

## § 1254. Research, investigations, training, and information

**[FWPCA § 104]**

### (a) Establishment of national programs; cooperation; investigations; water quality surveillance system; reports

The Administrator shall establish national programs for the prevention, reduction, and elimination of pollution and as part of such programs shall—

(1) in cooperation with other Federal, State, and local agencies, conduct and promote the coordination and acceleration of, research, investigations, experiments, training, demonstrations, surveys, and studies relating to the causes, effects, extent, prevention, reduction, and elimination of pollution;

(2) encourage, cooperate with, and render technical services to pollution control agencies and other appropriate public or private agencies, institutions, and organizations, and individuals, including the general public, in the conduct of activities referred to in paragraph (1) of this subsection;

(3) conduct, in cooperation with State water pollution control agencies and other interested agencies, organizations and persons, public investigations concerning the pollution of any navigable waters, and report on the results of such investigations;

(4) establish advisory committees composed of recognized experts in various aspects of pollution and representatives of the public to assist in the examination and evaluation of research progress and proposals and to avoid duplication of research;

(5) in cooperation with the States, and their political subdivisions, and other Federal agencies establish, equip, and maintain a water quality surveillance system for the purpose of monitoring the quality of the navigable waters and ground waters and the contiguous zone and the oceans and the Administrator shall, to the extent practicable, conduct such surveillance by utilizing the resources of the National Aeronautics and Space Administration, the National Oceanic and Atmospheric Administration, the United States Geological Survey, and the Coast Guard, and shall report on such quality in the report required under subsection (a) of section 1375 of this title; and

(6) initiate and promote the coordination and acceleration of research designed to develop the most effective practicable tools and techniques for measuring the social and economic costs and benefits of activities which are subject to regulation under this chapter; and shall transmit a report on the results of such research to the Congress not later than January 1, 1974.

### (b) Authorized activities of Administrator

In carrying out the provisions of subsection (a) of this section the Administrator is authorized to—

(1) collect and make available, through publications and other appropriate means, the results of and other information, including appropriate recommendations by him in connection therewith, pertaining to such research and other activities referred to in paragraph (1) of subsection (a) of this section;

(2) cooperate with other Federal departments and agencies, State water pollution control agencies, interstate agencies, other public and private agencies, institutions, organizations, industries involved, and individuals, in the preparation and conduct of such research and other activities referred to in paragraph (1) of subsection (a) of this section;

(3) make grants to State water pollution control agencies, interstate agencies, other public or nonprofit private agencies, institutions, organizations, and individuals, for purposes stated in paragraph (1) of subsection (a) of this section;

(4) contract with public or private agencies, institutions, organizations, and individuals, without regard to section 3324(a) and (b) of Title 31 and section 5 of Title 41, referred to in paragraph (1) of subsection (a) of this section;

(5) establish and maintain research fellowships at public or nonprofit private educational institutions or research organizations;

(6) collect and disseminate, in cooperation with other Federal departments and agencies, and with other public or private agencies, institutions, and organizations having related responsibilities, basic data on chemical, physical, and biological effects of varying water quality and other information per-

taining to pollution and the prevention, reduction, and elimination thereof; and

(7) develop effective and practical processes, methods, and prototype devices for the prevention, reduction, and elimination of pollution.

**(c) Research and studies on harmful effects of pollutants; cooperation with Secretary of Health and Human Services**

In carrying out the provisions of subsection (a) of this section the Administrator shall conduct research on, and survey the results of other scientific studies on, the harmful effects on the health or welfare of persons caused by pollutants. In order to avoid duplication of effort, the Administrator shall, to the extent practicable, conduct such research in cooperation with and through the facilities of the Secretary of Health and Human Services.

**(d) Sewage treatment; identification and measurement of effects of pollutants; augmented streamflow**

In carrying out the provisions of this section the Administrator shall develop and demonstrate under varied conditions (including conducting such basic and applied research, studies, and experiments as may be necessary):

(1) Practicable means of treating municipal sewage, and other waterborne wastes to implement the requirements of section 1281 of this title;

(2) Improved methods and procedures to identify and measure the effects of pollutants, including those pollutants created by new technological developments; and

(3) Methods and procedures for evaluating the effects on water quality of augmented streamflows to control pollution not susceptible to other means of prevention, reduction, or elimination.

**(e) Field laboratory and research facilities**

The Administrator shall establish, equip, and maintain field laboratory and research facilities, including, but not limited to, one to be located in the northeastern area of the United States, one in the Middle Atlantic area, one in the southeastern area, one in the midwestern area, one in the southwestern area, one in the Pacific Northwest, and one in the State of Alaska, for the conduct of research, investigations, experiments, field demonstrations and studies, and training relating to the prevention, reduction and elimination of pollution. Insofar as practicable, each such facility shall be located near institutions of higher learning in which graduate training in such research might be carried out. In conjunction with the development of criteria under section 1343 of this title, the Administrator shall construct the facilities authorized for the National Marine Water Quality Laboratory established under this subsection.

**(f) Great Lakes water quality research**

The Administrator shall conduct research and technical development work, and make studies, with respect to the quality of the waters of the Great Lakes, including an analysis of the present and projected future water quality of the Great Lakes under varying conditions of waste treatment and disposal, an evaluation of the water quality needs of those to be served by such waters, an evaluation of municipal, industrial, and vessel waste treatment and disposal practices with respect to such waters, and a study of alternate means of solving pollution problems (including additional waste treatment measures) with respect to such waters.

**(g) Treatment works pilot training programs; employment needs forecasting; training projects and grants; research fellowships; technical training; report to the President and transmittal to Congress**

(1) For the purpose of providing an adequate supply of trained personnel to operate and maintain existing and future treatment works and related activities, and for the purpose of enhancing substantially the proficiency of those engaged in such activities, the Administrator shall finance pilot programs, in cooperation with State and interstate agencies, municipalities, educational institutions, and other organizations and individuals, of manpower development and training and retraining of persons in, on entering into, the field of operation and maintenance of treatment works and related activities. Such program and any funds expended for such a program shall supplement, not supplant, other manpower and training programs and funds available for the purposes of this paragraph. The Administrator is authorized, under such terms and conditions as he deems appropriate, to enter into agreements with one or more States, acting jointly or severally, or with other public or private agencies or institutions for the development and implementation of such a program.

(2) The Administrator is authorized to enter into agreements with public and private agencies and institutions, and individuals to develop and maintain an effective system for forecasting the supply of, and demand for, various professional and other occupational categories needed for the prevention, reduction, and elimination of pollution in each region, State, or area of the United States and, from time to time, to publish the results of such forecasts.

(3) In furtherance of the purposes of this chapter, the Administrator is authorized to—

(A) make grants to public or private agencies and institutions and to individuals for training projects, and provide for the conduct of training by contract with public or private agencies and institutions and with individuals without regard to section 3324(a) and (b) of Title 31 and section 5 of Title 41;

(B) establish and maintain research fellowships in the Environmental Protection Agency with such stipends and allowances, including traveling and subsistence expenses, as he may deem necessary to procure the assistance of the most promising research fellows; and

(C) provide, in addition to the program established under paragraph (1) of this subsection, training in technical matters relating to the causes, prevention, reduction, and elimination of pollution for personnel of public agencies and other persons with suitable qualifications.

(4) The Administrator shall submit, through the President, a report to the Congress not later than December 31, 1973, summarizing the actions taken under this subsection and the effectiveness of such actions, and setting forth the number of persons trained, the occupational categories for which training was provided, the effectiveness of other Federal, State, and local training programs in this field, together with estimates of future needs, recommendations on improving training programs, and such other information and recommendations, including legislative recommendations, as he deems appropriate.

**(h) Lake pollution**

The Administrator is authorized to enter into contracts with, or make grants to, public or private agencies and organizations and individuals for (A) the purpose of developing and demonstrating new or improved methods for the prevention, removal, reduction, and elimination of pollution in lakes, including the undesirable effects of nutrients and vegetation, and (B) the construction of publicly owned research facilities for such purpose.

**(i) Oil pollution control studies**

The Administrator, in cooperation with the Secretary of the Department in which the Coast Guard is operating, shall—

(1) engage in such research, studies, experiments, and demonstrations as he deems appropriate, relative to the removal of oil from any waters and to the prevention, control, and elimination of oil and hazardous substances pollution;

(2) publish from time to time the results of such activities; and

(3) from time to time, develop and publish in the Federal Register specifications and other technical information on the various chemical compounds used in the control of oil and hazardous substances spills.

In carrying out this subsection, the Administrator may enter into contracts with, or make grants to, public or private agencies and organizations and individuals.

**(j) Solid waste disposal equipment for vessels**

The Secretary of the department in which the Coast Guard is operating shall engage in such research, studies, experiments, and demonstrations as he deems appropriate relative to equipment which is to be installed on board a vessel and is designed to receive, retain, treat, or discharge human body wastes and the wastes from toilets and other receptacles intended to receive or retain body wastes with particular emphasis on equipment to be installed on small recreational vessels. The Secretary of the department in which the Coast Guard is operating shall report to Congress the results of such research, studies, experiments, and demonstrations prior to the effective date of any regulations established under section 1322 of this title. In carrying out this subsection the Secretary of the department in which the Coast Guard is operating may enter into contracts with, or make grants to, public or private organizations and individuals.

**(k) Land acquisition**

In carrying out the provisions of this section relating to the conduct by the Administrator of demonstration projects and the development of field laboratories and research facilities, the Administrator may acquire land and interests therein by purchase, with appropriated or donated funds, by donation, or by exchange for acquired or public lands under his jurisdiction which he classifies as suitable for disposition. The values of the properties so exchanged either shall be approximately equal, or if they are not approximately equal, the values shall be equalized by the payment of cash to the grantor or to the Administrator as the circumstances require.

**(*l*) Collection and dissemination of scientific knowledge on effects and control of pesticides in water**

(1) The Administrator shall, after consultation with appropriate local, State, and Federal agencies, public and private organizations, and interested individuals, as soon as practicable but not later than January 1, 1973, develop and issue to the States for the purpose of carrying out this chapter the latest scientific knowledge available in indicating the kind and extent of effects on health and welfare which may be expected from the presence of pesticides in the water in varying quantities. He shall revise and add to such information whenever necessary to reflect developing scientific knowledge.

(2) The President shall, in consultation with appropriate local, State, and Federal agencies, public and

private organizations, and interested individuals, conduct studies and investigations of methods to control the release of pesticides into the environment which study shall include examination of the persistency of pesticides in the water environment and alternatives thereto. The President shall submit reports, from time to time, on such investigations to Congress together with his recommendations for any necessary legislation.

**(m) Waste oil disposal study**

(1) The Administrator shall, in an effort to prevent degradation of the environment from the disposal of waste oil, conduct a study of (A) the generation of used engine, machine, cooling, and similar waste oil, including quantities generated, the nature and quality of such oil, present collecting methods and disposal practices, and alternate uses of such oil; (B) the long-term, chronic biological effects of the disposal of such waste oil; and (C) the potential market for such oils, including the economic and legal factors relating to the sale of products made from such oils, the level of subsidy, if any, needed to encourage the purchase by public and private nonprofit agencies of products from such oil, and the practicability of Federal procurement, on a priority basis, of products made from such oil. In conducting such study, the Administrator shall consult with affected industries and other persons.

(2) The Administrator shall report the preliminary results of such study to Congress within six months after October 18, 1972, and shall submit a final report to Congress within 18 months after such date.

**(n) Comprehensive studies of effects of pollution on estuaries and estuarine zones**

(1) The Administrator shall, in cooperation with the Secretary of the Army, the Secretary of Agriculture, the Water Resources Council, and with other appropriate Federal, State, interstate, or local public bodies and private organizations, institutions, and individuals, conduct and promote, and encourage contributions to, continuing comprehensive studies of the effects of pollution, including sedimentation, in the estuaries and estuarine zones of the United States on fish and wildlife, on sport and commercial fishing, on recreation, on water supply and water power, and on other beneficial purposes. Such studies shall also consider the effect of demographic trends, the exploitation of mineral resources and fossil fuels, land and industrial development, navigation, flood and erosion control, and other uses of estuaries and estuarine zones upon the pollution of the waters therein.

(2) In conducting such studies, the Administrator shall assemble, coordinate, and organize all existing pertinent information on the Nation's estuaries and estuarine zones; carry out a program of investigations and surveys to supplement existing information in representative estuaries and estuarine zones; and identify the problems and areas where further research and study are required.

(3) The Administrator shall submit to Congress, from time to time, reports of the studies authorized by this subsection but at least one such report during any six-year period. Copies of each such report shall be made available to all interested parties, public and private.

(4) For the purpose of this subsection, the term "estuarine zones" means an environmental system consisting of an estuary and those transitional areas which are consistently influenced or affected by water from an estuary such as, but not limited to, salt marshes, coastal and intertidal areas, bays, harbors, lagoons, inshore waters, and channels, and the term "estuary" means all or part of the mouth of a river or stream or other body of water having unimpaired natural connection with open sea and within which the sea water is measurably diluted with fresh water derived from land drainage.

**(*o*) Methods of reducing total flow of sewage and unnecessary water consumption; reports**

(1) The Administrator shall conduct research and investigations on devices, systems, incentives, pricing policy, and other methods of reducing the total flow of sewage, including, but not limited to, unnecessary water consumption in order to reduce the requirements for, and the costs of, sewage and waste treatment services. Such research and investigations shall be directed to develop devices, systems, policies, and methods capable of achieving the maximum reduction of unnecessary water consumption.

(2) The Administrator shall report the preliminary results of such studies and investigations to the Congress within one year after October 18, 1972, and annually thereafter in the report required under subsection (a) of section 1375 of this title. Such report shall include recommendations for any legislation that may be required to provide for the adoption and use of devices, systems, policies, or other methods of reducing water consumption and reducing the total flow of sewage. Such report shall include an estimate of the benefits to be derived from adoption and use of such devices, systems, policies, or other methods and also shall reflect estimates of any increase in private, public, or other cost that would be occasioned thereby.

**(p) Agricultural pollution**

In carrying out the provisions of subsection (a) of this section the Administrator shall, in cooperation with the Secretary of Agriculture, other Federal agencies, and the States, carry out a comprehensive study and research program to determine new and improved methods and the better application of existing methods of preventing, reducing, and eliminating pollution from agriculture, including the legal, economic, and other implications of the use of such methods.

### (q) Sewage in rural areas; national clearinghouse for alternative treatment information; clearinghouse on small flows

(1) The Administrator shall conduct a comprehensive program of research and investigation and pilot project implementation into new and improved methods of preventing, reducing, storing, collecting, treating, or otherwise eliminating pollution from sewage in rural and other areas where collection of sewage in conventional, communitywide sewage collection systems is impractical, uneconomical, or otherwise infeasible, or where soil conditions or other factors preclude the use of septic tank and drainage field systems.

(2) The Administrator shall conduct a comprehensive program of research and investigation and pilot project implementation into new and improved methods for the collection and treatment of sewage and other liquid wastes combined with the treatment and disposal of solid wastes.

(3) The Administrator shall establish, either within the Environmental Protection Agency, or through contract with an appropriate public or private non-profit organization, a national clearinghouse which shall (A) receive reports and information resulting from research, demonstrations, and other projects funded under this chapter related to paragraph (1) of this subsection and to subsection (e)(2) of section 1255 of this title; (B) coordinate and disseminate such reports and information for use by Federal and State agencies, municipalities, institutions, and persons in developing new and improved methods pursuant to this subsection; and (C) provide for the collection and dissemination of reports and information relevant to this subsection from other Federal and State agencies, institutions, universities, and persons.

#### (4) Small flows clearinghouse

Notwithstanding section 1285(d) of this title, from amounts that are set aside for a fiscal year under section 1285(i) of this title and are not obligated by the end of the 24-month period of availability for such amounts under section 1285(d) of this title, the Administrator shall make available $1,000,000 or such unobligated amount, whichever is less, to support a national clearinghouse within the Environmental Protection Agency to collect and disseminate information on small flows of sewage and innovative or alternative wastewater treatment processes and techniques, consistent with paragraph (3). This paragraph shall apply with respect to amounts set aside under section 1285(i) of this title for which the 24-month period of availability referred to in the preceding sentence ends on or after September 30, 1986.

### (r) Research grants to colleges and universities

The Administrator is authorized to make grants to colleges and universities to conduct basic research into the structure and function of freshwater aquatic ecosystems, and to improve understanding of the ecological characteristics necessary to the maintenance of the chemical, physical, and biological integrity of freshwater aquatic ecosystems.

### (s) River Study Centers

The Administrator is authorized to make grants to one or more institutions of higher education (regionally located and to be designated as "River Study Centers") for the purpose of conducting and reporting on interdisciplinary studies on the nature of river systems, including hydrology, biology, ecology, economics, the relationship between river uses and land uses, and the effects of development within river basins on river systems and on the value of water resources and water related activities. No such grant in any fiscal year shall exceed $1,000,000.

### (t) Thermal discharges

The Administrator shall, in cooperation with State and Federal agencies and public and private organizations, conduct continuing comprehensive studies of the effects and methods of control of thermal discharges. In evaluating alternative methods of control the studies shall consider (1) such data as are available on the latest available technology, economic feasibility including cost-effectiveness analysis, and (2) the total impact on the environment, considering not only water quality but also air quality, land use, and effective utilization and conservation of freshwater and other natural resources. Such studies shall consider methods of minimizing adverse effects and maximizing beneficial effects of thermal discharges. The results of these studies shall be reported by the Administrator as soon as practicable, but not later than 270 days after October 18, 1972, and shall be made available to the public and the States, and considered as they become available by the Administrator in carrying out section 1326 of this title and by the States in proposing thermal water quality standards.

### (u) Authorization of appropriations

There is authorized to be appropriated (1) not to exceed $100,000,000 per fiscal year for the fiscal year ending June 30, 1973, the fiscal year ending June 30, 1974, and the fiscal year ending June 30, 1975, not to exceed $14,039,000 for the fiscal year ending September 30, 1980, not to exceed $20,697,000 for the fiscal year ending September 30, 1981, not to exceed $22,770,000 for the fiscal year ending September 30, 1982, such sums as may be necessary for fiscal years 1983 through 1985, and not to exceed $22,770,000 per fiscal year for each of the fiscal years 1986 through 1990, for carrying out the provisions of this section, other than subsections (g)(1) and (2), (p), (r), and (t) of this section, except that such authorizations are not for any research, development, or demonstration activity pursuant to such provisions; (2) not to exceed $7,500,000 for fiscal years 1973, 1974, and 1975, $2,000,000 for fiscal year 1977, $3,000,000 for fiscal year 1978, $3,000,000 for fiscal year 1979, $3,000,000 for fiscal year 1980, $3,000,000 for fiscal year 1981, $3,000,000 for fiscal year 1982, such sums as may be necessary for fiscal years 1983 through 1985, and $3,000,000 per fiscal year for each of the fiscal years 1986 through 1990, for carrying out the provisions of subsection (g)(1) of this section; (3) not to exceed $2,500,000 for fiscal years 1973, 1974, and 1975, $1,000,000 for fiscal year 1977, $1,500,000 for fiscal year 1978, $1,500,000 for fiscal year 1979, $1,500,000 for fiscal year 1980, $1,500,000 for fiscal year 1981, $1,500,000 for fiscal year 1982, such sums as may be necessary for fiscal years 1983 through 1985, and $1,500,000 per fiscal year for each of the fiscal years 1986 through 1990, for carrying out the provisions of subsection (g)(2) of this section; (4) not to exceed $10,000,000 for each of the fiscal years ending June 30, 1973, June 30, 1974, and June 30, 1975, for carrying out the provisions of subsection (p) of this section; (5) not to exceed $15,000,000 per fiscal year for the fiscal years ending June 30, 1973, June 30, 1974, and June 30, 1975, for carrying out the provisions of subsection (r) of this section; and (6) not to exceed $10,000,000 per fiscal year for the fiscal years ending June 30, 1973, June 30, 1974, and June 30, 1975, for carrying out the provisions of subsection (t) of this section.

**(v) Studies concerning pathogen indicators in coastal recreation waters**

Not later than 18 months after October 10, 2000, after consultation and in cooperation with appropriate Federal, State, tribal, and local officials (including local health officials), the Administrator shall initiate, and, not later than 3 years after October 10, 2000, shall complete, in cooperation with the heads of other Federal agencies, studies to provide additional information for use in developing—

(1) an assessment of potential human health risks resulting from exposure to pathogens in coastal recreation waters, including nongastrointestinal effects;

(2) appropriate and effective indicators for improving detection in a timely manner in coastal recreation waters of the presence of pathogens that are harmful to human health;

(3) appropriate, accurate, expeditious, and cost-effective methods (including predictive models) for detecting in a timely manner in coastal recreation waters the presence of pathogens that are harmful to human health; and

(4) guidance for State application of the criteria for pathogens and pathogen indicators to be published under section 1314(a)(9) of this title to account for the diversity of geographic and aquatic conditions.

(June 30, 1948, c. 758, Title I, § 104, as added Oct. 18, 1972, Pub.L. 92–500, § 2, 86 Stat. 819, and amended Dec. 28, 1973, Pub.L. 93–207, § 1(1), 87 Stat. 906; Jan. 2, 1975, Pub.L. 93–592, § 1, 88 Stat. 1924; Dec. 27, 1977, Pub.L. 95–217, §§ 4(a), (b), 6, 7, 91 Stat. 1566, 1567; Nov. 2, 1978, Pub.L. 95–576, § 1(a), 92 Stat. 2467; Oct. 17, 1979, Pub.L. 96–88, Title V, § 509(b), 93 Stat. 695; Oct. 21, 1980, Pub.L. 96–483, § 1(a), 94 Stat. 2360; Feb. 4, 1987, Pub.L. 100–4, Title I, §§ 101(a), 102, 101 Stat. 8, 9; Nov. 13, 1991, Pub.L. 102–154, Title I, 105 Stat. 1000; May 18, 1992, Pub.L. 102–285, § 10(a), 106 Stat. 171; Nov. 10, 1998, Pub.L. 105–362, Title V, § 501(a)(1), (d)(2)(A), 112 Stat. 3283, 3284; Oct. 10, 2000, Pub.L. 106–284, § 3(a), 114 Stat. 871; Nov. 27, 2002, Pub.L. 107–303, Title III, § 302(b)(1), 116 Stat. 2361.)

## HISTORICAL AND STATUTORY NOTES

### Codifications

In subsecs. (b)(4) and (g)(3)(A), "section 3324(a) and (b) of Title 31" was substituted for reference to section 3648 of the Revised Statutes [31 U.S.C.A. § 529] on authority of Pub.L. 97–258, § 4(b), Sept. 13, 1982, 96 Stat. 1067, the first section of which enacted Title 31, Money and Finance.

### Effective and Applicability Provisions

2002 Acts

Pub.L. 107–303, Title III, § 302(b), Nov. 27, 2002, 116 Stat. 2361, provided that:

"(1) **In general.**—Effective November 10, 1998, section 501 of the Federal Reports Elimination Act of 1998 (Public Law 105–362; 112 Stat. 3283) [Pub.L. 105–362, Title V, § 501, Nov. 10, 1998, 112 Stat. 3283, see Tables for complete classification] is amended by striking subsections (a), (b), (c), and (d) [amending this section and 33 U.S.C.A. §§ 1266, 1285, 1290, 1324, 1329, 1330, and 1375].

"(2) **Applicability.**—The Federal Water Pollution Control Act (33 U.S.C. 1254(n)(3)) shall be applied and administered on and after the date of enactment of this Act [Nov. 27, 2002] as if the amendments made by subsections (a), (b), (c), and (d) of section 501 of the Federal Reports Elimination Act of 1998 (Public Law 105–362; 112 Stat. 3283) [Pub.L. 105–362, Title V, § 501(a) to (d), Nov. 10, 1998, 112 Stat. 3283, amending this section and 33 U.S.C.A. §§ 1266, 1285, 1290, 1324, 1329, 1330, and 1375] had not been enacted."

### Change of Name

Pub.L. 102–285, § 10(a), May 18, 1992, 106 Stat. 171, redesignated the Geological Survey and provided that on and after May 18, 1992, it shall be known as the United States Geological Survey. An earlier statute [Pub.L. 102–154, Title I, Nov. 13, 1991, 105 Stat. 1000] had provided for the identical change of name effective on and after Nov. 13, 1991. See note under section 31 of Title 43, Public Lands.

"Secretary of Health and Human Services" was substituted for "Secretary of Health, Education, and Welfare" in subsec. (c) pursuant to section 509(b) of Pub.L. 96–88 which is classified to section 3508(b) of Title 20, Education.

**Transfer of Functions**

Enforcement functions of Secretary or other official in Department of Agriculture, insofar as they involve lands and programs under jurisdiction of that Department, related to compliance with this chapter with respect to pre-construction, construction, and initial operation of transportation system for Canadian and Alaskan natural gas were transferred to the Federal Inspector, Office of Federal Inspector for the Alaska Natural Gas Transportation System, until the first anniversary of date of initial operation of the Alaska Natural Gas Transportation System, see Reorg. Plan No. 1 of 1979, §§ 102(f), 203(a), 44 F.R. 33663, 33666, 93 Stat. 1373, 1376, effective July 1, 1979, set out in Appendix 1 to Title 5, Government Organization and Employees.

**Columbia River Basin System; Protection From Oil Spills and Discharges; Criteria for Evaluation and Report to Congress by Commandant of Coast Guard in Consultation With Federal, Etc., Agencies**

Pub. L. 95–308, § 8, June 30, 1978, 92 Stat. 359, set forth Congressional findings and declarations and evaluation criteria with respect to protection from oil spills and discharges and betterment of the Columbia River Basin system, with such evaluation by the Commandant of the Coast Guard to begin within 180 days after June 30, 1978, and immediate submission of the evaluation to appropriate Congressional committees.

**Contiguous Zone of United States**

For extension of contiguous zone of United States, see Proc. No. 7219, set out as a note under 43 U.S.C.A. § 1331.

## § 1254a. Research on effects of pollutants

In carrying out the provisions of section 1254(a) of this title, the Administrator shall conduct research on the harmful effects on the health and welfare of persons caused by pollutants in water, in conjunction with the United States Fish and Wildlife Service, the National Oceanic and Atmospheric Administration, and other Federal, State, and interstate agencies carrying on such research. Such research shall include, and shall place special emphasis on, the effect that bioaccumulation of these pollutants in aquatic species has upon reducing the value of aquatic commercial and sport industries. Such research shall further study methods to reduce and remove these pollutants from the relevant affected aquatic species so as to restore and enhance these valuable resources.

(Pub.L. 100–4, Title I, § 105, Feb. 4, 1987, 101 Stat. 15.)

### HISTORICAL AND STATUTORY NOTES

**Codifications**

Section was enacted as part of the Water Quality Act of 1987, and not as part of the Federal Water Pollution Control Act, which comprises this chapter.

**Definition**

Administrator means the Administrator of the Environmental Protection Agency, see section 1(d) of Pub.L. 100–4, set out as a note under 33 U.S.C.A. § 1251.

## § 1255. Grants for research and development

[FWPCA § 105]

**(a) Demonstration projects covering storm waters, advanced waste treatment and water purification methods, and joint treatment systems for municipal and industrial wastes**

The Administrator is authorized to conduct in the Environmental Protection Agency, and to make grants to any State, municipality, or intermunicipal or interstate agency for the purpose of assisting in the development of—

(1) any project which will demonstrate a new or improved method of preventing, reducing, and eliminating the discharge into any waters of pollutants from sewers which carry storm water or both storm water and pollutants; or

(2) any project which will demonstrate advanced waste treatment and water purification methods (including the temporary use of new or improved chemical additives which provide substantial immediate improvements to existing treatment processes), or new or improved methods of joint treatment systems for municipal and industrial wastes;

and to include in such grants such amounts as are necessary for the purpose of reports, plans, and specifications in connection therewith.

**(b) Demonstration projects for advanced treatment and environmental enhancement techniques to control pollution in river basins**

The Administrator is authorized to make grants to any State or States or interstate agency to demonstrate, in river basins or portions thereof, advanced treatment and environmental enhancement techniques to control pollution from all sources, within such basins or portions thereof, including nonpoint sources, together with in stream[1] water quality improvement techniques.

**(c) Research and demonstration projects for prevention of water pollution by industry**

In order to carry out the purposes of section 1311 of this title, the Administrator is authorized to (1) conduct in the Environmental Protection Agency, (2) make grants to persons, and (3) enter into contracts with persons, for research and demonstration projects for prevention of pollution of any waters by industry including, but not limited to, the prevention, reduction, and elimination of the discharge of pollutants. No grant shall be made for any project under this subsection unless the Administrator determines that such project will develop or demonstrate a new or improved method of treating industrial wastes or otherwise prevent pollution by industry, which method shall have industrywide application.

**(d) Accelerated and priority development of waste management and waste treatment methods and identification and measurement methods**

In carrying out the provisions of this section, the Administrator shall conduct, on a priority basis, an accelerated effort to develop, refine, and achieve practical application of:

(1) waste management methods applicable to point and nonpoint sources of pollutants to eliminate the discharge of pollutants, including, but not limited to, elimination of runoff of pollutants and the effects of pollutants from inplace or accumulated sources;

(2) advanced waste treatment methods applicable to point and nonpoint sources, including inplace or accumulated sources of pollutants, and methods for reclaiming and recycling water and confining pollutants so they will not migrate to cause water or other environmental pollution; and

(3) improved methods and procedures to identify and measure the effects of pollutants on the chemical, physical, and biological integrity of water, including those pollutants created by new technological developments.

**(e) Research and demonstration projects covering agricultural pollution and pollution from sewage in rural areas; dissemination of information**

(1) The Administrator is authorized to (A) make, in consultation with the Secretary of Agriculture, grants to persons for research and demonstration projects with respect to new and improved methods of preventing, reducing, and eliminating pollution from agriculture, and (B) disseminate, in cooperation with the Secretary of Agriculture, such information obtained under this subsection, section 1254(p) of this title, and section 1314 of this title as will encourage and enable the adoption of such methods in the agricultural industry.

(2) The Administrator is authorized, (A) in consultation with other interested Federal agencies, to make grants for demonstration projects with respect to new and improved methods of preventing, reducing, storing, collecting, treating, or otherwise eliminating pollution from sewage in rural and other areas where collection of sewage in conventional, community-wide sewage collection systems is impractical, uneconomical, or otherwise infeasible, or where soil conditions or other factors preclude the use of septic tank and drainage field systems, and (B) in cooperation with other interested Federal and State agencies, to disseminate such information obtained under this subsection as will encourage and enable the adoption of new and improved methods developed pursuant to this subsection.

**(f) Limitations**

Federal grants under subsection (a) of this section shall be subject to the following limitations:

(1) No grant shall be made for any project unless such project shall have been approved by the appropriate State water pollution control agency or agencies and by the Administrator;

(2) No grant shall be made for any project in an amount exceeding 75 per centum of cost thereof as determined by the Administrator; and

(3) No grant shall be made for any project unless the Administrator determines that such project will serve as a useful demonstration for the purpose set forth in clause (1) or (2) of subsection (a) of this section.

**(g) Maximum grants**

Federal grants under subsections (c) and (d) of this section shall not exceed 75 per centum of the cost of the project.

**(h) Authorization of appropriations**

For the purpose of this section there is authorized to be appropriated $75,000,000 per fiscal year for the fiscal year ending June 30, 1973, the fiscal year ending June 30, 1974, and the fiscal year ending June 30, 1975, and from such appropriations at least 10 per centum of the funds actually appropriated in each fiscal year shall be available only for the purposes of subsection (e) of this section.

**(i) Assistance for research and demonstration projects**

The Administrator is authorized to make grants to a municipality to assist in the costs of operating and maintaining a project which received a grant under this section, section 1254 of this title, or section 1263 of this title prior to December 27, 1977, so as to reduce the operation and maintenance costs borne by the recipients of services from such project to costs comparable to those for projects assisted under subchapter II of this chapter.

**(j) Assistance for recycle, reuse, and land treatment projects**

The Administrator is authorized to make a grant to any grantee who received an increased grant pursuant to section 1282(a)(2) of this title. Such grant may pay up to 100 per centum of the costs of technical evaluation of the operation of the treatment works, costs of training of persons (other than employees of the grantee), and costs of disseminating technical information on the operation of the treatment works.

(June 30, 1948, c. 758, Title I, § 105, as added Oct. 18, 1972, Pub.L. 92–500, § 2, 86 Stat. 825, and amended Jan. 2, 1975, Pub.L. 93–592, § 2, 88 Stat. 1925; Dec. 27, 1977, Pub.L. 95–217, §§ 8, 9, 91 Stat. 1568.)

[1] So in original.

### HISTORICAL AND STATUTORY NOTES

**Transfer of Functions**

Enforcement functions of Secretary or other official in Department of Agriculture, insofar as they involve lands and programs under jurisdiction of that Department, related to compliance with this chapter with respect to pre-construction, construction, and initial operation of transportation system for Canadian and Alaskan natural gas were transferred to the Federal Inspector, Office of Federal Inspector for the Alaska Natural Gas Transportation System, until the first anniversary of date of initial operation of the Alaska Natural Gas Transportation System, see Reorg. Plan No. 1 of 1979, §§ 102(f), 203(a), 44 F.R. 33663, 33666, 93 Stat. 1373, 1376, effective July 1, 1979, set out in Appendix 1 to Title 5, Government Organization and Employees.

## § 1256. Grants for pollution control programs

**[FWPCA § 106]**

**(a) Authorization of appropriations for State and interstate programs**

There are hereby authorized to be appropriated the following sums, to remain available until expended, to carry out the purposes of this section—

(1) $60,000,000 for the fiscal year ending June 30, 1973; and

(2) $75,000,000 for the fiscal year ending June 30, 1974, and the fiscal year ending June 30, 1975, $100,000,000 per fiscal year for the fiscal years 1977, 1978, 1979, and 1980, $75,000,000 per fiscal year for the fiscal years 1981 and 1982, such sums as may be necessary for fiscal years 1983 through 1985, and $75,000,000 per fiscal year for each of the fiscal years 1986 through 1990;

for grants to States and to interstate agencies to assist them in administering programs for the prevention, reduction, and elimination of pollution, including enforcement directly or through appropriate State law enforcement officers or agencies.

**(b) Allotments**

From the sums appropriated in any fiscal year, the Administrator shall make allotments to the several States and interstate agencies in accordance with regulations promulgated by him on the basis of the extent of the pollution problem in the respective States.

**(c) Maximum annual payments**

The Administrator is authorized to pay to each State and interstate agency each fiscal year either—

(1) the allotment of such State or agency for such fiscal year under subsection (b) of this section, or

(2) the reasonable costs as determined by the Administrator of developing and carrying out a pollution program by such State or agency during such fiscal year,

which ever amount is the lesser.

**(d) Limitations**

No grant shall be made under this section to any State or interstate agency for any fiscal year when the expenditure of non-Federal funds by such State or interstate agency during such fiscal year for the recurrent expenses of carrying out its pollution control program are less than the expenditure by such State or interstate agency of non-Federal funds for such recurrent program expenses during the fiscal year ending June 30, 1971.

**(e) Grants prohibited to States not establishing water quality monitoring procedures or adequate emergency and contingency plans**

Beginning in fiscal year 1974 the Administrator shall not make any grant under this section to any State which has not provided or is not carrying out as a part of its program—

(1) the establishment and operation of appropriate devices, methods, systems, and procedures necessary to monitor, and to compile and analyze data on (including classification according to eutrophic condition), the quality of navigable waters and to the extent practicable, ground waters including biological monitoring; and provision for annually updating such data and including it in the report required under section 1315 of this title;

(2) authority comparable to that in section 1364 of this title and adequate contingency plans to implement such authority.

**(f) Conditions**

Grants shall be made under this section on condition that—

(1) Such State (or interstate agency) files with the Administrator within one hundred and twenty days after October 18, 1972:

(A) a summary report of the current status of the State pollution control program, including the criteria used by the State in determining priority of treatment works; and

(B) such additional information, data, and reports as the Administrator may require.

(2) No federally assumed enforcement as defined in section 1319(a)(2) of this title is in effect with respect to such State or interstate agency.

(3) Such State (or interstate agency) submits within one hundred and twenty days after October 18, 1972, and before October 1 of each year thereafter for the Administrator's approval of its program for the prevention, reduction, and elimination of pollution in accordance with purposes and provisions of this chapter in such form and content as the Administrator may prescribe.

**(g) Reallotment of unpaid allotments**

Any sums allotted under subsection (b) of this section in any fiscal year which are not paid shall be reallotted by the Administrator in accordance with regulations promulgated by him.

(June 30, 1948, c. 758, Title I, § 106, as added Oct. 18, 1972, Pub.L. 92–500, § 2, 86 Stat. 827, and amended Jan. 2, 1975, Pub.L. 93–592, § 3, 88 Stat. 1925; Apr. 21, 1976, Pub.L. 94–273, § 3(20), 90 Stat. 377; Dec. 27, 1977, Pub.L. 95–217, § 4(c), 91 Stat. 1566; Oct. 21, 1980, Pub.L. 96–483, § 1(b), 94 Stat. 2360; Feb. 4, 1987, Pub.L. 100–4, Title I, § 101(b), 101 Stat. 9.)

## § 1257. Mine water pollution control demonstrations [FWPCA § 107]

### (a) Comprehensive approaches to elimination or control of mine water pollution

The Administrator in cooperation with the Appalachian Regional Commission and other Federal agencies is authorized to conduct, to make grants for, or to contract for, projects to demonstrate comprehensive approaches to the elimination or control of acid or other mine water pollution resulting from active or abandoned mining operations and other environmental pollution affecting water quality within all or part of a watershed or river basin, including siltation from surface mining. Such projects shall demonstrate the engineering and economic feasibility and practicality of various abatement techniques which will contribute substantially to effective and practical methods of acid or other mine water pollution elimination or control, and other pollution affecting water quality, including techniques that demonstrate the engineering and economic feasibility and practicality of using sewage sludge materials and other municipal wastes to diminish or prevent pollution affecting water quality from acid, sedimentation, or other pollutants and in such projects to restore affected lands to usefulness for forestry, agriculture, recreation, or other beneficial purposes.

### (b) Consistency of projects with objectives of Appalachian Regional Development Act of 1965

Prior to undertaking any demonstration project under this section in the Appalachian region (as defined in section 14102 of Title 40), the Appalachian Regional Commission shall determine that such demonstration project is consistent with the objectives of subtitle IV of Title 40.

### (c) Watershed selection

The Administrator, in selecting watersheds for the purposes of this section, shall be satisfied that the project area will not be affected adversely by the influx of acid or other mine water pollution from nearby sources.

### (d) Conditions upon Federal participation

Federal participation in such projects shall be subject to the conditions—

(1) that the State shall acquire any land or interests therein necessary for such project; and

(2) that the State shall provide legal and practical protection to the project area to insure against any activities which will cause future acid or other mine water pollution.

### (e) Authorization of appropriations

There is authorized to be appropriated $30,000,000 to carry out the provisions of this section, which sum shall be available until expended.

(June 30, 1948, c. 758, Title I, § 107, as added Oct. 18, 1972, Pub.L. 92–500, § 2, 86 Stat. 828.)

#### HISTORICAL AND STATUTORY NOTES

**References in Text**

Subtitle IV of Title 40, referred to in subsec. (b), is chapters 141, 143, 145, and 147 of Title 40, 40 U.S.C.A. §§ 14101 et seq., 14301 et seq., 14501 et seq., and 14701 et seq., respectively.

**Codifications**

In subsec. (b), "section 14102 of Title 40" substituted for "section 403 of the Appalachian Regional Development Act of 1965, as amended [40 App.U.S.C.A. § 403]" and "subtitle IV of Title 40" substituted for "the Appalachian Regional Development Act of 1965, as amended [40 App.U.S.C.A. § 1 et seq.]" on authority of Pub.L. 107–217, § 5(c), Aug. 21, 2002, 116 Stat. 1301, which is set out as a note preceding 40 U.S.C.A. § 101. Pub.L. 107–217, § 1, enacted Title 40 into positive law. The Appalachian Regional Development Act of 1965, is Pub.L. 89–4, Mar. 9, 1965, 79 Stat. 5, as amended, which was repealed by Pub.L. 107–217, § 6(b), Aug. 21, 2002, 116 Stat. 1317, and its substance reenacted as subtitle IV of Title 40, consisting of chapters 141, 143, 145, and 147 of Title 40, 40 U.S.C.A. §§ 14101 et seq., 14301 et seq., 14501 et seq., and 14701 et seq., respectively. Former 40 U.S.C.A. § 403 was reenacted as 40 U.S.C.A. § 14102.

## § 1257a. State demonstration programs for cleanup of abandoned mines for use as waste disposal sites; authorization of appropriations

The Administrator of the Environmental Protection Agency is authorized to make grants to States to undertake a demonstration program for the cleanup of State-owned abandoned mines which can be used as hazardous waste disposal sites. The State shall pay 10 per centum of project costs. At a minimum, the Administrator shall undertake projects under such program in the States of Ohio, Illinois, and West Virginia. There are authorized to be appropriated $10,000,000 per fiscal year for each of the fiscal years ending September 30, 1982, September 30, 1983, and September 30, 1984, to carry out this section. Such projects shall be undertaken in accordance with all applicable laws and regulations.

(Pub.L. 96–483, § 12, Oct. 21, 1980, 94 Stat. 2363.)

### HISTORICAL AND STATUTORY NOTES

**Codifications**

Section was not enacted as part of the Federal Water Pollution Control Act, which comprises this chapter.

## § 1258. Pollution control in the Great Lakes

**[FWPCA § 108]**

**(a) Demonstration projects**

The Administrator, in cooperation with other Federal departments, agencies, and instrumentalities is authorized to enter into agreements with any State, political subdivision, interstate agency, or other public agency, or combination thereof, to carry out one or more projects to demonstrate new methods and techniques and to develop preliminary plans for the elimination or control of pollution, within all or any part of the watersheds of the Great Lakes. Such projects shall demonstrate the engineering and economic feasibility and practicality of removal of pollutants and prevention of any polluting matter from entering into the Great Lakes in the future and other reduction and remedial techniques which will contribute substantially to effective and practical methods of pollution prevention, reduction, or elimination.

**(b) Conditions of Federal participation**

Federal participation in such projects shall be subject to the condition that the State, political subdivision, interstate agency, or other public agency, or combination thereof, shall pay not less than 25 per centum of the actual project costs, which payment may be in any form, including, but not limited to, land or interests therein that is needed for the project, and personal property or services the value of which shall be determined by the Administrator.

**(c) Authorization of appropriations**

There is authorized to be appropriated $20,000,000 to carry out the provisions of subsections (a) and (b) of this section, which sum shall be available until expended.

**(d) Lake Erie demonstration program**

(1) In recognition of the serious conditions which exist in Lake Erie, the Secretary of the Army, acting through the Chief of Engineers, is directed to design and develop a demonstration waste water management program for the rehabilitation and environmental repair of Lake Erie. Prior to the initiation of detailed engineering and design, the program, along with the specific recommendations of the Chief of Engineers, and recommendations for its financing, shall be submitted to the Congress for statutory approval. This authority is in addition to, and not in lieu of, other waste water studies aimed at eliminating pollution emanating from select sources around Lake Erie.

(2) This program is to be developed in cooperation with the Environmental Protection Agency, other interested departments, agencies, and instrumentalities of the Federal Government, and the States and their political subdivisions. This program shall set forth alternative systems for managing waste water on a regional basis and shall provide local and State governments with a range of choice as to the type of system to be used for the treatment of waste water. These alternative systems shall include both advanced waste treatment technology and land disposal systems including aerated treatment-spray irrigation technology and will also include provisions for the disposal of solid wastes, including sludge. Such program should include measures to control point sources of pollution, area sources of pollution, including acid-mine drainage, urban runoff and rural runoff, and in place sources of pollution, including bottom loads, sludge banks, and polluted harbor dredgings.

**(e) Authorization of appropriations for Lake Erie demonstration program**

There is authorized to be appropriated $5,000,000 to carry out the provisions of subsection (d) of this section, which sum shall be available until expended.

(June 30, 1948, c. 758, Title I, § 108, as added Oct. 18, 1972, Pub.L. 92–500, § 2, 86 Stat. 828.)

## § 1259. Training grants and contracts

**[FWPCA § 109]**

(a) The Administrator is authorized to make grants to or contracts with institutions of higher education, or combinations of such institutions, to assist them in planning, developing, strengthening, improving, or carrying out programs or projects for the preparation of undergraduate students to enter an occupation which involves the design, operation, and maintenance of treatment works, and other facilities whose purpose is water quality control. Such grants or contracts may include payment of all or part of the cost of programs or projects such as—

(A) planning for the development or expansion of programs or projects for training persons in the operation and maintenance of treatment works;

(B) training and retraining of faculty members;

(C) conduct of short-term or regular session institutes for study by persons engaged in, or preparing to engage in, the preparation of students preparing to enter an occupation involving the operation and maintenance of treatment works;

(D) carrying out innovative and experimental programs of cooperative education involving alternate periods of full-time or part-time academic study at the institution and periods of full-time or part-time employment involving the operation and maintenance of treatment works; and

(E) research into, and development of, methods of training students or faculty, including the preparation of teaching materials and the planning of curriculum.

(b)(1) The Administrator may pay 100 per centum of any additional cost of construction of treatment works required for a facility to train and upgrade waste treatment works operation and maintenance personnel and for the costs of other State treatment works operator training programs, including mobile training units, classroom rental, specialized instructors, and instructional material.

(2) The Administrator shall make no more than one grant for such additional construction in any State (to serve a group of States, where, in his judgment, efficient training programs require multi-State programs), and shall make such grant after consultation with and approval by the State or States on the basis of (A) the suitability of such facility for training operation and maintenance personnel for treatment works throughout such State or States; and (B) a commitment by the State agency or agencies to carry out at such facility a program of training approved by the Administrator. In any case where a grant is made to serve two or more States, the Administrator is authorized to make an additional grant for a supplemental facility in each such State.

(3) The Administrator may make such grant out of the sums allocated to a State under section 1285 of this title, except that in no event shall the Federal cost of any such training facilities exceed $500,000.

(4) The Administrator may exempt a grant under this section from any requirement under section 1284(a)(3) of this title. Any grantee who received a grant under this section prior to enactment of the Clean Water Act of 1977 shall be eligible to have its grant increased by funds made available under such Act.

(June 30, 1948, c. 758, Title I, § 109, as added Oct. 18, 1972, Pub.L. 92–500, § 2, 86 Stat. 829, and amended Dec. 27, 1977, Pub.L. 95–217, § 10, 91 Stat. 1568.)

### HISTORICAL AND STATUTORY NOTES

**References in Text**

Prior to the date of enactment of the Clean Water Act of 1977, referred to in subsec. (b)(4), means prior to the enactment of Pub.L. 95–217, Dec. 27, 1977, 91 Stat. 1566, which was approved Dec. 27, 1977.

Such Act, referred to in subsec. (b)(4), means Pub.L. 95–217, Dec. 27, 1977, 91 Stat. 1566, as amended, known as the Clean Water Act of 1977. For complete classification of this Act to the Code, see Short Title of 1977 Amendment note set out under section 1251 of this title and Tables volume.

## § 1260. Applications; allocation

**[FWPCA § 110]**

(1) A grant or contract authorized by section 1259 of this title may be made only upon application to the Administrator at such time or times and containing such information as he may prescribe, except that no such application shall be approved unless it—

(A) sets forth programs, activities, research, or development for which a grant is authorized under section 1259 of this title and describes the relation to any program set forth by the applicant in an application, if any, submitted pursuant to section 1261 of this title;

(B) provides such fiscal control and fund accounting procedures as may be necessary to assure proper disbursement of and accounting for Federal funds paid to the applicant under this section; and

(C) provides for making such reports, in such form and containing such information, as the Administrator may require to carry out his functions under this section, and for keeping such records and for affording such access thereto as the Administrator may find necessary to assure the correctness and verification of such reports.

(2) The Administrator shall allocate grants or contracts under section 1259 of this title in such manner as will most nearly provide an equitable distribution of the grants or contracts throughout the United States among institutions of higher education which show promise of being able to use funds effectively for the purpose of this section.

(3)(A) Payments under this section may be used in accordance with regulations of the Administrator, and subject to the terms and conditions set forth in an application approved under paragraph (1), to pay part of the compensation of students employed in connection with the operation and maintenance of treatment works, other than as an employee in connection with the operation and maintenance of treatment works or as an employee in any branch of the Government of the United States, as part of a program for which a grant has been approved pursuant to this section.

(B) Departments and agencies of the United States are encouraged, to the extent consistent with efficient administration, to enter into arrangements with institutions of higher education for the full-time, part-time, or temporary employment, whether in the competitive or excepted service, of students enrolled in programs set forth in applications approved under paragraph (1).

(June 30, 1948, c. 758, Title I, § 110, as added Oct. 18, 1972, Pub.L. 92–500, § 2, 86 Stat. 830.)

## § 1261. Scholarships

**[FWPCA § 111]**

(1) The Administrator is authorized to award scholarships in accordance with the provisions of this section for undergraduate study by persons who plan to enter an occupation involving the operation and maintenance of treatment works. Such scholarships shall be awarded for such periods as the Administrator may determine but not to exceed four academic years.

(2) The Administrator shall allocate scholarships under this section among institutions of higher education with programs approved under the provisions of this section for the use of individuals accepted into such programs in such manner and according to such plan as will insofar as practicable—

(A) provide an equitable distribution of such scholarships throughout the United States; and

(B) attract recent graduates of secondary schools to enter an occupation involving the operation and maintenance of treatment works.

(3) The Administrator shall approve a program of any institution of higher education for the purposes of this section only upon application by the institution and only upon his finding—

(A) that such program has a principal objective the education and training of persons in the operation and maintenance of treatment works;

(B) that such program is in effect and of high quality, or can be readily put into effect and may reasonably be expected to be of high quality;

(C) that the application describes the relation of such program to any program, activity, research, or development set forth by the applicant in an application, if any, submitted pursuant to section 1260 of this title; and

(D) that the application contains satisfactory assurances that (i) the institution will recommend to the Administrator for the award of scholarships under this section, for study in such program, only persons who have demonstrated to the satisfaction of the institution a serious intent, upon completing the program, to enter an occupation involving the operation and maintenance of treatment works, and (ii) the institution will make reasonable continuing efforts to encourage recipients of scholarships under this section, enrolled in such program, to enter occupations involving the operation and maintenance of treatment works upon completing the program.

(4)(A) The Administrator shall pay to persons awarded scholarships under this section such stipends (including such allowances for subsistence and other expenses for such persons and their dependents) as he may determine to be consistent with prevailing practices under comparable federally supported programs.

(B) The Administrator shall (in addition to the stipends paid to persons under paragraph (1)) pay to the institution of higher education at which such person is pursuing his course of study such amount as he may determine to be consistent with prevailing practices under comparable federally supported programs.

(5) A person awarded a scholarship under the provisions of this section shall continue to receive the payments provided in this section only during such periods as the Administrator finds that he is maintaining satisfactory proficiency and devoting full time to study or research in the field in which such scholarship was awarded in an institution of higher education, and is not engaging in gainful employment other than employment approved by the Administrator by or pursuant to regulation.

(6) The Administrator shall by regulation provide that any person awarded a scholarship under this section shall agree in writing to enter and remain in an occupation involving the design, operation, or maintenance of treatment works for such period after completion of his course of studies as the Administrator determines appropriate.

(June 30, 1948, c. 758, Title I, § 111, as added Oct. 18, 1972, Pub.L. 92–500, § 2, 86 Stat. 831.)

## § 1262. Definitions and authorizations

**[FWPCA § 112]**

(a) As used in sections 1259 through 1262 of this title—

(1) The term "institution of higher education" means an educational institution described in the first sentence of section 1001 of Title 20 (other than an institution of any agency of the United States) which is accredited by a nationally recognized accrediting agency or association approved by the Administrator for this purpose. For purposes of this subsection, the Administrator shall publish a list of nationally recognized accrediting agencies or associations which he determines to be reliable authority as to the quality of training offered.

(2) The term "academic year" means an academic year or its equivalent, as determined by the Administrator.

(b) The Administrator shall annually report his activities under sections 1259 through 1262 of this title, including recommendations for needed revisions in the provisions thereof.

**(c)** There are authorized to be appropriated $25,000,000 per fiscal year for the fiscal years ending June 30, 1973, June 30, 1974, and June 30, 1975, $6,000,000 for the fiscal year ending September 30, 1977, $7,000,000 for the fiscal year ending September 30, 1978, $7,000,000 for the fiscal year ending September 30, 1979, $7,000,000 for the fiscal year ending September 30, 1980, $7,000,000 for the fiscal year ending September 30, 1981, $7,000,000 for the fiscal year ending September 30, 1982, such sums as may be necessary for fiscal years 1983 through 1985, and $7,000,000 per fiscal year for each of the fiscal years 1986 through 1990, to carry out sections 1259 through 1262 of this title.

(June 30, 1948, c. 758, Title I, § 112, as added Oct. 18, 1972, Pub.L. 92–500, § 2, 86 Stat. 832, and amended Jan. 2, 1975, Pub.L. 93–592, § 4, 88 Stat. 1925; Dec. 27, 1977, Pub.L. 95–217, § 4(d), 91 Stat. 1566; Oct. 21, 1980, Pub.L. 96–483, § 1(c), 94 Stat. 2360; Feb. 4, 1987, Pub.L. 100–4, Title I, § 101(c), 101 Stat. 9; Oct. 7, 1998, Pub.L. 105–244, Title I, § 102(a)(11), Oct. 7, 1998.)

### HISTORICAL AND STATUTORY NOTES

**Effective and Applicability Provisions**

1998 Acts

Amendment by Pub.L. 105–244 effective Oct. 1, 1998, except as otherwise provided, see section 3 of Pub.L. 105–244, set out as a note under section 1001 of Title 20.

## § 1263. Alaska village demonstration projects [FWPCA § 113]

**(a) Central community facilities for safe water; elimination or control of pollution**

The Administrator is authorized to enter into agreements with the State of Alaska to carry out one or more projects to demonstrate methods to provide for central community facilities for safe water and elimination or control of pollution in those native villages of Alaska without such facilities. Such project shall include provisions for community safe water supply systems, toilets, bathing and laundry facilities, sewage disposal facilities, and other similar facilities, and educational and informational facilities and programs relating to health and hygiene. Such demonstration projects shall be for the further purpose of developing preliminary plans for providing such safe water and such elimination or control of pollution for all native villages in such State.

**(b) Utilization of personnel and facilities of Department of Health and Human Services**

In carrying out this section the Administrator shall cooperate with the Secretary of Health and Human Services for the purpose of utilizing such of the personnel and facilities of that Department as may be appropriate.

**(c) Omitted**

**(d) Authorization of appropriations**

There is authorized to be appropriated not to exceed $2,000,000 to carry out this section. In addition, there is authorized to be appropriated to carry out this section not to exceed $200,000 for the fiscal year ending September 30, 1978, and $220,000 for the fiscal year ending September 30, 1979.

**(e) Study to develop comprehensive program for achieving sanitation services; report to Congress**

The Administrator is authorized to coordinate with the Secretary of the Department of Health and Human Services, the Secretary of the Department of Housing and Urban Development, the Secretary of the Department of the Interior, the Secretary of the Department of Agriculture, and the heads of any other departments or agencies he may deem appropriate to conduct a joint study with representatives of the State of Alaska and the appropriate Native organizations (as defined in Public Law 92–203) to develop a comprehensive program for achieving adequate sanitation services in Alaska villages. This study shall be coordinated with the programs and projects authorized by sections 1254(q) and 1255(e)(2) of this title. The Administrator shall submit a report of the results of the study, together with appropriate supporting data and such recommendations as he deems desirable, to the Committee on Environment and Public Works of the Senate and to the Committee on Public Works and Transportation of the House of Representatives not later than December 31, 1979. The Administrator shall also submit recommended administrative actions, procedures, and any proposed legislation necessary to implement the recommendations of the study no later than June 30, 1980.

**(f) Technical, financial, and management assistance**

The Administrator is authorized to provide technical, financial and management assistance for operation and maintenance of the demonstration projects constructed under this section, until such time as the recommendations of subsection (e) of this section are implemented.

**(g) "Village" and "sanitation services" defined**

For the purpose of this section, the term "village" shall mean an incorporated or unincorporated community with a population of ten to six hundred people living within a two-mile radius. The term "sanitation services" shall mean water supply, sewage disposal, solid waste disposal and other services necessary to maintain generally accepted standards of personal hygiene and public health.

(June 30, 1948, c. 758, Title I, § 113, as added Oct. 18, 1972, Pub.L. 92–500, § 2, 86 Stat. 832, and amended Dec. 27, 1977, Pub.L. 95–217, § 11, 91 Stat. 1568; Oct. 17, 1979, Pub.L. 96–88, Title V, § 509(b), 93 Stat. 695.)

### HISTORICAL AND STATUTORY NOTES

**References in Text**

Public Law 92–203, referred to in subsec. (e), is Pub.L. 92–203, Dec. 18, 1971, 85 Stat. 688, as amended, known as the Alaska Native Claims Settlement Act, which is classified generally to chapter 33 (section 1601 et seq.) of Title 43, Public Lands. For complete classification of this Act to the Code, see Short Title note set out under section 1601 of Title 43 and Tables.

**Codifications**

Subsec. (c), authorized the Administrator to report to Congress the results of the demonstration project accompanied by his recommendations for the establishment of a statewide project not later than July 1, 1973.

**Change of Name**

"Secretary of Health and Human Services" was substituted for "Secretary of Health, Education, and Welfare" in subsec. (b), and "Secretary of the Department of Health and Human Services" was substituted for "Secretary of the Department of Health, Education, and Welfare" in subsec. (e), pursuant to section 509(b) of Pub. L. 96–88 which is classified to section 3508(b) of Title 20, Education.

Any reference in any provision of law enacted before Jan. 4, 1995, to the Committee on Public Works and Transportation of the House of Representatives treated as referring to the Committee on Transportation and Infrastructure of the House of Representatives, see section 1(a)(9) of Pub.L. 104–14, set out as a note preceding section 21 of Title 2, The Congress.

**Corps Capability Study, Alaska**

Pub.L. 104–303, Title IV, § 401, Oct. 12, 1996, 110 Stat. 3740, provided that: "Not later than 18 months after the date of the enactment of this Act [Oct. 12, 1996], the Secretary shall report to Congress on the advisability and capability of the Corps of Engineers to implement rural sanitation projects for rural and Native villages in Alaska."

## § 1263a. Grants to Alaska to improve sanitation in rural and Native villages

**(a) In general**

The Administrator of the Environmental Protection Agency may make grants to the State of Alaska for the benefit of rural and Native villages in Alaska to pay the Federal share of the cost of—

(1) the development and construction of public water systems and wastewater systems to improve the health and sanitation conditions in the villages; and

(2) training, technical assistance, and educational programs relating to the operation and management of sanitation services in rural and Native villages.

**(b) Federal share**

The Federal share of the cost of the activities described in subsection (a) of this section shall be 50 percent.

**(c) Administrative expenses**

The State of Alaska may use an amount not to exceed 4 percent of any grant made available under this subsection[1] for administrative expenses necessary to carry out the activities described in subsection (a) of this section.

**(d) Consultation with the State of Alaska**

The Administrator shall consult with the State of Alaska on a method of prioritizing the allocation of grants under subsection (a) of this section according to the needs of, and relative health and sanitation conditions in, each eligible village.

**(e) Authorization of appropriations**

There are authorized to be appropriated to carry out this section $40,000,000 for each of fiscal years 2001 through 2005.

(Pub.L. 104–182, Title III, § 303, Aug. 6, 1996, 110 Stat. 1683; Pub.L. 106–457, Title IX, § 903, Nov. 7, 2000, 114 Stat. 1982.)

[1] So in original. Probably should be "section".

### HISTORICAL AND STATUTORY NOTES

**Codifications**

Section was enacted as part of the Safe Drinking Water Act Amendments of 1996, and not as part of The Federal Water Pollution Control Act, which comprises this chapter.

**Effective and Applicability Provisions**

1996 Acts

Section effective Aug. 6, 1996, except as otherwise specifically provided, see section 2(b) of Pub.L. 104–182, set out as a note under section 300f of Title 42, The Public Health and Welfare.

## § 1264. Omitted

### HISTORICAL AND STATUTORY NOTES

**Codifications**

Section, Act June 30, 1948, c. 758, Title I, § 114, as added Oct. 18, 1972, Pub.L. 92–500, § 2, 86 Stat. 833, authorized the Administrator, in consultation with the Tahoe Regional Planning Agency, the Secretary of Agriculture, other Federal agencies, representatives of State and local governments, and members of the public, to conduct a thorough and complete study on the need of extending Federal oversight and control in order to preserve the fragile ecology of Lake Tahoe and to report the results of this study to Congress not later than one year after Oct. 18, 1972.

## § 1265. In-place toxic pollutants

[FWPCA § 115]

The Administrator is directed to identify the location of in-place pollutants with emphasis on toxic pollutants in harbors and navigable waterways and is authorized, acting through the Secretary of the Army, to make contracts for the removal and appropriate disposal of such materials from critical port and harbor areas. There is authorized to be appropriated

$15,000,000 to carry out the provisions of this section, which sum shall be available until expended.

(June 30, 1948, c. 758, Title I, § 115, as added Oct. 18, 1972, Pub.L. 92–500, § 2, 86 Stat. 833.)

## § 1266. Hudson River reclamation demonstration project

**[FWPCA § 116]**

(a) The Administrator is authorized to enter into contracts and other agreements with the State of New York to carry out a project to demonstrate methods for the selective removal of polychlorinated biphenyls contaminating bottom sediments of the Hudson River, treating such sediments as required, burying such sediments in secure landfills, and installing monitoring systems for such landfills. Such demonstration project shall be for the purpose of determining the feasibility of indefinite storage in secure landfills of toxic substances and of ascertaining the improvement of the rate of recovery of a toxic contaminated national waterway. No pollutants removed pursuant to this paragraph shall be placed in any landfill unless the Administrator first determines that disposal of the pollutants in such landfill would provide a higher standard of protection of the public health, safety, and welfare than disposal of such pollutants by any other method including, but not limited to, incineration or a chemical destruction process.

(b) The Administrator is authorized to make grants to the State of New York to carry out this section from funds allotted to such State under section 1285(a) of this title, except that the amount of any such grant shall be equal to 75 per centum of the cost of the project and such grant shall be made on condition that non-Federal sources provide the remainder of the cost of such project. The authority of this section shall be available until September 30, 1983. Funds allotted to the State of New York under section 1285(a) of this title shall be available under this subsection only to the extent that funds are not available, as determined by the Administrator, to the State of New York for the work authorized by this section under section 1265 or 1321 of this title or a comprehensive hazardous substance response and clean up fund. Any funds used under the authority of this subsection shall be deducted from any estimate of the needs of the State of New York prepared under section 1375(b) of this title. The Administrator may not obligate or expend more than $20,000,000 to carry out this section.

(June 30, 1948, c. 758, Title I, § 116, as added Oct. 21, 1980, Pub.L. 96–483, § 10, 94 Stat. 2363, and amended Nov. 10, 1998, Pub.L. 105–362, Title V, § 501(d)(2)(B), 112 Stat. 3284; Nov. 27, 2002, Pub.L. 107–303, Title III, § 302(b)(1), 116 Stat. 2361.)

### HISTORICAL AND STATUTORY NOTES

**Effective and Applicability Provisions**

2002 Acts

Effective November 10, 1998, section 501 of the Federal Reports Elimination Act of 1998 [Pub.L. 105–362, Title V, § 501, Nov. 10, 1998, 112 Stat. 3283] is amended by striking subsections (a), (b), (c), and (d) [amending this section and others, see Tables for complete classification]. The Federal Water Pollution Control Act (33 U.S.C.A. § 1254(n)(3)) shall be applied and administered on and after Nov. 27, 2002 as if the amendments made by subsections (a), (b), (c), and (d) of Pub.L. 105–362, § 501, had not been enacted, see Pub.L. 107–303, § 302(b)(2), set out as a note under 33 U.S.C.A. § 1254.

## § 1267. Chesapeake Bay

**[FWPCA § 117]**

**(a) Definitions**

In this section, the following definitions apply:

**(1) Administrative cost**

The term "administrative cost" means the cost of salaries and fringe benefits incurred in administering a grant under this section.

**(2) Chesapeake Bay Agreement**

The term "Chesapeake Bay Agreement" means the formal, voluntary agreements executed to achieve the goal of restoring and protecting the Chesapeake Bay ecosystem and the living resources of the Chesapeake Bay ecosystem and signed by the Chesapeake Executive Council.

**(3) Chesapeake Bay ecosystem**

The term "Chesapeake Bay ecosystem" means the ecosystem of the Chesapeake Bay and its watershed.

**(4) Chesapeake Bay Program**

The term "Chesapeake Bay Program" means the program directed by the Chesapeake Executive Council in accordance with the Chesapeake Bay Agreement.

**(5) Chesapeake Executive Council**

The term "Chesapeake Executive Council" means the signatories to the Chesapeake Bay Agreement.

**(6) Signatory jurisdiction**

The term "signatory jurisdiction" means a jurisdiction of a signatory to the Chesapeake Bay Agreement.

**(b) Continuation of Chesapeake Bay Program**

**(1) In general**

In cooperation with the Chesapeake Executive Council (and as a member of the Council), the

Administrator shall continue the Chesapeake Bay Program.

(2) **Program Office**

(A) **In general**

The Administrator shall maintain in the Environmental Protection Agency a Chesapeake Bay Program Office.

(B) **Function**

The Chesapeake Bay Program Office shall provide support to the Chesapeake Executive Council by—

(i) implementing and coordinating science, research, modeling, support services, monitoring, data collection, and other activities that support the Chesapeake Bay Program;

(ii) developing and making available, through publications, technical assistance, and other appropriate means, information pertaining to the environmental quality and living resources of the Chesapeake Bay ecosystem;

(iii) in cooperation with appropriate Federal, State, and local authorities, assisting the signatories to the Chesapeake Bay Agreement in developing and implementing specific action plans to carry out the responsibilities of the signatories to the Chesapeake Bay Agreement;

(iv) coordinating the actions of the Environmental Protection Agency with the actions of the appropriate officials of other Federal agencies and State and local authorities in developing strategies to—

(I) improve the water quality and living resources in the Chesapeake Bay ecosystem; and

(II) obtain the support of the appropriate officials of the agencies and authorities in achieving the objectives of the Chesapeake Bay Agreement; and

(v) implementing outreach programs for public information, education, and participation to foster stewardship of the resources of the Chesapeake Bay.

(c) **Interagency agreements**

The Administrator may enter into an interagency agreement with a Federal agency to carry out this section.

(d) **Technical assistance and assistance grants**

(1) **In general**

In cooperation with the Chesapeake Executive Council, the Administrator may provide technical assistance, and assistance grants, to nonprofit organizations, State and local governments, colleges, universities, and interstate agencies to carry out this section, subject to such terms and conditions as the Administrator considers appropriate.

(2) **Federal share**

(A) **In general**

Except as provided in subparagraph (B), the Federal share of an assistance grant provided under paragraph (1) shall be determined by the Administrator in accordance with guidance issued by the Administrator.

(B) **Small watershed grants program**

The Federal share of an assistance grant provided under paragraph (1) to carry out an implementing activity under subsection (g)(2) of this section shall not exceed 75 percent of eligible project costs, as determined by the Administrator.

(3) **Non-Federal share**

An assistance grant under paragraph (1) shall be provided on the condition that non-Federal sources provide the remainder of eligible project costs, as determined by the Administrator.

(4) **Administrative costs**

Administrative costs shall not exceed 10 percent of the annual grant award.

(e) **Implementation and monitoring grants**

(1) **In general**

If a signatory jurisdiction has approved and committed to implement all or substantially all aspects of the Chesapeake Bay Agreement, on the request of the chief executive of the jurisdiction, the Administrator—

(A) shall make a grant to the jurisdiction for the purpose of implementing the management mechanisms established under the Chesapeake Bay Agreement, subject to such terms and conditions as the Administrator considers appropriate; and

(B) may make a grant to a signatory jurisdiction for the purpose of monitoring the Chesapeake Bay ecosystem.

(2) **Proposals**

(A) **In general**

A signatory jurisdiction described in paragraph (1) may apply for a grant under this subsection for a fiscal year by submitting to the Administrator a comprehensive proposal to implement management mechanisms established under the Chesapeake Bay Agreement.

(B) Contents

A proposal under subparagraph (A) shall include—

(i) a description of proposed management mechanisms that the jurisdiction commits to take within a specified time period, such as reducing or preventing pollution in the Chesapeake Bay and its watershed or meeting applicable water quality standards or established goals and objectives under the Chesapeake Bay Agreement; and

(ii) the estimated cost of the actions proposed to be taken during the fiscal year.

(3) Approval

If the Administrator finds that the proposal is consistent with the Chesapeake Bay Agreement and the national goals established under section 1251(a) of this title, the Administrator may approve the proposal for an award.

(4) Federal share

The Federal share of a grant under this subsection shall not exceed 50 percent of the cost of implementing the management mechanisms during the fiscal year.

(5) Non-Federal share

A grant under this subsection shall be made on the condition that non-Federal sources provide the remainder of the costs of implementing the management mechanisms during the fiscal year.

(6) Administrative costs

Administrative costs shall not exceed 10 percent of the annual grant award.

(7) Reporting

On or before October 1 of each fiscal year, the Administrator shall make available to the public a document that lists and describes, in the greatest practicable degree of detail—

(A) all projects and activities funded for the fiscal year;

(B) the goals and objectives of projects funded for the previous fiscal year; and

(C) the net benefits of projects funded for previous fiscal years.

(f) Federal facilities and budget coordination

(1) Subwatershed planning and restoration

A Federal agency that owns or operates a facility (as defined by the Administrator) within the Chesapeake Bay watershed shall participate in regional and subwatershed planning and restoration programs.

(2) Compliance with Agreement

The head of each Federal agency that owns or occupies real property in the Chesapeake Bay watershed shall ensure that the property, and actions taken by the agency with respect to the property, comply with the Chesapeake Bay Agreement, the Federal Agencies Chesapeake Ecosystem Unified Plan, and any subsequent agreements and plans.

(3) Budget coordination

(A) In general

As part of the annual budget submission of each Federal agency with projects or grants related to restoration, planning, monitoring, or scientific investigation of the Chesapeake Bay ecosystem, the head of the agency shall submit to the President a report that describes plans for the expenditure of the funds under this section.

(B) Disclosure to the Council

The head of each agency referred to in subparagraph (A) shall disclose the report under that subparagraph with the Chesapeake Executive Council as appropriate.

(g) Chesapeake Bay Program

(1) Management strategies

The Administrator, in coordination with other members of the Chesapeake Executive Council, shall ensure that management plans are developed and implementation is begun by signatories to the Chesapeake Bay Agreement to achieve and maintain—

(A) the nutrient goals of the Chesapeake Bay Agreement for the quantity of nitrogen and phosphorus entering the Chesapeake Bay and its watershed;

(B) the water quality requirements necessary to restore living resources in the Chesapeake Bay ecosystem;

(C) the Chesapeake Bay Basinwide Toxins Reduction and Prevention Strategy goal of reducing or eliminating the input of chemical contaminants from all controllable sources to levels that result in no toxic or bioaccumulative impact on the living resources of the Chesapeake Bay ecosystem or on human health;

(D) habitat restoration, protection, creation, and enhancement goals established by Chesapeake Bay Agreement signatories for wetlands, riparian forests, and other types of habitat associated with the Chesapeake Bay ecosystem; and

(E) the restoration, protection, creation, and enhancement goals established by the Chesapeake Bay Agreement signatories for living resources associated with the Chesapeake Bay ecosystem.

**(2) Small watershed grants program**

The Administrator, in cooperation with the Chesapeake Executive Council, shall—

(A) establish a small watershed grants program as part of the Chesapeake Bay Program; and

(B) offer technical assistance and assistance grants under subsection (d) of this section to local governments and nonprofit organizations and individuals in the Chesapeake Bay region to implement—

(i) cooperative tributary basin strategies that address the water quality and living resource needs in the Chesapeake Bay ecosystem; and

(ii) locally based protection and restoration programs or projects within a watershed that complement the tributary basin strategies, including the creation, restoration, protection, or enhancement of habitat associated with the Chesapeake Bay ecosystem.

**(h) Study of Chesapeake Bay Program**

**(1) In general**

Not later than April 22, 2003, and every 5 years thereafter, the Administrator, in coordination with the Chesapeake Executive Council, shall complete a study and submit to Congress a comprehensive report on the results of the study.

**(2) Requirements**

The study and report shall—

(A) assess the state of the Chesapeake Bay ecosystem;

(B) compare the current state of the Chesapeake Bay ecosystem with its state in 1975, 1985, and 1995;

(C) assess the effectiveness of management strategies being implemented on November 7, 2000, and the extent to which the priority needs are being met;

(D) make recommendations for the improved management of the Chesapeake Bay Program either by strengthening strategies being implemented on November 7, 2000, or by adopting new strategies; and

(E) be presented in such a format as to be readily transferable to and usable by other watershed restoration programs.

**(i) Special study of living resource response**

**(1) In general**

Not later than 180 days after November 7, 2000, the Administrator shall commence a 5-year special study with full participation of the scientific community of the Chesapeake Bay to establish and expand understanding of the response of the living resources of the Chesapeake Bay ecosystem to improvements in water quality that have resulted from investments made through the Chesapeake Bay Program.

**(2) Requirements**

The study shall—

(A) determine the current status and trends of living resources, including grasses, benthos, phytoplankton, zooplankton, fish, and shellfish;

(B) establish to the extent practicable the rates of recovery of the living resources in response to improved water quality condition;

(C) evaluate and assess interactions of species, with particular attention to the impact of changes within and among trophic levels; and

(D) recommend management actions to optimize the return of a healthy and balanced ecosystem in response to improvements in the quality and character of the waters of the Chesapeake Bay.

**(j) Authorization of appropriations**

There is authorized to be appropriated to carry out this section $40,000,000 for each of fiscal years 2001 through 2005. Such sums shall remain available until expended.

(June 30, 1948, c. 758, Title I, § 117, as added Feb. 4, 1987, Pub.L. 100–4, Title I, § 103, 101 Stat. 10; Nov. 7, 2000, Pub.L. 106–457, Title II, § 203, 114 Stat. 1967.)

## HISTORICAL AND STATUTORY NOTES

**Codifications**

November 7, 2000, referred to in subsecs. (h)(2)(C), (D), and (i)(1), originally read "the date of enactment of this section", which was translated as meaning the date of enactment of Pub.L. 106–457, which amended this section generally, to reflect the probable intent of Congress.

**Findings and Purposes**

Pub.L. 106–457, Title II, § 202, Nov. 7, 2000, 114 Stat. 1967, provided that:

"(a) **Findings.**—Congress finds that—

"(1) the Chesapeake Bay is a national treasure and a resource of worldwide significance;

"(2) over many years, the productivity and water quality of the Chesapeake Bay and its watershed were diminished by pollution, excessive sedimentation, shoreline erosion, the impacts of population growth and development in the Chesapeake Bay watershed, and other factors;

"(3) the Federal Government (acting through the Administrator of the Environmental Protection Agency), the Governor of the State of Maryland, the Governor of the Commonwealth of Virginia, the Governor of the Commonwealth of Pennsylvania, the Chairperson of the Chesapeake Bay Commission, and the mayor of the District of Columbia, as Chesapeake Bay Agreement signatories, have committed to a comprehensive cooperative program to achieve improved water quality and improvements in the productivity of living resources of the Bay;

"(4) the cooperative program described in paragraph (3) serves as a national and international model for the management of estuaries; and

"(5) there is a need to expand Federal support for monitoring, management, and restoration activities in the Chesapeake Bay and the tributaries of the Bay in order to meet and further the original and subsequent goals and commitments of the Chesapeake Bay Program.

"**(b) Purposes.**—The purposes of this title [Pub.L. 106–457, Title II, Nov. 7, 2000, 114 Stat. 1957, amending this section and enacting this note] are—

"(1) to expand and strengthen cooperative efforts to restore and protect the Chesapeake Bay; and

"(2) to achieve the goals established in the Chesapeake Bay Agreement."

**Nutrient Loading Resulting from Dredged Material Disposal.**

Pub.L. 106–53, Title IV, § 457, Aug. 17, 1999, 113 Stat. 332, provided that:

"**(a) Study.**—The Secretary shall conduct a study of nutrient loading that occurs as a result of discharges of dredged material into open-water sites in the Chesapeake Bay.

"**(b) Report.**—Not later than 18 months after the date of enactment of this Act [Aug. 17, 1999], the Secretary shall submit to Congress a report on the results of the study."

## § 1268. Great Lakes

[FWPCA § 118]

### (a) Findings, purpose, and definitions

#### (1) Findings

The Congress finds that—

(A) the Great Lakes are a valuable national resource, continuously serving the people of the United States and other nations as an important source of food, fresh water, recreation, beauty, and enjoyment;

(B) the United States should seek to attain the goals embodied in the Great Lakes Water Quality Agreement of 1978, as amended by the Water Quality Agreement of 1987 and any other agreements and amendments, with particular emphasis on goals related to toxic pollutants; and

(C) the Environmental Protection Agency should take the lead in the effort to meet those goals, working with other Federal agencies and State and local authorities.

#### (2) Purpose

It is the purpose of this section to achieve the goals embodied in the Great Lakes Water Quality Agreement of 1978, as amended by the Water Quality Agreement of 1987 and any other agreements and amendments, through improved organization and definition of mission on the part of the Agency, funding of State grants for pollution control in the Great Lakes area, and improved accountability for implementation of such agreement.

#### (3) Definitions

For purposes of this section, the term—

(A) "Agency" means the Environmental Protection Agency;

(B) "Great Lakes" means Lake Ontario, Lake Erie, Lake Huron (including Lake St. Clair), Lake Michigan, and Lake Superior, and the connecting channels (Saint Mary's River, Saint Clair River, Detroit River, Niagara River, and Saint Lawrence River to the Canadian Border);

(C) "Great Lakes System" means all the streams, rivers, lakes, and other bodies of water within the drainage basin of the Great Lakes;

(D) "Program Office" means the Great Lakes National Program Office established by this section;

(E) "Research Office" means the Great Lakes Research Office established by subsection (d) of this section;

(F) "area of concern" means a geographic area located within the Great Lakes, in which beneficial uses are impaired and which has been officially designated as such under Annex 2 of the Great Lakes Water Quality Agreement;

(G) "Great Lakes States" means the States of Illinois, Indiana, Michigan, Minnesota, New York, Ohio, Pennsylvania, and Wisconsin;

(H) "Great Lakes Water Quality Agreement" means the bilateral agreement, between the United States and Canada which was signed in 1978 and amended by the Protocol of 1987;

(I) "Lakewide Management Plan" means a written document which embodies a systematic and comprehensive ecosystem approach to restoring and protecting the beneficial uses of the open waters of each of the Great Lakes, in accordance with article VI and Annex 2 of the Great Lakes Water Quality Agreement; and

(J) "Remedial Action Plan" means a written document which embodies a systematic and comprehensive ecosystem approach to restoring and protecting the beneficial uses of areas of concern, in accordance with article VI and Annex 2 of the Great Lakes Water Quality Agreement.

### (b) Great Lakes National Program Office

The Great Lakes National Program Office (previously established by the Administrator) is hereby established within the Agency. The Program Office shall be headed by a Director who, by reason of management experience and technical expertise relating to the Great Lakes, is highly qualified to direct the development of programs and plans on a variety of Great Lakes issues. The Great Lakes National Program Office shall be located in a Great Lakes State.

### (c) Great Lakes management

**(1) Functions**

The Program Office shall—

**(A)** in cooperation with appropriate Federal, State, tribal, and international agencies, and in accordance with section 1251(e) of this title, develop and implement specific action plans to carry out the responsibilities of the United States under the Great Lakes Water Quality Agreement of 1978, as amended by the Water Quality Agreement of 1987 and any other agreements and amendments,;[1]

**(B)** establish a Great Lakes system-wide surveillance network to monitor the water quality of the Great Lakes, with specific emphasis on the monitoring of toxic pollutants;

**(C)** serve as the liaison with, and provide information to, the Canadian members of the International Joint Commission and the Canadian counterpart to the Agency;

**(D)** coordinate actions of the Agency (including actions by headquarters and regional offices thereof) aimed at improving Great Lakes water quality; and

**(E)** coordinate actions of the Agency with the actions of other Federal agencies and State and local authorities, so as to ensure the input of those agencies and authorities in developing water quality strategies and obtain the support of those agencies and authorities in achieving the objectives of such agreement.

**(2) Great Lakes water quality guidance**

**(A)** By June 30, 1991, the Administrator, after consultation with the Program Office, shall publish in the Federal Register for public notice and comment proposed water quality guidance for the Great Lakes System. Such guidance shall conform with the objectives and provisions of the Great Lakes Water Quality Agreement, shall be no less restrictive than the provisions of this chapter and national water quality criteria and guidance, shall specify numerical limits on pollutants in ambient Great Lakes waters to protect human health, aquatic life, and wildlife, and shall provide guidance to the Great Lakes States on minimum water quality standards, antidegradation policies, and implementation procedures for the Great Lakes System.

**(B)** By June 30, 1992, the Administrator, in consultation with the Program Office, shall publish in the Federal Register, pursuant to this section and the Administrator's authority under this chapter, final water quality guidance for the Great Lakes System.

**(C)** Within two years after such Great Lakes guidance is published, the Great Lakes States shall adopt water quality standards, antidegradation policies, and implementation procedures for waters within the Great Lakes System which are consistent with such guidance. If a Great Lakes State fails to adopt such standards, policies, and procedures, the Administrator shall promulgate them not later than the end of such two-year period. When reviewing any Great Lakes State's water quality plan, the agency shall consider the extent to which the State has complied with the Great Lakes guidance issued pursuant to this section.

**(3) Remedial action plans**

**(A)** For each area of concern for which the United States has agreed to draft a Remedial Action Plan, the Program Office shall ensure that the Great Lakes State in which such area of concern is located—

**(i)** submits a Remedial Action Plan to the Program Office by June 30, 1991;

**(ii)** submits such Remedial Action Plan to the International Joint Commission by January 1, 1992; and

**(iii)** includes such Remedial Action Plans within the State's water quality plan by January 1, 1993.

**(B)** For each area of concern for which Canada has agreed to draft a Remedial Action Plan, the Program Office shall, pursuant to subparagraph (c)(1)(C) of this section, work with Canada to assure the submission of such Remedial Action Plans to the International Joint Commission by June 30, 1991, and to finalize such Remedial Action Plans by January 1, 1993.

**(C)** For any area of concern designated as such subsequent to November 16, 1990, the Program Office shall (i) if the United States has agreed to draft the Remedial Action Plan, ensure that the Great Lakes State in which such area of concern is located submits such Plan to the Program Office within two years of the area's designation, submits it to the International Joint Commission no later than six months after submitting it to the Program Office, and includes such Plan in the State's water quality plan no later than one year after submitting it to the Commission; and (ii) if Canada has agreed to draft the Remedial Action Plan, work with Canada, pursuant to subparagraph (c)(1)(C) of this section, to ensure the submission of such Plan to the International Joint Commission within two years of the area's designation and the finalization of such Plan no later than eighteen months after submitting it to such Commission.

**(D)** The Program Office shall compile formal comments on individual Remedial Action Plans made by the International Joint Commission pursuant to section 4(d) of Annex 2 of the Great Lakes Water Quality Agreement and, upon request by a member of the public, shall make such comments available for inspection and copying. The Program Office shall also make available, upon request, formal comments made by the Environmental Protection Agency on individual Remedial Action Plans.

**(E) Report**

Not later than 1 year after the date of enactment of this subparagraph, the Administrator shall submit to Congress a report on such actions, time periods, and resources as are necessary to fulfill the duties of the Agency relating to oversight of Remedial Action Plans under—

**(i)** this paragraph; and

**(ii)** the Great Lakes Water Quality Agreement.

**(4) Lakewide Management Plans**

The Administrator, in consultation with the Program Office shall—

**(A)** by January 1, 1992, publish in the Federal Register a proposed Lakewide Management Plan for Lake Michigan and solicit public comments;

**(B)** by January 1, 1993, submit a proposed Lakewide Management Plan for Lake Michigan to the International Joint Commission for review; and

**(C)** by January 1, 1994, publish in the Federal Register a final Lakewide Management Plan for Lake Michigan and begin implementation.

Nothing in this subparagraph shall preclude the simultaneous development of Lakewide Management Plans for the other Great Lakes.

**(5) Spills of oil and hazardous materials**

The Program Office, in consultation with the Coast Guard, shall identify areas within the Great Lakes which are likely to experience numerous or voluminous spills of oil or other hazardous materials from land based facilities, vessels, or other sources and, in consultation with the Great Lakes States, shall identify weaknesses in Federal and State programs and systems to prevent and respond to such spills. This information shall be included on at least a biennial basis in the report required by this section.

**(6) 5–year plan and program**

The Program Office shall develop, in consultation with the States, a five-year plan and program for reducing the amount of nutrients introduced into the Great Lakes. Such program shall incorporate any management program for reducing nutrient runoff from nonpoint sources established under section 1329 of this title and shall include a program for monitoring nutrient runoff into, and ambient levels in, the Great Lakes.

**(7) 5–year study and demonstration projects**

**(A)** The Program Office shall carry out a five-year study and demonstration projects relating to the control and removal of toxic pollutants in the Great Lakes, with emphasis on the removal of toxic pollutants from bottom sediments. In selecting locations for conducting demonstration projects under this paragraph, priority consideration shall be given to projects at the following locations: Saginaw Bay, Michigan; Sheboygan Harbor, Wisconsin; Grand Calumet River, Indiana; Ashtabula River, Ohio; and Buffalo River, New York.

**(B)** The Program Office shall—

**(i)** by December 31, 1990, complete chemical, physical, and biological assessments of the contaminated sediments at the locations selected for the study and demonstration projects;

**(ii)** by December 31, 1990, announce the technologies that will be demonstrated at each location and the numerical standard of protection intended to be achieved at each location;

**(iii)** by December 31, 1992, complete full or pilot scale demonstration projects on site at each location of promising technologies to remedy contaminated sediments; and

**(iv)** by December 31, 1993, issue a final report to Congress on its findings.

**(C)** The Administrator, after providing for public review and comment, shall publish information concerning the public health and environmental consequences of contaminants in Great Lakes sediment. Information published pursuant to this subparagraph shall include specific numerical limits to protect health, aquatic life, and wildlife from the bioaccumulation of toxins. The Administrator shall, at a minimum, publish information pursuant to this subparagraph within 2 years of November 16, 1990.

**(8) Administrator's responsibility**

The Administrator shall ensure that the Program Office enters into agreements with the various organizational elements of the Agency involved in Great Lakes activities and the appropriate State agencies specifically delineating—

**(A)** the duties and responsibilities of each such element in the Agency with respect to the Great Lakes;

**(B)** the time periods for carrying out such duties and responsibilities; and

**(C)** the resources to be committed to such duties and responsibilities.

**(9) Budget item**

The Administrator shall, in the Agency's annual budget submission to Congress, include a funding request for the Program Office as a separate budget line item.

**(10) Omitted**

**(11) Omitted**

**(12) Remediation of sediment contamination in areas of concern**

**(A) In general**

In accordance with this paragraph, the Administrator, acting through the Program Office, may carry out projects that meet the requirements of subparagraph (B).

**(B) Eligible projects**

A project meets the requirements of this subparagraph if the project is to be carried out in an area of concern located wholly or partially in the United States and the project—

(i) monitors or evaluates contaminated sediment;

(ii) subject to subparagraph (D), implements a plan to remediate contaminated sediment; or

(iii) prevents further or renewed contamination of sediment.

**(C) Priority**

In selecting projects to carry out under this paragraph, the Administrator shall give priority to a project that—

(i) constitutes remedial action for contaminated sediment;

(ii)(I) has been identified in a Remedial Action Plan submitted under paragraph (3); and

(II) is ready to be implemented;

(iii) will use an innovative approach, technology, or technique that may provide greater environmental benefits, or equivalent environmental benefits at a reduced cost; or

(iv) includes remediation to be commenced not later than 1 year after the date of receipt of funds for the project.

**(D) Limitation**

The Administrator may not carry out a project under this paragraph for remediation of contaminated sediments located in an area of concern—

(i) if an evaluation of remedial alternatives for the area of concern has not been conducted, including a review of the short-term and long-term effects of the alternatives on human health and the environment; or

(ii) if the Administrator determines that the area of concern is likely to suffer significant further or renewed contamination from existing sources of pollutants causing sediment contamination following completion of the project.

**(E) Non-Federal share**

**(i) In general**

The non-Federal share of the cost of a project carried out under this paragraph shall be at least 35 percent.

**(ii) In-kind contributions**

The non-Federal share of the cost of a project carried out under this paragraph may include the value of in-kind services contributed by a non-Federal sponsor.

**(iii) Non-Federal share**

The non-Federal share of the cost of a project carried out under this paragraph—

(I) may include monies paid pursuant to, or the value of any in-kind service performed under, an administrative order on consent or judicial consent decree; but

(II) may not include any funds paid pursuant to, or the value of any in-kind service performed under, a unilateral administrative order or court order.

**(iv) Operation and maintenance**

The non-Federal share of the cost of the operation and maintenance of a project carried out under this paragraph shall be 100 percent.

**(F) Maintenance of effort**

The Administrator may not carry out a project under this paragraph unless the non-Federal sponsor enters into such agreements with the Administrator as the Administrator may require to ensure that the non-Federal sponsor will maintain its aggregate expenditures from all other sources for remediation programs in the area of concern in which the project is located at or above the average level of such expenditures in the 2 fiscal years preceding the date on which the project is initiated.

**(G) Coordination**

In carrying out projects under this paragraph, the Administrator shall coordinate with the Secretary of the Army, and with the Governors of States in which the projects are located, to ensure that Federal and State assistance for remediation in areas of concern is used as efficiently as practicable.

**(H) Authorization of appropriations**

**(i) In general**

In addition to other amounts authorized under this section, there is authorized to be appropriated to carry out this paragraph $50,000,000 for each of fiscal years 2004 through 2008.

**(ii) Availability**

Funds made available under clause (i) shall remain available until expended.

**(13) Public information program**

**(A) In general**

The Administrator, acting through the Program Office and in coordination with States, Indian tribes, local governments, and other entities, may carry out a public information program to provide information relating to the remediation of contaminated sediment to the public in areas of concern that are located wholly or partially in the United States.

**(B) Authorization of appropriations**

There is authorized to be appropriated to carry out this paragraph $1,000,000 for each of fiscal years 2004 through 2008.

**(d) Great Lakes research**

**(1) Establishment of Research Office**

There is established within the National Oceanic and Atmospheric Administration the Great Lakes Research Office.

**(2) Identification of issues**

The Research Office shall identify issues relating to the Great Lakes resources on which research is needed. The Research Office shall submit a report to Congress on such issues before the end of each fiscal year which shall identify any changes in the Great Lakes system with respect to such issues.

**(3) Inventory**

The Research Office shall identify and inventory Federal, State, university, and tribal environmental research programs (and, to the extent feasible, those of private organizations and other nations) relating to the Great Lakes system, and shall update that inventory every four years.

**(4) Research exchange**

The Research Office shall establish a Great Lakes research exchange for the purpose of facilitating the rapid identification, acquisition, retrieval, dissemination, and use of information concerning research projects which are ongoing or completed and which affect the Great Lakes System.

**(5) Research program**

The Research Office shall develop, in cooperation with the Coordination Office, a comprehensive environmental research program and data base for the Great Lakes system. The data base shall include, but not be limited to, data relating to water quality, fisheries, and biota.

**(6) Monitoring**

The Research Office shall conduct, through the Great Lakes Environmental Research Laboratory, the National Sea Grant College program, other Federal laboratories, and the private sector, appropriate research and monitoring activities which address priority issues and current needs relating to the Great Lakes.

**(7) Location**

The Research Office shall be located in a Great Lakes State.

**(e) Research and management coordination**

**(1) Joint plan**

Before October 1 of each year, the Program Office and the Research Office shall prepare a joint research plan for the fiscal year which begins in the following calendar year.

**(2) Contents of plan**

Each plan prepared under paragraph (1) shall—

**(A)** identify all proposed research dedicated to activities conducted under the Great Lakes Water Quality Agreement of 1978, as amended by the Water Quality Agreement of 1987 and any other agreements and amendments,;[1]

**(B)** include the Agency's assessment of priorities for research needed to fulfill the terms of such Agreement; and

**(C)** identify all proposed research that may be used to develop a comprehensive environmental data base for the Great Lakes System and establish priorities for development of such data base.

**(3) Health research report**

**(A)** Not later than September 30, 1994, the Program Office, in consultation with the Research Office, the Agency for Toxic Substances and Disease Registry, and Great Lakes States shall submit to the Congress a report assessing the adverse effects of water pollutants in the Great Lakes System on the health of persons in Great Lakes States and the health of fish, shellfish, and wildlife in the Great Lakes System. In conducting research in support of this report, the Administrator may, where appropriate, provide for research to be conducted under cooperative agreements with Great Lakes States.

**(B)** There is authorized to be appropriated to the Administrator to carry out this section not to exceed $3,000,000 for each of fiscal years 1992, 1993, and 1994.

**(f) Interagency cooperation**

The head of each department, agency, or other instrumentality of the Federal Government which is engaged in, is concerned with, or has authority over programs relating to research, monitoring, and planning to maintain, enhance, preserve, or rehabilitate the environmental quality and natural resources of the Great Lakes, including the Chief of Engineers of the Army, the Chief of the Soil Conservation Service, the Commandant of the Coast Guard, the Director of the Fish and Wildlife Service, and the Administrator of the National Oceanic and Atmospheric Administration, shall submit an annual report to the Administrator with respect to the activities of that agency or office affecting compliance with the Great Lakes Water Quality Agreement of 1978, as amended by the Water Quality Agreement of 1987 and any other agreements and amendments,.[1]

**(g) Relationship to existing Federal and State laws and international treaties**

Nothing in this section shall be construed—

**(1)** to affect the jurisdiction, powers, or prerogatives of any department, agency, or officer of the Federal Government or of any State government, or of any tribe, nor any powers, jurisdiction, or prerogatives of any international body created by treaty with authority relating to the Great Lakes; or

**(2)** to affect any other Federal or State authority that is being used or may be used to facilitate the cleanup and protection of the Great Lakes.

**(h) Authorizations of Great Lakes appropriations**

There are authorized to be appropriated to the Administrator to carry out this section not to exceed—

**(1)** $11,000,000 per fiscal year for the fiscal years 1987, 1988, 1989, and 1990, and $25,000,000 for fiscal year 1991;

**(2)** such sums as are necessary for each of fiscal years 1992 through 2003; and

**(3)** $25,000,000 for each of fiscal years 2004 through 2008.

(June 30, 1948, c. 758, Title I, § 118, as added Feb. 4, 1987, Pub.L. 100–4, Title I, § 104, 101 Stat. 11, and amended Nov. 18, 1988, Pub.L. 100–688, Title I, § 1008, 102 Stat. 4151; Nov. 16, 1990, Pub.L. 101–596, Title I, §§ 101–106, 104 Stat. 3000–3004; Nov. 27, 2002, Pub.L. 107–303, Title I, §§ 102, 103, 104, 105, 116 Stat. 2355, 2356, 2357, 2358.)

[1] So in original.

## HISTORICAL AND STATUTORY NOTES

**References in Text**

The date of enactment of this subparagraph, referred to in subsec. (c)(3)(E), is Nov. 27, 2002, the date of enactment of Pub.L. 107–303, 116 Stat. 2355, which enacted such subparagraph (E).

**Codifications**

November 16, 1990, referred to in subsec. (c)(3)(C), (7)(C), was in the original "the enactment of this Act", and "the date of the enactment of this title" which were translated as meaning the date of enactment of Pub.L. 101–596, Title I of which enacted subsec. (c)(3), (7)(C), to reflect the probable intent of Congress.

Subsec. (c)(10) of this section, which required the Administrator to submit a comprehensive annual report to Congress on implementation of the Great Lakes Water Quality Agreement of 1978 and certain related matters, terminated, effective May 15, 2000, pursuant to section 3003 of Pub.L. 104–66, as amended, set out as a note under 31 U.S.C.A. § 1113. See, also, page 163 of House Document No. 103–7.

Subsec. (c)(11), as added by Pub.L. 101–596, § 104, which provided for development and implementation of plans for Great Lakes confined disposal facilities, expired by its provisions as of Nov. 16, 1991.

**Great Lakes Remedial Action Plans and Sediment Remediation**

Pub.L. 101–640, Title IV, § 401, Nov. 28, 1990, 104 Stat. 4644, as amended Pub.L. 104–303, Title V, § 515, Oct. 12, 1996, 110 Stat. 3763; Pub.L. 106–53, Title V, § 505, Aug. 17, 1999, 113 Stat. 338; Pub.L. 106–541, Title III, § 344, Dec. 11, 2000, 114 Stat. 2613, provided that:

**"(a) Great Lakes remedial action plans.—**

**"(1) In general.**—The Secretary may provide technical, planning, and engineering assistance to State and local governments and nongovernmental entities designated by a State or local government in the development and implementation of remedial action plans for Areas of Concern in the Great Lakes identified under the Great Lakes Water Quality Agreement of 1978.

**"(2) Non-Federal share.—**

**(A) In general.**—Non-Federal interests shall contribute, in cash or by providing in-kind contributions, 35 percent of costs of activities for which assistance is provided under paragraph (1).

**"(B) Contributions by entities.**—Nonprofit public or private entities may contribute all or a portion of the non–Federal share.

**"(b) Sediment remediation projects.—**

**"(1) In general.**—The Secretary, in consultation with the Administrator of the Environmental Protection Agency (acting through the Great Lakes National Program Office), may conduct pilot- and full-scale projects of promising technologies to remediate contaminated sediments in freshwater coastal regions in the Great Lakes basin. The Secretary shall conduct not fewer than 3 full-scale projects under this subsection.

**"(2) Site selection for projects.**—In selecting the sites for the technology projects, the Secretary shall give priority consideration to Saginaw Bay, Michigan, Sheboygan Harbor, Wisconsin, Grand Calumet River, Indiana, Ashtabula River, Ohio, Buffalo River, New York, and Duluth–Superior Harbor, Minnesota and Wisconsin.

**"(3) Non–Federal share.**—Non–Federal interests shall contribute 35 percent of costs of projects under this subsection. Such costs may be paid in cash or by providing in-kind contributions.

"(c) **Authorization of appropriations.**—There is authorized to be appropriated to the Secretary to carry out this section $10,000,000 for each of fiscal years 2001 through 2006."

## § 1269. Long Island Sound

**[FWPCA § 119]**

### (a) Office of Management Conference of the Long Island Sound Study

The Administrator shall continue the Management Conference of the Long Island Sound Study (hereinafter referred to as the "Conference") as established pursuant to section 1330 of this title, and shall establish an office (hereinafter referred to as the "Office") to be located on or near Long Island Sound.

### (b) Administration and staffing of Office

The Office shall be headed by a Director, who shall be detailed by the Administrator, following consultation with the Administrators of EPA regions I and II, from among the employees of the Agency who are in civil service. The Administrator shall delegate to the Director such authority and detail such additional staff as may be necessary to carry out the duties of the Director under this section.

### (c) Duties of Office

The Office shall assist the Management Conference of the Long Island Sound Study in carrying out its goals. Specifically, the Office shall—

(1) assist and support the implementation of the Comprehensive Conservation and Management Plan for Long Island Sound developed pursuant to section 1330 of this title, including efforts to establish, within the process for granting watershed general permits, a system for promoting innovative methodologies and technologies that are cost-effective and consistent with the goals of the Plan;

(2) conduct or commission studies deemed necessary for strengthened implementation of the Comprehensive Conservation and Management Plan including, but not limited to—

(A) population growth and the adequacy of wastewater treatment facilities,

(B) the use of biological methods for nutrient removal in sewage treatment plants,

(C) contaminated sediments, and dredging activities,

(D) nonpoint source pollution abatement and land use activities in the Long Island Sound watershed,

(E) wetland protection and restoration,

(F) atmospheric deposition of acidic and other pollutants into Long Island Sound,

(G) water quality requirements to sustain fish, shellfish, and wildlife populations, and the use of indicator species to assess environmental quality,

(H) State water quality programs, for their adequacy pursuant to implementation of the Comprehensive Conservation and Management Plan, and

(I) options for long-term financing of wastewater treatment projects and water pollution control programs.

(3) coordinate the grant, research and planning programs authorized under this section;

(4) coordinate activities and implementation responsibilities with other Federal agencies which have jurisdiction over Long Island Sound and with national and regional marine monitoring and research programs established pursuant to the Marine Protection, Research, and Sanctuaries Act [16 U.S.C.A. §§ 1431 et seq., 1447 et seq.; 33 U.S.C.A. §§ 1401 et seq., 2801 et seq.];

(5) provide administrative and technical support to the conference;

(6) collect and make available to the public publications, and other forms of information the conference determines to be appropriate, relating to the environmental quality of Long Island Sound;

(7) not more than two years after the date of the issuance of the final Comprehensive Conservation and Management Plan for Long Island Sound under section 1330 of this title, and biennially thereafter, issue a report to the Congress which—

(A) summarizes the progress made by the States in implementing the Comprehensive Conservation and Management Plan;

(B) summarizes any modifications to the Comprehensive Conservation and Management Plan in the twelve-month period immediately preceding such report; and

(C) incorporates specific recommendations concerning the implementation of the Comprehensive Conservation and Management Plan; and

(8) convene conferences and meetings for legislators from State governments and political subdivisions thereof for the purpose of making recommendations for coordinating legislative efforts to facilitate the environmental restoration of Long Island Sound and the implementation of the Comprehensive Conservation and Management Plan.

### (d) Grants

(1) The Administrator is authorized to make grants for projects and studies which will help implement the Long Island Sound Comprehensive Conservation and Management Plan. Special emphasis shall be given to implementation, research and planning, enforcement, and citizen involvement and education.

(2) State, interstate, and regional water pollution control agencies, and other public or nonprofit private agencies, institutions, and organizations held to be eligible for grants pursuant to this subsection.

(3) Citizen involvement and citizen education grants under this subsection shall not exceed 95 per centum of the costs of such work. All other grants under this subsection shall not exceed 50 per centum of the research, studies, or work. All grants shall be made on the condition that the non-Federal share of such costs are provided from non-Federal sources.

**(e) Assistance to distressed communities**

**(1) Eligible communities**

For the purposes of this subsection, a distressed community is any community that meets affordability criteria established by the State in which the community is located, if such criteria are developed after public review and comment.

**(2) Priority**

In making assistance available under this section for the upgrading of wastewater treatment facilities, the Administrator may give priority to a distressed community.

**(f) Authorizations**

(1) There is authorized to be appropriated to the Administrator for the implementation of this section, other than subsection (d) of this section, such sums as may be necessary for each of the fiscal years 2001 through 2005.

(2) There is authorized to be appropriated to the Administrator for the implementation of subsection (d) of this section not to exceed $40,000,000 for each of fiscal years 2001 through 2005.

(June 30, 1948, c. 758, Title I, § 119, as added Nov. 16, 1990, Pub.L. 101–596, Title II, § 202, 104 Stat. 3004, and amended Oct. 12, 1996, Pub.L. 104–303, Title IV, § 583, 110 Stat. 3791; Nov. 7, 2000, Pub.L. 106–457, Title IV, §§ 402 to 404, 114 Stat. 1973.)

### HISTORICAL AND STATUTORY NOTES

**References in Text**

The Marine Protection, Research, and Sanctuaries Act, referred to in subsec. (c)(4), probably means the Marine Protection, Research and Sanctuaries Act of 1972, Pub.L. 92–532, Oct. 23, 1972, 86 Stat. 1052, as amended, which is classified principally to chapters 32 and 32A of Title 16 [16 U.S.C.A. §§ 1431 et seq., 1447 et seq.] and chapters 27 and 41 of this title [33 U.S.C.A. §§ 1401 et seq. 2801 et seq.] See Short Title note set out under 33 U.S.C.A § 1401 and Tables for complete classification.

**Termination of Reporting Requirements**

For termination, effective May 15, 2000, of provisions in subsec. (c)(7) of this section relating to issuing a biennial report to Congress, see section 3003 of Pub.L. 104–66, as amended, set out as a note under 31 U.S.C.A. § 1113, and page 163 of House Document No. 103–7.

## § 1270. Lake Champlain Basin Program [FWPCA § 120]

**(a) Establishment**

**(1) In general**

There is established a Lake Champlain Management Conference to develop a comprehensive pollution prevention, control, and restoration plan for Lake Champlain. The Administrator shall convene the management conference within ninety days of November 16, 1990.

**(2) Implementation**

The Administrator—

(A) may provide support to the State of Vermont, the State of New York, and the New England Interstate Water Pollution Control Commission for the implementation of the Lake Champlain Basin Program; and

(B) shall coordinate actions of the Environmental Protection Agency under subparagraph (A) with the actions of other appropriate Federal agencies.";

**(b) Membership**

The Members of the Management Conference shall be comprised of—

(1) the Governors of the States of Vermont and New York;

(2) each interested Federal agency, not to exceed a total of five members;

(3) the Vermont and New York Chairpersons of the Vermont, New York, Quebec Citizens Advisory Committee for the Environmental Management of Lake Champlain;

(4) four representatives of the State legislature of Vermont;

(5) four representatives of the State legislature of New York;

(6) six persons representing local governments having jurisdiction over any land or water within the Lake Champlain basin, as determined appropriate by the Governors; and

(7) eight persons representing affected industries, nongovernmental organizations, public and private educational institutions, and the general public, as determined appropriate by the trigovernmental Citizens Advisory Committee for the Environmental Management of Lake Champlain, but not to be current members of the Citizens Advisory Committee.

**(c) Technical Advisory Committee**

(1) The Management Conference shall, not later than one hundred and twenty days after November 16, 1990, appoint a Technical Advisory Committee.

(2) Such Technical Advisory Committee shall consist of officials of: appropriate departments and agencies of the Federal Government; the State governments of New York and Vermont; and governments of political subdivisions of such States; and public and private research institutions.

**(d) Research program**

The Management Conference shall establish a multi-disciplinary environmental research program for Lake Champlain. Such research program shall be planned and conducted jointly with the Lake Champlain Research Consortium.

**(e) Pollution prevention, control, and restoration plan**

(1) Not later than three years after November 16, 1990, the Management Conference shall publish a pollution prevention, control, and restoration plan for Lake Champlain.

(2) The Plan developed pursuant to this section shall—

(A) identify corrective actions and compliance schedules addressing point and nonpoint sources of pollution necessary to restore and maintain the chemical, physical, and biological integrity of water quality, a balanced, indigenous population of shellfish, fish and wildlife, recreational, and economic activities in and on the lake;

(B) incorporate environmental management concepts and programs established in State and Federal plans and programs in effect at the time of the development of such plan;

(C) clarify the duties of Federal and State agencies in pollution prevention and control activities, and to the extent allowable by law, suggest a timetable for adoption by the appropriate Federal and State agencies to accomplish such duties within a reasonable period of time;

(D) describe the methods and schedules for funding of programs, activities, and projects identified in the Plan, including the use of Federal funds and other sources of funds;

(E) include a strategy for pollution prevention and control that includes the promotion of pollution prevention and management practices to reduce the amount of pollution generated in the Lake Champlain basin; and

(F) be reviewed and revised, as necessary, at least once every 5 years, in consultation with the Administrator and other appropriate Federal agencies.

(3) The Administrator, in cooperation with the Management Conference, shall provide for public review and comment on the draft Plan. At a minimum, the Management Conference shall conduct one public meeting to hear comments on the draft plan in the State of New York and one such meeting in the State of Vermont.

(4) Not less than one hundred and twenty days after the publication of the Plan required pursuant to this section, the Administrator shall approve such plan if the plan meets the requirements of this section and the Governors of the States of New York and Vermont concur.

(5) Upon approval of the plan, such plan shall be deemed to be an approved management program for the purposes of section 1329(h) of this title and such plan shall be deemed to be an approved comprehensive conservation and management plan pursuant to section 1330 of this title.

**(f) Grant assistance**

(1) The Administrator may, in consultation with participants in the Lake Champlain Basin Program, make grants to State, interstate, and regional water pollution control agencies, and public or nonprofit agencies, institutions, and organizations.

(2) Grants under this subsection shall be made for assisting research, surveys, studies, and modeling and technical and supporting work necessary for the development and implementation of the Plan.

(3) The amount of grants to any person under this subsection for a fiscal year shall not exceed 75 per centum of the costs of such research, survey, study and work and shall be made available on the condition that non-Federal share of such costs are provided from non-Federal sources.

(4) The Administrator may establish such requirements for the administration of grants as he determines to be appropriate.

**(g) Definitions**

In this section:

**(1) Lake Champlain Basin Program**

The term "Lake Champlain Basin Program" means the coordinated efforts among the Federal Government, State governments, and local governments to implement the Plan.

**(2) Lake Champlain drainage basin**

The term "Lake Champlain drainage basin" means all or part of Clinton, Franklin, Hamilton, Warren, Essex, and Washington counties in the State of New York and all or part of Franklin, Grand Isle, Chittenden, Addison, Rutland, Bennington, Lamoille, Orange, Washington, Orleans, and

Caledonia counties in Vermont, that contain all of the streams, rivers, lakes, and other bodies of water, including wetlands, that drain into Lake Champlain.

(3) Plan

The term "Plan" means the plan developed under subsection (e) of this section.

**(h) No effect on certain authority**

Nothing in this section—

(1) affects the jurisdiction or powers of—

(A) any department or agency of the Federal Government or any State government; or

(B) any international organization or entity related to Lake Champlain created by treaty or memorandum to which the United States is a signatory;

(2) provides new regulatory authority for the Environmental Protection Agency; or

(3) affects section 304 of the Great Lakes Critical Programs Act of 1990 (Public Law 101–596; 33 U.S.C. 1270 note).

**(i) Authorization**

There are authorized to be appropriated to the Environmental Protection Agency to carry out this section—

(1) $2,000,000 for each of fiscal years 1991, 1992, 1993, 1994, and 1995;

(2) such sums as are necessary for each of fiscal years 1996 through 2003; and

(3) $11,000,000 for each of fiscal years 2004 through 2008.

(June 30, 1948, c. 758, Title I, § 120, as added Nov. 16, 1990, Pub.L. 101–596, Title III, § 303, 104 Stat. 3006, and amended Nov. 27, 2002, Pub.L. 107–303, Title II, § 202, 116 Stat. 2358.)

## HISTORICAL AND STATUTORY NOTES

**References in Text**

Section 304 of the Great Lakes Critical Programs Act of 1990, referred to in subsec. (h)(3), is section 304 of Pub.L. 101–596, Nov. 16, 1990, 104 Stat. 3008, which is set out as a note under this section.

**Federal Program Coordination**

Section 304 of Pub.L. 101–596, as amended Pub.L. 104–127, Title III, § 336(a)(2)(F), Apr. 4, 1996, 110 Stat. 1005, provided that:

"**(a) Designation of Lake Champlain as a priority area under the Environmental Quality Incentives Program.—**

"(1) **In general.**—Notwithstanding any other provision of law, the Lake Champlain basin, as defined under section 120(h) of the Federal Water Pollution Control Act [section 1270(h) of this title], shall be designated by the Secretary of Agriculture as a priority area under the environmental quality incentives program established under part IV of subchapter IV of chapter 58 of Title 16.

"(2) **Technical assistance reimbursement.**—To carry out the purposes of this subsection, the technical assistance reimbursement from the Agricultural Stabilization and Conservation Service authorized under the Soil Conservation and Domestic Allotment Act [section 590a of Title 16], shall be increased from 5 per centum to 10 per centum.

"(3) **Comprehensive agricultural monitoring.**—The Secretary, in consultation with the Management Conference and appropriate State and Federal agencies, shall develop a comprehensive agricultural monitoring and evaluation network for all major drainages within the Lake Champlain basin.

"(4) **Allocation of funds.**—In allocating funds under this subsection, the Secretary of Agriculture shall consult with the Management Conference established under section 120 of the Federal Water Pollution Control Act [section 1270 of this title] and to the extent allowable by law, allocate funds to those agricultural enterprises located at sites that the Management Conference determines to be priority sites, on the basis of a concern for ensuring implementation of nonpoint source pollution controls throughout the Lake Champlain basin.

"**(b) Cooperation of the United States Geological Survey of the Department of the Interior.**—For the purpose of enhancing and expanding basic data collection and monitoring in operation in the Lake Champlain basin, as defined under section 120 of the Federal Water Pollution Control Act [section 1270 of this title], the Secretary of the Interior, acting through the heads of water resources divisions of the New York and New England districts of the United States Geological Survey, shall—

"(1) in cooperation with appropriate universities and private research institutions, and the appropriate officials of the appropriate departments and agencies of the States of New York and Vermont, develop an integrated geographic information system of the Lake Champlain basin;

"(2) convert all partial recording sites in the Lake Champlain basin to continuous monitoring stations with full gauging capabilities and status; and

"(3) establish such additional continuous monitoring station sites in the Lake Champlain basin as are necessary to carry out basic data collection and monitoring, as defined by the Secretary of the Interior, including groundwater mapping, and water quality and sediment data collection.

"**(c) Cooperation of the United States Fish and Wildlife Service of the Department of the Interior.—**

"(1) **Resource conservation program.**—The Secretary of the Interior, acting through the United States Fish and Wildlife Service, in cooperation with the Lake Champlain Fish and Wildlife Management Cooperative and the Management Conference established pursuant to this subsection shall—

"(A) establish and implement a fisheries resources restoration, development and conservation program, including dedicating a level of hatchery production within the Lake Champlain basin at or above the level that existed immediately preceding the date of enactment of this Act [Nov. 16, 1990]; and

"(B) conduct a wildlife species and habitat assessment survey in the Lake Champlain basin, including—

"(i) a survey of Federal threatened and endangered species, listed or proposed for listing under the Endangered Species Act of 1973 (16 U.S.C. 1531 et seq.), New York State and State of Vermont threatened and endangered species and other species of special concern, migratory nongame species of management concern, and national resources plan species;

"(ii) a survey of wildlife habitats such as islands, wetlands, and riparian areas; and

"(iii) a survey of migratory bird populations breeding, migrating and wintering within the Lake Champlain basin.

"(2) To accomplish the purposes of paragraph (1), the Director of the United States Fish and Wildlife Service is authorized to carry out activities related to—

"(A) controlling sea lampreys and other nonindigenous aquatic animal nuisances;

"(B) improving the health of fishery resources;

"(C) conducting investigations about and assessing the status of fishery resources, and disseminating that information to all interested parties; and

"(D) conducting and periodically updating a survey of the fishery resources and their habitats and food chains in the Lake Champlain basin.

"(d) **Authorizations.**—(1) There is authorized to be appropriated to the Department of Agriculture $2,000,000 for each of fiscal years 1991, 1992, 1993, 1994, and 1995 to carry out subsection (a) of this section.

"(2) There is authorized to be appropriated to the Department of Interior $1,000,000 for each of fiscal years 1991, 1992, 1993, 1994, and 1995 to carry out subsections (b) and (c) of this section."

## § 1271. Sediment survey and monitoring

[NCSAMA § 503]

### (a) Survey

#### (1) In general

The Administrator, in consultation with the Administrator of the National Oceanic and Atmospheric Administration and the Secretary, shall conduct a comprehensive national survey of data regarding aquatic sediment quality in the United States. The Administrator shall compile all existing information on the quantity, chemical and physical composition, and geographic location of pollutants in aquatic sediment, including the probable source of such pollutants and identification of those sediments which are contaminated pursuant to section 501(b)(4).

#### (2) Report

Not later than 24 months after October 31, 1992, the Administrator shall report to the Congress the findings, conclusions, and recommendations of such survey, including recommendations for actions necessary to prevent contamination of aquatic sediments and to control sources of contamination.

### (b) Monitoring

#### (1) In general

The Administrator, in consultation with the Administrator of the National Oceanic and Atmospheric Administration and the Secretary, shall conduct a comprehensive and continuing program to assess aquatic sediment quality. The program conducted pursuant to this subsection shall, at a minimum—

(A) identify the location of pollutants in aquatic sediment;

(B) identify the extent of pollutants in sediment and those sediments which are contaminated pursuant to section 501(b)(4);

(C) establish methods and protocols for monitoring the physical, chemical, and biological effects of pollutants in aquatic sediment and of contaminated sediment;

(D) develop a system for the management, storage, and dissemination of data concerning aquatic sediment quality;

(E) provide an assessment of aquatic sediment quality trends over time;

(F) identify locations where pollutants in sediment may pose a threat to the quality of drinking water supplies, fisheries resources, and marine habitats; and

(G) establish a clearing house for information on technology, methods, and practices available for the remediation, decontamination, and control of sediment contamination.

#### (2) Report

The Administrator shall submit to Congress a report on the findings of the monitoring under paragraph (1) on the date that is 2 years after the date specified in subsection (a)(2) of this section and biennially thereafter.

(Pub.L. 102–580, Title V, § 503, Oct. 31, 1992, 106 Stat. 4865.)

### HISTORICAL AND STATUTORY NOTES

**References in Text**

Section 501(b)(4), referred to in subsecs. (a)(1) and (b)(1)(B), is section 501(b)(4) of Pub.L. 102–580, Title V, Oct. 31, 1992, 106 Stat. 4864, which is classified in a note entitled "Definitions" and set out under this section.

**Codifications**

Section was enacted as part of the Water Resources Development Act of 1992 and the National Contaminated Sediment Assessment and Management Act, and not as part of the Federal Water Pollution Control Act, which comprises this chapter.

**Short Title**

1992 Acts

Section 501(a) of Pub.L. 102–580 provided that: "This title [Pub.L. 102–580, Title V, Oct. 31, 1992, 106 Stat. 4864, which enacted this section, amended sections 1412, 1413, 1414, 1415, 1416, 1420 and 1421 of this title, and enacted provisions set out as notes under section 1271 of this title; for distribution of Pub.L. 102–580 to the Code, see Short Title note set out under section 2201 of this title and Tables] may be cited as the 'National Contaminated Sediment Assessment and Management Act'."

**"Secretary" Defined**

Secretary means the Secretary of the Army, see section 2 of Pub.L. 100–676, set out as a note under 33 U.S.C.A. § 2201.

**Authorization of Appropriations**

Section 509(b) of Pub.L. 102–580 provided that: "There is authorized to be appropriated to the Administrator to carry out sections 502 [set out as a note under this section] and 503 [this section] such sums as may be necessary."

**Availability of Contaminated Sediments Information**

Section 327 of Pub.L. 102–580 directed the Secretary to conduct a national study on information currently available on contaminated sediments of surface waters of United States, compile information obtained in such study for the purpose of identifying the location and nature of contaminated sediments in the Nation, and, not later than 1 year after Oct. 31, 1992, to transmit to the Committee on Public Works and Transportation of the House of Representatives and the Committee on Environment and Public Works of the Senate a report on the results of the study.

**Definitions**

Section 501(b) of Pub.L. 102–580 provided that: "For the purposes of sections 502 [set out as a note under this section] and 503 of this title [this section]—

"(1) the term 'aquatic sediment' means sediment underlying the navigable waters of the United States;

"(2) the term 'navigable waters' has the same meaning as in section 502(7) of the Federal Water Pollution Control Act (33 U.S.C. 1362(7) [section 1362(7) of this title]);

"(3) the term 'pollutant' has the same meaning as in section 502(6) of the Federal Water Pollution Control Act (33 U.S.C. 1362(6) [section 1362(6) of this title]); except that such term does not include dredge spoil, rock, sand, or cellar dirt;

"(4) the term 'contaminated sediment' means aquatic sediment which—

"(A) contains chemical substances in excess of appropriate geochemical, toxicological or sediment quality criteria or measures; or

"(B) is otherwise considered by the Administrator to pose a threat to human health or the environment; and

"(5) the term 'Administrator' means the Administrator of the Environmental Protection Agency."

**National Contaminated Sediment Task Force**

Section 502 of Pub.L. 102–580 provided that:

**"Sec. 502. National contaminated sediment task force.**

"(a) **Establishment.**—There is established a National Contaminated Sediment Task Force (hereinafter referred to in this section as the 'Task Force'). The Task Force shall—

"(1) advise the Administrator and the Secretary in the implementation of this title [Pub.L. 102–580, Title V, Oct. 31, 1992, 106 Stat. 4864, which enacted this section, amended sections 1412, 1413, 1414, 1415, 1416, 1420 and 1421 of this title, and enacted provisions set out as notes under section 1271 of this title; for distribution of Pub.L. 102–580 to the Code, see Short Title note set out under section 2201 of this title and Tables];

"(2) review and comment on reports concerning aquatic sediment quality and the extent and seriousness of aquatic sediment contamination throughout the Nation;

"(3) review and comment on programs for the research and development of aquatic sediment restoration methods, practices, and technologies;

"(4) review and comment on the selection of pollutants for development of aquatic sediment criteria and the schedule for the development of such criteria;

"(5) advise appropriate officials in the development of guidelines for restoration of contaminated sediment;

"(6) make recommendations to appropriate officials concerning practices and measures—

"(A) to prevent the contamination of aquatic sediments; and

"(B) to control sources of sediment contamination; and

"(7) review and assess the means and methods for locating and constructing permanent, cost-effective long-term disposal sites for the disposal of dredged material that is not suitable for ocean dumping (as determined under the Marine Protection, Research, and Sanctuaries Act of 1972 (33 U.S.C. 1401 et seq.) [section 1401 et seq. of this title]).

"(b) Membership.—

"(1) **In general.**—The membership of the Task Force shall include 1 representative of each of the following:

"(A) The Administrator.

"(B) The Secretary.

"(C) The National Oceanic and Atmospheric Administration.

"(D) The United States Fish and Wildlife Service.

"(E) The Geological Survey.

"(F) The Department of Agriculture.

"(2) **Additional members.**—Additional members of the Task Force shall be jointly selected by the Administrator and the Secretary, and shall include—

"(A) not more than 3 representatives of States;

"(B) not more than 3 representatives of ports, agriculture, and manufacturing; and

"(C) not more than 3 representatives of public interest organizations with a demonstrated interest in aquatic sediment contamination.

"(3) **Cochairmen.**—The Administrator and the Secretary shall serve as cochairmen of the Task Force.

"(4) **Clerical and technical assistance.**—Such clerical and technical assistance as may be necessary to discharge the duties of the Task Force shall be provided by the personnel of the Environmental Protection Agency and the Army Corps of Engineers.

"(5) **Compensation for additional members.**—The additional members of the Task Force selected under paragraph (2) shall, while attending meetings or conferences of the Task Force, be compensated at a rate to be fixed by the cochairmen, but not to exceed the daily equivalent of the base rate of pay in effect for grade GS–15 of the General Schedule under section 5332 of title 5, United

States Code [section 5332 of Title 5, Government Organization and Employees], for each day (including travel time) during which they are engaged in the actual performance of duties vested in the Task Force. While away from their homes or regular places of business in the performance of services for the Task Force, such members shall be allowed travel expenses, including per diem in lieu of subsistence, in the same manner as persons employed intermittently in the Government service are allowed expenses under section 5703(b) of title 5, United States Code [section 5703(b) of Title 5].

"(c) **Report.**—Within 2 years after the date of the enactment of this Act [Oct. 31, 1992], the Task Force shall submit to Congress a report stating the findings and recommendations of the Task Force."

## § 1271a. Research and development program

**(a) In general**

In coordination with other Federal, State, and local officials, the Administrator of the Environmental Protection Agency may conduct research on the development and use of innovative approaches, technologies, and techniques for the remediation of sediment contamination in areas of concern that are located wholly or partially in the United States.

**(b) Authorization of appropriations**

**(1) In general**

In addition to amounts authorized under other laws, there is authorized to be appropriated to carry out this section $3,000,000 for each of fiscal years 2004 through 2008.

**(2) Availability**

Funds appropriated under paragraph (1) shall remain available until expended.

(Pub.L. 107–303, Title I, § 106, Nov. 27, 2002, 116 Stat. 2358.)

### HISTORICAL AND STATUTORY NOTES

**Codifications**

Section was enacted as part of the Great Lakes and Lake Champlain Act of 2002 and as part of the Great Lakes Legacy Act of 2002 and not as part of the Federal Water Pollution Control Act which otherwise comprises this chapter.

## § 1272. Environmental dredging

**(a) Operation and maintenance of navigation projects**

Whenever necessary to meet the requirements of the Federal Water Pollution Control Act [33 U.S.C.A. § 1251 et seq.], the Secretary, in consultation with the Administrator of the Environmental Protection Agency, may remove and remediate, as part of operation and maintenance of a navigation project, contaminated sediments outside the boundaries of and adjacent to the navigation channel.

**(b) Nonproject specific**

**(1) In general**

The Secretary may remove and remediate contaminated sediments from the navigable waters of the United States for the purpose of environmental enhancement and water quality improvement if such removal and remediation is requested by a non-Federal sponsor and the sponsor agrees to pay 35 percent of the cost of such removal and remediation.

**(2) Maximum amount**

The Secretary may not expend more than $50,000,000 in a fiscal year to carry out this subsection.

**(c) Joint plan requirement**

The Secretary may only remove and remediate contaminated sediments under subsection (b) of this section in accordance with a joint plan developed by the Secretary and interested Federal, State, and local government officials. Such plan must include an opportunity for public comment, a description of the work to be undertaken, the method to be used for dredged material disposal, the roles and responsibilities of the Secretary and non-Federal sponsors, and identification of sources of funding.

**(d) Disposal costs**

Costs of disposal of contaminated sediments removed under this section shall be a [1] shared as a cost of construction.

**(e) Limitation on statutory construction**

Nothing in this section shall be construed to affect the rights and responsibilities of any person under the Comprehensive Environmental Response, Compensation, and Liability Act of 1980 [42 U.S.C.A. § 9601 et seq.].

**(f) Priority work**

In carrying out this section, the Secretary shall give priority to work in the following areas:

(1) Brooklyn Waterfront, New York.

(2) Buffalo Harbor and River, New York.

(3) Ashtabula River, Ohio.

(4) Mahoning River, Ohio.

(5) Lower Fox River, Wisconsin.

(6) Passaic River and Newark Bay, New Jersey.

(7) Snake Creek, Bixby, Oklahoma.

(8) Willamette River, Oregon.

**(g) Nonprofit entities**

Notwithstanding section 1962d–5b of Title 42, for any project carried out under this section, a non-

Federal sponsor may include a nonprofit entity, with the consent of the affected local government.

Pub.L. 101–640, Title III, § 312, Nov. 28, 1990, 104 Stat. 4639; Pub.L. 104–303, Title II, § 205, Oct. 12, 1996, 110 Stat. 3679; Pub.L. 106–53, Title II, § 224, Aug. 17, 1999, 113 Stat. 297; Pub.L. 106–541, Title II, § 210(a), Dec. 11, 2000, 114 Stat. 2592.)

1 So in original.

### HISTORICAL AND STATUTORY NOTES

**References in Text**

The Federal Water Pollution Control Act, as amended, referred to in text, probably means Act June 30, 1948, c. 758, as amended generally by Pub.L. 92–500, § 2, Oct. 18, 1972, 86 Stat. 816, which is classified generally to this chapter 26 (section 1251 et seq.). For complete classification of this Act to the Code, see Short Title note set out under section 1251 of this title and Tables.

The Comprehensive Environmental Response, Compensation, and Liability Act, as amended, referred to in subsec. (e), is Pub.L. 96–510, Dec. 11, 1980, 94 Stat. 2767, as amended, which is classified principally to chapter 103 (section 9601 et seq.) of Title 42, The Public Health and Welfare. For complete classification of this Act to the Code, see Short Title note set out under section 9601 of Title 42 and Tables.

**Codifications**

Section was formerly set out as a note under section 1252 of this title.

Section was enacted as part of the Water Resources Development Act of 1990 and not as part of the Federal Water Pollution Control Act, which comprises this chapter.

## § 1273. Lake Pontchartrain Basin

[FWPCA § 121]

**(a) Establishment of Restoration Program**

The Administrator shall establish within the Environmental Protection Agency the Lake Pontchartrain Basin Restoration Program.

**(b) Purpose**

The purpose of the program shall be to restore the ecological health of the Basin by developing and funding restoration projects and related scientific and public education projects.

**(c) Duties**

In carrying out the program, the Administrator shall—

(1) provide administrative and technical assistance to a management conference convened for the Basin under section 1330 of this title;

(2) assist and support the activities of the management conference, including the implementation of recommendations of the management conference;

(3) support environmental monitoring of the Basin and research to provide necessary technical and scientific information;

(4) develop a comprehensive research plan to address the technical needs of the program;

(5) coordinate the grant, research, and planning programs authorized under this section; and

(6) collect and make available to the public publications, and other forms of information the management conference determines to be appropriate, relating to the environmental quality of the Basin.

**(d) Grants**

The Administrator may make grants—

(1) for restoration projects and studies recommended by a management conference convened for the Basin under section 1330 of this title; and

(2) for public education projects recommended by the management conference.

**(e) Definitions**

In this section, the following definitions apply:

**(1) Basin**

The term "Basin" means the Lake Pontchartrain Basin, a 5,000 square mile watershed encompassing 16 parishes in the State of Louisiana and 4 counties in the State of Mississippi.

**(2) Program**

The term "program" means the Lake Pontchartrain Basin Restoration Program established under subsection (a) of this section.

**(f) Authorization of appropriations**

**(1) In general**

There is authorized to be appropriated to carry out this section $20,000,000 for each of fiscal years 2001 through 2005. Such sums shall remain available until expended.

**(2) Public education projects**

Not more than 15 percent of the amount appropriated pursuant to paragraph (1) in a fiscal year may be expended on grants for public education projects under subsection (d)(2) of this section.

(June 30, 1948, c. 758, Title I, § 121, as added Nov. 7, 2000, Pub.L. 106–457, Title V, § 502, 114 Stat. 1973.)

### HISTORICAL AND STATUTORY NOTES

**Codifications**

Another § 121 of the Federal Water Pollution Control Act, which was added by of Pub.L. 106–554, § 1(a)(4) [Div. B, Title I, § 112(b)], was classified to section 1274 of this title.

## § 1274. Wet weather watershed pilot projects

[FWPCA § 121]

**(a) In general**

The Administrator, in coordination with the States, may provide technical assistance and grants for treatment works to carry out pilot projects relating to the following areas of wet weather discharge control:

**(1) Watershed management of wet weather discharges**

The management of municipal combined sewer overflows, sanitary sewer overflows, and stormwater discharges, on an integrated watershed or subwatershed basis for the purpose of demonstrating the effectiveness of a unified wet weather approach.

**(2) Stormwater best management practices**

The control of pollutants from municipal separate storm sewer systems for the purpose of demonstrating and determining controls that are cost-effective and that use innovative technologies in reducing such pollutants from stormwater discharges.

**(b) Administration**

The Administrator, in coordination with the States, shall provide municipalities participating in a pilot project under this section the ability to engage in innovative practices, including the ability to unify separate wet weather control efforts under a single permit.

**(c) Funding**

**(1) In general**

There is authorized to be appropriated to carry out this section $10,000,000 for fiscal year 2002, $15,000,000 for fiscal year 2003, and $20,000,000 for fiscal year 2004. Such funds shall remain available until expended.

**(2) Stormwater**

The Administrator shall make available not less than 20 percent of amounts appropriated for a fiscal year pursuant to this subsection to carry out the purposes of subsection (a)(2) of this section.

**(3) Administrative expenses**

The Administrator may retain not to exceed 4 percent of any amounts appropriated for a fiscal year pursuant to this subsection for the reasonable and necessary costs of administering this section.

**(d) Report to Congress**

Not later than 5 years after December 21, 2000, the Administrator shall transmit to Congress a report on the results of the pilot projects conducted under this section and their possible application nationwide.

(June 30, 1948, c. 758, Title I, § 121, as added Dec. 21, 2000, Pub.L. 106–554, § 1(a)(4) [Div. B, Title I, § 112(b)], 114 Stat. 2763, 2763A–225.)

### HISTORICAL AND STATUTORY NOTES

**Codifications**

Another § 121 of the Federal Water Pollution Control Act, which was added by § 502 of Pub.L. 106–457, was classified to section 1273 of this title.

## SUBCHAPTER II—GRANTS FOR CONSTRUCTION OF TREATMENT WORKS

## § 1281. Congressional declaration of purpose

**[FWPCA § 201]**

**(a) Development and implementation of waste treatment management plans and practices**

It is the purpose of this subchapter to require and to assist the development and implementation of waste treatment management plans and practices which will achieve the goals of this chapter.

**(b) Application of technology: confined disposal of pollutants; consideration of advanced techniques**

Waste treatment management plans and practices shall provide for the application of the best practicable waste treatment technology before any discharge into receiving waters, including reclaiming and recycling of water, and confined disposal of pollutants so they will not migrate to cause water or other environmental pollution and shall provide for consideration of advanced waste treatment techniques.

**(c) Waste treatment management area and scope**

To the extent practicable, waste treatment management shall be on an areawide basis and provide control or treatment of all point and nonpoint sources of pollution, including in place or accumulated pollution sources.

**(d) Waste treatment management construction of revenue producing facilities**

The Administrator shall encourage waste treatment management which results in the construction of revenue producing facilities providing for—

(1) the recycling of potential sewage pollutants through the production of agriculture, silviculture, or aquaculture products, or any combination thereof;

(2) the confined and contained disposal of pollutants not recycled;

(3) the reclamation of wastewater; and

(4) the ultimate disposal of sludge in a manner that will not result in environmental hazards.

**(e) Waste treatment management integration of facilities**

The Administrator shall encourage waste treatment management which results in integrating facilities for sewage treatment and recycling with facilities to treat, dispose of, or utilize other industrial and municipal wastes, including but not limited to solid waste and waste heat and thermal discharges. Such integrated facilities shall be designed and operated to produce revenues in excess of capital and operation and maintenance costs and such revenues shall be used by the designated regional management agency to aid in financing other environmental improvement programs.

**(f) Waste treatment management "open space" and recreational considerations**

The Administrator shall encourage waste treatment management which combines "open space" and recreational considerations with such management.

**(g) Grants to construct publicly owned treatment works**

(1) The Administrator is authorized to make grants to any State, municipality, or intermunicipal or interstate agency for the construction of publicly owned treatment works. On and after October 1, 1984, grants under this subchapter shall be made only for projects for secondary treatment or more stringent treatment, or any cost effective alternative thereto, new interceptors and appurtenances, and infiltration-in-flow correction. Notwithstanding the preceding sentences, the Administrator may make grants on and after October 1, 1984, for (A) any project within the definition set forth in section 1292(2) of this title, other than for a project referred to in the preceding sentence, and (B) any purpose for which a grant may be made under sections[1] 1329(h) and (i) of this title (including any innovative and alternative approaches for the control of nonpoint sources of pollution), except that not more than 20 per centum (as determined by the Governor of the State) of the amount allotted to a State under section 1285 of this title for any fiscal year shall be obligated in such State under authority of this sentence.

(2) The Administrator shall not make grants from funds authorized for any fiscal year beginning after June 30, 1974, to any State, municipality, or intermunicipal or interstate agency for the erection, building, acquisition, alteration, remodeling, improvement, or extension of treatment works unless the grant applicant has satisfactorily demonstrated to the Administrator that—

(A) alternative waste management techniques have been studied and evaluated and the works proposed for grant assistance will provide for the application of the best practicable waste treatment technology over the life of the works consistent with the purposes of this subchapter; and

(B) as appropriate, the works proposed for grant assistance will take into account and allow to the extent practicable the application of technology at a later date which will provide for the reclaiming or recycling of water or otherwise eliminate the discharge of pollutants.

(3) The Administrator shall not approve any grant after July 1, 1973, for treatment works under this section unless the applicant shows to the satisfaction of the Administrator that each sewer collection system discharging into such treatment works is not subject to excessive infiltration.

(4) The Administrator is authorized to make grants to applicants for treatment works grants under this section for such sewer system evaluation studies as may be necessary to carry out the requirements of paragraph (3) of this subsection. Such grants shall be made in accordance with rules and regulations promulgated by the Administrator. Initial rules and regulations shall be promulgated under this paragraph not later than 120 days after October 18, 1972.

(5) The Administrator shall not make grants from funds authorized for any fiscal year beginning after September 30, 1978, to any State, municipality, or intermunicipal or interstate agency for the erection, building, acquisition, alteration, remodeling, improvement, or extension of treatment works unless the grant applicant has satisfactorily demonstrated to the Administrator that innovative and alternative wastewater treatment processes and techniques which provide for the reclaiming and reuse of water, otherwise eliminate the discharge of pollutants, and utilize recycling techniques, land treatment, new or improved methods of waste treatment management for municipal and industrial waste (discharged into municipal systems) and the confined disposal of pollutants, so that pollutants will not migrate to cause water or other environmental pollution, have been fully studied and evaluated by the applicant taking into account subsection (d) of this section and taking into account and allowing to the extent practicable the more efficient use of energy and resources.

(6) The Administrator shall not make grants from funds authorized for any fiscal year beginning after September 30, 1978, to any State, municipality, or intermunicipal or interstate agency for the erection, building, acquisition, alteration, remodeling, improvement, or extension of treatment works unless the grant applicant has satisfactorily demonstrated to the Administrator that the applicant has analyzed the potential recreation and open space opportunities in the planning of the proposed treatment works.

**(h) Grants to construct privately owned treatment works**

A grant may be made under this section to construct a privately owned treatment works serving one or more principal residences or small commercial establishments constructed prior to, and inhabited on, December 27, 1977, where the Administrator finds that—

(1) a public body otherwise eligible for a grant under subsection (g) of this section has applied on

behalf of a number of such units and certified that public ownership of such works is not feasible;

(2) such public body has entered into an agreement with the Administrator which guarantees that such treatment works will be properly operated and maintained and will comply with all other requirements of section 1284 of this title and includes a system of charges to assure that each recipient of waste treatment services under such a grant will pay its proportionate share of the cost of operation and maintenance (including replacement); and

(3) the total cost and environmental impact of providing waste treatment services to such residences or commercial establishments will be less than the cost of providing a system of collection and central treatment of such wastes.

**(i) Waste treatment management methods, processes, and techniques to reduce energy requirements**

The Administrator shall encourage waste treatment management methods, processes, and techniques which will reduce total energy requirements.

**(j) Grants for treatment works utilizing processes and techniques of guidelines under section 1314(d)(3) of this title**

The Administrator is authorized to make a grant for any treatment works utilizing processes and techniques meeting the guidelines promulgated under section 1314(d)(3) of this title, if the Administrator determines it is in the public interest and if in the cost effectiveness study made of the construction grant application for the purpose of evaluating alternative treatment works, the life cycle cost of the treatment works for which the grant is to be made does not exceed the life cycle cost of the most cost effective alternative by more than 15 per centum.

**(k) Limitation on use of grants for publicly owned treatment works**

No grant made after November 15, 1981, for a publicly owned treatment works, other than for facility planning and the preparation of construction plans and specifications, shall be used to treat, store, or convey the flow of any industrial user into such treatment works in excess of a flow per day equivalent to fifty thousand gallons per day of sanitary waste. This subsection shall not apply to any project proposed by a grantee which is carrying out an approved project to prepare construction plans and specifications for a facility to treat wastewater, which received its grant approval before May 15, 1980. This subsection shall not be in effect after November 15, 1981.

**(*l*) Grants for facility plans, or plans, specifications, and estimates for proposed project for construction of treatment works; limitations, allotments, advances, etc.**

(1) After December 29, 1981, Federal grants shall not be made for the purpose of providing assistance solely for facility plans, or plans, specifications, and estimates for any proposed project for the construction of treatment works. In the event that the proposed project receives a grant under this section for construction, the Administrator shall make an allowance in such grant for non-Federal funds expended during the facility planning and advanced engineering and design phase at the prevailing Federal share under section 1282(a) of this title, based on the percentage of total project costs which the Administrator determines is the general experience for such projects.

(2)(A) Each State shall use a portion of the funds allotted to such State each fiscal year, but not to exceed 10 per centum of such funds, to advance to potential grant applicants under this subchapter the costs of facility planning or the preparation of plans, specifications, and estimates.

(B) Such an advance shall be limited to the allowance for such costs which the Administrator establishes under paragraph (1) of this subsection, and shall be provided only to a potential grant applicant which is a small community and which in the judgment of the State would otherwise be unable to prepare a request for a grant for construction costs under this section.

(C) In the event a grant for construction costs is made under this section for a project for which an advance has been made under this paragraph, the Administrator shall reduce the amount of such grant by the allowance established under paragraph (1) of this subsection. In the event no such grant is made, the State is authorized to seek repayment of such advance on such terms and conditions as it may determine.

**(m) Grants for State of California projects**

(1) Notwithstanding any other provisions of this subchapter, the Administrator is authorized to make a grant from any funds otherwise allotted to the State of California under section 1285 of this title to the project (and in the amount) specified in Order WQG 81-1 of the California State Water Resources Control Board.

(2) Notwithstanding any other provision of this chapter, the Administrator shall make a grant from any funds otherwise allotted to the State of California to the city of Eureka, California, in connection with project numbered C-06-2772, for the purchase of one hundred and thirty-nine acres of property as environmental mitigation for siting of the proposed treatment plant.

(3) Notwithstanding any other provision of this chapter, the Administrator shall make a grant from any funds otherwise allotted to the State of California to the city of San Diego, California, in connection with that city's aquaculture sewage process (total resources recovery system) as an innovative and alternative waste treatment process.

**(n) Water quality problems; funds, scope, etc.**

(1) On and after October 1, 1984, upon the request of the Governor of an affected State, the Administrator is authorized to use funds available to such State under section 1285 of this title to address water quality problems due to the impacts of discharges from combined storm water and sanitary sewer overflows, which are not otherwise eligible under this subsection, where correction of such discharges is a major priority for such State.

(2) Beginning fiscal year 1983, the Administrator shall have available $200,000,000 per fiscal year in addition to those funds authorized in section 1287 of this title to be utilized to address water quality problems of marine bays and estuaries subject to lower levels of water quality due to the impacts of discharges from combined storm water and sanitary sewer overflows from adjacent urban complexes, not otherwise eligible under this subsection. Such sums may be used as deemed appropriate by the Administrator as provided in paragraphs (1) and (2) of this subsection, upon the request of and demonstration of water quality benefits by the Governor of an affected State.

**(*o*) Capital financing plan**

The Administrator shall encourage and assist applicants for grant assistance under this subchapter to develop and file with the Administrator a capital financing plan which, at a minimum—

(1) projects the future requirements for waste treatment services within the applicant's jurisdiction for a period of no less than ten years;

(2) projects the nature, extent, timing, and costs of future expansion and reconstruction of treatment works which will be necessary to satisfy the applicant's projected future requirements for waste treatment services; and

(3) sets forth with specificity the manner in which the applicant intends to finance such future expansion and reconstruction.

**(p) Time limit on resolving certain disputes**

In any case in which a dispute arises with respect to the awarding of a contract for construction of treatment works by a grantee of funds under this subchapter and a party to such dispute files an appeal with the Administrator under this subchapter for resolution of such dispute, the Administrator shall make a final decision on such appeal within 90 days of the filing of such appeal.

(June 30, 1948, c. 758, Title II, § 201, as added Oct. 18, 1972, Pub.L. 92–500, § 2, 86 Stat. 833, and amended Dec. 27, 1977, Pub.L. 95–217, §§ 12–16, 91 Stat. 1569, 1570; Oct. 21, 1980, Pub.L. 96–483, §§ 2(d), 3, 94 Stat. 2361; Dec. 29, 1981, Pub.L. 97–117, §§ 2(a), 3(a), 4–6, 10(c), 95 Stat. 1623–1626; Feb. 4, 1987, Pub.L. 100–4, Title II, § 201, Title III, § 316(c), 101 Stat. 15, 60.)

[1] So in original. Probably should be "section".

## HISTORICAL AND STATUTORY NOTES

**Effective and Applicability Provisions**

1980 Acts

Section 2(g) of Pub.L. 96–483, provided that: "The amendments made by this section [amending sections 1281, 1284, and 1293 of this title enacting provisions set out as notes under section 1284 of this title, and amending provisions set out as a note under section 1284 of this title] shall take effect on December 27, 1977."

**Environmental Protection Agency State and Tribal Assistance Grants**

Pub.L. 105–174, Title III, May 1, 1998, 112 Stat. 92, provided, in part, that: "Notwithstanding any other provision of law, eligible recipients of the funds appropriated to the Environmental Protection Agency in the State and Tribal Assistance Grants account since fiscal year 1997 and hereafter for multi-media or single media grants, other than Performance Partnership Grants authorized pursuant to Public Law 104–134 and Public Law 105–65, for pollution prevention, control, and abatement and related activities have been and shall be those entities eligible for grants under the Agency's organic statutes."

**Grants to Indian Tribes for Pollution Prevention, Control and Abatement**

Pub.L. 105–65, Title III, Oct. 27, 1997, 111 Stat. 1373, provided in part that: "$745,000,000 for grants to States, federally recognized tribes, and air pollution control agencies for multi-media or single media pollution prevention, control and abatement and related activities pursuant to the provisions set forth under this heading in Public Law 104–134 [Omnibus Consolidated Recissions and Appropriations Act of 1996, Pub.L. 104–134, April 26, 1996, 111 Stat. 1321, for classification of which see Tables], provided that eligible recipients of these funds and the funds made available for this purpose since fiscal year 1996 and hereafter include States, federally recognized tribes, interstate agencies, tribal consortia, and air pollution control agencies, as provided in authorizing statutes, subject to such terms and conditions as the Administrator shall establish, and for making grants under section 103 of the Clean Air Act [section 7403 of Title 42] for particulate matter monitoring and data collection activities:"

**Multi–media or Single Media Pollution Control Prevention**

Pub.L. 105–65, Title III, Oct. 27, 1997, 111 Stat. 1374, provided in part that: "hereafter from funds appropriated under this heading, the Administrator is authorized to make grants to federally recognized Indian governments for the development of multi-media environmental programs: That, hereafter, the funds available under this heading for grants to States, federally recognized tribes, and air pollution control agencies for multi-media or single media pollution prevention, control and abatement and related activities may also be used for the direct implementation by the Federal Government of a program required by law in the absence of an acceptable State or tribal program:"

Similar provisions were contained in the following prior Acts:

Pub.L. 104–204, Title III, Sept. 26, 1996, 110 Stat. 2912.

Pub.L. 104–134, Title I, § 101(e), [Title III] April 26, 1996, 110 Stat. 1321–299, renumbered Title I, Pub.L. 104–140, § 1(a), May 2, 1996, 110 Stat. 1327.

Pub.L. 103–327, Title III, Sept. 28, 1994, 108 Stat. 2320.

Pub.L. 103–124, Title III, Oct. 28, 1993, 107 Stat. 1293.

Pub.L. 102–389, Title III, Oct. 6, 1992, 106 Stat. 1597.

Pub.L. 102–139, Title III, Oct. 28, 1991, 105 Stat. 762.

Pub.L. 101–507, Title III, Nov. 5, 1990, 104 Stat. 1372.

**Privatization of Infrastructure Assets**

Pub.L. 104–303, Title V, § 586, Oct. 12, 1996, 110 Stat. 3791, provided that:

"**(a) In general.**—Notwithstanding the provisions of title II of the Federal Water Pollution Control Act (33 U.S.C. 1281 et seq.) [Act June 30, 1948, c. 758, for complete classification to the Code, see Short Title note under section 1251 of this title], Executive Order 12803 [set out as a note under section 601 of Title 5, Government Organization and Employees], or any other law or authority, an entity that received Federal grant assistance for an infrastructure asset under the Federal Water Pollution Control Act shall not be required to repay any portion of the grant upon the lease or concession of the asset only if—

"(1) ownership of the asset remains with the entity that received the grant; and

"(2) the Administrator of the Environmental Protection Agency determines that the lease or concession furthers the purposes of such Act and approves the lease or concession.

"**(b) Limitation.**—The Administrator shall not approve a total of more than 5 leases and concessions under this section [this note]."

**Grants to States to Administer Completion and Closeout of Construction Grants Program**

Pub.L. 104–204, Title III, Sept. 26, 1996, 110 Stat. 2912, provided: "That notwithstanding any other provision of law, beginning in fiscal year 1997 the Administrator may make grants to States, from funds available for obligation in the State under title II of the Federal Water Pollution Control Act [this subchapter], as amended, for administering the completion and closeout of the State's construction grants program, based on a budget annually negotiated with the State."

**Wastewater Assistance to Colonias**

Pub.L. 104–182, Title III, § 307, Aug. 6, 1996, 110 Stat. 1688, provided that:

"**(a) Definitions.**—As used in this section:

"**(1) Border State.**—The term 'border State' means Arizona, California, New Mexico, and Texas.

"**(2) Eligible community.**—The term 'eligible community' means a low-income community with economic hardship that—

"**(A)** is commonly referred to as a colonia;

"**(B)** is located along the United States–Mexico border (generally in an unincorporated area); and

"**(C)** lacks basic sanitation facilities such as household plumbing or a proper sewage disposal system.

"**(3) Treatment works.**—The term 'treatment works' has the meaning provided in section 212(2) of the Federal Water Pollution Control Act (33 U.S.C. 1292(2)) [section 1292(2) of this title].

"**(b) Grants for wastewater assistance.**—The Administrator of the Environmental Protection Agency and the heads of other appropriate Federal agencies are authorized to award grants to a border State to provide assistance to eligible communities for the planning, design, and construction or improvement of sewers, treatment works, and appropriate connections for wastewater treatment.

"**(c) Use of funds.**—Each grant awarded pursuant to subsection (b) shall be used to provide assistance to one or more eligible communities with respect to which the residents are subject to a significant health risk (as determined by the Administrator or the head of the Federal agency making the grant) attributable to the lack of access to an adequate and affordable treatment works for wastewater.

"**(d) Cost sharing.**—The amount of a grant awarded pursuant to this section shall not exceed 50 percent of the costs of carrying out the project that is the subject of the grant.

"**(e) Authorization of appropriations.**—There are authorized to be appropriated to carry out this section $25,000,000 for each of the fiscal years 1997 through 1999."

[Provisions effective Aug. 6, 1996, see section 2(b) of Pub.L. 104–182, set out as a note under section 300f of Title 42, The Public Health and Welfare.]

**Authorization to Make Grants to Indian Tribes for Pollution Prevention, Control and Abatement**

Pub.L. 104–134, Title I, § 101(e)[Title III], Apr. 26, 1996, 110 Stat. 1321–299; renumbered Title I Pub.L. 104–140, § 1(a), May 2, 1996, 110 Stat. 1327, provided in part: "That beginning in fiscal year 1996 and each fiscal year thereafter, and notwithstanding any other provision of law, the Administrator is authorized to make grants annually from funds appropriated under this heading, subject to such terms and conditions as the Administrator shall establish, to any State or federally recognized Indian tribe for multimedia or single media pollution prevention, control and abatement and related environmental activities at the request of the Governor or other appropriate State official or the tribe[.]"

**State Management of Construction Grant Activities**

Pub.L. 104–134, Title I, § 101(e)[Title III], Apr. 26, 1996, 110 Stat. 1321–299; renumbered Title I Pub.L. 104–140, § 1(a), May 2, 1996, 110 Stat. 1327, provided in part: "That of the funds appropriated in the Construction Grants and Water Infrastructure/State Revolving Funds accounts since the appropriation for the fiscal year ending September 30, 1992, and hereafter, for making grants for wastewater treatment works construction projects, portions may be provided by the recipients to States for managing construction grant activities, on condition that the States agree to reimburse the recipients from State funding sources[.]"

**Grants to Trust Territory of the Pacific Islands, American Samoa, Guam, the Northern Mariana Islands, and the Virgin Islands; Waiver by Administrator of Limitations Relating to Collector Sewers**

Pub.L. 99–396, § 12(b), Aug. 27, 1986, 100 Stat. 841, provided that: "In awarding grants to the Trust Territory of the Pacific Islands, American Samoa, Guam, the Northern Mariana Islands and the Virgin Islands under section 201(g)(1) of the Clean Water Act (33 U.S.C. 1251 et seq.) [subsec. (g)(1) of this section], the Administrator of the Environmental Protection Agency may waive limitations regarding grant eligibility for sewerage facilities and related appurtenances, insofar as such limitations relate to collector sewers, based upon a determination that applying such limitations could hinder the alleviation of threats to public health and water quality. In making such a determination, the Administrator shall take into consideration the public health and water quality benefits to be derived and the availability of alternate funding sources. The Administrator shall not award grants under this section for the operation and maintenance of sewerage facilities, for construction of facilities which are not an essential component of the sewerage facilities, or any other activities or facilities which are not concerned with the management of wastewater to alleviate threats to public health and water quality."

**Environmental Financing Authority**

Section 12 of Pub.L. 92–500, as amended by Pub.L. 97–258, § 4(b), Sept. 13, 1982, 96 Stat. 1067, provided that:

"**(a) [Short Title]** This section may be cited as the 'Environmental Financing Act of 1972.'

"**(b) [Establishment]** There is hereby created a body corporate to be known as the Environmental Financing Authority, which shall have succession until dissolved by Act of Congress. The Authority shall be subject to the general supervision and direction of the Secretary of the Treasury. The Authority shall be an instrumentality of the United States Government and shall maintain such offices as may be necessary or appropriate in the conduct of its business.

"**(c) [Congressional Declaration of Purpose]** The purpose of this section is to assure that inability to borrow necessary funds on reasonable terms does not prevent any State or local public body from carrying out any project for construction of waste treatment works determined eligible for assistance pursuant to subsection (e) of this section.

"**(d) [Board of Directors]** (1) The Authority shall have a Board of Directors consisting of five persons, one of whom shall be the Secretary of the Treasury or his designee as Chairman of the Board, and four of whom shall be appointed by the President from among the officers or employees of the Authority or of any department or agency of the United States Government.

"(2) The Board of Directors shall meet at the call of its Chairman. The Board shall determine the general policies which shall govern the operations of the Authority. The Chairman of the Board shall select and effect the appointment of qualified persons to fill the offices as may be provided for in the bylaws, with such executive functions, powers, and duties as may be prescribed by the bylaws or by the Board of Directors, and such persons shall be the executive officers of the Authority and shall discharge all such executive functions, powers, and duties. The members of the Board, as such, shall not receive compensation for their services.

"**(e) [Purchase of State and Local Obligations]** (1) Until July 1, 1975, the Authority is authorized to make commitments to purchase, and to purchase on terms and conditions determined by the Authority, any obligation or participation therein which is issued by a State or local public body to finance the non-Federal share of the cost of any project for the construction of waste treatment works which the Administrator of the Environmental Protection Agency has determined to be eligible for Federal financial assistance under the Federal Water Pollution Control Act [this chapter].

"(2) No commitment shall be entered into, and no purchase shall be made, unless the Administrator of the Environmental Protection Agency (A) has certified that the public body is unable to obtain on reasonable terms sufficient credit to finance its actual needs; (B) has approved the project as eligible under the Federal Water Pollution Control Act [this chapter]; and (C) has agreed to guarantee timely payment of principal and interest on the obligation. The Administrator is authorized to guarantee such timely payments and to issue regulations as he deems necessary and proper to protect such guarantees. Appropriations are hereby authorized to be made to the Administrator in such sums as are necessary to make payments under such guarantees, and such payments are authorized to be made from such appropriations.

"(3) No purchase shall be made of obligations issued to finance projects, the permanent financing of which occurred prior to the enactment of this section [Oct. 18, 1972].

"(4) Any purchase by the Authority shall be upon such terms and conditions as to yield a return at a rate determined by the Secretary of the Treasury taking into consideration (A) the current average yield on outstanding marketable obligations of the United States of comparable maturity or in its stead whenever the Authority has sufficient of its own long-term obligations outstanding, the current average yield on outstanding obligations of the Authority of comparable maturity; and (B) the market yields on municipal bonds.

"(5) The Authority is authorized to charge fees for its commitments and other services adequate to cover all expenses and to provide for the accumulation of reasonable contingency reserves and such fees shall be included in the aggregate project costs.

"**(f) [Initial Capital]** To provide initial capital to the Authority the Secretary of the Treasury is authorized to advance the funds necessary for this purpose. Each such advance shall be upon such terms and conditions as to yield a return at a rate not less than a rate determined by the Secretary of the Treasury taking into consideration the current average yield on outstanding marketable obligations of the United States of comparable maturities. Interest payments on such advances may be deferred, at the discretion of the Secretary, but any such deferred payments shall themselves bear interest at the rate specified in this section. There is authorized to be appropriated not to exceed $100,000,000, which shall be available for the purposes of this subsection.

"**(g) [Issuance of Obligations]** (1) The Authority is authorized, with the approval of the Secretary of the Treasury, to issue and have outstanding obligations having such maturities and bearing such rate or rates of interest as may be determined by the Authority. Such obligations may be redeemable at the option of the Authority before maturity in such manner as may be stipulated therein.

"(h) [Interest Differential] The Secretary of the Treasury is authorized and directed to make annual payments to the Authority in such amounts as are necessary to equal the amount by which the dollar amount of interest expense accrued by the Authority on account of its obligations exceeds the dollar amount of interest income accrued by the Authority on account of obligations purchased by it pursuant to subsection (e) of this section.

"(i) [Powers] The Authority shall have power—

"(1) to sue and be sued, complain and defend, in its corporate name;

"(2) to adopt, alter, and use a corporate seal, which shall be judicially noticed;

"(3) to adopt, amend, and repeal by-laws, rules, and regulations as may be necessary for the conduct of its business;

"(4) to conduct its business, carry on its operations, and have offices and exercise the powers granted by this section in any State without regard to any qualification or similar statute in any State;

"(5) to lease, purchase, or otherwise acquire, own, hold, improve, use, or otherwise deal in and with any property, real, personal, or mixed, or any interest therein, wherever situated;

"(6) to accept gifts or donations of services, or of property, real, personal, or mixed, tangible or intangible, in aid of any of the purposes of the Authority;

"(7) to sell, convey, mortgage, pledge, lease, exchange, and otherwise dispose of its property and assets;

"(8) to appoint such officers, attorneys, employees, and agents as may be required, to define their duties, to fix and to pay such compensation for their services as may be determined, subject to the civil service and classification laws, to require bonds for them and pay the premium thereof; and

"(9) to enter into contracts, to execute instruments, to incur liabilities, and to do all things as are necessary or incidental to the proper management of its affairs and the proper conduct of its business.

"(j) [Tax Exemptions; Exceptions] The Authority, its property, its franchise, capital, reserves, surplus, security holdings, and other funds, and its income shall be exempt from all taxation now or hereafter imposed by the United States or by any State or local taxing authority; except that (A) any real property and any tangible personal property of the Authority shall be subject to Federal, State, and local taxation to the same extent according to its value as other such property is taxed, and (B) any and all obligations issued by the Authority shall be subject both as to principal and interest to Federal, State, and local taxation to the same extent as the obligations of private corporations are taxed.

"(k) [Nature of Obligations] All obligations issued by the Authority shall be lawful investments, and may be accepted as security for all fiduciary, trust, and public funds, the investment or deposit of which shall be under authority or control of the United States or of any officer or officers thereof. All obligations issued by the Authority pursuant to this section shall be deemed to be exempt securities within the meaning of laws administered by the Securities and Exchange Commission, to the same extent as securities which are issued by the United States.

"(*l*) [Preparation of Obligations by Secretary of Treasury] In order to furnish obligations for delivery by the Authority, the Secretary of the Treasury is authorized to prepare such obligations in such form as the Authority may approve, such obligations when prepared to be held in the Treasury subject to delivery upon order by the Authority. The engraved plates, dies, bed pieces, and so forth, executed in connection therewith, shall remain in the custody of the Secretary of the Treasury. The Authority shall reimburse the Secretary of the Treasury for any expenditures made in the preparation, custody, and delivery of such obligations.

"(m) [Annual Report to Congress] The Authority shall, as soon as practicable after the end of each fiscal year, transmit to the President and the Congress an annual report of its operations and activities.

"(n) [Subsec. (n) amended section 24 of Title 12, Banks and Banking, and is not set out herein.]

"(*o*) [Financial Controls] The budget and audit provisions of chapter 91 of title 31 shall be applicable to the Environmental Financing Authority in the same manner as they are applied to the wholly owned Government corporations. (As amended Pub.L. 97–258, § 4(b), Sept. 13, 1982, 96 Stat. 1067.)

"(p) [Subsec. (p) amended section 711 of Title 31, Money and Finance, and is not set out herein.]"

## § 1281a. Total treatment system funding

Notwithstanding any other provision of law, in any case where the Administrator of the Environmental Protection Agency finds that the total of all grants made under section 1281 of this title for the same treatment works exceeds the actual construction costs for such treatment works (as defined in this chapter) such excess amount shall be a grant of the Federal share (as defined in this chapter) of the cost of construction of a sewage collection system if—

(1) such sewage collection system was constructed as part of the same total treatment system as the treatment works for which such grants under section 1281 of this title were approved, and

(2) an application for assistance for the construction of such sewage collection system was filed in accordance with section 3102 of Title 42 before all such grants under section 1281 of this title were made and such grant under section 3102 of Title 42 could not be approved due to lack of funding under such section 3102 of Title 42.

The total of all grants for sewage collection systems made under this section shall not exceed $2,800,000. (Pub.L. 95–217, § 78, Dec. 27, 1977, 91 Stat. 1611.)

### HISTORICAL AND STATUTORY NOTES

**References in Text**

Section 3102 of title 42, referred to in par. (2), was omitted from the Code pursuant to 42 U.S.C.A. § 5316, which terminated the authority to make grants or loans under that section after Jan. 1, 1975.

**Codifications**

Section was enacted as part of the Clean Water Act of 1977, Pub.L. 95–217, and not as part of the Federal Water Pollution Control Act, June 30, 1948, c. 758, as added Oct. 18, 1972, Pub.L. 92–500, 86 Stat. 816, which comprises this chapter.

## § 1281b. Availability of Farmers Home Administration funds for non-Federal share

Notwithstanding any other provision of law, Federal assistance made available by the Farmers Home Administration to any political subdivision of a State may be used to provide the non-Federal share of the cost of any construction project carried out under section 1281 of this title.

(Pub.L. 100–4, Title II, § 202(f), Feb. 4, 1987, 101 Stat. 16.)

### HISTORICAL AND STATUTORY NOTES

**Codifications**

Section was enacted as part of the Water Quality Act of 1987, and not as part of the Federal Water Pollution Control Act, which comprises this chapter.

## § 1282. Federal share

**[FWPCA § 202]**

### (a) Amount of grants for treatment works

(1) The amount of any grant for treatment works made under this chapter from funds authorized for any fiscal year beginning after June 30, 1971, and ending before October 1, 1984, shall be 75 per centum of the cost of construction thereof (as approved by the Administrator), and for any fiscal year beginning on or after October 1, 1984, shall be 55 per centum of the cost of construction thereof (as approved by the Administrator), unless modified to a lower percentage rate uniform throughout a State by the Governor of that State with the concurrence of the Administrator. Within ninety days after October 21, 1980, the Administrator shall issue guidelines for concurrence in any such modification, which shall provide for the consideration of the unobligated balance of sums allocated to the State under section 1285 of this title, the need for assistance under this subchapter in such State, and the availability of State grant assistance to replace the Federal share reduced by such modification. The payment of any such reduced Federal share shall not constitute an obligation on the part of the United States or a claim on the part of any State or grantee to reimbursement for the portion of the Federal share reduced in any such State. Any grant (other than for reimbursement) made prior to October 18, 1972, from any funds authorized for any fiscal year beginning after June 30, 1971, shall, upon the request of the applicant, be increased to the applicable percentage under this section. Notwithstanding the first sentence of this paragraph, in any case where a primary, secondary, or advanced waste treatment facility or its related interceptors or a project for infiltration-in-flow correction has received a grant for erection, building, acquisition, alteration, remodeling, improvement, extension, or correction before October 1, 1984, all segments and phases of such facility, interceptors, and project for infiltration-in-flow correction shall be eligible for grants at 75 per centum of the cost of construction thereof for any grant made pursuant to a State obligation which obligation occurred before October 1, 1990. Notwithstanding the first sentence of this paragraph, in the case of a project for which an application for a grant under this subchapter has been made to the Administrator before October 1, 1984, and which project is under judicial injunction on such date prohibiting its construction, such project shall be eligible for grants at 75 percent of the cost of construction thereof. Notwithstanding the first sentence of this paragraph, in the case of the Wyoming Valley Sanitary Authority project mandated by judicial order under a proceeding begun prior to October 1, 1984, and a project for wastewater treatment for Altoona, Pennsylvania, such projects shall be eligible for grants at 75 percent of the cost of construction thereof.

(2) The amount of any grant made after September 30, 1978, and before October 1, 1981, for any eligible treatment works or significant portion thereof utilizing innovative or alternative wastewater treatment processes and techniques referred to in section 1281(g)(5) of this title shall be 85 per centum of the cost of construction thereof, unless modified by the Governor of the State with the concurrence of the Administrator to a percentage rate no less than 15 per centum greater than the modified uniform percentage rate in which the Administrator has concurred pursuant to paragraph (1) of this subsection. The amount of any grant made after September 30, 1981, for any eligible treatment works or unit processes and techniques thereof utilizing innovative or alternative wastewater treatment processes and techniques referred to in section 1281(g)(5) of this title shall be a percentage of the cost of construction thereof equal to 20 per centum greater than the percentage in effect under paragraph (1) of this subsection for such works or unit processes and techniques, but in no event greater than 85 per centum of the cost of construction thereof. No grant shall be made under this paragraph for construction of a treatment works in any State unless the proportion of the State contribution to the non-Federal share of construction costs for all treatment works in such State receiving a grant under this paragraph is the same as or greater than the proportion of the State contribution (if any) to the non-Federal share of construction costs for all treatment works receiving

grants in such State under paragraph (1) of this subsection.

(3) In addition to any grant made pursuant to paragraph (2) of this subsection, the Administrator is authorized to make a grant to fund all of the costs of the modification or replacement of any facilities constructed with a grant made pursuant to paragraph (2) if the Administrator finds that such facilities have not met design performance specifications unless such failure is attributable to negligence on the part of any person and if such failure has significantly increased capital or operating and maintenance expenditures. In addition, the Administrator is authorized to make a grant to fund all of the costs of the modification or replacement of biodisc equipment (rotating biological contactors) in any publicly owned treatment works if the Administrator finds that such equipment has failed to meet design performance specifications, unless such failure is attributable to negligence on the part of any person, and if such failure has significantly increased capital or operating and maintenance expenditures.

(4) For the purposes of this section, the term "eligible treatment works" means those treatment works in each State which meet the requirements of section 1281(g)(5) of this title and which can be fully funded from funds available for such purpose in such State.

**(b) Amount of grants for construction of treatment works not commenced prior to July 1, 1971**

The amount of the grant for any project approved by the Administrator after January 1, 1971, and before July 1, 1971, for the construction of treatment works, the actual erection, building or acquisition of which was not commenced prior to July 1, 1971, shall, upon the request of the applicant, be increased to the applicable percentage under subsection (a) of this section for grants for treatment works from funds for fiscal years beginning after June 30, 1971, with respect to the cost of such actual erection, building, or acquisition. Such increased amount shall be paid from any funds allocated to the State in which the treatment works is located without regard to the fiscal year for which such funds were authorized. Such increased amount shall be paid for such project only if—

(1) a sewage collection system that is a part of the same total waste treatment system as the treatment works for which such grant was approved is under construction or is to be constructed for use in conjunction with such treatment works, and if the cost of such sewage collection system exceeds the cost of such treatment works, and

(2) the State water pollution control agency or other appropriate State authority certifies that the quantity of available ground water will be insufficient, inadequate, or unsuitable for public use, including the ecological preservation and recreational use of surface water bodies, unless effluents from publicly-owned treatment works after adequate treatment are returned to the ground water consistent with acceptable technological standards.

**(c) Availability of sums allotted to Puerto Rico**

Notwithstanding any other provision of law, sums allotted to the Commonwealth of Puerto Rico under section 1285 of this title for fiscal year 1981 shall remain available for obligation for the fiscal year for which authorized and for the period of the next succeeding twenty-four months. Such sums and any unobligated funds available to Puerto Rico from allotments for fiscal years ending prior to October 1, 1981, shall be available for obligation by the Administrator of the Environmental Protection Agency only to fund the following systems: Aguadilla, Arecibo, Mayaguez, Carolina, and Camuy Hatillo. These funds may be used by the Commonwealth of Puerto Rico to fund the non-Federal share of the costs of such projects. To the extent that these funds are used to pay the non-Federal share, the Commonwealth of Puerto Rico shall repay to the Environmental Protection Agency such amounts on terms and conditions developed and approved by the Administrator in consultation with the Governor of the Commonwealth of Puerto Rico. Agreement on such terms and conditions, including the payment of interest to be determined by the Secretary of the Treasury, shall be reached prior to the use of these funds for the Commonwealth's non-Federal share. No Federal funds awarded under this provision shall be used to replace local governments funds previously expended on these projects.

(June 30, 1948, c. 758, Title II, § 202, as added Oct. 18, 1972, Pub.L. 92–500, § 2, 86 Stat. 834, and amended Dec. 27, 1977, Pub.L. 95–217, § 17, 91 Stat. 1571; Oct. 21, 1980, Pub.L. 96–483, § 9, 94 Stat. 2362; Dec. 29, 1981, Pub.L. 97–117, §§ 7, 8(a), (b), 95 Stat. 1625; Oct. 19, 1982, Pub.L. 97–357, Title V, § 501, 96 Stat. 1712; Feb. 4, 1987, Pub.L. 100–4, Title II, § 202(a)–(d), 101 Stat. 15, 16.)

### HISTORICAL AND STATUTORY NOTES

**Promulgation of Federal Shares**

Act July 9, 1956, c. 518, § 4, 70 Stat. 507, authorized the Surgeon General to promulgate Federal shares under the Federal Water Pollution Control Grant Program as soon as possible after July 9, 1956, in the manner specified in the Water Pollution Control Act, Act June 30, 1948, c. 758, 62 Stat. 1155, and provided that such shares were to be conclusive for the purposes of section 5 of Act June 30, 1948.

## § 1283. Plans, specifications, estimates, and payments

**[FWPCA § 203]**

**(a) Submission; contractual nature of approval by Administrator; agreement on eligible costs; single grant**

(1) Each applicant for a grant shall submit to the Administrator for his approval, plans, specifications, and estimates for each proposed project for the construction of treatment works for which a grant is applied for under section 1281(g)(1) of this title from funds allotted to the State under section 1285 of this title and which otherwise meets the requirements of this chapter. The Administrator shall act upon such plans, specifications, and estimates as soon as practicable after the same have been submitted, and his approval of any such plans, specifications, and estimates shall be deemed a contractual obligation of the United States for the payment of its proportional contribution to such project.

**(2) Agreement on eligible costs**

**(A) Limitation on modifications**

Before taking final action on any plans, specifications, and estimates submitted under this subsection after the 60th day following February 4, 1987, the Administrator shall enter into a written agreement with the applicant which establishes and specifies which items of the proposed project are eligible for Federal payments under this section. The Administrator may not later modify such eligibility determinations unless they are found to have been made in violation of applicable Federal statutes and regulations.

**(B) Limitation on effect**

Eligibility determinations under this paragraph shall not preclude the Administrator from auditing a project pursuant to section 1361 of this title, or other authority, or from withholding or recovering Federal funds for costs which are found to be unreasonable, unsupported by adequate documentation, or otherwise unallowable under applicable Federal cost principles, or which are incurred on a project which fails to meet the design specifications or effluent limitations contained in the grant agreement and permit pursuant to section 1342 of this title for such project.

(3) In the case of a treatment works that has an estimated total cost of $8,000,000 or less (as determined by the Administrator), and the population of the applicant municipality is twenty-five thousand or less (according to the most recent United States census), upon completion of an approved facility plan, a single grant may be awarded for the combined Federal share of the cost of preparing construction plans and specifications, and the building and erection of the treatment works.

**(b) Periodic payments**

The Administrator shall, from time to time as the work progresses, make payments to the recipient of a grant for costs of construction incurred on a project. These payments shall at no time exceed the Federal share of the cost of construction incurred to the date of the voucher covering such payment plus the Federal share of the value of the materials which have been stockpiled in the vicinity of such construction in conformity to plans and specifications for the project.

**(c) Final payments**

After completion of a project and approval of the final voucher by the Administrator, he shall pay out of the appropriate sums the unpaid balance of the Federal share payable on account of such project.

**(d) Projects eligible**

Nothing in this chapter shall be construed to require, or to authorize the Administrator to require, that grants under this chapter for construction of treatment works be made only for projects which are operable units usable for sewage collection, transportation, storage, waste treatment, or for similar purposes without additional construction.

**(e) Technical and legal assistance in administration and enforcement of contracts; intervention in civil actions**

At the request of a grantee under this subchapter, the Administrator is authorized to provide technical and legal assistance in the administration and enforcement of any contract in connection with treatment works assisted under this subchapter, and to intervene in any civil action involving the enforcement of such a contract.

**(f) Design/build projects**

**(1) Agreement**

Consistent with State law, an applicant who proposes to construct waste water treatment works may enter into an agreement with the Administrator under this subsection providing for the preparation of construction plans and specifications and the erection of such treatment works, in lieu of proceeding under the other provisions of this section.

**(2) Limitation on projects**

Agreements under this subsection shall be limited to projects under an approved facility plan which projects are—

**(A)** treatment works that have an estimated total cost of $8,000,000 or less; and

**(B)** any of the following types of waste water treatment systems: aerated lagoons, trickling filters, stabilization ponds, land application systems, sand filters, and subsurface disposal systems.

**(3) Required terms**

An agreement entered into under this subsection shall—

(A) set forth an amount agreed to as the maximum Federal contribution to the project, based upon a competitively bid document of basic design data and applicable standard construction specifications and a determination of the federally eligible costs of the project at the applicable Federal share under section 1282 of this title;

(B) set forth dates for the start and completion of construction of the treatment works by the applicant and a schedule of payments of the Federal contribution to the project;

(C) contain assurances by the applicant that (i) engineering and management assistance will be provided to manage the project; (ii) the proposed treatment works will be an operable unit and will meet all the requirements of this subchapter; and (iii) not later than 1 year after the date specified as the date of completion of construction of the treatment works, the treatment works will be operating so as to meet the requirements of any applicable permit for such treatment works under section 1342 of this title;

(D) require the applicant to obtain a bond from the contractor in an amount determined necessary by the Administrator to protect the Federal interest in the project; and

(E) contain such other terms and conditions as are necessary to assure compliance with this subchapter (except as provided in paragraph (4) of this subsection).

**(4) Limitation on application**

Subsections (a), (b), and (c) of this section shall not apply to grants made pursuant to this subsection.

**(5) Reservation to assure compliance**

The Administrator shall reserve a portion of the grant to assure contract compliance until final project approval as defined by the Administrator. If the amount agreed to under paragraph (3)(A) exceeds the cost of designing and constructing the treatment works, the Administrator shall reallot the amount of the excess to the State in which such treatment works are located for the fiscal year in which such audit is completed.

**(6) Limitation on obligations**

The Administrator shall not obligate more than 20 percent of the amount allotted to a State for a fiscal year under section 1285 of this title for grants pursuant to this subsection.

**(7) Allowance**

The Administrator shall determine an allowance for facilities planning for projects constructed under this subsection in accordance with section 1281(*l*) of this title.

**(8) Limitation on Federal contributions**

In no event shall the Federal contribution for the cost of preparing construction plans and specifications and the building and erection of treatment works pursuant to this subsection exceed the amount agreed upon under paragraph (3).

**(9) Recovery action**

In any case in which the recipient of a grant made pursuant to this subsection does not comply with the terms of the agreement entered into under paragraph (3), the Administrator is authorized to take such action as may be necessary to recover the amount of the Federal contribution to the project.

**(10) Prevention of double benefits**

A recipient of a grant made pursuant to this subsection shall not be eligible for any other grants under this subchapter for the same project.

(June 30, 1948, c. 758, Title II, § 203, as added Oct. 18, 1972, Pub.L. 92–500, § 2, 86 Stat. 835, and amended Jan. 2, 1974, Pub.L. 93–243, § 2, 87 Stat. 1069; Dec. 27, 1977, Pub.L. 95–217, §§ 18, 19, 91 Stat. 1571, 1572; Oct. 21, 1980, Pub.L. 96–483, § 6, 94 Stat. 2362; Dec. 29, 1981, Pub.L. 97–117, § 9, 95 Stat. 1626; Feb. 4, 1987, Pub.L. 100–4, Title II, §§ 203, 204, 101 Stat. 16, 17.)

## § 1284. Limitations and conditions

**[FWPCA § 204]**

**(a) Determinations by Administrator**

Before approving grants for any project for any treatment works under section 1281(g)(1) of this title the Administrator shall determine—

(1) that any required areawide waste treatment management plan under section 1288 of this title (A) is being implemented for such area and the proposed treatment works are included in such plan, or (B) is being developed for such area and reasonable progress is being made toward its implementation and the proposed treatment works will be included in such plan;

(2) that (A) the State in which the project is to be located (i) is implementing any required plan under section 1313(e) of this title and the proposed treatment works are in conformity with such plan, or (ii) is developing such a plan and the proposed treatment works will be in conformity with such plan, and (B) such State is in compliance with section 1315(b) of this title;

(3) that such works have been certified by the appropriate State water pollution control agency as entitled to priority over such other works in the State in accordance with any applicable State plan under section 1313(e) of this title, except that any priority list developed pursuant to section 1313 (e)(3)(H) of this title may be modified by such State

in accordance with regulations promulgated by the Administrator to give higher priority for grants for the Federal share of the cost of preparing construction drawings and specifications for any treatment works utilizing processes and techniques meeting the guidelines promulgated under section 1314(d)(3) of this title and for grants for the combined Federal share of the cost of preparing construction drawings and specifications and the building and erection of any treatment works meeting the requirements of the next to last sentence of section 1283(a) of this title which utilizes processes and techniques meeting the guidelines promulgated under section 1314(d)(3) of this title.[1]

(4) that the applicant proposing to construct such works agrees to pay the non-Federal costs of such works and has made adequate provisions satisfactory to the Administrator for assuring proper and efficient operation, including the employment of trained management and operations personnel, and the maintenance of such works in accordance with a plan of operation approved by the State water pollution control agency or, as appropriate, the interstate agency, after construction thereof;

(5) that the size and capacity of such works relate directly to the needs to be served by such works, including sufficient reserve capacity. The amount of reserve capacity provided shall be approved by the Administrator on the basis of a comparison of the cost of constructing such reserves as a part of the works to be funded and the anticipated cost of providing expanded capacity at a date when such capacity will be required, after taking into account, in accordance with regulations promulgated by the Administrator, efforts to reduce total flow of sewage and unnecessary water consumption. The amount of reserve capacity eligible for a grant under this subchapter shall be determined by the Administrator taking into account the projected population and associated commercial and industrial establishments within the jurisdiction of the applicant to be served by such treatment works as identified in an approved facilities plan, an areawide plan under section 1288 of this title, or an applicable municipal master plan of development. For the purpose of this paragraph, section 1288 of this title, and any such plan, projected population shall be determined on the basis of the latest information available from the United States Department of Commerce or from the States as the Administrator, by regulation, determines appropriate. Beginning October 1, 1984, no grant shall be made under this subchapter to construct that portion of any treatment works providing reserve capacity in excess of existing needs (including existing needs of residential, commercial, industrial, and other users) on the date of approval of a grant for the erection, building, acquisition, alteration, remodeling, improvement, or extension of a project for secondary treatment or more stringent treatment or new interceptors and appurtenances, except that in no event shall reserve capacity of a facility and its related interceptors to which this subsection applies be in excess of existing needs on October 1, 1990. In any case in which an applicant proposes to provide reserve capacity greater than that eligible for Federal financial assistance under this subchapter, the incremental costs of the additional reserve capacity shall be paid by the applicant;

(6) that no specification for bids in connection with such works shall be written in such a manner as to contain proprietary, exclusionary, or discriminatory requirements other than those based upon performance, unless such requirements are necessary to test or demonstrate a specific thing or to provide for necessary interchangeability of parts and equipment. When in the judgment of the grantee, it is impractical or uneconomical to make a clear and accurate description of the technical requirements, a "brand name or equal" description may be used as a means to define the performance or other salient requirements of a procurement, and in doing so the grantee need not establish the existence of any source other than the brand or source so named.

**(b) Additional determinations; issuance of guidelines; approval by Administrator; system of charges**

(1) Notwithstanding any other provision of this subchapter, the Administrator shall not approve any grant for any treatment works under section 1281(g)(1) of this title after March 1, 1973, unless he shall first have determined that the applicant (A) has adopted or will adopt a system of charges to assure that each recipient of waste treatment services within the applicant's jurisdiction, as determined by the Administrator, will pay its proportionate share (except as otherwise provided in this paragraph) of the costs of operation and maintenance (including replacement) of any waste treatment services provided by the applicant; and (B) has legal, institutional, managerial, and financial capability to insure adequate construction, operation, and maintenance of treatment works throughout the applicant's jurisdiction, as determined by the Administrator. In any case where an applicant which, as of December 27, 1977, uses a system of dedicated ad valorem taxes and the Administrator determines that the applicant has a system of charges which results in the distribution of operation and maintenance costs for treatment works within the applicant's jurisdiction, to each user class, in proportion to the contribution to the total cost of operation and maintenance of such works by each user class (taking into account total waste water loading of such

works, the constituent elements of the wastes, and other appropriate factors), and such applicant is otherwise in compliance with clause (A) of this paragraph with respect to each industrial user, then such dedicated ad valorem tax system shall be deemed to be the user charge system meeting the requirements of clause (A) of this paragraph for the residential user class and such small non-residential user classes as defined by the Administrator. In defining small non-residential users, the Administrator shall consider the volume of wastes discharged into the treatment works by such users and the constituent elements of such wastes as well as such other factors as he deems appropriate. A system of user charges which imposes a lower charge for low-income residential users (as defined by the Administrator) shall be deemed to be a user charge system meeting the requirements of clause (A) of this paragraph if the Administrator determines that such system was adopted after public notice and hearing.

(2) The Administrator shall, within one hundred and eighty days after October 18, 1972, and after consultation with appropriate State, interstate, municipal, and intermunicipal agencies, issue guidelines applicable to payment of waste treatment costs by industrial and nonindustrial recipients of waste treatment services which shall establish (A) classes of users of such services, including categories of industrial users; (B) criteria against which to determine the adequacy of charges imposed on classes and categories of users reflecting all factors that influence the cost of waste treatment, including strength, volume, and delivery flow rate characteristics of waste; and (C) model systems and rates of user charges typical of various treatment works serving municipal-industrial communities.

(3) Approval by the Administrator of a grant to an interstate agency established by interstate compact for any treatment works shall satisfy any other requirement that such works be authorized by Act of Congress.

(4) A system of charges which meets the requirement of clause (A) of paragraph (1) of this subsection may be based on something other than metering the sewage or water supply flow of residential recipients of waste treatment services, including ad valorem taxes. If the system of charges is based on something other than metering the Administrator shall require (A) the applicant to establish a system by which the necessary funds will be available for the proper operation and maintenance of the treatment works; and (B) the applicant to establish a procedure under which the residential user will be notified as to that portion of his total payment which will be allocated to the cost of the waste treatment services.

**(c) Applicability of reserve capacity restrictions to primary, secondary, or advanced waste treatment facilities or related interceptors**

The next to the last sentence of paragraph (5) of subsection (a) of this section shall not apply in any case where a primary, secondary, or advanced waste treatment facility or its related interceptors has received a grant for erection, building, acquisition, alteration, remodeling, improvement, or extension before October 1, 1984, and all segments and phases of such facility and interceptors shall be funded based on a 20-year reserve capacity in the case of such facility and a 20-year reserve capacity in the case of such interceptors, except that, if a grant for such interceptors has been approved prior to December 29, 1981, such interceptors shall be funded based on the approved reserve capacity not to exceed 40 years.

**(d) Engineering requirements; certification by owner and operator; contractual assurances, etc.**

(1) A grant for the construction of treatment works under this subchapter shall provide that the engineer or engineering firm supervising construction or providing architect engineering services during construction shall continue its relationship to the grant applicant for a period of one year after the completion of construction and initial operation of such treatment works. During such period such engineer or engineering firm shall supervise operation of the treatment works, train operating personnel, and prepare curricula and training material for operating personnel. Costs associated with the implementation of this paragraph shall be eligible for Federal assistance in accordance with this subchapter.

(2) On the date one year after the completion of construction and initial operation of such treatment works, the owner and operator of such treatment works shall certify to the Administrator whether or not such treatment works meet the design specifications and effluent limitations contained in the grant agreement and permit pursuant to section 1342 of this title for such works. If the owner and operator of such treatment works cannot certify that such treatment works meet such design specifications and effluent limitations, any failure to meet such design specifications and effluent limitations shall be corrected in a timely manner, to allow such affirmative certification, at other than Federal expense.

(3) Nothing in this section shall be construed to prohibit a grantee under this subchapter from requiring more assurances, guarantees, or indemnity or other contractual requirements from any party to a contract pertaining to a project assisted under this subchapter, than those provided under this subsection.

(June 30, 1948, c. 758, Title II, § 204, as added Oct. 18, 1972, Pub.L. 92–500, § 2, 86 Stat. 835, and amended Dec. 27, 1977, Pub.L. 95–217, §§ 20–24, 91 Stat. 1572, 1573; Oct. 21, 1980, Pub.L. 96–483, § 2(a), (b), 94 Stat. 2360, 2361; Dec. 29, 1981, Pub.L. 97–117, §§ 10(a), (b), 11, 12, 95 Stat. 1626, 1627; Feb. 4, 1987, Pub.L. 100–4, Title II, § 205(a)–(c), 101 Stat. 18.)

[1] So in original. The period probably should be a semicolon.

### HISTORICAL AND STATUTORY NOTES

**Effective and Applicability Provisions**

1987 Acts

Section 205(d) of Pub.L. 100–4 provided that: "This section [amending subsecs. (a)(1), (2), and (b)(1) of this section] shall take effect on the date of the enactment of this Act [Feb. 4, 1987], except that the amendments made by subsections (a) [amending subsec. (a)(1) of this section] and (b) [amending subsec. (a)(2) of this section] shall take effect on the last day of the two-year period beginning on such date of enactment [Feb. 4, 1987]."

1980 Acts

Amendment by Pub.L. 96–483 effective Dec. 27, 1977, see section 2(g) of Pub.L. 96–483, set out as a note under section 1281 of this title.

**Elimination of Inapplicable Conditions or Requirements From Certain Grants**

Section 2(c) of Pub.L. 96–483 provided that: "The Administrator of the Environmental Protection Agency shall take such action as may be necessary to remove from any grant made under section 201(g)(1) of the Federal Water Pollution Control Act [section 1281(g)(1) of this title] after March 1, 1973, and prior to the date of enactment of this Act [Oct. 21, 1980], any condition or requirement no longer applicable as a result of the repeals made by subsections (a) and (b) of this section [amending subsec. (b) of this section] or release any grant recipient of the obligations established by such conditions or other requirement."

Section 2(c) of Pub.L. 96–483, set out above, effective Dec. 27, 1977, see section 2(g) of Pub.L. 96–483, set out as a note under section 1281 of this title.

**Cost Recovery; Suspension of Grant Requirements That Industrial Users Make Payments**

Section 75 of Pub.L. 95–217, as amended by Pub.L. 96–148, § 1(a), (b), Dec. 16, 1979, 93 Stat. 1088; Pub.L. 96–483, § 2(f), Oct. 21, 1980, 94 Stat. 2361 authorized the Administrator of the Environmental Protection Agency to study and report to Congress not later than the last day of the twelfth month which begins after Dec. 27, 1977, cost recovery procedures from industrial users of treatment works to the extent construction costs are attributable to the Federal share of the cost of construction.

## § 1285. Allotment of grant funds

### [FWPCA § 205]

**(a) Funds for fiscal years during period June 30, 1972, and September 30, 1977; determination of amount**

Sums authorized to be appropriated pursuant to section 1287 of this title for each fiscal year beginning after June 30, 1972, and before September 30, 1977, shall be allotted by the Administrator not later than the January 1st immediately preceding the beginning of the fiscal year for which authorized, except that the allotment for fiscal year 1973 shall be made not later than 30 days after October 18, 1972. Such sums shall be allotted among the States by the Administrator in accordance with regulations promulgated by him, in the ratio that the estimated cost of constructing all needed publicly owned treatment works in each State bears to the estimated cost of construction of all needed publicly owned treatment works in all of the States. For the fiscal years ending June 30, 1973, and June 30, 1974, such ratio shall be determined on the basis of table III of House Public Works Committee Print No. 92–50. For the fiscal year ending June 30, 1975, such ratio shall be determined one-half on the basis of table I of House Public Works Committee Print Numbered 93–28 and one-half on the basis of table II of such print, except that no State shall receive an allotment less than that which it received for the fiscal year ending June 30, 1972, as set forth in table III of such print. Allotments for fiscal years which begin after the fiscal year ending June 30, 1975, shall be made only in accordance with a revised cost estimate made and submitted to Congress in accordance with section 1375(b) of this title and only after such revised cost estimate shall have been approved by law specifically enacted after October 18, 1972.

**(b) Availability and use of funds allotted for fiscal years during period June 30, 1972, and September 30, 1977; reallotment**

(1) Any sums allotted to a State under subsection (a) of this section shall be available for obligation under section 1283 of this title on and after the date of such allotment. Such sums shall continue available for obligation in such State for a period of one year after the close of the fiscal year for which such sums are authorized. Any amounts so allotted which are not obligated by the end of such one-year period shall be immediately reallotted by the Administrator, in accordance with regulations promulgated by him, generally on the basis of the ratio used in making the last allotment of sums under this section. Such reallotted sums shall be added to the last allotments made to the States. Any sum made available to a State by reallotment under this subsection shall be in addition to any funds otherwise allotted to such State for grants under this subchapter during any fiscal year.

(2) Any sums which have been obligated under section 1283 of this title and which are released by the payment of the final voucher for the project shall be immediately credited to the State to which such sums were last allotted. Such released sums shall be added to the amounts last allotted to such State and shall be immediately available for obligation in the same manner and to the same extent as such last allotment.

**(c) Funds for fiscal years during period October 1, 1977, and September 30, 1981; funds for fiscal years 1982 to 1990; determination of amount**

(1) Sums authorized to be appropriated pursuant to section 1287 of this title for the fiscal years during the period beginning October 1, 1977, and ending Septem-

ber 30, 1981, shall be allotted for each such year by the Administrator not later than the tenth day which begins after December 27, 1977. Notwithstanding any other provision of law, sums authorized for the fiscal years ending September 30, 1978, September 30, 1979, September 30, 1980, and September 30, 1981, shall be allotted in accordance with table 3 of Committee Print Numbered 95–30 of the Committee on Public Works and Transportation of the House of Representatives.

(2) Sums authorized to be appropriated pursuant to section 1287 of this title for the fiscal years 1982, 1983, 1984, and 1985 shall be allotted for each such year by the Administrator not later than the tenth day which begins after December 29, 1981. Notwithstanding any other provision of law, sums authorized for the fiscal year ending September 30, 1982, shall be allotted in accordance with table 3 of Committee Print Numbered 95–30 of the Committee on Public Works and Transportation of the House of Representatives. Sums authorized for the fiscal years ending September 30, 1983, September 30, 1984, September 30, 1985, and September 30, 1986, shall be allotted in accordance with the following table:

| States | Fiscal years 1983 through 1985 [1] |
|---|---|
| Alabama | .011398 |
| Alaska | .006101 |
| Arizona | .006885 |
| Arkansas | .006668 |
| California | .072901 |
| Colorado | .008154 |
| Connecticut | .012487 |
| Delaware | .004965 |
| District of Columbia | .004965 |
| Florida | .034407 |
| Georgia | .017234 |
| Hawaii | .007895 |
| Idaho | .004965 |
| Illinois | .046101 |
| Indiana | .024566 |
| Iowa | .013796 |
| Kansas | .009201 |
| Kentucky | .012973 |
| Louisiana | .011205 |
| Maine | .007788 |
| Maryland | .024653 |
| Massachusetts | .034608 |
| Michigan | .043829 |
| Minnesota | .018735 |
| Mississippi | .009184 |
| Missouri | .028257 |
| Montana | .004965 |
| Nebraska | .005214 |
| Nevada | .004965 |
| New Hampshire | .010186 |
| New Jersey | .041654 |
| New Mexico | .004965 |
| New York | .113097 |
| North Carolina | .018396 |
| North Dakota | .004965 |
| Ohio | .057383 |
| Oklahoma | .008235 |
| Oregon | .011515 |
| Pennsylvania | .040377 |
| Rhode Island | .006750 |
| South Carolina | .010442 |
| South Dakota | .004965 |
| Tennessee | .014807 |
| Texas | .038726 |
| Utah | .005371 |
| Vermont | .004965 |
| Virginia | .020861 |
| Washington | .017726 |
| West Virginia | .015890 |
| Wisconsin | .027557 |
| Wyoming | .004965 |
| Samoa | .000915 |
| Guam | .000662 |
| Northern Marianas | .000425 |
| Puerto Rico | .013295 |
| Pacific Trust Territories | .001305 |
| Virgin Islands | .000531 |
| United States totals | .999996 |

**(3) Fiscal years 1987–1990**

Sums authorized to be appropriated pursuant to section 1287 of this title for the fiscal years 1987, 1988, 1989, and 1990 shall be allotted for each such year by the Administrator not later than the 10th day which begins after February 4, 1987. Sums authorized for such fiscal years shall be allotted in accordance with the following table:

| States: | |
|---|---|
| Alabama | .011309 |
| Alaska | .006053 |
| Arizona | .006831 |
| Arkansas | .006616 |
| California | .072333 |
| Colorado | .008090 |
| Connecticut | .012390 |
| Delaware | .004965 |
| District of Columbia | .004965 |
| Florida | .034139 |
| Georgia | .017100 |
| Hawaii | .007833 |

| States: | |
|---|---|
| Idaho | .004965 |
| Illinois | .045741 |
| Indiana | .024374 |
| Iowa | .013688 |
| Kansas | .009129 |
| Kentucky | .012872 |
| Louisiana | .011118 |
| Maine | .007829 |
| Maryland | .024461 |
| Massachusetts | .034338 |
| Michigan | .043487 |
| Minnesota | .018589 |
| Mississippi | .009112 |
| Missouri | .028037 |
| Montana | .004965 |
| Nebraska | .005173 |
| Nevada | .004965 |
| New Hampshire | .010107 |
| New Jersey | .041329 |
| New Mexico | .004965 |
| New York | .111632 |
| North Carolina | .018253 |
| North Dakota | .004965 |
| Ohio | .056936 |
| Oklahoma | .008171 |
| Oregon | .011425 |
| Pennsylvania | .040062 |
| Rhode Island | .006791 |
| South Carolina | .010361 |
| South Dakota | .004965 |
| Tennessee | .014692 |
| Texas | .046226 |
| Utah | .005329 |
| Vermont | .004965 |
| Virginia | .020698 |
| Washington | .017588 |
| West Virginia | .015766 |
| Wisconsin | .027342 |
| Wyoming | .004965 |
| American Samoa | .000908 |
| Guam | .000657 |
| Northern Marianas | .000422 |
| Puerto Rico | .013191 |
| Pacific Trust Territories | .001295 |
| Virgin Islands | .000527 |

**(d) Availability and use of funds; reallotment**

Sums allotted to the States for a fiscal year shall remain available for obligation for the fiscal year for which authorized and for the period of the next succeeding twelve months. The amount of any allotment not obligated by the end of such twenty-four-month period shall be immediately reallotted by the Administrator on the basis of the same ratio as applicable to sums allotted for the then current fiscal year, except that none of the funds reallotted by the Administrator for fiscal year 1978 and for fiscal years thereafter shall be allotted to any State which failed to obligate any of the funds being reallotted. Any sum made available to a State by reallotment under this subsection shall be in addition to any funds otherwise allotted to such State for grants under this subchapter during any fiscal year.

**(e) Minimum allotment; additional appropriations; ratio of amount available**

For the fiscal years 1978, 1979, 1980, 1981, 1982, 1983, 1984, 1985, 1986, 1987, 1988, 1989, and 1990, no State shall receive less than one-half of 1 per centum of the total allotment under subsection (c) of this section, except that in the case of Guam, Virgin Islands, American Samoa, and the Trust Territories not more than thirty-three one-hundredths of 1 per centum in the aggregate shall be allotted to all four of these jurisdictions. For the purpose of carrying out this subsection there are authorized to be appropriated, subject to such amounts as are provided in appropriation Acts, not to exceed $75,000,000 for each of fiscal years 1978, 1979, 1980, 1981, 1982, 1983, 1984, 1985, 1986, 1987, 1988, 1989, and 1990. If for any fiscal year the amount appropriated under authority of this subsection is less than the amount necessary to carry out this subsection, the amount each State receives under this subsection for such year shall bear the same ratio to the amount such State would have received under this subsection in such year if the amount necessary to carry it out had been appropriated as the amount appropriated for such year bears to the amount necessary to carry out this subsection for such year.

**(f) Omitted**

**(g) Reservation of funds; State management assistance**

(1) The Administrator is authorized to reserve each fiscal year not to exceed 2 per centum of the amount authorized under section 1287 of this title for purposes of the allotment made to each State under this section on or after October 1, 1977, except in the case of any fiscal year beginning on or after October 1, 1981, and ending before October 1, 1994, in which case the percentage authorized to be reserved shall not exceed 4 per centum.[2] or $400,000 whichever amount is the greater. Sums so reserved shall be available for making grants to such State under paragraph (2) of this subsection for the same period as sums are available from such allotment under subsection (d) of this section, and any such grant shall be available for obligation only during such period. Any grant made from sums reserved under this subsection which has not been obligated by the end of the period for which available shall be added to the amount last allotted to such State under this section and shall be immediately available for obligation in the same manner and to the same extent as such last allotment. Sums authorized

to be reserved by this paragraph shall be in addition to and not in lieu of any other funds which may be authorized to carry out this subsection.

(2) The Administrator is authorized to grant to any State from amounts reserved to such State under this subsection, the reasonable costs of administering any aspects of sections 1281, 1283, 1284, and 1292 of this title the responsibility for administration of which the Administrator has delegated to such State. The Administrator may increase such grant to take into account the reasonable costs of administering an approved program under section 1342 or 1344 of this title, administering a state wide waste treatment management planning program under section 1288(b)(4) of this title, and managing waste treatment construction grants for small communities.

**(h) Alternate systems for small communities**

The Administrator shall set aside from funds authorized for each fiscal year beginning on or after October 1, 1978, a total (as determined by the Governor of the State) of not less than 4 percent nor more than 7½ percent of the sums allotted to any State with a rural population of 25 per centum or more of the total population of such State, as determined by the Bureau of the Census. The Administrator may set aside no more than 7½ percent of the sums allotted to any other State for which the Governor requests such action. Such sums shall be available only for alternatives to conventional sewage treatment works for municipalities having a population of three thousand five hundred or less, or for the highly dispersed sections of larger municipalities, as defined by the Administrator.

**(i) Set-aside for innovative and alternative projects**

Not less than ½ of 1 percent of funds allotted to a State for each of the fiscal years ending September 30, 1979, through September 30, 1990, under subsection (c) of this section shall be expended only for increasing the Federal share of grants for construction of treatment works utilizing innovative processes and techniques pursuant to section 1282(a)(2) of this title. Including the expenditures authorized by the preceding sentence, a total of 2 percent of the funds allotted to a State for each of the fiscal years ending September 30, 1979, and September 30, 1980, and 3 percent of the funds allotted to a State for the fiscal year ending September 30, 1981, under subsection (c) of this section shall be expended only for increasing grants for construction of treatment works pursuant to section 1282(a)(2) of this title. Including the expenditures authorized by the first sentence of this subsection, a total (as determined by the Governor of the State) of not less than 4 percent nor more than 7½ percent of the funds allotted to such State under subsection (c) of this section for each of the fiscal years ending September 30, 1982, through September 30, 1990, shall be expended only for increasing the Federal share of grants for construction of treatment works pursuant to section 1282(a)(2) of this title.

**(j) Water quality management plan; reservation of funds for nonpoint source management**

(1) The Administrator shall reserve each fiscal year not to exceed 1 per centum of the sums allotted and available for obligation to each State under this section for each fiscal year beginning on or after October 1, 1981, or $100,000, whichever amount is the greater.

(2) Such sums shall be used by the Administrator to make grants to the States to carry out water quality management planning, including, but not limited to—

(A) identifying most cost effective and locally acceptable facility and non-point measures to meet and maintain water quality standards;

(B) developing an implementation plan to obtain State and local financial and regulatory commitments to implement measures developed under subparagraph (A);

(C) determining the nature, extent, and causes of water quality problems in various areas of the State and interstate region, and reporting on these annually; and

(D) determining those publicly owned treatment works which should be constructed with assistance under this subchapter, in which areas and in what sequence, taking into account the relative degree of effluent reduction attained, the relative contributions to water quality of other point or nonpoint sources, and the consideration of alternatives to such construction, and implementing section 1313(e) of this title.

(3) In carrying out planning with grants made under paragraph (2) of this subsection, a State shall develop jointly with local, regional, and interstate entities, a plan for carrying out the program and give funding priority to such entities and designated or undesignated public comprehensive planning organizations to carry out the purposes of this subsection. In giving such priority, the State shall allocate at least 40 percent of the amount granted to such State for a fiscal year under paragraph (2) of this subsection to regional public comprehensive planning organizations in such State and appropriate interstate organizations for the development and implementation of the plan described in this paragraph. In any fiscal year for which the Governor, in consultation with such organizations and with the approval of the Administrator, determines that allocation of at least 40 percent of such amount to such organizations will not result in significant participation by such organizations in water quality management planning and not significantly assist in development and implementation of the plan described in this paragraph and achieving the goals of

this chapter, the allocation to such organization may be less than 40 percent of such amount.

(4) All activities undertaken under this subsection shall be in coordination with other related provisions of this chapter.

**(5) Nonpoint source reservation**

In addition to the sums reserved under paragraph (1), the Administrator shall reserve each fiscal year for each State 1 percent of the sums allotted and available for obligation to such State under this section for each fiscal year beginning on or after October 1, 1986, or $100,000, whichever is greater, for the purpose of carrying out section 1329 of this title. Sums so reserved in a State in any fiscal year for which such State does not request the use of such sums, to the extent such sums exceed $100,000, may be used by such State for other purposes under this subchapter.

**(k) New York City Convention Center**

The Administrator shall allot to the State of New York from sums authorized to be appropriated for the fiscal year ending September 30, 1982, an amount necessary to pay the entire cost of conveying sewage from the Convention Center of the city of New York to the Newtown sewage treatment plant, Brooklyn-Queens area, New York. The amount allotted under this subsection shall be in addition to and not in lieu of any other amounts authorized to be allotted to such State under this chapter.

**(l) Marine estuary reservation**

**(1) Reservation of funds**

**(A) General rule**

Prior to making allotments among the States under subsection (c) of this section, the Administrator shall reserve funds from sums appropriated pursuant to section 1287 of this title for each fiscal year beginning after September 30, 1986.

**(B) Fiscal years 1987 and 1988**

For each of fiscal years 1987 and 1988 the reservation shall be 1 percent of the sums appropriated pursuant to section 1287 of this title for such fiscal year.

**(C) Fiscal years 1989 and 1990**

For each of fiscal years 1989 and 1990 the reservation shall be 1½ percent of the funds appropriated pursuant to section 1287 of this title for such fiscal year.

**(2) Use of funds**

Of the sums reserved under this subsection, two-thirds shall be available to address water quality problems of marine bays and estuaries subject to lower levels of water quality due to the impacts of discharges from combined storm water and sanitary sewer overflows from adjacent urban complexes, and one-third shall be available for the implementation of section 1330 of this title, relating to the national estuary program.

**(3) Period of availability**

Sums reserved under this subsection shall be subject to the period of availability for obligation established by subsection (d) of this section.

**(4) Treatment of certain body of water**

For purposes of this section and section 1281(n) of this title, Newark Bay, New Jersey, and the portion of the Passaic River up to Little Falls, in the vicinity of Beatties Dam, shall be treated as a marine bay and estuary.

**(m) Discretionary deposits into State water pollution control revolving funds**

**(1) From construction grant allotments**

In addition to any amounts deposited in a water pollution control revolving fund established by a State under subchapter VI of this chapter, upon request of the Governor of such State, the Administrator shall make available to the State for deposit, as capitalization grants, in such fund in any fiscal year beginning after September 30, 1986, such portion of the amounts allotted to such State under this section for such fiscal year as the Governor considers appropriate; except that (A) in fiscal year 1987, such deposit may not exceed 50 percent of the amounts allotted to such State under this section for such fiscal year, and (B) in fiscal year 1988, such deposit may not exceed 75 percent of the amounts allotted to such State under this section for this fiscal year.

**(2) Notice requirement**

The Governor of a State may make a request under paragraph (1) for a deposit into the water pollution control revolving fund of such State—

(A) in fiscal year 1987 only if no later than 90 days after February 4, 1987, and

(B) in each fiscal year thereafter only if 90 days before the first day of such fiscal year,

the State provides notice of its intent to make such deposit.

**(3) Exception**

Sums reserved under section 1285(j) of this title shall not be available for obligation under this subsection.

(June 30, 1948, c. 758, Title II, § 205, as added Oct. 18, 1972, Pub.L. 92–500, § 2, 86 Stat. 837, and amended Jan. 2, 1974, Pub.L. 93–243, § 1, 87 Stat. 1069; Dec. 27, 1977, Pub.L. 95–217, §§ 25, 26(a), 27, 28, 91 Stat. 1574, 1575; Oct. 21, 1980, Pub.L. 96–483, § 11, 94 Stat. 2363; Dec. 29, 1981, Pub.L. 97–117, §§ 8(c), 13 to 16, 95 Stat. 1625, 1627 to 1629; Feb. 4, 1987, Pub.L. 100–4, Title II, §§ 206(a) to (c), 207 to 210, 212(b), Title III, § 316(d), 101 Stat. 19 to 21, 27, 60; Nov. 10, 1998, Pub.L. 105–362, Title V, § 501(d)(2)(C), 112 Stat. 3284; Nov. 27, 2002, Pub.L. 107–303, Title III, § 302(b)(1), 116 Stat. 2361.)

[1] So in original. Probably should be "1986".
[2] So in original. Probably should be a comma.

### HISTORICAL AND STATUTORY NOTES

**Codifications**

Subsec. (f) provided that sums made available for obligation between Jan. 1, 1975, and Mar. 1, 1975, be available for obligation until Sept. 30, 1978.

**Effective and Applicability Provisions**

2002 Acts

Effective November 10, 1998, section 501 of the Federal Reports Elimination Act of 1998 [Pub.L. 105–362, Title V, § 501, Nov. 10, 1998, 112 Stat. 3283] is amended by striking subsections (a), (b), (c), and (d) [amending this section and others, see Tables for complete classification]. The Federal Water Pollution Control Act (33 U.S.C.A. § 1254(n)(3)) shall be applied and administered on and after Nov. 27, 2002 as if the amendments made by subsections (a), (b), (c), and (d) of Pub.L. 105–362, § 501, had not been enacted, see Pub.L. 107–303, § 302(b)(2), set out as a note under 33 U.S.C.A. § 1254.

**Change of Name**

Any reference in any provision of law enacted before Jan. 4, 1995, to the Committee on Public Works and Transportation of the House of Representatives treated as referring to the Committee on Transportation and Infrastructure of the House of Representatives, see section 1(a)(9) of Pub.L. 104–14, set out as a note preceding section 21 of Title 2, The Congress.

**Termination of Trust Territory of the Pacific Islands**

For termination of Trust Territory of the Pacific Islands, see note set out preceding 48 U.S.C.A. § 1681.

**Period of July 1, 1975, through September, 30, 1976, Considered as One Year**

Period of July 1, 1975, through Sept. 30, 1976, considered as one year for purposes of subsec. (b)(1) of this section, see section 206(5) of Pub.L. 94–274, Title II, Apr. 21, 1976, 90 Stat. 394, set out as an note under section 246 of Title 42, The Public Health and Welfare.

**Limitation on Authorization of Appropriations and Allotment to States for Fiscal Year 1982**

Pub.L. 97–35, Title XVIII, § 1801(b), Aug. 13, 1981, 95 Stat. 764, authorized an appropriation to the Administrator of the Environmental Protection Agency for the fiscal year ending Sept. 30, 1982, not to exceed $40,000,000 to carry out section 1285(g) of this title. The Administrator was to make such authorization available to the States in accordance with such section 1285(g) in the same manner and to the same extent as would be the case if $2,000,000,000 had been authorized under section 1287 of this title, using the same allotment table as was applicable to the fiscal year ending Sept. 30, 1981.

**Availability of Allotted Sums in Subsequent Years; Reallotment of Unobligated Sums**

Section 7 of Pub.L. 96–483 provided that: "Notwithstanding section 205(d) of the Federal Water Pollution Control Act (33 U.S.C. 1285) [subsec. (d) of this section], sums allotted to the States for the fiscal year 1979 shall remain available for obligation for the fiscal year for which authorized and for the period of the next succeeding twenty-four months. The amount of any allotment not obligated by the end of such thirty-six month period shall be immediately reallotted by the Administrator on the basis of the same ratio as applicable to sums allotted for the then current fiscal year, except that none of the funds reallotted by the Administrator for fiscal year 1979 shall be allotted to any State which failed to obligate any of the funds being reallotted. Any sum made available to a State by reallotment under this section shall be in addition to any funds otherwise allotted to such State for grants under title II of the Federal Water Pollution Control Act [this subchapter] during any fiscal year. This section shall take effect on September 30, 1980."

**Period of July 1, 1975, through September 30, 1976, Considered as One Year**

Period of July 1, 1975, through Sept. 30, 1976, considered as one year for purposes of subsec. (b)(1) of this section, see section 206(5) of Pub.L. 94–274, Title II, Apr. 21, 1976, 90 Stat. 394, set out as a note under section 289c–2 of Title 42, The Public Health and Welfare.

## § 1286. Reimbursement and advanced construction

### [FWPCA § 206]

#### (a) Publicly owned treatment works construction initiated after June 30, 1966, but before July 1, 1973; reimbursement formula

Any publicly owned treatment works in a State on which construction was initiated after June 30, 1966, but before July 1, 1973, which was approved by the appropriate State water pollution control agency and which the Administrator finds meets the requirements of section 1158 of this title in effect at the time of the initiation of construction shall be reimbursed a total amount equal to the difference between the amount of Federal financial assistance, if any, received under such section 1158 of this title for such project and 50 per centum of the cost of such project, or 55 per centum of the project cost where the Administrator also determines that such treatment works was constructed in conformity with a comprehensive metropolitan treatment plan as described in section 1158(f) of this title as in effect immediately prior to October 18, 1972. Nothing in this subsection shall result in any such works receiving Federal grants from all sources in excess of 80 per centum of the cost of such project.

#### (b) Publicly owned treatment works construction initiated between June 30, 1956, and June 30, 1966; reimbursement formula

Any publicly owned treatment works constructed with or eligible for Federal financial assistance under this Act in a State between June 30, 1956, and June 30, 1966, which was approved by the State water pollution control agency and which the Administrator finds meets the requirements of section 1158 of this title prior to October 18, 1972 but which was constructed without assistance under such section 1158 of this title or which received such assistance in an amount less than 30 per centum of the cost of such project shall qualify for payments and reimbursement of State or local funds used for such project from sums allocated to such State under this section in an amount which shall not exceed the difference between the amount of such assistance, if any, received for such project and 30 per centum of the cost of such project.

**(c) Application for reimbursement**

No publicly owned treatment works shall receive any payment or reimbursement under subsection (a) or (b) of this section unless an application for such assistance is filed with the Administrator within the one year period which begins on October 18, 1972. Any application filed within such one year period may be revised from time to time, as may be necessary.

**(d) Allocation of funds**

The Administrator shall allocate to each qualified project under subsection (a) of this section each fiscal year for which funds are appropriated under subsection (e) of this section an amount which bears the same ratio to the unpaid balance of the reimbursement due such project as the total of such funds for such year bears to the total unpaid balance of reimbursement due all such approved projects on the date of enactment of such appropriation. The Administrator shall allocate to each qualified project under subsection (b) of this section each fiscal year for which funds are appropriated under subsection (e) of this section an amount which bears the same ratio to the unpaid balance of the reimbursement due such project as the total of such funds for such year bears to the total unpaid balance of reimbursement due all such approved projects on the date of enactment of such appropriation.

**(e) Authorization of appropriations**

There is authorized to be appropriated to carry out subsection (a) of this section not to exceed $2,600,000,000 and, to carry out subsection (b) of this section, not to exceed $750,000,000. The authorizations contained in this subsection shall be the sole source of funds for reimbursements authorized by this section.

**(f) Additional funds**

**(1)** In any case where a substantial portion of the funds allotted to a State for the current fiscal year under this subchapter have been obligated under section 1281(g) of this title, or will be so obligated in a timely manner (as determined by the Administrator), and there is construction of any treatment works project without the aid of Federal funds and in accordance with all procedures and all requirements applicable to treatment works projects, except those procedures and requirements which limit construction of projects to those constructed with the aid of previously allotted Federal funds, the Administrator, upon his approval of an application made under this subsection therefor, is authorized to pay the Federal share of the cost of construction of such project when additional funds are allotted to the State under this subchapter if prior to the construction of the project the Administrator approves plans, specifications, and estimates therefor in the same manner as other treatment works projects. The Administrator may not approve an application under this subsection unless an authorization is in effect for the first fiscal year in the period for which the application requests payment and such requested payment for that fiscal year does not exceed the State's expected allotment from such authorization. The Administrator shall not be required to make such requested payment for any fiscal year—

**(A)** to the extent that such payment would exceed such State's allotment of the amount appropriated for such fiscal year; and

**(B)** unless such payment is for a project which, on the basis of an approved funding priority list of such State, is eligible to receive such payment based on the allotment and appropriation for such fiscal year.

To the extent that sufficient funds are not appropriated to pay the full Federal share with respect to a project for which obligations under the provisions of this subsection have been made, the Administrator shall reduce the Federal share to such amount less than 75 per centum as such appropriations do provide.

**(2)** In determining the allotment for any fiscal year under this subchapter, any treatment works project constructed in accordance with this section and without the aid of Federal funds shall not be considered completed until an application under the provisions of this subsection with respect to such project has been approved by the Administrator, or the availability of funds from which this project is eligible for reimbursement has expired, whichever first occurs.

(June 30, 1948, c. 758, Title II, § 206, as added Oct. 18, 1972, Pub.L. 92–500, § 2, 86 Stat. 838, and amended Dec. 28, 1973, Pub.L. 93–207, § 1(2), 87 Stat. 906; Dec. 27, 1977, Pub.L. 95–217, § 29(a), 91 Stat. 1576; Oct. 21, 1980, Pub.L. 96–483, § 5, 94 Stat. 2361.)

## HISTORICAL AND STATUTORY NOTES

**References in Text**

Section 1158 of this title, referred to in subsecs. (a) and (b), refers to section 8 of Act June 30, 1948, c. 758, 62 Stat. 1158, prior to the supersedure and reenactment of Act June 30, 1948, by Act Oct. 18, 1972, Pub.L. 92–500, 86 Stat. 816. Provisions of section 1158 of this title are now covered by this subchapter.

This Act, referred to in subsec. (b), means Act June 30, 1948, c. 758, 62 Stat. 1155, prior to the supersedure and reenactment of Act June 30, 1948 by Act Oct. 18, 1972, Pub.L. 92–500, 86 Stat. 816. Act June 30, 1948, c. 758, as added by Act Oct. 18, 1972, Pub.L. 92–500, 86 Stat. 816, enacted this chapter.

**Applications for Assistance for Publicly Owned Treatment Works Where Grants Were Made Before July 2, 1972, and on Which Construction Was Initiated Before July 1, 1973**

Section 29(b) of Pub. L. 95–217 provided that applications for assistance for publicly owned treatment works for which a grant was made under this chapter before July 1, 1972, and on which construction was initiated before July 1, 1973, be filed not later than the ninetieth day after Dec. 27, 1977.

**Application for Assistance**

Section 2 of Pub.L. 93–207 provided that notwithstanding the requirements of subsec. (c) of this section, applications for assistance under this section could have been filed with the Administrator until Jan. 31, 1974.

**Allocation of Construction Grants Appropriated for the Year Ending June 30, 1973; Interim Payments; Limitations**

Section 3 of Pub.L. 93–207 provided that: "Funds available for reimbursement under Public Law 92–399 [making appropriations for Agriculture-Environmental and Consumer protection programs for the fiscal year ending June 30, 1973] shall be allocated in accordance with subsection (d) of section 206 of the Federal Water Pollution Control Act (86 Stat. 838) [subsec. (d) of this section], pro rata among all projects eligible under subsection (a) of such section 206 [subsec. (a) of this section] for which applications have been submitted and approved by the Administrator pursuant to such Act [this chapter]. Notwithstanding the provisions of subsection (d) of such section 206, (1) the Administrator is authorized to make interim payments to each such project for which an application has been approved on the basis of estimates of maximum pro rata entitlement of all applicants under section 206(a) and (2) for the purpose of determining allocation of sums available under Public Law 92–399, the unpaid balance of reimbursement due such projects shall be computed as of January 31, 1974. Upon completion by the Administrator of his audit and approval of all projects for which an application has been filed under subsection (a) of such section 206, the Administrator shall, within the limits of appropriated funds, allocate to each such qualified project the amount remaining, if any, of its total entitlement. Amounts allocated to projects which are later determined to be in excess of entitlement shall be available for reallocation, until expended, to other qualified projects under subsection (a) of such section 206. In no event, however, shall any payments exceed the Federal share of the cost of construction incurred to the date of the voucher covering such payment plus the Federal share of the value of the materials which have been stockpiled in the vicinity of such construction in conformity to plans and specifications for the project."

## § 1287. Authorization of appropriations

**[FWPCA § 207]**

There is authorized to be appropriated to carry out this subchapter, other than sections 1286(e), 1288 and 1289 of this title, for the fiscal year ending June 30, 1973, not to exceed $5,000,000,000, for the fiscal year ending June 30, 1974, not to exceed $6,000,000,000, and for the fiscal year ending June 30, 1975, not to exceed $7,000,000,000, and subject to such amounts as are provided in appropriation Acts, for the fiscal year ending September 30, 1977, $1,000,000,000 for the fiscal year ending September 30, 1978, $4,500,000,000 and for the fiscal years ending September 30, 1979, September 30, 1980, not to exceed $5,000,000,000; for the fiscal year ending September 30, 1981, not to exceed $2,548,837,000; and for the fiscal years ending September 30, 1982, September 30, 1983, September 30, 1984, and September 30, 1985, not to exceed $2,400,000,000 per fiscal year; and for each of the fiscal years ending September 30, 1986, September 30, 1987, and September 30, 1988, not to exceed $2,400,000,000; and for each of the fiscal years ending September 30, 1989, and September 30, 1990, not to exceed $1,200,000,000.

(June 30, 1948, c. 758, Title II, § 207, as added Oct. 18, 1972, Pub.L. 92–500, § 2, 86 Stat. 839, and amended Dec. 28, 1973, Pub.L. 93–207, § 1(3), 87 Stat. 906; Dec. 27, 1977, Pub.L. 95–217, § 30, 91 Stat. 1576; Aug. 13, 1981, Pub.L. 97–35, Title XVIII, § 1801(a), 95 Stat. 764; Dec. 29, 1981, Pub.L. 97–117, § 17, 95 Stat. 1630; Feb. 4, 1987, Pub.L. 100–4, Title II, § 211, 101 Stat. 21.)

### HISTORICAL AND STATUTORY NOTES

**Additional Authorization of Appropriations**

Pub.L. 94–369, title III, § 301, July 22, 1976, 90 Stat. 1011, provided for authorization to carry out this subchapter, other than sections 1286, 1288, and 1289, for the fiscal year ending Sept. 30, 1977, not to exceed $700,000,000, which sum (subject to amounts provided in appropriation Acts) was to be allotted to each State listed in column 1 of table IV contained in House Public Works and Transportation Committee Print numbered 94–25 in accordance with the percentages provided for such State (if any) in column 5 of such table, and such sum to be in addition to, and not in lieu of, any funds otherwise authorized and to be available until expended.

## § 1288. Areawide waste treatment management

**[FWPCA § 208]**

**(a) Identification and designation of areas having substantial water quality control problems**

For the purpose of encouraging and facilitating the development and implementation of areawide waste treatment management plans—

(1) The Administrator, within ninety days after October 18, 1972, and after consultation with appropriate Federal, State, and local authorities, shall by regulation publish guidelines for the identification of those areas which, as a result of urban-industrial concentrations or other factors, have substantial water quality control problems.

(2) The Governor of each State, within sixty days after publication of the guidelines issued pursuant to paragraph (1) of this subsection, shall identify each area within the State which, as a result of urban-industrial concentrations or other factors, has substantial water quality control problems. Not later than one hundred and twenty days following such identification and after consultation with appropriate elected and other officials of local governments having jurisdiction in such areas, the Governor shall designate (A) the boundaries of each such area, and (B) a single representative organization, including elected officials from local governments or their designees, capable of developing effective areawide waste treatment management plans for such area. The Governor may in the same manner at any later time identify any additional area (or modify an existing area) for which he determines areawide waste treatment management to be appropriate, designate the boundaries of such area, and designate an organization capable of developing effective areawide waste treatment management plans for such area.

(3) With respect to any area which, pursuant to the guidelines published under paragraph (1) of this subsection, is located in two or more States, the Governors of the respective States shall consult and cooperate in carrying out the provisions of paragraph (2), with a view toward designating the boundaries of the interstate area having common water quality control problems and for which areawide waste treatment management plans would be most effective, and toward designating, within one hundred and eighty days after publication of guidelines issued pursuant to paragraph (1) of this subsection, of a single representative organization capable of developing effective areawide waste treatment management plans for such area.

(4) If a Governor does not act, either by designating or determining not to make a designation under paragraph (2) of this subsection, within the time required by such paragraph, or if, in the case of an interstate area, the Governors of the States involved do not designate a planning organization within the time required by paragraph (3) of this subsection, the chief elected officials of local governments within an area may by agreement designate (A) the boundaries for such an area, and (B) a single representative organization including elected officials from such local governments, or their designees, capable of developing an areawide waste treatment management plan for such area.

(5) Existing regional agencies may be designated under paragraphs (2), (3), and (4) of this subsection.

(6) The State shall act as a planning agency for all portions of such State which are not designated under paragraphs (2), (3), or (4) of this subsection.

(7) Designations under this subsection shall be subject to the approval of the Administrator.

**(b) Planning process**

**(1)(A)** Not later than one year after the date of designation of any organization under subsection (a) of this section such organization shall have in operation a continuing areawide waste treatment management planning process consistent with section 1281 of this title. Plans prepared in accordance with this process shall contain alternatives for waste treatment management, and be applicable to all wastes generated within the area involved. The initial plan prepared in accordance with such process shall be certified by the Governor and submitted to the Administrator not later than two years after the planning process is in operation.

**(B)** For any agency designated after 1975 under subsection (a) of this section and for all portions of a State for which the State is required to act as the planning agency in accordance with subsection (a)(6) of this section, the initial plan prepared in accordance with such process shall be certified by the Governor and submitted to the Administrator not later than three years after the receipt of the initial grant award authorized under subsection (f) of this section.

(2) Any plan prepared under such process shall include, but not be limited to—

**(A)** the identification of treatment works necessary to meet the anticipated municipal and industrial waste treatment needs of the area over a twenty-year period, annually updated (including an analysis of alternative waste treatment systems), including any requirements for the acquisition of land for treatment purposes; the necessary waste water collection and urban storm water runoff systems; and a program to provide the necessary financial arrangements for the development of such treatment works, and an identification of open space and recreation opportunities that can be expected to result from improved water quality, including consideration of potential use of lands associated with treatment works and increased access to water-based recreation;

**(B)** the establishment of construction priorities for such treatment works and time schedules for the initiation and completion of all treatment works;

**(C)** the establishment of a regulatory program to—

**(i)** implement the waste treatment management requirements of section 1281(c) of this title,

**(ii)** regulate the location, modification, and construction of any facilities within such area which may result in any discharge in such area, and

(iii) assure that any industrial or commercial wastes discharged into any treatment works in such area meet applicable pretreatment requirements;

(D) the identification of those agencies necessary to construct, operate, and maintain all facilities required by the plan and otherwise to carry out the plan;

(E) the identification of the measures necessary to carry out the plan (including financing), the period of time necessary to carry out the plan, the costs of carrying out the plan within such time, and the economic, social, and environmental impact of carrying out the plan within such time;

(F) a process to (i) identify, if appropriate, agriculturally and silviculturally related nonpoint sources of pollution, including return flows from irrigated agriculture, and their cumulative effects, runoff from manure disposal areas, and from land used for livestock and crop production, and (ii) set forth procedures and methods (including land use requirements) to control to the extent feasible such sources;

(G) a process to (i) identify, if appropriate, mine-related sources of pollution including new, current, and abandoned surface and underground mine runoff, and (ii) set forth procedures and methods (including land use requirements) to control to the extent feasible such sources;

(H) a process to (i) identify construction activity related sources of pollution, and (ii) set forth procedures and methods (including land use requirements) to control to the extent feasible such sources;

(I) a process to (i) identify, if appropriate, salt water intrusion into rivers, lakes, and estuaries resulting from reduction of fresh water flow from any cause, including irrigation, obstruction, ground water extraction, and diversion, and (ii) set forth procedures and methods to control such intrusion to the extent feasible where such procedures and methods are otherwise a part of the waste treatment management plan;

(J) a process to control the disposition of all residual waste generated in such area which could affect water quality; and

(K) a process to control the disposal of pollutants on land or in subsurface excavations within such area to protect ground and surface water quality.

(3) Areawide waste treatment management plans shall be certified annually by the Governor or his designee (or Governors or their designees, where more than one State is involved) as being consistent with applicable basin plans and such areawide waste treatment management plans shall be submitted to the Administrator for his approval.

(4)(A) Whenever the Governor of any State determines (and notifies the Administrator) that consistency with a statewide regulatory program under section 1313 of this title so requires, the requirements of clauses (F) through (K) of paragraph (2) of this subsection shall be developed and submitted by the Governor to the Administrator for approval for application to a class or category of activity throughout such State.

(B) Any program submitted under subparagraph (A) of this paragraph which, in whole or in part, is to control the discharge or other placement of dredged or fill material into the navigable waters shall include the following:

(i) A consultation process which includes the State agency with primary jurisdiction over fish and wildlife resources.

(ii) A process to identify and manage the discharge or other placement of dredged or fill material which adversely affects navigable waters, which shall complement and be coordinated with a State program under section 1344 of this title conducted pursuant to this chapter.

(iii) A process to assure that any activity conducted pursuant to a best management practice will comply with the guidelines established under section 1344(b)(1) of this title, and sections 1317 and 1343 of this title.

(iv) A process to assure that any activity conducted pursuant to a best management practice can be terminated or modified for cause including, but not limited to, the following:

(I) violation of any condition of the best management practice;

(II) change in any activity that requires either a temporary or permanent reduction or elimination of the discharge pursuant to the best management practice.

(v) A process to assure continued coordination with Federal and Federal-State water-related planning and reviewing processes, including the National Wetlands Inventory.

(C) If the Governor of a State obtains approval from the Administrator of a statewide regulatory program which meets the requirements of subparagraph (B) of this paragraph and if such State is administering a permit program under section 1344 of this title, no person shall be required to obtain an individual permit pursuant to such section, or to comply with a general permit issued pursuant to such section, with respect to any appropriate activity within such State for which a best management practice has been approved by the Administrator under the program approved by the Administrator pursuant to this paragraph.

**(D)(i)** Whenever the Administrator determines after public hearing that a State is not administering a program approved under this section in accordance with the requirements of this section, the Administrator shall so notify the State, and if appropriate corrective action is not taken within a reasonable time, not to exceed ninety days, the Administrator shall withdraw approval of such program. The Administrator shall not withdraw approval of any such program unless he shall first have notified the State, and made public, in writing, the reasons for such withdrawal.

**(ii)** In the case of a State with a program submitted and approved under this paragraph, the Administrator shall withdraw approval of such program under this subparagraph only for a substantial failure of the State to administer its program in accordance with the requirements of this paragraph.

**(c) Regional operating agencies**

**(1)** The Governor of each State, in consultation with the planning agency designated under subsection (a) of this section, at the time a plan is submitted to the Administrator, shall designate one or more waste treatment management agencies (which may be an existing or newly created local, regional, or State agency or political subdivision) for each area designated under subsection (a) of this section and submit such designations to the Administrator.

**(2)** The Administrator shall accept any such designation, unless, within 120 days of such designation, he finds that the designated management agency (or agencies) does not have adequate authority—

**(A)** to carry out appropriate portions of an areawide waste treatment management plan developed under subsection (b) of this section;

**(B)** to manage effectively waste treatment works and related facilities serving such area in conformance with any plan required by subsection (b) of this section;

**(C)** directly or by contract, to design and construct new works, and to operate and maintain new and existing works as required by any plan developed pursuant to subsection (b) of this section;

**(D)** to accept and utilize grants, or other funds from any source, for waste treatment management purposes;

**(E)** to raise revenues, including the assessment of waste treatment charges;

**(F)** to incur short- and long-term indebtedness;

**(G)** to assure in implementation of an areawide waste treatment management plan that each participating community pays its proportionate share of treatment costs;

**(H)** to refuse to receive any wastes from any municipality or subdivision thereof, which does not comply with any provisions of an approved plan under this section applicable to such area; and

**(I)** to accept for treatment industrial wastes.

**(d) Conformity of works with area plan**

After a waste treatment management agency having the authority required by subsection (c) of this section has been designated under such subsection for an area and a plan for such area has been approved under subsection (b) of this section, the Administrator shall not make any grant for construction of a publicly owned treatment works under section 1281(g)(1) of this title within such area except to such designated agency and for works in conformity with such plan.

**(e) Permits not to conflict with approved plans**

No permit under section 1342 of this title shall be issued for any point source which is in conflict with a plan approved pursuant to subsection (b) of this section.

**(f) Grants**

**(1)** The Administrator shall make grants to any agency designated under subsection (a) of this section for payment of the reasonable costs of developing and operating a continuing areawide waste treatment management planning process under subsection (b) of this section.

**(2)** For the two-year period beginning on the date the first grant is made under paragraph (1) of this subsection to an agency, if such first grant is made before October 1, 1977, the amount of each such grant to such agency shall be 100 per centum of the costs of developing and operating a continuing areawide waste treatment management planning process under subsection (b) of this section, and thereafter the amount granted to such agency shall not exceed 75 per centum of such costs in each succeeding one-year period. In the case of any other grant made to an agency under such paragraph (1) of this subsection, the amount of such grant shall not exceed 75 per centum of the costs of developing and operating a continuing areawide waste treatment management planning process in any year.

**(3)** Each applicant for a grant under this subsection shall submit to the Administrator for his approval each proposal for which a grant is applied for under this subsection. The Administrator shall act upon such proposal as soon as practicable after it has been submitted, and his approval of that proposal shall be deemed a contractual obligation of the United States for the payment of its contribution to such proposal, subject to such amounts as are provided in appropriation Acts. There is authorized to be appropriated to carry out this subsection not to exceed $50,000,000 for the fiscal year ending June 30, 1973, not to exceed $100,000,000 for the fiscal year ending June 30, 1974, not to exceed $150,000,000 per fiscal year for the fiscal years ending June 30, 1975, September 30, 1977, September 30, 1978, September 30, 1979, and September 30, 1980, not to exceed $100,000,000 per fiscal year for the fiscal years ending September 30, 1981, and September 30, 1982, and such sums as may be necessary for fiscal years 1983 through 1990.

**(g) Technical assistance by Administrator**

The Administrator is authorized, upon request of the Governor or the designated planning agency, and without reimbursement, to consult with, and provide technical assistance to, any agency designated under subsection (a) of this section in the development of areawide waste treatment management plans under subsection (b) of this section.

**(h) Technical assistance by Secretary of the Army**

(1) The Secretary of the Army, acting through the Chief of Engineers, in cooperation with the Administrator is authorized and directed, upon request of the Governor or the designated planning organization, to consult with, and provide technical assistance to, any agency designed [1] under subsection (a) of this section in developing and operating a continuing areawide waste treatment management planning process under subsection (b) of this section.

(2) There is authorized to be appropriated to the Secretary of the Army, to carry out this subsection, not to exceed $50,000,000 per fiscal year for the fiscal years ending June 30, 1973, and June 30, 1974.

**(i) State best management practices program**

(1) The Secretary of the Interior, acting through the Director of the United States Fish and Wildlife Service, shall, upon request of the Governor of a State, and without reimbursement, provide technical assistance to such State in developing a statewide program for submission to the Administrator under subsection (b)(4)(B) of this section and in implementing such program after its approval.

(2) There is authorized to be appropriated to the Secretary of the Interior $6,000,000 to complete the National Wetlands Inventory of the United States, by December 31, 1981, and to provide information from such Inventory to States as it becomes available to assist such States in the development and operation of programs under this chapter.

**(j) Agricultural cost sharing**

(1) The Secretary of Agriculture, with the concurrence of the Administrator, and acting through the Soil Conservation Service and such other agencies of the Department of Agriculture as the Secretary may designate, is authorized and directed to establish and administer a program to enter into contracts, subject to such amounts as are provided in advance by appropriation acts, of not less than five years nor more than ten years with owners and operators having control of rural land for the purpose of installing and maintaining measures incorporating best management practices to control nonpoint source pollution for improved water quality in those States or areas for which the Administrator has approved a plan under subsection (b) of this section where the practices to which the contracts apply are certified by the management agency designated under subsection (c)(1) of this section to be consistent with such plans and will result in improved water quality. Such contracts may be entered into during the period ending not later than September 31, 1988. Under such contracts the land owner or operator shall agree—

(i) to effectuate a plan approved by a soil conservation district, where one exists, under this section for his farm, ranch, or other land substantially in accordance with the schedule outlined therein unless any requirement thereof is waived or modified by the Secretary;

(ii) to forfeit all rights to further payments or grants under the contract and refund to the United States all payments and grants received thereunder, with interest, upon his violation of the contract at any stage during the time he has control of the land if the Secretary, after considering the recommendations of the soil conservation district, where one exists, and the Administrator, determines that such violation is of such a nature as to warrant termination of the contract, or to make refunds or accept such payment adjustments as the Secretary may deem appropriate if he determines that the violation by the owner or operator does not warrant termination of the contract;

(iii) upon transfer of his right and interest in the farm, ranch, or other land during the contract period to forfeit all rights to further payments or grants under the contract and refund to the United States all payments or grants received thereunder, with interest, unless the transferee of any such land agrees with the Secretary to assume all obligations of the contract;

(iv) not to adopt any practice specified by the Secretary on the advice of the Administrator in the contract as a practice which would tend to defeat the purposes of the contract;

(v) to such additional provisions as the Secretary determines are desirable and includes in the contract to effectuate the purposes of the program or to facilitate the practical administration of the program.

(2) In return for such agreement by the landowner or operator the Secretary shall agree to provide technical assistance and share the cost of carrying out those conservation practices and measures set forth in the contract for which he determines that cost sharing is appropriate and in the public interest and which are approved for cost sharing by the agency designated to implement the plan developed under subsection (b) of this section. The portion of such cost (including labor) to be shared shall be that part which the Secretary determines is necessary and appropriate to effectuate the installation of the water quality management practices and measures under the contract, but not to exceed 50 per centum of the total cost of the measures set forth in the contract; except the Secretary may increase the matching cost share where he determines that (1) the main benefits to be derived from the measures are related to improving offsite water quality, and (2) the matching share requirement would place a burden on the landowner which would probably prevent him from participating in the program.

(3) The Secretary may terminate any contract with a landowner or operator by mutual agreement with the owner or operator if the Secretary determines that such termination would be in the public interest, and may agree to such modification of contracts previously entered into as he may determine to be desirable to carry out the purposes of the program or facilitate the practical administration thereof or to accomplish equitable treatment with respect to other conservation, land use, or water quality programs.

(4) In providing assistance under this subsection the Secretary will give priority to those areas and sources that have the most significant effect upon water quality. Additional investigations or plans may be made, where necessary, to supplement approved water quality management plans, in order to determine priorities.

(5) The Secretary shall, where practicable, enter into agreements with soil conservation districts, State soil and water conservation agencies, or State water quality agencies to administer all or part of the program established in this subsection under regulations developed by the Secretary. Such agreements shall provide for the submission of such reports as the Secretary deems necessary, and for payment by the United States of such portion of the costs incurred in the administration of the program as the Secretary may deem appropriate.

(6) The contracts under this subsection shall be entered into only in areas where the management agency designated under subsection (c)(1) of this section assures an adequate level of participation by owners and operators having control of rural land in such areas. Within such areas the local soil conservation district, where one exists, together with the Secretary of Agriculture, will determine the priority of assistance among individual land owners and operators to assure that the most critical water quality problems are addressed.

(7) The Secretary, in consultation with the Administrator and subject to section 1314(k) of this title, shall, not later than September 30, 1978, promulgate regulations for carrying out this subsection and for support and cooperation with other Federal and non-Federal agencies for implementation of this subsection.

(8) This program shall not be used to authorize or finance projects that would otherwise be eligible for assistance under the terms of Public Law 83–566 [16 U.S.C.A. § 1001 et seq.].

(9) There are hereby authorized to be appropriated to the Secretary of Agriculture $200,000,000 for fiscal year 1979, $400,000,000 for fiscal year 1980, $100,000,000 for fiscal year 1981, $100,000,000 for fiscal year 1982, and such sums as may be necessary for fiscal years 1983 through 1990, to carry out this subsection. The program authorized under this subsection shall be in addition to, and not in substitution of, other programs in such area authorized by this or any other public law.

(June 30, 1948, c. 758, Title II, § 208, as added Oct. 18, 1972, Pub.L. 92–500, § 2, 86 Stat. 839, and amended Dec. 27, 1977, Pub.L. 95–217, §§ 4(e), 31, 32, 33(a), 34, 35, 91 Stat. 1566, 1576–1579; Oct. 21, 1980, Pub.L. 96–483, § 1(d), (e), 94 Stat. 2360; Feb. 4, 1987, Pub.L. 100–4, Title I, § 101(d), (e), 101 Stat. 9.)

[1] So in original. Probably should be "designated".

## HISTORICAL AND STATUTORY NOTES

**References in Text**

Public Law 83–566, referred to in subsec. (j)(8), is Act Aug. 4, 1954, c. 656, 68 Stat. 666, as amended, known as the Watershed Protection and Flood Prevention Act, which is classified generally to chapter 18 (section 1001 et seq.) of Title 16, Conservation. For complete classification of this Act to the Code, see Short Title note set out under section 1001 of Title 16 and Tables.

**Transfer of Functions**

Enforcement functions of Secretary or other official in Department of Agriculture, insofar as they involve lands and programs under jurisdiction of that Department, related to compliance with this chapter with respect to pre-construction, construction, and initial operation of transportation system for Canadian and Alaskan natural gas were transferred to the Federal Inspector, Office of Federal Inspector for the Alaska Natural Gas Transportation System, until the first anniversary of date of initial operation of the Alaska Natural Gas Transportation System, see Reorg. Plan No. 1 of 1979, §§ 102(f), 203(a), 44 F.R. 33663, 33666, 93 Stat. 1373, 1376, effective July 1, 1979, set out in Appendix 1 to Title 5, Government Organization and Employees.

## § 1289. Basin planning

[FWPCA § 209]

### (a) Preparation of Level B plans

The President, acting through the Water Resources Council, shall, as soon as practicable, prepare a Level B plan under the Water Resources Planning Act [42 U.S.C.A. § 1962 et seq.] for all basins in the United States. All such plans shall be completed not later than January 1, 1980, except that priority in the preparation of such plans shall be given to those basins and portions thereof which are within those areas designated under paragraphs (2), (3), and (4) of subsection (a) of section 1288 of this title.

### (b) Omitted

### (c) Authorization of appropriations

There is authorized to be appropriated to carry out this section not to exceed $200,000,000.

(June 30, 1948, c. 758, Title II, § 209, as added Oct. 18, 1972, Pub.L. 92–500, § 2, 86 Stat. 843.)

#### HISTORICAL AND STATUTORY NOTES

**References in Text**

The Water Resources Planning Act, referred to in subsec. (a), is Pub.L. 89–80, July 22, 1965, 79 Stat. 244, as amended, which is classified generally to chapter 19B (section 1962 et seq.) of Title 42, The Public Health and Welfare. For complete classification of this Act to the Code, see Short Title note set out under section 1962 of Title 42 and Tables.

**Codifications**

Subsec. (b) of this section, which required the President, acting through the Water Resources Council, to report annually to Congress on progress being made in carrying out this section, terminated, effective May 15, 2000, pursuant to section 3003 of Pub.L. 104–66, as amended, set out as a note under 31 U.S.C.A. § 1113. See, also, page 195 of House Document No. 103–7.

## § 1290. Annual survey

[FWPCA § 210]

The Administrator shall annually make a survey to determine the efficiency of the operation and maintenance of treatment works constructed with grants made under this chapter, as compared to the efficiency planned at the time the grant was made. The results of such annual survey shall be included in the report required under section 1375(a) of this title.

(June 30, 1948, c. 758, Title II, § 210, as added Oct. 18, 1972, Pub.L. 92–500, § 2, 86 Stat. 843, and amended Nov. 10, 1998, Pub.L. 105–362, Title V, § 501(d)(2)(D), 112 Stat. 3284; Nov. 27, 2002, Pub.L. 107–303, Title III, § 302(b)(1), 116 Stat. 2361.)

#### HISTORICAL AND STATUTORY NOTES

**Effective and Applicability Provisions**

2002 Acts

Effective November 10, 1998, section 501 of the Federal Reports Elimination Act of 1998 [Pub.L. 105–362, Title V, § 501, Nov. 10, 1998, 112 Stat. 3283] is amended by striking subsections (a), (b), (c), and (d) [amending this section and others, see Tables for complete classification]. The Federal Water Pollution Control Act (33 U.S.C.A. § 1254(n)(3)) shall be applied and administered on and after Nov. 27, 2002 as if the amendments made by subsections (a), (b), (c), and (d) of Pub.L. 105–362, § 501, had not been enacted, see Pub.L. 107–303, § 302(b)(2), set out as a note under 33 U.S.C.A. § 1254.

## § 1291. Sewage collection systems

[FWPCA § 211]

### (a) Existing and new systems

No grant shall be made for a sewage collection system under this subchapter unless such grant (1) is for replacement or major rehabilitation of an existing collection system and is necessary to the total integrity and performance of the waste treatment works servicing such community, or (2) is for a new collection system in an existing community with sufficient existing or planned capacity adequately to treat such collected sewage and is consistent with section 1281 of this title.

### (b) Use of population density as test

If the Administrator uses population density as a test for determining the eligibility of a collector sewer for assistance it shall be only for the purpose of evaluating alternatives and determining the needs for such system in relation to ground or surface water quality impact.

### (c) Pollutant discharges from separate storm sewer systems

No grant shall be made under this subchapter from funds authorized for any fiscal year during the period beginning October 1, 1977, and ending September 30, 1990, for treatment works for control of pollutant discharges from separate storm sewer systems.

(June 30, 1948, c. 758, Title II, § 211, as added Oct. 18, 1972, Pub.L. 92–500, § 2, 86 Stat. 843, and amended Dec. 27, 1977, Pub.L. 95–217, § 36, 91 Stat. 1581; Dec. 29, 1981, Pub.L. 97–117, § 2(b), 95 Stat. 1623; Feb. 4, 1987, Pub.L. 100–4, Title II, § 206(d), 101 Stat. 20.)

## § 1292. Definitions

[FWPCA § 212]

As used in this subchapter—

(1) The term "construction" means any one or more of the following: preliminary planning to determine the feasibility of treatment works, engineering, architectural, legal, fiscal, or economic investigations or studies, surveys, designs, plans, working drawings, specifications, procedures, field testing of innovative or alternative waste water

treatment processes and techniques meeting guidelines promulgated under section 1314(d)(3) of this title, or other necessary actions, erection, building, acquisition, alteration, remodeling, improvement, or extension of treatment works, or the inspection or supervision of any of the foregoing items.

(2)(A) The term "treatment works" means any devices and systems used in the storage, treatment, recycling, and reclamation of municipal sewage or industrial wastes of a liquid nature to implement section 1281 of this title, or necessary to recycle or reuse water at the most economical cost over the estimated life of the works, including intercepting sewers, outfall sewers, sewage collection systems, pumping, power, and other equipment, and their appurtenances; extensions, improvements, remodeling, additions, and alterations thereof; elements essential to provide a reliable recycled supply such as standby treatment units and clear well facilities; and any works, including site acquisition of the land that will be an integral part of the treatment process (including land used for the storage of treated wastewater in land treatment systems prior to land application) or is used for ultimate disposal of residues resulting from such treatment.

**(B)** In addition to the definition contained in subparagraph (A) of this paragraph, "treatment works" means any other method or system for preventing, abating, reducing, storing, treating, separating, or disposing of municipal waste, including storm water runoff, or industrial waste, including waste in combined storm water and sanitary sewer systems. Any application for construction grants which includes wholly or in part such methods or systems shall, in accordance with guidelines published by the Administrator pursuant to subparagraph (C) of this paragraph, contain adequate data and analysis demonstrating such proposal to be, over the life of such works, the most cost efficient alternative to comply with sections 1311 or 1312 of this title, or the requirements of section 1281 of this title.

**(C)** For the purposes of subparagraph (B) of this paragraph, the Administrator shall, within one hundred and eighty days after October 18, 1972, publish and thereafter revise no less often than annually, guidelines for the evaluation of methods, including cost-effective analysis, described in subparagraph (B) of this paragraph.

(3) The term "replacement" as used in this subchapter means those expenditures for obtaining and installing equipment, accessories, or appurtenances during the useful life of the treatment works necessary to maintain the capacity and performance for which such works are designed and constructed.

(June 30, 1948, c. 758, Title II, § 212, as added Oct. 18, 1972, Pub.L. 92–500, § 2, 86 Stat. 844, and amended Dec. 27, 1977, Pub.L. 95–217, § 37, 91 Stat. 1581; Dec. 29, 1981, Pub.L. 97–117, § 8(d), 95 Stat. 1626.)

## § 1293. Loan guarantees

**[FWPCA § 213]**

### (a) State or local obligations issued exclusively to Federal Financing Bank for publicly owned treatment works; determination of eligibility of project by Administrator

Subject to the conditions of this section and to such terms and conditions as the Administrator determines to be necessary to carry out the purposes of this subchapter, the Administrator is authorized to guarantee, and to make commitments to guarantee, the principal and interest (including interest accruing between the date of default and the date of the payment in full of the guarantee) of any loan, obligation, or participation therein of any State, municipality, or intermunicipal or interstate agency issued directly and exclusively to the Federal Financing Bank to finance that part of the cost of any grant-eligible project for the construction of publicly owned treatment works not paid for with Federal financial assistance under this subchapter (other than this section), which project the Administrator has determined to be eligible for such financial assistance under this subchapter, including, but not limited to, projects eligible for reimbursement under section 1286 of this title.

### (b) Conditions for issuance

No guarantee, or commitment to make a guarantee, may be made pursuant to this section—

(1) unless the Administrator certifies that the issuing body is unable to obtain on reasonable terms sufficient credit to finance its actual needs without such guarantee; and

(2) unless the Administrator determines that there is a reasonable assurance of repayment of the loan, obligation, or participation therein.

A determination of whether financing is available at reasonable rates shall be made by the Secretary of the Treasury with relationship to the current average yield on outstanding marketable obligations of municipalities of comparable maturity.

### (c) Fees for application investigation and issuance of commitment guarantee

The Administrator is authorized to charge reasonable fees for the investigation of an application for a guarantee and for the issuance of a commitment to make a guarantee.

**(d) Commitment for repayment**

The Administrator, in determining whether there is a reasonable assurance of repayment, may require a commitment which would apply to such repayment. Such commitment may include, but not be limited to, any funds received by such grantee from the amounts appropriated under section 1286 of this title.

(June 30, 1948, c. 758, Title II, § 213, as added Oct. 19, 1976, Pub.L. 94–558, 90 Stat. 2639, and amended Oct. 21, 1980, Pub.L. 96–483, § 2(e), 94 Stat. 2361.)

### HISTORICAL AND STATUTORY NOTES

**Effective and Applicability Provisions**

1980 Acts

Amendment by Pub.L. 96–483 effective Dec. 27, 1977, see section 2(g) of Pub.L. 96–483, set out as a note under section 1281 of this title.

## § 1293a. Contained spoil disposal facilities

**(a) Construction, operation, and maintenance; period; conditions; requirements**

The Secretary of the Army, acting through the Chief of Engineers, is authorized to construct, operate, and maintain, subject to the provisions of subsection (c) of this section, contained spoil disposal facilities of sufficient capacity for a period not to exceed ten years, to meet the requirements of this section. Before establishing each such facility, the Secretary of the Army shall obtain the concurrence of appropriate local governments and shall consider the views and recommendations of the Administrator of the Environmental Protection Agency and shall comply with requirements of section 1171 of this title, and of the National Environmental Policy Act of 1969 [42 U.S.C.A. § 4321 et seq.]. Section 401 of this title shall not apply to any facility authorized by this section.

**(b) Time for establishment; consideration of area needs; requirements**

The Secretary of the Army, acting through the Chief of Engineers, shall establish the contained spoil disposal facilities authorized in subsection (a) of this section at the earliest practicable date, taking into consideration the views and recommendations of the Administrator of the Environmental Protection Agency as to those areas which, in the Administrator's judgment, are most urgently in need of such facilities and pursuant to the requirements of the National Environmental Policy Act of 1969 [42 U.S.C.A. § 4321 et seq.] and the Federal Water Pollution Control Act [33 U.S.C.A. § 1251 et seq.].

**(c) Written agreement requirement; terms of agreement**

Prior to construction of any such facility, the appropriate State or States, interstate agency, municipality, or other appropriate political subdivision of the State shall agree in writing to (1) furnish all lands, easements, and rights-of-way necessary for the construction, operation, and maintenance of the facility; (2) contribute to the United States 25 per centum of the construction costs, such amount to be payable either in cash prior to construction, in installments during construction, or in installments, with interest at a rate to be determined by the Secretary of the Treasury, as of the beginning of the fiscal year in which construction is initiated, on the basis of the computed average interest rate payable by the Treasury upon its outstanding marketable public obligations, which are neither due or callable for redemption for fifteen years from date of issue; (3) hold and save the United States free from damages due to construction, operation, and maintenance of the facility; and (4) except as provided in subsection (f) of this section, maintain the facility after completion of its use for disposal purposes in a manner satisfactory to the Secretary of the Army.

**(d) Waiver of construction costs contribution from non-Federal interests; findings of participation in waste treatment facilities for general geographical area and compliance with water quality standards; waiver of payments in event of written agreement before occurrence of findings**

The requirement for appropriate non-Federal interest or interests to furnish an agreement to contribute 25 per centum of the construction costs as set forth in subsection (c) of this section shall be waived by the Secretary of the Army upon a finding by the Administrator of the Environmental Protection Agency that for the area to which such construction applies, the State or States involved, interstate agency, municipality, and other appropriate political subdivision of the State and industrial concerns are participating in and in compliance with an approved plan for the general geographical area of the dredging activity for construction, modification, expansion, or rehabilitation of waste treatment facilities and the Administrator has found that applicable water quality standards are not being violated. In the event such findings occur after the appropriate non-Federal interest or interests have entered into the agreement required by subsection (c) of this section, any payments due after the date of such findings as part of the required local contribution of 25 per centum of the construction costs shall be waived by the Secretary of the Army.

**(e) Federal payment of costs for disposal of dredged spoil from project**

Notwithstanding any other provision of law, all costs of disposal of dredged spoil from the project for the Great Lakes connecting channels, Michigan, shall be borne by the United States.

**(f) Title to lands, easements, and rights-of-way; retention by non-Federal interests; conveyance of facilities; agreement of transferee**

The participating non-Federal interest or interests shall retain title to all lands, easements, and rights-of-way furnished by it pursuant to subsection (c) of this section. A spoil disposal facility owned by a non-Federal interest or interests may be conveyed to another party only after completion of the facility's use for disposal purposes and after the transferee agrees in writing to use or maintain the facility in a manner which the Secretary of the Army determines to be satisfactory.

**(g) Federal licenses or permits; charges; remission of charge**

Any spoil disposal facilities constructed under the provisions of this section shall be made available to Federal licensees or permittees upon payment of an appropriate charge for such use. Twenty-five per centum of such charge shall be remitted to the participating non-Federal interest or interests except for those excused from contributing to the construction costs under subsections (d) and (e) of this section.

**(h) Provisions applicable to Great Lakes and their connecting channels**

This section, other than subsection (i), shall be applicable only to the Great Lakes and their connecting channels.

**(i) Research, study, and experimentation program relating to dredged spoil extended to navigable waters, etc.; cooperative program; scope of program; utilization of facilities and personnel of Federal agency**

The Chief of Engineers, under the direction of the Secretary of the Army, is hereby authorized to extend to all navigable waters, connecting channels, tributary streams, other waters of the United States and waters contiguous to the United States, a comprehensive program of research, study, and experimentation relating to dredged spoil. This program shall be carried out in cooperation with other Federal and State agencies, and shall include, but not be limited to, investigations on the characteristics of dredged spoil, and alternative methods of its disposal. To the extent that such study shall include the effects of such dredge spoil on water quality, the facilities and personnel of the Environmental Protection Agency shall be utilized.

**(j) Period for depositing dredged materials**

The Secretary of the Army, acting through the Chief of Engineers, is authorized to continue to deposit dredged materials into a contained spoil disposal facility constructed under this section until the Secretary determines that such facility is no longer needed for such purpose or that such facility is completely full.

**(k) Study and monitoring program**

**(1) Study**

The Secretary of the Army, acting through the Chief of Engineers, shall conduct a study of the materials disposed of in contained spoil disposal facilities constructed under this section for the purpose of determining whether or not toxic pollutants are present in such facilities and for the purpose of determining the concentration levels of each of such pollutants in such facilities.

**(2) Report**

Not later than 1 year after November 17, 1988, the Secretary shall transmit to Congress a report on the results of the study conducted under paragraph (1).

**(3) Inspection and monitoring program**

The Secretary shall conduct a program to inspect and monitor contained spoil disposal facilities constructed under this section for the purpose of determining whether or not toxic pollutants are leaking from such facilities.

**(4) Toxic pollutant defined**

For purposes of this subsection, the term "toxic pollutant" means those toxic pollutants referred to in section 1311(b)(2)(C) and 1311(b)(2)(D) of this title and such other pollutants as the Secretary, in consultation with the Administrator of the Environmental Protection Agency, determines are appropriate based on their effects on human health and the environment.

(Pub.L. 91–611, Title I, § 123, Dec. 31, 1970, 84 Stat. 1823; Pub.L. 93–251, Title I, § 23, Mar. 7, 1974, 88 Stat. 20; Pub.L. 100–676, § 24, Nov. 17, 1988, 102 Stat. 4027.)

**HISTORICAL AND STATUTORY NOTES**

**References in Text**

Section 1171 of this title, referred to in subsec. (a), was omitted as superseded.

The National Environmental Policy Act of 1969, referred to in subsecs. (a) and (b), is Pub.L. 91–190, Jan. 1, 1970, 83 Stat. 852, as amended, which is classified generally to chapter 55 (section 4321 et seq.) of Title 42, The Public Health and Welfare. For complete classification of this Act to the Code, see Short Title note set out under section 4321 of Title 42 and Tables volume.

The Federal Water Pollution Control Act, referred to in subsec. (b), is Act June 30, 1948, c. 758, as amended generally by Pub.L. 92–500, § 2, Oct. 18, 1972, 86 Stat. 816, which is classified generally to chapter 26 (section 1251 et seq.) of this title. For complete classification of this Act to the Code, see Short Title note set out under section 1251 of this title and Tables volume.

**Codifications**

Section was formerly classified to section 1165a of this title.

Section was not enacted as part of the Federal Water Pollution Control Act, which comprises this chapter.

**Great Lakes Confined Disposal Facilities**

Pub.L. 104–303, Title V, § 513, Oct. 12, 1996, 110 Stat. 3762, provided that:

"(a) **Assessment.**—Pursuant to the responsibilities of the Secretary under section 123 of the River and Harbor Act of 1970 (33 U.S.C. 1293a) [this section], the Secretary shall conduct an assessment of the general conditions of confined disposal facilities in the Great Lakes.

"(b) **Report.**—Not later than 3 years after the date of the enactment of this Act [Oct. 12, 1996], the Secretary shall transmit to Congress a report on the results of the assessment conducted under subsection (a), including the following:

"(1) A description of the cumulative effects of confined disposal facilities in the Great Lakes.

"(2) Recommendations for specific remediation actions for each confined disposal facility in the Great Lakes.

"(3) An evaluation of, and recommendations for, confined disposal facility management practices and technologies to conserve capacity at such facilities and to minimize adverse environmental effects at such facilities throughout the Great Lakes system."

## § 1294. Public information and education on recycling and reuse of wastewater, use of land treatment, and reduction of wastewater volume

**[FWPCA § 214]**

The Administrator shall develop and operate within one year of December 27, 1977, a continuing program of public information and education on recycling and reuse of wastewater (including sludge), the use of land treatment, and methods for the reduction of wastewater volume.

(June 30, 1948, c. 758, Title II, § 214, as added Dec. 27, 1977, Pub.L. 95–217, § 38, 91 Stat. 1581.)

## § 1295. Requirements for American materials

**[FWPCA § 215]**

Notwithstanding any other provision of law, no grant for which application is made after February 1, 1978, shall be made under this subchapter for any treatment works unless only such unmanufactured articles, materials, and supplies as have been mined or produced in the United States, and only such manufactured articles, materials, and supplies as have been manufactured in the United States, substantially all from articles, materials, or supplies mined, produced, or manufactured, as the case may be, in the United States will be used in such treatment works. This section shall not apply in any case where the Administrator determines, based upon those factors the Administrator deems relevant, including the available resources of the agency, it to be inconsistent with the public interest (including multilateral government procurement agreements) or the cost to be unreasonable, or if articles, materials, or supplies of the class or kind to be used or the articles, materials, or supplies from which they are manufactured are not mined, produced, or manufactured, as the case may be, in the United States in sufficient and reasonably available commercial quantities and of a satisfactory quality.

(June 30, 1948, c. 758, Title II, § 215, as added Dec. 27, 1977, Pub.L. 95–217, § 39, 91 Stat. 1581.)

## § 1296. Determination of priority of projects

**[FWPCA § 216]**

Notwithstanding any other provision of this chapter, the determination of the priority to be given each category of projects for construction of publicly owned treatment works within each State shall be made solely by that State, except that if the Administrator, after a public hearing, determines that a specific project will not result in compliance with the enforceable requirements of this chapter, such project shall be removed from the State's priority list and such State shall submit a revised priority list. These categories shall include, but not be limited to (A) secondary treatment, (B) more stringent treatment, (C) infiltration-in-flow correction, (D) major sewer system rehabilitation, (E) new collector sewers and appurtenances, (F) new interceptors and appurtenances, and (G) correction of combined sewer overflows. Not less than 25 per centum of funds allocated to a State in any fiscal year under this subchapter for construction of publicly owned treatment works in such State shall be obligated for those types of projects referred to in clauses (D), (E), (F), and (G) of this section, if such projects are on such State's priority list for that year and are otherwise eligible for funding in that fiscal year. It is the policy of Congress that projects for wastewater treatment and management undertaken with Federal financial assistance under this chapter by any State, municipality, or intermunicipal or interstate agency shall be projects which, in the estimation of the State, are designed to achieve optimum water quality management, consistent with the public health and water quality goals and requirements of this chapter.

(June 30, 1948, c. 758, Title II, § 216, as added Dec. 27, 1977, Pub.L. 95–217, § 40, 91 Stat. 1582, and amended Dec. 29, 1981, Pub.L. 97–117, § 18, 95 Stat. 1630.)

## § 1297. Guidelines for cost-effectiveness analysis

**[FWPCA § 217]**

Any guidelines for cost-effectiveness analysis published by the Administrator under this subchapter shall provide for the identification and selection of cost effective alternatives to comply with the objective and goals of this chapter and sections 1281(b), 1281(d), 1281(g)(2)(A), and 1311(b)(2)(B) of this title.

(June 30, 1948, c. 758, Title II, § 217, as added Dec. 27, 1977, Pub.L. 95–217, § 41, 91 Stat. 1582.)

## § 1298. Cost effectiveness

**[FWPCA § 218]**

**(a) Congressional statement of policy**

It is the policy of Congress that a project for waste treatment and management undertaken with Federal financial assistance under this chapter by any State, municipality, or intermunicipal or interstate agency shall be considered as an overall waste treatment system for waste treatment and management, and shall be that system which constitutes the most economical and cost-effective combination of devices and systems used in the storage, treatment, recycling, and reclamation of municipal sewage or industrial wastes of a liquid nature to implement section 1281 of this title, or necessary to recycle or reuse water at the most economical cost over the estimated life of the works, including intercepting sewers, outfall sewers, sewage collection systems, pumping power, and other equipment, and their appurtenances; extension, improvements, remodeling, additions, and alterations thereof; elements essential to provide a reliable recycled supply such as standby treatment units and clear well facilities; and any works, including site acquisition of the land that will be an integral part of the treatment process (including land use for the storage of treated wastewater in land treatment systems prior to land application) or which is used for ultimate disposal of residues resulting from such treatment; water efficiency measures and devices; and any other method or system for preventing, abating, reducing, storing, treating, separating, or disposing of municipal waste, including storm water runoff, or industrial waste, including waste in combined storm water and sanitary sewer systems; to meet the requirements of this chapter.

**(b) Determination by Administrator as prerequisite to approval of grant**

In accordance with the policy set forth in subsection (a) of this section, before the Administrator approves any grant to any State, municipality, or intermunicipal or interstate agency for the erection, building, acquisition, alteration, remodeling, improvement, or extension of any treatment works the Administrator shall determine that the facilities plan of which such treatment works are a part constitutes the most economical and cost-effective combination of treatment works over the life of the project to meet the requirements of this chapter, including, but not limited to, consideration of construction costs, operation, maintenance, and replacement costs.

**(c) Value engineering review**

In furtherance of the policy set forth in subsection (a) of this section, the Administrator shall require value engineering review in connection with any treatment works, prior to approval of any grant for the erection, building, acquisition, alteration, remodeling, improvement, or extension of such treatment works, in any case in which the cost of such erection, building, acquisition, alteration, remodeling, improvement, or extension is projected to be in excess of $10,000,000. For purposes of this subsection, the term "value engineering review" means a specialized cost control technique which uses a systematic and creative approach to identify and to focus on unnecessarily high cost in a project in order to arrive at a cost saving without sacrificing the reliability or efficiency of the project.

**(d) Projects affected**

This section applies to projects for waste treatment and management for which no treatment works including a facilities plan for such project have received Federal financial assistance for the preparation of construction plans and specifications under this chapter before December 29, 1981.

(June 30, 1948, c. 758, Title II, § 218, as added Dec. 29, 1981, Pub.L. 97–117, § 19, 95 Stat. 1630.)

## § 1299. State certification of projects

**[FWPCA § 219]**

Whenever the Governor of a State which has been delegated sufficient authority to administer the construction grant program under this subchapter in that State certifies to the Administrator that a grant application meets applicable requirements of Federal and State law for assistance under this subchapter, the Administrator shall approve or disapprove such application within 45 days of the date of receipt of such application. If the Administrator does not approve or disapprove such application within 45 days of receipt, the application shall be deemed approved. If the Administrator disapproves such application the Administrator shall state in writing the reasons for such disapproval. Any grant approved or deemed approved under this section shall be subject to amounts provided in appropriation Acts.

(June 30, 1948, c. 758, Title II, § 219, as added Dec. 29, 1981, Pub.L. 97–117, § 20, 95 Stat. 1631.)

## § 1300. Pilot program for alternative water source projects

**[FWPCA § 220]**

**(a) Policy**

Nothing in this section shall be construed to affect the application of section 1251(g) of this title and all of the provisions of this section shall be carried out in accordance with the provisions of section 1251(g) of this title.

**(b) In general**

The Administrator may establish a pilot program to make grants to State, interstate, and intrastate water resource development agencies (including water management districts and water supply authorities), local government agencies, private utilities, and nonprofit entities for alternative water source projects to meet critical water supply needs.

**(c) Eligible entity**

The Administrator may make grants under this section to an entity only if the entity has authority under State law to develop or provide water for municipal, industrial, and agricultural uses in an area of the State that is experiencing critical water supply needs.

**(d) Selection of projects**

**(1) Limitation**

A project that has received funds under the reclamation and reuse program conducted under the Reclamation Projects Authorization and Adjustment Act of 1992 (43 U.S.C. 390h et seq.) shall not be eligible for grant assistance under this section.

**(2) Additional consideration**

In making grants under this section, the Administrator shall consider whether the project is located within the boundaries of a State or area referred to in section 391 of Title 43, and within the geographic scope of the reclamation and reuse program conducted under the Reclamation Projects Authorization and Adjustment Act of 1992 (43 U.S.C. 390h et seq.).

**(3) Geographical distribution**

Alternative water source projects selected by the Administrator under this section shall reflect a variety of geographical and environmental conditions.

**(e) Committee resolution procedure**

**(1) In general**

No appropriation shall be made for any alternative water source project under this section, the total Federal cost of which exceeds $3,000,000, if such project has not been approved by a resolution adopted by the Committee on Transportation and Infrastructure of the House of Representatives or the Committee on Environment and Public Works of the Senate.

**(2) Requirements for securing consideration**

For purposes of securing consideration of approval under paragraph (1), the Administrator shall provide to a committee referred to in paragraph (1) such information as the committee requests and the non-Federal sponsor shall provide to the committee information on the costs and relative needs for the alternative water source project.

**(f) Uses of grants**

Amounts from grants received under this section may be used for engineering, design, construction, and final testing of alternative water source projects designed to meet critical water supply needs. Such amounts may not be used for planning, feasibility studies or for operation, maintenance, replacement, repair, or rehabilitation.

**(g) Cost sharing**

The Federal share of the eligible costs of an alternative water source project carried out using assistance made available under this section shall not exceed 50 percent.

**(h) Reports**

On or before September 30, 2004, the Administrator shall transmit to Congress a report on the results of the pilot program established under this section, including progress made toward meeting the critical water supply needs of the participants in the pilot program.

**(i) Definitions**

In this section, the following definitions apply:

**(1) Alternative water source project**

The term "alternative water source project" means a project designed to provide municipal, industrial, and agricultural water supplies in an environmentally sustainable manner by conserving, managing, reclaiming, or reusing water or wastewater or by treating wastewater. Such term does not include water treatment or distribution facilities.

**(2) Critical water supply needs**

The term "critical water supply needs" means existing or reasonably anticipated future water supply needs that cannot be met by existing water supplies, as identified in a comprehensive statewide or regional water supply plan or assessment projected over a planning period of at least 20 years.

**(j) Authorization of appropriations**

There is authorized to be appropriated to carry out this section a total of $75,000,000 for fiscal years 2002 through 2004. Such sums shall remain available until expended.

(June 30, 1948, c. 758, Title II, § 220, as added Nov. 7, 2000, Pub.L. 106–457, Title VI, § 602, 114 Stat. 1975.)

HISTORICAL AND STATUTORY NOTES

**References in Text**

The Reclamation Projects Authorization and Adjustment Act of 1992, referred to in subsec. (d)(1), (2), is Pub.L. 102–575, Oct. 30, 1992, 106 Stat. 4600, as amended. Provisions relating to the reclamation and reuse program are classified principally to 43 U.S.C.A. § 390h et seq. See Short Title of 1992 Amendment note set out under 43 U.S.C.A. § 371 and Tables for complete classification.

Section 1 of the Reclamation Act of June 17, 1902, referred to in subsec. (d)(2), probably means Act June 17, 1902, c. 1093, § 1, 32 Stat. 388, which is classified to section 391 of Title 43.

## § 1301. Sewer overflow control grants [FWPCA § 221]

**(a) In general**

In any fiscal year in which the Administrator has available for obligation at least $1,350,000,000 for the purposes of section 1381 of this title—

(1) the Administrator may make grants to States for the purpose of providing grants to a municipality or municipal entity for planning, design, and construction of treatment works to intercept, transport, control, or treat municipal combined sewer overflows and sanitary sewer overflows; and

(2) subject to subsection (g) of this section, the Administrator may make a direct grant to a municipality or municipal entity for the purposes described in paragraph (1).

**(b) Prioritization**

In selecting from among municipalities applying for grants under subsection (a) of this section, a State or the Administrator shall give priority to an applicant that—

(1) is a municipality that is a financially distressed community under subsection (c) of this section;

(2) has implemented or is complying with an implementation schedule for the nine minimum controls specified in the CSO control policy referred to in section 1342(q)(1) of this title and has begun implementing a long-term municipal combined sewer overflow control plan or a separate sanitary sewer overflow control plan;

(3) is requesting a grant for a project that is on a State's intended use plan pursuant to section 1386(c) of this title; or

(4) is an Alaska Native Village.

**(c) Financially distressed community**

**(1) Definition**

In subsection (b) of this section, the term "financially distressed community" means a community that meets affordability criteria established by the State in which the community is located, if such criteria are developed after public review and comment.

**(2) Consideration of impact on water and sewer rates**

In determining if a community is a distressed community for the purposes of subsection (b) of this section, the State shall consider, among other factors, the extent to which the rate of growth of a community's tax base has been historically slow such that implementing a plan described in subsection (b)(2) of this section would result in a significant increase in any water or sewer rate charged by the community's publicly owned wastewater treatment facility.

**(3) Information to assist States**

The Administrator may publish information to assist States in establishing affordability criteria under paragraph (1).

**(d) Cost-sharing**

The Federal share of the cost of activities carried out using amounts from a grant made under subsection (a) of this section shall be not less than 55 percent of the cost. The non-Federal share of the cost may include, in any amount, public and private funds and in-kind services, and may include, notwithstanding section 1383(h) of this title, financial assistance, including loans, from a State water pollution control revolving fund.

**(e) Administrative reporting requirements**

If a project receives grant assistance under subsection (a) of this section and loan assistance from a State water pollution control revolving fund and the loan assistance is for 15 percent or more of the cost of the project, the project may be administered in accordance with State water pollution control revolving fund administrative reporting requirements for the purposes of streamlining such requirements.

**(f) Authorization of appropriations**

There is authorized to be appropriated to carry out this section $750,000,000 for each of fiscal years 2002 and 2003. Such sums shall remain available until expended.

**(g) Allocation of funds**

**(1) Fiscal year 2002**

Subject to subsection (h) of this section, the Administrator shall use the amounts appropriated to carry out this section for fiscal year 2002 for making grants to municipalities and municipal entities under subsection (a)(2) of this section, in accordance with the criteria set forth in subsection (b) of this section.

**(2) Fiscal year 2003**

Subject to subsection (h) of this section, the Administrator shall use the amounts appropriated to carry out this section for fiscal year 2003 as follows:

**(A)** Not to exceed $250,000,000 for making grants to municipalities and municipal entities under subsection (a)(2) of this section, in accordance with the criteria set forth in subsection (b) of this section.

**(B)** All remaining amounts for making grants to States under subsection (a)(1) of this section, in accordance with a formula to be established by the Administrator, after providing notice and an opportunity for public comment, that allocates to each State a proportional share of such amounts based on the total needs of the State for municipal combined sewer overflow controls and sanitary sewer overflow controls identified in the most recent survey conducted pursuant to section 1375(b)(1) of this title.

**(h) Administrative expenses**

Of the amounts appropriated to carry out this section for each fiscal year—

**(1)** the Administrator may retain an amount not to exceed 1 percent for the reasonable and necessary costs of administering this section; and

**(2)** the Administrator, or a State, may retain an amount not to exceed 4 percent of any grant made to a municipality or municipal entity under subsection (a) of this section, for the reasonable and necessary costs of administering the grant.

**(i) Reports**

Not later than December 31, 2003, and periodically thereafter, the Administrator shall transmit to Congress a report containing recommended funding levels for grants under this section. The recommended funding levels shall be sufficient to ensure the continued expeditious implementation of municipal combined sewer overflow and sanitary sewer overflow controls nationwide.

(June 30, 1948, c. 758, Title II, § 221, as added Pub.L. 106–554, § 1(a)(4) [Div. B, Title I, § 112(c)], Dec. 21, 2000, 114 Stat. 2763, 2763A–225.)

**HISTORICAL AND STATUTORY NOTES**

**References in Text**

Section 1375 of this title, referred to in subsec. (g)(2)(B), was amended by Pub.L. 105–362, Title V, § 501(d)(1), Nov. 10, 1998, 112 Stat. 3283, and, as so amended, no longer contains subsections.

**Information on CSOS and SSOS.—**

Pub.L. 106–554, § 1(a)(4) [Div. B, Title I, § 112(d)], Dec. 21, 2000, 114 Stat. 2763, 2763a-227, provided that:

"(1) **Report to Congress.**—Not later than 3 years after December 21, 2000, the Administrator of the Environmental Protection Agency shall transmit to Congress a report summarizing—

"(A) the extent of the human health and environmental impacts caused by municipal combined sewer overflows and sanitary sewer overflows, including the location of discharges causing such impacts, the volume of pollutants discharged, and the constituents discharged;

"(B) the resources spent by municipalities to address these impacts; and

"(C) an evaluation of the technologies used by municipalities to address these impacts.

"(2) **Technology clearinghouse.**—After transmitting a report under paragraph (1), the Administrator shall maintain a clearinghouse of cost- effective and efficient technologies for addressing human health and environmental impacts due to municipal combined sewer overflows and sanitary sewer overflows."

## SUBCHAPTER III—STANDARDS AND ENFORCEMENT

## § 1311. Effluent limitations

**[FWPCA § 301]**

**(a) Illegality of pollutant discharges except in compliance with law**

Except as in compliance with this section and sections 1312, 1316, 1317, 1328, 1342, and 1344 of this title, the discharge of any pollutant by any person shall be unlawful.

**(b) Timetable for achievement of objectives**

In order to carry out the objective of this chapter there shall be achieved—

**(1)(A)** not later than July 1, 1977, effluent limitations for point sources, other than publicly owned treatment works, (i) which shall require the application of the best practicable control technology currently available as defined by the Administrator pursuant to section 1314(b) of this title, or (ii) in the case of a discharge into a publicly owned treatment works which meets the requirements of subparagraph (B) of this paragraph, which shall require compliance with any applicable pretreatment requirements and any requirements under section 1317 of this title; and

**(B)** for publicly owned treatment works in existence on July 1, 1977, or approved pursuant to section 1283 of this title prior to June 30, 1974 (for which construction must be completed within four years of approval), effluent limitations based upon secondary treatment as defined by the Administrator pursuant to section 1314(d)(1) of this title; or,

**(C)** not later than July 1, 1977, any more stringent limitation, including those necessary to meet water quality standards, treatment standards, or schedules of compliance, established pursuant to any State law or regulations (under authority preserved by section 1370 of this title) or any other Federal law or regulation, or required to implement any applicable water quality standard established pursuant to this chapter.

**(2)(A)** for pollutants identified in subparagraphs (C), (D), and (F) of this paragraph, effluent limitations for categories and classes of point sources, other than publicly owned treatment works, which (i) shall require application of the best available technology economically achievable for such category or class, which will result in reasonable further progress toward the national goal of eliminating the discharge of all pollutants, as determined in accordance with regulations issued by the Administrator pursuant to section 1314(b)(2) of this title, which such effluent limitations shall require the elimination of discharges of all pollutants if the Administrator finds, on the basis of information available to him (including information developed pursuant to section 1325 of this title), that such elimination is technologically and economically achievable for a category or class of point sources as determined in accordance with regulations issued by the Administrator pursuant to section 1314(b)(2) of this title, or (ii) in the case of the introduction of a pollutant into a publicly owned treatment works which meets the requirements of subparagraph (B) of this paragraph, shall require compliance with any applicable pretreatment requirements and any other requirement under section 1317 of this title;

**(B)** Repealed. Pub.L. 97–117, § 21(b), Dec. 29, 1981, 95 Stat. 1632.

**(C)** with respect to all toxic pollutants referred to in table 1 of Committee Print Numbered 95–30 of the Committee on Public Works and Transportation of the House of Representatives compliance with effluent limitations in accordance with subparagraph (A) of this paragraph as expeditiously as practicable but in no case later than three years after the date such limitations are promulgated under section 1314(b) of this title, and in no case later than March 31, 1989;

**(D)** for all toxic pollutants listed under paragraph (1) of subsection (a) of section 1317 of this title which are not referred to in subparagraph (C) of this paragraph compliance with effluent limitations in accordance with subparagraph (A) of this paragraph as expeditiously as practicable, but in no case later than three years after the date such limitations are promulgated under section 1314(b) of this title, and in no case later than March 31, 1989;

**(E)** as expeditiously as practicable but in no case later than three years after the date such limitations are promulgated under section 1314(b) of this title, and in no case later than March 31, 1989, compliance with effluent limitations for categories and classes of point sources, other than publicly owned treatment works, which in the case of pollutants identified pursuant to section 1314(a)(4) of this title shall require application of the best conventional pollutant control technology as determined in accordance with regulations issued by the Administrator pursuant to section 1314(b)(4) of this title; and

**(F)** for all pollutants (other than those subject to subparagraphs (C), (D), or (E) of this paragraph) compliance with effluent limitations in accordance with subparagraph (A) of this paragraph as expeditiously as practicable but in no case later than 3 years after the date such limitations are established, and in no case later than March 31, 1989.

**(3)(A)** for effluent limitations under paragraph (1)(A)(i) of this subsection promulgated after January 1, 1982, and requiring a level of control substantially greater or based on fundamentally different control technology than under permits for an industrial category issued before such date, compliance as expeditiously as practicable but in no case later than three years after the date such limitations are promulgated under section 1314(b) of this title, and in no case later than March 31, 1989; and

**(B)** for any effluent limitation in accordance with paragraph (1)(A)(i), (2)(A)(i), or (2)(E) of this subsection established only on the basis of section 1342(a)(1) of this title in a permit issued after February 4, 1987, compliance as expeditiously as practicable but in no case later than three years after the date such limitations are established, and in no case later than March 31, 1989.

### (c) Modification of timetable

The Administrator may modify the requirements of subsection (b)(2)(A) of this section with respect to any point source for which a permit application is filed after July 1, 1977, upon a showing by the owner or operator of such point source satisfactory to the Administrator that such modified requirements (1) will represent the maximum use of technology within the economic capability of the owner or operator; and (2) will result in reasonable further progress toward the elimination of the discharge of pollutants.

### (d) Review and revision of effluent limitations

Any effluent limitation required by paragraph (2) of subsection (b) of this section shall be reviewed at least every five years and, if appropriate, revised pursuant to the procedure established under such paragraph.

### (e) All point discharge source application of effluent limitations

Effluent limitations established pursuant to this section or section 1312 of this title shall be applied to all point sources of discharge of pollutants in accordance with the provisions of this chapter.

**(f) Illegality of discharge of radiological, chemical, or biological warfare agents, high-level radioactive waste, or medical waste**

Notwithstanding any other provisions of this chapter it shall be unlawful to discharge any radiological, chemical, or biological warfare agent, any high-level radioactive waste, or any medical waste, into the navigable waters.

**(g) Modifications for certain nonconventional pollutants**

**(1) General authority**

The Administrator, with the concurrence of the State, may modify the requirements of subsection (b)(2)(A) of this section with respect to the discharge from any point source of ammonia, chlorine, color, iron, and total phenols (4AAP) (when determined by the Administrator to be a pollutant covered by subsection (b)(2)(F) of this section) and any other pollutant which the Administrator lists under paragraph (4) of this subsection.

**(2) Requirements for granting modifications**

A modification under this subsection shall be granted only upon a showing by the owner or operator of a point source satisfactory to the Administrator that—

(A) such modified requirements will result at a minimum in compliance with the requirements of subsection (b)(1)(A) or (C) of this section, whichever is applicable;

(B) such modified requirements will not result in any additional requirements on any other point or nonpoint source; and

(C) such modification will not interfere with the attainment or maintenance of that water quality which shall assure protection of public water supplies, and the protection and propagation of a balanced population of shellfish, fish, and wildlife, and allow recreational activities, in and on the water and such modification will not result in the discharge of pollutants in quantities which may reasonably be anticipated to pose an unacceptable risk to human health or the environment because of bioaccumulation, persistency in the environment, acute toxicity, chronic toxicity (including carcinogenicity, mutagenicity or teratogenicity), or synergistic propensities.

**(3) Limitation on authority to apply for subsection (c) modification**

If an owner or operator of a point source applies for a modification under this subsection with respect to the discharge of any pollutant, such owner or operator shall be eligible to apply for modification under subsection (c) of this section with respect to such pollutant only during the same time period as he is eligible to apply for a modification under this subsection.

**(4) Procedures for listing additional pollutants**

**(A) General authority**

Upon petition of any person, the Administrator may add any pollutant to the list of pollutants for which modification under this section is authorized (except for pollutants identified pursuant to section 1314(a)(4) of this title, toxic pollutants subject to section 1317(a) of this title, and the thermal component of discharges) in accordance with the provisions of this paragraph.

**(B) Requirements for listing**

**(i) Sufficient information**

The person petitioning for listing of an additional pollutant under this subsection shall submit to the Administrator sufficient information to make the determinations required by this subparagraph.

**(ii) Toxic criteria determination**

The Administrator shall determine whether or not the pollutant meets the criteria for listing as a toxic pollutant under section 1317(a) of this title.

**(iii) Listing as toxic pollutant**

If the Administrator determines that the pollutant meets the criteria for listing as a toxic pollutant under section 1317(a) of this title, the Administrator shall list the pollutant as a toxic pollutant under section 1317(a) of this title.

**(iv) Nonconventional criteria determination**

If the Administrator determines that the pollutant does not meet the criteria for listing as a toxic pollutant under such section and determines that adequate test methods and sufficient data are available to make the determinations required by paragraph (2) of this subsection with respect to the pollutant, the Administrator shall add the pollutant to the list of pollutants specified in paragraph (1) of this subsection for which modifications are authorized under this subsection.

**(C) Requirements for filing of petitions**

A petition for listing of a pollutant under this paragraph—

(i) must be filed not later than 270 days after the date of promulgation of an applicable effluent guideline under section 1314 of this title;

(ii) may be filed before promulgation of such guideline; and

(iii) may be filed with an application for a modification under paragraph (1) with respect to the discharge of such pollutant.

**(D) Deadline for approval of petition**

A decision to add a pollutant to the list of pollutants for which modifications under this subsection are authorized must be made within 270 days after the date of promulgation of an applicable effluent guideline under section 1314 of this title.

**(E) Burden of proof**

The burden of proof for making the determinations under subparagraph (B) shall be on the petitioner.

**(5) Removal of pollutants**

The Administrator may remove any pollutant from the list of pollutants for which modifications are authorized under this subsection if the Administrator determines that adequate test methods and sufficient data are no longer available for determining whether or not modifications may be granted with respect to such pollutant under paragraph (2) of this subsection.

**(h) Modification of secondary treatment requirements**

The Administrator, with the concurrence of the State, may issue a permit under section 1342 of this title which modifies the requirements of subsection (b)(1)(B) of this section with respect to the discharge of any pollutant from a publicly owned treatment works into marine waters, if the applicant demonstrates to the satisfaction of the Administrator that—

(1) there is an applicable water quality standard specific to the pollutant for which the modification is requested, which has been identified under section 1314(a)(6) of this title;

(2) the discharge of pollutants in accordance with such modified requirements will not interfere, alone or in combination with pollutants from other sources, with the attainment or maintenance of that water quality which assures protection of public water supplies and the protection and propagation of a balanced, indigenous population of shellfish, fish, and wildlife, and allows recreational activities, in and on the water;

(3) the applicant has established a system for monitoring the impact of such discharge on a representative sample of aquatic biota, to the extent practicable, and the scope of such monitoring is limited to include only those scientific investigations which are necessary to study the effects of the proposed discharge;

(4) such modified requirements will not result in any additional requirements on any other point or nonpoint source;

(5) all applicable pretreatment requirements for sources introducing waste into such treatment works will be enforced;

(6) in the case of any treatment works serving a population of 50,000 or more, with respect to any toxic pollutant introduced into such works by an industrial discharger for which pollutant there is no applicable pretreatment requirement in effect, sources introducing waste into such works are in compliance with all applicable pretreatment requirements, the applicant will enforce such requirements, and the applicant has in effect a pretreatment program which, in combination with the treatment of discharges from such works, removes the same amount of such pollutant as would be removed if such works were to apply secondary treatment to discharges and if such works had no pretreatment program with respect to such pollutant;

(7) to the extent practicable, the applicant has established a schedule of activities designed to eliminate the entrance of toxic pollutants from nonindustrial sources into such treatment works;

(8) there will be no new or substantially increased discharges from the point source of the pollutant to which the modification applies above that volume of discharge specified in the permit;

(9) the applicant at the time such modification becomes effective will be discharging effluent which has received at least primary or equivalent treatment and which meets the criteria established under section 1314(a)(1) of this title after initial mixing in the waters surrounding or adjacent to the point at which such effluent is discharged.

For the purposes of this subsection the phrase "the discharge of any pollutant into marine waters" refers to a discharge into deep waters of the territorial sea or the waters of the contiguous zone, or into saline estuarine waters where there is strong tidal movement and other hydrological and geological characteristics which the Administrator determines necessary to allow compliance with paragraph (2) of this subsection, and section 1251(a)(2) of this title. For the purposes of paragraph (9), "primary or equivalent treatment" means treatment by screening, sedimentation, and skimming adequate to remove at least 30 percent of the biological oxygen demanding material and of the suspended solids in the treatment works influent, and disinfection, where appropriate. A municipality which applies secondary treatment shall be eligible to receive a permit pursuant to this subsection which modifies the requirements of subsection (b)(1)(B) of this section with respect to the discharge of any pollutant from any treatment works owned by such municipality into marine waters. No permit issued under this subsection shall authorize the discharge of sewage sludge into marine waters. In order for a permit to be issued under this subsection for the discharge of a pollutant into marine waters, such marine waters must exhibit characteristics assuring that water providing dilution does not contain significant amounts of previously discharged effluent from such treatment works. No permit issued under this subsection shall authorize the discharge of any pollutant into saline estuarine waters which at the time of application do not support a balanced indigenous population of shellfish, fish and wildlife, or allow recreation in and on the waters or which exhibit ambient water quality below applicable water quality standards adopted for the protection of public water supplies, shellfish, fish and wildlife or recreational activities or such other standards necessary to assure support and protection of such uses. The prohibition contained in the preceding sentence shall apply without regard to the presence or absence of a causal relationship between such characteristics and the applicant's current or proposed discharge. Notwithstanding any other provisions of this subsection, no permit may be issued under this subsection for discharge of a pollutant into the New York Bight Apex consisting of the ocean waters of the Atlantic Ocean westward of 73 degrees 30 minutes west longitude and northward of 40 degrees 10 minutes north latitude.

**(i) Municipal time extensions**

**(1)** Where construction is required in order for a planned or existing publicly owned treatment works to achieve limitations under subsection (b)(1)(B) or (b)(1)(C) of this section, but (A) construction cannot be completed within the time required in such subsection, or (B) the United States has failed to make financial assistance under this chapter available in time to achieve such limitations by the time specified in such subsection, the owner or operator of such treatment works may request the Administrator (or if appropriate the State) to issue a permit pursuant to section 1342 of this title or to modify a permit issued pursuant to that section to extend such time for compliance. Any such request shall be filed with the Administrator (or if appropriate the State) within 180 days after February 4, 1987. The Administrator (or if appropriate the State) may grant such request and issue or modify such a permit, which shall contain a schedule of compliance for the publicly owned treatment works based on the earliest date by which such financial assistance will be available from the United States and construction can be completed, but in no event later than July 1, 1988, and shall contain such other terms and conditions, including those necessary to carry out subsections (b) through (g) of section 1281 of this title, section 1317 of this title, and such interim effluent limitations applicable to that treatment works as the Administrator determines are necessary to carry out the provisions of this chapter.

**(2)(A)** Where a point source (other than a publicly owned treatment works) will not achieve the requirements of subsections (b)(1)(A) and (b)(1)(C) of this section and—

**(i)** if a permit issued prior to July 1, 1977, to such point source is based upon a discharge into a publicly owned treatment works; or

**(ii)** if such point source (other than a publicly owned treatment works) had before July 1, 1977, a contract (enforceable against such point source) to discharge into a publicly owned treatment works; or

**(iii)** if either an application made before July 1, 1977, for a construction grant under this chapter for a publicly owned treatment works, or engineering or architectural plans or working drawings made before July 1, 1977, for a publicly owned treatment works, show that such point source was to discharge into such publicly owned treatment works,

and such publicly owned treatment works is presently unable to accept such discharge without construction, and in the case of a discharge to an existing publicly owned treatment works, such treatment works has an extension pursuant to paragraph (1) of this subsection, the owner or operator of such point source may request the Administrator (or if appropriate the State) to issue or modify such a permit pursuant to such section 1342 of this title to extend such time for compliance. Any such request shall be filed with the Administrator (or if appropriate the State) within 180 days after December 27, 1977, or the filing of a request by the appropriate publicly owned treatment works under paragraph (1) of this subsection, whichever is later. If the Administrator (or if appropriate the State) finds that the owner or operator of such point source has acted in good faith, he may grant such request and issue or modify such a permit, which shall contain a schedule of compliance for the point source to achieve the requirements of subsections (b)(1)(A) and (C) of this section and shall contain such other terms and conditions, including pretreatment and interim effluent limitations and water conservation requirements applicable to that point source, as the Administrator determines are necessary to carry out the provisions of this chapter.

**(B)** No time modification granted by the Administrator (or if appropriate the State) pursuant to paragraph (2)(A) of this subsection shall extend beyond the earliest date practicable for compliance or beyond the date of any extension granted to the appropriate publicly owned treatment works pursuant to paragraph (1) of this subsection, but in no event shall it extend beyond July 1, 1988; and no such time modification shall be granted unless (i) the publicly owned treatment works will be in operation and available to the point source before July 1, 1988, and will meet the requirements of subsections (b)(1)(B) and (C) of this section after receiving the discharge from that point source; and (ii) the point source and the publicly owned treatment works have entered into an enforceable contract requiring the point source to discharge into the publicly owned treatment works, the owner or operator of such point source to pay the costs required under section 1284 of this title, and the publicly owned treatment works to accept the discharge from the point source; and (iii) the permit for such point source requires that point source to meet all requirements under section 1317(a) and (b) of this title during the period of such time modification.

**(j) Modification procedures**

(1) Any application filed under this section for a modification of the provisions of—

**(A)** subsection (b)(1)(B) of this section under subsection (h) of this section shall be filed not later that[1] the 365th day which begins after December 29, 1981, except that a publicly owned treatment works which prior to December 31, 1982, had a contractual arrangement to use a portion of the capacity of an ocean outfall operated by another publicly owned treatment works which has applied for or received modification under subsection (h) of this section, may apply for a modification of subsection (h) of this section in its own right not later than 30 days after February 4, 1987, and except as provided in paragraph (5);

**(B)** subsection (b)(2)(A) of this section as it applies to pollutants identified in subsection (b)(2)(F) of this section shall be filed not later than 270 days after the date of promulgation of an applicable effluent guideline under section 1314 of this title or not later than 270 days after December 27, 1977, whichever is later.

(2) Subject to paragraph (3) of this section, any application for a modification filed under subsection (g) of this section shall not operate to stay any requirement under this chapter, unless in the judgment of the Administrator such a stay or the modification sought will not result in the discharge of pollutants in quantities which may reasonably be anticipated to pose an unacceptable risk to human health or the environment because of bioaccumulation, persistency in the environment, acute toxicity, chronic toxicity (including carcinogenicity, mutagenicity, or teratogenicity), or synergistic propensities, and that there is a substantial likelihood that the applicant will succeed on the merits of such application. In the case of an application filed under subsection (g) of this section, the Administrator may condition any stay granted under this paragraph on requiring the filing of a bond or other appropriate security to assure timely compliance with the requirements from which a modification is sought.

**(3) Compliance requirements under subsection (g)**

**(A) Effect of filing**

An application for a modification under subsection (g) of this section and a petition for listing of a pollutant as a pollutant for which modifications are authorized under such subsection shall not stay the requirement that the person seeking such modification or listing comply with effluent limitations under this chapter for all pollutants not the subject of such application or petition.

**(B) Effect of disapproval**

Disapproval of an application for a modification under subsection (g) of this section shall not stay the requirement that the person seeking such modification comply with all applicable effluent limitations under this chapter.

**(4) Deadline for subsection (g) decision**

An application for a modification with respect to a pollutant filed under subsection (g) of this section must be approved or disapproved not later than 365 days after the date of such filing; except that in any case in which a petition for listing such pollutant as a pollutant for which modifications are authorized under such subsection is approved, such application must be approved or disapproved not later than 365 days after the date of approval of such petition.

**(5) Extension of application deadline**

**(A) In general**

In the 180–day period beginning on October 31, 1994, the city of San Diego, California, may apply for a modification pursuant to subsection (h) of this section of the requirements of subsection (b)(1)(B) of this section with respect to biological oxygen demand and total suspended solids in the effluent discharged into marine waters.

**(B) Application**

An application under this paragraph shall include a commitment by the applicant to implement a waste water reclamation program that, at a minimum, will—

**(i)** achieve a system capacity of 45,000,000 gallons of reclaimed waste water per day by January 1, 2010; and

**(ii)** result in a reduction in the quantity of suspended solids discharged by the applicant into the marine environment during the period of the modification.

**(C) Additional conditions**

The Administrator may not grant a modification pursuant to an application submitted under this paragraph unless the Administrator determines that such modification will result in removal of not less than 58 percent of the biological oxygen demand (on an annual average) and not less than 80 percent of total suspended solids (on a monthly average) in the discharge to which the application applies.

**(D) Preliminary decision deadline**

The Administrator shall announce a preliminary decision on an application submitted under this paragraph not later than 1 year after the date the application is submitted.

**(k) Innovative technology**

In the case of any facility subject to a permit under section 1342 of this title which proposes to comply with the requirements of subsection (b)(2)(A) or (b)(2)(E) of this section by replacing existing production capacity with an innovative production process which will result in an effluent reduction significantly greater than that required by the limitation otherwise applicable to such facility and moves toward the national goal of eliminating the discharge of all pollutants, or with the installation of an innovative control technique that has a substantial likelihood for enabling the facility to comply with the applicable effluent limitation by achieving a significantly greater effluent reduction than that required by the applicable effluent limitation and moves toward the national goal of eliminating the discharge of all pollutants, or by achieving the required reduction with an innovative system that has the potential for significantly lower costs than the systems which have been determined by the Administrator to be economically achievable, the Administrator (or the State with an approved program under section 1342 of this title, in consultation with the Administrator) may establish a date for compliance under subsection (b)(2)(A) or (b)(2)(E) of this section no later than two years after the date for compliance with such effluent limitation which would otherwise be applicable under such subsection, if it is also determined that such innovative system has the potential for industrywide application.

**(*l*) Toxic pollutants**

Other than as provided in subsection (n) of this section, the Administrator may not modify any requirement of this section as it applies to any specific pollutant which is on the toxic pollutant list under section 1317(a)(1) of this title.

**(m) Modification of effluent limitation requirements for point sources**

(1) The Administrator, with the concurrence of the State, may issue a permit under section 1342 of this title which modifies the requirements of subsections (b)(1)(A) and (b)(2)(E) of this section, and of section 1343 of this title, with respect to effluent limitations to the extent such limitations relate to biochemical oxygen demand and pH from discharges by an industrial discharger in such State into deep waters of the territorial seas, if the applicant demonstrates and the Administrator finds that—

(A) the facility for which modification is sought is covered at the time of the enactment of this subsection by National Pollutant Discharge Elimination System permit number CA0005894 or CA0005282;

(B) the energy and environmental costs of meeting such requirements of subsections (b)(1)(A) and (b)(2)(E) of this section and section 1343 of this title exceed by an unreasonable amount the benefits to be obtained, including the objectives of this chapter;

(C) the applicant has established a system for monitoring the impact of such discharges on a representative sample of aquatic biota;

(D) such modified requirements will not result in any additional requirements on any other point or nonpoint source;

(E) there will be no new or substantially increased discharges from the point source of the pollutant to which the modification applies above that volume of discharge specified in the permit;

(F) the discharge is into waters where there is strong tidal movement and other hydrological and geological characteristics which are necessary to allow compliance with this subsection and section 1251(a)(2) of this title;

(G) the applicant accepts as a condition to the permit a contractural[2] obligation to use funds in the amount required (but not less than $250,000 per year for ten years) for research and development of water pollution control technology, including but not limited to closed cycle technology;

(H) the facts and circumstances present a unique situation which, if relief is granted, will not establish a precedent or the relaxation of the requirements of this chapter applicable to similarly situated discharges; and

(I) no owner or operator of a facility comparable to that of the applicant situated in the United States has demonstrated that it would be put at a competitive disadvantage to the applicant (or the parent company or any subsidiary thereof) as a result of the issuance of a permit under this subsection.

(2) The effluent limitations established under a permit issued under paragraph (1) shall be sufficient to implement the applicable State water quality standards, to assure the protection of public water supplies and protection and propagation of a balanced, indigenous population of shellfish, fish, fauna, wildlife, and other aquatic organisms, and to allow recreational activities in and on the water. In setting such limitations, the Administrator shall take into account any seasonal variations and the need for an adequate margin of safety, considering the lack of essential knowledge concerning the relationship between effluent limitations and water quality and the lack of essential knowledge of the effects of discharges on beneficial uses of the receiving waters.

(3) A permit under this subsection may be issued for a period not to exceed five years, and such a permit may be renewed for one additional period not to exceed five years upon a demonstration by the applicant and a finding by the Administrator at the time of application for any such renewal that the provisions of this subsection are met.

(4) The Administrator may terminate a permit issued under this subsection if the Administrator determines that there has been a decline in ambient water quality of the receiving waters during the period of the permit even if a direct cause and effect relationship cannot be shown: *Provided*, That if the effluent from a source with a permit issued under this subsection is contributing to a decline in ambient water quality of the receiving waters, the Administrator shall terminate such permit.

**(n) Fundamentally different factors**

**(1) General rule**

The Administrator, with the concurrence of the State, may establish an alternative requirement under subsection (b)(2) of this section or section 1317(b) of this title for a facility that modifies the requirements of national effluent limitation guidelines or categorical pretreatment standards that would otherwise be applicable to such facility, if the owner or operator of such facility demonstrates to the satisfaction of the Administrator that—

**(A)** the facility is fundamentally different with respect to the factors (other than cost) specified in section 1314(b) or 1314(g) of this title and considered by the Administrator in establishing such national effluent limitation guidelines or categorical pretreatment standards;

**(B)** the application—

**(i)** is based solely on information and supporting data submitted to the Administrator during the rulemaking for establishment of the applicable national effluent limitation guidelines or categorical pretreatment standard specifically raising the factors that are fundamentally different for such facility; or

**(ii)** is based on information and supporting data referred to in clause (i) and information and supporting data the applicant did not have a reasonable opportunity to submit during such rulemaking;

**(C)** the alternative requirement is no less stringent than justified by the fundamental difference; and

**(D)** the alternative requirement will not result in a non-water quality environmental impact which is markedly more adverse than the impact considered by the Administrator in establishing such national effluent limitation guideline or categorical pretreatment standard.

**(2) Time limit for applications**

An application for an alternative requirement which modifies the requirements of an effluent limitation or pretreatment standard under this subsection must be submitted to the Administrator within 180 days after the date on which such limitation or standard is established or revised, as the case may be.

**(3) Time limit for decision**

The Administrator shall approve or deny by final agency action an application submitted under this subsection within 180 days after the date such application is filed with the Administrator.

**(4) Submission of information**

The Administrator may allow an applicant under this subsection to submit information and supporting data until the earlier of the date the application is approved or denied or the last day that the Administrator has to approve or deny such application.

**(5) Treatment of pending applications**

For the purposes of this subsection, an application for an alternative requirement based on fundamentally different factors which is pending on February 4, 1987, shall be treated as having been submitted to the Administrator on the 180th day following February 4, 1987. The applicant may amend the application to take into account the provisions of this subsection.

**(6) Effect of submission of application**

An application for an alternative requirement under this subsection shall not stay the applicant's obligation to comply with the effluent limitation guideline or categorical pretreatment standard which is the subject of the application.

**(7) Effect of denial**

If an application for an alternative requirement which modifies the requirements of an effluent limitation or pretreatment standard under this subsection is denied by the Administrator, the applicant must comply with such limitation or standard as established or revised, as the case may be.

**(8) Reports**

By January 1, 1997, and January 1 of every odd-numbered year thereafter, the Administrator shall submit to the Committee on Environment and Public Works of the Senate and the Committee on Transportation and Infrastructure of the House of Representatives a report on the status of applications for alternative requirements which modify the requirements of effluent limitations under section 1311 or 1314 of this title or any national categorical pretreatment standard under section 1317(b) of this title filed before, on, or after February 4, 1987.

**(*o*) Application fees**

The Administrator shall prescribe and collect from each applicant fees reflecting the reasonable administrative costs incurred in reviewing and processing applications for modifications submitted to the Administrator pursuant to subsections (c), (g), (i), (k), (m), and (n) of this section, section 1314(d)(4) of this title, and section 1326(a) of this title. All amounts collected by the Administrator under this subsection shall be deposited into a special fund of the Treasury entitled "Water Permits and Related Services" which shall thereafter be available for appropriation to carry out activities of the Environmental Protection Agency for which such fees were collected.

**(p) Modified permit for coal remining operations**

**(1) In general**

Subject to paragraphs (2) through (4) of this subsection, the Administrator, or the State in any case which the State has an approved permit program under section 1342(b) of this title, may issue a permit under section 1342 of this title which modifies the requirements of subsection (b)(2)(A) of this section with respect to the pH level of any pre-existing discharge, and with respect to pre-existing discharges of iron and manganese from the remined area of any coal remining operation or with respect to the pH level or level of iron or manganese in any pre-existing discharge affected by the remining operation. Such modified requirements shall apply the best available technology economically achievable on a case-by-case basis, using best professional judgment, to set specific numerical effluent limitations in each permit.

**(2) Limitations**

The Administrator or the State may only issue a permit pursuant to paragraph (1) if the applicant demonstrates to the satisfaction of the Administrator or the State, as the case may be, that the coal remining operation will result in the potential for improved water quality from the remining operation but in no event shall such a permit allow the pH level of any discharge, and in no event shall such a permit allow the discharges of iron and manganese, to exceed the levels being discharged from the remined area before the coal remining operation begins. No discharge from, or affected by, the remining operation shall exceed State water quality standards established under section 1313 of this title.

**(3) Definitions**

For purposes of this subsection—

**(A) Coal remining operation**

The term "coal remining operation" means a coal mining operation which begins after February 4, 1987 at a site on which coal mining was conducted before August 3, 1977.

**(B) Remined area**

The term "remined area" means only that area of any coal remining operation on which coal mining was conducted before August 3, 1977.

**(C) Pre-existing discharge**

The term "pre-existing discharge" means any discharge at the time of permit application under this subsection.

**(4) Applicability of strip mining laws**

Nothing in this subsection shall affect the application of the Surface Mining Control and Reclamation Act of 1977 [30 U.S.C.A. § 1201 et seq.] to any coal remining operation, including the application of such Act to suspended solids.

(June 30, 1948, c. 758, Title III, § 301, as added Oct. 18, 1972, Pub.L. 92–500, § 2, 86 Stat. 844, and amended Dec. 27, 1977, Pub.L. 95–217, §§ 42–47, 53(c), 91 Stat. 1582–1586, 1590; Dec. 29, 1981, Pub.L. 97–117, §§ 21, 22(a)–(d), 95 Stat. 1631, 1632; Jan. 8, 1983, Pub.L. 97–440, 96 Stat. 2289; Feb. 4, 1987, Pub.L. 100–4, Title III, §§ 301(a) to (e), 302(a) to (d), 303(a), (b)(1), (c) to (f), 304(a), 305, 306(a), (b), 307, 101 Stat. 29–37; Nov. 18, 1988, Pub.L. 100–688, Title III, § 3202(b), 102 Stat. 4154; Oct. 31, 1994, Pub.L. 103–431, § 2, 108 Stat. 4396; Dec. 21, 1995, Pub.L. 104–66, Title II, § 2021(b), 109 Stat. 727.)

1 So in original. Probably should be "than".

2 So in original. Probably should be "contractual".

## HISTORICAL AND STATUTORY NOTES

### References in Text

The Surface Mining Control and Reclamation Act of 1977, referred to in subsec. (p)(4), is Pub.L. 95–87, Aug. 3, 1977, 91 Stat. 445, as amended, which is classified generally to chapter 25 (section 1201 et seq.) of Title 30, Mineral Lands and Mining. For complete classification of this Act to the Code, see Short Title note set out under section 1201 of Title 30 and Tables.

### Change of Name

Any reference in any provision of law enacted before Jan. 4, 1995, to the Committee on Public Works and Transportation of the House of Representatives treated as referring to the Committee on Transportation and Infrastructure of the House of Representatives, see section 1(a)(9) of Pub.L. 104–14, set out as a note preceding section 21 of Title 2, The Congress.

### Effective and Applicability Provisions

1987 Acts

Section 302(e) of Pub.L. 100–4 provided that:

"(1) **General Rule.**—Except as provided in paragraph (2), the amendments made by this section [amending subsecs. (g) and (j) of this section] shall apply to all requests for modifications under section 301(g) of the Federal Water Pollution Control Act [subsec. (g) of this section] pending on the date of the enactment of this Act [Feb. 4, 1987] and shall not have the effect of extending the deadline established in section 301(j)(1)(B) of such Act [subsec. (j)(1)(B) of this section].

"(2) **Exception.**—The amendments made by this section [amending subsecs. (g) and (j) of this section] shall not affect any application for a modification with respect to the discharge of ammonia, chlorine, color, iron, or total phenols (4AAP) under section 301(g) of the Federal Water Pollution Control Act [subsec. (g) of this section] pending on the date of the enactment of this Act [Feb. 4, 1987]; except that the Administrator must approve or disapprove such application not later than 365 days after the date of such enactment [Feb. 4, 1987]."

Section 303(b)(2) of Pub.L. 100–4 provided that: "The amendment made by subsection (b) [amending subsec. (h)(3) of this section] shall only apply to modifications and renewals of modifications which are tentatively or finally approved after the date of the enactment of this Act [Feb. 4, 1987]."

Section 303(g) of Pub.L. 100–4 provided that: "The amendments made by subsections (a) [amending subsec. (h)(2) of this section], (c) [enacting subsec. (h)(6) of this section and redesignating former subsec. (h)(6) and (7) as (h)(7) and (8) ], (d) [enacting subsec. (h)(9) of this section and inserting provision defining primary and equivalent treatment in provision following subsec. (h)(9) ], and (e) [inserting provision relating to issuance of permit to discharge pollutants into marine waters in provision following subsec. (h)(9) ] of this section shall not apply to an application for a permit under section 301(h) of the Federal Water Pollution Control Act [subsec. (h) of this title] which has been tentatively or finally approved by the Administrator before the date of the enactment of this Act [Feb. 4, 1987]; except that such amendments shall apply to all renewals of such permits after such date of enactment."

Section 304(b) of Pub.L. 100–4 provided that: "The amendment made by subsection (a) [amending subsec. (i)(1) of this section] shall not apply to those treatment works which are subject to a compliance schedule established before the date of the enactment of this Act [Feb. 4, 1987] by a court order or a final administrative order."

1981 Acts

Section 22(e) of Pub.L. 97–117 provided that: "The amendments made by this section [amending subsecs. (h) and (j)(1)(A) of this section] shall take effect on the date of enactment of this Act [Dec. 29, 1981], except that no applicant, other than the city of Avalon, California, who applies after the date of enactment of this Act for a permit pursuant to subsection (h) of section 301 of the Federal Water Pollution Control Act [subsec. (h) of this section] which modifies the requirements of subsection (b)(1)(B) of section 301 of such Act [subsec. (b)(1)(B) of this section] shall receive such permit during the one-year period which begins on the date of enactment of this Act."

### Phosphate Fertilizer Effluent Limitation

Amendment by section 306(a), (b) of Pub.L. 100–4 not to be construed (A) to require the Administrator to permit the discharge of gypsum or gypsum waste into the navigable waters, (B) to affect the procedures and standards applicable to the Administrator in issuing permits under section 1342(a)(1)(B) of this title, and (C) to affect the authority of any State to deny or condition certification under section 1314 of this title with respect to the issuance of permits under section 1342(a)(1)(B) of this title, see section 306(c) of Pub.L. 100–4, set out as a note under 33 U.S.C.A. § 1342.

### Territorial Sea and Contiguous Zone of United States

For extension of territorial sea and contiguous zone of United States, see Proc. No. 5928 and Proc. No. 7219, respectively, set out as notes under 43 U.S.C.A. § 1331.

### Deadlines for Regulations for Certain Toxic Pollutants

Section 301(f) of Pub.L. 100–4 provided that: "The Administrator shall promulgate final regulations establishing effluent limitations in accordance with sections 301(b)(2)(A) and 307(b)(1) of the Federal Water Pollution Control Act [subsec. (b)(2)(A) of this section and section 1317(b)(1) of this title] for all toxic pollutants referred to in table 1 of Committee Print Numbered 95–30 of the Committee on Public Works and Transportation of the House of Representatives which are discharged from the categories of point sources in accordance with the following table:

| "Category | Date by which the final regulation shall be promulgated |
|---|---|
| "Organic chemicals and plastics and synthetic fibers | December 31, 1986. |
| "Pesticides | December 31, 1986." |

[Any reference in any provision of law enacted before Jan. 4, 1995, to the Committee on Public Works and Transportation of the House of Representatives treated as referring to the Committee on Transportation and Infrastructure of the House of Representatives, see section 1(a)(9) of Pub.L. 104–14, set out as a note preceding section 21 of Title 2, The Congress.]

**Discharges From Point Sources in United States Virgin Islands Attributable to Manufacture of Rum; Exemption From Federal Water Pollution Control Requirements; Conditions**

Pub. L. 98–67, Title II, § 214(g), Aug. 5, 1983, 97 Stat. 393, provided that:

"Any discharge from a point source in the United States Virgin Islands in existence on the date of the enactment of this subsection [Aug. 5, 1983] which discharge is attributable to the manufacture of rum (as defined in paragraphs (3) of section 7652(c) of the Internal Revenue Code of 1954 [section 7652(c)(3) of Title 26, Internal Revenue Code] ) shall not be subject to the requirements of section 301 [this section] (other than toxic pollutant discharges), section 306 [section 1316 of this title] or section 403 [section 1343 of this title] of the Federal Water Pollution Control Act if—

"(1) such discharge occurs at least one thousand five hundred feet into the territorial sea from the line of ordinary low water from that portion of the coast which is in direct contact with the sea, and

"(2) the Governor of the United States Virgin Islands determines that such discharge will not interfere with the attainment or maintenance of that water quality which shall assure protection of public water supplies, and the protection and propagation of a balanced population of shellfish, fish, and wildlife, and allow recreational activities, in and on the water and will not result in the discharge of pollutants in quantities which may reasonably be anticipated to pose an unacceptable risk to human health or the environment because of bioaccumulation, persistency in the environment, acute toxicity, chronic toxicity (including carcinogenicity, mutagenicity, or teratogenicity), or synergistic propensities."

**Certain Municipal Compliance Deadlines Unaffected; Exception**

Section 21(a) of Pub.L. 97–117 provided in part that: "The amendment made by this subsection [amending subsec. (i)(1) and (2)(B) of this section] shall not be interpreted or applied to extend the date for compliance with section 301(b)(1)(B) or (C) of the Federal Water Pollution Control Act [subsec. (b)(1)(B) or (C) of this section] beyond schedules for compliance in effect as of the date of enactment of this Act [Dec. 29, 1981], except in cases where reductions in the amount of financial assistance under this Act [Pub.L. 97–117, see Short Title of 1981 Amendment set out under section 1251 of this title] or changed conditions affecting the rate of construction beyond the control of the owner or operator will make it impossible to complete construction by July 1, 1983."

## § 1312. Water quality related effluent limitations

[FWPCA § 302]

### (a) Establishment

Whenever, in the judgment of the Administrator or as identified under section 1314(*l*) of this title, discharges of pollutants from a point source or group of point sources, with the application of effluent limitations required under section 1311(b)(2) of this title, would interfere with the attainment or maintenance of that water quality in a specific portion of the navigable waters which shall assure protection of public health, public water supplies, agricultural and industrial uses, and the protection and propagation of a balanced population of shellfish, fish and wildlife, and allow recreational activities in and on the water, effluent limitations (including alternative effluent control strategies) for such point source or sources shall be established which can reasonably be expected to contribute to the attainment or maintenance of such water quality.

### (b) Modifications of effluent limitations

#### (1) Notice and hearing

Prior to establishment of any effluent limitation pursuant to subsection (a) of this section, the Administrator shall publish such proposed limitation and within 90 days of such publication hold a public hearing.

#### (2) Permits

##### (A) No reasonable relationship

The Administrator, with the concurrence of the State, may issue a permit which modifies the effluent limitations required by subsection (a) of this section for pollutants other than toxic pollutants if the applicant demonstrates at such hearing that (whether or not technology or other alternative control strategies are available) there is no reasonable relationship between the economic and social costs and the benefits to be obtained (including attainment of the objective of this chapter) from achieving such limitation.

##### (B) Reasonable progress

The Administrator, with the concurrence of the State, may issue a permit which modifies the effluent limitations required by subsection (a) of this section for toxic pollutants for a single period not to exceed 5 years if the applicant demonstrates to the satisfaction of the Administrator that such modified requirements (i) will represent the maximum degree of control within the economic capability of the owner and operator of the source, and (ii) will result in reasonable further progress beyond the requirements of section 1311(b)(2) of this title toward the requirements of subsection (a) of this section.

### (c) Delay in application of other limitations

The establishment of effluent limitations under this section shall not operate to delay the application of any effluent limitation established under section 1311 of this title.

(June 30, 1948, c. 758, Title III, § 302, as added Oct. 18, 1972, Pub.L. 92–500, § 2, 86 Stat. 846, and amended Feb. 4, 1987, Pub.L. 100–4, Title III, § 308(e), 101 Stat. 39.)

## § 1313. Water quality standards and implementation plans

[FWPCA § 303]

### (a) Existing water quality standards

(1) In order to carry out the purpose of this chapter, any water quality standard applicable to interstate waters which was adopted by any State and submitted to, and approved by, or is a waiting approval by, the Administrator pursuant to this Act as in effect immediately prior to October 18, 1972, shall remain in effect unless the Administrator determined that such standard is not consistent with the applicable requirements of this Act as in effect immediately prior to October 18, 1972. If the Administrator makes such a determination he shall, within three months after October 18, 1972, notify the State and specify the changes needed to meet such requirements. If such changes are not adopted by the State within ninety days after the date of such notification, the Administrator shall promulgate such changes in accordance with subsection (b) of this section.

(2) Any State which, before October 18, 1972, has adopted, pursuant to its own law, water quality standards applicable to intrastate waters shall submit such standards to the Administrator within thirty days after October 18, 1972. Each such standard shall remain in effect, in the same manner and to the same extent as any other water quality standard established under this chapter unless the Administrator determines that such standard is inconsistent with the applicable requirements of this Act as in effect immediately prior to October 18, 1972. If the Administrator makes such a determination he shall not later than the one hundred and twentieth day after the date of submission of such standards, notify the State and specify the changes needed to meet such requirements. If such changes are not adopted by the State within ninety days after such notification, the Administrator shall promulgate such changes in accordance with subsection (b) of this section.

(3)(A) Any State which prior to October 18, 1972, has not adopted pursuant to its own laws water quality standards applicable to intrastate waters shall, not later than one hundred and eighty days after October 18, 1972, adopt and submit such standards to the Administrator.

(B) If the Administrator determines that any such standards are consistent with the applicable requirements of this Act as in effect immediately prior to October 18, 1972, he shall approve such standards.

(C) If the Administrator determines that any such standards are not consistent with the applicable requirements of this Act as in effect immediately prior to October 18, 1972, he shall, not later than the ninetieth day after the date of submission of such standards, notify the State and specify the changes to meet such requirements. If such changes are not adopted by the State within ninety days after the date of notification, the Administrator shall promulgate such standards pursuant to subsection (b) of this section.

### (b) Proposed regulations

(1) The Administrator shall promptly prepare and publish proposed regulations setting forth water quality standards for a State in accordance with the applicable requirements of this Act as in effect immediately prior to October 18, 1972, if—

(A) the State fails to submit water quality standards within the times prescribed in subsection (a) of this section.

(B) a water quality standard submitted by such State under subsection (a) of this section is determined by the Administrator not to be consistent with the applicable requirements of subsection (a) of this section.

(2) The Administrator shall promulgate any water quality standard published in a proposed regulation not later than one hundred and ninety days after the date he publishes any such proposed standard, unless prior to such promulgation, such State has adopted a water quality standard which the Administrator determines to be in accordance with subsection (a) of this section.

### (c) Review; revised standards; publication

(1) The Governor of a State or the State water pollution control agency of such State shall from time to time (but at least once each three year period beginning with October 18, 1972) hold public hearings for the purpose of reviewing applicable water quality standards and, as appropriate, modifying and adopting standards. Results of such review shall be made available to the Administrator.

(2)(A) Whenever the State revises or adopts a new standard, such revised or new standard shall be submitted to the Administrator. Such revised or new water quality standard shall consist of the designated uses of the navigable waters involved and the water quality criteria for such waters based upon such uses. Such standards shall be such as to protect the public health or welfare, enhance the quality of water and serve the purposes of this chapter. Such standards shall be established taking into consideration their use and value for public water supplies, propagation of fish and wildlife, recreational purposes, and agricultural, industrial, and other purposes, and also taking into consideration their use and value for navigation.

(B) Whenever a State reviews water quality standards pursuant to paragraph (1) of this subsection, or revises or adopts new standards pursuant to this paragraph, such State shall adopt criteria for all toxic pollutants listed pursuant to section 1317(a)(1) of this title for which criteria have been published under section 1314(a) of this title, the discharge or presence of which in the affected waters could reasonably be expected to interfere with those designated uses adopted by the State, as necessary to support such designated uses. Such criteria shall be specific numerical criteria for such toxic pollutants. Where such numerical criteria are not available, whenever a State reviews water quality standards pursuant to paragraph (1), or revises or adopts new standards pursuant to this paragraph, such State shall adopt criteria based on biological monitoring or assessment methods consistent with information published pursuant to section 1314(a)(8) of this title. Nothing in this section shall be construed to limit or delay the use of effluent limitations or other permit conditions based on or involving biological monitoring or assessment methods or previously adopted numerical criteria.

**(3)** If the Administrator, within sixty days after the date of submission of the revised or new standard, determines that such standard meets the requirements of this chapter, such standard shall thereafter be the water quality standard for the applicable waters of that State. If the Administrator determines that any such revised or new standard is not consistent with the applicable requirements of this chapter, he shall not later than the ninetieth day after the date of submission of such standard notify the State and specify the changes to meet such requirements. If such changes are not adopted by the State within ninety days after the date of notification, the Administrator shall promulgate such standard pursuant to paragraph (4) of this subsection.

**(4)** The Administrator shall promptly prepare and publish proposed regulations setting forth a revised or new water quality standard for the navigable waters involved—

**(A)** if a revised or new water quality standard submitted by such State under paragraph (3) of this subsection for such waters is determined by the Administrator not to be consistent with the applicable requirements of this chapter, or

**(B)** in any case where the Administrator determines that a revised or new standard is necessary to meet the requirements of this chapter.

The Administrator shall promulgate any revised or new standard under this paragraph not later than ninety days after he publishes such proposed standards, unless prior to such promulgation, such State has adopted a revised or new water quality standard which the Administrator determines to be in accordance with this chapter.

**(d) Identification of areas with insufficient controls; maximum daily load; certain effluent limitations revision**

**(1)(A)** Each State shall identify those waters within its boundaries for which the effluent limitations required by section 1311(b)(1)(A) and section 1311(b)(1)(B) of this title are not stringent enough to implement any water quality standard applicable to such waters. The State shall establish a priority ranking for such waters, taking into account the severity of the pollution and the uses to be made of such waters.

**(B)** Each State shall identify those waters or parts thereof within its boundaries for which controls on thermal discharges under section 1311 of this title are not stringent enough to assure protection and propagation of a balanced indigenous population of shellfish, fish, and wildlife.

**(C)** Each State shall establish for the waters identified in paragraph (1)(A) of this subsection, and in accordance with the priority ranking, the total maximum daily load, for those pollutants which the Administrator identifies under section 1314(a)(2) of this title as suitable for such calculation. Such load shall be established at a level necessary to implement the applicable water quality standards with seasonal variations and a margin of safety which takes into account any lack of knowledge concerning the relationship between effluent limitations and water quality.

**(D)** Each State shall estimate for the waters identified in paragraph (1)(B) of this subsection the total maximum daily thermal load required to assure protection and propagation of a balanced, indigenous population of shellfish, fish, and wildlife. Such estimates shall take into account the normal water temperatures, flow rates, seasonal variations, existing sources of heat input, and the dissipative capacity of the identified waters or parts thereof. Such estimates shall include a calculation of the maximum heat input that can be made into each such part and shall include a margin of safety which takes into account any lack of knowledge concerning the development of thermal water quality criteria for such protection and propagation in the identified waters or parts thereof.

**(2)** Each State shall submit to the Administrator from time to time, with the first such submission not later than one hundred and eighty days after the date of publication of the first identification of pollutants under section 1314(a)(2)(D) of this title, for his approval the waters identified and the loads established under paragraphs (1)(A), (1)(B), (1)(C), and (1)(D) of this subsection. The Administrator shall either approve or disapprove such identification and load not later than thirty days after the date of submission. If the Administrator approves such identification and load, such State shall incorporate them into its current plan under subsection (e) of this section. If the Administrator disapproves such identification and load, he shall not later than thirty days after the date of such disapproval identify such waters in such State and establish such loads for such waters as he determines necessary to implement the water quality standards applicable to such waters and upon such identification and establishment the State shall incorporate them into its current plan under subsection (e) of this section.

(3) For the specific purpose of developing information, each State shall identify all waters within its boundaries which it has not identified under paragraph (1)(A) and (1)(B) of this subsection and estimate for such waters the total maximum daily load with seasonal variations and margins of safety, for those pollutants which the Administrator identifies under section 1314(a)(2) of this title as suitable for such calculation and for thermal discharges, at a level that would assure protection and propagation of a balanced indigenous population of fish, shellfish, and wildlife.

**(4) Limitations on revision of certain effluent limitations**

**(A) Standard not attained**

For waters identified under paragraph (1)(A) where the applicable water quality standard has not yet been attained, any effluent limitation based on a total maximum daily load or other waste load allocation established under this section may be revised only if (i) the cumulative effect of all such revised effluent limitations based on such total maximum daily load or waste load allocation will assure the attainment of such water quality standard, or (ii) the designated use which is not being attained is removed in accordance with regulations established under this section.

**(B) Standard attained**

For waters identified under paragraph (1)(A) where the quality of such waters equals or exceeds levels necessary to protect the designated use for such waters or otherwise required by applicable water quality standards, any effluent limitation based on a total maximum daily load or other waste load allocation established under this section, or any water quality standard established under this section, or any other permitting standard may be revised only if such revision is subject to and consistent with the antidegradation policy established under this section.

**(e) Continuing planning process**

(1) Each State shall have a continuing planning process approved under paragraph (2) of this subsection which is consistent with this chapter.

(2) Each State shall submit not later than 120 days after October 18, 1972, to the Administrator for his approval a proposed continuing planning process which is consistent with this chapter. Not later than thirty days after the date of submission of such a process the Administrator shall either approve or disapprove such process. The Administrator shall from time to time review each State's approved planning process for the purpose of insuring that such planning process is at all times consistent with this chapter. The Administrator shall not approve any State permit program under subchapter IV of this chapter for any State which does not have an approved continuing planning process under this section.

(3) The Administrator shall approve any continuing planning process submitted to him under this section which will result in plans for all navigable waters within such State, which include, but are not limited to, the following:

(A) effluent limitations and schedules of compliance at least as stringent as those required by section 1311(b)(1), section 1311(b)(2), section 1316, and section 1317 of this title, and at least as stringent as any requirements contained in any applicable water quality standard in effect under authority of this section;

(B) the incorporation of all elements of any applicable area-wide waste management plans under section 1288 of this title, and applicable basin plans under section 1289 of this title;

(C) total maximum daily load for pollutants in accordance with subsection (d) of this section;

(D) procedures for revision;

(E) adequate authority for intergovernmental cooperation;

(F) adequate implementation, including schedules of compliance, for revised or new water quality standards, under subsection (c) of this section;

(G) controls over the disposition of all residual waste from any water treatment processing;

(H) an inventory and ranking, in order of priority, of needs for construction of waste treatment works required to meet the applicable requirements of sections 1311 and 1312 of this title.

**(f) Earlier compliance**

Nothing in this section shall be construed to affect any effluent limitation, or schedule of compliance required by any State to be implemented prior to the dates set forth in sections 1311(b)(1) and 1311(b)(2) of this title nor to preclude any State from requiring compliance with any effluent limitation or schedule of compliance at dates earlier than such dates.

**(g) Heat standards**

Water quality standards relating to heat shall be consistent with the requirements of section 1326 of this title.

**(h) Thermal water quality standards**

For the purposes of this chapter the term "water quality standards" includes thermal water quality standards.

**(i) Coastal recreation water quality criteria**

**(1) Adoption by States**

**(A) Initial criteria and standards**

Not later than 42 months after October 10, 2000, each State having coastal recreation waters shall adopt and submit to the Administrator water quality criteria and standards for the coastal recreation waters of the State for those pathogens and pathogen indicators for which the Administrator has published criteria under section 1314(a) of this title.

**(B) New or revised criteria and standards**

Not later than 36 months after the date of publication by the Administrator of new or revised water quality criteria under section 1314(a)(9) of this title, each State having coastal recreation waters shall adopt and submit to the Administrator new or revised water quality standards for the coastal recreation waters of the State for all pathogens and pathogen indicators to which the new or revised water quality criteria are applicable.

**(2) Failure of States to adopt**

**(A) In general**

If a State fails to adopt water quality criteria and standards in accordance with paragraph (1)(A) that are as protective of human health as the criteria for pathogens and pathogen indicators for coastal recreation waters published by the Administrator, the Administrator shall promptly propose regulations for the State setting forth revised or new water quality standards for pathogens and pathogen indicators described in paragraph (1)(A) for coastal recreation waters of the State.

**(B) Exception**

If the Administrator proposes regulations for a State described in subparagraph (A) under subsection (c)(4)(B) of this section, the Administrator shall publish any revised or new standard under this subsection not later than 42 months after October 10, 2000.

**(3) Applicability**

Except as expressly provided by this subsection, the requirements and procedures of subsection (c) of this section apply to this subsection, including the requirement in subsection (c)(2)(A) of this section that the criteria protect public health and welfare.

(June 30, 1948, c. 758, Title III, § 303, as added Oct. 18, 1972, Pub.L. 92–500, § 2, 86 Stat. 846, and amended Feb. 4, 1987, Pub.L. 100–4, Title III, § 308(d), Title IV, § 404(b), 101 Stat. 39, 68; Oct. 10, 2000, Pub.L. 106–284, § 2, 114 Stat. 870.)

### HISTORICAL AND STATUTORY NOTES

**References in Text**

This Act, referred to in subsecs. (a)(1), (2), (3)(B), (C), (b)(1), means Act June 30, 1948, c. 758, 62 Stat. 1155, prior to the supersedure and reenactment of Act June 30, 1948 by Act Oct. 18, 1972, Pub.L. 92–500, 86 Stat. 816. Act June 30, 1948, c. 758, as added by Act Oct. 18, 1972, Pub.L. 92–500, 86 Stat. 816, enacted this chapter.

## § 1313a. Revised water quality standards

The review, revision, and adoption or promulgation of revised or new water quality standards pursuant to section 303(c) of the Federal Water Pollution Control Act [33 U.S.C.A. § 1313(c)] shall be completed by the date three years after December 29, 1981. No grant shall be made under title II of the Federal Water Pollution Control Act [33 U.S.C.A. § 1281 et seq.] after such date until water quality standards are reviewed and revised pursuant to section 303(c), except where the State has in good faith submitted such revised water quality standards and the Administrator has not acted to approve or disapprove such submission within one hundred and twenty days of receipt.

(Pub.L. 97–117, § 24, Dec. 29, 1981, 95 Stat. 1632.)

### HISTORICAL AND STATUTORY NOTES

**References in Text**

The Federal Water Pollution Control Act, referred to in text, is Act June 30, 1948, c. 758, as amended generally by Pub.L. 92–500, § 2, Oct. 18, 1972, 86 Stat. 816. Title II of the Federal Water Pollution Control Act is classified generally to subchapter II (section 1281 et seq.) of this chapter. For complete classification of this Act to the Code, see Short Title note set out under section 1251 of this title and Tables.

**Codifications**

Section was enacted as part of the Municipal Wastewater Treatment Construction Grant Amendments of 1981, and not as part of the Federal Water Pollution Control Act, which comprises this chapter.

## § 1314. Information and guidelines

[FWPCA § 304]

**(a) Criteria development and publication**

(1) The Administrator, after consultation with appropriate Federal and State agencies and other interested persons, shall develop and publish, within one

year after October 18, 1972 (and from time to time thereafter revise) criteria for water quality accurately reflecting the latest scientific knowledge (A) on the kind and extent of all identifiable effects on health and welfare including, but not limited to, plankton, fish, shellfish, wildlife, plant life, shorelines, beaches, esthetics, and recreation which may be expected from the presence of pollutants in any body of water, including ground water; (B) on the concentration and dispersal of pollutants, or their byproducts, through biological, physical, and chemical processes; and (C) on the effects of pollutants on biological community diversity, productivity, and stability, including information on the factors affecting rates of eutrophication and rates of organic and inorganic sedimentation for varying types of receiving waters.

(2) The Administrator, after consultation with appropriate Federal and State agencies and other interested persons, shall develop and publish, within one year after October 18, 1972 (and from time to time thereafter revise) information (A) on the factors necessary to restore and maintain the chemical, physical, and biological integrity of all navigable waters, ground waters, waters of the contiguous zone, and the oceans; (B) on the factors necessary for the protection and propagation of shellfish, fish, and wildlife for classes and categories of receiving waters and to allow recreational activities in and on the water; and (C) on the measurement and classification of water quality; and (D) for the purpose of section 1313 of this title, on and the identification of pollutants suitable for maximum daily load measurement correlated with the achievement of water quality objectives.

(3) Such criteria and information and revisions thereof shall be issued to the States and shall be published in the Federal Register and otherwise made available to the public.

(4) The Administrator shall, within 90 days after December 27, 1977, and from time to time thereafter, publish and revise as appropriate information identifying conventional pollutants, including but not limited to, pollutants classified as biological oxygen demanding, suspended solids, fecal coliform, and pH. The thermal component of any discharge shall not be identified as a conventional pollutant under this paragraph.

(5)(A) The Administrator, to the extent practicable before consideration of any request under section 1311(g) of this title and within six months after December 27, 1977, shall develop and publish information on the factors necessary for the protection of public water supplies, and the protection and propagation of a balanced population of shellfish, fish and wildlife, and to allow recreational activities, in and on the water.

(B) The Administrator, to the extent practicable before consideration of any application under section 1311(h) of this title and within six months after December 27, 1977, shall develop and publish information on the factors necessary for the protection of public water supplies, and the protection and propagation of a balanced indigenous population of shellfish, fish and wildlife, and to allow recreational activities, in and on the water.

(6) The Administrator shall, within three months after December 27, 1977, and annually thereafter, for purposes of section 1311(h) of this title publish and revise as appropriate information identifying each water quality standard in effect under this chapter or State law, the specific pollutants associated with such water quality standard, and the particular waters to which such water quality standard applies.

**(7) Guidance to states**

The Administrator, after consultation with appropriate State agencies and on the basis of criteria and information published under paragraphs (1) and (2) of this subsection, shall develop and publish, within 9 months after February 4, 1987, guidance to the States on performing the identification required by subsection (*l*)(1) of this section.

**(8) Information on water quality criteria**

The Administrator, after consultation with appropriate State agencies and within 2 years after February 4, 1987, shall develop and publish information on methods for establishing and measuring water quality criteria for toxic pollutants on other bases than pollutant-by-pollutant criteria, including biological monitoring and assessment methods.

**(9) Revised criteria for coastal recreation waters**

**(A) In general**

Not later than 5 years after October 10, 2000, after consultation and in cooperation with appropriate Federal, State, tribal, and local officials (including local health officials), the Administrator shall publish new or revised water quality criteria for pathogens and pathogen indicators (including a revised list of testing methods, as appropriate), based on the results of the studies conducted under section 1254(v) of this title, for the purpose of protecting human health in coastal recreation waters.

**(B) Reviews**

Not later than the date that is 5 years after the date of publication of water quality criteria under this paragraph, and at least once every 5 years thereafter, the Administrator shall review and, as necessary, revise the water quality criteria.

**(b) Effluent limitation guidelines**

For the purpose of adopting or revising effluent limitations under this chapter the Administrator shall, after consultation with appropriate Federal and State agencies and other interested persons, publish within one year of October 18, 1972, regulations, providing guidelines for effluent limitations, and, at least annually thereafter, revise, if appropriate, such regulations. Such regulations shall—

(1)(A) identify, in terms of amounts of constituents and chemical, physical, and biological characteristics of pollutants, the degree of effluent reduction attainable through the application of the best practicable control technology currently available for classes and categories of point sources (other than publicly owned treatment works); and

(B) specify factors to be taken into account in determining the control measures and practices to be applicable to point sources (other than publicly owned treatment works) within such categories or classes. Factors relating to the assessment of best practicable control technology currently available to comply with subsection (b)(1) of section 1311 of this title shall include consideration of the total cost of application of technology in relation to the effluent reduction benefits to be achieved from such application, and shall also take into account the age of equipment and facilities involved, the process employed, the engineering aspects of the application of various types of control techniques, process changes, non-water quality environmental impact (including energy requirements), and such other factors as the Administrator deems appropriate;

(2)(A) identify, in terms of amounts of constituents and chemical, physical, and biological characteristics of pollutants, the degree of effluent reduction attainable through the application of the best control measures and practices achievable including treatment techniques, process and procedure innovations, operating methods, and other alternatives for classes and categories of point sources (other than publicly owned treatment works); and

(B) specify factors to be taken into account in determining the best measures and practices available to comply with subsection (b)(2) of section 1311 of this title to be applicable to any point source (other than publicly owned treatment works) within such categories or classes. Factors relating to the assessment of best available technology shall take into account the age of equipment and facilities involved, the process employed, the engineering aspects of the application of various types of control techniques, process changes, the cost of achieving such effluent reduction, non-water quality environmental impact (including energy requirements), and such other factors as the Administrator deems appropriate;

(3) identify control measures and practices available to eliminate the discharge of pollutants from categories and classes of point sources, taking into account the cost of achieving such elimination of the discharge of pollutants; and

(4)(A) identify, in terms of amounts of constituents and chemical, physical, and biological characteristics of pollutants, the degree of effluent reduction attainable through the application of the best conventional pollutant control technology (including measures and practices) for classes and categories of point sources (other than publicly owned treatment works); and

(B) specify factors to be taken into account in determining the best conventional pollutant control technology measures and practices to comply with section 1311(b)(2)(E) of this title to be applicable to any point source (other than publicly owned treatment works) within such categories or classes. Factors relating to the assessment of best conventional pollutant control technology (including measures and practices) shall include consideration of the reasonableness of the relationship between the costs of attaining a reduction in effluents and the effluent reduction benefits derived, and the comparison of the cost and level of reduction of such pollutants from the discharge from publicly owned treatment works to the cost and level of reduction of such pollutants from a class or category of industrial sources, and shall take into account the age of equipment and facilities involved, the process employed, the engineering aspects of the application of various types of control techniques, process changes, non-water quality environmental impact (including energy requirements), and such other factors as the Administrator deems appropriate.

### (c) Pollution discharge elimination procedures

The Administrator, after consultation, with appropriate Federal and State agencies and other interested persons, shall issue to the States and appropriate water pollution control agencies within 270 days after October 18, 1972 (and from time to time thereafter) information on the processes, procedures, or operating methods which result in the elimination or reduction of the discharge of pollutants to implement standards of performance under section 1316 of this title. Such information shall include technical and other data, including costs, as are available on alternative methods of elimination or reduction of the discharge of pollutants. Such information, and revisions thereof, shall be published in the Federal Register and otherwise shall be made available to the public.

### (d) Secondary treatment information; alternative waste treatment management techniques; innovative and alternative wastewater treatment processes; facilities deemed equivalent of secondary treatment

(1) The Administrator, after consultation with appropriate Federal and State agencies and other interested persons, shall publish within sixty days after October 18, 1972 (and from time to time thereafter) information, in terms of amounts of constituents and chemical, physical, and biological characteristics of pollutants, on the degree of effluent reduction attainable through the application of secondary treatment.

(2) The Administrator, after consultation with appropriate Federal and State agencies and other interested persons, shall publish within nine months after October 18, 1972 (and from time to time thereafter) information on alternative waste treatment management techniques and systems available to implement section 1281 of this title.

(3) The Administrator, after consultation with appropriate Federal and State agencies and other interested persons, shall promulgate within one hundred and eighty days after December 27, 1977, guidelines for identifying and evaluating innovative and alternative wastewater treatment processes and techniques referred to in section 1281(g)(5) of this title.

(4) For the purposes of this subsection, such biological treatment facilities as oxidation ponds, lagoons, and ditches and trickling filters shall be deemed the equivalent of secondary treatment. The Administrator shall provide guidance under paragraph (1) of this subsection on design criteria for such facilities, taking into account pollutant removal efficiencies and, consistent with the objectives of this chapter, assuring that water quality will not be adversely affected by deeming such facilities as the equivalent of secondary treatment.

**(e) Best management practices for industry**

The Administrator, after consultation with appropriate Federal and State agencies and other interested persons, may publish regulations, supplemental to any effluent limitations specified under subsections (b) and (c) of this section for a class or category of point sources, for any specific pollutant which the Administrator is charged with a duty to regulate as a toxic or hazardous pollutant under section 1317(a)(1) or 1321 of this title, to control plant site runoff, spillage or leaks, sludge or waste disposal, and drainage from raw material storage which the Administrator determines are associated with or ancillary to the industrial manufacturing or treatment process within such class or category of point sources and may contribute significant amounts of such pollutants to navigable waters. Any applicable controls established under this subsection shall be included as a requirement for the purposes of section 1311, 1312, 1316, 1317, or 1343 of this title, as the case may be, in any permit issued to a point source pursuant to section 1342 of this title.

**(f) Identification and evaluation of nonpoint sources of pollution; processes, procedures, and methods to control pollution**

The Administrator, after consultation with appropriate Federal and State agencies and other interested persons, shall issue to appropriate Federal agencies, the States, water pollution control agencies, and agencies designated under section 1288 of this title, within one year after October 18, 1972 (and from time to time thereafter) information including (1) guidelines for identifying and evaluating the nature and extent of nonpoint sources of pollutants, and (2) processes, procedures, and methods to control pollution resulting from—

(A) agricultural and silvicultural activities, including runoff from fields and crop and forest lands;

(B) mining activities, including runoff and siltation from new, currently operating, and abandoned surface and underground mines;

(C) all construction activity, including runoff from the facilities resulting from such construction;

(D) the disposal of pollutants in wells or in subsurface excavations;

(E) salt water intrusion resulting from reductions of fresh water flow from any cause, including extraction of ground water, irrigation, obstruction, and diversion; and

(F) changes in the movement, flow, or circulation of any navigable waters or ground waters, including changes caused by the construction of dams, levees, channels, causeways, or flow diversion facilities.

Such information and revisions thereof shall be published in the Federal Register and otherwise made available to the public.

**(g) Guidelines for pretreatment of pollutants**

(1) For the purpose of assisting States in carrying out programs under section 1342 of this title, the Administrator shall publish, within one hundred and twenty days after October 18, 1972, and review at least annually thereafter and, if appropriate, revise guidelines for pretreatment of pollutants which he determines are not susceptible to treatment by publicly owned treatment works. Guidelines under this subsection shall be established to control and prevent the discharge into the navigable waters, the contiguous zone, or the ocean (either directly or through publicly owned treatment works) of any pollutant which interferes with, passes through, or otherwise is incompatible with such works.

(2) When publishing guidelines under this subsection, the Administrator shall designate the category or categories of treatment works to which the guidelines shall apply.

**(h) Test procedures guidelines**

The Administrator shall, within one hundred and eighty days from October 18, 1972, promulgate guidelines establishing test procedures for the analysis of pollutants that shall include the factors which must be provided in any certification pursuant to section 1341 of this title or permit application pursuant to section 1342 of this title.

**(i) Guidelines for monitoring, reporting, enforcement, funding, personnel, and manpower**

The Administrator shall (1) within sixty days after October 18, 1972, promulgate guidelines for the purpose of establishing uniform application forms and other minimum requirements for the acquisition of information from owners and operators of point-sources of discharge subject to any State program under section 1342 of this title, and (2) within sixty days from October 18, 1972, promulgate guidelines establishing the minimum procedural and other elements of any State program under section 1342 of this title, which shall include:

(A) monitoring requirements;

(B) reporting requirements (including procedures to make information available to the public);

(C) enforcement provisions; and

(D) funding, personnel qualifications, and manpower requirements (including a requirement that no board or body which approves permit applications or portions thereof shall include, as a member, any person who receives, or has during the previous two years received, a significant portion of his income directly or indirectly from permit holders or applicants for a permit).

**(j) Lake restoration guidance manual**

The Administrator shall, within 1 year after February 4, 1987, and biennially thereafter, publish and disseminate a lake restoration guidance manual describing methods, procedures, and processes to guide State and local efforts to improve, restore, and enhance water quality in the Nation's publicly owned lakes.

**(k) Agreements with Secretaries of Agriculture, Army, and the Interior to provide maximum utilization of programs to achieve and maintain water quality; transfer of funds; authorization of appropriations**

(1) The Administrator shall enter into agreements with the Secretary of Agriculture, the Secretary of the Army, and the Secretary of the Interior, and the heads of such other departments, agencies, and instrumentalities of the United States as the Administrator determines, to provide for the maximum utilization of other Federal laws and programs for the purpose of achieving and maintaining water quality through appropriate implementation of plans approved under section 1288 of this title and nonpoint source pollution management programs approved under section 1329 of this title.

(2) The Administrator is authorized to transfer to the Secretary of Agriculture, the Secretary of the Army, and the Secretary of the Interior and the heads of such other departments, agencies, and instrumentalities of the United States as the Administrator determines, any funds appropriated under paragraph (3) of this subsection to supplement funds otherwise appropriated to programs authorized pursuant to any agreement under paragraph (1).

(3) There is authorized to be appropriated to carry out the provisions of this subsection, $100,000,000 per fiscal year for the fiscal years 1979 through 1983 and such sums as may be necessary for fiscal years 1984 through 1990.

**(*l*) Individual control strategies for toxic pollutants**

**(1) State list of navigable waters and development of strategies**

Not later than 2 years after February 4, 1987, each State shall submit to the Administrator for review, approval, and implementation under this subsection—

(A) a list of those waters within the State which after the application of effluent limitations required under section 1311(b)(2) of this title cannot reasonably be anticipated to attain or maintain (i) water quality standards for such waters reviewed, revised, or adopted in accordance with section 1313(c)(2)(B) of this title, due to toxic pollutants, or (ii) that water quality which shall assure protection of public health, public water supplies, agricultural and industrial uses, and the protection and propagation of a balanced population of shellfish, fish and wildlife, and allow recreational activities in and on the water;

(B) a list of all navigable waters in such State for which the State does not expect the applicable standard under section 1313 of this title will be achieved after the requirements of sections 1311(b), 1316, and 1317(b) of this title are met, due entirely or substantially to discharges from point sources of any toxic pollutants listed pursuant to section 1317(a) of this title;

(C) for each segment of the navigable waters included on such lists, a determination of the specific point sources discharging any such toxic pollutant which is believed to be preventing or impairing such water quality and the amount of each such toxic pollutant discharged by each such source; and

(D) for each such segment, an individual control strategy which the State determines will produce a reduction in the discharge of toxic pollutants from point sources identified by the State under this paragraph through the establishment of effluent limitations under section 1342 of this title and water quality standards under section 1313(c)(2)(B) of this title, which reduction is sufficient, in combination with existing controls on point and nonpoint sources of pollution, to achieve the applicable water quality standard as soon as possible, but not later than 3 years after the date of the establishment of such strategy.

**(2) Approval or disapproval**

Not later than 120 days after the last day of the 2-year period referred to in paragraph (1), the Administrator shall approve or disapprove the control strategies submitted under paragraph (1) by any State.

**(3) Administrator's action**

If a State fails to submit control strategies in accordance with paragraph (1) or the Administrator does not approve the control strategies submitted by such State in accordance with paragraph (1), then, not later than 1 year after the last day of the period referred to in paragraph (2), the Administrator, in cooperation with such State and after notice and opportunity for public comment, shall implement the requirements of paragraph (1) in such State. In the implementation of such requirements, the Administrator shall, at a minimum, consider for listing under this subsection any navigable waters for which any person submits a petition to the Administrator for listing not later than 120 days after such last day.

**(m) Schedule for review of Guidelines**

**(1) Publication**

Within 12 months after February 4, 1987, and biennially thereafter, the Administrator shall publish in the Federal Register a plan which shall—

**(A)** establish a schedule for the annual review and revision of promulgated effluent guidelines, in accordance with subsection (b) of this section;

**(B)** identify categories of sources discharging toxic or nonconventional pollutants for which guidelines under subsection (b)(2) of this section and section 1316 of this title have not previously been published; and

**(C)** establish a schedule for promulgation of effluent guidelines for categories identified in subparagraph (B), under which promulgation of such guidelines shall be no later than 4 years after February 4, 1987, for categories identified in the first published plan or 3 years after the publication of the plan for categories identified in later published plans.

**(2) Public review**

The Administrator shall provide for public review and comment on the plan prior to final publication.

(June 30, 1948, c. 758, Title III, § 304, as added Oct. 18, 1972, Pub.L. 92–500, § 2, 86 Stat. 850, and amended Dec. 27, 1977, Pub.L. 95–217, §§ 48–51, 62(b), 91 Stat. 1587, 1588, 1598; Dec. 29, 1981, Pub.L. 97–117, § 23, 95 Stat. 1632; Feb. 4, 1987, Pub.L. 100–4, Title I, § 101(f), Title III, §§ 308(a), (c), (f), 315(c), 316(e), 101 Stat. 9, 38–40, 52, 61; Oct. 10, 2000, Pub.L. 106–284, § 3(b), 114 Stat. 871.)

## HISTORICAL AND STATUTORY NOTES

**References in Text**

December 27, 1977, referred to in subsec. (d)(3), was in the original "the date of enactment of this subsection", and has been editorially translated as December 27, 1977, the date of enactment of Pub.L. 95–217, which added par. (3) to subsec. (d), as the probable intent of Congress.

**Codifications**

Section 50 of Pub.L. 95–217 provided in part that, upon the enactment of subsec. (e) of this section by Pub.L. 95–217 and the concurrent redesignation of former subsecs. (e) to (j) of this section as (f) to (k), respectively, all references to former subsecs. (e) to (j) be changed to (f) to (k), respectively.

**Transfer of Functions**

Enforcement functions of Secretary or other official in Department of Agriculture, insofar as they involve lands and programs under jurisdiction of that Department, relating to compliance with this chapter with respect to pre-construction, construction, and initial operation of transportation system for Canadian and Alaskan natural gas were transferred to the Federal Inspector, Office of Federal Inspector for the Alaska Natural Gas Transportation System, until the first anniversary of the date of initial operation of the Alaska Natural Gas Transportation System, see Reorg. Plan No. 1 of 1979, §§ 102(f), 203(a), 44 F.R. 33663, 33666, 93 Stat. 1373, 1376, effective July 1, 1979, set out in Appendix 1 to Title 5, Government Organization and Employees.

**Contiguous Zone of United States**

For extension of contiguous zone of United States, see Proc. No. 7219, set out as a note under 43 U.S.C.A. § 1331.

**Review of Effluent Guidelines Promulgated Prior to December 27, 1977**

Section 73 of Pub.L. 95–217 provided that: "Within 90 days after the date of enactment of this Act [Dec. 27, 1977], the Administrator shall review every effluent guideline promulgated prior to the date of enactment of this Act which is final or interim final (other than those applicable to industrial categories listed in table 2 of Committee Print Numbered 95–30 of the Committee on Public Works and Transportation of the House of Representatives) and which applies to those pollutants identified pursuant to section 304(a)(4) of the Federal Water Pollution Control Act [subsec. (a)(4) of this section]. The Administrator shall review every guideline applicable to industrial categories listed in such table 2 on or before July 1, 1980. Upon completion of each such review the Administrator is authorized to make such adjustments in any such guidelines as may be necessary to carry out section 304(b)(4) of such Act [subsec. (b)(4) of this section]. The

Administrator shall publish the results of each such review, including, with respect to each such guideline, the determination to adjust or not to adjust such guideline. Any such determination by the Administrator shall be final except that if, on judicial review in accordance with section 509 of such Act [section 1369 of this title], it is determined that the Administrator either did not comply with the requirements of this section or the determination of the Administrator was based on arbitrary and capricious action in applying section 304(b)(4) of such Act [subsec. (b)(4) of this section] to such guideline, the Administrator shall make a further review and redetermination of any such guideline."

[Any reference in any provision of law enacted before Jan. 4, 1995, to the Committee on Public Works and Transportation of the House of Representatives treated as referring to the Committee on Transportation and Infrastructure of the House of Representatives, see section 1(a)(9) of Pub.L. 104–14, set out as a note preceding section 21 of Title 2, The Congress].

## § 1315. State reports on water quality

### [FWPCA § 305]

(a) Omitted

**(b)(1)** Each State shall prepare and submit to the Administrator by April 1, 1975, and shall bring up to date by April 1, 1976, and biennially thereafter, a report which shall include—

**(A)** a description of the water quality of all navigable waters in such State during the preceding year, with appropriate supplemental descriptions as shall be required to take into account seasonal, tidal, and other variations, correlated with the quality of water required by the objective of this chapter (as identified by the Administrator pursuant to criteria published under section 1314(a) of this title) and the water quality described in subparagraph (B) of this paragraph;

**(B)** an analysis of the extent to which all navigable waters of such State provide for the protection and propagation of a balanced population of shellfish, fish, and wildlife, and allow recreational activities in and on the water;

**(C)** an analysis of the extent to which the elimination of the discharge of pollutants and a level of water quality which provides for the protection and propagation of a balanced population of shellfish, fish, and wildlife and allows recreational activities in and on the water, have been or will be achieved by the requirements of this chapter, together with recommendations as to additional action necessary to achieve such objectives and for what waters such additional action is necessary;

**(D)** an estimate of (i) the environmental impact, (ii) the economic and social costs necessary to achieve the objective of this chapter in such State, (iii) the economic and social benefits of such achievement, and (iv) an estimate of the date of such achievement; and

**(E)** a description of the nature and extent of nonpoint sources of pollutants, and recommendations as to the programs which must be undertaken to control each category of such sources, including an estimate of the costs of implementing such programs.

(2) Omitted.

(June 30, 1948, c. 758, Title III, § 305, as added Oct. 18, 1972, Pub.L. 92–500, § 2, 86 Stat. 853, and amended Dec. 27, 1977, Pub.L. 95–217, § 52, 91 Stat. 1589.)

### HISTORICAL AND STATUTORY NOTES

**Codifications**

Subsec. (a) authorized the Administrator, in cooperation with the States and Federal agencies, to prepare a report describing the specific quality, during 1973, of all navigable waters and waters of the contiguous zone, including an inventory of all point sources of discharge of pollutants into these waters, and identifying those navigable waters capable of supporting fish and wildlife populations and allowing recreational activities, those which could reasonably be expected to attain this level by 1977 or 1983, and those which could attain this level sooner, and submit this report to Congress on or before Jan. 1, 1974.

Subsec. (b)(2) of this section, which required the Administrator to transmit to Congress biennially the State reports submitted to the Administrator under subsec. (b)(1) of this section, together with an analysis of the reports, terminated, effective May 15, 2000, pursuant to section 3003 of Pub.L. 104–66, as amended, set out as a note under 31 U.S.C.A. § 1113. See, also, page 165 of House Document No. 103–7.

## § 1316. National standards of performance

### [FWPCA § 306]

**(a) Definitions**

For purposes of this section:

(1) The term "standard of performance" means a standard for the control of the discharge of pollutants which reflects the greatest degree of effluent reduction which the Administrator determines to be achievable through application of the best available demonstrated control technology, processes, operating methods, or other alternatives, including, where practicable, a standard permitting no discharge of pollutants.

(2) The term "new source" means any source, the construction of which is commenced after the publication of proposed regulations prescribing a standard of performance under this section which will be applicable to such source, if such standard is thereafter promulgated in accordance with this section.

(3) The term "source" means any building, structure, facility, or installation from which there is or may be the discharge of pollutants.

(4) The term "owner or operator" means any person who owns, leases, operates, controls, or supervises a source.

(5) The term "construction" means any placement, assembly, or installation of facilities or equipment (including contractual obligations to purchase such facilities or equipment) at the premises where such equipment will be used, including preparation work at such premises.

**(b) Categories of sources; Federal standards of performance for new sources**

(1)(A) The Administrator shall, within ninety days after October 18, 1972, publish (and from time to time thereafter shall revise) a list of categories of sources, which shall, at the minimum, include:

pulp and paper mills;

paperboard, builders paper and board mills;

meat product and rendering processing;

dairy product processing;

grain mills;

canned and preserved fruits and vegetables processing;

canned and preserved seafood processing;

sugar processing;

textile mills;

cement manufacturing;

feedlots;

electroplating;

organic chemicals manufacturing;

inorganic chemicals manufacturing;

plastic and synthetic materials manufacturing;

soap and detergent manufacturing;

fertilizer manufacturing;

petroleum refining;

iron and steel manufacturing;

nonferrous metals manufacturing;

phosphate manufacturing;

steam electric powerplants;

ferroalloy manufacturing;

leather tanning and finishing;

glass and asbestos manufacturing;

rubber processing; and

timber products processing.

(B) As soon as practicable, but in no case more than one year, after a category of sources is included in a list under subparagraph (A) of this paragraph, the Administrator shall propose and publish regulations establishing Federal standards of performance for new sources within such category. The Administrator shall afford interested persons an opportunity for written comment on such proposed regulations. After considering such comments, he shall promulgate, within one hundred and twenty days after publication of such proposed regulations, such standards with such adjustments as he deems appropriate. The Administrator shall, from time to time, as technology and alternatives change, revise such standards following the procedure required by this subsection for promulgation of such standards. Standards of performance, or revisions thereof, shall become effective upon promulgation. In establishing or revising Federal standards of performance for new sources under this section, the Administrator shall take into consideration the cost of achieving such effluent reduction, and any non-water quality, environmental impact and energy requirements.

(2) The Administrator may distinguish among classes, types, and sizes within categories of new sources for the purpose of establishing such standards and shall consider the type of process employed (including whether batch or continuous).

(3) The provisions of this section shall apply to any new source owned or operated by the United States.

**(c) State enforcement of standards of performance**

Each State may develop and submit to the Administrator a procedure under State law for applying and enforcing standards of performance for new sources located in such State. If the Administrator finds that the procedure and the law of any State require the application and enforcement of standards of performance to at least the same extent as required by this section, such State is authorized to apply and enforce such standards of performance (except with respect to new sources owned or operated by the United States).

**(d) Protection from more stringent standards**

Notwithstanding any other provision of this chapter, any point source the construction of which is commenced after October 18, 1972, and which is so constructed as to meet all applicable standards of performance shall not be subject to any more stringent standard of performance during a ten-year period beginning on the date of completion of such construction or during the period of depreciation or amortization of such facility for the purposes of section 167 or 169 (or both) of Title 26, whichever period ends first.

**(e) Illegality of operation of new sources in violation of applicable standards of performance**

After the effective date of standards of performance promulgated under this section, it shall be unlawful for any owner or operator of any new source to operate such source in violation of any standard of performance applicable to such source.

(June 30, 1948, c. 758, Title III, § 306, as added Oct. 18, 1972, Pub.L. 92–500, § 2, 86 Stat. 854.)

### HISTORICAL AND STATUTORY NOTES

**Exemption For Discharges From Point Sources in United States Virgin Islands Attributable to Manufacture of Rum; Conditions**

Discharges from point sources in the United States Virgin Islands in existence on Aug. 5, 1983, attributable to the manufacture of rum not to be subject to the requirements of this section under certain conditions, see section 214(g) of Pub.L. 98–67, set out as a note under section 1311 of this title.

**Exemption for Fort Allen in Puerto Rico**

For provisions relating to the prohibition of an exemption from this section for Fort Allen in Puerto Rico, in its use as temporary housing for Haitian refugees, see section 1–101 of Ex. Ord. No. 12327, Oct. 1, 1981, 46 F.R. 48893, set out as a note under section 2601 of Title 22, Foreign Relations and Intercourse.

## § 1317. Toxic and pretreatment effluent standards

### [FWPCA § 307]

### (a) Toxic pollutant list; revision; hearing; promulgation of standards; effective date; consultation

(1) On and after December 27, 1977, the list of toxic pollutants or combination of pollutants subject to this chapter shall consist of those toxic pollutants listed in table 1 of Committee Print Numbered 95–30 of the Committee on Public Works and Transportation of the House of Representatives, and the Administrator shall publish, not later than the thirtieth day after December 27, 1977, that list. From time to time thereafter, the Administrator may revise such list and the Administrator is authorized to add to or remove from such list any pollutant. The Administrator in publishing any revised list, including the addition or removal of any pollutant from such list, shall take into account toxicity of the pollutant, its persistence, degradability, the usual or potential presence of the affected organisms in any waters, the importance of the affected organisms, and the nature and extent of the effect of the toxic pollutant on such organisms. A determination of the Administrator under this paragraph shall be final except that if, on judicial review, such determination was based on arbitrary and capricious action of the Administrator, the Administrator shall make a redetermination.

(2) Each toxic pollutant listed in accordance with paragraph (1) of this subsection shall be subject to effluent limitations resulting from the application of the best available technology economically achievable for the applicable category or class of point sources established in accordance with sections 1311(b)(2)(A) and 1314(b)(2) of this title. The Administrator, in his discretion, may publish in the Federal Register a proposed effluent standard (which may include a prohibition) establishing requirements for a toxic pollutant which, if an effluent limitation is applicable to a class or category of point sources, shall be applicable to such category or class only if such standard imposes more stringent requirements. Such published effluent standard (or prohibition) shall take into account the toxicity of the pollutant, its persistence, degradability, the usual or potential presence of the affected organisms in any waters, the importance of the affected organisms and the nature and extent of the effect of the toxic pollutant on such organisms, and the extent to which effective control is being or may be achieved under other regulatory authority. The Administrator shall allow a period of not less than sixty days following publication of any such proposed effluent standard (or prohibition) for written comment by interested persons on such proposed standard. In addition, if within thirty days of publication of any such proposed effluent standard (or prohibition) any interested person so requests, the Administrator shall hold a public hearing in connection therewith. Such a public hearing shall provide an opportunity for oral and written presentations, such cross-examination as the Administrator determines is appropriate on disputed issues of material fact, and the transcription of a verbatim record which shall be available to the public. After consideration of such comments and any information and material presented at any public hearing held on such proposed standard or prohibition, the Administrator shall promulgate such standard (or prohibition) with such modification as the Administrator finds are justified. Such promulgation by the Administrator shall be made within two hundred and seventy days after publication of proposed standard (or prohibition). Such standard (or prohibition) shall be final except that if, on judicial review, such standard was not based on substantial evidence, the Administrator shall promulgate a revised standard. Effluent limitations shall be established in accordance with sections 1311(b)(2)(A) and 1314(b)(2) of this title for every toxic pollutant referred to in table 1 of Committee Print Numbered 95–30 of the Committee on Public Works and Transportation of the House of Representatives as soon as practicable after December 27, 1977, but no later than July 1, 1980. Such effluent limitations or effluent standards (or prohibitions) shall be established for every other toxic pollutant listed under paragraph (1) of this subsection as soon as practicable after it is so listed.

(3) Each such effluent standard (or prohibition) shall be reviewed and, if appropriate, revised at least every three years.

(4) Any effluent standard promulgated under this section shall be at that level which the Administrator determines provides an ample margin of safety.

(5) When proposing or promulgating any effluent standard (or prohibition) under this section, the Administrator shall designate the category or categories of sources to which the effluent standard (or prohibition) shall apply. Any disposal of dredged material may be included in such a category of sources after consultation with the Secretary of the Army.

(6) Any effluent standard (or prohibition) established pursuant to this section shall take effect on such date or dates as specified in the order promulgating such standard, but in no case, more than one year from the date of such promulgation. If the Administrator determines that compliance within one year from the date of promulgation is technologically infeasible for a category of sources, the Administrator may establish the effective date of the effluent standard (or prohibition) for such category at the earliest date upon which compliance can be feasibly attained by sources within such category, but in no event more than three years after the date of such promulgation.

(7) Prior to publishing any regulations pursuant to this section the Administrator shall, to the maximum extent practicable within the time provided, consult with appropriate advisory committees, States, independent experts, and Federal departments and agencies.

**(b) Pretreatment standards; hearing; promulgation; compliance period; revision; application to State and local laws**

(1) The Administrator shall, within one hundred and eighty days after October 18, 1972, and from time to time thereafter, publish proposed regulations establishing pretreatment standards for introduction of pollutants into treatment works (as defined in section 1292 of this title) which are publicly owned for those pollutants which are determined not to be susceptible to treatment by such treatment works or which would interfere with the operation of such treatment works. Not later than ninety days after such publication, and after opportunity for public hearing, the Administrator shall promulgate such pretreatment standards. Pretreatment standards under this subsection shall specify a time for compliance not to exceed three years from the date of promulgation and shall be established to prevent the discharge of any pollutant through treatment works (as defined in section 1292 of this title) which are publicly owned, which pollutant interferes with, passes through, or otherwise is incompatible with such works. If, in the case of any toxic pollutant under subsection (a) of this section introduced by a source into a publicly owned treatment works, the treatment by such works removes all or any part of such toxic pollutant and the discharge from such works does not violate that effluent limitation or standard which would be applicable to such toxic pollutant if it were discharged by such source other than through a publicly owned treatment works, and does not prevent sludge use or disposal by such works in accordance with section 1345 of this title, then the pretreatment requirements for the sources actually discharging such toxic pollutant into such publicly owned treatment works may be revised by the owner or operator of such works to reflect the removal of such toxic pollutant by such works.

(2) The Administrator shall, from time to time, as control technology, processes, operating methods, or other alternatives change, revise such standards following the procedure established by this subsection for promulgation of such standards.

(3) When proposing or promulgating any pretreatment standard under this section, the Administrator shall designate the category or categories of sources to which such standard shall apply.

(4) Nothing in this subsection shall affect any pretreatment requirement established by any State or local law not in conflict with any pretreatment standard established under this subsection.

**(c) New sources of pollutants into publicly owned treatment works**

In order to insure that any source introducing pollutants into a publicly owned treatment works, which source would be a new source subject to section 1316 of this title if it were to discharge pollutants, will not cause a violation of the effluent limitations established for any such treatment works, the Administrator shall promulgate pretreatment standards for the category of such sources simultaneously with the promulgation of standards of performance under section 1316 of this title for the equivalent category of new sources. Such pretreatment standards shall prevent the discharge of any pollutant into such treatment works, which pollutant may interfere with, pass through, or otherwise be incompatible with such works.

**(d) Operation in violation of standards unlawful**

After the effective date of any effluent standard or prohibition or pretreatment standard promulgated under this section, it shall be unlawful for any owner or operator of any source to operate any source in violation of any such effluent standard or prohibition or pretreatment standard.

**(e) Compliance date extension for innovative pretreatment systems**

In the case of any existing facility that proposes to comply with the pretreatment standards of subsection (b) of this section by applying an innovative system that meets the requirements of section 1311(k) of this title, the owner or operator of the publicly owned treatment works receiving the treated effluent from such facility may extend the date for compliance with the applicable pretreatment standard established under this section for a period not to exceed 2 years—

(1) if the Administrator determines that the innovative system has the potential for industrywide application, and

(2) if the Administrator (or the State in consultation with the Administrator, in any case in which the State has a pretreatment program approved by the Administrator)—

(A) determines that the proposed extension will not cause the publicly owned treatment works to be in violation of its permit under section 1342 of this title or of section 1345 of this title or to contribute to such a violation, and

(B) concurs with the proposed extension.

(June 30, 1948, c. 758, Title III, § 307, as added Oct. 18, 1972, Pub.L. 92–500, § 2, 86 Stat. 856, and amended Dec. 27, 1977, Pub.L. 95–217, §§ 53(a), (b), 54(a), 91 Stat. 1589–1591; Feb. 4, 1987, Pub.L. 100–4, Title III, § 309(a), 101 Stat. 41.)

### HISTORICAL AND STATUTORY NOTES

**Change of Name**

Any reference in any provision of law enacted before Jan. 4, 1995, to the Committee on Public Works and Transportation of the House of Representatives treated as referring to the Committee on Transportation and Infrastructure of the House of Representatives, see section 1(a)(9) of Pub.L. 104–14, set out as a note preceding section 21 of Title 2, The Congress.

**Increase in EPA Employees**

Section 309(b) of Pub.L. 100–4 provided that: "The Administrator shall take such actions as may be necessary to increase the number of employees of the Environmental Protection Agency in order to effectively implement pretreatment requirements under section 307 of the Federal Water Pollution Control Act [this section]."

**Exemption for Fort Allen in Puerto Rico**

For provisions relating to the prohibition of an exemption from this section for Fort Allen in Puerto Rico, in its use as temporary housing for Haitian refugees, see section 1–101 of Ex. Ord. No. 12327, Oct. 1, 1981, 46 F.R. 48893, set out as a note under section 2601 of Title 22, Foreign Relations and Intercourse.

## § 1318. Records and reports; inspections

[FWPCA § 308]

**(a) Maintenance; monitoring equipment; entry; access to information**

Whenever required to carry out the objective of this chapter, including but not limited to (1) developing or assisting in the development of any effluent limitation, or other limitation, prohibition, or effluent standard, pretreatment standard, or standard of performance under this chapter; (2) determining whether any person is in violation of any such effluent limitation, or other limitation, prohibition or effluent standard, pretreatment standard, or standard of performance; (3) any requirement established under this section; or (4) carrying out sections 1315, 1321, 1342, 1344 (relating to State permit programs), 1345, and 1364 of this title—

(A) the Administrator shall require the owner or operator of any point source to (i) establish and maintain such records, (ii) make such reports, (iii) install, use, and maintain such monitoring equipment or methods (including where appropriate, biological monitoring methods), (iv) sample such effluents (in accordance with such methods, at such locations, at such intervals, and in such manner as the Administrator shall prescribe), and (v) provide such other information as he may reasonably require; and

(B) the Administrator or his authorized representative (including an authorized contractor acting as a representative of the Administrator), upon presentation of his credentials—

(i) shall have a right of entry to, upon, or through any premises in which an effluent source is located or in which any records required to be maintained under clause (A) of this subsection are located, and

(ii) may at reasonable times have access to and copy any records, inspect any monitoring equipment or method required under clause (A), and sample any effluents which the owner or operator of such source is required to sample under such clause.

**(b) Availability to public; trade secrets exception; penalty for disclosure of confidential information**

Any records, reports, or information obtained under this section (1) shall, in the case of effluent data, be related to any applicable effluent limitations, toxic, pretreatment, or new source performance standards, and (2) shall be available to the public, except that upon a showing satisfactory to the Administrator by any person that records, reports, or information, or particular part thereof (other than effluent data), to which the Administrator has access under this section, if made public would divulge methods or processes entitled to protection as trade secrets of such person, the Administrator shall consider such record, report, or information, or particular portion thereof confidential in accordance with the purposes of section 1905 of Title 18. Any authorized representative of the Administrator (including an authorized contractor acting as a representative of the Administrator) who knowingly or willfully publishes, divulges, discloses, or makes known in any manner or to any extent not authorized by law any information which is required to be considered confidential under this subsection shall be fined not more than $1,000 or imprisoned not more than 1 year, or both. Nothing in this subsection shall prohibit the Administrator or an authorized representative of the Administrator (including any authorized contractor acting as a representative of the Administrator) from disclosing records, reports, or information to other officers, employees, or authorized representatives of the United States concerned with carrying out this chapter or when relevant in any proceeding under this chapter.

**(c) Application of State law**

Each State may develop and submit to the Administrator procedures under State law for inspection, monitoring, and entry with respect to point sources located in such State. If the Administrator finds that the procedures and the law of any State relating to inspection, monitoring, and entry are applicable to at least the same extent as those required by this section, such State is authorized to apply and enforce its procedures for inspection, monitoring, and entry with respect to point sources located in such State (except with respect to point sources owned or operated by the United States).

**(d) Access by Congress**

Notwithstanding any limitation contained in this section or any other provision of law, all information reported to or otherwise obtained by the Administrator (or any representative of the Administrator) under this chapter shall be made available, upon written request of any duly authorized committee of Congress, to such committee.

(June 30, 1948, c. 758, Title III, § 308, as added Oct. 18, 1972, Pub.L. 92–500, § 2, 86 Stat. 858, and amended Dec. 27, 1977, Pub.L. 95–217, § 67(c)(1), 91 Stat. 1606; Feb. 4, 1987, Pub.L. 100–4, Title III, § 310, Title IV, § 406(d)(1), 101 Stat. 41, 73.)

## § 1319. Enforcement

**[FWPCA § 309]**

**(a) State enforcement; compliance orders**

(1) Whenever, on the basis of any information available to him, the Administrator finds that any person is in violation of any condition or limitation which implements section 1311, 1312, 1316, 1317, 1318, 1328, or 1345 of this title in a permit issued by a State under an approved permit program under section 1342 or 1344 of this title, he shall proceed under his authority in paragraph (3) of this subsection or he shall notify the person in alleged violation and such State of such finding. If beyond the thirtieth day after the Administrator's notification the State has not commenced appropriate enforcement action, the Administrator shall issue an order requiring such person to comply with such condition or limitation or shall bring a civil action in accordance with subsection (b) of this section.

(2) Whenever, on the basis of information available to him, the Administrator finds that violations of permit conditions or limitations as set forth in paragraph (1) of this subsection are so widespread that such violations appear to result from a failure of the State to enforce such permit conditions or limitations effectively, he shall so notify the State. If the Administrator finds such failure extends beyond the thirtieth day after such notice, he shall give public notice of such finding. During the period beginning with such public notice and ending when such State satisfies the Administrator that it will enforce such conditions and limitations (hereafter referred to in this section as the period of "federally assumed enforcement"), except where an extension has been granted under paragraph (5)(B) of this subsection, the Administrator shall enforce any permit condition or limitation with respect to any person—

(A) by issuing an order to comply with such condition or limitation, or

(B) by bringing a civil action under subsection (b) of this section.

(3) Whenever on the basis of any information available to him the Administrator finds that any person is in violation of section 1311, 1312, 1316, 1317, 1318, 1328, or 1345 of this title, or is in violation of any permit condition or limitation implementing any of such sections in a permit issued under section 1342 of this title by him or by a State or in a permit issued under section 1344 of this title by a State, he shall issue an order requiring such person to comply with such section or requirement, or he shall bring a civil action in accordance with subsection (b) of this section.

(4) A copy of any order issued under this subsection shall be sent immediately by the Administrator to the State in which the violation occurs and other affected States. In any case in which an order under this subsection (or notice to a violator under paragraph (1) of this subsection) is issued to a corporation, a copy of such order (or notice) shall be served on any appropriate corporate officers. An order issued under this subsection relating to a violation of section 1318 of this title shall not take effect until the person to whom it is issued has had an opportunity to confer with the Administrator concerning the alleged violation.

(5)(A) Any order issued under this subsection shall be by personal service, shall state with reasonable specificity the nature of the violation, and shall specify a time for compliance not to exceed thirty days in the case of a violation of an interim compliance schedule or operation and maintenance requirement and not to exceed a time the Administrator determines to be reasonable in the case of a violation of a final deadline, taking into account the seriousness of the violation and any good faith efforts to comply with applicable requirements.

(B) The Administrator may, if he determines (i) that any person who is a violator of, or any person who is otherwise not in compliance with, the time requirements under this chapter or in any permit issued under this chapter, has acted in good faith, and has made a commitment (in the form of contracts or other securities) of necessary resources to achieve compliance by the earliest possible date after July 1, 1977, but not later than April 1, 1979; (ii) that any extension under this provision will not result in the imposition of any additional controls on any other point or nonpoint source; (iii) that an application for a permit under section 1342 of this title was filed for such person prior to December 31, 1974; and (iv) that the facilities necessary for compliance with such requirements are under construction, grant an extension of the date referred to in section 1311(b)(1)(A) of this title to a date which will achieve compliance at the earliest time possible but not later than April 1, 1979.

(6) Whenever, on the basis of information available to him, the Administrator finds (A) that any person is in violation of section 1311(b)(1)(A) or (C) of this title, (B) that such person cannot meet the requirements for a time extension under section 1311(i)(2) of this title, and (C) that the most expeditious and appropriate means of compliance with this chapter by such person is to discharge into a publicly owned treatment works, then, upon request of such person, the Administrator may issue an order requiring such person to comply with this chapter at the earliest date practicable, but not later than July 1, 1983, by discharging into a publicly owned treatment works if such works concur with such order. Such order shall include a schedule of compliance.

**(b) Civil actions**

The Administrator is authorized to commence a civil action for appropriate relief, including a permanent or temporary injunction, for any violation for which he is authorized to issue a compliance order under subsection (a) of this section. Any action under this subsection may be brought in the district court of the United States for the district in which the defendant is located or resides or is doing business, and such court shall have jurisdiction to restrain such violation and to require compliance. Notice of the commencement of such action shall be given immediately to the appropriate State.

**(c) Criminal penalties**

**(1) Negligent violations**

Any person who—

(A) negligently violates section 1311, 1312, 1316, 1317, 1318, 1321(b)(3), 1328, or 1345 of this title, or any permit condition or limitation implementing any of such sections in a permit issued under section 1342 of this title by the Administrator or by a State, or any requirement imposed in a pretreatment program approved under section 1342(a)(3) or 1342(b)(8) of this title or in a permit issued under section 1344 of this title by the Secretary of the Army or by a State; or

(B) negligently introduces into a sewer system or into a publicly owned treatment works any pollutant or hazardous substance which such person knew or reasonably should have known could cause personal injury or property damage or, other than in compliance with all applicable Federal, State, or local requirements or permits, which causes such treatment works to violate any effluent limitation or condition in any permit issued to the treatment works under section 1342 of this title by the Administrator or a State;

shall be punished by a fine of not less than $2,500 nor more than $25,000 per day of violation, or by imprisonment for not more than 1 year, or by both. If a conviction of a person is for a violation committed after a first conviction of such person under this paragraph, punishment shall be by a fine of not more than $50,000 per day of violation, or by imprisonment of not more than 2 years, or by both.

**(2) Knowing violations**

Any person who—

(A) knowingly violates section 1311, 1312, 1316, 1317, 1318, 1321(b)(3), 1328, or 1345 of this title, or any permit condition or limitation implementing any of such sections in a permit issued under section 1342 of this title by the Administrator or by a State, or any requirement imposed in a pretreatment program approved under section 1342(a)(3) or 1342(b)(8) of this title or in a permit issued under section 1344 of this title by the Secretary of the Army or by a State; or

(B) knowingly introduces into a sewer system or into a publicly owned treatment works any pollutant or hazardous substance which such person knew or reasonably should have known could cause personal injury or property damage or, other than in compliance with all applicable Federal, State, or local requirements or permits, which causes such treatment works to violate any effluent limitation or condition in a permit issued to the treatment works under section 1342 of this title by the Administrator or a State;

shall be punished by a fine of not less than $5,000 nor more than $50,000 per day of violation, or by imprisonment for not more than 3 years, or by both. If a conviction of a person is for a violation committed after a first conviction of such person under this paragraph, punishment shall be by a fine of not more than $100,000 per day of violation, or by imprisonment of not more than 6 years, or by both.

**(3) Knowing endangerment**

**(A) General rule**

Any person who knowingly violates section 1311, 1312, 1313, 1316, 1317, 1318, 1321(b)(3), 1328, or 1345 of this title, or any permit condition or limitation implementing any of such sections in a permit issued under section 1342 of this title by the Administrator or by a State, or in a permit issued under section 1344 of this title by the Secretary of the Army or by a State, and who knows at that time that he thereby places another person in imminent danger of death or serious bodily injury, shall, upon conviction, be subject to a fine of not more than $250,000 or imprisonment of not more than 15 years, or both. A person which is an organization shall, upon conviction of violating this subparagraph, be subject to a fine of not more than $1,000,000. If a conviction of a person is for a violation committed after a first conviction of such person under this paragraph, the maximum punishment shall be doubled with respect to both fine and imprisonment.

**(B) Additional provisions**

For the purpose of subparagraph (A) of this paragraph—

**(i)** in determining whether a defendant who is an individual knew that his conduct placed another person in imminent danger of death or serious bodily injury—

**(I)** the person is responsible only for actual awareness or actual belief that he possessed; and

**(II)** knowledge possessed by a person other than the defendant but not by the defendant himself may not be attributed to the defendant;

except that in proving the defendant's possession of actual knowledge, circumstantial evidence may be used, including evidence that the defendant took affirmative steps to shield himself from relevant information;

**(ii)** it is an affirmative defense to prosecution that the conduct charged was consented to by the person endangered and that the danger and conduct charged were reasonably foreseeable hazards of—

**(I)** an occupation, a business, or a profession; or

**(II)** medical treatment or medical or scientific experimentation conducted by professionally approved methods and such other person had been made aware of the risks involved prior to giving consent;

and such defense may be established under this subparagraph by a preponderance of the evidence;

**(iii)** the term "organization" means a legal entity, other than a government, established or organized for any purpose, and such term includes a corporation, company, association, firm, partnership, joint stock company, foundation, institution, trust, society, union, or any other association of persons; and

**(iv)** the term "serious bodily injury" means bodily injury which involves a substantial risk of death, unconsciousness, extreme physical pain, protracted and obvious disfigurement, or protracted loss or impairment of the function of a bodily member, organ, or mental faculty.

**(4) False statements**

Any person who knowingly makes any false material statement, representation, or certification in any application, record, report, plan, or other document filed or required to be maintained under this chapter or who knowingly falsifies, tampers with, or renders inaccurate any monitoring device or method required to be maintained under this chapter, shall upon conviction, be punished by a fine of not more than $10,000, or by imprisonment for not more than 2 years, or by both. If a conviction of a person is for a violation committed after a first conviction of such person under this paragraph, punishment shall be by a fine of not more than $20,000 per day of violation, or by imprisonment of not more than 4 years, or by both.

**(5) Treatment of single operational upset**

For purposes of this subsection, a single operational upset which leads to simultaneous violations of more than one pollutant parameter shall be treated as a single violation.

**(6) Responsible corporate officer as "person"**

For the purpose of this subsection, the term "person" means, in addition to the definition contained in section 1362(5) of this title, any responsible corporate officer.

**(7) Hazardous substance defined**

For the purpose of this subsection, the term "hazardous substance" means (A) any substance designated pursuant to section 1321(b)(2)(A) of this title, (B) any element, compound, mixture, solution, or substance designated pursuant to section 9602 of Title 42, (C) any hazardous waste having the characteristics identified under or listed pursuant to section 3001 of the Solid Waste Disposal Act [42 U.S.C.A. § 6921] (but not including any waste the regulation of which under the Solid Waste Disposal Act [42 U.S.C.A. § 6901 et seq.] has been suspended by Act of Congress), (D) any toxic pollutant listed under section 1317(a) of this title, and (E) any imminently hazardous chemical substance or mixture with respect to which the Administrator has taken action pursuant to section 2606 of Title 15.

**(d) Civil penalties; factors considered in determining amount**

Any person who violates section 1311, 1312, 1316, 1317, 1318, 1328, or 1345 of this title, or any permit condition or limitation implementing any of such sections in a permit issued under section 1342 of this title by the Administrator, or by a State, ,[1] or in a permit issued under section 1344 of this title by a State, or any requirement imposed in a pretreatment program approved under section 1342(a)(3) or 1342(b)(8) of this title, and any person who violates any order issued by the Administrator under subsection (a) of this section, shall be subject to a civil penalty not to exceed $25,000 per day for each violation. In determining the amount of a civil penalty the court shall consider the seriousness of the violation or violations, the economic benefit (if any) resulting from the violation, any history of such violations, any good-faith efforts to comply with the applicable requirements, the economic impact of the penalty on the violator, and such other matters as justice may require. For purposes of this subsection, a single operational upset which leads to simultaneous violations of more than one pollutant parameter shall be treated as a single violation.

**(e) State liability for judgments and expenses**

Whenever a municipality is a party to a civil action brought by the United States under this section, the State in which such municipality is located shall be joined as a party. Such State shall be liable for payment of any judgment, or any expenses incurred as a result of complying with any judgment, entered against the municipality in such action to the extent that the laws of that State prevent the municipality from raising revenues needed to comply with such judgment.

**(f) Wrongful introduction of pollutant into treatment works**

Whenever, on the basis of any information available to him, the Administrator finds that an owner or operator of any source is introducing a pollutant into a treatment works in violation of subsection (d) of section 1317 of this title, the Administrator may notify the owner or operator of such treatment works and the State of such violation. If the owner or operator of the treatment works does not commence appropriate enforcement action within 30 days of the date of such notification, the Administrator may commence a civil action for appropriate relief, including but not limited to, a permanent or temporary injunction, against the owner or operator of such treatment works. In any such civil action the Administrator shall join the owner or operator of such source as a party to the action. Such action shall be brought in the district court of the United States in the district in which the treatment works is located. Such court shall have jurisdiction to restrain such violation and to require the owner or operator of the treatment works and the owner or operator of the source to take such action as may be necessary to come into compliance with this chapter. Notice of commencement of any such action shall be given to the State. Nothing in this subsection shall be construed to limit or prohibit any other authority the Administrator may have under this chapter.

**(g) Administrative penalties**

**(1) Violations**

Whenever on the basis of any information available—

**(A)** the Administrator finds that any person has violated section 1311, 1312, 1316, 1317, 1318, 1328, or 1345 of this title, or has violated any permit condition or limitation implementing any of such sections in a permit issued under section 1342 of this title by the Administrator or by a State, or in a permit issued under section 1344 of this title by a State, or

**(B)** the Secretary of the Army (hereinafter in this subsection referred to as the "Secretary") finds that any person has violated any permit condition or limitation in a permit issued under section 1344 of this title by the Secretary,

the Administrator or Secretary, as the case may be, may, after consultation with the State in which the violation occurs, assess a class I civil penalty or a class II civil penalty under this subsection.

**(2) Classes of penalties**

**(A) Class I**

The amount of a class I civil penalty under paragraph (1) may not exceed $10,000 per violation, except that the maximum amount of any class I civil penalty under this subparagraph shall not exceed $25,000. Before issuing an order assessing a civil penalty under this subparagraph, the Administrator or the Secretary, as the case may be, shall give to the person to be assessed such penalty written notice of the Administrator's or Secretary's proposal to issue such order and the opportunity to request, within 30 days of the date the notice is received by such person, a hearing on the proposed order. Such hearing shall not be subject to section 554 or 556 of Title 5, but shall provide a reasonable opportunity to be heard and to present evidence.

**(B) Class II**

The amount of a class II civil penalty under paragraph (1) may not exceed $10,000 per day for each day during which the violation continues; except that the maximum amount of any class II civil penalty under this subparagraph shall not exceed $125,000. Except as otherwise provided in this subsection, a class II civil penalty shall be assessed and collected in the same manner, and subject to the same provisions, as in the case of civil penalties assessed and collected after notice and opportunity for a hearing on the record in accordance with section 554 of Title 5. The Administrator and the Secretary may issue rules for discovery procedures for hearings under this subparagraph.

**(3) Determining amount**

In determining the amount of any penalty assessed under this subsection, the Administrator or the Secretary, as the case may be, shall take into account the nature, circumstances, extent and gravity of the violation, or violations, and, with respect to the violator, ability to pay, any prior history of such violations, the degree of culpability, economic benefit or savings (if any) resulting from the violation, and such other matters as justice may require. For purposes of this subsection, a single operational upset which leads to simultaneous violations of more than one pollutant parameter shall be treated as a single violation.

**(4) Rights of interested persons**

**(A) Public notice**

Before issuing an order assessing a civil penalty under this subsection the Administrator or Secretary, as the case may be, shall provide public notice of and reasonable opportunity to comment on the proposed issuance of such order.

**(B) Presentation of evidence**

Any person who comments on a proposed assessment of a penalty under this subsection shall be given notice of any hearing held under this subsection and of the order assessing such penalty. In any hearing held under this subsection, such person shall have a reasonable opportunity to be heard and to present evidence.

**(C) Rights of interested persons to a hearing**

If no hearing is held under paragraph (2) before issuance of an order assessing a penalty under this subsection, any person who commented on the proposed assessment may petition, within 30 days after the issuance of such order, the Administrator or Secretary, as the case may be, to set aside such order and to provide a hearing on the penalty. If the evidence presented by the petitioner in support of the petition is material and was not considered in the issuance of the order, the Administrator or Secretary shall immediately set aside such order and provide a hearing in accordance with paragraph (2)(A) in the case of a class I civil penalty and paragraph (2)(B) in the case of a class II civil penalty. If the Administrator or Secretary denies a hearing under this subparagraph, the Administrator or Secretary shall provide to the petitioner, and publish in the Federal Register, notice of and the reasons for such denial.

**(5) Finality of order**

An order issued under this subsection shall become final 30 days after its issuance unless a petition for judicial review is filed under paragraph (8) or a hearing is requested under paragraph (4)(C). If such a hearing is denied, such order shall become final 30 days after such denial.

**(6) Effect of order**

**(A) Limitation on actions under other sections**

Action taken by the Administrator or the Secretary, as the case may be, under this subsection shall not affect or limit the Administrator's or Secretary's authority to enforce any provision of this chapter; except that any violation—

(i) with respect to which the Administrator or the Secretary has commenced and is diligently prosecuting an action under this subsection,

(ii) with respect to which a State has commenced and is diligently prosecuting an action under a State law comparable to this subsection, or

(iii) for which the Administrator, the Secretary, or the State has issued a final order not subject to further judicial review and the violator has paid a penalty assessed under this subsection, or such comparable State law, as the case may be,

shall not be the subject of a civil penalty action under subsection (d) of this section or section 1321(b) of this title or section 1365 of this title.

**(B) Applicability of limitation with respect to citizen suits**

The limitations contained in subparagraph (A) on civil penalty actions under section 1365 of this title shall not apply with respect to any violation for which—

(i) a civil action under section 1365(a)(1) of this title has been filed prior to commencement of an action under this subsection, or

(ii) notice of an alleged violation of section 1365(a)(1) of this title has been given in accordance with section 1365(b)(1)(A) of this title prior to commencement of an action under this subsection and an action under section 1365(a)(1) of this title with respect to such alleged violation is filed before the 120th day after the date on which such notice is given.

**(7) Effect of action on compliance**

No action by the Administrator or the Secretary under this subsection shall affect any person's obligation to comply with any section of this chapter or with the terms and conditions of any permit issued pursuant to section 1342 or 1344 of this title.

**(8) Judicial review**

Any person against whom a civil penalty is assessed under this subsection or who commented on the proposed assessment of such penalty in accordance with paragraph (4) may obtain review of such assessment—

(A) in the case of assessment of a class I civil penalty, in the United States District Court for the District of Columbia or in the district in which the violation is alleged to have occurred, or

(B) in the case of assessment of a class II civil penalty, in United States Court of Appeals for the District of Columbia Circuit or for any other circuit in which such person resides or transacts business,

by filing a notice of appeal in such court within the 30-day period beginning on the date the civil penalty order is issued and by simultaneously sending a copy of such notice by certified mail to the Administrator or the Secretary, as the case may be, and the Attorney General. The Administrator or the Secretary shall promptly file in such court a certified copy of the record on which the order was issued. Such court shall not set aside or remand such order unless there is not substantial evidence in the record, taken as a whole, to support the finding of a violation or unless the Administrator's or Secretary's assessment of the penalty constitutes an abuse of discretion and shall not impose additional civil penalties for the same violation unless the Administrator's or Secretary's assessment of the penalty constitutes an abuse of discretion.

**(9) Collection**

If any person fails to pay an assessment of a civil penalty—

(A) after the order making the assessment has become final, or

(B) after a court in an action brought under paragraph (8) has entered a final judgment in favor of the Administrator or the Secretary, as the case may be,

the Administrator or the Secretary shall request the Attorney General to bring a civil action in an appropriate district court to recover the amount assessed (plus interest at currently prevailing rates from the date of the final order or the date of the final judgment, as the case may be). In such an action, the validity, amount, and appropriateness of such penalty shall not be subject to review. Any person who fails to pay on a timely basis the amount of an assessment of a civil penalty as described in the first sentence of this paragraph shall be required to pay, in addition to such amount and interest, attorneys fees and costs for collection proceedings and a quarterly nonpayment penalty for each quarter during which such failure to pay persists. Such nonpayment penalty shall be in an amount equal to 20 percent of the aggregate amount of such person's penalties and nonpayment penalties which are unpaid as of the beginning of such quarter.

**(10) Subpoenas**

The Administrator or Secretary, as the case may be, may issue subpoenas for the attendance and testimony of witnesses and the production of relevant papers, books, or documents in connection with hearings under this subsection. In case of contumacy or refusal to obey a subpoena issued pursuant to this paragraph and served upon any person, the district court of the United States for any district in which such person is found, resides, or transacts business, upon application by the United States and after notice to such person, shall have jurisdiction to issue an order requiring such person to appear and give testimony before the administrative law judge or to appear and produce documents before the administrative law judge, or both, and any failure to obey such order of the court may be punished by such court as a contempt thereof.

**(11) Protection of existing procedures**

Nothing in this subsection shall change the procedures existing on the day before February 4, 1987, under other subsections of this section for issuance and enforcement of orders by the Administrator.

(June 30, 1948, c. 758, Title III, § 309, as added Oct. 18, 1972, Pub.L. 92–500, § 2, 86 Stat. 859, and amended Dec. 27, 1977, Pub.L. 95–217, §§ 54(b), 55, 56, 67(c)(2), 91 Stat. 1591, 1592, 1606; Feb. 4, 1987, Pub.L. 100–4, Title III, §§ 312, 313(a)(1), (b)(1), (c), 314(a), 101 Stat. 42, 45, 46; Aug. 18, 1990, Pub.L. 101–380, Title IV, § 4301(c), 104 Stat. 537.)

1 So in original.

## HISTORICAL AND STATUTORY NOTES

**References in Text**

The Solid Waste Disposal Act, referred to in subsec. (c)(7) is Title II of Pub.L. 89–272, as amended generally by Pub.L. 94–580, § 2, Oct. 21, 1976, 90 Stat. 2795, which is classified generally to chapter 82 (section 6901 et seq.) of Title 42, The Public Health and Welfare. Section 3001 of the Solid Waste

Disposal Act is classified to section 6921 of Title 42. For complete classification of this Act to the Code, see Short Title note set out under section 6901 of Title 42 and Tables.

**Savings Provision**

Section 313(a)(2) of Pub.L. 100–4 provided that: "No State shall be required before July 1, 1988, to modify a permit program approved or submitted under section 402 of the Federal Water Pollution Control Act [section 1342 of this title] as a result of the amendment made by paragraph (1) [amending subsec. (d) of this section by inserting reference to requirements imposed in a pretreatment program approved under section 1342(a)(3) or (b)(8) of this title]."

**Deposit of Certain Penalties Into Oil Spill Liability Trust Fund**

Penalties paid pursuant to this section and sections 1321 and 1501 et seq., respectively, of this title, deposited in the Oil Spill Liability Trust Fund created under section 9509 of Title 26, Internal Revenue Code, see section 4304 of Pub.L. 101–380, set out as a note under section 9509 of Title 26.

**Increased Penalties Not Required Under State Programs**

Section 313(b)(2) of Pub.L. 100–4 provided that: "The Federal Water Pollution Control Act [this chapter] shall not be construed as requiring a State to have a civil penalty for violations described in section 309(d) of such Act [subsec. (d) of this section] which has the same monetary amount as the civil penalty established by such section, as amended by paragraph (1) [amending subsec. (d) of this section by increasing the penalty to $25,000]. Nothing in this paragraph shall affect the Administrator's authority to establish or adjust by regulation a minimum acceptable State civil penalty."

**Actions by Surgeon General Relating to Interstate Pollution**

Act July 9, 1956, c. 518, § 5, 70 Stat. 507, provided that actions by the Surgeon General with respect to water pollutants under section 2(d) of Act June 30, 1948, c. 758, 62 Stat. 1155, as in effect prior to July 9, 1956, which had been completed prior to such date, would still be subject to the terms of section 2(d) of Act June 30, 1948, in effect prior to the July 9, 1956 amendment, but that actions with respect to such pollutants would nevertheless subsequently be possible in accordance with the terms of Act June 30, 1948, as amended by Act July 9, 1956.

## § 1320. International pollution abatement

### [FWPCA § 310]

**(a) Hearing; participation by foreign nations**

Whenever the Administrator, upon receipts of reports, surveys, or studies from any duly constituted international agency, has reason to believe that pollution is occurring which endangers the health or welfare of persons in a foreign country, and the Secretary of State requests him to abate such pollution, he shall give formal notification thereof to the State water pollution control agency of the State or States in which such discharge or discharges originate and to the appropriate interstate agency, if any. He shall also promptly call such a hearing, if he believes that such pollution is occurring in sufficient quantity to warrant such action, and if such foreign country has given the United States essentially the same rights with respect to the prevention and control of pollution occurring in that country as is given that country by this subsection. The Administrator, through the Secretary of State, shall invite the foreign country which may be adversely affected by the pollution to attend and participate in the hearing, and the representative of such country shall, for the purpose of the hearing and any further proceeding resulting from such hearing, have all the rights of a State water pollution control agency. Nothing in this subsection shall be construed to modify, amend, repeal, or otherwise affect the provisions of the 1909 Boundary Waters Treaty between Canada and the United States or the Water Utilization Treaty of 1944 between Mexico and the United States (59 Stat. 1219), relative to the control and abatement of pollution in waters covered by those treaties.

**(b) Functions and responsibilities of Administrator not affected**

The calling of a hearing under this section shall not be construed by the courts, the Administrator, or any person as limiting, modifying, or otherwise affecting the functions and responsibilities of the Administrator under this section to establish and enforce water quality requirements under this chapter.

**(c) Hearing board; composition; findings of fact; recommendations; implementation of board's decision**

The Administrator shall publish in the Federal Register a notice of a public hearing before a hearing board of five or more persons appointed by the Administrator. A majority of the members of the board and the chairman who shall be designated by the Administrator shall not be officers or employees of Federal, State, or local governments. On the basis of the evidence presented at such hearing, the board shall within sixty days after completion of the hearing make findings of fact as to whether or not such pollution is occurring and shall thereupon by decision, incorporating its findings therein, make such recommendations to abate the pollution as may be appropriate and shall transmit such decision and the record of the hearings to the Administrator. All such decisions shall be public. Upon receipt of such decision, the Administrator shall promptly implement the board's decision in accordance with the provisions of this chapter.

**(d) Report by alleged polluter**

In connection with any hearing called under this subsection, the board is authorized to require any person whose alleged activities result in discharges causing or contributing to pollution to file with it in such forms as it may prescribe, a report based on existing data, furnishing such information as may reasonably be required as to the character, kind, and quantity of such discharges and the use of facilities or other means to prevent or reduce such discharges by the person filing such a report. Such report shall be made under oath or otherwise, as the board may prescribe, and shall be filed with the board within such reasonable period as it may prescribe, unless additional time is granted by it. Upon a showing satisfactory to the board by the person filing such report that such report or portion thereof (other than effluent data), to which the Administrator has access under this section, if made public would divulge trade secrets or secret processes of such person, the board shall consider such report or portion thereof confidential for the purposes of section 1905 of Title 18. If any person required to file any report under this paragraph shall fail to do so within the time fixed by the board for filing the same, and such failure shall continue for thirty days after notice of such default, such person shall forfeit to the United States the sum of $1,000 for each and every day of the continuance of such failure, which forfeiture shall be payable into the Treasury of the United States, and shall be recoverable in a civil suit in the name of the United States in the district court of the United States where such person has his principal office or in any district in which he does business. The Administrator may upon application therefor remit or mitigate any forfeiture provided for under this subsection.

**(e) Compensation of board members**

Board members, other than officers or employees of Federal, State, or local governments, shall be for each day (including travel-time) during which they are performing board business, entitled to receive compensation at a rate fixed by the Administrator but not in excess of the maximum rate of pay for grade GS–18, as provided in the General Schedule under section 5332 of Title 5, and shall, notwithstanding the limitations of sections 5703 and 5704 of Title 5, be fully reimbursed for travel, subsistence and related expenses.

**(f) Enforcement proceedings**

When any such recommendation adopted by the Administrator involves the institution of enforcement proceedings against any person to obtain the abatement of pollution subject to such recommendation, the Administrator shall institute such proceedings if he believes that the evidence warrants such proceedings. The district court of the United States shall consider and determine de novo all relevant issues, but shall receive in evidence the record of the proceedings before the conference or hearing board. The court shall have jurisdiction to enter such judgment and orders enforcing such judgment as it deems appropriate or to remand such proceedings to the Administrator for such further action as it may direct.

(June 30, 1948, c. 758, Title III, § 310, as added Oct. 18, 1972, Pub.L. 92–500, § 2, 86 Stat. 860.)

### HISTORICAL AND STATUTORY NOTES

**References in Other Laws to GS–16, 17, or 18 Pay Rates**

References in laws to the rates of pay for GS–16, 17, or 18, or to maximum rates of pay under the General Schedule, to be considered references to rates payable under specified sections of Title 5, see section 529 [Title I, § 101(c)(1)] of Pub.L. 101–509, set out in a note under 5 U.S.C.A. § 5376.

## § 1321. Oil and hazardous substance liability

**[FWPCA § 311]**

**(a) Definitions**

For the purpose of this section, the term—

(1) "oil" means oil of any kind or in any form, including, but not limited to, petroleum, fuel oil, sludge, oil refuse, and oil mixed with wastes other than dredged spoil;

(2) "discharge" includes, but is not limited to, any spilling, leaking, pumping, pouring, emitting, emptying or dumping, but excludes (A) discharges in compliance with a permit under section 1342 of this title, (B) discharges resulting from circumstances identified and reviewed and made a part of the public record with respect to a permit issued or modified under section 1342 of this title, and subject to a condition in such permit,,[1] (C) continuous or anticipated intermittent discharges from a point source, identified in a permit or permit application under section 1342 of this title, which are caused by events occurring within the scope of relevant operating or treatment systems, and (D) discharges incidental to mechanical removal authorized by the President under subsection (c) of this section;

(3) "vessel" means every description of watercraft or other artificial contrivance used, or capable of being used, as a means of transportation on water other than a public vessel;

(4) "public vessel" means a vessel owned or bareboat-chartered and operated by the United States, or by a State or political subdivision thereof, or by a foreign nation, except when such vessel is engaged in commerce;

(5) "United States" means the States, the District of Columbia, the Commonwealth of Puerto Rico, the Commonwealth of the Northern Mariana Islands, Guam, American Samoa, the Virgin Islands, and the Trust Territory of the Pacific Islands;

(6) "owner or operator" means (A) in the case of a vessel, any person owning, operating, or chartering by demise, such vessel, and (B) in the case of an onshore facility, and an offshore facility, any person

owning or operating such onshore facility or offshore facility, and (C) in the case of any abandoned offshore facility, the person who owned or operated such facility immediately prior to such abandonment;

(7) "person" includes an individual, firm, corporation, association, and a partnership;

(8) "remove" or "removal" refers to containment and removal of the oil or hazardous substances from the water and shorelines or the taking of such other actions as may be necessary to prevent, minimize, or mitigate damage to the public health or welfare, including, but not limited to, fish, shellfish, wildlife, and public and private property, shorelines, and beaches;

(9) "contiguous zone" means the entire zone established or to be established by the United States under article 24 of the Convention on the Territorial Sea and the Contiguous Zone;

(10) "onshore facility" means any facility (including, but not limited to, motor vehicles and rolling stock) of any kind located in, on, or under, any land within the United States other than submerged land;

(11) "offshore facility" means any facility of any kind located in, on, or under, any of the navigable waters of the United States, and any facility of any kind which is subject to the jurisdiction of the United States and is located in, on, or under any other waters, other than a vessel or a public vessel;

(12) "act of God" means an act occasioned by an unanticipated grave natural disaster;

(13) "barrel" means 42 United States gallons at 60 degrees Fahrenheit;

(14) "hazardous substance" means any substance designated pursuant to subsection (b)(2) of this section;

(15) "inland oil barge" means a non-self-propelled vessel carrying oil in bulk as cargo and certificated to operate only in the inland waters of the United States, while operating in such waters;

(16) "inland waters of the United States" means those waters of the United States lying inside the baseline from which the territorial sea is measured and those waters outside such baseline which are a part of the Gulf Intracoastal Waterway;

(17) "otherwise subject to the jurisdiction of the United States" means subject to the jurisdiction of the United States by virtue of United States citizenship, United States vessel documentation or numbering, or as provided for by international agreement to which the United States is a party;

(18) "Area Committee" means an Area Committee established under subsection (j) of this section;

(19) "Area Contingency Plan" means an Area Contingency Plan prepared under subsection (j) of this section;

(20) "Coast Guard District Response Group" means a Coast Guard District Response Group established under subsection (j) of this section;

(21) "Federal On-Scene Coordinator" means a Federal On-Scene Coordinator designated in the National Contingency Plan;

(22) "National Contingency Plan"means the National Contingency Plan prepared and published under subsection (d) of this section;

(23) "National Response Unit" means the National Response Unit established under subsection (j) of this section;

(24) "worst case discharge" means—

(A) in the case of a vessel, a discharge in adverse weather conditions of its entire cargo; and

(B) in the case of an offshore facility or onshore facility, the largest foreseeable discharge in adverse weather conditions; and.

(25) 'removal costs" means—

(A) the costs of removal of oil or a hazardous substance that are incurred after it is discharged; and

(B) in any case in which there is a substantial threat of a discharge of oil or a hazardous substance, the costs to prevent, minimize, or mitigate that threat.

**(b) Congressional declaration of policy against discharges of oil or hazardous substances; designation of hazardous substances; study of higher standard of care incentives and report to Congress; liability; penalties; civil actions: penalty limitations, separate offenses, jurisdiction, mitigation of damages and costs, recovery of removal costs, alternative remedies, and withholding clearance of vessels**

(1) The Congress hereby declares that it is the policy of the United States that there should be no discharges of oil or hazardous substances into or upon the navigable waters of the United States, adjoining shorelines, or into or upon the waters of the contiguous zone, or in connection with activities under the Outer Continental Shelf Lands Act [43 U.S.C.A. § 1331 et seq.] or the Deepwater Port Act of 1974 [33 U.S.C.A. § 1501 et seq.], or which may affect natural resources belonging to, appertaining to, or under the exclusive management authority of the United States (including resources under the Magnuson-Stevens Fishery Conservation and Management Act [16 U.S.C.A. § 1801 et seq.]).

(2)(A) The Administrator shall develop, promulgate, and revise as may be appropriate, regulations designating as hazardous substances, other than oil as defined in this section, such elements and compounds which, when discharged in any quantity into or upon the navigable waters of the United States or adjoining shorelines or the waters of the contiguous zone or in connection with activities under the Outer Continental Shelf Lands Act [43 U.S.C.A. § 1331 et seq.] or the Deepwater Port Act of 1974 [33 U.S.C.A. § 1501 et seq.], or which may affect natural resources belonging to, appertaining to, or under the exclusive management authority of the United States (including resources under the Magnuson-Stevens Fishery Conservation and Management Act [16 U.S.C.A. § 1801 et seq.] ), present an imminent and substantial danger to the public health or welfare, including, but not limited to, fish, shellfish, wildlife, shorelines, and beaches.

**(B)** The Administrator shall within 18 months after the date of enactment of this paragraph, conduct a study and report to the Congress on methods, mechanisms, and procedures to create incentives to achieve a higher standard of care in all aspects of the management and movement of hazardous substances on the part of owners, operators, or persons in charge of onshore facilities, offshore facilities, or vessels. The Administrator shall include in such study (1) limits of liability, (2) liability for third party damages, (3) penalties and fees, (4) spill prevention plans, (5) current practices in the insurance and banking industries, and (6) whether the penalty enacted in subclause (bb) of clause (iii) of subparagraph (B) of subsection (b)(2) of section 311 of Public Law 92–500 should be enacted.

(3) The discharge of oil or hazardous substances (i) into or upon the navigable waters of the United States, adjoining shorelines, or into or upon the waters of the contiguous zone, or (ii) in connection with activities under the Outer Continental Shelf Lands Act [43 U.S.C.A. § 1331 et seq.] or the Deepwater Port Act of 1974 [33 U.S.C.A. § 1501 et seq.], or which may affect natural resources belonging to, appertaining to, or under the exclusive management authority of the United States (including resources under the Magnuson-Stevens Fishery Conservation and Management Act [16 U.S.C.A. § 1801 et seq.] ), in such quantities as may be harmful as determined by the President under paragraph (4) of this subsection, is prohibited, except (A) in the case of such discharges into the waters of the contiguous zone or which may affect natural resources belonging to, appertaining to, or under the exclusive management authority of the United States (including resources under the Magnuson-Stevens Fishery Conservation and Management Act), where permitted under the Protocol of 1978 Relating to the International Convention for the Prevention of Pollution from Ships, 1973, and (B) where permitted in quantities and at times and locations or under such circumstances or conditions as the President may, by regulation, determine not to be harmful. Any regulations issued under this subsection shall be consistent with maritime safety and with marine and navigation laws and regulations and applicable water quality standards.

(4) The President shall by regulation determine for the purposes of this section those quantities of oil and any hazardous substances the discharge of which may be harmful to the public health or welfare or the environment of the United States, including but not limited to fish, shellfish, wildlife, and public and private property, shorelines, and beaches.

(5) Any person in charge of a vessel or of an onshore facility or an offshore facility shall, as soon as he has knowledge of any discharge of oil or a hazardous substance from such vessel or facility in violation of paragraph (3) of this subsection, immediately notify the appropriate agency of the United States Government of such discharge. The Federal agency shall immediately notify the appropriate State agency of any State which is, or may reasonably be expected to be, affected by the discharge of oil or a hazardous substance. Any such person (A) in charge of a vessel from which oil or a hazardous substance is discharged in violation of paragraph (3)(i) of this subsection, or (B) in charge of a vessel from which oil or a hazardous substance is discharged in violation of paragraph (3)(ii) of this subsection and who is otherwise subject to the jurisdiction of the United States at the time of the discharge, or (C) in charge of an onshore facility or an offshore facility, who fails to notify immediately such agency of such discharge shall, upon conviction, be fined in accordance with Title 18, or imprisoned for not more than 5 years, or both. Notification received pursuant to this paragraph shall not be used against any such natural person in any criminal case, except a prosecution for perjury or for giving a false statement.

**(6) Administrative penalties**

**(A) Violations**

Any owner, operator, or person in charge of any vessel, onshore facility, or offshore facility—

**(i)** from which oil or a hazardous substance is discharged in violation of paragraph (3), or

**(ii)** who fails or refuses to comply with any regulation issued under subsection (j) of this section to which that owner, operator, or person in charge is subject,

may be assessed a class I or class II civil penalty by the Secretary of the department in which the Coast Guard is operating or the Administrator.

**(B) Classes of penalties**

**(i) Class I**

The amount of a class I civil penalty under subparagraph (A) may not exceed $10,000 per violation, except that the maximum amount of any class I civil penalty under this subparagraph shall not exceed $25,000. Before assessing a civil penalty under this clause, the Administrator or Secretary, as the case may be, shall give to the person to be assessed such penalty written notice of the Administrator's or Secretary's proposal to assess the penalty and the opportunity to request, within 30 days of the date the notice is received by such person, a hearing on the proposed penalty. Such hearing shall not be subject to section 554 or 556 of Title 5, but shall provide a reasonable opportunity to be heard and to present evidence.

**(ii) Class II**

The amount of a class II civil penalty under subparagraph (A) may not exceed $10,000 per day for each day during which the violation continues; except that the maximum amount of any class II civil penalty under this subparagraph shall not exceed $125,000. Except as otherwise provided in this subsection, a class II civil penalty shall be assessed and collected in the same manner, and subject to the same provisions, as in the case of civil penalties assessed and collected after notice and opportunity for a hearing on the record in accordance with section 554 of Title 5. The Administrator and Secretary may issue rules for discovery procedures for hearings under this paragraph.

**(C) Rights of interested persons**

**(i) Public notice**

Before issuing an order assessing a class II civil penalty under this paragraph the Administrator or Secretary, as the case may be, shall provide public notice of and reasonable opportunity to comment on the proposed issuance of such order.

**(ii) Presentation of evidence**

Any person who comments on a proposed assessment of a class II civil penalty under this paragraph shall be given notice of any hearing held under this paragraph and of the order assessing such penalty. In any hearing held under this paragraph, such person shall have a reasonable opportunity to be heard and to present evidence.

**(iii) Rights of interested persons to a hearing**

If no hearing is held under subparagraph (B) before issuance of an order assessing a class II civil penalty under this paragraph, any person who commented on the proposed assessment may petition, within 30 days after the issuance of such order, the Administrator or Secretary, as the case may be, to set aside such order and to provide a hearing on the penalty. If the evidence presented by the petitioner in support of the petition is material and was not considered in the issuance of the order, the Administrator or Secretary shall immediately set aside such order and provide a hearing in accordance with subparagraph (B)(ii). If the Administrator or Secretary denies a hearing under this clause, the Administrator or Secretary shall provide to the petitioner, and publish in the Federal Register, notice of and the reasons for such denial.

**(D) Finality of order**

An order assessing a class II civil penalty under this paragraph shall become final 30 days after its issuance unless a petition for judicial review is filed under subparagraph (G) or a hearing is requested under subparagraph (C)(iii). If such a hearing is denied, such order shall become final 30 days after such denial.

**(E) Effect of order**

Action taken by the Administrator or Secretary, as the case may be, under this paragraph shall not affect or limit the Administrator's or Secretary's authority to enforce any provision of this chapter; except that any violation—

(i) with respect to which the Administrator or Secretary has commenced and is diligently prosecuting an action to assess a class II civil penalty under this paragraph, or

(ii) for which the Administrator or Secretary has issued a final order assessing a class II civil penalty not subject to further judicial review and the violator has paid a penalty assessed under this paragraph,

shall not be the subject of a civil penalty action under section 1319(d), 1319(g), or 1365 of this Title or under paragraph (7).

**(F) Effect of action on compliance**

No action by the Administrator or Secretary under this paragraph shall affect any person's obligation to comply with any section of this chapter.

**(G) Judicial review**

Any person against whom a civil penalty is assessed under this paragraph or who commented on the proposed assessment of such penalty in accordance with subparagraph (C) may obtain review of such assessment—

(i) in the case of assessment of a class I civil penalty, in the United States District Court for the District of Columbia or in the district in which the violation is alleged to have occurred, or

(ii) in the case of assessment of a class II civil penalty, in United States Court of Appeals for the District of Columbia Circuit or for any other circuit in which such person resides or transacts business,

by filing a notice of appeal in such court within the 30-day period beginning on the date the civil penalty order is issued and by simultaneously sending a copy of such notice by certified mail to the Administrator or Secretary, as the case may be, and the Attorney General. The Administrator or Secretary shall promptly file in such court a certified copy of the record on which the order was issued. Such court shall not set aside or remand such order unless there is not substantial evidence in the record, taken as a whole, to support the finding of a violation or unless the Administrator's or Secretary's assessment of the penalty constitutes an abuse of discretion and shall not impose additional civil penalties for the same violation unless the Administrator's or Secretary's assessment of the penalty constitutes an abuse of discretion.

**(H) Collection**

If any person fails to pay an assessment of a civil penalty—

(i) after the assessment has become final, or

(ii) after a court in an action brought under subparagraph (G) has entered a final judgment in favor of the Administrator or Secretary, as the case may be,

the Administrator or Secretary shall request the Attorney General to bring a civil action in an appropriate district court to recover the amount assessed (plus interest at currently prevailing rates from the date of the final order or the date of the final judgment, as the case may be). In such an action, the validity, amount, and appropriateness of such penalty shall not be subject to review. Any person who fails to pay on a timely basis the amount of an assessment of a civil penalty as described in the first sentence of this subparagraph shall be required to pay, in addition to such amount and interest, attorneys fees and costs for collection proceedings and a quarterly nonpayment penalty for each quarter during which such failure to pay persists. Such nonpayment penalty shall be in an amount equal to 20 percent of the aggregate amount of such person's penalties and nonpayment penalties which are unpaid as of the beginning of such quarter.

**(I) Subpoenas**

The Administrator or Secretary, as the case may be, may issue subpoenas for the attendance and testimony of witnesses and the production of relevant papers, books, or documents in connection with hearings under this paragraph. In case of contumacy or refusal to obey a subpoena issued pursuant to this subparagraph and served upon any person, the district court of the United States for any district in which such person is found, resides, or transacts business, upon application by the United States and after notice to such person, shall have jurisdiction to issue an order requiring such person to appear and give testimony before the administrative law judge or to appear and produce documents before the administrative law judge, or both, and any failure to obey such order of the court may be punished by such court as a contempt thereof.

**(7) Civil penalty action**

**(A) Discharge, generally**

Any person who is the owner, operator, or person in charge of any vessel, onshore facility, or offshore facility from which oil or a hazardous substance is discharged in violation of paragraph (3), shall be subject to a civil penalty in an amount up to $25,000 per day of violation or an amount up to $1,000 per barrel of oil or unit of reportable quantity of hazardous substances discharged.

**(B) Failure to remove or comply**

Any person described in subparagraph (A) who, without sufficient cause—

(i) fails to properly carry out removal of the discharge under an order of the President pursuant to subsection (c) of this section; or

(ii) fails to comply with an order pursuant to subsection (e)(1)(B) of this section;

shall be subject to a civil penalty in an amount up to $25,000 per day of violation or an amount up to 3 times the costs incurred by the Oil Spill Liability Trust Fund as a result of such failure.

**(C) Failure to comply with regulation**

Any person who fails or refuses to comply with any regulation issued under subsection (j) of this section shall be subject to a civil penalty in an amount up to $25,000 per day of violation.

**(D) Gross negligence**

In any case in which a violation of paragraph (3) was the result of gross negligence or willful misconduct of a person described in subparagraph (A), the person shall be subject to a civil penalty of not less than $100,000, and not more than $3,000 per barrel of oil or unit of reportable quantity of hazardous substance discharged.

**(E) Jurisdiction**

An action to impose a civil penalty under this paragraph may be brought in the district court of the United States for the district in which the defendant is located, resides, or is doing business, and such court shall have jurisdiction to assess such penalty.

**(F) Limitation**

A person is not liable for a civil penalty under this paragraph for a discharge if the person has been assessed a civil penalty under paragraph (6) for the discharge.

**(8) Determination of amount**

In determining the amount of a civil penalty under paragraphs (6) and (7), the Administrator, Secretary, or the court, as the case may be, shall consider the seriousness of the violation or violations, the economic benefit to the violator, if any, resulting from the violation, the degree of culpability involved, any other penalty for the same incident, any history of prior violations, the nature, extent, and degree of success of any efforts of the violator to minimize or mitigate the effects of the discharge, the economic impact of the penalty on the violator, and any other matters as justice may require.

**(9) Mitigation of damage**

In addition to establishing a penalty for the discharge of oil or a hazardous substance, the Administrator or the Secretary of the department in which the Coast Guard is operating may act to mitigate the damage to the public health or welfare caused by such discharge. The cost of such mitigation shall be deemed a cost incurred under subsection (c) of this section for the removal of such substance by the United States Government.

**(10) Recovery of removal costs**

Any costs of removal incurred in connection with a discharge excluded by subsection (a)(2)(C) of this section shall be recoverable from the owner or operator of the source of the discharge in an action brought under section 1319(b) of this Title.

**(11) Limitation**

Civil penalties shall not be assessed under both this section and section 1319 of this Title for the same discharge.

**(12) Withholding clearance**

If any owner, operator, or person in charge of a vessel is liable for a civil penalty under this subsection, or if reasonable cause exists to believe that the owner, operator, or person in charge may be subject to a civil penalty under this subsection, the Secretary of the Treasury, upon the request of the Secretary of the department in which the Coast Guard is operating or the Administrator, shall with respect to such vessel refuse or revoke—

(A) the clearance required by section 91 of the Appendix to Title 46;

(B) a permit to proceed under section 313 of the Appendix to Title 46; and

(C) a permit to depart required under section 1443 of Title 19;

as applicable. Clearance or a permit refused or revoked under this paragraph may be granted upon the filing of a bond or other surety satisfactory to the Secretary of the department in which the Coast Guard is operating or the Administrator.

**(c) Federal removal authority**

**(1) General removal requirement**

(A) The President shall, in accordance with the National Contingency Plan and any appropriate Area Contingency Plan, ensure effective and immediate removal of a discharge, and mitigation or prevention of a substantial threat of a discharge, of oil or a hazardous substance—

(i) into or on the navigable waters;

(ii) on the adjoining shorelines to the navigable waters;

(iii) into or on the waters of the exclusive economic zone; or

(iv) that may affect natural resources belonging to, appertaining to, or under the exclusive management authority of the United States.

(B) In carrying out this paragraph, the President may—

(i) remove or arrange for the removal of a discharge, and mitigate or prevent a substantial threat of a discharge, at any time;

(ii) direct or monitor all Federal, State, and private actions to remove a discharge; and

(iii) remove and, if necessary, destroy a vessel discharging, or threatening to discharge, by whatever means are available.

**(2) Discharge posing substantial threat to public health or welfare**

(A) If a discharge, or a substantial threat of a discharge, of oil or a hazardous substance from a vessel, offshore facility, or onshore facility is of such a size or character as to be a substantial threat to the public health or welfare of the United States (including but not limited to fish, shellfish, wildlife, other natural resources, and the public and private beaches and shorelines of the United States), the President shall direct all Federal, State, and private actions to remove the discharge or to mitigate or prevent the threat of the discharge.

(B) In carrying out this paragraph, the President may, without regard to any other provision of law governing contracting procedures or employment of personnel by the Federal Government—

(i) remove or arrange for the removal of the discharge, or mitigate or prevent the substantial threat of the discharge; and

(ii) remove and, if necessary, destroy a vessel discharging, or threatening to discharge, by whatever means are available.

(3) **Actions in accordance with National Contingency Plan**

(A) Each Federal agency, State, owner or operator, or other person participating in efforts under this subsection shall act in accordance with the National Contingency Plan or as directed by the President.

(B) An owner or operator participating in efforts under this subsection shall act in accordance with the National Contingency Plan and the applicable response plan required under subsection (j) of this section, or as directed by the President, except that the owner or operator may deviate from the applicable response plan if the President or the Federal On–Scene Coordinator determines that deviation from the response plan would provide for a more expeditious or effective response to the spill or mitigation of its environmental effects.

(4) **Exemption from liability**

(A) A person is not liable for removal costs or damages which result from actions taken or omitted to be taken in the course of rendering care, assistance, or advice consistent with the National Contingency Plan or as otherwise directed by the President relating to a discharge or a substantial threat of a discharge of oil or a hazardous substance.

(B) Subparagraph (A) does not apply—

(i) to a responsible party;

(ii) to a response under the Comprehensive Environmental Response, Compensation, and Liability Act of 1980 (42 U.S.C. 9601 et seq.);

(iii) with respect to personal injury or wrongful death; or

(iv) if the person is grossly negligent or engages in willful misconduct.

(C) A responsible party is liable for any removal costs and damages that another person is relieved of under subparagraph (A).

(5) **Obligation and liability of owner or operator not affected**

Nothing in this subsection affects—

(A) the obligation of an owner or operator to respond immediately to a discharge, or the threat of a discharge, of oil; or

(B) the liability of a responsible party under the Oil Pollution Act of 1990 [33 U.S.C.A. § 2701 et seq.].

(6) **"Responsible party" defined**

For purposes of this subsection, the term "responsible party" has the meaning given that term under section 1001 of the Oil Pollution Act of 1990 [33 U.S.C.A. § 2701].

(d) **National Contingency Plan**

(1) **Preparation by President**

The President shall prepare and publish a National Contingency Plan for removal of oil and hazardous substances pursuant to this section.

(2) **Contents**

The National Contingency Plan shall provide for efficient, coordinated, and effective action to minimize damage from oil and hazardous substance discharges, including containment, dispersal, and removal of oil and hazardous substances, and shall include, but not be limited to, the following:

(A) Assignment of duties and responsibilities among Federal departments and agencies in coordination with State and local agencies and port authorities including, but not limited to, water pollution control and conservation and trusteeship of natural resources (including conservation of fish and wildlife).

(B) Identification, procurement, maintenance, and storage of equipment and supplies.

(C) Establishment or designation of Coast Guard strike teams, consisting of—

(i) personnel who shall be trained, prepared, and available to provide necessary services to carry out the National Contingency Plan;

(ii) adequate oil and hazardous substance pollution control equipment and material; and

(iii) a detailed oil and hazardous substance pollution and prevention plan, including measures to protect fisheries and wildlife.

(D) A system of surveillance and notice designed to safeguard against as well as ensure earliest possible notice of discharges of oil and hazardous substances and imminent threats of such discharges to the appropriate State and Federal agencies.

(E) Establishment of a national center to provide coordination and direction for operations in carrying out the Plan.

(F) Procedures and techniques to be employed in identifying, containing, dispersing, and removing oil and hazardous substances.

(G) A schedule, prepared in cooperation with the States, identifying—

(i) dispersants, other chemicals, and other spill mitigating devices and substances, if any, that may be used in carrying out the Plan,

(ii) the waters in which such dispersants, other chemicals, and other spill mitigating devices and substances may be used, and

(iii) the quantities of such dispersant, other chemicals, or other spill mitigating device or substance which can be used safely in such waters,

which schedule shall provide in the case of any dispersant, chemical, spill mitigating device or substance, or waters not specifically identified in such schedule that the President, or his delegate, may, on a case-by-case basis, identify the dispersants, other chemicals, and other spill mitigating devices and substances which may be used, the waters in which they may be used, and the quantities which can be used safely in such waters.

**(H)** A system whereby the State or States affected by a discharge of oil or hazardous substance may act where necessary to remove such discharge and such State or States may be reimbursed in accordance with the Oil Pollution Act of 1990 [33 U.S.C.A. § 2701 et seq.], in the case of any discharge of oil from a vessel or facility, for the reasonable costs incurred for that removal, from the Oil Spill Liability Trust Fund.

**(I)** Establishment of criteria and procedures to ensure immediate and effective Federal identification of, and response to, a discharge, or the threat of a discharge, that results in a substantial threat to the public health or welfare of the United States, as required under subsection (c)(2) of this section.

**(J)** Establishment of procedures and standards for removing a worst case discharge of oil, and for mitigating or preventing a substantial threat of such a discharge.

**(K)** Designation of the Federal official who shall be the Federal On–Scene Coordinator for each area for which an Area Contingency Plan is required to be prepared under subsection (j) of this section.

**(L)** Establishment of procedures for the coordination of activities of—

**(i)** Coast Guard strike teams established under subparagraph (C);

**(ii)** Federal On–Scene Coordinators designated under subparagraph (K);

**(iii)** District Response Groups established under subsection (j) of this section; and

**(iv)** Area Committees established under subsection (j) of this section.

**(M)** A fish and wildlife response plan, developed in consultation with the United States Fish and Wildlife Service, the National Oceanic and Atmospheric Administration, and other interested parties (including State fish and wildlife conservation officials), for the immediate and effective protection, rescue, and rehabilitation of, and the minimization of risk of damage to, fish and wildlife resources and their habitat that are harmed or that may be jeopardized by a discharge.

**(3) Revisions and amendments**

The President may, from time to time, as the President deems advisable, revise or otherwise amend the National Contingency Plan.

**(4) Actions in accordance with National Contingency Plan**

After publication of the National Contingency Plan, the removal of oil and hazardous substances and actions to minimize damage from oil and hazardous substance discharges shall, to the greatest extent possible, be in accordance with the National Contingency Plan.

**(e) Civil enforcement**

**(1) Orders protecting public health**

In addition to any action taken by a State or local government, when the President determines that there may be an imminent and substantial threat to the public health or welfare of the United States, including fish, shellfish, and wildlife, public and private property, shorelines, beaches, habitat, and other living and nonliving natural resources under the jurisdiction or control of the United States, because of an actual or threatened discharge of oil or a hazardous substance from a vessel or facility in violation of subsection (b) of this section, the President may—

**(A)** require the Attorney General to secure any relief from any person, including the owner or operator of the vessel or facility, as may be necessary to abate such endangerment; or

**(B)** after notice to the affected State, take any other action under this section, including issuing administrative orders, that may be necessary to protect the public health and welfare.

**(2) Jurisdiction of district courts**

The district courts of the United States shall have jurisdiction to grant any relief under this subsection that the public interest and the equities of the case may require.

**(f) Liability for actual costs of removal**

(1) Except where an owner or operator can prove that a discharge was caused solely by (A) an act of God, (B) an act of war, (C) negligence on the part of the United States Government, or (D) an act or omission of a third party without regard to whether any such act or omission was or was not negligent, or any combination of the foregoing clauses, such owner or operator of any vessel from which oil or a hazardous substance is discharged in violation of subsection (b)(3) of this section shall, notwithstanding any other provision of law, be liable to the United States Government for the actual costs incurred under subsection (c) of this section for the removal of such oil or substance by the United States Government in an amount not to exceed, in the case of an inland oil barge $125 per gross ton of such barge, or $125,000, whichever is greater, and in the case of any other vessel, $150 per gross ton of such vessel (or, for a vessel carrying oil or hazardous substances as cargo,

$250,000), whichever is greater, except that where the United States can show that such discharge was the result of willful negligence or willful misconduct within the privity and knowledge of the owner, such owner or operator shall be liable to the United States Government for the full amount of such costs. Such costs shall constitute a maritime lien on such vessel which may be recovered in an action in rem in the district court of the United States for any district within which any vessel may be found. The United States may also bring an action against the owner or operator of such vessel in any court of competent jurisdiction to recover such costs.

(2) Except where an owner or operator of an onshore facility can prove that a discharge was caused solely by (A) an act of God, (B) an act of war, (C) negligence on the part of the United States Government, or (D) an act or omission of a third party without regard to whether any such act or omission was or was not negligent, or any combination of the foregoing clauses, such owner or operator of any such facility from which oil or a hazardous substance is discharged in violation of subsection (b)(3) of this section shall be liable to the United States Government for the actual costs incurred under subsection (c) of this section for the removal of such oil or substance by the United States Government in an amount not to exceed $50,000,000, except that where the United States can show that such discharge was the result of willful negligence or willful misconduct within the privity and knowledge of the owner, such owner or operator shall be liable to the United States Government for the full amount of such costs. The United States may bring an action against the owner or operator of such facility in any court of competent jurisdiction to recover such costs. The Administrator is authorized, by regulation, after consultation with the Secretary of Commerce and the Small Business Administration, to establish reasonable and equitable classifications of those onshore facilities having a total fixed storage capacity of 1,000 barrels or less which he determines because of size, type, and location do not present a substantial risk of the discharge of oil or a hazardous substance in violation of subsection (b)(3) of this section, and apply with respect to such classifications differing limits of liability which may be less than the amount contained in this paragraph.

(3) Except where an owner or operator of an offshore facility can prove that a discharge was caused solely by (A) an act of God, (B) an act of war, (C) negligence on the part of the United States Government, or (D) an act or omission of a third party without regard to whether any such act or omission was or was not negligent, or any combination of the foregoing clauses, such owner or operator of any such facility from which oil or a hazardous substance is discharged in violation of subsection (b)(3) of this section shall, notwithstanding any other provision of law, be liable to the United States Government for the actual costs incurred under subsection (c) of this section for the removal of such oil or substance by the United States Government in an amount not to exceed $50,000,000, except that where the United States can show that such discharge was the result of willful negligence or willful misconduct within the privity and knowledge of the owner, such owner or operator shall be liable to the United States Government for the full amount of such costs. The United States may bring an action against the owner or operator of such a facility in any court of competent jurisdiction to recover such costs.

(4) The costs of removal of oil or a hazardous substance for which the owner or operator of a vessel or onshore or offshore facility is liable under subsection (f) of this section shall include any costs or expenses incurred by the Federal Government or any State government in the restoration or replacement of natural resources damaged or destroyed as a result of a discharge of oil or a hazardous substance in violation of subsection (b) of this section.

(5) The President, or the authorized representative of any State, shall act on behalf of the public as trustee of the natural resources to recover for the costs of replacing or restoring such resources. Sums recovered shall be used to restore, rehabilitate, or acquire the equivalent of such natural resources by the appropriate agencies of the Federal Government, or the State government.

**(g) Third party liability**

Where the owner or operator of a vessel (other than an inland oil barge) carrying oil or hazardous substances as cargo or an onshore or offshore facility which handles or stores oil or hazardous substances in bulk, from which oil or a hazardous substance is discharged in violation of subsection (b) of this section, alleges that such discharge was caused solely by an act or omission of a third party, such owner or operator shall pay to the United States Government the actual costs incurred under subsection (c) of this section for removal of such oil or substance and shall be entitled by subrogation to all rights of the United States Government to recover such costs from such third party under this subsection. In any case where an owner or operator of a vessel, of an onshore facility, or of an offshore facility, from which oil or a hazardous substance is discharged in violation of subsection (b)(3) of this section, proves that such discharge of oil or hazardous substance was caused solely by an act or omission of a third party, or was caused solely by such an act or omission in combination with an act of God, an act of war, or negligence on the part of the United States Government, such third party shall, notwithstanding any other provision of law, be liable to the United States Government for the actual costs incurred under subsection (c) of this section for removal of such oil or substance by the United States Government, except where such third party can prove that such discharge was caused solely by (A) an act of God, (B) an act of war, (C) negligence on the part of the United States Government, or (D) an act or omission of another party without regard to whether such act or omission was or was not negligent, or any combination of the foregoing clauses. If such third party was the owner or operator of a vessel which caused the discharge of oil or a hazardous substance in violation of subsection (b)(3) of this section, the liability of such third party under this subsection shall not exceed, in the case of an inland oil barge $125 per gross ton of such barge, or $125,000, whichever is greater, and in the case of any other vessel, $150 per gross ton of such vessel (or, for a vessel carrying oil or hazardous substances as cargo, $250,000), whichever is greater. In any other case the liability of such third party shall not exceed the limitation which would have been applicable to the owner or operator of the vessel or the onshore or offshore facility from which the discharge actually occurred if such owner or operator were liable. If the United States can show that the discharge of oil or a hazardous substance in violation of subsection (b)(3) of this section was the result of willful negligence or willful misconduct within the privity and knowledge of such third party, such third party shall be liable to the United States Government for the full amount of such removal costs. The United States may bring an action against the third party in any court of competent jurisdiction to recover such removal costs.

**(h) Rights against third parties who caused or contributed to discharge**

The liabilities established by this section shall in no way affect any rights which (1) the owner or operator of a vessel or of an onshore facility or an offshore facility may have against any third party whose acts may in any way have caused or contributed to such discharge, or (2) The United States Government may have against any third party whose actions may in any way have caused or contributed to the discharge of oil or hazardous substance.

**(i) Recovery of removal costs**

In any case where an owner or operator of a vessel or an onshore facility or an offshore facility from which oil or a hazardous substance is discharged in violation of subsection (b)(3) of this section acts to remove such oil or substance in accordance with regulations promulgated pursuant to this section, such owner or operator shall be entitled to recover the reasonable costs incurred in such removal upon establishing, in a suit which may be brought against the United States Government in the United States Court of Federal Claims, that such discharge was caused solely by (A) an act of God, (B) an act of war, (C) negligence on the part of the United States Government, or (D) an act or omission of a third party without regard to whether such act or omission was or was not negligent, or of any combination of the foregoing causes.

**(j) National Response System**

**(1) In general**

Consistent with the National Contingency Plan required by subsection (c)(2) of this section, as soon as practicable after October 18, 1972, and from time to time thereafter, the President shall issue regulations consistent with maritime safety and with marine and navigation laws (A) establishing methods and procedures for removal of discharged oil and hazardous substances, (B) establishing criteria for the development and implementation of local and regional oil and hazardous substance removal contingency plans, (C) establishing procedures, methods, and equipment and other requirements for equipment to prevent discharges of oil and hazardous substances from vessels and from onshore facilities and offshore facilities, and to contain such discharges, and (D) governing the inspection of vessels carrying cargoes of oil and hazardous substances and the inspection of such cargoes in order to reduce the likelihood of discharges of oil from vessels in violation of this section.

**(2) National Response Unit**

The Secretary of the department in which the Coast Guard is operating shall establish a National Response Unit at Elizabeth City, North Carolina. The Secretary, acting through the National Response Unit—

**(A)** shall compile and maintain a comprehensive computer list of spill removal resources, personnel, and equipment that is available worldwide and within the areas designated by the President pursuant to paragraph (4), and of information regarding previous spills, including data from universities, research institutions, State governments, and other nations, as appropriate, which shall be disseminated as appropriate to response groups and area committees, and which shall be available to Federal and State agencies and the public;

**(B)** shall provide technical assistance, equipment, and other resources requested by a Federal On–Scene Coordinator;

**(C)** shall coordinate use of private and public personnel and equipment to remove a worst case discharge, and to mitigate or prevent a substantial threat of such a discharge, from a vessel, offshore facility, or onshore facility operating in or near an area designated by the President pursuant to paragraph (4);

(D) may provide technical assistance in the preparation of Area Contingency Plans required under paragraph (4);

(E) shall administer Coast Guard strike teams established under the National Contingency Plan;

(F) shall maintain on file all Area Contingency Plans approved by the President under this subsection; and

(G) shall review each of those plans that affects its responsibilities under this subsection.

**(3) Coast Guard District Response Groups**

(A) The Secretary of the department in which the Coast Guard is operating shall establish in each Coast Guard district a Coast Guard District Response Group.

(B) Each Coast Guard District Response Group shall consist of—

(i) the Coast Guard personnel and equipment, including firefighting equipment, of each port within the district;

(ii) additional prepositioned equipment; and

(iii) a district response advisory staff.

(C) Coast Guard district response groups—

(i) shall provide technical assistance, equipment, and other resources when required by a Federal On–Scene Coordinator;

(ii) shall maintain all Coast Guard response equipment within its district;

(iii) may provide technical assistance in the preparation of Area Contingency Plans required under paragraph (4); and

(iv) shall review each of those plans that affect its area of geographic responsibility.

**(4) Area Committees and Area Contingency Plans**

(A) There is established for each area designated by the President an Area Committee comprised of members appointed by the President from qualified personnel of Federal, State, and local agencies.

(B) Each Area Committee, under the direction of the Federal On–Scene Coordinator for its area, shall—

(i) prepare for its area the Area Contingency Plan required under subparagraph (C);

(ii) work with State and local officials to enhance the contingency planning of those officials and to assure preplanning of joint response efforts, including appropriate procedures for mechanical recovery, dispersal, shoreline cleanup, protection of sensitive environmental areas, and protection, rescue, and rehabilitation of fisheries and wildlife; and

(iii) work with State and local officials to expedite decisions for the use of dispersants and other mitigating substances and devices.

(C) Each Area Committee shall prepare and submit to the President for approval an Area Contingency Plan for its area. The Area Contingency Plan shall—

(i) when implemented in conjunction with the National Contingency Plan, be adequate to remove a worst case discharge, and to mitigate or prevent a substantial threat of such a discharge, from a vessel, offshore facility, or onshore facility operating in or near the area;

(ii) describe the area covered by the plan, including the areas of special economic or environmental importance that might be damaged by a discharge;

(iii) describe in detail the responsibilities of an owner or operator and of Federal, State, and local agencies in removing a discharge, and in mitigating or preventing a substantial threat of a discharge;

(iv) list the equipment (including firefighting equipment), dispersants or other mitigating substances and devices, and personnel available to an owner or operator and Federal, State, and local agencies, to ensure an effective and immediate removal of a discharge, and to ensure mitigation or prevention of a substantial threat of a discharge;

(v) compile a list of local scientists, both inside and outside Federal Government service, with expertise in the environmental effects of spills of the types of oil typically transported in the area, who may be contacted to provide information or, where appropriate, participate in meetings of the scientific support team convened in response to a spill, and describe the procedures to be followed for obtaining an expedited decision regarding the use of dispersants;

(vi) describe in detail how the plan is integrated into other Area Contingency Plans and vessel, offshore facility, and onshore facility response plans approved under this subsection, and into operating procedures of the National Response Unit;

(vii) include any other information the President requires; and

(viii) be updated periodically by the Area Committee.

(D) The President shall—

(i) review and approve Area Contingency Plans under this paragraph; and

(ii) periodically review Area Contingency Plans so approved.

**(5) Tank vessel and facility response plans**

**(A)** The President shall issue regulations which require an owner or operator of a tank vessel or facility described in subparagraph (B) to prepare and submit to the President a plan for responding, to the maximum extent practicable, to a worst case discharge, and to a substantial threat of such a discharge, of oil or a hazardous substance.

**(B)** The tank vessels and facilities referred to in subparagraph (A) are the following:

(i) A tank vessel, as defined under section 2101 of Title 46.

(ii) An offshore facility.

(iii) An onshore facility that, because of its location, could reasonably be expected to cause substantial harm to the environment by discharging into or on the navigable waters, adjoining shorelines, or the exclusive economic zone.

**(C)** A response plan required under this paragraph shall—

(i) be consistent with the requirements of the National Contingency Plan and Area Contingency Plans;

(ii) identify the qualified individual having full authority to implement removal actions, and require immediate communications between that individual and the appropriate Federal official and the persons providing personnel and equipment pursuant to clause (iii);

(iii) identify, and ensure by contract or other means approved by the President the availability of, private personnel and equipment necessary to remove to the maximum extent practicable a worst case discharge (including a discharge resulting from fire or explosion), and to mitigate or prevent a substantial threat of such a discharge;

(iv) describe the training, equipment testing, periodic unannounced drills, and response actions of persons on the vessel or at the facility, to be carried out under the plan to ensure the safety of the vessel or facility and to mitigate or prevent the discharge, or the substantial threat of a discharge;

(v) be updated periodically; and

(vi) be resubmitted for approval of each significant change.

**(D)** With respect to any response plan submitted under this paragraph for an onshore facility that, because of its location, could reasonably be expected to cause significant and substantial harm to the environment by discharging into or on the navigable waters or adjoining shorelines or the exclusive economic zone, and with respect to each response plan submitted under this paragraph for a tank vessel or offshore facility, the President shall—

(i) promptly review such response plan;

(ii) require amendments to any plan that does not meet the requirements of this paragraph;

(iii) approve any plan that meets the requirements of this paragraph; and

(iv) review each plan periodically thereafter.

**(E)** A tank vessel, offshore facility, or onshore facility required to prepare a response plan under this subsection may not handle, store, or transport oil unless—

(i) in the case of a tank vessel, offshore facility, or onshore facility for which a response plan is reviewed by the President under subparagraph (D), the plan has been approved by the President; and

(ii) the vessel or facility is operating in compliance with the plan.

**(F)** Notwithstanding subparagraph (E), the President may authorize a tank vessel, offshore facility, or onshore facility to operate without a response plan approved under this paragraph, until not later than 2 years after the date of the submission to the President of a plan for the tank vessel or facility, if the owner or operator certifies that the owner or operator has ensured by contract or other means approved by the President the availability of private personnel and equipment necessary to respond, to the maximum extent practicable, to a worst case discharge or a substantial threat of such a discharge.

**(G)** The owner or operator of a tank vessel, offshore facility, or onshore facility may not claim as a defense to liability under title I of the Oil Pollution Act of 1990 [33 U.S.C.A. § 2701 et seq.] that the owner or operator was acting in accordance with an approved response plan.

**(H)** The Secretary shall maintain, in the Vessel Identification System established under chapter 125 of Title 46, the dates of approval and review of a response plan under this paragraph for each tank vessel that is a vessel of the United States.

**(6) Equipment requirements and inspection**

Not later than 2 years after August 18, 1990, the President shall require—

**(A)** periodic inspection of containment booms, skimmers, vessels, and other major equipment used to remove discharges; and

**(B)** vessels operating on navigable waters and carrying oil or a hazardous substance in bulk as cargo to carry appropriate removal equipment that employs the best technology economically feasible and that is compatible with the safe operation of the vessel.

**(7) Area drills**

The President shall periodically conduct drills of removal capability, without prior notice, in areas for which Area Contingency Plans are required under this subsection and under relevant tank vessel and facility response plans. The drills may include participation by Federal, State, and local agencies, the owners and operators of vessels and facilities in the area, and private industry. The President may publish annual reports on these drills, including assessments of the effectiveness of the plans and a list of amendments made to improve plans.

**(8) United States Government not liable**

The United States Government is not liable for any damages arising from its actions or omissions relating to any response plan required by this section.

**(k) Repealed. Pub.L. 101–380, Title I, § 2002(b)(2), Aug. 18, 1990, 104 Stat. 507**

**(*l*) Administration**

The President is authorized to delegate the administration of this section to the heads of those Federal departments, agencies, and instrumentalities which he determines to be appropriate. Each such department, agency, and instrumentality, in order to avoid duplication of effort, shall, whenever appropriate, utilize the personnel, services, and facilities of other Federal departments, agencies, and instrumentalities.

**(m) Administrative provisions**

**(1) For vessels**

Anyone authorized by the President to enforce the provisions of this section with respect to any vessel may, except as to public vessels—

**(A)** board and inspect any vessel upon the navigable waters of the United States or the waters of the contiguous zone,

**(B)** with or without a warrant, arrest any person who in the presence or view of the authorized person violates the provisions of this section or any regulation issued thereunder, and

**(C)** execute any warrant or other process issued by an officer or court of competent jurisdiction.

**(2) For facilities**

**(A) Recordkeeping**

Whenever required to carry out the purposes of this section, the Administrator or the Secretary of the Department in which the Coast Guard is operating shall require the owner or operator of a facility to which this section applies to establish and maintain such records, make such reports, install, use, and maintain such monitoring equipment and methods, and provide such other information as the Administrator or Secretary, as the case may be, may require to carry out the objectives of this section.

**(B) Entry and inspection**

Whenever required to carry out the purposes of this section, the Administrator or the Secretary of the Department in which the Coast Guard is operating or an authorized representative of the Administrator or Secretary, upon presentation of appropriate credentials, may—

**(i)** enter and inspect any facility to which this section applies, including any facility at which any records are required to be maintained under subparagraph (A); and

**(ii)** at reasonable times, have access to and copy any records, take samples, and inspect any monitoring equipment or methods required under subparagraph (A).

**(C) Arrests and execution of warrants**

Anyone authorized by the Administrator or the Secretary of the department in which the Coast Guard is operating to enforce the provisions of this section with respect to any facility may—

**(i)** with or without a warrant, arrest any person who violates the provisions of this section or any regulation issued thereunder in the presence or view of the person so authorized; and

**(ii)** execute any warrant or process issued by an officer or court of competent jurisdiction.

**(D) Public access**

Any records, reports, or information obtained under this paragraph shall be subject to the same public access and disclosure requirements which are applicable to records, reports, and information obtained pursuant to section 1318 of this title.

**(n) Jurisdiction**

The several district courts of the United States are invested with jurisdiction for any actions, other than actions pursuant to subsection (i)(1) of this section, arising under this section. In the case of Guam and the Trust Territory of the Pacific Islands, such actions may be brought in the district court of Guam, and in the case of the Virgin Islands such actions may be brought in the district court of the Virgin Islands. In the case of American Samoa and the Trust Territory of the Pacific Islands, such actions may be brought in the District Court of the United States for the District of Hawaii and such court shall have jurisdiction of such actions. In the case of the Canal Zone, such actions may be brought in the United States District Court for the District of the Canal Zone.

**(*o*) Obligation for damages unaffected; local authority not preempted; existing Federal authority not modified or affected**

**(1)** Nothing in this section shall affect or modify in any way the obligations of any owner or operator of any vessel, or of any owner or operator of any onshore facility or offshore facility to any person or agency under any provision of law for damages to any publicly owned or privately owned property resulting from a discharge of any oil or hazardous substance or from the removal of any such oil or hazardous substance.

(2) Nothing in this section shall be construed as preempting any State or political subdivision thereof from imposing any requirement or liability with respect to the discharge of oil or hazardous substance into any waters within such State, or with respect to any removal activities related to such discharge.

(3) Nothing in this section shall be construed as affecting or modifying any other existing authority of any Federal department, agency, or instrumentality, relative to onshore or offshore facilities under this chapter or any other provision of law, or to affect any State or local law not in conflict with this section.

**(p) Repealed. Pub.L. 101–380, Title II, § 2002(b)(4), Aug. 18, 1990, 104 Stat. 507**

**(q) Establishment of maximum limit of liability with respect to onshore or offshore facilities**

The President is authorized to establish, with respect to any class or category of onshore or offshore facilities, a maximum limit of liability under subsections (f)(2) and (3) of this section of less than $50,000,000, but not less than $8,000,000.

**(r) Liability limitations not to limit liability under other legislation**

Nothing in this section shall be construed to impose, or authorize the imposition of, any limitation on liability under the Outer Continental Shelf Lands Act [43 U.S.C.A. § 1331 et seq.] or the Deepwater Port Act of 1974 [33 U.S.C.A. § 1501 et seq.].

**(s) Oil Spill Liability Trust Fund**

The Oil Spill Liability Trust Fund established under section 9509 of Title 26 shall be available to carry out subsections (b), (c), (d), (j), and (*l*) of this section as those subsections apply to discharges, and substantial threats of discharges, of oil. Any amounts received by the United States under this section shall be deposited in the Oil Spill Liability Trust Fund.

(June 30, 1948, c. 758, Title III, § 311, as added Oct. 18, 1972, Pub.L. 92–500, § 2, 86 Stat. 862, and amended Dec. 28, 1973, Pub.L. 93–207, § 1(4), 87 Stat. 906; Dec. 27, 1977, Pub.L. 95–217, §§ 57, 58(a)–(g), (i), (k)–(m), 91 Stat. 1593–1596; Nov. 2, 1978, Pub.L. 95–576, § 1(b), 92 Stat. 2467; Oct. 21, 1980, Pub.L. 96–478, § 13(b), 94 Stat. 2303; Oct. 21, 1980, Pub.L. 96–483, § 8, 94 Stat. 2362; Dec. 22, 1980, Pub.L. 96–561, Title II, § 238(b), 94 Stat. 3300; Apr. 2, 1982, Pub.L. 97–164, Title I, § 161(5), 96 Stat. 49; Feb. 4, 1987, Pub.L. 100–4, Title V, § 502(b), 101 Stat. 75; Aug. 18, 1990, Pub.L. 101–380, Title II, § 2002(b), Title IV, §§ 4201(a), (b), (b)[(c)], 4202(a), (c), 4204, 4301(a), (b), 4305, 4306, 104 Stat. 507, 523 to 527, 532, 533, 540, 541; Oct. 6, 1992, Pub.L. 102–388, Title III, § 349, 106 Stat. 1554; Oct. 29, 1992, Pub.L. 102–572, Title IX, § 902(b)(1), 106 Stat. 4516; Sept. 30, 1996, Pub.L. 104–208, Div. A, Title I, § 101(a) [Title II, § 211(b)], 110 Stat. 3009–41; Oct. 19, 1996, Pub.L. 104–324, Title XI, §§ 1143, 1144, 110 Stat. 3992; Nov. 13, 1998, Pub.L. 105–383, Title IV, § 411, 112 Stat. 3432.)

[1] So in original. The second comma should probably be deleted.

## HISTORICAL AND STATUTORY NOTES

**References in Text**

The Outer Continental Shelf Lands Act, referred to in subsecs. (b)(1), (2)(A), (3), and (r), is Act Aug. 7, 1953, c. 345, 67 Stat. 462, as amended, which is classified generally to subchapter III (section 1331 et seq.) of chapter 29 of Title 43, Public Lands. For complete classification of this Act to the Code, see Short Title note set out under section 1331 of Title 43 and Tables.

The Deepwater Port Act of 1974, referred to in subsecs. (b)(1), (2)(A), (3), and (r), is Pub.L. 93–627, Jan. 3, 1975, 88 Stat. 2126, as amended, which is classified generally to chapter 29 (section 1501 et seq.) of this title. For complete classification of this Act to the Code, see Short Title note set out under section 1501 of this title and Tables volume.

The Magnuson–Stevens Fishery Conservation and Management Act, referred to in subsec. (b)(1), (2)(A), and (3), is Pub. L. 94–265, Apr. 13, 1976, 90 Stat. 331, as amended, which is classified principally to chapter 38 (section 1801 et seq.) of Title 16, Conservation. For complete classification of this Act to the Code, see Short Title note set out under section 1801 of Title 16 and Tables.

The date of enactment of this paragraph, referred to in subsec. (b)(2)(B), probably means the date of enactment of Pub. L. 95–576, which amended subsec. (b)(2)(B) and which was approved Nov. 2, 1978.

Section 313 of the Appendix to Title 46, referred to in subsec. (b)(12)(B), was repealed by Pub.L. 103–182, Title VI, § 690(a)(21), Dec. 8, 1993, 107 Stat. 2223.

The penalty enacted in subclause (bb) of clause (iii) of subparagraph (B) of subsection (b)(2) of section 311 of Public Law 92–500, referred to in subsec. (b)(2)(B), probably means the penalty provision of subsec. (b)(2)(B)(iii)(bb) of this section as added by Pub.L. 92–500, § 2, Oct. 18, 1972, 86 Stat. 864, prior to the amendment to subsec. (b)(2)(B) by section 1(b)(3) of Pub.L. 95–576. Prior to amendment, subsec. (b)(2)(B)(iii)(bb) read as follows: "a penalty determined by the number of units discharged multiplied by the amount established for such unit under clause (iv) of this subparagraph, but such penalty shall not be more than $5,000,000 in the case of a discharge from a vessel and $500,000 in the case of a discharge from an onshore or offshore facility."

The Comprehensive Environmental Response, Compensation, and Liability Act of 1980, referred to in subsec. (c)(4)(B)(ii), is Pub.L. 96–510, Dec. 11, 1980, 94 Stat. 2767, as amended, which is principally classified to chapter 103 (section 9601 et seq.) of Title 42, The Public Health and Welfare. For complete classification of this Act to the Code, see Short Title note set out under section 9601 of Title 42 and Tables.

The Oil Pollution Act of 1990, referred to in subsecs. (c)(5)(B), (c)(6), (d)(2)(H) and (j)(5)(G), is Pub.L. 101–380, Aug. 18, 1990, 104 Stat. 484, which is principally classified to chapter 40 (section 2701 et seq.) of this title. Section 1001 of the Act is classified to section 2701 of this title. For complete classification of this Act to the Code, see Short Title note set out under section 2701 of this title and Tables.

**Codifications**

"Not later than 2 years after August 18, 1990", appearing in subsec. (j)(6), was, in the original, "not later than 2 years after the date of enactment of this section", and was editorially translated according to the probable intent of Congress in enacting subsec. (j)(6) by Pub.L. 101–380, 104 Stat. 484, which was approved Aug. 18, 1990.

**Effective and Applicability Provisions**

1996 Acts

Amendment by Pub.L. 104–208, Div. A, Title I, § 101(a) [Title II, § 211(b)], Sept. 30, 1996, 110 Stat. 3009–41, effective 15 days after Oct. 11, 1996, see Pub.L. 104–208, Div. A, Title I, § 101(a) [Title II, § 211(b)], Sept. 30, 1996, 110 Stat. 3009–41, set out as a note under section 1801 of Title 16, Conservation.

1992 Acts

Amendment by Title IX of Pub.L. 102–572 effective Oct. 29, 1992, see section 911 of Pub.L. 102–572, set out as a note under section 171 of Title 28, Judiciary and Judicial Procedure.

1982 Acts

Amendment by Pub. L. 97–164 effective Oct. 1, 1982, see section 402 of Pub. L. 97–164, set out as a note under section 171 of Title 28, Judiciary and Judicial Procedure.

1980 Acts

Amendment by Pub.L. 96–561 effective 15 days after Dec. 22, 1980, see section 238 of Pub.L. 96–561, set out as a Short Title note under section 1801 of Title 16, Conservation.

Amendment by Pub.L. 96–478 effective Oct. 2, 1983, see section 14(a) of Pub.L. 96–478, set out as a note under section 1901 of this title.

1977 Acts

Section 58(h) of Pub.L. 95–217 provided that: "The amendments made by paragraphs (5) and (6) of subsection (d) of this section [substituting '$50,000,000' for '$8,000,000' in subsec. (f)(2) and substituting '$50,000,000' for '$8,000,000' in subsec. (f)(3) of this section] shall take effect 180 days after the date of enactment of the Clean Water Act of 1977 [Dec. 27, 1977]."

**Change of Name**

References to United States Claims Court deemed to refer to United States Court of Federal Claims and references to Claims Court deemed to refer to Court of Federal Claims, see section 902(b) of Pub.L. 102–572, set out as a note under section 171 of Title 28, Judiciary and Judicial Procedure.

**Transfer of Functions**

Enforcement functions of Administrator or other official of the Environmental Protection Agency under this section relating to spill prevention, containment and countermeasure plans with respect to pre-construction, construction, and initial operation of transportation system for Canadian and Alaskan natural gas were transferred to the Federal Inspector, Office of Federal Inspector for the Alaska Natural Gas Transportation System, until the first anniversary of the date of initial operation of the Alaska Natural Gas Transportation System, see Reorg. Plan No. 1 of 1979, §§ 102(a), 203(a), 44 F.R. 33663, 33666, 93 Stat. 1373, 1376, effective July 1, 1979, set out in Appendix 1 to Title 5, Government Organization and Employees.

**Delegation of Functions**

Functions of the President under subsec. (p)(1)–(2), as incorporated by reference in section 1653(c)(3) of Title 43, Public Lands, relating to the demonstration of financial responsibility for vessels carrying oil loaded from the Trans-Alaska pipeline, delegated to the Secretary of the Department in which the Coast Guard is operating, see Ex. Ord. No. 12418, § 4, May 5, 1983, 48 F.R. 20891.

**Termination of Trust Territory of the Pacific Islands**

For termination of Trust Territory of the Pacific Islands, see note set out preceding 48 U.S.C.A. § 1681.

**Termination of United States District Court for the District of the Canal Zone**

For termination of the United States District Court for the District of the Canal Zone at end of the "transition period", being the 30-month period beginning Oct. 1, 1979, and ending midnight Mar. 31, 1982, see Paragraph 5 of Article XI of the Panama Canal Treaty of 1977 and sections 2101 and 2201 to 2203 of Pub.L. 96–70, Title II, Sept. 27, 1979, 93 Stat. 493, formerly classified to 22 U.S.C.A. §§ 3831 and 3841 to 3843, respectively.

**Territorial Sea and Contiguous Zone of United States**

For extension of territorial sea and contiguous zone of United States, see Proc. No. 5928 and Proc. No. 7219, respectively, set out as notes under 43 U.S.C.A. § 1331.

**Deposit of Certain Penalties Into Oil Spill Liability Trust Fund**

Penalties paid pursuant to this section and sections 1319(c) and 1501 et seq., respectively, of this title, deposited in the Oil Spill Liability Trust Fund created under section 9509 of Title 26, Internal Revenue Code, see section 4304 of Pub.L. 101–380, set out as a note under section 9509 of Title 26.

**Report on Oil Spill Responder Immunity**

Pub.L. 107–295, Title IV, § 440, Nov. 25, 2002, 116 Stat. 2130, provided that:

"**(a) Report to Congress.**—Not later than January 1, 2004, the Secretary of the department in which the Coast Guard is operating, jointly with the Secretary of Commerce and the Secretary of the Interior, and after consultation with the Administrator of the Environmental Protection Agency and the Attorney General, shall submit a report to the Committee on Commerce, Science, and Transportation of the Senate and the Committee on Transportation and Infrastructure of the House of Representatives on the immunity from criminal and civil penalties provided under existing law of a private responder (other than a responsible party) in the case of the incidental take of federally listed fish or wildlife that results from, but is not the purpose of, carrying out an otherwise lawful activity conducted by that responder during an oil spill removal activity where the responder was acting in a manner consistent with the National Contingency Plan or as otherwise directed by the Federal On–Scene Coordinator for the spill, and on the circumstances under which such penalties have been or could be imposed on a private responder. The report shall take into consideration the procedures under the Inter–Agency Memorandum for addressing incidental takes.

"**(b) Definitions.**—In this section—

"(1) the term 'Federal On–Scene Coordinator' has the meaning given that term in section 311 of the Federal Water Pollution Control Act (33 U.S.C. 1321);

"(2) the term 'incidental take' has the meaning given that term in the Inter–Agency Memorandum;

"(3) the term 'Inter-Agency Memorandum' means the Inter–Agency Memorandum of Agreement Regarding Oil Spill Planning and Response Activities under the Federal Water Pollution Control Act's National Oil and Hazardous Substances Pollution Contingency Plan [40 C.F.R. § 300.1 et seq.] and the Endangered Species Act [Pub.L. 93–205, Dec. 28, 1973, 87 Stat. 884, as amended, which is classified principally to 16 U.S.C.A. § 1531 et seq.; see Tables for complete classification], effective on July 22, 2001;

"(4) the terms 'National Contingency Plan', 'removal', and 'responsible party' have the meanings given those terms under section 1001 of the Oil Pollution Act of 1990 (33 U.S.C. 2701); and

"(5) the term 'private responder' means a nongovernmental entity or individual that is carrying out an oil spill removal activity at the direction of a Federal agency or a responsible party."

**Implementation of National Planning and Response System**

Section 4202(b) of Pub.L. 101–380 provided that:

"(1) **Area Committees and Contingency Plans.**—(A) Not later than 6 months after the date of the enactment of this Act [Aug. 18, 1990], the President shall designate the areas for which Area Committees are established under section 311(j)(4) of the Federal Water Pollution Control Act [subsec. (j)(4) of this section], as amended by this Act. In designating such areas, the President shall ensure that all navigable waters, adjoining shorelines, and waters of the exclusive economic zone are subject to an Area Contingency Plan under that section.

"(B) Not later than 18 months after the date of the enactment of this Act [Aug. 18, 1990], each Area Committee established under that section [subsec. (j)(4) of this section] shall submit to the President the Area Contingency Plan required under that section.

"(C) Not later than 24 months after the date of the enactment of this Act [Aug. 18, 1990], the President shall—

"(i) promptly review each plan;

"(ii) require amendments to any plan that does not meet the requirements of section 311(j)(4) of the Federal Water Pollution Control Act [subsec. (j)(4) of this section]; and

"(iii) approve each plan that meets the requirements of that section.

"(2) **National Response Unit.**—Not later than one year after the date of the enactment of this Act [Aug. 18, 1990], the Secretary of the department in which the Coast Guard is operating shall establish a National Response Unit in accordance with section 311(j)(2) of the Federal Water Pollution Control Act, as amended by this Act [subsec. (j)(2) of this section].

"(3) **Coast Guard District Response Groups.**—Not later than 1 year after the date of the enactment of this Act [Aug. 18, 1990], the Secretary of the department in which the Coast Guard is operating shall establish Coast Guard District Response Groups in accordance with section 311(j)(3) of the Federal Water Pollution Control Act, as amended by this Act [subsec. (j)(3) of this section].

"(4) **Tank vessel and facility response plans; transition provision; effective date of prohibition.**—(A) Not later than 24 months after the date of the enactment of this Act [Aug. 18, 1990], the President shall issue regulations for tank vessel and facility response plans under section 311(j)(5) of the Federal Water Pollution Control Act, as amended by this Act [subsec. (j)(5) of this section].

"(B) During the period beginning 30 months after the date of the enactment of this paragraph [Aug. 18, 1990], and ending 36 months after that date of enactment, a tank vessel or facility for which a response plan is required to be prepared under section 311(j)(5) of the Federal Water Pollution Control Act, [subsec. (j)(5) of this section], as amended by this Act, may not handle, store, or transport oil unless the owner or operator thereof has submitted such a plan to the President.

"(C) Subparagraph (E) of section 311(j)(5) of the Federal Water Pollution Control Act [subsec. (j)(5) of this section], as amended by this Act, shall take effect 36 months after the date of the enactment of this Act [Aug. 18, 1990]."

**Oil Spill Liability Under Oil Pollution Act of 1990**

Section 2002(a) of Pub.L. 101–380 provided that: "Subsections (f), (g), (h), and (i) of section 311 of the Federal Water Pollution Control Act (33 U.S.C. 1321) [subsecs. (f), (g), (h), and (i) of this section] shall not apply with respect to any incident for which liability is established under section 1002 of this Act [section 2702 of this title]."

**Transfer to Oil Spill Liability Trust Fund of Moneys Remaining in Revolving Fund Upon Its Repeal**

Section 2002(b)(2) of Pub.L. 101–380 provided that: "Subsection (k) [of this section] is repealed. Any amounts remaining in the revolving fund established under that subsection shall be deposited in the [Oil Spill Liability Trust] Fund. The [Oil Spill Liability Trust] Fund shall assume all liability incurred by the revolving fund established under that subsection."

**Revision of National Contingency Plan**

Section 4201(c) of Pub.L. 101–380 provided that: "Not later than one year after the date of the enactment of this Act [Aug. 18, 1990], the President shall revise and republish the National Contingency Plan prepared under section 311(c)(2) of the Federal Water Pollution Control Act [subsec. (c)(2) of this section] (as in effect immediately before the date of the enactment of this Act [Aug. 18, 1990] ) to implement the amendments made by this section [amending subsecs. (a), (c), and (d) of this section] and section 4202 [amending subsecs. (j) and (*o* ) of this section]."

**Designation of Federal Trustees for Natural Resources**

For designation by the President, in accordance with subsec. (f)(5) of this section, of the Secretaries of Defense, Interior, Agriculture, Commerce and Energy as among those to be designated in the National Contingency Plan as Federal Trustees for natural resources, see section 1(c) of Ex. Ord. No. 12580, Jan. 23, 1987, 52 F.R. 2923, set out as a note under section 9615 of Title 42, The Public Health and Welfare.

**Allowable Delay in Establishing Financial Responsibility for Increases in Amounts Under 1977 Amendment**

Section 58(j) of Pub.L. 95–217 provided that: "No vessel subject to the increased amounts which result from the amendments made by subsections (d)(2), (d)(3), and (d)(4) of this section [amending subsecs. (f)(1), (g), and (p)(1) of this section] shall be required to establish any evidence of financial responsibility under section 311(p) of the Federal Water Pollution Control Act [subsec. (p) of this section] for such increased amounts before October 1, 1978."

## § 1322. Marine sanitation devices

[FWPCA § 312]

### (a) Definitions

For the purpose of this section, the term—

(1) "new vessel" includes every description of watercraft or other artificial contrivance used, or capable of being used, as a means of transportation on the navigable waters, the construction of which is initiated after promulgation of standards and regulations under this section;

(2) "existing vessel" includes every description of watercraft or other artificial contrivance used, or capable of being used, as a means of transportation on the navigable waters, the construction of which is initiated before promulgation of standards and regulations under this section;

(3) "public vessel" means a vessel owned or bareboat chartered and operated by the United States, by a State or political subdivision thereof, or by a foreign nation, except when such vessel is engaged in commerce;

(4) "United States" includes the States, the District of Columbia, the Commonwealth of Puerto Rico, the Virgin Islands, Guam, American Samoa, the Canal Zone, and the Trust Territory of the Pacific Islands;

(5) "marine sanitation device" includes any equipment for installation on board a vessel which is designed to receive, retain, treat, or discharge sewage, and any process to treat such sewage;

(6) "sewage" means human body wastes and the wastes from toilets and other receptacles intended to receive or retain body wastes except that, with respect to commercial vessels on the Great Lakes, such term shall include graywater;

(7) "manufacturer" means any person engaged in the manufacturing, assembling, or importation of marine sanitation devices or of vessels subject to standards and regulations promulgated under this section;

(8) "person" means an individual, partnership, firm, corporation, association, or agency of the United States, but does not include an individual on board a public vessel;

(9) "discharge" includes, but is not limited to, any spilling, leaking, pumping, pouring, emitting, emptying or dumping;

(10) "commercial vessels" means those vessels used in the business of transporting property for compensation or hire, or in transporting property in the business of the owner, lessee, or operator of the vessel;

(11) "graywater" means galley, bath, and shower water;

(12) "discharge incidental to the normal operation of a vessel"—

(A) means a discharge, including—

(i) graywater, bilge water, cooling water, weather deck runoff, ballast water, oil water separator effluent, and any other pollutant discharge from the operation of a marine propulsion system, shipboard maneuvering system, crew habitability system, or installed major equipment, such as an aircraft carrier elevator or a catapult, or from a protective, preservative, or absorptive application to the hull of the vessel; and

(ii) a discharge in connection with the testing, maintenance, and repair of a system described in clause (i) whenever the vessel is waterborne; and

(B) does not include—

(i) a discharge of rubbish, trash, garbage, or other such material discharged overboard;

(ii) an air emission resulting from the operation of a vessel propulsion system, motor driven equipment, or incinerator; or

(iii) a discharge that is not covered by part 122.3 of title 40, Code of Federal Regulations (as in effect on February 10, 1996);

(13) "marine pollution control device" means any equipment or management practice, for installation or use on board a vessel of the Armed Forces, that is—

(A) designed to receive, retain, treat, control, or discharge a discharge incidental to the normal operation of a vessel; and

(B) determined by the Administrator and the Secretary of Defense to be the most effective equipment or management practice to reduce the environmental impacts of the discharge consistent with the considerations set forth in subsection (n)(2)(B) of this section; and

(14) "vessel of the Armed Forces" means—

(A) any vessel owned or operated by the Department of Defense, other than a time or voyage chartered vessel; and

(B) any vessel owned or operated by the Department of Transportation that is designated by the Secretary of the department in which the Coast Guard is operating as a vessel equivalent to a vessel described in subparagraph (A).

### (b) Federal standards of performance

(1) As soon as possible, after October 18, 1972, and subject to the provisions of section 1254(j) of this title, the Administrator, after consultation with the Secre-

tary of the department in which the Coast Guard is operating, after giving appropriate consideration to the economic costs involved, and within the limits of available technology, shall promulgate Federal standards of performance for marine sanitation devices (hereafter in this section referred to as "standards") which shall be designed to prevent the discharge of untreated or inadequately treated sewage into or upon the navigable waters from new vessels and existing vessels, except vessels not equipped with installed toilet facilities. Such standards and standards established under subsection (c)(1)(B) of this section shall be consistent with maritime safety and the marine and navigation laws and regulations and shall be coordinated with the regulations issued under this subsection by the Secretary of the department in which the Coast Guard is operating. The Secretary of the department in which the Coast Guard is operating shall promulgate regulations, which are consistent with standards promulgated under this subsection and subsection (c) of this section and with maritime safety and the marine and navigation laws and regulations governing the design, construction, installation, and operation of any marine sanitation device on board such vessels.

(2) Any existing vessel equipped with a marine sanitation device on the date of promulgation of initial standards and regulations under this section, which device is in compliance with such initial standards and regulations, shall be deemed in compliance with this section until such time as the device is replaced or is found not to be in compliance with such initial standards and regulations.

**(c) Initial standards; effective dates; revision; waiver**

(1)(A) Initial standards and regulations under this section shall become effective for new vessels two years after promulgation; and for existing vessels five years after promulgation. Revisions of standards and regulations shall be effective upon promulgation, unless another effective date is specified, except that no revision shall take effect before the effective date of the standard or regulation being revised.

(B) The Administrator shall, with respect to commercial vessels on the Great Lakes, establish standards which require at a minimum the equivalent of secondary treatment as defined under section 1314(d) of this title. Such standards and regulations shall take effect for existing vessels after such time as the Administrator determines to be reasonable for the upgrading of marine sanitation devices to attain such standard.

(2) The Secretary of the department in which the Coast Guard is operating with regard to his regulatory authority established by this section, after consultation with the Administrator, may distinguish among classes, type, and sizes of vessels as well as between new and existing vessels, and may waive applicability of standards and regulations as necessary or appropriate for such classes, types, and sizes of vessels (including existing vessels equipped with marine sanitation devices on the date of promulgation of the initial standards required by this section), and, upon application, for individual vessels.

**(d) Vessels owned and operated by the United States**

The provisions of this section and the standards and regulations promulgated hereunder apply to vessels owned and operated by the United States unless the Secretary of Defense finds that compliance would not be in the interest of national security. With respect to vessels owned and operated by the Department of Defense, regulations under the last sentence of subsection (b)(1) of this section and certifications under subsection (g)(2) of this section shall be promulgated and issued by the Secretary of Defense.

**(e) Pre-promulgation consultation**

Before the standards and regulations under this section are promulgated, the Administrator and the Secretary of the department in which the Coast Guard is operating shall consult with the Secretary of State; the Secretary of Health and Human Services; the Secretary of Defense; the Secretary of the Treasury; the Secretary of Commerce; other interested Federal agencies; and the States and industries interested; and otherwise comply with the requirements of section 553 of Title 5.

**(f) Regulation by States or political subdivisions thereof; complete prohibition upon discharge of sewage**

(1)(A) Except as provided in subparagraph (B), after the effective date of the initial standards and regulations promulgated under this section, no State or political subdivision thereof shall adopt or enforce any statute or regulation of such State or political subdivision with respect to the design, manufacture, or installation or use of any marine sanitation device on any vessel subject to the provisions of this section.

(B) A State may adopt and enforce a statute or regulation with respect to the design, manufacture, or installation or use of any marine sanitation device on a houseboat, if such statute or regulation is more stringent than the standards and regulations promulgated under this section. For purposes of this paragraph, the term "houseboat" means a vessel which, for a period of time determined by the State in which the vessel is located, is used primarily as a residence and is not used primarily as a means of transportation.

(2) If, after promulgation of the initial standards and regulations and prior to their effective date, a

vessel is equipped with a marine sanitation device in compliance with such standards and regulations and the installation and operation of such device is in accordance with such standards and regulations, such standards and regulations shall, for the purposes of paragraph (1) of this subsection, become effective with respect to such vessel on the date of such compliance.

(3) After the effective date of the initial standards and regulations promulgated under this section, if any State determines that the protection and enhancement of the quality of some or all of the waters within such State require greater environmental protection, such State may completely prohibit the discharge from all vessels of any sewage, whether treated or not, into such waters, except that no such prohibition shall apply until the Administrator determines that adequate facilities for the safe and sanitary removal and treatment of sewage from all vessels are reasonably available for such water to which such prohibition would apply. Upon application of the State, the Administrator shall make such determination within 90 days of the date of such application.

(4)(A) If the Administrator determines upon application by a State that the protection and enhancement of the quality of specified waters within such State requires such a prohibition, he shall by regulation completely prohibit the discharge from a vessel of any sewage (whether treated or not) into such waters.

(B) Upon application by a State, the Administrator shall, by regulation, establish a drinking water intake zone in any waters within such State and prohibit the discharge of sewage from vessels within that zone.

**(g) Sales limited to certified devices; certification of test device; recordkeeping; reports**

(1) No manufacturer of a marine sanitation device shall sell, offer for sale, or introduce or deliver for introduction in interstate commerce, or import into the United States for sale or resale any marine sanitation device manufactured after the effective date of the standards and regulations promulgated under this section unless such device is in all material respects substantially the same as a test device certified under this subsection.

(2) Upon application of the manufacturer, the Secretary of the department in which the Coast Guard is operating shall so certify a marine sanitation device if he determines, in accordance with the provisions of this paragraph, that it meets the appropriate standards and regulations promulgated under this section. The Secretary of the department in which the Coast Guard is operating shall test or require such testing of the device in accordance with procedures set forth by the Administrator as to standards of performance and for such other purposes as may be appropriate. If the Secretary of the department in which the Coast Guard is operating determines that the device is satisfactory from the standpoint of safety and any other requirements of maritime law or regulation, and after consideration of the design, installation, operation, material, or other appropriate factors, he shall certify the device. Any device manufactured by such manufacturer which is in all material respects substantially the same as the certified test device shall be deemed to be in conformity with the appropriate standards and regulations established under this section.

(3) Every manufacturer shall establish and maintain such records, make such reports, and provide such information as the Administrator or the Secretary of the department in which the Coast Guard is operating may reasonably require to enable him to determine whether such manufacturer has acted or is acting in compliance with this section and regulations issued thereunder and shall, upon request of an officer or employee duly designated by the Administrator or the Secretary of the department in which the Coast Guard is operating, permit such officer or employee at reasonable times to have access to and copy such records. All information reported to or otherwise obtained by the Administrator or the Secretary of the department in which the Coast Guard is operating or their representatives pursuant to this subsection which contains or relates to a trade secret or other matter referred to in section 1905 of Title 18 shall be considered confidential for the purpose of that section, except that such information may be disclosed to other officers or employees concerned with carrying out this section. This paragraph shall not apply in the case of the construction of a vessel by an individual for his own use.

**(h) Sale and resale of properly equipped vessels; operability of certified marine sanitation devices**

After the effective date of standards and regulations promulgated under this section, it shall be unlawful—

(1) for the manufacturer of any vessel subject to such standards and regulations to manufacture for sale, to sell or offer for sale, or to distribute for sale or resale any such vessel unless it is equipped with a marine sanitation device which is in all material respects substantially the same as the appropriate test device certified pursuant to this section;

(2) for any person, prior to the sale or delivery of a vessel subject to such standards and regulations to the ultimate purchaser, wrongfully to remove or render inoperative any certified marine sanitation device or element of design of such device installed in such vessel;

(3) for any person to fail or refuse to permit access to or copying of records or to fail to make

reports or provide information required under this section; and

(4) for a vessel subject to such standards and regulations to operate on the navigable waters of the United States, if such vessel is not equipped with an operable marine sanitation device certified pursuant to this section.

**(i) Jurisdiction to restrain violations; contempts**

The district courts of the United States shall have jurisdictions to restrain violations of subsection (g)(1) of this section and subsections (h)(1) through (3) of this section. Actions to restrain such violations shall be brought by, and in, the name of the United States. In case of contumacy or refusal to obey a subpena served upon any person under this subsection, the district court of the United States for any district in which such person is found or resides or transacts business, upon application by the United States and after notice to such person, shall have jurisdiction to issue an order requiring such person to appear and give testimony or to appear and produce documents, and any failure to obey such order of the court may be punished by such court as a contempt thereof.

**(j) Penalties**

Any person who violates subsection (g)(1) of this section, clause (1) or (2) of subsection (h) of this section, or subsection (n)(8) of this section shall be liable to a civil penalty of not more than $5,000 for each violation. Any person who violates clause (4) of subsection (h) of this section or any regulation issued pursuant to this section shall be liable to a civil penalty of not more than $2,000 for each violation. Each violation shall be a separate offense. The Secretary of the department in which the Coast Guard is operating may assess and compromise any such penalty. No penalty shall be assessed until the person charged shall have been given notice and an opportunity for a hearing on such charge. In determining the amount of the penalty, or the amount agreed upon in compromise, the gravity of the violation, and the demonstrated good faith of the person charged in attempting to achieve rapid compliance, after notification of a violation, shall be considered by said Secretary.

**(k) Enforcement authority**

The provisions of this section shall be enforced by the Secretary of the department in which the Coast Guard is operating and he may utilize by agreement, with or without reimbursement, law enforcement officers or other personnel and facilities of the Administrator, other Federal agencies, or the States to carry out the provisions of this section. The provisions of this section may also be enforced by a State.

**(*l*) Boarding and inspection of vessels; execution of warrants and other process**

Anyone authorized by the Secretary of the department in which the Coast Guard is operating to enforce the provisions of this section may, except as to public vessels, (1) board and inspect any vessel upon the navigable waters of the United States and (2) execute any warrant or other process issued by an officer or court of competent jurisdiction.

**(m) Enforcement in United States possessions**

In the case of Guam and the Trust Territory of the Pacific Islands, actions arising under this section may be brought in the district court of Guam, and in the case of the Virgin Islands such actions may be brought in the district court of the Virgin Islands. In the case of American Samoa and the Trust Territory of the Pacific Islands, such actions may be brought in the District Court of the United States for the District of Hawaii and such court shall have jurisdiction of such actions. In the case of the Canal Zone, such actions may be brought in the District Court for the District of the Canal Zone.

**(n) Uniform National Discharge Standards for Vessels of Armed Forces**

**(1) Applicability**

This subsection shall apply to vessels of the Armed Forces and discharges, other than sewage, incidental to the normal operation of a vessel of the Armed Forces, unless the Secretary of Defense finds that compliance with this subsection would not be in the national security interests of the United States.

**(2) Determination of discharges required to be controlled by marine pollution control devices**

**(A) In general**

The Administrator and the Secretary of Defense, after consultation with the Secretary of the department in which the Coast Guard is operating, the Secretary of Commerce, and interested States, shall jointly determine the discharges incidental to the normal operation of a vessel of the Armed Forces for which it is reasonable and practicable to require use of a marine pollution control device to mitigate adverse impacts on the marine environment. Notwithstanding subsection (a)(1) of section 553 of Title 5, the Administrator and the Secretary of Defense shall promulgate the determinations in accordance with such section. The Secretary of Defense shall require the use of a marine pollution control device on board a vessel of the Armed Forces in any case in which it is determined that the use of such a device is reasonable and practicable.

(B) Considerations

In making a determination under subparagraph (A), the Administrator and the Secretary of Defense shall take into consideration—

(i) the nature of the discharge;

(ii) the environmental effects of the discharge;

(iii) the practicability of using the marine pollution control device;

(iv) the effect that installation or use of the marine pollution control device would have on the operation or operational capability of the vessel;

(v) applicable United States law;

(vi) applicable international standards; and

(vii) the economic costs of the installation and use of the marine pollution control device.

(3) Performance standards for marine pollution control devices

(A) In general

For each discharge for which a marine pollution control device is determined to be required under paragraph (2), the Administrator and the Secretary of Defense, in consultation with the Secretary of the department in which the Coast Guard is operating, the Secretary of State, the Secretary of Commerce, other interested Federal agencies, and interested States, shall jointly promulgate Federal standards of performance for each marine pollution control device required with respect to the discharge. Notwithstanding subsection (a)(1) of section 553 of Title 5, the Administrator and the Secretary of Defense shall promulgate the standards in accordance with such section.

(B) Considerations

In promulgating standards under this paragraph, the Administrator and the Secretary of Defense shall take into consideration the matters set forth in paragraph (2)(B).

(C) Classes, types, and sizes of vessels

The standards promulgated under this paragraph may—

(i) distinguish among classes, types, and sizes of vessels;

(ii) distinguish between new and existing vessels; and

(iii) provide for a waiver of the applicability of the standards as necessary or appropriate to a particular class, type, age, or size of vessel.

(4) Regulations for use of marine pollution control devices

The Secretary of Defense, after consultation with the Administrator and the Secretary of the department in which the Coast Guard is operating, shall promulgate such regulations governing the design, construction, installation, and use of marine pollution control devices on board vessels of the Armed Forces as are necessary to achieve the standards promulgated under paragraph (3).

(5) Deadlines; effective date

(A) Determinations

The Administrator and the Secretary of Defense shall—

(i) make the initial determinations under paragraph (2) not later than 2 years after February 10, 1996; and

(ii) every 5 years—

(I) review the determinations; and

(II) if necessary, revise the determinations based on significant new information.

(B) Standards

The Administrator and the Secretary of Defense shall—

(i) promulgate standards of performance for a marine pollution control device under paragraph (3) not later than 2 years after the date of a determination under paragraph (2) that the marine pollution control device is required; and

(ii) every 5 years—

(I) review the standards; and

(II) if necessary, revise the standards, consistent with paragraph (3)(B) and based on significant new information.

(C) Regulations

The Secretary of Defense shall promulgate regulations with respect to a marine pollution control device under paragraph (4) as soon as practicable after the Administrator and the Secretary of Defense promulgate standards with respect to the device under paragraph (3), but not later than 1 year after the Administrator and the Secretary of Defense promulgate the standards. The regulations promulgated by the Secretary of Defense under paragraph (4) shall become effective upon promulgation unless another effective date is specified in the regulations.

(D) Petition for review

The Governor of any State may submit a petition requesting that the Secretary of Defense and the Administrator review a determination under paragraph (2) or a standard under paragraph (3), if there is significant new information, not considered previously, that could reasonably result in a change to the particular determination or standard after consideration of the matters set forth in paragraph (2)(B). The petition shall be accompanied by the scientific and technical information on which the petition is based. The Administrator and the Secretary of Defense shall grant or deny the petition not later than 2 years after the date of receipt of the petition.

**(6) Effect on other laws**

**(A) Prohibition on regulation by States or political subdivisions of States**

Beginning on the effective date of—

(i) a determination under paragraph (2) that it is not reasonable and practicable to require use of a marine pollution control device regarding a particular discharge incidental to the normal operation of a vessel of the Armed Forces; or

(ii) regulations promulgated by the Secretary of Defense under paragraph (4);

except as provided in paragraph (7), neither a State nor a political subdivision of a State may adopt or enforce any statute or regulation of the State or political subdivision with respect to the discharge or the design, construction, installation, or use of any marine pollution control device required to control discharges from a vessel of the Armed Forces.

**(B) Federal laws**

This subsection shall not affect the application of section 1321 of this title to discharges incidental to the normal operation of a vessel.

**(7) Establishment of State no-discharge zones**

**(A) State prohibition**

**(i) In general**

After the effective date of—

(I) a determination under paragraph (2) that it is not reasonable and practicable to require use of a marine pollution control device regarding a particular discharge incidental to the normal operation of a vessel of the Armed Forces; or

(II) regulations promulgated by the Secretary of Defense under paragraph (4);

if a State determines that the protection and enhancement of the quality of some or all of the waters within the State require greater environmental protection, the State may prohibit 1 or more discharges incidental to the normal operation of a vessel, whether treated or not treated, into the waters. No prohibition shall apply until the Administrator makes the determinations described in subclauses (II) and (III) of subparagraph (B)(i).

**(ii) Documentation**

To the extent that a prohibition under this paragraph would apply to vessels of the Armed Forces and not to other types of vessels, the State shall document the technical or environmental basis for the distinction.

**(B) Prohibition by the Administrator**

**(i) In general**

Upon application of a State, the Administrator shall by regulation prohibit the discharge from a vessel of 1 or more discharges incidental to the normal operation of a vessel, whether treated or not treated, into the waters covered by the application if the Administrator determines that—

(I) the protection and enhancement of the quality of the specified waters within the State require a prohibition of the discharge into the waters;

(II) adequate facilities for the safe and sanitary removal of the discharge incidental to the normal operation of a vessel are reasonably available for the waters to which the prohibition would apply; and

(III) the prohibition will not have the effect of discriminating against a vessel of the Armed Forces by reason of the ownership or operation by the Federal Government, or the military function, of the vessel.

**(ii) Approval or disapproval**

The Administrator shall approve or disapprove an application submitted under clause (i) not later than 90 days after the date on which the application is submitted to the Administrator. Notwithstanding clause (i)(II), the Administrator shall not disapprove an application for the sole reason that there are not adequate facilities to remove any discharge incidental to the normal operation of a vessel from vessels of the Armed Forces.

**(C) Applicability to foreign flagged vessels**

A prohibition under this paragraph—

(i) shall not impose any design, construction, manning, or equipment standard on a foreign flagged vessel engaged in innocent passage unless the prohibition implements a generally accepted international rule or standard; and

(ii) that relates to the prevention, reduction, and control of pollution shall not apply to a foreign flagged vessel engaged in transit passage unless the prohibition implements an applicable international regulation regarding the discharge of oil, oily waste, or any other noxious substance into the waters.

**(8) Prohibition relating to vessels of the Armed Forces**

After the effective date of the regulations promulgated by the Secretary of Defense under paragraph (4), it shall be unlawful for any vessel of the Armed Forces subject to the regulations to—

(A) operate in the navigable waters of the United States or the waters of the contiguous zone, if the vessel is not equipped with any required marine pollution control device meeting standards established under this subsection; or

(B) discharge overboard any discharge incidental to the normal operation of a vessel in waters with respect to which a prohibition on the discharge has been established under paragraph (7).

**(9) Enforcement**

This subsection shall be enforceable, as provided in subsections (j) and (k) of this section, against any agency of the United States responsible for vessels of the Armed Forces notwithstanding any immunity asserted by the agency.

(June 30, 1948, c. 758, Title III, § 312, as added Oct. 18, 1972, Pub.L. 92–500, § 2, 86 Stat. 871, and amended Dec. 27, 1977, Pub.L. 95–217, § 59, 91 Stat. 1596; Oct. 17, 1979, Pub.L. 96–88, Title V, § 509(b), 93 Stat. 695; Feb. 4, 1987, Pub.L. 100–4, Title III, § 311, 101 Stat. 42; Feb. 10, 1996, Pub.L. 104–106, Div. A, Title III, § 325(b) to (c)(2), 110 Stat. 254.)

## HISTORICAL AND STATUTORY NOTES

**References in Text**

For definition of Canal Zone, referred to in subsecs. (a)(4) and (m), see section 3602(b) of Title 22, Foreign Relations and Intercourse.

**Change of Name**

"Secretary of Health and Human Services" was substituted for "Secretary of Health, Education, and Welfare" in subsec. (e) pursuant to section 509(b) of Pub.L. 96–88 which is classified to section 3508(b) of Title 20, Education.

**Termination of Trust Territory of the Pacific Islands**

For termination of Trust Territory of the Pacific Islands, see note set out preceding 48 U.S.C.A. § 1681.

**Termination of United States District Court for the District of the Canal Zone**

For termination of the United States District Court for the District of the Canal Zone at end of the "transition period", being the 30-month period beginning Oct. 1, 1979, and ending midnight Mar. 31, 1982, see Paragraph 5 of Article XI of the Panama Canal Treaty of 1977 and sections 2101 and 2201 to 2203 of Pub.L. 96–70, Title II, Sept. 27, 1979, 93 Stat. 493, formerly classified to 22 U.S.C.A. §§ 3831 and 3841 to 3843, respectively.

**Contiguous Zone of United States**

For extension of contiguous zone of United States, see Proc. No. 7219, set out as a note under 43 U.S.C.A. § 1331.

**Purposes of National Discharge Standards**

Section 325(a) of Pub.L. 104–106 provided that: "The purposes of this section [section 325 of Pub.L. 104–106, which enacted subsec. (n) of this section, amended subsecs. (a) and (j) of this section and section 1362(6)(A) of this title, and enacted provisions set out as a note under this section] are to—

"(1) enhance the operational flexibility of vessels of the Armed Forces domestically and internationally;

"(2) stimulate the development of innovative vessel pollution control technology; and

"(3) advance the development by the United States Navy of environmentally sound ships."

**Cooperation in National Discharge Standards Development**

Section 325(d) of Pub.L. 104–106 provided that: "The Administrator of the Environmental Protection Agency and the Secretary of Defense may, by mutual agreement, with or without reimbursement, provide for the use of information, reports, personnel, or other resources of the Environmental Protection Agency or the Department of Defense to carry out section 312(n) of the Federal Water Pollution Control Act (as added by subsection (b) [subsec. (n) of this section]), including the use of the resources—

"(1) to determine—

"(A) the nature and environmental effect of discharges incidental to the normal operation of a vessel of the Armed Forces;

"(B) the practicability of using marine pollution control devices on vessels of the Armed Forces; and

"(C) the effect that installation or use of marine pollution control devices on vessels of the Armed Forces would have on the operation or operational capability of the vessels; and

"(2) to establish performance standards for marine pollution control devices on vessels of the Armed Forces."

**Construction, Renovation, Operation, and Maintenance of Pumpout Stations and Waste Reception Facilities**

Pub.L. 102–587, Title V, Subtitle F, § 5601 et seq., Nov. 4, 1992, 106 Stat. 5086, provided that:

**"Sec. 5601. Short title.**

"This subtitle [subtitle F, §§ 5601 to 5608, of Title V of Pub.L. 102–587, amending sections 777c and 777g of Title 16, Conservation and enacting this note] may be cited as the 'Clean Vessel Act of 1992'.

**"Sec. 5602. Findings; purpose.**

"(a) **Findings.**—The Congress finds the following:

"(1) The discharge of untreated sewage by vessels is prohibited under Federal law in all areas within the navigable waters of the United States.

"(2) The discharge of treated sewage by vessels is prohibited under either Federal or State law in many of the United States bodies of water where recreational boaters operate.

"(3) There is currently an inadequate number of pumpout stations for type III marine sanitation devices where recreational vessels normally operate.

"(4) Sewage discharged by recreational vessels because of an inadequate number of pumpout stations is a substantial contributor to localized degradation of water quality in the United States.

"(b) **Purpose.**—The purpose of this subtitle is to provide funds to States for the construction, renovation, operation, and maintenance of pumpout stations and waste reception facilities.

**"Sec. 5603. Determination and plan regarding State marine sanitation device pumpout station needs.**

"(a) **Survey.**—Within 3 months after the notification under section 5605(b), each coastal State shall conduct a survey to determine—

"(1) the number and location of all operational pumpout stations and waste reception facilities at public and private marinas, mooring areas, docks, and other boating access facilities within the coastal zone of the State; and

"(2) the number of recreational vessels in the coastal waters of the State with type III marine sanitation devices or portable toilets, and the areas of those coastal waters where those vessels congregate.

"(b) **Plan.** Within 6 months after the notification under section 5605(b), and based on the survey conducted under subsection (a), each coastal State shall—

"(1) develop and submit to the Secretary of the Interior a plan for any construction or renovation of pumpout stations and waste reception facilities that are necessary to ensure that, based on the guidance issued under section 5605(a), there are pumpout stations and waste reception facilities in the State that are adequate and reasonably available to meet the needs of recreational vessels using the coastal waters of the State; and

"(2) submit to the Secretary of the Interior with that plan a list of all stations and facilities in the coastal zone of the State which are operational on the date of submittal.

"(c) **Plan approval.**—

"(1) **In general.**—Not later than 60 days after a plan is submitted by a State under subsection (b), the Secretary of the Interior shall approve or disapprove the plan, based on—

"(A) the adequacy of the survey conducted by the State under subsection (a); and

"(B) the ability of the plan, based on the guidance issued under section 5605(a), to meet the construction and renovation needs of the recreational vessels identified in the survey.

"(2) **Notification of State; modification.**—The Secretary of the Interior shall promptly notify the affected Governor of the approval or disapproval of a plan. If a plan is disapproved, the Secretary of the Interior shall recommend necessary modifications and return the plan to the affected Governor.

"(3) **Resubmittal.**—Not later than 60 days after receiving a plan returned by the Secretary of the Interior, the Governor shall make the appropriate changes and resubmit the plan.

"(d) **Indication of stations and facilities on NOAA charts.**—

"(1) **In general.**—The Under Secretary of Commerce for Oceans and Atmosphere shall indicate, on charts published by the National Oceanic and Atmospheric Administration for the use of operators of recreational vessels, the locations of pumpout stations and waste reception facilities.

"(2) **Notification of NOAA.**—

"(A) **Lists of stations and facilities.**—The Secretary of the Interior shall transmit to the Under Secretary of Commerce for Oceans and Atmosphere each list of operational stations and facilities submitted by a State under subsection (b)(2), by not later than 30 days after the date of receipt of that list.

"(B) **Completion of project.**—The Director of the United States Fish and Wildlife Service shall notify the Under Secretary of the location of each station or facility at which a construction or renovation project is completed by a State with amounts made available under the Act of August 9, 1950 (16 U.S.C. 777a et seq.), as amended by this subtitle [section 777 et seq. of Title 16, Conservation], by not later than 30 days after the date of notification by a State of the completion of the project.

**"Sec. 5604. Funding.**

"(a) **[Omitted.** Subsec. (a) amended section 777c of Title 16, Conservation]

"(b) **[Omitted.** Subsec. (b) amended section 777g of Title 16, Conservation]

"(c) **Grant program.**—

"(1) **Matching grants.**—The Secretary of the Interior may obligate an amount not to exceed the amount made available under section 4(b)(2) of the Act of August 9, 1950 (16 U.S.C. 777c(b)(2), as amended by this Act) [section 777c(b)(2) of Title 16], to make grants to—

"(A) coastal States to pay not more than 75 percent of the cost to a coastal State of—

"(i) conducting a survey under section 5603(a);

"(ii) developing and submitting a plan and accompanying list under section 5603(b);

"(iii) constructing and renovating pumpout stations and waste reception facilities; and

"(iv) conducting a program to educate recreational boaters about the problem of human body waste discharges from vessels and inform them of the location of pumpout stations and waste reception facilities.

"(B) inland States, which can demonstrate to the Secretary of the Interior that there are an inadequate number of pumpout stations and waste reception facilities to meet the needs of recreational vessels in the waters of that State, to pay 75 percent of the cost to that State of—

"(i) constructing and renovating pumpout stations and waste reception facilities in the inland State; and

"(ii) conducting a program to educate recreational boaters about the problem of human body waste discharges from vessels and inform them of the location of pumpout stations and waste reception facilities.

"(2) **Priority.**—In awarding grants under this subsection, the Secretary of the Interior shall give priority consideration to grant applications that—

"(A) in coastal States, propose constructing and renovating pumpout stations and waste reception facilities in accordance with a coastal State's plan approved under section 5603(c);

"(B) provide for public/private partnership efforts to develop and operate pumpout stations and waste receptions facilities; and

"(C) propose innovative ways to increase the availability and use of pumpout stations and waste reception facilities.

"**(d) Disclaimer.**—Nothing in this subtitle shall be interpreted to preclude a State from carrying out the provisions of this subtitle with funds other than those described in this section.

**"Sec. 5605. Guidance and notification.**

"**(a) Issuance of guidance.**—Not later than 3 months after the date of the enactment of this subtitle [Nov. 4, 1992], the Secretary of the Interior shall, after consulting with the Administrator of the Environmental Protection Agency, the Under Secretary of Commerce for Oceans and Atmosphere, and the Commandant of the Coast Guard, issue for public comment pumpout station and waste reception facility guidance. The Secretary of the Interior shall finalize the guidance not later than 6 months after the date of enactment of this subtitle [Nov. 4, 1992]. The guidance shall include—

"(1) guidance regarding the types of pumpout stations and waste reception facilities that may be appropriate for construction, renovation, operation, or maintenance with amounts available under the Act of August 9, 1950 (16 U.S.C. 777a et seq.) [section 777 et seq. of Title 16], as amended by this subtitle, and appropriate location of the stations and facilities within a marina or boatyard;

"(2) guidance defining what constitutes adequate and reasonably available pumpout stations and waste reception facilities in boating areas;

"(3) guidance on appropriate methods for disposal of vessel sewage from pumpout stations and waste reception facilities;

"(4) guidance on appropriate connector fittings to facilitate the sanitary and expeditious discharge of sewage from vessels;

"(5) guidance on the waters most likely to be affected by the discharge of sewage from vessels; and

"(6) other information that is considered necessary to promote the establishment of pumpout facilities to reduce sewage discharges from vessels and to protect United States waters.

"**(b) Notification.**—Not later than one month after the guidance issued under subsection (a) is finalized, the Secretary of the Interior shall provide notification in writing to the fish and wildlife, water pollution control, and coastal zone management authorities of each State, of—

"(1) the availability of amounts under the Act of August 9, 1950 (16 U.S.C. 777a et seq.) [section 777 et seq. of Title 16] to implement the Clean Vessel Act of 1992 [subtitle F of Title V of Pub.L. 102–587 amending sections 777c and 777g of Title 16 and enacting this note]; and

"(2) the guidance developed under subsection (a).

**"Sec. 5606. Effect on State funding eligibility.**

"This subtitle shall not be construed or applied to jeopardize any funds available to a coastal State under the Act of August 9, 1950 (16 U.S.C. 777a et seq.) [section 777 et seq. of Title 16], if the coastal State is, in good faith, pursuing a survey and plan designed to meet the purposes of this subtitle.

**"Sec. 5607. Applicability.**

"The requirements of section 5603 shall not apply to a coastal State if within six months after the date of enactment of this subtitle [Nov. 4, 1992] the Secretary of the Interior certifies that—

"(1) the State has developed and is implementing a plan that will ensure that there will be pumpout stations and waste reception facilities adequate to meet the needs of recreational vessels in the coastal waters of the State; or

"(2) existing pumpout stations and waste reception facilities in the coastal waters of the State are adequate to meet those needs.

**"Sec. 5608. Definitions.**

"For the purposes of this subtitle the term:

"(1) 'coastal State'—

"(A) means a State of the United States in, or bordering on the Atlantic, Pacific, or Arctic Ocean; the Gulf of Mexico; Long Island Sound; or one or more of the Great Lakes;

"(B) includes Puerto Rico, the Virgin Islands, Guam, the Commonwealth of the Northern Mariana Islands, and American Samoa; and

"(C) does not include a State for which the ratio of the number of recreational vessels in the State numbered under chapter 123 of title 46, United States Code [section 12301 et seq. of Title 46, Shipping], to number of miles of shoreline (as that term is defined in section 926.2(d) of title 15, Code of Federal Regulations, as in effect on January 1, 1991), is less than one.

"(2) 'coastal waters' means—

"(A) in the Great Lakes area, the waters within the territorial jurisdiction of the United States consisting of the Great Lakes, their connecting waters, harbors, roadsteads, and estuary-type areas such as bays, shallows, and marshes; and

"(B) in other areas, those waters, adjacent to the shorelines, which contain a measurable percentage of sea water, including sounds, bay, lagoons, bayous, ponds, and estuaries.

"(3) 'coastal zone' has the same meaning that term has in section 304(1) of the Coastal Zone Management Act of 1972 (16 U.S.C. 1453(1)) [section 1453(1) of Title 16];

"(4) 'inland State' means a State which is not a coastal state;

"(5) 'type III marine sanitation device' means any equipment for installation on board a vessel which is specifically designed to receive, retain, and discharge human body wastes;

"(6) 'pumpout station' means a facility that pumps or receives human body wastes out of type III marine sanitation devices installed on board vessels;

"(7) 'recreational vessel' means a vessel—

"(A) manufactured for operation, or operated, primarily for pleasure; or

"(B) leased, rented, or chartered to another for the latter's pleasure; and

"(8) 'waste reception facility' means a facility specifically designed to receive wastes from portable toilets carried on vessels, and does not include lavatories."

## § 1323. Federal facilities pollution control [FWPCA § 313]

**(a)** Each department, agency, or instrumentality of the executive, legislative, and judicial branches of the Federal Government (1) having jurisdiction over any property or facility, or (2) engaged in any activity resulting, or which may result, in the discharge or runoff of pollutants, and each officer, agent, or employee thereof in the performance of his official duties, shall be subject to, and comply with, all Federal, State, interstate, and local requirements, administrative authority, and process and sanctions respecting the control and abatement of water pollution in the same manner, and to the same extent as any nongovernmental entity including the payment of reasonable service charges. The preceding sentence shall apply (A) to any requirement whether substantive or procedural (including any recordkeeping or reporting requirement, any requirement respecting permits and any other requirement, whatsoever), (B) to the exercise of any Federal, State, or local administrative authority, and (C) to any process and sanction, whether enforced in Federal, State, or local courts or in any other manner. This subsection shall apply notwithstanding any immunity of such agencies, officers, agents, or employees under any law or rule of law. Nothing in this section shall be construed to prevent any department, agency, or instrumentality of the Federal Government, or any officer, agent, or employee thereof in the performance of his official duties, from removing to the appropriate Federal district court any proceeding to which the department, agency, or instrumentality or officer, agent, or employee thereof is subject pursuant to this section, and any such proceeding may be removed in accordance with section 1441 et seq. of Title 28. No officer, agent, or employee of the United States shall be personally liable for any civil penalty arising from the performance of his official duties, for which he is not otherwise liable, and the United States shall be liable only for those civil penalties arising under Federal law or imposed by a State or local court to enforce an order or the process of such court. The President may exempt any effluent source of any department, agency, or instrumentality in the executive branch from compliance with any such a requirement if he determines it to be in the paramount interest of the United States to do so; except that no exemption may be granted from the requirements of section 1316 or 1317 of this title. No such exemptions shall be granted due to lack of appropriation unless the President shall have specifically requested such appropriation as a part of the budgetary process and the Congress shall have failed to make available such requested appropriation. Any exemption shall be for a period not in excess of one year, but additional exemptions may be granted for periods of not to exceed one year upon the President's making a new determination. The President shall report each January to the Congress all exemptions from the requirements of this section granted during the preceding calendar year, together with his reason for granting such exemption. In addition to any such exemption of a particular effluent source, the President may, if he determines it to be in the paramount interest of the United States to do so, issue regulations exempting from compliance with the requirements of this section any weaponry, equipment, aircraft, vessels, vehicles, or other classes or categories of property, and access to such property, which are owned or operated by the Armed Forces of the United States (including the Coast Guard) or by the National Guard of any State and which are uniquely military in nature. The President shall reconsider the need for such regulations at three-year intervals.

**(b)(1)** The Administrator shall coordinate with the head of each department, agency, or instrumentality of the Federal Government having jurisdiction over any property or facility utilizing federally owned wastewater facilities to develop a program of cooperation for utilizing wastewater control systems utilizing those innovative treatment processes and techniques for which guidelines have been promulgated under section 1314(d)(3) of this title. Such program shall include an inventory of property and facilities which could utilize such processes and techniques.

**(2)** Construction shall not be initiated for facilities for treatment of wastewater at any Federal property or facility after September 30, 1979, if alternative methods for wastewater treatment at such property or facility utilizing innovative treatment processes and techniques, including but not limited to methods utilizing recycle and reuse techniques and land treatment are not utilized, unless the life cycle cost of the alternative treatment works exceeds the life cycle cost of the most cost effective alternative by more than 15 per centum. The Administrator may waive the application of this paragraph in any case where the Administrator determines it to be in the public interest, or that compliance with this paragraph would interfere with the orderly compliance with conditions of a permit issued pursuant to section 1342 of this title.

(June 30, 1948, c. 758, Title III, § 313, as added Oct. 18, 1972, Pub.L. 92–500, § 2, 86 Stat. 875, and amended Dec. 27, 1977, Pub.L. 95–217, §§ 60, 61(a), 91 Stat. 1597, 1598.)

### HISTORICAL AND STATUTORY NOTES

**Marine Guidance Systems**

Pub.L. 105–383, Title IV, § 425(b), Nov. 13, 1998, 112 Stat. 3441, provided that: "The Secretary of Transportation shall, within 12 months after the date of the enactment of this Act [Nov. 13, 1998], evaluate and report to the Congress on the suitability of marine sector laser lighting, cold cathode lighting, and ultraviolet enhanced vision technologies for use in guiding marine vessels and traffic."

**Exemption for Fort Allen in Puerto Rico**

For provisions relating to the exemption for Fort Allen in Puerto Rico, in its use as temporary housing for Haitian refugees, from compliance with provisions of this chapter relating to effluent sources located at Fort Allen, with exceptions, see sections 1–101 and 1–105 of Ex. Ord. No. 12327, Oct. 1, 1981, 46 F.R. 48893, set out as a note under section 2601 of Title 22, Foreign Relations and Intercourse.

**Federal Compliance with Pollution Control Standards**

For provisions relating to the responsibility of the head of each Executive agency for compliance with applicable pollution control standards, see Ex. Ord. No. 12088, Oct. 13, 1978, 43 F.R. 47707, set out as a note under section 4321 of Title 42, The Public Health and Welfare.

## § 1324. Clean lakes

**[FWPCA § 314]**

### (a) Establishment and scope of program

#### (1) State program requirements

Each State on a biennial basis shall prepare and submit to the Administrator for his approval—

(A) an identification and classification according to eutrophic condition of all publicly owned lakes in such State;

(B) a description of procedures, processes, and methods (including land use requirements), to control sources of pollution of such lakes;

(C) a description of methods and procedures, in conjunction with appropriate Federal agencies, to restore the quality of such lakes;

(D) methods and procedures to mitigate the harmful effects of high acidity, including innovative methods of neutralizing and restoring buffering capacity of lakes and methods of removing from lakes toxic metals and other toxic substances mobilized by high acidity;

(E) a list and description of those publicly owned lakes in such State for which uses are known to be impaired, including those lakes which are known not to meet applicable water quality standards or which require implementation of control programs to maintain compliance with applicable standards and those lakes in which water quality has deteriorated as a result of high acidity that may reasonably be due to acid deposition; and

(F) an assessment of the status and trends of water quality in lakes in such State, including but not limited to, the nature and extent of pollution loading from point and nonpoint sources and the extent to which the use of lakes is impaired as a result of such pollution, particularly with respect to toxic pollution.

#### (2) Submission as part of 1315(b)(1) report

The information required under paragraph (1) shall be included in the report required under section 1315(b)(1) of this title, beginning with the report required under such section by April 1, 1988.

#### (3) Report of Administrator

Not later than 180 days after receipt from the States of the biennial information required under paragraph (1), the Administrator shall submit to the Committee on Public Works and Transportation of the House of Representatives and the Committee on Environment and Public Works of the Senate a report on the status of water quality in lakes in the United States, including the effectiveness of the methods and procedures described in paragraph (1)(D).

#### (4) Eligibility requirement

Beginning after April 1, 1988, a State must have submitted the information required under paragraph (1) in order to receive grant assistance under this section.

### (b) Financial assistance to States

The Administrator shall provide financial assistance to States in order to carry out methods and procedures approved by him under subsection (a) of this section. The Administrator shall provide financial assistance to States to prepare the identification and classification surveys required in subsection (a)(1) of this section.

### (c) Maximum amount of grant; authorization of appropriations

(1) The amount granted to any State for any fiscal year under subsection (b) of this section shall not exceed 70 per centum of the funds expended by such State in such year for carrying out approved methods and procedures under subsection (a) of this section.

(2) There is authorized to be appropriated $50,000,000 for each of fiscal years 2001 through 2005 for grants to States under subsection (b) of this section which such sums shall remain available until expended. The Administrator shall provide for an equitable distribution of such sums to the States with approved methods and procedures under subsection (a) of this section.

### (d) Demonstration program

#### (1) General requirements

The Administrator is authorized and directed to establish and conduct at locations throughout the Nation a lake water quality demonstration program. The program shall, at a minimum—

(A) develop cost effective technologies for the control of pollutants to preserve or enhance lake water quality while optimizing multiple lakes uses;

(B) control nonpoint sources of pollution which are contributing to the degradation of water quality in lakes;

(C) evaluate the feasibility of implementing regional consolidated pollution control strategies;

(D) demonstrate environmentally preferred techniques for the removal and disposal of contaminated lake sediments;

(E) develop improved methods for the removal of silt, stumps, aquatic growth, and other obstructions which impair the quality of lakes;

(F) construct and evaluate silt traps and other devices or equipment to prevent or abate the deposit of sediment in lakes; and

(G) demonstrate the costs and benefits of utilizing dredged material from lakes in the reclamation of despoiled land.

(2) **Geographical requirements**

Demonstration projects authorized by this subsection shall be undertaken to reflect a variety of geographical and environmental conditions. As a priority, the Administrator shall undertake demonstration projects at Lake Champlain, New York and Vermont; Lake Houston, Texas; Beaver Lake, Arkansas; Greenwood Lake and Belcher Creek, New Jersey; Deal Lake, New Jersey; Alcyon Lake, New Jersey; Gorton's Pond, Rhode Island; Lake Washington, Rhode Island; Lake Bomoseen, Vermont; Sauk Lake, Minnesota; Otsego Lake, New York; Oneida Lake, New York; Raystown Lake, Pennsylvania; Swan Lake, Itasca County, Minnesota; Walker Lake, Nevada; Lake Tahoe, California and Nevada; Ten Mile Lakes, Oregon; Woahink Lake, Oregon; Highland Lake, Connecticut; Lily Lake, New Jersey; Strawbridge Lake, New Jersey; Baboosic Lake, New Hampshire; French Pond, New Hampshire; Dillon Reservoir, Ohio; Tohopekaliga Lake, Florida; Lake Apopka, Florida; Lake George, New York; Lake Wallenpaupack, Pennsylvania; Lake Allatoona, Georgia; and Lake Worth, Texas.

(3) **Reports**

Notwithstanding section 3003 of the Federal Reports Elimination and Sunset Act of 1995 (31 U .S.C. 1113 note; 109 Stat. 734–736), by January 1, 1997, and January 1 of every odd-numbered year thereafter, the Administrator shall report to the Committee on Transportation and Infrastructure of the House of Representatives and the Committee on Environment and Public Works of the Senate on work undertaken pursuant to this subsection. Upon completion of the program authorized by this subsection, the Administrator shall submit to such committees a final report on the results of such program, along with recommendations for further measures to improve the water quality of the Nation's lakes.

(4) **Authorization of appropriations**

(A) **In general**

There is authorized to be appropriated to carry out this subsection not to exceed $40,000,000 for fiscal years beginning after September 30, 1986, to remain available until expended.

(B) **Special authorizations**

(i) **Amount**

There is authorized to be appropriated to carry out subsection (b) of this section with respect to subsection (a)(1)(D) of this section not to exceed $25,000,000 for fiscal years beginning after September 30, 1986, to remain available until expended.

(ii) **Distribution of funds**

The Administrator shall provide for an equitable distribution of sums appropriated pursuant to this subparagraph among States carrying out approved methods and procedures. Such distribution shall be based on the relative needs of each such State for the mitigation of the harmful effects on lakes and other surface waters of high acidity that may reasonably be due to acid deposition or acid mine drainage.

(iii) **Grants as additional assistance**

The amount of any grant to a State under this subparagraph shall be in addition to, and not in lieu of, any other Federal financial assistance.

(June 30, 1948, c. 758, Title III, § 314, as added Oct. 18, 1972, Pub.L. 92–500, § 2, 86 Stat. 875, and amended Dec. 27, 1977, Pub.L. 95–217, §§ 4(f), 62(a), 91 Stat. 1567, 1598; Oct. 21, 1980, Pub.L. 96–483, § 1(f), 94 Stat. 2360; Feb. 4, 1987, Pub.L. 100–4, Title I, § 101(g), Title III, § 315(a), (b), (d), 101 Stat. 9, 49, 50, 52; Nov. 16, 1990, Pub.L. 101–596, Title III, § 302, 104 Stat. 3006; Dec. 21, 1995, Pub.L. 104–66, Title II, § 2021(c), 109 Stat. 727; Nov. 10, 1998, Pub.L. 105–362, Title V, § 501(b), 112 Stat. 3283; Nov. 7, 2000, Pub.L. 106–457, Title VII, §§ 701, 702, 114 Stat. 1976; Nov. 27, 2002, Pub.L. 107–303, Title III, § 302(b)(1), 116 Stat. 2361.)

### HISTORICAL AND STATUTORY NOTES

**References in Text**

Section 3003 of the Federal Reports Elimination and Sunset Act of 1995, referred to in subsec. (d)(3), is Pub.L. 104–66, Title III, § 3003, Dec. 21, 1995, 109 Stat. 734, which is set out as a note under section 1113 of Title 31.

**Effective and Applicability Provisions**

2002 Acts

Effective November 10, 1998, section 501 of the Federal Reports Elimination Act of 1998 [Pub.L. 105–362, Title V, § 501, Nov. 10, 1998, 112 Stat. 3283] is amended by striking subsections (a), (b), (c), and (d) [amending this section and others, see Tables for complete classification]. The Federal Water Pollution Control Act (33 U.S.C.A. § 1254(n)(3)) shall be applied and administered on and after Nov. 27, 2002 as if the amendments made by subsections (a), (b), (c), and (d) of Pub.L. 105–362, § 501, had not been enacted, see Pub.L. 107–303, § 302(b)(2), set out as a note under 33 U.S.C.A. § 1254.

**Change of Name**

Any reference in any provision of law enacted before Jan. 4, 1995, to the Committee on Public Works and Transportation of the House of Representatives treated as referring to the Committee on Transportation and Infrastructure of the House of Representatives, see section 1(a)(9) of Pub.L. 104–14, set out as a note preceding section 21 of Title 2, The Congress.

## § 1325. National Study Commission

**[FWPCA § 315]**

### (a) Establishment

There is established a National Study Commission, which shall make a full and complete investigation and study of all of the technological aspects of achieving, and all aspects of the total economic, social, and environmental effects of achieving or not achieving, the effluent limitations and goals set forth for 1983 in section 1311(b)(2) of this title.

### (b) Membership; chairman

Such Commission shall be composed of fifteen members, including five members of the Senate, who are members of the Environment and Public Works committee, appointed by the President of the Senate, five members of the House, who are members of the Public Works and Transportation committee, appointed by the Speaker of the House, and five members of the public appointed by the President. The Chairman of such Commission shall be elected from among its members.

### (c) Contract authority

In the conduct of such study, the Commission is authorized to contract with the National Academy of Sciences and the National Academy of Engineering (acting through the National Research Council), the National Institute of Ecology, Brookings Institution, and other nongovernmental entities, for the investigation of matters within their competence.

### (d) Cooperation of departments, agencies, and instrumentalities of executive branch

The heads of the departments, agencies and instrumentalities of the executive branch of the Federal Government shall cooperate with the Commission in carrying out the requirements of this section, and shall furnish to the Commission such information as the Commission deems necessary to carry out this section.

### (e) Report to Congress

A report shall be submitted to the Congress of the results of such investigation and study, together with recommendations, not later than three years after October 18, 1972.

### (f) Compensation and allowances

The members of the Commission who are not officers or employees of the United States, while attending conferences or meetings of the Commission or while otherwise serving at the request of the Chairman shall be entitled to receive compensation at a rate not in excess of the maximum rate of pay for Grade GS–18, as provided in the General Schedule under section 5332 of Title 5, including traveltime and while away from their homes or regular places of business they may be allowed travel expenses, including per diem in lieu of subsistence as authorized by law for persons in the Government service employed intermittently.

### (g) Appointment of personnel

In addition to authority to appoint personnel subject to the provisions of Title 5 governing appointments in the competitive service, and to pay such personnel in accordance with the provisions of chapter 51 and subchapter III of chapter 53 of such title relating to classification and General Schedule pay rates, the Commission shall have authority to enter into contracts with private or public organizations who shall furnish the Commission with such administrative and technical personnel as may be necessary to carry out the purpose of this section. Personnel furnished by such organizations under this subsection are not, and shall not be considered to be, Federal employees for any purposes, but in the performance of their duties shall be guided by the standards which apply to employees of the legislative branches under rules 41 and 43 of the Senate and House of Representatives, respectively.

### (h) Authorization of appropriation

There is authorized to be appropriated, for use in carrying out this section, not to exceed $17,250,000.

(June 30, 1948, c. 758, Title III, § 315, as added Oct. 18, 1972, Pub.L. 92–500, § 2, 86 Stat. 875, and amended Dec. 28, 1973, Pub.L. 93–207, § 1(5), 87 Stat. 906; Jan. 2, 1975, Pub.L. 93–592, § 5, 88 Stat. 1925; Mar. 23, 1976, Pub.L. 94–238, 90 Stat. 250; H.Res. 988, Oct. 8, 1974; S.Res. 4, Feb. 4, 1977.)

### HISTORICAL AND STATUTORY NOTES

**References in Text**

Travel expenses, including per diem in lieu of subsistence as authorized by law, referred to in subsec. (f), probably refers to the allowances authorized by section 5703 of Title 5, Government Organization and Employees.

The General Schedule, referred to in subsec. (g), is set out under section 5332 of Title 5.

The Rules of the House of Representatives for the One Hundred Sixth Congress were adopted and amended generally by House Resolution No. 5, One Hundred Sixth Congress, Jan. 6, 1999. Provisions formerly appearing in rule 43, referred to in subsec. (g), were contained in rule XXIV, which was subsequently renumbered Rule XXIII by House Resolution No. 5, One Hundred Seventh Congress, Jan. 3, 2001.

**Change of Name**

The Committee on Public Works of the Senate was abolished and replaced by the Committee on Environment and Public Works of the Senate, effective Feb. 11, 1977. See Rule XXV of the Standing Rules of the Senate, as amended by Senate Resolution 4 (popularly cited as the "Committee System Reorganization Amendments of 1977"), approved Feb. 4, 1977.

Any reference in any provision of law enacted before Jan. 4, 1995, to the Committee on Public Works and Transportation of the House of Representatives treated as referring to the Committee on Transportation and Infrastructure of the House of Representatives, see section 1(a)(9) of Pub.L. 104–14, set out as a note preceding section 21 of Title 2, The Congress.

The Committee on Public Works of the House of Representatives was changed to the Committee on Public Works and Transportation of the House of Representatives, effective Jan. 3, 1975, by House Resolution 988, 93d Congress.

**References in Other Laws to GS–16, 17, or 18 Pay Rates**

References in laws to the rates of pay for GS–16, 17, or 18, or to maximum rates of pay under the General Schedule, to be considered references to rates payable under specified sections of Title 5, see section 529 [Title I, § 101(c)(1)] of Pub.L. 101–509, set out in a note under 5 U.S.C.A. § 5376.

## § 1326. Thermal discharges

**[FWPCA § 316]**

### (a) Effluent limitations that will assure protection and propagation of balanced, indigenous population of shellfish, fish, and wildlife

With respect to any point source otherwise subject to the provisions of section 1311 of this title or section 1316 of this title, whenever the owner or operator of any such source, after opportunity for public hearing, can demonstrate to the satisfaction of the Administrator (or, if appropriate, the State) that any effluent limitation proposed for the control of the thermal component of any discharge from such source will require effluent limitations more stringent than necessary to assure the projection and propagation of a balanced, indigenous population of shellfish, fish, and wildlife in and on the body of water into which the discharge is to be made, the Administrator (or, if appropriate, the State) may impose an effluent limitation under such sections for such plant, with respect to the thermal component of such discharge (taking into account the interaction of such thermal component with other pollutants), that will assure the protection and propagation of a balanced, indigenous population of shellfish, fish, and wildlife in and on that body of water.

### (b) Cooling water intake structures

Any standard established pursuant to section 1311 of this title or section 1316 of this title and applicable to a point source shall require that the location, design, construction, and capacity of cooling water intake structures reflect the best technology available for minimizing adverse environmental impact.

### (c) Period of protection from more stringent effluent limitations following discharge point source modification commenced after October 18, 1972

Notwithstanding any other provision of this chapter, any point source of a discharge having a thermal component, the modification of which point source is commenced after October 18, 1972, and which, as modified, meets effluent limitations established under section 1311 of this title or, if more stringent, effluent limitations established under section 1313 of this title and which effluent limitations will assure protection and propagation of a balanced, indigenous population of shellfish, fish, and wildlife in or on the water into which the discharge is made, shall not be subject to any more stringent effluent limitation with respect to the thermal component of its discharge during a ten year period beginning on the date of completion of such modification or during the period of depreciation or amortization of such facility for the purpose of section 167 or 169 (or both) of Title 26, whichever period ends first.

(June 30, 1948, c. 758, Title III, § 316, as added Oct. 18, 1972, Pub.L. 92–500, § 2, 86 Stat. 876, and amended Oct. 22, 1986, Pub.L. 99–514, § 2, 100 Stat. 2095.)

## § 1327. Omitted

### HISTORICAL AND STATUTORY NOTES

**Codifications**

Section, Act June 30, 1948, c. 758, Title III, § 317, as added Oct. 18, 1972, Pub.L. 92–500, § 2, 86 Stat. 877, authorized the Administrator to investigate and study the feasibility of alternate methods of financing the cost of preventing, controlling, and abating pollution as directed by the Water Quality Improvement Act of 1970 and to report to Congress, not later than two years after Oct. 18, 1972, the results of his investigation and study accompanied by his recommendations for financing these programs for the fiscal years beginning after 1976.

## § 1328. Aquaculture

[FWPCA § 318]

### (a) Authority to permit discharge of specific pollutants

The Administrator is authorized, after public hearings, to permit the discharge of a specific pollutant or pollutants under controlled conditions associated with an approved aquaculture project under Federal or State supervision pursuant to section 1342 of this title.

### (b) Procedures and guidelines

The Administrator shall by regulation establish any procedures and guidelines which the Administrator deems necessary to carry out this section. Such regulations shall require the application to such discharge of each criterion, factor, procedure, and requirement applicable to a permit issued under section 1342 of this title, as the Administrator determines necessary to carry out the objective of this chapter.

### (c) State administration

Each State desiring to administer its own permit program within its jurisdiction for discharge of a specific pollutant or pollutants under controlled conditions associated with an approved aquaculture project may do so if upon submission of such program the Administrator determines such program is adequate to carry out the objective of this chapter.

(June 30, 1948, c. 758, Title III, § 318, as added Oct. 18, 1972, Pub.L. 92–500, § 2, 86 Stat. 877, and amended Dec. 27, 1977, Pub.L. 95–217, § 63, 91 Stat. 1599.)

## § 1329. Nonpoint source management programs

[FWPCA § 319]

### (a) State assessment reports

#### (1) Contents

The Governor of each State shall, after notice and opportunity for public comment, prepare and submit to the Administrator for approval, a report which—

(A) identifies those navigable waters within the State which, without additional action to control nonpoint sources of pollution, cannot reasonably be expected to attain or maintain applicable water quality standards or the goals and requirements of this chapter;

(B) identifies those categories and subcategories of nonpoint sources or, where appropriate, particular nonpoint sources which add significant pollution to each portion of the navigable waters identified under subparagraph (A) in amounts which contribute to such portion not meeting such water quality standards or such goals and requirements;

(C) describes the process, including intergovernmental coordination and public participation, for identifying best management practices and measures to control each category and subcategory of nonpoint sources and, where appropriate, particular nonpoint sources identified under subparagraph (B) and to reduce, to the maximum extent practicable, the level of pollution resulting from such category, subcategory, or source; and

(D) identifies and describes State and local programs for controlling pollution added from nonpoint sources to, and improving the quality of, each such portion of the navigable waters, including but not limited to those programs which are receiving Federal assistance under subsections (h) and (i) of this section.

#### (2) Information used in preparation

In developing the report required by this section, the State (A) may rely upon information developed pursuant to sections 1288, 1313(e), 1314(f), 1315(b), and 1324 of this title, and other information as appropriate, and (B) may utilize appropriate elements of the waste treatment management plans developed pursuant to sections 1288(b) and 1313 of this title, to the extent such elements are consistent with and fulfill the requirements of this section.

### (b) State management programs

#### (1) In general

The Governor of each State, for that State or in combination with adjacent States, shall, after notice and opportunity for public comment, prepare and submit to the Administrator for approval a management program which such State proposes to implement in the first four fiscal years beginning after the date of submission of such management program for controlling pollution added from nonpoint sources to the navigable waters within the State and improving the quality of such waters.

#### (2) Specific contents

Each management program proposed for implementation under this subsection shall include each of the following:

(A) An identification of the best management practices and measures which will be undertaken to reduce pollutant loadings resulting from each category, subcategory, or particular nonpoint source designated under paragraph (1)(B), taking into account the impact of the practice on ground water quality.

(B) An identification of programs (including, as appropriate, nonregulatory or regulatory programs for enforcement, technical assistance, financial assistance, education, training, technology transfer, and demonstration projects) to achieve implementation of the best management practices by the categories, subcategories, and particular nonpoint sources designated under subparagraph (A).

**(C)** A schedule containing annual milestones for (i) utilization of the program implementation methods identified in subparagraph (B), and (ii) implementation of the best management practices identified in subparagraph (A) by the categories, subcategories, or particular nonpoint sources designated under paragraph (1)(B). Such schedule shall provide for utilization of the best management practices at the earliest practicable date.

**(D)** A certification of the attorney general of the State or States (or the chief attorney of any State water pollution control agency which has independent legal counsel) that the laws of the State or States, as the case may be, provide adequate authority to implement such management program or, if there is not such adequate authority, a list of such additional authorities as will be necessary to implement such management program. A schedule and commitment by the State or States to seek such additional authorities as expeditiously as practicable.

**(E)** Sources of Federal and other assistance and funding (other than assistance provided under subsections (h) and (i) of this section) which will be available in each of such fiscal years for supporting implementation of such practices and measures and the purposes for which such assistance will be used in each of such fiscal years.

**(F)** An identification of Federal financial assistance programs and Federal development projects for which the State will review individual assistance applications or development projects for their effect on water quality pursuant to the procedures set forth in Executive Order 12372 as in effect on September 17, 1983, to determine whether such assistance applications or development projects would be consistent with the program prepared under this subsection; for the purposes of this subparagraph, identification shall not be limited to the assistance programs or development projects subject to Executive Order 12372 but may include any programs listed in the most recent Catalog of Federal Domestic Assistance which may have an effect on the purposes and objectives of the State's nonpoint source pollution management program.

**(3) Utilization of local and private experts**

In developing and implementing a management program under this subsection, a State shall, to the maximum extent practicable, involve local public and private agencies and organizations which have expertise in control of nonpoint sources of pollution.

**(4) Development on watershed basis**

A State shall, to the maximum extent practicable, develop and implement a management program under this subsection on a watershed-by-watershed basis within such State.

**(c) Administrative provisions**

**(1) Cooperation requirement**

Any report required by subsection (a) of this section and any management program and report required by subsection (b) of this section shall be developed in cooperation with local, substate regional, and interstate entities which are actively planning for the implementation of nonpoint source pollution controls and have either been certified by the Administrator in accordance with section 1288 of this title, have worked jointly with the State on water quality management planning under section 1285(j) of this title, or have been designated by the State legislative body or Governor as water quality management planning agencies for their geographic areas.

**(2) Time period for submission of reports and management programs**

Each report and management program shall be submitted to the Administrator during the 18-month period beginning on February 4, 1987.

**(d) Approval or disapproval of reports and management programs**

**(1) Deadline**

Subject to paragraph (2), not later than 180 days after the date of submission to the Administrator of any report or management program under this section (other than subsections (h), (i), and (k) of this section), the Administrator shall either approve or disapprove such report or management program, as the case may be. The Administrator may approve a portion of a management program under this subsection. If the Administrator does not disapprove a report, management program, or portion of a management program in such 180-day period, such report, management program, or portion shall be deemed approved for purposes of this section.

**(2) Procedure for disapproval**

If, after notice and opportunity for public comment and consultation with appropriate Federal and State agencies and other interested persons, the Administrator determines that—

**(A)** the proposed management program or any portion thereof does not meet the requirements of subsection (b)(2) of this section or is not likely to satisfy, in whole or in part, the goals and requirements of this chapter;

(B) adequate authority does not exist, or adequate resources are not available, to implement such program or portion;

(C) the schedule for implementing such program or portion is not sufficiently expeditious; or

(D) the practices and measures proposed in such program or portion are not adequate to reduce the level of pollution in navigable waters in the State resulting from nonpoint sources and to improve the quality of navigable waters in the State;

the Administrator shall within 6 months of the receipt of the proposed program notify the State of any revisions or modifications necessary to obtain approval. The State shall thereupon have an additional 3 months to submit its revised management program and the Administrator shall approve or disapprove such revised program within three months of receipt.

**(3) Failure of State to submit report**

If a Governor of a State does not submit the report required by subsection (a) of this section within the period specified by subsection (c)(2) of this section, the Administrator shall, within 30 months after February 4, 1987, prepare a report for such State which makes the identifications required by paragraphs (1)(A) and (1)(B) of subsection (a) of this section. Upon completion of the requirement of the preceding sentence and after notice and opportunity for comment, the Administrator shall report to Congress on his actions pursuant to this section.

**(e) Local management programs; technical assistance**

If a State fails to submit a management program under subsection (b) of this section or the Administrator does not approve such a management program, a local public agency or organization which has expertise in, and authority to, control water pollution resulting from nonpoint sources in any area of such State which the Administrator determines is of sufficient geographic size may, with approval of such State, request the Administrator to provide, and the Administrator shall provide, technical assistance to such agency or organization in developing for such area a management program which is described in subsection (b) of this section and can be approved pursuant to subsection (d) of this section. After development of such management program, such agency or organization shall submit such management program to the Administrator for approval. If the Administrator approves such management program, such agency or organization shall be eligible to receive financial assistance under subsection (h) of this section for implementation of such management program as if such agency or organization were a State for which a report submitted under subsection (a) of this section and a management program submitted under subsection (b) of this section were approved under this section. Such financial assistance shall be subject to the same terms and conditions as assistance provided to a State under subsection (h) of this section.

**(f) Technical assistance for States**

Upon request of a State, the Administrator may provide technical assistance to such State in developing a management program approved under subsection (b) of this section for those portions of the navigable waters requested by such State.

**(g) Interstate management conference**

**(1) Convening of conference; notification; purpose**

If any portion of the navigable waters in any State which is implementing a management program approved under this section is not meeting applicable water quality standards or the goals and requirements of this chapter as a result, in whole or in part, of pollution from nonpoint sources in another State, such State may petition the Administrator to convene, and the Administrator shall convene, a management conference of all States which contribute significant pollution resulting from nonpoint sources to such portion. If, on the basis of information available, the Administrator determines that a State is not meeting applicable water quality standards or the goals and requirements of this chapter as a result, in whole or in part, of significant pollution from nonpoint sources in another State, the Administrator shall notify such States. The Administrator may convene a management conference under this paragraph not later than 180 days after giving such notification, whether or not the State which is not meeting such standards requests such conference. The purpose of such conference shall be to develop an agreement among such States to reduce the level of pollution in such portion resulting from nonpoint sources and to improve the water quality of such portion. Nothing in such agreement shall supersede or abrogate rights to quantities of water which have been established by interstate water compacts, Supreme Court decrees, or State water laws. This subsection shall not apply to any pollution which is subject to the Colorado River Basin Salinity Control Act [43 U.S.C.A. § 1571 et seq.]. The requirement that the Administrator convene a management conference shall not be subject to the provisions of section 1365 of this title.

**(2) State management program requirement**

To the extent that the States reach agreement through such conference, the management programs of the States which are parties to such agreements and which contribute significant pollution to the navigable waters or portions thereof not meeting applicable water quality standards or goals and requirements of this chapter will be revised to reflect such agreement. Such management programs shall be consistent with Federal and State law.

### (h) Grant program

#### (1) Grants for implementation of management programs

Upon application of a State for which a report submitted under subsection (a) of this section and a management program submitted under subsection (b) of this section is approved under this section, the Administrator shall make grants, subject to such terms and conditions as the Administrator considers appropriate, under this subsection to such State for the purpose of assisting the State in implementing such management program. Funds reserved pursuant to section 1285(j)(5) of this title may be used to develop and implement such management program.

#### (2) Applications

An application for a grant under this subsection in any fiscal year shall be in such form and shall contain such other information as the Administrator may require, including an identification and description of the best management practices and measures which the State proposes to assist, encourage, or require in such year with the Federal assistance to be provided under the grant.

#### (3) Federal share

The Federal share of the cost of each management program implemented with Federal assistance under this subsection in any fiscal year shall not exceed 60 percent of the cost incurred by the State in implementing such management program and shall be made on condition that the non-Federal share is provided from non-Federal sources.

#### (4) Limitation on grant amounts

Notwithstanding any other provision of this subsection, not more than 15 percent of the amount appropriated to carry out this subsection may be used to make grants to any one State, including any grants to any local public agency or organization with authority to control pollution from nonpoint sources in any area of such State.

#### (5) Priority for effective mechanisms

For each fiscal year beginning after September 30, 1987, the Administrator may give priority in making grants under this subsection, and shall give consideration in determining the Federal share of any such grant, to States which have implemented or are proposing to implement management programs which will—

(A) control particularly difficult or serious nonpoint source pollution problems, including, but not limited to, problems resulting from mining activities;

(B) implement innovative methods or practices for controlling nonpoint sources of pollution, including regulatory programs where the Administrator deems appropriate;

(C) control interstate nonpoint source pollution problems; or

(D) carry out ground water quality protection activities which the Administrator determines are part of a comprehensive nonpoint source pollution control program, including research, planning, ground water assessments, demonstration programs, enforcement, technical assistance, education, and training to protect ground water quality from nonpoint sources of pollution.

#### (6) Availability for obligation

The funds granted to each State pursuant to this subsection in a fiscal year shall remain available for obligation by such State for the fiscal year for which appropriated. The amount of any such funds not obligated by the end of such fiscal year shall be available to the Administrator for granting to other States under this subsection in the next fiscal year.

#### (7) Limitation on use of funds

States may use funds from grants made pursuant to this section for financial assistance to persons only to the extent that such assistance is related to the costs of demonstration projects.

#### (8) Satisfactory progress

No grant may be made under this subsection in any fiscal year to a State which in the preceding fiscal year received a grant under this subsection unless the Administrator determines that such State made satisfactory progress in such preceding fiscal year in meeting the schedule specified by such State under subsection (b)(2) of this section.

#### (9) Maintenance of effort

No grant may be made to a State under this subsection in any fiscal year unless such State enters into such agreements with the Administrator as the Administrator may require to ensure that such State will maintain its aggregate expenditures from all other sources for programs for controlling pollution added to the navigable waters in such State from nonpoint sources and improving the quality of such waters at or above the average level of such expenditures in its two fiscal years preceding February 4, 1987.

**(10) Request for information**

The Administrator may request such information, data, and reports as he considers necessary to make the determination of continuing eligibility for grants under this section.

**(11) Reporting and other requirements**

Each State shall report to the Administrator on an annual basis concerning (A) its progress in meeting the schedule of milestones submitted pursuant to subsection (b)(2)(C) of this section, and (B) to the extent that appropriate information is available, reductions in nonpoint source pollutant loading and improvements in water quality for those navigable waters or watersheds within the State which were identified pursuant to subsection (a)(1)(A) of this section resulting from implementation of the management program.

**(12) Limitation on administrative costs**

For purposes of this subsection, administrative costs in the form of salaries, overhead, or indirect costs for services provided and charged against activities and programs carried out with a grant under this subsection shall not exceed in any fiscal year 10 percent of the amount of the grant in such year, except that costs of implementing enforcement and regulatory activities, education, training, technical assistance, demonstration projects, and technology transfer programs shall not be subject to this limitation.

**(i) Grants for protecting groundwater quality**

**(1) Eligible applicants and activities**

Upon application of a State for which a report submitted under subsection (a) of this section and a plan submitted under subsection (b) of this section is approved under this section, the Administrator shall make grants under this subsection to such State for the purpose of assisting such State in carrying out groundwater quality protection activities which the Administrator determines will advance the State toward implementation of a comprehensive nonpoint source pollution control program. Such activities shall include, but not be limited to, research, planning, groundwater assessments, demonstration programs, enforcement, technical assistance, education and training to protect the quality of groundwater and to prevent contamination of groundwater from nonpoint sources of pollution.

**(2) Applications**

An application for a grant under this subsection shall be in such form and shall contain such information as the Administrator may require.

**(3) Federal share; maximum amount**

The Federal share of the cost of assisting a State in carrying out groundwater protection activities in any fiscal year under this subsection shall be 50 percent of the costs incurred by the State in carrying out such activities, except that the maximum amount of Federal assistance which any State may receive under this subsection in any fiscal year shall not exceed $150,000.

**(4) Report**

The Administrator shall include in each report transmitted under subsection (m) of this section a report on the activities and programs implemented under this subsection during the preceding fiscal year.

**(j) Authorization of appropriations**

There is authorized to be appropriated to carry out subsections (h) and (i) of this section not to exceed $70,000,000 for fiscal year 1988, $100,000,000 per fiscal year for each of fiscal years 1989 and 1990, and $130,000,000 for fiscal year 1991; except that for each of such fiscal years not to exceed $7,500,000 may be made available to carry out subsection (i) of this section. Sums appropriated pursuant to this subsection shall remain available until expended.

**(k) Consistency of other programs and projects with management programs**

The Administrator shall transmit to the Office of Management and Budget and the appropriate Federal departments and agencies a list of those assistance programs and development projects identified by each State under subsection (b)(2)(F) of this section for which individual assistance applications and projects will be reviewed pursuant to the procedures set forth in Executive Order 12372 as in effect on September 17, 1983. Beginning not later than sixty days after receiving notification by the Administrator, each Federal department and agency shall modify existing regulations to allow States to review individual development projects and assistance applications under the identified Federal assistance programs and shall accommodate, according to the requirements and definitions of Executive Order 12372, as in effect on September 17, 1983, the concerns of the State regarding the consistency of such applications or projects with the State nonpoint source pollution management program.

**(*l*) Collection of information**

The Administrator shall collect and make available, through publications and other appropriate means, information pertaining to management practices and implementation methods, including, but not limited to, (1) information concerning the costs and relative efficiencies of best management practices for reducing nonpoint source pollution; and (2) available data concerning the relationship between water quality and implementation of various management practices to control nonpoint sources of pollution.

**(m) Reports of Administrator**

**(1) Annual reports**

Not later than January 1, 1988, and each January 1 thereafter, the Administrator shall transmit to the Committee on Public Works and Transportation of the House of Representatives and the Committee on Environment and Public Works of the Senate, a report for the preceding fiscal year on the activities and programs implemented under this section and the progress made in reducing pollution in the navigable waters resulting from nonpoint sources and improving the quality of such waters.

**(2) Final report**

Not later than January 1, 1990, the Administrator shall transmit to Congress a final report on the activities carried out under this section. Such report, at a minimum, shall—

(A) describe the management programs being implemented by the States by types and amount of affected navigable waters, categories and subcategories of nonpoint sources, and types of best management practices being implemented;

(B) describe the experiences of the States in adhering to schedules and implementing best management practices;

(C) describe the amount and purpose of grants awarded pursuant to subsections (h) and (i) of this section;

(D) identify, to the extent that information is available, the progress made in reducing pollutant loads and improving water quality in the navigable waters;

(E) indicate what further actions need to be taken to attain and maintain in those navigable waters (i) applicable water quality standards, and (ii) the goals and requirements of this chapter;

(F) include recommendations of the Administrator concerning future programs (including enforcement programs) for controlling pollution from nonpoint sources; and

(G) identify the activities and programs of departments, agencies, and instrumentalities of the United States which are inconsistent with the management programs submitted by the States and recommend modifications so that such activities and programs are consistent with and assist the States in implementation of such management programs.

**(n) Set aside for administrative personnel**

Not less than 5 percent of the funds appropriated pursuant to subsection (j) of this section for any fiscal year shall be available to the Administrator to maintain personnel levels at the Environmental Protection Agency at levels which are adequate to carry out this section in such year.

(June 30, 1948, c. 758, Title III, § 319, as added Feb. 4, 1987, Pub.L. 100–4, Title III, § 316(a), 101 Stat. 52; Nov. 10, 1998, Pub.L. 105–362, Title V, § 501(c), 112 Stat. 3283, and amended Nov. 27, 2002, Pub.L. 107–303, Title III, § 302(b)(1), 116 Stat. 2361.)

### HISTORICAL AND STATUTORY NOTES

**References in Text**

Executive Order 12372, referred to in subsecs. (b)(2)(F) and (k), is Ex. Ord. No. 12372, July 14, 1982, 47 F.R. 30959, as amended, which is set out as a note under section 6506 of Title 31, Money and Finance.

The Colorado River Basin Salinity Control Act, referred to in subsec. (g)(1), is Pub.L. 93–320, June 24, 1974, 88 Stat. 266, as amended, which is classified principally to chapter 32A (section 1571 et seq.) of Title 43, Public Lands. For complete classification of this Act to the Code, see Short Title note set out under section 1571 of Title 43 and Tables.

**Effective and Applicability Provisions**

2002 Acts

Effective November 10, 1998, section 501 of the Federal Reports Elimination Act of 1998 [Pub.L. 105–362, Title V, § 501, Nov. 10, 1998, 112 Stat. 3283] is amended by striking subsections (a), (b), (c), and (d) [amending this section and others, see Tables for complete classification]. The Federal Water Pollution Control Act (33 U.S.C.A. § 1254(n)(3)) shall be applied and administered on and after Nov. 27, 2002 as if the amendments made by subsections (a), (b), (c), and (d) of Pub.L. 105–362, § 501, had not been enacted, see Pub.L. 107–303, § 302(b)(2), set out as a note under 33 U.S.C.A. § 1254.

**Change of Name**

Any reference in any provision of law enacted before Jan. 4, 1995, to the Committee on Public Works and Transportation of the House of Representatives treated as referring to the Committee on Transportation and Infrastructure of the House of Representatives, see section 1(a)(9) of Pub.L. 104–14, set out as a note preceding section 21 of Title 2, The Congress.

## § 1330. National estuary program

**[FWPCA § 320]**

**(a) Management conference**

**(1) Nomination of estuaries**

The Governor of any State may nominate to the Administrator an estuary lying in whole or in part within the State as an estuary of national significance and request a management conference to develop a comprehensive management plan for the estuary. The nomination shall document the need for the conference, the likelihood of success, and information relating to the factors in paragraph (2).

(2) **Convening of conference**

(A) **In general**

In any case where the Administrator determines, on his own initiative or upon nomination of a State under paragraph (1), that the attainment or maintenance of that water quality in an estuary which assures protection of public water supplies and the protection and propagation of a balanced, indigenous population of shellfish, fish, and wildlife, and allows recreational activities, in and on the water, requires the control of point and nonpoint sources of pollution to supplement existing controls of pollution in more than one State, the Administrator shall select such estuary and convene a management conference.

(B) **Priority consideration**

The Administrator shall give priority consideration under this section to Long Island Sound, New York and Connecticut; Narragansett Bay, Rhode Island; Buzzards Bay, Massachusetts; Massachusetts Bay, Massachusetts (including Cape Cod Bay and Boston Harbor); Puget Sound, Washington; New York-New Jersey Harbor, New York and New Jersey; Delaware Bay, Delaware and New Jersey; Delaware Inland Bays, Delaware; Albemarle Sound, North Carolina; Sarasota Bay, Florida; San Francisco Bay, California; Santa Monica Bay, California; Galveston Bay, Texas; Barataria-Terrebonne Bay estuary complex, Louisiana; Indian River Lagoon, Florida; Lake Pontchartrain Basin, Louisiana and Mississippi; and Peconic Bay, New York.

(3) **Boundary dispute exception**

In any case in which a boundary between two States passes through an estuary and such boundary is disputed and is the subject of an action in any court, the Administrator shall not convene a management conference with respect to such estuary before a final adjudication has been made of such dispute.

(b) **Purposes of conference**

The purposes of any management conference convened with respect to an estuary under this subsection shall be to—

(1) assess trends in water quality, natural resources, and uses of the estuary;

(2) collect, characterize, and assess data on toxics, nutrients, and natural resources within the estuarine zone to identify the causes of environmental problems;

(3) develop the relationship between the inplace loads and point and nonpoint loadings of pollutants to the estuarine zone and the potential uses of the zone, water quality, and natural resources;

(4) develop a comprehensive conservation and management plan that recommends priority corrective actions and compliance schedules addressing point and nonpoint sources of pollution to restore and maintain the chemical, physical, and biological integrity of the estuary, including restoration and maintenance of water quality, a balanced indigenous population of shellfish, fish and wildlife, and recreational activities in the estuary, and assure that the designated uses of the estuary are protected;

(5) develop plans for the coordinated implementation of the plan by the States as well as Federal and local agencies participating in the conference;

(6) monitor the effectiveness of actions taken pursuant to the plan; and

(7) review all Federal financial assistance programs and Federal development projects in accordance with the requirements of Executive Order 12372, as in effect on September 17, 1983, to determine whether such assistance program or project would be consistent with and further the purposes and objectives of the plan prepared under this section.

For purposes of paragraph (7), such programs and projects shall not be limited to the assistance programs and development projects subject to Executive Order 12372, but may include any programs listed in the most recent Catalog of Federal Domestic Assistance which may have an effect on the purposes and objectives of the plan developed under this section.

(c) **Members of conference**

The members of a management conference convened under this section shall include, at a minimum, the Administrator and representatives of—

(1) each State and foreign nation located in whole or in part in the estuarine zone of the estuary for which the conference is convened;

(2) international, interstate, or regional agencies or entities having jurisdiction over all or a significant part of the estuary;

(3) each interested Federal agency, as determined appropriate by the Administrator;

(4) local governments having jurisdiction over any land or water within the estuarine zone, as determined appropriate by the Administrator; and

(5) affected industries, public and private educational institutions, and the general public, as determined appropriate by the Administrator.

(d) **Utilization of existing data**

In developing a conservation and management plan under this section, the management conference shall survey and utilize existing reports, data, and studies relating to the estuary that have been developed by or made available to Federal, interstate, State, and local agencies.

**(e) Period of conference**

A management conference convened under this section shall be convened for a period not to exceed 5 years. Such conference may be extended by the Administrator, and if terminated after the initial period, may be reconvened by the Administrator at any time thereafter, as may be necessary to meet the requirements of this section.

**(f) Approval and implementation of plans**

**(1) Approval**

Not later than 120 days after the completion of a conservation and management plan and after providing for public review and comment, the Administrator shall approve such plan if the plan meets the requirements of this section and the affected Governor or Governors concur.

**(2) Implementation**

Upon approval of a conservation and management plan under this section, such plan shall be implemented. Funds authorized to be appropriated under subchapters II and VI of this chapter and section 1329 of this title may be used in accordance with the applicable requirements of this chapter to assist States with the implementation of such plan.

**(g) Grants**

**(1) Recipients**

The Administrator is authorized to make grants to State, interstate, and regional water pollution control agencies and entities, State coastal zone management agencies, interstate agencies, other public or nonprofit private agencies, institutions, organizations, and individuals.

**(2) Purposes**

Grants under this subsection shall be made to pay for activities necessary for the development and implementation of a comprehensive conservation and management plan under this section.

**(3) Federal share**

The Federal share of a grant to any person (including a State, interstate, or regional agency or entity) under this subsection for a fiscal year—

(A) shall not exceed—

(i) 75 percent of the annual aggregate costs of the development of a comprehensive conservation and management plan; and

(ii) 50 percent of the annual aggregate costs of the implementation of the plan; and

(B) shall be made on condition that the non-Federal share of the costs are provided from non-Federal sources.

**(h) Grant reporting**

Any person (including a State, interstate, or regional agency or entity) that receives a grant under subsection (g) of this section shall report to the Administrator not later than 18 months after receipt of such grant and biennially thereafter on the progress being made under this section.

**(i) Authorization of appropriations**

There are authorized to be appropriated to the Administrator not to exceed $35,000,000 for each of fiscal years 2001 through 2005 for—

(1) expenses related to the administration of management conferences under this section, not to exceed 10 percent of the amount appropriated under this subsection;

(2) making grants under subsection (g) of this section; and

(3) monitoring the implementation of a conservation and management plan by the management conference or by the Administrator, in any case in which the conference has been terminated.

The Administrator shall provide up to $5,000,000 per fiscal year of the sums authorized to be appropriated under this subsection to the Administrator of the National Oceanic and Atmospheric Administration to carry out subsection (j) of this section.

**(j) Research**

**(1) Programs**

In order to determine the need to convene a management conference under this section or at the request of such a management conference, the Administrator shall coordinate and implement, through the National Marine Pollution Program Office and the National Marine Fisheries Service of the National Oceanic and Atmospheric Administration, as appropriate, for one or more estuarine zones—

(A) a long-term program of trend assessment monitoring measuring variations in pollutant concentrations, marine ecology, and other physical or biological environmental parameters which may affect estuarine zones, to provide the Administrator the capacity to determine the potential and actual effects of alternative management strategies and measures;

(B) a program of ecosystem assessment assisting in the development of (i) baseline studies which determine the state of estuarine zones and the effects of natural and anthropogenic changes, and (ii) predictive models capable of translating information on specific discharges or general pollutant loadings within estuarine zones into a set of probable effects on such zones;

(C) a comprehensive water quality sampling program for the continuous monitoring of nutrients, chlorine, acid precipitation dissolved oxygen, and potentially toxic pollutants (including organic chemicals and metals) in estuarine zones, after consultation with interested State, local, interstate, or international agencies and review and analysis of all environmental sampling data presently collected from estuarine zones; and

(D) a program of research to identify the movements of nutrients, sediments and pollutants through estuarine zones and the impact of nutrients, sediments, and pollutants on water quality, the ecosystem, and designated or potential uses of the estuarine zones.

**(2) Omitted**

**(k) Definitions**

For purposes of this section, the terms "estuary" and "estuarine zone" have the meanings such terms have in section 1254(n)(4) of this title, except that the term "estuarine zone" shall also include associated aquatic ecosystems and those portions of tributaries draining into the estuary up to the historic height of migration of anadromous fish or the historic head of tidal influence, whichever is higher.

(June 30, 1948, c. 758, Title III, § 320, as added Feb. 4, 1987, Pub.L. 100–4, Title III, § 317(b), 101 Stat. 61, and amended Dec. 22, 1987, Pub.L. 100–202, Title II, § 101(f), 101 Stat. 1329–197; Nov. 14, 1988, Pub.L. 100–653, Title X, § 1004, 102 Stat. 3836; Nov. 18, 1988, Pub.L. 100–688, Title II, § 2001, 102 Stat. 4152; Nov. 10, 1998, Pub.L. 105–362, Title V, § 501(a)(2), 112 Stat. 3283; Nov. 7, 2000, Pub.L. 106–457, Title III, §§ 301 to 303, 114 Stat. 1972; Nov. 27, 2002, Pub.L. 107–303, Title III, § 302(b)(1), 116 Stat. 2361.)

## HISTORICAL AND STATUTORY NOTES

**References in Text**

Executive Order 12372, referred to in subsec. (b). is Ex. Ord. No. 12372, July 14, 1982, 47 F.R. 30959, as amended, which is set out as a note under section 6506 of Title 31, Money and Finance.

**Codifications**

Pub.L. 100–653 and section 2001(1) of Pub.L. 100–688 made an identical amendment to subsection (a)(2)(B).

Subsec. (j)(2) of this section, which required the Administrator, in cooperation with the Administrator of the National Oceanic and Atmospheric Administration, to submit to Congress no less often than biennially a comprehensive report on activities authorized under subsec. (j) of this section, terminated, effective May 15, 2000, pursuant to section 3003 of Pub.L. 104–66, as amended, set out as a note under 31 U.S.C.A. § 1113. See, also, page 162 of House Document No. 103–7.

**Effective and Applicability Provisions**

2002 Acts

Effective November 10, 1998, section 501 of the Federal Reports Elimination Act of 1998 [Pub.L. 105–362, Title V, § 501, Nov. 10, 1998, 112 Stat. 3283] is amended by striking subsections (a), (b), (c), and (d) [amending this section and others, see Tables for complete classification]. The Federal Water Pollution Control Act (33 U.S.C.A. § 1254(n)(3)) shall be applied and administered on and after Nov. 27, 2002 as if the amendments made by subsections (a), (b), (c), and (d) of Pub.L. 105–362, § 501, had not been enacted, see Pub.L. 107–303, § 302(b)(2), set out as a note under 33 U.S.C.A. § 1254.

**Massachusetts Bay Protection; Massachusetts Bay Defined**

Section 1002 of Pub.L. 100–653 provided that: "For purposes of this title [amending subsec. (a)(2)(B) of this section and enacting note provisions under sections 1251 and 1330 of this title], the term 'Massachusetts Bay' includes Massachusetts Bay, Cape Cod Bay, and Boston Harbor, consisting of an area extending from Cape Ann, Massachusetts south to the northern reach of Cape Cod, Massachusetts."

**Massachusetts Bay Protection; Congressional Findings and Purpose**

Section 1003 of Pub.L. 100–653 provided that:

"(a) **Findings.**—The Congress finds and declares that—

"(1) Massachusetts Bay comprises a single major estuarine and oceanographic system extending from Cape Ann, Massachusetts south to the northern reaches of Cape Cod, encompassing Boston Harbor, Massachusetts Bay, and Cape Cod Bay;

"(2) several major riverine systems, including the Charles, Neoponset, and Mystic Rivers, drain the watersheds of eastern Massachusetts into the Bay;

"(3) the shorelines of Massachusetts Bay, first occupied in the middle 1600's, are home to over 4 million people and support a thriving industrial and recreational economy;

"(4) Massachusetts Bay supports important commercial fisheries, including lobsters, finfish, and shellfisheries, and is home to or frequented by several endangered species and marine mammals;

"(5) Massachusetts Bay also constitutes an important recreational resource, providing fishing, swimming, and boating opportunities to the region;

"(6) rapidly expanding coastal populations and pollution pose increasing threats to the long-term health and integrity of Massachusetts Bay;

"(7) while the cleanup of Boston Harbor will contribute significantly to improving the overall environmental quality of Massachusetts Bay, expanded efforts encompassing the entire ecosystem will be necessary to ensure its long-term health;

"(8) the concerted efforts of all levels of Government, the private sector, and the public at large will be necessary to protect and enhance the environmental integrity of Massachusetts Bay; and

"(9) the designation of Massachusetts Bay as an Estuary of National Significance and the development of a comprehensive plan for protecting and restoring the Bay may contribute significantly to its long-term health and environmental integrity.

"(b) **Purpose.**—The purpose of this title [amending subsec. (a)(2)(B) of this section and enacting note provisions under sections 1251 and 1330 of this title] is to protect and enhance the environmental quality of Massachusetts Bay by providing for its designation as an Estuary of National Significance and by providing for the preparation of a comprehensive restoration plan for the Bay."

**Massachusetts Bay Protection; Funding Sources**

Section 1005 of Pub.L. 100–653 provided that: "Within one year of enactment [Nov. 14, 1988], the Administrator of the United States Environmental Protection Agency, and the Governor of Massachusetts shall undertake to identify and make available sources of funding to support activities pertaining to Massachusetts Bay undertaken pursuant to or authorized by section 320 of the Clean Water Act [this section], and shall make every effort to coordinate existing research, monitoring or control efforts with such activities."

**Purposes and Policies of National Estuary Program**

Section 317(a) of Pub.L. 100–4 provided that:

"(1) **Findings.**—Congress finds and declares that—

"(A) the Nation's estuaries are of great importance for fish and wildlife resources and recreation and economic opportunity;

"(B) maintaining the health and ecological integrity of these estuaries is in the national interest;

"(C) increasing coastal population, development, and other direct and indirect uses of these estuaries threaten their health and ecological integrity;

"(D) long-term planning and management will contribute to the continued productivity of these areas, and will maximize their utility to the Nation; and

"(E) better coordination among Federal and State programs affecting estuaries will increase the effectiveness and efficiency of the national effort to protect, preserve, and restore these areas.

"(2) **Purposes.**—The purposes of this section [enacting this section and enacting this provision] are to—

"(A) identify nationally significant estuaries that are threatened by pollution, development, or overuse;

"(B) promote comprehensive planning for, and conservation and management of, nationally significant estuaries;

"(C) encourage the preparation of management plans for estuaries of national significance; and

"(D) enhance the coordination of estuarine research."

## SUBCHAPTER IV—PERMITS AND LICENSES

## § 1341. Certification

### [FWPCA § 401]

### (a) Compliance with applicable requirements; application; procedures; license suspension

(1) Any applicant for a Federal license or permit to conduct any activity including, but not limited to, the construction or operation of facilities, which may result in any discharge into the navigable waters, shall provide the licensing or permitting agency a certification from the State in which the discharge originates or will originate, or, if appropriate, from the interstate water pollution control agency having jurisdiction over the navigable waters at the point where the discharge originates or will originate, that any such discharge will comply with the applicable provisions of sections 1311, 1312, 1313, 1316, and 1317 of this title. In the case of any such activity for which there is not an applicable effluent limitation or other limitation under sections 1311(b) and 1312 of this title, and there is not an applicable standard under sections 1316 and 1317 of this title, the State shall so certify, except that any such certification shall not be deemed to satisfy section 1371(c) of this title. Such State or interstate agency shall establish procedures for public notice in the case of all applications for certification by it and, to the extent it deems appropriate, procedures for public hearings in connection with specific applications. In any case where a State or interstate agency has no authority to give such a certification, such certification shall be from the Administrator. If the State, interstate agency, or Administrator, as the case may be, fails or refuses to act on a request for certification, within a reasonable period of time (which shall not exceed one year) after receipt of such request, the certification requirements of this subsection shall be waived with respect to such Federal application. No license or permit shall be granted until the certification required by this section has been obtained or has been waived as provided in the preceding sentence. No license or permit shall be granted if certification has been denied by the State, interstate agency, or the Administrator, as the case may be.

(2) Upon receipt of such application and certification the licensing or permitting agency shall immediately notify the Administrator of such application and certification. Whenever such a discharge may affect, as determined by the Administrator, the quality of the waters of any other State, the Administrator within thirty days of the date of notice of application for such Federal license or permit shall so notify such other State, the licensing or permitting agency, and the applicant. If, within sixty days after receipt of such notification, such other State determines that such discharge will affect the quality of its waters so as to violate any water quality requirements in such State, and within such sixty-day period notifies the Administrator and the licensing or permitting agency in writing of its objection to the issuance of such license or permit and requests a public hearing on such objection, the licensing or permitting agency shall hold such a hearing. The Administrator shall at such hearing submit his evaluation and recommendations with respect to any such objection to the licensing or permitting agency. Such agency, based upon the recommendations of such State, the Administrator, and upon any additional evidence, if any, presented to the agency at the hearing, shall condition such license or permit in such manner as may be necessary to insure compliance with applicable water quality requirements. If the imposition of conditions cannot insure such compli-

ance such agency shall not issue such license or permit.

(3) The certification obtained pursuant to paragraph (1) of this subsection with respect to the construction of any facility shall fulfill the requirements of this subsection with respect to certification in connection with any other Federal license or permit required for the operation of such facility unless, after notice to the certifying State, agency, or Administrator, as the case may be, which shall be given by the Federal agency to whom application is made for such operating license or permit, the State, or if appropriate, the interstate agency or the Administrator, notifies such agency within sixty days after receipt of such notice that there is no longer reasonable assurance that there will be compliance with the applicable provisions of sections 1311, 1312, 1313, 1316, and 1317 of this title because of changes since the construction license or permit certification was issued in (A) the construction or operation of the facility, (B) the characteristics of the waters into which such discharge is made, (C) the water quality criteria applicable to such waters or (D) applicable effluent limitations or other requirements. This paragraph shall be inapplicable in any case where the applicant for such operating license or permit has failed to provide the certifying State, or, if appropriate, the interstate agency or the Administrator, with notice of any proposed changes in the construction or operation of the facility with respect to which a construction license or permit has been granted, which changes may result in violation of section 1311, 1312, 1313, 1316, or 1317 of this title.

(4) Prior to the initial operation of any federally licensed or permitted facility or activity which may result in any discharge into the navigable waters and with respect to which a certification has been obtained pursuant to paragraph (1) of this subsection, which facility or activity is not subject to a Federal operating license or permit, the licensee or permittee shall provide an opportunity for such certifying State, or, if appropriate, the interstate agency or the Administrator to review the manner in which the facility or activity shall be operated or conducted for the purposes of assuring that applicable effluent limitations or other limitations or other applicable water quality requirements will not be violated. Upon notification by the certifying State, or if appropriate, the interstate agency or the Administrator that the operation of any such federally licensed or permitted facility or activity will violate applicable effluent limitations or other limitations or other water quality requirements such Federal agency may, after public hearing, suspend such license or permit. If such license or permit is suspended, it shall remain suspended until notification is received from the certifying State, agency, or Administrator, as the case may be, that there is reasonable assurance that such facility or activity will not violate the applicable provisions of section 1311, 1312, 1313, 1316, or 1317 of this title.

(5) Any Federal license or permit with respect to which a certification has been obtained under paragraph (1) of this subsection may be suspended or revoked by the Federal agency issuing such license or permit upon the entering of a judgment under this chapter that such facility or activity has been operated in violation of the applicable provisions of section 1311, 1312, 1313, 1316, or 1317 of this title.

(6) Except with respect to a permit issued under section 1342 of this title, in any case where actual construction of a facility has been lawfully commenced prior to April 3, 1970, no certification shall be required under this subsection for a license or permit issued after April 3, 1970, to operate such facility, except that any such license or permit issued without certification shall terminate April 3, 1973, unless prior to such termination date the person having such license or permit submits to the Federal agency which issued such license or permit a certification and otherwise meets the requirements of this section.

**(b) Compliance with other provisions of law setting applicable water quality requirements**

Nothing in this section shall be construed to limit the authority of any department or agency pursuant to any other provision of law to require compliance with any applicable water quality requirements. The Administrator shall, upon the request of any Federal department or agency, or State or interstate agency, or applicant, provide, for the purpose of this section, any relevant information on applicable effluent limitations, or other limitations, standards, regulations, or requirements, or water quality criteria, and shall, when requested by any such department or agency or State or interstate agency, or applicant, comment on any methods to comply with such limitations, standards, regulations, requirements, or criteria.

**(c) Authority of Secretary of the Army to permit use of spoil disposal areas by Federal licensees or permittees**

In order to implement the provisions of this section, the Secretary of the Army, acting through the Chief of Engineers, is authorized, if he deems it to be in the public interest, to permit the use of spoil disposal areas under his jurisdiction by Federal licensees or permittees, and to make an appropriate charge for such use. Moneys received from such licensees or permittees shall be deposited in the Treasury as miscellaneous receipts.

**(d) Limitations and monitoring requirements of certification**

Any certification provided under this section shall set forth any effluent limitations and other limitations, and monitoring requirements necessary to assure that any applicant for a Federal license or permit will comply with any applicable effluent limitations and other limitations, under section 1311 or 1312 of this title, standard of performance under section 1316 of this title, or prohibition, effluent standard, or pretreatment standard under section 1317 of this title, and with any other appropriate requirement of State law set forth in such certification, and shall become a condition on any Federal license or permit subject to the provisions of this section.

(June 30, 1948, c. 758, Title IV, § 401, as added Oct. 18, 1972, Pub.L. 92–500, § 2, 86 Stat. 877, and amended Dec. 27, 1977, Pub.L. 95–217, §§ 61(b), 64, 91 Stat. 1598, 1599.)

### HISTORICAL AND STATUTORY NOTES

**Administration of Refuse Act Permit Program**

Administration of Refuse Act Permit Program to regulate discharge of pollutants and other refuse matter into navigable waters of the United States or their tributaries, see Ex. Ord. No. 11574, Dec. 23, 1970, 35 F.R. 19627, set out as a note under section 407 of this title.

## § 1342. National pollutant discharge elimination system

**[FWPCA § 402]**

### (a) Permits for discharge of pollutants

(1) Except as provided in sections 1328 and 1344 of this title, the Administrator may, after opportunity for public hearing, issue a permit for the discharge of any pollutant, or combination of pollutants, notwithstanding section 1311(a) of this title, upon condition that such discharge will meet either (A) all applicable requirements under sections 1311, 1312, 1316, 1317, 1318, and 1343 of this title, or (B) prior to the taking of necessary implementing actions relating to all such requirements, such conditions as the Administrator determines are necessary to carry out the provisions of this chapter.

(2) The Administrator shall prescribe conditions for such permits to assure compliance with the requirements of paragraph (1) of this subsection, including conditions on data and information collection, reporting, and such other requirements as he deems appropriate.

(3) The permit program of the Administrator under paragraph (1) of this subsection, and permits issued thereunder, shall be subject to the same terms, conditions, and requirements as apply to a State permit program and permits issued thereunder under subsection (b) of this section.

(4) All permits for discharges into the navigable waters issued pursuant to section 407 of this title shall be deemed to be permits issued under this subchapter, and permits issued under this subchapter shall be deemed to be permits issued under section 407 of this title, and shall continue in force and effect for their term unless revoked, modified, or suspended in accordance with the provisions of this chapter.

(5) No permit for a discharge into the navigable waters shall be issued under section 407 of this title after October 18, 1972. Each application for a permit under section 407 of this title, pending on October 18, 1972, shall be deemed to be an application for a permit under this section. The Administrator shall authorize a State, which he determines has the capability of administering a permit program which will carry out the objective of this chapter to issue permits for discharges into the navigable waters within the jurisdiction of such State. The Administrator may exercise the authority granted him by the preceding sentence only during the period which begins on October 18, 1972, and ends either on the ninetieth day after the date of the first promulgation of guidelines required by section 1314(i)(2) of this title, or the date of approval by the Administrator of a permit program for such State under subsection (b) of this section, whichever date first occurs, and no such authorization to a State shall extend beyond the last day of such period. Each such permit shall be subject to such conditions as the Administrator determines are necessary to carry out the provisions of this chapter. No such permit shall issue if the Administrator objects to such issuance.

### (b) State permit programs

At any time after the promulgation of the guidelines required by subsection (i)(2) of section 1314 of this title, the Governor of each State desiring to administer its own permit program for discharges into navigable waters within its jurisdiction may submit to the Administrator a full and complete description of the program it proposes to establish and administer under State law or under an interstate compact. In addition, such State shall submit a statement from the attorney general (or the attorney for those State water pollution control agencies which have independent legal counsel), or from the chief legal officer in the case of an interstate agency, that the laws of such State, or the interstate compact, as the case may be, provide adequate authority to carry out the described program. The Administrator shall approve each such submitted program unless he determines that adequate authority does not exist:

(1) To issue permits which—

(A) apply, and insure compliance with, any applicable requirements of sections 1311, 1312, 1316, 1317, and 1343 of this title;

(B) are for fixed terms not exceeding five years; and

(C) can be terminated or modified for cause including, but not limited to, the following:

(i) violation of any condition of the permit;

(ii) obtaining a permit by misrepresentation, or failure to disclose fully all relevant facts;

(iii) change in any condition that requires either a temporary or permanent reduction or elimination of the permitted discharge;

(D) control the disposal of pollutants into wells;

(2)(A) To issue permits which apply, and insure compliance with, all applicable requirements of section 1318 of this title; or

(B) To inspect, monitor, enter, and require reports to at least the same extent as required in section 1318 of this title;

(3) To insure that the public, and any other State the waters of which may be affected, receive notice of each application for a permit and to provide an opportunity for public hearing before a ruling on each such application;

(4) To insure that the Administrator receives notice of each application (including a copy thereof) for a permit;

(5) To insure that any State (other than the permitting State), whose waters may be affected by the issuance of a permit may submit written recommendations to the permitting State (and the Administrator) with respect to any permit application and, if any part of such written recommendations are not accepted by the permitting State, that the permitting State will notify such affected State (and the Administrator) in writing of its failure to so accept such recommendations together with its reasons for so doing;

(6) To insure that no permit will be issued if, in the judgment of the Secretary of the Army acting through the Chief of Engineers, after consultation with the Secretary of the department in which the Coast Guard is operating, anchorage and navigation of any of the navigable waters would be substantially impaired thereby;

(7) To abate violations of the permit or the permit program, including civil and criminal penalties and other ways and means of enforcement;

(8) To insure that any permit for a discharge from a publicly owned treatment works includes conditions to require the identification in terms of character and volume of pollutants of any significant source introducing pollutants subject to pretreatment standards under section 1317(b) of this title into such works and a program to assure compliance with such pretreatment standards by each such source, in addition to adequate notice to the permitting agency of (A) new introductions into such works of pollutants from any source which would be a new source as defined in section 1316 of this title if such source were discharging pollutants, (B) new introductions of pollutants into such works from a source which would be subject to section 1311 of this title if it were discharging such pollutants, or (C) a substantial change in volume or character of pollutants being introduced into such works by a source introducing pollutants into such works at the time of issuance of the permit. Such notice shall include information on the quality and quantity of effluent to be introduced into such treatment works and any anticipated impact of such change in the quantity or quality of effluent to be discharged from such publicly owned treatment works; and

(9) To insure that any industrial user of any publicly owned treatment works will comply with sections 1284(b), 1317, and 1318 of this title.

**(c) Suspension of Federal program upon submission of State program; withdrawal of approval of State program; return of State program to Administrator**

(1) Not later than ninety days after the date on which a State has submitted a program (or revision thereof) pursuant to subsection (b) of this section, the Administrator shall suspend the issuance of permits under subsection (a) of this section as to those discharges subject to such program unless he determines that the State permit program does not meet the requirements of subsection (b) of this section or does not conform to the guidelines issued under section 1314(i)(2) of this title. If the Administrator so determines, he shall notify the State of any revisions or modifications necessary to conform to such requirements or guidelines.

(2) Any State permit program under this section shall at all times be in accordance with this section and guidelines promulgated pursuant to section 1314(i)(2) of this title.

(3) Whenever the Administrator determines after public hearing that a State is not administering a program approved under this section in accordance with requirements of this section, he shall so notify the State and, if appropriate corrective action is not taken within a reasonable time, not to exceed ninety days, the Administrator shall withdraw approval of such program. The Administrator shall not withdraw approval of any such program unless he shall first have notified the State, and made public, in writing, the reasons for such withdrawal.

**(4) Limitations on partial permit program returns and withdrawals.**

A State may return to the Administrator administration,[1] and the Administrator may withdraw under paragraph (3) of this subsection approval, of—

(A) a State partial permit program approved under subsection (n)(3) of this section only if the entire permit program being administered by the State department or agency at the time is returned or withdrawn; and

(B) a State partial permit program approved under subsection (n)(4) of this section only if an entire phased component of the permit program being administered by the State at the time is returned or withdrawn.

## (d) Notification of Administrator

(1) Each State shall transmit to the Administrator a copy of each permit application received by such State and provide notice to the Administrator of every action related to the consideration of such permit application, including each permit proposed to be issued by such State.

(2) No permit shall issue (A) if the Administrator within ninety days of the date of his notification under subsection (b)(5) of this section objects in writing to the issuance of such permit, or (B) if the Administrator within ninety days of the date of transmittal of the proposed permit by the State objects in writing to the issuance of such permit as being outside the guidelines and requirements of this chapter. Whenever the Administrator objects to the issuance of a permit under this paragraph such written objection shall contain a statement of the reasons for such objection and the effluent limitations and conditions which such permit would include if it were issued by the Administrator.

(3) The Administrator may, as to any permit application, waive paragraph (2) of this subsection.

(4) In any case where, after December 27, 1977, the Administrator, pursuant to paragraph (2) of this subsection, objects to the issuance of a permit, on request of the State, a public hearing shall be held by the Administrator on such objection. If the State does not resubmit such permit revised to meet such objection within 30 days after completion of the hearing, or, if no hearing is requested within 90 days after the date of such objection, the Administrator may issue the permit pursuant to subsection (a) of this section for such source in accordance with the guidelines and requirements of this chapter.

## (e) Waiver of notification requirement

In accordance with guidelines promulgated pursuant to subsection (i)(2) of section 1314 of this title, the Administrator is authorized to waive the requirements of subsection (d) of this section at the time he approves a program pursuant to subsection (b) of this section for any category (including any class, type, or size within such category) of point sources within the State submitting such program.

## (f) Point source categories

The Administrator shall promulgate regulations establishing categories of point sources which he determines shall not be subject to the requirements of subsection (d) of this section in any State with a program approved pursuant to subsection (b) of this section. The Administrator may distinguish among classes, types, and sizes within any category of point sources.

## (g) Other regulations for safe transportation, handling, carriage, storage, and stowage of pollutants

Any permit issued under this section for the discharge of pollutants into the navigable waters from a vessel or other floating craft shall be subject to any applicable regulations promulgated by the Secretary of the department in which the Coast Guard is operating, establishing specifications for safe transportation, handling, carriage, storage, and stowage of pollutants.

## (h) Violation of permit conditions; restriction or prohibition upon introduction of pollutant by source not previously utilizing treatment works

In the event any condition of a permit for discharges from a treatment works (as defined in section 1292 of this title) which is publicly owned is violated, a State with a program approved under subsection (b) of this section or the Administrator, where no State program is approved or where the Administrator determines pursuant to section 1319(a) of this title that a State with an approved program has not commenced appropriate enforcement action with respect to such permit, may proceed in a court of competent jurisdiction to restrict or prohibit the introduction of any pollutant into such treatment works by a source not utilizing such treatment works prior to the finding that such condition was violated.

## (i) Federal enforcement not limited

Nothing in this section shall be construed to limit the authority of the Administrator to take action pursuant to section 1319 of this title.

## (j) Public information

A copy of each permit application and each permit issued under this section shall be available to the public. Such permit application or permit, or portion thereof, shall further be available on request for the purpose of reproduction.

## (k) Compliance with permits

Compliance with a permit issued pursuant to this section shall be deemed compliance, for purposes of sections 1319 and 1365 of this title, with sections 1311, 1312, 1316, 1317, and 1343 of this title, except any standard imposed under section 1317 of this title for a toxic pollutant injurious to human health. Until December 31, 1974, in any case where a permit for discharge has been applied for pursuant to this section, but final administrative disposition of such application has not been made, such discharge shall not be a violation of (1) section 1311, 1316, or 1342 of this title, or (2) section 407 of this title, unless the Administrator or other plaintiff proves that final administrative disposition of such application has not been made because of the failure of the applicant to furnish information reasonably required or requested in order to process the application. For the 180-day period beginning on October 18, 1972, in the case of any point source discharging any pollutant or combination of pollutants immediately prior to such date which source is not subject to section 407 of this title, the discharge by such source shall not be a violation of this chapter if such a source applies for a permit for discharge pursuant to this section within such 180-day period.

**(*l*) Limitation on permit requirement**

**(1) Agricultural return flows**

The Administrator shall not require a permit under this section for discharges composed entirely of return flows from irrigated agriculture, nor shall the Administrator directly or indirectly, require any State to require such a permit.

**(2) Stormwater runoff from oil, gas, and mining operations**

The Administrator shall not require a permit under this section, nor shall the Administrator directly or indirectly require any State to require a permit, for discharges of stormwater runoff from mining operations or oil and gas exploration, production, processing, or treatment operations or transmission facilities, composed entirely of flows which are from conveyances or systems of conveyances (including but not limited to pipes, conduits, ditches, and channels) used for collecting and conveying precipitation runoff and which are not contaminated by contact with, or do not come into contact with, any overburden, raw material, intermediate products, finished product, byproduct, or waste products located on the site of such operations.

**(m) Additional pretreatment of conventional pollutants not required**

To the extent a treatment works (as defined in section 1292 of this title) which is publicly owned is not meeting the requirements of a permit issued under this section for such treatment works as a result of inadequate design or operation of such treatment works, the Administrator, in issuing a permit under this section, shall not require pretreatment by a person introducing conventional pollutants identified pursuant to section 1314(a)(4) of this title into such treatment works other than pretreatment required to assure compliance with pretreatment standards under subsection (b)(8) of this section and section 1317(b)(1) of this title. Nothing in this subsection shall affect the Administrator's authority under sections 1317 and 1319 of this title, affect State and local authority under sections 1317(b)(4) and 1370 of this title, relieve such treatment works of its obligations to meet requirements established under this chapter, or otherwise preclude such works from pursuing whatever feasible options are available to meet its responsibility to comply with its permit under this section.

**(n) Partial permit program**

**(1) State submission**

The Governor of a State may submit under subsection (b) of this section a permit program for a portion of the discharges into the navigable waters in such State.

**(2) Minimum coverage**

A partial permit program under this subsection shall cover, at a minimum, administration of a major category of the discharges into the navigable waters of the State or a major component of the permit program required by subsection (b) of this section.

**(3) Approval of major category partial permit programs**

The Administrator may approve a partial permit program covering administration of a major category of discharges under this subsection if—

**(A)** such program represents a complete permit program and covers all of the discharges under the jurisdiction of a department or agency of the State; and

**(B)** the Administrator determines that the partial program represents a significant and identifiable part of the State program required by subsection (b) of this section.

**(4) Approval of major component partial permit programs**

The Administrator may approve under this subsection a partial and phased permit program covering administration of a major component (including discharge categories) of a State permit program required by subsection (b) of this section if—

**(A)** the Administrator determines that the partial program represents a significant and identifiable part of the State program required by subsection (b) of this section; and

**(B)** the State submits, and the Administrator approves, a plan for the State to assume administration by phases of the remainder of the State program required by subsection (b) of this section by a specified date not more than 5 years after submission of the partial program under this subsection and agrees to make all reasonable efforts to assume such administration by such date.

**(*o*) Anti-backsliding**

**(1) General prohibition**

In the case of effluent limitations established on the basis of subsection (a)(1)(B) of this section, a permit may not be renewed, reissued, or modified on the basis of effluent guidelines promulgated under section 1314(b) of this title subsequent to the original issuance of such permit, to contain effluent limitations which are less stringent than the comparable effluent limitations in the previous permit. In the case of effluent limitations established on the basis of section 1311(b)(1)(C) or section 1313(d) or (e) of this title, a permit may not be renewed, reissued, or modified to contain effluent limitations which are less stringent than the comparable effluent limitations in the previous permit except in compliance with section 1313(d)(4) of this title.

**(2) Exceptions**

A permit with respect to which paragraph (1) applies may be renewed, reissued, or modified to contain a less stringent effluent limitation applicable to a pollutant if—

(A) material and substantial alterations or additions to the permitted facility occurred after permit issuance which justify the application of a less stringent effluent limitation;

(B)(i) information is available which was not available at the time of permit issuance (other than revised regulations, guidance, or test methods) and which would have justified the application of a less stringent effluent limitation at the time of permit issuance; or

(ii) the Administrator determines that technical mistakes or mistaken interpretations of law were made in issuing the permit under subsection (a)(1)(B) of this section;

(C) a less stringent effluent limitation is necessary because of events over which the permittee has no control and for which there is no reasonably available remedy;

(D) the permittee has received a permit modification under section 1311(c), 1311(g), 1311(h), 1311(i), 1311(k), 1311(n), or 1326(a) of this title; or

(E) the permittee has installed the treatment facilities required to meet the effluent limitations in the previous permit and has properly operated and maintained the facilities but has nevertheless been unable to achieve the previous effluent limitations, in which case the limitations in the reviewed, reissued, or modified permit may reflect the level of pollutant control actually achieved (but shall not be less stringent than required by effluent guidelines in effect at the time of permit renewal, reissuance, or modification).

Subparagraph (B) shall not apply to any revised waste load allocations or any alternative grounds for translating water quality standards into effluent limitations, except where the cumulative effect of such revised allocations results in a decrease in the amount of pollutants discharged into the concerned waters, and such revised allocations are not the result of a discharger eliminating or substantially reducing its discharge of pollutants due to complying with the requirements of this chapter or for reasons otherwise unrelated to water quality.

**(3) Limitations**

In no event may a permit with respect to which paragraph (1) applies be renewed, reissued, or modified to contain an effluent limitation which is less stringent than required by effluent guidelines in effect at the time the permit is renewed, reissued, or modified. In no event may such a permit to discharge into waters be renewed, reissued, or modified to contain a less stringent effluent limitation if the implementation of such limitation would result in a violation of a water quality standard under section 1313 of this title applicable to such waters.

**(p) Municipal and industrial stormwater discharges**

**(1) General rule**

Prior to October 1, 1994, the Administrator or the State (in the case of a permit program approved under this section) shall not require a permit under this section for discharges composed entirely of stormwater.

**(2) Exceptions**

Paragraph (1) shall not apply with respect to the following stormwater discharges:

(A) A discharge with respect to which a permit has been issued under this section before February 4, 1987.

(B) A discharge associated with industrial activity.

(C) A discharge from a municipal separate storm sewer system serving a population of 250,000 or more.

(D) A discharge from a municipal separate storm sewer system serving a population of 100,000 or more but less than 250,000.

(E) A discharge for which the Administrator or the State, as the case may be, determines that the stormwater discharge contributes to a violation of a water quality standard or is a significant contributor of pollutants to waters of the United States.

**(3) Permit requirements**

**(A) Industrial discharges**

Permits for discharges associated with industrial activity shall meet all applicable provisions of this section and section 1311 of this title.

(B) **Municipal discharge**

Permits for discharges from municipal storm sewers—

(i) may be issued on a system- or jurisdiction-wide basis;

(ii) shall include a requirement to effectively prohibit non-stormwater discharges into the storm sewers; and

(iii) shall require controls to reduce the discharge of pollutants to the maximum extent practicable, including management practices, control techniques and system, design and engineering methods, and such other provisions as the Administrator or the State determines appropriate for the control of such pollutants.

(4) **Permit application requirements**

(A) **Industrial and large municipal discharges**

Not later than 2 years after February 4, 1987, the Administrator shall establish regulations setting forth the permit application requirements for stormwater discharges described in paragraphs (2)(B) and (2)(C). Applications for permits for such discharges shall be filed no later than 3 years after February 4, 1987. Not later than 4 years after February 4, 1987, the Administrator or the State, as the case may be, shall issue or deny each such permit. Any such permit shall provide for compliance as expeditiously as practicable, but in no event later than 3 years after the date of issuance of such permit.

(B) **Other municipal discharges**

Not later than 4 years after February 4, 1987, the Administrator shall establish regulations setting forth the permit application requirements for stormwater discharges described in paragraph (2)(D). Applications for permits for such discharges shall be filed no later than 5 years after February 4, 1987. Not later than 6 years after February 4, 1987, the Administrator or the State, as the case may be, shall issue or deny each such permit. Any such permit shall provide for compliance as expeditiously as practicable, but in no event later than 3 years after the date of issuance of such permit.

(5) **Studies**

The Administrator, in consultation with the States, shall conduct a study for the purposes of—

(A) identifying those stormwater discharges or classes of stormwater discharges for which permits are not required pursuant to paragraphs (1) and (2) of this subsection;

(B) determining, to the maximum extent practicable, the nature and extent of pollutants in such discharges; and

(C) establishing procedures and methods to control stormwater discharges to the extent necessary to mitigate impacts on water quality.

Not later than October 1, 1988, the Administrator shall submit to Congress a report on the results of the study described in subparagraphs (A) and (B). Not later than October 1, 1989, the Administrator shall submit to Congress a report on the results of the study described in subparagraph (C).

(6) **Regulations**

Not later than October 1, 1993, the Administrator, in consultation with State and local officials, shall issue regulations (based on the results of the studies conducted under paragraph (5)) which designate stormwater discharges, other than those discharges described in paragraph (2), to be regulated to protect water quality and shall establish a comprehensive program to regulate such designated sources. The program shall, at a minimum, (A) establish priorities, (B) establish requirements for State stormwater management programs, and (C) establish expeditious deadlines. The program may include performance standards, guidelines, guidance, and management practices and treatment requirements, as appropriate.

(q) **Combined sewer overflows**

(1) **Requirement for permits, orders, and decrees**

Each permit, order, or decree issued pursuant to this chapter after December 21, 2000 for a discharge from a municipal combined storm and sanitary sewer shall conform to the Combined Sewer Overflow Control Policy signed by the Administrator on April 11, 1994 (in this subsection referred to as the "CSO control policy").

(2) **Water quality and designated use review guidance**

Not later than July 31, 2001, and after providing notice and opportunity for public comment, the Administrator shall issue guidance to facilitate the conduct of water quality and designated use reviews for municipal combined sewer overflow receiving waters.

(3) **Report**

Not later than September 1, 2001, the Administrator shall transmit to Congress a report on the progress made by the Environmental Protection Agency, States, and municipalities in implementing and enforcing the CSO control policy.

(June 30, 1948, c. 758, Title IV, § 402, as added Oct. 18, 1972, Pub.L. 92–500, § 2, 86 Stat. 880, and amended Dec. 27, 1977, Pub.L. 95–217, §§ 33(c), 50, 54(c)(1), 65, 66, 91 Stat. 1577, 1588, 1591, 1599, 1600; Feb. 4, 1987, Pub.L. 100–4, Title IV, §§ 401 to 404(a), (c), formerly (d), 405, 101 Stat. 65 to 67, 69; Oct. 31, 1992, Pub.L. 102–580, Title III, § 364, 106 Stat. 4862; Dec. 21, 1995, Pub.L. 104–66, Title II, § 2021(e)(2), 109 Stat. 727; Dec. 21, 2000, Pub.L. 106–554, § 1(a)(4) [Div. B, Title I, § 112(a)], 114 Stat. 2763, 2763A–224.)

[1] So in original.

### HISTORICAL AND STATUTORY NOTES

**References in Text**

This chapter, referred to in subsec. (q), originally read "this Act", meaning the Federal Water Pollution Control Act, June 30, 1948, c. 758, 62 Stat. 1155, which is classified principally to this chapter. See Tables for complete classification.

**Transfer of Functions**

Enforcement functions of Administrator or other official of the Environmental Protection Agency under this section relating to compliance with national pollutant discharge elimination system permits with respect to pre-construction, construction, and initial operation of transportation system for Canadian and Alaskan natural gas were transferred to the Federal Inspector, Office of Federal Inspector for the Alaska Natural Gas Transportation System, until the first anniversary of the date of initial operation of the Alaska Natural Gas Transportation System, see Reorg. Plan No. 1 of 1979, §§ 102(a), 203(a), 44 F.R. 33663, 33666, 93 Stat. 1373, 1376, effective July 1, 1979, set out in Appendix 1 to Title 5, Government Organization and Employees.

**Stormwater Permit Requirements**

Pub.L. 102–240, Title I, § 1068, Dec. 18, 1991, 105 Stat. 2007, provided that:

"**(a) General rule.**—Notwithstanding the requirements of sections 402(p)(2)(B), (C), and (D) of the Federal Water Pollution Control Act [subsec. (p)(2)(B), (C), and (D) of this section], permit application deadlines for stormwater discharges associated with industrial activities from facilities that are owned or operated by a municipality shall be established by the Administrator of the Environmental Protection Agency (hereinafter in this section referred to as the 'Administrator') pursuant to the requirements of this section.

"**(b) Permit applications.**—

"**(1) Individual applications.**—The Administrator shall require individual permit applications for discharges described in subsection (a) on or before October 1, 1992; except that any municipality that has participated in a timely part I group application for an industrial activity discharging stormwater that is denied such participation in a group application or for which a group application is denied shall not be required to submit an individual application until the 180th day following the date on which the denial is made.

"**(2) Group applications.**—With respect to group applications for permits for discharges described in subsection (a), the Administrator shall require—

"**(A)** part I applications on or before September 30, 1991, except that any municipality with a population of less than 250,000 shall not be required to submit a part I application before May 18, 1992; and

"**(B)** part II applications on or before October 1, 1992, except that any municipality with a population of less than 250,000 shall not be required to submit a part II application before May 17, 1993.

"**(c) Municipalities with less than 100,000 population.**—The Administrator shall not require any municipality with a population of less than 100,000 to apply for or obtain a permit for any stormwater discharge associated with an industrial activity other than an airport, powerplant, or uncontrolled sanitary landfill owned or operated by such municipality before October 1, 1992, unless such permit is required by section 402(p)(2)(A) or (E) of the Federal Water Pollution Control Act [subsec. (p)(2)(A) or (E) of this section].

"**(d) Uncontrolled sanitary landfill defined.**—For the purposes of this section, the term 'uncontrolled sanitary landfill' means a landfill or open dump, whether in operation or closed, that does not meet the requirements for run-on and run-off controls established pursuant to subtitle D of the Solid Waste Disposal Act [section 6941 et seq. of Title 42, The Public Health and Welfare].

"**(e) Limitation on statutory construction.**—Nothing in this section shall be construed to affect any application or permit requirement, including any deadline, to apply for or obtain a permit for stormwater discharges subject to section 402(p)(2)(A) or (E) of the Federal Water Pollution Control Act [subsec. (p)(2)(A) or (E) of this section].

"**(f) Regulations.**—The Administrator shall issue final regulations with respect to general permits for stormwater discharges associated with industrial activity on or before February 1, 1992."

**Phosphate Fertilizer Effluent Limitation**

Section 306(c) of Pub.L. 100–4 provided that:

"**(1) Issuance of permit.**—As soon as possible after the date of the enactment of this Act [Feb. 4, 1987], but not later than 180 days after such date of enactment [Feb. 4, 1987], the Administrator shall issue permits under section 402(a)(1)(B) of the Federal Water Pollution Control Act [subsec. (a)(1)(B) of this section] with respect to facilities—

"**(A)** which were under construction on or before April 8, 1974, and

"**(B)** for which the Administrator is proposing to revise the applicability of the effluent limitation established under section 301(b) of such Act [section 1311(b) of this title] for phosphate subcategory of the fertilizer manufacturing point source category to exclude such facilities.

"**(2) Limitations on statutory construction.**—Nothing in this section shall be construed—

"**(A)** to require the Administrator to permit the discharge of gypsum or gypsum waste into the navigable waters,

"**(B)** to affect the procedures and standards applicable to the Administrator in issuing permits under section 402(a)(1)(B) of the Federal Water Pollution Control Act [subsec. (a)(1)(B) of this section], and

"**(C)** to affect the authority of any State to deny or condition certification under section 401 of such Act [section 1341 of this title] with respect to the issuance of permits under section 402(a)(1)(B) of such Act [subsec. (a)(1)(B) of this section]."

**Log Transfer Facilities**

Section 407 of Pub.L. 100–4 provided that:

"**(a) Agreement.**—The Administrator and Secretary of the Army shall enter into an agreement regarding coordination of permitting for log transfer facilities to designate a lead agency and to process permits required under sections 402 and 404 of the Federal Water Pollution Control Act [this section and section 1344 of this title], where both such sections apply, for discharges associated with the construction and operation of log transfer facilities. The Administrator and Secretary are authorized to act in accordance with the terms of such agreement to assure that, to the maximum extent practicable, duplication, needless paperwork and delay in the issuance of permits, and inequitable enforcement between and among facilities in different States, shall be eliminated.

"(b) **Applications and permits before October 22, 1985.**—Where both of sections 402 and 404 of the Federal Water Pollution Control Act [this section and section 1344 of this title] apply, log transfer facilities which have received a permit under section 404 of such Act [section 1344 of this title] before October 22, 1985, shall not be required to submit a new application for a permit under section 402 of such Act [this section]. If the Administrator determines that the terms of a permit issued on or before October 22, 1985, under section 404 of such Act [section 1344 of this title] satisfies the applicable requirements of sections 301, 302, 306, 307, 308, and 403 of such Act [sections 1311, 1312, 1316, 1317, 1318, and 1343 of this title] a separate application for a permit under section 402 of such Act [this section] shall not thereafter be required. In any case where the Administrator demonstrates, after an opportunity for a hearing, that the terms of a permit issued on or before October 22, 1985, under section 404 of such Act [section 1344 of this title] do not satisfy the applicable requirements of sections 301, 302, 306, 307, 308, and 403 of such Act [sections 1311, 1312, 1316, 1317, 1318, and 1343 of this title], modifications to the existing permit under section 404 of such Act [section 1344 of this title] to incorporate such applicable requirements shall be issued by the Administrator as an alternative to issuance of a separate new permit under section 402 of such Act [this section].

"(c) **Log transfer facility defined.**—For the purposes of this section, the term 'log transfer facility' means a facility which is constructed in whole or in part in waters of the United States and which is utilized for the purpose of transferring commercially harvested logs to or from a vessel or log raft, including the formation of a log raft."

**Allowable Delay in Modifying Existing Approved State Permit Programs to Conform to 1977 Amendment**

Section 54(c)(2) of Pub.L. 95–217 provided that any State permit program approved under this section before Dec. 27, 1977, which required modification to conform to the amendment made by section 54(c)(1) of Pub.L. 95–217, which amended subsec. (b)(8) of this section, not be required to be modified before the end of the one year period which began on Dec. 27, 1977, unless in order to make the required modification a State must amend or enact a law in which case such modification not be required for such State before the end of the two year period which began on Dec. 27, 1977.

## § 1343. Ocean discharge criteria

### [FWPCA § 403]

### (a) Issuance of permits

No permit under section 1342 of this title for a discharge into the territorial sea, the waters of the contiguous zone, or the oceans shall be issued, after promulgation of guidelines established under subsection (c) of this section, except in compliance with such guidelines. Prior to the promulgation of such guidelines, a permit may be issued under such section 1342 of this title if the Administrator determines it to be in the public interest.

### (b) Waiver

The requirements of subsection (d) of section 1342 of this title may not be waived in the case of permits for discharges into the territorial sea.

### (c) Guidelines for determining degradation of waters

(1) The Administrator shall, within one hundred and eighty days after October 18, 1972 (and from time to time thereafter), promulgate guidelines for determining the degradation of the waters of the territorial seas, the contiguous zone, and the oceans, which shall include:

(A) the effect of disposal of pollutants on human health or welfare, including but not limited to plankton, fish, shellfish, wildlife, shorelines, and beaches;

(B) the effect of disposal of pollutants on marine life including the transfer, concentration, and dispersal of pollutants or their byproducts through biological, physical, and chemical processes; changes in marine ecosystem diversity, productivity, and stability; and species and community population changes;

(C) the effect of disposal, of pollutants on esthetic, recreation, and economic values;

(D) the persistence and permanence of the effects of disposal of pollutants;

(E) the effect of the disposal at varying rates, of particular volumes and concentrations of pollutants;

(F) other possible locations and methods of disposal or recycling of pollutants including land-based alternatives; and

(G) the effect on alternate uses of the oceans, such as mineral exploitation and scientific study.

(2) In any event where insufficient information exists on any proposed discharge to make a reasonable judgment on any of the guidelines established pursuant to this subsection no permit shall be issued under section 1342 of this title.

(June 30, 1948, c. 758, Title IV, § 403, as added Oct. 18, 1972, Pub.L. 92–500, § 2, 86 Stat. 883.)

### HISTORICAL AND STATUTORY NOTES

**Territorial Sea and Contiguous Zone of United States**

For extension of territorial sea and contiguous zone of United States, see Proc. No. 5928 and Proc. No. 7219, respectively, set out as notes under 43 U.S.C.A. § 1331.

**Discharges from Point Sources in United States Virgin Islands Attributable to Manufacture of Rum; Exemption; Conditions**

Discharges from point sources in the United States Virgin Islands in existence on Aug. 5, 1983, attributable to the manufacture of rum not to be subject to the requirements of this section under certain conditions, see section 214(g) of Pub.L. 98–67, set out as a note under section 1311 of this title.

## § 1344. Permits for dredged or fill material

### [FWPCA § 404]

**(a) Discharge into navigable waters at specified disposal sites**

The Secretary may issue permits, after notice and opportunity for public hearings for the discharge of dredged or fill material into the navigable waters at specified disposal sites. Not later than the fifteenth day after the date an applicant submits all the information required to complete an application for a permit under this subsection, the Secretary shall publish the notice required by this subsection.

**(b) Specification for disposal sites**

Subject to subsection (c) of this section, each such disposal site shall be specified for each such permit by the Secretary (1) through the application of guidelines developed by the Administrator, in conjunction with the Secretary, which guidelines shall be based upon criteria comparable to the criteria applicable to the territorial seas, the contiguous zone, and the ocean under section 1343(c) of this title, and (2) in any case where such guidelines under clause (1) alone would prohibit the specification of a site, through the application additionally of the economic impact of the site on navigation and anchorage.

**(c) Denial or restriction of use of defined areas as disposal sites**

The Administrator is authorized to prohibit the specification (including the withdrawal of specification) of any defined area as a disposal site, and he is authorized to deny or restrict the use of any defined area for specification (including the withdrawal of specification) as a disposal site, whenever he determines, after notice and opportunity for public hearings, that the discharge of such materials into such area will have an unacceptable adverse effect on municipal water supplies, shellfish beds and fishery areas (including spawning and breeding areas), wildlife, or recreational areas. Before making such determination, the Administrator shall consult with the Secretary. The Administrator shall set forth in writing and make public his findings and his reasons for making any determination under this subsection.

**(d) "Secretary" defined**

The term "Secretary" as used in this section means the Secretary of the Army, acting through the Chief of Engineers.

**(e) General permits on State, regional, or nationwide basis**

(1) In carrying out his functions relating to the discharge of dredged or fill material under this section, the Secretary may, after notice and opportunity for public hearing, issue general permits on a State, regional, or nationwide basis for any category of activities involving discharges of dredged or fill material if the Secretary determines that the activities in such category are similar in nature, will cause only minimal adverse environmental effects when performed separately, and will have only minimal cumulative adverse effect on the environment. Any general permit issued under this subsection shall (A) be based on the guidelines described in subsection (b)(1) of this section, and (B) set forth the requirements and standards which shall apply to any activity authorized by such general permit.

(2) No general permit issued under this subsection shall be for a period of more than five years after the date of its issuance and such general permit may be revoked or modified by the Secretary if, after opportunity for public hearing, the Secretary determines that the activities authorized by such general permit have an adverse impact on the environment or such activities are more appropriately authorized by individual permits.

**(f) Non-prohibited discharge of dredged or fill material**

(1) Except as provided in paragraph (2) of this subsection, the discharge of dredged or fill material—

(A) from normal farming, silviculture, and ranching activities such as plowing, seeding, cultivating, minor drainage, harvesting for the production of food, fiber, and forest products, or upland soil and water conservation practices;

(B) for the purpose of maintenance, including emergency reconstruction of recently damaged parts, of currently serviceable structures such as dikes, dams, levees, groins, riprap, breakwaters, causeways, and bridge abutments or approaches, and transportation structures;

(C) for the purpose of construction or maintenance of farm or stock ponds or irrigation ditches, or the maintenance of drainage ditches;

(D) for the purpose of construction of temporary sedimentation basins on a construction site which does not include placement of fill material into the navigable waters;

(E) for the purpose of construction or maintenance of farm roads or forest roads, or temporary roads for moving mining equipment, where such roads are constructed and maintained, in accordance with best management practices, to assure that flow and circulation patterns and chemical and biological characteristics of the navigable waters are not impaired, that the reach of the navigable waters is not reduced, and that any adverse effect on the aquatic environment will be otherwise minimized;

(F) resulting from any activity with respect to which a State has an approved program under section 1288(b)(4) of this title which meets the requirements of subparagraphs (B) and (C) of such section,

is not prohibited by or otherwise subject to regulation under this section or section 1311(a) or 1342 of this title (except for effluent standards or prohibitions under section 1317 of this title).

(2) Any discharge of dredged or fill material into the navigable waters incidental to any activity having as its purpose bringing an area of the navigable waters into a use to which it was not previously subject, where the flow or circulation of navigable waters may be impaired or the reach of such waters be reduced, shall be required to have a permit under this section.

**(g) State administration**

(1) The Governor of any State desiring to administer its own individual and general permit program for the discharge of dredged or fill material into the navigable waters (other than those waters which are presently used, or are susceptible to use in their natural condition or by reasonable improvement as a means to transport interstate or foreign commerce shoreward to their ordinary high water mark, including all waters which are subject to the ebb and flow of the tide shoreward to their mean high water mark, or mean higher high water mark on the west coast, including wetlands adjacent thereto) within its jurisdiction may submit to the Administrator a full and complete description of the program it proposes to establish and administer under State law or under an interstate compact. In addition, such State shall submit a statement from the attorney general (or the attorney for those State agencies which have independent legal counsel), or from the chief legal officer in the case of an interstate agency, that the laws of such State, or the interstate compact, as the case may be, provide adequate authority to carry out the described program.

(2) Not later than the tenth day after the date of the receipt of the program and statement submitted by any State under paragraph (1) of this subsection, the Administrator shall provide copies of such program and statement to the Secretary and the Secretary of the Interior, acting through the Director of the United States Fish and Wildlife Service.

(3) Not later than the ninetieth day after the date of the receipt by the Administrator of the program and statement submitted by any State, under paragraph (1) of this subsection, the Secretary and the Secretary of the Interior, acting through the Director of the United States Fish and Wildlife Service, shall submit any comments with respect to such program and statement to the Administrator in writing.

**(h) Determination of State's authority to issue permits under State program; approval; notification; transfers to State program**

(1) Not later than the one-hundred-twentieth day after the date of the receipt by the Administrator of a program and statement submitted by any State under paragraph (1) of this subsection, the Administrator shall determine, taking into account any comments submitted by the Secretary and the Secretary of the Interior, acting through the Director of the United States Fish and Wildlife Service, pursuant to subsection (g) of this section, whether such State has the following authority with respect to the issuance of permits pursuant to such program:

(A) To issue permits which—

(i) apply, and assure compliance with, any applicable requirements of this section, including, but not limited to, the guidelines established under subsection (b)(1) of this section, and sections 1317 and 1343 of this title;

(ii) are for fixed terms not exceeding five years; and

(iii) can be terminated or modified for cause including, but not limited to, the following:

(I) violation of any condition of the permit;

(II) obtaining a permit by misrepresentation, or failure to disclose fully all relevant facts;

(III) change in any condition that requires either a temporary or permanent reduction or elimination of the permitted discharge.

(B) To issue permits which apply, and assure compliance with, all applicable requirements of section 1318 of this title, or to inspect, monitor, enter, and require reports to at least the same extent as required in section 1318 of this title.

(C) To assure that the public, and any other State the waters of which may be affected, receive notice of each application for a permit and to provide an opportunity for public hearing before a ruling on each such application.

(D) To assure that the Administrator receives notice of each application (including a copy thereof) for a permit.

(E) To assure that any State (other than the permitting State), whose waters may be affected by the issuance of a permit may submit written recommendations to the permitting State (and the Administrator) with respect to any permit application and, if any part of such written recommendations are not accepted by the permitting State, that the permitting State will notify such affected State (and the Administrator) in writing of its failure to so accept such recommendations together with its reasons for so doing.

**(F)** To assure that no permit will be issued if, in the judgment of the Secretary, after consultation with the Secretary of the department in which the Coast Guard is operating, anchorage and navigation of any of the navigable waters would be substantially impaired thereby.

**(G)** To abate violations of the permit or the permit program, including civil and criminal penalties and other ways and means of enforcement.

**(H)** To assure continued coordination with Federal and Federal-State water-related planning and review processes.

**(2)** If, with respect to a State program submitted under subsection (g)(1) of this section, the Administrator determines that such State—

**(A)** has the authority set forth in paragraph (1) of this subsection, the Administrator shall approve the program and so notify (i) such State and (ii) the Secretary, who upon subsequent notification from such State that it is administering such program, shall suspend the issuance of permits under subsections (a) and (e) of this section for activities with respect to which a permit may be issued pursuant to such State program; or

**(B)** does not have the authority set forth in paragraph (1) of this subsection, the Administrator shall so notify such State, which notification shall also describe the revisions or modifications necessary so that such State may resubmit such program for a determination by the Administrator under this subsection.

**(3)** If the Administrator fails to make a determination with respect to any program submitted by a State under subsection (g)(1) of this section within one-hundred-twenty days after the date of the receipt of such program, such program shall be deemed approved pursuant to paragraph (2)(A) of this subsection and the Administrator shall so notify such State and the Secretary who, upon subsequent notification from such State that it is administering such program, shall suspend the issuance of permits under subsection (a) and (e) of this section for activities with respect to which a permit may be issued by such State.

**(4)** After the Secretary receives notification from the Administrator under paragraph (2) or (3) of this subsection that a State permit program has been approved, the Secretary shall transfer any applications for permits pending before the Secretary for activities with respect to which a permit may be issued pursuant to such State program to such State for appropriate action.

**(5)** Upon notification from a State with a permit program approved under this subsection that such State intends to administer and enforce the terms and conditions of a general permit issued by the Secretary under subsection (e) of this section with respect to activities in such State to which such general permit applies, the Secretary shall suspend the administration and enforcement of such general permit with respect to such activities.

**(i) Withdrawal of approval**

Whenever the Administrator determines after public hearing that a State is not administering a program approved under subsection (h)(2)(A) of this section, in accordance with this section, including, but not limited to, the guidelines established under subsection (b)(1) of this section, the Administrator shall so notify the State, and, if appropriate corrective action is not taken within a reasonable time, not to exceed ninety days after the date of the receipt of such notification, the Administrator shall (1) withdraw approval of such program until the Administrator determines such corrective action has been taken, and (2) notify the Secretary that the Secretary shall resume the program for the issuance of permits under subsections (a) and (e) of this section for activities with respect to which the State was issuing permits and that such authority of the Secretary shall continue in effect until such time as the Administrator makes the determination described in clause (1) of this subsection and such State again has an approved program.

**(j) Copies of applications for State permits and proposed general permits to be transmitted to Administrator**

Each State which is administering a permit program pursuant to this section shall transmit to the Administrator (1) a copy of each permit application received by such State and provide notice to the Administrator of every action related to the consideration of such permit application, including each permit proposed to be issued by such State, and (2) a copy of each proposed general permit which such State intends to issue. Not later than the tenth day after the date of the receipt of such permit application or such proposed general permit, the Administrator shall provide copies of such permit application or such proposed general permit to the Secretary and the Secretary of the Interior, acting through the Director of the United States Fish and Wildlife Service. If the Administrator intends to provide written comments to such State with respect to such permit application or such proposed general permit, he shall so notify such State not later than the thirtieth day after the date of the receipt of such application or such proposed general permit and provide such written comments to such State, after consideration of any comments made in writing with respect to such application or such proposed general permit by the Secretary and the Secretary of the Interior, acting through the Director of the United States Fish and Wildlife Service, not later than the ninetieth day after the date of such receipt. If such State is so notified by the Administrator, it shall not issue the proposed permit until after the receipt of such comments from the Administrator, or after such ninetieth day, whichever first occurs. Such State shall not issue such proposed permit after such ninetieth day if it has received such written comments in which the Administrator objects (A) to the issuance of such proposed permit and such proposed permit is one that has been submitted to the Administrator pursuant to subsection (h)(1)(E) of this section, or (B) to the issuance of such proposed permit as being outside the requirements of this section, including, but not limited to, the guidelines developed under subsection (b)(1) of this section unless it modifies such proposed permit in accordance with such comments. Whenever the Administrator objects to the issuance of a permit under the preceding sentence such written objection shall contain a statement of the reasons for such objection and the conditions which such permit would include if it were issued by the Administrator. In any case where the Administrator objects to the issuance of a permit, on request of the State, a public hearing shall be held by the Administrator on such objection. If the State does not resubmit such permit revised to meet such objection within 30 days after completion of the hearing or, if no hearing is requested within 90 days after the date of such objection, the Secretary may issue the permit pursuant to subsection (a) or (e) of this section, as the case may be, for such source in accordance with the guidelines and requirements of this chapter.

**(k) Waiver**

In accordance with guidelines promulgated pursuant to subsection (i)(2) of section 1314 of this title, the Administrator is authorized to waive the requirements of subsection (j) of this section at the time of the approval of a program pursuant to subsection (h)(2)(A) of this section for any category (including any class, type, or size within such category) of discharge within the State submitting such program.

**(*l*) Categories of discharges not subject to requirements**

The Administrator shall promulgate regulations establishing categories of discharges which he determines shall not be subject to the requirements of subsection (j) of this section in any State with a program approved pursuant to subsection (h)(2)(A) of this section. The Administrator may distinguish among classes, types, and sizes within any category of discharges.

**(m) Comments on permit applications or proposed general permits by Secretary of the Interior acting through Director of United States Fish and Wildlife Service**

Not later than the ninetieth day after the date on which the Secretary notifies the Secretary of the Interior, acting through the Director of the United States Fish and Wildlife Service that (1) an application for a permit under subsection (a) of this section has been received by the Secretary, or (2) the Secretary proposes to issue a general permit under subsection (e) of this section, the Secretary of the Interior, acting through the Director of the United States Fish and Wildlife Service, shall submit any comments with respect to such application or such proposed general permit in writing to the Secretary.

**(n) Enforcement authority not limited**

Nothing in this section shall be construed to limit the authority of the Administrator to take action pursuant to section 1319 of this title.

**(*o*) Public availability of permits and permit applications**

A copy of each permit application and each permit issued under this section shall be available to the public. Such permit application or portion thereof, shall further be available on request for the purpose of reproduction.

**(p) Compliance**

Compliance with a permit issued pursuant to this section, including any activity carried out pursuant to a general permit issued under this section, shall be deemed compliance, for purposes of sections 1319 and 1365 of this title, with sections 1311, 1317, and 1343 of this title.

**(q) Minimization of duplication, needless paperwork, and delays in issuance; agreements**

Not later than the one-hundred-eightieth day after December 27, 1977, the Secretary shall enter into agreements with the Administrator, the Secretaries of the Departments of Agriculture, Commerce, Interior, and Transportation, and the heads of other appropriate Federal agencies to minimize, to the maximum extent practicable, duplication, needless paperwork, and delays in the issuance of permits under this section. Such agreements shall be developed to assure that, to the maximum extent practicable, a decision with respect to an application for a permit under subsection (a) of this section will be made not later than the ninetieth day after the date the notice for such application is published under subsection (a) of this section.

**(r) Federal projects specifically authorized by Congress**

The discharge of dredged or fill material as part of the construction of a Federal project specifically authorized by Congress, whether prior to or on or after December 27, 1977, is not prohibited by or otherwise subject to regulation under this section, or a State program approved under this section, or section 1311(a) or 1342 of this title (except for effluent standards or prohibitions under section 1317 of this title), if information on the effects of such discharge, including consideration of the guidelines developed under subsection (b)(1) of this section, is included in an environmental impact statement for such project pursuant to the National Environmental Policy Act of 1969 [42 U.S.C.A. § 4321 et seq.] and such environmental impact statement has been submitted to Congress before the actual discharge of dredged or fill material in connection with the construction of such project and prior to either authorization of such project or an appropriation of funds for such construction.

**(s) Violation of permits**

(1) Whenever on the basis of any information available to him the Secretary finds that any person is in violation of any condition or limitation set forth in a permit issued by the Secretary under this section, the Secretary shall issue an order requiring such person to comply with such condition or limitation, or the Secretary shall bring a civil action in accordance with paragraph (3) of this subsection.

(2) A copy of any order issued under this subsection shall be sent immediately by the Secretary to the State in which the violation occurs and other affected States. Any order issued under this subsection shall be by personal service and shall state with reasonable specificity the nature of the violation, specify a time for compliance, not to exceed thirty days, which the Secretary determines is reasonable, taking into account the seriousness of the violation and any good faith efforts to comply with applicable requirements. In any case in which an order under this subsection is issued to a corporation, a copy of such order shall be served on any appropriate corporate officers.

(3) The Secretary is authorized to commence a civil action for appropriate relief, including a permanent or temporary injunction for any violation for which he is authorized to issue a compliance order under paragraph (1) of this subsection. Any action under this paragraph may be brought in the district court of the United States for the district in which the defendant is located or resides or is doing business, and such court shall have jurisdiction to restrain such violation and to require compliance. Notice of the commencement of such acton[1] shall be given immediately to the appropriate State.

(4) Any person who violates any condition or limitation in a permit issued by the Secretary under this section, and any person who violates any order issued by the Secretary under paragraph (1) of this subsection, shall be subject to a civil penalty not to exceed $25,000 per day for each violation. In determining the amount of a civil penalty the court shall consider the seriousness of the violation or violations, the economic benefit (if any) resulting from the violation, any history of such violations, any good-faith efforts to comply with the applicable requirements, the economic impact of the penalty on the violator, and such other matters as justice may require.

**(t) Navigable waters within State jurisdiction**

Nothing in this section shall preclude or deny the right of any State or interstate agency to control the discharge of dredged or fill material in any portion of the navigable waters within the jurisdiction of such State, including any activity of any Federal agency, and each such agency shall comply with such State or interstate requirements both substantive and procedural to control the discharge of dredged or fill material to the same extent that any person is subject to such requirements. This section shall not be construed as affecting or impairing the authority of the Secretary to maintain navigation.

(June 30, 1948, c. 758, Title IV, § 404, as added Oct. 18, 1972, Pub.L. 92–500, § 2, 86 Stat. 884, and amended Dec. 27, 1977, Pub.L. 95–217, § 67(a), (b), 91 Stat. 1600; Feb. 4, 1987, Pub.L. 100–4, Title III, § 313(d), 101 Stat. 45.)

[1] So in original. Probably should be "action".

## HISTORICAL AND STATUTORY NOTES

**References in Text**

The National Environmental Policy Act of 1969, referred to in subsec. (r), is Pub.L. 91–190, Jan. 1, 1970, 83 Stat. 852, as amended, which is classified generally to chapter 55 (section 4321 et seq.) of Title 42, the Public Health and Welfare. For complete classification of this Act to the Code, see Short Title note set out under section 4321 of Title 42 and Tables .

**Transfer of Functions**

Enforcement functions of Administrator or other official of the Environmental Protection Agency and of Secretary or other official in Department of Interior relating to review of the Corps of Engineers' dredged and fill material permits and such functions of Secretary of the Army, Chief of Engineers, or other official in Corps of Engineers of the United States Army relating to compliance with dredged and fill material permits issued under this section with respect to pre-construction, construction, and initial operation of transportation system for Canadian and Alaskan natural gas were transferred to the Federal Inspector, Office of Federal Inspector for the Alaska Natural Gas Transportation System, until the first anniversary of the date of initial operation of the Alaska Natural Gas Transportation System, see Reorg. Plan No. 1 of 1979, §§ 102(a), (b), (e), 203(a), 44 F.R. 33663, 33666, 93 Stat. 1373, 1376, effective July 1, 1979, set out in

Appendix 1 to Title 5, Government Organization and Employees.

**Mitigation and Mitigation Banking Regulations**

Pub.L. 108–136, Div. A, Title III, § 314(b), Nov. 24, 2003, 117 Stat. 1431, provided that:

"(1) To ensure opportunities for Federal agency participation in mitigation banking, the Secretary of the Army, acting through the Chief of Engineers, shall issue regulations establishing performance standards and criteria for the use, consistent with section 404 of the Federal Water Pollution Control Act (33 U.S.C. 1344) [this section], of on-site, off-site, and in-lieu fee mitigation and mitigation banking as compensation for lost wetlands functions in permits issued by the Secretary of the Army under such section. To the maximum extent practicable, the regulatory standards and criteria shall maximize available credits and opportunities for mitigation, provide flexibility for regional variations in wetland conditions, functions and values, and apply equivalent standards and criteria to each type of compensatory mitigation.

"(2) Final regulations shall be issued not later than two years after the date of the enactment of this Act [Nov. 24, 2003]."

**Contiguous Zone of United States**

For extension of contiguous zone of United States, see Proc. No. 7219, set out as a note under 43 U.S.C.A. § 1331.

**Regulatory Program**

Pub.L. 106–377, § 1(a)(2) [Title I], Oct. 27, 2000, 114 Stat. 1441, 1441A–63, provided in part that: "For expenses necessary for administration of laws pertaining to regulation of navigable waters and wetlands, $125,000,000, to remain available until expended: *Provided*, That the Secretary of the Army, acting through the Chief of Engineers, is directed to use funds appropriated herein to: (1) by March 1, 2001, supplement the report, Cost Analysis For the 1999 Proposal to Issue and Modify Nationwide Permits, to reflect the Nationwide Permits actually issued on March 9, 2000, including changes in the acreage limits, preconstruction notification requirements and general conditions between the rule proposed on July 21, 1999, and the rule promulgated and published in the Federal Register; (2) after consideration of the cost analysis for the 1999 proposal to issue and modify nationwide permits and the supplement prepared pursuant to this Act [Pub.L. 106–377, Oct. 27, 2000, 114 Stat. 1441] and by September 30, 2001, prepare, submit to Congress and publish in the Federal Register a Permit Processing Management Plan by which the Corps of Engineers will handle the additional work associated with all projected increases in the number of individual permit applications and preconstruction notifications related to the new and replacement permits and general conditions. The Permit Processing Management Plan shall include specific objective goals and criteria by which the Corps of Engineers' progress towards reducing any permit backlog can be measured; (3) beginning on December 31, 2001, and on a biannual basis thereafter, report to Congress and publish in the Federal Register, an analysis of the performance of its program as measured against the criteria set out in the Permit Processing Management Plan; (4) implement a 1-year pilot program to publish quarterly on the U.S. Army Corps of Engineer's Regulatory Program website all Regulatory Analysis and Management Systems (RAMS) data for the South Pacific Division and North Atlantic Division beginning within 30 days of the enactment of this Act [Oct. 27, 2000]; and (5) publish in Division Office websites all findings, rulings, and decisions rendered under the administrative appeals process for the Corps of Engineers Regulatory Program as established in Public Law 106–60: *Provided further*, That, through the period ending on September 30, 2003, the Corps of Engineers shall allow any appellant to keep a verbatim record of the proceedings of the appeals conference under the aforementioned administrative appeals process: *Provided further*, That within 30 days of the enactment of this Act [Oct. 27, 2000], the Secretary of the Army, acting through the Chief of Engineers, shall require all U.S. Army Corps of Engineers Divisions and Districts to record the date on which a section 404 individual permit application or nationwide permit notification is filed with the Corps of Engineers: *Provided further*, That the Corps of Engineers, when reporting permit processing times, shall track both the date a permit application is first received and the date the application is considered complete, as well as the reason that the application is not considered complete upon first submission."

**Authority to Delegate to State of Washington Functions of the Secretary Relating to Lake Chelan, Washington**

Section 76 of Pub.L. 95–217 provided that: "The Secretary of the Army, acting through the Chief of Engineers, is authorized to delegate to the State of Washington upon its request all or any part of those functions vested in such Secretary by section 404 of the Federal Water Pollution Control Act [this section] and by sections 9, 10, and 13 of the Act of March 3, 1899 [sections 401, 403, and 407 of this title], relating to Lake Chelan, Washington, if the Secretary determines (1) that such State has the authority, responsibility, and capability to carry out such functions, and (2) that such delegation is in the public interest. Such delegation shall be subject to such terms and conditions as the Secretary deems necessary, including, but not limited to, suspension and revocation for cause of such delegation."

## § 1345. Disposal or use of sewage sludge

**[FWPCA § 405]**

### (a) Permit

Notwithstanding any other provision of this chapter or of any other law, in any case where the disposal of sewage sludge resulting from the operation of a treatment works as defined in section 1292 of this title (including the removal of in-place sewage sludge from one location and its deposit at another location) would result in any pollutant from such sewage sludge entering the navigable waters, such disposal is prohibited except in accordance with a permit issued by the Administrator under section 1342 of this title.

### (b) Issuance of permit; regulations

The Administrator shall issue regulations governing the issuance of permits for the disposal of sewage sludge subject to subsection (a) of this section and section 1342 of this title. Such regulations shall require the application to such disposal of each criterion, factor, procedure, and requirement applicable to a permit issued under section 1342 of this title.

**(c) State permit program**

Each State desiring to administer its own permit program for disposal of sewage sludge subject to subsection (a) of this section within its jurisdiction may do so in accordance with section 1342 of this title.

**(d) Regulations**

**(1) Regulations**

The Administrator, after consultation with appropriate Federal and State agencies and other interested persons, shall develop and publish, within one year after December 27, 1977, and from time to time thereafter, regulations providing guidelines for the disposal of sludge and the utilization of sludge for various purposes. Such regulations shall—

(A) identify uses for sludge, including disposal;

(B) specify factors to be taken into account in determining the measures and practices applicable to each such use or disposal (including publication of information on costs);

(C) identify concentrations of pollutants which interfere with each such use or disposal.

The Administrator is authorized to revise any regulation issued under this subsection.

**(2) Identification and regulation of toxic pollutants**

**(A) On basis of available information**

**(i) Proposed regulations**

Not later than November 30, 1986,[1] the Administrator shall identify those toxic pollutants which, on the basis of available information on their toxicity, persistence, concentration, mobility, or potential for exposure, may be present in sewage sludge in concentrations which may adversely affect public health or the environment, and propose regulations specifying acceptable management practices for sewage sludge containing each such toxic pollutant and establishing numerical limitations for each such pollutant for each use identified under paragraph (1)(A).

**(ii) Final regulations**

Not later than August 31, 1987, and after opportunity for public hearing, the Administrator shall promulgate the regulations required by subparagraph (A)(i).

**(B) Others**

**(i) Proposed regulations**

Not later than July 31, 1987, the Administrator shall identify those toxic pollutants not identified under subparagraph (A)(i) which may be present in sewage sludge in concentrations which may adversely affect public health or the environment, and propose regulations specifying acceptable management practices for sewage sludge containing each such toxic pollutant and establishing numerical limitations for each pollutant for each such use identified under paragraph (1)(A).

**(ii) Final regulations**

Not later than June 15, 1988, the Administrator shall promulgate the regulations required by subparagraph (B)(i).

**(C) Review**

From time to time, but not less often than every 2 years, the Administrator shall review the regulations promulgated under this paragraph for the purpose of identifying additional toxic pollutants and promulgating regulations for such pollutants consistent with the requirements of this paragraph.

**(D) Minimum standards; compliance date**

The management practices and numerical criteria established under subparagraphs (A), (B), and (C) shall be adequate to protect public health and the environment from any reasonably anticipated adverse effects of each pollutant. Such regulations shall require compliance as expeditiously as practicable but in no case later than 12 months after their publication, unless such regulations require the construction of new pollution control facilities, in which case the regulations shall require compliance as expeditiously as practicable but in no case later than two years from the date of their publication.

**(3) Alternative standards**

For purposes of this subsection, if, in the judgment of the Administrator, it is not feasible to prescribe or enforce a numerical limitation for a pollutant identified under paragraph (2), the Administrator may instead promulgate a design, equipment, management practice, or operational standard, or combination thereof, which in the Administrator's judgment is adequate to protect public health and the environment from any reasonably anticipated adverse effects of such pollutant. In the event the Administrator promulgates a design or equipment standard under this subsection, the Administrator shall include as part of such standard such requirements as will assure the proper operation and maintenance of any such element of design or equipment.

(4) Conditions on permits

Prior to the promulgation of the regulations required by paragraph (2), the Administrator shall impose conditions in permits issued to publicly owned treatment works under section 1342 of this title or take such other measures as the Administrator deems appropriate to protect public health and the environment from any adverse effects which may occur from toxic pollutants in sewage sludge.

(5) Limitation on statutory construction

Nothing in this section is intended to waive more stringent requirements established by this chapter or any other law.

(e) Manner of sludge disposal

The determination of the manner of disposal or use of sludge is a local determination, except that it shall be unlawful for any person to dispose of sludge from a publicly owned treatment works or any other treatment works treating domestic sewage for any use for which regulations have been established pursuant to subsection (d) of this section, except in accordance with such regulations.

(f) Implementation of regulations

(1) Through section 1342 permits

Any permit issued under section 1342 of this title to a publicly owned treatment works or any other treatment works treating domestic sewage shall include requirements for the use and disposal of sludge that implement the regulations established pursuant to subsection (d) of this section, unless such requirements have been included in a permit issued under the appropriate provisions of subtitle C of the Solid Waste Disposal Act [42 U.S.C.A. § 6921 et seq.], part C of the Safe Drinking Water Act [42 U.S.C.A. § 300h et seq.], the Marine Protection, Research, and Sanctuaries Act of 1972 [33 U.S.C.A. § 1401 et seq.], or the Clean Air Act [42 U.S.C.A. § 7401 et seq.], or under State permit programs approved by the Administrator, where the Administrator determines that such programs assure compliance with any applicable requirements of this section. Not later than December 15, 1986,[2] the Administrator shall promulgate procedures for approval of State programs pursuant to this paragraph.

(2) Through other permits

In the case of a treatment works described in paragraph (1) that is not subject to section 1342 of this title and to which none of the other above listed permit programs nor approved State permit authority apply, the Administrator may issue a permit to such treatment works solely to impose requirements for the use and disposal of sludge that implement the regulations established pursuant to subsection (d) of this section. The Administrator shall include in the permit appropriate requirements to assure compliance with the regulations established pursuant to subsection (d) of this section. The Administrator shall establish procedures for issuing permits pursuant to this paragraph.

(g) Studies and projects

(1) Grant program; information gathering

The Administrator is authorized to conduct or initiate scientific studies, demonstration projects, and public information and education projects which are designed to promote the safe and beneficial management or use of sewage sludge for such purposes as aiding the restoration of abandoned mine sites, conditioning soil for parks and recreation areas, agricultural and horticultural uses, and other beneficial purposes. For the purposes of carrying out this subsection, the Administrator may make grants to State water pollution control agencies, other public or nonprofit agencies, institutions, organizations, and individuals. In cooperation with other Federal departments and agencies, other public and private agencies, institutions, and organizations, the Administrator is authorized to collect and disseminate information pertaining to the safe and beneficial use of sewage sludge.

(2) Authorization of appropriations

For the purposes of carrying out the scientific studies, demonstration projects, and public information and education projects authorized in this section, there is authorized to be appropriated for fiscal years beginning after September 30, 1986, not to exceed $5,000,000.

(June 30, 1948, c. 758, Title IV, § 405, as added Oct. 18, 1972, Pub.L. 92–500, § 2, 86 Stat. 884, and amended Dec. 27, 1977, Pub.L. 95–217, §§ 54(d), 68, 91 Stat. 1591, 1606; Feb. 4, 1987, Pub.L. 100–4, Title IV, § 406(a)-(c), (f), 101 Stat. 71, 72, 74.)

[1] So in original. Subsec. (d)(2) was enacted by Pub.L. 100–4, which was approved Feb. 4, 1987.

[2] So in original. Subsec. (f) was enacted by Pub.L. 100–4, which was approved Feb. 4, 1987.

## HISTORICAL AND STATUTORY NOTES

**References in Text**

The Solid Waste Disposal Act, referred to in subsec. (f)(1), is Title II of Pub.L. 89–272, Oct. 20, 1965, 79 Stat. 997, as amended generally by Pub.L. 94–580, § 2, Oct. 21, 1976, 90 Stat. 2795. Subtitle C of the Solid Waste Disposal Act is classified generally to subchapter III (section 6921 et seq.) of chapter 82 of Title 42, The Public Health and Welfare. For complete classification of this Act to the Code, see Short Title note set out under section 6901 of Title 42 and Tables.

The Safe Drinking Water Act, referred to in subsec. (f)(1), is Pub.L. 93–523, Dec. 16, 1974, 88 Stat. 1660, as amended. Part C of the Safe Drinking Water Act is classified generally to part C (section 300h et seq.) of subchapter XII of chapter 6A of Title 42, The Public Health and Welfare. For complete classification of this Act to the Code, see Short Title of 1974 Amendments note set out under section 201 of Title 42 and Tables.

The Marine Protection, Research, and Sanctuaries Act of 1972, referred to in subsec. (f)(1), is Pub.L. 92–532, Oct. 23, 1972, 86 Stat. 1052, as amended, which is classified principally to chapter 27 (section 1401 et seq.) of this title. For complete classification of this Act to the Code, see Short Title note set out under section 1401 of this title and Tables.

The Clean Air Act, referred to in subsec. (f)(1), is Act July 14, 1955, c. 360, as amended generally by Pub.L. 88–206, Dec. 17, 1963, 77 Stat. 392, and later by Pub.L. 95–95, Aug. 7, 1977, 91 Stat. 685. The Clean Air Act was originally classified to chapter 15B (section 1857 et seq.) of Title 42, The Public Health and Welfare. On enactment of Pub.L. 95–95, the Act was reclassified to chapter 85 (section 7401 et seq.) of Title 42. For complete classification of this Act to the Code, see short Title note set out under section 7401 of Title 42 and Tables.

**Removal Credits**

Section 406(e) of Pub.L. 100–4 provided that:

"The part of the decision of Natural Resources Defense Council, Inc. v. U.S. Environmental Protection Agency, No. 84–3530 (3d Cir.1986), which addresses section 405(d) of the Federal Water Pollution Control Act [subsec. (d) of this section] is stayed until August 31, 1987, with respect to—

"(1) those publicly owned treatment works the owner or operator of which received authority to revise pretreatment requirements under section 307(b)(1) of such Act [section 1317(b)(1) of this title] before the date of the enactment of this section [Feb. 4, 1987], and

"(2) those publicly owned treatment works the owner or operator of which has submitted an application for authority to revise pretreatment requirements under such section 307(b)(1) [section 1317(b)(1) of this title] which application is pending on such date of enactment [Feb. 4, 1987] and is approved before August 31, 1987.

The Administrator shall not authorize any other removal credits under such Act [this chapter] until the Administrator issues the regulations required by paragraph (2)(A)(ii) of section 405(d) of such Act, as amended by subsection (a) of this section [subsec. (d)(2)(A)(ii) of this section]."

## § 1346. Coastal recreation water quality monitoring and notification

**[FWPCA § 406]**

**(a) Monitoring and notification**

**(1) In general**

Not later than 18 months after October 10, 2000, after consultation and in cooperation with appropriate Federal, State, tribal, and local officials (including local health officials), and after providing public notice and an opportunity for comment, the Administrator shall publish performance criteria for—

**(A)** monitoring and assessment (including specifying available methods for monitoring) of coastal recreation waters adjacent to beaches or similar points of access that are used by the public for attainment of applicable water quality standards for pathogens and pathogen indicators; and

**(B)** the prompt notification of the public, local governments, and the Administrator of any exceeding of or likelihood of exceeding applicable water quality standards for coastal recreation waters described in subparagraph (A).

**(2) Level of protection**

The performance criteria referred to in paragraph (1) shall provide that the activities described in subparagraphs (A) and (B) of that paragraph shall be carried out as necessary for the protection of public health and safety.

**(b) Program development and implementation grants**

**(1) In general**

The Administrator may make grants to States and local governments to develop and implement programs for monitoring and notification for coastal recreation waters adjacent to beaches or similar points of access that are used by the public.

**(2) Limitations**

**(A) In general**

The Administrator may award a grant to a State or a local government to implement a monitoring and notification program if—

**(i)** the program is consistent with the performance criteria published by the Administrator under subsection (a) of this section;

**(ii)** the State or local government prioritizes the use of grant funds for particular coastal recreation waters based on the use of the water and the risk to human health presented by pathogens or pathogen indicators;

**(iii)** the State or local government makes available to the Administrator the factors used to prioritize the use of funds under clause (ii);

**(iv)** the State or local government provides a list of discrete areas of coastal recreation waters that are subject to the program for monitoring and notification for which the grant is provided that specifies any coastal recreation waters for which fiscal constraints will prevent consistency with the performance criteria under subsection (a) of this section; and

**(v)** the public is provided an opportunity to review the program through a process that provides for public notice and an opportunity for comment.

**(B) Grants to local governments**

The Administrator may make a grant to a local government under this subsection for implementation of a monitoring and notification program only if, after the 1-year period beginning on the date of publication of performance criteria under subsection (a)(1) of this section, the Administrator determines that the State is not implementing a program that meets the requirements of this subsection, regardless of whether the State has received a grant under this subsection.

**(3) Other requirements**

**(A) Report**

A State recipient of a grant under this subsection shall submit to the Administrator, in such format and at such intervals as the Administrator determines to be appropriate, a report that describes—

(i) data collected as part of the program for monitoring and notification as described in subsection (c) of this section; and

(ii) actions taken to notify the public when water quality standards are exceeded.

**(B) Delegation**

A State recipient of a grant under this subsection shall identify each local government to which the State has delegated or intends to delegate responsibility for implementing a monitoring and notification program consistent with the performance criteria published under subsection (a) of this section (including any coastal recreation waters for which the authority to implement a monitoring and notification program would be subject to the delegation).

**(4) Federal share**

**(A) In general**

The Administrator, through grants awarded under this section, may pay up to 100 percent of the costs of developing and implementing a program for monitoring and notification under this subsection.

**(B) Non-Federal share**

The non-Federal share of the costs of developing and implementing a monitoring and notification program may be—

(i) in an amount not to exceed 50 percent, as determined by the Administrator in consultation with State, tribal, and local government representatives; and

(ii) provided in cash or in kind.

**(c) Content of State and local government programs**

As a condition of receipt of a grant under subsection (b) of this section, a State or local government program for monitoring and notification under this section shall identify—

(1) lists of coastal recreation waters in the State, including coastal recreation waters adjacent to beaches or similar points of access that are used by the public;

(2) in the case of a State program for monitoring and notification, the process by which the State may delegate to local governments responsibility for implementing the monitoring and notification program;

(3) the frequency and location of monitoring and assessment of coastal recreation waters based on—

(A) the periods of recreational use of the waters;

(B) the nature and extent of use during certain periods;

(C) the proximity of the waters to known point sources and nonpoint sources of pollution; and

(D) any effect of storm events on the waters;

(4)(A) the methods to be used for detecting levels of pathogens and pathogen indicators that are harmful to human health; and

(B) the assessment procedures for identifying short-term increases in pathogens and pathogen indicators that are harmful to human health in coastal recreation waters (including increases in relation to storm events);

(5) measures for prompt communication of the occurrence, nature, location, pollutants involved, and extent of any exceeding of, or likelihood of exceeding, applicable water quality standards for pathogens and pathogen indicators to—

(A) the Administrator, in such form as the Administrator determines to be appropriate; and

(B) a designated official of a local government having jurisdiction over land adjoining the coastal recreation waters for which the failure to meet applicable standards is identified;

(6) measures for the posting of signs at beaches or similar points of access, or functionally equivalent communication measures that are sufficient to give notice to the public that the coastal recreation waters are not meeting or are not expected to meet applicable water quality standards for pathogens and pathogen indicators; and

(7) measures that inform the public of the potential risks associated with water contact activities in the coastal recreation waters that do not meet applicable water quality standards.

**(d) Federal agency programs**

Not later than 3 years after October 10, 2000, each Federal agency that has jurisdiction over coastal recreation waters adjacent to beaches or similar points of access that are used by the public shall develop and implement, through a process that provides for public notice and an opportunity for comment, a monitoring and notification program for the coastal recreation waters that—

(1) protects the public health and safety;

(2) is consistent with the performance criteria published under subsection (a) of this section;

(3) includes a completed report on the information specified in subsection (b)(3)(A) of this section, to be submitted to the Administrator; and

(4) addresses the matters specified in subsection (c) of this section.

**(e) Database**

The Administrator shall establish, maintain, and make available to the public by electronic and other means a national coastal recreation water pollution occurrence database that provides—

(1) the data reported to the Administrator under subsections (b)(3)(A)(i) and (d)(3) of this section; and

(2) other information concerning pathogens and pathogen indicators in coastal recreation waters that—

(A) is made available to the Administrator by a State or local government, from a coastal water quality monitoring program of the State or local government; and

(B) the Administrator determines should be included.

**(f) Technical assistance for monitoring floatable material**

The Administrator shall provide technical assistance to States and local governments for the development of assessment and monitoring procedures for floatable material to protect public health and safety in coastal recreation waters.

**(g) List of waters**

**(1) In general**

Beginning not later than 18 months after the date of publication of performance criteria under subsection (a) of this section, based on information made available to the Administrator, the Administrator shall identify, and maintain a list of, discrete coastal recreation waters adjacent to beaches or similar points of access that are used by the public that—

(A) specifies any waters described in this paragraph that are subject to a monitoring and notification program consistent with the performance criteria established under subsection (a) of this section; and

(B) specifies any waters described in this paragraph for which there is no monitoring and notification program (including waters for which fiscal constraints will prevent the State or the Administrator from performing monitoring and notification consistent with the performance criteria established under subsection (a) of this section).

**(2) Availability**

The Administrator shall make the list described in paragraph (1) available to the public through—

(A) publication in the Federal Register; and

(B) electronic media.

**(3) Updates**

The Administrator shall update the list described in paragraph (1) periodically as new information becomes available.

**(h) EPA implementation**

In the case of a State that has no program for monitoring and notification that is consistent with the performance criteria published under subsection (a) of this section after the last day of the 3-year period beginning on the date on which the Administrator lists waters in the State under subsection (g)(1)(B) of this section, the Administrator shall conduct a monitoring and notification program for the listed waters based on a priority ranking established by the Administrator using funds appropriated for grants under subsection (i) of this section—

(1) to conduct monitoring and notification; and

(2) for related salaries, expenses, and travel.

**(i) Authorization of appropriations**

There is authorized to be appropriated for making grants under subsection (b) of this section, including implementation of monitoring and notification programs by the Administrator under subsection (h), $30,000,000 for each of fiscal years 2001 through 2005.

(June 30, 1948, c. 758, Title IV, § 406, as added Oct. 10, 2000, Pub.L. 106–284, § 4, 114 Stat. 872.)

## SUBCHAPTER V—GENERAL PROVISIONS

### § 1361. Administration [FWPCA § 501]

**(a) Authority of Administrator to prescribe regulations**

The Administrator is authorized to prescribe such regulations as are necessary to carry out his functions under this chapter.

**(b) Utilization of other agency officers and employees**

The Administrator, with the consent of the head of any other agency of the United States, may utilize such officers and employees of such agency as may be found necessary to assist in carrying out the purposes of this chapter.

**(c) Recordkeeping**

Each recipient of financial assistance under this chapter shall keep such records as the Administrator shall prescribe, including records which fully disclose the amount and disposition by such recipient of the proceeds of such assistance, the total cost of the project or undertaking in connection with which such assistance is given or used, and the amount of that portion of the cost of the project or undertaking supplied by other sources, and such other records as will facilitate effective audit.

**(d) Audit**

The Administrator and the Comptroller General of the United States, or any of their duly authorized representatives, shall have access, for the purpose of audit and examination, to any books, documents, papers, and records of the recipients that are pertinent to the grants received under this chapter. For the purpose of carrying out audits and examinations with respect to recipients of Federal assistance under this chapter, the Administrator is authorized to enter into noncompetitive procurement contracts with independent State audit organizations, consistent with chapter 75 of Title 31. Such contracts may only be entered into to the extent and in such amounts as may be provided in advance in appropriation Acts.

**(e) Awards for outstanding technological achievement or innovative processes, methods, or devices in waste treatment and pollution abatement programs**

(1) It is the purpose of this subsection to authorize a program which will provide official recognition by the United States Government to those industrial organizations and political subdivisions of States which during the preceding year demonstrated an outstanding technological achievement or an innovative process, method, or device in their waste treatment and pollution abatement programs. The Administrator shall, in consultation with the appropriate State water pollution control agencies, establish regulations under which such recognition may be applied for and granted, except that no applicant shall be eligible for an award under this subsection if such applicant is not in total compliance with all applicable water quality requirements under this chapter, or otherwise does not have a satisfactory record with respect to environmental quality.

(2) The Administrator shall award a certificate or plaque of suitable design to each industrial organization or political subdivision which qualifies for such recognition under regulations established under this subsection.

(3) The President of the United States, the Governor of the appropriate State, the Speaker of the House of Representatives, and the President pro tempore of the Senate shall be notified of the award by the Administrator and the awarding of such recognition shall be published in the Federal Register.

**(f) Detail of Environmental Protection Agency personnel to State water pollution control agencies**

Upon the request of a State water pollution control agency, personnel of the Environmental Protection Agency may be detailed to such agency for the purpose of carrying out the provisions of this chapter.

(June 30, 1948, c. 758, Title V, § 501, as added Oct. 18, 1972, Pub.L. 92–500, § 2, 86 Stat. 885, and amended Feb. 4, 1987, Pub.L. 100–4, Title V, § 501, 101 Stat. 75.)

### HISTORICAL AND STATUTORY NOTES

**Environmental Court Feasibility Study**

Section 9 of Pub.L. 92–500, authorized the President, acting through the Attorney General, to study the feasibility of establishing a separate court or court system with jurisdiction over environmental matters and required him to report the results of his study, together with his recommendations, to Congress not later than one year after Oct. 18, 1972.

**Transfer of Public Health Service Officers**

Pub.L. 89–234, § 2(b) to (k), Oct. 2, 1965, 79 Stat. 903, authorized the transfer of certain commissioned officers of the Public Health Service to classified positions in the Federal Water Pollution Control Administration, now the Environmental Protection Agency, where such transfer was requested within six months after the establishment of the Administration and made certain administrative provisions relating to pension and retirement rights of the transferees, sick leave benefits, group life insurance, and certain other miscellaneous provisions.

## § 1362. Definitions

**[FWPCA § 502]**

Except as otherwise specifically provided, when used in this chapter:

(1) The term "State water pollution control agency" means the State agency designated by the Governor having responsibility for enforcing State laws relating to the abatement of pollution.

(2) The term "interstate agency" means an agency of two or more States established by or pursuant to an agreement or compact approved by the Congress, or any other agency of two or more States, having substantial powers or duties pertaining to the control of pollution as determined and approved by the Administrator.

(3) The term "State" means a State, the District of Columbia, the Commonwealth of Puerto Rico, the Virgin Islands, Guam, American Samoa, the Commonwealth of the Northern Mariana Islands, and the Trust Territory of the Pacific Islands.

(4) The term "municipality" means a city, town, borough, county, parish, district, association, or other

public body created by or pursuant to State law and having jurisdiction over disposal of sewage, industrial wastes, or other wastes, or an Indian tribe or an authorized Indian tribal organization, or a designated and approved management agency under section 1288 of this title.

(5) The term "person" means an individual, corporation, partnership, association, State, municipality, commission, or political subdivision of a State, or any interstate body.

(6) The term "pollutant" means dredged spoil, solid waste, incinerator residue, sewage, garbage, sewage sludge, munitions, chemical wastes, biological materials, radioactive materials, heat, wrecked or discarded equipment, rock, sand, cellar dirt and industrial, municipal, and agricultural waste discharged into water. This term does not mean (A) "sewage from vessels or a discharge incidental to the normal operation of a vessel of the Armed Forces" within the meaning of section 1322 of this title; or (B) water, gas, or other material which is injected into a well to facilitate production of oil or gas, or water derived in association with oil or gas production and disposed of in a well, if the well used either to facilitate production or for disposal purposes is approved by authority of the State in which the well is located, and if such State determines that such injection or disposal will not result in the degradation of ground or surface water resources.

(7) The term "navigable waters" means the waters of the United States, including the territorial seas.

(8) The term "territorial seas" means the belt of the seas measured from the line of ordinary low water along that portion of the coast which is in direct contact with the open sea and the line marking the seaward limit of inland waters, and extending seaward a distance of three miles.

(9) The term "contiguous zone" means the entire zone established or to be established by the United States under article 24 of the Convention of the Territorial Sea and the Contiguous Zone.

(10) The term "ocean" means any portion of the high seas beyond the contiguous zone.

(11) The term "effluent limitation" means any restriction established by a State or the Administrator on quantities, rates, and concentrations of chemical, physical, biological, and other constituents which are discharged from point sources into navigable waters, the waters of the contiguous zone, or the ocean, including schedules of compliance.

(12) The term "discharge of a pollutant" and the term "discharge of pollutants" each means (A) any addition of any pollutant to navigable waters from any point source, (B) any addition of any pollutant to the waters of the contiguous zone or the ocean from any point source other than a vessel or other floating craft.

(13) The term "toxic pollutant" means those pollutants, or combinations of pollutants, including disease-causing agents, which after discharge and upon exposure, ingestion, inhalation or assimilation into any organism, either directly from the environment or indirectly by ingestion through food chains, will, on the basis of information available to the Administrator, cause death, disease, behavioral abnormalities, cancer, genetic mutations, physiological malfunctions (including malfunctions in reproduction) or physical deformations, in such organisms or their offspring.

(14) The term "point source" means any discernible, confined and discrete conveyance, including but not limited to any pipe, ditch, channel, tunnel, conduit, well, discrete fissure, container, rolling stock, concentrated animal feeding operation, or vessel or other floating craft, from which pollutants are or may be discharged. This term does not include agricultural stormwater discharges and return flows from irrigated agriculture.

(15) The term "biological monitoring" shall mean the determination of the effects on aquatic life, including accumulation of pollutants in tissue, in receiving waters due to the discharge of pollutants (A) by techniques and procedures, including sampling of organisms representative of appropriate levels of the food chain appropriate to the volume and the physical, chemical, and biological characteristics of the effluent, and (B) at appropriate frequencies and locations.

(16) The term "discharge" when used without qualification includes a discharge of a pollutant, and a discharge of pollutants.

(17) The term "schedule of compliance" means a schedule of remedial measures including an enforceable sequence of actions or operations leading to compliance with an effluent limitation, other limitation, prohibition, or standard.

(18) The term "industrial user" means those industries identified in the Standard Industrial Classification Manual, Bureau of the Budget, 1967, as amended and supplemented, under the category of "Division D—Manufacturing" and such other classes of significant waste producers as, by regulation, the Administrator deems appropriate.

(19) The term "pollution" means the man-made or man-induced alteration of the chemical, physical, biological, and radiological integrity of water.

(20) The term "medical waste" means isolation wastes; infectious agents; human blood and blood products; pathological wastes; sharps; body parts; contaminated bedding; surgical wastes and potentially contaminated laboratory wastes; dialysis wastes; and

such additional medical items as the Administrator shall prescribe by regulation.

(21) **Coastal recreation waters**

(A) **In general**

The term "coastal recreation waters" means—

(i) the Great Lakes; and

(ii) marine coastal waters (including coastal estuaries) that are designated under section 1313(c) of this title by a State for use for swimming, bathing, surfing, or similar water contact activities.

(B) **Exclusions**

The term "coastal recreation waters" does not include—

(i) inland waters; or

(ii) waters upstream of the mouth of a river or stream having an unimpaired natural connection with the open sea.

(22) **Floatable material**

(A) **In general**

The term "floatable material" means any foreign matter that may float or remain suspended in the water column.

(B) **Inclusions**

The term "floatable material" includes—

(i) plastic;

(ii) aluminum cans;

(iii) wood products;

(iv) bottles; and

(v) paper products.

(23) **Pathogen indicator**

The term "pathogen indicator" means a substance that indicates the potential for human infectious disease.

(June 30, 1948, c. 758, Title V, § 502, as added Oct. 18, 1972, Pub.L. 92–500, § 2, 86 Stat. 886, and amended Dec. 27, 1977, Pub.L. 95–217, § 33(b), 91 Stat. 1577; Feb. 4, 1987, Pub.L. 100–4, Title V, §§ 502(a), 503, 101 Stat. 75; Nov. 18, 1988, Pub.L. 100–688, Title III, § 3202(a), 102 Stat. 4154; Feb. 10, 1996, Pub.L. 104–106, Div. A, Title III, § 325(c)(3), 110 Stat. 259; Oct. 10, 2000, Pub.L. 106–284, § 5, 114 Stat. 875.)

### HISTORICAL AND STATUTORY NOTES

**Termination of Trust Territory of the Pacific Islands**

For termination of Trust Territory of the Pacific Islands, see note set out preceding 48 U.S.C.A. § 1681.

**Territorial Sea and Contiguous Zone of United States**

For extension of territorial sea and contiguous zone of United States, see Proc. No. 5928 and Proc. No. 7219, respectively, set out as notes under 43 U.S.C.A. § 1331.

**Term "Point Source" to Include Landfill Leachate Collection System**

Section 507 of Pub.L. 100–4 provided that: "For purposes of the Federal Water Pollution Control Act [this chapter], the term 'point source' includes a landfill leachate collection system."

## § 1363. Water Pollution Control Advisory Board

**[FWPCA § 503]**

(a) **Establishment; composition; terms of office**

(1) There is hereby established in the Environmental Protection Agency a Water Pollution Control Advisory Board, composed of the Administrator or his designee, who shall be Chairman, and nine members appointed by the President, none of whom shall be Federal officers or employees. The appointed members, having due regard for the purposes of this chapter, shall be selected from among representatives of various State, interstate, and local governmental agencies, of public or private interests contributing to, affected by, or concerned with pollution, and of other public and private agencies, organizations, or groups demonstrating an active interest in the field of pollution prevention and control, as well as other individuals who are expert in this field.

(2)(A) Each member appointed by the President shall hold office for a term of three years, except that (i) any member appointed to fill a vacancy occurring prior to the expiration of the term for which his predecessor was appointed shall be appointed for the remainder of such term, and (ii) the terms of office of the members first taking office after June 30, 1956, shall expire as follows: three at the end of one year after such date, three at the end of two years after such date, and three at the end of three years after such date, as designated by the President at the time of appointment, and (iii) the term of any member under the preceding provisions shall be extended until the date on which his successor's appointment is effective. None of the members appointed by the President shall be eligible for reappointment within one year after the end of his preceding term.

(B) The members of the Board who are not officers or employees of the United States, while attending conferences or meetings of the Board or while serving at the request of the Administrator, shall be entitled to receive compensation at a rate to be fixed by the Administrator, but not exceeding $100 per diem, including travel-time, and while away from their homes or regular places of business they may be allowed travel expenses, including per diem in lieu of subsistence, as authorized by law for persons in the Government service employed intermittently.

(b) **Functions**

The Board shall advise, consult with, and make recommendations to the Administrator on matters of policy relating to the activities and functions of the Administrator under this chapter.

### (c) Clerical and technical assistance

Such clerical and technical assistance as may be necessary to discharge the duties of the Board shall be provided from the personnel of the Environmental Protection Agency.

(June 30, 1948, c. 758, Title V, § 503, as added Oct. 18, 1972, Pub.L. 92–500, § 2, 86 Stat. 887.)

### HISTORICAL AND STATUTORY NOTES

**References in Text**

Travel expenses, including per diem in lieu of subsistence as authorized by law, referred to in subsec. (a)(2)(B), probably means the allowances authorized by section 5703 of Title 5, Government Organization and Employees.

**Continuation of Term of Office**

Pub.L. 87–88, § 6(c), July 20, 1961, 75 Stat. 207, provided that members of the Water Pollution Control Advisory Board holding office immediately preceding July 20, 1961 were to remain in office as members of the Board as established by section 6(a) of Pub.L. 87–88 until the expiration of the terms of office for which they were originally appointed.

**Terms of Office of Members of Water Pollution Control Advisory Board**

Act July 9, 1956, c. 518, § 3, 70 Stat. 507, provided that the terms of office of members of the Water Pollution Control Advisory Board, holding office on July 9, 1956, were to terminate at the close of business on that date.

**Termination of Advisory Boards**

Advisory Boards in existence on Jan. 5, 1973, to terminate not later than the expiration of the two-year period following Jan. 5, 1973, unless, in the case of a board established by the President or an officer of the Federal Government, such board is renewed by appropriate action prior to the expiration of such two-year period, or in the case of a Board established by the Congress, its duration is otherwise provided for by law, see sections 3(2) and 14 of Pub.L. 92–463, Oct. 6, 1972, 86 Stat. 770, 776, set out in Appendix 2 to Title 5, Government Organization and Employees.

## § 1364. Emergency powers

### [FWPCA § 504]

### (a) Emergency powers

Notwithstanding any other provision of this chapter, the Administrator upon receipt of evidence that a pollution source or combination of sources is presenting an imminent and substantial endangerment to the health of persons or to the welfare of persons where such endangerment is to the livelihood of such persons, such as inability to market shellfish, may bring suit on behalf of the United States in the appropriate district court to immediately restrain any person causing or contributing to the alleged pollution to stop the discharge of pollutants causing or contributing to such pollution or to take such other action as may be necessary.

### (b) Repealed. Pub.L. 96–510, Title III, § 304(a), Dec. 11, 1980, 94 Stat. 2809

(June 30, 1948, c. 758, Title V, § 504, as added Oct. 18, 1972, Pub.L. 92–500, § 2, 86 Stat. 888, and amended Dec. 27, 1977, Pub.L. 95–217, § 69, 91 Stat. 1607; Dec. 11, 1980, Pub.L. 96–510, Title III, § 304(a), 94 Stat. 2809.)

### HISTORICAL AND STATUTORY NOTES

**Effective and Applicability Provisions**

1980 Acts

Amendment by Pub.L. 96–510 effective Dec. 11, 1980, see section 9652 of Title 42, The Public Health and Welfare.

## § 1365. Citizen suits

### [FWPCA § 505]

### (a) Authorization; jurisdiction

Except as provided in subsection (b) of this section and section 1319(g)(6) of this title, any citizen may commence a civil action on his own behalf—

(1) against any person (including (i) the United States, and (ii) any other governmental instrumentality or agency to the extent permitted by the eleventh amendment to the Constitution) who is alleged to be in violation of (A) an effluent standard or limitation under this chapter or (B) an order issued by the Administrator or a State with respect to such a standard or limitation, or

(2) against the Administrator where there is alleged a failure of the Administrator to perform any act or duty under this chapter which is not discretionary with the Administrator.

The district courts shall have jurisdiction, without regard to the amount in controversy or the citizenship of the parties, to enforce such an effluent standard or limitation, or such an order, or to order the Administrator to perform such act or duty, as the case may be, and to apply any appropriate civil penalties under section 1319(d) of this title.

### (b) Notice

No action may be commenced—

(1) under subsection (a)(1) of this section—

(A) prior to sixty days after the plaintiff has given notice of the alleged violation (i) to the Administrator, (ii) to the State in which the alleged violation occurs, and (iii) to any alleged violator of the standard, limitation, or order, or

(B) if the Administrator or State has commenced and is diligently prosecuting a civil or criminal action in a court of the United States, or a State to require compliance with the standard, limitation, or order, but in any such action in a court of the United States any citizen may intervene as a matter of right.

(2) under subsection (a)(2) of this section prior to sixty days after the plaintiff has given notice of such action to the Administrator,

except that such action may be brought immediately after such notification in the case of an action under this section respecting a violation of sections 1316 and 1317(a) of this title. Notice under this subsection shall be given in such manner as the Administrator shall prescribe by regulation.

**(c) Venue; intervention by Administrator; United States interests protected**

(1) Any action respecting a violation by a discharge source of an effluent standard or limitation or an order respecting such standard or limitation may be brought under this section only in the judicial district in which such source is located.

(2) In such action under this section, the Administrator, if not a party, may intervene as a matter of right.

**(3) Protection of interests of United States**

Whenever any action is brought under this section in a court of the United States, the plaintiff shall serve a copy of the complaint on the Attorney General and the Administrator. No consent judgment shall be entered in an action in which the United States is not a party prior to 45 days following the receipt of a copy of the proposed consent judgment by the Attorney General and the Administrator.

**(d) Litigation costs**

The court, in issuing any final order in any action brought pursuant to this section, may award costs of litigation (including reasonable attorney and expert witness fees) to any prevailing or substantially prevailing party, whenever the court determines such award is appropriate. The court may, if a temporary restraining order or preliminary injunction is sought, require the filing of a bond or equivalent security in accordance with the Federal Rules of Civil Procedure.

**(e) Statutory or common law rights not restricted**

Nothing in this section shall restrict any right which any person (or class of persons) may have under any statute or common law to seek enforcement of any effluent standard or limitation or to seek any other relief (including relief against the Administrator or a State agency).

**(f) Effluent standard or limitation**

For purposes of this section, the term "effluent standard or limitation under this chapter" means (1) effective July 1, 1973, an unlawful act under subsection (a) of section 1311 of this title; (2) an effluent limitation or other limitation under section 1311 or 1312 of this title; (3) standard of performance under section 1316 of this title; (4) prohibition, effluent standard or pretreatment standards under section 1317 of this title; (5) certification under section 1341 of this title; (6) a permit or condition thereof issued under section 1342 of this title, which is in effect under this chapter (including a requirement applicable by reason of section 1323 of this title); or (7) a regulation under section 1345(d) of this title,. [1]

**(g) "Citizen" defined**

For the purposes of this section the term "citizen" means a person or persons having an interest which is or may be adversely affected.

**(h) Civil action by State Governors**

A Governor of a State may commence a civil action under subsection (a) of this section, without regard to the limitations of subsection (b) of this section, against the Administrator where there is alleged a failure of the Administrator to enforce an effluent standard or limitation under this chapter the violation of which is occurring in another State and is causing an adverse effect on the public health or welfare in his State, or is causing a violation of any water quality requirement in his State.

(June 30, 1948, c. 758, Title V, § 505, as added Oct. 18, 1972, Pub.L. 92–500, § 2, 86 Stat. 888, and amended Feb. 4, 1987, Pub.L. 100–4, Title III, § 314(c), Title IV, § 406(d)(2), Title V, §§ 504, 505(c), 101 Stat. 49, 73, 75, 76.)

[1] So in original.

### HISTORICAL AND STATUTORY NOTES

**References in Text**

The Federal Rules of Civil Procedure, referred to in subsec. (d), are classified generally to Title 28, Judiciary and Judicial Procedure.

## § 1366. Appearance

**[FWPCA § 506]**

The Administrator shall request the Attorney General to appear and represent the United States in any civil or criminal action instituted under this chapter to which the Administrator is a party. Unless the Attorney General notifies the Administrator within a reasonable time, that he will appear in a civil action, attorneys who are officers or employees of the Environmental Protection Agency shall appear and represent the United States in such action.

(June 30, 1948, c. 758, Title V, § 506, as added Oct. 18, 1972, Pub.L. 92–500, § 2, 86 Stat. 889.)

## § 1367. Employee protection

**[FWPCA § 507]**

**(a) Discrimination against persons filing, instituting, or testifying in proceedings under this chapter prohibited**

No person shall fire, or in any other way discriminate against, or cause to be fired or discriminated against, any employee or any authorized representative of employees by reason of the fact that such employee or representative has filed, instituted, or caused to be filed or instituted any proceeding under this chapter, or has testified or is about to testify in any proceeding resulting from the administration or enforcement of the provisions of this chapter.

**(b) Application for review; investigation; hearing; review**

Any employee or a representative of employees who believes that he has been fired or otherwise discriminated against by any person in violation of subsection (a) of this section may, within thirty days after such alleged violation occurs, apply to the Secretary of Labor for a review of such firing or alleged discrimination. A copy of the application shall be sent to such person who shall be the respondent. Upon receipt of such application, the Secretary of Labor shall cause such investigation to be made as he deems appropriate. Such investigation shall provide an opportunity for a public hearing at the request of any party to such review to enable the parties to present information relating to such alleged violation. The parties shall be given written notice of the time and place of the hearing at least five days prior to the hearing. Any such hearing shall be of record and shall be subject to section 554 of Title 5. Upon receiving the report of such investigation, the Secretary of Labor shall make findings of fact. If he finds that such violation did occur, he shall issue a decision, incorporating an order therein and his findings, requiring the party committing such violation to take such affirmative action to abate the violation as the Secretary of Labor deems appropriate, including, but not limited to, the rehiring or reinstatement of the employee or representative of employees to his former position with compensation. If he finds that there was no such violation, he shall issue an order denying the application. Such order issued by the Secretary of Labor under this subparagraph shall be subject to judicial review in the same manner as orders and decisions of the Administrator are subject to judicial review under this chapter.

**(c) Costs and expenses**

Whenever an order is issued under this section to abate such violation, at the request of the applicant, a sum equal to the aggregate amount of all costs and expenses (including the attorney's fees), as determined by the Secretary of Labor, to have been reasonably incurred by the applicant for, or in connection with, the institution and prosecution of such proceedings, shall be assessed against the person committing such violation.

**(d) Deliberate violations by employee acting without direction from his employer or his agent**

This section shall have no application to any employee who, acting without direction from his employer (or his agent) deliberately violates any prohibition of effluent limitation or other limitation under section 1311 or 1312 of this title, standards of performance under section 1316 of this title, effluent standard, prohibition or pretreatment standard under section 1317 of this title, or any other prohibition or limitation established under this chapter.

**(e) Investigations of employment reductions**

The Administrator shall conduct continuing evaluations of potential loss or shifts of employment which may result from the issuance of any effluent limitation or order under this chapter, including, where appropriate, investigating threatened plant closures or reductions in employment allegedly resulting from such limitation or order. Any employee who is discharged or laid-off, threatened with discharge or lay-off, or otherwise discriminated against by any person because of the alleged results of any effluent limitation or order issued under this chapter, or any representative of such employee, may request the Administrator to conduct a full investigation of the matter. The Administrator shall thereupon investigate the matter and, at the request of any party, shall hold public hearings on not less than five days notice, and shall at such hearings require the parties, including the employer involved, to present information relating to the actual or potential effect of such limitation or order on employment and on any alleged discharge, lay-off, or other discrimination and the detailed reasons or justification therefor. Any such hearing shall be of record and shall be subject to section 554 of Title 5. Upon receiving the report of such investigation, the Administrator shall make findings of fact as to the effect of such effluent limitation or order on employment and on the alleged discharge, lay-off, or discrimination and shall make such recommendations as he deems appropriate. Such report, findings, and recommendations shall be available to the public. Nothing in this subsection shall be construed to require or authorize the Administrator to modify or withdraw any effluent limitation or order issued under this chapter.

(June 30, 1948, c. 758, Title V, § 507, as added Oct. 18, 1972, Pub.L. 92–500, § 2, 86 Stat. 890.)

## § 1368. Federal procurement

**[FWPCA § 508]**

**(a) Contracts with violators prohibited**

No Federal agency may enter into any contract with any person, who has been convicted of any offense under section 1319(c) of this title, for the procurement of goods, materials, and services if such contract is to be performed at any facility at which the violation which gave rise to such conviction occurred, and if such facility is owned, leased, or supervised by such person. The prohibition in the preceding sentence shall continue until the Administrator certifies that the condition giving rise to such conviction has been corrected.

**(b) Notification of agencies**

The Administrator shall establish procedures to provide all Federal agencies with the notification necessary for the purposes of subsection (a) of this section.

**(c) Omitted**

**(d) Exemptions**

The President may exempt any contract, loan, or grant from all or part of the provisions of this section where he determines such exemption is necessary in the paramount interest of the United States and he shall notify the Congress of such exemption.

**(e) Omitted**

**(f) Contractor certification or contract clause in acquisition of commercial items**

(1) No certification by a contractor, and no contract clause, may be required in the case of a contract for the acquisition of commercial items in order to implement a prohibition or requirement of this section or a prohibition or requirement issued in the implementation of this section.

(2) In paragraph (1), the term "commercial item" has the meaning given such term in section 403(12) of Title 41.

(June 30, 1948, c. 758, Title V, § 508, as added Oct. 18, 1972, Pub.L. 92–500, § 2, 86 Stat. 891, and amended Oct. 13, 1994, Pub.L. 103–355, Title VIII, § 8301(a), 108 Stat. 3396.)

## HISTORICAL AND STATUTORY NOTES

**Codifications**

Subsec. (c) authorized the President to cause to be issued, not more than 180 days after October 18, 1972, an order (1) requiring each Federal agency authorized to enter into contracts or to extend Federal assistance by way of grant, loan, or contract, to effectuate the purpose and policy of this chapter, and (2) setting forth procedures, sanctions and penalties as the President determines necessary to carry out such requirement.

Subsec. (e) of this section, which required the President to annually report to Congress on measures taken in compliance with the purpose and intent of this section, terminated, effective May 15, 2000, pursuant to section 3003 of Pub.L. 104–66, as amended, set out as a note under 31 U.S.C.A. § 1113. See, also, page 20 of House Document No. 103–7.

**Effective and Applicability Provisions**

1994 Acts

Amendment by section 8301(a) of Pub.L. 103–355 effective Oct. 13, 1994, except as otherwise provided, see section 10001 of Pub.L. 103–355, set out as a note under section 251 of Title 41, Public Contracts.

**Administration of Chapter With Respect to Federal Contracts, Grants, or Loans**

For provisions concerning the administration of this chapter with respect to Federal contracts, grants, or loans, see Ex. Ord. No. 11738, Sept. 10, 1973, 38 F.R. 25161, set out as a note under section 7606 of Title 42, The Public Health and Welfare.

## § 1369. Administrative procedure and judicial review

[FWPCA § 509]

**(a) Subpenas**

(1) For purposes of obtaining information under section 1315 of this title, or carrying out section 1367(e) of this title, the Administrator may issue subpenas for the attendance and testimony of witnesses and the production of relevant papers, books, and documents, and he may administer oaths. Except for effluent data, upon a showing satisfactory to the Administrator that such papers, books, documents, or information or particular part thereof, if made public, would divulge trade secrets or secret processes, the Administrator shall consider such record, report, or information or particular portion thereof confidential in accordance with the purposes of section 1905 of Title 18, except that such paper, book, document, or information may be disclosed to other officers, employees, or authorized representatives of the United States concerned with carrying out this chapter, or when relevant in any proceeding under this chapter. Witnesses summoned shall be paid the same fees and mileage that are paid witnesses in the courts of the United States. In case of contumacy or refusal to obey a subpena served upon any person under this subsection, the district court of the United States for any district in which such person is found or resides or transacts business, upon application by the United States and after notice to such person, shall have jurisdiction to issue an order requiring such person to appear and give testimony before the Administrator, to appear and produce papers, books, and documents before the Administrator, or both, and any failure to obey such order of the court may be punished by such court as a contempt thereof.

(2) The district courts of the United States are authorized, upon application by the Administrator, to issue subpenas for attendance and testimony of witnesses and the production of relevant papers, books, and documents, for purposes of obtaining information under sections 1314(b) and (c) of this title. Any papers, books, documents, or other information or part thereof, obtained by reason of such a subpena shall be subject to the same requirements as are provided in paragraph (1) of this subsection.

**(b) Review of Administrator's actions; selection of court; fees**

(1) Review of the Administrator's action (A) in promulgating any standard of performance under section 1316 of this title, (B) in making any determination pursuant to section 1316(b)(1)(C) of this title, (C) in promulgating any effluent standard, prohibition, or pretreatment standard under section 1317 of this title, (D) in making any determination as to a State permit program submitted under section 1342(b) of this title, (E) in approving or promulgating any effluent limitation or other limitation under section 1311, 1312, 1316, or 1345 of this title, (F) in issuing or denying any permit under section 1342 of this title, and (G) in promulgating any individual control strategy under section 1314(*l*) of this title, may be had by any interested person in the Circuit Court of Appeals of the United States for the Federal judicial district in which such person resides or transacts business which is directly affected by such action upon application by such person. Any such application shall be made within 120 days from the date of such determination, approval, promulgation, issuance or denial, or after such date only if such application is based solely on grounds which arose after such 120th day.

(2) Action of the Administrator with respect to which review could have been obtained under paragraph (1) of this subsection shall not be subject to judicial review in any civil or criminal proceeding for enforcement.

**(3) Award of fees**

In any judicial proceeding under this subsection, the court may award costs of litigation (including reasonable attorney and expert witness fees) to any prevailing or substantially prevailing party whenever it determines that such award is appropriate.

**(c) Additional evidence**

In any judicial proceeding brought under subsection (b) of this section in which review is sought of a determination under this chapter required to be made on the record after notice and opportunity for hearing, if any party applies to the court for leave to adduce additional evidence, and shows to the satisfaction of the court that such additional evidence is material and that there were reasonable grounds for the failure to adduce such evidence in the proceeding before the Administrator, the court may order such additional evidence (and evidence in rebuttal thereof) to be taken before the Administrator, in such manner and upon such terms and conditions as the court may deem proper. The Administrator may modify his findings as to the facts, or make new findings, by reason of the additional evidence so taken and he shall file such modified or new findings, and his recommendation, if any, for the modification or setting aside of his original determination, with the return of such additional evidence.

(June 30, 1948, c. 758, Title V, § 509, as added Oct. 18, 1972, Pub.L. 92–500, § 2, 86 Stat. 891, and amended Dec. 28, 1973, Pub.L. 93–207, § 1(6), 87 Stat. 906; Feb. 4, 1987, Pub.L. 100–4, Title III, § 308(b), Title IV, § 406(d)(3), Title V, § 505(a), (b), 101 Stat. 39, 73, 75; Jan. 8, 1988, Pub.L. 100–236, § 2, 101 Stat. 1732.)

### HISTORICAL AND STATUTORY NOTES

**Effective and Applicability Provisions**

1988 Acts

Amendment to subsec. (b) of this section by Pub.L. 100–236 to take effect 180 days after Jan. 8, 1988, see section 3 of Pub.L. 100–236, set out as a note under section 2112 of Title 28, Judiciary and Judicial Procedure.

## § 1370. State authority

**[FWPCA § 510]**

Except as expressly provided in this chapter, nothing in this chapter shall (1) preclude or deny the right of any State or political subdivision thereof or interstate agency to adopt or enforce (A) any standard or limitation respecting discharges of pollutants, or (B) any requirement respecting control or abatement of pollution; except that if an effluent limitation, or other limitation, effluent standard, prohibition, pretreatment standard, or standard of performance is in effect under this chapter, such State or political subdivision or interstate agency may not adopt or enforce any effluent limitation, or other limitation, effluent standard, prohibition, pretreatment standard, or standard of performance which is less stringent than the effluent limitation, or other limitation, effluent standard, prohibition, pretreatment standard, or standard of performance under this chapter; or (2) be construed as impairing or in any manner affecting any right or jurisdiction of the States with respect to the waters (including boundary waters) of such States.

(June 30, 1948, c. 758, Title V, § 510, as added Oct. 18, 1972, Pub.L. 92–500, § 2, 86 Stat. 893.)

## § 1371. Authority under other laws and regulations

**[FWPCA § 511]**

**(a) Impairment of authority or functions of officials and agencies; treaty provisions**

This chapter shall not be construed as (1) limiting the authority or functions of any officer or agency of the United States under any other law or regulation not inconsistent with this chapter; (2) affecting or impairing the authority of the Secretary of the Army (A) to maintain navigation or (B) under the Act of March 3, 1899 (30 Stat. 1112); except that any permit issued under section 1344 of this title shall be conclusive as to the effect on water quality of any discharge resulting from any activity subject to section 403 of this title, or (3) affecting or impairing the provisions of any treaty of the United States.

**(b) Discharges of pollutants into navigable waters**

Discharges of pollutants into the navigable waters subject to the Rivers and Harbors Act of 1910 (36 Stat. 593; 33 U.S.C. 421) and the Supervisory Harbors Act of 1888 (25 Stat. 209; 33 U.S.C. 441–451b) shall be regulated pursuant to this chapter, and not subject to such Act of 1910 and the Act of 1888 except as to effect on navigation and anchorage.

**(c) Action of the Administrator deemed major Federal action; construction of the National Environmental Policy Act of 1969**

(1) Except for the provision of Federal financial assistance for the purpose of assisting the construction of publicly owned treatment works as authorized by section 1281 of this title, and the issuance of a permit under section 1342 of this title for the discharge of any pollutant by a new source as defined in section 1316 of this title, no action of the Administrator taken pursuant to this chapter shall be deemed a major Federal action significantly affecting the quality of the human environment within the meaning of the National Environmental Policy Act of 1969 (83 Stat. 852) [42 U.S.C.A. § 4321 et seq.]; and

(2) Nothing in the National Environmental Policy Act of 1969 (83 Stat. 852) shall be deemed to—

(A) authorize any Federal agency authorized to license or permit the conduct of any activity which may result in the discharge of a pollutant into the navigable waters to review any effluent limitation or other requirement established pursuant to this chapter or the adequacy of any certification under section 1341 of this title; or

(B) authorize any such agency to impose, as a condition precedent to the issuance of any license or permit, any effluent limitation other than any such limitation established pursuant to this chapter.

**(d) Consideration of international water pollution control agreements**

Notwithstanding this chapter or any other provision of law, the Administrator (1) shall not require any State to consider in the development of the ranking in order of priority of needs for the construction of treatment works (as defined in subchapter II of this chapter), any water pollution control agreement which may have been entered into between the United States and any other nation, and (2) shall not consider any such agreement in the approval of any such priority ranking.

(June 30, 1948, c. 758, Title V, § 511, as added Oct. 18, 1972, Pub.L. 92–500, § 2, 86 Stat. 893, and amended Jan. 2, 1974, Pub.L. 93–243, § 3, 87 Stat. 1069.)

### HISTORICAL AND STATUTORY NOTES

**References in Text**

The Act of March 3, 1899, referred to in subsec. (a), is Act Mar. 3, 1899, c. 425, 30 Stat. 1121, as amended, which enacted sections 401, 403, 404, 406, 407, 408, 409, 411 to 416, 418, 502, 549, and 687 of this title and amended section 686 of this title. For complete classification of this Act to the Code, see Tables.

The Rivers and Harbors Act of 1910, referred to in subsec. (b), probably means Act June 23, 1910, c. 359, 36 Stat. 593.

The Supervisory Harbors Act of 1888, referred to in subsec. (b), probably means Act June 29, 1888, c. 496, 25 Stat. 209, as amended, which is classified generally to subchapter III (section 441 et seq.) of chapter 9 of this title. For complete classification of this Act to the Code, see Tables .

The National Environmental Policy Act of 1969, referred to in subsec. (c), is Pub.L. 91–190, Jan. 1, 1970, 83 Stat. 852, as amended, which is classified generally to chapter 55 (section 4321 et seq.) of Title 42, The Public Health and Welfare. For complete classification of this Act to the Code, see Short Title note set out under section 4321 of Title 42 and Tables .

## § 1372. Labor standards

**[FWPCA § 513]**

The Administrator shall take such action as may be necessary to insure that all laborers and mechanics employed by contractors or subcontractors on treatment works for which grants are made under this chapter shall be paid wages at rates not less than those prevailing for the same type of work on similar construction in the immediate locality, as determined by the Secretary of Labor, in accordance with sections 3141 to 3144, 3146, 3147 of Title 40. The Secretary of Labor shall have, with respect to the labor standards specified in this subsection [1], the authority and functions set forth in Reorganization Plan Numbered 14 of 1950 (15 F.R. 3176) and section 3145 of Title 40.

(June 30, 1948, c. 758, Title V, § 513, as added Oct. 18, 1972, Pub.L. 92–500, § 2, 86 Stat. 894.)

[1] So in original. Probably should be "section".

### HISTORICAL AND STATUTORY NOTES

**References in Text**

Reorganization Plan Numbered 14 of 1950, referred to in text, is Reorg. Plan No. 14 of 1950, eff. May 24, 1950, 15 F.R. 3176, 64 Stat. 1267, which is set out in Appendix 1 of Title 5, Government Organization and Employees.

**Codifications**

In text, "sections 3141 to 3144, 3146, 3147 of Title 40" substituted for "the Davis–Bacon Act of March 3, 1931 (46 Stat. 1494; 40 U.S.C. 276a through 276a–5)" on authority of Pub.L. 107–217, § 5(c), Aug. 21, 2002, 116 Stat. 1301, which is set out as a note preceding 40 U.S.C.A. § 101. Pub.L. 107–217, § 1, enacted Title 40 into positive law. The Davis–Bacon Act is Act Mar. 3, 1931, c. 411, 46 Stat. 1494, which was classified to former 40 U.S.C.A. §§ 276a, 276a–1 to 276a–6, prior to being repealed by Pub.L. 107–217, § 6(b),

Aug. 21, 2002, 116 Stat. 1308, and its substance reenacted as 40 U.S.C.A. §§ 3141 to 3144, 3146, 3147.

In text, "section 3145 of Title 40" substituted for "section 276c of Title 40", which originally read "section 2 of the Act of June 13, 1934, as amended (48 Stat. 948; 40 U.S.C. 276c)", on authority of Pub.L. 107–217, § 5(c), Aug. 21, 2002, 116 Stat. 1301, which is set out as a note preceding 40 U.S.C.A. § 101. Pub.L. 107–217, § 1, enacted Title 40 into positive law. Section 2 of the Act of June 13, 1934, as amended, is Act June 13, 1934, c. 482, § 2, 48 Stat. 948, which was classified to former 40 U.S.C.A. § 276c prior to being repealed by Pub.L. 107–217, § 6(b), Aug. 21, 2002, 116 Stat. 1309, and its substance reenacted as 40 U.S.C.A. § 3145.

## § 1373. Public health agency coordination

[FWPCA § 514]

The permitting agency under section 1342 of this title shall assist the applicant for a permit under such section in coordinating the requirements of this chapter with those of the appropriate public health agencies.

(June 30, 1948, c. 758, Title V, § 514, as added Oct. 18, 1972, Pub.L. 92–500, § 2, 86 Stat. 894.)

## § 1374. Effluent Standards and Water Quality Information Advisory Committee

[FWPCA § 515]

### (a) Establishment; membership; term

(1) There is established on[1] Effluent Standards and Water Quality Information Advisory Committee, which shall be composed of a Chairman and eight members who shall be appointed by the Administrator within sixty days after October 18, 1972.

(2) All members of the Committee shall be selected from the scientific community, qualified by education, training, and experience to provide, assess, and evaluate scientific and technical information on effluent standards and limitations.

(3) Members of the Committee shall serve for a term of four years, and may be reappointed.

### (b) Action on proposed regulations

(1) No later than one hundred and eighty days prior to the date on which the Administrator is required to publish any proposed regulations required by section 1314(b) of this title, any proposed standard of performance for new sources required by section 1316 of this title, or any proposed toxic effluent standard required by section 1317 of this title, he shall transmit to the Committee a notice of intent to propose such regulations. The Chairman of the Committee within ten days after receipt of such notice may publish a notice of a public hearing by the Committee, to be held within thirty days.

(2) No later than one hundred and twenty days after receipt of such notice, the Committee shall transmit to the Administrator such scientific and technical information as is in its possession, including that presented at any public hearing, related to the subject matter contained in such notice.

(3) Information so transmitted to the Administrator shall constitute a part of the administrative record and comments on any proposed regulations or standards as information to be considered with other comments and information in making any final determinations.

(4) In preparing information for transmittal, the Committee shall avail itself of the technical and scientific services of any Federal agency, including the United States Geological Survey and any national environmental laboratories which may be established.

### (c) Secretary; legal counsel; compensation

(1) The Committee shall appoint and prescribe the duties of a Secretary, and such legal counsel as it deems necessary. The Committee shall appoint such other employees as it deems necessary to exercise and fulfill its powers and responsibilities. The compensation of all employees appointed by the Committee shall be fixed in accordance with chapter 51 and subchapter III of chapter 53 of Title 5.

(2) Members of the Committee shall be entitled to receive compensation at a rate to be fixed by the President but not in excess of the maximum rate of pay for grade GS–18, as provided in the General Schedule under section 5332 of Title 5.

### (d) Quorum; special panel

Five members of the Committee shall constitute a quorum, and official actions of the Committee shall be taken only on the affirmative vote of at least five members. A special panel composed of one or more members upon order of the Committee shall conduct any hearing authorized by this section and submit the transcript of such hearing to the entire Committee for its action thereon.

### (e) Rules

The Committee is authorized to make such rules as are necessary for the orderly transaction of its business.

(June 30, 1948, c. 758, Title V, § 515, as added Oct. 18, 1972, Pub.L. 92–500, § 2, 86 Stat. 894.)

[1] So in original. Probably should be "an".

### HISTORICAL AND STATUTORY NOTES

**Termination of Advisory Committees**

Advisory Committees in existence on Jan. 5, 1973, to terminate not later than the expiration of the two-year period following Jan. 5, 1973, unless, in the case of a committee established by the President or an officer of the Federal Government, such committee is renewed by appropriate action prior to the expiration of such two-year period, or in the case of a committee established by the Congress, its duration is otherwise provided by law, see section 14 of Pub.L. 92–463, Oct. 6, 1972, 86 Stat. 770, set out in Appendix 2 to Title 5, Government Organization and Employees.

**References in Other Laws to GS–16, 17, or 18 Pay Rates**

References in laws to the rates of pay for GS–16, 17, or 18, or to maximum rates of pay under the General Schedule, to be considered references to rates payable under specified sections of Title 5, see section 529 [Title I, § 101(c)(1)] of Pub.L. 101–509, set out in a note under 5 U.S.C.A. § 5376.

## § 1375. Reports to Congress; detailed estimates and comprehensive study on costs; State estimates

### [FWPCA § 516]

**(a) Implementation of chapter objectives; status and progress of programs**

Within ninety days following the convening of each session of Congress, the Administrator shall submit to the Congress a report, in addition to any other report required by this chapter, on measures taken toward implementing the objective of this chapter, including, but not limited to, (1) the progress and problems associated with developing comprehensive plans under section 1252 of this title, areawide plans under section 1288 of this title, basin plans under section 1289 of this title, and plans under section 1313(e) of this title; (2) a summary of actions taken and results achieved in the field of water pollution control research, experiments, studies, and related matters by the Administrator and other Federal agencies and by other persons and agencies under Federal grants or contracts; (3) the progress and problems associated with the development of effluent limitations and recommended control techniques; (4) the status of State programs, including a detailed summary of the progress obtained as compared to that planned under State program plans for development and enforcement of water quality requirements; (5) the identification and status of enforcement actions pending or completed under this chapter during the preceding year; (6) the status of State, interstate, and local pollution control programs established pursuant to, and assisted by, this chapter; (7) a summary of the results of the survey required to be taken under section 1290 of this title; (8) his activities including recommendations under sections 1259 through 1261 of this title; and (9) all reports and recommendations made by the Water Pollution Control Advisory Board."

**(b)(1)** The Administrator, in cooperation with the States, including water pollution control agencies and other water pollution control planning agencies, shall make (A) a detailed estimate of the cost of carrying out the provisions of this chapter; (B) a detailed estimate, biennially revised, of the cost of construction of all needed publicly owned treatment works in all of the States and of the cost of construction of all needed publicly owned treatment works in each of the States; (C) a comprehensive study of the economic impact on affected units of government of the cost of installation of treatment facilities; and (D) a comprehensive analysis of the national requirements for and the cost of treating municipal, industrial, and other effluent to attain the water quality objectives as established by this chapter or applicable State law. The Administrator shall submit such detailed estimate and such comprehensive study of such cost to the Congress no later than February 10 of each odd-numbered year. Whenever the Administrator, pursuant to this subsection, requests and receives an estimate of cost from a State, he shall furnish copies of such estimate together with such detailed estimate to Congress.

**(2)** Notwithstanding the second sentence of paragraph (1) of this subsection, the Administrator shall make a preliminary detailed estimate called for by subparagraph (B) of such paragraph and shall submit such preliminary detailed estimate to the Congress no later than September 3, 1974. The Administrator shall require each State to prepare an estimate of cost for such State, and shall utilize the survey form EPA–1, O.M.B. No. 158–R0017, prepared for the 1973 detailed estimate, except that such estimate shall include all costs of compliance with section 1281(g)(2)(A) of this title and water quality standards established pursuant to section 1313 of this title, and all costs of treatment works as defined in section 1292(2) of this title, including all eligible costs of constructing sewage collection systems and correcting excessive infiltration or inflow and all eligible costs of correcting combined storm and sanitary sewer problems and treating storm water flows. The survey form shall be distributed by the Administrator to each State no later than January 31, 1974."

**(c) Status of combined sewer overflows in municipal treatment works operations**

The Administrator shall submit to the Congress by October 1, 1978, a report on the status of combined sewer overflows in municipal treatment works operations. The report shall include (1) the status of any projects funded under this chapter to address combined sewer overflows (2) a listing by State of combined sewer overflow needs identified in the 1977 State priority listings, (3) an estimate for each applicable municipality of the number of years necessary, assuming an annual authorization and appropriation for the construction grants program of $5,000,000,000, to correct combined sewer overflow problems, (4) an analysis using representative municipalities faced with major combined sewer overflow needs, of the annual discharges of pollutants from overflows in comparison to treated effluent discharges, (5) an analysis of the technological alternatives available to municipalities to correct major combined sewer overflow problems, and (6) any recommendations of the Administrator for legislation to address the problem of combined sewer overflows, including whether a separate authorization and grant program should be established by the Congress to address combined sewer overflows.

**(d) Legislative recommendations on program requiring coordination between water supply and wastewater control plans as condition for construction grants; public hearing**

The Administrator, in cooperation with the States, including water pollution control agencies, and other water pollution control planning agencies, and water supply and water resources agencies of the States and the United States shall submit to Congress, within two years of December 27, 1977, a report with recommendations for legislation on a program to require coordination between water supply and wastewater control plans as a condition to grants for construction of treatment works under this chapter. No such report shall be submitted except after opportunity for public hearings on such proposed report.

**(e) State revolving fund report**

**(1) In general**

Not later than February 10, 1990, the Administrator shall submit to Congress a report on the financial status and operations of water pollution control revolving funds established by the States under subchapter VI of this chapter. The Administrator shall prepare such report in cooperation with the States, including water pollution control agencies and other water pollution control planning and financing agencies.

**(2) Contents**

The report under this subsection shall also include the following:

(A) an inventory of the facilities that are in significant noncompliance with the enforceable requirements of this chapter;

(B) an estimate of the cost of construction necessary to bring such facilities into compliance with such requirements;

(C) an assessment of the availability of sources of funds for financing such needed construction, including an estimate of the amount of funds available for providing assistance for such construction through September 30, 1999, from the water pollution control revolving funds established by the States under subchapter VI of this chapter;

(D) an assessment of the operations, loan portfolio, and loan conditions of such revolving funds;

(E) an assessment of the effect on user charges of the assistance provided by such revolving funds compared to the assistance provided with funds appropriated pursuant to section 1287 of this title; and

(F) an assessment of the efficiency of the operation and maintenance of treatment works constructed with assistance provided by such revolving funds compared to the efficiency of the operation and maintenance of treatment works constructed with assistance provided under section 1281 of this title.

(June 30, 1948, c. 758, Title V, § 516, as added Oct. 18, 1972, Pub.L. 92–500, § 2, 86 Stat. 895, and amended Jan. 2, 1974, Pub.L. 93–243, § 4, 87 Stat. 1069; Dec. 27, 1977, Pub.L. 95–217, §§ 70–72, 91 Stat. 1608, 1609; Feb. 4, 1987, Pub.L. 100–4, Title II, § 212(c), 101 Stat. 27; Dec. 21, 1995, Pub.L. 104–66, Title II, § 2021(d), 109 Stat. 727; Nov. 10, 1998, Pub.L. 105–362, Title V, § 501(d)(1), 112 Stat. 3283; Nov. 27, 2002, Pub.L. 107–303, Title III, § 302(b)(1), 116 Stat. 2361.)

## HISTORICAL AND STATUTORY NOTES

**Effective and Applicability Provisions**

2002 Acts

Effective November 10, 1998, section 501 of the Federal Reports Elimination Act of 1998 [Pub.L. 105–362, Title V, § 501, Nov. 10, 1998, 112 Stat. 3283] is amended by striking subsections (a), (b), (c), and (d) [amending this section and others, see Tables for complete classification]. The Federal Water Pollution Control Act (33 U.S.C.A. § 1254(n)(3)) shall be applied and administered on and after Nov. 27, 2002 as if the amendments made by subsections (a), (b), (c), and (d) of Pub.L. 105–362, § 501, had not been enacted, see Pub.L. 107–303, § 302(b)(2), set out as a note under 33 U.S.C.A. § 1254.

**Studies and Reports**

Pub.L. 100–4, Title III, § 308(g), Feb. 4, 1987, 101 Stat. 40, directed the Administrator to conduct a water quality improvement study and report the results of such study to specified Congressional committees not later than 2 years after Feb. 4, 1987.

Pub.L. 100–4, Title III, § 314(b), Feb. 4, 1987, 101 Stat. 49, directed that the Secretary of the Army and the Administrator each prepare a report on enforcement mechanisms and submit the reports to Congress not later than Dec. 1, 1988.

Pub.L. 100–4, Title IV, § 404(c), Feb. 4, 1987, 101 Stat. 69, which directed the Administrator to study the extent to which States have adopted water quality standards in accordance with section 1313a of this title and the extent to which modifications of permits issued under section 1342(a)(1)(B) of this title for the purpose of reflecting revisions of water quality standards be encouraged and to submit a report on such study to Congress not later than 2 years after Feb. 4, 1987, was repealed by Pub.L. 104–66, Title II, § 2021(e)(1), Dec. 21, 1995, 109 Stat. 727.

Pub.L. 100–4, Title V, § 516, Feb. 4, 1987, 101 Stat. 86, directed the Administrator to conduct a study of de minimis discharges and report the results of such study to specified Congressional committees not later than 1 year after Feb. 4, 1987.

Pub.L. 100–4, Title V, § 517, Feb. 4, 1987, 100 Stat. 86, directed the Administrator to conduct a study of effectiveness of innovative and alternative processes and techniques and report the results of such study to specified Congressional committees not later than 1 year after Feb. 4, 1987.

Pub.L. 100–4, Title V, § 518, Feb. 4, 1987, 101 Stat. 86, directed the Administrator to conduct a study of testing procedures and report the results of such study to specified Congressional committees not later than 1 year after Feb. 4, 1987.

Pub.L. 100–4, Title V, § 519, Feb. 4, 1987, 100 Stat. 87, directed the Administrator to conduct a study of pretreatment of toxic pollutants and report the results of such study to specified Congressional committees not later than 4 years after Feb. 4, 1987.

Pub.L. 100–4, Title V, § 520, Feb. 4, 1987, 101 Stat. 87, directed the Administrator, in conjunction with State and local agencies, to conduct studies of water pollution problems in aquifers and report the result of such studies to Congress not later than 2 years after Feb. 4, 1987.

Pub.L. 100–4, Title V, § 522, Feb. 4, 1987, 101 Stat. 88, directed the Administrator to conduct a study on sulfide corrosion and report the results of such study to specified Congressional committees not later than 1 year after Feb. 4, 1987.

Pub.L. 100–4, Title V, § 523, Feb. 4, 1987, 101 Stat. 89, directed the Administrator to conduct a study of rainfall induced infiltration into sewer systems and report the results of such study to Congress not later than 1 year after Feb. 4, 1987.

Pub.L. 100–4, Title V, § 524, Feb. 4, 1987, 101 Stat. 89, directed the Administrator to conduct a study of dam water quality and report the results of such study to Congress not later than Dec. 31, 1987.

Pub.L. 100–4, Title V, § 525, Feb. 4, 1987, 101 Stat. 89, directed the Administrator to conduct a study of pollution in Lake Pend Oreille, Idaho, and the Clark Fork River and its tributaries, Idaho, Montana, and Washington, and to report to Congress the findings and recommendations.

**Termination of Reporting Requirements**

For termination, effective May 15, 2000, of provisions in this section relating to the requirement that the Administrator submit detailed estimates and comprehensive studies to Congress no later than February 10 of each odd-numbered year, see section 3003 of Pub.L. 104–66, as amended, set out as a note under 31 U.S.C.A. § 1113, and pages 163 and 165 of House Document No. 103–7.

**Detailed Estimates, Comprehensive Study, and Comprehensive Analysis; Report to Congress not Later Than December 31, 1982**

Pub.L. 97–117, § 25, Dec. 29, 1981, 95 Stat. 1633, provided that the Administrator of the Environmental Protection Agency submit to the Congress, not later than December 31, 1982, a report containing the detailed estimates, comprehensive study, and comprehensive analysis required by section 1375(b) of this title, including an estimate of the total cost and the amount of Federal funds necessary for the construction of needed publicly owned treatment facilities, such report to reflect the changes made in the Federal water pollution control program by Pub.L. 97–117 [see Short Title of 1981 Amendment note set out under section 1251 of this title]. The Administrator was to give emphasis to the effects of the amendment made by section 2(a) of Pub.L. 97–117 [amending section 1281(g)(1) of this title] in addressing water quality needs adequately and appropriately.

**Study and Report to Congress by Secretary of Interior of Financing Water Pollution Prevention, Control, and Abatement Programs**

Pub.L. 91–224, Title I, § 109, Apr. 3, 1970, 34 Stat. 113, directed the Secretary of the Interior to conduct a full and complete investigation and study of the feasibility of all methods of financing the cost of preventing, controlling, and abating water pollution, other than methods authorized by existing law, with results of such investigation and study to be reported to Congress no later than Dec. 31, 1970, together with the recommendations of the Secretary for financing the programs for preventing, controlling, and abating water pollution for the fiscal years beginning after fiscal year 1971, including any necessary legislation.

**Termination of Advisory Boards**

Advisory Boards in existence on Jan. 5, 1973, to terminate not later than the expiration of the two-year period following Jan. 5, 1973, unless, in the case of a board established by the President or an officer of the Federal Government, such board is renewed by appropriate action prior to the expiration of such two-year period, or in the case of a board established by the Congress, its duration is otherwise provided by law, see sections 3(2) and 14 of Pub.L. 92–463, Oct. 6, 1972, 86 Stat. 770, 776, set out in Appendix 2 to Title 5, Government Organization and Employees.

## § 1375a. Report on coastal recreation waters

### (a) In general

Not later than 4 years after October 10, 2000, and every 4 years thereafter, the Administrator of the Environmental Protection Agency shall submit to Congress a report that includes—

(1) recommendations concerning the need for additional water quality criteria for pathogens and pathogen indicators and other actions that should be taken to improve the quality of coastal recreation waters;

(2) an evaluation of Federal, State, and local efforts to implement this Act, including the amendments made by this Act; and

(3) recommendations on improvements to methodologies and techniques for monitoring of coastal recreation waters.

### (b) Coordination

The Administrator of the Environmental Protection Agency may coordinate the report under this section with other reporting requirements under the Federal Water Pollution Control Act (33 U.S.C. 1251 et seq.).

(Pub.L. 106–284, § 7, Oct. 10, 2000, 114 Stat. 876.)

### HISTORICAL AND STATUTORY NOTES

**References in Text**

This Act, referred to in subsec. (a)(2), is Pub.L. 106–284, Oct. 10, 2000, 114 Stat. 870, which enacted this section and section 1346 of this title, amended sections 1254, 1313, 1314, 1362, and 1377 of this title, and enacted provisions set out as a note under section 1251 of this title.

The Federal Water Pollution Control Act, referred to in subsec. (b), is Act June 30, 1948, c. 758, as amended generally by Pub.L. 92–500, § 2, Oct. 18, 1972, 86 Stat. 816, which is classified principally to this chapter. For complete classification of this Act to the Code, see Short Title note set out under 33 U.S.C.A. § 1251 and Tables.

**Codifications**

This section was enacted as part of the Beaches Environmental Assessment and Coastal Health Act of 2000 and not as part of the Federal Water Pollution Control Act, which comprises this chapter.

## § 1376. Authorization of appropriations

**[FWPCA § 517]**

There are authorized to be appropriated to carry out this chapter, other than sections 1254, 1255, 1256(a), 1257, 1258, 1262, 1263, 1264, 1265, 1286, 1287, 1288(f) and (h), 1289, 1314, 1321(c), (d), (i), (*l*), and (k), 1324, 1325, and 1327 of this title, $250,000,000 for the fiscal year ending June 30, 1973, $300,000,000 for the fiscal year ending June 30, 1974, $350,000,000 for the fiscal year ending June 30, 1975, $100,000,000 for the fiscal year ending September 30, 1977, $150,000,000 for the fiscal year ending September 30, 1978, $150,000,000 for the fiscal year ending September 30, 1979, $150,000,000 for the fiscal year ending September 30, 1980, $150,000,000 for the fiscal year ending September 30, 1981, $161,000,000 for the fiscal year ending September 30, 1982, such sums as may be necessary for fiscal years 1983 through 1985, and $135,000,000 per fiscal year for each of the fiscal years 1986 through 1990.

(June 30, 1948, c. 758, Title V, § 517, as added Oct. 18, 1972, Pub.L. 92–500, § 2, 86 Stat. 896, and amended Dec. 27, 1977, Pub.L. 95–217, § 4(g), 91 Stat. 1567; Oct. 21, 1980, Pub.L. 96–483, § 1(g), 94 Stat. 2360; Feb. 4, 1987, Pub.L. 100–4, Title I, § 101(h), 101 Stat. 9.)

### HISTORICAL AND STATUTORY NOTES

**References in Text**

Section 1264 of this title, referred to in text, was omitted from the Code as executed.

Section 1321(k) of this title, referred to in text, was repealed by Pub.L. 101–380, Title II, § 2002(b)(2), Aug. 18, 1990, 104 Stat. 507.

**Authorization Approval for Funds Appropriated Before December 27, 1977, for Expenditures Through Fiscal Year Ending September 30, 1977**

Pub.L. 95–217, § 3, Dec. 27, 1977, 91 Stat. 1566, provided that funds appropriated before Dec. 27, 1977 for expenditure during the fiscal year ending June 30, 1976, the transition quarter ending September 30, 1976, and the fiscal year ending September 30, 1977, under authority of this chapter were authorized for those purposes for which appropriated.

## § 1377. Indian tribes

**[FWPCA § 518]**

**(a) Policy**

Nothing in this section shall be construed to affect the application of section 1251(g) of this title, and all of the provisions of this section shall be carried out in accordance with the provisions of such section 1251(g) of this title. Indian tribes shall be treated as States for purposes of such section 1251(g) of this title.

**(b) Assessment of sewage treatment needs; report**

The Administrator, in cooperation with the Director of the Indian Health Service, shall assess the need for sewage treatment works to serve Indian tribes, the degree to which such needs will be met through funds allotted to States under section 1285 of this title and priority lists under section 1296 of this title, and any obstacles which prevent such needs from being met. Not later than one year after February 4, 1987, the Administrator shall submit a report to Congress on the assessment under this subsection, along with recommendations specifying (1) how the Administrator intends to provide assistance to Indian tribes to develop waste treatment management plans and to construct treatment works under this chapter, and (2) methods by which the participation in and administration of programs under this chapter by Indian tribes can be maximized.

**(c) Reservation of funds**

The Administrator shall reserve each fiscal year beginning after September 30, 1986, before allotments to the States under section 1285(e) of this title, one-half of one percent of the sums appropriated under section 1287 of this title. Sums reserved under this subsection shall be available only for grants for the development of waste treatment management plans and for the construction of sewage treatment works to serve Indian tribes, as defined in subsection (h) of this section and former Indian reservations in Oklahoma (as determined by the Secretary of the Interior) and Alaska Native Villages as defined in Public Law 92–203 [43 U.S.C.A. § 1601 et seq.].

**(d) Cooperative agreements**

In order to ensure the consistent implementation of the requirements of this chapter, an Indian tribe and the State or States in which the lands of such tribe are located may enter into a cooperative agreement, subject to the review and approval of the Administrator, to jointly plan and administer the requirements of this chapter.

**(e) Treatment as States**

The Administrator is authorized to treat an Indian tribe as a State for purposes of subchapter II of this chapter and sections 1254, 1256, 1313, 1315, 1318, 1319, 1324, 1329, 1341, 1342, 1344, and 1346 of this title to the degree necessary to carry out the objectives of this section, but only if—

(1) the Indian tribe has a governing body carrying out substantial governmental duties and powers;

(2) the functions to be exercised by the Indian tribe pertain to the management and protection of water resources which are held by an Indian tribe, held by the United States in trust for Indians, held by a member of an Indian tribe if such property interest is subject to a trust restriction on alienation, or otherwise within the borders of an Indian reservation; and

(3) the Indian tribe is reasonably expected to be capable, in the Administrator's judgment, of carrying out the functions to be exercised in a manner consistent with the terms and purposes of this chapter and of all applicable regulations.

Such treatment as a State may include the direct provision of funds reserved under subsection (c) of this section to the governing bodies of Indian tribes, and the determination of priorities by Indian tribes, where not determined by the Administrator in cooperation with the Director of the Indian Health Service. The Administrator, in cooperation with the Director of the Indian Health Service, is authorized to make grants under subchapter II of this chapter in an amount not to exceed 100 percent of the cost of a project. Not later than 18 months after February 4, 1987, the Administrator shall, in consultation with Indian tribes, promulgate final regulations which specify how Indian tribes shall be treated as States for purposes of this chapter. The Administrator shall, in promulgating such regulations, consult affected States sharing common water bodies and provide a mechanism for the resolution of any unreasonable consequences that may arise as a result of differing water quality standards that may be set by States and Indian tribes located on common bodies of water. Such mechanism shall provide for explicit consideration of relevant factors including, but not limited to, the effects of differing water quality permit requirements on upstream and downstream dischargers, economic impacts, and present and historical uses and quality of the waters subject to such standards. Such mechanism should provide for the avoidance of such unreasonable consequences in a manner consistent with the objective of this chapter.

**(f) Grants for nonpoint source programs**

The Administrator shall make grants to an Indian tribe under section 1329 of this title as though such tribe was a State. Not more than one-third of one percent of the amount appropriated for any fiscal year under section 1329 of this title may be used to make grants under this subsection. In addition to the requirements of section 1329 of this title, an Indian tribe shall be required to meet the requirements of paragraphs (1), (2), and (3) of subsection (d)[1] of this section in order to receive such a grant.

**(g) Alaska Native organizations**

No provision of this chapter shall be construed to—

(1) grant, enlarge, or diminish, or in any way affect the scope of the governmental authority, if any, of any Alaska Native organization, including any federally-recognized tribe, traditional Alaska Native council, or Native council organized pursuant to the Act of June 18, 1934 (48 Stat. 987), over lands or persons in Alaska;

(2) create or validate any assertion by such organization or any form of governmental authority over lands or persons in Alaska; or

(3) in any way affect any assertion that Indian country, as defined in section 1151 of Title 18, exists or does not exist in Alaska.

**(h) Definitions**

For purposes of this section, the term—

(1) "Federal Indian reservation" means all land within the limits of any Indian reservation under the jurisdiction of the United States Government, notwithstanding the issuance of any patent, and including rights-of-way running through the reservation; and

(2) "Indian tribe" means any Indian tribe, band, group, or community recognized by the Secretary of the Interior and exercising governmental authority over a Federal Indian reservation.

(June 30, 1948, c. 758, Title V, § 518, as added Feb. 4, 1987, Pub.L. 100–4, Title V, § 506, 101 Stat. 76, and amended Nov. 1, 1988, Pub.L. 100–581, Title II, § 207, 102 Stat. 2940; Oct. 10, 2000, Pub.L. 106–284, § 6, 114 Stat. 876.)

[1] So in original. Probably should be subsection "(e)".

## HISTORICAL AND STATUTORY NOTES

**References in Text**

Pub.L. 92–203, referred to in subsec. (c), is Pub.L. 92–203, Dec. 18, 1971, 85 Stat. 688, as amended, popularly known as the "Alaska Native Claims Settlement Act", which is classified generally to chapter 33 (section 1601 et seq.) of Title 43, Public Lands. "Alaska Native Villages", also so referred, are defined in section 1602(c) of Title 43, defining "Native village". For complete classification of this Act to the Code, see Short Title note set out under section 1601 of Title 43 and Tables.

Act of June 18, 1934, referred to in subsec. (g)(1), is Act June 18, 1934, c. 576, 48 Stat. 984, as amended, popularly known as the Indian Reorganization Act, which enacted sections 461, 462, 463, 464, 465, 466 to 470, 471 to 473, 474,

475, 476 to 478, and 479 of Title 25, Indians. For complete classification of this Act to the Code, see Short Title note set out under section 461 of Title 25 and Tables.

**Codifications**

In original enactment, subsec. (f) contained a reference to "paragraphs (1), (2), and (3) of subsection (d)", which reference has been editorially changed to "subsection (e)" as the probable intent of Congress as such subsec. (e) and not subsec. (d) contains pars. (1), (2), and (3).

**Prior Provisions**

A prior section 518 of Act June 30, 1948, was renumbered as section 519 of Act June 30, 1948, and is set out as a note under section 1251 of this title.

**Grants to Indian Tribes**

Pub.L. 108–199, Div. G, Title III, Jan. 23, 2004, 118 Stat. 406, provided in part that: "For fiscal year 2004, and notwithstanding section 518(f) of the Act [Federal Water Pollution Control Act, section 518(f) of which is subsec. (f) of this section], the Administrator is authorized to use the amounts appropriated for any fiscal year under section 319 of that Act [33 U.S.C.A. § 1329] to make grants to Indian tribes pursuant to sections 319(h) [33 U.S.C.A. § 1329(h)] and 518(e) of that Act [subsec. (e) of this section]."

Similar provisions were contained in the following prior Appropriations Acts:

Pub.L. 108–7, Div. K, Title III, Feb. 20, 2003, 117 Stat. 511.

Pub.L. 107–73, Title III, Nov. 26, 2001, 115 Stat. 685.

Pub.L. 106–377, § 1(a)(1) [Title III], Oct. 27, 2000, 114 Stat. 1441, 1441A–43.

Pub.L. 106–74, Title III, Oct. 20, 1999, 113 Stat. 1083.

## SUBCHAPTER VI—STATE WATER POLLUTION CONTROL REVOLVING FUNDS

### § 1381. Grants to States for establishment of revolving funds

**[FWPCA § 601]**

**(a) General authority**

Subject to the provisions of this subchapter, the Administrator shall make capitalization grants to each State for the purpose of establishing a water pollution control revolving fund for providing assistance (1) for construction of treatment works (as defined in section 1292 of this title) which are publicly owned, (2) for implementing a management program under section 1329 of this title, and (3) for developing and implementing a conservation and management plan under section 1330 of this title.

**(b) Schedule of grant payments**

The Administrator and each State shall jointly establish a schedule of payments under which the Administrator will pay to the State the amount of each grant to be made to the State under this subchapter. Such schedule shall be based on the State's intended use plan under section 1386(c) of this title, except that—

(1) such payments shall be made in quarterly installments, and

(2) such payments shall be made as expeditiously as possible, but in no event later than the earlier of—

(A) 8 quarters after the date such funds were obligated by the State, or

(B) 12 quarters after the date such funds were allotted to the State.

(June 30, 1948, c. 758, Title VI, § 601, as added Feb. 4, 1987, Pub.L. 100–4, Title II, § 212(a), 101 Stat. 22.)

### § 1382. Capitalization grant agreements

**[FWPCA § 602]**

**(a) General rule**

To receive a capitalization grant with funds made available under this subchapter and section 1285(m) of this title, a State shall enter into an agreement with the Administrator which shall include but not be limited to the specifications set forth in subsection (b) of this section.

**(b) Specific requirements**

The Administrator shall enter into an agreement under this section with a State only after the State has established to the satisfaction of the Administrator that—

(1) the State will accept grant payments with funds to be made available under this subchapter and section 1285(m) of this title in accordance with a payment schedule established jointly by the Administrator under section 1381(b) of this title and will deposit all such payments in the water pollution control revolving fund established by the State in accordance with this subchapter;

(2) the State will deposit in the fund from State moneys an amount equal to at least 20 percent of the total amount of all capitalization grants which will be made to the State with funds to be made available under this subchapter and section 1285(m) of this title on or before the date on which each quarterly grant payment will be made to the State under this subchapter;

(3) the State will enter into binding commitments to provide assistance in accordance with the requirements of this subchapter in an amount equal to 120 percent of the amount of each such grant payment within 1 year after the receipt of such grant payment;

(4) all funds in the fund will be expended in an expeditious and timely manner;

(5) all funds in the fund as a result of capitalization grants under this subchapter and section 1285(m) of this title will first be used to assure maintenance of progress, as determined by the Governor of the State, toward compliance with enforceable deadlines, goals, and requirements of this chapter, including the municipal compliance deadline;

(6) treatment works eligible under section 1383(c)(1) of this title which will be constructed in whole or in part before fiscal year 1995 with funds directly made available by capitalization grants under this subchapter and section 1285(m) of this title will meet the requirements of, or otherwise be treated (as determined by the Governor of the State) under sections 1281(b), 1281(g)(1), 1281(g)(2), 1281(g)(3), 1281(g)(5), 1281(g)(6), 1281(n)(1), 1281(*o*), 1284(a)(1), 1284(a)(2), 1284(b)(1), 1284(d)(2), 1291, 1298, 1371(c)(1), and 1372 of this title in the same manner as treatment works constructed with assistance under subchapter II of this chapter;

(7) in addition to complying with the requirements of this subchapter, the State will commit or expend each quarterly grant payment which it will receive under this subchapter in accordance with laws and procedures applicable to the commitment or expenditure of revenues of the State;

(8) in carrying out the requirements of section 1386 of this title, the State will use accounting, audit, and fiscal procedures conforming to generally accepted government accounting standards;

(9) the State will require as a condition of making a loan or providing other assistance, as described in section 1383(d) of this title, from the fund that the recipient of such assistance will maintain project accounts in accordance with generally accepted government accounting standards; and

(10) the State will make annual reports to the Administrator on the actual use of funds in accordance with section 1386(d) of this title.

(June 30, 1948, c. 758, Title VI, § 602, as added Feb. 4, 1987, Pub.L. 100–4, Title II, § 212(a), 101 Stat. 22.)

## § 1383. Water pollution control revolving loan funds

[FWPCA § 603]

### (a) Requirements for obligation of grant funds

Before a State may receive a capitalization grant with funds made available under this subchapter and section 1285(m) of this title, the State shall first establish a water pollution control revolving fund which complies with the requirements of this section.

### (b) Administration

Each State water pollution control revolving fund shall be administered by an instrumentality of the State with such powers and limitations as may be required to operate such fund in accordance with the requirements and objectives of this chapter.

### (c) Projects eligible for assistance

The amounts of funds available to each State water pollution control revolving fund shall be used only for providing financial assistance (1) to any municipality, intermunicipal, interstate, or State agency for construction of publicly owned treatment works (as defined in section 1292 of this title), (2) for the implementation of a management program established under section 1329 of this title, and (3) for development and implementation of a conservation and management plan under section 1330 of this title. The fund shall be established, maintained, and credited with repayments, and the fund balance shall be available in perpetuity for providing such financial assistance.

### (d) Types of assistance

Except as otherwise limited by State law, a water pollution control revolving fund of a State under this section may be used only—

(1) to make loans, on the condition that—

(A) such loans are made at or below market interest rates, including interest free loans, at terms not to exceed 20 years;

(B) annual principal and interest payments will commence not later than 1 year after completion of any project and all loans will be fully amortized not later than 20 years after project completion;

(C) the recipient of a loan will establish a dedicated source of revenue for repayment of loans; and

(D) the fund will be credited with all payments of principal and interest on all loans;

(2) to buy or refinance the debt obligation of municipalities and intermunicipal and interstate agencies within the State at or below market rates, where such debt obligations were incurred after March 7, 1985;

(3) to guarantee, or purchase insurance for, local obligations where such action would improve credit market access or reduce interest rates;

(4) as a source of revenue or security for the payment of principal and interest on revenue or general obligation bonds issued by the State if the proceeds of the sale of such bonds will be deposited in the fund;

(5) to provide loan guarantees for similar revolving funds established by municipalities or intermunicipal agencies;

(6) to earn interest on fund accounts; and

(7) for the reasonable costs of administering the fund and conducting activities under this subchap-

ter, except that such amounts shall not exceed 4 percent of all grant awards to such fund under this subchapter.

**(e) Limitation to prevent double benefits**

If a State makes, from its water pollution revolving fund, a loan which will finance the cost of facility planning and the preparation of plans, specifications, and estimates for construction of publicly owned treatment works, the State shall ensure that if the recipient of such loan receives a grant under section 1281(g) of this title for construction of such treatment works and an allowance under section 1281(*l*)(1) of this title for non-Federal funds expended for such planning and preparation, such recipient will promptly repay such loan to the extent of such allowance.

**(f) Consistency with planning requirements**

A State may provide financial assistance from its water pollution control revolving fund only with respect to a project which is consistent with plans, if any, developed under sections 1285(j), 1288, 1313(e), 1329, and 1330 of this title.

**(g) Priority list requirement**

The State may provide financial assistance from its water pollution control revolving fund only with respect to a project for construction of a treatment works described in subsection (c)(1) of this section if such project is on the State's priority list under section 1296 of this title. Such assistance may be provided regardless of the rank of such project on such list.

**(h) Eligibility of non-Federal share of construction grant projects**

A State water pollution control revolving fund may provide assistance (other than under subsection (d)(1) of this section) to a municipality or intermunicipal or interstate agency with respect to the non-Federal share of the costs of a treatment works project for which such municipality or agency is receiving assistance from the Administrator under any other authority only if such assistance is necessary to allow such project to proceed.

(June 30, 1948, c. 758, Title VI, § 603, as added Feb. 4, 1987, Pub.L. 100–4, Title II, § 212(a), 101 Stat. 23.)

## § 1384. Allotment of funds

[FWPCA § 604]

**(a) Formula**

Sums authorized to be appropriated to carry out this section for each of fiscal years 1989 and 1990 shall be allotted by the Administrator in accordance with section 1285(c) of this title.

**(b) Reservation of funds for planning**

Each State shall reserve each fiscal year 1 percent of the sums allotted to such State under this section for such fiscal year, or $100,000, whichever amount is greater, to carry out planning under sections 1285(j) and 1313(e) of this title.

**(c) Allotment period**

**(1) Period of availability for grant award**

Sums allotted to a State under this section for a fiscal year shall be available for obligation by the State during the fiscal year for which sums are authorized and during the following fiscal year.

**(2) Reallotment of unobligated funds**

The amount of any allotment not obligated by the State by the last day of the 2-year period of availability established by paragraph (1) shall be immediately reallotted by the Administrator on the basis of the same ratio as is applicable to sums allotted under subchapter II of this chapter for the second fiscal year of such 2-year period. None of the funds reallotted by the Administrator shall be reallotted to any State which has not obligated all sums allotted to such State in the first fiscal year of such 2-year period.

(June 30, 1948, c. 758, Title VI, § 604, as added Feb. 4, 1987, Pub.L. 100–4, Title II, § 212(a), 101 Stat. 25.)

### HISTORICAL AND STATUTORY NOTES

**Use of Capitalization Grant Funds for Construction Grants**

Pub.L. 101–144, Title III, Nov. 9, 1989, 103 Stat. 858, as amended Pub.L. 101–302, Title II, May 25, 1990, 104 Stat. 238, provided in part: "That, notwithstanding any other provision of law, sums heretofore, herein or hereafter appropriated under this heading allotted for title VI capitalization grants to American Samoa, Commonwealth of the Northern Mariana Islands, Guam, the Republic of Palau (or its successor entity), Virgin Islands and the District of Columbia, may be used for title II construction grants at the request of the chief executive of each of the above named entities, and sums appropriated in fiscal year 1989 shall remain available for obligation until September 30, 1992."

## § 1385. Corrective action

[FWPCA § 605]

**(a) Notification of noncompliance**

If the Administrator determines that a State has not complied with its agreement with the Administrator under section 1382 of this title or any other requirement of this subchapter, the Administrator shall notify the State of such noncompliance and the necessary corrective action.

**(b) Withholding of payments**

If a State does not take corrective action within 60 days after the date a State receives notification of such action under subsection (a) of this section, the

Administrator shall withhold additional payments to the State until the Administrator is satisfied that the State has taken the necessary corrective action.

**(c) Reallotment of withheld payments**

If the Administrator is not satisfied that adequate corrective actions have been taken by the State within 12 months after the State is notified of such actions under subsection (a) of this section, the payments withheld from the State by the Administrator under subsection (b) of this section shall be made available for reallotment in accordance with the most recent formula for allotment of funds under this subchapter.

(June 30, 1948, c. 758, Title VI, § 605, as added Feb. 4, 1987, Pub.L. 100–4, Title II, § 212(a), 101 Stat. 25.)

## § 1386. Audits, reports, and fiscal controls; intended use plan

**[FWPCA § 606]**

**(a) Fiscal control and auditing procedures**

Each State electing to establish a water pollution control revolving fund under this subchapter shall establish fiscal controls and accounting procedures sufficient to assure proper accounting during appropriate accounting periods for—

(1) payments received by the fund;

(2) disbursements made by the fund; and

(3) fund balances at the beginning and end of the accounting period.

**(b) Annual Federal audits**

The Administrator shall, at least on an annual basis, conduct or require each State to have independently conducted reviews and audits as may be deemed necessary or appropriate by the Administrator to carry out the objectives of this section. Audits of the use of funds deposited in the water pollution revolving fund established by such State shall be conducted in accordance with the auditing procedures of the General Accounting Office, including chapter 75 of Title 31.

**(c) Intended use plan**

After providing for public comment and review, each State shall annually prepare a plan identifying the intended uses of the amounts available to its water pollution control revolving fund. Such intended use plan shall include, but not be limited to—

(1) a list of those projects for construction of publicly owned treatment works on the State's priority list developed pursuant to section 1296 of this title and a list of activities eligible for assistance under sections 1329 and 1330 of this title;

(2) a description of the short- and long-term goals and objectives of its water pollution control revolving fund;

(3) information on the activities to be supported, including a description of project categories, discharge requirements under subchapters III and IV of this chapter, terms of financial assistance, and communities served;

(4) assurances and specific proposals for meeting the requirements of paragraphs (3), (4), (5), and (6) of section 1382(b) of this title; and

(5) the criteria and method established for the distribution of funds.

**(d) Annual report**

Beginning the first fiscal year after the receipt of payments under this subchapter, the State shall provide an annual report to the Administrator describing how the State has met the goals and objectives for the previous fiscal year as identified in the plan prepared for the previous fiscal year pursuant to subsection (c) of this section, including identification of loan recipients, loan amounts, and loan terms and similar details on other forms of financial assistance provided from the water pollution control revolving fund.

**(e) Annual Federal oversight review**

The Administrator shall conduct an annual oversight review of each State plan prepared under subsection (c) of this section, each State report prepared under subsection (d) of this section, and other such materials as are considered necessary and appropriate in carrying out the purposes of this subchapter. After reasonable notice by the Administrator to the State or the recipient of a loan from a water pollution control revolving fund, the State or loan recipient shall make available to the Administrator such records as the Administrator reasonably requires to review and determine compliance with this subchapter.

**(f) Applicability of subchapter II provisions**

Except to the extent provided in this subchapter, the provisions of subchapter II of this chapter shall not apply to grants under this subchapter.

(June 30, 1948, c. 758, Title VI, § 606, as added Feb. 4, 1987, Pub.L. 100–4, Title II, § 212(a), 101 Stat. 25.)

## § 1387. Authorization of appropriations

**[FWPCA § 607]**

There is authorized to be appropriated to carry out the purposes of this subchapter the following sums:

(1) $1,200,000,000 per fiscal year for each of fiscal years 1989 and 1990;

(2) $2,400,000,000 for fiscal year 1991;

(3) $1,800,000,000 for fiscal year 1992;

(4) $1,200,000,000 for fiscal year 1993; and

(5) $600,000,000 for fiscal year 1994.

(June 30, 1948, c. 758, Title VI, § 607, as added Feb. 4, 1987, Pub.L. 100–4, Title II, § 212(a), 101 Stat. 26.)

# OCEAN DUMPING

## MARINE PROTECTION, RESEARCH, AND SANCTUARIES ACT OF 1972 [MPRSA § ____]

**(33 U.S.C.A. §§ 1401 to 1445)**

## CHAPTER 27—OCEAN DUMPING



**Related Provisions**

*See, also, Water Pollution Prevention and Control, 33 U.S.C.A. § 1251 et seq., ante; Ocean Pollution Research, 33 U.S.C.A. § 1701 et seq., post; Prevention of Pollution from Ships, 33 U.S.C.A. § 1901 et seq., post; and Water Resources Research, 42 U.S.C.A. § 10301 et seq., post.*

### § 1401. Congressional finding, policy, and declaration of purpose

**[MPRSA § 2]**

**(a) Dangers of unregulated dumping**

Unregulated dumping of material into ocean waters endangers human health, welfare, and amenities, and the marine environment, ecological systems, and economic potentialities.

**(b) Policy of regulation and prevention or limitation**

The Congress declares that it is the policy of the United States to regulate the dumping of all types of materials into ocean waters and to prevent or strictly limit the dumping into ocean waters of any material which would adversely affect human health, welfare, or amenities, or the marine environment, ecological systems, or economic potentialities.

**(c) Regulation of dumping and transportation for dumping purposes**

It is the purpose of this Act to regulate (1) the transportation by any person of material from the United States and, in the case of United States vessels, aircraft, or agencies, the transportation of material from a location outside the United States, when in either case the transportation is for the purpose of dumping the material into ocean waters, and (2) the dumping of material transported by any person from a location outside the United States, if the dumping occurs in the territorial sea or the contiguous zone of the United States.

(Pub.L. 92–532, § 2, Oct. 23, 1972, 86 Stat. 1052; Pub.L. 93–254, § 1(1), Mar. 22, 1974, 88 Stat. 50.)

#### HISTORICAL AND STATUTORY NOTES

**References in Text**

This Act, referred to in subsec. (c), means Pub. L. 92-532, which is classified principally to this chapter, chapter 41 of this title [33 U.S.C.A. § 2801 et seq.], and chapters 32 [16 U.S.C.A. § 1431 et seq.] and 32A [16 U.S.C.A. § 1447 et seq.] of Title 16.

**Effective and Applicability Provisions**

1974 Acts

Section 2 of Pub.L. 93–254 provided in part that amendment of subsecs. (b) and (c) of this section and sections 1402, 1411, and 1412(a), other than last sentence of subsec. (a), of this title, by Pub.L. 93–254 shall become effective Mar. 22, 1974.

**Short Title**

1988 Amendments

Pub.L. 100–688, Title I, § 1001, Nov. 18, 1988, 102 Stat. 4139, provided that: "This title [enacting sections 1414b and 1414c of this title, amending sections 1268 and 1412a of this title, repealing provisions formerly classified to section 1414a of this title, and amending provisions set out as a note under section 2267 of this title] may be cited as the 'Ocean Dumping Ban Act of 1988'."

1972 Acts

Section 1 of Pub.L. 92–532 provided: "That this Act [enacting this chapter and sections 1431 to 1434 of Title 16, Conservation] may be cited as the 'Marine Protection, Research, and Sanctuaries Act of 1972'."

**Territorial Sea and Contiguous Zone of United States**

For extension of territorial sea and contiguous zone of United States, see Proc. No. 5928 and Proc. No. 7219, respectively, set out as notes under 43 U.S.C.A. § 1331.

**Environmental Effects Abroad of Major Federal Actions**

For provisions relating to environmental effects abroad of major federal actions, see Ex. Ord. No. 12114, Jan. 4, 1979, 44 F.R. 1957, set out as a note under section 4321 of Title 42, The Public Health and Welfare.

**Federal Compliance with Pollution Control Standards**

For provisions relating to the responsibility of the head of each Executive agency for compliance with applicable pollution control standards, see Ex. Ord. No. 12088, Oct. 13, 1978, 43 F.R. 47707, set out as a note under section 4321 of Title 42, The Public Health and Welfare.

## § 1402. Definitions

### [MPRSA § 3]

For the purposes of this Act the term—

**(a)** "Administrator" means the Administrator of the Environmental Protection Agency.

**(b)** "Ocean waters" means those waters of the open seas lying seaward of the base line from which the territorial sea is measured, as provided for in the Convention on the Territorial Sea and the Contiguous Zone (15 UST 1606; TIAS 5639).

**(c)** "Material" means matter of any kind or description, including, but not limited to, dredged material, solid waste, incinerator residue, garbage, sewage, sewage sludge, munitions, radiological, chemical, and biological warfare agents, radioactive materials, chemicals, biological and laboratory waste, wreck or discarded equipment, rock, sand, excavation debris, and industrial, municipal, agricultural, and other waste; but such term does not mean sewage from vessels within the meaning of section 1322 of this title. Oil within the meaning of section 1321 of this title shall be included only to the extent that such oil is taken on board a vessel or aircraft for the purpose of dumping.

**(d)** "United States" includes the several States, the District of Columbia, the Commonwealth of Puerto Rico, the Canal Zone, the territories and possessions of the United States, and the Trust Territory of the Pacific Islands.

**(e)** "Person" means any private person or entity, or any officer, employee, agent, department, agency, or instrumentality of the Federal Government, of any State or local unit of government, or of any foreign government.

**(f)** "Dumping" means a disposition of material: *Provided,* That it does not mean a disposition of any effluent from any outfall structure to the extent that such disposition is regulated under the provisions of the Federal Water Pollution Control Act, as amended [33 U.S.C.A. § 1251 et seq.] under the provisions of section 407 of this title, or under the provisions of the Atomic Energy Act of 1954, as amended [42 U.S.C.A. § 2011 et seq.], nor does it mean a routine discharge of effluent incidental to the propulsion of, or operation of motor-driven equipment on, vessels: *Provided, further,* That it does not mean the construction of any fixed structure or artificial island nor the intentional placement of any device in ocean waters or on or in the submerged land beneath such waters, for a purpose other than disposal, when such construction or such placement is otherwise regulated by Federal or State law or occurs pursuant to an authorized Federal or State program: *And provided further,* That it does not include the deposit of oyster shells, or other materials when such deposit is made for the purpose of developing, maintaining, or harvesting fisheries resources and is otherwise regulated by Federal or State law or occurs pursuant to an authorized Federal or State program.

**(g)** "District court of the United States" includes the District Court of Guam, the District Court of the Virgin Islands, the District Court of Puerto Rico, the District Court of the Canal Zone, and in the case of American Samoa and the Trust Territory of the Pacific Islands, the District Court of the United States for the District of Hawaii, which court shall have jurisdiction over actions arising therein.

**(h)** "Secretary" means the Secretary of the Army.

**(i)** "Dredged material" means any material excavated or dredged from the navigable waters of the United States.

**(j)** "High-level radioactive waste" means the aqueous waste resulting from the operation of the first cycle solvent extraction system, or equivalent and the concentrated waste from subsequent extraction cycles, or equivalent, in a facility for reprocessing irradiated reactor fuels, or irradiated fuel from nuclear power reactors.

**(k)** "Medical waste" means isolation wastes; infectious agents; human blood and blood products; pathological wastes; sharps; body parts; contaminated bedding; surgical wastes and potentially contaminated laboratory wastes; dialysis wastes; and such additional medical items as the Administrator shall prescribe by regulation.

**(*l*)** "Transport" or "transportation" refers to the carriage and related handling of any material by a vessel, or by any other vehicle, including aircraft.

**(m)** "Convention" means the Convention on the Prevention of Marine Pollution by Dumping of Wastes and Other Matter.

(Pub.L. 92–532, § 3, Oct. 23, 1972, 86 Stat. 1052; Pub.L. 93–254, § 1(2), Mar. 22, 1974, 88 Stat. 50; Pub.L. 100–688, Title III, § 3201(a), Nov. 18, 1988, 102 Stat. 4153.)

## HISTORICAL AND STATUTORY NOTES

**References in Text**

This Act, referred to in text, means Pub. L. 92-532, which is classified principally to this chapter, chapter 41 of this title [33 U.S.C.A. § 2801 et seq.], and chapters 32 [16 U.S.C.A. § 1431 et seq.] and 32A [16 U.S.C.A. § 1447 et seq.] of Title 16.

For definition of Canal Zone, referred to in subsec. (d), see section 3602(b) of Title 22, Foreign Relations and Intercourse.

The Federal Water Pollution Control Act, as amended, referred to in subsec. (f), is Act June 30, 1948, c. 758, as amended generally by Pub.L. 92–500, § 2, Oct. 18, 1972, 86 Stat. 816, which is classified generally to chapter 26 (section 1251 et seq.) of this title. For complete classification of this Act to the Code, see Short Title note set out under section 1251 of this title and Tables.

The Atomic Energy Act of 1954, as amended, referred to in subsec. (f), is Act Aug. 30, 1954, c. 1073, § 1, 68 Stat. 919, as amended, which is classified principally to chapter 23 (section 2011 et seq.) of Title 42, The Public Health and Welfare. For complete classification of this Act to the Code, see Short Title note set out under section 2011 of Title 42 and Tables .

**Effective and Applicability Provisions**

1974 Acts

Amendment by Pub.L. 93–254 effective Mar. 22, 1974, see section 2 of Pub.L. 93–254, set out in part as a note under section 1401 of this title.

**Termination of Trust Territory of the Pacific Islands**

For termination of Trust Territory of the Pacific Islands, see note set out preceding 48 U.S.C.A. § 1681.

**Termination of United States District Court for the District of the Canal Zone**

For termination of the United States District Court for the District of the Canal Zone at end of the "transition period", being the 30-month period beginning Oct. 1, 1979, and ending midnight Mar. 31, 1982, see Paragraph 5 of Article XI of the Panama Canal Treaty of 1977 and sections 2101 and 2201 to 2203 of Pub.L. 96–70, Title II, Sept. 27, 1979, 93 Stat. 493, formerly classified to 22 U.S.C.A. §§ 3831 and 3841 to 3843, respectively.

**Territorial Sea and Contiguous Zone of United States**

For extension of territorial sea and contiguous zone of United States, see Proc. No. 5928 and Proc. No. 7219, respectively, set out as notes under 43 U.S.C.A. § 1331.

# SUBCHAPTER I—REGULATION

## § 1411. Prohibited acts [MPRSA § 101]

**(a)** Except as may be authorized by a permit issued pursuant to section 1412 or section 1413 of this title, and subject to regulations issued pursuant to section 1418 of this title,

**(1)** no person shall transport from the United States, and

**(2)** in the case of a vessel or aircraft registered in the United States or flying the United States flag or in the case of a United States department, agency, or instrumentality, no person shall transport from any location

any material for the purpose of dumping it into ocean waters.

**(b)** Except as may be authorized by a permit issued pursuant to section 1412 of this title, and subject to regulations issued pursuant to section 1418 of this title, no person shall dump any material transported from a location outside the United States (1) into the territorial sea of the United States, or (2) into a zone contiguous to the territorial sea of the United States, extending to a line twelve nautical miles seaward from the base line from which the breadth of the territorial sea is measured, to the extent that it may affect the territorial sea or the territory of the United States.

(Pub.L. 92–532, Title I, § 101, Oct. 23, 1972, 86 Stat. 1053; Pub.L. 93–254, § 1(3), Mar. 22, 1974, 88 Stat. 51.)

## HISTORICAL AND STATUTORY NOTES

**Effective and Applicability Provisions**

1974 Acts

Amendment by Pub.L. 93–254 effective Mar. 22, 1974, see section 2 of Pub.L. 93–254, set out in part as a note under section 1401 of this title.

1972 Acts

Section 110(a) of Title I of Pub.L. 92–532 provided that: "This title [this subchapter] shall take effect six months after the date of the enactment of this Act [Oct. 23, 1972]."

**Savings Provisions**

Section 110(b) of Title I of Pub.L. 92–532 provided that: "No legal action begun, or right of action accrued, prior to the effective date of this title [this subchapter] shall be affected by any provision of this title [this subchapter]."

**Territorial Sea and Contiguous Zone of United States**

For extension of territorial sea and contiguous zone of United States, see Proc. No. 5928 and Proc. No. 7219, respectively, set out as notes under 43 U.S.C.A. § 1331.

## § 1412. Dumping permit program

### [MPRSA § 102]

#### (a) Environmental Protection Agency permits

Except in relation to dredged material, as provided for in section 1413 of this title, and in relation to radiological, chemical, and biological warfare agents, high-level radioactive waste, and medical waste, for which no permit may be issued, the Administrator may issue permits, after notice and opportunity for public hearings, for the transportation from the United States or, in the case of an agency or instrumentality of the United States, or in the case of a vessel or aircraft registered in the United States or flying the United States flag, for the transportation from a location outside the United States, of material for the purpose of dumping it into ocean waters, or for the dumping of material into the waters described in section 1411(b) of this title, where the Administrator determines that such dumping will not unreasonably degrade or endanger human health, welfare, or amenities, or the marine environment, ecological systems, or economic potentialities. The Administrator shall establish and apply criteria for reviewing and evaluating such permit applications, and, in establishing or revising such criteria, shall consider, but not be limited in his consideration to, the following:

(A) The need for the proposed dumping.

(B) The effect of such dumping on human health and welfare, including economic, esthetic, and recreational values.

(C) The effect of such dumping on fisheries resources, plankton, fish, shellfish, wildlife, shore lines and beaches.

(D) The effect of such dumping on marine ecosystems, particularly with respect to—

(i) the transfer, concentration, and dispersion of such material and its byproducts through biological, physical, and chemical processes,

(ii) potential changes in marine ecosystem diversity, productivity, and stability, and

(iii) species and community population dynamics.

(E) The persistence and permanence of the effects of the dumping.

(F) The effect of dumping particular volumes and concentrations of such materials.

(G) Appropriate locations and methods of disposal or recycling, including land-based alternatives and the probable impact of requiring use of such alternate locations or methods upon considerations affecting the public interest.

(H) The effect on alternate uses of oceans, such as scientific study, fishing, and other living resource exploitation, and non-living resource exploitation.

(I) In designating recommended sites, the Administrator shall utilize wherever feasible locations beyond the edge of the Continental Shelf.

In establishing or revising such criteria, the Administrator shall consult with Federal, State, and local officials, and interested members of the general public, as may appear appropriate to the Administrator. With respect to such criteria as may affect the civil works program of the Department of the Army, the Administrator shall also consult with the Secretary. In reviewing applications for permits, the Administrator shall make such provision for consultation with interested Federal and State agencies as he deems useful or necessary. No permit shall be issued for a dumping of material which will violate applicable water quality standards. To the extent that he may do so without relaxing the requirements of this subchapter, the Administrator, in establishing or revising such criteria, shall apply the standards and criteria binding upon the United States under the Convention, including its Annexes.

#### (b) Permit categories

The Administrator may establish and issue various categories of permits, including the general permits described in section 1414(c) of this title.

#### (c) Designation of sites

##### (1) In general

The Administrator shall, in a manner consistent with the criteria established pursuant to subsection (a) of this section, designate sites or time periods for dumping. The Administrator shall designate sites or time periods for dumping that will mitigate adverse impact on the environment to the greatest extent practicable.

##### (2) Prohibitions regarding site or time period

In any case where the Administrator determines that, with respect to certain materials, it is necessary to prohibit dumping at a site or during a time period, the Administrator shall prohibit the dumping of such materials in such site or during such time period. This prohibition shall apply to any dumping at the site or during such time period. This prohibition shall apply to any dumping at the site or during the time period, including any dumping under section 1413(e) of this title.

##### (3) Dredged material disposal sites

In the case of dredged material disposal sites, the Administrator, in conjunction with the Secretary, shall develop a site management plan for each site designated pursuant to this section. In developing such plans, the Administrator and the Secretary shall provide opportunity for public comment. Such plans shall include, but not be limited to—

(A) a baseline assessment of conditions at the site;

(B) a program for monitoring the site;

(C) special management conditions or practices to be implemented at each site that are necessary for protection of the environment;

(D) consideration of the quantity of the material to be disposed of at the site, and the presence, nature, and bioavailability of the contaminants in the material;

(E) consideration of the anticipated use of the site over the long term, including the anticipated closure date for the site, if applicable, and any need for management of the site after the closure of the site; and

(F) a schedule for review and revision of the plan (which shall not be reviewed and revised less frequently than 10 years after adoption of the plan, and every 10 years thereafter).

**(4) General site management plan requirement; prohibitions**

After January 1, 1995, no site shall receive a final designation unless a management plan has been developed pursuant to this section. Beginning on January 1, 1997, no permit for dumping pursuant to this Act or authorization for dumping under section 1413(e) of this title shall be issued for a site (other than the site located off the coast of Newport Beach, California, which is known as "LA–3") unless such site has received a final designation pursuant to this subsection or an alternative site has been selected pursuant to section 1413(b) of this title. Beginning January 1, 2003, no permit for dumping pursuant to this Act or authorization for dumping under section 1413(e) of this title shall be issued for the site located off the coast of Newport Beach, California, which is known as "LA–3", unless such site has received a final designation pursuant to this subsection or an alternative site has been selected pursuant to section 1413(b) of this title.

**(5) Management plans for previously designated sites**

The Administrator shall develop a site management plan for any site designated prior to January 1, 1995, as expeditiously as practicable, but not later than January 1, 1997, giving priority consideration to management plans for designated sites that are considered to have the greatest impact on the environment.

**(d) Fish wastes**

No permit is required under this subchapter for the transportation for dumping or the dumping of fish wastes, except when deposited in harbors or other protected or enclosed coastal waters, or where the Administrator finds that such deposits could endanger health, the environment, or ecological systems in a specific location. Where the Administrator makes such a finding, such material may be deposited only as authorized by a permit issued by the Administrator under this section.

**(e) Foreign State permits; acceptance**

In the case of transportation of material, by an agency or instrumentality of the United States or by a vessel or aircraft registered in the United States or flying the United States flag, from a location in a foreign State Party to the Convention, a permit issued pursuant to the authority of that foreign State Party, in accordance with Convention requirements, and which otherwise could have been issued pursuant to subsection (a) of this section, shall be accepted, for the purposes of this subchapter, as if it were issued by the Administrator under the authority of this section: *Provided*, That in the case of an agency or instrumentality of the United States, no application shall be made for a permit to be issued pursuant to the authority of a foreign State Party to the Convention unless the Administrator concurs in the filing of such application.

(Pub.L. 92–532, Title I, § 102, Oct. 23, 1972, 86 Stat. 1054; Pub.L. 93–254, § 1(4), Mar. 22, 1974, 88 Stat. 51; Pub.L. 96–572, § 3, Dec. 22, 1980, 94 Stat. 3345; Pub.L. 100–688, Title III, § 3201(b), Nov. 18, 1988, 102 Stat. 4153; Pub.L. 102–580, Title V, § 506(a), Oct. 31, 1992, 106 Stat. 4868; Pub.L. 104–303, Title V, § 582, Oct. 12, 1996, 110 Stat. 3791; Pub.L. 106–53, Title V, § 562, Aug. 17, 1999, 113 Stat. 355.)

## HISTORICAL AND STATUTORY NOTES

**References in Text**

This Act, referred to in subsec. (c)(4), means Pub. L. 92-532, which is classified principally to this chapter, chapter 41 of this title [33 U.S.C.A. § 2801 et seq.], and chapters 32 [16 U.S.C.A. § 1431 et seq.] and 32A [16 U.S.C.A. § 1447 et seq.] of Title 16.

**Effective and Applicability Provisions**

1974 Acts

Section 2 of Pub.L. 93–254 provided in part that: "The amendments made by subparagraph 1(4)(A)(iii) and paragraph 1(4)(B) of this Act [enacting provision of subsec. (a) respecting application of standards by Administrator and subsec. (e) of this section] shall become effective on the date that the Convention on the Prevention of Marine Pollution by Dumping of Wastes and Other Matters enters into force for the United States." [The Convention entered into force for the United States Aug. 30, 1975.]

Amendment of subsec. (a) of this section, other than last sentence, by Pub.L. 93–254 effective Mar. 22, 1974, see section 2 of Pub.L. 93–254, set out in part as a note under section 1401 of this title.

1972 Acts

Section effective six months after Oct. 23, 1972, see section 110(a) of Pub.L. 92–532, set out as a note under section 1411 of this title.

## § 1412a. Emergency dumping of industrial waste

### (a) Emergency permits for dumping of industrial waste; issuance, etc.

Notwithstanding section 104B of the Marine Protection, Research, and Sanctuaries Act of 1972 [33 U.S.C.A. § 1414b], after December 31, 1981, the Administrator may issue emergency permits under Title I of such Act [33 U.S.C.A. § 1411 et seq.] for the dumping of industrial waste into ocean waters, or into waters described in such section 101(b) [33 U.S.C.A. § 1411(b)], if the Administrator determines that there has been demonstrated to exist an emergency, requiring the dumping of such waste, which poses an unacceptable risk relating to human health and admits of no other feasible solution. As used herein, "emergency" refers to situations requiring action with a marked degree of urgency.

### (b) "Industrial waste" defined

For purposes of this section, the term "industrial waste" means any solid, semisolid, or liquid waste generated by a manufacturing or processing plant.

(Pub.L. 95–153, § 4, Nov. 4, 1977, 91 Stat. 1255; Pub.L. 96–572, § 2, Dec. 22, 1980, 94 Stat. 3344; Pub.L. 100–688, Title I, § 1003(a), Nov. 18, 1988, 102 Stat. 4149.)

#### HISTORICAL AND STATUTORY NOTES

**References in Text**

The Marine Protection, Research, and Sanctuaries Act of 1972, referred to in subsec. (a), is Pub.L. 92–532, Oct. 23, 1972, 86 Stat. 1052, as amended. Title I of such Act of 1972 is classified generally to subchapter I (section 1411 et seq.) of this chapter. For complete classification of this Act to the Code, see Short Title note set out under section 1401 of this title and Tables.

Such section 101(b), referred to in subsec. (a), means section 101(b) of the Marine Protection, Research, and Sanctuaries Act of 1972, which is classified as 33 U.S.C.A. § 1411(b).

**Codifications**

Section was not enacted as part of the Marine Protection, Research, and Sanctuaries Act of 1972, which comprises this chapter.

## § 1413. Dumping permit program for dredged material

[MPRSA § 103]

### (a) Issuance by Secretary of the Army

Subject to the provisions of subsections (b), (c), and (d) of this section, the Secretary may issue permits, after notice and opportunity for public hearings, for the transportation of dredged material for the purpose of dumping it into ocean waters, where the Secretary determines that the dumping will not unreasonably degrade or endanger human health, welfare, or amenities, or the marine environment, ecological systems, or economic potentialities.

### (b) Independent determination of need for dumping, other methods of disposal, and appropriate locations; alternative sites

In making the determination required by subsection (a) of this section, the Secretary shall apply those criteria, established pursuant to section 1412(a) of this title, relating to the effects of the dumping. Based upon an evaluation of the potential effect of a permit denial on navigation, economic and industrial development, and foreign and domestic commerce of the United States, the Secretary shall make an independent determination as to the need for the dumping. The Secretary shall also make an independent determination as to other possible methods of disposal and as to appropriate locations for the dumping. In considering appropriate locations, he shall, to the maximum extent feasible, utilize the recommended sites designated by the Administrator pursuant to section 1412(c) of this title. In any case in which the use of a designated site is not feasible, the Secretary may, with the concurrence of the Administrator, select an alternative site. The criteria and factors established in section 1412(a) of this title relating to site selection shall be used in selecting the alternative site in a manner consistent with the application of such factors and criteria pursuant to section 1412(c) of this title. Disposal at or in the vicinity of an alternative site shall be limited to a period of not greater than 5 years unless the site is subsequently designated pursuant to section 1412(c) of this title; except that an alternative site may continue to be used for an additional period of time that shall not exceed 5 years if—

(1) no feasible disposal site has been designated by the Administrator;

(2) the continued use of the alternative site is necessary to maintain navigation and facilitate interstate or international commerce; and

(3) the Administrator determines that the continued use of the site does not pose an unacceptable risk to human health, aquatic resources, or the environment.

### (c) Concurrence by Administrator

#### (1) Notification

Prior to issuing a permit to any person under this section, the Secretary shall first notify the Administrator of the Secretary's intention to do so and provide necessary and appropriate information concerning the permit to the Administrator. Within 30 days of receiving such information, the Administrator shall review the information and request any additional information the Administrator deems necessary to evaluate the proposed permit.

(2) **Concurrence by Administrator**

Within 45 days after receiving from the Secretary all information the Administrator considers to be necessary to evaluate the proposed permit, the Administrator shall, in writing, concur with (either entirely or with conditions) or decline to concur with the determination of the Secretary as to compliance with the criteria, conditions, and restrictions established pursuant to sections 1412(a) and 1412(c) of this title relating to the environmental impact of the permit. The Administrator may request one 45–day extension in writing and the Secretary shall grant such request on receipt of the request.

(3) **Effect of concurrence**

In any case where the Administrator makes a determination to concur (with or without conditions) or to decline to concur within the time period specified in paragraph (2) the determination shall prevail. If the Administrator declines to concur in the determination of the Secretary no permit shall be issued. If the Administrator concurs with conditions the permit shall include such conditions. The Administrator shall state in writing the reasons for declining to concur or for the conditions of the concurrence.

(4) **Failure to act**

If no written documentation is made by the Administrator within the time period provided for in paragraph (2), the Secretary may issue the permit.

(5) **Compliance with criteria and restrictions**

Unless the Administrator grants a waiver pursuant to subsection (d) of this section, any permit issued by the Secretary shall require compliance with such criteria and restrictions.

**(d) Waiver of requirements**

If, in any case, the Secretary finds that, in the disposition of dredged material, there is no economically feasible method or site available other than a dumping site the utilization of which would result in non-compliance with the criteria established pursuant to section 1412(a) of this title relating to the effects of dumping or with the restrictions established pursuant to section 1412(c) of this title relating to critical areas, he shall so certify and request a waiver from the Administrator of the specific requirements involved. Within thirty days of the receipt of the waiver request, unless the Administrator finds that the dumping of the material will result in an unacceptably adverse impact on municipal water supplies, shell-fish beds, wildlife, fisheries (including spawning and breeding areas), or recreational areas, he shall grant the waiver.

**(e) Federal projects involving dredged material**

In connection with Federal projects involving dredged material, the Secretary may, in lieu of the permit procedure, issue regulations which will require the application to such projects of the same criteria, other factors to be evaluated, the same procedures, and the same requirements which apply to the issuance of permits under subsections (a), (b), (c), and (d) of this section and section 1414(a) and (d) of this title.

(Pub.L. 92–532, Title I, § 103, Oct. 23, 1972, 86 Stat. 1055; Pub.L. 102–580, Title V, §§ 504, 506(b), Oct. 31, 1992, 106 Stat. 4866, 4869.)

### HISTORICAL AND STATUTORY NOTES

**Effective and Applicability Provisions**

1972 Acts

Section effective six months after Oct. 23, 1972, see section 110(a) of Pub.L. 92–532, set out as a note under section 1411 of this title.

## § 1414. Permit conditions

**[MPRSA § 104]**

**(a) Designated and included conditions**

Permits issued under this subchapter shall designate and include (1) the type of material authorized to be transported for dumping or to be dumped; (2) the amount of material authorized to be transported for dumping or to be dumped; (3) the location where such transport for dumping will be terminated or where such dumping will occur; (4) such requirements, limitations, or conditions as are necessary to assure consistency with any site management plan approved pursuant to section 1412(c) of this title; (5) any special provisions deemed necessary by the Administrator or the Secretary, as the case may be, after consultation with the Secretary of the Department in which the Coast Guard is operating, for the monitoring and surveillance of the transportation or dumping; and (6) such other matters as the Administrator or the Secretary, as the case may be, deems appropriate. Permits issued under this subchapter shall be issued for a period of not to exceed 7 years.

**(b) Permit processing fees; reporting requirements**

The Administrator or the Secretary, as the case may be, may prescribe such processing fees for permits and such reporting requirements for actions taken pursuant to permits issued by him under this subchapter as he deems appropriate.

**(c) General permits**

Consistent with the requirements of sections 1412 and 1413 of this title, but in lieu of a requirement for specific permits in such case, the Administrator or the Secretary, as the case may be, may issue general permits for the transportation for dumping, or dumping, or both, of specified materials or classes of materials for which he may issue permits, which he determines will have a minimal adverse environmental impact.

**(d) Review**

Any permit issued under this subchapter shall be reviewed periodically and, if appropriate, revised. The Administrator or the Secretary, as the case may be, may limit or deny the issuance of permits, or he may alter or revoke partially or entirely the terms of permits issued by him under this subchapter, for the transportation for dumping, or for the dumping, or both, of specified materials or classes of materials, where he finds, based upon monitoring data from the dump site and surrounding area, that such materials cannot be dumped consistently with the criteria and other factors required to be applied in evaluating the permit application. No action shall be taken under this subsection unless the affected person or permittee shall have been given notice and opportunity for a hearing on such action as proposed.

**(e) Information for review and evaluation of applications**

The Administrator or the Secretary, as the case may be, shall require an applicant for a permit under this subchapter to provide such information as he may consider necessary to review and evaluate such application.

**(f) Public information**

Information received by the Administrator or the Secretary, as the case may be, as a part of any application or in connection with any permit granted under this subchapter shall be available to the public as a matter of public record, at every stage of the proceeding. The final determination of the Administrator or the Secretary, as the case may be, shall be likewise available.

**(g) Display of issued permits**

A copy of any permit issued under this subchapter shall be placed in a conspicuous place in the vessel which will be used for the transportation or dumping authorized by such permit, and an additional copy shall be furnished by the issuing official to the Secretary of the department in which the Coast Guard is operating, or its designee.

**(h) Low-level radioactive waste; research purposes**

Notwithstanding any provision of this subchapter to the contrary, during the two-year period beginning on January 6, 1983, no permit may be issued under this subchapter that authorizes the dumping of any low-level radioactive waste unless the Administrator of the Environmental Protection Agency determines—

(1) that the proposed dumping is necessary to conduct research—

(A) on new technology related to ocean dumping, or

(B) to determine the degree to which the dumping of such substance will degrade the marine environment;

(2) that the scale of the proposed dumping is limited to the smallest amount of such material and the shortest duration of time that is necessary to fulfill the purposes of the research, such that the dumping will have minimal adverse impact upon human health, welfare, and amenities, and the marine environment, ecological systems, economic potentialities, and other legitimate uses;

(3) after consultation with the Secretary of Commerce, that the potential benefits of such research will outweigh any such adverse impact; and

(4) that the proposed dumping will be preceded by appropriate baseline monitoring studies of the proposed dump site and its surrounding environment.

Each permit issued pursuant to this subsection shall be subject to such conditions and restrictions as the Administrator determines to be necessary to minimize possible adverse impacts of such dumping.

**(i) Radioactive Material Disposal Impact Assessment; Congressional approval**

(1) Two years after January 6, 1983, the Administrator may not issue a permit under this subchapter for the disposal of radioactive waste material until the applicant, in addition to complying with all other requirements of this subchapter, prepares, with respect to the site at which the disposal is proposed, a Radioactive Material Disposal Impact Assessment which shall include—

(A) a listing of all radioactive materials in each container to be disposed, the number of containers to be dumped, the structural diagrams of each container, the number of curies of each material in each container, and the exposure levels in rems at the inside and outside of each container;

(B) an analysis of the environmental impact of the proposed action, at the site at which the applicant desires to dispose of the material, upon human health and welfare and marine life;

(C) any adverse environmental effects at the site which cannot be avoided should the proposal be implemented;

(D) an analysis of the resulting environmental and economic conditions if the containers fail to contain the radioactive waste material when initially deposited at the specific site;

(E) a plan for the removal or containment of the disposed nuclear material if the container leaks or decomposes;

(F) a determination by each affected State whether the proposed action is consistent with its approved Coastal Zone Management Program;

(G) an analysis of the economic impact upon other users of marine resources;

(H) alternatives to the proposed action;

(I) comments and results of consultation with State officials and public hearings held in the coastal States that are nearest to the affected areas;

(J) a comprehensive monitoring plan to be carried out by the applicant to determine the full effect of the disposal on the marine environment, living resources, or human health, which plan shall include, but not be limited to, the monitoring of exterior container radiation samples, the taking of water and sediment samples, and fish and benthic animal samples, adjacent to the containers, and the acquisition of such other information as the Administrator may require; and

(K) such other information which the Administrator may require in order to determine the full effects of such disposal.

(2) The Administrator shall include, in any permit to which paragraph (1) applies, such terms and conditions as may be necessary to ensure that the monitoring plan required under paragraph (1)(J) is fully implemented, including the analysis by the Administrator of the samples required to be taken under the plan.

(3) The Administrator shall submit a copy of the assessment prepared under paragraph (1) with respect to any permit to the Committee on Merchant Marine and Fisheries of the House of Representatives and the Committee on Environment and Public Works of the Senate.

(4)(A) Upon a determination by the Administrator that a permit to which this subsection applies should be issued, the Administrator shall transmit such a recommendation to the House of Representatives and the Senate.

(B) No permit may be issued by the Administrator under this Act for the disposal of radioactive materials in the ocean unless the Congress, by approval of a resolution described in paragraph (D) within 90 days of continuous session of the Congress beginning on the date after the date of receipt by the Senate and the House of Representatives of such recommendation, authorizes the Administrator to grant a permit to dispose of radioactive material under this Act.

(C) For purposes of this subsection—

(1) continuity of session of the Congress is broken only by an adjournment sine die;

(2) the days on which either House is not in session because of an adjournment of more than three days to a day certain are excluded in the computation of the 90 day calendar period.

(D) For the purposes of this subsection, the term "resolution" means a joint resolution, the resolving clause of which is as follows: "That the House of Representatives and the Senate approve and authorize the Administrator of the Environmental Protection Agency to grant a permit to ______ under the Marine Protection, Research, and Sanctuaries Act of 1972 to dispose of radioactive materials in the ocean as recommended by the Administrator to the Congress on ______, 19___."; the first blank space therein to be filled with the appropriate applicant to dispose of nuclear material and the second blank therein to be filled with the date on which the Administrator submits the recommendation to the House of Representatives and the Senate.

(Pub.L. 92–532, Title I, § 104, Oct. 23, 1972, 86 Stat. 1056; Pub.L. 97–424, Title IV, § 424(a), Jan. 6, 1983, 96 Stat. 2165; Pub.L. 100–17, Title I, § 133(c)(1), Apr. 2, 1987, 101 Stat. 172; Pub.L. 102–580, Title V, § 507, Oct. 31, 1992, 106 Stat. 4869.)

## HISTORICAL AND STATUTORY NOTES

**References in Text**

This Act and the Marine Protection, Research, and Sanctuaries Act of 1972, referred to in subsec. (i)(4)(B), (D), is Pub.L. 92–532, Oct. 23, 1972, 86 Stat. 1052, as amended, which is classified generally to this chapter, chapter 41 of this title [33 U.S.C.A. § 2801 et seq.], and chapters 32 [16 U.S.C.A. § 1431 et seq.] and 32A [16 U.S.C.A. § 1447 et seq.] of Title 16. For complete classification of this Act to the Code, see Short Title note set out under 33 U.S.C.A. § 1401 and Tables.

**Effective and Applicability Provisions**

1972 Acts

Section effective six months after Oct. 23, 1972, see section 110(a) of Pub.L. 92–532, set out as a note under section 1411 of this title.

**Abolition of House Committee on Merchant Marine and Fisheries**

Committee on Merchant Marine and Fisheries of House of Representatives abolished and any reference in any provision of law enacted before Jan. 4, 1995, to the Committee on Merchant Marine and Fisheries of the House of Representatives treated as referring to the Committee on Agriculture of the House of Representatives, in the case of a provision of law relating to inspection of seafood or seafood products, the Committee on National Security of the House of Representatives, in the case of a provision of law relating to interoceanic canals, the Merchant Marine Academy and State Maritime Academies, or national security aspects of merchant marine, the Committee on Resources of the House of Representatives, in the case of a provision of law relating to fisheries, wildlife, international fishing agreements marine affairs (including coastal zone management) except for measures relating to oil and other pollution of navigable waters, or oceanography, the Committee on Science of the House of Representatives, in the case of a provision of law relating to marine research, and the Committee on Transportation and Infrastructure of the House of Representatives, in the case of a provision of law relating to a matter other than a matter described above, see section 1(b)(3) of Pub.L. 104–14, set out as a note preceding section 21 of Title 2, The Congress.

## § 1414a. Special provisions regarding certain dumping sites

**[MPRSA § 104A]**

**(a) New York Bight Apex**

(1) For purposes of this subsection—

(A) The term "Apex" means the New York Bight Apex consisting of the ocean waters of the Atlantic Ocean westward of 73 degrees 30 minutes west longitude and northward of 40 degrees 10 minutes north latitude.

(B) The term "Apex site" means that site within the Apex at which the dumping of municipal sludge occurred before October 1, 1983.

(C) The term "eligible authority" means any sewerage authority or other unit of State or local government that on November 2, 1983, was authorized under court order to dump municipal sludge at the Apex site.

(2) No person may apply for a permit under this subchapter in relation to the dumping of, or the transportation for purposes of dumping, municipal sludge within the Apex unless that person is an eligible authority.

(3) The Administrator may not issue, or renew, any permit under this subchapter that authorizes the dumping of, or the transportation for purposes of dumping, municipal sludge within the Apex after the earlier of—

(A) December 15, 1987; or

(B) the day determined by the Administrator to be the first day on which municipal sludge generated by eligible authorities can reasonably be dumped at a site designated under section 1412 of this title other than a site within the Apex.

**(b) Restriction on use of the 106-mile site**

The Administrator may not issue or renew any permit under this subchapter which authorizes any person, other than a person that is an eligible authority within the meaning of subsection (a)(1)(C) of this section, to dump, or to transport for the purposes of dumping, municipal sludge within the site designated under section 1412(c) of this title by the Administrator and known as the "106-Mile Ocean Waste Dump Site" (as described in 49 F.R. 19005).

(Pub.L. 92–532, Title I, § 104A, as added Pub.L. 99–662, Title XI, § 1172(b), Nov. 17, 1986, 100 Stat. 4259.)

### HISTORICAL AND STATUTORY NOTES

**Prior Provisions**

An identical section 104A, which was added to Pub.L. 92–532 by Pub.L. 100–4, Title V, § 508(b), Feb. 4, 1987, 101 Stat. 79 and also classified to this section, was repealed by Pub.L. 100–688, Title I, § 1002, Nov. 18, 1988, 102 Stat. 4139.

**Congressional Finding**

Section 1172(a) of Pub.L. 99–662 provided that: "The Congress finds that the New York Bight Apex is no longer a suitable location for the ocean dumping of municipal sludge."

[An identical provision was enacted by Pub.L. 100–4, Title V, § 508(a), Feb. 4, 1987, 101 Stat. 79.]

## § 1414b. Ocean dumping of sewage sludge and industrial waste

**[MPRSA § 104B]**

**(a) Termination of dumping**

**(1) Prohibitions on dumping**

Notwithstanding any other provision of law—

(A) on and after the 270th day after November 18, 1988, no person (including a person described in section 1414a(a)(1)(C) of this title) shall dump into ocean waters, or transport for the purpose of dumping into ocean waters, sewage sludge or industrial waste, unless such person—

(i) has entered into a compliance agreement or enforcement agreement which meets the requirements of subsection (c)(2) or (3) of this section, as applicable; and

(ii) has obtained a permit issued under section 1412 of this title which authorizes such transportation and dumping; and

(B) after December 31, 1991, it shall be unlawful for any person to dump into ocean waters, or to transport for the purposes of dumping into ocean waters, sewage sludge or industrial waste.

**(2) Prohibition on new entrants**

The Administrator shall not issue any permit under this Act which authorizes a person to dump into ocean waters, or to transport for the purposes of dumping into ocean waters, sewage sludge or industrial waste, unless that person was authorized by a permit issued under section 1412 of this title or by a court order to dump into ocean waters, or to transport for the purpose of dumping into ocean waters, sewage sludge or industrial waste on September 1, 1988.

**(b) Special dumping fees**

**(1) In general**

Subject to paragraph (4), any person who dumps into ocean waters, or transports for the purpose of dumping into ocean waters, sewage sludge or industrial waste shall be liable for a fee equal to—

**(A)** $100 for each dry ton (or equivalent) of sewage sludge or industrial waste transported or dumped by the person on or after the 270th day after November 18, 1988, and before January 1, 1990;

**(B)** $150 for each dry ton (or equivalent) of sewage sludge or industrial waste transported or dumped by the person on or after January 1, 1990, and before January 1, 1991; and

**(C)** $200 for each dry ton (or equivalent) of sewage sludge or industrial waste transported or dumped by the person on or after January 1, 1991, and before January 1, 1992.

**(2) Payment of fees**

Of the amount of fees under paragraph (1) for which a person is liable, such person—

**(A)** shall pay into a trust account established by the person in accordance with subsection (e) of this section a sum equal to 85 percent of such amount;

**(B)** shall pay to the Administrator a sum equal to $15 per dry ton (or equivalent) of sewage sludge and industrial waste transported or dumped by such person, for use for agency activities as provided in subsection (f)(1) of this section;

**(C)** subject to paragraph (5), shall pay into the Clean Oceans Fund established by the State in which the person is located a sum equal to 50 percent of the balance of such amount after application of subparagraphs (A) and (B); and

**(D)** subject to paragraph (5), shall pay to the State in which the person is located a sum equal to the balance of such amount after application of subparagraphs (A), (B), and (C), for deposit into the water pollution control revolving fund established by the State under title VI of the Federal Water Pollution Control Act [33 U.S.C.A. § 1381 et seq.], as provided in subsection (f)(2) of this section.

**(3) Schedule for payment**

Fees under this subsection shall be paid on a quarterly basis.

**(4) Waiver of fees**

**(A)** The Administrator shall waive all fees under this subsection, other than the portion of fees required to be paid to the Administrator under paragraph (2)(B) for agency activities, for any person who has entered into a compliance agreement which meets the requirements of subsection (c)(2) of this section.

**(B)** The Administrator shall reimpose fees under this subsection for a person for whom such fees are waived under subparagraph (A) if the Administrator determines that—

**(i)** the person has failed to comply with the terms of a compliance agreement which the person entered into under subsection (c)(2) of this section; and

**(ii)** such failure is likely to result in the person not being able to terminate by December 31, 1991, dumping of sewage sludge or industrial waste into ocean waters.

**(C)** The Administrator may waive fees reimposed for a person under subparagraph (B) if the Administrator determines that the person has returned to compliance with a compliance agreement which the person entered into under subsection (c)(2) of this section.

**(5) Payments prior to establishment of account**

**(A)** In any case in which a State has not established a Clean Oceans Fund or a water pollution control revolving fund under title VI of the Federal Water Pollution Control Act [33 U.S.C.A. § 1381 et seq.], fees required to be paid by a person in that State under paragraph (2)(C) or (D), as applicable, shall be paid to the Administrator.

**(B)** Amounts paid to the Administrator pursuant to this paragraph shall be held by the Administrator in escrow until the establishment of the fund into which such amounts are required to be paid under paragraph (2), or until the last day of the 1-year period beginning on the date of such payment, whichever is earlier, and thereafter—

**(i)** if such fund has been established, shall be paid by the Administrator into the fund; or

**(ii)** if such fund has not been established, shall revert to the general fund of the Treasury.

**(c) Compliance agreements and enforcement agreements**

**(1) In general**

As a condition of issuing a permit under section 1412 of this title which authorizes a person to transport or dump sewage sludge or industrial waste, the Administrator shall require that, before the issuance of such permit, the person and the State in which the person is located enter into with the Administrator—

**(A)** a compliance agreement which meets the requirements of paragraph (2); or

**(B)** an enforcement agreement which meets the requirements of paragraph (3).

**(2) Compliance agreements**

An agreement shall be a compliance agreement for purposes of this section only if—

**(A)** it includes a plan negotiated by the person, the State in which the person is located, and the Administrator that will, in the opinion of the Administrator, if adhered to by the person in good faith, result in the phasing out and termination of ocean dumping, and transportation for the purpose of ocean dumping, of sewage sludge and industrial waste by such person by not later than December 31, 1991, through the design, construction, and full implementation of an alternative system for the management of sewage sludge and industrial waste transported or dumped by the person;

**(B)** it includes a schedule which—

**(i)** in the opinion of the Administrator, specifies reasonable dates by which the person shall complete the various activities that are necessary for the timely implementation of the alternative system referred to in subparagraph (A); and

**(ii)** meets the requirements of paragraph (4);

**(C)** it requires the person to notify in a timely manner the Administrator and the Governor of the State of any problems the person has in complying with the schedule referred to in subparagraph (B);

**(D)** it requires the Administrator and the Governor of the State to evaluate on an ongoing basis the compliance of the person with the schedule referred to in subparagraph (B);

**(E)** it requires the person to pay in accordance with this section all fees and penalties the person is liable for under this section; and

**(F)** it authorizes the person to use interim measures before completion of the alternative system referred to in subparagraph (A).

**(3) Enforcement agreements**

An agreement shall be an enforcement agreement for purposes of this section only if—

**(A)** it includes a plan negotiated by the person, the State in which the person is located, and the Administrator that will, in the opinion of the Administrator, if adhered to by the person in good faith, result in the phasing out and termination of ocean dumping, and transportation for the purpose of ocean dumping, of sewage sludge and industrial waste by such person through the design, construction, and full implementation of an alternative system for the management of sewage sludge and industrial waste transported or dumped by the person;

**(B)** it includes a schedule which—

**(i)** in the opinion of the Administrator, specifies reasonable dates by which the person shall complete the various activities that are necessary for the timely implementation of the alternative system referred to in subparagraph (A); and

**(ii)** meets the requirements of paragraph (4);

**(C)** it requires the person to notify in a timely manner the Administrator and the Governor of the State of any problems the person has in complying with the schedule referred to in subparagraph (B);

**(D)** it requires the Administrator and the Governor of the State to evaluate on an ongoing basis the compliance of the person with the schedule referred to in subparagraph (B);

**(E)** it requires the person to pay in accordance with this section all fees and penalties the person is liable for under this section; and

**(F)** it authorizes the person to use interim measures before completion of the alternative system referred to in subparagraph (A).

**(4) Schedules**

A schedule included in a compliance agreement pursuant to paragraph (2)(B) or an enforcement agreement pursuant to paragraph (3)(B) shall establish deadlines for—

**(A)** preparation of engineering designs and related specifications for the alternative system referred to in paragraph (2)(A) or paragraph (3)(A), as applicable;

**(B)** compliance with appropriate Federal, State, and local statutes, regulations, and ordinances;

**(C)** site and equipment acquisitions for such alternative system;

**(D)** construction and testing of such alternative system;

**(E)** operation of such alternative system at full capacity; and

**(F)** any other activities, including interim measures, that the Administrator considers necessary or appropriate.

**(5) Clean oceans funds**

**(A)** Each State that is a party to a compliance agreement or an enforcement agreement under this subsection shall establish an interest bearing account, to be known as a Clean Oceans Fund, into which a person shall pay fees and penalties in accordance with subsections (b)(2)(C) and (d)(2)(C)(i) of this section, respectively.

**(B)** A State which establishes a Clean Oceans Fund pursuant to this paragraph shall allocate and pay from the fund each year, to each person in the

State which has entered into a compliance agreement or enforcement agreement under this subsection, a portion of amounts in the fund on the last day of that year which is equal to the sum of—

**(i)** amounts paid by the person into the fund in that year as fees pursuant to subsection (b)(2)(C) of this section and as penalties pursuant to subsection (d)(2)(C)(i) of this section;

**(ii)** amounts paid by the Administrator into the fund in that year as fees held in escrow for the person pursuant to subsection (b)(5)(B) of this section; and

**(iii)** interest on such amounts.

**(C)** Amounts allocated and paid to a person pursuant to subparagraph (B)—

**(i)** shall be used for the purposes described in subsection (e)(2)(B) of this section; and

**(ii)** may be used for matching Federal grants.

**(D)** A Clean Oceans Fund established by a State pursuant to this paragraph shall be subject to such accounting, reporting, and other requirements as may be established by the Administrator to assure accountability of payments into and out of the fund.

**(6) Public participation**

The Administrator shall provide an opportunity for public comment regarding the establishment and implementation of compliance agreements and enforcement agreements entered into pursuant to this section.

**(d) Penalties**

**(1) In general**

In lieu of any other civil penalty under this Act, any person who has entered into a compliance agreement or enforcement agreement under subsection (c) of this section and who dumps or transports sewage sludge or industrial waste in violation of subsection (a)(1)(B) of this section shall be liable for a civil penalty, to be assessed by the Administrator, as follows:

**(A)** For each dry ton (or equivalent) of sewage sludge or industrial waste dumped or transported by the person in violation of this subsection in calendar year 1992, $600.

**(B)** For each dry ton (or equivalent) of sewage sludge or industrial waste dumped or transported by the person in violation of this subsection in any year after calendar year 1992, a sum equal to—

**(i)** the amount of penalty per dry ton (or equivalent) for a violation occurring in the preceding calendar year, plus

**(ii)** a percentage of such amount equal to 10 percent of such amount, plus an additional 1 percent of such amount for each full calendar year since December 31, 1991.

**(2) Payment of penalty**

Of the amount of penalties under paragraph (1) for which a person is liable, such person—

**(A)** shall pay into a trust account established by the person in accordance with subsection (e) of this section a sum which is a percentage of such amount equal to—

**(i)** 90 percent of such amount, reduced by

**(ii)** 5 percent of such amount for each full calendar year since December 31, 1991;

**(B)** shall pay to the Administrator a sum equal to $15 per dry ton (or equivalent) of sewage sludge and industrial waste transported or dumped by such person in that year, for use for agency activities as provided in subsection (f)(1) of this section;

**(C)** for violations in any year before calendar year 1995—

**(i)** subject to paragraph (4), shall pay into the Clean Oceans Fund established by the State in which the person is located a sum equal to 50 percent of the balance of such amount; and

**(ii)** subject to paragraph (4), shall pay to the State in which the person is located a sum equal to the portion of such amount which is not paid as provided in subparagraphs (A), (B), and (C), for deposit into the water pollution control revolving fund established by the State under title VI of the Federal Water Pollution Control Act [33 U.S.C.A. § 1381 et seq.]; as provided in subsection (f)(2) of this section; and

**(D)** for violations in any year after calendar year 1994, shall pay to the State in which the person is located a sum equal to the balance of such amount, for use by the State for providing assistance under subsection (f)(3) of this section.

**(3) Schedule for payment**

Penalties under this subsection shall be paid on a quarterly basis.

**(4) Payments prior to establishment of account**

In any case in which a State has not established a Clean Oceans Fund or a water pollution control revolving fund under title VI of the Federal Water Pollution Control Act, penalties required to be paid by a person in that State under paragraph (2)(C)(i) or (ii), as applicable, shall be paid to the Administrator for holding and payment or reversion, as applicable, in the same manner as fees are held and paid or revert under subsection (b)(5) of this section.

**(e) Trust account**

**(1) In general**

A person who enters into a compliance agreement or an enforcement agreement under subsection (c) of this section shall establish a trust account for the payment and use of fees and penalties under this section.

**(2) Trust account requirements**

An account shall be a trust account for purposes of this subsection only if it meets, to the satisfaction of the Administrator, the following requirements:

**(A)** Amounts in the account may be used only with the concurrence of the person who establishes the account and the Administrator; except that the person may use amounts in the account for a purpose authorized by subparagraph (B) after 60 days after notification of the Administrator if the Administrator does not disapprove such use before the end of such 60-day period.

**(B)** Amounts in the account may be used only for projects which will identify, develop, and implement—

**(i)** an alternative system, and any interim measures, for the management of sewage sludge and industrial waste, including but not limited to any such system or measures utilizing resource recovery, recycling, thermal reduction, or composting techniques; or

**(ii)** improvements in pretreatment, treatment, and storage techniques for sewage sludge and industrial waste to facilitate the implementation of such alternative system or interim measures.

**(C)** Upon a finding by the Administrator that a person did not pay fees or penalties into an account as required by this section, or did not use amounts in the account in accordance with this subsection, the balance of the amounts in the account shall be paid to the State in which the person is located, for deposit into the water pollution control revolving fund established by the State under title VI of the Federal Water Pollution Control Act [33 U.S.C.A. § 1381 et seq.], as provided in subsection (f)(2) of this section.

**(3) Use of unexpended amounts**

Upon a determination by the Administrator that a person has terminated ocean dumping of sewage sludge or industrial waste, the balance of amounts in an account established by the person under this subsection shall be paid to the person for use—

**(A)** for debts incurred by the person in complying with this Act or the Federal Water Pollution Control Act [33 U.S.C.A. § 1251 et seq.];

**(B)** in meeting the requirements of the Federal Water Pollution Control Act (33 U.S.C. 1251 et seq.) which apply to the person, including operations and maintenance; and

**(C)** for matching Federal grants.

**(4) Use for matching Federal grants**

Amounts in a trust account under this subsection may be used for matching Federal grants.

**(f) Use of fees and penalties**

**(1) Agency activities**

Of the total amount of fees and penalties paid to the Administrator in a fiscal year pursuant to subsections (b)(2)(B) and (d)(2)(B) of this section, respectively—

**(A)** not to exceed one-third of such total amount shall be used by the Administrator for—

**(i)** costs incurred or expected to be incurred in undertaking activities directly associated with the issuance under this Act of permits for the transportation or dumping of sewage sludge and industrial waste, including the costs of any environmental assessment of the direct effects of dumping under the permits;

**(ii)** preparation of reports under subsection (i) of this section; and

**(iii)** such other research, studies, and projects the Administrator considers necessary for, and consistent with, the development and implementation of alternative systems for the management of sewage sludge and industrial waste;

**(B)** not to exceed one-third of such total amount shall be transferred to the Secretary of the department in which the Coast Guard is operating for use for—

**(i)** Coast Guard surveillance of transportation and dumping of sewage sludge and industrial waste subject to this Act; and

**(ii)** such enforcement activities conducted by the Coast Guard with respect to such transportation and dumping as may be necessary to ensure to the maximum extent practicable complete compliance with the requirements of this Act; and

**(C)** not to exceed one-third of such total amount shall be transferred to the Under Secretary of Commerce for Oceans and Atmosphere for use for—

**(i)** monitoring, research, and related activities consistent with the program developed pursuant to subsection (j)(1) of this section; and

**(ii)** preparing annual reports to the Congress pursuant to subsection (j)(4) which describe the results of such monitoring, research, and activities.

**(2) Deposits into State water pollution control revolving fund**

**(A)** Amounts paid to a State pursuant to subsection (b)(2)(D), (d)(2)(C)(ii), or (e)(2)(C) of this section shall be deposited into the water pollution control revolving fund established by the State pursuant to title VI of the Federal Water Pollution Control Act [33 U.S.C.A. § 1381 et seq.].

(B) Amounts deposited into a State water pollution control revolving fund pursuant to this paragraph—

(i) shall not be used by the State to provide assistance to the person who paid such amounts for development or implementation of any alternative system;

(ii) shall not be considered to be State matching amounts under title VI of the Federal Water Pollution Control Act; and

(iii) shall not be subject to State matching requirements under such title.

**(3) Penalty payments to States after 1994**

(A) Amounts paid to a State as penalties pursuant to subsection (d)(2)(D) of this section may be used by the State—

(i) for providing assistance to any person in the State—

(I) for implementing a management program under section 319 of the Federal Water Pollution Control Act [33 U.S.C.A. § 1329];

(II) for developing and implementing a conservation and management plan under section 320 of such [33 U.S.C.A. § 1330]; or

(III) for implementing technologies and management practices necessary for controlling pollutant inputs adversely affecting the New York Bight, as such inputs are identified in the New York Bight Restoration Plan prepared under section 2301 of the Marine Plastic Pollution Research and Control Act of 1987; and

(ii) for providing assistance to any person in the State who was not required to pay such penalties for construction of treatment works (as defined in section 212 of the Federal Water Pollution Control Act [33 U.S.C.A. § 1292]) which are publicly owned.

(B) Amounts paid to a State as penalties pursuant to subsection (d)(2)(D) of this section which are not used in accordance with subparagraph (A) shall be deposited into the water pollution control revolving fund established by the State under title VI of the Federal Water Pollution Control Act [33 U.S.C.A. § 1381 et seq.]. Amounts deposited into such a fund pursuant to this subparagraph—

(i) shall not be used by the State to provide assistance to the person who paid such amounts;

(ii) shall not be considered to be State matching amounts under title VI of the Federal Water Pollution Control Act [33 U.S.C.A. § 1381 et seq.]; and

(iii) shall not be subject to State matching requirements under such title.

**(4) Deposits into Treasury as offsetting collections**

Amounts of fees and penalties paid to the Administrator pursuant to subsection (b)(2)(B) or (d)(2)(B) of this section which are used by an agency in accordance with paragraph (1) shall be deposited into the Treasury as offsetting collections of the agency.

**(g) Enforcement**

**(1) In general**

Whenever, on the basis of any information available, the Administrator finds that a person is dumping or transporting sewage sludge or industrial waste in violation of subsection (a)(1) of this section, the Administrator shall issue an order requiring such person to terminate such dumping or transporting (as applicable) until such person—

(A) enters into a compliance agreement or an enforcement agreement under subsection (c) of this section; and

(B) obtains a permit under section 1412 of this title which authorizes such dumping or transporting.

**(2) Requirements of order**

Any order issued by the Administrator under this subsection—

(A) shall be delivered by personal service to the person named in the order;

(B) shall state with reasonable specificity the nature of the violation for which the order is issued; and

(C) shall require that the person named in the order, as a condition of dumping into ocean waters, or transporting for the purpose of dumping into ocean waters, sewage sludge or industrial waste—

(i) shall enter into a compliance agreement or an enforcement agreement under subsection (c) of this section; and

(ii) shall obtain a permit under section 1412 of this title which authorizes such dumping or transporting.

**(3) Actions**

The Administrator may request the Attorney General to commence a civil action for appropriate relief, including a temporary or permanent injunction and the imposition of civil penalties authorized by subsection (d)(1) of this section, for any violation of subsection (a)(1) of this section or of an order issued by the Administrator under this section. Such an action may be brought in the district court of the United States for the district in which the defendant is located, resides, or is doing business, and such court shall have jurisdiction to restrain such violation and require compliance with subsection (a)(1) of this section and any such order.

**(h) State progress reports**

**(1) In general**

The Governor of each State that is a party to a compliance agreement or an enforcement agreement under subsection (c) of this section shall submit to the Administrator on September 30 of 1989 and of every year thereafter until the Administrator determines that ocean dumping of sewage sludge and industrial waste by persons located in that State has terminated, a report which describes—

(A) the efforts of each person located in the State to comply with a compliance agreement or enforcement agreement entered into by the person pursuant to subsection (c) of this section, including the extent to which such person has complied with deadlines established by the schedule included in such agreement;

(B) activity of the State regarding permits for the construction and operation of each alternative system; and

(C) an accounting of amounts paid into and withdrawn from a Clean Oceans Fund established by the State.

**(2) Failure to submit report**

If a State fails to submit a report in accordance with this subsection, the Administrator shall withhold funds reserved for such State under section 205(g) of the Federal Water Pollution Control Act (33 U.S.C. 1285(g)). Funds withheld pursuant to this paragraph may, at the discretion of the Administrator, be restored to a State upon compliance with this subsection.

**(i) EPA progress reports**

**(1) In general**

Not later than December 31 of 1989 and of each year thereafter until the Administrator determines that ocean dumping of sewage sludge and industrial waste has terminated, the Administrator shall prepare and submit to the Congress a report on—

(A) progress being made by persons issued permits under section 1412 of this title for transportation or dumping of sewage sludge or industrial waste in developing alternative systems for managing sewage sludge and industrial waste;

(B) the efforts of each such person to comply with a compliance agreement or enforcement agreement entered into by the person pursuant to subsection (c) of this section, including the extent to which such person has complied with deadlines established by the schedule included in such agreement;

(C) progress being made by the Administrator and others in identifying and implementing alternative systems for the management of sewage sludge and industrial waste; and

(D) progress being made toward the termination of ocean dumping of sewage sludge and industrial waste.

**(2) Referral to Congressional committees**

Each report submitted to the Congress under this subsection shall be referred to each standing committee of the House of Representatives and of the Senate having jurisdiction over any part of the subject matter of the report.

**(j) Environmental monitoring**

**(1) In general**

The Administrator, in cooperation with the Under Secretary of Commerce for Oceans and Atmosphere, shall design a program for monitoring environmental conditions—

(A) at the Apex site (as that term is defined in section 1414a of this title);

(B) at the site designated by the Administrator under section 1412(c) of this title and known as the "106–Mile Ocean Waste Dump Site" (as described in 49 F.R. 19005);

(C) at the site at which industrial waste is dumped; and

(D) within the potential area of influence of the sewage sludge and industrial waste dumped at those sites.

**(2) Program requirements**

The program designed under paragraph (1) shall include, but is not limited to—

(A) sampling of an appropriate number of fish and shellfish species and other organisms to assess the effects of environmental conditions on living marine organisms in these areas; and

(B) use of satellite and other advanced technologies in conducting the program.

**(3) Monitoring activities**

The Administrator and the Under Secretary of Commerce for Oceans and Atmosphere shall each conduct monitoring activities consistent with the program designed under paragraph (1).

**(4) Omitted**

**(k) Definitions**

For purposes of this section—

(1) the term "alternative system" means any method for the management of sewage sludge or industrial waste which does not require a permit under this Act;

(2) the term "Clean Oceans Fund" means such a fund established by a State in accordance with subsection (c)(5);

(3) the term "excluded material" means—

(A) any dredged material discharged by the United States Army Corps of Engineers or discharged pursuant to a permit issued by the Secretary in accordance with section 1413 of this title; and

(B) any waste from a tuna cannery operation located in American Samoa or Puerto Rico discharged pursuant to a permit issued by the Administrator under section 1412 of this title;

(4) the term "industrial waste" means any solid, semisolid, or liquid waste generated by a manufacturing or processing plant, other than an excluded material;

(5) the term "interim measure" means any short-term method for the management of sewage sludge or industrial waste, which—

(A) is used before implementation of an alternative system; and

(B) does not require a permit under this Act; and

(6) the term "sewage sludge" means any solid, semisolid, or liquid waste generated by a wastewater treatment plant, other than an excluded material.

(Pub.L. 92–532, Title I, § 104B, as added Pub.L. 100–688, Title I, § 1002, Nov. 18, 1988, 102 Stat. 4139.)

HISTORICAL AND STATUTORY NOTES

**References in Text**

This Act, referred to in subsecs. (a)(2), (d)(1), (e)(3)(A), (f)(1)(A)(i), (B), and (k)(1), (5)(B), means Pub.L. 92–532, which is classified principally to this chapter, chapter 41 [33 U.S.C.A. § 2801 et seq.] of this title, and chapters 32 [16 U.S.C.A. § 1431 et seq.] and 32A [16 U.S.C.A. § 1447 et seq.] of Title 16.

The Federal Water Pollution Control Act, referred to in text, is Act June 30, 1948, c. 758, as amended generally by Pub.L. 92–500, § 2, Oct. 18, 1972, 86 Stat. 816, which is classified generally to chapter 26 (section 1251 et seq.) of this title. Title VI of that Act is classified to subchapter VI (Section 1381 et seq.) of chapter 26 of this title. For complete classification of this Act to the Code, see Short Title note set out under section 1251 of this title and Tables.

Subsection (j)(4) of this section, referred to in subsec. (f)(1)(C)(ii), was omitted from the Code. See Codifications note under this section.

Section 2301 of the Marine Plastic Pollution Research and Control Act of 1987, referred to in subsec. (f)(3)(A)(i)(III), is section 2301 of Pub.L. 100–220, Title II, Dec. 29, 1987, 101 Stat. 1467, set out as a note under section 2267 of this title.

**Codifications**

Subsec. (j)(4)(A) of this section directed the Administrator, in cooperation with the Under Secretary of Commerce for Oceans and Atmosphere, to submit to Congress a report describing the program designed pursuant to subsec. (j)(1) of this section not later than one year after Nov. 18, 1988.

Subsec. (j)(4)(B) of this section, which required the Administrator and the Under Secretary of Commerce for Oceans and Atmosphere to report annually to Congress on monitoring activities conducted under the program designed pursuant to subsec. (j)(1) of this section, terminated, effective May 15, 2000, pursuant to section 3003 of Pub.L. 104–66, as amended, set out as a note under 31 U.S.C.A. § 1113. See, also, page 148 of House Document No. 103–7.

## § 1414c. Prohibition on disposal of sewage sludge at landfills on Staten Island

[MPRSA § 104C]

**(a) In general**

No person shall dispose of sewage sludge at any landfill located on Staten Island, New York.

**(b) Exclusion from penalties**

**(1) In general**

Subject to paragraph (2), a person who violates this section shall not be subject to any penalty under this Act.

**(2) Injunction**

Paragraph (1) shall not prohibit the bringing of an action for, or the granting of, an injunction under section 1415 of this title with respect to a violation of this section.

**(c) "Sewage sludge" defined**

For purposes of this section, the term "sewage sludge" has the meaning such term has in section 1414b of this title.

(Pub.L. 92–532, Title I, § 104C, as added Pub.L. 100–688, Title I, § 1005, Nov. 18, 1988, 102 Stat. 4150.)

HISTORICAL AND STATUTORY NOTES

**References in Text**

This Act, referred to in subsec. (b)(1), means Pub.L. 92–532, which is classified principally to this chapter, chapter 41 [33 U.S.C.A. § 2801 et seq.] of this title, and chapters 32 [16 U.S.C.A. § 1431 et seq.] and 32A [16 U.S.C.A. § 1447 et seq.] of Title 16.

## § 1415. Penalties

[MPRSA § 105]

**(a) Assessment of civil penalty by Administrator; remission or mitigation; court action for appropriate relief**

Any person who violates any provision of this subchapter, or of the regulations promulgated under this subchapter, or a permit issued under this subchapter shall be liable to a civil penalty of not more than $50,000 for each violation to be assessed by the Administrator. In addition, any person who violates this subchapter or any regulation issued under this subchapter by engaging in activity involving the dumping of medical waste shall be liable for a civil penalty of not more than $125,000 for each violation, to be assessed by the Administrator after written notice and an opportunity for a hearing. No penalty shall be assessed until the person charged shall have been given notice and an opportunity for a hearing of such violation. In determining the amount of the penalty, the gravity of the violation, prior violations, and the demonstrated good faith of the person charged in attempting to achieve rapid compliance after notification of a violation shall be considered by said Administrator. For good cause shown, the Administrator may remit or mitigate such penalty. Upon failure of the offending party to pay the penalty, the Administrator may request the Attorney General to commence an action in the appropriate district court of the United States for such relief as may be appropriate.

**(b) Criminal penalties**

In addition to any action that may be brought under subsection (a) of this section—

(1) any person who knowingly violates any provision of this subchapter, any regulation promulgated under this subchapter, or a permit issued under this subchapter, shall be fined under Title 18 or imprisoned for not more than 5 years, or both; and

(2) any person who is convicted of such a violation pursuant to paragraph (1) shall forfeit to the United States—

(A) any property constituting or derived from any proceeds that the person obtained, directly or indirectly, as a result of such violation; and

(B) any of the property of the person which was used, or intended to be used in any manner or part, to commit or to facilitate the commission of the violation.

**(c) Separate offenses**

For the purpose of imposing civil penalties and criminal fines under this section, each day of a continuing violation shall constitute a separate offense as shall the dumping from each of several vessels, or other sources.

**(d) Injunctive relief**

The Attorney General or his delegate may bring actions for equitable relief to enjoin an imminent or continuing violation of this subchapter, of regulations promulgated under this subchapter, or of permits issued under this subchapter, and the district courts of the United States shall have jurisdiction to grant such relief as the equities of the case may require.

**(e) Liability of vessels in rem**

A vessel, except a public vessel within the meaning of section 13 of the Federal Water Pollution Control Act, as amended, used in a violation, shall be liable in rem for any civil penalty assessed or criminal fine imposed and may be proceeded against in any district court of the United States having jurisdiction thereof; but no vessel shall be liable unless it shall appear that one or more of the owners, or bareboat charterers, was at the time of the violation a consenting party or privy to such violation.

**(f) Revocation and suspension of permits**

If the provisions of any permit issued under section 1412 or 1413 of this title are violated, the Administrator or the Secretary, as the case may be, may revoke the permit or may suspend the permit for a specified period of time. No permit shall be revoked or suspended unless the permittee shall have been given notice and opportunity for a hearing on such violation and proposed suspension or revocation.

**(g) Civil suits by private persons**

(1) Except as provided in paragraph (2) of this subsection any person may commence a civil suit on his own behalf to enjoin any person, including the United States and any other governmental instrumentality or agency (to the extent permitted by the eleventh amendment to the Constitution), who is alleged to be in violation of any prohibition, limitation, criterion, or permit established or issued by or under this subchapter. The district courts shall have jurisdiction, without regard to the amount in controversy or the citizenship of the parties, to enforce such prohibition, limitation, criterion, or permit, as the case may be.

(2) No action may be commenced—

(A) prior to sixty days after notice of the violation has been given to the Administrator or to the Secretary, and to any alleged violator of the prohibition, limitation, criterion, or permit; or

(B) if the Attorney General has commenced and is diligently prosecuting a civil action in a court of the United States to require compliance with the prohibition, limitation, criterion, or permit; or

(C) if the Administrator has commenced action to impose a penalty pursuant to subsection (a) of this section, or if the Administrator, or the Secretary, has initiated permit revocation or suspension proceedings under subsection (f) of this section; or

(D) if the United States has commenced and is diligently prosecuting a criminal action in a court of the United States or a State to redress a violation of this subchapter.

(3)(A) Any suit under this subsection may be brought in the judicial district in which the violation occurs.

(B) In any such suit under this subsection in which the United States is not a party, the Attorney General, at the request of the Administrator or Secretary, may intervene on behalf of the United States as a matter of right.

(4) The court, in issuing any final order in any suit brought pursuant to paragraph (1) of this subsection may award costs of litigation (including reasonable attorney and expert witness fees) to any party, whenever the court determines such award is appropriate.

(5) The injunctive relief provided by this subsection shall not restrict any right which any person (or class of persons) may have under any statute or common law to seek enforcement of any standard or limitation or to seek any other relief (including relief against the Administrator, the Secretary, or a State agency).

**(h) Emergencies**

No person shall be subject to a civil penalty or to a criminal fine or imprisonment for dumping materials from a vessel if such materials are dumped in an emergency to safeguard life at sea. Any such emergency dumping shall be reported to the Administrator under such conditions as he may prescribe.

**(i) Seizure and forfeiture**

**(1) In general**

Any vessel used to commit an act for which a penalty is imposed under subsection (b) of this section shall be subject to seizure and forfeiture to the United States under procedures established for seizure and forfeiture of conveyances under sections 853 and 881 of Title 21.

**(2) Limitation on application**

This subsection does not apply to an act committed substantially in accordance with a compliance agreement or enforcement agreement entered into by the Administrator under section 1414b(c) of this title.

(Pub.L. 92–532, Title I, § 105, Oct. 23, 1972, 86 Stat. 1057; Pub.L. 100–688, Title III, § 3201(c), (d), Nov. 18, 1988, 102 Stat. 4153; Pub.L. 102–580, Title V, § 508, Oct. 31, 1992, 106 Stat. 4869.)

### HISTORICAL AND STATUTORY NOTES

**References in Text**

Section 13 of the Federal Water Pollution Control Act, referred to in subsec. (e), is section 13 of Act June 30, 1948, c. 758, as added by Act Apr. 3, 1970, Pub.L. 91–224, Title I, § 102, 84 Stat. 100, which was classified to section 1163 of this title and was superseded by Pub.L. 92–500, Oct. 18, 1972, 86 Stat. 816. See section 1322 of this title.

**Effective and Applicability Provisions**

1972 Acts

Section effective six months after Oct. 23, 1972, see section 110(a) of Pub.L. 92–532, set out as a note under section 1411 of this title.

## § 1416. Relationship to other laws

**[MPRSA § 106]**

**(a) Voiding of preexisting licenses**

After the effective date of this subchapter, all licenses, permits, and authorizations other than those issued pursuant to this subchapter shall be void and of no legal effect, to the extent that they purport to authorize any activity regulated by this subchapter, and whether issued before or after the effective date of this subchapter.

**(b) Actions under authority of Rivers and Harbors Act**

The provisions of subsection (a) of this section shall not apply to actions taken before the effective date of this subchapter under the authority of the Rivers and Harbors Act of 1899 (30 Stat. 1151), as amended (33 U.S.C. 401 et seq.).

**(c) Impairment of navigation**

Prior to issuing any permit under this subchapter, if it appears to the Administrator that the disposition of material, other than dredged material, may adversely affect navigation in the territorial sea of the United States, or in the approaches to any harbor of the United States, or may create an artificial island on the Outer Continental Shelf, the Administrator shall consult with the Secretary and no permit shall be issued if the Secretary determines that navigation will be unreasonably impaired.

**(d) State programs**

**(1) State rights preserved**

Except as expressly provided in this subsection, nothing in this subchapter shall preclude or deny the right of any State to adopt or enforce any requirements respecting dumping of materials into ocean waters within the jurisdiction of the State.

**(2) Federal projects**

In the case of a Federal project, a State may not adopt or enforce a requirement that is more stringent than a requirement under this subchapter if the Administrator finds that such requirement—

(A) is not supported by relevant scientific evidence showing the requirement to be protective of human health, aquatic resources, or the environment;

(B) is arbitrary or capricious; or

(C) is not applicable or is not being applied to all projects without regard to Federal, State, or private participation and the Secretary of the Army concurs in such finding.

**(3) Exemption from State requirements**

The President may exempt a Federal project from any State requirement respecting dumping of materials into ocean waters if it is in the paramount interest of the United States to do so.

**(4) Consideration of site of origin prohibited**

Any requirement respecting dumping of materials into ocean waters applied by a State shall be applied without regard to the site of origin of the material to be dumped.

**(e) Existing conservation programs not affected**

Nothing in this subchapter shall be deemed to affect in any manner or to any extent any provision of the Fish and Wildlife Coordination Act as amended (16 U.S.C. 661–666c).

**(f) Dumping of dredged material in Long Island Sound from any Federal, etc., project**

In addition to other provisions of law and not withstanding the specific exclusion relating to dredged material in the first sentence in section 1412(a) of this title, the dumping of dredged material in Long Island Sound from any Federal project (or pursuant to Federal authorization) or from a dredging project by a non-Federal applicant exceeding 25,000 cubic yards shall comply with the requirements of this subchapter.

**(g) Savings clause**

Nothing in this Act shall restrict, affect or modify the rights of any person (1) to seek damages or enforcement of any standard or limitation under State law, including State common law, or (2) to seek damages under other Federal law, including maritime tort law, resulting from noncompliance with any requirement of this Act or any permit under this Act.

(Pub.L. 92–532, Title I, § 106, Oct. 23, 1972, 86 Stat. 1058; Pub.L. 96–572, § 4, Dec. 22, 1980, 94 Stat. 3345; Pub.L. 99–499, Title I, § 127(d), Oct. 17, 1986, 100 Stat. 1693; Pub.L. 101–596, Title II, § 203, Nov. 16, 1990, 104 Stat. 3006; Pub.L. 102–580, Title V, § 505, Oct. 31, 1992, 106 Stat. 4867.)

## HISTORICAL AND STATUTORY NOTES

**References in Text**

The effective date of this subchapter, referred to in subsecs. (a) and (b), means the effective date of Title I of Pub.L. 92–532 which is six months after Oct. 23, 1972. See section 110(a) of Pub.L. 92–532, set out as a note under section 1411 of this title.

The Rivers and Harbors Act of 1899, referred to in subsec. (b), is Act Mar. 3, 1899, c. 425, 30 Stat. 1151, as amended, which enacted sections 401, 403, 404, 406 to 409, 411 to 416, 418, 502, 549, 686, and 687 of this title. For complete classification of this Act to the Code, see Tables volume.

The Fish and Wildlife Coordination Act, referred to in subsec. (e), is Act Mar. 10, 1934, c. 55, 48 Stat. 401, as amended, which is classified generally to sections 661 to 666c of Title 16, Conservation. For complete classification of this Act to the Code, see Short Title note set out under section 661 of Title 16 and Tables volume.

This Act, referred to in subsec. (g), means Pub.L. 92–532, which is classified principally to this chapter, chapter 41 [33 U.S.C.A. § 2801 et seq.] of this title, and chapters 32 [16 U.S.C.A. § 1431 et seq.] and 32A [16 U.S.C.A. § 1447 et seq.] of Title 16.

**Codifications**

Direction in Pub.L. 101–596, § 203, for substitution, in subsec. (g), of "the requirements of this subchapter" for all that follows "shall comply with" has been executed in subsec. (f) as reflecting Congressional intent by such substitution for "the criteria established pursuant to the second sentence of section 1412(a) of this title relating to the effects of dumping. Subsection (d) of this section shall not apply to this subsection."

**Effective and Applicability Provisions**

1986 Acts

Amendment by Pub.L. 99–499 effective Oct. 17, 1986, see section 4 of Pub.L. 99–499, set out as a note under section 9601 of Title 42, The Public Health and Welfare.

1972 Acts

Section effective six months after Oct. 23, 1972, see section 110(a) of Pub.L. 92–532, set out as a note under section 1411 of this title.

**Territorial Sea of United States**

For extension of territorial sea of United States, see Proc. No. 5928, set out as a note under 43 U.S.C.A. § 1331.

## § 1417. Enforcement

**[MPRSA § 107]**

**(a) Utilization of other departments, agencies, and instrumentalities**

The Administrator or the Secretary, as the case may be, may, whenever appropriate, utilize by agreement, the personnel, services and facilities of other Federal departments, agencies, and instrumentalities, or State agencies or instrumentalities, whether on a reimbursable or a nonreimbursable basis, in carrying out his responsibilities under this subchapter.

**(b) Delegation of review and evaluation authority**

The Administrator or the Secretary may delegate responsibility and authority for reviewing and evaluating permit applications, including the decision as to whether a permit will be issued, to an officer of his agency, or he may delegate, by agreement, such responsibility and authority to the heads of other Federal departments or agencies, whether on a reimbursable or nonreimbursable basis.

**(c) Surveillance and other enforcement activity**

The Secretary of the department in which the Coast Guard is operating shall conduct surveillance and other appropriate enforcement activity to prevent unlawful transportation of material for dumping, or unlawful dumping. Such enforcement activity shall include, but not be limited to, enforcement of regulations issued by him pursuant to section 1418 of this title, relating to safe transportation, handling, carriage, storage, and stowage. The Secretary of the Department in which the Coast Guard is operating shall supply to the Administrator and to the Attorney General, as appropriate, such information of enforcement activities and such evidentiary material assembled as they may require in carrying out their duties relative to penalty assessments, criminal prosecutions, or other actions involving litigation pursuant to the provisions of this subchapter.

(Pub.L. 92–532, Title I, § 107, Oct. 23, 1972, 86 Stat. 1059.)

### HISTORICAL AND STATUTORY NOTES

**Effective and Applicability Provisions**

1972 Acts

Section effective six months after Oct. 23, 1972, see section 110(a) of Pub.L. 92–532, set out as a note under section 1411 of this title.

## § 1418. Regulations

### [MPRSA § 108]

In carrying out the responsibilities and authority conferred by this subchapter, the Administrator, the Secretary, and the Secretary of the department in which the Coast Guard is operating are authorized to issue such regulations as they may deem appropriate.

(Pub.L. 92–532, Title I, § 108, Oct. 23, 1972, 86 Stat. 1059.)

### HISTORICAL AND STATUTORY NOTES

**Effective and Applicability Provisions**

1972 Acts

Section effective six months after Oct. 23, 1972, see section 110(a) of Pub.L. 92–532, set out as a note under section 1411 of this title.

## § 1419. International cooperation

### [MPRSA § 109]

The Secretary of State, in consultation with the Administrator, shall seek effective international action and cooperation to insure protection of the marine environment, and may, for this purpose, formulate, present, or support specific proposals in the United Nations and other component international organizations for the development of appropriate international rules and regulations in support of the policy of this Act.

(Pub.L. 92–532, Title I, § 109, Oct. 23, 1972, 86 Stat. 1060.)

### HISTORICAL AND STATUTORY NOTES

**References in Text**

This Act, referred to in text, means Pub.L. 92–532, which is classified principally to this chapter, chapter 41 [33 U.S.C.A. § 2801 et seq.] of this title, and chapters 32 [16 U.S.C.A. § 1431 et seq.] and 32A [16 U.S.C.A. § 1447 et seq.] of Title 16.

**Effective and Applicability Provisions**

1972 Acts

Section effective six months after Oct. 23, 1972, see section 110(a) of Pub.L. 92–532, set out as a note under section 1411 of this title.

## § 1420. Authorization of appropriations

### [MPRSA § 111]

There are authorized to be appropriated, for purposes of carrying out this subchapter, not to exceed $12,000,000 for fiscal year 1993 and not to exceed $14,000,000 for each of the fiscal years 1994, 1995, 1996, and 1997, to remain available until expended.

(Pub.L. 92–532, Title I, § 111, Oct. 23, 1972, 86 Stat. 1060; Pub.L. 93–472, Oct. 26, 1974, 88 Stat. 1430; Pub.L. 94–62, § 1, July 25, 1975, 89 Stat. 303; Pub.L. 94–326, § 1, June 30, 1976, 90 Stat. 725; Pub.L. 95–153, § 1, Nov. 4, 1977, 91 Stat. 1255; Pub.L. 96–572, § 1, Dec. 22, 1980, 94 Stat. 3344; Pub.L. 97–16, June 23, 1981, 95 Stat. 100; Pub.L. 100–536, Oct. 28, 1988, 102 Stat. 2710; Pub.L. 102–580, Title V, § 509(a), Oct. 31, 1992, 106 Stat. 4870.)

### HISTORICAL AND STATUTORY NOTES

**Effective and Applicability Provisions**

1972 Acts

Section effective six months after Oct. 23, 1972, see section 110(a) of Pub.L. 92–532, set out as a note under section 1411 of this title.

## § 1421. Omitted

### [MPRSA § 112]

### HISTORICAL AND STATUTORY NOTES

**Codifications**

Section, Pub.L. 92–532, Title I, § 112, Oct. 23, 1972, 86 Stat. 1060; Pub.L. 94-326, § 2, June 30, 1976, 90 Stat. 725; Pub.L. 96–470, Title II, § 209(f), Oct. 19, 1980, 94 Stat. 2245; Pub.L. 102–580, Title V, § 510, Oct. 31, 1992, 106 Stat. 4870, which required the Administrator of the Environmental Protection Agency to report annually to Congress on the administration of this subchapter, terminated, effective May 15, 2000, pursuant to section 3003 of Pub.L. 104–66, as amended, set out as a note under 31 U.S.C.A. § 1113. See, also, page 163 of House Document No. 103–7.

# SUBCHAPTER II—RESEARCH

## § 1441. Monitoring and research program

### [MPRSA § 201]

The Secretary of Commerce, in coordination with the Secretary of the Department in which the Coast Guard is operating and with the Administrator shall, within six months of October 23, 1972, initiate a comprehensive and continuing program of monitoring and research regarding the effects of the dumping of material into ocean waters or other coastal waters where the tide ebbs and flows or into the Great Lakes or their connecting waters.

(Pub.L. 92–532, Title II, § 201, Oct. 23, 1972, 86 Stat. 1060; Pub.L. 99–272, Title VI, § 6061, Apr. 7, 1986, 100 Stat. 131.)

## § 1442. Research program respecting possible long-range effects of pollution, overfishing, and man-induced changes of ocean ecosystems

**[MPRSA § 202]**

### (a) Secretary of Commerce

(1) The Secretary of Commerce, in close consultation with other appropriate Federal departments, agencies, and instrumentalities shall, within six months of October 23, 1972, initiate a comprehensive and continuing program of research with respect to the possible long-range effects of pollution, overfishing, and man-induced changes of ocean ecosystems. These responsibilities shall include the scientific assessment of damages to the natural resources from spills of petroleum or petroleum products. In carrying out such research, the Secretary of Commerce shall take into account such factors as existing and proposed international policies affecting oceanic problems, economic considerations involved in both the protection and the use of the oceans, possible alternatives to existing programs, and ways in which the health of the oceans may best be preserved for the benefit of succeeding generations of mankind.

(2) The Secretary of Commerce shall ensure that the program under this section complements, when appropriate, the activities undertaken by other Federal agencies pursuant to subchapter I of this chapter and section 1443 of this title. That program shall include but not be limited to—

(A) the development and assessment of scientific techniques to define and quantify the degradation of the marine environment;

(B) the assessment of the capacity of the marine environment to receive materials without degradation;

(C) continuing monitoring programs to assess the health of the marine environment, including but not limited to the monitoring of bottom oxygen concentrations, contaminant levels in biota, sediments, and the water column, diseases in fish and shellfish, and changes in types and abundance of indicator species;

(D) the development of methodologies, techniques, and equipment for disposal of waste materials to minimize degradation of the marine environment.

(3) The Secretary of Commerce shall ensure that the comprehensive and continuing research program conducted under this subsection is consistent with the comprehensive plan for ocean pollution research and development and monitoring prepared under section 1703 of this title.

### (b) Action with other nations

In carrying out his responsibilities under this section, the Secretary of Commerce, under the foreign policy guidance of the President and pursuant to international agreements and treaties made by the President with the advice and consent of the Senate, may act alone or in conjunction with any other nation or group of nations, and shall make known the results of his activities by such channels of communication as may appear appropriate.

### (c) Cooperation of other departments, agencies, and independent instrumentalities

Each department, agency, and independent instrumentality of the Federal Government is authorized and directed to cooperate with the Secretary of Commerce in carrying out the purposes of this section and, to the extent permitted by law, to furnish such information as may be requested.

### (d) Utilization of personnel, services, and facilities; inter-agency agreements

The Secretary of Commerce, in carrying out his responsibilities under this section, shall, to the extent feasible utilize the personnel, services, and facilities of other Federal departments, agencies, and instrumentalities (including those of the Coast Guard for monitoring purposes), and is authorized to enter into appropriate inter-agency agreements to accomplish this action.

(Pub.L. 92–532, Title II, § 202, Oct. 23, 1972, 86 Stat. 1060; Pub.L. 94–62, § 2, July 25, 1975, 89 Stat. 303; Pub.L. 96–381, § 3, Oct. 6, 1980, 94 Stat. 1524; Pub.L. 96–470, Title II, § 201(f), Oct. 19, 1980, 94 Stat. 2242; Pub.L. 99–272, Title VI, § 6062, Apr. 7, 1986, 100 Stat. 131; Pub.L. 100–627, Title I, § 101, Nov. 7, 1988, 102 Stat. 3213.)

### HISTORICAL AND STATUTORY NOTES

**References in Text**

Section 1703 of this title, referred to in subsec. (a)(3), was repealed by Pub.L. 102–567, Title II, § 204, Oct. 29, 1992, 106 Stat. 4282.

## § 1443. Research program respecting ocean dumping and other methods of waste disposal

**[MPRSA § 203]**

### (a) Cooperation with public authorities, agencies, and institutions, private agencies and institutions, and individuals

The Administrator of the Environmental Protection Agency shall—

(1) conduct research, investigations, experiments, training, demonstrations, surveys, and studies for the purpose of—

(A) determining means of minimizing or ending, as soon as possible after October 6, 1980, the dumping into ocean waters, or waters described in section 1411(b) of this title, of material which may unreasonably degrade or endanger human health, welfare, or amenities, or the marine environment, ecological systems, or economic potentialities, and

(B) developing disposal methods as alternatives to the dumping described in subparagraph (A); and

(2) encourage, cooperate with, promote the coordination of, and render financial and other assistance to appropriate public authorities, agencies, and institutions (whether Federal, State, interstate, or local) and appropriate private agencies, institutions, and individuals in the conduct of research and other activities described in paragraph (1).

**(b) Termination date for ocean dumping of sewage sludge not affected**

Nothing in this section shall be construed to affect in any way the December 31, 1981, termination date, established in section 1412a of this title, for the ocean dumping of sewage sludge.

**(c) Regional management plans for waste disposal**

The Administrator, in cooperation with the Secretary, the Secretary of Commerce, and other officials of appropriate Federal, State, and local agencies, shall assess the feasibility in coastal areas of regional management plans for the disposal of waste materials. Such plans should integrate where appropriate Federal, State, regional, and local waste disposal activities into a comprehensive regional disposal strategy. These plans should address, among other things—

(1) the sources, quantities, and types of materials that require and will require disposal;

(2) the environmental, economic, social, and human health factors (and the methods used to assess these factors) associated with disposal alternatives;

(3) the improvements in production processes, methods of disposal, and recycling to reduce the adverse effects associated with such disposal alternatives;

(4) the applicable laws and regulations governing waste disposal; and

(5) improvements in permitting processes to reduce administrative burdens.

**(d) Report on sewage disposal in New York metropolitan area**

The Administrator, in cooperation with the Secretary of Commerce, shall submit to the Congress and the President, not later than one year after April 7, 1986, a report on sewage sludge disposal in the New York City metropolitan region. The report shall—

(1) consider the factors listed in subsection (c) of this section as they relate to landfilling, incineration, ocean dumping, or any other feasible disposal or reuse/recycling option;

(2) include an assessment of the cost of these alternatives; and

(3) recommend such regulatory or legislative changes as may be necessary to reduce the adverse impacts associated with sewage sludge disposal.

(Pub.L. 92–532, Title II, § 203, Oct. 23, 1972, 86 Stat. 1061; Pub.L. 96–381, § 1, Oct. 6, 1980, 94 Stat. 1523; Pub.L. 99–272, Title VI, § 6063, Apr. 7, 1986, 100 Stat. 131.)

### HISTORICAL AND STATUTORY NOTES

**Codifications**

In subsec. (a)(1)(A), October 6, 1980, was substituted for "the date of the enactment of this section", which has been translated to reflect the probable intent of Congress as meaning the date of enactment of Pub.L. 96–381 which amended this section generally and which was approved Oct. 6, 1980.

## § 1444. Annual reports

**[MPRSA § 204]**

**(a) Report by Secretary of Commerce**

In March of each year, the Secretary of Commerce shall report to the Congress on his activities under this subchapter during the previous fiscal year. The report shall include—

(1) the Secretary's findings made under section 1441 of this title, including an evaluation of the short-term ecological effects and the social and economic factors involved with the dumping;

(2) the results of activities undertaken pursuant to section 1442 of this title;

(3) with the concurrence of the Administrator and after consulting with officials of other appropriate Federal agencies, an identification of the short- and long-term research requirements associated with activities under subchapter I of this chapter, and a description of how Federal research under this subchapter and subchapter I of this chapter will meet those requirements; and

(4) activities of the Department of Commerce under section 665 of Title 16.

**(b) Report by Administrator**

In March of each year, the Administrator shall report to the Congress on his activities during the previous fiscal year under section 1443 of this title.

**(c) Report by Under Secretary**

On October 31 of each year, the Under Secretary shall report to the Congress the specific programs that the National Oceanic and Atmospheric Administration and the Environmental Protection Agency carried out pursuant to this subchapter in the previous fiscal year, specifically listing the amount of funds allocated to those specific programs in the previous fiscal year.

(Pub.L. 92–532, Title II, § 204, Oct. 23, 1972, 86 Stat. 1061; Pub.L. 94–62, § 3, July 25, 1975, 89 Stat. 303; Pub.L. 94–326, § 3, June 30, 1976, 90 Stat. 725; Pub.L. 95–153, § 2, Nov. 4, 1977, 91 Stat. 1255; Pub.L. 96–381, § 2, Oct. 6, 1980, 94 Stat. 1523; Pub.L. 92–532, Title II, § 204, formerly § 205, as added Pub.L. 96–572, § 5, Dec. 22, 1980, 94 Stat. 3345; renumbered and amended Pub.L. 99–272, Title VI, § 6065, Apr. 7, 1986, 100 Stat. 132; Pub.L. 100–627, Title I, § 102, Nov. 7, 1988, 102 Stat. 3213.)

### HISTORICAL AND STATUTORY NOTES

**Prior Provisions**

A prior section 204 of Pub.L. 92–532, which was classified to this section, was renumbered section 205 and is classified to 33 U.S.C.A. § 1445.

## § 1445. Authorization of appropriations

### [MPRSA § 205]

There are authorized to be appropriated for the first fiscal year after October 23, 1972, and for the next two fiscal years thereafter such sums as may be necessary to carry out this subchapter, but the sums appropriated for any such fiscal year may not exceed $6,000,000. There are authorized to be appropriated not to exceed $1,500,000 for the transition period (July 1 through September 30, 1976), not to exceed $5,600,000 for fiscal year 1977, and not to exceed $6,500,000 for fiscal year 1978, not to exceed $11,396,000 for fiscal year 1981, not to exceed $12,000,000 for fiscal year 1982, not to exceed $10,635,000 for fiscal year 1986, not to exceed $11,114,000 for fiscal year 1987, not to exceed $13,500,000 for fiscal year 1989, and not to exceed $14,500,000 for fiscal year 1990.

(Pub.L. 92–532, Title II, § 205, as added Pub.L. 96–572, § 5, Dec. 22, 1980, 94 Stat. 3345; formerly § 204, Oct. 23, 1972, 86 Stat. 1061; Pub.L. 94–62, § 3, July 25, 1975, 89 Stat. 303; Pub.L. 94–326, § 3, June 30, 1976, 90 Stat. 725; Pub.L. 95–153, § 2, Nov. 4, 1977, 91 Stat. 1255; Pub.L. 96–381, § 2, Oct. 6, 1980, 94 Stat. 1523; renumbered and amended Pub.L. 99–272, Title VI, § 6064, Apr. 7, 1986, 100 Stat. 132; Pub.L. 100–627, Title I, § 103, Nov. 7, 1988, 102 Stat. 3213.)

### HISTORICAL AND STATUTORY NOTES

**Prior Provisions**

A prior section 205 of Pub.L. 92–532, which was classified to this section, was renumbered section 204 and is classified to 33 U.S.C.A. § 1444.

# PREVENTION OF POLLUTION FROM SHIPS

## ACT TO PREVENT POLLUTION FROM SHIPS [APPS § ______]

**(33 U.S.C.A. §§ 1901 to 1915)**

## CHAPTER 33—PREVENTION OF POLLUTION FROM SHIPS



**Related Provisions**

*See, also, Water Pollution Prevention and Control, 33 U.S.C.A. § 1251 et seq., ante; Ocean Dumping, 33 U.S.C.A. § 1401 et seq., ante; Ocean Pollution Research, 33 U.S.C.A. § 1701 et seq., ante; and Water Resources Research, see 42 U.S.C.A. § 10301 et seq., post.*

### § 1901. Definitions

[APPS § 2]

**(a)** Unless the context indicates otherwise, as used in this chapter—

**(1)** "Antarctica" means the area south of 60 degrees south latitude;

**(2)** "Antarctic Protocol" means the Protocol on Environmental Protection to the Antarctic Treaty, signed October 4, 1991, in Madrid, and all annexes thereto, and includes any future amendments thereto which have entered into force;

**(3)** "MARPOL Protocol" means the Protocol of 1978 relating to the International Convention for the Prevention of Pollution from Ships, 1973, and includes the Convention;

**(4)** "Convention" means the International Convention for the Prevention of Pollution from Ships, 1973, including Protocols I and II and Annexes I, II, and V thereto, including any modification or amendments to the Convention, Protocols, or Annexes which have entered into force for the United States;

**(5)** "discharge" and "garbage" and "harmful substance" and "incident" shall have the meanings provided in the Convention;

**(6)** "owner" means any person holding title to, or in the absence of title, any other indicia of ownership of, a ship or terminal, but does not include a person who, without participating in the management or operation of a ship or terminal, holds indicia of ownership primarily to protect a security interest in the ship or terminal;

**(7)** "operator" means—

**(a)** in the case of a ship, a charterer by demise or any other person, except the owner, who is responsible for the operation, manning, victualing, and supplying of the vessel, or

**(b)** in the case of a terminal, any person, except the owner, responsible for the operation of the terminal by agreement with the owner;

**(8)** "person" means an individual, firm, public or private corporation, partnership, association, State, municipality, commission, political subdivision of a State, or any interstate body;

**(9)** "Secretary" means the Secretary of the department in which the Coast Guard is operating;

**(10)** "ship" means a vessel of any type whatsoever, including hydrofoils, air-cushion vehicles, submersibles, floating craft whether self-propelled or not, and fixed or floating platforms;

**(11)** "submersible" means a submarine, or any other vessel designed to operate under water; and

**(12)** "terminal" means an onshore facility or an offshore structure located in the navigable waters of the United States or subject to the jurisdiction of the United States and used, or intended to be used, as a port or facility for the transfer or other handling of a harmful substance.

**(b)** For purposes of this chapter, the requirements of Annex V shall apply to the navigable waters of the United States, as well as to all other waters and vessels over which the United States has jurisdiction.

(c) For the purposes of this chapter, the requirements of Annex IV to the Antarctic Protocol shall apply in Antarctica to all vessels over which the United States has jurisdiction.

(Pub.L. 96–478, § 2, Oct. 21, 1980, 94 Stat. 2297; Pub.L. 100–220, Title II, § 2101, Dec. 29, 1987, 101 Stat. 1460; Pub.L. 103–160, Div. A, Title X, § 1003(f), Nov. 30, 1993, 107 Stat. 1748; Pub.L. 104–227, Title II, § 201(a), Oct. 2, 1996, 110 Stat. 3042.)

## HISTORICAL AND STATUTORY NOTES

### References in Text

This chapter, referred to in text, was in the original "this Act", meaning Pub.L. 96–478, Oct. 21, 1980, 94 Stat. 2297, known as the "Act to Prevent Pollution from Ships". For complete classification of this Act to the Code, see Short Title note below and Tables.

### Effective and Applicability Provisions

1987 Acts

Section 2002 of Pub.L. 100–220, provided that:

"**(a) In general.**—Except as provided in subsections (b) and (c), this title [see Short Title of 1987 Amendment note set out under this section] shall be effective on the date on which Annex V to the International Convention for the Prevention of Pollution from Ships, 1973, enters into force for the United States [such annex entered into force for the United States on Dec. 31, 1988].

"**(b) Exceptions.**—Sections 2001, 2002, 2003, 2108, 2202, 2203, 2204, and subtitle C of this title [enacting section 1912 of this title and provisions set out as notes under this section, section 2267 of this title, and section 6981 of Title 42, Public Health and Welfare] shall be effective on the date of the enactment of this title [Dec. 29, 1987].

"**(c) Issuance of regulations.**—

"**(1) In general.**—The authority to prescribe regulations pursuant to this title shall be effective on the date of enactment of this title [Dec. 29, 1987].

"**(2) Effective date of regulations.**—Any regulation prescribed pursuant to this title shall not be effective before the effective date of the provision of this title under which the regulation is prescribed."

1980 Acts

Section 14(a) and (b) of Pub.L. 96–478 provided:

"**(a)** Except as provided in subsection (b) of this section, this Act [see Short Title note below] is effective upon the date of enactment [Oct. 21, 1980], or on the date the MARPOL Protocol becomes effective as to the United States whichever is later. [The MARPOL Protocol became effective as to the United States Oct. 2, 1983.]

"**(b)** The Secretary and the heads of Federal departments shall have the authority to issue regulations, standards, and certifications under sections 3(c), 3(d), 4(b), 5(a), 6(a), 6(c) and 6(f) [sections 1902(c), (d), 1903(b), 1904(a), and 1905(a), (c), (f) of this title] effective on the date of enactment of this Act [Oct. 21, 1980]. Section 13(a)(2) [amending section 391a(3)(E) of Title 46, Shipping] is effective upon the date of enactment of this Act [Oct. 21, 1980]."

### Short Title

1987 Amendments

Section 2001 of Pub.L. 100–220, provided that: "This title [enacting section 1912 of this title, amending this section and sections 1902, 1903, 1905, 1907, 1908 and 1909 of this title, and enacting provisions set out as notes under this section and sections 1902 and 2267 of this title and section 6981 of Title 42, The Public Health and Welfare] may be cited as the 'Marine Plastic Pollution Research and Control Act of 1987'."

1980 Acts

Section 1 of Pub.L. 96–478 provided: "That this Act [enacting this chapter, amending section 1321 of this title and section 742c(c) of Title 16, Conservation, and section 391a of Title 46, Shipping, repealing sections 1001 to 1011 and 1013 to 1016 of this title, and enacting provisions set out as notes under section 1001 of this title, and section 742c of Title 16] may be cited as the 'Act to Prevent Pollution from Ships'."

### Dry Bulk Cargo Residue Disposal on the Great Lakes; Study and Regulations

Pub.L. 106–554, § 1(a)(4) [Div. A, § 1117(b), (c)], Dec. 21, 2000, 114 Stat. 2763, 2763A–209, provided that:

"**(b)** The Secretary shall conduct a study of the effectiveness of the United States 1997 Enforcement Policy for Cargo Residues on the Great Lakes ('Policy') by September 30, 2002.

"**(c)** The Secretary is authorized to promulgate regulations to implement and enforce a program to regulate incidental discharges from vessels of residues of non-hazardous and non-toxic dry bulk cargo into the waters of the Great Lakes, which takes into account the finding in the study required under subsection (b). This program shall be consistent with the Policy."

### Certain Alaskan Cruise Ship Operations

Pub.L. 106–554, § 1(a)(4) [Div. B, Title XIV, §§ 1401 to 1414], Dec. 21, 2000, 114 Stat. 2763, 2763A–315 to 2763A–322, provided that:

"**Sec. 1401. Purpose.**

"The purpose of this title [Pub.L. 106–554, § 1(a)(4) [Div. B, Title XIV, § 1401 et seq.], Dec. 21, 2000, 114 Stat. 2763, 2763a–315, enacting provisions set out as this note] is to:

"(1) Ensure that cruise vessels operating in the waters of the Alexander Archipelago and the navigable waters of the United States within the State of Alaska and within the Kachemak Bay National Estuarine Research Reserve comply with all applicable environmental laws, including, but not limited to, the Federal Water Pollution Control Act [Act June 30, 1948, ch. 758, 62 Stat. 1155], as amended (33 U.S.C. 1251 et seq.), the Act to Prevent Pollution from Ships, as amended (33 U.S.C. 1901 et seq.), and the protections contained within this title [this note].

"(2) Ensure that cruise vessels do not discharge untreated sewage within the waters of the Alexander Archipelago, the navigable waters of the United States in the State of Alaska, or within the Kachemak Bay National Estuarine Research Reserve.

"(3) Prevent the unregulated discharge of treated sewage and graywater while in ports in the State of Alaska or traveling near the shore in the Alexander Archipelago and the navigable waters of the United States in the State of Alaska or within the Kachemak Bay National Estuarine Research Reserve.

"(4) Ensure that discharges of sewage and graywater from cruise vessels operating in the Alexander Archipelago and the navigable waters of the United States in the State of Alaska or within the Kachemak Bay National Estuarine Research Reserve can be monitored for compliance with the requirements contained in this title [this note].

**"Sec. 1402. Applicability.**

"This title [this note] applies to all cruise vessels authorized to carry 500 or more passengers for hire.

**"Sec. 1403. Prohibition on discharge of untreated sewage.**

"No person shall discharge any untreated sewage from a cruise vessel into the waters of the Alexander Archipelago or the navigable waters of the United States within the State of Alaska or within the Kachemak Bay National Estuarine Research Reserve.

**"Sec. 1404. Limitations on discharge of treated sewage or graywater.**

"**(a)** No person shall discharge any treated sewage or graywater from a cruise vessel into the waters of the Alexander Archipelago or the navigable waters of the United States within the State of Alaska or within the Kachemak Bay National Estuarine Research Reserve unless—

"(1) the cruise vessel is underway and proceeding at a speed of not less than six knots;

"(2) the cruise vessel is not less than one nautical mile from the nearest shore, except in areas designated by the Secretary, in consultation with the State of Alaska;

"(3) the discharge complies with all applicable cruise vessel effluent standards established pursuant to this title [this note] and any other applicable law; and

"(4) the cruise vessel is not in an area where the discharge of treated sewage or graywater is prohibited.

"**(b)** The Administrator, in consultation with the Secretary, may promulgate regulations allowing the discharge of treated sewage or graywater, otherwise prohibited under paragraphs (a)(1) and (a)(2) of this section, where the discharge meets effluent standards determined by the Administrator as appropriate for discharges into the marine environment. In promulgating such regulations, the Administrator shall take into account the best available scientific information on the environmental effects of the regulated discharges. The effluent discharge standards promulgated under this section shall, at a minimum, be consistent with all relevant State of Alaska water quality standards in force at the time of the enactment of this title [Dec. 21, 2000].

"**(c)** Until such time as the administrator promulgates regulations under paragraph (b) of this section, treated sewage and graywater may be discharged from vessels subject to this title [this note] in circumstances otherwise prohibited under paragraphs (a)(1) and (a)(2) of this section, provided that—

"(1) the discharge satisfies the minimum level of effluent quality specified in 40 CFR 133.102, as in effect on the date of enactment of this section [Dec. 21, 2000];

"(2) the geometric mean of the samples from the discharge during any 30–day period does not exceed 20 fecal coliform/100 ml and not more than 10 percent of the samples exceed 40 fecal coliform/100 ml;

"(3) concentrations of total residual chlorine may not exceed 10.0 μg/l; and

"(4) prior to any such discharge occurring, the owner, operator or master, or other person in charge of a cruise vessel, can demonstrate test results from at least five samples taken from the vessel representative of the effluent to be discharged, on different days over a 30–day period, conducted in accordance with the guidelines promulgated by the Administrator in 40 CFR Part 136, which confirm that the water quality of the effluents proposed for discharge is in compliance with paragraphs (1), (2), and (3) of this subsection. To the extent not otherwise being done by the owner, operator, master or other person in charge of a cruise vessel pursuant to section 1406 [of this note], the owner, operator, master or other person in charge of a cruise vessel shall demonstrate continued compliance through periodic sampling. Such sampling and test results shall be considered environmental compliance records that must be made available for inspection pursuant to section 1406(d) of this title [this note].

**"Sec. 1405. Safety exception.**

"Sections 1403 and 1404 of this title [this note] shall not apply to discharges made for the purpose of securing the safety of the cruise vessel or saving life at sea, provided that all reasonable precautions have been taken for the purpose of preventing or minimizing the discharge.

**"Sec. 1406. Inspection and sampling regime.**

"**(a)** The Secretary shall incorporate into the commercial vessel examination program an inspection regime sufficient to verify that cruise vessels visiting ports in the State of Alaska or operating in the waters of the Alexander Archipelago or the navigable waters of the United States within the State of Alaska or within the Kachemak Bay National Estuarine Research Reserve are in full compliance with this title [this note], the Federal Water Pollution Control Act, as amended, and any regulations issued thereunder, other applicable Federal laws and regulations, and all applicable international treaty requirements.

"**(b)** The inspection regime shall, at a minimum, include—

"(1) examination of environmental compliance records and procedures; and

"(2) inspection of the functionality and proper operation of installed equipment for abatement and control of any discharge.

"**(c)** The inspection regime may—

"(1) include unannounced inspections of any aspect of cruise vessel operations, equipment or discharges pertinent to the verification under subsection (a) of this section; and

"(2) require the owner, operator or master, or other person in charge of a cruise vessel subject to this title [this note] to maintain and produce a logbook detailing the times, types, volumes or flow rates and locations of any discharges of sewage or graywater under this title [this note].

"**(d)** The inspection regime shall incorporate a plan for sampling and testing cruise vessel discharges to ensure that any discharges of sewage or graywater are in compliance with this title, the Federal Water Pollution Control Act, as amended, and any other applicable laws and regulations, and may require the owner, operator or master, or other person in charge of a cruise vessel subject to this title [this note] to conduct such samples or tests, and to produce any records of such sampling or testing at the request of the Secretary or Administrator.

**"Sec. 1407. Cruise vessel effluent standards.**

"Pursuant to this title [this note] and the authority of the Federal Water Pollution Control Act [Act June 30, 1948, c. 758, 62 Stat. 1155, which is classified to chapter 26 of title 33 (33 U.S.C.A. § 125 et seq.). See Tables for complete classification], as amended, the Administrator may promulgate effluent standards for treated sewage and graywater from cruise vessels operating in the waters of the Alexander Archipelago or the navigable waters of the United States within the State of Alaska or within the Kachemak Bay National Estuarine Research Reserve. Regulations implementing such standards shall take into account the best available scientific information on the environmental effects of the regulated discharges and the availability of new technologies for wastewater treatment. Until such time as the Administrator promulgates such effluent standards, treated sewage effluent discharges shall not have a fecal coliform bacterial count of greater than 200 per 100 milliliters nor suspended solids greater than 150 milligrams per liter.

**"Sec. 1408. Reports.**

"(a) Any owner, operator or master, or other person in charge of a cruise vessel who has knowledge of a discharge from the cruise vessel in violation of section 1403 or 1404 or pursuant to section 1405 of this title [this note], or any regulations promulgated thereunder, shall immediately report that discharge to the Secretary, who shall provide a copy to the Administrator upon request.

"(b) The Secretary may prescribe the form of reports required under this section.

**"Sec. 1409. Enforcement.**

"**(a) Administrative penalties.**—

"**(1) Violations.**—Any person who violates section 1403, 1404, 1408, or 1413 of this title [this note], or any regulations promulgated pursuant to this title [this note] may be assessed a class I or class II civil penalty by the Secretary or Administrator.

"**(2) Classes of penalties.**—

"**(A) Class I.**—The amount of a class I civil penalty under this section may not exceed $10,000 per violation, except that the maximum amount of any class I civil penalty under this section shall not exceed $25,000. Before assessing a civil penalty under this clause, the Secretary or Administrator, as the case may be, shall give to the person to be assessed such penalty written notice of the Secretary's or Administrator's proposal to assess the penalty and the opportunity to request, within 30 days of the date the notice is received by such person, a hearing on the proposed penalty. Such hearing shall not be subject to section 554 or 556 of title 5, but shall provide a reasonable opportunity to be heard and to present evidence.

"**(B) Class II.**—The amount of a class II civil penalty under this section may not exceed $10,000 per day for each day during which the violation continues, except that the maximum amount of any class II civil penalty under this section shall not exceed $125,000. Except as otherwise provided in this subsection, a class II civil penalty shall be assessed and collected in the same manner, and subject to the same provisions as in the case of civil penalties assessed and collected after notice and an opportunity for a hearing on the record in accordance with section 554 of title 5, United States Code. The Secretary and Administrator may issue rules for discovery procedures for hearings under this paragraph.

"**(3) Rights of interested persons.**—

"**(A) Public notice.**—Before issuing an order assessing a class II civil penalty under this section, the Secretary or Administrator, as the case may be, shall provide public notice of and reasonable opportunity to comment on the proposed issuance of each order.

"**(B) Presentation of evidence.**—Any person who comments on a proposed assessment of a class II civil penalty under this section shall be given notice of any hearing held under this paragraph and of the order assessing such penalty. In any hearing held under this paragraph, such person shall have a reasonable opportunity to be heard and present evidence.

"**(C) Rights of interested persons to a hearing.**—If no hearing is held under subsection (2) before issuance of an order assessing a class II civil penalty under this section, any person who commented on the proposed assessment may petition, within 30 days after the issuance of such order, the Administrator or Secretary, as the case may be, to set aside such order and to provide a hearing on the penalty. If the evidence presented by the petitioner in support of the petition is material and was not considered in the issuance of the order, the Administrator or Secretary shall immediately set aside such order and provide a hearing in accordance with subsection (2)( B). If the Administrator or Secretary denies a hearing under this clause, the Administrator or Secretary shall provide to the petitioner, and publish in the Federal Register, notice of and the reasons for such denial.

"**(4) Finality of order.**—An order assessing a class II civil penalty under this paragraph shall become final 30 days after its issuance unless a petition for judicial review is filed under subparagraph (6) or a hearing is requested under subsection (3)(C). If such a hearing is denied, such order shall become final 30 days after such denial.

"**(5) Effect of action on compliance.**—No action by the Administrator or Secretary under this paragraph shall affect any person's obligation to comply with any section of this title [this note].

"**(6) Judicial review.**—Any person against whom a civil penalty is assessed under this paragraph or who commented on the proposed assessment of such penalty in accordance with subsection (3) may obtain review of such assessment—

"(A) in the case of assessment of a class I civil penalty, in the United States District Court for the District of Columbia or in the District of Alaska; or

"(B) in the case of assessment of a class II civil penalty, in the United States Court of Appeals for the District of Columbia Circuit or for any other circuit in which such person resides or transacts business, by filing a notice of appeal in such court within the 30–day period beginning on the date the civil penalty order is issued and by simultaneously sending a copy of such notice by certified mail to the Administrator or Secretary, as the case may be, and the Attorney General. The Administrator or Secretary shall promptly file in such court a certified copy of the record on which the order was issued. Such court shall not set aside or remand such order unless there is not substantial evidence in the record, taken as a whole, to support the finding of a violation or unless the Administrator's or Secretary's assessment of the penalty constitutes an abuse of discretion and shall not impose additional civil penalties for the same violation unless the Administrator's or Secretary's assessment of the penalty constitutes an abuse of discretion.

"(7) **Collection.**—If any person fails to pay an assessment of a civil penalty—

"(A) after the assessment has become final, or

"(B) after a court in an action brought under subsection (6) has entered a final judgment in favor of the Administrator or Secretary, as the case may be, the Administrator or Secretary shall request the Attorney General to bring a civil action in an appropriate district court to recover the amount assessed (plus interest at currently prevailing rates from the date of the final order or the date of the final judgment, as the case may be). In such an action, the validity, amount, and appropriateness of such penalty shall not be subject to review. Any person who fails to pay on a timely basis the amount of an assessment of a civil penalty as described in the first sentence of this subparagraph shall be required to pay, in addition to such amount and interest, attorneys fees and costs for collection proceedings and a quarterly nonpayment penalty for each quarter during which such failure to pay persists. Such nonpayment penalty shall be in an amount equal to 20 percent of the aggregate amount of such person's penalties and nonpayment penalties which are unpaid as of the beginning of such quarter.

"(8) **Subpoenas.**—The Administrator or Secretary, as the case may be, may issue subpoenas for the attendance and testimony of witnesses and the production of relevant papers, books, or documents in connection with hearings under this section. In case of contumacy or refusal to obey a subpoena issued pursuant to this subsection and served upon any person, the district court of the United States for any district in which such person is found, resides, or transacts business, upon application by the United States and after notice to such person, shall have jurisdiction to issue an order requiring such person to appear and give testimony before the Administrator or Secretary or to appear and produce documents before the Administrator or Secretary, or both, and any failure to obey such order of the court may be punished by such court as a contempt thereof.

"(b) **Civil penalties.**—

"(1) **In general.**—Any person who violates section 1403, 1404, 1408, or 1413 of this title [this note], or any regulations promulgated pursuant to this title [this note] shall be subject to a civil penalty not to exceed $25,000 per day for each violation. Each day a violation continues constitutes a separate violation.

"(2) **Jurisdiction.**—An action to impose a civil penalty under this section may be brought in the district court of the United States for the district in which the defendant is located, resides, or transacts business, and such court shall have jurisdiction to assess such penalty.

"(3) **Limitation.**—A person is not liable for a civil judicial penalty under this paragraph for a violation if the person has been assessed a civil administrative penalty under paragraph (a) for the violation.

"(c) **Determination of amount.**—In determining the amount of a civil penalty under paragraphs (a) or (b) of this section, the court, the Secretary or the Administrator, as the case may be, shall consider the seriousness of the violation or violations, the economic benefit (if any) resulting from the violation, any history of such violations, any good-faith efforts to comply with the applicable requirements, the economic impact of the penalty on the violator, and other such matters as justice may require.

"(d) **Criminal penalties.**—

"(1) **Negligent violations.**—Any person who negligently violates section 1403, 1404, 1408, or 1413 of this title [of this note], or any regulations promulgated pursuant to this title [this note] commits a Class A misdemeanor.

"(2) **Knowing violations.**—Any person who knowingly violates section 1403, 1404, 1408, or 1413 of this title [this note], or any regulations promulgated pursuant to this title [this note] commits a Class D felony.

"(3) **False Statements.**—Any person who knowingly makes any false statement, representation, or certification in any record, report or other document filed or required to be maintained under this title [this note] or the regulations issued thereunder, or who falsifies, tampers with, or knowingly renders inaccurate any testing or monitoring device or method required to be maintained under this title [this note], or the regulations issued thereunder, commits a Class D felony.

"(e) **Awards.**—

"(1) The Secretary, the Administrator, or the court, when assessing any fines or civil penalties, as the case may be, may pay from any fines or civil penalties collected under this section an amount not to exceed one-half of the penalty or fine collected, to any individual who furnishes information which leads to the payment of the penalty or fine. If several individuals provide such information, the amount shall be divided equitably among such individuals. No officer or employee of the United States, the State of Alaska or any federally recognized Tribe who furnishes information or renders service in the performance of his or her official duties shall be eligible for payment under this subsection.

"(2) The Secretary, Administrator or the court, when assessing any fines or civil penalties, as the case may be, may pay, from any fines or civil penalties collected under this section, to the State of Alaska or to any federally recognized Tribe providing information or investigative assistance which leads to payment of the penalty or fine, an amount which reflects the level of information or investigative assistance provided. Should the State of Alaska or a federally recognized Tribe and an individual under paragraph (1) of this section be eligible for an award, the Secretary, the Administrator, or the court, as the case may be, shall divide the amount equitably.

"(f) **Liability in rem.**—A cruise vessel operated in violation of this title [this note] or the regulations issued thereunder is liable in rem for any fine imposed under subsection (d) of this section or for any civil penalty imposed under subsections (a) or (b) of this section, and may be proceeded against in the United States district court of any district in which the cruise vessel may be found.

"(g) **Compliance orders.**—

"(1) **In general.**—Whenever on the basis of any information available to him the Administrator finds that any person is in violation of section 1403, 1404, 1408, or 1413 of this title [of this note], or any regulations promulgated pursuant to this title [this note], the Administrator shall issue an order requiring such person to comply with such section or requirement, or shall bring a civil action in accordance with subsection (b).

"(2) **Copies of orders, service.**—A copy of any order issued under this subsection shall be sent immediately by the Administrator to the State of Alaska. In any case in which an order under this subsection is issued to a corporation, a copy of such order shall be served on any appropriate corporate officer. Any order issued under this subsection shall be by personal service, shall state with reasonable specificity the nature of the violation, and shall specify a time for compliance not to exceed 30 days in the case of a violation of an interim compliance schedule or operation and maintenance requirement and not to exceed a time the Administrator determines to be reasonable in the case of a violation of a final deadline, taking into account the seriousness of the violation and any good faith efforts to comply with applicable requirements.

"(h) **Civil actions.**—The Administrator is authorized to commence a civil action for appropriate relief, including a permanent or temporary injunction, for any violation for which he is authorized to issue a compliance order under this subsection. Any action under subsection (h) may be brought in the district court of the United States for the district in which the defendant is located or resides or is doing business, and such court shall have jurisdiction to restrain such violation and to require compliance. Notice of the commencement of such action shall be given immediately to the State of Alaska.

**"Sec. 1410. Designation of cruise vessel no-discharge zones.**

"If the State of Alaska determines that the protection and enhancement of the quality of some or all of the waters of the Alexander Archipelago or the navigable waters of the United States within the State of Alaska or within the Kachemak Bay National Estuarine Research Reserve require greater environmental protection, the State of Alaska may petition the Administrator to prohibit the discharge of graywater and sewage from cruise vessels operating in such waters. The establishment of such a prohibition shall be achieved in the same manner as the petitioning process and prohibition of the discharge of sewage pursuant to section 312(f) of the Federal Water Pollution Control Act [33 U.S.C.A. § 1312(f)], as amended, and the regulations promulgated thereunder.

**"Sec. 1411. Savings clause.**

"(a) Nothing in this title [this note] shall be construed as restricting, affecting, or amending any other law or the authority of any department, instrumentality, or agency of the United States.

"(b) Nothing in this title shall in any way affect or restrict, or be construed to affect or restrict, the authority of the State of Alaska or any political subdivision thereof—

"(1) to impose additional liability or additional requirements; or

"(2) to impose, or determine the amount of a fine or penalty (whether criminal or civil in nature) for any violation of law; relating to the discharge of sewage (whether treated or untreated) or graywater in the waters of the Alexander Archipelago and the navigable waters of the United States within the State of Alaska or within the Kachemak Bay National Estuarine Research Reserve.

**"Sec. 1412. Regulations.**

"The Secretary and the Administrator each may prescribe any regulations necessary to carry out the provisions of this title [this note].

**"Sec. 1413. Information gathering authority.**

"The authority of sections 308(a) and (b) of the Federal Water Pollution Control Act [33 U.S.C.A. § 1318(a),(b)], as amended, shall be available to the Administrator to carry out the provisions of this title [this note]. The Administrator and the Secretary shall minimize, to the extent practicable, duplication of or inconsistency with the inspection, sampling, testing, recordkeeping, and reporting requirements established by the Secretary under section 1406 of this title [this note].

**"Sec. 1414. Definitions.**

"In this title:

"(1) **Administrator.**—The term 'Administrator' means the Administrator of the United States Environmental Protection Agency.

"(2) **Cruise vessel.**—The term 'cruise vessel' means a passenger vessel as defined in section 2101(22) of title 46, United States Code. The term 'cruise vessel' does not include a vessel of the United States operated by the Federal Government or a vessel owned and operated by the government of a State.

"(3) **Discharge.**—The term 'discharge' means any release however caused from a cruise vessel, and includes any escape, disposal, spilling, leaking, pumping, emitting, or emptying.

"(4) **Graywater.**—The term 'graywater' means only galley, dishwasher, bath, and laundry waste water. The term does not include other wastes or waste streams.

"(5) **Navigable waters.**—The term 'navigable waters' has the same meaning as in section 502 of the Federal Water Pollution Control Act [33 U.S.C.A. § 1362], as amended.

"(6) **Person.**—The term 'person' means an individual, corporation, partnership, limited liability company, association, State, municipality, commission, or political subdivision of a State, or any federally recognized tribe.

"(7) **Secretary.**—The term 'Secretary' means the Secretary of the department in which the United States Coast Guard is operating.

"(8) **Sewage.**—The term 'sewage' means human body wastes and the wastes from toilets and other receptacles intended to receive or retain body waste.

"(9) **Treated sewage.**—The term 'treated sewage' means sewage meeting all applicable effluent limitation standards and processing requirements of the Federal Water Pollution Control Act, as amended and of this title [this note], and regulations promulgated under either.

"(10) **Untreated sewage.**—The term 'untreated sewage' means sewage that is not treated sewage.

"(11) **Waters of the Alexander Archipelago.**—The term 'waters of the Alexander Archipelago' means all waters under the sovereignty of the United States within or near Southeast Alaska, beginning at a point 58°11′41″N, 136°39′25″W [near Cape Spencer Light], thence southeasterly along a line three nautical miles seaward of the baseline from which the breadth of the territorial sea is measured in the Pacific Ocean and the Dixon Entrance, except where this line intersects geodesics connecting the following five pairs of points:

"(1) 58°05′17″N, 136°33′49″W and 58°11′41″N, 136°39′25″W [Cross Sound].

"(2) 56°09′40″N, 134°40′00″W and 55°49′15″N, 134°17′40″W [Chatham Strait].

"(3) 55°49′15″N, 134°17′40″W and 55°50′30″N, 133°54′15″W [Sumner Strait].

"(4) 54°41′30″N, 132°01′00″W and 54°51′30″N, 131°20′45″W [Clarence Strait].

"(5) 54°51′30″N, 131°20′45″W and 54°46′15″N, 130°52′00″W [Revillagigedo Channel].

"The portion of each such geodesic situated beyond three nautical miles from the baseline from which the breadth of the territorial sea is measured forms the outer limit of the waters of the Alexander Archipelago in those five locations."

**Savings Provision; Regulations in Effect Until Superseded**

Section 14(c) of Pub.L. 96–478 provided that: "Any rights or liabilities existing on the effective date of this Act [see Effective Date note above] shall not be affected by this enactment [see Short Title note above]. Any regulations or procedures promulgated or effected pursuant to the Oil Pollution Act, 1961, as amended [former section 1001 et seq. of this title], remain in effect until modified or superseded by regulations promulgated under the authority of the MARPOL Protocol or this Act."

**Preemption; Additional State Requirements**

Section 2003 of Pub.L. 100–220, provided that:

"(a) **Preemption.**—Except as specifically provided in this title [see Short Title of 1987 Amendment note set out under this section], nothing in this title shall be interpreted or construed to supersede or preempt any other provision of Federal or State law, either statutory or common.

"(b) **Additional state requirements.**—Nothing in this title shall be construed or interpreted as preempting any State from imposing any additional requirements."

## § 1902. Ships subject to preventive measures

**[APPS § 3]**

### (a) Included vessels

This chapter shall apply—

(1) to a ship of United States registry or nationality, or one operated under the authority of the United States, wherever located;

(2) with respect to Annexes I and II to the Convention, to a ship, other than a ship referred to in paragraph (1), while in the navigable waters of the United States;

(3) with respect to the requirements of Annex V to the Convention, to a ship, other than a ship referred to in paragraph (1), while in the navigable waters or the exclusive economic zone of the United States; and

(4) with respect to regulations prescribed under section 1905 of this title, any port or terminal in the United States.

### (b) Excluded vessels

(1) Except as provided in paragraph (2), this chapter shall not apply to—

(A) a warship, naval auxiliary, or other ship owned or operated by the United States when engaged in noncommercial service; or

(B) any other ship specifically excluded by the MARPOL Protocol or the Antarctic Protocol.

(2)(A) Notwithstanding any provision of the MARPOL Protocol, and subject to subparagraph (B) of this paragraph, the requirements of Annex V to the Convention shall apply as follows:

(i) After December 31, 1993, to all ships referred to in paragraph (1)(A) of this subsection other than those owned or operated by the Department of the Navy.

(ii) Except as provided in subsection (c) of this section, after December 31, 1998, to all ships referred to in paragraph (1)(A) of this subsection other than submersibles owned or operated by the Department of the Navy.

(iii) Except as provided in subsection (c) of this section, after December 31, 2008, to all ships referred to in paragraph (1)(A) of this subsection.

(B) This paragraph shall not apply during time of war or a declared national emergency.

### (c) Discharges in special areas

(1) Except as provided in paragraphs (2) and (3), not later than December 31, 2000, all surface ships owned or operated by the Department of the Navy, and not later than December 31, 2008, all submersibles owned or operated by the Department of the Navy, shall comply with the special area requirements of Regulation 5 of Annex V to the Convention.

(2)(A) Subject to subparagraph (B), any ship described in subparagraph (C) may discharge, without regard to the special area requirements of Regulation 5 of Annex V to the Convention, the following nonplastic, non-floating garbage:

(i) A slurry of seawater, paper, cardboard, or food waste that is capable of passing through a screen with openings no larger than 12 millimeters in diameter.

(ii) Metal and glass that have been shredded and bagged so as to ensure negative buoyancy.

(iii) With regard to a submersible, nonplastic garbage that has been compacted and weighted to ensure negative buoyancy.

(B)(i) Garbage described in subparagraph (A)(i) may not be discharged within 3 nautical miles of land.

(ii) Garbage described in clauses (ii) and (iii) of subparagraph (A) may not be discharged within 12 nautical miles of land.

(C) This paragraph applies to any ship that is owned or operated by the Department of the Navy that, as determined by the Secretary of the Navy—

(i) has unique military design, construction, manning, or operating requirements; and

(ii) cannot fully comply with the special area requirements of Regulation 5 of Annex V to the Convention because compliance is not technologically feasible or would impair the operations or operational capability of the ship.

(3)(A) Not later than December 31, 2000, the Secretary of the Navy shall prescribe and publish in the Federal Register standards to ensure that each ship described in subparagraph (B) is, to the maximum extent practicable without impairing the operations or operational capabilities of the ship, operated in a manner that is consistent with the special area requirements of Regulation 5 of Annex V to the Convention.

(B) Subparagraph (A) applies to surface ships that are owned or operated by the Department of the Navy that the Secretary plans to decommission during the period beginning on January 1, 2001, and ending on December 31, 2005.

(C) At the same time that the Secretary publishes standards under subparagraph (A), the Secretary shall publish in the Federal Register a list of the ships covered by subparagraph (B).

**(d) Regulations**

The Secretary shall prescribe regulations applicable to the ships of a country not a party to the MARPOL Protocol, including regulations conforming to and giving effect to the requirements of Annex V as they apply under subsection (a) of this section, to ensure that their treatment is not more favorable than that accorded ships to parties to the MARPOL Protocol.

**(e) Compliance by excluded vessels**

(1) The Secretary of the Navy shall develop and, as appropriate, support the development of technologies and practices for solid waste management aboard ships owned or operated by the Department of the Navy, including technologies and practices for the reduction of the waste stream generated aboard such ships, that are necessary to ensure the compliance of such ships with Annex V to the Convention on or before the dates referred to in subsections (b)(2)(A) and (c)(1) of this section.

(2) Notwithstanding any effective date of the application of this section to a ship, the provisions of Annex V to the Convention with respect to the disposal of plastic shall apply to ships equipped with plastic processors required for the long-term collection and storage of plastic aboard ships of the Navy upon the installation of such processors in such ships.

(3) Except when necessary for the purpose of securing the safety of the ship, the health of the ship's personnel, or saving life at sea, it shall be a violation of this chapter for a ship referred to in subsection (b)(1)(A) of this section that is owned or operated by the Department of the Navy:

(A) With regard to a submersible, to discharge buoyant garbage or plastic.

(B) With regard to a surface ship, to discharge plastic contaminated by food during the last 3 days before the ship enters port.

(C) With regard to a surface ship, to discharge plastic, except plastic that is contaminated by food, during the last 20 days before the ship enters port.

(4) The Secretary of Defense shall publish in the Federal Register:

(A) Each year, the amount and nature of the discharges in special areas, not otherwise authorized under this chapter, during the preceding year from ships referred to in subsection (b)(1)(A) of this section owned or operated by the Department of the Navy.

(B) Beginning on October 1, 1996, and each year thereafter until October 1, 1998, a list of the names of such ships equipped with plastic processors pursuant to section 1003(e) of the National Defense Authorization Act for Fiscal Year 1994.

**(f) Waiver authority**

The President may waive the effective dates of the requirements set forth in subsection (c) of this section and in subsection 1003(e) of the National Defense Authorization Act for Fiscal Year 1994 if the President determines it to be in the paramount interest of the United States to do so. Any such waiver shall be for a period not in excess of one year. The President shall submit to the Congress each January a report on all waivers from the requirements of this section granted during the preceding calendar year, together with the reasons for granting such waivers.

**(g) Noncommercial shipping standards**

The heads of Federal departments and agencies shall prescribe standards applicable to ships excluded from this chapter by subsection (b)(1) of this section and for which they are responsible. Standards prescribed under this subsection shall ensure, so far as is reasonable and practicable without impairing the operations or operational capabilities of such ships, that such ships act in a manner consistent with the MARPOL Protocol.

(Pub.L. 96–478, § 3, Oct. 21, 1980, 94 Stat. 2297; Pub.L. 100–220, Title II, § 2102, Dec. 29, 1987, 101 Stat. 1460; Pub.L. 103–160, Div. A, Title X, § 1003(a) to (d), Nov. 30, 1993, 107 Stat. 1745 to 1747; Pub.L. 104–201, Div. A, Title III, § 324(a), (d), Sept. 23, 1996, 110 Stat. 2480, 2481; Pub.L. 104–227, Title II, § 201(b), Oct. 2, 1996, 110 Stat. 3042; Pub.L. 105–261, Div. A, Title III, § 326, Oct. 17, 1998, 112 Stat. 1965.)

HISTORICAL AND STATUTORY NOTES

**References in Text**

This chapter, referred to in subsecs. (a), (b)(1), (e)(3), (4)(A), was in the original "this Act", meaning Pub.L. 96–478, Oct. 21, 1980, 94 Stat. 2297, known as the "Act to Prevent Pollution from Ships". For complete classification of this Act to the Code, see Short Title note set out under section 1901 of this title and Tables.

The National Defense Authorization Act for Fiscal Year 1994, referred to in subsecs. (e)(4)(B), (f), is Pub.L. 103–160, 107 Stat. 1547, which was enacted Nov. 30, 1993. Section 1003(e) of such Act is classified as a note under this section. For complete classification of this Act to the Code, see Tables.

**Effective and Applicability Provisions**

1987 Acts

Amendment by Pub.L. 100–220, effective on date on which Annex V to the International Convention for the Pollution from Ships, 1973, enters into force for the United States [such Annex entered into force for the United States on Dec. 31, 1988], see section 2002(a) of Pub.L. 100–220, set out as a note under section 1901 of this title.

1980 Acts

Subsecs. (a) and (b) effective Oct. 2, 1983, and subsecs. (c) and (d) effective Oct. 21, 1980, see section 14(a) and (b) of Pub.L. 96–478, set out as a note under section 1901 of this title.

**Installation Schedule for Plastics Processor Equipment Aboard Ships; Request for Proposals for Equipment**

Section 1003(e) of Pub.L. 103–160 provided that:

"(1) Not later than October 1, 1994, the Secretary of the Navy shall release a request for proposals for equipment (hereinafter in this subsection referred to as 'plastics processor') required for the long-term collection and storage of plastic aboard ships owned or operated by the Navy.

"(2) Not later than July 1, 1996, the Secretary shall install the first production unit of the plastics processor on board a ship owned or operated by the Navy.

"(3) Not later than March 1, 1997, the Secretary shall complete the installation of plastics processors on board not less than 25 percent of the ships owned or operated by the Navy that require plastics processors to comply with section 3 of the Act to Prevent Pollution from Ships, as amended by subsections (a), (b), and (c) of this section [this section].

"(4) Not later than July 1, 1997, the Secretary shall complete the installation of plastics processors on board not less than 50 percent of the ships owned or operated by the Navy that require processors to comply with section 3 of such Act, as amended by subsections (a), (b), and (c) of this section [this section].

"(5) Not later than July 1, 1998, the Secretary shall complete the installation of plastics processors on board not less than 75 percent of the ships owned or operated by the Navy that require processors to comply with section 3 of such Act, as amended by subsections (a), (b), and (c) of this section [this section].

"(6) Not later than December 31, 1998, the Secretary shall complete the installation of plastics processors on board all ships owned or operated by the Navy that require processors to comply with section 3 of such Act, as amended by subsections (a), (b), and (c) of this section [this section]."

**Compliance With Reporting Requirements**

Pub.L. 100–220, Title II, § 2201, Dec. 29, 1987, 101 Stat. 1460, as amended, formerly set out as a note under this section, was transferred and, as amended by Pub.L. 104–324, is now set out as section 1913 of this title.

## § 1902a. Discharge of agricultural cargo residue

Notwithstanding any other provision of law, the discharge from a vessel of any agricultural cargo residue material in the form of hold washings shall be governed exclusively by the provisions of the Act to Prevent Pollution from Ships (33 U.S.C. 1901 et seq.) that implement Annex V to the International Convention for the Prevention of Pollution from Ships.

(Pub.L. 107–295, Title II, § 204, Nov. 25, 2002, 116 Stat. 2094.)

HISTORICAL AND STATUTORY NOTES

**References in Text**

The Act to Prevent Pollution from Ships, referred to in text, is Pub.L. 96–478, Oct. 21, 1980, 94 Stat. 2297, as amended, which is classified principally to chapter 33 of this title, 33 U.S.C.A. § 1901 et seq. For complete classification, see Short Title note set out under 33 U.S.C.A. § 1901 and Tables.

**Codifications**

This section was enacted as part of the Maritime Transportation Security Act of 2002, Pub.L. 107–295, Nov. 25, 2002, 116 Stat. 2064, and not as part of the Act to Prevent Pollution from Ships (APPS), Pub.L. 96–478, Oct. 21, 1980, 94 Stat. 2297, which otherwise comprises this chapter.

## § 1903. Administration and enforcement

[APPS § 4]

**(a) Duty of Secretary; Annexes of Convention applicable to seagoing vessels**

Unless otherwise specified in this chapter, the Secretary shall administer and enforce the MARPOL Protocol, Annex IV to the Antarctic Protocol, and this chapter. In the administration and enforcement of the MARPOL Protocol and this chapter, Annexes I and II of the Convention apply only to seagoing ships.

**(b) Regulations; refuse record books; waste management plans; notification of crew and passengers**

(1) The Secretary shall prescribe any necessary or desired regulations to carry out the provisions of the MARPOL Protocol, Annex IV to the Antarctic Protocol, or this chapter.

(2) The Secretary of the department in which the Coast Guard is operating shall—

(A) prescribe regulations which—

(i) require certain ships described in section 1902(a)(1) of this title to maintain refuse record books and shipboard management plans, and to display placards which notify the crew and passengers of the requirements of Annex V to the Convention and of Annex IV to the Antarctic Protocol; and

(ii) specify the ships described in section 1902(a)(1) of this title to which the regulations apply;

(B) seek an international agreement or international agreements which apply requirements equivalent to those described in subparagraph (A)(i) to all vessels subject to Annex V to the Convention; and

(C) within 2 years after the effective date of this paragraph, report to the Congress—

(i) regarding activities of the Secretary under subparagraph (B); and

(ii) if the Secretary has not obtained agreements pursuant to subparagraph (B) regarding the desirability of applying the requirements described in subparagraph (A)(i) to all vessels described in section 1902(a) of this title which call at United States ports.

**(c) Utilization of personnel, facilities, or equipment of other Federal departments and agencies**

The Secretary may utilize by agreement, with or without reimbursement, personnel, facilities, or equipment of other Federal departments and agencies in administering the MARPOL Protocol, this chapter, or the regulations thereunder.

(Pub.L. 96–478, § 4, Oct. 21, 1980, 94 Stat. 2298; Pub.L. 100–220, Title II, § 2107, Dec. 29, 1987, 101 Stat. 1464; Pub.L. 104–227, Title II, § 201(c), Oct. 2, 1996, 110 Stat. 3042.)

### HISTORICAL AND STATUTORY NOTES

**References in Text**

This chapter, referred to in text, was in the original "this Act", meaning Pub.L. 96–478, Oct. 21, 1980, 94 Stat. 2297, known as the "Act to Prevent Pollution from Ships". For complete classification of this Act to the Code, see Tables.

Effective date of this paragraph, referred to in subsec. (b)(2)(C), refers to effective date of Amendment to this section by Pub.L. 100–220, which became effective on Dec. 31, 1988, the date on which Annex V to the International Convention for the Prevention of Pollution from Ships, 1973, entered into force for the United States, as provided in Effective Date of 1987 Amendment note, set out under section 1901 of this title.

**Effective and Applicability Provisions**

1987 Acts

Amendment by Pub.L. 100–220, effective on date on which Annex V to the International Convention for the Pollution from Ships, 1973, enters into force for the United States [such Annex entered into force for the United States on Dec. 31, 1988], see section 2002(a) of Pub.L. 100–220, set out as a note under section 1901 of this title.

1980 Acts

Subsecs. (a) and (c) effective Oct. 2 1983, and subsec. (b) effective Oct. 21, 1980, see section 14(a) and (b) of Pub.L. 96–478, set out under section 1901 of this title.

## § 1904. Certificates

**[APPS § 5]**

**(a) Issuance by authorized designees; restriction on issuance**

The Secretary shall designate those persons authorized to issue on behalf of the United States the certificates required by the MARPOL Protocol. A certificate required by the MARPOL Protocol shall not be issued to a ship which is registered in or of the nationality of a country which is not a party to the MARPOL Protocol.

**(b) Validity of foreign certificates**

A certificate issued by a country which is a party to the MARPOL Protocol has the same validity as a certificate issued by the Secretary under the authority of the MARPOL Protocol.

**(c) Location onboard vessel; inspection of vessels subject to jurisdiction of the United States**

A ship required by the MARPOL Protocol to have a certificate—

(1) shall carry a valid certificate onboard in the manner prescribed by the authority issuing the certificate; and

(2) is subject to inspection while in a port or terminal under the jurisdiction of the United States.

**(d) Onboard inspections; other Federal inspection authority unaffected**

An inspection conducted under subsection (c)(2) of this section is limited to verifying whether or not a valid certificate is onboard, unless clear grounds exist which reasonably indicate that the condition of the ship or its equipment does not substantially agree with the particulars of its certificate. This section shall not limit the authority of any official or employee of the United States under any other treaty, law, or regulation to board and inspect a ship or its equipment.

**(e) Detention orders; duration of detention; shipyard option**

In addition to the penalties prescribed in section 1908 of this title, a ship required by the MARPOL Protocol to have a certificate—

(1) which does not have a valid certificate onboard; or

(2) whose condition or whose equipment's condition does not substantially agree with the particulars of the certificate onboard;

shall be detained by order of the Secretary at the port or terminal where the violation is discovered until, in the opinion of the Secretary, the ship can proceed to sea without presenting an unreasonable threat of harm to the marine environment. The detention order may authorize the ship to proceed to the nearest appropriate available shipyard rather than remaining at the place where the violation was discovered.

**(f) Ship clearance or permits; refusal or revocation**

If a ship is under a detention order under this section, the Secretary of the Treasury, upon the request of the Secretary, may refuse or revoke—

(1) the clearance required by section 91 of Title 46 Appendix; or

(2) a permit to proceed under section 313 of Title 46 Appendix or section 1443 of Title 19.

**(g) Review of detention orders; petition; determination by Secretary**

A person whose ship is subject to a detention order under this section may petition the Secretary, in the manner prescribed by regulation, to review the detention order. Upon receipt of a petition under this subsection, the Secretary shall affirm, modify, or withdraw the detention order within the time prescribed by regulation.

**(h) Compensation for loss or damage**

A ship unreasonably detained or delayed by the Secretary acting under the authority of this chapter is entitled to compensation for any loss or damage suffered thereby.

(Pub.L. 96–478, § 5, Oct. 21, 1980, 94 Stat. 2298.)

### HISTORICAL AND STATUTORY NOTES

**References in Text**

Section 313 of Title 46 Appendix, referred to in subsec. (f)(2), was repealed by Pub.L. 103–182, Title VI, § 690(a)(21), Dec. 8, 1993, 107 Stat. 2223.

This chapter, referred to in subsec. (h), was in the original "this Act", meaning Pub.L. 96–478, Oct. 21, 1980, 94 Stat. 2297, known as the "Act to Prevent Pollution from Ships". For complete classification of this Act to the Code, see Tables.

**Codifications**

Section 1443 of Title 19, referred to in subsec. (f)(2), was in the original section 442 of the Tariff Act of 1930, as amended (19 U.S.C. 1443). Although section 442 of the Tariff Act of 1930, June 17, 1930, c. 497, title IV, 46 Stat. 713, is classified to section 1442 of Title 19, Customs Duties, the reference was translated to reflect the probable intent of Congress as section 1443 of Title 19 which is section 443 of the Tariff Act of 1930.

**Effective and Applicability Provisions**

1980 Acts

Subsec. (a) effective Oct. 21, 1980, and subsecs. (b) to (h) effective Oct. 2, 1983, see section 14(a) and (b) of Pub.L. 96–478, set out as a note under section 1901 of this title.

## § 1905. Pollution reception facilities

**[APPS § 6]**

**(a) Adequacy; criteria**

(1) The Secretary, after consultation with the Administrator of the Environmental Protection Agency, shall establish regulations setting criteria for determining the adequacy of a port's or terminal's reception facilities for mixtures containing oil or noxious liquid substances and shall establish procedures whereby a person in charge of a port or terminal may request the Secretary to certify that the port's or terminal's facilities for receiving the residues and mixtures containing oil or noxious liquid substance from seagoing ships are adequate.

(2) The Secretary, after consulting with appropriate Federal agencies, shall establish regulations setting criteria for determining the adequacy of reception facilities for garbage at a port or terminal, and stating such additional measures and requirements as are appropriate to ensure such adequacy. Persons in charge of ports and terminals shall provide reception facilities, or ensure that such facilities are available, for receiving garbage in accordance with those regulations.

**(b) Traffic considerations**

In determining the adequacy of reception facilities required by the MARPOL Protocol or the Antarctic Protocol at a port or terminal, and in establishing regulations under subsection (a) of this section, the Secretary may consider, among other things, the number and types of ships or seagoing ships using the port or terminal, including their principal trades.

**(c) Certificate; issuance; validity; inspection; review of suspension or revocation by Secretary**

(1) If reception facilities of a port or terminal meet the requirements of Annex I and Annex II to the Convention and the regulations prescribed under subsection (a)(1) of this section, the Secretary shall, after consultation with the Administrator of the Environmental Protection Agency, issue a certificate to that effect to the applicant.

(2)(A) Subject to subparagraph (B), if reception facilities of a port or terminal meet the requirements of Annex V to the Convention and the regulations prescribed under subsection (a)(2) of this section, the Secretary may, after consultation with appropriate Federal agencies, issue a certificate to that effect to the person in charge of the port or terminal.

(B) The Secretary may not issue a certificate attesting to the adequacy of reception facilities under this paragraph unless, prior to the issuance of the certificate, the Secretary conducts an inspection of the reception facilities of the port or terminal that is the subject of the certificate.

(C) The Secretary may, with respect to certificates issued under this paragraph prior to October 19, 1996, prescribe by regulation differing periods of validity for such certificates.

(3) A certificate issued under this subsection—

(A) is valid for the 5-year period beginning on the date of issuance of the certificate, except that if—

(i) the charge for operation of the port or terminal is transferred to a person or entity other than the person or entity that is the operator on the date of issuance of the certificate—

(I) the certificate shall expire on the date that is 30 days after the date of the transfer; and

(II) the new operator shall be required to submit an application for a certificate before a certificate may be issued for the port or terminal; or

(ii) the certificate is suspended or revoked by the Secretary, the certificate shall cease to be valid; and

(B) shall be available for inspection upon the request of the master, other person in charge, or agent of a ship using or intending to use the port or terminal.

(4) The suspension or revocation of a certificate issued under this subsection may be appealed to the Secretary and acted on by the Secretary in the manner prescribed by regulation.

**(d) Publication of list of certified ports or terminals**

(1) The Secretary shall maintain a list of ports or terminals with respect to which a certificate issued under this section—

(A) is in effect; or

(B) has been revoked or suspended.

(2) The Secretary shall make the list referred to in paragraph (1) available to the general public.

**(e) Entry; denial**

(1) Except in the case of force majeure, the Secretary shall deny entry to a seagoing ship required by the Convention or the Antarctic Protocol to retain onboard while at sea, residues and mixtures containing oil or noxious liquid substances, if—

(A) the port or terminal is one required by Annexes I and II of the Convention or Article 9 of Annex IV to the Antarctic Protocol or regulations hereunder to have adequate reception facilities; and

(B) the port or terminal does not hold a valid certificate issued by the Secretary under this section.

(2) The Secretary may deny the entry of a ship to a port or terminal required by regulations issued under this section to provide adequate reception facilities for garbage if the port or terminal is not in compliance with those regulations.

**(f) Surveys**

(1) The Secretary is authorized to conduct surveys of existing reception facilities in the United States to determine measures needed to comply with the MARPOL Protocol or the Antarctic Protocol.

(2) (A) [1] Not later than 18 months after October 19, 1996, the Secretary shall promulgate regulations that require the operator of each port or terminal that is subject to any requirement of the MARPOL Protocol relating to reception facilities to post a placard in a location that can easily be seen by port and terminal users. The placard shall state, at a minimum, that a user of a reception facility of the port or terminal should report to the Secretary any inadequacy of the reception facility.

(Pub.L. 96–478, § 6, Oct. 21, 1980, 94 Stat. 2299; Pub.L. 100–220, Title II, § 2103, Dec. 29, 1987, 101 Stat. 1461; Pub.L. 101–225, Title II, § 201(1), Dec. 12, 1989, 103 Stat. 1910; Pub.L. 104–227, Title II, § 201(d), Oct. 2, 1996, 110 Stat. 3043; Pub.L. 104–324, Title VIII, § 801, Oct. 19, 1996, 110 Stat. 3943.)

[1] So in original. No subpar. (B) was enacted.

## HISTORICAL AND STATUTORY NOTES

**Effective and Applicability Provisions**

1989 Acts

Amendment by Pub.L. 101–225 effective Dec. 12, 1989, see section 309 of Pub.L. 101–225, set out as a note under section 12101 of Title 46, shipping.

1987 Acts

Amendment by Pub.L. 100–220, effective on date on which Annex V to the International Convention for the Pollution from Ships, 1973, enters into force for the United States [such Annex entered into force for the United States on Dec. 31, 1988], see section 2002(a) of Pub.L. 100–220, set out as a note under section 1901 of this title.

1980 Acts

Subsecs. (a), (c), and (f) effective Oct. 21, 1980, and subsecs. (b), (d), and (e) effective Oct. 2, 1983, see section 14(a) and (b) of Pub.L. 96–478, set out as a note under section 1901 of this title.

## § 1906. Incidents involving ships

[APPS § 7]

**(a) Requirement to report incident**

The master, person in charge, owner, charterer, manager, or operator of a ship involved in an incident shall report the incident in the manner prescribed by Article 8 of the Convention in accordance with regulations promulgated by the Secretary for that purpose.

**(b) Discharge, probable discharge, or presence of oil**

The master or person in charge of—

(1) a ship of United States registry or nationality, or operated under the authority of the United States, wherever located;

(2) another ship while in the navigable waters of the United States; or

(3) a sea port or oil handling facility subject to the jurisdiction of the United States,

shall report a discharge, probable discharge, or presence of oil in the manner prescribed by Article 4 of the International Convention on Oil Pollution Preparedness, Response and Cooperation, 1990 (adopted at London, November 30, 1990), in accordance with regulations promulgated by the Secretary for that purpose.

(Pub.L. 96–478, § 7, Oct. 21, 1980, 94 Stat. 2300; Pub.L. 102–241, § 39, Dec. 19, 1991, 105 Stat. 2225.)

**HISTORICAL AND STATUTORY NOTES**

1980 Acts

House Report No. 96–1224, see 1980 U.S. Code Cong. and Adm. News, p. 4849.

1991 Acts

House Report No. 102–132, and Statement by President, see 1991 U.S. Code Cong. and Adm. News, p. 1867.

**Effective and Applicability Provisions**

1980 Acts

Section effective Oct. 2, 1983, see section 14(a) of Pub.L. 96–478, set out as a note under section 1901 of this title.

## § 1907. Violations

[APPS § 8]

**(a) General prohibition; cooperation and enforcement; detection and monitoring measures; reports; evidence**

It is unlawful to act in violation of the MARPOL Protocol, Annex IV to the Antarctic Protocol, this chapter, or the regulations issued thereunder. The Secretary shall cooperate with other parties to the MARPOL Protocol or to the Antarctic Protocol in the detection of violations and in enforcement of the MARPOL Protocol and Annex IV to the Antarctic Protocol. The Secretary shall use all appropriate and practical measures of detection and environmental monitoring, and shall establish adequate procedures for reporting violations and accumulating evidence.

**(b) Investigations; subpenas: issuance by Secretary, enforcement; action by Secretary; information to party**

Upon receipt of evidence that a violation has occurred, the Secretary shall cause the matter to be investigated. In any investigation under this section the Secretary may issue subpenas to require the attendance of any witness and the production of documents and other evidence. In case of refusal to obey a subpena issued to any person, the Secretary may request the Attorney General to invoke the aid of the appropriate district court of the United States to compel compliance. Upon completion of the investigation, the Secretary shall take the action required by the MARPOL Protocol or the Antarctic Protocol and whatever further action he considers appropriate under the circumstances. If the initial evidence was provided by a party to the MARPOL Protocol or the Antarctic Protocol, the Secretary, acting through the Secretary of State, shall inform that party of the action taken or proposed.

**(c) Ship inspections; reports to Secretary; additional action**

(1) This subsection applies to inspections relating to possible violations of Annex I or Annex II to the Convention, of Article 3 or Article 4 of Annex IV to the Antarctic Protocol, or of this chapter by any seagoing ship referred to in section 1902(a)(2) of this title.

(2) While at a port or terminal subject to the jurisdiction of the United States, a ship to which the MARPOL Protocol or the Antarctic Protocol applies may be inspected by the Secretary—

(A) to verify whether or not the ship has discharged a harmful substance in violation of the MARPOL Protocol, Annex IV to the Antarctic Protocol, or this chapter; or

(B) to comply with a request from a party to the MARPOL Protocol or the Antarctic Protocol for an investigation as to whether the ship may have discharged a harmful substance anywhere in violation of the MARPOL Protocol or Annex IV to the Antarctic Protocol. An investigation may be undertaken under this clause only when the requesting party has furnished sufficient evidence to allow the Secretary reasonably to believe that a discharge has occurred.

If an inspection under this subsection indicates that a violation has occurred, the investigating officer shall forward a report to the Secretary for appropriate action. The Secretary shall undertake to notify the master of the ship concerned and, acting in coordination with the Secretary of State, shall take any additional action required by Article 6 of the Convention.

**(d) Garbage disposal inspections; covered ships; enforcement actions**

(1) The Secretary may inspect a ship referred to in section 1902(a)(3) of this title to verify whether the ship has disposed of garbage in violation of Annex V to the Convention, Article 5 of Annex IV to the Antarctic Protocol, or this chapter.

(2) If an inspection under this subsection indicates that a violation has occurred, the Secretary may undertake enforcement action under section 1908 of this title.

**(e) Harmful substance or garbage disposal inspections; covered ships; enforcement actions**

(1) The Secretary may inspect at any time a ship of United States registry or nationality or operating under the authority of the United States to which the MARPOL Protocol or the Antarctic Protocol applies to verify whether the ship has discharged a harmful substance or disposed of garbage in violation of those Protocols or this chapter.

(2) If an inspection under this subsection indicates that a violation of the MARPOL Protocol, of Annex IV to the Antarctic Protocol, or of this chapter has occurred the Secretary may undertake enforcement action under section 1908 of this title.

**(f) Supplemental remedies and requirements; other provisions and available remedies unaffected**

Remedies and requirements of this chapter supplement and neither amend nor repeal any other provisions of law, except as expressly provided in this chapter. Nothing in this chapter shall limit, deny, amend, modify, or repeal any other remedy available to the United States or any other person, except as expressly provided in this chapter.

(Pub.L. 96–478, § 8, Oct. 21, 1980, 94 Stat. 2300; Pub.L. 100–220, Title II, § 2104, Dec. 29, 1987, 101 Stat. 1462; Pub.L. 101–225, Title II, § 201(2), (3), Dec. 12, 1989, 103 Stat. 1910; Pub.L. 104–227, Title II, § 201(e), Oct. 2, 1996, 110 Stat. 3043.)

### HISTORICAL AND STATUTORY NOTES

**References in text**

This chapter, referred to in text, was in the original "this Act", meaning Pub.L. 96–478, Oct. 21, 1980, 94 Stat. 2297, known as the "Act to Prevent Pollution from Ships". For complete classification of this Act to the Code, see Short Title note below and Tables.

**Effective and Applicability Provisions**

1989 Acts

Amendment by Pub.L. 101–225 effective Dec. 12, 1989, see section 309 of Pub.L. 101–225, set out as a note under section 12101 of Title 46, shipping.

1987 Acts

Amendment by Pub.L. 100–220, effective on date on which Annex V to the International Convention for the Pollution from Ships, 1973, enters into force for the United States [such Annex entered into force for the United States on Dec. 31, 1988], see section 2002(a) of Pub.L. 100–220, set out as a note under section 1901 of this title.

1980 Acts

Section effective Oct. 2, 1983, see section 14(a) of Pub.L. 96–478, set out as a note under section 1901 of this title.

## § 1908. Penalties for violations

[APPS § 9]

**(a) Criminal penalties; payment for information leading to conviction**

A person who knowingly violates the MARPOL Protocol,,[1] Annex IV to the Antarctic Protocol, this chapter, or the regulations issued thereunder commits a class D felony. In the discretion of the Court, an amount equal to not more than ½ of such fine may be paid to the person giving information leading to conviction.

**(b) Civil penalties; separate violations; assessment notice; considerations affecting amount, payment for information leading to assessment of penalty**

A person who is found by the Secretary, after notice and an opportunity for a hearing, to have—

(1) violated the MARPOL Protocol,,[1] Annex IV to the Antarctic Protocol, this chapter, or the regulations issued thereunder shall be liable to the United States for a civil penalty, not to exceed $25,000 for each violation; or

(2) made a false, fictitious, or fraudulent statement or representation in any matter in which a statement or representation is required to be made to the Secretary under the MARPOL Protocol,,[1] Annex IV to the Antarctic Protocol, this chapter, or the regulations thereunder, shall be liable to the United States for a civil penalty, not to exceed $5,000 for each statement or representation.

Each day of a continuing violation shall constitute a separate violation. The amount of the civil penalty shall be assessed by the Secretary, or his designee, by written notice. In determining the amount of the penalty, the Secretary shall take into account the nature, circumstances, extent, and gravity of the prohibited acts committed and, with respect to the violator, the degree of culpability, any history of prior offenses, ability to pay, and other matters as justice may require. An amount equal to not more than ½ of such penalties may be paid by the Secretary to the person giving information leading to the assessment of such penalties.

**(c) Abatement of civil penalties; collection by Attorney General**

The Secretary may compromise, modify, or remit, with or without conditions, any civil penalty which is subject to assessment or which has been assessed under this section. If any person fails to pay an assessment of a civil penalty after it has become final, the Secretary may refer the matter to the Attorney General of the United States for collection in any appropriate district court of the United States.

**(d) Liability in rem; district court jurisdiction**

A ship operated in violation of the MARPOL Protocol,,[1] Annex IV to the Antarctic Protocol, this chapter, or the regulations thereunder is liable in rem for any fine imposed under subsection (a) of this section or civil penalty assessed pursuant to subsection (b) of this section, and may be proceeded against in the United States district court of any district in which the ship may be found.

**(e) Ship clearance or permits; refusal or revocation; bond or other surety**

If any ship subject to the MARPOL Protocol, Annex IV to the Antarctic Protocol, or this chapter, its owner, operator, or person in charge is liable for a fine or civil penalty under this section, or if reasonable cause exists to believe that the ship, its owner, operator, or person in charge may be subject to a fine or civil penalty under this section, the Secretary of the Treasury, upon the request of the Secretary, shall refuse or revoke the clearance required by section 91 of the Appendix to Title 46. Clearance may be granted upon the filing of a bond or other surety satisfactory to the Secretary.

**(f) Referrals for appropriate action by foreign country**

Notwithstanding subsection (a), (b), or (d) of this section, if the violation is by a ship registered in or of the nationality of a country party to the MARPOL Protocol or the Antarctic Protocol, or one operated under the authority of a country party to the MARPOL Protocol or the Antarctic Protocol, the Secretary, acting in coordination with the Secretary of State, may refer the matter to the government of the country of the ship's registry or nationality, or under whose authority the ship is operating for appropriate action, rather than taking the actions required or authorized by this section.

(Pub.L. 96–478, § 9, Oct. 21, 1980, 94 Stat. 2301; Pub.L. 100–220, Title II, § 2105, Dec. 29, 1987, 101 Stat. 1463; Pub.L. 101–380, Title IV, § 4302(n), Aug. 18, 1990, 104 Stat. 539; Pub.L. 103–182, Title VI, § 688, Dec. 8, 1993, 107 Stat. 2222; Pub.L. 104–227, Title II, § 201(f), Oct. 2, 1996, 110 Stat. 3043.)

[1] So in original.

**HISTORICAL AND STATUTORY NOTES**

**References in Text**

This chapter, referred to in subsecs. (a), (b)(1), (2), and (d), was in the original "this Act", meaning Pub.L. 96–478, Oct. 21, 1980, 94 Stat. 2297, known as the "Act to Prevent Pollution from Ships". For complete classification of this Act to the Code, see Tables.

**Effective and Applicability Provisions**

1993 Acts

Amendment by section 688 of Pub.L. 103–182 effective Dec. 8, 1993, see section 692 of Pub.L. 103–182, set out as a note under section 58c of Title 19, Customs Duties.

1987 Acts

Amendment by Pub.L. 100–220, effective on date on which Annex V to the International Convention for the Pollution from Ships, 1973, enters into force for the United States [such Annex entered into force for the United States on Dec. 31, 1988], see section 2002(a) of Pub.L. 100–220, set out as a note under section 1901 of this title.

1980 Acts

Section effective Oct. 2, 1983, see section 14(a) of Pub.L. 96–478, set out as a note under section 1901 of this title.

## § 1909. MARPOL Protocol; proposed amendments

**[APPS § 10]**

**(a) Acceptance of certain amendments by the President**

A proposed amendment to the MARPOL Protocol received by the United States from the Secretary-General of the International Maritime Organization pursuant to Article VI of the MARPOL Protocol, may be accepted on behalf of the United States by the President following the advice and consent of the Senate, except as provided for in subsection (b) of this section.

**(b) Action on certain amendments by Secretary of State**

A proposed amendment to Annex I, II, or V to the Convention, appendices to those Annexes, or Protocol I of the Convention, received by the United States from the Secretary-General of the Inter-Governmental Maritime Organization pursuant to Article VI of the MARPOL Protocol, may be the subject of appropriate action on behalf of the United States by the Secretary of State following consultation with the Secretary, who shall inform the Secretary of State as to what action he considers appropriate at least 30 days prior to the expiration of the period specified in Article VI of the MARPOL Protocol during which objection may be made to any amendment received.

**(c) Declaration of nonacceptance by the Secretary of State**

Following consultation with the Secretary, the Secretary of State may make a declaration that the

United States does not accept an amendment proposed pursuant to Article VI of the MARPOL Protocol.

(Pub.L. 96–478, § 10, Oct. 21, 1980, 94 Stat. 2302; Pub.L. 100–220, Title II, § 2106, Dec. 29, 1987, 101 Stat. 1463.)

### HISTORICAL AND STATUTORY NOTES

**Effective and Applicability Provisions**

1987 Acts

Amendment by Pub.L. 100–220, effective on date on which Annex V to the International Convention for the Pollution from Ships, 1973, enters into force for the United States [such Annex entered into force for the United States on Dec. 31, 1988], see section 2002(a) of Pub.L. 100–220, set out as a note under section 1901 of this title.

1980 Acts

Section effective Oct. 2, 1983, see section 14(a) of Pub.L. 96–478, set out as a note under section 1901 of this title.

## § 1910. Legal actions

**[APPS § 11]**

**(a) Persons with adversely affected interests as plaintiffs; defendants**

Except as provided in subsection (b) of this section, any person having an interest which is, or can be, adversely affected, may bring an action on his own behalf—

(1) against any person alleged to be in violation of the provisions of this chapter, or regulations issued hereunder;

(2) against the Secretary where there is alleged a failure of the Secretary to perform any act or duty under this chapter which is not discretionary with the Secretary;

(3) against the Secretary of the Treasury where there is alleged a failure of the Secretary of the Treasury to take action under section 1908(e) of this title.

**(b) Commencement conditions**

No action may be commenced under subsection (a) of this section—

(1) prior to 60 days after the plaintiff has given notice, in writing and under oath, to the alleged violator, the Secretary concerned, and the Attorney General; or

(2) if the Secretary has commenced enforcement or penalty action with respect to the alleged violation and is conducting such procedures diligently.

**(c) Venue**

Any suit brought under this section shall be brought—

(1) in a case concerning an onshore facility or port, in the United States district court for the judicial district where the onshore facility or port is located;

(2) in a case concerning an offshore facility or offshore structure under the jurisdiction of the United States, in the United States district court for the judicial district nearest the offshore facility or offshore structure;

(3) in a case concerning a ship, in the United States district court for any judicial district wherein the ship or its owner or operator may be found; or

(4) in any case, in the District Court for the District of Columbia.

**(d) Costs; attorney fees; witness fees**

The court, in issuing any final order in any action brought pursuant to this section, may award costs of litigation (including reasonable attorney and expert witness fees) to any party including the Federal Government.

**(e) Federal intervention**

In any action brought under this section, if the Secretary or Attorney General are not parties of record, the United States, through the Attorney General, shall have the right to intervene.

(Pub.L. 96–478, § 11, Oct. 21, 1980, 94 Stat. 2302.)

### HISTORICAL AND STATUTORY NOTES

**References in Text**

This chapter, referred to in subsec. (a)(1) and (2), was in the original "this Act", meaning Pub.L. 96–478, Oct. 21, 1980, 94 Stat. 2297, known as the "Act to Prevent Pollution from Ships". For complete classification of this Act to the Code, see Tables.

**Effective and Applicability Provisions**

1980 Acts

Section effective Oct. 2, 1983, see section 14(a) of Pub.L. 96–478, set out as a note under section 1901 of this title.

## § 1911. Authority of Secretary under port and tanker safety program unaffected

**[APPS § 15]**

Nothing in this chapter shall be construed as limiting, diminishing, or otherwise restricting any of the authority of the Secretary under the Port and Tanker Safety Act of 1978.

(Pub.L. 96–478, § 15, Oct. 21, 1980, 94 Stat. 2303.)

### HISTORICAL AND STATUTORY NOTES

**References in Text**

This chapter, referred to in text, was in the original "this Act", meaning Pub.L. 96–478, Oct. 21, 1980, 94 Stat. 2297, known as the "Act to Prevent Pollution from Ships". For complete classification of this Act to the Code, see Tables.

The Port and Tanker Safety Act of 1978, referred to in text, is Pub.L. 95–474, Oct. 17, 1978, 92 Stat. 1471, which enacted sections 1225, 1228 to 1231, and 1232 of this title, amended sections 1221 to 1224, 1226, and 1227 of this title, and sections 214 and 391a of Title 46, Shipping, and enacted provisions set out as notes under sections 1221 and 1224 of this title and section 391a of Title 46. For complete classification of this Act to the Code, see Short Title of 1978 Amendments note set out under section 1221 of this title and Tables volume.

**Effective and Applicability Provisions**

1980 Acts

Section effective Oct. 2, 1983, see section 14(a) of Pub.L. 98–478, set out as a note under section 1901 of this title.

## § 1912. International law

[APPS § 17]

Any action taken under this chapter shall be taken in accordance with international law.

(Pub.L. 96–478, § 17, as added Pub.L. 100–220, Title II, § 2108, Dec. 29, 1987, 101 Stat. 1464.)

### HISTORICAL AND STATUTORY NOTES

**Effective and Applicability Provisions**

1987 Acts

Section effective Dec. 29, 1987, see section 2002(b) of Pub.L. 100–220, set out as a note under section 1901 of this title.

## § 1913. Compliance reports

### (a) In general

Within 1 year after the effective date of this section, and triennially thereafter, the Secretary of the department in which the Coast Guard is operating, in consultation with the Secretary of Agriculture and the Secretary of Commerce, shall report to the Congress regarding compliance with Annex V to the International Convention for the Prevention of Pollution from Ships, 1973, in United States waters and, not later than 1 year after October 19, 1996, and annually thereafter, shall publish in the Federal Register a list of the enforcement actions taken against any domestic or foreign ship (including any commercial or recreational ship) pursuant to the Act to Prevent Pollution from Ships (33 U.S.C. 1901 et seq.).

### (b) Report on inability to comply

Within 3 years after the effective date of this section, the head of each Federal agency that operates or contracts for the operation of any ship referred to in section 3(b)(1)(A) of the Act to Prevent Pollution from Ships [33 U.S.C.A. § 1902(b)(1)(A)] that may not be able to comply with the requirements of that section shall report to the Congress describing—

(1) the technical and operational impediments to achieving that compliance;

(2) an alternative schedule for achieving that compliance as rapidly as is technologically feasible;

(3) the ships operated or contracted for operation by the agency for which full compliance with section 3(b)(2)(A) [33 U.S.C.A. § 1902(b)(2)(A)] is not technologically feasible; and

(4) any other information which the agency head considers relevant and appropriate.

### (c) Congressional action

Upon receipt of the compliance report under subsection (b) of this section, the Congress shall modify the applicability of Annex V to ships referred to in section 3(b)(1)(A) of the Act to Prevent Pollution from Ships [33 U.S.C.A. § 1902(b)(1)(A)], as may be appropriate with respect to the requirements of Annex V to the Convention.

(Pub.L. 100–220, Title II, § 2201, Dec. 29, 1987, 101 Stat. 1464; Pub.L. 104–66, Title I, § 1121(c), Dec. 21, 1995, 109 Stat. 724; Pub.L. 104–324, Title VIII, § 802(a), Oct. 19, 1996, 110 Stat. 3944.)

### HISTORICAL AND STATUTORY NOTES

**References in Text**

For effective date of this section, referred to in subsecs. (a) and (b), see section 2002 of Pub.L. 100–220, set out as a note under section 1901 of this title.

The Act to Prevent Pollution from Ships, referred to in text, is Pub.L. 96–478, Oct. 21, 1980, 94 Stat. 2297, as amended, which is classified principally to this chapter [33 U.S.C.A. § 1901 et seq.]. For complete classification of this Act to the Code, see Short Title note set out under 33 U.S.C.A. § 1901 and Tables.

**Codifications**

Section was formerly set out as a note under section 1902 of this title.

Section was enacted as part of the Marine Plastic Pollution Research and Control Act of 1987 and as part of the United States-Japan Fishery Agreement Approval Act of 1987, and not as part of the Act to Prevent Pollution from Ships which comprises this chapter.

## § 1914. Coordination

### (a) Establishment of Marine Debris Coordinating Committee

The Secretary of Commerce shall establish a Marine Debris Coordinating Committee.

### (b) Membership

The Committee shall include a senior official from—

(1) the National Oceanic and Atmospheric Administration, who shall serve as the Chairperson of the Committee;

(2) the Environmental Protection Agency;

(3) the United States Coast Guard;

(4) the United States Navy; and

(5) such other Federal agencies that have an interest in ocean issues or water pollution preven-

tion and control as the Secretary of Commerce determines appropriate.

**(c) Meetings**

The Committee shall meet at least twice a year to provide a forum to ensure the coordination of national and international research, monitoring, education, and regulatory actions addressing the persistent marine debris problem.

**(d) Monitoring**

The Secretary of Commerce, acting through the Administrator of the National Oceanic and Atmospheric Administration, in cooperation with the Administrator of the Environmental Protection Agency, shall utilize the marine debris data derived under title V of the Marine Protection, Research, and Sanctuaries Act of 1972 (33 U.S.C. 2801 et seq.) to assist—

(1) the Committee in ensuring coordination of research, monitoring, education and regulatory actions; and

(2) the United States Coast Guard in assessing the effectiveness of this Act and the Act to Prevent Pollution from Ships [33 U.S.C.A. § 1901 et seq.] in ensuring compliance under section 1913 of this title.

(Pub.L. 100–220, Title II, § 2203, Dec. 29, 1987, 101 Stat. 1466; Pub.L. 104–324, Title VIII, § 802(b), Oct. 19, 1996, 110 Stat. 3944.)

### HISTORICAL AND STATUTORY NOTES

**References in Text**

The Marine Protection, Research, and Sanctuaries Act of 1972, referred to in subsec. (d), is Pub.L. 92–532, Oct. 23, 1972, 86 Stat. 1052, as amended. Title V of the Marine Protection, Research, and Sanctuaries Act of 1972, popularly known as the National Coastal Monitoring Act, is classified generally to chapter 41 (section 2801 et seq.) of this title. For complete classification of this Act to the Code, see Short Title note set out under section 1401 of this title and Tables.

This Act, referred to in subsec. (d)(2), is Pub.L. 100–200, Title II, Dec. 29, 1987, 101 Stat. 1460, known as the Marine Plastic Pollution Research and Control Act of 1987. For complete classification of this Act to the Code, see Short Title of 1987 Amendment note set out under section 1901 of this title and Tables.

The Act to Prevent Pollution from Ships, referred to in subsec. (d)(2), is Pub.L. 96–478, Oct. 21, 1980, 94 Stat. 2297, as amended, which is classified principally to this chapter (section 1901 et seq.). For complete classification of this Act to the Code, see Short Title note set out under section 1901 of this title and Tables.

**Codifications**

Section was enacted as part of the Marine Plastic Pollution Research and Control Act of 1987 and as part of the United States-Japan Fishery Agreement Approval Act of 1987, and not as part of the Act to Prevent Pollution from Ships which comprises this chapter.

## § 1915. Plastic pollution public education program

**(a) Outreach program**

**(1) In general**

Not later than April 1, 1988, the Administrator of the National Oceanic and Atmospheric Administration and the Administrator of the Environmental Protection Agency, in consultation with the Secretary of Transportation, shall jointly commence and thereafter conduct a public outreach program to educate the public (including recreational boaters, fishermen, and other users of the marine environment) regarding—

(A) the harmful effects of plastic pollution;

(B) the need to reduce such pollution;

(C) the need to recycle plastic materials;

(D) the need to reduce the quantity of plastic debris in the marine environment; and

(E) the requirements under this Act and the Act to Prevent Pollution from Ships (33 U.S.C. 1901 et seq.) with respect to ships and ports, and the authority of citizens to report violations of this Act and the Act to Prevent Pollution from Ships (33 U.S.C. 1901 et seq.).

**(2) Authorized activities**

**(A) Public outreach program**

A public outreach program under paragraph (1) may include—

(i) developing and implementing a voluntary boaters' pledge program;

(ii) workshops with interested groups;

(iii) public service announcements;

(iv) distribution of leaflets and posters; and

(v) any other means appropriate to educating the public.

**(B) Grants and cooperative agreements**

To carry out this section, the Secretary of the department in which the Coast Guard is operating, the Secretary of Commerce, and the Administrator of the Environmental Protection Agency are authorized to award grants, enter into cooperative agreements with appropriate officials of other Federal agencies and agencies of States and political subdivisions of States and with public and private entities, and provide other financial assistance to eligible recipients.

**(C) Consultation**

In developing outreach initiatives for groups that are subject to the requirements of this title and the Act to Prevent Pollution from Ships (33 U.S.C. 1901 et seq.), the Secretary of the department in which the Coast Guard is operating, in consultation with the Secretary of Commerce, acting through the Administrator of the National

Oceanic and Atmospheric Administration, and the Administrator of the Environmental Protection Agency, shall consult with—

(i) the heads of State agencies responsible for implementing State boating laws; and

(ii) the heads of other enforcement agencies that regulate boaters or commercial fishermen.

**(b) Citizen Pollution Patrols**

The Secretary of Commerce, along with the Administrator of the Environmental Protection Agency and the Secretary of the Department in which the Coast Guard is operating, shall conduct a program to encourage the formation of volunteer groups, to be designated as "Citizen Pollution Patrols", to assist in monitoring, reporting, cleanup, and prevention of ocean and shoreline pollution.

(Pub.L. 100–220, Title II, § 2204, Dec. 19, 1987, 101 Stat. 1466; Pub.L. 104–324, Title VIII, § 802(c), Oct. 19, 1996, 110 Stat. 3945.)

### HISTORICAL AND STATUTORY NOTES

**References in Text**

This Act, referred to in subsec. (a)(1)(E), is Pub.L. 100–200, Title II, Dec. 29, 1987, 101 Stat. 1460, known as the Marine Plastic Pollution Research and Control Act of 1987. For complete classification of this Act to the Code, see Short Title of 1987 Amendment note set out under section 1901 of this title and Tables.

The Act to Prevent Pollution from Ships, referred to in subsec. (a)(1)(E) and (2)(C), is Pub.L. 96–478, Oct. 21, 1980, 94 Stat. 2297, as amended, which is classified principally to this chapter (section 1901 et seq.). For complete classification of this Act to the Code, see Short Title note set out under section 1901 of this title and Tables.

This title, referred to in subsec. (a)(2)(C), is Title II of Pub.L. 100–220, see References in Text note above.

**Codifications**

Section was formerly set out as a note under section 6981 of Title 42, The Public Health and Welfare.

Section was enacted as part of the Marine Plastic Pollution Research and Control Act of 1987 and as part of the United States-Japan Fishery Agreement Approval Act of 1987, and not as part of the Act to Prevent Pollution from Ships which comprises this chapter.

## §§ 1916 to 2000. Reserved for future legislation

# SHORE PROTECTION

## SHORE PROTECTION ACT OF 1988 [SPA § ____]

**(33 U.S.C.A. §§ 2601 to 2623)**

## CHAPTER 39—SHORE PROTECTION FROM MUNICIPAL OR COMMERCIAL WASTE

SUBCHAPTER I—SHORE PROTECTION



### SUBCHAPTER I—SHORE PROTECTION

### § 2601. Definitions

**[SPA § 4101]**

In this chapter—

(1) "Administrator" means the Administrator of the Environmental Protection Agency.

(2) "coastal waters" means—

(A) the territorial sea of the United States;

(B) the Great Lakes and their connecting waters;

(C) the marine and estuarine waters of the United States up to the head of tidal influence; and

(D) the Exclusive Economic Zone as established by Presidential Proclamation Number 5030, dated March 10, 1983.

(3) "municipal or commercial waste" means solid waste (as defined in section 6903 of Title 42) except—

(A) solid waste identified and listed under section 6921 of Title 42;

(B) waste generated by the vessel during normal operations;

(C) debris solely from construction activities;

(D) sewage sludge subject to regulation under title I of the Marine Protection, Research, and Sanctuaries Act of 1972 (33 U.S.C. 1401 et seq.); and

(E) dredged or fill material subject to regulation under title I of the Marine Protection, Research, and Sanctuaries Act of 1972 (33 U.S.C. 1401 et seq.), the Federal Water Pollution Control Act (33 U.S.C. 1251 et seq.), or the Rivers and Harbors Appropriation Act of 1899 (33 U.S.C. 401 et seq.).

(4) "person" means an individual, trust, firm, joint stock company, corporation (including a government corporation), partnership, association, State, municipality, commission, political subdivision of a State, or any interstate body.

(5) "receiving facility" means a facility or operation where municipal or commercial waste is unloaded from a vessel.

(6) "United States", when used in a geographic sense, means the States of the United States, Puerto Rico, the District of Columbia, the Virgin Islands, American Samoa, Guam, the Northern Mariana Islands, and any other territory or possession of the United States.

(7) "waste source" means a facility or vessel from which municipal or commercial waste is loaded onto a vessel, including any rolling stock or motor vehicles from which that waste is directly loaded.

(Pub.L. 100–688, Title IV, § 4101, Nov. 18, 1988, 102 Stat. 4154.)

#### HISTORICAL AND STATUTORY NOTES

**References in Text**

Presidential Proclamation Number 5030, referred to in par. (2)(D), is set out under 16 U.S.C.A. § 1453.

The Marine Protection, Research, and Sanctuaries Act of 1972, referred to in par. (3)(D), (E), is Pub.L. 92–532, Oct. 23, 1972, 86 Stat. 1052, as amended. Title I of such Act of 1972 is classified generally to subchapter I (section 1411 et seq.) of chapter 27 of this title. For complete classification of this Act to the Code, see Short Title note set out under section 1401 of this title and Tables.

The Federal Water Pollution Control Act, referred to in par. (3)(E), is Act June 30, 1948, c. 758, as amended generally by Pub.L. 92–500, § 2, Oct. 18, 1972, 86 Stat. 816, which is classified generally to chapter 26 (section 1251 et seq.) of this title. For complete classification of this Act to the Code, see

Short Title note set out under section 1251 of this title and Tables.

The Rivers and Harbors Appropriation Act of 1899, referred to in par. (3)(E), also known as the Rivers and Harbors Act of 1899, is Act Mar. 3, 1899, c. 425, 30 Stat. 1151, as amended, which enacted sections 401, 403, 404, 406 to 409, 411 to 416, 418, 502, 549, 686, and 687 of this title. For complete classification of this Act to the Code, see Tables.

**Short Title**

1988 Acts

Section 4001 of Pub.L. 100–688 provided that: "This title [enacting this chapter and provisions set out as notes under sections 2602 and 2603 of this title] may be cited as the 'Shore Protection Act of 1988'."

**Territorial Sea of United States**

For extension of territorial sea of United States, see Proc. No. 5928, set out as a note under 43 U.S.C.A. § 1331.

## § 2602. Vessel permits and numbers

**[SPA § 4102]**

### (a) In general

A vessel (except a public vessel as defined in section 2101 of Title 46) may not transport municipal or commercial waste in coastal waters without—

(1) a permit for that vessel from the Secretary of Transportation; and

(2) displaying a number or other marking on the vessel as prescribed by the Secretary under chapter 123 or section 12502(b) of Title 46.

### (b) Permit applications

Application for a permit required by subsection (a) of this section shall be made by the vessel owner or operator and include—

(1) the name, address, and telephone number of the vessel owner and operator;

(2) the vessel's name and identification number;

(3) the vessel's area of operation;

(4) the vessel's transport capacity;

(5) a history of the types of cargo transported by that vessel during the previous year, including identifying the type of municipal or commercial waste transported as—

(A) municipal waste;
(B) commercial waste;
(C) medical waste; or
(D) waste of another character.

(6) any other information the Secretary may require; and

(7) an acknowledgment.

### (c) Effective date of permits

A permit issued under this section—

(1) is effective 30 days after the date on which it was issued;

(2) may be issued only for a period of not more than 5 years after the effective date of the permit;

(3) may be renewed for periods of not more than 5 years only by the vessel owner or operator that applied for the original permit; and

(4) is terminated when the vessel is sold.

### (d) Denial of permits

The Secretary may, or at the request of the Administrator shall, deny the issuance of a permit for any vessel if the owner or operator of the vessel has a record of a pattern of serious violations of—

(1) this subchapter;

(2) the Solid Waste Disposal Act (42 U.S.C. 6901 et seq.);

(3) the Marine Protection, Research, and Sanctuaries Act of 1972 [16 U.S.C.A. §§ 1431 et seq., 1447 et seq., 33 U.S.C.A. §§ 1401 et seq., 2801 et seq.];

(4) the Rivers and Harbors Appropriation Act of 1899 (33 U.S.C. 401 et seq.); or

(5) the Federal Water Pollution Control Act (33 U.S.C. 1251 et seq.).

### (e) Permit decision

The Secretary, after consultation with the Administrator, shall issue or deny a vessel permit under this section within 30 days after receiving a complete application. On denying the issuance of the permit for a vessel the Secretary shall—

(1) notify the applicant of the denial and the reasons for the denial; and

(2) provide an opportunity for a hearing on the denial.

### (f) Maintaining permit

**(1) In general**

The permit issued for a vessel under this chapter shall be maintained in a manner prescribed by the Secretary.

**(2) Endorsements**

If a vessel is a documented vessel, the Secretary may endorse a permit on the vessel's certificate of documentation.

### (g) Vessel information system

The Secretary may include information in a permit in the vessel information system maintained under chapter 125 of Title 46.

(Pub.L. 100–688, Title IV, § 4102, Nov. 18, 1988, 102 Stat. 4155.)

HISTORICAL AND STATUTORY NOTES

**References in Text**

The Solid Waste Disposal Act, referred to in subsec. (d)(2), is Title II of Pub.L. 89–272, as amended generally by Pub.L. 94–580, § 2, Oct. 21, 1976, 90 Stat. 2795, which is classified generally to chapter 82 (section 6901 et seq.) of Title 42, The Public Health and Welfare. For complete classification of this Act to the Code, see Short Title note set out under section 6901 of Title 42 and Tables.

The Marine Protection, Research, and Sanctuaries Act of 1972, referred to in subsec. (d)(3), is Pub.L. 92–532, Oct. 23, 1972, 86 Stat. 1052, as amended, which is classified principally to chapters 27 [33 U.S.C.A. § 1401 et seq.] and 41 [33 U.S.C.A. § 2801 et seq.] of this title and chapters 32 [16 U.S.C.A. § 1431 et seq.] and 32A [16 U.S.C.A. § 1447 et seq.] of Title 16. For complete classification, see Short Title note set out under 33 U.S.C.A. § 1401 and Tables.

The Rivers and Harbors Appropriation Act of 1899, referred to in subsec. (d)(4), also known as the Rivers and Harbors Act of 1899, is Act Mar. 3, 1899, c. 425, 30 Stat. 1151, as amended, which enacted sections 401, 403, 404, 406 to 409, 411 to 416, 418, 502, 549, 686, and 687 of this title. For complete classification of this Act to the Code, see Tables.

The Federal Water Pollution Control Act, referred to in subsec. (d)(5) is Act June 30, 1948, c. 758, as amended generally by Pub.L. 92–500, § 2, Oct. 18, 1972, 86 Stat. 816, which is classified generally to chapter 26 (section 1251 et seq.) of this title. For complete classification of this Act to the Code, see Short Title note set out under section 1251 of this title and Tables.

**Effective and Applicability Provisions**

1988 Acts

Section 4204(b) of Pub.L. 100–688 provided that: "Section 4102(a) of this Act [subsec. (a) of this section] is effective 240 days after the date of enactment of this Act [Nov. 18, 1988]."

**Availability of Applications**

Section 4204(a) of Pub.L. 100–688 provided that: "The Secretary shall make vessel applications for permits to be issued under section 4102 of this Act [this section] publicly available within 60 days after the date of enactment of this Act [Nov. 18, 1988]."

## § 2603. Waste handling practices

[SPA § 4103]

**(a) In general**

**(1) Loading**

The owner or operator of the waste source shall take all reasonable steps to assure that all municipal or commercial waste is loaded onto a vessel in a manner that assures that waste deposited in coastal waters is minimized.

**(2) Securing**

The owner or operator of a vessel shall assure that all municipal or commercial waste loaded onto the vessel is secured by netting or other means to assure that waste will not be deposited into coastal waters during transport.

**(3) Offloading**

The owner or operator of the receiving facility shall take all reasonable steps to assure that any municipal or commercial waste is offloaded from a vessel in a manner that assures that waste deposited into coastal waters is minimized.

**(4) Cleaning up**

The owner or operator of any waste source or receiving facility shall provide adequate control measures to clean up any municipal or commercial waste which is deposited into coastal waters.

**(b) Regulations**

The Administrator, in consultation with the Secretary of Transportation, shall prescribe regulations—

(1) requiring that waste sources, receiving facilities, and vessels provide the means and facilities to assure that the waste will not be deposited into coastal waters during loading, offloading, and transport;

(2) requiring, as appropriate, the submission and adoption by each responsible party of an operation and maintenance manual identifying procedures to be used to prevent, report, and clean up any deposit of municipal or commercial waste into coastal waters, including record keeping requirements; and

(3) if the Administrator determines that tracking systems are required to assure adequate enforcement of laws preventing the deposit of municipal or commercial waste into coastal waters, requiring installation of the appropriate systems within 18 months after the Administrator makes that determination.

(Pub.L. 100–688, Title IV, § 4103, Nov. 18, 1988, 102 Stat. 4156.)

HISTORICAL AND STATUTORY NOTES

**Effective and Applicability Provisions**

1988 Acts

Section 4204(c) of Pub.L. 100–688 provided that: "Section 4103 of this Act [this section] takes effect 60 days after the date of enactment of this Act [Nov. 18, 1988]."

## § 2604. Suspension, revocation, and injunctions

[SPA § 4104]

**(a) Suspension and revocation**

After notice and opportunity for a hearing, the Secretary of Transportation may, and at the request of the Administrator shall, suspend or revoke a permit issued to a vessel under this chapter for a violation of this chapter or a regulation prescribed under this chapter.

**(b) Injunctions**

The Secretary or the Administrator may bring a civil action to enjoin any operation in violation of this chapter or a regulation prescribed under this chapter in the district court of the United States for the district in which the violation occurred.

(Pub.L. 100–688, Title IV, § 4104, Nov. 18, 1988, 102 Stat. 4157.)

## § 2605. Enforcement

**[SPA § 4105]**

**(a) General authority**

The Secretary of Transportation shall enforce this chapter under section 89 of Title 14. The Secretary may authorize other officers or employees of the United States Government to enforce this chapter under that section.

**(b) Periodic examinations**

The Secretary shall conduct periodic examinations of vessels operating under this chapter transporting municipal or commercial waste to determine that each of these vessels has a permit issued under section 2602 of this title.

**(c) Refusal of clearance**

The Secretary of the Treasury may refuse the clearance required by section 91 of the Appendix to Title 46, to any vessel subject to this chapter which does not have a permit required under section 2602 of this title.

**(d) Denial of entry and detention**

If a vessel does not comply with this chapter, the Secretary of Transportation may—

(1) deny entry to any place in the United States; and

(2) detain at the place in the United States from which it is about to depart.

**(e) Persistent violators**

The Administrator shall conduct an investigation of the owner or operator of a vessel or facility if the owner has 5 or more separate violations during a 6–month period.

(Pub.L. 100–688, Title IV, § 4105, Nov. 18, 1988, 102 Stat. 4157.)

## § 2606. Subpena authority

**[SPA § 4106]**

**(a) General authority**

In an investigation under this chapter, the attendance and testimony of witnesses, including parties in interest, and the production of any evidence may be compelled by subpena. The subpena authority granted by this section is coextensive with that of a district court of the United States, in civil matters, for the district in which the investigation is conducted.

**(b) Subpena authority**

An official designated by the Secretary of Transportation or Administrator to conduct an investigation under this chapter may issue subpenas as provided in this section and administer oaths to witnesses.

**(c) Failure to comply**

When a person fails to obey a subpena issued under this section, the district court of the United States for the district in which the investigation is conducted or in which the person failing to obey is found, shall on proper application issue an order directing that person to comply with the subpena. The court may punish as contempt any disobedience of its order.

**(d) Witness fees**

A witness complying with a subpena issued under this section may be paid for actual travel and attendance at the rate provided for witnesses in the district courts of the United States.

(Pub.L. 100–688, Title IV, § 4106, Nov. 18, 1988, 102 Stat. 4157.)

### HISTORICAL AND STATUTORY NOTES

**References in Text**

This chapter, referred to in subsec. (b), originally read "this part" and was translated as reading "this title" to reflect the probable intent of Congress.

## § 2607. Fees

**[SPA § 4107]**

The Secretary of Transportation may collect a fee under section 9701 of Title 31 of not more than $1,000, from each person to whom a permit is issued under this subchapter for a permitting system and to maintain information.

(Pub.L. 100–688, Title IV, § 4107, Nov. 18, 1988, 102 Stat. 4158.)

## § 2608. Civil penalty procedures

**[SPA § 4108]**

**(a) General procedures**

After notice and an opportunity for a hearing, a person found by the Secretary of Transportation to have violated this chapter or a regulation prescribed under this chapter for which a civil penalty is provided, is liable to the United States Government for the civil penalty provided. The amount of the civil penalty shall be assessed by the Secretary by written notice. In determining the amount of the penalty, the

Secretary shall consider the nature, circumstances, extent, and gravity of the prohibited acts committed and, with respect to the violator, the degree of culpability, any history of prior offenses, ability to pay, and other matters that justice requires.

**(b) Compromising penalties**

The Secretary may compromise, modify, or remit, with or without consideration, a civil penalty under this chapter until the assessment is referred to the Attorney General.

**(c) Referral to the Attorney General**

If a person fails to pay an assessment of a civil penalty after it has become final, the Secretary may refer the matter to the Attorney General for collection in an appropriate district court of the United States.

**(d) Refund of penalty**

The Secretary may refund or remit a civil penalty collected under this chapter if—

(1) application has been made for refund or remission of the penalty within one year from the date of payment; and

(2) the Secretary finds that the penalty was unlawfully, improperly, or excessively imposed.

(Pub.L. 100–688, Title IV, § 4108, Nov. 18, 1988, 102 Stat. 4158.)

## § 2609. Penalties

[SPA § 4109]

**(a) General penalty**

Except as provided in subsection (b) of this section, a person violating this chapter is liable to the United States Government for a civil penalty of not more than $25,000. Each day of a continuing violation is a separate violation. A vessel involved in the violation also is liable in rem for the penalty.

**(b) Operating without a permit**

A person violating section 2602 of this title is liable to the United States Government for a civil penalty of not more than $10,000. Each day of a continuing violation is a separate violation. A vessel involved in the violation also is liable in rem for the penalty.

**(c) Criminal penalty**

Any person that knowingly violates, or that knowingly aids, abets, authorizes, or instigates a violation of this chapter, shall be fined under Title 18, imprisoned for not more than 3 years, or both.

**(d) Payments for information**

The court, the Secretary of Transportation, or the Administrator, as the case may be, may pay up to one-half of a fine or penalty to any person giving information leading to the assessment of the fine or penalty.

(Pub.L. 100–688, Title IV, § 4109, Nov. 18, 1988, 102 Stat. 4158.)

## SUBCHAPTER II—RELATED PROVISIONS

## § 2621. Study and recommendations

[SPA § 4201]

**(a) Study**

The Administrator, in consultation with the Secretary of Transportation, shall conduct a study to determine the need for, and effectiveness of additional tracking systems for vessels to assure that municipal or commercial waste is not deposited in coastal waters. In conducting this study, the Administrator shall use the data collected from its permitting and enforcement activities under this chapter. In determining the effectiveness of tracking systems, the Administrator shall rely on the information provided by the Secretary under subsection (b) of this section. The report shall include a recommendation whether additional tracking systems are needed. This study shall be submitted to Congress within 21 months after November 18, 1988.

**(b) Recommendations**

The Secretary shall provide recommendations to the Administrator concerning the various tracking systems that might be applicable to vessels transporting municipal or commercial waste which the Secretary currently is studying. The Secretary shall consider the relative effectiveness of various systems and the relative costs of the systems both to the United States Government and to the vessel owner.

(Pub.L. 100–688, § 4201, Nov. 18, 1988, 102 Stat. 4159.)

## § 2622. Relation to other laws

[SPA § 4202]

**(a) Effect on Federal and State laws**

This chapter does not affect the application of any other Federal or State law, statutory or common, including the Marine Protection, Research, and Sanctuaries Act of 1972 [16 U.S.C.A. §§ 1431 et seq., 1447 et seq., 33 U.S.C.A. §§ 1401 et seq., 2801 et seq.] and the Solid Waste Disposal Act (42 U.S.C. 6901 et seq.).

**(b) Effect on foreign vessels**

This chapter shall be carried out with respect to foreign vessels consistent with the obligations of the United States under international law.

(Pub.L. 100–688, Title IV, § 4202, Nov. 18, 1988, 102 Stat. 4159.)

### HISTORICAL AND STATUTORY NOTES

**References in Text**

The Marine Protection, Research, and Sanctuaries Act of 1972, referred to in subsec. (a), is Pub.L. 92–532, Oct. 23, 1972, 86 Stat. 1052, as amended, which is classified generally to chapters 27 [33 U.S.C.A. § 1401 et seq.] and 41 [33 U.S.C.A. § 2801 et seq.] of this title and chapters 32 [16 U.S.C.A. § 1431 et seq.] and 32A [16 U.S.C.A. § 1447 et seq.] of Title 16. For complete classification of this Act to the Code, see Short Title note set out under 33 U.S.C.A. § 1401 and Tables.

The Solid Waste Disposal Act, referred to in subsec. (a), is Title II of Pub.L. 89–272, Oct. 20, 1965, 79 Stat. 997, as amended generally by Pub.L. 94–580, § 2, Oct. 21, 1976, 90 Stat. 2795, which is classified principally to chapter 82 [42 U.S.C.A. § 6901 et seq.] of Title 42. For complete classification of this Act to the Code, see Short Title note set out under 42 U.S.C.A. § 6901 and Tables.

## § 2623. Authorization of appropriations

**[SPA § 4203]**

There are authorized to be appropriated $1,500,000 for each of the fiscal years 1989 and 1990, to carry out this chapter.

(Pub.L. 100–688, Title IV, § 4203, Nov. 18, 1988, 102 Stat. 4160.)

# OIL POLLUTION

## OIL POLLUTION ACT OF 1990 [OPA § ______]

(33 U.S.C.A. §§ 2701 to 2761)

## CHAPTER 40—OIL POLLUTION

SUBCHAPTER I—OIL POLLUTION LIABILITY AND COMPENSATION



### SUBCHAPTER I—OIL POLLUTION LIABILITY AND COMPENSATION

### § 2701. Definitions

[OPA § 1001]

For the purposes of this Act, the term—

(1) "act of God" means an unanticipated grave natural disaster or other natural phenomenon of an exceptional, inevitable, and irresistible character the effects of which could not have been prevented or avoided by the exercise of due care or foresight;

(2) "barrel" means 42 United States gallons at 60 degrees fahrenheit;

(3) "claim" means a request, made in writing for a sum certain, for compensation for damages or removal costs resulting from an incident;

(4) "claimant" means any person or government who presents a claim for compensation under this subchapter;

(5) "damages" means damages specified in section 2702(b) of this title, and includes the cost of assessing these damages;

(6) "deepwater port" is a facility licensed under the Deepwater Port Act of 1974 (33 U.S.C. 1501-1524);

(7) "discharge" means any emission (other than natural seepage), intentional or unintentional, and includes, but is not limited to, spilling, leaking, pumping, pouring, emitting, emptying, or dumping;

(8) "exclusive economic zone" means the zone established by Presidential Proclamation Numbered 5030, dated March 10, 1983, including the ocean waters of the areas referred to as "eastern special areas" in Article 3(1) of the Agreement between the United States of America and the Union of Soviet Socialist Republics on the Maritime Boundary, signed June 1, 1990;

(9) "facility" means any structure, group of structures, equipment, or device (other than a vessel) which is used for one or more of the following purposes: exploring for, drilling for, producing, storing, handling, transferring, processing, or transporting oil. This term includes any motor vehicle,

rolling stock, or pipeline used for one or more of these purposes;

(10) "foreign offshore unit" means a facility which is located, in whole or in part, in the territorial sea or on the continental shelf of a foreign country and which is or was used for one or more of the following purposes: exploring for, drilling for, producing, storing, handling, transferring, processing, or transporting oil produced from the seabed beneath the foreign country's territorial sea or from the foreign country's continental shelf;

(11) "Fund" means the Oil Spill Liability Trust Fund, established by section 9509 of Title 26;

(12) "gross ton" has the meaning given that term by the Secretary under part J of Title 46;

(13) "guarantor" means any person, other than the responsible party, who provides evidence of financial responsibility for a responsible party under this Act;

(14) "incident" means any occurrence or series of occurrences having the same origin, involving one or more vessels, facilities, or any combination thereof, resulting in the discharge or substantial threat of discharge of oil;

(15) "Indian tribe" means any Indian tribe, band, nation, or other organized group or community, but not including any Alaska Native regional or village corporation, which is recognized as eligible for the special programs and services provided by the United States to Indians because of their status as Indians and has governmental authority over lands belonging to or controlled by the tribe;

(16) "lessee" means a person holding a leasehold interest in an oil or gas lease on lands beneath navigable waters (as that term is defined in section 1301(a) of Title 43) or on submerged lands of the Outer Continental Shelf, granted or maintained under applicable State law or the Outer Continental Shelf Lands Act (43 U.S.C. 1331 et seq.);

(17) "liable" or "liability" shall be construed to be the standard of liability which obtains under section 1321 of this title;

(18) "mobile offshore drilling unit" means a vessel (other than a self-elevating lift vessel) capable of use as an offshore facility;

(19) "National Contingency Plan" means the National Contingency Plan prepared and published under section 1321(d) of this title or revised under section 105 of the Comprehensive Environmental Response, Compensation, and Liability Act (42 U.S.C. 9605);

(20) "natural resources" includes land, fish, wildlife, biota, air, water, ground water, drinking water supplies, and other such resources belonging to, managed by, held in trust by, appertaining to, or otherwise controlled by the United States (including the resources of the exclusive economic zone), any State or local government or Indian tribe, or any foreign government;

(21) "navigable waters" means the waters of the United States, including the territorial sea;

(22) "offshore facility" means any facility of any kind located in, on, or under any of the navigable waters of the United States, and any facility of any kind which is subject to the jurisdiction of the United States and is located in, on, or under any other waters, other than a vessel or a public vessel;

(23) "oil" means oil of any kind or in any form, including petroleum, fuel oil, sludge, oil refuse, and oil mixed with wastes other than dredged spoil, but does not include any substance which is specifically listed or designated as a hazardous substance under subparagraphs (A) through (F) of section 101(14) of the Comprehensive Environmental Response, Compensation, and Liability Act (42 U.S.C. 9601) and which is subject to the provisions of that Act [42 U.S.C.A. § 9601 et seq.];

(24) "onshore facility" means any facility (including, but not limited to, motor vehicles and rolling stock) of any kind located in, on, or under, any land within the United States other than submerged land;

(25) the term "Outer Continental Shelf facility" means an offshore facility which is located, in whole or in part, on the Outer Continental Shelf and is or was used for one or more of the following purposes: exploring for, drilling for, producing, storing, handling, transferring, processing, or transporting oil produced from the Outer Continental Shelf;

(26) "owner or operator" means (A) in the case of a vessel, any person owning, operating, or chartering by demise, the vessel, and (B) in the case of an onshore facility, and an offshore facility, any person owning or operating such onshore facility or offshore facility, and (C) in the case of any abandoned offshore facility, the person who owned or operated such facility immediately prior to such abandonment;

(27) "person" means an individual, corporation, partnership, association, State, municipality, commission, or political subdivision of a State, or any interstate body;

(28) "permittee" means a person holding an authorization, license, or permit for geological exploration issued under section 11 of the Outer Continental Shelf Lands Act (43 U.S.C. 1340) or applicable State law;

(29) "public vessel" means a vessel owned or bareboat chartered and operated by the United

States, or by a State or political subdivision thereof, or by a foreign nation, except when the vessel is engaged in commerce;

(30) "remove" or "removal" means containment and removal of oil or a hazardous substance from water and shorelines or the taking of other actions as may be necessary to minimize or mitigate damage to the public health or welfare, including, but not limited to, fish, shellfish, wildlife, and public and private property, shorelines, and beaches;

(31) "removal costs" means the costs of removal that are incurred after a discharge of oil has occurred or, in any case in which there is a substantial threat of a discharge of oil, the costs to prevent, minimize, or mitigate oil pollution from such an incident;

(32) "responsible party" means the following:

**(A) Vessels**

In the case of a vessel, any person owning, operating, or demise chartering the vessel.

**(B) Onshore facilities**

In the case of an onshore facility (other than a pipeline), any person owning or operating the facility, except a Federal agency, State, municipality, commission, or political subdivision of a State, or any interstate body, that as the owner transfers possession and right to use the property to another person by lease, assignment, or permit.

**(C) Offshore facilities**

In the case of an offshore facility (other than a pipeline or a deepwater port licensed under the Deepwater Port Act of 1974 (33 U.S.C. 1501 et seq.)), the lessee or permittee of the area in which the facility is located or the holder of a right of use and easement granted under applicable State law or the Outer Continental Shelf Lands Act (43 U.S.C. 1301–1356) for the area in which the facility is located (if the holder is a different person than the lessee or permittee), except a Federal agency, State, municipality, commission, or political subdivision of a State, or any interstate body, that as owner transfers possession and right to use the property to another person by lease, assignment, or permit.

**(D) Deepwater ports**

In the case of a deepwater port licensed under the Deepwater Port Act of 1974 (33 U.S.C. 1501–1524), the licensee.

**(E) Pipelines**

In the case of a pipeline, any person owning or operating the pipeline.

**(F) Abandonment**

In the case of an abandoned vessel, onshore facility, deepwater port, pipeline, or offshore facility, the persons who would have been responsible parties immediately prior to the abandonment of the vessel or facility.

(33) "Secretary" means the Secretary of the department in which the Coast Guard is operating;

(34) "tank vessel" means a vessel that is constructed or adapted to carry, or that carries, oil or hazardous material in bulk as cargo or cargo residue, and that—

(A) is a vessel of the United States;

(B) operates on the navigable waters; or

(C) transfers oil or hazardous material in a place subject to the jurisdiction of the United States;

(35) "territorial seas" means the belt of the seas measured from the line of ordinary low water along that portion of the coast which is in direct contact with the open sea and the line marking the seaward limit of inland waters, and extending seaward a distance of 3 miles;

(36) "United States" and "State" mean the several States of the United States, the District of Columbia, the Commonwealth of Puerto Rico, Guam, American Samoa, the United States Virgin Islands, the Commonwealth of the Northern Marianas, and any other territory or possession of the United States; and

(37) "vessel" means every description of watercraft or other artificial contrivance used, or capable of being used, as a means of transportation on water, other than a public vessel.

(Pub.L. 101–380, Title I, § 1001, Aug. 18, 1990, 104 Stat. 486; Pub.L. 105–383, Title III, § 307(a), Nov. 13, 1998, 112 Stat. 3421.)

## HISTORICAL AND STATUTORY NOTES

**References in Text**

This Act, referred to in text, is Pub.L. 101–380, Aug. 18, 1990, 104 Stat. 484, as amended, known as the Oil Pollution Act of 1990, which is classified principally to this chapter. For complete classification to the Code, see Short Title note under this section and Tables.

The Deepwater Port Act of 1974, referred to in pars. (6) and (32), is Pub.L. 93–627, Jan. 3, 1975, 88 Stat. 2126, as amended, which is classified generally to chapter 29 (§ 1501 et seq.) of this title. For complete classification of this Act to the Code, see Short Title note set out under section 1501 of this title and Tables.

The Outer Continental Shelf Lands Act, referred to in pars. (16), (28), and (32), is Act Aug. 7, 1953, c. 345, 67 Stat.

462, as amended, which is classified generally to subchapter III (§ 1331 et seq.) of chapter 29 of Title 43, Public Lands. For complete classification of this Act to the Code, see Short Title note set out under section 1331 of Title 43 and Tables.

Reference in par. (19) to the amendment of section 1321(d) of this title "by this Act" refers to the amendment by Pub.L. 101–380, Aug. 18, 1990, 104 Stat. 484.

The Comprehensive Environmental Response, Compensation, and Liability Act of 1980, referred to in pars. (19) and (23), is Pub.L. 96–510, Dec. 11, 1980, 94 Stat. 2767, as amended, which is classified principally to chapter 103 (§ 9601 et seq.) of Title 42, The Public Health and Welfare. section 101(14) of that Act, also referred to in par. (23), is section 101(14) of Pub.L. 96–510, Title I, Dec. 11, 1980, 94 Stat. 2767, as amended, which is classified to section 9601(14) of Title 42.

**Effective and Applicability Provisions**

1990 Acts

Section 1020 of Pub.L. 101–380 provided that: "This Act [probably refers to title I of Pub.L. 101–380 which enacted this subchapter] shall apply to an incident occurring after the date of the enactment of this Act [Aug. 18, 1990]."

**Short Title**

1995 Amendments

Pub.L. 104–55, § 1, Nov. 20, 1995, 109 Stat. 546, provided that: "This Act [enacting section 2720 of this title, and amending sections 2704 and 2716 of this title] may be cited as the 'Edible Oil Regulatory Reform Act'."

1990 Amendments

Pub.L. 101–646, Title IV, § 4001, Nov. 29, 1990, 104 Stat. 4788, as amended Pub.L. 104–332, § 2(h)(1), Oct. 26, 1996, 110 Stat. 4091, provided that: "This title [amending section 2761 of this title] may be cited as the 'Great Lakes Oil Pollution Research and Development Act'."

Pub.L. 101–537, Title II, § 2001, Nov. 8, 1990, 104 Stat. 2375, provided that: "This title [amending section 2761 of this title] may be cited as the 'Great Lakes Oil Pollution Research and Development Act'."

1990 Acts

Section 1 of Pub.L. 101–380 provided that: "This Act [enacting this chapter and sections 1642 and 1656 of Title 43, Public Lands, section 3703a of Title 46, Shipping, and section 1274a of the Appendix to Title 46; amending sections 1223, 1228, 1232, 1236, 1319, 1321, 1481, 1486, 1503, 1514, and 1908 of this title, section 3145 of Title 16, Conservation, section 401 note of Title 23, Highways, sections 4612 and 9509 of Title 26, Internal Revenue Code, sections 1334, 1350, and 1653 of Title 43, sections 2101, 2302, 3318, 3715, 3718, 5116, 6101, 7101, 7106, 7107, 7109, 7302, 7502, 7503, 7505, 7701, 7702, 7703, 8101, 8104, 8502, 8503, 8702, 9101, 9302, 9308, and 12106 of Title 46, and section 1274 of the Appendix to Title 46; repealing section 1517 of this title and sections 1811, 1811 note, and 1812 to 1824 of Title 43; and enacting provisions set out as notes under sections 1203, 1223, and 1321 of this title, section 92 of Title 14, Coast Guard, section 9509 of Title 26, sections 1334, 1651, and 1653 of Title 43, sections 3703, 3703a, and 7106 of Title 46, and section 1295 of the Appendix to Title 46] may be cited as the 'Oil Pollution Act of 1990'."

## § 2702. Elements of liability

**[OPA § 1002]**

**(a) In general**

Notwithstanding any other provision or rule of law, and subject to the provisions of this Act, each responsible party for a vessel or a facility from which oil is discharged, or which poses the substantial threat of a discharge of oil, into or upon the navigable waters or adjoining shorelines or the exclusive economic zone is liable for the removal costs and damages specified in subsection (b) of this section that result from such incident.

**(b) Covered removal costs and damages**

**(1) Removal costs**

The removal costs referred to in subsection (a) of this section are—

**(A)** all removal costs incurred by the United States, a State, or an Indian tribe under subsection (c), (d), (e), or (*l*) of section 1321 of this title under the Intervention on the High Seas Act (33 U.S.C. 1471 et seq.), or under State law; and

**(B)** any removal costs incurred by any person for acts taken by the person which are consistent with the National Contingency Plan.

**(2) Damages**

The damages referred to in subsection (a) of this section are the following:

**(A) Natural resources**

Damages for injury to, destruction of, loss of, or loss of use of, natural resources, including the reasonable costs of assessing the damage, which shall be recoverable by a United States trustee, a State trustee, an Indian tribe trustee, or a foreign trustee.

**(B) Real or personal property**

Damages for injury to, or economic losses resulting from destruction of, real or personal property, which shall be recoverable by a claimant who owns or leases that property.

**(C) Subsistence use**

Damages for loss of subsistence use of natural resources, which shall be recoverable by any claimant who so uses natural resources which have been injured, destroyed, or lost, without regard to the ownership or management of the resources.

**(D) Revenues**

Damages equal to the net loss of taxes, royalties, rents, fees, or net profit shares due to the injury, destruction, or loss of real property, personal property, or natural resources, which shall be recoverable by the Government of the United States, a State, or a political subdivision thereof.

**(E) Profits and earning capacity**

Damages equal to the loss of profits or impairment of earning capacity due to the injury, destruction, or loss of real property, personal property, or natural resources, which shall be recoverable by any claimant.

**(F) Public services**

Damages for net costs of providing increased or additional public services during or after removal activities, including protection from fire, safety, or health hazards, caused by a discharge of oil, which shall be recoverable by a State, or a political subdivision of a State.

**(c) Excluded discharges**

This subchapter does not apply to any discharge—

(1) permitted by a permit issued under Federal, State, or local law;

(2) from a public vessel; or

(3) from an onshore facility which is subject to the Trans-Alaska Pipeline Authorization Act (43 U.S.C. 1651 et seq.).

**(d) Liability of third parties**

**(1) In general**

**(A) Third party treated as responsible party**

Except as provided in subparagraph (B), in any case in which a responsible party establishes that a discharge or threat of a discharge and the resulting removal costs and damages were caused solely by an act or omission of one or more third parties described in section 2703(a)(3) of this title (or solely by such an act or omission in combination with an act of God or an act of war), the third party or parties shall be treated as the responsible party or parties for purposes of determining liability under this subchapter.

**(B) Subrogation of responsible party**

If the responsible party alleges that the discharge or threat of a discharge was caused solely by an act or omission of a third party, the responsible party—

(i) in accordance with section 2713 of this title, shall pay removal costs and damages to any claimant; and

(ii) shall be entitled by subrogation to all rights of the United States Government and the claimant to recover removal costs or damages from the third party or the Fund paid under this subsection.

**(2) Limitation applied**

**(A) Owner or operator of vessel or facility**

If the act or omission of a third party that causes an incident occurs in connection with a vessel or facility owned or operated by the third party, the liability of the third party shall be subject to the limits provided in section 2704 of this title as applied with respect to the vessel or facility.

**(B) Other cases**

In any other case, the liability of a third party or parties shall not exceed the limitation which would have been applicable to the responsible party of the vessel or facility from which the discharge actually occurred if the responsible party were liable.

(Pub.L. 101–380, Title I, § 1002, Aug. 18, 1990, 104 Stat. 489.)

**HISTORICAL AND STATUTORY NOTES**

**References in Text**

This Act, referred to in subsec. (a), is Pub.L. 101–380, Aug. 18, 1990, 104 Stat. 484, as amended, known as the Oil Pollution Act of 1990, which is classified principally to this chapter. For complete classification to the Code, see Short Title note under 33 U.S.C.A. § 2701 and Tables.

Reference in subsec. (b)(1)(A) to the amendment of section 1321 of this title "by this Act" refers to amendment by Pub.L. 101–380, Aug. 18, 1990, 104 Stat. 484.

The Intervention on the High Seas Act, referred to in subsec. (b)(1)(A), is Pub.L. 93–248, Feb. 5, 1974, 88 Stat. 8, as amended, which is classified generally to chapter 28 (§ 1471 et seq.) of this title. For complete classification of this Act to the Code, see Short Title note set out under section 1471 of this title and Tables.

The Trans-Alaska Pipeline Authorization Act, referred to in subsec. (c)(3), is title II of Pub.L. 93–153, Nov. 16, 1973, 87 Stat. 584, which is classified to chapter 34 (§ 1651 et seq.) of Title 43, Public Lands. For complete classification of this Act to the Code, see Short Title note set out under section 1651 of Title 43 and Tables.

**Effective and Applicability Provisions**

1990 Acts

Section applicable to incidents occurring after Aug. 18, 1990, see section 1020 of Pub.L. 101–380, set out as a note under section 2701 of this title.

## § 2703. Defenses to liability

**[OPA § 1003]**

**(a) Complete defenses**

A responsible party is not liable for removal costs or damages under section 2702 of this title if the responsible party establishes, by a preponderance of the evidence, that the discharge or substantial threat of a discharge of oil and the resulting damages or removal costs were caused solely by—

(1) an act of God;

(2) an act of war;

(3) an act or omission of a third party, other than an employee or agent of the responsible party or a third party whose act or omission occurs in connection with any contractual relationship with the responsible party (except where the sole contractual arrangement arises in connection with carriage by a common carrier by rail), if the responsible party establishes, by a preponderance of the evidence, that the responsible party—

(A) exercised due care with respect to the oil concerned, taking into consideration the characteristics of the oil and in light of all relevant facts and circumstances; and

(B) took precautions against foreseeable acts or omissions of any such third party and the foreseeable consequences of those acts or omissions; or

(4) any combination of paragraphs (1), (2), and (3).

**(b) Defenses as to particular claimants**

A responsible party is not liable under section 2702 of this title to a claimant, to the extent that the incident is caused by the gross negligence or willful misconduct of the claimant.

**(c) Limitation on complete defense**

Subsection (a) of this section does not apply with respect to a responsible party who fails or refuses—

(1) to report the incident as required by law if the responsible party knows or has reason to know of the incident;

(2) to provide all reasonable cooperation and assistance requested by a responsible official in connection with removal activities; or

(3) without sufficient cause, to comply with an order issued under subsection (c) or (e) of section 1321 of this title or the Intervention on the High Seas Act (33 U.S.C. 1471 et seq.).

(Pub.L. 101–380, Title I, § 1003, Aug. 18, 1990, 104 Stat. 491.)

## HISTORICAL AND STATUTORY NOTES

**References in Text**

Reference in subsec. (c)(3), to the amendment of section 1321 of this title "by this Act" refers to amendment by Pub.L. 101–380, Aug. 18, 1990, 104 Stat. 484.

The Intervention on the High Seas Act, referred to in subsec. (c)(3), is Pub.L. 93–248, Feb. 5, 1974, 88 Stat. 8, as amended, which is classified generally to chapter 28 (§ 1471 et seq.) of this title. For complete classification of this Act to the Code, see Short Title note set out under section 1471 of this title and Tables.

**Effective and Applicability Provisions**

1990 Acts

Section applicable to incidents occurring after Aug. 18, 1990, see section 1020 of Pub.L. 101–380, set out as a note under section 2701 of this title.

## § 2704. Limits on liability

**[OPA § 1004]**

**(a) General rule**

Except as otherwise provided in this section, the total of the liability of a responsible party under section 2702 of this title and any removal costs incurred by, or on behalf of, the responsible party, with respect to each incident shall not exceed—

(1) for a tank vessel, the greater of—

(A) $1,200 per gross ton; or

(B)(i) in the case of a vessel greater than 3,000 gross tons, $10,000,000; or

(ii) in the case of a vessel of 3,000 gross tons or less, $2,000,000;

(2) for any other vessel, $600 per gross ton or $500,000, whichever is greater;

(3) for an offshore facility except a deepwater port, the total of all removal costs plus $75,000,000; and

(4) for any onshore facility and a deepwater port, $350,000,000.

**(b) Division of liability for mobile offshore drilling units**

**(1) Treated first as tank vessel**

For purposes of determining the responsible party and applying this Act and except as provided in paragraph (2), a mobile offshore drilling unit which is being used as an offshore facility is deemed to be a tank vessel with respect to the discharge, or the substantial threat of a discharge, of oil on or above the surface of the water.

**(2) Treated as facility for excess liability**

To the extent that removal costs and damages from any incident described in paragraph (1) exceed the amount for which a responsible party is liable (as that amount may be limited under subsection (a)(1) of this section), the mobile offshore drilling unit is deemed to be an offshore facility. For purposes of applying subsection (a)(3) of this section, the amount specified in that subsection shall be reduced by the amount for which the responsible party is liable under paragraph (1).

**(c) Exceptions**

**(1) Acts of responsible party**

Subsection (a) of this section does not apply if the incident was proximately caused by—

(A) gross negligence or willful misconduct of, or

(B) the violation of an applicable Federal safety, construction, or operating regulation by,

the responsible party, an agent or employee of the responsible party, or a person acting pursuant to a contractual relationship with the responsible party (except where the sole contractual arrangement arises in connection with carriage by a common carrier by rail).

**(2) Failure or refusal of responsible party**

Subsection (a) of this section does not apply if the responsible party fails or refuses—

(A) to report the incident as required by law and the responsible party knows or has reason to know of the incident;

(B) to provide all reasonable cooperation and assistance requested by a responsible official in connection with removal activities; or

(C) without sufficient cause, to comply with an order issued under subsection (c) or (e) of section 1321 of this title or the Intervention on the High Seas Act (33 U.S.C. 1471 et seq.).

**(3) OCS facility or vessel**

Notwithstanding the limitations established under subsection (a) of this section and the defenses of section 2703 of this title, all removal costs incurred by the United States Government or any State or local official or agency in connection with a discharge or substantial threat of a discharge of oil from any Outer Continental Shelf facility or a vessel carrying oil as cargo from such a facility shall be borne by the owner or operator of such facility or vessel.

**(4) Certain tank vessels**

Subsection (a)(1) of this section shall not apply to—

(A) a tank vessel on which the only oil carried as cargo is an animal fat or vegetable oil, as those terms are used in section 2720 of this title; and

(B) a tank vessel that is designated in its certificate of inspection as an oil spill response vessel (as that term is defined in section 2101 of Title 46) and that is used solely for removal.

**(d) Adjusting limits of liability**

**(1) Onshore facilities**

Subject to paragraph (2), the President may establish by regulation, with respect to any class or category of onshore facility, a limit of liability under this section of less than $350,000,000, but not less than $8,000,000, taking into account size, storage capacity, oil throughput, proximity to sensitive areas, type of oil handled, history of discharges, and other factors relevant to risks posed by the class or category of facility.

**(2) Deepwater ports and associated vessels**

**(A) Study**

The Secretary shall conduct a study of the relative operational and environmental risks posed by the transportation of oil by vessel to deepwater ports (as defined in section 1502 of this title) versus the transportation of oil by vessel to other ports. The study shall include a review and analysis of offshore lightering practices used in connection with that transportation, an analysis of the volume of oil transported by vessel using those practices, and an analysis of the frequency and volume of oil discharges which occur in connection with the use of those practices.

**(B) Report**

Not later than 1 year after August 18, 1990, the Secretary shall submit to the Congress a report on the results of the study conducted under subparagraph (A).

**(C) Rulemaking proceeding**

If the Secretary determines, based on the results of the study conducted under this[1] subparagraph (A), that the use of deepwater ports in connection with the transportation of oil by vessel results in a lower operational or environmental risk than the use of other ports, the Secretary shall initiate, not later than the 180th day following the date of submission of the report to the Congress under subparagraph (B), a rulemaking proceeding to lower the limits of liability under this section for deepwater ports as the Secretary determines appropriate. The Secretary may establish a limit of liability of less than $350,000,000, but not less than $50,000,000, in accordance with paragraph (1).

**(3) Periodic reports**

The President shall, within 6 months after August 18, 1990, and from time to time thereafter, report to the Congress on the desirability of adjusting the limits of liability specified in subsection (a) of this section.

**(4) Adjustment to reflect Consumer Price Index**

The President shall, by regulations issued not less often than every 3 years, adjust the limits of liability specified in subsection (a) of this section to reflect significant increases in the Consumer Price Index.

(Pub.L. 101–380, Title I, § 1004, Aug. 18, 1990, 104 Stat. 491; Pub.L. 104–55, § 2(d)(1), Nov. 20, 1995, 109 Stat. 546; Pub.L. 105–383, Title IV, § 406, Nov. 13, 1998, 112 Stat. 3429.)

[1] So in original. The word "this" probably should not appear.

HISTORICAL AND STATUTORY NOTES

**References in Text**

This Act, referred to in subsec. (b)(1), is Pub.L. 101–380, Aug. 18, 1990, 104 Stat. 484, as amended, known as the Oil Pollution Act of 1990, which is classified principally to this chapter. For complete classification to the Code, see Short Title note under 33 U.S.C.A. § 2701 and Tables.

Reference in subsec. (c)(2)(C) to the amendment of section 1321 of this title "by this Act" refers to amendment by Pub.L. 101–380, Aug. 18, 1990, 104 Stat. 484.

The Intervention on the High Seas Act, referred to in subsec. (c)(2)(C), is Pub.L. 93–248, Feb. 5, 1974, 88 Stat. 8, as amended, which is classified generally to chapter 28 (§ 1471 et seq.) of this title. For complete classification of this Act to the Code, see Short Title note set out under section 1471 of this title and Tables.

The Deepwater Port Act of 1974, referred to in subsec. (d)(2)(A), is Pub.L. 93–627, Jan. 3, 1975, 88 Stat. 2126, as amended, which is classified generally to chapter 29 (§ 1501 et seq.) of this title. For complete classification of this Act to the Code, see Short Title note set out under section 1501 of this title and Tables.

**Effective and Applicability Provisions**

1990 Acts

Section applicable to incidents occurring after Aug. 18, 1990, see section 1020 of Pub.L. 101–380, set out as a note under section 2701 of this title.

**Delegation of Functions**

The functions vested in the President by subsec. (d) of this section respecting the establishment of limits of liability, with respect to classes or categories of non-transportation-related onshore facilities, the reporting to Congress on the desirability of adjusting limits of liability with respect to non-transportation-related onshore facilities, and the adjustment of limits of liability to reflect significant increases in the Consumer Price Index with respect to non-transportation-related onshore facilities, are delegated to the Administrator of the Environmental Protection Agency, acting in consultation with the Secretary of Transportation, the Secretary of Energy, and the Attorney General, see Ex. Ord. No. 12777, Oct. 18, 1991, 56 F.R. 54757, set out as a note under section 1321 of this title.

The functions vested in the President by subsec.(d) of this section respecting the establishment of limits of liability, with respect to classes or categories of transportation-related onshore facilities, the reporting to Congress on the desirability of adjusting limits of liability, with respect to vessels or transportation-related onshore facilities and deepwater ports subject to chapter 29 [section 1501 et seq.] of this title , and the adjustment of limits of liability to reflect significant increases in the Consumer Price Index with respect to vessels or transportation-related onshore facilities and deepwater ports subject to chapter 29 of this title, are delegated to the Secretary of Transportation, see Ex. Ord. No. 12777, Oct. 18, 1991, 56 F.R. 54757, set out as a note under section 1321 of this title.

The functions vested in the President by subsec. (d) of this section, respecting the reporting to Congress on the desirability of adjusting limits of liability with respect to offshore facilities, including associated pipelines, other than deepwater ports subject to chapter 29 [section 1501 et seq.] of this title, and the adjustment of limits of liability to reflect significant increases in the Consumer Price Index with respect to offshore facilities, including associated pipelines, other than deepwater ports subject to chapter 29 of this title, are delegated to the Secretary of the Interior, see Ex. Ord. No. 122777, Oct. 18, 1991, 56 F.R. 54757, set out as a note under section 1321 of this title.

## § 2705. Interest; partial payment of claims

[OPA § 1005]

### (a) General rule

The responsible party or the responsible party's guarantor is liable to a claimant for interest on the amount paid in satisfaction of a claim under this Act for the period described in subsection (b) of this section. The responsible party shall establish a procedure for the payment or settlement of claims for interim, short-term damages. Payment or settlement of a claim for interim, short-term damages representing less than the full amount of damages to which the claimant ultimately may be entitled shall not preclude recovery by the claimant for damages not reflected in the paid or settled partial claim.

### (b) Period

#### (1) In general

Except as provided in paragraph (2), the period for which interest shall be paid is the period beginning on the 30th day following the date on which the claim is presented to the responsible party or guarantor and ending on the date on which the claim is paid.

#### (2) Exclusion of period due to offer by guarantor

If the guarantor offers to the claimant an amount equal to or greater than that finally paid in satisfaction of the claim, the period described in paragraph (1) does not include the period beginning on the date the offer is made and ending on the date the offer is accepted. If the offer is made within 60 days after the date on which the claim is presented under section 2713(a) of this title, the period described in paragraph (1) does not include any period before the offer is accepted.

#### (3) Exclusion of periods in interests of justice

If in any period a claimant is not paid due to reasons beyond the control of the responsible party or because it would not serve the interests of justice, no interest shall accrue under this section during that period.

#### (4) Calculation of interest

The interest paid under this section shall be calculated at the average of the highest rate for commercial and finance company paper of maturities of 180 days or less obtaining on each of the days included within the period for which interest must be paid to the claimant, as published in the Federal Reserve Bulletin.

**(5) Interest not subject to liability limits**

**(A) In general**

Interest (including prejudgment interest) under this paragraph is in addition to damages and removal costs for which claims may be asserted under section 2702 of this title and shall be paid without regard to any limitation of liability under section 2704 of this title.

**(B) Payment by guarantor**

The payment of interest under this subsection by a guarantor is subject to section 2716(g) of this title.

(Pub.L. 101–380, Title I, § 1005, Aug. 18, 1990, 104 Stat. 493; Pub.L. 104–324, Title XI, § 1142(a), Oct. 19, 1996, 110 Stat. 3991.)

### HISTORICAL AND STATUTORY NOTES

**References in Text**

This Act, referred to in subsec. (a), is Pub.L. 101–380, Aug. 18, 1990, 104 Stat. 484, as amended, known as the Oil Pollution Act of 1990, which is classified principally to this chapter. For complete classification to the Code, see Short Title note under 33 U.S.C.A. § 2701 and Tables.

**Effective and Applicability Provisions**

1990 Acts

Section applicable to incidents occurring after Aug. 18, 1990, see section 1020 of Pub.L. 101–380, set out as a note under section 2701 of this title.

## § 2706. Natural resources

**[OPA § 1006]**

**(a) Liability**

In the case of natural resource damages under section 2702(b)(2)(A) of this title, liability shall be—

(1) to the United States Government for natural resources belonging to, managed by, controlled by, or appertaining to the United States;

(2) to any State for natural resources belonging to, managed by, controlled by, or appertaining to such State or political subdivision thereof;

(3) to any Indian tribe for natural resources belonging to, managed by, controlled by, or appertaining to such Indian tribe; and

(4) in any case in which section 2707 of this title applies, to the government of a foreign country for natural resources belonging to, managed by, controlled by, or appertaining to such country.

**(b) Designation of trustees**

**(1) In general**

The President, or the authorized representative of any State, Indian tribe, or foreign government, shall act on behalf of the public, Indian tribe, or foreign country as trustee of natural resources to present a claim for and to recover damages to the natural resources.

**(2) Federal trustees**

The President shall designate the Federal officials who shall act on behalf of the public as trustees for natural resources under this Act.

**(3) State trustees**

The Governor of each State shall designate State and local officials who may act on behalf of the public as trustee for natural resources under this Act and shall notify the President of the designation.

**(4) Indian tribe trustees**

The governing body of any Indian tribe shall designate tribal officials who may act on behalf of the tribe or its members as trustee for natural resources under this Act and shall notify the President of the designation.

**(5) Foreign trustees**

The head of any foreign government may designate the trustee who shall act on behalf of that government as trustee for natural resources under this Act.

**(c) Functions of trustees**

**(1) Federal trustees**

The Federal officials designated under subsection (b)(2) of this section—

(A) shall assess natural resource damages under section 2702(b)(2)(A) of this title for the natural resources under their trusteeship;

(B) may, upon request of and reimbursement from a State or Indian tribe and at the Federal officials' discretion, assess damages for the natural resources under the State's or tribe's trusteeship; and

(C) shall develop and implement a plan for the restoration, rehabilitation, replacement, or acquisition of the equivalent, of the natural resources under their trusteeship.

**(2) State trustees**

The State and local officials designated under subsection (b)(3) of this section—

(A) shall assess natural resource damages under section 2702(b)(2)(A) of this title for the purposes of this Act for the natural resources under their trusteeship; and

(B) shall develop and implement a plan for the restoration, rehabilitation, replacement, or acquisition of the equivalent, of the natural resources under their trusteeship.

(3) **Indian tribe trustees**

The tribal officials designated under subsection (b)(4) of this section—

(A) shall assess natural resource damages under section 2702(b)(2)(A) of this title for the purposes of this Act for the natural resources under their trusteeship; and

(B) shall develop and implement a plan for the restoration, rehabilitation, replacement, or acquisition of the equivalent, of the natural resources under their trusteeship.

(4) **Foreign trustees**

The trustees designated under subsection (b)(5) of this section—

(A) shall assess natural resource damages under section 2702(b)(2)(A) of this title for the purposes of this Act for the natural resources under their trusteeship; and

(B) shall develop and implement a plan for the restoration, rehabilitation, replacement, or acquisition of the equivalent, of the natural resources under their trusteeship.

(5) **Notice and opportunity to be heard**

Plans shall be developed and implemented under this section only after adequate public notice, opportunity for a hearing, and consideration of all public comment.

(d) **Measure of damages**

(1) **In general**

The measure of natural resource damages under section 2702(b)(2)(A) of this title is—

(A) the cost of restoring, rehabilitating, replacing, or acquiring the equivalent of, the damaged natural resources;

(B) the diminution in value of those natural resources pending restoration; plus

(C) the reasonable cost of assessing those damages.

(2) **Determine costs with respect to plans**

Costs shall be determined under paragraph (1) with respect to plans adopted under subsection (c) of this section.

(3) **No double recovery**

There shall be no double recovery under this Act for natural resource damages, including with respect to the costs of damage assessment or restoration, rehabilitation, replacement, or acquisition for the same incident and natural resource.

(e) **Damage assessment regulations**

(1) **Regulations**

The President, acting through the Under Secretary of Commerce for Oceans and Atmosphere and in consultation with the Administrator of the Environmental Protection Agency, the Director of the United States Fish and Wildlife Service, and the heads of other affected agencies, not later than 2 years after August 18, 1990, shall promulgate regulations for the assessment of natural resource damages under section 2702(b)(2)(A) of this title resulting from a discharge of oil for the purpose of this Act.

(2) **Rebuttable presumption**

Any determination or assessment of damages to natural resources for the purposes of this Act made under subsection (d) of this section by a Federal, State, or Indian trustee in accordance with the regulations promulgated under paragraph (1) shall have the force and effect of a rebuttable presumption on behalf of the trustee in any administrative or judicial proceeding under this Act.

(f) **Use of recovered sums**

Sums recovered under this Act by a Federal, State, Indian, or foreign trustee for natural resource damages under section 2702(b)(2)(A) of this title shall be retained by the trustee in a revolving trust account, without further appropriation, for use only to reimburse or pay costs incurred by the trustee under subsection (c) of this section with respect to the damaged natural resources. Any amounts in excess of those required for these reimbursements and costs shall be deposited in the Fund.

(g) **Compliance**

Review of actions by any Federal official where there is alleged to be a failure of that official to perform a duty under this section that is not discretionary with that official may be had by any person in the district court in which the person resides or in which the alleged damage to natural resources occurred. The court may award costs of litigation (including reasonable attorney and expert witness fees) to any prevailing or substantially prevailing party. Nothing in this subsection shall restrict any right which any person may have to seek relief under any other provision of law.

(Pub.L. 101–380, Title I, § 1006, Aug. 18, 1990, 104 Stat. 494.)

### HISTORICAL AND STATUTORY NOTES

**References in Text**

This Act, referred to in text, is Pub.L. 101–380, Aug. 18, 1990, 104 Stat. 484, as amended, known as the Oil Pollution Act of 1990, which is classified principally to this chapter. For complete classification to the Code, see Short Title note under 33 U.S.C.A. § 2701 and Tables.

**Effective and Applicability Provisions**

1990 Acts

Section applicable to incidents occurring after Aug. 18, 1990, see section 1020 of Pub.L. 101–380, set out as a note under section 2701 of this title.

**Delegation of Functions**

The functions vested in the President by section 2752 (b) of this title respecting making amounts, not to exceed $50,000,000 and subject to normal budget controls, in any fiscal year, available from the Fund (i) to carry out section 1321(c) of this title, and (ii) to initiate the assessment of natural resources damages required under this section are delegated to the Secretary of the Department in which the Coast Guard is operating, with such Secretary required to make amounts available from the Fund to initiate the assessment of natural resources damages exclusively to the Federal trustees designated in the NCP [National Contingency Plan], who are in turn directed to allocate such amounts among all trustees required to assess natural resources damages under this section, see Ex. Ord. No. 12777, Oct. 18, 1991, 56 F.R. 54757, set out as a note under section 1321 of this title.

The functions vested in the President by subsec. (b)(3),(4) of this section respecting the receipt of designations of State and Indian tribe trustees for natural resources are delegated to the Administrator of the Environmental Protection Agency, see Ex. Ord. No. 12777, Oct. 18, 1991, 56 F.R. 54757, set out as a note under section 1321 of this title.

**NOAA Oil and Hazardous Substance Spill Cost Reimbursement**

Pub.L. 102–567, Title II, § 205, Oct. 29, 1992, 106 Stat. 4282, provided that:

"(a) **Treatment of amounts received as reimbursement of expenses.**—Notwithstanding any other provision of law, amounts received by the United States as reimbursement of expenses related to oil or hazardous substance spill response activities, or natural resource damage assessment, restoration, rehabilitation, replacement, or acquisition activities, conducted (or to be conducted) by the National Oceanic and Atmospheric Administration—

"(1) shall be deposited into the Fund;

"(2) shall be available, without fiscal year limitation and without apportionment, for use in accordance with the law under which the activities are conducted; and

"(3) shall not be considered to be an augmentation of appropriations.

"(b) **Application.**—Subsection (a) shall apply to amounts described in subsection (a) that are received—

"(1) after the date of the enactment of this Act [Oct. 29, 1992]; or

"(2) with respect to the oil spill associated with the grounding of the EXXON VALDEZ.

"(c) **Definitions.**—For purposes of this section—

"(1) the term 'Fund' means the Damage Assessment and Restoration Revolving Fund of the National Oceanic and Atmospheric Administration referred to in title I of Public Law 101–515 under the heading 'National Oceanic and Atmospheric Administration' (104 Stat. 2105) [Pub.L. 101–515, Title I (part), Nov. 5, 1990, 104 Stat. 2105, which is not classified to the Code]; and

"(2) the term 'expenses' includes incremental and base salaries, ships, aircraft, and associated indirect costs, except the term does not include base salaries and benefits of National Oceanic and Atmospheric Administration Support Coordinators."

**Damage Assessment and Restoration Revolving Fund; Deposits; Availability; Transfer**

Pub.L. 101–515, Title I, Nov. 5, 1990, 104 Stat. 2105, provided in part that: "Notwithstanding any other provision of law, in fiscal year 1991 and thereafter, sums provided by any party or governmental entity for natural resource damage assessment, response or restoration activities conducted or to be conducted by the National Oceanic and Atmospheric Administration as a result of any injury to the marine environment and/or resources for which the National Oceanic and Atmospheric Administration acts as trustee of said marine environment and/or resources, shall be deposited in the Damage Assessment and Restoration Revolving Fund and said funds so deposited shall remain available until expended: *Provided further*, That for purposes of obligation and expenditure in fiscal year 1991 and thereafter, sums available in the Damage Assessment and Restoration Revolving Fund may be transferred, upon the approval of the Secretary of Commerce or his delegate, to the Operations, Research, and Facilities appropriation of the National Oceanic and Atmospheric Administration."

**Designation of Federal Trustees for Natural Resources**

For designation by the President, in accordance with subsec. (b)(1),(2) of this section, of the Secretaries of Defense, Interior, Agriculture, Commerce and Energy as among those to be designated in the National Contingency Plan as Federal trustees for natural resources, with additional provisions for the designation of Lead Administrative Trustees,see section 1(c) of Ex. Ord. No. 12580, Jan. 23, 1987, 52 F.R. 2923, as amended, set out as a note under section 9615 of Title 42, The Public Health and Welfare.

## § 2707. Recovery by foreign claimants

**[OPA § 1007]**

**(a) Required showing by foreign claimants**

**(1) In general**

In addition to satisfying the other requirements of this Act, to recover removal costs or damages resulting from an incident a foreign claimant shall demonstrate that—

(A) the claimant has not been otherwise compensated for the removal costs or damages; and

(B) recovery is authorized by a treaty or executive agreement between the United States and the claimant's country, or the Secretary of State, in consultation with the Attorney General and other appropriate officials, has certified that the claimant's country provides a comparable remedy for United States claimants.

**(2) Exceptions**

Paragraph (1)(B) shall not apply with respect to recovery by a resident of Canada in the case of an incident described in subsection (b)(4) of this section.

**(b) Discharges in foreign countries**

A foreign claimant may make a claim for removal costs and damages resulting from a discharge, or substantial threat of a discharge, of oil in or on the territorial sea, internal waters, or adjacent shoreline of a foreign country, only if the discharge is from—

(1) an Outer Continental Shelf facility or a deepwater port;

(2) a vessel in the navigable waters;

(3) a vessel carrying oil as cargo between 2 places in the United States; or

(4) a tanker that received the oil at the terminal of the pipeline constructed under the Trans-Alaska Pipeline Authorization Act (43 U.S.C. 1651 et seq.), for transportation to a place in the United States, and the discharge or threat occurs prior to delivery of the oil to that place.

**(c) "Foreign claimant" defined**

In this section, the term "foreign claimant" means—

(1) a person residing in a foreign country;

(2) the government of a foreign country; and

(3) an agency or political subdivision of a foreign country.

(Pub.L. 101–380, Title I, § 1007, Aug. 18, 1990, 104 Stat. 496.)

### HISTORICAL AND STATUTORY NOTES

**References in Text**

This Act, referred to in subsec. (a)(1), is Pub.L. 101–380, Aug. 18, 1990, 104 Stat. 484, as amended, known as the Oil Pollution Act of 1990, which is classified principally to this chapter. For complete classification to the Code, see Short Title note under 33 U.S.C.A. § 2701 and Tables.

The Trans-Alaska Pipeline Authorization Act, referred to in subsec. (b)(4), is title II of Pub.L. 93–153, Nov. 16, 1973, 87 Stat. 584, which is classified to chapter 34 (§ 1651 et seq.) of Title 43, Public Lands. For complete classification of this Act to the Code, see Short Title note set out under section 1651 of Title 43 and Tables.

**Effective and Applicability Provisions**

1990 Acts

Section applicable to incidents occurring after Aug. 18, 1990, see section 1020 of Pub.L. 101–380, set out as a note under section 2701 of this title.

## § 2708. Recovery by responsible party

[OPA § 1008]

**(a) In general**

The responsible party for a vessel or facility from which oil is discharged, or which poses the substantial threat of a discharge of oil, may assert a claim for removal costs and damages under section 2713 of this title only if the responsible party demonstrates that—

(1) the responsible party is entitled to a defense to liability under section 2703 of this title; or

(2) the responsible party is entitled to a limitation of liability under section 2704 of this title.

**(b) Extent of recovery**

A responsible party who is entitled to a limitation of liability may assert a claim under section 2713 of this title only to the extent that the sum of the removal costs and damages incurred by the responsible party plus the amounts paid by the responsible party, or by the guarantor on behalf of the responsible party, for claims asserted under section 2713 of this title exceeds the amount to which the total of the liability under section 2702 of this title and removal costs and damages incurred by, or on behalf of, the responsible party is limited under section 2704 of this title.

(Pub.L. 101–380, Title I, § 1008, Aug. 18, 1990, 104 Stat. 497.)

### HISTORICAL AND STATUTORY NOTES

**Effective and Applicability Provisions**

1990 Acts

Section applicable to incidents occurring after Aug. 18, 1990, see section 1020 of Pub.L. 101–380, set out as a note under section 2701 of this title.

## § 2709. Contribution

[OPA § 1009]

A person may bring a civil action for contribution against any other person who is liable or potentially liable under this Act or another law. The action shall be brought in accordance with section 2717 of this title.

(Pub.L. 101–380, Title I, § 1009, Aug. 18, 1990, 104 Stat. 497.)

### HISTORICAL AND STATUTORY NOTES

**References in Text**

This Act, referred to in text, is Pub.L. 101–380, Aug. 18, 1990, 104 Stat. 484, as amended, known as the Oil Pollution Act of 1990, which is classified principally to this chapter. For complete classification to the Code, see Short Title note under 33 U.S.C.A. § 2701 and Tables.

**Effective and Applicability Provisions**

1990 Acts

Section applicable to incidents occurring after Aug. 18, 1990, see section 1020 of Pub.L. 101–380, set out as a note under section 2701 of this title.

## § 2710. Indemnification agreements

[OPA § 1010]

**(a) Agreements not prohibited**

Nothing in this Act prohibits any agreement to insure, hold harmless, or indemnify a party to such agreement for any liability under this Act.

**(b) Liability not transferred**

No indemnification, hold harmless, or similar agreement or conveyance shall be effective to transfer liability imposed under this Act from a responsible party or from any person who may be liable for an incident under this Act to any other person.

**(c) Relationship to other causes of action**

Nothing in this Act, including the provisions of subsection (b) of this section, bars a cause of action that a responsible party subject to liability under this Act, or a guarantor, has or would have, by reason of subrogation or otherwise, against any person.

(Pub.L. 101–380, Title I, § 1010, Aug. 18, 1990, 104 Stat. 498.)

#### HISTORICAL AND STATUTORY NOTES

**References in Text**

This Act, referred to in text, is Pub.L. 101–380, Aug. 18, 1990, 104 Stat. 484, as amended, known as the Oil Pollution Act of 1990, which is classified principally to this chapter. For complete classification to the Code, see Short Title note under 33 U.S.C.A. § 2701 and Tables.

**Effective and Applicability Provisions**

1990 Acts

Section applicable to incidents occurring after Aug. 18, 1990, see section 1020 of Pub.L. 101–380, set out as a note under section 2701 of this title.

### § 2711. Consultation on removal actions

**[OPA § 1011]**

The President shall consult with the affected trustees designated under section 2706 of this title on the appropriate removal action to be taken in connection with any discharge of oil. For the purposes of the National Contingency Plan, removal with respect to any discharge shall be considered completed when so determined by the President in consultation with the Governor or Governors of the affected States. However, this determination shall not preclude additional removal actions under applicable State law.

(Pub.L. 101–380, Title I, § 1011, Aug. 18, 1990, 104 Stat. 498.)

#### HISTORICAL AND STATUTORY NOTES

**Effective and Applicability Provisions**

1990 Acts

Section applicable to incidents occurring after Aug. 18, 1990, see section 1020 of Pub.L. 101–380, set out as a note under section 2701 of this title.

**Delegation of Functions**

The functions vested in the President by this section, respecting an effective and immediate removal or arrangement for removal of a discharge and mitigation or prevention of a substantial threat of a discharge of oil or a hazardous substance, the direction and monitoring of all Federal, State and private actions, the removal and destruction of a vessel the issuance of directions consulting with affected trustees, and removal completion determinations, are delegated to the Administrator of the Environmental Protection Agency for the inland zone and to the Secretary of the Department in which the Coast Guard is operating for the coastal zone, see Ex. Ord. No. 12777, Oct. 18, 1991, 56 F.R. 54757, set out as a note under section 1321 of this title.

### § 2712. Uses of Fund

**[OPA § 1012]**

**(a) Uses generally**

The Fund shall be available to the President for—

(1) the payment of removal costs, including the costs of monitoring removal actions, determined by the President to be consistent with the National Contingency Plan—

(A) by Federal authorities; or

(B) by a Governor or designated State official under subsection (d) of this section;

(2) the payment of costs incurred by Federal, State, or Indian tribe trustees in carrying out their functions under section 2706 of this title for assessing natural resource damages and for developing and implementing plans for the restoration, rehabilitation, replacement, or acquisition of the equivalent of damaged resources determined by the President to be consistent with the National Contingency Plan;

(3) the payment of removal costs determined by the President to be consistent with the National Contingency Plan as a result of, and damages resulting from, a discharge, or a substantial threat of a discharge, of oil from a foreign offshore unit;

(4) the payment of claims in accordance with section 2713 of this title for uncompensated removal costs determined by the President to be consistent with the National Contingency Plan or uncompensated damages;

(5) the payment of Federal administrative, operational, and personnel costs and expenses reasonably necessary for and incidental to the implementation, administration, and enforcement of this Act (including, but not limited to, sections 1004(d)(2), 1006(e), 4107, 4110, 4111, 4112, 4117, 5006, 8103, and Title IV) and subsections (b), (c), (d), (j), and (*l*) of section 1321 of this title, with respect to prevention, removal, and enforcement related to oil discharges, provided that—

(A) not more than $25,000,000 in each fiscal year shall be available to the Secretary for operating expenses incurred by the Coast Guard;

(B) not more than $30,000,000 each year through the end of fiscal year 1992 shall be available to establish the National Response System under section 1321(j) of this title including the purchase and prepositioning of oil spill removal equipment; and

(C) not more than $27,250,000 in each fiscal year shall be available to carry out subchapter IV of this chapter.

**(b) Defense to liability for Fund**

The Fund shall not be available to pay any claim for removal costs or damages to a particular claimant, to the extent that the incident, removal costs, or damages are caused by the gross negligence or willful misconduct of that claimant.

**(c) Obligation of Fund by Federal officials**

The President may promulgate regulations designating one or more Federal officials who may obligate money in accordance with subsection (a) of this section.

**(d) Access to Fund by State officials**

**(1) Immediate removal**

In accordance with regulations promulgated under this section, the President, upon the request of the Governor of a State or pursuant to an agreement with a State under paragraph (2), may obligate the Fund for payment in an amount not to exceed $250,000 for removal costs consistent with the National Contingency Plan required for the immediate removal of a discharge, or the mitigation or prevention of a substantial threat of a discharge, of oil.

**(2) Agreements**

**(A) In general**

The President shall enter into an agreement with the Governor of any interested State to establish procedures under which the Governor or a designated State official may receive payments from the Fund for removal costs pursuant to paragraph (1).

**(B) Terms**

Agreements under this paragraph—

(i) may include such terms and conditions as may be agreed upon by the President and the Governor of a State;

(ii) shall provide for political subdivisions of the State to receive payments for reasonable removal costs; and

(iii) may authorize advance payments from the Fund to facilitate removal efforts.

**(e) Regulations**

The President shall—

(1) not later than 6 months after August 18, 1990, publish proposed regulations detailing the manner in which the authority to obligate the Fund and to enter into agreements under this subsection shall be exercised; and

(2) not later than 3 months after the close of the comment period for such proposed regulations, promulgate final regulations for that purpose.

**(f) Rights of subrogation**

Payment of any claim or obligation by the Fund under this Act shall be subject to the United States Government acquiring by subrogation all rights of the claimant or State to recover from the responsible party.

**(g) Audits**

The Comptroller General shall audit all payments, obligations, reimbursements, and other uses of the Fund, to assure that the Fund is being properly administered and that claims are being appropriately and expeditiously considered. The Comptroller General shall submit to the Congress an interim report one year after August 18, 1990. The Comptroller General shall thereafter audit the Fund as is appropriate. Each Federal agency shall cooperate with the Comptroller General in carrying out this subsection.

**(h) Period of limitations for claims**

**(1) Removal costs**

No claim may be presented under this subchapter for recovery of removal costs for an incident unless the claim is presented within 6 years after the date of completion of all removal actions for that incident.

**(2) Damages**

No claim may be presented under this section for recovery of damages unless the claim is presented within 3 years after the date on which the injury and its connection with the discharge in question were reasonably discoverable with the exercise of due care, or in the case of natural resource damages under section 2702(b)(2)(A) of this title, if later, the date of completion of the natural resources damage assessment under section 2706(e) of this title.

**(3) Minors and incompetents**

The time limitations contained in this subsection shall not begin to run—

(A) against a minor until the earlier of the date when such minor reaches 18 years of age or the date on which a legal representative is duly appointed for the minor, or

(B) against an incompetent person until the earlier of the date on which such incompetent's incompetency ends or the date on which a legal representative is duly appointed for the incompetent.

**(i) Limitation on payment for same costs**

In any case in which the President has paid an amount from the Fund for any removal costs or damages specified under subsection (a) of this section, no other claim may be paid from the Fund for the same removal costs or damages.

**(j) Obligation in accordance with plan**

**(1) In general**

Except as provided in paragraph (2), amounts may be obligated from the Fund for the restoration, rehabilitation, replacement, or acquisition of natural resources only in accordance with a plan adopted under section 2706(c) of this title.

**(2) Exception**

Paragraph (1) shall not apply in a situation requiring action to avoid irreversible loss of natural resources or to prevent or reduce any continuing danger to natural resources or similar need for emergency action.

**(k) Preference for private persons in area affected by discharge**

**(1) In general**

In the expenditure of Federal funds for removal of oil, including for distribution of supplies, construction, and other reasonable and appropriate activities, under a contract or agreement with a private person, preference shall be given, to the extent feasible and practicable, to private persons residing or doing business primarily in the area affected by the discharge of oil.

**(2) Limitation**

This subsection shall not be considered to restrict the use of Department of Defense resources.

(Pub.L. 101–380, Title I, § 1012, Aug. 18, 1990, 104 Stat. 498.)

## HISTORICAL AND STATUTORY NOTES

**References in Text**

This Act, referred to in subsecs. (a)(5) and (f), is Pub.L. 101–380, Aug. 18, 1990, 104 Stat. 484, known as the Oil Pollution Act of 1990, which is classified principally to this chapter. Sections 1004(d)(2) and 1006(e) are classified to 33 U.S.C.A. §§ 2704(d)(2) and 2706(e), respectively. Section 4107 amended 33 U.S.C.A. § 1223 and enacted provisions set out as a note under 33 U.S.C.A. § 1223. Sections 4110 and 4111 enacted provisions set out as notes under 46 U.S.C.A. § 3703. Section 4112 is not classified to the Code. Section 4117 enacted provisions set out as a note under 46 U.S.C.A. § 1295, Appendix. Section 5006 is classified to 33 U.S.C.A. § 2736. Section 8103 enacted provisions set out as a note under 43 U.S.C.A. § 1651. Title VII is classified to subchapter IV of this chapter [33 U.S.C.A. § 2761 et seq.]. For complete classification of this Act to the Code, see Short Title note set out under 33 U.S.C.A. § 2701 and Tables.

References in subsec. (a)(5) to the amendment of section 1321 of this title "by this Act" refer to amendment by Pub.L. 101–380, Aug. 18, 1990, 104 Stat. 484.

**Effective and Applicability Provisions**

1990 Acts

Section applicable to incidents occurring after Aug. 18, 1990, see section 1020 of Pub.L. 101–380, set out as a note under section 2701 of this title.

**Delegation of Functions**

Memorandum of the President of Aug. 24, 1990, 55 F.R. 35291, delegating certain authorities of the President under this section and section 2752 of this title, was revoked by Ex. Ord. No. 12777, Oct. 18, 1991, 56 F.R. 54757, set out as a note under section 1321 of this title.

The functions vested in the President by subsec. (a)(1), (3), and (4) of this section respecting payment of removal costs and claims and determining consistency with the National Contingency Plan (NCP) are delegated to the Secretary or the Department in which the Coast Guard is operating, see Ex. Ord. No. 12777, Oct. 18, 1991, 56 F.R. 54757, set out as a note under section 1321 of this title.

[The functions vested in the President by subsec. (a) of this section, respecting the payment of costs, damages, and claims, delegated by Ex. Ord. No. 12777 to the Secretary of the Department in which the Coast Guard is operating, include, *inter alia*, the authority to process, settle, and administratively adjudicate such costs, damages, and claims, regardless of amount.]

The functions vested in the President by subsec.(a)(2) of this section, respecting the payment of costs and determining consistency with the NCP, are delegated to the Federal trustees designated in the NCP [National Contingency Plan], see Ex. Ord. No. 12777, Oct. 18, 1991, 56 F.R. 54757, set out as a note under section 1321 of this title.

The functions vested in the President by subsec. (a)(5) of this section, respecting the payment of costs and expenses of departments and agencies having responsibility for the implementation, administration, and enforcement of the Oil Pollution Act of 1990 [Pub.L. 101–380, Aug. 18, 1990, 104 Stat. 484. See Tables for classification] are delegated to each head of such department and agency, see Ex. Ord. No. 12777, Oct. 18, 1991, 56 F.R. 54757, set out as a note under section 1321 of this title.

The functions vested in the President by subsec. (c) of this section, respecting designation of Federal officials who may obligate money, are delegated to each head of the departments and agencies to whom functions have been delegated under section 7(a) of this order for the purpose of carrying out such functions, see Ex. Ord. No. 12777, Oct. 18, 1991, 56 F.R. 54757, set out as a note under section 1321 of this title.

The functions vested in the President by subsecs. (d) and (e) of this section, respecting the obligation of the Trust Fund on the request of a Governor or pursuant to an agreement with a State, entrance into agreements with States, agreement upon terms and conditions, and the promulgation of regulations concerning such obligation and entrance into such agreement, are delegated to the Secretary of the Department in which the Coast Guard is operating, in consultation with the Administrator of the Environmental Protection Agency, see Ex. Ord. No. 12777, Oct. 18, 1991, 56 F.R. 54757, set out as a note under section 1321 of this title.

## § 2713. Claims procedure

**[OPA § 1013]**

**(a) Presentation**

Except as provided in subsection (b) of this section, all claims for removal costs or damages shall be presented first to the responsible party or guarantor of the source designated under section 2714(a) of this title.

**(b) Presentation to Fund**

**(1) In general**

Claims for removal costs or damages may be presented first to the Fund—

**(A)** if the President has advertised or otherwise notified claimants in accordance with section 2714(c) of this title;

**(B)** by a responsible party who may assert a claim under section 2708 of this title;

**(C)** by the Governor of a State for removal costs incurred by that State; or

**(D)** by a United States claimant in a case where a foreign offshore unit has discharged oil causing damage for which the Fund is liable under section 2712(a) of this title.

**(2) Limitation on presenting claim**

No claim of a person against the Fund may be approved or certified during the pendency of an action by the person in court to recover costs which are the subject of the claim.

**(c) Election**

If a claim is presented in accordance with subsection (a) of this section and—

(1) each person to whom the claim is presented denies all liability for the claim, or

(2) the claim is not settled by any person by payment within 90 days after the date upon which (A) the claim was presented, or (B) advertising was begun pursuant to section 2714(b) of this title, whichever is later,

the claimant may elect to commence an action in court against the responsible party or guarantor or to present the claim to the Fund.

**(d) Uncompensated damages**

If a claim is presented in accordance with this section, including a claim for interim, short-term damages representing less than the full amount of damages to which the claimant ultimately may be entitled, and full and adequate compensation is unavailable, a claim for the uncompensated damages and removal costs may be presented to the Fund.

**(e) Procedure for claims against Fund**

The President shall promulgate, and may from time to time amend, regulations for the presentation, filing, processing, settlement, and adjudication of claims under this Act against the Fund.

(Pub.L. 101–380, Title I, § 1013, Aug. 18, 1990, 104 Stat. 501; Pub.L. 104–324, Title XI, § 1142(b), Oct. 19, 1996, 110 Stat. 3991.)

### HISTORICAL AND STATUTORY NOTES

**References in Text**

This Act, referred to in subsec. (e), is Pub.L. 101–380, Aug. 18, 1990, 104 Stat. 484, as amended, known as the Oil Pollution Act of 1990, which is classified principally to this chapter. For complete classification to the Code, see Short Title note under 33 U.S.C.A. § 2701 and Tables.

**Effective and Applicability Provisions**

1990 Acts

Section applicable to incidents occurring after Aug. 18, 1990, see section 1020 of Pub.L. 101–380, set out as a note under section 2701 of this title.

**Delegation of Functions**

The functions vested in the President by subsec.(e) of this section, respecting the promulgation and amendment of regulations for the presentation, filing, processing, settlement, and adjudication of claims under this subchapter against the Trust Fund, are delegated to the Secretary of the Department in which the Coast Guard is operating, in consultation with the Attorney General, see Ex. Ord. No. 12777, Oct. 18, 1991, 56 F.R. 54757, set out as a note under section 1321 of this title.

## § 2714. Designation of source and advertisement

[OPA § 1014]

**(a) Designation of source and notification**

When the President receives information of an incident, the President shall, where possible and appropriate, designate the source or sources of the discharge or threat. If a designated source is a vessel or a facility, the President shall immediately notify the responsible party and the guarantor, if known, of that designation.

**(b) Advertisement by responsible party or guarantor**

(1) If a responsible party or guarantor fails to inform the President, within 5 days after receiving notification of a designation under subsection (a) of this section, of the party's or the guarantor's denial of the designation, such party or guarantor shall advertise the designation and the procedures by which claims may be presented, in accordance with regulations promulgated by the President. Advertisement under the preceding sentence shall begin no later than 15 days after the date of the designation made under subsection (a) of this section. If advertisement is not otherwise made in accordance with this subsection, the President shall promptly and at the expense of the responsible party or the guarantor involved, advertise

the designation and the procedures by which claims may be presented to the responsible party or guarantor. Advertisement under this subsection shall continue for a period of no less than 30 days.

(2) An advertisement under paragraph (1) shall state that a claimant may present a claim for interim, short-term damages representing less than the full amount of damages to which the claimant ultimately may be entitled and that payment of such a claim shall not preclude recovery for damages not reflected in the paid or settled partial claim.

**(c) Advertisement by President**

If

(1) the responsible party and the guarantor both deny a designation within 5 days after receiving notification of a designation under subsection (a) of this section,

(2) the source of the discharge or threat was a public vessel, or

(3) the President is unable to designate the source or sources of the discharge or threat under subsection (a) of this section,

the President shall advertise or otherwise notify potential claimants of the procedures by which claims may be presented to the Fund.

(Pub.L. 101–380, Title I, § 1014, Aug. 18, 1990, 104 Stat. 501; Pub.L. 104–324, Title XI, § 1142(c), Oct. 19, 1996, 110 Stat. 3991.)

### HISTORICAL AND STATUTORY NOTES

**Effective and Applicability Provisions**

1990 Acts

Section applicable to incidents occurring after Aug. 18, 1990, see section 1020 of Pub.L. 101–380, set out as a note under section 2701 of this title.

**Delegation of Functions**

The functions vested in the President by this section, respecting designation of sources of discharges or threats, notification to responsible parties, promulgation of regulations respecting advertisements, the advertisement of designation, and notification of claims procedures, are delegated to the Secretary of the Department in which the Coast Guard is operating, see Ex. Ord. No. 12777, Oct. 18, 1991, 56 F.R. 54757, set out as a note under section 1321 of this title.

## § 2715. Subrogation

**[OPA § 1015]**

**(a) In general**

Any person, including the Fund, who pays compensation pursuant to this Act to any claimant for removal costs or damages shall be subrogated to all rights, claims, and causes of action that the claimant has under any other law.

**(b) Interim damages**

**(1) In general**

If a responsible party, a guarantor, or the Fund has made payment to a claimant for interim, short-term damages representing less than the full amount of damages to which the claimant ultimately may be entitled, subrogation under subsection (a) of this section shall apply only with respect to the portion of the claim reflected in the paid interim claim.

**(2) Final damages**

Payment of such a claim shall not foreclose a claimant's right to recovery of all damages to which the claimant otherwise is entitled under this Act or under any other law.

**(c) Actions on behalf of Fund**

At the request of the Secretary, the Attorney General shall commence an action on behalf of the Fund to recover any compensation paid by the Fund to any claimant pursuant to this Act, and all costs incurred by the Fund by reason of the claim, including interest (including prejudgment interest), administrative and adjudicative costs, and attorney's fees. Such an action may be commenced against any responsible party or (subject to section 2716 of this title) guarantor, or against any other person who is liable, pursuant to any law, to the compensated claimant or to the Fund, for the cost or damages for which the compensation was paid. Such an action shall be commenced against the responsible foreign government or other responsible party to recover any removal costs or damages paid from the Fund as the result of the discharge, or substantial threat of discharge, of oil from a foreign offshore unit.

(Pub.L. 101–380, Title I, § 1015, Aug. 18, 1990, 104 Stat. 502; Pub.L. 104–324, Title XI, § 1142(d), Oct. 19, 1996, 110 Stat. 3991.)

### HISTORICAL AND STATUTORY NOTES

**References in Text**

This Act, referred to in text, is Pub.L. 101–380, Aug. 18, 1990, 104 Stat. 484, as amended, known as the Oil Pollution Act of 1990, which is classified principally to this chapter. For complete classification to the Code, see Short Title note under 33 U.S.C.A. § 2701 and Tables.

**Effective and Applicability Provisions**

1990 Acts

Section applicable to incidents occurring after Aug. 18, 1990, see section 1020 of Pub.L. 101–380, set out as a note under section 2701 of this title.

## § 2716. Financial responsibility

**[OPA § 1016]**

**(a) Requirement**

The responsible party for—

(1) any vessel over 300 gross tons (except a non-self-propelled vessel that does not carry oil as cargo or fuel) using any place subject to the jurisdiction of the United States; or

(2) any vessel using the waters of the exclusive economic zone to transship or lighter oil destined for a place subject to the jurisdiction of the United States;

shall establish and maintain, in accordance with regulations promulgated by the Secretary, evidence of financial responsibility sufficient to meet the maximum amount of liability to which the responsible party could be subjected under section 2704(a) or (d) of this title, in a case where the responsible party would be entitled to limit liability under that section. If the responsible party owns or operates more than one vessel, evidence of financial responsibility need be established only to meet the amount of the maximum liability applicable to the vessel having the greatest maximum liability.

**(b) Sanctions**

**(1) Withholding clearance**

The Secretary of the Treasury shall withhold or revoke the clearance required by section 91 of the Appendix to Title 46 of any vessel subject to this section that does not have the evidence of financial responsibility required for the vessel under this section.

**(2) Denying entry to or detaining vessels**

The Secretary may—

(A) deny entry to any vessel to any place in the United States, or to the navigable waters, or

(B) detain at the place,

any vessel that, upon request, does not produce the evidence of financial responsibility required for the vessel under this section.

**(3) Seizure of vessel**

Any vessel subject to the requirements of this section which is found in the navigable waters without the necessary evidence of financial responsibility for the vessel shall be subject to seizure by and forfeiture to the United States.

**(c) Offshore facilities**

**(1) In general**

**(A) Evidence of financial responsibility required**

Except as provided in paragraph (2), a responsible party with respect to an offshore facility that—

(i)(I) is located seaward of the line of ordinary low water along that portion of the coast that is in direct contact with the open sea and the line marking the seaward limit of inland waters; or

(II) is located in coastal inland waters, such as bays or estuaries, seaward of the line of ordinary low water along that portion of the coast that is not in direct contact with the open sea;

(ii) is used for exploring for, drilling for, producing, or transporting oil from facilities engaged in oil exploration, drilling, or production; and

(iii) has a worst-case oil spill discharge potential of more than 1,000 barrels of oil (or a lesser amount if the President determines that the risks posed by such facility justify it),

shall establish and maintain evidence of financial responsibility in the amount required under subparagraph (B) or (C), as applicable.

**(B) Amount required generally**

Except as provided in subparagraph (C), the amount of financial responsibility for offshore facilities that meet the criteria of subparagraph (A) is—

(i) $35,000,000 for an offshore facility located seaward of the seaward boundary of a State; or

(ii) $10,000,000 for an offshore facility located landward of the seaward boundary of a State.

**(C) Greater amount**

If the President determines that an amount of financial responsibility for a responsible party greater than the amount required by subparagraph (B) is justified based on the relative operational, environmental, human health, and other risks posed by the quantity or quality of oil that is explored for, drilled for, produced, or transported by the responsible party, the evidence of financial responsibility required shall be for an amount determined by the President not exceeding $150,000,000.

**(D) Multiple facilities**

In a case in which a person is a responsible party for more than one facility subject to this subsection, evidence of financial responsibility need be established only to meet the amount applicable to the facility having the greatest financial responsibility requirement under this subsection.

**(E) Definition**

For the purpose of this paragraph, the seaward boundary of a State shall be determined in accordance with section 1301(b) of Title 43.

(2) **Deepwater ports**

Each responsible party with respect to a deepwater port shall establish and maintain evidence of financial responsibility sufficient to meet the maximum amount of liability to which the responsible party could be subjected under section 2704(a) of this title in a case where the responsible party would be entitled to limit liability under that section. If the Secretary exercises the authority under section 2704(d)(2) of this title to lower the limit of liability for deepwater ports, the responsible party shall establish and maintain evidence of financial responsibility sufficient to meet the maximum amount of liability so established. In a case in which a person is the responsible party for more than one deepwater port, evidence of financial responsibility need be established only to meet the maximum liability applicable to the deepwater port having the greatest maximum liability.

(e)[1] **Methods of financial responsibility**

Financial responsibility under this section may be established by any one, or by any combination, of the following methods which the Secretary (in the case of a vessel) or the President (in the case of a facility) determines to be acceptable: evidence of insurance, surety bond, guarantee, letter of credit, qualification as a self-insurer, or other evidence of financial responsibility. Any bond filed shall be issued by a bonding company authorized to do business in the United States. In promulgating requirements under this section, the Secretary or the President, as appropriate, may specify policy or other contractual terms, conditions, or defenses which are necessary, or which are unacceptable, in establishing evidence of financial responsibility to effectuate the purposes of this Act.

(f) **Claims against guarantor**

(1) **In general**

Subject to paragraph (2), a claim for which liability may be established under section 2702 of this title may be asserted directly against any guarantor providing evidence of financial responsibility for a responsible party liable under that section for removal costs and damages to which the claim pertains. In defending against such a claim, the guarantor may invoke—

(A) all rights and defenses which would be available to the responsible party under this Act;

(B) any defense authorized under subsection (e) of this section; and

(C) the defense that the incident was caused by the willful misconduct of the responsible party.

The guarantor may not invoke any other defense that might be available in proceedings brought by the responsible party against the guarantor.

(2) **Further requirement**

A claim may be asserted pursuant to paragraph (1) directly against a guarantor providing evidence of financial responsibility under subsection (c)(1) of this section with respect to an offshore facility only if—

(A) the responsible party for whom evidence of financial responsibility has been provided has denied or failed to pay a claim under this Act on the basis of being insolvent, as defined under section 101(32) of Title 11, and applying generally accepted accounting principles;

(B) the responsible party for whom evidence of financial responsibility has been provided has filed a petition for bankruptcy under Title 11; or

(C) the claim is asserted by the United States for removal costs and damages or for compensation paid by the Fund under this Act, including costs incurred by the Fund for processing compensation claims.

(3) **Rulemaking authority**

Not later than 1 year after October 19, 1996, the President shall promulgate regulations to establish a process for implementing paragraph (2) in a manner that will allow for the orderly and expeditious presentation and resolution of claims and effectuate the purposes of this Act.

(g) **Limitation on guarantor's liability**

Nothing in this Act shall impose liability with respect to an incident on any guarantor for damages or removal costs which exceed, in the aggregate, the amount of financial responsibility which that guarantor has provided for a responsible party pursuant to this section. The total liability of the guarantor on direct action for claims brought under this Act with respect to an incident shall be limited to that amount.

(h) **Continuation of regulations**

Any regulation relating to financial responsibility, which has been issued pursuant to any provision of law repealed or superseded by this Act, and which is in effect on the date immediately preceding the effective date of this Act, is deemed and shall be construed to be a regulation issued pursuant to this section. Such a regulation shall remain in full force and effect unless and until superseded by a new regulation issued under this section.

(i) **Unified certificate**

The Secretary may issue a single unified certificate of financial responsibility for purposes of this Act and any other law.

(Pub.L. 101–380, Title I, § 1016, Aug. 18, 1990, 104 Stat. 502; Pub.L. 104–55, § 2(d)(2), Nov. 20, 1995, 109 Stat. 547; Pub.L. 104–324, Title XI, § 1125(a), Oct. 19, 1996, 110 Stat. 3981.)

[1] So in original. No subsec. (d) was enacted.

HISTORICAL AND STATUTORY NOTES

**References in Text**

This Act, referred to in text, is Pub.L. 101–380, Aug. 18, 1990, 104 Stat. 484, as amended, known as the Oil Pollution Act of 1990, which is classified principally to this chapter. For complete classification to the Code, see Short Title note under 33 U.S.C.A. § 2701 and Tables.

Reference in subsec. (h) to the "effective date of this Act" probably refers to the date of enactment of Pub.L. 101–380 which was approved on Aug. 18, 1990.

**Effective and Applicability Provisions**

1996 Acts

Section 1125(b) of Pub.L. 104–324 provided that: "The amendment made by subsection (a)(2) [amending subsec. (f) of this section] shall not apply to any final rule issued before the date of enactment of this section [Oct. 19, 1996]."

1990 Acts

Section applicable to incidents occurring after Aug. 18, 1990, see section 1020 of Pub.L. 101–380, set out as a note under section 2701 of this title.

**Delegation of Functions**

The functions vested in the President by subsec.(e) of this section, respecting (in the case of offshore facilities other than deepwater ports) the issuance of regulations concerning financial responsibility, the determination of acceptable methods of financial responsibility, and the specification of necessary or unacceptable terms, conditions, or defenses, are delegated to the Secretary of the Interior, see Ex. Ord. No. 12777, Oct. 18, 1991, 56 F.R. 54757, set out as a note under section 1321 of this title.

The functions vested in the President by subsec. (e) of this section, respecting (in the case of deepwater ports) the issuance of regulations concerning financial responsibility, the determination of acceptable methods of financial responsibility, and the specification of necessary or unacceptable terms, conditions, or defenses, are delegated to the Secretary of Transportation, see Ex. Ord. No. 12777, Oct. 18, 1991, 56 F.R. 54757, set out as a note under section 1321 of this title.

## § 2716a. Financial responsibility civil penalties

[OPA § 4303]

### (a) Administrative

Any person who, after notice and an opportunity for a hearing, is found to have failed to comply with the requirements of section 2716 of this title or the regulations issued under that section, or with a denial or detention order issued under subsection (c)(2) of that section, shall be liable to the United States for a civil penalty, not to exceed $25,000 per day of violation. The amount of the civil penalty shall be assessed by the President by written notice. In determining the amount of the penalty, the President shall take into account the nature, circumstances, extent, and gravity of the violation, the degree of culpability, any history of prior violation, ability to pay, and such other matters as justice may require. The President may compromise, modify, or remit, with or without conditions, any civil penalty which is subject to imposition or which had been imposed under this paragraph. If any person fails to pay an assessed civil penalty after it has become final, the President may refer the matter to the Attorney General for collection.

### (b) Judicial

In addition to, or in lieu of, assessing a penalty under subsection (a) of this section, the President may request the Attorney General to secure such relief as necessary to compel compliance with this[1] section 2716 of this title, including a judicial order terminating operations. The district courts of the United States shall have jurisdiction to grant any relief as the public interest and the equities of the case may require.

(Pub.L. 101–380, Title IV, § 4303, Aug. 18, 1990, 104 Stat. 539.)

[1] So in original. The word "this " probably should not appear.

HISTORICAL AND STATUTORY NOTES

**Codifications**

Section was not enacted as part of title I of Pub.L. 101–380 which comprises this subchapter.

**Effective and Applicability Provisions**

1990 Acts

Incidents occurring after Aug. 18, 1990, as constituting the basis for violations of section 2716 of this title for which penalties are assessed under this section, see section 1020 of Pub.L. 101–380, set out as a note under section 2701 of this title.

**Delegation of Functions**

The functions vested in the President by this section, respecting (in cases involving vessels) the assessment of civil penalties, the compromising, modification or remission, with or without condition, and the referral for collection of such imposed penalties, and requests to the Attorney General to secure necessary judicial relief, are delegated to the Secretary of the Department in which the Coast Guard is operating, see Ex. Ord. No. 12777, Oct. 18, 1991, 56 F.R. 54757, set out as a note under section 1321 of this title.

The functions vested in the President by this section, respecting (in cases involving offshore facilities other than deepwater ports) the assessment of civil penalties, the compromising, modification or remission, with or without condition, and the referral for collection of such imposed penalties, and requests to the Attorney General to secure necessary judicial relief, are delegated to the Secretary of the Interior, see Ex. Ord. No. 12777, Oct. 18, 1991, 56 F.R. 54757, set out as a note under section 1321 of this title.

The functions vested in the President by this section, respecting (in cases involving deepwater ports) the assessment of civil penalties, the compromising, modification or remission, with or without condition, and the referral for collection of such imposed penalties, and requests to the Attorney General to secure necessary judicial relief, are delegated to the Secretary of Transportation, see Ex. Ord. No. 12777, Oct. 18, 1991, 56 F.R. 54757, set out as a note under section 1321 of this title.

## § 2717. Litigation, jurisdiction, and venue

[OPA § 1017]

### (a) Review of regulations

Review of any regulation promulgated under this Act may be had upon application by any interested person only in the Circuit Court of Appeals of the United States for the District of Columbia. Any such application shall be made within 90 days from the date of promulgation of such regulations. Any matter with respect to which review could have been obtained under this subsection shall not be subject to judicial review in any civil or criminal proceeding for enforcement or to obtain damages or recovery of response costs.

### (b) Jurisdiction

Except as provided in subsections (a) and (c) of this section, the United States district courts shall have exclusive original jurisdiction over all controversies arising under this Act, without regard to the citizenship of the parties or the amount in controversy. Venue shall lie in any district in which the discharge or injury or damages occurred, or in which the defendant resides, may be found, has its principal office, or has appointed an agent for service of process. For the purposes of this section, the Fund shall reside in the District of Columbia.

### (c) State court jurisdiction

A State trial court of competent jurisdiction over claims for removal costs or damages, as defined under this Act, may consider claims under this Act or State law and any final judgment of such court (when no longer subject to ordinary forms of review) shall be recognized, valid, and enforceable for all purposes of this Act.

### (d) Assessment and collection of tax

The provisions of subsections (a), (b), and (c) of this section shall not apply to any controversy or other matter resulting from the assessment or collection of any tax, or to the review of any regulation promulgated under Title 26.

### (e) Savings provision

Nothing in this subchapter shall apply to any cause of action or right of recovery arising from any incident which occurred prior to August 18, 1990. Such claims shall be adjudicated pursuant to the law applicable on the date of the incident.

### (f) Period of limitations

#### (1) Damages

Except as provided in paragraphs (3) and (4), an action for damages under this Act shall be barred unless the action is brought within 3 years after—

**(A)** the date on which the loss and the connection of the loss with the discharge in question are reasonably discoverable with the exercise of due care, or

**(B)** in the case of natural resource damages under section 2702(b)(2)(A) of this title, the date of completion of the natural resources damage assessment under section 2706(c) of this title.

#### (2) Removal costs

An action for recovery of removal costs referred to in section 2702(b)(1) of this title must be commenced within 3 years after completion of the removal action. In any such action described in this subsection, the court shall enter a declaratory judgment on liability for removal costs or damages that will be binding on any subsequent action or actions to recover further removal costs or damages. Except as otherwise provided in this paragraph, an action may be commenced under this subchapter for recovery of removal costs at any time after such costs have been incurred.

#### (3) Contribution

No action for contribution for any removal costs or damages may be commenced more than 3 years after—

**(A)** the date of judgment in any action under this Act for recovery of such costs or damages, or

**(B)** the date of entry of a judicially approved settlement with respect to such costs or damages.

#### (4) Subrogation

No action based on rights subrogated pursuant to this Act by reason of payment of a claim may be commenced under this Act more than 3 years after the date of payment of such claim.

#### (5) Commencement

The time limitations contained herein shall not begin to run—

**(A)** against a minor until the earlier of the date when such minor reaches 18 years of age or the date on which a legal representative is duly appointed for such minor, or

**(B)** against an incompetent person until the earlier of the date on which such incompetent's incompetency ends or the date on which a legal representative is duly appointed for such incompetent.

(Pub.L. 101–380, Title I, § 1017, Aug. 18, 1990, 104 Stat. 504.)

### HISTORICAL AND STATUTORY NOTES

**References in Text**

This Act, referred to in text, is Pub.L. 101–380, Aug. 18, 1990, 104 Stat. 484, as amended, known as the Oil Pollution Act of 1990, which is classified principally to this chapter.

For complete classification to the Code, see Short Title note under 33 U.S.C.A. § 2701 and Tables.

**Effective and Applicability Provisions**

1990 Acts

Section applicable to incidents occurring after Aug. 18, 1990, see section 1020 of Pub.L. 101-380, set out as a note under section 2701 of this title.

## § 2718. Relationship to other law

**[OPA § 1018]**

**(a) Preservation of State authorities; Solid Waste Disposal Act**

Nothing in this Act or the Act of March 3, 1851 shall—

(1) affect, or be construed or interpreted as preempting, the authority of any State or political subdivision thereof from imposing any additional liability or requirements with respect to—

(A) the discharge of oil or other pollution by oil within such State; or

(B) any removal activities in connection with such a discharge; or

(2) affect, or be construed or interpreted to affect or modify in any way the obligations or liabilities of any person under the Solid Waste Disposal Act (42 U.S.C. 6901 et seq.) or State law, including common law.

**(b) Preservation of State funds**

Nothing in this Act or in section 9509 of Title 26 shall in any way affect, or be construed to affect, the authority of any State—

(1) to establish, or to continue in effect, a fund any purpose of which is to pay for costs or damages arising out of, or directly resulting from, oil pollution or the substantial threat of oil pollution; or

(2) to require any person to contribute to such a fund.

**(c) Additional requirements and liabilities; penalties**

Nothing in this Act, the Act of March 3, 1851 (46 U.S.C. 183 et seq.), or section 9509 of Title 26, shall in any way affect, or be construed to affect, the authority of the United States or any State or political subdivision thereof—

(1) to impose additional liability or additional requirements; or

(2) to impose, or to determine the amount of, any fine or penalty (whether criminal or civil in nature) for any violation of law;

relating to the discharge, or substantial threat of a discharge, of oil.

**(d) Federal employee liability**

For purposes of section 2679(b)(2)(B) of Title 28, nothing in this Act shall be construed to authorize or create a cause of action against a Federal officer or employee in the officer's or employee's personal or individual capacity for any act or omission while acting within the scope of the officer's or employee's office or employment.

(Pub.L. 101-380, Title I, § 1018, Aug. 18, 1990, 104 Stat. 505.)

### HISTORICAL AND STATUTORY NOTES

**References in Text**

This Act, referred to in text, is Pub.L. 101-380, Aug. 18, 1990, 104 Stat. 484, as amended, known as the Oil Pollution Act of 1990, which is classified principally to this chapter. For complete classification to the Code, see Short Title note under 33 U.S.C.A. § 2701 and Tables.

Reference in subsecs. (a) and (c) to "the Act of March 3, 1851" probably is a reference to Act March 3, 1851, c. 43, 9 Stat. 635, entitled "An Act to limit the liability of shipowners, and for other purposes", which is now covered by section 181 et seq. of the Appendix to Title 46, Shipping.

The Solid Waste Disposal Act, referred to in subsec. (a)(2), is title II of Pub.L. 89-272, Oct. 20, 1965, 79 Stat. 997, as amended generally by Pub.L. 94-580, § 2, Oct. 21, 1976, 90 Stat. 2795, which is classified generally to chapter 82 (§ 6901 et seq.) of Title 42, The Public Health and Welfare. For complete classification of this Act to the Code, see Short Title note set out under section 6901 of Title 42 and Tables.

**Effective and Applicability Provisions**

1990 Acts

Section applicable to incidents occurring after Aug. 18, 1990, see section 1020 of Pub.L. 101-380, set out as a note under section 2701 of this title.

**Report on Vessel Safety and Ability to Meet Legal Obligations**

Pub.L. 102-241, § 32, Dec. 19, 1991, 105 Stat. 2222, provided that: "Not later than one year after the date of enactment of this Act [Dec. 19, 1991], the Secretary of Transportation shall report to Congress on the effect of section 1018 of the Oil Pollution Act of 1990 (Public Law 101-380; 104 Stat. 484) [this section] on the safety of vessels being used to transport oil and the capability of owners and operators to meet their legal obligations in the event of an oil spill."

## § 2719. State financial responsibility

**[OPA § 1019]**

A State may enforce, on the navigable waters of the State, the requirements for evidence of financial responsibility under section 2716 of this title.

(Pub.L. 101-380, Title I, § 1019, Aug. 18, 1990, 104 Stat. 506.)

### HISTORICAL AND STATUTORY NOTES

**Effective and Applicability Provisions**

1990 Acts

Section applicable to incidents occurring after Aug. 18, 1990, see section 1020 of Pub.L. 101-380, set out as a note under section 2701 of this title.

## § 2720. Differentiation among fats, oils, and greases

### (a) In general

Except as provided in subsection (c) of this section, in issuing or enforcing any regulation or establishing any interpretation or guideline relating to the transportation, storage, discharge, release, emission, or disposal of a fat, oil, or grease under any Federal law, the head of that Federal agency shall—

(1) differentiate between and establish separate classes for—

(A) animal fats and oils and greases, and fish and marine mammal oils, within the meaning of paragraph (2) of section 61(a) of Title 13, and oils of vegetable origin, including oils from the seeds, nuts, and kernels referred to in paragraph (1)(A) of that section; and

(B) other oils and greases, including petroleum; and

(2) apply standards to different classes of fats and oils based on considerations in subsection (b) of this section.

### (b) Considerations

In differentiating between the class of fats, oils, and greases described in subsection (a)(1)(A) of this section and the class of oils and greases described in subsection (a)(1)(B) of this section, the head of the Federal agency shall consider differences in the physical, chemical, biological, and other properties, and in the environmental effects, of the classes.

### (c) Exception

The requirements of this Act shall not apply to the Food and Drug Administration and the Food Safety and Inspection Service.

### (d) Omitted

(Pub.L. 104–55, § 2, Nov. 20, 1995, 109 Stat. 546.)

### HISTORICAL AND STATUTORY NOTES

**References in Text**

This Act, referred to in subsec. (c), is Pub.L. 104–55, Nov. 20, 1995, 109 Stat. 546, which enacted this section, amended sections 2704 and 2716 of this title, and enacted provisions set out as a note under section 2701 of this title. For complete classification of this Act to the Code, see Short Title note set out under section 2701 of this title and Tables.

**Codifications**

Section was enacted as part of the Edible Oil Regulatory Reform Act [Pub.L. 104–55] and not as part of the Oil Pollution Act of 1990 [Pub.L. 101–380] which enacted this chapter.

Section 2 of Pub.L. 104–55, which enacted this section, consisted in the original of subsecs. (a) to (d). Section 2(d) of Pub.L. 104–55, which has been omitted from the text of this section, amended sections 2704(a)(1) and 2716(a) of this title.

**Interpretations or Guidelines under the Edible Oil Regulatory Reform Act**

Pub.L. 105–277, Div. A, § 101(g) [Title III, § 343], Oct. 21, 1998, 112 Stat. 2681–473, provided that:

"**(a)** None of the funds made available by this Act or subsequent Acts may be used by the Coast Guard to issue, implement, or enforce a regulation or to establish an interpretation or guideline under the Edible Oil Regulatory Reform Act (Public Law 104–55), or the amendments made by that Act [Pub.L. 104–55, Nov. 20, 1995, 109 Stat. 546, enacting this section and amending sections 2704 and 2716 of this title], that does not recognize and provide for, with respect to fats, oils, and greases (as described in that Act, or the amendments made by that Act) differences in—

"(1) physical, chemical, biological and other relevant properties; and

"(2) environmental effects.

"**(b)** Not later than March 31, 1999, the Secretary of Transportation shall issue regulations amending 33 CFR 154 to comply with the requirements of Public Law 104–55 [Edible Oil Regulatory Reform Act, Pub.L. 104–55, Nov. 20, 1995, 109 Stat. 546, enacting this section and amending sections 2704 and 2716 of this title]."

**Administrative Provision**

Pub.L. 105–276, Title III, Oct. 21, 1998, 112 Stat. 2499, provided in part that: "Not later than March 31, 1999, the Administrator of the Environmental Protection Agency shall issue regulations amending 40 C.F.R. 112 to comply with the requirements of the Edible Oil Regulatory Reform Act (Public Law 104–55). Such regulations shall differentiate between and establish separate classes for animal fats and oils and greases, and fish and marine mammal oils (as described in that Act), and other oils and greases, and shall apply standards to such different classes of fats and oils based on differences in the physical, chemical, biological, and other properties, and in the environmental effects, of the classes. None of the funds made available by this Act [Pub.L. 105–276, Oct. 21, 1998, 112 Stat. 2461, for classification of which, see Tables] or in subsequent Acts may be used by the Environmental Protection Agency to issue or to establish an interpretation or guidance relating to fats, oils, and greases (as described in Public Law 104–55) that does not comply with the requirements of the Edible Oil Regulatory Reform Act."

**Sense of Congress on the Implementation of Regulations Regarding Animal Fats and Vegetable Oils**

Pub.L. 104–324, Title XI, § 1130, Oct. 19, 1996, 110 Stat. 3985, provided that:

"**(a) Sense of Congress.**—It is the sense of Congress that, in an effort to reduce unnecessary regulatory burdens, a regulation issued or enforced and an interpretation or guideline established pursuant to Public Law 104–55 [Nov. 20, 1995, 109 Stat. 546] should in any manner possible recognize and provide for the differences in the physical, chemical, biological, and other properties, and in the environmental effects, of the classes of fats, oils, and greases described under that law.

"**(b) Report.**—Within 60 days after the date of enactment of this section [Oct. 19, 1996] and on January 1 of each year thereafter, the Secretary of Transportation shall submit a report to Congress on the extent to which the implementation by the United States Coast Guard of regulations issued or enforced, or interpretations or guidelines established, pursuant to Public Law 104–55, carry out the intent of Congress and recognize and provide for the differences in the physical, chemical, biological, and other properties, and in the environmental effects, of the classes of fats, oils, and greases described under that law."

## SUBCHAPTER II—PRINCE WILLIAM SOUND PROVISIONS

### § 2731. Oil Spill Recovery Institute

**[OPA § 5001]**

**(a) Establishment of Institute**

The Secretary of Commerce shall provide for the establishment of a Prince William Sound Oil Spill Recovery Institute (hereinafter in this section referred to as the "Institute") through the Prince William Sound Science and Technology Institute located in Cordova, Alaska.

**(b) Functions**

The Institute shall conduct research and carry out educational and demonstration projects designed to—

(1) identify and develop the best available techniques, equipment, and materials for dealing with oil spills in the arctic and subarctic marine environment; and

(2) complement Federal and State damage assessment efforts and determine, document, assess, and understand the long-range effects of Arctic or Subarctic oil spills on the natural resources of Prince William Sound and its adjacent waters (as generally depicted on the map entitled "EXXON VALDEZ oil spill dated March 1990"), and the environment, the economy, and the lifestyle and well-being of the people who are dependent on them, except that the Institute shall not conduct studies or make recommendations on any matter which is not directly related to Arctic or Subarctic oil spills or the effects thereof.

**(c) Advisory board**

**(1) In general**

The policies of the Institute shall be determined by an advisory board, composed of 16 members appointed as follows:

(A) One representative appointed by each of the Commissioners of Fish and Game, Environmental Conservation, and Natural Resources of the State of Alaska, all of whom shall be State employees.

(B) One representative appointed by each of the Secretaries of Commerce, the Interior, and Transportation, who shall be Federal employees.

(C) Two representatives from the fishing industry appointed by the Governor of the State of Alaska from among residents of communities in Alaska that were affected by the EXXON VALDEZ oil spill, who shall serve terms of 2 years each. Interested organizations from within the fishing industry may submit the names of qualified individuals for consideration by the Governor.

(D) Two Alaska Natives who represent Native entities affected by the EXXON VALDEZ oil spill, at least one of whom represents an entity located in Prince William Sound, appointed by the Governor of Alaska from a list of 4 qualified individuals submitted by the Alaska Federation of Natives, who shall serve terms of 2 years each.

(E) Two representatives from the oil and gas industry to be appointed by the Governor of the State of Alaska who shall serve terms of 2 years each. Interested organizations from within the oil and gas industry may submit the names of qualified individuals for consideration by the Governor.

(F) Two at-large representatives from among residents of communities in Alaska that were affected by the EXXON VALDEZ oil spill who are knowledgeable about the marine environment and wildlife within Prince William Sound, and who shall serve terms of 2 years each, appointed by the remaining members of the Advisory Board. Interested parties may submit the names of qualified individuals for consideration by the Advisory Board.

(G) One nonvoting representative of the Institute of Marine Science.

(H) One nonvoting representative appointed by the Prince William Sound Science and Technology Institute.

**(2) Chairman**

The representative of the Secretary of Commerce shall serve as Chairman of the Advisory Board.

**(3) Policies**

Policies determined by the Advisory Board under this subsection shall include policies for the conduct and support, through contracts and grants awarded on a nationally competitive basis, of research, projects, and studies to be supported by the Institute in accordance with the purposes of this section.

**(4) Scientific review**

The Advisory Board may request a scientific review of the research program every five years by the National Academy of Sciences which shall perform the review, if requested, as part of its responsibilities under section 2761(b)(2) of this title.

**(d) Scientific and technical committee**

(1) **In general**

The Advisory Board shall establish a scientific and technical committee, composed of specialists in matters relating to oil spill containment and cleanup technology, arctic and subarctic marine ecology, and the living resources and socioeconomics of Prince William Sound and its adjacent waters, from the University of Alaska, the Institute of Marine Science, the Prince William Sound Science and Technology Institute, and elsewhere in the academic community.

(2) **Functions**

The Scientific and Technical Committee shall provide such advice to the Advisory Board as the Advisory Board shall request, including recommendations regarding the conduct and support of research, projects, and studies in accordance with the purposes of this section. The Advisory Board shall not request, and the Committee shall not provide, any advice which is not directly related to Arctic or Subarctic oil spills or the effects thereof.

(e) **Director**

The Institute shall be administered by a Director appointed by the Advisory Board. The Prince William Sound Science and Technology Institute and the Scientific and Technical Committee may each submit independent recommendations for the Advisory Board's consideration for appointment as Director. The Director may hire such staff and incur such expenses on behalf of the Institute as are authorized by the Advisory Board.

(f) **Evaluation**

The Secretary of Commerce may conduct an ongoing evaluation of the activities of the Institute to ensure that funds received by the Institute are used in a manner consistent with this section.

(g) **Audit**

The Comptroller General of the United States, and any of his or her duly authorized representatives, shall have access, for purposes of audit and examination, to any books, documents, papers, and records of the Institute and its administering agency that are pertinent to the funds received and expended by the Institute and its administering agency.

(h) **Status of employees**

Employees of the Institute shall not, by reason of such employment, be considered to be employees of the Federal Government for any purpose.

(i) **Termination**

The authorization in section 2736(b) of this title providing funding for the Institute shall terminate September 30, 2012.

(j) **Use of funds**

No funds made available to carry out this section may be used to initiate litigation. No funds made available to carry out this section may be used for the acquisition of real property (including buildings) or construction of any building. No more than 20 percent of funds made available to carry out this section may be used to lease necessary facilities and to administer the Institute. The Advisory Board may compensate its Federal representatives for their reasonable travel costs. None of the funds authorized by this section shall be used for any purpose other than the functions specified in subsection (b) of this section.

(k) **Research**

The Institute shall publish and make available to any person upon request the results of all research, educational, and demonstration projects conducted by the Institute. The Administrator shall provide a copy of all research, educational, and demonstration projects conducted by the Institute to the National Oceanic and Atmospheric Administration.

(*l*) **"Prince William Sound and its adjacent waters" defined**

In this section, the term "Prince William Sound and its adjacent waters" means such sound and waters as generally depicted on the map entitled "EXXON VALDEZ oil spill dated March 1990".

(Pub.L. 101–380, Title V, § 5001, Aug. 18, 1990, 104 Stat. 542; Pub.L. 104–324, Title XI, § 1102(a), Oct. 19, 1996, 110 Stat. 3964; Pub.L. 107–295, Title IV, § 427, Nov. 25, 2002, 116 Stat. 2127.)

**HISTORICAL AND STATUTORY NOTES**

**Termination of Advisory Boards**

Advisory boards established after Jan. 5, 1973, to terminate not later than the expiration of the 2-year period beginning on the date of their establishment, unless, in the case of a board established by the President or an officer of the Federal Government, such board is renewed by appropriate action prior to the expiration of such 2-year period, or in the case of a board established by Congress, its duration is otherwise provided for by law. See sections 3(2) and 14 of Pub.L. 92–463, Oct. 6, 1972, 86 Stat. 770, 776, set out in the Appendix to Title 5.

## § 2732. Terminal and tanker oversight and monitoring

**[OPA § 5002]**

(a) **Short title and findings**

(1) **Short title**

This section may be cited as the "Oil Terminal and Oil Tanker Environmental Oversight and Monitoring Act of 1990".

(2) **Findings**

The Congress finds that—

(A) the March 24, 1989, grounding and rupture of the fully loaded oil tanker, the EXXON VALDEZ, spilled 11 million gallons of crude oil in Prince William Sound, an environmentally sensitive area;

(B) many people believe that complacency on the part of the industry and government personnel responsible for monitoring the operation of the Valdez terminal and vessel traffic in Prince William Sound was one of the contributing factors to the EXXON VALDEZ oil spill;

(C) one way to combat this complacency is to involve local citizens in the process of preparing, adopting, and revising oil spill contingency plans;

(D) a mechanism should be established which fosters the long-term partnership of industry, government, and local communities in overseeing compliance with environmental concerns in the operation of crude oil terminals;

(E) such a mechanism presently exists at the Sullom Voe terminal in the Shetland Islands and this terminal should serve as a model for others;

(F) because of the effective partnership that has developed at Sullom Voe, Sullom Voe is considered the safest terminal in Europe;

(G) the present system of regulation and oversight of crude oil terminals in the United States has degenerated into a process of continual mistrust and confrontation;

(H) only when local citizens are involved in the process will the trust develop that is necessary to change the present system from confrontation to consensus;

(I) a pilot program patterned after Sullom Voe should be established in Alaska to further refine the concepts and relationships involved; and

(J) similar programs should eventually be established in other major crude oil terminals in the United States because the recent oil spills in Texas, Delaware, and Rhode Island indicate that the safe transportation of crude oil is a national problem.

**(b) Demonstration programs**

**(1) Establishment**

There are established 2 Oil Terminal and Oil Tanker Environmental Oversight and Monitoring Demonstration Programs (hereinafter referred to as "Programs") to be carried out in the State of Alaska.

**(2) Advisory function**

The function of these Programs shall be advisory only.

**(3) Purpose**

The Prince William Sound Program shall be responsible for environmental monitoring of the terminal facilities in Prince William Sound and the crude oil tankers operating in Prince William Sound. The Cook Inlet Program shall be responsible for environmental monitoring of the terminal facilities and crude oil tankers operating in Cook Inlet located South of the latitude at Point Possession and North of the latitude at Amatuli Island, including offshore facilities in Cook Inlet.

**(4) Suits barred**

No program, association, council, committee or other organization created by this section may sue any person or entity, public or private, concerning any matter arising under this section except for the performance of contracts.

**(c) Oil Terminal Facilities and Oil Tanker Operations Association**

**(1) Establishment**

There is established an Oil Terminal Facilities and Oil Tanker Operations Association (hereinafter in this section referred to as the "Association") for each of the Programs established under subsection (b) of this section.

**(2) Membership**

Each Association shall be comprised of 4 individuals as follows:

(A) One individual shall be designated by the owners and operators of the terminal facilities and shall represent those owners and operators.

(B) One individual shall be designated by the owners and operators of the crude oil tankers calling at the terminal facilities and shall represent those owners and operators.

(C) One individual shall be an employee of the State of Alaska, shall be designated by the Governor of the State of Alaska, and shall represent the State government.

(D) One individual shall be an employee of the Federal Government, shall be designated by the President, and shall represent the Federal Government.

**(3) Responsibilities**

Each Association shall be responsible for reviewing policies relating to the operation and maintenance of the oil terminal facilities and crude oil tankers which affect or may affect the environment in the vicinity of their respective terminals. Each Association shall provide a forum among the owners and operators of the terminal facilities, the owners and operators of crude oil tankers calling at those facilities, the United States, and the State of Alaska to discuss and to make recommendations concerning all permits, plans, and site-specific regulations governing the activities and actions of the terminal facilities which affect or may affect the environment in the vicinity of the terminal facilities and of crude oil tankers calling at those facilities.

**(4) Designation of existing organization**

The Secretary may designate an existing nonprofit organization as an Association under this subsection if the organization is organized to meet the purposes of this section and consists of at least the individuals listed in paragraph (2).

**(d) Regional Citizens' Advisory Councils**

**(1) Membership**

There is established a Regional Citizens' Advisory Council (hereinafter in this section referred to as the "Council") for each of the programs established by subsection (b) of this section.

**(2) Membership**

Each Council shall be composed of voting members and nonvoting members, as follows:

**(A) Voting members**

Voting members shall be Alaska residents and, except as provided in clause (vii) of this paragraph, shall be appointed by the Governor of the State of Alaska from a list of nominees provided by each of the following interests, with one representative appointed to represent each of the following interests, taking into consideration the need for regional balance on the Council:

**(i)** Local commercial fishing industry organizations, the members of which depend on the fisheries resources of the waters in the vicinity of the terminal facilities.

**(ii)** Aquaculture associations in the vicinity of the terminal facilities.

**(iii)** Alaska Native Corporations and other Alaska Native organizations the members of which reside in the vicinity of the terminal facilities.

**(iv)** Environmental organizations the members of which reside in the vicinity of the terminal facilities.

**(v)** Recreational organizations the members of which reside in or use the vicinity of the terminal facilities.

**(vi)** The Alaska State Chamber of Commerce, to represent the locally based tourist industry.

**(vii)(I)** For the Prince William Sound Terminal Facilities Council, one representative selected by each of the following municipalities: Cordova, Whittier, Seward, Valdez, Kodiak, the Kodiak Island Borough, and the Kenai Peninsula Borough.

**(II)** For the Cook Inlet Terminal Facilities Council, one representative selected by each of the following municipalities: Homer, Seldovia, Anchorage, Kenai, Kodiak, the Kodiak Island Borough, and the Kenai Peninsula Borough.

**(B) Nonvoting members**

One ex-officio, nonvoting representative shall be designated by, and represent, each of the following:

**(i)** The Environmental Protection Agency.

**(ii)** The Coast Guard.

**(iii)** The National Oceanic and Atmospheric Administration.

**(iv)** The United States Forest Service.

**(v)** The Bureau of Land Management.

**(vi)** The Alaska Department of Environmental Conservation.

**(vii)** The Alaska Department of Fish and Game.

**(viii)** The Alaska Department of Natural Resources.

**(ix)** The Division of Emergency Services, Alaska Department of Military and Veterans Affairs.

**(3) Terms**

**(A) Duration of Councils**

The term of the Councils shall continue throughout the life of the operation of the Trans-Alaska Pipeline System and so long as oil is transported to or from Cook Inlet.

**(B) Three years**

The voting members of each Council shall be appointed for a term of 3 years except as provided for in subparagraph (C).

**(C) Initial appointments**

The terms of the first appointments shall be as follows:

**(i)** For the appointments by the Governor of the State of Alaska, one-third shall serve for 3 years, one-third shall serve for 2 years, and one-third shall serve for one year.

**(ii)** For the representatives of municipalities required by subsection (d)(2)(A)(vii) of this section, a drawing of lots among the appointees shall determine that one-third of that group serves for 3 years, one-third serves for 2 years, and the remainder serves for 1 year.

**(4) Self-governing**

Each Council shall elect its own chairperson, select its own staff, and make policies with regard to its internal operating procedures. After the initial organizational meeting called by the Secretary under subsection (i) of this section, each Council shall be self-governing.

**(5) Dual membership and conflicts of interest prohibited**

(A) No individual selected as a member of the Council shall serve on the Association.

(B) No individual selected as a voting member of the Council shall be engaged in any activity which might conflict with such individual carrying out his functions as a member thereof.

**(6) Duties**

Each Council shall—

(A) provide advice and recommendations to the Association on policies, permits, and site-specific regulations relating to the operation and maintenance of terminal facilities and crude oil tankers which affect or may affect the environment in the vicinity of the terminal facilities;

(B) monitor through the committee established under subsection (e) of this section, the environmental impacts of the operation of the terminal facilities and crude oil tankers;

(C) monitor those aspects of terminal facilities' and crude oil tankers' operations and maintenance which affect or may affect the environment in the vicinity of the terminal facilities;

(D) review through the committee established under subsection (f) of this section, the adequacy of oil spill prevention and contingency plans for the terminal facilities and the adequacy of oil spill prevention and contingency plans for crude oil tankers, operating in Prince William Sound or in Cook Inlet;

(E) provide advice and recommendations to the Association on port operations, policies and practices;

(F) recommend to the Association—

(i) standards and stipulations for permits and site-specific regulations intended to minimize the impact of the terminal facilities' and crude oil tankers' operations in the vicinity of the terminal facilities;

(ii) modifications of terminal facility operations and maintenance intended to minimize the risk and mitigate the impact of terminal facilities, operations in the vicinity of the terminal facilities and to minimize the risk of oil spills;

(iii) modifications of crude oil tanker operations and maintenance in Prince William Sound and Cook Inlet intended to minimize the risk and mitigate the impact of oil spills; and

(iv) modifications to the oil spill prevention and contingency plans for terminal facilities and for crude oil tankers in Prince William Sound and Cook Inlet intended to enhance the ability to prevent and respond to an oil spill; and

(G) create additional committees of the Council as necessary to carry out the above functions, including a scientific and technical advisory committee to the Prince William Sound Council.

**(7) No estoppel**

No Council shall be held liable under State or Federal law for costs or damages as a result of rendering advice under this section. Nor shall any advice given by a voting member of a Council, or program representative or agent, be grounds for estopping the interests represented by the voting Council members from seeking damages or other appropriate relief.

**(8) Scientific work**

In carrying out its research, development and monitoring functions, each Council is authorized to conduct its own scientific research and shall review the scientific work undertaken by or on behalf of the terminal operators or crude oil tanker operators as a result of a legal requirement to undertake that work. Each Council shall also review the relevant scientific work undertaken by or on behalf of any government entity relating to the terminal facilities or crude oil tankers. To the extent possible, to avoid unnecessary duplication, each Council shall coordinate its independent scientific work with the scientific work performed by or on behalf of the terminal operators and with the scientific work performed by or on behalf of the operators of the crude oil tankers.

**(e) Committee for Terminal and Oil Tanker Operations and Environmental Monitoring**

**(1) Monitoring Committee**

Each Council shall establish standing Terminal and Oil Tanker Operations and Environmental Monitoring Committee (hereinafter in this section referred to as the "Monitoring Committee") to devise and manage a comprehensive program of monitoring the environmental impacts of the operations of terminal facilities and of crude oil tankers while operating in Prince William Sound and Cook Inlet. The membership of the Monitoring Committee shall be made up of members of the Council, citizens, and recognized scientific experts selected by the Council.

**(2) Duties**

In fulfilling its responsibilities, the Monitoring Committee shall—

(A) advise the Council on a monitoring strategy that will permit early detection of environmental impacts of terminal facility operations and crude oil tanker operations while in Prince William Sound and Cook Inlet;

(B) develop monitoring programs and make recommendations to the Council on the implementation of those programs;

(C) at its discretion, select and contract with universities and other scientific institutions to carry out specific monitoring projects authorized by the Council pursuant to an approved monitoring strategy;

(D) complete any other tasks assigned by the Council; and

(E) provide written reports to the Council which interpret and assess the results of all monitoring programs.

**(f) Committee for Oil Spill Prevention, Safety, and Emergency Response**

**(1) Technical Oil Spill Committee**

Each Council shall establish a standing technical committee (hereinafter referred to as "Oil Spill Committee") to review and assess measures designed to prevent oil spills and the planning and preparedness for responding to, containing, cleaning up, and mitigating impacts of oil spills. The membership of the Oil Spill Committee shall be made up of members of the Council, citizens, and recognized technical experts selected by the Council.

**(2) Duties**

In fulfilling its responsibilities, the Oil Spill Committee shall—

(A) periodically review the respective oil spill prevention and contingency plans for the terminal facilities and for the crude oil tankers while in Prince William Sound or Cook Inlet, in light of new technological developments and changed circumstances;

(B) monitor periodic drills and testing of the oil spill contingency plans for the terminal facilities and for crude oil tankers while in Prince William Sound and Cook Inlet;

(C) study wind and water currents and other environmental factors in the vicinity of the terminal facilities which may affect the ability to prevent, respond to, contain, and clean up an oil spill;

(D) identify highly sensitive areas which may require specific protective measures in the event of a spill in Prince William Sound or Cook Inlet;

(E) monitor developments in oil spill prevention, containment, response, and cleanup technology;

(F) periodically review port organization, operations, incidents, and the adequacy and maintenance of vessel traffic service systems designed to assure safe transit of crude oil tankers pertinent to terminal operations;

(G) periodically review the standards for tankers bound for, loading at, exiting from, or otherwise using the terminal facilities;

(H) complete any other tasks assigned by the Council; and

(I) provide written reports to the Council outlining its findings and recommendations.

**(g) Agency cooperation**

On and after the expiration of the 180–day period following August 18, 1990, each Federal department, agency, or other instrumentality shall, with respect to all permits, site-specific regulations, and other matters governing the activities and actions of the terminal facilities which affect or may affect the vicinity of the terminal facilities, consult with the appropriate Council prior to taking substantive action with respect to the permit, site-specific regulation, or other matter. This consultation shall be carried out with a view to enabling the appropriate Association and Council to review the permit, site-specific regulation, or other matters and make appropriate recommendations regarding operations, policy or agency actions. Prior consultation shall not be required if an authorized Federal agency representative reasonably believes that an emergency exists requiring action without delay.

**(h) Recommendations of Council**

In the event that the Association does not adopt, or significantly modifies before adoption, any recommendation of the Council made pursuant to the authority granted to the Council in subsection (d) of this section, the Association shall provide to the Council, in writing, within 5 days of its decision, notice of its decision and a written statement of reasons for its rejection or significant modification of the recommendation.

**(i) Administrative actions**

Appointments, designations, and selections of individuals to serve as members of the Associations and Councils under this section shall be submitted to the Secretary prior to the expiration of the 120–day period following August 18, 1990. On or before the expiration of the 180–day period following August 18, 1990, the Secretary shall call an initial meeting of each Association and Council for organizational purposes.

**(j) Location and compensation**

**(1) Location**

Each Association and Council established by this section shall be located in the State of Alaska.

**(2) Compensation**

No member of an Association or Council shall be compensated for the member's services as a member of the Association or Council, but shall be allowed travel expenses, including per diem in lieu of subsistence, at a rate established by the Association or Council not to exceed the rates authorized for employees of agencies under sections 5702 and 5703 of Title 5. However, each Council may enter into contracts to provide compensation and expenses to members of the committees created under subsections (d), (e), and (f) of this section.

**(k) Funding**

**(1) Requirement**

Approval of the contingency plans required of owners and operators of the Cook Inlet and Prince William Sound terminal facilities and crude oil tankers while operating in Alaskan waters in commerce with those terminal facilities shall be effective only so long as the respective Association and Council for a facility are funded pursuant to paragraph (2).

**(2) Prince William Sound program**

The owners or operators of terminal facilities or crude oil tankers operating in Prince William Sound shall provide, on an annual basis, an aggregate amount of not more than $2,000,000, as determined by the Secretary. Such amount—

**(A)** shall provide for the establishment and operation on the environmental oversight and monitoring program in Prince William Sound;

**(B)** shall be adjusted annually by the Anchorage Consumer Price Index; and

**(C)** may be adjusted periodically upon the mutual consent of the owners or operators of terminal facilities or crude oil tankers operating in Prince William Sound and the Prince William Sound terminal facilities Council.

**(3) Cook Inlet program**

The owners or operators of terminal facilities, offshore facilities, or crude oil tankers operating in Cook Inlet shall provide, on an annual basis, an aggregate amount of not more than $1,000,000, as determined by the Secretary. Such amount—

**(A)** shall provide for the establishment and operation of the environmental oversight and monitoring program in Cook Inlet;

**(B)** shall be adjusted annually by the Anchorage Consumer Price Index; and

**(C)** may be adjusted periodically upon the mutual consent of the owners or operators of terminal facilities, offshore facilities, or crude oil tankers operating in Cook Inlet and the Cook Inlet Council.

**(*l*) Reports**

**(1) Associations and Councils**

Prior to the expiration of the 36-month period following August 18, 1990, each Association and Council established by this section shall report to the President and the Congress concerning its activities under this section, together with its recommendations.

**(2) GAO**

Prior to the expiration of the 36-month period following August 18, 1990, the General Accounting Office shall report to the President and the Congress as to the handling of funds, including donated funds, by the entities carrying out the programs under this section, and the effectiveness of the demonstration programs carried out under this section, together with its recommendations.

**(m) Definitions**

As used in this section, the term—

(1) "terminal facilities" means—

**(A)** in the case of the Prince William Sound Program, the entire oil terminal complex located in Valdez, Alaska, consisting of approximately 1,000 acres including all buildings, docks (except docks owned by the City of Valdez if those docks are not used for loading of crude oil), pipes, piping, roads, ponds, tanks, crude oil tankers only while at the terminal dock, tanker escorts owned or operated by the operator of the terminal, vehicles, and other facilities associated with, and necessary for, assisting tanker movement of crude oil into and out of the oil terminal complex; and

**(B)** in the case of the Cook Inlet Program, the entire oil terminal complex including all buildings, docks, pipes, piping, roads, ponds, tanks, vessels, vehicles, crude oil tankers only while at the terminal dock, tanker escorts owned or operated by the operator of the terminal, emergency spill response vessels owned or operated by the operator of the terminal, and other facilities associated with, and necessary for, assisting tanker movement of crude oil into and out of the oil terminal complex;

(2) "crude oil tanker" means a tanker (as that term is defined under section 2101 of Title 46)—

**(A)** in the case of the Prince William Sound Program, calling at the terminal facilities for the purpose of receiving and transporting oil to refineries, operating north of Middleston Island and bound for or exiting from Prince William Sound; and

**(B)** in the case of the Cook Inlet Program, calling at the terminal facilities for the purpose of receiving and transporting oil to refineries and operating in Cook Inlet and the Gulf of Alaska north of Amatuli Island, including tankers transiting to Cook Inlet from Prince William Sound;

(3) "vicinity of the terminal facilities" means that geographical area surrounding the environment of terminal facilities which is directly affected or may

be directly affected by the operation of the terminal facilities; and

(4) "Secretary" means the Secretary of Transportation.

### (n) Savings clause

#### (1) Regulatory authority

Nothing in this section shall be construed as modifying, repealing, superseding, or preempting any municipal, State or Federal law or regulation, or in any way affecting litigation arising from oil spills or the rights and responsibilities of the United States or the State of Alaska, or municipalities thereof, to preserve and protect the environment through regulation of land, air, and water uses, of safety, and of related development. The monitoring provided for by this section shall be designed to help assure compliance with applicable laws and regulations and shall only extend to activities—

(A) that would affect or have the potential to affect the vicinity of the terminal facilities and the area of crude oil tanker operations included in the Programs; and

(B) are subject to the United States or State of Alaska, or municipality thereof, law, regulation, or other legal requirement.

#### (2) Recommendations

This subsection is not intended to prevent the Association or Council from recommending to appropriate authorities that existing legal requirements should be modified or that new legal requirements should be adopted.

### (*o*) Alternative voluntary advisory group in lieu of Council

The requirements of subsections (c) through (*l*) of this section, as such subsections apply respectively to the Prince William Sound Program and the Cook Inlet Program, are deemed to have been satisfied so long as the following conditions are met:

#### (1) Prince William Sound

With respect to the Prince William Sound Program, the Alyeska Pipeline Service Company or any of its owner companies enters into a contract for the duration of the operation of the Trans–Alaska Pipeline System with the Alyeska Citizens Advisory Committee in existence on August 18, 1990, or a successor organization, to fund that Committee or organization on an annual basis in the amount provided for by subsection (k)(2)(A) of this section and the President annually certifies that the Committee or organization fosters the general goals and purposes of this section and is broadly representative of the communities and interests in the vicinity of the terminal facilities and Prince William Sound.

#### (2) Cook Inlet

With respect to the Cook Inlet Program, the terminal facilities, offshore facilities, or crude oil tanker owners and operators enter into a contract with a voluntary advisory organization to fund that organization on an annual basis and the President annually certifies that the organization fosters the general goals and purposes of this section and is broadly representative of the communities and interests in the vicinity of the terminal facilities and Cook Inlet.

(Pub.L. 101–380, Title V, § 5002, Aug. 18, 1990, 104 Stat. 544.)

## HISTORICAL AND STATUTORY NOTES

**Delegation of Functions**

The function vested in the President by subsec. (c)(2)(D) of this section, respecting the designating of an employee of the Federal Government who shall represent the Federal Government on the Oil Terminal Facilities and Oil Tanker Operations Associations, is delegated to the Secretary of Transportation, see Ex. Ord. No. 12777, Oct. 18, 1991, 56 F.R. 54757, set out as a note under section 1321 of this title.

The functions vested in the President by subsec. (*o*) of this section, respecting the annual certification of alternative voluntary advisory groups, are delegated to the Secretary of Transportation, see Ex. Ord. No. 12777, Oct. 18, 1991, 56 F.R. 54757, set out as a note under section 1321 of this title.

## CERTIFICATION OF PRESIDENT

**Mar. 21, 1991, 56 F.R. 12439**

PRINCE WILLIAM SOUND REGIONAL CITIZENS ADVISORY COMMITTEE

By the authority vested in me as President by the Constitution and the laws of the United States of America, including section 5002(*o*)(1) of the Oil Pollution Act of 1990 (Public Law 101–380, 104 Stat. 552) [subsec. (*o*)(1) of this section], I hereby certify for the year 1991 the following:

(1) that the Prince William Sound Regional Citizens Advisory Committee fosters the general goals and purposes of section 5002 of the Oil Pollution Act of 1990 [this section] for the year 1991; and

(2) that the Prince William Sound Regional Citizens Advisory Committee is broadly representative of the communities and interests in the vicinity of the terminal facilities and Prince William Sound.

This certification shall be published in the **Federal Register.**

GEORGE BUSH

**Aug. 6, 1991, 56 F.R. 37819**

By the authority vested in me as President by the Constitution and the laws of the United States of America, including section 5002(*o*)(2) of the Oil Pollution Act of 1990 [subsec. (*o*)(2) of this section], I hereby certify for the year 1991 the following:

(1) that the Cook Inlet Regional Citizens Advisory Council has met the general goals and purposes of section 5002 of the Oil Pollution Act of 1990 [this section] for the year 1991; and

(2) that the Cook Inlet Regional Citizens Advisory Council is broadly representative of the communities and interests in the vicinity of the terminal facilities and offshore facilities in Cook Inlet.

This certification shall be published in the **Federal Register.**

GEORGE BUSH

## § 2733. Bligh Reef light

**[OPA § 5003]**

The Secretary of Transportation shall within one year after August 18, 1990, install and ensure operation of an automated navigation light on or adjacent to Bligh Reef in Prince William Sound, Alaska, of sufficient power and height to provide long-range warning of the location of Bligh Reef.

(Pub.L. 101–380, Title V, § 5003, Aug. 18, 1990, 104 Stat. 553.)

## § 2734. Vessel traffic service system

**[OPA § 5004]**

The Secretary of Transportation shall within one year after August 18, 1990—

(1) acquire, install, and operate such additional equipment (which may consist of radar, closed circuit television, satellite tracking systems, or other shipboard dependent surveillance), train and locate such personnel, and issue such final regulations as are necessary to increase the range of the existing VTS system in the Port of Valdez, Alaska, sufficiently to track the locations and movements of tank vessels carrying oil from the Trans-Alaska Pipeline when such vessels are transiting Prince William Sound, Alaska, and to sound an audible alarm when such tankers depart from designated navigation routes; and

(2) submit to the Committee on Commerce, Science, and Transportation of the Senate and the Committee on Transportation and Infrastructure of the House of Representatives a report on the feasibility and desirability of instituting positive control of tank vessel movements in Prince William Sound by Coast Guard personnel using the Port of Valdez, Alaska, VTS system, as modified pursuant to paragraph (1).

(Pub.L. 101–380, Title V, § 5004, Aug. 18, 1990, 104 Stat. 553; Pub.L. 107–295, Title IV, § 408(b)(2), Nov. 25, 2002, 116 Stat. 2117.)

### HISTORICAL AND STATUTORY NOTES

**Abolition of House Committee on Merchant Marine and Fisheries**

Committee on Merchant Marine and Fisheries of House of Representatives abolished and any reference in any provision of law enacted before Jan. 4, 1995, to the Committee on Merchant Marine and Fisheries of the House of Representatives treated as referring to the Committee on Agriculture of the House of Representatives, in the case of a provision of law relating to inspection of seafood or seafood products, the Committee on National Security of the House of Representatives, in the case of a provision of law relating to interoceanic canals, the Merchant Marine Academy and State Maritime Academies, or national security aspects of merchant marine, the Committee on Resources of the House of Representatives, in the case of a provision of law relating to fisheries, wildlife, international fishing agreements marine affairs (including coastal zone management) except for measures relating to oil and other pollution of navigable waters, or oceanography, the Committee on Science of the House of Representatives, in the case of a provision of law relating to marine research, and the Committee on Transportation and Infrastructure of the House of Representatives, in the case of a provision of law relating to a matter other than a matter described above, see section 1(b)(3) of Pub.L. 104–14, set out as a note preceding section 21 of Title 2, The Congress.

## § 2735. Equipment and personnel requirements under tank vessel and facility response plans

**[OPA § 5005]**

### (a) In general

In addition to the requirements for response plans for vessels established by section 1321(j) of this title a response plan for a tanker loading cargo at a facility permitted under the Trans-Alaska Pipeline Authorization Act (43 U.S.C. 1651 et seq.), and a response plan for such a facility, shall provide for—

(1) prepositioned oil spill containment and removal equipment in communities and other strategic locations within the geographic boundaries of Prince William Sound, including escort vessels with skimming capability; barges to receive recovered oil; heavy duty sea boom, pumping, transferring, and lightering equipment; and other appropriate removal equipment for the protection of the environment, including fish hatcheries;

(2) the establishment of an oil spill removal organization at appropriate locations in Prince William Sound, consisting of trained personnel in sufficient numbers to immediately remove, to the maximum extent practicable, a worst case discharge or a discharge of 200,000 barrels of oil, whichever is greater;

(3) training in oil removal techniques for local residents and individuals engaged in the cultivation or production of fish or fish products in Prince William Sound;

(4) practice exercises not less than 2 times per year which test the capacity of the equipment and personnel required under this paragraph; and

(5) periodic testing and certification of equipment required under this paragraph, as required by the Secretary.

**(b) Definitions**

In this section—

(1) the term "Prince William Sound" means all State and Federal waters within Prince William Sound, Alaska, including the approach to Hinchenbrook Entrance out to and encompassing Seal Rocks; and

(2) the term "worst case discharge" means—

(A) in the case of a vessel, a discharge in adverse weather conditions of its entire cargo; and

(B) in the case of a facility, the largest foreseeable discharge in adverse weather conditions.

(Pub.L. 101–380, Title V, § 5005, Aug. 18, 1990, 104 Stat. 553; Pub.L. 102–388, Title III, § 354, Oct. 6, 1992, 106 Stat. 1555.)

### HISTORICAL AND STATUTORY NOTES

**References in Text**

Reference in subsec. (a) to the amendment of section 1321(j) of this title "by this Act" refers to the amendment by Pub.L. 101–380, Aug. 18, 1990, 104 Stat. 484.

The Trans-Alaska Pipeline Authorization Act, referred to in subsec. (a), is title II of Pub.L. 93–153, Nov. 16, 1973, 87 Stat. 584, which is classified to chapter 34 (§ 1651 et seq.) of Title 43, Public Lands. For complete classification of this Act to the Code, see Short Title note set out under section 1651 of Title 43 and Tables.

## § 2736. Funding

[OPA § 5006]

**(a) Sections 2731, 2733, and 2734**

Amounts in the Fund shall be available, without further appropriations and without fiscal year limitation, to carry out section 2731 of this title in the amount as determined in subsection (b) of this section, and to carry out sections 2733 and 2734 of this title, in an amount not to exceed $5,000,000.

**(b) Use of interest only**

The amount of funding to be made available annually to carry out section 2731 of this title shall be the interest produced by the Fund's investment of the $22,500,000 remaining funding authorized for the Prince William Sound Oil Spill Recovery Institute and currently deposited in the Fund and invested by the Secretary of the Treasury in income producing securities along with other funds comprising the Fund. The National Pollution Funds Center shall transfer all such accrued interest, including the interest earned from the date funds in the Trans-Alaska Liability Pipeline Fund were transferred into the Oil Spill Liability Trust Fund pursuant to section 8102(a)(2)(B)(ii), to the Prince William Sound Oil Spill Recovery Institute annually, beginning 60 days after October 19, 1996.

**(c) [1] Use for section 2712**

Beginning with the eleventh year following October 19, 1996, the funding authorized for the Prince William Sound Oil Spill Recovery Institute and deposited in the Fund shall thereafter be made available for purposes of section 2712 of this title in Alaska.

**(c) [1] Section 2738**

Amounts in the Fund shall be available, without further appropriation and without fiscal year limitation, to carry out section 2738(b) of this title, in an amount not to exceed $5,000,000 of which up to 3,000,000 may be used for the lease payment to the Alaska SeaLife Center under section 2738(b)(2) of this title: *Provided*, That the entire amount is designated by the Congress as an emergency requirement pursuant to section 251(b)(2)(A) of the Balanced Budget and Emergency Deficit Control Act of 1985, as amended [2 U.S.C.A. § 901(b)(2)(A)]: *Provided further*, That the entire amount shall be available only to the extent an official budget request that includes designation of the entire amount of the request as an emergency requirement as defined in the Balanced Budget and Emergency Deficit Control Act of 1985, as amended, is transmitted by the President to the Congress.

(Pub.L. 101–380, Title V, § 5006, Aug. 18, 1990, 104 Stat. 554; Pub.L. 104–324, Title XI, § 1102(b), Oct. 19, 1996, 110 Stat. 3965; Pub.L. 106–246, Div. B, Title II, § 2204(2), July 13, 2000, 114 Stat. 547; Pub.L. 106–554, § 1(a)(4) [Div. B, Title I, § 144(c)(1)(C)], Dec. 21, 2000, 114 Stat. 2763, 2763A–239.)

[1] So in original. Two subsecs. (c) have been enacted.

### HISTORICAL AND STATUTORY NOTES

**References in Text**

Section 8102(a)(2)(B)(ii), referred to in subsec. (b), is section 8102(a)(2)(B)(ii) of Pub.L. 101–380, Aug. 18, 1990, 104 Stat. 565, which is set out as a note under section 1653 of Title 43, Public Lands.

The Balanced Budget and Emergency Deficit Control Act of 1985, referred to in subsec. (c), also known as the BBEDCA and the Gramm-Rudman-Hollings Act, is Pub.L. 99–177, Title II, Dec. 12, 1985, 99 Stat. 1038, as amended, which is classified generally to subchapter I of chapter 20 of Title 2 (2 U.S.C.A. § 901 et seq.). For complete classification of this Act to the Code, see Tables.

## § 2737. Limitation

[OPA § 5007]

Notwithstanding any other law, tank vessels that have spilled more than 1,000,000 gallons of oil into the marine environment after March 22, 1989, are prohibited from operating on the navigable waters of Prince William Sound, Alaska.

(Pub.L. 101–380, Title V, § 5007, Aug. 18, 1990, 104 Stat. 554.)

## § 2738. North Pacific Marine Research Institute

[OPA § 5008]

### (a) Institute established

The Secretary of Commerce shall establish a North Pacific Marine Research Institute (hereafter in this section referred to as the "Institute") to be administered at the Alaska SeaLife Center by the North Pacific Research Board.

### (b) Functions

The Institute shall—

(1) conduct research and carry out education and demonstration projects on or relating to the North Pacific marine ecosystem with particular emphasis on marine mammal, sea bird, fish, and shellfish populations in the Bering Sea and Gulf of Alaska including populations located in or near Kenai Fjords National Park and the Alaska Maritime National Wildlife Refuge; and

(2) lease, maintain, operate, and upgrade the necessary research equipment and related facilities necessary to conduct such research at the Alaska SeaLife Center.

### (c) Evaluation and audit

The Secretary of Commerce may periodically evaluate the activities of the Institute to ensure that funds received by the Institute are used in a manner consistent with this section. The Federal Advisory Committee Act (5 U.S.C. App. 2) shall not apply to the Institute.

### (d) Status of employees

Employees of the Institute shall not, by reason of such employment, be considered to be employees of the Federal Government for any purpose.

### (e) Use of funds

No funds made available to carry out this section may be used to initiate litigation, or for the acquisition of real property (other than facilities leased at the Alaska SeaLife Center). No more than 10 percent of the funds made available to carry out subsection (b)(1) of this section may be used to administer the Institute. The administrative funds of the Institute and the administrative funds of the North Pacific Research Board created under Public Law 105–83 may be used to jointly administer such programs at the discretion of the North Pacific Research Board.

### (f) Availability of research

The Institute shall publish and make available to any person on request the results of all research, educational, and demonstration projects conducted by the Institute. The Institute shall provide a copy of all research, educational, and demonstration projects conducted by the Institute to the National Park Service, the United States Fish and Wildlife Service, and the National Oceanic and Atmospheric Administration.

(Pub.L. 101–380, Title V, § 5008, as added Pub.L. 106–246, Div. B, Title II, § 2204(1), July 13, 2000, 114 Stat. 546; Pub.L. 106–554, § 1(a)(4) [Div. B, Title I, § 144(c)(1)(A), (B)], Dec. 21, 2000, 114 Stat. 2763, 2763A–239.)

#### HISTORICAL AND STATUTORY NOTES

**References in Text**

The Federal Advisory Committee Act, referred to in subsec. (c), is Pub.L. 92–463, Oct. 6, 1972, 86 Stat. 770, as amended, which is set out as Appendix 2 to Title 5.

Pub.L. 105–83, referred to in subsec. (e), is Department of the Interior and Related Agencies Appropriations Act, 1998, Pub.L. 105–83, Nov. 14, 1997, 111 Stat. 1543. See Tables for complete classification.

# SUBCHAPTER III—MISCELLANEOUS

## § 2751. Savings provisions

[OPA § 6001]

### (a) Cross-references

A reference to a law replaced by this Act, including a reference in a regulation, order, or other law, is deemed to refer to the corresponding provision of this Act.

### (b) Continuation of regulations

An order, rule, or regulation in effect under a law replaced by this Act continues in effect under the corresponding provision of this Act until repealed, amended, or superseded.

### (c) Rule of construction

An inference of legislative construction shall not be drawn by reason of the caption or catch line of a provision enacted by this Act.

### (d) Actions and rights

Nothing in this Act shall apply to any rights and duties that matured, penalties that were incurred, and proceedings that were begun before August 18, 1990, except as provided by this section, and shall be adjudicated pursuant to the law applicable on the date prior to August 18, 1990.

### (e) Admiralty and maritime law

Except as otherwise provided in this Act, this Act does not affect—

(1) admiralty and maritime law; or

(2) the jurisdiction of the district courts of the United States with respect to civil actions under admiralty and maritime jurisdiction, saving to suit-

ors in all cases all other remedies to which they are otherwise entitled.

(Pub.L. 101–380, Title VI, § 6001, Aug. 18, 1990, 104 Stat. 554.)

### HISTORICAL AND STATUTORY NOTES

**References in Text**

This Act, referred to in text, is Pub.L. 101–380, Aug. 18, 1990, 104 Stat. 484, as amended, known as the Oil Pollution Act of 1990, which is classified principally to this chapter. For complete classification to the Code, see Short Title note under 33 U.S.C.A. § 2701 and Tables.

## § 2752. Annual appropriations

**[OPA § 6002]**

**(a) Required**

Except as provided in subsection (b) of this section, amounts in the Fund shall be available only as provided in annual appropriation Acts.

**(b) Exceptions**

Subsection (a) of this section shall not apply to sections[1] 2706(f), 2712(a)(4), or 2736 of this title, and shall not apply to an amount not to exceed $50,000,000 in any fiscal year which the President may make available from the Fund to carry out section 1321(c) of this title and to initiate the assessment of natural resources damages required under section 2706 of this title. To the extent that such amount is not adequate, the Coast Guard may obtain an advance from the Fund of such sums as may be necessary, up to a maximum of $100,000,000, and within 30 days shall notify Congress of the amount advanced and the facts and circumstances necessitating the advance. Amounts advanced shall be repaid to the Fund when, and to the extent that, removal costs are recovered by the Coast Guard from responsible parties for the discharge or substantial threat of discharge. Sums to which this subsection applies shall remain available until expended.

(Pub.L. 101–380, Title VI, § 6002, Aug. 18, 1990, 104 Stat. 555; Pub.L. 104–324, Title XI, § 1102(c)(1), Oct. 19, 1996, 110 Stat. 3966; Pub.L. 107–295, Title III, § 323, Nov. 25, 2002, 116 Stat. 2104.)

[1] So in original. Probably should be "section".

### HISTORICAL AND STATUTORY NOTES

**References in Text**

Reference in subsec. (b) to the amendment of section 1321(c) of this title "by this Act" refers to the amendment by Pub.L. 101–380, Aug. 18, 1990, 104 Stat. 484.

**Delegation of Functions**

The functions vested in the President by subsec. (b) of this section respecting making amounts, not to exceed $50,000,000 and subject to normal budget controls, in any fiscal year, available from the Fund (i) to carry out section 1321(c) of this title, and (ii) to initiate the assessment of natural resources damages required under section 2706 of this title are delegated to the Secretary of the Department in which the Coast Guard is operating, with such Secretary required to make amounts available from the Fund to initiate the assessment of natural resources damages exclusively to the Federal trustees designated in the NCP [National Contingency Plan], who are in turn directed to allocate such amounts among all trustees required to assess natural resources damages under section 2706 of this title,see Ex. Ord. No. 12777, Oct. 18, 1991, 56 F.R. 54757, set out as a note under section 1321 of this title.

## § 2753. Repealed. Pub.L. 104–134, Title I, § 101(c)[Title I, § 109], Apr. 26, 1996, 110 Stat. 1321–177; renumbered Title I Pub.L. 104–140, § 1(a), May 2, 1996, 110 Stat. 1327

**[OPA § 6003]**

### HISTORICAL AND STATUTORY NOTES

Section, Pub.L. 101–380, Title VI, § 6003, Aug. 18, 1990, 104 Stat. 555, related to protection of the Outer Banks of North Carolina.

# SUBCHAPTER IV—OIL POLLUTION RESEARCH AND DEVELOPMENT PROGRAM

## § 2761. Oil pollution research and development program

**[OPA § 7001]**

**(a) Interagency Coordinating Committee on Oil Pollution Research**

**(1) Establishment**

There is established an Interagency Coordinating Committee on Oil Pollution Research (hereinafter in this section referred to as the "Interagency Committee").

**(2) Purposes**

The Interagency Committee shall coordinate a comprehensive program of oil pollution research, technology development, and demonstration among the Federal agencies, in cooperation and coordination with industry, universities, research institutions, State governments, and other nations, as appropriate, and shall foster cost-effective research mechanisms, including the joint funding of research.

**(3) Membership**

The Interagency Committee shall include representatives from the Department of Commerce (including the National Oceanic and Atmospheric Administration and the National Institute of Standards and Technology), the Department of Energy, the Department of the Interior (including the Minerals Management Service and the United States Fish and Wildlife Service), the Department of Transportation (including the United States Coast Guard, the Maritime Administration, and the Research and Special Projects Administration), the Department of Defense (including the Army Corps of Engineers and the Navy), the Environmental Protection Agency, the National Aeronautics and Space Administration, and the United States Fire Administration in the Federal Emergency Management Agency, as well as such other Federal agencies as the President may designate.

A representative of the Department of Transportation shall serve as Chairman.

**(b) Oil pollution research and technology plan**

**(1) Implementation plan**

Within 180 days after August 18, 1990, the Interagency Committee shall submit to Congress a plan for the implementation of the oil pollution research, development, and demonstration program established pursuant to subsection (c) of this section. The research plan shall—

(A) identify agency roles and responsibilities;

(B) assess the current status of knowledge on oil pollution prevention, response, and mitigation technologies and effects of oil pollution on the environment;

(C) identify significant oil pollution research gaps including an assessment of major technological deficiencies in responses to past oil discharges;

(D) establish research priorities and goals for oil pollution technology development related to prevention, response, mitigation, and environmental effects;

(E) estimate the resources needed to conduct the oil pollution research and development program established pursuant to subsection (c) of this section, and timetables for completing research tasks; and

(F) identify, in consultation with the States, regional oil pollution research needs and priorities for a coordinated, multidisciplinary program of research at the regional level.

**(2) Advice and guidance**

The Chairman, through the Department of Transportation, shall contract with the National Academy of Sciences to—

(A) provide advice and guidance in the preparation and development of the research plan; and

(B) assess the adequacy of the plan as submitted, and submit a report to Congress on the conclusions of such assessment.

The National Institute of Standards and Technology shall provide the Interagency Committee with advice and guidance on issues relating to quality assurance and standards measurements relating to its activities under this section.

**(c) Oil pollution research and development program**

**(1) Establishment**

The Interagency Committee shall coordinate the establishment, by the agencies represented on the Interagency Committee, of a program for conducting oil pollution research and development, as provided in this subsection.

**(2) Innovative oil pollution technology**

The program established under this subsection shall provide for research, development, and demonstration of new or improved technologies which are effective in preventing or mitigating oil discharges and which protect the environment, including—

(A) development of improved designs for vessels and facilities, and improved operational practices;

(B) research, development, and demonstration of improved technologies to measure the ullage of a vessel tank, prevent discharges from tank vents, prevent discharges during lightering and bunkering operations, contain discharges on the deck of a vessel, prevent discharges through the use of vacuums in tanks, and otherwise contain discharges of oil from vessels and facilities;

(C) research, development, and demonstration of new or improved systems of mechanical, chemical, biological, and other methods (including the use of dispersants, solvents, and bioremediation) for the recovery, removal, and disposal of oil, including evaluation of the environmental effects of the use of such systems;

(D) research and training, in consultation with the National Response Team, to improve industry's and Government's ability to quickly and effectively remove an oil discharge, including the long-term use, as appropriate, of the National Spill Control School in Corpus Christi, Texas, and the Center for Marine Training and Safety in Galveston, Texas;

(E) research to improve information systems for decisionmaking, including the use of data from coastal mapping, baseline data, and other data related to the environmental effects of oil discharges, and cleanup technologies;

(F) development of technologies and methods to protect public health and safety from oil discharges, including the population directly exposed to an oil discharge;

(G) development of technologies, methods, and standards for protecting removal personnel, including training, adequate supervision, protective equipment, maximum exposure limits, and decontamination procedures;

(H) research and development of methods to restore and rehabilitate natural resources damaged by oil discharges;

(I) research to evaluate the relative effectiveness and environmental impacts of bioremediation technologies; and

(J) the demonstration of a satellite-based, dependent surveillance vessel traffic system in Narragansett Bay to evaluate the utility of such system in reducing the risk of oil discharges from vessel collisions and groundings in confined waters.

**(3) Oil pollution technology evaluation**

The program established under this subsection shall provide for oil pollution prevention and mitigation technology evaluation including—

(A) the evaluation and testing of technologies developed independently of the research and development program established under this subsection;

(B) the establishment, where appropriate, of standards and testing protocols traceable to national standards to measure the performance of oil pollution prevention or mitigation technologies; and

(C) the use, where appropriate, of controlled field testing to evaluate real-world application of oil discharge prevention or mitigation technologies.

**(4) Oil pollution effects research**

(A) The Committee shall establish a research program to monitor and evaluate the environmental effects of oil discharges. Such program shall include the following elements:

(i) The development of improved models and capabilities for predicting the environmental fate, transport, and effects of oil discharges.

(ii) The development of methods, including economic methods, to assess damages to natural resources resulting from oil discharges.

(iii) The identification of types of ecologically sensitive areas at particular risk to oil discharges and the preparation of scientific monitoring and evaluation plans, one for each of several types of ecological conditions, to be implemented in the event of major oil discharges in such areas.

(iv) The collection of environmental baseline data in ecologically sensitive areas at particular risk to oil discharges where such data are insufficient.

(B) The Department of Commerce in consultation with the Environmental Protection Agency shall monitor and scientifically evaluate the long-term environmental effects of oil discharges if—

(i) the amount of oil discharged exceeds 250,000 gallons;

(ii) the oil discharge has occurred on or after January 1, 1989; and

(iii) the Interagency Committee determines that a study of the long-term environmental effects of the discharge would be of significant scientific value, especially for preventing or responding to future oil discharges.

Areas for study may include the following sites where oil discharges have occurred: the New York/New Jersey Harbor area, where oil was discharged by an Exxon underwater pipeline, the T/B CIBRO SAVANNAH, and the M/V BT NAUTILUS; Narragansett Bay where oil was discharged by the WORLD PRODIGY; the Houston Ship Channel where oil was discharged by the RACHEL B; the Delaware River, where oil was discharged by the PRESIDENTE RIVERA, and Huntington Beach, California, where oil was discharged by the AMERICAN TRADER.

(C) Research conducted under this paragraph by, or through, the United States Fish and Wildlife Service shall be directed and coordinated by the National Wetland Research Center.

**(5) Marine simulation research**

The program established under this subsection shall include research on the greater use and application of geographic and vessel response simulation models, including the development of additional data bases and updating of existing data bases using, among others, the resources of the National Maritime Research Center. It shall include research and vessel simulations for—

(A) contingency plan evaluation and amendment;

(B) removal and strike team training;

(C) tank vessel personnel training; and

(D) those geographic areas where there is a significant likelihood of a major oil discharge.

**(6) Demonstration projects**

The United States Coast Guard, in conjunction with other such agencies in the Department of Transportation as the Secretary of Transportation may designate, shall conduct 4 port oil pollution minimization demonstration projects, one each with (A) the Port Authority of New York and New Jersey, (B) the Ports of Los Angeles and Long Beach, California, (C) the Port of New Orleans, Louisiana, and (D) ports on the Great Lakes, for the purpose of developing and demonstrating integrated port oil pollution prevention and cleanup systems which utilize the information and implement the improved practices and technologies developed from the research, development, and demonstration program established in this section. Such systems shall utilize improved technologies and management practices for reducing the risk of oil discharges, including, as appropriate, improved data access, computerized tracking of oil shipments, improved vessel tracking and navigation systems, advanced technology to monitor pipeline and tank conditions, improved oil spill response capability, improved capability to predict the flow and effects of oil discharges in both the inner and outer harbor areas for the purposes of making infrastructure decisions, and such other activities necessary to achieve the purposes of this section.

**(7) Simulated environmental testing**

Agencies represented on the Interagency Committee shall ensure the long-term use and operation of the Oil and Hazardous Materials Simulated Environmental Test Tank (OHMSETT) Research Center in New Jersey for oil pollution technology testing and evaluations.

**(8) Regional research program**

**(A)** Consistent with the research plan in subsection (b) of this section, the Interagency Committee shall coordinate a program of competitive grants to universities or other research institutions, or groups of universities or research institutions, for the purposes of conducting a coordinated research program related to the regional aspects of oil pollution, such as prevention, removal, mitigation, and the effects of discharged oil on regional environments. For the purposes of this paragraph, a region means a Coast Guard district as set out in part 3 of title 33, Code of Federal Regulations (1989).

**(B)** The Interagency Committee shall coordinate the publication by the agencies represented on the Interagency Committee of a solicitation for grants under this subsection. The application shall be in such form and contain such information as may be required in the published solicitation. The applications shall be reviewed by the Interagency Committee, which shall make recommendations to the appropriate granting agency represented on the Interagency Committee for awarding the grant. The granting agency shall award the grants recommended by the Interagency Committee unless the agency decides not to award the grant due to budgetary or other compelling considerations and publishes its reasons for such a determination in the Federal Register. No grants may be made by any agency from any funds authorized for this paragraph unless such grant award has first been recommended by the Interagency Committee.

**(C)** Any university or other research institution, or group of universities or research institutions, may apply for a grant for the regional research program established by this paragraph. The applicant must be located in the region, or in a State a part of which is in the region, for which the project is proposed as part of the regional research program. With respect to a group application, the entity or entities which will carry out the substantial portion of the proposed research must be located in the region, or in a State a part of which is in the region, for which the project is proposed as part of the regional research program.

**(D)** The Interagency Committee shall make recommendations on grants in such a manner as to ensure an appropriate balance within a region among the various aspects of oil pollution research, including prevention, removal, mitigation, and the effects of discharged oil on regional environments. In addition, the Interagency Committee shall make recommendations for grants based on the following criteria:

**(i)** There is available to the applicant for carrying out this paragraph demonstrated research resources.

**(ii)** The applicant demonstrates the capability of making a significant contribution to regional research needs.

**(iii)** The projects which the applicant proposes to carry out under the grant are consistent with the research plan under subsection (b)(1)(F) of this section and would further the objectives of the research and development program established in this section.

**(E)** Grants provided under this paragraph shall be for a period up to 3 years, subject to annual review by the granting agency, and provide not more than 80 percent of the costs of the research activities carried out in connection with the grant.

**(F)** No funds made available to carry out this subsection may be used for the acquisition of real property (including buildings) or construction of any building.

**(G)** Nothing in this paragraph is intended to alter or abridge the authority under existing law of any Federal agency to make grants, or enter into contracts or cooperative agreements, using funds other than those authorized in this Act for the purposes of carrying out this paragraph.

**(9) Funding**

For each of the fiscal years 1991, 1992, 1993, 1994, and 1995, $6,000,000 of amounts in the Fund shall be available to carry out the regional research program in paragraph (8), such amounts to be available in equal amounts for the regional research program in each region; except that if the agencies represented on the Interagency Committee determine that regional research needs exist which cannot be addressed within such funding limits, such agencies may use their authority under paragraph (10) to make additional grants to meet such needs. For the purposes of this paragraph, the research program carried out by the Prince William Sound Oil Spill Recovery Institute established under section 2731 of this title, shall not be eligible to receive grants under this paragraph until the authorization for funding under section 2736(b) of this title expires.

**(10) Grants**

In carrying out the research and development program established under this subsection, the agencies represented on the Interagency Committee may enter into contracts and cooperative agreements and make grants to universities, research institutions, and other persons. Such contracts, cooperative agreements, and grants shall address research and technology priorities set forth in the oil pollution research plan under subsection (b) of this section.

**(11)** In carrying out research under this section, the Department of Transportation shall continue to utilize the resources of the Research and Special Programs Administration of the Department of Transportation, to the maximum extent practicable.

**(d) International cooperation**

In accordance with the research plan submitted under subsection (b) of this section, the Interagency Committee shall coordinate and cooperate with other nations and foreign research entities in conducting oil pollution research, development, and demonstration activities, including controlled field tests of oil discharges.

**(e) Omitted**

**(f) Funding**

Not to exceed $22,000,000 of amounts in the Fund shall be available annually to carry out this section except for subsection (c)(8) of this section. Of such sums—

**(1)** funds authorized to be appropriated to carry out the activities under subsection (c)(4) of this section shall not exceed $5,000,000 for fiscal year 1991 or $3,500,000 for any subsequent fiscal year; and

**(2)** not less than $3,000,000 shall be available for carrying out the activities in subsection (c)(6) of this section for fiscal years 1992, 1993, 1994, and 1995.

All activities authorized in this section, including subsection (c)(8) of this section, are subject to appropriations.

(Pub.L. 101–380, Title VII, § 7001, Aug. 18, 1990, 104 Stat. 559; Pub.L. 101–537, Title II, § 2002, Nov. 18, 1990, 104 Stat. 2375; Pub.L. 101–646, Title IV, § 4002, Nov. 29, 1990, 104 Stat. 4788; Pub.L. 104–324, Title XI, §§ 1102(c)(2), 1108, Oct. 19, 1996, 110 Stat. 3966, 3968; Pub.L. 104–332, § 2(h)(1), (2), Oct. 26, 1996, 110 Stat. 4091.)

### HISTORICAL AND STATUTORY NOTES

**References in Text**

This Act, referred to in subsec. (c)(8)(G), is Pub.L. 101–380, Aug. 18, 1990, 104 Stat. 484, as amended, known as the Oil Pollution Act of 1990, which is classified principally to this chapter. For complete classification to the Code, see Short Title note under 33 U.S.C.A. § 2701 and Tables.

**Codifications**

Identical amendments were made by Pub.L. 101–537 and Pub.L. 101–646 to subsecs. (c)(6), (f) and (f)(2).

Subsec. (e) of this section, which required the Chairman of the Interagency Coordinating Committee on Oil Pollution Research to submit a biennial report to Congress on activities carried out and activities proposed to be carried out under this section, terminated, effective May 15, 2000, pursuant to section 3003 of Pub.L. 104–66, as amended, set out as a note under 31 U.S.C.A. § 1113. See, also, page 175 of House Document No. 103–7.

**Delegation of Functions**

The function vested in the President by subsec. (a)(3) of this section, respecting the appointment of Federal agencies to membership on the Interagency Coordinating Committee on Oil Pollution Research, is delegated to the Secretary of Transportation, see Ex. Ord. No. 12777, Oct. 18, 1991, 56 F.R. 54757, set out as a note under section 1321 of this title.

# NATIONAL COASTAL MONITORING

**(33 U.S.C.A. §§ 2801 to 2805)**

## CHAPTER 41—NATIONAL COASTAL MONITORING



### § 2801. Purposes

The purposes of this chapter are to—

(1) establish a comprehensive national program for consistent monitoring of the Nation's coastal ecosystems;

(2) establish long-term water quality assessment and monitoring programs for high priority coastal waters that will enhance the ability of Federal, State, and local authorities to develop and implement effective remedial programs for those waters;

(3) establish a system for reviewing and evaluating the scientific, analytical, and technological means that are available for monitoring the environmental quality of coastal ecosystems;

(4) establish methods for identifying uniform indicators of coastal ecosystem quality;

(5) provide for periodic, comprehensive reports to Congress concerning the quality of the Nation's coastal ecosystems;

(6) establish a coastal environment information program to distribute coastal monitoring information;

(7) provide state [1] programs authorized under the Coastal Zone Management Act of 1972 (16 U.S.C. 1451 et seq.) with information necessary to design land use plans and coastal zone regulations that will contribute to the protection of coastal ecosystems; and

(8) provide certain water pollution control programs authorized under the Federal Water Pollution Control Act (33 U.S.C. 1251 et seq.) with information necessary to design and implement effective coastal water pollution controls.

(Pub.L. 92–532, Title V, § 501, as added Pub.L. 102–567, Title V, § 501, Oct. 29, 1992, 106 Stat. 4293.)

[1] So in original. Probably should be capitalized.

#### HISTORICAL AND STATUTORY NOTES

**References in Text**

The Coastal Zone Management Act of 1972, referred to in par. (7), is Title III of Pub.L. 89–454, as added by Pub.L. 92–583, Oct. 27, 1972, 86 Stat. 1280, as amended, which is classified generally to chapter 33 (section 1451 et seq.) of Title 16, Conservation. For complete classification of this Act to the Code, see Short Title note set out under section 1451 of Title 16 and Tables.

The Federal Water Pollution Control Act, referred to in par. (8), is Act June 30, 1948, c. 758, as amended generally by Pub.L. 92–500, § 2, Oct. 18, 1972, 86 Stat. 816, which is classified generally to chapter 26 (section 1251 et seq.) of this title. For complete classification of this Act to the Code, see Short Title note set out under section 1251 of this title and Tables.

**Short Title**

Title V of Pub.L. 92–532, which comprises this chapter, is popularly known as the "National Coastal Monitoring Act".

### § 2802. Definitions

For the purposes of this chapter, the term—

(1) "Administrator" means the Administrator of the Environmental Protection Agency;

(2) "coastal ecosystem" means a system of interacting biological, chemical, and physical components throughout the water column, water surface, and benthic environment of coastal waters;

(3) "coastal water quality" means the physical, chemical and biological parameters that relate to the health and integrity of coastal ecosystems;

(4) "coastal water quality monitoring" means a continuing program of measurement, analysis, and synthesis to identify and quantify coastal water quality conditions and trends to provide a technical basis for decisionmaking;

(5) "coastal waters" means waters of the Great Lakes, including their connecting waters and those portions of rivers, streams, and other bodies of water having unimpaired connection with the open sea up to the head of tidal influence, including wetlands, intertidal areas, bays, harbors, and lagoons, including waters of the territorial sea of the United States and the contiguous zone" [1]; and

(6) "Under Secretary" means Under Secretary of Commerce for Oceans and Atmosphere.

(Pub.L. 92–532, Title V, § 502, as added Pub.L. 102–567, Title V, § 501, Oct. 29, 1992, 106 Stat. 4294.)

[1] So in original. The closing quotation marks preceding the semicolon probably should not appear.

### HISTORICAL AND STATUTORY NOTES

**Territorial Sea and Contiguous Zone of United States**

For extension of territorial sea and contiguous zone of United States, see Proc. No. 5928 and Proc. No. 7219, respectively, set out as notes under 43 U.S.C.A. § 1331.

## § 2803. Comprehensive Coastal Water Quality Monitoring Program

**(a) Authority; joint implementation**

(1) The Administrator and the Under Secretary, in conjunction with other Federal, State, and local authorities, shall jointly develop and implement a program for the long-term collection, assimilation, and analysis of scientific data designed to measure the environmental quality of the Nation's coastal ecosystems pursuant to this section. Monitoring conducted pursuant to this section shall be coordinated with relevant monitoring programs conducted by the Administrator, Under Secretary, and other Federal, State, and local authorities.

(2) Primary leadership for the monitoring program activities conducted by the Environmental Protection Agency pursuant to this section shall be located at the Environmental Research Laboratory in Narragansett, Rhode Island.

**(b) Program elements**

The Comprehensive Coastal Water Quality Monitoring Program shall include, but not be limited to—

(1) identification and analysis of the status of environmental quality in the Nation's coastal ecosystems, including but not limited to, assessment of—

(A) ambient water quality, including contaminant levels in relation to criteria and standards issued pursuant to title III or [1] the Federal Water Pollution Control Act (33 U.S.C. 1311 et seq.);

(B) benthic environmental quality, including analysis of contaminant levels in sediments in relation to criteria and standards issued pursuant to title III of the Federal Water Pollution Control Act (33 U.S.C. 1311 et seq.); and

(C) health and quality of living resources.

(2) identification of sources of environmental degradation affecting the Nation's coastal ecosystems;

(3) assessment of the impact of governmental programs and management strategies and measures designed to abate or prevent the environmental degradation of the Nation's coastal ecosystems;

(4) assessment of the accumulation of floatables along coastal shorelines;

(5) analysis of expected short-term and long-term trends in the environmental quality of the Nation's coastal ecosystems; and

(6) the development and implementation of intensive coastal water quality monitoring programs in accordance with subsection (d) of this section.

**(c) Monitoring guidelines and protocols**

**(1) Guidelines**

Not later than 18 months after October 29, 1992, the Administrator and the Under Secretary shall jointly issue coastal water quality monitoring guidelines to assist in the development and implementation of coastal water quality monitoring programs. The guidelines shall—

(A) provide an appropriate degree of uniformity among the coastal water quality monitoring methods and data while preserving the flexibility of monitoring programs to address specific needs;

(B) establish scientifically valid monitoring methods that will—

(i) provide simplified methods to survey and assess the water quality and ecological health of coastal waters;

(ii) identify and quantify through more intensive efforts the severity of existing or anticipated problems in selected coastal waters;

(iii) identify and quantify sources of pollution that cause or contribute to those problems, including point and nonpoint sources; and

(iv) evaluate over time the effectiveness of efforts to reduce or eliminate pollution from those sources;

(C) provide for data compatibility to enable data to be efficiently stored and shared by various users; and

(D) identify appropriate physical, chemical, and biological indicators of the health and quality of coastal ecosystems.

**(2) Technical protocols**

Guidelines issued under paragraph (1) shall include protocols for—

(A) designing statistically valid coastal water quality monitoring networks and monitoring surveys, including assessment of the accumulation of floatables.

(B) sampling and analysis, including appropriate physical and chemical parameters, living resource parameters, and sediment analysis techniques; and

(C) quality control, quality assessment, and data consistency and management.

**(3) Periodic review**

The Administrator and the Under Secretary shall periodically review the guidelines and protocols issued under this subsection to evaluate their effectiveness, the degree to which they continue to answer program objectives and provide an appropriate degree of uniformity while taking local conditions into account, and any need to modify or supplement them with new guidelines and protocols, as needed.

**(4) Discharge permit data**

The Administrator or a State permitting authority shall ensure that compliance monitoring conducted pursuant to section 402(a)(2) of the Federal Water Pollution Control Act (33 U.S.C. 1342(a)(2)) for permits for discharges to coastal waters is consistent with the guidelines issued under this subsection. Any modifications of discharge permits necessary to implement this subsection shall be deemed to be minor modifications of such permit. Nothing in this subsection requires dischargers to conduct monitoring other than compliance monitoring pursuant to permits under section 402(a)(2) of the Federal Water Pollution Control Act (33 U.S.C. 1342(a)(2)).

**(d) Intensive coastal water quality monitoring programs**

**(1) In general**

The Comprehensive Coastal Water Quality Monitoring Program established pursuant to this section shall include intensive coastal water quality monitoring programs developed under this subsection.

**(2) Designation of intensive monitoring areas**

Not later than 24 months after October 29, 1992, and periodically thereafter, the Administrator and the Under Secretary shall, based on recommendations by the National Research Council, jointly designate coastal areas to be intensively monitored.

**(3) Identification of suitable coastal areas**

(A) The Administrator and the Under Secretary shall contract with the National Research Council to conduct a study to identify coastal areas suitable for the establishment of intensive coastal monitoring programs. In identifying these coastal areas, the National Research Council shall consider areas that—

(i) are representatives of coastal ecosystems throughout the United States;

(ii) will provide information to assess the status and trends of coastal water quality nationwide; and

(iii) would benefit from intensive water quality monitoring because of local management needs.

(B) In making recommendations under this paragraph, the National Research Council shall consult with Regional Research Boards established pursuant to Title IV of this Act [16 U.S.C.A. § 1447 et seq.].

(C) The National Research Council shall, within 18 months of October 29, 1992, submit a report to the Administrator and the Under Secretary listing areas suitable for intensive monitoring.

(D) The Administrator and the Under Secretary, in conjunction with other Federal, State, and local authorities, shall develop and implement multi-year programs of intensive monitoring for Massachusetts and Cape Cod Bays, the Gulf of Maine, the Chesapeake Bay, the Hudson-Raritan Estuary, and each area jointly designated by the Administrator and the Under Secretary pursuant to paragraph (2).

**(4) Intensive coastal water quality monitoring programs**

Each intensive coastal water quality monitoring program developed pursuant to this subsection shall—

(A) identify water quality conditions and problems and provide information to assist in improving coastal water quality;

(B) clearly state the goals and objectives of the monitoring program and their relationship to the water quality objectives for coastal waters covered by the program;

(C) identify the water quality and biological parameters of the monitoring program and their relationship to these goals and objectives;

(D) describe the types of monitoring networks, surveys and other activities to be used to achieve these goals and objectives, using where appropriate the guidelines issued under subsection (c) of this section;

(E) survey existing Federal, State, and local coastal monitoring activities and private compliance monitoring activities in or on the coastal waters covered by the program, describe the relationship of the program to those other monitoring activities, and integrate them, as appropriate, into the intensive monitoring program;

(F) describe the data management and quality control components of the program;

(G) specify the implementation requirements for the program, including—

(i) the lead Federal, State, or regional authority that will administer the program;

(ii) the public and private parties that will implement the program;

(iii) a detailed schedule for program implementation;

(iv) all Federal and State responsibilities for implementing the program; and

(v) the changes in Federal, State, and local monitoring programs necessary to implement the program;

(H) estimate the costs to Federal and State governments, and other participants, of implementing the monitoring program; and

(I) describe the methods to assess periodically the success of the monitoring program in meeting its goals and objectives, and the manner in which the program may be modified from time-to-time.

**(5) Criteria for monitoring Massachusetts and Cape Cod Bays**

In addition to the criteria listed in paragraph (4), the intensive monitoring program for Massachusetts and Cape Cod Bays shall establish baseline data on environmental phenomena (such as quantity of bacteria and quality of indigenous species, and swimmability) and determine the ecological impacts resulting from major point source discharges.

**(6) Memorandum of Understanding**

Prior to implementing any intensive coastal water quality monitoring program under this subsection, the Administrator and the Under Secretary shall enter into a Memorandum of Understanding to implement the intensive coastal water quality monitoring programs and may extend the memorandum [2] of Understanding to include other appropriate Federal agencies. The Memorandum of Understanding shall identify the monitoring and reporting responsibilities of each agency and shall encourage the coordination of monitoring activities.

**(7) Implementation**

(A) The Administrator, the Under Secretary, and the Governor of each State having waters subject to an intensive coastal water quality monitoring program developed pursuant to this subsection shall ensure compliance with that program.

(B) The Administrator and the Under Secretary are authorized to enter into cooperative agreements to provide financial assistance to non-Federal agencies and institutions to support implementation of intensive monitoring programs under this subsection. Federal financial assistance may only be provided on the condition that not less than fifty percent of the costs of the monitoring to be conducted by a non-Federal agency or institution is provided from non-Federal funds.

**(e) Comprehensive Implementation Strategy**

**(1) In general**

Within 1 year after October 29, 1992, the Administrator and the Under Secretary shall jointly submit to Congress a Comprehensive Implementation Strategy identifying the current and planned activities to implement the Comprehensive Coastal Monitoring Program pursuant to this section.

**(2) Consultation**

The Administrator and the Under Secretary shall consult with the National Academy of Sciences, the Director of the United States Fish and Wildlife Service, the Director of the Minerals Management Service, the Commandant of the Coast Guard, the Secretary of the Navy, the Secretary of Agriculture, the heads of any other relevant Federal or regional agencies, and the Governors of coastal States in developing the Strategy.

**(3) Public comment**

Not less than 3 months before submitting the Strategy to Congress, the Administrator and the Under Secretary shall jointly publish a draft version of the Strategy in the Federal Register and shall solicit public comments regarding the Strategy.

**(4) Memorandum of Understanding**

Within 1 year after submission of the Strategy under paragraph (1), the Administrator and the Under Secretary shall enter into a Memorandum of Understanding with appropriate Federal agencies necessary to effect the coordination of Federal coastal monitoring programs. The Memorandum of Understanding shall identify the monitoring and reporting responsibilities of each agency and shall encourage the coordination of monitoring activities where possible.

(Pub.L. 92–532, Title V, § 503, as added Pub.L. 102–567, Title V, § 501, Oct. 29, 1992, 106 Stat. 4294.)

[1] So in original. Probably should be "of".

[2] So in original. Probably should be capitalized.

## HISTORICAL AND STATUTORY NOTES

**References in Text**

The Federal Water Pollution Control Act, referred to in text, is Act June 30, 1948, c. 758, as amended generally by Pub.L. 92–500, § 2, Oct. 18, 1972, 86 Stat. 816, which is classified generally to chapter 26 (section 1251 et seq.) of this title. For complete classification of this Act to the Code, see Short Title note set out under section 1251 of this title and Tables.

Title IV of this Act, referred to in subsec. (d)(3)(B), is Title IV of Pub.L. 92–532 which is classified principally to chapter 32A of Title 16 [33 U.S.C.A. § 1447 et seq.].

## § 2804. Report to Congress

On September 30 of each other year beginning in 1993, the Administrator and the Under Secretary shall jointly submit to the Committee on Commerce, Science, and Transportation and the Committee on Environment and Public Works of the Senate and the Committee on Merchant Marine and Fisheries and the Committee on Public Works and Transportation of the House of Representatives a report describing the condition of the Nation's coastal ecosystems, including the following:

(1) an assessment of the status and health of the Nation's coastal ecosystems;

(2) an evaluation of environmental trends in coastal ecosystems;

(3) identification of sources of enironmental[1] degradation affecting coastal ecosystems;

(4) an assessment of the extent to which floatables degrade coastal ecosystems, including trends in the accumulation of floatables and the threat posed by floatables to aquatic life;

(5) an assessment of the impact of government programs designed to abate the degradation of coastal ecosystems:[2]

(6) an evaluation of the adequacy of monitoring programs and identification of any additional program elements which may be needed; and

(7) a summary of monitoring results in areas monitored under subsection[3] 2803(d) of this title.

(Pub.L. 92–532, Title V, § 504, as added Pub.L. 102–567, Title V, § 501, Oct. 29, 1992, 106 Stat. 4299.)

[1] So in original. Probably should be "environmental".

[2] So in original. Probably should be a semicolon.

[3] So in original. Probably should be "section".

### HISTORICAL AND STATUTORY NOTES

**Codifications**

Reference in par. (7) to "subsection" 2803(d) of this title has been translated as "section" 2803(d) of this title as the probable intent of Congress.

**Change of Name**

Any reference in any provision of law enacted before Jan. 4, 1995, to the Committee on Public Works and Transportation of the House of Representatives treated as referring to the Committee on Transportation and Infrastructure of the House of Representatives, see section 1(a)(9) of Pub.L. 104–14, set out as a note preceding section 21 of Title 2, The Congress.

**Abolition of House Committee on Merchant Marine and Fisheries**

Committee on Merchant Marine and Fisheries of House of Representatives abolished and any reference in any provision of law enacted before Jan. 4, 1995, to the Committee on Merchant Marine and Fisheries of the House of Representatives treated as referring to the Committee on Agriculture of the House of Representatives, in the case of a provision of law relating to inspection of seafood or seafood products, the Committee on National Security of the House of Representatives, in the case of a provision of law relating to interoceanic canals, the Merchant Marine Academy and State Maritime Academies, or national security aspects of merchant marine, the Committee on Resources of the House of Representatives, in the case of a provision of law relating to fisheries, wildlife, international fishing agreements marine affairs (including coastal zone management) except for measures relating to oil and other pollution of navigable waters, or oceanography, the Committee on Science of the House of Representatives, in the case of a provision of law relating to marine research, and the Committee on Transportation and Infrastructure of the House of Representatives, in the case of a provision of law relating to a matter other than a matter described above, see section 1(b)(3) of Pub.L. 104–14, set out as a note preceding section 21 of Title 2, The Congress.

## § 2805. Authorization of appropriations

### (a) NOAA authorization

For development and implementation of programs under this chapter, including financial assistance to non-Federal agencies and institutions to support implementation of intensive monitoring programs under section 2803(d) of this title, there is authorized to be appropriated to the Under Secretary amounts not to exceed $5,000,000 for fiscal year 1993, $8,000,000 for fiscal year 1994, $10,000,000 for fiscal year 1995, and $12,000,000 for fiscal year 1996.

### (b) EPA authorization

For development and implementation of programs under this chapter, including financial assistance to non-Federal agencies and institutions to support implementation of intensive monitoring programs under section 2803(d) of this title, there is authorized to be appropriated to the Administrator amounts not to exceed $5,000,000 for fiscal year 1993, $8,000,000 for fiscal year 1994, and $10,000,000 for fiscal year 1995, and $12,000,000 for fiscal year 1996.

(Pub.L. 92–532, Title V, § 505, as added Pub.L. 102–567, Title V, § 501, Oct. 29, 1992, 106 Stat. 4299.)

# NATIONAL OCEANIC AND ATMOSPHERIC ADMINISTRATION COMMISSIONED OFFICER CORPS

(33 U.S.C.A. §§ 3001 to 3076)

## CHAPTER 43—NATIONAL OCEANIC AND ATMOSPHERIC ADMINISTRATION COMMISSIONED OFFICER CORPS



### SUBCHAPTER I—GENERAL PROVISIONS

### § 3001. Commissioned officer corps

There shall be in the National Oceanic and Atmospheric Administration a commissioned officer corps.

(Pub.L. 107–372, Title II, § 211, Dec. 19, 2002, 116 Stat. 3082.)

#### HISTORICAL AND STATUTORY NOTES

**Short Title**

2002 Acts

Pub.L. 107–372, Title II, § 201, Dec. 19, 2002, 116 Stat. 3082, provided that: "This title [enacting this chapter, 33 U.S.C.A. §§ 3001 to 3076, amending 10 U.S.C.A. § 1406 and 22 U.S.C.A. § 2396, repealing 33 U.S.C.A. §§ 853a to 853j, 853j–1, 853k, 853*l*, 853*o*, 853p to 853r, 853t 853v, 857–1 to 857–5, 854, 855, 856, 857, 857a, 858, 864, and 874, and 38 U.S.C.A. § 101, amending provisions set out as a note under 10 U.S.C.A. § 1293, and repealing provisions set out as notes under 33 U.S.C.A. §§ 853a and 857–1] may be cited as the 'National Oceanic and Atmospheric Administration Commissioned Officer Corps Act of 2002'."

### § 3002. Definitions

**(a) Applicability of definitions in Title 10**

Except as provided in subsection (b) of this section, the definitions provided in section 101 of Title 10 apply to the provisions of this chapter.

**(b) Additional definitions**

In this chapter:

**(1) Active duty**

The term "active duty" means full-time duty in the active service of a uniformed service.

**(2) Grade**

The term "grade" means a step or degree, in a graduated scale of office or rank, that is established and designated as a grade by law or regulation.

**(3) Officer**

The term "officer" means an officer of the commissioned corps.

**(4) Flag officer**

The term "flag officer" means an officer serving in, or having the grade of, vice admiral, rear admiral, or rear admiral (lower half).

**(5) Secretary**

The term "Secretary" means the Secretary of Commerce.

**(6) Administration**

The term "Administration" means the National Oceanic and Atmospheric Administration.

(Pub.L. 107–372, Title II, § 212, Dec. 19, 2002, 116 Stat. 3082.)

### HISTORICAL AND STATUTORY NOTES

**References in Text**

This chapter, referred to in text, originally read "this title", meaning Title II of Pub.L. 107–372, known as the National Oceanic and Atmospheric Administration Commissioned Officer Corps Act of 2002, Pub.L. 107–372, Title II, §§ 201 to 272, Dec. 19, 2002, 116 Stat. 3082, which enacted this chapter.

## § 3003. Authorized number on the active list

**(a) Annual strength on active list**

The annual strength of the commissioned corps in officers on the lineal list of active duty officers of the corps shall be prescribed by law.

**(b) Lineal list**

The Secretary shall maintain a list, known as the "lineal list", of officers on active duty. Officers shall be carried on the lineal list by grade and, within grade, by seniority in grade.

(Pub.L. 107–372, Title II, § 213, Dec. 19, 2002, 116 Stat. 3083.)

## § 3004. Strength and distribution in grade

**(a) Relative rank; proportion**

Of the total authorized number of officers on the lineal list of the commissioned corps, there are authorized numbers in permanent grade, in relative rank with officers of the Navy, in proportions as follows:

(1) 8 in the grade of captain.

(2) 14 in the grade of commander.

(3) 19 in the grade of lieutenant commander.

(4) 23 in the grade of lieutenant.

(5) 18 in the grade of lieutenant (junior grade).

(6) 18 in the grade of ensign.

**(b) Computation of number in grade**

**(1) In general**

Subject to paragraph (2), whenever a final fraction occurs in computing the authorized number of officers in a grade, the nearest whole number shall be taken, and if the fraction is one-half the next higher whole number shall be taken.

**(2) Limitation on increase in total number**

The total number of officers on the lineal list authorized by law may not be increased as the result of the computations prescribed in this section, and if necessary the number of officers in the lowest grade shall be reduced accordingly.

**(c) Preservation of grade and pay, etc.**

No officer may be reduced in grade or pay or separated from the commissioned corps as the result of a computation made to determine the authorized number of officers in the various grades.

**(d) Filling of vacancies; additional numbers**

Nothing in this section may be construed as requiring the filling of any vacancy or as prohibiting additional numbers in any grade to compensate for vacancies existing in higher grades.

**(e) Temporary increase in numbers**

The total number of officers authorized by law to be on the lineal list during a fiscal year may be temporarily exceeded so long as the average number on that list during that fiscal year does not exceed the authorized number.

(Pub.L. 107–372, Title II, § 214, Dec. 19, 2002, 116 Stat. 3083.)

## § 3005. Authorized number for fiscal years 2003 through 2005

There are authorized to be on the lineal list of the commissioned corps of the National Oceanic and Atmospheric Administration—

(1) 270 officers for fiscal year 2003;

(2) 285 officers for fiscal year 2004; and

(3) 299 officers for fiscal year 2005.

(Pub.L. 107–372, Title II, § 215, Dec. 19, 2002, 116 Stat. 3084.)

## SUBCHAPTER II—APPOINTMENT AND PROMOTION OF OFFICERS

### § 3021. Original appointments

**(a) In general**

**(1) Grades**

Original appointments may be made in the grades of ensign, lieutenant (junior grade), and lieutenant.

**(2) Qualifications**

Under regulations prescribed by the Secretary, such an appointment may be given only to a person who—

(A) meets the qualification requirements specified in paragraphs (1) through (4) of section 532(a) of Title 10; and

(B) has such other special qualifications as the Secretary may prescribe by regulation.

**(3) Examination**

A person may be given such an appointment only after passage of a mental and physical examination given in accordance with regulations prescribed by the Secretary.

**(4) Revocation of Commission of officers found not qualified**

The President may revoke the commission of any officer appointed under this section during the officer's first three years of service if the officer is found not qualified for the service. Any such revocation shall be made under regulations prescribed by the President.

**(b) Lineal list**

Each person appointed under this section shall be placed on the lineal list in a position commensurate with that person's age, education, and experience, in accordance with regulations prescribed by the Secretary.

**(c) Service credit upon original appointment in grade above ensign**

**(1) In general**

For the purposes of basic pay, a person appointed under this section in the grade of lieutenant shall be credited as having, on the date of that appointment, three years of service, and a person appointed under this section in the grade of lieutenant (junior grade) shall be credited as having, as of the date of that appointment, 1½ years of service.

**(2) Higher credit under other law**

If a person appointed under this section is entitled to credit for the purpose of basic pay under any other provision of law that would exceed the amount of credit authorized by paragraph (1), that person shall be credited with that amount of service in lieu of the credit authorized by paragraph (1).

(Pub.L. 107–372, Title II, § 221, Dec. 19, 2002, 116 Stat. 3084.)

### § 3022. Personnel boards

**(a) Convening**

At least once a year and at such other times as the Secretary determines necessary, the Secretary shall convene a personnel board. A personnel board shall consist of not less than five officers on the lineal list in the permanent grade of commander or above.

**(b) Duties**

Each personnel board shall—

(1) recommend to the Secretary such changes in the lineal list as the board may determine; and

(2) make selections and recommendations to the Secretary and President for the appointment, promotion, separation, continuation, and retirement of officers as prescribed in this subchapter and subchapter III of this chapter.

**(c) Action on recommendations not acceptable**

In a case in which any recommendation by a board convened under subsection (a) of this section is not accepted by the Secretary or the President, the board shall make such further recommendations as are acceptable.

(Pub.L. 107–372, Title II, § 222, Dec. 19, 2002, 116 Stat. 3085.)

#### HISTORICAL AND STATUTORY NOTES

**References in Text**

This subchapter, referred to in subsec. (b)(2), originally read "this subtitle", meaning Subtitle B of Title II of Pub.L. 107–372, known as the National Oceanic and Atmospheric Administration Commissioned Officer Corps Act of 2002, Pub.L. 107–372, Title II, Subtitle B, §§ 221 to 232, Dec. 19, 2002, 116 Stat. 3084, which enacted this subchapter.

Subchapter III, referred to in subsec. (b)(2), originally read "subtitle C", meaning Subtitle C of Title II of Pub.L. 107–372, known as the National Oceanic and Atmospheric Administration Commissioned Officer Corps Act of 2002, Pub.L. 107–372, Title II, Subtitle C, §§ 241 to 249, Dec. 19, 2002, 116 Stat. 3088, which enacted Subchapter III of Chapter 43 of this title, which is classified as 33 U.S.C.A. § 3041 et seq.

### § 3023. Promotion of ensigns to grade of lieutenant (junior grade)

**(a) In general**

An officer in the permanent grade of ensign shall be promoted to and appointed in the grade of lieutenant (junior grade) upon completion of three years of service. The authorized number of officers in the grade of lieutenant (junior grade) shall be temporarily increased as necessary to authorize such appointment.

**(b) Separation of ensigns found not fully qualified**

If an officer in the permanent grade of ensign is at any time found not fully qualified, the officer's commission shall be revoked and the officer shall be separated from the commissioned service.

(Pub.L. 107–372, Title II, § 223, Dec. 19, 2002, 116 Stat. 3085.)

## § 3024. Promotion by selection to permanent grades above lieutenant (junior grade)

Promotion to fill vacancies in each permanent grade above the grade of lieutenant (junior grade) shall be made by selection from the next lower grade upon recommendation of the personnel board.

(Pub.L. 107–372, Title II, § 224, Dec. 19, 2002, 116 Stat. 3085.)

## § 3025. Length of service for promotion purposes

**(a) General rule**

Each officer shall be assumed to have, for promotion purposes, at least the same length of service as any other officer below that officer on the lineal list.

**(b) Exception**

Notwithstanding subsection (a) of this section, an officer who has lost numbers shall be assumed to have, for promotion purposes, no greater service than the officer next above such officer in such officer's new position on the lineal list.

(Pub.L. 107–372, Title II, § 225, Dec. 19, 2002, 116 Stat. 3085.)

## § 3026. Appointments and promotions to permanent grades

Appointments in and promotions to all permanent grades shall be made by the President, by and with the advice and consent of the Senate.

(Pub.L. 107–372, Title II, § 226, Dec. 19, 2002, 116 Stat. 3085.)

## § 3027. General qualification of officers for promotion to higher permanent grade

No officer may be promoted to a higher permanent grade on the active list until the officer has passed a satisfactory mental and physical examination in accordance with regulations prescribed by the Secretary.

(Pub.L. 107–372, Title II, § 227, Dec. 19, 2002, 116 Stat. 3085.)

## § 3028. Positions of importance and responsibility

**(a) Designation of positions**

The Secretary may designate positions in the Administration as being positions of importance and responsibility for which it is appropriate that officers of the Administration, if serving in those positions, serve in the grade of vice admiral, rear admiral, or rear admiral (lower half), as designated by the Secretary for each position.

**(b) Assignment of officers to designated positions**

The Secretary may assign officers to positions designated under subsection (a) of this section.

**(c) Director of NOAA corps and office of marine and aviation operations**

The Secretary shall designate one position under this section as responsible for oversight of the vessel and aircraft fleets and for the administration of the commissioned officer corps. That position shall be filled by an officer on the lineal list serving in or above the grade of rear admiral (lower half). For the specific purpose of administering the commissioned officer corps, that position shall carry the title of Director of the National Oceanic and Atmospheric Administration Commissioned Officer Corps. For the specific purpose of administering the vessel and aircraft fleets, that position shall carry the title of Director of the Office of Marine and Aviation Operations.

**(d) Grade**

**(1) Temporary appointment to grade designated for position**

An officer assigned to a position under this section while so serving has the grade designated for that position, if appointed to that grade by the President, by and with the advice and consent of the Senate.

**(2) Reversion to permanent grade**

An officer who has served in a grade above captain, upon termination of the officer's assignment to the position for which that appointment was made, shall, unless appointed or assigned to another position for which a higher grade is designated, revert to the grade and number the officer would have occupied but for serving in a grade above that of captain. In such a case, the officer shall be an extra number in that grade.

**(e) Number of officers appointed**

**(1) Overall limit**

The total number of officers serving on active duty at any one time in the grade of rear admiral (lower half) or above may not exceed four.

**(2) Limit by grade**

The number of officers serving on active duty under appointments under this section may not exceed—

**(A)** one in the grade of vice admiral;

**(B)** two in the grade of rear admiral; and

(C) two in the grade of rear admiral (lower half).

**(f) Pay and allowances**

An officer appointed to a grade under this section, while serving in that grade, shall have the pay and allowances of the grade to which appointed.

**(g) Effect of appointment**

An appointment of an officer under this section—

(1) does not vacate the permanent grade held by the officer; and

(2) creates a vacancy on the active list.

(Pub.L. 107–372, Title II, § 228, Dec. 19, 2002, 116 Stat. 3086.)

## § 3029. Temporary appointments and promotions generally

**(a) Ensign**

Temporary appointments in the grade of ensign may be made by the President alone. Each such temporary appointment terminates at the close of the next regular session of the Congress unless the Senate sooner gives its advice and consent to the appointment.

**(b) Lieutenant (junior grade)**

Officers in the permanent grade of ensign may be temporarily promoted to and appointed in the grade of lieutenant (junior grade) by the President alone whenever vacancies exist in higher grades.

**(c) Any one grade**

When determined by the Secretary to be in the best interest of the service, officers in any permanent grade may be temporarily promoted one grade by the President alone. Any such temporary promotion terminates upon the transfer of the officer to a new assignment.

(Pub.L. 107–372, Title II, § 229, Dec. 19, 2002, 116 Stat. 3087.)

## § 3030. Temporary appointment or advancement of commissioned officers in time of war or national emergency

**(a) In general**

Officers of the Administration shall be subject in like manner and to the same extent as personnel of the Navy to all laws authorizing temporary appointment or advancement of commissioned officers in time of war or national emergency.

**(b) Limitations**

Subsection (a) of this section shall be applied subject to the following limitations:

(1) A commissioned officer in the service of a military department under section 3061 of this title may, upon the recommendation of the Secretary of the military department concerned, be temporarily promoted to a higher rank or grade.

(2) A commissioned officer in the service of the Administration may be temporarily promoted to fill vacancies in ranks and grades caused by the transfer of commissioned officers to the service and jurisdiction of a military department under section 3061 of this title.

(3) Temporary appointments may be made in all grades to which original appointments in the Administration are authorized, except that the number of officers holding temporary appointments may not exceed the number of officers transferred to a military department under section 3061 of this title.

(Pub.L. 107–372, Title II, § 230, Dec. 19, 2002, 116 Stat. 3087.)

## § 3031. Pay and allowances; date of acceptance of promotion

**(a) Acceptance and date of promotion**

An officer of the commissioned corps who is promoted to a higher grade—

(1) is deemed for all purposes to have accepted the promotion upon the date the promotion is made by the President, unless the officer expressly declines the promotion; and

(2) shall receive the pay and allowances of the higher grade from that date unless the officer is entitled under another provision of law to receive the pay and allowances of the higher grade from an earlier date.

**(b) Oath of office**

An officer who subscribed to the oath of office required by section 3331 of Title 5 shall not be required to renew such oath or to take a new oath upon promotion to a higher grade, if the service of the officer after the taking of such oath is continuous.

(Pub.L. 107–372, Title II, § 231, Dec. 19, 2002, 116 Stat. 3087.)

## § 3032. Service credit as deck officer or junior engineer for promotion purposes

For purposes of promotion, there shall be counted in addition to active commissioned service, service as deck officer or junior engineer.

(Pub.L. 107–372, Title II, § 232, Dec. 19, 2002, 116 Stat. 3088.)

## § 3033. Suspension during war or emergency

In time of emergency declared by the President or by the Congress, and in time of war, the President is authorized, in the President's discretion, to suspend the operation of all or any part of the provisions of law pertaining to promotion of commissioned officers of the Administration.

(Pub.L. 107–372, Title II, § 233, Dec. 19, 2002, 116 Stat. 3088.)

## SUBCHAPTER III—SEPARATION AND RETIREMENT OF OFFICERS

### § 3041. Involuntary retirement or separation

**(a) Transfer of officers to retired list; separation from service**

As recommended by a personnel board convened under section 3022 of this title—

(1) an officer in the permanent grade of captain or commander may be transferred to the retired list; and

(2) an officer in the permanent grade of lieutenant commander, lieutenant, or lieutenant (junior grade) who is not qualified for retirement may be separated from the service.

**(b) Computations**

In any fiscal year, the total number of officers selected for retirement or separation under subsection (a) of this section plus the number of officers retired for age may not exceed the whole number nearest 4 percent of the total number of officers authorized to be on the active list, except as otherwise provided by law.

**(c) Effective date of retirements and separations**

A retirement or separation under subsection (a) of this section shall take effect on the first day of the sixth month beginning after the date on which the Secretary approves the retirement or separation, except that if the officer concerned requests an earlier retirement or separation date, the date shall be as determined by the Secretary.

(Pub.L. 107–372, Title II, § 241, Dec. 19, 2002, 116 Stat. 3088.)

### § 3042. Separation pay

**(a) Authorization of payment**

An officer who is separated under section 3041(a)(2) of this title and who has completed more than three years of continuous active service immediately before that separation is entitled to separation pay computed under subsection (b) of this section unless the Secretary determines that the conditions under which the officer is separated do not warrant payment of that pay.

**(b) Amount of separation pay**

**(1) Six or more years**

In the case of an officer who has completed six or more years of continuous active service immediately before that separation, the amount of separation pay to be paid to the officer under this section is 10 percent of the product of—

(A) the years of active service creditable to the officer; and

(B) 12 times the monthly basic pay to which the officer was entitled at the time of separation.

**(2) Three to six years**

In the case of an officer who has completed three or more but fewer than six years of continuous active service immediately before that separation, the amount of separation pay to be paid to the officer under this section is one-half of the amount computed under paragraph (1).

**(c) Other conditions, requirements, and administrative provisions**

The provisions of subsections (f), (g), and (h) of section 1174 of Title 10 shall apply to separation pay under this section in the same manner as such provisions apply to separation pay under that section.

(Pub.L. 107–372, Title II, § 242, Dec. 19, 2002, 116 Stat. 3088.)

### § 3043. Mandatory retirement for age

**(a) Officers below grade of rear admiral (lower half)**

Unless retired or separated earlier, each officer on the lineal list of the commissioned corps who is serving in a grade below the grade of rear admiral (lower half) shall be retired on the first day of the month following the month in which the officer becomes 62 years of age.

**(b) Flag officers**

Notwithstanding subsection (a) of this section, the President may defer the retirement of an officer serving in a position that carries a grade above captain for such period as the President considers advisable, but such a deferment may not extend beyond the first day of the month following the month in which the officer becomes 64 years of age.

(Pub.L. 107–372, Title II, § 243, Dec. 19, 2002, 116 Stat. 3089.)

### § 3044. Retirement for length of service

An officer who has completed 20 years of service, of which at least 10 years was service as a commissioned officer, may at any time thereafter, upon application by such officer and in the discretion of the President, be placed on the retired list.

(Pub.L. 107–372, Title II, § 244, Dec. 19, 2002, 116 Stat. 3089.)

### § 3045. Computation of retired pay

**(a) Officers first becoming members before September 8, 1980**

Each officer on the retired list who first became a member of a uniformed service before September 8, 1980, shall receive retired pay at the rate determined by multiplying—

(1) the retired pay base determined under section 1406(g) of Title 10; by

(2) 2½ percent of the number of years of service that may be credited to the officer under section 1405 of Title 10 as if the officer's service were service as a member of the Armed Forces.

The retired pay so computed may not exceed 75 percent of the retired pay base.

**(b) Officers first becoming members on or after September 8, 1980**

Each officer on the retired list who first became a member of a uniformed service on or after September 8, 1980, shall receive retired pay at the rate determined by multiplying—

(1) the retired pay base determined under section 1407 of Title 10; by

(2) the retired pay multiplier determined under section 1409 of Title 10 for the number of years of service that may be credited to the officer under section 1405 of Title 10 as if the officer's service were service as a member of the Armed Forces.

**(c) Treatment of full and fractional parts of months in computing years of service**

**(1) In general**

In computing the number of years of service of an officer for the purposes of subsection (a) of this section—

(A) each full month of service that is in addition to the number of full years of service creditable to the officer shall be credited as 1/12 of a year; and

(B) any remaining fractional part of a month shall be disregarded.

**(2) Rounding**

Retired pay computed under this section, if not a multiple of $1, shall be rounded to the next lower multiple of $1.

(Pub.L. 107–372, Title II, § 245, Dec. 19, 2002, 116 Stat. 3089.)

## § 3046. Retired grade and retired pay

Each officer retired pursuant to law shall be placed on the retired list with the highest grade satisfactorily held by that officer while on active duty including active duty pursuant to recall, under permanent or temporary appointment, and shall receive retired pay based on such highest grade, if—

(1) the officer's performance of duty in such highest grade has been satisfactory, as determined by the Secretary of the department or departments under whose jurisdiction the officer served; and

(2) unless retired for disability, the officer's length of service in such highest grade is no less than that required by the Secretary of officers retiring under permanent appointment in that grade.

(Pub.L. 107–372, Title II, § 246, Dec. 19, 2002, 116 Stat. 3090.)

## § 3047. Retired rank and pay held pursuant to other laws unaffected

Nothing in this subchapter shall prevent an officer from being placed on the retired list with the highest rank and with the highest retired pay to which the officer is entitled under any other provision of law.

(Pub.L. 107–372, Title II, § 247, Dec. 19, 2002, 116 Stat. 3090.)

### HISTORICAL AND STATUTORY NOTES

**References in Text**

This subchapter, referred to in text, originally read "this subtitle", meaning Subtitle C of Title II of Pub.L. 107–372, known as the National Oceanic and Atmospheric Administration Commissioned Officer Corps Act of 2002, Pub.L. 107–372, Title II, Subtitle C, §§ 241 to 249, Dec. 19, 2002, 116 Stat. 3088, which enacted this subchapter.

## § 3048. Continuation on active duty; deferral of retirement

The provisions of subchapter IV of chapter 36 of Title 10 relating to continuation on active duty and deferral of retirement shall apply to commissioned officers of the Administration.

(Pub.L. 107–372, Title II, § 248, Dec. 19, 2002, 116 Stat. 3090.)

### HISTORICAL AND STATUTORY NOTES

**References in Text**

Subchapter IV of chapter 36 of Title 10, referred to in text, is 10 U.S.C.A. § 637 et seq.

## § 3049. Recall to active duty

The provisions of chapter 39 of Title 10, relating to recall of retired officers to active duty, including the limitations on such recalls, shall apply to commissioned officers of the Administration.

(Pub.L. 107–372, Title II, § 249, Dec. 19, 2002, 116 Stat. 3090.)

### HISTORICAL AND STATUTORY NOTES

**References in Text**

Chapter 39 of Title 10, referred to in text, is 10 U.S.C.A. § 671 et seq.

## SUBCHAPTER IV—SERVICE OF OFFICERS WITH THE MILITARY DEPARTMENTS

### § 3061. Cooperation with and transfer to military departments

**(a) Transfers of resources and officers during national emergency**

**(1) Transfers authorized**

The President may, whenever in the judgment of the President a sufficient national emergency exists, transfer to the service and jurisdiction of a military department such vessels, equipment, stations, and officers of the Administration as the President considers to be in the best interest of the country.

**(2) Responsibility for funding of transferred resources and officers**

After any such transfer all expenses connected therewith shall be defrayed out of the appropriations for the department to which the transfer is made.

**(3) Return of transferred resources and officers**

Such transferred vessels, equipment, stations, and officers shall be returned to the Administration when the national emergency ceases, in the opinion of the President.

**(4) Rule of construction**

Nothing in this section shall be construed as transferring the Administration or any of its functions from the Department of Commerce except in time of national emergency and to the extent provided in this section.

**(b) Limitation on transfer of officers**

This section does not authorize the transfer of an officer of the Administration to a military department if the accession or retention of that officer in that military department is otherwise not authorized by law.

**(c) Status of transferred officers**

An officer of the Administration transferred under this section, shall, while under the jurisdiction of a military department, have proper military status and shall be subject to the laws, regulations, and orders for the government of the Army, Navy, or Air Force, as the case may be, insofar as the same may be applicable to persons whose retention permanently in the military service of the United States is not contemplated by law.

(Pub.L. 107–372, Title IV, § 251, Dec. 19, 2002, 116 Stat. 3090.)

### § 3062. Relative rank of officers when serving with Army, Navy, or Air Force

When serving with the Army, Navy, or Air Force, an officer of the Administration shall rank with and after officers of corresponding grade in the Army, Navy, or Air Force of the same length of service in grade. Nothing in this subchapter shall be construed to affect or alter an officer's rates of pay and allowances when not assigned to military duty.

(Pub.L. 107–372, Title IV, § 252, Dec. 19, 2002, 116 Stat. 3091.)

#### HISTORICAL AND STATUTORY NOTES

**References in Text**

This subchapter, referred to in text, originally read "this subtitle", meaning Subtitle D of Title II of Pub.L. 107–372, known as the National Oceanic and Atmospheric Administration Commissioned Officer Corps Act of 2002, Pub.L. 107–372, Title II, Subtitle D, §§ 251 to 253, Dec. 19, 2002, 116 Stat. 3090, which enacted this subchapter.

### § 3063. Rules and regulations when cooperating with military departments

**(a) Joint regulations**

The Secretary of Defense and the Secretary of Commerce shall jointly prescribe regulations—

(1) governing the duties to be performed by the Administration in time of war; and

(2) providing for the cooperation of the Administration with the military departments in time of peace in preparation for its duties in time of war.

**(b) Approval**

Regulations under subsection (a) of this section shall not be effective unless approved by each of those Secretaries.

**(c) Communications**

Regulations under subsection (a) of this section may provide procedures for making reports and communications between a military department and the Administration.

(Pub.L. 107–372, Title IV, § 253, Dec. 19, 2002, 116 Stat. 3091.)

## SUBCHAPTER V—RIGHTS AND BENEFITS

### § 3071. Applicability of certain provisions of Title 10

**(a) Provisions made applicable to the corps**

The rules of law that apply to the Armed Forces under the following provisions of Title 10, as those provisions are in effect from time to time, apply also to the commissioned officer corps of the Administration:

(1) Chapter 40, relating to leave.

(2) Section 533(b), relating to constructive service.

(3) Section 716, relating to transfers between the armed forces and to and from National Oceanic and Atmospheric Administration.

(4) Section 1035, relating to deposits of savings.

(5) Section 1036, relating to transportation and travel allowances for escorts for dependents of members.

(6) Section 1052, relating to reimbursement for adoption expenses.

(7) Section 1174a, relating to special separation benefits (except that benefits under subsection (b)(2)(B) of such section are subject to the availability of appropriations for such purpose and are provided at the discretion of the Secretary of Commerce).

(8) Chapter 61, relating to retirement or separation for physical disability.

(9) Chapter 69, relating to retired grade, except sections 1370, 1375, and 1376.

(10) Chapter 71, relating to computation of retired pay.

(11) Chapter 73, relating to annuities based on retired or retainer pay.

(12) Subchapter II of chapter 75, relating to death benefits.

(13) Section 2634, relating to transportation of motor vehicles for members on permanent change of station.

(14) Sections 2731 and 2735, relating to property loss incident to service.

(15) Section 2771, relating to final settlement of accounts of deceased members.

(16) Such other provisions of subtitle A of that title as may be adopted for applicability to the commissioned officer corps of the National Oceanic and Atmospheric Administration by any other provision of law.

**(b) References**

The authority vested by Title 10 in the "military departments", "the Secretary concerned", or "the Secretary of Defense" with respect to the provisions of law referred to in subsection (a) of this section shall be exercised, with respect to the commissioned officer corps of the Administration, by the Secretary of Commerce or the Secretary's designee.

(Pub.L. 107–372, Title II, § 261, Dec. 19, 2002, 116 Stat. 3091.)

### HISTORICAL AND STATUTORY NOTES

**References in Text**

Chapter 40, referred to in subsec. (a)(1), means Chapter 40 of Title 10, 10 U.S.C.A. § 701 et seq.

Chapter 61, referred to in subsec. (a)(8), means Chapter 61 of Title 10, 10 U.S.C.A. § 1201 et seq.

Chapter 69, referred to in subsec. (a)(9), means Chapter 69 of Title 10, 10 U.S.C.A. § 1370 et seq.

Chapter 71, referred to in subsec. (a)(10), means Chapter 71 of Title 10, 10 U.S.C.A. § 1401 et seq.

Chapter 73, referred to in subsec. (a)(11), means Chapter 73 of Title 10, 10 U.S.C.A. § 1431 et seq.

Subchapter II of Chapter 75, referred to in subsec. (a)(12), means Subchapter II of Chapter 75 of Title 10, 10 U.S.C.A. § 1475 et seq.

Subtitle A of that title, referred to in subsec. (a)(16), means Subtitle A of Title 10, 10 U.S.C.A. § 101 et seq.

## § 3072. Eligibility for veterans benefits and other rights, privileges, immunities, and benefits under certain provisions of law

**(a) In general**

Active service of officers of the Administration shall be deemed to be active military service for the purposes of all rights, privileges, immunities, and benefits under the following:

(1) Laws administered by the Secretary of Veterans Affairs.

(2) The Servicemembers Civil Relief Act (50 App. U.S.C.A. § 501 et seq.).

(3) Section 410 of Title 42, as in effect before September 1, 1950.

**(b) Exercise of authority**

In the administration of the laws and regulations referred to in subsection (a) of this section, with respect to the Administration, the authority vested in the Secretary of Defense and the Secretaries of the military departments and their respective departments shall be exercised by the Secretary of Commerce.

(Pub.L. 107–372, Title II, § 262, Dec. 19, 2002, 116 Stat. 3092; Pub.L. 108–189, § 2(g), Dec. 19, 2003, 117 Stat. 2866.)

### HISTORICAL AND STATUTORY NOTES

**References in Text**

The Servicemembers Civil Relief Act, referred to in subsec. (a)(2), is Act Oct. 17, 1940, c. 888, as amended by Pub.L. 108–189, § 1, Dec. 19, 2003, 117 Stat. 2835, which is classified as 50 App. U.S.C.A. § 501 et seq. For complete classification, see 50 App. U.S.C.A. § 501 and Tables.

**Effective and Applicability Provisions**

2003 Acts

Amendments by Pub.L. 108–189 applicable to any case that is not final before Dec. 19, 2003, see Pub.L. 108–189, § 3, set out as a note under 50 App. U.S.C.A. § 501.

## § 3073. Medical and dental care

The Secretary may provide medical and dental care, including care in private facilities, for personnel of the Administration entitled to that care by law or regulation.

(Pub.L. 107–372, Title II, § 263, Dec. 19, 2002, 116 Stat. 3093.)

## § 3074. Commissary privileges

### (a) Extension of privilege

Commissioned officers, ships' officers, and members of crews of vessels of the Administration shall be permitted to purchase commissary and quartermaster supplies as far as available from the Armed Forces at the prices charged officers and enlisted members of the Armed Forces.

### (b) Sales of rations, stores, uniforms, and related equipment

The Secretary may purchase ration supplies for messes, stores, uniforms, accouterments, and related equipment for sale aboard ship and shore stations of the Administration to members of the uniformed services and to personnel assigned to such ships or shore stations. Sales shall be in accordance with regulations prescribed by the Secretary, and proceeds therefrom shall, as far as is practicable, fully reimburse the appropriations charged without regard to fiscal year.

### (c) Surviving spouses' rights

Rights extended to members of the uniformed services in this section are extended to their surviving spouses and to such others as are designated by the Secretary concerned.

(Pub.L. 107–372, Title II, § 264, Dec. 19, 2002, 116 Stat. 3093.)

## § 3075. Authority to use appropriated funds for transportation and reimbursement of certain items

### (a) Transportation of effects of deceased officers

In the case of an officer who dies on active duty, the Secretary may provide, from appropriations made available to the Administration, transportation (including packing, unpacking, crating, and uncrating) of personal and household effects of that officer to the official residence of record of that officer. However, upon application by the dependents of such an officer, such transportation may be provided to such other location as may be determined by the Secretary.

### (b) Reimbursement for supplies furnished by officers to distressed and shipwrecked persons

Under regulations prescribed by the Secretary, appropriations made available to the Administration may be used to reimburse an officer for food, clothing, medicines, and other supplies furnished by the officer—

(1) for the temporary relief of distressed persons in remote localities; or

(2) to shipwrecked persons who are temporarily provided for by the officer.

(Pub.L. 107–372, Title II, § 265, Dec. 19, 2002, 116 Stat. 3093.)

## § 3076. Presentation of United States flag upon retirement

### (a) Presentation of flag upon retirement

Upon the release of a commissioned officer from active commissioned service for retirement, the Secretary shall present a United States flag to the officer.

### (b) Multiple presentations not authorized

An officer is not eligible for presentation of a flag under subsection (a) of this section if the officer has previously been presented a flag under this section or any other provision of law providing for the presentation of a United States flag incident to release from active service for retirement.

### (c) No cost to recipient

The presentation of a flag under this section shall be at no cost to the recipient.

(Pub.L. 107–372, Title II, § 266, Dec. 19, 2002, 116 Stat. 3093.)

# TITLE 42

# THE PUBLIC HEALTH AND WELFARE

## SAFETY OF PUBLIC WATER SYSTEMS

## PUBLIC HEALTH SERVICE ACT (TITLE XIV) [PHSA § ____]

**(42 U.S.C.A. §§ 300f to 300j–26)**

## CHAPTER 6A—PUBLIC HEALTH SERVICE

### SUBCHAPTER XII—SAFETY OF PUBLIC WATER SYSTEMS



**Complete Annotation Materials, see Title 42 U.S.C.A.**

**Related Provisions**

*See, also, Water Pollution Prevention and Control, 33 U.S.C.A. § 1251 et seq., ante; and Water Resources Research, 42 U.S.C.A. § 10301 et seq., post.*

# CHAPTER 6A—PUBLIC HEALTH SERVICE

## SUBCHAPTER XII—SAFETY OF PUBLIC WATER SYSTEMS

### PART A—DEFINITIONS

### § 300f. Definitions

**[PHSA § 1401]**

For purposes of this subchapter:

**(1)** The term "primary drinking water regulation" means a regulation which—

**(A)** applies to public water systems;

**(B)** specifies contaminants which, in the judgment of the Administrator, may have any adverse effect on the health of persons;

**(C)** specifies for each such contaminant either—

**(i)** a maximum contaminant level, if, in the judgment of the Administrator, it is economically and technologically feasible to ascertain the level of such contaminant in water in public water systems, or

**(ii)** if, in the judgment of the Administrator, it is not economically or technologically feasible to so ascertain the level of such contaminant, each treatment technique known to the Administrator which leads to a reduction in the level of such contaminant sufficient to satisfy the requirements of section 300g–1 of this title; and

**(D)** contains criteria and procedures to assure a supply of drinking water which dependably complies with such maximum contaminant levels; including accepted methods for quality control and testing procedures to insure compliance with such levels and to insure proper operation and maintenance of the system, and requirements as to (i) the minimum quality of water which may be taken into the system and (ii) siting for new facilities for public water systems.

At any time after promulgation of a regulation referred to in this paragraph, the Administrator may add equally effective quality control and testing procedures by guidance published in the Federal Register. Such procedures shall be treated as an alternative for public water systems to the quality control and testing procedures listed in the regulation.

**(2)** The term "secondary drinking water regulation" means a regulation which applies to public water systems and which specifies the maximum contaminant levels which, in the judgment of the Administrator, are requisite to protect the public welfare. Such regulations may apply to any contaminant in drinking water (A) which may adversely affect the odor or appearance of such water and consequently may cause a substantial number of the persons served by the public water system providing such water to discontinue its use, or (B) which may otherwise adversely affect the public welfare. Such regulations may vary according to geographic and other circumstances.

**(3)** The term "maximum contaminant level" means the maximum permissible level of a contaminant in water which is delivered to any user of a public water system.

**(4) Public water system.—**

**(A) In general.**—The term "public water system" means a system for the provision to the public of water for human consumption through pipes or other constructed conveyances, if such system has at least fifteen service connections or regularly serves at least twenty-five individuals. Such term includes (i) any collection, treatment, storage, and distribution facilities under control of the operator of such system and used primarily in connection with such system, and (ii) any collection or pretreatment storage facilities not under such control which are used primarily in connection with such system.

**(B) Connections.—**

**(i) In general.**—For purposes of subparagraph (A), a connection to a system that delivers water by a constructed conveyance other than a pipe shall not be considered a connection, if—

**(I)** the water is used exclusively for purposes other than residential uses (consisting of drinking, bathing, and cooking, or other similar uses);

**(II)** the Administrator or the State (in the case of a State exercising primary enforcement responsibility for public water systems) determines that alternative water to achieve the equivalent level of public health protection provided by the applicable national primary drinking water regulation is provided for residential or similar uses for drinking and cooking; or

**(III)** the Administrator or the State (in the case of a State exercising primary enforcement responsibility for public water systems) determines that the water provided for residential or similar uses for drinking, cooking, and bathing is centrally treated or treated at the point of entry by the provider, a pass-through entity, or the user to achieve the equivalent level of protection provided by the applicable national primary drinking water regulations.

**(ii) Irrigation districts.**—An irrigation district in existence prior to May 18, 1994, that provides primarily agricultural service through a piped water system with only incidental residential or similar use shall not be considered to be a public water system if the system or the residential or similar users of the system comply with subclause (II) or (III) of clause (i).

**(C) Transition period.**—A water supplier that would be a public water system only as a result of modifications made to this paragraph by the Safe Drinking Water Act Amendments of 1996 shall not be considered a public water system for purposes of the Act until the date that is two years after August 6, 1996. If a water supplier does not serve 15 service connections (as defined in subparagraphs (A) and (B)) or 25 people at any time after the conclusion of the 2-year period, the water supplier shall not be considered a public water system.

**(5)** The term "supplier of water" means any person who owns or operates a public water system.

**(6)** The term "contaminant" means any physical, chemical, biological, or radiological substance or matter in water.

**(7)** The term "Administrator" means the Administrator of the Environmental Protection Agency.

**(8)** The term "Agency" means the Environmental Protection Agency.

**(9)** The term "Council" means the National Drinking Water Advisory Council established under section 300j-5 of this title.

**(10)** The term "municipality" means a city, town, or other public body created by or pursuant to State law, or an Indian Tribe.

**(11)** The term "Federal agency" means any department, agency, or instrumentality of the United States.

**(12)** The term "person" means an individual, corporation, company, association, partnership, State, municipality, or Federal agency (and includes officers, employees, and agents of any corporation, company, association, State, municipality, or Federal agency).

**(13)(A)** Except as provided in subparagraph (B), the term "State" includes, in addition to the several States, only the District of Columbia, Guam, the Commonwealth of Puerto Rico, the Northern Mariana Islands, the Virgin Islands, American Samoa, and the Trust Territory of the Pacific Islands.

**(B)** For purposes of section 300j-12 of this title, the term "State" means each of the 50 States, the District of Columbia, and the Commonwealth of Puerto Rico.

**(14)** The term "Indian Tribe" means any Indian tribe having a Federally recognized governing body carrying out substantial governmental duties and powers over any area. For purposes of section 300j-12 of this title, the term includes any Native village (as defined in section 1602(c) of Title 43).

**(15) Community water system.**—The term "community water system" means a public water system that—

**(A)** serves at least 15 service connections used by year-round residents of the area served by the system; or

**(B)** regularly serves at least 25 year-round residents.

**(16) Noncommunity water system.**—The term "noncommunity water system" means a public water system that is not a community water system.

(July 1, 1944, c. 373, Title XIV, § 1401, as added Dec. 16, 1974, Pub.L. 93-523, § 2(a), 88 Stat. 1661, and amended June 23, 1976, Pub.L. 94-317, Title III, § 301(b)(2), 90 Stat. 707; Oct. 12, 1976, Pub.L. 94-484, Title IX, § 905(b)(1), 90 Stat. 2325; Nov. 16, 1977, Pub.L. 95-190, § 8(b), 91 Stat. 1397; June 19, 1986, Pub.L. 99-339, Title III, § 302(b), 100 Stat. 666; Aug. 6, 1996, Pub.L. 104-182, Title I, § 101(a), (b)(1), 110 Stat. 1615, 1616.)

## HISTORICAL AND STATUTORY NOTES

### References in Text

The Safe Drinking Water Act Amendments of 1996, referred to in par. (4)(C), is Pub.L. 104-182, Aug. 6, 1996, 110 Stat. 1613. The modifications made by such Act to par. (4) are the amendments made by Pub.L. 104-182, Title I, § 101(b)(1), Aug. 6, 1996, 110 Stat. 1616; see 1996 Amendments note set out under this section. For complete classification of this Act to the Code, see Short Title note set out under section 201 of this title and Tables.

### Effective and Applicability Provisions

1996 Acts

Section 2(b) of Pub.L. 104-182 provided that: "Except as otherwise specified in this Act [Pub.L. 104-182, Aug. 6, 1996, 110 Stat. 1613, for classification of which to the Code, see Short Title of 1996 Amendments note, set out under section 201 of this title] or in the amendments made by this Act, this

Act and the amendments made by this Act shall take effect on the date of enactment of this Act [Aug. 6, 1996]".

**Short Title**

1996 Amendments

For short title of Pub.L. 104–182, which amended this subchapter, as the "Safe Drinking Water Act Amendments of 1996", see section 1(a) of Pub.L. 104–182, set out as a note under section 201 of this title.

1986 Amendments

For short title of Pub.L. 99–339, which amended this subchapter, as the "Safe Drinking Water Act Amendments of 1986", see section 1 of Pub.L. 99–339, set out as a note under section 201 of this title.

1977 Amendments

For Short Title of Pub.L. 95–190, which amended this subchapter, see Short Title of 1977 Amendments note set out under section 201 of this title.

1974 Acts

For Short Title of Pub.L. 93–523, which enacted this subchapter, as the "Safe Drinking Water Act of 1974", see section 1 of Pub.L. 93–523, as amended, set out as a Short Title of 1974 Amendments note under section 201 of this title.

**Termination of Trust Territory of the Pacific Islands**

For termination of Trust Territory of the Pacific Islands, see note set out preceding 48 U.S.C.A. § 1681.

**Effect of Public Law 104–182 on Federal Water Pollution Control Act**

Section 2(c) of Pub.L. 104–182 provided that: "Except for the provisions of section 302 (relating to transfers of funds) [section 302 of Pub.L. 104–182, set out as a note under section 300j–12 of this title], nothing in this Act [Pub.L. 104–182, Aug. 6, 1996, 110 Stat. 1613, for classification of which to the Code, see Short Title of 1996 Amendments note, set out under section 201 of this title] or in any amendments made by this Act to title XIV of the Public Health Service Act (commonly known as the 'Safe Drinking Water Act') [this subchapter] or any other law shall be construed by the Administrator of the Environmental Protection Agency or the courts as affecting, modifying, expanding, changing, or altering—

"(1) the provisions of the Federal Water Pollution Control Act [Act June 30, 1948, c. 758, as amended generally by Pub.L. 92–500, § 2, Oct. 18, 1972, 86 Stat. 816, also known as the Clean Water Act, which is classified generally to chapter 26 (section 1251 et seq.) of Title 33, Navigation and Navigable Waters];

"(2) the duties and responsibilities of the Administrator under that Act; or

"(3) the regulation or control of point or nonpoint sources of pollution discharged into waters covered by that Act. The Administrator shall identify in the agency's annual budget all funding and full-time equivalents administering such title XIV [this subchapter] separately from funding and staffing for the Federal Water Pollution Control Act."

**Congressional Findings**

Section 3 of Pub.L. 104–182 provided that: "The Congress finds that—

"(1) safe drinking water is essential to the protection of public health;

"(2) because the requirements of the Safe Drinking Water Act (42 U.S.C. 300f et seq.) [this subchapter] now exceed the financial and technical capacity of some public water systems, especially many small public water systems, the Federal Government needs to provide assistance to communities to help the communities meet Federal drinking water requirements;

"(3) the Federal Government commits to maintaining and improving its partnership with the States in the administration and implementation of the Safe Drinking Water Act [this subchapter];

"(4) States play a central role in the implementation of safe drinking water programs, and States need increased financial resources and appropriate flexibility to ensure the prompt and effective development and implementation of drinking water programs;

"(5) the existing process for the assessment and selection of additional drinking water contaminants needs to be revised and improved to ensure that there is a sound scientific basis for setting priorities in establishing drinking water regulations;

"(6) procedures for assessing the health effects of contaminants establishing drinking water standards should be revised to provide greater opportunity for public education and participation;

"(7) in considering the appropriate level of regulation for contaminants in drinking water, risk assessment, based on sound and objective science, and benefit-cost analysis are important analytical tools for improving the efficiency and effectiveness of drinking water regulations to protect human health;

"(8) more effective protection of public health requires—

"(A) a Federal commitment to set priorities that will allow scarce Federal, State, and local resources to be targeted toward the drinking water problems of greatest public health concern;

"(B) maximizing the value of the different and complementary strengths and responsibilities of the Federal and State governments in those States that have primary enforcement responsibility for the Safe Drinking Water Act [this subchapter]; and

"(C) prevention of drinking water contamination through well-trained system operators, water systems with adequate managerial, technical, and financial capacity, and enhanced protection of source waters of public water systems;

"(9) compliance with the requirements of the Safe Drinking Water Act [this subchapter] continues to be a concern at public water systems experiencing technical and financial limitations, and Federal, State, and local governments need more resources and more effective authority to attain the objectives of the Safe Drinking Water Act; and

"(10) consumers served by public water systems should be provided with information on the source of the water they are drinking and its quality and safety, as well as prompt notification of any violation of drinking water regulations."

**GAO Study**

Section 101(b)(2) of Pub.L. 104-182 provided that: "The Comptroller General of the United States shall undertake a study to—

"(A) ascertain the numbers and locations of individuals and households relying for their residential water needs, including drinking, bathing, and cooking (or other similar uses) on irrigation water systems, mining water systems, industrial water systems, or other water systems covered by section 1401(4)(B) of the Safe Drinking Water Act [par. (4)(B) of this section] that are not public water systems subject to the Safe Drinking Water Act [this subchapter];

"(B) determine the sources and costs and affordability (to users and systems) of water used by such populations for their residential water needs; and

"(C) review State and water system compliance with the exclusion provisions of section 1401(4)(B) of such Act [par. (4)(B) of this section]. The Comptroller General shall submit a report to the Congress within 3 years after the date of enactment of this Act [Aug. 6, 1996] containing the results of such study."

**Federal Compliance With Pollution Control Standards**

For provisions relating to the responsibility of the head of each Executive agency for compliance with applicable pollution control standards, see Ex. Ord. No. 12088, Oct. 13, 1978, 43 F.R. 47707, set out as a note under § 4321 of this title.

**Safe Drinking Water Amendments of 1977 as Not Affecting Authority of Administrator With Respect to Contaminants**

Section 3(e)(2) of Pub.L. 95-190 provided that: "Nothing in this Act [see Short Title of 1977 Amendment note set out under section 201 of this title] shall be construed to alter or affect the Administrator's authority or duty under title 14 of the Public Health Service Act [this subchapter] to promulgate regulations or take other action with respect to any contaminant."

**Safe Drinking Water Amendments of 1977 Restrictions on Appropriations for Research**

Section 2(e) of Pub.L. 95-190 provided that: "Nothing in this Act [see Short Title of 1977 Amendment note set out under section 201 of this title] shall be construed to authorize the appropriation of any amount for research under title XIV of the Public Health Service Act [this subchapter] (relating to safe drinking water)."

**Rural Water Survey; Report to President and Congress; Authorization of Appropriations**

Section 3 of Pub.L. 93-523, as amended by Pub.L. 95-190, §§ 2(d), 3(d), Nov. 16, 1977, 91 Stat. 1393, 1394, directed the Administrator of the Environmental Protection Agency, after consultation with the Secretary of Agriculture and the several States, to enter into arrangements with public or private entities to conduct a survey of the quantity, quality, and availability of rural drinking water supplies, which survey was to include, but not be limited to, the consideration of the number of residents in each rural area who presently are being inadequately served by a public or private drinking water supply system, or by an individual home drinking water supply system, or who presently have limited or otherwise inadequate access to drinking water, or who, due to the absence or inadequacy of a drinking water supply system, are exposed to an increased health hazard, and who have experienced incidents or chronic or acute illness, which may be attributed to the inadequacy of a drinking water supply system. Since the survey was to be completed within eighteen months of Dec. 16, 1974 and a final report thereon submitted, not later than six months after the completion of the survey, to the President and to the Congress, the provision was omitted from the Code as executed.

**Termination of Advisory Committees**

Pub.L. 93-641, § 6, Jan. 4, 1975, 88 Stat. 2275, set out as a note under section 217a of this title, provided that an advisory committee established pursuant to the Public Health Service Act [this chapter] shall terminate at such time as may be specifically prescribed by an Act of Congress enacted after Jan. 4, 1975.

## PART B—PUBLIC WATER SYSTEMS

## § 300g. Coverage

**[PHSA § 1411]**

Subject to sections 300g-4 and 300g-5 of this title, national primary drinking water regulations under this part shall apply to each public water system in each State; except that such regulations shall not apply to a public water system—

(1) which consists only of distribution and storage facilities (and does not have any collection and treatment facilities);

(2) which obtains all of its water from, but is not owned or operated by, a public water system to which such regulations apply;

(3) which does not sell water to any person; and

(4) which is not a carrier which conveys passengers in interstate commerce.

(July 1, 1944, c. 373, Title XIV, § 1411, as added Dec. 16, 1974, Pub.L. 93-523, § 2(a), 88 Stat. 1662.)

## § 300g-1. National drinking water regulations

**[PHSA § 1412]**

### (a) National primary drinking water regulations; maximum contaminant level goals; simultaneous publication of regulations and goals

(1) Effective on June 19, 1986, each national interim or revised primary drinking water regulation promulgated under this section before June 19, 1986, shall be deemed to be a national primary drinking water regulation under subsection (b) of this section. No such regulation shall be required to comply with the standards set forth in subsection (b)(4) of this section unless such regulation is amended to establish a different maximum contaminant level after June 19, 1986.

(2) After June 19, 1986, each recommended maximum contaminant level published before June 19,

1986, shall be treated as a maximum contaminant level goal.

(3) Whenever a national primary drinking water regulation is proposed under subsection (b) of this section for any contaminant, the maximum contaminant level goal for such contaminant shall be proposed simultaneously. Whenever a national primary drinking water regulation is promulgated under subsection (b) of this section for any contaminant, the maximum contaminant level goal for such contaminant shall be published simultaneously.

(4) Paragraph (3) shall not apply to any recommended maximum contaminant level published before June 19, 1986.

**(b) Standards**

**(1) Identification of contaminants for listing**

**(A) General authority**

The Administrator shall, in accordance with the procedures established by this subsection, publish a maximum contaminant level goal and promulgate a national primary drinking water regulation for a contaminant (other than a contaminant referred to in paragraph (2) for which a national primary drinking water regulation has been promulgated as of August 6, 1996) if the Administrator determines that—

(i) the contaminant may have an adverse effect on the health of persons;

(ii) the contaminant is known to occur or there is a substantial likelihood that the contaminant will occur in public water systems with a frequency and at levels of public health concern; and

(iii) in the sole judgment of the Administrator, regulation of such contaminant presents a meaningful opportunity for health risk reduction for persons served by public water systems.

**(B) Regulation of unregulated contaminants**

**(i) Listing of contaminants for consideration**

(I) Not later than 18 months after August 6, 1996, and every 5 years thereafter, the Administrator, after consultation with the scientific community, including the Science Advisory Board, after notice and opportunity for public comment, and after considering the occurrence data base established under section 300j–4(g) of this title, shall publish a list of contaminants which, at the time of publication, are not subject to any proposed or promulgated national primary drinking water regulation, which are known or anticipated to occur in public water systems, and which may require regulation under this subchapter.

(II) The unregulated contaminants considered under subclause (I) shall include, but not be limited to, substances referred to in section 9601(14) of this title, and substances registered as pesticides under the Federal Insecticide, Fungicide, and Rodenticide Act [7 U.S.C.A. § 136 et seq.].

(III) The Administrator's decision whether or not to select an unregulated contaminant for a list under this clause shall not be subject to judicial review.

**(ii) Determination to regulate**

(I) Not later than 5 years after August 6, 1996, and every 5 years thereafter, the Administrator shall, after notice of the preliminary determination and opportunity for public comment, for not fewer than 5 contaminants included on the list published under clause (i), make determinations of whether or not to regulate such contaminants.

(II) A determination to regulate a contaminant shall be based on findings that the criteria of clauses (i), (ii), and (iii) of subparagraph (A) are satisfied. Such findings shall be based on the best available public health information, including the occurrence data base established under section 300j–4(g) of this title.

(III) The Administrator may make a determination to regulate a contaminant that does not appear on a list under clause (i) if the determination to regulate is made pursuant to subclause (II).

(IV) A determination under this clause not to regulate a contaminant shall be considered final agency action and subject to judicial review.

**(iii) Review**

Each document setting forth the determination for a contaminant under clause (ii) shall be available for public comment at such time as the determination is published.

**(C) Priorities**

In selecting unregulated contaminants for consideration under subparagraph (B), the Administrator shall select contaminants that present the greatest public health concern. The Administrator, in making such selection, shall take into consideration, among other factors of public health concern, the effect of such contaminants upon subgroups that comprise a meaningful portion of the general population (such as infants, children, pregnant women, the elderly, individuals with a history of serious illness, or other subpopulations) that are identifiable as being at greater risk of adverse health effects due to exposure to contaminants in drinking water than the general population.

**(D) Urgent threats to public health**

The administrator may promulgate an interim national primary drinking water regulation for a contaminant without making a determination for the contaminant under paragraph (4)(C), or completing the analysis under paragraph (3)(C), to address an urgent threat to public health as determined by the Administrator after consultation with and written response to any comments provided by the Secretary of Health and Human Services, acting through the director of the Centers for Disease Control and Prevention or the director of the National Institutes of Health. A determination for any contaminant in accordance with paragraph (4)(C) subject to an interim regulation under this subparagraph shall be issued, and a completed analysis meeting the requirements of paragraph (3)(C) shall be published, not later than 3 years after the date on which the regulation is promulgated and the regulation shall be repromulgated, or revised if appropriate, not later than 5 years after that date.

**(E) Regulation**

For each contaminant that the Administrator determines to regulate under subparagraph (B), the Administrator shall publish maximum contaminant level goals and promulgate, by rule, national primary drinking water regulations under this subsection. The Administrator shall propose the maximum contaminant level goal and national primary drinking water regulation for a contaminant not later than 24 months after the determination to regulate under subparagraph (B), and may publish such proposed regulation concurrent with the determination to regulate. The Administrator shall publish a maximum contaminant level goal and promulgate a national primary drinking water regulation within 18 months after the proposal thereof. The Administrator, by notice in the Federal Register, may extend the deadline for such promulgation for up to 9 months.

**(F) Health advisories and other actions**

The Administrator may publish health advisories (which are not regulations) or take other appropriate actions for contaminants not subject to any national primary drinking water regulation.

**(2) Schedules and deadlines**

**(A) In general**

In the case of the contaminants listed in the Advance Notice of Proposed Rulemaking published in volume 47, Federal Register, page 9352, and in volume 48, Federal Register, page 45502, the Administrator shall publish maximum contaminant level goals and promulgate national primary drinking water regulations—

**(i)** not later than 1 year after June 19, 1986, for not fewer than 9 of the listed contaminants;

**(ii)** not later than 2 years after June 19, 1986, for not fewer than 40 of the listed contaminants; and

**(iii)** not later than 3 years after June 19, 1986, for the remainder of the listed contaminants.

**(B) Substitution of contaminants**

If the Administrator identifies a drinking water contaminant the regulation of which, in the judgment of the Administrator, is more likely to be protective of public health (taking into account the schedule for regulation under subparagraph (A)) than a contaminant referred to in subparagraph (A), the Administrator may publish a maximum contaminant level goal and promulgate a national primary drinking water regulation for the identified contaminant in lieu of regulating the contaminant referred to in subparagraph (A). Substitutions may be made for not more than 7 contaminants referred to in subparagraph (A). Regulation of a contaminant identified under this subparagraph shall be in accordance with the schedule applicable to the contaminant for which the substitution is made.

**(C) Disinfectants and disinfection byproducts**

The Administrator shall promulgate an Interim Enhanced Surface Water Treatment Rule, a Final Enhanced Surface Water Treatment Rule, a Stage I Disinfectants and Disinfection Byproducts Rule, and a Stage II Disinfectants and Disinfection Byproducts Rule in accordance with the schedule published in volume 59, Federal Register, page 6361 (February 10, 1994), in table III.13 of the proposed Information Collection Rule. If a delay occurs with respect to the promulgation of any rule in the schedule referred to in this subparagraph, all subsequent rules shall be completed as expeditiously as practicable but no later than a revised date that reflects the interval or intervals for the rules in the schedule.

**(3) Risk assessment, management, and communication**

**(A) Use of science in decisionmaking**

In carrying out this section, and, to the degree that an Agency action is based on science, the Administrator shall use—

(i) the best available, peer-reviewed science and supporting studies conducted in accordance with sound and objective scientific practices; and

(ii) data collected by accepted methods or best available methods (if the reliability of the method and the nature of the decision justifies use of the data).

**(B) Public information**

In carrying out this section, the Administrator shall ensure that the presentation of information on public health effects is comprehensive, informative, and understandable. The Administrator shall, in a document made available to the public in support of a regulation promulgated under this section, specify, to the extent practicable—

(i) each population addressed by any estimate of public health effects;

(ii) the expected risk or central estimate of risk for the specific populations;

(iii) each appropriate upper-bound or lower-bound estimate of risk;

(iv) each significant uncertainty identified in the process of the assessment of public health effects and studies that would assist in resolving the uncertainty; and

(v) peer-reviewed studies known to the Administrator that support, are directly relevant to, or fail to support any estimate of public health effects and the methodology used to reconcile inconsistencies in the scientific data.

**(C) Health risk reduction and cost analysis**

**(i) Maximum contaminant levels**

When proposing any national primary drinking water regulation that includes a maximum contaminant level, the Administrator shall, with respect to a maximum contaminant level that is being considered in accordance with paragraph (4) and each alternative maximum contaminant level that is being considered pursuant to paragraph (5) or (6)(A), publish, seek public comment on, and use for the purposes of paragraphs (4), (5), and (6) an analysis of each of the following:

(I) Quantifiable and nonquantifiable health risk reduction benefits for which there is a factual basis in the rulemaking record to conclude that such benefits are likely to occur as the result of treatment to comply with each level.

(II) Quantifiable and nonquantifiable health risk reduction benefits for which there is a factual basis in the rulemaking record to conclude that such benefits are likely to occur from reductions in co-occurring contaminants that may be attributed solely to compliance with the maximum contaminant level, excluding benefits resulting from compliance with other proposed or promulgated regulations.

(III) Quantifiable and nonquantifiable costs for which there is a factual basis in the rulemaking record to conclude that such costs are likely to occur solely as a result of compliance with the maximum contaminant level, including monitoring, treatment, and other costs and excluding costs resulting from compliance with other proposed or promulgated regulations.

(IV) The incremental costs and benefits associated with each alternative maximum contaminant level considered.

(V) The effects of the contaminant on the general population and on groups within the general population such as infants, children, pregnant women, the elderly, individuals with a history of serious illness, or other subpopulations that are identified as likely to be at greater risk of adverse health effects due to exposure to contaminants in drinking water than the general population.

(VI) Any increased health risk that may occur as the result of compliance, including risks associated with co-occurring contaminants.

(VII) Other relevant factors, including the quality and extent of the information, the uncertainties in the analysis supporting subclauses (I) through (VI), and factors with respect to the degree and nature of the risk.

**(ii) Treatment techniques**

When proposing a national primary drinking water regulation that includes a treatment technique in accordance with paragraph (7)(A), the Administrator shall publish and seek public comment on an analysis of the health risk reduction benefits and costs likely to be experienced as the result of compliance with the treatment technique and alternative treatment techniques that are being considered, taking into account, as appropriate, the factors described in clause (i).

**(iii) Approaches to measure and value benefits**

The Administrator may identify valid approaches for the measurement and valuation of benefits under this subparagraph, including approaches to identify consumer willingness to pay for reductions in health risks from drinking water contaminants.

(iv) **Authorization**

There are authorized to be appropriated to the Administrator, acting through the Office of Ground Water and Drinking Water, to conduct studies, assessments, and analyses in support of regulations or the development of methods, $35,000,000 for each of fiscal years 1996 through 2003.

(4) **Goals and standards**

(A) **Maximum contaminant level goals**

Each maximum contaminant level goal established under this subsection shall be set at the level at which no known or anticipated adverse effects on the health of persons occur and which allows an adequate margin of safety.

(B) **Maximum contaminant levels**

Except as provided in paragraphs (5) and (6), each national primary drinking water regulation for a contaminant for which a maximum contaminant level goal is established under this subsection shall specify a maximum contaminant level for such contaminant which is as close to the maximum contaminant level goal as is feasible.

(C) **Determination**

At the time the Administrator proposes a national primary drinking water regulation under this paragraph, the Administrator shall publish a determination as to whether the benefits of the maximum contaminant level justify, or do not justify, the costs based on the analysis conducted under paragraph (3)(C).

(D) **Definition of feasible**

For the purposes of this subsection, the term "feasible" means feasible with the use of the best technology, treatment techniques and other means which the Administrator finds, after examination for efficacy under field conditions and not solely under laboratory conditions, are available (taking cost into consideration). For the purpose of this paragraph, granular activated carbon is feasible for the control of synthetic organic chemicals, and any technology, treatment technique, or other means found to be the best available for the control of synthetic organic chemicals must be at least as effective in controlling synthetic organic chemicals as granular activated carbon.

(E) **Feasible technologies**

(i) **In general**

Each national primary drinking water regulation which establishes a maximum contaminant level shall list the technology, treatment techniques, and other means which the Administrator finds to be feasible for purposes of meeting such maximum contaminant level, but a regulation under this subsection shall not require that any specified technology, treatment technique, or other means be used for purposes of meeting such maximum contaminant level.

(ii) **List of technologies for small systems**

The Administrator shall include in the list any technology, treatment technique, or other means that is affordable, as determined by the Administrator in consultation with the States, for small public water systems serving—

(I) a population of 10,000 or fewer but more than 3,300;

(II) a population of 3,300 or fewer but more than 500; and

(III) a population of 500 or fewer but more than 25,

and that achieves compliance with the maximum contaminant level or treatment technique, including packaged or modular systems and point-of-entry or point-of-use treatment units. Point-of-entry and point-of-use treatment units shall be owned, controlled and maintained by the public water system or by a person under contract with the public water system to ensure proper operation and maintenance and compliance with the maximum contaminant level or treatment technique and equipped with mechanical warnings to ensure that customers are automatically notified of operational problems. The Administrator shall not include in the list any point-of-use treatment technology, treatment technique, or other means to achieve compliance with a maximum contaminant level or treatment technique requirement for a microbial contaminant (or an indicator of a microbial contaminant). If the American National Standards Institute has issued product standards applicable to a specific type of point-of-entry or point-of-use treatment unit, individual units of that type shall not be accepted for compliance with a maximum contaminant level or treatment technique requirement unless they are independently certified in accordance with such standards. In listing any technology, treatment technique, or other means pursuant to this clause, the Administrator shall consider the quality of the source water to be treated.

(iii) **List of technologies that achieve compliance**

Except as provided in clause (v), not later than 2 years after August 6, 1996, and after consultation with the States, the Administrator shall issue a list of technologies that achieve compliance with the maximum contaminant level or treatment technique for each category of public water systems described in subclauses (I), (II), and (III) of clause (ii) for each national primary drinking water regulation promulgated prior to June 19, 1986.

(iv) **Additional technologies**

The Administrator may, at any time after a national primary drinking water regulation has been promulgated, supplement the list of technologies describing additional or new or innovative treatment technologies that meet the requirements of this paragraph for categories of small public water systems described in subclauses (I), (II), and (III) of clause (ii) that are subject to the regulation.

(v) **Technologies that meet surface water treatment rules**

Within one year after August 6, 1996, the Administrator shall list technologies that meet the Surface Water Treatment Rule for each category of public water systems described in subclauses (I), (II), and (III) of clause (ii).

(5) **Additional health risk considerations**

(A) **In general**

Notwithstanding paragraph (4), the Administrator may establish a maximum contaminant level for a contaminant at a level other than the feasible level, if the technology, treatment techniques, and other means used to determine the feasible level would result in an increase in the health risk from drinking water by—

(i) increasing the concentration of other contaminants in drinking water; or

(ii) interfering with the efficacy of drinking water treatment techniques or processes that are used to comply with other national primary drinking water regulations.

(B) **Establishment of level**

If the Administrator establishes a maximum contaminant level or levels or requires the use of treatment techniques for any contaminant or contaminants pursuant to the authority of this paragraph—

(i) the level or levels or treatment techniques shall minimize the overall risk of adverse health effects by balancing the risk from the contaminant and the risk from other contaminants the concentrations of which may be affected by the use of a treatment technique or process that would be employed to attain the maximum contaminant level or levels; and

(ii) the combination of technology, treatment techniques, or other means required to meet the level or levels shall not be more stringent than is feasible (as defined in paragraph (4)(D)).

(6) **Additional health risk reduction and cost considerations**

(A) **In general**

Notwithstanding paragraph (4), if the Administrator determines based on an analysis conducted under paragraph (3)(C) that the benefits of a maximum contaminant level promulgated in accordance with paragraph (4) would not justify the costs of complying with the level, the Administrator may, after notice and opportunity for public comment, promulgate a maximum contaminant level for the contaminant that maximizes health risk reduction benefits at a cost that is justified by the benefits.

(B) **Exception**

The Administrator shall not use the authority of this paragraph to promulgate a maximum contaminant level for a contaminant, if the benefits of compliance with a national primary drinking water regulation for the contaminant that would be promulgated in accordance with paragraph (4) experienced by—

(i) persons served by large public water systems; and

(ii) persons served by such other systems as are unlikely, based on information provided by the States, to receive a variance under section 300g-4(e) of this title (relating to small system variances);

would justify the costs to the systems of complying with the regulation. This subparagraph shall not apply if the contaminant is found almost exclusively in small systems eligible under section 300g-4(e) of this title for a small system variance.

(C) **Disinfectants and disinfection byproducts**

The Administrator may not use the authority of this paragraph to establish a maximum contaminant level in a Stage I or Stage II national primary drinking water regulation (as described in paragraph (2)(C)) for contaminants that are disinfectants or disinfection byproducts, or to establish a maximum contaminant level or treatment technique requirement for the control of cryptosporidium. The authority of this paragraph may be used to establish regulations for the use of disinfection by systems relying on ground water sources as required by paragraph (8).

**(D) Judicial review**

A determination by the Administrator that the benefits of a maximum contaminant level or treatment requirement justify or do not justify the costs of complying with the level shall be reviewed by the court pursuant to section 300j–7 of this title only as part of a review of a final national primary drinking water regulation that has been promulgated based on the determination and shall not be set aside by the court under that section unless the court finds that the determination is arbitrary and capricious.

(7)**(A)** The Administrator is authorized to promulgate a national primary drinking water regulation that requires the use of a treatment technique in lieu of establishing a maximum contaminant level, if the Administrator makes a finding that it is not economically or technologically feasible to ascertain the level of the contaminant. In such case, the Administrator shall identify those treatment techniques which, in the Administrator's judgment, would prevent known or anticipated adverse effects on the health of persons to the extent feasible. Such regulations shall specify each treatment technique known to the Administrator which meets the requirements of this paragraph, but the Administrator may grant a variance from any specified treatment technique in accordance with section 300g–4(a)(3) of this title.

**(B)** Any schedule referred to in this subsection for the promulgation of a national primary drinking water regulation for any contaminant shall apply in the same manner if the regulation requires a treatment technique in lieu of establishing a maximum contaminant level.

**(C)(i)** Not later than 18 months after June 19, 1986, the Administrator shall propose and promulgate national primary drinking water regulations specifying criteria under which filtration (including coagulation and sedimentation, as appropriate) is required as a treatment technique for public water systems supplied by surface water sources. In promulgating such rules, the Administrator shall consider the quality of source waters, protection afforded by watershed management, treatment practices (such as disinfection and length of water storage) and other factors relevant to protection of health.

**(ii)** In lieu of the provisions of section 300g–4 of this title the Administrator shall specify procedures by which the State determines which public water systems within its jurisdiction shall adopt filtration under the criteria of clause (i). The State may require the public water system to provide studies or other information to assist in this determination. The procedures shall provide notice and opportunity for public hearing on this determination. If the State determines that filtration is required, the State shall prescribe a schedule for compliance by the public water system with the filtration requirement. A schedule shall require compliance within 18 months of a determination made under clause (iii).

**(iii)** Within 18 months from the time that the Administrator establishes the criteria and procedures under this subparagraph, a State with primary enforcement responsibility shall adopt any necessary regulations to implement this subparagraph. Within 12 months of adoption of such regulations the State shall make determinations regarding filtration for all the public water systems within its jurisdiction supplied by surface waters.

**(iv)** If a State does not have primary enforcement responsibility for public water systems, the Administrator shall have the same authority to make the determination in clause (ii) in such State as the State would have under that clause. Any filtration requirement or schedule under this subparagraph shall be treated as if it were a requirement of a national primary drinking water regulation.

**(v)** As an additional alternative to the regulations promulgated pursuant to clauses (i) and (iii), including the criteria for avoiding filtration contained in 40 CFR 141.71, a State exercising primary enforcement responsibility for public water systems may, on a case-by-case basis, and after notice and opportunity for public comment, establish treatment requirements as an alternative to filtration in the case of systems having uninhabited, undeveloped watersheds in consolidated ownership, and having control over access to, and activities in, those watersheds, if the State determines (and the Administrator concurs) that the quality of the source water and the alternative treatment requirements established by the State ensure greater removal or inactivation efficiencies of pathogenic organisms for which national primary drinking water regulations have been promulgated or that are of public health concern than would be achieved by the combination of filtration and chlorine disinfection (in compliance with this section).

**(8) Disinfection**

At any time after the end of the 3–year period that begins on August 6, 1996, but not later than the date on which the Administrator promulgates a

Stage II rulemaking for disinfectants and disinfection byproducts (as described in paragraph (2)(C)), the Administrator shall also promulgate national primary drinking water regulations requiring disinfection as a treatment technique for all public water systems, including surface water systems and, as necessary, ground water systems. After consultation with the States, the Administrator shall (as part of the regulations) promulgate criteria that the Administrator, or a State that has primary enforcement responsibility under section 300g–2 of this title, shall apply to determine whether disinfection shall be required as a treatment technique for any public water system served by ground water. The Administrator shall simultaneously promulgate a rule specifying criteria that will be used by the Administrator (or delegated State authorities) to grant variances from this requirement according to the provisions of sections 300g–4(a)(1)(B) and 300g–4(a)(3) of this title. In implementing section 300j–1(e) of this title the Administrator or the delegated State authority shall, where appropriate, give special consideration to providing technical assistance to small public water systems in complying with the regulations promulgated under this paragraph.

**(9) Review and revision**

The Administrator shall, not less often than every 6 years, review and revise, as appropriate, each national primary drinking water regulation promulgated under this subchapter. Any revision of a national primary drinking water regulation shall be promulgated in accordance with this section, except that each revision shall maintain, or provide for greater, protection of the health of persons.

**(10) Effective date**

A national primary drinking water regulation promulgated under this section (and any amendment thereto) shall take effect on the date that is 3 years after the date on which the regulation is promulgated unless the Administrator determines that an earlier date is practicable, except that the Administrator, or a State (in the case of an individual system), may allow up to 2 additional years to comply with a maximum contaminant level or treatment technique if the Administrator or State (in the case of an individual system) determines that additional time is necessary for capital improvements.

(11) No national primary drinking water regulation may require the addition of any substance for preventive health care purposes unrelated to contamination of drinking water.

**(12) Certain contaminants**

**(A) Arsenic**

**(i) Schedule and standard**

Notwithstanding the deadlines set forth in paragraph (1), the Administrator shall promulgate a national primary drinking water regulation for arsenic pursuant to this subsection, in accordance with the schedule established by this paragraph.

**(ii) Study plan**

Not later than 180 days after August 6, 1996, the Administrator shall develop a comprehensive plan for study in support of drinking water rulemaking to reduce the uncertainty in assessing health risks associated with exposure to low levels of arsenic. In conducting such study, the Administrator shall consult with the National Academy of Sciences, other Federal agencies, and interested public and private entities.

**(iii) Cooperative agreements**

In carrying out the study plan, the Administrator may enter into cooperative agreements with other Federal agencies, State and local governments, and other interested public and private entities.

**(iv) Proposed regulations**

The Administrator shall propose a national primary drinking water regulation for arsenic not later than January 1, 2000.

**(v) Final regulations**

Not later than January 1, 2001, after notice and opportunity for public comment, the Administrator shall promulgate a national primary drinking water regulation for arsenic.

**(vi) Authorization**

There are authorized to be appropriated $2,500,000 for each of fiscal years 1997 through 2000 for the studies required by this paragraph.

**(B) Sulfate**

**(i) Additional study**

Prior to promulgating a national primary drinking water regulation for sulfate, the Administrator and the Director of the Centers for Disease Control and Prevention shall jointly conduct an additional study to establish a reliable dose-response relationship for the adverse human health effects that may result from exposure to sulfate in drinking water, including the health effects that may be experienced by groups within the general population (including infants and travelers) that are potentially at greater risk of adverse health effects as the result of such exposure. The study shall be conducted in consultation with interested States, shall be based on the best available, peer-reviewed science and supporting studies conducted in accordance with sound and objective scientific practices, and shall be completed not later than 30 months after August 6, 1996.

**(ii) Determination**

The Administrator shall include sulfate among the 5 or more contaminants for which a determination is made pursuant to paragraph (3)(B) not later than 5 years after August 6, 1996.

**(iii) Proposed and final rule**

Notwithstanding the deadlines set forth in paragraph (2), the Administrator may, pursuant to the authorities of this subsection and after notice and opportunity for public comment, promulgate a final national primary drinking water regulation for sulfate. Any such regulation shall include requirements for public notification and options for the provision of alternative water supplies to populations at risk as a means of complying with the regulation in lieu of a best available treatment technology or other means.

**(13) Radon in drinking water**

**(A) National primary drinking water regulation**

Notwithstanding paragraph (2), the Administrator shall withdraw any national primary drinking water regulation for radon proposed prior to August 6, 1996, and shall propose and promulgate a regulation for radon under this section, as amended by the Safe Drinking Water Act Amendments of 1996.

**(B) Risk assessment and studies**

**(i) Assessment by NAS**

Prior to proposing a national primary drinking water regulation for radon, the Administrator shall arrange for the National Academy of Sciences to prepare a risk assessment for radon in drinking water using the best available science in accordance with the requirements of paragraph (3). The risk assessment shall consider each of the risks associated with exposure to radon from drinking water and consider studies on the health effects of radon at levels and under conditions likely to be experienced through residential exposure. The risk assessment shall be peer-reviewed.

**(ii) Study of other measures**

The Administrator shall arrange for the National Academy of Sciences to prepare an assessment of the health risk reduction benefits associated with various mitigation measures to reduce radon levels in indoor air. The assessment may be conducted as part of the risk assessment authorized by clause (i) and shall be used by the Administrator to prepare the guidance and approve State programs under subparagraph (G).

**(iii) Other organization**

If the National Academy of Sciences declines to prepare the risk assessment or studies required by this subparagraph, the Administrator shall enter into a contract or cooperative agreement with another independent, scientific organization to prepare such assessments or studies.

**(C) Health risk reduction and cost analysis**

Not later than 30 months after August 6, 1996, the Administrator shall publish, and seek public comment on, a health risk reduction and cost analysis meeting the requirements of paragraph (3)(C) for potential maximum contaminant levels that are being considered for radon in drinking water. The Administrator shall include a response to all significant public comments received on the analysis with the preamble for the proposed rule published under subparagraph (D).

**(D) Proposed regulation**

Not later than 36 months after August 6, 1996, the Administrator shall propose a maximum contaminant level goal and a national primary drinking water regulation for radon pursuant to this section.

**(E) Final regulation**

Not later than 12 months after the date of the proposal under subparagraph (D), the Administrator shall publish a maximum contaminant level goal and promulgate a national primary drinking water regulation for radon pursuant to this section based on the risk assessment prepared pursuant to subparagraph (B) and the health risk reduction and cost analysis published pursuant to subparagraph (C). In considering the risk assessment and the health risk reduction and cost analysis in connection with the promulgation of such a standard, the Administrator shall take into account the costs and benefits of control programs for radon from other sources.

**(F) Alternative maximum contaminant level**

If the maximum contaminant level for radon in drinking water promulgated pursuant to subparagraph (E) is more stringent than necessary to reduce the contribution to radon in indoor air from drinking water to a concentration that is equivalent to the national average concentration of radon in outdoor air, the Administrator shall, simultaneously with the promulgation of such level, promulgate an alternative maximum contaminant level for radon that would result in a contribution of radon from drinking water to radon levels in indoor air equivalent to the national average concentration of radon in outdoor air. If the Administrator promulgates an alternative maximum contaminant level under this subparagraph, the Administrator shall, after notice and opportunity for public comment and in consultation with the States, publish guidelines for State programs, including criteria for multimedia measures to mitigate radon levels in indoor air, to be used by the States in preparing programs under subparagraph (G). The guidelines shall take into account data from existing radon mitigation programs and the assessment of mitigation measures prepared under subparagraph (B).

**(G) Multimedia radon mitigation programs**

**(i) In general**

A State may develop and submit a multimedia program to mitigate radon levels in indoor air for approval by the Administrator under this subparagraph. If, after notice and the opportunity for public comment, such program is approved by the Administrator, public water systems in the State may comply with the alternative maximum contaminant level promulgated under subparagraph (F) in lieu of the maximum contaminant level in the national primary drinking water regulation promulgated under subparagraph (E).

**(ii) Elements of programs**

State programs may rely on a variety of mitigation measures including public education, testing, training, technical assistance, remediation grant and loan or incentive programs, or other regulatory or nonregulatory measures. The effectiveness of elements in State programs shall be evaluated by the Administrator based on the assessment prepared by the National Academy of Sciences under subparagraph (B) and the guidelines published by the Administrator under subparagraph (F).

**(iii) Approval**

The Administrator shall approve a State program submitted under this paragraph if the health risk reduction benefits expected to be achieved by the program are equal to or greater than the health risk reduction benefits that would be achieved if each public water system in the State complied with the maximum contaminant level promulgated under subparagraph (E). The Administrator shall approve or disapprove a program submitted under this paragraph within 180 days of receipt. A program that is not disapproved during such period shall be deemed approved. A program that is disapproved may be modified to address the objections of the Administrator and be resubmitted for approval.

**(iv) Review**

The Administrator shall periodically, but not less often than every 5 years, review each multimedia mitigation program approved under this subparagraph to determine whether it continues to meet the requirements of clause (iii) and shall, after written notice to the State and an opportunity for the State to correct any deficiency in the program, withdraw approval of programs that no longer comply with such requirements.

**(v) Extension**

If, within 90 days after the promulgation of an alternative maximum contaminant level under subparagraph (F), the Governor of a State submits a letter to the Administrator committing to develop a multimedia mitigation program under this subparagraph, the effective date of the national primary drinking water regulation for radon in the State that would be applicable under paragraph (10) shall be extended for a period of 18 months.

**(vi) Local programs**

In the event that a State chooses not to submit a multimedia mitigation program for approval under this subparagraph or has submitted a program that has been disapproved, any public water system in the State may submit a program for approval by the Administrator according to the same criteria, conditions, and approval process that would apply to a State program. The Administrator shall approve a multimedia mitigation program if the health risk reduction benefits expected to be achieved by the program are equal to or greater than the health risk reduction benefits that would result from compliance by the public water system with the maximum contaminant level for radon promulgated under subparagraph (E).

(14) **Recycling of filter backwash**

The Administrator shall promulgate a regulation to govern the recycling of filter backwash water within the treatment process of a public water system. The Administrator shall promulgate such regulation not later than 4 years after August 6, 1996, unless such recycling has been addressed by the Administrator's Enhanced Surface Water Treatment Rule prior to such date.

(15) **Variance technologies**

(A) **In general**

At the same time as the Administrator promulgates a national primary drinking water regulation for a contaminant pursuant to this section, the Administrator shall issue guidance or regulations describing the best treatment technologies, treatment techniques, or other means (referred to in this paragraph as "variance technology") for the contaminant that the Administrator finds, after examination for efficacy under field conditions and not solely under laboratory conditions, are available and affordable, as determined by the Administrator in consultation with the States, for public water systems of varying size, considering the quality of the source water to be treated. The Administrator shall identify such variance technologies for public water systems serving—

(i) a population of 10,000 or fewer but more than 3,300;

(ii) a population of 3,300 or fewer but more than 500; and

(iii) a population of 500 or fewer but more than 25,

if, considering the quality of the source water to be treated, no treatment technology is listed for public water systems of that size under paragraph (4)(E). Variance technologies identified by the Administrator pursuant to this paragraph may not achieve compliance with the maximum contaminant level or treatment technique requirement of such regulation, but shall achieve the maximum reduction or inactivation efficiency that is affordable considering the size of the system and the quality of the source water. The guidance or regulations shall not require the use of a technology from a specific manufacturer or brand.

(B) **Limitation**

The Administrator shall not identify any variance technology under this paragraph, unless the Administrator has determined, considering the quality of the source water to be treated and the expected useful life of the technology, that the variance technology is protective of public health.

(C) **Additional information**

The Administrator shall include in the guidance or regulations identifying variance technologies under this paragraph any assumptions supporting the public health determination referred to in subparagraph (B), where such assumptions concern the public water system to which the technology may be applied, or its source waters. The Administrator shall provide any assumptions used in determining affordability, taking into consideration the number of persons served by such systems. The Administrator shall provide as much reliable information as practicable on performance, effectiveness, limitations, costs, and other relevant factors including the applicability of variance technology to waters from surface and underground sources.

(D) **Regulations and guidance**

Not later than 2 years after August 6, 1996, and after consultation with the States, the Administrator shall issue guidance or regulations under subparagraph (A) for each national primary drinking water regulation promulgated prior to August 6, 1996, for which a variance may be granted under section 300g–4(e) of this title. The Administrator may, at any time after a national primary drinking water regulation has been promulgated, issue guidance or regulations describing additional variance technologies. The Administrator shall, not less often than every 7 years, or upon receipt of a petition supported by substantial information, review variance technologies identified under this paragraph. The Administrator shall issue revised guidance or regulations if new or innovative variance technologies become available that meet the requirements of this paragraph and achieve an equal or greater reduction or inactivation efficiency than the variance technologies previously identified under this subparagraph. No public water system shall be required to replace a variance technology during the useful life of the technology for the sole reason that a more efficient variance technology has been listed under this subparagraph.

(c) **Secondary regulations; publication of proposed regulations; promulgation; amendments**

The Administrator shall publish proposed national secondary drinking water regulations within 270 days after December 16, 1974. Within 90 days after publication of any such regulation, he shall promulgate such regulation with such modifications as he deems appropriate. Regulations under this subsection may be amended from time to time.

### (d) Regulations; public hearings; administrative consultations

Regulations under this section shall be prescribed in accordance with section 553 of Title 5 (relating to rulemaking), except that the Administrator shall provide opportunity for public hearing prior to promulgation of such regulations. In proposing and promulgating regulations under this section, the Administrator shall consult with the Secretary and the National Drinking Water Advisory Council.

### (e) Science Advisory Board comments

The Administrator shall request comments from the Science Advisory Board (established under the Environmental Research, Development, and Demonstration Act of 1978) prior to proposal of a maximum contaminant level goal and national primary drinking water regulation. The Board shall respond, as it deems appropriate, within the time period applicable for promulgation of the national primary drinking water standard concerned. This subsection shall, under no circumstances, be used to delay final promulgation of any national primary drinking water standard.

(July 1, 1944, c. 373, Title XIV, § 1412, as added Dec. 16, 1974, Pub.L. 93–523, § 2(a), 88 Stat. 1662, and amended Nov. 16, 1977, Pub.L. 95–190, §§ 3(c), 12(a), 91 Stat. 1394, 1398; June 19, 1986, Pub.L. 99–339, Title I, § 101(a) to (c)(1), (d), (e), 100 Stat. 642 to 646; Aug. 6, 1996, Pub.L. 104–182, Title I, §§ 102(a), (c)(2), 103, 104(a), (c), 105 to 111(a), Title V, § 501(a)(1), (2), 110 Stat. 1617, 1621, 1623, 1625 to 1631, 1691.)

## HISTORICAL AND STATUTORY NOTES

**References in Text**

The Federal Insecticide, Fungicide, and Rodenticide Act, referred to in subsec. (b)(1)(B)(i)(II), is Act June 25, 1947, c. 125, as amended generally by Pub.L. 92–516, Oct. 21, 1972, 86 Stat. 973, which is classified generally to subchapter II (section 136 et seq.) of chapter 6 of Title 7, Agriculture. For complete classification of this Act to the Code, see Short Title note set out under section 136 of Title 7 and Tables.

The Safe Drinking Water Act Amendments of 1996, referred to in subsec. (b)(13)(A), is Pub.L. 104–182, Aug. 6, 1996, 110 Stat. 1613, which is classified principally to this subchapter. For complete classification of such Act to the Code, see Short Title of 1996 Amendments note set out under section 201 of this title and Tables.

The Environmental Research, Development, and Demonstration Act of 1978, referred to in subsec. (e), is Pub.L. 95–155, Nov. 8, 1977, 91 Stat. 1257, which enacted sections 300j–3a, 4361a, 4361b, 4363, 4364, 4365, 4366, and 4367 of this title. Section 4365 of this title established the Science Advisory Board. For complete classification of this Act to the Code, see Tables.

**Effective and Applicability Provisions**

1996 Acts

Amendment by Pub.L. 104–182 effective Aug. 6, 1996, except as otherwise specifically provided, see section 2(b) of Pub.L. 104–182, set out as a note under section 300f of this title.

**National Regulation For Arsenic In Primary Drinking Water**

Pub.L. 106–377, § 1(a)(1) [Title III], Oct. 27, 2000, 114 Stat. 1441, 1441A–41, provided in part: "That notwithstanding section 1412(b)(12)(A)(v) of the Safe Drinking Water Act [subsec. (b)(12)(A)(v) of this section], as amended, the Administrator shall promulgate a national primary drinking water regulation for arsenic not later than June 22, 2001."

**Applicability of Prior Requirements**

Section 102(b) of Pub.L. 104–182 provided that: "The requirements of subparagraphs (C) and (D) of section 1412(b)(3) of the Safe Drinking Water Act as in effect before the date of enactment of this Act [former subsec. (b)(3)(C) and (D) of this section, as in effect prior to Aug. 6, 1996], and any obligation to promulgate regulations pursuant to such subparagraphs not promulgated as of the date of enactment of this Act [Aug. 6, 1996], are superseded by the amendments made by subsection (a) [amending subsec. (b) of this section]."

**Disinfectants and Disinfection Byproducts**

Section 104(b) of Pub.L. 104–182 provided that: "The Administrator of the Environmental Protection Agency may use the authority of section 1412(b)(5) of the Safe Drinking Water Act (as amended by this Act) [subsec. (b)(5) of this section] to promulgate the Stage I and Stage II Disinfectants and Disinfection Byproducts Rules as proposed in volume 59, Federal Register, page 38668 (July 29, 1994). The considerations used in the development of the July 29, 1994, proposed national primary drinking water regulation on disinfectants and disinfection byproducts shall be treated as consistent with such section 1412(b)(5) [subsec. (b)(5) of this section] for purposes of such Stage I and Stage II rules."

# § 300g–2. State primary enforcement responsibility

## [PHSA § 1413]

### (a) In general

For purposes of this subchapter, a State has primary enforcement responsibility for public water systems during any period for which the Administrator determines (pursuant to regulations prescribed under subsection (b) of this section) that such State—

(1) has adopted drinking water regulations that are no less stringent than the national primary drinking water regulations promulgated by the Administrator under subsections (a) and (b) of section 300g–1 of this title not later than 2 years after the date on which the regulations are promulgated by the Administrator, except that the Administrator may provide for an extension of not more than 2 years if, after submission and review of appropriate,

adequate documentation from the State, the Administrator determines that the extension is necessary and justified;

(2) has adopted and is implementing adequate procedures for the enforcement of such State regulations, including conducting such monitoring and making such inspections as the Administrator may require by regulation;

(3) will keep such records and make such reports with respect to its activities under paragraphs (1) and (2) as the Administrator may require by regulation;

(4) if it permits variances or exemptions, or both, from the requirements of its drinking water regulations which meet the requirements of paragraph (1), permits such variances and exemptions under conditions and in a manner which is not less stringent than the conditions under, and the manner in which variances and exemptions may be granted under sections 300g–4 and 300g–5 of this title;

(5) has adopted and can implement an adequate plan for the provision of safe drinking water under emergency circumstances including earthquakes, floods, hurricanes, and other natural disasters, as appropriate; and

(6) has adopted authority for administrative penalties (unless the constitution of the State prohibits the adoption of the authority) in a maximum amount—

(A) in the case of a system serving a population of more than 10,000, that is not less than $1,000 per day per violation; and

(B) in the case of any other system, that is adequate to ensure compliance (as determined by the State);

except that a State may establish a maximum limitation on the total amount of administrative penalties that may be imposed on a public water system per violation.

**(b) Regulations**

(1) The Administrator shall, by regulation (proposed within 180 days of December 16, 1974), prescribe the manner in which a State may apply to the Administrator for a determination that the requirements of paragraphs (1), (2), (3), and (4) of subsection (a) of this section are satisfied with respect to the State, the manner in which the determination is made, the period for which the determination will be effective, and the manner in which the Administrator may determine that such requirements are no longer met. Such regulations shall require that before a determination of the Administrator that such requirements are met or are no longer met with respect to a State may become effective, the Administrator shall notify such State of the determination and the reasons therefor and shall provide an opportunity for public hearing on the determination. Such regulations shall be promulgated (with such modifications as the Administrator deems appropriate) within 90 days of the publication of the proposed regulations in the Federal Register. The Administrator shall promptly notify in writing the chief executive officer of each State of the promulgation of regulations under this paragraph. Such notice shall contain a copy of the regulations and shall specify a State's authority under this subchapter when it is determined to have primary enforcement responsibility for public water systems.

(2) When an application is submitted in accordance with the Administrator's regulations under paragraph (1), the Administrator shall within 90 days of the date on which such application is submitted (A) make the determination applied for, or (B) deny the application and notify the applicant in writing of the reasons for his denial.

**(c) Interim primary enforcement authority**

A State that has primary enforcement authority under this section with respect to each existing national primary drinking water regulation shall be considered to have primary enforcement authority with respect to each new or revised national primary drinking water regulation during the period beginning on the effective date of a regulation adopted and submitted by the State with respect to the new or revised national primary drinking water regulation in accordance with subsection (b)(1) of this section and ending at such time as the Administrator makes a determination under subsection (b)(2)(B) of this section with respect to the regulation.

(July 1, 1944, c. 373, Title XIV, § 1413, as added Dec. 16, 1974, Pub.L. 93–523, § 2(a), 88 Stat. 1665, and amended June 19, 1986, Pub.L. 99–339, Title I, § 101(c)(2), 100 Stat. 646; Aug. 6, 1996, Pub.L. 104–182, Title I, §§ 112, 113(b), 110 Stat. 1633, 1635.)

### HISTORICAL AND STATUTORY NOTES

**Effective and Applicability Provisions**

1996 Acts

Amendment by Pub.L. 104–182 effective Aug. 6, 1996, except as otherwise specifically provided, see section 2(b) of Pub.L. 104–182, set out as a note under section 300f of this title.

## § 300g–3. Enforcement of drinking water regulations
## [PHSA § 1414]

**(a) Notice to State and public water system; issuance of administrative order; civil action**

(1)(A) Whenever the Administrator finds during a period during which a State has primary enforcement responsibility for public water systems (within the meaning of section 300g–2(a) of this title) that any public water system—

(i) for which a variance under section 300g–4 or an exemption under section 300g–5 of this title is not in effect, does not comply with any applicable requirement, or

(ii) for which a variance under section 300g–4 or an exemption under section 300g–5 of this title is in effect, does not comply with any schedule or other requirement imposed pursuant thereto,

he shall so notify the State and such public water system and provide such advice and technical assistance to such State and public water system as may be appropriate to bring the system into compliance with the requirement by the earliest feasible time.

**(B)** If, beyond the thirtieth day after the Administrator's notification under subparagraph (A), the State has not commenced appropriate enforcement action, the Administrator shall issue an order under subsection (g) of this section requiring the public water system to comply with such applicable requirement or the Administrator shall commence a civil action under subsection (b) of this section.

**(2) Enforcement in nonprimacy States**

**(A) In general**

If, on the basis of information available to the Administrator, the Administrator finds, with respect to a period in which a State does not have primary enforcement responsibility for public water systems, that a public water system in the State—

(i) for which a variance under section 300g–4 of this title or an exemption under section 300g–5 of this title is not in effect, does not comply with any applicable requirement; or

(ii) for which a variance under section 300g–4 of this title or an exemption under section 300g–5 of this title is in effect, does not comply with any schedule or other requirement imposed pursuant to the variance or exemption;

the Administrator shall issue an order under subsection (g) of this section requiring the public water system to comply with the requirement, or commence a civil action under subsection (b) of this section.

**(B) Notice**

If the Administrator takes any action pursuant to this paragraph, the Administrator shall notify an appropriate local elected official, if any, with jurisdiction over the public water system of the action prior to the time that the action is taken.

**(b) Judicial determinations in appropriate Federal district courts; civil penalties; separate violations**

The Administrator may bring a civil action in the appropriate United States district court to require compliance with any applicable requirement with an order issued under subsection (g) of this section, or with any schedule or other requirement imposed pursuant to a variance or exemption granted under section 300g–4 or 300g–5 of this title if—

(1) authorized under paragraph (1) or (2) of subsection (a) of this section, or

(2) if requested by (A) the chief executive officer of the State in which is located the public water system which is not in compliance with such regulation or requirement, or (B) the agency of such State which has jurisdiction over compliance by public water systems in the State with national primary drinking water regulations or State drinking water regulations.

The court may enter, in an action brought under this subsection, such judgment as protection of public health may require, taking into consideration the time necessary to comply and the availability of alternative water supplies; and, if the court determines that there has been a violation of the regulation or schedule or other requirement with respect to which the action was brought, the court may, taking into account the seriousness of the violation, the population at risk, and other appropriate factors, impose on the violator a civil penalty of not to exceed $25,000 for each day in which such violation occurs.

**(c) Notice to persons served**

**(1) In general**

Each owner or operator of a public water system shall give notice of each of the following to the persons served by the system:

**(A)** Notice of any failure on the part of the public water system to—

(i) comply with an applicable maximum contaminant level or treatment technique requirement of, or a testing procedure prescribed by, a national primary drinking water regulation; or

(ii) perform monitoring required by section 300j–4(a) of this title.

**(B)** If the public water system is subject to a variance granted under subsection (a)(1)(A), (a)(2), or (e) of section 300g–4 of this title for an inability to meet a maximum contaminant level requirement or is subject to an exemption granted under section 300g–5 of this title, notice of—

(i) the existence of the variance or exemption; and

(ii) any failure to comply with the requirements of any schedule prescribed pursuant to the variance or exemption.

**(C)** Notice of the concentration level of any unregulated contaminant for which the Administrator has required public notice pursuant to paragraph (2)(E).

**(2) Form, manner, and frequency of notice**

**(A) In general**

The Administrator shall, by regulation, and after consultation with the States, prescribe the manner, frequency, form, and content for giving notice under this subsection. The regulations shall—

(i) provide for different frequencies of notice based on the differences between violations that are intermittent or infrequent and violations that are continuous or frequent; and

(ii) take into account the seriousness of any potential adverse health effects that may be involved.

**(B) State requirements**

**(i) In general**

A State may, by rule, establish alternative notification requirements—

(I) with respect to the form and content of notice given under and in a manner in accordance with subparagraph (C); and

(II) with respect to the form and content of notice given under subparagraph (D).

**(ii) Contents**

The alternative requirements shall provide the same type and amount of information as required pursuant to this subsection and regulations issued under subparagraph (A).

**(iii) Relationship to section 300g–2**

Nothing in this subparagraph shall be construed or applied to modify the requirements of section 300g–2 of this title.

**(C) Violations with potential to have serious adverse effects on human health**

Regulations issued under subparagraph (A) shall specify notification procedures for each violation by a public water system that has the potential to have serious adverse effects on human health as a result of short-term exposure. Each notice of violation provided under this subparagraph shall—

(i) be distributed as soon as practicable after the occurrence of the violation, but not later than 24 hours after the occurrence of the violation;

(ii) provide a clear and readily understandable explanation of—

(I) the violation;

(II) the potential adverse effects on human health;

(III) the steps that the public water system is taking to correct the violation; and

(IV) the necessity of seeking alternative water supplies until the violation is corrected;

(iii) be provided to the Administrator or the head of the State agency that has primary enforcement responsibility under section 300g–2 of this title as soon as practicable, but not later than 24 hours after the occurrence of the violation; and

(iv) as required by the State agency in general regulations of the State agency, or on a case-by-case basis after the consultation referred to in clause (iii), considering the health risks involved—

(I) be provided to appropriate broadcast media;

(II) be prominently published in a newspaper of general circulation serving the area not later than 1 day after distribution of a notice pursuant to clause (i) or the date of publication of the next issue of the newspaper; or

(III) be provided by posting or door-to-door notification in lieu of notification by means of broadcast media or newspaper.

**(D) Written notice**

**(i) In general**

Regulations issued under subparagraph (A) shall specify notification procedures for violations other than the violations covered by subparagraph (C). The procedures shall specify that a public water system shall provide written notice to each person served by the system by notice (I) in the first bill (if any) prepared after the date of occurrence of the violation, (II) in an annual report issued not later than 1 year after the date of occurrence of the violation, or (III) by mail or direct delivery as soon as practicable, but not later than 1 year after the date of occurrence of the violation.

**(ii) Form and manner of notice**

The Administrator shall prescribe the form and manner of the notice to provide a clear and readily understandable explanation of the violation, any potential adverse health effects, and the steps that the system is taking to seek alternative water supplies, if any, until the violation is corrected.

**(E) Unregulated contaminants**

The Administrator may require the owner or operator of a public water system to give notice to the persons served by the system of the concentration levels of an unregulated contaminant required to be monitored under section 300j–4(a) of this title.

(3) **Reports**

(A) **Annual report by State**

(i) **In general**

Not later than January 1, 1998, and annually thereafter, each State that has primary enforcement responsibility under section 300g–2 of this title shall prepare, make readily available to the public, and submit to the Administrator an annual report on violations of national primary drinking water regulations by public water systems in the State, including violations with respect to (I) maximum contaminant levels, (II) treatment requirements, (III) variances and exemptions, and (IV) monitoring requirements determined to be significant by the Administrator after consultation with the States.

(ii) **Distribution**

The State shall publish and distribute summaries of the report and indicate where the full report is available for review.

(B) **Annual report by Administrator**

Not later than July 1, 1998, and annually thereafter, the Administrator shall prepare and make available to the public an annual report summarizing and evaluating reports submitted by States pursuant to subparagraph (A) and notices submitted by public water systems serving Indian Tribes provided to the Administrator pursuant to subparagraph (C) or (D) of paragraph (2) and making recommendations concerning the resources needed to improve compliance with this subchapter. The report shall include information about public water system compliance on Indian reservations and about enforcement activities undertaken and financial assistance provided by the Administrator on Indian reservations, and shall make specific recommendations concerning the resources needed to improve compliance with this subchapter on Indian reservations.

(4) **Consumer confidence reports by community water systems**

(A) **Annual reports to consumers**

The Administrator, in consultation with public water systems, environmental groups, public interest groups, risk communication experts, and the States, and other interested parties, shall issue regulations within 24 months after August 6, 1996, to require each community water system to mail to each customer of the system at least once annually a report on the level of contaminants in the drinking water purveyed by that system (referred to in this paragraph as a "consumer confidence report"). Such regulations shall provide a brief and plainly worded definition of the terms "maximum contaminant level goal", "maximum contaminant level", "variances", and "exemptions" and brief statements in plain language regarding the health concerns that resulted in regulation of each regulated contaminant. The regulations shall also include a brief and plainly worded explanation regarding contaminants that may reasonably be expected to be present in drinking water, including bottled water. The regulations shall also provide for an Environmental Protection Agency toll-free hotline that consumers can call for more information and explanation.

(B) **Contents of report**

The consumer confidence reports under this paragraph shall include, but not be limited to, each of the following:

(i) Information on the source of the water purveyed.

(ii) A brief and plainly worded definition of the terms "maximum contaminant level goal", "maximum contaminant level", "variances", and "exemptions" as provided in the regulations of the Administrator.

(iii) If any regulated contaminant is detected in the water purveyed by the public water system, a statement setting forth (I) the maximum contaminant level goal, (II) the maximum contaminant level, (III) the level of such contaminant in such water system, and (IV) for any regulated contaminant for which there has been a violation of the maximum contaminant level during the year concerned, the brief statement in plain language regarding the health concerns that resulted in regulation of such contaminant, as provided by the Administrator in regulations under subparagraph (A).

(iv) Information on compliance with national primary drinking water regulations, as required by the Administrator, and notice if the system is operating under a variance or exemption and the basis on which the variance or exemption was granted.

(v) Information on the levels of unregulated contaminants for which monitoring is required under section 300j–4(a)(2) of this title (including levels of cryptosporidium and radon where States determine they may be found).

(vi) A statement that the presence of contaminants in drinking water does not necessarily indicate that the drinking water poses a health risk and that more information about contaminants and potential health effects can be obtained by calling the Environmental Protection Agency hotline.

A public water system may include such additional information as it deems appropriate for public education. The Administrator may, for not more than 3 regulated contaminants other than those referred to in subclause (IV) of clause (iii), require a consumer confidence report under this paragraph to include the brief statement in plain language regarding the health concerns that resulted in regulation of the contaminant or contaminants concerned, as provided by the Administrator in regulations under subparagraph (A).

**(C) Coverage**

The Governor of a State may determine not to apply the mailing requirement of subparagraph (A) to a community water system serving fewer than 10,000 persons. Any such system shall—

**(i)** inform, in the newspaper notice required by clause (iii) or by other means, its customers that the system will not be mailing the report as required by subparagraph (A);

**(ii)** make the consumer confidence report available upon request to the public; and

**(iii)** publish the report referred to in subparagraph (A) annually in one or more local newspapers serving the area in which customers of the system are located.

**(D) Alternative to publication**

For any community water system which, pursuant to subparagraph (C), is not required to meet the mailing requirement of subparagraph (A) and which serves 500 persons or fewer, the community water system may elect not to comply with clause (i) or (iii) of subparagraph (C). If the community water system so elects, the system shall, at a minimum—

**(i)** prepare an annual consumer confidence report pursuant to subparagraph (B); and

**(ii)** provide notice at least once per year to each of its customers by mail, by door-to-door delivery, by posting or by other means authorized by the regulations of the Administrator that the consumer confidence report is available upon request.

**(E) Alternative form and content**

A State exercising primary enforcement responsibility may establish, by rule, after notice and public comment, alternative requirements with respect to the form and content of consumer confidence reports under this paragraph.

**(d) Notice of noncompliance with secondary drinking water regulations**

Whenever, on the basis of information available to him, the Administrator finds that within a reasonable time after national secondary drinking water regulations have been promulgated, one or more public water systems in a State do not comply with such secondary regulations, and that such noncompliance appears to result from a failure of such State to take reasonable action to assure that public water systems throughout such State meet such secondary regulations, he shall so notify the State.

**(e) State authority to adopt or enforce laws or regulations respecting drinking water regulations or public water systems unaffected**

Nothing in this subchapter shall diminish any authority of a State or political subdivision to adopt or enforce any law or regulation respecting drinking water regulations or public water systems, but no such law or regulation shall relieve any person of any requirement otherwise applicable under this subchapter.

**(f) Notice and public hearing; availability of recommendations transmitted to State and public water system**

If the Administrator makes a finding of noncompliance (described in subparagraph (A) or (B) of subsection (a)(1) of this section) with respect to a public water system in a State which has primary enforcement responsibility, the Administrator may, for the purpose of assisting that State in carrying out such responsibility and upon the petition of such State or public water system or persons served by such system, hold, after appropriate notice, public hearings for the purpose of gathering information from technical or other experts, Federal, State, or other public officials, representatives of such public water system, persons served by such system, and other interested persons on—

**(1)** the ways in which such system can within the earliest feasible time be brought into compliance with the regulation or requirement with respect to which such finding was made, and

**(2)** the means for the maximum feasible protection of the public health during any period in which such system is not in compliance with a national primary drinking water regulation or requirement applicable to a variance or exemption.

On the basis of such hearings the Administrator shall issue recommendations which shall be sent to such State and public water system and shall be made available to the public and communications media.

**(g) Administrative order requiring compliance; notice and hearing; civil penalty; civil actions**

(1) In any case in which the Administrator is authorized to bring a civil action under this section or under section 300j–4 of this title with respect to any applicable requirement, the Administrator also may issue an order to require compliance with such applicable requirement.

(2) An order issued under this subsection shall not take effect, in the case of a State having primary enforcement responsibility for public water systems in that State, until after the Administrator has provided the State with an opportunity to confer with the Administrator regarding the order. A copy of any order issued under this subsection shall be sent to the appropriate State agency of the State involved if the State has primary enforcement responsibility for public water systems in that State. Any order issued under this subsection shall state with reasonable specificity the nature of the violation. In any case in which an order under this subsection is issued to a corporation, a copy of such order shall be issued to appropriate corporate officers.

(3)(A) Any person who violates, or fails or refuses to comply with, an order under this subsection shall be liable to the United States for a civil penalty of not more than $25,000 per day of violation.

(B) In a case in which a civil penalty sought by the Administrator under this paragraph does not exceed $5,000, the penalty shall be assessed by the Administrator after notice and opportunity for a public hearing (unless the person against whom the penalty is assessed requests a hearing on the record in accordance with section 554 of Title 5). In a case in which a civil penalty sought by the Administrator under this paragraph exceeds $5,000, but does not exceed $25,000, the penalty shall be assessed by the Administrator after notice and opportunity for a hearing on the record in accordance with section 554 of Title 5.

(C) Whenever any civil penalty sought by the Administrator under this subsection for a violation of an applicable requirement exceeds $25,000, the penalty shall be assessed by a civil action brought by the Administrator in the appropriate United States district court (as determined under the provisions of Title 28).

(D) If any person fails to pay an assessment of a civil penalty after it has become a final and unappealable order, or after the appropriate court of appeals has entered final judgment in favor of the Administrator, the Attorney General shall recover the amount for which such person is liable in any appropriate district court of the United States. In any such action, the validity and appropriateness of the final order imposing the civil penalty shall not be subject to review.

**(h) Consolidation incentive**

**(1) In general**

An owner or operator of a public water system may submit to the State in which the system is located (if the State has primary enforcement responsibility under section 300g–2 of this title) or to the Administrator (if the State does not have primary enforcement responsibility) a plan (including specific measures and schedules) for—

(A) the physical consolidation of the system with 1 or more other systems;

(B) the consolidation of significant management and administrative functions of the system with 1 or more other systems; or

(C) the transfer of ownership of the system that may reasonably be expected to improve drinking water quality.

**(2) Consequences of approval**

If the state or the administrator approves a plan pursuant to paragraph (1), no enforcement action shall be taken pursuant to this part with respect to a specific violation identified in the approved plan prior to the date that is the earlier of the date on which consolidation is completed according to the plan or the date that is 2 years after the plan is approved.

**(i) "Applicable requirement" defined**

In this section, the term "applicable requirement" means—

(1) a requirement of section 300g–1, 300g–3, 300g–4, 300g–5, 300g–6 [1] 300i–2, 300j, or 300j–4 of this title;

(2) a regulation promulgated pursuant to a section referred to in paragraph (1);

(3) a schedule or requirement imposed pursuant to a section referred to in paragraph (1); and

(4) a requirement of, or permit issued under, an applicable State program for which the Administrator has made a determination that the requirements of section 300g–2 of this title have been satisfied, or an applicable State program approved pursuant to this part.

(July 1, 1944, c. 373, Title XIV, § 1414, as added Dec. 16, 1974, Pub.L. 93–523, § 2(a), 88 Stat. 1666, and amended Nov. 16, 1977, Pub.L. 95–190, § 12(b), 91 Stat. 1398; June 19, 1986, Pub.L. 99–339, Title I, §§ 102, 103, 100 Stat. 647, 648; Aug. 6, 1996, Pub.L. 104–182, Title I, §§ 113(a), 114(a), 110 Stat. 1634, 1636; June 12, 2002, Pub.L. 107–188, Title IV, § 403(1), 116 Stat. 687.)

[1] So in original. Probably should be followed by a comma.

## HISTORICAL AND STATUTORY NOTES

**Effective and Applicability Provisions**

1996 Acts

Amendment by Pub.L. 104–182 effective Aug. 6, 1996, except as otherwise specifically provided, see section 2(b) of Pub.L. 104–182, set out as a note under section 300f of this title.

## § 300g–4. Variances

**[PHSA § 1415]**

**(a) Characteristics of raw water sources; specific treatment technique; notice to Administrator, reasons for variance; compliance, enforcement; approval or revision of schedules and revocation of variances; review of variances and schedules; publication in Federal Register, notice and results of review; notice to State; considerations respecting abuse of discretion in granting variances or failing to prescribe schedules; State corrective action; authority of Administrator in a State without primary enforcement responsibility; alternative treatment techniques**

Notwithstanding any other provision of this part, variances from national primary drinking water regulations may be granted as follows:

**(1)(A)** A State which has primary enforcement responsibility for public water systems may grant one or more variances from an applicable national primary drinking water regulation to one or more public water systems within its jurisdiction which, because of characteristics of the raw water sources which are reasonably available to the systems, cannot meet the requirements respecting the maximum contaminant levels of such drinking water regulation. A variance may be issued to a system on condition that the system install the best technology, treatment techniques, or other means, which the Administrator finds are available (taking costs into consideration), and based upon an evaluation satisfactory to the State that indicates that alternative sources of water are not reasonably available to the system. The Administrator shall propose and promulgate his finding of the best available technology, treatment techniques or other means available for each contaminant for purposes of this subsection at the time he proposes and promulgates a maximum contaminant level for each such contaminant. The Administrator's finding of best available technology, treatment techniques or other means for purposes of this subsection may vary depending on the number of persons served by the system or for other physical conditions related to engineering feasibility and costs of compliance with maximum contaminant levels as considered appropriate by the Administrator. Before a State may grant a variance under this subparagraph, the State must find that the variance will not result in an unreasonable risk to health. If a State grants a public water system a variance under this subparagraph, the State shall prescribe at the the [1] time the variance is granted, a schedule for—

(i) compliance (including increments of progress) by the public water system with each contaminant level requirement with respect to which the variance was granted, and

(ii) implementation by the public water system of such additional control measures as the State may require for each contaminant, subject to such contaminant level requirement, during the period ending on the date compliance with such requirement is required.

Before a schedule prescribed by a State pursuant to this subparagraph may take effect, the State shall provide notice and opportunity for a public hearing on the schedule. A notice given pursuant to the preceding sentence may cover the prescribing of more than one such schedule and a hearing held pursuant to such notice shall include each of the schedules covered by the notice. A schedule prescribed pursuant to this subparagraph for a public water system granted a variance shall require compliance by the system with each contaminant level requirement with respect to which the variance was granted as expeditiously as practicable (as the State may reasonably determine).

**(B)** A State which has primary enforcement responsibility for public water systems may grant to one or more public water systems within its jurisdiction one or more variances from any provision of a national primary drinking water regulation which requires the use of a specified treatment technique with respect to a contaminant if the public water system applying for the variance demonstrates to the satisfaction of the State that such treatment technique is not necessary to protect the health of persons because of the nature of the raw water source of such system. A variance granted under this subparagraph shall be conditioned on such monitoring and other requirements as the Administrator may prescribe.

**(C)** Before a variance proposed to be granted by a State under subparagraph (A) or (B) may take effect, such State shall provide notice and opportunity for public hearing on the proposed variance. A notice given pursuant to the preceding sentence may cover the granting of more than one variance and a hearing held pursuant to such notice shall include each of the variances covered by the notice. The State shall promptly notify the Administrator of all variances granted by it. Such notification shall contain the reason for the variance (and in the case of a variance under subparagraph (A), the basis for the finding required by that subparagraph before the granting of the variance) and documentation of the need for the variance.

(D) Each public water system's variance granted by a State under subparagraph (A) shall be conditioned by the State upon compliance by the public water system with the schedule prescribed by the State pursuant to that subparagraph. The requirements of each schedule prescribed by a State pursuant to that subparagraph shall be enforceable by the State under its laws. Any requirement of a schedule on which a variance granted under that subparagraph is conditioned may be enforced under section 300g–3 of this title as if such requirement was part of a national primary drinking water regulation.

(E) Each schedule prescribed by a State pursuant to subparagraph (A) shall be deemed approved by the Administrator unless the variance for which it was prescribed is revoked by the Administrator under subparagraph (G) or the schedule is revised by the Administrator under such subparagraph.

(F) Not later than 18 months after the effective date of the interim national primary drinking water regulations the Administrator shall complete a comprehensive review of the variances granted under subparagraph (A) (and schedules prescribed pursuant thereto) and under subparagraph (B) by the States during the one-year period beginning on such effective date. The Administrator shall conduct such subsequent reviews of variances and schedules as he deems necessary to carry out the purposes of this subchapter, but each subsequent review shall be completed within each 3–year period following the completion of the first review under this subparagraph. Before conducting any review under this subparagraph, the Administrator shall publish notice of the proposed review in the Federal Register. Such notice shall (i) provide information respecting the location of data and other information respecting the variances to be reviewed (including data and other information concerning new scientific matters bearing on such variances), and (ii) advise of the opportunity to submit comments on the variances reviewed and on the need for continuing them. Upon completion of any such review, the Administrator shall publish in the Federal Register the results of his review together with findings responsive to comments submitted in connection with such review.

(G)(i) If the Administrator finds that a State has, in a substantial number of instances, abused its discretion in granting variances under subparagraph (A) or (B) or that in a substantial number of cases the State has failed to prescribe schedules in accordance with subparagraph (A), the Administrator shall notify the State of his findings. In determining if a State has abused its discretion in granting variances in a substantial number of instances, the Administrator shall consider the number of persons who are affected by the variances and if the requirements applicable to the granting of the variances were complied with. A notice under this clause shall—

(I) identify each public water system with respect to which the finding was made,

(II) specify the reasons for the finding, and

(III) as appropriate, propose revocations of specific variances or propose revised schedules or other requirements for specific public water systems granted variances, or both.

(ii) The Administrator shall provide reasonable notice and public hearing on the provisions of each notice given pursuant to clause (i) of this subparagraph. After a hearing on a notice pursuant to such clause, the Administrator shall (I) rescind the finding for which the notice was given and promptly notify the State of such rescission, or (II) promulgate (with such modifications as he deems appropriate) such variance revocations and revised schedules or other requirements proposed in such notice as he deems appropriate. Not later than 180 days after the date a notice is given pursuant to clause (i) of this subparagraph, the Administrator shall complete the hearing on the notice and take the action required by the preceding sentence.

(iii) If a State is notified under clause (i) of this subparagraph of a finding of the Administrator made with respect to a variance granted a public water system within that State or to a schedule or other requirement for a variance and if, before a revocation of such variance or a revision of such schedule or other requirement promulgated by the Administrator takes effect, the State takes corrective action with respect to such variance or schedule or other requirement which the Administrator determines makes his finding inapplicable to such variance or schedule or other requirement, the Administrator shall rescind the application of his finding to that variance or schedule or other requirement. No variance revocation or revised schedule or other requirement may take effect before the expiration of 90 days following the date of the notice in which the revocation or revised schedule or other requirement was proposed.

(2) If a State does not have primary enforcement responsibility for public water systems, the Administrator shall have the same authority to grant variances in such State as the State would have under paragraph (1) if it had primary enforcement responsibility.

(3) The Administrator may grant a variance from any treatment technique requirement of a national primary drinking water regulation upon a showing by any person that an alternative treatment technique not included in such requirement is at least as efficient in lowering the level of the contaminant

with respect to which such requirement was prescribed. A variance under this paragraph shall be conditioned on the use of the alternative treatment technique which is the basis of the variance.

**(b) Enforcement of schedule or other requirement**

Any schedule or other requirement on which a variance granted under paragraph (1)(B) or (2) of subsection (a) of this section is conditioned may be enforced under section 300g–3 of this title as if such schedule or other requirement was part of a national primary drinking water regulation.

**(c) Applications for variances; regulations: reasonable time for acting**

If an application for a variance under subsection (a) of this section is made, the State receiving the application or the Administrator, as the case may be, shall act upon such application within a reasonable period (as determined under regulations prescribed by the Administrator) after the date of its submission.

**(d) "Treatment technique requirement" defined**

For purposes of this section, the term "treatment technique requirement" means a requirement in a national primary drinking water regulation which specifies for a contaminant (in accordance with section 300f(1)(C)(ii) of this title) each treatment technique known to the Administrator which leads to a reduction in the level of such contaminant sufficient to satisfy the requirements of section 300g–1(b) of this title.

**(e) Small system variances**

**(1) In general**

A State exercising primary enforcement responsibility for public water systems under section 300g–2 of this title (or the Administrator in nonprimacy States) may grant a variance under this subsection for compliance with a requirement specifying a maximum contaminant level or treatment technique contained in a national primary drinking water regulation to—

**(A)** public water systems serving 3,300 or fewer persons; and

**(B)** with the approval of the Administrator pursuant to paragraph (9), public water systems serving more than 3,300 persons but fewer than 10,000 persons,

if the variance meets each requirement of this subsection.

**(2) Availability of variances**

A public water system may receive a variance pursuant to paragraph (1), if—

**(A)** the Administrator has identified a variance technology under section 300g–1(b)(15) of this title that is applicable to the size and source water quality conditions of the public water system;

**(B)** the public water system installs, operates, and maintains, in accordance with guidance or regulations issued by the Administrator, such treatment technology, treatment technique, or other means; and

**(C)** the State in which the system is located determines that the conditions of paragraph (3) are met.

**(3) Conditions for granting variances**

A variance under this subsection shall be available only to a system—

**(A)** that cannot afford to comply, in accordance with affordability criteria established by the Administrator (or the State in the case of a State that has primary enforcement responsibility under section 300g–2 of this title), with a national primary drinking water regulation, including compliance through—

**(i)** treatment;

**(ii)** alternative source of water supply; or

**(iii)** restructuring or consolidation (unless the Administrator (or the State in the case of a State that has primary enforcement responsibility under section 300g–2 of this title) makes a written determination that restructuring or consolidation is not practicable); and

**(B)** for which the Administrator (or the State in the case of a State that has primary enforcement responsibility under section 300g–2 of this title) determines that the terms of the variance ensure adequate protection of human health, considering the quality of the source water for the system and the removal efficiencies and expected useful life of the treatment technology required by the variance.

**(4) Compliance schedules**

A variance granted under this subsection shall require compliance with the conditions of the variance not later than 3 years after the date on which the variance is granted, except that the Administrator (or the State in the case of a State that has primary enforcement responsibility under section 300g–2 of this title) may allow up to 2 additional years to comply with a variance technology, secure an alternative source of water, restructure or consolidate if the Administrator (or the State) determines that additional time is necessary for capital improvements, or to allow for financial assistance provided pursuant to section 300j–12 of this title or any other Federal or State program.

**(5) Duration of variances**

The Administrator (or the State in the case of a State that has primary enforcement responsibility under section 300g–2 of this title) shall review each variance granted under this subsection not less often than every 5 years after the compliance date established in the variance to determine whether the system remains eligible for the variance and is conforming to each condition of the variance.

**(6) Ineligibility for variances**

A variance shall not be available under this subsection for—

**(A)** any maximum contaminant level or treatment technique for a contaminant with respect to which a national primary drinking water regulation was promulgated prior to January 1, 1986; or

**(B)** a national primary drinking water regulation for a microbial contaminant (including a bacterium, virus, or other organism) or an indicator or treatment technique for a microbial contaminant.

**(7) Regulations and guidance**

**(A) In general**

Not later than 2 years after August 6, 1996, and in consultation with the States, the Administrator shall promulgate regulations for variances to be granted under this subsection. The regulations shall, at a minimum, specify—

**(i)** procedures to be used by the Administrator or a State to grant or deny variances, including requirements for notifying the Administrator and consumers of the public water system that a variance is proposed to be granted (including information regarding the contaminant and variance) and requirements for a public hearing on the variance before the variance is granted;

**(ii)** requirements for the installation and proper operation of variance technology that is identified (pursuant to section 300g–1(b)(15) of this title) for small systems and the financial and technical capability to operate the treatment system, including operator training and certification;

**(iii)** eligibility criteria for a variance for each national primary drinking water regulation, including requirements for the quality of the source water (pursuant to section 300g–1(b)(15)(A) of this title); and

**(iv)** information requirements for variance applications.

**(B) Affordability criteria**

Not later than 18 months after August 6, 1996, the Administrator, in consultation with the States and the Rural Utilities Service of the Department of Agriculture, shall publish information to assist the States in developing affordability criteria. The affordability criteria shall be reviewed by the States not less often than every 5 years to determine if changes are needed to the criteria.

**(8) Review by the Administrator**

**(A) In general**

The Administrator shall periodically review the program of each State that has primary enforcement responsibility for public water systems under section 300g–2 of this title with respect to variances to determine whether the variances granted by the State comply with the requirements of this subsection. With respect to affordability, the determination of the Administrator shall be limited to whether the variances granted by the State comply with the affordability criteria developed by the State.

**(B) Notice and publication**

If the Administrator determines that variances granted by a State are not in compliance with affordability criteria developed by the State and the requirements of this subsection, the Administrator shall notify the State in writing of the deficiencies and make public the determination.

**(9) Approval of variances**

A State proposing to grant a variance under this subsection to a public water system serving more than 3,300 and fewer than 10,000 persons shall submit the variance to the Administrator for review and approval prior to the issuance of the variance. The Administrator shall approve the variance if it meets each of the requirements of this subsection. The Administrator shall approve or disapprove the variance within 90 days. If the Administrator disapproves a variance under this paragraph, the Administrator shall notify the State in writing of the reasons for disapproval and the variance may be resubmitted with modifications to address the objections stated by the Administrator.

**(10) Objections to variances**

**(A) By the Administrator**

The Administrator may review and object to any variance proposed to be granted by a State, if the objection is communicated to the State not later than 90 days after the State proposes to grant the variance. If the Administrator objects to the granting of a variance, the Administrator shall notify the State in writing of each basis for the objection and propose a modification to the variance to resolve the concerns of the Administrator. The State shall make the recommended modification or respond in writing to each objection. If the State issues the variance without resolving the concerns of the Administrator, the Administrator may overturn the State decision to grant the variance if the Administrator determines that the State decision does not comply with this subsection.

**(B) Petition by consumers**

Not later than 30 days after a State exercising primary enforcement responsibility for public water systems under section 300g–2 of this title proposes to grant a variance for a public water system, any person served by the system may petition the Administrator to object to the granting of a variance. The Administrator shall respond to the petition and determine whether to object to the variance under subparagraph (A) not later than 60 days after the receipt of the petition.

**(C) Timing**

No variance shall be granted by a State until the later of the following:

(i) 90 days after the State proposes to grant a variance.

(ii) If the Administrator objects to the variance, the date on which the State makes the recommended modifications or responds in writing to each objection.

(July 1, 1944, c. 373, Title XIV, § 1415, as added Dec. 16, 1974, Pub.L. 93–523, § 2(a), 88 Stat. 1669, and amended June 19, 1986, Pub.L. 99–339, Title I, § 104, 100 Stat. 649; Aug. 6, 1996, Pub.L. 104–182, Title I, §§ 102(c)(1), 115, 116, Title V, § 501(a)(3), 110 Stat. 1621, 1641, 1691.)

[1] So in original.

### HISTORICAL AND STATUTORY NOTES

**Effective and Applicability Provisions**

1996 Acts

Amendment by Pub.L. 104–182 effective Aug. 6, 1996, except as otherwise specifically provided, see section 2(b) of Pub.L. 104–182, set out as a note under section 300f of this title.

## § 300g–5. Exemptions

**[PHSA § 1416]**

**(a) Requisite findings**

A State which has primary enforcement responsibility may exempt any public water system within the State's jurisdiction from any requirement respecting a maximum contaminant level or any treatment technique requirement, or from both, of an applicable national primary drinking water regulation upon a finding that—

(1) due to compelling factors (which may include economic factors, including qualification of the public water system as a system serving a disadvantaged community pursuant to section 300j–12(d) of this title), the public water system is unable to comply with such contaminant level or treatment technique requirement, or to implement measures to develop an alternative source of water supply,

(2) the public water system was in operation on the effective date of such contaminant level or treatment technique requirement, or, for a system that was not in operation by that date, only if no reasonable alternative source of drinking water is available to such new system,

(3) the granting of the exemption will not result in an unreasonable risk to health;[1] and

(4) management or restructuring changes (or both) cannot reasonably be made that will result in compliance with this subchapter or, if compliance cannot be achieved, improve the quality of the drinking water.

**(b) Compliance schedule and implementation of control measures; notice and hearing; dates for compliance with schedule; compliance, enforcement; approval or revision of schedules and revocation of exemptions**

(1) If a State grants a public water system an exemption under subsection (a) of this section, the State shall prescribe, at the time the exemption is granted, a schedule for—

(A) compliance (including increments of progress or measures to develop an alternative source of water supply) by the public water system with each contaminant level requirement or treatment technique requirement with respect to which the exemption was granted, and

(B) implementation by the public water system of such control measures as the State may require for each contaminant, subject to such contaminant level requirement or treatment technique requirement, during the period ending on the date compliance with such requirement is required.

Before a schedule prescribed by a State pursuant to this subsection may take effect, the State shall provide notice and opportunity for a public hearing on the schedule. A notice given pursuant to the preceding sentence may cover the prescribing of more than one such schedule and a hearing held pursuant to such notice shall include each of the schedules covered by the notice.

(2)(A) A schedule prescribed pursuant to this subsection for a public water system granted an exemption under subsection (a) of this section shall require compliance by the system with each contaminant level and treatment technique requirement with respect to which the exemption was granted as expeditiously as practicable (as the State may reasonably determine) but not later than 3 years after the otherwise applicable compliance date established in section 300g–1(b)(10) of this title.

(B) No exemption shall be granted unless the public water system establishes that—

(i) the system cannot meet the standard without capital improvements which cannot be completed prior to the date established pursuant to section 300g–1(b)(10) of this title;

(ii) in the case of a system which needs financial assistance for the necessary improvements, the system has entered into an agreement to obtain such financial assistance or assistance pursuant to section 300j–12 of this title, or any other Federal or State program is reasonably likely to be available within the period of the exemption; or

(iii) the system has entered into an enforceable agreement to become a part of a regional public water system; and

the system is taking all practicable steps to meet the standard.

(C) In the case of a system which does not serve more than a population of 3,300 and which needs financial assistance for the necessary improvements, an exemption granted under clause (i) or (ii) of subparagraph (B) may be renewed for one or more additional 2-year periods, but not to exceed a total of 6 years, if the system establishes that it is taking all practicable steps to meet the requirements of subparagraph (B).

(D) Limitation

A public water system may not receive an exemption under this section if the system was granted a variance under section 300g–4(e) of this title.

(3) Each public water system's exemption granted by a State under subsection (a) of this section shall be conditioned by the State upon compliance by the public water system with the schedule prescribed by the State pursuant to this subsection. The requirements of each schedule prescribed by a State pursuant to this subsection shall be enforceable by the State under its laws. Any requirement of a schedule on which an exemption granted under this section is conditioned may be enforced under section 300g–3 of this title as if such requirement was part of a national primary drinking water regulation.

(4) Each schedule prescribed by a State pursuant to this subsection shall be deemed approved by the Administrator unless the exemption for which it was prescribed is revoked by the Administrator under subsection (d)(2) of this section or the schedule is revised by the Administrator under such subsection.

**(c) Notice to Administrator; reasons for exemption**

Each State which grants an exemption under subsection (a) of this section shall promptly notify the Administrator of the granting of such exemption. Such notification shall contain the reasons for the exemption (including the basis for the finding required by subsection (a)(3) of this section before the exemption may be granted) and document the need for the exemption.

**(d) Review of exemptions and schedules; publication in Federal Register, notice and results of review; notice to State; considerations respecting abuse of discretion in granting exemptions or failing to prescribe schedules; State corrective action**

(1) Not later than 18 months after the effective date of the interim national primary drinking water regulations the Administrator shall complete a comprehensive review of the exemptions granted (and schedules prescribed pursuant thereto) by the States during the one-year period beginning on such effective date. The Administrator shall conduct such subsequent reviews of exemptions and schedules as he deems necessary to carry out the purposes of this subchapter, but each subsequent review shall be completed within each 3-year period following the completion of the first review under this subparagraph. Before conducting any review under this subparagraph, the Administrator shall publish notice of the proposed review in the Federal Register. Such notice shall (A) provide information respecting the location of data and other information respecting the exemptions to be reviewed (including data and other information concerning new scientific matters bearing on such exemptions), and (B) advise of the opportunity to submit comments on the exemptions reviewed and on the need for continuing them. Upon completion of any such review, the Administrator shall publish in the Federal Register the results of his review, together with findings responsive to comments submitted in connection with such review.

(2)(A) If the Administrator finds that a State has, in a substantial number of instances, abused its discretion in granting exemptions under subsection (a) of this section or failed to prescribe schedules in accordance with subsection (b) of this section, the Administrator shall notify the State of his findings. In determining if a State has abused its discretion in granting exemptions in a substantial number of instances, the Administrator shall consider the number of persons who are affected by the exemptions and if the requirements applicable to the granting of the exemptions were complied with. A notice under this subparagraph shall—

(i) identify each exempt public water system with respect to which the finding was made,

(ii) specify the reasons for the finding, and

(iii) as appropriate, propose revocations of specific exemptions or propose revised schedules for specific exempt public water systems, or both.

(B) The Administrator shall provide reasonable notice and public hearing on the provisions of each notice given pursuant to subparagraph (A). After a hearing on notice pursuant to subparagraph (A), the Administrator shall (i) rescind the finding for which the notice was given and promptly notify the State of such rescission, or (ii) promulgate (with such modifications as he deems appropriate) such exemption revocations and revised schedules proposed in such notice as he deems appropriate. Not later than 180 days after the date a notice is given pursuant to subparagraph (A), the Administrator shall complete the hearing on the notice and take the action required by the preceding sentence.

(C) If a State is notified under subparagraph (A) of a finding of the Administrator made with respect to an exemption granted a public water system within that State or to a schedule prescribed pursuant to such an exemption and if before a revocation of such exemption or a revision of such schedule promulgated by the Administrator takes effect the State takes corrective action with respect to such exemption or schedule which the Administrator determines makes his finding inapplicable to such exemption or schedule, the Administrator shall rescind the application of his finding to that exemption or schedule. No exemption revocation or revised schedule may take effect before the expiration of 90 days following the date of the notice in which the revocation or revised schedule was proposed.

**(e) "Treatment technique requirement" defined**

For purposes of this section, the term "treatment technique requirement" means a requirement in a national primary drinking water regulation which specifies for a contaminant (in accordance with section 300f(1)(C)(ii) of this title) each treatment technique known to the Administrator which leads to a reduction in the level of such contaminant sufficient to satisfy the requirements of section 300g–1(b) of this title.

**(f) Authority of Administrator in a State without primary enforcement responsibility**

If a State does not have primary enforcement responsibility for public water systems, the Administrator shall have the same authority to exempt public water systems in such State from maximum contaminant level requirements and treatment technique requirements under the same conditions and in the same manner as the State would be authorized to grant exemptions under this section if it had primary enforcement responsibility.

**(g) Applications for exemptions; regulations; reasonable time for acting**

If an application for an exemption under this section is made, the State receiving the application or the Administrator, as the case may be, shall act upon such application within a reasonable period (as determined under regulations prescribed by the Administrator) after the date of its submission.

(July 1, 1944, c. 373, Title XIV, § 1416, as added Dec. 16, 1974, Pub.L. 93–523, § 2(a), 88 Stat. 1672, and amended Nov. 16, 1977, Pub.L. 95–190, § 10(a), 91 Stat. 1398; Dec. 5, 1980, Pub.L. 96–502, §§ 1, 4(b), 94 Stat. 2737, 2738; June 19, 1986, Pub.L. 99–339, Title I, §§ 101(c)(4), 105, 100 Stat. 646, 649; Aug. 6, 1996, Pub.L. 104–182, Title I, § 117(a), 110 Stat. 1644.)

[1] So in original. Semicolon probably should be a comma.

### HISTORICAL AND STATUTORY NOTES

**Effective and Applicability Provisions**

1996 Acts

Amendment by Pub.L. 104–182 effective Aug. 6, 1996, except as otherwise specifically provided, see section 2(b) of Pub.L. 104–182, set out as a note under section 300f of this title.

## § 300g–6. Prohibition on use of lead pipes, solder, and flux

**[PHSA § 1417]**

**(a) In general**

**(1) Prohibitions**

**(A) In general**

No person may use any pipe, any pipe or plumbing fitting or fixture, any solder, or any flux, after June 19, 1986, in the installation or repair of—

(i) any public water system; or

(ii) any plumbing in a residential or nonresidential facility providing water for human consumption,

that is not lead free (within the meaning of subsection (d) of this section).

**(B) Leaded joints**

Subparagraph (A) shall not apply to leaded joints necessary for the repair of cast iron pipes.

**(2) Public notice requirements**

**(A) In general**

Each owner or operator of a public water system shall identify and provide notice to persons that may be affected by lead contamination of their drinking water where such contamination results from either or both of the following:

(i) The lead content in the construction materials of the public water distribution system.

(ii) Corrosivity of the water supply sufficient to cause leaching of lead.

The notice shall be provided in such manner and form as may be reasonably required by the Administrator. Notice under this paragraph shall be provided notwithstanding the absence of a violation of any national drinking water standard.

**(B) Contents of notice**

Notice under this paragraph shall provide a clear and readily understandable explanation of—

(i) the potential sources of lead in the drinking water,

(ii) potential adverse health effects,

(iii) reasonably available methods of mitigating known or potential lead content in drinking water,

(iv) any steps the system is taking to mitigate lead content in drinking water, and

(v) the necessity for seeking alternative water supplies, if any.

**(3) Unlawful acts**

Effective 2 years after August 6, 1996, it shall be unlawful—

(A) for any person to introduce into commerce any pipe, or any pipe or plumbing fitting or fixture, that is not lead free, except for a pipe that is used in manufacturing or industrial processing;

(B) for any person engaged in the business of selling plumbing supplies, except manufacturers, to sell solder or flux that is not lead free; or

(C) for any person to introduce into commerce any solder or flux that is not lead free unless the solder or flux bears a prominent label stating that it is illegal to use the solder or flux in the installation or repair of any plumbing providing water for human consumption.

**(b) State enforcement**

**(1) Enforcement of prohibition**

The requirements of subsection (a)(1) of this section shall be enforced in all States effective 24 months after June 19, 1986. States shall enforce such requirements through State or local plumbing codes, or such other means of enforcement as the State may determine to be appropriate.

**(2) Enforcement of public notice requirements**

The requirements of subsection (a)(2) of this section shall apply in all States effective 24 months after June 19, 1986.

**(c) Penalties**

If the Administrator determines that a State is not enforcing the requirements of subsection (a) of this section as required pursuant to subsection (b) of this section, the Administrator may withhold up to 5 percent of Federal funds available to that State for State program grants under section 300j–2(a) of this title.

**(d) "Lead free" defined**

For purposes of this section, the term "lead free"—

(1) when used with respect to solders and flux refers to solders and flux containing not more than 0.2 percent lead;

(2) when used with respect to pipes and pipe fittings refers to pipes and pipe fittings containing not more than 8.0 percent lead; and

(3) when used with respect to plumbing fittings and fixtures, refers to plumbing fittings and fixtures in compliance with standards established in accordance with subsection (e) of this section.

**(e) Plumbing fittings and fixtures**

**(1) In general**

The Administrator shall provide accurate and timely technical information and assistance to qualified third-party certifiers in the development of voluntary standards and testing protocols for the leaching of lead from new plumbing fittings and fixtures that are intended by the manufacturer to dispense water for human ingestion.

**(2) Standards**

**(A) In general**

If a voluntary standard for the leaching of lead is not established by the date that is 1 year after August 6, 1996, the Administrator shall, not later than 2 years after August 6, 1996, promulgate regulations setting a health-effects-based performance standard establishing maximum leaching levels from new plumbing fittings and fixtures that are intended by the manufacturer to dispense water for human ingestion. The standard shall become effective on the date that is 5 years after the date of promulgation of the standard.

**(B) Alternative requirement**

If regulations are required to be promulgated under subparagraph (A) and have not been promulgated by the date that is 5 years after August 6, 1996, no person may import, manufacture, process, or distribute in commerce a new plumbing fitting or fixture, intended by the manufacturer to dispense water for human ingestion, that contains more than 4 percent lead by dry weight.

(July 1, 1944, c. 373, Title XIV, § 1417, as added June 19, 1986, Pub.L. 99–339, Title I, § 109(a)(1), 100 Stat. 651, and amended Aug. 6, 1996, Pub.L. 104–182, Title I, § 118, Title V, § 501(f)(1), 110 Stat. 1645, 1691.)

## HISTORICAL AND STATUTORY NOTES

**Effective and Applicability Provisions**

1996 Acts

Amendment by Pub.L. 104–182 effective Aug. 6, 1996, except as otherwise specifically provided, see section 2(b) of Pub.L. 104–182, set out as a note under section 300f of this title.

**Ban on Lead Water Pipes, Solder and Flux in Department of Veterans Affairs and HUD Insured or Assisted Property**

Section 109(c) of Pub.L. 99–339, as amended by Pub.L. 102–54, § 13(q)(2), June 13, 1991, 105 Stat. 279, provided that:

"(1) **Prohibition.**—The Secretary of Housing and Urban Development and the Secretary of Veterans Affairs may not insure or guarantee a mortgage or furnish assistance with respect to newly constructed residential property which contains a potable water system unless such system uses only lead free pipe, solder, and flux.

"(2) **Definition of Lead Free.**—For purposes of paragraph (1) the term 'lead free'—

"(A) when used with respect to solders and flux refers to solders and flux containing not more than 0.2 percent lead, and

"(B) when used with respect to pipes and pipe fittings refers to pipes and pipe fittings containing not more than 8.0 percent lead.

"(3) **Effective Date.**—Paragraph (1) shall become effective 24 months after the enactment of this Act [June 19, 1986]."

**Notification to States**

Section 109(b) of Pub.L. 99–339 provided that: "The Administrator of the Environmental Protection Agency shall notify all States with respect to the requirements of section 1417 of the Public Health Service Act [this section] within 90 days after the enactment of this Act [June 19, 1986]."

## § 300g–7. Monitoring of contaminants

**[PHSA § 1418]**

### (a) Interim monitoring relief authority

#### (1) In general

A State exercising primary enforcement responsibility for public water systems may modify the monitoring requirements for any regulated or unregulated contaminants for which monitoring is required other than microbial contaminants (or indicators thereof), disinfectants and disinfection byproducts or corrosion byproducts for an interim period to provide that any public water system serving 10,000 persons or fewer shall not be required to conduct additional quarterly monitoring during an interim relief period for such contaminants if—

(A) monitoring, conducted at the beginning of the period for the contaminant concerned and certified to the State by the public water system, fails to detect the presence of the contaminant in the ground or surface water supplying the public water system; and

(B) the State, considering the hydrogeology of the area and other relevant factors, determines in writing that the contaminant is unlikely to be detected by further monitoring during such period.

#### (2) Termination; timing of monitoring

The interim relief period referred to in paragraph (1) shall terminate when permanent monitoring relief is adopted and approved for such State, or at the end of 36 months after August 6, 1996, whichever comes first. In order to serve as a basis for interim relief, the monitoring conducted at the beginning of the period must occur at the time determined by the State to be the time of the public water system's greatest vulnerability to the contaminant concerned in the relevant ground or surface water, taking into account in the case of pesticides the time of application of the pesticide for the source water area and the travel time for the pesticide to reach such waters and taking into account, in the case of other contaminants, seasonality of precipitation and contaminant travel time.

### (b) Permanent monitoring relief authority

#### (1) In general

Each State exercising primary enforcement responsibility for public water systems under this subchapter and having an approved source water assessment program may adopt, in accordance with guidance published by the Administrator, tailored alternative monitoring requirements for public water systems in such State (as an alternative to the monitoring requirements for chemical contaminants set forth in the applicable national primary drinking water regulations) where the State concludes that (based on data available at the time of adoption concerning susceptibility, use, occurrence, or wellhead protection, or from the State's drinking water source water assessment program) such alternative monitoring would provide assurance that it complies with the Administrator's guidelines. The State program must be adequate to assure compliance with, and enforcement of, applicable national primary drinking water regulations. Alternative monitoring shall not apply to regulated microbiological contaminants (or indicators thereof), disinfectants and disinfection byproducts, or corrosion byproducts. The preceding sentence is not intended to limit other authority of the Administrator under other provisions of this subchapter to grant monitoring flexibility.

#### (2) Guidelines

##### (A) In general

The Administrator shall issue, after notice and comment and at the same time as guidelines are issued for source water assessment under section

300j–13 of this title, guidelines for States to follow in proposing alternative monitoring requirements under paragraph (1) for chemical contaminants. The Administrator shall publish such guidelines in the Federal Register. The guidelines shall assure that the public health will be protected from drinking water contamination. The guidelines shall require that a State alternative monitoring program apply on a contaminant-by-contaminant basis and that, to be eligible for such alternative monitoring program, a public water system must show the State that the contaminant is not present in the drinking water supply or, if present, it is reliably and consistently below the maximum contaminant level.

**(B) Definition**

For purposes of subparagraph (A), the phrase "reliably and consistently below the maximum contaminant level" means that, although contaminants have been detected in a water supply, the State has sufficient knowledge of the contamination source and extent of contamination to predict that the maximum contaminant level will not be exceeded. In determining that a contaminant is reliably and consistently below the maximum contaminant level, States shall consider the quality and completeness of data, the length of time covered and the volatility or stability of monitoring results during that time, and the proximity of such results to the maximum contaminant level. Wide variations in the analytical results, or analytical results close to the maximum contaminant level, shall not be considered to be reliably and consistently below the maximum contaminant level.

**(3) Effect of detection of contaminants**

The guidelines issued by the Administrator under paragraph (2) shall require that if, after the monitoring program is in effect and operating, a contaminant covered by the alternative monitoring program is detected at levels at or above the maximum contaminant level or is no longer reliably or consistently below the maximum contaminant level, the public water system must either—

**(A)** demonstrate that the contamination source has been removed or that other action has been taken to eliminate the contamination problem; or

**(B)** test for the detected contaminant pursuant to the applicable national primary drinking water regulation.

**(4) States not exercising primary enforcement responsibility**

The Governor of any State not exercising primary enforcement responsibility under section 300g–2 of this title on August 6, 1996, may submit to the Administrator a request that the Administrator modify the monitoring requirements established by the Administrator and applicable to public water systems in that State. After consultation with the Governor, the Administrator shall modify the requirements for public water systems in that State if the request of the Governor is in accordance with each of the requirements of this subsection that apply to alternative monitoring requirements established by States that have primary enforcement responsibility. A decision by the Administrator to approve a request under this clause shall be for a period of 3 years and may subsequently be extended for periods of 5 years.

**(c) Treatment as NPDWR**

All monitoring relief granted by a State to a public water system for a regulated contaminant under subsection (a) or (b) of this section shall be treated as part of the national primary drinking water regulation for that contaminant.

**(d) Other monitoring relief**

Nothing in this section shall be construed to affect the authority of the States under applicable national primary drinking water regulations to alter monitoring requirements through waivers or other existing authorities. The Administrator shall periodically review and, as appropriate, revise such authorities.

(July 1, 1944, c. 373, Title XIV, § 1418, as added Aug. 6, 1996, Pub.L. 104–182, Title I, § 125(b), 110 Stat. 1654.)

**HISTORICAL AND STATUTORY NOTES**

**Effective and Applicability Provisions**

1996 Acts

Section effective Aug. 6, 1996, except as otherwise specifically provided, see section 2(b) of Pub.L. 104–182, set out as a note under section 300f of this title.

## § 300g–8. Operator certification

**[PHSA § 1419]**

**(a) Guidelines**

Not later than 30 months after August 6, 1996, and in cooperation with the States, the Administrator shall publish guidelines in the Federal Register, after notice and opportunity for comment from interested persons, including States and public water systems, specifying minimum standards for certification (and recertification) of the operators of community and nontransient noncommunity public water systems. Such guidelines shall take into account existing State programs, the complexity of the system, and other factors aimed at providing an effective program at reasonable cost to States and public water systems, taking into account the size of the system.

**(b) State programs**

Beginning 2 years after the date on which the Administrator publishes guidelines under subsection (a) of this section, the Administrator shall withhold 20 percent of the funds a State is otherwise entitled to receive under section 300j–12 of this title unless the State has adopted and is implementing a program for the certification of operators of community and nontransient noncommunity public water systems that meets the requirements of the guidelines published pursuant to subsection (a) of this section or that has been submitted in compliance with subsection (c) of this section and that has not been disapproved.

**(c) Existing programs**

For any State exercising primary enforcement responsibility for public water systems or any other State which has an operator certification program, the guidelines under subsection (a) of this section shall allow the State to enforce such program in lieu of the guidelines under subsection (a) of this section if the State submits the program to the Administrator within 18 months after the publication of the guidelines unless the Administrator determines (within 9 months after the State submits the program to the Administrator) that such program is not substantially equivalent to such guidelines. In making this determination, an existing State program shall be presumed to be substantially equivalent to the guidelines, notwithstanding program differences, based on the size of systems or the quality of source water, providing the State program meets the overall public health objectives of the guidelines. If disapproved, the program may be resubmitted within 6 months after receipt of notice of disapproval.

**(d) Expense reimbursement**

**(1) In general**

The Administrator shall provide reimbursement for the costs of training, including an appropriate per diem for unsalaried operators, and certification for persons operating systems serving 3,300 persons or fewer that are required to undergo training pursuant to this section.

**(2) State grants**

The reimbursement shall be provided through grants to States with each State receiving an amount sufficient to cover the reasonable costs for training all such operators in the State, as determined by the Administrator, to the extent required by this section. Grants received by a State pursuant to this paragraph shall first be used to provide reimbursement for training and certification costs of persons operating systems serving 3,300 persons or fewer. If a State has reimbursed all such costs, the State may, after notice to the Administrator, use any remaining funds from the grant for any of the other purposes authorized for grants under section 300j–12 of this title.

**(3) Authorization**

There are authorized to be appropriated to the Administrator to provide grants for reimbursement under this section $30,000,000 for each of fiscal years 1997 through 2003.

**(4) Reservation**

If the appropriation made pursuant to paragraph (3) for any fiscal year is not sufficient to satisfy the requirements of paragraph (1), the Administrator shall, prior to any other allocation or reservation, reserve such sums as necessary from the funds appropriated pursuant to section 300j–12(m) of this title to provide reimbursement for the training and certification costs mandated by this subsection.

(July 1, 1944, c. 373, Title XIV, § 1419, as added Aug. 6, 1996, Pub.L. 104–182, Title I, § 123, 110 Stat. 1652.)

### HISTORICAL AND STATUTORY NOTES

**Effective and Applicability Provisions**

1996 Acts

Section effective Aug. 6, 1996, except as otherwise specifically provided, see section 2(b) of Pub.L. 104–182, set out as a note under section 300f of this title.

## § 300g–9. Capacity development

**[PHSA § 1420]**

**(a) State authority for new systems**

A State shall receive only 80 percent of the allotment that the State is otherwise entitled to receive under section 300j–12 of this title (relating to State loan funds) unless the State has obtained the legal authority or other means to ensure that all new community water systems and new nontransient, noncommunity water systems commencing operation after October 1, 1999, demonstrate technical, managerial, and financial capacity with respect to each national primary drinking water regulation in effect, or likely to be in effect, on the date of commencement of operations.

**(b) Systems in significant noncompliance**

**(1) List**

Beginning not later than 1 year after August 6, 1996, each State shall prepare, periodically update, and submit to the Administrator a list of community water systems and nontransient, noncommunity water systems that have a history of significant noncompliance with this subchapter (as defined in guidelines issued prior to August 6, 1996, or any revisions of the guidelines that have been made in consultation with the States) and, to the extent practicable, the reasons for noncompliance.

(2) **Report**

Not later than 5 years after August 6, 1996, and as part of the capacity development strategy of the State, each State shall report to the Administrator on the success of enforcement mechanisms and initial capacity development efforts in assisting the public water systems listed under paragraph (1) to improve technical, managerial, and financial capacity.

(3) **Withholding**

The list and report under this subsection shall be considered part of the capacity development strategy of the State required under subsection (c) of this section for purposes of the withholding requirements of section 300j–12(a)(1)(G)(i) of this title (relating to State loan funds).

**(c) Capacity development strategy**

(1) **In general**

Beginning 4 years after August 6, 1996, a State shall receive only—

(A) 90 percent in fiscal year 2001;

(B) 85 percent in fiscal year 2002; and

(C) 80 percent in each subsequent fiscal year,

of the allotment that the State is otherwise entitled to receive under section 300j–12 of this title (relating to State loan funds), unless the State is developing and implementing a strategy to assist public water systems in acquiring and maintaining technical, managerial, and financial capacity.

(2) **Content**

In preparing the capacity development strategy, the State shall consider, solicit public comment on, and include as appropriate—

(A) the methods or criteria that the State will use to identify and prioritize the public water systems most in need of improving technical, managerial, and financial capacity;

(B) a description of the institutional, regulatory, financial, tax, or legal factors at the Federal, State, or local level that encourage or impair capacity development;

(C) a description of how the State will use the authorities and resources of this subchapter or other means to—

(i) assist public water systems in complying with national primary drinking water regulations;

(ii) encourage the development of partnerships between public water systems to enhance the technical, managerial, and financial capacity of the systems; and

(iii) assist public water systems in the training and certification of operators;

(D) a description of how the State will establish a baseline and measure improvements in capacity with respect to national primary drinking water regulations and State drinking water law; and

(E) an identification of the persons that have an interest in and are involved in the development and implementation of the capacity development strategy (including all appropriate agencies of Federal, State, and local governments, private and nonprofit public water systems, and public water system customers).

(3) **Report**

Not later than 2 years after the date on which a State first adopts a capacity development strategy under this subsection, and every 3 years thereafter, the head of the State agency that has primary responsibility to carry out this subchapter in the State shall submit to the Governor a report that shall also be available to the public on the efficacy of the strategy and progress made toward improving the technical, managerial, and financial capacity of public water systems in the State.

(4) **Review**

The decisions of the State under this section regarding any particular public water system are not subject to review by the Administrator and may not serve as the basis for withholding funds under section 300j–12 of this title.

**(d) Federal assistance**

(1) **In general**

The Administrator shall support the States in developing capacity development strategies.

(2) **Informational assistance**

(A) **In general**

Not later than 180 days after August 6, 1996, the Administrator shall—

(i) conduct a review of State capacity development efforts in existence on August 6, 1996, and publish information to assist States and public water systems in capacity development efforts; and

(ii) initiate a partnership with States, public water systems, and the public to develop information for States on recommended operator certification requirements.

(B) **Publication of information**

The Administrator shall publish the information developed through the partnership under subparagraph (A)(ii) not later than 18 months after August 6, 1996.

### (3) Promulgation of drinking water regulations

In promulgating a national primary drinking water regulation, the Administrator shall include an analysis of the likely effect of compliance with the regulation on the technical, financial, and managerial capacity of public water systems.

### (4) Guidance for new systems

Not later than 2 years after August 6, 1996, the Administrator shall publish guidance developed in consultation with the States describing legal authorities and other means to ensure that all new community water systems and new nontransient, noncommunity water systems demonstrate technical, managerial, and financial capacity with respect to national primary drinking water regulations.

## (e) Variances and exemptions

Based on information obtained under subsection (c)(3) of this section, the Administrator shall, as appropriate, modify regulations concerning variances and exemptions for small public water systems to ensure flexibility in the use of the variances and exemptions. Nothing in this subsection shall be interpreted, construed, or applied to affect or alter the requirements of section 300g–4 or 300g–5 of this title.

## (f) Small public water systems technology assistance centers

### (1) Grant program

The Administrator is authorized to make grants to institutions of higher learning to establish and operate small public water system technology assistance centers in the United States.

### (2) Responsibilities of the centers

The responsibilities of the small public water system technology assistance centers established under this subsection shall include the conduct of training and technical assistance relating to the information, performance, and technical needs of small public water systems or public water systems that serve Indian Tribes.

### (3) Applications

Any institution of higher learning interested in receiving a grant under this subsection shall submit to the Administrator an application in such form and containing such information as the Administrator may require by regulation.

### (4) Selection criteria

The Administrator shall select recipients of grants under this subsection on the basis of the following criteria:

(A) The small public water system technology assistance center shall be located in a State that is representative of the needs of the region in which the State is located for addressing the drinking water needs of small and rural communities or Indian Tribes.

(B) The grant recipient shall be located in a region that has experienced problems, or may reasonably be foreseen to experience problems, with small and rural public water systems.

(C) The grant recipient shall have access to expertise in small public water system technology management.

(D) The grant recipient shall have the capability to disseminate the results of small public water system technology and training programs.

(E) The projects that the grant recipient proposes to carry out under the grant are necessary and appropriate.

(F) The grant recipient has regional support beyond the host institution.

### (5) Consortia of States

At least 2 of the grants under this subsection shall be made to consortia of States with low population densities.

### (6) Authorization of appropriations

There are authorized to be appropriated to make grants under this subsection $2,000,000 for each of the fiscal years 1997 through 1999, and $5,000,000 for each of the fiscal years 2000 through 2003.

## (g) Environmental finance centers

### (1) In general

The Administrator shall provide initial funding for one or more university-based environmental finance centers for activities that provide technical assistance to State and local officials in developing the capacity of public water systems. Any such funds shall be used only for activities that are directly related to this subchapter.

### (2) National capacity development clearinghouse

The Administrator shall establish a national public water system capacity development clearinghouse to receive and disseminate information with respect to developing, improving, and maintaining financial and managerial capacity at public water systems. The Administrator shall ensure that the clearinghouse does not duplicate other federally supported clearinghouse activities.

### (3) Capacity development techniques

The Administrator may request an environmental finance center funded under paragraph (1) to develop and test managerial, financial, and institutional techniques for capacity development. The techniques may include capacity assessment methodologies, manual and computer based public water system rate models and capital planning models, public water system consolidation procedures, and regionalization models.

**(4) Authorization of appropriations**

There are authorized to be appropriated to carry out this subsection $1,500,000 for each of the fiscal years 1997 through 2003.

**(5) Limitation**

No portion of any funds made available under this subsection may be used for lobbying expenses.

(July 1, 1944, c. 373, Title XIV, § 1420, as added Aug. 6, 1996, Pub.L. 104–182, Title I, § 119, 110 Stat. 1647.)

**HISTORICAL AND STATUTORY NOTES**

**References in Text**

This subchapter, referred to in subsec. (b)(1), originally read "this title", meaning Title XIV of Act July 1, 1944, c. 373, Title XIV, § 1401 et seq., as added Dec. 16, 1974, Pub.L. 93–523, § 2(a), 88 Stat. 1661, and amended, which enacted this subchapter.

**Effective and Applicability Provisions**

1996 Acts

Section effective Aug. 6, 1996, except as otherwise specifically provided, see section 2(b) of Pub.L. 104–182, set out as a note under section 300f of this title.

## PART C—PROTECTION OF UNDERGROUND SOURCES OF DRINKING WATER

## § 300h. Regulations for State programs

**[PHSA § 1421]**

**(a) Publication of proposed regulations; promulgation; amendments; public hearings; administrative consultations**

(1) The Administrator shall publish proposed regulations for State underground injection control programs within 180 days after December 16, 1974. Within 180 days after publication of such proposed regulations, he shall promulgate such regulations with such modifications as he deems appropriate. Any regulation under this subsection may be amended from time to time.

(2) Any regulation under this section shall be proposed and promulgated in accordance with section 553 of Title 5 (relating to rulemaking), except that the Administrator shall provide opportunity for public hearing prior to promulgation of such regulations. In proposing and promulgating regulations under this section, the Administrator shall consult with the Secretary, the National Drinking Water Advisory Council, and other appropriate Federal entities and with interested State entities.

**(b) Minimum requirements; restrictions**

(1) Regulations under subsection (a) of this section for State underground injection programs shall contain minimum requirements for effective programs to prevent underground injection which endangers drinking water sources within the meaning of subsection (d)(2) of this section. Such regulations shall require that a State program, in order to be approved under section 300h–1 of this title—

(A) shall prohibit, effective on the date on which the applicable underground injection control program takes effect, any underground injection in such State which is not authorized by a permit issued by the State (except that the regulations may permit a State to authorize underground injection by rule);

(B) shall require (i) in the case of a program which provides for authorization of underground injection by permit, that the applicant for the permit to inject must satisfy the State that the underground injection will not endanger drinking water sources, and (ii) in the case of a program which provides for such an authorization by rule, that no rule may be promulgated which authorizes any underground injection which endangers drinking water sources;

(C) shall include inspection, monitoring, recordkeeping, and reporting requirements; and

(D) shall apply (i) as prescribed by section 300j–6(b) of this title, to underground injections by Federal agencies, and (ii) to underground injections by any other person whether or not occurring on property owned or leased by the United States.

(2) Regulations of the Administrator under this section for State underground injection control programs may not prescribe requirements which interfere with or impede—

(A) the underground injection of brine or other fluids which are brought to the surface in connection with oil or natural gas production or natural gas storage operations, or

(B) any underground injection for the secondary or tertiary recovery of oil or natural gas,

unless such requirements are essential to assure that underground sources of drinking water will not be endangered by such injection.

(3)(A) The regulations of the Administrator under this section shall permit or provide for consideration of varying geologic, hydrological, or historical conditions in different States and in different areas within a State.

(B)(i) In prescribing regulations under this section the Administrator shall, to the extent feasible, avoid promulgation of requirements which would unnecessarily disrupt State underground injection control programs which are in effect and being enforced in a substantial number of States.

(ii) For the purpose of this subparagraph, a regulation prescribed by the Administrator under this section shall be deemed to disrupt a State underground injection control program only if it would be infeasible to comply with both such regulation and the State underground injection control program.

(iii) For the purpose of this subparagraph, a regulation prescribed by the Administrator under this section shall be deemed unnecessary only if, without such regulation, underground sources of drinking water will not be endangered by an underground injection.

(C) Nothing in this section shall be construed to alter or affect the duty to assure that underground sources of drinking water will not be endangered by any underground injection.

**(c) Temporary permits; notice and hearing**

(1) The Administrator may, upon application of the Governor of a State which authorizes underground injection by means of permits, authorize such State to issue (without regard to subsection (b)(1)(B)(i) of this section) temporary permits for underground injection which may be effective until the expiration of four years after December 16, 1974, if—

(A) the Administrator finds that the State has demonstrated that it is unable and could not reasonably have been able to process all permit applications within the time available;

(B) the Administrator determines the adverse effect on the environment of such temporary permits is not unwarranted;

(C) such temporary permits will be issued only with respect to injection wells in operation on the date on which such State's permit program approved under this part first takes effect and for which there was inadequate time to process its permit application; and

(D) the Administrator determines the temporary permits require the use of adequate safeguards established by rules adopted by him.

(2) The Administrator may, upon application of the Governor of a State which authorizes underground injection by means of permits, authorize such State to issue (without regard to subsection (b)(1)(B)(i) of this section), but after reasonable notice and hearing, one or more temporary permits each of which is applicable to a particular injection well and to the underground injection of a particular fluid and which may be effective until the expiration of four years after December 16, 1974, if the State finds, on the record of such hearing—

(A) that technology (or other means) to permit safe injection of the fluid in accordance with the applicable underground injection control program is not generally available (taking costs into consideration);

(B) that injection of the fluid would be less harmful to health than the use of other available means of disposing of waste or producing the desired product; and

(C) that available technology or other means have been employed (and will be employed) to reduce the volume and toxicity of the fluid and to minimize the potentially adverse effect of the injection on the public health.

**(d) "Underground injection" defined; underground injection endangerment of drinking water sources**

For purposes of this part:

(1) The term "underground injection" means the subsurface emplacement of fluids by well injection. Such term does not include the underground injection of natural gas for purposes of storage.

(2) Underground injection endangers drinking water sources if such injection may result in the presence in underground water which supplies or can reasonably be expected to supply any public water system of any contaminant, and if the presence of such contaminant may result in such system's not complying with any national primary drinking water regulation or may otherwise adversely affect the health of persons.

(July 1, 1944, c. 373, Title XIV, § 1421, as added Dec. 16, 1974, Pub.L. 93–523, § 2(a), 88 Stat. 1674, and amended Nov. 16, 1977, Pub.L. 95–190, § 6(b), 91 Stat. 1396; Dec. 5, 1980, Pub.L. 96–502, §§ 3, 4(c), 94 Stat. 2738; June 19, 1986, Pub.L. 99–339, Title II, § 201(a), 100 Stat. 653; Aug. 6, 1996, Pub.L. 104–182, Title V, § 501(b)(1), 110 Stat. 1691.)

### HISTORICAL AND STATUTORY NOTES

**References in Text**

Section 300j–6(b) of this title, referred to in subsec. (b)(1)(D), was repealed, and a new section 300j–6(b) relating to administrative penalty orders was added by Pub.L. 104–182, title I, § 129(a), Aug. 6, 1996, 110 Stat. 1660.

**Effective and Applicability Provisions**

1996 Acts

Amendment by Pub.L. 104–182 effective Aug. 6, 1996, except as otherwise specifically provided, see section 2(b) of Pub.L. 104–182, set out as a note under section 300f of this title.

## § 300h–1. State primary enforcement responsibility

**[PHSA § 1422]**

**(a) List of States in need of a control program; amendment of list**

Within 180 days after December 16, 1974, the Administrator shall list in the Federal Register each State for which in his judgment a State underground injection control program may be necessary to assure that underground injection will not endanger drinking water sources. Such list may be amended from time to time.

**(b) State applications; notice to Administrator of compliance with revised or added requirements; approval or disapproval by Administrator; duration of State primary enforcement responsibility; public hearing**

**(1)(A)** Each State listed under subsection (a) of this section shall within 270 days after the date of promulgation of any regulation under section 300h of this title (or, if later, within 270 days after such State is first listed under subsection (a) of this section) submit to the Administrator an application which contains a showing satisfactory to the Administrator that the State—

**(i)** has adopted after reasonable notice and public hearings, and will implement, an underground injection control program which meets the requirements of regulations in effect under section 300h of this title; and

**(ii)** will keep such records and make such reports with respect to its activities under its underground injection control program as the Administrator may require by regulation.

The Administrator may, for good cause, extend the date for submission of an application by any State under this subparagraph for a period not to exceed an additional 270 days.

**(B)** Within 270 days of any amendment of a regulation under section 300h of this title revising or adding any requirement respecting State underground injection control programs, each State listed under subsection (a) of this section shall submit (in such form and manner as the Administrator may require) a notice to the Administrator containing a showing satisfactory to him that the State underground injection control program meets the revised or added requirement.

(2) Within ninety days after the State's application under paragraph (1)(A) or notice under paragraph (1)(B) and after reasonable opportunity for presentation of views, the Administrator shall by rule either approve, disapprove, or approve in part and disapprove in part, the State's underground injection control program.

(3) If the Administrator approves the State's program under paragraph (2), the State shall have primary enforcement responsibility for underground water sources until such time as the Administrator determines, by rule, that such State no longer meets the requirements of clause (i) or (ii) of paragraph (1)(A) of this subsection.

(4) Before promulgating any rule under paragraph (2) or (3) of this subsection, the Administrator shall provide opportunity for public hearing respecting such rule.

**(c) Program by Administrator for State without primary enforcement responsibility; restrictions**

If the Administrator disapproves a State's program (or part thereof) under subsection (b)(2) of this section, if the Administrator determines under subsection (b)(3) of this section that a State no longer meets the requirements of clause (i) or (ii) of subsection (b)(1)(A) of this section, or if a State fails to submit an application or notice before the date of expiration of the period specified in subsection (b)(1) of this section, the Administrator shall by regulation within 90 days after the date of such disapproval, determination, or expiration (as the case may be) prescribe (and may from time to time by regulation revise) a program applicable to such State meeting the requirements of section 300h(b) of this title. Such program may not include requirements which interfere with or impede—

**(1)** the underground injection of brine or other fluids which are brought to the surface in connection with oil or natural gas production or natural gas storage operations, or

**(2)** any underground injection for the secondary or tertiary recovery of oil or natural gas,

unless such requirements are essential to assure that underground sources of drinking water will not be endangered by such injection. Such program shall apply in such State to the extent that a program adopted by such State which the Administrator determines meets such requirements is not in effect. Before promulgating any regulation under this section, the Administrator shall provide opportunity for public hearing respecting such regulation.

**(d) "Applicable underground injection control program" defined**

For purposes of this subchapter, the term "applicable underground injection control program" with respect to a State means the program (or most recent amendment thereof) (1) which has been adopted by the State and which has been approved under subsection (b) of this section, or (2) which has been prescribed by the Administrator under subsection (c) of this section.

**(e) Primary enforcement responsibility by Indian Tribe**

An Indian Tribe may assume primary enforcement responsibility for underground injection control under this section consistent with such regulations as the Administrator has prescribed pursuant to this part and section 300j–11 of this title. The area over which such Indian Tribe exercises governmental jurisdiction need not have been listed under subsection (a) of this section, and such Tribe need not submit an application to assume primary enforcement responsibility within the 270–day deadline noted in subsection (b)(1)(A) of this section. Until an Indian Tribe assumes primary enforcement responsibility, the currently applicable underground injection control program shall continue to apply. If an applicable underground injection control program does not exist for an Indian Tribe, the Administrator shall prescribe such a program pursuant to subsection (c) of this section, and consistent with section 300h(b) of this title, within 270 days after June 19, 1986, unless an Indian Tribe first obtains approval to assume primary enforcement responsibility for underground injection control.

(July 1, 1944, c. 373, Title XIV, § 1422, as added Dec. 16, 1974, Pub.L. 93–523, § 2(a), 88 Stat. 1676, and amended Nov. 16, 1977, Pub.L. 95–190, § 6(a), 91 Stat. 1396; June 19, 1986, Pub.L. 99–339, Title II, § 201(a), Title III, § 302(c), 100 Stat. 653, 666.)

## § 300h–2. Enforcement of program

**[PHSA § 1423]**

**(a) Notice to State and violator; issuance of administrative order; civil action**

(1) Whenever the Administrator finds during a period during which a State has primary enforcement responsibility for underground water sources (within the meaning of section 300h–1(b)(3) of this title or section 300h–4(c) of this title) that any person who is subject to a requirement of an applicable underground injection control program in such State is violating such requirement, he shall so notify the State and the person violating such requirement. If beyond the thirtieth day after the Administrator's notification the State has not commenced appropriate enforcement action, the Administrator shall issue an order under subsection (c) of this section requiring the person to comply with such requirement or the Administrator shall commence a civil action under subsection (b) of this section.

(2) Whenever the Administrator finds during a period during which a State does not have primary enforcement responsibility for underground water sources that any person subject to any requirement of any applicable underground injection control program in such State is violating such requirement, the Administrator shall issue an order under subsection (c) of this section requiring the person to comply with such requirement or the Administrator shall commence a civil action under subsection (b) of this section.

**(b) Civil and criminal actions**

Civil actions referred to in paragraphs (1) and (2) of subsection (a) of this section shall be brought in the appropriate United States district court. Such court shall have jurisdiction to require compliance with any requirement of an applicable underground injection program or with an order issued under subsection (c) of this section. The court may enter such judgment as protection of public health may require. Any person who violates any requirement of an applicable underground injection control program or an order requiring compliance under subsection (c) of this section—

(1) shall be subject to a civil penalty of not more than $25,000 for each day of such violation, and

(2) if such violation is willful, such person may, in addition to or in lieu of the civil penalty authorized by paragraph (1), be imprisoned for not more than 3 years, or fined in accordance with Title 18, or both.

**(c) Administrative orders**

(1) In any case in which the Administrator is authorized to bring a civil action under this section with respect to any regulation or other requirement of this part other than those relating to—

(A) the underground injection of brine or other fluids which are brought to the surface in connection with oil or natural gas production, or

(B) any underground injection for the secondary or tertiary recovery of oil or natural gas,

the Administrator may also issue an order under this subsection either assessing a civil penalty of not more than $10,000 for each day of violation for any past or current violation, up to a maximum administrative penalty of $125,000, or requiring compliance with such regulation or other requirement, or both.

(2) In any case in which the Administrator is authorized to bring a civil action under this section with respect to any regulation, or other requirement of this part relating to—

(A) the underground injection of brine or other fluids which are brought to the surface in connection with oil or natural gas production, or

(B) any underground injection for the secondary or tertiary recovery of oil or natural gas,

the Administrator may also issue an order under this subsection either assessing a civil penalty of not more than $5,000 for each day of violation for any past or current violation, up to a maximum administrative penalty of $125,000, or requiring compliance with such regulation or other requirement, or both.

(3)(A) An order under this subsection shall be issued by the Administrator after opportunity (provided in accordance with this subparagraph) for a hearing. Before issuing the order, the Administrator shall give to the person to whom it is directed written notice of the Administrator's proposal to issue such order and the opportunity to request, within 30 days of the date the notice is received by such person, a hearing on the order. Such hearing shall not be subject to section 554 or 556 of Title 5, but shall provide a reasonable opportunity to be heard and to present evidence.

**(B)** The Administrator shall provide public notice of, and reasonable opportunity to comment on, any proposed order.

**(C)** Any citizen who comments on any proposed order under subparagraph (B) shall be given notice of any hearing under this subsection and of any order. In any hearing held under subparagraph (A), such citizen shall have a reasonable opportunity to be heard and to present evidence.

**(D)** Any order issued under this subsection shall become effective 30 days following its issuance unless an appeal is taken pursuant to paragraph (6).

**(4)(A)** Any order issued under this subsection shall state with reasonable specificity the nature of the violation and may specify a reasonable time for compliance.

**(B)** In assessing any civil penalty under this subsection, the Administrator shall take into account appropriate factors, including (i) the seriousness of the violation; (ii) the economic benefit (if any) resulting from the violation; (iii) any history of such violations; (iv) any good-faith efforts to comply with the applicable requirements; (v) the economic impact of the penalty on the violator; and (vi) such other matters as justice may require.

**(5)** Any violation with respect to which the Administrator has commenced and is diligently prosecuting an action, or has issued an order under this subsection assessing a penalty, shall not be subject to an action under subsection (b) of this section or section 300h-3(c) or 300j-8 of this title, except that the foregoing limitation on civil actions under section 300j-8 of this title shall not apply with respect to any violation for which—

**(A)** a civil action under section 300j-8(a)(1) of this title has been filed prior to commencement of an action under this subsection, or

**(B)** a notice of violation under section 300j-8(b)(1) of this title has been given before commencement of an action under this subsection and an action under section 300j-8(a)(1) of this title is filed before 120 days after such notice is given.

**(6)** Any person against whom an order is issued or who commented on a proposed order pursuant to paragraph (3) may file an appeal of such order with the United States District Court for the District of Columbia or the district in which the violation is alleged to have occurred. Such an appeal may only be filed within the 30-day period beginning on the date the order is issued. Appellant shall simultaneously send a copy of the appeal by certified mail to the Administrator and to the Attorney General. The Administrator shall promptly file in such court a certified copy of the record on which such order was imposed. The district court shall not set aside or remand such order unless there is not substantial evidence on the record, taken as a whole, to support the finding of a violation or, unless the Administrator's assessment of penalty or requirement for compliance constitutes an abuse of discretion. The district court shall not impose additional civil penalties for the same violation unless the Administrator's assessment of a penalty constitutes an abuse of discretion. Notwithstanding section 300j-7(a)(2) of this title, any order issued under paragraph (3) shall be subject to judicial review exclusively under this paragraph.

**(7)** If any person fails to pay an assessment of a civil penalty—

**(A)** after the order becomes effective under paragraph (3), or

**(B)** after a court, in an action brought under paragraph (6), has entered a final judgment in favor of the Administrator,

the Administrator may request the Attorney General to bring a civil action in an appropriate district court to recover the amount assessed (plus costs, attorneys' fees, and interest at currently prevailing rates from the date the order is effective or the date of such final judgment, as the case may be). In such an action, the validity, amount, and appropriateness of such penalty shall not be subject to review.

**(8)** The Administrator may, in connection with administrative proceedings under this subsection, issue subpoenas compelling the attendance and testimony of witnesses and subpoenas duces tecum, and may request the Attorney General to bring an action to enforce any subpoena under this section. The district courts shall have jurisdiction to enforce such subpoenas and impose sanction.

**(d) State authority to adopt or enforce laws or regulations respecting underground injection unaffected**

Nothing in this subchapter shall diminish any authority of a State or political subdivision to adopt or enforce any law or regulation respecting underground injection but no such law or regulation shall relieve any person of any requirement otherwise applicable under this subchapter.

(July 1, 1944, c. 373, Title XIV, § 1423, as added Dec. 16, 1974, Pub.L. 93-523, § 2(a), 88 Stat. 1677, and amended Dec. 5, 1980, Pub.L. 96-502, § 2(b), 94 Stat. 2738; June 19, 1986, Pub.L. 99-339, Title II, § 202, 100 Stat. 654.)

## § 300h-3. Interim regulation of underground injections

[PHSA § 1424]

### (a) Necessity for well operation permit; designation of one aquifer areas

(1) Any person may petition the Administrator to have an area of a State (or States) designated as an area in which no new underground injection well may be operated during the period beginning on the date of the designation and ending on the date on which the applicable underground injection control program covering such area takes effect unless a permit for the operation of such well has been issued by the Administrator under subsection (b) of this section. The Administrator may so designate an area within a State if he finds that the area has one aquifer which is the sole or principal drinking water source for the area and which, if contaminated, would create a significant hazard to public health.

(2) Upon receipt of a petition under paragraph (1) of this subsection, the Administrator shall publish it in the Federal Register and shall provide an opportunity to interested persons to submit written data, views, or arguments thereon. Not later than the 30th day following the date of the publication of a petition under this paragraph in the Federal Register, the Administrator shall either make the designation for which the petition is submitted or deny the petition.

### (b) Well operation permits; publication in Federal Register; notice and hearing; issuance or denial; conditions for issuance

(1) During the period beginning on the date an area is designated under subsection (a) of this section and ending on the date the applicable underground injection control program covering such area takes effect, no new underground injection well may be operated in such area unless the Administrator has issued a permit for such operation.

(2) Any person may petition the Administrator for the issuance of a permit for the operation of such a well in such an area. A petition submitted under this paragraph shall be submitted in such manner and contain such information as the Administrator may require by regulation. Upon receipt of such a petition, the Administrator shall publish it in the Federal Register. The Administrator shall give notice of any proceeding on a petition and shall provide opportunity for agency hearing. The Administrator shall act upon such petition on the record of any hearing held pursuant to the preceding sentence respecting such petition. Within 120 days of the publication in the Federal Register of a petition submitted under this paragraph, the Administrator shall either issue the permit for which the petition was submitted or shall deny its issuance.

(3) The Administrator may issue a permit for the operation of a new underground injection well in an area designated under subsection (a) of this section only if he finds that the operation of such well will not cause contamination of the aquifer of such area so as to create a significant hazard to public health. The Administrator may condition the issuance of such a permit upon the use of such control measures in connection with the operation of such well, for which the permit is to be issued, as he deems necessary to assure that the operation of the well will not contaminate the aquifer of the designated area in which the well is located so as to create a significant hazard to public health.

### (c) Civil penalties; separate violations; penalties for willful violations; temporary restraining order or injunction

Any person who operates a new underground injection well in violation of subsection (b) of this section, (1) shall be subject to a civil penalty of not more than $5,000 for each day in which such violation occurs, or (2) if such violation is willful, such person may, in lieu of the civil penalty authorized by clause (1), be fined not more than $10,000 for each day in which such violation occurs. If the Administrator has reason to believe that any person is violating or will violate subsection (b) of this section, he may petition the United States district court to issue a temporary restraining order or injunction (including a mandatory injunction) to enforce such subsection.

### (d) "New underground injection well" defined

For purposes of this section, the term "new underground injection well" means an underground injection well whose operation was not approved by appropriate State and Federal agencies before December 16, 1974.

### (e) Areas with one aquifer; publication in Federal Register; commitments for Federal financial assistance

If the Administrator determines, on his own initiative or upon petition, that an area has an aquifer which is the sole or principal drinking water source for the area and which, if contaminated, would create a significant hazard to public health, he shall publish notice of that determination in the Federal Register. After the publication of any such notice, no commitment for Federal financial assistance (through a grant, contract, loan guarantee, or otherwise) may be entered into for any project which the Administrator determines may contaminate such aquifer through a recharge zone so as to create a significant hazard to public health, but a commitment for Federal financial assistance may, if authorized under another provision of law, be entered into to plan or design the project to assure that it will not so contaminate the aquifer. (July 1, 1944, c. 373, Title XIV, § 1424, as added Dec. 16, 1974, Pub.L. 93–523, § 2(a), 88 Stat. 1678.)

## § 300h–4. Optional demonstration by States relating to oil or natural gas

[PHSA § 1425]

**(a) Approval of State underground injection control program; alternative showing of effectiveness of program by State**

For purposes of the Administrator's approval or disapproval under section 300h–1 of this title of that portion of any State underground injection control program which relates to—

(1) the underground injection of brine or other fluids which are brought to the surface in connection with oil or natural gas production or natural gas storage operations, or

(2) any underground injection for the secondary or tertiary recovery of oil or natural gas,

in lieu of the showing required under subparagraph (A) of section 300h–1(b)(1) of this title the State may demonstrate that such portion of the State program meets the requirements of subparagraphs (A) through (D) of section 300h(b)(1) of this title and represents an effective program (including adequate recordkeeping and reporting) to prevent underground injection which endangers drinking water sources.

**(b) Revision or amendment of requirements of regulation; showing of effectiveness of program by State**

If the Administrator revises or amends any requirement of a regulation under section 300h of this title relating to any aspect of the underground injection referred to in subsection (a) of this section, in the case of that portion of a State underground injection control program for which the demonstration referred to in subsection (a) of this section has been made, in lieu of the showing required under section 300h–1(b)(1)(B) of this title the State may demonstrate that, with respect to that aspect of such underground injection, the State program meets the requirements of subparagraphs (A) through (D) of section 300h(b)(1) of this title and represents an effective program (including adequate recordkeeping and reporting) to prevent underground injection which endangers drinking water sources.

**(c) Primary enforcement responsibility of State; voiding by Administrator under duly promulgated rule**

(1) Section 300h–1(b)(3) of this title shall not apply to that portion of any State underground injection control program approved by the Administrator pursuant to a demonstration under subsection (a) of this section (and under subsection (b) of this section where applicable).

(2) If pursuant to such a demonstration, the Administrator approves such portion of the State program, the State shall have primary enforcement responsibility with respect to that portion until such time as the Administrator determines, by rule, that such demonstration is no longer valid. Following such a determination, the Administrator may exercise the authority of subsection (c) of section 300h–1 of this title in the same manner as provided in such subsection with respect to a determination described in such subsection.

(3) Before promulgating any rule under paragraph (2), the Administrator shall provide opportunity for public hearing respecting such rule.

(July 1, 1944, c. 373, Title XIV, § 1425, as added Dec. 5, 1980, Pub.L. 96–502, § 2(a), 94 Stat. 2737, and amended June 19, 1986, Pub.L. 99–339, Title II, § 201(a), 100 Stat. 653.)

## § 300h–5. Regulation of State programs

[PHSA § 1426]

Not later than 18 months after June 19, 1986, the Administrator shall modify regulations issued under this chapter for Class I injection wells to identify monitoring methods, in addition to those in effect on November 1, 1985, including groundwater monitoring. In accordance with such regulations, the Administrator, or delegated State authority, shall determine the applicability of such monitoring methods, wherever appropriate, at locations and in such a manner as to provide the earliest possible detection of fluid migration into, or in the direction of, underground sources of drinking water from such wells, based on its assessment of the potential for fluid migration from the injection zone that may be harmful to human health or the environment. For purposes of this subsection, a class I injection well is defined in accordance with 40 CFR 146.05 as in effect on November 1, 1985.

(July 1, 1944, c. 373, Title XIV, § 1426, as added June 19, 1986, Pub.L. 99–339, Title II, § 201(b), 100 Stat. 653, and amended Dec. 21, 1995, Pub.L. 104–66, Title II, § 2021(f), 109 Stat. 727; Aug. 6, 1996, Pub.L. 104–182, Title V, § 501(f)(2), 110 Stat. 1691.)

### HISTORICAL AND STATUTORY NOTES

**Effective and Applicability Provisions**

1996 Acts

Amendment by Pub.L. 104–182 effective Aug. 6, 1996, except as otherwise specifically provided, see section 2(b) of Pub.L. 104–182, set out as a note under section 300f of this title.

## § 300h–6. Sole source aquifer demonstration program

[PHSA § 1427]

### (a) Purpose

The purpose of this section is to establish procedures for development, implementation, and assessment of demonstration programs designed to protect critical aquifer protection areas located within areas designated as sole or principal source aquifers under section 300h–3(e) of this title.

### (b) "Critical aquifer protection area" defined

For purposes of this section, the term "critical aquifer protection area" means either of the following:

(1) All or part of an area located within an area for which an application or designation as a sole or principal source aquifer pursuant to section 300h–3(e) of this title, has been submitted and approved by the Administrator and which satisfies the criteria established by the Administrator under subsection (d) of this section.

(2) All or part of an area which is within an aquifer designated as a sole source aquifer as of June 19, 1986, and for which an areawide ground water quality protection plan has been approved under section 208 of the Clean Water Act [33 U.S.C.A. § 1288] prior to June 19, 1986.

### (c) Application

Any State, municipal or local government or political subdivision thereof or any planning entity (including any interstate regional planning entity) that identifies a critical aquifer protection area over which it has authority or jurisdiction may apply to the Administrator for the selection of such area for a demonstration program under this section. Any applicant shall consult with other government or planning entities with authority or jurisdiction in such area prior to application. Applicants, other than the Governor, shall submit the application for a demonstration program jointly with the Governor.

### (d) Criteria

Not later than 1 year after June 19, 1986, the Administrator shall, by rule, establish criteria for identifying critical aquifer protection areas under this section. In establishing such criteria, the Administrator shall consider each of the following:

(1) The vulnerability of the aquifer to contamination due to hydrogeologic characteristics.

(2) The number of persons or the proportion of population using the ground water as a drinking water source.

(3) The economic, social and environmental benefits that would result to the area from maintenance of ground water of high quality.

(4) The economic, social and environmental costs that would result from degradation of the quality of the ground water.

### (e) Contents of application

An application submitted to the Administrator by any applicant for a demonstration program under this section shall meet each of the following requirements:

(1) The application shall propose boundaries for the critical aquifer protection area within its jurisdiction.

(2) The application shall designate or, if necessary, establish a planning entity (which shall be a public agency and which shall include representation of elected local and State governmental officials) to develop a comprehensive management plan (hereinafter in this section referred to as the "plan") for the critical protection area. Where a local government planning agency exists with adequate authority to carry out this section with respect to any proposed critical protection area, such agency shall be designated as the planning entity.

(3) The application shall establish procedures for public participation in the development of the plan, for review, approval, and adoption of the plan, and for assistance to municipalities and other public agencies with authority under State law to implement the plan.

(4) The application shall include a hydrogeologic assessment of surface and ground water resources within the critical protection area.

(5) The application shall include a comprehensive management plan for the proposed protection area.

(6) The application shall include the measures and schedule proposed for implementation of such plan.

### (f) Comprehensive plan

(1) The objective of a comprehensive management plan submitted by an applicant under this section shall be to maintain the quality of the ground water in the critical protection area in a manner reasonably expected to protect human health, the environment and ground water resources. In order to achieve such objective, the plan may be designed to maintain, to the maximum extent possible, the natural vegetative and hydrogeological conditions. Each of the following elements shall be included in such a protection plan:

(A) A map showing the detailed boundary of the critical protection area.

(B) An identification of existing and potential point and nonpoint sources of ground water degradation.

(C) An assessment of the relationship between activities on the land surface and ground water quality.

(D) Specific actions and management practices to be implemented in the critical protection area to prevent adverse impacts on ground water quality.

(E) Identification of authority adequate to implement the plan, estimates of program costs, and sources of State matching funds.

(2) Such plan may also include the following:

(A) A determination of the quality of the existing ground water recharged through the special protection area and the natural recharge capabilities of the special protection area watershed.

(B) Requirements designed to maintain existing underground drinking water quality or improve underground drinking water quality if prevailing conditions fail to meet drinking water standards, pursuant to this chapter and State law.

(C) Limits on Federal, State, and local government, financially assisted activities and projects which may contribute to degradation of such ground water or any loss of natural surface and subsurface infiltration of purification capability of the special protection watershed.

(D) A comprehensive statement of land use management including emergency contingency planning as it pertains to the maintenance of the quality of underground sources of drinking water or to the improvement of such sources if necessary to meet drinking water standards pursuant to this chapter and State law.

(E) Actions in the special protection area which would avoid adverse impacts on water quality, recharge capabilities, or both.

(F) Consideration of specific techniques, which may include clustering, transfer of development rights, and other innovative measures sufficient to achieve the objectives of this section.

(G) Consideration of the establishment of a State institution to facilitate and assist funding a development transfer credit system.

(H) A program for State and local implementation of the plan described in this subsection in a manner that will insure the continued, uniform, consistent protection of the critical protection area in accord with the purposes of this section.

(I) Pollution abatement measures, if appropriate.

**(g) Plans under section 208 of Clean Water Act**

A plan approved before June 19, 1986, under section 208 of the Clean Water Act [33 U.S.C.A. § 1288] to protect a sole source aquifer designated under section 300h–3(e) of this title shall be considered a comprehensive management plan for the purposes of this section.

**(h) Consultation and hearings**

During the development of a comprehensive management plan under this section, the planning entity shall consult with, and consider the comments of, appropriate officials of any municipality and State or Federal agency which has jurisdiction over lands and waters within the special protection area, other concerned organizations and technical and citizen advisory committees. The planning entity shall conduct public hearings at places within the special protection area for the purpose of providing the opportunity to comment on any aspect of the plan.

**(i) Approval or disapproval**

Within 120 days after receipt of an application under this section, the Administrator shall approve or disapprove the application. The approval or disapproval shall be based on a determination that the critical protection area satisfies the criteria established under subsection (d) of this section and that a demonstration program for the area would provide protection for ground water quality consistent with the objectives stated in subsection (f) of this section. The Administrator shall provide to the Governor a written explanation of the reasons for the disapproval of any such application. Any petitioner may modify and resubmit any application which is not approved. Upon approval of an application, the Administrator may enter into a cooperative agreement with the applicant to establish a demonstration program under this section.

**(j) Grants and reimbursement**

Upon entering a cooperative agreement under subsection (i) of this section, the Administrator may provide to the applicant, on a matching basis, a grant of 50 per centum of the costs of implementing the plan established under this section. The Administrator may also reimburse the applicant of an approved plan up to 50 per centum of the costs of developing such plan, except for plans approved under section 208 of the Clean Water Act [33 U.S.C.A. § 1288]. The total amount of grants under this section for any one aquifer, designated under section 300h–3(e) of this title, shall not exceed $4,000,000 in any one fiscal year.

**(k) Activities funded under other law**

No funds authorized under this section may be used to fund activities funded under other sections of this chapter or the Clean Water Act [33 U.S.C.A. § 1251 et seq.], the Solid Waste Disposal Act [42 U.S.C.A. § 6901 et seq.], the Comprehensive Environmental Response, Compensation, and Liability Act of 1980 [42 U.S.C.A. § 9601 et seq.] or other environmental laws.

**(*l*) Savings provision**

Nothing under this section shall be construed to amend, supersede or abrogate rights to quantities of water which have been established by interstate water compacts, Supreme Court decrees, or State water laws; or any requirement imposed or right provided under any Federal or State environmental or public health statute.

**(m) Authorization of appropriations**

There are authorized to be appropriated to carry out this section not more than the following amounts:

| Fiscal year: | *Amount* |
|---|---|
| 1987 | $10,000,000 |
| 1988 | 15,000,000 |
| 1989 | 17,500,000 |
| 1990 | 17,500,000 |
| 1991 | 17,500,000 |
| 1992–2003 | 15,000,000. |

Matching grants under this section may also be used to implement or update any water quality management plan for a sole or principal source aquifer approved (before June 19, 1986) by the Administrator under section 208 of the Federal Water Pollution Control Act [33 U.S.C.A. § 1288].

(July 1, 1944, c. 373, Title XIV, § 1427, as added and amended June 19, 1986, Pub.L. 99–339, Title II, § 203, Title III, § 301(f), 100 Stat. 657, 664; Dec. 21, 1995, Pub.L. 104–66, Title II, § 2021(g), 109 Stat. 727; Aug. 6, 1996, Pub.L. 104–182, Title I, § 120(a), Title V, § 501(b)(2), (f)(3), 110 Stat. 1650, 1691.)

### HISTORICAL AND STATUTORY NOTES

**References in Text**

The Clean Water Act, referred to in subsec. (k), is Act June 30, 1948, c. 758, as amended generally by Pub.L. 92–500, § 2, Oct. 18, 1972, 86 Stat. 816, also known as the Federal Water Pollution Control Act, which is classified generally to chapter 26 (section 1251 et seq.) of Title 33, Navigation and Navigable Waters. For complete classification of this Act to the Code, see Short Title note set out under section 1251 of Title 33 and Tables.

The Solid Waste Disposal Act, referred to in subsec. (k) is Title II of Pub.L. 89–272, Oct. 20, 1965, 79 Stat. 997, as amended generally by Pub.L. 94–580, § 2, Oct. 21, 1976, 90 Stat. 2795, which is classified generally to chapter 82 (section 6901 et seq.) of this title. For complete classification of this Act to the Code, see Short Title note set out under section 6901 of this title and Tables.

The Comprehensive Environmental Response, Compensation, and Liability Act of 1980, referred to in subsec. (k), is Pub.L. 96–510, Dec. 11, 1980, 94 Stat. 2767, as amended, which is classified principally to chapter 103 (section 9601 et seq.) of this title. For complete classification of this Act to the Code, see Short Title note set out under section 9601 of this title and Tables.

**Effective and Applicability Provisions**

1996 Acts

Amendment by Pub.L. 104–182 effective Aug. 6, 1996, except as otherwise specifically provided, see section 2(b) of Pub.L. 104–182, set out as a note under section 300f of this title.

## § 300h–7. State programs to establish wellhead protection areas

**[PHSA § 1428]**

**(a) State programs**

The Governor or Governor's designee of each State shall, within 3 years of June 19, 1986, adopt and submit to the Administrator a State program to protect wellhead areas within their jurisdiction from contaminants which may have any adverse effect on the health of persons. Each State program under this section shall, at a minimum—

(1) specify the duties of State agencies, local governmental entities, and public water supply systems with respect to the development and implementation of programs required by this section;

(2) for each wellhead, determine the wellhead protection area as defined in subsection (e) of this section based on all reasonably available hydrogeologic information on ground water flow, recharge and discharge and other information the State deems necessary to adequately determine the wellhead protection area;

(3) identify within each wellhead protection area all potential anthropogenic sources of contaminants which may have any adverse effect on the health of persons;

(4) describe a program that contains, as appropriate, technical assistance, financial assistance, implementation of control measures, education, training, and demonstration projects to protect the water supply within wellhead protection areas from such contaminants;

(5) include contingency plans for the location and provision of alternate drinking water supplies for each public water system in the event of well or wellfield contamination by such contaminants; and

(6) include a requirement that consideration be given to all potential sources of such contaminants within the expected wellhead area of a new water well which serves a public water supply system.

**(b) Public participation**

To the maximum extent possible, each State shall establish procedures, including but not limited to the establishment of technical and citizens' advisory committees, to encourage the public to participate in developing the protection program for wellhead areas and source water assessment programs under section 300j–13 of this title. Such procedures shall include notice and opportunity for public hearing on the State program before it is submitted to the Administrator.

**(c) Disapproval**

**(1) In general**

If, in the judgment of the Administrator, a State program or portion thereof under subsection (a) of this section is not adequate to protect public water systems as required by subsection (a) of this section or a State program under section 300j–13 of this title or section 300g–7(b) of this title does not meet the applicable requirements of section 300j–13 of this title or section 300g–7(b) of this title, the Administrator shall disapprove such program or portion thereof. A State program developed pursuant to subsection (a) of this section shall be deemed to be adequate unless the Administrator determines, within 9 months of the receipt of a State program, that such program (or portion thereof) is inadequate for the purpose of protecting public water systems as required by this section from contaminants that may have any adverse effect on the health of persons. A State program developed pursuant to section 300j–13 of this title or section 300g–7(b) of this title shall be deemed to meet the applicable requirements of section 300j–13 of this title or section 300g–7(b) of this title unless the Administrator determines within 9 months of the receipt of the program that such program (or portion thereof) does not meet such requirements. If the Administrator determines that a proposed State program (or any portion thereof) is disapproved, the Administrator shall submit a written statement of the reasons for such determination to the Governor of the State.

**(2) Modification and resubmission**

Within 6 months after receipt of the Administrator's written notice under paragraph (1) that any proposed State program (or portion thereof) is disapproved, the Governor or Governor's designee, shall modify the program based upon the recommendations of the Administrator and resubmit the modified program to the Administrator.

**(d) Federal assistance**

After the date 3 years after June 19, 1986, no State shall receive funds authorized to be appropriated under this section except for the purpose of implementing the program and requirements of paragraphs (4) and (6) of subsection (a) of this section.

**(e) "Wellhead protection area" defined**

As used in this section, the term "wellhead protection area" means the surface and subsurface area surrounding a water well or wellfield, supplying a public water system, through which contaminants are reasonably likely to move toward and reach such water well or wellfield. The extent of a wellhead protection area, within a State, necessary to provide protection from contaminants which may have any adverse effect on the health of persons is to be determined by the State in the program submitted under subsection (a) of this section. Not later than one year after June 19, 1986, the Administrator shall issue technical guidance which States may use in making such determinations. Such guidance may reflect such factors as the radius of influence around a well or wellfield, the depth of drawdown of the water table by such well or wellfield at any given point, the time or rate of travel of various contaminants in various hydrologic conditions, distance from the well or wellfield, or other factors affecting the likelihood of contaminants reaching the well or wellfield, taking into account available engineering pump tests or comparable data, field reconnaissance, topographic information, and the geology of the formation in which the well or wellfield is located.

**(f) Prohibitions**

**(1) Activities under other laws**

No funds authorized to be appropriated under this section may be used to support activities authorized by the Federal Water Pollution Control Act [33 U.S.C.A. § 1251 et seq.], the Solid Waste Disposal Act [42 U.S.C.A. § 6901 et seq.], the Comprehensive Environmental Response, Compensation, and Liability Act of 1980 [42 U.S.C.A. § 9601 et seq.], or other sections of this chapter.

**(2) Individual sources**

No funds authorized to be appropriated under this section may be used to bring individual sources of contamination into compliance.

**(g) Implementation**

Each State shall make every reasonable effort to implement the State wellhead area protection program under this section within 2 years of submitting the program to the Administrator. Each State shall submit to the Administrator a biennial status report describing the State's progress in implementing the program. Such report shall include amendments to the State program for water wells sited during the biennial period.

**(h) Federal agencies**

Each department, agency, and instrumentality of the executive, legislative, and judicial branches of the Federal Government having jurisdiction over any potential source of contaminants identified by a State program pursuant to the provisions of subsection (a)(3) of this section shall be subject to and comply with all requirements of the State program developed according to subsection (a)(4) of this section applicable to such potential source of contaminants, both substantive and procedural, in the same manner, and to the same extent, as any other person is subject to such requirements, including payment of reasonable charges and fees. The President may exempt any potential source under the jurisdiction of any department, agency, or instrumentality in the executive branch if the President determines it to be in the paramount interest of the United States to do so. No such exemption shall be granted due to the lack of an appropriation unless the President shall have specifically requested such appropriation as part of the budgetary process and the Congress shall have failed to make available such requested appropriations.

**(i) Additional requirement**

**(1) In general**

In addition to the provisions of subsection (a) of this section, States in which there are more than 2,500 active wells at which annular injection is used as of January 1, 1986, shall include in their State program a certification that a State program exists and is being adequately enforced that provides protection from contaminants which may have any adverse effect on the health of persons and which are associated with the annular injection or surface disposal of brines associated with oil and gas production.

**(2) "Annular injection" defined**

For purposes of this subsection, the term "annular injection" means the reinjection of brines associated with the production of oil or gas between the production and surface casings of a conventional oil or gas producing well.

**(3) Review**

The Administrator shall conduct a review of each program certified under this subsection.

**(4) Disapproval**

If a State fails to include the certification required by this subsection or if in the judgment of the Administrator the State program certified under this subsection is not being adequately enforced, the Administrator shall disapprove the State program submitted under subsection (a) of this section.

**(j) Coordination with other laws**

Nothing in this section shall authorize or require any department, agency, or other instrumentality of the Federal Government or State or local government to apportion, allocate or otherwise regulate the withdrawal or beneficial use of ground or surface waters, so as to abrogate or modify any existing rights to water established pursuant to State or Federal law, including interstate compacts.

**(k) Authorization of appropriations**

Unless the State program is disapproved under this section, the Administrator shall make grants to the State for not less than 50 or more than 90 percent of the costs incurred by a State (as determined by the Administrator) in developing and implementing each State program under this section. For purposes of making such grants there is authorized to be appropriated not more than the following amounts:

| Fiscal year: | *Amount* |
|---|---|
| 1987 | $20,000,000 |
| 1988 | 20,000,000 |
| 1989 | 35,000,000 |
| 1990 | 35,000,000 |
| 1991 | 35,000,000 |
| 1992–2003 | 30,000,000. |

(July 1, 1944, c. 373, Title XIV, § 1428, as added and amended June 19, 1986, Pub.L. 99–339, Title II, § 205, Title III, § 301(e), 100 Stat. 660, 664; Aug. 6, 1996, Pub.L. 104–182, Title I, §§ 120(b), 132(b), Title V, § 501(f)(4), 110 Stat. 1650, 1674, 1692.

## HISTORICAL AND STATUTORY NOTES

**References in Text**

The Federal Water Pollution Control Act, referred to in subsec. (f)(1), is Act June 30, 1948, c. 758, as amended generally by Pub.L. 92–500, § 2, Oct. 18, 1972, 86 Stat. 816, which is classified generally to chapter 26 (section 1251 et seq.) of Title 33, Navigation and Navigable Waters. For complete classification of this Act to the Code, see Short Title note set out under section 1251 of Title 33 and Tables.

The Solid Waste Disposal Act, referred to in subsec. (f)(1), is Title II of Pub.L. 89–272, as amended generally by Pub.L. 94–580, § 2, Oct. 21, 1976, 90 Stat. 2795, which is classified generally to chapter 82 (section 6901 et seq.) of this title. For complete classification of this Act to the Code, see Short Title note set out under section 6901 of this title and Tables.

The Comprehensive Environmental Response, Compensation, and Liability Act of 1980, referred to in subsec. (f)(1), is Pub.L. 96–510, Dec. 11, 1980, 94 Stat. 2767, as amended, which is classified principally to chapter 103 (section 9601 et seq.) of this title. For complete classification of this Act to the Code, see Short Title note set out under section 9601 of this title and Tables.

**Effective and Applicability Provisions**

1996 Acts

Amendment by Pub.L. 104–182 effective Aug. 6, 1996, except as otherwise specifically provided, see section 2(b) of Pub.L. 104–182, set out as a note under section 300f of this title.

## § 300h–8. State ground water protection grants

**[PHSA § 1429]**

**(a) In general**

The Administrator may make a grant to a State for the development and implementation of a State program to ensure the coordinated and comprehensive protection of ground water resources within the State.

**(b) Guidance**

Not later than 1 year after August 6, 1996, and annually thereafter, the Administrator shall publish guidance that establishes procedures for application for State ground water protection program assistance and that identifies key elements of State ground water protection programs.

**(c) Conditions of grants**

**(1) In general**

The Administrator shall award grants to States that submit an application that is approved by the Administrator. The Administrator shall determine the amount of a grant awarded pursuant to this paragraph on the basis of an assessment of the extent of ground water resources in the State and the likelihood that awarding the grant will result in sustained and reliable protection of ground water quality.

**(2) Innovative program grants**

The Administrator may also award a grant pursuant to this subsection for innovative programs proposed by a State for the prevention of ground water contamination.

**(3) Allocation of funds**

The Administrator shall, at a minimum, ensure that, for each fiscal year, not less than 1 percent of funds made available to the Administrator by appropriations to carry out this section are allocated to each State that submits an application that is approved by the Administrator pursuant to this section.

**(4) Limitation on grants**

No grant awarded by the Administrator may be used for a project to remediate ground water contamination.

**(d) Amount of grants**

The amount of a grant awarded pursuant to paragraph (1) shall not exceed 50 percent of the eligible costs of carrying out the ground water protection program that is the subject of the grant (as determined by the Administrator) for the 1-year period beginning on the date that the grant is awarded. The State shall pay a State share to cover the costs of the ground water protection program from State funds in an amount that is not less than 50 percent of the cost of conducting the program.

**(e) Evaluations and reports**

Not later than 3 years after August 6, 1996, and every 3 years thereafter, the Administrator shall evaluate the State ground water protection programs that are the subject of grants awarded pursuant to this section and report to the Congress on the status of ground water quality in the United States and the effectiveness of State programs for ground water protection.

**(f) Authorization of appropriations**

There are authorized to be appropriated to carry out this section $15,000,000 for each of fiscal years 1997 through 2003.

(July 1, 1944, c. 373, Title XIV, § 1429, as added Aug. 6, 1996, Pub.L. 104–182, Title I, § 131, 110 Stat. 1672.)

### HISTORICAL AND STATUTORY NOTES

**Effective and Applicability Provisions**

1996 Acts

Section effective Aug. 6, 1996, except as otherwise specifically provided, see section 2(b) of Pub.L. 104–182, set out as a note under section 300f of this title.

## Part D—Emergency Powers

## § 300i. Emergency powers

**[PHSA § 1431]**

**(a) Actions authorized against imminent and substantial endangerment to health**

Notwithstanding any other provision of this subchapter, the Administrator, upon receipt of information that a contaminant which is present in or is likely to enter a public water system or an underground source of drinking water, or that there is a threatened or potential terrorist attack (or other intentional act designed to disrupt the provision of safe drinking water or to impact adversely the safety of drinking water supplied to communities and individuals), which may present an imminent and substantial endangerment to the health of persons, and that appropriate State and local authorities have not acted to protect the health of such persons, may take such actions as he may deem necessary in order to protect the health of such persons. To the extent he determines it to be practicable in light of such imminent endangerment, he shall consult with the State and local authorities in order to confirm the correctness of the information on which action proposed to be taken under this subsection is based and to ascertain the action which such authorities are or will be taking. The action which the Administrator may take may include (but shall not be limited to) (1) issuing such orders as may be necessary to protect the health of persons who are or may be users of such system (including travelers), including orders requiring the provision of alternative water supplies by persons who caused or contributed to the endangerment, and (2) commencing a civil action for appropriate relief, including a restraining order or permanent or temporary injunction.

**(b) Penalties for violations; separate offenses**

Any person who violates or fails or refuses to comply with any order issued by the Administrator under subsection (a)(1) of this section may, in an action brought in the appropriate United States district court to enforce such order, be subject to a civil penalty of not to exceed $15,000 for each day in which such violation occurs or failure to comply continues.

(July 1, 1944, c. 373, Title XIV, § 1431, as added Dec. 16, 1974, Pub.L. 93–523, § 2(a), 88 Stat. 1680, and amended June 19, 1986, Pub.L. 99–339, Title II, § 204, 100 Stat. 660; Aug. 6, 1996, Pub.L. 104–182, Title I, § 113(d), 110 Stat. 1636; June 12, 2002, Pub.L. 107–188, Title IV, § 403(2), 116 Stat. 687.)

### HISTORICAL AND STATUTORY NOTES

**Effective and Applicability Provisions**

1996 Acts

Amendment by Pub.L. 104–182 effective Aug. 6, 1996, except as otherwise specifically provided, see section 2(b) of Pub.L. 104–182, set out as a note under section 300f of this title.

## § 300i–1. Tampering with public water systems

### [PHSA § 1432]

**(a) Tampering**

Any person who tampers with a public water system shall be imprisoned for not more than 20 years, or fined in accordance with Title 18, or both.

**(b) Attempt or threat**

Any person who attempts to tamper, or makes a threat to tamper, with a public drinking water system be imprisoned for not more than 10 years, or fined in accordance with Title 18, or both.

**(c) Civil penalty**

The Administrator may bring a civil action in the appropriate United States district court (as determined under the provisions of Title 28) against any person who tampers, attempts to tamper, or makes a threat to tamper with a public water system. The court may impose on such person a civil penalty of not more than $1,000,000 for such tampering or not more than $100,000 for such attempt or threat.

**(d) "Tamper" defined**

For purposes of this section, the term "tamper" means—

(1) to introduce a contaminant into a public water system with the intention of harming persons; or

(2) to otherwise interfere with the operation of a public water system with the intention of harming persons.

(July 1, 1944, c. 373, Title XIV, § 1432, as added June 19, 1986, Pub.L. 99–339, Title I, § 108, 100 Stat. 651, and amended Aug. 6, 1996, Pub.L. 104–182, Title V, § 501(f)(5), 110 Stat. 1692; June 12, 2002, Pub.L. 107–188, Title IV, § 403(3), 116 Stat. 687.)

### HISTORICAL AND STATUTORY NOTES

**Effective and Applicability Provisions**

1996 Acts

Amendment by Pub.L. 104–182 effective Aug. 6, 1996, except as otherwise specifically provided, see section 2(b) of Pub.L. 104–182, set out as a note under section 300f of this title.

## § 300i–2. Terrorist and other intentional acts

### [PHSA § 1433]

**(a) Vulnerability assessments**

(1) Each community water system serving a population of greater than 3,300 persons shall conduct an assessment of the vulnerability of its system to a terrorist attack or other intentional acts intended to substantially disrupt the ability of the system to provide a safe and reliable supply of drinking water. The vulnerability assessment shall include, but not be limited to, a review of pipes and constructed conveyances, physical barriers, water collection, pretreatment, treatment, storage and distribution facilities, electronic, computer or other automated systems which are utilized by the public water system, the use, storage, or handling of various chemicals, and the operation and maintenance of such system. The Administrator, not later than August 1, 2002, after consultation with appropriate departments and agencies of the Federal Government and with State and local governments, shall provide baseline information to community water systems required to conduct vulnerability assessments regarding which kinds of terrorist attacks or other intentional acts are the probable threats to—

(A) substantially disrupt the ability of the system to provide a safe and reliable supply of drinking water; or

(B) otherwise present significant public health concerns.

(2) Each community water system referred to in paragraph (1) shall certify to the Administrator that the system has conducted an assessment complying with paragraph (1) and shall submit to the Administrator a written copy of the assessment. Such certification and submission shall be made prior to:

(A) March 31, 2003, in the case of systems serving a population of 100,000 or more.

(B) December 31, 2003, in the case of systems serving a population of 50,000 or more but less than 100,000.

(C) June 30, 2004, in the case of systems serving a population greater than 3,300 but less than 50,000.

(3) Except for information contained in a certification under this subsection identifying the system submitting the certification and the date of the certification, all information provided to the Administrator under this subsection and all information derived

therefrom shall be exempt from disclosure under section 552 of Title 5.

(4) No community water system shall be required under State or local law to provide an assessment described in this section to any State, regional, or local governmental entity solely by reason of the requirement set forth in paragraph (2) that the system submit such assessment to the Administrator.

(5) Not later than November 30, 2002, the Administrator, in consultation with appropriate Federal law enforcement and intelligence officials, shall develop such protocols as may be necessary to protect the copies of the assessments required to be submitted under this subsection (and the information contained therein) from unauthorized disclosure. Such protocols shall ensure that—

(A) each copy of such assessment, and all information contained in or derived from the assessment, is kept in a secure location;

(B) only individuals designated by the Administrator may have access to the copies of the assessments; and

(C) no copy of an assessment, or part of an assessment, or information contained in or derived from an assessment shall be available to anyone other than an individual designated by the Administrator.

At the earliest possible time prior to November 30, 2002, the Administrator shall complete the development of such protocols for the purpose of having them in place prior to receiving any vulnerability assessments from community water systems under this subsection.

(6)(A) Except as provided in subparagraph (B), any individual referred to in paragraph (5)(B) who acquires the assessment submitted under paragraph (2), or any reproduction of such assessment, or any information derived from such assessment, and who knowingly or recklessly reveals such assessment, reproduction, or information other than—

(i) to an individual designated by the Administrator under paragraph (5),

(ii) for purposes of section 300j–4 of this title or for actions under section 300i of this title, or

(iii) for use in any administrative or judicial proceeding to impose a penalty for failure to comply with this section,

shall upon conviction be imprisoned for not more than one year or fined in accordance with the provisions of chapter 227 of Title 18, applicable to class A misdemeanors, or both, and shall be removed from Federal office or employment.

(B) Notwithstanding subparagraph (A), an individual referred to in paragraph (5)(B) who is an officer or employee of the United States may discuss the contents of a vulnerability assessment submitted under this section with a State or local official.

(7) Nothing in this section authorizes any person to withhold any information from Congress or from any committee or subcommittee of Congress.

### (b) Emergency response plan

Each community water system serving a population greater than 3,300 shall prepare or revise, where necessary, an emergency response plan that incorporates the results of vulnerability assessments that have been completed. Each such community water system shall certify to the Administrator, as soon as reasonably possible after the enactment of this section, but not later than 6 months after the completion of the vulnerability assessment under subsection (a) of this section, that the system has completed such plan. The emergency response plan shall include, but not be limited to, plans, procedures, and identification of equipment that can be implemented or utilized in the event of a terrorist or other intentional attack on the public water system. The emergency response plan shall also include actions, procedures, and identification of equipment which can obviate or significantly lessen the impact of terrorist attacks or other intentional actions on the public health and the safety and supply of drinking water provided to communities and individuals. Community water systems shall, to the extent possible, coordinate with existing Local Emergency Planning Committees established under the Emergency Planning and Community Right-to-Know Act (42 U.S.C. 11001 et seq.) when preparing or revising an emergency response plan under this subsection.

### (c) Record maintenance

Each community water system shall maintain a copy of the emergency response plan completed pursuant to subsection (b) of this section for 5 years after such plan has been certified to the Administrator under this section.

### (d) Guidance to small public water systems

The Administrator shall provide guidance to community water systems serving a population of less than 3,300 persons on how to conduct vulnerability assessments, prepare emergency response plans, and address threats from terrorist attacks or other intentional actions designed to disrupt the provision of safe drinking water or significantly affect the public health or significantly affect the safety or supply of drinking water provided to communities and individuals.

### (e) Funding

(1) There are authorized to be appropriated to carry out this section not more than $160,000,000 for the

fiscal year 2002 and such sums as may be necessary for the fiscal years 2003 through 2005.

(2) The Administrator, in coordination with State and local governments, may use funds made available under paragraph (1) to provide financial assistance to community water systems for purposes of compliance with the requirements of subsections (a) and (b) of this section and to community water systems for expenses and contracts designed to address basic security enhancements of critical importance and significant threats to public health and the supply of drinking water as determined by a vulnerability assessment conducted under subsection (a) of this section. Such basic security enhancements may include, but shall not be limited to the following:

(A) the purchase and installation of equipment for detection of intruders;

(B) the purchase and installation of fencing, gating, lighting, or security cameras;

(C) the tamper-proofing of manhole covers, fire hydrants, and valve boxes;

(D) the rekeying of doors and locks;

(E) improvements to electronic, computer, or other automated systems and remote security systems;

(F) participation in training programs, and the purchase of training manuals and guidance materials, relating to security against terrorist attacks;

(G) improvements in the use, storage, or handling of various chemicals; and

(H) security screening of employees or contractor support services.

Funding under this subsection for basic security enhancements shall not include expenditures for personnel costs, or monitoring, operation, or maintenance of facilities, equipment, or systems.

(3) The Administrator may use not more than $5,000,000 from the funds made available under paragraph (1) to make grants to community water systems to assist in responding to and alleviating any vulnerability to a terrorist attack or other intentional acts intended to substantially disrupt the ability of the system to provide a safe and reliable supply of drinking water (including sources of water for such systems) which the Administrator determines to present an immediate and urgent security need.

(4) The Administrator may use not more than $5,000,000 from the funds made available under paragraph (1) to make grants to community water systems serving a population of less than 3,300 persons for activities and projects undertaken in accordance with the guidance provided to such systems under subsection (d) of this section.

(July 1, 1944, c. 373, Title XIV, § 1433, as added June 12, 2002, Pub.L. 107-188, Title IV, § 401, 116 Stat. 682.)

### HISTORICAL AND STATUTORY NOTES

**References in Text**

Chapter 227 of Title 18, referred to in subsec. (a)(6)(A)(ii), is 18 U.S.C.A. § 3551 et seq.

The Emergency Planning and Community Right-to-Know Act, referred to in subsec. (b), probably means the Emergency Planning and Community Right-to-Know Act of 1986, Title III of Pub.L. 99-499, Oct. 17, 1986, 100 Stat. 1728, which is classified principally to chapter 116 of this title, 42 U.S.C.A. § 11001 et seq. For complete classification of this Act to the Code, see Short Title of 1986 Amendments note set out under 42 U.S.C.A. § 11001 and Tables.

## § 300i-3. Contaminant prevention, detection and response

**[PHSA § 1434]**

**(a) In general**

The Administrator, in consultation with the Centers for Disease Control and, after consultation with appropriate departments and agencies of the Federal Government and with State and local governments, shall review (or enter into contracts or cooperative agreements to provide for a review of) current and future methods to prevent, detect and respond to the intentional introduction of chemical, biological or radiological contaminants into community water systems and source water for community water systems, including each of the following:

(1) Methods, means and equipment, including real time monitoring systems, designed to monitor and detect various levels of chemical, biological, and radiological contaminants or indicators of contaminants and reduce the likelihood that such contaminants can be successfully introduced into public water systems and source water intended to be used for drinking water.

(2) Methods and means to provide sufficient notice to operators of public water systems, and individuals served by such systems, of the introduction of chemical, biological or radiological contaminants and the possible effect of such introduction on public health and the safety and supply of drinking water.

(3) Methods and means for developing educational and awareness programs for community water systems.

(4) Procedures and equipment necessary to prevent the flow of contaminated drinking water to individuals served by public water systems.

(5) Methods, means, and equipment which could negate or mitigate deleterious effects on public

health and the safety and supply caused by the introduction of contaminants into water intended to be used for drinking water, including an examination of the effectiveness of various drinking water technologies in removing, inactivating, or neutralizing biological, chemical, and radiological contaminants.

(6) Biomedical research into the short-term and long-term impact on public health of various chemical, biological and radiological contaminants that may be introduced into public water systems through terrorist or other intentional acts.

**(b) Funding**

For the authorization of appropriations to carry out this section, see section 300i–4(e) of this title.

(July 1, 1944, c. 373, Title XIV, § 1434, as added June 12, 2002, Pub.L. 107–188, Title IV, § 402, 116 Stat. 685.)

## § 300i–4. Supply disruption prevention, detection and response

**[PHSA § 1435]**

**(a) Disruption of supply or safety**

The Administrator, in coordination with the appropriate departments and agencies of the Federal Government, shall review (or enter into contracts or cooperative agreements to provide for a review of) methods and means by which terrorists or other individuals or groups could disrupt the supply of safe drinking water or take other actions against water collection, pretreatment, treatment, storage and distribution facilities which could render such water significantly less safe for human consumption, including each of the following:

(1) Methods and means by which pipes and other constructed conveyances utilized in public water systems could be destroyed or otherwise prevented from providing adequate supplies of drinking water meeting applicable public health standards.

(2) Methods and means by which collection, pretreatment, treatment, storage and distribution facilities utilized or used in connection with public water systems and collection and pretreatment storage facilities used in connection with public water systems could be destroyed or otherwise prevented from providing adequate supplies of drinking water meeting applicable public health standards.

(3) Methods and means by which pipes, constructed conveyances, collection, pretreatment, treatment, storage and distribution systems that are utilized in connection with public water systems could be altered or affected so as to be subject to cross-contamination of drinking water supplies.

(4) Methods and means by which pipes, constructed conveyances, collection, pretreatment, treatment, storage and distribution systems that are utilized in connection with public water systems could be reasonably protected from terrorist attacks or other acts intended to disrupt the supply or affect the safety of drinking water.

(5) Methods and means by which information systems, including process controls and supervisory control and data acquisition and cyber systems at community water systems could be disrupted by terrorists or other groups.

**(b) Alternative sources**

The review under this section shall also include a review of the methods and means by which alternative supplies of drinking water could be provided in the event of the destruction, impairment or contamination of public water systems.

**(c) Requirements and considerations**

In carrying out this section and section 300i–3 of this title—

(1) the Administrator shall ensure that reviews carried out under this section reflect the needs of community water systems of various sizes and various geographic areas of the United States; and

(2) the Administrator may consider the vulnerability of, or potential for forced interruption of service for, a region or service area, including community water systems that provide service to the National Capital area.

**(d) Information sharing**

As soon as practicable after reviews carried out under this section or section 300i–3 of this title have been evaluated, the Administrator shall disseminate, as appropriate as determined by the Administrator, to community water systems information on the results of the project through the Information Sharing and Analysis Center, or other appropriate means.

**(e) Funding**

There are authorized to be appropriated to carry out this section and section 300i–3 of this title not more than $15,000,000 for the fiscal year 2002 and such sums as may be necessary for the fiscal years 2003 through 2005.

(July 1, 1944, c. 373, Title XIV, § 1435, as added June 12, 2002, Pub.L. 107–188, Title IV, § 402, 116 Stat. 686.)

PART E—GENERAL PROVISIONS

## § 300j. Assurances of availability of adequate supplies of chemicals necessary for treatment of water

**[PHSA § 1441]**

**(a) Certification of need application**

If any person who uses chlorine, activated carbon, lime, ammonia, soda ash, potassium permanganate, caustic soda, or other chemical or substance for the purpose of treating water in any public water system or in any public treatment works determines that the amount of such chemical or substance necessary to effectively treat such water is not reasonably available to him or will not be so available to him when required for the effective treatment of such water, such person may apply to the Administrator for a certification (hereinafter in this section referred to as a "certification of need") that the amount of such chemical or substance which such person requires to effectively treat such water is not reasonably available to him or will not be so available when required for the effective treatment of such water.

**(b) Application requirements; publication in Federal Register; waiver; certification, issuance or denial**

(1) An application for a certification of need shall be in such form and submitted in such manner as the Administrator may require and shall (A) specify the persons the applicant determines are able to provide the chemical or substance with respect to which the application is submitted, (B) specify the persons from whom the applicant has sought such chemical or substance, and (C) contain such other information as the Administrator may require.

(2) Upon receipt of an application under this section, the Administrator shall (A) publish in the Federal Register a notice of the receipt of the application and a brief summary of it, (B) notify in writing each person whom the President or his delegate (after consultation with the Administrator) determines could be made subject to an order required to be issued upon the issuance of the certification of need applied for in such application, and (C) provide an opportunity for the submission of written comments on such application. The requirements of the preceding sentence of this paragraph shall not apply when the Administrator for good cause finds (and incorporates the finding with a brief statement of reasons therefor in the order issued) that waiver of such requirements is necessary in order to protect the public health.

(3) Within 30 days after—

(A) the date a notice is published under paragraph (2) in the Federal Register with respect to an application submitted under this section for the issuance of a certification of need, or

(B) the date on which such application is received if as authorized by the second sentence of such paragraph no notice is published with respect to such application,

the Administrator shall take action either to issue or deny the issuance of a certification of need.

**(c) Certification of need; issuance; executive orders; implementation of orders; equitable apportionment of orders; factors considered**

(1) If the Administrator finds that the amount of a chemical or substance necessary for an applicant under an application submitted under this section to effectively treat water in a public water system or in a public treatment works is not reasonably available to the applicant or will not be so available to him when required for the effective treatment of such water, the Administrator shall issue a certification of need. Not later than seven days following the issuance of such certification, the President or his delegate shall issue an order requiring the provision to such person of such amounts of such chemical or substance as the Administrator deems necessary in the certification of need issued for such person. Such order shall apply to such manufacturers, producers, processors, distributors, and repackagers of such chemical or substance as the President or his delegate deems necessary and appropriate, except that such order may not apply to any manufacturer, producer, or processor of such chemical or substance who manufactures, produces, or processes (as the case may be) such chemical or substance solely for its own use. Persons subject to an order issued under this section shall be given a reasonable opportunity to consult with the President or his delegate with respect to the implementation of the order.

(2) Orders which are to be issued under paragraph (1) to manufacturers, producers, and processors of a chemical or substance shall be equitably apportioned, as far as practicable, among all manufacturers, producers, and processors of such chemical or substance; and orders which are to be issued under paragraph (1) to distributors and repackagers of a chemical or substance shall be equitably apportioned, as far as practicable, among all distributors and repackagers of such chemical or substance. In apportioning orders issued under paragraph (1) to manufacturers, producers, processors, distributors, and repackagers of chlorine, the President or his delegate shall, in carrying out the requirements of the preceding sentence, consider—

(A) the geographical relationships and established commercial relationships between such manufacturers, producers, processors, distributors, and repackagers and the persons for whom the orders are issued;

(B) in the case of orders to be issued to producers of chlorine, the (i) amount of chlorine historically supplied by each such producer to treat water in public water systems and public treatment works, and (ii) share of each such producer of the total annual production of chlorine in the United States; and

(C) such other factors as the President or his delegate may determine are relevant to the apportionment of orders in accordance with the requirements of the preceding sentence.

(3) Subject to subsection (f) of this section, any person for whom a certification of need has been issued under this subsection may upon the expiration of the order issued under paragraph (1) upon such certification apply under this section for additional certifications.

**(d) Breach of contracts; defense**

There shall be available as a defense to any action brought for breach of contract in a Federal or State court arising out of delay or failure to provide, sell, or offer for sale or exchange a chemical or substance subject to an order issued pursuant to subsection (c)(1) of this section, that such delay or failure was caused solely by compliance with such order.

**(e) Penalties for noncompliance with orders; temporary restraining orders and preliminary or permanent injunctions**

(1) Whoever knowingly fails to comply with any order issued pursuant to subsection (c)(1) of this section shall be fined not more than $5,000 for each such failure to comply.

(2) Whoever fails to comply with any order issued pursuant to subsection (c)(1) of this section shall be subject to a civil penalty of not more than $2,500 for each such failure to comply.

(3) Whenever the Administrator or the President or his delegate has reason to believe that any person is violating or will violate any order issued pursuant to subsection (c)(1) of this section, he may petition a United States district court to issue a temporary restraining order or preliminary or permanent injunction (including a mandatory injunction) to enforce the provision of such order.

**(f) Termination date**

No certification of need or order issued under this section may remain in effect for more than one year.

(July 1, 1944, c. 373, Title XIV, § 1441, as added Dec. 16, 1974, Pub.L. 93–523, § 2(a), 88 Stat. 1680, and amended Nov. 16, 1977, Pub.L. 95–190, § 7, 91 Stat. 1396; Sept. 6, 1979, Pub.L. 96–63, § 3, 93 Stat. 411; June 19, 1986, Pub.L. 99–339, Title III, § 301(d), 100 Stat. 664; Aug. 6, 1996, Pub.L. 104–182, Title V, § 501(c), 110 Stat. 1691.)

### HISTORICAL AND STATUTORY NOTES

**Effective and Applicability Provisions**

1996 Acts

Amendment by Pub.L. 104–182 effective Aug. 6, 1996, except as otherwise specifically provided, see section 2(b) of Pub.L. 104–182, set out as a note under section 300f of this title.

## § 300j–1. Research, technical assistance, information, training of personnel

[PHSA § 1442]

**(a) Specific powers and duties of Administrator**

(1) The Administrator may conduct research, studies, and demonstrations relating to the causes, diagnosis, treatment, control, and prevention of physical and mental diseases and other impairments of man resulting directly or indirectly from contaminants in water, or to the provision of a dependably safe supply of drinking water, including—

(A) improved methods (i) to identify and measure the existence of contaminants in drinking water (including methods which may be used by State and local health and water officials), and (ii) to identify the source of such contaminants;

(B) improved methods to identify and measure the health effects of contaminants in drinking water;

(C) new methods of treating raw water to prepare it for drinking, so as to improve the efficiency of water treatment and to remove contaminants from water;

(D) improved methods for providing a dependably safe supply of drinking water, including improvements in water purification and distribution, and methods of assessing the health related hazards of drinking water; and

(E) improved methods of protecting underground water sources of public water systems from contamination.

(2) Information and research facilities—

In carrying out this subchapter, the Administrator is authorized to—

(A) collect and make available information pertaining to research, investigations, and demonstrations with respect to providing a dependably safe supply of drinking water, together with appropriate recommendations in connection with the information; and

(B) make available research facilities of the Agency to appropriate public authorities, institutions, and individuals engaged in studies and research relating to this subchapter.

(3) The Administrator shall carry out a study of polychlorinated biphenyl contamination of actual or potential sources of drinking water, contamination of such sources by other substances known or suspected to be harmful to public health, the effects of such contamination, and means of removing, treating, or otherwise controlling such contamination. To assist in carrying out this paragraph, the Administrator is authorized to make grants to public agencies and private nonprofit institutions.

(4) The Administrator shall conduct a survey and study of—

(A) disposal of waste (including residential waste) which may endanger underground water which supplies, or can reasonably be expected to supply, any public water systems, and

(B) means of control of such waste disposal.

Not later than one year after December 16, 1974, he shall transmit to the Congress the results of such survey and study, together with such recommendations as he deems appropriate.

(5) The Administrator shall carry out a study of methods of underground injection which do not result in the degradation of underground drinking water sources.

(6) The Administrator shall carry out a study of methods of preventing, detecting, and dealing with surface spills of contaminants which may degrade underground water sources for public water systems.

(7) The Administrator shall carry out a study of virus contamination of drinking water sources and means of control of such contamination.

(8) The Administrator shall carry out a study of the nature and extent of the impact on underground water which supplies or can reasonably be expected to supply public water systems of (A) abandoned injection or extraction wells; (B) intensive application of pesticides and fertilizers in underground water recharge areas; and (C) ponds, pools, lagoons, pits, or other surface disposal of contaminants in underground water recharge areas.

(9) The Administrator shall conduct a comprehensive study of public water supplies and drinking water sources to determine the nature, extent, sources of and means of control of contamination by chemicals or other substances suspected of being carcinogenic. Not later than six months after December 16, 1974, he shall transmit to the Congress the initial results of such study, together with such recommendations for further review and corrective action as he deems appropriate.

(10) The Administrator shall carry out a study of the reaction of chlorine and humic acids and the effects of the contaminants which result from such reaction on public health and on the safety of drinking water, including any carcinogenic effect.

**(b) Emergency situations**

The Administrator is authorized to provide technical assistance and to make grants to States, or publicly owned water systems to assist in responding to and alleviating any emergency situation affecting public water systems (including sources of water for such systems) which the Administrator determines to present substantial danger to the public health. Grants provided under this subsection shall be used only to support those actions which (i) are necessary for preventing, limiting or mitigating danger to the public health in such emergency situation and (ii) would not, in the judgment of the Administrator, be taken without such emergency assistance. The Administrator may carry out the program authorized under this subparagraph as part of, and in accordance with the terms and conditions of, any other program of assistance for environmental emergencies which the Administrator is authorized to carry out under any other provision of law. No limitation on appropriations for any such other program shall apply to amounts appropriated under this subsection.

**(c) Establishment of training programs and grants for training; training fees**

The Administrator shall—

(1) provide training for, and make grants for training (including postgraduate training) of (A) personnel of State agencies which have primary enforcement responsibility and of agencies or units of local government to which enforcement responsibilities have been delegated by the State, and (B) personnel who manage or operate public water systems, and

(2) make grants for postgraduate training of individuals (including grants to educational institutions for traineeships) for purposes of qualifying such individuals to work as personnel referred to in paragraph (1).

(3) make grants to, and enter into contracts with, any public agency, educational institution, and any other organization, in accordance with procedures prescribed by the Administrator, under which he may pay all or part of the costs (as may be determined by the Administrator) of any project or activity which is designed—

(A) to develop, expand, or carry out a program (which may combine training education and employment) for training persons for occupations involving the public health aspects of providing safe drinking water;

(B) to train inspectors and supervisory personnel to train or supervise persons in occupations involving the public health aspects of providing safe drinking water; or

(C) to develop and expand the capability of programs of States and municipalities to carry out the purposes of this subchapter (other than by carrying out State programs of public water system supervision or underground water source protection (as defined in section 300j–2(c) of this title) ).

Reasonable fees may be charged for training provided under paragraph (1)(B) to persons other than personnel of State or local agencies but such training shall be provided to personnel of State or local agencies without charge.

**(d)** There are authorized to be appropriated to carry out subsection (b) of this section not more than $35,000,000 for the fiscal year 2002 and such sums as may be necessary for each fiscal year thereafter.

**(e) Technical assistance**

The Administrator may provide technical assistance to small public water systems to enable such systems to achieve and maintain compliance with applicable national primary drinking water regulations. Such assistance may include circuit-rider and multi-State regional technical assistance programs, training, and preliminary engineering evaluations. The Administrator shall ensure that technical assistance pursuant to this subsection is available in each State. Each nonprofit organization receiving assistance under this subsection shall consult with the State in which the assistance is to be expended or otherwise made available before using assistance to undertake activities to carry out this subsection. There are authorized to be appropriated to the Administrator to be used for such technical assistance $15,000,000 for each of the fiscal years 1997 through 2003. No portion of any State loan fund established under section 300j–12 of this title (relating to State loan funds) and no portion of any funds made available under this subsection may be used for lobbying expenses. Of the total amount appropriated under this subsection, 3 percent shall be used for technical assistance to public water systems owned or operated by Indian Tribes.

(July 1, 1944, c. 373, Title XIV, § 1442, as added Dec. 16, 1974, Pub.L. 93–523, § 2(a), 88 Stat. 1682, and amended Nov. 16, 1977, Pub.L. 95–190, §§ 2(a), 3(a), (b), (e)(1), 4, 9, 10(b), 13, 91 Stat. 1393–1395, 1397–1399; Sept. 6, 1979, Pub.L. 96–63, § 1, 93 Stat. 411; Dec. 5, 1980, Pub.L. 96–502, § 5, 94 Stat. 2738; June 19, 1986, Pub.L. 99–339, Title I, § 107, Title III, §§ 301(a), (g), 304(a), 100 Stat. 651, 663, 665, 667; Dec. 21, 1995, Pub.L. 104–66, Title II, § 2021(h), 109 Stat. 727; Aug. 6, 1996, Pub.L. 104–182, Title I, §§ 121, 122, 110 Stat. 1651; June 12, 2002, Pub.L. 107–188, Title IV, § 403(4), 116 Stat. 687.)

### HISTORICAL AND STATUTORY NOTES

**Codifications**

Section 121(1) of Pub.L. 104–182, which directed that this section be amended by redesignating subsec. (b)(3) as subsec. (d)(3), was executed, as the probable intent of Congress, by redesignating such subsec. (b)(3) as subsec. (c)(3). Former subsec. (d) was redesignated as subsec. (c) by section 2021(h) of Pub.L. 104–66. See 1996 Amendments notes set out under this section.

**Effective and Applicability Provisions**

1996 Acts

Amendment by Pub.L. 104–182 effective Aug. 6, 1996, except as otherwise specifically provided, see section 2(b) of Pub.L. 104–182, set out as a note under section 300f of this title.

**Comparative Health Effects Assessment**

Section 304(b) of Pub.L. 99–339, provided that: "The Administrator of the Environmental Protection Agency shall conduct a comparative health effects assessment, using available data, to compare the public health effects (both positive and negative) associated with water treatment chemicals and their byproducts to the public health effects associated with contaminants found in public water supplies. Not later than 18 months after the date of the enactment of this Act [June 19, 1986], the Administrator shall submit a report to the Congress setting forth the results of such assessment."

**National Center for Ground Water Research**

Section 203 of Pub.L. 104–182 provided that: "The Administrator of the Environmental Protection Agency, acting through the Robert S. Kerr Environmental Research Laboratory, is authorized to reestablish a partnership between the Laboratory and the National Center for Ground Water Research, a university consortium, to conduct research, training, and technology transfer for ground water quality protection and restoration. No funds are authorized by this section."

**Scientific Research Review**

Section 202 of Pub.L. 104–182 provided that:

"**(a) In general.**—The Administrator shall—

"(1) develop a strategic plan for drinking water research activities throughout the Environmental Protection Agency (in this section referred to as the 'Agency');

"(2) integrate that strategic plan into ongoing Agency planning activities; and

"(3) review all Agency drinking water research to ensure the research—

"(A) is of high quality; and

"(B) does not duplicate any other research being conducted by the Agency.

"**(b) Plan.**—The Administrator shall transmit the plan to the Committees on Commerce and Science of the House of Representatives and the Committee on Environment and Public Works of the Senate and the plan shall be made available to the public."

## § 300j–2. Grants for State programs

**[PHSA § 1443]**

**(a) Public water systems supervision programs; applications for grants; allotment of sums; waiver of grant restrictions; notice of approval or disapproval of application; authorization of appropriations**

**(1)** From allotments made pursuant to paragraph (4), the Administrator may make grants to States to carry out public water system supervision programs.

**(2)** No grant may be made under paragraph (1) unless an application therefor has been submitted to the Administrator in such form and manner as he may require. The Administrator may not approve an application of a State for its first grant under paragraph (1) unless he determines that the State—

(A) has established or will establish within one year from the date of such grant a public water system supervision program, and

(B) will, within that one year, assume primary enforcement responsibility for public water systems within the State.

No grant may be made to a State under paragraph (1) for any period beginning more than one year after the date of the State's first grant unless the State has assumed and maintains primary enforcement responsibility for public water systems within the State. The prohibitions contained in the preceding two sentences shall not apply to such grants when made to Indian Tribes.

(3) A grant under paragraph (1) shall be made to cover not more than 75 per centum of the grant recipient's costs (as determined under regulations of the Administrator) in carrying out, during the one-year period beginning on the date the grant is made, a public water system supervision program.

(4) In each fiscal year the Administrator shall, in accordance, with regulations, allot the sums appropriated for such year under paragraph (5) among the States on the basis of population, geographical area, number of public water systems, and other relevant factors. No State shall receive less than 1 per centum of the annual appropriation for grants under paragraph (1): *Provided*, That the Administrator may, by regulation, reduce such percentage in accordance with the criteria specified in this paragraph: *And provided further*, That such percentage shall not apply to grants allotted to Guam, American Samoa, or the Virgin Islands.

(5) The prohibition contained in the last sentence of paragraph (2) may be waived by the Administrator with respect to a grant to a State through fiscal year 1979 but such prohibition may only be waived if, in the judgment of the Administrator—

(A) the State is making a diligent effort to assume and maintain primary enforcement responsibility for public water systems within the State;

(B) the State has made significant progress toward assuming and maintaining such primary enforcement responsibility; and

(C) there is reason to believe the State will assume such primary enforcement responsibility by October 1, 1979.

The amount of any grant awarded for the fiscal years 1978 and 1979 pursuant to a waiver under this paragraph may not exceed 75 per centum of the allotment which the State would have received for such fiscal year if it had assumed and maintained such primary enforcement responsibility. The remaining 25 per centum of the amount allotted to such State for such fiscal year shall be retained by the Administrator, and the Administrator may award such amount to such State at such time as the State assumes such responsibility before the beginning of fiscal year 1980. At the beginning of each fiscal years [1] 1979 and 1980 the amounts retained by the Administrator for any preceding fiscal year and not awarded by the beginning of fiscal year 1979 or 1980 to the States to which such amounts were originally allotted may be removed from the original allotment and reallotted for fiscal year 1979 or 1980 (as the case may be) to States which have assumed primary enforcement responsibility by the beginning of such fiscal year.

(6) The Administrator shall notify the State of the approval or disapproval of any application for a grant under this section—

(A) within ninety days after receipt of such application, or

(B) not later than the first day of the fiscal year for which the grant application is made,

whichever is later.

**(7) Authorization**

For the purpose of making grants under paragraph (1), there are authorized to be appropriated $100,000,000 for each of fiscal years 1997 through 2003.

**(8) Reservation of funds by the Administrator**

If the Administrator assumes the primary enforcement responsibility of a State public water system supervision program, the Administrator may reserve from funds made available pursuant to this subsection an amount equal to the amount that would otherwise have been provided to the State pursuant to this subsection. The Administrator shall use the funds reserved pursuant to this paragraph to ensure the full and effective administration of a public water system supervision program in the State.

**(9) State loan funds**

**(A) Reservation of funds**

For any fiscal year for which the amount made available to the Administrator by appropriations to carry out this subsection is less than the amount that the Administrator determines is necessary to supplement funds made available pursuant to paragraph (8) to ensure the full and effective administration of a public water system supervision program in a State, the Administrator may reserve from the funds made available to the State under section 300j–12 of this title (relating to State loan funds) an amount that is equal to the amount of the shortfall. This paragraph shall not apply to any State not exercising primary enforcement responsibility for public water systems as of August 6, 1996.

**(B) Duty of Administrator**

If the Administrator reserves funds from the allocation of a State under subparagraph (A), the Administrator shall carry out in the State each of the activities that would be required of the State if the State had primary enforcement authority under section 300g–2 of this title.

**(b) Underground water source protection programs; applications for grants; allotment of sums; authorization of appropriations**

(1) From allotments made pursuant to paragraph (4), the Administrator may make grants to States to carry out underground water source protection programs.

(2) No grant may be made under paragraph (1) unless an application therefor has been submitted to the Administrator in such form and manner as he may require. No grant may be made to any State under paragraph (1) unless the State has assumed primary enforcement responsibility within two years after the date the Administrator promulgates regulations for State underground injection control programs under section 300h of this title. The prohibition contained in the preceding sentence shall not apply to such grants when made to Indian Tribes.

(3) A grant under paragraph (1) shall be made to cover not more than 75 per centum of the grant recipient's costs (as determined under regulations of the Administrator) in carrying out, during the one-year period beginning on the date the grant is made, an underground water source protection program.

(4) In each fiscal year the Administrator shall, in accordance with regulations, allot the sums appropriated for such year under paragraph (5) among the States on the basis of population, geographical area, and other relevant factors.

(5) For purposes of making grants under paragraph (1) there are authorized to be appropriated $5,000,000 for the fiscal year ending June 30, 1976, $7,500,000 for the fiscal year ending June 30, 1977, $10,000,000 for each of the fiscal years 1978 and 1979, $7,795,000 for the fiscal year ending September 30, 1980, $18,000,000 for the fiscal year ending September 30, 1981, and $21,000,000 for the fiscal year ending September 30, 1982. For the purpose of making grants under paragraph (1) there are authorized to be appropriated not more than the following amounts:

| Fiscal year: | *Amount* |
|---|---|
| 1987 | $19,700,000 |
| 1988 | 19,700,000 |
| 1989 | 20,850,000 |
| 1990 | 20,850,000 |
| 1991 | 20,850,000 |
| 1992–2003 | 15,000,000 |

**(c) Definitions**

For purposes of this section:

(1) The term "public water system supervision program" means a program for the adoption and enforcement of drinking water regulations (with such variances and exemptions from such regulations under conditions and in a manner which is not less stringent than the conditions under, and the manner in, which variances and exemptions may be granted under sections 300g–4 and 300g–5 of this title) which are no less stringent than the national primary drinking water regulations under section 300g–1 of this title, and for keeping records and making reports required by section 300g–2(a)(3) of this title.

(2) The term "underground water source protection program" means a program for the adoption and enforcement of a program which meets the requirements of regulations under section 300h of this title, and for keeping records and making reports required by section 300h–1(b)(1)(A)(ii) of this title. Such term includes, where applicable, a program which meets the requirements of section 300h–4 of this title.

**(d) New York City watershed protection program**

**(1) In general**

The Administrator is authorized to provide financial assistance to the State of New York for demonstration projects implemented as part of the watershed program for the protection and enhancement of the quality of source waters of the New York City water supply system, including projects that demonstrate, assess, or provide for comprehensive monitoring and surveillance and projects necessary to comply with the criteria for avoiding filtration contained in 40 CFR 141.71. Demonstration projects which shall be eligible for financial assistance shall be certified to the Administrator by the State of New York as satisfying the purposes of this subsection. In certifying projects to the Administrator, the State of New York shall give priority to monitoring projects that have undergone peer review.

**(2) Report**

Not later than 5 years after the date on which the Administrator first provides assistance pursuant to this paragraph, the Governor of the State of New York shall submit a report to the Administrator on the results of projects assisted.

**(3) Matching requirements**

Federal assistance provided under this subsection shall not exceed 50 percent of the total cost of the protection program being carried out for any particular watershed or ground water recharge area.

(4) **Authorization**

There are authorized to be appropriated to the Administrator to carry out this subsection for each of fiscal years 1997 through 2003, $15,000,000 for the purpose of providing assistance to the State of New York to carry out paragraph (1).

(July 1, 1944, c. 373, Title XIV, § 1443, as added Dec. 16, 1974, Pub.L. 93-523, § 2(a), 88 Stat. 1684, and amended Nov. 16, 1977, Pub.L. 95-190, §§ 2(b), (c), 5(a), 91 Stat. 1393, 1395; Sept. 6, 1979, Pub.L. 96-63, § 2, 93 Stat. 411; Dec. 5, 1980, Pub.L. 96-502, §§ 2(c), 4(d), 94 Stat. 2738; June 19, 1986, Pub.L. 99-339, Title III, §§ 301(b), (c), 302(d), 100 Stat. 664, 666; Aug. 6, 1996, Pub.L. 104-182, Title I, §§ 120(c), 124, 128, 110 Stat. 1651, 1653, 1659.)

1 So in original. Probably should be "year".

**HISTORICAL AND STATUTORY NOTES**

**Effective and Applicability Provisions**

1996 Acts

Amendment by Pub.L. 104-182 effective Aug. 6, 1996, except as otherwise specifically provided, see section 2(b) of Pub.L. 104-182, set out as a note under section 300f of this title.

## § 300j-3. Special project grants and guaranteed loans

**[PHSA § 1444]**

(a) **Special study and demonstration project grants**

The Administrator may make grants to any person for the purposes of—

(1) assisting in the development and demonstration (including construction) of any project which will demonstrate a new or improved method, approach, or technology, for providing a dependably safe supply of drinking water to the public; and

(2) assisting in the development and demonstration (including construction) of any project which will investigate and demonstrate health implications involved in the reclamation, recycling, and reuse of waste waters for drinking and the processes and methods for the preparation of safe and acceptable drinking water.

(b) **Limitations**

Grants made by the Administrator under this section shall be subject to the following limitations:

(1) Grants under this section shall not exceed 66⅔ per centum of the total cost of construction of any facility and 75 per centum of any other costs, as determined by the Administrator.

(2) Grants under this section shall not be made for any project involving the construction or modification of any facilities for any public water system in a State unless such project has been approved by the State agency charged with the responsibility for safety of drinking water (or if there is no such agency in a State, by the State health authority).

(3) Grants under this section shall not be made for any project unless the Administrator determines, after consulting the National Drinking Water Advisory Council, that such project will serve a useful purpose relating to the development and demonstration of new or improved techniques, methods, or technologies for the provision of safe water to the public for drinking.

(4) Priority for grants under this section shall be given where there are known or potential public health hazards which require advanced technology for the removal of particles which are too small to be removed by ordinary treatment technology.

(c) **Authorization of appropriations**

For the purposes of making grants under subsections (a) and (b) of this section there are authorized to be appropriated $7,500,000 for the fiscal year ending June 30, 1975; and $7,500,000 for the fiscal year ending June 30, 1976; and $10,000,000 for the fiscal year ending June 30, 1977.

(d) **Loan guarantees to public water systems; conditions; indebtedness limitation; regulations**

The Administrator during the fiscal years ending June 30, 1975, and June 30, 1976, shall carry out a program of guaranteeing loans made by private lenders to small public water systems for the purpose of enabling such systems to meet national primary drinking water regulations prescribed under section 300g-1 of this title. No such guarantee may be made with respect to a system unless (1) such system cannot reasonably obtain financial assistance necessary to comply with such regulations from any other source, and (2) the Administrator determines that any facilities constructed with a loan guaranteed under this subsection is not likely to be made obsolete by subsequent changes in primary regulations. The aggregate amount of indebtedness guaranteed with respect to any system may not exceed $50,000. The aggregate amount of indebtedness guaranteed under this subsection may not exceed $50,000,000. The Administrator shall prescribe regulations to carry out this subsection.

(July 1, 1944, c. 373, Title XIV, § 1444, as added Dec. 16, 1974, Pub.L. 93-523, § 2(a), 88 Stat. 1685, and amended June 19, 1986, Pub.L. 99-339, Title I, § 101(c)(3), 100 Stat. 646.)

## § 300j-3a. Grants to public sector agencies

(a) **Assistance for development and demonstration projects**

The Administrator of the Environmental Protection Agency shall offer grants to public sector agencies for the purposes of—

(1) assisting in the development and demonstration (including construction) of any project which will demonstrate a new or improved method, ap-

proach, or technology for providing a dependably safe supply of drinking water to the public; and

(2) assisting in the development and demonstration (including construction) of any project which will investigate and demonstrate health and conservation implications involved in the reclamation, recycling, and reuse of wastewaters for drinking and agricultural use or the processes and methods for the preparation of safe and acceptable drinking water.

**(b) Limitations**

Grants made by the Administrator under this section shall be subject to the following limitations:

(1) Grants under this section shall not exceed 66⅔ per centum of the total cost of construction of any facility and 75 per centum of any other costs, as determined by the Administrator.

(2) Grants under this section shall not be made for any project involving the construction or modification of any facilities for any public water system in a State unless such project has been approved by the State agency charged with the responsibility for safety of drinking water (or if there is no such agency in a State, by the State health authority).

(3) Grants under this section shall not be made for any project unless the Administrator determines, after consultation, that such project will serve a useful purpose relating to the development and demonstration of new or improved techniques, methods, or technologies for the provision of safe water to the public for drinking.

**(c) Authorization of appropriations**

There are authorized to be appropriated for the purposes of this section $25,000,000 for fiscal year 1978.

(Pub.L. 95–155, § 5, Nov. 8, 1977, 91 Stat. 1258; Pub.L. 95–477, § 7(a)(1), Oct. 18, 1978, 92 Stat. 1511.)

### HISTORICAL AND STATUTORY NOTES

**Codifications**

Section was enacted as part of the Environmental Research, Development, and Demonstration Authorization Act of 1978, and not as part of the Public Health Service Act, which comprises this chapter.

**Effective and Applicability Provisions**

1978 Acts

Section 7(a)(2) of Pub.L. 95–477 provided that: "This subsection [amending this section] shall become effective October 1, 1978."

## § 300j–3b. Contaminant standards or treatment technique guidelines

(1) Not later than nine months after October 18, 1978, the Administrator shall promulgate guidelines establishing supplemental standards or treatment technique requirements for microbiological, viral, radiological, organic, and inorganic contaminants, which guidelines shall be conditions, as provided in paragraph (2), of any grant for a demonstration project for water reclamation, recycling, and reuse funded under section 300j–3a of this title or under section 300j–3(a)(2) of this title, where such project involves direct human consumption of treated wastewater. Such guidelines shall provide for sufficient control of each such contaminant, such that in the Administrator's judgment, no adverse effects on the health of persons may reasonably be anticipated to occur, allowing an adequate margin of safety.

(2) A grant referred to in paragraph (1) for a project which involves direct human consumption of treated wastewater may be awarded on or after the date of promulgation of guidelines under this section only if the applicant demonstrates to the satisfaction of the Administrator that the project—

(A) will comply with all national primary drinking water regulations under section 300g–1 of this title;

(B) will comply with all guidelines under this section; and

(C) will in other respects provide safe drinking water.

Any such grant awarded before the date of promulgation of such guidelines shall be conditioned on the applicant's agreement to comply to the maximum feasible extent with such guidelines as expeditiously as practicable following the date of promulgation thereof.

(3) Guidelines under this section may, in the discretion of the Administrator—

(A) be nationally and uniformly applicable to all projects funded under section 300j–3a of this title or section 300j–1(a)(2) of this title;

(B) vary for different classes or categories of such projects (as determined by the Administrator);

(C) be established and applicable on a project-by-project basis; or

(D) any combination of the above.

(4) Nothing in this section shall be construed to prohibit or delay the award of any grant referred to in paragraph (1) prior to the date of promulgation of such guidelines.

(Pub.L. 95–477, § 7(b), Oct. 18, 1978, 92 Stat. 1511.)

### HISTORICAL AND STATUTORY NOTES

**References in Text**

Section 300j–1(a)(2) of this title, referred to in par. (3)(A), was amended by Pub.L. 104–182, title I, § 121(3), (4)(A), Aug. 6, 1996, 110 Stat. 1651, to redesignate par. (2)(B) as subsec. (b) of section 300j–1, strike par. (2)(A), and add a new par. (2) relating to information and research facilities.

**Codifications**

Section was enacted as part of the Environmental Research, Development, and Demonstration Authorization Act of 1979, and not as part of the Public Health Service Act which comprises this chapter.

## § 300j–3c. National assistance program for water infrastructure and watersheds

**(a) Technical and financial assistance**

The Administrator of the Environmental Protection Agency may provide technical and financial assistance in the form of grants to States (1) for the construction, rehabilitation, and improvement of water supply systems, and (2) consistent with nonpoint source management programs established under section 1329 of Title 33, for source water quality protection programs to address pollutants in navigable waters for the purpose of making such waters usable by water supply systems.

**(b) Limitation**

Not more than 30 percent of the amounts appropriated to carry out this section in a fiscal year may be used for source water quality protection programs described in subsection (a)(2) of this section.

**(c) Condition**

As a condition to receiving assistance under this section, a State shall ensure that such assistance is carried out in the most cost-effective manner, as determined by the State.

**(d) Authorization of appropriations**

**(1) Unconditional authorization**

There are authorized to be appropriated to carry out this section $25,000,000 for each of fiscal years 1997 through 2003. Such sums shall remain available until expended.

**(2) Conditional authorization**

In addition to amounts authorized under paragraph (1), there are authorized to be appropriated to carry out this section $25,000,000 for each of fiscal years 1997 through 2003, provided that such authorization shall be in effect for a fiscal year only if at least 75 percent of the total amount of funds authorized to be appropriated for such fiscal year by section 300j–12(m) of this title are appropriated.

**(e) Acquisition of lands**

Assistance provided with funds made available under this section may be used for the acquisition of lands and other interests in lands; however, nothing in this section authorizes the acquisition of lands or other interests in lands from other than willing sellers.

**(f) Federal share**

The Federal share of the cost of activities for which grants are made under this section shall be 50 percent.

**(g) Definitions**

In this section, the following definitions apply:

**(1) State**

The term "State" means a State, the District of Columbia, the Commonwealth of Puerto Rico, the Virgin Islands, Guam, American Samoa, and the Commonwealth of the Northern Mariana Islands.

**(2) Water supply system**

The term "water supply system" means a system for the provision to the public of piped water for human consumption if such system has at least 15 service connections or regularly serves at least 25 individuals and a draw and fill system for the provision to the public of water for human consumption. Such term does not include a system owned by a Federal agency. Such term includes (A) any collection, treatment, storage, and distribution facilities under control of the operator of such system and used primarily in connection with such system, and (B) any collection or pretreatment facilities not under such control that are used primarily in connection with such system.

(Pub.L. 104–182, Title IV, § 401, Aug. 6, 1996, 110 Stat. 1690.)

### HISTORICAL AND STATUTORY NOTES

**Codifications**

Section was enacted as part of the Safe Drinking Water Act Amendments of 1996, and not as part of the Safe Drinking Water Act, which comprises this subchapter, nor as part of the Public Health Service Act, which comprises this chapter.

**Effective and Applicability Provisions**

1996 Acts

Section effective Aug. 6, 1996, except as otherwise specifically provided, see section 2(b) of Pub.L. 104–182, set out as a note under section 300f of this title.

## § 300j–4. Records and inspections

**[PHSA § 1445]**

**(a) Provision of information to Administrator; monitoring program for unregulated contaminants**

(1)(A) Every person who is subject to any requirement of this subchapter or who is a grantee, shall establish and maintain such records, make such reports, conduct such monitoring, and provide such information as the Administrator may reasonably require by regulation to assist the Administrator in establishing regulations under this subchapter, in determining whether such person has acted or is acting in compliance with this subchapter, in administering any program of financial assistance under this subchapter, in evaluating the health risks of unregulated contaminants, or in advising the public of such risks. In requiring a public water system to monitor under this subsection, the Administrator may take into consideration the system size and the contaminants likely to be found in the system's drinking water.

**(B)** Every person who is subject to a national primary drinking water regulation under section 300g–1 of this title shall provide such information as the Administrator may reasonably require, after consultation with the State in which such person is located if such State has primary enforcement responsibility for public water systems, on a case-by-case basis, to determine whether such person has acted or is acting in compliance with this subchapter.

**(C)** Every person who is subject to a national primary drinking water regulation under section 300g–1 of this title shall provide such information as the Administrator may reasonably require to assist the Administrator in establishing regulations under section 300g–1 of this title, after consultation with States and suppliers of water. The Administrator may not require under this subparagraph the installation of treatment equipment or process changes, the testing of treatment technology, or the analysis or processing of monitoring samples, except where the Administrator provides the funding for such activities. Before exercising this authority, the Administrator shall first seek to obtain the information by voluntary submission.

**(D)** The Administrator shall not later than 2 years after August 6, 1996, after consultation with public health experts, representatives of the general public, and officials of State and local governments, review the monitoring requirements for not fewer than 12 contaminants identified by the Administrator, and promulgate any necessary modifications.

**(2) Monitoring program for unregulated contaminants**

**(A) Establishment**

The Administrator shall promulgate regulations establishing the criteria for a monitoring program for unregulated contaminants. The regulations shall require monitoring of drinking water supplied by public water systems and shall vary the frequency and schedule for monitoring requirements for systems based on the number of persons served by the system, the source of supply, and the contaminants likely to be found, ensuring that only a representative sample of systems serving 10,000 persons or fewer are required to monitor.

**(B) Monitoring program for certain unregulated contaminants**

**(i) Initial list**

Not later than 3 years after August 6, 1996, and every 5 years thereafter, the Administrator shall issue a list pursuant to subparagraph (A) of not more than 30 unregulated contaminants to be monitored by public water systems and to be included in the national drinking water occurrence data base maintained pursuant to subsection (g) of this section.

**(ii) Governors' petition**

The Administrator shall include among the list of contaminants for which monitoring is required under this paragraph each contaminant recommended in a petition signed by the Governor of each of 7 or more States, unless the Administrator determines that the action would prevent the listing of other contaminants of a higher public health concern.

**(C) Monitoring plan for small and medium systems**

**(i) In general**

Based on the regulations promulgated by the Administrator, each State may develop a representative monitoring plan to assess the occurrence of unregulated contaminants in public water systems that serve a population of 10,000 or fewer in that State. The plan shall require monitoring for systems representative of different sizes, types, and geographic locations in the State.

**(ii) Grants for small system costs**

From funds reserved under section 300j–12(*o*) of this title or appropriated under subparagraph (H), the Administrator shall pay the reasonable cost of such testing and laboratory analysis as are necessary to carry out monitoring under the plan.

**(D) Monitoring results**

Each public water system that conducts monitoring of unregulated contaminants pursuant to this paragraph shall provide the results of the monitoring to the primary enforcement authority for the system.

**(E) Notification**

Notification of the availability of the results of monitoring programs required under paragraph (2)(A) shall be given to the persons served by the system.

**(F) Waiver of monitoring requirement**

The Administrator shall waive the requirement for monitoring for a contaminant under this paragraph in a State, if the State demonstrates that the criteria for listing the contaminant do not apply in that State.

**(G) Analytical methods**

The State may use screening methods approved by the Administrator under subsection (i) of this section in lieu of monitoring for particular contaminants under this paragraph.

**(H) Authorization of appropriations**

There are authorized to be appropriated to carry out this paragraph $10,000,000 for each of the fiscal years 1997 through 2003.

**(b) Entry of establishments, facilities, or other property; inspections; conduct of certain tests; audit and examination of records; entry restrictions; prohibition against informing of a proposed entry**

(1) Except as provided in paragraph (2), the Administrator, or representatives of the Administrator duly designated by him, upon presenting appropriate credentials and a written notice to any supplier of water or other person subject to (A) a national primary drinking water regulation prescribed under section 300g–1 of this title, (B) an applicable underground injection control program, or (C) any requirement to monitor an unregulated contaminant pursuant to subsection (a) of this section, or person in charge of any of the property of such supplier or other person referred to in clause (A), (B), or (C), is authorized to enter any establishment, facility, or other property of such supplier or other person in order to determine whether such supplier or other person has acted or is acting in compliance with this subchapter, including for this purpose, inspection, at reasonable times, of records, files, papers, processes, controls, and facilities, or in order to test any feature of a public water system, including its raw water source. The Administrator or the Comptroller General (or any representative designated by either) shall have access for the purpose of audit and examination to any records, reports, or information of a grantee which are required to be maintained under subsection (a) of this section or which are pertinent to any financial assistance under this subchapter.

(2) No entry may be made under the first sentence of paragraph (1) in an establishment, facility, or other property of a supplier of water or other person subject to a national primary drinking water regulation if the establishment, facility, or other property is located in a State which has primary enforcement responsibility for public water systems unless, before written notice of such entry is made, the Administrator (or his representative) notifies the State agency charged with responsibility for safe drinking water of the reasons for such entry. The Administrator shall, upon a showing by the State agency that such an entry will be detrimental to the administration of the State's program of primary enforcement responsibility, take such showing into consideration in determining whether to make such entry. No State agency which receives notice under this paragraph of an entry proposed to be made under paragraph (1) may use the information contained in the notice to inform the person whose property is proposed to be entered of the proposed entry; and if a State agency so uses such information, notice to the agency under this paragraph is not required until such time as the Administrator determines the agency has provided him satisfactory assurances that it will no longer so use information contained in a notice under this paragraph.

**(c) Penalty**

Whoever fails or refuses to comply with any requirement of subsection (a) of this section or to allow the Administrator, the Comptroller General, or representatives of either, to enter and conduct any audit or inspection authorized by subsection (b) of this section shall be subject to a civil penalty of not to exceed $25,000.

**(d) Confidential information; trade secrets and secret processes; information disclosure; "information required under this section" defined**

(1) Subject to paragraph (2), upon a showing satisfactory to the Administrator by any person that any information required under this section from such person, if made public, would divulge trade secrets or secret processes of such person, the Administrator shall consider such information confidential in accordance with the purposes of section 1905 of Title 18. If the applicant fails to make a showing satisfactory to the Administrator, the Administrator shall give such applicant thirty days' notice before releasing the information to which the application relates (unless the public health or safety requires an earlier release of such information).

(2) Any information required under this section (A) may be disclosed to other officers, employees, or authorized representatives of the United States concerned with carrying out this subchapter or to committees of the Congress, or when relevant in any proceeding under this subchapter, and (B) shall be disclosed to the extent it deals with the level of contaminants in drinking water. For purposes of this subsection the term "information required under this section" means any papers, books, documents, or information, or any particular part thereof, reported to

or otherwise obtained by the Administrator under this section.

**(e) "Grantee" and "person" defined**

For purposes of this section, (1) the term "grantee" means any person who applies for or receives financial assistance, by grant, contract, or loan guarantee under this subchapter, and (2) the term "person" includes a Federal agency.

**(f) Information regarding drinking water coolers**

The Administrator may utilize the authorities of this section for purposes of part F of this subchapter. Any person who manufactures, imports, sells, or distributes drinking water coolers in interstate commerce shall be treated as a supplier of water for purposes of applying the provisions of this section in the case of persons subject to part F of this subchapter.

**(g) Occurrence data base**

**(1) In general**

Not later than 3 years after August 6, 1996, the Administrator shall assemble and maintain a national drinking water contaminant occurrence data base, using information on the occurrence of both regulated and unregulated contaminants in public water systems obtained under subsection (a)(1)(A) of this section or subsection (a)(2) of this section and reliable information from other public and private sources.

**(2) Public input**

In establishing the occurrence data base, the Administrator shall solicit recommendations from the Science Advisory Board, the States, and other interested parties concerning the development and maintenance of a national drinking water contaminant occurrence data base, including such issues as the structure and design of the data base, data input parameters and requirements, and the use and interpretation of data.

**(3) Use**

The data shall be used by the Administrator in making determinations under section 300g–1(b)(1) of this title with respect to the occurrence of a contaminant in drinking water at a level of public health concern.

**(4) Public recommendations**

The Administrator shall periodically solicit recommendations from the appropriate officials of the National Academy of Sciences and the States, and any person may submit recommendations to the Administrator, with respect to contaminants that should be included in the national drinking water contaminant occurrence data base, including recommendations with respect to additional unregulated contaminants that should be listed under subsection (a)(2) of this section. Any recommendation submitted under this clause shall be accompanied by reasonable documentation that—

**(A)** the contaminant occurs or is likely to occur in drinking water; and

**(B)** the contaminant poses a risk to public health.

**(5) Public availability**

The information from the data base shall be available to the public in readily accessible form.

**(6) Regulated contaminants**

With respect to each contaminant for which a national primary drinking water regulation has been established, the data base shall include information on the detection of the contaminant at a quantifiable level in public water systems (including detection of the contaminant at levels not constituting a violation of the maximum contaminant level for the contaminant).

**(7) Unregulated contaminants**

With respect to contaminants for which a national primary drinking water regulation has not been established, the data base shall include—

**(A)** monitoring information collected by public water systems that serve a population of more than 10,000, as required by the Administrator under subsection (a) of this section;

**(B)** monitoring information collected from a representative sampling of public water systems that serve a population of 10,000 or fewer; and

**(C)** other reliable and appropriate monitoring information on the occurrence of the contaminants in public water systems that is available to the Administrator.

**(h) Availability of information on small system technologies**

For purposes of sections 300g–1(b)(4)(E) and 300g–4(e) of this title (relating to small system variance program), the Administrator may request information on the characteristics of commercially available treatment systems and technologies, including the effectiveness and performance of the systems and technologies under various operating conditions. The Administrator may specify the form, content, and submission date of information to be submitted by manufacturers, States, and other interested persons for the purpose of considering the systems and technologies in the development of regulations or guidance under sections 300g–1(b)(4)(E) and 300g–4(e) of this title.

**(i) Screening methods**

The Administrator shall review new analytical methods to screen for regulated contaminants and may approve such methods as are more accurate or cost-effective than established reference methods for use in compliance monitoring.

(July 1, 1944, c. 373, Title XIV, § 1445, as added Dec. 16, 1974, Pub.L. 93–523, § 2(a), 88 Stat. 1686, and amended Nov. 16, 1977, Pub.L. 95–190, § 12(c), (d), 91 Stat. 1398; June 19, 1986, Pub.L. 99–339, Title I, § 106, Title III, § 301(h), 100 Stat. 650, 665; Oct. 31, 1988, Pub.L. 100–572, § 5, 102 Stat. 2889; Aug. 6, 1996, Pub.L. 104–182, Title I, §§ 111(b), 125(a), (c), (d), 126, 110 Stat. 1633, 1653, 1656, 1658.)

HISTORICAL AND STATUTORY NOTES

**Effective and Applicability Provisions**

1996 Acts

Amendment by Pub.L. 104–182 effective Aug. 6, 1996, except as otherwise specifically provided, see section 2(b) of Pub.L. 104–182, set out as a note under section 300f of this title.

## § 300j–5. National Drinking Water Advisory Council

[PHSA § 1446]

**(a) Establishment; membership; representation of interests; term of office, vacancies; reappointment**

There is established a National Drinking Water Advisory Council which shall consist of fifteen members appointed by the Administrator after consultation with the Secretary. Five members shall be appointed from the general public; five members shall be appointed from appropriate State and local agencies concerned with water hygiene and public water supply; and five members shall be appointed from representatives of private organizations or groups demonstrating an active interest in the field of water hygiene and public water supply, of which two such members shall be associated with small, rural public water systems. Each member of the Council shall hold office for a term of three years, except that—

(1) any member appointed to fill a vacancy occurring prior to the expiration of the term for which his predecessor was appointed shall be appointed for the remainder of such term; and

(2) the terms of the members first taking office shall expire as follows: Five shall expire three years after December 16, 1974, five shall expire two years after such date, and five shall expire one year after such date, as designated by the Administrator at the time of appointment.

The members of the Council shall be eligible for reappointment.

**(b) Functions**

The Council shall advise, consult with, and make recommendations to, the Administrator on matters relating to activities, functions, and policies of the Agency under this subchapter.

**(c) Compensation and allowances; travel expenses**

Members of the Council appointed under this section shall, while attending meetings or conferences of the Council or otherwise engaged in business of the Council, receive compensation and allowances at a rate to be fixed by the Administrator, but not exceeding the daily equivalent of the annual rate of basic pay in effect for grade GS–18 of the General Schedule for each day (including traveltime) during which they are engaged in the actual performance of duties vested in the Council. While away from their homes or regular places of business in the performance of services for the Council, members of the Council shall be allowed travel expenses, including per diem in lieu of subsistence, in the same manner as persons employed intermittently in the Government service are allowed expenses under section 5703(b) of Title 5.

**(d) Advisory committee termination provision inapplicable**

Section 14(a) of the Federal Advisory Committee Act (relating to termination) shall not apply to the Council.

(July 1, 1944, c. 373, Title XIV, § 1446, as added Dec. 16, 1974, Pub.L. 93–523, § 2(a), 88 Stat. 1688, and amended Aug. 6, 1996, Pub.L. 104–182, Title I, § 127, 110 Stat. 1659.)

HISTORICAL AND STATUTORY NOTES

**References in Text**

The General Schedule, referred to in subsec. (c), is set out under section 5332 of Title 5, Government Organization and Employees.

Section 5703 of Title 5, referred to in subsec. (c), was amended generally by Pub.L. 94–22, § 4, May 19, 1975, 89 Stat. 85, and as so amended does not contain a subsec. (b).

Section 14(a) of the Federal Advisory Committee Act, referred to in subsec. (d), is § 14(a) of Pub.L.92–463, Oct. 6, 1972, 86 Stat. 776, which is set out in Appendix 2 to Title 5, Government Organization and Employees.

**Codifications**

Section 127 of Pub.L. 104–182, which directed that section 1446(a) of the Public Health Service Act (subsec. (a) of this section) be amended by inserting ", of which two such members shall be associated with small, rural public water systems" before the period at the end of the second sentence, was executed to subsec. (a) of this section, despite parenthetical reference to "42 U.S.C. 300j–6(a)", as the probable intent of Congress. See 1996 Amendments note set out under this section.

**Effective and Applicability Provisions**

1996 Acts

Amendment by Pub.L. 104–182 effective Aug. 6, 1996, except as otherwise specifically provided, see section 2(b) of Pub.L. 104–182, set out as a note under section 300f of this title.

**Termination of Advisory Committees**

Pub.L. 93–641, § 6, Jan. 4, 1975, 88 Stat. 2275, set out as a note under § 217a of this title, provided that an advisory committee established pursuant to the Public Health Service Act [this chapter] shall terminate at such time as may be specifically prescribed by an Act of Congress enacted after Jan. 4, 1975.

## § 300j–6. Federal agencies

[PHSA § 1447]

### (a) In general

Each department, agency, and instrumentality of the executive, legislative, and judicial branches of the Federal Government—

(1) owning or operating any facility in a wellhead protection area;

(2) engaged in any activity at such facility resulting, or which may result, in the contamination of water supplies in any such area;

(3) owning or operating any public water system; or

(4) engaged in any activity resulting, or which may result in, underground injection which endangers drinking water (within the meaning of section 300h(d)(2) of this title),

shall be subject to, and comply with, all Federal, State, interstate, and local requirements, both substantive and procedural (including any requirement for permits or reporting or any provisions for injunctive relief and such sanctions as may be imposed by a court to enforce such relief), respecting the protection of such wellhead areas, respecting such public water systems, and respecting any underground injection in the same manner and to the same extent as any person is subject to such requirements, including the payment of reasonable service charges. The Federal, State, interstate, and local substantive and procedural requirements referred to in this subsection include, but are not limited to, all administrative orders and all civil and administrative penalties and fines, regardless of whether such penalties or fines are punitive or coercive in nature or are imposed for isolated, intermittent, or continuing violations. The United States hereby expressly waives any immunity otherwise applicable to the United States with respect to any such substantive or procedural requirement (including, but not limited to, any injunctive relief, administrative order or civil or administrative penalty or fine referred to in the preceding sentence, or reasonable service charge). The reasonable service charges referred to in this subsection include, but are not limited to, fees or charges assessed in connection with the processing and issuance of permits, renewal of permits, amendments to permits, review of plans, studies, and other documents, and inspection and monitoring of facilities, as well as any other nondiscriminatory charges that are assessed in connection with a Federal, State, interstate, or local regulatory program respecting the protection of wellhead areas or public water systems or respecting any underground injection. Neither the United States, nor any agent, employee, or officer thereof, shall be immune or exempt from any process or sanction of any State or Federal Court[1] with respect to the enforcement of any such injunctive relief. No agent, employee, or officer of the United States shall be personally liable for any civil penalty under any Federal, State, interstate, or local law concerning the protection of wellhead areas or public water systems or concerning underground injection with respect to any act or omission within the scope of the official duties of the agent, employee, or officer. An agent, employee, or officer of the United States shall be subject to any criminal sanction (including, but not limited to, any fine or imprisonment) under any Federal or State requirement adopted pursuant to this subchapter, but no department, agency, or instrumentality of the executive, legislative, or judicial branch of the Federal Government shall be subject to any such sanction. The President may exempt any facility of any department, agency, or instrumentality in the executive branch from compliance with such a requirement if he determines it to be in the paramount interest of the United States to do so. No such exemption shall be granted due to lack of appropriation unless the President shall have specifically requested such appropriation as a part of the budgetary process and the Congress shall have failed to make available such requested appropriation. Any exemption shall be for a period not in excess of 1 year, but additional exemptions may be granted for periods not to exceed 1 year upon the President's making a new determination. The President shall report each January to the Congress all exemptions from the requirements of this section granted during the preceding calendar year, together with his reason for granting each such exemption.

### (b) Administrative penalty orders

#### (1) In general

If the Administrator finds that a Federal agency has violated an applicable requirement under this subchapter, the Administrator may issue a penalty order assessing a penalty against the Federal agency.

#### (2) Penalties

The Administrator may, after notice to the agency, assess a civil penalty against the agency in an amount not to exceed $25,000 per day per violation.

#### (3) Procedure

Before an administrative penalty order issued under this subsection becomes final, the Administrator shall provide the agency an opportunity to confer with the Administrator and shall provide the agency notice and an opportunity for a hearing on the record in accordance with chapters 5 and 7 of Title 5.

**(4) Public review**

**(A) In general**

Any interested person may obtain review of an administrative penalty order issued under this subsection. The review may be obtained in the United States District Court for the District of Columbia or in the United States District Court for the district in which the violation is alleged to have occurred by the filing of a complaint with the court within the 30–day period beginning on the date the penalty order becomes final. The person filing the complaint shall simultaneously send a copy of the complaint by certified mail to the Administrator and the Attorney General.

**(B) Record**

The Administrator shall promptly file in the court a certified copy of the record on which the order was issued.

**(C) Standard of review**

The court shall not set aside or remand the order unless the court finds that there is not substantial evidence in the record, taken as a whole, to support the finding of a violation or that the assessment of the penalty by the Administrator constitutes an abuse of discretion.

**(D) Prohibition on additional penalties**

The court may not impose an additional civil penalty for a violation that is subject to the order unless the court finds that the assessment constitutes an abuse of discretion by the Administrator.

**(c) Limitation on State use of funds collected from Federal Government**

Unless a State law in effect on August 6, 1996, or a State constitution requires the funds to be used in a different manner, all funds collected by a State from the Federal Government from penalties and fines imposed for violation of any substantive or procedural requirement referred to in subsection (a) of this section shall be used by the State only for projects designed to improve or protect the environment or to defray the costs of environmental protection or enforcement.

**(d) Indian rights and sovereignty as unaffected; "Federal agency" defined**

(1) Nothing in the Safe Drinking Water Amendments of 1977 shall be construed to alter or affect the status of American Indian lands or water rights nor to waive any sovereignty over Indian lands guaranteed by treaty or statute.

(2) For the purposes of this chapter, the term "Federal agency" shall not be construed to refer to or include any American Indian tribe, nor to the Secretary of the Interior in his capacity as trustee of Indian lands.

**(e) Washington Aqueduct**

The Secretary of the Army shall not pass the cost of any penalty assessed under this subchapter on to any customer, user, or other purchaser of drinking water from the Washington Aqueduct system, including finished water from the Dalecarlia or McMillan treatment plant.

(July 1, 1944, c. 373, Title XIV, § 1447, as added Dec. 16, 1974, Pub.L. 93–523, § 2(a), 88 Stat. 1688, and amended Nov. 16, 1977, Pub.L. 95–190, § 8(a), (d), 91 Stat. 1396, 1397; Aug. 6, 1996, Pub.L. 104–182, Title I, § 129(a), (c), 110 Stat. 1660, 1662.)

1 So in original. Probably should not be capitalized.

**HISTORICAL AND STATUTORY NOTES**

**References in Text**

The Safe Drinking Water Amendments of 1977, referred to in subsec. (d)(1), is Pub.L. 95–190, Nov. 16, 1977, 91 Stat. 1393. For complete classification of this Act to the Code, see Short Title of 1977 Amendment note set out under section 201 of this title and Tables.

**Effective and Applicability Provisions**

1996 Acts

Amendment by Pub.L. 104–182 effective Aug. 6, 1996, except as otherwise specifically provided, see section 2(b) of Pub.L. 104–182, set out as a note under section 300f of this title.

## § 300j–7. Judicial review

**[PHSA § 1448]**

**(a) Courts of appeals; petition for review; actions respecting regulations; filing period; grounds arising after expiration of filing period; exclusiveness of remedy**

A petition for review of—

(1) actions pertaining to the establishment of national primary drinking water regulations (including maximum contaminant level goals) may be filed only in the United States Court of Appeals for the District of Columbia circuit; and

(2) any other final action of the Administrator under this chapter may be filed in the circuit in which the petitioner resides or transacts business which is directly affected by the action.

Any such petition shall be filed within the 45–day period beginning on the date of the promulgation of the regulation or any other final Agency action with respect to which review is sought or on the date of the determination with respect to which review is sought, and may be filed after the expiration of such 45–day period if the petition is based solely on grounds arising after the expiration of such period. Action of the Administrator with respect to which review could have been obtained under this subsection shall not be subject to judicial review in any civil or criminal proceeding for enforcement or in any civil action to enjoin enforcement. In any petition concerning the assessment of a civil penalty pursuant to section 300g–3(g)(3)(B) of this title, the petitioner shall simultaneously send a copy of the complaint by certified mail to the Administrator and the Attorney General. The court shall set aside and remand the penalty order if the court finds that there is not substantial evidence in the record to support the finding of a violation or that the assessment of the penalty by the Administrator constitutes an abuse of discretion.

**(b) District courts; petition for review; actions respecting variances or exemptions; filing period; grounds arising after expiration of filing period; exclusiveness of remedy**

The United States district courts shall have jurisdiction of actions brought to review (1) the granting of, or the refusing to grant, a variance or exemption under section 300g–4 or 300g–5 of this title or (2) the requirements of any schedule prescribed for a variance or exemption under such section or the failure to prescribe such a schedule. Such an action may only be brought upon a petition for review filed with the court within the 45–day period beginning on the date the action sought to be reviewed is taken or, in the case of a petition to review the refusal to grant a variance or exemption or the failure to prescribe a schedule, within the 45–day period beginning on the date action is required to be taken on the variance, exemption, or schedule, as the case may be. A petition for such review may be filed after the expiration of such period if the petition is based solely on grounds arising after the expiration of such period. Action with respect to which review could have been obtained under this subsection shall not be subject to judicial review in any civil or criminal proceeding for enforcement or in any civil action to enjoin enforcement.

**(c) Judicial order for additional evidence before Administrator; modified or new findings; recommendation for modification or setting aside of original determination**

In any judicial proceeding in which review is sought of a determination under this subchapter required to be made on the record after notice and opportunity for hearing, if any party applies to the court for leave to adduce additional evidence and shows to the satisfaction of the court that such additional evidence is material and that there were reasonable grounds for the failure to adduce such evidence in the proceeding before the Administrator, the court may order such additional evidence (and evidence in rebuttal thereof) to be taken before the Administrator, in such manner and upon such terms and conditions as the court may deem proper. The Administrator may modify his findings as to the facts, or make new findings, by reason of the additional evidence so taken, and he shall file such modified or new findings, and his recommendation, if any, for the modification or setting aside of his original determination, with the return of such additional evidence.

(July 1, 1944, c. 373, Title XIV, § 1448, as added Dec. 16, 1974, Pub.L. 93–523, § 2(a), 88 Stat. 1689, and amended June 19, 1986, Pub.L. 99–339, Title III, § 303, 100 Stat. 667; Aug. 6, 1996, Pub.L. 104–182, Title I, § 113(c), 110 Stat. 1636.)

### HISTORICAL AND STATUTORY NOTES

**Effective and Applicability Provisions**

1996 Acts

Amendment by Pub.L. 104–182 effective Aug. 6, 1996, except as otherwise specifically provided, see section 2(b) of Pub.L. 104–182, set out as a note under section 300f of this title.

## § 300j–8. Citizen's civil action

**[PHSA § 1449]**

**(a) Persons subject to civil action; jurisdiction of enforcement proceedings**

Except as provided in subsection (b) of this section, any person may commence a civil action on his own behalf—

(1) against any person (including (A) the United States, and (B) any other governmental instrumentality or agency to the extent permitted by the eleventh amendment to the Constitution) who is alleged to be in violation of any requirement prescribed by or under this subchapter;

(2) against the Administrator where there is alleged a failure of the Administrator to perform any act or duty under this subchapter which is not discretionary with the Administrator; or

(3) for the collection of a penalty by the United States Government (and associated costs and interest) against any Federal agency that fails, by the date that is 18 months after the effective date of a final order to pay a penalty assessed by the Administrator under section 300h–8(b)[1] of this title, to pay the penalty.

No action may be brought under paragraph (1) against a public water system for a violation of a requirement prescribed by or under this subchapter which occurred within the 27-month period beginning on the first day of the month in which this subchapter is enacted. The United States district courts shall have jurisdiction, without regard to the amount in controversy or the citizenship of the parties, to enforce in an action brought under this subsection any requirement prescribed by or under this subchapter or to order the Administrator to perform an act or duty described in paragraph (2), as the case may be.

**(b) Conditions for commencement of civil action; notice**

No civil action may be commenced—

(1) under subsection (a)(1) of this section respecting violation of a requirement prescribed by or under this subchapter—

(A) prior to sixty days after the plaintiff has given notice of such violation (i) to the Administrator, (ii) to any alleged violator of such requirement and (iii) to the State in which the violation occurs, or

(B) if the Administrator, the Attorney General, or the State has commenced and is diligently prosecuting a civil action in a court of the United States to require compliance with such requirement, but in any such action in a court of the United States any person may intervene as a matter of right; or

(2) under subsection (a)(2) of this section prior to sixty days after the plaintiff has given notice of such action to the Administrator; or

(3) under subsection (a)(3) of this section prior to 60 days after the plaintiff has given notice of such action to the Attorney General and to the Federal agency.

Notice required by this subsection shall be given in such manner as the Administrator shall prescribe by regulation. No person may commence a civil action under subsection (a) of this section to require a State to prescribe a schedule under section 300g-4 or 300g-5 of this title for a variance or exemption, unless such person shows to the satisfaction of the court that the State has in a substantial number of cases failed to prescribe such schedules.

**(c) Intervention of right**

In any action under this section, the Administrator or the Attorney General, if not a party, may intervene as a matter of right.

**(d) Costs; attorney fees; expert witness fees; filing of bond**

The court, in issuing any final order in any action brought under subsection (a) of this section, may award costs of litigation (including reasonable attorney and expert witness fees) to any party whenever the court determines such an award is appropriate. The court may, if a temporary restraining order or preliminary injunction is sought, require the filing of a bond or equivalent security in accordance with the Federal Rules of Civil Procedure.

**(e) Availability of other relief**

Nothing in this section shall restrict any right which any person (or class of persons) may have under any statute or common law to seek enforcement of any requirement prescribed by or under this subchapter or to seek any other relief. Nothing in this section or in any other law of the United States shall be construed to prohibit, exclude, or restrict any State or local government from—

(1) bringing any action or obtaining any remedy or sanction in any State or local court, or

(2) bringing any administrative action or obtaining any administrative remedy or sanction,

against any agency of the United States under State or local law to enforce any requirement respecting the provision of safe drinking water or respecting any underground injection control program. Nothing in this section shall be construed to authorize judicial review of regulations or orders of the Administrator under this subchapter, except as provided in section 300j-7 of this title. For provisions providing for application of certain requirements to such agencies in the same manner as to nongovernmental entities, see section 300j-6 of this title.

(July 1, 1944, c. 373, Title XIV, § 1449, as added Dec. 16, 1974, Pub.L. 93-523, § 2(a), 88 Stat. 1690, and amended Nov. 16, 1977, Pub.L. 95-190, § 8(c), 91 Stat. 1397; Aug. 6, 1996, Pub.L. 104-182, Title I, § 129(b), 110 Stat. 1662.)

[1] So in original. Probably should be "300j-6(b)".

### HISTORICAL AND STATUTORY NOTES

**References in Text**

The Federal Rules of Civil Procedure, referred to in subsec. (d), are set out in Title 28, Judiciary and Judicial Procedure.

**Effective and Applicability Provisions**

1996 Acts

Amendment by Pub.L. 104-182 effective Aug. 6, 1996, except as otherwise specifically provided, see section 2(b) of Pub.L. 104-182, set out as a note under section 300f of this title.

## § 300j-9. General provisions

**[PHSA § 1450]**

**(a) Regulations; delegation of functions**

(1) The Administrator is authorized to prescribe such regulations as are necessary or appropriate to carry out his functions under this subchapter.

(2) The Administrator may delegate any of his functions under this subchapter (other than prescribing regulations) to any officer or employee of the Agency.

**(b) Utilization of officers and employees of Federal agencies**

The Administrator, with the consent of the head of any other agency of the United States, may utilize such officers and employees of such agency as he deems necessary to assist him in carrying out the purposes of this subchapter.

**(c) Assignment of Agency personnel to State or interstate agencies**

Upon the request of a State or interstate agency, the Administrator may assign personnel of the Agency to such State or interstate agency for the purposes of carrying out the provisions of this subchapter.

**(d) Payments of grants; adjustments; advances; reimbursement; installments; conditions; eligibility for grants; "nonprofit agency or institution" defined**

**(1)** The Administrator may make payments of grants under this subchapter (after necessary adjustment on account of previously made underpayments or overpayments) in advance or by way of reimbursement, and in such installments and on such conditions as he may determine.

**(2)** Financial assistance may be made available in the form of grants only to individuals and nonprofit agencies or institutions. For purposes of this paragraph, the term "nonprofit agency or institution" means an agency or institution no part of the net earnings of which inure, or may lawfully inure, to the benefit of any private shareholder or individual.

**(e) Labor standards**

The Administrator shall take such action as may be necessary to assure compliance with provisions of sections 3141 to 3144, 3146, 3147 of Title 40. The Secretary of Labor shall have, with respect to the labor standards specified in this subsection, the authority and functions set forth in Reorganization Plan Numbered 14 of 1950 (15 F.R. 3176; 64 Stat. 1267) and section 3145 of Title 40.

**(f) Appearance and representation of Administrator through Attorney General or attorney appointees**

The Administrator shall request the Attorney General to appear and represent him in any civil action instituted under this subchapter to which the Administrator is a party. Unless, within a reasonable time, the Attorney General notifies the Administrator that he will appear in such action, attorneys appointed by the Administrator shall appear and represent him.

**(g) Authority of Administrator under other provisions unaffected**

The provisions of this subchapter shall not be construed as affecting any authority of the Administrator under part G of subchapter II of this chapter.

**(h) Reports to Congressional committees; review by Office of Management and Budget: submittal of comments to Congressional committees**

Not later than April 1 of each year, the Administrator shall submit to the Committee on Commerce, Science, and Transportation of the Senate and the Committee on Energy and Commerce of the House of Representatives a report respecting the activities of the Agency under this subchapter and containing such recommendations for legislation as he considers necessary. The report of the Administrator under this subsection which is due not later than April 1, 1975, and each subsequent report of the Administrator under this subsection shall include a statement on the actual and anticipated cost to public water systems in each State of compliance with the requirements of this subchapter. The Office of Management and Budget may review any report required by this subsection before its submission to such committees of Congress, but the Office may not revise any such report, require any revision in any such report, or delay its submission beyond the day prescribed for its submission, and may submit to such committees of Congress its comments respecting any such report.

**(i) Discrimination prohibition; filing of complaint; investigation; orders of Secretary; notice and hearing; settlements; attorneys' fees; judicial review; filing of petition; procedural requirements; stay of orders; exclusiveness of remedy; civil actions for enforcement of orders; appropriate relief; mandamus proceedings; prohibition inapplicable to undirected but deliberate violations**

**(1)** No employer may discharge any employee or otherwise discriminate against any employee with respect to his compensation, terms, conditions, or privileges of employment because the employee (or any person acting pursuant to a request of the employee) has—

**(A)** commenced, caused to be commenced, or is about to commence or cause to be commenced a proceeding under this subchapter or a proceeding for the administration or enforcement of drinking water regulations or underground injection control programs of a State,

**(B)** testified or is about to testify in any such proceeding, or

**(C)** assisted or participated or is about to assist or participate in any manner in such a proceeding or in any other action to carry out the purposes of this subchapter.

**(2)(A)** Any employee who believes that he has been discharged or otherwise discriminated against by any person in violation of paragraph (1) may, within 30

days after such violation occurs, file (or have any person file on his behalf) a complaint with the Secretary of Labor (hereinafter in this subsection referred to as the "Secretary") alleging such discharge or discrimination. Upon receipt of such a complaint, the Secretary shall notify the person named in the complaint of the filing of the complaint.

**(B)(i)** Upon receipt of a complaint filed under subparagraph (A), the Secretary shall conduct an investigation of the violation alleged in the complaint. Within 30 days of the receipt of such complaint, the Secretary shall complete such investigation and shall notify in writing the complainant (and any person acting in his behalf) and the person alleged to have committed such violation of the results of the investigation conducted pursuant to this subparagraph. Within 90 days of the receipt of such complaint the Secretary shall, unless the proceeding on the complaint is terminated by the Secretary on the basis of a settlement entered into by the Secretary and the person alleged to have committed such violation, issue an order either providing the relief prescribed by clause (ii) or denying the complaint. An order of the Secretary shall be made on the record after notice and opportunity for agency hearing. The Secretary may not enter into a settlement terminating a proceeding on a complaint without the participation and consent of the complainant.

**(ii)** If in response to a complaint filed under subparagraph (A) the Secretary determines that a violation of paragraph (1) has occurred, the Secretary shall order (I) the person who committed such violation to take affirmative action to abate the violation, (II) such person to reinstate the complainant to his former position together with the compensation (including back pay), terms, conditions, and privileges of his employment, (III) compensatory damages, and (IV) where appropriate, exemplary damages. If such an order is issued, the Secretary, at the request of the complainant, shall assess against the person against whom the order is issued a sum equal to the aggregate amount of all costs and expenses (including attorneys' fees) reasonably incurred, as determined by the Secretary, by the complainant for, or in connection with, the bringing of the complaint upon which the order was issued.

**(3)(A)** Any person adversely affected or aggrieved by an order issued under paragraph (2) may obtain review of the order in the United States Court of Appeals for the circuit in which the violation, with respect to which the order was issued, allegedly occurred. The petition for review must be filed within sixty days from the issuance of the Secretary's order. Review shall conform to chapter 7 of Title 5. The commencement of proceedings under this subparagraph shall not, unless ordered by the court, operate as a stay of the Secretary's order.

**(B)** An order of the Secretary with respect to which review could have been obtained under subparagraph (A) shall not be subject to judicial review in any criminal or other civil proceeding.

**(4)** Whenever a person has failed to comply with an order issued under paragraph (2)(B), the Secretary shall file a civil action in the United States District Court for the district in which the violation was found to occur to enforce such order. In actions brought under this paragraph, the district courts shall have jurisdiction to grant all appropriate relief including, but not limited to, injunctive relief, compensatory, and exemplary damages.

**(5)** Any nondiscretionary duty imposed by this section is enforceable in mandamus proceeding brought under section 1361 of Title 28.

**(6)** Paragraph (1) shall not apply with respect to any employee who, acting without direction from his employer (or the employer's agent), deliberately causes a violation of any requirement of this subchapter.

(July 1, 1944, c. 373, Title XIV, § 1450, as added Dec. 16, 1974, Pub.L. 93–523, § 2(a), 88 Stat. 1691, and amended S.Res. 4, Feb. 4, 1977; H.Res. 549, Mar. 25, 1980; Nov. 8, 1984, Pub.L. 98–620, Title IV, § 402(38), 98 Stat. 3360; Nov. 2, 1994, Pub.L. 103–437, § 15(a)(2), 108 Stat. 4591.)

## HISTORICAL AND STATUTORY NOTES

### References in Text

Reorganization Plan Numbered 14 of 1950 (15 F.R. 3176; 64 Stat. 1267), referred to in subsec. (e), is set out in Appendix 1 to Title 5, Government Organization and Employees.

Part G of subchapter II of this chapter, referred to in subsec. (g), is classified to section 264 et seq. of this title.

### Codifications

In subsec. (e), "sections 3141 to 3144, 3146, 3147 of Title 40" substituted for "the Act of March 3, 1931 (known as the Davis–Bacon Act; 40 U.S.C. 276a—276a–5)" on authority of Pub.L. 107–217, § 5(c), Aug. 21, 2002, 116 Stat. 1301, which is set out as a note preceding 40 U.S.C.A. § 101. Pub.L. 107–217, § 1, enacted Title 40 into positive law. The Davis–Bacon Act is Act Mar. 3, 1931, c. 411, 46 Stat. 1494, which was classified to former 40 U.S.C.A. §§ 276a, 276a–1 to 276a–6, prior to being repealed by Pub.L. 107–217, § 6(b), Aug. 21, 2002, 116 Stat. 1308, and its substance reenacted as 40 U.S.C.A. §§ 3141 to 3144, 3146, 3147.

In subsec. (e), "section 3145 of Title 40" substituted for "section 276c of Title 40", which originally read "section 2 of the Act of June 13, 1934 (40 U.S.C. 276c)", on authority of Pub.L. 107–217, § 5(c), Aug. 21, 2002, 116 Stat. 1301, which is set out as a note preceding 40 U.S.C.A. § 101. Pub.L. 107–217, § 1, enacted Title 40 into positive law. Section 2 of the Act of June 13, 1934, as amended, is Act June 13, 1934, c. 482, § 2, 48 Stat. 948, which was classified to former 40 U.S.C.A. § 276c prior to being repealed by Pub.L. 107–217, § 6(b), Aug. 21, 2002, 116 Stat. 1309, and its substance reenacted as 40 U.S.C.A. § 3145.

**Effective and Applicability Provisions**

1984 Acts

Amendment by Pub.L. 98–620 not to apply to cases pending on Nov. 8, 1984, see section 403 of Pub.L. 98–620, set out as a note under section 1657 of Title 28, Judiciary and Judicial Procedure.

**Change of Name**

Any reference in any provision of law enacted before Jan. 4, 1995, to the Committee on Energy and Commerce of the House of Representatives treated as referring to the Committee on Commerce of the House of Representatives, except that any reference in any provision of law enacted before Jan. 4, 1995, to the Committee on Energy and Commerce of the House of Representatives treated as referring to the Committee on Agriculture of the House of Representatives, in the case of a provision of law relating to inspection of seafood or seafood products, the Committee on Banking and Financial Services of the House of Representatives, in the case of a provision of law relating to bank capital markets activities generally or to depository institution securities activities generally, and the Committee on Transportation and Infrastructure of the House of Representatives, in the case of a provision of law relating to railroads, railway labor, or railroad retirement and unemployment (except revenue measures related thereto), see section 1(a)(4) and (c)(1) of Pub.L. 104–14, set out as a note preceding section 21 of Title 2, The Congress.

The Committee on Commerce of the Senate was abolished and replaced by the Committee on Commerce, Science, and Transportation of the Senate, effective Feb. 11, 1977. See Rule XXV of the Standing Rules of the Senate, as amended by Senate Resolution 4 (popularly cited as the "Committee System Reorganization Amendments of 1977"), approved Feb. 4, 1977.

The name of the Committee on Interstate and Foreign Commerce of the House of Representatives was changed to Committee on Energy and Commerce immediately prior to noon on Jan. 3, 1981, by House Resolution 549, Ninety-sixth Congress, Mar. 25, 1980.

## § 300j–10. Appointment of scientific, etc., personnel by Administrator of Environmental Protection Agency for implementation of responsibilities; compensation

To the extent that the Administrator of the Environmental Protection Agency deems such action necessary to the discharge of his functions under Title XIV of the Public Health Service Act [42 U.S.C.A. § 300f et seq.] (relating to safe drinking water) and under other provisions of law, he may appoint personnel to fill not more than thirty scientific, engineering, professional, legal, and administrative positions within the Environmental Protection Agency without regard to the civil service laws and may fix the compensation of such personnel not in excess of the maximum rate payable for GS–18 of the General Schedule under section 5332 of Title 5.

(Pub.L. 95–190, § 11(b), Nov. 16, 1977, 91 Stat. 1398.)

**HISTORICAL AND STATUTORY NOTES**

**References in Text**

The Public Health Service Act, referred to in text, is Act July 1, 1944, c. 373, 58 Stat. 682, as amended. Title XIV of the Public Health Service Act is classified generally to this subchapter (section 300f et seq.). For complete classification of this Act to the Code, see Short Title note set out under section 201 of this title and Tables.

The civil service laws, referred to in text, are set out in Title 5, Government Organization and Employees. See, particularly, section 3301 et seq. of Title 5.

**Codifications**

Section was enacted as part of the Safe Drinking Water Amendments of 1977 and not as part of the Public Health Service Act, which comprises this chapter.

## § 300j–11. Indian Tribes

**[PHSA § 1451]**

**(a) In general**

Subject to the provisions of subsection (b) of this section, the Administrator—

(1) is authorized to treat Indian Tribes as States under this subchapter,

(2) may delegate to such Tribes primary enforcement responsibility for public water systems and for underground injection control, and

(3) may provide such Tribes grant and contract assistance to carry out functions provided by this subchapter.

**(b) EPA regulations**

**(1) Specific provisions**

The Administrator shall, within 18 months after June 19, 1986, promulgate final regulations specifying those provisions of this subchapter for which it is appropriate to treat Indian Tribes as States. Such treatment shall be authorized only if:

(A) the Indian Tribe is recognized by the Secretary of the Interior and has a governing body carrying out substantial governmental duties and powers;

(B) the functions to be exercised by the Indian Tribe are within the area of the Tribal Government's jurisdiction; and

(C) the Indian Tribe is reasonably expected to be capable, in the Administrator's judgment, of carrying out the functions to be exercised in a manner consistent with the terms and purposes of this subchapter and of all applicable regulations.

**(2) Provisions where treatment as State inappropriate**

For any provision of this subchapter where treatment of Indian Tribes as identical to States is inappropriate, administratively infeasible or otherwise inconsistent with the purposes of this subchapter, the Administrator may include in the regulations promulgated under this section, other means for administering such provision in a manner that will achieve the purpose of the provision. Nothing in this section shall be construed to allow Indian Tribes to assume or maintain primary enforcement responsibility for public water systems or for underground injection control in a manner less protective of the health of persons than such responsibility may be assumed or maintained by a State. An Indian tribe [1] shall not be required to exercise criminal enforcement jurisdiction for purposes of complying with the preceding sentence.

(July 1, 1944, c. 373, Title XIV, § 1451, as added June 19, 1986, Pub.L. 99–339, Title III, § 302(a), 100 Stat. 665; and amended Aug. 6, 1996, Pub.L. 104–182, Title V, § 501(f)(6), 110 Stat. 1692.)

[1] So in original. Probably should be "Tribe".

HISTORICAL AND STATUTORY NOTES

**Effective and Applicability Provisions**

1996 Acts

Amendment by Pub.L. 104–182 effective Aug. 6, 1996, except as otherwise specifically provided, see section 2(b) of Pub.L. 104–182, set out as a note under section 300f of this title.

## § 300j–12. State revolving loan funds

**[PHSA § 1452]**

### (a) General authority

#### (1) Grants to States to establish State loan funds

**(A) In general**

The Administrator shall offer to enter into agreements with eligible States to make capitalization grants, including letters of credit, to the States under this subsection to further the health protection objectives of this subchapter, promote the efficient use of fund resources, and for other purposes as are specified in this subchapter.

**(B) Establishment of fund**

To be eligible to receive a capitalization grant under this section, a State shall establish a drinking water treatment revolving loan fund (referred to in this section as a "State loan fund") and comply with the other requirements of this section. Each grant to a State under this section shall be deposited in the State loan fund established by the State, except as otherwise provided in this section and in other provisions of this subchapter. No funds authorized by other provisions of this subchapter to be used for other purposes specified in this subchapter shall be deposited in any State loan fund.

**(C) Extended period**

The grant to a State shall be available to the State for obligation during the fiscal year for which the funds are authorized and during the following fiscal year, except that grants made available from funds provided prior to fiscal year 1997 shall be available for obligation during each of the fiscal years 1997 and 1998.

**(D) Allotment formula**

Except as otherwise provided in this section, funds made available to carry out this section shall be allotted to States that have entered into an agreement pursuant to this section (other than the District of Columbia) in accordance with—

(i) for each of fiscal years 1995 through 1997, a formula that is the same as the formula used to distribute public water system supervision grant funds under section 300j–2 of this title in fiscal year 1995, except that the minimum proportionate share established in the formula shall be 1 percent of available funds and the formula shall be adjusted to include a minimum proportionate share for the State of Wyoming and the District of Columbia; and

(ii) for fiscal year 1998 and each subsequent fiscal year, a formula that allocates to each State the proportional share of the State needs identified in the most recent survey conducted pursuant to subsection (h) of this section, except that the minimum proportionate share provided to each State shall be the same as the minimum proportionate share provided under clause (i).

**(E) Reallotment**

The grants not obligated by the last day of the period for which the grants are available shall be reallotted according to the appropriate criteria set forth in subparagraph (D), except that the Administrator may reserve and allocate 10 percent of the remaining amount for financial assistance to Indian Tribes in addition to the amount allotted under subsection (i) of this section and none of the funds reallotted by the Administrator shall be reallotted to any State that has not obligated all sums allotted to the State pursuant to this section during the period in which the sums were available for obligation.

**(F) Nonprimacy States**

The State allotment for a State not exercising primary enforcement responsibility for public water systems shall not be deposited in any such fund but shall be allotted by the Administrator under this subparagraph. Pursuant to section 300j–2(a)(9)(A) of this title such sums allotted under this subparagraph shall be reserved as needed by the Administrator to exercise primary enforcement responsibility under this subchapter in such State and the remainder shall be reallotted to States exercising primary enforcement responsibility for public water systems for deposit in such funds. Whenever the Administrator makes a final determination pursuant to section 300g–2(b) of this title that the requirements of section 300g–2(a) of this title are no longer being met by a State, additional grants for such State under this subchapter shall be immediately terminated by the Administrator. This subparagraph shall not apply to any State not exercising primary enforcement responsibility for public water systems as of August 6, 1996.

**(G) Other programs**

**(i) New system capacity**

Beginning in fiscal year 1999, the Administrator shall withhold 20 percent of each capitalization grant made pursuant to this section to a State unless the State has met the requirements of section 300g–9(a) of this title (relating to capacity development) and shall withhold 10 percent for fiscal year 2001, 15 percent for fiscal year 2002, and 20 percent for fiscal year 2003 if the State has not complied with the provisions of section 300g–9(c) of this title (relating to capacity development strategies). Not more than a total of 20 percent of the capitalization grants made to a State in any fiscal year may be withheld under the preceding provisions of this clause. All funds withheld by the Administrator pursuant to this clause shall be reallotted by the Administrator on the basis of the same ratio as is applicable to funds allotted under subparagraph (D). None of the funds reallotted by the Administrator pursuant to this paragraph shall be allotted to a State unless the State has met the requirements of section 300g–9 of this title (relating to capacity development).

**(ii) Operator certification**

The Administrator shall withhold 20 percent of each capitalization grant made pursuant to this section unless the State has met the requirements of 300g–8[1] of this title (relating to operator certification). All funds withheld by the Administrator pursuant to this clause shall be reallotted by the Administrator on the basis of the same ratio as applicable to funds allotted under subparagraph (D). None of the funds reallotted by the Administrator pursuant to this paragraph shall be allotted to a State unless the State has met the requirements of section 300g–8 of this title (relating to operator certification).

**(2) Use of funds**

Except as otherwise authorized by this subchapter, amounts deposited in a State loan fund, including loan repayments and interest earned on such amounts, shall be used only for providing loans or loan guarantees, or as a source of reserve and security for leveraged loans, the proceeds of which are deposited in a State loan fund established under paragraph (1), or other financial assistance authorized under this section to community water systems and nonprofit noncommunity water systems, other than systems owned by Federal agencies. Financial assistance under this section may be used by a public water system only for expenditures (not including monitoring, operation, and maintenance expenditures) of a type or category which the Administrator has determined, through guidance, will facilitate compliance with national primary drinking water regulations applicable to the system under section 300g–1 of this title or otherwise significantly further the health protection objectives of this subchapter. The funds may also be used to provide loans to a system referred to in section 300f(4)(B) of this title for the purpose of providing the treatment described in section 300f(4)(B)(i)(III) of this title. The funds shall not be used for the acquisition of real property or interests therein, unless the acquisition is integral to a project authorized by this paragraph and the purchase is from a willing seller. Of the amount credited to any State loan fund established under this section in any fiscal year, 15 percent shall be available solely for providing loan assistance to public water systems which regularly serve fewer than 10,000 persons to the extent such funds can be obligated for eligible projects of public water systems.

**(3) Limitation**

**(A) In general**

Except as provided in subparagraph (B), no assistance under this section shall be provided to a public water system that—

(i) does not have the technical, managerial, and financial capability to ensure compliance with the requirements of this subchapter; or

(ii) is in significant noncompliance with any requirement of a national primary drinking water regulation or variance.

**(B) Restructuring**

A public water system described in subparagraph (A) may receive assistance under this section if—

(i) the use of the assistance will ensure compliance; and

(ii) if subparagraph (A)(i) applies to the system, the owner or operator of the system agrees to undertake feasible and appropriate changes in operations (including ownership, management, accounting, rates, maintenance, consolidation, alternative water supply, or other procedures) if the State determines that the measures are necessary to ensure that the system has the technical, managerial, and financial capability to comply with the requirements of this subchapter over the long term.

**(C) Review**

Prior to providing assistance under this section to a public water system that is in significant noncompliance with any requirement of a national primary drinking water regulation or variance, the State shall conduct a review to determine whether subparagraph (A)(i) applies to the system.

**(b) Intended use plans**

**(1) In general**

After providing for public review and comment, each State that has entered into a capitalization agreement pursuant to this section shall annually prepare a plan that identifies the intended uses of the amounts available to the State loan fund of the State.

**(2) Contents**

An intended use plan shall include—

(A) a list of the projects to be assisted in the first fiscal year that begins after the date of the plan, including a description of the project, the expected terms of financial assistance, and the size of the community served;

(B) the criteria and methods established for the distribution of funds; and

(C) a description of the financial status of the State loan fund and the short-term and long-term goals of the State loan fund.

**(3) Use of funds**

**(A) In general**

An intended use plan shall provide, to the maximum extent practicable, that priority for the use of funds be given to projects that—

(i) address the most serious risk to human health;

(ii) are necessary to ensure compliance with the requirements of this subchapter (including requirements for filtration); and

(iii) assist systems most in need on a per household basis according to State affordability criteria.

**(B) List of projects**

Each State shall, after notice and opportunity for public comment, publish and periodically update a list of projects in the State that are eligible for assistance under this section, including the priority assigned to each project and, to the extent known, the expected funding schedule for each project.

**(c) Fund management**

Each State loan fund under this section shall be established, maintained, and credited with repayments and interest. The fund corpus shall be available in perpetuity for providing financial assistance under this section. To the extent amounts in the fund are not required for current obligation or expenditure, such amounts shall be invested in interest bearing obligations.

**(d) Assistance for disadvantaged communities**

**(1) Loan subsidy**

Notwithstanding any other provision of this section, in any case in which the State makes a loan pursuant to subsection (a)(2) of this section to a disadvantaged community or to a community that the State expects to become a disadvantaged community as the result of a proposed project, the State may provide additional subsidization (including forgiveness of principal).

**(2) Total amount of subsidies**

For each fiscal year, the total amount of loan subsidies made by a State pursuant to paragraph (1) may not exceed 30 percent of the amount of the capitalization grant received by the State for the year.

**(3) "Disadvantaged community" defined**

In this subsection, the term "disadvantaged community" means the service area of a public water system that meets affordability criteria established after public review and comment by the State in which the public water system is located. The Administrator may publish information to assist States in establishing affordability criteria.

**(e) State contribution**

Each agreement under subsection (a) of this section shall require that the State deposit in the State loan fund from State moneys an amount equal to at least 20 percent of the total amount of the grant to be made to the State on or before the date on which the grant payment is made to the State, except that a State shall not be required to deposit such amount into the fund prior to the date on which each grant payment is made for fiscal years 1994, 1995, 1996, and 1997 if the State deposits the State contribution amount into the State loan fund prior to September 30, 1999.

**(f) Types of assistance**

Except as otherwise limited by State law, the amounts deposited into a State loan fund under this section may be used only—

(1) to make loans, on the condition that—

(A) the interest rate for each loan is less than or equal to the market interest rate, including an interest free loan;

(B) principal and interest payments on each loan will commence not later than 1 year after completion of the project for which the loan was made, and each loan will be fully amortized not later than 20 years after the completion of the project, except that in the case of a disadvantaged community (as defined in subsection (d)(3) of this section), a State may provide an extended term for a loan, if the extended term—

(i) terminates not later than the date that is 30 years after the date of project completion; and

(ii) does not exceed the expected design life of the project;

(C) the recipient of each loan will establish a dedicated source of revenue (or, in the case of a privately owned system, demonstrate that there is adequate security) for the repayment of the loan; and

(D) the State loan fund will be credited with all payments of principal and interest on each loan;

(2) to buy or refinance the debt obligation of a municipality or an intermunicipal or interstate agency within the State at an interest rate that is less than or equal to the market interest rate in any case in which a debt obligation is incurred after July 1, 1993;

(3) to guarantee, or purchase insurance for, a local obligation (all of the proceeds of which finance a project eligible for assistance under this section) if the guarantee or purchase would improve credit market access or reduce the interest rate applicable to the obligation;

(4) as a source of revenue or security for the payment of principal and interest on revenue or general obligation bonds issued by the State if the proceeds of the sale of the bonds will be deposited into the State loan fund; and

(5) to earn interest on the amounts deposited into the State loan fund.

**(g) Administration of State loan funds**

**(1) Combined financial administration**

Notwithstanding subsection (c) of this section, a State may (as a convenience and to avoid unnecessary administrative costs) combine, in accordance with State law, the financial administration of a State loan fund established under this section with the financial administration of any other revolving fund established by the State if otherwise not prohibited by the law under which the State loan fund was established and if the Administrator determines that—

(A) the grants under this section, together with loan repayments and interest, will be separately accounted for and used solely for the purposes specified in subsection (a) of this section; and

(B) the authority to establish assistance priorities and carry out oversight and related activities (other than financial administration) with respect to assistance remains with the State agency having primary responsibility for administration of the State program under section 300g–2 of this title, after consultation with other appropriate State agencies (as determined by the State): *Provided,* That in nonprimacy States eligible to receive assistance under this section, the Governor shall determine which State agency will have authority to establish priorities for financial assistance from the State loan fund.

**(2) Cost of administering fund**

Each State may annually use up to 4 percent of the funds allotted to the State under this section to cover the reasonable costs of administration of the programs under this section, including the recovery of reasonable costs expended to establish a State loan fund which are incurred after August 6, 1996, and to provide technical assistance to public water systems within the State. For fiscal year 1995 and each fiscal year thereafter, each State may use up to an additional 10 percent of the funds allotted to the State under this section—

(A) for public water system supervision programs under section 300j–2(a) of this title;

(B) to administer or provide technical assistance through source water protection programs;

(C) to develop and implement a capacity development strategy under section 300g–9(c) of this title; and

(D) for an operator certification program for purposes of meeting the requirements of section 300g–8 of this title,

if the State matches the expenditures with at least an equal amount of State funds. At least half of the match must be additional to the amount expended by the State for public water supervision in fiscal year 1993. An additional 2 percent of the funds annually allotted to each State under this section may be used by the State to provide technical assistance to public water systems serving 10,000 or fewer persons in the State. Funds utilized under subparagraph (B) shall not be used for enforcement actions.

**(3) Guidance and regulations**

The Administrator shall publish guidance and promulgate regulations as may be necessary to carry out the provisions of this section, including—

(A) provisions to ensure that each State commits and expends funds allotted to the State under this section as efficiently as possible in accordance with this subchapter and applicable State laws;

(B) guidance to prevent waste, fraud, and abuse; and

(C) guidance to avoid the use of funds made available under this section to finance the expansion of any public water system in anticipation of future population growth.

The guidance and regulations shall also ensure that the States, and public water systems receiving assistance under this section, use accounting, audit, and fiscal procedures that conform to generally accepted accounting standards.

**(4) State report**

Each State administering a loan fund and assistance program under this subsection shall publish and submit to the Administrator a report every 2 years on its activities under this section, including the findings of the most recent audit of the fund and the entire State allotment. The Administrator shall periodically audit all State loan funds established by, and all other amounts allotted to, the States pursuant to this section in accordance with procedures established by the Comptroller General.

**(h) Needs survey**

The Administrator shall conduct an assessment of water system capital improvement needs of all eligible public water systems in the United States and submit a report to the Congress containing the results of the assessment within 180 days after August 6, 1996, and every 4 years thereafter.

**(i) Indian Tribes**

**(1) In general**

1½ percent of the amounts appropriated annually to carry out this section may be used by the Administrator to make grants to Indian Tribes and Alaska Native villages that have not otherwise received either grants from the Administrator under this section or assistance from State loan funds established under this section. The grants may only be used for expenditures by tribes and villages for public water system expenditures referred to in subsection (a)(2) of this section.

**(2) Use of funds**

Funds reserved pursuant to paragraph (1) shall be used to address the most significant threats to public health associated with public water systems that serve Indian Tribes, as determined by the Administrator in consultation with the Director of the Indian Health Service and Indian Tribes.

**(3) Alaska Native villages**

In the case of a grant for a project under this subsection in an Alaska Native village, the Administrator is also authorized to make grants to the State of Alaska for the benefit of Native villages. An amount not to exceed 4 percent of the grant amount may be used by the State of Alaska for project management.

**(4) Needs assessment**

The Administrator, in consultation with the Director of the Indian Health Service and Indian Tribes, shall, in accordance with a schedule that is consistent with the needs surveys conducted pursuant to subsection (h) of this section, prepare surveys and assess the needs of drinking water treatment facilities to serve Indian Tribes, including an evaluation of the public water systems that pose the most significant threats to public health.

**(j) Other areas**

Of the funds annually available under this section for grants to States, the Administrator shall make allotments in accordance with section 300j–2(a)(4) of this title for the Virgin Islands, the Commonwealth of the Northern Mariana Islands, American Samoa, and Guam. The grants allotted as provided in this subsection may be provided by the Administrator to the governments of such areas, to public water systems in such areas, or to both, to be used for the public water system expenditures referred to in subsection (a)(2) of this section. The grants, and grants for the District of Columbia, shall not be deposited in State loan funds. The total allotment of grants under this section for all areas described in this subsection in any fiscal year shall not exceed 0.33 percent of the aggregate amount made available to carry out this section in that fiscal year.

**(k) Other authorized activities**

**(1) In general**

Notwithstanding subsection (a)(2) of this section, a State may take each of the following actions:

(A) Provide assistance, only in the form of a loan, to one or more of the following:

(i) Any public water system described in subsection (a)(2) of this section to acquire land or a conservation easement from a willing seller or grantor, if the purpose of the acquisition is to protect the source water of the system from contamination and to ensure compliance with national primary drinking water regulations.

**(ii)** Any community water system to implement local, voluntary source water protection measures to protect source water in areas delineated pursuant to section 300j–13 of this title, in order to facilitate compliance with national primary drinking water regulations applicable to the system under section 300g–1 of this title or otherwise significantly further the health protection objectives of this subchapter. Funds authorized under this clause may be used to fund only voluntary, incentive-based mechanisms.

**(iii)** Any community water system to provide funding in accordance with section 300j–14(a)(1)(B)(i) of this title.

**(B)** Provide assistance, including technical and financial assistance, to any public water system as part of a capacity development strategy developed and implemented in accordance with section 300g–9(c) of this title.

**(C)** Make expenditures from the capitalization grant of the State for fiscal years 1996 and 1997 to delineate and assess source water protection areas in accordance with section 300j–13 of this title, except that funds set aside for such expenditure shall be obligated within 4 fiscal years.

**(D)** Make expenditures from the fund for the establishment and implementation of wellhead protection programs under section 300h–7 of this title.

**(2) Limitation**

For each fiscal year, the total amount of assistance provided and expenditures made by a State under this subsection may not exceed 15 percent of the amount of the capitalization grant received by the State for that year and may not exceed 10 percent of that amount for any one of the following activities:

**(A)** To acquire land or conservation easements pursuant to paragraph (1)(A)(i).

**(B)** To provide funding to implement voluntary, incentive-based source water quality protection measures pursuant to clauses (ii) and (iii) of paragraph (1)(A).

**(C)** To provide assistance through a capacity development strategy pursuant to paragraph (1)(B).

**(D)** To make expenditures to delineate or assess source water protection areas pursuant to paragraph (1)(C).

**(E)** To make expenditures to establish and implement wellhead protection programs pursuant to paragraph (1)(D).

**(3) Statutory construction**

Nothing in this section creates or conveys any new authority to a State, political subdivision of a State, or community water system for any new regulatory measure, or limits any authority of a State, political subdivision of a State or community water system.

**(*l*) Savings**

The failure or inability of any public water system to receive funds under this section or any other loan or grant program, or any delay in obtaining the funds, shall not alter the obligation of the system to comply in a timely manner with all applicable drinking water standards and requirements of this subchapter.

**(m) Authorization of appropriations**

There are authorized to be appropriated to carry out the purposes of this section $599,000,000 for the fiscal year 1994 and $1,000,000,000 for each of the fiscal years 1995 through 2003. To the extent amounts authorized to be appropriated under this subsection in any fiscal year are not appropriated in that fiscal year, such amounts are authorized to be appropriated in a subsequent fiscal year (prior to the fiscal year 2004). Such sums shall remain available until expended.

**(n) Health effects studies**

From funds appropriated pursuant to this section for each fiscal year, the Administrator shall reserve $10,000,000 for health effects studies on drinking water contaminants authorized by the Safe Drinking Water Act Amendments of 1996. In allocating funds made available under this subsection, the Administrator shall give priority to studies concerning the health effects of cryptosporidium (as authorized by section 300j–18(c) of this title), disinfection byproducts (as authorized by section 300j–18(c) of this title), and arsenic (as authorized by section 300g–1(b)(12)(A) of this title), and the implementation of a plan for studies of subpopulations at greater risk of adverse effects (as authorized by section 300j–18(a) of this title).

**(*o*) Monitoring for unregulated contaminants**

From funds appropriated pursuant to this section for each fiscal year beginning with fiscal year 1998, the Administrator shall reserve $2,000,000 to pay the costs of monitoring for unregulated contaminants under section 300j–4(a)(2)(C) of this title.

**(p) Demonstration project for State of Virginia**

Notwithstanding the other provisions of this section limiting the use of funds deposited in a State loan fund from any State allotment, the State of Virginia may, as a single demonstration and with the approval of the Virginia General Assembly and the Administrator, conduct a program to demonstrate alternative approaches to intergovernmental coordination to assist in the financing of new drinking water facilities in the following rural communities in southwestern Virginia where none exists on August 6, 1996, and where such communities are experiencing economic hardship: Lee County, Wise County, Scott County, Dickenson County, Russell County, Buchanan County, Tazewell County, and the city of Norton, Virginia. The funds allotted to that State and deposited in the State loan fund may be loaned to a regional endowment fund for the purpose set forth in this subsection under a plan to be approved by the Administrator. The plan may include an advisory group that includes representatives of such counties.

### (q) Small system technical assistance

The Administrator may reserve up to 2 percent of the total funds appropriated pursuant to subsection (m) of this section for each of the fiscal years 1997 through 2003 to carry out the provisions of section 300j–1(e) of this title (relating to technical assistance for small systems), except that the total amount of funds made available for such purpose in any fiscal year through appropriations (as authorized by section 300j–1(e) of this title) and reservations made pursuant to this subsection shall not exceed the amount authorized by section 300j–1(e) of this title.

### (r) Evaluation

The Administrator shall conduct an evaluation of the effectiveness of the State loan funds through fiscal year 2001. The evaluation shall be submitted to the Congress at the same time as the President submits to the Congress, pursuant to section 1108 of Title 31, an appropriations request for fiscal year 2003 relating to the budget of the Environmental Protection Agency.

(July 1, 1944, c. 373, Title XIV, § 1452, as added Aug. 6, 1996, Pub.L. 104–182, Title I, § 130, 110 Stat. 1662.)

1 So in original. Probably should be preceded by "section".

## HISTORICAL AND STATUTORY NOTES

**References in Text**

The Safe Drinking Water Act Amendments of 1996, referred to in subsec. (n), is Pub.L. 104–182, Aug. 6, 1996, 110 Stat. 1613. For complete classification of this Act to the Code, see Short Title note set out under section 201 of this title and Tables.

**Effective and Applicability Provisions**

1996 Acts

Section effective Aug. 6, 1996, except as otherwise specifically provided, see section 2(b) of Pub.L. 104–182, set out as a note under section 300f of this title.

**Transfer of Funds**

Pub.L. 104–182, Title III, § 302, Aug. 6, 1996, 110 Stat. 1683, provided that:

"**(a) In general.**—Notwithstanding any other provision of law, at any time after the date 1 year after a State establishes a State loan fund pursuant to section 1452 of the Safe Drinking Water Act [this section] but prior to fiscal year 2002, a Governor of the State may—

"(1) reserve up to 33 percent of a capitalization grant made pursuant to such section 1452 [this section] and add the funds reserved to any funds provided to the State pursuant to section 601 of the Federal Water Pollution Control Act (33 U.S.C. 1381) [section 1381 of Title 33, Navigation and Navigable Waters]; and

"(2) reserve in any year a dollar amount up to the dollar amount that may be reserved under paragraph (1) for that year from capitalization grants made pursuant to section 601 of such Act (33 U.S.C. 1381) [section 1381 of Title 33] and add the reserved funds to any funds provided to the State pursuant to section 1452 of the Safe Drinking Water Act [this section].

"**(b) Report.**—Not later than 4 years after the date of enactment of this Act [Aug. 6, 1996], the Administrator shall submit a report to the Congress regarding the implementation of this section, together with the Administrator's recommendations, if any, for modifications or improvement.

"**(c) State match.**—Funds reserved pursuant to this section shall not be considered to be a State match of a capitalization grant required pursuant to section 1452 of the Safe Drinking Water Act [this section] or the Federal Water Pollution Control Act (33 U.S.C. 1251 et seq.) [section 1251 et seq. of Title 33]."

**State and Tribal Assistance Grants**

Pub.L. 108–199, Div. G, Title III, Jan. 23, 2004, 118 Stat. 406, provided in part that: "For fiscal year 2004, State authority under section 302(a) of Public Law 104–182 [Pub.L. 104–182, Title III, § 302(a), Aug. 6, 1996, 110 Stat. 1683, which is set out as a note under this section] shall remain in effect."

Similar provisions were contained in the following prior appropriation Acts:

Pub.L. 108–7, Div. K, Title III, Feb. 20, 2003, 117 Stat. 512.

Pub.L. 107–73, Title III, Nov. 26, 2001, 115 Stat. 685.

**Combining Fund Assets For Enhancement of Lending Capacity**

Pub.L. 105–276, Title III, Oct. 21, 1998, 112 Stat. 2498, provided in part: "That, consistent with section 1452(g) of the Safe Drinking Water Act (42 U.S.C.A. § 300j–12(g)), section 302 of the Safe Drinking Water Act Amendments of 1996 (Public Law 104–182) (set out as a note below) and the accompanying joint explanatory statement of the committee of conference (H. Rept. No. 104–741 to accompany S. 1316, the Safe Drinking Water Act Amendments of 1996), and notwithstanding any other provision of law, beginning in fiscal year 1999 and thereafter, States may combine the assets of State Revolving Funds (SRFs) established under section 1452 of the Safe Drinking Water Act, as amended, and title VI of the Federal Water Pollution Control Act (33 U.S.C.A. § 381 et seq.), as amended, as security for bond issues to enhance the lending capacity of one or both SRFs, but not to acquire the state match for either program, provided that revenues from the bonds are allocated to the purposes of the Safe Drinking Water Act (this subchapter) and the Federal Water Pollution Control Act (33 U.S.C.A. § 1251 et seq.) in the same portion as the funds are used as security for the bonds."

## § 300j–13. Source water quality assessment

**[PHSA § 1453]**

### (a) Source water assessment

#### (1) Guidance

Within 12 months after August 6, 1996, after notice and comment, the Administrator shall publish guidance for States exercising primary enforcement responsibility for public water systems to carry out directly or through delegation (for the protection and benefit of public water systems and for the support of monitoring flexibility) a source water assessment program within the State's boundaries. Each State adopting modifications to monitoring requirements pursuant to section 300g–7(b) of this title shall, prior to adopting such modifications, have an approved source water assessment program under this section and shall carry out the program either directly or through delegation.

#### (2) Program requirements

A source water assessment program under this subsection shall—

(A) delineate the boundaries of the assessment areas in such State from which one or more public water systems in the State receive supplies of drinking water, using all reasonably available hydrogeologic information on the sources of the supply of drinking water in the State and the water flow, recharge, and discharge and any other reliable information as the State deems necessary to adequately determine such areas; and

(B) identify for contaminants regulated under this subchapter for which monitoring is required under this subchapter (or any unregulated contaminants selected by the State, in its discretion, which the State, for the purposes of this subsection, has determined may present a threat to public health), to the extent practical, the origins within each delineated area of such contaminants to determine the susceptibility of the public water systems in the delineated area to such contaminants.

#### (3) Approval, implementation, and monitoring relief

A State source water assessment program under this subsection shall be submitted to the Administrator within 18 months after the Administrator's guidance is issued under this subsection and shall be deemed approved 9 months after the date of such submittal unless the Administrator disapproves the program as provided in section 300h–7(c) of this title. States shall begin implementation of the program immediately after its approval. The Administrator's approval of a State program under this subsection shall include a timetable, established in consultation with the State, allowing not more than 2 years for completion after approval of the program. Public water systems seeking monitoring relief in addition to the interim relief provided under section 300g–7(a) of this title shall be eligible for monitoring relief, consistent with section 300g–7(b) of this title, upon completion of the assessment in the delineated source water assessment area or areas concerned.

#### (4) Timetable

The timetable referred to in paragraph (3) shall take into consideration the availability to the State of funds under section 300j–12 of this title (relating to State loan funds) for assessments and other relevant factors. The Administrator may extend any timetable included in a State program approved under paragraph (3) to extend the period for completion by an additional 18 months.

#### (5) Demonstration project

The Administrator shall, as soon as practicable, conduct a demonstration project, in consultation with other Federal agencies, to demonstrate the most effective and protective means of assessing and protecting source waters serving large metropolitan areas and located on Federal lands.

#### (6) Use of other programs

To avoid duplication and to encourage efficiency, the program under this section may make use of any of the following:

(A) Vulnerability assessments, sanitary surveys, and monitoring programs.

(B) Delineations or assessments of ground water sources under a State wellhead protection program developed pursuant to this section.

(C) Delineations or assessments of surface or ground water sources under a State pesticide management plan developed pursuant to the Pesticide and Ground Water State Management Plan Regulation (subparts I and J of part 152 of title 40, Code of Federal Regulations), promulgated under section 136a(d) of Title 7.

(D) Delineations or assessments of surface water sources under a State watershed initiative or to satisfy the watershed criterion for determining if filtration is required under the Surface Water Treatment Rule (section 141.70 of title 40, Code of Federal Regulations).

(E) Delineations or assessments of surface or ground water sources under programs or plans pursuant to the Federal Water Pollution Control Act [33 U.S.C.A. § 1251 et seq.].

**(7) Public availability**

The State shall make the results of the source water assessments conducted under this subsection available to the public.

**(b) Approval and disapproval**

For provisions relating to program approval and disapproval, see section 300h–7(c) of this title.

(July 1, 1944, c. 373, Title XIV, § 1453, as added Aug. 6, 1996, Pub.L. 104–182, Title I, § 132(a), 110 Stat. 1673.)

### HISTORICAL AND STATUTORY NOTES

**References in Text**

The Federal Water Pollution Control Act, referred to in subsec. (a)(6)(E), is Act June 30, 1948, c. 758, 62 Stat. 155, as amended, also known as the Clean Water Act, which is classified generally to chapter 26 (section 1251 et seq.) of Title 33, Navigation and Navigable Waters. For complete classification of this Act to the Code, see Short Title note set out under section 1251 of Title 33 and Tables.

**Effective and Applicability Provisions**

1996 Acts

Section effective Aug. 6, 1996, except as otherwise specifically provided, see section 2(b) of Pub.L. 104–182, set out as a note under section 300f of this title.

## § 300j–14. Source water petition program [PHSA § 1454]

**(a) Petition program**

**(1) In general**

**(A) Establishment**

A State may establish a program under which an owner or operator of a community water system in the State, or a municipal or local government or political subdivision of a State, may submit a source water quality protection partnership petition to the State requesting that the State assist in the local development of a voluntary, incentive-based partnership, among the owner, operator, or government and other persons likely to be affected by the recommendations of the partnership, to—

**(i)** reduce the presence in drinking water of contaminants that may be addressed by a petition by considering the origins of the contaminants, including to the maximum extent practicable the specific activities that affect the drinking water supply of a community;

**(ii)** obtain financial or technical assistance necessary to facilitate establishment of a partnership, or to develop and implement recommendations of a partnership for the protection of source water to assist in the provision of drinking water that complies with national primary drinking water regulations with respect to contaminants addressed by a petition; and

**(iii)** develop recommendations regarding voluntary and incentive-based strategies for the long-term protection of the source water of community water systems.

**(B) Funding**

Each State may—

**(i)** use funds set aside pursuant to section 300j–12(k)(1)(A)(iii) of this title by the State to carry out a program described in subparagraph (A), including assistance to voluntary local partnerships for the development and implementation of partnership recommendations for the protection of source water such as source water quality assessment, contingency plans, and demonstration projects for partners within a source water area delineated under section 300j–13(a) of this title; and

**(ii)** provide assistance in response to a petition submitted under this subsection using funds referred to in subsection (b)(2)(B) of this section.

**(2) Objectives**

The objectives of a petition submitted under this subsection shall be to—

**(A)** facilitate the local development of voluntary, incentive-based partnerships among owners and operators of community water systems, governments, and other persons in source water areas; and

**(B)** obtain assistance from the State in identifying resources which are available to implement the recommendations of the partnerships to address the origins of drinking water contaminants that may be addressed by a petition (including to the maximum extent practicable the specific activities contributing to the presence of the contaminants) that affect the drinking water supply of a community.

**(3) Contaminants addressed by a petition**

A petition submitted to a State under this subsection may address only those contaminants—

**(A)** that are pathogenic organisms for which a national primary drinking water regulation has been established or is required under section 300g–1 of this title; or

**(B)** for which a national primary drinking water regulation has been promulgated or proposed and that are detected by adequate monitoring methods in the source water at the intake structure or in any collection, treatment, storage, or distribution facilities by the community water systems at levels—

(i) above the maximum contaminant level; or

(ii) that are not reliably and consistently below the maximum contaminant level.

**(4) Contents**

A petition submitted under this subsection shall, at a minimum—

**(A)** include a delineation of the source water area in the State that is the subject of the petition;

**(B)** identify, to the maximum extent practicable, the origins of the drinking water contaminants that may be addressed by a petition (including to the maximum extent practicable the specific activities contributing to the presence of the contaminants) in the source water area delineated under section 300j–13 of this title;

**(C)** identify any deficiencies in information that will impair the development of recommendations by the voluntary local partnership to address drinking water contaminants that may be addressed by a petition;

**(D)** specify the efforts made to establish the voluntary local partnership and obtain the participation of—

(i) the municipal or local government or other political subdivision of the State with jurisdiction over the source water area delineated under section 300j–13 of this title; and

(ii) each person in the source water area delineated under section 300j–13 of this title—

(I) who is likely to be affected by recommendations of the voluntary local partnership; and

(II) whose participation is essential to the success of the partnership;

**(E)** outline how the voluntary local partnership has or will, during development and implementation of recommendations of the voluntary local partnership, identify, recognize and take into account any voluntary or other activities already being undertaken by persons in the source water area delineated under section 300j–13 of this title under Federal or State law to reduce the likelihood that contaminants will occur in drinking water at levels of public health concern; and

**(F)** specify the technical, financial, or other assistance that the voluntary local partnership requests of the State to develop the partnership or to implement recommendations of the partnership.

**(b) Approval or disapproval of petitions**

**(1) In general**

After providing notice and an opportunity for public comment on a petition submitted under subsection (a) of this section, the State shall approve or disapprove the petition, in whole or in part, not later than 120 days after the date of submission of the petition.

**(2) Approval**

The State may approve a petition if the petition meets the requirements established under subsection (a) of this section. The notice of approval shall, at a minimum, include for informational purposes—

**(A)** an identification of technical, financial, or other assistance that the State will provide to assist in addressing the drinking water contaminants that may be addressed by a petition based on—

(i) the relative priority of the public health concern identified in the petition with respect to the other water quality needs identified by the State;

(ii) any necessary coordination that the State will perform of the program established under this section with programs implemented or planned by other States under this section; and

(iii) funds available (including funds available from a State revolving loan fund established under title VI of the Federal Water Pollution Control Act (33 U.S.C. 1381 et seq.)) or section 300j–12 of this title;

**(B)** a description of technical or financial assistance pursuant to Federal and State programs that is available to assist in implementing recommendations of the partnership in the petition, including—

(i) any program established under the Federal Water Pollution Control Act (33 U.S.C. 1251 et seq.);

(ii) the program established under section 1455b of Title 16;

(iii) the agricultural water quality protection program established under chapter 2 of subtitle D of title XII of the Food Security Act of 1985 (16 U.S.C. 3838 et seq.);

(iv) the sole source aquifer protection program established under section 300h–6 of this title;

(v) the community wellhead protection program established under section 300h–7 of this title;

(vi) any pesticide or ground water management plan;

(vii) any voluntary agricultural resource management plan or voluntary whole farm or whole ranch management plan developed and implemented under a process established by the Secretary of Agriculture; and

(viii) any abandoned well closure program; and

(C) a description of activities that will be undertaken to coordinate Federal and State programs to respond to the petition.

(3) **Disapproval**

If the State disapproves a petition submitted under subsection (a) of this section, the State shall notify the entity submitting the petition in writing of the reasons for disapproval. A petition may be resubmitted at any time if—

(A) new information becomes available;

(B) conditions affecting the source water that is the subject of the petition change; or

(C) modifications are made in the type of assistance being requested.

(c) **Grants to support State programs**

(1) **In general**

The Administrator may make a grant to each State that establishes a program under this section that is approved under paragraph (2). The amount of each grant shall not exceed 50 percent of the cost of administering the program for the year in which the grant is available.

(2) **Approval**

In order to receive grant assistance under this subsection, a State shall submit to the Administrator for approval a plan for a source water quality protection partnership program that is consistent with the guidance published under subsection (d) of this section. The Administrator shall approve the plan if the plan is consistent with the guidance published under subsection (d) of this section.

(d) **Guidance**

(1) **In general**

Not later than 1 year after August 6, 1996, the Administrator, in consultation with the States, shall publish guidance to assist—

(A) States in the development of a source water quality protection partnership program; and

(B) municipal or local governments or political subdivisions of a State and community water systems in the development of source water quality protection partnerships and in the assessment of source water quality.

(2) **Contents of the guidance**

The guidance shall, at a minimum—

(A) recommend procedures for the approval or disapproval by a State of a petition submitted under subsection (a) of this section;

(B) recommend procedures for the submission of petitions developed under subsection (a) of this section;

(C) recommend criteria for the assessment of source water areas within a State; and

(D) describe technical or financial assistance pursuant to Federal and State programs that is available to address the contamination of sources of drinking water and to develop and respond to petitions submitted under subsection (a) of this section.

(e) **Authorization of appropriations**

There are authorized to be appropriated to carry out this section $5,000,000 for each of the fiscal years 1997 through 2003. Each State with a plan for a program approved under subsection (b) of this section shall receive an equitable portion of the funds available for any fiscal year.

(f) **Statutory construction**

Nothing in this section—

(1)(A) creates or conveys new authority to a State, political subdivision of a State, or community water system for any new regulatory measure; or

(B) limits any authority of a State, political subdivision, or community water system; or

(2) precludes a community water system, municipal or local government, or political subdivision of a government from locally developing and carrying out a voluntary, incentive-based, source water quality protection partnership to address the origins of drinking water contaminants of public health concern.

(July 1, 1944, c. 373, Title XIV, § 1454, as added Aug. 6, 1996, Pub.L. 104–182, Title I, § 133(a), 110 Stat. 1675.)

### HISTORICAL AND STATUTORY NOTES

**References in Text**

The Federal Water Pollution Control Act, referred to in subsec. (b)(2)(A)(iii) and (B)(i), is Act June 30, 1948, c. 758, 62 Stat. 1155, as amended, also known as the Clean Water Act, which is classified generally to chapter 26 (section 1251 et seq.) of Title 33, Navigation and Navigable Waters. Title VI of such Act is classified to subchapter VI (section 1381 et seq.) of chapter 26 of Title 33. For complete classification of this Act to the Code, see Short Title note set out under section 1251 of Title 33 and Tables.

Chapter 2 of Subtitle D of Title XII of the Food Security Act of 1985, referred to in subsec. (b)(2)(B)(iii), is section 1238 et seq. of Title XII of Pub.L. 99–198, as added, which is classified generally to part II (section 3838 et seq.) of subchapter IV of chapter 58 of Title 16, Conservation.

**Effective and Applicability Provisions**

1996 Acts

Section effective Aug. 6, 1996, except as otherwise specifically provided, see section 2(b) of Pub.L. 104–182, set out as a note under section 300f of this title.

## § 300j–15. Water conservation plan

**[PHSA § 1455]**

(a) **Guidelines**

Not later than 2 years after August 6, 1996, the Administrator shall publish in the Federal Register guidelines for water conservation plans for public water systems serving fewer than 3,300 persons, public water systems serving between 3,300 and 10,000 persons, and public water systems serving more than 10,000 persons, taking into consideration such factors as water availability and climate.

**(b) Loans or grants**

Within 1 year after publication of the guidelines under subsection (a) of this section, a State exercising primary enforcement responsibility for public water systems may require a public water system, as a condition of receiving a loan or grant from a State loan fund under section 300j–12 of this title, to submit with its application for such loan or grant a water conservation plan consistent with such guidelines.

(July 1, 1944, c. 373, Title XIV, § 1455, as added Aug. 6, 1996, Pub.L. 104–182, Title I, § 134, 110 Stat. 1679.)

### HISTORICAL AND STATUTORY NOTES

**Effective and Applicability Provisions**

1996 Acts

Section effective Aug. 6, 1996, except as otherwise specifically provided, see section 2(b) of Pub.L. 104–182, set out as a note under section 300f of this title.

## § 300j–16. Assistance to colonias

[PHSA § 1456]

**(a) Definitions**

As used in this section:

**(1) Border State**

The term "border State" means Arizona, California, New Mexico, and Texas.

**(2) Eligible community**

The term "eligible community" means a low-income community with economic hardship that—

(A) is commonly referred to as a colonia;

(B) is located along the United States–Mexico border (generally in an unincorporated area); and

(C) lacks a safe drinking water supply or adequate facilities for the provision of safe drinking water for human consumption.

**(b) Grants to alleviate health risks**

The Administrator of the Environmental Protection Agency and the heads of other appropriate Federal agencies are authorized to award grants to a border State to provide assistance to eligible communities to facilitate compliance with national primary drinking water regulations or otherwise significantly further the health protection objectives of this subchapter.

**(c) Use of funds**

Each grant awarded pursuant to subsection (b) of this section shall be used to provide assistance to one or more eligible communities with respect to which the residents are subject to a significant health risk (as determined by the Administrator or the head of the Federal agency making the grant) attributable to the lack of access to an adequate and affordable drinking water supply system.

**(d) Cost sharing**

The amount of a grant awarded pursuant to this section shall not exceed 50 percent of the costs of carrying out the project that is the subject of the grant.

**(e) Authorization of appropriations**

There are authorized to be appropriated to carry out this section $25,000,000 for each of the fiscal years 1997 through 1999.

(July 1, 1944, c. 373, Title XIV, § 1456, as added Aug. 6, 1996, Pub.L. 104–182, Title I, § 135, 110 Stat. 1679.)

### HISTORICAL AND STATUTORY NOTES

**Effective and Applicability Provisions**

1996 Acts

Section effective Aug. 6, 1996, except as otherwise specifically provided, see section 2(b) of Pub.L. 104–182, set out as a note under section 300f of this title.

## § 300j–17. Estrogenic substances screening program

[PHSA § 1457]

In addition to the substances referred to in section 346a(p)(3)(B) of Title 21 the Administrator may provide for testing under the screening program authorized by section 346a(p) of Title 21, in accordance with the provisions of section 346a(p) of Title 21, of any other substance that may be found in sources of drinking water if the Administrator determines that a substantial population may be exposed to such substance.

(July 1, 1994, c. 373, Title XIV, § 1457, as added Aug. 6, 1996, Pub.L. 104–182, Title I, § 136, 110 Stat. 1680.)

### HISTORICAL AND STATUTORY NOTES

**Effective and Applicability Provisions**

1996 Acts

Section effective Aug. 6, 1996, except as otherwise specifically provided, see section 2(b) of Pub.L. 104–182, set out as a note under section 300f of this title.

## § 300j–18. Drinking water studies

[PHSA § 1458]

**(a) Subpopulations at greater risk**

### (1) In general

The Administrator shall conduct a continuing program of studies to identify groups within the general population that may be at greater risk than the general population of adverse health effects from exposure to contaminants in drinking water. The study shall examine whether and to what degree infants, children, pregnant women, the elderly, individuals with a history of serious illness, or other subpopulations that can be identified and characterized are likely to experience elevated health risks, including risks of cancer, from contaminants in drinking water.

### (2) Report

Not later than 4 years after August 6, 1996, and periodically thereafter as new and significant information becomes available, the Administrator shall report to the Congress on the results of the studies.

## (b) Biological mechanisms

The Administrator shall conduct biomedical studies to—

(1) understand the mechanisms by which chemical contaminants are absorbed, distributed, metabolized, and eliminated from the human body, so as to develop more accurate physiologically based models of the phenomena;

(2) understand the effects of contaminants and the mechanisms by which the contaminants cause adverse effects (especially noncancer and infectious effects) and the variations in the effects among humans, especially subpopulations at greater risk of adverse effects, and between test animals and humans; and

(3) develop new approaches to the study of complex mixtures, such as mixtures found in drinking water, especially to determine the prospects for synergistic or antagonistic interactions that may affect the shape of the dose-response relationship of the individual chemicals and microbes, and to examine noncancer endpoints and infectious diseases, and susceptible individuals and subpopulations.

## (c) Studies on harmful substances in drinking water

### (1) Development of studies

The Administrator shall, not later than 180 days after August 6, 1996, and after consultation with the Secretary of Health and Human Services, the Secretary of Agriculture, and, as appropriate, the heads of other Federal agencies, conduct the studies described in paragraph (2) to support the development and implementation of the most current version of each of the following:

(A) Enhanced Surface Water Treatment Rule (59 Fed.Reg. 38832 (July 29, 1994)).

(B) Disinfectant and Disinfection Byproducts Rule (59 Fed.Reg. 38668 (July 29, 1994)).

(C) Ground Water Disinfection Rule (availability of draft summary announced at (57 Fed.Reg. 33960; July 31, 1992)).

### (2) Contents of studies

The studies required by paragraph (1) shall include, at a minimum, each of the following:

(A) Toxicological studies and, if warranted, epidemiological studies to determine what levels of exposure from disinfectants and disinfection byproducts, if any, may be associated with developmental and birth defects and other potential toxic end points.

(B) Toxicological studies and, if warranted, epidemiological studies to quantify the carcinogenic potential from exposure to disinfection byproducts resulting from different disinfectants.

(C) The development of dose-response curves for pathogens, including cryptosporidium and the Norwalk virus.

### (3) Authorization of appropriations

There are authorized to be appropriated to carry out this subsection $12,500,000 for each of fiscal years 1997 through 2003.

## (d) Waterborne disease occurrence study

### (1) System

The Director of the Centers for Disease Control and Prevention, and the Administrator shall jointly—

(A) within 2 years after August 6, 1996, conduct pilot waterborne disease occurrence studies for at least 5 major United States communities or public water systems; and

(B) within 5 years after August 6, 1996, prepare a report on the findings of the pilot studies, and a national estimate of waterborne disease occurrence.

### (2) Training and education

The Director and Administrator shall jointly establish a national health care provider training and public education campaign to inform both the professional health care provider community and the general public about waterborne disease and the symptoms that may be caused by infectious agents, including microbial contaminants. In developing such a campaign, they shall seek comment from interested groups and individuals, including scientists, physicians, State and local governments, environmental groups, public water systems, and vulnerable populations.

**(3) Funding**

There are authorized to be appropriated for each of the fiscal years 1997 through 2001, $3,000,000 to carry out this subsection. To the extent funds under this subsection are not fully appropriated, the Administrator may use not more than $2,000,000 of the funds from amounts reserved under section 300j–12(n) of this title for health effects studies for purposes of this subsection. The Administrator may transfer a portion of such funds to the Centers for Disease Control and Prevention for such purposes.

(July 1, 1944, c. 373, Title XIV, § 1458, as added Aug. 6, 1996, Pub.L. 104–182, Title I, § 137, 110 Stat. 1680.)

### HISTORICAL AND STATUTORY NOTES

**Effective and Applicability Provisions**

1996 Acts

Section effective Aug. 6, 1996, except as otherwise specifically provided, see section 2(b) of Pub.L. 104–182, set out as a note under section 300f of this title.

**Public Health Assessment of Exposure to Perchlorate**

Pub.L. 108–136, Div. A, Title III, § 323, Nov. 24, 2003, 117 Stat. 1440, provided that:

"(a) **Epidemiological study of exposure to perchlorate.**—The Secretary of Defense shall provide for an independent epidemiological study of exposure to perchlorate in drinking water. The entity conducting the study shall—

"(1) assess the incidence of thyroid disease and measurable effects of thyroid function in relation to exposure to perchlorate;

"(2) ensure that the study is of sufficient scope and scale to permit the making of meaningful conclusions of the measurable public health threat associated with exposure to perchlorate, especially the threat to sensitive subpopulations; and

"(3) examine thyroid function, including measurements of urinary iodine and thyroid hormone levels, in a sufficient number of pregnant women, neonates, and infants exposed to perchlorate in drinking water and match measurements of perchlorate levels in the drinking water of each study participant in order to permit the development of meaningful conclusions on the public health threat to individuals exposed to perchlorate.

"(b) **Review of effects of perchlorate on endocrine system.**—The Secretary shall provide for an independent review of the effects of perchlorate on the human endocrine system. The entity conducting the review shall assess—

"(1) available data on human exposure to perchlorate, including clinical data and data on exposure of sensitive subpopulations, and the levels at which health effects were observed; and

"(2) available data on other substances that have endocrine effects similar to perchlorate to which the public is frequently exposed.

"(c) **Performance of study and review.**—(1) The Secretary shall provide for the performance of the study under subsection (a) [of this note] through the Centers for Disease Control and Prevention, the National Institutes of Health, or another Federal entity with experience in environmental toxicology selected by the Secretary.

"(2) The Secretary shall provide for the performance of the review under subsection (b) [of this note] through the Centers for Disease Control and Prevention, the National Institutes of Health, or another appropriate Federal research entity with experience in human endocrinology selected by the Secretary. The Secretary shall ensure that the panel conducting the review is composed of individuals with expertise in human endocrinology.

"(d) **Reporting requirements.**—Not later than June 1, 2005, the Federal entities conducting the study and review under this section [this note] shall submit to the Secretary reports containing the results of the study and review."

## Part F—Additional Requirements to Regulate Safety of Drinking Water

## § 300j–21. Definitions

**[PHSA § 1461]**

As used in this part—

**(1) Drinking water cooler**

The term "drinking water cooler" means any mechanical device affixed to drinking water supply plumbing which actively cools water for human consumption.

**(2) Lead free**

The term "lead free" means, with respect to a drinking water cooler, that each part or component of the cooler which may come in contact with drinking water contains not more than 8 percent lead, except that no drinking water cooler which contains any solder, flux, or storage tank interior surface which may come in contact with drinking water shall be considered lead free if the solder, flux, or storage tank interior surface contains more than 0.2 percent lead. The Administrator may establish more stringent requirements for treating any part or component of a drinking water cooler as lead free for purposes of this part whenever he determines that any such part may constitute an important source of lead in drinking water.

**(3) Local educational agency**

The term "local educational agency" means—

(A) any local educational agency as defined in section 7801 of Title 20,

(B) the owner of any private, nonprofit elementary or secondary school building, and

(C) the governing authority of any school operating under the defense dependent's education system provided for under the Defense Dependent's Education Act of 1978 (20 U.S.C. 921 and following).

**(4) Repair**

The term "repair" means, with respect to a drinking water cooler, to take such corrective action as is necessary to ensure that water cooler is lead free.

**(5) Replacement**

The term "replacement", when used with respect to a drinking water cooler, means the permanent removal of the water cooler and the installation of a lead free water cooler.

**(6) School**

The term "school" means any elementary school or secondary school as defined in section 7801 of Title 20 and any kindergarten or day care facility.

**(7) Lead-lined tank**

The term "lead-lined tank" means a water reservoir container in a drinking water cooler which container is constructed of lead or which has an interior surface which is not lead free.

(July 1, 1944, c. 373, Title XIV, § 1461, as added Oct. 31, 1988, Pub.L. 100–572, § 2(a), 102 Stat. 2884, and amended Oct. 20, 1994, Pub.L. 103–382, Title III, § 391(p), 108 Stat. 4024; Aug. 6, 1996, Pub.L. 104–182, Title V, § 501(f)(7), 110 Stat. 1692, Jan. 8, 2002, Pub.L. 107–110, Title X, § 1076(x), 115 Stat. 2093.)

### HISTORICAL AND STATUTORY NOTES

**References in Text**

The Defense Dependent's Education Act of 1978, referred to in par. (3)(C), probably means the Defense Dependents' Education Act of 1978, Title XIV of Pub.L. 95–561, Nov. 1, 1978, 92 Stat. 2365, as amended, which is classified principally to chapter 25A (§ 921 et seq.) of Title 20. For complete classification of this Act to the Code, see Short Title note set out under section 921 of Title 20 and Tables.

**Codifications**

Section 391(p) of Pub.L. 103–382 directed amendment of "section 1461 of the Safe Water Drinking Act (42 U.S.C. 300j–21(6))", section 1461 is classified to this section, section 1461(6) is classified to par. (6) of this section. Par. (1) of section 391(p) of Pub.L. 103–382 directed amendment of subpar. (A) of par. (3), which was executed to subpar. (A) of par. (3) of this section as the probable intent of Congress.

**Effective and Applicability Provisions**

2002 Acts

Except as otherwise provided, amendments by Pub.L. 107–110 effective Jan. 8, 2002, see Pub.L. 107–110, § 5, set out as a note under 20 U.S.C.A. § 6301.

1996 Acts

Amendment by Pub.L. 104–182 effective Aug. 6, 1996, except as otherwise specifically provided, see section 2(b) of Pub.L. 104–182, set out as a note under section 300f of this title.

## § 300j–22. Recall of drinking water coolers with lead-lined tanks

**[PHSA § 1462]**

For purposes of the Consumer Product Safety Act [15 U.S.C.A. § 2051 et seq.], all drinking water coolers identified by the Administrator on the list under section 300j–23 of this title as having a lead-lined tank shall be considered to be imminently hazardous consumer products within the meaning of section 12 of such Act [15 U.S.C.A. § 2061]. After notice and opportunity for comment, including a public hearing, the Consumer Product Safety Commission shall issue an order requiring the manufacturers and importers of such coolers to repair, replace, or recall and provide a refund for such coolers within 1 year after October 31, 1988. For purposes of enforcement, such order shall be treated as an order under section 15(d) of that Act) [15 U.S.C.A. § 2064(d)].

(July 1, 1944, c. 373, Title XIV, § 1462, as added Oct. 31, 1988, Pub.L. 100–572, § 2(a), 102 Stat. 2885, and amended Aug. 6, 1996, Pub.L. 104–182, Title V, § 501(f)(8), 110 Stat. 1692.)

### HISTORICAL AND STATUTORY NOTES

**References in Text**

The Consumer Product Safety Act, referred to in text, is Pub.L. 92–573, Oct. 27, 1972, 86 Stat. 1207, as amended, which is classified generally to chapter 47 (section 2051 et seq.) of Title 15, Commerce and Trade. For complete classification of this Act to the Code, see Short Title note set out under section 2051 of Title 15 and Tables.

**Effective and Applicability Provisions**

1996 Acts

Amendment by Pub.L. 104–182 effective Aug. 6, 1996, except as otherwise specifically provided, see section 2(b) of Pub.L. 104–182, set out as a note under section 300f of this title.

## § 300j–23. Drinking water coolers containing lead

**[PHSA § 1463]**

**(a) Publication of lists**

The Administrator shall, after notice and opportunity for public comment, identify each brand and model of drinking water cooler which is not lead free, including each brand and model of drinking water cooler which has a lead-lined tank. For purposes of identifying the brand and model of drinking water coolers under this subsection, the Administrator shall use the best information available to the Environmental Protection Agency. Within 100 days after October 31, 1988, the Administrator shall publish a list of each brand and model of drinking water cooler identified under this subsection. Such list shall separately identify each brand and model of cooler which has a lead-lined tank. The Administrator shall continue to gather information regarding lead in drinking water coolers and shall revise and republish the list from time to time as may be appropriate as new information or analysis becomes available regarding lead contamination in drinking water coolers.

**(b) Prohibition**

No person may sell in interstate commerce, or manufacture for sale in interstate commerce, any drinking water cooler listed under subsection (a) of this section or any other drinking water cooler which is not lead free, including a lead-lined drinking water cooler.

**(c) Criminal penalty**

Any person who knowingly violates the prohibition contained in subsection (b) of this section shall be imprisoned for not more than 5 years, or fined in accordance with Title 18, or both.

**(d) Civil penalty**

The Administrator may bring a civil action in the appropriate United States District Court (as determined under the provisions of Title 28) to impose a civil penalty on any person who violates subsection (b) of this section. In any such action the court may impose on such person a civil penalty of not more than $5,000 ($50,000 in the case of a second or subsequent violation).

(July 1, 1944, c. 373, Title XIV, § 1463, as added Oct. 31, 1988, Pub.L. 100–572, § 2(a), 102 Stat. 2885, and amended Aug. 6, 1996, Pub.L. 104–182, Title V, § 501(f)(9), 110 Stat. 1692.)

### HISTORICAL AND STATUTORY NOTES

**Effective and Applicability Provisions**

1996 Acts

Amendment by Pub.L. 104–182 effective Aug. 6, 1996, except as otherwise specifically provided, see section 2(b) of Pub.L. 104–182, set out as a note under section 300f of this title.

## § 300j–24. Lead contamination in school drinking water

**[PHSA § 1464]**

**(a) Distribution of drinking water cooler list**

Within 100 days after October 31, 1988, the Administrator shall distribute to the States a list of each brand and model of drinking water cooler identified and listed by the Administrator under section 300j–23(a) of this title.

**(b) Guidance document and testing protocol**

The Administrator shall publish a guidance document and a testing protocol to assist schools in determining the source and degree of lead contamination in school drinking water supplies and in remedying such contamination. The guidance document shall include guidelines for sample preservation. The guidance document shall also include guidance to assist States, schools, and the general public in ascertaining the levels of lead contamination in drinking water coolers and in taking appropriate action to reduce or eliminate such contamination. The guidance document shall contain a testing protocol for the identification of drinking water coolers which contribute to lead contamination in drinking water. Such document and protocol may be revised, republished and redistributed as the Administrator deems necessary. The Administrator shall distribute the guidance document and testing protocol to the States within 100 days after October 31, 1988.

**(c) Dissemination to schools, etc.**

Each State shall provide for the dissemination to local educational agencies, private nonprofit elementary or secondary schools and to day care centers of the guidance document and testing protocol published under subsection (b) of this section, together with the list of drinking water coolers published under section 300j–23(a) of this title.

**(d) Remedial action program**

**(1) Testing and remedying lead contamination**

Within 9 months after October 31, 1988, each State shall establish a program, consistent with this section, to assist local educational agencies in testing for, and remedying, lead contamination in drinking water from coolers and from other sources of lead contamination at schools under the jurisdiction of such agencies.

**(2) Public availability**

A copy of the results of any testing under paragraph (1) shall be available in the administrative offices of the local educational agency for inspection by the public, including teachers, other school personnel, and parents. The local educational agency shall notify parent, teacher, and employee organizations of the availability of such testing results.

**(3) Coolers**

In the case of drinking water coolers, such program shall include measures for the reduction or elimination of lead contamination from those water coolers which are not lead free and which are located in schools. Such measures shall be adequate to ensure that within 15 months after October 31, 1988, all such water coolers in schools under the jurisdiction of such agencies are repaired, replaced, permanently removed, or rendered inoperable unless the cooler is tested and found (within the limits of testing accuracy) not to contribute lead to drinking water.

(July 1, 1944, c. 373, Title XIV, § 1464, as added Oct. 31, 1988, Pub.L. 100–572, § 2(a), 102 Stat. 2886, and amended Aug. 6, 1996, Pub.L. 104–182, Title V, § 501(f)(10), 110 Stat. 1692.)

### HISTORICAL AND STATUTORY NOTES

**Effective and Applicability Provisions**

1996 Acts

Amendment by Pub.L. 104–182 effective Aug. 6, 1996, except as otherwise specifically provided, see section 2(b) of Pub.L. 104–182, set out as a note under section 300f of this title.

## § 300j–25. Federal assistance for State programs regarding lead contamination in school drinking water

**[PHSA § 1465]**

**(a) School drinking water programs**

The Administrator shall make grants to States to establish and carry out State programs under section 300j–24 of this title to assist local educational agencies in testing for, and remedying, lead contamination in drinking water from drinking water coolers and from other sources of lead contamination at schools under the jurisdiction of such agencies. Such grants may be used by States to reimburse local educational agencies for expenses incurred after October 31, 1988, for such testing and remedial action.

**(b) Limits**

Each grant under this section shall be used by the State for testing water coolers in accordance with section 300j–24 of this title, for testing for lead contamination in other drinking water supplies under section 300j–24 of this title, or for remedial action under State programs under section 300j–24 of this title. Not more than 5 percent of the grant may be used for program administration.

**(c) Authorization of appropriations**

There are authorized to be appropriated to carry out this section not more than $30,000,000 for fiscal year 1989, $30,000,000 for fiscal year 1990, and $30,000,000 for fiscal year 1991.

(July 1, 1944, c. 373, Title XIV, § 1465, as added Oct. 31, 1988, Pub.L. 100–572, § 2(a), 102 Stat. 2887, and amended Aug. 6, 1996, Pub.L. 104–182, Title V, § 501(d), (f)(11), 110 Stat. 1691, 1692.)

### HISTORICAL AND STATUTORY NOTES

**Effective and Applicability Provisions**

1996 Acts

Amendment by Pub.L. 104–182 effective Aug. 6, 1996, except as otherwise specifically provided, see section 2(b) of Pub.L. 104–182, set out as a note under section 300f of this title.

## § 300j–26. Certification of testing laboratories

The Administrator of the Environmental Protection Agency shall assure that programs for the certification of testing laboratories which test drinking water supplies for lead contamination certify only those laboratories which provide reliable accurate testing. The Administrator (or the State in the case of a State to which certification authority is delegated under this subsection [1]) shall publish and make available to the public upon request the list of laboratories certified under this subsection [1].

(Pub.L. 100–572, § 4, Oct. 31, 1988, 102 Stat. 2889.)

[1] So in original. Probably should be "section".

### HISTORICAL AND STATUTORY NOTES

**Codifications**

Section enacted as part of the Lead Contamination Control Act of 1988, and not as part of the Public Health Service Act, which comprises this chapter, or of the Safe Drinking Water Act, which comprises this subchapter.

# DEVELOPMENT AND CONTROL OF ATOMIC ENERGY

## ATOMIC ENERGY ACT OF 1954 [AEA § ______]

## LOW–LEVEL RADIOACTIVE WASTE POLICY ACT [LLRWPA § ______]

**(42 U.S.C.A. §§ 2014, 2021 to 2021j, 2022, 2111, 2113, 2114)**

## CHAPTER 23—DEVELOPMENT AND CONTROL OF ATOMIC ENERGY

DIVISION A—ATOMIC ENERGY

SUBCHAPTER I—GENERAL PROVISIONS



SUBCHAPTER VII—BYPRODUCT MATERIALS



DIVISION A—ATOMIC ENERGY

SUBCHAPTER I—GENERAL PROVISIONS

### § 2014. Definitions

**[AEA § 11]**

The intent of Congress in the definitions as given in this section should be construed from the words or phrases used in the definitions. As used in this chapter:

**(a)** The term "agency of the United States" means the executive branch of the United States, or any Government agency, or the legislative branch of the United States, or any agency, committee, commission, office, or other establishment in the legislative branch, or the judicial branch of the United States, or any office, agency, committee, commission, or other establishment in the judicial branch.

**(b)** The term "agreement for cooperation" means any agreement with another nation or regional defense organization authorized or permitted by sections 2074, 2077, 2094, 2112, 2121(c), 2133, 2134, or 2164 of this title, and made pursuant to section 2153 of this title.

**(c)** The term "atomic energy" means all forms of energy released in the course of nuclear fission or nuclear transformation.

**(d)** The term "atomic weapon" means any device utilizing atomic energy, exclusive of the means for transporting or propelling the device (where such means is a separable and divisible part of the device), the principal purpose of which is for use as, or for development of, a weapon, a weapon prototype, or a weapon test device.

**(e)** The term "byproduct material" means (1) any radioactive material (except special nuclear material) yielded in or made radioactive by exposure to the radiation incident to the process of producing or utilizing special nuclear material, and (2) the tailings or wastes produced by the extraction or concentration of uranium or thorium from any ore processed primarily for its source material content.

**(f)** The term "Commission" means the Atomic Energy Commission.

**(g)** The term "common defense and security" means the common defense and security of the United States.

**(h)** The term "defense information" means any information in any category determined by any Government agency authorized to classify information, as being information respecting, relating to, or affecting the national defense.

**(i)** The term "design" means (1) specifications, plans, drawings, blueprints, and other items of like nature; (2) the information contained therein; or (3) the research and development data pertinent to the information contained therein.

**(j)** The term "extraordinary nuclear occurrence" means any event causing a discharge or dispersal of source, special nuclear, or byproduct material from its intended place of confinement in amounts offsite, or causing radiation levels offsite, which the Nuclear Regulatory Commission or the Secretary of Energy, as appropriate, determines to be substantial, and which the Nuclear Regulatory Commission or the Secretary of Energy, as appropriate, determines has resulted or will probably result in substantial damages to persons offsite or property offsite. Any determination by the Nuclear Regulatory Commission or the Secretary of Energy, as appropriate, that such an event has, or has not, occurred shall be final and conclusive, and no other official or any court shall have power or jurisdiction to review any such determination. The Nuclear Regulatory Commission or the Secretary of Energy, as appropriate, shall establish criteria in writing setting forth the basis upon which such determination shall be made. As used in this subsection, "offsite" means away from "the location" or "the contract location" as defined in the applicable Nuclear Regulatory Commission or the Secretary of Energy, as appropriate, indemnity agreement, entered into pursuant to section 2210 of this title.

**(k)** The term "financial protection" means the ability to respond in damages for public liability and to meet the costs of investigating and defending claims and settling suits for such damages.

**(*l*)** The term "Government agency" means any executive department, commission, independent establishment, corporation, wholly or partly owned by the United States of America which is an instrumentality of the United States, or any board, bureau, division, service, office, officer, authority, administration, or other establishment in the executive branch of the Government.

**(m)** The term "indemnitor" means (1) any insurer with respect to his obligations under a policy of insurance furnished as proof of financial protection; (2) any licensee, contractor or other person who is obligated under any other form of financial protection, with respect to such obligations; and (3) the Nuclear Regulatory Commission or the Secretary of Energy, as appropriate, with respect to any obligation undertaken by it in an indemnity agreement entered into pursuant to section 2210 of this title.

**(n)** The term "international arrangement" means any international agreement hereafter approved by the Congress or any treaty during the time such agreement or treaty is in full force and effect, but does not include any agreement for cooperation.

**(*o*)** The term "Energy Committees" means the Committee on Energy and Natural Resources of the Senate and the Committee on Energy and Commerce of the House of Representatives.

**(p)** The term "licensed activity" means an activity licensed pursuant to this chapter and covered by the provisions of section 2210(a) of this title.

**(q)** The term "nuclear incident" means any occurrence, including an extraordinary nuclear occurrence, within the United States causing, within or outside the United States, bodily injury, sickness, disease, or death, or loss of or damage to property, or loss of use of property, arising out of or resulting from the radioactive, toxic, explosive, or other hazardous properties of source, special nuclear, or byproduct material: *Provided, however,* That as the term is used in section 2210(*l*) of this title, it shall include any such occurrence outside the United States: *And provided further,* That as the term is used in section 2210(d) of this title, it shall include any such occurrence outside the United States if such occurrence involves source, special nuclear, or byproduct material owned by, and used by or under contract with, the United States: *And provided further,* That as the term is used in section 2210(c) of this title, it shall include any such occurrence outside both the United States and any other nation if such occurrence arises out of or results from the radioactive, toxic, explosive, or other hazardous properties of source, special nuclear, or byproduct material licensed pursuant to subchapters V, VI, VII, and IX of this division, which is used in connection with the operation of a licensed stationary production or utilization facility or which moves outside the territorial limits of the United States in transit from one person licensed by the Nuclear Regulatory Commission to another person licensed by the Nuclear Regulatory Commission.

**(r)** The term "operator" means any individual who manipulates the controls of a utilization or production facility.

**(s)** The term "person" means (1) any individual, corporation, partnership, firm, association, trust, estate, public or private institution, group, Government agency other than the Commission, any State or any political subdivision of, or any political entity within a State, any foreign government or nation or any political subdivision of any such government or nation, or other entity; and (2) any legal successor, representative, agent, or agency of the foregoing.

**(t)** The term "person indemnified" means (1) with respect to a nuclear incident occurring within the United States or outside the United States as the term is used in section 2210(c) of this title, and with respect to any nuclear incident in connection with the design, development, construction, operation, repair, maintenance, or use of the nuclear ship Savannah, the person with whom an indemnity agreement is executed or who is required to maintain financial protection, and any other person who may be liable for public liability or (2) with respect to any other nuclear incident occurring outside the United States, the person with whom an indemnity agreement is executed and any other person who may be liable for public liability by reason of his activities under any contract with the Secretary of Energy or any project to which indemnification under the provisions of section 2210(d) of this title has been extended or under any subcontract, purchase order, or other agreement, of any tier, under any such contract or project.

**(u)** The term "produce", when used in relation to special nuclear material, means (1) to manufacture, make, produce, or refine special nuclear material; (2) to separate special nuclear material from other substances in which such material may be contained; or (3) to make or to produce new special nuclear material.

**(v)** The term "production facility" means (1) any equipment or device determined by rule of the Commission to be capable of the production of special nuclear material in such quantity as to be of significance to the common defense and security, or in such manner as to affect the health and safety of the public; or (2) any important component part especially designed for such equipment or device as determined by the Commission. Except with respect to the export of a uranium enrichment production facility, such term as used in subchapters IX and XV of this division shall not include any equipment or device (or important component part especially designed for such equipment or device) capable of separating the isotopes of uranium or enriching uranium in the isotope 235.

**(w)** The term "public liability" means any legal liability arising out of or resulting from a nuclear incident or precautionary evacuation (including all reasonable additional costs incurred by a State, or a political subdivision of a State, in the course of responding to a nuclear incident or a precautionary evacuation), except: (i) claims under State or Federal workmen's compensation acts of employees of persons indemnified who are employed at the site of and in connection with the activity where the nuclear incident occurs; (ii) claims arising out of an act of war; and (iii) whenever used in subsections (a), (c), and (k) of section 2210 of this title, claims for loss of, or damage to, or loss of use of property which is located at the site of and used in connection with the licensed activity where the nuclear incident occurs. "Public liability" also includes damage to property of persons indemnified: *Provided,* That such property is covered under the terms of the financial protection required, except property which is located at the site of and used in connection with the activity where the nuclear incident occurs.

**(x)** The term "research and development" means (1) theoretical analysis, exploration, or experimentation; or (2) the extension of investigative findings and theories of a scientific or technical nature into practical application for experimental and demonstration purposes, including the experimental production and testing of models, devices, equipment, materials, and processes.

**(y)** The term "Restricted Data" means all data concerning (1) design, manufacture, or utilization of atomic weapons; (2) the production of special nuclear material; or (3) the use of special nuclear material in the production of energy, but shall not include data declassified or removed from the Restricted Data category pursuant to section 2162 of this title.

**(z)** The term "source material" means (1) uranium, thorium, or any other material which is determined by the Commission pursuant to the provisions of section 2091 of this title to be source material; or (2) ores containing one or more of the foregoing materials, in such concentration as the Commission may by regulation determine from time to time.

**(aa)** The term "special nuclear material" means (1) plutonium, uranium enriched in the isotope 233 or in the isotope 235, and any other material which the Commission, pursuant to the provisions of section 2071 of this title, determines to be special nuclear material, but does not include source material; or (2) any material artificially enriched by any of the foregoing, but does not include source material.

**(bb)** The term "United States" when used in a geographical sense includes all territories and possessions of the United States, the Canal Zone and Puerto Rico.

**(cc)** The term "utilization facility" means (1) any equipment or device, except an atomic weapon, determined by rule of the Commission to be capable of making use of special nuclear material in such quantity as to be of significance to the common defense and security, or in such manner as to affect the health and safety of the public, or peculiarly adapted for making use of atomic energy in such quantity as to be of significance to the common defense and security, or in such manner as to affect the health and safety of the public; or (2) any important component part especially designed for such equipment or device as determined by the Commission.

**(dd)** The terms "high-level radioactive waste" and "spent nuclear fuel" have the meanings given such terms in section 10101 of this title.

**(ee)** The term "transuranic waste" means material contaminated with elements that have an atomic number greater than 92, including neptunium, plutonium, americium, and curium, and that are in concentrations greater than 10 nanocuries per gram, or in such other concentrations as the Nuclear Regulatory Commission may prescribe to protect the public health and safety.

**(ff)** The term "nuclear waste activities", as used in section 2210 of this title, means activities subject to an agreement of indemnification under subsection (d) of such section, that the Secretary of Energy is authorized to undertake, under this chapter or any other law, involving the storage, handling, transportation, treatment, or disposal of, or research and development on, spent nuclear fuel, high-level radioactive waste, or transuranic waste, including (but not limited to) activities authorized to be carried out under the Waste Isolation Pilot Project under section 213 of Public Law 96–164 (93 Stat. 1265).

**(gg)** The term "precautionary evacuation" means an evacuation of the public within a specified area near a nuclear facility, or the transportation route in the case of an accident involving transportation of source material, special nuclear material, byproduct material, high-level radioactive waste, spent nuclear fuel, or transuranic waste to or from a production or utilization facility, if the evacuation is—

**(1)** the result of any event that is not classified as a nuclear incident but that poses imminent danger of bodily injury or property damage from the radiological properties of source material, special nuclear material, byproduct material, high-level radioactive waste, spent nuclear fuel, or transuranic waste, and causes an evacuation; and

**(2)** initiated by an official of a State or a political subdivision of a State, who is authorized by State law to initiate such an evacuation and who reasonably determined that such an evacuation was necessary to protect the public health and safety.

**(hh)** The term "public liability action", as used in section 2210 of this title, means any suit asserting public liability. A public liability action shall be deemed to be an action arising under section 2210 of this title, and the substantive rules for decision in such action shall be derived from the law of the State in which the nuclear incident involved occurs, unless such law is inconsistent with the provisions of such section.

**(jj)** [1] Legal Costs

As used in section 2210 of this title, the term "legal costs" means the costs incurred by a plaintiff or a defendant in initiating, prosecuting, investigating, settling, or defending claims or suits for damage arising under such section.

(Aug. 1, 1946, c. 724, Title I, § 11, as added Aug. 30, 1954, c. 1073, § 1, 68 Stat. 922, and amended Aug. 6, 1956, c. 1015, § 1, 70 Stat. 1069; Sept. 2, 1957, Pub.L. 85–256, § 3, 71 Stat. 576; Aug. 8, 1958, Pub.L. 85–602, § 1, 72 Stat. 525; Sept. 6, 1961, Pub.L. 87–206, §§ 2, 3, 75 Stat. 476; Aug. 29, 1962, Pub.L. 87–615, §§ 4, 5, 76 Stat. 410; Oct. 13, 1966, Pub.L. 89–645, § 1(a), 80 Stat. 891; Dec. 31, 1975, Pub.L. 94–197, § 1, 89 Stat. 1111; Nov. 8, 1978, Pub.L. 95–604, Title II, § 201, 92 Stat. 3033; Aug. 20, 1988, Pub.L. 100–408, §§ 4(b), 5(a), (b), 11(b), (d)(2), 16(a)(1), (b)(1), (2), (d)(1)–(3), 102 Stat. 1069, 1070, 1076, 1078–1080; Nov. 15, 1990, Pub.L. 101–575, § 5(a), 104 Stat. 2835; renumbered Title I, and amended Oct. 24, 1992, Pub.L. 102–486, Title IX, § 902(a)(8), Title XI, § 1102, 106 Stat. 2944, 2955; Nov. 2, 1994, Pub.L. 103–437, § 15(f)(1), 108 Stat. 4592; Apr. 26, 1996, Pub.L. 104–134, Title III, § 3116(b)(1), 110 Stat. 1321–349.)

[1] So in original. No subsec. (ii) has been enacted.

## HISTORICAL AND STATUTORY NOTES

### References in Text

The Waste Isolation Pilot Project under section 213 of Pub.L. 96–164, referred to in subsec. (ff), is the Waste Isolation Pilot Plant in the Delaware Basin of southeast New Mexico, authorized under Pub.L. 96–164, Title II, § 213, Dec. 29, 1979, 93 Stat. 1265. Section 213 of Pub.L. 96–164 was not classified to the Code.

### Codifications

Section 3116(b)(1) of Pub.L. 104–134, which directed that subsec. (v) of this section be amended by striking out "or the construction and operation of a uranium enrichment facility using Atomic Vapor Laser Isotope Separation technology", was executed, as the probable intent of Congress, by striking out "or the construction and operation of a uranium enrichment production facility using Atomic Vapor Laser Isotope Separation technology", as former phrase did not appear in text. See 1996 Amendments note set out under this section.

### Effective and Applicability Provisions

1988 Acts

Section 20 of Pub.L. 100–408 provided that:

"**(a)** Except as provided in subsection (b), the amendments made by this Act [enacting section 2282a of this title, amending this section and sections 2210 and 2273 of this title, and enacting provisions set out as notes under sections 2011 and 2210 of this title] shall become effective on the date of the enactment of this Act [Aug. 20, 1988] and shall be applicable with respect to nuclear incidents occurring on or after such date.

"**(b)(1)** The amendments made by section 11 [enacting subsec. (hh) and (jj) of this section and section 2210(m)(3) of this title and amending section 2210(m)(2) and (*o*) of this title] shall apply to nuclear incidents occurring before, on, or after the date of the enactment of this Act [Aug. 20, 1988].

"**(2)(A)** Section 234A of the Atomic Energy Act of 1954 [section 2282a of this title] shall not apply to any violation occurring before the date of the enactment of this Act [Aug. 20, 1988].

"**(B)** Section 223 c. of the Atomic Energy Act of 1954 [section 2273(c) of this title] shall not apply to any violation occurring before the date of enactment of this Act [Aug. 20, 1988]."

1978 Acts

Section 208 of Pub.L. 95–604 provided that: "Except as otherwise provided in this title [section 202(b) of Title II, set out as note under section 2113 of this title] the amendments made by this title [enacting sections 2022 and 2114 of this title, amending this section and sections 2021, 2111, and 2201 of this title, and enacting note provisions under sections 2021 and 2113 of this title] shall take effect on the date of the enactment of this Act [Nov. 8, 1978]."

**Change of Name**

Any reference in any provision of law enacted before Jan. 4, 1995, to the Committee on Energy and Commerce of the House of Representatives treated as referring to the Committee on Commerce of the House of Representatives, except that any reference in any provision of law enacted before Jan. 4, 1995, to the Committee on Energy and Commerce of the House of Representatives treated as referring to the Committee on Agriculture of the House of Representatives, in the case of a provision of law relating to inspection of seafood or seafood products, the Committee on Banking and Financial Services of the House of Representatives, in the case of a provision of law relating to bank capital markets activities generally or to depository institution securities activities generally, and the Committee on Transportation and Infrastructure of the House of Representatives, in the case of a provision of law relating to railroads, railway labor, or railroad retirement and unemployment (except revenue measures related thereto), see section 1(a)(4) and (c)(1) of Pub.L. 104–14, set out as a note preceding section 21 of Title 2, The Congress.

**Transfer of Functions**

All functions of the Nuclear Regulatory Commission, including those pertaining to an emergency concerning a particular facility or materials licensed or regulated by the Commission, are transferred to the Chairman of the Nuclear Regulatory Commission, with the exception of those functions relating to policy formation, rulemaking, and orders and adjudications, which are to be retained by the Commission, pursuant to Reorg. Plan No. 1 of 1980, 45 F.R. 40561, 94 Stat. 3585, set out as a note under section 5841 of this title.

The Atomic Energy Commission was abolished and all functions of the Commission, the Chairman, members of the Commission, and the officers and components of the Commission were transferred to and vested in the Nuclear Regulatory Commission and the Administrator of the Energy Research and Development Administration, with certain exceptions, by Pub.L. 93–438, Oct. 11, 1974, 88 Stat. 1233. See sections 5814 and 5841 of this title. The functions vested by law in the Energy Research and Development Administration or in the Administrator, officers, and components of the Energy Research and Development Administration were transferred to and vested in the Secretary of Energy, unless otherwise specifically provided, as part of the creation of the Department of Energy by Pub.L. 95–91, Aug. 4, 1977, 91 Stat. 565. See sections 7151(a) and 7293 of this title.

**Prior Provisions**

Provisions similar to those comprising this section were contained in section 18 of Act Aug. 1, 1946, c. 724, 60 Stat. 774, which was classified to section 1818 of this title, prior to the complete amendment and renumbering of Act Aug. 1, 1946 by Act Aug. 30, 1954.

**Abolition of the Joint Committee on Atomic Energy**

The Joint Committee on Atomic Energy, referred to in subsec. (c), was abolished by section 2258 of this title and references to the Joint Committee are deemed, on or after Sept. 20, 1977, to refer to the committees of the Senate or House of Representatives which, under the rules of the Senate or House, have jurisdiction over the subject matter with records and files of the Joint Committee being transferred to the respective committees of the House or Senate.

## § 2021. Cooperation with States

[AEA § 274]

**(a) Purpose**

It is the purpose of this section—

(1) to recognize the interests of the States in the peaceful uses of atomic energy, and to clarify the respective responsibilities under this chapter of the States and the Commission with respect to the regulation of byproduct, source, and special nuclear materials;

(2) to recognize the need, and establish programs for, cooperation between the States and the Commission with respect to control of radiation hazards associated with use of such materials;

(3) to promote an orderly regulatory pattern between the Commission and State governments with respect to nuclear development and use and regulation of byproduct, source, and special nuclear materials;

(4) to establish procedures and criteria for discontinuance of certain of the Commission's regulatory responsibilities with respect to byproduct, source, and special nuclear materials, and the assumption thereof by the States;

(5) to provide for coordination of the development of radiation standards for the guidance of Federal agencies and cooperation with the States; and

(6) to recognize that, as the States improve their capabilities to regulate effectively such materials, additional legislation may be desirable.

**(b) Agreements with States**

Except as provided in subsection (c) of this section, the Commission is authorized to enter into agreements with the Governor of any State providing for discontinuance of the regulatory authority of the Commission under subchapters V, VI, and VII of this division, and section 2201 of this title, with respect to any one or more of the following materials within the State—

(1) byproduct materials as defined in section 2014(e)(1) of this title;

(2) byproduct materials as defined in section 2014(e)(2) of this title;

(3) source materials;

(4) special nuclear materials in quantities not sufficient to form a critical mass.

During the duration of such an agreement it is recognized that the State shall have authority to regulate the materials covered by the agreement for the protection of the public health and safety from radiation hazards.

### (c) Commission regulation of certain activities

No agreement entered into pursuant to subsection (b) of this section shall provide for discontinuance of any authority and the Commission shall retain authority and responsibility with respect to regulation of—

(1) the construction and operation of any production or utilization facility or any uranium enrichment facility;

(2) the export from or import into the United States of byproduct, source, or special nuclear material, or of any production or utilization facility;

(3) the disposal into the ocean or sea of byproduct, source, or special nuclear waste materials as defined in regulations or orders of the Commission;

(4) the disposal of such other byproduct, source, or special nuclear material as the Commission determines by regulation or order should, because of the hazards or potential hazards thereof, not be so disposed of without a license from the Commission.

The Commission shall also retain authority under any such agreement to make a determination that all applicable standards and requirements have been met prior to termination of a license for byproduct material, as defined in section 2014(e)(2) of this title. Notwithstanding any agreement between the Commission and any State pursuant to subsection (b) of this section, the Commission is authorized by rule, regulation, or order to require that the manufacturer, processor, or producer of any equipment, device, commodity, or other product containing source, byproduct, or special nuclear material shall not transfer possession or control of such product except pursuant to a license issued by the Commission.

### (d) Conditions

The Commission shall enter into an agreement under subsection (b) of this section with any State if—

(1) The [1] Governor of that State certifies that the State has a program for the control of radiation hazards adequate to protect the public health and safety with respect to the materials within the State covered by the proposed agreement, and that the State desires to assume regulatory responsibility for such materials; and

(2) the Commission finds that the State program is in accordance with the requirements of subsection (*o*) of this section and in all other respects compatible with the Commission's program for the regulation of such materials, and that the State program is adequate to protect the public health and safety with respect to the materials covered by the proposed agreement.

### (e) Publication in Federal Register; comment of interested persons

(1) Before any agreement under subsection (b) of this section is signed by the Commission, the terms of the proposed agreement and of proposed exemptions pursuant to subsection (f) of this section shall be published once each week for four consecutive weeks in the Federal Register; and such opportunity for comment by interested persons on the proposed agreement and exemptions shall be allowed as the Commission determines by regulation or order to be appropriate.

(2) Each proposed agreement shall include the proposed effective date of such proposed agreement or exemptions. The agreement and exemptions shall be published in the Federal Register within thirty days after signature by the Commission and the Governor.

### (f) Exemptions

The Commission is authorized and directed, by regulation or order, to grant such exemptions from the licensing requirements contained in subchapters V, VI, and VII of this division, and from its regulations applicable to licensees as the Commission finds necessary or appropriate to carry out any agreement entered into pursuant to subsection (b) of this section.

### (g) Compatible radiation standards

The Commission is authorized and directed to cooperate with the States in the formulation of standards for protection against hazards of radiation to assure that State and Commission programs for protection against hazards of radiation will be coordinated and compatible.

### (h) Consultative, advisory, and miscellaneous functions of Administrator of Environmental Protection Agency

The Administrator of the Environmental Protection Agency shall consult qualified scientists and experts in radiation matters, including the President of the National Academy of Sciences, the Chairman of the National Committee on Radiation Protection and Measurement, and qualified experts in the field of biology and medicine and in the field of health physics. The Special Assistant to the President for Science and Technology, or his designee, is authorized to attend meetings with, participate in the deliberations of, and to advise the Administrator. The Administrator shall advise the President with respect to radiation matters, directly or indirectly affecting health, including guidance for all Federal agencies in the formulation of radiation standards and in the establishment and execution of programs of cooperation with States. The Administrator shall also perform such other functions as the President may assign to him by Executive order.

**(i) Inspections and other functions; training and other assistance**

The Commission in carrying out its licensing and regulatory responsibilities under this chapter is authorized to enter into agreements with any State, or group of States, to perform inspections or other functions on a cooperative basis as the Commission deems appropriate. The Commission is also authorized to provide training, with or without charge, to employees of, and such other assistance to, any State or political subdivision thereof or group of States as the Commission deems appropriate. Any such provision or assistance by the Commission shall take into account the additional expenses that may be incurred by a State as a consequence of the State's entering into an agreement with the Commission pursuant to subsection (b) of this section.

**(j) Reserve power to terminate or suspend agreements; emergency situations; State nonaction on causes of danger; authority exercisable only during emergency and commensurate with danger**

(1) The Commission, upon its own initiative after reasonable notice and opportunity for hearing to the State with which an agreement under subsection (b) of this section has become effective, or upon request of the Governor of such State, may terminate or suspend all or part of its agreement with the State and reassert the licensing and regulatory authority vested in it under this chapter, if the Commission finds that (1) such termination or suspension is required to protect the public health and safety, or (2) the State has not complied with one or more of the requirements of this section. The Commission shall periodically review such agreements and actions taken by the States under the agreements to ensure compliance with the provisions of this section.

(2) The Commission, upon its own motion or upon request of the Governor of any State, may, after notifying the Governor, temporarily suspend all or part of its agreement with the State without notice or hearing if, in the judgment of the Commission:

(A) an emergency situation exists with respect to any material covered by such an agreement creating danger which requires immediate action to protect the health or safety of persons either within or outside the State, and

(B) the State has failed to take steps necessary to contain or eliminate the cause of the danger within a reasonable time after the situation arose.

A temporary suspension under this paragraph shall remain in effect only for such time as the emergency situation exists and shall authorize the Commission to exercise its authority only to the extent necessary to contain or eliminate the danger.

**(k) State regulation of activities for certain purposes**

Nothing in this section shall be construed to affect the authority of any State or local agency to regulate activities for purposes other than protection against radiation hazards.

**(*l*) Commission regulated activities; notice of filing; hearing**

With respect to each application for Commission license authorizing an activity as to which the Commission's authority is continued pursuant to subsection (c) of this section, the Commission shall give prompt notice to the State or States in which the activity will be conducted of the filing of the license application; and shall afford reasonable opportunity for State representatives to offer evidence, interrogate witnesses, and advise the Commission as to the application without requiring such representatives to take a position for or against the granting of the application.

**(m) Limitation of agreements and exemptions**

No agreement entered into under subsection (b) of this section, and no exemption granted pursuant to subsection (f) of this section, shall affect the authority of the Commission under section 2201(b) or (i) of this title to issue rules, regulations, or orders to protect the common defense and security, to protect restricted data or to guard against the loss or diversion of special nuclear material. For purposes of section 2201(i) of this title, activities covered by exemptions granted pursuant to subsection (f) of this section shall be deemed to constitute activities authorized pursuant to this chapter; and special nuclear material acquired by any person pursuant to such an exemption shall be deemed to have been acquired pursuant to section 2073 of this title.

**(n) "State" and "agreement" defined**

As used in this section, the term "State" means any State, Territory, or possession of the United States, the Canal Zone, Puerto Rico, and the District of Columbia. As used in this section, the term "agreement" includes any amendment to any agreement.

**(*o*) State compliance requirements: compliance with section 2113(b) of this title and health and environmental protection standards; procedures for licenses, rulemaking, and li-**

**cense impact analysis; amendment of agreements for transfer of State collected funds; proceedings duplication restriction; alternative requirements**

In the licensing and regulation of byproduct material, as defined in section 2014(e)(2) of this title, or of any activity which results in the production of byproduct material as so defined under an agreement entered into pursuant to subsection (b) of this section, a State shall require—

(1) compliance with the requirements of subsection (b) of section 2113 of this title (respecting ownership of byproduct material and land), and

(2) compliance with standards which shall be adopted by the State for the protection of the public health, safety, and the environment from hazards associated with such material which are equivalent, to the extent practicable, or more stringent than, standards adopted and enforced by the Commission for the same purpose, including requirements and standards promulgated by the Commission and the Administrator of the Environmental Protection Agency pursuant to sections 2113, 2114, and 2022 of this title, and

(3) procedures which—

(A) in the case of licenses, provide procedures under State law which include—

(i) an opportunity, after public notice, for written comments and a public hearing, with a transcript,

(ii) an opportunity for cross examination, and

(iii) a written determination which is based upon findings included in such determination and upon the evidence presented during the public comment period and which is subject to judicial review;

(B) in the case of rulemaking, provide an opportunity for public participation through written comments or a public hearing and provide for judicial review of the rule;

(C) require for each license which has a significant impact on the human environment a written analysis (which shall be available to the public before the commencement of any such proceedings) of the impact of such license, including any activities conducted pursuant thereto, on the environment, which analysis shall include—

(i) an assessment of the radiological and nonradiological impacts to the public health of the activities to be conducted pursuant to such license;

(ii) an assessment of any impact on any waterway and groundwater resulting from such activities;

(iii) consideration of alternatives, including alternative sites and engineering methods, to the activities to be conducted pursuant to such license; and

(iv) consideration of the long-term impacts, including decommissioning, decontamination, and reclamation impacts, associated with activities to be conducted pursuant to such license, including the management of any byproduct material, as defined by section 2014(e)(2) of this title; and

(D) prohibit any major construction activity with respect to such material prior to complying with the provisions of subparagraph (C).

If any State under such agreement imposes upon any licensee any requirement for the payment of funds to such State for the reclamation or long-term maintenance and monitoring of such material, and if transfer to the United States of such material is required in accordance with section 2113(b) of this title, such agreement shall be amended by the Commission to provide that such State shall transfer to the United States upon termination of the license issued to such licensee the total amount collected by such State from such licensee for such purpose. If such payments are required, they must be sufficient to ensure compliance with the standards established by the Commission pursuant to section 2201(x) of this title. No State shall be required under paragraph (3) to conduct proceedings concerning any license or regulation which would duplicate proceedings conducted by the Commission. In adopting requirements pursuant to paragraph (2) of this subsection with respect to sites at which ores are processed primarily for their source material content or which are used for the disposal of byproduct material as defined in section 2014(e)(2) of this title, the State may adopt alternatives (including, where appropriate, site-specific alternatives) to the requirements adopted and enforced by the Commission for the same purpose if, after notice and opportunity for public hearing, the Commission determines that such alternatives will achieve a level of stabilization and containment of the sites concerned, and a level of protection for public health, safety, and the environment from radiological and nonradiological hazards associated with such sites, which is equivalent to, to the extent practicable, or more stringent than the level which would be achieved by standards and requirements adopted and enforced by the Commission for the same purpose and any final standards promulgated by the Administrator of the Environmental Protection Agency in accordance with section 2022 of this title. Such alternative State requirements may take into account local or regional conditions, including geology, topography, hydrology and meteorology.

(Aug. 1, 1946, c. 724, Title I, § 274, as added Sept. 23, 1959, Pub.L. 86–373, § 1, 73 Stat. 688, and amended 1970 Reorg. Plan No. 3, §§ 2(a)(7), 6(2), eff. Dec. 2, 1970, 35 F.R. 15623, 84 Stat. 2086; Nov. 8, 1978, Pub.L. 95–604, Title II, § 204(a)–(e)(1), (f), 92 Stat. 3036–3038; June 30, 1980, Pub.L. 96–295, Title II, § 205, 94 Stat. 787; Jan. 4, 1983, Pub.L. 97–415, § 19(a), 96 Stat. 2078; renumbered Title I and amended Oct. 24, 1992, Pub.L. 102–486, Title IX, § 902(a)(6), (8), 106 Stat. 2944.)

[1] So in original. Probably should read "the".

## HISTORICAL AND STATUTORY NOTES

### Codifications

In subsec. (h) of this section, provisions for the establishment of a Federal Radiation Council and for the designation of its Chairman and members have been omitted and the Administrator of the Environmental Protection Agency has been substituted for the Council as the person charged with the responsibility of carrying out the functions of the Council pursuant to Reorg. Plan No. 3 of 1970, §§ 2(a)(7), 6(2), eff. Dec. 2, 1970, 35 F.R. 15623, 84 Stat. 2086, set out in Appendix 1 to Title 5, Government Organization and Employees, which abolished the Federal Radiation Council and transferred its functions to the Administrator of the Environmental Protection Administration.

### Effective and Applicability Provisions

1978 Acts

Section 204(e)(2) of Pub.L. 95–604, as added by Pub.L. 96–106, § 22(d), Nov. 9, 1979, 93 Stat. 800, provided that: "The provisions of the amendment made by paragraph (1) of this subsection (which adds a new subsection *o* to section 274 of the Atomic Energy Act of 1954 [this section] ) shall apply only to the maximum extent practicable during the three-year period beginning on the date of the enactment of this Act [Nov. 8, 1978]."

Amendment by Pub.L. 95–604 effective Nov. 8, 1978, see section 208 of Pub.L. 95–604, set out as a note under section 2014 of this title.

### Transfer of Functions

All functions of the Nuclear Regulatory Commission, including those pertaining to an emergency concerning a particular facility or materials licensed or regulated by the Commission, are transferred to the Chairman of the Nuclear Regulatory Commission, with the exception of those functions relating to policy formation, rulemaking, and orders and adjudications, which are to be retained by the Commission, pursuant to Reorg. Plan No. 1 of 1980, 45 F.R. 40561, 94 Stat. 3585, set out as a note under section 5841 of this title.

The Atomic Energy Commission was abolished and all functions under this section were transferred to the Nuclear Regulatory Commission and the Administrator of the Energy Research and Development Administration by sections 5814 and 5841 of this title. The Energy Research and Development Administration was terminated and functions vested by law in the Administrator thereof were transferred to the Secretary of Energy (unless otherwise specifically provided) by sections 7151(a) and 7293 of this title.

### Abolition of the Atomic Energy Commission

The Atomic Energy Commission was abolished and all functions of the Commission, the Chairman, members of the Commission, and the officers and components of the Commission were transferred to and vested in the Nuclear Regulatory Commission and the Administrator of the Energy Research and Development Administration, with certain exceptions, by Pub.L. 93–438, Oct. 11, 1974, 88 Stat. 1233. See section 5814 of this title. The functions vested by law in the Energy Research and Development Administration or in the Administrator, officers, and components of the Energy Research and Development Administration were transferred to and vested in the Secretary of Energy, unless otherwise specifically provided, as part of the creation of the Department of Energy by Pub.L. 95–91, Aug. 4, 1977, 91 Stat. 565. See section 7151 of this title.

### Federal Compliance with Pollution Control Standards

For provisions relating to the responsibility of the head of each Executive agency for compliance with applicable pollution control standards, see Ex. Ord. No. 12088, Oct. 13, 1978, 43 F.R. 47707, set out under section 4321 of this title.

### Radiation Policy Council

For provisions relating to the establishment of the Radiation Policy Council, see Ex. Ord. No. 12194, Feb. 21, 1980, 45 F.R. 12209.

### State Authorities and Agreements Respecting Byproduct Material; Entry and Effective and Applicability Provisions of Agreements

Section 204(g), (h) of Pub.L. 95–604, as amended by Pub.L. 96–106, § 22(a), (b), Nov. 9, 1979, 93 Stat. 799; Pub. L. 97–415, § 19(b), Jan. 4, 1983, 96 Stat. 2079, provided that:

**"(g)** Nothing in any amendment made by this section [adding subsec. (a) and amending subsecs. (b), (c), (d)(2), (j), and (n) of this section] shall preclude any State from exercising any other authority as permitted under the Atomic Energy Act of 1954 [this chapter] respecting any byproduct material, as defined in section 11e.(2) of the Atomic Energy Act of 1954 [section 2014(e)(2) of this title].

**"(h)(1)** During the three-year period beginning on the date of the enactment of this Act [Nov. 8, 1978], notwithstanding any other provision of this title [enacting section 2113 of this title and amending sections 2014 and 2021 of this title], any State may exercise any authority under State law (including authority exercised pursuant to an agreement entered into pursuant to section 274 of the Atomic Energy Act of 1954 [this section] ) respecting (A) byproduct material, as defined in section 11e. (2) of the Atomic Energy Act of 1954 [section 2014(e)(2) of this title], or (B) any activity which results in the production of byproduct material as so defined, in the same manner and to the same extent as permitted before the date of the enactment of this Act [Nov. 8, 1978], except that such State authority shall be exercised in a manner which, to the extent practicable, is consistent with the requirements of section 274*o* of the Atomic Energy Act of 1954 [subsec. (*o*) of this section] (as added by section 204(e) of this Act). The Commission shall have the authority to ensure that such section 274*o*, is implemented by any such State to the extent practicable during the three-year period beginning on the date of the enactment of this Act. Nothing in this section shall be construed to preclude the Commission or the Administrator of the Environmental Protection Agency from taking such action under section 275 of the Atomic Energy Act of 1954 [section 2022 of this title] as may be necessary to implement title I of this Act [section 7911 et seq. of this title].

"(2) An agreement entered into with any State as permitted under section 274 of the Atomic Energy Act of 1954 [this section] with respect to byproduct material as defined in section 11e.(2) of such Act [section 2014(e)(2) of this title], may be entered into at any time after the date of the enactment of this Act [Nov. 8, 1978] but no such agreement may take effect before the date three years after the date of the enactment of this Act [Nov. 8, 1978].

"(3) Notwithstanding any other provision of this title [enacting sections 2022 and 2113 of this title, amending sections 2014, 2021, 2111, and 2201 of this title, and adding provisions set out as notes under sections 2014, 2021, 2113, and 2114 of this title], where a State assumes or has assumed, pursuant to an agreement entered into under section 274 b. of the Atomic Energy Act of 1954 [subsec. (b) of this section], authority over any activity which results in the production of byproduct material, as defined in section 11e. (2) of such Act [section 2014(e)(2) of this title], the Commission shall not, until the end of the three-year period beginning on the date of the enactment of this Act [Nov. 8, 1978], have licensing authority over such byproduct material produced in any activity covered by such agreement, unless the agreement is terminated, suspended, or amended to provide for such Federal licensing. If, at the end of such three-year period, a State has not entered into such an agreement with respect to byproduct material, as defined in section 11e. (2) of the Atomic Energy Act of 1954, the Commission shall have authority over such byproduct material: *Provided, however*, That, in the case of a State which has exercised any authority under State law pursuant to an agreement entered into under section 274 of the Atomic Energy Act of 1954 [this section], the State authority over such byproduct material may be terminated, and the Commission authority over such material may be exercised, only after compliance by the Commission with the same procedures as are applicable in the case of termination of agreements under section 274j of the Atomic Energy Act of 1954 [subsec. (j) of this section]."

## § 2021a. Storage or disposal facility planning

### (a) Planning

Any person, agency, or other entity proposing to develop a storage or disposal facility, including a test disposal facility, for high-level radioactive wastes, non-high-level radioactive wastes including transuranium contaminated wastes, or irradiated nuclear reactor fuel, shall notify the Commission as early as possible after the commencement of planning for a particular proposed facility. The Commission shall in turn notify the Governor and the State legislature of the State of proposed situs whenever the Commission has knowledge of such proposal.

### (b) Independent State review

The Commission is authorized and directed to prepare a report on means for improving the opportunities for State participation in the process for siting, licensing, and developing nuclear waste storage or disposal facilities. Such report shall include detailed consideration of a program to provide grants through the Commission to any State, and the advisability of such a program, for the purpose of conducting an independent State review of any proposal to develop a nuclear waste storage or disposal facility identified in subsection (a) of this section within such State. On or before March 1, 1979, the Commission shall submit the report to the Congress including recommendations for improving the opportunities for State participation together with any necessary legislative proposals.

(Pub.L. 95–601, § 14, Nov. 6, 1978, 92 Stat. 2953.)

### HISTORICAL AND STATUTORY NOTES

**References in Text**

Commission, referred to in text, probably means the Nuclear Regulatory Commission in view of the fact that this section was enacted as part of the act authorizing appropriations for the Nuclear Regulatory Commission for fiscal year 1979. The Atomic Energy Commission was abolished and its functions were transferred to the Nuclear Regulatory Commission by sections 5814 and 5841 of this title.

**Codifications**

Section was enacted as part of an act authorizing appropriations to the Nuclear Regulatory Commission for fiscal year 1979, and not as part of the Atomic Energy Act of 1954 which comprises this chapter.

**Funding for the West Valley Demonstration Project**

Pub.L. 107–66, Title III, Nov. 12, 2001, 115 Stat. 503, provided that: "That funding for the West Valley Demonstration Project shall be reduced in subsequent fiscal years to the minimum necessary to maintain the project in a safe and stable condition, unless, not later than September 30, 2002, the Secretary: (1) provides written notification to the Committees on Appropriations of the House of Representatives and the Senate that agreement has been reached with the State of New York on the final scope of Federal activities at the West Valley site and on the respective Federal and State cost shares for those activities; (2) submits a written copy of that agreement to the Committees on Appropriations of the House of Representatives and the Senate; and (3) provides a written certification that the Federal actions proposed in the agreement will be in full compliance with all relevant Federal statutes and are in the best interest of the Federal Government".

**Plan For Permanent Disposal of Waste From Atomic Energy Defense Activities; Submission of Plan to Congress Not Later Than June 30, 1983**

Pub.L. 97–90, Title II, § 213, Dec. 4, 1981, 95 Stat. 1171, provided that:

"(a) The President shall submit to the Committees on Armed Services of the Senate and of the House of Representatives not later than June 30, 1983, a report which sets forth his plans for the permanent disposal of high-level and transuranic wastes resulting from atomic energy defense activities.

"(b) Such report shall include, but not be limited to, for each State in which such wastes are stored in interim storage facilities on the date of enactment of this Act [Dec. 4, 1981]—

"(1) specific estimates of amounts planned for expenditure in each of the next five fiscal years to achieve the permanent disposal of such wastes and general estimates of amounts planned for expenditure in fiscal years thereafter to achieve such purpose; and

"(2) a thorough and detailed program management plan for the disposal of such wastes, including but not limited to—

"(A) an explicit schedule for decisions regarding the further processing and permanent disposal of such wastes;

"(B) a general description of new facilities likely to be required to achieve such permanent disposal; and

"(C) identification of all major program objectives, milestones, key events, and critical path items."

[Any reference in any provision of law enacted before Jan. 4, 1995, to the Committee on Armed Services of the House of Representatives treated as referring to the Committee on National Security of the House of Representatives, see section 1(a)(1) of Pub.L. 104–14, set out as a note preceding section 21 of Title 2, The Congress.]

**West Valley Demonstration Project; Radioactive Waste Management; Project Activities; Public Hearings; Review of Project and Consultations; Authorization of Appropriations; Report to Congress**

Pub.L. 96–368, §§ 1 to 6, Oct. 1, 1980, 94 Stat. 1347, 1349, as amended Pub.L. 102–154, Title I, Nov. 13, 1991, 105 Stat. 1000; Pub.L. 102–285, § 10(a), May 18, 1992, 106 Stat. 171, provided that:

"**Section 1.** This Act may be cited as the 'West Valley Demonstration Project Act'.

"**Sec. 2.** (a) The Secretary shall carry out, in accordance with this Act, a high level radioactive waste management demonstration project at the Western New York Service Center in West Valley, New York, for the purpose of demonstrating solidification techniques which can be used for preparing high level radioactive waste for disposal. Under the project the Secretary shall carry out the following activities:

"(1) The Secretary shall solidify, in a form suitable for transportation and disposal, the high level radioactive waste at the Center by vitrification or by such other technology which the Secretary determines to be the most effective for solidification.

"(2) The Secretary shall develop containers suitable for the permanent disposal of the high level radioactive waste solidified at the Center.

"(3) The Secretary shall, as soon as feasible, transport, in accordance with applicable provisions of law, the waste solidified at the Center to an appropriate Federal repository for permanent disposal.

"(4) The Secretary shall, in accordance with applicable licensing requirements, dispose of low level radioactive waste and transuranic waste produced by the solidification of the high level radioactive waste under the project.

"(5) The Secretary shall decontaminate and decommission—

"(A) the tanks and other facilities of the Center in which the high level radioactive waste solidified under the project was stored,

"(B) the facilities used in the solidification of the waste, and

"(C) any material and hardware used in connection with the project,

in accordance with such requirements as the Commission may prescribe.

"(b) Before undertaking the project and during the fiscal year ending September 30, 1981, the Secretary shall carry out the following:

"(1) The Secretary shall hold in the vicinity of the Center public hearings to inform the residents of the area in which the Center is located of the activities proposed to be undertaken under the project and to receive their comments on the project.

"(2) The Secretary shall consider the various technologies available for the solidification and handling of high level radioactive waste taking into account the unique characteristics of such waste at the Center.

"(3) The Secretary shall—

"(A) undertake detailed engineering and cost estimates for the project,

"(B) prepare a plan for the safe removal of the high level radioactive waste at the Center for the purposes of solidification and include in the plan provisions respecting the safe breaching of the tanks in which the waste is stored, operating equipment to accomplish the removal, and sluicing techniques,

"(C) conduct appropriate safety analyses of the project, and

"(D) prepare required environmental impact analyses of the project.

"(4) The Secretary shall enter into a cooperative agreement with the State in accordance with the Federal Grant and Cooperative Agreement Act of 1977 [see section 6301 et seq. of Title 31, Money and Finance] under which the State will carry out the following:

"(A) The State will make available to the Secretary the facilities of the Center and the high level radioactive waste at the Center which are necessary for the completion of the project. The facilities and the waste shall be made available without the transfer of title and for such period as may be required for completion of the project.

"(B) The Secretary shall provide technical assistance in securing required license amendments.

"(C) The State shall pay 10 per centum of the costs of the project, as determined by the Secretary. In determining the costs of the project, the Secretary shall consider the value of the use of the Center for the project. The State may not use Federal funds to pay its share of the cost of the project, but may use the perpetual care fund to pay such share.

"(D) Submission jointly by the Department of Energy and the State of New York of an application for a licensing amendment as soon as possible with the Nuclear Regulatory Commission providing for the demonstration.

"(c) Within one year from the date of the enactment of this Act [Oct. 1, 1980], the Secretary shall enter into an agreement with the Commission to establish arrangements for review and consultation by the Commission with respect to the project: *Provided*, That review and consultation by the Commission pursuant to this subsection shall be conducted informally by the Commission and shall not include nor require formal procedures or actions by the Commission pursuant to the Atomic Energy Act of 1954, as amended [this chapter], the Energy Reorganization Act of 1974, as amended [section 5801 et seq. of this title], or any other law. The agreement shall provide for the following:

"(1) The Secretary shall submit to the Commission, for its review and comment, a plan for the solidification of the high level radioactive waste at the Center, the removal of the waste for purposes of its solidification, the preparation of the waste for disposal, and the decontamination of the facilities to be used in solidifying the waste. In preparing its comments on the plan, the Commission shall specify with precision its objections to any provision of the plan. Upon submission of a plan to the Commission, the Secretary shall publish a notice in the Federal Register of the submission of the plan and of its availability for public inspection, and, upon receipt of the comments of the Commission respecting a plan, the Secretary shall publish a notice in the Federal Register of the receipt of the comments and of the availability of the comments for public inspection. If the Secretary does not revise the plan to meet objections specified in the comments of the Commission, the Secretary shall publish in the Federal Register a detailed statement for not so revising the plan.

"(2) The Secretary shall consult with the Commission with respect to the form in which the high level radioactive waste at the Center shall be solidified and the containers to be used in the permanent disposal of such waste.

"(3) The Secretary shall submit to the Commission safety analysis reports and such other information as the Commission may require to identify and danger to the public health and safety which may be presented by the project.

"(4) The Secretary shall afford the Commission access to the Center to enable the Commission to monitor the activities under the project for the purpose of assuring the public health and safety.

"(d) In carrying out the project, the Secretary shall consult with the Administrator of the Environmental Protection Agency, the Secretary of Transportation, the Director of the United States Geological Survey, and the commercial operator of the Center.

"Sec. 3. (a) There are authorized to be appropriated to the Secretary for the project not more than $5,000,000 for the fiscal year ending September 30, 1981.

"(b) The total amount obligated for the project by the Secretary shall be 90 per centum of the costs of the project.

"(c) The authority of the Secretary to enter into contracts under this Act shall be effective for any fiscal year only to such extent or in such amounts as are provided in advance by appropriation Acts.

"Sec. 4. Not later than February 1, 1981, and on February 1 of each calendar year thereafter during the term of the project, the Secretary shall transmit to the Speaker of the House of Representatives and the President pro tempore of the Senate an up-to-date report containing a detailed description of the activities of the Secretary in carrying out the project, including agreements entered into and the costs incurred during the period reported on and the activities to be undertaken in the next fiscal year and the estimated costs thereof.

"Sec. 5. (a) Other than the costs and responsibilities established by this Act for the project, nothing in this Act shall be construed as affecting any rights, obligations, or liabilities of the commercial operator of the Center, the State, or any person, as is appropriate, arising under the Atomic Energy Act of 1954 [this chapter] or under any other law, contract, or agreement for the operation, maintenance, or decontamination of any facility or property at the Center or for any wastes at the Center. Nothing in this Act shall be construed as affecting any applicable licensing requirement of the Atomic Energy Act of 1954 [this chapter] or the Energy Reorganization Act of 1974 [section 5801 et seq. of this title]. This Act shall not apply or be extended to any facility or property at the Center which is not used in conducting the project. This Act may not be construed to expand or diminish the rights of the Federal Government.

"(b) This Act does not authorize the Federal Government to acquire title to any high level radioactive waste at the Center or to the Center or any portion thereof.

"Sec. 6. For purposes of this Act:

"(1) The term 'Secretary' means the Secretary of Energy.

"(2) The term 'Commission' means the Nuclear Regulatory Commission.

"(3) The term 'State' means the State of New York.

"(4) The term 'high level radioactive waste' means the high level radioactive waste which was produced by the reprocessing at the Center of spent nuclear fuel. Such term includes both liquid wastes which are produced directly in reprocessing, dry solid material derived from such liquid waste, and such other material as the Commission designates as high level radioactive waste for purposes of protecting the public health and safety.

"(5) The term 'transuranic waste' means material contaminated with elements which have an atomic number greater than 92, including neptunium, plutonium, americium, and curium, and which are in concentrations greater than 10 nanocuries per gram, or in such other concentrations as the Commission may prescribe to protect the public health and safety.

"(6) The term 'low level radioactive waste' means radioactive waste not classified as high level radioactive waste, transuranic waste, or byproduct material as defined in section 11 e. (2) of the Atomic Energy Act of 1954 [section 2014(e)(2) of this title].

"(7) The term 'project' means the project prescribed by section 2(a).

"(8) The term 'Center' means the Western New York Service Center in West Valley, New York."

## § 2021b. Definitions

**[LLRWPA § 2]**

For purposes of sections 2021b to 2021j of this title:

**(1) Agreement State**

The term "agreement State" means a State that—

(A) has entered into an agreement with the Nuclear Regulatory Commission under section 2021 of this title; and

**(B)** has authority to regulate the disposal of low-level radioactive waste under such agreement.

**(2) Allocation**

The term "allocation" means the assignment of a specific amount of low-level radioactive waste disposal capacity to a commercial nuclear power reactor for which access is required to be provided by sited States subject to the conditions specified under sections 2021b to 2021j of this title.

**(3) Commercial nuclear power reactor**

The term "commercial nuclear power reactor" means any unit of a civilian light-water moderated utilization facility required to be licensed under section 2133 or 2134(b) of this title.

**(4) Compact**

The term "compact" means a compact entered into by two or more States pursuant to sections 2021b to 2021j of this title.

**(5) Compact commission**

The term "compact commission" means the regional commission, committee, or board established in a compact to administer such compact.

**(6) Compact region**

The term "compact region" means the area consisting of all States that are members of a compact.

**(7) Disposal**

The term "disposal" means the permanent isolation of low-level radioactive waste pursuant to the requirements established by the Nuclear Regulatory Commission under applicable laws, or by an agreement State if such isolation occurs in such agreement State.

**(8) Generate**

The term "generate", when used in relation to low-level radioactive waste, means to produce low-level radioactive waste.

**(9) Low-level radioactive waste**

The term "low-level radioactive waste" means radioactive material that—

**(A)** is not high-level radioactive waste, spent nuclear fuel, or byproduct material (as defined in section 2014(e)(2) of this title); and

**(B)** the Nuclear Regulatory Commission, consistent with existing law and in accordance with paragraph (A), classifies as low-level radioactive waste.

**(10) Non-sited compact region**

The term "non-sited compact region" means any compact region that is not a sited compact region.

**(11) Regional disposal facility**

The term "regional disposal facility" means a non-Federal low-level radioactive waste disposal facility in operation on January 1, 1985, or subsequently established and operated under a compact.

**(12) Secretary**

The term "Secretary" means the Secretary of Energy.

**(13) Sited compact region**

The term "sited compact region" means a compact region in which there is located one of the regional disposal facilities at Barnwell, in the State of South Carolina; Richland, in the State of Washington; or Beatty, in the State of Nevada.

**(14) State**

The term "State" means any State of the United States, the District of Columbia, and the Commonwealth of Puerto Rico.

(Pub.L. 96–573, § 2, as added Pub.L. 99–240, Title I, § 102, Jan. 15, 1986, 99 Stat. 1842.)

## HISTORICAL AND STATUTORY NOTES

**Codifications**

Section was not enacted as part of the Atomic Energy Act of 1954 which comprises this chapter, but as part of the Low-Level Radioactive Waste Policy Act.

**Prior Provisions**

A prior section 2021b, Pub.L. 96–573, § 2, Dec. 22, 1980, 94 Stat. 3347, which related to definitions respecting low-level radioactive waste policy as used in former sections 2021b to 2021d of this title, was repealed by Pub.L. 99–240, Title I, § 102, Jan. 15, 1986, 99 Stat. 1842.

**Short Title**

1986 Acts

Section 101 of Title I of Pub.L. 99–240 provided that: "This Title [enacting sections 2021b to 2021j of this title, repealing former sections 2021b to 2021d of this title, enacting a provision set out as a note under this section, and repealing a provision set out as a note under this section] may be cited as the 'Low-Level Radioactive Waste Policy Amendments Act of 1985'."

Section 1 of Pub.L. 96–573 as added by Pub.L. 99–240, Title I, § 102, Jan. 15, 1986, 99 Stat. 1842, provided that: "This Act [enacting sections 2021b to 2021j of this title] may be cited as the 'Low-Level Radioactive Waste Policy Act'."

A prior section 1 of Pub.L. 96–573, which provided that Pub.L. 96–573, enacting former sections 2021b to 2021d of this title, be cited as the "Low-Level Radioactive Waste Policy Act", was repealed by Pub.L. 99–240, Title I, § 102, Jan. 15, 1986, 99 Stat. 1842.

## § 2021c. Responsible for disposal of low-level radioactive waste

[LLRWPA § 3]

**(a) State responsibilities**

(1) Each State shall be responsible for providing, either by itself or in cooperation with other States, for the disposal of—

(A) low-level radioactive waste generated within the State (other than by the Federal Government) that consists of or contains class A, B, or C radioactive waste as defined by section 61.55 of title 10, Code of Federal Regulations, as in effect on January 26, 1983;

(B) low-level radioactive waste described in subparagraph (A) that is generated by the Federal Government except such waste that is—

(i) owned or generated by the Department of Energy;

(ii) owned or generated by the United States Navy as a result of the decommissioning of vessels of the United States Navy; or

(iii) owned or generated as a result of any research, development, testing, or production of any atomic weapon; and

(C) low-level radioactive waste described in subparagraphs (A) and (B) that is generated outside of the State and accepted for disposal in accordance with sections [1] 2021e or 2021f of this title.

(2) No regional disposal facility may be required to accept for disposal any material—

(A) that is not low-level radioactive waste as defined by section 61.55 of title 10, Code of Federal Regulations, as in effect on January 26, 1983, or

(B) identified under the Formerly Utilized Sites Remedial Action Program.

Nothing in this paragraph shall be deemed to prohibit a State, subject to the provisions of its compact, or a compact region from accepting for disposal any material identified in subparagraph (A) or (B).

**(b) Federal Government responsibilities**

(1) The Federal Government shall be responsible for the disposal of—

(A) low-level radioactive waste owned or generated by the Department of Energy;

(B) low-level radioactive waste owned or generated by the United States Navy as a result of the decommissioning of vessels of the United States Navy;

(C) low-level radioactive waste owned or generated by the Federal Government as a result of any research, development, testing, or production of any atomic weapon; and

(D) any other low-level radioactive waste with concentrations of radionuclides that exceed the limits established by the Commission for class C radioactive waste, as defined by section 61.55 of title 10, Code of Federal Regulations, as in effect on January 26, 1983.

(2) All radioactive waste designated a Federal responsibility pursuant to subparagraph (b)(1)(D) that results from activities licensed by the Nuclear Regulatory Commission under this chapter, shall be disposed of in a facility licensed by the Nuclear Regulatory Commission that the Commission determines is adequate to protect the public health and safety.

(3) Not later than 12 months after January 15, 1986, the Secretary shall submit to the Congress a comprehensive report setting forth the recommendations of the Secretary for ensuring the safe disposal of all radioactive waste designated a Federal responsibility pursuant to subparagraph (b)(1)(D). Such report shall include—

(A) an identification of the radioactive waste involved, including the source of such waste, and the volume, concentration, and other relevant characteristics of such waste;

(B) an identification of the Federal and non-Federal options for disposal of such radioactive waste;

(C) a description of the actions proposed to ensure the safe disposal of such radioactive waste;

(D) a description of the projected costs of undertaking such actions;

(E) an identification of the options for ensuring that the beneficiaries of the activities resulting in the generation of such radioactive wastes bear all reasonable costs of disposing of such wastes; and

(F) an identification of any statutory authority required for disposal of such waste.

(4) The Secretary may not dispose of any radioactive waste designated a Federal responsibility pursuant to paragraph (b)(1)(D) that becomes a Federal responsibility for the first time pursuant to such paragraph until ninety days after the report prepared pursuant to paragraph (3) has been submitted to the Congress.

(Pub.L. 96–573, § 3, as added Pub.L. 99–240, Title I, § 102, Jan. 15, 1986, 99 Stat. 1843.)

[1] So in original. Probably should be "section".

### HISTORICAL AND STATUTORY NOTES

**References in Text**

This chapter, referred to in subsec. (b)(2), is the Atomic Energy Act of 1954, Aug. 30, 1954, c. 1073, 68 Stat. 919, as amended, which is classified generally to chapter 23 (section 2011 et seq.) of this title. For complete classification of this

Act to the Code, see Short Title note set out under section 2011 of this title and Tables.

January 15, 1986, referred to in subsec. (b)(3), was in the original "the date of enactment of this Act" and was translated as meaning the date of enactment of Pub.L. 99–240 as the probable intent of Congress.

**Codifications**

Section was not enacted as part of the Atomic Energy Act of 1954 which comprises this chapter but as part of the Low-Level Radioactive Waste Policy Act.

**Prior Provisions**

A prior section 2021c, Pub.L. 96–573, § 3, Dec. 22, 1980, 94 Stat. 3347, which related to the application of low-level radioactive compacts, was repealed by Pub.L. 99–240, Title I, § 102, Jan. 15, 1986, 99 Stat. 1842. See section 2021d of this title.

## § 2021d. Regional compacts for disposal of low-level radioactive waste

**[LLRWPA § 4]**

**(a) In general**

**(1) Federal policy**

It is the policy of the Federal Government that the responsibilities of the States under section 2021c of this title for the disposal of low-level radioactive waste can be most safely and effectively managed on a regional basis.

**(2) Interstate compacts**

To carry out the policy set forth in paragraph (1), the States may enter into such compacts as may be necessary to provide for the establishment and operation of regional disposal facilities for low-level radioactive waste.

**(b) Applicability to Federal activities**

**(1) In general**

**(A) Activities of the Secretary**

Except as provided in subparagraph (B), no compact or action taken under a compact shall be applicable to the transportation, management, or disposal of any low-level radioactive waste designated in section 2021c(a)(1)(B)(i)–(iii) of this title.

**(B) Federal low-level radioactive waste disposed of at non-Federal facilities**

Low-level radioactive waste owned or generated by the Federal Government that is disposed of at a regional disposal facility or non-Federal disposal facility within a State that is not a member of a compact shall be subject to the same conditions, regulations, requirements, fees, taxes, and surcharges imposed by the compact commission, and by the State in which such facility is located, in the same manner and to the same extent as any low-level radioactive waste not generated by the Federal Government.

**(2) Federal low-level radioactive waste disposal facilities**

Any low-level radioactive waste disposal facility established or operated exclusively for the disposal of low-level radioactive waste owned or generated by the Federal Government shall not be subject to any compact or any action taken under a compact.

**(3) Effect of compacts on Federal law**

Nothing contained in sections 2021b to 2021j of this title or any compact may be construed to confer any new authority on any compact commission or State—

**(A)** to regulate the packaging, generation, treatment, storage, disposal, or transportation of low-level radioactive waste in a manner incompatible with the regulations of the Nuclear Regulatory Commission or inconsistent with the regulations of the Department of Transportation;

**(B)** to regulate health, safety, or environmental hazards from source material, byproduct material, or special nuclear material;

**(C)** to inspect the facilities of licensees of the Nuclear Regulatory Commission;

**(D)** to inspect security areas or operations at the site of the generation of any low-level radioactive waste by the Federal Government, or to inspect classified information related to such areas or operations; or

**(E)** to require indemnification pursuant to the provisions of chapter 171 of Title 28 (commonly referred to as the Federal Tort Claims Act), or section 2210 of this title, whichever is applicable.

**(4) Federal authority**

Except as expressly provided in sections 2021b to 2021j of this title, nothing contained in sections 2021b to 2021j of this title or any compact may be construed to limit the applicability of any Federal law or to diminish or otherwise impair the jurisdiction of any Federal agency, or to alter, amend, or otherwise affect any Federal law governing the judicial review of any action taken pursuant to any compact.

**(5) State authority preserved**

Except as expressly provided in sections 2021b to 2021j of this title, nothing contained in sections 2021b to 2021j of this title expands, diminishes, or otherwise affects State law.

**(c) Restricted use of regional disposal facilities**

Any authority in a compact to restrict the use of the regional disposal facilities under the compact to the disposal of low-level radioactive waste generated within the compact region shall not take effect before each of the following occurs:

(1) January 1, 1986; and

(2) the Congress by law consents to the compact.

**(d) Congressional review**

Each compact shall provide that every 5 years after the compact has taken effect the Congress may by law withdraw its consent.

(Pub.L. 96–573, § 4, as added Pub.L. 99–240, Title I, § 102, Jan. 15, 1986, 99 Stat. 1845.)

## HISTORICAL AND STATUTORY NOTES

**References in Text**

The Federal Tort Claims Act, referred to in subsec. (b)(3)(E), is classified generally to section 1346(b) and chapter 171 (section 2671 et seq.) of Title 28, Judiciary and Judicial Procedure.

**Codifications**

Section was not enacted as part of the Atomic Energy Act of 1954 which comprises this chapter, but as part of the Low–Level Radioactive Waste Policy Act.

**Prior Provisions**

A prior section 2021d, Pub.L. 96–573, § 4, Dec. 22, 1980, 94 Stat. 3348, which related to the policy of the Federal government concerning low-level radioactive waste disposal, implementation of that policy, and a report to Congress and the States to assist in carrying out the policy, was repealed by Pub.L. 99–240, Title I, § 102, Jan. 15, 1986, 99 Stat. 1842.

**Texas Low-Level Radioactive Waste Disposal Compact Consent Act**

Pub.L. 105–236, §§ 1–5, Sept. 20, 1998, 112 Stat. 1542, provided that:

**"Section 1. Short Title.**

"This Act [this note] may be cited as the 'Texas Low–Level Radioactive Waste Disposal Compact Consent Act'.

**"Sec. 2. Congressional Finding.**

"The Congress finds that the compact set forth in section 5 [of this note] is in furtherance of the Low–Level Radioactive Waste Policy Act (42 U.S.C. 2021b et seq.).

**"Sec. 3. Conditions of Consent to Compact.**

"The consent of the Congress to the compact set forth in section 5 [of this note]—

"(1) shall become effective on the date of the enactment of this Act [Sept. 20, 1998];

"(2) is granted subject to the provisions of the Low–Level Radioactive Waste Policy Act (42 U.S.C. 2021b et seq.); and

"(3) is granted only for so long as the regional commission established in the compact complies with all of the provisions of such Act.

**"Sec. 4. Congressional review.**

"The Congress may alter, amend, or repeal this Act [this note] with respect to the compact set forth in section 5 [of this note] after the expiration of the 10–year period following the date of the enactment of this Act [Sept. 20, 1998], and at such intervals thereafter as may be provided in such compact.

**"Sec. 5. Texas Low-Level Radioactive Waste Compact.**

**"(a) Consent of Congress.**—In accordance with section 4(a)(2) of the Low–Level Radioactive Waste Policy Act (42 U.S.C. 2021d(a)(2)), the consent of Congress is given to the States of Texas, Maine, and Vermont to enter into the compact set forth in subsection (b).

**"(b) Text of compact.**—The compact reads substantially as follows:

**Appalachian States Low-Level Radioactive Waste Compact Consent Act**

Pub.L. 100–319, May 19, 1988, 102 Stat. 471, provided that:

**"Section 1. Short Title.**

"This Act may be cited as the 'Appalachian States Low–Level Radioactive Waste Compact Consent Act'.

**"Sec. 2. Congressional Finding.**

The Congress finds that the compact set forth in section 5 is in furtherance of the Low–Level Radioactive Waste Policy Act [42 U.S.C.A. §§ 2021b to 2021j].

**"Sec. 3. Conditions of Consent to Compact.**

"The consent of the Congress to the compact set forth in section 5—

"(1) shall become effective on the date of the enactment of this Act [May 19,1988],

"(2) is granted subject to the provisions of the Low–Level Radioactive Waste Policy Act [42 U.S.C.A. §§ 2021b to 2021j], and

"(3) is granted only for so long as the Appalachian States Low–Level Radioactive Waste Commission, advisory committees, and regional boards established in the compact comply with all the provisions of such Act.

**"Sec. 4. Congressional Review.**

"The Congress may alter, amend, or repeal this Act with respect to the compact set forth in section 5 after the expiration of the 10-year period following the date of the enactment of this Act [May 19, 1988], and at such intervals thereafter as may be provided for in such compact.

**"Sec. 5. Appalachian States Low-Level Radioactive Waste Compact.**

"In accordance with section 4(a)(2) of the Low–Level Radioactive Waste Policy Act (42 U.S.C. 2021d(A)(2)) [subsec. (a)(2) of this section], the consent of Congress is given to the States of Pennsylvania, West Virginia, and any eligible States as defined in Article 5(A) of the Appalachian States Low–Level Radioactive Waste Compact to enter into such compact. Such compact is substantially as follows:

**Central Midwest Interstate Low-Level Radioactive Waste Compact Amendments Consent Act of 1994**

Pub.L. 103–439, Nov. 2, 1994, 108 Stat. 4607, provided that:

**"Section 1. Short Title.**

"This Act may be cited as the 'Central Midwest Interstate Low–Level Radioactive Waste Compact Amendments Consent Act of 1994'.

**"Sec. 2. Conditions of Consent to Compact Amendments.**

"The consent of the Congress to the compact amendments set forth in section 3—

"(1) shall become effective on the date of the enactment of this Act [Nov. 2, 1994];

"(2) is granted subject to the provisions of the Low–Level Radioactive Waste Policy Act (42 U.S.C. 2021b et seq.); and

"(3) is granted only for so long as the regional commission established in the amended compact complies with all of the provisions of such Act.

**"Sec. 3. Consent of Congress to Compact Amendments.**

"In accordance with section 4(a)(2) of the Low–Level Radioactive Waste Policy Act (42 U.S.C. 2021d(a)(2)), the consent of the Congress is hereby given to amendments made by the States of Illinois and Kentucky to the Central Midwest Interstate Low–Level Radioactive Waste Compact, which compact was consented to by the Congress in section 224 of the Omnibus Low–Level Radioactive Waste Interstate Compact Consent Act (Public Law 99–240; 42 U.S.C. 2021 note). The amendments to which such consent is given are substantially as follows:

**Omnibus Low–Level Radioactive Waste Interstate Compact Consent Act**

Pub.L. 99–240, Title II, Jan. 15, 1986, 99 Stat. 1859, provided that:

**"Sec. 201. Short Title.**

"This Title may be cited as the 'Omnibus Low–Level Radioactive Waste Interstate Compact Consent Act'.

**"Subtitle A—General Provisions**

**"Sec. 211. Congressional Finding.**

"The Congress hereby finds that each of the compacts set forth in subtitle B is in furtherance of the Low–Level Radioactive Waste Policy Act [42 U.S.C.A. §§ 2021b to 2021j].

**"Sec. 212. Conditions of Consent to Compacts.**

"The consent of the Congress to each of the compacts set forth in subtitle B—

"(1) shall become effective on the date of the enactment of this Act [Jan. 15, 1986];

"(2) is granted subject to the provisions of the Low–Level Radioactive Waste Policy Act, as amended [42 U.S.C.A. §§ 2021b to 2021j]; and

"(3) is granted only for so long as the regional commission, committee, or board established in the compact complies with all of the provisions of such Act.

**"Sec. 213. Congressional Review.**

"The Congress may alter, amend, or repeal this Act with respect to any compact set forth in subtitle B after the expiration of the 10-year period following the date of the enactment of this Act [Jan. 15, 1986], and at such intervals thereafter as may be provided in such compact.

**"Subtitle B—Congressional Consent to Compacts**

**"Sec. 221. Northwest Interstate Compact on Low–Level Radioactive Waste Management.**

"The consent of Congress is hereby given to the states of Alaska, Hawaii, Idaho, Montana, Oregon, Utah, Washington, and Wyoming to enter into the Northwest Interstate Compact on Low–level Radioactive Waste Management, and to each and every part and article thereof. Such compact reads substantially as follows:

**"Sec. 222. Central Interstate Low–Level Radioactive Waste Compact.**

"The consent of Congress is hereby given to the states of Arkansas, Iowa, Kansas, Louisiana, Minnesota, Missouri, Nebraska, North Dakota, and Oklahoma to enter into the Central Interstate Low–Level Radioactive Waste Compact, and to each and every part and article thereof. Such compact reads substantially as follows:

**"Sec. 223. Southeast Interstate Low–Level Radioactive Waste Management Compact.**

"In accordance with section 4(a)(2) of the Low–Level Radioactive Waste Policy Act (42 U.S.C. 2021d(a)(2)) [subsec. (a)(2) of this section], the consent of the Congress is hereby given to the States of Alabama, Florida, Georgia, Mississippi, North Carolina, South Carolina, Tennessee, and Virginia to enter into the Southeast Interstate Low–Level Radioactive Waste Management Compact. Such compact is substantially as follows:

**"Sec. 224. Central Midwest Interstate Low–Level Radioactive Waste Compact.**

"In accordance with section 4(a)(2) of the Low–Level Radioactive Waste Policy Act (42 U.S.C. 2021d(a)(2)) [subsec. (a)(2) of this section], the consent of the Congress hereby is given to the States of Illinois and Kentucky to enter into the Central Midwest Interstate Low–Level Radioactive Waste Compact. Such compact is substantially as follows:

**"Sec. 225. Midwest Interstate Low–Level Radioactive Waste Management Compact.**

"The consent of Congress is hereby given to the States of Iowa, Indiana, Michigan, Minnesota, Missouri, Ohio, and Wisconsin to enter into the Midwest Interstate Compact on Low–Level Radioactive Waste Management. Such compact is as follows:

**"Sec. 226. Rocky Mountain Low–Level Radioactive Waste Compact.**

"In accordance with section 4(a)(2) of the Low–Level Radioactive Waste Policy Act (42 U.S.C. 2021d(a)(2)) [subsec. (a)(2) of this section], the consent of the Congress hereby is given to the States of Arizona, Colorado, Nevada, New Mexico, Utah, and Wyoming to enter into the Rocky Mountain Interstate Low–Level Radioactive Waste Compact. Such compact is substantially as follows:

**"Sec. 227. Northeast Interstate Low–Level Radioactive Waste Management Compact.**

"In accordance with section 4(a)(2) of the Low–Level Radioactive Waste Policy Act [subsec. (a)(2) of this section], the consent of the Congress is hereby given to the States of Connecticut, New Jersey, Delaware, and Maryland to enter into the Northeast Interstate Low–Level Radioactive Waste Management Compact. Such compact is substantially as follows:

**Southwestern Low–Level Radioactive Waste Disposal Compact Consent Act**

Pub.L. 100–712, §§ 1–5, Nov. 23, 1988, 102 Stat. 4773, provided that:

**"Section 1. Short title.**

"This Act may be cited as the 'Southwestern Low–Level Radioactive Waste Disposal Compact Consent Act'.

**"Sec. 2. Congressional finding.**

"The Congress finds that the compact set forth in section 5 is in furtherance of the Low–Level Radioactive Waste Policy Act [42 U.S.C.A. §§ 2021b to 2021j].

**"Sec. 3. Conditions of consent to compact.**

"The consent of the Congress to the compact set forth in section 5—

"(1) shall become effective on the date of the enactment of this Act [November 23, 1988];

"(2) is granted subject to the provisions of the Low-Level Radioactive Waste Policy Act [42 U.S.C.A. §§ 2021b to 2021j]; and

"(3) is granted only for so long as the regional commission established in the compact complies with all of the provisions of such Act.

**"Sec. 4. Congressional review.**

"The Congress may alter, amend, or repeal this Act with respect to the compact set forth in section 5 after the expiration of the 10-year period following the date of enactment of this Act [November 23, 1988], and at such intervals thereafter as may be provided in such compact.

**"Sec. 5. Southwestern Low-Level Radioactive Waste Compact.**

"In accordance with section 4(a)(2) of the Low-Level Radioactive Waste Policy Act (42 U.S.C. 2021d(a)(2)) [subsec. (a)(2) of this section], the consent of Congress is given to the states of Arizona, California, and any eligible states, as defined in article VII of the Southwestern Low-Level Radioactive Waste Disposal Compact, to enter into such compact. Such compact is substantially as follows:

## § 2021e. Limited availability of certain regional disposal facilities during transition and licensing periods

[LLRWPA § 5]

### (a) Availability of disposal capacity

#### (1) Pressurized water and boiling water reactors

During the seven-year period beginning January 1, 1986 and ending December 31, 1992, subject to the provisions of subsections (b) through (g) of this section, each State in which there is located a regional disposal facility referred to in paragraphs (1) through (3) of subsection (b) of this section shall make disposal capacity available for low-level radioactive waste generated by pressurized water and boiling water commercial nuclear power reactors in accordance with the allocations established in subsection (c) of this section.

#### (2) Other sources of low-level radioactive waste

During the seven-year period beginning January 1, 1986 and ending December 31, 1992, subject to the provisions of subsections (b) through (g) of this section, each State in which there is located a regional disposal facility referred to in paragraphs (1) through (3) of subsection (b) of this section shall make disposal capacity available for low-level radioactive waste generated by any source not referred to in paragraph (1).

#### (3) Allocation of disposal capacity

**(A)** During the seven-year period beginning January 1, 1986 and ending December 31, 1992, low-level radioactive waste generated within a sited compact region shall be accorded priority under this section in the allocation of available disposal capacity at a regional disposal facility referred to in paragraphs (1) through (3) of subsection (b) of this section and located in the sited compact region in which such waste is generated.

**(B)** Any State in which a regional disposal facility referred to in paragraphs (1) through (3) of subsection (b) of this section is located may, subject to the provisions of its compact, prohibit the disposal at such facility of low-level radioactive waste generated outside of the compact region if the disposal of such waste in any given calendar year, together with all other low-level radioactive waste disposed of at such facility within that same calendar year, would result in that facility disposing of a total annual volume of low-level radioactive waste in excess of 100 per centum of the average annual volume for such facility designated in subsection (b) of this section: *Provided, however,* That in the event that all three States in which regional disposal facilities referred to in paragraphs (1) through (3) of subsection (b) of this section act to prohibit the disposal of low-level radioactive waste pursuant to this subparagraph, each such State shall, in accordance with any applicable procedures of its compact, permit, as necessary, the disposal of additional quantities of such waste in increments of 10 per centum of the average annual volume for each such facility designated in subsection (b) of this section.

**(C)** Nothing in this paragraph shall require any disposal facility or State referred to in paragraphs (1) through (3) of subsection (b) of this section to accept for disposal low-level radioactive waste in excess of the total amounts designated in subsection (b) of this section.

#### (4) Cessation of operation of low-level radioactive waste disposal facility

No provision of this section shall be construed to obligate any State referred to in paragraphs (1) through (3) of subsection (b) of this section to accept low-level radioactive waste from any source in the event that the regional disposal facility located in such State ceases operations.

### (b) Limitations

The availability of disposal capacity for low-level radioactive waste from any source shall be subject to the following limitations:

#### (1) Barnwell, South Carolina

The State of South Carolina, in accordance with the provisions of its compact, may limit the volume of low-level radioactive waste accepted for disposal at the regional disposal facility located at Barnwell, South Carolina to a total of 8,400,000 cubic feet of low-level radioactive waste during the 7-year period beginning January 1, 1986, and ending December 31, 1992 (as based on an average annual volume of 1,200,000 cubic feet of low-level radioactive waste).

**(2) Richland, Washington**

The State of Washington, in accordance with the provisions of its compact, may limit the volume of low-level radioactive waste accepted for disposal at the regional disposal facility located at Richland, Washington to a total of 9,800,000 cubic feet of low-level radioactive waste during the 7-year period beginning January 1, 1986, and ending December 31, 1992 (as based on an average annual volume of 1,400,000 cubic feet of low-level radioactive waste).

**(3) Beatty, Nevada**

The State of Nevada, in accordance with the provisions of its compact, may limit the volume of low-level radioactive waste accepted for disposal at the regional disposal facility located at Beatty, Nevada to a total of 1,400,000 cubic feet of low-level radioactive waste during the 7-year period beginning January 1, 1986, and ending December 31, 1992 (as based on an average annual volume of 200,000 cubic feet of low-level radioactive waste).

**(c) Commercial nuclear power reactor allocations**

**(1) Amount**

Subject to the provisions of subsections (a) through (g) of this section each commercial nuclear power reactor shall upon request receive an allocation of low-level radioactive waste disposal capacity (in cubic feet) at the facilities referred to in subsection (b) of this section during the 4-year transition period beginning January 1, 1986, and ending December 31, 1989, and during the 3-year licensing period beginning January 1, 1990, and ending December 31, 1992, in an amount calculated by multiplying the appropriate number from the following table by the number of months remaining in the applicable period as determined under paragraph (2).

| Reactor Type | 4-year Transition Period | | 3-year Licensing Period | |
|---|---|---|---|---|
| | In Sited Region | All Other Locations | In Sited Region | All Other Locations |
| PWR | 1027 | 871 | 934 | 685 |
| BWR | 2300 | 1951 | 2091 | 1533 |

**(2) Method of calculation**

For purposes of calculating the aggregate amount of disposal capacity available to a commercial nuclear power reactor under this subsection, the number of months shall be computed beginning with the first month of the applicable period, or the sixteenth month after receipt of a full power operating license, whichever occurs later.

**(3) Unused allocations**

Any unused allocation under paragraph (1) received by a reactor during the transition period or the licensing period may be used at any time after such reactor receives its full power license or after the beginning of the pertinent period, whichever is later, but not in any event after December 31, 1992, or after commencement of operation of a regional disposal facility in the compact region or State in which such reactor is located, whichever occurs first.

**(4) Transferability**

Any commercial nuclear power reactor in a State or compact region that is in compliance with the requirements of subsection (e) of this section may assign any disposal capacity allocated to it under this subsection to any other person in each State or compact region. Such assignment may be for valuable consideration and shall be in writing, copies of which shall be filed at the affected compact commissions and States, along with the assignor's unconditional written waiver of the disposal capacity being assigned.

**(5) Unusual volumes**

**(A)** The Secretary may, upon petition by the owner or operator of any commercial nuclear power reactor, allocate to such reactor disposal capacity in excess of the amount calculated under paragraph (1) if the Secretary finds and states in writing his reasons for so finding that making additional capacity available for such reactor through this paragraph is required to permit unusual or unexpected operating, maintenance, repair or safety activities.

**(B)** The Secretary may not make allocations pursuant to subparagraph (A) that would result in the acceptance for disposal of more than 800,000 cubic feet of low-level radioactive waste or would result in the total of the allocations made pursuant to this subsection exceeding 11,900,000 cubic feet over the entire seven-year interim access period.

**(6) Limitation**

During the seven-year interim access period referred to in subsection (a) of this section, the disposal facilities referred to in subsection (b) of this section shall not be required to accept more than

11,900,000 cubic feet of low-level radioactive waste generated by commercial nuclear power reactors.

**(d) Use of surcharge funds for milestone incentives; consequences of failure to meet disposal deadline**

**(1) Surcharges**

The disposal of any low-level radioactive waste under this section (other than low-level radioactive waste generated in a sited compact region) may be charged a surcharge by the State in which the applicable regional disposal facility is located, in addition to the fees and surcharges generally applicable for disposal of low-level radioactive waste in the regional disposal facility involved. Except as provided in subsection (e)(2) of this section, such surcharges shall not exceed—

(A) in 1986 and 1987, $10 per cubic foot of low-level radioactive waste;

(B) in 1988 and 1989, $20 per cubic foot of low-level radioactive waste; and

(C) in 1990, 1991, and 1992, $40 per cubic foot of low-level radioactive waste.

**(2) Milestone incentives**

**(A) Escrow account**

Twenty-five per centum of all surcharge fees received by a State pursuant to paragraph (1) during the seven-year period referred to in subsection (a) of this section shall be transferred on a monthly basis to an escrow account held by the Secretary. The Secretary shall deposit all funds received in a special escrow account. The funds so deposited shall not be the property of the United States. The Secretary shall act as trustee for such funds and shall invest them in interest-bearing United States Government Securities with the highest available yield. Such funds shall be held by the Secretary until—

(i) paid or repaid in accordance with subparagraph (B) or (C); or

(ii) paid to the State collecting such fees in accordance with subparagraph (F).

**(B) Payments**

**(i) July 1, 1986.**—The twenty-five per centum of any amount collected by a State under paragraph (1) for low-level radioactive waste disposed of under this section during the period beginning on January 15, 1986, and ending June 30, 1986, and transferred to the Secretary under subparagraph (A), shall be paid by the Secretary in accordance with subparagraph (D) if the milestone described in subsection (e)(1)(A) of this section is met by the State in which such waste originated.

**(ii) January 1, 1988.**—The twenty-five per centum of any amount collected by a State under paragraph (1) for low-level radioactive waste disposed of under this section during the period beginning July 1, 1986 and ending December 31, 1987, and transferred to the Secretary under subparagraph (A), shall be paid by the Secretary in accordance with subparagraph (D) if the milestone described in subsection (e)(1)(B) of this section is met by the State in which such waste originated (or its compact region, where applicable).

**(iii) January 1, 1990.**—The twenty-five per centum of any amount collected by a State under paragraph (1) for low-level radioactive waste disposed of under this section during the period beginning January 1, 1988 and ending December 31, 1989, and transferred to the Secretary under subparagraph (A), shall be paid by the Secretary in accordance with subparagraph (D) if the milestone described in subsection (e)(1)(C) of this section is met by the State in which such waste originated (or its compact region, where applicable).

**(iv)** The twenty-five per centum of any amount collected by a State under paragraph (1) for low-level radioactive waste disposed of under this section during the period beginning January 1, 1990 and ending December 31, 1992, and transferred to the Secretary under subparagrah[1] (A), shall be paid by the Secretary in accordance with subparagraph (D) if, by January 1, 1993, the State in which such waste originated (or its compact region, where applicable) is able to provide for the disposal of all low-level radioactive waste generated within such State or compact region.

**(C) Failure to meet January 1, 1993 deadline**

If, by January 1, 1993, a State (or, where applicable, a compact region) in which low-level radioactive waste is generated is unable to provide for the disposal of all such waste generated within such State or compact region—

(i) each State in which such waste is generated, upon the request of the generator or owner of the waste, shall take title to the waste, shall be obligated to take possession of the waste, and shall be liable for all damages directly or indirectly incurred by such generator or owner as a consequence of the failure of the State to take possession of the waste as soon after January 1, 1993 as the generator or owner notifies the State that the waste is available for shipment; or

(ii) if such State elects not to take title to, take possession of, and assume liability for such waste, pursuant to clause (i), twenty-five per centum of any amount collected by a State under paragraph (1) for low-level radioactive waste disposed of under this section during the period beginning January 1, 1990 and ending December 31, 1992 shall be repaid, with interest, to each generator from whom such surcharge was collected. Repayments made pursuant to this clause shall be made on a monthly basis, with the first such repayment beginning on February 1, 1993, in an amount equal to one thirty-sixth of the total amount required to be repaid pursuant to this clause, and shall continue until the State (or, where applicable, compact region) in which such low-level radioactive waste is generated is able to provide for the disposal of all such waste generated within such State or compact region or until January 1, 1996, whichever is earlier.

If a State in which low-level radioactive waste is generated elects to take title to, take possession of, and assume liability for such waste pursuant to clause (i), such State shall be paid such amounts as are designated in subparagraph (B)(iv). If a State (or, where applicable, a compact region) in which low-level radioactive waste is generated provides for the disposal of such waste at any time after January 1, 1993 and prior to January 1, 1996, such State (or, where applicable, compact region) shall be paid in accordance with subparagraph (D) a lump sum amount equal to twenty-five per centum of any amount collected by a State under paragraph (1): *Provided, however,* That such payment shall be adjusted to reflect the remaining number of months between January 1, 1993 and January 1, 1996 for which such State (or, where applicable, compact region) provides for the disposal of such waste. If a State (or, where applicable, a compact region) in which low-level radioactive waste is generated is unable to provide for the disposal of all such waste generated within such State or compact region by January 1, 1996, each State in which such waste is generated, upon the request of the generator or owner of the waste, shall take title to the waste, be obligated to take possession of the waste, and shall be liable for all damages directly or indirectly incurred by such generator or owner as a consequence of the failure of the State to take possession of the waste as soon after January 1, 1996, as the generator or owner notifies the State that the waste is available for shipment.

**(D) Recipients of payments**

The payments described in subparagraphs (B) and (C) shall be paid within thirty days after the applicable date—

(i) if the State in which such waste originated is not a member of a compact region, to such State;

(ii) if the State in which such waste originated is a member of the compact region, to the compact commission serving such State.

**(E) Uses of payments**

**(i) Limitations**

Any amount paid under subparagraphs (B) or (C) may only be used to—

(I) establish low-level radioactive waste disposal facilities;

(II) mitigate the impact of low-level radioactive waste disposal facilities on the host State;

(III) regulate low-level radioactive waste disposal facilities; or

(IV) ensure the decommissioning, closure, and care during the period of institutional control of low-level radioactive waste disposal facilities.

**(ii) Reports**

**(I) Recipient**

Any State or compact commission receiving a payment under subparagraphs (B) or (C) shall, on December 31 of each year in which any such funds are expended, submit a report to the Department of Energy itemizing any such expenditures.

**(II) Department of Energy**

Not later than six months after receiving the reports under subclause (I), the Secretary shall submit to the Congress a summary of all such reports that shall include an assessment of the compliance of each such State or compact commission with the requirements of clause (i).

**(F) Payment to States**

Any amount collected by a State under paragraph (1) that is placed in escrow under subparagraph (A) and not paid to a State or compact commission under subparagraphs (B) and (C) or not repaid to a generator under subparagraph (C) shall be paid from such escrow account to such State collecting such payment under paragraph (1). Such payment shall be made not later than 30 days after a determination of ineligibility for a refund is made.

(G) **Penalty surcharges**

No rebate shall be made under this subsection of any surcharge or penalty surcharge paid during a period of noncompliance with subsection (e)(1) of this section.

**(e) Requirements for access to regional disposal facilities**

**(1) Requirements for non-sited compact regions and non-member States**

Each non-sited compact region, or State that is not a member of a compact region that does not have an operating disposal facility, shall comply with the following requirements:

(A) By July 1, 1986, each such non-member State shall ratify compact legislation or, by the enactment of legislation or the certification of the Governor, indicate its intent to develop a site for the location of a low-level radioactive waste disposal facility within such State.

(B) By January 1, 1988

(i) each non-sited compact region shall identify the State in which its low-level radioactive waste disposal facility is to be located, or shall have selected the developer for such facility and the site to be developed, and each compact region or the State in which its low-level radioactive waste disposal facility is to be located shall develop a siting plan for such facility providing detailed procedures and a schedule for establishing a facility location and preparing a facility license application and shall delegate authority to implement such plan;

(ii) each non-member State shall develop a siting plan providing detailed procedures and a schedule for establishing a facility location and preparing a facility license application for a low-level radioactive waste disposal facility and shall delegate authority to implement such plan; and

(iii) The siting plan required pursuant to this paragraph shall include a description of the optimum way to attain operation of the low-level radioactive waste disposal facility involved, within the time period specified in sections 2021b to 2021j of this title. Such plan shall include a description of the objectives and a sequence of deadlines for all entities required to take action to implement such plan, including, to the extent practicable, an identification of the activities in which a delay in the start, or completion, of such activities will cause a delay in beginning facility operation. Such plan shall also identify, to the extent practicable, the process for (1) screening for broad siting areas; (2) identifying and evaluating specific candidate sites; and (3) characterizing the preferred site(s), completing all necessary environmental assessments, and preparing a license application for submission to the Nuclear Regulatory Commission or an Agreement State.

(C) By January 1, 1990

(i) a complete application (as determined by the Nuclear Regulatory Commission or the appropriate agency of an agreement State) shall be filed for a license to operate a low-level radioactive waste disposal facility within each non-sited compact region or within each non-member State; or

(ii) the Governor (or, for any State without a Governor, the chief executive officer) of any State that is not a member of a compact region in compliance with clause (i), or has not complied with such clause by its own actions, shall provide a written certification to the Nuclear Regulatory Commission, that such State will be capable of providing for, and will provide for, the storage, disposal, or management of any low-level radioactive waste generated within such State and requiring disposal after December 31, 1992, and include a description of the actions that will be taken to ensure that such capacity exists.

(D) By January 1, 1992, a complete application (as determined by the Nuclear Regulatory Commission or the appropriate agency of an agreement State) shall be filed for a license to operate a low-level radioactive waste disposal facility within each non-sited compact region or within each non-member State.

(E) The Nuclear Regulatory Commission shall transmit any certification received under subparagraph (C) to the Congress and publish any such certification in the Federal Register.

(F) Any State may, subject to all applicable provisions, if any, of any applicable compact, enter into an agreement with the compact commission of a region in which a regional disposal facility is located to provide for the disposal of all low-level radioactive waste generated within such State, and, by virtue of such agreement, may, with the approval of the State in which the regional disposal facility is located, be deemed to be in compliance with subparagraphs (A), (B), (C), and (D).

**(2) Penalties for failure to comply**

**(A) By July 1, 1986**

If any State fails to comply with subparagraph (1)(A)—

(i) any generator of low-level radioactive waste within such region or non-member State shall, for the period beginning July 1, 1986, and ending December 31, 1986, be charged 2 times the surcharge otherwise applicable under subsection (d) of this section; and

(ii) on or after January 1, 1987, any low-level radioactive waste generated within such region or non-member State may be denied access to the regional disposal facilities referred to in paragraphs (1) through (3) of subsection (b) of this section.

**(B) By January 1, 1988**

If any non-sited compact region or non-member State fails to comply with paragraph (1)(B)—

(i) any generator of low-level radioactive waste within such region or non-member State shall—

(I) for the period beginning January 1, 1988, and ending June 30, 1988, be charged 2 times the surcharge otherwise applicable under subsection (d) of this section; and

(II) for the period beginning July 1, 1988, and ending December 31, 1988, be charged 4 times the surcharge otherwise applicable under subsection (d) of this section; and

(ii) on or after January 1, 1989, any low-level radioactive waste generated within such region or non-member State may be denied access to the regional disposal facilities referred to in paragraphs (1) through (3) of subsection (b) of this section.

**(C) By January 1, 1990**

If any non-sited compact region or non-member State fails to comply with paragraph (1)(C), any low-level radioactive waste generated within such region or non-member State may be denied access to the regional disposal facilities referred to in paragraphs (1) through (3) of subsection (b) of this section.

**(D) By January 1, 1992**

If any non-sited compact region or non-member State fails to comply with paragraph (1)(D), any generator of low-level radioactive waste within such region or non-member State shall, for the period beginning January 1, 1992 and ending upon the filing of the application described in paragraph (1)(D), be charged 3 times the surcharge otherwise applicable under subsection (d) of this section.

**(3) Denial of access**

No denial or suspension of access to a regional disposal facility under paragraph (2) may be based on the source, class, or type of low-level radioactive waste.

**(4) Restoration of suspended access; penalties for failure to comply**

Any access to a regional disposal facility that is suspended under paragraph (2) shall be restored after the non-sited compact region or non-member State involved complies with such requirement. Any payment of surcharge penalties pursuant to paragraph (2) for failure to comply with the requirements this section shall be terminated after the non-sited compact region or non-member State involved complies with such requirements.

**(f) Monitoring of compliance and denial of access to non–Federal facilities for noncompliance; information requirements of certain States; proprietary information**

**(1) Administration**

Each State and compact commission in which a regional disposal facility referred to in paragraphs (1) through (3) of subsection (b) of this section is located shall have authority—

(A) to monitor compliance with the limitations, allocations, and requirements established in this section; and

(B) to deny access to any non-Federal low-level radioactive waste disposal facilities within its borders to any low-level radioactive waste that—

(i) is in excess of the limitations or allocations established in this section; or

(ii) is not required to be accepted due to the failure of a compact region or State to comply with the requirements of subsection (e)(1) of this section.

**(2) Availability of information during interim access period**

(A) The States of South Carolina, Washington, and Nevada may require information from disposal facility operators, generators, intermediate handlers, and the Department of Energy that is reasonably necessary to monitor the availability of disposal capacity, the use and assignment of allocations and the applicability of surcharges.

(B) The States of South Carolina, Washington, and Nevada may, after written notice followed by a period of at least 30 days, deny access to disposal capacity to any generator or intermediate handler who fails to provide information under subparagraph (A).

(C) Proprietary information.—

(i) Trade secrets, proprietary and other confidential information shall be made available to a State under this subsection upon request only if such State—

(I) consents in writing to restrict the dissemination of the information to those who are directly involved in monitoring under subparagraph (A) and who have a need to know;

(II) accepts liability for wrongful disclosure; and

(III) demonstrates that such information is essential to such monitoring.

(ii) The United States shall not be liable for the wrongful disclosure by any individual or State of any information provided to such individual or State under this subsection.

(iii) Whenever any individual or State has obtained possession of information under this subsection, the individual shall be subject to the same provisions of law with respect to the disclosure of such information as would apply to an officer or employee of the United States or of any department or agency thereof and the State shall be subject to the same provisions of law with respect to the disclosure of such information as would apply to the United States or any department or agency thereof. No State or State officer or employee who receives trade secrets, proprietary information, or other confidential information under sections 2021b to 2021j of this title may be required to disclose such information under State law.

**(g) Nondiscrimination**

Except as provided in subsections (b) through (e) of this section, low-level radioactive waste disposed of under this section shall be subject without discrimination to all applicable legal requirements of the compact region and State in which the disposal facility is located as if such low-level radioactive waste were generated within such compact region.

(Pub.L. 96–573, § 5, as added Pub.L. 99–240, Title I, § 102, Jan. 15, 1986, 99 Stat. 1846.)

[1] So in original. Probably should be "subparagraph".

### HISTORICAL AND STATUTORY NOTES

**Codifications**

Section was not enacted as part of the Atomic Energy Act of 1954 which comprises this chapter but as part of the Low-Level Radioactive Waste Policy Act.

## § 2021f. Emergency access

**[LLRWPA § 6]**

**(a) In general**

The Nuclear Regulatory Commission may grant emergency access to any regional disposal facility or non-Federal disposal facility within a State that is not a member of a compact for specific low-level radioactive waste, if necessary to eliminate an immediate and serious threat to the public health and safety or the common defense and security. The procedure for granting emergency access shall be as provided in this section.

**(b) Request for emergency access**

Any generator of low-level radioactive waste, or any Governor (or, for any State without a Governor, the chief executive officer of the State) on behalf of any generator or generators located in his or her State, may request that the Nuclear Regulatory Commission grant emergency access to a regional disposal facility or a non-Federal disposal facility within a State that is not a member of a compact for specific low-level radioactive waste. Any such request shall contain any information and certifications the Nuclear Regulatory Commission may require.

**(c) Determination of Nuclear Regulatory Commission**

**(1) Required determination**

Not later than 45 days after receiving a request under subsection (b) of this section, the Nuclear Regulatory Commission shall determine whether—

(A) emergency access is necessary because of an immediate and serious threat to the public health and safety or the common defense and security; and

(B) the threat cannot be mitigated by any alternative consistent with the public health and safety, including storage of low-level radioactive waste at the site of generation or in a storage facility obtaining access to a disposal facility by voluntary agreement, purchasing disposal capacity available for assignment pursuant to section 2021e(c) of this title or ceasing activities that generate low-level radioactive waste.

**(2) Required notification**

If the Nuclear Regulatory Commission makes the determinations required in paragraph (1) in the affirmative, it shall designate an appropriate non-Federal disposal facility or facilities, and notify the Governor (or chief executive officer) of the State in which such facility is located and the appropriate compact commission that emergency access is required. Such notification shall specifically describe the low-level radioactive waste as to source, physical and radiological characteristics, and the minimum volume and duration, not exceeding 180 days, necessary to alleviate the immediate threat to public health and safety or the common defense and security. The Nuclear Regulatory Commission shall also notify the Governor (or chief executive officer) of the State in which the low-level radioactive waste requiring emergency access was generated that emergency access has been granted and that, pursuant to subsection (e) of this section, no extension of emergency access may be granted absent diligent State action during the period of the initial grant.

**(d) Temporary emergency access**

Upon determining that emergency access is necessary because of an immediate and serious threat to the public health and safety or the common defense and security, the Nuclear Regulatory Commission may at its discretion grant temporary emergency access, pending its determination whether the threat could be mitigated by any alternative consistent with the public health and safety. In granting access under this subsection, the Nuclear Regulatory Commission shall provide the same notification and information required under subsection (c) of this section. Absent a determination that no alternative consistent with the public health and safety would mitigate the threat, access granted under this subsection shall expire 45 days after the granting of temporary emergency access under this subsection.

**(e) Extension of emergency access**

The Nuclear Regulatory Commission may grant one extension of emergency access beyond the period provided in subsection (c) of this section, if it determines that emergency access continues to be necessary because of an immediate and serious threat to the public health and safety or the common defense and security that cannot be mitigated by any alternative consistent with the public health and safety, and that the generator of low-level radioactive waste granted emergency access and the State in which such low-level radioactive waste was generated have diligently though unsuccessfully acted during the period of the initial grant to eliminate the need for emergency access. Any extension granted under this subsection shall be for the minimum volume and duration the Nuclear Regulatory Commission finds necessary to eliminate the immediate threat to public health and safety or the common defense and security, and shall not in any event exceed 180 days.

**(f) Reciprocal access**

Any compact region or State not a member of a compact that provides emergency access to non-Federal disposal facilities within its borders shall be entitled to reciprocal access to any subsequently operating non-Federal disposal facility that serves the State or compact region in which low-level radioactive waste granted emergency access was generated. The compact commission or State having authority to approve importation of low-level radioactive waste to the disposal facility to which emergency access was granted shall designate for reciprocal access an equal volume of low-level radioactive waste having similar characteristics to that provided emergency access.

**(g) Approval by compact commission**

Any grant of access under this section shall be submitted to the compact commission for the region in which the designated disposal facility is located for such approval as may be required under the terms of its compact. Any such compact commission shall act to approve emergency access not later than 15 days after receiving notification from the Nuclear Regulatory Commission, or reciprocal access not later than 15 days after receiving notification from the appropriate authority under subsection (f) of this section.

**(h) Limitations**

No State shall be required to provide emergency or reciprocal access to any regional disposal facility within its borders for low-level radioactive waste not meeting criteria established by the license or license agreement of such facility, or in excess of the approved capacity of such facility, or to delay the closing of any such facility pursuant to plans established before receiving a request for emergency or reciprocal access. No State shall, during any 12-month period, be required to provide emergency or reciprocal access to any regional disposal facility within its borders for more than 20 percent of the total volume of low-level radioactive waste accepted for disposal at such facility during the previous calendar year.

**(i) Volume reduction and surcharges**

Any low-level radioactive waste delivered for disposal under this section shall be reduced in volume to the maximum extent practicable and shall be subject to surcharges established in sections 2021b to 2021j of this title.

**(j) Deduction from allocation**

Any volume of low-level radioactive waste granted emergency or reciprocal access under this section, if generated by any commercial nuclear power reactor, shall be deducted from the low-level radioactive waste volume allocable under section 2021e(c) of this title.

**(k) Agreement States**

Any agreement under section 2021 of this title shall not be applicable to the determinations of the Nuclear Regulatory Commission under this section.

(Pub.L. 96–573, § 6, as added Pub.L. 99–240, Title I, § 102, Jan. 15, 1986, 99 Stat. 1855.)

## HISTORICAL AND STATUTORY NOTES

**Codifications**

Section was not enacted as part of the Atomic Energy Act of 1954 which comprises this chapter but as part of the Low-Level Radioactive Waste Policy Act.

## § 2021g. Responsibilities of Department of Energy

**[LLRWPA § 7]**

**(a) Financial and technical assistance**

The Secretary shall, to the extent provided in appropriations Act, provide to those compact regions, host States, and nonmember States detemined[1] by the Secretary to require assistance for purposes of carrying out sections 2021b to 2021j of this title—

(1) continuing technical assistance to assist them in fulfilling their responsibilities under sections 2021b to 2021j of this title. Such technical assistance shall include, but not be limited to, technical guidelines for site selection, alternative technologies for low-level radioactive waste disposal, volume reduction options, management techniques to reduce low-level waste generation, transportation practices for shipment of low-level wastes, health and safety considerations in the storage, shipment and disposal of low-level radioactive wastes, and establishment of a computerized database to monitor the management of low-level radioactive wastes; and

(2) through the end of fiscal year 1993, financial assistance to assist them in fulfilling their responsibilities under sections 2021b to 2021j of this title.

**(b) Omitted**

(Pub.L. 96–573, § 7, as added Pub.L. 99–240, Title I, § 102, Jan. 15, 1986, 99 Stat. 1858.)

[1] So in original. Probably should be "determined".

**HISTORICAL AND STATUTORY NOTES**

**Codifications**

Section was not enacted as part of the Atomic Energy Act of 1954 which comprises this chapter but as part of the Low-Level Radioactive Waste Policy Act.

Subsec. (b) of this section, which required the Secretary to prepare and submit to Congress on an annual basis a report on low—level waste disposal, terminated, effective May 15, 2000, pursuant to section 3003 of Pub.L. 104–66, as amended, set out as a note under 31 U.S.C.A. § 1113. See, also, item 2 on page 84 of House Document No. 103–97.

## § 2021h. Alternative disposal methods

**[LLRWPA § 8]**

**(a) Methods other than shallow land burial**

Not later than 12 months after January 15, 1986, the Nuclear Regulatory Commission shall, in consultation with the States and other interested persons, identify methods for the disposal of low-level radioactive waste other than shallow land burial, and establish and publish technical guidance regarding licensing of facilities that use such methods.

**(b) Technical information and requirements**

Not later than 24 months after January 15, 1986, the Commission shall, in consultation with the States and other interested persons, identify and publish all relevant technical information regarding the methods identified pursuant to subsection (a) of this section that a State or compact must provide to the Commission in order to pursue such methods, together with the technical requirements that such facilities must meet, in the judgment of the Commission, if pursued as an alternative to shallow land burial. Such technical information and requirements shall include, but need not be limited to, site suitability, site design, facility operation, disposal site closure, and environmental monitoring, as necessary to meet the performance objectives established by the Commission for a licensed low-level radioactive waste disposal facility. The Commission shall specify and publish such requirements in a manner and form deemed appropriate by the Commission.

(Pub.L. 96–573, § 8, as added Pub.L. 99–240, Title I, § 102, Jan. 15, 1986, 99 Stat. 1858.)

**HISTORICAL AND STATUTORY NOTES**

**Codifications**

Section was not enacted as part of the Atomic Energy Act of 1954 which comprises this chapter but as part of the Low-Level Radioactive Waste Policy Act.

## § 2021i. Licensing review and approval

**[LLRWPA § 9]**

In order to ensure the timely development of new low-level radioactive waste disposal facilities, the Nuclear Regulatory Commission or, as appropriate, agreement States, shall consider an application for a disposal facility license in accordance with the laws applicable to such application, except that the Commission and the agreement state [1] shall—

(1) not later than 12 months after January 15, 1986, establish procedures and develop the technical capability for processing applications for such licenses;

(2) to the extent practicable, complete all activities associated with the review and processing of any application for such a license (except for public hearings) no later than 15 months after the date of receipt of such application; and

(3) to the extent practicable, consolidate all required technical and environmental reviews and public hearings.

(Pub.L. 96–573, § 9, as added Pub.L. 99–240, Title I, § 102, Jan. 15, 1986, 99 Stat. 1859.)

[1] So in original. Probably should be "States".

**HISTORICAL AND STATUTORY NOTES**

**Codifications**

Section was not enacted as part of the Atomic Energy Act of 1954 which comprises this chapter but as part of the Low-Level Radioactive Waste Policy Act.

## § 2021j. Radioactive waste below regulatory concern

**[LLRWPA § 10]**

**(a) Standards and procedures**

Not later than 6 months after January 15, 1986, the Commission shall establish standards and procedures, pursuant to existing authority, and develop the technical capability for considering and acting upon petitions to exempt specific radioactive waste streams from regulation by the Commission due to the presence of radionuclides in such waste streams in sufficiently low concentrations or quantities as to be below regulatory concern.

**(b) Submission of supporting information**

The standards and procedures established by the Commission pursuant to subsection (a) of this section shall set forth all information required to be submitted to the Commission by licensees in support of such petitions, including, but not limited to—

(1) a detailed description of the waste materials, including their origin, chemical composition, physical state, volume, and mass; and

(2) the concentration or contamination levels, half-lives, and identities of the radionuclides present.

Such standards and procedures shall provide that, upon receipt of a petition to exempt a specific radioactive waste stream from regulation by the Commission, the Commission shall determine in an expeditious manner whether the concentration or quantity of radionuclides present in such waste stream requires regulation by the Commission in order to protect the public health and safety. Where the Commission determines that regulation of a radioactive waste stream is not necessary to protect the public health and safety, the Commission shall take such steps as may be necessary, in an expeditious manner, to exempt the disposal of such radioactive waste from regulation by the Commission.

(Pub.L. 96–573, § 10, as added Pub.L. 99–240, Title I, § 102, Jan. 15, 1986, 99 Stat. 1859.)

### HISTORICAL AND STATUTORY NOTES

**Codifications**

Section was not enacted as part of the Atomic Energy Act of 1954 which comprises this chapter but as part of the Low-Level Radioactive Waste Policy Act.

## § 2022. Health and environmental standards for uranium mill tailings

[AEA § 275]

**(a) Promulgation and revision of rules for protection from hazards at inactive or depository sites**

As soon as practicable, but not later than October 1, 1982, the Administrator of the Environmental Protection Agency (hereinafter referred to in this section as the "Administrator") shall, by rule, promulgate standards of general application (including standards applicable to licenses under section 104(h) of the Uranium Mill Tailings Radiation Control Act of 1978 [42 U.S.C.A. § 7914(h)]) for the protection of the public health, safety, and the environment from radiological and nonradiological hazards associated with residual radioactive materials (as defined in section 101 of the Uranium Mill Tailings Radiation Control Act of 1978 [42 U.S.C.A. § 7911]) located at inactive uranium mill tailings sites and depository sites for such materials selected by the Secretary of Energy, pursuant to Title I of the Uranium Mill Tailings Radiation Control Act of 1978 [42 U.S.C.A. § 7911 et seq.]. Standards promulgated pursuant to this subsection shall, to the maximum extent practicable, be consistent with the requirements of the Solid Waste Disposal Act, as amended [42 U.S.C.A. § 6901 et seq.]. In establishing such standards, the Administrator shall consider the risk to the public health, safety, and the environment, the environmental and economic costs of applying such standards, and such other factors as the Administrator determines to be appropriate. The Administrator may periodically revise any standard promulgated pursuant to this subsection. After October 1, 1982, if the Administrator has not promulgated standards in final form under this subsection, any action of the Secretary of Energy under title I of the Uranium Mill Tailings Radiation Control Act of 1978 which is required to comply with, or be taken in accordance with, standards of the Administrator shall comply with, or be taken in accordance with, the standards proposed by the Administrator under this subsection until such time as the Administrator promulgates such standards in final form.

**(b) Promulgation and revision of rules for protection from hazards at processing or disposal sites**

(1) As soon as practicable, but not later than October 31, 1982, the Administrator shall, by rule, propose, and within 11 months thereafter promulgate in final form, standards of general application for the protection of the public health, safety, and the environment from radiological and nonradiological hazards associated with the processing and with the possession, transfer, and disposal of byproduct material, as defined in section 2014(e)(2) of this title, at sites at which ores are processed primarily for their source material content or which are used for the disposal of such byproduct material. If the Administrator fails to promulgate standards in final form under this subsection by October 1, 1983, the authority of the Administrator to promulgate such standards shall terminate, and the Commission may take actions under this chapter without regard to any provision of this chapter requiring such actions to comply with, or be taken in accordance with, standards promulgated by the Administrator. In any such case, the Commission shall promulgate, and from time to time revise, any such standards of

general application which the Commission deems necessary to carry out its responsibilities in the conduct of its licensing activities under this chapter. Requirements established by the Commission under this chapter with respect to byproduct material as defined in section 2014(e)(2) of this title shall conform to such standards. Any requirements adopted by the Commission respecting such byproduct material before promulgation by the Commission of such standards shall be amended as the Commission deems necessary to conform to such standards in the same manner as provided in subsection (f)(3) of this section. Nothing in this subsection shall be construed to prohibit or suspend the implementation or enforcement by the Commission of any requirement of the Commission respecting byproduct material as defined in section 2014(e)(2) of this title pending promulgation by the Commission of any such standard of general application. In establishing such standards, the Administrator shall consider the risk to the public health, safety, and the environment, the environmental and economic costs of applying such standards, and such other factors as the Administrator determines to be appropriate.

(2) Such generally applicable standards promulgated pursuant to this subsection for nonradiological hazards shall provide for the protection of human health and the environment consistent with the standards required under subtitle C of the Solid Waste Disposal Act, as amended [42 U.S.C.A. § 6921 et seq.], which are applicable to such hazards: *Provided, however,* That no permit issued by the Administrator is required under this chapter or the Solid Waste Disposal Act, as amended [42 U.S.C.A. § 6901 et seq.], for the processing, possession, transfer, or disposal of byproduct material, as defined in section 2014(e)(2) of this title. The Administrator may periodically revise any standard promulgated pursuant to this subsection. Within three years after such revision of any such standard, the Commission and any State permitted to exercise authority under section 2021(b)(2) of this title shall apply such revised standard in the case of any license for byproduct material as defined in section 2014(e)(2) of this title or any revision thereof.

**(c) Publication in Federal Register; notice and hearing; consultations; judicial review; time for petition; venue; copy to Administrator; record; administrative jurisdiction; review by Supreme Court; effective date of rule**

(1) Before the promulgation of any rule pursuant to this section, the Administrator shall publish the proposed rule in the Federal Register, together with a statement of the research, analysis, and other available information in support of such proposed rule, and provide a period of public comment of at least thirty days for written comments thereon and an opportunity, after such comment period and after public notice, for any interested person to present oral data, views, and arguments at a public hearing. There shall be a transcript of any such hearing. The Administrator shall consult with the Commission and the Secretary of Energy before promulgation of any such rule.

(2) Judicial review of any rule promulgated under this section may be obtained by any interested person only upon such person filing a petition for review within sixty days after such promulgation in the United States court of appeals for the Federal judicial circuit in which such person resides or has his principal place of business. A copy of the petition shall be forthwith transmitted by the clerk of court to the Administrator. The Administrator thereupon shall file in the court the written submissions to, and transcript of, the written or oral proceedings on which such rule was based as provided in section 2112 of Title 28. The court shall have jurisdiction to review the rule in accordance with chapter 7 of Title 5 and to grant appropriate relief as provided in such chapter. The judgment of the court affirming, modifying, or setting aside, in whole or in part, any such rule shall be final, subject to judicial review by the Supreme Court of the United States upon certiorari or certification as provided in section 1254 of Title 28.

(3) Any rule promulgated under this section shall not take effect earlier than sixty calendar days after such promulgation.

**(d) Federal and State implementation and enforcement**

Implementation and enforcement of the standards promulgated pursuant to subsection (b) of this section shall be the responsibility of the Commission in the conduct of its licensing activities under this chapter. States exercising authority pursuant to section 2021(b)(2) of this title shall implement and enforce such standards in accordance with subsection (*o*) of such section.

**(e) Other authorities of Administrator unaffected**

Nothing in this chapter applicable to byproduct material, as defined in section 2014(e)(2) of this title, shall affect the authority of the Administrator under the Clean Air Act of 1970, as amended [42 U.S.C.A. § 7401 et seq.], or the Federal Water Pollution Control Act, as amended [33 U.S.C.A. § 1251 et seq.].

**(f) Implementation or enforcement of Uranium Mill Licensing Requirements**

(1) Prior to January 1, 1983, the Commission shall not implement or enforce the provisions of the Uranium Mill Licensing Requirements published as final rules at 45 Federal Register 65521 to 65538 on October 3, 1980 (hereinafter in this subsection referred to as the "October 3 regulations"). After December 31,

1982, the Commission is authorized to implement and enforce the provisions of such October 3 regulations (and any subsequent modifications or additions to such regulations which may be adopted by the Commission), except as otherwise provided in paragraphs (2) and (3) of this subsection.

**(2)** Following the proposal by the Administrator of standards under subsection (b) of this section, the Commission shall review the October 3 regulations, and, not later than 90 days after the date of such proposal, suspend implementation and enforcement of any provision of such regulations which the Commission determines after notice and opportunity for public comment to require a major action or major commitment by licensees which would be unnecessary if—

**(A)** the standards proposed by the Administrator are promulgated in final form without modification, and

**(B)** the Commission's requirements are modified to conform to such standards.

Such suspension shall terminate on the earlier of April 1, 1984 or the date on which the Commission amends the October 3 regulations to conform to final standards promulgated by the Administrator under subsection (b) of this section. During the period of such suspension, the Commission shall continue to regulate byproduct material (as defined in section 2014(e)(2) of this title) under this chapter on a licensee-by-licensee basis as the Commission deems necessary to protect public health, safety, and the environment.

**(3)** Not later than 6 months after the date on which the Administrator promulgates final standards pursuant to subsection (b) of this section, the Commission shall, after notice and opportunity for public comment, amend the October 3 regulations, and adopt such modifications, as the Commission deems necessary to conform to such final standards of the Administrator.

**(4)** Nothing in this subsection may be construed as affecting the authority or responsibility of the Commission under section 2114 of this title to promulgate regulations to protect the public health and safety and the environment.

(Aug. 1, 1946, c. 724, Title I, § 275, as added Nov. 8, 1978, Pub.L. 95–604, Title II, § 206(a), 92 Stat. 3039, and amended Jan. 4, 1983, Pub.L. 97–415, §§ 18(a), 22(b), 96 Stat. 2077, 2080; renumbered Title I, Oct. 24, 1992, Pub.L. 102–486, Title IX, § 902(a)(8), 106 Stat. 2944.)

### HISTORICAL AND STATUTORY NOTES

**References in Text**

The Uranium Mill Tailings Radiation Control Act of 1978, referred to in subsec. (a), is Pub.L. 95–604, Nov. 8, 1978, 92 Stat. 3021. Title I of such act is classified generally to subchapter I (section 7911 et seq.) of chapter 88 of this title. For complete classification of this act to the Code, see Short Title note set out under section 7901 of this title and Tables.

The Solid Waste Disposal Act, as amended, referred to in subsecs. (a) and (b)(2), is Title II of Pub.L. 89–272, as amended generally by Pub.L. 94–580, § 2, Oct. 21, 1976, 90 Stat. 2795, which is classified generally to chapter 82 (section 6901 et seq.) of this title. Subtitle C of the Solid Waste Disposal Act is classified generally to subchapter III (section 6921 et seq.) of chapter 82 of this title. For complete classification of this Act to the Code, see Short Title note set out under section 6901 of this title and Tables.

The Clean Air Act of 1970, as amended, referred to in subsec. (e), probably means the Clean Air Act, which is Act July 14, 1955, c. 360, as amended generally by Pub.L. 88–206, Dec. 17, 1963, 77 Stat. 392, and later by Pub.L. 95–95, Aug. 7, 1977, 91 Stat. 685. The Clean Air Act was originally classified to chapter 15B (section 1857 et seq.) of this title. On enactment of Pub.L. 95–95, the Act was reclassified to chapter 85 (section 7401 et seq.) of this title. For complete classification of this Act to the Code, see Short Title note set out under section 7401 of this title and Tables.

The Federal Water Pollution Control Act, as amended, referred to in subsec. (e), is Act June 30, 1948, c. 758, as amended generally by Pub.L. 92–500, § 2, Oct. 18, 1972, 86 Stat. 816, which is classified generally to chapter 26 (section 1251 et seq.) of Title 33, Navigation and Navigable Waters. For complete classification of this Act to the Code, see Short Title note set out under section 1251 of Title 33 and Tables.

**Effective and Applicability Provisions**

1978 Acts

Section effective Nov. 8, 1978, see section 208 of Pub.L. 95–604, set out as a note under section 2014 of this title.

**Transfer of Functions**

The Atomic Energy Commission was abolished and all functions of the Commission, the Chairman, the members of the Commission, and the officers and components of the Commission under this section were transferred to and vested in the Nuclear Regulatory Commission by sections 5814 and 5841 of this title.

## SUBCHAPTER VII—BYPRODUCT MATERIALS

### HISTORICAL AND STATUTORY NOTES

**Prior Provisions**

Provisions similar to those comprising this subchapter were contained in section 5 of Act Aug. 1, 1946, c. 724, 60 Stat. 760 (formerly classified to section 1805 of this title) prior to the complete amendment and renumbering of Act Aug. 1, 1946 by Act Aug. 30, 1954, c. 1073, 68 Stat. 921.

## § 2111. Domestic distribution; license; price limitations

**[AEA § 81]**

No person may transfer or receive in interstate commerce, manufacture, produce, transfer, acquire, own, possess, import, or export any byproduct material, except to the extent authorized by this section, section 2112 or section 2114 of this title. The Commission is authorized to issue general or specific licenses to applicants seeking to use byproduct material for research or development purposes, for medical therapy, industrial uses, agricultural uses, or such other useful applications as may be developed. The Commission may distribute, sell, loan, or lease such byproduct material as it owns to qualified applicants with or without charge: *Provided, however*, That, for byproduct material to be distributed by the Commission for a charge, the Commission shall establish prices on such equitable basis as, in the opinion of the Commission, (a) will provide reasonable compensation to the Government for such material, (b) will not discourage the use of such material or the development of sources of supply of such material independent of the Commission, and (c) will encourage research and development. In distributing such material, the Commission shall give preference to applicants proposing to use such material either in the conduct of research and development or in medical therapy. The Commission shall not permit the distribution of any byproduct material to any licensee, and shall recall or order the recall of any distributed material from any licensee, who is not equipped to observe or who fails to observe such safety standards to protect health as may be established by the Commission or who uses such material in violation of law or regulation of the Commission or in a manner other than as disclosed in the application therefor or approved by the Commission. The Commission is authorized to establish classes of byproduct material and to exempt certain classes or quantities of material or kinds of uses or users from the requirements for a license set forth in this section when it makes a finding that the exemption of such classes or quantities of such material or such kinds of uses or users will not constitute an unreasonable risk to the common defense and security and to the health and safety of the public.

(Aug. 1, 1946, c. 724, Title I, § 81, as added Aug. 30, 1954, c. 1073, § 1, 68 Stat. 935, and amended Aug. 17, 1974, Pub.L. 93–377, § 4, 88 Stat. 475; Nov. 8, 1978, Pub.L. 95–604, Title II, § 205(b), 92 Stat. 3039; renumbered Title I, Oct. 24, 1992, Pub.L. 102–486, Title IX, § 902(a)(8), 106 Stat. 2944.)

### HISTORICAL AND STATUTORY NOTES

**Effective and Applicability Provisions**

1978 Acts

Amendment by Pub.L. 95–604 effective Nov. 8, 1978, see section 208 of Pub.L. 95–604, set out a note under section 2014 of this title.

**Transfer of Functions**

For transfer of certain functions from the Nuclear Regulatory Commission to the Chairman thereof, see Reorg. Plan No. 1 of 1980, 45 F.R. 40561, 94 Stat. 3585, set out under section 5841 of this title.

The Atomic Energy Commission was abolished and all functions under these sections relating to distribution of byproduct material were transferred to the Administrator of the Energy Research and Development Administration and the functions relating to licensing transferred to the Nuclear Regulatory Commission by sections 5814 and 5841 of this title. The Energy Research and Development Administration was terminated and functions vested by law in the Administrator thereof were transferred to the Secretary of Energy (unless otherwise specifically provided) by sections 7151(a) and 7293 of this title.

**Prior Provisions**

Provisions similar to this section were contained in section 1805(c)(2) of this title prior to the general amendment and renumbering of Act Aug. 1, 1946 by Act Aug. 30, 1954, c. 1073, 68 Stat. 921.

## § 2113. Ownership and custody of certain byproduct material and disposal sites

**[AEA § 83]**

**(a) Specific assurances in license for pretermination actions**

Any license issued or renewed after the effective date of this section under section 2092 or section 2111 of this title for any activity which results in the production of any byproduct material, as defined in section 2014(e)(2) of this title, shall contain such terms and conditions as the Commission determines to be necessary to assure that, prior to termination of such license—

(1) the licensee will comply with decontamination, decommissioning, and reclamation standards prescribed by the Commission for sites (A) at which ores were processed primarily for their source material content and (B) at which such byproduct material is deposited, and

(2) ownership of any byproduct material, as defined in section 2014(e)(2) of this title, which resulted from such licensed activity shall be transferred to (A) the United States or (B) in the State in which such activity occurred if such State exercises the option under subsection (b)(1) of this section to acquire land used for the disposal of byproduct material.

Any license which is in effect on the effective date of this section and which is subsequently terminated without renewal shall comply with paragraphs (1) and (2) upon termination.

**(b) Transfer of title; health and environmental protection through maintenance of property and materials; use of surface or subsurface estates; first refusal rights of transferor; maintenance, monitoring, and emergency measures and other authorized action; licensee-transferor liability for fraud or negligence; administrative and legal costs limitation; government retransfers under section 7914(h) of this title**

(1)(A) The Commission shall require by rule, regulation, or order that prior to the termination of any license which is issued after the effective date of this section, title to the land, including any interests therein (other than land owned by the United States or by a State) which is used for the disposal of any byproduct material, as defined by section 2014(e)(2) of this title, pursuant to such license shall be transferred to—

(i) the United States, or

(ii) the State in which such land is located, at the option of such State,

unless the Commission determines prior to such termination that transfer of title to such land and such byproduct material is not necessary or desirable to protect the public health, safety, or welfare or to minimize or eliminate danger to life or property. Such determination shall be made in accordance with section 2231 of this title. Notwithstanding any other provision of law or any such determination, such property and materials shall be maintained pursuant to a license issued by the Commission pursuant to section 2111 of this title in such manner as will protect the public health, safety, and the environment.

(B) If the Commission determines by order that use of the surface or subsurface estates, or both, of the land transferred to the United States or to a State under subparagraph (A) would not endanger the public health, safety, welfare, or environment, the Commission, pursuant to such regulations as it may prescribe, shall permit the use of the surface or subsurface estates, or both, of such land in a manner consistent with the provisions of this section. If the Commission permits such use of such land, it shall provide the person who transferred such land with the right of first refusal with respect to such use of such land.

(2) If transfer to the United States of title to such byproduct material and such land is required under this section, the Secretary of Energy or any Federal agency designated by the President shall, following the Commission's determination of compliance under subsection (c) of this section, assume title and custody of such byproduct material and land transferred as provided in this subsection. Such Secretary or Federal agency shall maintain such material and land in such manner as will protect the public health and safety and the environment. Such custody may be transferred to another officer or instrumentality of the United States only upon approval of the President.

(3) If transfer to a State of title to such byproduct material is required in accordance with this subsection, such State shall, following the Commission's determination of compliance under subsection (d) of this section, assume title and custody of such byproduct material and land transferred as provided in this subsection. Such State shall maintain such material and land in such manner as will protect the public health, safety, and the environment.

(4) In the case of any such license under section 2092 of this title, which was in effect on the effective date of this section, the Commission may require, before the termination of such license, such transfer of land and interests therein (as described in paragraph (1) of this subsection) to the United States or a State in which such land is located, at the option of such State, as may be necessary to protect the public health, welfare, and the environment from any effects associated with such byproduct material. In exercising the authority of this paragraph, the Commission shall take into consideration the status of the ownership of such land and interests therein and the ability of the licensee to transfer title and custody thereof to the United States or a State.

(5) The Commission may, pursuant to a license, or by rule or order, require the Secretary or other Federal agency or State having custody of such property and materials to undertake such monitoring, maintenance, and emergency measures as are necessary to protect the public health and safety and such other actions as the Commission deems necessary to comply with the standards promulgated pursuant to section 2114 of this title. The Secretary or such other Federal agency is authorized to carry out maintenance, monitoring, and emergency measures, but shall take no other action pursuant to such license, rule or order, with respect to such property and materials unless expressly authorized by Congress after November 8, 1978.

(6) The transfer of title to land or byproduct materials, as defined in section 2014(e)(2) of this title, to a State or the United States pursuant to this subsection shall not relieve any licensee of liability for any fraudulent or negligent acts done prior to such transfer.

(7) Material and land transferred to the United States or a State in accordance with this subsection shall be transferred without cost to the United States or a State (other than administrative and legal costs incurred in carrying out such transfer). Subject to the provisions of paragraph (1)(B) of this subsection, the United States or a State shall not transfer title to material or property acquired under this subsection to any person, unless such transfer is in the same manner as provided under section 7914(h) of this title.

(8) The provisions of this subsection respecting transfer of title and custody to land shall not apply in the case of lands held in trust by the United States for any Indian tribe or lands owned by such Indian tribe subject to a restriction against alienation imposed by the United States. In the case of such lands which are used for the disposal of byproduct material, as defined in section 2014(e)(2) of this title, the licensee shall be required to enter into such arrangements with the Commission as may be appropriate to assure the

long-term maintenance and monitoring of such lands by the United States.

**(c) Compliance with applicable standards and license requirements; determination upon termination of license**

Upon termination on[1] any license to which this section applies, the Commission shall determine whether or not the licensee has complied with all applicable standards and requirements under such license.

(Aug. 1, 1946, c. 724, Title I, § 83, as added Nov. 8, 1978, Pub.L. 95–604, Title II, § 202(a), 92 Stat. 3033, and amended Nov. 9, 1979, Pub.L. 96–106, § 22(c), (e), 93 Stat. 800; renumbered Title I, Oct. 24, 1992, Pub.L. 102–486, Title IX, § 902(a)(8), 106 Stat. 2944.)

[1] So in original. Probably should be "of".

## HISTORICAL AND STATUTORY NOTES

**References in Text**

Effective date of this section, referred to in subsecs. (a) and (b)(1)(A), (4), as being three years after Nov. 8, 1978, see section 202(b) of Pub.L. 95–604, set out as an Effective Date note under this section.

**Effective and Applicability Provisions**

1978 Acts

Section 202(b) of Pub.L. 95–604 provided that: "This section [enacting this section] shall be effective three years after the enactment of this Act [Nov. 8, 1978]."

**Transfer of Functions**

The Atomic Energy Commission was abolished and all functions were transferred to the Nuclear Regulatory Commission and the Administrator of the Energy Research and Development Administration by sections 5814 and 5841 of this title. The Energy Research and Development Administration was terminated and functions vested by law in the Administrator thereof were transferred to the Secretary of Energy (unless otherwise specifically provided) by sections 7151(a) and 7293 of this title.

**Consolidation of Licenses and Procedures**

Section 209 of Pub.L. 95–604 provided that: "The Nuclear Regulatory Commission shall consolidate, to the maximum extent practicable, licenses and licensing procedures under amendments made by this title [enacting sections 2021(*o*), 2022, 2113, 2114, and 2201(x) of this title, amending sections 2014(e), 2021(b), (c), (d)(2), (j), (n), and 2111 of this title, and enacting note provisions under sections 2014, 2021, and 2113 of this title] with licenses and licensing procedures under other authorities contained in the Atomic Energy Act of 1954 [this chapter]."

[Provision effective Nov. 8, 1978, see section 208 of Pub.L. 95–604, set out as an Effective and Applicability Provisions of 1978 Acts note under section 2014 of this title.]

## § 2114. Authorities of Commission respecting certain byproduct material

[AEA § 84]

**(a) Management function**

The Commission shall insure that the management of any byproduct material, as defined in section 2014(e)(2) of this title, is carried out in such manner as—

(1) the Commission deems appropriate to protect the public health and safety and the environment from radiological and non-radiological hazards associated with the processing and with the possession and transfer of such material, taking into account the risk to the public health, safety, and the environment, with due consideration of the economic costs and such other factors as the Commission determines to be appropriate,,[1]

(2) conforms with applicable general standards promulgated by the Administrator of the Environmental Protection Agency under section 2022 of this title, and

(3) conforms to general requirements established by the Commission, with the concurrence of the Administrator, which are, to the maximum extent practicable, at least comparable to requirements applicable to the possession, transfer, and disposal of similar hazardous material regulated by the Administrator under the Solid Waste Disposal Act, as amended [42 U.S.C.A. § 6901 et seq.].

**(b) Rules, regulations, or orders for certain activities; civil penalty**

In carrying out its authority under this section, the Commission is authorized to—

(1) by rule, regulation, or order require persons, officers, or instrumentalities exempted from licensing under section 2111 of this title to conduct monitoring, perform remedial work, and to comply with such other measures as it may deem necessary or desirable to protect health or to minimize danger to life or property, and in connection with the disposal or storage of such byproduct material; and

(2) make such studies and inspections and to conduct such monitoring as may be necessary.

Any violation by any person other than the United States or any officer or employee of the United States or a State of any rule, regulation, or order or licensing provision, of the Commission established under this section or section 2113 of this title shall be subject to a civil penalty in the same manner and in the same amount as violations subject to a civil penalty under section 2282 of this title. Nothing in this section affects any authority of the Commission under any other provision of this chapter.

**(c) Alternative requirements or proposals**

In the case of sites at which ores are processed primarily for their source material content or which are used for the disposal of byproduct material as defined in section 2014(e)(2) of this title, a licensee may propose alternatives to specific requirements adopted and enforced by the Commission under this chapter. Such alternative proposals may take into account local or regional conditions, including geology, topography, hydrology and meteorology. The Commission may treat such alternatives as satisfying Commission requirements if the Commission determines that such alternatives will achieve a level of stabilization and containment of the sites concerned, and a level of protection for public health, safety, and the environment from radiological and nonradiological hazards associated with such sites, which is equivalent to, to the extent practicable, or more stringent than the level which would be achieved by standards and requirements adopted and enforced by the Commission for the same purpose and any final standards promulgated by the Administrator of the Environmental Protection Agency in accordance with section 2022 of this title.

(Aug. 1, 1946, c. 724, Title I, § 84, as added Nov. 8, 1978, Pub.L. 95–604, Title II, § 205(a), 92 Stat. 3039, and amended Jan. 4, 1983, Pub.L. 97–415, §§ 20, 22(a), 96 Stat. 2079, 2080; renumbered Title I, Oct. 24, 1992, Pub.L. 102–486, Title IX, § 902(a)(8), 106 Stat. 2944.)

1 So in original.

## HISTORICAL AND STATUTORY NOTES

### References in Text

The Solid Waste Disposal Act, as amended, referred to in subsec. (a)(3), is Title II of Pub.L. 89–272, as amended generally by Pub.L. 94–580, § 2, Oct. 21, 1976, 90 Stat. 2795, which is classified generally to chapter 82 (section 6901 et seq.) of this title. For complete classification of this Act to the Code, see Short Title note set out under section 6901 of this title and Tables.

### Effective and Applicability Provisions

1978 Acts

Section effective Nov. 8, 1978, see section 208 of Pub.L. 95–604, set out as a note under section 2014 of this title.

### Transfer of Functions

The Atomic Energy Commission was abolished and all functions were transferred to the Nuclear Regulatory Commission and the Administrator of the Energy Research and Development Administration by sections 5814 and 5841 of this title. The Energy Research and Development Administration was terminated and functions vested by law in the Administrator thereof were transferred to the Secretary of Energy (unless otherwise specifically provided) by sections 7151(a) and 7293 of this title.

# NATIONAL ENVIRONMENTAL POLICY

## NATIONAL ENVIRONMENTAL POLICY ACT OF 1969 [NEPA § ____]

**(42 U.S.C.A. §§ 4321 to 4370f)**

## CHAPTER 55—NATIONAL ENVIRONMENTAL POLICY



## § 4321. Congressional declaration of purpose

**[NEPA § 2]**

The purposes of this chapter are: To declare a national policy which will encourage productive and enjoyable harmony between man and his environment; to promote efforts which will prevent or eliminate damage to the environment and biosphere and stimulate the health and welfare of man; to enrich the understanding of the ecological systems and natural resources important to the Nation; and to establish a Council on Environmental Quality.

(Pub.L. 91–190, § 2, Jan. 1, 1970, 83 Stat. 852.)

### HISTORICAL AND STATUTORY NOTES

**Transfer of Functions**

Enforcement functions of Secretary or other official in Department of Interior related to compliance with system activities requiring coordination and approval under this chapter, and enforcement functions of Secretary or other official in Department of Agriculture, insofar as they involve lands and programs under jurisdiction of that Department, related to compliance with this chapter with respect to preconstruction, construction, and initial operation of transportation system for Canadian and Alaskan natural gas transferred to Federal Inspector, Office of Federal Inspector for Alaska Natural Gas Transportation System, until first anniversary of date of initial operation of Alaska Natural Gas Transportation System, see Reorg. Plan No. 1 of 1979, §§ 102(e), (f), 203(a), 44 F.R. 33663, 33666, 93 Stat. 1373, 1376, effective July 1, 1979, set out in Appendix 1 to Title 5, Government Organization and Employees. Office of Federal Inspector for the Alaska Natural Gas Transportation System abolished and functions and authority vested in Inspector transferred to Secretary of Energy by section 3012(b) of Pub.L. 102–486, set out as an Abolition of Office of Federal Inspector note under section 719e of Title 15, Commerce and Trade.

**Short Title**

1970 Acts

Section 1 of Pub.L. 91–190 provided: "That this Act [enacting this chapter] may be cited as the 'National Environmental Policy Act of 1969'."

**Necessity of Military Low–Level Flight Training to Protect National Security and Enhance Military Readiness.**

Pub.L. 106–398, § 1 [Div. A, Title III, § 317], Oct. 30, 2000, 114 Stat. 1654, 1654A–57, provided that: "Nothing in the National Environmental Policy Act of 1969 (42 U.S.C. 4321 et seq.) [Pub.L. 91–190, Jan. 1, 1970, 83 Stat. 852, which is classified principally to this chapter; see Tables for complete classification] or the regulations implementing such law shall require the Secretary of Defense or the Secretary of a military department to prepare a programmatic, nation-wide environmental impact statement for low-level flight training as a precondition to the use by the Armed Forces of an airspace for the performance of low-level training flights."

**Emergency Preparedness Functions**

For assignment of certain emergency preparedness functions to the Administrator of the Environmental Protection Agency, see Parts 1, 2, and 16 of Ex. Ord. No. 12656, Nov. 18, 1988, 53 F.R. 47491, set out as a note under section 2251 of Appendix to Title 50, War and National Defense.

**Pollution Prosecution**

Pub.L. 101–593, Title II, Nov. 16, 1990, 104 Stat. 2962, provided that:

**"Sec. 201. Short Title**

"This title [this note] may be cited as the 'Pollution Prosecution Act of 1990'.

**"Sec. 202. EPA Office of Criminal Investigation**

"(a) The Administrator of the Environmental Protection Agency (hereinafter referred to as the 'Administrator') shall increase the number of criminal investigators assigned to the Office of Criminal Investigations by such numbers as may be necessary to assure that the number of criminal investigators assigned to the office—

"(1) for the period October 1, 1991, through September 30, 1992, is not less than 72;

"(2) for the period October 1, 1992, through September 30, 1993, is not less than 110;

"(3) for the period October 1, 1993, through September 30, 1994, is not less than 123;

"(4) for the period October 1, 1994, through September 30, 1995, is not less than 160;

"(5) beginning October 1, 1995, is not less than 200.

"(b) For fiscal year 1991 and in each of the following 4 fiscal years, the Administrator shall, during each such fiscal year, provide increasing numbers of additional support staff to the Office of Criminal Investigations.

"(c) The head of the Office of Criminal Investigations shall be a position in the competitive service as defined in 2102 of title 5 U.S.C. [section 2102 of Title 5, Government Organization and Employees] or a career reserve position as defined in 3132(A) of title 5 U.S.C. [section 3132(A) of Title 5] and the head of such office shall report directly, without intervening review or approval, to the Assistant Administrator for Enforcement.

**"Sec. 203. Civil Investigators**

"The Administrator, as soon as practicable following the date of the enactment of this Act [Nov. 16, 1990], but no later than September 30, 1991, shall increase by fifty the number of civil investigators assigned to assist the Office of Enforcement in developing and prosecuting civil and administrative actions and carrying out its other functions.

**"Sec. 204. National Training Institute**

"The Administrator shall, as soon as practicable but no later than September 30, 1991 establish within the Office of Enforcement the National Enforcement Training Institute. It shall be the function of the Institute, among others, to train Federal, State, and local lawyers, inspectors, civil and criminal investigators, and technical experts in the enforcement of the Nation's environmental laws.

**"Sec. 205. Authorization**

"For the purposes of carrying out the provisions of this Act, there is authorized to be appropriated to the Environmental Protection Agency $13,000,000 for fiscal year 1991, $18,000,000 for fiscal year 1992, $20,000,000 for fiscal year 1993, $26,000,000 for fiscal year 1994, and $33,000,000 for fiscal year 1995."

## SUBCHAPTER I—POLICIES AND GOALS

### § 4331. Congressional declaration of national environmental policy

**[NEPA § 101]**

**(a)** The Congress, recognizing the profound impact of man's activity on the interrelations of all components of the natural environment, particularly the profound influences of population growth, high-density urbanization, industrial expansion, resource exploitation, and new and expanding technological advances and recognizing further the critical importance of restoring and maintaining environmental quality to the overall welfare and development of man, declares that it is the continuing policy of the Federal Government, in cooperation with State and local governments, and other concerned public and private organizations, to use all practicable means and measures, including financial and technical assistance, in a manner calculated to foster and promote the general welfare, to create and maintain conditions under which man and nature can exist in productive harmony, and fulfill the social, economic, and other requirements of present and future generations of Americans.

**(b)** In order to carry out the policy set forth in this chapter, it is the continuing responsibility of the Federal Government to use all practicable means, consistent with other essential considerations of national policy, to improve and coordinate Federal plans, functions, programs, and resources to the end that the Nation may—

**(1)** fulfill the responsibilities of each generation as trustee of the environment for succeeding generations;

**(2)** assure for all Americans safe, healthful, productive, and esthetically and culturally pleasing surroundings;

**(3)** attain the widest range of beneficial uses of the environment without degradation, risk to health or safety, or other undesirable and unintended consequences;

**(4)** preserve important historic, cultural, and natural aspects of our national heritage, and maintain, wherever possible, an environment which supports diversity and variety of individual choice;

**(5)** achieve a balance between population and resource use which will permit high standards of living and a wide sharing of life's amenities; and

**(6)** enhance the quality of renewable resources and approach the maximum attainable recycling of depletable resources.

**(c)** The Congress recognizes that each person should enjoy a healthful environment and that each person has a responsibility to contribute to the preservation and enhancement of the environment.

(Pub.L. 91–190, Title I, § 101, Jan. 1, 1970, 83 Stat. 852.)

## HISTORICAL AND STATUTORY NOTES

**Commission on Population Growth and the American Future**

Pub.L. 91–213, §§ 1 to 9, Mar. 16, 1970, 84 Stat. 67–69, established the Commission on Population Growth and the American Future to conduct and sponsor such studies and research and make such recommendations as might be necessary to provide information and education to all levels of government in the United States, and to our people regarding a broad range of problems associated with population growth and their implications for America's future; prescribed the composition of the Commission; provided for the appointment of its members, and the designation of a Chairman and Vice Chairman; required a majority of the members of the Commission to constitute a quorum, but allowed a lesser number to conduct hearings; prescribed the compensation of members of the Commission; required the Commission to conduct an inquiry into certain prescribed aspects of population growth in the United States and its foreseeable social consequences; provided for the appointment of an Executive Director and other personnel and prescribed their compensation; authorized the Commission to enter into contracts with public agencies, private firms, institutions, and individuals for the conduct of research and surveys, the preparation of reports, and other activities necessary to the discharge of its duties, and to request from any Federal department or agency any information and assistance it deems necessary to carry out its functions; required the General Services Administration to provide administrative services for the Commission on a reimbursable basis; required the Commission to submit an interim report to the President and the Congress one year after it was established and to submit its final report two years after Mar. 16, 1970; terminated the Commission sixty days after the date of the submission of its final report; and authorized to be appropriated, out of any money in the Treasury not otherwise appropriated, such amounts as might be necessary to carry out the provisions of Pub.L. 91–213.

## § 4332. Cooperation of agencies; reports; availability of information; recommendations; international and national coordination of efforts

**[NEPA § 102]**

The Congress authorizes and directs that, to the fullest extent possible: (1) the policies, regulations, and public laws of the United States shall be interpreted and administered in accordance with the policies set forth in this chapter, and (2) all agencies of the Federal Government shall—

**(A)** utilize a systematic, interdisciplinary approach which will insure the integrated use of the natural and social sciences and the environmental design arts in planning and in decisionmaking which may have an impact on man's environment;

**(B)** identify and develop methods and procedures, in consultation with the Council on Environmental Quality established by subchapter II of this chapter, which will insure that presently unquantified environmental amenities and values may be given appropriate consideration in decisionmaking along with economic and technical considerations;

**(C)** include in every recommendation or report on proposals for legislation and other major Federal actions significantly affecting the quality of the human environment, a detailed statement by the responsible official on—

**(i)** the environmental impact of the proposed action,

**(ii)** any adverse environmental effects which cannot be avoided should the proposal be implemented,

**(iii)** alternatives to the proposed action,

**(iv)** the relationship between local short-term uses of man's environment and the maintenance and enhancement of long-term productivity, and

(v) any irreversible and irretrievable commitments of resources which would be involved in the proposed action should it be implemented.

Prior to making any detailed statement, the responsible Federal official shall consult with and obtain the comments of any Federal agency which has jurisdiction by law or special expertise with respect to any environmental impact involved. Copies of such statement and the comments and views of the appropriate Federal, State, and local agencies, which are authorized to develop and enforce environmental standards, shall be made available to the President, the Council on Environmental Quality and to the public as provided by section 552 of Title 5, and shall accompany the proposal through the existing agency review processes;

**(D)** Any detailed statement required under subparagraph (C) after January 1, 1970, for any major Federal action funded under a program of grants to States shall not be deemed to be legally insufficient solely by reason of having been prepared by a State agency or official, if:

**(i)** the State agency or official has statewide jurisdiction and has the responsibility for such action,

**(ii)** the responsible Federal official furnishes guidance and participates in such preparation,

**(iii)** the responsible Federal official independently evaluates such statement prior to its approval and adoption, and

**(iv)** after January 1, 1976, the responsible Federal official provides early notification to, and solicits the views of, any other State or any Federal land management entity of any action or any alternative thereto which may have significant impacts upon such State or affected Federal land management entity and, if there is any disagreement on such impacts, prepares a written assessment of such impacts and views for incorporation into such detailed statement.

The procedures in this subparagraph shall not relieve the Federal official of his responsibilities for the scope, objectivity, and content of the entire statement or of any other responsibility under this chapter; and further, this subparagraph does not affect the legal sufficiency of statements prepared by State agencies with less than statewide jurisdiction.[1]

**(E)** study, develop, and describe appropriate alternatives to recommended courses of action in any proposal which involves unresolved conflicts concerning alternative uses of available resources;

**(F)** recognize the worldwide and long-range character of environmental problems and, where consistent with the foreign policy of the United States, lend appropriate support to initiatives, resolutions, and programs designed to maximize international cooperation in anticipating and preventing a decline in the quality of mankind's world environment;

**(G)** make available to States, counties, municipalities, institutions, and individuals, advice and information useful in restoring, maintaining, and enhancing the quality of the environment;

**(H)** initiate and utilize ecological information in the planning and development of resource-oriented projects; and

**(I)** assist the Council on Environmental Quality established by subchapter II of this chapter.

(Pub.L. 91–190, Title I, § 102, Jan. 1, 1970, 83 Stat. 853; Pub.L. 94–83, Aug. 9, 1975, 89 Stat. 424.)

[1] So in original. The period probably should be a semicolon.

### HISTORICAL AND STATUTORY NOTES

**Certain Commercial Space Launch Activities**

Pub.L. 104–88, Title IV, § 401, Dec. 29, 1995, 109 Stat. 955, provided that: "The licensing of a launch vehicle or launch site operator (including any amendment, extension, or renewal of the license) under chapter 701 of title 49, United States Code [section 70101 et seq. of Title 49, Transportation], shall not be considered a major Federal action for purposes of section 102(C) of the National Environmental Policy Act of 1969 (42 U.S.C. 4332(C)) if—

"(1) the Department of the Army has issued a permit for the activity; and

"(2) the Army Corps of Engineers has found that the activity has no significant impact."

[Section 401 of Pub.L. 104–88 effective Jan. 1, 1996, see section 2 of Pub.L. 104–88, set out as a note under section 701 of Title 49, Transportation.]

## § 4333. Conformity of administrative procedures to national environmental policy

**[NEPA § 103]**

All agencies of the Federal Government shall review their present statutory authority, administrative regulations, and current policies and procedures for the purpose of determining whether there are any deficiencies or inconsistencies therein which prohibit full compliance with the purposes and provisions of this chapter and shall propose to the President not later than July 1, 1971, such measures as may be necessary to bring their authority and policies into conformity with the intent, purposes, and procedures set forth in this chapter.

(Pub.L. 91–190, Title I, § 103, Jan. 1, 1970, 83 Stat. 854.)

## § 4334. Other statutory obligations of agencies

**[NEPA § 104]**

Nothing in section 4332 or 4333 of this title shall in any way affect the specific statutory obligations of any Federal agency (1) to comply with criteria or standards of environmental quality, (2) to coordinate or consult with any other Federal or State agency, or (3) to act, or refrain from acting contingent upon the recommendations or certification of any other Federal or State agency.

(Pub.L. 91–190, Title I, § 104, Jan. 1, 1970, 83 Stat. 854.)

## § 4335. Efforts supplemental to existing authorizations

**[NEPA § 105]**

The policies and goals set forth in this chapter are supplementary to those set forth in existing authorizations of Federal agencies.

(Pub.L. 91–190, Title I, § 105, Jan. 1, 1970, 83 Stat. 854.)

# SUBCHAPTER II—COUNCIL ON ENVIRONMENTAL QUALITY

## § 4341. Omitted

### HISTORICAL AND STATUTORY NOTES

**Codifications**

Section, Pub.L. 91–190, Title II, § 201, Jan. 1, 1970, 83 Stat. 854, which required the President to transmit to Congress annually an Environmental Quality Report, terminated, effective May 15, 2000, pursuant to Pub.L. 104–66, § 3003, as amended, set out as a note under 31 U.S.C.A. § 1113. See, also, item 1 on page 41 of House Document No. 103–7.

## § 4342. Establishment; membership; Chairman; appointments

**[NEPA § 202]**

There is created in the Executive Office of the President a Council on Environmental Quality (hereinafter referred to as the "Council"). The Council shall be composed of three members who shall be appointed by the President to serve at his pleasure, by and with the advice and consent of the Senate. The President shall designate one of the members of the Council to serve as Chairman. Each member shall be a person who, as a result of his training, experience, and attainments, is exceptionally well qualified to analyze and interpret environmental trends and information of all kinds; to appraise programs and activities of the Federal Government in the light of the policy set forth in subchapter I of this chapter; to be conscious of and responsive to the scientific, economic, social, esthetic, and cultural needs and interests of the Nation; and to formulate and recommend national policies to promote the improvement of the quality of the environment.

(Pub.L. 91–190, Title II, § 202, Jan. 1, 1970, 83 Stat. 854.)

### HISTORICAL AND STATUTORY NOTES

**Council on Environmental Quality**

Pub.L. 108–199, Div. G, Title III, Jan. 23, 2004, 118 Stat. 408, provided in part that: "Notwithstanding section 202 of the National Environmental Policy Act of 1970 [sic; probably means section 202 of the National Environmental Policy Act of 1969, which enacted this section], the Council shall consist of one member, appointed by the President, by and with the advice and consent of the Senate, serving as chairman and exercising all powers, functions, and duties of the Council."

Similar provisions were contained in the following prior appropriations Acts:

Pub.L. 108–7, Div. K, Title I, Feb. 20, 2003, 117 Stat. 514.

Pub.L. 107–73, Title III, Nov. 26, 2001, 115 Stat. 686.

Pub.L. 106–377, § 1(a)(1) [Title III], Oct. 27, 2000, 114 Stat. 1441, 1441A–45.

Pub.L. 106–74, Title III, Oct. 20, 1999, 113 Stat. 1084.

Pub.L. 105–276, Title III, Oct. 21, 1998, 112 Stat. 2500.

Pub.L. 105–65, Title III, Oct. 27, 1997, 111 Stat. 1375.

## § 4343. Employment of personnel, experts and consultants

**[NEPA § 203]**

**(a)** The Council may employ such officers and employees as may be necessary to carry out its functions under this chapter. In addition, the Council may employ and fix the compensation of such experts and consultants as may be necessary for the carrying out of its functions under this chapter, in accordance with section 3109 of Title 5 (but without regard to the last sentence thereof).

**(b)** Notwithstanding section 1342 of Title 31, the Council may accept and employ voluntary and uncompensated services in furtherance of the purposes of the Council.

(Pub.L. 91–190, Title II, § 203, Jan. 1, 1970, 83 Stat. 855; Pub.L. 94–52, § 2, July 3, 1975, 89 Stat. 258; Pub.L. 97–258, § 4(b), Sept. 13, 1982, 96 Stat. 1067.)

### HISTORICAL AND STATUTORY NOTES

**Codifications**

In subsec. (b), "section 1342 of Title 31" was substituted for "section 3679(b) of the Revised Statutes (31 U.S.C. 665(b))" on authority of Pub.L. 97–258, § 4(b), Sept. 13, 1982, 96 Stat. 1067, the first section of which enacted Title 31, Money and Finance.

## § 4344. Duties and functions

**[NEPA § 204]**

It shall be the duty and function of the Council—

**(1)** to assist and advise the President in the preparation of the Environmental Quality Report required by section 4341 of this title;

**(2)** to gather timely and authoritative information concerning the conditions and trends in the quality of the environment both current and prospective, to analyze and interpret such information for the purpose of determining whether such conditions and trends are interfering, or are likely to interfere, with the achievement of the policy set forth in subchapter I of this chapter, and to compile and submit to the President studies relating to such conditions and trends;

(3) to review and appraise the various programs and activities of the Federal Government in the light of the policy set forth in subchapter I of this chapter for the purpose of determining the extent to which such programs and activities are contributing to the achievement of such policy, and to make recommendations to the President with respect thereto;

(4) to develop and recommend to the President national policies to foster and promote the improvement of environmental quality to meet the conservation, social, economic, health, and other requirements and goals of the Nation;

(5) to conduct investigations, studies, surveys, research, and analyses relating to ecological systems and environmental quality;

(6) to document and define changes in the natural environment, including the plant and animal systems, and to accumulate necessary data and other information for a continuing analysis of these changes or trends and an interpretation of their underlying causes;

(7) to report at least once each year to the President on the state and condition of the environment; and

(8) to make and furnish such studies, reports thereon, and recommendations with respect to matters of policy and legislation as the President may request.

(Pub.L. 91–190, Title II, § 204, Jan. 1, 1970, 83 Stat. 855.)

### HISTORICAL AND STATUTORY NOTES

**References in Text**

Section 4341 of this title, referred to in par. (1), was omitted from the Code.

**Transfer of Functions**

So much of the functions of the Council on Environmental Quality under par. (4) of this section as pertains to ecological systems was transferred to the Administrator of the Environmental Protection Agency by 1970 Reorg. Plan No. 3, Section 2(a)(5), eff. Dec. 2, 1970, 35 F.R. 15623, 84 Stat. 2086, set out under section 4321 of this title.

## § 4345. Consultation with Citizens' Advisory Committee on Environmental Quality and other representatives

**[NEPA § 205]**

In exercising its powers, functions, and duties under this chapter, the Council shall—

(1) consult with the Citizens' Advisory Committee on Environmental Quality established by Executive Order numbered 11472, dated May 29, 1969, and with such representatives of science, industry, agriculture, labor, conservation organizations, State and local governments and other groups, as it deems advisable; and

(2) utilize, to the fullest extent possible, the services, facilities, and information (including statistical information) of public and private agencies and organizations, and individuals, in order that duplication of effort and expense may be avoided, thus assuring that the Council's activities will not unnecessarily overlap or conflict with similar activities authorized by law and performed by established agencies.

(Pub.L. 91–190, Title II, § 205, Jan. 1, 1970, 83 Stat. 855.)

### HISTORICAL AND STATUTORY NOTES

**References in Text**

Executive Order numbered 11472, dated May 29, 1969, referred to in par. (1), is set out as a note under section 4321 of this title.

**Citizens' Advisory Committee on Environmental Quality**

For provisions relating to termination of Citizens' Advisory Committee on Environmental Quality, see Ex. Ord. No. 12007, Aug. 22, 1977, 42 F.R. 42839, set out as a note under section 14 of the Federal Advisory Committee Act in Appendix 2 to Title 5, Government Organization and Employees.

## § 4346. Tenure and compensation of members

**[NEPA § 206]**

Members of the Council shall serve full time and the Chairman of the Council shall be compensated at the rate provided for Level II of the Executive Schedule Pay Rates (5 U.S.C. 5313). The other members of the Council shall be compensated at the rate provided for Level IV or [1] the Executive Schedule Pay Rates (5 U.S.C. 5315).

(Pub.L. 91–190, Title II, § 206, Jan. 1, 1970, 83 Stat. 856.)

[1] So in original. Probably should be "of".

## § 4346a. Travel reimbursement by private organizations and Federal, State, and local governments

**[NEPA § 207]**

The Council may accept reimbursements from any private nonprofit organization or from any department, agency, or instrumentality of the Federal Government, any State, or local government, for the reasonable travel expenses incurred by an officer or employee of the Council in connection with his attendance at any conference, seminar, or similar meeting conducted for the benefit of the Council.

(Pub.L. 91–190, Title II, § 207, as added Pub.L. 94–52, § 3, July 3, 1975, 89 Stat. 258.)

## § 4346b. Expenditures in support of international activities

**[NEPA § 208]**

The Council may make expenditures in support of its international activities, including expenditures for: (1) international travel; (2) activities in implementation of international agreements; and (3) the support of international exchange programs in the United States and in foreign countries.

(Pub.L. 91–190, Title II, § 208, as added Pub.L. 94–52, § 3, July 3, 1975, 89 Stat. 258.)

## § 4347. Authorization of appropriations

**[NEPA § 209]**

There are authorized to be appropriated to carry out the provisions of this chapter not to exceed $300,000 for fiscal year 1970, $700,000 for fiscal year 1971, and $1,000,000 for each fiscal year thereafter.

(Pub.L. 91–190, Title II, § 209, formerly § 207, Jan. 1, 1970, 83 Stat. 856; renumbered § 209, Pub.L. 94–52, § 3, July 3, 1975, 89 Stat. 258.)

# SUBCHAPTER III—MISCELLANEOUS PROVISIONS

## § 4361. Repealed. Pub.L. 104–66, Title II, § 2021(k)(1), Dec. 21, 1995, 109 Stat. 728

### HISTORICAL AND STATUTORY NOTES

Section, Pub.L. 94–475, § 5, Oct. 11, 1976, 90 Stat. 2071, related to a plan for research, development, and demonstration.

## § 4361a. Repealed. Pub.L. 104–66, Title II, § 2021(k)(2), Dec. 21, 1995, 109 Stat. 728

### HISTORICAL AND STATUTORY NOTES

Section, Pub.L. 95–155, § 4, Nov. 8, 1977, 91 Stat. 1258, related to budget projections in annual revisions of the plan for research, development, and demonstration.

## § 4361b. Implementation by Administrator of Environmental Protection Agency of recommendations of "CHESS" Investigative Report; waiver; inclusion of status of implementation requirements in annual revisions of plan for research, development, and demonstration

The Administrator of the Environmental Protection Agency shall implement the recommendations of the report prepared for the House Committee on Science and Technology entitled "The Environmental Protection Agency Research Program with primary emphasis on the Community Health and Environmental Surveillance System (CHESS): An Investigative Report", unless for any specific recommendation he determines (1) that such recommendation has been implemented, (2) that implementation of such recommendation would not enhance the quality of the research, or (3) that implementation of such recommendation will require funding which is not available. Where such funding is not available, the Administrator shall request the required authorization or appropriation for such implementation. The Administrator shall report the status of such implementation in each annual revision of the five-year plan transmitted to the Congress under section 4361 of this title.

(Pub.L. 95–155, § 10, Nov. 8, 1977, 91 Stat. 1262.)

### HISTORICAL AND STATUTORY NOTES

**References in Text**

Section 4361 of this title, referred to in text, was repealed by Pub.L. 104–66, Title II, § 2021(k)(1), Dec. 21, 1995, 109 Stat. 728.

**Codifications**

Section was enacted as part of the Environmental Research, Development, and Demonstration Authorization Act of 1978, and not as part of the National Environmental Policy Act of 1969, which comprises this chapter.

## § 4361c. Staff management

**(a) Appointments for educational programs**

(1) The Administrator is authorized to select and appoint up to 75 full-time permanent staff members in the Office of Research and Development to pursue full-time educational programs for the purpose of (A) securing an advanced degree or (B) securing academic training, for the purpose of making a career change in order to better carry out the Agency's research mission.

(2) The Administrator shall select and appoint staff members for these assignments according to rules and criteria promulgated by him. The Agency may continue to pay the salary and benefits of the appointees as well as reasonable and appropriate relocation expenses and tuition.

(3) The term of each appointment shall be for up to one year, with a single renewal of up to one year in appropriate cases at the discretion of the Administrator.

(4) Staff members appointed to this program shall not count against any Agency personnel ceiling during the term of their appointment.

**(b) Post-doctoral research fellows**

(1) The Administrator is authorized to appoint up to 25 Post-doctoral Research Fellows in accordance with the provisions of section 213.3102(aa) of title 5 of the Code of Federal Regulations.

(2) Persons holding these appointments shall not count against any personnel ceiling of the Agency.

**(c) Non-Government research associates**

(1) The Administrator is authorized and encouraged to utilize research associates from outside the Federal Government in conducting the research, development, and demonstration programs of the Agency.

(2) These persons shall be selected and shall serve according to rules and criteria promulgated by the Administrator.

**(d) Women and minority groups**

For all programs in this section, the Administrator shall place special emphasis on providing opportunities for education and training of women and minority groups.

(Pub.L. 95–477, § 6, Oct. 18, 1978, 92 Stat. 1510.)

### HISTORICAL AND STATUTORY NOTES

**Codifications**

Section was enacted as part of the Environmental Research, Development, and Demonstration Authorization Act of 1969, and not as part of the National Environmental Policy Act of 1969, which comprises this chapter.

**Environmental Protection Agency**

Pub.L. 108–7, Div. K, Title III, Feb. 20, 2003, 117 Stat. 509, provided in part that: "The Office of Research and Development of the Environmental Protection Agency may hereafter [on or after Feb. 20, 2003] contract directly with individuals or indirectly with institutions or nonprofit organizations, without regard to 41 U.S.C. 5, for the temporary or intermittent personal services of students or recent graduates, who shall be considered employees for the purposes of chapters 57 and 81 of title 5, United States Code [5 U.S.C.A. §§ 5701 et seq. and 8101 et seq.], relating to compensation for travel and work injuries, and chapter 171 of title 28, United States Code [28 U.S.C.A. § 2671 et seq.], relating to tort claims, but shall not be considered to be Federal employees for any other purposes."

## § 4362. Interagency cooperation on prevention of environmental cancer and heart and lung disease

(a) Not later than three months after August 7, 1977, there shall be established a Task Force on Environmental Cancer and Heart and Lung Disease (hereinafter referred to as the "Task Force"). The Task Force shall include representatives of the Environmental Protection Agency, the National Cancer Institute, the National Heart, Lung, and Blood Institute, the National Institute of Occupational Safety and Health, and the National Institute on Environmental Health Sciences, and shall be chaired by the Administrator (or his delegate).

(b) The Task Force shall—

(1) recommend a comprehensive research program to determine and quantify the relationship between environmental pollution and human cancer and heart and lung disease;

(2) recommend comprehensive strategies to reduce or eliminate the risks of cancer or such other diseases associated with environmental pollution;

(3) recommend research and such other measures as may be appropriate to prevent or reduce the incidence of environmentally related cancer and heart and lung diseases;

(4) coordinate research by, and stimulate cooperation between, the Environmental Protection Agency, the Department of Health and Human Services, and such other agencies as may be appropriate to prevent environmentally related cancer and heart and lung diseases; and

(5) report to Congress, not later than one year after August 7, 1977, and annually thereafter, on the problems and progress in carrying out this section.

(Pub.L. 95–95, Title IV, § 402, Aug. 7, 1977, 91 Stat. 791; Pub.L. 96–88, Title V, § 509(b), Oct. 17, 1979, 93 Stat. 695.)

### HISTORICAL AND STATUTORY NOTES

**Codifications**

Section was enacted as part of the Clean Air Act Amendments of 1977 and not as part of the National Environmental Policy Act of 1969, which comprises this chapter.

**Effective and Applicability Provisions**

1977 Acts

Section effective Aug. 7, 1977, except as otherwise expressly provided, see section 406(d) of Pub.L. 95–95, set out as a note under section 7401 of this title.

**Change of Name**

"Department of Health and Human Services" was substituted for "Department of Health, Education, and Welfare" in subsec. (b)(4), pursuant to section 509(b) of Pub.L. 96–88, which is classified to section 3508(b) of Title 20, Education.

## § 4362a. Membership of Task Force on Environmental Cancer and Heart and Lung Disease

The Director of the National Center for Health Statistics and the head of the Center for Disease Control (or the successor to such entity) shall each serve as members of the Task Force on Environmental Cancer and Heart and Lung Disease established under section 4362 of this title.

(Pub.L. 95–623, § 9, Nov. 9, 1978, 92 Stat. 3455.)

### HISTORICAL AND STATUTORY NOTES

**Codifications**

Section was enacted as part of the Health Services Research, Health Statistics, and Health Care Technology Act of 1978 and not as part of the National Environmental Policy Act of 1969, which comprises this chapter.

**Change of Name**

Centers for Disease Control changed to Centers for Disease Control and Prevention by Pub.L. 102–531, Title III, § 312, Oct. 27, 1992, 106 Stat. 3504.

## § 4363. Continuing and long-term environmental research and development

The Administrator of the Environmental Protection Agency shall establish a separately identified program of continuing, long-term environmental research and development for each activity listed in section 2(a) of this Act. Unless otherwise specified by law, at least 15 per centum of funds appropriated to the Administrator for environmental research and development for each activity listed in section 2(a) of this Act shall be obligated and expended for such long-term environmental research and development under this section.

(Pub.L. 96–569, § 2(f), Dec. 22, 1980, 94 Stat. 3337.)

### HISTORICAL AND STATUTORY NOTES

**References in Text**

Section 2(a) of this Act, referred to in text, is section 2(a) of Pub.L. 96–569, Dec. 22, 1980, 94 Stat. 3335, which was not classified to the Code.

**Codifications**

Section was enacted as part of the Environmental Research, Development and Demonstration Authorization Act of 1981, and not as part of the National Environmental Policy Act of 1969, which comprises this chapter.

**Similar Provisions**

Provisions similar to this section were contained in the following prior authorization acts:

Pub.L. 96–229, § 2(e), Apr. 7, 1980, 94 Stat. 327.

Pub.L. 95–155, § 6, Nov. 8, 1977, 91 Stat. 1259.

## § 4363a. Pollution control technologies demonstrations

(1) The Administrator shall continue to be responsible for conducting and shall continue to conduct full-scale demonstrations of energy-related pollution control technologies as necessary in his judgment to fulfill the provisions of the Clean Air Act as amended [42 U.S.C.A. § 7401 et seq.], the Federal Water Pollution Control Act as amended [33 U.S.C.A. § 1251 et seq.], and other pertinent pollution control statutes.

(2) Energy-related environmental protection projects authorized to be administered by the Environmental Protection Agency under this Act shall not be transferred administratively to the Department of Energy or reduced through budget amendment. No action shall be taken through administrative or budgetary means to diminish the ability of the Environmental Protection Agency to initiate such projects.

(Pub.L. 96–229, § 2(d), Apr. 7, 1980, 94 Stat. 327.)

### HISTORICAL AND STATUTORY NOTES

**References in Text**

The Clean Air Act as amended, referred to in par. (1), is Act July 14, 1955, c. 360, as amended generally by Pub.L. 88–206, Dec. 17, 1963, 77 Stat. 392, and later by Pub.L. 95–95, Aug. 7, 1977, 91 Stat. 685. The Clean Air Act was originally classified to chapter 15B (section 1857 et seq.) of this title. On enactment of Pub.L. 95–95, the Act was reclassified to chapter 85 (section 7401 et seq.) of this title. For complete classification of this Act to the Code, see Short Title note set out under section 7401 of this title and Tables.

The Federal Water Pollution Control Act as amended, referred to in par. (1), is Act June 30, 1948, c. 758, as amended generally by Pub.L. 92–500, § 2, Oct. 18, 1972, 86 Stat. 816, which is classified generally to chapter 26 (section 1251 et seq.) of Title 33, Navigation and Navigable Waters. For complete classification of this Act to the Code, see Short Title note set out under section 1251 of Title 33 and Tables.

This Act, referred to in par. (2), is Pub.L. 96–229, Apr. 7, 1980, 94 Stat. 325, known as the Environmental Research, Development, and Demonstration Authorization Act of 1980, which enacted sections 4363, 4363a, 4369a, and 4370 of this title. For complete classification of this Act to the Code, see Tables.

**Codifications**

Section was enacted as part of the Environmental Research, Development, and Demonstration Authorization Act of 1980, and not as part of the National Environmental Policy Act of 1969, which comprises this chapter.

**Similar Provisions**

Provisions similar to this section were contained in the following prior authorization act:

Pub.L. 95–477, § 2(d), Oct. 18, 1978, 92 Stat. 1508.

## § 4364. Expenditure of funds for research and development related to regulatory program activities

### (a) Coordination, etc., with research needs and priorities of program offices and Environmental Protection Agency

The Administrator of the Environmental Protection Agency shall assure that the expenditure of any funds appropriated pursuant to this Act or any other provision of law for environmental research and development related to regulatory program activities shall be coordinated with and reflect the research needs and priorities of the program offices, as well as the overall research needs and priorities of the Agency, including those defined in the five-year research plan.

### (b) Program offices subject to coverage

For purposes of subsection (a) of this section, the appropriate program offices are—

(1) the Office of Air and Waste Management, for air quality activities;

(2) the Office of Water and Hazardous Materials, for water quality activities and water supply activities;

(3) the Office of Pesticides, for environmental effects of pesticides;

(4) the Office of Solid Waste, for solid waste activities;

(5) the Office of Toxic Substances, for toxic substance activities;

(6) the Office of Radiation Programs, for radiation activities; and

(7) the Office of Noise Abatement and Control, for noise activities.

**(c) Report to Congress; contents**

The Administrator shall submit to the President and the Congress a report concerning the most appropriate means of assuring, on a continuing basis, that the research efforts of the Agency reflect the needs and priorities of the regulatory program offices, while maintaining a high level of scientific quality. Such report shall be submitted on or before March 31, 1978.

(Pub.L. 95–155, § 7, Nov. 8, 1977, 91 Stat. 1259.)

**HISTORICAL AND STATUTORY NOTES**

**References in Text**

This Act, referred to in subsec. (a), is the Environmental Research, Development, and Demonstration Authorization Act of 1978, Pub.L. 95–155, Nov. 8, 1977, 91 Stat. 1257. For distribution in the Code of such Act see Tables.

**Codifications**

Section was enacted as part of the Environmental Research, Development, and Demonstration Authorization Act of 1978, and not as part of the National Environmental Policy Act of 1969, which comprises this chapter.

## § 4365. Science Advisory Board

**(a) Establishment; requests for advice by Administrator of Environmental Protection Agency and Congressional committees**

The Administrator of the Environmental Protection Agency shall establish a Science Advisory Board which shall provide such scientific advice as may be requested by the Administrator, the Committee on Environment and Public Works of the United States Senate, or the Committee on Science, Space, and Technology, on Energy and Commerce, or on Public Works and Transportation of the House of Representatives.

**(b) Membership; Chairman; meetings; qualifications of members**

Such Board shall be composed of at least nine members, one of whom shall be designated Chairman, and shall meet at such times and places as may be designated by the Chairman of the Board in consultation with the Administrator. Each member of the Board shall be qualified by education, training, and experience to evaluate scientific and technical information on matters referred to the Board under this section.

**(c) Proposed environmental criteria document, standard, limitation, or regulation; functions respecting in conjunction with Administrator**

(1) The Administrator, at the time any proposed criteria document, standard, limitation, or regulation under the Clean Air Act [42 U.S.C.A. § 7401 et seq.], the Federal Water Pollution Control Act [33 U.S.C.A. § 1251 et seq.], the Resource, Conservation and Recovery Act of 1976 [42 U.S.C.A. § 6901 et seq.], the Noise Control Act [42 U.S.C.A. § 4901 et seq.], the Toxic Substances Control Act [15 U.S.C.A. § 2601 et seq.], or the Safe Drinking Water Act [42 U.S.C.A. § 300f et seq.], or under any other authority of the Administrator, is provided to any other Federal agency for formal review and comment, shall make available to the Board such proposed criteria document, standard, limitation, or regulation, together with relevant scientific and technical information in the possession of the Environmental Protection Agency on which the proposed action is based.

(2) The Board may make available to the Administrator, within the time specified by the Administrator, its advice and comments on the adequacy of the scientific and technical basis of the proposed criteria document, standard, limitation, or regulation, together with any pertinent information in the Board's possession.

**(d) Utilization of technical and scientific capabilities of Federal agencies and national environmental laboratories for determining adequacy of scientific and technical basis of proposed criteria document, etc.**

In preparing such advice and comments, the Board shall avail itself of the technical and scientific capabilities of any Federal agency, including the Environmental Protection Agency and any national environmental laboratories.

**(e) Member committees and investigative panels; establishment; chairmenship**

The Board is authorized to constitute such member committees and investigative panels as the Administrator and the Board find necessary to carry out this section. Each such member committee or investigative panel shall be chaired by a member of the Board.

**(f) Appointment and compensation of secretary and other personnel; compensation of members**

(1) Upon the recommendation of the Board, the Administrator shall appoint a secretary, and such other employees as deemed necessary to exercise and fulfill the Board's powers and responsibilities. The compensation of all employees appointed under this paragraph shall be fixed in accordance with chapter 51 and subchapter III of chapter 53 of Title 5.

(2) Members of the Board may be compensated at a rate to be fixed by the President but not in excess of the maximum rate of pay for grade GS–18, as provided in the General Schedule under section 5332 of Title 5.

**(g) Consultation and coordination with Scientific Advisory Panel**

In carrying out the functions assigned by this section, the Board shall consult and coordinate its activities with the Scientific Advisory Panel established by the Administrator pursuant to section 136w(d) of Title 7.

(Pub.L. 95–155, § 8, Nov. 8, 1977, 91 Stat. 1260; H.Res. 549, Mar. 25, 1980; Pub.L. 96–569, § 3, Dec. 22, 1980, 94 Stat. 3337; Pub.L. 103–437, § 15(*o*), Nov. 2, 1994, 108 Stat. 4593; Pub.L. 104–66, Title II, § 2021(k)(3), Dec. 21, 1995, 109 Stat. 728.)

## HISTORICAL AND STATUTORY NOTES

**References in Text**

The Clean Air Act, referred to in subsec. (c)(1), is Act July 14, 1955, c. 360, as amended generally by Pub.L. 88–206, Dec. 17, 1963, 77 Stat. 392, and later by Pub.L. 95–95, Aug. 7, 1977, 91 Stat. 685. The Clean Air Act was originally classified to chapter 15B (section 1857 et seq.) of this title. On enactment of Pub.L. 95–95, the Act was reclassified to chapter 85 (section 7401 et seq.) of this title. For complete classification of this Act to the Code, see Short Title note set out under section 7401 of this title and Tables.

The Federal Water Pollution Control Act, referred to in subsec. (c)(1), is Act June 30, 1948, c. 758, as amended generally by Pub.L. 92–500, § 2, Oct. 18, 1972, 86 Stat. 816, which is classified generally to chapter 26 (section 1251 et seq.) of Title 33, Navigation and Navigable Waters. For complete classification of this Act to the Code, see Short Title note set out under section 1251 of Title 33 and Tables.

The Resource, Conservation and Recovery Act of 1976, referred to in subsec. (c)(1), probably means the Resource Conservation and Recovery Act of 1976, Pub.L. 94–580, Oct. 21, 1976, 90 Stat. 2796, as amended, which is classified generally to chapter 82 (section 6901 et seq.) of this title. For complete classification of this Act to the Code, see Short Title note set out under section 6901 of this title and Tables.

The Noise Control Act, referred to in subsec. (c)(1), probably means the Noise Control Act of 1972, Pub.L. 92–574, Oct. 27, 1972, 86 Stat. 1234, as amended, which is classified principally to chapter 65 (section 4901 et seq.) of this title. For complete classification of this Act to the Code, see Short Title note set out under section 4901 of this title and Tables.

The Toxic Substances Control Act, referred to in subsec. (c)(1), is Pub.L. 94–469, Oct. 11, 1976, 90 Stat. 2003, as amended, which is classified generally to chapter 53 (section 2601 et seq.) of Title 15, Commerce and Trade. For complete classification of this Act to the Code, see Short Title note set out under section 2601 of Title 15 and Tables.

The Safe Drinking Water Act, referred to in subsec. (c)(1), is Pub.L. 93–523, Dec. 16, 1974, 88 Stat. 1660, as amended, which is classified principally to subchapter XII (section 300f et seq.) of chapter 6A of this title. For complete classification of this Act to the Code, see Short Title of 1974 Amendments note set out under section 201 of this title and Tables.

**Codifications**

Section was enacted as part of the Environmental Research, Development, and Demonstration Authorization Act of 1978, and not as part of the National Environmental Policy Act of 1969, which comprises this chapter.

Amendment to subsec. (a) by section 15(*o*)(1) of Pub.L. 103–437, which directed the substitution of "Committee on Science, Space, and Technology, on Energy and Commerce, or on" for "Committees on Science and Technology, Interstate and Foreign Commerce, or" was executed by substituting "Committee on Science, Space, and Technology, on Energy and Commerce, or on" for "Committees on Science and Technology, Energy and Commerce, or", as the probable intent of Congress.

**Change of Name**

Any reference in any provision of law enacted before Jan. 4, 1995, to the Committee on Energy and Commerce of the House of Representatives treated as referring to the Committee on Commerce of the House of Representatives, except that any reference in any provision of law enacted before Jan. 4, 1995, to the Committee on Energy and Commerce of the House of Representatives treated as referring to the Committee on Agriculture of the House of Representatives, in the case of a provision of law relating to inspection of seafood or seafood products, the Committee on Banking and Financial Services of the House of Representatives, in the case of a provision of law relating to bank capital markets activities generally or to depository institution securities activities generally, and the Committee on Transportation and Infrastructure of the House of Representatives, in the case of a provision of law relating to railroads, railway labor, or railroad retirement and unemployment (except revenue measures related thereto), see section 1(a)(4) and (c)(1) of Pub.L. 104–14, set out as a note preceding section 21 of Title 2, The Congress.

Any reference in any provision of law enacted before Jan. 4, 1995, to the Committee on Science, Space, and Technology of the House of Representatives treated as referring to the Committee on Science of the House of Representatives, see section 1(a)(10) of Pub.L. 104–14, set out as a note preceding section 21 of Title 2, The Congress.

Any reference in any provision of law enacted before Jan. 4, 1995, to the Committee on Public Works and Transportation of the House of Representatives treated as referring to the Committee on Transportation and Infrastructure of the House of Representatives, see section 1(a)(9) of Pub.L. 104–14, set out as a note preceding section 21 of Title 2, The Congress.

**References in Other Laws to GS–16, 17, or 18 Pay Rates**

References in laws to the rates of pay for GS–16, 17, or 18, or to maximum rates of pay under the General Schedule, to be considered references to rates payable under specified sections of Title 5, Government Organization and Employees, see section 529 [Title I, § 101(c)(1) ] of Pub.L. 101–509, set out in a note under section 5376 of Title 5.

**Termination of Advisory Boards**

Advisory boards established after Jan. 5, 1973, to terminate not later than the expiration of the 2–year period beginning on the date of their establishment, unless, in the case of a board established by the President or an officer of the Federal Government, such board is renewed by appropriate action prior to the expiration of such 2–year period, or in the case of a board established by the Congress, its duration is otherwise provided for by law. See sections 3(2) and 14 of Pub.L. 92–463, Oct. 6, 1972, 86 Stat. 770, 776, set out in Appendix 2 to Title 5, Government Organization and Employees.

## § 4366. Identification and coordination of research, development, and demonstration activities

### (a) Consultation and cooperation of Administrator of Environmental Protection Agency with heads of Federal agencies; inclusion of activities in annual revisions of plan for research, etc.

The Administrator of the Environmental Protection Agency, in consultation and cooperation with the heads of other Federal agencies, shall take such actions on a continuing basis as may be necessary or appropriate—

(1) to identify environmental research, development, and demonstration activities, within and outside the Federal Government, which may need to be more effectively coordinated in order to minimize unnecessary duplication of programs, projects, and research facilities;

(2) to determine the steps which might be taken under existing law, by him and by the heads of such other agencies, to accomplish or promote such coordination, and to provide for or encourage the taking of such steps; and

(3) to determine the additional legislative actions which would be needed to assure such coordination to the maximum extent possible.

The Administrator shall include in each annual revision of the five-year plan provided for by section 4361 of this title a full and complete report on the actions taken and determinations made during the preceding year under this subsection, and may submit interim reports on such actions and determinations at such other times as he deems appropriate.

### (b) Coordination of programs by Administrator

The Administrator of the Environmental Protection Agency shall coordinate environmental research, development, and demonstration programs of such Agency with the heads of other Federal agencies in order to minimize unnecessary duplication of programs, projects, and research facilities.

### (c) Joint study by Council on Environmental Quality in consultation with Office of Science and Technology Policy for coordination of activities; report to President and Congress; report by President to Congress on implementation of joint study and report

(1) In order to promote the coordination of environmental research and development activities, and to assure that the action taken and methods used (under subsection (a) of this section and otherwise) to bring about such coordination will be as effective as possible for that purpose, the Council on Environmental Quality in consultation with the Office of Science and Technology Policy shall promptly undertake and carry out a joint study of all aspects of the coordination of environmental research and development. The Chairman of the Council shall prepare a report on the results of such study, together with such recommendations (including legislative recommendations) as he deems appropriate, and shall submit such report to the President and the Congress not later than May 31, 1978.

(2) Not later than September 30, 1978, the President shall report to the Congress on steps he has taken to implement the recommendations included in the report under paragraph (1), including any recommendations he may have for legislation.

(Pub.L. 95–155, § 9, Nov. 8, 1977, 91 Stat. 1261.)

### HISTORICAL AND STATUTORY NOTES

**References in Text**

Section 4361 of this title, referred to in subsec. (a), was repealed by Pub.L. 104–66, title II, § 2021(k)(1), Dec. 21, 1995, 109 Stat. 728.

**Codifications**

Section was enacted as part of the Environmental Research, Development, and Demonstration Authorization Act of 1978, and not as part of the National Environmental Policy Act of 1969, which comprises this chapter.

**Coordination of Environmental Research, Development, and Demonstration Efforts; Study and Report**

Pub.L. 95–477, § 3(c), Oct. 18, 1978, 92 Stat. 1509, authorized to be appropriated to the Environmental Protection Agency for the fiscal year 1979, $1,000,000, and for the fiscal year 1980, $1,000,000, for a study and report, under a contract let by the Administrator, to be conducted outside the Federal Government, on coordination of the Federal Government's efforts in environmental research, development, and demonstration, and the application of the results of such efforts to environmental problems, with the report on the study submitted to the President, the Administrator, and the Congress within two years after Oct. 18, 1978, accompanied by recommendations for action by the President, the Administrator, other agencies, or the Congress, as may be appropriate.

## § 4366a. Omitted

### HISTORICAL AND STATUTORY NOTES

**Codifications**

Section, Pub.L. 101–617, § 4, Nov. 16, 1990, 104 Stat. 3287, which related to development of a data base of environmental research articles indexed by geographic location, expired 10 years after Nov. 16, 1990, pursuant to section 6 of Pub.L. 101–617, formerly set out as a note under this section.

**Termination Date**

Pub.L. 101–617, § 6, Nov. 16, 1990, 104 Stat. 3287, provided that Pub.L. 101–617, which enacted this section and provisions formerly set out under this section, was to expire 10 years after Nov. 16, 1990.

**Short Title; Findings; Purpose; Authorization**

Pub.L. 101–617, §§ 1 to 3, Nov. 16, 1990, 104 Stat. 3287, which provided that Pub.L. 101–617, which enacted this section and provisions formerly set out under this section, could be cited as the "Environmental Research Geographic Location Information Act", and further provided for findings, purpose to develop a data base of environmental research articles indexed by geographic location, and authorization of appropriations, expired 10 years after Nov. 16, 1990, pursuant to section 6 of Pub.L. 101–617, formerly set out as a note under this section.

## § 4367. Reporting requirements of financial interests of officers and employees of Environmental Protection Agency

**(a) Covered officers and employees**

Each officer or employee of the Environmental Protection Agency who—

(1) performs any function or duty under this Act; and

(2) has any known financial interest in any person who applies for or receives grants, contracts, or other forms of financial assistance under this Act,

shall, beginning on February 1, 1978, annually file with the Administrator a written statement concerning all such interests held by such officer or employee during the preceding calendar year. Such statement shall be available to the public.

**(b) Implementation of requirements by Administrator**

The Administrator shall—

(1) act within ninety days after November 8, 1977—

(A) to define the term "known financial interest" for purposes of subsection (a) of this section; and

(B) to establish the methods by which the requirement to file written statements specified in subsection (a) of this section will be monitored and enforced, including appropriate provision for the filing by such officers and employees of such statements and the review by the Administrator of such statements; and

(2) Omitted.

**(c) Exemption of positions by Administrator**

In the rules prescribed under subsection (b) of this section, the Administrator may identify specific positions of a nonpolicymaking nature within the Administration and provide that officers or employees occupying such positions shall be exempt from the requirements of this section.

**(d) Violations; penalties**

Any officer or employee who is subject to, and knowingly violates, this section, shall be fined not more than $2,500 or imprisoned not more than one year, or both.

(Pub.L. 95–155, § 12, Nov. 8, 1977, 91 Stat. 1263.)

### HISTORICAL AND STATUTORY NOTES

**References in Text**

This Act, referred to in subsec. (a)(1), (2), is Pub.L. 95–155, Nov. 8, 1977, 91 Stat. 1257, as amended, known as the Environmental Research, Development, and Demonstration Authorization Act of 1978, which to the extent classified to the Code enacted sections 300j–3a, 4361a, 4361b, and 4363 to 4367 of this title. For complete classification of this Act to the Code, see Tables.

**Codifications**

Section was enacted as part of the Environmental Research, Development, and Demonstration Authorization Act of 1978, and not as part of the National Environmental Policy Act of 1969, which comprises this chapter.

Subsec. (b)(2) of this section, which required the Administrator to report to Congress on June 1 of each calendar year with respect to such disclosures and the actions taken in regard thereto during the preceding calendar year, terminated, effective May 15, 2000, pursuant to section 3003 of Pub.L. 104–66, as amended, set out as a note under 31 U.S.C.A. § 1113. See, also, item 9 on page 164 of House Document No. 103–7.

## § 4368. Grants to qualified citizens groups

(1) There is authorized to be appropriated to the Environmental Protection Agency, for grants to qualified citizens groups in States and regions, $3,000,000.

(2) Grants under this section may be made for the purpose of supporting and encouraging participation by qualified citizens groups in determining how scientific, technological, and social trends and changes affect the future environment and quality of life of an area, and for setting goals and identifying measures for improvement.

(3) The term "qualified citizens group" shall mean a nonprofit organization of citizens having an area based focus, which is not single-issue oriented and which can demonstrate a prior record of interest and involvement in goal-setting and research concerned with

improving the quality of life, including plans to identify, protect and enhance significant natural and cultural resources and the environment.

(4) A citizens group shall be eligible for assistance only if certified by the Governor in consultation with the State legislature as a bonafide organization entitled to receive Federal assistance to pursue the aims of this program. The group shall further demonstrate its capacity to employ usefully the funds for the purposes of this program and its broad-based representative nature.

(5) After an initial application for assistance under this section has been approved, the Administrator may make grants on an annual basis, on condition that the Governor recertify the group and that the applicant submits to the Administrator annually—

(A) an evaluation of the progress made during the previous year in meeting the objectives for which the grant was made;

(B) a description of any changes in the objectives of the activities; and

(C) a description of the proposed activities for the succeeding one year period.

(6) A grant made under this program shall not exceed 75 per centum of the estimated cost of the project or program for which the grant is made, and no group shall receive more than $50,000 in any one year.

(7) No financial assistance provided under this section shall be used to support lobbying or litigation by any recipient group.

(Pub.L. 95–477, § 3(d), Oct. 18, 1978, 92 Stat. 1509.)

### HISTORICAL AND STATUTORY NOTES

**References in Text**

This section, referred to in par. (5), means section 3 of Pub.L. 95–477, in its entirety, subsec. (d) of which enacted this section, subsecs. (a) and (b) of which were not classified to the Code, and subsec. (c) of which is set out as a note under section 4366 of this title.

**Codifications**

Section was enacted as part of the Environmental Research, Development, and Demonstration Authorization Act of 1979, and not as part of the National Environmental Policy Act of 1969, which comprises this chapter.

## § 4368a. Utilization of talents of older Americans in projects of pollution prevention, abatement, and control

### (a) Technical assistance to environmental agencies

Notwithstanding any other provision of law relating to Federal grants and cooperative agreements, the Administrator of the Environmental Protection Agency is authorized to make grants to, or enter into cooperative agreements with, private nonprofit organizations designated by the Secretary of Labor under title V of the Older Americans Act of 1965 [42 U.S.C.A. § 3056 et seq.] to utilize the talents of older Americans in programs authorized by other provisions of law administered by the Administrator (and consistent with such provisions of law) in providing technical assistance to Federal, State, and local environmental agencies for projects of pollution prevention, abatement, and control. Funding for such grants or agreements may be made available from such programs or through title V of the Older Americans Act of 1965 [42 U.S.C.A. § 3056 et seq.] and subtitle D of title I of the Workforce Investment Act of 1998 [29 U.S.C.A. § 2911 et seq.].

### (b) Pre-award certifications

Prior to awarding any grant or agreement under subsection (a) of this section, the applicable Federal, State, or local environmental agency shall certify to the Administrator that such grants or agreements will not—

(1) result in the displacement of individuals currently employed by the environmental agency concerned (including partial displacement through reduction of nonovertime hours, wages, or employment benefits);

(2) result in the employment of any individual when any other person is in a layoff status from the same or substantially equivalent job within the jurisdiction of the environmental agency concerned; or

(3) affect existing contracts for services.

### (c) Prior appropriation Acts

Grants or agreements awarded under this section shall be subject to prior appropriation Acts.

(Pub.L. 98–313, § 2, June 12, 1984, 98 Stat. 235; Pub.L. 105–277, Div. A, § 101(f) [Title VIII, § 405(d)(35), (f)(27)], Oct. 21, 1998, 112 Stat. 2681–426, 2681–434.)

### HISTORICAL AND STATUTORY NOTES

**References in Text**

Title V of the Older Americans Act of 1965, referred to in subsec. (a), is Title V of Pub.L. 89–73, July 14, 1965, 79 Stat. 218, as amended, which is known as the "Older Americans Community Service Employment Act" and which is classified to subchapter IX (section 3056 et seq.) of chapter 35 of this title. For complete classification of the Act to the Code, see Short Title note set out under section 3001 of this title and Tables.

Subtitle D of title I of the Workforce Investment Act of 1998, is Subtitle D (sections 166 to 174) of title I of Pub.L. 105–220, Aug. 7, 1998, 112 Stat. 1021, which is classified generally to subchapter IV (section 2911 et seq.) of chapter 30 of Title 29. For complete classification of this Act to the Code, see Tables.

**Codifications**

Section was enacted as part of the Environmental Programs Assistance Act of 1984, and not as part of the National Environmental Policy Act of 1969, which comprises this chapter.

**Effective and Applicability Provisions**

1998 Acts

Amendment by section 101(f) [Title VIII, § 405(f)(27)] of Pub.L. 105–277 shall take effect July 1, 2000, see section 101(f) [Title VIII, § 405(g)(2)(B)] of Pub.L. 105–277, set out as a note under section 3502 of Title 5.

Amendment by section 101(f) [Title VIII, § 405(d)(35)] of Pub.L. 105–277 effective Oct. 21, 1998, see section 101(f) [Title VIII, § 405(g)(1)] of Pub.L. 105–277, set out as a note under section 3502 of Title 5.

**Change of Name**

Effective August 7, 1998, all references in any provision of law (other than 18 U.S.C.A. § 665) to the Comprehensive Employment and Training Act, or the Job Training Partnership Act, deemed to refer to the Workforce Investment Act of 1998 (Pub.L. 105–220, Aug. 7, 1998, 112 Stat. 936), see section 2940 of Title 29.

All references in any other provision of law to a provision of the Comprehensive Employment and Training Act, or of the Job Training Partnership Act, deemed to refer to the corresponding provision of Title I of the Workforce Investment Act of 1998 (Pub.L. 105–220, Title I, §§ 101 to 199A, Aug. 7, 1998, 112 Stat. 936 [29 U.S.C.A. § 2801 et seq.]), see section 199A(c) of Pub.L. 105–220, set out as a note under section 2940 of Title 29.

**Short Title**

1984 Acts

Section 1 of Pub.L. 98–313 provided that: "This Act [enacting this section] may be cited as the 'Environmental Programs Assistance Act of 1984'."

## § 4368b. General assistance program

### (a) Short title

This section may be cited as the "Indian Environmental General Assistance Program Act of 1992".

### (b) Purposes

The purposes of this section are to—

(1) provide general assistance grants to Indian tribal governments and intertribal consortia to build capacity to administer environmental regulatory programs that may be delegated by the Environmental Protection Agency on Indian lands; and

(2) provide technical assistance from the Environmental Protection Agency to Indian tribal governments and intertribal consortia in the development of multimedia programs to address environmental issues on Indian lands.

### (c) Definitions

For purposes of this section:

(1) The term "Indian tribal government" means any Indian tribe, band, nation, or other organized group or community, including any Alaska Native village or regional or village corporation (as defined in, or established pursuant to, the Alaska Native Claims Settlement Act (43 U.S.C.A. § 1601, et seq.)), which is recognized as eligible for the special services provided by the United States to Indians because of their status as Indians.

(2) The term "intertribal consortia" or "intertribal consortium" means a partnership between two or more Indian tribal governments authorized by the governing bodies of those tribes to apply for and receive assistance pursuant to this section.

(3) The term "Administrator" means the Administrator of the Environmental Protection Agency.

### (d) General assistance program

(1) The Administrator of the Environmental Protection Agency shall establish an Indian Environmental General Assistance Program that provides grants to eligible Indian tribal governments or intertribal consortia to cover the costs of planning, developing, and establishing environmental protection programs consistent with other applicable provisions of law providing for enforcement of such laws by Indian tribes on Indian lands.

(2) Each grant awarded for general assistance under this subsection for a fiscal year shall be no less than $75,000, and no single grant may be awarded to an Indian tribal government or intertribal consortium for more than 10 percent of the funds appropriated under subsection (h) of this section.

(3) The term of any general assistance award made under this subsection may exceed one year. Any awards made pursuant to this section shall remain available until expended. An Indian tribal government or intertribal consortium may receive a general assistance grant for a period of up to four years in each specific media area.

### (e) No reduction in amounts

In no case shall the award of a general assistance grant to an Indian tribal government or intertribal consortium under this section result in a reduction of Environmental Protection Agency grants for environmental programs to that tribal government or consortium. Nothing in this section shall preclude an Indian tribal government or intertribal consortium from receiving individual media grants or cooperative agreements. Funds provided by the Environmental Protection Agency through the general assistance program shall be used by an Indian tribal government or intertribal consortium to supplement other funds provided by the Environmental Protection Agency through individual media grants or cooperative agreements.

**(f) Expenditure of general assistance**

Any general assistance under this section shall be expended for the purpose of planning, developing, and establishing the capability to implement programs administered by the Environmental Protection Agency and specified in the assistance agreement. Purposes and programs authorized under this section shall include the development and implementation of solid and hazardous waste programs for Indian lands. An Indian tribal government or intertribal consortium receiving general assistance pursuant to this section shall utilize such funds for programs and purposes to be carried out in accordance with the terms of the assistance agreement. Such programs and general assistance shall be carried out in accordance with the purposes and requirements of applicable provisions of law, including the Solid Waste Disposal Act (42 U.S.C. 6901 et seq.).

**(g) Procedures**

(1) Within 12 months following October 24, 1992, the Administrator shall promulgate regulations establishing procedures under which an Indian tribal government or intertribal consortium may apply for general assistance grants under this section.

(2) The Administrator shall publish regulations issued pursuant to this section in the Federal Register.

(3) The Administrator shall establish procedures for accounting, auditing, evaluating, and reviewing any programs or activities funded in whole or in part for a general assistance grant under this section.

**(h) Authorization**

There are authorized to be appropriated to carry out the provisions of this section, such sums as may be necessary for each of the fiscal years 1993, 1994, 1995, 1996, 1997, and 1998.

**(i) Report to Congress**

The Administrator shall transmit an annual report to the appropriate Committees of the Congress with jurisdiction over the applicable environmental laws and Indian tribes describing which Indian tribes or intertribal consortia have been granted approval by the Administrator pursuant to law to enforce certain environmental laws and the effectiveness of any such enforcement.

(Pub.L. 95–134, Title V, § 502, as added Pub.L. 102–497, § 11, Oct. 24, 1992, 106 Stat. 3258, and amended Pub.L. 103–155, Nov. 24, 1993, 107 Stat. 1523; Pub.L. 104–233, § 1, Oct. 2, 1996, 110 Stat. 3057.)

**HISTORICAL AND STATUTORY NOTES**

**References in Text**

The Alaska Native Claims Settlement Act, referred to in subsec. (c)(1), is Pub.L. 92–203, Dec. 18, 1971, 85 Stat. 688, as amended, which is classified generally to chapter 33 (section 1601 et seq.) of Title 43, Public Lands. For complete classification of this Act to the Code, see Short Title note set out under section 1601 of Title 43 and Tables.

The Solid Waste Disposal Act, referred to in subsec. (f), is Title II of Pub.L. 89–272, Oct. 20, 1965, 79 Stat. 997, as amended generally by Pub.L. 94–580, § 2, Oct. 21, 1976, 90 Stat. 2795, which is classified generally to chapter 82 (section 6901 et seq.) of this title. For complete classification of this Act to the Code, see Short Title note set out under section 6901 of this title and Tables.

**Codifications**

Section was enacted as part of the Indian Environmental General Assistance Program Act of 1992 and as part of the Omnibus Territories Act of 1977, and not as part of the National Environmental Policy Act of 1969, which comprises this chapter.

## § 4369. Miscellaneous reports

**(a) Availability to Congressional committees**

All reports to or by the Administrator relevant to the Agency's program of research, development, and demonstration shall promptly be made available to the Committee on Science, Space, and Technology of the House of Representatives and the Committee on Environment and Public Works of the Senate, unless otherwise prohibited by law.

**(b) Transmittal of jurisdictional information**

The Administrator shall keep the Committee on Science, Space, and Technology of the House of Representatives and the Committee on Environment and Public Works of the Senate fully and currently informed with respect to matters falling within or related to the jurisdiction of the committees.

**(c) Comment by Government agencies and the public**

The reports provided for in section 5910 of this title shall be made available to the public for comment, and to the heads of affected agencies for comment and, in the case of recommendations for action, for response.

**(d) Transmittal of research information to the Department of Energy**

For the purpose of assisting the Department of Energy in planning and assigning priorities in research development and demonstration activities related to environmental control technologies, the Administrator shall actively make available to the Department all information on research activities and results of research programs of the Environmental Protection Agency.

(Pub.L. 95–477, § 5, Oct. 18, 1978, 92 Stat. 1510; Pub.L. 103–437, § 15(c)(6), Nov. 2, 1994, 108 Stat. 4592.)

HISTORICAL AND STATUTORY NOTES

**References in Text**

Section 5910 of this title, referred to in subsec. (c), was repealed by Pub.L. 104–66, title II, § 2021(i), Dec. 21, 1995, 109 Stat. 727.

**Codifications**

Section was enacted as part of the Environmental Research, Development, and Demonstration Authorization Act of 1979, and not as part of the National Environmental Policy Act of 1969, which comprises this chapter.

**Change of Name**

Any reference in any provision of law enacted before Jan. 4, 1995, to the Committee on Science, Space, and Technology of the House of Representatives treated as referring to the Committee on Science of the House of Representatives, see section 1(a)(10) of Pub.L. 104–14, set out as a note preceding section 21 of Title 2, The Congress.

## § 4369a. Reports on environmental research and development activities of the Agency

**(a) Reports to keep Congressional committees fully and currently informed**

The Administrator shall keep the appropriate committees of the House and the Senate fully and currently informed about all aspects of the environmental research and development activities of the Environmental Protection Agency.

**[(b) Omitted]**

(Pub.L. 96–229, § 4, Apr. 7, 1980, 94 Stat. 328.)

HISTORICAL AND STATUTORY NOTES

**Codifications**

Section was enacted as part of the Environmental Research, Development, and Demonstration Authorization Act of 1980, and not as part of the National Environmental Policy Act of 1969, which comprises this chapter.

Subsec. (b) of this section, which required the Administrator to annually make available to the appropriate committees of Congress sufficient copies of a report fully describing funds requested and the environmental research and development activities to be carried out with these funds, terminated, effective May 15, 2000, pursuant to section 3003 of Pub.L. 104–66, as amended, set out as a note under 31 U.S.C.A. § 1113. See also, item 24 on page 163 of House Document No. 103–7.

## § 4370. Reimbursement for use of facilities

**(a) Authority to allow outside groups or individuals to use research and test facilities; reimbursement**

The Administrator is authorized to allow appropriate use of special Environmental Protection Agency research and test facilities by outside groups or individuals and to receive reimbursement or fees for costs incurred thereby when he finds this to be in the public interest. Such reimbursement or fees are to be used by the Agency to defray the costs of use by outside groups or individuals.

**(b) Rules and regulations**

The Administrator may promulgate regulations to cover such use of Agency facilities in accordance with generally accepted accounting, safety, and laboratory practices.

**(c) Waiver of reimbursement by Administrator**

When he finds it is in the public interest the Administrator may waive reimbursement or fees for outside use of Agency facilities by nonprofit private or public entities.

(Pub.L. 96–229, § 5, Apr. 7, 1980, 94 Stat. 328.)

HISTORICAL AND STATUTORY NOTES

**Codifications**

Section was enacted as part of the Environmental Research, Development, and Demonstration Authorization Act of 1980, and not as part of the National Environmental Policy Act of 1969, which comprises this chapter.

## § 4370a. Assistant Administrators of Environmental Protection Agency; appointment; duties

(a) The President, by and with the advice and consent of the Senate, may appoint three Assistant Administrators of the Environmental Protection Agency in addition to—

(1) the five Assistant Administrators provided for in section 1(d) of Reorganization Plan Numbered 3 of 1970 (5 U.S.C. Appendix);

(2) the Assistant Administrator provided by section 2625(g) of Title 15; and

(3) the Assistant Administrator provided by section 6911a of this title.

(b) Each Assistant Administrator appointed under subsection (a) of this section shall perform such duties as the Administrator of the Environmental Protection Agency may prescribe.

(Pub.L. 98–80, § 1, Aug. 23, 1983, 97 Stat. 485.)

HISTORICAL AND STATUTORY NOTES

**References in Text**

Reorganization Plan Numbered 3 of 1970, referred to in subsec. (a)(1), is set out in Appendix 1 to Title 5, Government Organization and Employees, and also as a note under section 4321 of this title.

**Codifications**

Section was not enacted as part of the National Environmental Policy Act of 1969, which comprises this chapter.

## § 4370b. Availability of fees and charges to carry out Agency programs

Notwithstanding any other provision of law, after September 30, 1990, amounts deposited in the Licensing and Other Services Fund from fees and charges assessed and collected by the Administrator for services and activities carried out pursuant to the statutes administered by the Environmental Protection Agency shall thereafter be available to carry out the Agency's activities in the programs for which the fees or charges are made.

(Pub.L. 101–144, Title III, Nov. 9, 1989, 103 Stat. 858.)

#### HISTORICAL AND STATUTORY NOTES

**Codifications**

Section was enacted as part of the Departments of Veterans Affairs and Housing and Urban Development, and Independent Agencies Appropriations Act, 1990, and not as part of the National Environmental Policy Act of 1969, which comprises this chapter.

## § 4370c. Environmental Protection Agency fees

### (a) Assessment and collection

The Administrator of the Environmental Protection Agency shall, by regulation, assess and collect fees and charges for services and activities carried out pursuant to laws administered by the Environmental Protection Agency.

### (b) Amount of fees and charges

Fees and charges assessed pursuant to this section shall be in such amounts as may be necessary to ensure that the aggregate amount of fees and charges collected pursuant to this section, in excess of the amount of fees and charges collected under current law—

(1) in fiscal year 1991, is not less than $28,000,000; and

(2) in each of fiscal years 1992, 1993, 1994, and 1995, is not less than $38,000,000.

### (c) Limitation on fees and charges

(1) The maximum aggregate amount of fees and charges in excess of the amounts being collected under current law which may be assessed and collected pursuant to this section in a fiscal year—

(A) for services and activities carried out pursuant ot [1] the Federal Water Pollution Control Act [33 U.S.C.A. § 1251 et seq.] is $10,000,000; and

(B) for services and activities in programs within the jurisdiction of the House Committee on Energy and Commerce and administered by the Environmental Protection Agency through the Administrator, shall be limited to such sums collected as of November 5, 1990, pursuant to sections 2625(b) and 2665(e)(2) of Title 15, and such sums specifically authorized by the Clean Air Act Amendments of 1990.

(2) Any remaining amounts required to be collected under this section shall be collected from services and programs administered by the Environmental Protection Agency other than those specified in subparagraphs (A) and (B) of paragraph (1).

### (d) Rule of construction

Nothing in this section increases or diminishes the authority of the Administrator to promulgate regulations pursuant to section 9701 of Title 31.

### (e) Uses of fees

Fees and charges collected pursuant to this section shall be deposited into a special account for environmental services in the Treasury of the United States. Subject to appropriation Acts, such funds shall be available to the Environmental Protection Agency to carry out the activities for which such fees and charges are collected. Such funds shall remain available until expended.

(Pub.L. 101–508, Title VI, § 6501, Nov. 5, 1990, 104 Stat. 1388–320.)

[1] So in original. Probably should be "to".

#### HISTORICAL AND STATUTORY NOTES

**References in Text**

The Federal Water Pollution Control Act, referred to in subsec. (c)(1)(A), is Act June 30, 1948, c. 758, 62 Stat. 1155, as amended generally by Pub.L. 92–500, § 2, Oct. 18, 1972, 86 Stat. 816, which is classified generally to chapter 26 (section 1251 et seq.) of Title 33. For complete classification of this Act to the Code, see Short Title note set out under section 1251 of Title 33 and Tables.

The Clean Air Act Amendments of 1990, referred to in subsec. (c)(1)(B), is Pub.L. 101–549, Nov. 15, 1990, 104 Stat. 2399, which is classified principally to chapter 85 (section 7401 et seq.) of this title. For complete classification of this Act to the Code, see Tables.

Section 2665(e)(2) of title 15, referred to in subsec. (c)(1)(B), was redesignated section 2655(d)(2) of title 15, by Pub.L. 104–66, title II, § 2021(*l*)(2), Dec. 21, 1995, 109 Stat. 728.

**Codifications**

In subsec. (d), "section 9701 of Title 31" was in the original "the Independent Office Appropriations Act (31 U.S.C. 9701)" and substitution was made as if it read for "title V of the Independent Offices Appropriation Act of 1952" on authority of Pub.L. 97–258, § 4(b), Sept. 13, 1982, 96 Stat. 1067, the first section of which enacted Title 31, Money and Finance.

Section was enacted as part of the Omnibus Budget Reconciliation Act of 1990, and not as part of the National Environmental Policy Act of 1969, which comprises this chapter.

**Change of Name**

Any reference in any provision of law enacted before Jan. 4, 1995, to the Committee on Energy and Commerce of the House of Representatives treated as referring to the Committee on Commerce of the House of Representatives, except that any reference in any provision of law enacted before Jan. 4, 1995, to the Committee on Energy and Commerce of the House of Representatives treated as referring to the

Committee on Agriculture of the House of Representatives, in the case of a provision of law relating to inspection of seafood or seafood products, the Committee on Banking and Financial Services of the House of Representatives, in the case of a provision of law relating to bank capital markets activities generally or to depository institution securities activities generally, and the Committee on Transportation and Infrastructure of the House of Representatives, in the case of a provision of law relating to railroads, railway labor, or railroad retirement and unemployment (except revenue measures related thereto), see section 1(a)(4) and (c)(1) of Pub.L. 104–14, set out as a note preceding section 21 of Title 2, The Congress.

## § 4370d. Percentage of Federal funding for organizations owned by economically and socially disadvantaged individuals

The Administrator of the Environmental Protection Agency shall, on and after October 6, 1992, to the fullest extent possible, ensure that at least 8 per centum of Federal funding for prime and subcontracts awarded in support of authorized programs, including grants, loans, and contracts for wastewater treatment and leaking underground storage tanks grants, be made available to business concerns or other organizations owned or controlled by socially and economically disadvantaged individuals (within the meaning of section 637(a)(5) and (6) of Title 15), including historically black colleges and universities. For purposes of this section, economically and socially disadvantaged individuals shall be deemed to include women.

(Pub.L. 102–389, Title III, Oct. 6, 1992, 106 Stat. 1602.)

### HISTORICAL AND STATUTORY NOTES

**Codifications**

Section was enacted as part of the Departments of Veterans Affairs and Housing and Urban Development, and Independent Agencies Appropriations Act, 1993, and not as part of the National Environmental Policy Act of 1969, which comprises this chapter.

## § 4370e. Working Capital Fund in Treasury

There is hereby established in the Treasury a "Working capital fund", to be available without fiscal year limitation for expenses and equipment necessary for the maintenance and operation of such administrative services as the Administrator determines may be performed more advantageously as central services: *Provided,* That any inventories, equipment, and other assets pertaining to the services to be provided by such fund, either on hand or on order, less the related liabilities or unpaid obligations, and any appropriations made hereafter for the purpose of providing capital, shall be used to capitalize such fund: *Provided further,* That such fund shall be paid in advance or reimbursed from funds available to the Agency and other Federal agencies for which such centralized services are performed, at rates which will return in full all expenses of operation, including accrued leave, depreciation of fund plant and equipment, amortization of automated data processing (ADP) software and systems (either acquired or donated), and an amount necessary to maintain a reasonable operating reserve, as determined by the Administrator: *Provided further,* That such fund shall provide services on a competitive basis: *Provided further,* That an amount not to exceed four percent of the total annual income to such fund may be retained in the fund for fiscal year 1997 and each fiscal year thereafter, to remain available until expended, to be used for the acquisition of capital equipment and for the improvement and implementation of Agency financial management, ADP, and other support systems: *Provided further,* That no later than thirty days after the end of each fiscal year amounts in excess of this reserve limitation shall be transferred to the Treasury.

(Pub.L. 104–204, Title III, Sept. 26, 1996, 110 Stat. 2912; Pub.L. 105–65, Title III, Oct. 27, 1997, 111 Stat. 1374; Pub.L. 105–276, Title III, Oct. 21, 1998, 112 Stat. 2499.)

### HISTORICAL AND STATUTORY NOTES

**Codifications**

Section was enacted as part of the Departments of Veterans Affairs and Housing and Urban Development, and Independent Agencies Appropriations Act, 1997, and not as part of the National Environmental Policy Act of 1969, which comprises this chapter.

Section was formerly set out as a note under section 501 of Title 31.

Pub.L. 105–276, Title III, Oct. 21, 1998, 112 Stat. 2499 instructed that "or reimbursed" be inserted after the phrase "that such fund shall be paid in advance". This instruction was executed by inserting the language after the phrase "That such fund shall be paid in advance" as the probable intent of Congress.

## § 4370f. Availability of funds after expiration of period for liquidating obligations

For fiscal year 2001 and thereafter, the obligated balances of sums available in multiple-year appropriations accounts shall remain available through the seventh fiscal year after their period of availability has expired for liquidating obligations made during the period of availability.

(Pub.L. 106–377, § 1(a)(1) [Title III], Oct. 27, 2000, 114 Stat. 1441, 1441A–44.)

# ENVIRONMENTAL QUALITY IMPROVEMENT

## ENVIRONMENTAL QUALITY IMPROVEMENT ACT OF 1970 [EQIA § ____]

**(42 U.S.C.A. §§ 4371 to 4375)**

## CHAPTER 56—ENVIRONMENTAL QUALITY IMPROVEMENT



### § 4371. Congressional findings, declarations, and purposes

**[EQIA § 202]**

(a) The Congress finds—

(1) that man has caused changes in the environment;

(2) that many of these changes may affect the relationship between man and his environment; and

(3) that population increases and urban concentration contribute directly to pollution and the degradation of our environment.

(b)(1) The Congress declares that there is a national policy for the environment which provides for the enhancement of environmental quality. This policy is evidenced by statutes heretofore enacted relating to the prevention, abatement, and control of environmental pollution, water and land resources, transportation, and economic and regional development.

(2) The primary responsibility for implementing this policy rests with State and local government.

(3) The Federal Government encourages and supports implementation of this policy through appropriate regional organizations established under existing law.

(c) The purposes of this chapter are—

(1) to assure that each Federal department and agency conducting or supporting public works activities which affect the environment shall implement the policies established under existing law; and

(2) to authorize an Office of Environmental Quality, which, notwithstanding any other provision of law, shall provide the professional and administrative staff for the Council on Environmental Quality established by Public Law 91–190.

(Pub.L. 91–224, Title II, § 202, Apr. 3, 1970, 84 Stat. 114.)

#### HISTORICAL AND STATUTORY NOTES

**References in Text**

Public Law 91–190, referred to in subsec. (c)(2), is Pub.L. 91–190, Jan. 1, 1970, 83 Stat. 852, as amended, known as the National Environmental Policy Act of 1969, which is classified generally to chapter 55 (section 4321 et seq.) of this title. For complete classification of this Act to the Code, see Short Title note set out under section 4321 of this title and Tables.

**Short Title**

1970 Acts

Section 201 of Pub.L. 91–224 provided that: "This title [enacting this chapter] may be cited as the 'Environmental Quality Improvement Act of 1970'."

### § 4372. Office of Environmental Quality

**[EQIA § 203]**

**(a) Establishment; Director; Deputy Director**

There is established in the Executive Office of the President an office to be known as the Office of Environmental Quality (hereafter in this chapter referred to as the "Office"). The Chairman of the Council on Environmental Quality established by Public Law 91–190 shall be the Director of the Office. There shall be in the Office a Deputy Director who shall be appointed by the President, by and with the advice and consent of the Senate.

**(b) Compensation of Deputy Director**

The compensation of the Deputy Director shall be fixed by the President at a rate not in excess of the annual rate of compensation payable to the Deputy Director of the Office of Management and Budget.

**(c) Employment of personnel, experts, and consultants; compensation**

The Director is authorized to employ such officers and employees (including experts and consultants) as may be necessary to enable the Office to carry out its functions under this chapter and Public Law 91–190, except that he may employ no more than ten specialists and other experts without regard to the provisions of Title 5, governing appointments in the competitive service, and pay such specialists and experts without regard to the provisions of chapter 51 and subchapter III of chapter 53 of such title relating to classification and General Schedule pay rates, but no such specialist or expert shall be paid at a rate in excess of the maximum rate for GS–18 of the General Schedule under section 5332 of Title 5.

**(d) Duties and functions of Director**

In carrying out his functions the Director shall assist and advise the President on policies and programs of the Federal Government affecting environmental quality by—

(1) providing the professional and administrative staff and support for the Council on Environmental Quality established by Public Law 91–190;

(2) assisting the Federal agencies and departments in appraising the effectiveness of existing and proposed facilities, programs, policies, and activities of the Federal Government, and those specific major projects designated by the President which do not require individual project authorization by Congress, which affect environmental quality;

(3) reviewing the adequacy of existing systems for monitoring and predicting environmental changes in order to achieve effective coverage and efficient use of research facilities and other resources;

(4) promoting the advancement of scientific knowledge of the effects of actions and technology on the environment and encourage the development of the means to prevent or reduce adverse effects that endanger the health and well-being of man;

(5) assisting in coordinating among the Federal departments and agencies those programs and activities which affect, protect, and improve environmental quality;

(6) assisting the Federal departments and agencies in the development and interrelationship of environmental quality criteria and standards established through the Federal Government;

(7) collecting, collating, analyzing, and interpreting data and information on environmental quality, ecological research, and evaluation.

**(e) Authority of Director to contract**

The Director is authorized to contract with public or private agencies, institutions, and organizations and with individuals without regard to section 3324(a) and (b) of Title 31 and section 5 of Title 41 in carrying out his functions.

(Pub.L. 91–224, Title II, § 203, Apr. 3, 1970, 84 Stat. 114; 1970 Reorg. Plan No. 2, § 102, eff. July 1, 1970, 35 F.R. 7959, 84 Stat. 2085; Pub.L. 97–258, § 4(b), Sept. 13, 1982, 96 Stat. 1067.)

### HISTORICAL AND STATUTORY NOTES

**References in Text**

Public Law 91–190, referred to in subsecs. (a), (c), and (d), is Pub.L. 91–190, Jan. 1, 1970, 83 Stat. 852, as amended, known as the National Environmental Policy Act of 1969, which is classified generally to chapter 55 (section 4321 et seq.) of this title. For complete classification of this Act to the Code, see Short Title note set out under section 4321 of this title and Tables.

The provisions of Title 5, governing appointments in the competitive service, referred to in subsec. (c), are classified to section 3301 et seq. of Title 5, Government Organization and Employees.

The General Schedule, referred to in subsec. (c), is set out under section 5332 of Title 5.

**Codifications**

In subsec. (e), "section 3324(a) and (b) of Title 31" was substituted for reference to section 3648 of the Revised Statutes (31 U.S.C. 529) on authority of Pub.L. 97–258, § 4(b), Sept. 13, 1982, 96 Stat. 1067, the first section of which enacted Title 31, Money and Finance.

**Transfer of Functions**

All functions vested by law (including reorganization plan) in the Bureau of the Budget or the Director of the Bureau of the Budget were transferred to the President of the United States by section 101 of 1970 Reorg. Plan No. 2, eff. July 1, 1970, 35 F.R. 7959, 84 Stat. 2085. Section 102 of 1970 Reorg. Plan No. 2 redesignated the Bureau of the Budget as the Office of Management and Budget and the offices of Director of the Bureau of the Budget, Deputy Director of the Bureau of the Budget, and Assistant Directors of the Bureau of the Budget as Director of the Office of Management and Budget, Deputy Director of the Office of Management and Budget, and Assistant Directors of the Office of Management and Budget, respectively. Section 103 of 1970 Reorg. Plan No. 2 transferred all records, property, personnel, and funds of the Bureau to the Office of Management and Budget. See Part I of 1970 Reorganization Plan No. 2, set out in Appendix 1 to Title 5, Government Organization and Employees.

**References in Other Laws to GS–16, 17, or 18 Pay Rates**

References in laws to the rates of pay for GS–16, 17, or 18, or to maximum rates of pay under the General Schedule, to be considered references to rates payable under specified sections of Title 5, Government Organization and Employees, see section 529 [Title I, § 101(c)(1) ] of Pub.L. 101–509, set out in a note under section 5376 of Title 5.

## § 4373. Referral of Environmental Quality Reports to standing committees having jurisdiction

**[EQIA § 204]**

Each Environmental Quality Report required by Public Law 91–190 shall, upon transmittal to Congress, be referred to each standing committee having jurisdiction over any part of the subject matter of the Report.

(Pub.L. 91–224, Title II, § 204, Apr. 3, 1970, 84 Stat. 115.)

HISTORICAL AND STATUTORY NOTES

**References in Text**

Public Law 91–190, referred to in text, is Pub.L. 91–190, Jan. 1, 1970, 83 Stat. 852, as amended, known as the National Environmental Policy Act of 1969, which is classified generally to chapter 55 (section 4321 et seq.) of this title. For complete classification of this Act to the Code, see Short Title note set out under section 4321 of this title and Tables.

## § 4374. Authorization of appropriations

[EQIA § 205]

There are hereby authorized to be appropriated for the operations of the Office of Environmental Quality and the Council on Environmental Quality not to exceed the following sums for the following fiscal years which sums are in addition to those contained in Public Law 91–190:

**(a)** $2,126,000 for the fiscal year ending September 30, 1979.

**(b)** $3,000,000 for each of the fiscal years ending September 30, 1980, and September 30, 1981.

**(c)** $44,000 for the fiscal years ending September 30, 1982, 1983, and 1984.

**(d)** $480,000 for each of the fiscal years ending September 30, 1985 and September 30, 1986.

(Pub.L. 91–224, Title II, § 205, Apr. 3, 1970, 84 Stat. 115; Pub.L. 93–36, May 18, 1973, 87 Stat. 72; Pub.L. 94–52, § 1, July 3, 1975, 89 Stat. 258; Pub.L. 94–298, May 29, 1976, 90 Stat. 587; Pub.L. 95–300, June 26, 1978, 92 Stat. 342; Pub.L. 97–350, § 1, Oct. 18, 1982, 96 Stat. 1661; Pub.L. 98–581, § 1, Oct. 30, 1984, 98 Stat. 3093.)

HISTORICAL AND STATUTORY NOTES

**References in Text**

Pub.L. 91–190, referred to in text, is Pub.L. 91–190, Jan. 1, 1970, 83 Stat. 852, as amended, known as the National Environmental Policy Act of 1969, which is classified generally to chapter 55 (section 4321 et seq.) of this title. For complete classification of this Act to the Code, see Short Title note set out under section 4321 of this title and Tables.

## § 4375. Office of Environmental Quality Management Fund

[EQIA § 206]

**(a) Establishment; financing of study contracts and Federal interagency environmental projects**

There is established an Office of Environmental Quality Management Fund (hereinafter referred to as the "Fund") to receive advance payments from other agencies or accounts that may be used solely to finance—

(1) study contracts that are jointly sponsored by the Office and one or more other Federal agencies; and

(2) Federal interagency environmental projects (including task forces) in which the Office participates.

**(b) Study contract or project initiative**

Any study contract or project that is to be financed under subsection (a) of this section may be initiated only with the approval of the Director.

**(c) Regulations**

The Director shall promulgate regulations setting forth policies and procedures for operation of the Fund.

(Pub.L. 91–224, Title II, § 206, as added Pub.L. 98–581, § 2, Oct. 30, 1984, 98 Stat. 3093.)

# NOISE CONTROL

## NOISE CONTROL ACT OF 1972 [NCA § ____]

**(42 U.S.C.A. §§ 4901 to 4918)**

## CHAPTER 65—NOISE CONTROL



**Related Provisions**

*See, also, Abatement of Aviation Noise, 49 U.S.C.A. App. § 2101 et seq., post.*

### § 4901. Congressional findings and statement of policy

**[NCA § 2]**

(a) The Congress finds—

(1) that inadequately controlled noise presents a growing danger to the health and welfare of the Nation's population, particularly in urban areas;

(2) that the major sources of noise include transportation vehicles and equipment, machinery, appliances, and other products in commerce; and

(3) that, while primary responsibility for control of noise rests with State and local governments, Federal action is essential to deal with major noise sources in commerce control of which require national uniformity of treatment.

(b) The Congress declares that it is the policy of the United States to promote an environment for all Americans free from noise that jeopardizes their health or welfare. To that end, it is the purpose of this chapter to establish a means for effective coordination of Federal research and activities in noise control, to authorize the establishment of Federal noise emission standards for products distributed in commerce, and to provide information to the public respecting the noise emission and noise reduction characteristics of such products.

(Pub.L. 92–574, § 2, Oct. 27, 1972, 86 Stat. 1234.)

**HISTORICAL AND STATUTORY NOTES**

**Short Title**

1978 Amendments

Pub.L. 95–609, § 1, Nov. 8, 1978, 92 Stat. 3079, provided: "That this Act [amending sections 4905, 4910, 4913, 4918, 6901, 6903, 6907, 6913, 6922, 6923, 6925 to 6928, 6947, 6961, 6962, 6964, 6972, 6973, 6977, and 6981 to 6984 of this title] may be cited as the 'Quiet Communities Act of 1978'."

1972 Acts

Section 1 of Pub.L. 92–574 provided that: "This Act [which enacted this chapter, and enacted provisions set out as notes under this section] may be cited as the 'Noise Control Act of 1972'."

**Federal Compliance With Pollution Control Standards**

For provisions relating to the responsibility of the head of each Executive agency for compliance with applicable pollution control standards, see Ex. Ord. No. 12088, Oct. 13, 1978, 43 F.R. 47707, set out as a note under section 4321 of this title.

### § 4902. Definitions

**[NCA § 3]**

For purposes of this chapter:

(1) The term "Administrator" means the Administrator of the Environmental Protection Agency.

(2) The term "person" means an individual, corporation, partnership, or association, and (except as provided in sections 4910(e) and 4911(a) of this title) includes any officer, employee, department, agency, or instrumentality of the United States, a State, or any political subdivision of a State.

(3) The term "product" means any manufactured article or goods or component thereof; except that such term does not include—

(A) any aircraft, aircraft engine, propeller, or appliance, as such terms are defined in section 40102(a) of Title 49; or

(B) (i) any military weapons or equipment which are designed for combat use; (ii) any rockets or equipment which are designed for research, experimental, or developmental work to be performed by the National Aeronautics and Space Administration; or (iii) to the extent provided by regulations of the Administrator, any other machinery or equipment designed for use in experimental work done by or for the Federal Government.

(4) The term "ultimate purchaser" means the first person who in good faith purchases a product for purposes other than resale.

(5) The term "new product" means (A) a product the equitable or legal title of which has never been transferred to an ultimate purchaser, or (B) a product which is imported or offered for importation into the United States and which is manufactured after the effective date of a regulation under section 4905 or 4907 of this title which would have been applicable to such product had it been manufactured in the United States.

(6) The term "manufacturer" means any person engaged in the manufacturing or assembling of new products, or the importing of new products for resale, or who acts for, and is controlled by, any such person in connection with the distribution of such products.

(7) The term "commerce" means trade, traffic, commerce, or transportation—

(A) between a place in a State and any place outside thereof, or

(B) which affects trade, traffic, commerce, or transportation described in subparagraph (A).

(8) The term "distribute in commerce" means sell in, offer for sale in, or introduce or deliver for introduction into, commerce.

(9) The term "State" includes the District of Columbia, the Commonwealth of Puerto Rico, the Virgin Islands, American Samoa, Guam, and the Trust Territory of the Pacific Islands.

(10) The term "Federal agency" means an executive agency (as defined in section 105 of Title 5) and includes the United States Postal Service.

(11) The term "environmental noise" means the intensity, duration, and the character of sounds from all sources.

(Pub.L. 92–574, § 3, Oct. 27, 1972, 86 Stat. 1234.)

## § 4903. Federal programs

[NCA § 4]

### (a) Furtherance of Congressional policy

The Congress authorizes and directs that Federal agencies shall, to the fullest extent consistent with their authority under Federal laws administered by them, carry out the programs within their control in such a manner as to further the policy declared in section 4901(b) of this title.

### (b) Presidential authority to exempt activities or facilities from compliance requirements

Each department, agency, or instrumentality of the executive, legislative, and judicial branches of the Federal Government—

(1) having jurisdiction over any property or facility, or

(2) engaged in any activity resulting, or which may result, in the emission of noise,

shall comply with Federal, State, interstate, and local requirements respecting control and abatement of environmental noise to the same extent that any person is subject to such requirements. The President may exempt any single activity or facility, including noise emission sources or classes thereof, of any department, agency, or instrumentality in the executive branch from compliance with any such requirement if he determines it to be in the paramount interest of the United States to do so; except that no exemption, other than for those products referred to in section 4902(3)(B) of this title, may be granted from the requirements of sections 4905, 4916, and 4917 of this title. No such exemption shall be granted due to lack of appropriation unless the President shall have specifically requested such appropriation as a part of the budgetary process and the Congress shall have failed to make available such requested appropriation. Any exemption shall be for a period not in excess of one year, but additional exemptions may be granted for periods of not to exceed one year upon the President's making a new determination. The President shall report each January to the Congress all exemptions from the requirements of this section granted during the preceding calendar year, together with his reason for granting such exemption.

### (c) Coordination of programs of Federal agencies; standards and regulations; status reports

(1) The Administrator shall coordinate the programs of all Federal agencies relating to noise research and noise control. Each Federal agency shall, upon request, furnish to the Administrator such information as he may reasonably require to determine the nature, scope, and results of the noise-research and noise-control programs of the agency.

(2) Each Federal agency shall consult with the Administrator in prescribing standards or regulations respecting noise. If at any time the Administrator has reason to believe that a standard or regulation, or any proposed standard or regulation, of any Federal agency respecting noise does not protect the public

health and welfare to the extent he believes to be required and feasible, he may request such agency to review and report to him on the advisability of revising such standard or regulation to provide such protection. Any such request may be published in the Federal Register and shall be accompanied by a detailed statement of the information on which it is based. Such agency shall complete the requested review and report to the Administrator within such time as the Administrator specifies in the request, but such time specified may not be less than ninety days from the date the request was made. The report shall be published in the Federal Register and shall be accompanied by a detailed statement of the findings and conclusions of the agency respecting the revision of its standard or regulation. With respect to the Federal Aviation Administration, section 44715 of Title 49 shall apply in lieu of this paragraph.

(3) On the basis of regular consultation with appropriate Federal agencies, the Administrator shall compile and publish, from time to time, a report on the status and progress of Federal activities relating to noise research and noise control. This report shall describe the noise-control programs of each Federal agency and assess the contributions of those programs to the Federal Government's overall efforts to control noise.

(Pub.L. 92–574, § 4, Oct. 27, 1972, 86 Stat. 1235.)

## § 4904. Identification of major noise sources

**[NCA § 5]**

### (a) Development and publication of criteria

(1) The Administrator shall, after consultation with appropriate Federal agencies and within nine months of October 27, 1972, develop and publish criteria with respect to noise. Such criteria shall reflect the scientific knowledge most useful in indicating the kind and extent of all identifiable effects on the public health or welfare which may be expected from differing quantities and qualities of noise.

(2) The Administrator shall, after consultation with appropriate Federal agencies and within twelve months of October 27, 1972, publish information on the levels of environmental noise the attainment and maintenance of which in defined areas under various conditions are requisite to protect the public health and welfare with an adequate margin of safety.

### (b) Compilation and publication of reports on noise sources and control technology

The Administrator shall, after consultation with appropriate Federal agencies, compile and publish a report or series of reports (1) identifying products (or classes of products) which in his judgment are major sources of noise, and (2) giving information on techniques for control of noise from such products, including available data on the technology, costs, and alternative methods of noise control. The first such report shall be published not later than eighteen months after October 27, 1972.

### (c) Supplemental criteria and reports

The Administrator shall from time to time review and, as appropriate, revise or supplement any criteria or reports published under this section.

### (d) Publication in Federal Register

Any report (or revision thereof) under subsection (b)(1) of this section identifying major noise sources shall be published in the Federal Register. The publication or revision under this section of any criteria or information on control techniques shall be announced in the Federal Register, and copies shall be made available to the general public.

(Pub.L. 92–574, § 5, Oct. 27, 1972, 86 Stat. 1236.)

## § 4905. Noise emission standards for products distributed in commerce

**[NCA § 6]**

### (a) Proposed regulations

(1) The Administrator shall publish proposed regulations, meeting the requirements of subsection (c) of this section, for each product—

(A) which is identified (or is part of a class identified) in any report published under section 4904(b)(1) of this title as a major source of noise,

(B) for which, in his judgment, noise emission standards are feasible, and

(C) which falls in one of the following categories:

(i) Construction equipment.

(ii) Transportation equipment (including recreational vehicles and related equipment).

(iii) Any motor or engine (including any equipment of which an engine or motor is an integral part).

(iv) Electrical or electronic equipment.

(2)(A) Initial proposed regulations under paragraph (1) shall be published not later than eighteen months after October 27, 1972, and shall apply to any product described in paragraph (1) which is identified (or is a part of a class identified) as a major source of noise in any report published under section 4904(b)(1) of this title on or before the date of publication of such initial proposed regulations.

(B) In the case of any product described in paragraph (1) which is identified (or is part of a class identified) as a major source of noise in a report published under section 4904(b)(1) of this title after publication of the initial proposed regulations under subparagraph (A) of this paragraph, regulations under paragraph (1) for such product shall be proposed and published by the Administrator not later than eighteen months after such report is published.

(3) After proposed regulations respecting a product have been published under paragraph (2), the Administrator shall, unless in his judgment noise emission standards are not feasible for such product, prescribe regulations, meeting the requirements of subsection (c) of this section, for such product—

(A) not earlier than six months after publication of such proposed regulations, and

(B) not later than—

(i) twenty-four months after October 27, 1972, in the case of a product subject to proposed regulations published under paragraph (2)(A), or

(ii) in the case of any other product, twenty-four months after the publication of the report under section 4904(b)(1) of this title identifying it (or a class of products of which it is a part) as a major source of noise.

**(b) Authority to publish regulations not otherwise required**

The Administrator may publish proposed regulations, meeting the requirements of subsection (c) of this section, for any product for which he is not required by subsection (a) of this section to prescribe regulations but for which, in his judgment, noise emission standards are feasible and are requisite to protect the public health and welfare. Not earlier than six months after the date of publication of such proposed regulations respecting such product, he may prescribe regulations, meeting the requirements of subsection (c) of this section, for such product.

**(c) Contents of regulations; appropriate consideration of other standards; participation by interested persons; revision**

(1) Any regulation prescribed under subsection (a) or (b) of this section (and any revision thereof) respecting a product shall include a noise emission standard which shall set limits on noise emissions from such product and shall be a standard which in the Administrator's judgment, based on criteria published under section 4904 of this title, is requisite to protect the public health and welfare, taking into account the magnitude and conditions of use of such product (alone or in combination with other noise sources), the degree of noise reduction achievable through the application of the best available technology, and the cost of compliance. In establishing such a standard for any product, the Administrator shall give appropriate consideration to standards under other laws designed to safeguard the health and welfare of persons, including any standards under chapter 301 of title 49, the Clean Air Act [42 U.S.C.A. § 7401 et seq.], and the Federal Water Pollution Control Act [33 U.S.C.A. § 1251 et seq.]. Any such noise emission standards shall be a performance standard. In addition, any regulation under subsection (a) or (b) of this section (and any revision thereof) may contain testing procedures necessary to assure compliance with the emission standard in such regulation, and may contain provisions respecting instructions of the manufacturer for the maintenance, use, or repair of the product.

(2) After publication of any proposed regulations under this section, the Administrator shall allow interested persons an opportunity to participate in rulemaking in accordance with the first sentence of section 553(c) of Title 5.

(3) The Administrator may revise any regulation prescribed by him under this section by (A) publication of proposed revised regulations, and (B) the promulgation, not earlier than six months after the date of such publication, of regulations making the revision; except that a revision which makes only technical or clerical corrections in a regulation under this section may be promulgated earlier than six months after such date if the Administrator finds that such earlier promulgation is in the public interest.

**(d) Warranty by manufacturer of conformity of product with regulations; transfer of cost obligation from manufacturer to dealer prohibited**

(1) On and after the effective date of any regulation prescribed under subsection (a) or (b) of this section, the manufacturer of each new product to which such regulation applies shall warrant to the ultimate purchaser and each subsequent purchaser that such product is designed, built, and equipped so as to conform at the time of sale with such regulation.

(2) Any cost obligation of any dealer incurred as a result of any requirement imposed by paragraph (1) of this subsection shall be borne by the manufacturer. The transfer of any such cost obligation from a manufacturer to any dealer through franchise or other agreement is prohibited.

(3) If a manufacturer includes in any advertisement a statement respecting the cost or value of noise emission control devices or systems, such manufacturer shall set forth in such statement the cost or value attributed to such devices or systems by the Secretary of Labor (through the Bureau of Labor Statistics). The Secretary of Labor, and his representatives, shall have the same access for this purpose to the books, documents, papers, and records of a manufacturer as the Comptroller General has to those of a recipient of assistance for purposes of section 311 of the Clean Air Act [42 U.S.C.A. § 7611].

**(e) State and local regulations**

(1) No State or political subdivision thereof may adopt or enforce—

(A) with respect to any new product for which a regulation has been prescribed by the Administrator under this section, any law or regulation which sets a limit on noise emissions from such new product and which is not identical to such regulation of the Administrator; or

(B) with respect to any component incorporated into such new product by the manufacturer of such product, any law or regulation setting a limit on noise emissions from such component when so incorporated.

(2) Subject to sections 4916 and 4917 of this title, nothing in this section precludes or denies the right of any State or political subdivision thereof to establish and enforce controls on environmental noise (or one or more sources thereof) through the licensing, regulation, or restriction of the use, operation, or movement of any product or combination of products.

**(f) Publication of notice of receipt of revision petitions and proposed revised regulations**

At any time after the promulgation of regulations respecting a product under this section, a State or political subdivision thereof may petition the Administrator to revise such standard on the grounds that a more stringent standard under subsection (c) of this section is necessary to protect the public health and welfare. The Administration shall publish notice of receipt of such petition in the Federal Register and shall within ninety days of receipt of such petition respond by (1) publication of proposed revised regulations in accordance with subsection (c)(3) of this section, or (2) publication in the Federal Register of a decision not to publish such proposed revised regulations at that time, together with a detailed explanation for such decision.

(Pub.L. 92–574, § 6, Oct. 27, 1972, 86 Stat. 1237; Pub.L. 95–609, § 5, Nov. 8, 1978, 92 Stat. 3081.)

### HISTORICAL AND STATUTORY NOTES

**References in Text**

Chapter 301 of title 49, referred to in subsec.(c)(1), is 49 U.S.C.A. § 30101 et seq.

The Clean Air Act, referred to in subsec. (c)(1), is Act July 14, 1955, c. 360, as amended generally by Pub.L. 88–206, Dec. 17, 1963, 77 Stat. 392, and later by Pub.L. 95–95, Aug. 7, 1977, 91 Stat. 685. The Clean Air Act was originally classified to chapter 15B (section 1857 et seq.) of this title. On enactment of Pub.L. 95–95, the Act was reclassified to chapter 85 (section 7401 et seq.) of this title. For complete classification of this Act to the Code, see Short Title of 1955 Acts note set out under section 7401 of this title and Tables.

The Federal Water Pollution Control Act, referred to in subsec. (c)(1), is Act June 30, 1948, c. 758, as amended generally by Pub.L. 92–500, § 2, Oct. 18, 1972, 86 Stat. 816, which is classified generally to chapter 26 (section 1251 et seq.) of Title 33, Navigation and Navigable Waters. For complete classification of this Act to the Code, see Short Title note set out under section 1251 of Title 33 and Tables.

## § 4906. Omitted

### HISTORICAL AND STATUTORY NOTES

**Codifications**

Section, Pub.L. 92–574, § 7(a), Oct. 27, 1972, 86 Stat. 1239, related to a study by the Administrator of the adequacy of noise controls, noise emission standards, and measures available to control such noise, the results of such study to be reported to the appropriate committees of Congress within nine months after Oct. 27, 1972.

## § 4907. Labeling

[NCA § 8]

**(a) Regulations**

The Administrator shall by regulation designate any product (or class thereof)—

(1) which emits noise capable of adversely affecting the public health or welfare; or

(2) which is sold wholly or in part on the basis of its effectiveness in reducing noise.

**(b) Manner of notice; form; methods and units of measurement**

For each product (or class thereof) designated under subsection (a) of this section the Administrator shall by regulation require that notice be given to the prospective user of the level of the noise the product emits, or of its effectiveness in reducing noise, as the case may be. Such regulations shall specify (1) whether such notice shall be affixed to the product or to the outside of its container, or to both, at the time of its sale to the ultimate purchaser or whether such notice shall be given to the prospective user in some other manner, (2) the form of the notice, and (3) the methods and units of measurement to be used. Section 4905(c)(2) of this title shall apply to the prescribing of any regulation under this section.

**(c) State regulation of product labeling**

This section does not prevent any State or political subdivision thereof from regulating product labeling or information respecting products in any way not in conflict with regulations prescribed by the Administrator under this section.

(Pub.L. 92–574, § 8, Oct. 27, 1972, 86 Stat. 1241.)

## § 4908. Imports

[NCA § 9]

The Secretary of the Treasury shall, in consultation with the Administrator, issue regulations to carry out the provisions of this chapter with respect to new products imported or offered for importation.

(Pub.L. 92–574, § 9, Oct. 27, 1972, 86 Stat. 1242.)

## § 4909. Prohibited acts

[NCA § 10]

**(a)** Except as otherwise provided in subsection (b) of this section, the following acts or the causing thereof are prohibited:

(1) In the case of a manufacturer, to distribute in commerce any new product manufactured after the effective date of a regulation prescribed under section 4905 of this title which is applicable to such product, except in conformity with such regulation.

(2) (A) The removal or rendering inoperative by any person, other than for purposes of maintenance, repair, or replacement, of any device or element of design incorporated into any product in compliance with regulations under section 4905 of this title, prior to its sale or delivery to the ultimate purchaser or while it is in use, or (B) the use of a product after such device or element of design has been removed or rendered inoperative by any person.

(3) In the case of a manufacturer, to distribute in commerce any new product manufactured after the effective date of a regulation prescribed under section 4907(b) of this title (requiring information respecting noise) which is applicable to such product, except in conformity with such regulation.

(4) The removal by any person of any notice affixed to a product or container pursuant to regulations prescribed under section 4907(b) of this title, prior to sale of the product to the ultimate purchaser.

(5) The importation into the United States by any person of any new product in violation of a regulation prescribed under section 4908 of this title which is applicable to such product.

(6) The failure or refusal by any person to comply with any requirement of section 4910(d) or 4912(a) of this title or regulations prescribed under section 4912(a), 4916, or 4917 of this title.

**(b)(1)** For the purpose of research, investigations, studies, demonstrations, or training, or for reasons of national security, the Administrator may exempt for a specified period of time any product, or class thereof, from paragraphs (1), (2), (3), and (5) of subsection (a) of this section, upon such terms and conditions as he may find necessary to protect the public health or welfare.

(2) Paragraphs (1), (2), (3), and (4) of subsection (a) of this section shall not apply with respect to any product which is manufactured solely for use outside any State and which (and the container of which) is labeled or otherwise marked to show that it is manufactured solely for use outside any State; except that such paragraphs shall apply to such product if it is in fact distributed in commerce for use in any State.

(Pub.L. 92–574, § 10, Oct. 27, 1972, 86 Stat. 1242.)

## § 4910. Enforcement

[NCA § 11]

### (a) Criminal penalties

(1) Any person who willfully or knowingly violates paragraph (1), (3), (5), or (6) of subsection (a) of section 4909 of this title shall be punished by a fine of not more than $25,000 per day of violation, or by imprisonment for not more than one year, or by both. If the conviction is for a violation committed after a first conviction of such person under this subsection, punishment shall be by a fine of not more than $50,000 per day of violation, or by imprisonment for not more than two years, or by both.

(2) Any person who violates paragraph (1), (3), (5), or (6) of subsection (a) of section 4909 of this title shall be subject to a civil penalty not to exceed $10,000 per day of such violation.

### (b) Separate violations

For the purpose of this section, each day of violation of any paragraph of section 4909(a) of this title shall constitute a separate violation of that section.

### (c) Actions to restrain violations

The district courts of the United States shall have jurisdiction of actions brought by and in the name of the United States to restrain any violations of section 4909(a) of this title.

### (d) Orders issued to protect public health and welfare; notice; opportunity for hearing

(1) Whenever any person is in violation of section 4909(a) of this title, the Administrator may issue an order specifying such relief as he determines is necessary to protect the public health and welfare.

(2) Any order under this subsection shall be issued only after notice and opportunity for a hearing in accordance with section 554 of Title 5.

### (e) "Person" defined

The term "person," as used in this section, does not include a department, agency, or instrumentality of the United States.

(Pub.L. 92–574, § 11, Oct. 27, 1972, 86 Stat. 1242; Pub.L. 95–609, § 4, Nov. 8, 1978, 92 Stat. 3081).

## § 4911. Citizen suits

[NCA § 12]

### (a) Authority to commence suits

Except as provided in subsection (b) of this section, any person (other than the United States) may commence a civil action on his own behalf—

(1) against any person (including (A) the United States, and (B) any other governmental instrumentality or agency to the extent permitted by the eleventh amendment to the Constitution) who is alleged to be in violation of any noise control requirement (as defined in subsection (e)[1] of this section), or

(2) against—

(A) the Administrator of the Environmental Protection Agency where there is alleged a failure of such Administrator to perform any act or duty under this chapter which is not discretionary with such Administrator, or

(B) the Administrator of the Federal Aviation Administration where there is alleged a failure of such Administrator to perform any act or duty under section 44715 of Title 49 which is not discretionary with such Administrator.

The district courts of the United States shall have jurisdiction, without regard to the amount in controversy, to restrain such person from violating such noise control requirement or to order such Administrator to perform such act or duty, as the case may be.

**(b) Notice**

No action may be commenced—

(1) under subsection (a)(1) of this section—

(A) prior to sixty days after the plaintiff has given notice of the violation (i) to the Administrator of the Environmental Protection Agency (and to the Federal Aviation Administrator in the case of a violation of a noise control requirement under such section 44715 of Title 49) and (ii) to any alleged violator of such requirement, or

(B) if an Administrator has commenced and is diligently prosecuting a civil action to require compliance with the noise control requirement, but in any such action in a court of the United States any person may intervene as a matter of right, or

(2) under subsection (a)(2) of this section prior to sixty days after the plaintiff has given notice to the defendant that he will commence such action.

Notice under this subsection shall be given in such manner as the Administrator of the Environmental Protection Agency shall prescribe by regulation.

**(c) Intervention**

In an action under this section, the Administrator of the Environmental Protection Agency, if not a party, may intervene as a matter of right. In an action under this section respecting a noise control requirement under section 44715 of Title 49, the Administrator of the Federal Aviation Administration, if not a party, may also intervene as a matter of right.

**(d) Litigation costs**

The court, in issuing any final order in any action brought pursuant to subsection (a) of this section, may award costs of litigation (including reasonable attorney and expert witness fees) to any party, whenever the court determines such an award is appropriate.

**(e) Other common law or statutory rights of action**

Nothing in this section shall restrict any right which any person (or class of persons) may have under any statute or common law to seek enforcement of any noise control requirement or to seek any other relief (including relief against an Administrator).

**(f) "Noise control requirement" defined**

For purposes of this section, the term "noise control requirement" means paragraph (1), (2), (3), (4), or (5) of section 4909(a) of this title, or a standard, rule, or regulation issued under section 4916 or 4917 of this title or under section 44715 of Title 49.

(Pub.L. 92–574, § 12, Oct. 27, 1972, 86 Stat. 1243.)

1 So in original. Probably should be subsection "(f)".

## § 4912. Records, reports, and information

[NCA § 13]

**(a) Duties of manufacturers of products**

Each manufacturer of a product to which regulations under section 4905 or 4907 of this title apply shall—

(1) establish and maintain such records, make such reports, provide such information, and make such tests, as the Administrator may reasonably require to enable him to determine whether such manufacturer has acted or is acting in compliance with this chapter,

(2) upon request of an officer or employee duly designated by the Administrator, permit such officer or employee at reasonable times to have access to such information and the results of such tests and to copy such records, and

(3) to the extent required by regulations of the Administrator, make products coming off the assembly line or otherwise in the hands of the manufacturer available for testing by the Administrator.

**(b) Confidential information; disclosure**

(1) All information obtained by the Administrator or his representatives pursuant to subsection (a) of this section, which information contains or relates to a trade secret or other matter referred to in section 1905 of Title 18, shall be considered confidential for the purpose of that section, except that such information may be disclosed to other Federal officers or

employees, in whose possession it shall remain confidential, or when relevant to the matter in controversy in any proceeding under this chapter.

(2) Nothing in this subsection shall authorize the withholding of information by the Administrator, or by any officers or employees under his control, from the duly authorized committees of the Congress.

**(c) Violations and penalties**

Any person who knowingly makes any false statement, representation, or certification in any application, record, report, plan, or other document filed or required to be maintained under this chapter or who falsifies, tampers with, or knowingly renders inaccurate any monitoring device or method required to be maintained under this chapter, shall upon conviction be punished by a fine of not more than $10,000, or by imprisonment for not more than six months, or by both.

(Pub.L. 92–574, § 13, Oct. 27, 1972, 86 Stat. 1244.)

## § 4913. Quiet communities, research, and public information

[NCA § 14]

To promote the development of effective State and local noise control programs, to provide an adequate Federal noise control research program designed to meet the objectives of this chapter, and to otherwise carry out the policy of this chapter, the Administrator shall, in cooperation with other Federal agencies and through the use of grants, contracts, and direct Federal actions—

**(a)** develop and disseminate information and educational materials to all segments of the public on the public health and other effects of noise and the most effective means for noise control, through the use of materials for school curricula, volunteer organizations, radio and television programs, publication, and other means;

**(b)** conduct or finance research directly or with any public or private organization or any person on the effects, measurement, and control of noise, including but not limited to—

(1) investigation of the psychological and physiological effects of noise on humans and the effects of noise on domestic animals, wildlife, and property, and the determination of dose/response relationships suitable for use in decisionmaking, with special emphasis on the nonauditory effects of noise;

(2) investigation, development, and demonstration of noise control technology for products subject to possible regulation under sections 4905 and 4907 of this title and section 44715 of Title 49;

(3) investigation, development, and demonstration of monitoring equipment and other technology especially suited for use by State and local noise control programs;

(4) investigation of the economic impact of noise on property and human activities; and

(5) investigation and demonstration of the use of economic incentives (including emission charges) in the control of noise;

**(c)** administer a nationwide Quiet Communities Program which shall include, but not be limited to—

(1) grants to States, local governments, and authorized regional planning agencies for the purpose of—

(A) identifying and determining the nature and extent of the noise problem within the subject jurisdiction;

(B) planning, developing, and establishing a noise control capacity in such jurisdiction, including purchasing initial equipment;

(C) developing abatement plans for areas around major transportation facilities (including airports, highways, and rail yards) and other major stationary sources of noise, and, where appropriate, for the facility or source itself; and,

(D) evaluating techniques for controlling noise (including institutional arrangements) and demonstrating the best available techniques in such jurisdiction;

(2) purchase of monitoring and other equipment for loan to State and local noise control programs to meet special needs or assist in the beginning implementation of a noise control program or project;

(3) development and implementation of a quality assurance program for equipment and monitoring procedures of State and local noise control programs to help communities assure that their data collection activities are accurate;

(4) conduct of studies and demonstrations to determine the resource and personnel needs of States and local governments required for the establishment and implementation of effective noise abatement and control programs; and

(5) development of education and training materials and programs, including national and regional workshops, to support State and local noise abatement and control programs;

except that no actions, plans or programs hereunder shall be inconsistent with existing Federal authority under this chapter to regulate sources of noise in interstate commerce;

**(d)** develop and implement a national noise environmental assessment program to identify trends in noise exposure and response, ambient levels, and compliance data and to determine otherwise the effectiveness of noise abatement actions through the collection of physical, social, and human response data;

**(e)** establish regional technical assistance centers which use the capabilities of university and private organizations to assist State and local noise control programs;

**(f)** provide technical assistance to State and local governments to facilitate their development and enforcement of noise control, including direct onsite assistance of agency or other personnel with technical expertise, and preparation of model State or local legislation for noise control; and

**(g)** provide for the maximum use in programs assisted under this section of senior citizens and persons eligible for participation in programs under the Older Americans Act [42 U.S.C.A. § 3001 et seq.].

(Pub.L. 92–574, § 14, Oct. 27, 1972, 86 Stat. 1244; Pub.L. 95–609, § 2, Nov. 8, 1978, 92 Stat. 3079.)

### HISTORICAL AND STATUTORY NOTES

**References in Text**

The Older Americans Act, referred to in subsec. (g), probably means the Older Americans Act of 1965, Pub.L. 89–73, July 14, 1965, 79 Stat. 218, as amended, which is classified generally to chapter 35 (section 3001 et seq.) of this title. For complete classification of this Act to the Code, see Short Title of 1965 Acts note set out under section 3001 of this title and Tables.

## § 4914. Development of low-noise-emission products

[NCA § 15]

**(a) Definitions**

For the purpose of this section:

(1) The term "Committee" means the Low-Noise-Emission Product Advisory Committee.

(2) The term "Federal Government" includes the legislative, executive, and judicial branches of the Government of the United States, and the government of the District of Columbia.

(3) The term "low-noise-emission product" means any product which emits noise in amounts significantly below the levels specified in noise emission standards under regulations applicable under section 4905 of this title at the time of procurement to that type of product.

(4) The term "retail price" means (A) the maximum statutory price applicable to any type of product; or (B) in any case where there is no applicable maximum statutory price, the most recent procurement price paid for any type of product.

**(b) Certification of products; Low-Noise-Emission Product Advisory Committee**

(1) The Administrator shall determine which products qualify as low-noise-emission products in accordance with the provisions of this section.

(2) The Administrator shall certify any product—

**(A)** for which a certification application has been filed in accordance with paragraph (5)(A) of this subsection;

**(B)** which is a low-noise-emission product as determined by the Administrator; and

**(C)** which he determines is suitable for use as a substitute for a type of product at that time in use by agencies of the Federal Government.

(3) The Administrator may establish a Low-Noise-Emission Product Advisory Committee to assist him in determining which products qualify as low-noise-emission products for purposes of this section. The Committee shall include the Administrator or his designee, a representative of the National Institute of Standards and Technology, and representatives of such other Federal agencies and private individuals as the Administrator may deem necessary from time to time. Any member of the Committee not employed on a full-time basis by the United States may receive the daily equivalent of the annual rate of basic pay in effect for Grade GS–18 of the General Schedule for each day such member is engaged upon work of the Committee. Each member of the Committee shall be reimbursed for travel expenses, including per diem in lieu of subsistence as authorized by section 5703 of Title 5 for persons in the Government service employed intermittently.

(4) Certification under this section shall be effective for a period of one year from the date of issuance.

(5)(A) Any person seeking to have a class or model of product certified under this section shall file a certification application in accordance with regulations prescribed by the Administrator.

**(B)** The Administrator shall publish in the Federal Register a notice of each application received.

**(C)** The Administrator shall make determinations for the purpose of this section in accordance with procedures prescribed by him by regulation.

**(D)** The Administrator shall conduct whatever investigation is necessary, including actual inspection of the product at a place designated in regulations prescribed under subparagraph (A).

**(E)** The Administrator shall receive and evaluate written comments and documents from interested persons in support of, or in opposition to, certification of the class or model of product under consideration.

**(F)** Within ninety days after the receipt of a properly filed certification application the Administrator shall determine whether such product is a low-noise-emission product for purposes of this section. If the

Administrator determines that such product is a low-noise-emission product, then within one hundred and eighty days of such determination the Administrator shall reach a decision as to whether such product is a suitable substitute for any class or classes of products presently being purchased by the Federal Government for use by its agencies.

(G) Immediately upon making any determination or decision under subparagraph (F), the Administrator shall publish in the Federal Register notice of such determination or decision, including reasons therefor.

**(c) Federal procurement of low-noise-emission products**

(1) Certified low-noise-emission products shall be acquired by purchase or lease by the Federal Government for use by the Federal Government in lieu of other products if the Administrator of General Services determines that such certified products have procurement costs which are no more than 125 per centum of the retail price of the least expensive type of product for which they are certified substitutes.

(2) Data relied upon by the Administrator in determining that a product is a certified low-noise-emission product shall be incorporated in any contract for the procurement of such product.

**(d) Product selection**

The procuring agency shall be required to purchase available certified low-noise-emission products which are eligible for purchase to the extent they are available before purchasing any other products for which any low-noise-emission product is a certified substitute. In making purchasing selections between competing eligible certified low-noise-emission products, the procuring agency shall give priority to any class or model which does not require extensive periodic maintenance to retain its low-noise-emission qualities or which does not involve operating costs significantly in excess of those products for which it is a certified substitute.

**(e) Waiver of statutory price limitations**

For the purpose of procuring certified low-noise-emission products any statutory price limitations shall be waived.

**(f) Tests of noise emissions from products purchased by Federal Government**

The Administrator shall, from time to time as he deems appropriate, test the emissions of noise from certified low-noise-emission products purchased by the Federal Government. If at any time he finds that the noise-emission levels exceed the levels on which certification under this section was based, the Administrator shall give the supplier of such product written notice of this finding, issue public notice of it, and give the supplier an opportunity to make necessary repairs, adjustments, or replacements. If no such repairs, adjustments, or replacements are made within a period to be set by the Administrator, he may order the supplier to show cause why the product involved should be eligible for recertification.

**(g) Authorization of appropriations**

There are authorized to be appropriated for paying additional amounts for products pursuant to, and for carrying out the provisions of, this section, $1,000,000 for the fiscal year ending June 30, 1973, and $2,000,000 for each of the two succeeding fiscal years, $2,200,000 for the fiscal year ending June 30, 1976, $550,000 for the transition period of July 1, 1976, through September 30, 1976, and $2,420,000 for the fiscal year ending September 30, 1977.

**(h) Promulgation of procedures**

The Administrator shall promulgate the procedures required to implement this section within one hundred and eighty days after October 27, 1972.

(Pub.L. 92–574, § 15, Oct. 27, 1972, 86 Stat. 1245; Pub.L. 94–301, § 1, May 31, 1976, 90 Stat. 590; Pub.L. 100–418, Title V, § 5115(c), Aug. 23, 1988, 102 Stat. 1433.)

## HISTORICAL AND STATUTORY NOTES

**References in Text**

The General Schedule, referred to in subsec. (b)(3), is set out under section 5332 of Title 5, Government Organization and Employees.

**References in Other Laws to GS–16, 17, or 18 Pay Rates**

References in laws to the rates of pay for GS–16, 17, or 18, or to maximum rates of pay under the General Schedule, to be considered references to rates payable under specified sections of Title 5, Government Organization and Employees, see section 529 [Title I, § 101(c)(1) ] of Pub.L. 101–509, set out in a note under section 5376 of Title 5.

**Termination of Advisory Committees**

Advisory committees in existence on Jan. 5, 1973, to terminate not later than the expiration of the two-year period following Jan. 5, 1973, unless, in the case of a committee established by the President or an officer of the Federal Government, such committee is renewed by appropriate action prior to the expiration of such two-year period, or in the case of a committee established by the Congress, its duration is otherwise provided by law. A committee established after Jan. 5, 1973, to terminate not later than the expiration of the two-year period beginning on the date of its establishment unless in the case of a committee established by the President or an officer of the federal government, such committee is renewed by appropriate action prior to the end of such period, or in the case of a committee established by the Congress, its duration is otherwise provided by law, see section 14 of Pub.L. 92–463, Oct. 6, 1972, 86 Stat. 776, set out in Appendix 2 to Title 5, Government Organization and Employees.

## § 4915. Judicial review

[NCA § 16]

### (a) Petition for review

A petition for review of action of the Administrator of the Environmental Protection Agency in promulgating any standard or regulation under sections 4905, 4916, or 4917 of this title or any labeling regulation under section 4907 of this title may be filed only in the United States Court of Appeals for the District of Columbia Circuit, and a petition for review of action of the Administrator of the Federal Aviation Administration in promulgating any standard or regulation under section 44715 of Title 49 may be filed only in such court. Any such petition shall be filed within ninety days from the date of such promulgation, or after such date if such petition is based solely on grounds arising after such ninetieth day. Action of either Administrator with respect to which review could have been obtained under this subsection shall not be subject to judicial review in civil or criminal proceedings for enforcement.

### (b) Additional evidence

If a party seeking review under this chapter applies to the court for leave to adduce additional evidence, and shows to the satisfaction of the court that the information is material and was not available at the time of the proceeding before the Administrator of such Agency or Administration (as the case may be), the court may order such additional evidence (and evidence in rebuttal thereof) to be taken before such Administrator, and to be adduced upon the hearing, in such manner and upon such terms and conditions as the court may deem proper. Such Administrator may modify his findings as to the facts, or make new findings, by reason of the additional evidence so taken, and he shall file with the court such modified or new findings, and his recommendation, if any, for the modification or setting aside of his original order, with the return of such additional evidence.

### (c) Stay of agency action

With respect to relief pending review of an action by either Administrator, no stay of an agency action may be granted unless the reviewing court determines that the party seeking such stay is (1) likely to prevail on the merits in the review proceeding and (2) will suffer irreparable harm pending such proceeding.

### (d) Subpenas

For the purpose of obtaining information to carry out this chapter, the Administrator of the Environmental Protection Agency may issue subpenas for the attendance and testimony of witnesses and the production of relevant papers, books, and documents, and he may administer oaths. Witnesses summoned shall be paid the same fees and mileage that are paid witnesses in the courts of the United States. In cases of contumacy or refusal to obey a subpena served upon any person under this subsection, the district court of the United States for any district in which such person is found or resides or transacts business, upon application by the United States and after notice to such person, shall have jurisdiction to issue an order requiring such person to appear and give testimony before the Administrator, to appear and produce papers, books, and documents before the Administrator, or both, and any failure to obey such order of the court may be punished by such court as a contempt thereof.

(Pub.L. 92–574, § 16, Oct. 27, 1972, 86 Stat. 1247.)

## § 4916. Railroad noise emission standards

[NCA § 17]

### (a) Regulations; standards; consultation with Secretary of Transportation

(1) Within nine months after October 27, 1972, the Administrator shall publish proposed noise emission regulations for surface carriers engaged in interstate commerce by railroad. Such proposed regulations shall include noise emission standards setting such limits on noise emissions resulting from operation of the equipment and facilities of surface carriers engaged in interstate commerce by railroad which reflect the degree of noise reduction achievable through the application of the best available technology, taking into account the cost of compliance. These regulations shall be in addition to any regulations that may be proposed under section 4905 of this title.

(2) Within ninety days after the publication of such regulations as may be proposed under paragraph (1) of this subsection, and subject to the provisions of section 4915 of this title, the Administrator shall promulgate final regulations. Such regulations may be revised, from time to time, in accordance with this subsection.

(3) Any standard or regulation, or revision thereof, proposed under this subsection shall be promulgated only after consultation with the Secretary of Transportation in order to assure appropriate consideration for safety and technological availability.

(4) Any regulation or revision thereof promulgated under this subsection shall take effect after such period as the Administrator finds necessary, after consultation with the Secretary of Transportation, to permit the development and application of the requisite technology, giving appropriate consideration to the cost of compliance within such period.

### (b) Regulations to insure compliance with noise emission standards

The Secretary of Transportation, after consultation with the Administrator, shall promulgate regulations to insure compliance with all standards promulgated by the Administrator under this section. The Secretary of Transportation shall carry out such regulations through the use of his powers and duties of enforcement and inspection authorized by the Safety Appliance Acts [45 U.S.C.A. § 1 et seq.], subtitle IV of Title 49, and the Department of Transportation Act. Regulations promulgated under this section shall be subject to the provisions of sections 4909, 4910, 4911, and 4915 of this title.

**(c) State and local standards and controls**

(1) Subject to paragraph (2) but notwithstanding any other provision of this chapter, after the effective date of a regulation under this section applicable to noise emissions resulting from the operation of any equipment or facility of a surface carrier engaged in interstate commerce by railroad, no State or political subdivision thereof may adopt or enforce any standard applicable to noise emissions resulting from the operation of the same equipment or facility of such carrier unless such standard is identical to a standard applicable to noise emissions resulting from such operation prescribed by any regulation under this section.

(2) Nothing in this section shall diminish or enhance the rights of any State or political subdivision thereof to establish and enforce standards or controls on levels of environmental noise, or to control, license, regulate, or restrict the use, operation, or movement of any product if the Administrator, after consultation with the Secretary of Transportation, determines that such standard, control, license, regulation, or restriction is necessitated by special local conditions and is not in conflict with regulations promulgated under this section.

**(d) "Carrier" and "railroad" defined**

The terms "carrier" and "railroad" as used in this section shall have the same meaning as the term "railroad carrier" has in section 20102 of Title 49.

(Pub.L. 92–574, § 17, Oct. 27, 1972, 86 Stat. 1248; Pub.L. 104–287, § 6(i), Oct. 11, 1996, 110 Stat. 3399.)

### HISTORICAL AND STATUTORY NOTES

**References in Text**

The Safety Appliance Acts, referred to in subsec. (b), are Act Mar. 2, 1893, c. 196, 27 Stat. 531, which enacted former sections 1 to 7 of Title 45, Railroads, Act Mar. 2, 1903, c. 976, 32 Stat. 943, which enacted former sections 8, 9, and 10 of Title 45, and Act Apr. 14, 1910, c. 160, 36 Stat. 298, which enacted former sections 11 to 16 of Title 45.

The Department of Transportation Act, referred to in subsec. (b), is Pub.L. 89–670, Oct. 15, 1966, 80 Stat. 931, as amended, which was classified principally to sections 1651 to 1660 of former Title 49, Transportation. The Act was substantially repealed and the provisions thereof reenacted in Title 49, Transportation, by Pub.L. 97–449, Jan. 12, 1983, 96 Stat. 2413, and Pub.L. 103–272, July 5, 1994, 108 Stat. 745. The Act was also repealed by Pub.l. 104–287, § 7(5), Oct. 11, 1996, 110 Stat. 3400. For disposition of sections of former Title 49, see Table at the beginning of Title 49.

**Codifications**

"Subtitle IV of Title 49" was substituted in subsec. (b) for "the Interstate Commerce Act", on authority of Pub.L. 95–473, § 3(b), Oct. 17, 1978, 92 Stat. 1466, the first section of which enacted subtitle IV of Title 49, Transportation.

## § 4917. Motor carrier noise emission standards [NCA § 18]

**(a) Regulations; standards; consultation with Secretary of Transportation**

(1) Within nine months after October 27, 1972, the Administrator shall publish proposed noise emission regulations for motor carriers engaged in interstate commerce. Such proposed regulations shall include noise emission standards setting such limits on noise emissions resulting from operation of motor carriers engaged in interstate commerce which reflect the degree of noise reduction achievable through the application of the best available technology, taking into account the cost of compliance. These regulations shall be in addition to any regulations that may be proposed under section 4905 of this title.

(2) Within ninety days after the publication of such regulations as may be proposed under paragraph (1) of this subsection, and subject to the provisions of section 4915 of this title, the Administrator shall promulgate final regulations. Such regulations may be revised from time to time, in accordance with this subsection.

(3) Any standard or regulation, or revision thereof, proposed under this subsection shall be promulgated only after consultation with the Secretary of Transportation in order to assure appropriate consideration for safety and technological availability.

(4) Any regulation or revision thereof promulgated under this subsection shall take effect after such period as the Administrator finds necessary, after consultation with the Secretary of Transportation, to permit the development and application of the requisite technology, giving appropriate consideration to the cost of compliance within such period.

**(b) Regulations to insure compliance with noise emission standards**

The Secretary of Transportation, after consultation with the Administrator shall promulgate regulations to insure compliance with all standards promulgated by the Administrator under this section. The Secretary of Transportation shall carry out such regulations through the use of his powers and duties of enforcement and inspection authorized by subtitle IV of Title

49 and the Department of Transportation Act. Regulations promulgated under this section shall be subject to the provisions of sections 4909, 4910, 4911, and 4915 of this title.

**(c) State and local standards and controls**

(1) Subject to paragraph (2) of this subsection but notwithstanding any other provision of this chapter, after the effective date of a regulation under this section applicable to noise emissions resulting from the operation of any motor carrier engaged in interstate commerce, no State or political subdivision thereof may adopt or enforce any standard applicable to the same operation of such motor carrier, unless such standard is identical to a standard applicable to noise emissions resulting from such operation prescribed by any regulation under this section.

(2) Nothing in this section shall diminish or enhance the rights of any State or political subdivision thereof to establish and enforce standards or controls on levels of environmental noise, or to control, license, regulate, or restrict the use, operation, or movement of any product if the Administrator, after consultation with the Secretary of Transportation, determines that such standard, control, license, regulation, or restriction is necessitated by special local conditions and is not in conflict with regulations promulgated under this section.

**(d) "Motor carrier" defined**

For purposes of this section, the term "motor carrier" includes a motor carrier and motor private carrier as those terms are defined in section 13102 of Title 49.

(Pub.L. 92–574, § 18, Oct. 27, 1972, 86 Stat. 1249; Pub.L. 104–88, Title III, § 339, Dec. 29, 1995, 109 Stat. 955.)

### HISTORICAL AND STATUTORY NOTES

**References in Text**

The Department of Transportation Act, referred to in subsec. (b), is Pub.L. 89–670, Oct. 15, 1966, 80 Stat. 931, as amended, which was classified principally to sections 1651 to 1660 of former Title 49, Transportation. The Act was substantially repealed and the provisions thereof reenacted in Title 49, Transportation, by Pub.L. 97–449, Jan. 12, 1983, 96 Stat. 2413, and Pub.L. 103–272, July 5, 1994, 108 Stat. 745. The Act was also repealed by Pub.l. 104–287, § 7(5), Oct. 11, 1996, 110 Stat. 3400. For disposition of sections of former Title 49, see Table at the beginning of Title 49.

**Codifications**

"Subtitle IV of Title 49" was substituted in subsec. (b) for "Interstate Commerce Act" and in subsec. (d) "section 10102 of Title 49" was substituted for "paragraphs (14), (15), and (17) of section 203(a) of the Interstate Commerce Act (49 U.S.C. 303(a) )" on authority of Pub.L. 95–473, § 3(b), Oct. 17, 1978, 92 Stat. 1466, the first section of which enacted subtitle IV of Title 49, Transportation.

**Effective and Applicability Provisions**

1995 Acts

Amendment of this section by Pub.L. 104–88 effective Jan. 1, 1996, see section 2 of Pub.L. 104–88, set out as a note under section 701 of Title 49, Transportation.

## § 4918. Authorization of appropriations

**[NCA § 19]**

There are authorized to be appropriated to carry out this chapter (other than for research and development) $15,000,000 for the fiscal year ending September 30, 1979.

(Pub.L. 92–574, § 19, Oct. 27, 1972, 86 Stat. 1250; Pub.L. 94–301, § 2, May 31, 1976, 90 Stat. 590; Pub.L. 95–609, § 6, Nov. 8, 1978, 92 Stat. 3081.)

# SOLID WASTE DISPOSAL

## SOLID WASTE DISPOSAL ACT [SWDA § ____]

**(42 U.S.C.A. §§ 6901 to 6992k)**

## CHAPTER 82—SOLID WASTE DISPOSAL

## SUBCHAPTER I—GENERAL PROVISIONS

### § 6901. Congressional findings

**[SWDA § 1002]**

**(a) Solid waste**

The Congress finds with respect to solid waste—

(1) that the continuing technological progress and improvement in methods of manufacture, packaging, and marketing of consumer products has resulted in an ever-mounting increase, and in a change in the characteristics, of the mass material discarded by the purchaser of such products;

(2) that the economic and population growth of our Nation, and the improvements in the standard of living enjoyed by our population, have required increased industrial production to meet our needs, and have made necessary the demolition of old buildings, the construction of new buildings, and the provision of highways and other avenues of transportation, which, together with related industrial, commercial, and agricultural operations, have resulted in a rising tide of scrap, discarded, and waste materials;

(3) that the continuing concentration of our population in expanding metropolitan and other urban areas has presented these communities with serious financial, management, intergovernmental, and technical problems in the disposal of solid wastes resulting from the industrial, commercial, domestic, and other activities carried on in such areas;

(4) that while the collection and disposal of solid wastes should continue to be primarily the function of State, regional, and local agencies, the problems of waste disposal as set forth above have become a matter national in scope and in concern and necessitate Federal action through financial and technical assistance and leadership in the development, demonstration, and application of new and improved methods and processes to reduce the amount of waste and unsalvageable materials and to provide for proper and economical solid waste disposal practices.

**(b) Environment and health**

The Congress finds with respect to the environment and health, that—

(1) although land is too valuable a national resource to be needlessly polluted by discarded materials, most solid waste is disposed of on land in open dumps and sanitary landfills;

(2) disposal of solid waste and hazardous waste in or on the land without careful planning and management can present a danger to human health and the environment;

(3) as a result of the Clean Air Act [42 U.S.C.A. § 7401 et seq.], the Water Pollution Control Act [33 U.S.C.A. § 1251 et seq.], and other Federal and State laws respecting public health and the environment, greater amounts of solid waste (in the form of sludge and other pollution treatment residues) have been created. Similarly, inadequate and environmentally unsound practices for the disposal or use of solid waste have created greater amounts of air and water pollution and other problems for the environment and for health;

(4) open dumping is particularly harmful to health, contaminates drinking water from underground and surface supplies, and pollutes the air and the land;

(5) the placement of inadequate controls on hazardous waste management will result in substantial risks to human health and the environment;

(6) if hazardous waste management is improperly performed in the first instance, corrective action is likely to be expensive, complex, and time consuming;

(7) certain classes of land disposal facilities are not capable of assuring long-term containment of certain hazardous wastes, and to avoid substantial risk to human health and the environment, reliance on land disposal should be minimized or eliminated, and land disposal, particularly landfill and surface impoundment, should be the least favored method for managing hazardous wastes; and

(8) alternatives to existing methods of land disposal must be developed since many of the cities in the United States will be running out of suitable solid waste disposal sites within five years unless immediate action is taken.

**(c) Materials**

The Congress finds with respect to materials, that—

(1) millions of tons of recoverable material which could be used are needlessly buried each year;

(2) methods are available to separate usable materials from solid waste; and

(3) the recovery and conservation of such materials can reduce the dependence of the United States on foreign resources and reduce the deficit in its balance of payments.

**(d) Energy**

The Congress finds with respect to energy, that—

(1) solid waste represents a potential source of solid fuel, oil, or gas that can be converted into energy;

(2) the need exists to develop alternative energy sources for public and private consumption in order to reduce our dependence on such sources as petroleum products, natural gas, nuclear and hydroelectric generation; and

(3) technology exists to produce usable energy from solid waste.

(Pub.L. 89–272, Title II, § 1002, as added Pub.L. 94–580, § 2, Oct. 21, 1976, 90 Stat. 2796, and amended Pub.L. 95–609, § 7(a), Nov. 8, 1978, 92 Stat. 3081; Pub.L. 98–616, Title I, § 101(a), Nov. 8, 1984, 98 Stat. 3224.)

## HISTORICAL AND STATUTORY NOTES

**References in Text**

The Clean Air Act, referred to in subsec. (b)(3), is Act July 14, 1955, c. 360, as amended generally by Pub.L. 88–206, Dec. 17, 1963, 77 Stat. 392, and later by Pub.L. 95–95, Aug. 7, 1977, 91 Stat. 685. The Clean Air Act was originally classified to chapter 15B (section 1857 et seq.) of this title. On enactment of Pub.L. 95–95, the Act was reclassified to chapter 85 (section 7401 et seq.) of this title. For complete classification of this Act to the Code, see Short Title of 1955 Acts note set out under section 7401 of this title and Tables.

The Water Pollution Control Act, referred to in subsec. (b)(3), is Act June 30, 1948, c. 758, as amended generally by Pub.L. 92–500, § 2, Oct. 18, 1972, 86 Stat. 816, which is classified generally to chapter 26 (section 1251 et seq.) of Title 33, Navigation and Navigable Waters. For complete classification of this Act to the Code, see Short Title note set out under section 1251 of Title 33 and Tables.

**Codifications**

The statutory system governing the disposal of solid wastes set out in this chapter is found in Pub.L. 89–272, Title II, as amended in its entirety and completely revised by section 2 of Pub.L. 94–580, Oct. 21, 1976, 90 Stat. 2795. See Short Title of 1965 Acts note under this section.

The Act, as set out in this chapter, carries a statutory credit showing the sections as having been added by Pub.L. 94–580, without reference to amendments to the Act between its original enactment in 1965 and its complete revision in 1976. The Act, as originally enacted in 1965, was classified to section 3251 et seq. of this title. For a recapitulation of the provisions of the Act as originally enacted, see notes in chapter 39 of this title [section 3251 et seq. of this title] where the Act was originally set out.

**Short Title**

1996 Amendments

Pub.L. 104–119, § 1, Mar. 26, 1996, 110 Stat. 830, provided that: "This Act [amending sections 6921, 6924, 6925, 6947 and 6949a of this title, and enacting provisions set out as a note under section 6949a of this title] may be cited as the 'Land Disposal Program Flexibility Act of 1996'."

1992 Amendments

Pub.L. 102–386, Title I, § 101, Oct. 6, 1992, 106 Stat. 1505, provided that: "This title [enacting sections 6908, 6939c, 6939d, 6939e, and 6965 of this title, amending sections 6903, 6924, 6927, and 6961 of this title, and enacting provisions set out as notes under sections 6939c and 6961 of this title] may be cited as the 'Federal Facility Compliance Act of 1992'."

1988 Amendments

Pub.L. 100–582, § 1, Nov. 1, 1988, 102 Stat. 2950, provided that: "This Act [enacting section 6903(40) and sections 6992 to 6992k of this title (subchapter X of this chapter) and section 3063 of Title 18, Crimes and Criminal Procedure] may be cited as the 'Medical Waste Tracking Act of 1988'."

1984 Amendments

Section 1 of Pub.L. 98–616 provided that: "This Act [enacting sections 6917, 6936 to 6939a, 6949a, 6979a, 6979b, and 6991 to 6991i of this title, amending this section and sections 6902, 6905, 6912, 6915, 6916, 6921 to 6930, 6931, 6932, 6933, 6935, 6941 to 6945, 6948, 6956, 6962, 6972, 6973, 6976, 6982 and 6984 of this title and enacting provisions set out as notes under sections 6905, 6921 and 6926 of this title] may be cited as 'The Hazardous and Solid Waste Amendments of 1984'."

1980 Amendments

Pub.L. 96–482, § 1, Oct. 21, 1980, 94 Stat. 2334, provided: "This Act [enacting sections 6933, 6934, 6941a, 6955, and 6956 of this title, amending sections 6903, 6905, 6911, 6912, 6916, 6921, 6922, 6924, 6925, 6927 to 6931, 6941 to 6943, 6945, 6946, 6948, 6949, 6952, 6953, 6962, 6963, 6964, 6971, 6973, 6974, 6976, 6979, and 6982 of this title; and enacting and repealing provisions set out as a note under section 6981 of this title] may be cited as the 'Solid Waste Disposal Act Amendments of 1980'."

Pub.L. 96–463, § 1, Oct. 15, 1980, 94 Stat. 2055, provided: "This Act [enacting sections 6901a, 6914a and 6932 of this title, amending sections 6903, 6943 and 6948 of this title, and enacting provisions set out as notes under sections 6363 and 6932 of this title] may be cited as the 'Used Oil Recycling Act of 1980'."

1976 Amendments

Section 1 of Pub.L. 94–580 provided that: "This Act [enacting this chapter and provisions set out as notes under this section and section 6981 of this title] may be cited as the 'Resource Conservation and Recovery Act of 1976'."

1965 Acts

Section 1001 of Pub.L. 89–272, as added Pub.L. 94–580, § 2, Oct. 21, 1976, 90 Stat. 2795, provided in part that: "This title [Title II of Pub.L. 89–272, enacting this chapter] may be cited as the 'Solid Waste Disposal Act'."

**Prior Provisions**

Provisions similar to this section were contained in section 3251 of this title, prior to the complete revision of the Solid Waste Disposal Act by Pub.L. 94–580.

**Federal Compliance with Pollution Control Standards**

For provisions relating to the responsibility of the head of each Executive agency for compliance with applicable pollution control standards, see Ex. Ord. No. 12088, Oct. 13, 1978, 43 F.R. 47707, set out as a note under section 4321 of this title.

**National Commission on Materials Policy**

Pub.L. 91–512, Title II, §§ 201 to 206, Oct. 26, 1970, 84 Stat. 1234, known as the "National Materials Policy Act of 1970", provided for the establishment of the National Commission on Materials Policy to make a full investigation and study for the purpose of developing a national materials policy to utilize present resources and technology more efficiently and to anticipate the future materials requirements of the Nation and the world, the Commission to submit to the President and Congress a report on its findings and recommendations no later than June 30, 1973, ninety days after the submission of which it should cease to exist.

## § 6901a. Congressional findings: used oil recycling

The Congress finds and declares that—

(1) used oil is a valuable source of increasingly scarce energy and materials;

(2) technology exists to re-refine, reprocess, reclaim, and otherwise recycle used oil;

(3) used oil constitutes a threat to public health and the environment when reused or disposed of improperly; and

that, therefore, it is in the national interest to recycle used oil in a manner which does not constitute a threat to public health and the environment and which conserves energy and materials.

(Pub.L. 96–463, § 2, Oct. 15, 1980, 94 Stat. 2055.)

### HISTORICAL AND STATUTORY NOTES

**Codifications**

Section was not enacted as part of the Solid Waste Disposal Act, which comprises this chapter, but was enacted as part of the Used Oil Recycling Act of 1980.

## § 6902. Objectives and national policy

### [SWDA § 1003]

**(a) Objectives**

The objectives of this chapter are to promote the protection of health and the environment and to conserve valuable material and energy resources by—

(1) providing technical and financial assistance to State and local governments and interstate agencies for the development of solid waste management plans (including resource recovery and resource conservation systems) which will promote improved solid waste management techniques (including more effective organizational arrangements), new and improved methods of collection, separation, and recovery of solid waste, and the environmentally safe disposal of nonrecoverable residues;

(2) providing training grants in occupations involving the design, operation, and maintenance of solid waste disposal systems;

(3) prohibiting future open dumping on the land and requiring the conversion of existing open dumps to facilities which do not pose a danger to the environment or to health;

(4) assuring that hazardous waste management practices are conducted in a manner which protects human health and the environment;

(5) requiring that hazardous waste be properly managed in the first instance thereby reducing the need for corrective action at a future date;

(6) minimizing the generation of hazardous waste and the land disposal of hazardous waste by encouraging process substitution, materials recovery, properly conducted recycling and reuse, and treatment;

(7) establishing a viable Federal-State partnership to carry out the purposes of this chapter and insuring that the Administrator will, in carrying out the provisions of subchapter III of this chapter, give a high priority to assisting and cooperating with States in obtaining full authorization of State programs under subchapter III of this chapter;

(8) providing for the promulgation of guidelines for solid waste collection, transport, separation, recovery, and disposal practices and systems;

(9) promoting a national research and development program for improved solid waste management and resource conservation techniques, more effective organizational arrangements, and new and improved methods of collection, separation, and recovery, and recycling of solid wastes and environmentally safe disposal of nonrecoverable residues;

(10) promoting the demonstration, construction, and application of solid waste management, resource recovery, and resource conservation systems which preserve and enhance the quality of air, water, and land resources; and

(11) establishing a cooperative effort among the Federal, State, and local governments and private enterprise in order to recover valuable materials and energy from solid waste.

**(b) National policy**

The Congress hereby declares it to be the national policy of the United States that, wherever feasible, the generation of hazardous waste is to be reduced or eliminated as expeditiously as possible. Waste that is nevertheless generated should be treated, stored, or disposed of so as to minimize the present and future threat to human health and the environment.

(Pub.L. 89–272, Title II, § 1003, as added Pub.L. 94–580, § 2, Oct. 21, 1976, 90 Stat. 2798, and amended Pub.L 98–616, Title I, § 101(b), Nov. 8, 1984, 98 Stat. 3224.)

**HISTORICAL AND STATUTORY NOTES**

**Prior Provisions**

Provisions similar to this section were contained in section 3251 of this title, prior to the complete revision of the Solid Waste Disposal Act by Pub.L. 94–580.

## § 6903. Definitions

**[SWDA § 1004]**

As used in this chapter:

(1) The term "Administrator" means the Administrator of the Environmental Protection Agency.

(2) The term "construction," with respect to any project of construction under this chapter, means (A) the erection or building of new structures and acquisition of lands or interests therein, or the acquisition, replacement, expansion, remodeling, alteration, modernization, or extension of existing structures, and (B) the acquisition and installation of initial equipment of, or required in connection with, new or newly acquired structures or the expanded, remodeled, altered, modernized or extended part of existing structures (including trucks and other motor vehicles, and tractors, cranes, and other machinery) necessary for the proper utilization and operation of the facility after completion of the project; and includes preliminary planning to determine the economic and engineering feasibility and the public health and safety aspects of the project, the engineering, architectural, legal, fiscal, and economic investigations and studies, and any surveys, designs, plans, working drawings, specifications, and other action necessary for the carrying out of the project, and (C) the inspection and supervision of the process of carrying out the project to completion.

(2A) The term "demonstration" means the initial exhibition of a new technology process or practice or a significantly new combination or use of technologies, processes or practices, subsequent to the development stage, for the purpose of proving technological feasibility and cost effectiveness.

(3) The term "disposal" means the discharge, deposit, injection, dumping, spilling, leaking, or placing of any solid waste or hazardous waste into or on any land or water so that such solid waste or hazardous waste or any constituent thereof may enter the environment or be emitted into the air or discharged into any waters, including ground waters.

(4) The term "Federal agency" means any department, agency, or other instrumentality of the Federal Government, any independent agency or establishment of the Federal Government including any Government corporation, and the Government Printing Office.

(5) The term "hazardous waste" means a solid waste, or combination of solid wastes, which because

of its quantity, concentration, or physical, chemical, or infectious characteristics may—

(A) cause, or significantly contribute to an increase in mortality or an increase in serious irreversible, or incapacitating reversible, illness; or

(B) pose a substantial present or potential hazard to human health or the environment when improperly treated, stored, transported, or disposed of, or otherwise managed.

(6) The term "hazardous waste generation" means the act or process of producing hazardous waste.

(7) The term "hazardous waste management" means the systematic control of the collection, source separation, storage, transportation, processing, treatment, recovery, and disposal of hazardous wastes.

(8) For purposes of Federal financial assistance (other than rural communities assistance), the term "implementation" does not include the acquisition, leasing, construction, or modification of facilities or equipment or the acquisition, leasing, or improvement of land.

(9) The term "intermunicipal agency" means an agency established by two or more municipalities with responsibility for planning or administration of solid waste.

(10) The term "interstate agency" means an agency of two or more municipalities in different States, or an agency established by two or more States, with authority to provide for the management of solid wastes and serving two or more municipalities located in different States.

(11) The term "long-term contract" means, when used in relation to solid waste supply, a contract of sufficient duration to assure the viability of a resource recovery facility (to the extent that such viability depends upon solid waste supply).

(12) The term "manifest" means the form used for identifying the quantity, composition, and the origin, routing, and destination of hazardous waste during its transportation from the point of generation to the point of disposal, treatment, or storage.

(13) The term "municipality" (A) means a city, town, borough, county, parish, district, or other public body created by or pursuant to State law, with responsibility for the planning or administration of solid waste management, or an Indian tribe or authorized tribal organization or Alaska Native village or organization, and (B) includes any rural community or unincorporated town or village or any other public entity for which an application for assistance is made by a State or political subdivision thereof.

(14) The term "open dump" means any facility or site where solid waste is disposed of which is not a sanitary landfill which meets the criteria promulgated under section 6944 of this title and which is not a facility for disposal of hazardous waste.

(15) The term "person" means an individual, trust, firm, joint stock company, corporation (including a government corporation), partnership, association, State, municipality, commission, political subdivision of a State, or any interstate body and shall include each department, agency, and instrumentality of the United States.

(16) The term "procurement item" means any device, good, substance, material, product, or other item whether real or personal property which is the subject of any purchase, barter, or other exchange made to procure such item.

(17) The term "procuring agency" means any Federal agency, or any State agency or agency of a political subdivision of a State which is using appropriated Federal funds for such procurement, or any person contracting with any such agency with respect to work performed under such contract.

(18) The term "recoverable" refers to the capability and likelihood of being recovered from solid waste for a commercial or industrial use.

(19) The term "recovered material" means waste material and byproducts which have been recovered or diverted from solid waste, but such term does not include those materials and byproducts generated from, and commonly reused within, an original manufacturing process.

(20) The term "recovered resources" means material or energy recovered from solid waste.

(21) The term "resource conservation" means reduction of the amounts of solid waste that are generated, reduction of overall resource consumption, and utilization of recovered resources.

(22) The term "resource recovery" means the recovery of material or energy from solid waste.

(23) The term "resource recovery system" means a solid waste management system which provides for collection, separation, recycling, and recovery of solid wastes, including disposal of nonrecoverable waste residues.

(24) The term "resource recovery facility" means any facility at which solid waste is processed for the purpose of extracting, converting to energy, or otherwise separating and preparing solid waste for reuse.

(25) The term "regional authority" means the authority established or designated under section 6946 of this title.

(26) The term "sanitary landfill" means a facility for the disposal of solid waste which meets the criteria published under section 6944 of this title.

(26A) The term "sludge" means any solid, semisolid or liquid waste generated from a municipal, commercial, or industrial wastewater treatment plant, water supply treatment plant, or air pollution control facility or any other such waste having similar characteristics and effects.

**(27)** The term "solid waste" means any garbage, refuse, sludge from a waste treatment plant, water supply treatment plant, or air pollution control facility and other discarded material, including solid, liquid, semisolid, or contained gaseous material resulting from industrial, commercial, mining, and agricultural operations, and from community activities, but does not include solid or dissolved material in domestic sewage, or solid or dissolved materials in irrigation return flows or industrial discharges which are point sources subject to permits under section 1342 of Title 33, or source, special nuclear, or byproduct material as defined by the Atomic Energy Act of 1954, as amended (68 Stat. 923) [42 U.S.C.A. § 2011 et seq.].

**(28)** The term "solid waste management" means the systematic administration of activities which provide for the collection, source separation, storage, transportation, transfer, processing, treatment, and disposal of solid waste.

**(29)** The term "solid waste management facility" includes—

**(A)** any resource recovery system or component thereof,

**(B)** any system, program, or facility for resource conservation, and

**(C)** any facility for the collection, source separation, storage, transportation, transfer, processing, treatment or disposal of solid wastes, including hazardous wastes, whether such facility is associated with facilities generating such wastes or otherwise.

**(30)** The terms "solid waste planning", "solid waste management", and "comprehensive planning" include planning or management respecting resource recovery and resource conservation.

**(31)** The term "State" means any of the several States, the District of Columbia, the Commonwealth of Puerto Rico, the Virgin Islands, Guam, American Samoa, and the Commonwealth of the Northern Mariana Islands.

**(32)** The term "State authority" means the agency established or designated under section 6947 of this title.

**(33)** The term "storage", when used in connection with hazardous waste, means the containment of hazardous waste, either on a temporary basis or for a period of years, in such a manner as not to constitute disposal of such hazardous waste.

**(34)** The term "treatment", when used in connection with hazardous waste, means any method, technique, or process, including neutralization, designed to change the physical, chemical, or biological character or composition of any hazardous waste so as to neutralize such waste or so as to render such waste nonhazardous, safer for transport, amenable for recovery, amenable for storage, or reduced in volume. Such term includes any activity or processing designed to change the physical form or chemical composition of hazardous waste so as to render it nonhazardous.

**(35)** The term "virgin material" means a raw material, including previously unused copper, aluminum, lead, zinc, iron, or other metal or metal ore, any undeveloped resource that is, or with new technology will become, a source of raw materials.

**(36)** The term "used oil" means any oil which has been—

**(A)** refined from crude oil,

**(B)** used, and

**(C)** as a result of such use, contaminated by physical or chemical impurities.

**(37)** The term "recycled oil" means any used oil which is reused, following its original use, for any purpose (including the purpose for which the oil was originally used). Such term includes oil which is re-refined, reclaimed, burned, or reprocessed.

**(38)** The term "lubricating oil" means the fraction of crude oil which is sold for purposes of reducing friction in any industrial or mechanical device. Such term includes re-refined oil.

**(39)** The term "re-refined oil" means used oil from which the physical and chemical contaminants acquired through previous use have been removed through a refining process.

**(40)** Except as otherwise provided in this paragraph, the term "medical waste" means any solid waste which is generated in the diagnosis, treatment, or immunization of human beings or animals, in research pertaining thereto, or in the production or testing of biologicals. Such term does not include any hazardous waste identified or listed under subchapter III of this chapter or any household waste as defined in regulations under subchapter III of this chapter.

**(41)** The term "mixed waste" means waste that contains both hazardous waste and source, special nuclear, or by-product material subject to the Atomic Energy Act of 1954 (42 U.S.C. 2011 et seq.).

(Pub.L. 89–272, Title II, § 1004, as added Pub.L. 94–580, § 2, Oct. 21, 1976, 90 Stat. 2798, and amended Pub.L. 95–609, § 7(b), Nov. 8, 1978, 92 Stat. 3081; Pub.L. 96–463, § 3, Oct. 15, 1980, 94 Stat. 2055; Pub.L. 96–482, § 2, Oct. 21, 1980, 94 Stat. 2334; Pub.L. 100–582, § 3, Nov. 1, 1988, 102 Stat. 2958; Pub.L. 102–386, Title I, §§ 103, 105(b), Oct. 6, 1992, 106 Stat. 1507, 1512.)

HISTORICAL AND STATUTORY NOTES

**References in Text**

The Atomic Energy Act of 1954, as amended, referred to in pars. (27) and (41), is Act Aug. 30, 1954, c. 1073, § 1, 68 Stat. 919, as amended, which is classified principally to chapter 23 (section 2011 et seq.) of this title. For complete classification of this Act to the Code, see Short Title note set out under section 2011 of this title and Tables.

**Transfer of Functions**

Enforcement functions of Administrator or other official of the Environmental Protection Agency related to compliance with resource conservation and recovery permits used under this chapter with respect to preconstruction, construction, and initial operation of transportation system for Canadian and Alaskan natural gas were transferred to the Federal inspector, Office of Federal Inspector for the Alaska Natural Gas Transportation System, until the first anniversary of date of initial operation of the Alaska Natural Gas Transportation System, see Reorg. Plan No. 1 of 1979, eff. July 1, 1979, §§ 102(a), 203(a), 44 F.R. 33663, 33666, 93 Stat. 1373, 1376, set out in Appendix 1 to Title 5, Government Organization and Employees. Office of Federal Inspector for the Alaska Natural Gas Transportation System abolished and functions and authority vested in Inspector transferred to Secretary of Energy by section 3012(b) of Pub.L. 102–486, set out as an Abolition of Office of Federal Inspector note under section 719e of Title 15, Commerce and Trade.

**Prior Provisions**

Provisions similar to this section were contained in section 3252 of this title, prior to the complete revision of the Solid Waste Disposal Act by Pub.L. 94–580.

## § 6904. Governmental cooperation

[SWDA § 1005]

**(a) Interstate cooperation**

The provisions of this chapter to be carried out by States may be carried out by interstate agencies and provisions applicable to States may apply to interstate regions where such agencies and regions have been established by the respective States and approved by the Administrator. In any such case, action required to be taken by the Governor of a State, respecting regional designation shall be required to be taken by the Governor of each of the respective States with respect to so much of the interstate region as is within the jurisdiction of that State.

**(b) Consent of Congress to compacts**

The consent of the Congress is hereby given to two or more States to negotiate and enter into agreements or compacts, not in conflict with any law or treaty of the United States, for—

(1) cooperative effort and mutual assistance for the management of solid waste or hazardous waste (or both) and the enforcement of their respective laws relating thereto, and

(2) the establishment of such agencies, joint or otherwise, as they may deem desirable for making effective such agreements or compacts.

No such agreement or compact shall be binding or obligatory upon any State a party thereto unless it is agreed upon by all parties to the agreement and until it has been approved by the Administrator and the Congress.

(Pub.L. 89–272, Title II, § 1005, as added Pub.L. 94–580, § 2, Oct. 21, 1976, 90 Stat. 2801.)

HISTORICAL AND STATUTORY NOTES

**Transfer of Functions**

For transfer of certain enforcement functions of Administrator or other official of the Environmental Protection Agency under this chapter to Federal Inspector, Office of Federal Inspector for the Alaska Natural Gas Transportation System, see note set out under section 6903 of this title.

## § 6905. Application of chapter and integration with other Acts

[SWDA § 1006]

**(a) Application of chapter**

Nothing in this chapter shall be construed to apply to (or to authorize any State, interstate, or local authority to regulate) any activity or substance which is subject to the Federal Water Pollution Control Act [33 U.S.C.A. § 1251 et seq.], the Safe Drinking Water Act [42 U.S.C.A. § 300f et seq.], the Marine Protection, Research and Sanctuaries Act of 1972 [16 U.S.C.A. §§ 1431 et seq., 1447 et seq., 33 U.S.C.A. §§ 1401 et seq., 2801 et seq.], or the Atomic Energy Act of 1954 [42 U.S.C.A. § 2011 et seq.] except to the extent that such application (or regulation) is not inconsistent with the requirements of such Acts.

**(b) Integration with other Acts**

(1) The Administrator shall integrate all provisions of this chapter for purposes of administration and enforcement and shall avoid duplication, to the maximum extent practicable, with the appropriate provisions of the Clean Air Act [42 U.S.C.A. § 7401 et seq.], the Federal Water Pollution Control Act [33 U.S.C.A. § 1251 et seq.], the Federal Insecticide, Fungicide, and Rodenticide Act [7 U.S.C.A. § 136 et seq.], the Safe Drinking Water Act [42 U.S.C.A. § 300f et seq.], the Marine Protection, Research and Sanctuaries Act of 1972 [16 U.S.C.A. §§ 1431 et seq.,1447 et seq., 33 U.S.C.A. §§ 1401 et seq., 2801 et seq.], and such other Acts of Congress as grant regulatory authority to the Administrator. Such integration shall be effected only to the extent that it can be done in a manner consistent with the goals and policies expressed in this chapter and in the other acts referred to in this subsection.

(2)(A) As promptly as practicable after November 8, 1984, the Administrator shall submit a report describing—

(i) the current data and information available on emissions of polychlorinated dibenzo-p-dioxins from resource recovery facilities burning municipal solid waste;

(ii) any significant risks to human health posed by these emissions; and

(iii) operating practices appropriate for controlling these emissions.

(B) Based on the report under subparagraph (A) and on any future information on such emissions, the Administrator may publish advisories or guidelines regarding the control of dioxin emissions from such facilities. Nothing in this paragraph shall be construed to preempt or otherwise affect the authority of the Administrator to promulgate any regulations under the Clean Air Act [42 U.S.C.A. § 7401 et seq.] regarding emissions of polychlorinated dibenzo-p-dioxins.

(3) Notwithstanding any other provisions of law, in developing solid waste plans, it is the intention of this chapter that in determining the size of a waste-to-energy facility, adequate provisions shall be given to the present and reasonably anticipated future needs, including those needs created by thorough implementation of section 6962(h) of this title, of the recycling and resource recovery interests within the area encompassed by the solid waste plan.

**(c) Integration with the Surface Mining Control and Reclamation Act of 1977**

(1) No later than 90 days after October 21, 1980, the Administrator shall review any regulations applicable to the treatment, storage, or disposal of any coal mining wastes or overburden promulgated by the Secretary of the Interior under the Surface Mining and Reclamation Act of 1977 [30 U.S.C.A. § 1201 et seq.]. If the Administrator determines that any requirement of final regulations promulgated under any section of subchapter III of this chapter relating to mining wastes or overburden is not adequately addressed in such regulations promulgated by the Secretary, the Administrator shall promptly transmit such determination, together with suggested revisions and supporting documentation, to the Secretary.

(2) The Secretary of the Interior shall have exclusive responsibility for carrying out any requirement of subchapter III of this chapter with respect to coal mining wastes or overburden for which a surface coal mining and reclamation permit is issued or approved under the Surface Mining Control and Reclamation Act of 1977 [30 U.S.C.A. § 1201 et seq.]. The Secretary shall, with the concurrence of the Administrator, promulgate such regulations as may be necessary to carry out the purposes of this subsection and shall integrate such regulations with regulations promulgated under the Surface Mining Control and Reclamation Act of 1977.

(Pub.L. 89–272, Title II, § 1006, as added Pub.L. 94–580, § 2, Oct. 21, 1976, 90 Stat. 2802, and amended Pub.L. 96–482, § 3, Oct. 21, 1980, 94 Stat. 2334; Pub.L. 98–616, Title I, § 102, Title V, § 501(f)(2), Nov. 8, 1984, 98 Stat. 3225, 3276.)

## HISTORICAL AND STATUTORY NOTES

**References in Text**

The Federal Water Pollution Control Act, referred to in subsecs. (a) and (b), is Act June 30, 1948, c. 758, as amended generally by Pub.L. 92–500, § 2, Oct. 18, 1972, 86 Stat. 816, which is classified generally to chapter 26 (section 1251 et seq.) of Title 33, Navigation and Navigable Waters. For complete classification of this Act to the Code, see Short Title note set out under section 1251 of Title 33 and Tables.

The Safe Drinking Water Act, referred to in subsecs. (a) and (b), is Pub.L. 93–523, Dec. 16, 1974, 88 Stat. 1660, as amended, which is classified principally to subchapter XII (section 300f et seq.) of chapter 6A of this title. For complete classification of this Act to the Code see Short Title note set out under section 201 of this title and Tables.

The Marine Protection, Research and Sanctuaries Act of 1972, referred to in subsecs. (a) and (b), is Pub.L. 92–532, Oct. 23, 1972, 86 Stat. 1052, as amended, which enacted chapters 32 (section 1431 et seq.) and 32A (section 1447 et seq.) of Title 16, Conservation and chapters 27 (section 1401 et seq.) and 41 (section 2801 et seq.) of Title 33, Navigation and Navigable Waters. For complete classification of this Act to the Code, see Short Title note set out under section 1401 of Title 33 and Tables.

The Atomic Energy Act of 1954, as amended, referred to in subsec. (a), is Act Aug. 30, 1954, c. 1073, § 1, 68 Stat. 919, which is classified principally to chapter 23 (section 2011 et seq.) of this title. For complete classification of this Act to the Code, see Short Title note set out under section 2011 of this title and Tables.

The Clean Air Act, as amended, referred to in subsec. (b)(1), (2)(B), is Act July 14, 1955, c. 360, as amended generally by Pub.L. 88–206, Dec. 17, 1963, 77 Stat. 392, and later by Pub.L. 95–95, Aug. 7, 1977, 91 Stat. 685. The Clean Air Act was originally classified to chapter 15B (section 1857 et seq.) of this title. On enactment of Pub.L. 95–95, the Act was reclassified to chapter 85 (section 7401 et seq.) of this title. For complete classification of this Act to the Code, see Short Title of 1955 Acts note set out under section 7401 of this title and Tables.

The Federal Insecticide, Fungicide, and Rodenticide Act, referred to in subsec. (b), is Act June 25, 1947, c. 125, as amended generally by Pub.L. 92–516, Oct. 21, 1972, 86 Stat. 973, which is classified generally to subchapter II (section 136 et seq.) of chapter 6 of Title 7, Agriculture. For complete classification of this Act to the Code, see Short Title note set out under section 136 of Title 7 and Tables.

The Surface Mining and Reclamation Act of 1977, referred to in subsec. (c)(1), is probably the Surface Mining Control and Reclamation Act of 1977, which is referred to in subsec. (c)(2), which is Pub.L. 95–87, Aug. 3, 1977, 91 Stat. 448, as amended, which is classified generally to chapter 25 (section 1201 et seq.) of Title 30, Mineral Lands and Mining. For complete classification of this Act to the Code, see Short Title note set out under section 1201 of Title 30 and Tables.

**Transfer of Functions**

For transfer of certain enforcement functions of Administrator or other official of the Environmental Protection Agency under this chapter to Federal Inspector, Office of Federal Inspector for the Alaska Natural Gas Transportation System, see note set out under section 6903 of this title.

**Prior Provisions**

Provisions similar to this section were contained in section 3257 of this title, prior to the complete revision of the Solid Waste Disposal Act by Pub.L. 94–580.

**Uranium Mill Tailings**

Section 703 of Pub.L. 98–616 provided that: "Nothing in the Hazardous and Solid Waste Amendments of 1984 [see Short Title of 1984 Amendments note set out under section 6901 of this title] shall be construed to affect, modify, or amend the Uranium Mill Tailings Radiation Control Act of 1978 [Pub.L. 95–604, see Short Title of 1978 Acts note set out under section 7901 of this title]."

## § 6906. Financial disclosure

[SWDA § 1007]

**(a) Statement**

Each officer or employee of the Administrator who—

(1) performs any function or duty under this chapter; and

(2) has any known financial interest in any person who applies for or receives financial assistance under this chapter

shall, beginning on February 1, 1977, annually file with the Administrator a written statement concerning all such interests held by such officer or employee during the preceding calendar year. Such statement shall be available to the public.

**(b) Action by Administrator**

The Administrator shall—

(1) act within ninety days after October 21, 1976—

(A) to define the term "known financial interest" for purposes of subsection (a) of this section; and

(B) to establish the methods by which the requirement to file written statements specified in subsection (a) of this section will be monitored and enforced, including appropriate provision for the filing by such officers and employees of such statements and the review by the Administrator of such statements; and

(2) report to the Congress on June 1, 1978, and of each succeeding calendar year with respect to such disclosures and the actions taken in regard thereto during the preceding calendar year.

**(c) Exemption**

In the rules prescribed under subsection (b) of this section, the Administrator may identify specific positions within the Environmental Protection Agency which are of a nonpolicy-making nature and provide that officers or employees occupying such positions shall be exempt from the requirements of this section.

**(d) Penalty**

Any officer or employee who is subject to, and knowingly violates, this section shall be fined not more than $2,500 or imprisoned not more than one year, or both.

(Pub.L. 89–272, Title II, § 1007, as added Pub.L. 94–580, § 2, Oct. 21, 1976, 90 Stat. 2802.)

### HISTORICAL AND STATUTORY NOTES

**Transfer of Functions**

For transfer of certain enforcement functions of Administrator or other official of the Environmental Protection Agency under this chapter to Federal Inspector, Office of Federal Inspector for the Alaska Natural Gas Transportation System, see note set out under section 6903 of this title.

**Termination of Reporting Requirements**

For termination, effective May 15, 2000, of reporting provisions in subsec. (b)(2) of this section, see section 3003 of Pub.L. 104–66, as amended, set out as a note under 31 U.S.C.A. § 1113, and the 14th item on page 164 of House Document No. 103–7.

## § 6907. Solid waste management information and guidelines

[SWDA § 1008]

**(a) Guidelines**

Within one year of October 21, 1976, and from time to time thereafter, the Administrator shall, in cooperation with appropriate Federal, State, municipal, and intermunicipal agencies, and in consultation with other interested persons, and after public hearings, develop and publish suggested guidelines for solid waste management. Such suggested guidelines shall—

(1) provide a technical and economic description of the level of performance that can be attained by various available solid waste management practices (including operating practices) which provide for the protection of public health and the environment;

(2) not later than two years after October 21, 1976, describe levels of performance, including appropriate methods and degrees of control, that provide at a minimum for (A) protection of public health and welfare; (B) protection of the quality of ground waters and surface waters from leachates; (C) protection of the quality of surface waters from runoff through compliance with effluent limitations under the Federal Water Pollution Control Act, as amended [33 U.S.C.A. § 1251 et seq.]; (D) protec-

tion of ambient air quality through compliance with new source performance standards or requirements of air quality implementation plans under the Clean Air Act, as amended [42 U.S.C.A. § 7401 et seq.]; (E) disease and vector control; (F) safety; and (G) esthetics; and

(3) provide minimum criteria to be used by the States to define those solid waste management practices which constitute the open dumping of solid waste or hazardous waste and are to be prohibited under subchapter IV of this chapter.

Where appropriate, such suggested guidelines also shall include minimum information for use in deciding the adequate location, design, and construction of facilities associated with solid waste management practices, including the consideration of regional, geographic, demographic, and climatic factors.

### (b) Notice

The Administrator shall notify the Committee on Environment and Public Works of the Senate and the Committee on Energy and Commerce of the House of Representatives a reasonable time before publishing any suggested guidelines or proposed regulations under this chapter of the content of such proposed suggested guidelines or proposed regulations under this chapter.

(Pub.L. 89–272, Title II, § 1008, as added Pub.L. 94–580, § 2, Oct. 21, 1976, 90 Stat. 2803, and amended S.Res. 4, Feb. 4, 1977; Pub.L. 95–609, § 7(c), (d), Nov. 8, 1978, 92 Stat. 3081; H.Res. 549, Mar. 25, 1980; Pub.L. 103–437, § 15(r), Nov. 2, 1994, 108 Stat. 4594.)

## HISTORICAL AND STATUTORY NOTES

**References in Text**

The Federal Water Pollution Control Act, referred to in subsec. (a)(2), is Act June 30, 1948, c. 758, as amended generally by Pub.L. 92–500, § 2, Oct. 18, 1972, 86 Stat. 816, which is classified generally to chapter 26 (section 1251 et seq.) of Title 33, Navigation and Navigable Waters. For complete classification of this Act to the Code, see Short Title note set out under section 1251 of Title 33 and Tables.

The Clean Air Act, as amended, referred to in subsec. (a)(2), is Act July 14, 1955, c. 360, as amended generally by Pub.L. 88–206, Dec. 17, 1963, 77 Stat. 392, and later by Pub.L. 95–95, Aug. 7, 1977, 91 Stat. 685. The Clean Air Act was originally classified to chapter 15B (section 1857 et seq.) of this title. On enactment of Pub.L. 95–95, the Act was reclassified to chapter 85 (section 7401 et seq.) of this title. For complete classification of this Act to the Code, see Short Title of 1955 Acts note set out under section 7401 of this title and Tables.

**Codifications**

Subchapter IV of this chapter, referred to in subsec. (a)(3), was in the original "subtitle D of this Act". Reference to subtitle D of this Act probably means subtitle D of Title II of this Act (Pub.L. 89–272), as added by Pub.L. 94–580, which is known as the Solid Waste Disposal Act and which is classified generally to subchapter IV (section 6941 et seq.) of this chapter.

**Change of Name**

The Committee on Public Works of the Senate, was abolished and replaced by the Committee on Environment and Public Works of the Senate, effective Feb. 11, 1977. See Rule XXV of the Standing Rules of the Senate, as amended by Senate Resolution 4 (popularly cited as the "Committee System Reorganization Amendments of 1977"), approved Feb. 4, 1977.

Any reference in any provision of law enacted before Jan. 4, 1995, to the Committee on Energy and Commerce of the House of Representatives treated as referring to the Committee on Commerce of the House of Representatives, except that any reference in any provision of law enacted before Jan. 4, 1995, to the Committee on Energy and Commerce of the House of Representatives treated as referring to the Committee on Agriculture of the House of Representatives, in the case of a provision of law relating to inspection of seafood or seafood products, the Committee on Banking and Financial Services of the House of Representatives, in the case of a provision of law relating to bank capital markets activities generally or to depository institution securities activities generally, and the Committee on Transportation and Infrastructure of the House of Representatives, in the case of a provision of law relating to railroads, railway labor, or railroad retirement and unemployment (except revenue measures related thereto), see section 1(a)(4) and (c)(1) of Pub.L. 104–14, set out as a note preceding section 21 of Title 2, The Congress.

The name of the Committee on Interstate and Foreign Commerce of the House of Representatives was changed, in subsec. (b), to Committee on Energy and Commerce immediately prior to noon on Jan. 3, 1981, by House Resolution 549, Ninety-sixth Congress, Mar. 25, 1980.

**Transfer of Functions**

For transfer of certain enforcement functions of Administrator or other official of the Environmental Protection Agency under this chapter to Federal Inspector, Office of Federal Inspector for the Alaska Natural Gas Transportation System, see note set out under section 6903 of this title.

**Prior Provisions**

Provisions similar to this section were contained in section 3254c of this title, prior to the complete revision of the Solid Waste Disposal Act by Pub.L. 94–580.

## § 6908. Small town environmental planning

**[FFCA § 109]**

### (a) Establishment

The Administrator of the Environmental Protection Agency (hereafter referred to as the "Administrator") shall establish a program to assist small communities in planning and financing environmental facilities. The program shall be known as the "Small Town Environmental Planning Program".

### (b) Small Town Environmental Planning Task Force

(1) The Administrator shall establish a Small Town Environmental Planning Task Force which shall be composed of representatives of small towns from different areas of the United States, Federal and State governmental agencies, and public interest groups. The Administrator shall terminate the Task Force not later than 2 years after the establishment of the Task Force.

(2) The Task Force shall—

(A) identify regulations developed pursuant to Federal environmental laws which pose significant compliance problems for small towns;

(B) identify means to improve the working relationship between the Environmental Protection Agency (hereafter referred to as the Agency) and small towns;

(C) review proposed regulations for the protection of the environmental and public health and suggest revisions that could improve the ability of small towns to comply with such regulations;

(D) identify means to promote regionalization of environmental treatment systems and infrastructure serving small towns to improve the economic condition of such systems and infrastructure; and

(E) provide such other assistance to the Administrator as the Administrator deems appropriate.

**(c) Identification of environmental requirements**

(1) Not later than 6 months after October 6, 1992, the Administrator shall publish a list of requirements under Federal environmental and public health statutes (and the regulations developed pursuant to such statutes) applicable to small towns. Not less than annually, the Administrator shall make such additions and deletions to and from the list as the Administrator deems appropriate.

(2) The Administrator shall, as part of the Small Town Environmental Planning Program under this section, implement a program to notify small communities of the regulations identified under paragraph (1) and of future regulations and requirements through methods that the Administrator determines to be effective to provide information to the greatest number of small communities, including any of the following:

(A) Newspapers and other periodicals.

(B) Other news media.

(C) Trade, municipal, and other associations that the Administrator determines to be appropriate.

(D) Direct mail.

**(d) Small Town Ombudsman**

The Administrator shall establish and staff an Office of the Small Town Ombudsman. The Office shall provide assistance to small towns in connection with the Small Town Environmental Planning Program and other business with the Agency. Each regional office shall identify a small town contact. The Small Town Ombudsman and the regional contacts also may assist larger communities, but only if first priority is given to providing assistance to small towns.

**(e) Multi-media permits**

(1) The Administrator shall conduct a study of establishing a multi-media permitting program for small towns. Such evaluation shall include an analysis of—

(A) environmental benefits and liabilities of a multi-media permitting program;

(B) the potential of using such a program to coordinate a small town's environmental and public health activities; and

(C) the legal barriers, if any, to the establishment of such a program.

(2) Within 3 years after October 6, 1992, the Administrator shall report to Congress on the results of the evaluation performed in accordance with paragraph (1). Included in this report shall be a description of the activities conducted pursuant to subsections (a) through (d) of this section.

**(f) "Small town" defined**

For purposes of this section, the term "small town" means an incorporated or unincorporated community (as defined by the Administrator) with a population of less than 2,500 individuals.

**(g) Authorization**

There is authorized to be appropriated the sum of $500,000 to implement this section.

(Pub.L. 102–386, Title I, § 109, Oct. 6, 1992, 106 Stat. 1515.)

**HISTORICAL AND STATUTORY NOTES**

**Codifications**

Section was enacted as part of the Federal Facility Compliance Act of 1992 and not as part of the Solid Waste Disposal Act, which comprises this chapter.

## § 6908a. Agreements with Indian tribes

On and after October 21, 1998, the Administrator is authorized to enter into assistance agreements with Federally [1] recognized Indian tribes on such terms and conditions as the Administrator deems appropriate for the development and implementation of programs to manage hazardous waste, and underground storage tanks.

(Pub.L. 105–276, Title III, Oct. 21, 1998, 112 Stat. 2499.)

[1] So in original. Probably should not be capitalized.

# SUBCHAPTER II—OFFICE OF SOLID WASTE; AUTHORITIES OF THE ADMINISTRATOR

## § 6911. Office of Solid Waste and Interagency Coordinating Committee [SWDA § 2001]

**(a) Office of Solid Waste**

The Administrator shall establish within the Environmental Protection Agency an Office of Solid Waste (hereinafter referred to as the "Office") to be headed by an Assistant Administrator of the Environmental Protection Agency. The duties and responsibilities (other than duties and responsibilities relating to research and development) of the Administrator under this chapter (as modified by applicable reorganization plans) shall be carried out through the Office.

**(b) Interagency Coordinating Committee**

**(1)** There is hereby established an Interagency Coordinating Committee on Federal Resource Conservation and Recovery Activities which shall have the responsibility for coordinating all activities dealing with resource conservation and recovery from solid waste carried out by the Environmental Protection Agency, the Department of Energy, the Department of Commerce, and all other Federal agencies which conduct such activities pursuant to this chapter or any other Act. For purposes of this subsection, the term "resource conservation and recovery activities" shall include, but not be limited to, all research, development and demonstration projects on resource conservation or energy, or material, recovery from solid waste, and all technical or financial assistance for State or local planning for, or implementation of, projects related to resource conservation or energy or material, recovery from solid waste. The Committee shall be chaired by the Administrator of the Environmental Protection Agency or such person as the Administrator may designate. Members of the Committee shall include representatives of the Department of Energy, the Department of Commerce, the Department of the Treasury, and each other Federal agency which the Administrator determines to have programs or responsibilities affecting resource conservation or recovery.

**(2)** The Interagency Coordinating Committee shall include oversight of the implementation of—

**(A)** the May 1979 Memorandum of Understanding on Energy Recovery from Municipal Solid Waste between the Environmental Protection Agency and the Department of Energy;

**(B)** the May 30, 1978, Interagency Agreement between the Department of Commerce and the Environmental Protection Agency on the Implementation[1] of the Resource Conservation and Recovery Act [42 U.S.C.A. § 6901 et seq.]; and

**(C)** any subsequent agreements between these agencies or other Federal agencies which address Federal resource recovery or conservation activities.

(3) Omitted

(Pub.L. 89–272, Title II, § 2001, as added Pub.L. 94–580, § 2, Oct. 21, 1976, 90 Stat. 2804, and amended Pub.L. 96–482, § 4(c), Oct. 21, 1980, 94 Stat. 2335; Pub.L. 96–510, Title III, § 307(a), Dec. 11, 1980, 94 Stat. 2810.)

[1] So in original. Probably should not be capitalized.

### HISTORICAL AND STATUTORY NOTES

**References in Text**

The Resource Conservation and Recovery Act, referred to in subsec. (b)(2)(B), is Pub.L. 94–580, § 1, Oct. 21, 1976, 90 Stat. 2795, which is classified generally to this chapter. For complete classification of this Act to the Code, see Short Title of 1976 Acts note set out under section 6901 of this title and Tables.

**Codifications**

Subsection (b)(3) of this section, which required the Interagency Coordinating Committee to submit to Congress on March 1 of each year, a five-year action plan for Federal resource conservation or recovery activities, terminated, effective May 15, 2000, pursuant to section 3003 of Pub.L. 104–66, as amended, set out as a note under 31 U.S.C.A. § 1113. See, also, the 2nd item on page 175 of House Document No. 103–7.

**Effective and Applicability Provisions**

1980 Acts

Section 307(c) of Pub.L. 96–510 provided that: "The amendment made by subsection (a) [amending this section] shall become effective ninety days after the date of the enactment of this Act [Dec. 11, 1980]."

**Transfer of Functions**

For transfer of certain enforcement functions of Administrator or other official of the Environmental Protection Agency under this chapter to Federal Inspector, Office of Federal Inspector for the Alaska Natural Gas Transportation System, see note set out under section 6903 of this title.

## § 6911a. Assistant Administrator of Environmental Protection Agency; appointment, etc.

The Assistant Administrator of the Environmental Protection Agency appointed to head the Office of Solid Waste shall be in addition to the five Assistant Administrators of the Environmental Protection Agency provided for in section 1(d) of Reorganization Plan Numbered 3 of 1970 and the additional Assistant Administrator provided by the Toxic Substances Control Act [15 U.S.C.A. § 2601 et seq.], shall be appointed by the President by and with the advice and consent of the Senate.

(Pub.L. 96–510, Title III, § 307(b), Dec. 11, 1980, 94 Stat. 2810; Pub.L. 98–80, § 2(c)(2)(B), Aug. 23, 1983, 97 Stat. 485.)

### HISTORICAL AND STATUTORY NOTES

**References in Text**

Reorganization Plan Numbered 3 of 1970, referred to in text, is set out in Appendix 1 to Title 5, Government Organization and Employees.

The Toxic Substances Control Act, referred to in text, is Pub.L. 94–469, Oct. 11, 1976, 90 Stat. 2003, as amended, which is classified generally to chapter 53 (section 2601 et seq.) of Title 15, Commerce and Trade. For complete classification of this Act to the Code, see Short Title note set out under section 2601 of Title 15 and Tables.

**Codifications**

Section was enacted as part of the Comprehensive Environmental Response, Compensation, and Liability Act of 1980, and not as part of the Solid Waste Disposal Act which comprises this chapter.

**Effective and Applicability Provisions**

1980 Acts

Section effective Dec. 11, 1980, see section 9652 of this title.

## § 6912. Authorities of Administrator

**[SWDA § 2002]**

### (a) Authorities

In carrying out this chapter, the Administrator is authorized to—

(1) prescribe, in consultation with Federal, State, and regional authorities, such regulations as are necessary to carry out his functions under this chapter;

(2) consult with or exchange information with other Federal agencies undertaking research, development, demonstration projects, studies, or investigations relating to solid waste;

(3) provide technical and financial assistance to States or regional agencies in the development and implementation of solid waste plans and hazardous waste management programs;

(4) consult with representatives of science, industry, agriculture, labor, environmental protection and consumer organizations, and other groups, as he deems advisable;

(5) utilize the information, facilities, personnel and other resources of Federal agencies, including the National Institute of Standards and Technology and the National Bureau of the Census, on a reimbursable basis, to perform research and analyses and conduct studies and investigations related to resource recovery and conservation and to otherwise carry out the Administrator's functions under this chapter; and

(6) to delegate to the Secretary of Transportation the performance of any inspection or enforcement function under this chapter relating to the transportation of hazardous waste where such delegation would avoid unnecessary duplication of activity and would carry out the objectives of this chapter and of chapter 51 of Title 49.

### (b) Revision of regulations

Each regulation promulgated under this chapter shall be reviewed and, where necessary, revised not less frequently than every three years.

### (c) Criminal investigations

In carrying out the provisions of this chapter, the Administrator, and duly-designated agents and employees of the Environmental Protection Agency, are authorized to initiate and conduct investigations under the criminal provisions of this chapter, and to refer the results of these investigations to the Attorney General for prosecution in appropriate cases.

(Pub.L. 89–272, Title II, § 2002, as added Pub.L. 94–580, § 2, Oct. 21, 1976, 90 Stat. 2804, and amended Pub.L. 96–482, § 5, Oct. 21, 1980, 94 Stat. 2335; Pub.L. 98–616, Title IV, § 403(d)(4), Nov. 8, 1984, 98 Stat. 3272; Pub.L. 100–418, Title V, § 5115(c), Aug. 23, 1988, 102 Stat. 1433.)

**HISTORICAL AND STATUTORY NOTES**

**References in Text**

Chapter 51 of Title 49, referred to in subsec. (a)(6), is 49 U.S.C.A. § 5101 et seq.

**Transfer of Functions**

For transfer of certain enforcement functions of Administrator or other official of the Environmental Protection Agency under this chapter to Federal Inspector, Office of Federal Inspector for the Alaska Natural Gas Transportation System, see note set out under section 6903 of this title.

## § 6913. Resource Recovery and Conservation Panels

**[SWDA § 2003]**

The Administrator shall provide teams of personnel, including Federal, State, and local employees or contractors (hereinafter referred to as "Resource Conservation and Recovery Panels") to provide Federal agencies, States and local governments upon request with technical assistance on solid waste management, resource recovery, and resource conservation. Such teams shall include technical, marketing, financial, and institutional specialists, and the services of such teams shall be provided without charge to States or local governments.

(Pub.L. 89–272, Title II, § 2003, as added Pub.L. 94–580, § 2, Oct. 21, 1976, 90 Stat. 2804, and amended Pub.L. 95–609, § 7(e), Nov. 8, 1978, 92 Stat. 3081.)

**HISTORICAL AND STATUTORY NOTES**

**Transfer of Functions**

For transfer of certain enforcement functions of Administrator or other official of the Environmental Protection Agency under this chapter to Federal Inspector, Office of Federal Inspector for the Alaska Natural Gas Transportation System, see note set out under section 6903 of this title.

## § 6914. Grants for discarded tire disposal

[SWDA § 2004]

### (a) Grants

The Administrator shall make available grants equal to 5 percent of the purchase price of tire shredders (including portable shredders attached to tire collection trucks) to those eligible applicants best meeting criteria promulgated under this section. An eligible applicant may be any private purchaser, public body, or public-private joint venture. Criteria for receiving grants shall be promulgated under this section and shall include the policy to offer any private purchaser the first option to receive a grant, the policy to develop widespread geographic distribution of tire shredding facilities, the need for such facilities within a geographic area, and the projected risk and viability of any such venture. In the case of an application under this section from a public body, the Administrator shall first make a determination that there are no private purchasers interested in making an application before approving a grant to a public body.

### (b) Authorization of appropriations

There is authorized to be appropriated $750,000 for each of the fiscal years 1978 and 1979 to carry out this section.

(Pub.L. 89–272, Title II, § 2004, as added Pub.L. 94–580, § 2, Oct. 21, 1976, 90 Stat. 2805.)

#### HISTORICAL AND STATUTORY NOTES

**Transfer of Functions**

For transfer of certain enforcement functions of Administrator or other official of the Environmental Protection Agency under this chapter to Federal Inspector, Office of Federal Inspector for the Alaska Natural Gas Transportation System, see note set out under section 6903 of this title.

## § 6914a. Labeling of lubricating oil

[SWDA § 2005]

For purposes of any provision of law which requires the labeling of commodities, lubricating oil shall be treated as lawfully labeled only if it bears the following statement, prominently displayed:

"DON'T POLLUTE—CONSERVE RESOURCES; RETURN USED OIL TO COLLECTION CENTERS".

(Pub.L. 89–272, Title II, § 2005, as added Pub.L. 96–463, § 4(a), Oct. 15, 1980, 94 Stat. 2056.)

#### HISTORICAL AND STATUTORY NOTES

**Prior Provisions**

A prior section 2005 of Pub.L. 89–272 was renumbered section 2006 and is classified to section 6915 of this title.

## § 6914b. Degradable plastic ring carriers; definitions

As used in this title—

(1) the term "regulated item" means any plastic ring carrier device that contains at least one hole greater than 1¾ inches in diameter which is made, used, or designed for the purpose of packaging, transporting, or carrying multipackaged cans or bottles, and which is of a size, shape, design, or type capable, when discarded, of becoming entangled with fish or wildlife; and

(2) the term "naturally degradable material" means a material which, when discarded, will be reduced to environmentally benign subunits under the action of normal environmental forces, such as, among others, biological decomposition, photodegradation, or hydrolysis.

(Pub.L. 100–556, Title I, § 102, Oct. 28, 1988, 102 Stat. 2779.)

#### HISTORICAL AND STATUTORY NOTES

**References in Text**

This title, referred to in text, is Title I of Pub.L. 100–556, Oct. 28, 1988, 102 Stat. 2779, which enacted sections 6914b and 6914b–1 of this title, and provisions set out as a note under section 6914b of this title. For complete classification of this title to the Code, see Tables.

**Codifications**

Section was not enacted as part of the Solid Waste Disposal Act which comprises this chapter.

**Congressional Findings**

Section 101 of Pub.L. 100–556 provided that: "The Congress finds that—

"(1) plastic ring carrier devices have been found in large quantities in the marine environment;

"(2) fish and wildlife have been known to have become entangled in plastic ring carriers;

"(3) nondegradable plastic ring carrier devices can remain intact in the marine environment for decades, posing a threat to fish and wildlife; and

"(4) 16 States have enacted laws requiring that plastic ring carrier devices be made from degradable material in order to reduce litter and to protect fish and wildlife."

## § 6914b–1. Regulation of plastic ring carriers

Not later than 24 months after October 28, 1988 (unless the Administrator of the Environmental Protection Agency determines that it is not feasible or that the byproducts of degradable regulated items present a greater threat to the environment than nondegradable regulated items), the Administrator of the Environmental Protection Agency shall require, by regulation, that any regulated item intended for use in the United States shall be made of naturally degradable material which, when discarded, decomposes within a period established by such regulation. The period within which decomposition must occur after being discarded shall be the shortest period of time consistent with the intended use of the item and the physical integrity required for such use. Such regulation shall allow a reasonable time for affected parties to come into compliance, including the use of existing inventories.

(Pub.L. 100–556, Title I, § 103, Oct. 28, 1988, 102 Stat. 2779.)

### HISTORICAL AND STATUTORY NOTES

**Codifications**

Section was not enacted as part of the Solid Waste Disposal Act which comprises this chapter.

## § 6915. Annual report

[SWDA § 2006]

The Administrator shall transmit to the Congress and the President, not later than ninety days after the end of each fiscal year, a comprehensive and detailed report on all activities of the Office during the preceding fiscal year. Each such report shall include—

(1) a statement of specific and detailed objectives for the activities and programs conducted and assisted under this chapter;

(2) statements of the Administrator's conclusions as to the effectiveness of such activities and programs in meeting the stated objectives and the purposes of this chapter, measured through the end of such fiscal year;

(3) a summary of outstanding solid waste problems confronting the Administrator, in order of priority;

(4) recommendations with respect to such legislation which the Administrator deems necessary or desirable to assist in solving problems respecting solid waste;

(5) all other information required to be submitted to the Congress pursuant to any other provision of this chapter; and

(6) the Administrator's plans for activities and programs respecting solid waste during the next fiscal year.

(Pub.L. 89–272, Title II, § 2006, formerly § 2005, as added Pub.L. 94–580, § 2, Oct. 21, 1976, 90 Stat. 2805, and renumbered Pub.L. 96–463, § 4(a), Oct. 15, 1980, 94 Stat. 2056; Pub.L. 98–616, Title V, § 502(b), Nov. 8, 1984, 98 Stat. 3276.)

### HISTORICAL AND STATUTORY NOTES

**Transfer of Functions**

For transfer of certain enforcement functions of Administrator or other official of the Environmental Protection Agency under this chapter to Federal Inspector, Office of Federal Inspector for the Alaska Natural Gas Transportation System, see note set out under section 6903 of this title.

**Prior Provisions**

A prior section 2006 of Pub.L. 89–272 was renumbered section 2007 and is classified to section 6916 of this title.

**Termination of Reporting Requirements**

For termination, effective May 15, 2000, of provisions of this section relating to transmittal of annual report to Congress, see section 3003 of Pub.L. 104–66, as amended, set out as a note under 31 U.S.C.A. § 1113, and the 19th item on page 164 of House Document No. 103–7.

## § 6916. General authorization

[SWDA § 2007]

**(a) General administration**

There are authorized to be appropriated to the Administrator for the purpose of carrying out the provisions of this chapter, $35,000,000 for the fiscal year ending September 30, 1977, $38,000,000 for the fiscal year ending September 30, 1978, $42,000,000 for the fiscal year ending September 30, 1979, $70,000,000 for the fiscal year ending September 30, 1980, $80,000,000 for the fiscal year ending September 30, 1981, $80,000,000 for the fiscal year ending September 30, 1982, $70,000,000 for the fiscal year ending September 30, 1985, $80,000,000 for the fiscal year ending September 30, 1986, $80,000,000 for the fiscal year ending September 30, 1987, and $80,000,000 for the fiscal year 1988.

**(b) Resource Recovery and Conservation Panels**

Not less than 20 percent of the amount appropriated under subsection (a) of this section, or $5,000,000 per fiscal year, whichever is less, shall be used only for purposes of Resource Recovery and Conservation Panels established under section 6913 of this title (including travel expenses incurred by such panels in carrying out their functions under this chapter).

**(c) Hazardous waste**

Not less than 30 percent of the amount appropriated under subsection (a) of this section shall be used only for purposes of carrying out subchapter III of this chapter (relating to hazardous waste) other than section 6931 of this title.

**(d) State and local support**

Not less than 25 per centum of the total amount appropriated under this chapter, up to the amount authorized in section 6948(a)(1) of this title, shall be used only for purposes of support to State, regional, local, and interstate agencies in accordance with subchapter IV of this chapter other than section 6948(a)(2) or 6949 of this title.

**(e) Criminal investigators**

There is authorized to be appropriated to the Administrator $3,246,000 for the fiscal year 1985, $2,408,300 for the fiscal year 1986, $2,529,000 for the fiscal year 1987, and $2,529,000 for the fiscal year 1988 to be used—

(1) for additional officers or employees of the Environmental Protection Agency authorized by the Administrator to conduct criminal investigations (to investigate, or supervise the investigation of, any activity for which a criminal penalty is provided) under this chapter; and

(2) for support costs for such additional officers or employees.

**(f) Underground storage tanks**

(1) There are authorized to be appropriated to the Administrator for the purpose of carrying out the provisions of subchapter IX of this chapter (relating to regulation of underground storage tanks), $10,000,000 for each of the fiscal years 1985 through 1988.

(2) There is authorized to be appropriated $25,000,000 for each of the fiscal years 1985 through 1988 to be used to make grants to the States for purposes of assisting the States in the development and implementation of approved State underground storage tank release detection, prevention, and correction programs under subchapter IX of this chapter.

(Pub.L. 89–272, Title II, § 2007, formerly § 2006, as added Pub.L. 94–580, § 2, Oct. 21, 1976, 90 Stat. 2805, renumbered Pub.L. 96–463, § 4(a), Oct. 15, 1980, 94 Stat. 2055, and amended Pub.L. 96–482, §§ 6, 31(a), Oct. 21, 1980, 94 Stat. 2336, 2352; Pub.L. 98–616, § 2(a), (i), Nov. 8, 1984, 98 Stat. 3222, 3223.)

### HISTORICAL AND STATUTORY NOTES

**Transfer of Functions**

For transfer of certain enforcement functions of Administrator or other official of the Environmental Protection Agency under this chapter to Federal Inspector, Office of Federal Inspector for the Alaska Natural Gas Transportation System, see note set out under section 6903 of this title.

## § 6917. Office of Ombudsman

**[SWDA § 2008]**

**(a) Establishment; functions**

The Administrator shall establish an Office of Ombudsman, to be directed by an Ombudsman. It shall be the function of the Office of Ombudsman to receive individual complaints, grievances, requests for information submitted by any person with respect to any program or requirement under this chapter.

**(b) Authority to render assistance**

The Ombudsman shall render assistance with respect to the complaints, grievances, and requests submitted to the Office of Ombudsman, and shall make appropriate recommendations to the Administrator.

**(c) Effect on procedures for grievances, appeals, or administrative matters**

The establishment of the Office of Ombudsman shall not affect any procedures for grievances, appeals, or administrative matters in any other provision of this chapter, any other provision of law, or any Federal regulation.

**(d) Termination**

The Office of the Ombudsman shall cease to exist 4 years after November 8, 1984.

(Pub.L. 89–272, Title II, § 2008, as added Pub.L. 98–616, Title I, § 103(a), Nov. 8, 1984, 98 Stat. 3225.)

# SUBCHAPTER III—HAZARDOUS WASTE MANAGEMENT

## § 6921. Identification and listing of hazardous waste

**[SWDA § 3001]**

**(a) Criteria for identification or listing**

Not later than eighteen months after October 21, 1976, the Administrator shall, after notice and opportunity for public hearing, and after consultation with appropriate Federal and State agencies, develop and promulgate criteria for identifying the characteristics of hazardous waste, and for listing hazardous waste, which should be subject to the provisions of this subchapter, taking into account toxicity, persistence, and degradability in nature, potential for accumulation in tissue, and other related factors such as flammability, corrosiveness, and other hazardous characteristics. Such criteria shall be revised from time to time as may be appropriate.

**(b) Identification and listing**

(1) Not later than eighteen months after October 21, 1976, and after notice and opportunity for public hearing, the Administrator shall promulgate regulations identifying the characteristics of hazardous waste, and listing particular hazardous wastes (within the meaning of section 6903(5) of this title), which shall be subject to the provisions of this subchapter. Such regulations shall be based on the criteria promulgated under subsection (a) of this section and shall be revised from time to time thereafter as may be appropriate. The Administrator, in cooperation with the Agency for Toxic Substances and Disease Registry and the National Toxicology Program, shall also identify or list those hazardous wastes which shall be subject to the provisions of this subchapter solely because of the presence in such wastes of certain constituents (such as identified carcinogens, mutagens, or teratagens [1]) at levels in excess of levels which endanger human health.

(2)(A) Notwithstanding the provisions of paragraph (1) of this subsection, drilling fluids, produced waters, and other wastes associated with the exploration, development, or production of crude oil or natural gas or geothermal energy shall be subject only to existing State or Federal regulatory programs in lieu of this subchapter until at least 24 months after October 21, 1980, and after promulgation of the regulations in accordance with subparagraphs (B) and (C) of this paragraph. It is the sense of the Congress that such State or Federal programs should include, for waste disposal sites which are to be closed, provisions requiring at least the following:

**(i)** The identification through surveying, platting, or other measures, together with recordation of such information on the public record, so as to assure that the location where such wastes are disposed of can be located in the future; except however, that no such surveying, platting, or other measure identifying the location of a disposal site for drilling fluids and associated wastes shall be required if the distance from the disposal site to the surveyed or platted location to the associated well is less than two hundred lineal feet; and

**(ii)** A chemical and physical analysis of a produced water and a composition of a drilling fluid suspected to contain a hazardous material, with such information to be acquired prior to closure and to be placed on the public record.

**(B)** Not later than six months after completion and submission of the study required by section 6982(m) of this title, the Administrator shall, after public hearings and opportunity for comment, determine either to promulgate regulations under this subchapter for drilling fluids, produced waters, and other wastes associated with the exploration, development, or production of crude oil or natural gas or geothermal energy or that such regulations are unwarranted. The Administrator shall publish his decision in the Federal Register accompanied by an explanation and justification of the reasons for it. In making the decision under this paragraph, the Administrator shall utilize the information developed or accumulated pursuant to the study required under section 6982(m) of this title.

**(C)** The Administrator shall transmit his decision, along with any regulations, if necessary, to both Houses of Congress. Such regulations shall take effect only when authorized by Act of Congress.

**(3)(A)** Notwithstanding the provisions of paragraph (1) of this subsection, each waste listed below shall, except as provided in subparagraph (B) of this paragraph, be subject only to regulation under other applicable provisions of Federal or State law in lieu of this subchapter until at least six months after the date of submission of the applicable study required to be conducted under subsection (f), (n), (*o*), or (p) of section 6982 of this title and after promulgation of regulations in accordance with subparagraph (C) of this paragraph:

**(i)** Fly ash waste, bottom ash waste, slag waste, and flue gas emission control waste generated primarily from the combustion of coal or other fossil fuels.

**(ii)** Solid waste from the extraction, beneficiation, and processing of ores and minerals, including phosphate rock and overburden from the mining of uranium ore.

**(iii)** Cement kiln dust waste.

**(B)(i)** Owners and operators of disposal sites for wastes listed in subparagraph (A) may be required by the Administrator, through regulations prescribed under authority of section 6912 of this title—

**(I)** as to disposal sites for such wastes which are to be closed, to identify the locations of such sites through surveying, platting, or other measures, together with recordation of such information on the public record, to assure that the locations where such wastes are disposed of are known and can be located in the future, and

**(II)** to provide chemical and physical analysis and composition of such wastes, based on available information, to be placed on the public record.

**(ii)(I)** In conducting any study under subsection (f), (n), (*o*), or (p), of section 6982 of this title, any officer, employee, or authorized representative of the Environmental Protection Agency, duly designated by the Administrator, is authorized, at reasonable times and as reasonably necessary for the purposes of such study, to enter any establishment where any waste subject to such study is generated, stored, treated, disposed of, or transported from; to inspect, take samples, and conduct monitoring and testing; and to have access to and copy records relating to such waste. Each such inspection shall be commenced and completed with reasonable promptness. If the officer, employee, or authorized representative obtains any samples prior to leaving the premises, he shall give to the owner, operator, or agent in charge a receipt describing the sample obtained and if requested a portion of each such sample equal in volume or weight to the portion retained. If any analysis is made of such samples, or monitoring and testing performed, a copy of the results shall be furnished promptly to the owner, operator, or agent in charge.

**(II)** Any records, reports, or information obtained from any person under subclause (I) shall be available to the public, except that upon a showing satisfactory to the Administrator by any person that records, reports, or information, or particular part thereof, to which the Administrator has access under this subparagraph if made public, would divulge information entitled to protection under section 1905 of Title 18, the

Administrator shall consider such information or particular portion thereof confidential in accordance with the purposes of that section, except that such record, report, document, or information may be disclosed to other officers, employees, or authorized representatives of the United States concerned with carrying out this chapter. Any person not subject to the provisions of section 1905 of Title 18 who knowingly and willfully divulges or discloses any information entitled to protection under this subparagraph shall, upon conviction, be subject to a fine of not more than $5,000 or to imprisonment not to exceed one year, or both.

**(iii)** The Administrator may prescribe regulations, under the authority of this chapter, to prevent radiation exposure which presents an unreasonable risk to human health from the use in construction or land reclamation (with or without revegetation) of (I) solid waste from the extraction, beneficiation, and processing of phosphate rock or (II) overburden from the mining of uranium ore.

**(iv)** Whenever on the basis of any information the Administrator determines that any person is in violation of any requirement of this subparagraph, the Administrator shall give notice to the violator of his failure to comply with such requirement. If such violation extends beyond the thirtieth day after the Administrator's notification, the Administrator may issue an order requiring compliance within a specified time period or the Administrator may commence a civil action in the United States district court in the district in which the violation occurred for appropriate relief, including a temporary or permanent injunction.

**(C)** Not later than six months after the date of submission of the applicable study required to be conducted under subsection (f), (n), (*o*), or (p), of section 6982 of this title, the Administrator shall, after public hearings and opportunity for comment, either determine to promulgate regulations under this subchapter for each waste listed in subparagraph (A) of this paragraph or determine that such regulations are unwarranted. The Administrator shall publish his determination, which shall be based on information developed or accumulated pursuant to such study, public hearings, and comment, in the Federal Register accompanied by an explanation and justification of the reasons for it.

**(c) Petition by State Governor**

At any time after the date eighteen months after October 21, 1976, the Governor of any State may petition the Administrator to identify or list a material as a hazardous waste. The Administrator shall act upon such petition within ninety days following his receipt thereof and shall notify the Governor of such action. If the Administrator denies such petition because of financial considerations, in providing such notice to the Governor he shall include a statement concerning such considerations.

**(d) Small quantity generator waste**

**(1)** By March 31, 1986, the Administrator shall promulgate standards under sections 6922, 6923, and 6924 of this title for hazardous waste generated by a generator in a total quantity of hazardous waste greater than one hundred kilograms but less than one thousand kilograms during a calendar month.

**(2)** The standards referred to in paragraph (1), including standards applicable to the legitimate use, reuse, recycling, and reclamation of such wastes, may vary from the standards applicable to hazardous waste generated by larger quantity generators, but such standards shall be sufficient to protect human health and the environment.

**(3)** Not later than two hundred and seventy days after November 8, 1984, any hazardous waste which is part of a total quantity generated by a generator generating greater than one hundred kilograms but less than one thousand kilograms during one calendar month and which is shipped off the premises on which such waste is generated shall be accompanied by a copy of the Environmental Protection Agency Uniform Hazardous Waste Manifest form signed by the generator. This form shall contain the following information:

**(A)** the name and address of the generator of the waste;

**(B)** the United States Department of Transportation description of the waste, including the proper shipping name, hazard class, and identification number (UN/NA), if applicable;

**(C)** the number and type of containers;

**(D)** the quantity of waste being transported; and

**(E)** the name and address of the facility designated to receive the waste.

If subparagraph (B) is not applicable, in lieu of the description referred to in such subparagraph (B), the form shall contain the Environmental Protection Agency identification number, or a generic description of the waste, or a description of the waste by hazardous waste characteristic. Additional requirements related to the manifest form shall apply only if determined necessary by the Administrator to protect human health and the environment.

**(4)** The Administrator's responsibility under this subchapter to protect human health and the environment may require the promulgation of standards under this subchapter for hazardous wastes which are generated by any generator who does not generate more than one hundred kilograms of hazardous waste in a calendar month.

(5) Until the effective date of standards required to be promulgated under paragraph (1), any hazardous waste identified or listed under this section generated by any generator during any calendar month in a total quantity greater than one hundred kilograms but less than one thousand kilograms, which is not treated, stored, or disposed of at a hazardous waste treatment, storage, or disposal facility with a permit under section 6925 of this title, shall be disposed of only in a facility which is permitted, licensed, or registered by a State to manage municipal or industrial solid waste.

(6) Standards promulgated as provided in paragraph (1) shall, at a minimum, require that all treatment, storage, or disposal of hazardous wastes generated by generators referred to in paragraph (1) shall occur at a facility with interim status or a permit under this subchapter, except that onsite storage of hazardous waste generated by a generator generating a total quantity of hazardous waste greater than one hundred kilograms, but less than one thousand kilograms during a calendar month, may occur without the requirement of a permit for up to one hundred and eighty days. Such onsite storage may occur without the requirement of a permit for not more than six thousand kilograms for up to two hundred and seventy days if such generator must ship or haul such waste over two hundred miles.

(7)(A) Nothing in this subsection shall be construed to affect or impair the validity of regulations promulgated by the Secretary of Transportation pursuant to chapter 51 of Title 49.

(B) Nothing in this subsection shall be construed to affect, modify, or render invalid any requirements in regulations promulgated prior to January 1, 1983 applicable to any acutely hazardous waste identified or listed under this section which is generated by any generator during any calendar month in a total quantity less than one thousand kilograms.

(8) Effective March 31, 1986, unless the Administrator promulgates standards as provided in paragraph (1) of this subsection prior to such date, hazardous waste generated by any generator in a total quantity greater than one hundred kilograms but less than one thousand kilograms during a calendar month shall be subject to the following requirements until the standards referred to in paragraph (1) of this subsection have become effective:

(A) the notice requirements of paragraph (3) of this subsection shall apply and in addition, the information provided in the form shall include the name of the waste transporters and the name and address of the facility designated to receive the waste;

(B) except in the case of the onsite storage referred to in paragraph (6) of this subsection, the treatment, storage, or disposal of such waste shall occur at a facility with interim status or a permit under this subchapter;

(C) generators of such waste shall file manifest exception reports as required of generators producing greater amounts of hazardous waste per month except that such reports shall be filed by January 31, for any waste shipment occurring in the last half of the preceding calendar year, and by July 31, for any waste shipment occurring in the first half of the calendar year; and

(D) generators of such waste shall retain for three years a copy of the manifest signed by the designated facility that has received the waste.

Nothing in this paragraph shall be construed as a determination of the standards appropriate under paragraph (1).

(9) The last sentence of section 6930(b) of this title shall not apply to regulations promulgated under this subsection.

**(e) Specified wastes**

(1) Not later than 6 months after November 8, 1984, the Administrator shall, where appropriate, list under subsection (b)(1) of this section, additional wastes containing chlorinated dioxins or chlorinated-dibenzofurans. Not later than one year after November 8, 1984, the Administrator shall, where appropriate, list under subsection (b)(1) of this section wastes containing remaining halogenated dioxins and halogenated-dibenzofurans.

(2) Not later than fifteen months after November 8, 1984, the Administrator shall make a determination of whether or not to list under subsection (b)(1) of this section the following wastes: Chlorinated Aliphatics, Dioxin, Dimethyl Hydrazine, TDI (toluene diisocyanate), Carbamates, Bromacil, Linuron, Organo-bromines, solvents, refining wastes, chlorinated aromatics, dyes and pigments, inorganic chemical industry wastes, lithium batteries, coke byproducts, paint production wastes, and coal slurry pipeline effluent.

**(f) Delisting procedures**

(1) When evaluating a petition to exclude a waste generated at a particular facility from listing under this section, the Administrator shall consider factors (including additional constituents) other than those for which the waste was listed if the Administrator has a reasonable basis to believe that such additional factors could cause the waste to be a hazardous waste. The Administrator shall provide notice and opportunity for comment on these additional factors before granting or denying such petition.

(2)(A) To the maximum extent practicable the Administrator shall publish in the Federal Register a proposal to grant or deny a petition referred to in paragraph (1) within twelve months after receiving a complete application to exclude a waste generated at a particular facility from being regulated as a hazardous waste and shall grant or deny such a petition within twenty-four months after receiving a complete application.

**(B)** The temporary granting of such a petition prior to November 8, 1984, without the opportunity for public comment and the full consideration of such comments shall not continue for more than twenty-four months after November 8, 1984. If a final decision to grant or deny such a petition has not been promulgated after notice and opportunity for public comment within the time limit prescribed by the preceding sentence, any such temporary granting of such petition shall cease to be in effect.

**(g) EP toxicity**

Not later than twenty-eight months after November 8, 1984, the Administrator shall examine the deficiencies of the extraction procedure toxicity characteristic as a predictor of the leaching potential of wastes and make changes in the extraction procedure toxicity characteristic, including changes in the leaching media, as are necessary to insure that it accurately predicts the leaching potential of wastes which pose a threat to human health and the environment when mismanaged.

**(h) Additional characteristics**

Not later than two years after November 8, 1984, the Administrator shall promulgate regulations under this section identifying additional characteristics of hazardous waste, including measures or indicators of toxicity.

**(i) Clarification of household waste exclusion**

A resource recovery facility recovering energy from the mass burning of municipal solid waste shall not be deemed to be treating, storing, disposing of, or otherwise managing hazardous wastes for the purposes of regulation under this subchapter, if—

**(1)** such facility—

**(A)** receives and burns only—

**(i)** household waste (from single and multiple dwellings, hotels, motels, and other residential sources), and

**(ii)** solid waste from commercial or industrial sources that does not contain hazardous waste identified or listed under this section, and

**(B)** does not accept hazardous wastes identified or listed under this section, and

**(2)** the owner or operator of such facility has established contractual requirements or other appropriate notification or inspection procedures to assure that hazardous wastes are not received at or burned in such facility.

(Pub.L. 89–272, Title II, § 3001, as added Pub.L. 94–580, § 2, Oct. 21, 1976, 90 Stat. 2806, and amended Pub.L. 96–482, § 7, Oct. 21, 1980, 94 Stat. 2336; Pub.L. 98–616, Title II, §§ 221(a), 222, 223(a), Nov. 8, 1984, 98 Stat. 3248, 3251, 3252; Pub.L. 104–119, § 4(1), Mar. 26, 1996, 110 Stat. 833.)

[1] So in original. Probably should be "teratogens".

## HISTORICAL AND STATUTORY NOTES

**References in Text**

Chapter 51 of Title 49, referred to in subsec.(d)(7)(A), is 49 U.S.C.A. § 5101 et seq.

**Transfer of Functions**

For transfer of certain enforcement functions of Administrator or other official of the Environmental Protection Agency under this chapter to Federal Inspector, Office of Federal Inspector for the Alaska Natural Gas Transportation System, see note set out under section 6903 of this title.

**Administrative Burdens; Small Quantity Generators; Retention of Current System; Report to Congress**

Section 221(e) of Pub.L. 98–616 provided that: "The Administrator of the Environmental Protection Agency, in conjunction with the Secretary of Transportation, shall prepare and submit to the Congress a report on the feasibility of easing the administrative burden on small quantity generators, increasing compliance with statutory and regulatory requirements, and simplifying enforcement efforts through a program of licensing hazardous waste transporters to assume the responsibilities of small quantity generators relating to the preparation of manifests and associated recordkeeping and reporting requirements. The report shall examine the appropriate licensing requirements under such a program including the need for financial assurances by licensed transporters and shall make recommendations on provisions and requirements for such a program including the appropriate division of responsibilities between the Department of Transportation and the Environmental Protection Administration. Such report shall be submitted to the Congress not later than April 1, 1987."

**Ash Management and Disposal**

Pub.L. 101–549, Title III, § 306, Nov. 15, 1990, 104 Stat. 2584, provided that: "For a period of 2 years after the date of enactment of the Clean Air Act Amendments of 1990 [Nov. 15, 1990], ash from solid waste incineration units burning municipal waste shall not be regulated by the Administrator of the Environmental Protection Agency pursuant to section 3001 of the Solid Waste Disposal Act [this section]. Such reference and limitation shall not be construed to prejudice, endorse or otherwise affect any activity by the Administrator following the 2-year period from the date of enactment of the Clean Air Act Amendments of 1990 [Nov. 15, 1990]."

**Educational Institutions; Accumulation, Storage and Disposal of Hazardous Wastes; Study**

Section 221(f) of Pub.L. 98–616, as amended Pub.L. 107–110, Title X, § 1076(aa), Jan. 8, 2002, 115 Stat. 2093, provided that:

"(1) The Administrator of the Environmental Protection Agency shall, in consultation with the Secretary of Education, the States, and appropriate educational associations, conduct a comprehensive study of problems associated with the accumulation, storage and disposal of hazardous wastes from educational institutions. The study shall include an investigation of the feasibility and availability of environmentally sound methods for the treatment, storage or disposal of hazardous waste from such institutions, taking into account the types and quantities of such waste which are generated by these institutions, and the nonprofit nature of these institutions.

"(2) The Administrator shall submit a report to the Congress containing the findings of the study carried out under paragraph (1) not later than April 1, 1987.

"(3) For purposes of this subsection—

"(A) the term 'hazardous waste' means hazardous waste which is listed or identified under Section 3001 of the Solid Waste Disposal Act [this section];

"(B) the term 'educational institution' includes, but shall not be limited to,

"(i) secondary schools as defined in section 9101 of the Elementary and Secondary Education Act of 1965 [20 U.S.C.A. § 7801]; and

"(ii) institutions of higher education as defined in section 1201(a) of the Higher Education Act of 1965 [section 1141(a) of Title 20]."

[Except as otherwise provided, amendments by Pub.L. 107–110 effective Jan. 8, 2002, see Pub.L. 107–110, § 5, set out as a note under 20 U.S.C.A. § 6301.]

**Regulation Under the Solid Waste Disposal Act**

Pub.L. 99–499, Title I, § 124(b), Oct. 17, 1986, 100 Stat. 1689, provided that: "Unless the Administrator of the Environmental Protection Agency promulgates regulations under subtitle C of the Solid Waste Disposal Act [this subchapter] addressing the extraction of wastes from landfills as part of the process of recovering methane from such landfills, the owner and operator of equipment used to recover methane from a landfill shall not be deemed to be managing, generating, transporting, treating, storing, or disposing of hazardous or liquid wastes within the meaning of that subtitle. If the aqueous or hydrocarbon phase of the condensate or any other waste material removed from the gas recovered from the landfill meets any of the characteristics identified under section 3001 of subtitle C of the Solid Waste Disposal Act [this section], the preceding sentence shall not apply and such condensate phase or other waste material shall be deemed a hazardous waste under that subtitle, and shall be regulated accordingly."

**Small Quantity Generator Waste; Administrator of Environmental Protection Agency; Information and Education; Waste Generators**

Section 221(b) of Pub.L. 98–616 provided that: "The Administrator of the Environmental Protection Agency shall undertake activities to inform and educate the waste generators of their responsibilities under the amendments made by this section [enacting subsec. (d) of this section] during the period within thirty months after the enactment of the Hazardous and Solid Waste Amendments of 1984 [Nov. 8, 1984] to help assure compliance."

**Study of Existing Manifest System for Hazardous Wastes as Applicable to Small Quantity Generators; Submittal to Congress**

Section 221(d) of Pub.L. 98–616 provided that: "The Administrator of the Environmental Protection Agency shall cause to be studied the existing manifest system for hazardous wastes as it applies to small quantity generators and recommend whether the current system shall be retained or whether a new system should be introduced. The study shall include an analysis of the cost versus the benefits of the system studied as well as an analysis of the ease of retrieving and collating information and identifying a given substance. Finally, any new proposal shall include a list of those standards that are necessary to protect human health and the environment. Such study shall be submitted to the Congress not later than April 1, 1987."

## § 6922. Standards applicable to generators of hazardous waste

### [SWDA § 3002]

**(a) In general**

Not later than eighteen months after October 21, 1976, and after notice and opportunity for public hearings and after consultation with appropriate Federal and State agencies, the Administrator shall promulgate regulations establishing such standards, applicable to generators of hazardous waste identified or listed under this subchapter, as may be necessary to protect human health and the environment. Such standards shall establish requirements respecting—

(1) recordkeeping practices that accurately identify the quantities of such hazardous waste generated, the constituents thereof which are significant in quantity or in potential harm to human health or the environment, and the disposition of such wastes;

(2) labeling practices for any containers used for the storage, transport, or disposal of such hazardous waste such as will identify accurately such waste;

(3) use of appropriate containers for such hazardous waste;

(4) furnishing of information on the general chemical composition of such hazardous waste to persons transporting, treating, storing, or disposing of such wastes;

(5) use of a manifest system and any other reasonable means necessary to assure that all such hazardous waste generated is designated for treatment, storage, or disposal in, and arrives at, treatment, storage, or disposal facilities (other than facilities on the premises where the waste is generated) for which a permit has been issued as provided in this subchapter, or pursuant to title I of the Marine Protection, Research, and Sanctuaries Act (86 Stat. 1052) [33 U.S.C.A. § 1411 et seq.]; and

(6) submission of reports to the Administrator (or the State agency in any case in which such

agency carries out a permit program pursuant to this subchapter) at least once every two years, setting out—

(A) the quantities and nature of hazardous waste identified or listed under this subchapter that he has generated during the year;

(B) the disposition of all hazardous waste reported under subparagraph (A);

(C) the efforts undertaken during the year to reduce the volume and toxicity of waste generated; and

(D) the changes in volume and toxicity of waste actually achieved during the year in question in comparison with previous years, to the extent such information is available for years prior to November 8, 1984.

**(b) Waste minimization**

Effective September 1, 1985, the manifest required by subsection (a)(5) of this section shall contain a certification by the generator that—

(1) the generator of the hazardous waste has a program in place to reduce the volume or quantity and toxicity of such waste to the degree determined by the generator to be economically practicable; and

(2) the proposed method of treatment, storage, or disposal is that practicable method currently available to the generator which minimizes the present and future threat to human health and the environment.

(Pub.L. 89–272, Title II, § 3002, as added Pub.L. 94–580, § 2, Oct. 21, 1976, 90 Stat. 2806, and amended Pub.L. 95–609, § 7(f), Nov. 8, 1978, 92 Stat. 3082; Pub.L. 96–482, § 8, Oct. 21, 1980, 94 Stat. 2338; Pub.L. 98–616, Title II, § 224(a), Nov. 8, 1984, 98 Stat. 3252.)

### HISTORICAL AND STATUTORY NOTES

**References in Text**

The Marine Protection, Research, and Sanctuaries Act, referred to in subsec. (a)(5), probably means the Marine Protection, Research, and Sanctuaries Act of 1972, Pub.L. 92–532, Oct. 23, 1972, 86 Stat. 1052, as amended. Title I of the Marine Protection, Research, and Sanctuaries Act of 1972 is classified generally to subchapter I (section 1411 et seq.) of chapter 27 of Title 33, Navigation and Navigable Waters. For complete classification of this Act to the Code, see Short Title note set out under section 1401 of Title 33 and Tables.

**Transfer of Functions**

For transfer of certain enforcement functions of Administrator or other official of the Environmental Protection Agency under this chapter to Federal Inspector, Office of Federal Inspector for the Alaska Natural Gas Transportation System, see note set out under section 6903 of this title.

## § 6923. Standards applicable to transporters of hazardous waste

**[SWDA § 3003]**

**(a) Standards**

Not later than eighteen months after October 21, 1976, and after opportunity for public hearings, the Administrator, after consultation with the Secretary of Transportation and the States, shall promulgate regulations establishing such standards, applicable to transporters of hazardous waste identified or listed under this subchapter, as may be necessary to protect human health and the environment. Such standards shall include but need not be limited to requirements respecting—

(1) recordkeeping concerning such hazardous waste transported, and their source and delivery points;

(2) transportation of such waste only if properly labeled;

(3) compliance with the manifest system referred to in section 6922(5) of this title; and

(4) transportation of all such hazardous waste only to the hazardous waste treatment, storage, or disposal facilities which the shipper designates on the manifest form to be a facility holding a permit issued under this subchapter, or pursuant to title I of the Marine Protection, Research, and Sanctuaries Act (86 Stat. 1052) [33 U.S.C.A. § 1411 et seq.].

**(b) Coordination with regulations of Secretary of Transportation**

In case of any hazardous waste identified or listed under this subchapter which is subject to chapter 51 of Title 49, the regulations promulgated by the Administrator under this section shall be consistent with the requirements of such Act and the regulations thereunder. The Administrator is authorized to make recommendations to the Secretary of Transportation respecting the regulations of such hazardous waste under the Hazardous Materials Transportation Act and for addition of materials to be covered by such Act.

**(c) Fuel from hazardous waste**

Not later than two years after November 8, 1984, and after opportunity for public hearing, the Administrator shall promulgate regulations establishing standards, applicable to transporters of fuel produced (1) from any hazardous waste identified or listed under section 6921 of this title, or (2) from any hazardous waste identified or listed under section 6921 of this title and any other material, as may be necessary to protect human health and the environment. Such standards may include any of the requirements set forth in paragraphs (1) through (4) of subsection (a) of this section as may be appropriate.

(Pub.L. 89–272, Title II, § 3003, as added Pub.L. 94–580, § 2, Oct. 21, 1976, 90 Stat. 2807, and amended Pub.L. 95–609, § 7(g), Nov. 8, 1978, 92 Stat. 3082; Pub.L. 98–616, Title II, § 204(b)(2), Nov. 8, 1984, 98 Stat. 3238.)

### HISTORICAL AND STATUTORY NOTES

**References in Text**

Section 6922(5) of this title, referred to in subsec. (a)(3), was redesignated section 6922(a)(5) of this title, by Pub.L. 98–616, Title II, § 224(a)(1), Nov. 8, 1984, 98 Stat. 3253.

The Marine Protection, Research, and Sanctuaries Act, referred to in subsec. (a)(4), probably means the Marine Protection, Research, and Sanctuaries Act of 1972, Pub.L. 92–532, Oct. 23, 1972, 86 Stat. 1052, as amended. Title I of the Marine Protection, Research, and Sanctuaries Act of 1972 is classified generally to subchapter I (section 1411 et seq.) of chapter 27 of Title 33, Navigation and Navigable Waters. For complete classification of this Act to the Code, see Short Title note set out under section 1401 of Title 33 and Tables.

Chapter 51 of Title 49, referred to in subsec. (b), is 49 U.S.C.A. § 5101 et seq.

**Transfer of Functions**

For transfer of certain enforcement functions of Administrator or other official of the Environmental Protection Agency under this chapter to Federal Inspector, Office of Federal Inspector for the Alaska Natural Gas Transportation System, see note set out under section 6903 of this title.

## § 6924. Standards applicable to owners and operators of hazardous waste treatment, storage, and disposal facilities

[SWDA § 3004]

### (a) In general

Not later than eighteen months after October 21, 1976, and after opportunity for public hearings and after consultation with appropriate Federal and State agencies, the Administrator shall promulgate regulations establishing such performance standards, applicable to owners and operators of facilities for the treatment, storage, or disposal of hazardous waste identified or listed under this subchapter, as may be necessary to protect human health and the environment. In establishing such standards the Administrator shall, where appropriate, distinguish in such standards between requirements appropriate for new facilities and for facilities in existence on the date of promulgation of such regulations. Such standards shall include, but need not be limited to, requirements respecting—

(1) maintaining records of all hazardous wastes identified or listed under this chapter which is treated, stored, or disposed of, as the case may be, and the manner in which such wastes were treated, stored, or disposed of;

(2) satisfactory reporting, monitoring, and inspection and compliance with the manifest system referred to in section 6922(5) of this title;

(3) treatment, storage, or disposal of all such waste received by the facility pursuant to such operating methods, techniques, and practices as may be satisfactory to the Administrator;

(4) the location, design, and construction of such hazardous waste treatment, disposal, or storage facilities;

(5) contingency plans for effective action to minimize unanticipated damage from any treatment, storage, or disposal of any such hazardous waste;

(6) the maintenance of operation of such facilities and requiring such additional qualifications as to ownership, continuity of operation, training for personnel, and financial responsibility (including financial responsibility for corrective action) as may be necessary or desirable; and

(7) compliance with the requirements of section 6925 of this title respecting permits for treatment, storage, or disposal.

No private entity shall be precluded by reason of criteria established under paragraph (6) from the ownership or operation of facilities providing hazardous waste treatment, storage, or disposal services where such entity can provide assurances of financial responsibility and continuity of operation consistent with the degree and duration of risks associated with the treatment, storage, or disposal of specified hazardous waste.

### (b) Salt dome formations, salt bed formations, underground mines and caves

(1) Effective on November 8, 1984, the placement of any noncontainerized or bulk liquid hazardous waste in any salt dome formation, salt bed formation, underground mine, or cave is prohibited until such time as—

(A) the Administrator has determined, after notice and opportunity for hearings on the record in the affected areas, that such placement is protective of human health and the environment;

(B) the Administrator has promulgated performance and permitting standards for such facilities under this subchapter, and;

(C) a permit has been issued under section 6925(c) of this title for the facility concerned.

(2) Effective on November 8, 1984, the placement of any hazardous waste other than a hazardous waste referred to in paragraph (1) in a salt dome formation, salt bed formation, underground mine, or cave is prohibited until such time as a permit has been issued under section 6925(c) of this title for the facility concerned.

(3) No determination made by the Administrator under subsection (d), (e), or (g) of this section regarding any hazardous waste to which such subsection (d), (e), or (g) of this section applies shall affect the prohibition contained in paragraph (1) or (2) of this subsection.

(4) Nothing in this subsection shall apply to the Department of Energy Waste Isolation Pilot Project in New Mexico.

**(c) Liquids in landfills**

(1) Effective 6 months after November 8, 1984, the placement of bulk or noncontainerized liquid hazardous waste or free liquids contained in hazardous waste (whether or not absorbents have been added) in any landfill is prohibited. Prior to such date the requirements (as in effect on April 30, 1983) promulgated under this section by the Administrator regarding liquid hazardous waste shall remain in force and effect to the extent such requirements are applicable to the placement of bulk or noncontainerized liquid hazardous waste, or free liquids contained in hazardous waste, in landfills.

(2) Not later than fifteen months after November 8, 1984, the Administrator shall promulgate final regulations which—

**(A)** minimize the disposal of containerized liquid hazardous waste in landfills, and

**(B)** minimize the presence of free liquids in containerized hazardous waste to be disposed of in landfills.

Such regulations shall also prohibit the disposal in landfills of liquids that have been absorbed in materials that biodegrade or that release liquids when compressed as might occur during routine landfill operations. Prior to the date on which such final regulations take effect, the requirements (as in effect on April 30, 1983) promulgated under this section by the Administrator shall remain in force and effect to the extent such requirements are applicable to the disposal of containerized liquid hazardous waste, or free liquids contained in hazardous waste, in landfills.

(3) Effective twelve months after November 8, 1984, the placement of any liquid which is not a hazardous waste in a landfill for which a permit is required under section 6925(c) of this title or which is operating pursuant to interim status granted under section 6925(e) of this title is prohibited unless the owner or operator of such landfill demonstrates to the Administrator, or the Administrator determines, that—

**(A)** the only reasonably available alternative to the placement in such landfill is placement in a landfill or unlined surface impoundment, whether or not permitted under section 6925(c) of this title or operating pursuant to interim status under section 6925(e) of this title, which contains, or may reasonably be anticipated to contain, hazardous waste; and

**(B)** placement in such owner or operator's landfill will not present a risk of contamination of any underground source of drinking water.

As used in subparagraph (B), the term "underground source of drinking water" has the same meaning as provided in regulations under the Safe Drinking Water Act (title XIV of the Public Health Service Act) [42 U.S.C.A. § 300f et seq.].

(4) No determination made by the Administrator under subsection (d), (e), or (g) of this section regarding any hazardous waste to which such subsection (d), (e), or (g) of this section applies shall affect the prohibition contained in paragraph (1) of this subsection.

**(d) Prohibitions on land disposal of specified wastes**

(1) Effective 32 months after November 8, 1984 (except as provided in subsection (f) of this section with respect to underground injection into deep injection wells), the land disposal of the hazardous wastes referred to in paragraph (2) is prohibited unless the Administrator determines the prohibition on one or more methods of land disposal of such waste is not required in order to protect human health and the environment for as long as the waste remains hazardous, taking into account—

**(A)** the long-term uncertainties associated with land disposal,

**(B)** the goal of managing hazardous waste in an appropriate manner in the first instance, and

**(C)** the persistence, toxicity, mobility, and propensity to bioaccumulate of such hazardous wastes and their hazardous constituents.

For the purposes of this paragraph, a method of land disposal may not be determined to be protective of human health and the environment for a hazardous waste referred to in paragraph (2) (other than a hazardous waste which has complied with the pretreatment regulations promulgated under subsection (m) of this section), unless, upon application by an interested person, it has been demonstrated to the Administrator, to a reasonable degree of certainty, that there will be no migration of hazardous constituents from the disposal unit or injection zone for as long as the wastes remain hazardous.

(2) Paragraph (1) applies to the following hazardous wastes listed or identified under section 6921 of this title:

**(A)** Liquid hazardous wastes, including free liquids associated with any solid or sludge, containing free cyanides at concentrations greater than or equal to 1,000 mg/l.

**(B)** Liquid hazardous wastes, including free liquids associated with any solid or sludge, containing the following metals (or elements) or compounds of these metals (or elements) at concentrations greater than or equal to those specified below:

**(i)** arsenic and/or compounds (as As) 500 mg/l;

**(ii)** cadmium and/or compounds (as Cd) 100 mg/l;

**(iii)** chromium (VI and/or compounds (as Cr VI)) 500 mg/l;

**(iv)** lead and/or compounds (as Pb) 500 mg/l;

**(v)** mercury and/or compounds (as Hg) 20 mg/l;

**(vi)** nickel and/or compounds (as Ni) 134 mg/l;

**(vii)** selenium and/or compounds (as Se) 100 mg/l; and

**(viii)** thallium and/or compounds (as Th) 130 mg/l.

**(C)** Liquid hazardous waste having a pH less than or equal to two (2.0).

**(D)** Liquid hazardous wastes containing polychlorinated biphenyls at concentrations greater than or equal to 50 ppm.

**(E)** Hazardous wastes containing halogenated organic compounds in total concentration greater than or equal to 1,000 mg/kg.

When necessary to protect human health and the environment, the Administrator shall substitute more stringent concentration levels than the levels specified in subparagraphs (A) through (E).

**(3)** During the period ending forty-eight months after November 8, 1984, this subsection shall not apply to any disposal of contaminated soil or debris resulting from a response action taken under section 9604 or 9606 of this title or a corrective action required under this subchapter.

**(e) Solvents and dioxins**

**(1)** Effective twenty-four months after November 8, 1984 (except as provided in subsection (f) of this section with respect to underground injection into deep injection wells), the land disposal of the hazardous wastes referred to in paragraph (2) is prohibited unless the Administrator determines the prohibition of one or more methods of land disposal of such waste is not required in order to protect human health and the environment for as long as the waste remains hazardous, taking into account the factors referred to in subparagraph (A) through (C) of subsection (d)(1) of this section. For the purposes of this paragraph, a method of land disposal may not be determined to be protective of human health and the environment for a hazardous waste referred to in paragraph (2) (other than a hazardous waste which has complied with the pretreatment regulations promulgated under subsection (m) of this section), unless upon application by an interested person it has been demonstrated to the Administrator, to a reasonable degree of certainty, that there will be no migration of hazardous constituents from the disposal unit or injection zone for as long as the wastes remain hazardous.

**(2)** The hazardous wastes to which the prohibition under paragraph (1) applies are as follows—

**(A)** dioxin-containing hazardous wastes numbered F020, F021, F022, and F023 (as referred to in the proposed rule published by the Administrator in the Federal Register for April 4, 1983), and

**(B)** those hazardous wastes numbered F001, F002, F003, F004, and F005 in regulations promulgated by the Administrator under section 6921 of this title (40 C.F.R. 261.31 (July 1, 1983)), as those regulations are in effect on July 1, 1983.

**(3)** During the period ending forty-eight months after November 8, 1984, this subsection shall not apply to any disposal of contaminated soil or debris resulting from a response action taken under section 9604 or 9606 of this title or a corrective action required under this subchapter.

**(f) Disposal into deep injection wells; specified subsection (d) wastes; solvents and dioxins**

**(1)** Not later than forty-five months after November 8, 1984, the Administrator shall complete a review of the disposal of all hazardous wastes referred to in paragraph (2) of subsection (d) of this section and in paragraph (2) of subsection (e) of this section by underground injection into deep injection wells.

**(2)** Within forty-five months after November 8, 1984, the Administrator shall make a determination regarding the disposal by underground injection into deep injection wells of the hazardous wastes referred to in paragraph (2) of subsection (d) of this section and the hazardous wastes referred to in paragraph (2) of subsection (e) of this section. The Administrator shall promulgate final regulations prohibiting the disposal of such wastes into such wells if it may reasonably be determined that such disposal may not be protective of human health and the environment for as long as the waste remains hazardous, taking into account the factors referred to in subparagraphs (A) through (C) of subsection (d)(1) of this section. In promulgating such regulations, the Administrator shall consider each hazardous waste referred to in paragraph (2) of subsection (d) of this section or in paragraph (2) of subsection (e) of this section which is prohibited from disposal into such wells by any State.

**(3)** If the Administrator fails to make a determination under paragraph (2) for any hazardous waste referred to in paragraph (2) of subsection (d) of this section or in paragraph (2) of subsection (e) of this section within forty-five months after November 8, 1984, such hazardous waste shall be prohibited from disposal into any deep injection well.

(4) As used in this subsection, the term "deep injection well" means a well used for the underground injection of hazardous waste other than a well to which section 6979a(a) of this title applies.

**(g) Additional land disposal prohibition determinations**

(1) Not later than twenty-four months after November 8, 1984, the Administrator shall submit a schedule to Congress for—

(A) reviewing all hazardous wastes listed (as of November 8, 1984) under section 6921 of this title other than those wastes which are referred to in subsection (d) or (e) of this section; and

(B) taking action under paragraph (5) of this subsection with respect to each such hazardous waste.

(2) The Administrator shall base the schedule on a ranking of such listed wastes considering their intrinsic hazard and their volume such that decisions regarding the land disposal of high volume hazardous wastes with high intrinsic hazard shall, to the maximum extent possible, be made by the date forty-five months after November 8, 1984. Decisions regarding low volume hazardous wastes with lower intrinsic hazard shall be made by the date sixty-six months after November 8, 1984.

(3) The preparation and submission of the schedule under this subsection shall not be subject to the Paperwork Reduction Act of 1980. No hearing on the record shall be required for purposes of preparation or submission of the schedule. The schedule shall not be subject to judicial review.

(4) The schedule under this subsection shall require that the Administrator shall promulgate regulations in accordance with paragraph (5) or make a determination under paragraph (5)—

(A) for at least one-third of all hazardous wastes referred to in paragraph (1) by the date forty-five months after November 8, 1984;

(B) for at least two-thirds of all such listed wastes by the date fifty-five months after November 8, 1984; and

(C) for all such listed wastes and for all hazardous wastes identified under 6921 of this title [1] by the date sixty-six months after November 8, 1984.

In the case of any hazardous waste identified or listed under section 6921 of this title after November 8, 1984, the Administrator shall determine whether such waste shall be prohibited from one or more methods of land disposal in accordance with paragraph (5) within six months after the date of such identification or listing.

(5) Not later than the date specified in the schedule published under this subsection, the Administrator shall promulgate final regulations prohibiting one or more methods of land disposal of the hazardous wastes listed on such schedule except for methods of land disposal which the Administrator determines will be protective of human health and the environment for as long as the waste remains hazardous, taking into account the factors referred to in subparagraphs (A) through (C) of subsection (d)(1) of this section. For the purposes of this paragraph, a method of land disposal may not be determined to be protective of human health and the environment (except with respect to a hazardous waste which has complied with the pretreatment regulations promulgated under subsection (m) of this section) unless, upon application by an interested person, it has been demonstrated to the Administrator, to a reasonable degree of certainty, that there will be no migration of hazardous constituents from the disposal unit or injection zone for as long as the wastes remain hazardous.

(6)(A) If the Administrator fails (by the date forty-five months after November 8, 1984) to promulgate regulations or make a determination under paragraph (5) for any hazardous waste which is included in the first one-third of the schedule published under this subsection, such hazardous waste may be disposed of in a landfill or surface impoundment only if—

(i) such facility is in compliance with the requirements of subsection (*o*) of this section which are applicable to new facilities (relating to minimum technological requirements); and

(ii) prior to such disposal, the generator has certified to the Administrator that such generator has investigated the availability of treatment capacity and has determined that the use of such landfill or surface impoundment is the only practical alternative to treatment currently available to the generator.

The prohibition contained in this subparagraph shall continue to apply until the Administrator promulgates regulations or makes a determination under paragraph (5) for the waste concerned.

(B) If the Administrator fails (by the date 55 months after November 8, 1984) to promulgate regulations or make a determination under paragraph (5) for any hazardous waste which is included in the first two-thirds of the schedule published under this subsection, such hazardous waste may be disposed of in a landfill or surface impoundment only if—

(i) such facility is in compliance with the requirements of subsection (*o*) of this section which are applicable to new facilities (relating to minimum technological requirements); and

**(ii)** prior to such disposal, the generator has certified to the Administrator that such generator has investigated the availability of treatment capacity and has determined that the use of such landfill or surface impoundment is the only practical alternative to treatment currently available to the generator.

The prohibition contained in this subparagraph shall continue to apply until the Administrator promulgates regulations or makes a determination under paragraph (5) for the waste concerned.

**(C)** If the Administrator fails to promulgate regulations, or make a determination under paragraph (5) for any hazardous waste referred to in paragraph (1) within 66 months after November 8, 1984, such hazardous waste shall be prohibited from land disposal.

**(7)** Solid waste identified as hazardous based solely on one or more characteristics shall not be subject to this subsection, any prohibitions under subsection (d), (e), or (f) of this section, or any requirement promulgated under subsection (m) of this section (other than any applicable specific methods of treatment, as provided in paragraph (8)) if the waste—

**(A)** is treated in a treatment system that subsequently discharges to waters of the United States pursuant to a permit issued under section 1342 of Title 33, treated for the purposes of the pretreatment requirements of section 1317 of Title 33, or treated in a zero discharge system that, prior to any permanent land disposal, engages in treatment that is equivalent to treatment required under section 1342 of Title 33 for discharges to waters of the United States, as determined by the Administrator; and

**(B)** no longer exhibits a hazardous characteristic prior to management in any land-based solid waste management unit.

**(8)** Solid waste that otherwise qualifies under paragraph (7) shall nevertheless be required to meet any applicable specific methods of treatment specified for such waste by the Administrator under subsection (m) of this section, including those specified in the rule promulgated by the Administrator June 1, 1990, prior to management in a land-based unit as part of a treatment system specified in paragraph (7)(A). No solid waste may qualify under paragraph (7) that would generate toxic gases, vapors, or fumes due to the presence of cyanide when exposed to pH conditions between 2.0 and 12.5.

**(9)** Solid waste identified as hazardous based on one or more characteristics alone shall not be subject to this subsection, any prohibitions under subsection (d), (e), or (f) of this section, or any requirement promulgated under subsection (m) of this section if the waste no longer exhibits a hazardous characteristic at the point of injection in any Class I injection well permitted under section 300h–1 of this title.

**(10)** Not later than five years after March 26, 1996, the Administrator shall complete a study of hazardous waste managed pursuant to paragraph (7) or (9) to characterize the risks to human health or the environment associated with such management. In conducting this study, the Administrator shall evaluate the extent to which risks are adequately addressed under existing State or Federal programs and whether unaddressed risks could be better addressed under such laws or programs. Upon receipt of additional information or upon completion of such study and as necessary to protect human health and the environment, the Administrator may impose additional requirements under existing Federal laws, including subsection (m)(1) of this section, or rely on other State or Federal programs or authorities to address such risks. In promulgating any treatment standards pursuant to subsection (m)(1) of this section under the previous sentence, the Administrator shall take into account the extent to which treatment is occurring in land-based units as part of a treatment system specified in paragraph (7)(A).

**(11)** Nothing in paragraph (7) or (9) shall be interpreted or applied to restrict any inspection or enforcement authority under the provisions of this chapter.

**(h) Variance from land disposal prohibitions**

**(1)** A prohibition in regulations under subsection (d), (e), (f), or (g) of this section shall be effective immediately upon promulgation.

**(2)** The Administrator may establish an effective date different from the effective date which would otherwise apply under subsection (d), (e), (f), or (g) of this section with respect to a specific hazardous waste which is subject to a prohibition under subsection (d), (e), (f), or (g) of this section or under regulations under subsection (d), (e), (f), or (g) of this section. Any such other effective date shall be established on the basis of the earliest date on which adequate alternative treatment, recovery, or disposal capacity which protects human health and the environment will be available. Any such other effective date shall in no event be later than 2 years after the effective date of the prohibition which would otherwise apply under subsection (d), (e), (f), or (g) of this section.

**(3)** The Administrator, after notice and opportunity for comment and after consultation with appropriate State agencies in all affected States, may on a case-by-case basis grant an extension of the effective date which would otherwise apply under subsection (d), (e), (f), or (g) of this section or under paragraph (2) for up to one year, where the applicant demonstrates that there is a binding contractual commitment to construct or otherwise provide such alternative capacity but due to circumstances beyond the control of such applicant such alternative capacity cannot reasonably be made available by such effective date. Such extension shall be renewable once for no more than one additional year.

(4) Whenever another effective date (hereinafter referred to as a "variance") is established under paragraph (2), or an extension is granted under paragraph (3), with respect to any hazardous waste, during the period for which such variance or extension is in effect, such hazardous waste may be disposed of in a landfill or surface impoundment only if such facility is in compliance with the requirements of subsection (*o*) of this section.

**(i) Publication of determination**

If the Administrator determines that a method of land disposal will be protective of human health and the environment, he shall promptly publish in the Federal Register notice of such determination, together with an explanation of the basis for such determination.

**(j) Storage of hazardous waste prohibited from land disposal**

In the case of any hazardous waste which is prohibited from one or more methods of land disposal under this section (or under regulations promulgated by the Administrator under any provision of this section) the storage of such hazardous waste is prohibited unless such storage is solely for the purpose of the accumulation of such quantities of hazardous waste as are necessary to facilitate proper recovery, treatment or disposal.

**(k) "Land disposal" defined**

For the purposes of this section, the term "land disposal", when used with respect to a specified hazardous waste, shall be deemed to include, but not be limited to, any placement of such hazardous waste in a landfill, surface impoundment, waste pile, injection well, land treatment facility, salt dome formation, salt bed formation, or underground mine or cave.

**(*l*) Ban on dust suppression**

The use of waste or used oil or other material, which is contaminated or mixed with dioxin or any other hazardous waste identified or listed under section 6921 of this title (other than a waste identified solely on the basis of ignitability), for dust suppression or road treatment is prohibited.

**(m) Treatment standards for wastes subject to land disposal prohibition**

(1) Simultaneously with the promulgation of regulations under subsection (d), (e), (f), or (g) of this section prohibiting one or more methods of land disposal of a particular hazardous waste, and as appropriate thereafter, the Administrator shall, after notice and an opportunity for hearings and after consultation with appropriate Federal and State agencies, promulgate regulations specifying those levels or methods of treatment, if any, which substantially diminish the toxicity of the waste or substantially reduce the likelihood of migration of hazardous constituents from the waste so that short-term and long-term threats to human health and the environment are minimized.

(2) If such hazardous waste has been treated to the level or by a method specified in regulations promulgated under this subsection, such waste or residue thereof shall not be subject to any prohibition promulgated under subsection (d), (e), (f), or (g) of this section and may be disposed of in a land disposal facility which meets the requirements of this subchapter. Any regulation promulgated under this subsection for a particular hazardous waste shall become effective on the same date as any applicable prohibition promulgated under subsection (d), (e), (f), or (g) of this section.

**(n) Air emissions**

Not later than thirty months after November 8, 1984, the Administrator shall promulgate such regulations for the monitoring and control of air emissions at hazardous waste treatment, storage, and disposal facilities, including but not limited to open tanks, surface impoundments, and landfills, as may be necessary to protect human health and the environment.

**(*o*) Minimum technological requirements**

(1) The regulations under subsection (a) of this section shall be revised from time to time to take into account improvements in the technology of control and measurement. At a minimum, such regulations shall require, and a permit issued pursuant to section 6925(c) of this title after November 8, 1984, by the Administrator or a State shall require—

(A) for each new landfill or surface impoundment, each new landfill or surface impoundment unit at an existing facility, each replacement of an existing landfill or surface impoundment unit, and each lateral expansion of an existing landfill or surface impoundment unit, for which an application for a final determination regarding issuance of a permit under section 6925(c) of this title is received after November 8, 1984—

(i) the installation of two or more liners and a leachate collection system above (in the case of a landfill) and between such liners; and

(ii) ground water monitoring; and

(B) for each incinerator which receives a permit under section 6925(c) of this title after November 8, 1984, the attainment of the minimum destruction and removal efficiency required by regulations in effect on June 24, 1982.

The requirements of this paragraph shall apply with respect to all waste received after the issuance of the permit.

(2) Paragraph (1)(A)(i) shall not apply if the owner or operator demonstrates to the Administrator, and the Administrator finds for such landfill or surface impoundment, that alternative design and operating practices, together with location characteristics, will prevent the migration of any hazardous constituents into the ground water or surface water at least as effectively as such liners and leachate collection systems.

(3) The double-liner requirement set forth in paragraph (1)(A)(i) may be waived by the Administrator for any monofill, if—

(A) such monofill contains only hazardous wastes from foundry furnace emission controls or metal casting molding sand,

(B) such wastes do not contain constituents which would render the wastes hazardous for reasons other than the Extraction Procedure ("EP") toxicity characteristics set forth in regulations under this subchapter, and

(C) such monofill meets the same requirements as are applicable in the case of a waiver under section 6925(j)(2) or (4) of this title.

(4)(A) Not later than thirty months after November 8, 1984, the Administrator shall promulgate standards requiring that new landfill units, surface impoundment units, waste piles, underground tanks and land treatment units for the storage, treatment, or disposal of hazardous waste identified or listed under section 6921 of this title shall be required to utilize approved leak detection systems.

(B) For the purposes of subparagraph (A)—

(i) the term "approved leak detection system" means a system or technology which the Administrator determines to be capable of detecting leaks of hazardous constituents at the earliest practicable time; and

(ii) the term "new units" means units on which construction commences after the date of promulgation of regulations under this paragraph.

(5)(A) The Administrator shall promulgate regulations or issue guidance documents implementing the requirements of paragraph (1)(A) within two years after November 8, 1984.

(B) Until the effective date of such regulations or guidance documents, the requirement for the installation of two or more liners may be satisfied by the installation of a top liner designed, operated, and constructed of materials to prevent the migration of any constituent into such liner during the period such facility remains in operation (including any post-closure monitoring period), and a lower liner designed, operated [2] and constructed to prevent the migration of any constituent through such liner during such period. For the purpose of the preceding sentence, a lower liner shall be deemed to satisfy such requirement if it is constructed of at least a 3-foot thick layer of recompacted clay or other natural material with a permeability of no more than $1 \times 10^{-7}$ centimeter per second.

(6) Any permit under section 6925 of this title which is issued for a landfill located within the State of Alabama shall require the installation of two or more liners and a leachate collection system above and between such liners, notwithstanding any other provision of this chapter.

(7) In addition to the requirements set forth in this subsection, the regulations referred to in paragraph (1) shall specify criteria for the acceptable location of new and existing treatment, storage, or disposal facilities as necessary to protect human health and the environment. Within 18 months after November 8, 1984, the Administrator shall publish guidance criteria identifying areas of vulnerable hydrogeology.

**(p) Ground water monitoring**

The standards under this section concerning ground water monitoring which are applicable to surface impoundments, waste piles, land treatment units, and landfills shall apply to such a facility whether or not—

(1) the facility is located above the seasonal high water table;

(2) two liners and a leachate collection system have been installed at the facility; or

(3) the owner or operator inspects the liner (or liners) which has been installed at the facility.

This subsection shall not be construed to affect other exemptions or waivers from such standards provided in regulations in effect on November 8, 1984, or as may be provided in revisions to those regulations, to the extent consistent with this subsection. The Administrator is authorized on a case-by-case basis to exempt from ground water monitoring requirements under this section (including subsection (*o*) of this section) any engineered structure which the Administrator finds does not receive or contain liquid waste (nor waste containing free liquids), is designed and operated to exclude liquid from precipitation or other runoff, utilizes multiple leak detection systems within the outer layer of containment, and provides for continuing operation and maintenance of these leak detection systems during the operating period, closure, and the period required for post-closure monitoring and for which the Administrator concludes on the basis of such findings that there is a reasonable certainty hazardous constituents will not migrate beyond the outer layer of containment prior to the end of the period required for post-closure monitoring.

**(q) Hazardous waste used as fuel**

**(1)** Not later than two years after November 8, 1984, and after notice and opportunity for public hearing, the Administrator shall promulgate regulations establishing such—

**(A)** standards applicable to the owners and operators of facilities which produce a fuel—

**(i)** from any hazardous waste identified or listed under section 6921 of this title, or

**(ii)** from any hazardous waste identified or listed under section 6921 of this title and any other material;

**(B)** standards applicable to the owners and operators of facilities which burn, for purposes of energy recovery, any fuel produced as provided in subparagraph (A) or any fuel which otherwise contains any hazardous waste identified or listed under section 6921 of this title; and

**(C)** standards applicable to any person who distributes or markets any fuel which is produced as provided in subparagraph (A) or any fuel which otherwise contains any hazardous waste identified or listed under section 6921 of this title;

as may be necessary to protect human health and the environment. Such standards may include any of the requirements set forth in paragraphs (1) through (7) of subsection (a) of this section as may be appropriate. Nothing in this subsection shall be construed to affect or impair the provisions of section 6921(b)(3) of this title. For purposes of this subsection, the term "hazardous waste listed under section 6921 of this title" includes any commercial chemical product which is listed under section 6921 of this title and which, in lieu of its original intended use, is (i) produced for use as (or as a component of) a fuel, (ii) distributed for use as a fuel, or (iii) burned as a fuel.

**(2)(A)** This subsection, subsection (r) of this section, and subsection (s) of this section shall not apply to petroleum refinery wastes containing oil which are converted into petroleum coke at the same facility at which such wastes were generated, unless the resulting coke product would exceed one or more characteristics by which a substance would be identified as a hazardous waste under section 6921 of this title.

**(B)** The Administrator may exempt from the requirements of this subsection, subsection (r) of this section, or subsection (s) of this section facilities which burn de minimis quantities of hazardous waste as fuel, as defined by the Administrator, if the wastes are burned at the same facility at which such wastes are generated; the waste is burned to recover useful energy, as determined by the Administrator on the basis of the design and operating characteristics of the facility and the heating value and other characteristics of the waste; and the waste is burned in a type of device determined by the Administrator to be designed and operated at a destruction and removal efficiency sufficient such that protection of human health and environment is assured.

**(C)(i)** After November 8, 1984, and until standards are promulgated and in effect under paragraph (2) of this subsection, no fuel which contains any hazardous waste may be burned in any cement kiln which is located within the boundaries of any incorporated municipality with a population greater than five hundred thousand (based on the most recent census statistics) unless such kiln fully complies with regulations (as in effect on November 8, 1984) under this subchapter which are applicable to incinerators.

**(ii)** Any person who knowingly violates the prohibition contained in clause (i) shall be deemed to have violated section 6928(d)(2) of this title.

**(r) Labeling**

**(1)** Notwithstanding any other provision of law, until such time as the Administrator promulgates standards under subsection (q) of this section specifically superceding this requirement, it shall be unlawful for any person who is required to file a notification in accordance with paragraph (1) or (3) of section 6930 of this title to distribute or market any fuel which is produced from any hazardous waste identified or listed under section 6921 of this title, or any fuel which otherwise contains any hazardous waste identified or listed under section 6921 of this title if the invoice or the bill of sale fails—

**(A)** to bear the following statement: "WARNING: THIS FUEL CONTAINS HAZARDOUS WASTES", and

**(B)** to list the hazardous wastes contained therein.

Beginning ninety days after November 8, 1984, such statement shall be located in a conspicuous place on every such invoice or bill of sale and shall appear in conspicuous and legible type in contrast by typography, layouts, or color with other printed matter on the invoice or bill of sale.

**(2)** Unless the Administrator determines otherwise as may be necessary to protect human health and the environment, this subsection shall not apply to fuels produced from petroleum refining waste containing oil if—

**(A)** such materials are generated and reinserted onsite into the refining process;

**(B)** contaminants are removed; and

**(C)** such refining waste containing oil is converted along with normal process streams into petroleum-derived fuel products at a facility at which crude oil is refined into petroleum products and which is classified as a number SIC 2911 facility under the Office of Management and Budget Standard Industrial Classification Manual.

(3) Unless the Administrator determines otherwise as may be necessary to protect human health and the environment, this subsection shall not apply to fuels produced from oily materials, resulting from normal petroleum refining, production and transportation practices, if (A) contaminants are removed; and (B) such oily materials are converted along with normal process streams into petroleum-derived fuel products at a facility at which crude oil is refined into petroleum products and which is classified as a number SIC 2911 facility under the Office of Management and Budget Standard Industrial Classification Manual.

**(s) Recordkeeping**

Not later than fifteen months after November 8, 1984, the Administrator shall promulgate regulations requiring that any person who is required to file a notification in accordance with subparagraph (1), (2), or (3), of section 6930(a) of this title shall maintain such records regarding fuel blending, distribution, or use as may be necessary to protect human health and the environment.

**(t) Financial responsibility provisions**

(1) Financial responsibility required by subsection (a) of this section may be established in accordance with regulations promulgated by the Administrator by any one, or any combination, of the following: insurance, guarantee, surety bond, letter of credit, or qualification as a self-insurer. In promulgating requirements under this section, the Administrator is authorized to specify policy or other contractual terms, conditions, or defenses which are necessary or are unacceptable in establishing such evidence of financial responsibility in order to effectuate the purposes of this chapter.

(2) In any case where the owner or operator is in bankruptcy, reorganization, or arrangement pursuant to the Federal Bankruptcy Code or where (with reasonable diligence) jurisdiction in any State court or any Federal Court cannot be obtained over an owner or operator likely to be solvent at the time of judgment, any claim arising from conduct for which evidence of financial responsibility must be provided under this section may be asserted directly against the guarantor providing such evidence of financial responsibility. In the case of any action pursuant to this subsection, such guarantor shall be entitled to invoke all rights and defenses which would have been available to the owner or operator if any action had been brought against the owner or operator by the claimant and which would have been available to the guarantor if an action had been brought against the guarantor by the owner or operator.

(3) The total liability of any guarantor shall be limited to the aggregate amount which the guarantor has provided as evidence of financial responsibility to the owner or operator under this chapter. Nothing in this subsection shall be construed to limit any other State or Federal statutory, contractual or common law liability of a guarantor to its owner or operator including, but not limited to, the liability of such guarantor for bad faith either in negotiating or in failing to negotiate the settlement of any claim. Nothing in this subsection shall be construed to diminish the liability of any person under section 9607 or 9611 of this title or other applicable law.

(4) For the purpose of this subsection, the term "guarantor" means any person, other than the owner or operator, who provides evidence of financial responsibility for an owner or operator under this section.

**(u) Continuing releases at permitted facilities**

Standards promulgated under this section shall require, and a permit issued after November 8, 1984, by the Administrator or a State shall require, corrective action for all releases of hazardous waste or constituents from any solid waste management unit at a treatment, storage, or disposal facility seeking a permit under this subchapter, regardless of the time at which waste was placed in such unit. Permits issued under section 6925 of this title shall contain schedules of compliance for such corrective action (where such corrective action cannot be completed prior to issuance of the permit) and assurances of financial responsibility for completing such corrective action.

**(v) Corrective action beyond facility boundary**

As promptly as practicable after November 8, 1984, the Administrator shall amend the standards under this section regarding corrective action required at facilities for the treatment, storage, or disposal, of hazardous waste listed or identified under section 6921 of this title to require that corrective action be taken beyond the facility boundary where necessary to protect human health and the environment unless the owner or operator of the facility concerned demonstrates to the satisfaction of the Administrator that, despite the owner or operator's best efforts, the owner or operator was unable to obtain the necessary permission to undertake such action. Such regulations shall take effect immediately upon promulgation, notwithstanding section 6930(b) of this title, and shall apply to—

(1) all facilities operating under permits issued under subsection (c) of this section, and

(2) all landfills, surface impoundments, and waste pile units (including any new units, replacements of existing units, or lateral expansions of existing

units) which receive hazardous waste after July 26, 1982.

Pending promulgation of such regulations, the Administrator shall issue corrective action orders for facilities referred to in paragraphs (1) and (2), on a case-by-case basis, consistent with the purposes of this subsection.

**(w) Underground tanks**

Not later than March 1, 1985, the Administrator shall promulgate final permitting standards under this section for underground tanks that cannot be entered for inspection. Within forty-eight months after November 8, 1984, such standards shall be modified, if necessary, to cover at a minimum all requirements and standards described in section 6991b of this title.

**(x) Mining and other special wastes**

If (1) solid waste from the extraction, beneficiation or processing of ores and minerals, including phosphate rock and overburden from the mining of uranium, (2) fly ash waste, bottom ash waste, slag waste, and flue gas emission control waste generated primarily from the combustion of coal or other fossil fuels, or (3) cement kiln dust waste, is subject to regulation under this subchapter, the Administrator is authorized to modify the requirements of subsections (c), (d), (e), (f), (g), (*o*), and (u) of this section and section 6925(j) of this title, in the case of landfills or surface impoundments receiving such solid waste, to take into account the special characteristics of such wastes, the practical difficulties associated with implementation of such requirements, and site-specific characteristics, including but not limited to the climate, geology, hydrology and soil chemistry at the site, so long as such modified requirements assure protection of human health and the environment.

**(y) Munitions**

(1) Not later than 6 months after October 6, 1992, the Administrator shall propose, after consulting with the Secretary of Defense and appropriate State officials, regulations identifying when military munitions become hazardous waste for purposes of this subchapter and providing for the safe transportation and storage of such waste. Not later than 24 months after October 6, 1992, and after notice and opportunity for comment, the Administrator shall promulgate such regulations. Any such regulations shall assure protection of human health and the environment.

(2) For purposes of this subsection, the term "military munitions" includes chemical and conventional munitions.

(Pub.L. 89–272, Title II, § 3004, as added Pub.L. 94–580, § 2, Oct. 21, 1976, 90 Stat. 2807, and amended Pub.L. 96–482, § 9, Oct. 21, 1980, 94 Stat. 2338; Pub.L. 98–616, Title II, §§ 201(a), 202(a), 203, 204(b)(1), 205 to 209, Nov. 8, 1984, 98 Stat. 3226, 3233, 3234, 3236, 3238 to 3240; Pub.L. 102–386, Title I, § 107, Oct. 6, 1992, 106 Stat. 1513; Pub.L. 104–119, §§ 2, 4(2) to (5), Mar. 26, 1996, 110 Stat. 830, 833.)

[1] So in original. Probably should be "section 6921 of this title".
[2] So in original. Probably should be followed by a comma.

### HISTORICAL AND STATUTORY NOTES

**References in Text**

Section 6922(5) of this title, referred to in subsec. (a)(2), was redesignated section 6922(a)(5) of this title, by Pub.L. 98–616, Title II, § 224(a)(1), Nov. 8, 1984, 98 Stat. 3253.

The Safe Drinking Water Act, referred to in subsec. (c)(3), is Pub.L. 93–523, Dec. 16, 1974, 88 Stat. 1660, as amended, which is classified principally to subchapter XII (section 300f et seq.) of chapter 6A of this title. For complete classification of this Act to the Code, see Short Title of 1974 Amendments note set out under section 201 of this title and Tables.

Section 6979a of this title, referred to in subsec. (f)(4), was in the original a reference to section 7010 of Pub.L. 89–272, which was renumbered section 3020 of Pub.L. 89–272 by Pub.L. 99–339, Title II, § 201(c), June 19, 1986, 100 Stat. 654, and transferred to section 6939b of this title.

The Paperwork Reduction Act of 1980, referred to in subsec. (g)(3), is Pub. L. 96–511, Dec. 11, 1980, 94 Stat. 2812, as amended, which was classified principally to chapter 35 of Title 44, 44 U.S.C.A. § 3501 et seq., prior to the general amendment of that chapter by Pub. L. 104–13, § 2, May 22, 1995, 109 Stat. 163. For complete classification, see Short Title of 1980 Amendment note set out under 44 U.S.C.A. § 101 and Tables.

The Federal Bankruptcy Code, referred to in subsec. (t)(2), probably means a reference to Title 11, Bankruptcy.

**Transfer of Functions**

For transfer of certain enforcement functions of Administrator or other official of the Environmental Protection Agency under this chapter to Federal Inspector, Office of Federal Inspector for the Alaska Natural Gas Transportation System, see note set out under section 6903 of this title.

## § 6925. Permits for treatment, storage, or disposal of hazardous waste

**[SWDA § 3005]**

**(a) Permit requirements**

Not later than eighteen months after October 21, 1976, the Administrator shall promulgate regulations requiring each person owning or operating an existing facility or planning to construct a new facility for the treatment, storage, or disposal of hazardous waste identified or listed under this subchapter to have a permit issued pursuant to this section. Such regulations shall take effect on the date provided in section 6930 of this title and upon and after such date the treatment, storage, or disposal of any such hazardous waste and the construction of any new facility for the treatment, storage, or disposal of any such hazardous waste is prohibited except in accordance with such a permit. No permit shall be required under this section in order to construct a facility if such facility is constructed pursuant to an approval issued by the Administrator under section 2605(e) of Title 15 for the incineration of polychlorinated biphenyls and any person owning or operating such a facility may, at any time after operation or construction of such facility has begun, file an application for a permit pursuant to this section authorizing such facility to incinerate hazardous waste identified or listed under this subchapter.

**(b) Requirements of permit application**

Each application for a permit under this section shall contain such information as may be required under regulations promulgated by the Administrator, including information respecting—

(1) estimates with respect to the composition, quantities, and concentrations of any hazardous waste identified or listed under this subchapter, or combinations of any such hazardous waste and any other solid waste, proposed to be disposed of, treated, transported, or stored, and the time, frequency, or rate of which such waste is proposed to be disposed of, treated, transported, or stored; and

(2) the site at which such hazardous waste or the products of treatment of such hazardous waste will be disposed of, treated, transported to, or stored.

**(c) Permit issuance**

(1) Upon a determination by the Administrator (or a State, if applicable), of compliance by a facility for which a permit is applied for under this section with the requirements of this section and section 6924 of this title, the Administrator (or the State) shall issue a permit for such facilities. In the event permit applicants propose modification of their facilities, or in the event the Administrator (or the State) determines that modifications are necessary to conform to the requirements under this section and section 6924 of this title, the permit shall specify the time allowed to complete the modifications.

(2)(A)(i) Not later than the date four years after November 8, 1984, in the case of each application under this subsection for a permit for a land disposal facility which was submitted before such date, the Administrator shall issue a final permit pursuant to such application or issue a final denial of such application.

(ii) Not later than the date five years after November 8, 1984, in the case of each application for a permit under this subsection for an incinerator facility which was submitted before such date, the Administrator shall issue a final permit pursuant to such application or issue a final denial of such application.

(B) Not later than the date eight years after November 8, 1984, in the case of each application for a permit under this subsection for any facility (other than a facility referred to in subparagraph (A)) which was submitted before such date, the Administrator shall issue a final permit pursuant to such application or issue a final denial of such application.

(C) The time periods specified in this paragraph shall also apply in the case of any State which is administering an authorized hazardous waste program under section 6926 of this title. Interim status under subsection (e) of this section shall terminate for each facility referred to in subparagraph (A)(ii) or (B) on the expiration of the five- or eight-year period referred to in subparagraph (A) or (B), whichever is applicable, unless the owner or operator of the facility applies for a final determination regarding the issuance of a permit under this subsection within—

(i) two years after November 8, 1984 (in the case of a facility referred to in subparagraph (A)(ii)), or

(ii) four years after November 8, 1984 (in the case of a facility referred to in subparagraph (B)).

(3) Any permit under this section shall be for a fixed term, not to exceed 10 years in the case of any land disposal facility, storage facility, or incinerator or other treatment facility. Each permit for a land disposal facility shall be reviewed five years after date of issuance or reissuance and shall be modified as necessary to assure that the facility continues to comply with the currently applicable requirements of this section and section 6924 of this title. Nothing in this subsection shall preclude the Administrator from reviewing and modifying a permit at any time during its term. Review of any application for a permit renewal shall consider improvements in the state of control and measurement technology as well as changes in applicable regulations. Each permit issued under this section shall contain such terms and conditions as the Administrator (or the State) determines necessary to protect human health and the environment.

**(d) Permit revocation**

Upon a determination by the Administrator (or by a State, in the case of a State having an authorized hazardous waste program under section 6926 of this title) of noncompliance by a facility having a permit under this chapter with the requirements of this section or section 6924 of this title, the Administrator (or State, in the case of a State having an authorized hazardous waste program under section 6926 of this title) shall revoke such permit.

**(e) Interim status**

(1) Any person who—

(A) owns or operates a facility required to have a permit under this section which facility—

(i) was in existence on November 19, 1980, or

(ii) is in existence on the effective date of statutory or regulatory changes under this chapter that render the facility subject to the requirement to have a permit under this section,

(B) has complied with the requirements of section 6930(a) of this title, and

(C) has made an application for a permit under this section,

shall be treated as having been issued such permit until such time as final administrative disposition of such application is made, unless the Administrator or other plaintiff proves that final administrative disposition of such application has not been made because of the failure of the applicant to furnish information reasonably required or requested in order to process the application. This paragraph shall not apply to any facility which has been previously denied a permit under this section or if authority to operate the facility under this section has been previously terminated.

(2) In the case of each land disposal facility which has been granted interim status under this subsection before November 8, 1984, interim status shall terminate on the date twelve months after November 8, 1984, unless the owner or operator of such facility—

(A) applies for a final determination regarding the issuance of a permit under subsection (c) of this section for such facility before the date twelve months after November 8, 1984; and

(B) certifies that such facility is in compliance with all applicable groundwater monitoring and financial responsibility requirements.

(3) In the case of each land disposal facility which is in existence on the effective date of statutory or regulatory changes under this chapter that render the facility subject to the requirement to have a permit under this section and which is granted interim status under this subsection, interim status shall terminate on the date twelve months after the date on which the facility first becomes subject to such permit requirement unless the owner or operator of such facility—

(A) applies for a final determination regarding the issuance of a permit under subsection (c) of this section for such facility before the date twelve months after the date on which the facility first becomes subject to such permit requirement; and

(B) certifies that such facility is in compliance with all applicable groundwater monitoring and financial responsibility requirements.

### (f) Coal mining wastes and reclamation permits

Notwithstanding subsection (a) through (e) of this section, any surface coal mining and reclamation permit covering any coal mining wastes or overburden which has been issued or approved under the Surface Mining Control and Reclamation Act of 1977 [30 U.S.C.A. § 1201 et seq.] shall be deemed to be a permit issued pursuant to this section with respect to the treatment, storage, or disposal of such wastes or overburden. Regulations promulgated by the Administrator under this subchapter shall not be applicable to treatment, storage, or disposal of coal mining wastes and overburden which are covered by such a permit.

### (g) Research, development, and demonstration permits

(1) The Administrator may issue a research, development, and demonstration permit for any hazardous waste treatment facility which proposes to utilize an innovative and experimental hazardous waste treatment technology or process for which permit standards for such experimental activity have not been promulgated under this subchapter. Any such permit shall include such terms and conditions as will assure protection of human health and the environment. Such permits—

(A) shall provide for the construction of such facilities, as necessary, and for operation of the facility for not longer than one year (unless renewed as provided in paragraph (4)), and

(B) shall provide for the receipt and treatment by the facility of only those types and quantities of hazardous waste which the Administrator deems necessary for purposes of determining the efficacy and performance capabilities of the technology or process and the effects of such technology or process on human health and the environment, and

(C) shall include such requirements as the Administrator deems necessary to protect human health and the environment (including, but not limited to, requirements regarding monitoring, operation, insurance or bonding, financial reponsibility,[1] closure, and remedial action), and such requirements as the Administrator deems necessary regarding testing and providing of information to the Administrator with respect to the operation of the facility.

The Administrator may apply the criteria set forth in this paragraph in establishing the conditions of each permit without separate establishment of regulations implementing such criteria.

(2) For the purpose of expediting review and issuance of permits under this subsection, the Administrator may, consistent with the protection of human health and the environment, modify or waive permit application and permit issuance requirements established in the Administrator's general permit regulations except that there may be no modification or waiver of regulations regarding financial responsibility (including insurance) or of procedures established under section 6974(b)(2) of this title regarding public participation.

(3) The Administrator may order an immediate termination of all operations at the facility at any time he determines that termination is necessary to protect human health and the environment.

(4) Any permit issued under this subsection may be renewed not more than three times. Each such renewal shall be for a period of not more than 1 year.

**(h) Waste minimization**

Effective September 1, 1985, it shall be a condition of any permit issued under this section for the treatment, storage, or disposal of hazardous waste on the premises where such waste was generated that the permittee certify, no less often than annually, that—

(1) the generator of the hazardous waste has a program in place to reduce the volume or quantity and toxicity of such waste to the degree determined by the generator to be economically practicable; and

(2) the proposed method of treatment, storage, or disposal is that practicable method currently available to the generator which minimizes the present and future threat to human health and the environment.

**(i) Interim status facilities receiving wastes after July 26, 1982**

The standards concerning ground water monitoring, unsaturated zone monitoring, and corrective action, which are applicable under section 6924 of this title to new landfills, surface impoundments, land treatment units, and waste-pile units required to be permitted under subsection (c) of this section shall also apply to any landfill, surface impoundment, land treatment unit, or waste-pile unit qualifying for the authorization to operate under subsection (e) of this section which receives hazardous waste after July 26, 1982.

**(j) Interim status surface impoundments**

(1) Except as provided in paragraph (2), (3), or (4), each surface impoundment in existence on November 8, 1984, and qualifying for the authorization to operate under subsection (e) of this section shall not receive, store, or treat hazardous waste after the date four years after November 8, 1984, unless such surface impoundment is in compliance with the requirements of section 6924(*o*)(1)(A) of this title which would apply to such impoundment if it were new.

(2) Paragraph (1) of this subsection shall not apply to any surface impoundment which (A) has at least one liner, for which there is no evidence that such liner is leaking; (B) is located more than one-quarter mile from an underground source of drinking water; and (C) is in compliance with generally applicable ground water monitoring requirements for facilities with permits under subsection (c) of this section.

(3) Paragraph (1) of this subsection shall not apply to any surface impoundment which (A) contains treated waste water during the secondary or subsequent phases of an aggressive biological treatment facility subject to a permit issued under section 1342 of Title 33 (or which holds such treated waste water after treatment and prior to discharge); (B) is in compliance with generally applicable ground water monitoring requirements for facilities with permits under subsection (c) of this section; and (C)(i) is part of a facility in compliance with section 1311(b)(2) of Title 33, or (ii) in the case of a facility for which no effluent guidelines required under section 1314(b)(2) of Title 33 are in effect and no permit under section 1342(a)(1) of Title 33 implementing section 1311(b)(2) of Title 33 has been issued, is part of a facility in compliance with a permit under section 1342 of Title 33, which is achieving significant degradation of toxic pollutants and hazardous constituents contained in the untreated waste stream and which has identified those toxic pollutants and hazardous constituents in the untreated waste stream to the appropriate permitting authority.

(4) The Administrator (or the State, in the case of a State with an authorized program), after notice and opportunity for comment, may modify the requirements of paragraph (1) for any surface impoundment if the owner or operator demonstrates that such surface impoundment is located, designed and operated so as to assure that there will be no migration of any hazardous constitutent [2] into ground water or surface water at any future time. The Administrator or the State shall take into account locational criteria established under section 6924(*o*)(7) of this title.

(5) The owner or operator of any surface impoundment potentially subject to paragraph (1) who has reason to believe that on the basis of paragraph (2), (3), or (4) such surface impoundment is not required to comply with the requirements of paragraph (1), shall apply to the Administrator (or the State, in the case of a State with an authorized program) not later than twenty-four months after November 8, 1984, for a determination of the applicability of paragraph (1) (in the case of paragraph (2) or (3)) or for a modification of the requirements of paragraph (1) (in the case of paragraph (4)), with respect to such surface impoundment. Such owner or operator shall provide, with such application, evidence pertinent to such decision, including:

(A) an application for a final determination regarding the issuance of a permit under subsection (c) of this section for such facility, if not previously submitted;

(B) evidence as to compliance with all applicable ground water monitoring requirements and the information and analysis from such monitoring;

(C) all reasonably ascertainable evidence as to whether such surface impoundment is leaking; and

(D) in the case of applications under paragraph (2) or (3), a certification by a registered professional engineer with academic training and experience in ground water hydrology that—

**(i)** under paragraph (2), the liner of such surface impoundment is designed, constructed, and operated in accordance with applicable requirements, such surface impoundment is more than one-quarter mile from an underground source of drinking water and there is no evidence such liner is leaking; or

**(ii)** under paragraph (3), based on analysis of those toxic pollutants and hazardous constituents that are likely to be present in the untreated waste stream, such impoundment satisfies the conditions of paragraph (3).

In the case of any surface impoundment for which the owner or operator fails to apply under this paragraph within the time provided by this paragraph or paragraph (6), such surface impoundment shall comply with paragraph (1) notwithstanding paragraph (2), (3), or (4). Within twelve months after receipt of such application and evidence and not later than thirty-six months after November 8, 1984, and after notice and opportunity to comment, the Administrator (or, if appropriate, the State) shall advise such owner or operator on the applicability of paragraph (1) to such surface impoundment or as to whether and how the requirements of paragraph (1) shall be modified and applied to such surface impoundment.

**(6)(A)** In any case in which a surface impoundment becomes subject to paragraph (1) after November 8, 1984, due to the promulgation of additional listings or characteristics for the identification of hazardous waste under section 6921 of this title, the period for compliance in paragraph (1) shall be four years after the date of such promulgation, the period for demonstrations under paragraph (4) and for submission of evidence under paragraph (5) shall be not later than twenty-four months after the date of such promulgation, and the period for the Administrator (or if appropriate, the State) to advise such owners or operators under paragraph (5) shall be not later than thirty-six months after the date of promulgation.

**(B)** In any case in which a surface impoundment is initially determined to be excluded from the requirements of paragraph (1) but due to a change in condition (including the existence of a leak) no longer satisfies the provisions of paragraph (2), (3), or (4) and therefore becomes subject to paragraph (1), the period for compliance in paragraph (1) shall be two years after the date of discovery of such change of condition, or in the case of a surface impoundment excluded under paragraph (3) three years after such date of discovery.

**(7)(A)** The Administrator shall study and report to the Congress on the number, range of size, construction, likelihood of hazardous constituents migrating into ground water, and potential threat to human health and the environment of existing surface impoundments excluded by paragraph (3) from the requirements of paragraph (1). Such report shall address the need, feasibility, and estimated costs of subjecting such existing surface impoundments to the requirements of paragraph (1).

**(B)** In the case of any existing surface impoundment or class of surface impoundments from which the Administrator (or the State, in the case of a State with an authorized program) determines hazardous constituents are likely to migrate into ground water, the Administrator (or if appropriate, the State) is authorized to impose such requirements as may be necessary to protect human health and the environment, including the requirements of section 6924(*o*) of this title which would apply to such impoundments if they were new.

**(C)** In the case of any surface impoundment excluded by paragraph (3) from the requirements of paragraph (1) which is subsequently determined to be leaking, the Administrator (or, if appropriate, the State) shall require compliance with paragraph (1), unless the Administrator (or, if appropriate, the State) determines that such compliance is not necessary to protect human health and the environment.

**(8)** In the case of any surface impoundment in which the liners and leak detection system have been installed pursuant to the requirements of paragraph (1) and in good faith compliance with section 6924(*o*) of this title and the Administrator's regulations and guidance documents governing liners and leak detection systems, no liner or leak detection system which is different from that which was so installed pursuant to paragraph (1) shall be required for such unit by the Administrator when issuing the first permit under this section to such facility. Nothing in this paragraph shall preclude the Administrator from requiring installation of a new liner when the Administrator has reason to believe that any liner installed pursuant to the requirements of this subsection is leaking.

**(9)** In the case of any surface impoundment which has been excluded by paragraph (2) on the basis of a liner meeting the definition under paragraph (12)(A)(ii), at the closure of such impoundment the Administrator shall require the owner or operator of such impoundment to remove or decontaminate all waste residues, all contaminated liner material, and contaminated soil to the extent practicable. If all contaminated soil is not removed or decontaminated, the owner or operator of such impoundment shall be required to comply with appropriate post-closure requirements, including but not limited to ground water monitoring and corrective action.

**(10)** Any incremental cost attributable to the requirements of this subsection or section 6924(*o*) of this title shall not be considered by the Administrator (or the State, in the case of a State with an authorized program under section 1342 of Title 33)—

(A) in establishing effluent limitations and standards under section 1311, 1314, 1316, 1317, or 1342 of Title 33 based on effluent limitations guidelines and standards promulgated any time before twelve months after November 8, 1984; or

(B) in establishing any other effluent limitations to carry out the provisions of section 1311, 1317, or 1342 of Title 33 on or before October 1, 1986.

(11)(A) If the Administrator allows a hazardous waste which is prohibited from one or more methods of land disposal under subsection (d), (e), or (g) of section 6924 of this title (or under regulations promulgated by the Administrator under such subsections) to be placed in a surface impoundment (which is operating pursuant to interim status) for storage or treatment, such impoundment shall meet the requirements that are applicable to new surface impoundments under section 6924(*o*)(1) of this title, unless such impoundment meets the requirements of paragraph (2) or (4).

(B) In the case of any hazardous waste which is prohibited from one or more methods of land disposal under subsection (d), (e), or (g) of section 6924 of this title (or under regulations promulgated by the Administrator under such subsection) the placement or maintenance of such hazardous waste in a surface impoundment for treatment is prohibited as of the effective date of such prohibition unless the treatment residues which are hazardous are, at a minimum, removed for subsequent management within one year of the entry of the waste into the surface impoundment.

(12)(A) For the purposes of paragraph (2)(A) of this subsection, the term "liner" means—

(i) a liner designed, constructed, installed, and operated to prevent hazardous waste from passing into the liner at any time during the active life of the facility; or

(ii) a liner designed, constructed, installed, and operated to prevent hazardous waste from migrating beyond the liner to adjacent subsurface soil, ground water, or surface water at any time during the active life of the facility.

(B) For the purposes of this subsection, the term "aggressive biological treatment facility" means a system of surface impoundments in which the initial impoundment of the secondary treatment segment of the facility utilizes intense mechanical aeration to enhance biological activity to degrade waste water pollutants and

(i) the hydraulic retention time in such initial impoundment is no longer than 5 days under normal operating conditions, on an annual average basis;

(ii) the hydraulic retention time in such initial impoundment is no longer than thirty days under normal operating conditions, on an annual average basis: *Provided,* That the sludge in such impoundment does not constitute a hazardous waste as identified by the extraction procedure toxicity characteristic in effect on November 8, 1984; or

(iii) such system utilizes activated sludge treatment in the first portion of secondary treatment.

(C) For the purposes of this subsection, the term "underground source or[3] drinking water" has the same meaning as provided in regulations under the Safe Drinking Water Act (title XIV of the Public Health Service Act) [42 U.S.C.A. § 300f et seq.].

(13) The Administrator may modify the requirements of paragraph (1) in the case of a surface impoundment for which the owner or operator, prior to October 1, 1984, has entered into, and is in compliance with, a consent order, decree, or agreement with the Administrator or a State with an authorized program mandating corrective action with respect to such surface impoundment that provides a degree of protection of human health and the environment which is at a minimum equivalent to that provided by paragraph (1).

(Pub.L. 89–272, Title II, § 3005, as added Pub.L. 94–580, § 2, Oct. 21, 1976, 90 Stat. 2808, and amended Pub.L. 95–609, § 7(h), Nov. 8, 1978, 92 Stat. 3082; Pub.L. 96–482, §§ 10, 11, Oct. 21, 1980, 94 Stat. 2338; Pub.L. 98–616, Title II, §§ 211 to 213(a), (c), 214(a), 215, 224(b), 243(c), Nov. 8, 1984, 98 Stat. 3240 to 3243, 3253, 3261; Pub.L. 104–119, § 4(6), (7), Mar. 26, 1996, 110 Stat. 833.)

1 So in original. Probably should be "responsibility".

2 So in original. Probably should be "constituent".

3 So in original. Probably should be "of".

## HISTORICAL AND STATUTORY NOTES

### References in Text

The Surface Mining Control and Reclamation Act of 1977, referred to in subsec. (f), is Pub.L. 95–87, Aug. 3, 1977, 91 Stat. 445, as amended, which is classified generally to chapter 25 (section 1201 et seq.) of Title 30, Mineral Lands and Mining. For complete classification of this Act to the Code, see Short Title note set out under section 1201 of Title 30 and Tables.

The Safe Drinking Water Act, referred to in subsec. (j)(12)(C), is Pub.L. 93–523, Dec. 16, 1974, 88 Stat. 1660, as amended, which is classified generally to subchapter XII (section 300f et seq.) of chapter 6A of this title. For complete classification of this Act to the Code, see Short Title of 1974 Amendments note set out under section 201 of this title and Tables.

### Transfer of Functions

For transfer of certain enforcement functions of Administrator or other official of the Environmental Protection Agency under this chapter to Federal Inspector, Office of Federal Inspector for the Alaska Natural Gas Transportation System, see note set out under section 6903 of this title.

## § 6926. Authorized State hazardous waste programs

[SWDA § 3006]

### (a) Federal guidelines

Not later than eighteen months after October 21, 1976, the Administrator, after consultation with State authorities, shall promulgate guidelines to assist States in the Development of State hazardous waste programs.

### (b) Authorization of State program

Any State which seeks to administer and enforce a hazardous waste program pursuant to this subchapter may develop and, after notice and opportunity for public hearing, submit to the Administrator an application, in such form as he shall require, for authorization of such program. Within ninety days following submission of an application under this subsection, the Administrator shall issue a notice as to whether or not he expects such program to be authorized, and within ninety days following such notice (and after opportunity for public hearing) he shall publish his findings as to whether or not the conditions listed in items (1), (2), and (3) below have been met. Such State is authorized to carry out such program in lieu of the Federal program under this subchapter in such State and to issue and enforce permits for the storage, treatment, or disposal of hazardous waste (and to enforce permits deemed to have been issued under section 6935(d)(1) of this title) unless, within ninety days following submission of the application the Administrator notifies such State that such program may not be authorized and, within ninety days following such notice and after opportunity for public hearing, he finds that (1) such State program is not equivalent to the Federal program under this subchapter, (2) such program is not consistent with the Federal or State programs applicable in other States, or (3) such program does not provide adequate enforcement of compliance with the requirements of this subchapter. In authorizing a State program, the Administrator may base his findings on the Federal program in effect one year prior to submission of a State's application or in effect on January 26, 1983, whichever is later.

### (c) Interim authorization

(1) Any State which has in existence a hazardous waste program pursuant to State law before the date ninety days after the date of promulgation of regulations under sections 6922, 6923, 6924, and 6925 of this title, may submit to the Administrator evidence of such existing program and may request a temporary authorization to carry out such program under this subchapter. The Administrator shall, if the evidence submitted shows the existing State program to be substantially equivalent to the Federal program under this subchapter, grant an interim authorization to the State to carry out such program in lieu of the Federal program pursuant to this subchapter for a period ending no later than January 31, 1986.

(2) The Administrator shall, by rule, establish a date for the expiration of interim authorization under this subsection.

(3) Pending interim or final authorization of a State program for any State which reflects the amendments made by the Hazardous and Solid Waste Amendments of 1984, the State may enter into an agreement with the Administrator under which the State may assist in the administration of the requirements and prohibitions which take effect pursuant to such Amendments.

(4) In the case of a State permit program for any State which is authorized under subsection (b) of this section or under this subsection, until such program is amended to reflect the amendments made by the Hazardous and Solid Waste Amendments of 1984 and such program amendments receive interim or final authorization, the Administrator shall have the authority in such State to issue or deny permits or those portions of permits affected by the requirements and prohibitions established by the Hazardous and Solid Waste Amendments of 1984. The Administrator shall coordinate with States the procedures for issuing such permits.

### (d) Effect of State permit

Any action taken by a State under a hazardous waste program authorized under this section shall have the same force and effect as action taken by the Administrator under this subchapter.

### (e) Withdrawal of authorization

Whenever the Administrator determines after public hearing that a State is not administering and enforcing a program authorized under this section in accordance with requirements of this section, he shall so notify the State and, if appropriate corrective action is not taken within a reasonable time, not to exceed ninety days, the Administrator shall withdraw authorization of such program and establish a Federal program pursuant to this subchapter. The Administrator shall not withdraw authorization of any such program unless he shall first have notified the State, and made public, in writing, the reasons for such withdrawal.

### (f) Availability of information

No State program may be authorized by the Administrator under this section unless—

(1) such program provides for the public availability of information obtained by the State regarding facilities and sites for the treatment, storage, and disposal of hazardous waste; and

(2) such information is available to the public in substantially the same manner, and to the same degree, as would be the case if the Administrator was carrying out the provisions of this subchapter in such State.

**(g) Amendments made by 1984 act**

(1) Any requirement or prohibition which is applicable to the generation, transportation, treatment, storage, or disposal of hazardous waste and which is imposed under this subchapter pursuant to the amendments made by the Hazardous and Solid Waste Amendments of 1984 shall take effect in each State having an interim or finally authorized State program on the same date as such requirement takes effect in other States. The Administrator shall carry out such requirement directly in each such State unless the State program is finally authorized (or is granted interim authorization as provided in paragraph (2)) with respect to such requirement.

(2) Any State which, before November 8, 1984, has an existing hazardous waste program which has been granted interim or final authorization under this section may submit to the Administrator evidence that such existing program contains (or has been amended to include) any requirement which is substantially equivalent to a requirement referred to in paragraph (1) and may request interim authorization to carry out that requirement under this subchapter. The Administrator shall, if the evidence submitted shows the State requirement to be substantially equivalent to the requirement referred to in paragraph (1), grant an interim authorization to the State to carry out such requirement in lieu of direct administration in the State by the Administrator of such requirement.

**(h) State programs for used oil**

In the case of used oil which is not listed or identified under this subchapter as a hazardous waste but which is regulated under section 6935 of this title, the provisions of this section regarding State programs shall apply in the same manner and to the same extent as such provisions apply to hazardous waste identified or listed under this subchapter.

(Pub.L. 89–272, Title II, § 3006, as added Pub.L. 94–580, § 2, Oct. 21, 1976, 90 Stat. 2809, and amended Pub.L. 95–609, § 7(i), Nov. 8, 1978, 92 Stat. 3082; Pub.L. 98–616, Title II, §§ 225, 226(a), 227, 228, 241(b)(2), Nov. 8, 1984, 98 Stat. 3254, 3255, 3260; Pub.L. 99–499, Title II, § 205(j), Oct. 17, 1986, 100 Stat. 1703.)

### HISTORICAL AND STATUTORY NOTES

**References in Text**

Section 6935(d)(1) of this title, referred to in subsec. (b), was in the original a reference to section 3012(d)(1) of Pub.L. 89–272, which was renumbered section 3014(d)(1) of Pub.L. 89–272 by Pub.L. 98–616 and is classified to section 6935(d)(1) of this title.

The Hazardous and Solid Waste Amendments of 1984, referred to in subsecs. (c)(3), (4), and (g), is Pub.L. 98–616, Nov. 8, 1984, 98 Stat. 3221, which amended this chapter. For complete classification of this Act to the Code, see Short Title of 1984 Amendments note set out under section 6901 of this title and Tables.

**Effective and Applicability Provisions**

1986 Acts

Amendment by Pub.L. 99–499 effective Oct. 17, 1986, see section 4 of Pub.L. 99–499, set out as a note under section 9601 of this title.

1984 Acts

Section 226(b) of Pub.L. 98–616 provided that: "The amendment made by subsection (a) [enacting subsec. (f) of this section] shall apply with respect to State programs authorized under section 3006 [this section] before, on, or after the date of the enactment of the Hazardous and Solid Waste Amendments of 1984 [Nov. 8, 1984]."

**Transfer of Functions**

For transfer of certain enforcement functions of Administrator or other official of the Environmental Protection Agency under this chapter to Federal Inspector, Office of Federal Inspector for the Alaska Natural Gas Transportation System, see note set out under section 6903 of this title.

## § 6927. Inspections

**[SWDA § 3007]**

**(a) Access entry**

For purposes of developing or assisting in the development of any regulation or enforcing the provisions of this chapter, any person who generates, stores, treats, transports, disposes of, or otherwise handles or has handled hazardous wastes shall, upon request of any officer, employee or representative of the Environmental Protection Agency, duly designated by the Administrator, or upon request of any duly designated officer, employee or representative of a State having an authorized hazardous waste program, furnish information relating to such wastes and permit such person at all reasonable times to have access to, and to copy all records relating to such wastes. For the purposes of developing or assisting in the development of any regulation or enforcing the provisions of this chapter, such officers, employees or representatives are authorized—

(1) to enter at reasonable times any establishment or other place where hazardous wastes are or have been generated, stored, treated, disposed of, or transported from;

(2) to inspect and obtain samples from any person of any such wastes and samples of any containers or labeling for such wastes.

Each such inspection shall be commenced and completed with reasonable promptness. If the officer, employee or representative obtains any samples, prior to leaving the premises, he shall give to the owner, operator, or agent in charge a receipt describing the sample obtained and if requested a portion of each such sample equal in volume or weight to the portion retained. If any analysis is made of such samples, a copy of the results of such analysis shall be furnished promptly to the owner, operator, or agent in charge.

**(b) Availability to public**

(1) Any records, reports, or information (including records, reports, or information obtained by representatives of the Environmental Protection Agency) obtained from any person under this section shall be available to the public, except that upon a showing satisfactory to the Administrator (or the State, as the case may be) by any person that records, reports, or information, or particular part thereof, to which the Administrator (or the State, as the case may be) or any officer, employee or representative thereof has access under this section if made public, would divulge information entitled to protection under section 1905 of Title 18, such information or particular portion thereof shall be considered confidential in accordance with the purposes of that section, except that such record, report, document, or information may be disclosed to other officers, employees, or authorized representatives of the United States concerned with carrying out this chapter, or when relevant in any proceeding under this chapter.

(2) Any person not subject to the provisions of section 1905 of Title 18 who knowingly and willfully divulges or discloses any information entitled to protection under this subsection shall, upon conviction, be subject to a fine of not more than $5,000 or to imprisonment not to exceed one year, or both.

(3) In submitting data under this chapter, a person required to provide such data may—

(A) designate the data which such person believes is entitled to protection under this subsection, and

(B) submit such designated data separately from other data submitted under this chapter.

A designation under this paragraph shall be made in writing and in such manner as the Administrator may prescribe.

(4) Notwithstanding any limitation contained in this section or any other provision of law, all information reported to, or otherwise obtained by, the Administrator (or any representative of the Administrator) under this chapter shall be made available, upon written request of any duly authorized committee of the Congress, to such committee.

**(c) Federal facility inspections**

The Administrator shall undertake on an annual basis a thorough inspection of each facility for the treatment, storage, or disposal of hazardous waste which is owned or operated by a department, agency, or instrumentality of the United States to enforce its compliance with this subchapter and the regulations promulgated thereunder. Any State with an authorized hazardous waste program also may conduct an inspection of any such facility for purposes of enforcing the facility's compliance with the State hazardous waste program. The records of such inspections shall be available to the public as provided in subsection (b) of this section. The department, agency, or instrumentality owning or operating each such facility shall reimburse the Environmental Protection Agency for the costs of the inspection of the facility. With respect to the first inspection of each such facility occurring after October 6, 1992, the Administrator shall conduct a comprehensive ground water monitoring evaluation at the facility, unless such an evaluation was conducted during the 12–month period preceding October 6, 1992.

**(d) State-operated facilities**

The Administrator shall annually undertake a thorough inspection of every facility for the treatment, storage, or disposal of hazardous waste which is operated by a State or local government for which a permit is required under section 6925 of this title. The records of such inspection shall be available to the public as provided in subsection (b) of this section.

**(e) Mandatory inspections**

(1) The Administrator (or the State in the case of a State having an authorized hazardous waste program under this subchapter) shall commence a program to thoroughly inspect every facility for the treatment, storage, or disposal of hazardous waste for which a permit is required under section 6925 of this title no less often than every two years as to its compliance with this subchapter (and the regulations promulgated under this subchapter). Such inspections shall commence not later than twelve months after November 8, 1984. The Administrator shall, after notice and opportunity for public comment, promulgate regulations governing the minimum frequency and manner of such inspections, including the manner in which records of such inspections shall be maintained and the manner in which reports of such inspections shall be filed. The Administrator may distinguish between classes and categories of facilities commensurate with the risks posed by each class or category.

(2) Not later than six months after November 8, 1984, the Administrator shall submit to the Congress a report on the potential for inspections of hazardous waste treatment, storage, or disposal facilities by nongovernmental inspectors as a supplement to inspections conducted by officers, employees, or representatives of the Environmental Protection Agency or States having authorized hazardous waste programs

or operating under a cooperative agreement with the Administrator. Such report shall be prepared in cooperation with the States, insurance companies offering environmental impairment insurance, independent companies providing inspection services, and other such groups as appropriate. Such report shall contain recommendations on provisions and requirements for a program of private inspections to supplement governmental inspections.

(Pub.L. 89–272, Title II, § 3007, as added Pub.L. 94–580, § 2, Oct. 21, 1976, 90 Stat. 2810, and amended Pub.L. 95–609, § 7(j), Nov. 8, 1978, 92 Stat. 3082; Pub.L. 96–482, § 12, Oct. 21, 1980, 94 Stat. 2339; Pub.L. 98–616, Title II, §§ 229 to 231, Title V, § 502(a), Nov. 8, 1984, 98 Stat. 3255, 3256, 3276; Pub.L. 102–386, Title I, § 104, Oct. 6, 1992, 106 Stat. 1507.)

### HISTORICAL AND STATUTORY NOTES

**Codifications**

Amendment by section 12(b)(4) of Pub.L. 96–482, directing that subsec. (b) of this section be amended by inserting "(including records, reports, or information obtained by representatives of the Environmental Protection Agency)", without specifying where in text such phrase be inserted, could not be executed.

**Transfer of Functions**

For transfer of certain enforcement functions of Administrator or other official of the Environmental Protection Agency under this chapter to Federal Inspector, Office of Federal Inspector for the Alaska Natural Gas Transportation System, see note set out under section 6903 of this title.

## § 6928. Federal enforcement

[SWDA § 3008]

### (a) Compliance orders

(1) Except as provided in paragraph (2), whenever on the basis of any information the Administrator determines that any person has violated or is in violation of any requirement of this subchapter, the Administrator may issue an order assessing a civil penalty for any past or current violation, requiring compliance immediately or within a specified time period, or both, or the Administrator may commence a civil action in the United States district court in the district in which the violation occurred for appropriate relief, including a temporary or permanent injunction.

(2) In the case of a violation of any requirement of this subchapter where such violation occurs in a State which is authorized to carry out a hazardous waste program under section 6926 of this title, the Administrator shall give notice to the State in which such violation has occurred prior to issuing an order or commencing a civil action under this section.

(3) Any order issued pursuant to this subsection may include a suspension or revocation of any permit issued by the Administrator or a State under this subchapter and shall state with reasonable specificity the nature of the violation. Any penalty assessed in the order shall not exceed $25,000 per day of noncompliance for each violation of a requirement of this subchapter. In assessing such a penalty, the Administrator shall take into account the seriousness of the violation and any good faith efforts to comply with applicable requirements.

### (b) Public hearing

Any order issued under this section shall become final unless, no later than thirty days after the order is served, the person or persons named therein request a public hearing. Upon such request the Administrator shall promptly conduct a public hearing. In connection with any proceeding under this section the Administrator may issue subpenas for the attendance and testimony of witnesses and the production of relevant papers, books, and documents, and may promulgate rules for discovery procedures.

### (c) Violation of compliance orders

If a violator fails to take corrective action within the time specified in a compliance order, the Administrator may assess a civil penalty of not more than $25,000 for each day of continued noncompliance with the order and the Administrator may suspend or revoke any permit issued to the violator (whether issued by the Administrator or the State).

### (d) Criminal penalties

Any person who—

(1) knowingly transports or causes to be transported any hazardous waste identified or listed under this subchapter to a facility which does not have a permit under this subchapter, or pursuant to title I of the Marine Protection, Research, and Sanctuaries Act (86 Stat. 1052) [33 U.S.C.A. § 1411 et seq.],

(2) knowingly treats, stores, or disposes of any hazardous waste identified or listed under this subchapter—

(A) without a permit under this subchapter or pursuant to title I of the Marine Protection, Research, and Sanctuaries Act (86 Stat. 1052) [33 U.S.C.A. § 1411 et seq.]; or

(B) in knowing violation of any material condition or requirement of such permit; or

(C) in knowing violation of any material condition or requirement of any applicable interim status regulations or standards;

(3) knowingly omits material information or makes any false material statement or representation in any application, label, manifest, record, report, permit, or other document filed, maintained, or used for purposes of compliance with regulations promulgated by the Administrator (or by a State in the case of an authorized State program) under this subchapter;

(4) knowingly generates, stores, treats, transports, disposes of, exports, or otherwise handles any hazardous waste or any used oil not identified or listed as a hazardous waste under this subchapter (whether such activity took place before or takes place after November 8, 1984) and who knowingly destroys, alters, conceals, or fails to file any record, application, manifest, report, or other document required to be maintained or filed for purposes of compliance with regulations promulgated by the Administrator (or by a State in the case of an authorized State program) under this subchapter;

(5) knowingly transports without a manifest, or causes to be transported without a manifest, any hazardous waste or any used oil not identified or listed as a hazardous waste under this subchapter required by regulations promulgated under this subchapter (or by a State in the case of a State program authorized under this subchapter) to be accompanied by a manifest;

(6) knowingly exports a hazardous waste identified or listed under this subchapter (A) without the consent of the receiving country or, (B) where there exists an international agreement between the United States and the government of the receiving country establishing notice, export, and enforcement procedures for the transportation, treatment, storage, and disposal of hazardous wastes, in a manner which is not in conformance with such agreement; or

(7) knowingly stores, treats, transports, or causes to be transported, disposes of, or otherwise handles any used oil not identified or listed as a hazardous waste under this subchapter—

(A) in knowing violation of any material condition or requirement of a permit under this subchapter; or

(B) in knowing violation of any material condition or requirement of any applicable regulations or standards under this chapter;

shall, upon conviction, be subject to a fine of not more than $50,000 for each day of violation, or imprisonment not to exceed two years (five years in the case of a violation of paragraph (1) or (2)), or both. If the conviction is for a violation committed after a first conviction of such person under this paragraph, the maximum punishment under the respective paragraph shall be doubled with respect to both fine and imprisonment.

**(e) Knowing endangerment**

Any person who knowingly transports, treats, stores, disposes of, or exports any hazardous waste identified or listed under this subchapter or used oil not identified or listed as a hazardous waste under this subchapter in violation of paragraph (1), (2), (3), (4), (5), (6), or (7) of subsection (d) of this section who knows at that time that he thereby places another person in imminent danger of death or serious bodily injury, shall, upon conviction, be subject to a fine of not more than $250,000 or imprisonment for not more than fifteen years, or both. A defendant that is an organization shall, upon conviction of violating this subsection, be subject to a fine of not more than $1,000,000.

**(f) Special rules**

For the purposes of subsection (e) of this section—

(1) A person's state of mind is knowing with respect to—

(A) his conduct, if he is aware of the nature of his conduct;

(B) an existing circumstance, if he is aware or believes that the circumstance exists; or

(C) a result of his conduct, if he is aware or believes that his conduct is substantially certain to cause danger of death or serious bodily injury.

(2) In determining whether a defendant who is a natural person knew that his conduct placed another person in imminent danger of death or serious bodily injury—

(A) the person is responsible only for actual awareness or actual belief that he possessed; and

(B) knowledge possessed by a person other than the defendant but not by the defendant himself may not be attributed to the defendant;

*Provided*, That in proving the defendant's possession of actual knowledge, circumstantial evidence may be used, including evidence that the defendant took affirmative steps to shield himself from relevant information.

(3) It is an affirmative defense to a prosecution that the conduct charged was consented to by the person endangered and that the danger and conduct charged were reasonably foreseeable hazards of—

(A) an occupation, a business, or a profession; or

(B) medical treatment or medical or scientific experimentation conducted by professionally approved methods and such other person had been made aware of the risks involved prior to giving consent.

The defendant may establish an affirmative defense under this subsection by a preponderance of the evidence.

(4) All general defenses, affirmative defenses, and bars to prosecution that may apply with respect to other Federal criminal offenses may apply under subsection (e) of this section and shall be determined by the courts of the United States according to the principles of common law as they may be interpreted in the light of reason and experience. Concepts of justification and excuse applicable un-

der this section may be developed in the light of reason and experience.

(5) The term "organization" means a legal entity, other than a government, established or organized for any purpose, and such term includes a corporation, company, association, firm, partnership, joint stock company, foundation, institution, trust, society, union, or any other association of persons.

(6) The term "serious bodily injury" means—

(A) bodily injury which involves a substantial risk of death;

(B) unconsciousness;

(C) extreme physical pain;

(D) protracted and obvious disfigurement; or

(E) protracted loss or impairment of the function of a bodily member, organ, or mental faculty.

**(g) Civil penalty**

Any person who violates any requirement of this subchapter shall be liable to the United States for a civil penalty in an amount not to exceed $25,000 for each such violation. Each day of such violation shall, for purposes of this subsection, constitute a separate violation.

**(h) Interim status corrective action orders**

(1) Whenever on the basis of any information the Administrator determines that there is or has been a release of hazardous waste into the environment from a facility authorized to operate under section 6925(e) of this title, the Administrator may issue an order requiring corrective action or such other response measure as he deems necessary to protect human health or the environment or the Administrator may commence a civil action in the United States district court in the district in which the facility is located for appropriate relief, including a temporary or permanent injunction.

(2) Any order issued under this subsection may include a suspension or revocation of authorization to operate under section 6925(e) of this title, shall state with reasonable specificity the nature of the required corrective action or other response measure, and shall specify a time for compliance. If any person named in an order fails to comply with the order, the Administrator may assess, and such person shall be liable to the United States for, a civil penalty in an amount not to exceed $25,000 for each day of noncompliance with the order.

(Pub.L. 89–272, Title II, § 3008, as added Pub.L. 94–580, § 2, Oct. 21, 1976, 90 Stat. 2811, and amended Pub.L. 95–609, § 7(k), Nov. 8, 1978, 92 Stat. 3082; Pub.L. 96–482, § 13, Oct. 21, 1980, 94 Stat. 2339; Pub.L. 98–616, Title II, §§ 232, 233, 245(c), Title IV, § 403(d)(1) to (3), Nov. 8, 1984, 98 Stat. 3256, 3257, 3264, 3272; Pub.L. 99–499, Title II, § 205(i), Oct. 17, 1986, 100 Stat. 1703.)

### HISTORICAL AND STATUTORY NOTES

**References in Text**

The Marine Protection, Research, and Sanctuaries Act, referred to in subsec. (d)(1) and (2)(A), probably means the Marine Protection, Research, and Sanctuaries Act of 1972, Pub.L. 92–532, Oct. 23, 1972, 86 Stat. 1052, as amended. Title I of the Marine Protection, Research, and Sanctuaries Act of 1972 is classified generally to subchapter I (section 1411 et seq.) of chapter 27 of Title 33, Navigation and Navigable Waters. For complete classification of this Act to the Code, see Short Title note set out under section 1401 of Title 33 and Tables.

**Effective and Applicability Provisions**

1986 Acts

Amendment by Pub.L. 99–499 effective Oct. 17, 1986, see section 4 of Pub.L. 99–499, set out as a note under section 9601 of this title.

**Transfer of Functions**

For transfer of certain enforcement functions of Administrator or other official of the Environmental Protection Agency under this chapter to Federal Inspector, Office of Federal Inspector for the Alaska Natural Gas Transportation System, see note set out under section 6903 of this title.

## § 6929. Retention of State authority

**[SWDA § 3009]**

Upon the effective date of regulations under this subchapter no State or political subdivision may impose any requirements less stringent than those authorized under this subchapter respecting the same matter as governed by such regulations, except that if application of a regulation with respect to any matter under this subchapter is postponed or enjoined by the action of any court, no State or political subdivision shall be prohibited from acting with respect to the same aspect of such matter until such time as such regulation takes effect. Nothing in this chapter shall be construed to prohibit any State or political subdivision thereof from imposing any requirements, including those for site selection, which are more stringent than those imposed by such regulations. Nothing in this chapter (or in any regulation adopted under this chapter) shall be construed to prohibit any State from requiring that the State be provided with a copy of each manifest used in connection with hazardous waste which is generated within that State or transported to a treatment, storage, or disposal facility within that State.

(Pub.L. 89–272, Title II, § 3009, as added Pub.L. 94–580, § 2, Oct. 21, 1976, 90 Stat. 2812, and amended Pub.L. 96–482, § 14, Oct. 21, 1980, 94 Stat. 2342; Pub.L. 98–616, Title II, § 213(b), Nov. 8, 1984, 98 Stat. 3242.)

## § 6930. Effective date

**[SWDA § 3010]**

**(a) Preliminary notification**

Not later than ninety days after promulgation of regulations under section 6921 of this title identifying by its characteristics or listing any substance as hazardous waste subject to this subchapter, any person generating or transporting such substance or owning or operating a facility for treatment, storage, or disposal of such substance shall file with the Administrator (or with States having authorized hazardous waste permit programs under section 6926 of this title) a notification stating the location and general description of such activity and the identified or listed hazardous wastes handled by such person. Not later than fifteen months after November 8, 1984—

(1) the owner or operator of any facility which produces a fuel (A) from any hazardous waste identified or listed under section 6921 of this title, (B) from such hazardous waste identified or listed under section 6921 of this title and any other material, (C) from used oil, or (D) from used oil and any other material;

(2) the owner or operator of any facility (other than a single- or two-family residence) which burns for purposes of energy recovery any fuel produced as provided in paragraph (1) or any fuel which otherwise contains used oil or any hazardous waste identified or listed under section 6921 of this title; and

(3) any person who distributes or markets any fuel which is produced as provided in paragraph (1) or any fuel which otherwise contains used oil or any hazardous waste identified or listed under section 6921 of this title[1]

shall file with the Administrator (and with the State in the case of a State with an authorized hazardous waste program) a notification stating the location and general description of the facility, together with a description of the identified or listed hazardous waste involved and, in the case of a facility referred to in paragraph (1) or (2), a description of the production or energy recovery activity carried out at the facility and such other information as the Administrator deems necessary. For purposes of the preceding provisions, the term "hazardous waste listed under section 6921 of this title" also includes any commercial chemical product which is listed under section 6921 of this title and which, in lieu of its original intended use, is (i) produced for use as (or as a component of) a fuel, (ii) distributed for use as a fuel, or (iii) burned as a fuel. Notification shall not be required under the second sentence of this subsection in the case of facilities (such as residential boilers) where the Administrator determines that such notification is not necessary in order for the Administrator to obtain sufficient information respecting current practices of facilities using hazardous waste for energy recovery. Nothing in this subsection shall be construed to affect or impair the provisions of section 6921(b)(3) of this title. Nothing in this subsection shall affect regulatory determinations under section 6935 of this title. In revising any regulation under section 6921 of this title identifying additional characteristics of hazardous waste or listing any additional substance as hazardous waste subject to this subchapter, the Administrator may require any person referred to in the preceding provisions to file with the Administrator (or with States having authorized hazardous waste permit programs under section 6926 of this title) the notification described in the preceding provisions. Not more than one such notification shall be required to be filed with respect to the same substance. No identified or listed hazardous waste subject to this subchapter may be transported, treated, stored, or disposed of unless notification has been given as required under this subsection.

**(b) Effective date of regulation**

The regulations under this subchapter respecting requirements applicable to the generation, transportation, treatment, storage, or disposal of hazardous waste (including requirements respecting permits for such treatment, storage, or disposal) shall take effect on the date six months after the date of promulgation thereof (or six months after the date of revision in the case of any regulation which is revised after the date required for promulgation thereof). At the time a regulation is promulgated, the Administrator may provide for a shorter period prior to the effective date, or an immediate effective date for:

(1) a regulation with which the Administrator finds the regulated community does not need six months to come into compliance;

(2) a regulation which responds to an emergency situation; or

(3) other good cause found and published with the regulation.

(Pub.L. 89–272, Title II, § 3010, as added Pub.L. 94–580, § 2, Oct. 21, 1976, 90 Stat. 2812, and amended Pub.L. 96–482, § 15, Oct. 21, 1980, 94 Stat. 2342; Pub.L. 98–616, Title II, §§ 204(a), 234, Nov. 8, 1984, 98 Stat. 3235, 3258.)

[1] So in original. Probably should be followed by a semicolon.

### HISTORICAL AND STATUTORY NOTES

**Transfer of Functions**

For transfer of certain enforcement functions of Administrator or other official of the Environmental Protection Agency under this chapter to Federal Inspector, Office of Federal Inspector for the Alaska Natural Gas Transportation System, see note set out under section 6903 of this title.

## § 6931. Authorization of assistance to States

**[SWDA § 3011]**

**(a) Authorization of appropriations**

There is authorized to be appropriated $25,000,000 for each of the fiscal years 1978 and 1979[1] $20,000,000 for fiscal year 1980, $35,000,000 for fiscal year 1981, $40,000,000 for the fiscal year 1982, $55,000,000 for the fiscal year 1985, $60,000,000 for the fiscal year 1986, $60,000,000 for the fiscal year 1987, and $60,000,000 for the fiscal year 1988 to be used to make grants to the States for purposes of assisting the States in the development and implementation of authorized State hazardous waste programs.

**(b) Allocation**

Amounts authorized to be appropriated under subsection (a) of this section shall be allocated among the States on the basis of regulations promulgated by the Administrator, after consultation with the States, which take into account, the extent to which hazardous waste is generated, transported, treated, stored, and disposed of within such State, the extent of exposure of human beings and the environment within such State to such waste, and such other factors as the Administrator deems appropriate.

**(c) Activities included**

State hazardous waste programs for which grants may be made under subsection (a) of this section may include (but shall not be limited to) planning for hazardous waste treatment, storage and disposal facilities, and the development and execution of programs to protect health and the environment from inactive facilities which may contain hazardous waste.

(Pub.L. 89–272, Title II, § 3011, as added Pub.L. 94–580, § 2, Oct. 21, 1976, 90 Stat. 2812, and amended Pub.L. 96–482, §§ 16, 31(b), Oct. 21, 1980, 94 Stat. 2342, 2352; Pub.L. 98–616, § 2(b), Nov. 8, 1984, 98 Stat. 3222.)

[1] So in original. Probably should be followed by a comma.

### HISTORICAL AND STATUTORY NOTES

**Transfer of Functions**

For transfer of certain enforcement functions of Administrator or other official of the Environmental Protection Agency under this chapter to Federal Inspector, Office of Federal Inspector for the Alaska Natural Gas Transportation System, see note set out under section 6903 of this title.

## § 6932. Transferred

### HISTORICAL AND STATUTORY NOTES

**Codifications**

Section 6932, Pub.L. 89–272, Title II, § 3012, as added Pub.L. 96–463, § 7(a), Oct. 15, 1980, 94 Stat. 2057, was redesignated section 3014 of Pub.L. 89–272, by Pub.L. 98–616, Title V, § 502(g)(1), Nov. 8, 1984, 98 Stat. 3277, and was transferred to section 6935 of this title.

## § 6933. Hazardous waste site inventory

[SWDA § 3012]

**(a) State inventory programs**

Each State shall, as expeditiously as practicable, undertake a continuing program to compile, publish, and submit to the Administrator an inventory describing the location of each site within such State at which hazardous waste has at any time been stored or disposed of. Such inventory shall contain—

(1) a description of the location of the sites at which any such storage or disposal has taken place before the date on which permits are required under section 6925 of this title for such storage or disposal;

(2) such information relating to the amount, nature, and toxicity of the hazardous waste at each such site as may be practicable to obtain and as may be necessary to determine the extent of any health hazard which may be associated with such site;

(3) the name and address, or corporate headquarters of, the owner of each such site, determined as of the date of preparation of the inventory;

(4) an identification of the types or techniques of waste treatment or disposal which have been used at each such site; and

(5) information concerning the current status of the site, including information respecting whether or not hazardous waste is currently being treated or disposed of at such site (and if not, the date on which such activity ceased) and information respecting the nature of any other activity currently carried out at such site.

For purposes of assisting the States in compiling information under this section, the Administrator shall make available to each State undertaking a program under this section such information as is available to him concerning the items specified in paragraphs (1) through (5) with respect to the sites within such State, including such information as the Administrator is able to obtain from other agencies or departments of the United States and from surveys and studies carried out by any committee or subcommittee of the Congress. Any State may exercise the authority of section 6927 of this title for purposes of this section in the same manner and to the same extent as provided in such section in the case of States having an authorized hazardous waste program, and any State may by order require any person to submit such information as may be necessary to compile the data referred to in paragraphs (1) through (5).

**(b) Environmental Protection Agency program**

If the Administrator determines that any State program under subsection (a) of this section is not adequately providing information respecting the sites in such State referred to in subsection (a) of this section, the Administrator shall notify the State. If within ninety days following such notification, the

State program has not been revised or amended in such manner as will adequately provide such information, the Administrator shall carry out the inventory program in such State. In any such case—

(1) the Administrator shall have the authorities provided with respect to State programs under subsection (a) of this section;

(2) the funds allocated under subsection (c) of this section for grants to States under this section may be used by the Administrator for carrying out such program in such State; and

(3) no further expenditure may be made for grants to such State under this section until such time as the Administrator determines that such State is carrying out, or will carry out, an inventory program which meets the requirements of this section.

**(c) Grants**

(1) Upon receipt of an application submitted by any State to carry out a program under this section, the Administrator may make grants to the States for purposes of carrying out such a program. Grants under this section shall be allocated among the several States by the Administrator based upon such regulations as he prescribes to carry out the purposes of this section. The Administrator may make grants to any State which has conducted an inventory program which effectively carried out the purposes of this section before October 21, 1980, to reimburse such State for all, or any portion of, the costs incurred by such State in conducting such program.

(2) There are authorized to be appropriated to carry out this section $25,000,000 for each of the fiscal years 1985 through 1988.

**(d) No impediment to immediate remedial action**

Nothing in this section shall be construed to provide that the Administrator or any State should, pending completion of the inventory required under this section, postpone undertaking any enforcement or remedial action with respect to any site at which hazardous waste has been treated, stored, or disposed of.

(Pub.L. 89–272, Title II, § 3012, as added Pub.L. 96–482, § 17(a), Oct. 21, 1980, 94 Stat. 2342, and amended Pub.L. 98–616, § 2(c), Nov. 8, 1984, 98 Stat. 3222.)

### HISTORICAL AND STATUTORY NOTES

**Codifications**

Another section 3012 of Pub.L. 89–272, providing for restrictions on recycled oil, was enacted by Pub.L. 96–463, § 7(a), Oct. 15, 1980, 94 Stat. 2057, was redesignated section 3014 of Pub.L. 89–272, and is classified to section 6935 of this title.

**Transfer of Functions**

For transfer of certain enforcement functions of Administrator or other official of the Environmental Protection Agency under this chapter to Federal Inspector, Office of Federal Inspector for the Alaska Natural Gas Transportation System, see note set out under section 6903 of this title.

## § 6934. Monitoring, analysis, and testing

**[SWDA § 3013]**

**(a) Authority of Administrator**

If the Administrator determines, upon receipt of any information, that—

(1) the presence of any hazardous waste at a facility or site at which hazardous waste is, or has been, stored, treated, or disposed of, or

(2) the release of any such waste from such facility or site

may present a substantial hazard to human health or the environment, he may issue an order requiring the owner or operator of such facility or site to conduct such monitoring, testing, analysis, and reporting with respect to such facility or site as the Administrator deems reasonable to ascertain the nature and extent of such hazard.

**(b) Previous owners and operators**

In the case of any facility or site not in operation at the time a determination is made under subsection (a) of this section with respect to the facility or site, if the Administrator finds that the owner of such facility or site could not reasonably be expected to have actual knowledge of the presence of hazardous waste at such facility or site and of its potential for release, he may issue an order requiring the most recent previous owner or operator of such facility or site who could reasonably be expected to have such actual knowledge to carry out the actions referred to in subsection (a) of this section.

**(c) Proposal**

An order under subsection (a) or (b) of this section shall require the person to whom such order is issued to submit to the Administrator within 30 days from the issuance of such order a proposal for carrying out the required monitoring, testing, analysis, and reporting. The Administrator may, after providing such person with an opportunity to confer with the Administrator respecting such proposal, require such person to carry out such monitoring, testing, analysis, and reporting in accordance with such proposal, and such modifications in such proposal as the Administrator deems reasonable to ascertain the nature and extent of the hazard.

**(d) Monitoring, etc., carried out by Administrator**

(1) If the Administrator determines that no owner or operator referred to in subsection (a) or (b) of this section is able to conduct monitoring, testing, analysis, or reporting satisfactory to the Administrator, if the

Administrator deems any such action carried out by an owner or operator to be unsatisfactory, or if the Administrator cannot initially determine that there is an owner or operator referred to in subsection (a) or (b) of this section who is able to conduct such monitoring, testing, analysis, or reporting, he may—

(A) conduct monitoring, testing, or analysis (or any combination thereof) which he deems reasonable to ascertain the nature and extent of the hazard associated with the site concerned, or

(B) authorize a State or local authority or other person to carry out any such action,

and require, by order, the owner or operator referred to in subsection (a) or (b) of this section to reimburse the Administrator or other authority or person for the costs of such activity.

(2) No order may be issued under this subsection requiring reimbursement of the costs of any action carried out by the Administrator which confirms the results of an order issued under subsection (a) or (b) of this section.

(3) For purposes of carrying out this subsection, the Administrator or any authority or other person authorized under paragraph (1), may exercise the authorities set forth in section 6927 of this title.

**(e) Enforcement**

The Administrator may commence a civil action against any person who fails or refuses to comply with any order issued under this section. Such action shall be brought in the United States district court in which the defendant is located, resides, or is doing business. Such court shall have jurisdiction to require compliance with such order and to assess a civil penalty of not to exceed $5,000 for each day during which such failure or refusal occurs.

(Pub.L. 89–272, Title II, § 3013, as added Pub.L. 96–482, § 17(a), Oct. 21, 1980, 94 Stat. 2344.)

### HISTORICAL AND STATUTORY NOTES

**Transfer of Functions**

For transfer of certain enforcement functions of Administrator or other official of the Environmental Protection Agency under this chapter to Federal Inspector, Office of Federal Inspector for the Alaska Natural Gas Transportation System, see note set out under section 6903 of this title.

## § 6935. Restrictions on recycled oil

[SWDA § 3014]

**(a) In general**

Not later than one year after October 15, 1980, the Administrator shall promulgate regulations establishing such performance standards and other requirements as may be necessary to protect the public health and the environment from hazards associated with recycled oil. In developing such regulations, the Administrator shall conduct an analysis of the economic impact of the regulations on the oil recycling industry. The Administrator shall ensure that such regulations do not discourage the recovery or recycling of used oil, consistent with the protection of human health and the environment.

**(b) Identification or listing of used oil as hazardous waste**

Not later than twelve months after November 8, 1984, the Administrator shall propose whether to list or identify used automobile and truck crankcase oil as hazardous waste under section 6921 of this title. Not later than twenty-four months after November 8, 1984, the Administrator shall make a final determination whether to list or identify used automobile and truck crankcase oil and other used oil as hazardous wastes under section 6921 of this title.

**(c) Used oil which is recycled**

(1) With respect to generators and transporters of used oil identified or listed as a hazardous waste under section 6921 of this title, the standards promulgated under section[1] 6921(d), 6922, and 6923 of this title shall not apply to such used oil if such used oil is recycled.

(2)(A) In the case of used oil which is exempt under paragraph (1), not later than twenty-four months after November 8, 1984, the Administrator shall promulgate such standards under this subsection regarding the generation and transportation of used oil which is recycled as may be necessary to protect human health and the environment. In promulgating such regulations with respect to generators, the Administrator shall take into account the effect of such regulations on environmentally acceptable types of used oil recycling and the effect of such regulations on small quantity generators and generators which are small businesses (as defined by the Administrator).

(B) The regulations promulgated under this subsection shall provide that no generator of used oil which is exempt under paragraph (1) from the standards promulgated under section [1] 6921(d), 6922, and 6923 of this title shall be subject to any manifest requirement or any associated recordkeeping and reporting requirement with respect to such used oil if such generator—

(i) either—

(I) enters into an agreement or other arrangement (including an agreement or arrangement with an independent transporter or with an agent of the recycler) for delivery of such used oil to a recycling facility which has a permit under section 6925(c) of this title (or for which a valid permit is deemed to be in effect under subsection (d) of this section), or

(II) recycles such used oil at one or more facilities of the generator which has such a permit under section 6925 of this title (or for which a valid permit is deemed to have been issued under subsection (d) of this section);

(ii) such used oil is not mixed by the generator with other types of hazardous wastes; and

(iii) the generator maintains such records relating to such used oil, including records of agreements or other arrangements for delivery of such used oil to any recycling facility referred to in clause (i)(I), as the Administrator deems necessary to protect human health and the environment.

(3) The regulations under this subsection regarding the transportation of used oil which is exempt from the standards promulgated under section[1] 6921(d), 6922, and 6923 of this title under paragraph (1) shall require the transporters of such used oil to deliver such used oil to a facility which has a valid permit under section 6925 of this title or which is deemed to have a valid permit under subsection (d) of this section. The Administrator shall also establish other standards for such transporters as may be necessary to protect human health and the environment.

## (d) Permits

(1) The owner or operator of a facility which recycles used oil which is exempt under subsection (c)(1) of this section, shall be deemed to have a permit under this subsection for all such treatment or recycling (and any associated tank or container storage) if such owner and operator comply with standards promulgated by the Administrator under section 6924 of this title; except that the Administrator may require such owners and operators to obtain an individual permit under section 6925(c) of this title if he determines that an individual permit is necessary to protect human health and the environment.

(2) Notwithstanding any other provision of law, any generator who recycles used oil which is exempt under subsection (c)(1) of this section shall not be required to obtain a permit under section 6925(c) of this title with respect to such used oil until the Administrator has promulgated standards under section 6924 of this title regarding the recycling of such used oil.

(Pub.L. 89–272, Title II, § 3014, formerly § 3012, as added Pub.L. 96–463, § 7(a), Oct. 15, 1980, 94 Stat. 2057, and renumbered § 3014 and amended Pub.L. 98–616, Title II, §§ 241(a), 242, Title V, § 502(g)(1), Nov. 8, 1984, 98 Stat. 3258, 3260, 3277.)

[1] So in original. Probably should be "sections".

### HISTORICAL AND STATUTORY NOTES

**Codifications**

Section was formerly classified to section 6932 of this title.

**Transfer of Functions**

For transfer of certain enforcement functions of Administrator or other official of the Environmental Protection Agency under this chapter to Federal Inspector, Office of Federal Inspector for the Alaska Natural Gas Transportation System, see note set out under section 6903 of this title.

## § 6936. Expansion during interim status [SWDA § 3015]

### (a) Waste piles

The owner or operator of a waste pile qualifying for the authorization to operate under section 6925(e) of this title shall be subject to the same requirements for liners and leachate collection systems or equivalent protection provided in regulations promulgated by the Administrator under section 6924 of this title before October 1, 1982, or revised under section 6924(*o*) of this title (relating to minimum technological requirements), for new facilities receiving individual permits under subsection (c) of section 6925 of this title, with respect to each new unit, replacement of an existing unit, or lateral expansion of an existing unit that is within the waste management area identified in the permit application submitted under section 6925 of this title, and with respect to waste received beginning six months after November 8, 1984.

### (b) Landfills and surface impoundments

(1) The owner or operator of a landfill or surface impoundment qualifying for the authorization to operate under section 6925(e) of this title shall be subject to the requirements of section 6924(*o*) of this title (relating to minimum technological requirements), with respect to each new unit, replacement of an existing unit, or lateral expansion of an existing unit that is within the waste management area identified in the permit application submitted under this section, and with respect to waste received beginning 6 months after November 8, 1984.

(2) The owner or operator of each unit referred to in paragraph (1) shall notify the Administrator (or the State, if appropriate) at least sixty days prior to receiving waste. The Administrator (or the State) shall require the filing, within six months of receipt of such notice, of an application for a final determination regarding the issuance of a permit for each facility submitting such notice.

(3) In the case of any unit in which the liner and leachate collection system has been installed pursuant to the requirements of this section and in good faith compliance with the Administrator's regulations and guidance documents governing liners and leachate collection systems, no liner or leachate collection system which is different from that which was so installed pursuant to this section shall be required for such unit by the Administrator when issuing the first permit

under section 6925 of this title to such facility, except that the Administrator shall not be precluded from requiring installation of a new liner when the Administrator has reason to believe that any liner installed pursuant to the requirements of this section is leaking. The Administrator may, under section 6924 of this title, amend the requirements for liners and leachate collection systems required under this section as may be necessary to provide additional protection for human health and the environment.

(Pub.L. 89–272, Title II, § 3015, as added Pub.L. 98–616, Title II, § 243(a), Nov. 8, 1984, 98 Stat. 3260.)

## § 6937. Inventory of Federal agency hazardous waste facilities

**[SWDA § 3016]**

### (a) Program requirement; submission; availability; contents

Each Federal agency shall undertake a continuing program to compile, publish, and submit to the Administrator (and to the State in the case of sites in States having an authorized hazardous waste program) an inventory of each site which the Federal agency owns or operates or has owned or operated at which hazardous waste is stored, treated, or disposed of or has been disposed of at any time. The inventory shall be submitted every two years beginning January 31, 1986. Such inventory shall be available to the public as provided in section 6927(b) of this title. Information previously submitted by a Federal agency under section 9603 of this title, or under section 6925 or 6930 of this title, or under this section need not be resubmitted except that the agency shall update any previous submission to reflect the latest available data and information. The inventory shall include each of the following:

(1) A description of the location of each site at which any such treatment, storage, or disposal has taken place before the date on which permits are required under section 6925 of this title for such storage, treatment, or disposal, and where hazardous waste has been disposed, a description of hydrogeology of the site and the location of withdrawal wells and surface water within one mile of the site.

(2) Such information relating to the amount, nature, and toxicity of the hazardous waste in each site as may be necessary to determine the extent of any health hazard which may be associated with any site.

(3) Information on the known nature and extent of environmental contamination at each site, including a description of the monitoring data obtained.

(4) Information concerning the current status of the site, including information respecting whether or not hazardous waste is currently being treated, stored, or disposed of at such site (and if not, the date on which such activity ceased) and information respecting the nature of any other activity currently carried out at such site.

(5) A list of sites at which hazardous waste has been disposed and environmental monitoring data has not been obtained, and the reasons for the lack of monitoring data at each site.

(6) A description of response actions undertaken or contemplated at contaminated sites.

(7) An identification of the types of techniques of waste treatment, storage, or disposal which have been used at each site.

(8) The name and address and responsible Federal agency for each site, determined as of the date of preparation of the inventory.

### (b) Environmental Protection Agency program

If the Administrator determines that any Federal agency under subsection (a) of this section is not adequately providing information respecting the sites referred to in subsection (a) of this section, the Administrator shall notify the chief official of such agency. If within ninety days following such notification, the Federal agency has not undertaken a program to adequately provide such information, the Administrator shall carry out the inventory program for such agency.

(Pub.L. 89–272, Title II, § 3016, as added Pub.L. 98–616, Title II, § 244, Nov. 8, 1984, 98 Stat. 3261.)

## § 6938. Export of hazardous wastes

**[SWDA § 3017]**

### (a) In general

Beginning twenty-four months after November 8, 1984, no person shall export any hazardous waste identified or listed under this subchapter unless [1]

(1)(A) such person has provided the notification required in subsection (c) of this section,

(B) the government of the receiving country has consented to accept such hazardous waste,

(C) a copy of the receiving country's written consent is attached to the manifest accompanying each waste shipment, and

(D) the shipment conforms with the terms of the consent of the government of the receiving country required pursuant to subsection (e) of this section, or

(2) the United States and the government of the receiving country have entered into an agreement as provided for in subsection (f) of this section and the shipment conforms with the terms of such agreement.

### (b) Regulations

Not later than twelve months after November 8, 1984, the Administrator shall promulgate the regulations necessary to implement this section. Such regulations shall become effective one hundred and eighty days after promulgation.

**(c) Notification**

Any person who intends to export a hazardous waste identified or listed under this subchapter beginning twelve months after November 8, 1984, shall, before such hazardous waste is scheduled to leave the United States, provide notification to the Administrator. Such notification shall contain the following information:

(1) the name and address of the exporter;

(2) the types and estimated quantities of hazardous waste to be exported;

(3) the estimated frequency or rate at which such waste is to be exported; and the period of time over which such waste is to be exported;

(4) the ports of entry;

(5) a description of the manner in which such hazardous waste will be transported to and treated, stored, or disposed in the receiving country; and

(6) the name and address of the ultimate treatment, storage or disposal facility.

**(d) Procedures for requesting consent of receiving country**

Within thirty days of the Administrator's receipt of a complete notification under this section, the Secretary of State, acting on behalf of the Administrator, shall—

(1) forward a copy of the notification to the government of the receiving country;

(2) advise the government that United States law prohibits the export of hazardous waste unless the receiving country consents to accept the hazardous waste;

(3) request the government to provide the Secretary with a written consent or objection to the terms of the notification; and

(4) forward to the government of the receiving country a description of the Federal regulations which would apply to the treatment, storage, and disposal of the hazardous waste in the United States.

**(e) Conveyance of written consent to exporter**

Within thirty days of receipt by the Secretary of State of the receiving country's written consent or objection (or any subsequent communication withdrawing a prior consent or objection), the Administrator shall forward such a consent, objection, or other communication to the exporter.

**(f) International agreements**

Where there exists an international agreement between the United States and the government of the receiving country establishing notice, export, and enforcement procedures for the transportation, treatment, storage, and disposal of hazardous wastes, only the requirements of subsections (a)(2) and (g) of this section shall apply.

**(g) Reports**

After November 8, 1984, any person who exports any hazardous waste identified or listed under section 6921 of this title shall file with the Administrator no later than March 1 of each year, a report summarizing the types, quantities, frequency, and ultimate destination of all such hazardous waste exported during the previous calendar year.

**(h) Other standards**

Nothing in this section shall preclude the Administrator from establishing other standards for the export of hazardous wastes under section 6922 of this title or section 6923 of this title.

(Pub.L. 89–272, Title II, § 3017, as added Pub.L. 98–616, Title II, § 245(a), Nov. 8, 1984, 98 Stat. 3262.)

1 So in original.

## § 6939. Domestic sewage

**[SWDA § 3018]**

**(a) Report**

The Administrator shall, not later than 15 months after November 8, 1984, submit a report to the Congress concerning those substances identified or listed under section 6921 of this title which are not regulated under this subchapter by reason of the exclusion for mixtures of domestic sewage and other wastes that pass through a sewer system to a publicly owned treatment works. Such report shall include the types, size and number of generators which dispose of such substances in this manner, the types and quantities disposed of in this manner, and the identification of significant generators, wastes, and waste constituents not regulated under existing Federal law or regulated in a manner sufficient to protect human health and the environment.

**(b) Revisions of regulations**

Within eighteen months after submitting the report specified in subsection (a) of this section, the Administrator shall revise existing regulations and promulgate such additional regulations pursuant to this subchapter (or any other authority of the Administrator, including section 1317 of Title 33) as are necessary to assure that substances identified or listed under section 6921 of this title which pass through a sewer system to a publicly owned treatment works are adequately controlled to protect human health and the environment.

**(c) Report on wastewater lagoons**

The Administrator shall, within thirty-six months after November 8, 1984, submit a report to Congress concerning wastewater lagoons at publicly owned treatment works and their effect on groundwater quality. Such report shall include—

(1) the number and size of such lagoons;

(2) the types and quantities of waste contained in such lagoons;

(3) the extent to which such waste has been or may be released from such lagoons and contaminate ground water; and

(4) available alternatives for preventing or controlling such releases.

The Administrator may utilize the authority of sections 6927 and 6934 of this title for the purpose of completing such report.

**(d) Application of sections 6927 and 6930**

The provisions of sections 6927 and 6930 of this title shall apply to solid or dissolved materials in domestic sewage to the same extent and in the same manner as such provisions apply to hazardous waste.

(Pub.L. 89–272, Title II, § 3018, as added Pub.L. 98–616, Title II, § 246(a), Nov. 8, 1984, 98 Stat. 3264.)

## § 6939a. Exposure information and health assessments

**[SWDA § 3019]**

**(a) Exposure information**

Beginning on the date nine months after November 8, 1984, each application for a final determination regarding a permit under section 6925(c) of this title for a landfill or surface impoundment shall be accompanied by information reasonably ascertainable by the owner or operator on the potential for the public to be exposed to hazardous wastes or hazardous constituents through releases related to the unit. At a minimum, such information must address:

(1) reasonably foreseeable potential releases from both normal operations and accidents at the unit, including releases associated with transportation to or from the unit;

(2) the potential pathways of human exposure to hazardous wastes or constituents resulting from the releases described under paragraph (1); and

(3) the potential magnitude and nature of the human exposure resulting from such releases.

The owner or operator of a landfill or surface impoundment for which an application for such a final determination under section 6925(c) of this title has been submitted prior to November 8, 1984, shall submit the information required by this subsection to the Administrator (or the State, in the case of a State with an authorized program) no later than the date nine months after November 8, 1984.

**(b) Health assessments**

(1) The Administrator (or the State, in the case of a State with an authorized program) shall make the information required by subsection (a) of this section, together with other relevant information, available to the Agency for Toxic Substances and Disease Registry established by section 9604(i) of this title.

(2) Whenever in the judgment of the Administrator, or the State (in the case of a State with an authorized program), a landfill or a surface impoundment poses a substantial potential risk to human health, due to the existence of releases of hazardous constituents, the magnitude of contamination with hazardous constituents which may be the result of a release, or the magnitude of the population exposed to such release or contamination, the Administrator or the State (with the concurrence of the Administrator) may request the Administrator of the Agency for Toxic Substances and Disease Registry to conduct a health assessment in connection with such facility and take other appropriate action with respect to such risks as authorized by section 9604(b) and (i) of this title. If funds are provided in connection with such request the Administrator of such Agency shall conduct such health assessment.

**(c) Members of the public**

Any member of the public may submit evidence of releases of or exposure to hazardous constituents from such a facility, or as to the risks or health effects associated with such releases or exposure, to the Administrator of the Agency for Toxic Substances and Disease Registry, the Administrator, or the State (in the case of a State with an authorized program).

**(d) Priority**

In determining the order in which to conduct health assessments under this subsection, the Administrator of the Agency for Toxic Substances and Disease Registry shall give priority to those facilities or sites at which there is documented evidence of release of hazardous constituents, at which the potential risk to human health appears highest, and for which in the judgment of the Administrator of such Agency existing health assessment data is inadequate to assess the potential risk to human health as provided in subsection (f) of this section.

**(e) Periodic reports**

The Administrator of such Agency shall issue periodic reports which include the results of all the assessments carried out under this section. Such assessments or other activities shall be reported after appropriate peer review.

**(f) "Health assessments" defined**

For the purposes of this section, the term "health assessments" shall include preliminary assessments of the potential risk to human health posed by individual sites and facilities subject to this section, based on such factors as the nature and extent of contamination, the existence of potential for pathways of human exposure (including ground or surface water contamination, air emissions, and food chain contamination), the size and potential susceptibility of the community within the likely pathways of exposure, the comparison of expected human exposure levels to the short-term and long-term health effects associated with identified contaminants and any available recommended exposure or tolerance limits for such contaminants, and the comparison of existing morbidity and mortality data on diseases that may be associated with the observed levels of exposure. The assessment shall include an evaluation of the risks to the potentially affected population from all sources of such contaminants, including known point or nonpoint sources other than the site or facility in question. A purpose of such preliminary assessments shall be to help determine whether full-scale health or epidemiological studies and medical evaluations of exposed populations shall be undertaken.

**(g) Cost recovery**

In any case in which a health assessment performed under this section discloses the exposure of a population to the release of a hazardous substance, the costs of such health assessment may be recovered as a cost of response under section 9607 of this title from persons causing or contributing to such release of such hazardous substance or, in the case of multiple releases contributing to such exposure, to all such release.

(Pub.L. 89–272, Title II, § 3019, as added Pub.L. 98–616, Title II, § 247(a), Nov. 8, 1984, 98 Stat. 3265.)

## § 6939b. Interim control of hazardous waste injection

**[SWDA § 3020]**

**(a) Underground source of drinking water**

No hazardous waste may be disposed of by underground injection—

(1) into a formation which contains (within one-quarter mile of the well used for such underground injection) an underground source of drinking water; or

(2) above such a formation.

The prohibitions established under this section shall take effect 6 months after November 8, 1984, except in the case of any State in which identical or more stringent prohibitions are in effect before such date under the Safe Drinking Water Act [42 U.S.C.A. § 300f et seq.].

**(b) Actions under Comprehensive Environmental Response, Compensation, and Liability Act**

Subsection (a) of this section shall not apply to the injection of contaminated ground water into the aquifer from which it was withdrawn, if—

(1) such injection is—

(A) a response action taken under section 9604 or 9606 of this title, or

(B) part of corrective action required under this chapter [1]

intended to clean up such contamination;

(2) such contaminated ground water is treated to substantially reduce hazardous constituents prior to such injection; and

(3) such response action or corrective action will, upon completion, be sufficient to protect human health and the environment.

**(c) Enforcement**

In addition to enforcement under the provisions of this chapter, the prohibitions established under paragraphs (1) and (2) of subsection (a) of this section shall be enforceable under the Safe Drinking Water Act [42 U.S.C.A. § 300f et seq.] in any State—

(1) which has adopted identical or more stringent prohibitions under part C of the Safe Drinking Water Act [42 U.S.C.A. § 300h et seq.] and which has assumed primary enforcement responsibility under that Act [42 U.S.C.A. § 300f et seq.] for enforcement of such prohibitions; or

(2) in which the Administrator has adopted identical or more stringent prohibitions under the Safe Drinking Water Act [42 U.S.C.A. § 300f et seq.] and is exercising primary enforcement responsibility under that Act [42 U.S.C.A. § 300f et seq.] for enforcement of such prohibitions.

**(d) Definitions**

The terms "primary enforcement responsibility", "underground source of drinking water", "formation" and "well" have the same meanings as provided in regulations of the Administrator under the Safe Drinking Water Act [42 U.S.C.A. § 300f et seq.]. The term "Safe Drinking Water Act" means title XIV of the Public Health Service Act.

(Pub.L. 89–272, Title II, § 3020, formerly § 7010, as added Pub.L. 98–616, Title IV, § 405(a), Nov. 8, 1984, 98 Stat. 3273; renumbered § 3020 and amended Pub.L. 99–339, Title II, § 201(c), June 19, 1986, 100 Stat. 654.)

[1] So in original. Probably should be followed by a comma.

HISTORICAL AND STATUTORY NOTES

**References in Text**

Title XIV of the Public Health Service Act, referred to in subsec. (d), is Title XIV of Act July 1, 1944, as added Dec. 16, 1974, Pub. L. 93–523, 2(a), 88 Stat. 1660, as amended, known as the Safe Drinking Water Act, which is classified principally to subchapter XII of chapter 6A of this title, 42 U.S.C.A. § 300f et seq. Part C of the Act is classified generally to part C of subchapter XII of chapter 6A of this title, 42 U.S.C.A. § 300h et seq. For complete classification, see Short Title note set out under 42 U.S.C.A. § 201 of this title and Tables.

**Codifications**

Section was formerly classified to section 6979a of this title, prior to renumbering by section 201(c)(2) of Pub.L. 99–339.

## § 6939c. Mixed waste inventory reports and plan

[SWDA § 3021]

**(a) Mixed waste inventory reports**

**(1) Requirement**

Not later than 180 days after October 6, 1992, the Secretary of Energy shall submit to the Administrator and to the Governor of each State in which the Department of Energy stores or generates mixed wastes the following reports:

(A) A report containing a national inventory of all such mixed wastes, regardless of the time they were generated, on a State-by-State basis.

(B) A report containing a national inventory of mixed waste treatment capacities and technologies.

**(2) Inventory of wastes**

The report required by paragraph (1)(A) shall include the following:

(A) A description of each type of mixed waste at each Department of Energy facility in each State, including, at a minimum, the name of the waste stream.

(B) The amount of each type of mixed waste currently stored at each Department of Energy facility in each State, set forth separately by mixed waste that is subject to the land disposal prohibition requirements of section 6924 of this title and mixed waste that is not subject to such prohibition requirements.

(C) An estimate of the amount of each type of mixed waste the Department expects to generate in the next 5 years at each Department of Energy facility in each State.

(D) A description of any waste minimization actions the Department has implemented at each Department of Energy facility in each State for each mixed waste stream.

(E) The EPA hazardous waste code for each type of mixed waste containing waste that has been characterized at each Department of Energy facility in each State.

(F) An inventory of each type of waste that has not been characterized by sampling and analysis at each Department of Energy facility in each State.

(G) The basis for the Department's determination of the applicable hazardous waste code for each type of mixed waste at each Department of Energy facility and a description of whether the determination is based on sampling and analysis conducted on the waste or on the basis of process knowledge.

(H) A description of the source of each type of mixed waste at each Department of Energy facility in each State.

(I) The land disposal prohibition treatment technology or technologies specified for the hazardous waste component of each type of mixed waste at each Department of Energy facility in each State.

(J) A statement of whether and how the radionuclide content of the waste alters or affects use of the technologies described in subparagraph (I).

**(3) Inventory of treatment capacities and technologies**

The report required by paragraph (1)(B) shall include the following:

(A) An estimate of the available treatment capacity for each waste described in the report required by paragraph (1)(A) for which treatment technologies exist.

(B) A description, including the capacity, number and location, of each treatment unit considered in calculating the estimate under subparagraph (A).

(C) A description, including the capacity, number and location, of any existing treatment unit that was not considered in calculating the estimate under subparagraph (A) but that could, alone or in conjunction with other treatment units, be used to treat any of the wastes described in the report required by paragraph (1)(A) to meet the requirements of regulations promulgated pursuant to section 6924(m) of this title.

(D) For each unit listed in subparagraph (C), a statement of the reasons why the unit was not included in calculating the estimate under subparagraph (A).

(E) A description, including the capacity, number, location, and estimated date of availability, of each treatment unit currently proposed to increase the treatment capacities estimated under subparagraph (A).

**(F)** For each waste described in the report required by paragraph (1)(A) for which the Department has determined no treatment technology exists, information sufficient to support such determination and a description of the technological approaches the Department anticipates will need to be developed to treat the waste.

**(4) Comments and revisions**

Not later than 90 days after the date of the submission of the reports by the Secretary of Energy under paragraph (1), the Administrator and each State which received the reports shall submit any comments they may have concerning the reports to the Department of Energy. The Secretary of Energy shall consider and publish the comments prior to publication of the final report.

**(5) Requests for additional information**

Nothing in this subsection limits or restricts the authority of States or the Administrator to request additional information from the Secretary of Energy.

**(b) Plan for development of treatment capacities and technologies**

**(1) Plan requirement**

**(A)(i)** For each facility at which the Department of Energy generates or stores mixed wastes, except any facility subject to a permit, agreement, or order described in clause (ii), the Secretary of Energy shall develop and submit, as provided in paragraph (2), a plan for developing treatment capacities and technologies to treat all of the facility's mixed wastes, regardless of the time they were generated, to the standards promulgated pursuant to section 6924(m) of this title.

**(ii)** Clause (i) shall not apply with respect to any facility subject to any permit establishing a schedule for treatment of such wastes, or any existing agreement or administrative or judicial order governing the treatment of such wastes, to which the State is a party.

**(B)** Each plan shall contain the following:

**(i)** For mixed wastes for which treatment technologies exist, a schedule for submitting all applicable permit applications, entering into contracts, initiating construction, conducting systems testing, commencing operations, and processing backlogged and currently generated mixed wastes.

**(ii)** For mixed wastes for which no treatment technologies exist, a schedule for identifying and developing such technologies, identifying the funding requirements for the identification and development of such technologies, submitting treatability study exemptions, and submitting research and development permit applications.

**(iii)** For all cases where the Department proposes radionuclide separation of mixed wastes, or materials derived from mixed wastes, it shall provide an estimate of the volume of waste generated by each case of radionuclide separation, the volume of waste that would exist or be generated without radionuclide separation, the estimated costs of waste treatment and disposal if radionuclide separation is used compared to the estimated costs if it is not used, and the assumptions underlying such waste volume and cost estimates.

**(C)** A plan required under this subsection may provide for centralized, regional, or on-site treatment of mixed wastes, or any combination thereof.

**(2) Review and approval of plan**

**(A)** For each facility that is located in a State (i) with authority under State law to prohibit land disposal of mixed waste until the waste has been treated and (ii) with both authority under State law to regulate the hazardous components of mixed waste and authorization from the Environmental Protection Agency under section 6926 of this title to regulate the hazardous components of mixed waste, the Secretary of Energy shall submit the plan required under paragraph (1) to the appropriate State regulatory officials for their review and approval, modification, or disapproval. In reviewing the plan, the State shall consider the need for regional treatment facilities. The State shall consult with the Administrator and any other State in which a facility affected by the plan is located and consider public comments in making its determination on the plan. The State shall approve, approve with modifications, or disapprove the plan within 6 months after receipt of the plan.

**(B)** For each facility located in a State that does not have the authority described in subparagraph (A), the Secretary shall submit the plan required under paragraph (1) to the Administrator of the Environmental Protection Agency for review and approval, modification, or disapproval. A copy of the plan also shall be provided by the Secretary to the State in which such facility is located. In reviewing the plan, the Administrator shall consider the need for regional treatment facilities. The Administrator shall consult with the State or States in which any facility affected by the plan is located and consider public comments in making a determination on the plan. The Administrator shall approve, approve with modifications, or disapprove the plan within 6 months after receipt of the plan.

**(C)** Upon the approval of a plan under this paragraph by the Administrator or a State, the Administrator shall issue an order under section 6928(a) of this title, or the State shall issue an order under appropriate State authority, requiring compliance with the approved plan.

**(3) Public participation**

Upon submission of a plan by the Secretary of Energy to the Administrator or a State, and before approval of the plan by the Administrator or a State, the Administrator or State shall publish a notice of the availability of the submitted plan and make such submitted plan available to the public on request.

**(4) Revisions of plan**

If any revisions of an approved plan are proposed by the Secretary of Energy or required by the Administrator or a State, the provisions of paragraphs (2) and (3) shall apply to the revisions in the same manner as they apply to the original plan.

**(5) Waiver of plan requirement**

**(A)** A State may waive the requirement for the Secretary of Energy to develop and submit a plan under this subsection for a facility located in the State if the State (i) enters into an agreement with the Secretary of Energy that addresses compliance at that facility with section 6924(j) of this title with respect to mixed waste, and (ii) issues an order requiring compliance with such agreement and which is in effect.

**(B)** Any violation of an agreement or order referred to in subparagraph (A) is subject to the waiver of sovereign immunity contained in section 6961(a) of this title.

**(c) Schedule and progress reports**

**(1) Schedule**

Not later than 6 months after October 6, 1992, the Secretary of Energy shall publish in the Federal Register a schedule for submitting the plans required under subsection (b) of this section.

**(2) Progress reports**

**(A)** Not later than the deadlines specified in subparagraph (B), the Secretary of Energy shall submit to the Committee on Environment and Public Works of the Senate and the Committee on Energy and Commerce of the House of Representatives a progress report containing the following:

**(i)** An identification, by facility, of the plans that have been submitted to States or the Administrator of the Environmental Protection Agency pursuant to subsection (b) of this section.

**(ii)** The status of State and Environmental Protection Agency review and approval of each such plan.

**(iii)** The number of orders requiring compliance with such plans that are in effect.

**(iv)** For the first 2 reports required under this paragraph, an identification of the plans required under such subsection (b) of this section that the Secretary expects to submit in the 12-month period following submission of the report.

**(B)** The Secretary of Energy shall submit a report under subparagraph (A) not later than 12 months after October 6, 1992, 24 months after October 6, 1992, and 36 months after October 6, 1992.

(Pub.L. 89–272, Title II, § 3021, as added Pub.L. 102–386, Title I, § 105(a)(1), Oct. 6, 1992, 106 Stat. 1508.)

## HISTORICAL AND STATUTORY NOTES

**Change of Name**

Any reference in any provision of law enacted before Jan. 4, 1995, to the Committee on Energy and Commerce of the House of Representatives treated as referring to the Committee on Commerce of the House of Representatives, except that any reference in any provision of law enacted before Jan. 4, 1995, to the Committee on Energy and Commerce of the House of Representatives treated as referring to the Committee on Agriculture of the House of Representatives, in the case of a provision of law relating to inspection of seafood or seafood products, the Committee on Banking and Financial Services of the House of Representatives, in the case of a provision of law relating to bank capital markets activities generally or to depository institution securities activities generally, and the Committee on Transportation and Infrastructure of the House of Representatives, in the case of a provision of law relating to railroads, railway labor, or railroad retirement and unemployment (except revenue measures related thereto), see section 1(a)(4) and (c)(1) of Pub.L. 104–14, set out as a note preceding section 21 of Title 2, The Congress.

**GAO Report**

Section 105(c) of Pub.L. 102–386 provided that:

"**(1) Requirement.**—Not later than 18 months after the date of the enactment of this Act [Oct. 6, 1992], the Comptroller General shall submit to Congress a report on the Department of Energy's progress in complying with section 3021(b) of the Solid Waste Disposal Act [subsec. (b) of this section].

"**(2) Matters to be included.**—The report required under paragraph (1) shall contain, at a minimum, the following:

"**(A)** The Department of Energy's progress in submitting to the States or the Administrator of the Environmental Protection Agency a plan for each facility for which a plan is required under section 3021(b) of the Solid Waste Disposal Act [subsec. (b) of this section] and the status of State or Environmental Protection Agency review and approval of each such plan.

"**(B)** The Department of Energy's progress in entering into orders requiring compliance with any such plans that have been approved.

"**(C)** An evaluation of the completeness and adequacy of each such plan as of the date of submission of the report required under paragraph (1).

"**(D)** An identification of any recurring problems among the Department of Energy's submitted plans.

"(E) A description of treatment technologies and capacity that have been developed by the Department of Energy since the date of the enactment of this Act [Oct. 6, 1992] and a list of the wastes that are expected to be treated by such technologies and the facilities at which the wastes are generated or stored.

"(F) The progress made by the Department of Energy in characterizing its mixed waste streams at each such facility by sampling and analysis.

"(G) An identification and analysis of additional actions that the Department of Energy must take to—

"(i) complete submission of all plans required under such section 3021(b) [subsec. (b) of this section] for all such facilities;

"(ii) obtain the adoption of orders requiring compliance with all such plans; and

"(iii) develop mixed waste treatment capacity and technologies."

## § 6939d. Public vessels

**[SWDA § 3022]**

### (a) Waste generated on public vessels

Any hazardous waste generated on a public vessel shall not be subject to the storage, manifest, inspection, or recordkeeping requirements of this chapter until such waste is transferred to a shore facility, unless—

(1) the waste is stored on the public vessel for more than 90 days after the public vessel is placed in reserve or is otherwise no longer in service; or

(2) the waste is transferred to another public vessel within the territorial waters of the United States and is stored on such vessel or another public vessel for more than 90 days after the date of transfer.

### (b) Computation of storage period

For purposes of subsection (a) of this section, the 90–day period begins on the earlier of—

(1) the date on which the public vessel on which the waste was generated is placed in reserve or is otherwise no longer in service; or

(2) the date on which the waste is transferred from the public vessel on which the waste was generated to another public vessel within the territorial waters of the United States;

and continues, without interruption, as long as the waste is stored on the original public vessel (if in reserve or not in service) or another public vessel.

### (c) Definitions

For purposes of this section:

(1) The term "public vessel" means a vessel owned or bareboat chartered and operated by the United States, or by a foreign nation, except when the vessel is engaged in commerce.

(2) The terms "in reserve" and "in service" have the meanings applicable to those terms under section 7293 and sections 7304 through 7308 of Title 10 and regulations prescribed under those sections.

### (d) Relationship to other law

Nothing in this section shall be construed as altering or otherwise affecting the provisions of section 7311 of Title 10.

(Pub.L. 89–272, Title II, § 3022, as added Pub.L. 102–386, Title I, § 106(a), Oct. 6, 1992, 106 Stat. 1513.)

## § 6939e. Federally owned treatment works

**[SWDA § 3023]**

### (a) In general

For purposes of section 6903(27) of this title, the phrase "but does not include solid or dissolved material in domestic sewage" shall apply to any solid or dissolved material introduced by a source into a federally owned treatment works if—

(1) such solid or dissolved material is subject to a pretreatment standard under section 1317 of Title 33, and the source is in compliance with such standard;

(2) for a solid or dissolved material for which a pretreatment standard has not been promulgated pursuant to section 1317 of Title 33, the Administrator has promulgated a schedule for establishing such a pretreatment standard which would be applicable to such solid or dissolved material not later than 7 years after October 6, 1992, such standard is promulgated on or before the date established in the schedule, and after the effective date of such standard the source is in compliance with such standard;

(3) such solid or dissolved material is not covered by paragraph (1) or (2) and is not prohibited from land disposal under subsections[1] (d), (e), (f), or (g) of section 6924 of this title because such material has been treated in accordance with section 6924(m) of this title; or

(4) notwithstanding paragraphs[1] (1), (2), or (3), such solid or dissolved material is generated by a household or person which generates less than 100 kilograms of hazardous waste per month unless such solid or dissolved material would otherwise be an acutely hazardous waste and subject to standards, regulations, or other requirements under this chapter notwithstanding the quantity generated.

### (b) Prohibition

It is unlawful to introduce into a federally owned treatment works any pollutant that is a hazardous waste.

### (c) Enforcement

(1) Actions taken to enforce this section shall not require closure of a treatment works if the hazardous waste is removed or decontaminated and such removal or decontamination is adequate, in the discretion of the Administrator or, in the case of an authorized State, of the State, to protect human health and the environment.

(2) Nothing in this subsection shall be construed to prevent the Administrator or an authorized State from ordering the closure of a treatment works if the Administrator or State determines such closure is necessary for protection of human health and the environment.

(3) Nothing in this subsection shall be construed to affect any other enforcement authorities available to the Administrator or a State under this subchapter.

**(d) "Federally owned treatment works" defined**

For purposes of this section, the term "federally owned treatment works" means a facility that is owned and operated by a department, agency, or instrumentality of the Federal Government treating wastewater, a majority of which is domestic sewage, prior to discharge in accordance with a permit issued under section 1342 of Title 33.

**(e) Savings clause**

Nothing in this section shall be construed as affecting any agreement, permit, or administrative or judicial order, or any condition or requirement contained in such an agreement, permit, or order, that is in existence on October 6, 1992, and that requires corrective action or closure at a federally owned treatment works or solid waste management unit or facility related to such a treatment works.

(Pub.L. 89–272, Title II, § 3023, as added Pub.L. 102–386, Title I, § 108(a), Oct. 6, 1992, 106 Stat. 1514.)

1 So in original. Probably should be singular.

## SUBCHAPTER IV—STATE OR REGIONAL SOLID WASTE PLANS

### § 6941. Objectives of subchapter

**[SWDA § 4001]**

The objectives of this subchapter are to assist in developing and encouraging methods for the disposal of solid waste which are environmentally sound and which maximize the utilization of valuable resources including energy and materials which are recoverable from solid waste and to encourage resource conservation. Such objectives are to be accomplished through Federal technical and financial assistance to States or regional authorities for comprehensive planning pursuant to Federal guidelines designed to foster cooperation among Federal, State, and local governments and private industry. In developing such comprehensive plans, it is the intention of this chapter that in determining the size of the waste-to-energy facility, adequate provision shall be given to the present and reasonably anticipated future needs, including those needs created by thorough implementation of section 6962(h) of this title, of the recycling and resource recovery interest within the area encompassed by the planning process.

(Pub.L. 89–272, Title II, § 4001, as added Pub.L. 94–580, § 2, Oct. 21, 1976, 90 Stat. 2813, and amended Pub.L. 96–482, § 32(b), Oct. 21, 1980, 94 Stat. 2353; Pub.L. 98–616, Title III, § 301(a), Title V, § 501(f)(1), Nov. 8, 1984, 98 Stat. 3267, 3276.)

#### HISTORICAL AND STATUTORY NOTES

**Prior Provisions**

Provisions similar to this section were contained in section 3254 of this title, prior to the complete revision of the Solid Waste Disposal Act by Pub.L. 94–580.

### § 6941a. Energy and materials conservation and recovery; Congressional findings

The Congress finds that—

(1) significant savings could be realized by conserving materials in order to reduce the volume or quantity of material which ultimately becomes waste;

(2) solid waste contains valuable energy and material resources which can be recovered and used thereby conserving increasingly scarce and expensive fossil fuels and virgin materials;

(3) the recovery of energy and materials from municipal waste, and the conservation of energy and materials contributing to such waste streams, can have the effect of reducing the volume of the municipal waste stream and the burden of disposing of increasing volumes of solid waste;

(4) the technology to conserve resources exists and is commercially feasible to apply;

(5) the technology to recover energy and materials from solid waste is of demonstrated commercial feasibility; and

(6) various communities throughout the nation have different needs and different potentials for conserving resources and for utilizing techniques for the recovery of energy and materials from waste, and Federal assistance in planning and implementing such energy and materials conservation and recovery programs should be available to all such communities on an equitable basis in relation to their needs and potential.

(Pub.L. 96–482, § 32(a), Oct. 21, 1980, 94 Stat. 2353.)

HISTORICAL AND STATUTORY NOTES

**Codifications**

Section was enacted as part of the Solid Waste Disposal Act Amendments of 1980, and not as part of the Solid Waste Disposal Act which comprises this chapter.

## § 6942. Federal guidelines for plans

[SWDA § 4002]

**(a) Guidelines for identification of regions**

For purposes of encouraging and facilitating the development of regional planning for solid waste management, the Administrator, within one hundred and eighty days after October 21, 1976, and after consultation with appropriate Federal, State, and local authorities, shall by regulation publish guidelines for the identification of those areas which have common solid waste management problems and are appropriate units for planning regional solid waste management services. Such guidelines shall consider—

(1) the size and location of areas which should be included,

(2) the volume of solid waste which should be included, and

(3) the available means of coordinating regional planning with other related regional planning and for coordination of such regional planning into the State plan.

**(b) Guidelines for State plans**

Not later than eighteen months after October 21, 1976, and after notice and hearing, the Administrator shall, after consultation with appropriate Federal, State, and local authorities, promulgate regulations containing guidelines to assist in the development and implementation of State solid waste management plans (hereinafter in this chapter referred to as "State plans"). The guidelines shall contain methods for achieving the objectives specified in section 6941 of this title. Such guidelines shall be reviewed from time to time, but not less frequently than every three years, and revised as may be appropriate.

**(c) Considerations for State plan guidelines**

The guidelines promulgated under subsection (b) of this section shall consider—

(1) the varying regional, geologic, hydrologic, climatic, and other circumstances under which different solid waste practices are required in order to insure the reasonable protection of the quality of the ground and surface waters from leachate contamination, the reasonable protection of the quality of the surface waters from surface runoff contamination, and the reasonable protection of ambient air quality;

(2) characteristics and conditions of collection, storage, processing, and disposal operating methods, techniques and practices, and location of facilities where such operating methods, techniques, and practices are conducted, taking into account the nature of the material to be disposed;

(3) methods for closing or upgrading open dumps for purposes of eliminating potential health hazards;

(4) population density, distribution, and projected growth;

(5) geographic, geologic, climatic, and hydrologic characteristics;

(6) the type and location of transportation;

(7) the profile of industries;

(8) the constituents and generation rates of waste;

(9) the political, economic, organizational, financial, and management problems affecting comprehensive solid waste management;

(10) types of resource recovery facilities and resource conservation systems which are appropriate; and

(11) available new and additional markets for recovered material and energy and energy resources recovered from solid waste as well as methods for conserving such materials and energy.

(Pub.L. 89–272, Title II, § 4002, as added Pub.L. 94–580, § 2, Oct. 21, 1976, 90 Stat. 2813, and amended Pub.L. 96–482, § 32(c), Oct. 21, 1980, 94 Stat. 2353.)

HISTORICAL AND STATUTORY NOTES

**Transfer of Functions**

For transfer of certain enforcement functions of Administrator or other official of the Environmental Protection Agency under this chapter to Federal Inspector, Office of Federal Inspector for the Alaska Natural Gas Transportation System, see note set out under section 6903 of this title.

## § 6943. Requirements for approval of plans

[SWDA § 4003]

**(a) Minimum requirements**

In order to be approved under section 6947 of this title, each State plan must comply with the following minimum requirements—

(1) The plan shall identify (in accordance with section 6946(b) of this title) (A) the responsibilities of State, local, and regional authorities in the implementation of the State plan, (B) the distribution of Federal funds to the authorities responsible for development and implementation of the State plan, and (C) the means for coordinating regional planning and implementation under the State plan.

(2) The plan shall, in accordance with sections 6944(b) and 6945(a) of this title, prohibit the establishment of new open dumps within the State, and contain requirements that all solid waste (including

solid waste originating in other States, but not including hazardous waste) shall be (A) utilized for resource recovery or (B) disposed of in sanitary landfills (within the meaning of section 6944(a) of this title) or otherwise disposed of in an environmentally sound manner.

(3) The plan shall provide for the closing or upgrading of all existing open dumps within the State pursuant to the requirements of section 6945 of this title.

(4) The plan shall provide for the establishment of such State regulatory powers as may be necessary to implement the plan.

(5) The plan shall provide that no State or local government within the State shall be prohibited under State or local law from negotiating and entering into long-term contracts for the supply of solid waste to resource recovery facilities, from entering into long-term contracts for the operation of such facilities, or from securing long-term markets for material and energy recovered from such facilities or for conserving materials or energy by reducing the volume of waste.

(6) The plan shall provide for such resource conservation or recovery and for the disposal of solid waste in sanitary landfills or any combination of practices so as may be necessary to use or dispose of such waste in a manner that is environmentally sound.

**(b) Discretionary plan provisions relating to recycled oil**

Any State plan submitted under this subchapter may include, at the option of the State, provisions to carry out each of the following:

(1) Encouragement, to the maximum extent feasible and consistent with the protection of the public health and the environment, of the use of recycled oil in all appropriate areas of State and local government.

(2) Encouragement of persons contracting with the State to use recycled oil to the maximum extent feasible, consistent with protection of the public health and the environment.

(3) Informing the public of the uses of recycled oil.

(4) Establishment and implementation of a program (including any necessary licensing of persons and including the use, where appropriate, of manifests) to assure that used oil is collected, transported, treated, stored, reused, and disposed of, in a manner which does not present a hazard to the public health or the environment.

Any plan submitted under this chapter before October 15, 1980, may be amended, at the option of the State, at any time after such date to include any provision referred to in this subsection.

**(c) Energy and materials conservation and recovery feasibility planning and assistance**

(1) A State which has a plan approved under this subchapter or which has submitted a plan for such approval shall be eligible for assistance under section 6948(a)(3) of this title if the Administrator determines that under such plan the State will—

(A) analyze and determine the economic and technical feasibility of facilities and programs to conserve resources which contribute to the waste stream or to recover energy and materials from municipal waste;

(B) analyze the legal, institutional, and economic impediments to the development of systems and facilities for conservation of energy or materials which contribute to the waste stream or for the recovery of energy and materials from municipal waste and make recommendations to appropriate governmental authorities for overcoming such impediments;

(C) assist municipalities within the State in developing plans, programs, and projects to conserve resources or recover energy and materials from municipal waste; and

(D) coordinate the resource conservation and recovery planning under subparagraph (C).

(2) The analysis referred to in paragraph (1)(A) shall include—

(A) the evaluation of, and establishment of priorities among, market opportunities for industrial and commercial users of all types (including public utilities and industrial parks) to utilize energy and materials recovered from municipal waste;

(B) comparisons of the relative costs of energy recovered from municipal waste in relation to the costs of energy derived from fossil fuels and other sources;

(C) studies of the transportation and storage problems and other problems associated with the development of energy and materials recovery technology, including curbside source separation;

(D) the evaluation and establishment of priorities among ways of conserving energy or materials which contribute to the waste stream;

(E) comparison of the relative total costs between conserving resources and disposing of or recovering such waste; and

(F) studies of impediments to resource conservation or recovery, including business practices, transportation requirements, or storage difficulties.

Such studies and analyses shall also include studies of other sources of solid waste from which energy and materials may be recovered or minimized.

**(d) Size of waste-to-energy facilities**

Notwithstanding any of the above requirements, it is the intention of this chapter and the planning process developed pursuant to this chapter that in determining the size of the waste-to-energy facility, adequate provision shall be given to the present and reasonably anticipated future needs of the recycling and resource recovery interest within the area encompassed by the planning process.

(Pub.L. 89–272, Title II, § 4003, as added Pub.L. 94–580, § 2, Oct. 21, 1976, 90 Stat. 2814, and amended Pub.L. 96–463, § 5(a), (b), Oct. 15, 1980, 94 Stat. 2056; Pub.L. 96–482, §§ 18, 32(d), Oct. 21, 1980, 94 Stat. 2345, 2353; Pub.L. 98–616, Title III, § 301(b), Title V, § 502(h), Nov. 8, 1984, 98 Stat. 3267, 3277.)

### HISTORICAL AND STATUTORY NOTES

**Codifications**

Another section 5(b) of Pub.L. 96–463 amended section 6948 of this title.

## § 6944. Criteria for sanitary landfills; sanitary landfills required for all disposal

**[SWDA § 4004]**

**(a) Criteria for sanitary landfills**

Not later than one year after October 21, 1976, after consultation with the States, and after notice and public hearings, the Administrator shall promulgate regulations containing criteria for determining which facilities shall be classified as sanitary landfills and which shall be classified as open dumps within the meaning of this chapter. At a minimum, such criteria shall provide that a facility may be classified as a sanitary landfill and not an open dump only if there is no reasonable probability of adverse effects on health or the environment from disposal of solid waste at such facility. Such regulations may provide for the classification of the types of sanitary landfills.

**(b) Disposal required to be in sanitary landfills, etc.**

For purposes of complying with section 6943(2) of this title each State plan shall prohibit the establishment of open dumps and contain a requirement that disposal of all solid waste within the State shall be in compliance with such section 6943(2) of this title.

**(c) Effective date**

The prohibition contained in subsection (b) of this section shall take effect on the date six months after the date of promulgation of regulations under subsection (a) of this section.

(Pub.L. 89–272, Title II, § 4004, as added Pub.L. 94–580, § 2, Oct. 21, 1976, 90 Stat. 2815, and amended Pub.L. 98–616, Title III, § 302(b), Nov. 8, 1984, 98 Stat. 3268.)

### HISTORICAL AND STATUTORY NOTES

**References in Text**

Section 6943(2) of this title, referred to in subsec. (b), was redesignated section 6943(a)(2) of this title by Pub.L. 96–463, § 5(b), Oct. 15, 1980, 94 Stat. 2056, and Pub.L. 96–482, § 32(d)(2), Oct. 21, 1980, 94 Stat. 2353.

**Transfer of Functions**

For transfer of certain enforcement functions of Administrator or other official of the Environmental Protection Agency under this chapter to Federal Inspector, Office of Federal Inspector for the Alaska Natural Gas Transportation System, see note set out under section 6903 of this title.

## § 6945. Upgrading of open dumps

**[SWDA § 4005]**

**(a) Closing or upgrading of existing open dumps**

Upon promulgation of criteria under section 6907(a)(3) of this title, any solid waste management practice or disposal of solid waste or hazardous waste which constitutes the open dumping of solid waste or hazardous waste is prohibited, except in the case of any practice or disposal of solid waste under a timetable or schedule for compliance established under this section. The prohibition contained in the preceding sentence shall be enforceable under section 6972 of this title against persons engaged in the act of open dumping. For purposes of complying with section 6943(a)(2) and 6943(a)(3) of this title, each State plan shall contain a requirement that all existing disposal facilities or sites for solid waste in such State which are open dumps listed in the inventory under subsection (b) of this section shall comply with such measures as may be promulgated by the Administrator to eliminate health hazards and minimize potential health hazards. Each such plan shall establish, for any entity which demonstrates that it has considered other public or private alternatives for solid waste management to comply with the prohibition on open dumping and is unable to utilize such alternatives to so comply, a timetable or schedule for compliance for such practice or disposal of solid waste which specifies a schedule of remedial measures, including an enforceable sequence of actions or operations, leading to compliance with the prohibition on open dumping of solid waste within a reasonable time (not to exceed 5 years from the date of publication of criteria under section 6907(a)(3) of this title).

**(b) Inventory**

To assist the States in complying with section 6943(a)(3) of this title, not later than one year after promulgation of regulations under section 6944 of this title, the Administrator, with the cooperation of the Bureau of the Census shall publish an inventory of all disposal facilities or sites in the United States which are open dumps within the meaning of this chapter.

**(c) Control of hazardous disposal**

**(1)(A)** Not later than 36 months after November 8, 1984, each State shall adopt and implement a permit program or other system of prior approval and conditions to assure that each solid waste management facility within such State which may receive hazardous household waste or hazardous waste due to the provision of section 6921(d) of this title for small quantity generators (otherwise not subject to the requirement for a permit under section 6925 of this title) will comply with the applicable criteria promulgated under section 6944(a) and 6907(a)(3) of this title.

**(B)** Not later than eighteen months after the promulgation of revised criteria under subsection[1] 6944(a) of this title (as required by section 6949a(c) of this title), each State shall adopt and implement a permit program or other system or[2] prior approval and conditions, to assure that each solid waste management facility within such State which may receive hazardous household waste or hazardous waste due to the provision of section 6921(d) of this title for small quantity generators (otherwise not subject to the requirement for a permit under section 6925 of this title) will comply with the criteria revised under section 6944(a) of this title.

**(C)** The Administrator shall determine whether each State has developed an adequate program under this paragraph. The Administrator may make such a determination in conjunction with approval, disapproval or partial approval of a State plan under section 6947 of this title.

**(2)(A)** In any State that the Administrator determines has not adopted an adequate program for such facilities under paragraph (1)(B) by the date provided in such paragraph, the Administrator may use the authorities available under sections 6927 and 6928 of this title to enforce the prohibition contained in subsection (a) of this section with respect to such facilities.

**(B)** For purposes of this paragraph, the term "requirement of this subchapter" in section 6928 of this title shall be deemed to include criteria promulgated by the Administrator under sections 6907(a)(3) and 6944(a) of this title, and the term "hazardous wastes" in section 6927 of this title shall be deemed to include solid waste at facilities that may handle hazardous household wastes or hazardous wastes from small quantity generators.

(Pub.L. 89–272, Title II, § 4005, as added Pub.L. 94–580, § 2, Oct. 21, 1976, 90 Stat. 2815, and amended Pub.L. 96–482, § 19(a), (b), Oct. 21, 1980, 94 Stat. 2345; Pub.L. 98–616, Title III, § 302(c), Title IV, § 403(c), Title V, § 502(c), Nov. 8, 1984, 98 Stat. 3268, 3272, 3276.)

[1] So in original. Probably should be "section".

[2] So in original. Probably should be "of".

### HISTORICAL AND STATUTORY NOTES

**Codifications**

Another section 19(b) of Pub.L. 96–482 amended section 6946 of this title.

**Transfer of Functions**

For transfer of certain enforcement functions of Administrator or other official of the Environmental Protection Agency under this chapter to Federal Inspector, Office of Federal Inspector for the Alaska Natural Gas Transportation System, see note set out under section 6903 of this title.

## § 6946. Procedure for development and implementation of State plan

[SWDA § 4006]

**(a) Identification of regions**

Within one hundred and eighty days after publication of guidelines under section 6942(a) of this title (relating to identification of regions), the Governor of each State, after consultation with local elected officials, shall promulgate regulations based on such guidelines identifying the boundaries of each area within the State which, as a result of urban concentrations, geographic conditions, markets, and other factors, is appropriate for carrying out regional solid waste management. Such regulations may be modified from time to time (identifying additional or different regions) pursuant to such guidelines.

**(b) Identification of State and local agencies and responsibilities**

**(1)** Within one hundred and eighty days after the Governor promulgates regulations under subsection (a) of this section, for purposes of facilitating the development and implementation of a State plan which will meet the minimum requirements of section 6943 of this title, the State, together with appropriate elected officials of general purpose units of local government, shall jointly (A) identify an agency to develop the State plan and identify one or more agencies to implement such plan, and (B) identify which solid waste management activities will, under such State plan, be planned for and carried out by the State and which such management activities will, under such State plan, be planned for and carried out by a regional or local authority or a combination of regional or local and State authorities. If a multi-functional regional agency authorized by State law to conduct solid waste planning and management (the members of which are appointed by the Governor) is in existence on October 21, 1976, the Governor shall identify such authority for purposes of carrying out within such region clause (A) of this paragraph. Where feasible, designation of the agency for the affected area designated under section 1288 of Title 33 shall be considered. A State agency identified under this paragraph shall be established or designated by the Governor of such State. Local or regional agencies identified under this paragraph shall be composed of individuals at least a majority of whom are elected local officials.

(2) If planning and implementation agencies are not identified and designated or established as required under paragraph (1) for any affected area, the governor shall, before the date two hundred and seventy days after promulgation of regulations under subsection (a) of this section, establish or designate a State agency to develop and implement the State plan for such area.

**(c) Interstate regions**

(1) In the case of any region which, pursuant to the guidelines published by the Administrator under section 6942(a) of this title (relating to identification of regions), would be located in two or more States, the Governors of the respective States, after consultation with local elected officials, shall consult, cooperate, and enter into agreements identifying the boundaries of such region pursuant to subsection (a) of this section.

(2) Within one hundred and eighty days after an interstate region is identified by agreement under paragraph (1), appropriate elected officials of general purpose units of local government within such region shall jointly establish or designate an agency to develop a plan for such region. If no such agency is established or designated within such period by such officials, the Governors of the respective States may, by agreement, establish or designate for such purpose a single representative organization including elected officials of general purpose units of local government within such region.

(3) Implementation of interstate regional solid waste management plans shall be conducted by units of local government for any portion of a region within their jurisdiction, or by multijurisdictional agencies or authorities designated in accordance with State law, including those designated by agreement by such units of local government for such purpose. If no such unit, agency, or authority is so designated, the respective Governors shall designate or establish a single interstate agency to implement such plan.

(4) For purposes of this subchapter, so much of an interstate regional plan as is carried out within a particular State shall be deemed part of the State plan for such State.

(Pub.L. 89–272, Title II, § 4006, as added Pub.L. 94–580, § 2, Oct. 21, 1976, 90 Stat. 2816, and amended Pub.L. 96–482, § 19(b), Oct. 21, 1980, 94 Stat. 2345.)

### HISTORICAL AND STATUTORY NOTES

**Codifications**

Another section 19(b) of Pub.L. 96–482 amended section 6945 of this title.

**Transfer of Functions**

For transfer of certain enforcement functions of Administrator or other official of the Environmental Protection Agency under this chapter to Federal Inspector, Office of Federal Inspector for the Alaska Natural Gas Transportation System, see note set out under section 6903 of this title.

## § 6947. Approval of State plan; Federal assistance

**[SWDA § 4007]**

**(a) Plan approval**

The Administrator shall, within six months after a State plan has been submitted for approval, approve or disapprove the plan. The Administrator shall approve a plan if he determines that—

(1) it meets the requirements of paragraphs (1), (2), (3), and (5) of section 6943(a) of this title; and

(2) it contains provision for revision of such plan, after notice and public hearing, whenever the Administrator, by regulation, determines—

(A) that revised regulations respecting minimum requirements have been promulgated under paragraphs (1), (2), (3), and (5) of section 6943(a) of this title with which the State plan is not in compliance;

(B) that information has become available which demonstrates the inadequacy of the plan to effectuate the purposes of this subchapter; or

(C) that such revision is otherwise necessary.

The Administrator shall review approved plans from time to time and if he determines that revision or corrections are necessary to bring such plan into compliance with the minimum requirements promulgated under section 6943 of this title (including new or revised requirements), he shall, after notice and opportunity for public hearing, withdraw his approval of such plan. Such withdrawal of approval shall cease to be effective upon the Administrator's determination that such complies with such minimum requirements.

**(b) Eligibility of States for Federal financial assistance**

(1) The Administrator shall approve a State application for financial assistance under this subchapter, and make grants to such State, if such State and local and regional authorities within such State have complied with the requirements of section 6946 of this title within the period required under such section and if such State has a State plan which has been approved by the Administrator under this subchapter.

(2) The Administrator shall approve a State application for financial assistance under this subchapter, and make grants to such State, for fiscal years 1978 and 1979 if the Administrator determines that the State plan continues to be eligible for approval under subsection (a) of this section and is being implemented by the State.

(3) Upon withdrawal of approval of a State plan under subsection (a) of this section, the Administrator shall withhold Federal financial and technical assistance under this subchapter (other than such technical assistance as may be necessary to assist in obtaining the reinstatement of approval) until such time as such approval is reinstated.

**(c) Existing activities**

Nothing in this subchapter shall be construed to prevent or affect any activities respecting solid waste planning or management which are carried out by State, regional, or local authorities unless such activities are inconsistent with a State plan approved by the Administrator under this subchapter.

(Pub.L. 89–272, Title II, § 4007, as added Pub.L. 94–580, § 2, Oct. 21, 1976, 90 Stat. 2817, and amended Pub.L. 95–609, § 7(*l*), Nov. 8, 1978, 92 Stat. 3082; Pub.L. 104–119, § 4(8), Mar. 26, 1996, 110 Stat. 833.)

### HISTORICAL AND STATUTORY NOTES

**References in Text**

Paragraphs (1), (2), (3), and (5) of section 6943 of this title, referred to in subsec. (a)(1), (2)(A), were redesignated as the same paragraphs of section 6943(a) of this title by Pub.L. 96–463, § 5(b), Oct. 15, 1980, 94 Stat. 2056, and Pub.L. 96–482, § 32(d)(2), Oct. 21, 1980, 94 Stat. 2353.

**Transfer of Functions**

For transfer of certain enforcement functions of Administrator or other official of the Environmental Protection Agency under this chapter to Federal Inspector, Office of Federal Inspector for the Alaska Natural Gas Transportation System, see note set out under section 6903 of this title.

## § 6948. Federal assistance

**[SWDA § 4008]**

**(a) Authorization of Federal financial assistance**

(1) There are authorized to be appropriated $30,000,000 for fiscal year 1978, $40,000,000 for fiscal year 1979, $20,000,000 for fiscal year 1980, $15,000,000 for fiscal year 1981, $20,000,000 for the fiscal year 1982, and $10,000,000 for each of the fiscal years 1985 through 1988 for purposes of financial assistance to States and local, regional, and interstate authorities for the development and implementation of plans approved by the Administrator under this subchapter (other than the provisions of such plans referred to in section 6943(b) of this title, relating to feasibility planning for municipal waste energy and materials conservation and recovery).

(2)(A) The Administrator is authorized to provide financial assistance to States, counties, municipalities, and intermunicipal agencies and State and local public solid waste management authorities for implementation of programs to provide solid waste management, resource recovery, and resource conservation services and hazardous waste management. Such assistance shall include assistance for facility planning and feasibility studies; expert consultation; surveys and analyses of market needs; marketing of recovered resources; technology assessments; legal expenses; construction feasibility studies; source separation projects; and fiscal or economic investigations or studies; but such assistance shall not include any other element of construction, or any acquisition of land or interest in land, or any subsidy for the price of recovered resources. Agencies assisted under this subsection shall consider existing solid waste management and hazardous waste management services and facilities as well as facilities proposed for construction.

(B) An applicant for financial assistance under this paragraph must agree to comply with respect to the project or program assisted with the applicable requirements of section 6945 of this title and subchapter III of this chapter and apply applicable solid waste management practices, methods, and levels of control consistent with any guidelines published pursuant to section 6907 of this title. Assistance under this paragraph shall be available only for programs certified by the State to be consistent with any applicable State or areawide solid waste management plan or program. Applicants for technical and financial assistance under this section shall not preclude or foreclose consideration of programs for the recovery of recyclable materials through source separation or other resource recovery techniques.

(C) There are authorized to be appropriated $15,000,000 for each of the fiscal years 1978 and 1979 for purposes of this section. There are authorized to be appropriated $10,000,000 for fiscal year 1980, $10,000,000 for fiscal year 1981, $10,000,000 for fiscal year 1982, and $10,000,000 for each of the fiscal years 1985 through 1988 for purposes of this paragraph.

(D) There are authorized—

(i) to be made available $15,000,000 out of funds appropriated for fiscal year 1985, and

(ii) to be appropriated for each of the fiscal years 1986 though[1] 1988, $20,000,000[2]

for grants to States (and where appropriate to regional, local, and interstate agencies) to implement programs requiring compliance by solid waste management facilities with the criteria promulgated under section 6944(a) of this title and section 6907(a)(3) of this title and with the provisions of section 6945 of this title. To the extent practicable, such programs shall require such compliance not later than thirty-six months after November 8, 1984.

(3)(A) There is authorized to be appropriated for the fiscal year beginning October 1, 1981, and for each fiscal year thereafter before October 1, 1986, $4,000,000 for purposes of making grants to States to carry out section 6943(b) of this title. No amount may be appropriated for such purposes for the fiscal year beginning on October 1, 1986, or for any fiscal year thereafter.

(B) Assistance provided by the Administrator under this paragraph shall be used only for the purposes specified in section 6943(b) of this title. Such assistance may not be used for purposes of land acquisition, final facility design, equipment purchase, construction, startup or operation activities.

(C) Where appropriate, any State receiving assistance under this paragraph may make all or any part of such assistance available to municipalities within the State to carry out the activities specified in section 6943(b)(1)(A) and (B) of this title.

**(b) State allotment**

The sums appropriated in any fiscal year under subsection (a)(1) of this section shall be allotted by the Administrator among all States, in the ratio that the population in each State bears to the population in all of the States, except that no State shall receive less than one-half of 1 per centum of the sums so allotted in any fiscal year. No State shall receive any grant under this section during any fiscal year when its expenditures of non-Federal funds for other than non-recurrent expenditures for solid waste management control programs will be less than its expenditures were for such programs during fiscal year 1975, except that such funds may be reduced by an amount equal to their proportionate share of any general reduction of State spending ordered by the Governor or legislature of such State. No State shall receive any grant for solid waste management programs unless the Administrator is satisfied that such grant will be so used as to supplement and, to the extent practicable, increase the level of State, local, regional, or other non-Federal funds that would in the absence of such grant be made available for the maintenance of such programs.

**(c) Distribution of Federal financial assistance within the State**

The Federal assistance allotted to the States under subsection (b) of this section shall be allocated by the State receiving such funds to State, local, regional, and interstate authorities carrying out planning and implementation of the State plan. Such allocation shall be based upon the responsibilities of the respective parties as determined pursuant to section 6946(b) of this title.

**(d) Technical assistance**

(1) The Administrator may provide technical assistance to State and local governments for purposes of developing and implementing State plans. Technical assistance respecting resource recovery and conservation may be provided through resource recovery and conservation panels, established in the Environmental Protection Agency under subchapter II of this chapter, to assist the State and local governments with respect to particular resource recovery and conservation projects under consideration and to evaluate their effect on the State plan.

(2) In carrying out this subsection, the Administrator may, upon request, provide technical assistance to States to assist in the removal or modification of legal, institutional, economic, and other impediments to the recycling of used oil. Such impediments may include laws, regulations, and policies, including State procurement policies, which are not favorable to the recycling of used oil.

(3) In carrying out this subsection, the Administrator is authorized to provide technical assistance to States, municipalities, regional authorities, and intermunicipal agencies upon request, to assist in the removal or modification of legal, institutional, and economic impediments which have the effect of impeding the development of systems and facilities to recover energy and materials from municipal waste or to conserve energy or materials which contribute to the waste stream. Such impediments may include—

(A) laws, regulations, and policies, including State and local procurement policies, which are not favorable to resource conservation and recovery policies, systems, and facilities;

(B) impediments to the financing of facilities to conserve or recover energy and materials from municipal waste through the exercise of State and local authority to issue revenue bonds and the use of State and local credit assistance; and

(C) impediments to institutional arrangements necessary to undertake projects for the conservation or recovery of energy and materials from municipal waste, including the creation of special districts, authorities, or corporations where necessary having the power to secure the supply of waste of a project, to conserve resources, to implement the project, and to undertake related activities.

**(e) Special communities**

(1) The Administrator, in cooperation with State and local officials, shall identify local governments within the United States (A) having a solid waste disposal facility (i) which is owned by the unit of local government, (ii) for which an order has been issued by the State to cease receiving solid waste for treatment, storage, or disposal, and (iii) which is subject to a

State-approved end-use recreation plan, and (B) which are located over an aquifer which is the source of drinking water for any person or public water system and which has serious environmental problems resulting from the disposal of such solid waste, including possible methane migration.

(2) There is authorized to be appropriated to the Administrator $2,500,000 for the fiscal year 1980 and $1,500,000 for each of the fiscal years 1981 and 1982 to make grants to be used for containment and stabilization of solid waste located at the disposal sites referred to in paragraph (1). Not more than one community in any State shall be eligible for grants under this paragraph and not more than one project in any State shall be eligible for such grants. No unit of local government shall be eligible for grants under this paragraph with respect to any site which exceeds 65 acres in size.

**(f) Assistance to States for discretionary program for recycled oil**

(1) The Administrator may make grants to States, which have a State plan approved under section 6947 of this title, or which have submitted a State plan for approval under such section, if such plan includes the discretionary provisions described in section 6943(b) of this title. Grants under this subsection shall be for purposes of assisting the State in carrying out such discretionary provisions. No grant under this subsection may be used for construction or for the acquisition of land or equipment.

(2) Grants under this subsection shall be allotted among the States in the same manner as provided in the first sentence of subsection (b) of this section.

(3) No grant may be made under this subsection unless an application therefor is submitted to, and approved by, the Administrator. The application shall be in such form, be submitted in such manner, and contain such information as the Administrator may require.

(4) For purposes of making grants under this subsection, there are authorized to be appropriated $5,000,000 for fiscal year 1982, $5,000,000 for fiscal year 1983, and $5,000,000 for each of the fiscal years 1985 through 1988.

**(g) Assistance to municipalities for energy and materials conservation and recovery planning activities**

(1) The Administrator is authorized to make grants to municipalities, regional authorities, and intermunicipal agencies to carry out activities described in subparagraphs (A) and (B) of section 6943(b)(1) of this title. Such grants may be made only pursuant to an application submitted to the Administrator by the municipality which application has been approved by the State and determined by the State to be consistent with any State plan approved or submitted under this subchapter or any other appropriate planning carried out by the State.

(2) There is authorized to be appropriated for the fiscal year beginning October 1, 1981, and for each fiscal year thereafter before October 1, 1986, $8,000,000 for purposes of making grants to municipalities under this subsection. No amount may be appropriated for such purposes for the fiscal year beginning on October 1, 1986, or for any fiscal year thereafter.

(3) Assistance provided by the Administrator under this subsection shall be used only for the purposes specified in paragraph (1). Such assistance may not be used for purposes of land acquisition, final facility design, equipment purchase, construction, startup or operation activities.

(Pub.L. 89–272, Title II, § 4008, as added Pub.L. 94–580, § 2, Oct. 21, 1976, 90 Stat. 2818, and amended Pub.L. 96–463, §§ 5(b), 6, Oct. 15, 1980, 94 Stat. 2057; Pub.L. 96–482, §§ 20, 31(c), (d), 32(e), (f), Oct. 21, 1980, 94 Stat. 2345, 2352, 2354, 2355; Pub.L. 98–616, § 2(d) to (g), (k), Title V, § 502(d), (e), Nov. 8, 1984, 98 Stat. 3222, 3223, 3276.)

1 So in original. Probably should be "through".

2 So in original. Probably should be followed by a comma.

## HISTORICAL AND STATUTORY NOTES

**References in Text**

Section 6943(b) of this title, referred to in subsecs. (a)(1), (3), and (g)(1), was redesignated section 6943(c) of this title by Pub.L. 98–616, Title V, § 502(h), Nov. 8, 1984, 98 Stat. 3277.

**Codifications**

Section 2(d) to (g) of Pub.L. 98–616, cited in the credit to this section, appears to contain a typographical error in that the text of subsec. "(f)(1)" of such section 2 is also shown as the text of subsec. (f)(1) of section 2007 of the Solid Waste Disposal Act (as added by section 2(i) of Pub.L. 98–616). Subsec. (f) of section 2, as set out in the Conference Report (H.Rept. 98–1133) to accompany H.R. 2867 (which became Pub.L. 98–616) read:

"(f) Section 4008(e)(2) of the Solid Waste Disposal Act (relating to special communities) is amended by striking out 'and $1,500,000 for each of the fiscal years 1981 and 1982' and substituting ', $1,500,000 for each of the fiscal years 1981 and 1982, and $500,000 for each of the fiscal years 1985 through 1988'."

Another section 5(b) of Pub.L. 96–463 amended section 6943 of this title.

**Transfer of Functions**

For transfer of certain enforcement functions of Administrator or other official of the Environmental Protection Agency under this chapter to Federal Inspector, Office of Federal Inspector for the Alaska Natural Gas Transportation System, see note set out under section 6903 of this title.

## § 6949. Rural communities assistance

[SWDA § 4009]

### (a) In general

The Administrator shall make grants to States to provide assistance to municipalities with a population of five thousand or less, or counties with a population of ten thousand or less or less than twenty persons per square mile and not within a metropolitan area, for solid waste management facilities (including equipment) necessary to meet the requirements of section 6945 of this title or restrictions on open burning or other requirements arising under the Clean Air Act [42 U.S.C.A. § 7401 et seq.] or the Federal Water Pollution Control Act [33 U.S.C.A. § 1251 et seq.]. Such assistance shall only be available—

(1) to any municipality or county which could not feasibly be included in a solid waste management system or facility serving an urbanized, multijurisdictional area because of its distance from such systems;

(2) where existing or planned solid waste management services or facilities are unavailable or insufficient to comply with the requirements of section 6945 of this title; and

(3) for systems which are certified by the State to be consistent with any plans or programs established under any State or areawide planning process.

### (b) Allotment

The Administrator shall allot the sums appropriated to carry out this section in any fiscal year among the States in accordance with regulations promulgated by him on the basis of the average of the ratio which the population of rural areas of each State bears to the total population of rural areas of all the States, the ratio which the population of counties in each State having less than twenty persons per square mile bears to the total population of such counties in all the States, and the ratio which the population of such low-density counties in each State having 33 per centum or more of all families with incomes not in excess of 125 per centum of the poverty level bears to the total population of such counties in all the States.

### (c) Limit

The amount of any grant under this section shall not exceed 75 per centum of the costs of the project. No assistance under this section shall be available for the acquisition of land or interests in land.

### (d) Authorization of appropriations

There are authorized to be appropriated $25,000,000 for each of the fiscal years 1978 and 1979 to carry out this section. There are authorized to be appropriated $10,000,000 for the fiscal year 1980 and $15,000,000 for each of the fiscal years 1981 and 1982 to carry out this section.

(Pub.L. 89–272, Title II, § 4009, as added Pub.L. 94–580, § 2, Oct. 21, 1976, 90 Stat. 2819, and amended Pub.L. 96–482, § 31(e), Oct. 21, 1980, 94 Stat. 2353.)

#### HISTORICAL AND STATUTORY NOTES

**References in Text**

The Clean Air Act, referred to in subsec. (a), is Act July 14, 1955, c. 360, as amended generally by Pub.L. 88–206, Dec. 17, 1963, 77 Stat. 392, and later by Pub.L. 95–95, Aug. 7, 1977, 91 Stat. 685. The Clean Air Act was originally classified to chapter 15B (section 1857 et seq.) of this title. On enactment of Pub.L. 95–95, the Act was reclassified to chapter 85 (section 7401 et seq.) of this title. For complete classification of this Act to the Code, see Short Title of 1955 Acts note set out under section 7401 of this title and Tables.

The Federal Water Pollution Control Act, referred to in subsec. (a), is Act June 30, 1948, c. 758, as amended generally by Pub.L. 92–500, § 2, Oct. 18, 1972, 86 Stat. 816, which is classified generally to chapter 26 (section 1251 et seq.) of Title 33, Navigation and Navigable Waters. For complete classification of this Act to the Code, see Short Title note set out under section 1251 of Title 33 and Tables.

**Transfer of Functions**

For transfer of certain enforcement functions of Administrator or other official of the Environmental Protection Agency under this chapter to Federal Inspector, Office of Federal Inspector for the Alaska Natural Gas Transportation System, see note set out under section 6903 of this title.

## § 6949a. Adequacy of certain guidelines and criteria

[SWDA § 4010]

### (a) Study

The Administrator shall conduct a study of the extent to which the guidelines and criteria under this chapter (other than guidelines and criteria for facilities to which subchapter III of this chapter applies) which are applicable to solid waste management and disposal facilities, including, but not limited to landfills and surface impoundments, are adequate to protect human health and the environment from ground water contamination. Such study shall include a detailed assessment of the degree to which the criteria under section 6907(a) of this title and the criteria under section 6944 of this title regarding monitoring, prevention of contamination, and remedial action are adequate to protect ground water and shall also include recommendation with respect to any additional enforcement authorities which the Administrator, in consultation with the Attorney General, deems necessary for such purposes.

### (b) Report

Not later than thirty-six months after November 8, 1984, the Administrator shall submit a report to the Congress setting forth the results of the study required under this section, together with any recommendations made by the Administrator on the basis of such study.

**(c) Revisions of guidelines and criteria**

**(1) In general**

Not later than March 31, 1988, the Administrator shall promulgate revisions of the criteria promulgated under paragraph (1) of section 6944(a) of this title and under section 6907(a)(3) of this title for facilities that may receive hazardous household wastes or hazardous wastes from small quantity generators under section 6921(d) of this title. The criteria shall be those necessary to protect human health and the environment and may take into account the practicable capability of such facilities. At a minimum such revisions for facilities potentially receiving such wastes should require ground water monitoring as necessary to detect contamination, establish criteria for the acceptable location of new or existing facilities, and provide for corrective action as appropriate.

**(2) Additional revisions**

Subject to paragraph (3), the requirements of the criteria described in paragraph (1) relating to ground water monitoring shall not apply to an owner or operator of a new municipal solid waste landfill unit, an existing municipal solid waste landfill unit, or a lateral expansion of a municipal solid waste landfill unit, that disposes of less than 20 tons of municipal solid waste daily, based on an annual average, if—

(A) there is no evidence of ground water contamination from the municipal solid waste landfill unit or expansion; and

(B) the municipal solid waste landfill unit or expansion serves—

(i) a community that experiences an annual interruption of at least 3 consecutive months of surface transportation that prevents access to a regional waste management facility; or

(ii) a community that has no practicable waste management alternative and the landfill unit is located in an area that annually receives less than or equal to 25 inches of precipitation.

**(3) Protection of ground water resources**

**(A) Monitoring requirement**

A State may require ground water monitoring of a solid waste landfill unit that would otherwise be exempt under paragraph (2) if necessary to protect ground water resources and ensure compliance with a State ground water protection plan, where applicable.

**(B) Methods**

If a State requires ground water monitoring of a solid waste landfill unit under subparagraph (A), the State may allow the use of a method other than the use of ground water monitoring wells to detect a release of contamination from the unit.

**(C) Corrective action**

If a State finds a release from a solid waste landfill unit, the State shall require corrective action as appropriate.

**(4) No-migration exemption**

**(A) In general**

Ground water monitoring requirements may be suspended by the Director of an approved State for a landfill operator if the operator demonstrates that there is no potential for migration of hazardous constituents from the unit to the uppermost aquifer during the active life of the unit and the post-closure care period.

**(B) Certification**

A demonstration under subparagraph (A) shall be certified by a qualified ground-water scientist and approved by the Director of an approved State.

**(C) Guidance**

Not later than 6 months after March 26, 1996, the Administrator shall issue a guidance document to facilitate small community use of the no migration[1] exemption under this paragraph.

**(5) Alaska Native villages**

Upon certification by the Governor of the State of Alaska that application of the requirements described in paragraph (1) to a solid waste landfill unit of a Native village (as defined in section 1602 of Title 43) or unit that is located in or near a small, remote Alaska village would be infeasible, or would not be cost-effective, or is otherwise inappropriate because of the remote location of the unit, the State may exempt the unit from some or all of those requirements. This paragraph shall apply only to solid waste landfill units that dispose of less than 20 tons of municipal solid waste daily, based on an annual average.

**(6) Further revisions of guidelines and criteria**

Recognizing the unique circumstances of small communities, the Administrator shall, not later than two years after March 26, 1996, promulgate revisions to the guidelines and criteria promulgated under this subchapter to provide additional flexibility to approved States to allow landfills that receive 20 tons or less of municipal solid waste per day, based on an annual average, to use alternative frequencies of daily cover application, frequencies of methane gas monitoring, infiltration layers for final cover, and means for demonstrating financial assurance: Provided, That such alternative requirements take into account climatic and hydrogeologic conditions and are protective of human health and environment.

(Pub.L. 89–272, Title II, § 4010, as added Pub.L. 98–616, Title III, § 302(a)(1), Nov. 8, 1984, 98 Stat. 3267, and amended Pub.L. 104–119, § 3(a), Mar. 26, 1996, 110 Stat. 831.)

[1] So in original. Probably should be "no-migration".

### HISTORICAL AND STATUTORY NOTES

**Codifications**

Section 1602 of Title 43, appearing in subsec. (c)(5), was in the original section 3 of the Alaska Native Claims Settlement Act (16 U.S.C. 1602), which is section 3 of Pub.L. 92–203, Dec. 18, 1971, 85 Stat. 688, as amended, and is classified to section 1602 of Title 43, Public Lands. Translation was made to section 1602 of Title 43 as the probable intent of Congress.

Not later than two years after March 26, 1996, appearing in subsec. (c)(6), was in the original not later than two years after enactment of this provision. Such provision was enacted by Pub.L. 104–119, 110 Stat. 830, which was approved Mar. 26, 1996; translation to this date was made as the probable intent of Congress.

**Reinstatement of Regulatory Exemption**

Section 3(b) of Pub.L. 104–119 provided that: "It is the intent of section 4010(c)(2) of the Solid Waste Disposal Act, as added by subsection (a) [subsec. (c)(2) of this section], to immediately reinstate subpart E of part 258 of title 40, Code of Federal Regulations, as added by the final rule published at 56 Federal Register 50798 on October 9, 1991."

## SUBCHAPTER V—DUTIES OF THE SECRETARY OF COMMERCE IN RESOURCE AND RECOVERY

## § 6951. Functions

[SWDA § 5001]

The Secretary of Commerce shall encourage greater commercialization of proven resource recovery technology by providing—

(1) accurate specifications for recovered materials;

(2) stimulation of development of markets for recovered materials;

(3) promotion of proven technology; and

(4) a forum for the exchange of technical and economic data relating to resource recovery facilities.

(Pub.L. 89–272, Title II, § 5001, as added Pub.L. 94–580, § 2, Oct. 21, 1976, 90 Stat. 2820.)

## § 6952. Development of specifications for secondary materials

[SWDA § 5002]

The Secretary of Commerce, acting through the National Institute of Standards and Technology, and in conjunction with national standards-setting organizations in resource recovery, shall, after public hearings, and not later than two years after September 1, 1979, publish guidelines for the development of specifications for the classification of materials recovered from waste which were destined for disposal. The specifications shall pertain to the physical and chemical properties and characteristics of such materials with regard to their use in replacing virgin materials in various industrial, commercial, and governmental uses. In establishing such guidelines the Secretary shall also, to the extent feasible, provide such information as may be necessary to assist Federal agencies with procurement of items containing recovered materials. The Secretary shall continue to cooperate with national standards-setting organizations, as may be necessary, to encourage the publication, promulgation and updating of standards for recovered materials and for the use of recovered materials in various industrial, commercial, and governmental uses.

(Pub.L. 89–272, Title II, § 5002, as added Pub.L. 94–580, § 2, Oct. 21, 1976, 90 Stat. 2820, and amended Pub.L. 96–482, § 21(a), Oct. 21, 1980, 94 Stat. 2346; Pub.L. 100–418, Title V, § 5115(c), Aug. 23, 1988, 102 Stat. 1433.)

## § 6953. Development of markets for recovered materials

[SWDA § 5003]

The Secretary of Commerce shall within two years after September 1, 1979, take such actions as may be necessary to—

(1) identify the geographical location of existing or potential markets for recovered materials;

(2) identify the economic and technical barriers to the use of recovered materials; and

(3) encourage the development of new uses for recovered materials.

(Pub.L. 89–272, Title II, § 5003, as added Pub.L. 94–580, § 2, Oct. 21, 1976, 90 Stat. 2821, and amended Pub.L. 96–482, § 21(b), Oct. 21, 1980, 94 Stat. 2346.)

## § 6954. Technology promotion

[SWDA § 5004]

The Secretary of Commerce is authorized to evaluate the commercial feasibility of resource recovery facilities and to publish the results of such evaluation, and to develop a data base for purposes of assisting persons in choosing such a system.

(Pub.L. 89–272, Title II, § 5004, as added Pub.L. 94–580, § 2, Oct. 21, 1976, 90 Stat. 2821.)

## § 6955. Marketing policies, establishment; nondiscrimination requirement

[SWDA § 5005]

In establishing any policies which may affect the development of new markets for recovered materials and in making any determination concerning whether or not to impose monitoring or other controls on any marketing or transfer of recovered materials, the Secretary of Commerce may consider whether to establish the same or similar policies or impose the same or similar monitoring or other controls on virgin materials.

(Pub.L. 89–272, Title II, § 5005, as added Pub.L. 96–482, § 21(c)(1), Oct. 21, 1980, 94 Stat. 2346.)

## § 6956. Authorization of appropriations

[SWDA § 5006]

There are authorized to be appropriated to the Secretary of Commerce $5,000,000 for each of fiscal years 1980, 1981, and 1982 and $1,500,000 for each of the fiscal years 1985 through 1988 to carry out the purposes of this subchapter.

(Pub.L. 89–272, Title II, § 5006, as added Pub.L. 96–482, § 31(f)(1), Oct. 21, 1980, 94 Stat. 2353, and amended Pub.L. 98–616, § 2(h), Nov. 8, 1984, 98 Stat. 3223.)

# SUBCHAPTER VI—FEDERAL RESPONSIBILITIES

## § 6961. Application of Federal, State, and local law to Federal facilities

[SWDA § 6001]

### (a) In general

Each department, agency, and instrumentality of the executive, legislative, and judicial branches of the Federal Government (1) having jurisdiction over any solid waste management facility or disposal site, or (2) engaged in any activity resulting, or which may result, in the disposal or management of solid waste or hazardous waste shall be subject to, and comply with, all Federal, State, interstate, and local requirements, both substantive and procedural (including any requirement for permits or reporting or any provisions for injunctive relief and such sanctions as may be imposed by a court to enforce such relief), respecting control and abatement of solid waste or hazardous waste disposal and management in the same manner, and to the same extent, as any person is subject to such requirements, including the payment of reasonable service charges. The Federal, State, interstate, and local substantive and procedural requirements referred to in this subsection include, but are not limited to, all administrative orders and all civil and administrative penalties and fines, regardless of whether such penalties or fines are punitive or coercive in nature or are imposed for isolated, intermittent, or continuing violations. The United States hereby expressly waives any immunity otherwise applicable to the United States with respect to any such substantive or procedural requirement (including, but not limited to, any injunctive relief, administrative order or civil or administrative penalty or fine referred to in the preceding sentence, or reasonable service charge). The reasonable service charges referred to in this subsection include, but are not limited to, fees or charges assessed in connection with the processing and issuance of permits, renewal of permits, amendments to permits, review of plans, studies, and other documents, and inspection and monitoring of facilities, as well as any other nondiscriminatory charges that are assessed in connection with a Federal, State, interstate, or local solid waste or hazardous waste regulatory program. Neither the United States, nor any agent, employee, or officer thereof, shall be immune or exempt from any process or sanction of any State or Federal Court with respect to the enforcement of any such injunctive relief. No agent, employee, or officer of the United States shall be personally liable for any civil penalty under any Federal, State, interstate, or local solid or hazardous waste law with respect to any act or omission within the scope of the official duties of the agent, employee, or officer. An agent, employee, or officer of the United States shall be subject to any criminal sanction (including, but not limited to, any fine or imprisonment) under any Federal or State solid or hazardous waste law, but no department, agency, or instrumentality of the executive, legislative, or judicial branch of the Federal Government shall be subject to any such sanction. The President may exempt any solid waste management facility of any department, agency, or instrumentality in the executive branch from compliance with such a requirement if he determines it to be in the paramount interest of the United States to do so. No such exemption shall be granted due to lack of appropriation unless the President shall have specifically requested such appropriation as a part of the budgetary process and the Congress shall have failed to make available such requested appropriation. Any exemption shall be for a period not in excess of one year, but additional exemptions may be granted for periods not to exceed one year upon the President's making a new determination. The President shall report each January to the Congress all exemptions from the requirements of this section granted during the preceding calendar year, together with his reason for granting each such exemption.

### (b) Administrative enforcement actions

(1) The Administrator may commence an administrative enforcement action against any department, agency, or instrumentality of the executive, legislative, or judicial branch of the Federal Government pursu-

ant to the enforcement authorities contained in this chapter. The Administrator shall initiate an administrative enforcement action against such a department, agency, or instrumentality in the same manner and under the same circumstances as an action would be initiated against another person. Any voluntary resolution or settlement of such an action shall be set forth in a consent order.

(2) No administrative order issued to such a department, agency, or instrumentality shall become final until such department, agency, or instrumentality has had the opportunity to confer with the Administrator.

### (c) Limitation on State use of funds collected from Federal Government

Unless a State law in effect on October 6, 1992, or a State constitution requires the funds to be used in a different manner, all funds collected by a State from the Federal Government from penalties and fines imposed for violation of any substantive or procedural requirement referred to in subsection (a) of this section shall be used by the State only for projects designed to improve or protect the environment or to defray the costs of environmental protection or enforcement.

(Pub.L. 89–272, Title II, § 6001, as added Pub.L. 94–580, § 2, Oct. 21, 1976, 90 Stat. 2821, and amended Pub.L. 95–609, § 7(m), Nov. 8, 1978, 92 Stat. 3082; Pub.L. 102–386, Title I, § 102(a), (b), Oct. 6, 1992, 106 Stat. 1505, 1506.)

## HISTORICAL AND STATUTORY NOTES

**Effective and Applicability Provisions**

1992 Acts

Section 102(c) of Pub.L. 102–386 provided that:

"**(1) In general.**—Except as otherwise provided in paragraphs (2) and (3), the amendments made by subsection (a) [amending subsec. (a) of this section] shall take effect upon the date of the enactment of this Act [Oct. 6, 1992].

"**(2) Delayed effective date for certain mixed waste.**—Until the date that is 3 years after the date of the enactment of this Act [Oct. 6, 1992], the waiver of sovereign immunity contained in section 6001(a) of the Solid Waste Disposal Act with respect to civil, criminal, and administrative penalties and fines (as added by the amendments made by subsection (a) [subsec. (a) of this section]) shall not apply to departments, agencies, and instrumentalities of the executive branch of the Federal Government for violations of section 3004(j) of the Solid Waste Disposal Act [section 6924(j) of this title] involving storage of mixed waste that is not subject to an existing agreement, permit, or administrative or judicial order, so long as such waste is managed in compliance with all other applicable requirements.

"**(3) Effective date for certain mixed waste.**—(A) Except as provided in subparagraph (B), after the date that is 3 years after the date of the enactment of this Act [Oct. 6, 1992], the waiver of sovereign immunity contained in section 6001(a) of the Solid Waste Disposal Act with respect to civil, criminal, and administrative penalties and fines (as added by the amendments made by subsection (a) [subsec. (a) of this section]) shall apply to departments, agencies, and instrumentalities of the executive branch of the Federal Government for violations of section 3004(j) of the Solid Waste Disposal Act [section 6924(j) of this title] involving storage of mixed waste.

"(B) With respect to the Department of Energy, the waiver of sovereign immunity referred to in subparagraph (A) shall not apply after the date that is 3 years after the date of the enactment of this Act [Oct. 6, 1992] for violations of section 3004(j) of such Act [section 6924(j) of this title] involving storage of mixed waste, so long as the Department of Energy is in compliance with both—

"(i) a plan that has been submitted and approved pursuant to section 3021(b) of the Solid Waste Disposal Act [section 6939c(b) of this title] and which is in effect; and

"(ii) an order requiring compliance with such plan which has been issued pursuant to such section 3021(b) [section 6939c(b) of this title] and which is in effect.

"**(4) Application of waiver to agreements and orders.**—The waiver of sovereign immunity contained in section 6001(a) of the Solid Waste Disposal Act (as added by the amendments made by subsection (a) [subsec. (a) of this section]) shall take effect on the date of the enactment of this Act [Oct. 6, 1992] with respect to any agreement, permit, or administrative or judicial order existing on such date of enactment [Oct. 6, 1992] (and any subsequent modifications to such an agreement, permit, or order), including, without limitation, any provision of an agreement, permit, or order that addresses compliance with section 3004(j) of such Act [section 6924(j) of this title] with respect to mixed waste.

"**(5) Agreement or order.**—Except as provided in paragraph (4), nothing in this Act [see Short Title of 1992 Amendments note set out under section 6901 of this title] shall be construed to alter, modify, or change in any manner any agreement, permit, or administrative or judicial order, including, without limitation, any provision of an agreement, permit, or order—

"(i) that addresses compliance with section 3004(j) of the Solid Waste Disposal Act [section 6924(j) of this title] with respect to mixed waste;

"(ii) that is in effect on the date of enactment of this Act [Oct. 6, 1992]; and

"(iii) to which a department, agency, or instrumentality of the executive branch of the Federal Governmental is a party."

**Termination of Reporting Requirements**

For termination, effective May 15, 2000, of provisions in subsec. (a) of this section requiring the President to report annually to Congress, see section 3003 of Pub.L. 104–66, as amended, set out as a note under 31 U.S.C.A. § 1113, and the 8th item on page 20 of House Document No. 103–7.

## § 6962. Federal procurement

[SWDA § 6002]

### (a) Application of section

Except as provided in subsection (b) of this section, a procuring agency shall comply with the requirements set forth in this section and any regulations issued under this section, with respect to any purchase or acquisition of a procurement item where the purchase price of the item exceeds $10,000 or where the quantity of such items or of functionally equivalent items purchased or acquired in the course of the preceding fiscal year was $10,000 or more.

**(b) Procurement subject to other law**

Any procurement, by any procuring agency, which is subject to regulations of the Administrator under section 6964 of this title (as promulgated before October 21, 1976, under comparable provisions of prior law) shall not be subject to the requirements of this section to the extent that such requirements are inconsistent with such regulations.

**(c) Requirements**

(1) After the date specified in applicable guidelines prepared pursuant to subsection (e) of this section, each procuring agency which procures any items designated in such guidelines shall procure such items composed of the highest percentage of recovered materials practicable (and in the case of paper, the highest percentage of the postconsumer recovered materials referred to in subsection (h)(1) of this section practicable), consistent with maintaining a satisfactory level of competition, considering such guidelines. The decision not to procure such items shall be based on a determination that such procurement items—

(A) are not reasonably available within a reasonable period of time;

(B) fail to meet the performance standards set forth in the applicable specifications or fail to meet the reasonable performance standards of the procuring agencies; or

(C) are only available at an unreasonable price. Any determination under subparagraph (B) shall be made on the basis of the guidelines of the National Institute of Standards and Technology in any case in which such material is covered by such guidelines.

(2) Agencies that generate heat, mechanical, or electrical energy from fossil fuel in systems that have the technical capability of using energy or fuels derived from solid waste as a primary or supplementary fuel shall use such capability to the maximum extent practicable.

(3)(A) After the date specified in any applicable guidelines prepared pursuant to subsection (e) of this section, contracting officers shall require that vendors:

(i) certify that the percentage of recovered materials to be used in the performance of the contract will be at least the amount required by applicable specifications or other contractual requirements and

(ii) estimate the percentage of the total material utilized for the performance of the contract which is recovered materials.

(B) Clause (ii) of subparagraph (A) applies only to a contract in an amount greater than $100,000.

**(d) Specifications**

All Federal agencies that have the responsibility for drafting or reviewing specifications for procurement items procured by Federal agencies shall—

(1) as expeditiously as possible but in any event no later than eighteen months after November 8, 1984, eliminate from such specifications—

(A) any exclusion of recovered materials and

(B) any requirement that items be manufactured from virgin materials; and

(2) within one year after the date of publication of applicable guidelines under subsection (e) of this section, or as otherwise specified in such guidelines, assure that such specifications require the use of recovered materials to the maximum extent possible without jeopardizing the intended end use of the item.

**(e) Guidelines**

The Administrator, after consultation with the Administrator of General Services, the Secretary of Commerce (acting through the National Institute of Standards and Technology), and the Public Printer, shall prepare, and from time to time revise, guidelines for the use of procuring agencies in complying with the requirements of this section. Such guidelines shall—

(1) designate those items which are or can be produced with recovered materials and whose procurement by procuring agencies will carry out the objectives of this section, and in the case of paper, provide for maximizing the use of post consumer recovered materials referred to in subsection (h)(1) of this section; and

(2) set forth recommended practices with respect to the procurement of recovered materials and items containing such materials and with respect to certification by vendors of the percentage of recovered materials used,

and shall provide information as to the availability, relative price, and performance of such materials and items and where appropriate shall recommend the level of recovered material to be contained in the procured product. The Administrator shall prepare final guidelines for paper within one hundred and eighty days after November 8, 1984, and for three additional product categories (including tires) by October 1, 1985. In making the designation under paragraph (1), the Administrator shall consider, but is not limited in his considerations, to—

(A) the availability of such items;

(B) the impact of the procurement of such items by procuring agencies on the volume of solid waste which must be treated, stored or disposed of;

(C) the economic and technological feasibility of producing and using such items; and

(D) other uses for such recovered materials.

**(f) Procurement of services**

A procuring agency shall, to the maximum extent practicable, manage or arrange for the procurement of solid waste management services in a manner which maximizes energy and resource recovery.

**(g) Executive Office**

The Office of Procurement Policy in the Executive Office of the President, in cooperation with the Administrator, shall implement the requirements of this section. It shall be the responsibility of the Office of Procurement Policy to coordinate this policy with other policies for Federal procurement, in such a way as to maximize the use of recovered resources, and to, every two years beginning in 1984, report to the Congress on actions taken by Federal agencies and the progress made in the implementation of this section, including agency compliance with subsection (d) of this section.

**(h) "Recovered materials" defined**

As used in this section, in the case of paper products, the term "recovered materials" includes—

(1) postconsumer materials such as—

(A) paper, paperboard, and fibrous wastes from retail stores, office buildings, homes, and so forth, after they have passed through their end-usage as a consumer item, including: used corrugated boxes; old newspapers; old magazines; mixed waste paper; tabulating cards; and used cordage; and

(B) all paper, paperboard, and fibrous wastes that enter and are collected from municipal solid waste, and

(2) manufacturing, forest residues, and other wastes such as—

(A) dry paper and paperboard waste generated after completion of the papermaking process (that is, those manufacturing operations up to and including the cutting and trimming of the paper machine reel into smaller rolls or rough sheets) including: envelope cuttings, bindery trimmings, and other paper and paperboard waste, resulting from printing, cutting, forming, and other converting operations; bag, box, and carton manufacturing wastes; and butt rolls, mill wrappers, and rejected unused stock; and

(B) finished paper and paperboard from obsolete inventories of paper and paperboard manufacturers, merchants, wholesalers, dealers, printers, converters, or others;

(C) fibrous byproducts of harvesting, manufacturing, extractive, or wood-cutting processes, flax, straw, linters, bagasse, slash, and other forest residues;

(D) wastes generated by the conversion of goods made from fibrous material (that is, waste rope from cordage manufacture, textile mill waste, and cuttings); and

(E) fibers recovered from waste water which otherwise would enter the waste stream.

**(i) Procurement program**

(1) Within one year after the date of publication of applicable guidelines under subsection (e) of this section, each procuring agency shall develop an affirmative procurement program which will assure that items composed of recovered materials will be purchased to the maximum extent practicable and which is consistent with applicable provisions of Federal procurement law.

(2) Each affirmative procurement program required under this subsection shall, at a minimum, contain—

(A) a recovered materials preference program;

(B) an agency promotion program to promote the preference program adopted under subparagraph (A);

(C) a program for requiring estimates of the total percentage of recovered material utilized in the performance of a contract; certification of minimum recovered material content actually utilized, where appropriate; and reasonable verification procedures for estimates and certifications; and

(D) annual review and monitoring of the effectiveness of an agency's affirmative procurement program.

In the case of paper, the recovered materials preference program required under subparagraph (A) shall provide for the maximum use of the post consumer recovered materials referred to in subsection (h)(1) of this section.

(3) In developing the preference program, the following options shall be considered for adoption:

(A) Case-by-Case Policy Development: Subject to the limitations of subsection (c)(1) (A) through (C) of this section, a policy of awarding contracts to the vendor offering an item composed of the highest percentage of recovered materials practicable (and in the case of paper, the highest percentage of the post consumer recovered materials referred to in subsection (h)(1) of this section). Subject to such limitations, agencies may make an award to a vendor offering items with less than the maximum recovered materials content.

(B) Minimum Content Standards: Minimum recovered materials content specifications which are set in such a way as to assure that the recovered materials content (and in the case of paper, the content of post consumer materials referred to in subsection (h)(1) of this section) required is the maximum available without jeopardizing the intended end use of the item, or violating the limitations of subsection (c)(1) (A) through (C) of this section.

Procuring agencies shall adopt one of the options set forth in subparagraphs (A) and (B) or a substantially equivalent alternative, for inclusion in the affirmative procurement program.

(Pub.L. 89–272, Title II, § 6002, as added Pub.L. 94–580, § 2, Oct. 21, 1976, 90 Stat. 2822, and amended Pub.L. 95–609, § 7(n), Nov. 8, 1978, 92 Stat. 3082; Pub.L. 96–482, § 22, Oct. 21, 1980, 94 Stat. 2346; Pub.L. 97–375, Title I, § 102, Dec. 21, 1982, 96 Stat. 1819; Pub.L. 98–616, Title V, § 501(a)–(e), Nov. 8, 1984, 98 Stat. 3274–3276; Pub.L. 100–418, Title V, § 5115(c), Aug. 23, 1988, 102 Stat. 1433; Pub.L. 102–393, Title VI, § 630, Oct. 6, 1992, 106 Stat. 1773; Pub.L. 103–355, Title I, § 1554(1), Title IV, § 4104(e), Oct. 13, 1994, 108 Stat. 3300, 3342.)

### HISTORICAL AND STATUTORY NOTES

**Effective and Applicability Provisions**

1994 Acts

Amendment by section 1554(1) of Pub.L. 103–355 effective Oct. 13, 1994, and applicable on and after such date; amendment by section 4104(e) of Pub.L. 103–355 effective Oct. 13, 1994, except as otherwise provided, see section 10001 of Pub.L. 103–355, set out as a note under section 251 of Title 41, Public Contracts.

**Transfer of Functions**

For transfer of certain enforcement functions of Administrator or other official of the Environmental Protection Agency under this chapter to Federal Inspector, Office of Federal Inspector for the Alaska Natural Gas Transportation System, see note set out under section 6903 of this title.

**Federal Acquisition, Recycling, and Waste Prevention**

Executive agency heads to develop and implement affirmative procurement programs in accordance with this section and Ex. Ord. No. 12873, and specifications, standards, and product descriptions inconsistent with this section or Ex. Ord. No. 12873 to be revised, see Ex. Ord. No. 12873, §§ 402, 501(a), Oct. 20, 1993, 58 F.R. 54914, 54915, set out as a note under section 6961 of this title.

**Procurement Preference for U.S. Made Remanufactured or Recycled Toner Cartridges**

Pub.L. 103–123, Title IV, § 401, Oct. 28, 1993, 107 Stat. 1238, which provided in part that a Federal agency, when purchasing toner cartridges, give preference to remanufactured toner cartridges made in the U.S. by small businesses and to recycled toner cartridges, unless such cartridges do not exist, the cost is greater than new cartridges, or sufficient quantities are not available, but authorizing the purchase of one or more new cartridges as a part of an initial printer or copier acquisition, and providing that such purchasing preference directives shall not affect current law with respect to Organizations for the Blind or Other Severely Handicapped, was repealed by Pub.L. 103–355, Title I, § 1554(2), Title X, § 10001, Oct. 13, 1994, 108 Stat. 3300, 3404, effective Oct. 13, 1994, and applicable on and after such date.

## § 6963. Cooperation with Environmental Protection Agency

**[SWDA § 6003]**

### (a) General rule

All Federal agencies shall assist the Administrator in carrying out his functions under this chapter and shall promptly make available all requested information concerning past or present Agency waste management practices and past or present Agency owned, leased, or operated solid or hazardous waste facilities. This information shall be provided in such format as may be determined by the Administrator.

### (b) Information relating to energy and materials conservation and recovery

The Administrator shall collect, maintain, and disseminate information concerning the market potential of energy and materials recovered from solid waste, including materials obtained through source separation, and information concerning the savings potential of conserving resources contributing to the waste stream. The Administrator shall identify the regions in which the increased substitution of such energy for energy derived from fossil fuels and other sources is most likely to be feasible, and provide information on the technical and economic aspects of developing integrated resource conservation or recovery systems which provide for the recovery of source-separated materials to be recycled or the conservation of resources. The Administrator shall utilize the authorities of subsection (a) of this section in carrying out this subsection.

(Pub.L. 89–272, Title II, § 6003, as added Pub.L. 94–580, § 2, Oct. 21, 1976, 90 Stat. 2823, and amended Pub.L. 96–482, § 32(g), Oct. 21, 1980, 94 Stat. 2355.)

### HISTORICAL AND STATUTORY NOTES

**Transfer of Functions**

For transfer of certain enforcement functions of Administrator or other official of the Environmental Protection Agency under this chapter to Federal Inspector, Office of Federal Inspector for the Alaska Natural Gas Transportation System, see note set out under section 6903 of this title.

## § 6964. Applicability of solid waste disposal guidelines to Executive agencies

**[SWDA § 6004]**

### (a) Compliance

(1) If—

(A) an Executive agency (as defined in section 105 of Title 5) or any unit of the legislative branch of the Federal Government has jurisdiction over any real property or facility the operation or administration of which involves such agency in solid waste management activities, or

(B) such an agency enters into a contract with any person for the operation by such person of any Federal property or facility, and the performance of such contract involves such person in solid waste management activities,

then such agency shall insure compliance with the guidelines recommended under section 6907 of this title and the purposes of this chapter in the operation or administration of such property or facility, or the performance of such contract, as the case may be.

(2) Each Executive agency or any unit of the legislative branch of the Federal Government which conducts any activity—

(A) which generates solid waste, and

(B) which, if conducted by a person other than such agency, would require a permit or license from such agency in order to dispose of such solid waste,

shall insure compliance with such guidelines and the purposes of this chapter in conducting such activity.

(3) Each Executive agency which permits the use of Federal property for purposes of disposal of solid waste shall insure compliance with such guidelines and the purposes of this chapter in the disposal of such waste.

(4) The President or the Committee on House Oversight of the House of Representatives and the Committee on Rules and Administration of the Senate with regard to any unit of the legislative branch of the Federal Government shall prescribe regulations to carry out this subsection.

**(b) Licenses and permits**

Each Executive agency which issues any license or permit for disposal of solid waste shall, prior to the issuance of such license or permit, consult with the Administrator to insure compliance with guidelines recommended under section 6907 of this title and the purposes of this chapter.

(Pub.L. 89–272, Title II, § 6004, as added Pub.L. 94–580, § 2, Oct. 21, 1976, 90 Stat. 2823, and amended Pub.L. 95–609, § 7(*o*), Nov. 8, 1978, 92 Stat. 3083; Pub.L. 96–482, § 23, Oct. 21, 1980, 94 Stat. 2347; Pub.L. 104–186, Title II, § 222(2), Aug. 20, 1996, 110 Stat. 1751.)

### HISTORICAL AND STATUTORY NOTES

**Transfer of Functions**

For transfer of certain enforcement functions of Administrator or other official of the Environmental Protection Agency under this chapter to Federal Inspector, Office of Federal Inspector for the Alaska Natural Gas Transportation System, see note set out under section 6903 of this title.

**Prior Provisions**

Prior to the complete revision of the Solid Waste Disposal Act by Pub.L. 94–580, provisions similar to this section were contained in section 211 of that Act, which was classified to section 3254e of this title. See note thereunder.

## § 6965. Chief Financial Officer report

The Chief Financial Officer of each affected agency shall submit to Congress an annual report containing, to the extent practicable, a detailed description of the compliance activities undertaken by the agency for mixed waste streams, and an accounting of the fines and penalties imposed on the agency for violations involving mixed waste.

(Pub.L. 102–386, Title I, § 110, Oct. 6, 1992, 106 Stat. 1516.)

### HISTORICAL AND STATUTORY NOTES

**Codifications**

Section was enacted as part of the Federal Facility Compliance Act of 1992 and not as part of the Solid Waste Disposal Act, which comprises this chapter.

## SUBCHAPTER VII—MISCELLANEOUS PROVISIONS

## § 6971. Employee protection

[SWDA § 7001]

**(a) General**

No person shall fire, or in any other way discriminate against, or cause to be fired or discriminated against, any employee or any authorized representative of employees by reason of the fact that such employee or representative has filed, instituted, or caused to be filed or instituted any proceeding under this chapter or under any applicable implementation plan, or has testified or is about to testify in any proceeding resulting from the administration or enforcement of the provisions of this chapter or of any applicable implementation plan.

**(b) Remedy**

Any employee or a representative of employees who believes that he has been fired or otherwise discriminated against by any person in violation of subsection (a) of this section may, within thirty days after such alleged violation occurs, apply to the Secretary of Labor for a review of such firing or alleged discrimination. A copy of the application shall be sent to such person who shall be the respondent. Upon receipt of such application, the Secretary of Labor shall cause such investigation to be made as he deems appropriate. Such investigation shall provide an opportunity for a public hearing at the request of any party to such review to enable the parties to present information relating to such alleged violation. The parties shall be given written notice of the time and place of the hearing at least five days prior to the hearing. Any such hearing shall be of record and shall be subject to section 554 of Title 5. Upon receiving the report of such investigation, the Secretary of Labor shall make findings of fact. If he finds that such violation did occur, he shall issue a decision, incorporating an order therein and his findings, requiring the party committing such violation to take such affirmative action to abate the violation as the Secretary of Labor deems appropriate, including, but not limited to, the rehiring or reinstatement of the employee or representative of employees to his former position with compensation. If he finds that there was no such violation, he shall issue an order denying the application. Such order issued by the Secretary of Labor under this subparagraph shall be subject to judicial review in the same manner as orders and decisions of the Administrator or subject to judicial review under this chapter.

**(c) Costs**

Whenever an order is issued under this section to abate such violation, at the request of the applicant, a sum equal to the aggregate amount of all costs and expenses (including the attorney's fees) as determined by the Secretary of Labor, to have been reasonably incurred by the applicant for, or in connection with, the institution and prosecution of such proceedings, shall be assessed against the person committing such violation.

**(d) Exception**

This section shall have no application to any employee who, acting without direction from his employer (or his agent) deliberately violates any requirement of this chapter.

**(e) Employment shifts and loss**

The Administrator shall conduct continuing evaluations of potential loss or shifts of employment which may result from the administration or enforcement of the provisions of this chapter and applicable implementation plans, including, where appropriate, investigating threatened plant closures or reductions in employment allegedly resulting from such administration or enforcement. Any employee who is discharged, or laid off, threatened with discharge or layoff, or otherwise discriminated against by any person because of the alleged results of such administration or enforcement, or any representative of such employee, may request the Administrator to conduct a full investigation of the matter. The Administrator shall thereupon investigate the matter and, at the request of any party, shall hold public hearings on not less than five days' notice, and shall at such hearings require the parties, including the employer involved, to present information relating to the actual or potential effect of such administration or enforcement on employment and on any alleged discharge, layoff, or other discrimination and the detailed reasons or justification therefor. Any such hearing shall be of record and shall be subject to section 554 of Title 5. Upon receiving the report of such investigation, the Administrator shall make findings of fact as to the effect of such administration or enforcement on employment and on the alleged discharge, layoff, or discrimination and shall make such recommendations as he deems appropriate. Such report, findings, and recommendations shall be available to the public. Nothing in this subsection shall be construed to require or authorize the Administrator or any State to modify or withdraw any standard, limitation, or any other requirement of this chapter or any applicable implementation plan.

**(f) Occupational safety and health**

In order to assist the Secretary of Labor and the Director of the National Institute for Occupational Safety and Health in carrying out their duties under the Occupational Safety and Health Act of 1970 [29 U.S.C.A. § 651 et seq.], the Administrator shall—

(1) provide the following information, as such information becomes available, to the Secretary and the Director:

(A) the identity of any hazardous waste generation, treatment, storage, disposal facility or site where cleanup is planned or underway;

(B) information identifying the hazards to which persons working at a hazardous waste generation, treatment, storage, disposal facility or site or otherwise handling hazardous waste may be exposed, the nature and extent of the exposure, and methods to protect workers from such hazards; and

(C) incidents of worker injury or harm at a hazardous waste generation, treatment, storage or disposal facility or site; and

(2) notify the Secretary and the Director of the Administrator's receipt of notifications under section 6930 or reports under sections 6922, 6923, and 6924 of this title and make such notifications and reports available to the Secretary and the Director.

(Pub.L. 89–272, Title II, § 7001, as added Pub.L. 94–580, § 2, Oct. 21, 1976, 90 Stat. 2824, and amended Pub.L. 96–482, § 24, Oct. 21, 1980, 94 Stat. 2347.)

## HISTORICAL AND STATUTORY NOTES

**References in Text**

The Occupational Safety and Health Act of 1970, referred to in subsec. (f), is Pub.L. 91–596, Dec. 29, 1970, 84 Stat. 1590, as amended, which is classified principally to chapter 15 (section 651 et seq.) of Title 29, Labor. For complete classification of this Act to the Code, see Short Title note set out under section 651 of Title 29 and Tables.

**Transfer of Functions**

For transfer of certain enforcement functions of Administrator or other official of the Environmental Protection Agency under this chapter to Federal Inspector, Office of Federal Inspector for the Alaska Natural Gas Transportation System, see note set out under section 6903 of this title.

## § 6972. Citizen suits

**[SWDA § 7002]**

**(a) In general**

Except as provided in subsection (b) or (c) of this section, any person may commence a civil action on his own behalf—

**(1)(A)** against any person (including (a) the United States, and (b) any other governmental instrumentality or agency, to the extent permitted by the eleventh amendment to the Constitution) who is alleged to be in violation of any permit, standard, regulation, condition, requirement, prohibition, or order which has become effective pursuant to this chapter; or

**(B)** against any person, including the United States and any other governmental instrumentality or agency, to the extent permitted by the eleventh amendment to the Constitution, and including any past or present generator, past or present transporter, or past or present owner or operator of a treatment, storage, or disposal facility, who has contributed or who is contributing to the past or present handling, storage, treatment, transportation, or disposal of any solid or hazardous waste which may present an imminent and substantial endangerment to health or the environment; or

**(2)** against the Administrator where there is alleged a failure of the Administrator to perform any act or duty under this chapter which is not discretionary with the Administrator.

Any action under paragraph (a)(1) of this subsection shall be brought in the district court for the district in which the alleged violation occurred or the alleged endangerment may occur. Any action brought under paragraph (a)(2) of this subsection may be brought in the district court for the district in which the alleged violation occurred or in the District Court of the District of Columbia. The district court shall have jurisdiction, without regard to the amount in controversy or the citizenship of the parties, to enforce the permit, standard, regulation, condition, requirement, prohibition, or order, referred to in paragraph (1)(A), to restrain any person who has contributed or who is contributing to the past or present handling, storage, treatment, transportation, or disposal of any solid or hazardous waste referred to in paragraph (1)(B), to order such person to take such other action as may be necessary, or both, or to order the Administrator to perform the act or duty referred to in paragraph (2), as the case may be, and to apply any appropriate civil penalties under section 6928(a) and (g) of this title.

**(b) Actions prohibited**

**(1)** No action may be commenced under subsection (a)(1)(A) of this section—

**(A)** prior to 60 days after the plaintiff has given notice of the violation to—

**(i)** the Administrator;

**(ii)** the State in which the alleged violation occurs; and

**(iii)** to any alleged violator of such permit, standard, regulation, condition, requirement, prohibition, or order,

except that such action may be brought immediately after such notification in the case of an action under this section respecting a violation of subchapter III of this chapter; or

**(B)** if the Administrator or State has commenced and is diligently prosecuting a civil or criminal action in a court of the United States or a State to require compliance with such permit, standard, regulation, condition, requirement, prohibition, or order.

In any action under subsection (a)(1)(A) of this section in a court of the United States, any person may intervene as a matter of right.

**(2)(A)** No action may be commenced under subsection (a)(1)(B) of this section prior to ninety days after the plaintiff has given notice of the endangerment to—

**(i)** the Administrator;

**(ii)** the State in which the alleged endangerment may occur;

**(iii)** any person alleged to have contributed or to be contributing to the past or present handling, storage, treatment, transportation, or disposal of any solid or hazardous waste referred to in subsection (a)(1)(B) of this section,

except that such action may be brought immediately after such notification in the case of an action under this section respecting a violation of subchapter III of this chapter.

**(B)** No action may be commenced under subsection (a)(1)(B) of this section if the Administrator, in order to restrain or abate acts or conditions which may have contributed or are contributing to the activities which may present the alleged endangerment—

**(i)** has commenced and is diligently prosecuting an action under section 6973 of this title or under section 106 of the Comprehensive Environmental Response, Compensation and Liability Act of 1980 [42 U.S.C.A. § 9606], [1]

(ii) is actually engaging in a removal action under section 104 of the Comprehensive Environmental Response, Compensation and Liability Act of 1980 [42 U.S.C.A. § 9604];

(iii) has incurred costs to initiate a Remedial Investigation and Feasibility Study under section 104 of the Comprehensive Environmental Response, Compensation and Liability Act of 1980 [42 U.S.C.A. § 9604] and is diligently proceeding with a remedial action under that Act [42 U.S.C.A. § 9601 et seq.]; or

(iv) has obtained a court order (including a consent decree) or issued an administrative order under section 106 of the Comprehensive Environmental Response, Compensation and Liability Act of 980 [2] [42 U.S.C.A. § 9606] or section 6973 of this title pursuant to which a responsible party is diligently conducting a removal action, Remedial Investigation and Feasibility Study (RIFS), or proceeding with a remedial action.

In the case of an administrative order referred to in clause (iv), actions under subsection (a)(1)(B) of this section are prohibited only as to the scope and duration of the administrative order referred to in clause (iv).

(C) No action may be commenced under subsection (a)(1)(B) of this section if the State, in order to restrain or abate acts or conditions which may have contributed or are contributing to the activities which may present the alleged endangerment—

(i) has commenced and is diligently prosecuting an action under subsection (a)(1)(B) of this section;

(ii) is actually engaging in a removal action under section 104 of the Comprehensive Environmental Response, Compensation and Liability Act of 1980 [42 U.S.C.A. § 9604]; or

(iii) has incurred costs to initiate a Remedial Investigation and Feasibility Study under section 104 of the Comprehensive Environmental Response, Compensation and Liability Act of 1980 [42 U.S.C.A. § 9604] and is diligently proceeding with a remedial action under that Act [42 U.S.C.A. § 9601 et seq.].

(D) No action may be commenced under subsection (a)(1)(B) of this section by any person (other than a State or local government) with respect to the siting of a hazardous waste treatment, storage, or a disposal facility, nor to restrain or enjoin the issuance of a permit for such facility.

(E) In any action under subsection (a)(1)(B) of this section in a court of the United States, any person may intervene as a matter of right when the applicant claims an interest relating to the subject of the action and he is so situated that the disposition of the action may, as a practical matter, impair or impede his ability to protect that interest, unless the Administrator or the State shows that the applicant's interest is adequately represented by existing parties.

(F) Whenever any action is brought under subsection (a)(1)(B) of this section in a court of the United States, the plaintiff shall serve a copy of the complaint on the Attorney General of the United States and with the Administrator.

**(c) Notice**

No action may be commenced under paragraph (a)(2) of this section prior to sixty days after the plaintiff has given notice to the Administrator that he will commence such action, except that such action may be brought immediately after such notification in the case of an action under this section respecting a violation of subchapter III of this chapter. Notice under this subsection shall be given in such manner as the Administrator shall prescribe by regulation. Any action respecting a violation under this chapter may be brought under this section only in the judicial district in which such alleged violation occurs.

**(d) Intervention**

In any action under this section the Administrator, if not a party, may intervene as a matter of right.

**(e) Costs**

The court, in issuing any final order in any action brought pursuant to this section or section 6976 of this title, may award costs of litigation (including reasonable attorney and expert witness fees) to the prevailing or substantially prevailing party, whenever the court determines such an award is appropriate. The court may, if a temporary restraining order or preliminary injunction is sought, require the filing of a bond or equivalent security in accordance with the Federal Rules of Civil Procedure.

**(f) Other rights preserved**

Nothing in this section shall restrict any right which any person (or class of persons) may have under any statute or common law to seek enforcement of any standard or requirement relating to the management of solid waste or hazardous waste, or to seek any other relief (including relief against the Administrator or a State agency).

**(g) Transporters**

A transporter shall not be deemed to have contributed or to be contributing to the handling, storage, treatment, or disposal, referred to in subsection (a)(1)(B) of this section taking place after such solid waste or hazardous waste has left the possession or control of such transporter, if the transportation of such waste was under a sole contractual arrangement arising from a published tariff and acceptance for carriage by common carrier by rail and such transporter has exercised due care in the past or present handling, storage, treatment, transportation and disposal of such waste.

(Pub.L. 89–272, Title II, § 7002, as added Pub.L. 94–580, § 2, Oct. 21, 1976, 90 Stat. 2825, and amended Pub.L. 95–609, § 7(p), Nov. 8, 1978, 92 Stat. 3083; Pub.L. 98–616, Title IV, § 401, Nov. 8, 1984, 98 Stat. 3268.)

[1] So in original. The comma probably should be a semicolon.

[2] So in original. Probably should be "1980".

### HISTORICAL AND STATUTORY NOTES

**References in Text**

That Act, referred to in subsec. (b)(2)(B)(iii), (C)(iii), means Pub.L. 96–510, Dec. 11, 1980, 94 Stat. 2767, as amended, known as the Comprehensive Environmental Response, Compensation, and Liability Act of 1980, which is classified principally to chapter 103 (section 9601 et seq.) of this title. For complete classification of this Act to the Code, see Short Title of 1980 Acts note set out under section 9601 of this title and Tables.

The Federal Rules of Civil Procedure, referred to in subsec. (e), are set out in the Appendix to Title 28, Judiciary and Judicial Procedure.

**Transfer of Functions**

For transfer of certain enforcement functions of Administrator or other official of the Environmental Protection Agency under this chapter to Federal Inspector, Office of Federal Inspector for the Alaska Natural Gas Transportation System, see note set out under section 6903 of this title.

## § 6973. Imminent hazard

[SWDA § 7003]

### (a) Authority of Administrator

Notwithstanding any other provision of this chapter, upon receipt of evidence that the past or present handling, storage, treatment, transportation or disposal of any solid waste or hazardous waste may present an imminent and substantial endangerment to health or the environment, the Administrator may bring suit on behalf of the United States in the appropriate district court against any person (including any past or present generator, past or present transporter, or past or present owner or operator of a treatment, storage, or disposal facility) who has contributed or who is contributing to such handling, storage, treatment, transportation or disposal to restrain such person from such handling, storage, treatment, transportation, or disposal, to order such person to take such other action as may be necessary, or both. A transporter shall not be deemed to have contributed or to be contributing to such handling, storage, treatment, or disposal taking place after such solid waste or hazardous waste has left the possession or control of such transporter if the transportation of such waste was under a sole contractural[1] arrangement arising from a published tariff and acceptance for carriage by common carrier by rail and such transporter has exercised due care in the past or present handling, storage, treatment, transportation and disposal of such waste. The Administrator shall provide notice to the affected State of any such suit. The Administrator may also, after notice to the affected State, take other action under this section including, but not limited to, issuing such orders as may be necessary to protect public health and the environment.

### (b) Violations

Any person who willfully violates, or fails or refuses to comply with, any order of the Administrator under subsection (a) of this section may, in an action brought in the appropriate United States district court to enforce such order, be fined not more than $5,000 for each day in which such violation occurs or such failure to comply continues.

### (c) Immediate notice

Upon receipt of information that there is hazardous waste at any site which has presented an imminent and substantial endangerment to human health or the environment, the Administrator shall provide immediate notice to the appropriate local government agencies. In addition, the Administrator shall require notice of such endangerment to be promptly posted at the site where the waste is located.

### (d) Public participation in settlements

Whenever the United States or the Administrator proposes to covenant not to sue or to forbear from suit or to settle any claim arising under this section, notice, and opportunity for a public meeting in the affected area, and a reasonable opportunity to comment on the proposed settlement prior to its final entry shall be afforded to the public. The decision of the United States or the Administrator to enter into or not to enter into such Consent Decree, covenant or agreement shall not constitute a final agency action subject to judicial review under this chapter or chapter 7 of Title 5.

(Pub.L. 89–272, Title II, § 7003, as added Pub.L. 94–580, § 2, Oct. 21, 1976, 90 Stat. 2826, and amended Pub.L. 95–609, § 7(q), Nov. 8, 1978, 92 Stat. 3083; Pub.L. 96–482, § 25, Oct. 21, 1980, 94 Stat. 2348; Pub.L. 98–616, Title IV, §§ 402, 403(a), 404, Nov. 8, 1984, 98 Stat. 3271, 3273.)

[1] So in original. Probably should be "contractual".

### HISTORICAL AND STATUTORY NOTES

**Codifications**

In subsec. (d), "chapter 7 of Title 5" was substituted for "the Administrative Procedure Act" on authority of Pub.L. 89–554, § 7(b), Sept. 6, 1966, 80 Stat. 631, the first section of which enacted Title 5, Government Organization and Employees.

**Transfer of Functions**

For transfer of certain enforcement functions of Administrator or other official of the Environmental Protection

Agency under this chapter to Federal Inspector, Office of Federal Inspector for the Alaska Natural Gas Transportation System, see note set out under section 6903 of this title.

## § 6974. Petition for regulations; public participation

**[SWDA § 7004]**

### (a) Petition

Any person may petition the Administrator for the promulgation, amendment, or repeal of any regulation under this chapter. Within a reasonable time following receipt of such petition, the Administrator shall take action with respect to such petition and shall publish notice of such action in the Federal Register, together with the reasons therefor.

### (b) Public participation

(1) Public participation in the development, revision, implementation, and enforcement of any regulation, guideline, information, or program under this chapter shall be provided for, encouraged, and assisted by the Administrator and the States. The Administrator, in cooperation with the States, shall develop and publish minimum guidelines for public participation in such processes.

(2) Before the issuing of a permit to any person with any respect to any facility for the treatment, storage, or disposal of hazardous wastes under section 6925 of this title, the Administrator shall—

(A) cause to be published in major local newspapers of general circulation and broadcast over local radio stations notice of the agency's intention to issue such permit, and

(B) transmit in writing notice of the agency's intention to issue such permit to each unit of local government having jurisdiction over the area in which such facility is proposed to be located and to each State agency having any authority under State law with respect to the construction or operation of such facility.

If within 45 days the Administrator receives written notice of opposition to the agency's intention to issue such permit and a request for a hearing, or if the Administrator determines on his own initiative, he shall hold an informal public hearing (including an opportunity for presentation of written and oral views) on whether he should issue a permit for the proposed facility. Whenever possible the Administrator shall schedule such hearing at a location convenient to the nearest population center to such proposed facility and give notice in the aforementioned manner of the date, time, and subject matter of such hearing. No State program which provides for the issuance of permits referred to in this paragraph may be authorized by the Administrator under section 6926 of this title unless such program provides for the notice and hearing required by the paragraph.

(Pub.L. 89–272, Title II, § 7004, as added Pub.L. 94–580, § 2, Oct. 21, 1976, 90 Stat. 2826, and amended Pub.L. 96–482, § 26, Oct. 21, 1980, 94 Stat. 2348.)

### HISTORICAL AND STATUTORY NOTES

**Transfer of Functions**

For transfer of certain enforcement functions of Administrator or other official of the Environmental Protection Agency under this chapter to Federal Inspector, Office of Federal Inspector for the Alaska Natural Gas Transportation System, see note set out under section 6903 of this title.

## § 6975. Separability

**[SWDA § 7005]**

If any provision of this chapter, or the application of any provision of this chapter to any person or circumstance, is held invalid, the application of such provision to other persons or circumstances, and the remainder of this chapter, shall not be affected thereby.

(Pub.L. 89–272, Title II, § 7005, as added Pub.L. 94–580, § 2, Oct. 21, 1976, 90 Stat. 2827.)

## § 6976. Judicial review

**[SWDA § 7006]**

### (a) Review of final regulations and certain petitions

Any judicial review of final regulations promulgated pursuant to this chapter and the Administrator's denial of any petition for the promulgation, amendment, or repeal of any regulation under this chapter shall be in accordance with sections 701 through 706 of Title 5, except that—

(1) a petition for review of action of the Administrator in promulgating any regulation, or requirement under this chapter or denying any petition for the promulgation, amendment or repeal of any regulation under this chapter may be filed only in the United States Court of Appeals for the District of Columbia, and such petition shall be filed within ninety days from the date of such promulgation or denial, or after such date if such petition for review is based solely on grounds arising after such ninetieth day; action of the Administrator with respect to which review could have been obtained under this subsection shall not be subject to judicial review in civil or criminal proceedings for enforcement; and

(2) in any judicial proceeding brought under this section in which review is sought of a determination under this chapter required to be made on the record after notice and opportunity for hearing, if a party seeking review under this chapter applies to the court for leave to adduce additional evidence, and shows to the satisfaction of the court that the information is material and that there were reason-

able grounds for the failure to adduce such evidence in the proceeding before the Administrator, the court may order such additional evidence (and evidence in rebuttal thereof) to be taken before the Administrator, and to be adduced upon the hearing in such manner and upon such terms and conditions as the court may deem proper; the Administrator may modify his findings as to the facts, or make new findings, by reason of the additional evidence so taken, and he shall file with the court such modified or new findings and his recommendation, if any, for the modification or setting aside of his original order, with the return of such additional evidence.

**(b) Review of certain actions under sections 6925 and 6926 of this title**

Review of the Administrator's action (1) in issuing, denying, modifying, or revoking any permit under section 6925 of this title (or in modifying or revoking any permit which is deemed to have been issued under section 6935(d)(1) of this title), or (2) in granting, denying, or withdrawing authorization or interim authorization under section 6926 of this title, may be had by any interested person in the Circuit Court of Appeals of the United States for the Federal judicial district in which such person resides or transacts such business upon application by such person. Any such application shall be made within ninety days from the date of such issuance, denial, modification, revocation, grant, or withdrawal, or after such date only if such application is based solely on grounds which arose after such ninetieth day. Action of the Administrator with respect to which review could have been obtained under this subsection shall not be subject to judicial review in civil or criminal proceedings for enforcement. Such review shall be in accordance with sections 701 through 706 of Title 5.

(Pub.L. 89–272, Title II, § 7006, as added Pub.L. 94–580, § 2, Oct. 21, 1976, 90 Stat. 2827, and amended Pub.L. 96–482, § 27, Oct. 21, 1980, 94 Stat. 2349; Pub.L. 98–616, Title II, § 241(b)(1), Title IV, § 403(d)(5), Nov. 8, 1984, 98 Stat. 3259, 3273.)

### HISTORICAL AND STATUTORY NOTES

**References in Text**

Section 6935(d)(1) of this title, referred to in subsec. (b), was in the original a reference to section 3012(d)(1) of Pub.L. 89–272, which was renumbered section 3014(d)(1) of Pub.L. 89–272 by Pub.L. 98–616 and is classified to section 6935(d)(1) of this title.

**Transfer of Functions**

For transfer of certain enforcement functions of Administrator or other official of the Environmental Protection Agency under this chapter to Federal Inspector, Office of Federal Inspector for the Alaska Natural Gas Transportation System, see note set out under section 6903 of this title.

## § 6977. Grants or contracts for training projects

**[SWDA § 7007]**

**(a) General authority**

The Administrator is authorized to make grants to, and contracts with any eligible organization. For purposes of this section the term "eligible organization" means a State or interstate agency, a municipality, educational institution, and any other organization which is capable of effectively carrying out a project which may be funded by grant under subsection (b) of this section.

**(b) Purposes**

(1) Subject to the provisions of paragraph (2), grants or contracts may be made to pay all or a part of the costs, as may be determined by the Administrator, of any project operated or to be operated by an eligible organization, which is designed—

(A) to develop, expand, or carry out a program (which may combine training, education, and employment) for training persons for occupations involving the management, supervision, design, operation, or maintenance of solid waste management and resource recovery equipment and facilities; or

(B) to train instructors and supervisory personnel to train or supervise persons in occupations involving the design, operation, and maintenance of solid waste management and resource recovery equipment and facilities.

(2) A grant or contract authorized by paragraph (1) of this subsection may be made only upon application to the Administrator at such time or times and containing such information as he may prescribe, except that no such application shall be approved unless it provides for the same procedures and reports (and access to such reports and to other records) as required by section 3254a(b)(4) and (5) of this title (as in effect before October 21, 1976) with respect to applications made under such section (as in effect before October 21, 1976).

(Pub.L. 89–272, Title II, § 7007, as added Pub.L. 94–580, § 2, Oct. 21, 1976, 90 Stat. 2827, and amended Pub.L. 95–609, § 7(r), Nov. 8, 1978, 92 Stat. 3083; Pub.L. 105–362, § 501(f), Title V, Nov. 10, 1998, 112 Stat. 3284.)

### HISTORICAL AND STATUTORY NOTES

**References in Text**

Section 3254a(b)(4) and (5) of this title, referred to in subsec. (b)(2), was in the original, "section 207(b)(4) and (5)", meaning section 207(b)(4) and (5) of the Solid Waste Disposal Act, which was omitted in the general revision of the Solid Waste Disposal Act by Pub.L. 94–580 on Oct. 21, 1976.

**Transfer of Functions**

For transfer of certain enforcement functions of Administrator or other official of the Environmental Protection

Agency under this chapter to Federal Inspector, Office of Federal Inspector for the Alaska Natural Gas Transportation System, see note set out under section 6903 of this title.

**Prior Provisions**

Provisions similar to this section were contained in section 3254d of this title, prior to the complete revision of the Solid Waste Disposal Act by Pub.L. 94–580.

## § 6978. Payments

**[SWDA § 7008]**

**(a) General rule**

Payments of grants under this chapter may be made (after necessary adjustment on account of previously made underpayments or overpayments) in advance or by way of reimbursement, and in such installments and on such conditions as the Administrator may determine.

**(b) Prohibition**

No grant may be made under this chapter to any private profitmaking organization.

(Pub.L. 89–272, Title II, § 7008, as added Pub.L. 94–580, § 2, Oct. 21, 1976, 90 Stat. 2828.)

### HISTORICAL AND STATUTORY NOTES

**Transfer of Functions**

For transfer of certain enforcement functions of Administrator or other official of the Environmental Protection Agency under this chapter to Federal Inspector, Office of Federal Inspector for the Alaska Natural Gas Transportation System, see note set out under section 6903 of this title.

**Prior Provisions**

Provisions similar to this section were contained in section 3258 of this title, prior to the complete revision of the Solid Waste Disposal Act by Pub.L. 94–580.

## § 6979. Labor standards

**[SWDA § 7009]**

No grant for a project of construction under this chapter shall be made unless the Administrator finds that the application contains or is supported by reasonable assurance that all laborers and mechanics employed by contractors or subcontractors on projects of the type covered by sections 3141 to 3144, 3146, 3147 of Title 40, will be paid wages at rates not less than those prevailing on similar work in the locality as determined by the Secretary of Labor in accordance with that Act; and the Secretary of Labor shall have with respect to the labor standards specified in this section the authority and functions set forth in Reorganization Plan Numbered 14 of 1950 (15 F.R. 3176) and section 3145 of Title 40.

(Pub.L. 89–272, Title II, § 7009, as added Pub.L. 94–580, § 2, Oct. 21, 1976, 90 Stat. 2828, and amended Pub.L. 96–482, § 28, Oct. 21, 1980, 94 Stat. 2349.)

### HISTORICAL AND STATUTORY NOTES

**References in Text**

Reorganization Plan No. 14 of 1950, referred to in text, is set out in Appendix 1 to Title 5, Government Organization and Employees.

**Codifications**

In text, "sections 3141 to 3144, 3146, 3147 of Title 40" substituted for "the Davis–Bacon Act, as amended (40 U.S.C. 276a to 276a–5)" on authority of Pub.L. 107–217, § 5(c), Aug. 21, 2002, 116 Stat. 1301, which is set out as a note preceding 40 U.S.C.A. § 101. Pub.L. 107–217, § 1, enacted Title 40 into positive law. The Davis–Bacon Act is Act Mar. 3, 1931, c. 411, 46 Stat. 1494, which was classified to former 40 U.S.C.A. §§ 276a, 276a–1 to 276a–6, prior to being repealed by Pub.L. 107–217, § 6(b), Aug. 21, 2002, 116 Stat. 1308, and its substance reenacted as 40 U.S.C.A. §§ 3141 to 3144, 3146, 3147.

In text, "section 3145 of Title 40" substituted for "section 276c of Title 40", which originally read "section 2 of the Act of June 1, 1934, as amended (40 U.S.C. 276c)", on authority of Pub.L. 107–217, § 5(c), Aug. 21, 2002, 116 Stat. 1301, which is set out as a note preceding 40 U.S.C.A. § 101. Pub.L. 107–217, § 1, enacted Title 40 into positive law. Act June 13, 1934, c. 482, 48 Stat. 948, was classified to former 40 U.S.C.A. § 276c prior to being repealed by Pub.L. 107–217, § 6(b), Aug. 21, 2002, 116 Stat. 1309, and its substance reenacted as 40 U.S.C.A. § 3145.

**Prior Provisions**

Provisions similar to this section were contained in section 3256 of this title, prior to the complete revision of the Solid Waste Disposal Act by Pub.L. 94–580.

## § 6979a. Transferred

### HISTORICAL AND STATUTORY NOTES

**Codifications**

Section, Pub.L. 89–272, Title II, § 7010, as added Pub.L. 98–616, Title IV, § 405(a), Nov. 8, 1984, 98 Stat. 3273, and amended Pub.L. 99–339, Title II, § 201(c)(1), June 19, 1986, 100 Stat. 654, was renumbered section 3020 of Pub.L. 89–272 by Pub.L. 99–339 Title II, § 201(c)(2), June 19, 1986, 100 Stat. 654, and transferred to section 6939b of this title.

## § 6979b. Law enforcement authority

**[SWDA § 7010]**

The Attorney General of the United States shall, at the request of the Administrator and on the basis of a showing of need, deputize qualified employees of the Environmental Protection Agency to serve as special deputy United States marshals in criminal investigations with respect to violations of the criminal provisions of this chapter.

(Pub.L. 89–272, Title II, § 7010, formerly § 7012, as added Pub.L. 98–616, Title IV, § 403(b)(1), Nov. 8, 1984, 98 Stat. 3272, and renumbered § 7010, Pub.L. 99–339, Title II, § 201(c)(2), June 19, 1986, 100 Stat. 654.)

### HISTORICAL AND STATUTORY NOTES

**Prior Provisions**

A prior section 7010 of Pub.L. 89–272, which was classified to section 6979a of this title, was redesignated as section 3020 of Pub.L. 89–272 by section 201(c)(2) of Pub.L. 99–339, and transferred to section 6939b of this title.

## SUBCHAPTER VIII—RESEARCH, DEVELOPMENT, DEMONSTRATION, AND INFORMATION

## § 6981. Research, demonstration, training, and other activities

[SWDA § 8001]

### (a) General authority

The Administrator, alone or after consultation with the Secretary of Energy, shall conduct, and encourage, cooperate with, and render financial and other assistance to appropriate public (whether Federal, State, interstate, or local) authorities, agencies, and institutions, private agencies and institutions, and individuals in the conduct of, and promote the coordination of, research, investigations, experiments, training, demonstrations, surveys, public education programs, and studies relating to—

(1) any adverse health and welfare effects of the release into the environment of material present in solid waste, and methods to eliminate such effects;

(2) the operation and financing of solid waste management programs;

(3) the planning, implementation, and operation of resource recovery and resource conservation systems and hazardous waste management systems, including the marketing of recovered resources;

(4) the production of usable forms of recovered resources, including fuel, from solid waste;

(5) the reduction of the amount of such waste and unsalvageable waste materials;

(6) the development and application of new and improved methods of collecting and disposing of solid waste and processing and recovering materials and energy from solid wastes;

(7) the identification of solid waste components and potential materials and energy recoverable from such waste components;

(8) small scale and low technology solid waste management systems, including but not limited to, resource recovery source separation systems;

(9) methods to improve the performance characteristics of resources recovered from solid waste and the relationship of such performance characteristics to available and potentially available markets for such resources;

(10) improvements in land disposal practices for solid waste (including sludge) which may reduce the adverse environmental effects of such disposal and other aspects of solid waste disposal on land, including means for reducing the harmful environmental effects of earlier and existing landfills, means for restoring areas damaged by such earlier or existing landfills, means for rendering landfills safe for purposes of construction and other uses, and techniques of recovering materials and energy from landfills;

(11) methods for the sound disposal of, or recovery of resources, including energy, from, sludge (including sludge from pollution control and treatment facilities, coal slurry pipelines, and other sources);

(12) methods of hazardous waste management, including methods of rendering such waste environmentally safe; and

(13) any adverse effects on air quality (particularly with regard to the emission of heavy metals) which result from solid waste which is burned (either alone or in conjunction with other substances) for purposes of treatment, disposal or energy recovery.

### (b) Management program

(1)(A) In carrying out his functions pursuant to this chapter, and any other Federal legislation respecting solid waste or discarded material research, development, and demonstrations, the Administrator shall establish a management program or system to insure the coordination of all such activities and to facilitate and accelerate the process of development of sound new technology (or other discoveries) from the research phase, through development, and into the demonstration phase.

(B) The Administrator shall (i) assist, on the basis of any research projects which are developed with assistance under this chapter or without Federal assistance, the construction of pilot plant facilities for the purpose of investigating or testing the technological feasibility of any promising new fuel, energy, or resource recovery or resource conservation method or technology; and (ii) demonstrate each such method and technology that appears justified by an evaluation at such pilot plant stage or at a pilot plant stage developed without Federal assistance. Each such demonstration shall incorporate new or innovative technical advances or shall apply such advances to different circumstances and conditions, for the purpose of evaluating design concepts or to test the performance, efficiency, and economic feasibility of a particular method or technology under actual operating conditions. Each such demonstration shall be so planned and designed that, if successful, it can be expanded or utilized directly as a full-scale operational fuel, energy, or resource recovery or resource conservation facility.

(2) Any energy-related research, development, or demonstration project for the conversion including bioconversion, of solid waste carried out by the Environmental Protection Agency or by the Secretary of Energy pursuant to this chapter or any other Act shall be administered in accordance with the May 7, 1976, Interagency Agreement between the Environmental Protection Agency and the Energy Research and Development Administration on the Development of Energy from Solid Wastes and specifically, that in accordance with this agreement, (A) for those energy-related projects of mutual interest, planning will be conducted jointly by the Environmental Protection Agency and the Secretary of Energy, following which project responsibility will be assigned to one agency; (B) energy-related portions of projects for recovery of synthetic fuels or other forms of energy from solid waste shall be the responsibility of the Secretary of Energy; (C) the Environmental Protection Agency shall retain responsibility for the environmental, economic, and institutional aspects of solid waste projects and for assurance that such projects are consistent with any applicable suggested guidelines published pursuant to section 6907 of this title, and any applicable State or regional solid waste management plan; and (D) any activities undertaken under provisions of sections 6982 and 6983 of this title as related to energy; as related to energy or synthetic fuels recovery from waste; or as related to energy conservation shall be accomplished through coordination and consultation with the Secretary of Energy.

**(c) Authorities**

(1) In carrying out subsection (a) of this section respecting solid waste research, studies, development, and demonstration, except as otherwise specifically provided in section 6984(d) of this title, the Administrator may make grants to or enter into contracts (including contracts for construction) with, public agencies and authorities or private persons.

(2) Contracts for research, development, or demonstrations or for both (including contracts for construction) shall be made in accordance with and subject to the limitations provided with respect to research contracts of the military departments in section 2353 of Title 10, except that the determination, approval, and certification required thereby shall be made by the Administrator.

(3) Any invention made or conceived in the course of, or under, any contract under this chapter shall be subject to section 9 of the Federal Nonnuclear Energy Research and Development Act of 1974 [42 U.S.C.A. § 5908] to the same extent and in the same manner as inventions made or conceived in the course of contracts under such Act [42 U.S.C.A. § 5901 et seq.], except that in applying such section, the Environmental Protection Agency shall be substituted for the Secretary of Energy and the words "solid waste" shall be substituted for the word "energy" where appropriate.

(4) For carrying out the purpose of this chapter the Administrator may detail personnel of the Environmental Protection Agency to agencies eligible for assistance under this section.

(Pub.L. 89–272, Title II, § 8001, as added Pub.L. 94–580, § 2, Oct. 21, 1976, 90 Stat. 2829, and amended Pub.L. 95–91, Title III, § 301, Title VII, §§ 703, 707, Aug. 4, 1977, 91 Stat. 577, 606, 607; Pub.L. 95–609, § 7(s), Nov. 8, 1978, 92 Stat. 3083.)

## HISTORICAL AND STATUTORY NOTES

**References in Text**

Such Act, referred to in subsec. (c)(3), means the Federal Nonnuclear Energy Research and Development Act of 1974, which is Pub.L. 93–577, Dec. 31, 1974, 88 Stat. 1878, as amended, and which is classified generally to chapter 74 (section 5901 et seq.) of this title. For complete classification of this Act to the Code, see Short Title of 1974 Acts note set out under section 5901 of this title and Tables.

**Transfer of Functions**

For transfer of certain enforcement functions of Administrator or other official of the Environmental Protection Agency under this chapter to Federal Inspector, Office of Federal Inspector for the Alaska Natural Gas Transportation System, see note set out under section 6903 of this title.

"Secretary of Energy" was substituted for "Administrator of the Federal Energy Administration, the Administrator of the Energy Research and Development Administration, or the Chairman of the Federal Power Commission" in subsec. (a) and for "Energy Research and Development Administration" in subsecs. (b)(2) and (c)(3) pursuant to sections 301, 703, and 707 of Pub.L. 95–91, which are classified to sections 7151, 7293, and 7297 of this title and which terminated the Federal Energy Administration and the Energy Research and Development Administration and transferred their functions and the functions of the Administrators thereof (with certain exceptions) to the Secretary of Energy and terminated the Federal Power Commission and transferred its functions and the functions of the Chairman thereof (with certain exceptions) to the Secretary of Energy.

**Prior Provisions**

Provisions similar to this section were contained in section 3253 of this title, prior to the complete revision of the Solid Waste Disposal Act by Pub.L. 94–580.

**EPA Study of Methods to Reduce Plastic Pollution**

Pub.L. 100–220, Title II, § 2202, Dec. 29, 1987, 101 Stat. 1465, authorized the Administrator of the Environmental Agency, in consultation with the Secretary of Commerce, to conduct a study of the adverse effects of the improper disposal of plastic articles on the environment and waste disposal, and various methods to reduce or eliminate such adverse effects, and directed the Administrator, within 18 months after Dec. 29, 1987, to report the results of this study to Congress.

**Leachate Control Research Program in Delaware**

Section 4 of Pub.L. 94–580 directed the Administrator of the Environmental Protection Agency, in order to demonstrate effective means of dealing with contamination of public water supplies by leachate from abandoned or other landfills, to provide technical and financial assistance for a research program, designed by the New Castle County areawide waste treatment management program, to control leachate from Llangollen Landfill in New Castle County, Delaware, and provided up to $200,000 in each of the fiscal years 1978 and 1979 for the operating costs of a counter-pumping program to contain the leachate from the Llangollen Landfill during the period of this study.

**National Advisory Commission on Resource Conservation and Recovery**

Pub.L. 96–482, § 33, Oct. 21, 1980, 94 Stat. 2356, as amended Pub.L. 105–362, Title V, § 501(g), Nov. 10, 1998, 112 Stat. 3284, provided for the establishment, membership, functions, etc., of a National Advisory Commission on Resource Conservation and Recovery, directed the Commission to submit an interim report for legislative and administrative actions relating to this chapter on Feb. 15, 1982, and upon the expiration of the two-year period beginning on the date when all initial members of the Commission have been appointed or the date initial funds become available, whichever is later, to transmit a final report to the President and Congress containing a detailed statement of the findings and conclusions of the Commission, and terminated the Commission 30 days after the submission of its final report.

**Plastic Pollution Public Education Program**

Pub.L. 100–220, Title II, § 2204, Dec. 29, 1987, 101 Stat. 1466, formerly set out as a note under this section was transferred and, as amended by Pub.L. 104–324, is now set out as section 1915 of Title 33, Navigation and Navigable Waters.

**Solid Waste Cleanup on Federal Lands in Alaska; Study and Report to Congressional Committees**

Pub.L. 94–580, § 3, Oct. 21, 1976, 90 Stat. 2829, providing for study of procedures for removal of solid waste from Federal lands in Alaska and submission of a Presidential Report to Senate Committee on Public Lands and House Committee on Interstate and Foreign Commerce no later than one year after Oct. 21, 1976, and implementing recommendations to such committees within six months thereafter, was repealed by Pub.L. 96–482, § 30, Oct. 21, 1980, 94 Stat. 2352.

## § 6982. Special studies; plans for research, development, and demonstrations

**[SWDA § 8002]**

### (a) Glass and plastic

The Administrator shall undertake a study and publish a report on resource recovery from glass and plastic waste, including a scientific, technological, and economic investigation of potential solutions to implement such recovery.

### (b) Composition of waste stream

The Administrator shall undertake a systematic study of the composition of the solid waste stream and of anticipated future changes in the composition of such stream and shall publish a report containing the results of such study and quantitatively evaluating the potential utility of such components.

### (c) Priorities study

For purposes of determining priorities for research on recovery of materials and energy from solid waste and developing materials and energy recovery research, development, and demonstration strategies, the Administrator shall review, and make a study of, the various existing and promising techniques of energy recovery from solid waste (including, but not limited to, waterwall furnace incinerators, dry shredded fuel systems, pyrolysis, densified refuse-derived fuel systems, anerobic digestion, and fuel and feedstock preparation systems). In carrying out such study the Administrator shall investigate with respect to each such technique—

(1) the degree of public need for the potential results of such research, development, or demonstration,

(2) the potential for research, development, and demonstration without Federal action, including the degree of restraint on such potential posed by the risks involved, and

(3) the magnitude of effort and period of time necessary to develop the technology to the point where Federal assistance can be ended.

### (d) Small-scale and low technology study

The Administrator shall undertake a comprehensive study and analysis of, and publish a report on, systems of small-scale and low technology solid waste management, including household resource recovery and resource recovery systems which have special application to multiple dwelling units and high density housing and office complexes. Such study and analysis shall include an investigation of the degree to which such systems could contribute to energy conservation.

### (e) Front-end source separation

The Administrator shall undertake research and studies concerning the compatibility of front-end source separation systems with high technology resource recovery systems and shall publish a report containing the results of such research and studies.

### (f) Mining waste

The Administrator, in consultation with the Secretary of the Interior, shall conduct a detailed and comprehensive study on the adverse effects of solid wastes from active and abandoned surface and underground mines on the environment, including, but not limited to, the effects of such wastes on humans, water, air, health, welfare, and natural resources, and on the adequacy of means and measures currently employed by the mining industry, Government agencies, and others to dispose of and utilize such solid wastes and to prevent or substantially mitigate such adverse effects. Such study shall include an analysis of—

(1) the sources and volume of discarded material generated per year from mining;

(2) present disposal practices;

(3) potential dangers to human health and the environment from surface runoff of leachate and air pollution by dust;

(4) alternatives to current disposal methods;

(5) the cost of those alternatives in terms of the impact on mine product costs; and

(6) potential for use of discarded material as a secondary source of the mine product.

In furtherance of this study, the Administrator shall, as he deems appropriate, review studies and other actions of other Federal agencies concerning such wastes with a view toward avoiding duplication of effort and the need to expedite such study. Not later than thirty-six months after October 21, 1980, the Administrator shall publish a report of such study and shall include appropriate findings and recommendations for Federal and non-Federal actions concerning such effects. Such report shall be submitted to the Committee on Environment and Public Works of the United States Senate and the Committee on Energy and Commerce of the United States House of Representatives.

**(g) Sludge**

The Administrator shall undertake a comprehensive study and publish a report on sludge. Such study shall include an analysis of—

(1) what types of solid waste (including but not limited to sewage and pollution treatment residues and other residues from industrial operations such as extraction of oil from shale, liquefaction and gasification of coal and coal slurry pipeline operations) shall be classified as sludge;

(2) the effects of air and water pollution legislation on the creation of large volumes of sludge;

(3) the amounts of sludge originating in each State and in each industry producing sludge;

(4) methods of disposal of such sludge, including the cost, efficiency, and effectiveness of such methods;

(5) alternative methods for the use of sludge, including agricultural applications of sludge and energy recovery from sludge; and

(6) methods to reclaim areas which have been used for the disposal of sludge or which have been damaged by sludge.

**(h) Tires**

The Administrator shall undertake a study and publish a report respecting discarded motor vehicle tires which shall include an analysis of the problems involved in the collection, recovery of resources including energy, and use of such tires.

**(i) Resource recovery facilities**

The Administrator shall conduct research and report on the economics of, and impediments, to the effective functioning of resource recovery facilities.

**(j) Resource Conservation Committee**

(1) The Administrator shall serve as Chairman of a Committee composed of himself, the Secretary of Commerce, the Secretary of Labor, the Chairman of the Council on Environmental Quality, the Secretary of Treasury, the Secretary of the Interior, the Secretary of Energy, the Chairman of the Council of Economic Advisors, and a representative of the Office of Management and Budget, which shall conduct a full and complete investigation and study of all aspects of the economic, social, and environmental consequences of resource conservation with respect to—

(A) the appropriateness of recommended incentives and disincentives to foster resource conservation;

(B) the effect of existing public policies (including subsidies and economic incentives and disincentives, percentage depletion allowances, capital gains treatment and other tax incentives and disincentives) upon resource conservation, and the likely effect of the modification or elimination of such incentives and disincentives upon resource conservation;

(C) the appropriateness and feasibility of restricting the manufacture or use of categories of consumer products as a resource conservation strategy;

(D) the appropriateness and feasibility of employing as a resource conservation strategy the imposition of solid waste management charges on consumer products, which charges would reflect the costs of solid waste management services, litter pickup, the value of recoverable components of such product, final disposal, and any social value associated with the nonrecycling or uncontrolled disposal of such product; and

(E) the need for further research, development, and demonstration in the area of resource conservation.

(2) The study required in paragraph (1)(D) may include pilot scale projects, and shall consider and evaluate alternative strategies with respect to—

(A) the product categories on which such charges would be imposed;

(B) the appropriate state in the production of such consumer product at which to levy such charge;

(C) appropriate criteria for establishing such charges for each consumer product category;

(D) methods for the adjustment of such charges to reflect actions such as recycling which would reduce the overall quantities of solid waste requiring disposal; and

(E) procedures for amending, modifying, or revising such charges to reflect changing conditions.

(3) The design for the study required in paragraph (1) of this subsection shall include timetables for the completion of the study. A preliminary report putting forth the study design shall be sent to the President and the Congress within six months following October 21, 1976, and followup reports shall be sent six months thereafter. Each recommendation resulting from the study shall include at least two alternatives to the proposed recommendation.

(4) The results of such investigation and study, including recommendations, shall be reported to the President and the Congress not later than two years after October 21, 1976.

(5) There are authorized to be appropriated not to exceed $2,000,000 to carry out this subsection.

**(k) Airport landfills**

The Administrator shall undertake a comprehensive study and analysis of and publish a report on systems to alleviate the hazards to aviation from birds congregating and feeding on landfills in the vicinity of airports.

**(*l*) Completion of research and studies**

The Administrator shall complete the research and studies, and submit the reports, required under subsections (b), (c), (d), (e), (f), (g), and (k) of this section not later than October 1, 1978. The Administrator shall complete the research and studies, and submit the reports, required under subsections (a), (h), and (i) of this section not later than October 1, 1979. Upon completion, each study specified in subsections (a) through (k) of this section, the Administrator shall prepare a plan for research, development, and demonstration respecting the findings of the study and shall submit any legislative recommendations resulting from such study to appropriate committees of Congress.

**(m) Drilling fluids, produced waters, and other wastes associated with the exploration, development, or production of crude oil or natural gas or geothermal energy**

(1) The Administrator shall conduct a detailed and comprehensive study and submit a report on the adverse effects, if any, of drilling fluids, produced waters, and other wastes associated with the exploration, development, or production of crude oil or natural gas or geothermal energy on human health and the environment, including, but not limited to, the effects of such wastes on humans, water, air, health, welfare, and natural resources and on the adequacy of means and measures currently employed by the oil and gas and geothermal drilling and production industry, Government agencies, and others to dispose of and utilize such wastes and to prevent or substantially mitigate such adverse effects. Such study shall include an analysis of—

(A) the sources and volume of discarded material generated per year from such wastes;

(B) present disposal practices;

(C) potential danger to human health and the environment from the surface runoff or leachate;

(D) documented cases which prove or have caused danger to human health and the environment from surface runoff or leachate;

(E) alternatives to current disposal methods;

(F) the cost of such alternatives; and

(G) the impact of those alternatives on the exploration for, and development and production of, crude oil and natural gas or geothermal energy.

In furtherance of this study, the Administrator shall, as he deems appropriate, review studies and other actions of other Federal agencies concerning such wastes with a view toward avoiding duplication of effort and the need to expedite such study. The Administrator shall publish a report of such study and shall include appropriate findings and recommendations for Federal and non-Federal actions concerning such effects.

(2) The Administrator shall complete the research and study and submit the report required under paragraph (1) not later than twenty-four months from October 21, 1980. Upon completion of the study, the Administrator shall prepare a summary of the findings of the study, a plan for research, development, and demonstration respecting the findings of the study, and shall submit the findings and the study, along with any recommendations resulting from such study, to the Committee on Environment and Public Works of the United States Senate and the Committee on Energy and Commerce of the United States House of Representatives.

(3) There are authorized to be appropriated not to exceed $1,000,000 to carry out the provisions of this subsection.

**(n) Materials generated from the combustion of coal and other fossil fuels**

The Administrator shall conduct a detailed and comprehensive study and submit a report on the adverse effects on human health and the environment, if any, of the disposal and utilization of fly ash waste, bottom ash waste, slag waste, flue gas emission control waste, and other byproduct materials generated primarily from the combustion of coal or other fossil fuels. Such study shall include an analysis of—

(1) the source and volumes of such material generated per year;

(2) present disposal and utilization practices;

(3) potential danger, if any, to human health and the environment from the disposal and reuse of such materials;

(4) documented cases in which danger to human health or the environment from surface runoff or leachate has been proved;

(5) alternatives to current disposal methods;

(6) the costs of such alternatives;

(7) the impact of those alternatives on the use of coal and other natural resources; and

(8) the current and potential utilization of such materials.

In furtherance of this study, the Administrator shall, as he deems appropriate, review studies and other actions of other Federal and State agencies concerning such material and invite participation by other concerned parties, including industry and other Federal and State agencies, with a view toward avoiding duplication of effort. The Administrator shall publish a report on such study, which shall include appropriate findings, not later than twenty-four months after October 21, 1980. Such study and findings shall be submitted to the Committee on Environment and Public Works of the United States Senate and the Committee on Energy and Commerce of the United States House of Representatives.

**(*o*) Cement kiln dust waste**

The Administrator shall conduct a detailed and comprehensive study of the adverse effects on human health and the environment, if any, of the disposal of cement kiln dust waste. Such study shall include an analysis of—

(1) the source and volumes of such materials generated per year;

(2) present disposal practices;

(3) potential danger, if any, to human health and the environment from the disposal of such materials;

(4) documented cases in which danger to human health or the environment has been proved;

(5) alternatives to current disposal methods;

(6) the costs of such alternatives;

(7) the impact of those alternatives on the use of natural resources; and

(8) the current and potential utilization of such materials.

In furtherance of this study, the Administrator shall, as he deems appropriate, review studies and other actions of other Federal and State agencies concerning such waste or materials and invite participation by other concerned parties, including industry and other Federal and State agencies, with a view toward avoiding duplication of effort. The Administrator shall publish a report of such study, which shall include appropriate findings, not later than thirty-six months after October 21, 1980. Such report shall be submitted to the Committee on Environment and Public Works of the United States Senate and the Committee on Energy and Commerce of the United States House of Representatives.

**(p) Materials generated from extraction, beneficiation, and processing of ores and minerals, including phosphate rock and overburden from uranium mining**

The Administrator shall conduct a detailed and comprehensive study on the adverse effects on human health and the environment, if any, of the disposal and utilization of solid waste from the extraction, beneficiation, and processing of ores and minerals, including phosphate rock and overburden from uranium mining. Such study shall be conducted in conjunction with the study of mining wastes required by subsection (f) of this section and shall include an analysis of—

(1) the source and volumes of such materials generated per year;

(2) present disposal and utilization practices;

(3) potential danger, if any, to human health and the environment from the disposal and reuse of such materials;

(4) documented cases in which danger to human health or the environment has been proved;

(5) alternatives to current disposal methods;

(6) the costs of such alternatives;

(7) the impact of those alternatives on the use of phosphate rock and uranium ore, and other natural resources; and

(8) the current and potential utilization of such materials.

In furtherance of this study, the Administrator shall, as he deems appropriate, review studies and other actions of other Federal and State agencies concerning such waste or materials and invite participation by other concerned parties, including industry and other Federal and State agencies, with a view toward avoiding duplication of effort. The Administrator shall publish a report of such study, which shall include appropriate findings, in conjunction with the publication of the report of the study of mining wastes required to be conducted under subsection (f) of this section. Such report and findings shall be submitted to the Committee on Environment and Public Works of the United States Senate and the Committee on Energy and Commerce of the United States House of Representatives.

**(q) Authorization of appropriations**

There are authorized to be appropriated not to exceed $8,000,000 for the fiscal years 1978 and 1979 to carry out this section other than subsection (j) of this section.

**(r) Minimization of hazardous waste**

The Administrator shall compile, and not later than October 1, 1986, submit to the Congress, a report on the feasibility and desirability of establishing standards of performance or of taking other additional actions under this chapter to require the generators of hazardous waste to reduce the volume or quantity and toxicity of the hazardous waste they generate, and of establishing with respect to hazardous wastes required management practices or other requirements to assure such wastes are managed in ways that minimize present and future risks to human health and the environment. Such report shall include any recommendations for legislative changes which the Administrator determines are feasible and desirable to implement the national policy established by section 6902 of this title.

**(s) Extending landfill life and reusing landfilled areas**

The Administrator shall conduct detailed, comprehensive studies of methods to extend the useful life of sanitary landfills and to better use sites in which filled or closed landfills are located. Such studies shall address—

(1) methods to reduce the volume of materials before placement in landfills;

(2) more efficient systems for depositing waste in landfills;

(3) methods to enhance the rate of decomposition of solid waste in landfills, in a safe and environmentally acceptable manner;

(4) methane production from closed landfill units;

(5) innovative uses of closed landfill sites, including use for energy production such as solar or wind energy and use for metals recovery;

(6) potential for use of sewage treatment sludge in reclaiming landfilled areas; and

(7) methods to coordinate use of a landfill owned by one municipality by nearby municipalities, and to establish equitable rates for such use, taking into account the need to provide future landfill capacity to replace that so used.

The Administrator is authorized to conduct demonstrations in the areas of study provided in this subsection. The Administrator shall periodically report on the results of such studies, with the first such report not later than October 1, 1986. In carrying out this subsection, the Administrator need not duplicate other studies which have been completed and may rely upon information which has previously been compiled.

(Pub.L. 89–272, Title II, § 8002, as added Pub.L. 94–580, § 2, Oct. 21, 1976, 90 Stat. 2831, and amended Pub.L. 95–609, § 7(t), Nov. 8, 1978, 92 Stat. 3083; H.Res. 549, Mar. 25, 1980; Pub.L. 96–482, § 29, Oct. 21, 1980, 94 Stat. 2349; Pub.L. 98–616, Title II, § 224(c), Title VII, § 702, Nov. 8, 1984, 98 Stat. 3253, 3289.)

## HISTORICAL AND STATUTORY NOTES

**Change of Name**

The name of the Committee on Interstate and Foreign Commerce of the House of Representatives was changed to Committee on Energy and Commerce immediately prior to noon on Jan. 3, 1981, by House Resolution 549, Ninety-sixth Congress, Mar. 25, 1980.

Any reference in any provision of law enacted before Jan. 4, 1995, to the Committee on Energy and Commerce of the House of Representatives treated as referring to the Committee on Commerce of the House of Representatives, except that any reference in any provision of law enacted before Jan. 4, 1995, to the Committee on Energy and Commerce of the House of Representatives treated as referring to the Committee on Agriculture of the House of Representatives, in the case of a provision of law relating to inspection of seafood or seafood products, the Committee on Banking and Financial Services of the House of Representatives, in the case of a provision of law relating to bank capital markets activities generally or to depository institution securities activities generally, and the Committee on Transportation and Infrastructure of the House of Representatives, in the case of a provision of law relating to railroads, railway labor, or railroad retirement and unemployment (except revenue measures related thereto), see section 1(a)(4) and (c)(1) of Pub.L. 104–14, set out as a note preceding section 21 of Title 2, The Congress.

**Transfer of Functions**

For transfer of certain enforcement functions of Administrator or other official of the Environmental Protection Agency under this chapter to Federal Inspector, Office of Federal Inspector for the Alaska Natural Gas Transportation System, see note set out under section 6903 of this title.

## § 6983. Coordination, collection, and dissemination of information

**[SWDA § 8003]**

### (a) Information

The Administrator shall develop, collect, evaluate, and coordinate information on—

(1) methods and costs of the collection of solid waste;

(2) solid waste management practices, including data on the different management methods and the cost, operation, and maintenance of such methods;

(3) the amounts and percentages of resources (including energy) that can be recovered from solid waste by use of various solid waste management practices and various technologies;

(4) methods available to reduce the amount of solid waste that is generated;

(5) existing and developing technologies for the recovery of energy or materials from solid waste and the costs, reliability, and risks associated with such technologies;

(6) hazardous solid waste, including incidents of damage resulting from the disposal of hazardous solid wastes; inherently and potentially hazardous solid wastes; methods of neutralizing or properly disposing of hazardous solid wastes; facilities that properly dispose of hazardous wastes;

(7) methods of financing resource recovery facilities or, sanitary landfills, or hazardous solid waste treatment facilities, whichever is appropriate for the entity developing such facility or landfill (taking into account the amount of solid waste reasonably expected to be available to such entity);

(8) the availability of markets for the purchase of resources, either materials or energy, recovered from solid waste; and

(9) research and development projects respecting solid waste management.

### (b) Library

(1) The Administrator shall establish and maintain a central reference library for (A) the materials collected pursuant to subsection (a) of this section and (B) the actual performance and cost effectiveness records and other data and information with respect to—

(i) the various methods of energy and resource recovery from solid waste,

(ii) the various systems and means of resource conservation,

(iii) the various systems and technologies for collection, transport, storage, treatment, and final disposition of solid waste, and

(iv) other aspects of solid waste and hazardous solid waste management.

Such central reference library shall also contain, but not be limited to, the model codes and model accounting systems developed under this section, the information collected under subsection (d) of this section, and, subject to any applicable requirements of confidentiality, information respecting any aspect of solid waste provided by officers and employees of the Environmental Protection Agency which has been acquired by them in the conduct of their functions under this chapter and which may be of value to Federal, State, and local authorities and other persons.

(2) Information in the central reference library shall, to the extent practicable, be collated, analyzed, verified, and published and shall be made available to State and local governments and other persons at reasonable times and subject to such reasonable charges as may be necessary to defray expenses of making such information available.

### (c) Model accounting system

In order to assist State and local governments in determining the cost and revenues associated with the collection and disposal of solid waste and with resource recovery operations, the Administrator shall develop and publish a recommended model cost and revenue accounting system applicable to the solid waste management functions of State and local governments. Such system shall be in accordance with generally accepted accounting principles. The Administrator shall periodically, but not less frequently than once every five years, review such accounting system and revise it as necessary.

### (d) Model codes

The Administrator is authorized, in cooperation with appropriate State and local agencies, to recommend model codes, ordinances, and statutes, providing for sound solid waste management.

### (e) Information programs

(1) The Administrator shall implement a program for the rapid dissemination of information on solid waste management, hazardous waste management, resource conservation, and methods of resource recovery from solid waste, including the results of any relevant research, investigations, experiments, surveys, studies, or other information which may be useful in the implementation of new or improved solid waste management practices and methods and infor-

mation on any other technical, managerial, financial, or market aspect of resource conservation and recovery facilities.

(2) The Administrator shall develop and implement educational programs to promote citizen understanding of the need for environmentally sound solid waste management practices.

**(f) Coordination**

In collecting and disseminating information under this section, the Administrator shall coordinate his actions and cooperate to the maximum extent possible with State and local authorities.

**(g) Special restriction**

Upon request, the full range of alternative technologies, programs or processes deemed feasible to meet the resource recovery or resource conservation needs of a jurisdiction shall be described in such a manner as to provide a sufficient evaluative basis from which the jurisdiction can make its decisions, but no officer or employee of the Environmental Protection Agency shall, in an official capacity, lobby for or otherwise represent an agency position in favor of resource recovery or resource conservation, as a policy alternative for adoption into ordinances, codes, regulations, or law by any State or political subdivision thereof.

(Pub.L. 89–272, Title II, § 8003, as added Pub.L. 94–580, § 2, Oct. 21, 1976, 90 Stat. 2834, and amended Pub.L. 95–609, § 7(u), Nov. 8, 1978, 92 Stat. 3083.)

### HISTORICAL AND STATUTORY NOTES

**Transfer of Functions**

For transfer of certain enforcement functions of Administrator or other official of the Environmental Protection Agency under this chapter to Federal Inspector, Office of Federal Inspector for the Alaska Natural Gas Transportation System, see note set out under section 6903 of this title.

## § 6984. Full-scale demonstration facilities

**[SWDA § 8004]**

**(a) Authority**

The Administrator may enter into contracts with public agencies or authorities or private persons for the construction and operation of a full-scale demonstration facility under this chapter, or provide financial assistance in the form of grants to a full-scale demonstration facility under this chapter only if the Administrator finds that—

(1) such facility or proposed facility will demonstrate at full scale a new or significantly improved technology or process, a practical and significant improvement in solid waste management practice, or the technological feasibility and cost effectiveness of an existing, but unproven technology, process, or practice, and will not duplicate any other Federal, State, local, or commercial facility which has been constructed or with respect to which construction has begun (determined as of the date action is taken by the Administrator under this chapter),

(2) such contract or assistance meets the requirements of section 6981 of this title and meets other applicable requirements of this chapter,

(3) such facility will be able to comply with the guidelines published under section 6907 of this title and with other laws and regulations for the protection of health and the environment,

(4) in the case of a contract for construction or operation, such facility is not likely to be constructed or operated by State, local, or private persons or in the case of an application for financial assistance, such facility is not likely to receive adequate financial assistance from other sources, and

(5) any Federal interest in, or assistance to, such facility will be disposed of or terminated, with appropriate compensation, within such period of time as may be necessary to carry out the basic objectives of this chapter.

**(b) Time limitation**

No obligation may be made by the Administrator for financial assistance under this subchapter for any full-scale demonstration facility after the date ten years after October 21, 1976. No expenditure of funds for any such full-scale demonstration facility under this subchapter may be made by the Administrator after the date fourteen years after October 21, 1976.

**(c) Cost sharing**

(1) Wherever practicable, in constructing, operating, or providing financial assistance under this subchapter to a full-scale demonstration facility, the Administrator shall endeavor to enter into agreements and make other arrangements for maximum practicable cost sharing with other Federal, State, and local agencies, private persons, or any combination thereof.

(2) The Administrator shall enter into arrangements, wherever practicable and desirable, to provide monitoring of full-scale solid waste facilities (whether or not constructed or operated under this chapter) for purposes of obtaining information concerning the performance, and other aspects, of such facilities. Where the Administrator provides only monitoring and evaluation instruments or personnel (or both) or funds for such instruments or personnel and provides no other financial assistance to a facility, notwithstanding section 6981(c)(3) of this title, title to any invention made or conceived of in the course of developing, constructing, or operating such facility shall not be required to vest in the United States and patents respecting such invention shall not be required to be issued to the United States.

**(d) Prohibition**

After October 21, 1976, the Administrator shall not construct or operate any full-scale facility (except by contract with public agencies or authorities or private persons).

(Pub.L. 89–272, Title II, § 8004, as added Pub.L. 94–580, § 2, Oct. 21, 1976, 90 Stat. 2836, and amended Pub.L. 95–609, § 7(v), Nov. 8, 1978, 92 Stat. 3084; Pub.L. 98–616, Title V, § 502(f), Nov. 8, 1984, 98 Stat. 3276.)

### HISTORICAL AND STATUTORY NOTES

**Transfer of Functions**

For transfer of certain enforcement functions of Administrator or other official of the Environmental Protection Agency under this chapter to Federal Inspector, Office of Federal Inspector for the Alaska Natural Gas Transportation System, see note set out under section 6903 of this title.

## § 6985. Special study and demonstration projects on recovery of useful energy and materials

[SWDA § 8005]

**(a) Studies**

The Administrator shall conduct studies and develop recommendations for administrative or legislative action on—

(1) means of recovering materials and energy from solid waste, recommended uses of such materials and energy for national or international welfare, including identification of potential markets for such recovered resources, the impact of distribution of such resources on existing markets, and potentials for energy conservation through resource conservation and resource recovery;

(2) actions to reduce waste generation which have been taken voluntarily or in response to governmental action, and those which practically could be taken in the future, and the economic, social, and environmental consequences of such actions;

(3) methods of collection, separation, and containerization which will encourage efficient utilization of facilities and contribute to more effective programs of reduction, reuse, or disposal of wastes;

(4) the use of Federal procurement to develop market demand for recovered resources;

(5) recommended incentives (including Federal grants, loans, and other assistance) and disincentives to accelerate the reclamation or recycling of materials from solid wastes, with special emphasis on motor vehicle hulks;

(6) the effect of existing public policies, including subsidies and economic incentives and disincentives, percentage depletion allowances, capital gains treatment and other tax incentives and disincentives, upon the recycling and reuse of materials, and the likely effect of the modification or elimination of such incentives and disincentives upon the reuse, recycling and conservation of such materials;

(7) the necessity and method of imposing disposal or other charges on packaging, containers, vehicles, and other manufactured goods, which charges would reflect the cost of final disposal, the value of recoverable components of the item, and any social costs associated with nonrecycling or uncontrolled disposal of such items; and

(8) the legal constraints and institutional barriers to the acquisition of land needed for solid waste management, including land for facilities and disposal sites;

(9) in consultation with the Secretary of Agriculture, agricultural waste management problems and practices, the extent of reuse and recovery of resources in such wastes, the prospects for improvement, Federal, State, and local regulations governing such practices, and the economic, social, and environmental consequences of such practices; and

(10) in consultation with the Secretary of the Interior, mining waste management problems, and practices, including an assessment of existing authorities, technologies, and economics, and the environmental and public health consequences of such practices.

**(b) Demonstration**

The Administrator is also authorized to carry out demonstration projects to test and demonstrate methods and techniques developed pursuant to subsection (a) of this section.

**(c) Application of other sections**

Section 6981(b) and (c) of this title shall be applicable to investigations, studies, and projects carried out under this section.

(Pub.L. 89–272, Title II, § 8005, as added Pub.L. 94–580, § 2, Oct. 21, 1976, 90 Stat. 2837.)

### HISTORICAL AND STATUTORY NOTES

**Transfer of Functions**

For transfer of certain enforcement functions of Administrator or other official of the Environmental Protection Agency under this chapter to Federal Inspector, Office of Federal Inspector for the Alaska Natural Gas Transportation System, see note set out under section 6903 of this title.

**Prior Provisions**

Provisions similar to this section were contained in section 3253a of this title, prior to the complete revision of the Solid Waste Disposal Act by Pub.L. 94–580.

## § 6986. Grants for resource recovery systems and improved solid waste disposal facilities

[SWDA § 8006]

**(a) Authority**

The Administrator is authorized to make grants pursuant to this section to any State, municipal, or interstate or intermunicipal agency for the demonstration of resource recovery systems or for the construction of new or improved solid waste disposal facilities.

**(b) Conditions**

(1) Any grant under this section for the demonstration of a resource recovery system may be made only if it (A) is consistent with any plans which meet the requirements of subchapter IV of this chapter; (B) is consistent with the guidelines recommended pursuant to section 6907 of this title; (C) is designed to provide area-wide resource recovery systems consistent with the purposes of this chapter, as determined by the Administrator, pursuant to regulations promulgated under subsection (d) of this section; and (D) provides an equitable system for distributing the costs associated with construction, operation, and maintenance of any resource recovery system among the users of such system.

(2) The Federal share for any project to which paragraph (1) applies shall not be more than 75 percent.

**(c) Limitations**

(1) A grant under this section for the construction of a new or improved solid waste disposal facility may be made only if—

(A) a State or interstate plan for solid waste disposal has been adopted which applies to the area involved, and the facility to be constructed (i) is consistent with such plan, (ii) is included in a comprehensive plan for the area involved which is satisfactory to the Administrator for the purposes of this chapter, and (iii) is consistent with the guidelines recommended under section 6907 of this title, and

(B) the project advances the state of the art by applying new and improved techniques in reducing the environmental impact of solid waste disposal, in achieving recovery of energy or resources, or in recycling useful materials.

(2) The Federal share for any project to which paragraph (1) applies shall be not more than 50 percent in the case of a project serving an area which includes only one municipality, and not more than 75 percent in any other case.

**(d) Regulations**

(1) The Administrator shall promulgate regulations establishing a procedure for awarding grants under this section which—

(A) provides that projects will be carried out in communities of varying sizes, under such conditions as will assist in solving the community waste problems of urban-industrial centers, metropolitan regions, and rural areas, under representative geographic and environmental conditions; and

(B) provides deadlines for submission of, and action on, grant requests.

(2) In taking action on applications for grants under this section, consideration shall be given by the Administrator (A) to the public benefits to be derived by the construction and the propriety of Federal aid in making such grant; (B) to the extent applicable, to the economic and commercial viability of the project (including contractual arrangements with the private sector to market any resources recovered); (C) to the potential of such project for general application to community solid waste disposal problems; and (D) to the use by the applicant of comprehensive regional or metropolitan area planning.

**(e) Additional limitations**

A grant under this section—

(1) may be made only in the amount of the Federal share of (A) the estimated total design and construction costs, plus (B) in the case of a grant to which subsection (b)(1) of this section applies, the first-year operation and maintenance costs;

(2) may not be provided for land acquisition or (except as otherwise provided in paragraph (1)(B) ) for operating or maintenance costs;

(3) may not be made until the applicant has made provision satisfactory to the Administrator for proper and efficient operation and maintenance of the project (subject to paragraph (1)(B) ); and

(4) may be made subject to such conditions and requirements, in addition to those provided in this section, as the Administrator may require to properly carry out his functions pursuant to this chapter.

For purposes of paragraph (1), the non-Federal share may be in any form, including, but not limited to, lands or interests therein needed for the project or personal property or services, the value of which shall be determined by the Administrator.

**(f) Single State**

(1) Not more than 15 percent of the total of funds authorized to be appropriated for any fiscal year to carry out this section shall be granted under this section for projects in any one State.

(2) The Administrator shall prescribe by regulation the manner in which this subection[1] shall apply to a grant under this section for a project in an area which includes all or part of more than one State.

(Pub.L. 89–272, Title II, § 8006, as added Pub.L. 94–580, § 2, Oct. 21, 1976, 90 Stat. 2838.)

1 So in original. Probably should be "subsection".

HISTORICAL AND STATUTORY NOTES

**Transfer of Functions**

For transfer of certain enforcement functions of Administrator or other official of the Environmental Protection Agency under this chapter to Federal Inspector, Office of Federal Inspector for the Alaska Natural Gas Transportation System, see note set out under section 6903 of this title.

**Prior Provisions**

Provisions similar to this section were contained in section 3254b of this title, prior to the complete revision of the Solid Waste Disposal Act by Pub.L. 94–580.

## § 6987. Authorization of appropriations

**[SWDA § 8007]**

There are authorized to be appropriated not to exceed $35,000,000 for the fiscal year 1978 to carry out the purposes of this subchapter (except for section 6982 of this title).

(Pub.L. 89–272, Title II, § 8007, as added Pub.L. 94–580, § 2, Oct. 21, 1976, 90 Stat. 2839.)

HISTORICAL AND STATUTORY NOTES

**Prior Provisions**

Provisions similar to this section were contained in section 3259 of this title, prior to the complete revision of the Solid Waste Disposal Act by Pub.L. 94–580.

# SUBCHAPTER IX—REGULATION OF UNDERGROUND STORAGE TANKS

## § 6991. Definitions and exemptions

**[SWDA § 9001]**

For the purposes of this subchapter—

(1) The term "underground storage tank" means any one or combination of tanks (including underground pipes connected thereto) which is used to contain an accumulation of regulated substances, and the volume of which (including the volume of the underground pipes connected thereto) is 10 per centum or more beneath the surface of the ground. Such term does not include any—

(A) farm or residential tank of 1,100 gallons or less capacity used for storing motor fuel for noncommercial purposes,

(B) tank used for storing heating oil for consumptive use on the premises where stored,

(C) septic tank,

(D) pipeline facility (including gathering lines)—

(i) which is regulated under chapter 601 of Title 49, or

(ii) which is an intrastate pipeline facility regulated under State laws as provided in chapter 601 of Title 49,

and which is determined by the Secretary to be connected to a pipeline or to be operated or intended to be capable of operating at pipeline pressure or as an integral part of a pipeline,

(E) surface impoundment, pit, pond, or lagoon,

(F) storm water or waste water collection system,

(G) flow-through process tank,

(H) liquid trap or associated gathering lines directly related to oil or gas production and gathering operations, or

(I) storage tank situated in an underground area (such as a basement, cellar, mineworking, drift, shaft, or tunnel) if the storage tank is situated upon or above the surface of the floor.

The term "underground storage tank" shall not include any pipes connected to any tank which is described in subparagraphs (A) through (I).

(2) The term "regulated substance" means—

(A) any substance defined in section 9601(14) of this title (but not including any substance regulated as a hazardous waste under subchapter III of this chapter), and

(B) petroleum.

(3) The term "owner" means—

(A) in the case of an underground storage tank in use on November 8, 1984, or brought into use after that date, any person who owns an underground storage tank used for the storage, use, or dispensing of regulated sustances,[1] and

(B) in the case of any underground storage tank in use before November 8, 1984, but no longer in use on November 8, 1984, any person who owned such tank immediately before the discontinuation of its use.

(4) The term "operator" means any person in control of, or having responsibility for, the daily operation of the underground storage tank.

(5) The term "release" means any spilling, leaking, emitting, discharging, escaping, leaching, or disposing from an underground storage tank into ground water, surface water or subsurface soils.

(6) The term "person" has the same meaning as provided in section 6903(15) of this title, except that such term includes a consortium, a joint venture, and a commercial entity, and the United States Government.

(7) The term "nonoperational storage tank" means any underground storage tank in which regulated substances will not be deposited or from which regulated substances will not be dispensed after November 8, 1984.

(8) The term "petroleum" means petroleum, including crude oil or any fraction thereof which is liquid at standard conditions of temperature and

pressure (60 degrees Fahrenheit and 14.7 pounds per square inch absolute).

(Pub.L. 89–272, Title II, § 9001, as added Pub.L. 98–616, Title VI, § 601(a), Nov. 8, 1984, 98 Stat. 3277, and amended Pub.L. 99–499, Title II, § 205(a), Oct. 17, 1986, 100 Stat. 1696; Pub.L. 102–508, Title III, § 302, Oct. 24, 1992, 106 Stat. 3307; Pub.L. 103–429, § 7(d), Oct. 31, 1994, 108 Stat. 4389.)

[1] So in original. Probably should be "substances,".

## HISTORICAL AND STATUTORY NOTES

### Effective and Applicability Provisions

1986 Acts

Amendment by Pub.L. 99–499 effective Oct. 17, 1986, see section 4 of Pub.L. 99–499, set out as a note under section 9601 of this title.

### Aboveground Storage Tank Grant Program

Pub.L. 106–554, § 1(a)(4) [Div. B, Title XII, § 1201], Dec. 21, 2000, 114 Stat. 2763, 2763A–313, provided that:

"(a) **Definitions.**—In this provision:

"(1) **Aboveground storage tank.**—The term 'aboveground storage tank' means any tank or combination of tanks (including any connected pipe)—

"(A) that is used to contain an accumulation of regulated substances; and

"(B) the volume of which (including the volume of any connected pipe) is located wholly above the surface of the ground.

"(2) **Administrator.**—The term 'Administrator' means the Administrator of the Environmental Protection Agency.

"(3) **Denali Commission.**—The term 'Denali Commission' means the commission established by section 303(a) of the Denali Commission Act of 1998 (42 U.S.C. 3121 note).

"(4) **Federal environmental law.**—The term 'Federal environmental law' means—

"(A) the Oil Pollution Control Act of 1990 [Oil Pollution Act of 1990, Pub.L. 101–380, Aug. 18, 1990, 104 Stat. 484] (33 U.S.C. 2701 et seq.);

"(B) the Comprehensive Environmental Response, Compensation, and Liability Act of 1980 [Pub.L. 96–510, Dec. 11, 1980, 94 Stat. 2767] (42 U.S.C. 9601 et seq.);

"(C) the Solid Waste Disposal Act [Pub.L. 89–272, Title II, Oct. 20, 1965, 79 Stat. 997](42 U.S.C. 6901 et seq.);

"(D) the Federal Water Pollution Control Act [Act June 30, 1948, ch. 758, 62 Stat. 1155] (33 U.S.C. 1251 et seq.); or

"(E) any other Federal law that is applicable to the release into the environment of a regulated substance, as determined by the Administrator.

"(5) **Native village.**—The term 'Native village' has the meaning given the term in section 11(b) in Public Law 92–203 (85 Stat. 688) [43 U.S.C.A. § 1601(b)].

"(6) **Program.**—The term 'program' means the Aboveground Storage Tank Grant Program established by subsection (b)(1).

"(7) **Regulated substance.**—The term 'regulated substance' has the meaning given the term in section 9001 of the Solid Waste Disposal Act (42 U.S.C. 6991).

"(8) **State.**—The term 'State' means the State of Alaska.

"(b) **Establishment.**—

"(1) **In general.**—There is established a grant program to be known as the 'Aboveground Storage Tank Grant Program'.

"(2) **Grants.**—Under the program, the Administrator shall award a grant to—

"(A) the State, on behalf of a Native village; or

"(B) the Denali Commission.

"(c) **Use of grants.**—The State or the Denali Commission shall use the funds of a grant under subsection (b) to repair, upgrade, or replace one or more aboveground storage tanks that—

"(1) leaks or poses an imminent threat of leaking, as certified by the Administrator, the Commandant of the Coast Guard, or any other appropriate Federal or State agency (as determined by the Administrator); and

"(2) Is located in a native village—

"(A) the median household income of which is less than 80 percent of the median household income in the State;

"(B) That is located—

"(i) Within the boundaries of—

"(I) a unit of the National Park System;

"(II) a unit of the National Wildlife Refuge System; or

"(III) a National Forest; or

"(ii) on public land under the administrative jurisdiction of the Bureau of Land Management; or

"(C) that receives payments from the Federal Government under chapter 69 of title 31, United States Code (commonly known as 'payments in lieu of taxes').

"(d) **Reports.**—Not later than 1 year after the date on which the State or the Denali Commission receives a grant under subsection (c), and annually thereafter, the State or the Denali Commission, as the case may be, shall submit a report describing each project completed with grant funds and any projects planned for the following year, to—

"(1) the Administrator;

"(2) the Committee on Resources of the House of Representatives;

"(3) the Committee on Environment and Public Works of the Senate;

"(4) the Committee on Appropriations of the House of Representatives; and

"(5) the Committee on Appropriations of the Senate.

"(e) **Authorization of appropriations.**—There are authorized to be appropriated to carry out this Act [Pub.L. 106–554, § 1(a)(4), Dec. 21, 2000, 114 Stat. 2763, 2763A–313], to remain available until expended—

"(1) $20,000,000 for fiscal year 2001; and

"(2) such sums as are necessary for each fiscal year thereafter."

## § 6991a. Notification

[SWDA § 9002]

### (a) Underground storage tanks

(1) Within 18 months after November 8, 1984, each owner of an underground storage tank shall notify the State or local agency or department designated pursuant to subsection (b)(1) of this section of the existence of such tank, specifying the age, size, type, location, and uses of such tank.

(2)(A) For each underground storage tank taken out of operation after January 1, 1974, the owner of such tank shall, within eighteen months after November 8, 1984, notify the State or local agency, or department designated pursuant to subsection (b)(1) of this section of the existence of such tanks (unless the owner knows the tank subsequently was removed from the ground). The owner of a tank taken out of operation on or before January 1, 1974, shall not be required to notify the State or local agency under this subsection.

(B) Notice under subparagraph (A) shall specify, to the extent known to the owner—

(i) the date the tank was taken out of operation,

(ii) the age of the tank on the date taken out of operation,

(iii) the size, type and location of the tank, and

(iv) the type and quantity of substances left stored in such tank on the date taken out of operation.

(3) Any owner which brings into use an underground storage tank after the initial notification period specified under paragraph (1), shall notify the designated State or local agency or department within thirty days of the existence of such tank, specifying the age, size, type, location and uses of such tank.

(4) Paragraphs (1) through (3) of this subsection shall not apply to tanks for which notice was given pursuant to section 9603(c) of this title.

(5) Beginning thirty days after the Administrator prescribes the form of notice pursuant to subsection (b)(2) of this section and for eighteen months thereafter, any person who deposits regulated substances in an underground storage tank shall reasonably notify the owner or operator of such tank of the owner's notification requirements pursuant to this subsection.

(6) Beginning thirty days after the Administrator issues new tank performance standards pursuant to section 6991b(e) of this title, any person who sells a tank intended to be used as an underground storage tank shall notify the purchaser of such tank of the owner's notification requirements pursuant to this subsection.

### (b) Agency designation

(1) Within one hundred and eighty days after November 8, 1984, the Governors of each State shall designate the appropriate State agency or department or local agencies or departments to receive the notifications under subsection (a)(1), (2), or (3) of this section.

(2) Within twelve months after November 8, 1984, the Administrator, in consultation with State and local officials designated pursuant to subsection (b)(1) of this section, and after notice and opportunity for public comment, shall prescribe the form of the notice and the information to be included in the notifications under subsection (a)(1), (2), or (3) of this section. In prescribing the form of such notice, the Administrator shall take into account the effect on small businesses and other owners and operators.

### (c) State inventories

Each State shall make 2 separate inventories of all underground storage tanks in such State containing regulated substances. One inventory shall be made with respect to petroleum and one with respect to other regulated substances. In making such inventories, the State shall utilize and aggregate the data in the notification forms submitted pursuant to subsections (a) and (b) of this section. Each State shall submit such aggregated data to the Administrator not later than 270 days after October 17, 1986.

(Pub.L. 89–272, Title II, § 9002, as added Pub.L. 98–616, Title VI, § 601(a), Nov. 8, 1984, 98 Stat. 3278, and amended Pub.L. 99–499, Title II, § 205(b), Oct. 17, 1986, 100 Stat. 1696.)

#### HISTORICAL AND STATUTORY NOTES

**Effective and Applicability Provisions**

1986 Acts

Amendment by Pub.L. 99–499, effective Oct. 17, 1986, see section 4 of Pub.L. 99–499, set out as a note under section 9601 of this title.

## § 6991b. Release detection, prevention, and correction regulations

[SWDA § 9003]

### (a) Regulations

The Administrator, after notice and opportunity for public comment, and at least three months before the effective dates specified in subsection (f) of this section, shall promulgate release detection, prevention, and correction regulations applicable to all owners and operators of underground storage tanks, as may be necessary to protect human health and the environment.

### (b) Distinctions in regulations

In promulgating regulations under this section, the Administrator may distinguish between types, classes, and ages of underground storage tanks. In making such distinctions, the Administrator may take into consideration factors, including, but not limited to: location of the tanks, soil and climate conditions, uses of the tanks, history of maintenance, age of the tanks, current industry recommended practices, national consensus codes, hydrogeology, water table, size of the tanks, quantity of regulated substances periodically deposited in or dispensed from the tank, the technical capability of the owners and operators, and the compatibility of the regulated substance and the materials of which the tank is fabricated.

**(c) Requirements**

The regulations promulgated pursuant to this section shall include, but need not be limited to, the following requirements respecting all underground storage tanks—

(1) requirements for maintaining a leak detection system, an inventory control system together with tank testing, or a comparable system or method designed to identify releases in a manner consistent with the protection of human health and the environment;

(2) requirements for maintaining records of any monitoring or leak detection system or inventory control system or tank testing or comparable system;

(3) requirements for reporting of releases and corrective action taken in response to a release from an underground storage tank;

(4) requirements for taking corrective action in response to a release from an underground storage tank;

(5) requirements for the closure of tanks to prevent future releases of regulated substances into the environment; and

(6) requirements for maintaining evidence of financial responsibility for taking corrective action and compensating third parties for bodily injury and property damage caused by sudden and nonsudden accidental releases arising from operating an underground storage tank.

**(d) Financial responsibility**

(1) Financial responsibility required by this subsection may be established in accordance with regulations promulgated by the Administrator by any one, or any combination, of the following: insurance, guarantee, surety bond, letter of credit, qualification as a self-insurer or any other method satisfactory to the Administrator. In promulgating requirements under this subsection, the Administrator is authorized to specify policy or other contractual terms, conditions, or defenses which are necessary or are unacceptable in establishing such evidence of financial responsibility in order to effectuate the purposes of this subchapter.

(2) In any case where the owner or operator is in bankruptcy, reorganization, or arrangement pursuant to the Federal Bankruptcy Code or where with reasonable diligence jurisdiction in any State court of the Federal Courts cannot be obtained over an owner or operator likely to be solvent at the time of judgment, any claim arising from conduct for which evidence of financial responsibility must be provided under this subsection may be asserted directly against the guarantor providing such evidence of financial responsibility. In the case of any action pursuant to this paragraph such guarantor shall be entitled to invoke all rights and defenses which would have been available to the owner or operator if any action had been brought against the owner or operator by the claimant and which would have been available to the guarantor if an action had been brought against the guarantor by the owner or operator.

(3) The total liability of any guarantor shall be limited to the aggregate amount which the guarantor has provided as evidence of financial responsibility to the owner or operator under this section. Nothing in this subsection shall be construed to limit any other State or Federal statutory, contractual or common law liability of a guarantor to its owner or operator including, but not limited to, the liability of such guarantor for bad faith either in negotiating or in failing to negotiate the settlement of any claim. Nothing in this subsection shall be construed to diminish the liability of any person under section 9607 or 9611 of this title or other applicable law.

(4) For the purpose of this subsection, the term "guarantor" means any person, other than the owner or operator, who provides evidence of financial responsibility for an owner or operator under this subsection.

(5)(A) The Administrator, in promulgating financial responsibility regulations under this section, may establish an amount of coverage for particular classes or categories of underground storage tanks containing petroleum which shall satisfy such regulations and which shall not be less than $1,000,000 for each occurrence with an appropriate aggregate requirement.

(B) The Administrator may set amounts lower than the amounts required by subparagraph (A) of this paragraph for underground storage tanks containing petroleum which are at facilities not engaged in petroleum production, refining, or marketing and which are not used to handle substantial quantities of petroleum.

(C) In establishing classes and categories for purposes of this paragraph, the Administrator may consider the following factors:

(i) The size, type, location, storage, and handling capacity of underground storage tanks in the class or category and the volume of petroleum handled by such tanks.

(ii) The likelihood of release and the potential extent of damage from any release from underground storage tanks in the class or category.

(iii) The economic impact of the limits on the owners and operators of each such class or category, particularly relating to the small business segment of the petroleum marketing industry.

(iv) The availability of methods of financial responsibility in amounts greater than the amount established by this paragraph.

(v) Such other factors as the Administrator deems pertinent.

(D) The Administrator may suspend enforcement of the financial responsibility requirements for a particular class or category of underground storage tanks or in a particular State, if the Administrator makes a determination that methods of financial responsibility satisfying the requirements of this subsection are not generally available for underground storage tanks in that class or category, and—

(i) steps are being taken to form a risk retention group for such class of tanks; or

(ii) such State is taking steps to establish a fund pursuant to section 6991c(c)(1) of this title to be submitted as evidence of financial responsibility.

A suspension by the Administrator pursuant to this paragraph shall extend for a period not to exceed 180 days. A determination to suspend may be made with respect to the same class or category or for the same State at the end of such period, but only if substantial progress has been made in establishing a risk retention group, or the owners or operators in the class or category demonstrate, and the Administrator finds, that the formation of such a group is not possible and that the State is unable or unwilling to establish such a fund pursuant to clause (ii).

**(e) New tank performance standards**

The Administrator shall, not later than three months prior to the effective date specified in subsection (f) of this section, issue performance standards for underground storage tanks brought into use on or after the effective date of such standards. The performance standards for new underground storage tanks shall include, but need not be limited to, design, construction, installation, release detection, and compatibility standards.

**(f) Effective dates**

(1) Regulations issued pursuant to subsection [1] (c) and (d) of this section, and standards issued pursuant to subsection (e) of this section, for underground storage tanks containing regulated substances defined in section 6991(2)(B) of this title (petroleum, including crude oil or any fraction thereof which is liquid at standard conditions of temperature and pressure) shall be effective not later than thirty months after November 8, 1984.

(2) Standards issued pursuant to subsection (e) of this section (entitled "New Tank Performance Standards") for underground storage tanks containing regulated substances defined in section 6991(2)(A) of this title shall be effective not later than thirty-six months after November 8, 1984.

(3) Regulations issued pursuant to subsection (c) of this section (entitled "Requirements") and standards issued pursuant to subsection (d) of this section (entitled "Financial Responsibility") for underground storage tanks containing regulated substances defined in section 6991(2)(A) of this title shall be effective not later than forty-eight months after November 8, 1984.

**(g) Interim prohibition**

(1) Until the effective date of the standards promulgated by the Administrator under subsection (e) of this section and after one hundred and eighty days after November 8, 1984, no person may install an underground storage tank for the purpose of storing regulated substances unless such tank (whether of single or double wall construction)—

(A) will prevent releases due to corrosion or structural failure for the operational life of the tank;

(B) is cathodically protected against corrosion, constructed of noncorrosive material, steel clad with a noncorrosive material, or designed in a manner to prevent the release or threatened release of any stored substance; and

(C) the material used in the construction or lining of the tank is compatible with the substance to be stored.

(2) Notwithstanding paragraph (1), if soil tests conducted in accordance with ASTM Standard G57–78, or another standard approved by the Administrator, show that soil resistivity in an installation location is 12,000 ohm/cm or more (unless a more stringent standard is prescribed by the Administrator by rule), a storage tank without corrosion protection may be installed in that location during the period referred to in paragraph (1).

**(h) EPA response program for petroleum**

**(1) Before regulations**

Before the effective date of regulations under subsection (c) of this section, the Administrator (or a State pursuant to paragraph (7)) is authorized to—

(A) require the owner or operator of an underground storage tank to undertake corrective action with respect to any release of petroleum when the Administrator (or the State) determines that such corrective action will be done properly and promptly by the owner or operator of the underground storage tank from which the release occurs; or

**(B)** undertake corrective action with respect to any release of petroleum into the environment from an underground storage tank if such action is necessary, in the judgment of the Administrator (or the State), to protect human health and the environment.

The corrective action undertaken or required under this paragraph shall be such as may be necessary to protect human health and the environment. The Administrator shall use funds in the Leaking Underground Storage Tank Trust Fund for payment of costs incurred for corrective action under subparagraph (B), enforcement action under subparagraph (A), and cost recovery under paragraph (6) of this subsection. Subject to the priority requirements of paragraph (3), the Administrator (or the State) shall give priority in undertaking such actions under subparagraph (B) to cases where the Administrator (or the State) cannot identify a solvent owner or operator of the tank who will undertake action properly.

**(2) After regulations**

Following the effective date of regulations under subsection (c) of this section, all actions or orders of the Administrator (or a State pursuant to paragraph (7)) described in paragraph (1) of this subsection shall be in conformity with such regulations. Following such effective date, the Administrator (or the State) may undertake corrective action with respect to any release of petroleum into the environment from an underground storage tank only if such action is necessary, in the judgment of the Administrator (or the State), to protect human health and the environment and one or more of the following situations exists:

**(A)** No person can be found, within 90 days or such shorter period as may be necessary to protect human health and the environment, who is—

**(i)** an owner or operator of the tank concerned,

**(ii)** subject to such corrective action regulations, and

**(iii)** capable of carrying out such corrective action properly.

**(B)** A situation exists which requires prompt action by the Administrator (or the State) under this paragraph to protect human health and the environment.

**(C)** Corrective action costs at a facility exceed the amount of coverage required by the Administrator pursuant to the provisions of subsections (c) and (d)(5) of this section and, considering the class or category of underground storage tank from which the release occurred, expenditures from the Leaking Underground Storage Tank Trust Fund are necessary to assure an effective corrective action.

**(D)** The owner or operator of the tank has failed or refused to comply with an order of the Administrator under this subsection or section 6991e of this title or with the order of a State under this subsection to comply with the corrective action regulations.

**(3) Priority of corrective actions**

The Administrator (or a State pursuant to paragraph (7)) shall give priority in undertaking corrective actions under this subsection, and in issuing orders requiring owners or operators to undertake such actions, to releases of petroleum from underground storage tanks which pose the greatest threat to human health and the environment.

**(4) Corrective action orders**

The Administrator is authorized to issue orders to the owner or operator of an underground storage tank to carry out subparagraph (A) of paragraph (1) or to carry out regulations issued under subsection (c)(4) of this section. A State acting pursuant to paragraph (7) of this subsection is authorized to carry out subparagraph (A) of paragraph (1) only until the State's program is approved by the Administrator under section 6991c of this title. Such orders shall be issued and enforced in the same manner and subject to the same requirements as orders under section 6991e of this title.

**(5) Allowable corrective actions**

The corrective actions undertaken by the Administrator (or a State pursuant to paragraph (7)) under paragraph (1) or (2) may include temporary or permanent relocation of residents and alternative household water supplies. In connection with the performance of any corrective action under paragraph (1) or (2), the Administrator may undertake an exposure assessment as defined in paragraph (10) of this subsection or provide for such an assessment in a cooperative agreement with a State pursuant to paragraph (7) of this subsection. The costs of any such assessment may be treated as corrective action for purposes of paragraph (6), relating to cost recovery.

**(6) Recovery of costs**

**(A) In general**

Whenever costs have been incurred by the Administrator, or by a State pursuant to paragraph (7), for undertaking corrective action or enforcement action with respect to the release of petroleum from an underground storage tank, the owner or operator of such tank shall be liable to the Administrator or the State for such costs.

The liability under this paragraph shall be construed to be the standard of liability which obtains under section 1321 of Title 33.

**(B) Recovery**

In determining the equities for seeking the recovery of costs under subparagraph (A), the Administrator (or a State pursuant to paragraph (7) of this subsection) may consider the amount of financial responsibility required to be maintained under subsections (c) and (d)(5) of this section and the factors considered in establishing such amount under subsection (d)(5) of this section.

**(C) Effect on liability**

**(i) No transfers of liability**

No indemnification, hold harmless, or similar agreement or conveyance shall be effective to transfer from the owner or operator of any underground storage tank or from any person who may be liable for a release or threat of release under this subsection, to any other person the liability imposed under this subsection. Nothing in this subsection shall bar any agreement to insure, hold harmless, or indemnify a party to such agreement for any liability under this section.

**(ii) No bar to cause of action**

Nothing in this subsection, including the provisions of clause (i) of this subparagraph, shall bar a cause of action that an owner or operator or any other person subject to liability under this section, or a guarantor, has or would have, by reason of subrogation or otherwise against any person.

**(D) Facility**

For purposes of this paragraph, the term "facility" means, with respect to any owner or operator, all underground storage tanks used for the storage of petroleum which are owned or operated by such owner or operator and located on a single parcel of property (or on any contiguous or adjacent property).

**(7) State authorities**

**(A) General**

A State may exercise the authorities in paragraphs (1) and (2) of this subsection, subject to the terms and conditions of paragraphs (3), (5), (9), (10), and (11), and including the authorities of paragraphs (4), (6), and (8) of this subsection if—

(i) the Administrator determines that the State has the capabilities to carry out effective corrective actions and enforcement activities; and

(ii) the Administrator enters into a cooperative agreement with the State setting out the actions to be undertaken by the State.

The Administrator may provide funds from the Leaking Underground Storage Tank Trust Fund for the reasonable costs of the State's actions under the cooperative agreement.

**(B) Cost share**

Following the effective date of the regulations under subsection (c) of this section, the State shall pay 10 per centum of the cost of corrective actions undertaken either by the Administrator or by the State under a cooperative agreement, except that the Administrator may take corrective action at a facility where immediate action is necessary to respond to an imminent and substantial endangerment to human health or the environment if the State fails to pay the cost share.

**(8) Emergency procurement powers**

Notwithstanding any other provision of law, the Administrator may authorize the use of such emergency procurement powers as he deems necessary.

**(9) Definition of owner or operator**

**(A) In general**

As used in this subchapter, the terms "owner" and "operator" do not include a person that, without participating in the management of an underground storage tank and otherwise not engaged in petroleum production, refining, or marketing, holds indicia of ownership primarily to protect the person's security interest.

**(B) Security interest holders**

The provisions regarding holders of security interests in subparagraphs (E) through (G) of section 9601(20) of this title and the provisions regarding fiduciaries at section 9607(n) of this title shall apply in determining a person's liability as an owner or operator of an underground storage tank for the purposes of this subchapter.

**(C) Effect on rule**

Nothing in subparagraph (B) shall be construed as modifying or affecting the final rule issued by the Administrator on September 7, 1995 (60 Fed. Reg. 46,692), or as limiting the authority of the Administrator to amend the final rule, in accordance with applicable law. The final rule in effect on September 30, 1996, shall prevail over any inconsistent provision regarding holders of security interests in subparagraphs (E) through (G) of section 9601(20) of this title or any inconsistent provision regarding fiduciaries in section 9607(n) of this title. Any amendment to the final rule shall be consistent with the provisions regarding holders of security interests in subparagraphs (E) through (G) of section 9601(20) of this title and the provisions regarding fiduciaries in section 9607(n) of this title. This subparagraph does not preclude judicial review of any amendment of the final rule made after September 30, 1996.

**(10) Definition of exposure assessment**

As used in this subsection, the term "exposure assessment" means an assessment to determine the extent of exposure of, or potential for exposure of, individuals to petroleum from a release from an underground storage tank based on such factors as the nature and extent of contamination and the existence of or potential for pathways of human exposure (including ground or surface water contamination, air emissions, and food chain contamination), the size of the community within the likely pathways of exposure, and the comparison of expected human exposure levels to the short-term and long-term health effects associated with identified contaminants and any available recommended exposure or tolerance limits for such contaminants. Such assessment shall not delay corrective action to abate immediate hazards or reduce exposure.

**(11) Facilities without financial responsibility**

At any facility where the owner or operator has failed to maintain evidence of financial responsibility in amounts at least equal to the amounts established by subsection (d)(5)(A) of this section (or a lesser amount if such amount is applicable to such facility as a result of subsection (d)(5)(B) of this section) for whatever reason the Administrator shall expend no monies from the Leaking Underground Storage Tank Trust Fund to clean up releases at such facility pursuant to the provisions of paragraph (1) or (2) of this subsection. At such facilities the Administrator shall use the authorities provided in subparagraph (A) of paragraph (1) and paragraph (4) of this subsection and section 6991e of this title to order corrective action to clean up such releases. States acting pursuant to paragraph (7) of this subsection shall use the authorities provided in subparagraph (A) of paragraph (1) and paragraph (4) of this subsection to order corrective action to clean up such releases. Notwithstanding the provisions of this paragraph, the Administrator may use monies from the fund to take the corrective actions authorized by paragraph (5) of this subsection to protect human health at such facilities and shall seek full recovery of the costs of all such actions pursuant to the provisions of paragraph (6)(A) of this subsection and without consideration of the factors in paragraph (6)(B) of this subsection. Nothing in this paragraph shall prevent the Administrator (or a State pursuant to paragraph (7) of this subsection) from taking corrective action at a facility where there is no solvent owner or operator or where immediate action is necessary to respond to an imminent and substantial endangerment of human health or the environment.

(Pub.L. 89–272, Title II, § 9003, as added Pub.L. 98–616, Title VI, § 601(a), Nov. 8, 1984, 98 Stat. 3279, and amended Pub.L. 99–499, Title II, § 205(c), (d), Oct. 17, 1986, 100 Stat. 1697, 1698; Pub.L. 104–208, Div. A, Title II, § 2503, Sept. 30, 1996, 110 Stat. 3009–468.)

[1] So in original. Probably should be "subsections".

## HISTORICAL AND STATUTORY NOTES

**References in Text**

The Federal Bankruptcy Code, referred to in subsec. (d)(2), probably means a reference to Title 11, Bankruptcy.

**Effective and Applicability Provisions**

1996 Acts

Pub.L. 104–208, Div. A, Title II, § 2505, Sept. 30, 1996, 110 Stat. 3009–469, provided that: "The amendments made by this subtitle [Pub.L. 104–208, Div. A, Title II, Subtitle E, § 2501 et seq., Sept. 30, 1996, 110 Stat. 3009–462, amending this section and sections 9601 and 9607 of this title] shall be applicable with respect to any claim that has not been finally adjudicated as of the date of enactment of this Act [Sept. 30, 1996]."

1986 Acts

Amendment by Pub.L. 99–499 effective Oct. 17, 1986, see section 4 of Pub.L. 99–499, set out as a note under section 9601 of this title.

**Leaking Underground Storage Tank Program**

Pub.L. 105–276, Title III, Oct. 21, 1998, 112 Stat. 2497, provided in part: "That hereafter, the Administrator is authorized to enter into assistance agreements with Federally recognized Indian tribes on such terms and conditions as the Administrator deems appropriate for the same purposes as are set forth in section 9003(h)(7) of the Resource Conservation and Recovery Act [subsec. (h)(7) of this section]."

**Pollution Liability Insurance**

Section 205(h) of Pub.L. 99–499 provided that:

"(1) **Study.**—The Comptroller General shall conduct a study of the availability of pollution liability insurance, leak insurance, and contamination insurance for owners and operators of petroleum storage and distribution facilities. The study shall assess the current and projected extent to which private insurance can contribute to the financial responsibility of owners and operators of underground storage tanks and the ability of owners and operators of underground storage tanks to maintain financial responsibility through other methods. The study shall consider the experience of owners and operators of marine vessels in getting insurance for their liabilities under the Federal Water Pollution Control Act [33 U.S.C.A. § 1251 et seq.] and the operation of the Water Quality Insurance Syndicate.

"(2) **Report.**—The Comptroller General shall report the findings under this subsection to the Congress within 15 months after the enactment of this subsection [eff. Oct. 17, 1986]. Such report shall include recommendations for legislative or administrative changes that will enable owners and operators of underground storage tanks to maintain financial responsibility sufficient to provide all clean-up costs and damages that may result from reasonably foreseeable releases and events."

## § 6991c. Approval of State programs [SWDA § 9004]

### (a) Elements of State program

Beginning 30 months after November 8, 1984, any State may,[1] submit an underground storage tank release detection, prevention, and correction program for review and approval by the Administrator. The program may cover tanks used to store regulated substances referred to in [2] 6991(2)(A) or (B) or both of this title. A State program may be approved by the Administrator under this section only if the State demonstrates that the State program includes the following requirements and standards and provides for adequate enforcement of compliance with such requirements and standards—

(1) requirements for maintaining a leak detection system, an inventory control system together with tank testing, or a comparable system or method designed to identify releases in a manner consistent with the protection of human health and the environment;

(2) requirements for maintaining records of any monitoring or leak detection system or inventory control system or tank testing system;

(3) requirements for reporting of any releases and corrective action taken in response to a release from an underground storage tank;

(4) requirements for taking corrective action in response to a release from an underground storage tank;

(5) requirements for the closure of tanks to prevent future releases of regulated substances into the environment;

(6) requirements for maintaining evidence of financial responsibility for taking corrective action and compensating third parties for bodily injury and property damage caused by sudden and nonsudden accidental releases arising from operating an underground storage tank;

(7) standards of performance for new underground storage tanks; and

(8) requirements—

(A) for notifying the appropriate State agency or department (or local agency or department) designated according to section 6991a(b)(1) of this title of the existence of any operational or non-operational underground storage tank; and

(B) for providing the information required on the form issued pursuant to section 6991a(b)(2) of this title.

### (b) Federal standards

(1) A State program submitted under this section may be approved only if the requirements under paragraphs (1) through (7) of subsection (a) of this section are no less stringent than the corresponding requirements standards promulgated by the Administrator pursuant to section 6991b(a) of this title.

(2)(A) A State program may be approved without regard to whether or not the requirements referred to in paragraphs (1), (2), (3), and (5) of subsection (a) of this section are less stringent than the corresponding standards under section 6991b(a) of this title during the one-year period commencing on the date of promulgation of regulations under section 6991b(a) of this title if State regulatory action but no State legislative action is required in order to adopt a State program.

(B) If such State legislative action is required, the State program may be approved without regard to whether or not the requirements referred to in paragraphs (1), (2), (3), and (5) of subsection (a) of this section are less stringent than the corresponding standards under section 6991b(a) of this title during the two-year period commencing on the date of promulgation of regulations under section 6991b(a) of this title (and during an additional one-year period after such legislative action if regulations are required to be promulgated by the State pursuant to such legislative action).

### (c) Financial responsibility

(1) Corrective action and compensation programs administered by State or local agencies or departments may be submitted for approval under subsection (a)(6) of this section as evidence of financial responsibility.

(2) Financial responsibility required by this subsection may be established in accordance with regulations promulgated by the Administrator by any one, or any combination, of the following: insurance, guarantee, surety bond, letter of credit, qualification as a self-insurer or any other method satisfactory to the Administrator. In promulgating requirements under this subsection, the Administrator is authorized to specify policy or other contractual terms including the amount of coverage required for various classes and categories of underground storage tanks pursuant to section 6991b(d)(5) of this title, conditions, or defenses which are necessary or are unacceptable in establishing such evidence of financial responsibility in order to effectuate the purposes of this subchapter.

(3) In any case where the owner or operator is in bankruptcy, reorganization, or arrangement pursuant

to the Federal Bankruptcy Code or where with reasonable diligence jurisdiction in any State court of the Federal courts cannot be obtained over an owner or operator likely to be solvent at the time of judgment, any claim arising from conduct for which evidence of financial responsibility must be provided under this subsection may be asserted directly against the guarantor providing such evidence of financial responsibility. In the case of any action pursuant to this paragraph such guarantor shall be entitled to invoke all rights and defenses which would have been available to the owner or operator if any action had been brought against the owner or operator by the claimant and which would have been available to the guarantor if an action had been brought against the guarantor by the owner or operator.

(4) The total liability of any guarantor shall be limited to the aggregate amount which the guarantor has provided as evidence of financial responsibility to the owner or operator under this section. Nothing in this subsection shall be construed to limit any other State or Federal statutory, contractual or common law liability of a guarantor to its owner or operator including, but not limited to, the liability of such guarantor for bad faith either in negotiating or in failing to negotiate the settlement of any claim. Nothing in this subsection shall be construed to diminish the liability of any person under section 9607 or 9611 of this title or other applicable law.

(5) For the purpose of this subsection, the term "guarantor" means any person, other than the owner or operator, who provides evidence of financial responsibility for an owner or operator under this subsection.

**(d) EPA determination**

(1) Within one hundred and eighty days of the date of receipt of a proposed State program, the Administrator shall, after notice and opportunity for public comment, make a determination whether the State's program complies with the provisions of this section and provides for adequate enforcement of compliance with the requirements and standards adopted pursuant to this section.

(2) If the Administrator determines that a State program complies with the provisions of this section and provides for adequate enforcement of compliance with the requirements and standards adopted pursuant to this section, he shall approve the State program in lieu of the Federal program and the State shall have primary enforcement responsibility with respect to requirements of its program.

**(e) Withdrawal of authorization**

Whenever the Administrator determines after public hearing that a State is not administering and enforcing a program authorized under this subchapter in accordance with the provisions of this section, he shall so notify the State. If appropriate action is not taken within a reasonable time, not to exceed one hundred and twenty days after such notification, the Administrator shall withdraw approval of such program and reestablish the Federal program pursuant to this subchapter.

(Pub.L. 89–272, Title II, § 9004, as added Pub.L. 98–616, Title VI, § 601(a), Nov. 8, 1984, 98 Stat. 3282, and amended Pub.L. 99–499, Title II, § 205(e), Oct. 17, 1986, 100 Stat. 1702.)

[1] So in original.

[2] So in original. Probably should be followed by "section".

### HISTORICAL AND STATUTORY NOTES

**References in Text**

The Federal Bankruptcy Code, referred to in subsec. (c)(3), probably means a reference to Title 11, Bankruptcy.

**Effective and Applicability Provisions**

1986 Acts

Amendment by Pub.L. 99–499 effective Oct. 17, 1986, see section 4 of Pub.L. 99–499, set out as a note under section 9601 of this title.

## § 6991d. Inspections, monitoring, testing, and corrective action

**[SWDA § 9005]**

**(a) Furnishing information**

For the purposes of developing or assisting in the development of any regulation, conducting any study [1] taking any corrective action, or enforcing the provisions of this subchapter, any owner or operator of an underground storage tank (or any tank subject to study under section 6991h of this title that is used for storing regulated substances) shall, upon request of any officer, employee or representative of the Environmental Protection Agency, duly designated by the Administrator, or upon request of any duly designated officer, employee, or representative of a State acting pursuant to subsection (h)(7) of section 6991b of this title or with an approved program, furnish information relating to such tanks, their associated equipment, their contents, conduct monitoring or testing, permit such officer at all reasonable times to have access to, and to copy all records relating to such tanks and permit such officer to have access for corrective action. For the purposes of developing or assisting in the development of any regulation, conducting any study, taking corrective action, or enforcing the provisions of this subchapter, such officers, employees, or representatives are authorized—

(1) to enter at reasonable times any establishment or other place where an underground storage tank is located;

(2) to inspect and obtain samples from any person of any regulated substances contained in such tank;

(3) to conduct monitoring or testing of the tanks, associated equipment, contents, or surrounding soils, air, surface water or ground water; and

(4) to take corrective action.

Each such inspection shall be commenced and completed with reasonable promptness.

**(b) Confidentiality**

(1) Any records, reports, or information obtained from any persons under this section shall be available to the public, except that upon a showing satisfactory to the Administrator (or the State, as the case may be) by any person that records, reports, or information, or a particular part thereof, to which the Administrator (or the State, as the case may be) or any officer, employee, or representative thereof has access under this section if made public, would divulge information entitled to protection under section 1905 of Title 18, such information or particular portion thereof shall be considered confidential in accordance with the purposes of that section, except that such record, report, document, or information may be disclosed to other officers, employees, or authorized representatives of the United States concerned with carrying out this chapter, or when relevent[2] in any proceeding under this chapter.

(2) Any person not subject to the provisions of section 1905 of Title 18 who knowingly and willfully divulges or discloses any information entitled to protection under this subsection shall, upon conviction, be subject to a fine of not more than $5,000 or to imprisonment not to exceed one year, or both.

(3) In submitting data under this subchapter, a person required to provide such data may—

(A) designate the data which such person believes is entitled to protection under this subsection, and

(B) submit such designated data separately from other data submitted under this subchapter.

A designation under this paragraph shall be made in writing and in such manner as the Administrator may prescribe.

(4) Notwithstanding any limitation contained in this section or any other provision of law, all information reported to, or otherwise obtained, by the Administrator (or any representative of the Administrator) under this chapter shall be made available, upon written request of any duly authorized committee of the Congress, to such committee (including records, reports, or information obtained by representatives of the Evironmental[3] Protection Agency).

(Pub.L. 89–272, Title II, § 9005, as added Pub.L. 98–616, Title VI, § 601(a), Nov. 8, 1984, 98 Stat. 3284, and amended Pub.L. 99–499, Title II, § 205(f), Oct. 17, 1986, 100 Stat. 1702.)

[1] So in original. Probably should be followed by a comma.
[2] So in original. Probably should be "relevant".
[3] So in original. Probably should be "Environmental".

### HISTORICAL AND STATUTORY NOTES

**Effective and Applicability Provisions**

1986 Acts

Amendment by Pub.L. 99–499 effective Oct. 17, 1986, see section 4 of Pub.L. 99–499, set out as a note under section 9601 of this title.

## § 6991e. Federal enforcement

**[SWDA § 9006]**

**(a) Compliance orders**

(1) Except as provided in paragraph (2), whenever on the basis of any information, the Administrator determines that any person is in violation of any requirement of this subchapter, the Administrator may issue an order requiring compliance within a reasonable specified time period or the Administrator may commence a civil action in the United States district court in which the violation occurred for appropriate relief, including a temporary or permanent injunction.

(2) In the case of a violation of any requirement of this subchapter where such violation occurs in a State with a program approved under section 6991c of this title, the Administrator shall give notice to the State in which such violation has occurred prior to issuing an order or commencing a civil action under this section.

(3) If a violator fails to comply with an order under this subsection within the time specified in the order, he shall be liable for a civil penalty of not more than $25,000 for each day of continued noncompliance.

**(b) Procedure**

Any order issued under this section shall become final unless, no later than thirty days after the order is served, the person or persons named therein request a public hearing. Upon such request the Administrator shall promptly conduct a public hearing. In connection with any proceeding under this section the Administrator may issue subpoenas for the attendance and testimony of witnesses and the production of relevant papers, books, and documents, and may promulgate rules for discovery procedures.

**(c) Contents of order**

Any order issued under this section shall state with reasonable specificity the nature of the violation, specify a reasonable time for compliance, and assess a penalty, if any, which the Administrator determines is reasonable taking into account the seriousness of the violation and any good faith efforts to comply with the applicable requirements.

**(d) Civil penalties**

(1) Any owner who knowingly fails to notify or submits false information pursuant to section 6991a(a) of this title shall be subject to a civil penalty not to exceed $10,000 for each tank for which notification is not given or false information is submitted.

(2) Any owner or operator of an underground storage tank who fails to comply with—

(A) any requirement or standard promulgated by the Administrator under section 6991b of this title;

(B) any requirement or standard of a State program approved pursuant to section 6991c of this title; or

(C) the provisions of section 6991b(g) of this title (entitled "Interim Prohibition")

shall be subject to a civil penalty not to exceed $10,000 for each tank for each day of violation.

(Pub.L. 89–272, Title II, § 9006, as added Pub.L. 98–616, Title VI, § 601(a), Nov. 8, 1984, 98 Stat. 3285.)

## § 6991f. Federal facilities

[SWDA § 9007]

**(a) Application of subchapter**

Each department, agency, and instrumentality of the executive, legislative, and judicial branches of the Federal Government having jurisdiction over any underground storage tank shall be subject to and comply with all Federal, State, interstate, and local requirements, applicable to such tank, both substantive and procedural, in the same manner, and to the same extent, as any other person is subject to such requirements, including payment of reasonable service charges. Neither the United States, nor any agent, employee, or officer thereof, shall be immune or exempt from any process or sanction of any State or Federal court with respect to the enforcement of any such injunctive relief.

**(b) Presidential exemption**

The President may exempt any underground storage tanks of any department, agency, or instrumentality in the executive branch from compliance with such a requirement if he determines it to be in the paramount interest of the United States to do so. No such exemption shall be granted due to lack of appropriation unless the President shall have specifically requested such appropriation as a part of the budgetary process and the Congress shall have failed to make available such requested appropriations. Any exemption shall be for a period not in excess of one year, but additional exemptions may be granted for periods not to exceed one year upon the President's making a new determination. The President shall report each January to the Congress all exemptions from the requirements of this section granted during the preceding calendar year, together with his reason for granting each such exemption.

(Pub.L. 89–272, Title II, § 9007, as added Pub.L. 98–616, Title VI, § 601(a), Nov. 8, 1984, 98 Stat. 3286.)

### HISTORICAL AND STATUTORY NOTES

**Termination of Reporting Requirements**

For termination, effective May 15, 2000, of provisions in subsec. (b) of this section requiring the President to report annually to Congress, see section 3003 of Pub.L. 104–66, as amended, set out as a note under 31 U.S.C.A. § 1113, and the 9th item on page 20 of House Document No. 103–7.

## § 6991g. State authority

[SWDA § 9008]

Nothing in this subchapter shall preclude or deny any right of any State or political subdivision thereof to adopt or enforce any regulation, requirement, or standard of performance respecting underground storage tanks that is more stringent than a regulation, requirement, or standard of performance in effect under this subchapter or to impose any additional liability with respect to the release of regulated substances within such State or political subdivision.

(Pub.L. 89–272, Title II, § 9008, as added Pub.L. 98–616, Title VI, § 601(a), Nov. 8, 1984, 98 Stat. 3286, and amended Pub.L. 99–499, Title II, § 205(g), Oct. 17, 1986, 100 Stat. 1702.)

### HISTORICAL AND STATUTORY NOTES

**Effective and Applicability Provisions**

1986 Acts

Amendment by Pub.L. 99–499 effective Oct. 17, 1986, see section 4 of Pub.L. 99–499, set out as a note under section 9601 of this title.

## § 6991h. Study of underground storage tanks

[SWDA § 9009]

**(a) Petroleum tanks**

Not later than twelve months after November 8, 1984, the Administrator shall complete a study of underground storage tanks used for the storage of regulated substances defined in section 6991(2)(B) of this title.

**(b) Other tanks**

Not later than thirty-six months after November 8, 1984, the Administrator shall complete a study of all other underground storage tanks.

**(c) Elements of studies**

The studies under subsections (a) and (b) of this section shall include an assessment of the ages, types (including methods of manufacture, coatings, protection systems, the compatibility of the construction materials and the installation methods) and locations (including the climate of the locations) of such tanks;

soil conditions, water tables, and the hydrogeology of tank locations; the relationship between the foregoing factors and the likelihood of releases from underground storage tanks; the effectiveness and costs of inventory systems, tank testing, and leak detection systems; and such other factors as the Administrator deems appropriate.

**(d) Farm and heating oil tanks**

Not later than thirty-six months after November 8, 1984, the Administrator shall conduct a study regarding the tanks referred to in section 6991(1)(A) and (B) of this title. Such study shall include estimates of the number and location of such tanks and an analysis of the extent to which there may be releases or threatened releases from such tanks into the environment.

**(e) Reports**

Upon completion of the studies authorized by this section, the Administrator shall submit reports to the President and to the Congress containing the results of the studies and recommendations respecting whether or not such tanks should be subject to the preceding provisions of this subchapter.

**(f) Reimbursement**

(1) If any owner or operator (excepting an agency, department, or instrumentality of the United States Government, a State or a political subdivision thereof) shall incur costs, including the loss of business opportunity, due to the closure or interruption of operation of an underground storage tank solely for the purpose of conducting studies authorized by this section, the Administrator shall provide such person fair and equitable reimbursement for such costs.

(2) All claims for reimbursement shall be filed with the Administrator not later than ninety days after the closure or interruption which gives rise to the claim.

(3) Reimbursements made under this section shall be from funds appropriated by the Congress pursuant to the authorization contained in section 6916(g) of this title.

(4) For purposes of judicial review, a determination by the Administrator under this subsection shall be considered final agency action.

(Pub.L. 89–272, Title II, § 9009, as added Pub.L. 98–616, Title VI, § 601(a), Nov. 8, 1984, 98 Stat. 3287.)

### HISTORICAL AND STATUTORY NOTES

**References in Text**

Section 6916(g) of this title, referred to in subsec. (f)(3), probably means section 6916(f) of this title, which authorizes appropriations for this subchapter. There is no subsec. (g) of that section.

## § 6991i. Authorization of appropriations

**[SWDA § 9010]**

For authorization of appropriations to carry out this subchapter, see section 6916(g) of this title.

(Pub.L. 89–272, Title II, § 9010, as added Pub.L. 98–616, Title VI, § 601(a), Nov. 8, 1984, 98 Stat. 3287.)

### HISTORICAL AND STATUTORY NOTES

**References in Text**

Section 6916(g) of this title, referred to in text, probably means section 6916(f) of this title, which authorizes appropriations for this subchapter. There is no subsec. (g) of that section.

# SUBCHAPTER X—DEMONSTRATION MEDICAL WASTE TRACKING PROGRAM

## § 6992. Scope of demonstration program for medical waste

**[SWDA § 11001]**

**(a) Covered States**

The States within the demonstration program established under this subchapter for tracking medical wastes shall be New York, New Jersey, Connecticut, the States contiguous to the Great Lakes and any State included in the program through the petition procedure described in subsection (c) of this section, except for any of such States in which the Governor notifies the Administrator under subsection (b) of this section that such State shall not be covered by the program.

**(b) Opt out**

(1) If the Governor of any State covered under subsection (a) of this section which is not contiguous to the Atlantic Ocean notifies the Administrator that such State elects not to participate in the demonstration program, the Administrator shall remove such State from the program.

(2) If the Governor of any other State covered under subsection (a) of this section notifies the Administrator that such State has implemented a medical waste tracking program that is no less stringent than the demonstration program under this subchapter and that such State elects not to participate in the demonstration program, the Administrator shall, if the Administrator determines that such State program is no less stringent than the demonstration program under this subchapter, remove such State from the demonstration program.

(3) Notifications under paragraphs (1) or (2) shall be submitted to the Administrator no later than 30 days after the promulgation of regulations implementing the demonstration program under this subchapter.

**(c) Petition in**

The Governor of any State may petition the Administrator to be included in the demonstration program and the Administrator may, in his discretion, include any such State. Such petition may not be made later than 30 days after promulgation of regulations establishing the demonstration program under this subchapter, and the Administrator shall determine whether to include the State within 30 days after receipt of the State's petition.

**(d) Expiration of demonstration program**

The demonstration program shall expire on the date 24 months after the effective date of the regulations under this subchapter.

(Pub.L. 89–272, Title II, § 11001, as added Pub.L. 100–582, § 2(a), Nov. 1, 1988, 102 Stat. 2950.)

## § 6992a. Listing of medical wastes

**[SWDA § 11002]**

**(a) List**

Not later than 6 months after November 1, 1988, the Administrator shall promulgate regulations listing the types of medical waste to be tracked under the demonstration program. Except as provided in subsection (b) of this section, such list shall include, but need not be limited to, each of the following types of solid waste:

(1) Cultures and stocks of infectious agents and associated biologicals, including cultures from medical and pathological laboratories, cultures and stocks of infectious agents from research and industrial laboratories, wastes from the production of biologicals, discarded live and attenuated vaccines, and culture dishes and devices used to transfer, inoculate, and mix cultures.

(2) Pathological wastes, including tissues, organs, and body parts that are removed during surgery or autopsy.

(3) Waste human blood and products of blood, including serum, plasma, and other blood components.

(4) Sharps that have been used in patient care or in medical, research, or industrial laboratories, including hypodermic needles, syringes, pasteur pipettes, broken glass, and scalpel blades.

(5) Contaminated animal carcasses, body parts, and bedding of animals that were exposed to infectious agents during research, production of biologicals, or testing of pharmaceuticals.

(6) Wastes from surgery or autopsy that were in contact with infectious agents, including soiled dressings, sponges, drapes, lavage tubes, drainage sets, underpads, and surgical gloves.

(7) Laboratory wastes from medical, pathological, pharmaceutical, or other research, commercial, or industrial laboratories that were in contact with infectious agents, including slides and cover slips, disposable gloves, laboratory coats, and aprons.

(8) Dialysis wastes that were in contact with the blood of patients undergoing hemodialysis, including contaminated disposable equipment and supplies such as tubing, filters, disposable sheets, towels, gloves, aprons, and laboratory coats.

(9) Discarded medical equipment and parts that were in contact with infectious agents.

(10) Biological waste and discarded materials contaminated with blood, excretion, excudates [1] or secretion from human beings or animals who are isolated to protect others from communicable diseases.

(11) Such other waste material that results from the administration of medical care to a patient by a health care provider and is found by the Administrator to pose a threat to human health or the environment.

**(b) Exclusions from list**

The Administrator may exclude from the list under this section any categories or items described in paragraphs (6) through (10) of subsection (a) of this section which he determines do not pose a substantial present or potential hazard to human health or the environment when improperly treated, stored, transported, disposed of, or otherwise managed.

(Pub.L. 89–272, Title II, § 11002, as added Pub.L. 100–582, § 2(a), Nov. 1, 1988, 102 Stat. 2951.)

[1] So in original. Probably should be "exudates".

## § 6992b. Tracking of medical waste

**[SWDA § 11003]**

**(a) Demonstration program**

Not later than 6 months after November 1, 1988, the Administrator shall promulgate regulations establishing a program for the tracking of the medical waste listed in section 6992a of this title which is generated in a State subject to the demonstration program. The program shall (1) provide for tracking of the transportation of the waste from the generator to the disposal facility, except that waste that is incinerated need not be tracked after incineration, (2) include a system for providing the generator of the waste with assurance that the waste is received by the disposal facility, (3) use a uniform form for tracking in each of the demonstration States, and (4) include the following requirements:

(A) A requirement for segregation of the waste at the point of generation where practicable.

(B) A requirement for placement of the waste in containers that will protect waste handlers and the public from exposure.

(C) A requirement for appropriate labeling of containers of the waste.

**(b) Small quantities**

In the program under subsection (a) of this section, the Administrator may establish an exemption for generators of small quantities of medical waste listed under section 6992a of this title, except that the Administrator may not exempt from the program any person who, or facility that, generates 50 pounds or more of such waste in any calendar month.

**(c) On-site incinerators**

Concurrently with the promulgation of regulations under subsection (a) of this section, the Administrator shall promulgate a recordkeeping and reporting requirement for any generator in a demonstration State of medical waste listed in section 6992a of this title that (1) incinerates medical waste listed in section 6992a of this title on site and (2) does not track such waste under the regulations promulgated under subsection (a) of this section. Such requirement shall require the generator to report to the Administrator on the volume and types of medical waste listed in section 6992a of this title that the generator incinerated on site during the 6 months following the effective date of the requirements of this subsection.

**(d) Type of medical waste and types of generators**

For each of the requirements of this section, the regulations may vary for different types of medical waste and for different types of medical waste generators.

(Pub.L. 89–272, Title II, § 11003, as added Pub.L. 100–582, § 2(a), Nov. 1, 1988, 102 Stat. 2952.)

## § 6992c. Inspections

[SWDA § 11004]

**(a) Requirements for access**

For purposes of developing or assisting in the development of any regulation or report under this subchapter or enforcing any provision of this subchapter, any person who generates, stores, treats, transports, disposes of, or otherwise handles or has handled medical waste shall, upon request of any officer, employee, or representative of the Environmental Protection Agency duly designated by the Administrator, furnish information relating to such waste, including any tracking forms required to be maintained under section 6992b of this title, conduct monitoring or testing, and permit such person at all reasonable times to have access to, and to copy, all records relating to such waste. For such purposes, such officers, employees, or representatives are authorized to—

(1) enter at reasonable times any establishment or other place where medical wastes are or have been generated, stored, treated, disposed of, or transported from;

(2) conduct monitoring or testing; and

(3) inspect and obtain samples from any person of any such wastes and samples of any containers or labeling for such wastes.

**(b) Procedures**

Each inspection under this section shall be commenced and completed with reasonable promptness. If the officer, employee, or representative obtains any samples, prior to leaving the premises he shall give to the owner, operator, or agent in charge a receipt describing the sample obtained and, if requested, a portion of each such sample equal in volume or weight to the portion retained if giving such an equal portion is feasible. If any analysis is made of such samples, a copy of the results of such analysis shall be furnished promptly to the owner, operator, or agent in charge of the premises concerned.

**(c) Availability to public**

The provisions of section 6927(b) of this title shall apply to records, reports, and information obtained under this section in the same manner and to the same extent as such provisions apply to records, reports, and information obtained under section 6927 of this title.

(Pub.L. 89–272, Title II, § 11004, as added Pub.L. 100–582, § 2(a), Nov. 1, 1988, 102 Stat. 2952.)

## § 6992d. Enforcement

[SWDA § 11005]

**(a) Compliance orders**

**(1) Violations**

Whenever on the basis of any information the Administrator determines that any person has violated, or is in violation of, any requirement or prohibition in effect under this subchapter (including any requirement or prohibition in effect under regulations under this subchapter) (A) the Administrator may issue an order (i) assessing a civil penalty for any past or current violation, (ii) requiring compliance immediately or within a specified time period, or (iii) both, or (B) the Administrator may commence a civil action in the United States district court in the district in which the violation occurred for appropriate relief, including a temporary or permanent injunction. Any order issued pursuant to this subsection shall state with reasonable specificity the nature of the violation.

**(2) Orders assessing penalties**

Any penalty assessed in an order under this subsection shall not exceed $25,000 per day of noncompliance for each violation of a requirement or prohibition in effect under this subchapter. In assessing such a penalty, the Administrator shall take into account the seriousness of the violation and any good faith efforts to comply with applicable requirements.

**(3) Public hearing**

Any order issued under this subsection shall become final unless, not later than 30 days after issuance of the order, the persons named therein request a public hearing. Upon such request, the Administrator shall promptly conduct a public hearing. In connection with any proceeding under this section, the Administrator may issue subpoenas for the production of relevant papers, books, and documents, and may promulgate rules for discovery procedures.

**(4) Violation of compliance orders**

In the case of an order under this subsection requiring compliance with any requirement of or regulation under this subchapter, if a violator fails to take corrective action within the time specified in an order, the Administrator may assess a civil penalty of not more than $25,000 for each day of continued noncompliance with the order.

**(b) Criminal penalties**

Any person who—

(1) knowingly violates the requirements of or regulations under this subchapter;

(2) knowingly omits material information or makes any false material statement or representation in any label, record, report, or other document filed, maintained, or used for purposes of compliance with this subchapter or regulations thereunder; or

(3) knowingly generates, stores, treats, transports, disposes of, or otherwise handles any medical waste (whether such activity took place before or takes place after November 1, 1988) and who knowingly destroys, alters, conceals, or fails to file any record, report, or other document required to be maintained or filed for purposes of compliance with this subchapter or regulations thereunder

shall, upon conviction, be subject to a fine of not more than $50,000 for each day of violation, or imprisonment not to exceed 2 years (5 years in the case of a violation of paragraph (1)). If the conviction is for a violation committed after a first conviction of such person under this paragraph, the maximum punishment under the respective paragraph shall be doubled with respect to both fine and imprisonment.

**(c) Knowing endangerment**

Any person who knowingly violates any provision of subsection (b) of this section who knows at that time that he thereby places another person in imminent danger of death or serious bodily injury, shall upon conviction be subject to a fine of not more than $250,000 or imprisonment for not more than 15 years, or both. A defendant that is an organization shall, upon conviction under this subsection, be subject to a fine of not more than $1,000,000. The terms of this paragraph shall be interpreted in accordance with the rules provided under section 6928(f) of this title.

**(d) Civil penalties**

Any person who violates any requirement of or regulation under this subchapter shall be liable to the United States for a civil penalty in an amount not to exceed $25,000 for each such violation. Each day of such violation shall, for purposes of this section, constitute a separate violation.

**(e) Civil penalty policy**

Civil penalties assessed by the United States or by the States under this subchapter shall be assessed in accordance with the Administrator's "RCRA Civil Penalty Policy", as such policy may be amended from time to time.

(Pub.L. 89–272, Title II, § 11005, as added Pub.L. 100–582, § 2(a), Nov. 1, 1988, 102 Stat. 2953.)

## § 6992e. Federal facilities

**[SWDA § 11006]**

**(a) In general**

Each department, agency, and instrumentality of the executive, legislative, and judicial branches of the Federal Government in a demonstration State (1) having jurisdiction over any solid waste management facility or disposal site at which medical waste is disposed of or otherwise handled, or (2) engaged in any activity resulting, or which may result, in the disposal, management, or handling of medical waste shall be subject to, and comply with, all Federal, State, interstate, and local requirements, both substantive and procedural (including any requirement for permits or reporting or any provisions for injunctive relief and such sanctions as may be imposed by a court to enforce such relief), respecting control and abatement of medical waste disposal and management in the same manner, and to the same extent, as any person is subject to such requirements, including the payment of reasonable service charges. The Federal, State, interstate, and local substantive and procedural requirements referred to in this subsection include, but are not limited to, all administrative orders, civil, criminal, and administrative penalties, and other sanctions, including injunctive relief, fines, and imprisonment. Neither the United States, nor any agent, employee, or officer thereof, shall be immune or exempt from any process or sanction of any State or Federal court with respect to the enforcement of any such order, penalty, or other sanction. For purposes of enforcing any such substantive or procedural requirement (including, but not limited to, any injunctive relief, administrative order, or civil, criminal, administrative penalty, or other sanction), against any such department, agency, or instrumentality, the United States hereby expressly waives any immunity otherwise applicable to the United States. The President may exempt any department, agency, or instrumentality in the executive branch from compliance with such a requirement if he determines it to be in the paramount interest of the United States to do so. No such exemption shall be granted due to lack of appropriation unless the President shall have specifically requested such appropriation as a part of the budgetary process and the Congress shall have failed to make available such requested appropriation. Any exemption shall be for a period not in excess of one year, but additional exemptions may be granted for periods not to exceed one year upon the President's making a new determination. The President shall report each January to the Congress all exemptions from the requirements of this section granted during the preceding calendar year, together with his reason for granting each such exemption.

**(b) "Person" defined**

For purposes of this chapter, the term "person" shall be treated as including each department, agency, and instrumentality of the United States.

(Pub.L. 89–272, Title II, § 11006, as added Pub.L. 100–582, § 2(a), Nov. 1, 1988, 102 Stat. 2954.)

#### HISTORICAL AND STATUTORY NOTES

**Termination of Reporting Requirements**

For termination, effective May 15, 2000, of provisions in subsec. (a) of this section requiring the President to report annually to Congress, see section 3003 of Pub.L. 104–66, as amended, set out as a note under 31 U.S.C.A. § 1113, and the 10th item on page 20 of House Document No. 103–7.

## § 6992f. Relationship to State law

**[SWDA § 11007]**

**(a) State inspections and enforcement**

A State may conduct inspections under 6992c of this title [1] and take enforcement actions under section 6992d of this title against any person, including any person who has imported medical waste into a State in violation of the requirements of, or regulations under, this subchapter, to the same extent as the Administrator. At the time a State initiates an enforcement action under section 6992d of this title against any person, the State shall notify the Administrator in writing.

**(b) Retention of State authority**

Nothing in this subchapter shall—

(1) preempt any State or local law; or

(2) except as provided in subsection (c) of this section, otherwise affect any State or local law or the authority of any State or local government to adopt or enforce any State or local law.

**(c) State forms**

Any State or local law which requires submission of a tracking form from any person subject to this subchapter shall require that the form be identical in content and format to the form required under section 6992b of this title, except that a State may require the submission of other tracking information which is supplemental to the information required on the form required under section 6992b of this title through additional sheets or such other means as the State deems appropriate.

(Pub.L. 89–272, Title II, § 11007, as added Pub.L. 100–582, § 2(a), Nov. 1, 1988, 102 Stat. 2955.)

1 The phrase "under 6992c" should read "under section 6992c".

## § 6992g. Repealed. Pub.L. 105–362, Title V, § 501(h)(1)(A), Nov. 10, 1998

#### HISTORICAL AND STATUTORY NOTES

Section Pub.L. 89–272, Title II, § 11008, as added Pub.L. 100–582, § 2(a), Nov. 1, 1988, 102 Stat. 2956, repealed by Pub.L. 105–362, Title V, § 501(h)(1)(A), Nov. 10, 1998, 112 Stat. 3284, related to reports to Congress.

## § 6992h. Health impacts report

**[SWDA § 11009]**

Within 24 months after November 1, 1988, the Administrator of the Agency for Toxic Substances and Disease Registry shall prepare for Congress a report on the health effects of medical waste, including each of the following—

(1) A description of the potential for infection or injury from the segregation, handling, storage, treatment, or disposal of medical wastes.

(2) An estimate of the number of people injured or infected annually by sharps, and the nature and seriousness of those injuries or infections.

(3) An estimate of the number of people infected annually by other means related to waste segregation, handling, storage, treatment, or disposal, and the nature and seriousness of those infections.

(4) For diseases possibly spread by medical waste, including Acquired Immune Deficiency Syndrome and hepatitis B, an estimate of what percent-

age of the total number of cases nationally may be traceable to medical wastes.

(Pub.L. 89–272, Title II, § 11008, formerly § 11009, as added Pub.L. 100–582, § 2(a), Nov. 1, 1988, 102 Stat. 295, renumbered § 11008, Pub.L. 105–362, Title V, § 501(h)(1)(B), Nov. 10, 1998, 112 Stat. 3284.)

## § 6992i. General provisions

**[SWDA § 11010]**

**(a) Consultation**

(1) In promulgating regulations under this subchapter, the Administrator shall consult with the affected States and may consult with other interested parties.

(2) The Administrator shall also consult with the International Joint Commission to determine how to monitor the disposal of medical waste emanating from Canada.

**(b) Public comment**

In the case of the regulations required by this subchapter to be promulgated within 9 months after November 1, 1988, the Administrator may promulgate such regulations in interim final form without prior opportunity for public comment, but the Administrator shall provide an opportunity for public comment on the interim final rule. The promulgation of such regulations shall not be subject to the Paperwork Reduction Act of 1980.

**(c) Relationship to subchapter III**

Nothing in this subchapter shall affect the authority of the Administrator to regulate medical waste, including medical waste listed under section 6992a of this title, under subchapter III of this chapter.

(Pub.L. 89–272, Title II, § 11009, formerly § 11010, as added Pub.L. 100–582, § 2(a), Nov. 1, 1988, 102 Stat. 2957, renumbered § 11009, Pub.L. 105–362, Title V, § 501(h)(1)(B), Nov. 10, 1998, 112 Stat. 3284.)

### HISTORICAL AND STATUTORY NOTES

**References in Text**

The Paperwork Reduction Act of 1980, referred to in subsec. (b), is Pub. L. 96–511, Dec. 11, 1980, 94 Stat. 2812, as amended, which was classified principally to chapter 35 of Title 44, 44 U.S.C.A. § 3501 et seq., prior to the general amendment of that chapter by Pub. L. 104–13, § 2, May 22, 1995, 109 Stat. 163. For complete classification, see Short Title of 1980 Amendment note set out under 44 U.S.C.A. § 101 and Tables.

## § 6992j. Effective date

**[SWDA § 11011]**

The regulations promulgated under this subchapter shall take effect within 90 days after promulgation, except that, at the time of promulgation, the Administrator may provide for a shorter period prior to the effective date if he finds the regulated community does not need 90 days to come into compliance.

(Pub.L. 89–272, Title II, § 11010, formerly § 11011, as added Pub.L. 100–582, § 2(a), Nov. 1, 1988, 102 Stat. 2958, renumbered § 11010, Pub.L. 105–362, Title V, § 501(h)(1)(B), Nov. 10, 1998, 112 Stat. 3284.)

## § 6992k. Authorization of appropriations

**[SWDA § 11012]**

There are authorized to be appropriated to the Administrator such sums as may be necessary for each of the fiscal years 1989 through 1991 for purposes of carrying out activities under this subchapter.

(Pub.L. 89–272, Title II, § 11011, formerly § 11012, as added Pub.L. 100–582, § 2(a), Nov. 1, 1988, 102 Stat. 2958, renumbered § 11011, Pub.L. 105–362, Title V, § 501(h)(1)(B), Nov. 10, 1998, 112 Stat. 3284.)

## §§ 6993 to 7000. Reserved for future legislation

# AIR POLLUTION PREVENTION AND CONTROL

## CLEAN AIR ACT [CAA § ______]

**(42 U.S.C.A. §§ 7401 to 7671q)**

## CHAPTER 85—AIR POLLUTION PREVENTION AND CONTROL

## SUBCHAPTER I—PROGRAMS AND ACTIVITIES

### PART A—AIR QUALITY AND EMISSIONS LIMITATIONS

#### HISTORICAL AND STATUTORY NOTES

**Codifications**

Act July 14, 1955, c. 360, 69 Stat. 322, as amended, known as the Clean Air Act, which was formerly classified to chapter 15B (section 1857 et seq.) of this title, was completely revised by Pub.L. 95–95, Aug. 7, 1977, 91 Stat. 685, and was reclassified to this chapter.

## § 7401. Congressional findings and declaration of purpose

[CAA § 101]

**(a) Findings**

The Congress finds—

(1) that the predominant part of the Nation's population is located in its rapidly expanding metropolitan and other urban areas, which generally cross the boundary lines of local jurisdictions and often extend into two or more States;

(2) that the growth in the amount and complexity of air pollution brought about by urbanization, industrial development, and the increasing use of motor vehicles, has resulted in mounting dangers to the public health and welfare, including injury to agricultural crops and livestock, damage to and the deterioration of property, and hazards to air and ground transportation;

(3) that air pollution prevention (that is, the reduction or elimination, through any measures, of the amount of pollutants produced or created at the source) and air pollution control at its source is the primary responsibility of States and local governments; and

(4) that Federal financial assistance and leadership is essential for the development of cooperative Federal, State, regional, and local programs to prevent and control air pollution.

**(b) Declaration**

The purposes of this subchapter are—

(1) to protect and enhance the quality of the Nation's air resources so as to promote the public health and welfare and the productive capacity of its population;

(2) to initiate and accelerate a national research and development program to achieve the prevention and control of air pollution;

(3) to provide technical and financial assistance to State and local governments in connection with the development and execution of their air pollution prevention and control programs; and

(4) to encourage and assist the development and operation of regional air pollution prevention and control programs.

**(c) Pollution prevention**

A primary goal of this chapter is to encourage or otherwise promote reasonable Federal, State, and local governmental actions, consistent with the provisions of this chapter, for pollution prevention.

(July 14, 1955, c. 360, Title I, § 101, formerly § 1, as added Dec. 17, 1963, Pub.L. 88–206, § 1, 77 Stat. 392, and renumbered § 101 and amended Oct. 20, 1965, Pub.L. 89–272, Title I, § 101(2), (3), 79 Stat. 992; Nov. 21, 1967, Pub.L. 90–148, § 2, 81 Stat. 485; Nov. 15, 1990, Pub.L. 101–549, Title I, § 108(k), 104 Stat. 2468.)

#### HISTORICAL AND STATUTORY NOTES

**Codifications**

Section was formerly classified to section 1857 of this title.

**Effective and Applicability Provisions**

1990 Acts

Section 711(b) of Pub.L. 101–549 provided that:

"(1) Except as otherwise expressly provided, the amendments made by this Act [Pub.L. 101–549, Nov. 15, 1990, 104 Stat. 2399, popularly known as the Clean Air Act Amendments of 1990, for distribution of this Act to the Code see Tables] shall be effective on the date of enactment of this Act [Nov. 15, 1990].

"(2) The Administrator's authority to assess civil penalties under section 205(c) of the Clean Air Act, as amended by this Act, [section 7524(c) of this title], shall apply to violations that occur or continue on or after the date of enactment of this Act [Nov. 15, 1990]. Civil penalties for violations that occur prior to such date and do not continue after such date shall be assessed in accordance with the provisions of the Clean Air Act [this chapter] in effect immediately prior to the date of enactment of this Act.

"(3) The civil penalties prescribed under sections 205(a) and 211(d)(1) of the Clean Air Act, as amended by this Act [sections 7524(a) and 7545(d)(1) of this title], shall apply to violations that occur on or after the date of enactment of this Act [Nov. 15, 1990]. Violations that occur prior to such date shall be subject to the civil penalty provisions prescribed in sections 205(a) and 211(d) of the Clean Air Act in effect immediately prior to the enactment of this Act. The injunctive authority prescribed under section 211(d)(2) of the Clean Air Act, as amended by this Act [section 7545(d)(2) of this title], shall apply to violations that occur or continue on or after the date of enactment of this Act [Nov. 15, 1990].

"(4) For purposes of paragraphs (2) and (3), where the date of a violation cannot be determined it will be assumed to be the date on which the violation is discovered."

1977 Acts

Section 406 of Pub.L. 95–95, as amended by Pub.L. 95–190, § 14(b)(6), Nov. 16, 1977, 91 Stat. 1405, provided that:

"**(a)** No suit, action, or other proceeding lawfully commenced by or against the Administrator or any other officer or employee of the United States in his official capacity or in relation to the discharge of his official duties under the Clean Air Act [this chapter], as in effect immediately prior to the date of enactment of this Act [Aug. 7, 1977] shall abate by reason of the taking effect of the amendments made by this Act [see Short Title of 1977 Acts note under this section]. The court may, on its own motion or that of any party made at any time within twelve months after such taking effect, allow the same to be maintained by or against the Administrator or such officer or employee.

"**(b)** All rules, regulations, orders, determinations, contracts, certifications, authorizations, delegations or other actions duly issued, made, or taken by or pursuant to the Clean Air Act [this chapter], as in effect immediately prior to the date of enactment of this Act [Aug. 7, 1977], and pertaining to any functions, powers, requirements, and duties under the Clean Air Act, as in effect immediately prior to the date of enactment of this Act, and not suspended by the Administrator or the courts, shall continue in full force and effect after the date of enactment of this Act until modified or rescinded in accordance with the Clean Air Act as amended by this Act [see Short Title of 1977 Acts note under this section].

"**(c)** Nothing in this Act [see Short Title of 1977 Acts note under this section] nor any action taken pursuant to this Act shall in any way affect any requirement of an approved implementation plan in effect under section 110 of the Clean Air Act [section 7410 of this title] or any other provision of the Act in effect under the Clean Air Act before the date of enactment of this section [Aug. 7, 1977] until modified or rescinded in accordance with the Clean Air Act [this chapter] as amended by this Act [see Short Title of 1977 Acts note under this section].

"**(d)(1)** Except as otherwise expressly provided, the amendments made by this Act [see Short Title of 1977 Acts note under this section] shall be effective on date of enactment [Aug. 7, 1977].

"(2) Except as otherwise expressly provided, each State required to revise its applicable implementation plan by reason of any amendment made by this Act [see Short Title of 1977 Acts note under this section] shall adopt and submit to the Administrator of the Environmental Protection Administration such plan revision before the later of the date—

"**(A)** one year after the date of enactment of this Act [Aug. 7, 1977], or

"**(B)** nine months after the date of promulgation by the Administrator of the Environmental Protection Administration of any regulations under an amendment made by this Act [see Short Title of 1977 Acts note under this section] which are necessary for the approval of such plan revision".

**Transfer of Functions**

Reorg. Plan No. 3 of 1970, § 2(a)(3), eff. Dec. 2, 1970, 35 F.R. 15623, 84 Stat. 2086, transferred to the Administrator of the Environmental Protection Agency the functions vested by law in the Secretary of Health, Education, and Welfare or in the Department of Health, Education, and Welfare which are administered through the Environmental Health Service, including the functions exercised by the National Air Pollution Control Administration, and the Environmental Control Administration's Bureau of Solid Waste Management, Bureau of Water Hygiene, and Bureau of Radiological Health, except insofar as the functions carried out by the Bureau of Radiological Health pertain to regulation of radiation from consumer products, including electronic product radiation, radiation as used in the healing arts, occupational exposure to radiation, and research, technical assistance, and training related to radiation from consumer products, radiation as used in the healing arts, and occupational exposure to radiation.

**Savings Provisions**

Section 711(a) of Pub.L. 101–549 provided that: "Except as otherwise expressly provided in this Act [Pub.L. 101–549, Nov. 15, 1990, 104 Stat. 2399, popularly known as the Clean Air Act Amendments of 1990, for distribution of this Act to the Code see Tables], no suit, action, or other proceeding lawfully commenced by the Administrator or any other officer or employee of the United States in his official capacity or in relation to the discharge of his official duties under the Clean Air Act [this chapter], as in effect immediately prior to the date of enactment of this Act, [Nov. 15, 1990], shall abate by reason of the taking effect of the amendments made by this Act."

**Prior Provisions**

Provisions similar to those comprising this section were contained in a prior section 1857 of this title, Act July 14, 1955, c. 360, § 1, 69 Stat. 322, prior to the general amendment of this chapter by Pub.L. 88–206.

**Short Title**

1999 Amendments

Pub.L. 106–40, § 1, Aug. 5, 1999, 113 Stat. 207, provided that: This Act [amending section 7412 of this title, and enacting provisions set out as notes under section 7412 of this title] may be cited as the 'Chemical Safety Information, Site Security and Fuels Regulatory Relief Act'."

1998 Amendments

Pub.L. 105–286, § 1, Oct. 27, 1998, 112 Stat. 2773, provided that: "This Act [amending section 7511b of this title, and enacting provisions set out as notes under section 7511b of this title] may be cited as the 'Border Smog Reduction Act of 1998'."

1990 Amendments

Pub.L. 101–549, Nov. 15, 1990, 104 Stat. 2399, is popularly known as the "Clean Air Act Amendments of 1990". See Tables for classification.

1981 Amendments

Pub.L. 97–23, § 1, July 17, 1981, 95 Stat. 139, provided: "That this Act [amending sections 7410 and 7413 of this title] may be cited as the 'Steel Industry Compliance Extension Act of 1981'."

1977 Amendments

Pub.L. 95–95, § 1, Aug. 7, 1977, 91 Stat. 685, provided that: "This Act [enacting sections 4362, 7419 to 7428, 7450 to 7459, 7470 to 7479, 7491, 7501 to 7508, 7548, 7549, 7551, 7617 to 7625, and 7626 of this title, amending sections 7403, 7405, 7407 to 7415, 7417, 7418, 7521 to 7525, 7541, 7543, 7544, 7545, 7550, 7571, 7601 to 7605, 7607, 7612, 7613, and 7616 of this title, repealing section 1857c–10 of this title and enacting provisions set out as notes under this section and sections 7403, 7422, 7470, 7479, 7502, 7521, 7548, and 7621 of this title and section 792 of Title 15, Commerce and Trade] may be cited as the 'Clean Air Act Amendments of 1977'."

1970 Amendments

Pub.L. 91–604, § 1, Dec. 31, 1970, 84 Stat. 1676, provided: "That this Act [amending this chapter generally] may be cited as the 'Clean Air Amendments of 1970'."

Section 401 of Act July 14, 1955, as added Dec. 31, 1970, Pub.L. 91–604, § 14, 84 Stat. 1709, provided that: "This title [subchapter IV of this chapter] may be cited as the 'Noise Pollution and Abatement Act of 1970'."

1967 Amendments

Section 1 of Pub.L. 90–148 provided: "That this Act [amending this chapter generally] may be cited as the 'Air Quality Act of 1967'."

1966 Amendments

Pub.L. 89–675, § 1, Oct. 15, 1966, 80 Stat. 954, provided: "That this Act [amending sections 7405 and 7616 of this title and repealing section 1857f–8 of this title] may be cited as the 'Clean Air Act Amendments of 1966'."

1965 Amendments

Section 201 of Act July 14, 1955, as added by Pub.L. 89–272, Title I, § 101(8), Oct. 20, 1965, 79 Stat. 992, and amended by Pub.L. 90–148, § 2, Nov. 2, 1967, 81 Stat. 499, provided that: "This title [subchapter II of this chapter] may be cited as the 'National Emission Standards Act'." Prior to its amendment by Pub.L. 90–148, Title II of Act July 14, 1955, was known as the "Motor Vehicle Air Pollution Control Act".

1963 Acts

Section 317, formerly section 14, of Act July 14, 1955, as added by section 1 of Pub.L. 88–206, renumbered section 307 by section 101(4) of Pub.L. 89–272, renumbered section 310 by section 2 of Pub.L. 90–148, and renumbered section 317 by Pub.L. 91–604, § 12(a), Dec. 31, 1970, 84 Stat. 1705, provided that: "This Act [this chapter] may be cited as the 'Clean Air Act'."

**Federal Compliance with Pollution Control Standards**

For provisions relating to the responsibility of the head of each Executive agency for compliance with applicable pollution control standards, see Ex. Ord. No. 12088, Oct. 13, 1978, 43 F.R. 47707, as amended, set out as a note under section 4321 of this title.

**Impact on Small Communities**

Section 810 of Pub.L. 101–549 provided that: "Before implementing a provision of this Act [Pub.L. 101–549, Nov. 15, 1990, 104 Stat. 2399, popularly known as the Clean Air Act Amendments of 1990, for distribution of this Act to the Code, see Tables], the Administrator of the Environmental Protection Agency shall consult with the Small Communities Coordinator of the Environmental Protection Agency to determine the impact of such provision on small communities, including the estimated cost of compliance with such provision."

**List of Chemical Contaminants From Environmental Pollution Found in Human Tissue**

Pub.L. 95–95, Title IV, § 403(c), Aug. 7, 1977, 91 Stat. 792, provided that, not later than twelve months after Aug. 7, 1977, the Administrator of the Environmental Protection Agency was to publish throughout the United States a list of all known chemical contaminants resulting from environmental pollution which had been found in human tissue including blood, urine, breast milk, and all other human tissue, and that, not later than eighteen months after Aug. 7, 1977, the Administrator was to publish in the same manner an explanation of what was known about the manner in which the chemicals had entered the environment and thereafter human tissue, and, further, that the Administrator, in consultation with National Institutes of Health, the National Center for Health Statistics, and the National Center for Health Services Research and Development, if feasible, was to conduct an epidemiological study to demonstrate the relationship between levels of chemicals in the environment and in human tissue.

**National Industrial Pollution Control Council**

For provisions relating to the establishment of the National Industrial Pollution Control Council, see Ex. Ord. No. 11523, Apr. 9, 1970, 35 F.R. 5993, set out as a note under section 4321 of this title.

**Radon Assessment and Mitigation**

Pub.L. 99–499, Title I, § 118(k), Oct. 17, 1986, 100 Stat. 1659, as amended Pub.L. 105–362, Title V, § 501(i), Nov. 10, 1998, 112 Stat. 3284, provided that:

**"(1) National assessment of radon gas.**—No later than one year after the enactment of this Act [Oct. 17, 1986], the Administrator shall submit to the Congress a report which shall, to the extent possible—

"(A) identify the locations in the United States where radon is found in structures where people normally live or work, including educational institutions;

"(B) assess the levels of radon gas that are present in such structures;

"(C) determine the level of radon gas and radon daughters which poses a threat to human health and assess for each location identified under subparagraph (A) the extent of the threat to human health;

"(D) determine methods of reducing or eliminating the threat to human health of radon gas and radon daughters; and

"(E) include guidance and public information materials based on the findings or research of mitigating radon.

**"(2) Radon mitigation demonstration program.—**

**"(A) Demonstration program.**—The Administrator shall conduct a demonstration program to test methods and technologies of reducing or eliminating radon gas and radon daughters where it poses a threat to human health. The Administrator shall take into consideration any demonstration program underway in the Reading Prong of Pennsylvania, New Jersey, and New York and at other sites prior to enactment. The demonstration program under this section shall be conducted in the Reading Prong, and at such other sites as the Administrator considers appropriate.

**"(B) Liability.**—Liability, if any, for persons undertaking activities pursuant to the radon mitigation demonstration program authorized under this subsection shall be determined under principles of existing law.

**"(3) Construction of section.**—Nothing in this subsection shall be construed to authorize the Administrator to carry out any regulatory program or any activity other than research, development, and related reporting, information dissemination, and coordination activities specified in this subsection. Nothing in paragraph (1) or (2) shall be construed to limit the authority of the Administrator or of any other agency or instrumentality of the United States under any other authority of law."

**Radon Gas and Indoor Air Quality Research**

Pub.L. 99–499, Title IV, §§ 401 to 405, Oct. 17, 1986, 100 Stat. 1758, provided that:

**"Sec. 401. Short title.**

"This title may be cited as the 'Radon Gas and Indoor Air Quality Research Act of 1986'.

**"Sec. 402. Findings.**

"The Congress finds that:

"(1) High levels of radon gas pose a serious health threat in structures in certain areas of the country.

"(2) Various scientific studies have suggested that exposure to radon, including exposure to naturally occurring radon and indoor air pollutants, poses a public health risk.

"(3) Existing Federal radon and indoor air pollutant research programs are fragmented and underfunded.

"(4) An adequate information base concerning exposure to radon and indoor air pollutants should be developed by the appropriate Federal agencies.

**"Sec. 403. Radon gas and indoor air quality research program.**

**"(a) Design of program.**—The Administrator of the Environmental Protection Agency shall establish a research program with respect to radon gas and indoor air quality. Such program shall be designed to—

"(1) gather data and information on all aspects of indoor air quality in order to contribute to the understanding of health problems associated with the existence of air pollutants in the indoor environment;

"(2) coordinate Federal, State, local, and private research and development efforts relating to the improvement of indoor air quality; and

"(3) assess appropriate Federal Government actions to mitigate the environmental and health risks associated with indoor air quality problems.

**"(b) Program requirements.**—The research program required under this section shall include—

"(1) research and development concerning the identification, characterization, and monitoring of the sources and levels of indoor air pollution, including radon, which includes research and development relating to—

"(A) the measurement of various pollutant concentrations and their strengths and sources,

"(B) high-risk building types, and

"(C) instruments for indoor air quality data collection;

"(2) research relating to the effects of indoor air pollution and radon on human health;

"(3) research and development relating to control technologies or other mitigation measures to prevent or abate indoor air pollution (including the development, evaluation, and testing of individual and generic control devices and systems);

"(4) demonstration of methods for reducing or eliminating indoor air pollution and radon, including sealing, venting, and other methods that the Administrator determines may be effective;

"(5) research, to be carried out in conjunction with the Secretary of Housing and Urban Development, for the purpose of developing—

"(A) methods for assessing the potential for radon contamination of new construction, including (but not limited to) consideration of the moisture content of soil, porosity of soil, and radon content of soil; and

"(B) design measures to avoid indoor air pollution; and

"(6) the dissemination of information to assure the public availability of the findings of the activities under this section.

**"(c) Advisory committees.**—The Administrator shall establish a committee comprised of individuals representing Federal agencies concerned with various aspects of indoor air quality and an advisory group comprised of individuals representing the States, the scientific community, industry, and public interest organizations to assist him in carrying out the research program for radon gas and indoor air quality.

**"(d) Implementation plan.**—Not later than 90 days after the enactment of this Act[Oct. 17, 1986], the Administrator shall submit to the Congress a plan for implementation of the research program under this section. Such plan shall also be submitted to the EPA Science Advisory Board, which shall, within a reasonable period of time, submit its comments on such plan to Congress.

"(e) **Report.**—Not later than 2 years after the enactment of this Act [Oct. 17, 1986], the Administrator shall submit to Congress a report respecting his activities under this section and making such recommendations as appropriate.

**"Sec. 404. Construction of title.**

"Nothing in this title shall be construed to authorize the Administrator to carry out any regulatory program or any activity other than research, development, and related reporting, information dissemination, and coordination activities specified in this title. Nothing in this title shall be construed to limit the authority of the Administrator or of any other agency or instrumentality of the United States under any other authority of law.

**"Sec. 405. Authorizations.**

"There are authorized to be appropriated to carry out the activities under this title and under section 118(k) of the Superfund Amendments and Reauthorization Act of 1986 (relating to radon gas assessment and demonstration program) not to exceed $5,000,000 for each of the fiscal years 1987, 1988, and 1989. Of such sums appropriated in fiscal years 1987 and 1988, two-fifths shall be reserved for the implementation of section 118(k)(2)."

**Railroad Emission Study**

Pub.L. 95–95, Title IV, § 404, Aug. 7, 1977, 91 Stat. 793, as amended H.Res. 549, Mar. 25, 1980, directed the Administrator of the Environmental Protection Agency to conduct a study and investigation of emissions of air pollutants from railroad locomotives, locomotive engines, and secondary power sources on railroad rolling stock in order to determine the extent to which such emissions affect air quality in air quality control regions throughout the United States, the technological feasibility and the current state of technology for controlling such emissions, and the status and effect of current and proposed State and local regulations affecting such emissions, and, within one hundred and eighty days after commencing such study and investigation, to submit a report of such study and investigation, together with recommendations for appropriate legislation, to the Senate Committee on Environment and Public Works and the House Committee on Energy and Commerce.

[Any reference in any provision of law enacted before Jan. 4, 1995, to the Committee on Energy and Commerce of the House of Representatives treated as referring to the Committee on Commerce of the House of Representatives, except that any reference in any provision of law enacted before Jan. 4, 1995, to the Committee on Energy and Commerce of the House of Representatives treated as referring to the Committee on Agriculture of the House of Representatives, in the case of a provision of law relating to inspection of seafood or seafood products, the Committee on Banking and Financial Services of the House of Representatives, in the case of a provision of law relating to bank capital markets activities generally or to depository institution securities activities generally, and the Committee on Transportation and Infrastructure of the House of Representatives, in the case of a provision of law relating to railroads, railway labor, or railroad retirement and unemployment (except revenue measures related thereto), see section 1(a)(4) and (c)(1) of Pub.L. 104–14, set out as a note preceding section 21 of Title 2, The Congress.]

**Spill Control Technology**

Pub.L. 99–499, Title I, § 118(n), Oct. 17, 1986, 100 Stat. 1660, provided that:

"(1) **Establishment of program.**—Within 180 days of enactment of this subsection [Oct. 17, 1986], the Secretary of the United States Department of Energy is directed to carry out a program of testing and evaluation of technologies which may be utilized in responding to liquefied gaseous and other hazardous substance spills at the Liquefied Gaseous Fuels Spill Test Facility that threaten public health or the environment.

"(2) **Technology transfer.**—In carrying out the program established under this subsection, the Secretary shall conduct a technology transfer program that, at a minimum—

"(A) documents and archives spill control technology;

"(B) investigates and analyzes significant hazardous spill incidents;

"(C) develops and provides generic emergency action plans;

"(D) documents and archives spill test results;

"(E) develops emergency action plans to respond to spills;

"(F) conducts training of spill response personnel; and

"(G) establishes safety standards for personnel engaged in spill response activities.

"(3) **Contracts and grants.**—The Secretary is directed to enter into contracts and grants with a nonprofit organization in Albany County, Wyoming, that is capable of providing the necessary technical support and which is involved in environmental activities related to such hazardous substance related emergencies.

"(4) **Use of site.**—The Secretary shall arrange for the use of the Liquefied Gaseous Fuels Spill Test Facility to carry out the provisions of this subsection."

**Study and Report Concerning Economic Approaches to Controlling Air Pollution**

Pub.L. 95–95, Title IV, § 405, Aug. 7, 1977, 91 Stat. 794, directed the Administrator of the Environmental Protection Agency, in conjunction with the Council of Economic Advisors, to undertake a study and assessment of economic measures for the control of air pollution which could strengthen the effectiveness of existing methods of controlling air pollution, provide incentives to abate air pollution to a greater degree than was required by existing provisions of the Clean Air Act, and serve as the primary incentive for controlling air pollution problems not addressed by any provision of the Clean Air Act, and, not later than two years after Aug. 7, 1977, to conclude the study and assessment and submit a report containing the results thereof to the President and to the Congress.

**Study of Odors and Odorous Emissions**

Pub.L. 95–95, Title IV, § 403(b), Aug. 7, 1977, 91 Stat. 792, provided that the Administrator of the Environmental Protection Agency conduct a study and report to the Congress not later than Jan. 1, 1979, on the effects on public health and welfare of odors or odorous emissions, the sources of such emissions, the technology or other measures available for control of such emissions and the costs of such technology or measures, and the costs and benefits of alternative measures or strategies to abate such emissions.

**Study on Regional Air Quality**

Pub.L. 95–95, Title IV, § 403(d), Aug. 7, 1977, 91 Stat. 793, directed the Administrator of the Environmental Protection Agency to conduct a study of air quality in various areas throughout the country including the gulf coast region, with such study to include analysis of liquid and solid aerosols and other fine particulate matter and the contribution of such substances to visibility and public health problems in such areas."

## § 7402. Cooperative activities

[CAA § 102]

### (a) Interstate cooperation; uniform State laws; State compacts

The Administrator shall encourage cooperative activities by the States and local governments for the prevention and control of air pollution; encourage the enactment of improved and, so far as practicable in the light of varying conditions and needs, uniform State and local laws relating to the prevention and control of air pollution; and encourage the making of agreements and compacts between States for the prevention and control of air pollution.

### (b) Federal cooperation

The Administrator shall cooperate with and encourage cooperative activities by all Federal departments and agencies having functions relating to the prevention and control of air pollution, so as to assure the utilization in the Federal air pollution control program of all appropriate and available facilities and resources within the Federal Government.

### (c) Consent of Congress to compacts

The consent of the Congress is hereby given to two or more States to negotiate and enter into agreements or compacts, not in conflict with any law or treaty of the United States, for (1) cooperative effort and mutual assistance for the prevention and control of air pollution and the enforcement of their respective laws relating thereto, and (2) the establishment of such agencies, joint or otherwise, as they may deem desirable for making effective such agreements or compacts. No such agreement or compact shall be binding or obligatory upon any State a party thereto unless and until it has been approved by Congress. It is the intent of Congress that no agreement or compact entered into between States after November 21, 1967, which relates to the control and abatement of air pollution in an air quality control region, shall provide for participation by a State which is not included (in whole or in part) in such air quality control region.

(July 14, 1955, c. 360, Title I, § 102, formerly § 2, as added Dec. 17, 1963, Pub.L. 88–206, § 1, 77 Stat. 393, renumbered § 102, Oct. 20, 1965, Pub.L. 89–272, Title I, § 101(3), 79 Stat. 992, and amended Nov. 21, 1967, Pub.L. 90–148, § 2, 81 Stat. 485; Dec. 31, 1970, Pub.L. 91–604, § 15(c)(2), 84 Stat. 1713.)

### HISTORICAL AND STATUTORY NOTES

**Codifications**

Section was formerly classified to section 1857a of this title.

**Prior Provisions**

Provisions similar to those comprising the first clause of subsec. (a) of this section were contained in subsec. (b)(1) of a prior section 1857a of this title, Act July 14, 1955, c. 360, § 2, 69 Stat. 322, prior to the general amendment of this chapter by Pub.L. 88–206.

## § 7403. Research, investigation, training, and other activities

[CAA § 103]

### (a) Research and development program for prevention and control of air pollution

The Administrator shall establish a national research and development program for the prevention and control of air pollution and as part of such program shall—

(1) conduct, and promote the coordination and acceleration of, research, investigations, experiments, demonstrations, surveys, and studies relating to the causes, effects (including health and welfare effects), extent, prevention, and control of air pollution;

(2) encourage, cooperate with, and render technical services and provide financial assistance to air pollution control agencies and other appropriate public or private agencies, institutions, and organizations, and individuals in the conduct of such activities;

(3) conduct investigations and research and make surveys concerning any specific problem of air pollution in cooperation with any air pollution control agency with a view to recommending a solution of such problem, if he is requested to do so by such agency or if, in his judgment, such problem may affect any community or communities in a State other than that in which the source of the matter causing or contributing to the pollution is located;

(4) establish technical advisory committees composed of recognized experts in various aspects of air pollution to assist in the examination and evaluation of research progress and proposals and to avoid duplication of research, and

(5) conduct and promote coordination and acceleration of training for individuals relating to the causes, effects, extent, prevention, and control of air pollution.

### (b) Authorized activities of Administrator in establishing research and development program

In carrying out the provisions of the preceding subsection the Administrator is authorized to—

(1) collect and make available, through publications and other appropriate means, the results of and other information, including appropriate recommendations by him in connection therewith, pertaining to such research and other activities;

(2) cooperate with other Federal departments and agencies, with air pollution control agencies, with other public and private agencies, institutions, and organizations, and with any industries involved, in the preparation and conduct of such research and other activities;

(3) make grants to air pollution control agencies, to other public or nonprofit private agencies, institutions, and organizations, and to individuals, for purposes stated in subsection (a)(1) of this section;

(4) contract with public or private agencies, institutions, and organizations, and with individuals, without regard to section 3324(a) and (b) of Title 31 and section 5 of Title 41;

(5) establish and maintain research fellowships, in the Environmental Protection Agency and at public or nonprofit private educational institutions or research organizations;

(6) collect and disseminate, in cooperation with other Federal departments and agencies, and with other public or private agencies, institutions, and organizations having related responsibilities, basic data on chemical, physical, and biological effects of varying air quality and other information pertaining to air pollution and the prevention and control thereof;

(7) develop effective and practical processes, methods, and prototype devices for the prevention or control of air pollution; and

(8) construct facilities, provide equipment, and employ staff as necessary to carry out this chapter.

In carrying out the provisions of subsection (a) of this section, the Administrator shall provide training for, and make training grants to, personnel of air pollution control agencies and other persons with suitable qualifications and make grants to such agencies, to other public or nonprofit private agencies, institutions, and organizations for the purposes stated in subsection (a)(5) of this section. Reasonable fees may be charged for such training provided to persons other than personnel of air pollution control agencies but such training shall be provided to such personnel of air pollution control agencies without charge.

**(c) Air pollutant monitoring, analysis, modeling, and inventory research**

In carrying out subsection (a) of this section, the Administrator shall conduct a program of research, testing, and development of methods for sampling, measurement, monitoring, analysis, and modeling of air pollutants. Such program shall include the following elements:

(1) Consideration of individual, as well as complex mixtures of, air pollutants and their chemical transformations in the atmosphere.

(2) Establishment of a national network to monitor, collect, and compile data with quantification of certainty in the status and trends of air emissions, deposition, air quality, surface water quality, forest condition, and visibility impairment, and to ensure the comparability of air quality data collected in different States and obtained from different nations.

(3) Development of improved methods and technologies for sampling, measurement, monitoring, analysis, and modeling to increase understanding of the sources of ozone percursors [1], ozone formation, ozone transport, regional influences on urban ozone, regional ozone trends, and interactions of ozone with other pollutants. Emphasis shall be placed on those techniques which—

(A) improve the ability to inventory emissions of volatile organic compounds and nitrogen oxides that contribute to urban air pollution, including anthropogenic and natural sources;

(B) improve the understanding of the mechanism through which anthropogenic and biogenic volatile organic compounds react to form ozone and other oxidants; and

(C) improve the ability to identify and evaluate region-specific prevention and control options for ozone pollution.

(4) Submission of periodic reports to the Congress, not less than once every 5 years, which evaluate and assess the effectiveness of air pollution control regulations and programs using monitoring and modeling data obtained pursuant to this subsection.

**(d) Environmental health effects research**

(1) The Administrator, in consultation with the Secretary of Health and Human Services, shall conduct a research program on the short-term and long-term effects of air pollutants, including wood smoke, on human health. In conducting such research program the Administrator—

(A) shall conduct studies, including epidemiological, clinical, and laboratory and field studies, as necessary to identify and evaluate exposure to and effects of air pollutants on human health;

(B) may utilize, on a reimbursable basis, the facilities of existing Federal scientific laboratories and research centers; and

(C) shall consult with other Federal agencies to ensure that similar research being conducted in other agencies is coordinated to avoid duplication.

(2) In conducting the research program under this subsection, the Administrator shall develop methods and techniques necessary to identify and assess the risks to human health from both routine and accidental exposures to individual air pollutants and combinations thereof. Such research program shall include the following elements:

(A) The creation of an Interagency Task Force to coordinate such program. The Task Force shall include representatives of the National Institute for Environmental Health Sciences, the Environmental Protection Agency, the Agency for Toxic Substances and Disease Registry, the National Toxicology Program, the National Institute of Standards and Technology, the National Science Foundation, the Surgeon General, and the Department of Energy. This Interagency Task Force shall be chaired by a representative of the Environmental Protection Agency and shall convene its first meeting within 60 days after November 15, 1990.

(B) An evaluation, within 12 months after November 15, 1990, of each of the hazardous air pollutants listed under section 7412(b) of this title, to decide, on the basis of available information, their relative priority for preparation of environmental health assessments pursuant to subparagraph (C). The evaluation shall be based on reasonably anticipated toxicity to humans and exposure factors such as frequency of occurrence as an air pollutant and volume of emissions in populated areas. Such evaluation shall be reviewed by the Interagency Task Force established pursuant to subparagraph (A).

(C) Preparation of environmental health assessments for each of the hazardous air pollutants referred to in subparagraph (B), beginning 6 months after the first meeting of the Interagency Task Force and to be completed within 96 months thereafter. No fewer than 24 assessments shall be completed and published annually. The assessments shall be prepared in accordance with guidelines developed by the Administrator in consultation with the Interagency Task Force and the Science Advisory Board of the Environmental Protection Agency. Each such assessment shall include—

(i) an examination, summary, and evaluation of available toxicological and epidemiological information for the pollutant to ascertain the levels of human exposure which pose a significant threat to human health and the associated acute, subacute, and chronic adverse health effects;

(ii) a determination of gaps in available information related to human health effects and exposure levels; and

(iii) where appropriate, an identification of additional activities, including toxicological and inhalation testing, needed to identify the types or levels of exposure which may present significant risk of adverse health effects in humans.

**(e) Ecosystem research**

In carrying out subsection (a) of this section, the Administrator, in cooperation, where appropriate, with the Under Secretary of Commerce for Oceans and Atmosphere, the Director of the Fish and Wildlife Service, and the Secretary of Agriculture, shall conduct a research program to improve understanding of the short-term and long-term causes, effects, and trends of ecosystems damage from air pollutants on ecosystems. Such program shall include the following elements:

(1) Identification of regionally representative and critical ecosystems for research.

(2) Evaluation of risks to ecosystems exposed to air pollutants, including characterization of the causes and effects of chronic and episodic exposures to air pollutants and determination of the reversibility of those effects.

(3) Development of improved atmospheric dispersion models and monitoring systems and networks for evaluating and quantifying exposure to and effects of multiple environmental stresses associated with air pollution.

(4) Evaluation of the effects of air pollution on water quality, including assessments of the short-term and long-term ecological effects of acid deposition and other atmospherically derived pollutants on surface water (including wetlands and estuaries) and groundwater.

(5) Evaluation of the effects of air pollution on forests, materials, crops, biological diversity, soils, and other terrestrial and aquatic systems exposed to air pollutants.

(6) Estimation of the associated economic costs of ecological damage which have occurred as a result of exposure to air pollutants.

Consistent with the purpose of this program, the Administrator may use the estuarine research reserves established pursuant to section 1461 of Title 16 to carry out this research.

**(f) Liquefied Gaseous Fuels Spill Test Facility**

(1) The Administrator, in consultation with the Secretary of Energy and the Federal Coordinating Council for Science, Engineering, and Technology, shall oversee an experimental and analytical research effort, with the experimental research to be carried out at the Liquefied Gaseous Fuels Spill Test Facility. In consultation with the Secretary of Energy, the Administrator shall develop a list of chemicals and a schedule for field testing at the Facility. Analysis of a minimum of 10 chemicals per year shall be carried out, with the selection of a minimum of 2 chemicals for

field testing each year. Highest priority shall be given to those chemicals that would present the greatest potential risk to human health as a result of an accidental release—

(A) from a fixed site; or

(B) related to the transport of such chemicals.

(2) The purpose of such research shall be to—

(A) develop improved predictive models for atmospheric dispersion which at a minimum—

(i) describe dense gas releases in complex terrain including man-made structures or obstacles with variable winds;

(ii) improve understanding of the effects of turbulence on dispersion patterns; and

(iii) consider realistic behavior of aerosols by including physicochemical reactions with water vapor, ground deposition, and removal by water spray;

(B) evaluate existing and future atmospheric dispersion models by—

(i) the development of a rigorous, standardized methodology for dense gas models; and

(ii) the application of such methodology to current dense gas dispersion models using data generated from field experiments; and

(C) evaluate the effectiveness of hazard mitigation and emergency response technology for fixed site and transportation related accidental releases of toxic chemicals.

Models pertaining to accidental release shall be evaluated and improved periodically for their utility in planning and implementing evacuation procedures and other mitigative strategies designed to minimize human exposure to hazardous air pollutants released accidentally.

(3) The Secretary of Energy shall make available to interested persons (including other Federal agencies and businesses) the use of the Liquefied Gaseous Fuels Spill Test Facility to conduct research and other activities in connection with the activities described in this subsection.

### (g) Pollution prevention and emissions control

In carrying out subsection (a) of this section, the Administrator shall conduct a basic engineering research and technology program to develop, evaluate, and demonstrate nonregulatory strategies and technologies for air pollution prevention. Such strategies and technologies shall be developed with priority on those pollutants which pose a significant risk to human health and the environment, and with opportunities for participation by industry, public interest groups, scientists, and other interested persons in the development of such strategies and technologies. Such program shall include the following elements:

(1) Improvements in nonregulatory strategies and technologies for preventing or reducing multiple air pollutants, including sulfur oxides, nitrogen oxides, heavy metals, PM–10 (particulate matter), carbon monoxide, and carbon dioxide, from stationary sources, including fossil fuel power plants. Such strategies and technologies shall include improvements in the relative cost effectiveness and long-range implications of various air pollutant reduction and nonregulatory control strategies such as energy conservation, including end-use efficiency, and fuel-switching to cleaner fuels. Such strategies and technologies shall be considered for existing and new facilities.

(2) Improvements in nonregulatory strategies and technologies for reducing air emissions from area sources.

(3) Improvements in nonregulatory strategies and technologies for preventing, detecting, and correcting accidental releases of hazardous air pollutants.

(4) Improvements in nonregulatory strategies and technologies that dispose of tires in ways that avoid adverse air quality impacts.

Nothing in this subsection shall be construed to authorize the imposition on any person of air pollution control requirements. The Administrator shall consult with other appropriate Federal agencies to ensure coordination and to avoid duplication of activities authorized under this subsection.

### (h) NIEHS studies

(1) The Director of the National Institute of Environmental Health Sciences may conduct a program of basic research to identify, characterize, and quantify risks to human health from air pollutants. Such research shall be conducted primarily through a combination of university and medical school-based grants, as well as through intramural studies and contracts.

(2) The Director of the National Institute of Environmental Health Sciences shall conduct a program for the education and training of physicians in environmental health.

(3) The Director shall assure that such programs shall not conflict with research undertaken by the Administrator.

(4) There are authorized to be appropriated to the National Institute of Environmental Health Sciences such sums as may be necessary to carry out the purposes of this subsection.

### (i) Coordination of research

The Administrator shall develop and implement a plan for identifying areas in which activities authorized under this section can be carried out in conjunction with other Federal ecological and air pollution research efforts. The plan, which shall be submitted to Congress within 6 months after November 15, 1990, shall include—

(1) an assessment of ambient monitoring stations and networks to determine cost effective ways to expand monitoring capabilities in both urban and rural environments;

(2) a consideration of the extent of the feasibility and scientific value of conducting the research program under subsection (e) of this section to include consideration of the effects of atmospheric processes and air pollution effects; and

(3) a methodology for evaluating and ranking pollution prevention technologies, such as those developed under subsection (g) of this section, in terms of their ability to reduce cost effectively the emissions of air pollutants and other airborne chemicals of concern.

Not later than 2 years after November 15, 1990, and every 4 years thereafter, the Administrator shall report to Congress on the progress made in implementing the plan developed under this subsection, and shall include in such report any revisions of the plan.

**(j) Continuation of national acid precipitation assessment program**

(1) The acid precipitation research program set forth in the Acid Precipitation Act of 1980 [42 U.S.C.A. § 8901 et seq.] shall be continued with modifications pursuant to this subsection.

(2) The Acid Precipitation Task Force shall consist of the Administrator of the Environmental Protection Agency, the Secretary of Energy, the Secretary of the Interior, the Secretary of Agriculture, the Administrator of the National Oceanic and Atmospheric Administration, the Administrator of the National Aeronautics and Space Administration, and such additional members as the President may select. The President shall appoint a chairman for the Task Force from among its members within 30 days after November 15, 1990.

(3) The responsibilities of the Task Force shall include the following:

(A) Review of the status of research activities conducted to date under the comprehensive research plan developed pursuant to the Acid Precipitation Act of 1980 [42 U.S.C.A. § 8901 et seq.], and development of a revised plan that identifies significant research gaps and establishes a coordinated program to address current and future research priorities. A draft of the revised plan shall be submitted by the Task Force to Congress within 6 months after November 15, 1990. The plan shall be available for public comment during the 60 day period after its submission, and a final plan shall be submitted by the President to the Congress within 45 days after the close of the comment period.

(B) Coordination with participating Federal agencies, augmenting the agencies' research and monitoring efforts and sponsoring additional research in the scientific community as necessary to ensure the availability and quality of data and methodologies needed to evaluate the status and effectiveness of the acid deposition control program. Such research and monitoring efforts shall include, but not be limited to—

(i) continuous monitoring of emissions of precursors of acid deposition;

(ii) maintenance, upgrading, and application of models, such as the Regional Acid Deposition Model, that describe the interactions of emissions with the atmosphere, and models that describe the response of ecosystems to acid deposition; and

(iii) analysis of the costs, benefits, and effectiveness of the acid deposition control program.

(C) Publication and maintenance of a National Acid Lakes Registry that tracks the condition and change over time of a statistically representative sample of lakes in regions that are known to be sensitive to surface water acidification.

(D) Submission every two years of a unified budget recommendation to the President for activities of the Federal Government in connection with the research program described in this subsection.

(E) Beginning in 1992 and biennially thereafter, submission of a report to Congress describing the results of its investigations and analyses. The reporting of technical information about acid deposition shall be provided in a format that facilitates communication with policymakers and the public. The report shall include—

(i) actual and projected emissions and acid deposition trends;

(ii) average ambient concentrations of acid deposition percursors[1] and their transformation products;

(iii) the status of ecosystems (including forests and surface waters), materials, and visibility affected by acid deposition;

(iv) the causes and effects of such deposition, including changes in surface water quality and forest and soil conditions;

(v) the occurrence and effects of episodic acidification, particularly with respect to high elevation watersheds; and

(vi) the confidence level associated with each conclusion to aid policymakers in use of the information.

(F) Beginning in 1996, and every 4 years thereafter, the report under subparagraph (E) shall include—

(i) the reduction in deposition rates that must be achieved in order to prevent adverse ecological effects; and

(ii) the costs and benefits of the acid deposition control program created by subchapter IV–A of this chapter.

## (k) Air pollution conferences

If, in the judgment of the Administrator, an air pollution problem of substantial significance may result from discharge or discharges into the atmosphere, the Administrator may call a conference concerning this potential air pollution problem to be held in or near one or more of the places where such discharge or discharges are occurring or will occur. All interested persons shall be given an opportunity to be heard at such conference, either orally or in writing, and shall be permitted to appear in person or by representative in accordance with procedures prescribed by the Administrator. If the Administrator finds, on the basis of the evidence presented at such conference, that the discharge or discharges if permitted to take place or continue are likely to cause or contribute to air pollution subject to abatement under this part, the Administrator shall send such findings, together with recommendations concerning the measures which the Administrator finds reasonable and suitable to prevent such pollution, to the person or persons whose actions will result in the discharge or discharges involved; to air pollution agencies of the State or States and of the municipality or municipalities where such discharge or discharges will originate; and to the interstate air pollution control agency, if any, in the jurisdictional area of which any such municipality is located. Such findings and recommendations shall be advisory only, but shall be admitted together with the record of the conference, as part of the proceedings under subsections (b), (c), (d), (e), and (f) of section 7408 of this title.

(July 14, 1955, c. 360, Title I, § 103, formerly § 3, as added Dec. 17, 1963, Pub.L. 88–206, § 1, 77 Stat. 394, and renumbered § 103 and amended Oct. 20, 1965, Pub.L. 89–272, Title I, §§ 101(3), 103, 79 Stat. 992, 996; Nov. 21, 1967, Pub.L. 90–148, § 2, 81 Stat. 486; Dec. 31, 1970, Pub.L. 91–604, §§ 2(a), 4(b)(2), 15(a)(2), (c)(2), 84 Stat. 1676, 1689, 1710, 1713; Aug. 7, 1977, Pub.L. 95–95, Title I, § 101(a), (b), 91 Stat. 686, 687; Nov. 15, 1990, Pub.L. 101–549, Title IX, § 901(a) to (c), 104 Stat. 2700 to 2703.)

[1] So in original. Probably should be "precursors".

## HISTORICAL AND STATUTORY NOTES

### References in Text

The Acid Precipitation Act of 1980, referred to in subsec. (j)(1) and (3)(A), is Title VII of Pub.L. 96–294, June 30, 1980, 94 Stat. 770, which is classified generally to chapter 97 (section 8901 et seq.) of this title. For complete classification of this Act to the Code, see Short Title of 1980 Acts note set out under section 8901 of this title and Tables.

### Codifications

Section was formerly classified to section 1857b of this title.

In subsec. (b)(4), "section 3324(a) and (b) of Title 31" was substituted for reference to section 3648 of the Revised Statutes (31 U.S.C. 529) on authority of Pub.L. 97–258, § 4(b), Sept. 13, 1982, 96 Stat. 1067, the first section of which enacted Title 31, Money and Finance.

### Effective and Applicability Provisions

1990 Acts

Amendment by Pub.L. 101–549 effective Nov. 15, 1990, except as otherwise provided, see section 711(b) of Pub.L. 101–549, set out as a note under section 7401 of this title.

1977 Acts

Amendment by Pub.L. 95–95 effective Aug. 7, 1977, except as otherwise expressly provided, see section 406(d) of Pub.L. 95–95, set out as a note under section 7401 of this title.

### Savings Provisions

Suits, actions or proceedings commenced under this chapter as in effect prior to Nov. 15, 1990, not to abate by reason of the taking effect of amendments by Pub.L. 101–549, except as otherwise provided for, see section 711(a) of Pub.L. 101–549, set out as a note under section 7401 of this title.

### Prior Provisions

Provisions similar to those comprising subsec. (a)(3) of this section were contained in subsec. (a) of a prior section 1857b of this title, Act July 14, 1955, c. 360, § 3, 69 Stat. 322, as amended Oct. 9, 1962, Pub.L. 87–761, § 2, 76 Stat. 760, prior to the general amendment of this chapter by Pub.L. 88–206.

Provisions similar to those comprising this section were contained in prior sections 1857a to 1857d of this title, Act July 14, 1955, c. 360, §§ 2 to 5, 69 Stat. 322 (section 1857b as amended Oct. 9, 1962, Pub.L. 87–761, § 2, 76 Stat. 760; section 1857d as amended Sept. 22, 1959, Pub.L. 86–365, § 1, 73 Stat. 646 and Oct. 9, 1962, Pub.L. 87–761, § 1, 76 Stat. 760), prior to the general amendment of this chapter by Pub.L. 88–206.

### Pilot Design Program

Pub.L. 106–246, Div. B, Title II, § 2603, July 13, 2000, 114 Stat. 558, provided that:

"(a) The Administrator of the Environmental Protection Agency shall make a grant for the purpose of carrying out the first year of a 2–year program to implement in five metropolitan areas pilot design programs developed under section 365(a)(2) of the Department of Transportation and Related Agencies Appropriations Act, 2000 (113 Stat. 1028–1029) [Pub.L. 106–69, Title III, § 365(a)(2), Oct. 9, 1999, 113 Stat. 1028, which is not classified to the Code].

"(b) The Administrator shall ensure that each pilot design program is implemented in accordance with recommendations developed by the National Telecommuting and Air Quality Steering Committee, in consultation with the local design teams.

"(c) Grants received under subsection (a) may be used for—

"(1) protocol development in the five metropolitan areas;

"(2) marketing of the telecommute, emissions reduction, pollution credits strategy and recruitment of participating employers; and

"(3) data gathering on emissions reductions.

"(d) In addition to the grant under subsection (a), for the purpose of carrying out the second year of the 2-year program referred to in subsection (a), the administrator shall—

"(1) make a grant of $750,000 to the National Environmental Policy Institute (a nonprofit private entity incorporated under the laws of and located in the District of Columbia); and

"(2) make grants totaling $1,250,000 to local agencies within the five metropolitan areas referred to in subsection (a).

"(e) Not later than 360 days from first day of the second year of the 2-year program referred to in subsection (a), the Administrator shall transmit to Congress a report on the results of the program.

"(f) The Administrator shall carry out this section in collaboration with the Secretary of Transportation.

"(g) There is appropriated to the Department of Transportation, 'Office of the Assistant Secretary for Policy', $2,000,000 to carry out this section . Such amounts shall be transferred to and administered by the Environmental Protection Agency and shall remain available until expended: *Provided,* That the entire amount is designated by the Congress as an emergency requirement pursuant to section 251(b)(2)(A) of the Balanced Budget and Emergency Deficit Control Act of 1985 [2 U.S.C.A. § 901(b)(2)(A)], as amended: *Provided further,* That the entire amount shall be available only to the extent an official budget request for a specific dollar amount, that includes designation of the entire amount of the request as an emergency requirement as defined by such Act, is transmitted by the President to the Congress."

**Assessment of International Air Pollution Control Technologies**

Section 901(e) of Pub.L. 101-549 directed Administrator of the Environmental Protection Agency to conduct a study that compares international air pollution control technologies of selected industrialized countries to determine if there exist air pollution control technologies in countries outside the United States that may have beneficial applications to this Nation's air pollution control efforts, including, with respect to each country studied, the topics of urban air quality, motor vehicle emissions, toxic air emissions, and acid deposition, and within 2 years after Nov. 15, 1990, submit to Congress a report detailing the results of such study.

**Consultation With Committee on Science and Technology of House of Representatives**

Section 101(c) of Pub.L. 95-95 provided that: "The Administrator of the Environmental Protection Agency shall consult with the House Committee on Science and Technology on the environmental and atmospheric research, development, and demonstration aspects of this Act [see Short Title of 1977 Acts note set out under section 7401 of this title]. In addition, the reports and studies required by this Act that relate to research, development, and demonstration issues shall be transmitted to the Committee on Science and Technology at the same time they are made available to other committees of the Congress."

**Modification or Rescission of Rules, Regulations, Orders, Determinations, Contracts, Certifications, Authorizations, Delegations, and Other Actions**

All rules, regulations, orders, determinations, contracts, certifications, authorizations, delegations, or other actions duly issued, made, or taken by or pursuant to Act July 14, 1955, the Clean Air Act, as in effect immediately prior to the date of enactment of Pub.L. 95-95 [Aug. 7, 1977] to continue in full force and effect until modified or rescinded in accordance with Act July 14, 1955, as amended by Pub.L. 95-95 [this chapter], see section 406(b) of Pub.L. 95-95, set out as an Effective Date of 1977 Acts note under section 7401 of this title.

**National Acid Lakes Registry**

Section 405 of Pub.L. 101-549 provided that: "The Administrator of the Environmental Protection Agency shall create a National Acid Lakes Registry that shall list, to the extent practical, all lakes that are known to be acidified due to acid deposition, and shall publish such list within one year of the enactment of this Act [Nov. 15, 1990]. Lakes shall be added to the registry as they become acidic or as data becomes available to show they are acidic. Lakes shall be deleted from the registry as they become nonacidic."

**Study of Substances Discharged From Exhausts of Motor Vehicles**

Pub.L. 86-493, June 8, 1960, 74 Stat. 162, directed the Surgeon General of the Public Health Service to conduct a thorough study for the purposes of determining, with respect to the various substances discharged from the exhausts of motor vehicles, the amounts and kinds of such substances which, from the standpoint of human health, it is safe for motor vehicles to discharge into the atmosphere under the various conditions under which such vehicles may operate. Not later than two years after June 8, 1960, the Surgeon General was required to submit to Congress a report on the results of the study, together with such recommendations, if any, based upon the findings made in such study, as he deemed necessary for the protection of the public health.

**Termination of Advisory Committees**

Advisory Committees in existence on Jan. 5, 1973, to terminate not later than the expiration of the two-year period following Jan. 5, 1973, unless, in the case of a committee established by the President or an officer of the Federal Government, such committee is renewed by appropriate action prior to the expiration of such two-year period, or in the case of a committee established by the Congress, its duration is otherwise provided by law, see section 14 of Pub.L. 92-463, Oct. 6, 1972, 86 Stat. 776, set out in Appendix 2 to Title 5, Government Organization and Employees.

**Western States Acid Deposition Research**

Section 901(g) of Pub.L. 101-549 provided that:

"(1) The Administrator of the Environmental Protection Agency shall sponsor monitoring and research and submit to Congress annual and periodic assessment reports on—

"(A) the occurrence and effects of acid deposition on surface waters located in that part of the United States west of the Mississippi River;

"(B) the occurrence and effects of acid deposition on high elevation ecosystems (including forests, and surface waters); and

"(C) the occurrence and effects of episodic acidification, particularly with respect to high elevation watersheds.

"(2) The Administrator of the Environmental Protection Agency shall analyze data generated from the studies conducted under paragraph (1), data from the Western Lakes Survey, and other appropriate research and utilize predictive modeling techniques that take into account the unique geographic, climatological, and atmospheric conditions which exist in the western United States to determine the potential occurrence and effects of acid deposition due to any projected increases in the emission of sulfur dioxide and nitrogen oxides in that part of the United States located west of the Mississippi River. The Administrator shall include the results of the project conducted under this paragraph in the reports issued to Congress under paragraph (1)."

## § 7404. Research relating to fuels and vehicles

### [CAA § 104]

### (a) Research programs; grants; contracts; pilot and demonstration plants; byproducts research

The Administrator shall give special emphasis to research and development into new and improved methods, having industry-wide application, for the prevention and control of air pollution resulting from the combustion of fuels. In furtherance of such research and development he shall—

(1) conduct and accelerate research programs directed toward development of improved, cost-effective techniques for—

(A) control of combustion byproducts of fuels,

(B) removal of potential air pollutants from fuels prior to combustion,

(C) control of emissions from the evaporation of fuels,

(D) improving the efficiency of fuels combustion so as to decrease atmospheric emissions, and

(E) producing synthetic or new fuels which, when used, result in decreased atmospheric emissions.

(2) provide for Federal grants to public or nonprofit agencies, institutions, and organizations and to individuals, and contracts with public or private agencies, institutions, or persons, for payment of (A) part of the cost of acquiring, constructing, or otherwise securing for research and development purposes, new or improved devices or methods having industrywide application of preventing or controlling discharges into the air of various types of pollutants; (B) part of the cost of programs to develop low emission alternatives to the present internal combustion engine; (C) the cost to purchase vehicles and vehicle engines, or portions thereof, for research, development, and testing purposes; and (D) carrying out the other provisions of this section, without regard to section 3324(a) and (b) of Title 31 and section 5 of Title 41: *Provided,* That research or demonstration contracts awarded pursuant to this subsection (including contracts for construction) may be made in accordance with, and subject to the limitations provided with respect to research contracts of the military departments in, section 2353 of Title 10, except that the determination, approval, and certification required thereby shall be made by the Administrator; *Provided further,* That no grant may be made under this paragraph in excess of $1,500,000;

(3) determine, by laboratory and pilot plant testing, the results of air pollution research and studies in order to develop new or improved processes and plant designs to the point where they can be demonstrated on a large and practical scale;

(4) construct, operate, and maintain, or assist in meeting the cost of the construction, operation, and maintenance of new or improved demonstration plants or processes which have promise of accomplishing the purposes of this chapter;

(5) study new or improved methods for the recovery and marketing of commercially valuable byproducts resulting from the removal of pollutants.

### (b) Powers of Administrator in establishing research and development programs

In carrying out the provisions of this section, the Administrator may—

(1) conduct and accelerate research and development of cost-effective instrumentation techniques to facilitate determination of quantity and quality of air pollutant emissions, including, but not limited to, automotive emissions;

(2) utilize, on a reimbursable basis, the facilities of existing Federal scientific laboratories;

(3) establish and operate necessary facilities and test sites at which to carry on the research, testing, development, and programming necessary to effectuate the purposes of this section;

(4) acquire secret processes, technical data, inventions, patent applications, patents, licenses, and an interest in lands, plants, and facilities, and other property or rights by purchase, license, lease, or donation; and

(5) cause on-site inspections to be made of promising domestic and foreign projects, and cooperate and participate in their development in instances in which the purposes of the chapter will be served thereby.

### (c) Clean alternative fuels

The Administrator shall conduct a research program to identify, characterize, and predict air emissions related to the production, distribution, storage, and use of clean alternative fuels to determine the risks and benefits to human health and the environment relative to those from using conventional gasoline and diesel fuels. The Administrator shall consult with other Federal agencies to ensure coordination and to avoid duplication of activities authorized under this subsection.

(July 14, 1955, c. 360, Title I, § 104, as added Nov. 21, 1967, Pub.L. 90–148, § 2, 81 Stat. 487, and amended Dec. 5, 1969, Pub.L. 91–137, 83 Stat. 283; Dec. 31, 1970, Pub.L. 91–604, §§ 2(b), (c), 13(a), 15(c)(2), 84 Stat. 1676, 1677, 1709, 1713; Apr. 9, 1973, Pub.L. 93–15, § 1(a), 87 Stat. 11; June 22, 1974, Pub.L. 93–319, § 13(a), 88 Stat. 265; Sept. 13, 1982, Pub.L. 97–258, § 4(b), 96 Stat. 1067; Nov. 15, 1990, Pub.L. 101–549, Title IX, § 901(d), 104 Stat. 2706.)

### HISTORICAL AND STATUTORY NOTES

**Codifications**

Section was formerly classified to section 1857b–1 of this title.

In subsec. (a)(2), "section 3324(a) and (b) of Title 31" was substituted for reference to section 3648 of the Revised Statutes (31 U.S.C. 529) on authority of Pub.L. 97–258, § 4(b), Sept. 13, 1982, 96 Stat. 1067, the first section of which enacted Title 31, Money and Finance.

**Effective and Applicability Provisions**

1990 Acts

Amendment by Pub.L. 101–549 effective Nov. 15, 1990, except as otherwise provided, see section 711(b) of Pub.L. 101–549, set out as a note under section 7401 of this title.

**Savings Provisions**

Suits, actions or proceedings commenced under this chapter as in effect prior to Nov. 15, 1990, not to abate by reason of the taking effect of amendments by Pub.L. 101–549, except as otherwise provided for, see section 711(a) of Pub.L. 101–549, set out as a note under section 7401 of this title.

**Prior Provisions**

A prior section 104 of Act July 14, 1955, was renumbered section 105 by Pub.L. 90–148 and is set out as section 7405 of this title.

**Combustion of Contaminated Used Oil in Ships**

Section 813 of Pub.L. 101–549 provided that: "Within 2 years after the enactment of the Clean Air Act Amendments of 1990 [Nov. 15, 1990], the Administrator of the Environmental Protection Agency shall complete a study and submit a report to Congress evaluating the health and environmental impacts of the combustion of contaminated used oil in ships, the reasons for using such oil for such purposes, the alternatives to such use, the costs of such alternatives, and other relevant factors and impacts. In preparing such study, the Administrator shall obtain the view and comments of all interested persons and shall consult with the Secretary of Transportation and the Secretary of the department in which the Coast Guard is operating."

**Extension to Aug. 31, 1970 of Authorization Period for Fiscal Year 1970**

Pub.L. 91–316, July 10, 1970, 84 Stat. 416, provided in part that the authorization contained in section 104(c) of the Clean Air Act [subsec. (c) of this section] for the fiscal year ending June 30, 1970, should remain available through Aug. 31, 1970, notwithstanding any provisions of this section.

**Hydrogen Fuel Cell Vehicle Study and Test Program**

Section 807 of Pub.L. 101–549 provided that: "The Administrator of the Environmental Protection Agency, in conjunction with the National Aeronautics and Space Administration and the Department of Energy, shall conduct a study and test program on the development of a hydrogen fuel cell electric vehicle. The study and test program shall determine how best to transfer existing NASA hydrogen fuel cell technology into the form of a mass-producible, cost effective hydrogen fuel cell vehicle. Such study and test program shall include at a minimum a feasibility-design study, the construction of a prototype, and a demonstration. This study and test program should be completed and a report submitted to Congress within 3 years after the enactment of the Clean Air Act Amendments of 1990 [Nov. 15, 1990]. This study and test program should be performed in the university or universities which are best exhibiting the facilities and expertise to develop such a fuel cell vehicle."

## § 7405. Grants for support of air pollution planning and control programs

[CAA § 105]

### (a) Amounts; limitations; assurances of plan development capability

**(1)(A)** The Administrator may make grants to air pollution control agencies, within the meaning of paragraph (1), (2), (3), (4), or (5) of section 7602 of this title, in an amount up to three-fifths of the cost of implementing programs for the prevention and control of air pollution or implementation of national primary and secondary ambient air quality standards. For the purpose of this section, "implementing" means any activity related to the planning, developing, establishing, carrying-out, improving, or maintaining of such programs.

**(B)** Subject to subsections (b) and (c) of this section, an air pollution control agency which receives a grant under subparagraph (A) and which contributes less than the required two-fifths minimum shall have 3 years following November 15, 1990, in which to contribute such amount. If such an agency fails to meet and maintain this required level, the Administrator shall reduce the amount of the Federal contribution accordingly.

**(C)** With respect to any air quality control region or portion thereof for which there is an applicable implementation plan under section 7410 of this title, grants under subparagraph (A) may be made only to air pollution control agencies which have substantial responsibilities for carrying out such applicable implementation plan.

**(2)** Before approving any grant under this subsection to any air pollution control agency within the meaning of sections 7602(b)(2) and 7602(b)(4) of this title, the Administrator shall receive assurances that such agency provides for adequate representation of appropriate State, interstate, local, and (when appropriate) international, interests in the air quality control region.

(3) Before approving any planning grant under this subsection to any air pollution control agency within the meaning of sections 7602(b)(2) and 7602(b)(4) of this title, the Administrator shall receive assurances that such agency has the capability of developing a comprehensive air quality plan for the air quality control region, which plan shall include (when appropriate) a recommended system of alerts to avert and reduce the risk of situations in which there may be imminent and serious danger to the public health or welfare from air pollutants and the various aspects relevant to the establishment of air quality standards for such air quality control region, including the concentration of industries, other commercial establishments, population and naturally occurring factors which shall affect such standards.

**(b) Terms and conditions; regulations; factors for consideration; State expenditure limitations**

(1) From the sums available for the purposes of subsection (a) of this section for any fiscal year, the Administrator shall from time to time make grants to air pollution control agencies upon such terms and conditions as the Administrator may find necessary to carry out the purpose of this section. In establishing regulations for the granting of such funds the Administrator shall, so far as practicable, give due consideration to (A) the population, (B) the extent of the actual or potential air pollution problem, and (C) the financial need of the respective agencies.

(2) Not more than 10 per centum of the total of funds appropriated or allocated for the purposes of subsection (a) of this section shall be granted for air pollution control programs in any one State. In the case of a grant for a program in an area crossing State boundaries, the Administrator shall determine the portion of such grant that is chargeable to the percentage limitation under this subsection for each State into which such area extends. Subject to the provisions of paragraph (1) of this subsection, no State shall have made available to it for application less than one-half of 1 per centum of the annual appropriation for grants under this section for grants to agencies within such State.

**(c) Maintenance of effort**

(1) No agency shall receive any grant under this section during any fiscal year when its expenditures of non-Federal funds for recurrent expenditures for air pollution control programs will be less than its expenditures were for such programs during the preceding fiscal year. In order for the Administrator to award grants under this section in a timely manner each fiscal year, the Administrator shall compare an agency's prospective expenditure level to that of its second preceding fiscal year. The Administrator shall revise the current regulations which define applicable nonrecurrent and recurrent expenditures, and in so doing, give due consideration to exempting an agency from the limitations of this paragraph and subsection (a) of this section due to periodic increases experienced by that agency from time to time in its annual expenditures for purposes acceptable to the Administrator for that fiscal year.

(2) The Administrator may still award a grant to an agency not meeting the requirements of paragraph (*l*)[1] of this subsection if the Administrator, after notice and opportunity for public hearing, determines that a reduction in expenditures is attributable to a non-selective reduction in the expenditures in the programs of all Executive branch agencies of the applicable unit of Government. No agency shall receive any grant under this section with respect to the maintenance of a program for the prevention and control of air pollution unless the Administrator is satisfied that such a grant will be so used to supplement and, to the extent practicable, increase the level of State, local, or other non-Federal funds. No grants shall be made under this section until the Administrator has consulted with the appropriate official as designated by the Governor or Governors of the State or States affected.

**(d) Reduction of payments; availability of reduced amounts; reduced amount as deemed paid to agency for purpose of determining amount of grant**

The Administrator, with the concurrence of any recipient of a grant under this section, may reduce the payments to such recipient by the amount of the pay, allowances, traveling expenses, and any other costs in connection with the detail of any officer or employee to the recipient under section 7601 of this title, when such detail is for the convenience of, and at the request of, such recipient and for the purpose of carrying out the provisions of this chapter. The amount by which such payments have been reduced shall be available for payment of such costs by the Administrator, but shall, for the purpose of determining the amount of any grant to a recipient under subsection (a) of this section, be deemed to have been paid to such agency.

**(e) Notice and opportunity for hearing when affected by adverse action**

No application by a State for a grant under this section may be disapproved by the Administrator without prior notice and opportunity for a public hearing in the affected State, and no commitment or obligation of any funds under any such grant may be revoked or reduced without prior notice and opportunity for a public hearing in the affected State (or in one of the affected States if more than one State is affected).

(July 14, 1955, c. 360, Title I, § 105, formerly § 4, as added Dec. 17, 1963, Pub.L. 88–206, § 1, 77 Stat. 395; renumbered § 104 and amended Oct. 20, 1965, Pub.L. 89–272, Title I, § 101(2)–(4), 79 Stat. 992; Oct. 15, 1966, Pub.L. 89–675, § 3, 80 Stat. 954; renumbered § 105 and amended Nov. 21, 1967, Pub.L. 90–148, § 2, 81 Stat. 489; Dec. 31, 1970, Pub.L. 91–604, §§ 3(a), (b)(1), 15(c)(2), 84 Stat. 1677, 1713; Aug. 7, 1977, Pub.L. 95–95, Title I, § 102, Title III, § 305(b), 91 Stat. 687, 776; Nov. 15, 1990, Pub.L. 101–549, Title VIII, § 802(a)–(e), 104 Stat. 2687, 2688.)

1 So in original. Probably should be paragraph "(1)".

### HISTORICAL AND STATUTORY NOTES

**Codifications**

Section was formerly classified to section 1857c of this title.

**Effective and Applicability Provisions**

1990 Acts

Amendment by Pub.L. 101–549 effective Nov. 15, 1990, except as otherwise provided, see section 711(b) of Pub.L. 101–549, set out as a note under section 7401 of this title.

1977 Acts

Amendment by Pub.L. 95–95 effective Aug. 7, 1977, except as otherwise expressly provided, see section 406(d) of Pub.L. 95–95, set out as a note under section 7401 of this title.

**Savings Provisions**

Suits, actions or proceedings commenced under this chapter as in effect prior to Nov. 15, 1990, not to abate by reason of the taking effect of amendments by Pub.L. 101–549, except as otherwise provided for, see section 711(a) of Pub.L. 101–549, set out as a note under section 7401 of this title.

**Prior Provisions**

A prior section 105 of Act July 14, 1955 was renumbered section 108 by Pub.L. 90–148, and is set out as section 7415 of this title.

A prior section 4 of Act July 14, 1955, c. 360, 69 Stat. 322, which was classified to a prior section 1857c of this title, related to the preparation of reports and recommendations prior to the general amendment by Pub.L. 88–206. See section 7403 of this title.

Provisions similar to those comprising subsecs. (a) and (b) of this section were contained in a prior section 1857d of this title, Act July 14, 1955, c. 360, § 5, 69 Stat. 322, as amended Sept. 22, 1959, Pub.L. 86–365, § 1, 73 Stat. 646; Oct. 9, 1962, Pub.L. 87–761, § 1, 76 Stat. 760, prior to the general amendment by Pub.L. 88–206.

**Modification or Rescission of Rules, Regulations, Orders, Determinations, Contracts, Certifications, Authorizations, Delegations, and Other Actions**

All rules, regulations, orders, determinations, contracts, certifications, authorizations, delegations, or other actions duly issued, made, or taken by or pursuant to Act July 14, 1955, the Clean Air Act, as in effect immediately prior to the date of enactment of Pub.L. 95–95 [Aug. 7, 1977] to continue in full force and effect until modified or rescinded in accordance with Act July 14, 1955, as amended by Pub.L. 95–95 [this chapter], see section 406(b) of Pub.L. 95–95, set out as an Effective Date of 1977 Acts note under section 7401 of this title.

## § 7406. Interstate air quality agencies; program cost limitations

**[CAA § 106]**

For the purpose of developing implementation plans for any interstate air quality control region designated pursuant to section 7407 of this title or of implementing section 7506a of this title (relating to control of interstate air pollution) or section 7511c of this title (relating to control of interstate ozone pollution), the Administrator is authorized to pay, for two years, up to 100 per centum of the air quality planning program costs of any commission established under section 7506a of this title (relating to control of interstate air pollution) or section 7511c of this title (relating to control of interstate ozone pollution) or any agency designated by the Governors of the affected States, which agency shall be capable of recommending to the Governors plans for implementation of national primary and secondary ambient air quality standards and shall include representation from the States and appropriate political subdivisions within the air quality control region. After the initial two-year period the Administrator is authorized to make grants to such agency or such commission in an amount up to three-fifths of the air quality implementation program costs of such agency or commission.

(July 14, 1955, c. 360, Title I, § 106, as added Nov. 21, 1967, Pub.L. 90–148, § 2, 81 Stat. 490, and amended Dec. 31, 1970, Pub.L. 91–604, § 3(c), 84 Stat. 1677; Nov. 15, 1990, Pub.L. 101–549, Title I, § 102(f)(2), Title VIII, § 802(f), 104 Stat. 2420, 2688.)

### HISTORICAL AND STATUTORY NOTES

**Codifications**

Section was formerly classified to section 1857c–1 of this title.

**Effective and Applicability Provisions**

1990 Acts

Amendment by Pub.L. 101–549 effective Nov. 15, 1990, except as otherwise provided, see section 711(b) of Pub.L. 101–549, set out as a note under section 7401 of this title.

**Savings Provisions**

Suits, actions or proceedings commenced under this chapter as in effect prior to Nov. 15, 1990, not to abate by reason of the taking effect of amendments by Pub.L. 101–549, except as otherwise provided for, see section 711(a) of Pub.L. 101–549, set out as a note under section 7401 of this title.

**Prior Provisions**

A prior section 106 of Act July 14, 1955, was renumbered section 117 by Pub.L. 91–604 and is set out as section 7417 of this title.

## § 7407. Air quality control regions

**[CAA § 107]**

### (a) Responsibility of each State for air quality; submission of implementation plan

Each State shall have the primary responsibility for assuring air quality within the entire geographic area comprising such State by submitting an implementation plan for such State which will specify the manner in which national primary and secondary ambient air quality standards will be achieved and maintained within each air quality control region in such State.

### (b) Designated regions

For purposes of developing and carrying out implementation plans under section 7410 of this title—

(1) an air quality control region designated under this section before December 31, 1970, or a region designated after such date under subsection (c) of this section, shall be an air quality control region; and

(2) the portion of such State which is not part of any such designated region shall be an air quality control region, but such portion may be subdivided by the State into two or more air quality control regions with the approval of the Administrator.

### (c) Authority of Administrator to designate regions; notification of Governors of affected States

The Administrator shall, within 90 days after December 31, 1970, after consultation with appropriate State and local authorities, designate as an air quality control region any interstate area or major intrastate area which he deems necessary or appropriate for the attainment and maintenance of ambient air quality standards. The Administrator shall immediately notify the Governors of the affected States of any designation made under this subsection.

### (d) Designations

#### (1) Designations generally

##### (A) Submission by Governors of initial designations following promulgation of new or revised standards

By such date as the Administrator may reasonably require, but not later than 1 year after promulgation of a new or revised national ambient air quality standard for any pollutant under section 7409 of this title, the Governor of each State shall (and at any other time the Governor of a State deems appropriate the Governor may) submit to the Administrator a list of all areas (or portions thereof) in the State, designating as—

(i) nonattainment, any area that does not meet (or that contributes to ambient air quality in a nearby area that does not meet) the national primary or secondary ambient air quality standard for the pollutant,

(ii) attainment, any area (other than an area identified in clause (i)) that meets the national primary or secondary ambient air quality standard for the pollutant, or

(iii) unclassifiable, any area that cannot be classified on the basis of available information as meeting or not meeting the national primary or secondary ambient air quality standard for the pollutant.

The Administrator may not require the Governor to submit the required list sooner than 120 days after promulgating a new or revised national ambient air quality standard.

##### (B) Promulgation by EPA of designations

(i) Upon promulgation or revision of a national ambient air quality standard, the Administrator shall promulgate the designations of all areas (or portions thereof) submitted under subparagraph (A) as expeditiously as practicable, but in no case later than 2 years from the date of promulgation of the new or revised national ambient air quality standard. Such period may be extended for up to one year in the event the Administrator has insufficient information to promulgate the designations.

(ii) In making the promulgations required under clause (i), the Administrator may make such modifications as the Administrator deems necessary to the designations of the areas (or portions thereof) submitted under subparagraph (A) (including to the boundaries of such areas or portions thereof). Whenever the Administrator intends to make a modification, the Administrator shall notify the State and provide such State with an opportunity to demonstrate why any proposed modification is inappropriate. The Administrator shall give such notification no later than 120 days before the date the Administrator promulgates the designation, including any modification thereto. If the Governor fails to submit the list in whole or in part, as required under subparagraph (A), the Administrator shall promulgate the designation that the Administrator deems appropriate for any area (or portion thereof) not designated by the State.

(iii) If the Governor of any State, on the Governor's own motion, under subparagraph (A), submits a list of areas (or portions thereof) in the State designated as nonattainment, attainment, or unclassifiable, the Administrator shall act on such designations in accordance with the procedures under paragraph (3) (relating to redesignation).

**(iv)** A designation for an area (or portion thereof) made pursuant to this subsection shall remain in effect until the area (or portion thereof) is redesignated pursuant to paragraph (3) or (4).

**(C) Designations by operation of law**

**(i)** Any area designated with respect to any air pollutant under the provisions of paragraph (1)(A), (B), or (C) of this subsection (as in effect immediately before November 15, 1990) is designated, by operation of law, as a nonattainment area for such pollutant within the meaning of subparagraph (A)(i).

**(ii)** Any area designated with respect to any air pollutant under the provisions of paragraph (1)(E) (as in effect immediately before November 15, 1990) is designated by operation of law, as an attainment area for such pollutant within the meaning of subparagraph (A)(ii).

**(iii)** Any area designated with respect to any air pollutant under the provisions of paragraph (1)(D) (as in effect immediately before November 15, 1990) is designated, by operation of law, as an unclassifiable area for such pollutant within the meaning of subparagraph (A)(iii).

**(2) Publication of designations and redesignations**

**(A)** The Administrator shall publish a notice in the Federal Register promulgating any designation under paragraph (1) or (5), or announcing any designation under paragraph (4), or promulgating any redesignation under paragraph (3).

**(B)** Promulgation or announcement of a designation under paragraph (1), (4) or (5) shall not be subject to the provisions of sections 553 through 557 of Title 5 (relating to notice and comment), except nothing herein shall be construed as precluding such public notice and comment whenever possible.

**(3) Redesignation**

**(A)** Subject to the requirements of subparagraph (E), and on the basis of air quality data, planning and control considerations, or any other air quality-related considerations the Administrator deems appropriate, the Administrator may at any time notify the Governor of any State that available information indicates that the designation of any area or portion of an area within the State or interstate area should be revised. In issuing such notification, which shall be public, to the Governor, the Administrator shall provide such information as the Administrator may have available explaining the basis for the notice.

**(B)** No later than 120 days after receiving a notification under subparagraph (A), the Governor shall submit to the Administrator such redesignation, if any, of the appropriate area (or areas) or portion thereof within the State or interstate area, as the Governor considers appropriate.

**(C)** No later than 120 days after the date described in subparagraph (B) (or paragraph (1)(B)(iii)), the Administrator shall promulgate the redesignation, if any, of the area or portion thereof, submitted by the Governor in accordance with subparagraph (B), making such modifications as the Administrator may deem necessary, in the same manner and under the same procedure as is applicable under clause (ii) of paragraph (1)(B), except that the phrase "60 days" shall be substituted for the phrase "120 days" in that clause. If the Governor does not submit, in accordance with subparagraph (B), a redesignation for an area (or portion thereof) identified by the Administrator under subparagraph (A), the Administrator shall promulgate such redesignation, if any, that the Administrator deems appropriate.

**(D)** The Governor of any State may, on the Governor's own motion, submit to the Administrator a revised designation of any area or portion thereof within the State. Within 18 months of receipt of a complete State redesignation submittal, the Administrator shall approve or deny such redesignation. The submission of a redesignation by a Governor shall not affect the effectiveness or enforceability of the applicable implementation plan for the State.

**(E)** The Administrator may not promulgate a redesignation of a nonattainment area (or portion thereof) to attainment unless—

**(i)** the Administrator determines that the area has attained the national ambient air quality standard;

**(ii)** the Administrator has fully approved the applicable implementation plan for the area under section 7410(k) of this title;

**(iii)** the Administrator determines that the improvement in air quality is due to permanent and enforceable reductions in emissions resulting from implementation of the applicable implementation plan and applicable Federal air pollutant control regulations and other permanent and enforceable reductions;

**(iv)** the Administrator has fully approved a maintenance plan for the area as meeting the requirements of section 7505a of this title; and

**(v)** the State containing such area has met all requirements applicable to the area under section 7410 of this title and part D of this subchapter.

**(F)** The Administrator shall not promulgate any redesignation of any area (or portion thereof) from nonattainment to unclassifiable.

**(4) Nonattainment designations for ozone, carbon monoxide and particulate matter (PM–10)**

**(A) Ozone and carbon monoxide**

**(i)** Within 120 days after November 15, 1990, each Governor of each State shall submit to the Administrator a list that designates, affirms or reaffirms the designation of, or redesignates (as the case may be), all areas (or portions thereof) of the Governor's State as attainment, nonattainment, or unclassifiable with respect to the national ambient air quality standards for ozone and carbon monoxide.

**(ii)** No later than 120 days after the date the Governor is required to submit the list of areas (or portions thereof) required under clause (i) of this subparagraph, the Administrator shall promulgate such designations, making such modifications as the Administrator may deem necessary, in the same manner, and under the same procedure, as is applicable under clause (ii) of paragraph (1)(B), except that the phrase "60 days" shall be substituted for the phrase "120 days" in that clause. If the Governor does not submit, in accordance with clause (i) of this subparagraph, a designation for an area (or portion thereof), the Administrator shall promulgate the designation that the Administrator deems appropriate.

**(iii)** No nonattainment area may be redesignated as an attainment area under this subparagraph.

**(iv)** Notwithstanding paragraph (1)(C)(ii) of this subsection, if an ozone or carbon monoxide nonattainment area located within a metropolitan statistical area or consolidated metropolitan statistical area (as established by the Bureau of the Census) is classified under part D of this subchapter as a Serious, Severe, or Extreme Area, the boundaries of such area are hereby revised (on the date 45 days after such classification) by operation of law to include the entire metropolitan statistical area or consolidated metropolitan statistical area, as the case may be, unless within such 45-day period the Governor (in consultation with State and local air pollution control agencies) notifies the Administrator that additional time is necessary to evaluate the application of clause (v). Whenever a Governor has submitted such a notice to the Administrator, such boundary revision shall occur on the later of the date 8 months after such classification or 14 months after November 15, 1990, unless the Governor makes the finding referred to in clause (v), and the Administrator concurs in such finding, within such period. Except as otherwise provided in this paragraph, a boundary revision under this clause or clause (v) shall apply for purposes of any State implementation plan revision required to be submitted after November 15, 1990.

**(v)** Whenever the Governor of a State has submitted a notice under clause (iv), the Governor, in consultation with State and local air pollution control agencies, shall undertake a study to evaluate whether the entire metropolitan statistical area or consolidated metropolitan statistical area should be included within the nonattainment area. Whenever a Governor finds and demonstrates to the satisfaction of the Administrator, and the Administrator concurs in such finding, that with respect to a portion of a metropolitan statistical area or consolidated metropolitan statistical area, sources in the portion do not contribute significantly to violation of the national ambient air quality standard, the Administrator shall approve the Governor's request to exclude such portion from the nonattainment area. In making such finding, the Governor and the Administrator shall consider factors such as population density, traffic congestion, commercial development, industrial development, meteorological conditions, and pollution transport.

**(B) PM–10 designations**

By operation of law, until redesignation by the Administrator pursuant to paragraph (3)—

**(i)** each area identified in 52 Federal Register 29383 (Aug. 7, 1987) as a Group I area (except to the extent that such identification was modified by the Administrator before November 15, 1990) is designated nonattainment for PM–10;

**(ii)** any area containing a site for which air quality monitoring data show a violation of the national ambient air quality standard for PM–10 before January 1, 1989 (as determined under part 50, appendix K of title 40 of the Code of Federal Regulations) is hereby designated nonattainment for PM–10; and

**(iii)** each area not described in clause (i) or (ii) is hereby designated unclassifiable for PM–10.

Any designation for particulate matter (measured in terms of total suspended particulates) that the Administrator promulgated pursuant to this subsection (as in effect immediately before November 15, 1990) shall remain in effect for purposes of implementing the maximum allowable increases in concentrations of particulate matter (measured in terms of total suspended particulates) pursuant to section 7473(b) of this title, until the Administrator determines that such designation is no longer necessary for that purpose.

(5) **Designations for lead**

The Administrator may, in the Administrator's discretion at any time the Administrator deems appropriate, require a State to designate areas (or portions thereof) with respect to the national ambient air quality standard for lead in effect as of November 15, 1990, in accordance with the procedures under subparagraphs (A) and (B) of paragraph (1), except that in applying subparagraph (B)(i) of paragraph (1) the phrase "2 years from the date of promulgation of the new or revised national ambient air quality standard" shall be replaced by the phrase "1 year from the date the Administrator notifies the State of the requirement to designate areas with respect to the standard for lead".

(6) **Designations**

(A) **Submission**

Notwithstanding any other provision of law, not later than February 15, 2004, the Governor of each State shall submit designations referred to in paragraph (1) for the July 1997 $PM_{2.5}$ national ambient air quality standards for each area within the State, based on air quality monitoring data collected in accordance with any applicable Federal reference methods for the relevant areas.

(B) **Promulgation**

Notwithstanding any other provision of law, not later than December 31, 2004, the Administrator shall, consistent with paragraph (1), promulgate the designations referred to in subparagraph (A) for each area of each State for the July 1997 $PM_{2.5}$ national ambient air quality standards.

(7) **Implementation plan for regional haze**

(A) **In general**

Notwithstanding any other provision of law, not later than 3 years after the date on which the Administrator promulgates the designations referred to in paragraph (6)(B) for a State, the State shall submit, for the entire State, the State implementation plan revisions to meet the requirements promulgated by the Administrator under section 169B(e)(1) (referred to in this paragraph as "regional haze requirements").

(B) **No preclusion of other provisions**

Nothing in this paragraph precludes the implementation of the agreements and recommendations stemming from the Grand Canyon Visibility Transport Commission Report dated June 1996, including the submission of State implementation plan revisions by the States of Arizona, California, Colorado, Idaho, Nevada, New Mexico, Oregon, Utah, or Wyoming by December 31, 2003, for implementation of regional haze requirements applicable to those States.

(e) **Redesignation of air quality control regions**

(1) Except as otherwise provided in paragraph (2), the Governor of each State is authorized, with the approval of the Administrator, to redesignate from time to time the air quality control regions within such State for purposes of efficient and effective air quality management. Upon such redesignation, the list under subsection (d) of this section shall be modified accordingly.

(2) In the case of an air quality control region in a State, or part of such region, which the Administrator finds may significantly affect air pollution concentrations in another State, the Governor of the State in which such region, or part of a region, is located may redesignate from time to time the boundaries of so much of such air quality control region as is located within such State only with the approval of the Administrator and with the consent of all Governors of all States which the Administrator determines may be significantly affected.

(3) No compliance date extension granted under section 7413(d)(5) of this title (relating to coal conversion) shall cease to be effective by reason of the regional limitation provided in section 7413(d)(5) of this title if the violation of such limitation is due solely to a redesignation of a region under this subsection.

(July 14, 1955, c. 360, Title I, § 107, as added Dec. 31, 1970, Pub.L. 91–604, § 4(a), 84 Stat. 1678, and amended Aug. 7, 1977, Pub.L. 95–95, Title I, § 103, 91 Stat. 687; Nov. 15, 1990, Pub.L. 101–549, Title I, § 101(a), 104 Stat. 2399; Jan. 23, 2004, Pub.L. 108–199, Div. G, Title IV, § 425(a), 118 Stat. 417.)

## HISTORICAL AND STATUTORY NOTES

**References in Text**

Section 7413 of this title, referred to in subsec. (e)(3), was amended generally by Pub.L. 101–549, Title VII, § 701, Nov. 15, 1990, 104 Stat. 2672, and, as so amended, subsec. (d) of section 7413 no longer relates to final compliance orders.

**Codifications**

Section was formerly classified to section 1857c–2 of this title.

**Effective and Applicability Provisions**

1990 Acts

Amendment by Pub.L. 101–549 effective Nov. 15, 1990, except as otherwise provided, see section 711(b) of Pub.L. 101–549, set out as a note under section 7401 of this title.

1977 Acts

Amendment by Pub.L. 95–95 effective Aug. 7, 1977, except as otherwise expressly provided, see section 406(d) of Pub.L. 95–95, set out as a note under section 7401 of this title.

**Savings Provisions**

Suits, actions or proceedings commenced under this chapter as in effect prior to Nov. 15, 1990, not to abate by reason of the taking effect of amendments by Pub.L. 101–549, except as otherwise provided for, see section 711(a) of Pub.L. 101–549, set out as a note under section 7401 of this title.

Suits, actions, and other proceedings lawfully commenced by or against the Administrator or any other officer or employee of the United States in his official capacity or in relation to the discharge of his official duties under Act July 14, 1955, the Clean Air Act, as in effect immediately prior to the enactment of Pub.L. 95–95 [Aug. 7, 1977], not to abate by reason of the taking effect of Pub.L. 95–95, see section 406(a) of Pub.L. 95–95, set out as an Effective and Applicability Provisions of 1977 Acts note under section 7401 of this title.

**Prior Provisions**

A prior section 107 of Act July 14, 1955, as added Nov. 21, 1967, Pub.L. 90–148, § 2, 81 Stat. 490, which was classified to section 1857c–2 of this title, related to air quality control regions and was repealed by Pub.L. 91–604.

Another prior section 107 of Act July 14, 1955, as added Dec. 17, 1963, Pub.L. 88–206, § 1, 77 Stat. 399; renumbered § 107, Oct. 25, 1965, Pub.L. 89–272, Title I, § 101(3), 79 Stat. 992; renumbered § 111 and amended Nov. 21, 1967, Pub.L. 90–148, § 2, 81 Stat. 499; renumbered § 118 and amended Dec. 31, 1970, Pub.L. 91–604, §§ 4(a), 5, 84 Stat. 1678, 1689; Aug. 7, 1977, Pub.L. 95–95, Title I, § 116, 91 Stat. 711; Nov. 15, 1990, Pub.L. 101–549, Title I, § 101(e), Title II, § 235, Title III, § 302(d), 104 Stat. 2409, 2530, 2574, is classified to section 7418 of this title.

**Relationship to Transportation Equity Act for the 21st Century**

Pub.L. 108–199, Div. G, Title IV, § 425(b), Jan. 23, 2004, 118 Stat. 417, provided that: "Except as provided in paragraphs (6) and (7) of section 107(d) of the Clean Air Act (as added by subsection (a) [subsec. (d)(6), (7) of this section]), section 6101, subsections (a) and (b) of section 6102, and section 6103 of the Transportation Equity Act for the 21st Century (42 U.S.C. 7407 note; 112 Stat. 463), as in effect on the day before the date of enactment of this Act [Departments of Veterans Affairs and Housing and Urban Development, and Independent Agencies Appropriations Act, 2004, Pub.L. 108–199, Div.G, Jan. 23, 2004, 118 Stat. § 363 was enacted on Jan. 23, 2004, see Tables for complete classification], shall remain in effect."

**Ozone and Particulate Matter Standards**

Pub.L. 105–178, Title VI, June 9, 1998, 112 Stat. 463, provided that:

"**Sec. 6101. Findings and purpose.**

"(a) The Congress finds that—

"(1) there is a lack of air quality monitoring data for fine particle levels, measured as $PM_{2.5}$ in the United States and the States should receive full funding for the monitoring efforts;

"(2) such data would provide a basis for designating areas as attainment or nonattainment for any $PM_{2.5}$ national ambient air quality standards pursuant to the standards promulgated in July 1997;

"(3) the President of the United States directed the Administrator of the Environmental Protection Agency (referred to in this title [this note] as the 'Administrator') in a memorandum dated July 16, 1997, to complete the next periodic review of the particulate matter national ambient air quality standards by July 2002 in order to determine 'whether to revise or maintain the standards';

"(4) the Administrator has stated that 3 years of air quality monitoring data for fine particle levels, measured as $PM_{2.5}$ and performed in accordance with any applicable Federal reference methods, is appropriate for designating areas as attainment or nonattainment pursuant to the July 1997 promulgated standards; and

"(5) the Administrator has acknowledged that in drawing boundaries for attainment and nonattainment areas for the July 1997 ozone national air quality standards, Governors would benefit from considering implementation guidance from EPA on drawing area boundaries.

"(b) The purposes of this title are—

"(1) to ensure that 3 years of air quality monitoring data regarding fine particle levels are gathered for use in the determination of area attainment or nonattainment designations respecting any $PM_{2.5}$ national ambient air quality standards;

"(2) to ensure that the Governors have adequate time to consider implementation guidance from EPA on drawing area boundaries prior to submitting area designations respecting the July 1997 ozone national ambient air quality standards;

"(3) to ensure that the schedule for implementation of the July 1997 revisions of the ambient air quality standards for particulate matter and the schedule for the Environmental Protection Agency's visibility regulations related to regional haze are consistent with the timetable for implementation of such particulate matter standards as set forth in the President's Implementation Memorandum dated July 16, 1997.

"**Sec. 6102. Particulate matter monitoring program.**

"(a) Through grants under section 103 of the Clean Air Act [section 7403 of this title] the Administrator of the Environmental Protection Agency shall use appropriated funds no later than fiscal year 2000 to fund 100 percent of the cost of the establishment, purchase, operation and maintenance of a $PM_{2.5}$ monitoring network necessary to implement the national ambient air quality standards for $PM_{2.5}$ under section 109 of the Clean Air Act. This implementation shall not result in a diversion or reprogramming of funds from other Federal, State or local Clean Air Act activities. Any funds previously diverted or reprogrammed from section 105 Clean Air Act [section 7405 of this title] grants for $PM_{2.5}$ monitors must be restored to State or local air programs in fiscal year 1999.

"(b) EPA and the States, consistent with their respective authorities under the Clean Air Act [Act July 14, 1955, ch. 360, 69 Stat. 322, which is classified generally to section 7401 et seq. of this title], shall ensure that the national network (designated in subsection (a)) which consists of the $PM_{2.5}$ monitors necessary to implement the national ambient air quality standards is established by December 31, 1999.

"(c)(1) The Governors shall be required to submit designations referred to in section 107(d)(1) of the Clean Air Act [subsec. (d)(1) of this section] for each area following promulgation of the July 1997 $PM_{2.5}$ national ambient air quality standard within 1 year after receipt of 3 years of air quality monitoring data performed in accordance with any applicable Federal reference methods for the relevant areas. Only data from the monitoring network designated in subsection (a) and other Federal reference method $PM_{2.5}$ monitors shall be considered for such designations. Nothing in the previous sentence shall be construed as affecting the Governor's authority to designate an area initially as nonattainment, and the Administrator's authority to promulgate the designation of an area as nonattainment, under section 107(d)(1) of the Clean Air Act [subsec. (d)(1) of this section], based on its contribution to ambient air quality in a nearby nonattainment area.

"(2) For any area designated as nonattainment for the July 1997 $PM_{2.5}$ national ambient air quality standard in accordance with the schedule set forth in this section, notwithstanding the time limit prescribed in paragraph (2) of section 169B(e) of the Clean Air Act [section 7492(e)(2) of this title], the Administrator shall require State implementation plan revisions referred to in such paragraph (2) to be submitted at the same time as State implementation plan revisions referred to in section 172 of the Clean Air Act [section 7502 of this title] implementing the revised national ambient air quality standard for fine particulate matter are required to be submitted. For any area designated as attainment or unclassifiable for such standard, the Administrator shall require the State implementation plan revisions referred to in such paragraph (2) to be submitted 1 year after the area has been so designated. The preceding provisions of this paragraph shall not preclude the implementation of the agreements and recommendations set forth in the Grand Canyon Visibility Transport Commission Report dated June 1996.

"**(d)** The Administrator shall promulgate the designations referred to in section 107(d)(1) of the Clean Air Act [subsec. (d)(1) of this section] for each area following promulgation of the July 1997 $PM_{2.5}$ national ambient air quality standard by the earlier of 1 year after the initial designations required under subsection (c)(1) are required to be submitted or December 31, 2005.

"**(e)** The Administrator shall conduct a field study of the ability of the $PM_{2.5}$ Federal Reference Method to differentiate those particles that are larger than 2.5 micrograms in diameter. This study shall be completed and provided to the Committee on Commerce of the House of Representatives and the Committee on Environment and Public Works of the United States Senate no later than 2 years from the date of enactment of this Act [June 9, 1998].

"**Sec. 6103. Ozone designation requirements.**

"**(a)** The Governors shall be required to submit the designations referred to in section 107(d)(1) of the Clean Air Act [subsec. (d)(1) of this section] within 2 years following the promulgation of the July 1997 ozone national ambient air quality standards.

"**(b)** The Administrator shall promulgate final designations no later than 1 year after the designations required under subsection (a) are required to be submitted.

"**Sec. 6104. Additional provisions.**

"Nothing in sections 6101 through 6103 [set out above in this note] shall be construed by the Administrator of Environmental Protection Agency or any court, State, or person to affect any pending litigation or to be a ratification of the ozone or $PM_{2.5}$ standards."

**Modification or Rescission of Rules, Regulations, Orders, Determinations, Contracts, Certifications, Authorizations, Delegations, and Other Actions**

All rules, regulations, orders, determinations, contracts, certifications, authorizations, delegations, or other actions duly issued, made, or taken by or pursuant to Act July 14, 1955, the Clean Air Act, as in effect immediately prior to the date of enactment of Pub.L. 95–95 [Aug. 7, 1977] to continue in full force and effect until modified or rescinded in accordance with Act July 14, 1955, as amended by Pub.L. 95–95 [this chapter], see section 406(b) of Pub.L. 95–95, set out as an Effective and Applicability Provisions of 1977 Acts note under section 7401 of this title.

## § 7408. Air quality criteria and control techniques

[CAA § 108]

### (a) Air pollutant list; publication and revision by Administrator; issuance of air quality criteria for air pollutants

**(1)** For the purpose of establishing national primary and secondary ambient air quality standards, the Administrator shall within 30 days after December 31, 1970, publish, and shall from time to time thereafter revise, a list which includes each air pollutant—

**(A)** emissions of which, in his judgment, cause or contribute to air pollution which may reasonably be anticipated to endanger public health or welfare;

**(B)** the presence of which in the ambient air results from numerous or diverse mobile or stationary sources; and

**(C)** for which air quality criteria had not been issued before December 31, 1970, but for which he plans to issue air quality criteria under this section.

**(2)** The Administrator shall issue air quality criteria for an air pollutant within 12 months after he has included such pollutant in a list under paragraph (1). Air quality criteria for an air pollutant shall accurately reflect the latest scientific knowledge useful in indicating the kind and extent of all identifiable effects on public health or welfare which may be expected from the presence of such pollutant in the ambient air, in varying quantities. The criteria for an air pollutant, to the extent practicable, shall include information on—

**(A)** those variable factors (including atmospheric conditions) which of themselves or in combination with other factors may alter the effects on public health or welfare of such air pollutant;

**(B)** the types of air pollutants which, when present in the atmosphere, may interact with such pollutant to produce an adverse effect on public health or welfare; and

**(C)** any known or anticipated adverse effects on welfare.

**(b) Issuance by Administrator of information on air pollution control techniques; standing consulting committees for air pollutants; establishment; membership**

(1) Simultaneously with the issuance of criteria under subsection (a) of this section, the Administrator shall, after consultation with appropriate advisory committees and Federal departments and agencies, issue to the States and appropriate air pollution control agencies information on air pollution control techniques, which information shall include data relating to the cost of installation and operation, energy requirements, emission reduction benefits, and environmental impact of the emission control technology. Such information shall include such data as are available on available technology and alternative methods of prevention and control of air pollution. Such information shall also include data on alternative fuels, processes, and operating methods which will result in elimination or significant reduction of emissions.

(2) In order to assist in the development of information on pollution control techniques, the Administrator may establish a standing consulting committee for each air pollutant included in a list published pursuant to subsection (a)(1) of this section, which shall be comprised of technically qualified individuals representative of State and local governments, industry, and the academic community. Each such committee shall submit, as appropriate, to the Administrator information related to that required by paragraph (1).

**(c) Review, modification, and reissuance of criteria or information**

The Administrator shall from time to time review, and, as appropriate, modify, and reissue any criteria or information on control techniques issued pursuant to this section. Not later than six months after August 7, 1977, the Administrator shall revise and reissue criteria relating to concentrations of $NO_2$ over such period (not more than three hours) as he deems appropriate. Such criteria shall include a discussion of nitric and nitrous acids, nitrites, nitrates, nitrosamines, and other carcinogenic and potentially carcinogenic derivatives of oxides of nitrogen.

**(d) Publication in Federal Register; availability of copies for general public**

The issuance of air quality criteria and information on air pollution control techniques shall be announced in the Federal Register and copies shall be made available to the general public.

**(e) Transportation planning and guidelines**

The Administrator shall, after consultation with the Secretary of Transportation, and after providing public notice and opportunity for comment, and with State and local officials, within nine months after November 15, 1990, and periodically thereafter as necessary to maintain a continuous transportation-air quality planning process, update the June 1978 Transportation-Air Quality Planning Guidelines and publish guidance on the development and implementation of transportation and other measures necessary to demonstrate and maintain attainment of national ambient air quality standards. Such guidelines shall include information on—

(1) methods to identify and evaluate alternative planning and control activities;

(2) methods of reviewing plans on a regular basis as conditions change or new information is presented;

(3) identification of funds and other resources necessary to implement the plan, including interagency agreements on providing such funds and resources;

(4) methods to assure participation by the public in all phases of the planning process; and

(5) such other methods as the Administrator determines necessary to carry out a continuous planning process.

**(f) Information regarding processes, procedures, and methods to reduce or control pollutants in transportation; reduction of mobile source related pollutants; reduction of impact on public health**

(1) The Administrator shall publish and make available to appropriate Federal, State, and local environmental and transportation agencies not later than one year after November 15, 1990, and from time to time thereafter—

(A) information prepared, as appropriate, in consultation with the Secretary of Transportation, and after providing public notice and opportunity for comment, regarding the formulation and emission reduction potential of transportation control measures related to criteria pollutants and their precursors, including, but not limited to—

(i) programs for improved public transit;

(ii) restriction of certain roads or lanes to, or construction of such roads or lanes for use by, passenger buses or high occupancy vehicles;

(iii) employer-based transportation management plans, including incentives;

(iv) trip-reduction ordinances;

(v) traffic flow improvement programs that achieve emission reductions;

(vi) fringe and transportation corridor parking facilities serving multiple occupancy vehicle programs or transit service;

(vii) programs to limit or restrict vehicle use in downtown areas or other areas of emission concentration particularly during periods of peak use;

(viii) programs for the provision of all forms of high-occupancy, shared-ride services;

(ix) programs to limit portions of road surfaces or certain sections of the metropolitan area to the use of non-motorized vehicles or pedestrian use, both as to time and place;

(x) programs for secure bicycle storage facilities and other facilities, including bicycle lanes, for the convenience and protection of bicyclists, in both public and private areas;

(xi) programs to control extended idling of vehicles;

(xii) programs to reduce motor vehicle emissions, consistent with subchapter II of this chapter, which are caused by extreme cold start conditions;

(xiii) employer-sponsored programs to permit flexible work schedules;

(xiv) programs and ordinances to facilitate non-automobile travel, provision and utilization of mass transit, and to generally reduce the need for single-occupant vehicle travel, as part of transportation planning and development efforts of a locality, including programs and ordinances applicable to new shopping centers, special events, and other centers of vehicle activity;

(xv) programs for new construction and major reconstructions of paths, tracks or areas solely for the use by pedestrian or other non-motorized means of transportation when economically feasible and in the public interest. For purposes of this clause, the Administrator shall also consult with the Secretary of the Interior; and

(xvi) program to encourage the voluntary removal from use and the marketplace of pre-1980 model year light duty vehicles and pre-1980 model light duty trucks.

(B) information on additional methods or strategies that will contribute to the reduction of mobile source related pollutants during periods in which any primary ambient air quality standard will be exceeded and during episodes for which an air pollution alert, warning, or emergency has been declared;

(C) information on other measures which may be employed to reduce the impact on public health or protect the health of sensitive or susceptible individuals or groups; and

(D) information on the extent to which any process, procedure, or method to reduce or control such air pollutant may cause an increase in the emissions or formation of any other pollutant.

(2) In publishing such information the Administrator shall also include an assessment of—

(A) the relative effectiveness of such processes, procedures, and methods;

(B) the potential effect of such processes, procedures, and methods on transportation systems and the provision of transportation services; and

(C) the environmental, energy, and economic impact of such processes, procedures, and methods.

**(g) Assessment of risks to ecosystems**

The Administrator may assess the risks to ecosystems from exposure to criteria air pollutants (as identified by the Administrator in the Administrator's sole discretion).

**(h) RACT/BACT/LAER clearinghouse**

The Administrator shall make information regarding emission control technology available to the States and to the general public through a central database. Such information shall include all control technology information received pursuant to State plan provisions requiring permits for sources, including operating permits for existing sources.

(July 14, 1955, c. 360, Title I, § 108, as added Dec. 31, 1970, Pub.L. 91–604, § 4(a), 84 Stat. 1678, and amended Aug. 7, 1977, Pub.L. 95–95, Title I, §§ 104, 105, Title IV, § 401(a), 91 Stat. 689, 790; Nov. 15, 1990, Pub.L. 101–549, Title I, §§ 108(a) to (c), (*o*), 111, 104 Stat. 2465, 2466, 2469, 2470; Nov. 10, 1998, Pub.L. 105–362, Title XV, § 1501(b), 112 Stat. 3294.)

## HISTORICAL AND STATUTORY NOTES

**Codifications**

Section was formerly classified to section 1857c–3 of this title.

Reference in subsec. (e) in the original to "enactment of the Clean Air Act Amendments of 1989" has been codified as "November 15, 1990" as manifesting Congressional intent in the date of the enactment of Pub.L. 101–549, Nov. 15, 1990, 104 Stat. 2399, popularly known as the Clean Air Act Amendments of 1990.

**Effective and Applicability Provisions**

1990 Acts

Amendment by Pub.L. 101–549 effective Nov. 15, 1990, except as otherwise provided, see section 711(b) of Pub.L. 101–549, set out as a note under section 7401 of this title.

1977 Acts

Amendment by Pub.L. 95–95 effective Aug. 7, 1977, except as otherwise expressly provided, see section 406(d) of Pub.L. 95–95, set out as a note under section 7401 of this title.

**Savings Provisions**

Suits, actions or proceedings commenced under this chapter as in effect prior to Nov. 15, 1990, not to abate by reason of the taking effect of amendments by Pub.L. 101–549, except as otherwise provided for, see section 711(a) of Pub.L. 101–549, set out as a note under section 7401 of this title.

**Prior Provisions**

A prior section 108 of Act July 14, 1955, was renumbered section 115 by Pub.L. 91–604 and is set out as section 7415 of this title.

**Modification or Rescission of Rules, Regulations, Orders, Determinations, Contracts, Certifications, Authorizations, Delegations, and Other Actions**

All rules, regulations, orders, determinations, contracts, certifications, authorizations, delegations, or other actions duly issued, made, or taken by or pursuant to Act July 14, 1955, the Clean Air Act, as in effect immediately prior to the date of enactment of Pub.L. 95–95 [Aug. 7, 1977] to continue in full force and effect until modified or rescinded in accordance with Act July 14, 1955, as amended by Pub.L. 95–95 [this chapter], see section 406(b) of Pub.L. 95–95, set out as an Effective and Applicability Provisions of 1977 Acts note under section 7401 of this title.

## § 7409. National primary and secondary ambient air quality standards

**[CAA § 109]**

### (a) Promulgation

(1) The Administrator—

(A) within 30 days after December 31, 1970, shall publish proposed regulations prescribing a national primary ambient air quality standard and a national secondary ambient air quality standard for each air pollutant for which air quality criteria have been issued prior to such date; and

(B) after a reasonable time for interested persons to submit written comments thereon (but no later than 90 days after the initial publication of such proposed standards) shall by regulation promulgate such proposed national primary and secondary ambient air quality standards with such modifications as he deems appropriate.

(2) With respect to any air pollutant for which air quality criteria are issued after December 31, 1970, the Administrator shall publish, simultaneously with the issuance of such criteria and information, proposed national primary and secondary ambient air quality standards for any such pollutant. The procedure provided for in paragraph (1)(B) of this subsection shall apply to the promulgation of such standards.

### (b) Protection of public health and welfare

(1) National primary ambient air quality standards, prescribed under subsection (a) of this section shall be ambient air quality standards the attainment and maintenance of which in the judgment of the Administrator, based on such criteria and allowing an adequate margin of safety, are requisite to protect the public health. Such primary standards may be revised in the same manner as promulgated.

(2) Any national secondary ambient air quality standard prescribed under subsection (a) of this section shall specify a level of air quality the attainment and maintenance of which in the judgment of the Administrator, based on such criteria, is requisite to protect the public welfare from any known or anticipated adverse effects associated with the presence of such air pollutant in the ambient air. Such secondary standards may be revised in the same manner as promulgated.

### (c) National primary ambient air quality standard for nitrogen dioxide

The Administrator shall, not later than one year after August 7, 1977, promulgate a national primary ambient air quality standard for $NO_2$ concentrations over a period of not more than 3 hours unless, based on the criteria issued under section 7408(c) of this title, he finds that there is no significant evidence that such a standard for such a period is requisite to protect public health.

### (d) Review and revision of criteria and standards; independent scientific review committee; appointment; advisory functions

(1) Not later than December 31, 1980, and at five-year intervals thereafter, the Administrator shall complete a thorough review of the criteria published under section 7408 of this title and the national ambient air quality standards promulgated under this section and shall make such revisions in such criteria and standards and promulgate such new standards as may be appropriate in accordance with section 7408 of this title and subsection (b) of this section. The Administrator may review and revise criteria or promulgate new standards earlier or more frequently than required under this paragraph.

(2)(A) The Administrator shall appoint an independent scientific review committee composed of seven members including at least one member of the National Academy of Sciences, one physician, and one person representing State air pollution control agencies.

(B) Not later than January 1, 1980, and at five-year intervals thereafter, the committee referred to in subparagraph (A) shall complete a review of the criteria published under section 7408 of this title and the national primary and secondary ambient air quality standards promulgated under this section and shall recommend to the Administrator any new national ambient air quality standards and revisions of existing criteria and standards as may be appropriate under section 7408 of this title and subsection (b) of this section.

(C) Such committee shall also (i) advise the Administrator of areas in which additional knowledge is required to appraise the adequacy and basis of existing, new, or revised national ambient air quality standards, (ii) describe the research efforts necessary to provide the required information, (iii) advise the Administrator on the relative contribution to air pollution concentrations of natural as well as anthropogenic activity, and (iv) advise the Administrator of any adverse public health, welfare, social, economic, or energy effects which may result from various strategies for attainment and maintenance of such national ambient air quality standards.

(July 14, 1955, c. 360, Title I, § 109, as added Dec. 31, 1970, Pub.L. 91–604, § 4(a), 84 Stat. 1679, and amended Aug. 7, 1977, Pub.L. 95–95, Title I, § 106, 91 Stat. 691.)

### HISTORICAL AND STATUTORY NOTES

**Codifications**

Section was formerly classified to section 1857c–4 of this title.

**Effective and Applicability Provisions**

1977 Acts

Amendment by Pub.L. 95–95 effective Aug. 7, 1977, except as otherwise expressly provided, see section 406(d) of Pub.L. 95–95, set out as a note under section 7401 of this title.

**Prior Provisions**

A prior section 109 of Act July 14, 1955, was renumbered section 116 by Pub.L. 91–604 and is set out as section 7416 of this title.

**Modification or Rescission of Rules, Regulations, Orders, Determinations, Contracts, Certifications, Authorizations, Delegations, and Other Actions**

All rules, regulations, orders, determinations, contracts, certifications, authorizations, delegations, or other actions duly issued, made, or taken by or pursuant to Act July 14, 1955, the Clean Air Act, as in effect immediately prior to the date of enactment of Pub.L. 95–95 [Aug. 7, 1977] to continue in full force and effect until modified or rescinded in accordance with Act July 14, 1955, as amended by Pub.L. 95–95 [this chapter], see section 406(b) of Pub.L. 95–95, set out as an Effective and Applicability Provisions of 1977 Acts note under section 7401 of this title.

**Role of Secondary Standards**

Pub.L. 101–549, Title VIII, § 817, Nov. 15, 1990, 104 Stat. 2697, provided that:

"(a) **Report.**—The Administrator shall request the National Academy of Sciences to prepare a report to the Congress on the role of national secondary ambient air quality standards in protecting welfare and the environment. The report shall:

"(1) include information on the effects on welfare and the environment which are caused by ambient concentrations of pollutants listed pursuant to section 108 [section 7408 of this title] and other pollutants which may be listed;

"(2) estimate welfare and environmental costs incurred as a result of such effects;

"(3) examine the role of secondary standards and the State implementation planning process in preventing such effects;

"(4) determine ambient concentrations of each such pollutant which would be adequate to protect welfare and the environment from such effects;

"(5) estimate the costs and other impacts of meeting secondary standards; and

"(6) consider other means consistent with the goals and objectives of the Clean Air Act [this chapter] which may be more effective than secondary standards in preventing or mitigating such effects.

"**(b) Submission to Congress; comments; authorization.**—(1) The report shall be transmitted to the Congress not later than 3 years after the date of enactment of the Clean Air Act Amendments of 1990 [Nov. 15, 1990].

"(2) At least 90 days before issuing a report the Administrator shall provide an opportunity for public comment on the proposed report. The Administrator shall include in the final report a summary of the comments received on the proposed report.

"(3) There are authorized to be appropriated such sums as are necessary to carry out this section."

**Termination of Advisory Committees**

Advisory committees established after Jan. 5, 1973, to terminate not later than the expiration of the two-year period beginning on the date of their establishment, unless, in the case of a committee established by the President or an officer of the Federal Government, such committee is renewed by appropriate action prior to the expiration of such two-year period, or in the case of a committee established by the Congress, its duration is otherwise provided for by law, see section 14 of Pub.L. 92–463, Oct. 6, 1972, 86 Stat. 776, set out in Appendix 2 to Title 5, Government Organization and Employees.

## § 7410. State implementation plans for national primary and secondary ambient air quality standards

**[CAA § 110]**

### (a) Adoption of plan by State; submission to Administrator; content of plan; revision; new sources; indirect source review program; supplemental or intermittent control systems

(1) Each State shall, after reasonable notice and public hearings, adopt and submit to the Administrator, within 3 years (or such shorter period as the Administrator may prescribe) after the promulgation of a national primary ambient air quality standard (or any revision thereof) under section 7409 of this title for any air pollutant, a plan which provides for implementation, maintenance, and enforcement of such primary standard in each air quality control region (or portion thereof) within such State. In addition, such State shall adopt and submit to the Administrator (either as a part of a plan submitted under the preceding sentence or separately) within 3 years (or such shorter period as the Administrator may prescribe) after the promulgation of a national ambient air quality secondary standard (or revision thereof), a plan which provides for implementation, maintenance, and enforcement of such secondary standard in each air quality control region (or portion thereof) within such State. Unless a separate public hearing is provided,

each State shall consider its plan implementing such secondary standard at the hearing required by the first sentence of this paragraph.

(2) Each implementation plan submitted by a State under this chapter shall be adopted by the State after reasonable notice and public hearing. Each such plan shall—

(A) include enforceable emission limitations and other control measures, means, or techniques (including economic incentives such as fees, marketable permits, and auctions of emissions rights), as well as schedules and timetables for compliance, as may be necessary or appropriate to meet the applicable requirements of this chapter;

(B) provide for establishment and operation of appropriate devices, methods, systems, and procedures necessary to—

(i) monitor, compile, and analyze data on ambient air quality, and

(ii) upon request, make such data available to the Administrator;

(C) include a program to provide for the enforcement of the measures described in subparagraph (A), and regulation of the modification and construction of any stationary source within the areas covered by the plan as necessary to assure that national ambient air quality standards are achieved, including a permit program as required in parts C and D of this subchapter;

(D) contain adequate provisions—

(i) prohibiting, consistent with the provisions of this subchapter, any source or other type of emissions activity within the State from emitting any air pollutant in amounts which will—

(I) contribute significantly to nonattainment in, or interfere with maintenance by, any other State with respect to any such national primary or secondary ambient air quality standard, or

(II) interfere with measures required to be included in the applicable implementation plan for any other State under part C of this subchapter to prevent significant deterioration of air quality or to protect visibility,

(ii) insuring compliance with the applicable requirements of sections 7426 and 7415 of this title (relating to interstate and international pollution abatement);

(E) provide (i) necessary assurances that the State (or, except where the Administrator deems inappropriate, the general purpose local government or governments, or a regional agency designated by the State or general purpose local governments for such purpose) will have adequate personnel, funding, and authority under State (and, as appropriate, local) law to carry out such implementation plan (and is not prohibited by any provision of Federal or State law from carrying out such implementation plan or portion thereof), (ii) requirements that the State comply with the requirements respecting State boards under section 7428 of this title, and (iii) necessary assurances that, where the State has relied on a local or regional government, agency, or instrumentality for the implementation of any plan provision, the State has responsibility for ensuring adequate implementation of such plan provision;

(F) require, as may be prescribed by the Administrator—

(i) the installation, maintenance, and replacement of equipment, and the implementation of other necessary steps, by owners or operators of stationary sources to monitor emissions from such sources,

(ii) periodic reports on the nature and amounts of emissions and emissions-related data from such sources, and

(iii) correlation of such reports by the State agency with any emission limitations or standards established pursuant to this chapter, which reports shall be available at reasonable times for public inspection;

(G) provide for authority comparable to that in section 7603 of this title and adequate contingency plans to implement such authority;

(H) provide for revision of such plan—

(i) from time to time as may be necessary to take account of revisions of such national primary or secondary ambient air quality standard or the availability of improved or more expeditious methods of attaining such standard, and

(ii) except as provided in paragraph (3)(C), whenever the Administrator finds on the basis of information available to the Administrator that the plan is substantially inadequate to attain the national ambient air quality standard which it implements or to otherwise comply with any additional requirements established under this chapter;

(I) in the case of a plan or plan revision for an area designated as a nonattainment area, meet the applicable requirements of part D of this subchapter (relating to nonattainment areas);

(J) meet the applicable requirements of section 7421 of this title (relating to consultation), section 7427 of this title (relating to public notification), and part C of this subchapter (relating to prevention of significant deterioration of air quality and visibility protection);

(K) provide for—

(i) the performance of such air quality modeling as the Administrator may prescribe for the purpose of predicting the effect on ambient air quality of any emissions of any air pollutant for which the Administrator has established a national ambient air quality standard, and

(ii) the submission, upon request, of data related to such air quality modeling to the Administrator;

**(L)** require the owner or operator of each major stationary source to pay to the permitting authority, as a condition of any permit required under this chapter, a fee sufficient to cover—

(i) the reasonable costs of reviewing and acting upon any application for such a permit, and

(ii) if the owner or operator receives a permit for such source, the reasonable costs of implementing and enforcing the terms and conditions of any such permit (not including any court costs or other costs associated with any enforcement action),

until such fee requirement is superseded with respect to such sources by the Administrator's approval of a fee program under subchapter V of this chapter; and

**(M)** provide for consultation and participation by local political subdivisions affected by the plan.

**(3)(A)** Repealed. Pub.L. 101–549, Title I, § 101(d)(1), Nov. 15, 1990, 104 Stat. 2409

**(B)** As soon as practicable, the Administrator shall, consistent with the purposes of this chapter and the Energy Supply and Environmental Coordination Act of 1974 [15 U.S.C.A. § 791 et seq.], review each State's applicable implementation plans and report to the State on whether such plans can be revised in relation to fuel burning stationary sources (or persons supplying fuel to such sources) without interfering with the attainment and maintenance of any national ambient air quality standard within the period permitted in this section. If the Administrator determines that any such plan can be revised, he shall notify the State that a plan revision may be submitted by the State. Any plan revision which is submitted by the State shall, after public notice and opportunity for public hearing, be approved by the Administrator if the revision relates only to fuel burning stationary sources (or persons supplying fuel to such sources), and the plan as revised complies with paragraph (2) of this subsection. The Administrator shall approve or disapprove any revision no later than three months after its submission.

**(C)** Neither the State, in the case of a plan (or portion thereof) approved under this subsection, nor the Administrator, in the case of a plan (or portion thereof) promulgated under subsection (c) of this section, shall be required to revise an applicable implementation plan because one or more exemptions under section 7418 of this title (relating to Federal facilities), enforcement orders under section 7413(d) of this title, suspensions under subsection (f) or (g) of this section (relating to temporary energy or economic authority), orders under section 7419 of this title (relating to primary nonferrous smelters), or extensions of compliance in decrees entered under section 7413(e) of this title (relating to iron- and steel-producing operations) have been granted, if such plan would have met the requirements of this section if no such exemptions, orders, or extensions had been granted.

**(4)** Repealed. Pub.L. 101–549, Title I, § 101(d)(2), Nov. 15, 1990, 104 Stat. 2409

**(5)(A)(i)** Any State may include in a State implementation plan, but the Administrator may not require as a condition of approval of such plan under this section, any indirect source review program. The Administrator may approve and enforce, as part of an applicable implementation plan, an indirect source review program which the State chooses to adopt and submit as part of its plan.

**(ii)** Except as provided in subparagraph (B), no plan promulgated by the Administrator shall include any indirect source review program for any air quality control region, or portion thereof.

**(iii)** Any State may revise an applicable implementation plan approved under this subsection to suspend or revoke any such program included in such plan, provided that such plan meets the requirements of this section.

**(B)** The Administrator shall have the authority to promulgate, implement and enforce regulations under subsection (c) of this section respecting indirect source review programs which apply only to federally assisted highways, airports, and other major federally assisted indirect sources and federally owned or operated indirect sources.

**(C)** For purposes of this paragraph, the term "indirect source" means a facility, building, structure, installation, real property, road, or highway which attracts, or may attract, mobile sources of pollution. Such term includes parking lots, parking garages, and other facilities subject to any measure for management of parking supply (within the meaning of subsection (c)(2)(D)(ii) of this section), including regulation of existing off-street parking but such term does not include new or existing on-street parking. Direct emissions sources or facilities at, within, or associated with, any indirect source shall not be deemed indirect sources for the purpose of this paragraph.

**(D)** For purposes of this paragraph the term "indirect source review program" means the facility-by-facility review of indirect sources of air pollution, including such measures as are necessary to assure, or assist in assuring, that a new or modified indirect source will not attract mobile sources of air pollution, the emissions from which would cause or contribute to air pollution concentrations—

(i) exceeding any national primary ambient air quality standard for a mobile source-related air pollutant after the primary standard attainment date, or

(ii) preventing maintenance of any such standard after such date.

(E) For purposes of this paragraph and paragraph (2)(B), the term "transportation control measure" does not include any measure which is an "indirect source review program".

(6) No State plan shall be treated as meeting the requirements of this section unless such plan provides that in the case of any source which uses a supplemental, or intermittent control system for purposes of meeting the requirements of an order under section 7413(d) of this title or section 7419 of this title (relating to primary nonferrous smelter orders), the owner or operator of such source may not temporarily reduce the pay of any employee by reason of the use of such supplemental or intermittent or other dispersion dependent control system.

**(b) Extension of period for submission of plans**

The Administrator may, wherever he determines necessary, extend the period for submission of any plan or portion thereof which implements a national secondary ambient air quality standard for a period not to exceed 18 months from the date otherwise required for submission of such plan.

**(c) Preparation and publication by Administrator of proposed regulations setting forth implementation plan; transportation regulations study and report; parking surcharge; suspension authority; plan implementation**

(1) The Administrator shall promulgate a Federal implementation plan at any time within 2 years after the Administrator—

(A) finds that a State has failed to make a required submission or finds that the plan or plan revision submitted by the State does not satisfy the minimum criteria established under subsection (k)(1)(A) of this section, or

(B) disapproves a State implementation plan submission in whole or in part,

unless the State corrects the deficiency, and the Administrator approves the plan or plan revision, before the Administrator promulgates such Federal implementation plan.

(2)(A) Repealed. Pub.L. 101–549, Title I, § 101(d)(3)(A), Nov. 15, 1990, 104 Stat. 2409

(B) No parking surcharge regulation may be required by the Administrator under paragraph (1) of this subsection as a part of an applicable implementation plan. All parking surcharge regulations previously required by the Administrator shall be void upon June 22, 1974. This subparagraph shall not prevent the Administrator from approving parking surcharges if they are adopted and submitted by a State as part of an applicable implementation plan. The Administrator may not condition approval of any implementation plan submitted by a State on such plan's including a parking surcharge regulation.

(C) Repealed. Pub.L. 101–549, Title I, § 101(d)(3)(B), Nov. 15, 1990, 104 Stat. 2409

(D) For purposes of this paragraph—

(i) The term "parking surcharge regulation" means a regulation imposing or requiring the imposition of any tax, surcharge, fee, or other charge on parking spaces, or any other area used for the temporary storage of motor vehicles.

(ii) The term "management of parking supply" shall include any requirement providing that any new facility containing a given number of parking spaces shall receive a permit or other prior approval, issuance of which is to be conditioned on air quality considerations.

(iii) The term "preferential bus/carpool lane" shall include any requirement for the setting aside of one or more lanes of a street or highway on a permanent or temporary basis for the exclusive use of buses or carpools, or both.

(E) No standard, plan, or requirement, relating to management of parking supply or preferential bus/carpool lanes shall be promulgated after June 22, 1974, by the Administrator pursuant to this section, unless such promulgation has been subjected to at least one public hearing which has been held in the area affected and for which reasonable notice has been given in such area. If substantial changes are made following public hearings, one or more additional hearings shall be held in such area after such notice.

(3) Upon application of the chief executive officer of any general purpose unit of local government, if the Administrator determines that such unit has adequate authority under State or local law, the Administrator may delegate to such unit the authority to implement and enforce within the jurisdiction of such unit any part of a plan promulgated under this subsection. Nothing in this paragraph shall prevent the Administrator from implementing or enforcing any applicable provision of a plan promulgated under this subsection.

(4) Repealed. Pub.L. 101–549, Title I, § 101(d)(3)(C), Nov. 15, 1990, 104 Stat. 2409

(5)(A) Any measure in an applicable implementation plan which requires a toll or other charge for the use of a bridge located entirely within one city shall be eliminated from such plan by the Administrator upon application by the Governor of the State, which application shall include a certification by the Governor that he will revise such plan in accordance with subparagraph (B).

**(B)** In the case of any applicable implementation plan with respect to which a measure has been eliminated under subparagraph (A), such plan shall, not later than one year after August 7, 1977, be revised to include comprehensive measures to:

**(i)** establish, expand, or improve public transportation measures to meet basic transportation needs, as expeditiously as is practicable; and

**(ii)** implement transportation control measures necessary to attain and maintain national ambient air quality standards,

and such revised plan shall, for the purpose of implementing such comprehensive public transportation measures, include requirements to use (insofar as is necessary) Federal grants, State or local funds, or any combination of such grants and funds as may be consistent with the terms of the legislation providing such grants and funds. Such measures shall, as a substitute for the tolls or charges eliminated under subparagraph (A), provide for emissions reductions equivalent to the reductions which may reasonably be expected to be achieved through the use of the tolls or charges eliminated.

**(C)** Any revision of an implementation plan for purposes of meeting the requirements of subparagraph (B) shall be submitted in coordination with any plan revision required under part D of this subchapter.

**(d), (e) Repealed. Pub.L. 101-549, Title I, § 101(d)(4), (5), Nov. 15, 1990, 104 Stat. 2409**

**(f) National or regional energy emergencies; determination by President**

**(1)** Upon application by the owner or operator of a fuel burning stationary source, and after notice and opportunity for public hearing, the Governor of the State in which such source is located may petition the President to determine that a national or regional energy emergency exists of such severity that—

**(A)** a temporary suspension of any part of the applicable implementation plan or of any requirement under section 7651j of this title (concerning excess emissions penalties or offsets) may be necessary, and

**(B)** other means of responding to the energy emergency may be inadequate.

Such determination shall not be delegable by the President to any other person. If the President determines that a national or regional energy emergency of such severity exists, a temporary emergency suspension of any part of an applicable implementation plan or of any requirement under section 7651j of this title (concerning excess emissions penalties or offsets) adopted by the State may be issued by the Governor of any State covered by the President's determination under the condition specified in paragraph (2) and may take effect immediately.

**(2)** A temporary emergency suspension under this subsection shall be issued to a source only if the Governor of such State finds that—

**(A)** there exists in the vicinity of such source a temporary energy emergency involving high levels of unemployment or loss of necessary energy supplies for residential dwellings; and

**(B)** such unemployment or loss can be totally or partially alleviated by such emergency suspension.

Not more than one such suspension may be issued for any source on the basis of the same set of circumstances or on the basis of the same emergency.

**(3)** A temporary emergency suspension issued by a Governor under this subsection shall remain in effect for a maximum of four months or such lesser period as may be specified in a disapproval order of the Administrator, if any. The Administrator may disapprove such suspension if he determines that it does not meet the requirements of paragraph (2).

**(4)** This subsection shall not apply in the case of a plan provision or requirement promulgated by the Administrator under subsection (c) of this section, but in any such case the President may grant a temporary emergency suspension for a four month period of any such provision or requirement if he makes the determinations and findings specified in paragraphs (1) and (2).

**(5)** The Governor may include in any temporary emergency suspension issued under this subsection a provision delaying for a period identical to the period of such suspension any compliance schedule (or increment of progress) to which such source is subject under section 1857c–10 of this title, as in effect before August 7, 1977, or section 7413(d) of this title, upon a finding that such source is unable to comply with such schedule (or increment) solely because of the conditions on the basis of which a suspension was issued under this subsection.

**(g) Governor's authority to issue temporary emergency suspensions**

**(1)** In the case of any State which has adopted and submitted to the Administrator a proposed plan revision which the State determines—

**(A)** meets the requirements of this section, and

**(B)** is necessary (i) to prevent the closing for one year or more of any source of air pollution, and (ii) to prevent substantial increases in unemployment which would result from such closing, and

which the Administrator has not approved or disapproved under this section within 12 months of submission of the proposed plan revision, the Governor may issue a temporary emergency suspension of the part of the applicable implementation plan for such State which is proposed to be revised with respect to such source. The determination under subparagraph (B) may not be made with respect to a source which would close without regard to whether or not the proposed plan revision is approved.

(2) A temporary emergency suspension issued by a Governor under this subsection shall remain in effect for a maximum of four months or such lesser period as may be specified in a disapproval order of the Administrator. The Administrator may disapprove such suspension if he determines that it does not meet the requirements of this subsection.

(3) The Governor may include in any temporary emergency suspension issued under this subsection a provision delaying for a period identical to the period of such suspension any compliance schedule (or increment of progress) to which such source is subject under section 1857c–10 of this title as in effect before August 7, 1977, or under section 7413(d) of this title upon a finding that such source is unable to comply with such schedule (or increment) solely because of the conditions on the basis of which a suspension was issued under this subsection.

**(h) Publication of comprehensive document for each State setting forth requirements of applicable implementation plan**

(1) Not later than 5 years after November 15, 1990, and every 3 years thereafter, the Administrator shall assemble and publish a comprehensive document for each State setting forth all requirements of the applicable implementation plan for such State and shall publish notice in the Federal Register of the availability of such documents.

(2) The Administrator may promulgate such regulations as may be reasonably necessary to carry out the purpose of this subsection.

**(i) Modification of requirements prohibited**

Except for a primary nonferrous smelter order under section 7419 of this title, a suspension under subsection (f) or (g) of this section (relating to emergency suspensions), an exemption under section 7418 of this title (relating to certain Federal facilities), an order under section 7413(d) of this title (relating to compliance orders), a plan promulgation under subsection (c) of this section, or a plan revision under subsection (a)(3) of this section, no order, suspension, plan revision, or other action modifying any requirement of an applicable implementation plan may be taken with respect to any stationary source by the State or by the Administrator.

**(j) Technological systems of continuous emission reduction on new or modified stationary sources; compliance with performance standards**

As a condition for issuance of any permit required under this subchapter, the owner or operator of each new or modified stationary source which is required to obtain such a permit must show to the satisfaction of the permitting authority that the technological system of continuous emission reduction which is to be used will enable such source to comply with the standards of performance which are to apply to such source and that the construction or modification and operation of such source will be in compliance with all other requirements of this chapter.

**(k) Environmental Protection Agency action on plan submissions**

**(1) Completeness of plan submissions**

**(A) Completeness criteria**

Within 9 months after November 15, 1990, the Administrator shall promulgate minimum criteria that any plan submission must meet before the Administrator is required to act on such submission under this subsection. The criteria shall be limited to the information necessary to enable the Administrator to determine whether the plan submission complies with the provisions of this chapter.

**(B) Completeness finding**

Within 60 days of the Administrator's receipt of a plan or plan revision, but no later than 6 months after the date, if any, by which a State is required to submit the plan or revision, the Administrator shall determine whether the minimum criteria established pursuant to subparagraph (A) have been met. Any plan or plan revision that a State submits to the Administrator, and that has not been determined by the Administrator (by the date 6 months after receipt of the submission) to have failed to meet the minimum criteria established pursuant to subparagraph (A), shall on that date be deemed by operation of law to meet such minimum criteria.

**(C) Effect of finding of incompleteness**

Where the Administrator determines that a plan submission (or part thereof) does not meet the minimum criteria established pursuant to subparagraph (A), the State shall be treated as not having made the submission (or, in the Administrator's discretion, part thereof).

**(2) Deadline for action**

Within 12 months of a determination by the Administrator (or a determination deemed by operation of law) under paragraph (1) that a State has submitted a plan or plan revision (or, in the Administrator's discretion, part thereof) that meets the minimum criteria established pursuant to paragraph (1), if applicable (or, if those criteria are not applicable, within 12 months of submission of the plan or revision), the Administrator shall act on the submission in accordance with paragraph (3).

**(3) Full and partial approval and disapproval**

In the case of any submittal on which the Administrator is required to act under paragraph (2), the Administrator shall approve such submittal as a whole if it meets all of the applicable requirements of this chapter. If a portion of the plan revision meets all the applicable requirements of this chapter, the Administrator may approve the plan revision in part and disapprove the plan revision in part. The plan revision shall not be treated as meeting the requirements of this chapter until the Administrator approves the entire plan revision as complying with the applicable requirements of this chapter.

**(4) Conditional approval**

The Administrator may approve a plan revision based on a commitment of the State to adopt specific enforceable measures by a date certain, but not later than 1 year after the date of approval of the plan revision. Any such conditional approval shall be treated as a disapproval if the State fails to comply with such commitment.

**(5) Calls for plan revisions**

Whenever the Administrator finds that the applicable implementation plan for any area is substantially inadequate to attain or maintain the relevant national ambient air quality standard, to mitigate adequately the interstate pollutant transport described in section 7506a of this title or section 7511c of this title, or to otherwise comply with any requirement of this chapter, the Administrator shall require the State to revise the plan as necessary to correct such inadequacies. The Administrator shall notify the State of the inadequacies, and may establish reasonable deadlines (not to exceed 18 months after the date of such notice) for the submission of such plan revisions. Such findings and notice shall be public. Any finding under this paragraph shall, to the extent the Administrator deems appropriate, subject the State to the requirements of this chapter to which the State was subject when it developed and submitted the plan for which such finding was made, except that the Administrator may adjust any dates applicable under such requirements as appropriate (except that the Administrator may not adjust any attainment date prescribed under part D of this subchapter, unless such date has elapsed).

**(6) Corrections**

Whenever the Administrator determines that the Administrator's action approving, disapproving, or promulgating any plan or plan revision (or part thereof), area designation, redesignation, classification, or reclassification was in error, the Administrator may in the same manner as the approval, disapproval, or promulgation revise such action as appropriate without requiring any further submission from the State. Such determination and the basis thereof shall be provided to the State and public.

**(*l*) Plan revisions**

Each revision to an implementation plan submitted by a State under this chapter shall be adopted by such State after reasonable notice and public hearing. The Administrator shall not approve a revision of a plan if the revision would interfere with any applicable requirement concerning attainment and reasonable further progress (as defined in section 7501 of this title), or any other applicable requirement of this chapter.

**(m) Sanctions**

The Administrator may apply any of the sanctions listed in section 7509(b) of this title at any time (or at any time after) the Administrator makes a finding, disapproval, or determination under paragraphs (1) through (4), respectively, of section 7509(a) of this title in relation to any plan or plan item (as that term is defined by the Administrator) required under this chapter, with respect to any portion of the State the Administrator determines reasonable and appropriate, for the purpose of ensuring that the requirements of this chapter relating to such plan or plan item are met. The Administrator shall, by rule, establish criteria for exercising his authority under the previous sentence with respect to any deficiency referred to in section 7509(a) of this title to ensure that, during the 24–month period following the finding, disapproval, or determination referred to in section 7509(a) of this title, such sanctions are not applied on a statewide basis where one or more political subdivisions covered by the applicable implementation plan are principally responsible for such deficiency.

**(n) Savings clauses**

**(1) Existing plan provisions**

Any provision of any applicable implementation plan that was approved or promulgated by the Administrator pursuant to this section as in effect before November 15, 1990, shall remain in effect as part of such applicable implementation plan, except to the extent that a revision to such provision is approved or promulgated by the Administrator pursuant to this chapter.

**(2) Attainment dates**

For any area not designated nonattainment, any plan or plan revision submitted or required to be submitted by a State—

**(A)** in response to the promulgation or revision of a national primary ambient air quality standard in effect on November 15, 1990, or

**(B)** in response to a finding of substantial inadequacy under subsection (a)(2) of this section (as in effect immediately before November 15, 1990),

shall provide for attainment of the national primary ambient air quality standards within 3 years of November 15, 1990, or within 5 years of issuance of such finding of substantial inadequacy, whichever is later.

**(3) Retention of construction moratorium in certain areas**

In the case of an area to which, immediately before November 15, 1990, the prohibition on construction or modification of major stationary sources prescribed in subsection (a)(2)(I) of this section (as in effect immediately before November 15, 1990) applied by virtue of a finding of the Administrator that the State containing such area had not submitted an implementation plan meeting the requirements of section 7502(b)(6) of this title (relating to establishment of a permit program) (as in effect immediately before November 15, 1990) or 7502(a)(1) of this title (to the extent such requirements relate to provision for attainment of the primary national ambient air quality standard for sulfur oxides by December 31, 1982) as in effect immediately before November 15, 1990, no major stationary source of the relevant air pollutant or pollutants shall be constructed or modified in such area until the Administrator finds that the plan for such area meets the applicable requirements of section 7502(c)(5) of this title (relating to permit programs) or subpart 5 of part D of this subchapter (relating to attainment of the primary national ambient air quality standard for sulfur dioxide), respectively.

**(*o*) Indian tribes**

If an Indian tribe submits an implementation plan to the Administrator pursuant to section 7601(d) of this title, the plan shall be reviewed in accordance with the provisions for review set forth in this section for State plans, except as otherwise provided by regulation promulgated pursuant to section 7601(d)(2) of this title. When such plan becomes effective in accordance with the regulations promulgated under section 7601(d) of this title, the plan shall become applicable to all areas (except as expressly provided otherwise in the plan) located within the exterior boundaries of the reservation, notwithstanding the issuance of any patent and including rights-of-way running through the reservation.

**(p) Reports**

Any State shall submit, according to such schedule as the Administrator may prescribe, such reports as the Administrator may require relating to emission reductions, vehicle miles traveled, congestion levels, and any other information the Administrator may deem necessary to assess the development effectiveness, need for revision, or implementation of any plan or plan revision required under this chapter.

(July 14, 1955, c. 360, Title I, § 110, as added Dec. 31, 1970, Pub.L. 91–604, § 4(a), 84 Stat. 1680, and amended June 22, 1974, Pub.L. 93–319, § 4, 88 Stat. 256; S.Res. 4, Feb. 4, 1977; Aug. 7, 1977, Pub.L. 95–95, Title I, §§ 107, 108, 91 Stat. 691, 693; Nov. 16, 1977, Pub.L. 95–190, § 14(a)(1)–(6), 91 Stat. 1399; July 17, 1981, Pub.L. 97–23, § 3, 95 Stat. 142; Nov. 15, 1990, Pub.L. 101–549, Title I, §§ 101(b)–(d), 102(h), 107(c), 108(d), Title IV, § 412, 104 Stat. 2404–2408, 2422, 2464, 2466, 2634.)

## HISTORICAL AND STATUTORY NOTES

**References in Text**

The Energy Supply and Environmental Coordination Act of 1974, referred to in subsec. (a)(3)(B), is Pub.L. 93–319, June 22, 1974, 88 Stat. 246, as amended, which is classified principally to chapter 16C (section 791 et seq.) of Title 15, Commerce and Trade. For complete classification of this Act to the Code, see Short Title note set out under section 791 of Title 15 and Tables.

Section 7413 of this title, referred to in subsecs. (a)(3)(C), (6), (f)(5), (g)(3), and (i), was amended generally by Pub.L. 101–549, Title VII, § 701, Nov. 15, 1990, 104 Stat. 2672, and, as so amended, subsecs. (d) and (e) of section 7413 no longer relate to final compliance orders and steel industry compliance extension, respectively.

Section 1857c–10 of this title, as in effect before August 7, 1977, referred to in subsecs. (f)(5) and (g)(3), was in the original "section 119, as in effect before the date of the enactment of this paragraph", meaning section 119 of Act July 14, 1955, c. 360, Title I, as added June 22, 1974, Pub.L. 93–319, § 3, 88 Stat. 248, (which was classified to section 1857c–10 of this title) as in effect prior to the enactment of subsecs. (f)(5) and (g)(3) of this section by Pub.L. 95–95, § 107, Aug. 7, 1977, 91 Stat. 691, effective Aug. 7, 1977. Section 112(b)(1) of Pub.L. 95–95 repealed section 119 of Act July 14, 1955, c. 360, Title I, as added by Pub.L. 93–319, and provided that all references to such section 119 in any subsequent enactment which supersedes Pub.L. 93–319 shall be construed to refer to section 113(d) of the Clean Air Act and to paragraph (5) thereof in particular which is classified to section 7413(d)(5) of this title. Section 7413 of this title was subsequently amended generally by Pub.L. 101–549, Title VII, § 701, Nov. 15, 1990, 104 Stat. 2672, see note above. Section 117(b) of Pub.L. 95–95 added a new section 119 of Act July 14, 1955, which is classified to section 7419 of this title.

**Codifications**

Section was formerly classified to section 1857c–5 of this title.

**Effective and Applicability Provisions**

1990 Acts

Amendment by Pub.L. 101–549 effective Nov. 15, 1990, except as otherwise provided, see section 711(b) of Pub.L. 101–549, set out as a note under section 7401 of this title.

1977 Acts

Amendment by Pub.L. 95–95 effective Aug. 7, 1977, except as otherwise expressly provided, see section 406(d) of Pub.L. 95–95, set out as a note under section 7401 of this title.

**Change of Name**

The Committee on Public Works of the Senate was abolished and replaced by the Committee on Environment and Public Works of the Senate, effective Feb. 11, 1977. See Rule XXV of the Standing Rules of the Senate, as amended by Senate Resolution 4 (popularly cited as the "Committee System Reorganization Amendments of 1977"), approved Feb. 4, 1977.

**Transfer of Functions**

The 'Federal Energy Administrator', for purposes of this chapter, to mean the Administrator of the Federal Energy Administration established by Pub.L. 93-2q75, May 7, 1974, 88 Stat. 97, which is classified to section 761 et seq. of Title 15. Commerce and Trade, but with the term to mean any officer of the United States designated as such by the President until the Federal Energy Administrator takes office and after the Federal Energy Administration ceases to exist, see section 798 of Title 15. The Federal Energy Administration was terminated and functions vested by law in the Administrator thereof were transferred to the Secretary of Energy (unless otherwise specifically provided) by sections 7151(a) and 7293 of this title.

**Savings Provisions**

Suits, actions or proceedings commenced under this chapter as in effect prior to Nov. 15, 1990, not to abate by reason of the taking effect of amendments by Pub.L. 101–549, except as otherwise provided for, see section 711(a) of Pub.L. 101–549, set out as a note under section 7401 of this title.

Suits, actions and other proceedings lawfully commenced by or against the Administrator or any other officer or employee of the United States in his official capacity or in relation to the discharge of his official duties under Act July 14, 1955, the Clean Air Act, as in effect immediately prior to the enactment of Pub.L. 95–95 [Aug. 7, 1977], not to abate by reason of the taking effect of Pub.L. 95–95, see section 406(a) of Pub.L. 95–95, set out as an Effective and Applicability Provisions of 1977 Acts note under section 7401 of this title.

Section 16 of Pub.L. 91–604 provided that:

"(a)(1) Any implementation plan adopted by any State and submitted to the Secretary of Health, Education, and Welfare, or to the Administrator pursuant to the Clean Air Act [this chapter] prior to enactment of this Act [Dec. 31, 1970] may be approved under section 110 of the Clean Air Act [this section] (as amended by this Act) [Pub.L. 91–604] and shall remain in effect, unless the Administrator determines that such implementation plan, or any portion thereof, is not consistent with the applicable requirements of the Clean Air Act [this chapter] (as amended by this Act) and will not provide for the attainment of national primary ambient air quality standards in the time required by such Act. If the Administrator so determines, he shall, within 90 days after promulgation of any national ambient air quality standards pursuant to section 109(a) of the Clean Air Act [section 7409(a) of this title], notify the State and specify in what respects changes are needed to meet the additional requirements of such Act, including requirements to implement national secondary ambient air quality standards. If such changes are not adopted by the State after public hearings and within six months after such notification, the Administrator shall promulgate such changes pursuant to section 110(c) of such Act [subsec. (c) of this section].

"(2) The amendments made by section 4(b) [amending sections 7403 and 7415 of this title] shall not be construed as repealing or modifying the powers of the Administrator with respect to any conference convened under section 108(d) of the Clean Air Act [section 7415 of this title] before the date of enactment of this Act [Dec. 31, 1970].

"(b) Regulations or standards issued under title II of the Clean Air Act [subchapter II of this chapter] prior to the enactment of this Act [Dec. 31, 1970] shall continue in effect until revised by the Administrator consistent with the purposes of such Act [this chapter]."

**Prior Provisions**

A prior section 110 of Act July 14, 1955, was renumbered section 117 by Pub.L. 91–604 and is set out as section 7417 of this title.

**Modification or Rescission of Implementation Plans Approved and In Effect Prior to Aug. 7, 1977**

Nothing in the Clean Air Act Amendments of 1977 [Pub.L. 95–95] to affect any requirement of an approved implementation plan under this section or any other provision in effect under this chapter before Aug. 7, 1977, until modified or rescinded in accordance with this chapter as amended by the Clean Air Act Amendments of 1977, see section 406(c) of Pub.L. 95–95, set out as an Effective and Applicability Provisions of 1977 Acts note under section 7401 of this title.

**Modification or Rescission of Rules, Regulations, Orders, Determinations, Contracts, Certifications, Authorizations, Delegations, and Other Actions**

All rules, regulations, orders, determinations, contracts, certifications, authorizations, delegations or other actions duly issued, made, or taken by or pursuant to Act July 14, 1955, the Clean Air Act, as in effect immediately prior to the date of enactment of Pub.L. 95–95 [Aug. 7, 1977] to continue in full force and effect until modified or rescinded in accordance with Act July 14, 1955, as amended by Pub.L. 95–95 [this chapter], see section 406(b) of Pub.L. 95–95, set out as an Effective and Applicability Provisions of 1977 Acts note under section 7401 of this title.

## § 7411. Standards of performance for new stationary sources

[CAA § 111]

### (a) Definitions

For purposes of this section:

(1) The term "standard of performance" means a standard for emissions of air pollutants which reflects the degree of emission limitation achievable through the application of the best system of emission reduction which (taking into account the cost of achieving such reduction and any nonair quality health and environmental impact and energy requirements) the Administrator determines has been adequately demonstrated.

(2) The term "new source" means any stationary source, the construction or modification of which is commenced after the publication of regulations (or, if earlier, proposed regulations) prescribing a standard of performance under this section which will be applicable to such source.

(3) The term "stationary source" means any building, structure, facility, or installation which emits or may emit any air pollutant. Nothing in subchapter II of this chapter relating to nonroad engines shall be construed to apply to stationary internal combustion engines.

(4) The term "modification" means any physical change in, or change in the method of operation of, a stationary source which increases the amount of any air pollutant emitted by such source or which results in the emission of any air pollutant not previously emitted.

(5) The term "owner or operator" means any person who owns, leases, operates, controls, or supervises a stationary source.

(6) The term "existing source" means any stationary source other than a new source.

(7) The term "technological system of continuous emission reduction" means—

(A) a technological process for production or operation by any source which is inherently low-polluting or nonpolluting, or

(B) a technological system for continuous reduction of the pollution generated by a source before such pollution is emitted into the ambient air, including precombustion cleaning or treatment of fuels.

(8) A conversion to coal (A) by reason of an order under section 2(a) of the Energy Supply and Environmental Coordination Act of 1974 [15 U.S.C.A. § 792(a) ] or any amendment thereto, or any subsequent enactment which supersedes such Act [15 U.S.C.A. § 791 et seq.], or (B) which qualifies under section 7413(d)(5)(A)(ii) of this title, shall not be deemed to be a modification for purposes of paragraphs (2) and (4) of this subsection.

**(b) List of categories of stationary sources; standards of performance; information on pollution control techniques; sources owned or operated by United States; particular systems; revised standards**

(1)(A) The Administrator shall, within 90 days after December 31, 1970, publish (and from time to time thereafter shall revise) a list of categories of stationary sources. He shall include a category of sources in such list if in his judgment it causes, or contributes significantly to, air pollution which may reasonably be anticipated to endanger public health or welfare.

(B) Within one year after the inclusion of a category of stationary sources in a list under subparagraph (A), the Administrator shall publish proposed regulations, establishing Federal standards of performance for new sources within such category. The Administrator shall afford interested persons an opportunity for written comment on such proposed regulations. After considering such comments, he shall promulgate, within one year after such publication, such standards with such modifications as he deems appropriate. The Administrator shall, at least every 8 years, review and, if appropriate, revise such standards following the procedure required by this subsection for promulgation of such standards. Notwithstanding the requirements of the previous sentence, the Administrator need not review any such standard if the Administrator determines that such review is not appropriate in light of readily available information on the efficacy of such standard. Standards of performance or revisions thereof shall become effective upon promulgation. When implementation and enforcement of any requirement of this chapter indicate that emission limitations and percent reductions beyond those required by the standards promulgated under this section are achieved in practice, the Administrator shall, when revising standards promulgated under this section, consider the emission limitations and percent reductions achieved in practice.

(2) The Administrator may distinguish among classes, types, and sizes within categories of new sources for the purpose of establishing such standards.

(3) The Administrator shall, from time to time, issue information on pollution control techniques for categories of new sources and air pollutants subject to the provisions of this section.

(4) The provisions of this section shall apply to any new source owned or operated by the United States.

(5) Except as otherwise authorized under subsection (h) of this section, nothing in this section shall be construed to require, or to authorize the Administrator to require, any new or modified source to install and operate any particular technological system of continuous emission reduction to comply with any new source standard of performance.

(6) The revised standards of performance required by enactment of subsection (a)(1)(A)(i) and (ii) of this

section shall be promulgated not later than one year after August 7, 1977. Any new or modified fossil fuel fired stationary source which commences construction prior to the date of publication of the proposed revised standards shall not be required to comply with such revised standards.

**(c) State implementation and enforcement of standards of performance**

(1) Each State may develop and submit to the Administrator a procedure for implementing and enforcing standards of performance for new sources located in such State. If the Administrator finds the State procedure is adequate, he shall delegate to such State any authority he has under this chapter to implement and enforce such standards.

(2) Nothing in this subsection shall prohibit the Administrator from enforcing any applicable standard of performance under this section.

**(d) Standards of performance for existing sources; remaining useful life of source**

(1) The Administrator shall prescribe regulations which shall establish a procedure similar to that provided by section 7410 of this title under which each State shall submit to the Administrator a plan which (A) establishes standards of performance for any existing source for any air pollutant (i) for which air quality criteria have not been issued or which is not included on a list published under section 7408(a) of this title or emitted from a source category which is regulated under section 7412 of this title but (ii) to which a standard of performance under this section would apply if such existing source were a new source, and (B) provides for the implementation and enforcement of such standards of performance. Regulations of the Administrator under this paragraph shall permit the State in applying a standard of performance to any particular source under a plan submitted under this paragraph to take into consideration, among other factors, the remaining useful life of the existing source to which such standard applies.

(2) The Administrator shall have the same authority—

(A) to prescribe a plan for a State in cases where the State fails to submit a satisfactory plan as he would have under section 7410(c) of this title in the case of failure to submit an implementation plan, and

(B) to enforce the provisions of such plan in cases where the State fails to enforce them as he would have under sections 7413 and 7414 of this title with respect to an implementation plan.

In promulgating a standard of performance under a plan prescribed under this paragraph, the Administrator shall take into consideration, among other factors, remaining useful lives of the sources in the category of sources to which such standard applies.

**(e) Prohibited acts**

After the effective date of standards of performance promulgated under this section, it shall be unlawful for any owner or operator of any new source to operate such source in violation of any standard of performance applicable to such source.

**(f) New source standards of performance**

(1) For those categories of major stationary sources that the Administrator listed under subsection (b)(1)(A) of this section before November 15, 1990, and for which regulations had not been proposed by the Administrator by November 15, 1990, the Administrator shall—

(A) propose regulations establishing standards of performance for at least 25 percent of such categories of sources within 2 years after November 15, 1990;

(B) propose regulations establishing standards of performance for at least 50 percent of such categories of sources within 4 years after November 15, 1990; and

(C) propose regulations for the remaining categories of sources within 6 years after November 15, 1990.

(2) In determining priorities for promulgating standards for categories of major stationary sources for the purpose of paragraph (1), the Administrator shall consider—

(A) the quantity of air pollutant emissions which each such category will emit, or will be designed to emit;

(B) the extent to which each such pollutant may reasonably be anticipated to endanger public health or welfare; and

(C) the mobility and competitive nature of each such category of sources and the consequent need for nationally applicable new source standards of performance.

(3) Before promulgating any regulations under this subsection or listing any category of major stationary sources as required under this subsection, the Administrator shall consult with appropriate representatives of the Governors and of State air pollution control agencies.

**(g) Revision of regulations**

(1) Upon application by the Governor of a State showing that the Administrator has failed to specify in regulations under subsection (f)(1) of this section any category of major stationary sources required to be specified under such regulations, the Administrator

shall revise such regulations to specify any such category.

(2) Upon application of the Governor of a State, showing that any category of stationary sources which is not included in the list under subsection (b)(1)(A) of this section contributes significantly to air pollution which may reasonably be anticipated to endanger public health or welfare (notwithstanding that such category is not a category of major stationary sources), the Administrator shall revise such regulations to specify such category of stationary sources.

(3) Upon application of the Governor of a State showing that the Administrator has failed to apply properly the criteria required to be considered under subsection (f)(2) of this section, the Administrator shall revise the list under subsection (b)(1)(A) of this section to apply properly such criteria.

(4) Upon application of the Governor of a State showing that—

(A) a new, innovative, or improved technology or process which achieves greater continuous emission reduction has been adequately demonstrated for any category of stationary sources, and

(B) as a result of such technology or process, the new source standard of performance in effect under this section for such category no longer reflects the greatest degree of emission limitation achievable through application of the best technological system of continuous emission reduction which (taking into consideration the cost of achieving such emission reduction, and any non-air quality health and environmental impact and energy requirements) has been adequately demonstrated,

the Administrator shall revise such standard of performance for such category accordingly.

(5) Unless later deadlines for action of the Administrator are otherwise prescribed under this section, the Administrator shall, not later than three months following the date of receipt of any application by a Governor of a State, either—

(A) find that such application does not contain the requisite showing and deny such application, or

(B) grant such application and take the action required under this subsection.

(6) Before taking any action required by subsection (f) of this section or by this subsection, the Administrator shall provide notice and opportunity for public hearing.

### (h) Design, equipment, work practice, or operational standard; alternative emission limitation

(1) For purposes of this section, if in the judgment of the Administrator, it is not feasible to prescribe or enforce a standard of performance, he may instead promulgate a design, equipment, work practice, or operational standard, or combination thereof, which reflects the best technological system of continuous emission reduction which (taking into consideration the cost of achieving such emission reduction, and any non-air quality health and environmental impact and energy requirements) the Administrator determines has been adequately demonstrated. In the event the Administrator promulgates a design or equipment standard under this subsection, he shall include as part of such standard such requirements as will assure the proper operation and maintenance of any such element of design or equipment.

(2) For the purpose of this subsection, the phrase "not feasible to prescribe or enforce a standard of performance" means any situation in which the Administrator determines that (A) a pollutant or pollutants cannot be emitted through a conveyance designed and constructed to emit or capture such pollutant, or that any requirement for, or use of, such a conveyance would be inconsistent with any Federal, State, or local law, or (B) the application of measurement methodology to a particular class of sources is not practicable due to technological or economic limitations.

(3) If after notice and opportunity for public hearing, any person establishes to the satisfaction of the Administrator that an alternative means of emission limitation will achieve a reduction in emissions of any air pollutant at least equivalent to the reduction in emissions of such air pollutant achieved under the requirements of paragraph (1), the Administrator shall permit the use of such alternative by the source for purposes of compliance with this section with respect to such pollutant.

(4) Any standard promulgated under paragraph (1) shall be promulgated in terms of standard of performance whenever it becomes feasible to promulgate and enforce such standard in such terms.

(5) Any design, equipment, work practice, or operational standard, or any combination thereof, described in this subsection shall be treated as a standard of performance for purposes of the provisions of this chapter (other than the provisions of subsection (a) of this section and this subsection).

### (i) Country elevators

Any regulations promulgated by the Administrator under this section applicable to grain elevators shall not apply to country elevators (as defined by the Administrator) which have a storage capacity of less than two million five hundred thousand bushels.

### (j) Innovative technological systems of continuous emission reduction

(1)(A) Any person proposing to own or operate a new source may request the Administrator for one or more waivers from the requirements of this section for such source or any portion thereof with respect to any air pollutant to encourage the use of an innovative technological system or systems of continuous emission reduction. The Administrator may, with the consent of the Governor of the State in which the source is to be located, grant a waiver under this paragraph, if the Administrator determines after notice and opportunity for public hearing, that—

(i) the proposed system or systems have not been adequately demonstrated,

(ii) the proposed system or systems will operate effectively and there is a substantial likelihood that such system or systems will achieve greater continuous emission reduction than that required to be achieved under the standards of performance which would otherwise apply, or achieve at least an equivalent reduction at lower cost in terms of energy, economic, or nonair quality environmental impact,

(iii) the owner or operator of the proposed source has demonstrated to the satisfaction of the Administrator that the proposed system will not cause or contribute to an unreasonable risk to public health, welfare, or safety in its operation, function, or malfunction, and

(iv) the granting of such waiver is consistent with the requirements of subparagraph (C).

In making any determination under clause (ii), the Administrator shall take into account any previous failure of such system or systems to operate effectively or to meet any requirement of the new source performance standards. In determining whether an unreasonable risk exists under clause (iii), the Administrator shall consider, among other factors, whether and to what extent the use of the proposed technological system will cause, increase, reduce, or eliminate emissions of any unregulated pollutants; available methods for reducing or eliminating any risk to public health, welfare, or safety which may be associated with the use of such system; and the availability of other technological systems which may be used to conform to standards under this section without causing or contributing to such unreasonable risk. The Administrator may conduct such tests and may require the owner or operator of the proposed source to conduct such tests and provide such information as is necessary to carry out clause (iii) of this subparagraph. Such requirements shall include a requirement for prompt reporting of the emission of any unregulated pollutant from a system if such pollutant was not emitted, or was emitted in significantly lesser amounts without use of such system.

(B) A waiver under this paragraph shall be granted on such terms and conditions as the Administrator determines to be necessary to assure—

(i) emissions from the source will not prevent attainment and maintenance of any national ambient air quality standards, and

(ii) proper functioning of the technological system or systems authorized.

Any such term or condition shall be treated as a standard of performance for the purposes of subsection (e) of this section and section 7413 of this title.

(C) The number of waivers granted under this paragraph with respect to a proposed technological system of continuous emission reduction shall not exceed such number as the Administrator finds necessary to ascertain whether or not such system will achieve the conditions specified in clauses (ii) and (iii) of subparagraph (A).

(D) A waiver under this paragraph shall extend to the sooner of—

(i) the date determined by the Administrator, after consultation with the owner or operator of the source, taking into consideration the design, installation, and capital cost of the technological system or systems being used, or

(ii) the date on which the Administrator determines that such system has failed to—

(I) achieve at least an equivalent continuous emission reduction to that required to be achieved under the standards of performance which would otherwise apply, or

(II) comply with the condition specified in paragraph (1)(A)(iii),

and that such failure cannot be corrected.

(E) In carrying out subparagraph (D)(i), the Administrator shall not permit any waiver for a source or portion thereof to extend beyond the date—

(i) seven years after the date on which any waiver is granted to such source or portion thereof, or

(ii) four years after the date on which such source or portion thereof commences operation,

whichever is earlier.

(F) No waiver under this subsection shall apply to any portion of a source other than the portion on which the innovative technological system or systems of continuous emission reduction is used.

(2)(A) If a waiver under paragraph (1) is terminated under clause (ii) of paragraph (1)(D), the Administrator shall grant an extension of the requirements of this section for such source for such minimum period as may be necessary to comply with the applicable standard of performance under this section. Such period shall not extend beyond the date three years from the time such waiver is terminated.

**(B)** An extension granted under this paragraph shall set forth emission limits and a compliance schedule containing increments of progress which require compliance with the applicable standards of performance as expeditiously as practicable and include such measures as are necessary and practicable in the interim to minimize emissions. Such schedule shall be treated as a standard of performance for purposes of subsection (e) of this section and section 7413 of this title.

(July 14, 1955, c. 360, Title I, § 111, as added Dec. 31, 1970, Pub.L. 91–604, § 4(a), 84 Stat. 1683, and amended Nov. 18, 1971, Pub.L. 92–157, Title III, § 302(f), 85 Stat. 464; Aug. 7, 1977, Pub.L. 95–95, Title I, § 109(a)–(d)(1), (e), (f), Title IV, § 401(b), 91 Stat. 697 to 703, 791; Nov. 16, 1977, Pub.L. 95–190, § 14(a)(7) to (9), 91 Stat. 1399; Nov. 9, 1978, Pub.L. 95–623, § 13(a), 92 Stat. 3457; Nov. 15, 1990, Pub.L. 101–549, Title I, § 108(e) to (g), Title III, § 302(a), (b), Title IV, § 403(a), 104 Stat. 2467, 2574, 2631.)

## HISTORICAL AND STATUTORY NOTES

### References in Text

Such Act, referred to in subsec. (a)(8), means Pub.L. 93–319, June 22, 1974, 88 Stat. 246, as amended, known as the Energy Supply and Environmental Coordination Act of 1974, which is classified principally to chapter 16C (section 791 et seq.) of Title 15, Commerce and Trade. For complete classification of this Act to the Code, see Short Title note set out under section 791 of Title 15 and Tables.

Section 7413 of this title, referred to in subsec. (a)(8), was amended generally by Pub.L. 101–549, Title VII, § 701, Nov. 15, 1990, 104 Stat. 2672, and, as so amended, subsec. (d) of section 7413 no longer relates to final compliance orders.

Subsec. (a)(1) of this section, referred to in subsec. (b)(6), was amended generally by Pub.L. 101–549, Title IV, § 403(a), Nov. 15, 1990, 104 Stat. 2631, and, as so amended, no longer contains subpars.

### Codifications

Section was formerly classified to section 1857c–6 of this title.

### Effective and Applicability Provisions

1990 Acts

Amendment by Pub.L. 101–549 effective Nov. 15, 1990, except as otherwise provided, see section 711(b) of Pub.L. 101–549, set out as a note under section 7401 of this title.

1977 Acts

Amendment by Pub.L. 95–95 effective Aug. 7, 1977, except as otherwise expressly provided, see section 406(d) of Pub.L. 95–95, set out as a note under section 7401 of this title.

### Transfer of Functions

Enforcement functions of Administrator or other official in Environmental Protection Agency related to compliance with new source performance standards under this section with respect to pre-construction, construction, and initial operation of transportation system for Canadian and Alaskan natural gas transferred to Federal Inspector, Office of Federal Inspector for the Alaska Natural Gas Transportation System, until first anniversary of date of initial operation of Alaska Natural Gas Transportation System, see Reorg. Plan No. 1 of 1979, eff. July 1, 1979, §§ 102(a), 203(a), 44 F.R. 33663, 33666, 93 Stat. 1373, 1376, set out in Appendix 1 to Title 5, Government Organization and Employees Office of Federal Inspector for the Alaska Natural Gas Transportation System abolished and functions and authority vested in Inspector transferred to Secretary of Energy by section 3012(b) of Pub.L. 102–486, set out as an Abolition of Office of Federal Inspector note under section 719e of Title 15, Commerce and Trade.

### Savings Provisions

Suits, actions or proceedings commenced under this chapter as in effect prior to Nov. 15, 1990, not to abate by reason of the taking effect of amendments by Pub.L. 101–549, except as otherwise provided for, see section 711(a) of Pub.L. 101–549, set out as a note under section 7401 of this title.

Suits, actions, and other proceedings lawfully commenced by or against the Administrator or any other officer or employee of the United States in his official capacity or in relation to the discharge of his official duties under Act July 14, 1955, the Clean Air Act, as in effect immediately prior to the enactment of Pub.L. 95–95 [Aug. 7, 1977], not to abate by reason of the taking effect of Pub.L. 95–95, see section 406(a) of Pub.L. 95–95, set out as an Effective and Applicability Provisions note under section 7401 of this title.

### Prior Provisions

A prior section 111 of Act July 14, 1955, was renumbered section 118 by Pub.L. 91–604, and is set out as section 7418 of this title.

### Modification or Rescission of Rules, Regulations, Orders, Determinations, Contracts, Certifications, Authorizations, Delegations, and Other Actions

All rules, regulations, orders, determinations, contracts, certifications, authorizations, delegations, or other actions duly issued, made, or taken by or pursuant to Act July 14, 1955, the Clean Air Act, as in effect immediately prior to the date of enactment of Pub.L. 95–95 [Aug. 7, 1977] to continue in full force and effect until modified or rescinded in accordance with Act July 14, 1955, as amended by Pub.L. 95–95 [this chapter], see section 406(b) of Pub.L. 95–95, set out as an Effective Date note under section 7401 of this title.

### Revised Regulations; Applicability

Section 403(b), (c) of Pub.L. 101–549 provided that:

"**(b) Revised regulations.**—Not later than three years after the date of enactment of the Clean Air Act Amendments of 1990 [Nov. 15, 1990], the Administrator shall promulgate revised regulations for standards of performance for new fossil fuel fired electric utility units commencing construction after the date on which such regulations are proposed that, at a minimum, require any source subject to such revised standards to emit sulfur dioxide at a rate not greater than would have resulted from compliance by such source with the applicable standards of performance under this section [amending sections 9411 and 7479 of this title] prior to such revision.

"**(c) Applicability.**—The provisions of subsections (a) [amending subsec. (a)(1) of this section] and (b) [subsec. (b) of this note] apply only so long as the provisions of section 403(e) of the Clean Air Act [section 7651b(e) of this title] remain in effect."

## § 7412. Hazardous air pollutants [CAA § 112]

### (a) Definitions

For purposes of this section, except subsection (r) of this section—

#### (1) Major source

The term "major source" means any stationary source or group of stationary sources located within a contiguous area and under common control that emits or has the potential to emit considering controls, in the aggregate, 10 tons per year or more of any hazardous air pollutant or 25 tons per year or more of any combination of hazardous air pollutants. The Administrator may establish a lesser quantity, or in the case of radionuclides different criteria, for a major source than that specified in the previous sentence, on the basis of the potency of the air pollutant, persistence, potential for bioaccumulation, other characteristics of the air pollutant, or other relevant factors.

#### (2) Area source

The term "area source" means any stationary source of hazardous air pollutants that is not a major source. For purposes of this section, the term "area source" shall not include motor vehicles or nonroad vehicles subject to regulation under subchapter II of this chapter.

#### (3) Stationary source

The term "stationary source" shall have the same meaning as such term has under section 7411(a) of this title.

#### (4) New source

The term "new source" means a stationary source the construction or reconstruction of which is commenced after the Administrator first proposes regulations under this section establishing an emission standard applicable to such source.

#### (5) Modification

The term "modification" means any physical change in, or change in the method of operation of, a major source which increases the actual emissions of any hazardous air pollutant emitted by such source by more than a de minimis amount or which results in the emission of any hazardous air pollutant not previously emitted by more than a de minimis amount.

#### (6) Hazardous air pollutant

The term "hazardous air pollutant" means any air pollutant listed pursuant to subsection (b) of this section.

#### (7) Adverse environmental effect

The term "adverse environmental effect" means any significant and widespread adverse effect, which may reasonably be anticipated, to wildlife, aquatic life, or other natural resources, including adverse impacts on populations of endangered or threatened species or significant degradation of environmental quality over broad areas.

#### (8) Electric utility steam generating unit

The term "electric utility steam generating unit" means any fossil fuel fired combustion unit of more than 25 megawatts that serves a generator that produces electricity for sale. A unit that cogenerates steam and electricity and supplies more than one-third of its potential electric output capacity and more than 25 megawatts electrical output to any utility power distribution system for sale shall be considered an electric utility steam generating unit.

#### (9) Owner or operator

The term "owner or operator" means any person who owns, leases, operates, controls, or supervises a stationary source.

#### (10) Existing source

The term "existing source" means any stationary source other than a new source.

#### (11) Carcinogenic effect

Unless revised, the term "carcinogenic effect" shall have the meaning provided by the Administrator under Guidelines for Carcinogenic Risk Assessment as of the date of enactment. Any revisions in the existing Guidelines shall be subject to notice and opportunity for comment.

### (b) List of pollutants

#### (1) Initial list

The Congress establishes for purposes of this section a list of hazardous air pollutants as follows:

| CAS number | Chemical name |
|---|---|
| 75070 | Acetaldehyde |
| 60355 | Acetamide |
| 75058 | Acetonitrile |
| 98862 | Acetophenone |
| 53963 | 2–Acetylaminofluorene |
| 107028 | Acrolein |
| 79061 | Acrylamide |
| 79107 | Acrylic acid |
| 107131 | Acrylonitrile |
| 107051 | Allyl chloride |
| 92671 | 4–Aminobiphenyl |
| 62533 | Aniline |
| 90040 | o-Anisidine |
| 1332214 | Asbestos |
| 71432 | Benzene (including benzene from gasoline) |

| CAS number | Chemical name |
|---|---|
| 92875 | Benzidine |
| 98077 | Benzotrichloride |
| 100447 | Benzyl chloride |
| 92524 | Biphenyl |
| 117817 | Bis(2–ethylhexyl)phthalate (DEHP) |
| 542881 | Bis(chloromethyl)ether |
| 75252 | Bromoform |
| 106990 | 1,3–Butadiene |
| 156627 | Calcium cyanamide |
| 105602 | Caprolactam |
| 133062 | Captan |
| 63252 | Carbaryl |
| 75150 | Carbon disulfide |
| 56235 | Carbon tetrachloride |
| 463581 | Carbonyl sulfide |
| 120809 | Catechol |
| 133904 | Chloramben |
| 57749 | Chlordane |
| 7782505 | Chlorine |
| 79118 | Chloroacetic acid |
| 532274 | 2–Chloroacetophenone |
| 108907 | Chlorobenzene |
| 510156 | Chlorobenzilate |
| 67663 | Chloroform |
| 107302 | Chloromethyl methyl ether |
| 126998 | Chloroprene |
| 1319773 | Cresols/Cresylic acid (Isomers and mixture) |
| 95487 | o-Cresol |
| 108394 | m-Cresol |
| 106445 | p-Cresol |
| 98828 | Cumene |
| 94757 | 2,4–D, salts and esters |
| 3547044 | DDE |
| 334883 | Diazomethane |
| 132649 | Dibenzofurans |
| 96128 | 1,2–Dibromo–3–chloropropane |
| 84742 | Dibutylphthalate |
| 106467 | 1,4–Dichlorobenzene(p) |
| 91941 | 3,3–Dichlorobenzidene |
| 111444 | Dichloroethyl ether (Bis(2–chloroethyl)ether) |
| 542756 | 1,3–Dichloropropene |
| 62737 | Dichlorvos |
| 111422 | Diethanolamine |
| 121697 | N,N–Diethyl aniline (N,N–Dimethylaniline) |
| 64675 | Diethyl sulfate |
| 119904 | 3,3–Dimethoxybenzidine |
| 60117 | Dimethyl aminoazobenzene |
| 119937 | 3,3′–Dimethyl benzidine |
| 79447 | Dimethyl carbamoyl chloride |
| 68122 | Dimethyl formamide |
| 57147 | 1,1–Dimethyl hydrazine |
| 131113 | Dimethyl phthalate |
| 77781 | Dimethyl sulfate |
| 534521 | 4,6–Dinitro-o-cresol, and salts |
| 51285 | 2,4–Dinitrophenol |
| 121142 | 2,4–Dinitrotoluene |
| 123911 | 1,4–Dioxane (1,4–Diethyleneoxide) |
| 122667 | 1,2–Diphenylhydrazine |
| 106898 | Epichlorohydrin (1–Chloro–2,3–epoxypropane) |
| 106887 | 1,2–Epoxybutane |
| 140885 | Ethyl acrylate |
| 100414 | Ethyl benzene |

| CAS number | Chemical name |
|---|---|
| 51796 | Ethyl carbamate (Urethane) |
| 75003 | Ethyl chloride (Chloroethane) |
| 106934 | Ethylene dibromide (Dibromoethane) |
| 107062 | Ethylene dichloride (1,2–Dichloroethane) |
| 107211 | Ethylene glycol |
| 151564 | Ethylene imine (Aziridine) |
| 75218 | Ethylene oxide |
| 96457 | Ethylene thiourea |
| 75343 | Ethylidene dichloride (1,1–Dichloroethane) |
| 50000 | Formaldehyde |
| 76448 | Heptachlor |
| 118741 | Hexachlorobenzene |
| 87683 | Hexachlorobutadiene |
| 77474 | Hexachlorocyclopentadiene |
| 67721 | Hexachloroethane |
| 822060 | Hexamethylene–1,6–diisocyanate |
| 680319 | Hexamethylphosphoramide |
| 110543 | Hexane |
| 302012 | Hydrazine |
| 7647010 | Hydrochloric acid |
| 7664393 | Hydrogen fluoride (Hydrofluoric acid) |
| 123319 | Hydroquinone |
| 78591 | Isophorone |
| 58899 | Lindane (all isomers) |
| 108316 | Maleic anhydride |
| 67561 | Methanol |
| 72435 | Methoxychlor |
| 74839 | Methyl bromide (Bromomethane) |
| 74873 | Methyl chloride (Chloromethane) |
| 71556 | Methyl chloroform (1,1,1–Trichloroethane) |
| 78933 | Methyl ethyl ketone (2–Butanone) |
| 60344 | Methyl hydrazine |
| 74884 | Methyl iodide (Iodomethane) |
| 108101 | Methyl isobutyl ketone (Hexone) |
| 624839 | Methyl isocyanate |
| 80626 | Methyl methacrylate |
| 1634044 | Methyl tert butyl ether |
| 101144 | 4,4–Methylene bis(2–chloroaniline) |
| 75092 | Methylene chloride (Dichloromethane) |
| 101688 | Methylene diphenyl diisocyanate (MDI) |
| 101779 | 4,4′–Methylenedianiline |
| 91203 | Naphthalene |
| 98953 | Nitrobenzene |
| 92933 | 4–Nitrobiphenyl |
| 100027 | 4–Nitrophenol |
| 79469 | 2–Nitropropane |
| 684935 | N–Nitroso–N–methylurea |
| 62759 | N–Nitrosodimethylamine |
| 59892 | N–Nitrosomorpholine |
| 56382 | Parathion |
| 82688 | Pentachloronitrobenzene (Quintobenzene) |
| 87865 | Pentachlorophenol |
| 108952 | Phenol |
| 106503 | p-Phenylenediamine |
| 75445 | Phosgene |
| 7803512 | Phosphine |
| 7723140 | Phosphorus |
| 85449 | Phthalic anhydride |
| 1336363 | Polychlorinated biphenyls (Aroclors) |
| 1120714 | 1,3–Propane sultone |
| 57578 | beta-Propiolactone |
| 123386 | Propionaldehyde |

| CAS number | Chemical name |
|---|---|
| 114261 | Propoxur (Baygon) |
| 78875 | Propylene dichloride (1,2–Dichloropropane) |
| 75569 | Propylene oxide |
| 75558 | 1,2–Propylenimine (2–Methyl aziridine) |
| 91225 | Quinoline |
| 106514 | Quinone |
| 100425 | Styrene |
| 96093 | Styrene oxide |
| 1746016 | 2,3,7,8–Tetrachlorodibenzo-p-dioxin |
| 79345 | 1,1,2,2–Tetrachloroethane |
| 127184 | Tetrachloroethylene (Perchloroethylene) |
| 7550450 | Titanium tetrachloride |
| 108883 | Toluene |
| 95807 | 2,4–Toluene diamine |
| 584849 | 2,4–Toluene diisocyanate |
| 95534 | o-Toluidine |
| 8001352 | Toxaphene (chlorinated camphene) |
| 120821 | 1,2,4–Trichlorobenzene |
| 79005 | 1,1,2–Trichloroethane |
| 79016 | Trichloroethylene |
| 95954 | 2,4,5–Trichlorophenol |
| 88062 | 2,4,6–Trichlorophenol |
| 121448 | Triethylamine |
| 1582098 | Trifluralin |
| 540841 | 2,2,4–Trimethylpentane |
| 108054 | Vinyl acetate |
| 593602 | Vinyl bromide |
| 75014 | Vinyl chloride |
| 75354 | Vinylidene chloride (1,1–Dichloroethylene) |
| 1330207 | Xylenes (isomers and mixture) |
| 95476 | o-Xylenes |
| 108383 | m-Xylenes |
| 106423 | p-Xylenes |
| 0 | Antimony Compounds |
| 0 | Arsenic Compounds (inorganic including arsine) |
| 0 | Beryllium Compounds |
| 0 | Cadmium Compounds |
| 0 | Chromium Compounds |
| 0 | Cobalt Compounds |
| 0 | Coke Oven Emissions |
| 0 | Cyanide Compounds [1] |
| 0 | Glycol ethers [2] |
| 0 | Lead Compounds |
| 0 | Manganese Compounds |
| 0 | Mercury Compounds |
| 0 | Fine mineral fibers [3] |
| 0 | Nickel Compounds |
| 0 | Polycylic Organic Matter [4] |
| 0 | Radionuclides (including radon) [5] |
| 0 | Selenium Compounds |

NOTE: For all listings above which contain the word "compounds" and for glycol ethers, the following applies: Unless otherwise specified, these listings are defined as including any unique chemical substance that contains the named chemical (i.e., antimony, arsenic, etc.) as part of that chemical's infrastructure.

[1] X'CN where X = H' or any other group where a formal dissociation may occur. For example KCN or $Ca(CN)_2$

[2] Includes mono- and di- ethers of ethylene glycol, diethylene glycol, and triethylene glycol $R\text{–}(OCH_2CH_2)_n\text{–}OR'$ where

n = 1, 2, or 3
R = alkyl or aryl groups
R' = R, H, or groups which, when removed, yield glycol ethers with the structure: $R\text{–}(OCH_2CH)_n\text{–}OH$. Polymers are excluded from the glycol category.

[3] Includes mineral fiber emissions from facilities manufacturing or processing glass, rock, or slag fibers (or other mineral derived fibers) of average diameter 1 micrometer or less.

[4] Includes organic compounds with more than one benzene ring, and which have a boiling point greater than or equal to 100°C.

[5] A type of atom which spontaneously undergoes radioactive decay.

### (2) Revision of the list

The Administrator shall periodically review the list established by this subsection and publish the results thereof and, where appropriate, revise such list by rule, adding pollutants which present, or may present, through inhalation or other routes of exposure, a threat of adverse human health effects (including, but not limited to, substances which are known to be, or may reasonably be anticipated to be, carcinogenic, mutagenic, teratogenic, neurotoxic, which cause reproductive dysfunction, or which are acutely or chronically toxic) or adverse environmental effects whether through ambient concentrations, bioaccumulation, deposition, or otherwise, but not including releases subject to regulation under subsection (r) of this section as a result of emissions to the air. No air pollutant which is listed under section 7408(a) of this title may be added to the list under this section, except that the prohibition of this sentence shall not apply to any pollutant which independently meets the listing criteria of this paragraph and is a precursor to a pollutant which is listed under section 7408(a) of this title or to any pollutant which is in a class of pollutants listed under such section. No substance, practice, process or activity regulated under subchapter VI of this chapter shall be subject to regulation under this section solely due to its adverse effects on the environment.

### (3) Petitions to modify the list

**(A)** Beginning at any time after 6 months after November 15, 1990, any person may petition the Administrator to modify the list of hazardous air pollutants under this subsection by adding or deleting a substance or, in case of listed pollutants without CAS numbers (other than coke oven emissions, mineral fibers, or polycyclic organic matter) removing certain unique substances. Within 18 months after receipt of a petition, the Administrator shall either grant or deny the petition by publishing a written explanation of the reasons for the Administrator's decision. Any such petition shall include a showing by the petitioner that there is adequate data on the health or environmental defects [1] of the pollutant or other evidence adequate to support the petition. The Administrator may not deny a petition solely on the basis of inadequate resources or time for review.

(B) The Administrator shall add a substance to the list upon a showing by the petitioner or on the Administrator's own determination that the substance is an air pollutant and that emissions, ambient concentrations, bioaccumulation or deposition of the substance are known to cause or may reasonably be anticipated to cause adverse effects to human health or adverse environmental effects.

(C) The Administrator shall delete a substance from the list upon a showing by the petitioner or on the Administrator's own determination that there is adequate data on the health and environmental effects of the substance to determine that emissions, ambient concentrations, bioaccumulation or deposition of the substance may not reasonably be anticipated to cause any adverse effects to the human health or adverse environmental effects.

(D) The Administrator shall delete one or more unique chemical substances that contain a listed hazardous air pollutant not having a CAS number (other than coke oven emissions, mineral fibers, or polycyclic organic matter) upon a showing by the petitioner or on the Administrator's own determination that such unique chemical substances that contain the named chemical of such listed hazardous air pollutant meet the deletion requirements of subparagraph (C). The Administrator must grant or deny a deletion petition prior to promulgating any emission standards pursuant to subsection (d) of this section applicable to any source category or subcategory of a listed hazardous air pollutant without a CAS number listed under subsection (b) of this section for which a deletion petition has been filed within 12 months of November 15, 1990.

**(4) Further information**

If the Administrator determines that information on the health or environmental effects of a substance is not sufficient to make a determination required by this subsection, the Administrator may use any authority available to the Administrator to acquire such information.

**(5) Test methods**

The Administrator may establish, by rule, test measures and other analytic procedures for monitoring and measuring emissions, ambient concentrations, deposition, and bioaccumulation of hazardous air pollutants.

**(6) Prevention of significant deterioration**

The provisions of part C of this subchapter (prevention of significant deterioration) shall not apply to pollutants listed under this section.

**(7) Lead**

The Administrator may not list elemental lead as a hazardous air pollutant under this subsection.

**(c) List of source categories**

**(1) In general**

Not later than 12 months after November 15, 1990, the Administrator shall publish, and shall from time to time, but no less often than every 8 years, revise, if appropriate, in response to public comment or new information, a list of all categories and subcategories of major sources and area sources (listed under paragraph (3)) of the air pollutants listed pursuant to subsection (b) of this section. To the extent practicable, the categories and subcategories listed under this subsection shall be consistent with the list of source categories established pursuant to section 7411 of this title and part C of this subchapter. Nothing in the preceding sentence limits the Administrator's authority to establish subcategories under this section, as appropriate.

**(2) Requirement for emissions standards**

For the categories and subcategories the Administrator lists, the Administrator shall establish emissions standards under subsection (d) of this section, according to the schedule in this subsection and subsection (e) of this section.

**(3) Area sources**

The Administrator shall list under this subsection each category or subcategory of area sources which the Administrator finds presents a threat of adverse effects to human health or the environment (by such sources individually or in the aggregate) warranting regulation under this section. The Administrator shall, not later than 5 years after November 15, 1990, and pursuant to subsection (k)(3)(B) of this section, list, based on actual or estimated aggregate emissions of a listed pollutant or pollutants, sufficient categories or subcategories of area sources to ensure that area sources representing 90 percent of the area source emissions of the 30 hazardous air pollutants that present the greatest threat to public health in the largest number of urban areas are subject to regulation under this section. Such regulations shall be promulgated not later than 10 years after November 15, 1990.

**(4) Previously regulated categories**

The Administrator may, in the Administrator's discretion, list any category or subcategory of sources previously regulated under this section as in effect before November 15, 1990.

(5) **Additional categories**

In addition to those categories and subcategories of sources listed for regulation pursuant to paragraphs (1) and (3), the Administrator may at any time list additional categories and subcategories of sources of hazardous air pollutants according to the same criteria for listing applicable under such paragraphs. In the case of source categories and subcategories listed after publication of the initial list required under paragraph (1) or (3), emission standards under subsection (d) of this section for the category or subcategory shall be promulgated within 10 years after November 15, 1990, or within 2 years after the date on which such category or subcategory is listed, whichever is later.

(6) **Specific pollutants**

With respect to alkylated lead compounds, polycyclic organic matter, hexachlorobenzene, mercury, polychlorinated biphenyls, 2,3,7,8–tetrachlorodibenzofurans and 2,3,7,8–tetrachlorodibenzo-p-dioxin, the Administrator shall, not later than 5 years after November 15, 1990, list categories and subcategories of sources assuring that sources accounting for not less than 90 per centum of the aggregate emissions of each such pollutant are subject to standards under subsection (d)(2) or (d)(4) of this section. Such standards shall be promulgated not later than 10 years after November 15, 1990. This paragraph shall not be construed to require the Administrator to promulgate standards for such pollutants emitted by electric utility steam generating units.

(7) **Research facilities**

The Administrator shall establish a separate category covering research or laboratory facilities, as necessary to assure the equitable treatment of such facilities. For purposes of this section, "research or laboratory facility" means any stationary source whose primary purpose is to conduct research and development into new processes and products, where such source is operated under the close supervision of technically trained personnel and is not engaged in the manufacture of products for commercial sale in commerce, except in a de minimis manner.

(8) **Boat manufacturing**

When establishing emissions standards for styrene, the Administrator shall list boat manufacturing as a separate subcategory unless the Administrator finds that such listing would be inconsistent with the goals and requirements of this chapter.

(9) **Deletions from the list**

**(A)** Where the sole reason for the inclusion of a source category on the list required under this subsection is the emission of a unique chemical substance, the Administrator shall delete the source category from the list if it is appropriate because of action taken under either subparagraphs (C) or (D) of subsection (b)(3) of this section.

**(B)** The Administrator may delete any source category from the list under this subsection, on petition of any person or on the Administrator's own motion, whenever the Administrator makes the following determination or determinations, as applicable:

**(i)** In the case of hazardous air pollutants emitted by sources in the category that may result in cancer in humans, a determination that no source in the category (or group of sources in the case of area sources) emits such hazardous air pollutants in quantities which may cause a lifetime risk of cancer greater than one in one million to the individual in the population who is most exposed to emissions of such pollutants from the source (or group of sources in the case of area sources).

**(ii)** In the case of hazardous air pollutants that may result in adverse health effects in humans other than cancer or adverse environmental effects, a determination that emissions from no source in the category or subcategory concerned (or group of sources in the case of area sources) exceed a level which is adequate to protect public health with an ample margin of safety and no adverse environmental effect will result from emissions from any source (or from a group of sources in the case of area sources).

The Administrator shall grant or deny a petition under this paragraph within 1 year after the petition is filed.

(d) **Emission standards**

(1) **In general**

The Administrator shall promulgate regulations establishing emission standards for each category or subcategory of major sources and area sources of hazardous air pollutants listed for regulation pursuant to subsection (c) of this section in accordance with the schedules provided in subsections (c) and (e) of this section. The Administrator may distinguish among classes, types, and sizes of sources within a category or subcategory in establishing such standards except that, there shall be no delay in the compliance date for any standard applicable to any source under subsection (i) of this section as the result of the authority provided by this sentence.

(2) **Standards and methods**

Emissions standards promulgated under this subsection and applicable to new or existing sources of hazardous air pollutants shall require the maximum degree of reduction in emissions of the hazardous air pollutants subject to this section (including a prohibition on such emissions, where achievable) that the Administrator, taking into consideration the cost of achieving such emission reduction, and any non-air quality health and environmental impacts and energy requirements, determines is achievable for new or existing sources in the category or subcategory to which such emission standard applies, through application of measures, processes, methods, systems or techniques including, but not limited to, measures which—

(A) reduce the volume of, or eliminate emissions of, such pollutants through process changes, substitution of materials or other modifications,

(B) enclose systems or processes to eliminate emissions,

(C) collect, capture or treat such pollutants when released from a process, stack, storage or fugitive emissions point,

(D) are design, equipment, work practice, or operational standards (including requirements for operator training or certification) as provided in subsection (h) of this section, or

(E) are a combination of the above.

None of the measures described in subparagraphs (A) through (D) shall, consistent with the provisions of section 7414(c) of this title, in any way compromise any United States patent or United States trademark right, or any confidential business information, or any trade secret or any other intellectual property right.

**(3) New and existing sources**

The maximum degree of reduction in emissions that is deemed achievable for new sources in a category or subcategory shall not be less stringent than the emission control that is achieved in practice by the best controlled similar source, as determined by the Administrator. Emission standards promulgated under this subsection for existing sources in a category or subcategory may be less stringent than standards for new sources in the same category or subcategory but shall not be less stringent, and may be more stringent than—

(A) the average emission limitation achieved by the best performing 12 percent of the existing sources (for which the Administrator has emissions information), excluding those sources that have, within 18 months before the emission standard is proposed or within 30 months before such standard is promulgated, whichever is later, first achieved a level of emission rate or emission reduction which complies, or would comply if the source is not subject to such standard, with the lowest achievable emission rate (as defined by section 7501 of this title) applicable to the source category and prevailing at the time, in the category or subcategory for categories and subcategories with 30 or more sources, or

(B) the average emission limitation achieved by the best performing 5 sources (for which the Administrator has or could reasonably obtain emissions information) in the category or subcategory for categories or subcategories with fewer than 30 sources.

**(4) Health threshold**

With respect to pollutants for which a health threshold has been established, the Administrator may consider such threshold level, with an ample margin of safety, when establishing emission standards under this subsection.

**(5) Alternative standard for area sources**

With respect only to categories and subcategories of area sources listed pursuant to subsection (c) of this section, the Administrator may, in lieu of the authorities provided in paragraph (2) and subsection (f) of this section, elect to promulgate standards or requirements applicable to sources in such categories or subcategories which provide for the use of generally available control technologies or management practices by such sources to reduce emissions of hazardous air pollutants.

**(6) Review and revision**

The Administrator shall review, and revise as necessary (taking into account developments in practices, processes, and control technologies), emission standards promulgated under this section no less often than every 8 years.

**(7) Other requirements preserved**

No emission standard or other requirement promulgated under this section shall be interpreted, construed or applied to diminish or replace the requirements of a more stringent emission limitation or other applicable requirement established pursuant to section 7411 of this title, part C or D of this subchapter, or other authority of this chapter or a standard issued under State authority.

**(8) Coke ovens**

(A) Not later than December 31, 1992, the Administrator shall promulgate regulations establishing emission standards under paragraphs (2) and (3) of this subsection for coke oven batteries. In establishing such standards, the Administrator shall evaluate—

(i) the use of sodium silicate (or equivalent) luting compounds to prevent door leaks, and other operating practices and technologies for their effectiveness in reducing coke oven emissions, and their suitability for use on new and existing coke oven batteries, taking into account costs and reasonable commercial door warranties; and

**(ii)** as a basis for emission standards under this subsection for new coke oven batteries that begin construction after the date of proposal of such standards, the Jewell design Thompson non-recovery coke oven batteries and other non-recovery coke oven technologies, and other appropriate emission control and coke production technologies, as to their effectiveness in reducing coke oven emissions and their capability for production of steel quality coke.

Such regulations shall require at a minimum that coke oven batteries will not exceed 8 per centum leaking doors, 1 per centum leaking lids, 5 per centum leaking offtakes, and 16 seconds visible emissions per charge, with no exclusion for emissions during the period after the closing of self-sealing oven doors. Notwithstanding subsection (i) of this section, the compliance date for such emission standards for existing coke oven batteries shall be December 31, 1995.

**(B)** The Administrator shall promulgate work practice regulations under this subsection for coke oven batteries requiring, as appropriate—

**(i)** the use of sodium silicate (or equivalent) luting compounds, if the Administrator determines that use of sodium silicate is an effective means of emissions control and is achievable, taking into account costs and reasonable commercial warranties for doors and related equipment; and

**(ii)** door and jam cleaning practices.

Notwithstanding subsection (i) of this section, the compliance date for such work practice regulations for coke oven batteries shall be not later than the date 3 years after November 15, 1990.

**(C)** For coke oven batteries electing to qualify for an extension of the compliance date for standards promulgated under subsection (f) of this section in accordance with subsection (i)(8) of this section, the emission standards under this subsection for coke oven batteries shall require that coke oven batteries not exceed 8 per centum leaking doors, 1 per centum leaking lids, 5 per centum leaking offtakes, and 16 seconds visible emissions per charge, with no exclusion for emissions during the period after the closing of self-sealing doors. Notwithstanding subsection (i) of this section, the compliance date for such emission standards for existing coke oven batteries seeking an extension shall be not later than the date 3 years after November 15, 1990.

#### (9) Sources licensed by the Nuclear Regulatory Commission

No standard for radionuclide emissions from any category or subcategory of facilities licensed by the Nuclear Regulatory Commission (or an Agreement State) is required to be promulgated under this section if the Administrator determines, by rule, and after consultation with the Nuclear Regulatory Commission, that the regulatory program established by the Nuclear Regulatory Commission pursuant to the Atomic Energy Act [42 U.S.C.A. § 2011 et seq.] for such category or subcategory provides an ample margin of safety to protect the public health. Nothing in this subsection shall preclude or deny the right of any State or political subdivision thereof to adopt or enforce any standard or limitation respecting emissions of radionuclides which is more stringent than the standard or limitation in effect under section 7411 of this title or this section.

#### (10) Effective date

Emission standards or other regulations promulgated under this subsection shall be effective upon promulgation.

### (e) Schedule for standards and review

#### (1) In general

The Administrator shall promulgate regulations establishing emission standards for categories and subcategories of sources initially listed for regulation pursuant to subsection (c)(1) of this section as expeditiously as practicable, assuring that—

**(A)** emission standards for not less than 40 categories and subcategories (not counting coke oven batteries) shall be promulgated not later than 2 years after November 15, 1990;

**(B)** emission standards for coke oven batteries shall be promulgated not later than December 31, 1992;

**(C)** emission standards for 25 per centum of the listed categories and subcategories shall be promulgated not later than 4 years after November 15, 1990;

**(D)** emission standards for an additional 25 per centum of the listed categories and subcategories shall be promulgated not later than 7 years after November 15, 1990; and

**(E)** emission standards for all categories and subcategories shall be promulgated not later than 10 years after November 15, 1990.

#### (2) Priorities

In determining priorities for promulgating standards under subsection (d) of this section, the Administrator shall consider—

**(A)** the known or anticipated adverse effects of such pollutants on public health and the environment;

**(B)** the quantity and location of emissions or reasonably anticipated emissions of hazardous air pollutants that each category or subcategory will emit; and

(C) the efficiency of grouping categories or subcategories according to the pollutants emitted, or the processes or technologies used.

**(3) Published schedule**

Not later than 24 months after November 15, 1990, and after opportunity for comment, the Administrator shall publish a schedule establishing a date for the promulgation of emission standards for each category and subcategory of sources listed pursuant to subsection (c)(1) and (3) of this section which shall be consistent with the requirements of paragraphs (1) and (2). The determination of priorities for the promulgation of standards pursuant to this paragraph is not a rulemaking and shall not be subject to judicial review, except that, failure to promulgate any standard pursuant to the schedule established by this paragraph shall be subject to review under section 7604 of this title.

**(4) Judicial review**

Notwithstanding section 7607 of this title, no action of the Administrator adding a pollutant to the list under subsection (b) of this section or listing a source category or subcategory under subsection (c) of this section shall be a final agency action subject to judicial review, except that any such action may be reviewed under such section 7607 of this title when the Administrator issues emission standards for such pollutant or category.

**(5) Publicly owned treatment works**

The Administrator shall promulgate standards pursuant to subsection (d) of this section applicable to publicly owned treatment works (as defined in title II of the Federal Water Pollution Control Act [33 U.S.C.A. § 1281 et seq.]) not later than 5 years after November 15, 1990.

**(f) Standard to protect health and environment**

**(1) Report**

Not later than 6 years after November 15, 1990, the Administrator shall investigate and report, after consultation with the Surgeon General and after opportunity for public comment, to Congress on—

(A) methods of calculating the risk to public health remaining, or likely to remain, from sources subject to regulation under this section after the application of standards under subsection (d) of this section;

(B) the public health significance of such estimated remaining risk and the technologically and commercially available methods and costs of reducing such risks;

(C) the actual health effects with respect to persons living in the vicinity of sources, any available epidemiological or other health studies, risks presented by background concentrations of hazardous air pollutants, any uncertainties in risk assessment methodology or other health assessment technique, and any negative health or environmental consequences to the community of efforts to reduce such risks; and

(D) recommendations as to legislation regarding such remaining risk.

**(2) Emission standards**

(A) If Congress does not act on any recommendation submitted under paragraph (1), the Administrator shall, within 8 years after promulgation of standards for each category or subcategory of sources pursuant to subsection (d) of this section, promulgate standards for such category or subcategory if promulgation of such standards is required in order to provide an ample margin of safety to protect public health in accordance with this section (as in effect before November 15, 1990) or to prevent, taking into consideration costs, energy, safety, and other relevant factors, an adverse environmental effect. Emission standards promulgated under this subsection shall provide an ample margin of safety to protect public health in accordance with this section (as in effect before November 15, 1990), unless the Administrator determines that a more stringent standard is necessary to prevent, taking into consideration costs, energy, safety, and other relevant factors, an adverse environmental effect. If standards promulgated pursuant to subsection (d) of this section and applicable to a category or subcategory of sources emitting a pollutant (or pollutants) classified as a known, probable or possible human carcinogen do not reduce lifetime excess cancer risks to the individual most exposed to emissions from a source in the category or subcategory to less than one in one million, the Administrator shall promulgate standards under this subsection for such source category.

(B) Nothing in subparagraph (A) or in any other provision of this section shall be construed as affecting, or applying to the Administrator's interpretation of this section, as in effect before November 15, 1990, and set forth in the Federal Register of September 14, 1989 (54 Federal Register 38044).

(C) The Administrator shall determine whether or not to promulgate such standards and, if the Administrator decides to promulgate such standards, shall promulgate the standards 8 years after promulgation of the standards under subsection (d) of this section for each source category or subcategory concerned. In the case of categories or subcategories for which standards under subsection (d) of this section are required to be promulgated within 2 years after November 15, 1990, the Administrator shall have 9 years after promulgation of the standards under subsection (d) of this section to make the determination under the preceding sentence and, if required, to promulgate the standards under this paragraph.

**(3) Effective date**

Any emission standard established pursuant to this subsection shall become effective upon promulgation.

**(4) Prohibition**

No air pollutant to which a standard under this subsection applies may be emitted from any stationary source in violation of such standard, except that in the case of an existing source—

**(A)** such standard shall not apply until 90 days after its effective date, and

**(B)** the Administrator may grant a waiver permitting such source a period of up to 2 years after the effective date of a standard to comply with the standard if the Administrator finds that such period is necessary for the installation of controls and that steps will be taken during the period of the waiver to assure that the health of persons will be protected from imminent endangerment.

**(5) Area sources**

The Administrator shall not be required to conduct any review under this subsection or promulgate emission limitations under this subsection for any category or subcategory of area sources that is listed pursuant to subsection (c)(3) of this section and for which an emission standard is promulgated pursuant to subsection (d)(5) of this section.

**(6) Unique chemical substances**

In establishing standards for the control of unique chemical substances of listed pollutants without CAS numbers under this subsection, the Administrator shall establish such standards with respect to the health and environmental effects of the substances actually emitted by sources and direct transformation byproducts of such emissions in the categories and subcategories.

**(g) Modifications**

**(1) Offsets**

**(A)** A physical change in, or change in the method of operation of, a major source which results in a greater than de minimis increase in actual emissions of a hazardous air pollutant shall not be considered a modification, if such increase in the quantity of actual emissions of any hazardous air pollutant from such source will be offset by an equal or greater decrease in the quantity of emissions of another hazardous air pollutant (or pollutants) from such source which is deemed more hazardous, pursuant to guidance issued by the Administrator under subparagraph (B). The owner or operator of such source shall submit a showing to the Administrator (or the State) that such increase has been offset under the preceding sentence.

**(B)** The Administrator shall, after notice and opportunity for comment and not later than 18 months after November 15, 1990, publish guidance with respect to implementation of this subsection. Such guidance shall include an identification, to the extent practicable, of the relative hazard to human health resulting from emissions to the ambient air of each of the pollutants listed under subsection (b) of this section sufficient to facilitate the offset showing authorized by subparagraph (A). Such guidance shall not authorize offsets between pollutants where the increased pollutant (or more than one pollutant in a stream of pollutants) causes adverse effects to human health for which no safety threshold for exposure can be determined unless there are corresponding decreases in such types of pollutant(s).

**(2) Construction, reconstruction and modifications**

**(A)** After the effective date of a permit program under subchapter V of this chapter in any State, no person may modify a major source of hazardous air pollutants in such State, unless the Administrator (or the State) determines that the maximum achievable control technology emission limitation under this section for existing sources will be met. Such determination shall be made on a case-by-case basis where no applicable emissions limitations have been established by the Administrator.

**(B)** After the effective date of a permit program under subchapter V of this chapter in any State, no person may construct or reconstruct any major source of hazardous air pollutants, unless the Administrator (or the State) determines that the maximum achievable control technology emission limitation under this section for new sources will be met. Such determination shall be made on a case-by-case basis where no applicable emission limitations have been established by the Administrator.

**(3) Procedures for modifications**

The Administrator (or the State) shall establish reasonable procedures for assuring that the requirements applying to modifications under this section are reflected in the permit.

**(h) Work practice standards and other requirements**

**(1) In general**

For purposes of this section, if it is not feasible in the judgment of the Administrator to prescribe or enforce an emission standard for control of a hazardous air pollutant or pollutants, the Administrator may, in lieu thereof, promulgate a design, equipment, work practice, or operational standard, or combination thereof, which in the Administrator's judgment is consistent with the provisions of subsection (d) or (f) of this section. In the event the Administrator promulgates a design or equipment standard under this subsection, the Administrator shall include as part of such standard such requirements as will assure the proper operation and maintenance of any such element of design or equipment.

**(2) Definition**

For the purpose of this subsection, the phrase "not feasible to prescribe or enforce an emission standard" means any situation in which the Administrator determines that—

**(A)** a hazardous air pollutant or pollutants cannot be emitted through a conveyance designed and constructed to emit or capture such pollutant, or that any requirement for, or use of, such a conveyance would be inconsistent with any Federal, State or local law, or

**(B)** the application of measurement methodology to a particular class of sources is not practicable due to technological and economic limitations.

**(3) Alternative standard**

If after notice and opportunity for comment, the owner or operator of any source establishes to the satisfaction of the Administrator that an alternative means of emission limitation will achieve a reduction in emissions of any air pollutant at least equivalent to the reduction in emissions of such pollutant achieved under the requirements of paragraph (1), the Administrator shall permit the use of such alternative by the source for purposes of compliance with this section with respect to such pollutant.

**(4) Numerical standard required**

Any standard promulgated under paragraph (1) shall be promulgated in terms of an emission standard whenever it is feasible to promulgate and enforce a standard in such terms.

**(i) Schedule for compliance**

**(1) Preconstruction and operating requirements**

After the effective date of any emission standard, limitation, or regulation under subsection (d), (f) or (h) of this section, no person may construct any new major source or reconstruct any existing major source subject to such emission standard, regulation or limitation unless the Administrator (or a State with a permit program approved under subchapter V of this chapter) determines that such source, if properly constructed, reconstructed and operated, will comply with the standard, regulation or limitation.

**(2) Special rule**

Notwithstanding the requirements of paragraph (1), a new source which commences construction or reconstruction after a standard, limitation or regulation applicable to such source is proposed and before such standard, limitation or regulation is promulgated shall not be required to comply with such promulgated standard until the date 3 years after the date of promulgation if—

**(A)** the promulgated standard, limitation or regulation is more stringent than the standard, limitation or regulation proposed; and

**(B)** the source complies with the standard, limitation, or regulation as proposed during the 3-year period immediately after promulgation.

**(3) Compliance schedule for existing sources**

**(A)** After the effective date of any emissions standard, limitation or regulation promulgated under this section and applicable to a source, no person may operate such source in violation of such standard, limitation or regulation except, in the case of an existing source, the Administrator shall establish a compliance date or dates for each category or subcategory of existing sources, which shall provide for compliance as expeditiously as practicable, but in no event later than 3 years after the effective date of such standard, except as provided in subparagraph (B) and paragraphs (4) through (8).

**(B)** The Administrator (or a State with a program approved under subchapter V of this chapter) may issue a permit that grants an extension permitting an existing source up to 1 additional year to comply with standards under subsection (d) of this section if such additional period is necessary for the installation of controls. An additional extension of up to 3 years may be added for mining waste operations, if the 4-year compliance time is insufficient to dry and cover mining waste in order to reduce emissions of any pollutant listed under subsection (b) of this section.

**(4) Presidential exemption**

The President may exempt any stationary source from compliance with any standard or limitation under this section for a period of not more than 2 years if the President determines that the technology to implement such standard is not available and that it is in the national security interests of the United States to do so. An exemption under this paragraph may be extended for 1 or more additional periods, each period not to exceed 2 years. The President shall report to Congress with respect to each exemption (or extension thereof) made under this paragraph.

**(5) Early reduction**

**(A)** The Administrator (or a State acting pursuant to a permit program approved under subchapter V of this chapter) shall issue a permit allowing an existing source, for which the owner or operator demonstrates that the source has achieved a reduction of 90 per centum or more in emissions of hazardous air pollutants (95 per centum in the case of hazardous air pollutants which are particulates) from the source, to meet an alternative emission limitation reflecting such reduction in lieu of an emission limitation promulgated under subsection (d) of this section for a period of 6 years from the compliance date for the otherwise applicable standard, provided that such reduction is achieved before the otherwise applicable standard under subsection (d) of this section is first proposed. Nothing in this paragraph shall preclude a State from requiring reductions in excess of those specified in this subparagraph as a condition of granting the extension authorized by the previous sentence.

**(B)** An existing source which achieves the reduction referred to in subparagraph (A) after the proposal of an applicable standard but before January 1, 1994, may qualify under subparagraph (A), if the source makes an enforceable commitment to achieve such reduction before the proposal of the standard. Such commitment shall be enforceable to the same extent as a regulation under this section.

**(C)** The reduction shall be determined with respect to verifiable and actual emissions in a base year not earlier than calendar year 1987, provided that, there is no evidence that emissions in the base year are artificially or substantially greater than emissions in other years prior to implementation of emissions reduction measures. The Administrator may allow a source to use a baseline year of 1985 or 1986 provided that the source can demonstrate to the satisfaction of the Administrator that emissions data for the source reflects verifiable data based on information for such source, received by the Administrator prior to November 15, 1990, pursuant to an information request issued under section 7414 of this title.

**(D)** For each source granted an alternative emission limitation under this paragraph there shall be established by a permit issued pursuant to subchapter V of this chapter an enforceable emission limitation for hazardous air pollutants reflecting the reduction which qualifies the source for an alternative emission limitation under this paragraph. An alternative emission limitation under this paragraph shall not be available with respect to standards or requirements promulgated pursuant to subsection (f) of this section and the Administrator shall, for the purpose of determining whether a standard under subsection (f) of this section is necessary, review emissions from sources granted an alternative emission limitation under this paragraph at the same time that other sources in the category or subcategory are reviewed.

**(E)** With respect to pollutants for which high risks of adverse public health effects may be associated with exposure to small quantities including, but not limited to, chlorinated dioxins and furans, the Administrator shall by regulation limit the use of offsetting reductions in emissions of other hazardous air pollutants from the source as counting toward the 90 per centum reduction in such high-risk pollutants qualifying for an alternative emissions limitation under this paragraph.

**(6) Other reductions**

Notwithstanding the requirements of this section, no existing source that has installed—

**(A)** best available control technology (as defined in section 7479(3) of this title), or

**(B)** technology required to meet a lowest achievable emission rate (as defined in section 7501 of this title),

prior to the promulgation of a standard under this section applicable to such source and the same pollutant (or stream of pollutants) controlled pursuant to an action described in subparagraph (A) or (B) shall be required to comply with such standard under this section until the date 5 years after the date on which such installation or reduction has been achieved, as determined by the Administrator. The Administrator may issue such rules and guidance as are necessary to implement this paragraph.

**(7) Extension for new sources**

A source for which construction or reconstruction is commenced after the date an emission standard applicable to such source is proposed pursuant to subsection (d) of this section but before the date an emission standard applicable to such source is proposed pursuant to subsection (f) of this section shall not be required to comply with the emission standard under subsection (f) of this section until the date 10 years after the date construction or reconstruction is commenced.

**(8) Coke ovens**

**(A)** Any coke oven battery that complies with the emission limitations established under subsection (d)(8)(C) of this section, subparagraph (B), and subparagraph (C), and complies with the provisions of subparagraph (E), shall not be required to achieve emission limitations promulgated under subsection (f) of this section until January 1, 2020.

(B)(i) Not later than December 31, 1992, the Administrator shall promulgate emission limitations for coke oven emissions from coke oven batteries. Notwithstanding paragraph (3) of this subsection, the compliance date for such emission limitations for existing coke oven batteries shall be January 1, 1998. Such emission limitations shall reflect the lowest achievable emission rate as defined in section 7501 of this title for a coke oven battery that is rebuilt or a replacement at a coke oven plant for an existing battery. Such emission limitations shall be no less stringent than—

(I) 3 per centum leaking doors (5 per centum leaking doors for six meter batteries);

(II) 1 per centum leaking lids;

(III) 4 per centum leaking offtakes; and

(IV) 16 seconds visible emissions per charge,

with an exclusion for emissions during the period after the closing of self-sealing oven doors (or the total mass emissions equivalent). The rulemaking in which such emission limitations are promulgated shall also establish an appropriate measurement methodology for determining compliance with such emission limitations, and shall establish such emission limitations in terms of an equivalent level of mass emissions reduction from a coke oven battery, unless the Administrator finds that such a mass emissions standard would not be practicable or enforceable. Such measurement methodology, to the extent it measures leaking doors, shall take into consideration alternative test methods that reflect the best technology and practices actually applied in the affected industries, and shall assure that the final test methods are consistent with the performance of such best technology and practices.

(ii) If the Administrator fails to promulgate such emission limitations under this subparagraph prior to the effective date of such emission limitations, the emission limitations applicable to coke oven batteries under this subparagraph shall be—

(I) 3 per centum leaking doors (5 per centum leaking doors for six meter batteries);

(II) 1 per centum leaking lids;

(III) 4 per centum leaking offtakes; and

(IV) 16 seconds visible emissions per charge,

or the total mass emissions equivalent (if the total mass emissions equivalent is determined to be practicable and enforceable), with no exclusion for emissions during the period after the closing of self-sealing oven doors.

(C) Not later than January 1, 2007, the Administrator shall review the emission limitations promulgated under subparagraph (B) and revise, as necessary, such emission limitations to reflect the lowest achievable emission rate as defined in section 7501 of this title at the time for a coke oven battery that is rebuilt or a replacement at a coke oven plant for an existing battery. Such emission limitations shall be no less stringent than the emission limitation promulgated under subparagraph (B). Notwithstanding paragraph (2) of this subsection, the compliance date for such emission limitations for existing coke oven batteries shall be January 1, 2010.

(D) At any time prior to January 1, 1998, the owner or operator of any coke oven battery may elect to comply with emission limitations promulgated under subsection (f) of this section by the date such emission limitations would otherwise apply to such coke oven battery, in lieu of the emission limitations and the compliance dates provided under subparagraphs (B) and (C) of this paragraph. Any such owner or operator shall be legally bound to comply with such emission limitations promulgated under subsection (f) of this section with respect to such coke oven battery as of January 1, 2003. If no such emission limitations have been promulgated for such coke oven battery, the Administrator shall promulgate such emission limitations in accordance with subsection (f) of this section for such coke oven battery.

(E) Coke oven batteries qualifying for an extension under subparagraph (A) shall make available not later than January 1, 2000, to the surrounding communities the results of any risk assessment performed by the Administrator to determine the appropriate level of any emission standard established by the Administrator pursuant to subsection (f) of this section.

(F) Notwithstanding the provisions of this section, reconstruction of any source of coke oven emissions qualifying for an extension under this paragraph shall not subject such source to emission limitations under subsection (f) of this section more stringent than those established under subparagraphs (B) and (C) until January 1, 2020. For the purposes of this subparagraph, the term "reconstruction" includes the replacement of existing coke oven battery capacity with new coke oven batteries of comparable or lower capacity and lower potential emissions.

**(j) Equivalent emission limitation by permit**

**(1) Effective date**

The requirements of this subsection shall apply in each State beginning on the effective date of a permit program established pursuant to subchapter V of this chapter in such State, but not prior to the date 42 months after November 15, 1990.

**(2) Failure to promulgate a standard**

In the event that the Administrator fails to promulgate a standard for a category or subcategory of major sources by the date established pursuant to subsection (e)(1) and (3) of this section, and beginning 18 months after such date (but not prior to the effective date of a permit program under subchapter V of this chapter), the owner or operator of any major source in such category or subcategory shall submit a permit application under paragraph (3) and such owner or operator shall also comply with paragraphs (5) and (6).

**(3) Applications**

By the date established by paragraph (2), the owner or operator of a major source subject to this subsection shall file an application for a permit. If the owner or operator of a source has submitted a timely and complete application for a permit required by this subsection, any failure to have a permit shall not be a violation of paragraph (2), unless the delay in final action is due to the failure of the applicant to timely submit information required or requested to process the application. The Administrator shall not later than 18 months after November 15, 1990, and after notice and opportunity for comment, establish requirements for applications under this subsection including a standard application form and criteria for determining in a timely manner the completeness of applications.

**(4) Review and approval**

Permit applications submitted under this subsection shall be reviewed and approved or disapproved according to the provisions of section 7661d of this title. In the event that the Administrator (or the State) disapproves a permit application submitted under this subsection or determines that the application is incomplete, the applicant shall have up to 6 months to revise the application to meet the objections of the Administrator (or the State).

**(5) Emission limitation**

The permit shall be issued pursuant to subchapter V of this chapter and shall contain emission limitations for the hazardous air pollutants subject to regulation under this section and emitted by the source that the Administrator (or the State) determines, on a case-by-case basis, to be equivalent to the limitation that would apply to such source if an emission standard had been promulgated in a timely manner under subsection (d) of this section. In the alternative, if the applicable criteria are met, the permit may contain an emissions limitation established according to the provisions of subsection (i)(5) of this section. For purposes of the preceding sentence, the reduction required by subsection (i)(5)(A) of this section shall be achieved by the date on which the relevant standard should have been promulgated under subsection (d) of this section. No such pollutant may be emitted in amounts exceeding an emission limitation contained in a permit immediately for new sources and, as expeditiously as practicable, but not later than the date 3 years after the permit is issued for existing sources or such other compliance date as would apply under subsection (i) of this section.

**(6) Applicability of subsequent standards**

If the Administrator promulgates an emission standard that is applicable to the major source prior to the date on which a permit application is approved, the emission limitation in the permit shall reflect the promulgated standard rather than the emission limitation determined pursuant to paragraph (5), provided that the source shall have the compliance period provided under subsection (i) of this section. If the Administrator promulgates a standard under subsection (d) of this section that would be applicable to the source in lieu of the emission limitation established by permit under this subsection after the date on which the permit has been issued, the Administrator (or the State) shall revise such permit upon the next renewal to reflect the standard promulgated by the Administrator providing such source a reasonable time to comply, but no longer than 8 years after such standard is promulgated or 8 years after the date on which the source is first required to comply with the emissions limitation established by paragraph (5), whichever is earlier.

**(k) Area source program**

**(1) Findings and purpose**

The Congress finds that emissions of hazardous air pollutants from area sources may individually, or in the aggregate, present significant risks to public health in urban areas. Considering the large number of persons exposed and the risks of carcinogenic and other adverse health effects from hazardous air pollutants, ambient concentrations characteristic of large urban areas should be reduced to levels substantially below those currently experienced. It is the purpose of this subsection to achieve a substantial reduction in emissions of hazardous air pollutants from area sources and an equivalent reduction in the public health risks associated with such sources including a reduction of not less than 75 per centum in the incidence of cancer attributable to emissions from such sources.

**(2) Research program**

The Administrator shall, after consultation with State and local air pollution control officials, conduct a program of research with respect to sources of hazardous air pollutants in urban areas and shall include within such program—

(A) ambient monitoring for a broad range of hazardous air pollutants (including, but not limited to, volatile organic compounds, metals, pesticides and products of incomplete combustion) in a representative number of urban locations;

(B) analysis to characterize the sources of such pollution with a focus on area sources and the contribution that such sources make to public health risks from hazardous air pollutants; and

(C) consideration of atmospheric transformation and other factors which can elevate public health risks from such pollutants.

Health effects considered under this program shall include, but not be limited to, carcinogenicity, mutagenicity, teratogenicity, neurotoxicity, reproductive dysfunction and other acute and chronic effects including the role of such pollutants as precursors of ozone or acid aerosol formation. The Administrator shall report the preliminary results of such research not later than 3 years after November 15, 1990.

**(3) National strategy**

(A) Considering information collected pursuant to the monitoring program authorized by paragraph (2), the Administrator shall, not later than 5 years after November 15, 1990, and after notice and opportunity for public comment, prepare and transmit to the Congress a comprehensive strategy to control emissions of hazardous air pollutants from area sources in urban areas.

(B) The strategy shall—

(i) identify not less than 30 hazardous air pollutants which, as the result of emissions from area sources, present the greatest threat to public health in the largest number of urban areas and that are or will be listed pursuant to subsection (b) of this section, and

(ii) identify the source categories or subcategories emitting such pollutants that are or will be listed pursuant to subsection (c) of this section. When identifying categories and subcategories of sources under this subparagraph, the Administrator shall assure that sources accounting for 90 per centum or more of the aggregate emissions of each of the 30 identified hazardous air pollutants are subject to standards pursuant to subsection (d) of this section.

(C) The strategy shall include a schedule of specific actions to substantially reduce the public health risks posed by the release of hazardous air pollutants from area sources that will be implemented by the Administrator under the authority of this or other laws (including, but not limited to, the Toxic Substances Control Act [15 U.S.C.A. § 2601 et seq.], the Federal Insecticide, Fungicide and Rodenticide Act [7 U.S.C.A. § 136 et seq.] and the Resource Conservation and Recovery Act [42 U.S.C.A. § 6901 et seq.]) or by the States. The strategy shall achieve a reduction in the incidence of cancer attributable to exposure to hazardous air pollutants emitted by stationary sources of not less than 75 per centum, considering control of emissions of hazardous air pollutants from all stationary sources and resulting from measures implemented by the Administrator or by the States under this or other laws.

(D) The strategy may also identify research needs in monitoring, analytical methodology, modeling or pollution control techniques and recommendations for changes in law that would further the goals and objectives of this subsection.

(E) Nothing in this subsection shall be interpreted to preclude or delay implementation of actions with respect to area sources of hazardous air pollutants under consideration pursuant to this or any other law and that may be promulgated before the strategy is prepared.

(F) The Administrator shall implement the strategy as expeditiously as practicable assuring that all sources are in compliance with all requirements not later than 9 years after November 15, 1990.

(G) As part of such strategy the Administrator shall provide for ambient monitoring and emissions modeling in urban areas as appropriate to demonstrate that the goals and objectives of the strategy are being met.

**(4) Areawide activities**

In addition to the national urban air toxics strategy authorized by paragraph (3), the Administrator shall also encourage and support areawide strategies developed by State or local air pollution control agencies that are intended to reduce risks from emissions by area sources within a particular urban area. From the funds available for grants under this section, the Administrator shall set aside not less than 10 per centum to support areawide strategies addressing hazardous air pollutants emitted by area sources and shall award such funds on a demonstration basis to those States with innovative and effective strategies. At the request of State or local air pollution control officials, the Administrator shall prepare guidelines for control technologies or management practices which may be applicable to various categories or subcategories of area sources.

**(5) Report**

The Administrator shall report to the Congress at intervals not later than 8 and 12 years after November 15, 1990, on actions taken under this subsection and other parts of this chapter to reduce the risk to public health posed by the release of hazardous air pollutants from area sources. The reports shall also identify specific metropolitan areas that continue to experience high risks to public health as the result of emissions from area sources.

**(*l*) State programs**

**(1) In general**

Each State may develop and submit to the Administrator for approval a program for the implementation and enforcement (including a review of enforcement delegations previously granted) of emission standards and other requirements for air pollutants subject to this section or requirements for the prevention and mitigation of accidental releases pursuant to subsection (r) of this section. A program submitted by a State under this subsection may provide for partial or complete delegation of the Administrator's authorities and responsibilities to implement and enforce emissions standards and prevention requirements but shall not include authority to set standards less stringent than those promulgated by the Administrator under this chapter.

**(2) Guidance**

Not later than 12 months after November 15, 1990, the Administrator shall publish guidance that would be useful to the States in developing programs for submittal under this subsection. The guidance shall also provide for the registration of all facilities producing, processing, handling or storing any substance listed pursuant to subsection (r) of this section in amounts greater than the threshold quantity. The Administrator shall include as an element in such guidance an optional program begun in 1986 for the review of high-risk point sources of air pollutants including, but not limited to, hazardous air pollutants listed pursuant to subsection (b) of this section.

**(3) Technical assistance**

The Administrator shall establish and maintain an air toxics clearinghouse and center to provide technical information and assistance to State and local agencies and, on a cost recovery basis, to others on control technology, health and ecological risk assessment, risk analysis, ambient monitoring and modeling, and emissions measurement and monitoring. The Administrator shall use the authority of section 7403 of this title to examine methods for preventing, measuring, and controlling emissions and evaluating associated health and ecological risks. Where appropriate, such activity shall be conducted with not-for-profit organizations. The Administrator may conduct research on methods for preventing, measuring and controlling emissions and evaluating associated health and environment risks. All information collected under this paragraph shall be available to the public.

**(4) Grants**

Upon application of a State, the Administrator may make grants, subject to such terms and conditions as the Administrator deems appropriate, to such State for the purpose of assisting the State in developing and implementing a program for submittal and approval under this subsection. Programs assisted under this paragraph may include program elements addressing air pollutants or extremely hazardous substances other than those specifically subject to this section. Grants under this paragraph may include support for high-risk point source review as provided in paragraph (2) and support for the development and implementation of areawide area source programs pursuant to subsection (k) of this section.

**(5) Approval or disapproval**

Not later than 180 days after receiving a program submitted by a State, and after notice and opportunity for public comment, the Administrator shall either approve or disapprove such program. The Administrator shall disapprove any program submitted by a State, if the Administrator determines that—

**(A)** the authorities contained in the program are not adequate to assure compliance by all sources within the State with each applicable standard, regulation or requirement established by the Administrator under this section;

**(B)** adequate authority does not exist, or adequate resources are not available, to implement the program;

**(C)** the schedule for implementing the program and assuring compliance by affected sources is not sufficiently expeditious; or

**(D)** the program is otherwise not in compliance with the guidance issued by the Administrator under paragraph (2) or is not likely to satisfy, in whole or in part, the objectives of this chapter.

If the Administrator disapproves a State program, the Administrator shall notify the State of any revisions or modifications necessary to obtain approval. The State may revise and resubmit the proposed program for review and approval pursuant to the provisions of this subsection.

**(6) Withdrawal**

Whenever the Administrator determines, after public hearing, that a State is not administering and enforcing a program approved pursuant to this subsection in accordance with the guidance published pursuant to paragraph (2) or the requirements of paragraph (5), the Administrator shall so notify the State and, if action which will assure prompt compliance is not taken within 90 days, the Administrator shall withdraw approval of the program. The Administrator shall not withdraw approval of any program unless the State shall have been notified and the reasons for withdrawal shall have been stated in writing and made public.

**(7) Authority to enforce**

Nothing in this subsection shall prohibit the Administrator from enforcing any applicable emission standard or requirement under this section.

**(8) Local program**

The Administrator may, after notice and opportunity for public comment, approve a program developed and submitted by a local air pollution control agency (after consultation with the State) pursuant to this subsection and any such agency implementing an approved program may take any action authorized to be taken by a State under this section.

**(9) Permit authority**

Nothing in this subsection shall affect the authorities and obligations of the Administrator or the State under subchapter V of this chapter.

**(m) Atmospheric deposition to Great Lakes and coastal waters**

**(1) Deposition assessment**

The Administrator, in cooperation with the Under Secretary of Commerce for Oceans and Atmosphere, shall conduct a program to identify and assess the extent of atmospheric deposition of hazardous air pollutants (and in the discretion of the Administrator, other air pollutants) to the Great Lakes, the Chesapeake Bay, Lake Champlain and coastal waters. As part of such program, the Administrator shall—

(A) monitor the Great Lakes, the Chesapeake Bay, Lake Champlain and coastal waters, including monitoring of the Great Lakes through the monitoring network established pursuant to paragraph (2) of this subsection and designing and deploying an atmospheric monitoring network for coastal waters pursuant to paragraph (4);

(B) investigate the sources and deposition rates of atmospheric deposition of air pollutants (and their atmospheric transformation precursors);

(C) conduct research to develop and improve monitoring methods and to determine the relative contribution of atmospheric pollutants to total pollution loadings to the Great Lakes, the Chesapeake Bay, Lake Champlain, and coastal waters;

(D) evaluate any adverse effects to public health or the environment caused by such deposition (including effects resulting from indirect exposure pathways) and assess the contribution of such deposition to violations of water quality standards established pursuant to the Federal Water Pollution Control Act [33 U.S.C.A. § 1251 et seq.] and drinking water standards established pursuant to the Safe Drinking Water Act [42 U.S.C.A. § 300f et seq.]; and

(E) sample for such pollutants in biota, fish, and wildlife of the Great Lakes, the Chesapeake Bay, Lake Champlain and coastal waters and characterize the sources of such pollutants.

**(2) Great Lakes monitoring network**

The Administrator shall oversee, in accordance with Annex 15 of the Great Lakes Water Quality Agreement, the establishment and operation of a Great Lakes atmospheric deposition network to monitor atmospheric deposition of hazardous air pollutants (and in the Administrator's discretion, other air pollutants) to the Great Lakes.

(A) As part of the network provided for in this paragraph, and not later than December 31, 1991, the Administrator shall establish in each of the 5 Great Lakes at least 1 facility capable of monitoring the atmospheric deposition of hazardous air pollutants in both dry and wet conditions.

(B) The Administrator shall use the data provided by the network to identify and track the movement of hazardous air pollutants through the Great Lakes, to determine the portion of water pollution loadings attributable to atmospheric deposition of such pollutants, and to support development of remedial action plans and other management plans as required by the Great Lakes Water Quality Agreement.

(C) The Administrator shall assure that the data collected by the Great Lakes atmospheric deposition monitoring network is in a format compatible with databases sponsored by the International Joint Commission, Canada, and the several States of the Great Lakes region.

**(3) Monitoring for the Chesapeake Bay and Lake Champlain**

The Administrator shall establish at the Chesapeake Bay and Lake Champlain atmospheric deposition stations to monitor deposition of hazardous air pollutants (and in the Administrator's discretion, other air pollutants) within the Chesapeake Bay and Lake Champlain watersheds. The Administrator shall determine the role of air deposition in the pollutant loadings of the Chesapeake Bay and Lake Champlain, investigate the sources of air pollutants deposited in the watersheds, evaluate the health and environmental effects of such pollutant loadings, and shall sample such pollutants in biota, fish and wildlife within the watersheds, as necessary to characterize such effects.

**(4) Monitoring for coastal waters**

The Administrator shall design and deploy atmospheric deposition monitoring networks for coastal waters and their watersheds and shall make any information collected through such networks available to the public. As part of this effort, the Administrator shall conduct research to develop and improve deposition monitoring methods, and to determine the relative contribution of atmospheric pollutants to pollutant loadings. For purposes of this subsection, "coastal waters" shall mean estuaries selected pursuant to section 320(a)(2)(A) of the Federal Water Pollution Control Act [33 U.S.C.A. § 1330(a)(2)(A) ] or listed pursuant to section 320(a)(2)(B) of such Act [33 U.S.C.A. § 1330(a)(2)(B) ] or estuarine research reserves designated pursuant to section 1461 of Title 16.

**(5) Report**

Within 3 years of November 15, 1990, and biennially thereafter, the Administrator, in cooperation with the Under Secretary of Commerce for Oceans and Atmosphere, shall submit to the Congress a report on the results of any monitoring, studies, and investigations conducted pursuant to this subsection. Such report shall include, at a minimum, an assessment of—

**(A)** the contribution of atmospheric deposition to pollution loadings in the Great Lakes, the Chesapeake Bay, Lake Champlain and coastal waters;

**(B)** the environmental and public health effects of any pollution which is attributable to atmospheric deposition to the Great Lakes, the Chesapeake Bay, Lake Champlain and coastal waters;

**(C)** the source or sources of any pollution to the Great Lakes, the Chesapeake Bay, Lake Champlain and coastal waters which is attributable to atmospheric deposition;

**(D)** whether pollution loadings in the Great Lakes, the Chesapeake Bay, Lake Champlain or coastal waters cause or contribute to exceedances [2] of drinking water standards pursuant to the Safe Drinking Water Act [42 U.S.C.A. § 300f et seq.] or water quality standards pursuant to the Federal Water Pollution Control Act [33 U.S.C.A. § 1251 et seq.] or, with respect to the Great Lakes, exceedances [2] of the specific objectives of the Great Lakes Water Quality Agreement; and

**(E)** a description of any revisions of the requirements, standards, and limitations pursuant to this chapter and other applicable Federal laws as are necessary to assure protection of human health and the environment.

**(6) Additional regulation**

As part of the report to Congress, the Administrator shall determine whether the other provisions of this section are adequate to prevent serious adverse effects to public health and serious or widespread environmental effects, including such effects resulting from indirect exposure pathways, associated with atmospheric deposition to the Great Lakes, the Chesapeake Bay, Lake Champlain and coastal waters of hazardous air pollutants (and their atmospheric transformation products). The Administrator shall take into consideration the tendency of such pollutants to bioaccumulate. Within 5 years after November 15, 1990, the Administrator shall, based on such report and determination, promulgate, in accordance with this section, such further emission standards or control measures as may be necessary and appropriate to prevent such effects, including effects due to bioaccumulation and indirect exposure pathways. Any requirements promulgated pursuant to this paragraph with respect to coastal waters shall only apply to the coastal waters of the States which are subject to section 7627(a) of this title.

**(n) Other provisions**

**(1) Electric utility steam generating units**

**(A)** The Administrator shall perform a study of the hazards to public health reasonably anticipated to occur as a result of emissions by electric utility steam generating units of pollutants listed under subsection (b) of this section after imposition of the requirements of this chapter. The Administrator shall report the results of this study to the Congress within 3 years after November 15, 1990. The Administrator shall develop and describe in the Administrator's report to Congress alternative control strategies for emissions which may warrant regulation under this section. The Administrator shall regulate electric utility steam generating units under this section, if the Administrator finds such regulation is appropriate and necessary after considering the results of the study required by this subparagraph.

**(B)** The Administrator shall conduct, and transmit to the Congress not later than 4 years after November 15, 1990, a study of mercury emissions from electric utility steam generating units, municipal waste combustion units, and other sources, including area sources. Such study shall consider the rate and mass of such emissions, the health and environmental effects of such emissions, technologies which are available to control such emissions, and the costs of such technologies.

**(C)** The National Institute of Environmental Health Sciences shall conduct, and transmit to the Congress not later than 3 years after November 15, 1990, a study to determine the threshold level of mercury exposure below which adverse human health effects are not expected to occur. Such study shall include a threshold for mercury concentrations in the tissue of fish which may be consumed (including consumption by sensitive populations) without adverse effects to public health.

(2) **Coke oven production technology study**

(A) The Secretary of the Department of Energy and the Administrator shall jointly undertake a 6-year study to assess coke oven production emission control technologies and to assist in the development and commercialization of technically practicable and economically viable control technologies which have the potential to significantly reduce emissions of hazardous air pollutants from coke oven production facilities. In identifying control technologies, the Secretary and the Administrator shall consider the range of existing coke oven operations and battery design and the availability of sources of materials for such coke ovens as well as alternatives to existing coke oven production design.

(B) The Secretary and the Administrator are authorized to enter into agreements with persons who propose to develop, install and operate coke production emission control technologies which have the potential for significant emissions reductions of hazardous air pollutants provided that Federal funds shall not exceed 50 per centum of the cost of any project assisted pursuant to this paragraph.

(C) On completion of the study, the Secretary shall submit to Congress a report on the results of the study and shall make recommendations to the Administrator identifying practicable and economically viable control technologies for coke oven production facilities to reduce residual risks remaining after implementation of the standard under subsection (d) of this section.

(D) There are authorized to be appropriated $5,000,000 for each of the fiscal years 1992 through 1997 to carry out the program authorized by this paragraph.

(3) **Publicly owned treatment works**

The Administrator may conduct, in cooperation with the owners and operators of publicly owned treatment works, studies to characterize emissions of hazardous air pollutants emitted by such facilities, to identify industrial, commercial and residential discharges that contribute to such emissions and to demonstrate control measures for such emissions. When promulgating any standard under this section applicable to publicly owned treatment works, the Administrator may provide for control measures that include pretreatment of discharges causing emissions of hazardous air pollutants and process or product substitutions or limitations that may be effective in reducing such emissions. The Administrator may prescribe uniform sampling, modeling and risk assessment methods for use in implementing this subsection.

(4) **Oil and gas wells; pipeline facilities**

(A) Notwithstanding the provisions of subsection (a) of this section, emissions from any oil or gas exploration or production well (with its associated equipment) and emissions from any pipeline compressor or pump station shall not be aggregated with emissions from other similar units, whether or not such units are in a contiguous area or under common control, to determine whether such units or stations are major sources, and in the case of any oil or gas exploration or production well (with its associated equipment), such emissions shall not be aggregated for any purpose under this section.

(B) The Administrator shall not list oil and gas production wells (with its associated equipment) as an area source category under subsection (c) of this section, except that the Administrator may establish an area source category for oil and gas production wells located in any metropolitan statistical area or consolidated metropolitan statistical area with a population in excess of 1 million, if the Administrator determines that emissions of hazardous air pollutants from such wells present more than a negligible risk of adverse effects to public health.

(5) **Hydrogen sulfide**

The Administrator is directed to assess the hazards to public health and the environment resulting from the emission of hydrogen sulfide associated with the extraction of oil and natural gas resources. To the extent practicable, the assessment shall build upon and not duplicate work conducted for an assessment pursuant to section 8002(m) of the Solid Waste Disposal Act [42 U.S.C.A. § 6982(m) ] and shall reflect consultation with the States. The assessment shall include a review of existing State and industry control standards, techniques and enforcement. The Administrator shall report to the Congress within 24 months after November 15, 1990, with the findings of such assessment, together with any recommendations, and shall, as appropriate, develop and implement a control strategy for emissions of hydrogen sulfide to protect human health and the environment, based on the findings of such assessment, using authorities under this chapter including sections [3] 7411 of this title and this section.

(6) **Hydrofluoric acid**

Not later than 2 years after November 15, 1990, the Administrator shall, for those regions of the country which do not have comprehensive health and safety regulations with respect to hydrofluoric acid, complete a study of the potential hazards of hydrofluoric acid and the uses of hydrofluoric acid in industrial and commercial applications to public health and the environment considering a range of events including worst-case accidental releases and shall make recommendations to the Congress for the reduction of such hazards, if appropriate.

**(7) RCRA facilities**

In the case of any category or subcategory of sources the air emissions of which are regulated under subtitle C of the Solid Waste Disposal Act [42 U.S.C.A. § 6921 et seq.], the Administrator shall take into account any regulations of such emissions which are promulgated under such subtitle and shall, to the maximum extent practicable and consistent with the provisions of this section, ensure that the requirements of such subtitle and this section are consistent.

**(*o*) National Academy of Sciences study**

**(1) Request of the Academy**

Within 3 months of November 15, 1990, the Administrator shall enter into appropriate arrangements with the National Academy of Sciences to conduct a review of—

**(A)** risk assessment methodology used by the Environmental Protection Agency to determine the carcinogenic risk associated with exposure to hazardous air pollutants from source categories and subcategories subject to the requirements of this section; and

**(B)** improvements in such methodology.

**(2) Elements to be studied**

In conducting such review, the National Academy of Sciences should consider, but not be limited to, the following—

**(A)** the techniques used for estimating and describing the carcinogenic potency to humans of hazardous air pollutants; and

**(B)** the techniques used for estimating exposure to hazardous air pollutants (for hypothetical and actual maximally exposed individuals as well as other exposed individuals).

**(3) Other health effects of concern**

To the extent practicable, the Academy shall evaluate and report on the methodology for assessing the risk of adverse human health effects other than cancer for which safe thresholds of exposure may not exist, including, but not limited to, inheritable genetic mutations, birth defects, and reproductive dysfunctions.

**(4) Report**

A report on the results of such review shall be submitted to the Senate Committee on Environment and Public Works, the House Committee on Energy and Commerce, the Risk Assessment and Management Commission established by section 303 of the Clean Air Act Amendments of 1990 and the Administrator not later than 30 months after November 15, 1990.

**(5) Assistance**

The Administrator shall assist the Academy in gathering any information the Academy deems necessary to carry out this subsection. The Administrator may use any authority under this chapter to obtain information from any person, and to require any person to conduct tests, keep and produce records, and make reports respecting research or other activities conducted by such person as necessary to carry out this subsection.

**(6) Authorization**

Of the funds authorized to be appropriated to the Administrator by this chapter, such amounts as are required shall be available to carry out this subsection.

**(7) Guidelines for carcinogenic risk assessment**

The Administrator shall consider, but need not adopt, the recommendations contained in the report of the National Academy of Sciences prepared pursuant to this subsection and the views of the Science Advisory Board, with respect to such report. Prior to the promulgation of any standard under subsection (f) of this section, and after notice and opportunity for comment, the Administrator shall publish revised Guidelines for Carcinogenic Risk Assessment or a detailed explanation of the reasons that any recommendations contained in the report of the National Academy of Sciences will not be implemented. The publication of such revised Guidelines shall be a final Agency action for purposes of section 7607 of this title.

**(p) Mickey Leland National Urban Air Toxics Research Center**

**(1) Establishment**

The Administrator shall oversee the establishment of a National Urban Air Toxics Research Center, to be located at a university, a hospital, or other facility capable of undertaking and maintaining similar research capabilities in the areas of epidemiology, oncology, toxicology, pulmonary medicine, pathology, and biostatistics. The center shall be known as the Mickey Leland National Urban Air Toxics Research Center. The geographic site of the National Urban Air Toxics Research Center should be further directed to Harris County, Texas, in order to take full advantage of the well developed scientific community presence on-site at the Texas Medical Center as well as the extensive data previously compiled for the comprehensive monitoring system currently in place.

**(2) Board of Directors**

The National Urban Air Toxics Research Center shall be governed by a Board of Directors to be comprised of 9 members, the appointment of which shall be allocated pro rata among the Speaker of the House, the Majority Leader of the Senate and the President. The members of the Board of Directors shall be selected based on their respective academic and professional backgrounds and expertise in matters relating to public health, environmental pollution and industrial hygiene. The duties of the Board of Directors shall be to determine policy and research guidelines, submit views from center sponsors and the public and issue periodic reports of center findings and activities.

**(3) Scientific Advisory Panel**

The Board of Directors shall be advised by a Scientific Advisory Panel, the 13 members of which shall be appointed by the Board, and to include eminent members of the scientific and medical communities. The Panel membership may include scientists with relevant experience from the National Institute of Environmental Health Sciences, the Center for Disease Control, the Environmental Protection Agency, the National Cancer Institute, and others, and the Panel shall conduct peer review and evaluate research results. The Panel shall assist the Board in developing the research agenda, reviewing proposals and applications, and advise on the awarding of research grants.

**(4) Funding**

The center shall be established and funded with both Federal and private source funds.

**(q) Savings provision**

**(1) Standards previously promulgated**

Any standard under this section in effect before the date of enactment of the Clean Air Act Amendments of 1990 [Nov. 15, 1990] shall remain in force and effect after such date unless modified as provided in this section before the date of enactment of such Amendments or under such Amendments. Except as provided in paragraph (4), any standard under this section which has been promulgated, but has not taken effect, before such date shall not be affected by such Amendments unless modified as provided in this section before such date or under such Amendments. Each such standard shall be reviewed and, if appropriate, revised, to comply with the requirements of subsection (d) of this section within 10 years after the date of enactment of the Clean Air Act Amendments of 1990. If a timely petition for review of any such standard under section 7607 of this title is pending on such date of enactment, the standard shall be upheld if it complies with this section as in effect before that date. If any such standard is remanded to the Administrator, the Administrator may in the Administrator's discretion apply either the requirements of this section, or those of this section as in effect before the date of enactment of the Clean Air Act Amendments of 1990.

**(2) Special rule**

Notwithstanding paragraph (1), no standard shall be established under this section, as amended by the Clean Air Act Amendments of 1990, for radionuclide emissions from (A) elemental phosphorous plants, (B) grate calcination elemental phosphorous plants, (C) phosphogypsum stacks, or (D) any subcategory of the foregoing. This section, as in effect prior to the date of enactment of the Clean Air Act Amendments of 1990 [November 15, 1990], shall remain in effect for radionuclide emissions from such plants and stacks.

**(3) Other categories**

Notwithstanding paragraph (1), this section, as in effect prior to the date of enactment of the Clean Air Act Amendments of 1990 [Nov. 15, 1990], shall remain in effect for radionuclide emissions from non-Department of Energy Federal facilities that are not licensed by the Nuclear Regulatory Commission, coal-fired utility and industrial boilers, underground uranium mines, surface uranium mines, and disposal of uranium mill tailings piles, unless the Administrator, in the Administrator's discretion, applies the requirements of this section as modified by the Clean Air Act Amendments of 1990 to such sources of radionuclides.

**(4) Medical facilities**

Notwithstanding paragraph (1), no standard promulgated under this section prior to November 15, 1990, with respect to medical research or treatment facilities shall take effect for two years following November 15, 1990, unless the Administrator makes a determination pursuant to a rulemaking under subsection (d)(9) of this section. If the Administrator determines that the regulatory program established by the Nuclear Regulatory Commission for such facilities does not provide an ample margin of safety to protect public health, the requirements of this section shall fully apply to such facilities. If the Administrator determines that such regulatory program does provide an ample margin of safety to protect the public health, the Administrator is not required to promulgate a standard under this section for such facilities, as provided in subsection (d)(9) of this section.

**(r) Prevention of accidental releases**

**(1) Purpose and general duty**

It shall be the objective of the regulations and programs authorized under this subsection to prevent the accidental release and to minimize the consequences of any such release of any substance listed pursuant to paragraph (3) or any other extremely hazardous substance. The owners and operators of stationary sources producing, processing, handling or storing such substances have a general duty in the same manner and to the same extent as section 654 of Title 29 to identify hazards which may result from such releases using appropriate hazard assessment techniques, to design and maintain a safe facility taking such steps as are necessary to prevent releases, and to minimize the consequences of accidental releases which do occur. For purposes of this paragraph, the provisions of section 7604 of this title shall not be available to any person or otherwise be construed to be applicable to this paragraph. Nothing in this section shall be interpreted, construed, implied or applied to create any liability or basis for suit for compensation for bodily injury or any other injury or property damages to any person which may result from accidental releases of such substances.

**(2) Definitions**

**(A)** The term "accidental release" means an unanticipated emission of a regulated substance or other extremely hazardous substance into the ambient air from a stationary source.

**(B)** The term "regulated substance" means a substance listed under paragraph (3).

**(C)** The term "stationary source" means any buildings, structures, equipment, installations or substance emitting stationary activities (i) which belong to the same industrial group, (ii) which are located on one or more contiguous properties, (iii) which are under the control of the same person (or persons under common control), and (iv) from which an accidental release may occur.

**(D)** The term "retail facility" means a stationary source at which more than one-half of the income is obtained from direct sales to end users or at which more than one-half of the fuel sold, by volume, is sold through a cylinder exchange program.

**(3) List of substances**

The Administrator shall promulgate not later than 24 months after November 15, 1990, an initial list of 100 substances which, in the case of an accidental release, are known to cause or may reasonably be anticipated to cause death, injury, or serious adverse effects to human health or the environment. For purposes of promulgating such list, the Administrator shall use, but is not limited to, the list of extremely hazardous substances published under the Emergency Planning and Community Right-to-Know Act of 1986 [42 U.S.C.A. § 11001 et seq.], with such modifications as the Administrator deems appropriate. The initial list shall include chlorine, anhydrous ammonia, methyl chloride, ethylene oxide, vinyl chloride, methyl isocyanate, hydrogen cyanide, ammonia, hydrogen sulfide, toluene diisocyanate, phosgene, bromine, anhydrous hydrogen chloride, hydrogen fluoride, anhydrous sulfur dioxide, and sulfur trioxide. The initial list shall include at least 100 substances which pose the greatest risk of causing death, injury, or serious adverse effects to human health or the environment from accidental releases. Regulations establishing the list shall include an explanation of the basis for establishing the list. The list may be revised from time to time by the Administrator on the Administrator's own motion or by petition and shall be reviewed at least every 5 years. No air pollutant for which a national primary ambient air quality standard has been established shall be included on any such list. No substance, practice, process, or activity regulated under subchapter VI of this chapter shall be subject to regulations under this subsection. The Administrator shall establish procedures for the addition and deletion of substances from the list established under this paragraph consistent with those applicable to the list in subsection (b) of this section.

**(4) Factors to be considered**

In listing substances under paragraph (3), the Administrator—

**(A)** shall consider—

**(i)** the severity of any acute adverse health effects associated with accidental releases of the substance;

**(ii)** the likelihood of accidental releases of the substance; and

**(iii)** the potential magnitude of human exposure to accidental releases of the substance; and

**(B)** shall not list a flammable substance when used as a fuel or held for sale as a fuel at a retail facility under this subsection solely because of the explosive or flammable properties of the substance, unless a fire or explosion caused by the substance will result in acute adverse health effects from human exposure to the substance, including the unburned fuel or its combustion byproducts, other than those caused by the heat of the fire or impact of the explosion.

**(5) Threshold quantity**

At the time any substance is listed pursuant to paragraph (3), the Administrator shall establish by rule, a threshold quantity for the substance, taking into account the toxicity, reactivity, volatility, dispersibility, combustibility, or flammability of the substance and the amount of the substance which, as a result of an accidental release, is known to cause or may reasonably be anticipated to cause death, injury or serious adverse effects to human health for which the substance was listed. The Administrator is authorized to establish a greater threshold quantity for, or to exempt entirely, any substance that is a nutrient used in agriculture when held by a farmer.

**(6) Chemical Safety Board**

**(A)** There is hereby established an independent safety board to be known as the Chemical Safety and Hazard Investigation Board.

**(B)** The Board shall consist of 5 members, including a Chairperson, who shall be appointed by the President, by and with the advice and consent of the Senate. Members of the Board shall be appointed on the basis of technical qualification, professional standing, and demonstrated knowledge in the fields of accident reconstruction, safety engineering, human factors, toxicology, or air pollution regulation. The terms of office of members of the Board shall be 5 years. Any member of the Board, including the Chairperson, may be removed for inefficiency, neglect of duty, or malfeasance in office. The Chairperson shall be the Chief Executive Officer of the Board and shall exercise the executive and administrative functions of the Board.

**(C)** The Board shall—

**(i)** investigate (or cause to be investigated), determine and report to the public in writing the facts, conditions, and circumstances and the cause or probable cause of any accidental release resulting in a fatality, serious injury or substantial property damages;

**(ii)** issue periodic reports to the Congress, Federal, State and local agencies, including the Environmental Protection Agency and the Occupational Safety and Health Administration, concerned with the safety of chemical production, processing, handling and storage, and other interested persons recommending measures to reduce the likelihood or the consequences of accidental releases and proposing corrective steps to make chemical production, processing, handling and storage as safe and free from risk of injury as is possible and may include in such reports proposed rules or orders which should be issued by the Administrator under the authority of this section or the Secretary of Labor under the Occupational Safety and Health Act [29 U.S.C.A. § 651 et seq.] to prevent or minimize the consequences of any release of substances that may cause death, injury or other serious adverse effects on human health or substantial property damage as the result of an accidental release; and

**(iii)** establish by regulation requirements binding on persons for reporting accidental releases into the ambient air subject to the Board's investigatory jurisdiction. Reporting releases to the National Response Center, in lieu of the Board directly, shall satisfy such regulations. The National Response Center shall promptly notify the Board of any releases which are within the Board's jurisdiction.

**(D)** The Board may utilize the expertise and experience of other agencies.

**(E)** The Board shall coordinate its activities with investigations and studies conducted by other agencies of the United States having a responsibility to protect public health and safety. The Board shall enter into a memorandum of understanding with the National Transportation Safety Board to assure coordination of functions and to limit duplication of activities which shall designate the National Transportation Safety Board as the lead agency for the investigation of releases which are transportation related. The Board shall not be authorized to investigate marine oil spills, which the National Transportation Safety Board is authorized to investigate. The Board shall enter into a memorandum of understanding with the Occupational Safety and Health Administration so as to limit duplication of activities. In no event shall the Board forego an investigation where an accidental release causes a fatality or serious injury among the general public, or had the potential to cause substantial property damage or a number of deaths or injuries among the general public.

**(F)** The Board is authorized to conduct research and studies with respect to the potential for accidental releases, whether or not an accidental release has occurred, where there is evidence which indicates the presence of a potential hazard or hazards. To the extent practicable, the Board shall conduct such studies in cooperation with other Federal agencies having emergency response authorities, State and local governmental agencies and associations and organizations from the industrial, commercial, and nonprofit sectors.

**(G)** No part of the conclusions, findings, or recommendations of the Board relating to any accidental release or the investigation thereof shall be admitted as evidence or used in any action or suit for damages arising out of any matter mentioned in such report.

**(H)** Not later than 18 months after November 15, 1990, the Board shall publish a report accompanied by recommendations to the Administrator on the use of hazard assessments in preventing the occurrence and minimizing the consequences of accidental releases of extremely hazardous substances. The recommendations shall include a list of extremely hazardous substances which are not regulated substances (including threshold quantities for such substances) and categories of stationary sources for which hazard assessments would be an appropriate measure to aid in the prevention of accidental releases and to minimize the consequences of those releases that do occur. The recommendations shall also include a description of the information and analysis which would be appropriate to include in any hazard assessment. The Board shall also make recommendations with respect to the role of risk management plans as required by paragraph (8)(B)[4] in preventing accidental releases. The Board may from time to time review and revise its recommendations under this subparagraph.

(I) Whenever the Board submits a recommendation with respect to accidental releases to the Administrator, the Administrator shall respond to such recommendation formally and in writing not later than 180 days after receipt thereof. The response to the Board's recommendation by the Administrator shall indicate whether the Administrator will—

(i) initiate a rulemaking or issue such orders as are necessary to implement the recommendation in full or in part, pursuant to any timetable contained in the recommendation;

(ii) decline to initiate a rulemaking or issue orders as recommended.

Any determination by the Administrator not to implement a recommendation of the Board or to implement a recommendation only in part, including any variation from the schedule contained in the recommendation, shall be accompanied by a statement from the Administrator setting forth the reasons for such determination.

(J) The Board may make recommendations with respect to accidental releases to the Secretary of Labor. Whenever the Board submits such recommendation, the Secretary shall respond to such recommendation formally and in writing not later than 180 days after receipt thereof. The response to the Board's recommendation by the Administrator shall indicate whether the Secretary will—

(i) initiate a rulemaking or issue such orders as are necessary to implement the recommendation in full or in part, pursuant to any timetable contained in the recommendation;

(ii) decline to initiate a rulemaking or issue orders as recommended.

Any determination by the Secretary not to implement a recommendation or to implement a recommendation only in part, including any variation from the schedule contained in the recommendation, shall be accompanied by a statement from the Secretary setting forth the reasons for such determination.

(K) Within 2 years after November 15, 1990, the Board shall issue a report to the Administrator of the Environmental Protection Agency and to the Administrator of the Occupational Safety and Health Administration recommending the adoption of regulations for the preparation of risk management plans and general requirements for the prevention of accidental releases of regulated substances into the ambient air (including recommendations for listing substances under paragraph (3)) and for the mitigation of the potential adverse effect on human health or the environment as a result of accidental releases which should be applicable to any stationary source handling any regulated substance in more than threshold amounts. The Board may include proposed rules or orders which should be issued by the Administrator under authority of this subsection or by the Secretary of Labor under the Occupational Safety and Health Act [29 U.S.C.A. § 651 et seq.]. Any such recommendations shall be specific and shall identify the regulated substance or class of regulated substances (or other substances) to which the recommendations apply. The Administrator shall consider such recommendations before promulgating regulations required by paragraph (7)(B).

(L) The Board, or upon authority of the Board, any member thereof, any administrative law judge employed by or assigned to the Board, or any officer or employee duly designated by the Board, may for the purpose of carrying out duties authorized by subparagraph (C)—

(i) hold such hearings, sit and act at such times and places, administer such oaths, and require by subpoena or otherwise attendance and testimony of such witnesses and the production of evidence and may require by order that any person engaged in the production, processing, handling, or storage of extremely hazardous substances submit written reports and responses to requests and questions within such time and in such form as the Board may require; and

(ii) upon presenting appropriate credentials and a written notice of inspection authority, enter any property where an accidental release causing a fatality, serious injury or substantial property damage has occurred and do all things therein necessary for a proper investigation pursuant to subparagraph (C) and inspect at reasonable times records, files, papers, processes, controls, and facilities and take such samples as are relevant to such investigation.

Whenever the Administrator or the Board conducts an inspection of a facility pursuant to this subsection, employees and their representatives shall have the same rights to participate in such inspections as provided in the Occupational Safety and Health Act [29 U.S.C.A. § 651 et seq.].

**(M)** In addition to that described in subparagraph (L), the Board may use any information gathering authority of the Administrator under this chapter, including the subpoena power provided in section 7607(a)(1) of this title.

**(N)** The Board is authorized to establish such procedural and administrative rules as are necessary to the exercise of its functions and duties. The Board is authorized without regard to section 5 of Title 41 to enter into contracts, leases, cooperative agreements or other transactions as may be necessary in the conduct of the duties and functions of the Board with any other agency, institution, or person.

**(O)** After the effective date of any reporting requirement promulgated pursuant to subparagraph (C)(iii) it shall be unlawful for any person to fail to report any release of any extremely hazardous substance as required by such subparagraph. The Administrator is authorized to enforce any regulation or requirements established by the Board pursuant to subparagraph (C)(iii) using the authorities of sections 7413 and 7414 of this title. Any request for information from the owner or operator of a stationary source made by the Board or by the Administrator under this section shall be treated, for purposes of sections 7413, 7414, 7416, 7420, 7603, 7604 and 7607 of this title and any other enforcement provisions of this chapter, as a request made by the Administrator under section 7414 of this title and may be enforced by the Chairperson of the Board or by the Administrator as provided in such section.

**(P)** The Administrator shall provide to the Board such support and facilities as may be necessary for operation of the Board.

**(Q)** Consistent with subsection (G)[5] and section 7414(c) of this title any records, reports or information obtained by the Board shall be available to the Administrator, the Secretary of Labor, the Congress and the public, except that upon a showing satisfactory to the Board by any person that records, reports, or information, or particular part thereof (other than release or emissions data) to which the Board has access, if made public, is likely to cause substantial harm to the person's competitive position, the Board shall consider such record, report, or information or particular portion thereof confidential in accordance with section 1905 of Title 18, except that such record, report, or information may be disclosed to other officers, employees, and authorized representatives of the United States concerned with carrying out this chapter or when relevant under any proceeding under this chapter. This subparagraph does not constitute authority to withhold records, reports, or information from the Congress.

**(R)** Whenever the Board submits or transmits any budget estimate, budget request, supplemental budget request, or other budget information, legislative recommendation, prepared testimony for congressional hearings, recommendation or study to the President, the Secretary of Labor, the Administrator, or the Director of the Office of Management and Budget, it shall concurrently transmit a copy thereof to the Congress. No report of the Board shall be subject to review by the Administrator or any Federal agency or to judicial review in any court. No officer or agency of the United States shall have authority to require the Board to submit its budget requests or estimates, legislative recommendations, prepared testimony, comments, recommendations or reports to any officer or agency of the United States for approval or review prior to the submission of such recommendations, testimony, comments or reports to the Congress. In the performance of their functions as established by this chapter, the members, officers and employees of the Board shall not be responsible to or subject to supervision or direction, in carrying out any duties under this subsection, of any officer or employee or agent of the Environmental Protection Agency, the Department of Labor or any other agency of the United States except that the President may remove any member, officer or employee of the Board for inefficiency, neglect of duty or malfeasance in office. Nothing in this section shall affect the application of Title 5 to officers or employees of the Board.

**(S)** The Board shall submit an annual report to the President and to the Congress which shall include, but not be limited to, information on accidental releases which have been investigated by or reported to the Board during the previous year, recommendations for legislative or administrative action which the Board has made, the actions which have been taken by the Administrator or the Secretary of Labor or the heads of other agencies to implement such recommendations, an identification of priorities for study and investigation in the succeeding year, progress in the development of risk-reduction technologies and the response to and implementation of significant research findings on chemical safety in the public and private sector.

**(7) Accident prevention**

**(A)** In order to prevent accidental releases of regulated substances, the Administrator is authorized to promulgate release prevention, detection, and correction requirements which may include monitoring, record-keeping, reporting, training, vapor recovery, secondary containment, and other design, equipment, work practice, and operational requirements. Regulations promulgated under this paragraph may make distinctions between various types, classes, and kinds of facilities, devices and systems taking into consideration factors including, but not limited to, the size, location, process, process controls, quantity of substances handled, potency of substances, and response capabilities present at any stationary source. Regulations promulgated pursuant to this subparagraph shall have an effective date, as determined by the Administrator, assuring compliance as expeditiously as practicable.

**(B)(i)** Within 3 years after November 15, 1990, the Administrator shall promulgate reasonable regulations and appropriate guidance to provide, to the greatest extent practicable, for the prevention and detection of accidental releases of regulated substances and for response to such releases by the owners or operators of the sources of such releases. The Administrator shall utilize the expertise of the Secretaries of Transportation and Labor in promulgating such regulations. As appropriate, such regulations shall cover the use, operation, repair, replacement, and maintenance of equipment to monitor, detect, inspect, and control such releases, including training of persons in the use and maintenance of such equipment and in the conduct of periodic inspections. The regulations shall include procedures and measures for emergency response after an accidental release of a regulated substance in order to protect human health and the environment. The regulations shall cover storage, as well as operations. The regulations shall, as appropriate, recognize differences in size, operations, processes, class and categories of sources and the voluntary actions of such sources to prevent such releases and respond to such releases. The regulations shall be applicable to a stationary source 3 years after the date of promulgation, or 3 years after the date on which a regulated substance present at the source in more than threshold amounts is first listed under paragraph (3), whichever is later.

**(ii)** The regulations under this subparagraph shall require the owner or operator of stationary sources at which a regulated substance is present in more than a threshold quantity to prepare and implement a risk management plan to detect and prevent or minimize accidental releases of such substances from the stationary source, and to provide a prompt emergency response to any such releases in order to protect human health and the environment. Such plan shall provide for compliance with the requirements of this subsection and shall also include each of the following:

**(I)** a hazard assessment to assess the potential effects of an accidental release of any regulated substance. This assessment shall include an estimate of potential release quantities and a determination of downwind effects, including potential exposures to affected populations. Such assessment shall include a previous release history of the past 5 years, including the size, concentration, and duration of releases, and shall include an evaluation of worst case accidental releases;

**(II)** a program for preventing accidental releases of regulated substances, including safety precautions and maintenance, monitoring and employee training measures to be used at the source; and

**(III)** a response program providing for specific actions to be taken in response to an accidental release of a regulated substance so as to protect human health and the environment, including procedures for informing the public and local agencies responsible for responding to accidental releases, emergency health care, and employee training measures.

At the time regulations are promulgated under this subparagraph, the Administrator shall promulgate guidelines to assist stationary sources in the preparation of risk management plans. The guidelines shall, to the extent practicable, include model risk management plans.

**(iii)** The owner or operator of each stationary source covered by clause (ii) shall register a risk management plan prepared under this subparagraph with the Administrator before the effective date of regulations under clause (i) in such form and manner as the Administrator shall, by rule, require. Plans prepared pursuant to this subparagraph shall also be submitted to the Chemical Safety and Hazard Investigation Board, to the State in which the stationary source is located, and to any local agency or entity having responsibility for planning for or responding to accidental releases which may occur at such source, and shall be available to the public under section 7414(c) of this title. The Administrator shall establish, by rule, an auditing system to regularly review and, if necessary, require revision in risk management plans to assure that the plans comply with this subparagraph. Each such plan shall be updated periodically as required by the Administrator, by rule.

**(C)** Any regulations promulgated pursuant to this subsection shall to the maximum extent practicable, consistent with this subsection, be consistent with the recommendations and standards established by the American Society of Mechanical Engineers (ASME), the American National Standards

Institute (ANSI) or the American Society of Testing Materials (ASTM). The Administrator shall take into consideration the concerns of small business in promulgating regulations under this subsection.

(D) In carrying out the authority of this paragraph, the Administrator shall consult with the Secretary of Labor and the Secretary of Transportation and shall coordinate any requirements under this paragraph with any requirements established for comparable purposes by the Occupational Safety and Health Administration or the Department of Transportation. Nothing in this subsection shall be interpreted, construed or applied to impose requirements affecting, or to grant the Administrator, the Chemical Safety and Hazard Investigation Board, or any other agency any authority to regulate (including requirements for hazard assessment), the accidental release of radionuclides arising from the construction and operation of facilities licensed by the Nuclear Regulatory Commission.

(E) After the effective date of any regulation or requirement imposed under this subsection, it shall be unlawful for any person to operate any stationary source subject to such regulation or requirement in violation of such regulation or requirement. Each regulation or requirement under this subsection shall for purposes of sections 7413, 7414, 7416, 7420, 7604, and 7607 of this title and other enforcement provisions of this chapter, be treated as a standard in effect under subsection (d) of this section.

(F) Notwithstanding the provisions of subchapter V of this chapter or this section, no stationary source shall be required to apply for, or operate pursuant to, a permit issued under such subchapter solely because such source is subject to regulations or requirements under this subsection.

(G) In exercising any authority under this subsection, the Administrator shall not, for purposes of section 653(b)(1) of Title 29, be deemed to be exercising statutory authority to prescribe or enforce standards or regulations affecting occupational safety and health.

**(H) Public access to off-site consequence analysis information**

**(i) Definitions**

In this subparagraph:

(I) Covered person

The term "covered person" means—

**(aa)** an officer or employee of the United States;

**(bb)** an officer or employee of an agent or contractor of the Federal Government;

**(cc)** an officer or employee of a State or local government;

**(dd)** an officer or employee of an agent or contractor of a State or local government;

**(ee)** an individual affiliated with an entity that has been given, by a State or local government, responsibility for preventing, planning for, or responding to accidental releases;

**(ff)** an officer or employee or an agent or contractor of an entity described in item (ee); and

**(gg)** a qualified researcher under clause (vii).

(II) Official use

The term "official use" means an action of a Federal, State, or local government agency or an entity referred to in subclause (I)(ee) intended to carry out a function relevant to preventing, planning for, or responding to accidental releases.

(III) Off-site consequence analysis information

The term "off-site consequence analysis information" means those portions of a risk management plan, excluding the executive summary of the plan, consisting of an evaluation of 1 or more worst-case release scenarios or alternative release scenarios, and any electronic data base created by the Administrator from those portions.

(IV) Risk management plan

The term "risk management plan" means a risk management plan submitted to the Administrator by an owner or operator of a stationary source under subparagraph (B)(iii).

**(ii) Regulations**

Not later than 1 year after the date of enactment of this subparagraph, the President shall—

(I) assess—

**(aa)** the increased risk of terrorist and other criminal activity associated with the posting of off-site consequence analysis information on the Internet; and

**(bb)** the incentives created by public disclosure of off-site consequence analysis information for reduction in the risk of accidental releases; and

(II) based on the assessment under subclause (I), promulgate regulations governing the distribution of off-site consequence analysis information in a manner that, in the opinion of the President, minimizes the likelihood of accidental releases and the risk described in subclause (I)(aa) and the likelihood of harm to public health and welfare, and—

**(aa)** allows access by any member of the public to paper copies of off-site consequence analysis information for a limited number of stationary sources located anywhere in the United States, without any geographical restriction;

**(bb)** allows other public access to off-site consequence analysis information as appropriate;

**(cc)** allows access for official use by a covered person described in any of items (cc) through (ff) of clause (i)(I) (referred to in this subclause as a 'State or local covered person') to off-site consequence analysis information relating to stationary sources located in the person's State;

**(dd)** allows a State or local covered person to provide, for official use, off-site consequence analysis information relating to stationary sources located in the person's State to a State or local covered person in a contiguous State; and

**(ee)** allows a State or local covered person to obtain for official use, by request to the Administrator, off-site consequence analysis information that is not available to the person under item (cc).

**(iii) Availability under freedom of information act**

**(I)** First year

Off-site consequence analysis information, and any ranking of stationary sources derived from the information, shall not be made available under section 552 of Title 5, during the 1-year period beginning on the date of enactment of this subparagraph.

**(II)** After first year

If the regulations under clause (ii) are promulgated on or before the end of the period described in subclause (I), off-site consequence analysis information covered by the regulations, and any ranking of stationary sources derived from the information, shall not be made available under section 552 of Title 5, after the end of that period.

**(III)** Applicability

Subclauses (I) and (II) apply to off-site consequence analysis information submitted to the Administrator before, on, or after the date of enactment of this subparagraph.

**(iv) Availability of information during transition period**

The Administrator shall make off-site consequence analysis information available to covered persons for official use in a manner that meets the requirements of items (cc)through (ee) of clause (ii)(II), and to the public in a form that does not make available any information concerning the identity or location of stationary sources, during the period—

**(I)** beginning on the date of enactment of this subparagraph; and

**(II)** ending on the earlier of the date of promulgation of the regulations under clause (ii) or the date that is 1 year after the date of enactment of this subparagraph.

**(v) Prohibition on unauthorized disclosure of information by covered persons**

**(I)** In general

Beginning on the date of enactment of this subparagraph, a covered person shall not disclose to the public off-site consequence analysis information in any form, or any statewide or national ranking of identified stationary sources derived from such information, except as authorized by this subparagraph (including the regulations promulgated under clause (ii)). After the end of the 1-year period beginning on the date of enactment of this subparagraph, if regulations have not been promulgated under clause (ii), the preceding sentence shall not apply.

**(II)** Criminal penalties

Notwithstanding section 7413 of this title, a covered person that willfully violates a restriction or prohibition established by this subparagraph (including the regulations promulgated under clause (ii)) shall, upon conviction, be fined for an infraction under section 3571 of Title 18, (but shall not be subject to imprisonment) for each unauthorized disclosure of off-site consequence analysis information, except that subsection (d) of such section 3571 shall not apply to a case in which the offense results in pecuniary loss unless the defendant knew that such loss would occur. The disclosure of off-site consequence analysis information for each specific stationary source shall be considered a separate offense. The total of all penalties that may be imposed on a single person or organization under this item shall not exceed $1,000,000 for violations committed during any 1 calendar year.

**(III)** Applicability

If the owner or operator of a stationary source makes off-site consequence analysis information relating to that stationary source available to the public without restriction—

(**aa**) subclauses (I) and (II) shall not apply with respect to the information; and

(**bb**) the owner or operator shall notify the Administrator of the public availability of the information.

(**IV**) List

The Administrator shall maintain and make publicly available a list of all stationary sources that have provided notification under subclause (III)(bb).

**(vi) Notice**

The Administrator shall provide notice of the definition of official use as provided in clause (i)(III) and examples of actions that would and would not meet that definition, and notice of the restrictions on further dissemination and the penalties established by this Act to each covered person who receives off-site consequence analysis information under clause (iv) and each covered person who receives off-site consequence analysis information for an official use under the regulations promulgated under clause (ii).

**(vii) Qualified researchers**

(**I**) In general

Not later than 180 days after the date of enactment of this subparagraph, the Administrator, in consultation with the Attorney General, shall develop and implement a system for providing off-site consequence analysis information, including facility identification, to any qualified researcher, including a qualified researcher from industry or any public interest group.

(**II**) Limitation on dissemination

The system shall not allow the researcher to disseminate, or make available on the Internet, the off-site consequence analysis information, or any portion of the off-site consequence analysis information, received under this clause.

**(viii) Read-only information technology system**

In consultation with the Attorney General and the heads of other appropriate Federal agencies, the Administrator shall establish an information technology system that provides for the availability to the public of off-site consequence analysis information by means of a central data base under the control of the Federal Government that contains information that users may read, but that provides no means by which an electronic or mechanical copy of the information may be made.

**(ix) Voluntary industry accident prevention standards**

The Environmental Protection Agency, the Department of Justice, and other appropriate agencies may provide technical assistance to owners and operators of stationary sources and participate in the development of voluntary industry standards that will help achieve the objectives set forth in paragraph (1).

**(x) Effect on State or local law**

(**I**) In general

Subject to subclause (II), this subparagraph (including the regulations promulgated under this subparagraph) shall supersede any provision of State or local law that is inconsistent with this subparagraph (including the regulations).

(**II**) Availability of information under State law

Nothing in this subparagraph precludes a State from making available data on the off-site consequences of chemical releases collected in accordance with State law.

**(xi) Report**

(**I**) In general

Not later than 3 years after the date of enactment of this subparagraph, the Attorney General, in consultation with appropriate State, local, and Federal Government agencies, affected industry, and the public, shall submit to Congress a report that describes the extent to which regulations promulgated under this paragraph have resulted in actions, including the design and maintenance of safe facilities, that are effective in detecting, preventing, and minimizing the consequences of releases of regulated substances that may be caused by criminal activity. As part of this report, the Attorney General, using available data to the extent possible, and a sampling of covered stationary sources selected at the discretion of the Attorney General, and in consultation with appropriate State, local, and Federal governmental agencies, affected industry, and the public, shall review the vulnerability of covered stationary sources to criminal and terrorist activity, current industry practices regarding site security, and security of transportation of regulated substances. The Attorney General shall submit this report, containing the results of the review, together with recommendations, if any, for reducing vulnerability of covered stationary sources to criminal and terrorist activity, to the Committee on Commerce of the United States House of Representatives and the Committee on Environment and Public Works of the United States Senate and other relevant committees of Congress.

(**II**) Interim report

Not later than 12 months after the date of enactment of this subparagraph, the Attorney General shall submit to the Committee on Commerce of the United States House of Representatives and the Committee on Environment and Public Works of the United States Senate, and other relevant committees of Congress, an interim report that includes, at a minimum—

**(aa)** the preliminary findings under subclause (I);

**(bb)** the methods used to develop the findings; and

**(cc)** an explanation of the activities expected to occur that could cause the findings of the report under subclause (I) to be different than the preliminary findings.

**(III)** Availability of information

Information that is developed by the Attorney General or requested by the Attorney General and received from a covered stationary source for the purpose of conducting the review under subclauses(I) and (II) shall be exempt from disclosure under section 552 of Title 5, if such information would pose a threat to national security.

**(xii) Scope**

This subparagraph—

**(I)** applies only to covered persons; and

**(II)** does not restrict the dissemination of off-site consequence analysis information by any covered person in any manner or form except in the form of a risk management plan or an electronic data base created by the Administrator from off-site consequence analysis information.

**(xiii) Authorization of appropriations**

There are authorized to be appropriated to the Administrator and the Attorney General such sums as are necessary to carry out this subparagraph (including the regulations promulgated under clause (ii)), to remain available until expended.

**(8) Research on hazard assessments**

The Administrator may collect and publish information on accident scenarios and consequences covering a range of possible events for substances listed under paragraph (3). The Administrator shall establish a program of long-term research to develop and disseminate information on methods and techniques for hazard assessment which may be useful in improving and validating the procedures employed in the preparation of hazard assessments under this subsection.

**(9) Order authority**

**(A)** In addition to any other action taken, when the Administrator determines that there may be an imminent and substantial endangerment to the human health or welfare or the environment because of an actual or threatened accidental release of a regulated substance, the Administrator may secure such relief as may be necessary to abate such danger or threat, and the district court of the United States in the district in which the threat occurs shall have jurisdiction to grant such relief as the public interest and the equities of the case may require. The Administrator may also, after notice to the State in which the stationary source is located, take other action under this paragraph including, but not limited to, issuing such orders as may be necessary to protect human health. The Administrator shall take action under section 7603 of this title rather than this paragraph whenever the authority of such section is adequate to protect human health and the environment.

**(B)** Orders issued pursuant to this paragraph may be enforced in an action brought in the appropriate United States district court as if the order were issued under section 7603 of this title.

**(C)** Within 180 days after November 15, 1990, the Administrator shall publish guidance for using the order authorities established by this paragraph. Such guidance shall provide for the coordinated use of the authorities of this paragraph with other emergency powers authorized by section 9606 of this title, sections 311(c), 308, 309 and 504(a) of the Federal Water Pollution Control Act [33 U.S.C.A. §§ 1321(c), 1318, 1319 and 1364(a) ], sections 3007, 3008, 3013, and 7003 of the Solid Waste Disposal Act [42 U.S.C.A. §§ 6927, 6928, 6934, and 6973], sections 1445 and 1431 of the Safe Drinking Water Act [42 U.S.C.A. §§ 300j–4 and 300i], sections 5 and 7 of the Toxic Substances Control Act [15 U.S.C.A. §§ 2604, 2606], and sections 7413, 7414, and 7603 of this title.

**(10) Presidential review**

The President shall conduct a review of release prevention, mitigation and response authorities of the various Federal agencies and shall clarify and coordinate agency responsibilities to assure the most effective and efficient implementation of such authorities and to identify any deficiencies in authority or resources which may exist. The President may utilize the resources and solicit the recommendations of the Chemical Safety and Hazard Investigation Board in conducting such review. At the conclusion of such review, but not later than 24 months after November 15, 1990, the President shall transmit a message to the Congress on the release prevention, mitigation and response activities of the Federal Government making such recommendations for change in law as the President may deem appropriate. Nothing in this paragraph shall be interpreted, construed or applied to authorize the President to modify or reassign release prevention, mitigation or response authorities otherwise established by law.

**(11) State authority**

Nothing in this subsection shall preclude, deny or limit any right of a State or political subdivision thereof to adopt or enforce any regulation, requirement, limitation or standard (including any procedural requirement) that is more stringent than a regulation, requirement, limitation or standard in effect under this subsection or that applies to a substance not subject to this subsection.

**(s) Periodic report**

Not later than January 15, 1993 and every 3 years thereafter, the Administrator shall prepare and transmit to the Congress a comprehensive report on the measures taken by the Agency and by the States to implement the provisions of this section. The Administrator shall maintain a database on pollutants and sources subject to the provisions of this section and shall include aggregate information from the database in each annual report. The report shall include, but not be limited to—

(1) a status report on standard-setting under subsections (d) and (f) of this section;

(2) information with respect to compliance with such standards including the costs of compliance experienced by sources in various categories and subcategories;

(3) development and implementation of the national urban air toxics program; and

(4) recommendations of the Chemical Safety and Hazard Investigation Board with respect to the prevention and mitigation of accidental releases.

(July 14, 1955, c. 360, Title I, § 112, as added Dec. 31, 1970, Pub.L. 91–604, § 4(a), 84 Stat. 1685, and amended Aug. 7, 1977, Pub.L. 95–95, Title I, §§ 109(d)(2), 110, Title IV, § 401(c), 91 Stat. 701, 703, 791; Nov. 9, 1978, Pub.L. 95–623, § 13(b), 92 Stat. 3458; Nov. 15, 1990, Pub.L. 101–549, Title III, § 301, 104 Stat. 2531; Dec. 4, 1991, Pub.L. 102–187, 105 Stat. 1285; Nov. 10, 1998, Pub.L. 105–362, Title IV, § 402(b), 112 Stat. 3283; Aug. 5, 1999, Pub.L. 106–40, §§ 2, 3(a), 113 Stat. 207.)

[1] So in original. Probably should be "effects".

[2] So in original.

[3] So in original. Probably should be "section".

[4] So in original. Probably should be paragraph "(7)(B)".

[5] So in original. Probably should be "subparagraph".

## HISTORICAL AND STATUTORY NOTES

**References in Text**

The date of enactment, referred to in subsec. (a)(11), probably means the date of enactment of Pub.L. 101–549, which amended this section generally and was approved Nov. 15, 1990.

The Atomic Energy Act of 1954, referred to in subsec. (d)(9), is Act Aug. 30, 1954, c. 1073, 68 Stat. 919, as amended, which is classified generally to chapter 23 (section 2011 et seq.) of this title. For complete classification of this Act to the Code, see Short Title of 1954 Acts note set out under section 2011 of this title and Tables.

The Federal Water Pollution Control Act, referred to in subsecs. (e)(5), (m)(1)(D), (m)(4), (m)(5)(D) and (r)(9)(C), is Act June 30, 1948, c. 758, as amended generally by Pub.L. 92–500, § 2, Oct. 18, 1972, 86 Stat. 816, which is classified generally to chapter 26 (section 1251 et seq.) of Title 33, Navigation and Navigable Waters. Title II of the Federal Water Pollution Control Act, referred to in subsec. (e)(5), is classified generally to subchapter II (section 1281 et seq.) of Title 33. Section 320 of such Act, referred to in subsec. (m)(4), is classified to section 1330 of Title 33. Sections 308, 309, 311(c) and 504(a) of such Act, referred to in subsec. (r)(9)(C), are classified to sections 1318, 1319, 1321(c) and 1364(a), respectively, of Title 33. For complete classification of this Act to the Code, see Short Title note set out under section 1251 of Title 33 and Tables.

The Toxic Substances Control Act, referred to in subsecs. (k)(3)(C) and (r)(9)(C), is Pub.L. 94–469, Oct. 11, 1976, 90 Stat. 2003, as amended, which is classified generally to chapter 53 (section 2601 et seq.) of Title 15, Commerce and Trade. Sections 5 and 7 of such Act, referred to in subsec. (r)(9)(C), are classified to sections 2604 and 2606, respectively, of Title 15. For complete classification of this Act to the Code, see Short Title note set out under section 2601 of Title 15 and Tables.

The Federal Insecticide, Fungicide, and Rodenticide Act, referred to in subsec. (k)(3)(C), is Act June 25, 1947, c. 125, as amended generally by Pub.L. 92–516, Oct. 21, 1972, 86 Stat. 973, which is classified generally to subchapter II (section 136 et seq.) of chapter 6 of Title 7, Agriculture. For complete classification of this Act to the Code, see Short Title note set out under section 136 of Title 7 and Tables.

The Resource Conservation and Recovery Act of 1976, referred to in subsec. (k)(3)(C), is Pub.L. 94–580, Oct. 21, 1976, 90 Stat. 2796, as amended, which is classified generally to chapter 82 (section 6901 et seq.) of this title. For complete classification of this Act to the Code, see Short Title of 1976 Acts note set out under section 6901 of this title and Tables.

The Safe Drinking Water Act, referred to in subsecs. (m)(1)(D), (m)(5)(D), and (r)(9)(C), is Pub.L. 93–523, Dec. 16, 1974, 88 Stat. 1660, as amended, which is classified principally to subchapter XII (section 300f et seq.) of chapter 6A of this title. Sections 1431 and 1445 of such Act, referred to in subsec. (r)(9)(C), are classified to sections 300i and 300j–4 of this title, respectively. For complete classification of this Act to the Code see Short Title of 1974 Amendments note set out under section 201 of this title and Tables.

The Solid Waste Disposal Act, referred to in subsecs. (n)(5), (n)(7), and (r)(9)(C), is Title II of Pub.L. 89–272, Oct. 20, 1965, 79 Stat. 997, as amended generally by Pub.L.

94–580, § 2, Oct. 21, 1976, 90 Stat. 2795, which is classified generally to chapter 82 (section 6901 et seq.) of this title. Section 8002(m) of the Solid Waste Disposal Act, referred to in subsec. (n)(5), is classified to section 6982(m) of this title. Subtitle C of such Act, referred to in subsec. (n)(7), is classified generally to subchapter III (section 6921 et seq.) of chapter 82 of this title. Sections 3007, 3008, 3013 and 7003 of such Act, referred to in subsec. (r)(9)(C), are classified to sections 6927, 6928, 6934 and 6973, respectively, of this title. For complete classification of this Act to the Code, see Short Title of 1976 Acts note set out under section 6901 of this title and Tables.

The Clean Air Act Amendments of 1990, referred to in subsecs. (*o*)(4), (q)(1), (q)(2) and (q)(3), is Pub.L. 101–549, Nov. 15, 1990, 104 Stat. 2399. Section 303 of such Act, referred to in subsec. (*o*)(4), is set out as a note under this section. For complete classification of this Act to the Code, see Tables.

The date of enactment of the Clean Air Act Amendments of 1990, referred to in subsec. (q)(1) to (3), is the date of enactment of Pub.L. 101–549, Nov. 15, 1990, 104 Stat. 2399, which was approved Nov. 15, 1990.

The Emergency Planning and Community Right-to-Know Act of 1986, referred to in subsec. (r)(3), is Title III of Pub.L. 99–499, Oct. 17, 1986, 100 Stat. 1728, which is classified generally to chapter 116 (section 11001 et seq.) of this title. For complete classification of this Act to the Code, see Short Title of 1986 Amendments note set out under section 11001 of this title and Tables.

The Occupational Safety and Health Act of 1970, referred to in subsecs. (r)(6)(C)(ii), (r)(6)(K), and (L) is Pub.L. 91–596, Dec. 29, 1970, 84 Stat. 1590, as amended, which is classified principally to chapter 15 (section 651 et seq.) of Title 29, Labor. For complete classification of this Act to the Code, see Short Title note set out under section 651 of Title 29 and Tables.

The date of enactment of this subparagraph, referred to in subpar. (r)(7)(H), means the date of enactment of Pub.L. 106–40, 113 Stat. 207, which amended par. (r)(4) and enacted subpar. (r)(7)(H), and enacted note provisions under this section and section 7401 of this title, and was approved Aug. 5, 1999.

This Act, referred to in subpar. (r)(7)(H), is the Chemical Safety Information Site Security and Fuels Regulatory Relief Act, Pub.L. 106–40, Aug. 5, 1999, 113 Stat. 207, which amended this section and enacted note provisions set out under this section and section 7401 of this title.

### Codifications

Section was formerly classified to section 1857c–7 of this title.

### Effective and Applicability Provisions

1990 Acts

Amendment by Pub.L. 101–549 effective Nov. 15, 1990, except as otherwise provided, see section 711(b) of Pub.L. 101–549, set out as a note under section 7401 of this title.

1977 Acts

Amendment by Pub.L. 95–95 effective Aug. 7, 1977, except as otherwise expressly provided, see section 406(d) of Pub.L. 95–95, set out as a note under section 7401 of this title.

### Change of Name

Any reference in any provision of law enacted before Jan. 4, 1995, to the Committee on Energy and Commerce of the House of Representatives treated as referring to the Committee on Commerce of the House of Representatives, except that any reference in any provision of law enacted before Jan. 4, 1995, to the Committee on Energy and Commerce of the House of Representatives treated as referring to the Committee on Agriculture of the House of Representatives, in the case of a provision of law relating to inspection of seafood or seafood products, the Committee on Banking and Financial Services of the House of Representatives, in the case of a provision of law relating to bank capital markets activities generally or to depository institution securities activities generally, and the Committee on Transportation and Infrastructure of the House of Representatives, in the case of a provision of law relating to railroads, railway labor, or railroad retirement and unemployment (except revenue measures related thereto), see section 1(a)(4) and (c)(1) of Pub.L. 104–14, set out as a note preceding section 21 of Title 2, The Congress.

### Savings Provisions

Suits, actions or proceedings commenced under this chapter as in effect prior to Nov. 15, 1990, not to abate by reason of the taking effect of amendments by Pub.L. 101–549, except as otherwise provided for, see section 711(a) of Pub.L. 101–549, set out as a note under section 7401 of this title.

Suits, actions, and other proceedings lawfully commenced by or against the Administrator or any other officer or employee of the United States in his official capacity or in relation to the discharge of his official duties under Act July 14, 1955, the Clean Air Act, as in effect immediately prior to the enactment of Pub.L. 95–95 [Aug. 7, 1977], not to abate by reason of the taking effect of Pub.L. 95–95, see section 406(a) of Pub.L. 95–95, set out as an Effective and Applicability Provisions of 1977 Acts note under section 7401 of this title.

### Modification or Rescission of Rules, Regulations, Orders, Determinations, Contracts, Certifications, Authorizations, Delegations, and Other Actions

All rules, regulations, orders, determinations, contracts, certifications, authorizations, delegations, or other actions duly issued, made, or taken by or pursuant to Act July 14, 1955, the Clean Air Act, as in effect immediately prior to the date of enactment of Pub.L. 95–95 [Aug. 7, 1977] to continue in full force and effect until modified or rescinded in accordance with Act July 14, 1955, as amended by Pub.L. 95–95 [this chapter], see section 406(b) of Pub.L. 95–95, set out as an Effective and Applicability Provisions of 1977 Acts note under section 7401 of this title.

### Public Meeting During Moratorium Period

Pub.L. 106–40, § 4, Aug. 5, 1999, 113 Stat. 214, provided that:

"**(a) In General.**—Not later than 180 days after the date of enactment of this Act [August 5, 1999], each owner or operator of a stationary source covered by section 112(r)(7)(B)(ii) of the Clean Air Act [42 U.S.C.A. § 7412(r)(7)(B)(ii)] shall convene a public meeting, after reasonable public notice, in order to describe and discuss the local implications of the risk management plan submitted by the stationary source pursuant to section 112(r)(7)(B)(iii) of the Clean Air Act [42 U.S.C.A. § 7412(r)(7)(B)(iii)], including a summary of the off-site consequence analysis portion of the plan. Two or more stationary sources may conduct a joint meeting. In lieu of conducting such a meeting, small business stationary sources as defined in section 507(c)(1) of the Clean Air Act [42 U.S.C.A. § 7661f(c)(1)] may comply with this section by publicly posting a summary of the off-site consequence analysis information for their facility not later than 180 days after the enactment of this Act [August 5, 1999]. Not later than 10 months after the date of enactment of this Act [August 5, 1999], each such owner or operator shall send a certification to the director of the Federal Bureau of Investigation stating that such meeting has been held, or that such summary has been posted, within 1 year prior to, or within 6 months after, the date of the enactment of this Act [August 5, 1999]. This section shall not apply to sources that employ only Program 1 processes within the meaning of regulations promulgated under section 112(r)(7)(B)(i) of the Clean Air Act [42 U.S.C.A. § 7412(r)(7)(B)(i)].

"**(b) Enforcement.**—The Administrator of the Environmental Protection Agency may bring an action in the appropriate United States district court against any person who fails or refuses to comply with the requirements of this section, and such court may issue such orders, and take such other actions, as may be necessary to require compliance with such requirements."

**Reevaluation of Regulations**

Pub.L. 106–40, § 3(c), Aug. 5, 1999, 113 Stat. 213, provided that:

"The President shall reevaluate the regulations promulgated under this section within 6 years after the enactment of this Act [Chemical Safety Information, Site Security and Fuels Regulatory Relief Act, Pub. L. 106–40, Aug. 5, 1999, 113 Stat. 207]. If the President determines not to modify such regulations, the President shall publish a notice in the Federal Register stating that such reevaluation has been completed and that a determination has been made not to modify the regulations. Such notice shall include an explanation of the basis of such decision."

**Reports**

Pub.L. 106–40, § 3(b), Aug. 5, 1999, 113 Stat. 213, provided that:

"**(1) Definition Of Accidental Release.**—In this subsection, the term 'accidental release' has the meaning given the term in section 112(r)(2) of the Clean Air Act (42 U.S.C. 7412(r)(2)).

"**(2) Report On Status Of Certain Amendments.**—Not later than 2 years after the date of enactment of this Act [August 5, 1999], the Comptroller General of the United States shall submit to Congress a report on the status of the development of amendments to the National Fire Protection Association Code for Liquefied Petroleum Gas that will result in the provision of information to local emergency response personnel concerning the off-site effects of accidental releases of substances exempted from listing under section 112(r)(4)(B) of the Clean Air Act [42 U.S.C.A. § 7412(r)(4)(B)] (as added by section 3) [sic; probably should be section 2 of Pub.L. 106–40, Aug. 5, 1999, 113 Stat. 207, which added subsec. (r)(4)(B)].

"**(3) Report On Compliance With Certain Information Submission Requirements.**—Not later than 3 years after the date of enactment of this Act [August 5, 1999], the Comptroller General of the United States shall submit to Congress a report that—

"**(A)** describes the level of compliance with Federal and State requirements relating to the submission to local emergency response personnel of information intended to help the local emergency response personnel respond to chemical accidents or related environmental or public health threats; and

"**(B)** contains an analysis of the adequacy of the information required to be submitted and the efficacy of the methods for delivering the information to local emergency response personnel."

**Risk Assessment and Management Commission**

Section 303 of Pub.L. 101–549 provided that:

"**(a) Establishment.**—There is hereby established a Risk Assessment and Management Commission (hereafter referred to in this section as the "Commission"), which shall commence proceedings not later than 18 months after the date of enactment of the Clean Air Act Amendments of 1990 [Nov. 15, 1990] and which shall make a full investigation of the policy implications and appropriate uses of risk assessment and risk management in regulatory programs under various Federal laws to prevent cancer and other chronic human health effects which may result from exposure to hazardous substances.

"**(b) Charge.**—The Commission shall consider—

"**(1)** the report of the National Academy of Sciences authorized by section 112(*o*) of the Clean Air Act [subsec. (*o*) of this section], the use and limitations of risk assessment in establishing emission or effluent standards, ambient standards, exposure standards, acceptable concentration levels, tolerances or other environmental criteria for hazardous substances that present a risk of carcinogenic effects or other chronic health effects and the suitability of risk assessment for such purposes;

"**(2)** the most appropriate methods for measuring and describing cancer risks or risks of other chronic health effects from exposure to hazardous substances considering such alternative approaches as the lifetime risk of cancer or other effects to the individual or individuals most exposed to emissions from a source or sources on both an actual and worst case basis, the range of such risks, the total number of health effects avoided by exposure reductions, effluent standards, ambient standards, exposures standards, acceptable concentration levels, tolerances and other environmental criteria, reductions in the number of persons exposed at various levels of risk, the incidence of cancer, and other public health factors;

"**(3)** methods to reflect uncertainties in measurement and estimation techniques, the existence of synergistic or antagonistic effects among hazardous substances, the accuracy of extrapolating human health risks from animal exposure data, and the existence of unquantified direct or indirect effects on human health in risk assessment studies;

"**(4)** risk management policy issues including the use of lifetime cancer risks to individuals most exposed, incidence of cancer, the cost and technical feasibility of exposure reduction measures and the use of site-specific actual exposure information in setting emissions standards and other limitations applicable to sources of exposure to hazardous substances; and

"(5) and comment on the degree to which it is possible or desirable to develop a consistent risk assessment methodology, or a consistent standard of acceptable risk, among various Federal programs.

"(c) **Membership.**—Such Commission shall be composed of ten members who shall have knowledge or experience in fields of risk assessment or risk management, including three members to be appointed by the President, two members to be appointed by the Speaker of the House of Representatives, one member to be appointed by the Minority Leader of the House of Representatives, two members to be appointed by the Majority Leader of the Senate, one member to be appointed by the Minority Leader of the Senate, and one member to be appointed by the President of the National Academy of Sciences. Appointments shall be made not later than 18 months after the date of enactment of the Clean Air Act Amendments of 1990 [Nov. 15, 1990].

"(d) **Assistance from agencies.**—The Administrator of the Environmental Protection Agency and the heads of all other departments, agencies, and instrumentalities of the executive branch of the Federal Government shall, to the maximum extent practicable, assist the Commission in gathering such information as the Commission deems necessary to carry out this section subject to other provisions of law.

"(e) **Staff and contracts.**—

"(1) In the conduct of the study required by this section, the Commission is authorized to contract (in accordance with Federal contract law) with nongovernmental entities that are competent to perform research or investigations within the Commission's mandate, and to hold public hearings, forums, and workshops to enable full public participation.

"(2) The Commission may appoint and fix the pay of such staff as it deems necessary in accordance with the provisions of title 5, United States Code [Title 5, Government Organization and Employees]. The Commission may request the temporary assignment of personnel from the Environmental Protection Agency or other Federal agencies.

"(3) The members of the Commission who are not officers or employees of the United States, while attending conferences or meetings of the Commission or while otherwise serving at the request of the Chair, shall be entitled to receive compensation at a rate not in excess of the maximum rate of pay for Grade GS–18, as provided in the General Schedule under section 5332 of title 5 of the United States Code [section 5332 of Title 5], including travel time, and while away from their homes or regular places of business they may be allowed travel expenses, including per diem in lieu of subsistence as authorized by law for persons in the Government service employed intermittently.

"(f) **Report.**—A report containing the results of all Commission studies and investigations under this section, together with any appropriate legislative recommendations or administrative recommendations, shall be made available to the public for comment not later than 42 months after the date of enactment of the Clean Air Act Amendments of 1990 [Nov. 15, 1990] and shall be submitted to the President and to the Congress not later than 48 months after such date of enactment. In the report, the Commission shall make recommendations with respect to the appropriate use of risk assessment and risk management in Federal regulatory programs to prevent cancer or other chronic health effects which may result from exposure to hazardous substances. The Commission shall cease to exist upon the date determined by the Commission, but not later than 9 months after the submission of such report.

"(g) **Authorization.**—There are authorized to be appropriated such sums as are necessary to carry out the activities of the Commission established by this section."

## § 7413. Federal enforcement

**[CAA § 113]**

### (a) In general

#### (1) Order to comply with SIP

Whenever, on the basis of any information available to the Administrator, the Administrator finds that any person has violated or is in violation of any requirement or prohibition of an applicable implementation plan or permit, the Administrator shall notify the person and the State in which the plan applies of such finding. At any time after the expiration of 30 days following the date on which such notice of a violation is issued, the Administrator may, without regard to the period of violation (subject to section 2462 of Title 28)—

(A) issue an order requiring such person to comply with the requirements or prohibitions of such plan or permit,

(B) issue an administrative penalty order in accordance with subsection (d) of this section, or

(C) bring a civil action in accordance with subsection (b) of this section.

#### (2) State failure to enforce SIP or permit program

Whenever, on the basis of information available to the Administrator, the Administrator finds that violations of an applicable implementation plan or an approved permit program under subchapter V of this chapter are so widespread that such violations appear to result from a failure of the State in which the plan or permit program applies to enforce the plan or permit program effectively, the Administrator shall so notify the State. In the case of a permit program, the notice shall be made in accordance with subchapter V of this chapter. If the Administrator finds such failure extends beyond the 30th day after such notice (90 days in the case of such permit program), the Administrator shall give public notice of such finding. During the period beginning with such public notice and ending when such State satisfies the Administrator that it will enforce such plan or permit program (hereafter referred to in this section as "period of federally assumed enforcement"), the Administrator may enforce any requirement or prohibition of such plan or permit program with respect to any person by—

(A) issuing an order requiring such person to comply with such requirement or prohibition,

(B) issuing an administrative penalty order in accordance with subsection (d) of this section, or

(C) bringing a civil action in accordance with subsection (b) of this section.

**(3) EPA enforcement of other requirements**

Except for a requirement or prohibition enforceable under the preceding provisions of this subsection, whenever, on the basis of any information available to the Administrator, the Administrator finds that any person has violated, or is in violation of, any other requirement or prohibition of this subchapter, section 7603 of this title, subchapter IV–A, subchapter V, or subchapter VI of this chapter, including, but not limited to, a requirement or prohibition of any rule, plan, order, waiver, or permit promulgated, issued, or approved under those provisions or subchapters, or for the payment of any fee owed to the United States under this chapter (other than subchapter II of this chapter), the Administrator may—

(A) issue an administrative penalty order in accordance with subsection (d) of this section,

(B) issue an order requiring such person to comply with such requirement or prohibition,

(C) bring a civil action in accordance with subsection (b) of this section or section 7605 of this title, or

(D) request the Attorney General to commence a criminal action in accordance with subsection (c) of this section.

**(4) Requirements for orders**

An order issued under this subsection (other than an order relating to a violation of section 7412 of this title) shall not take effect until the person to whom it is issued has had an opportunity to confer with the Administrator concerning the alleged violation. A copy of any order issued under this subsection shall be sent to the State air pollution control agency of any State in which the violation occurs. Any order issued under this subsection shall state with reasonable specificity the nature of the violation and specify a time for compliance which the Administrator determines is reasonable, taking into account the seriousness of the violation and any good faith efforts to comply with applicable requirements. In any case in which an order under this subsection (or notice to a violator under paragraph (1)) is issued to a corporation, a copy of such order (or notice) shall be issued to appropriate corporate officers. An order issued under this subsection shall require the person to whom it was issued to comply with the requirement as expeditiously as practicable, but in no event longer than one year after the date the order was issued, and shall be nonrenewable. No order issued under this subsection shall prevent the State or the Administrator from assessing any penalties nor otherwise affect or limit the State's or the United States authority to enforce under other provisions of this chapter, nor affect any person's obligations to comply with any section of this chapter or with a term or condition of any permit or applicable implementation plan promulgated or approved under this chapter.

**(5) Failure to comply with new source requirements**

Whenever, on the basis of any available information, the Administrator finds that a State is not acting in compliance with any requirement or prohibition of the chapter relating to the construction of new sources or the modification of existing sources, the Administrator may—

(A) issue an order prohibiting the construction or modification of any major stationary source in any area to which such requirement applies;[1]

(B) issue an administrative penalty order in accordance with subsection (d) of this section, or

(C) bring a civil action under subsection (b) of this section.

Nothing in this subsection shall preclude the United States from commencing a criminal action under subsection (c) of this section at any time for any such violation.

**(b) Civil judicial enforcement**

The Administrator shall, as appropriate, in the case of any person that is the owner or operator of an affected source, a major emitting facility, or a major stationary source, and may, in the case of any other person, commence a civil action for a permanent or temporary injunction, or to assess and recover a civil penalty of not more than $25,000 per day for each violation, or both, in any of the following instances:

(1) Whenever such person has violated, or is in violation of, any requirement or prohibition of an applicable implementation plan or permit. Such an action shall be commenced (A) during any period of federally assumed enforcement, or (B) more than 30 days following the date of the Administrator's notification under subsection (a)(1) of this section that such person has violated, or is in violation of, such requirement or prohibition.

(2) Whenever such person has violated, or is in violation of, any other requirement or prohibition of this subchapter, section 7603 of this title, subchapter IV–A, subchapter V, or subchapter VI of this chapter, including, but not limited to, a requirement or prohibition of any rule, order, waiver or permit

promulgated, issued, or approved under this chapter, or for the payment of any fee owed the United States under this chapter (other than subchapter II of this chapter).

(3) Whenever such person attempts to construct or modify a major stationary source in any area with respect to which a finding under subsection (a)(5) of this section has been made.

Any action under this subsection may be brought in the district court of the United States for the district in which the violation is alleged to have occurred, or is occurring, or in which the defendant resides, or where the defendant's principal place of business is located, and such court shall have jurisdiction to restrain such violation, to require compliance, to assess such civil penalty, to collect any fees owed the United States under this chapter (other than subchapter II of this chapter) and any noncompliance assessment and nonpayment penalty owed under section 7420 of this title, and to award any other appropriate relief. Notice of the commencement of such action shall be given to the appropriate State air pollution control agency. In the case of any action brought by the Administrator under this subsection, the court may award costs of litigation (including reasonable attorney and expert witness fees) to the party or parties against whom such action was brought if the court finds that such action was unreasonable.

**(c) Criminal penalties**

(1) Any person who knowingly violates any requirement or prohibition of an applicable implementation plan (during any period of federally assumed enforcement or more than 30 days after having been notified under subsection (a)(1) of this section by the Administrator that such person is violating such requirement or prohibition), any order under subsection (a) of this section, requirement or prohibition of section 7411(e) of this title (relating to new source performance standards), section 7412 of this title, section 7414 of this title (relating to inspections, etc.), section 7429 of this title (relating to solid waste combustion), section 7475(a) of this title (relating to preconstruction requirements), an order under section 7477 of this title (relating to preconstruction requirements), an order under section 7603 of this title (relating to emergency orders), section 7661a(a) or 7661b(c) of this title (relating to permits), or any requirement or prohibition of subchapter IV–A of this chapter (relating to acid deposition control), or subchapter VI of this chapter (relating to stratospheric ozone control), including a requirement of any rule, order, waiver, or permit promulgated or approved under such sections or subchapters, and including any requirement for the payment of any fee owed the United States under this chapter (other than subchapter II of this chapter) shall, upon conviction, be punished by a fine pursuant to Title 18, or by imprisonment for not to exceed 5 years, or both. If a conviction of any person under this paragraph is for a violation committed after a first conviction of such person under this paragraph, the maximum punishment shall be doubled with respect to both the fine and imprisonment.

(2) Any person who knowingly—

**(A)** makes any false material statement, representation, or certification in, or omits material information from, or knowingly alters, conceals, or fails to file or maintain any notice, application, record, report, plan, or other document required pursuant to this chapter to be either filed or maintained (whether with respect to the requirements imposed by the Administrator or by a State);

**(B)** fails to notify or report as required under this chapter; or

**(C)** falsifies, tampers with, renders inaccurate, or fails to install any monitoring device or method required to be maintained or followed under this chapter [2]

shall, upon conviction, be punished by a fine pursuant to Title 18, or by imprisonment for not more than 2 years, or both. If a conviction of any person under this paragraph is for a violation committed after a first conviction of such person under this paragraph, the maximum punishment shall be doubled with respect to both the fine and imprisonment.

(3) Any person who knowingly fails to pay any fee owed the United States under this subchapter, subchapter III, IV–A, V, or VI of this chapter shall, upon conviction, be punished by a fine pursuant to Title 18, or by imprisonment for not more than 1 year, or both. If a conviction of any person under this paragraph is for a violation committed after a first conviction of such person under this paragraph, the maximum punishment shall be doubled with respect to both the fine and imprisonment.

(4) Any person who negligently releases into the ambient air any hazardous air pollutant listed pursuant to section 7412 of this title or any extremely hazardous substance listed pursuant to section 11002(a)(2) of this title that is not listed in section 7412 of this title, and who at the time negligently places another person in imminent danger of death or serious bodily injury shall, upon conviction, be punished by a fine under Title 18, or by imprisonment for not more than 1 year, or both. If a conviction of any person under this paragraph is for a violation committed after a first conviction of such person under this paragraph, the maximum punishment shall be doubled with respect to both the fine and imprisonment.

**(5)(A)** Any person who knowingly releases into the ambient air any hazardous air pollutant listed pursuant to section 7412 of this title or any extremely hazardous substance listed pursuant to section 11002(a)(2) of this title that is not listed in section 7412 of this title, and who knows at the time that he thereby places another person in imminent danger of death or serious bodily injury shall, upon conviction, be punished by a fine under Title 18, or by imprisonment of not more than 15 years, or both. Any person committing such violation which is an organization shall, upon conviction under this paragraph, be subject to a fine of not more than $1,000,000 for each violation. If a conviction of any person under this paragraph is for a violation committed after a first conviction of such person under this paragraph, the maximum punishment shall be doubled with respect to both the fine and imprisonment. For any air pollutant for which the Administrator has set an emissions standard or for any source for which a permit has been issued under subchapter V of this chapter, a release of such pollutant in accordance with that standard or permit shall not constitute a violation of this paragraph or paragraph (4).

(B) In determining whether a defendant who is an individual knew that the violation placed another person in imminent danger of death or serious bodily injury—

(i) the defendant is responsible only for actual awareness or actual belief possessed; and

(ii) knowledge possessed by a person other than the defendant, but not by the defendant, may not be attributed to the defendant;

except that in proving a defendant's possession of actual knowledge, circumstantial evidence may be used, including evidence that the defendant took affirmative steps to be shielded from relevant information.

(C) It is an affirmative defense to a prosecution that the conduct charged was freely consented to by the person endangered and that the danger and conduct charged were reasonably foreseeable hazards of—

(i) an occupation, a business, or a profession; or

(ii) medical treatment or medical or scientific experimentation conducted by professionally approved methods and such other person had been made aware of the risks involved prior to giving consent.

The defendant may establish an affirmative defense under this subparagraph by a preponderance of the evidence.

(D) All general defenses, affirmative defenses, and bars to prosecution that may apply with respect to other Federal criminal offenses may apply under subparagraph (A) of this paragraph and shall be determined by the courts of the United States according to the principles of common law as they may be interpreted in the light of reason and experience. Concepts of justification and excuse applicable under this section may be developed in the light of reason and experience.

(E) The term "organization" means a legal entity, other than a government, established or organized for any purpose, and such term includes a corporation, company, association, firm, partnership, joint stock company, foundation, institution, trust, society, union, or any other association of persons.

(F) The term "serious bodily injury" means bodily injury which involves a substantial risk of death, unconsciousness, extreme physical pain, protracted and obvious disfigurement or protracted loss or impairment of the function of a bodily member, organ, or mental faculty.

(6) For the purpose of this subsection, the term "person" includes, in addition to the entities referred to in section 7602(e) of this title, any responsible corporate officer.

**(d) Administrative assessment of civil penalties**

(1) The Administrator may issue an administrative order against any person assessing a civil administrative penalty of up to $25,000, per day of violation, whenever, on the basis of any available information, the Administrator finds that such person—

(A) has violated or is violating any requirement or prohibition of an applicable implementation plan (such order shall be issued (i) during any period of federally assumed enforcement, or (ii) more than thirty days following the date of the Administrator's notification under subsection (a)(1) of this section of a finding that such person has violated or is violating such requirement or prohibition); or

(B) has violated or is violating any other requirement or prohibition of this subchapter or subchapter III, IV–A, V, or VI of this chapter, including, but not limited to, a requirement or prohibition of any rule, order, waiver, permit, or plan promulgated, issued, or approved under this chapter, or for the payment of any fee owed the United States under this chapter (other than subchapter II of this chapter); or

(C) attempts to construct or modify a major stationary source in any area with respect to which a finding under subsection (a)(5) of this section has been made.

The Administrator's authority under this paragraph shall be limited to matters where the total penalty sought does not exceed $200,000 and the first alleged date of violation occurred no more than 12 months prior to the initiation of the administrative action, except where the Administrator and the Attorney General jointly determine that a matter involving a larger penalty amount or longer period of violation is appropriate for administrative penalty action. Any such determination by the Administrator and the Attorney General shall not be subject to judicial review.

(2)(A) An administrative penalty assessed under paragraph (1) shall be assessed by the Administrator by an order made after opportunity for a hearing on the record in accordance with sections 554 and 556 of Title 5. The Administrator shall issue reasonable rules for discovery and other procedures for hearings under this paragraph. Before issuing such an order, the Administrator shall give written notice to the person to be assessed an administrative penalty of the Administrator's proposal to issue such order and provide such person an opportunity to request such a hearing on the order, within 30 days of the date the notice is received by such person.

(B) The Administrator may compromise, modify, or remit, with or without conditions, any administrative penalty which may be imposed under this subsection.

(3) The Administrator may implement, after consultation with the Attorney General and the States, a field citation program through regulations establishing appropriate minor violations for which field citations assessing civil penalties not to exceed $5,000 per day of violation may be issued by officers or employees designated by the Administrator. Any person to whom a field citation is assessed may, within a reasonable time as prescribed by the Administrator through regulation, elect to pay the penalty assessment or to request a hearing on the field citation. If a request for a hearing is not made within the time specified in the regulation, the penalty assessment in the field citation shall be final. Such hearing shall not be subject to section 554 or 556 of Title 5, but shall provide a reasonable opportunity to be heard and to present evidence. Payment of a civil penalty required by a field citation shall not be a defense to further enforcement by the United States or a State to correct a violation, or to assess the statutory maximum penalty pursuant to other authorities in the chapter, if the violation continues.

(4) Any person against whom a civil penalty is assessed under paragraph (3) of this subsection or to whom an administrative penalty order is issued under paragraph (1) of this subsection may seek review of such assessment in the United States District Court for the District of Columbia or for the district in which the violation is alleged to have occurred, in which such person resides, or where such person's principal place of business is located, by filing in such court within 30 days following the date the administrative penalty order becomes final under paragraph (2), the assessment becomes final under paragraph (3), or a final decision following a hearing under paragraph (3) is rendered, and by simultaneously sending a copy of the filing by certified mail to the Administrator and the Attorney General. Within 30 days thereafter, the Administrator shall file in such court a certified copy, or certified index, as appropriate, of the record on which the administrative penalty order or assessment was issued. Such court shall not set aside or remand such order or assessment unless there is not substantial evidence in the record, taken as a whole, to support the finding of a violation or unless the order or penalty assessment constitutes an abuse of discretion. Such order or penalty assessment shall not be subject to review by any court except as provided in this paragraph. In any such proceedings, the United States may seek to recover civil penalties ordered or assessed under this section.

(5) If any person fails to pay an assessment of a civil penalty or fails to comply with an administrative penalty order—

(A) after the order or assessment has become final, or

(B) after a court in an action brought under paragraph (4) has entered a final judgment in favor of the Administrator,

the Administrator shall request the Attorney General to bring a civil action in an appropriate district court to enforce the order or to recover the amount ordered or assessed (plus interest at rates established pursuant to section 6621(a)(2) of Title 26 from the date of the final order or decision or the date of the final judgment, as the case may be). In such an action, the validity, amount, and appropriateness of such order or assessment shall not be subject to review. Any person who fails to pay on a timely basis a civil penalty ordered or assessed under this section shall be required to pay, in addition to such penalty and interest, the United States enforcement expenses, including but not limited to attorneys fees and costs incurred by the United States for collection proceedings and a quarterly nonpayment penalty for each quarter during which such failure to pay persists. Such nonpayment penalty shall be 10 percent of the aggregate amount of such person's outstanding penalties and nonpayment penalties accrued as of the beginning of such quarter.

**(e) Penalty assessment criteria**

(1) In determining the amount of any penalty to be assessed under this section or section 7604(a) of this title, the Administrator or the court, as appropriate, shall take into consideration (in addition to such other factors as justice may require) the size of the business, the economic impact of the penalty on the business, the violator's full compliance history and good faith efforts to comply, the duration of the violation as established by any credible evidence (including evidence other than the applicable test method), payment by the violator of penalties previously assessed for the same violation, the economic benefit of noncompliance, and the seriousness of the violation. The court shall

not assess penalties for noncompliance with administrative subpoenas under section 7607(a) of this title, or actions under section 7414 of this title, where the violator had sufficient cause to violate or fail or refuse to comply with such subpoena or action.

(2) A penalty may be assessed for each day of violation. For purposes of determining the number of days of violation for which a penalty may be assessed under subsection (b) or (d)(1) of this section, or section 7604(a) of this title, or an assessment may be made under section 7420 of this title, where the Administrator or an air pollution control agency has notified the source of the violation, and the plaintiff makes a prima facie showing that the conduct or events giving rise to the violation are likely to have continued or recurred past the date of notice, the days of violation shall be presumed to include the date of such notice and each and every day thereafter until the violator establishes that continuous compliance has been achieved, except to the extent that the violator can prove by a preponderance of the evidence that there were intervening days during which no violation occurred or that the violation was not continuing in nature.

**(f) Awards**

The Administrator may pay an award, not to exceed $10,000, to any person who furnishes information or services which lead to a criminal conviction or a judicial or administrative civil penalty for any violation of this subchapter or subchapter III, IV–A, V, or VI of this chapter enforced under this section. Such payment is subject to available appropriations for such purposes as provided in annual appropriation Acts. Any officer, or employee of the United States or any State or local government who furnishes information or renders service in the performance of an official duty is ineligible for payment under this subsection. The Administrator may, by regulation, prescribe additional criteria for eligibility for such an award.

**(g) Settlements; public participation**

At least 30 days before a consent order or settlement agreement of any kind under this chapter to which the United States is a party (other than enforcement actions under this section, section 7420 of this title, or subchapter II of this chapter, whether or not involving civil or criminal penalties, or judgments subject to Department of Justice policy on public participation) is final or filed with a court, the Administrator shall provide a reasonable opportunity by notice in the Federal Register to persons who are not named as parties or intervenors to the action or matter to comment in writing. The Administrator or the Attorney General, as appropriate, shall promptly consider any such written comments and may withdraw or withhold his consent to the proposed order or agreement if the comments disclose facts or considerations which indicate that such consent is inappropriate, improper, inadequate, or inconsistent with the requirements of this chapter. Nothing in this subsection shall apply to civil or criminal penalties under this chapter.

**(h) Operator**

For purposes of the provisions of this section and section 7420 of this title, the term "operator", as used in such provisions, shall include any person who is senior management personnel or a corporate officer. Except in the case of knowing and willful violations, such term shall not include any person who is a stationary engineer or technician responsible for the operation, maintenance, repair, or monitoring of equipment and facilities and who often has supervisory and training duties but who is not senior management personnel or a corporate officer. Except in the case of knowing and willful violations, for purposes of subsection (c)(4) of this section, the term "a person" shall not include an employee who is carrying out his normal activities and who is not a part of senior management personnel or a corporate officer. Except in the case of knowing and willful violations, for purposes of paragraphs (1), (2), (3), and (5) of subsection (c) of this section the term "a person" shall not include an employee who is carrying out his normal activities and who is acting under orders from the employer.

(July 14, 1955, c. 360, Title I, § 113, as added Dec. 31, 1970, Pub.L. 91–604, § 4(a), 84 Stat. 1686, and amended Nov. 18, 1971, Pub.L. 92–157, Title III, § 302(b), (c), 85 Stat. 464; June 22, 1974, Pub.L. 93–319, § 6(a)(1) to (3), 88 Stat. 259; Aug. 7, 1977, Pub.L. 95–95, Title I, §§ 111, 112(a), 91 Stat. 704, 705; Nov. 16, 1977, Pub.L. 95–190, § 14(a)(10) to (21), (b)(1), 91 Stat. 1400, 1404; July 17, 1981, Pub.L. 97–23, § 2, 95 Stat. 139; Nov. 15, 1990, Pub.L. 101–549, Title VII, § 701, 104 Stat. 2672.)

[1] So in original. The semicolon probably should be a comma.

[2] So in original. Probably should be followed by a comma.

## HISTORICAL AND STATUTORY NOTES

**Codifications**

Section was formerly classified to section 1857c–8 of this title.

**Effective and Applicability Provisions**

1990 Acts

Amendment by Pub.L. 101–549 effective Nov. 15, 1990, except as otherwise provided, see section 711(b) of Pub.L. 101–549, set out as a note under section 7401 of this title.

1977 Acts

Amendment by Pub.L. 95–95 effective Aug. 7, 1977, except as otherwise expressly provided, see section 406(d) of Pub.L. 95–95, set out as a note under section 7401 of this title.

**Transfer of Functions**

The Federal Power Commission was terminated and its functions, personnel, property, funds, etc. were transferred to the Secretary of Energy (except for certain functions which were transferred to the Federal Energy Regulatory Commission) by sections 7151(b), 7171(a), 7172(a), 7291, and 7293 of this title.

**Savings Provisions**

Suits, actions or proceedings commenced under this chapter as in effect prior to Nov. 15, 1990, not to abate by reason of the taking effect of amendments by Pub.L. 101–549, except as otherwise provided for, see section 711(a) of Pub.L. 101–549, set out as a note under section 7401 of this title.

Suits, actions, and other proceedings lawfully commenced by or against the Administrator or any other officer or employee of the United States in his official capacity or in relation to the discharge of his official duties under Act July 14, 1955, the Clean Air Act, as in effect immediately prior to the enactment of Pub.L. 95–95 [Aug. 7, 1977], not to abate by reason of the taking effect of Pub.L. 95–95, see section 406(a) of Pub.L. 95–95, set out as an Effective Date of 1977 Acts note under section 7401 of this title.

**Short Title**

1981 Amendments

Citation of Pub.L. 97–23, which enacted subsec. (e) of this section, as the "Steel Industry Compliance Extension Act of 1981", see section 1 of Pub.L. 97–23, set out as a note under section 7401 of this title.

**Modification or Rescission of Rules, Regulations, Orders, Determinations, Contracts, Certifications, Authorizations, Delegations, and Other Actions**

All rules, regulations, orders, determinations, contracts, certifications, authorizations, delegations, or other actions duly issued, made, or taken by or pursuant to Act July 14, 1955, the Clean Air Act, as in effect immediately prior to the date of enactment of Pub.L. 95–95 [Aug. 7, 1977] to continue in full force and effect until modified or rescinded in accordance with Act July 14, 1955, as amended by Pub.L. 95–95 [this chapter], see section 406(b) of Pub.L. 95–95, set out as an Effective Date of 1977 Acts note under section 7401 of this title.

## § 7414. Recordkeeping, inspections, monitoring, and entry

**[CAA § 114]**

### (a) Authority of Administrator or authorized representative

For the purpose (i) of developing or assisting in the development of any implementation plan under section 7410 or section 7411(d) of this title, any standard of performance under section 7411 of this title, any emission standard under section 7412 of this title,, [1] or any regulation of solid waste combustion under section 7429 of this title, or any regulation under section 7429 of this title (relating to solid waste combustion), (ii) of determining whether any person is in violation of any such standard or any requirement of such a plan, or (iii) carrying out any provision of this chapter (except a provision of subchapter II of this chapter with respect to a manufacturer of new motor vehicles or new motor vehicle engines)—

(1) the Administrator may require any person who owns or operates any emission source, who manufactures emission control equipment or process equipment, who the Administrator believes may have information necessary for the purposes set forth in this subsection, or who is subject to any requirement of this chapter (other than a manufacturer subject to the provisions of section 7525(c) or 7542 of this title with respect to a provision of subchapter II of this chapter) on a one-time, periodic or continuous basis to—

(A) establish and maintain such records;

(B) make such reports;

(C) install, use, and maintain such monitoring equipment, and use such audit procedures, or methods;

(D) sample such emissions (in accordance with such procedures or methods, at such locations, at such intervals, during such periods and in such manner as the Administrator shall prescribe);

(E) keep records on control equipment parameters, production variables or other indirect data when direct monitoring of emissions is impractical;

(F) submit compliance certifications in accordance with subsection (a)(3) of this section; and

(G) provide such other information as the Administrator may reasonably require; and

(2) the Administrator or his authorized representative, upon presentation of his credentials—

(A) shall have a right of entry to, upon, or through any premises of such person or in which any records required to be maintained under paragraph (1) of this section are located, and

(B) may at reasonable times have access to and copy any records, inspect any monitoring equipment or method required under paragraph (1), and sample any emissions which such person is required to sample under paragraph (1).[2]

(3) The [3] Administrator shall in the case of any person which is the owner or operator of a major stationary source, and may, in the case of any other person, require enhanced monitoring and submission of compliance certifications. Compliance certifications shall include (A) identification of the applicable requirement that is the basis of the certification, (B) the method used for determining the compliance status of the source, (C) the compliance status, (D) whether compliance is continuous or intermittent, (E) such other facts as the Administrator may require. Compliance certifications and monitoring data shall be subject to subsection (c) of this section. Submission of a compliance certification shall in no way limit the Administrator's authorities to investigate or otherwise implement this chapter. The Administrator shall promulgate

rules to provide guidance and to implement this paragraph within 2 years after November 15, 1990.

**(b) State enforcement**

(1) Each State may develop and submit to the Administrator a procedure for carrying out this section in such State. If the Administrator finds the State procedure is adequate, he may delegate to such State any authority he has to carry out this section.

(2) Nothing in this subsection shall prohibit the Administrator from carrying out this section in a State.

**(c) Availability of records, reports, and information to public; disclosure of trade secrets**

Any records, reports or information obtained under subsection (a) of this section shall be available to the public, except that upon a showing satisfactory to the Administrator by any person that records, reports, or information, or particular part thereof, (other than emission data) to which the Administrator has access under this section if made public, would divulge methods or processes entitled to protection as trade secrets of such person, the Administrator shall consider such record, report, or information or particular portion thereof confidential in accordance with the purposes of section 1905 of Title 18, except that such record, report, or information may be disclosed to other officers, employees, or authorized representatives of the United States concerned with carrying out this chapter or when relevant in any proceeding under this chapter.

**(d) Notice of proposed entry, inspection, or monitoring**

(1) In the case of any emission standard or limitation or other requirement which is adopted by a State, as part of an applicable implementation plan or as part of an order under section 7413(d) of this title, before carrying out an entry, inspection, or monitoring under paragraph (2) of subsection (a) of this section with respect to such standard, limitation, or other requirement, the Administrator (or his representatives) shall provide the State air pollution control agency with reasonable prior notice of such action, indicating the purpose of such action. No State agency which receives notice under this paragraph of an action proposed to be taken may use the information contained in the notice to inform the person whose property is proposed to be affected of the proposed action. If the Administrator has reasonable basis for believing that a State agency is so using or will so use such information, notice to the agency under this paragraph is not required until such time as the Administrator determines the agency will no longer so use information contained in a notice under this paragraph. Nothing in this section shall be construed to require notification to any State agency of any action taken by the Administrator with respect to any standard, limitation, or other requirement which is not part of an applicable implementation plan or which was promulgated by the Administrator under section 7410(c) of this title.

(2) Nothing in paragraph (1) shall be construed to provide that any failure of the Administrator to comply with the requirements of such paragraph shall be a defense in any enforcement action brought by the Administrator or shall make inadmissible as evidence in any such action any information or material obtained notwithstanding such failure to comply with such requirements.

(July 14, 1955, c. 360, Title I, § 114, as added Dec. 31, 1970, Pub.L. 91–604, § 4(a), 84 Stat. 1687, and amended June 22, 1974, Pub.L. 93–319, § 6(a)(4), 88 Stat. 259; Aug. 7, 1977, Pub.L. 95–95, Title I, §§ 109(d)(3), 113, Title III, § 305(d), 91 Stat. 701, 709, 776; Nov. 16, 1977, Pub.L. 95–190, § 14(a)(22), (23), 91 Stat. 1400; Nov. 15, 1990, Pub.L. 101–549, Title III, § 302(c), Title VII, § 702(a), (b), 104 Stat. 2574, 2680, 2681.)

[1] So in original.

[2] The period probably should be "; and".

[3] So in original. Probably should not be capitalized.

## HISTORICAL AND STATUTORY NOTES

**References in Text**

Section 7413(d) of this title, referred to in subsec. (d)(1), was amended generally by Pub.L. 101–549, Title VII, § 701, Nov. 15, 1990, 104 Stat. 2672, and, as so amended, no longer relates to final compliance orders.

**Codifications**

Section was formerly classified to section 1857c–9 of this title.

**Effective and Applicability Provisions**

1990 Acts

Amendment by Pub.L. 101–549 effective Nov. 15, 1990, except as otherwise provided, see section 711(b) of Pub.L. 101–549, set out as a note under section 7401 of this title.

1977 Acts

Amendment by Pub.L. 95–95 effective Aug. 7, 1977, except as otherwise expressly provided, see section 406(d) of Pub.L. 95–95, set out as a note under section 7401 of this title.

**Savings Provisions**

Suits, actions or proceedings commenced under this chapter as in effect prior to Nov. 15, 1990, not to abate by reason of the taking effect of amendments by Pub.L. 101–549, except as otherwise provided for, see section 711(a) of Pub.L. 101–549, set out as a note under section 7401 of this title.

**Modification or Rescission of Rules, Regulations, Orders, Determinations, Contracts, Certifications, Authorizations, Delegations, and Other Actions**

All rules, regulations, orders, determinations, contracts, certifications, authorizations, delegations, or other actions duly issued, made, or taken by or pursuant to Act July 14, 1955, the Clean Air Act, as in effect immediately prior to the date of enactment of Pub.L. 95–95 [Aug. 7, 1977] to continue in full force and effect until modified or rescinded in accordance with Act July 14, 1955, as amended by Pub.L. 95–95 [this chapter], see section 406(b) of Pub.L. 95–95, set out as an Effective Date of 1977 Acts note under section 7401 of this title.

**Pending Actions and Proceedings**

Suits, actions, and other proceedings lawfully commenced by or against the Administrator or any other officer or employee of the United States in his official capacity or in relation to the discharge of his official duties under Act July 14, 1955, the Clean Air Act, as in effect immediately prior to the enactment of Pub.L. 95–95 [Aug. 7, 1977], not to abate by reason of the taking effect of Pub.L. 95–95, see section 406(a) of Pub.L. 95–95, set out as an Effective and Applicability Provisions of 1977 Acts note under section 7401 of this title.

## § 7415. International air pollution

[CAA § 115]

### (a) Endangerment of public health or welfare in foreign countries from pollution emitted in United States

Whenever the Administrator, upon receipt of reports, surveys or studies from any duly constituted international agency has reason to believe that any air pollutant or pollutants emitted in the United States cause or contribute to air pollution which may reasonably be anticipated to endanger public health or welfare in a foreign country or whenever the Secretary of State requests him to do so with respect to such pollution which the Secretary of State alleges is of such a nature, the Administrator shall give formal notification thereof to the Governor of the State in which such emissions originate.

### (b) Prevention or elimination of endangerment

The notice of the Administrator shall be deemed to be a finding under section 7410(a)(2)(H)(ii) of this title which requires a plan revision with respect to so much of the applicable implementation plan as is inadequate to prevent or eliminate the endangerment referred to in subsection (a) of this section. Any foreign country so affected by such emission of pollutant or pollutants shall be invited to appear at any public hearing associated with any revision of the appropriate portion of the applicable implementation plan.

### (c) Reciprocity

This section shall apply only to a foreign country which the Administrator determines has given the United States essentially the same rights with respect to the prevention or control of air pollution occurring in that country as is given that country by this section.

### (d) Recommendations

Recommendations issued following any abatement conference conducted prior to August 7, 1977, shall remain in effect with respect to any pollutant for which no national ambient air quality standard has been established under section 7409 of this title unless the Administrator, after consultation with all agencies which were party to the conference, rescinds any such recommendation on grounds of obsolescence.

(July 14, 1955, c. 360, Title I, § 115, formerly § 5, as added Dec. 17, 1963, Pub.L. 88–206, § 1, 77 Stat. 396, renumbered § 105 and amended Oct. 20, 1965, Pub.L. 89–272, Title I, §§ 101(2), (3), 102, 79 Stat. 992, 995, renumbered § 108 and amended Nov. 21, 1967, Pub.L. 90–148, § 2, 81 Stat. 491, renumbered § 115 and amended Dec. 31, 1970, Pub.L. 91–604, §§ 4(a), (b)(2) to (10), 15(c)(2), 84 Stat. 1678, 1688, 1689, 1713; Aug. 7, 1977, Pub.L. 95–95, Title I, § 114, 91 Stat. 710.)

### HISTORICAL AND STATUTORY NOTES

**Codifications**

Section was formerly classified to section 1857d of this title.

**Effective and Applicability Provisions**

1977 Acts

Amendment by Pub.L. 95–95 effective Aug. 7, 1977, except as otherwise expressly provided, see section 406(d) of Pub.L. 95–95, set out as a note under section 7401 of this title.

**Prior Provisions**

A prior section 5 of Act July 14, 1955, c. 360, 69 Stat. 322, as amended Sept. 22, 1959, Pub.L. 86–365, § 1, 73 Stat. 646; Oct. 9, 1962, Pub.L. 87–761, § 1, 76 Stat. 760, which was classified to a prior section 1857d of this title prior to the general amendment of this chapter by Pub.L. 88–206, related to appropriations, grants-in-aid, and contracts.

**Modification or Rescission of Rules, Regulations, Orders, Determinations, Contracts, Certifications, Authorizations, Delegations, and Other Actions**

All rules, regulations, orders, determinations, contracts, certifications, authorizations, delegations, or other actions duly issued, made, or taken by or pursuant to Act July 14, 1955, the Clean Air Act, as in effect immediately prior to the date of enactment of Pub.L. 95–95 [Aug. 7, 1977] to continue in full force and effect until modified or rescinded in accordance with Act July 14, 1955, as amended by Pub.L. 95–95 [this chapter], see section 406(b) of Pub.L. 95–95, set out as an Effective and Applicability Provisions of 1977 Acts note under section 7401 of this title.

**United States—Canadian Negotiations on Air Quality**

Pub.L. 95–426, Title VI, § 612, Oct. 7, 1978, 92 Stat. 990, provided that:

"(a) The Congress finds that—

"(1) the United States and Canada share a common environment along a 5,500 mile border;

"(2) the United States and Canada are both becoming increasingly concerned about the effects of pollution, particularly that resulting from power generation facilities, since the facilities of each country affect the environment of the other;

"(3) the United States and Canada have subscribed to international conventions; have joined in the environmental work of the United Nations, the Organization for Economic Cooperation and Development, and other international environmental forums; and have entered into and implemented effectively the provisions of the historic Boundary Waters Treaty of 1909; and

"(4) the United States and Canada have a tradition of cooperative resolution of issues of mutual concern which is nowhere more evident than in the environmental area.

"(b) It is the sense of the Congress that the President should make every effort to negotiate a cooperative agreement with the Government of Canada aimed at preserving the mutual airshed of the United States and Canada so as to protect and enhance air resources and insure the attainment and maintenance of air quality protective of public health and welfare.

"(c) It is further the sense of the Congress that the President, through the Secretary of State working in concert with interested Federal agencies and the affected States, should take whatever diplomatic actions appear necessary to reduce or eliminate any undesirable impact upon the United States and Canada resulting from air pollution from any source."

Transboundary pollution in the Great Lakes: Do individual states have any role to play in its prevention? Steven M. Siros, 20 S.Ill.U.L.J. 287 (Winter 1996).

## § 7416. Retention of State authority

**[CAA § 116]**

Except as otherwise provided in sections 1857c–10(c), (e), and (f) (as in effect before August 7, 1977), 7543, 7545(c)(4), and 7573 of this title (preempting certain State regulation of moving sources) nothing in this chapter shall preclude or deny the right of any State or political subdivision thereof to adopt or enforce (1) any standard or limitation respecting emissions of air pollutants or (2) any requirement respecting control or abatement of air pollution; except that if an emission standard or limitation is in effect under an applicable implementation plan or under section 7411 or section 7412 of this title, such State or political subdivision may not adopt or enforce any emission standard or limitation which is less stringent than the standard or limitation under such plan or section.

(July 14, 1955, c. 360, Title I, § 116, formerly § 109, as added Nov. 21, 1967, Pub.L. 90–148, § 2, 81 Stat. 497, renumbered and amended Dec. 31, 1970, Pub.L. 91–604, § 4(a), (c), 84 Stat. 1678, 1689; June 22, 1974, Pub.L. 93–319, § 6(b), 88 Stat. 259; Nov. 16, 1977, Pub.L. 95–190, § 14(a)(24), 91 Stat. 1400.)

### HISTORICAL AND STATUTORY NOTES

**References in Text**

"1857c–10(c), (e), and (f) (as in effect before August 7, 1977)", referred to in text, was in the original "119(c), (e), and (f) (as in effect before the date of the enactment of the Clean Air Act Amendments of 1977)" meaning section 119 of Act July 14, 1955, c. 360, Title I, as added June 22, 1974, Pub.L. 93–319, § 3, 88 Stat. 248, (which was classified to section 1857c–10 of this title) as in effect prior to the enactment of Pub.L. 95–95, Aug. 7, 1977, 91 Stat. 691, effective Aug. 7, 1977. Section 112(b)(1) of Pub.L. 95–95 repealed section 119 of Act July 14, 1955, c. 360, Title I, as added by Pub.L. 93–319, and provided that all references to such section 119 in any subsequent enactment which supersedes Pub.L. 93–319 shall be construed to refer to section 113(d) of the Clean Air Act and to paragraph (5) thereof in particular which is classified to subsec. (d)(5) of section 7413 of this title. Section 7413 of this title was subsequently amended generally by Pub.L. 101–549, Title VII, § 701, Nov. 15, 1990, 104 Stat. 2672, and as so amended, no longer relates to final compliance orders. Section 117(b) of Pub.L. 95–95 added a new section 119 of Act July 14, 1955, which is classified to section 7419 of this title.

**Codifications**

Section was formerly classified to section 1857d–1 of this title.

**Modification or Rescission of Rules, Regulations, Orders, Determinations, Contracts, Certifications, Authorizations, Delegations, and Other Actions**

All rules, regulations, orders, determinations, contracts, certifications, authorizations, delegations, or other actions duly issued, made, or taken by or pursuant to Act July 14, 1955, the Clean Air Act, as in effect immediately prior to the date of enactment of Pub.L. 95–95 [Aug. 7, 1977] to continue in full force and effect until modified or rescinded in accordance with Act July 14, 1955, as amended by Pub.L. 95–95 [this chapter], see section 406(b) of Pub.L. 95–95, set out as an Effective and Applicability Provisions of 1977 Acts note under section 7401 of this title.

## § 7417. Advisory committees

**[CAA § 117]**

### (a) Establishment; membership

In order to obtain assistance in the development and implementation of the purposes of this chapter including air quality criteria, recommended control techniques, standards, research and development, and to encourage the continued efforts on the part of industry to improve air quality and to develop economically feasible methods for the control and abatement of air pollution, the Administrator shall from time to time establish advisory committees. Committee members shall include, but not be limited to, persons who are knowledgeable concerning air quality from the standpoint of health, welfare, economics or technology.

### (b) Compensation

The members of any other advisory committees appointed pursuant to this chapter who are not officers or employees of the United States while attending conferences or meetings or while otherwise serving at the request of the Administrator, shall be entitled to receive compensation at a rate to be fixed by the Administrator, but not exceeding $100 per diem, including traveltime, and while away from their homes or regular places of business they may be allowed travel expenses, including per diem in lieu of subsistence, as authorized by section 5703 of Title 5 for persons in the Government service employed intermittently.

**(c) Consultations by Administrator**

Prior to—

(1) issuing criteria for an air pollutant under section 7408(a)(2) of this title,

(2) publishing any list under section 7411(b)(1)(A) or section 7412(b)(1)(A) of this title,

(3) publishing any standard under section 7411 or section 7412 of this title, or

(4) publishing any regulation under section 7521(a) of this title,

the Administrator shall, to the maximum extent practicable within the time provided, consult with appropriate advisory committees, independent experts, and Federal departments and agencies.

(July 14, 1955, c. 360, Title I, § 117, formerly § 6, as added Dec. 17, 1963, Pub.L. 88–206, § 1, 77 Stat. 399, renumbered § 106, Oct. 20, 1965, Pub.L. 89–272, Title I, § 101(3), 79 Stat. 992, renumbered § 110 and amended Nov. 21, 1967, Pub.L. 90–148, § 2, 81 Stat. 498, renumbered § 117 and amended Dec. 31, 1970, Pub.L. 91–604, §§ 4(a), (d), 15(c)(2), 84 Stat. 1678, 1689, 1713; Aug. 7, 1977, Pub.L. 95–95, Title I, § 115, 91 Stat. 711; Nov. 9, 1978, Pub.L. 95–623, § 13(c), 92 Stat. 3458.)

## HISTORICAL AND STATUTORY NOTES

**References in Text**

Section 7412(b)(1), referred to in subsec. (c)(2), was amended generally by Pub.L. 101–549, Title III, § 301, Nov. 15, 1990, 104 Stat. 2531, and, as so amended, no longer contains a subpar. (A).

**Codifications**

Subsec. (c) was originally enacted as subsec. (f) but has been redesignated (c) for purposes of codification in view of the omission by Pub.L. 95–95 to redesignate subsec. (f) as (c) after repealing former subsecs. (a) and (b) and redesignating former subsecs. (d) and (e) as (a) and (b).

Section was formerly classified to section 1857e of this title.

**Effective and Applicability Provisions**

1977 Acts

Amendment by Pub.L. 95–95 effective Aug. 7, 1977, except as otherwise expressly provided, see section 406(d) of Pub.L. 95–95, set out as a note under section 7401 of this title.

**Prior Provisions**

A prior section 6 of Act July 14, 1955, c. 360, 69 Stat. 323, which was classified to a prior section 1857e of this title, prior to the general amendment of this chapter by Pub.L. 88–206, defined "State air pollution control agency", "local government air pollution control agency" and "State". See section 7602 of this title.

**Modification or Rescission of Rules, Regulations, Orders, Determinations, Contracts, Certifications, Authorizations, Delegations, and Other Actions**

All rules, regulations, orders, determinations, contracts, certifications, authorizations, delegations, or other actions duly issued, made, or taken by or pursuant to Act July 14, 1955, the Clean Air Act, as in effect immediately prior to the date of enactment of Pub.L. 95–95 [Aug. 7, 1977] to continue in full force and effect until modified or rescinded in accordance with Act July 14, 1955, as amended by Pub.L. 95–95 [this chapter], see section 406(b) of Pub.L. 95–95, set out as an Effective and Applicability Provisions of 1977 Acts note under section 7401 of this title.

**Termination of Advisory Committees**

Advisory committees in existence on Jan. 5, 1973, to terminate not later than the expiration of the two-year period following Jan. 5, 1973, unless, in the case of a committee established by the President or an officer of the Federal Government, such committee is renewed by appropriate action prior to the expiration of such two-year period, or in the case of a committee established by the Congress, its duration is otherwise provided by law. Advisory committees established after Jan. 5, 1973, to terminate not later than the expiration of the two-year period beginning on the date of their establishment, unless, in the case of a committee established by the President or an officer of the Federal Government, such committee is renewed by appropriate action prior to the expiration of such two-year period, or in the case of a committee established by the Congress, its duration is otherwise provided by law. See section 14 of Pub.L. 92–463, Oct. 6, 1972, 86 Stat. 776, set out in Appendix 2 to Title 5, Government Organization and Employees.

## § 7418. Control of pollution from Federal facilities

[CAA § 118]

**(a) General compliance**

Each department, agency, and instrumentality of the executive, legislative, and judicial branches of the Federal Government (1) having jurisdiction over any property or facility, or (2) engaged in any activity resulting, or which may result, in the discharge of air pollutants, and each officer, agent, or employee thereof, shall be subject to, and comply with, all Federal, State, interstate, and local requirements, administrative authority, and process and sanctions respecting the control and abatement of air pollution in the same manner, and to the same extent as any nongovernmental entity. The preceding sentence shall apply (A) to any requirement whether substantive or procedural (including any recordkeeping or reporting requirement, any requirement respecting permits and any other requirement whatsoever), (B) to any requirement to pay a fee or charge imposed by any State or local agency to defray the costs of its air pollution regulatory program, (C) to the exercise of any Federal, State, or local administrative authority, and (D) to any process and sanction, whether enforced in Federal, State, or local courts, or in any other manner.

This subsection shall apply notwithstanding any immunity of such agencies, officers, agents, or employees under any law or rule of law. No officer, agent, or employee of the United States shall be personally liable for any civil penalty for which he is not otherwise liable.

**(b) Exemption**

The President may exempt any emission source of any department, agency, or instrumentality in the executive branch from compliance with such a requirement if he determines it to be in the paramount interest of the United States to do so, except that no exemption may be granted from section 7411 of this title, and an exemption from section 7412 of this title may be granted only in accordance with section 7412(i)(4) of this title. No such exemption shall be granted due to lack of appropriation unless the President shall have specifically requested such appropriation as a part of the budgetary process and the Congress shall have failed to make available such requested appropriation. Any exemption shall be for a period not in excess of one year, but additional exemptions may be granted for periods of not to exceed one year upon the President's making a new determination. In addition to any such exemption of a particular emission source, the President may, if he determines it to be in the paramount interest of the United States to do so, issue regulations exempting from compliance with the requirements of this section any weaponry, equipment, aircraft, vehicles, or other classes or categories of property which are owned or operated by the Armed Forces of the United States (including the Coast Guard) or by the National Guard of any State and which are uniquely military in nature. The President shall reconsider the need for such regulations at three-year intervals. The President shall report each January to the Congress all exemptions from the requirements of this section granted during the preceding calendar year, together with his reason for granting each such exemption.

**(c) Government vehicles**

Each department, agency, and instrumentality of executive, legislative, and judicial branches of the Federal Government shall comply with all applicable provisions of a valid inspection and maintenance program established under the provisions of subpart 2 of part D of this subchapter or subpart 3 of part D of this subchapter except for such vehicles that are considered military tactical vehicles.

**(d) Vehicles operated on Federal installations**

Each department, agency, and instrumentality of executive, legislative, and judicial branches of the Federal Government having jurisdiction over any property or facility shall require all employees which operate motor vehicles on the property or facility to furnish proof of compliance with the applicable requirements of any vehicle inspection and maintenance program established under the provisions of subpart 2 of part D of this subchapter or subpart 3 of part D of this subchapter for the State in which such property or facility is located (without regard to whether such vehicles are registered in the State). The installation shall use one of the following methods to establish proof of compliance—

(1) presentation by the vehicle owner of a valid certificate of compliance from the vehicle inspection and maintenance program;

(2) presentation by the vehicle owner of proof of vehicle registration within the geographic area covered by the vehicle inspection and maintenance program (except for any program whose enforcement mechanism is not through the denial of vehicle registration);

(3) another method approved by the vehicle inspection and maintenance program administrator.

(July 14, 1955, c. 360, Title I, § 118, formerly § 7, as added Dec. 17, 1963, Pub.L. 88–206, § 1, 77 Stat. 399, renumbered § 107, Oct. 20, 1965, Pub.L. 89–272, Title I, § 101(3), 79 Stat. 992, renumbered § 111 and amended Nov. 21, 1967, Pub.L. 90–148, § 2, 81 Stat. 499, and renumbered § 118 and amended Dec. 31, 1970, Pub.L. 91–604, §§ 4(a), 5, 84 Stat. 1678, 1689; Aug. 7, 1977, Pub.L. 95–95, Title I, § 116, 91 Stat. 711; Nov. 15, 1990, Pub.L. 101–549, Title I, § 101(e), Title II, § 235, Title III, § 302(d), 104 Stat. 2409, 2530, 2574.)

## HISTORICAL AND STATUTORY NOTES

**Codifications**

Section was formerly classified to section 1857f of this title.

**Effective and Applicability Provisions**

1990 Acts

Amendment by Pub.L. 101–549 effective Nov. 15, 1990, except as otherwise provided, see section 711(b) of Pub.L. 101–549, set out as a note under section 7401 of this title.

1977 Acts

Amendment by Pub.L. 95–95 effective Aug. 7, 1977, except as otherwise expressly provided, see section 406(d) of Pub.L. 95–95, set out as a note under section 7401 of this title.

**Savings Provisions**

Suits, actions or proceedings commenced under this chapter as in effect prior to Nov. 15, 1990, not to abate by reason of the taking effect of amendments by Pub.L. 101–549, except as otherwise provided for, see section 711(a) of Pub.L. 101–549, set out as a note under section 7401 of this title.

**Prior Provisions**

A prior section 7 of Act July 14, 1955, c. 360, 69 Stat. 323, which was classified to a prior section 1857f of this title, related to research and experiments under other laws.

**Exemption for Fort Allen in Puerto Rico**

For provisions relating to the exemption for Fort Allen in Puerto Rico, in its use as temporary housing for Haitian refugees, from compliance with provisions of this chapter relating to emission sources located at Fort Allen, with exceptions, see sections 1–102 and 1–105 of Ex. Ord. No. 12327, Oct. 1, 1981, 46 F.R. 48893, set out as a note under section 2601 of Title 22, Foreign Relations and Intercourse.

**Modification or Rescission of Rules, Regulations, Orders, Determinations, Contracts, Certifications, Authorizations, Delegations, and Other Actions**

All rules, regulations, orders, determinations, contracts, certifications, authorizations, delegations, or other actions duly issued, made, or taken by or pursuant to Act July 14, 1955, the Clean Air Act, as in effect immediately prior to the date of enactment of Pub.L. 95–95 [Aug. 7, 1977] to continue in full force and effect until modified or rescinded in accordance with Act July 14, 1955, as amended by Pub.L. 95–95 [this chapter], see section 406(b) of Pub.L. 95–95, set out as an Effective and Applicability Provisions of 1977 Acts note under section 7401 of this title.

**Pending Actions and Proceedings**

Suits, actions, and other proceedings lawfully commenced by or against the Administrator or any other officer or employee of the United States in his official capacity or in relation to the discharge of his official duties under Act July 14, 1955, the Clean Air Act, as in effect immediately prior to the enactment of Pub.L. 95–95 [Aug. 7, 1977], not to abate by reason of the taking effect of Pub.L. 95–95, see section 406(a) of Pub.L. 95–95, set out as an Effective Date of 1977 Acts note under section 7401 of this title.

## § 7419. Primary nonferrous smelter orders

**[CAA § 119]**

### (a) Issuance; hearing; enforcement orders; statement of grounds for application; findings

(1) Upon application by the owner or operator of a primary nonferrous smelter, a primary nonferrous smelter order under subsection (b) of this section may be issued—

(A) by the Administrator, after thirty days' notice to the State, or

(B) by the State in which such source is located, but no such order issued by the State shall take effect until the Administrator determines that such order has been issued in accordance with the requirements of this chapter.

Not later than ninety days after submission by the State to the Administrator of notice of the issuance of a primary nonferrous smelter order under this section, the Administrator shall determine whether or not such order has been issued by the State in accordance with the requirements of this chapter. If the Administrator determines that such order has not been issued in accordance with such requirements, he shall conduct a hearing respecting the reasonably available control technology for primary nonferrous smelters.

(2)(A) An order issued under this section to a primary nonferrous smelter shall be referred to as a "primary nonferrous smelter order". No primary nonferrous smelter may receive both an enforcement order under section 7413(d) of this title and a primary nonferrous smelter order under this section.

(B) Before any hearing conducted under this section, in the case of an application made by the owner or operator of a primary nonferrous smelter for a second order under this section, the applicant shall furnish the Administrator (or the State as the case may be) with a statement of the grounds on which such application is based (including all supporting documents and information). The statement of the grounds for the proposed order shall be provided by the Administrator or the State in any case in which such State or Administrator is acting on its own initiative. Such statement (including such documents and information) shall be made available to the public for a thirty-day period before such hearing and shall be considered as part of such hearing. No primary nonferrous smelter order may be granted unless the applicant establishes that he meets the conditions required for the issuance of such order (or the Administrator or State establishes the meeting of such conditions when acting on their own initiative).

(C) Any decision with respect to the issuance of a primary nonferrous smelter order shall be accompanied by a concise statement of the findings and of the basis of such findings.

(3) For the purposes of sections 7410, 7604, and 7607 of this title, any order issued by the State and in effect pursuant to this subsection shall become part of the applicable implementation plan.

### (b) Prerequisites to issuance of orders

A primary nonferrous smelter order under this section may be issued to a primary nonferrous smelter if—

(1) such smelter is in existence on August 7, 1977;

(2) the requirement of the applicable implementation plan with respect to which the order is issued is an emission limitation or standard for sulfur oxides which is necessary and intended to be itself sufficient to enable attainment and maintenance of national primary and secondary ambient air quality standards for sulfur oxides; and

(3) such smelter is unable to comply with such requirement by the applicable date for compliance because no means of emission limitation applicable to such smelter which will enable it to achieve compliance with such requirement has been adequately demonstrated to be reasonably available (as determined by the Administrator, taking into account the cost of compliance, non-air quality health and environmental impact, and energy consideration).

### (c) Second orders

(1) A second order issued to a smelter under this section shall set forth compliance schedules containing increments of progress which require compliance with the requirement postponed as expeditiously as practicable. The increments of progress shall be limited to requiring compliance with subsection (d) of this section and, in the case of a second order, to procuring, installing, and operating the necessary means of emission limitation as expeditiously as practicable after the Administrator determines such means have been adequately demonstrated to be reasonably available within the meaning of subsection (b)(3) of this section.

(2) Not in excess of two primary nonferrous smelter orders may be issued under this section to any primary nonferrous smelter. The first such order issued to a smelter shall not result in the postponement of the requirement with respect to which such order is issued beyond January 1, 1983. The second such order shall not result in the postponement of such requirement beyond January 1, 1988.

**(d) Interim measures; continuous emission reduction technology**

(1)(A) Each primary nonferrous smelter to which an order is issued under this section shall be required to use such interim measures for the period during which such order is in effect as may be necessary in the judgment of the Administrator to assure attainment and maintenance of the national primary and secondary ambient air quality standards during such period, taking into account the aggregate effect on air quality of such order together with all variances, extensions, waivers, enforcement orders, delayed compliance orders and primary nonferrous smelter orders previously issued under this chapter.

(B) Such interim requirements shall include—

(i) a requirement that the source to which the order applies comply with such reporting requirements and conduct such monitoring as the Administrator determines may be necessary, and

(ii) such measures as the Administrator determines are necessary to avoid an imminent and substantial endangerment to health of persons.

(C) Such interim measures shall also, except as provided in paragraph (2), include continuous emission reduction technology. The Administrator shall condition the use of any such interim measures upon the agreement of the owner or operator of the smelter—

(i) to comply with such conditions as the Administrator determines are necessary to maximize the reliability and enforceability of such interim measures, as applied to the smelter, in attaining and maintaining the national ambient air quality standards to which the order relates, and

(ii) to commit reasonable resources to research and development of appropriate emission control technology.

(2) The requirement of paragraph (1) for the use of continuous emission reduction technology may be waived with respect to a particular smelter by the State or the Administrator, after notice and a hearing on the record, and upon a showing by the owner or operator of the smelter that such requirement would be so costly as to necessitate permanent or prolonged temporary cessation of operations of the smelter. Upon application for such waiver, the Administrator shall be notified and shall, within ninety days, hold a hearing on the record in accordance with section 554 of Title 5. At such hearing the Administrator shall require the smelter involved to present information relating to any alleged cessation of operations and the detailed reasons or justifications therefor. On the basis of such hearing the Administrator shall make findings of fact as to the effect of such requirement and on the alleged cessation of operations and shall make such recommendations as he deems appropriate. Such report, findings, and recommendations shall be available to the public, and shall be taken into account by the State or the Administrator in making the decision whether or not to grant such waiver.

(3) In order to obtain information for purposes of a waiver under paragraph (2), the Administrator may, on his own motion, conduct an investigation and use the authority of section 7621 of this title.

(4) In the case of any smelter which on August 7, 1977, uses continuous emission reduction technology and supplemental controls and which receives an initial primary nonferrous smelter order under this section, no additional continuous emission reduction technology shall be required as a condition of such order unless the Administrator determines, at any time, after notice and public hearing, that such additional continuous emission reduction technology is adequately demonstrated to be reasonably available for the primary nonferrous smelter industry.

**(e) Termination of orders**

At any time during which an order under this section applies, the Administrator may enter upon a public hearing respecting the availability of technology. Any order under this section shall be terminated if the Administrator determines on the record, after notice and public hearing, that the conditions upon which the order was based no longer exist. If the owner or operator of the smelter to which the order is issued demonstrates that prompt termination of such order would result in undue hardship, the termination shall become effective at the earliest practicable date on which such undue hardship would not result, but in no event later than the date required under subsection (c) of this section.

**(f) Violation of requirements**

If the Administrator determines that a smelter to which an order is issued under this section is in violation of any requirement of subsection (c) or (d) of this section, he shall—

(1) enforce such requirement under section 7413 of this title,

(2) (after notice and opportunity for public hearing) revoke such order and enforce compliance with the requirement with respect to which such order was granted,

(3) give notice of noncompliance and commence action under section 7420 of this title, or

(4) take any appropriate combination of such actions.

(July 14, 1955, c. 360, Title I, § 119, as added Aug. 7, 1977, Pub.L. 95–95, Title I, § 117(b), 91 Stat. 712, and amended Nov. 16, 1977, Pub.L. 95–190, § 14(a)(25) to (27), 91 Stat. 1401.)

### HISTORICAL AND STATUTORY NOTES

**References in Text**

Section 7413(d) of this title, referred to in subsec. (a)(2)(A), was amended generally by Pub.L. 101–549, Title VII, § 701, Nov. 15, 1990, 104 Stat. 2672, and, as so amended, no longer relates to final compliance orders.

**Effective and Applicability Provisions**

1977 Acts

Section effective Aug. 7, 1977, except as otherwise expressly provided, see section 406(d) of Pub.L. 95–95, set out as a note under section 7401 of this title.

**Prior Provisions**

A prior section 119 of Act July 14, 1955, c. 360, Title I, as added June 22, 1974, Pub.L. 93–319, § 3, 88 Stat. 248, which was classified to section 1857c–10 of this title, provided for the authority to deal with energy shortages. Such section 119 was repealed by Pub.L. 95–95, Title I, § 112(b)(1), Aug. 7, 1977, 91 Stat. 709, which provided that all references to such section 119 in any subsequent enactment which supersedes Pub.L. 93–319 shall be construed to refer to section 113(d) of the Clean Air Act and to paragraph (5) thereof in particular which is classified to section 7413(d)(5) of this title.

**Modification or Rescission of Rules, Regulations, Orders, Determinations, Contracts, Certifications, Authorizations, Delegations, and Other Actions**

All rules, regulations, orders, determinations, contracts, certifications, authorizations, delegations, or other actions duly issued, made, or taken by or pursuant to Act July 14, 1955, the Clean Air Act, as in effect immediately prior to the date of enactment of Pub.L. 95–95 [Aug. 7, 1977] to continue in full force and effect until modified or rescinded in accordance with Act July 14, 1955, as amended by Pub.L. 95–95 [this chapter], see section 406(b) of Pub.L. 95–95, set out as an Effective and Applicability Provisions of 1977 Acts note under section 7401 of this title.

## § 7420. Noncompliance penalty

[CAA § 120]

**(a) Assessment and collection**

**(1)(A)** Not later than 6 months after August 7, 1977, and after notice and opportunity for a public hearing, the Administrator shall promulgate regulations requiring the assessment and collection of a noncompliance penalty against persons referred to in paragraph (2)(A).

**(B)(i)** Each State may develop and submit to the Administrator a plan for carrying out this section in such State. If the Administrator finds that the State plan meets the requirements of this section, he may delegate to such State any authority he has to carry out this section.

**(ii)** Notwithstanding a delegation to a State under clause (i), the Administrator may carry out this section in such State under the circumstances described in subsection (b)(2)(B) of this section.

**(2)(A)** Except as provided in subparagraph (B) or (C) of this paragraph, the State or the Administrator shall assess and collect a noncompliance penalty against every person who owns or operates—

**(i)** a major stationary source (other than a primary nonferrous smelter which has received a primary nonferrous smelter order under section 7419 of this title), which is not in compliance with any emission limitation, emission standard or compliance schedule under any applicable implementation plan (whether or not such source is subject to a Federal or State consent decree), or

**(ii)** a stationary source which is not in compliance with an emission limitation, emission standard, standard of performance, or other requirement established under section 7411, 7477, 7603, or 7412 of this title, or

**(iii)** a stationary source which is not in compliance with any requirement of subchapter IV–A, V, or VI of this chapter, or

**(iv)** any source referred to in clause (i), (ii), or (iii) (for which an extension, order, or suspension referred to in subparagraph (B), or Federal or State consent decree is in effect), or a primary nonferrous smelter which has received a primary nonferrous smelter order under section 7419 of this title which is not in compliance with any interim emission control requirement or schedule of compliance under such extension, order, suspension, or consent decree.

For purposes of subsection (d)(2) of this section, in the case of a penalty assessed with respect to a source referred to in clause (iii) of this subparagraph, the costs referred to in such subsection (d)(2) shall be the economic value of noncompliance with the interim emission control requirement or the remaining steps in the schedule of compliance referred to in such clause.

**(B)** Notwithstanding the requirements of subparagraph (A)(i) and (ii), the owner or operator of any source shall be exempted from the duty to pay a noncompliance penalty under such requirements with respect to that source if, in accordance with the procedures in subsection (b)(5) of this section, the owner or operator demonstrates that the failure of such source to comply with any such requirement is due solely to—

**(i)** a conversion by such source from the burning of petroleum products or natural gas, or both, as the permanent primary energy source to the burning of coal pursuant to an order under section 7413(d)(5) of this title or section 1857c–10 of this title (as in effect before August 7, 1977);

**(ii)** in the case of a coal-burning source granted an extension under the second sentence of section 1857c–10(c)(1) of this title (as in effect before August 7, 1977), a prohibition from using petroleum products or natural gas or both, by reason of an order under the provisions of section 792(a) and (b) of Title 15 or under any legislation which amends or supersedes such provisions;

**(iii)** the use of innovative technology sanctioned by an enforcement order under section 7413(d)(4) of this title;

**(iv)** an inability to comply with any such requirement, for which inability the source has received an order under section 7413(d) of this title (or an order under section 7413 of this title issued before August 7, 1977) which has the effect of permitting a delay or violation of any requirement of this chapter (including a requirement of an applicable implementation plan) which inability results from reasons entirely beyond the control of the owner or operator of such source or of any entity controlling, controlled by, or under common control with the owner or operator of such source; or

**(v)** the conditions by reason of which a temporary emergency suspension is authorized under section 7410(f) or (g) of this title.

An exemption under this subparagraph shall cease to be effective if the source fails to comply with the interim emission control requirements or schedules of compliance (including increments of progress) under any such extension, order, or suspension.

**(C)** The Administrator may, after notice and opportunity for public hearing, exempt any source from the requirements of this section with respect to a particular instance of noncompliance if he finds that such instance of noncompliance is de minimis in nature and in duration.

**(b) Regulations**

Regulations under subsection (a) of this section shall—

**(1)** permit the assessment and collection of such penalty by the State if the State has a delegation of authority in effect under subsection (a)(1)(B)(i) of this section;

**(2)** provide for the assessment and collection of such penalty by the Administrator, if—

**(A)** the State does not have a delegation of authority in effect under subsection (a)(1)(B)(i) of this section, or

**(B)** the State has such a delegation in effect but fails with respect to any particular person or source to assess or collect the penalty in accordance with the requirements of this section;

**(3)** require the States, or in the event the States fail to do so, the Administrator, to give a brief but reasonably specific notice of noncompliance under this section to each person referred to in subsection (a)(2)(A) of this section with respect to each source owned or operated by such person which is not in compliance as provided in such subsection, not later than July 1, 1979, or thirty days after the discovery of such noncompliance, whichever is later;

**(4)** require each person to whom notice is given under paragraph (3) to—

**(A)** calculate the amount of the penalty owed (determined in accordance with subsection (d)(2) of this section) and the schedule of payments (determined in accordance with subsection (d)(3) of this section) for each such source and, within forty-five days after the issuance of such notice or after the denial of a petition under subparagraph (B), to submit that calculation and proposed schedule, together with the information necessary for an independent verification thereof, to the State and to the Administrator, or

**(B)** submit a petition, within forty-five days after the issuance of such notice, challenging such notice of noncompliance or alleging entitlement to an exemption under subsection (a)(2)(B) of this section with respect to a particular source;

**(5)** require the Administrator to provide a hearing on the record (within the meaning of subchapter II of chapter 5 of Title 5) and to make a decision on such petition (including findings of fact and conclusions of law) not later than ninety days after the receipt of any petition under paragraph (4)(B), unless the State agrees to provide a hearing which is substantially similar to such a hearing on the record and to make a decision on such petition (including such findings and conclusions) within such ninety-day period;

**(6)** **(A)** authorize the Administrator on his own initiative to review the decision of the State under paragraph (5) and disapprove it if it is not in accordance with the requirements of this section, and **(B)** require the Administrator to do so not later than sixty days after receipt of a petition under this subparagraph, notice, and public hearing and a showing by such petitioner that the State decision under paragraph (5) is not in accordance with the requirements of this section;

**(7)** require payment, in accordance with subsection (d) of this section, of the penalty by each person to whom notice of noncompliance is given under paragraph (3) with respect to each noncomplying source for which such notice is given unless there has been a final determination granting a petition under paragraph (4)(B) with respect to such source;

**(8)** authorize the State or the Administrator to adjust (and from time to time to readjust) the amount of the penalty assessment calculated or the payment schedule proposed by such owner or operator under paragraph (4), if the Administrator finds after notice and opportunity for a hearing on the record that the penalty or schedule does not meet the requirements of this section; and

**(9)** require a final adjustment of the penalty within 180 days after such source comes into compliance in accordance with subsection (d)(4) of this section.

In any case in which the State establishes a noncompliance penalty under this section, the State shall provide notice thereof to the Administrator. A noncompliance penalty established by a State under this section shall apply unless the Administrator, within ninety days after the date of receipt of notice of the State penalty assessment under this section, objects in writing to the amount of the penalty as less than would be required to comply with guidelines established by the Administrator. If the Administrator objects, he shall immediately establish a substitute noncompliance penalty applicable to such source.

**(c) Contract to assist in determining amount of penalty assessment or payment schedule**

If the owner or operator of any stationary source to whom a notice is issued under subsection (b)(3) of this section—

**(1)** does not submit a timely petition under subsection (b)(4)(B) of this section, or

**(2)** submits a petition under subsection (b)(4)(B) of this section which is denied, and

fails to submit a calculation of the penalty assessment, a schedule for payment, and the information necessary for independent verification thereof, the State (or the Administrator, as the case may be) may enter into a contract with any person who has no financial interest in the owner or operator of the source (or in any person controlling, controlled by or under common control with such source) to assist in determining the amount of the penalty assessment or payment schedule with respect to such source. The cost of carrying out such contract may be added to the penalty to be assessed against the owner or operator of such source.

**(d) Payment**

**(1)** All penalties assessed by the Administrator under this section shall be paid to the United States Treasury. All penalties assessed by the State under this section shall be paid to such State.

**(2)** The amount of the penalty which shall be assessed and collected with respect to any source under this section shall be equal to—

**(A)** the amount determined in accordance with regulations promulgated by the Administrator under subsection (a) of this section, which is no less than the economic value which a delay in compliance beyond July 1, 1979, may have for the owner of such source, including the quarterly equivalent of the capital costs of compliance and debt service over a normal amortization period, not to exceed ten years, operation and maintenance costs foregone as a result of noncompliance, and any additional economic value which such a delay may have for the owner or operator of such source, minus

**(B)** the amount of any expenditure made by the owner or operator of that source during any such quarter for the purpose of bringing that source into, and maintaining compliance with, such requirement, to the extent that such expenditures have not been taken into account in the calculation of the penalty under subparagraph (A).

To the extent that any expenditure under subparagraph (B) made during any quarter is not subtracted for such quarter from the costs under subparagraph (A), such expenditure may be subtracted for any subsequent quarter from such costs. In no event shall the amount paid be less than the quarterly payment minus the amount attributed to actual cost of construction.

**(3)(A)** The assessed penalty required under this section shall be paid in quarterly installments for the period of covered noncompliance. All quarterly payments (determined without regard to any adjustment or any subtraction under paragraph (2)(B) ) after the first payment shall be equal.

**(B)** The first payment shall be due on the date six months after the date of issuance of the notice of noncompliance under subsection (b)(3) of this section with respect to any source or on January 1, 1980, whichever is later. Such first payment shall be in the amount of the quarterly installment for the upcoming quarter, plus the amount owed for any preceding period within the period of covered noncompliance for such source.

(C) For the purpose of this section, the term "period of covered noncompliance" means the period which begins—

(i) two years after August 7, 1977, in the case of a source for which notice of noncompliance under subsection (b)(3) of this section is issued on or before the date two years after August 7, 1977, or

(ii) on the date of issuance of the notice of noncompliance under subsection (b)(3) of this section, in the case of a source for which such notice is issued after July 1, 1979,

and ending on the date on which such source comes into (or for the purpose of establishing the schedule of payments, is estimated to come into) compliance with such requirement.

(4) Upon making a determination that a source with respect to which a penalty has been paid under this section is in compliance and is maintaining compliance with the applicable requirement, the State (or the Administrator as the case may be) shall review the actual expenditures made by the owner or operator of such source for the purpose of attaining and maintaining compliance, and shall within 180 days after such source comes into compliance—

(A) provide reimbursement with interest (to be paid by the State or Secretary of the Treasury, as the case may be) at appropriate prevailing rates (as determined by the Secretary of the Treasury) for any overpayment by such person, or

(B) assess and collect an additional payment with interest at appropriate prevailing rates (as determined by the Secretary of the Treasury) for any underpayment by such person.

(5) Any person who fails to pay the amount of any penalty with respect to any source under this section on a timely basis shall be required to pay in addition a quarterly nonpayment penalty for each quarter during which such failure to pay persists. Such nonpayment penalty shall be in an amount equal to 20 percent of the aggregate amount of such person's penalties and nonpayment penalties with respect to such source which are unpaid as of the beginning of such quarter.

**(e) Judicial review**

Any action pursuant to this section, including any objection of the Administrator under the last sentence of subsection (b) of this section, shall be considered a final action for purposes of judicial review of any penalty under section 7607 of this title.

**(f) Other orders, payments, sanctions, or requirements**

Any orders, payments, sanctions, or other requirements under this section shall be in addition to any other permits, orders, payments, sanctions, or other requirements established under this chapter, and shall in no way affect any civil or criminal enforcement proceedings brought under any provision of this chapter or State or local law.

**(g) More stringent emission limitations or other requirements**

In the case of any emission limitation or other requirement approved or promulgated by the Administrator under this chapter after August 7, 1977, which is more stringent than the emission limitation or requirement for the source in effect prior to such approval or promulgation, if any, or where there was no emission limitation or requirement approved or promulgated before August 7, 1977, the date for imposition of the non-compliance penalty under this section, shall be either July 1, 1979, or the date on which the source is required to be in full compliance with such emission limitation or requirement, whichever is later, but in no event later than three years after the approval or promulgation of such emission limitation or requirement.

(July 14, 1955, c. 360, Title I, § 120, as added Aug. 7, 1977, Pub.L. 95–95, Title I, § 118, 91 Stat. 714, and amended Nov. 16, 1977, Pub.L. 95–190, § 14(a)(28) to (38), 91 Stat. 1401; Nov. 15, 1990, Pub.L. 101–549, Title VII, § 710(a), 104 Stat. 2684.)

## HISTORICAL AND STATUTORY NOTES

**References in Text**

Section 7413(d) of this title, referred to in subsec. (a)(2)(B), was amended generally by Pub.L. 101–549, Title VII, § 701, Nov. 15, 1990, 104 Stat. 2672, and, as so amended, no longer relates to final compliance orders.

Section 1857c–10 of this title (as in effect before August 7, 1977), referred to in subsec. (a)(2)(B)(i), was in the original "section 119 (as in effect before the date of the enactment of the Clean Air Act Amendments of 1977)", meaning section 119 of Act July 14, 1955, c. 360, Title I, as added June 22, 1974, Pub.L. 93–319, § 3, 88 Stat. 248, (which was classified to section 1857c–10 of this title) as in effect prior to the enactment of Pub.L. 95–95, Aug. 7, 1977, 91 Stat. 691, effective Aug. 7, 1977. Section 112(b)(1) of Pub.L. 95–95 repealed section 119 of Act July 14, 1955, c. 360, Title I, as added by Pub.L. 93–319, and provided that all references to such section 119 in any subsequent enactment which supersedes Pub.L. 93–319 shall be construed to refer to section 113(d) of the Clean Air Act and to paragraph (5) thereof in particular which is classified to subsec. (d)(5) of section 7413 of this title. Section 7413(d) of this title was subsequently amended generally by Pub.L. 101–549, Title VII, § 701, Nov. 15, 1990, 104 Stat. 2672, and, as so amended, no longer relates to final compliance orders. Section 117(b) of Pub.L. 95–95 added a new section 119 of Act July 14, 1955, which is classified to section 7419 of this title.

Section 1857c–10(c)(1) of this title (as in effect before August 7, 1977), referred to in subsec. (a)(2)(B)(ii), was in the original "section 119(c)(1) (as in effect before the date of the enactment of the Clean Air Act Amendments of 1977)."

**Effective and Applicability Provisions**

1990 Acts

Amendment by Pub.L. 101–549 effective Nov. 15, 1990, except as otherwise provided, see section 711(b) of Pub.L. 101–549, set out as a note under section 7401 of this title.

1977 Acts

Section effective Aug. 7, 1977, except as otherwise expressly provided, see section 406(d) of Pub.L. 95–95, set out as a note under section 7401 of this title.

**Savings Provisions**

Suits, actions or proceedings commenced under this chapter as in effect prior to Nov. 15, 1990, not to abate by reason of the taking effect of amendments by Pub.L. 101–549, except as otherwise provided for, see section 711(a) of Pub.L. 101–549, set out as a note under section 7401 of this title.

## § 7421. Consultation

[CAA § 121]

In carrying out the requirements of this chapter requiring applicable implementation plans to contain—

(1) any transportation controls, air quality maintenance plan requirements or preconstruction review of direct sources of air pollution, or

(2) any measure referred to—

(A) in part D of this subchapter (pertaining to nonattainment requirements), or

(B) in part C of this subchapter (pertaining to prevention of significant deterioration),

and in carrying out the requirements of section 7413(d) of this title (relating to certain enforcement orders), the State shall provide a satisfactory process of consultation with general purpose local governments, designated organizations of elected officials of local governments and any Federal land manager having authority over Federal land to which the State plan applies, effective with respect to any such requirement which is adopted more than one year after August 7, 1977, as part of such plan. Such process shall be in accordance with regulations promulgated by the Administrator to assure adequate consultation. The Administrator shall update as necessary the original regulations required and promulgated under this section (as in effect immediately before November 15, 1990) to ensure adequate consultation. Only a general purpose unit of local government, regional agency, or council of governments adversely affected by action of the Administrator approving any portion of a plan referred to in this subsection[1] may petition for judicial review of such action on the basis of a violation of the requirements of this section.

(July 14, 1955, c. 360, Title I, § 121, as added Aug. 7, 1977, Pub.L. 95–95, Title I, § 119, 91 Stat. 719, and amended Nov. 15, 1990, Pub.L. 101–549, Title I, § 108(h), 104 Stat. 2467.)

[1] So in original. Probably should be "section".

### HISTORICAL AND STATUTORY NOTES

**References in Text**

Section 7413(d) of this title, referred to in text, was amended generally by Pub.L. 101–549, Title VII, § 701, Nov. 15, 1990, 104 Stat. 2672, and, as so amended, no longer relates to final compliance orders.

**Effective and Applicability Provisions**

1990 Acts

Amendment by Pub.L. 101–549 effective Nov. 15, 1990, except as otherwise provided, see section 711(b) of Pub.L. 101–549, set out as a note under section 7401 of this title.

1977 Acts

Section effective Aug. 7, 1977, except as otherwise expressly provided, see section 406(d) of Pub.L. 95–95, set out as a note under section 7401 of this title.

**Savings Provisions**

Suits, actions or proceedings commenced under this chapter as in effect prior to Nov. 15, 1990, not to abate by reason of the taking effect of amendments by Pub.L. 101–549, except as otherwise provided for, see section 711(a) of Pub.L. 101–549, set out as a note under section 7401 of this title.

## § 7422. Listing of certain unregulated pollutants

[CAA § 122]

### (a) Radioactive pollutants, cadmium, arsenic, and polycyclic organic matter

Not later than one year after August 7, 1977 (two years for radioactive pollutants) and after notice and opportunity for public hearing, the Administrator shall review all available relevant information and determine whether or not emissions of radioactive pollutants (including source material, special nuclear material, and byproduct material), cadmium, arsenic and polycyclic organic matter into the ambient air will cause, or contribute to, air pollution which may reasonably be anticipated to endanger public health. If the Administrator makes an affirmative determination with respect to any such substance, he shall simultaneously with such determination include such substance in the list published under section 7408(a)(1) or 7412(b)(1)(A) of this title (in the case of a substance which, in the judgment of the Administrator, causes, or contributes to, air pollution which may reasonably be anticipated to result in an increase in mortality or an increase in serious irreversible, or incapacitating reversible, illness), or shall include each category of stationary sources emitting such substance in significant amounts in the list published under section 7411(b)(1)(A) of this title, or take any combination of such actions.

### (b) Revision authority

Nothing in subsection (a) of this section shall be construed to affect the authority of the Administrator to revise any list referred to in subsection (a) of this section with respect to any substance (whether or not enumerated in subsection (a) of this section).

**(c) Consultation with Nuclear Regulatory Commission; interagency agreement; notice and hearing**

(1) Before listing any source material, special nuclear, or byproduct material (or component or derivative thereof) as provided in subsection (a) of this section, the Administrator shall consult with the Nuclear Regulatory Commission.

(2) Not later than six months after listing any such material (or component or derivative thereof) the Administrator and the Nuclear Regulatory Commission shall enter into an interagency agreement with respect to those sources or facilities which are under the jurisdiction of the Commission. This agreement shall, to the maximum extent practicable consistent with this chapter, minimize duplication of effort and conserve administrative resources in the establishment, implementation, and enforcement of emission limitations, standards of performance, and other requirements and authorities (substantive and procedural) under this chapter respecting the emission of such material (or component or derivative thereof) from such sources or facilities.

(3) In case of any standard or emission limitation promulgated by the Administrator, under this chapter or by any State (or the Administrator) under any applicable implementation plan under this chapter, if the Nuclear Regulatory Commission determines, after notice and opportunity for public hearing that the application of such standard or limitation to a source or facility within the jurisdiction of the Commission would endanger public health or safety, such standard or limitation shall not apply to such facilities or sources unless the President determines otherwise within ninety days from the date of such finding.
(July 14, 1955, c. 360, Title I, § 122, as added Aug. 7, 1977, Pub.L. 95–95, Title I, § 120(a), 91 Stat. 720.)

### HISTORICAL AND STATUTORY NOTES

**References in Text**

Section 7412(b)(1), referred to in subsec. (a), was amended generally by Pub.L. 101–549, Title III, § 301, Nov. 15, 1990, 104 Stat. 2531, and, as so amended, no longer contains a subpar. (A).

**Effective and Applicability Provisions**

1977 Acts

Section effective Aug. 7, 1977, except as otherwise expressly provided, see section 406(d) of Pub.L. 95–95, set out as a note under section 7401 of this title.

**Transfer of Functions**

For transfer of certain functions from the Nuclear Regulatory Commission to the Chairman thereof, see Reorg. Plan No. 1 of 1980, 45 F.R. 40561, 94 Stat. 3585, set out as a note under section 5841 of this title.

**Study by Administrator of Environmental Protection Agency**

Section 120(b) of Pub.L. 95–95 provided that: "The Administrator of the Environmental Protection Agency shall conduct a study, in conjunction with other appropriate agencies, concerning the effect on the public health and welfare of sulfates, radioactive pollutants, cadmium, arsenic, and polycyclic organic matter which are present or may reasonably be anticipated to occur in the ambient air. Such study shall include a thorough investigation of how sulfates are formed and how to protect public health and welfare from the injurious effects, if any, of sulfates, cadmium, arsenic, and polycyclic organic matter."

## § 7423. Stack heights

**[CAA § 123]**

**(a) Heights in excess of good engineering practice; other dispersion techniques**

The degree of emission limitation required for control of any air pollutant under an applicable implementation plan under this subchapter shall not be affected in any manner by—

(1) so much of the stack height of any source as exceeds good engineering practice (as determined under regulations promulgated by the Administrator), or

(2) any other dispersion technique.

The preceding sentence shall not apply with respect to stack heights in existence before December 31, 1970, or dispersion techniques implemented before such date. In establishing an emission limitation for coal-fired steam electric generating units which are subject to the provisions of section 7418 of this title and which commenced operation before July 1, 1957, the effect of the entire stack height of stacks for which a construction contract was awarded before February 8, 1974, may be taken into account.

**(b) Dispersion technique**

For the purpose of this section, the term "dispersion technique" includes any intermittent or supplemental control of air pollutants varying with atmospheric conditions.

**(c) Regulations; good engineering practice**

Not later than six months after August 7, 1977, the Administrator, shall after notice and opportunity for public hearing, promulgate regulations to carry out this section. For purposes of this section, good engineering practice means, with respect to stack heights, the height necessary to insure that emissions from the stack do not result in excessive concentrations of any air pollutant in the immediate vicinity of the source as a result of atmospheric downwash, eddies and wakes which may be created by the source itself, nearby structures or nearby terrain obstacles (as determined by the Administrator). For purposes of this section such height shall not exceed two and a half times the height of such source unless the owner or operator of the source demonstrates, after notice and opportunity for public hearing, to the satisfaction of the Administrator, that a greater height is necessary as provided under the preceding sentence. In no event may the Administrator prohibit any increase in any stack height or restrict in any manner the stack height of any source.

(July 14, 1955, c. 360, Title I, § 123, as added Aug. 7, 1977, Pub.L. 95–95, Title I, § 121, 91 Stat. 721.)

### HISTORICAL AND STATUTORY NOTES

**Effective and Applicability Provisions**

1977 Acts

Section effective Aug. 7, 1977, except as otherwise expressly provided, see section 406(d) of Pub.L. 95–95, set out as a note under section 7401 of this title.

## § 7424. Assurance of adequacy of State plans

[CAA § 124]

### (a) State review of implementation plans which relate to major fuel burning sources

As expeditiously as practicable but not later than one year after August 7, 1977, each State shall review the provisions of its implementation plan which relate to major fuel burning sources and shall determine—

(1) the extent to which compliance with requirements of such plan is dependent upon the use by major fuel burning stationary sources of petroleum products or natural gas,

(2) the extent to which such plan may reasonably be anticipated to be inadequate to meet the requirements of this chapter in such State on a reliable and long-term basis by reason of its dependence upon the use of such fuels, and

(3) the extent to which compliance with the requirements of such plan is dependent upon use of coal or coal derivatives which is not locally or regionally available.

Each State shall submit the results of its review and its determination under this paragraph to the Administrator promptly upon completion thereof.

### (b) Plan revision

(1) Not later than eighteen months after August 7, 1977, the Administrator shall review the submissions of the States under subsection (a) of this section and shall require each State to revise its plan if, in the judgment of the Administrator, such plan revision is necessary to assure that such plan will be adequate to assure compliance with the requirements of this chapter in such State on a reliable and long-term basis, taking into account the actual or potential prohibitions on use of petroleum products or natural gas, or both, under any other authority of law.

(2) Before requiring a plan revision under this subsection, with respect to any State the Administrator shall take into account the report of the review conducted by such State under paragraph (1) and shall consult with the Governor of the State respecting such required revision.

(July 14, 1955, c. 360, Title I, § 124, as added Aug. 7, 1977, Pub.L. 95–95, Title I, § 122, 91 Stat. 722.)

### HISTORICAL AND STATUTORY NOTES

**Effective and Applicability Provisions**

1977 Acts

Section effective Aug. 7, 1977, except as otherwise expressly provided, see section 406(d) of Pub.L. 95–95, set out as a note under section 7401 of this title.

## § 7425. Measures to prevent economic disruption or unemployment

[CAA § 125]

### (a) Determination that action is necessary

After notice and opportunity for a public hearing—

(1) the Governor of any State in which a major fuel burning stationary source referred to in this subsection (or class or category thereof) is located,

(2) the Administrator, or

(3) the President (or his designee),

may determine that action under subsection (b) of this section is necessary to prevent or minimize significant local or regional economic disruption or unemployment which would otherwise result from use by such source (or class or category) of—

(A) coal or coal derivatives other than locally or regionally available coal,

(B) petroleum products,

(C) natural gas, or

(D) any combination of fuels referred to in subparagraphs (A) through (C),

to comply with the requirements of a State implementation plan.

### (b) Use of locally or regionally available coal or coal derivatives to comply with implementation plan requirements

Upon a determination under subsection (a) of this section—

(1) such Governor, with the written consent of the President or his designee,

(2) the President's designee with the written consent of such Governor, or

(3) the President

may by rule or order prohibit any such major fuel burning stationary source (or class or category thereof) from using fuels other than locally or regionally available coal or coal derivatives to comply with implementation plan requirements. In taking any action under this subsection, the Governor, the President, or the President's designee as the case may be, shall take into account, the final cost to the consumer of such an action.

**(c) Contracts; schedules**

The Governor, in the case of action under subsection (b)(1) of this section, or the Administrator, in the case of an action under subsection (b)(2) or (3) of this section shall, by rule or order, require each source to which such action applies to—

(1) enter into long-term contracts of at least ten years in duration (except as the President or his designee may otherwise permit or require by rule or order for good cause) for supplies of regionally available coal or coal derivatives,

(2) enter into contracts to acquire any additional means of emission limitation which the Administrator or the State determines may be necessary to comply with the requirements of this chapter while using such coal or coal derivatives as fuel, and

(3) comply with such schedules (including increments of progress), timetables and other requirements as may be necessary to assure compliance with the requirements of this chapter.

Requirements under this subsection shall be established simultaneously with, and as a condition of, any action under subsection (b) of this section.

**(d) Existing or new major fuel burning stationary sources**

This section applies only to existing or new major fuel burning stationary sources—

(1) which have the design capacity to produce 250,000,000 Btu's per hour (or its equivalent), as determined by the Administrator, and

(2) which are not in compliance with the requirements of an applicable implementation plan or which are prohibited from burning oil or natural gas, or both, under any other authority of law.

**(e) Actions not to be deemed modifications of major fuel burning stationary sources**

Except as may otherwise be provided by rule by the State or the Administrator for good cause, any action required to be taken by a major fuel burning stationary source under this section shall not be deemed to constitute a modification for purposes of section 7411(a)(2) and (4) of this title.

**(f) Treatment of prohibitions, rules, or orders as requirements or parts of plans under other provisions**

For purposes of sections 7413 and 7420 of this title a prohibition under subsection (b) of this section, and a corresponding rule or order under subsection (c) of this section, shall be treated as a requirement of section 7413 of this title. For purposes of any plan (or portion thereof) promulgated under section 7410(c) of this title, any rule or order under subsection (c) of this section corresponding to a prohibition under subsection (b) of this section, shall be treated as a part of such plan. For purposes of section 7413 of this title, a prohibition under subsection (b) of this section, applicable to any source, and a corresponding rule or order under subsection (c) of this section, shall be treated as part of the applicable implementation plan for the State in which subject source is located.

**(g) Delegation of Presidential authority**

The President may delegate his authority under this section to an officer or employee of the United States designated by him on a case-by-case basis or in any other manner he deems suitable.

**(h) "Locally or regionally available coal or coal derivatives" defined**

For the purpose of this section the term "locally or regionally available coal or coal derivatives" means coal or coal derivatives which is, or can in the judgment of the State or the Administrator feasibly be, mined or produced in the local or regional area (as determined by the Administrator) in which the major fuel burning stationary source is located.

(July 14, 1955, c. 360, Title I, § 125, as added Aug. 7, 1977, Pub.L. 95–95, Title I, § 122, 91 Stat. 722.)

### HISTORICAL AND STATUTORY NOTES

**Effective and Applicability Provisions**

1977 Acts

Section effective Aug. 7, 1977, except as otherwise expressly provided, see section 406(d) of Pub.L. 95–95, set out as a note under section 7401 of this title.

## § 7426. Interstate pollution abatement

**[CAA § 126]**

**(a) Written notice to all nearby States**

Each applicable implementation plan shall—

(1) require each major proposed new (or modified) source—

(A) subject to part C of this subchapter (relating to significant deterioration of air quality) or

(B) which may significantly contribute to levels of air pollution in excess of the national ambient air quality standards in any air quality control region outside the State in which such source intends to locate (or make such modification),

to provide written notice to all nearby States the air pollution levels of which may be affected by such source at least sixty days prior to the date on which commencement of construction is to be permitted by the State providing notice, and

(2) identify all major existing stationary sources which may have the impact described in paragraph (1) with respect to new or modified sources and provide notice to all nearby States of the identity of such sources not later than three months after August 7, 1977.

**(b) Petition for finding that major sources emit or would emit prohibited air pollutants**

Any State or political subdivision may petition the Administrator for a finding that any major source or group of stationary sources emits or would emit any air pollutant in violation of the prohibition of section 7410(a)(2)(D)(ii) of this title or this section. Within 60 days after receipt of any petition under this subsection and after public hearing, the Administrator shall make such a finding or deny the petition.

**(c) Violations; allowable continued operation**

Notwithstanding any permit which may have been granted by the State in which the source is located (or intends to locate), it shall be a violation of this section and the applicable implementation plan in such State—

(1) for any major proposed new (or modified) source with respect to which a finding has been made under subsection (b) of this section to be constructed or to operate in violation of the prohibition of section 7410(a)(2)(D)(ii) of this title or this section, or

(2) for any major existing source to operate more than three months after such finding has been made with respect to it.

The Administrator may permit the continued operation of a source referred to in paragraph (2) beyond the expiration of such three-month period if such source complies with such emission limitations and compliance schedules (containing increments of progress) as may be provided by the Administrator to bring about compliance with the requirements contained in section 7410(a)(2)(D)(ii) of this title or this section as expeditiously as practicable, but in no case later than three years after the date of such finding. Nothing in the preceding sentence shall be construed to preclude any such source from being eligible for an enforcement order under section 7413(d) of this title after the expiration of such period during which the Administrator has permitted continuous operation.

(July 14, 1955, c. 360, Title I, § 126, as added Aug. 7, 1977, Pub.L. 95–95, Title I, § 123, 91 Stat. 724, and amended Nov. 16, 1977, Pub.L. 95–190, § 14(a)(39), 91 Stat. 1401; Nov. 15, 1990, Pub.L. 101–549, Title I, § 109(a), 104 Stat. 2469.)

**HISTORICAL AND STATUTORY NOTES**

**References in Text**

Section 7413(d) of this title, referred to in subsec. (c), was amended generally by Pub.L. 101–549, Title VII, § 701, Nov. 15, 1990, 104 Stat. 2672, and, as so amended, no longer relates to final compliance orders.

**Effective and Applicability Provisions**

1990 Acts

Amendment by Pub.L. 101–549 effective Nov. 15, 1990, except as otherwise provided, see section 711(b) of Pub.L. 101–549, set out as a note under section 7401 of this title.

1977 Acts

Section effective Aug. 7, 1977, except as otherwise expressly provided, see section 406(d) of Pub.L. 95–95, set out as a note under section 7401 of this title.

**Savings Provisions**

Suits, actions or proceedings commenced under this chapter as in effect prior to Nov. 15, 1990, not to abate by reason of the taking effect of amendments by Pub.L. 101–549, except as otherwise provided for, see section 711(a) of Pub.L. 101–549, set out as a note under section 7401 of this title.

## § 7427. Public notification

[CAA § 127]

**(a) Warning signs; television, radio, or press notices or information**

Each State plan shall contain measures which will be effective to notify the public during any calendar [1] on a regular basis of instances or areas in which any national primary ambient air quality standard is exceeded or was exceeded during any portion of the preceding calendar year to advise the public of the health hazards associated with such pollution, and to enhance public awareness of the measures which can be taken to prevent such standards from being exceeded and the ways in which the public can participate in regulatory and other efforts to improve air quality. Such measures may include the posting of warning signs on interstate highway access points to metropolitan areas or television, radio, or press notices or information.

**(b) Grants**

The Administrator is authorized to make grants to States to assist in carrying out the requirements of subsection (a) of this section.

(July 14, 1955, c. 360, Title I, § 127, as added Aug. 7, 1977, Pub.L. 95–95, Title I, § 124, 91 Stat. 725.)

[1] So in original. Probably should be "calendar year".

**HISTORICAL AND STATUTORY NOTES**

**Effective and Applicability Provisions**

1977 Acts

Section effective Aug. 7, 1977, except as otherwise expressly provided, see section 406(d) of Pub.L. 95–95, set out as a note under section 7401 of this title.

## § 7428. State boards

[CAA § 128]

(a) [1] Not later than the date one year after August 7, 1977, each applicable implementation plan shall contain requirements that—

(1) any board or body which approves permits or enforcement orders under this chapter shall have at least a majority of members who represent the public interest and do not derive any significant portion of their income from persons subject to permits or enforcement orders under this chapter, and

(2) any potential conflicts of interest by members of such board or body or the head of an executive agency with similar powers be adequately disclosed.

A State may adopt any requirements respecting conflicts of interest for such boards or bodies or heads of executive agencies, or any other entities which are more stringent than the requirements of paragraph (1) and (2), and the Administrator shall approve any such more stringent requirements submitted as part of an implementation plan.

(July 14, 1955, c. 360, Title I, § 128, as added Aug. 7, 1977, Pub.L. 95–95, Title I, § 125, 91 Stat. 725.)

[1] So in original. Section enacted without a subsec. (b).

### HISTORICAL AND STATUTORY NOTES

**Effective and Applicability Provisions**

1977 Acts

Section effective Aug. 7, 1977, except as otherwise expressly provided, see section 406(d) of Pub.L. 95–95, set out as a note under section 7401 of this title.

## § 7429. Solid waste combustion

[CAA § 129]

### (a) New source performance standards

**(1) In general**

(A) The Administrator shall establish performance standards and other requirements pursuant to section 7411 of this title and this section for each category of solid waste incineration units. Such standards shall include emissions limitations and other requirements applicable to new units and guidelines (under section 7411(d) of this title and this section) and other requirements applicable to existing units.

(B) Standards under section 7411 of this title and this section applicable to solid waste incineration units with capacity greater than 250 tons per day combusting municipal waste shall be promulgated not later than 12 months after November 15, 1990. Nothing in this subparagraph shall alter any schedule for the promulgation of standards applicable to such units under section 7411 of this title pursuant to any settlement and consent decree entered by the Administrator before November 15, 1990: *Provided*, That, such standards are subsequently modified pursuant to the schedule established in this subparagraph to include each of the requirements of this section.

(C) Standards under section 7411 of this title and this section applicable to solid waste incineration units with capacity equal to or less than 250 tons per day combusting municipal waste and units combusting hospital waste, medical waste and infectious waste shall be promulgated not later than 24 months after November 15, 1990.

(D) Standards under section 7411 of this title and this section applicable to solid waste incineration units combusting commercial or industrial waste shall be proposed not later than 36 months after November 15, 1990, and promulgated not later than 48 months after November 15, 1990.

(E) Not later than 18 months after November 15, 1990, the Administrator shall publish a schedule for the promulgation of standards under section 7411 of this title and this section applicable to other categories of solid waste incineration units.

**(2) Emissions standard**

Standards applicable to solid waste incineration units promulgated under section 7411 of this title and this section shall reflect the maximum degree of reduction in emissions of air pollutants listed under section [1] (a)(4) that the Administrator, taking into consideration the cost of achieving such emission reduction, and any non-air quality health and environmental impacts and energy requirements, determines is achievable for new or existing units in each category. The Administrator may distinguish among classes, types (including mass-burn, refuse-derived fuel, modular and other types of units), and sizes of units within a category in establishing such standards. The degree of reduction in emissions that is deemed achievable for new units in a category shall not be less stringent than the emissions control that is achieved in practice by the best controlled similar unit, as determined by the Administrator. Emissions standards for existing units in a category may be less stringent than standards for new units in the same category but shall not be less stringent than the average emissions limitation achieved by the best performing 12 percent of units in the category (excluding units which first met lowest achievable emissions rates 18 months before the date such standards are proposed or 30 months before the date such standards are promulgated, whichever is later).

(3) **Control methods and technologies**

Standards under section 7411 of this title and this section applicable to solid waste incineration units shall be based on methods and technologies for removal or destruction of pollutants before, during, or after combustion, and shall incorporate for new units siting requirements that minimize, on a site specific basis, to the maximum extent practicable, potential risks to public health or the environment.

(4) **Numerical emissions limitations**

The performance standards promulgated under section 7411 of this title and this section and applicable to solid waste incineration units shall specify numerical emission limitations for the following substances or mixtures: particulate matter (total and fine), opacity (as appropriate), sulfur dioxide, hydrogen chloride, oxides of nitrogen, carbon monoxide, lead, cadmium, mercury, and dioxins and dibenzofurans. The Administrator may promulgate numerical emissions limitations or provide for the monitoring of postcombustion concentrations of surrogate substances, parameters or periods of residence time in excess of stated temperatures with respect to pollutants other than those listed in this paragraph.

(5) **Review and revision**

Not later than 5 years following the initial promulgation of any performance standards and other requirements under this section and section 7411 of this title applicable to a category of solid waste incineration units, and at 5 year intervals thereafter, the Administrator shall review, and in accordance with this section and section 7411 of this title, revise such standards and requirements.

(b) **Existing units**

(1) **Guidelines**

Performance standards under this section and section 7411 of this title for solid waste incineration units shall include guidelines promulgated pursuant to section 7411(d) of this title and this section applicable to existing units. Such guidelines shall include, as provided in this section, each of the elements required by subsection (a) of this section (emissions limitations, notwithstanding any restriction in section 7411(d) of this title regarding issuance of such limitations), subsection (c) of this section (monitoring), subsection (d) of this section (operator training), subsection (e) of this section (permits), and subsection (h)(4) [2] of this section (residual risk).

(2) **State plans**

Not later than 1 year after the Administrator promulgates guidelines for a category of solid waste incineration units, each State in which units in the category are operating shall submit to the Administrator a plan to implement and enforce the guidelines with respect to such units. The State plan shall be at least as protective as the guidelines promulgated by the Administrator and shall provide that each unit subject to the guidelines shall be in compliance with all requirements of this section not later than 3 years after the State plan is approved by the Administrator but not later than 5 years after the guidelines were promulgated. The Administrator shall approve or disapprove any State plan within 180 days of the submission, and if a plan is disapproved, the Administrator shall state the reasons for disapproval in writing. Any State may modify and resubmit a plan which has been disapproved by the Administrator.

(3) **Federal plan**

The Administrator shall develop, implement and enforce a plan for existing solid waste incineration units within any category located in any State which has not submitted an approvable plan under this subsection with respect to units in such category within 2 years after the date on which the Administrator promulgated the relevant guidelines. Such plan shall assure that each unit subject to the plan is in compliance with all provisions of the guidelines not later than 5 years after the date the relevant guidelines are promulgated.

(c) **Monitoring**

The Administrator shall, as part of each performance standard promulgated pursuant to subsection (a) of this section and section 7411 of this title, promulgate regulations requiring the owner or operator of each solid waste incineration unit—

(1) to monitor emissions from the unit at the point at which such emissions are emitted into the ambient air (or within the stack, combustion chamber or pollution control equipment, as appropriate) and at such other points as necessary to protect public health and the environment;

(2) to monitor such other parameters relating to the operation of the unit and its pollution control technology as the Administrator determines are appropriate; and

(3) to report the results of such monitoring.

Such regulations shall contain provisions regarding the frequency of monitoring, test methods and procedures validated on solid waste incineration units, and the form and frequency of reports containing the results of monitoring and shall require that any monitoring reports or test results indicating an exceedance of any standard under this section shall be reported separately and in a manner that facilitates review for purposes of enforcement actions. Such regulations shall require that copies of the results of such monitoring be maintained on file at the facility concerned and that copies shall be made available for inspection and copying by interested members of the public during business hours.

**(d) Operator training**

Not later than 24 months after November 15, 1990, the Administrator shall develop and promote a model State program for the training and certification of solid waste incineration unit operators and high-capacity fossil fuel fired plant operators. The Administrator may authorize any State to implement a model program for the training of solid waste incineration unit operators and high-capacity fossil fuel fired plant operators, if the State has adopted a program which is at least as effective as the model program developed by the Administrator. Beginning on the date 36 months after the date on which performance standards and guidelines are promulgated under subsection (a) of this section and section 7411 of this title for any category of solid waste incineration units it shall be unlawful to operate any unit in the category unless each person with control over processes affecting emissions from such unit has satisfactorily completed a training program meeting the requirements established by the Administrator under this subsection.

**(e) Permits**

Beginning (1) 36 months after the promulgation of a performance standard under subsection (a) of this section and section 7411 of this title applicable to a category of solid waste incineration units, or (2) the effective date of a permit program under subchapter V of this chapter in the State in which the unit is located, whichever is later, each unit in the category shall operate pursuant to a permit issued under this subsection and subchapter V of this chapter. Permits required by this subsection may be renewed according to the provisions of subchapter V of this chapter. Notwithstanding any other provision of this chapter, each permit for a solid waste incineration unit combusting municipal waste issued under this chapter shall be issued for a period of up to 12 years and shall be reviewed every 5 years after date of issuance or reissuance. Each permit shall continue in effect after the date of issuance until the date of termination, unless the Administrator or State determines that the unit is not in compliance with all standards and conditions contained in the permit. Such determination shall be made at regular intervals during the term of the permit, such intervals not to exceed 5 years, and only after public comment and public hearing. No permit for a solid waste incineration unit may be issued under this chapter by an agency, instrumentality or person that is also responsible, in whole or part, for the design and construction or operation of the unit. Notwithstanding any other provision of this subsection, the Administrator or the State shall require the owner or operator of any unit to comply with emissions limitations or implement any other measures, if the Administrator or the State determines that emissions in the absence of such limitations or measures may reasonably be anticipated to endanger public health or the environment. The Administrator's determination under the preceding sentence is a discretionary decision.

**(f) Effective date and enforcement**

**(1) New units**

Performance standards and other requirements promulgated pursuant to this section and section 7411 of this title and applicable to new solid waste incineration units shall be effective as of the date 6 months after the date of promulgation.

**(2) Existing units**

Performance standards and other requirements promulgated pursuant to this section and section 7411 of this title and applicable to existing solid waste incineration units shall be effective as expeditiously as practicable after approval of a State plan under subsection (b)(2) of this section (or promulgation of a plan by the Administrator under subsection (b)(3) of this section) but in no event later than 3 years after the State plan is approved or 5 years after the date such standards or requirements are promulgated, whichever is earlier.

**(3) Prohibition**

After the effective date of any performance standard, emission limitation or other requirement promulgated pursuant to this section and section 7411 of this title, it shall be unlawful for any owner or operator of any solid waste incineration unit to which such standard, limitation or requirement applies to operate such unit in violation of such limitation, standard or requirement or for any other person to violate an applicable requirement of this section.

**(4) Coordination with other authorities**

For purposes of sections 7411(e), 7413, 7414, 7416, 7420, 7603, 7604, 7607 of this title and other provisions for the enforcement of this chapter, each performance standard, emission limitation or other requirement established pursuant to this section by the Administrator or a State or local government, shall be treated in the same manner as a standard of performance under section 7411 of this title which is an emission limitation.

**(g) Definitions**

For purposes of section 306 of the Clean Air Act Amendments of 1990 and this section only—

**(1) Solid waste incineration unit**

The term "solid waste incineration unit" means a distinct operating unit of any facility which combusts any solid waste material from commercial or industrial establishments or the general public (including single and multiple residences, hotels, and motels). Such term does not include incinerators or other units required to have a permit under section 3005 of the Solid Waste Disposal Act [42 U.S.C.A. § 6925]. The term "solid waste incineration unit" does not include (A) materials recovery facilities (including primary or secondary smelters) which combust waste for the primary purpose of recovering metals, (B) qualifying small power production facilities, as defined in section 796(17)(C) of Title 16, or qualifying cogeneration facilities, as defined in section 796(18)(B) of Title 16, which burn homogeneous waste (such as units which burn tires or used oil, but not including refuse-derived fuel) for the production of electric energy or in the case of qualifying cogeneration facilities which burn homogeneous waste for the production of electric energy and steam or forms of useful energy (such as heat) which are used for industrial, commercial, heating or cooling purposes, or (C) air curtain incinerators provided that such incinerators only burn wood wastes, yard wastes and clean lumber and that such air curtain incinerators comply with opacity limitations to be established by the Administrator by rule.

**(2) New solid waste incineration unit**

The term "new solid waste incineration unit" means a solid waste incineration unit the construction of which is commenced after the Administrator proposes requirements under this section establishing emissions standards or other requirements which would be applicable to such unit or a modified solid waste incineration unit.

**(3) Modified solid waste incineration unit**

The term "modified solid waste incineration unit" means a solid waste incineration unit at which modifications have occurred after the effective date of a standard under subsection (a) of this section if (A) the cumulative cost of the modifications, over the life of the unit, exceed 50 per centum of the original cost of construction and installation of the unit (not including the cost of any land purchased in connection with such construction or installation) updated to current costs, or (B) the modification is a physical change in or change in the method of operation of the unit which increases the amount of any air pollutant emitted by the unit for which standards have been established under this section or section 7411 of this title.

**(4) Existing solid waste incineration unit**

The term "existing solid waste incineration unit" means a solid waste unit which is not a new or modified solid waste incineration unit.

**(5) Municipal waste**

The term "municipal waste" means refuse (and refuse-derived fuel) collected from the general public and from residential, commercial, institutional, and industrial sources consisting of paper, wood, yard wastes, food wastes, plastics, leather, rubber, and other combustible materials and non-combustible materials such as metal, glass and rock, provided that: (A) the term does not include industrial process wastes or medical wastes that are segregated from such other wastes; and (B) an incineration unit shall not be considered to be combusting municipal waste for purposes of section 7411 of this title or this section if it combusts a fuel feed stream, 30 percent or less of the weight of which is comprised, in aggregate, of municipal waste.

**(6) Other terms**

The terms "solid waste" and "medical waste" shall have the meanings established by the Administrator pursuant to the Solid Waste Disposal Act [42 U.S.C.A. § 6901 et seq.].

**(h) Other authority**

**(1) State authority**

Nothing in this section shall preclude or deny the right of any State or political subdivision thereof to adopt or enforce any regulation, requirement, limitation or standard relating to solid waste incineration units that is more stringent than a regulation, requirement, limitation or standard in effect under this section or under any other provision of this chapter.

**(2) Other authority under this chapter**

Nothing in this section shall diminish the authority of the Administrator or a State to establish any other requirements applicable to solid waste incineration units under any other authority of law, including the authority to establish for any air pollutant a national ambient air quality standard, except that no solid waste incineration unit subject to performance standards under this section and section 7411 of this title shall be subject to standards under section 7412(d) of this title.

**(3) Residual risk**

The Administrator shall promulgate standards under section 7412(f) of this title for a category of solid waste incineration units, if promulgation of such standards is required under section 7412(f) of this title. For purposes of this [3] preceding sentence only—

(A) the performance standards under subsection (a) of this section and section 7411 of this title applicable to a category of solid waste incineration units shall be deemed standards under section 7412(d)(2) of this title, and

(B) the Administrator shall consider and regulate, if required, the pollutants listed under subsection (a)(4) of this section and no others.

### (4) Acid rain

A solid waste incineration unit shall not be a utility unit as defined in subchapter IV–A of this chapter: *Provided,* That, more than 80 per centum of its annual average fuel consumption measured on a Btu basis, during a period or periods to be determined by the Administrator, is from a fuel (including any waste burned as a fuel) other than a fossil fuel.

### (5) Requirements of parts C and D

No requirement of an applicable implementation plan under section 7475 of this title (relating to construction of facilities in regions identified pursuant to section 7407(d)(1)(A)(ii) or (iii) of this title) or under section 7502(c)(5) of this title (relating to permits for construction and operation in nonattainment areas) may be used to weaken the standards in effect under this section.

(July 14, 1955, c. 360, Title I, § 129, as added Nov. 15, 1990, Pub.L. 101–549, Title III, § 305(a), 104 Stat. 2577.)

1 So in original. Probably should be "subsection".

2 So in original. Probably should be subsection "(h)(3)".

3 So in original. Probably should be "the".

## HISTORICAL AND STATUTORY NOTES

**References in Text**

Section 306 of the Clean Air Act Amendments of 1990, referred to in subsec. (g), probably means section 306 of Pub.L. 101–549, which is set out as a note under section 6921 of this title.

The Solid Waste Disposal Act, referred to in subsecs. (g)(1) and (6), is Title II of Pub.L. 89–272, Oct. 20, 1965, 79 Stat. 997, as amended generally by Pub.L. 94–580, § 2, Oct. 21, 1976, 90 Stat. 2795, which is classified generally to chapter 82 (section 6901 et seq.) of this title. Section 3005 of the Solid Waste Disposal Act, referred to in subsec. (g)(1), is classified to section 6925 of this title. For complete classification of this Act to the Code, see Short Title of 1965 Acts note set out under section 6901 of this title and Tables.

**Effective and Applicability Provisions**

1990 Acts

Section to take effect Nov. 15, 1990, except as otherwise provided, see section 711(b) of Pub.L. 101–549, set out as a note under section 7401 of this title.

**Savings Provisions**

Suits, actions or proceedings commenced under this chapter as in effect prior to Nov. 15, 1990, not to abate by reason of the taking effect of amendments by Pub.L. 101–549, except as otherwise provided for, see section 711(a) of Pub.L. 101–549, set out as a note under section 7401 of this title.

**Review of Acid Gas Scrubbing Requirements**

Section 305(c) of Pub.L. 101–549 provided that: "Prior to the promulgation of any performance standard for solid waste incineration units combusting municipal waste under section 111 [section 7411 of this title] or section 129 of the Clean Air Act [this section], the Administrator shall review the availability of acid gas scrubbers as a pollution control technology for small new units and for existing units (as defined in 54 Federal Register 52190 (December 20, 1989)[]), taking into account the provisions of subsection (a)(2) of section 129 of the Clean Air Act [subsec. (a)(2) of this section]."

## § 7430. Emission factors

[CAA § 130]

Within 6 months after November 15, 1990, and at least every 3 years thereafter, the Administrator shall review and, if necessary, revise, the methods ("emission factors") used for purposes of this chapter to estimate the quantity of emissions of carbon monoxide, volatile organic compounds, and oxides of nitrogen from sources of such air pollutants (including area sources and mobile sources). In addition, the Administrator shall establish emission factors for sources for which no such methods have previously been established by the Administrator. The Administrator shall permit any person to demonstrate improved emissions estimating techniques, and following approval of such techniques, the Administrator shall authorize the use of such techniques. Any such technique may be approved only after appropriate public participation. Until the Administrator has completed the revision required by this section, nothing in this section shall be construed to affect the validity of emission factors established by the Administrator before November 15, 1990.

(July 14, 1955, c. 360, Title I, § 130, as added Nov. 15, 1990, Pub.L. 101–549, Title VIII, § 804, 104 Stat. 2689.)

## HISTORICAL AND STATUTORY NOTES

**Effective and Applicability Provisions**

1990 Acts

Section to take effect Nov. 15, 1990, except as otherwise provided, see section 711(b) of Pub.L. 101–549, set out as a note under section 7401 of this title.

**Savings Provisions**

Suits, actions or proceedings commenced under this chapter as in effect prior to Nov. 15, 1990, not to abate by reason of the taking effect of amendments by Pub.L. 101–549, except as otherwise provided for, see section 711(a) of Pub.L. 101–549, set out as a note under section 7401 of this title.

## § 7431. Land use authority

[CAA § 131]

Nothing in this chapter constitutes an infringement on the existing authority of counties and cities to plan or control land use, and nothing in this chapter provides or transfers authority over such land use.

(July 14, 1955, c. 360, Title I, § 131, as added Nov. 15, 1990, Pub.L. 101–549, Title VIII, § 805, 104 Stat. 2689.)

### HISTORICAL AND STATUTORY NOTES

**Effective and Applicability Provisions**

1990 Acts

Section to take effect Nov. 15, 1990, except as otherwise provided, see section 711(b) of Pub.L. 101–549, set out as a note under section 7401 of this title.

**Savings Provisions**

Suits, actions or proceedings commenced under this chapter as in effect prior to Nov. 15, 1990, not to abate by reason of the taking effect of amendments by Pub.L. 101–549, except as otherwise provided for, see section 711(a) of Pub.L. 101–549, set out as a note under section 7401 of this title.

## §§ 7432 to 7449. Reserved for future legislation

### PART B—OZONE PROTECTION

## §§ 7450 to 7459. Repealed. Pub.L. 101–549, Title VI, § 601, Nov. 15, 1990, 104 Stat. 2648

### HISTORICAL AND STATUTORY NOTES

Section 7450, Act July 14, 1955, c. 360, Title I, § 150, as added Aug. 7, 1977, Pub.L. 95–95, Title I, § 126, 91 Stat. 725, set forth the Congressional declaration of purpose.

Section 7451, Act July 14, 1955, c. 360, Title I, § 151, as added Aug. 7, 1977, Pub.L. 95–95, Title I, § 126, 91 Stat. 726, set forth Congressional findings.

Section 7452, Act July 14, 1955, c. 360, Title I, § 152, as added Aug. 7, 1977, Pub.L. 95–95, Title I, § 126, 91 Stat. 726, set forth definitions applicable to this part.

Section 7453, Act July 14, 1955, c. 360, Title I, § 153, as added Aug. 7, 1977, Pub.L. 95–95, Title I, § 126, 91 Stat. 726, related to studies by the Environmental Protection Agency.

Section 7454, Act July 14, 1955, c. 360, Title I, § 154, as added Aug. 7, 1977, Pub.L. 95–95, Title I, § 126, 91 Stat. 728, and amended Pub.L. 96–88, Title V, § 509(b), Oct. 17, 1979, 93 Stat. 695, related to research and monitoring activities by Federal agencies.

Section 7455, Act July 14, 1955, c. 360, Title I, § 155, as added Aug. 7, 1977, Pub.L. 95–95, Title I, § 126, 91 Stat. 726, related to reports on the progress of regulation.

Section 7456, Act July 14, 1955, c. 360, Title I, § 156, as added Aug. 7, 1977, Pub.L. 95–95, Title I, § 126, 91 Stat. 729, authorized the President to enter into international agreements to foster cooperative research.

Section 7457, Act July 14, 1955, c. 360, Title I, § 157, as added Aug. 7, 1977, Pub.L. 95–95, Title I, § 126, 91 Stat. 729, related to promulgation of regulations.

Section 7458, Act July 14, 1955, c. 360, Title I, § 158, as added Aug. 7, 1977, Pub.L. 95–95, Title I, § 126, 91 Stat. 730, set forth other provisions of law that would be unaffected by the provisions of this part.

Section 7459, Act July 14, 1955, c. 360, Title I, § 159, as added Aug. 7, 1977, Pub.L. 95–95, Title I, § 126, 91 Stat. 730, related to the authority of the State to protect the stratosphere.

**Effective Date of Repeal**

Repeal of sections 7450 to 7459 effective Nov. 15, 1990, except as otherwise provided, see section 711(b) of Pub.L. 101–549, set out as a note under section 7401 of this title.

**Savings Provisions**

Suits, actions or proceedings commenced under this chapter as in effect prior to Nov. 15, 1990, not to abate by reason of the taking effect of amendments by Pub.L. 101–549, except as otherwise provided for, see section 711(a) of Pub.L. 101–549, set out as a note under section 7401 of this title.

**Similar Provisions**

For provisions relating to stratospheric ozone protection, see section 7671 et seq. of this title.

### PART C—PREVENTION OF SIGNIFICANT DETERIORATION OF AIR QUALITY

#### *Subpart I—Clean Air*

## § 7470. Congressional declaration of purpose [CAA § 160]

The purposes of this part are as follows:

(1) to protect public health and welfare from any actual or potential adverse effect which in the Administrator's judgment may reasonably be anticipate [1] to occur from air pollution or from exposures to pollutants in other media, which pollutants originate as emissions to the ambient air) [2], notwithstanding attainment and maintenance of all national ambient air quality standards;

(2) to preserve, protect, and enhance the air quality in national parks, national wilderness areas, national monuments, national seashores, and other areas of special national or regional natural, recreational, scenic, or historic value;

(3) to insure that economic growth will occur in a manner consistent with the preservation of existing clean air resources;

(4) to assure that emissions from any source in any State will not interfere with any portion of the applicable implementation plan to prevent significant deterioration of air quality for any other State; and

(5) to assure that any decision to permit increased air pollution in any area to which this section applies is made only after careful evaluation of all the consequences of such a decision and after

adequate procedural opportunities for informed public participation in the decisionmaking process.

(July 14, 1955, c. 360, Title I, § 160, as added Aug. 7, 1977, Pub.L. 95–95, Title I, § 127(a), 91 Stat. 731.)

[1] So in original. Probably should be "anticipated".

[2] So in original. Section was enacted without an opening parenthesis.

### HISTORICAL AND STATUTORY NOTES

**Effective and Applicability Provisions**

1977 Acts

Section effective Aug. 7, 1977, except as otherwise expressly provided, see section 406(d) of Pub.L. 95–95, set out as a note under section 7401 of this title.

**Guidance Document**

Section 127(c) of Pub.L. 95–95 provided that not later than 1 year after Aug. 7, 1977, the Administrator publish a guidance document to assist the States in carrying out their functions under part C of Title I of the Clean Air Act [this part] with respect to pollutants for which national ambient air quality standards are promulgated.

**Study and Report on Progress Made in Program Relating to Significant Deterioration of Air Quality**

Section 127(d) of Pub.L. 95–95 provided that not later than 2 years after Aug. 7, 1977, the Administrator shall complete a study and report to the Congress on the progress made in carrying out part C of Title I of the Clean Air Act [this part] and the problems associated with carrying out such section.

## § 7471. Plan requirements

[CAA § 161]

In accordance with the policy of section 7401(b)(1) of this title, each applicable implementation plan shall contain emission limitations and such other measures as may be necessary, as determined under regulations promulgated under this part, to prevent significant deterioration of air quality in each region (or portion thereof) designated pursuant to section 7407 of this title as attainment or unclassifiable.

(July 14, 1955, c. 360, Title I, § 161, as added Aug. 7, 1977, Pub.L. 95–95, Title I, § 127(a), 91 Stat. 731, and amended Nov. 15, 1990, Pub.L. 101–549, Title I, § 110(1), 104 Stat. 2470.)

### HISTORICAL AND STATUTORY NOTES

**Effective and Applicability Provisions**

1990 Acts

Amendment by Pub.L. 101–549 effective Nov. 15, 1990, except as otherwise provided, see section 711(b) of Pub.L. 101–549, set out as a note under section 7401 of this title.

1977 Acts

Section effective Aug. 7, 1977, except as otherwise expressly provided, see section 406(d) of Pub.L. 95–95, set out as a note under section 7401 of this title.

**Savings Provisions**

Suits, actions or proceedings commenced under this chapter as in effect prior to Nov. 15, 1990, not to abate by reason of the taking effect of amendments by Pub.L. 101–549, except as otherwise provided for, see section 711(a) of Pub.L. 101–549, set out as a note under section 7401 of this title.

## § 7472. Initial classifications

[CAA § 162]

**(a) Areas designated as class I**

Upon the enactment of this part, all—

(1) international parks,

(2) national wilderness areas which exceed 5,000 acres in size,

(3) national memorial parks which exceed 5,000 acres in size, and

(4) national parks which exceed six thousand acres in size,

and which are in existence on August 7, 1977, shall be class I areas and may not be redesignated. All areas which were redesignated as class I under regulations promulgated before August 7, 1977, shall be class I areas which may be redesignated as provided in this part. The extent of the areas designated as Class I under this section shall conform to any changes in the boundaries of such areas which have occurred subsequent to August 7, 1977, or which may occur subsequent to November 15, 1990.

**(b) Areas designated as class II**

All areas in such State designated pursuant to section 7407(d) of this title as attainment or unclassifiable which are not established as class I under subsection (a) of this section shall be class II areas unless redesignated under section 7474 of this title.

(July 14, 1955, c. 360, Title I, § 162, as added Aug. 7, 1977, Pub.L. 95–95, Title I, § 127(a), 91 Stat. 731, and amended Nov. 16, 1977, Pub.L. 95–190, § 14(a)(40), 91 Stat. 1401; Nov. 15, 1990, Pub.L. 101–549, Title I, §§ 108(m), 110(2), 104 Stat. 2469, 2470.)

### HISTORICAL AND STATUTORY NOTES

**Effective and Applicability Provisions**

1990 Acts

Amendment by Pub.L. 101–549 effective Nov. 15, 1990, except as otherwise provided, see section 711(b) of Pub.L. 101–549, set out as a note under section 7401 of this title.

1977 Acts

Section effective Aug. 7, 1977, except as otherwise expressly provided, see section 406(d) of Pub.L. 95–95, set out as a note under section 7401 of this title.

**Savings Provisions**

Suits, actions or proceedings commenced under this chapter as in effect prior to Nov. 15, 1990, not to abate by reason of the taking effect of amendments by Pub.L. 101–549, except as otherwise provided for, see section 711(a) of Pub.L. 101–549, set out as a note under section 7401 of this title.

## § 7473. Increments and ceilings

[CAA § 163]

### (a) Sulfur oxide and particulate matter; requirement that maximum allowable increases and maximum allowable concentrations not be exceeded

In the case of sulfur oxide and particulate matter, each applicable implementation plan shall contain measures assuring that maximum allowable increases over baseline concentrations of, and maximum allowable concentrations of, such pollutant shall not be exceeded. In the case of any maximum allowable increase (except an allowable increase specified under section 7475(d)(2)(C)(iv) of this title) for a pollutant based on concentrations permitted under national ambient air quality standards for any period other than an annual period, such regulations shall permit such maximum allowable increase to be exceeded during one such period per year.

### (b) Maximum allowable increases in concentrations over baseline concentrations

(1) For any class I area, the maximum allowable increase in concentrations of sulfur dioxide and particulate matter over the baseline concentration of such pollutants shall not exceed the following amounts:

| Pollutant | Maximum allowable increase (in micrograms per cubic meter) |
|---|---|
| Particulate matter: | |
| Annual geometric mean | 5 |
| Twenty-four-hour maximum | 10 |
| Sulfur dioxide: | |
| Annual arithmetic mean | 2 |
| Twenty-four-hour maximum | 5 |
| Three-hour maximum | 25 |

(2) For any class II area, the maximum allowable increase in concentrations of sulfur dioxide and particulate matter over the baseline concentration of such pollutants shall not exceed the following amounts:

| Pollutant | Maximum allowable increase (in micrograms per cubic meter) |
|---|---|
| Particulate matter: | |
| Annual geometric mean | 19 |
| Twenty-four-hour maximum | 37 |
| Sulfur dioxide: | |
| Annual arithmetic mean | 20 |
| Twenty-four-hour maximum | 91 |
| Three-hour maximum | 512 |

(3) For any class III area, the maximum allowable increase in concentrations of sulfur dioxide and particulate matter over the baseline concentration of such pollutants shall not exceed the following amounts:

| Pollutant | Maximum allowable increase (in micrograms per cubic meter) |
|---|---|
| Particulate matter: | |
| Annual geometric mean | 37 |
| Twenty-four-hour maximum | 75 |
| Sulfur dioxide: | |
| Annual arithmetic mean | 40 |
| Twenty-four-hour maximum | 182 |
| Three-hour maximum | 700 |

(4) The maximum allowable concentration of any air pollutant in any area to which this part applies shall not exceed a concentration for such pollutant for each period of exposure equal to—

(A) the concentration permitted under the national secondary ambient air quality standard, or

(B) the concentration permitted under the national primary ambient air quality standard,

whichever concentration is lowest for such pollutant for such period of exposure.

### (c) Orders or rules for determining compliance with maximum allowable increases in ambient concentrations of air pollutants

(1) In the case of any State which has a plan approved by the Administrator for purposes of carrying out this part, the Governor of such State may, after notice and opportunity for public hearing, issue orders or promulgate rules providing that for purposes of determining compliance with the maximum allowable increases in ambient concentrations of an air pollutant, the following concentrations of such pollutant shall not be taken into account:

(A) concentrations of such pollutant attributable to the increase in emissions from stationary sources which have converted from the use of petroleum products, or natural gas, or both, by reason of an order which is in effect under the provisions of sections 792(a) and (b) of Title 15 (or any subsequent legislation which supersedes such provisions) over the emissions from such sources before the effective date of such order.[1]

(B) the concentrations of such pollutant attributable to the increase in emissions from stationary sources which have converted from using natural gas by reason of a natural gas curtailment pursuant to a natural gas curtailment plan in effect pursuant to the Federal Power Act [16 U.S.C.A. § 791a et seq.] over the emissions from such sources before the effective date of such plan,

(C) concentrations of particulate matter attributable to the increase in emissions from construction or other temporary emission-related activities, and

(D) the increase in concentrations attributable to new sources outside the United States over the concentrations attributable to existing sources which are included in the baseline concentration determined in accordance with section 7479(4) of this title.

(2) No action taken with respect to a source under paragraph (1)(A) or (1)(B) shall apply more than five years after the effective date of the order referred to in paragraph (1)(A) or the plan referred to in paragraph (1)(B), whichever is applicable. If both such order and plan are applicable, no such action shall apply more than five years after the later of such effective dates.

(3) No action under this subsection shall take effect unless the Governor submits the order or rule providing for such exclusion to the Administrator and the Administrator determines that such order or rule is in compliance with the provisions of this subsection.

(July 14, 1955, c. 360, Title I, § 163, as added Aug. 7, 1977, Pub.L. 95–95, Title I, § 127(a), 91 Stat. 732, and amended Nov. 16, 1977, Pub.L. 95–190, § 14(a)(41), 91 Stat. 1401.)

[1] So in original. The period probably should be a comma.

### HISTORICAL AND STATUTORY NOTES

**References in Text**

The Federal Power Act, referred to in subsec. (c)(1)(B), is Act June 10, 1920, c. 285, 41 Stat. 1063, as amended, which is classified generally to chapter 12 (section 791a et seq.) of Title 16, Conservation. For complete classification of this Act to the Code, see section 791a of Title 16 and Tables.

**Effective and Applicability Provisions**

1977 Acts

Section effective Aug. 7, 1977, except as otherwise expressly provided, see section 406(d) of Pub.L. 95–95, set out as a note under section 7401 of this title.

## § 7474. Area redesignation

[CAA § 164]

### (a) Authority of States to redesignate areas

Except as otherwise provided under subsection (c) of this section, a State may redesignate such areas as it deems appropriate as class I areas. The following areas may be redesignated only as class I or II:

(1) an area which exceeds ten thousand acres in size and is a national monument, a national primitive area, a national preserve, a national recreation area, a national wild and scenic river, a national wildlife refuge, a national lakeshore or seashore, and

(2) a national park or national wilderness area established after August 7, 1977, which exceeds ten thousand acres in size.

The extent of the areas referred to in paragraph[1] (1) and (2) shall conform to any changes in the boundaries of such areas which have occurred subsequent to August 7, 1977, or which may occur subsequent to November 15, 1990. Any area (other than an area referred to in paragraph (1) or (2) or an area established as class I under the first sentence of section 7472(a) of this title) may be redesignated by the State as class III if—

(A) such redesignation has been specifically approved by the Governor of the State, after consultation with the appropriate Committees of the legislature if it is in session or with the leadership of the legislature if it is not in session (unless State law provides that such redesignation must be specifically approved by State legislation) and if general purpose units of local government representing a majority of the residents of the area so redesignated enact legislation (including for such units of local government resolutions where appropriate) concurring in the State's redesignation;

(B) such redesignation will not cause, or contribute to, concentrations of any air pollutant which exceed any maximum allowable increase or maximum allowable concentration permitted under the classification of any other area; and

(C) such redesignation otherwise meets the requirements of this part.

Subparagraph (A) of this paragraph shall not apply to area redesignations by Indian tribes.

### (b) Notice and hearing; notice to Federal land manager; written comments and recommendations; regulations; disapproval of redesignation

(1)(A) Prior to redesignation of any area under this part, notice shall be afforded and public hearings shall be conducted in areas proposed to be redesignated and in areas which may be affected by the proposed redesignation. Prior to any such public hearing a satisfactory description and analysis of the health, environmental, economic, social, and energy effects of the proposed redesignation shall be prepared and made available for public inspection and prior to any such redesignation, the description and analysis of such effects shall be reviewed and examined by the redesignating authorities.

(B) Prior to the issuance of notice under subparagraph (A) respecting the redesignation of any area under this subsection, if such area includes any Federal lands, the State shall provide written notice to the appropriate Federal land manager and afford adequate opportunity (but not in excess of 60 days) to confer with the State respecting the intended notice of redesignation and to submit written comments and recommendations with respect to such intended notice of redesignation. In redesignating any area under this section with respect to which any Federal land manager has submitted written comments and recommendations, the State shall publish a list of any inconsistency between such redesignation and such recommendations and an explanation of such inconsistency (together with the reasons for making such redesignation against the recommendation of the Federal land manager).

(C) The Administrator shall promulgate regulations not later than six months after August 7, 1977, to assure, insofar as practicable, that prior to any public hearing on redesignation of any area, there shall be available for public inspection any specific plans for any new or modified major emitting facility which may be permitted to be constructed and operated only if the area in question is designated or redesignated as class III.

(2) The Administrator may disapprove the redesignation of any area only if he finds, after notice and opportunity for public hearing, that such redesignation does not meet the procedural requirements of this section or is inconsistent with the requirements of section 7472(a) of this title or of subsection (a) of this section. If any such disapproval occurs, the classification of the area shall be that which was in effect prior to the redesignation which was disapproved.

**(c) Indian reservations**

Lands within the exterior boundaries of reservations of federally recognized Indian tribes may be redesignated only by the appropriate Indian governing body. Such Indian governing body shall be subject in all respect to the provisions of subsection (e) of this section.

**(d) Review of national monuments, primitive areas, and national preserves**

The Federal Land Manager shall review all national monuments, primitive areas, and national preserves, and shall recommend any appropriate areas for redesignation as class I where air quality related values are important attributes of the area. The Federal Land Manager shall report such recommendations, within [2] supporting analysis, to the Congress and the affected States within one year after August 7, 1977. The Federal Land Manager shall consult with the appropriate States before making such recommendations.

**(e) Resolution of disputes between State and Indian tribes**

If any State affected by the redesignation of an area by an Indian tribe or any Indian tribe affected by the redesignation of an area by a State disagrees with such redesignation of any area, or if a permit is proposed to be issued for any new major emitting facility proposed for construction in any State which the Governor of an affected State or governing body of an affected Indian tribe determines will cause or contribute to a cumulative change in air quality in excess of that allowed in this part within the affected State or tribal reservation, the Governor or Indian ruling body may request the Administrator to enter into negotiations with the parties involved to resolve such dispute. If requested by any State or Indian tribe involved, the Administrator shall make a recommendation to resolve the dispute and protect the air quality related values of the lands involved. If the parties involved do not reach agreement, the Administrator shall resolve the dispute and his determination, or the results of agreements reached through other means, shall become part of the applicable plan and shall be enforceable as part of such plan. In resolving such disputes relating to area redesignation, the Administrator shall consider the extent to which the lands involved are of sufficient size to allow effective air quality management or have air quality related values of such an area.

(July 14, 1955, c. 360, Title I, § 164, as added Aug. 7, 1977, Pub.L. 95–95, Title I, § 127(a), 91 Stat. 733, and amended Nov. 16, 1977, Pub.L. 95–190, § 14(a)(42), (43), 91 Stat. 1402; Nov. 15, 1990, Pub.L. 101–549, Title I, § 108(n), 104 Stat. 2469.)

[1] So in original. Probably should be "paragraphs".

[2] So in original. Probably should be "with".

### HISTORICAL AND STATUTORY NOTES

**Effective and Applicability Provisions**

1990 Acts

Amendment by Pub.L. 101–549 effective Nov. 15, 1990, except as otherwise provided, see section 711(b) of Pub.L. 101–549, set out as a note under section 7401 of this title.

1977 Acts

Section effective Aug. 7, 1977, except as otherwise expressly provided, see section 406(d) of Pub.L. 95–95, set out as a note under section 7401 of this title.

**Savings Provisions**

Suits, actions or proceedings commenced under this chapter as in effect prior to Nov. 15, 1990, not to abate by reason of the taking effect of amendments by Pub.L. 101–549, except as otherwise provided for, see section 711(a) of Pub.L. 101–549, set out as a note under section 7401 of this title.

## § 7475. Preconstruction requirements

[CAA § 165]

**(a) Major emitting facilities on which construction is commenced**

No major emitting facility on which construction is commenced after August 7, 1977, may be constructed in any area to which this part applies unless—

(1) a permit has been issued for such proposed facility in accordance with this part setting forth emission limitations for such facility which conform to the requirements of this part;

(2) the proposed permit has been subject to a review in accordance with this section, the required analysis has been conducted in accordance with regulations promulgated by the Administrator, and a public hearing has been held with opportunity for interested persons including representatives of the Administrator to appear and submit written or oral presentations on the air quality impact of such source, alternatives thereto, control technology requirements, and other appropriate considerations;

(3) the owner or operator of such facility demonstrates, as required pursuant to section 7410(j) of this title, that emissions from construction or operation of such facility will not cause, or contribute to, air pollution in excess of any (A) maximum allowable increase or maximum allowable concentration for any pollutant in any area to which this part applies more than one time per year, (B) national ambient air quality standard in any air quality control region, or (C) any other applicable emission standard or standard of performance under this chapter;

(4) the proposed facility is subject to the best available control technology for each pollutant subject to regulation under this chapter emitted from, or which results from, such facility;

(5) the provisions of subsection (d) of this section with respect to protection of class I areas have been complied with for such facility;

(6) there has been an analysis of any air quality impacts projected for the area as a result of growth associated with such facility;

(7) the person who owns or operates, or proposes to own or operate, a major emitting facility for which a permit is required under this part agrees to conduct such monitoring as may be necessary to determine the effect which emissions from any such facility may have, or is having, on air quality in any area which may be affected by emissions from such source; and

(8) in the case of a source which proposes to construct in a class III area, emissions from which would cause or contribute to exceeding the maximum allowable increments applicable in a class II area and where no standard under section 7411 of this title has been promulgated subsequent to August 7, 1977, for such source category, the Administrator has approved the determination of best available technology as set forth in the permit.

**(b) Exception**

The demonstration pertaining to maximum allowable increases required under subsection (a)(3) of this section shall not apply to maximum allowable increases for class II areas in the case of an expansion or modification of a major emitting facility which is in existence on August 7, 1977, whose allowable emissions of air pollutants, after compliance with subsection (a)(4) of this section, will be less than fifty tons per year and for which the owner or operator of such facility demonstrates that emissions of particulate matter and sulfur oxides will not cause or contribute to ambient air quality levels in excess of the national secondary ambient air quality standard for either of such pollutants.

**(c) Permit applications**

Any completed permit application under section 7410 of this title for a major emitting facility in any area to which this part applies shall be granted or denied not later than one year after the date of filing of such completed application.

**(d) Action taken on permit applications; notice; adverse impact on air quality related values; variance; emission limitations**

(1) Each State shall transmit to the Administrator a copy of each permit application relating to a major emitting facility received by such State and provide notice to the Administrator of every action related to the consideration of such permit.

(2)(A) The Administrator shall provide notice of the permit application to the Federal Land Manager and the Federal official charged with direct responsibility for management of any lands within a class I area which may be affected by emissions from the proposed facility.

(B) The Federal Land Manager and the Federal official charged with direct responsibility for management of such lands shall have an affirmative responsibility to protect the air quality related values (including visibility) of any such lands within a class I area and to consider, in consultation with the Administrator, whether a proposed major emitting facility will have an adverse impact on such values.

(C)(i) In any case where the Federal official charged with direct responsibility for management of any lands within a class I area or the Federal Land Manager of such lands, or the Administrator, or the Governor of an adjacent State containing such a class I area files a notice alleging that emissions from a proposed major emitting facility may cause or contribute to a change in the air quality in such area and identifying the potential adverse impact of such change, a permit shall not be issued unless the owner or operator of such facility demonstrates that emissions of particulate matter and sulfur dioxide will not cause or contribute to concentrations which exceed the maximum allowable increases for a class I area.

**(ii)** In any case where the Federal Land Manager demonstrates to the satisfaction of the State that the emissions from such facility will have an adverse impact on the air quality-related values (including visibility) of such lands, notwithstanding the fact that the change in air quality resulting from emissions from such facility will not cause or contribute to concentrations which exceed the maximum allowable increases for a class I area, a permit shall not be issued.

**(iii)** In any case where the owner or operator of such facility demonstrates to the satisfaction of the Federal Land Manager, and the Federal Land Manager so certifies, that the emissions from such facility will have no adverse impact on the air quality-related values of such lands (including visibility), notwithstanding the fact that the change in air quality resulting from emissions from such facility will cause or contribute to concentrations which exceed the maximum allowable increases for class I areas, the State may issue a permit.

**(iv)** In the case of a permit issued pursuant to clause (iii), such facility shall comply with such emission limitations under such permit as may be necessary to assure that emissions of sulfur oxides and particulates from such facility will not cause or contribute to concentrations of such pollutant which exceed the following maximum allowable increases over the baseline concentration for such pollutants:

| | Maximum allowable increase (in micrograms per cubic meter) |
|---|---|
| Particulate matter: | |
| Annual geometric mean | 19 |
| Twenty-four-hour maximum | 37 |
| Sulfur dioxide: | |
| Annual arithmetic mean | 20 |
| Twenty-four-hour maximum | 91 |
| Three-hour maximum | 325 |

**(D)(i)** In any case where the owner or operator of a proposed major emitting facility who has been denied a certification under subparagraph (C)(iii) demonstrates to the satisfaction of the Governor, after notice and public hearing, and the Governor finds, that the facility cannot be constructed by reason of any maximum allowable increase for sulfur dioxide for periods of twenty-four hours or less applicable to any class I area and, in the case of Federal mandatory class I areas, that a variance under this clause will not adversely affect the air quality related values of the area (including visibility), the Governor, after consideration of the Federal Land Manager's recommendation (if any) and subject to his concurrence, may grant a variance from such maximum allowable increase. If such variance is granted, a permit may be issued to such source pursuant to the requirements of this subparagraph.

**(ii)** In any case in which the Governor recommends a variance under this subparagraph in which the Federal Land Manager does not concur, the recommendations of the Governor and the Federal Land Manager shall be transmitted to the President. The President may approve the Governor's recommendation if he finds that such variance is in the national interest. No Presidential finding shall be reviewable in any court. The variance shall take effect if the President approves the Governor's recommendations. The President shall approve or disapprove such recommendation within ninety days after his receipt of the recommendations of the Governor and the Federal Land Manager.

**(iii)** In the case of a permit issued pursuant to this subparagraph, such facility shall comply with such emission limitations under such permit as may be necessary to assure that emissions of sulfur oxides from such facility will not (during any day on which the otherwise applicable maximum allowable increases are exceeded) cause or contribute to concentrations which exceed the following maximum allowable increases for such areas over the baseline concentration for such pollutant and to assure that such emissions will not cause or contribute to concentrations which exceed the otherwise applicable maximum allowable increases for periods of exposure of 24 hours or less on more than 18 days during any annual period:

MAXIMUM ALLOWABLE INCREASE
[In micrograms per cubic meter]

| Period of exposure | Low terrain areas | High terrain areas |
|---|---|---|
| 24-hr maximum | 36 | 62 |
| 3-hr maximum | 130 | 221 |

**(iv)** For purposes of clause (iii), the term "high terrain area" means with respect to any facility, any area having an elevation of 900 feet or more above the base of the stack of such facility, and the term "low terrain area" means any area other than a high terrain area.

### (e) Analysis; continuous air quality monitoring data; regulations; model adjustments

**(1)** The review provided for in subsection (a) of this section shall be preceded by an analysis in accordance with regulations of the Administrator, promulgated under this subsection, which may be conducted by the State (or any general purpose unit of local government) or by the major emitting facility applying for such permit, of the ambient air quality at the proposed site and in areas which may be affected by emissions from such facility for each pollutant subject to regulation under this chapter which will be emitted from such facility.

(2) Effective one year after August 7, 1977, the analysis required by this subsection shall include continuous air quality monitoring data gathered for purposes of determining whether emissions from such facility will exceed the maximum allowable increases or the maximum allowable concentration permitted under this part. Such data shall be gathered over a period of one calendar year preceding the date of application for a permit under this part unless the State, in accordance with regulations promulgated by the Administrator, determines that a complete and adequate analysis for such purposes may be accomplished in a shorter period. The results of such analysis shall be available at the time of the public hearing on the application for such permit.

(3) The Administrator shall within six months after August 7, 1977, promulgate regulations respecting the analysis required under this subsection which regulations—

(A) shall not require the use of any automatic or uniform buffer zone or zones,

(B) shall require an analysis of the ambient air quality, climate and meteorology, terrain, soils and vegetation, and visibility at the site of the proposed major emitting facility and in the area potentially affected by the emissions from such facility for each pollutant regulated under this chapter which will be emitted from, or which results from the construction or operation of, such facility, the size and nature of the proposed facility, the degree of continuous emission reduction which could be achieved by such facility, and such other factors as may be relevant in determining the effect of emissions from a proposed facility on any air quality control region,

(C) shall require the results of such analysis shall be available at the time of the public hearing on the application for such permit, and

(D) shall specify with reasonable particularity each air quality model or models to be used under specified sets of conditions for purposes of this part.

Any model or models designated under such regulations may be adjusted upon a determination, after notice and opportunity for public hearing, by the Administrator that such adjustment is necessary to take into account unique terrain or meteorological characteristics of an area potentially affected by emissions from a source applying for a permit required under this part.

(July 14, 1955, c. 360, Title I, § 165, as added Aug. 7, 1977, Pub.L. 95–95, Title I, § 127(a), 91 Stat. 735, and amended Nov. 16, 1977, Pub.L. 95–190, § 14(a)(44)–(51), 91 Stat. 1402.)

### HISTORICAL AND STATUTORY NOTES

**Effective and Applicability Provisions**

1977 Acts

Section effective Aug. 7, 1977, except as otherwise expressly provided, see section 406(d) of Pub.L. 95–95, set out as a note under section 7401 of this title.

## § 7476. Other pollutants

**[CAA § 166]**

**(a) Hydrocarbons, carbon monoxide, photochemical oxidants, and nitrogen oxides**

In the case of the pollutants hydrocarbons, carbon monoxide, photochemical oxidants, and nitrogen oxides, the Administrator shall conduct a study and not later than two years after August 7, 1977, promulgate regulations to prevent the significant deterioration of air quality which would result from the emissions of such pollutants. In the case of pollutants for which national ambient air quality standards are promulgated after August 7, 1977, he shall promulgate such regulations not more than 2 years after the date of promulgation of such standards.

**(b) Effective date of regulations**

Regulations referred to in subsection (a) of this section shall become effective one year after the date of promulgation. Within 21 months after such date of promulgation such plan revision shall be submitted to the Administrator who shall approve or disapprove the plan within 25 months after such date or promulgation in the same manner as required under section 7410 of this title.

**(c) Contents of regulations**

Such regulations shall provide specific numerical measures against which permit applications may be evaluated, a framework for stimulating improved control technology, protection of air quality values, and fulfill the goals and purposes set forth in section 7401 and section 7470 of this title.

**(d) Specific measures to fulfill goals and purposes**

The regulations of the Administrator under subsection (a) of this section shall provide specific measures at least as effective as the increments established in section 7473 of this title to fulfill such goals and purposes, and may contain air quality increments, emission density requirements, or other measures.

**(e) Area classification plan not required**

With respect to any air pollutant for which a national ambient air quality standard is established other than sulfur oxides or particulate matter, an area classification plan shall not be required under this section if the implementation plan adopted by the State and submitted for the Administrator's approval or promulgated by the Administrator under section 7410(c) of this title contains other provisions which when considered as a whole, the Administrator finds will carry out the purposes in section 7470 of this title at least as effectively as an area classification plan for such pollutant. Such other provisions referred to in the preceding sentence need not require the establishment of maximum allowable increases with respect to such pollutant for any area to which this section applies.

**(f) PM–10 increments**

The Administrator is authorized to substitute, for the maximum allowable increases in particulate matter specified in section 7473(b) of this title and section 7475(d)(2)(C)(iv) of this title, maximum allowable increases in particulate matter with an aerodynamic diameter smaller than or equal to 10 micrometers. Such substituted maximum allowable increases shall be of equal stringency in effect as those specified in the provisions for which they are substituted. Until the Administrator promulgates regulations under the authority of this subsection, the current maximum allowable increases in concentrations of particulate matter shall remain in effect.

(July 14, 1955, c. 360, Title I, § 166, as added Aug. 7, 1977, Pub.L. 95–95, Title I, § 127(a), 91 Stat. 739, and amended Nov. 15, 1990, Pub.L. 101–549, Title I, § 105(b), 104 Stat. 2462.)

### HISTORICAL AND STATUTORY NOTES

**Effective and Applicability Provisions**

1990 Acts

Amendment by Pub.L. 101–549 effective Nov. 15, 1990, except as otherwise provided, see section 711(b) of Pub.L. 101–549, set out as a note under section 7401 of this title.

1977 Acts

Section effective Aug. 7, 1977, except as otherwise expressly provided, see section 406(d) of Pub.L. 95–95, set out as a note under section 7401 of this title.

**Savings Provisions**

Suits, actions or proceedings commenced under this chapter as in effect prior to Nov. 15, 1990, not to abate by reason of the taking effect of amendments by Pub.L. 101–549, except as otherwise provided for, see section 711(a) of Pub.L. 101–549, set out as a note under section 7401 of this title.

## § 7477. Enforcement

**[CAA § 167]**

The Administrator shall, and a State may, take such measures, including issuance of an order, or seeking injunctive relief, as necessary to prevent the construction or modification of a major emitting facility which does not conform to the requirements of this part, or which is proposed to be constructed in any area designated pursuant to section 7407(d) of this title as attainment or unclassifiable and which is not subject to an implementation plan which meets the requirements of this part.

(July 14, 1955, c. 360, Title I, § 167, as added Aug. 7, 1977, Pub.L. 95–95, Title I, § 127(a), 91 Stat. 740, and amended Nov. 15, 1990, Pub.L. 101–549, Title I, § 110(3), Title VII, § 708, 104 Stat. 2470, 2684.)

### HISTORICAL AND STATUTORY NOTES

**Effective and Applicability Provisions**

1990 Acts

Amendment by Pub.L. 101–549 effective Nov. 15, 1990, except as otherwise provided, see section 711(b) of Pub.L. 101–549, set out as a note under section 7401 of this title.

1977 Acts

Section effective Aug. 7, 1977, except as otherwise expressly provided, see section 406(d) of Pub.L. 95–95, set out as a note under section 7401 of this title.

**Savings Provisions**

Suits, actions or proceedings commenced under this chapter as in effect prior to Nov. 15, 1990, not to abate by reason of the taking effect of amendments by Pub.L. 101–549, except as otherwise provided for, see section 711(a) of Pub.L. 101–549, set out as a note under section 7401 of this title.

## § 7478. Period before plan approval

**[CAA § 168]**

**(a) Existing regulations to remain in effect**

Until such time as an applicable implementation plan is in effect for any area, which plan meets the requirements of this part to prevent significant deterioration of air quality with respect to any air pollutant, applicable regulations under this chapter prior to August 7, 1977, shall remain in effect to prevent significant deterioration of air quality in any such area for any such pollutant except as otherwise provided in subsection (b) of this section.

**(b) Regulations deemed amended; construction commenced after June 1, 1975**

If any regulation in effect prior to August 7, 1977, to prevent significant deterioration of air quality would be inconsistent with the requirements of section 7472(a), section 7473(b) or section 7474(a) of this title, then such regulations shall be deemed amended so as to conform with such requirements. In the case of a facility on which construction was commenced (in accordance with the definition of "commenced" in section 7479(2) of this title) after June 1, 1975, and prior to August 7, 1977, the review and permitting of such facility shall be in accordance with the regulations for the prevention of significant deterioration in effect prior to August 7, 1977.

(July 14, 1955, c. 360, Title I, § 168, as added Aug. 7, 1977, Pub.L. 95–95, Title I, § 127(a), 91 Stat. 740, and amended Nov. 16, 1977, Pub.L. 95–190, § 14(a)(52), 91 Stat. 1402.)

### HISTORICAL AND STATUTORY NOTES

**Effective and Applicability Provisions**

1977 Acts

Section effective Aug. 7, 1977, except as otherwise expressly provided, see section 406(d) of Pub.L. 95–95, set out as a note under section 7401 of this title.

## § 7479. Definitions

[CAA § 169]

For purposes of this part—

(1) The term "major emitting facility" means any of the following stationary sources of air pollutants which emit, or have the potential to emit, one hundred tons per year or more of any air pollutant from the following types of stationary sources: fossil-fuel fired steam electric plants of more than two hundred and fifty million British thermal units per hour heat input, coal cleaning plants (thermal dryers), kraft pulp mills, Portland Cement plants, primary zinc smelters, iron and steel mill plants, primary aluminum ore reduction plants, primary copper smelters, municipal incinerators capable of charging more than fifty tons of refuse per day, hydrofluoric, sulfuric, and nitric acid plants, petroleum refineries, lime plants, phosphate rock processing plants, coke oven batteries, sulfur recovery plants, carbon black plants (furnace process), primary lead smelters, fuel conversion plants, sintering plants, secondary metal production facilities, chemical process plants, fossil-fuel boilers of more than two hundred and fifty million British thermal units per hour heat input, petroleum storage and transfer facilities with a capacity exceeding three hundred thousand barrels, taconite ore processing facilities, glass fiber processing plants, charcoal production facilities. Such term also includes any other source with the potential to emit two hundred and fifty tons per year or more of any air pollutant. This term shall not include new or modified facilities which are nonprofit health or education institutions which have been exempted by the State.

(2)(A) The term "commenced" as applied to construction of a major emitting facility means that the owner or operator has obtained all necessary preconstruction approvals or permits required by Federal, State, or local air pollution emissions and air quality laws or regulations and either has (i) begun, or caused to begin, a continuous program of physical on-site construction of the facility or (ii) entered into binding agreements or contractual obligations, which cannot be canceled or modified without substantial loss to the owner or operator, to undertake a program of construction of the facility to be completed within a reasonable time.

(B) The term "necessary preconstruction approvals or permits" means those permits or approvals, required by the permitting authority as a precondition to undertaking any activity under clauses (i) or (ii) of subparagraph (A) of this paragraph.

(C) The term "construction" when used in connection with any source or facility, includes the modification (as defined in section 7411(a) of this title) of any source or facility.

(3) The term "best available control technology" means an emission limitation based on the maximum degree of reduction of each pollutant subject to regulation under this chapter emitted from or which results from any major emitting facility, which the permitting authority, on a case-by-case basis, taking into account energy, environmental, and economic impacts and other costs, determines is achievable for such facility through application of production processes and available methods, systems, and techniques, including fuel cleaning, clean fuels, or treatment or innovative fuel combustion techniques for control of each such pollutant. In no event shall application of "best available control technology" result in emissions of any pollutants which will exceed the emissions allowed by any applicable standard established pursuant to section 7411 or 7412 of this title. Emissions from any source utilizing clean fuels, or any other means, to comply with this paragraph shall not be allowed to increase above levels that would have been required under this paragraph as it existed prior to November 15, 1990.

(4) The term "baseline concentration" means, with respect to a pollutant, the ambient concentration levels which exist at the time of the first application for a permit in an area subject to this part, based on air quality data available in the Environmental Protection Agency or a State air pollution control agency and on such monitoring data as the permit applicant is required to submit. Such ambient concentration levels shall take into account all projected emissions in, or which may affect, such area from any major emitting facility on which construction commenced prior to January 6, 1975, but which has not begun operation by the date of the baseline air quality concentration determination. Emissions of sulfur oxides and particulate matter from any major emitting facility on which construction commenced after January 6, 1975, shall not be included in the baseline and shall be counted against the maximum allowable increases in pollutant concentrations established under this part.

(July 14, 1955, c. 360, Title I, § 169, as added Aug. 7, 1977, Pub.L. 95–95, Title I, § 127(a), 91 Stat. 740, and amended Nov. 16, 1977, Pub.L. 95–190, § 14(a)(54), 91 Stat. 1402; Nov. 15, 1990, Pub.L. 101–549, Title III, § 305(b), Title IV, § 403(d), 104 Stat. 2583, 2631.)

HISTORICAL AND STATUTORY NOTES

**Effective and Applicability Provisions**

1990 Acts

Amendment by Pub.L. 101–549 effective Nov. 15, 1990, except as otherwise provided, see section 711(b) of Pub.L. 101–549, set out as a note under section 7401 of this title.

1977 Acts

Section effective Aug. 7, 1977, except as otherwise expressly provided, see section 406(d) of Pub.L. 95–95, set out as a note under section 7401 of this title.

**Savings Provisions**

Suits, actions or proceedings commenced under this chapter as in effect prior to Nov. 15, 1990, not to abate by reason of the taking effect of amendments by Pub.L. 101–549, except as otherwise provided for, see section 711(a) of Pub.L. 101–549, set out as a note under section 7401 of this title.

**Study of Major Emitting Facilities With Potential of Emitting 250 Tons Per Year**

Section 127(b) of Pub.L. 95–95 provided that within 1 year after Aug. 7, 1977, the Administrator report to the Congress on the consequences of that portion of the definition of "major emitting facility" under this subpart which applies to facilities with the potential to emit 250 hundred tons per year or more.

*Subpart II—Visibility Protection*

HISTORICAL AND STATUTORY NOTES

**Codifications**

As originally enacted, subpart II of part C of subchapter I of this chapter was added following section 7478 of this title. Pub.L. 95–190, § 14(a)(53), Nov. 16, 1977, 91 Stat. 1402, struck out subpart II and inserted such subpart following section 7479 of this title.

## § 7491. Visibility protection for Federal class I areas

[CAA § 169A]

**(a) Impairment of visibility; list of areas; study and report**

(1) Congress hereby declares as a national goal the prevention of any future, and the remedying of any existing, impairment of visibility in mandatory class I Federal areas which impairment results from manmade air pollution.

(2) Not later than six months after August 7, 1977, the Secretary of the Interior in consultation with other Federal land managers shall review all mandatory class I Federal areas and identify those where visibility is an important value of the area. From time to time the Secretary of the Interior may revise such identifications. Not later than one year after August 7, 1977, the Administrator shall, after consultation with the Secretary of the Interior, promulgate a list of mandatory class I Federal areas in which he determines visibility is an important value.

(3) Not later than eighteen months after August 7, 1977, the Administrator shall complete a study and report to Congress on available methods for implementing the national goal set forth in paragraph (1). Such report shall include recommendations for—

(A) methods for identifying, characterizing, determining, quantifying, and measuring visibility impairment in Federal areas referred to in paragraph (1), and

(B) modeling techniques (or other methods) for determining the extent to which manmade air pollution may reasonably be anticipated to cause or contribute to such impairment, and

(C) methods for preventing and remedying such manmade air pollution and resulting visibility impairment.

Such report shall also identify the classes or categories of sources and the types of air pollutants which, alone or in conjunction with other sources or pollutants, may reasonably be anticipated to cause or contribute significantly to impairment of visibility.

(4) Not later than twenty-four months after August 7, 1977, and after notice and public hearing, the Administrator shall promulgate regulations to assure (A) reasonable progress toward meeting the national goal specified in paragraph (1), and (B) compliance with the requirements of this section.

**(b) Regulations**

Regulations under subsection (a)(4) of this section shall—

(1) provide guidelines to the States, taking into account the recommendations under subsection (a)(3) of this section on appropriate techniques and methods for implementing this section (as provided in subparagraphs (A) through (C) of such subsection (a)(3) ), and

(2) require each applicable implementation plan for a State in which any area listed by the Administrator under subsection (a)(2) of this section is located (or for a State the emissions from which may reasonably be anticipated to cause or contribute to any impairment of visibility in any such area) to contain such emission limits, schedules of compliance and other measures as may be necessary to make reasonable progress toward meeting the national goal specified in subsection (a) of this section, including—

(A) except as otherwise provided pursuant to subsection (c) of this section, a requirement that each major stationary source which is in existence on August 7, 1977, but which has not been in operation for more than fifteen years as of such date, and which, as determined by the State (or the Administrator in the case of a plan promulgated under section 7410(c) of this title) emits any air pollutant which may reasonably be anticipated to cause or contribute to any impairment of visibility in any such area, shall procure, install, and operate, as expeditiously as practicable (and maintain thereafter) the best available retrofit technology, as determined by the State (or the Administrator in the case of a plan promulgated under section 7410(c) of this title) for controlling emissions from such source for the purpose of eliminating or reducing any such impairment, and

(B) a long-term (ten to fifteen years) strategy for making reasonable progress toward meeting the national goal specified in subsection (a) of this section.

In the case of a fossil-fuel fired generating powerplant having a total generating capacity in excess of 750 megawatts, the emission limitations required under this paragraph shall be determined pursuant to guidelines, promulgated by the Administrator under paragraph (1).

**(c) Exemptions**

(1) The Administrator may, by rule, after notice and opportunity for public hearing, exempt any major stationary source from the requirement of subsection (b)(2)(A) of this section, upon his determination that such source does not or will not, by itself or in combination with other sources, emit any air pollutant which may reasonably be anticipated to cause or contribute to a significant impairment of visibility in any mandatory class I Federal area.

(2) Paragraph (1) of this subsection shall not be applicable to any fossil-fuel fired powerplant with total design capacity of 750 megawatts or more, unless the owner or operator of any such plant demonstrates to the satisfaction of the Administrator that such powerplant is located at such distance from all areas listed by the Administrator under subsection (a)(2) of this section that such powerplant does not or will not, by itself or in combination with other sources, emit any air pollutant which may reasonably be anticipated to cause or contribute to significant impairment of visibility in any such area.

(3) An exemption under this subsection shall be effective only upon concurrence by the appropriate Federal land manager or managers with the Administrator's determination under this subsection.

**(d) Consultations with appropriate Federal land managers**

Before holding the public hearing on the proposed revision of an applicable implementation plan to meet the requirements of this section, the State (or the Administrator, in the case of a plan promulgated under section 7410(c) of this title) shall consult in person with the appropriate Federal land manager or managers and shall include a summary of the conclusions and recommendations of the Federal land managers in the notice to the public.

**(e) Buffer zones**

In promulgating regulations under this section, the Administrator shall not require the use of any automatic or uniform buffer zone or zones.

**(f) Nondiscretionary duty**

For purposes of section 7604(a)(2) of this title, the meeting of the national goal specified in subsection (a)(1) of this section by any specific date or dates shall not be considered a "nondiscretionary duty" of the Administrator.

**(g) Definitions**

For the purpose of this section—

(1) in determining reasonable progress there shall be taken into consideration the costs of compliance, the time necessary for compliance, and the energy and nonair quality environmental impacts of compliance, and the remaining useful life of any existing source subject to such requirements;

(2) in determining best available retrofit technology the State (or the Administrator in determining emission limitations which reflect such technology) shall take into consideration the costs of compliance, the energy and nonair quality environmental impacts of compliance, any existing pollution control technology in use at the source, the remaining useful life of the source, and the degree of improvement in visibility which may reasonably be anticipated to result from the use of such technology;

(3) the term "manmade air pollution" means air pollution which results directly or indirectly from human activities;

(4) the term "as expeditiously as practicable" means as expeditiously as practicable but in no event later than five years after the date of approval of a plan revision under this section (or the date of promulgation of such a plan revision in the case of action by the Administrator under section 7410(c) of this title for purposes of this section);

(5) the term "mandatory class I Federal areas" means Federal areas which may not be designated as other than class I under this part;

(6) the terms "visibility impairment" and "impairment of visibility" shall include reduction in visual range and atmospheric discoloration; and

(7) the term "major stationary source" means the following types of stationary sources with the potential to emit 250 tons or more of any pollutant: fossil-fuel fired steam electric plants of more than 250 million British thermal units per hour heat input, coal cleaning plants (thermal dryers), kraft pulp mills, Portland Cement plants, primary zinc

smelters, iron and steel mill plants, primary aluminum ore reduction plants, primary copper smelters, municipal incinerators capable of charging more than 250 tons of refuse per day, hydrofluoric, sulfuric, and nitric acid plants, petroleum refineries, lime plants, phosphate rock processing plants, coke oven batteries, sulfur recovery plants, carbon black plants (furnace process), primary lead smelters, fuel conversion plants, sintering plants, secondary metal production facilities, chemical process plants, fossil-fuel boilers of more than 250 million British thermal units per hour heat input, petroleum storage and transfer facilities with a capacity exceeding 300,000 barrels, taconite ore processing facilities, glass fiber processing plants, charcoal production facilities.

(July 14, 1955, c. 360, Title I, § 169A, as added Aug. 7, 1977, Pub.L. 95–95, Title I, § 128, 91 Stat. 742.)

### HISTORICAL AND STATUTORY NOTES

**Effective and Applicability Provisions**

1977 Acts

Section effective Aug. 7, 1977, except as otherwise expressly provided, see section 406(d) of Pub.L. 95–95, set out as a note under section 7401 of this title.

## § 7492. Visibility

**[CAA § 169B]**

### (a) Studies

(1) The Administrator, in conjunction with the National Park Service and other appropriate Federal agencies, shall conduct research to identify and evaluate sources and source regions of both visibility impairment and regions that provide predominantly clean air in class I areas. A total of $8,000,000 per year for 5 years is authorized to be appropriated for the Environmental Protection Agency and the other Federal agencies to conduct this research. The research shall include—

(A) expansion of current visibility related monitoring in class I areas;

(B) assessment of current sources of visibility impairing pollution and clean air corridors;

(C) adaptation of regional air quality models for the assessment of visibility;

(D) studies of atmospheric chemistry and physics of visibility.

(2) Based on the findings available from the research required in subsection (a)(1) of this section as well as other available scientific and technical data, studies, and other available information pertaining to visibility source-receptor relationships, the Administrator shall conduct an assessment and evaluation that identifies, to the extent possible, sources and source regions of visibility impairment including natural sources as well as source regions of clear air for class I areas. The Administrator shall produce interim findings from this study within 3 years after November 15, 1990.

### (b) Impacts of other provisions

Within 24 months after November 15, 1990, the Administrator shall conduct an assessment of the progress and improvements in visibility in class I areas that are likely to result from the implementation of the provisions of the Clean Air Act Amendments of 1990 other than the provisions of this section. Every 5 years thereafter the Administrator shall conduct an assessment of actual progress and improvement in visibility in class I areas. The Administrator shall prepare a written report on each assessment and transmit copies of these reports to the appropriate committees of Congress.

### (c) Establishment of visibility transport regions and commissions

#### (1) Authority to establish visibility transport regions

Whenever, upon the Administrator's motion or by petition from the Governors of at least two affected States, the Administrator has reason to believe that the current or projected interstate transport of air pollutants from one or more States contributes significantly to visibility impairment in class I areas located in the affected States, the Administrator may establish a transport region for such pollutants that includes such States. The Administrator, upon the Administrator's own motion or upon petition from the Governor of any affected State, or upon the recommendations of a transport commission established under subsection (b) of this section[1] may—

(A) add any State or portion of a State to a visibility transport region when the Administrator determines that the interstate transport of air pollutants from such State significantly contributes to visibility impairment in a class I area located within the transport region, or

(B) remove any State or portion of a State from the region whenever the Administrator has reason to believe that the control of emissions in that State or portion of the State pursuant to this section will not significantly contribute to the protection or enhancement of visibility in any class I area in the region.

#### (2) Visibility transport commissions

Whenever the Administrator establishes a transport region under subsection (c)(1) of this section, the Administrator shall establish a transport commission comprised of (as a minimum) each of the following members:

(A) the Governor of each State in the Visibility Transport Region, or the Governor's designee;

(B) The[2] Administrator or the Administrator's designee; and

(C) A[2] representative of each Federal agency charged with the direct management of each class I area or areas within the Visibility Transport Region.

**(3) Ex officio members**

All representatives of the Federal Government shall be ex officio members.

**(4) Federal Advisory Committee Act**

The visibility transport commissions shall be exempt from the requirements of the Federal Advisory Committee Act [5 U.S.C.A. App.].

**(d) Duties of visibility transport commissions**

A Visibility Transport Commission—

(1) shall assess the scientific and technical data, studies, and other currently available information, including studies conducted pursuant to subsection (a)(1) of this section, pertaining to adverse impacts on visibility from potential or projected growth in emissions from sources located in the Visibility Transport Region; and

(2) shall, within 4 years of establishment, issue a report to the Administrator recommending what measures, if any, should be taken under this chapter to remedy such adverse impacts. The report required by this subsection shall address at least the following measures:

(A) the establishment of clean air corridors, in which additional restrictions on increases in emissions may be appropriate to protect visibility in affected class I areas;

(B) the imposition of the requirements of part D of this subchapter affecting the construction of new major stationary sources or major modifications to existing sources in such clean air corridors specifically including the alternative siting analysis provisions of section 7503(a)(5) of this title; and

(C) the promulgation of regulations under section 7491 of this title to address long range strategies for addressing regional haze which impairs visibility in affected class I areas.

**(e) Duties of Administrator**

(1) The Administrator shall, taking into account the studies pursuant to subsection (a)(1) of this section and the reports pursuant to subsection (d)(2) of this section and any other relevant information, within eighteen months of receipt of the report referred to in subsection (d)(2) of this section, carry out the Administrator's regulatory responsibilities under section 7491 of this title, including criteria for measuring "reasonable progress" toward the national goal.

(2) Any regulations promulgated under section 7491 of this title pursuant to this subsection shall require affected States to revise within 12 months their implementation plans under section 7410 of this title to contain such emission limits, schedules of compliance, and other measures as may be necessary to carry out regulations promulgated pursuant to this subsection.

**(f) Grand Canyon visibility transport commission**

The Administrator pursuant to subsection (c)(1) of this section shall, within 12 months, establish a visibility transport commission for the region affecting the visibility of the Grand Canyon National Park.

(July 14, 1955, c. 360, Title I, § 169B, as added Nov. 15, 1990, Pub.L. 101–549, Title VIII, § 816, 104 Stat. 2695.)

[1] So in original. Words "subsection (b) of this section" probably should be "paragraph (2)".

[2] So in original. Probably should not be capitalized.

### HISTORICAL AND STATUTORY NOTES

**References in Text**

The Clean Air Act Amendments of 1990, referred to in subsec. (b), probably means Pub.L. 101–549, Nov. 15, 1990, 104 Stat. 2399. For complete classification of this Act to the Code, see Short Title of 1990 Amendments note set out under section 7401 of this title and Tables.

The Federal Advisory Committee Act, referred to in subsec. (c)(4), is Pub.L. 92–463, Oct. 6, 1972, 86 Stat. 770, as amended, which is set out in Appendix 2 to Title 5, Government Organization and Employees.

**Effective and Applicability Provisions**

1990 Acts

Section to take effect Nov. 15, 1990, except as otherwise provided, see section 711(b) of Pub.L. 101–549, set out as a note under section 7401 of this title.

**Savings Provisions**

Suits, actions or proceedings commenced under this chapter as in effect prior to Nov. 15, 1990, not to abate by reason of the taking effect of amendments by Pub.L. 101–549, except as otherwise provided for, see section 711(a) of Pub.L. 101–549, set out as a note under section 7401 of this title.

## PART D—PLAN REQUIREMENTS FOR NONATTAINMENT AREAS

### *Subpart 1—Nonattainment Areas in General*

## § 7501. Definitions

[CAA § 171]

For the purpose of this part—

**(1) Reasonable further progress**

The term "reasonable further progress" means such annual incremental reductions in emissions of the relevant air pollutant as are required by this part or may reasonably be required by the Administrator for the purpose of ensuring attainment of the applicable national ambient air quality standard by the applicable date.

**(2) Nonattainment area**

The term "nonattainment area" means, for any air pollutant, an area which is designated "nonattainment" with respect to that pollutant within the meaning of section 7407(d) of this title.

**(3) Lowest achievable emission rate**

The term "lowest achievable emission rate" means for any source, that rate of emissions which reflects—

(A) the most stringent emission limitation which is contained in the implementation plan of any State for such class or category of source, unless the owner or operator of the proposed source demonstrates that such limitations are not achievable, or

(B) the most stringent emission limitation which is achieved in practice by such class or category of source, whichever is more stringent.

In no event shall the application of this term permit a proposed new or modified source to emit any pollutant in excess of the amount allowable under applicable new source standards of performance.

**(4) Modifications; modified**

The terms "modifications" and "modified" mean the same as the term "modification" as used in section 7411(a)(4) of this title.

(July 14, 1955, c. 360, Title I, § 171, as added Aug. 7, 1977, Pub.L. 95–95, Title I, § 129(b), 91 Stat. 746, and amended Nov. 15, 1990, Pub.L. 101–549, Title I, § 102(a)(2), 104 Stat. 2412.)

### HISTORICAL AND STATUTORY NOTES

**Effective and Applicability Provisions**

1990 Acts

Amendment by Pub.L. 101–549 effective Nov. 15, 1990, except as otherwise provided, see section 711(b) of Pub.L. 101–549, set out as a note under section 7401 of this title.

1977 Acts

Section effective Aug. 7, 1977, except as otherwise expressly provided, see section 406(d) of Pub.L. 95–95, set out as a note under section 7401 of this title.

**Savings Provisions**

Suits, actions or proceedings commenced under this chapter as in effect prior to Nov. 15, 1990, not to abate by reason of the taking effect of amendments by Pub.L. 101–549, except as otherwise provided for, see section 711(a) of Pub.L. 101–549, set out as a note under section 7401 of this title.

## § 7502. Nonattainment plan provisions in general

[CAA § 172]

**(a) Classifications and attainment dates**

**(1) Classifications**

(A) On or after the date the Administrator promulgates the designation of an area as a nonattainment area pursuant to section 7407(d) of this title with respect to any national ambient air quality standard (or any revised standard, including a revision of any standard in effect on November 15, 1990), the Administrator may classify the area for the purpose of applying an attainment date pursuant to paragraph (2), and for other purposes. In determining the appropriate classification, if any, for a nonattainment area, the Administrator may consider such factors as the severity of nonattainment in such area and the availability and feasibility of the pollution control measures that the Administrator believes may be necessary to provide for attainment of such standard in such area.

(B) The Administrator shall publish a notice in the Federal Register announcing each classification under subparagraph (A), except the Administrator shall provide an opportunity for at least 30 days for written comment. Such classification shall not be subject to the provisions of sections 553 through 557 of Title 5 (concerning notice and comment) and shall not be subject to judicial review until the Administrator takes final action under subsection (k) or (*l*) of section 7410 of this title (concerning action on plan submissions) or section 7509 of this title (concerning sanctions) with respect to any plan submissions required by virtue of such classification.

(C) This paragraph shall not apply with respect to nonattainment areas for which classifications are specifically provided under other provisions of this part.

**(2) Attainment dates for nonattainment areas**

(A) The attainment date for an area designated nonattainment with respect to a national primary ambient air quality standard shall be the date by which attainment can be achieved as expeditiously as practicable, but no later than 5 years from the date such area was designated nonattainment under section 7407(d) of this title, except that the Administrator may extend the attainment date to the extent the Administrator determines appropriate, for a period no greater than 10 years from the date of designation as nonattainment, considering the severity of nonattainment and the availability and feasibility of pollution control measures.

(B) The attainment date for an area designated nonattainment with respect to a secondary national ambient air quality standard shall be the date by which attainment can be achieved as expeditiously as practicable after the date such area was designated nonattainment under section 7407(d) of this title.

(C) Upon application by any State, the Administrator may extend for 1 additional year (hereinafter referred to as the "Extension Year") the attainment date determined by the Administrator under subparagraph (A) or (B) if—

(i) the State has complied with all requirements and commitments pertaining to the area in the applicable implementation plan, and

(ii) in accordance with guidance published by the Administrator, no more than a minimal number of exceedances of the relevant national ambient air quality standard has occurred in the area in the year preceding the Extension Year.

No more than 2 one-year extensions may be issued under this subparagraph for a single nonattainment area.

(D) This paragraph shall not apply with respect to nonattainment areas for which attainment dates are specifically provided under other provisions of this part.

**(b) Schedule for plan submissions**

At the time the Administrator promulgates the designation of an area as nonattainment with respect to a national ambient air quality standard under section 7407(d) of this title, the Administrator shall establish a schedule according to which the State containing such area shall submit a plan or plan revision (including the plan items) meeting the applicable requirements of subsection (c) of this section and section 7410(a)(2) of this title. Such schedule shall at a minimum, include a date or dates, extending no later than 3 years from the date of the nonattainment designation, for the submission of a plan or plan revision (including the plan items) meeting the applicable requirements of subsection (c) of this section and section 7410(a)(2) of this title.

**(c) Nonattainment plan provisions**

The plan provisions (including plan items) required to be submitted under this part shall comply with each of the following:

**(1) In general**

Such plan provisions shall provide for the implementation of all reasonably available control measures as expeditiously as practicable (including such reductions in emissions from existing sources in the area as may be obtained through the adoption, at a minimum, of reasonably available control technology) and shall provide for attainment of the national primary ambient air quality standards.

**(2) RFP**

Such plan provisions shall require reasonable further progress.

**(3) Inventory**

Such plan provisions shall include a comprehensive, accurate, current inventory of actual emissions from all sources of the relevant pollutant or pollutants in such area, including such periodic revisions as the Administrator may determine necessary to assure that the requirements of this part are met.

**(4) Identification and quantification**

Such plan provisions shall expressly identify and quantify the emissions, if any, of any such pollutant or pollutants which will be allowed, in accordance with section 7503(a)(1)(B) of this title, from the construction and operation of major new or modified stationary sources in each such area. The plan shall demonstrate to the satisfaction of the Administrator that the emissions quantified for this purpose will be consistent with the achievement of reasonable further progress and will not interfere with attainment of the applicable national ambient air quality standard by the applicable attainment date.

**(5) Permits for new and modified major stationary sources**

Such plan provisions shall require permits for the construction and operation of new or modified major stationary sources anywhere in the nonattainment area, in accordance with section 7503 of this title.

**(6) Other measures**

Such plan provisions shall include enforceable emission limitations, and such other control measures, means or techniques (including economic incentives such as fees, marketable permits, and auctions of emission rights), as well as schedules and timetables for compliance, as may be necessary or appropriate to provide for attainment of such standard in such area by the applicable attainment date specified in this part.

**(7) Compliance with section 7410(a)(2)**

Such plan provisions shall also meet the applicable provisions of section 7410(a)(2) of this title.

**(8) Equivalent techniques**

Upon application by any State, the Administrator may allow the use of equivalent modeling, emission inventory, and planning procedures, unless the Administrator determines that the proposed techniques are, in the aggregate, less effective than the methods specified by the Administrator.

**(9) Contingency measures**

Such plan shall provide for the implementation of specific measures to be undertaken if the area fails to make reasonable further progress, or to attain the national primary ambient air quality standard by the attainment date applicable under this part. Such measures shall be included in the plan revision as contingency measures to take effect in any such case without further action by the State or the Administrator.

**(d) Plan revisions required in response to finding of plan inadequacy**

Any plan revision for a nonattainment area which is required to be submitted in response to a finding by the Administrator pursuant to section 7410(k)(5) of this title (relating to calls for plan revisions) must correct the plan deficiency (or deficiencies) specified by the Administrator and meet all other applicable plan requirements of section 7410 of this title and this part. The Administrator may reasonably adjust the dates otherwise applicable under such requirements to such revision (except for attainment dates that have not yet elapsed), to the extent necessary to achieve a consistent application of such requirements. In order to facilitate submittal by the States of adequate and approvable plans consistent with the applicable requirements of this chapter, the Administrator shall, as appropriate and from time to time, issue written guidelines, interpretations, and information to the States which shall be available to the public, taking into consideration any such guidelines, interpretations, or information provided before November 15, 1990.

**(e) Future modification of standard**

If the Administrator relaxes a national primary ambient air quality standard after November 15, 1990, the Administrator shall, within 12 months after the relaxation, promulgate requirements applicable to all areas which have not attained that standard as of the date of such relaxation. Such requirements shall provide for controls which are not less stringent than the controls applicable to areas designated nonattainment before such relaxation.

(July 14, 1955, c. 360, Title I, § 172, as added Aug. 7, 1977, Pub.L. 95–95, Title I, § 129(b), 91 Stat. 746, and amended Nov. 16, 1977, Pub.L. 95–190, § 14(a)(55), (56), 91 Stat. 1402; Nov. 15, 1990, Pub.L. 101–549, Title I, § 102(b), 104 Stat. 2412.)

## HISTORICAL AND STATUTORY NOTES

**Effective and Applicability Provisions**

1990 Acts

Amendment by Pub.L. 101–549 effective Nov. 15, 1990, except as otherwise provided, see section 711(b) of Pub.L. 101–549, set out as a note under section 7401 of this title.

1977 Acts

Section effective Aug. 7, 1977, except as otherwise expressly provided, see section 406(d) of Pub.L. 95–95, set out as a note under section 7401 of this title.

**Savings Provisions**

Suits, actions or proceedings commenced under this chapter as in effect prior to Nov. 15, 1990, not to abate by reason of the taking effect of amendments by Pub.L. 101–549, except as otherwise provided for, see section 711(a) of Pub.L. 101–549, set out as a note under section 7401 of this title.

**Nonattainment Areas**

Section 129(a) of Pub.L. 95–95, as amended Pub.L. 95–190, § 14(b)(2), (3), Nov. 16, 1977, 91 Stat. 1404, provided that:

"(1) Before July 1, 1979, the interpretative regulation of the Administrator of the Environmental Protection Agency published in 41 Federal Register 55524–30, December 21, 1976, as may be modified by rule of the Administrator, shall apply except that the baseline to be used for determination of appropriate emission offsets under such regulation shall be the applicable implementation plan of the State in effect at the time of application for a permit by a proposed major stationary source (within the meaning of section 302 of the Clean Air Act) [section 7602 of this title].

"(2) Before July 1, 1979, the requirements of the regulation referred to in paragraph (1) shall be waived by the Administrator with respect to any pollutant if he determines that the State has—

"(A) an inventory of emissions of the applicable pollutant for each nonattainment area (as defined in section 171 of the Clean Air Act) [section 7501 of this title] that identifies the type, quantity, and source of such pollutant so as to provide information sufficient to demonstrate that the requirements of subparagraph (C) are being met;

"(B) an enforceable permit program which—

"(i) requires new or modified major stationary sources to meet emission limitations at least as stringent as required under the permit requirements referred to in paragraphs (2) and (3) of section 173 of the Clean Air Act [section 7503 of this title] (relating to lowest achievable emission rate and compliance by other sources) and which assures compliance with the annual reduction requirements of subparagraph (C); and

"(ii) requires existing sources to achieve such reduction in emissions in the area as may be obtained through the adoption, at a minimum of reasonably available control technology, and

"(C) a program which requires reductions in total allowable emissions in the area prior to July 1, 1979, so as to provide for the same level of emission reduction as would result from the application of the regulation referred to in paragraph (1).

The Administrator shall terminate such waiver if in his judgment the reduction in emissions actually being attained is less than the reduction on which the waiver was conditioned pursuant to subparagraph (C), or if the Administrator determines that the State is no longer in compliance with any requirement of this paragraph. Upon application by the State, the Administrator may reinstate a waiver terminated under the preceding sentence if he is satisfied that such State is in compliance with all requirements of this subsection.

"(3) Operating permits may be issued to those applicants who were properly granted construction permits, in accordance with the law and applicable regulations in effect at the time granted, for construction of a new or modified source in areas exceeding national primary air quality standards on or before the date of the enactment of this Act [Aug. 7, 1977] if such construction permits were granted prior to the date of the enactment of this Act and the person issued any such permit is able to demonstrate that the emissions from the source will be within the limitations set forth in such construction permit."

**State Implementation Plan Revision**

Section 129(c) of Pub.L. 95–95, as amended Pub.L. 95–190, § 14(b)(4), Nov. 16, 1977, 91 Stat. 1405, provided that: "Notwithstanding the requirements of section 406(d)(2) [set out as an Effective and Applicability Provisions of 1977 Amendments note under section 7401 of this title] (relating to date required for submission of certain implementation plan revisions), for purposes of section 110(a)(2) of the Clean Air Act [section 7410(a)(2) of this title] each State in which there is any nonattainment area (as defined in part D of Title I of the Clean Air Act) [this part] shall adopt and submit an implementation plan revision which meets the requirements of section 110(a)(2)(I) [section 7410(a)(2)(I) of this title] and part D of Title I of the Clean Air Act [this part] not later than January 1, 1979. In the case of any State for which a plan revision adopted and submitted before such date has made the demonstration required under section 172(a)(2) of the Clean Air Act [subsec. (a)(2) of this section] (respecting impossibility of attainment before 1983), such State shall adopt and submit to the Administrator a plan revision before July 1, 1982, which meets the requirements of section 172(b) and (c) of such Act [subsecs. (b) and (c) of this section]."

## § 7503. Permit requirements

[CAA § 173]

### (a) In general

The permit program required by section 7502(b)(6) of this title shall provide that permits to construct and operate may be issued if—

(1) in accordance with regulations issued by the Administrator for the determination of baseline emissions in a manner consistent with the assumptions underlying the applicable implementation plan approved under section 7410 of this title and this part, the permitting agency determines that—

(A) by the time the source is to commence operation, sufficient offsetting emissions reductions have been obtained, such that total allowable emissions from existing sources in the region, from new or modified sources which are not major emitting facilities, and from the proposed source will be sufficiently less than total emissions from existing sources (as determined in accordance with the regulations under this paragraph) prior to the application for such permit to construct or modify so as to represent (when considered together with the plan provisions required under section 7502 of this title) reasonable further progress (as defined in section 7501 of this title); or

(B) in the case of a new or modified major stationary source which is located in a zone (within the nonattainment area) identified by the Administrator, in consultation with the Secretary of Housing and Urban Development, as a zone to which economic development should be targeted, that emissions of such pollutant resulting from the proposed new or modified major stationary source will not cause or contribute to emissions levels which exceed the allowance permitted for such pollutant for such area from new or modified major stationary sources under section 7502(c) of this title;

(2) the proposed source is required to comply with the lowest achievable emission rate;

(3) the owner or operator of the proposed new or modified source has demonstrated that all major stationary sources owned or operated by such person (or by any entity controlling, controlled by, or under common control with such person) in such State are subject to emission limitations and are in compliance, or on a schedule for compliance, with all applicable emission limitations and standards under this chapter; and [1]

(4) the Administrator has not determined that the applicable implementation plan is not being adequately implemented for the nonattainment area in which the proposed source is to be constructed or modified in accordance with the requirements of this part; and

(5) an analysis of alternative sites, sizes, production processes, and environmental control techniques for such proposed source demonstrates that benefits of the proposed source significantly outweigh the environmental and social costs imposed as a result of its location, construction, or modification.

Any emission reductions required as a precondition of the issuance of a permit under paragraph (1) shall be federally enforceable before such permit may be issued.

### (b) Prohibition on use of old growth allowances

Any growth allowance included in an applicable implementation plan to meet the requirements of section 7502(b)(5) of this title (as in effect immediately before November 15, 1990) shall not be valid for use in any area that received or receives a notice under section 7410(a)(2)(H)(ii) of this title (as in effect immediately before November 15, 1990) or under section 7410(k)(1) of this title that its applicable implementation plan containing such allowance is substantially inadequate.

### (c) Offsets

(1) The owner or operator of a new or modified major stationary source may comply with any offset requirement in effect under this part for increased emissions of any air pollutant only by obtaining emission reductions of such air pollutant from the same source or other sources in the same nonattainment area, except that the State may allow the owner or operator of a source to obtain such emission reductions in another nonattainment area if (A) the other area has an equal or higher nonattainment classification than the area in which the source is located and (B) emissions from such other area contribute to a violation of the national ambient air quality standard in the nonattainment area in which the source is located. Such emission reductions shall be, by the time a new or modified source commences operation, in effect and enforceable and shall assure that the total tonnage of increased emissions of the air pollutant from the new or modified source shall be offset by an equal or greater reduction, as applicable, in the actual emissions of such air pollutant from the same or other sources in the area.

(2) Emission reductions otherwise required by this chapter shall not be creditable as emissions reductions for purposes of any such offset requirement. Incidental emission reductions which are not otherwise required by this chapter shall be creditable as emission reductions for such purposes if such emission reductions meet the requirements of paragraph (1).

**(d) Control technology information**

The State shall provide that control technology information from permits issued under this section will be promptly submitted to the Administrator for purposes of making such information available through the RACT/BACT/LAER clearinghouse to other States and to the general public.

**(e) Rocket engines or motors**

The permitting authority of a State shall allow a source to offset by alternative or innovative means emission increases from rocket engine and motor firing, and cleaning related to such firing, at an existing or modified major source that tests rocket engines or motors under the following conditions:

(1) Any modification proposed is solely for the purpose of expanding the testing of rocket engines or motors at an existing source that is permitted to test such engines on November 15, 1990.

(2) The source demonstrates to the satisfaction of the permitting authority of the State that it has used all reasonable means to obtain and utilize offsets, as determined on an annual basis, for the emissions increases beyond allowable levels, that all available offsets are being used, and that sufficient offsets are not available to the source.

(3) The source has obtained a written finding from the Department of Defense, Department of Transportation, National Aeronautics and Space Administration or other appropriate Federal agency, that the testing of rocket motors or engines at the facility is required for a program essential to the national security.

(4) The source will comply with an alternative measure, imposed by the permitting authority, designed to offset any emission increases beyond permitted levels not directly offset by the source. In lieu of imposing any alternative offset measures, the permitting authority may impose an emissions fee to be paid to such authority of a State which shall be an amount no greater than 1.5 times the average cost of stationary source control measures adopted in that area during the previous 3 years. The permitting authority shall utilize the fees in a manner that maximizes the emissions reductions in that area.

(July 14, 1955, c. 360, Title I, § 173, as added Aug. 7, 1977, Pub.L. 95–95, Title I, § 129(b), 91 Stat. 748, and amended Nov. 16, 1977, Pub.L. 95–190, § 14(a)(57), (58), 91 Stat. 1403; Nov. 15, 1990, Pub.L. 101–549, Title I, § 102(c), 104 Stat. 2415.)

[1] So in original. The word "and" probably should not appear.

## HISTORICAL AND STATUTORY NOTES

### References in Text

Section 7502(b) of this title, referred to in subsec. (a), was amended generally by Pub.L. 101–549, Title I, § 102(b), Nov. 15, 1990, 104 Stat. 2412, and, as so amended, does not contain a par. (6). See section 7502(c)(5) of this title.

### Effective and Applicability Provisions

1990 Acts

Amendment by Pub.L. 101–549 effective Nov. 15, 1990, except as otherwise provided, see section 711(b) of Pub.L. 101–549, set out as a note under section 7401 of this title.

1977 Acts

Section effective Aug. 7, 1977, except as otherwise expressly provided, see section 406(d) of Pub.L. 95–95, set out as a note under section 7401 of this title.

### Savings Provisions

Suits, actions or proceedings commenced under this chapter as in effect prior to Nov. 15, 1990, not to abate by reason of the taking effect of amendments by Pub.L. 101–549, except as otherwise provided for, see section 711(a) of Pub.L. 101–549, set out as a note under section 7401 of this title.

### Failure to Attain National Primary Ambient Air Quality Standards Under the Clean Air Act

Pub.L. 100–202, § 101(f), [Title II], Dec. 22, 1987, 101 Stat. 1329–199, provided that: "No restriction or prohibition on construction, permitting, or funding under sections 110(a)(2)(I) [section 7410(a)(2)(I) of this title], 173(4) [par. (4) of this section], 176(a) [former section 7506(a) of this title], 176(b) [former section 7506(b) of this title], or 316 [section 7616 of this title] of the Clean Air Act shall be imposed or take effect during the period prior to August 31, 1988, by reason of (1) the failure of any nonattainment area to attain the national primary ambient air quality standard under the Clean Air Act [this chapter] for photochemical oxidants (ozone) or carbon monoxide (or both) by December 31, 1987, (2) the failure of any State to adopt and submit to the Administrator of the Environmental Protection Agency an implementation plan that meets the requirements of part D of Title I of such Act [this part] and provides for attainment of such standards by December 31, 1987, (3) the failure of any State or designated local government to implement the applicable implementation plan, or (4) any combination of the foregoing. During such period and consistent with the preceding sentence, the issuance of a permit (including required offsets) under section 173 of such Act [this section] for the construction or modification of a source in a nonattainment area shall not be denied solely or partially by reason of the reference contained in section 171(*l*) of such Act [section 7501(1) of this title] to the applicable date established in section 172(a) [section 7502(a) of this title]. This subsection [probably means the first 3 sentences of this note] shall not apply to any restriction or prohibition in effect under sections 110(a)(2)(I), 173(4), 176(a), 176(b), or 316 of such Act prior to the enactment of this section [Dec. 22, 1987]. Prior to August 31, 1988, the Administrator of the Environmental Protection Agency shall evaluate air quality data and make determinations with respect to which areas throughout the nation have attained, or failed to attain, either or both of the national primary ambient air quality standards referred to in subsection (a) [probably means the first 3 sentences of this note] and shall take appropriate steps to designate those areas failing to attain either or both of such standards as nonattainment areas within the meaning of part D of Title I of the Clean Air Act."

## § 7504. Planning procedures

[CAA § 174]

### (a) In general

For any ozone, carbon monoxide, or PM–10 nonattainment area, the State containing such area and elected officials of affected local governments shall, before the date required for submittal of the inventory described under sections 7511a(a)(1) and 7512a(a)(1) of this title, jointly review and update as necessary the planning procedures adopted pursuant to this subsection as in effect immediately before November 15, 1990, or develop new planning procedures pursuant to this subsection, as appropriate. In preparing such procedures the State and local elected officials shall determine which elements of a revised implementation plan will be developed, adopted, and implemented (through means including enforcement) by the State and which by local governments or regional agencies, or any combination of local governments, regional agencies, or the State. The implementation plan required by this part shall be prepared by an organization certified by the State, in consultation with elected officials of local governments and in accordance with the determination under the second sentence of this subsection. Such organization shall include elected officials of local governments in the affected area, and representatives of the State air quality planning agency, the State transportation planning agency, the metropolitan planning organization designated to conduct the continuing, cooperative and comprehensive transportation planning process for the area under section 134 of Title 23, the organization responsible for the air quality maintenance planning process under regulations implementing this chapter, and any other organization with responsibilities for developing, submitting, or implementing the plan required by this part. Such organization may be one that carried out these functions before November 15, 1990.

### (b) Coordination

The preparation of implementation plan provisions and subsequent plan revisions under the continuing transportation-air quality planning process described in section 7408(e) of this title shall be coordinated with the continuing, cooperative and comprehensive transportation planning process required under section 134 of Title 23, and such planning processes shall take into account the requirements of this part.

### (c) Joint planning

In the case of a nonattainment area that is included within more than one State, the affected States may jointly, through interstate compact or otherwise, undertake and implement all or part of the planning procedures described in this section.

(July 14, 1955, c. 360, Title I, § 174, as added Aug. 7, 1977, Pub.L. 95–95, Title I, § 129(b), 91 Stat. 748, and amended Nov. 15, 1990, Pub.L. 101–549, Title 1, § 102(d), 104 Stat. 2417.)

### HISTORICAL AND STATUTORY NOTES

**Effective and Applicability Provisions**

1990 Acts

Amendment by Pub.L. 101–549 effective Nov. 15, 1990, except as otherwise provided, see section 711(b) of Pub.L. 101–549, set out as a note under section 7401 of this title.

1977 Acts

Section effective Aug. 7, 1977, except as otherwise expressly provided, see section 406(d) of Pub.L. 95–95, set out as a note under section 7401 of this title.

**Savings Provisions**

Suits, actions or proceedings commenced under this chapter as in effect prior to Nov. 15, 1990, not to abate by reason of the taking effect of amendments by Pub.L. 101–549, except as otherwise provided for, see section 711(a) of Pub.L. 101–549, set out as a note under section 7401 of this title.

## § 7505. Environmental Protection Agency grants

[CAA § 175]

### (a) Plan revision development costs

The Administrator shall make grants to any organization of local elected officials with transportation or air quality maintenance planning responsibilities recognized by the State under section 7504(a) of this title for payment of the reasonable costs of developing a plan revision under this part.

**(b) Uses of grant funds**

The amount granted to any organization under subsection (a) of this section shall be 100 percent of any additional costs of developing a plan revision under this part for the first two fiscal years following receipt of the grant under this paragraph, and shall supplement any funds available under Federal law to such organization for transportation or air quality maintenance planning. Grants under this section shall not be used for construction.

(July 14, 1955, c. 360, Title I, § 175, as added Aug. 7, 1977, Pub.L. 95–95, Title I, § 129(b), 91 Stat. 749.)

### HISTORICAL AND STATUTORY NOTES

**Effective and Applicability Provisions**

1977 Acts

Section effective Aug. 7, 1977, except as otherwise expressly provided, see section 406(d) of Pub.L. 95–95, set out as a note under section 7401 of this title.

## § 7505a. Maintenance plans

[CAA § 175A]

**(a) Plan revision**

Each State which submits a request under section 7407(d) of this title for redesignation of a nonattainment area for any air pollutant as an area which has attained the national primary ambient air quality standard for that air pollutant shall also submit a revision of the applicable State implementation plan to provide for the maintenance of the national primary ambient air quality standard for such air pollutant in the area concerned for at least 10 years after the redesignation. The plan shall contain such additional measures, if any, as may be necessary to ensure such maintenance.

**(b) Subsequent plan revisions**

8 years after redesignation of any area as an attainment area under section 7407(d) of this title, the State shall submit to the Administrator an additional revision of the applicable State implementation plan for maintaining the national primary ambient air quality standard for 10 years after the expiration of the 10–year period referred to in subsection (a) of this section.

**(c) Nonattainment requirements applicable pending plan approval**

Until such plan revision is approved and an area is redesignated as attainment for any area designated as a nonattainment area, the requirements of this part shall continue in force and effect with respect to such area.

**(d) Contingency provisions**

Each plan revision submitted under this section shall contain such contingency provisions as the Administrator deems necessary to assure that the State will promptly correct any violation of the standard which occurs after the redesignation of the area as an attainment area. Such provisions shall include a requirement that the State will implement all measures with respect to the control of the air pollutant concerned which were contained in the State implementation plan for the area before redesignation of the area as an attainment area. The failure of any area redesignated as an attainment area to maintain the national ambient air quality standard concerned shall not result in a requirement that the State revise its State implementation plan unless the Administrator, in the Administrator's discretion, requires the State to submit a revised State implementation plan.

(July 14, 1955, c. 360, Title I, § 175A, as added Nov. 15, 1990, Pub.L. 101–549, Title I, § 102(e), 104 Stat. 2418.)

### HISTORICAL AND STATUTORY NOTES

**Effective and Applicability Provisions**

1990 Acts

Section to take effect Nov. 15, 1990, except as otherwise provided, see section 711(b) of Pub.L. 101–549, set out as a note under section 7401 of this title.

**Savings Provisions**

Suits, actions or proceedings commenced under this chapter as in effect prior to Nov. 15, 1990, not to abate by reason of the taking effect of amendments by Pub.L. 101–549, except as otherwise provided for, see section 711(a) of Pub.L. 101–549, set out as a note under section 7401 of this title.

## § 7506. Limitations on certain Federal assistance

[CAA § 176]

**(a), (b) Repealed. Pub.L. 101–549, Title I, § 110(4), Nov. 15, 1990, 104 Stat. 2470**

**(c) Activities not conforming to approved or promulgated plans**

(1) No department, agency, or instrumentality of the Federal Government shall engage in, support in any way or provide financial assistance for, license or permit, or approve, any activity which does not conform to an implementation plan after it has been approved or promulgated under section 7410 of this title. No metropolitan planning organization designated under section 134 of Title 23, shall give its approval to any project, program, or plan which does not conform to an implementation plan approved or promulgated under section 7410 of this title. The assurance of conformity to such an implementation

plan shall be an affirmative responsibility of the head of such department, agency, or instrumentality. Conformity to an implementation plan means—

(A) conformity to an implementation plan's purpose of eliminating or reducing the severity and number of violations of the national ambient air quality standards and achieving expeditious attainment of such standards; and

(B) that such activities will not—

(i) cause or contribute to any new violation of any standard in any area;

(ii) increase the frequency or severity of any existing violation of any standard in any area; or

(iii) delay timely attainment of any standard or any required interim emission reductions or other milestones in any area.

The determination of conformity shall be based on the most recent estimates of emissions, and such estimates shall be determined from the most recent population, employment, travel and congestion estimates as determined by the metropolitan planning organization or other agency authorized to make such estimates.

(2) Any transportation plan or program developed pursuant to Title 23 or chapter 53 of Title 49 shall implement the transportation provisions of any applicable implementation plan approved under this chapter applicable to all or part of the area covered by such transportation plan or program. No Federal agency may approve, accept or fund any transportation plan, program or project unless such plan, program or project has been found to conform to any applicable implementation plan in effect under this chapter. In particular—

(A) no transportation plan or transportation improvement program may be adopted by a metropolitan planning organization designated under Title 23 or chapter 53 of Title 49, or be found to be in conformity by a metropolitan planning organization until a final determination has been made that emissions expected from implementation of such plans and programs are consistent with estimates of emissions from motor vehicles and necessary emissions reductions contained in the applicable implementation plan, and that the plan or program will conform to the requirements of paragraph (1)(B);

(B) no metropolitan planning organization or other recipient of funds under Title 23 or chapter 53 of Title 49 shall adopt or approve a transportation improvement program of projects until it determines that such program provides for timely implementation of transportation control measures consistent with schedules included in the applicable implementation plan;

(C) a transportation project may be adopted or approved by a metropolitan planning organization or any recipient of funds designated under Title 23 or chapter 53 of Title 49, or found in conformity by a metropolitan planning organization or approved, accepted, or funded by the Department of Transportation only if it meets either the requirements of subparagraph (D) or the following requirements—

(i) such a project comes from a conforming plan and program;

(ii) the design concept and scope of such project have not changed significantly since the conformity finding regarding the plan and program from which the project derived; and

(iii) the design concept and scope of such project at the time of the conformity determination for the program was adequate to determine emissions.

(D) Any project not referred to in subparagraph (C) shall be treated as conforming to the applicable implementation plan only if it is demonstrated that the projected emissions from such project, when considered together with emissions projected for the conforming transportation plans and programs within the nonattainment area, do not cause such plans and programs to exceed the emission reduction projections and schedules assigned to such plans and programs in the applicable implementation plan.

(3) Until such time as the implementation plan revision referred to in paragraph (4)(C) is approved, conformity of such plans, programs, and projects will be demonstrated if—

(A) the transportation plans and programs—

(i) are consistent with the most recent estimates of mobile source emissions;

(ii) provide for the expeditious implementation of transportation control measures in the applicable implementation plan; and

(iii) with respect to ozone and carbon monoxide nonattainment areas, contribute to annual emissions reductions consistent with sections 7511a(b)(1) and 7512a(a)(7) of this title; and

(B) the transportation projects—

(i) come from a conforming transportation plan and program as defined in subparagraph (A) or for 12 months after November 15, 1990, from a transportation program found to conform within 3 years prior to November 15, 1990; and

(ii) in carbon monoxide nonattainment areas, eliminate or reduce the severity and number of violations of the carbon monoxide standards in the area substantially affected by the project.

With regard to subparagraph (B)(ii), such determination may be made as part of either the conformity determination for the transportation program or for the individual project taken as a whole during the environmental review phase of project development.

(4)(A) No later than one year after November 15, 1990, the Administrator shall promulgate criteria and procedures for determining conformity (except in the case of transportation plans, programs, and projects) of, and for keeping the Administrator informed about, the activities referred to in paragraph (1). No later than one year after November 15, 1990, the Administrator, with the concurrence of the Secretary of Transportation, shall promulgate criteria and procedures for demonstrating and assuring conformity in the case of transportation plans, programs, and projects. A suit may be brought against the Administrator and the Secretary of Transportation under section 7604 of this title to compel promulgation of such criteria and procedures and the Federal district court shall have jurisdiction to order such promulgation.

**(B)** The procedures and criteria shall, at a minimum—

**(i)** address the consultation procedures to be undertaken by metropolitan planning organizations and the Secretary of Transportation with State and local air quality agencies and State departments of transportation before such organizations and the Secretary make conformity determinations;

**(ii)** address the appropriate frequency for making conformity determinations, but in no case shall such determinations for transportation plans and programs be less frequent than every three years; and

**(iii)** address how conformity determinations will be made with respect to maintenance plans.

**(C)** Such procedures shall also include a requirement that each State shall submit to the Administrator and the Secretary of Transportation within 24 months of November 15, 1990, a revision to its implementation plan that includes criteria and procedures for assessing the conformity of any plan, program, or project subject to the conformity requirements of this subsection.

**(D)** Compliance with the rules of the Administrator for determining the conformity of transportation plans, programs, and projects funded or approved under Title 23 or chapter 53 of Title 49 to State or Federal implementation plans shall not be required for traffic signal synchronization projects prior to the funding, approval or implementation of such projects. The supporting regional emissions analysis for any conformity determination made with respect to a transportation plan, program, or project shall consider the effect on emissions of any such project funded, approved, or implemented prior to the conformity determination.

**(5) Applicability**

This subsection shall apply only with respect to—

**(A)** a nonattainment area and each pollutant for which the area is designated as a nonattainment area; and

**(B)** an area that was designated as a nonattainment area but that was later redesignated by the Administrator as an attainment area and that is required to develop a maintenance plan under section 7505a of this title with respect to the specific pollutant for which the area was designated nonattainment.

**(6)** Notwithstanding paragraph 5[1], this subsection shall not apply with respect to an area designated nonattainment under section 7407(d)(1) of this title until 1 year after that area is first designated nonattainment for a specific national ambient air quality standard. This paragraph only applies with respect to the national ambient air quality standard for which an area is newly designated nonattainment and does not affect the area's requirements with respect to all other national ambient air quality standards for which the area is designated nonattainment or has been redesignated from nonattainment to attainment with a maintenance plan pursuant to section 7505a of this title (including any pre-existing national ambient air quality standard for a pollutant for which a new or revised standard has been issued).

**(d) Priority of achieving and maintaining national primary ambient air quality standards**

Each department, agency, or instrumentality of the Federal Government having authority to conduct or support any program with air-quality related transportation consequences shall give priority in the exercise of such authority, consistent with statutory requirements for allocation among States or other jurisdictions, to the implementation of those portions of plans prepared under this section to achieve and maintain the national primary ambient air-quality standard. This paragraph extends to, but is not limited to, authority exercised under the Urban Mass Transportation Act, Title 23, and the Housing and Urban Development Act.

(July 14, 1955, c. 360, Title I, § 176, as added Aug. 7, 1977, Pub.L. 95–95, Title I, § 129(b), 91 Stat. 749, and amended Nov. 16, 1977, Pub.L. 95–190, § 14(a)(59), 91 Stat. 1403; Nov. 15, 1990, Pub.L. 101–549, Title I, §§ 101(f), 110(4), 104 Stat. 2409, 2470; Nov. 28, 1995, Pub.L. 104–59, Title III, § 305(b), 109 Stat. 580; Oct. 9, 1996, Pub.L. 104–260, § 1, 110 Stat. 3175; Oct. 27, 2000, Pub.L. 106–377, § 1(a)(1) [Title III], 114 Stat. 1441, 1441A–44.)

[1] So in original. Probably should be "paragraph 5".

### HISTORICAL AND STATUTORY NOTES

**References in Text**

Title 23, referred to in subsecs. (c) and (d), is Title 23, Highways.

The Housing and Urban Development Act, referred to in subsec. (d), may be the name for a series of Acts sharing the same name but enacted in different years by Pub.L. 89–117, Aug. 10, 1965, 79 Stat. 451, Pub.L. 90–448, Aug. 1, 1968, 82 Stat. 476, Pub.L. 91–152, Dec. 24, 1969, 83 Stat. 379, and Pub.L. 91–609, Dec. 31, 1970, 84 Stat. 1770, respectively. For complete classification of these Acts to the Code, see Short Title notes set out under section 1701 of Title 12 and Tables.

**Codifications**

In subsecs. (c)(2) and (d), "chapter 53 of title 49" was substituted for "the Urban Mass Transportation Act [49 App. USCA 1601 et seq.]" and in subsec. (c)(4)(D), same was substituted for the "Federal Transit Act" on authority of Pub.L. 103–272, § 6(b), July 5, 1994, 108 Stat. 1378 (the first section of which enacted subtitles II, III, and V to X of Title 49, Transportation) and Pub.L. 102–240, Title III, § 3003(b), Dec. 18, 1991, 105 Stat. 2088 (which provided that references in laws to the "Urban Mass Transportation Act of 1964" be deemed to be references to the "Federal Transit Act").

**Effective and Applicability Provisions**

1990 Acts

Amendment by Pub.L. 101–549 effective Nov. 15, 1990, except as otherwise provided, see section 711(b) of Pub.L. 101–549, set out as a note under section 7401 of this title.

1977 Acts

Section effective Aug. 7, 1977, except as otherwise expressly provided, see section 406(d) of Pub.L. 95–95, set out as a note under section 7401 of this title.

**Savings Provisions**

Suits, actions or proceedings commenced under this chapter as in effect prior to Nov. 15, 1990, not to abate by reason of the taking effect of amendments by Pub.L. 101–549, except as otherwise provided for, see section 711(a) of Pub.L. 101–549, set out as a note under section 7401 of this title.

## § 7506a. Interstate transport commissions

**[CAA § 176A]**

### (a) Authority to establish interstate transport regions

Whenever, on the Administrator's own motion or by petition from the Governor of any State, the Administrator has reason to believe that the interstate transport of air pollutants from one or more States contributes significantly to a violation of a national ambient air quality standard in one or more other States, the Administrator may establish, by rule, a transport region for such pollutant that includes such States. The Administrator, on the Administrator's own motion or upon petition from the Governor of any State, or upon the recommendation of a transport commission established under subsection (b) of this section, may—

(1) add any State or portion of a State to any region established under this subsection whenever the Administrator has reason to believe that the interstate transport of air pollutants from such State significantly contributes to a violation of the standard in the transport region, or

(2) remove any State or portion of a State from the region whenever the Administrator has reason to believe that the control of emissions in that State or portion of the State pursuant to this section will not significantly contribute to the attainment of the standard in any area in the region.

The Administrator shall approve or disapprove any such petition or recommendation within 18 months of its receipt. The Administrator shall establish appropriate proceedings for public participation regarding such petitions and motions, including notice and comment.

### (b) Transport commissions

#### (1) Establishment

Whenever the Administrator establishes a transport region under subsection (a) of this section, the Administrator shall establish a transport commission comprised of (at a minimum) each of the following members:

(A) The Governor of each State in the region or the designee of each such Governor.

(B) The Administrator or the Administrator's designee.

(C) The Regional Administrator (or the Administrator's designee) for each Regional Office for each Environmental Protection Agency Region affected by the transport region concerned.

(D) An air pollution control official representing each State in the region, appointed by the Governor.

Decisions of, and recommendations and requests to, the Administrator by each transport commission may be made only by a majority vote of all members other than the Administrator and the Regional Administrators (or designees thereof).

#### (2) Recommendations

The transport commission shall assess the degree of interstate transport of the pollutant or precursors to the pollutant throughout the transport region, assess strategies for mitigating the interstate pollution, and recommend to the Administrator such measures as the Commission determines to be necessary to ensure that the plans for the relevant States meet the requirements of section 7410(a)(2)(D) of this title. Such commission shall not be subject to the provisions of the Federal Advisory Committee Act (5 U.S.C. App.).

### (c) Commission requests

A transport commission established under subsection (b) of this section may request the Administrator to issue a finding under section 7410(k)(5) of this title that the implementation plan for one or more of the States in the transport region is substantially inadequate to meet the requirements of section 7410(a)(2)(D) of this title. The Administrator shall approve, disapprove, or partially approve and partially disapprove such a request within 18 months of its receipt and, to the extent the Administrator approves such request, issue the finding under section 7410(k)(5) of this title at the time of such approval. In acting on such request, the Administrator shall provide an opportunity for public participation and shall address each specific recommendation made by the commission. Approval or disapproval of such a request shall constitute final agency action within the meaning of section 7607(b) of this title.

(July 14, 1955, c. 360, Title I, § 176A, as added Nov. 15, 1990, Pub.L. 101–549, Title I, § 102(f)(1), 104 Stat. 2419.)

### HISTORICAL AND STATUTORY NOTES

**References in Text**

The Federal Advisory Committee Act, referred to in subsec. (b)(2), is Pub.L. 92–463, Oct. 6, 1972, 86 Stat. 770, as amended, which is set out in Appendix 2 to Title 5, Government Organization and Employees.

**Effective and Applicability Provisions**

1990 Acts

Section to take effect Nov. 15, 1990, except as otherwise provided, see section 711(b) of Pub.L. 101–549, set out as a note under section 7401 of this title.

**Savings Provisions**

Suits, actions or proceedings commenced under this chapter as in effect prior to Nov. 15, 1990, not to abate by reason of the taking effect of amendments by Pub.L. 101–549, except as otherwise provided for, see section 711(a) of Pub.L. 101–549, set out as a note under section 7401 of this title.

## § 7507. New motor vehicle emission standards in nonattainment areas

[CAA § 177]

Notwithstanding section 7543(a) of this title, any State which has plan provisions approved under this part may adopt and enforce for any model year standards relating to control of emissions from new motor vehicles or new motor vehicle engines and take such other actions as are referred to in section 7543(a) of this title respecting such vehicles if—

(1) such standards are identical to the California standards for which a waiver has been granted for such model year, and

(2) California and such State adopt such standards at least two years before commencement of such model year (as determined by regulations of the Administrator).

Nothing in this section or in subchapter II of this chapter shall be construed as authorizing any such State to prohibit or limit, directly or indirectly, the manufacture or sale of a new motor vehicle or motor vehicle engine that is certified in California as meeting California standards, or to take any action of any kind to create, or have the effect of creating, a motor vehicle or motor vehicle engine different than a motor vehicle or engine certified in California under California standards (a "third vehicle") or otherwise create such a "third vehicle".

(July 14, 1955, c. 360, Title I, § 177, as added Aug. 7, 1977, Pub.L. 95–95, Title I, § 129(b), 91 Stat. 750, and amended Nov. 15, 1990, Pub.L. 101–549, Title II, § 232, 104 Stat. 2529.)

### HISTORICAL AND STATUTORY NOTES

**Effective and Applicability Provisions**

1990 Acts

Amendment by Pub.L. 101–549 effective Nov. 15, 1990, except as otherwise provided, see section 711(b) of Pub.L. 101–549, set out as a note under section 7401 of this title.

1977 Acts

Section effective Aug. 7, 1977, except as otherwise expressly provided, see section 406(d) of Pub.L. 95–95, set out as a note under section 7401 of this title.

**Savings Provisions**

Suits, actions or proceedings commenced under this chapter as in effect prior to Nov. 15, 1990, not to abate by reason of the taking effect of amendments by Pub.L. 101–549, except as otherwise provided for, see section 711(a) of Pub.L. 101–549, set out as a note under section 7401 of this title.

## § 7508. Guidance documents

[CAA § 178]

The Administrator shall issue guidance documents under section 7408 of this title for purposes of assisting States in implementing requirements of this part respecting the lowest achievable emission rate. Such a document shall be published not later than nine months after August 7, 1977, and shall be revised at least every two years thereafter.

(July 14, 1955, c. 360, Title I, § 178, as added Aug. 7, 1977, Pub.L. 95–95, Title I, § 129(b), 91 Stat. 750.)

### HISTORICAL AND STATUTORY NOTES

**Effective and Applicability Provisions**

1977 Acts

Section effective Aug. 7, 1977, except as otherwise expressly provided, see section 406(d) of Pub.L. 95–95, set out as a note under section 7401 of this title.

## § 7509. Sanctions and consequences of failure to attain

[CAA § 179]

**(a) State failure**

For any implementation plan or plan revision required under this part (or required in response to a finding of substantial inadequacy as described in section 7410(k)(5) of this title), if the Administrator—

(1) finds that a State has failed, for an area designated nonattainment under section 7407(d) of this title, to submit a plan, or to submit 1 or more of

the elements (as determined by the Administrator) required by the provisions of this chapter applicable to such an area, or has failed to make a submission for such an area that satisfies the minimum criteria established in relation to any such element under section 7410(k) of this title,

(2) disapproves a submission under section 7410(k) of this title, for an area designated nonattainment under section 7407 of this title, based on the submission's failure to meet one or more of the elements required by the provisions of this chapter applicable to such an area,

(3)(A) determines that a State has failed to make any submission as may be required under this chapter, other than one described under paragraph (1) or (2), including an adequate maintenance plan, or has failed to make any submission, as may be required under this chapter, other than one described under paragraph (1) or (2), that satisfies the minimum criteria established in relation to such submission under section 7410(k)(1)(A) of this title, or

(B) disapproves in whole or in part a submission described under subparagraph (A), or

(4) finds that any requirement of an approved plan (or approved part of a plan) is not being implemented,

unless such deficiency has been corrected within 18 months after the finding, disapproval, or determination referred to in paragraphs (1), (2), (3), and (4), one of the sanctions referred to in subsection (b) of this section shall apply, as selected by the Administrator, until the Administrator determines that the State has come into compliance, except that if the Administrator finds a lack of good faith, sanctions under both paragraph (1) and paragraph (2) of subsection (b) of this section shall apply until the Administrator determines that the State has come into compliance. If the Administrator has selected one of such sanctions and the deficiency has not been corrected within 6 months thereafter, sanctions under both paragraph (1) and paragraph (2) of subsection (b) of this section shall apply until the Administrator determines that the State has come into compliance. In addition to any other sanction applicable as provided in this section, the Administrator may withhold all or part of the grants for support of air pollution planning and control programs that the Administrator may award under section 7405 of this title.

## (b) Sanctions

The sanctions available to the Administrator as provided in subsection (a) of this section are as follows:

### (1) Highway sanctions

(A) The Administrator may impose a prohibition, applicable to a nonattainment area, on the approval by the Secretary of Transportation of any projects or the awarding by the Secretary of any grants, under Title 23 other than projects or grants for safety where the Secretary determines, based on accident or other appropriate data submitted by the State, that the principal purpose of the project is an improvement in safety to resolve a demonstrated safety problem and likely will result in a significant reduction in, or avoidance of, accidents. Such prohibition shall become effective upon the selection by the Administrator of this sanction.

(B) In addition to safety, projects or grants that may be approved by the Secretary, notwithstanding the prohibition in subparagraph (A), are the following—

(i) capital programs for public transit;

(ii) construction or restriction of certain roads or lanes solely for the use of passenger buses or high occupancy vehicles;

(iii) planning for requirements for employers to reduce employee work-trip-related vehicle emissions;

(iv) highway ramp metering, traffic signalization, and related programs that improve traffic flow and achieve a net emission reduction;

(v) fringe and transportation corridor parking facilities serving multiple occupancy vehicle programs or transit operations;

(vi) programs to limit or restrict vehicle use in downtown areas or other areas of emission concentration particularly during periods of peak use, through road use charges, tolls, parking surcharges, or other pricing mechanisms, vehicle restricted zones or periods, or vehicle registration programs;

(vii) programs for breakdown and accident scene management, nonrecurring congestion, and vehicle information systems, to reduce congestion and emissions; and

(viii) such other transportation-related programs as the Administrator, in consultation with the Secretary of Transportation, finds would improve air quality and would not encourage single occupancy vehicle capacity.

In considering such measures, the State should seek to ensure adequate access to downtown, other commercial, and residential areas, and avoid increasing or relocating emissions and congestion rather than reducing them.

### (2) Offsets

In applying the emissions offset requirements of section 7503 of this title to new or modified sources or emissions units for which a permit is required under this part, the ratio of emission reductions to increased emissions shall be at least 2 to 1.

**(c) Notice of failure to attain**

(1) As expeditiously as practicable after the applicable attainment date for any nonattainment area, but not later than 6 months after such date, the Administrator shall determine, based on the area's air quality as of the attainment date, whether the area attained the standard by that date.

(2) Upon making the determination under paragraph (1), the Administrator shall publish a notice in the Federal Register containing such determination and identifying each area that the Administrator has determined to have failed to attain. The Administrator may revise or supplement such determination at any time based on more complete information or analysis concerning the area's air quality as of the attainment date.

**(d) Consequences for failure to attain**

(1) Within 1 year after the Administrator publishes the notice under subsection (c)(2) of this section (relating to notice of failure to attain), each State containing a nonattainment area shall submit a revision to the applicable implementation plan meeting the requirements of paragraph (2) of this subsection.

(2) The revision required under paragraph (1) shall meet the requirements of section 7410 of this title and section 7502 of this title. In addition, the revision shall include such additional measures as the Administrator may reasonably prescribe, including all measures that can be feasibly implemented in the area in light of technological achievability, costs, and any nonair quality and other air quality-related health and environmental impacts.

(3) The attainment date applicable to the revision required under paragraph (1) shall be the same as provided in the provisions of section 7502(a)(2) of this title, except that in applying such provisions the phrase "from the date of the notice under section 7509(c)(2) of this title" shall be substituted for the phrase "from the date such area was designated nonattainment under section 7407(d) of this title" and for the phrase "from the date of designation as nonattainment".

(July 14, 1955, c. 360, Title I, § 179, as added Nov. 15, 1990, Pub.L. 101–549, Title I, § 102(g), 104 Stat. 2420.)

### HISTORICAL AND STATUTORY NOTES

**References in Text**

Title 23, referred to in subsec. (b)(1)(A), is Title 23, Highways.

**Effective and Applicability Provisions**

1990 Acts

Section to take effect Nov. 15, 1990, except as otherwise provided, see section 711(b) of Pub.L. 101–549, set out as a note under section 7401 of this title.

**Savings Provisions**

Suits, actions or proceedings commenced under this chapter as in effect prior to Nov. 15, 1990, not to abate by reason of the taking effect of amendments by Pub.L. 101–549, except as otherwise provided for, see section 711(a) of Pub.L. 101–549, set out as a note under section 7401 of this title.

## § 7509a. International border areas

**[CAA § 179B]**

**(a) Implementation plans and revisions**

Notwithstanding any other provision of law, an implementation plan or plan revision required under this chapter shall be approved by the Administrator if—

(1) such plan or revision meets all the requirements applicable to it under the [1] chapter other than a requirement that such plan or revision demonstrate attainment and maintenance of the relevant national ambient air quality standards by the attainment date specified under the applicable provision of this chapter, or in a regulation promulgated under such provision, and

(2) the submitting State establishes to the satisfaction of the Administrator that the implementation plan of such State would be adequate to attain and maintain the relevant national ambient air quality standards by the attainment date specified under the applicable provision of this chapter, or in a regulation promulgated under such provision, but for emissions emanating from outside of the United States.

**(b) Attainment of ozone levels**

Notwithstanding any other provision of law, any State that establishes to the satisfaction of the Administrator that, with respect to an ozone nonattainment area in such State, such State would have attained the national ambient air quality standard for ozone by the applicable attainment date, but for emissions emanating from outside of the United States, shall not be subject to the provisions of section 7511(a)(2) or (5) of this title or section 7511d of this title.

**(c) Attainment of carbon monoxide levels**

Notwithstanding any other provision of law, any State that establishes to the satisfaction of the Administrator, with respect to a carbon monoxide nonattainment area in such State, that such State has attained the national ambient air quality standard for carbon monoxide by the applicable attainment date, but for emissions emanating from outside of the United States, shall not be subject to the provisions of section 7512(b)(2) or (9) [2] of this title.

**(d) Attainment of PM–10 levels**

Notwithstanding any other provision of law, any State that establishes to the satisfaction of the Administrator that, with respect to a PM–10 nonattainment area in such State, such State would have attained the national ambient air quality standard for carbon monoxide by the applicable attainment date, but for emissions emanating from outside the United States, shall not be subject to the provisions of section 7513(b)(2) of this title.

(July 14, 1955, c. 360, Title I, § 179B, as added Nov. 15, 1990, Pub.L. 101–549, Title VIII, § 818, 104 Stat. 2697.)

1 So in original. Probably should be "this".

2 So in original. Section 7512(b) of this title does not contain a par. (9).

### HISTORICAL AND STATUTORY NOTES

**Effective and Applicability Provisions**

1990 Acts

Section effective Nov. 15, 1990, except as otherwise provided, see section 711(b) of Pub.L. 101–549, set out as a note under section 7401 of this title.

**Savings Provisions**

Suits, actions or proceedings commenced under this chapter as in effect prior to Nov. 15, 1990, not to abate by reason of the taking effect of amendments by Pub.L. 101–549, except as otherwise provided for, see section 711(a) of Pub.L. 101–549, set out as a note under section 7401 of this title.

**Establishment of Program to Monitor and Improve Air Quality in Regions Along the Border Between the United States and Mexico**

Section 815 of Pub.L. 101–549 provided that:

"**(a) In general.**—The Administrator of the Environmental Protection Agency (hereinafter referred to as the 'Administrator') is authorized, in cooperation with the Department of State and the affected States, to negotiate with representatives of Mexico to authorize a program to monitor and improve air quality in regions along the border between the United States and Mexico. The program established under this section shall not extend beyond July 1, 1995.

"**(b) Monitoring and remediation.**—

"**(1) Monitoring.**—The monitoring component of the program conducted under this section shall identify and determine sources of pollutants for which national ambient air quality standards (hereinafter referred to as 'NAAQS') and other air quality goals have been established in regions along the border between the United States and Mexico. Any such monitoring component of the program shall include, but not be limited to, the collection of meteorological data, the measurement of air quality, the compilation of an emissions inventory, and shall be sufficient to the extent necessary to successfully support the use of a state-of-the-art mathematical air modeling analysis. Any such monitoring component of the program shall collect and produce data projecting the level of emission reductions necessary in both Mexico and the United States to bring about attainment of both primary and secondary NAAQS, and other air quality goals, in regions along the border in the United States. Any such monitoring component of the program shall include to the extent possible, data from monitoring programs undertaken by other parties.

"**(2) Remediation.**—The Administrator is authorized to negotiate with appropriate representatives of Mexico to develop joint remediation measures to reduce the level of airborne pollutants to achieve and maintain primary and secondary NAAQS, and other air quality goals, in regions along the border between the United States and Mexico. Such joint remediation measures may include, but not be limited to measures included in the Environmental Protection Agency's Control Techniques and Control Technology documents. Any such remediation program shall also identify those control measures implementation of which in Mexico would be expedited by the use of material and financial assistance of the United States.

"**(c) Annual reports.**—The Administrator shall, each year the program authorized in this section is in operation, report to Congress on the progress of the program in bringing nonattainment areas along the border of the United States into attainment with primary and secondary NAAQS. The report issued by the Administrator under this paragraph shall include recommendations on funding mechanisms to assist in implementation of monitoring and remediation efforts.

"**(d) Funding and personnel.**—The Administrator may, where appropriate, make available, subject to the appropriations, such funds, personnel, and equipment as may be necessary to implement the provisions of this section. In those cases where direct financial assistance of the United States is provided to implement monitoring and remediation programs in Mexico, the Administrator shall develop grant agreements with appropriate representatives of Mexico to assure the accuracy and completeness of monitoring data and the performance of remediation measures which are financed by the United States. With respect to any control measures within Mexico funded by the United States, the Administrator shall, to the maximum extent practicable, utilize resources of Mexico where such utilization would reduce costs to the United States. Such funding agreements shall include authorization for the Administrator to—

"(1) review and agree to plans for monitoring and remediation;

"(2) inspect premises, equipment and records to insure compliance with the agreements established under and the purposes set forth in this section; and

"(3) where necessary, develop grant agreements with affected States to carry out the provisions of this section."

### *Subpart 2—Additional Provisions for Ozone Nonattainment Areas*

## § 7511. Classifications and attainment dates [CAA § 181]

### (a) Classification and attainment dates for 1989 nonattainment areas

(1) Each area designated nonattainment for ozone pursuant to section 7407(d) of this title shall be classified at the time of such designation, under table 1, by operation of law, as a Marginal Area, a Moderate Area, a Serious Area, a Severe Area, or an Extreme

Area based on the design value for the area. The design value shall be calculated according to the interpretation methodology issued by the Administrator most recently before November 15, 1990. For each area classified under this subsection, the primary standard attainment date for ozone shall be as expeditiously as practicable but not later than the date provided in table 1.

TABLE 1

| Area class | Design value* | Primary standard attainment date** |
|---|---|---|
| Marginal | 0.121 up to 0.138 | 3 years after November 15, 1990 |
| Moderate | 0.138 up to 0.160 | 6 years after November 15, 1990 |
| Serious | 0.160 up to 0.180 | 9 years after November 15, 1990 |
| Severe | 0.180 up to 0.280 | 15 years after November 15, 1990 |
| Extreme | 0.280 and above | 20 years after November 15, 1990 |

* The design value is measured in parts per million (ppm).

** The primary standard attainment date is measured from November 15, 1990.

(2) Notwithstanding table 1, in the case of a severe area with a 1988 ozone design value between 0.190 and 0.280 ppm, the attainment date shall be 17 years (in lieu of 15 years) after November 15, 1990.

(3) At the time of publication of the notice under section 7407(d)(4) of this title (relating to area designations) for each ozone nonattainment area, the Administrator shall publish a notice announcing the classification of such ozone nonattainment area. The provisions of section 7502(a)(1)(B) of this title (relating to lack of notice and comment and judicial review) shall apply to such classification.

(4) If an area classified under paragraph (1) (Table 1) would have been classified in another category if the design value in the area were 5 percent greater or 5 percent less than the level on which such classification was based, the Administrator may, in the Administrator's discretion, within 90 days after the initial classification, by the procedure required under paragraph (3), adjust the classification to place the area in such other category. In making such adjustment, the Administrator may consider the number of exceedances of the national primary ambient air quality standard for ozone in the area, the level of pollution transport between the area and other affected areas, including both intrastate and interstate transport, and the mix of sources and air pollutants in the area.

(5) Upon application by any State, the Administrator may extend for 1 additional year (hereinafter referred to as the "Extension Year") the date specified in table 1 of paragraph (1) of this subsection if—

(A) the State has complied with all requirements and commitments pertaining to the area in the applicable implementation plan, and

(B) no more than 1 exceedance of the national ambient air quality standard level for ozone has occurred in the area in the year preceding the Extension Year.

No more than 2 one-year extensions may be issued under this paragraph for a single nonattainment area.

**(b) New designations and reclassifications**

**(1) New designations to nonattainment**

Any area that is designated attainment or unclassifiable for ozone under section 7407(d)(4) of this title, and that is subsequently redesignated to nonattainment for ozone under section 7407(d)(3) of this title, shall, at the time of the redesignation, be classified by operation of law in accordance with table 1 under subsection (a) of this section. Upon its classification, the area shall be subject to the same requirements under section 7410 of this title, subpart 1 of this part, and this subpart that would have applied had the area been so classified at the time of the notice under subsection (a)(3) of this section, except that any absolute, fixed date applicable in connection with any such requirement is extended by operation of law by a period equal to the length of time between November 15, 1990, and the date the area is classified under this paragraph.

**(2) Reclassification upon failure to attain**

(A) Within 6 months following the applicable attainment date (including any extension thereof) for an ozone nonattainment area, the Administrator shall determine, based on the area's design value (as of the attainment date), whether the area attained the standard by that date. Except for any Severe or Extreme area, any area that the Administrator finds has not attained the standard by that date shall be reclassified by operation of law in accordance with table 1 of subsection (a) of this section to the higher of—

(i) the next higher classification for the area, or

(ii) the classification applicable to the area's design value as determined at the time of the notice required under subparagraph (B).

No area shall be reclassified as Extreme under clause (ii).

(B) The Administrator shall publish a notice in the Federal Register, no later than 6 months following the attainment date, identifying each area that the Administrator has determined under subparagraph (A) as having failed to attain and identifying the reclassification, if any, described under subparagraph (A).

**(3) Voluntary reclassification**

The Administrator shall grant the request of any State to reclassify a nonattainment area in that State in accordance with table 1 of subsection (a) of this section to a higher classification. The Administrator shall publish a notice in the Federal Register of any such request and of action by the Administrator granting the request.

**(4) Failure of Severe Areas to attain standard**

(A) If any Severe Area fails to achieve the national primary ambient air quality standard for ozone by the applicable attainment date (including any extension thereof), the fee provisions under section 7511d of this title shall apply within the area, the percent reduction requirements of section 7511a(c)(2)(B) and (C) of this title (relating to reasonable further progress demonstration and $NO_x$ control) shall continue to apply to the area, and the State shall demonstrate that such percent reduction has been achieved in each 3-year interval after such failure until the standard is attained. Any failure to make such a demonstration shall be subject to the sanctions provided under this part.

(B) In addition to the requirements of subparagraph (A), if the ozone design value for a Severe Area referred to in subparagraph (A) is above 0.140 ppm for the year of the applicable attainment date, or if the area has failed to achieve its most recent milestone under section 7511a(g) of this title, the new source review requirements applicable under this subpart in Extreme Areas shall apply in the area and the term[1] "major source" and "major stationary source" shall have the same meaning as in Extreme Areas.

(C) In addition to the requirements of subparagraph (A) for those areas referred to in subparagraph (A) and not covered by subparagraph (B), the provisions referred to in subparagraph (B) shall apply after 3 years from the applicable attainment date unless the area has attained the standard by the end of such 3-year period.

(D) If, after November 15, 1990, the Administrator modifies the method of determining compliance with the national primary ambient air quality standard, a design value or other indicator comparable to 0.140 in terms of its relationship to the standard shall be used in lieu of 0.140 for purposes of applying the provisions of subparagraphs (B) and (C).

**(c) References to terms**

(1) Any reference in this subpart to a "Marginal Area", a "Moderate Area", a "Serious Area", a "Severe Area", or an "Extreme Area" shall be considered a reference to a Marginal Area, a Moderate Area, a Serious Area, a Severe Area, or an Extreme Area as respectively classified under this section.

(2) Any reference in this subpart to "next higher classification" or comparable terms shall be considered a reference to the classification related to the next higher set of design values in table 1.

(July 14, 1955, c. 360, Title I, § 181, as added Nov. 15, 1990, Pub.L. 101–549, Title I, § 103, 104 Stat. 2423.)

[1] So in original. Probably should be "terms".

## HISTORICAL AND STATUTORY NOTES

**Effective and Applicability Provisions**

1990 Acts

Section effective Nov. 15, 1990, except as otherwise provided, see section 711(b) of Pub.L. 101–549, set out as a note under section 7401 of this title.

**Savings Provisions**

Suits, actions or proceedings commenced under this chapter as in effect prior to Nov. 15, 1990, not to abate by reason of the taking effect of amendments by Pub.L. 101–549, except as otherwise provided for, see section 711(a) of Pub.L. 101–549, set out as a note under section 7401 of this title.

**Exemptions for Stripper Wells**

Section 819 of Pub.L. 101–549 provided that: "Notwithstanding any other provision of law, the amendments to the Clean Air Act [this chapter] made by section 103 of the Clean Air Act Amendments of 1990 [enacting sections 7511 to 7511f of this title] (relating to additional provisions for ozone nonattainment areas), by section 104 of such amendments [enacting sections 7512 and 7512a of this title] (relating to additional provisions for carbon monoxide nonattainment areas), by section 105 of such amendments [enacting sections 7513 to 7513b of this title and amending section 7476 of this title] (relating to additional provisions for PM–10 nonattainment areas), and by section 106 of such amendments [enacting sections 7514 and 7514a of this title] (relating to additional provisions for areas designated as nonattainment for sulfur oxides, nitrogen dioxide, and lead) shall not apply with respect to the production of and equipment used in the exploration, production, development, storage or processing of—

"(1) oil from a stripper well property, within the meaning of the June 1979 energy regulations (within the meaning of section 4996(b)(7) of the Internal Revenue Code of 1986 [26 U.S.C.A. § 4996(b)(7)], as in effect before the repeal of such section); and

"(2) stripper well natural gas, as defined in section 108(b) of the Natural Gas Policy Act of 1978 (15 U.S.C. 3318(b)) [section 3318(b) of Title 15, Commerce and Trade].[,]

except to the extent that provisions of such amendments cover areas designated as Serious pursuant to part D of title I of the Clean Air Act [this part] and having a population of 350,000 or more, or areas designated as Severe or Extreme pursuant to such part D."

## § 7511a. Plan submissions and requirements

[CAA § 182]

### (a) Marginal Areas

Each State in which all or part of a Marginal Area is located shall, with respect to the Marginal Area (or portion thereof, to the extent specified in this subsection), submit to the Administrator the State implementation plan revisions (including the plan items) described under this subsection except to the extent the State has made such submissions as of November 15, 1990.

**(1) Inventory**

Within 2 years after November 15, 1990, the State shall submit a comprehensive, accurate, current inventory of actual emissions from all sources, as described in section 7502(c)(3) of this title, in accordance with guidance provided by the Administrator.

**(2) Corrections to the State implementation plan**

Within the periods prescribed in this paragraph, the State shall submit a revision to the State implementation plan that meets the following requirements—

**(A) Reasonably available control technology corrections**

For any Marginal Area (or, within the Administrator's discretion, portion thereof) the State shall submit, within 6 months of the date of classification under section 7511(a) of this title, a revision that includes such provisions to correct requirements in (or add requirements to) the plan concerning reasonably available control technology as were required under section 7502(b) of this title (as in effect immediately before November 15, 1990), as interpreted in guidance issued by the Administrator under section 7408 of this title before November 15, 1990.

**(B) Savings clause for vehicle inspection and maintenance**

**(i)** For any Marginal Area (or, within the Administrator's discretion, portion thereof), the plan for which already includes, or was required by section 7502(b)(11)(B) of this title (as in effect immediately before November 15, 1990) to have included, a specific schedule for implementation of a vehicle emission control inspection and maintenance program, the State shall submit, immediately after November 15, 1990, a revision that includes any provisions necessary to provide for a vehicle inspection and maintenance program of no less stringency than that of either the program defined in House Report Numbered 95–294, 95th Congress, 1st Session, 281–291 (1977) as interpreted in guidance of the Administrator issued pursuant to section 7502(b)(11)(B) of this title (as in effect immediately before November 15, 1990) or the program already included in the plan, whichever is more stringent.

**(ii)** Within 12 months after November 15, 1990, the Administrator shall review, revise, update, and republish in the Federal Register the guidance for the States for motor vehicle inspection and maintenance programs required by this chapter, taking into consideration the Administrator's investigations and audits of such program. The guidance shall, at a minimum, cover the frequency of inspections, the types of vehicles to be inspected (which shall include leased vehicles that are registered in the nonattainment area), vehicle maintenance by owners and operators, audits by the State, the test method and measures, including whether centralized or decentralized, inspection methods and procedures, quality of inspection, components covered, assurance that a vehicle subject to a recall notice from a manufacturer has complied with that notice, and effective implementation and enforcement, including ensuring that any retesting of a vehicle after a failure shall include proof of corrective action and providing for denial of vehicle registration in the case of tampering or misfueling. The guidance which shall be incorporated in the applicable State implementation plans by the States shall provide the States with continued reasonable flexibility to fashion effective, reasonable, and fair programs for the affected consumer. No later than 2 years after the Administrator promulgates regulations under section 7521(m)(3) of this title (relating to emission control diagnostics), the State shall submit a revision to such program to meet any requirements that the Administrator may prescribe under that section.

**(C) Permit programs**

Within 2 years after November 15, 1990, the State shall submit a revision that includes each of the following:

**(i)** Provisions to require permits, in accordance with sections 7502(c)(5) and 7503 of this title, for the construction and operation of each new or modified major stationary source (with respect to ozone) to be located in the area.

**(ii)** Provisions to correct requirements in (or add requirements to) the plan concerning permit programs as were required under section 7502(b)(6) of this title (as in effect immediately before November 15, 1990), as interpreted in regulations of the Administrator promulgated as of November 15, 1990.

**(3) Periodic inventory**

**(A) General requirement**

No later than the end of each 3–year period after submission of the inventory under paragraph (1) until the area is redesignated to attainment, the State shall submit a revised inventory meeting the requirements of subsection (a)(1) of this section.

**(B) Emissions statements**

**(i)** Within 2 years after November 15, 1990, the State shall submit a revision to the State implementation plan to require that the owner or operator of each stationary source of oxides of nitrogen or volatile organic compounds provide the State with a statement, in such form as the Administrator may prescribe (or accept an equivalent alternative developed by the State), for classes or categories of sources, showing the actual emissions of oxides of nitrogen and volatile organic compounds from that source. The first such statement shall be submitted within 3 years after November 15, 1990. Subsequent statements shall be submitted at least every year thereafter. The statement shall contain a certification that the information contained in the statement is accurate to the best knowledge of the individual certifying the statement.

**(ii)** The State may waive the application of clause (i) to any class or category of stationary sources which emit less than 25 tons per year of volatile organic compounds or oxides of nitrogen if the State, in its submissions under subparagraphs[1] (1) or (3)(A), provides an inventory of emissions from such class or category of sources, based on the use of the emission factors established by the Administrator or other methods acceptable to the Administrator.

**(4) General offset requirement**

For purposes of satisfying the emission offset requirements of this part, the ratio of total emission reductions of volatile organic compounds to total increased emissions of such air pollutant shall be at least 1.1 to 1.

The Administrator may, in the Administrator's discretion, require States to submit a schedule for submitting any of the revisions or other items required under this subsection. The requirements of this subsection shall apply in lieu of any requirement that the State submit a demonstration that the applicable implementation plan provides for attainment of the ozone standard by the applicable attainment date in any Marginal Area. Section 7502(c)(9) of this title (relating to contingency measures) shall not apply to Marginal Areas.

**(b) Moderate Areas**

Each State in which all or part of a Moderate Area is located shall, with respect to the Moderate Area, make the submissions described under subsection (a) of this section (relating to Marginal Areas), and shall also submit the revisions to the applicable implementation plan described under this subsection.

**(1) Plan provisions for reasonable further progress**

**(A) General rule**

**(i)** By no later than 3 years after November 15, 1990, the State shall submit a revision to the applicable implementation plan to provide for volatile organic compound emission reductions, within 6 years after November 15, 1990, of at least 15 percent from baseline emissions, accounting for any growth in emissions after 1990. Such plan shall provide for such specific annual reductions in emissions of volatile organic compounds and oxides of nitrogen as necessary to attain the national primary ambient air quality standard for ozone by the attainment date applicable under this chapter. This subparagraph shall not apply in the case of oxides of nitrogen for those areas for which the Administrator determines (when the Administrator approves the plan or plan revision) that additional reductions of oxides of nitrogen would not contribute to attainment.

**(ii)** A percentage less than 15 percent may be used for purposes of clause (i) in the case of any State which demonstrates to the satisfaction of the Administrator that—

**(I)** new source review provisions are applicable in the nonattainment areas in the same manner and to the same extent as required under subsection (e) of this section in the case of Extreme Areas (with the exception that, in applying such provisions, the terms "major source" and "major stationary source" shall include (in addition to the sources described in section 7602 of this title) any stationary source or group of sources located within a contiguous area and under common control that emits, or has the potential to emit, at least 5 tons per year of volatile organic compounds);

**(II)** reasonably available control technology is required for all existing major sources (as defined in subclause (I)); and

**(III)** the plan reflecting a lesser percentage than 15 percent includes all measures that can feasibly be implemented in the area, in light of technological achievability.

To qualify for a lesser percentage under this clause, a State must demonstrate to the satisfaction of the Administrator that the plan for the area includes the measures that are achieved in practice by sources in the same source category in nonattainment areas of the next higher category.

**(B) Baseline emissions**

For purposes of subparagraph (A), the term "baseline emissions" means the total amount of actual VOC or $NO_x$ emissions from all anthropogenic sources in the area during the calendar year 1990, excluding emissions that would be eliminated under the regulations described in clauses (i) and (ii) of subparagraph (D).

**(C) General rule for creditability of reductions**

Except as provided under subparagraph (D), emissions reductions are creditable toward the 15 percent required under subparagraph (A) to the extent they have actually occurred, as of 6 years after November 15, 1990, from the implementation of measures required under the applicable implementation plan, rules promulgated by the Administrator, or a permit under subchapter V of this chapter.

**(D) Limits on creditability of reductions**

Emission reductions from the following measures are not creditable toward the 15 percent reductions required under subparagraph (A):

(i) Any measure relating to motor vehicle exhaust or evaporative emissions promulgated by the Administrator by January 1, 1990.

(ii) Regulations concerning Reid Vapor Pressure promulgated by the Administrator by November 15, 1990, or required to be promulgated under section 7545(h) of this title.

(iii) Measures required under subsection (a)(2)(A) of this section (concerning corrections to implementation plans prescribed under guidance by the Administrator).

(iv) Measures required under subsection (a)(2)(B) of this section to be submitted immediately after November 15, 1990 (concerning corrections to motor vehicle inspection and maintenance programs).

**(2) Reasonably available control technology**

The State shall submit a revision to the applicable implementation plan to include provisions to require the implementation of reasonably available control technology under section 7502(c)(1) of this title with respect to each of the following:

(A) Each category of VOC sources in the area covered by a CTG document issued by the Administrator between November 15, 1990, and the date of attainment.

(B) All VOC sources in the area covered by any CTG issued before November 15, 1990.

(C) All other major stationary sources of VOCs that are located in the area.

Each revision described in subparagraph (A) shall be submitted within the period set forth by the Administrator in issuing the relevant CTG document. The revisions with respect to sources described in subparagraphs (B) and (C) shall be submitted by 2 years after November 15, 1990, and shall provide for the implementation of the required measures as expeditiously as practicable but no later than May 31, 1995.

**(3) Gasoline vapor recovery**

**(A) General rule**

Not later than 2 years after November 15, 1990, the State shall submit a revision to the applicable implementation plan to require all owners or operators of gasoline dispensing systems to install and operate, by the date prescribed under subparagraph (B), a system for gasoline vapor recovery of emissions from the fueling of motor vehicles. The Administrator shall issue guidance as appropriate as to the effectiveness of such system. This subparagraph shall apply only to facilities which sell more than 10,000 gallons of gasoline per month (50,000 gallons per month in the case of an independent small business marketer of gasoline as defined in section 7625–1 [2] of this title).

**(B) Effective date**

The date required under subparagraph (A) shall be—

(i) 6 months after the adoption date, in the case of gasoline dispensing facilities for which construction commenced after November 15, 1990;

(ii) one year after the adoption date, in the case of gasoline dispensing facilities which dispense at least 100,000 gallons of gasoline per month, based on average monthly sales for the 2–year period before the adoption date; or

(iii) 2 years after the adoption date, in the case of all other gasoline dispensing facilities.

Any gasoline dispensing facility described under both clause (i) and clause (ii) shall meet the requirements of clause (i).

**(C) Reference to terms**

For purposes of this paragraph, any reference to the term "adoption date" shall be considered a reference to the date of adoption by the State of requirements for the installation and operation of a system for gasoline vapor recovery of emissions from the fueling of motor vehicles.

**(4) Motor vehicle inspection and maintenance**

For all Moderate Areas, the State shall submit, immediately after November 15, 1990, a revision to the applicable implementation plan that includes provisions necessary to provide for a vehicle inspection and maintenance program as described in subsection (a)(2)(B) of this section (without regard to whether or not the area was required by section 7502(b)(11)(B) of this title (as in effect immediately before November 15, 1990) to have included a specific schedule for implementation of such a program).

**(5) General offset requirement**

For purposes of satisfying the emission offset requirements of this part, the ratio of total emission reductions of volatile organic compounds to total increase emissions of such air pollutant shall be at least 1.15 to 1.

**(c) Serious Areas**

Except as otherwise specified in paragraph (4), each State in which all or part of a Serious Area is located shall, with respect to the Serious Area (or portion thereof, to the extent specified in this subsection), make the submissions described under subsection (b) of this section (relating to Moderate Areas), and shall also submit the revisions to the applicable implementation plan (including the plan items) described under this subsection. For any Serious Area, the terms "major source" and "major stationary source" include (in addition to the sources described in section 7602 of this title) any stationary source or group of sources located within a contiguous area and under common control that emits, or has the potential to emit, at least 50 tons per year of volatile organic compounds.

**(1) Enhanced monitoring**

In order to obtain more comprehensive and representative data on ozone air pollution, not later than 18 months after November 15, 1990, the Administrator shall promulgate rules, after notice and public comment, for enhanced monitoring of ozone, oxides of nitrogen, and volatile organic compounds. The rules shall, among other things, cover the location and maintenance of monitors. Immediately following the promulgation of rules by the Administrator relating to enhanced monitoring, the State shall commence such actions as may be necessary to adopt and implement a program based on such rules, to improve monitoring for ambient concentrations of ozone, oxides of nitrogen and volatile organic compounds and to improve monitoring of emissions of oxides of nitrogen and volatile organic compounds. Each State implementation plan for the area shall contain measures to improve the ambient monitoring of such air pollutants.

**(2) Attainment and reasonable further progress demonstrations**

Within 4 years after November 15, 1990, the State shall submit a revision to the applicable implementation plan that includes each of the following:

**(A) Attainment demonstration**

A demonstration that the plan, as revised, will provide for attainment of the ozone national ambient air quality standard by the applicable attainment date. This attainment demonstration must be based on photochemical grid modeling or any other analytical method determined by the Administrator, in the Administrator's discretion, to be at least as effective.

**(B) Reasonable further progress demonstration**

A demonstration that the plan, as revised, will result in VOC emissions reductions from the baseline emissions described in subsection (b)(1)(B) of this section equal to the following amount averaged over each consecutive 3–year period beginning 6 years after November 15, 1990, until the attainment date:

**(i)** at least 3 percent of baseline emissions each year; or

**(ii)** an amount less than 3 percent of such baseline emissions each year, if the State demonstrates to the satisfaction of the Administrator that the plan reflecting such lesser amount includes all measures that can feasibly be implemented in the area, in light of technological achievability.

To lessen the 3 percent requirement under clause (ii), a State must demonstrate to the satisfaction of the Administrator that the plan for the area includes the measures that are achieved in practice by sources in the same source category in nonattainment areas of the next higher classification. Any determination to lessen the 3 percent requirement shall be reviewed at each milestone under subsection (g) of this section and revised to reflect such new measures (if any) achieved in practice by sources in the same category in any State, allowing a reasonable time to implement such measures. The emission reductions described in this subparagraph shall be calculated in accordance with subsection (b)(1)(C) and (D) of this section (concerning creditability of reductions). The reductions creditable for the period beginning 6 years after November 15, 1990, shall include reductions that occurred before such period, computed in accordance with subsection (b)(1) of this section, that exceed the 15–percent amount of reductions required under subsection (b)(1)(A) of this section.

(C) $NO_x$ control

The revision may contain, in lieu of the demonstration required under subparagraph (B), a demonstration to the satisfaction of the Administrator that the applicable implementation plan, as revised, provides for reductions of emissions of VOC's and oxides of nitrogen (calculated according to the creditability provisions of subsection (b)(1)(C) and (D) of this section), that would result in a reduction in ozone concentrations at least equivalent to that which would result from the amount of VOC emission reductions required under subparagraph (B). Within 1 year after November 15, 1990, the Administrator shall issue guidance concerning the conditions under which $NO_x$ control may be substituted for VOC control or may be combined with VOC control in order to maximize the reduction in ozone air pollution. In accord with such guidance, a lesser percentage of VOCs may be accepted as an adequate demonstration for purposes of this subsection.

**(3) Enhanced vehicle inspection and maintenance program**

**(A) Requirement for submission**

Within 2 years after November 15, 1990, the State shall submit a revision to the applicable implementation plan to provide for an enhanced program to reduce hydrocarbon emissions and $NO_x$ emissions from in-use motor vehicles registered in each urbanized area (in the nonattainment area), as defined by the Bureau of the Census, with a 1980 population of 200,000 or more.

**(B) Effective date of State programs; guidance**

The State program required under subparagraph (A) shall take effect no later than 2 years from November 15, 1990, and shall comply in all respects with guidance published in the Federal Register (and from time to time revised) by the Administrator for enhanced vehicle inspection and maintenance programs. Such guidance shall include—

(i) a performance standard achievable by a program combining emission testing, including on-road emission testing, with inspection to detect tampering with emission control devices and misfueling for all light-duty vehicles and all light-duty trucks subject to standards under section 7521 of this title; and

(ii) program administration features necessary to reasonably assure that adequate management resources, tools, and practices are in place to attain and maintain the performance standard.

Compliance with the performance standard under clause (i) shall be determined using a method to be established by the Administrator.

**(C) State program**

The State program required under subparagraph (A) shall include, at a minimum, each of the following elements—

**(i)** Computerized emission analyzers, including on-road testing devices.

**(ii)** No waivers for vehicles and parts covered by the emission control performance warranty as provided for in section 7541(b) of this title unless a warranty remedy has been denied in writing, or for tampering-related repairs.

**(iii)** In view of the air quality purpose of the program, if, for any vehicle, waivers are permitted for emissions-related repairs not covered by warranty, an expenditure to qualify for the waiver of an amount of $450 or more for such repairs (adjusted annually as determined by the Administrator on the basis of the Consumer Price Index in the same manner as provided in subchapter V of this chapter).

**(iv)** Enforcement through denial of vehicle registration (except for any program in operation before November 15, 1990, whose enforcement mechanism is demonstrated to the Administrator to be more effective than the applicable vehicle registration program in assuring that noncomplying vehicles are not operated on public roads).

**(v)** Annual emission testing and necessary adjustment, repair, and maintenance, unless the State demonstrates to the satisfaction of the Administrator that a biennial inspection, in combination with other features of the program which exceed the requirements of this chapter, will result in emission reductions which equal or exceed the reductions which can be obtained through such annual inspections.

**(vi)** Operation of the program on a centralized basis, unless the State demonstrates to the satisfaction of the Administrator that a decentralized program will be equally effective. An electronically connected testing system, a licensing system, or other measures (or any combination thereof) may be considered, in accordance with criteria established by the Administrator, as equally effective for such purposes.

**(vii)** Inspection of emission control diagnostic systems and the maintenance or repair of malfunctions or system deterioration identified by or affecting such diagnostics systems.

Each State shall biennially prepare a report to the Administrator which assesses the emission reductions achieved by the program required under this paragraph based on data collected during inspection and repair of vehicles. The methods used to assess the emission reductions shall be those established by the Administrator.

**(4) Clean-fuel vehicle programs**

**(A)** Except to the extent that substitute provisions have been approved by the Administrator under subparagraph (B), the State shall submit to the Administrator, within 42 months of November 15, 1990, a revision to the applicable implementation plan for each area described under part C of subchapter II of this chapter to include such measures as may be necessary to ensure the effectiveness of the applicable provisions of the clean-fuel vehicle program prescribed under part C of subchapter II of this chapter, including all measures necessary to make the use of clean alternative fuels in clean-fuel vehicles (as defined in part C of subchapter II of this chapter) economic from the standpoint of vehicle owners. Such a revision shall also be submitted for each area that opts into the clean fuel-vehicle program as provided in part C of subchapter II of this chapter.

**(B)** The Administrator shall approve, as a substitute for all or a portion of the clean-fuel vehicle program prescribed under part C of subchapter II of this chapter, any revision to the relevant applicable implementation plan that in the Administrator's judgment will achieve long-term reductions in ozone-producing and toxic air emissions equal to those achieved under part C of subchapter II of this chapter, or the percentage thereof attributable to the portion of the clean-fuel vehicle program for which the revision is to substitute. The Administrator may approve such revision only if it consists exclusively of provisions other than those required under this chapter for the area. Any State seeking approval of such revision must submit the revision to the Administrator within 24 months of November 15, 1990. The Administrator shall approve or disapprove any such revision within 30 months of November 15, 1990. The Administrator shall publish the revision submitted by a State in the Federal Register upon receipt. Such notice shall constitute a notice of proposed rulemaking on whether or not to approve such revision and shall be deemed to comply with the requirements concerning notices of proposed rulemaking contained in sections 553 through 557 of Title 5 (related to notice and comment). Where the Administrator approves such revision for any area, the State need not submit the revision required by subparagraph (A) for the area with respect to the portions of the Federal clean-fuel vehicle program for which the Administrator has approved the revision as a substitute.

**(C)** If the Administrator determines, under section 7509 of this title, that the State has failed to submit any portion of the program required under subparagraph (A), then, in addition to any sanctions available under section 7509 of this title, the State may not receive credit, in any demonstration of attainment or reasonable further progress for the area, for any emission reductions from implementation of the corresponding aspects of the Federal clean-fuel vehicle requirements established in part C of subchapter II of this chapter.

**(5) Transportation control**

**(A)** [3] Beginning 6 years after November 15, 1990, and each third year thereafter, the State shall submit a demonstration as to whether current aggregate vehicle mileage, aggregate vehicle emissions, congestion levels, and other relevant parameters are consistent with those used for the area's demonstration of attainment. Where such parameters and emissions levels exceed the levels projected for purposes of the area's attainment demonstration, the State shall within 18 months develop and submit a revision of the applicable implementation plan that includes a transportation control measures program consisting of measures from, but not limited to, section 7408(f) of this title that will reduce emissions to levels that are consistent with emission levels projected in such demonstration. In considering such measures, the State should ensure adequate access to downtown, other commercial, and residential areas and should avoid measures that increase or relocate emissions and congestion rather than reduce them. Such revision shall be developed in accordance with guidance issued by the Administrator pursuant to section 7408(e) of this title and with the requirements of section 7504(b) of this title and shall include implementation and funding schedules that achieve expeditious emissions reductions in accordance with implementation plan projections.

**(6) De minimis rule**

The new source review provisions under this part shall ensure that increased emissions of volatile organic compounds resulting from any physical change in, or change in the method of operation of, a stationary source located in the area shall not be considered de minimis for purposes of determining the applicability of the permit requirements established by this chapter unless the increase in net emissions of such air pollutant from such source does not exceed 25 tons when aggregated with all other net increases in emissions from the source over any period of 5 consecutive calendar years which includes the calendar year in which such increase occurred.

**(7) Special rule for modifications of sources emitting less than 100 tons**

In the case of any major stationary source of volatile organic compounds located in the area (other than a source which emits or has the potential to emit 100 tons or more of volatile organic compounds per year), whenever any change (as described in section 7411(a)(4) of this title) at that source results in any increase (other than a de minimis increase) in emissions of volatile organic compounds from any discrete operation, unit, or other pollutant emitting activity at the source, such increase shall be considered a modification for purposes of section 7502(c)(5) of this title and section 7503(a) of this title, except that such increase shall not be considered a modification for such purposes if the owner or operator of the source elects to offset the increase by a greater reduction in emissions of volatile organic compounds concerned from other operations, units, or activities within the source at an internal offset ratio of at least 1.3 to 1. If the owner or operator does not make such election, such change shall be considered a modification for such purposes, but in applying section 7503(a)(2) of this title in the case of any such modification, the best available control technology (BACT), as defined in section 7479 of this title, shall be substituted for the lowest achievable emission rate (LAER). The Administrator shall establish and publish policies and procedures for implementing the provisions of this paragraph.

**(8) Special rule for modifications of sources emitting 100 tons or more**

In the case of any major stationary source of volatile organic compounds located in the area which emits or has the potential to emit 100 tons or more of volatile organic compounds per year, whenever any change (as described in section 7411(a)(4) of this title) at that source results in any increase (other than a de minimis increase) in emissions of volatile organic compounds from any discrete operation, unit, or other pollutant emitting activity at the source, such increase shall be considered a modification for purposes of section 7502(c)(5) of this title and section 7503(a) of this title, except that if the owner or operator of the source elects to offset the increase by a greater reduction in emissions of volatile organic compounds from other operations, units, or activities within the source at an internal offset ratio of at least 1.3 to 1, the requirements of section 7503(a)(2) of this title (concerning the lowest achievable emission rate (LAER)) shall not apply.

**(9) Contingency provisions**

In addition to the contingency provisions required under section 7502(c)(9) of this title, the plan revision shall provide for the implementation of specific measures to be undertaken if the area fails to meet any applicable milestone. Such measures shall be included in the plan revision as contingency measures to take effect without further action by the State or the Administrator upon a failure by the State to meet the applicable milestone.

**(10) General offset requirement**

For purposes of satisfying the emission offset requirements of this part, the ratio of total emission reductions of volatile organic compounds to total increase emissions of such air pollutant shall be at least 1.2 to 1.

Any reference to "attainment date" in subsection (b) of this section, which is incorporated by reference into this subsection, shall refer to the attainment date for serious areas.

**(d) Severe Areas**

Each State in which all or part of a Severe Area is located shall, with respect to the Severe Area, make the submissions described under subsection (c) of this section (relating to Serious Areas), and shall also submit the revisions to the applicable implementation plan (including the plan items) described under this subsection. For any Severe Area, the terms "major source" and "major stationary source" include (in addition to the sources described in section 7602 of this title) any stationary source or group of sources located within a contiguous area and under common control that emits, or has the potential to emit, at least 25 tons per year of volatile organic compounds.

**(1) Vehicle miles traveled**

**(A)** Within 2 years after November 15, 1990, the State shall submit a revision that identifies and adopts specific enforceable transportation control strategies and transportation control measures to offset any growth in emissions from growth in vehicle miles traveled or numbers of vehicle trips in such area and to attain reduction in motor vehicle emissions as necessary, in combination with other emission reduction requirements of this subpart, to comply with the requirements of subsection[4] (b)(2)(B) and (c)(2)(B) of this section (pertaining to periodic emissions reduction requirements). The State shall consider measures specified in section 7408(f) of this title, and choose from among and implement such measures as necessary to demonstrate attainment with the national ambient air quality standards; in considering such measures, the State should ensure adequate access to downtown, other commercial, and residential areas and should avoid measures that increase or relocate emissions and congestion rather than reduce them.

**(B)** The State may also, in its discretion, submit a revision at any time requiring employers in such area to implement programs to reduce work-related vehicle trips and miles travelled by employees. Such revision shall be developed in accordance with guidance issued by the Administrator pursuant to section 7408(f) of this title and may require that employers in such area increase average passenger occupancy per vehicle in commuting trips between home and the workplace during peak travel periods. The guidance of the Administrator may specify average vehicle occupancy rates which vary for locations within a nonattainment area (suburban, center city, business district) or among nonattainment areas reflecting existing occupancy rates and the availability of high occupancy modes. Any State required to submit a revision under this subparagraph (as in effect before December 23, 1995) containing provisions requiring employers to reduce work-related vehicle trips and miles travelled by employees may, in accordance with State law, remove such provisions from the implementation plan, or withdraw its submission, if the State notifies the Administrator, in writing, that the State has undertaken, or will undertake, one or more alternative methods that will achieve emission reductions equivalent to those to be achieved by the removed or withdrawn provisions.

**(2) Offset requirement**

For purposes of satisfying the offset requirements pursuant to this part, the ratio of total emission reductions of VOCs to total increased emissions of such air pollutant shall be at least 1.3 to 1, except that if the State plan requires all existing major sources in the nonattainment area to use best available control technology (as defined in section 7479(3) of this title) for the control of volatile organic compounds, the ratio shall be at least 1.2 to 1.

**(3) Enforcement under section 7511d**

By December 31, 2000, the State shall submit a plan revision which includes the provisions required under section 7511d of this title.

Any reference to the term "attainment date" in subsection (b) or (c) of this section, which is incorporated by reference into this subsection (d), shall refer to the attainment date for Severe Areas.

**(e) Extreme Areas**

Each State in which all or part of an Extreme Area is located shall, with respect to the Extreme Area, make the submissions described under subsection (d) of this section (relating to Severe Areas), and shall also submit the revisions to the applicable implementation plan (including the plan items) described under this subsection. The provisions of clause (ii) of subsection (c)(2)(B) of this section (relating to reductions of less than 3 percent), the provisions of paragraphs [5] (6), (7) and (8) of subsection (c) of this section (relating to de minimus rule and modification of sources), and the provisions of clause (ii) of subsection (b)(1)(A) of this section (relating to reductions of less than 15 percent) shall not apply in the case of an Extreme Area. For any Extreme Area, the terms "major source" and "major stationary source" includes (in addition to the sources described in section 7602 of this title) any stationary source or group of sources located within a contiguous area and under common control that emits, or has the potential to emit, at least 10 tons per year of volatile organic compounds.

**(1) Offset requirement**

For purposes of satisfying the offset requirements pursuant to this part, the ratio of total emission reductions of VOCs to total increased emissions of such air pollutant shall be at least 1.5 to 1, except that if the State plan requires all existing major sources in the nonattainment area to use best available control technology (as defined in section 7479(3) of this title) for the control of volatile organic compounds, the ratio shall be at least 1.2 to 1.

**(2) Modifications**

Any change (as described in section 7411(a)(4) of this title) at a major stationary source which results in any increase in emissions from any discrete operation, unit, or other pollutant emitting activity at the source shall be considered a modification for purposes of section 7502(c)(5) of this title and section 7503(a) of this title, except that for purposes of complying with the offset requirement pursuant to section 7503(a)(1) of this title, any such increase shall not be considered a modification if the owner or operator of the source elects to offset the increase by a greater reduction in emissions of the air pollutant concerned from other discrete operations, units, or activities within the source at an internal offset ratio of at least 1.3 to 1. The offset requirements of this part shall not be applicable in Extreme Areas to a modification of an existing source if such modification consists of installation of equipment required to comply with the applicable implementation plan, permit, or this chapter.

**(3) Use of clean fuels or advanced control technology**

For Extreme Areas, a plan revision shall be submitted within 3 years after November 15, 1990, to require, effective 8 years after November 15, 1990, that each new, modified, and existing electric utility and industrial and commercial boiler which emits more than 25 tons per year of oxides of nitrogen—

**(A)** burn as its primary fuel natural gas, methanol, or ethanol (or a comparably low polluting fuel), or

**(B)** use advanced control technology (such as catalytic control technology or other comparably effective control methods) for reduction of emissions of oxides of nitrogen.

For purposes of this subsection, the term "primary fuel" means the fuel which is used 90 percent or more of the operating time. This paragraph shall not apply during any natural gas supply emergency (as defined in title III of the Natural Gas Policy Act of 1978 [15 U.S.C.A. § 3361 et seq.] ).

**(4) Traffic control measures during heavy traffic hours**

For Extreme Areas, each implementation plan revision under this subsection may contain provisions establishing traffic control measures applicable during heavy traffic hours to reduce the use of high polluting vehicles or heavy-duty vehicles, notwithstanding any other provision of law.

**(5) New technologies**

The Administrator may, in accordance with section 7410 of this title, approve provisions of an implementation plan for an Extreme Area which anticipate development of new control techniques or improvement of existing control technologies, and an attainment demonstration based on such provisions, if the State demonstrates to the satisfaction of the Administrator that—

(A) such provisions are not necessary to achieve the incremental emission reductions required during the first 10 years after November 15, 1990; and

(B) the State has submitted enforceable commitments to develop and adopt contingency measures to be implemented as set forth herein if the anticipated technologies do not achieve planned reductions.

Such contingency measures shall be submitted to the Administrator no later than 3 years before proposed implementation of the plan provisions and approved or disapproved by the Administrator in accordance with section 7410 of this title. The contingency measures shall be adequate to produce emission reductions sufficient, in conjunction with other approved plan provisions, to achieve the periodic emission reductions required by subsection (b)(1) or (c)(2) of this section and attainment by the applicable dates. If the Administrator determines that an Extreme Area has failed to achieve an emission reduction requirement set forth in subsection (b)(1) or (c)(2) of this section, and that such failure is due in whole or part to an inability to fully implement provisions approved pursuant to this subsection, the Administrator shall require the State to implement the contingency measures to the extent necessary to assure compliance with subsections (b)(1) and (c)(2) of this section.

Any reference to the term "attainment date" in subsection (b), (c), or (d) of this section which is incorporated by reference into this subsection, shall refer to the attainment date for Extreme Areas.

**(f) $NO_x$ requirements**

(1) The plan provisions required under this subpart for major stationary sources of volatile organic compounds shall also apply to major stationary sources (as defined in section 7602 of this title and subsections (c), (d), and (e) of this section) of oxides of nitrogen. This subsection shall not apply in the case of oxides of nitrogen for those sources for which the Administrator determines (when the Administrator approves a plan or plan revision) that net air quality benefits are greater in the absence of reductions of oxides of nitrogen from the sources concerned. This subsection shall also not apply in the case of oxides of nitrogen for—

(A) nonattainment areas not within an ozone transport region under section 7511c of this title, if the Administrator determines (when the Administrator approves a plan or plan revision) that additional reductions of oxides of nitrogen would not contribute to attainment of the national ambient air quality standard for ozone in the area, or

(B) nonattainment areas within such an ozone transport region if the Administrator determines (when the Administrator approves a plan or plan revision) that additional reductions of oxides of nitrogen would not produce net ozone air quality benefits in such region.

The Administrator shall, in the Administrator's determinations, consider the study required under section 7511f of this title.

(2)(A) If the Administrator determines that excess reductions in emissions of $NO_x$ would be achieved under paragraph (1), the Administrator may limit the application of paragraph (1) to the extent necessary to avoid achieving such excess reductions.

(B) For purposes of this paragraph, excess reductions in emissions of $NO_x$ are emission reductions for which the Administrator determines that net air quality benefits are greater in the absence of such reductions. Alternatively, for purposes of this paragraph, excess reductions in emissions of $NO_x$ are, for—

(i) nonattainment areas not within an ozone transport region under section 7511c of this title, emission reductions that the Administrator determines would not contribute to attainment of the national ambient air quality standard for ozone in the area, or

(ii) nonattainment areas within such ozone transport region, emission reductions that the Administrator determines would not produce net ozone air quality benefits in such region.

(3) At any time after the final report under section 7511f of this title is submitted to Congress, a person may petition the Administrator for a determination under paragraph (1) or (2) with respect to any nonat-

tainment area or any ozone transport region under section 7511c of this title. The Administrator shall grant or deny such petition within 6 months after its filing with the Administrator.

**(g) Milestones**

**(1) Reductions in emissions**

6 years after November 15, 1990, and at intervals of every 3 years thereafter, the State shall determine whether each nonattainment area (other than an area classified as Marginal or Moderate) has achieved a reduction in emissions during the preceding intervals equivalent to the total emission reductions required to be achieved by the end of such interval pursuant to subsection (b)(1) of this section and the corresponding requirements of subsections (c)(2)(B) and (C), (d), and (e) of this section. Such reduction shall be referred to in this section as an applicable milestone.

**(2) Compliance demonstration**

For each nonattainment area referred to in paragraph (1), not later than 90 days after the date on which an applicable milestone occurs (not including an attainment date on which a milestone occurs in cases where the standard has been attained), each State in which all or part of such area is located shall submit to the Administrator a demonstration that the milestone has been met. A demonstration under this paragraph shall be submitted in such form and manner, and shall contain such information and analysis, as the Administrator shall require, by rule. The Administrator shall determine whether or not a State's demonstration is adequate within 90 days after the Administrator's receipt of a demonstration which contains the information and analysis required by the Administrator.

**(3) Serious and Severe Areas; State election**

If a State fails to submit a demonstration under paragraph (2) for any Serious or Severe Area within the required period or if the Administrator determines that the area has not met any applicable milestone, the State shall elect, within 90 days after such failure or determination—

**(A)** to have the area reclassified to the next higher classification,

**(B)** to implement specific additional measures adequate, as determined by the Administrator, to meet the next milestone as provided in the applicable contingency plan, or

**(C)** to adopt an economic incentive program as described in paragraph (4).

If the State makes an election under subparagraph (B), the Administrator shall, within 90 days after the election, review such plan and shall, if the Administrator finds the contingency plan inadequate, require further measures necessary to meet such milestone. Once the State makes an election, it shall be deemed accepted by the Administrator as meeting the election requirement. If the State fails to make an election required under this paragraph within the required 90-day period or within 6 months thereafter, the area shall be reclassified to the next higher classification by operation of law at the expiration of such 6-month period. Within 12 months after the date required for the State to make an election, the State shall submit a revision of the applicable implementation plan for the area that meets the requirements of this paragraph. The Administrator shall review such plan revision and approve or disapprove the revision within 9 months after the date of its submission.

**(4) Economic incentive program**

**(A)** An economic incentive program under this paragraph shall be consistent with rules published by the Administrator and sufficient, in combination with other elements of the State plan, to achieve the next milestone. The State program may include a nondiscriminatory system, consistent with applicable law regarding interstate commerce, of State established emissions fees or a system of marketable permits, or a system of State fees on sale or manufacture of products the use of which contributes to ozone formation, or any combination of the foregoing or other similar measures. The program may also include incentives and requirements to reduce vehicle emissions and vehicle miles traveled in the area, including any of the transportation control measures identified in section 7408(f) of this title.

**(B)** Within 2 years after November 15, 1990, the Administrator shall publish rules for the programs to be adopted pursuant to subparagraph (A). Such rules shall include model plan provisions which may be adopted for reducing emissions from permitted stationary sources, area sources, and mobile sources. The guidelines shall require that any revenues generated by the plan provisions adopted pursuant to subparagraph (A) shall be used by the State for any of the following:

**(i)** Providing incentives for achieving emission reductions.

**(ii)** Providing assistance for the development of innovative technologies for the control of ozone air pollution and for the development of lower-polluting solvents and surface coatings. Such assistance shall not provide for the payment of more than 75 percent of either the costs of any project to develop such a technology or the costs of development of a lower-polluting solvent or surface coating.

**(iii)** Funding the administrative costs of State programs under this chapter. Not more than 50 percent of such revenues may be used for purposes of this clause.

**(5) Extreme Areas**

If a State fails to submit a demonstration under paragraph (2) for any Extreme Area within the required period, or if the Administrator determines that the area has not met any applicable milestone, the State shall, within 9 months after such failure or determination, submit a plan revision to implement an economic incentive program which meets the requirements of paragraph (4). The Administrator shall review such plan revision and approve or disapprove the revision within 9 months after the date of its submission.

**(h) Rural transport areas**

(1) Notwithstanding any other provision of section 7511 of this title or this section, a State containing an ozone nonattainment area that does not include, and is not adjacent to, any part of a Metropolitan Statistical Area or, where one exists, a Consolidated Metropolitan Statistical Area (as defined by the United States Bureau of the Census), which area is treated by the Administrator, in the Administrator's discretion, as a rural transport area within the meaning of paragraph (2), shall be treated by operation of law as satisfying the requirements of this section if it makes the submissions required under subsection (a) of this section (relating to marginal areas).

(2) The Administrator may treat an ozone nonattainment area as a rural transport area if the Administrator finds that sources of VOC (and, where the Administrator determines relevant, $NO_x$) emissions within the area do not make a significant contribution to the ozone concentrations measured in the area or in other areas.

**(i) Reclassified areas**

Each State containing an ozone nonattainment area reclassified under section 7511(b)(2) of this title shall meet such requirements of subsections (b) through (d) of this section as may be applicable to the area as reclassified, according to the schedules prescribed in connection with such requirements, except that the Administrator may adjust any applicable deadlines (other than attainment dates) to the extent such adjustment is necessary or appropriate to assure consistency among the required submissions.

**(j) Multi-State ozone nonattainment areas**

**(1) Coordination among States**

Each State in which there is located a portion of a single ozone nonattainment area which covers more than one State (hereinafter in this section referred to as a "multi-State ozone nonattainment area") shall—

**(A)** take all reasonable steps to coordinate, substantively and procedurally, the revisions and implementation of State implementation plans applicable to the nonattainment area concerned; and

**(B)** use photochemical grid modeling or any other analytical method determined by the Administrator, in his discretion, to be at least as effective.

The Administrator may not approve any revision of a State implementation plan submitted under this part for a State in which part of a multi-State ozone nonattainment area is located if the plan revision for that State fails to comply with the requirements of this subsection.

**(2) Failure to demonstrate attainment**

If any State in which there is located a portion of a multi-State ozone nonattainment area fails to provide a demonstration of attainment of the national ambient air quality standard for ozone in that portion within the required period, the State may petition the Administrator to make a finding that the State would have been able to make such demonstration but for the failure of one or more other States in which other portions of the area are located to commit to the implementation of all measures required under this section (relating to plan submissions and requirements for ozone nonattainment areas). If the Administrator makes such finding, the provisions of section 7509 of this title (relating to sanctions) shall not apply, by reason of the failure to make such demonstration, in the portion of the multi-State ozone nonattainment area within the State submitting such petition.

(July 14, 1955, c. 360, Title I, § 182, as added Nov. 15, 1990, Pub.L. 101–549, Title I, § 103, 104 Stat. 2426, and amended Dec. 23, 1995, Pub.L. 104–70, § 1, 109 Stat. 773.)

1 So in original. Probably should be "subparagraph".
2 So in original. Probably should be section "7625".
3 So in original. No subpar. (B) has been enacted.
4 So in original. Probably should be "subsections".
5 So in original. Probably should be "paragraphs".

## HISTORICAL AND STATUTORY NOTES

**References in Text**

The Natural Gas Policy Act of 1978, referred to in subsec. (e)(3), is Pub.L. 95–621, Nov. 9, 1978, 92 Stat. 3350, as amended. Title III of the Natural Gas Policy Act of 1978 is classified to subchapter III (section 3361 et seq.) of chapter 60 of Title 15, Commerce and Trade. For complete classification of this Act to the Code, see Short Title note set out under section 3301 of Title 15 and Tables.

**Effective and Applicability Provisions**

1990 Acts

Section effective Nov. 15, 1990, except as otherwise provided, see section 711(b) of Pub.L. 101–549, set out as a note under section 7401 of this title.

**Savings Provisions**

Suits, actions or proceedings commenced under this chapter as in effect prior to Nov. 15, 1990, not to abate by reason of the taking effect of amendments by Pub.L. 101–549, except as otherwise provided for, see section 711(a) of Pub.L. 101–549, set out as a note under section 7401 of this title.

**Moratorium on Certain Emissions Testing Requirements**

Pub.L. 104–59, Title III, § 348, Nov. 28, 1995, 109 Stat. 617, provided that:

"(a) **In general.**—The Administrator of the Environmental Protection Agency (hereinafter in this section referred to as the 'Administrator') shall not require adoption or implementation by a State of a test-only I/M240 enhanced vehicle inspection and maintenance program as a means of compliance with section 182 or 187 of the Clean Air Act (42 U.S.C. 7511a; 7512a), but the Administrator may approve such a program if a State chooses to adopt the program as a means of compliance with such section.

"(b) **Limitation on plan disapproval.**—The Administrator shall not disapprove or apply an automatic discount to a State implementation plan revision under section 182 or 187 of the Clean Air Act (42 U.S.C. 7511a; 7512a) on the basis of a policy, regulation, or guidance providing for a discount of emissions credits because the inspection and maintenance program in such plan revision is decentralized or a test-and-repair program.

"(c) **Emissions reduction credits.**—

"(1) **State plan revision; approval.**—Within 120 days of the date of the enactment of this subsection [Nov. 28, 1995], a State may submit an implementation plan revision proposing an interim inspection and maintenance program under section 182 or 187 of the Clean Air Act (42 U.S.C. 7511a; 7512a). The Administrator shall approve the program based on the full amount of credits proposed by the State for each element of the program if the proposed credits reflect good faith estimates by the State and the revision is otherwise in compliance with such Act [this chapter]. If, within such 120-day period, the State submits to the Administrator proposed revisions to the implementation plan, has all of the statutory authority necessary to implement the revisions, and has proposed a regulation to make the revisions, the Administrator may approve the revisions without regard to whether or not such regulation has been issued as a final regulation by the State.

"(2) **Expiration of interim approval.**—The interim approval shall expire on the earlier of (A) the last day of the 18-month period beginning on the date of the interim approval, or (B) the date of final approval. The interim approval may not be extended.

"(3) **Final approval.**—The Administrator shall grant final approval of the revision based on the credits proposed by the State during or after the period of interim approval if data collected on the operation of the State program demonstrates that the credits are appropriate and the revision is otherwise in compliance with the Clean Air Act [this chapter].

"(4) **Basis of approval; no automatic discount.**—Any determination with respect to interim or full approval shall be based on the elements of the program and shall not apply any automatic discount because the program is decentralized or a test-and-repair program."

## § 7511b. Federal ozone measures

[CAA § 183]

**(a) Control techniques guidelines for VOC sources**

Within 3 years after November 15, 1990, the Administrator shall issue control techniques guidelines, in accordance with section 7408 of this title, for 11 categories of stationary sources of VOC emissions for which such guidelines have not been issued as of November 15, 1990, not including the categories referred to in paragraphs (3) and (4) of subsection (b) of this section. The Administrator may issue such additional control techniques guidelines as the Administrator deems necessary.

**(b) Existing and new CTGS**

(1) Within 36 months after November 15, 1990, and periodically thereafter, the Administrator shall review and, if necessary, update control technique guidance issued under section 7408 of this title before November 15, 1990.

(2) In issuing the guidelines the Administrator shall give priority to those categories which the Administrator considers to make the most significant contribution to the formation of ozone air pollution in ozone nonattainment areas, including hazardous waste treatment, storage, and disposal facilities which are permitted under subtitle C of the Solid Waste Disposal Act [42 U.S.C.A. § 6921 et seq.]. Thereafter the Administrator shall periodically review and, if necessary, revise such guidelines.

(3) Within 3 years after November 15, 1990, the Administrator shall issue control techniques guidelines in accordance with section 7408 of this title to reduce the aggregate emissions of volatile organic compounds into the ambient air from aerospace coatings and solvents. Such control techniques guidelines shall, at a minimum, be adequate to reduce aggregate emissions of volatile organic compounds into the ambient air from the application of such coatings and solvents to such level as the Administrator determines may be achieved through the adoption of best available control measures. Such control technology guidance shall provide for such reductions in such increments and on such schedules as the Administrator determines to be reasonable, but in no event later than 10 years after the final issuance of such control technology guidance. In developing control technology guidance under this subsection, the Administrator shall consult with the Secretary of Defense, the Secretary of Transportation, and the Administrator of the National Aeronautics and Space Administration with regard to the establishment of specifications for such coatings. In evaluating VOC reduction strategies, the guidance shall take into account the applicable requirements of section 7412 of this title and the need to protect stratospheric ozone.

(4) Within 3 years after November 15, 1990, the Administrator shall issue control techniques guidelines in accordance with section 7408 of this title to reduce the aggregate emissions of volatile organic compounds and PM–10 into the ambient air from paints, coatings, and solvents used in shipbuilding operations and ship repair. Such control techniques guidelines shall, at a minimum, be adequate to reduce aggregate emissions of volatile organic compounds and PM–10 into the ambient air from the removal or application of such paints, coatings, and solvents to such level as the Administrator determines may be achieved through the adoption of the best available control measures. Such control techniques guidelines shall provide for such reductions in such increments and on such schedules as the Administrator determines to be reasonable, but in no event later than 10 years after the final issuance of such control technology guidance. In developing control techniques guidelines under this subsection, the Administrator shall consult with the appropriate Federal agencies.

**(c) Alternative control techniques**

Within 3 years after November 15, 1990, the Administrator shall issue technical documents which identify alternative controls for all categories of stationary sources of volatile organic compounds and oxides of nitrogen which emit, or have the potential to emit 25 tons per year or more of such air pollutant. The Administrator shall revise and update such documents as the Administrator determines necessary.

**(d) Guidance for evaluating cost-effectiveness**

Within 1 year after November 15, 1990, the Administrator shall provide guidance to the States to be used in evaluating the relative cost-effectiveness of various options for the control of emissions from existing stationary sources of air pollutants which contribute to nonattainment of the national ambient air quality standards for ozone.

**(e) Control of emissions from certain sources**

**(1) Definitions**

For purposes of this subsection—

**(A) Best available controls**

The term "best available controls" means the degree of emissions reduction that the Administrator determines, on the basis of technological and economic feasibility, health, environmental, and energy impacts, is achievable through the application of the most effective equipment, measures, processes, methods, systems or techniques, including chemical reformulation, product or feedstock substitution, repackaging, and directions for use, consumption, storage, or disposal.

**(B) Consumer or commercial product**

The term "consumer or commercial product" means any substance, product (including paints, coatings, and solvents), or article (including any container or packaging) held by any person, the use, consumption, storage, disposal, destruction, or decomposition of which may result in the release of volatile organic compounds. The term does not include fuels or fuel additives regulated under section 7545 of this title, or motor vehicles, non-road vehicles, and non-road engines as defined under section 7550 of this title.

**(C) Regulated entities**

The term "regulated entities" means—

(i) manufacturers, processors, wholesale distributors, or importers of consumer or commercial products for sale or distribution in interstate commerce in the United States; or

(ii) manufacturers, processors, wholesale distributors, or importers that supply the entities listed under clause (i) with such products for sale or distribution in interstate commerce in the United States.

**(2) Study and report**

**(A) Study**

The Administrator shall conduct a study of the emissions of volatile organic compounds into the ambient air from consumer and commercial products (or any combination thereof) in order to—

(i) determine their potential to contribute to ozone levels which violate the national ambient air quality standard for ozone; and

(ii) establish criteria for regulating consumer and commercial products or classes or categories thereof which shall be subject to control under this subsection.

The study shall be completed and a report submitted to Congress not later than 3 years after November 15, 1990.

**(B) Consideration of certain factors**

In establishing the criteria under subparagraph (A)(ii), the Administrator shall take into consideration each of the following:

(i) The uses, benefits, and commercial demand of consumer and commercial products.

(ii) The health or safety functions (if any) served by such consumer and commercial products.

(iii) Those consumer and commercial products which emit highly reactive volatile organic compounds into the ambient air.

(iv) Those consumer and commercial products which are subject to the most cost-effective controls.

(v) The availability of alternatives (if any) to such consumer and commercial products which are of comparable costs, considering health, safety, and environmental impacts.

**(3) Regulations to require emission reductions**

**(A) In general**

Upon submission of the final report under paragraph (2), the Administrator shall list those categories of consumer or commercial products that the Administrator determines, based on the study, account for at least 80 percent of the VOC emissions, on a reactivity-adjusted basis, from consumer or commercial products in areas that violate the NAAQS for ozone. Credit toward the 80 percent emissions calculation shall be given for emission reductions from consumer or commercial products made after November 15, 1990. At such time, the Administrator shall divide the list into 4 groups establishing priorities for regulation based on the criteria established in paragraph (2). Every 2 years after promulgating such list, the Administrator shall regulate one group of categories until all 4 groups are regulated. The regulations shall require best available controls as defined in this section. Such regulations may exempt health use products for which the Administrator determines there is no suitable substitute. In order to carry out this section, the Administrator may, by regulation, control or prohibit any activity, including the manufacture or introduction into commerce, offering for sale, or sale of any consumer or commercial product which results in emission of volatile organic compounds into the ambient air.

**(B) Regulated entities**

Regulations under this subsection may be imposed only with respect to regulated entities.

**(C) Use of CTGS**

For any consumer or commercial product the Administrator may issue control techniques guidelines under this chapter in lieu of regulations required under subparagraph (A) if the Administrator determines that such guidance will be substantially as effective as regulations in reducing emissions of volatile organic compounds which contribute to ozone levels in areas which violate the national ambient air quality standard for ozone.

**(4) Systems of regulation**

The regulations under this subsection may include any system or systems of regulation as the Administrator may deem appropriate, including requirements for registration and labeling, self-monitoring and reporting, prohibitions, limitations, or economic incentives (including marketable permits and auctions of emissions rights) concerning the manufacture, processing, distribution, use, consumption, or disposal of the product.

**(5) Special fund**

Any amounts collected by the Administrator under such regulations shall be deposited in a special fund in the United States Treasury for licensing and other services, which thereafter shall be available until expended, subject to annual appropriation Acts, solely to carry out the activities of the Administrator for which such fees, charges, or collections are established or made.

**(6) Enforcement**

Any regulation established under this subsection shall be treated, for purposes of enforcement of this chapter, as a standard under section 7411 of this title and any violation of such regulation shall be treated as a violation of a requirement of section 7411(e) of this title.

**(7) State administration**

Each State may develop and submit to the Administrator a procedure under State law for implementing and enforcing regulations promulgated under this subsection. If the Administrator finds the State procedure is adequate, the Administrator shall approve such procedure. Nothing in this paragraph shall prohibit the Administrator from enforcing any applicable regulations under this subsection.

**(8) Size, etc.**

No regulations regarding the size, shape, or labeling of a product may be promulgated, unless the Administrator determines such regulations to be useful in meeting any national ambient air quality standard.

**(9) State consultation**

Any State which proposes regulations other than those adopted under this subsection shall consult with the Administrator regarding whether any other State or local subdivision has promulgated or is promulgating regulations on any products covered under this part. The Administrator shall establish a clearinghouse of information, studies, and regulations proposed and promulgated regarding products covered under this subsection and disseminate such information collected as requested by State or local subdivisions.

**(f) Tank vessel standards**

(1) **Schedule for standards**

(A) Within 2 years after November 15, 1990, the Administrator, in consultation with the Secretary of the Department in which the Coast Guard is operating, shall promulgate standards applicable to the emission of VOCs and any other air pollutant from loading and unloading of tank vessels (as that term is defined in section 2101 of Title 46) which the Administrator finds causes, or contributes to, air pollution that may be reasonably anticipated to endanger public health or welfare. Such standards shall require the application of reasonably available control technology, considering costs, any nonair-quality benefits, environmental impacts, energy requirements and safety factors associated with alternative control techniques. To the extent practicable such standards shall apply to loading and unloading facilities and not to tank vessels.

(B) Any regulation prescribed under this subsection (and any revision thereof) shall take effect after such period as the Administrator finds (after consultation with the Secretary of the department[1] in which the Coast Guard is operating) necessary to permit the development and application of the requisite technology, giving appropriate consideration to the cost of compliance within such period, except that the effective date shall not be more than 2 years after promulgation of such regulations.

(2) **Regulations on equipment safety**

Within 6 months after November 15, 1990, the Secretary of the Department in which the Coast Guard is operating shall issue regulations to ensure the safety of the equipment and operations which are to control emissions from the loading and unloading of tank vessels, under section 3703 of Title 46 and section 1225 of Title 33. The standards promulgated by the Administrator under paragraph (1) and the regulations issued by a State or political subdivision regarding emissions from the loading and unloading of tank vessels shall be consistent with the regulations regarding safety of the Department in which the Coast Guard is operating.

(3) **Agency authority**

(A) The Administrator shall ensure compliance with the tank vessel emission standards prescribed under paragraph (1)(A). The Secretary of the Department in which the Coast Guard is operating shall also ensure compliance with the tank vessel standards prescribed under paragraph (1)(A).

(B) The Secretary of the Department in which the Coast Guard is operating shall ensure compliance with the regulations issued under paragraph (2).

(4) **State or local standards**

After the Administrator promulgates standards under this section, no State or political subdivision thereof may adopt or attempt to enforce any standard respecting emissions from tank vessels subject to regulation under paragraph (1) unless such standard is no less stringent than the standards promulgated under paragraph (1).

(5) **Enforcement**

Any standard established under paragraph (1)(A) shall be treated, for purposes of enforcement of this chapter, as a standard under section 7411 of this title and any violation of such standard shall be treated as a violation of a requirement of section 7411(e) of this title.

(g) **Ozone design value study**

The Administrator shall conduct a study of whether the methodology in use by the Environmental Protection Agency as of November 15, 1990, for establishing a design value for ozone provides a reasonable indicator of the ozone air quality of ozone nonattainment areas. The Administrator shall obtain input from States, local subdivisions thereof, and others. The study shall be completed and a report submitted to Congress not later than 3 years after November 15, 1990. The results of the study shall be subject to peer and public review before submitting it to Congress.

(h) **Vehicles entering ozone nonattainment areas**

(1) **Authority regarding ozone inspection and maintenance testing**

(A) **In general**

No noncommercial motor vehicle registered in a foreign country and operated by a United States citizen or by an alien who is a permanent resident of the United States, or who holds a visa for the purposes of employment or educational study in the United States, may enter a covered ozone nonattainment area from a foreign country bordering the United States and contiguous to the nonattainment area more than twice in a single calendar-month period, if State law has requirements for the inspection and maintenance of such vehicles under the applicable implementation plan in the nonattainment area.

(B) **Applicability**

Subparagraph (A) shall not apply if the operator presents documentation at the United States border entry point establishing that the vehicle has complied with such inspection and maintenance requirements as are in effect and are applicable to motor vehicles of the same type and model year.

### (2) Sanctions for violations

The President may impose and collect from the operator of any motor vehicle who violates, or attempts to violate, paragraph (1) a civil penalty of not more than $200 for the second violation or attempted violation and $400 for the third and each subsequent violation or attempted violation.

### (3) State election

The prohibition set forth in paragraph (1) shall not apply in any State that elects to be exempt from the prohibition. Such an election shall take effect upon the President's receipt of written notice from the Governor of the State notifying the President of such election.

### (4) Alternative approach

The prohibition set forth in paragraph (1) shall not apply in a State, and the President may implement an alternative approach, if—

(A) The Governor of the State submits to the President a written description of an alternative approach to facilitate the compliance, by some or all foreign-registered motor vehicles, with the motor vehicle inspection and maintenance requirements that are—

(i) related to emissions of air pollutants;

(ii) in effect under the applicable implementation plan in the covered ozone nonattainment area; and

(iii) applicable to motor vehicles of the same types and model years as the foreign-registered motor vehicles; and

(B) the President approves the alternative approach as facilitating compliance with the motor vehicle inspection and maintenance requirements referred to in subparagraph (A).

### (5) Definition of covered ozone nonattainment area

In this section, the term "covered ozone nonattainment area" means a Serious Area, as classified under section 7511 of this title as of October 27, 1998.

(July 14, 1955, c. 360, Title I, § 183, as added Nov. 15, 1990, Pub.L. 101–549, Title I, § 103, 104 Stat. 2443, and amended Pub.L. 105–286, § 2, Oct. 27, 1998, 112 Stat. 2773.)

[1] So in original. Probably should be capitalized.

## HISTORICAL AND STATUTORY NOTES

**References in Text**

The Solid Waste Disposal Act, referred to in subsec. (b)(2), is Title II of Pub.L. 89–272, Oct. 20, 1965, 79 Stat. 997, as amended generally by Pub.L. 94–580, § 2, Oct. 21, 1976, 90 Stat. 2795. Subtitle C of the Solid Waste Disposal Act is classified generally to subchapter III (section 6921 et seq.) of chapter 82 of this title. For complete classification of this Act to the Code, see Short Title of 1965 Acts note set out under section 6901 of this title and Tables.

**Effective and Applicability Provisions**

1998 Acts

Pub.L. 105–286, § 3, provided that:

"(a) **In general.**—The amendment made by section 2 [amending this section] takes effect 180 days after the date of the enactment of this Act [Oct. 27, 1998]. Nothing in that amendment shall require action that is inconsistent with the obligations of the United States under any international agreement.

"(b) **Information.**—As soon as practicable after the date of enactment of this Act [Oct. 27, 1998], the appropriate agency of the United States shall distribute information to publicize the prohibition set forth in the amendment made by section 2 [amending this section]."

1990 Acts

Section effective Nov. 15, 1990, except as otherwise provided, see section 711(b) of Pub.L. 101–549, set out as a note under section 7401 of this title.

**Savings Provisions**

Suits, actions or proceedings commenced under this chapter as in effect prior to Nov. 15, 1990, not to abate by reason of the taking effect of amendments by Pub.L. 101–549, except as otherwise provided for, see section 711(a) of Pub.L. 101–549, set out as a note under section 7401 of this title.

## § 7511c. Control of interstate ozone air pollution

**[CAA § 184]**

### (a) Ozone transport regions

A single transport region for ozone (within the meaning of section 7506a(a) of this title), comprised of the States of Connecticut, Delaware, Maine, Maryland, Massachusetts, New Hampshire, New Jersey, New York, Pennsylvania, Rhode Island, Vermont, and the Consolidated Metropolitan Statistical Area that includes the District of Columbia, is hereby established by operation of law. The provisions of section 7506a(a)(1) and (2) of this title shall apply with respect to the transport region established under this section and any other transport region established for ozone, except to the extent inconsistent with the provisions of this section. The Administrator shall convene the commission required (under section 7506a(b) of this title) as a result of the establishment of such region within 6 months of November 15, 1990.

### (b) Plan provisions for States in ozone transport regions

(1) In accordance with section 7410 of this title, not later than 2 years after November 15, 1990 (or 9 months after the subsequent inclusion of a State in a transport region established for ozone), each State included within a transport region established for ozone shall submit a State implementation plan or

revision thereof to the Administrator which requires the following—

(A) that each area in such State that is in an ozone transport region, and that is a metropolitan statistical area or part thereof with a population of 100,000 or more comply with the provisions of section 7511a(c)(2)(A) of this title (pertaining to enhanced vehicle inspection and maintenance programs); and

(B) implementation of reasonably available control technology with respect to all sources of volatile organic compounds in the State covered by a control techniques guideline issued before or after November 15, 1990.

(2) Within 3 years after November 15, 1990, the Administrator shall complete a study identifying control measures capable of achieving emission reductions comparable to those achievable through vehicle refueling controls contained in section 7511a(b)(3) of this title, and such measures or such vehicle refueling controls shall be implemented in accordance with the provisions of this section. Notwithstanding other deadlines in this section, the applicable implementation plan shall be revised to reflect such measures within 1 year of completion of the study. For purposes of this section any stationary source that emits or has the potential to emit at least 50 tons per year of volatile organic compounds shall be considered a major stationary source and subject to the requirements which would be applicable to major stationary sources if the area were classified as a Moderate nonattainment area.

**(c) Additional control measures**

**(1) Recommendations**

Upon petition of any State within a transport region established for ozone, and based on a majority vote of the Governors on the Commission[1] (or their designees), the Commission [1] may, after notice and opportunity for public comment, develop recommendations for additional control measures to be applied within all or a part of such transport region if the commission determines such measures are necessary to bring any area in such region into attainment by the dates provided by this subpart. The commission shall transmit such recommendations to the Administrator.

**(2) Notice and review**

Whenever the Administrator receives recommendations prepared by a commission pursuant to paragraph (1) (the date of receipt of which shall hereinafter in this section be referred to as the "receipt date"), the Administrator shall—

(A) immediately publish in the Federal Register a notice stating that the recommendations are available and provide an opportunity for public hearing within 90 days beginning on the receipt date; and

(B) commence a review of the recommendations to determine whether the control measures in the recommendations are necessary to bring any area in such region into attainment by the dates provided by this subpart and are otherwise consistent with this chapter.

**(3) Consultation**

In undertaking the review required under paragraph (2)(B), the Administrator shall consult with members of the commission of the affected States and shall take into account the data, views, and comments received pursuant to paragraph (2)(A).

**(4) Approval and disapproval**

Within 9 months after the receipt date, the Administrator shall (A) determine whether to approve, disapprove, or partially disapprove and partially approve the recommendations; (B) notify the commission in writing of such approval, disapproval, or partial disapproval; and (C) publish such determination in the Federal Register. If the Administrator disapproves or partially disapproves the recommendations, the Administrator shall specify—

(i) why any disapproved additional control measures are not necessary to bring any area in such region into attainment by the dates provided by this subpart or are otherwise not consistent with the [2] chapter; and

(ii) recommendations concerning equal or more effective actions that could be taken by the commission to conform the disapproved portion of the recommendations to the requirements of this section.

**(5) Finding**

Upon approval or partial approval of recommendations submitted by a commission, the Administrator shall issue to each State which is included in the transport region and to which a requirement of the approved plan applies, a finding under section 7410(k)(5) of this title that the implementation plan for such State is inadequate to meet the requirements of section 7410(a)(2)(D) of this title. Such finding shall require each such State to revise its implementation plan to include the approved additional control measures within one year after the finding is issued.

**(d) Best available air quality monitoring and modeling**

For purposes of this section, not later than 6 months after November 15, 1990, the Administrator shall promulgate criteria for purposes of determining the contribution of sources in one area to concentrations of ozone in another area which is a nonattainment area for ozone. Such criteria shall require that the best available air quality monitoring and modeling techniques be used for purposes of making such determinations.

(July 14, 1955, c. 360, Title I, § 184, as added Nov. 15, 1990, Pub.L. 101–549, Title I, § 103, 104 Stat. 2448.)

[1] So in original. Probably should not be capitalized.

[2] So in original. Probably should be "this".

### HISTORICAL AND STATUTORY NOTES

**Effective and Applicability Provisions**

1990 Acts

Section effective Nov. 15, 1990, except as otherwise provided, see section 711(b) of Pub.L. 101–549, set out as a note under section 7401 of this title.

**Savings Provisions**

Suits, actions or proceedings commenced under this chapter as in effect prior to Nov. 15, 1990, not to abate by reason of the taking effect of amendments by Pub.L. 101–549, except as otherwise provided for, see section 711(a) of Pub.L. 101–549, set out as a note under section 7401 of this title.

## § 7511d. Enforcement for Severe and Extreme ozone nonattainment areas for failure to attain

**[CAA § 185]**

**(a) General rule**

Each implementation plan revision required under section 7511a(d) and (e) of this title (relating to the attainment plan for Severe and Extreme ozone nonattainment areas) shall provide that, if the area to which such plan revision applies has failed to attain the national primary ambient air quality standard for ozone by the applicable attainment date, each major stationary source of VOCs located in the area shall, except as otherwise provided under subsection (c) of this section, pay a fee to the State as a penalty for such failure, computed in accordance with subsection (b) of this section, for each calendar year beginning after the attainment date, until the area is redesignated as an attainment area for ozone. Each such plan revision should include procedures for assessment and collection of such fees.

**(b) Computation of fee**

**(1) Fee amount**

The fee shall equal $5,000, adjusted in accordance with paragraph (3), per ton of VOC emitted by the source during the calendar year in excess of 80 percent of the baseline amount, computed under paragraph (2).

**(2) Baseline amount**

For purposes of this section, the baseline amount shall be computed, in accordance with such guidance as the Administrator may provide, as the lower of the amount of actual VOC emissions ("actuals") or VOC emissions allowed under the permit applicable to the source (or, if no such permit has been issued for the attainment year, the amount of VOC emissions allowed under the applicable implementation plan ("allowables")) during the attainment year. Notwithstanding the preceding sentence, the Administrator may issue guidance authorizing the baseline amount to be determined in accordance with the lower of average actuals or average allowables, determined over a period of more than one calendar year. Such guidance may provide that such average calculation for a specific source may be used if that source's emissions are irregular, cyclical, or otherwise vary significantly from year to year.

**(3) Annual adjustment**

The fee amount under paragraph (1) shall be adjusted annually, beginning in the year beginning after 1990, in accordance with section 7661a(b)(3)(B)(v) of this title (relating to inflation adjustment).

**(c) Exception**

Notwithstanding any provision of this section, no source shall be required to pay any fee under subsection (a) of this section with respect to emissions during any year that is treated as an Extension Year under section 7511(a)(5) of this title.

**(d) Fee collection by Administrator**

If the Administrator has found that the fee provisions of the implementation plan do not meet the requirements of this section, or if the Administrator makes a finding that the State is not administering and enforcing the fee required under this section, the Administrator shall, in addition to any other action authorized under this subchapter, collect, in accordance with procedures promulgated by the Administrator, the unpaid fees required under subsection (a) of this section. If the Administrator makes such a finding under section 7509(a)(4) of this title, the Administrator may collect fees for periods before the determination, plus interest computed in accordance with section 6621(a)(2) of Title 26 (relating to computation of interest on underpayment of Federal taxes), to the extent the Administrator finds such fees have not been paid to the State. The provisions of clauses (ii) through (iii) of section 7661a(b)(3)(C) of this title (relating to penalties and use of the funds, respectively) shall apply with respect to fees collected under this subsection.

**(e) Exemptions for certain small areas**

For areas with a total population under 200,000 which fail to attain the standard by the applicable attainment date, no sanction under this section or under any other provision of this chapter shall apply if the area can demonstrate, consistent with guidance issued by the Administrator, that attainment in the area is prevented because of ozone or ozone precursors transported from other areas. The prohibition applies only in cases in which the area has met all requirements and implemented all measures applicable to the area under this chapter.

(July 14, 1955, c. 360, Title I, § 185, as added Nov. 15, 1990, Pub.L. 101–549, Title I, § 103, 104 Stat. 2450.)

HISTORICAL AND STATUTORY NOTES

**Effective and Applicability Provisions**

1990 Acts

Section effective Nov. 15, 1990, except as otherwise provided, see section 711(b) of Pub.L. 101–549, set out as a note under section 7401 of this title.

**Savings Provisions**

Suits, actions or proceedings commenced under this chapter as in effect prior to Nov. 15, 1990, not to abate by reason of the taking effect of amendments by Pub.L. 101–549, except as otherwise provided for, see section 711(a) of Pub.L. 101–549, set out as a note under section 7401 of this title.

## § 7511e. Transitional areas

[CAA § 185A]

If an area designated as an ozone nonattainment area as of November 15, 1990, has not violated the national primary ambient air quality standard for ozone for the 36–month period commencing on January 1, 1987, and ending on December 31, 1989, the Administrator shall suspend the application of the requirements of this subpart to such area until December 31, 1991. By June 30, 1992, the Administrator shall determine by order, based on the area's design value as of the attainment date, whether the area attained such standard by December 31, 1991. If the Administrator determines that the area attained the standard, the Administrator shall require, as part of the order, the State to submit a maintenance plan for the area within 12 months of such determination. If the Administrator determines that the area failed to attain the standard, the Administrator shall, by June 30, 1992, designate the area as nonattainment under section 7407(d)(4) of this title.

(July 14, 1955, c. 360, Title I, § 185A, as added Nov. 15, 1990, Pub.L. 101–549, Title I, § 103, 104 Stat. 2451.)

HISTORICAL AND STATUTORY NOTES

**Effective and Applicability Provisions**

1990 Acts

Section effective Nov. 15, 1990, except as otherwise provided, see section 711(b) of Pub.L. 101–549, set out as a note under section 7401 of this title.

**Savings Provisions**

Suits, actions or proceedings commenced under this chapter as in effect prior to Nov. 15, 1990, not to abate by reason of the taking effect of amendments by Pub.L. 101–549, except as otherwise provided for, see section 711(a) of Pub.L. 101–549, set out as a note under section 7401 of this title.

## § 7511f. $NO_x$ and VOC study

[CAA § 185B]

The Administrator, in conjunction with the National Academy of Sciences, shall conduct a study on the role of ozone precursors in tropospheric ozone formation and control. The study shall examine the roles of $NO_x$ and VOC emission reductions, the extent to which $NO_x$ reductions may contribute (or be counterproductive) to achievement of attainment in different nonattainment areas, the sensitivity of ozone to the control of $NO_x$, the availability and extent of controls for $NO_x$, the role of biogenic VOC emissions, and the basic information required for air quality models. The study shall be completed and a proposed report made public for 30 days comment within 1 year of November 15, 1990, and a final report shall be submitted to Congress within 15 months after November 15, 1990. The Administrator shall utilize all available information and studies, as well as develop additional information, in conducting the study required by this section.

(July 14, 1955, c. 360, Title I, § 185B, as added Nov. 15, 1990, Pub.L. 101–549, Title I, § 103, 104 Stat. 2452.)

HISTORICAL AND STATUTORY NOTES

**Effective and Applicability Provisions**

1990 Acts

Section effective Nov. 15, 1990, except as otherwise provided, see section 711(b) of Pub.L. 101–549, set out as a note under section 7401 of this title.

**Savings Provisions**

Suits, actions or proceedings commenced under this chapter as in effect prior to Nov. 15, 1990, not to abate by reason of the taking effect of amendments by Pub.L. 101–549, except as otherwise provided for, see section 711(a) of Pub.L. 101–549, set out as a note under section 7401 of this title.

*Subpart 3—Additional Provisions for Carbon Monoxide Nonattainment Areas*

## § 7512. Classification and attainment dates

[CAA § 186]

**(a) Classification by operation of law and attainment dates for nonattainment areas**

(1) Each area designated nonattainment for carbon monoxide pursuant to section 7407(d) of this title shall be classified at the time of such designation under table 1, by operation of law, as a Moderate Area or a Serious Area based on the design value for the area. The design value shall be calculated according to the interpretation methodology issued by the Administrator most recently before November 15, 1990. For each area classified under this subsection, the primary

standard attainment date for carbon monoxide shall be as expeditiously as practicable but not later than the date provided in table 1:

TABLE 3 [1]

| Area classification | Design value | Primary standard attainment date |
|---|---|---|
| Moderate | 9.1–16.4 ppm | December 31, 1995 |
| Serious | 16.5 and above | December 31, 2000 |

(2) At the time of publication of the notice required under section 7407 of this title (designating carbon monoxide nonattainment areas), the Administrator shall publish a notice announcing the classification of each such carbon monoxide nonattainment area. The provisions of section 7502(a)(1)(B) of this title (relating to lack of notice-and-comment and judicial review) shall apply with respect to such classification.

(3) If an area classified under paragraph (1), table 1, would have been classified in another category if the design value in the area were 5 percent greater or 5 percent less than the level on which such classification was based, the Administrator may, in the Administrator's discretion, within 90 days after November 15, 1990, by the procedure required under paragraph (2), adjust the classification of the area. In making such adjustment, the Administrator may consider the number of exceedances of the national primary ambient air quality standard for carbon monoxide in the area, the level of pollution transport between the area and the other affected areas, and the mix of sources and air pollutants in the area. The Administrator may make the same adjustment for purposes of paragraphs (2), (3), (6), and (7) of section 7512a(a) of this title.

(4) Upon application by any State, the Administrator may extend for 1 additional year (hereinafter in this subpart referred to as the "Extension Year") the date specified in table 1 of subsection (a) of this section if—

(A) the State has complied with all requirements and commitments pertaining to the area in the applicable implementation plan, and

(B) no more than one exceedance of the national ambient air quality standard level for carbon monoxide has occurred in the area in the year preceding the Extension Year.

No more than 2 one-year extensions may be issued under this paragraph for a single nonattainment area.

### (b) New designations and reclassifications

#### (1) New designations to nonattainment

Any area that is designated attainment or unclassifiable for carbon monoxide under section 7407(d)(4) of this title, and that is subsequently redesignated to nonattainment for carbon monoxide under section 7407(d)(3) of this title, shall, at the time of the redesignation, be classified by operation of law in accordance with table 1 under subsections (a)(1) and (a)(4) of this section. Upon its classification, the area shall be subject to the same requirements under section 7410 of this title, subpart 1 of this part, and this subpart that would have applied had the area been so classified at the time of the notice under subsection (a)(2) of this section, except that any absolute, fixed date applicable in connection with any such requirement is extended by operation of law by a period equal to the length of time between November 15, 1990, and the date the area is classified.

#### (2) Reclassification of Moderate Areas upon failure to attain

##### (A) General rule

Within 6 months following the applicable attainment date for a carbon monoxide nonattainment area, the Administrator shall determine, based on the area's design value as of the attainment date, whether the area has attained the standard by that date. Any Moderate Area that the Administrator finds has not attained the standard by that date shall be reclassified by operation of law in accordance with table 1 of subsection (a)(1) of this section as a Serious Area.

##### (B) Publication of notice

The Administrator shall publish a notice in the Federal Register, no later than 6 months following the attainment date, identifying each area that the Administrator has determined, under subparagraph (A), as having failed to attain and identifying the reclassification, if any, described under subparagraph (A).

### (c) References to terms

Any reference in this subpart to a "Moderate Area" or a "Serious Area" shall be considered a reference to a Moderate Area or a Serious Area, respectively, as classified under this section.

(July 14, 1955, c. 360, Title I, § 186, as added Nov. 15, 1990, Pub.L. 101–549, Title I, § 104, 104 Stat. 2452.)

[1] So in original. Probably should be "TABLE 1".

## HISTORICAL AND STATUTORY NOTES

### Effective and Applicability Provisions

1990 Acts

Section to take effect Nov. 15, 1990, except as otherwise provided, see section 711(b) of Pub.L. 101–549, set out as a note under section 7401 of this title.

### Savings Provisions

Suits, actions or proceedings commenced under this chapter as in effect prior to Nov. 15, 1990, not to abate by reason of the taking effect of amendments by Pub.L. 101–549, except as otherwise provided for, see section 711(a) of Pub.L. 101–549, set out as a note under section 7401 of this title.

## § 7512a. Plan submissions and requirements

[CAA § 187]

### (a) Moderate Areas

Each State in which all or part of a Moderate Area is located shall, with respect to the Moderate Area (or portion thereof, to the extent specified in guidance of the Administrator issued before November 15, 1990), submit to the Administrator the State implementation plan revisions (including the plan items) described under this subsection, within such periods as are prescribed under this subsection, except to the extent the State has made such submissions as of November 15, 1990:

#### (1) Inventory

No later than 2 years from November 15, 1990, the State shall submit a comprehensive, accurate, current inventory of actual emissions from all sources, as described in section 7502(c)(3) of this title, in accordance with guidance provided by the Administrator.

#### (2)(A) Vehicle miles traveled

No later than 2 years after November 15, 1990, for areas with a design value above 12.7 ppm at the time of classification, the plan revision shall contain a forecast of vehicle miles traveled in the nonattainment area concerned for each year before the year in which the plan projects the national ambient air quality standard for carbon monoxide to be attained in the area. The forecast shall be based on guidance which shall be published by the Administrator, in consultation with the Secretary of Transportation, within 6 months after November 15, 1990. The plan revision shall provide for annual updates of the forecasts to be submitted to the Administrator together with annual reports regarding the extent to which such forecasts proved to be accurate. Such annual reports shall contain estimates of actual vehicle miles traveled in each year for which a forecast was required.

#### (B) Special rule for Denver

Within 2 years after November 15, 1990, in the case of Denver, the State shall submit a revision that includes the transportation control measures as required in section 7511a(d)(1)(A) of this title except that such revision shall be for the purpose of reducing CO emissions rather than volatile organic compound emissions. If the State fails to include any such measure, the implementation plan shall contain an explanation of why such measure was not adopted and what emissions reduction measure was adopted to provide a comparable reduction in emissions, or reasons why such reduction is not necessary to attain the national primary ambient air quality standard for carbon monoxide.

#### (3) Contingency provisions

No later than 2 years after November 15, 1990, for areas with a design value above 12.7 ppm at the time of classification, the plan revision shall provide for the implementation of specific measures to be undertaken if any estimate of vehicle miles traveled in the area which is submitted in an annual report under paragraph (2) exceeds the number predicted in the most recent prior forecast or if the area fails to attain the national primary ambient air quality standard for carbon monoxide by the primary standard attainment date. Such measures shall be included in the plan revision as contingency measures to take effect without further action by the State or the Administrator if the prior forecast has been exceeded by an updated forecast or if the national standard is not attained by such deadline.

#### (4) Savings clause for vehicle inspection and maintenance provisions of the State implementation plan

Immediately after November 15, 1990, for any Moderate Area (or, within the Administrator's discretion, portion thereof), the plan for which is of the type described in section 7511a(a)(2)(B) of this title any provisions necessary to ensure that the applicable implementation plan includes the vehicle inspection and maintenance program described in section 7511a(a)(2)(B) of this title.

#### (5) Periodic inventory

No later than September 30, 1995, and no later than the end of each 3 year period thereafter, until the area is redesignated to attainment, a revised inventory meeting the requirements of subsection (a)(1) of this section.

#### (6) Enhanced vehicle inspection and maintenance

No later than 2 years after November 15, 1990, in the case of Moderate Areas with a design value greater than 12.7 ppm at the time of classification, a revision that includes provisions for an enhanced vehicle inspection and maintenance program as required in section 7511a(c)(3) of this title (concerning serious ozone nonattainment areas), except that such program shall be for the purpose of reducing carbon monoxide rather than hydrocarbon emissions.

#### (7) Attainment demonstration and specific annual emission reductions

In the case of Moderate Areas with a design value greater than 12.7 ppm at the time of classification, no later than 2 years after November 15, 1990, a revision to provide, and a demonstration that the plan as revised will provide, for attainment of the carbon monoxide NAAQS by the applicable attainment date and provisions for such specific annual emission reductions as are necessary to attain the standard by that date.

The Administrator may, in the Administrator's discretion, require States to submit a schedule for submitting any of the revisions or other items required under this subsection. In the case of Moderate Areas with a design value of 12.7 ppm or lower at the time of classification, the requirements of this subsection shall apply in lieu of any requirement that the State submit a demonstration that the applicable implementation plan provides for attainment of the carbon monoxide standard by the applicable attainment date.

**(b) Serious Areas**

**(1) In general**

Each State in which all or part of a Serious Area is located shall, with respect to the Serious Area, make the submissions (other than those required under subsection (a)(1)(B) [1] of this section) applicable under subsection (a) of this section to Moderate Areas with a design value of 12.7 ppm or greater at the time of classification, and shall also submit the revision and other items described under this subsection.

**(2) Vehicle miles traveled**

Within 2 years after November 15, 1990, the State shall submit a revision that includes the transportation control measures as required in section 7511a(d)(1) of this title except that such revision shall be for the purpose of reducing CO emissions rather than volatile organic compound emissions. In the case of any such area (other than an area in New York State) which is a covered area (as defined in section 7586(a)(2)(B) of this title) for purposes of the Clean Fuel Fleet program under part C of subchapter II of this chapter, if the State fails to include any such measure, the implementation plan shall contain an explanation of why such measure was not adopted and what emissions reduction measure was adopted to provide a comparable reduction in emissions, or reasons why such reduction is not necessary to attain the national primary ambient air quality standard for carbon monoxide.

**(3) Oxygenated gasoline**

**(A)** Within 2 years after November 15, 1990, the State shall submit a revision to require that gasoline sold, supplied, offered for sale or supply, dispensed, transported or introduced into commerce in the larger of—

**(i)** the Consolidated Metropolitan Statistical Area (as defined by the United States Office of Management and Budget) (CMSA) in which the area is located, or

**(ii)** if the area is not located in a CMSA, the Metropolitan Statistical Area (as defined by the United States Office of Management and Budget) in which the area is located,

be blended, during the portion of the year in which the area is prone to high ambient concentrations of carbon monoxide (as determined by the Administrator), with fuels containing such level of oxygen as is necessary, in combination with other measures, to provide for attainment of the carbon monoxide national ambient air quality standard by the applicable attainment date and maintenance of the national ambient air quality standard thereafter in the area. The revision shall provide that such requirement shall take effect no later than October 1, 1993, and shall include a program for implementation and enforcement of the requirement consistent with guidance to be issued by the Administrator.

**(B)** Notwithstanding subparagraph (A), the revision described in this paragraph shall not be required for an area if the State demonstrates to the satisfaction of the Administrator that the revision is not necessary to provide for attainment of the carbon monoxide national ambient air quality standard by the applicable attainment date and maintenance of the national ambient air quality standard thereafter in the area.

**(c) Areas with significant stationary source emissions of CO**

**(1) Serious Areas**

In the case of Serious Areas in which stationary sources contribute significantly to carbon monoxide levels (as determined under rules issued by the Administrator), the State shall submit a plan revision within 2 years after November 15, 1990, which provides that the term "major stationary source" includes (in addition to the sources described in section 7602 of this title) any stationary source which emits, or has the potential to emit, 50 tons per year or more of carbon monoxide.

**(2) Waivers for certain areas**

The Administrator may, on a case-by-case basis, waive any requirements that pertain to transportation controls, inspection and maintenance, or oxygenated fuels where the Administrator determines by rule that mobile sources of carbon monoxide do not contribute significantly to carbon monoxide levels in the area.

**(3) Guidelines**

Within 6 months after November 15, 1990, the Administrator shall issue guidelines for and rules determining whether stationary sources contribute significantly to carbon monoxide levels in an area.

**(d) CO milestone**

**(1) Milestone demonstration**

By March 31, 1996, each State in which all or part of a Serious Area is located shall submit to the Administrator a demonstration that the area has achieved a reduction in emissions of CO equivalent to the total of the specific annual emission reductions required by December 31, 1995. Such reductions shall be referred to in this subsection as the milestone.

**(2) Adequacy of demonstration**

A demonstration under this paragraph shall be submitted in such form and manner, and shall contain such information and analysis, as the Administrator shall require. The Administrator shall determine whether or not a State's demonstration is adequate within 90 days after the Administrator's receipt of a demonstration which contains the information and analysis required by the Administrator.

**(3) Failure to meet emission reduction milestone**

If a State fails to submit a demonstration under paragraph (1) within the required period, or if the Administrator notifies the State that the State has not met the milestone, the State shall, within 9 months after such a failure or notification, submit a plan revision to implement an economic incentive and transportation control program as described in section 7511a(g)(4) of this title. Such revision shall be sufficient to achieve the specific annual reductions in carbon monoxide emissions set forth in the plan by the attainment date.

**(e) Multi-State CO nonattainment areas**

**(1) Coordination among States**

Each State in which there is located a portion of a single nonattainment area for carbon monoxide which covers more than one State ("multi-State nonattainment area") shall take all reasonable steps to coordinate, substantively and procedurally, the revisions and implementation of State implementation plans applicable to the nonattainment area concerned. The Administrator may not approve any revision of a State implementation plan submitted under this part for a State in which part of a multi-State nonattainment area is located if the plan revision for that State fails to comply with the requirements of this subsection.

**(2) Failure to demonstrate attainment**

If any State in which there is located a portion of a multi-State nonattainment area fails to provide a demonstration of attainment of the national ambient air quality standard for carbon monoxide in that portion within the period required under this part the State may petition the Administrator to make a finding that the State would have been able to make such demonstration but for the failure of one or more other States in which other portions of the area are located to commit to the implementation of all measures required under this section (relating to plan submissions for carbon monoxide nonattainment areas). If the Administrator makes such finding, in the portion of the nonattainment area within the State submitting such petition, no sanction shall be imposed under section 7509 of this title or under any other provision of this chapter, by reason of the failure to make such demonstration.

**(f) Reclassified areas**

Each State containing a carbon monoxide nonattainment area reclassified under section 7512(b)(2) of this title shall meet the requirements of subsection (b) of this section, as may be applicable to the area as reclassified, according to the schedules prescribed in connection with such requirements, except that the Administrator may adjust any applicable deadlines (other than the attainment date) where such deadlines are shown to be infeasible.

**(g) Failure of Serious Area to attain standard**

If the Administrator determines under section 7512(b)(2) of this title that the national primary ambient air quality standard for carbon monoxide has not been attained in a Serious Area by the applicable attainment date, the State shall submit a plan revision for the area within 9 months after the date of such determination. The plan revision shall provide that a program of incentives and requirements as described in section 7511a(g)(4) of this title shall be applicable in the area, and such program, in combination with other elements of the revised plan, shall be adequate to reduce the total tonnage of emissions of carbon monoxide in the area by at least 5 percent per year in each year after approval of the plan revision and before attainment of the national primary ambient air quality standard for carbon monoxide.

(July 14, 1955, c. 360, Title I, § 187, as added Nov. 15, 1990, Pub.L. 101–549, Title I, § 104, 104 Stat. 2454.)

[1] So in original. Subsec. (a)(1) of this section does not contain a subpar. (B).

### HISTORICAL AND STATUTORY NOTES

**Effective and Applicability Provisions**

1990 Acts

Section to take effect Nov. 15, 1990, except as otherwise provided, see section 711(b) of Pub.L. 101–549, set out as a note under section 7401 of this title.

**Savings Provisions**

Suits, actions or proceedings commenced under this chapter as in effect prior to Nov. 15, 1990, not to abate by reason of the taking effect of amendments by Pub.L. 101–549, except as otherwise provided for, see section 711(a) of Pub.L. 101–549, set out as a note under section 7401 of this title.

**Moratorium on Certain Emissions Testing Requirements**

For provisions directing that the Administrator shall not require the adoption or implementation by a State of a test-only I/M240 enhanced vehicle inspection and maintenance program as a mean of compliance with this section, see section 348 of Pub.L. 104–59, set out as a note under section 7511a of this title.

*Subpart 4—Additional Provisions for Particulate Matter Nonattainment Areas*

## § 7513. Classifications and attainment dates

[CAA § 188]

### (a) Initial classifications

Every area designated nonattainment for PM–10 pursuant to section 7407(d) of this title shall be classified at the time of such designation, by operation of law, as a moderate PM–10 nonattainment area (also referred to in this subpart as a "Moderate Area") at the time of such designation. At the time of publication of the notice under section 7407(d)(4) of this title (relating to area designations) for each PM–10 nonattainment area, the Administrator shall publish a notice announcing the classification of such area. The provisions of section 7502(a)(1)(B) of this title (relating to lack of notice-and-comment and judicial review) shall apply with respect to such classification.

### (b) Reclassification as Serious

#### (1) Reclassification before attainment date

The Administrator may reclassify as a Serious PM–10 nonattainment area (identified in this subpart also as a "Serious Area") any area that the Administrator determines cannot practicably attain the national ambient air quality standard for PM–10 by the attainment date (as prescribed in subsection (c) of this section) for Moderate Areas. The Administrator shall reclassify appropriate areas as Serious by the following dates:

(A) For areas designated nonattainment for PM–10 under section 7407(d)(4) of this title, the Administrator shall propose to reclassify appropriate areas by June 30, 1991, and take final action by December 31, 1991.

(B) For areas subsequently designated nonattainment, the Administrator shall reclassify appropriate areas within 18 months after the required date for the State's submission of a SIP for the Moderate Area.

#### (2) Reclassification upon failure to attain

Within 6 months following the applicable attainment date for a PM–10 nonattainment area, the Administrator shall determine whether the area attained the standard by that date. If the Administrator finds that any Moderate Area is not in attainment after the applicable attainment date—

(A) the area shall be reclassified by operation of law as a Serious Area; and

(B) the Administrator shall publish a notice in the Federal Register no later than 6 months following the attainment date, identifying the area as having failed to attain and identifying the reclassification described under subparagraph (A).

### (c) Attainment dates

Except as provided under subsection (d) of this section, the attainment dates for PM–10 nonattainment areas shall be as follows:

#### (1) Moderate Areas

For a Moderate Area, the attainment date shall be as expeditiously as practicable but no later than the end of the sixth calendar year after the area's designation as nonattainment, except that, for areas designated nonattainment for PM–10 under section 7407(d)(4) of this title, the attainment date shall not extend beyond December 31, 1994.

#### (2) Serious Areas

For a Serious Area, the attainment date shall be as expeditiously as practicable but no later than the end of the tenth calendar year beginning after the area's designation as nonattainment, except that, for areas designated nonattainment for PM–10 under section 7407(d)(4) of this title, the date shall not extend beyond December 31, 2001.

### (d) Extension of attainment date for Moderate Areas

Upon application by any State, the Administrator may extend for 1 additional year (hereinafter referred to as the "Extension Year") the date specified in paragraph [1] (c)(1) if—

(1) the State has complied with all requirements and commitments pertaining to the area in the applicable implementation plan; and

(2) no more than one exceedance of the 24–hour national ambient air quality standard level for PM–10 has occurred in the area in the year preceding the Extension Year, and the annual mean concentration of PM–10 in the area for such year is less than or equal to the standard level.

No more than 2 one-year extensions may be issued under the subsection for a single nonattainment area.

### (e) Extension of attainment date for Serious Areas

Upon application by any State, the Administrator may extend the attainment date for a Serious Area beyond the date specified under subsection (c) of this section, if attainment by the date established under subsection (c) of this section would be impracticable, the State has complied with all requirements and commitments pertaining to that area in the implementation plan, and the State demonstrates to the satisfaction of the Administrator that the plan for that area includes the most stringent measures that are included in the implementation plan of any State or are achieved in practice in any State, and can feasibly be implemented in the area. At the time of such application, the State must submit a revision to the implementation plan that includes a demonstration of attainment by the most expeditious alternative date practicable. In determining whether to grant an extension, and the appropriate length of time for any such extension, the Administrator may consider the nature and extent of nonattainment, the types and numbers of sources or other emitting activities in the area (including the influence of uncontrollable natural sources and transboundary emissions from foreign countries), the population exposed to concentrations in excess of the standard, the presence and concentration of potentially toxic substances in the mix of particulate emissions in the area, and the technological and economic feasibility of various control measures. The Administrator may not approve an extension until the State submits an attainment demonstration for the area. The Administrator may grant at most one such extension for an area, of no more than 5 years.

**(f) Waivers for certain areas**

The Administrator may, on a case-by-case basis, waive any requirement applicable to any Serious Area under this subpart where the Administrator determines that anthropogenic sources of PM–10 do not contribute significantly to the violation of the PM–10 standard in the area. The Administrator may also waive a specific date for attainment of the standard where the Administrator determines that nonanthropogenic sources of PM–10 contribute significantly to the violation of the PM–10 standard in the area.

(July 14, 1955, c. 360, Title I, § 188, as added Nov. 15, 1990, Pub.L. 101–549, Title I, § 105(a), 104 Stat. 2458.)

[1] So in original. Probably should be "subsection".

### HISTORICAL AND STATUTORY NOTES

**Effective and Applicability Provisions**

1990 Acts

Section to take effect Nov. 15, 1990, except as otherwise provided, see section 711(b) of Pub.L. 101–549, set out as a note under section 7401 of this title.

**Savings Provisions**

Suits, actions or proceedings commenced under this chapter as in effect prior to Nov. 15, 1990, not to abate by reason of the taking effect of amendments by Pub.L. 101–549, except as otherwise provided for, see section 711(a) of Pub.L. 101–549, set out as a note under section 7401 of this title.

## § 7513a. Plan provisions and schedules for plan submissions

[CAA § 189]

**(a) Moderate Areas**

**(1) Plan provisions**

Each State in which all or part of a Moderate Area is located shall submit, according to the applicable schedule under paragraph (2), an implementation plan that includes each of the following:

**(A)** For the purpose of meeting the requirements of section 7502(c)(5) of this title, a permit program providing that permits meeting the requirements of section 7503 of this title are required for the construction and operation of new and modified major stationary sources of PM–10.

**(B)** Either (i) a demonstration (including air quality modeling) that the plan will provide for attainment by the applicable attainment date; or (ii) a demonstration that attainment by such date is impracticable.

**(C)** Provisions to assure that reasonably available control measures for the control of PM–10 shall be implemented no later than December 10, 1993, or 4 years after designation in the case of an area classified as moderate after November 15, 1990.

**(2) Schedule for plan submissions**

A State shall submit the plan required under subparagraph (1) no later than the following:

**(A)** Within 1 year of November 15, 1990, for areas designated nonattainment under section 7407(d)(4) of this title, except that the provision required under subparagraph (1)(A) shall be submitted no later than June 30, 1992.

**(B)** 18 months after the designation as nonattainment, for those areas designated nonattainment after the designations prescribed under section 7407(d)(4) of this title.

**(b) Serious Areas**

**(1) Plan provisions**

In addition to the provisions submitted to meet the requirements of paragraph [1] (a)(1) (relating to Moderate Areas), each State in which all or part of a Serious Area is located shall submit an implementation plan for such area that includes each of the following:

**(A)** A demonstration (including air quality modeling)—

**(i)** that the plan provides for attainment of the PM–10 national ambient air quality standard by the applicable attainment date, or

**(ii)** for any area for which the State is seeking, pursuant to section 7513(e) of this title, an extension of the attainment date beyond the date set forth in section 7513(c) of this title, that attainment by that date would be impracticable, and that the plan provides for attainment by the most expeditious alternative date practicable.

(B) Provisions to assure that the best available control measures for the control of PM–10 shall be implemented no later than 4 years after the date the area is classified (or reclassified) as a Serious Area.

**(2) Schedule for plan submissions**

A State shall submit the demonstration required for an area under paragraph (1)(A) no later than 4 years after reclassification of the area to Serious, except that for areas reclassified under section 7513(b)(2) of this title, the State shall submit the attainment demonstration within 18 months after reclassification to Serious. A State shall submit the provisions described under paragraph (1)(B) no later than 18 months after reclassification of the area as a Serious Area.

**(3) Major sources**

For any Serious Area, the terms "major source" and "major stationary source" include any stationary source or group of stationary sources located within a contiguous area and under common control that emits, or has the potential to emit, at least 70 tons per year of PM–10.

**(c) Milestones**

(1) Plan revisions demonstrating attainment submitted to the Administrator for approval under this subpart shall contain quantitative milestones which are to be achieved every 3 years until the area is redesignated attainment and which demonstrate reasonable further progress, as defined in section 7501(1) of this title, toward attainment by the applicable date.

(2) Not later than 90 days after the date on which a milestone applicable to the area occurs, each State in which all or part of such area is located shall submit to the Administrator a demonstration that all measures in the plan approved under this section have been implemented and that the milestone has been met. A demonstration under this subsection shall be submitted in such form and manner, and shall contain such information and analysis, as the Administrator shall require. The Administrator shall determine whether or not a State's demonstration under this subsection is adequate within 90 days after the Administrator's receipt of a demonstration which contains the information and analysis required by the Administrator.

(3) If a State fails to submit a demonstration under paragraph (2) with respect to a milestone within the required period or if the Administrator determines that the area has not met any applicable milestone, the Administrator shall require the State, within 9 months after such failure or determination to submit a plan revision that assures that the State will achieve the next milestone (or attain the national ambient air quality standard for PM–10, if there is no next milestone) by the applicable date.

**(d) Failure to attain**

In the case of a Serious PM–10 nonattainment area in which the PM–10 standard is not attained by the applicable attainment date, the State in which such area is located shall, after notice and opportunity for public comment, submit within 12 months after the applicable attainment date, plan revisions which provide for attainment of the PM–10 air quality standard and, from the date of such submission until attainment, for an annual reduction in PM–10 or PM–10 precursor emissions within the area of not less than 5 percent of the amount of such emissions as reported in the most recent inventory prepared for such area.

**(e) PM–10 precursors**

The control requirements applicable under plans in effect under this part for major stationary sources of PM–10 shall also apply to major stationary sources of PM–10 precursors, except where the Administrator determines that such sources do not contribute significantly to PM–10 levels which exceed the standard in the area. The Administrator shall issue guidelines regarding the application of the preceding sentence.

(July 14, 1955, c. 360, Title I, § 189, as added Nov. 15, 1990, Pub.L. 101–549, Title I, § 105(a), 104 Stat. 2460.)

[1] So in original. Probably should be "subsection".

### HISTORICAL AND STATUTORY NOTES

**Effective and Applicability Provisions**

1990 Acts

Section to take effect Nov. 15, 1990, except as otherwise provided, see section 711(b) of Pub.L. 101–549, set out as a note under section 7401 of this title.

**Savings Provisions**

Suits, actions or proceedings commenced under this chapter as in effect prior to Nov. 15, 1990, not to abate by reason of the taking effect of amendments by Pub.L. 101–549, except as otherwise provided for, see section 711(a) of Pub.L. 101–549, set out as a note under section 7401 of this title.

## § 7513b. Issuance of RACM and BACM guidance

[CAA § 190]

The Administrator shall issue, in the same manner and according to the same procedure as guidance is issued under section 7408(c) of this title, technical guidance on reasonably available control measures and best available control measures for urban fugitive dust, and emissions from residential wood combustion (including curtailments and exemptions from such curtailments) and prescribed silvicultural and agricultural burning, no later than 18 months following November 15, 1990. The Administrator shall also examine other categories of sources contributing to nonattainment of the PM–10 standard, and determine whether additional guidance on reasonably available control measures and best available control measures is needed, and issue any such guidance no later than 3 years after November 15, 1990. In issuing guidelines and making determinations under this section, the Administrator (in consultation with the State) shall take into account emission reductions achieved, or expected to be achieved, under subchapter IV–A of this chapter and other provisions of this chapter.

(July 14, 1955, c. 360, Title I, § 190, as added Nov. 15, 1990, Pub.L. 101–549, Title I, § 105(a), 104 Stat. 2462.)

### HISTORICAL AND STATUTORY NOTES

**References in Text**

Subchapter IV–A of this chapter, referred to in text, originally read "title IV", meaning Title IV of the Clean Air Act, July 14, 1955, c. 360, Title IV, as added Nov. 15, 1990, Pub.L. 101–549, Title IV, 104 Stat. 2584, which is classified as Subchapter IV–A of this chapter, 42 U.S.C.A. § 7651 et seq.

**Effective and Applicability Provisions**

1990 Acts

Section to take effect Nov. 15, 1990, except as otherwise provided, see section 711(b) of Pub.L. 101–549, set out as a note under section 7401 of this title.

**Savings Provisions**

Suits, actions or proceedings commenced under this chapter as in effect prior to Nov. 15, 1990, not to abate by reason of the taking effect of amendments by Pub.L. 101–549, except as otherwise provided for, see section 711(a) of Pub.L. 101–549, set out as a note under section 7401 of this title.

*Subpart 5—Additional Provisions for Areas Designated Nonattainment for Sulfur Oxides, Nitrogen Dioxide, or Lead*

## § 7514. Plan submission deadlines

[CAA § 191]

### (a) Submission

Any State containing an area designated or redesignated under section 7407(d) of this title as nonattainment with respect to the national primary ambient air quality standards for sulfur oxides, nitrogen dioxide, or lead subsequent to November 15, 1990, shall submit to the Administrator, within 18 months of the designation, an applicable implementation plan meeting the requirements of this part.

### (b) States lacking fully approved State implementation plans

Any State containing an area designated nonattainment with respect to national primary ambient air quality standards for sulfur oxides or nitrogen dioxide under section 7407(d)(1)(C)(i) of this title, but lacking a fully approved implementation plan complying with the requirements of this chapter (including this part) as in effect immediately before November 15, 1990, shall submit to the Administrator, within 18 months of November 15, 1990, an implementation plan meeting the requirements of subpart 1 (except as otherwise prescribed by section 7514a of this title).

(July 14, 1955, c. 360, Title I, § 191, as added Nov. 15, 1990, Pub.L. 101–549, Title I, § 106, 104 Stat. 2463.)

### HISTORICAL AND STATUTORY NOTES

**Effective and Applicability Provisions**

1990 Acts

Section to take effect Nov. 15, 1990, except as otherwise provided, see section 711(b) of Pub.L. 101–549, set out as a note under section 7401 of this title.

**Savings Provisions**

Suits, actions or proceedings commenced under this chapter as in effect prior to Nov. 15, 1990, not to abate by reason of the taking effect of amendments by Pub.L. 101–549, except as otherwise provided for, see section 711(a) of Pub.L. 101–549, set out as a note under section 7401 of this title.

## § 7514a. Attainment dates

[CAA § 192]

### (a) Plans under section 7514(a)

Implementation plans required under section 7514(a) of this title shall provide for attainment of the relevant primary standard as expeditiously as practicable but no later than 5 years from the date of the nonattainment designation.

### (b) Plans under section 7514(b)

Implementation plans required under section 7514(b) of this title shall provide for attainment of the relevant primary national ambient air quality standard within 5 years after November 15, 1990.

### (c) Inadequate plans

Implementation plans for nonattainment areas for sulfur oxides or nitrogen dioxide with plans that were approved by the Administrator before November 15, 1990, but, subsequent to such approval, were found by the Administrator to be substantially inadequate, shall provide for attainment of the relevant primary standard within 5 years from the date of such finding.

(July 14, 1955, c. 360, Title I, § 192, as added Nov. 15, 1990, Pub.L. 101–549, Title I, § 106, 104 Stat. 2463.)

### HISTORICAL AND STATUTORY NOTES

**Effective and Applicability Provisions**

1990 Acts

Section to take effect Nov. 15, 1990, except as otherwise provided, see section 711(b) of Pub.L. 101–549, set out as a note under section 7401 of this title.

**Savings Provisions**

Suits, actions or proceedings commenced under this chapter as in effect prior to Nov. 15, 1990, not to abate by reason of the taking effect of amendments by Pub.L. 101–549, except as otherwise provided for, see section 711(a) of Pub.L. 101–549, set out as a note under section 7401 of this title.

*Subpart 6—Savings Provisions*

## § 7515. General savings clause

[CAA § 193]

Each regulation, standard, rule, notice, order and guidance promulgated or issued by the Administrator under this chapter, as in effect before November 15, 1990, shall remain in effect according to its terms, except to the extent otherwise provided under this chapter, inconsistent with any provision of this chapter, or revised by the Administrator. No control requirement in effect, or required to be adopted by an order, settlement agreement, or plan in effect before November 15, 1990, in any area which is a nonattainment area for any air pollutant may be modified after November 15, 1990, in any manner unless the modification insures equivalent or greater emission reductions of such air pollutant.

(July 14, 1955, c. 360, Title I, § 193, as added Nov. 15, 1990, Pub.L. 101–549, Title I, § 108(*l*), 104 Stat. 2469.)

### HISTORICAL AND STATUTORY NOTES

**Effective and Applicability Provisions**

1990 Acts

Section to take effect Nov. 15, 1990, except as otherwise provided, see section 711(b) of Pub.L. 101–549, set out as a note under section 7401 of this title.

**Savings Provisions**

Suits, actions or proceedings commenced under this chapter as in effect prior to Nov. 15, 1990, not to abate by reason of the taking effect of amendments by Pub.L. 101–549, except as otherwise provided for, see section 711(a) of Pub.L. 101–549, set out as a note under section 7401 of this title.

# SUBCHAPTER II—EMISSION STANDARDS FOR MOVING SOURCES

## PART A—MOTOR VEHICLE EMISSION AND FUEL STANDARDS

## § 7521. Emission standards for new motor vehicles or new motor vehicle engines

[CAA § 202]

### (a) Authority of Administrator to prescribe by regulation

Except as otherwise provided in subsection (b) of this section—

(1) The Administrator shall by regulation prescribe (and from time to time revise) in accordance with the provisions of this section, standards applicable to the emission of any air pollutant from any class or classes of new motor vehicles or new motor vehicle engines, which in his judgment cause, or contribute to, air pollution which may reasonably be anticipated to endanger public health or welfare. Such standards shall be applicable to such vehicles and engines for their useful life (as determined under subsection (d) of this section, relating to useful life of vehicles for purposes of certification), whether such vehicles and engines are designed as complete systems or incorporate devices to prevent or control such pollution.

(2) Any regulation prescribed under paragraph (1) of this subsection (and any revision thereof) shall take effect after such period as the Administrator finds necessary to permit the development and application of the requisite technology, giving appropriate consideration to the cost of compliance within such period.

**(3)(A) In general**

(i) Unless the standard is changed as provided in subparagraph (B), regulations under paragraph (1) of this subsection applicable to emissions of hydrocarbons, carbon monoxide, oxides of nitrogen, and particulate matter from classes or categories of heavy-duty vehicles or engines manufactured during or after model year 1983 shall contain standards which reflect the greatest degree of emission reduction achievable through the application of technology which the Administrator determines will be available for the model year to which such standards apply, giving appropriate consideration to cost, energy, and safety factors associated with the application of such technology.

(ii) In establishing classes or categories of vehicles or engines for purposes of regulations under this paragraph, the Administrator may base such classes or categories on gross vehicle weight, horsepower, type of fuel used, or other appropriate factors.

**(B) Revised standards for heavy duty trucks**

(i) On the basis of information available to the Administrator concerning the effects of air pollutants emitted from heavy-duty vehicles or engines and from other sources of mobile source related pollutants on the public health and welfare, and taking costs into account, the Administrator may promulgate regulations under paragraph (1) of this subsection revising any standard promulgated under, or before the date of, the enactment of the Clean Air Act Amendments of 1990 (or previously revised under this subparagraph) and applicable to classes or categories of heavy-duty vehicles or engines.

(ii) Effective for the model year 1998 and thereafter, the regulations under paragraph (1) of this subsection applicable to emissions of oxides of nitrogen ($NO_x$) from gasoline and diesel-fueled heavy duty trucks shall contain standards which provide that such emissions may not exceed 4.0 grams per brake horsepower hour (gbh).

**(C) Lead time and stability**

Any standard promulgated or revised under this paragraph and applicable to classes or categories of heavy-duty vehicles or engines shall apply for a period of no less than 3 model years beginning no earlier than the model year commencing 4 years after such revised standard is promulgated.

**(D) Rebuilding practices**

The Administrator shall study the practice of rebuilding heavy-duty engines and the impact rebuilding has on engine emissions. On the basis of that study and other information available to the Administrator, the Administrator may prescribe requirements to control rebuilding practices, including standards applicable to emissions from any rebuilt heavy-duty engines (whether or not the engine is past its statutory useful life), which in the Administrator's judgment cause, or contribute to, air pollution which may reasonably be anticipated to endanger public health or welfare taking costs into account. Any regulation shall take effect after a period the Administrator finds necessary to permit the development and application of the requisite control measures, giving appropriate consideration to the cost of compliance within the period and energy and safety factors.

**(E) Motorcycles**

For purposes of this paragraph, motorcycles and motorcycle engines shall be treated in the same manner as heavy-duty vehicles and engines (except as otherwise permitted under section 7525(f)(1) of this title) unless the Administrator promulgates a rule reclassifying motorcycles as light-duty vehicles within the meaning of this section or unless the Administrator promulgates regulations under subsection (a) of this section applying standards applicable to the emission of air pollutants from motorcycles as a separate class or category. In any case in which such standards are promulgated for such emissions from motorcycles as a separate class or category, the Administrator, in promulgating such standards, shall consider the need to achieve equivalency of emission reductions between motorcycles and other motor vehicles to the maximum extent practicable.

**(4)(A)** Effective with respect to vehicles and engines manufactured after model year 1978, no emission control device, system, or element of design shall be used in a new motor vehicle or new motor vehicle engine for purposes of complying with requirements prescribed under this subchapter if such device, system, or element of design will cause or contribute to an unreasonable risk to public health, welfare, or safety in its operation or function.

**(B)** In determining whether an unreasonable risk exists under subparagraph (A), the Administrator shall consider, among other factors, (i) whether and to what extent the use of any device, system, or element of design causes, increases, reduces, or eliminates emissions of any unregulated pollutants; (ii) available methods for reducing or eliminating any risk to public health, welfare, or safety which may be associated with the use of such device, system, or element of design, and (iii) the availability of other devices, systems, or elements of design which may be used to conform to requirements prescribed under this subchapter without causing or contributing to such unreasonable risk. The Administrator shall include in the consideration required by this paragraph all relevant information developed pursuant to section 7548 of this title.

**(5)(A)** If the Administrator promulgates final regulations which define the degree of control required and the test procedures by which compliance could be determined for gasoline vapor recovery of uncontrolled emissions from the fueling of motor vehicles, the Administrator shall, after consultation with the Secretary of Transportation with respect to motor vehicle safety, prescribe, by regulation, fill pipe standards for new motor vehicles in order to insure effective connection between such fill pipe and any vapor recovery system which the Administrator determines may be required to comply with such vapor recovery regulations. In promulgating such standards the Administrator shall take into consideration limits on fill pipe diameter, minimum design criteria for nozzle retainer lips, limits on the location of the unleaded fuel restrictors, a minimum access zone surrounding a fill pipe, a minimum pipe or nozzle insertion angle, and such other factors as he deems pertinent.

**(B)** Regulations prescribing standards under subparagraph (A) shall not become effective until the introduction of the model year for which it would be feasible to implement such standards, taking into consideration the restraints of an adequate leadtime for design and production.

**(C)** Nothing in subparagraph (A) shall (i) prevent the Administrator from specifying different nozzle and fill neck sizes for gasoline with additives and gasoline without additives or (ii) permit the Administrator to require a specific location, configuration, modeling, or styling of the motor vehicle body with respect to the fuel tank fill neck or fill nozzle clearance envelope.

(D) For the purpose of this paragraph, the term "fill pipe" shall include the fuel tank fill pipe, fill neck, fill inlet, and closure.

**(6) Onboard vapor recovery**

Within 1 year after November 15, 1990, the Administrator shall, after consultation with the Secretary of Transportation regarding the safety of vehicle-based ("onboard") systems for the control of vehicle refueling emissions, promulgate standards under this section requiring that new light-duty vehicles manufactured beginning in the fourth model year after the model year in which the standards are promulgated and thereafter shall be equipped with such systems. The standards required under this paragraph shall apply to a percentage of each manufacturer's fleet of new light-duty vehicles beginning with the fourth model year after the model year in which the standards are promulgated. The percentage shall be as specified in the following table:

IMPLEMENTATION SCHEDULE FOR ONBOARD VAPOR RECOVERY REQUIREMENTS

| Model year commencing after standards promulgated | Percentage* |
|---|---|
| Fourth | 40 |
| Fifth | 80 |
| After Fifth | 100 |

*Percentages in the table refer to a percentage of the manufacturer's sales volume.

The standards shall require that such systems provide a minimum evaporative emission capture efficiency of 95 percent. The requirements of section 7511a(b)(3) of this title (relating to stage II gasoline vapor recovery) for areas classified under section 7511 of this title as moderate for ozone shall not apply after promulgation of such standards and the Administrator may, by rule, revise or waive the application of the requirements of such section 7511a(b)(3) of this title for areas classified under section 7511 of this title as Serious, Severe, or Extreme for ozone, as appropriate, after such time as the Administrator determines that onboard emissions control systems required under this paragraph are in widespread use throughout the motor vehicle fleet.

**(b) Emissions of carbon monoxide, hydrocarbons, and oxides of nitrogen; annual report to Congress; waiver of emission standards; research objectives**

(1)(A) The regulations under subsection (a) of this section applicable to emissions of carbon monoxide and hydrocarbons from light-duty vehicles and engines manufactured during model years 1977 through 1979 shall contain standards which provide that such emissions from such vehicles and engines may not exceed 1.5 grams per vehicle mile of hydrocarbons and 15.0 grams per vehicle mile of carbon monoxide. The regulations under subsection (a) of this section applicable to emissions of carbon monoxide from light-duty vehicles and engines manufactured during the model year 1980 shall contain standards which provide that such emissions may not exceed 7.0 grams per vehicle mile. The regulations under subsection (a) of this section applicable to emissions of hydrocarbons from light-duty vehicles and engines manufactured during or after model year 1980 shall contain standards which require a reduction of at least 90 percent from emissions of such pollutant allowable under the standards under this section applicable to light-duty vehicles and engines manufactured in model year 1970. Unless waived as provided in paragraph (5), regulations under subsection (a) of this section applicable to emissions of carbon monoxide from light-duty vehicles and engines manufactured during or after the model year 1981 shall contain standards which require a reduction of at least 90 percent from emissions of such pollutant allowable under the standards under this section applicable to light-duty vehicles and engines manufactured in model year 1970.

(B) The regulations under subsection (a) of this section applicable to emissions of oxides of nitrogen from light-duty vehicles and engines manufactured during model years 1977 through 1980 shall contain standards which provide that such emissions from such vehicles and engines may not exceed 2.0 grams per vehicle mile. The regulations under subsection (a) of this section applicable to emissions of oxides of nitrogen from light-duty vehicles and engines manufactured during the model year 1981 and thereafter shall contain standards which provide that such emissions from such vehicles and engines may not exceed 1.0 gram per vehicle mile. The Administrator shall prescribe standards in lieu of those required by the preceding sentence, which provide that emissions of oxides of nitrogen may not exceed 2.0 grams per vehicle mile for any light-duty vehicle manufactured during model years 1981 and 1982 by any manufacturer whose production, by corporate identity, for calendar year 1976 was less than three hundred thousand light-duty motor vehicles worldwide if the Administrator determines that—

(i) the ability of such manufacturer to meet emission standards in the 1975 and subsequent model years was, and is, primarily dependent upon technology developed by other manufacturers and purchased from such manufacturers; and

(ii) such manufacturer lacks the financial resources and technological ability to develop such technology.

(C) The Administrator may promulgate regulations under subsection (a)(1) of this section revising any standard prescribed or previously revised under this subsection, as needed to protect public health or welfare, taking costs, energy, and safety into account. Any revised standard shall require a reduction of emissions from the standard that was previously applicable. Any such revision under this subchapter may provide for a phase-in of the standard. It is the intent of Congress that the numerical emission standards specified in subsections (a)(3)(B)(ii), (g), (h), and (i) of this section shall not be modified by the Administrator after November 15, 1990, for any model year before the model year 2004.

(2) Emission standards under paragraph (1), and measurement techniques on which such standards are based (if not promulgated prior to November 15, 1990), shall be promulgated by regulation within 180 days after November 15, 1990.

(3) For purposes of this part—

(A)(i) The term "model year" with reference to any specific calendar year means the manufacturer's annual production period (as determined by the Administrator) which includes January 1 of such calendar year. If the manufacturer has no annual production period, the term "model year" shall mean the calendar year.

(ii) For the purpose of assuring that vehicles and engines manufactured before the beginning of a model year were not manufactured for purposes of circumventing the effective date of a standard required to be prescribed by subsection (b) of this section, the Administrator may prescribe regulations defining "model year" otherwise than as provided in clause (i).

(B) Repealed. Pub.L. 101–549, Title II, § 230(1), Nov. 15, 1990, 104 Stat. 2529.

(C) The term "heavy duty vehicle" means a truck, bus, or other vehicle manufactured primarily for use on the public streets, roads, and highways (not including any vehicle operated exclusively on a rail or rails) which has a gross vehicle weight (as determined under regulations promulgated by the Administrator) in excess of six thousand pounds. Such term includes any such vehicle which has special features enabling off-street or off-highway operation and use.

(3)[1] Upon the petition of any manufacturer, the Administrator, after notice and opportunity for public hearing, may waive the standard required under subparagraph (B) of paragraph (1) to not exceed 1.5 grams of oxides of nitrogen per vehicle mile for any class or category of light-duty vehicles or engines manufactured by such manufacturer during any period of up to four model years beginning after the model year 1980 if the manufacturer demonstrates that such waiver is necessary to permit the use of an innovative power train technology, or innovative emission control device or system, in such class or category of vehicles or engines and that such technology or system was not utilized by more than 1 percent of the light-duty vehicles sold in the United States in the 1975 model year. Such waiver may be granted only if the Administrator determines—

(A) that such waiver would not endanger public health,

(B) that there is a substantial likelihood that the vehicles or engines will be able to comply with the applicable standard under this section at the expiration of the waiver, and

(C) that the technology or system has a potential for long-term air quality benefit and has the potential to meet or exceed the average fuel economy standard applicable under the Energy Policy and Conservation Act [42 U.S.C.A. § 6201 et seq.] upon the expiration of the waiver.

No waiver under this subparagraph[2] granted to any manufacturer shall apply to more than 5 percent of such manufacturer's production or more than fifty thousand vehicles or engines, whichever is greater.

**(c) Feasibility study and investigation by National Academy of Sciences; reports to Administrator and Congress; availability of information**

(1) The Administrator shall undertake to enter into appropriate arrangements with the National Academy of Sciences to conduct a comprehensive study and investigation of the technological feasibility of meeting the emissions standards required to be prescribed by the Administrator by subsection (b) of this section.

(2) Of the funds authorized to be appropriated to the Administrator by this chapter, such amounts as are required shall be available to carry out the study and investigation authorized by paragraph (1) of this subsection.

(3) In entering into any arrangement with the National Academy of Sciences for conducting the study and investigation authorized by paragraph (1) of this subsection, the Administrator shall request the National Academy of Sciences to submit semiannual reports on the progress of its study and investigation to the Administrator and the Congress, beginning not later than July 1, 1971, and continuing until such study and investigation is completed.

(4) The Administrator shall furnish to such Academy at its request any information which the Academy deems necessary for the purpose of conducting the investigation and study authorized by paragraph (1) of this subsection. For the purpose of furnishing such information, the Administrator may use any authority he has under this chapter (A) to obtain information from any person, and (B) to require such person to

conduct such tests, keep such records, and make such reports respecting research or other activities conducted by such person as may be reasonably necessary to carry out this subsection.

**(d) Useful life of vehicles**

The Administrator shall prescribe regulations under which the useful life of vehicles and engines shall be determined for purposes of subsection (a)(1) of this section and section 7541 of this title. Such regulations shall provide that except where a different useful life period is specified in this subchapter useful life shall—

(1) in the case of light duty vehicles and light duty vehicle engines and light-duty trucks up to 3,750 lbs. LVW and up to 6,000 lbs. GVWR, be a period of use of five years or fifty thousand miles (or the equivalent), whichever first occurs, except that in the case of any requirement of this section which first becomes applicable after November 15, 1990, where the useful life period is not otherwise specified for such vehicles and engines, the period shall be 10 years or 100,000 miles (or the equivalent), whichever first occurs, with testing for purposes of in-use compliance under section 7541 of this title up to (but not beyond) 7 years or 75,000 miles (or the equivalent), whichever first occurs;

(2) in the case of any other motor vehicle or motor vehicle engine (other than motorcycles or motorcycle engines), be a period of use set forth in paragraph (1) unless the Administrator determines that a period of use of greater duration or mileage is appropriate; and

(3) in the case of any motorcycle or motorcycle engine, be a period of use the Administrator shall determine.

**(e) New power sources or propulsion systems**

In the event of a new power source or propulsion system for new motor vehicles or new motor vehicle engines is submitted for certification pursuant to section 7525(a) of this title, the Administrator may postpone certification until he has prescribed standards for any air pollutants emitted by such vehicle or engine which in his judgment cause, or contribute to, air pollution which may reasonably be anticipated to endanger the public health or welfare but for which standards have not been prescribed under subsection (a) of this section.

**(f) [3] High altitude regulations**

(1) The high altitude regulation in effect with respect to model year 1977 motor vehicles shall not apply to the manufacture, distribution, or sale of 1978 and later model year motor vehicles. Any future regulation affecting the sale or distribution of motor vehicles or engines manufactured before the model year 1984 in high altitude areas of the country shall take effect no earlier than model year 1981.

(2) Any such future regulation applicable to high altitude vehicles or engines shall not require a percentage of reduction in the emissions of such vehicles which is greater than the required percentage of reduction in emissions from motor vehicles as set forth in subsection (b) of this section. This percentage reduction shall be determined by comparing any proposed high altitude emission standards to high altitude emissions from vehicles manufactured during model year 1970. In no event shall regulations applicable to high altitude vehicles manufactured before the model year 1984 establish a numerical standard which is more stringent than that applicable to vehicles certified under non-high altitude conditions.

(3) Section 7607(d) of this title shall apply to any high altitude regulation referred to in paragraph (2) and before promulgating any such regulation, the Administrator shall consider and make a finding with respect to—

(A) the economic impact upon consumers, individual high altitude dealers, and the automobile industry of any such regulation, including the economic impact which was experienced as a result of the regulation imposed during model year 1977 with respect to high altitude certification requirements;

(B) the present and future availability of emission control technology capable of meeting the applicable vehicle and engine emission requirements without reducing model availability; and

(C) the likelihood that the adoption of such a high altitude regulation will result in any significant improvement in air quality in any area to which it shall apply.

**(g) Light-duty trucks up to 6,000 lbs. GVWR and light-duty vehicles; standards for model years after 1993**

**(1) NMHC, CO, and $NO_x$**

Effective with respect to the model year 1994 and thereafter, the regulations under subsection (a) of this section applicable to emissions of nonmethane hydrocarbons (NMHC), carbon monoxide (CO), and oxides of nitrogen ($NO_x$) from light-duty trucks (LDTs) of up to 6,000 lbs. gross vehicle weight rating (GVWR) and light-duty vehicles (LDVs) shall contain standards which provide that emissions from a percentage of each manufacturer's sales volume of such vehicles and trucks shall comply with the levels specified in table G. The percentage shall be as specified in the implementation schedule below:

TABLE G—EMISSION STANDARDS FOR NMHC, CO, AND $NO_x$ FROM LIGHT–DUTY TRUCKS OF UP TO 6,000 LBS. GVWR AND LIGHT–DUTY VEHICLES

| Vehicle type | Column A (5 yrs/50,000 mi) | | | Column B (10 yrs/100,000 mi) | | |
|---|---|---|---|---|---|---|
| | NMHC | CO | $NO_x$ | NMHC | CO | $NO_x$ |
| LDTs (0–3,750 lbs. LVW) and light-duty vehicles | 0.25 | 3.4 | 0.4* | 0.31 | 4.2 | 0.6* |
| LDTs (3,751–5,750 lbs. LVW) | 0.32 | 4.4 | 0.7** | 0.40 | 5.5 | 0.97 |

Standards are expressed in grams per mile (gpm).

For standards under column A, for purposes of certification under section 7525 of this title, the applicable useful life shall be 5 years or 50,000 miles (or the equivalent), whichever first occurs.

For standards under column B, for purposes of certification under section 7525 of this title, the applicable useful life shall be 10 years or 100,000 miles (or the equivalent), whichever first occurs.

* In the case of diesel-fueled LDTs (0–3,750 lvw) and light-duty vehicles, before the model year 2004, in lieu of the 0.4 and 0.6 standards for $NO_X$, the applicable standards for $NO_X$ shall be 1.0 gpm for a useful life of 5 years or 50,000 miles (or the equivalent), whichever first occurs, and 1.25 gpm for a useful life of 10 years or 100,000 miles (or the equivalent), whichever first occurs.

** This standard does not apply to diesel-fueled LDTs (3,751–5,750 lbs. LVW).

IMPLEMENTATION SCHEDULE FOR TABLE G STANDARDS

| Model year | Percentage * |
|---|---|
| 1994 | 40 |
| 1995 | 80 |
| after 1995 | 100 |

* Percentages in the table refer to a percentage of each manufacturer's sales volume.

### (2) PM Standard

Effective with respect to model year 1994 and thereafter in the case of light-duty vehicles, and effective with respect to the model year 1995 and thereafter in the case of light-duty trucks (LDTs) of up to 6,000 lbs. gross vehicle weight rating (GVWR), the regulations under subsection (a) of this section applicable to emissions of particulate matter (PM) from such vehicles and trucks shall contain standards which provide that such emissions from a percentage of each manufacturer's sales volume of such vehicles and trucks shall not exceed the levels specified in the table below. The percentage shall be as specified in the Implementation Schedule below.

PM STANDARD FOR LDTs OF UP TO 6,000 LBS. GVWR

| Useful life period | Standard |
|---|---|
| 5/50,000 | 0.80 gpm |
| 10/100,000 | 0.10 gpm |

The applicable useful life, for purposes of certification under section 7525 of this title and for purposes of in-use compliance under section 7541 of this title, shall be 5 years or 50,000 miles (or the equivalent), whichever first occurs, in the case of the 5/50,000 standard.

The applicable useful life, for purposes of certification under section 7525 of this title and for purposes of in-use compliance under section 7541 of this title, shall be 10 years or 100,000 miles (or the equivalent), whichever first occurs in the case of the 10/100,000 standard.

IMPLEMENTATION SCHEDULE FOR PM STANDARDS

| Model year | Light-duty vehicles | LDTs |
|---|---|---|
| 1994 | 40%* | .... |
| 1995 | 80%* | 40%* |
| 1996 | 100%* | 80%* |
| after 1996 | 100%* | 100%* |

* Percentages in the table refer to a percentage of each manufacturer's sales volume.

### (h) Light-duty trucks of more than 6,000 lbs. GVWR; standards for model years after 1995

Effective with respect to the model year 1996 and thereafter, the regulations under subsection (a) of this section applicable to emissions of nonmethane hydrocarbons (NMHC), carbon monoxide (CO), oxides of nitrogen ($NO_x$), and particulate matter (PM) from light-duty trucks (LDTs) of more than 6,000 lbs. gross vehicle weight rating (GVWR) shall contain standards which provide that emissions from a specified percentage of each manufacturer's sales volume of such trucks shall comply with the levels specified in table H. The specified percentage shall be 50 percent in model year 1996 and 100 percent thereafter.

TABLE H—EMISSION STANDARDS FOR NMHC AND CO FROM GASOLINE AND DIESEL FUELED LIGHT–DUTY TRUCKS OF MORE THAN 6,000 LBS. GVWR

| LDT Test weight | Column A (5 yrs/50,000 mi) | | | Column B (11 yrs/120,000 mi) | | | |
|---|---|---|---|---|---|---|---|
| | NMHC | CO | $NO_x$ | NMHC | CO | $NO_x$ | PM |
| 3,751–5,750 lbs. TW | 0.32 | 4.4 | 0.7* | 0.46 | 6.4 | 0.98 | 0.10 |
| Over 5,750 lbs. TW | 0.39 | 5.0 | 1.1* | 0.56 | 7.3 | 1.53 | 0.12 |

Standards are expressed in grams per mile (GPM).

For standards under column A, for purposes of certification under section 7525 of this title, the applicable useful life shall be 5 years or 50,000 miles (or the equivalent) whichever first occurs.

For standards under column B, for purposes of certification under section 7525 of this title, the applicable useful life shall be 11 years or 120,000 miles (or the equivalent), whichever first occurs.

* Not applicable to diesel-fueled LDTs.

**(i) Phase II study for certain light-duty vehicles and light-duty trucks**

(1) The Administrator, with the participation of the Office of Technology Assessment, shall study whether or not further reductions in emissions from light-duty vehicles and light-duty trucks should be required pursuant to this subchapter. The study shall consider whether to establish with respect to model years commencing after January 1, 2003, the standards and useful life period for gasoline and diesel-fueled light-duty vehicles and light-duty trucks with a loaded vehicle weight (LVW) of 3,750 lbs. or less specified in the following table:

TABLE 3—PENDING EMISSION STANDARDS FOR GASOLINE AND DIESEL FUELED LIGHT–DUTY VEHICLES AND LIGHT–DUTY TRUCKS 3,750 LBS. LVW OR LESS

| Pollutant | Emission level* |
|---|---|
| NMHC | 0.125 GPM |
| $NO_x$ | 0.2 GPM |
| CO | 1.7 GPM |

* Emission levels are expressed in grams per mile (GPM). For vehicles and engines subject to this subsection for purposes of subsection (d) of this section and any reference thereto, the useful life of such vehicles and engines shall be a period of 10 years or 100,000 miles (or the equivalent), whichever first occurs.

Such study shall also consider other standards and useful life periods which are more stringent or less stringent than those set forth in table 3 (but more stringent than those referred to in subsections (g) and (h) of this section).

**(2)(A)** As part of the study under paragraph (1), the Administrator shall examine the need for further reductions in emissions in order to attain or maintain the national ambient air quality standards, taking into consideration the waiver provisions of section 7543(b) of this title. As part of such study, the Administrator shall also examine—

**(i)** the availability of technology (including the costs thereof), in the case of light-duty vehicles and light-duty trucks with a loaded vehicle weight (LVW) of 3,750 lbs. or less, for meeting more stringent emission standards than those provided in subsections (g) and (h) of this section for model years commencing not earlier than after January 1, 2003, and not later than model year 2006, including the lead time and safety and energy impacts of meeting more stringent emission standards; and

**(ii)** the need for, and cost effectiveness of, obtaining further reductions in emissions from such light-duty vehicles and light-duty trucks, taking into consideration alternative means of attaining or maintaining the national primary ambient air quality standards pursuant to State implementation plans and other requirements of this chapter, including their feasibility and cost effectiveness.

**(B)** The Administrator shall submit a report to Congress no later than June 1, 1997, containing the results of the study under this subsection, including the results of the examination conducted under subparagraph (A). Before submittal of such report the Administrator shall provide a reasonable opportunity for public comment and shall include a summary of such comments in the report to Congress.

**(3)(A)** Based on the study under paragraph (1) the Administrator shall determine, by rule, within 3 calendar years after the report is submitted to Congress, but not later than December 31, 1999, whether—

**(i)** there is a need for further reductions in emissions as provided in paragraph (2)(A);

**(ii)** the technology for meeting more stringent emission standards will be available, as provided in paragraph (2)(A)(i), in the case of light-duty vehicles and light-duty trucks with a loaded vehicle weight (LVW) of 3,750 lbs. or less, for model years commencing not earlier than January 1, 2003, and not later than model year 2006, considering the factors listed in paragraph (2)(A)(i); and

(iii) obtaining further reductions in emissions from such vehicles will be needed and cost effective, taking into consideration alternatives as provided in paragraph (2)(A)(ii).

The rulemaking under this paragraph shall commence within 3 months after submission of the report to Congress under paragraph (2)(B).

**(B)** If the Administrator determines under subparagraph (A) that—

**(i)** there is no need for further reductions in emissions as provided in paragraph (2)(A);

**(ii)** the technology for meeting more stringent emission standards will not be available as provided in paragraph (2)(A)(i), in the case of light-duty vehicles and light-duty trucks with a loaded vehicle weight (LVW) of 3,750 lbs. or less, for model years commencing not earlier than January 1, 2003, and not later than model year 2006, considering the factors listed in paragraph (2)(A)(i); or

**(iii)** obtaining further reductions in emissions from such vehicles will not be needed or cost effective, taking into consideration alternatives as provided in paragraph (2)(A)(ii),

the Administrator shall not promulgate more stringent standards than those in effect pursuant to subsections (g) and (h) of this section. Nothing in this paragraph shall prohibit the Administrator from exercising the Administrator's authority under subsection (a) of this section to promulgate more stringent standards for light-duty vehicles and light-duty trucks with a loaded vehicle weight (LVW) of 3,750 lbs. or less at any other time thereafter in accordance with subsection (a) of this section.

**(C)** If the Administrator determines under subparagraph (A) that—

**(i)** there is a need for further reductions in emissions as provided in paragraph (2)(A);

**(ii)** the technology for meeting more stringent emission standards will be available, as provided in paragraph (2)(A)(i), in the case of light-duty vehicles and light-duty trucks with a loaded vehicle weight (LVW) of 3,750 lbs. or less, for model years commencing not earlier than January 1, 2003, and not later than model year 2006, considering the factors listed in paragraph (2)(A)(i); and

**(iii)** obtaining further reductions in emissions from such vehicles will be needed and cost effective, taking into consideration alternatives as provided in paragraph (2)(A)(ii),

the Administrator shall either promulgate the standards (and useful life periods) set forth in Table 3 in paragraph (1) or promulgate alternative standards (and useful life periods) which are more stringent than those referred to in subsections (g) and (h) of this section. Any such standards (or useful life periods) promulgated by the Administrator shall take effect with respect to any such vehicles or engines no earlier than the model year 2003 but not later than model year 2006, as determined by the Administrator in the rule.

**(D)** Nothing in this paragraph shall be construed by the Administrator or by a court as a presumption that any standards (or useful life period) set forth in Table 3 shall be promulgated in the rulemaking required under this paragraph. The action required of the Administrator in accordance with this paragraph shall be treated as a nondiscretionary duty for purposes of section 7604(a)(2) of this title (relating to citizen suits).

**(E)** Unless the Administrator determines not to promulgate more stringent standards as provided in subparagraph (B) or to postpone the effective date of standards referred to in Table 3 in paragraph (1) or to establish alternative standards as provided in subparagraph (C), effective with respect to model years commencing after January 1, 2003, the regulations under subsection (a) of this section applicable to emissions of nonmethane hydrocarbons (NMHC), oxides of nitrogen ($NO_x$), and carbon monoxide (CO) from motor vehicles and motor vehicle engines in the classes specified in Table 3 in paragraph (1) above shall contain standards which provide that emissions may not exceed the pending emission levels specified in Table 3 in paragraph (1).

**(j) Cold CO standard**

**(1) Phase I**

Not later than 12 months after November 15, 1990, the Administrator shall promulgate regulations under subsection (a) of this section applicable to emissions of carbon monoxide from 1994 and later model year light-duty vehicles and light-duty trucks when operated at 20 degrees Fahrenheit. The regulations shall contain standards which provide that emissions of carbon monoxide from a manufacturer's vehicles when operated at 20 degrees Fahrenheit may not exceed, in the case of light-duty vehicles, 10.0 grams per mile, and in the case of light-duty trucks, a level comparable in stringency to the standard applicable to light-duty vehicles. The standards shall take effect after model year 1993 according to a phase-in schedule which requires a percentage of each manufacturer's sales volume of light-duty vehicles and light-duty trucks to comply with applicable standards after model year 1993. The percentage shall be as specified in the following table:

PHASE-IN SCHEDULE FOR COLD START STANDARDS

| Model Year | Percentage |
|---|---|
| 1994 | 40 |
| 1995 | 80 |
| 1996 and after | 100 |

**(2) Phase II**

**(A)** Not later than June 1, 1997, the Administrator shall complete a study assessing the need for further reductions in emissions of carbon monoxide and the maximum reductions in such emissions achievable from model year 2001 and later model year light-duty vehicles and light-duty trucks when operated at 20 degrees Fahrenheit.

**(B)(i)** If as of June 1, 1997, 6 or more nonattainment areas have a carbon monoxide design value of 9.5 ppm or greater, the regulations under subsection (a)(1) of this section applicable to emissions of carbon monoxide from model year 2002 and later model year light-duty vehicles and light-duty trucks shall contain standards which provide that emissions of carbon monoxide from such vehicles and trucks when operated at 20 degrees Fahrenheit may not exceed 3.4 grams per mile (gpm) in the case of light-duty vehicles and 4.4 grams per mile (gpm) in the case of light-duty trucks up to 6,000 GVWR and a level comparable in stringency in the case of light-duty trucks 6,000 GVWR and above.

**(ii)** In determining for purposes of this subparagraph whether 6 or more nonattainment areas have a carbon monoxide design value of 9.5 ppm or greater, the Administrator shall exclude the areas of Steubenville, Ohio, and Oshkosh, Wisconsin.

**(3) Useful-life for phase I and phase II standards**

In the case of the standards referred to in paragraphs (1) and (2), for purposes of certification under section 7525 of this title and in-use compliance under section 7541 of this title, the applicable useful life period shall be 5 years or 50,000 miles, whichever first occurs, except that the Administrator may extend such useful life period (for purposes of section 7525 of this title, or section 7541 of this title, or both) if he determines that it is feasible for vehicles and engines subject to such standards to meet such standards for a longer useful life. If the Administrator extends such useful life period, the Administrator may make an appropriate adjustment of applicable standards for such extended useful life. No such extended useful life shall extend beyond the useful life period provided in regulations under subsection (d) of this section.

**(4) Heavy-duty vehicles and engines**

The Administrator may also promulgate regulations under subsection (a)(1) of this section applicable to emissions of carbon monoxide from heavy-duty vehicles and engines when operated at cold temperatures.

**(k) Control of evaporative emissions**

The Administrator shall promulgate (and from time to time revise) regulations applicable to evaporative emissions of hydrocarbons from all gasoline-fueled motor vehicles—

**(1)** during operation; and

**(2)** over 2 or more days of nonuse;

under ozone-prone summertime conditions (as determined by regulations of the Administrator). The regulations shall take effect as expeditiously as possible and shall require the greatest degree of emission reduction achievable by means reasonably expected to be available for production during any model year to which the regulations apply, giving appropriate consideration to fuel volatility, and to cost, energy, and safety factors associated with the application of the appropriate technology. The Administrator shall commence a rulemaking under this subsection within 12 months after November 15, 1990. If final regulations are not promulgated under this subsection within 18 months after November 15, 1990, the Administrator shall submit a statement to the Congress containing an explanation of the reasons for the delay and a date certain for promulgation of such final regulations in accordance with this chapter. Such date certain shall not be later than 15 months after the expiration of such 18 month deadline.

**(*l*) Mobile source-related air toxics**

**(1) Study**

Not later than 18 months after November 15, 1990, the Administrator shall complete a study of the need for, and feasibility of, controlling emissions of toxic air pollutants which are unregulated under this chapter and associated with motor vehicles and motor vehicle fuels, and the need for, and feasibility of, controlling such emissions and the means and measures for such controls. The study shall focus on those categories of emissions that pose the greatest risk to human health or about which significant uncertainties remain, including emissions of benzene, formaldehyde, and 1, 3 butadiene. The proposed report shall be available for public review and comment and shall include a summary of all comments.

**(2) Standards**

Within 54 months after November 15, 1990, the Administrator shall, based on the study under paragraph (1), promulgate (and from time to time revise) regulations under subsection (a)(1) of this section or section 7545(c)(1) of this title containing reasonable requirements to control hazardous air pollutants from motor vehicles and motor vehicle fuels. The regulations shall contain standards for such fuels or vehicles, or both, which the Administrator determines reflect the greatest degree of emission reduction achievable through the application of technology which will be available, taking into consideration the standards established under subsection (a) of this section, the availability and costs of the technology, and noise, energy, and safety factors, and lead time. Such regulations shall not be inconsistent with standards under subsection (a) of this section. The regulations shall, at a minimum, apply to emissions of benzene and formaldehyde.

**(m) Emissions control diagnostics**

**(1) Regulations**

Within 18 months after November 15, 1990, the Administrator shall promulgate regulations under subsection (a) of this section requiring manufacturers to install on all new light duty vehicles and light duty trucks diagnostics systems capable of—

**(A)** accurately identifying for the vehicle's useful life as established under this section, emission-related systems deterioration or malfunction, including, at a minimum, the catalytic converter and oxygen sensor, which could cause or result in failure of the vehicles to comply with emission standards established under this section,

**(B)** alerting the vehicle's owner or operator to the likely need for emission-related components or systems maintenance or repair,

**(C)** storing and retrieving fault codes specified by the Administrator, and

**(D)** providing access to stored information in a manner specified by the Administrator.

The Administrator may, in the Administrator's discretion, promulgate regulations requiring manufacturers to install such onboard diagnostic systems on heavy-duty vehicles and engines.

**(2) Effective date**

The regulations required under paragraph (1) of this subsection shall take effect in model year 1994, except that the Administrator may waive the application of such regulations for model year 1994 or 1995 (or both) with respect to any class or category of motor vehicles if the Administrator determines that it would be infeasible to apply the regulations to that class or category in such model year or years, consistent with corresponding regulations or policies adopted by the California Air Resources Board for such systems.

**(3) State inspection**

The Administrator shall by regulation require States that have implementation plans containing motor vehicle inspection and maintenance programs to amend their plans within 2 years after promulgation of such regulations to provide for inspection of onboard diagnostics systems (as prescribed by regulations under paragraph (1) of this subsection) and for the maintenance or repair of malfunctions or system deterioration identified by or affecting such diagnostics systems. Such regulations shall not be inconsistent with the provisions for warranties promulgated under section 7541(a) and (b) of this title.

**(4) Specific requirements**

In promulgating regulations under this subsection, the Administrator shall require—

**(A)** that any connectors through which the emission control diagnostics system is accessed for inspection, diagnosis, service, or repair shall be standard and uniform on all motor vehicles and motor vehicle engines;

**(B)** that access to the emission control diagnostics system through such connectors shall be unrestricted and shall not require any access code or any device which is only available from a vehicle manufacturer; and

**(C)** that the output of the data from the emission control diagnostics system through such connectors shall be usable without the need for any unique decoding information or device.

**(5) Information availability**

The Administrator, by regulation, shall require (subject to the provisions of section 7542(c) of this title regarding the protection of methods or processes entitled to protection as trade secrets) manufacturers to provide promptly to any person engaged in the repairing or servicing of motor vehicles or motor vehicle engines, and the Administrator for use by any such persons, with any and all information needed to make use of the emission control diagnostics system prescribed under this subsection and such other information including instructions for making emission related diagnosis and repairs. No such information may be withheld under section 7542(c) of this title if that information is provided (directly or indirectly) by the manufacturer to franchised dealers or other persons engaged in the repair, diagnosing, or servicing of motor vehicles or motor vehicle engines. Such information shall also be available to the Administrator, subject to section 7542(c) of this title, in carrying out the Administrator's responsibilities under this section.

**(f)[4] Model years after 1990**

For model years prior to model year 1994, the regulations under subsection (a) of this section applicable to buses other than those subject to standards under section 7554 of this title shall contain a standard which provides that emissions of particulate matter (PM) from such buses may not exceed the standards set forth in the following table:

**PM STANDARD FOR BUSES**

| Model year | Standard* |
|---|---|
| 1991 | 0.25 |
| 1992 | 0.25 |
| 1993 and thereafter | 0.10 |

* Standards are expressed in grams per brake horsepower hour (g/bhp/hr).

(July 14, 1955, c. 360, Title II, § 202, as added Oct. 20, 1965, Pub.L. 89–272, Title I, § 101(8), 79 Stat. 992, and amended Nov. 21, 1967, Pub.L. 90–148, § 2, 81 Stat. 499; Dec. 31, 1970, Pub.L. 91–604, § 6(a), 84 Stat. 1690; June 22, 1974, Pub.L. 93–319, § 5, 88 Stat. 258; Aug. 7, 1977, Pub.L. 95–95, Title II, §§ 201, 202(b), 213(b), 214(a), 215 to 217, 224(a), (b), (g), Title IV, § 401(d), 91 Stat. 751 to 753, 758 to 761, 765, 767, 769, 791; Nov. 16, 1977, Pub.L. 95–190, § 14(a)(60) to (65), (b)(5), 91 Stat. 1403, 1405; Nov. 15, 1990, Pub.L. 101–549, Title II, §§ 201 to 207, 227(b), 230(1) to (5), 104 Stat. 2472 to 2481, 2507, 2529.)

1 So in original. Probably should be "(4)".

2 So in original. Probably should be "paragraph".

3 Another subsec. (f) is set out following subsec. (m).

4 So in original. Probably should be (n).

## HISTORICAL AND STATUTORY NOTES

**References in Text**

The enactment of the Clean Air Act Amendments of 1990, referred to in subsec. (a)(3)(B), probably means the enactment of Pub.L. 101–549, Nov. 15, 1990, 104 Stat. 2399, which was approved Nov. 15, 1990. For complete classification of this Act to the Code, see Short Title of 1990 Amendments note set out under section 7401 of this title and Tables.

Section 7525(f)(1) of this title, referred to in subsec. (a)(3)(E), was redesignated section 7525(f) of this title by Pub.L. 101–549, Title II, § 230(8), Nov. 15, 1990, 104 Stat. 2529.

The Energy Policy and Conservation Act, referred to in subsec. (b)(3)(c), is Pub.L. 94–163, Dec. 22, 1975, 89 Stat. 871, as amended, which is classified principally to chapter 77 (section 6201 et seq.) of this title. For complete classification of this Act to the Code, see Short Title of 1975 Acts note set out under section 6201 of this title and Tables.

**Codifications**

Section was formerly classified to section 1857f–1 of this title.

**Effective and Applicability Provisions**

1990 Acts

Amendment by Pub.L. 101–549 effective Nov. 15, 1990, except as otherwise provided, see section 711(b) of Pub.L. 101–549, set out as a note under section 7401 of this title.

1977 Acts

Amendment by Pub.L. 95–95 effective Aug. 7, 1977, except as otherwise expressly provided, see section 406(d) of Pub.L. 95–95, set out as a note under section 7401 of this title.

**Savings Provisions**

Suits, actions or proceedings commenced under this chapter as in effect prior to Nov. 15, 1990, not to abate by reason of the taking effect of amendments by Pub.L. 101–549, except as otherwise provided for, see section 711(a) of Pub.L. 101–549, set out as a note under section 7401 of this title.

**Continuing Comprehensive Studies and Investigations by National Academy of Sciences**

Section 403(f) of Pub.L. 95–95 provided that: "The Administrator of the Environmental Protection Agency shall undertake to enter into appropriate arrangements with the National Academy of Sciences to conduct continuing comprehensive studies and investigations of the effects on public health and welfare of emissions subject to section 202(a) of the Clean Air Act [subsec. (a) of this section] (including sulfur compounds) and the technological feasibility of meeting emission standards required to be prescribed by the Administrator by section 202(b) of such Act [subsec. (b) of this section]. The Administrator shall report to the Congress within six months of the date of enactment of this section [Aug. 7, 1977] and each year thereafter regarding the status of the contractual arrangements and conditions necessary to implement this paragraph."

**Modification or Rescission of Rules, Regulations, Orders, Determinations, Contracts, Certifications, Authorizations, Delegations, and Other Actions**

All rules, regulations, orders, determinations, contracts, certifications, authorizations, delegations, or other actions duly issued, made, or taken by or pursuant to Act July 14, 1955, the Clean Air Act, as in effect immediately prior to the date of enactment of Pub.L. 95–95 [Aug. 7, 1977] to continue in full force and effect until modified or rescinded in accordance with Act July 14, 1955, as amended by Pub.L. 95–95 [this chapter], see section 406(b) of Pub.L. 95–95, set out as an Effective Date note under section 7401 of this title.

**Study of Carbon Monoxide Intrusion Into Sustained-Use Vehicles**

Section 226 of Pub.L. 95–95 provided that the Administrator, in conjunction with the Secretary of Transportation, study the problem of carbon monoxide intrusion into the passenger area of sustained-use motor vehicles and that within one year the Administrator report to the Congress respecting the results of such study.

**Study on Emission of Sulfur-Bearing Compounds From Motor Vehicles and Motor Vehicle and Aircraft Engines**

Section 403(g) of Pub.L. 95–95 provided that the Administrator of the Environmental Protection Agency conduct a study and report to the Congress by the date one year after Aug. 7, 1977, on the emission of sulfur-bearing compounds from motor vehicles and motor vehicle engines and aircraft engines.

**Study on Oxides of Nitrogen From Light Duty Vehicles**

Section 202(a) of Pub.L. 95–95 provided that the Administrator of the Environmental Protection Agency conduct a study of the public health implications of attaining an emission standard on oxides of nitrogen from light duty vehicles of 0.4 gram per vehicle mile, the cost and technological capability of attaining such standard, and the need for such a standard to protect public health or welfare and that the Administrator submit a report of such study to the Congress, together with recommendations not later than July 1, 1980.

## § 7522. Prohibited acts

### [CAA § 203]

### (a) Enumerated prohibitions

The following acts and the causing thereof are prohibited—

(1) in the case of a manufacturer of new motor vehicles or new motor vehicle engines for distribu-

tion in commerce, the sale, or the offering for sale, or the introduction, or delivery for introduction, into commerce, or (in the case of any person, except as provided by regulation of the Administrator), the importation into the United States, of any new motor vehicle or new motor vehicle engine, manufactured after the effective date of regulations under this part which are applicable to such vehicle or engine unless such vehicle or engine is covered by a certificate of conformity issued (and in effect) under regulations prescribed under this part or part C in the case of clean-fuel vehicles (except as provided in subsection (b) of this section);

**(2)(A)** for any person to fail or refuse to permit access to or copying of records or to fail to make reports or provide information required under section 7542 of this title;

**(B)** for any person to fail or refuse to permit entry, testing or inspection authorized under section 7525(c) of this title or section 7542 of this title;

**(C)** for any person to fail or refuse to perform tests, or have tests performed as required under section 7542 of this title;

**(D)** for any manufacturer to fail to make information available as provided by regulation under section 7521(m)(5) of this title;

**(3)(A)** for any person to remove or render inoperative any device or element of design installed on or in a motor vehicle or motor vehicle engine in compliance with regulations under this subchapter prior to its sale and delivery to the ultimate purchaser, or for any person knowingly to remove or render inoperative any such device or element of design after such sale and delivery to the ultimate purchaser; or

**(B)** for any person to manufacture or sell, or offer to sell, or install, any part or component intended for use with, or as part of, any motor vehicle or motor vehicle engine, where a principal effect of the part or component is to bypass, defeat, or render inoperative any device or element of design installed on or in a motor vehicle or motor vehicle engine in compliance with regulations under this subchapter, and where the person knows or should know that such part or component is being offered for sale or installed for such use or put to such use; or

**(4)** for any manufacturer of a new motor vehicle or new motor vehicle engine subject to standards prescribed under section 7521 of this title or part C of this subchapter—

**(A)** to sell or lease any such vehicle or engine unless such manufacturer has complied with (i) the requirements of section 7541(a) and (b) of this title with respect to such vehicle or engine, and unless a label or tag is affixed to such vehicle or engine in accordance with section 7541(c)(3) of this title, or (ii) the corresponding requirements of part C of this subchapter in the case of clean fuel vehicles unless the manufacturer has complied with the corresponding requirements of part C of this subchapter [1]

**(B)** to fail or refuse to comply with the requirements of section 7541(c) or (e) of this title, or the corresponding requirements of part C of this subchapter in the case of clean fuel vehicles [1]

**(C)** except as provided in subsection (c)(3) of section 7541 of this title and the corresponding requirements of part C of this subchapter in the case of clean fuel vehicles, to provide directly or indirectly in any communication to the ultimate purchaser or any subsequent purchaser that the coverage of any warranty under this chapter is conditioned upon use of any part, component, or system manufactured by such manufacturer or any person acting for such manufacturer or under his control, or conditioned upon service performed by any such person, or

**(D)** to fail or refuse to comply with the terms and conditions of the warranty under section 7541(a) or (b) of this title or the corresponding requirements of part C of this subchapter in the case of clean fuel vehicles with respect to any vehicle; or

**(5)** for any person to violate section 7553 of this title, 7554 of this title, or part C of this subchapter or any regulations under section 7553 of this title, 7554 of this title, or part C of this subchapter.

No action with respect to any element of design referred to in paragraph (3) (including any adjustment or alteration of such element) shall be treated as a prohibited act under such paragraph (3) if such action is in accordance with section 7549 of this title. Nothing in paragraph (3) shall be construed to require the use of manufacturer parts in maintaining or repairing any motor vehicle or motor vehicle engine. For the purposes of the preceding sentence, the term "manufacturer parts" means, with respect to a motor vehicle engine, parts produced or sold by the manufacturer of the motor vehicle or motor vehicle engine. No action with respect to any device or element of design referred to in paragraph (3) shall be treated as a prohibited act under that paragraph if (i) the action is for the purpose of repair or replacement of the device or element, or is a necessary and temporary procedure to repair or replace any other item and the device or element is replaced upon completion of the procedure, and (ii) such action thereafter results in the proper functioning of the device or element referred to in paragraph (3). No action with respect to any device or element of design referred to in paragraph (3) shall be treated as a prohibited act under that paragraph if the action is for the purpose of a conversion of a motor vehicle for use of a clean alternative fuel (as defined in this subchapter) and if such vehicle complies with the applicable standard under section 7521 of this title when operating on such fuel, and if in the case of a clean alternative fuel vehicle (as defined by rule by the Administrator), the device or element is replaced upon completion of the conversion procedure and such action results in proper functioning of the device or element when the motor vehicle operates on conventional fuel.

**(b) Exemptions; refusal to admit vehicle or engine into United States; vehicles or engines intended for export**

(1) The Administrator may exempt any new motor vehicle or new motor vehicle engine, from subsection (a) of this section, upon such terms and conditions as he may find necessary for the purpose of research, investigations, studies, demonstrations, or training, or for reasons of national security.

(2) A new motor vehicle or new motor vehicle engine offered for importation or imported by any person in violation of subsection (a) of this section shall be refused admission into the United States, but the Secretary of the Treasury and the Administrator may, by joint regulation, provide for deferring final determination as to admission and authorizing the delivery of such a motor vehicle or engine offered for import to the owner or consignee thereof upon such terms and conditions (including the furnishing of a bond) as may appear to them appropriate to insure that any such motor vehicle or engine will be brought into conformity with the standards, requirements, and limitations applicable to it under this part. The Secretary of the Treasury shall, if a motor vehicle or engine is finally refused admission under this paragraph, cause disposition thereof in accordance with the customs laws unless it is exported, under regulations prescribed by such Secretary, within ninety days of the date of notice of such refusal or such additional time as may be permitted pursuant to such regulations, except that disposition in accordance with the customs laws may not be made in such manner as may result, directly or indirectly, in the sale, to the ultimate consumer, of a new motor vehicle or new motor vehicle engine that fails to comply with applicable standards of the Administrator under this part.

(3) A new motor vehicle or new motor vehicle engine intended solely for export, and so labeled or tagged on the outside of the container and on the vehicle or engine itself, shall be subject to the provisions of subsection (a) of this section, except that if the country which is to receive such vehicle or engine has emission standards which differ from the standards prescribed under section 7521 of this title, then such vehicle or engine shall comply with the standards of such country which is to receive such vehicle or engine.

(July 14, 1955, c. 360, Title II, § 203, as added Oct. 20, 1965, Pub.L. 89–272, Title I, § 101(8), 79 Stat. 993, and amended Nov. 21, 1967, Pub.L. 90–148, § 2, 81 Stat. 499; Dec. 31, 1970, Pub.L. 91–604, §§ 7(a), 11(a)(2)(A), 15(c)(2), 84 Stat. 1693, 1705, 1713; Aug. 7, 1977, Pub.L. 95–95, Title II, §§ 206, 211(a), 218(a), (d), 219(a), (b), 91 Stat. 755, 757, 761, 762; Nov. 16, 1977, Pub.L. 95–190, § 14(a)(66)–(68), 91 Stat. 1403; Nov. 15, 1990, Pub.L. 101–549, Title II, §§ 228(a), (b), (e), 230(6), 104 Stat. 2507, 2511, 2529.)

[1] So in original. Probably should be followed by a comma.

### HISTORICAL AND STATUTORY NOTES

**Codifications**

Section was formerly classified to section 1857f–2 of this title.

**Effective and Applicability Provisions**

1990 Acts

Amendment by Pub.L. 101–549 effective Nov. 15, 1990, except as otherwise provided, see section 711(b) of Pub.L. 101–549, set out as a note under section 7401 of this title.

1977 Acts

Amendment by Pub.L. 95–95 effective Aug. 7, 1977, except as otherwise expressly provided, see section 406(d) of Pub.L. 95–95, set out as a note under section 7401 of this title.

**Savings Provisions**

Suits, actions or proceedings commenced under this chapter as in effect prior to Nov. 15, 1990, not to abate by reason of the taking effect of amendments by Pub.L. 101–549, except as otherwise provided for, see section 711(a) of Pub.L. 101–549, set out as a note under section 7401 of this title.

## § 7523. Actions to restrain violations [CAA § 204]

**(a) Jurisdiction**

The district courts of the United States shall have jurisdiction to restrain violations of section 7522(a) of this title.

**(b) Actions brought by or in name of United States; subpenas**

Actions to restrain such violations shall be brought by and in the name of the United States. In any such action, subpenas for witnesses who are required to attend a district court in any district may run into any other district.

(July 14, 1955, c. 360, Title II, § 204, as added Oct. 20, 1965, Pub.L. 89–272, Title I, § 101(8), 79 Stat. 994, and amended Nov. 21, 1967, Pub.L. 90–148, § 2, 81 Stat. 500; Dec. 31, 1970, Pub.L. 91–604, § 7(b), 84 Stat. 1694; Aug. 7, 1977, Pub.L. 95–95, Title II, § 218(b), 91 Stat. 761.)

### HISTORICAL AND STATUTORY NOTES

**Codifications**

Section was formerly classified to section 1857f–3 of this title.

**Effective and Applicability Provisions**

1977 Acts

Amendment by Pub.L. 95–95 effective Aug. 7, 1977, except as otherwise expressly provided, see section 406(d) of Pub.L. 95–95, set out as a note under section 7401 of this title.

**Pending Actions and Proceedings**

Suits, actions, and other proceedings lawfully commenced by or against the Administrator or any other officer or employee of the United States in his official capacity or in relation to the discharge of his official duties under Act July 14, 1955, the Clean Air Act, as in effect immediately prior to the enactment of Pub.L. 95–95 [Aug. 7, 1977], not to abate by reason of the taking effect of Pub.L. 95–95, see section 406(a) of Pub.L. 95–95, set out as an Effective Date of 1977 Acts note under section 7401 of this title.

## § 7524. Civil penalties

[CAA § 205]

### (a) Violations

Any person who violates sections[1] 7522(a)(1), 7522(a)(4), or 7522(a)(5) of this title or any manufacturer or dealer who violates section 7522(a)(3)(A) of this title shall be subject to a civil penalty of not more than $25,000. Any person other than a manufacturer or dealer who violates section 7522(a)(3)(A) of this title or any person who violates section 7522(a)(3)(B) of this title shall be subject to a civil penalty of not more than $2,500. Any such violation with respect to paragraph (1), (3)(A), or (4) of section 7522(a) of this title shall constitute a separate offense with respect to each motor vehicle or motor vehicle engine. Any such violation with respect to section 7522(a)(3)(B) of this title shall constitute a separate offense with respect to each part or component. Any person who violates section 7522(a)(2) of this title shall be subject to a civil penalty of not more than $25,000 per day of violation.

### (b) Civil actions

The Administrator may commence a civil action to assess and recover any civil penalty under subsection (a) of this section, section 7545(d) of this title, or section 7547(d) of this title. Any action under this subsection may be brought in the district court of the United States for the district in which the violation is alleged to have occurred or in which the defendant resides or has the Administrator's principal place of business, and the court shall have jurisdiction to assess a civil penalty. In determining the amount of any civil penalty to be assessed under this subsection, the court shall take into account the gravity of the violation, the economic benefit or savings (if any) resulting from the violation, the size of the violator's business, the violator's history of compliance with this subchapter, action taken to remedy the violation, the effect of the penalty on the violator's ability to continue in business, and such other matters as justice may require. In any such action, subpoenas for witnesses who are required to attend a district court in any district may run into any other district.

### (c) Administrative assessment of certain penalties

#### (1) Administrative penalty authority

In lieu of commencing a civil action under subsection (b) of this section, the Administrator may assess any civil penalty prescribed in subsection (a) of this section, section 7545(d) of this title, or section 7547(d) of this title, except that the maximum amount of penalty sought against each violator in a penalty assessment proceeding shall not exceed $200,000, unless the Administrator and the Attorney General jointly determine that a matter involving a larger penalty amount is appropriate for administrative penalty assessment. Any such determination by the Administrator and the Attorney General shall not be subject to judicial review. Assessment of a civil penalty under this subsection shall be by an order made on the record after opportunity for a hearing in accordance with sections 554 and 556 of Title 5. The Administrator shall issue reasonable rules for discovery and other procedures for hearings under this paragraph. Before issuing such an order, the Administrator shall give written notice to the person to be assessed an administrative penalty of the Administrator's proposal to issue such order and provide such person an opportunity to request such a hearing on the order, within 30 days of the date the notice is received by such person. The Administrator may compromise, or remit, with or without conditions, any administrative penalty which may be imposed under this section.

#### (2) Determining amount

In determining the amount of any civil penalty assessed under this subsection, the Administrator shall take into account the gravity of the violation, the economic benefit or savings (if any) resulting from the violation, the size of the violator's business, the violator's history of compliance with this subchapter, action taken to remedy the violation, the effect of the penalty on the violator's ability to continue in business, and such other matters as justice may require.

#### (3) Effect of Administrator's action

(A) Action by the Administrator under this subsection shall not affect or limit the Administrator's authority to enforce any provision of this chapter; except that any violation,

(i) with respect to which the Administrator has commenced and is diligently prosecuting an action under this subsection, or

(ii) for which the Administrator has issued a final order not subject to further judicial review and the violator has paid a penalty assessment under this subsection,

shall not be the subject of civil penalty action under subsection (b) of this section.

**(B)** No action by the Administrator under this subsection shall affect any person's obligation to comply with any section of this chapter.

**(4) Finality of order**

An order issued under this subsection shall become final 30 days after its issuance unless a petition for judicial review is filed under paragraph (5).

**(5) Judicial review**

Any person against whom a civil penalty is assessed in accordance with this subsection may seek review of the assessment in the United States District Court for the District of Columbia, or for the district in which the violation is alleged to have occurred, in which such person resides, or where such person's principal place of business is located, within the 30-day period beginning on the date a civil penalty order is issued. Such person shall simultaneously send a copy of the filing by certified mail to the Administrator and the Attorney General. The Administrator shall file in the court a certified copy, or certified index, as appropriate, of the record on which the order was issued within 30 days. The court shall not set aside or remand any order issued in accordance with the requirements of this subsection unless there is not substantial evidence in the record, taken as a whole, to support the finding of a violation or unless the Administrator's assessment of the penalty constitutes an abuse of discretion, and the court shall not impose additional civil penalties unless the Administrator's assessment of the penalty constitutes an abuse of discretion. In any proceedings, the United States may seek to recover civil penalties assessed under this section.

**(6) Collection**

If any person fails to pay an assessment of a civil penalty imposed by the Administrator as provided in this subsection—

**(A)** after the order making the assessment has become final, or

**(B)** after a court in an action brought under paragraph (5) has entered a final judgment in favor of the Administrator,

the Administrator shall request the Attorney General to bring a civil action in an appropriate district court to recover the amount assessed (plus interest at rates established pursuant to section 6621(a)(2) of Title 26 from the date of the final order or the date of the final judgment, as the case may be). In such an action, the validity, amount, and appropriateness of the penalty shall not be subject to review. Any person who fails to pay on a timely basis the amount of an assessment of a civil penalty as described in the first sentence of this paragraph shall be required to pay, in addition to that amount and interest, the United States' enforcement expenses, including attorneys fees and costs for collection proceedings, and a quarterly nonpayment penalty for each quarter during which such failure to pay persists. The nonpayment penalty shall be in an amount equal to 10 percent of the aggregate amount of that person's penalties and nonpayment penalties which are unpaid as of the beginning of such quarter.

(July 14, 1955, c. 360, Title II, § 205, as added Oct. 20, 1965, Pub.L. 89–272, Title I, § 101(8), 79 Stat. 994, and amended Nov. 21, 1967, Pub.L. 90–148, § 2, 81 Stat. 500; Dec. 31, 1970, Pub.L. 91–604, § 7(c), 84 Stat. 1694; Aug. 7, 1977, Pub.L. 95–95, Title II, § 219(c), 91 Stat. 762; Nov. 15, 1990, Pub.L. 101–549, Title II, § 228(c), 104 Stat. 2508.)

[1] So in original. Probably should be "section".

### HISTORICAL AND STATUTORY NOTES

**Codifications**

Section was formerly classified to section 1857f–4 of this title.

**Effective and Applicability Provisions**

1990 Acts

Amendment by Pub.L. 101–549 effective Nov. 15, 1990, except as otherwise provided, see section 711(b) of Pub.L. 101–549, set out as a note under section 7401 of this title.

1977 Acts

Amendment by Pub.L. 95–95 effective Aug. 7, 1977, except as otherwise expressly provided, see section 406(d) of Pub.L. 95–95, set out as a note under section 7401 of this title.

**Savings Provisions**

Suits, actions or proceedings commenced under this chapter as in effect prior to Nov. 15, 1990, not to abate by reason of the taking effect of amendments by Pub.L. 101–549, except as otherwise provided for, see section 711(a) of Pub.L. 101–549, set out as a note under section 7401 of this title.

## § 7525. Motor vehicle and motor vehicle engine compliance testing and certification

[CAA § 206]

**(a) Testing and issuance of certificate of conformity**

(1) The Administrator shall test, or require to be tested in such manner as he deems appropriate, any new motor vehicle or new motor vehicle engine submitted by a manufacturer to determine whether such vehicle or engine conforms with the regulations prescribed under section 7521 of this title. If such vehicle or engine conforms to such regulations, the Administrator shall issue a certificate of conformity upon

such terms, and for such period (not in excess of one year), as he may prescribe. In the case of any original equipment manufacturer (as defined by the Administrator in regulations promulgated before November 15, 1990) of vehicles or vehicle engines whose projected sales in the United States for any model year (as determined by the Administrator) will not exceed 300, the Administrator shall not require, for purposes of determining compliance with regulations under section 7521 of this title for the useful life of the vehicle or engine, operation of any vehicle or engine manufactured during such model year for more than 5,000 miles or 160 hours, respectively, unless the Administrator, by regulation, prescribes otherwise. The Administrator shall apply any adjustment factors that the Administrator deems appropriate to assure that each vehicle or engine will comply during its useful life (as determined under section 7521(d) of this title) with the regulations prescribed under section 7521 of this title.

(2) The Administrator shall test any emission control system incorporated in a motor vehicle or motor vehicle engine submitted to him by any person, in order to determine whether such system enables such vehicle or engine to conform to the standards required to be prescribed under section 7521(b) of this title. If the Administrator finds on the basis of such tests that such vehicle or engine conforms to such standards, the Administrator shall issue a verification of compliance with emission standards for such system when incorporated in vehicles of a class of which the tested vehicle is representative. He shall inform manufacturers and the National Academy of Sciences, and make available to the public, the results of such tests. Tests under this paragraph shall be conducted under such terms and conditions (including requirements for preliminary testing by qualified independent laboratories) as the Administrator may prescribe by regulations.

(3)(A) A certificate of conformity may be issued under this section only if the Administrator determines that the manufacturer (or in the case of a vehicle or engine for import, any person) has established to the satisfaction of the Administrator that any emission control device, system, or element of design installed on, or incorporated in, such vehicle or engine conforms to applicable requirements of section 7521(a)(4) of this title.

(B) The Administrator may conduct such tests and may require the manufacturer (or any such person) to conduct such tests and provide such information as is necessary to carry out subparagraph (A) of this paragraph. Such requirements shall include a requirement for prompt reporting of the emission of any unregulated pollutant from a system, device, or element of design if such pollutant was not emitted, or was emitted in significantly lesser amounts, from the vehicle or engine without use of the system, device, or element of design.

(4)(A) Not later than 12 months after November 15, 1990, the Administrator shall revise the regulations promulgated under this subsection to add test procedures capable of determining whether model year 1994 and later model year light-duty vehicles and light-duty trucks, when properly maintained and used, will pass the inspection methods and procedures established under section 7541(b) of this title for that model year, under conditions reasonably likely to be encountered in the conduct of inspection and maintenance programs, but which those programs cannot reasonably influence or control. The conditions shall include fuel characteristics, ambient temperature, and short (30 minutes or less) waiting periods before tests are conducted. The Administrator shall not grant a certificate of conformity under this subsection for any 1994 or later model year vehicle or engine that the Administrator concludes cannot pass the test procedures established under this paragraph.

(B) From time to time, the Administrator may revise the regulations promulgated under subparagraph (A), as the Administrator deems appropriate.

**(b) Testing procedures; hearing; judicial review; additional evidence**

(1) In order to determine whether new motor vehicles or new motor vehicle engines being manufactured by a manufacturer do in fact conform with the regulations with respect to which the certificate of conformity was issued, the Administrator is authorized to test such vehicles or engines. Such tests may be conducted by the Administrator directly or, in accordance with conditions specified by the Administrator, by the manufacturer.

(2)(A)(i) If, based on tests conducted under paragraph (1) on a sample of new vehicles or engines covered by a certificate of conformity, the Administrator determines that all or part of the vehicles or engines so covered do not conform with the regulations with respect to which the certificate of conformity was issued and with the requirements of section 7521(a)(4) of this title, he may suspend or revoke such certificate in whole or in part, and shall so notify the manufacturer. Such suspension or revocation shall apply in the case of any new motor vehicles or new motor vehicle engines manufactured after the date of such notification (or manufactured before such date if still in the hands of the manufacturer), and shall apply until such time as the Administrator finds that vehicles and engines manufactured by the manufacturer do conform to such regulations and requirements. If, during any period of suspension or revocation, the Administrator finds that a vehicle or engine actually conforms to such regulations and requirements, he shall issue a certificate of conformity applicable to such vehicle or engine.

**(ii)** If, based on tests conducted under paragraph (1) on any new vehicle or engine, the Administrator determines that such vehicle or engine does not conform with such regulations and requirements, he may suspend or revoke such certificate insofar as it applies to such vehicle or engine until such time as he finds such vehicle or engine actually so conforms with such regulations and requirements, and he shall so notify the manufacturer.

**(B)(i)** At the request of any manufacturer the Administrator shall grant such manufacturer a hearing as to whether the tests have been properly conducted or any sampling methods have been properly applied, and make a determination on the record with respect to any suspension or revocation under subparagraph (A); but suspension or revocation under subparagraph (A) shall not be stayed by reason of such hearing.

**(ii)** In any case of actual controversy as to the validity of any determination under clause (i), the manufacturer may at any time prior to the 60th day after such determination is made file a petition with the United States court of appeals for the circuit wherein such manufacturer resides or has his principal place of business for a judicial review of such determination. A copy of the petition shall be forthwith transmitted by the clerk of the court to the Administrator or other officer designated by him for that purpose. The Administrator thereupon shall file in the court the record of the proceedings on which the Administrator based his determination, as provided in section 2112 of Title 28.

**(iii)** If the petitioner applies to the court for leave to adduce additional evidence, and shows to the satisfaction of the court that such additional evidence is material and that there were reasonable grounds for the failure to adduce such evidence in the proceeding before the Administrator, the court may order such additional evidence (and evidence in rebuttal thereof) to be taken before the Administrator, in such manner and upon such terms and conditions as the court may deem proper. The Administrator may modify his findings as to the facts, or make new findings, by reason of the additional evidence so taken and he shall file such modified or new findings, and his recommendation, if any, for the modification or setting aside of his original determination, with the return of such additional evidence.

**(iv)** Upon the filing of the petition referred to in clause (ii), the court shall have jurisdiction to review the order in accordance with chapter 7 of Title 5 and to grant appropriate relief as provided in such chapter.

### (c) Inspection

For purposes of enforcement of this section, officers or employees duly designated by the Administrator, upon presenting appropriate credentials to the manufacturer or person in charge, are authorized (1) to enter, at reasonable times, any plant or other establishment of such manufacturer, for the purpose of conducting tests of vehicles or engines in the hands of the manufacturer, or (2) to inspect, at reasonable times, records, files, papers, processes, controls, and facilities used by such manufacturer in conducting tests under regulations of the Administrator. Each such inspection shall be commenced and completed with reasonable promptness.

### (d) Rules and regulations

The Administrator shall by regulation establish methods and procedures for making tests under this section.

### (e) Publication of test results

The Administrator shall make available to the public the results of his tests of any motor vehicle or motor vehicle engine submitted by a manufacturer under subsection (a) of this section as promptly as possible after December 31, 1970, and at the beginning of each model year which begins thereafter. Such results shall be described in such nontechnical manner as will reasonably disclose to prospective ultimate purchasers of new motor vehicles and new motor vehicle engines the comparative performance of the vehicles and engines tested in meeting the standards prescribed under section 7521 of this title.

### (f) High altitude regulations

All light duty [1] vehicles and engines manufactured during or after model year 1984 and all light-duty trucks manufactured during or after model year 1995 shall comply with the requirements of section 7521 of this title regardless of the altitude at which they are sold.

### (g) Nonconformance penalty

**(1)** In the case of any class or category of heavy-duty vehicles or engines to which a standard promulgated under section 7521(a) of this title applies, except as provided in paragraph (2), a certificate of conformity shall be issued under subsection (a) of this section and shall not be suspended or revoked under subsection (b) of this section for such vehicles or engines manufactured by a manufacturer notwithstanding the failure of such vehicles or engines to meet such standard if such manufacturer pays a nonconformance penalty as provided under regulations promulgated by the Administrator after notice and opportunity for public hearing. In the case of motorcycles to which such a standard applies, such a certificate may be issued notwithstanding such failure if the manufacturer pays such a penalty.

(2) No certificate of conformity may be issued under paragraph (1) with respect to any class or category of vehicle or engine if the degree by which the manufacturer fails to meet any standard promulgated under section 7521(a) of this title with respect to such class or category exceeds the percentage determined under regulations promulgated by the Administrator to be practicable. Such regulations shall require such testing of vehicles or engines being produced as may be necessary to determine the percentage of the classes or categories of vehicles or engines which are not in compliance with the regulations with respect to which a certificate of conformity was issued and shall be promulgated not later than one year after August 7, 1977.

(3) The regulations promulgated under paragraph (1) shall, not later than one year after August 7, 1977, provide for nonconformance penalties in amounts determined under a formula established by the Administrator. Such penalties under such formula—

(A) may vary from pollutant-to-pollutant;

(B) may vary by class or category or vehicle or engine;

(C) shall take into account the extent to which actual emissions of any air pollutant exceed allowable emissions under the standards promulgated under section 7521 of this title;

(D) shall be increased periodically in order to create incentives for the development of production vehicles or engines which achieve the required degree of emission reduction; and

(E) shall remove any competitive disadvantage to manufacturers whose engines or vehicles achieve the required degree of emission reduction (including any such disadvantage arising from the application of paragraph (4)).

(4) In any case in which a certificate of conformity has been issued under this subsection, any warranty required under section 7541(b)(2) of this title and any action under section 7541(c) of this title shall be required to be effective only for the emission levels which the Administrator determines that such certificate was issued and not for the emission levels required under the applicable standard.

(5) The authorities of section 7542(a) of this title shall apply, subject to the conditions of section 7542(b) of this title, for purposes of this subsection.

**(h) Review and revision of regulations**

Within 18 months after November 15, 1990, the Administrator shall review and revise as necessary the regulations under subsection [2] (a) and (b) of this section regarding the testing of motor vehicles and motor vehicle engines to insure that vehicles are tested under circumstances which reflect the actual current driving conditions under which motor vehicles are used, including conditions relating to fuel, temperature, acceleration, and altitude.

(July 14, 1955, c. 360, Title II, § 206, as added Dec. 31, 1970, Pub.L. 91–604, § 8(a), 84 Stat. 1694, and amended Aug. 7, 1977, Pub.L. 95–95, Title II, §§ 213(a), 214(b), (c), 220, 224(e), 91 Stat. 758–760, 762, 768; Nov. 16, 1977, Pub.L. 95–190, § 14(a)(69), 91 Stat. 1403; Nov. 15, 1990, Pub.L. 101–549, Title II, §§ 208, 230(7), (8), 104 Stat. 2483, 2529.)

[1] So in original. Probably should be "light-duty".

[2] So in original. Probably should be "subsections".

## HISTORICAL AND STATUTORY NOTES

**References in Text**

Section 7542 of this title, referred to in subsec. (g)(5), was amended generally by Pub.L. 101–549, Title II, § 211, Nov. 15, 1990, 104 Stat. 2487, and provisions formerly contained in section 7542(b) of this title are contained in section 7542(c).

**Codifications**

Section was formerly classified to section 1857f–5 of this title.

**Effective and Applicability Provisions**

1990 Acts

Amendment by Pub.L. 101–549 effective Nov. 15, 1990, except as otherwise provided, see section 711(b) of Pub.L. 101–549, set out as a note under section 7401 of this title.

1977 Acts

Amendment by Pub.L. 95–95 effective Aug. 7, 1977, except as otherwise expressly provided, see section 406(d) of Pub.L. 95–95, set out as a note under section 7401 of this title.

1970 Acts

Section 8(b) of Pub.L. 91–604 provided that: "The amendments made by this section [enacting this section and section 7541 of this title] shall not apply to vehicles or engines imported into the United States before the sixtieth day after the date of enactment of this Act [Dec. 31, 1970]."

**Savings Provisions**

Suits, actions or proceedings commenced under this chapter as in effect prior to Nov. 15, 1990, not to abate by reason of the taking effect of amendments by Pub.L. 101–549, except as otherwise provided for, see section 711(a) of Pub.L. 101–549, set out as a note under section 7401 of this title.

**Prior Provisions**

A prior section 206 of Act July 14, 1955, relating to the testing of motor vehicles and motor vehicle engines, was repealed by Pub.L. 91–604, § 8(a), Dec. 31, 1970, 84 Stat. 1694.

**Modification or Rescission of Rules, Regulations, Orders, Determinations, Contracts, Certifications, Authorizations, Delegations, and Other Actions**

All rules, regulations, orders, determinations, contracts, certifications, authorizations, delegations, or other actions duly issued, made, or taken by or pursuant to Act July 14, 1955, the Clean Air Act, as in effect immediately prior to the date of enactment of Pub.L. 95–95 [Aug. 7, 1977] to continue in full force and effect until modified or rescinded in accordance with Act July 14, 1955, as amended by Pub.L. 95–95 [this chapter], see section 406(b) of Pub.L. 95–95, set out as an Effective Date of 1977 Acts note under section 7401 of this title.

## § 7541. Compliance by vehicles and engines in actual use

**[CAA § 207]**

### (a) Warranty; certification; payment of replacement costs of parts, devices, or components designed for emission control

(1) Effective with respect to vehicles and engines manufactured in model years beginning more than 60 days after December 31, 1970, the manufacturer of each new motor vehicle and new motor vehicle engine shall warrant to the ultimate purchaser and each subsequent purchaser that such vehicle or engine is (A) designed, built, and equipped so as to conform at the time of sale with applicable regulations under section 7521 of this title, and (B) free from defects in materials and workmanship which cause such vehicle or engine to fail to conform with applicable regulations for its useful life (as determined under section 7521(d) of this title). In the case of vehicles and engines manufactured in the model year 1995 and thereafter such warranty shall require that the vehicle or engine is free from any such defects for the warranty period provided under subsection (i) of this section.

(2) In the case of a motor vehicle part or motor vehicle engine part, the manufacturer or rebuilder of such part may certify that use of such part will not result in a failure of the vehicle or engine to comply with emission standards promulgated under section 7521 of this title. Such certification shall be made only under such regulations as may be promulgated by the Administrator to carry out the purposes of subsection (b) of this section. The Administrator shall promulgate such regulations no later than two years following August 7, 1977.

(3) The cost of any part, device, or component of any light-duty vehicle that is designed for emission control and which in the instructions issued pursuant to subsection (c)(3) of this section is scheduled for replacement during the useful life of the vehicle in order to maintain compliance with regulations under section 7521 of this title, the failure of which shall not interfere with the normal performance of the vehicle, and the expected retail price of which, including installation costs, is greater than 2 percent of the suggested retail price of such vehicle, shall be borne or reimbursed at the time of replacement by the vehicle manufacturer and such replacement shall be provided without cost to the ultimate purchaser, subsequent purchaser, or dealer. The term "designed for emission control" as used in the preceding sentence means a catalytic converter, thermal reactor, or other component installed on or in a vehicle for the sole or primary purpose of reducing vehicle emissions (not including those vehicle components which were in general use prior to model year 1968 and the primary function of which is not related to emission control).

### (b) Testing methods and procedures

If the Administrator determines that (i) there are available testing methods and procedures to ascertain whether, when in actual use throughout its [1] the warranty period (as determined under subsection (i) of this section), each vehicle and engine to which regulations under section 7521 of this title apply complies with the emission standards of such regulations, (ii) such methods and procedures are in accordance with good engineering practices, and (iii) such methods and procedures are reasonably capable of being correlated with tests conducted under section 7525(a)(1) of this title, then—

(1) he shall establish such methods and procedures by regulation, and

(2) at such time as he determines that inspection facilities or equipment are available for purposes of carrying out testing methods and procedures established under paragraph (1), he shall prescribe regulations which shall require manufacturers to warrant the emission control device or system of each new motor vehicle or new motor vehicle engine to which a regulation under section 7521 of this title applies and which is manufactured in a model year beginning after the Administrator first prescribes warranty regulations under this paragraph (2). The warranty under such regulations shall run to the ultimate purchaser and each subsequent purchaser and shall provide that if—

(A) the vehicle or engine is maintained and operated in accordance with instructions under subsection (c)(3) of this section,

(B) it fails to conform at any time during its [1] the warranty period (as determined under subsection (i) of this section) to the regulations prescribed under section 7521 of this title, and

(C) such nonconformity results in the ultimate purchaser (or any subsequent purchaser) of such vehicle or engine having to bear any penalty or other sanction (including the denial of the right to use such vehicle or engine) under State or Federal law,

then such manufacturer shall remedy such nonconformity under such warranty with the cost thereof to be borne by the manufacturer. No such warranty shall be invalid on the basis of any part used in the maintenance or repair of a vehicle or engine if such part was certified as provided under subsection (a)(2) of this section.

### (c) Nonconforming vehicles; plan for remedying nonconformity; instructions for maintenance and use; label or tag

Effective with respect to vehicles and engines manufactured during model years beginning more than 60 days after December 31, 1970—

(1) If the Administrator determines that a substantial number of any class or category of vehicles or engines, although properly maintained and used, do not conform to the regulations prescribed under section 7521 of this title, when in actual use throughout their useful life (as determined under section 7521(d) of this title), he shall immediately notify the manufacturer thereof of such nonconformity, and he shall require the manufacturer to submit a plan for remedying the nonconformity of the vehicles or engines with respect to which such notification is given. The plan shall provide that the nonconformity of any such vehicles or engines which are properly used and maintained will be remedied at the expense of the manufacturer. If the manufacturer disagrees with such determination of nonconformity and so advises the Administrator, the Administrator shall afford the manufacturer and other interested persons an opportunity to present their views and evidence in support thereof at a public hearing. Unless, as a result of such hearing the Administrator withdraws such determination of nonconformity, he shall, within 60 days after the completion of such hearing, order the manufacturer to provide prompt notification of such nonconformity in accordance with paragraph (2).

(2) Any notification required by paragraph (1) with respect to any class or category of vehicles or engines shall be given to dealers, ultimate purchasers, and subsequent purchasers (if known) in such manner and containing such information as the Administrator may by regulations require.

(3)(A) The manufacturer shall furnish with each new motor vehicle or motor vehicle engine written instructions for the proper maintenance and use of the vehicle or engine by the ultimate purchaser and such instructions shall correspond to regulations which the Administrator shall promulgate. The manufacturer shall provide in boldface type on the first page of the written maintenance instructions notice that maintenance, replacement, or repair of the emission control devices and systems may be performed by any automotive repair establishment or individual using any automotive part which has been certified as provided in subsection (a)(2) of this section.

(B) The instruction under subparagraph (A) of this paragraph shall not include any condition on the ultimate purchaser's using, in connection with such vehicle or engine, any component or service (other than a component or service provided without charge under the terms of the purchase agreement) which is identified by brand, trade, or corporate name; or directly or indirectly distinguishing between service performed by the franchised dealers of such manufacturer or any other service establishments with which such manufacturer has a commercial relationship, and service performed by independent automotive repair facilities with which such manufacturer has no commercial relationship; except that the prohibition of this subsection may be waived by the Administrator if—

(i) the manufacturer satisfies the Administrator that the vehicle or engine will function properly only if the component or service so identified is used in connection with such vehicle or engine, and

(ii) the Administrator finds that such a waiver is in the public interest.

(C) In addition, the manufacturer shall indicate by means of a label or tag permanently affixed to such vehicle or engine that such vehicle or engine is covered by a certificate of conformity issued for the purpose of assuring achievement of emissions standards prescribed under section 7521 of this title. Such label or tag shall contain such other information relating to control of motor vehicle emissions as the Administrator shall prescribe by regulation.

**(4) Intermediate in-use standards**

**(A) Model years 1994 and 1995**

For light-duty trucks of up to 6,000 lbs. gross vehicle weight rating (GVWR) and light-duty vehicles which are subject to standards under table G of section 7521(g)(1) of this title in model years 1994 and 1995 (40 percent of the manufacturer's sales volume in model year 1994 and 80 percent in model year 1995), the standards applicable to NMHC, CO, and $NO_x$ for purposes of this subsection shall be those set forth in table A below in lieu of the standards for such air pollutants otherwise applicable under this subchapter.

TABLE A—INTERMEDIATE IN-USE STANDARDS LDTs UP TO 6,000 LBS. GVWR AND LIGHT-DUTY VEHICLES

| Vehicle type | NMHC | CO | $NO_x$ |
|---|---|---|---|
| Light-duty vehicles | 0.32 | 3.4 | 0.4* |
| LDT's (0–3,750 LVW) | 0.32 | 5.2 | 0.4* |
| LDT's (3,751–5,750 LVW) | 0.41 | 6.7 | 0.7* |

* Not applicable to diesel-fueled vehicles.

**(B) Model years 1996 and thereafter**

(i) In the model years 1996 and 1997, light-duty trucks (LDTs) up to 6,000 lbs. gross vehicle weight rating (GVWR) and light-duty vehicles which are not subject to final in-use standards under paragraph (5) (60 percent of the manufacturer's sales volume in model year 1996 and 20 percent in model year 1997) shall be subject to the standards set forth in table A of subparagraph (A) for NMHC, CO, and $NO_x$ for purposes of this subsection in lieu of those set forth in paragraph (5).

**(ii)** For LDTs of more than 6,000 lbs. GVWR—

**(I)** in model year 1996 which are subject to the standards set forth in Table H of section 7521(h) of this title (50%);

**(II)** in model year 1997 (100%); and

**(III)** in model year 1998 which are not subject to final in-use standards under paragraph (5) (50%);

the standards for NMHC, CO, and $NO_x$ for purposes of this subsection shall be those set forth in Table B below in lieu of the standards for such air pollutants otherwise applicable under this subchapter.

TABLE B—INTERMEDIATE IN-USE STANDARDS LDTs MORE THAN 6,000 LBS. GVWR

| Vehicle type | NMHC | CO | $NO_x$ |
|---|---|---|---|
| LDTs (3,751–5,750 lbs. TW) .... | 0.40 | 5.5 | 0.88* |
| LDTs (over 5,750 lbs. TW)...... | 0.49 | 6.2 | 1.38* |

* Not applicable to diesel-fueled vehicles.

**(C) Useful life**

In the case of the in-use standards applicable under this paragraph, for purposes of applying this subsection, the applicable useful life shall be 5 years or 50,000 miles or the equivalent (whichever first occurs).

**(5) Final in-use standards**

**(A)** After the model year 1995, for purposes of applying this subsection, in the case of the percentage specified in the implementation schedule below of each manufacturer's sales volume of light-duty trucks of up to 6,000 lbs. gross vehicle weight rating (GVWR) and light duty [2] vehicles, the standards for NMHC, CO, and $NO_x$ shall be as provided in Table G in section 7521(g) of this title, except that in applying the standards set forth in Table G for purposes of determining compliance with this subsection, the applicable useful life shall be (i) 5 years or 50,000 miles (or the equivalent) whichever first occurs in the case of standards applicable for purposes of certification at 50,000 miles; and (ii) 10 years or 100,000 miles (or the equivalent), whichever first occurs in the case of standards applicable for purposes of certification at 100,000 miles, except that no testing shall be done beyond 7 years or 75,000 miles, or the equivalent whichever first occurs.

LDTs UP TO 6,000 LBS. GVWR AND LIGHT-DUTY VEHICLE SCHEDULE FOR IMPLEMENTATION OF FINAL IN-USE STANDARDS

| Model year | Percent |
|---|---|
| 1996.......................... | 40 |
| 1997.......................... | 80 |
| 1998.......................... | 100 |

**(B)** After the model year 1997, for purposes of applying this subsection, in the case of the percentage specified in the implementation schedule below of each manufacturer's sales volume of light-duty trucks of more than 6,000 lbs. gross vehicle weight rating (GVWR), the standards for NMHC, CO, and $NO_x$ shall be as provided in Table H in section 7521(h) of this title, except that in applying the standards set forth in Table H for purposes of determining compliance with this subsection, the applicable useful life shall be (i) 5 years or 50,000 miles (or the equivalent) whichever first occurs in the case of standards applicable for purposes of certification at 50,000 miles; and (ii) 11 years or 120,000 miles (or the equivalent), whichever first occurs in the case of standards applicable for purposes of certification at 120,000 miles, except that no testing shall be done beyond 7 years or 90,000 miles (or the equivalent) whichever first occurs.

LDTs OF MORE THAN 6,000 LBS. GVWR IMPLEMENTATION SCHEDULE FOR IMPLEMENTATION OF FINAL IN-USE STANDARDS

| Model year | Percent |
|---|---|
| 1998.......................... | 50 |
| 1999.......................... | 100 |

**(6) Diesel vehicles; in-use useful life and testing**

**(A)** In the case of diesel-fueled light-duty trucks up to 6,000 lbs. GVWR and light-duty vehicles, the useful life for purposes of determining in-use compliance with the standards under section 7521(g) of this title for $NO_x$ shall be a period of 10 years or 100,000 miles (or the equivalent), whichever first occurs, in the case of standards applicable for purposes of certification at 100,000 miles, except that testing shall not be done for a period beyond 7 years or 75,000 miles (or the equivalent) whichever first occurs.

**(B)** In the case of diesel-fueled light-duty trucks of 6,000 lbs. GVWR or more, the useful life for purposes of determining in-use compliance with the standards under section 7521(h) of this title for $NO_x$ shall be a period of 11 years or 120,000 miles (or the equivalent), whichever first occurs, in the case of standards applicable for purposes of certification at 120,000 miles, except that testing shall not be done for a period beyond 7 years or 90,000 miles (or the equivalent) whichever first occurs.

**(d) Dealer costs borne by manufacturer**

Any cost obligation of any dealer incurred as a result of any requirement imposed by subsection (a), (b), or (c) of this section shall be borne by the manufacturer. The transfer of any such cost obligation from a manufacturer to any dealer through franchise or other agreement is prohibited.

**(e) Cost statement**

If a manufacturer includes in any advertisement a statement respecting the cost or value of emission control devices or systems, such manufacturer shall set forth in such statement the cost or value attributed to such devices or systems by the Secretary of Labor (through the Bureau of Labor Statistics). The Secretary of Labor, and his representatives, shall have the same access for this purpose to the books, documents, papers, and records of a manufacturer as the Comptroller General has to those of a recipient of assistance for purposes of section 7611 of this title.

**(f) Inspection after sale to ultimate purchaser**

Any inspection of a motor vehicle or a motor vehicle engine for purposes of subsection (c)(1) of this section, after its sale to the ultimate purchaser, shall be made only if the owner of such vehicle or engine voluntarily permits such inspection to be made, except as may be provided by any State or local inspection program.

**(g) Replacement and maintenance costs borne by owner**

For the purposes of this section, the owner of any motor vehicle or motor vehicle engine warranted under this section is responsible in the proper maintenance of such vehicle or engine to replace and to maintain, at his expense at any service establishment or facility of his choosing, such items as spark plugs, points, condensers, and any other part, item, or device related to emission control (but not designed for emission control under the terms of the last sentence of subsection (a)(3) of this section)),[3] unless such part, item, or device is covered by any warranty not mandated by this chapter.

**(h) Dealer certification**

(1) Upon the sale of each new light-duty motor vehicle by a dealer, the dealer shall furnish to the purchaser a certificate that such motor vehicle conforms to the applicable regulations under section 7521 of this title, including notice of the purchaser's rights under paragraph (2).

(2) If at any time during the period for which the warranty applies under subsection (b) of this section, a motor vehicle fails to conform to the applicable regulations under section 7521 of this title as determined under subsection (b) of this section such nonconformity shall be remedied by the manufacturer at the cost of the manufacturer pursuant to such warranty as provided in subsection (b)(2) of this section (without regard to subparagraph (C) thereof).

(3) Nothing in section 7543(a) of this title shall be construed to prohibit a State from testing, or requiring testing of, a motor vehicle after the date of sale of such vehicle to the ultimate purchaser (except that no new motor vehicle manufacturer or dealer may be required to conduct testing under this paragraph).

**(i) Warranty period**

**(1) In general**

For purposes of subsection (a)(1) of this section and subsection (b) of this section, the warranty period, effective with respect to new light-duty trucks and new light-duty vehicles and engines, manufactured in the model year 1995 and thereafter, shall be the first 2 years or 24,000 miles of use (whichever first occurs), except as provided in paragraph (2). For purposes of subsection (a)(1) of this section and subsection (b) of this section, for other vehicles and engines the warranty period shall be the period established by the Administrator by regulation (promulgated prior to November 15, 1990) for such purposes unless the Administrator subsequently modifies such regulation.

**(2) Specified major emission control components**

In the case of a specified major emission control component, the warranty period for new light-duty trucks and new light-duty vehicles and engines manufactured in the model year 1995 and thereafter for purposes of subsection (a)(1) of this section and subsection (b) of this section shall be 8 years or 80,000 miles of use (whichever first occurs). As used in this paragraph, the term "specified major emission control component" means only a catalytic converter, an electronic emissions control unit, and an onboard emissions diagnostic device, except that the Administrator may designate any other pollution control device or component as a specified major emission control component if—

(A) the device or component was not in general use on vehicles and engines manufactured prior to the model year 1990; and

(B) the Administrator determines that the retail cost (exclusive of installation costs) of such device or component exceeds $200 (in 1989 dollars), adjusted for inflation or deflation as calculated by the Administrator at the time of such determination.

For purposes of this paragraph, the term "onboard emissions diagnostic device" means any device installed for the purpose of storing or processing emissions related diagnostic information, but not including any parts or other systems which it monitors except specified major emissions control components. Nothing in this chapter shall be construed to provide that any part (other than a part referred to in the preceding sentence) shall be required to be warranted under this chapter for the period of 8 years or 80,000 miles referred to in this paragraph.

**(3) Instructions**

Subparagraph (A) of subsection (b)(2) of this section shall apply only where the Administrator has made a determination that the instructions concerned conform to the requirements of subsection (c)(3) of this section.

(July 14, 1955, c. 360, Title II, § 207, as added Dec. 31, 1970, Pub.L. 91–604, § 8(a), 84 Stat. 1696, and amended Aug. 7, 1977, Pub.L. 95–95, Title II, §§ 205, 208–210, 212, 91 Stat. 754–756, 758; Nov. 16, 1977, Pub.L. 95–190, § 14(a)(70)–(72), 91 Stat. 1403; Nov. 15, 1990, Pub.L. 101–549, Title II, §§ 209, 210, 230(9), 104 Stat. 2484, 2485, 2529.)

1 So in original. The word "its" probably should not appear.

2 So in original. Probably should be "light-duty".

3 So in original. The second closing parenthesis probably should not appear.

## HISTORICAL AND STATUTORY NOTES

**Codifications**

Section was formerly classified to section 1857f–5a of this title.

**Effective and Applicability Provisions**

1990 Acts

Amendment by sections 210 and 230(a) of Pub.L. 101–549 effective Nov. 15, 1990, except as otherwise provided, see section 711(b) of Pub.L. 101–549, set out as a note under section 7401 of this title.

Section 209 of Pub.L. 101–549, provided in part that the amendments made by such section [enacting subsec. (i) of this section and amending subsecs. (a) and (b) of this section] shall be effective with respect to new motor vehicles and engines manufactured in the model year 1995 and thereafter.

1977 Acts

Amendment by Pub.L. 95–95 effective Aug. 7, 1977, except as otherwise expressly provided, see section 406(d) of Pub.L. 95–95, set out as a note under section 7401 of this title.

1970 Acts

Section not applicable to vehicles or engines imported into the United States before the sixtieth day after Dec. 31, 1970, see section 8(b) of Pub.L. 91–604, set out as a note under section 7525 of this title.

**Savings Provisions**

Suits, actions or proceedings commenced under this chapter as in effect prior to Nov. 15, 1990, not to abate by reason of the taking effect of amendments by Pub.L. 101–549, except as otherwise provided for, see section 711(a) of Pub.L. 101–549, set out as a note under section 7401 of this title.

**Prior Provisions**

A prior section 207 of Act July 14, 1955, was renumbered section 208 by Pub.L. 91–604 and is set out as section 7542 of this title.

**Modification or Rescission of Rules, Regulations, Orders, Determinations, Contracts, Certifications, Authorizations, Delegations, and Other Actions**

All rules, regulations, orders, determinations, contracts, certifications, authorizations, delegations, or other actions duly issued, made, or taken by or pursuant to Act July 14, 1955, the Clean Air Act, as in effect immediately prior to the date of enactment of Pub.L. 95–95 [Aug. 7, 1977] to continue in full force and effect until modified or rescinded in accordance with Act July 14, 1955, as amended by Pub.L. 95–95 [this chapter], see section 406(b) of Pub.L. 95–95, set out as an Effective Date of 1977 Acts note under section 7401 of this title.

## § 7542. Information collection

**[CAA § 208]**

**(a) Manufacturer's responsibility**

Every manufacturer of new motor vehicles or new motor vehicle engines, and every manufacturer of new motor vehicle or engine parts or components, and other persons subject to the requirements of this part or part C of this subchapter, shall establish and maintain records, perform tests where such testing is not otherwise reasonably available under this part and part C of this subchapter (including fees for testing), make reports and provide information the Administrator may reasonably require to determine whether the manufacturer or other person has acted or is acting in compliance with this part and part C of this subchapter and regulations thereunder, or to otherwise carry out the provision of this part and part C of this subchapter, and shall, upon request of an officer or employee duly designated by the Administrator, permit such officer or employee at reasonable times to have access to and copy such records.

**(b) Enforcement authority**

For the purposes of enforcement of this section, officers or employees duly designated by the Administrator upon presenting appropriate credentials are authorized—

(1) to enter, at reasonable times, any establishment of the manufacturer, or of any person whom the manufacturer engages to perform any activity required by subsection (a) of this section, for the purposes of inspecting or observing any activity conducted pursuant to subsection (a) of this section, and

(2) to inspect records, files, papers, processes, controls, and facilities used in performing any activity required by subsection (a) of this section, by such manufacturer or by any person whom the manufacturer engages to perform any such activity.

**(c) Availability to public; trade secrets**

Any records, reports, or information obtained under this part or part C of this subchapter shall be available to the public, except that upon a showing satisfactory to the Administrator by any person that records, reports, or information, or a particular portion thereof (other than emission data), to which the Administrator has access under this section, if made public, would divulge methods or processes entitled to protection as trade secrets of that person, the Administrator shall consider the record, report, or information or particular portion thereof confidential in accordance with the purposes of section 1905 of Title 18. Any authorized representative of the Administrator shall be considered an employee of the United States for purposes of section 1905 of Title 18. Nothing in this section shall prohibit the Administrator or authorized representative of the Administrator from disclosing records, reports or information to other officers, employees or authorized representatives of the United States concerned with carrying out this chapter or when relevant in any proceeding under this chapter. Nothing in this section shall authorize the withholding of information by the Administrator or any officer or employee under the Administrator's control from the duly authorized committees of the Congress.

(July 14, 1955, c. 360, Title II, § 208, formerly § 207, as added Oct. 20, 1965, Pub.L. 89–272, Title I, § 101(8), 79 Stat. 994, amended Nov. 21, 1967, Pub.L. 90–148, § 2, 81 Stat. 501, renumbered and amended Dec. 31, 1970, Pub.L. 91–604, §§ 8(a), 10(a), 11(a)(2)(A), 15(c)(2), 84 Stat. 1694, 1700, 1705, 1713; Nov. 15, 1990, Pub.L. 101–549, Title II, § 211, 104 Stat. 2487.)

## HISTORICAL AND STATUTORY NOTES

**Codifications**

Section was formerly classified to section 1857f–6 of this title.

**Effective and Applicability Provisions**

1990 Acts

Amendment by Pub.L. 101–549 effective Nov. 15, 1990, except as otherwise provided, see section 711(b) of Pub.L. 101–549, set out as a note under section 7401 of this title.

**Savings Provisions**

Suits, actions or proceedings commenced under this chapter as in effect prior to Nov. 15, 1990, not to abate by reason of the taking effect of amendments by Pub.L. 101–549, except as otherwise provided for, see section 711(a) of Pub.L. 101–549, set out as a note under section 7401 of this title.

**Prior Provisions**

A prior section 208 of Act July 14, 1955, as added Nov. 21, 1967, Pub.L. 90–148, § 2, 81 Stat. 501, was renumbered section 209 by Pub.L. 91–604, and is set out as section 7543 of this title.

Another prior section 208 of Act July 14, 1955, forming a part of such Act as originally enacted, was renumbered section 212 by Pub.L. 90–148, renumbered section 213 by Pub.L. 91–604, renumbered section 214 by Pub.L. 93–319, section 10, June 22, 1974, 88 Stat. 261, and renumbered section 216 by Pub.L. 95–95, Title II, § 224(d), Aug. 7, 1977, 91 Stat. 767, and is set out as section 7550 of this title.

## § 7543. State standards

**[CAA § 209]**

**(a) Prohibition**

No State or any political subdivision thereof shall adopt or attempt to enforce any standard relating to the control of emissions from new motor vehicles or new motor vehicle engines subject to this part. No State shall require certification, inspection, or any other approval relating to the control of emissions from any new motor vehicle or new motor vehicle engine as condition precedent to the initial retail sale, titling (if any), or registration of such motor vehicle, motor vehicle engine, or equipment.

**(b) Waiver**

(1) The Administrator shall, after notice and opportunity for public hearing, waive application of this section to any State which has adopted standards (other than crankcase emission standards) for the control of emissions from new motor vehicles or new motor vehicle engines prior to March 30, 1966, if the State determines that the State standards will be, in the aggregate, at least as protective of public health and welfare as applicable Federal standards. No such waiver shall be granted if the Administrator finds that—

(A) the determination of the State is arbitrary and capricious,

(B) such State does not need such State standards to meet compelling and extraordinary conditions, or

(C) such State standards and accompanying enforcement procedures are not consistent with section 7521(a) of this title.

(2) If each State standard is at least as stringent as the comparable applicable Federal standard, such State standard shall be deemed to be at least as protective of health and welfare as such Federal standards for purposes of paragraph (1).

(3) In the case of any new motor vehicle or new motor vehicle engine to which State standards apply pursuant to a waiver granted under paragraph (1), compliance with such State standards shall be treated as compliance with applicable Federal standards for purposes of this subchapter.

**(c) Certification of vehicle parts or engine parts**

Whenever a regulation with respect to any motor vehicle part or motor vehicle engine part is in effect under section 7541(a)(2) of this title, no State or political subdivision thereof shall adopt or attempt to enforce any standard or any requirement of certification, inspection, or approval which relates to motor vehicle emissions and is applicable to the same aspect of such part. The preceding sentence shall not apply in the case of a State with respect to which a waiver is in effect under subsection (b) of this section.

**(d) Control, regulation, or restrictions on registered or licensed motor vehicles**

Nothing in this part shall preclude or deny to any State or political subdivision thereof the right otherwise to control, regulate, or restrict the use, operation, or movement of registered or licensed motor vehicles.

**(e) Nonroad engines or vehicles**

**(1) Prohibition on certain State standards**

No State or any political subdivision thereof shall adopt or attempt to enforce any standard or other requirement relating to the control of emissions from either of the following new nonroad engines or nonroad vehicles subject to regulation under this chapter—

**(A)** New engines which are used in construction equipment or vehicles or used in farm equipment or vehicles and which are smaller than 175 horsepower.

**(B)** New locomotives or new engines used in locomotives.

Subsection (b) of this section shall not apply for purposes of this paragraph.

**(2) Other nonroad engines or vehicles**

**(A)** In the case of any nonroad vehicles or engines other than those referred to in subparagraph (A) or (B) of paragraph (1), the Administrator shall, after notice and opportunity for public hearing, authorize California to adopt and enforce standards and other requirements relating to the control of emissions from such vehicles or engines if California determines that California standards will be, in the aggregate, at least as protective of public health and welfare as applicable Federal standards. No such authorization shall be granted if the Administrator finds that—

**(i)** the determination of California is arbitrary and capricious,

**(ii)** California does not need such California standards to meet compelling and extraordinary conditions, or

**(iii)** California standards and accompanying enforcement procedures are not consistent with this section.

**(B)** Any State other than California which has plan provisions approved under part D of subchapter I of this chapter may adopt and enforce, after notice to the Administrator, for any period, standards relating to control of emissions from nonroad vehicles or engines (other than those referred to in subparagraph (A) or (B) of paragraph (1)) and take such other actions as are referred to in subparagraph (A) of this paragraph respecting such vehicles or engines if—

**(i)** such standards and implementation and enforcement are identical, for the period concerned, to the California standards authorized by the Administrator under subparagraph (A), and

**(ii)** California and such State adopt such standards at least 2 years before commencement of the period for which the standards take effect.

The Administrator shall issue regulations to implement this subsection.

(July 14, 1955, c. 360, Title II, § 209, formerly § 208, as added Nov. 21, 1967, Pub.L. 90–148, § 2, 81 Stat. 501, renumbered and amended Dec. 31, 1970, Pub.L. 91–604, §§ 8(a), 11(a)(2)(A), 15(c)(2), 84 Stat. 1694, 1705, 1713; Aug. 7, 1977, Pub.L. 95–95, Title II, §§ 207, 221, 91 Stat. 755, 762; Nov. 15, 1990, Pub.L. 101–549, Title II, § 222(b), 104 Stat. 2502.)

## HISTORICAL AND STATUTORY NOTES

**Codifications**

Section was formerly classified to section 1857f–6a of this title.

**Effective and Applicability Provisions**

1990 Acts

Amendment by Pub.L. 101–549 effective Nov. 15, 1990, except as otherwise provided, see section 711(b) of Pub.L. 101–549, set out as a note under section 7401 of this title.

1977 Acts

Amendment by Pub.L. 95–95 effective Aug. 7, 1977, except as otherwise expressly provided, see section 406(d) of Pub.L. 95–95, set out as a note under section 7401 of this title.

**Savings Provisions**

Suits, actions or proceedings commenced under this chapter as in effect prior to Nov. 15, 1990, not to abate by reason of the taking effect of amendments by Pub.L. 101–549, except as otherwise provided for, see section 711(a) of Pub.L. 101–549, set out as a note under section 7401 of this title.

**Prior Provisions**

A prior section 209 of Act July 14, 1955, as added Nov. 21, 1967, Pub.L. 90–148, § 2, 81 Stat. 502, was renumbered section 210 by Pub.L. 91–604 and is classified to section 7544 of this title.

Another prior section 209 of Act July 14, 1955, c. 360, Title II, as added Oct. 20, 1965, Pub.L. 89–272, Title I, § 101(8), 79 Stat. 995, relating to appropriations for the fiscal years ending June 30, 1966, 1967, 1968, and 1969, was classified to prior section 1857f–8 of this title and was repealed by Pub.L. 89–675, § 2(b), Oct. 15, 1966, 80 Stat. 954.

**Modification or Rescission of Rules, Regulations, Orders, Determinations, Contracts, Certifications, Authorizations, Delegations, and Other Actions**

All rules, regulations, orders, determinations, contracts, certifications, authorizations, delegations, or other actions duly issued, made, or taken by or pursuant to Act July 14,

1955, the Clean Air Act, as in effect immediately prior to the date of enactment of Pub.L. 95–95 [Aug. 7, 1977] to continue in full force and effect until modified or rescinded in accordance with Act July 14, 1955, as amended by Pub.L. 95–95 [this chapter], see section 406(b) of Pub.L. 95–95, set out as an Effective Date of 1977 Acts note under section 7401 of this title.

## § 7544. State grants

[CAA § 210]

The Administrator is authorized to make grants to appropriate State agencies in an amount up to two-thirds of the cost of developing and maintaining effective vehicle emission devices and systems inspection and emission testing and control programs, except that—

(1) no such grant shall be made for any part of any State vehicle inspection program which does not directly relate to the cost of the air pollution control aspects of such a program;

(2) no such grant shall be made unless the Secretary of Transportation has certified to the Administrator that such program is consistent with any highway safety program developed pursuant to section 402 of Title 23; and

(3) no such grant shall be made unless the program includes provisions designed to insure that emission control devices and systems on vehicles in actual use have not been discontinued or rendered inoperative.

Grants may be made under this section by way of reimbursement in any case in which amounts have been expended by the State before the date on which any such grant was made.

(July 14, 1955, c. 360, Title II, § 210, formerly § 209, as added Nov. 21, 1967, Pub.L. 90–148, § 2, 81 Stat. 502, and renumbered and amended Dec. 31, 1970, Pub.L. 91–604, §§ 8(a), 10(b), 84 Stat. 1694, 1700; Aug. 7, 1977, Pub.L. 95–95, Title II, § 204, 91 Stat. 754.)

### HISTORICAL AND STATUTORY NOTES

**Codifications**

Section was formerly classified to section 1857f–6b of this title.

**Effective and Applicability Provisions**

1977 Acts

Amendment by Pub.L. 95–95 effective Aug. 7, 1977, except as otherwise expressly provided, see section 406(d) of Pub.L. 95–95, set out as a note under section 7401 of this title.

**Prior Provisions**

A prior section 210 of Act July 14, 1955, was renumbered section 211 by Pub.L. 91–604 and is set out as section 7545 of this title.

## § 7545. Regulation of fuels

[CAA § 211]

**(a) Authority of Administrator to regulate**

The Administrator may by regulation designate any fuel or fuel additive (including any fuel or fuel additive used exclusively in nonroad engines or nonroad vehicles) and, after such date or dates as may be prescribed by him, no manufacturer or processor of any such fuel or additive may sell, offer for sale, or introduce into commerce such fuel or additive unless the Administrator has registered such fuel or additive in accordance with subsection (b) of this section.

**(b) Registration requirement**

(1) For the purpose of registration of fuels and fuel additives, the Administrator shall require—

(A) the manufacturer of any fuel to notify him as to the commercial identifying name and manufacturer of any additive contained in such fuel; the range of concentration of any additive in the fuel; and the purpose-in-use of any such additive; and

(B) the manufacturer of any additive to notify him as to the chemical composition of such additive.

(2) For the purpose of registration of fuels and fuel additives, the Administrator may also require the manufacturer of any fuel or fuel additive—

(A) to conduct tests to determine potential public health effects of such fuel or additive (including, but not limited to, carcinogenic, teratogenic, or mutagenic effects), and

(B) to furnish the description of any analytical technique that can be used to detect and measure any additive in such fuel, the recommended range of concentration of such additive, and the recommended purpose-in-use of such additive, and such other information as is reasonable and necessary to determine the emissions resulting from the use of the fuel or additive contained in such fuel, the effect of such fuel or additive on the emission control performance of any vehicle, vehicle engine, nonroad engine or nonroad vehicle, or the extent to which such emissions affect the public health or welfare.

Tests under subparagraph (A) shall be conducted in conformity with test procedures and protocols established by the Administrator. The result of such tests shall not be considered confidential.

(3) Upon compliance with the provision of this subsection, including assurances that the Administrator will receive changes in the information required, the Administrator shall register such fuel or fuel additive.

**(c) Offending fuels and fuel additives; control; prohibition**

(1) The Administrator may, from time to time on the basis of information obtained under subsection (b) of this section or other information available to him, by regulation, control or prohibit the manufacture, introduction into commerce, offering for sale, or sale of any fuel or fuel additive for use in a motor vehicle, motor vehicle engine, or nonroad engine or nonroad vehicle (A) if in the judgment of the Administrator any emission product of such fuel or fuel additive causes, or contributes, to air pollution which may reasonably be anticipated to endanger the public health or welfare, or (B) if emission products of such fuel or fuel additive will impair to a significant degree the performance of any emission control device or system which is in general use, or which the Administrator finds has been developed to a point where in a reasonable time it would be in general use were such regulation to be promulgated.

(2)(A) No fuel, class of fuels, or fuel additive may be controlled or prohibited by the Administrator pursuant to clause (A) of paragraph (1) except after consideration of all relevant medical and scientific evidence available to him, including consideration of other technologically or economically feasible means of achieving emission standards under section 7521 of this title.

(B) No fuel or fuel additive may be controlled or prohibited by the Administrator pursuant to clause (B) of paragraph (1) except after consideration of available scientific and economic data, including a cost benefit analysis comparing emission control devices or systems which are or will be in general use and require the proposed control or prohibition with emission control devices or systems which are or will be in general use and do not require the proposed control or prohibition. On request of a manufacturer of motor vehicles, motor vehicle engines, fuels, or fuel additives submitted within 10 days of notice of proposed rulemaking, the Administrator shall hold a public hearing and publish findings with respect to any matter he is required to consider under this subparagraph. Such findings shall be published at the time of promulgation of final regulations.

(C) No fuel or fuel additive may be prohibited by the Administrator under paragraph (1) unless he finds, and publishes such finding, that in his judgment such prohibition will not cause the use of any other fuel or fuel additive which will produce emissions which will endanger the public health or welfare to the same or greater degree than the use of the fuel or fuel additive proposed to be prohibited.

(3)(A) For the purpose of obtaining evidence and data to carry out paragraph (2), the Administrator may require the manufacturer of any motor vehicle or motor vehicle engine to furnish any information which has been developed concerning the emissions from motor vehicles resulting from the use of any fuel or fuel additive, or the effect of such use on the performance of any emission control device or system.

(B) In obtaining information under subparagraph (A), section 7607(a) of this title (relating to subpenas) shall be applicable.

(4)(A) Except as otherwise provided in subparagraph (B) or (C), no State (or political subdivision thereof) may prescribe or attempt to enforce, for purposes of motor vehicle emission control, any control or prohibition respecting any characteristic or component of a fuel or fuel additive in a motor vehicle or motor vehicle engine—

(i) if the Administrator has found that no control or prohibition of the characteristic or component of a fuel or fuel additive under paragraph (1) is necessary and has published his finding in the Federal Register, or

(ii) if the Administrator has prescribed under paragraph (1) a control or prohibition applicable to such characteristic or component of a fuel or fuel additive, unless State prohibition or control is identical to the prohibition or control prescribed by the Administrator.

(B) Any State for which application of section 7543(a) of this title has at any time been waived under section 7543(b) of this title may at any time prescribe and enforce, for the purpose of motor vehicle emission control, a control or prohibition respecting any fuel or fuel additive.

(C) A State may prescribe and enforce, for purposes of motor vehicle emission control, a control or prohibition respecting the use of a fuel or fuel additive in a motor vehicle or motor vehicle engine if an applicable implementation plan for such State under section 7410 of this title so provides. The Administrator may approve such provision in an implementation plan, or promulgate an implementation plan containing such a provision, only if he finds that the State control or prohibition is necessary to achieve the national primary or secondary ambient air quality standard which the plan implements. The Administrator may find that a State control or prohibition is necessary to achieve that standard if no other measures that would bring about timely attainment exist, or if other measures exist and are technically possible to implement, but are unreasonable or impracticable. The Administrator may make a finding of necessity under this subparagraph even if the plan for the area does not contain an approved demonstration of timely attainment.

**(d) Penalties and injunctions**

**(1) Civil penalties**

Any person who violates subsection (a), (f), (g), (k), (*l*), (m), or (n) of this section or the regulations prescribed under subsection (c), (h), (i), (k), (*l*), (m), or (n) of this section or who fails to furnish any information or conduct any tests required by the Administrator under subsection (b) of this section shall be liable to the United States for a civil penalty of not more than the sum of $25,000 for every day of such violation and the amount of economic benefit or savings resulting from the violation. Any violation with respect to a regulation prescribed under subsection (c), (k), (*l*), or (m) of this section which establishes a regulatory standard based upon a multiday averaging period shall constitute a separate day of violation for each and every day in the averaging period. Civil penalties shall be assessed in accordance with subsections (b) and (c) of section 7524 of this title.

**(2) Injunctive authority**

The district courts of the United States shall have jurisdiction to restrain violations of subsections (a), (f), (g), (k), (*l*), (m), and (n) of this section and of the regulations prescribed under subsections (c), (h), (i), (k), (*l*), (m), and (n) of this section, to award other appropriate relief, and to compel the furnishing of information and the conduct of tests required by the Administrator under subsection (b) of this section. Actions to restrain such violations and compel such actions shall be brought by and in the name of the United States. In any such action, subpoenas for witnesses who are required to attend a district court in any district may run into any other district.

**(e) Testing of fuels and fuel additives**

(1) Not later than one year after August 7, 1977, and after notice and opportunity for a public hearing, the Administrator shall promulgate regulations which implement the authority under subsection (b)(2)(A) and (B) of this section with respect to each fuel or fuel additive which is registered on the date of promulgation of such regulations and with respect to each fuel or fuel additive for which an application for registration is filed thereafter.

(2) Regulations under subsection (b) of this section to carry out this subsection shall require that the requisite information be provided to the Administrator by each such manufacturer—

(A) prior to registration, in the case of any fuel or fuel additive which is not registered on the date of promulgation of such regulations; or

(B) not later than three years after the date of promulgation of such regulations, in the case of any fuel or fuel additive which is registered on such date.

(3) In promulgating such regulations, the Administrator may—

(A) exempt any small business (as defined in such regulations) from or defer or modify the requirements of, such regulations with respect to any such small business;

(B) provide for cost-sharing with respect to the testing of any fuel or fuel additive which is manufactured or processed by two or more persons or otherwise provide for shared responsibility to meet the requirements of this section without duplication; or

(C) exempt any person from such regulations with respect to a particular fuel or fuel additive upon a finding that any additional testing of such fuel or fuel additive would be duplicative of adequate existing testing.

**(f) New fuels and fuel additives**

(1)(A) Effective upon March 31, 1977, it shall be unlawful for any manufacturer of any fuel or fuel additive to first introduce into commerce, or to increase the concentration in use of, any fuel or fuel additive for general use in light duty motor vehicles manufactured after model year 1974 which is not substantially similar to any fuel or fuel additive utilized in the certification of any model year 1975, or subsequent model year, vehicle or engine under section 7525 of this title.

(B) Effective upon November 15, 1990, it shall be unlawful for any manufacturer of any fuel or fuel additive to first introduce into commerce, or to increase the concentration in use of, any fuel or fuel additive for use by any person in motor vehicles manufactured after model year 1974 which is not substantially similar to any fuel or fuel additive utilized in the certification of any model year 1975, or subsequent model year, vehicle or engine under section 7525 of this title.

(2) Effective November 30, 1977, it shall be unlawful for any manufacturer of any fuel to introduce into commerce any gasoline which contains a concentration of manganese in excess of .0625 grams per gallon of fuel, except as otherwise provided pursuant to a waiver under paragraph (4).

(3) Any manufacturer of any fuel or fuel additive which prior to March 31, 1977, and after January 1, 1974, first introduced into commerce or increased the concentration in use of a fuel or fuel additive that would otherwise have been prohibited under paragraph (1)(A) if introduced on or after March 31, 1977 shall, not later than September 15, 1978, cease to distribute such fuel or fuel additive in commerce. During the period beginning 180 days after August 7, 1977, and before September 15, 1978, the Administrator shall prohibit, or restrict the concentration of any fuel additive which he determines will cause or contribute to the failure of an emission control device or system (over the useful life of any vehicle in which such device or system is used) to achieve compliance

by the vehicle with the emission standards with respect to which it has been certified under section 7525 of this title.

(4) The Administrator, upon application of any manufacturer of any fuel or fuel additive, may waive the prohibitions established under paragraph (1) or (3) of this subsection or the limitation specified in paragraph (2) of this subsection, if he determines that the applicant has established that such fuel or fuel additive or a specified concentration thereof, and the emission products of such fuel or additive or specified concentration thereof, will not cause or contribute to a failure of any emission control device or system (over the useful life of any vehicle in which such device or system is used) to achieve compliance by the vehicle with the emission standards with respect to which it has been certified pursuant to section 7525 of this title. If the Administrator has not acted to grant or deny an application under this paragraph within one hundred and eighty days of receipt of such application, the waiver authorized by this paragraph shall be treated as granted.

(5) No action of the Administrator under this section may be stayed by any court pending judicial review of such action.

**(g) Misfueling**

(1) No person shall introduce, or cause or allow the introduction of, leaded gasoline into any motor vehicle which is labeled "unleaded gasoline only," which is equipped with a gasoline tank filler inlet designed for the introduction of unleaded gasoline, which is a 1990 or later model year motor vehicle, or which such person knows or should know is a vehicle designed solely for the use of unleaded gasoline.

(2) Beginning October 1, 1993, no person shall introduce or cause or allow the introduction into any motor vehicle of diesel fuel which such person knows or should know contains a concentration of sulfur in excess of 0.05 percent (by weight) or which fails to meet a cetane index minimum of 40 or such equivalent alternative aromatic level as prescribed by the Administrator under subsection (i)(2) of this section.

**(h) Reid Vapor Pressure requirements**

**(1) Prohibition**

Not later than 6 months after November 15, 1990, the Administrator shall promulgate regulations making it unlawful for any person during the high ozone season (as defined by the Administrator) to sell, offer for sale, dispense, supply, offer for supply, transport, or introduce into commerce gasoline with a Reid Vapor Pressure in excess of 9.0 pounds per square inch (psi). Such regulations shall also establish more stringent Reid Vapor Pressure standards in a nonattainment area as the Administrator finds necessary to generally achieve comparable evaporative emissions (on a per-vehicle basis) in nonattainment areas, taking into consideration the enforceability of such standards, the need of an area for emission control, and economic factors.

**(2) Attainment areas**

The regulations under this subsection shall not make it unlawful for any person to sell, offer for supply, transport, or introduce into commerce gasoline with a Reid Vapor Pressure of 9.0 pounds per square inch (psi) or lower in any area designated under section 7407 of this title as an attainment area. Notwithstanding the preceding sentence, the Administrator may impose a Reid vapor pressure requirement lower than 9.0 pounds per square inch (psi) in any area, formerly an ozone nonattainment area, which has been redesignated as an attainment area.

**(3) Effective date; enforcement**

The regulations under this subsection shall provide that the requirements of this subsection shall take effect not later than the high ozone season for 1992, and shall include such provisions as the Administrator determines are necessary to implement and enforce the requirements of this subsection.

**(4) Ethanol waiver**

For fuel blends containing gasoline and 10 percent denatured anhydrous ethanol, the Reid vapor pressure limitation under this subsection shall be one pound per square inch (psi) greater than the applicable Reid vapor pressure limitations established under paragraph (1); Provided, however, That a distributor, blender, marketer, reseller, carrier, retailer, or wholesale purchaser-consumer shall be deemed to be in full compliance with the provisions of this subsection and the regulations promulgated thereunder if it can demonstrate (by showing receipt of a certification or other evidence acceptable to the Administrator) that—

(A) the gasoline portion of the blend complies with the Reid vapor pressure limitations promulgated pursuant to this subsection;

(B) the ethanol portion of the blend does not exceed its waiver condition under subsection (f)(4) of this section; and

(C) no additional alcohol or other additive has been added to increase the Reid Vapor Pressure of the ethanol portion of the blend.

**(5) Areas covered**

The provisions of this subsection shall apply only to the 48 contiguous States and the District of Columbia.

**(i) Sulfur content requirements for diesel fuel**

(1) Effective October 1, 1993, no person shall manufacture, sell, supply, offer for sale or supply, dispense, transport, or introduce into commerce motor vehicle diesel fuel which contains a concentration of sulfur in excess of 0.05 percent (by weight) or which fails to meet a cetane index minimum of 40.

(2) Not later than 12 months after November 15, 1990, the Administrator shall promulgate regulations to implement and enforce the requirements of paragraph (1). The Administrator may require manufacturers and importers of diesel fuel not intended for use in motor vehicles to dye such fuel in a particular manner in order to segregate it from motor vehicle diesel fuel. The Administrator may establish an equivalent alternative aromatic level to the cetane index specification in paragraph (1).

(3) The sulfur content of fuel required to be used in the certification of 1991 through 1993 model year heavy-duty diesel vehicles and engines shall be 0.10 percent (by weight). The sulfur content and cetane index minimum of fuel required to be used in the certification of 1994 and later model year heavy-duty diesel vehicles and engines shall comply with the regulations promulgated under paragraph (2).

(4) The States of Alaska and Hawaii may be exempted from the requirements of this subsection in the same manner as provided in section 7625 [1] of this title. The Administrator shall take final action on any petition filed under section 7625 [1] of this title or this paragraph for an exemption from the requirements of this subsection, within 12 months from the date of the petition.

**(j) Lead substitute gasoline additives**

(1) After November 15, 1990, any person proposing to register any gasoline additive under subsection (a) of this section or to use any previously registered additive as a lead substitute may also elect to register the additive as a lead substitute gasoline additive for reducing valve seat wear by providing the Administrator with such relevant information regarding product identity and composition as the Administrator deems necessary for carrying out the responsibilities of paragraph (2) of this subsection (in addition to other information which may be required under subsection (b) of this section).

(2) In addition to the other testing which may be required under subsection (b) of this section, in the case of the lead substitute gasoline additives referred to in paragraph (1), the Administrator shall develop and publish a test procedure to determine the additives' effectiveness in reducing valve seat wear and the additives' tendencies to produce engine deposits and other adverse side effects. The test procedures shall be developed in cooperation with the Secretary of Agriculture and with the input of additive manufacturers, engine and engine components manufacturers, and other interested persons. The Administrator shall enter into arrangements with an independent laboratory to conduct tests of each additive using the test procedures developed and published pursuant to this paragraph. The Administrator shall publish the results of the tests by company and additive name in the Federal Register along with, for comparison purposes, the results of applying the same test procedures to gasoline containing 0.1 gram of lead per gallon in lieu of the lead substitute gasoline additive. The Administrator shall not rank or otherwise rate the lead substitute additives. Test procedures shall be established within 1 year after November 15, 1990. Additives shall be tested within 18 months of November 15, 1990, or 6 months after the lead substitute additives are identified to the Administrator, whichever is later.

(3) The Administrator may impose a user fee to recover the costs of testing of any fuel additive referred to in this subsection. The fee shall be paid by the person proposing to register the fuel additive concerned. Such fee shall not exceed $20,000 for a single fuel additive.

(4) There are authorized to be appropriated to the Administrator not more than $1,000,000 for the second full fiscal year after November 15, 1990, to establish test procedures and conduct engine tests as provided in this subsection. Not more than $500,000 per year is authorized to be appropriated for each of the 5 subsequent fiscal years.

(5) Any fees collected under this subsection shall be deposited in a special fund in the United States Treasury for licensing and other services which thereafter shall be available for appropriation, to remain available until expended, to carry out the Agency's activities for which the fees were collected.

**(k) Reformulated gasoline for conventional vehicles**

**(1) EPA regulations**

Within 1 year after November 15, 1990, the Administrator shall promulgate regulations under this section establishing requirements for reformulated gasoline to be used in gasoline-fueled vehicles in specified nonattainment areas. Such regulations shall require the greatest reduction in emissions of ozone forming volatile organic compounds (during the high ozone season) and emissions of toxic air pollutants (during the entire year) achievable through the reformulation of conventional gasoline, taking into consideration the cost of achieving such emission reductions, any nonair-quality and other air-quality related health and environmental impacts and energy requirements.

(2) **General requirements**

The regulations referred to in paragraph (1) shall require that reformulated gasoline comply with paragraph (3) and with each of the following requirements (subject to paragraph (7)):

(A) **$NO_x$ emissions**

The emissions of oxides of nitrogen ($NO_x$) from baseline vehicles when using the reformulated gasoline shall be no greater than the level of such emissions from such vehicles when using baseline gasoline. If the Administrator determines that compliance with the limitation on emissions of oxides of nitrogen under the preceding sentence is technically infeasible, considering the other requirements applicable under this subsection to such gasoline, the Administrator may, as appropriate to ensure compliance with this subparagraph, adjust (or waive entirely), any other requirements of this paragraph (including the oxygen content requirement contained in subparagraph (B)) or any requirements applicable under paragraph (3)(A).

(B) **Oxygen content**

The oxygen content of the gasoline shall equal or exceed 2.0 percent by weight (subject to a testing tolerance established by the Administrator) except as otherwise required by this chapter. The Administrator may waive, in whole or in part, the application of this subparagraph for any ozone nonattainment area upon a determination by the Administrator that compliance with such requirement would prevent or interfere with the attainment by the area of a national primary ambient air quality standard.

(C) **Benzene content**

The benzene content of the gasoline shall not exceed 1.0 percent by volume.

(D) **Heavy metals**

The gasoline shall have no heavy metals, including lead or manganese. The Administrator may waive the prohibition contained in this subparagraph for a heavy metal (other than lead) if the Administrator determines that addition of the heavy metal to the gasoline will not increase, on an aggregate mass or cancer-risk basis, toxic air pollutant emissions from motor vehicles.

(3) **More stringent of formula or performance standards**

The regulations referred to in paragraph (1) shall require compliance with the more stringent of either the requirements set forth in subparagraph (A) or the requirements of subparagraph (B) of this paragraph. For purposes of determining the more stringent provision, clause (i) and clause (ii) of subparagraph (B) shall be considered independently.

(A) **Formula**

(i) **Benzene**

The benzene content of the reformulated gasoline shall not exceed 1.0 percent by volume.

(ii) **Aromatics**

The aromatic hydrocarbon content of the reformulated gasoline shall not exceed 25 percent by volume.

(iii) **Lead**

The reformulated gasoline shall have no lead content.

(iv) **Detergents**

The reformulated gasoline shall contain additives to prevent the accumulation of deposits in engines or vehicle fuel supply systems.

(v) **Oxygen content**

The oxygen content of the reformulated gasoline shall equal or exceed 2.0 percent by weight (subject to a testing tolerance established by the Administrator) except as otherwise required by this chapter.

(B) **Performance standard**

(i) **VOC emissions**

During the high ozone season (as defined by the Administrator), the aggregate emissions of ozone forming volatile organic compounds from baseline vehicles when using the reformulated gasoline shall be 15 percent below the aggregate emissions of ozone forming volatile organic compounds from such vehicles when using baseline gasoline. Effective in calendar year 2000 and thereafter, 25 percent shall be substituted for 15 percent in applying this clause, except that the Administrator may adjust such 25 percent requirement to provide for a lesser or greater reduction based on technological feasibility, considering the cost of achieving such reductions in VOC emissions. No such adjustment shall provide for less than a 20 percent reduction below the aggregate emissions of such air pollutants from such vehicles when using baseline gasoline. The reductions required under this clause shall be on a mass basis.

(ii) Toxics

During the entire year, the aggregate emissions of toxic air pollutants from baseline vehicles when using the reformulated gasoline shall be 15 percent below the aggregate emissions of toxic air pollutants from such vehicles when using baseline gasoline. Effective in calendar year 2000 and thereafter, 25 percent shall be substituted for 15 percent in applying this clause, except that the Administrator may adjust such 25 percent requirement to provide for a lesser or greater reduction based on technological feasibility, considering the cost of achieving such reductions in toxic air pollutants. No such adjustment shall provide for less than a 20 percent reduction below the aggregate emissions of such air pollutants from such vehicles when using baseline gasoline. The reductions required under this clause shall be on a mass basis.

Any reduction greater than a specific percentage reduction required under this subparagraph shall be treated as satisfying such percentage reduction requirement.

**(4) Certification procedures**

**(A) Regulations**

The regulations under this subsection shall include procedures under which the Administrator shall certify reformulated gasoline as complying with the requirements established pursuant to this subsection. Under such regulations, the Administrator shall establish procedures for any person to petition the Administrator to certify a fuel formulation, or slate of fuel formulations. Such procedures shall further require that the Administrator shall approve or deny such petition within 180 days of receipt. If the Administrator fails to act within such 180–day period, the fuel shall be deemed certified until the Administrator completes action on the petition.

**(B) Certification; equivalency**

The Administrator shall certify a fuel formulation or slate of fuel formulations as complying with this subsection if such fuel or fuels—

**(i)** comply with the requirements of paragraph (2), and

**(ii)** achieve equivalent or greater reductions in emissions of ozone forming volatile organic compounds and emissions of toxic air pollutants than are achieved by a reformulated gasoline meeting the applicable requirements of paragraph (3).

**(C) EPA determination of emissions level**

Within 1 year after November 15, 1990, the Administrator shall determine the level of emissions of ozone forming volatile organic compounds and emissions of toxic air pollutants emitted by baseline vehicles when operating on baseline gasoline. For purposes of this subsection, within 1 year after November 15, 1990, the Administrator shall, by rule, determine appropriate measures of, and methodology for, ascertaining the emissions of air pollutants (including calculations, equipment, and testing tolerances).

**(5) Prohibition**

Effective beginning January 1, 1995, each of the following shall be a violation of this subsection:

**(A)** The sale or dispensing by any person of conventional gasoline to ultimate consumers in any covered area.

**(B)** The sale or dispensing by any refiner, blender, importer, or marketer of conventional gasoline for resale in any covered area, without (i) segregating such gasoline from reformulated gasoline, and (ii) clearly marking such conventional gasoline as "conventional gasoline, not for sale to ultimate consumer in a covered area".

Any refiner, blender, importer or marketer who purchases property segregated and marked conventional gasoline, and thereafter labels, represents, or wholesales such gasoline as reformulated gasoline shall also be in violation of this subsection. The Administrator may impose sampling, testing, and record-keeping requirements upon any refiner, blender, importer, or marketer to prevent violations of this section.

**(6) Opt-in areas**

**(A)** Upon the application of the Governor of a State, the Administrator shall apply the prohibition set forth in paragraph (5) in any area in the State classified under subpart 2 of part D of subchapter I of this chapter as a Marginal, Moderate, Serious, or Severe Area (without regard to whether or not the 1980 population of the area exceeds 250,000). In any such case, the Administrator shall establish an effective date for such prohibition as he deems appropriate, not later than January 1, 1995, or 1 year after such application is received, whichever is later. The Administrator shall publish such application in the Federal Register upon receipt.

**(B)** If the Administrator determines, on the Administrator's own motion or on petition of any person, after consultation with the Secretary of Energy, that there is insufficient domestic capacity to produce gasoline certified under this subsection, the Administrator shall, by rule, extend the effective date of such prohibition in Marginal, Moderate,

Serious, or Severe Areas referred to in subparagraph (A) for one additional year, and may, by rule, renew such extension for 2 additional one-year periods. The Administrator shall act on any petition submitted under this paragraph within 6 months after receipt of the petition. The Administrator shall issue such extensions for areas with a lower ozone classification before issuing any such extension for areas with a higher classification.

**(7) Credits**

**(A)** The regulations promulgated under this subsection shall provide for the granting of an appropriate amount of credits to a person who refines, blends, or imports and certifies a gasoline or slate of gasoline that—

**(i)** has an oxygen content (by weight) that exceeds the minimum oxygen content specified in paragraph (2);

**(ii)** has an aromatic hydrocarbon content (by volume) that is less than the maximum aromatic hydrocarbon content required to comply with paragraph (3); or

**(iii)** has a benzene content (by volume) that is less than the maximum benzene content specified in paragraph (2).

**(B)** The regulations described in subparagraph (A) shall also provide that a person who is granted credits may use such credits, or transfer all or a portion of such credits to another person for use within the same nonattainment area, for the purpose of complying with this subsection.

**(C)** The regulations promulgated under subparagraphs (A) and (B) shall ensure the enforcement of the requirements for the issuance, application, and transfer of the credits. Such regulations shall prohibit the granting or transfer of such credits for use with respect to any gasoline in a nonattainment area, to the extent the use of such credits would result in any of the following:

**(i)** An average gasoline aromatic hydrocarbon content (by volume) for the nonattainment (taking into account all gasoline sold for use in conventional gasoline-fueled vehicles in the nonattainment area) higher than the average fuel aromatic hydrocarbon content (by volume) that would occur in the absence of using any such credits.

**(ii)** An average gasoline oxygen content (by weight) for the nonattainment area (taking into account all gasoline sold for use in conventional gasoline-fueled vehicles in the nonattainment area) lower than the average gasoline oxygen content (by weight) that would occur in the absence of using any such credits.

**(iii)** An average benzene content (by volume) for the nonattainment area (taking into account all gasoline sold for use in conventional gasoline-fueled vehicles in the nonattainment area) higher than the average benzene content (by volume) that would occur in the absence of using any such credits.

**(8) Anti-dumping rules**

**(A) In general**

Within 1 year after November 15, 1990, the Administrator shall promulgate regulations applicable to each refiner, blender, or importer of gasoline ensuring that gasoline sold or introduced into commerce by such refiner, blender, or importer (other than reformulated gasoline subject to the requirements of paragraph (1)) does not result in average per gallon emissions (measured on a mass basis) of (i) volatile organic compounds, (ii) oxides of nitrogen, (iii) carbon monoxide, and (iv) toxic air pollutants in excess of such emissions of such pollutants attributable to gasoline sold or introduced into commerce in calendar year 1990 by that refiner, blender, or importer. Such regulations shall take effect beginning January 1, 1995.

**(B) Adjustments**

In evaluating compliance with the requirements of subparagraph (A), the Administrator shall make appropriate adjustments to insure that no credit is provided for improvement in motor vehicle emissions control in motor vehicles sold after the calendar year 1990.

**(C) Compliance determined for each pollutant independently**

In determining whether there is an increase in emissions in violation of the prohibition contained in subparagraph (A) the Administrator shall consider an increase in each air pollutant referred to in clauses (i) through (iv) as a separate violation of such prohibition, except that the Administrator shall promulgate regulations to provide that any increase in emissions of oxides of nitrogen resulting from adding oxygenates to gasoline may be offset by an equivalent or greater reduction (on a mass basis) in emissions of volatile organic compounds, carbon monoxide, or toxic air pollutants, or any combination of the foregoing.

**(D) Compliance period**

The Administrator shall promulgate an appropriate compliance period or appropriate compliance periods to be used for assessing compliance with the prohibition contained in subparagraph (A).

**(E) Baseline for determining compliance**

If the Administrator determines that no adequate and reliable data exists regarding the composition of gasoline sold or introduced into commerce by a refiner, blender, or importer in calendar year 1990, for such refiner, blender, or importer, baseline gasoline shall be substituted for such 1990 gasoline in determining compliance with subparagraph (A).

**(9) Emissions from entire vehicle**

In applying the requirements of this subsection, the Administrator shall take into account emissions from the entire motor vehicle, including evaporative, running, refueling, and exhaust emissions.

**(10) Definitions**

For purposes of this subsection—

**(A) Baseline vehicles**

The term "baseline vehicles" mean [2] representative model year 1990 vehicles.

**(B) Baseline gasoline**

**(i) Summertime**

The term "baseline gasoline" means in the case of gasoline sold during the high ozone period (as defined by the Administrator) a gasoline which meets the following specifications:

BASELINE GASOLINE FUEL PROPERTIES

| | |
|---|---|
| API Gravity | 57.4 |
| Sulfur, ppm | 339 |
| Benzene, % | 1.53 |
| RVP, psi | 8.7 |
| Octane, R + M/2 | 87.3 |
| IBP, F | 91 |
| 10%, F | 128 |
| 50%, F | 218 |
| 90%, F | 330 |
| End Point, F | 415 |
| Aromatics, % | 32.0 |
| Olefins, % | 9.2 |
| Saturates, % | 58.8 |

**(ii) Wintertime**

The Administrator shall establish the specifications of "baseline gasoline" for gasoline sold at times other than the high ozone period (as defined by the Administrator). Such specifications shall be the specifications of 1990 industry average gasoline sold during such period.

**(C) Toxic air pollutants**

The term "toxic air pollutants" means the aggregate emissions of the following:

Benzene
1,3 Butadiene
Polycyclic organic matter (POM)
Acetaldehyde
Formaldehyde.

**(D) Covered area**

The 9 ozone nonattainment areas having a 1980 population in excess of 250,000 and having the highest ozone design value during the period 1987 through 1989 shall be "covered areas" for purposes of this subsection. Effective one year after the reclassification of any ozone nonattainment area as a Severe ozone nonattainment area under section 7511(b) of this title, such Severe area shall also be a "covered area" for purposes of this subsection.

**(E) Reformulated gasoline**

The term "reformulated gasoline" means any gasoline which is certified by the Administrator under this section as complying with this subsection.

**(F) Conventional gasoline**

The term "conventional gasoline" means any gasoline which does not meet specifications set by a certification under this subsection.

**(*l*) Detergents**

Effective beginning January 1, 1995, no person may sell or dispense to an ultimate consumer in the United States, and no refiner or marketer may directly or indirectly sell or dispense to persons who sell or dispense to ultimate consumers in the United States any gasoline which does not contain additives to prevent the accumulation of deposits in engines or fuel supply systems. Not later than 2 years after November 15, 1990, the Administrator shall promulgate a rule establishing specifications for such additives.

**(m) Oxygenated fuels**

**(1) Plan revisions for CO nonattainment areas**

(A) Each State in which there is located all or part of an area which is designated under subchapter I of this chapter as a nonattainment area for carbon monoxide and which has a carbon monoxide design value of 9.5 parts per million (ppm) or above based on data for the 2–year period of 1988 and 1989 and calculated according to the most recent interpretation methodology issued by the Administrator prior to November 15, 1990, shall submit to the Administrator a State implementation plan revision under section 7410 of this title and part D of subchapter I of this chapter for such area which shall contain the provisions specified under this subsection regarding oxygenated gasoline.

**(B)** A plan revision which contains such provisions shall also be submitted by each State in which there is located any area which, for any 2–year period after 1989 has a carbon monoxide design value of 9.5 ppm or above. The revision shall be submitted within 18 months after such 2–year period.

**(2) Oxygenated gasoline in CO nonattainment areas**

Each plan revision under this subsection shall contain provisions to require that any gasoline sold, or dispensed, to the ultimate consumer in the carbon monoxide nonattainment area or sold or dispensed directly or indirectly by fuel refiners or marketers to persons who sell or dispense to ultimate consumers, in the larger of—

**(A)** the Consolidated Metropolitan Statistical Area (CMSA) in which the area is located, or

**(B)** if the area is not located in a CMSA, the Metropolitan Statistical Area in which the area is located,

be blended, during the portion of the year in which the area is prone to high ambient concentrations of carbon monoxide to contain not less than 2.7 percent oxygen by weight (subject to a testing tolerance established by the Administrator). The portion of the year in which the area is prone to high ambient concentrations of carbon monoxide shall be as determined by the Administrator, but shall not be less than 4 months. At the request of a State with respect to any area designated as nonattainment for carbon monoxide, the Administrator may reduce the period specified in the preceding sentence if the State can demonstrate that because of meteorological conditions, a reduced period will assure that there will be no exceedances of the carbon monoxide standard outside of such reduced period. For areas with a carbon monoxide design value of 9.5 ppm or more of [3] November 15, 1990, the revision shall provide that such requirement shall take effect no later than November 1, 1992 (or at such other date during 1992 as the Administrator establishes under the preceding provisions of this paragraph). For other areas, the revision shall provide that such requirement shall take effect no later than November 1 of the third year after the last year of the applicable 2–year period referred to in paragraph (1) (or at such other date during such third year as the Administrator establishes under the preceding provisions of this paragraph) and shall include a program for implementation and enforcement of the requirement consistent with guidance to be issued by the Administrator.

**(3) Waivers**

**(A)** The Administrator shall waive, in whole or in part, the requirements of paragraph (2) upon a demonstration by the State to the satisfaction of the Administrator that the use of oxygenated gasoline would prevent or interfere with the attainment by the area of a national primary ambient air quality standard (or a State or local ambient air quality standard) for any air pollutant other than carbon monoxide.

**(B)** The Administrator shall, upon demonstration by the State satisfactory to the Administrator, waive the requirement of paragraph (2) where the Administrator determines that mobile sources of carbon monoxide do not contribute significantly to carbon monoxide levels in an area.

**(C)(i)** Any person may petition the Administrator to make a finding that there is, or is likely to be, for any area, an inadequate domestic supply of, or distribution capacity for, oxygenated gasoline meeting the requirements of paragraph (2) or fuel additives (oxygenates) necessary to meet such requirements. The Administrator shall act on such petition within 6 months after receipt of the petition.

**(ii)** If the Administrator determines, in response to a petition under clause (i), that there is an inadequate supply or capacity described in clause (i), the Administrator shall delay the effective date of paragraph (2) for 1 year. Upon petition, the Administrator may extend such effective date for one additional year. No partial delay or lesser waiver may be granted under this clause.

**(iii)** In granting waivers under this subparagraph the Administrator shall consider distribution capacity separately from the adequacy of domestic supply and shall grant such waivers in such manner as will assure that, if supplies of oxygenated gasoline are limited, areas having the highest design value for carbon monoxide will have a priority in obtaining oxygenated gasoline which meets the requirements of paragraph (2).

**(iv)** As used in this subparagraph, the term distribution capacity includes capacity for transportation, storage, and blending.

**(4) Fuel dispensing systems**

Any person selling oxygenated gasoline at retail pursuant to this subsection shall be required under regulations promulgated by the Administrator to label the fuel dispensing system with a notice that the gasoline is oxygenated and will reduce the carbon monoxide emissions from the motor vehicle.

(5) **Guidelines for credit**

The Administrator shall promulgate guidelines, within 9 months after November 15, 1990, allowing the use of marketable oxygen credits from gasolines during that portion of the year specified in paragraph (2) with higher oxygen content than required to offset the sale or use of gasoline with a lower oxygen content than required. No credits may be transferred between nonattainment areas.

(6) **Attainment areas**

Nothing in this subsection shall be interpreted as requiring an oxygenated gasoline program in an area which is in attainment for carbon monoxide, except that in a carbon monoxide nonattainment area which is redesignated as attainment for carbon monoxide, the requirements of this subsection shall remain in effect to the extent such program is necessary to maintain such standard thereafter in the area.

(7) **Failure to attain CO standard**

If the Administrator determines under section 7512(b)(2) of this title that the national primary ambient air quality standard for carbon monoxide has not been attained in a Serious Area by the applicable attainment date, the State shall submit a plan revision for the area within 9 months after the date of such determination. The plan revision shall provide that the minimum oxygen content of gasoline referred to in paragraph (2) shall be 3.1 percent by weight unless such requirement is waived in accordance with the provisions of this subsection.

**(n) Prohibition on leaded gasoline for highway use**

After December 31, 1995, it shall be unlawful for any person to sell, offer for sale, supply, offer for supply, dispense, transport, or introduce into commerce, for use as fuel in any motor vehicle (as defined in section 7554(2) [4] of this title) any gasoline which contains lead or lead additives.

**(*o*) Fuel and fuel additive importers and importation**

For the purposes of this section, the term "manufacturer" includes an importer and the term "manufacture" includes importation.

(July 14, 1955, c. 360, Title II, § 211, formerly § 210, as added Nov. 21, 1967, Pub.L. 90–148, § 2, 81 Stat. 502, and renumbered and amended Dec. 31, 1970, Pub.L. 91–604, §§ 8(a), 9(a), 84 Stat. 1694, 1698; Nov. 18, 1971, Pub.L. 92–157, Title III, § 302(d), (e), 85 Stat. 464; Aug. 7, 1977, Pub.L. 95–95, Title II, §§ 222, 223, Title IV, § 401(e), 91 Stat. 762, 764, 791; Nov. 16, 1977, Pub.L. 95–190, § 14(a)(73), (74), 91 Stat. 1403, 1404; Nov. 15, 1990, Pub.L. 101–549, Title II, §§ 212 to 221, 228(d), 104 Stat. 2488 to 2500, 2510.)

[1] So in original. Probably should be section "7625–1".

[2] So in original. Probably should be "means".

[3] So in original. Probably should be "as of".

[4] So in original. Probably should be section "7550(2)".

## HISTORICAL AND STATUTORY NOTES

**Codifications**

Section was formerly classified to section 1857f–6c of this title.

**Effective and Applicability Provisions**

1990 Acts

Amendment by Pub.L. 101–549 effective Nov. 15, 1990, except as otherwise provided, see section 711(b) of Pub.L. 101–549, set out as a note under section 7401 of this title.

1977 Acts

Amendment by Pub.L. 95–95 effective Aug. 7, 1977, except as otherwise expressly provided, see section 406(d) of Pub.L. 95–95, set out as a note under section 7401 of this title.

**Savings Provisions**

Suits, actions or proceedings commenced under this chapter as in effect prior to Nov. 15, 1990, not to abate by reason of the taking effect of amendments by Pub.L. 101–549, except as otherwise provided for, see section 711(a) of Pub.L. 101–549, set out as a note under section 7401 of this title.

**Prior Provisions**

A prior section 211 of Act July 14, 1955, as added Nov. 21, 1967, Pub.L. 90–148, § 2, 81 Stat. 503, providing for a national emissions standards study, was set out as section 1857f–6d of this title and was repealed by Pub.L. 91–604, § 8(a), Dec. 31, 1970, 84 Stat. 1694.

**Agricultural Machinery: Study of Unleaded Fuel**

Pub.L. 99–198, Title XVII, § 1765, Dec. 23, 1985, 99 Stat. 1653, directed the Administrator of the Environmental Protection Agency and the Secretary of Agriculture to conduct jointly a study of the use of fuel containing lead additives and alternative lubricating additives in gasoline engines that are used in agricultural machinery and are designed to combust fuel containing such additives, with the results of the study to be published not later than January 1, 1987.

**Findings and Sense of Congress on Ethanol Usage**

Pub.L. 100–203, Title I, § 1508, Dec. 22, 1987, 101 Stat. 1330–29, provided that:

"(a) **Findings.**—Congress finds that—

"(1) the United States is dependent for a large and growing share of its energy needs on the Middle East at a time when world petroleum reserves are declining;

"(2) the burning of gasoline causes pollution;

"(3) ethanol can be blended with gasoline to produce a cleaner source of fuel;

"(4) ethanol can be produced from grain, a renewable resource that is in considerable surplus in the United States;

"(5) the conversion of grain into ethanol would reduce farm program costs and grain surpluses; and

"(6) increasing the quantity of motor fuels that contain at least 10 percent ethanol from current levels to 50 percent by 1992 would create thousands of new jobs in ethanol production facilities.

"(b) **Sense of Congress.**—It is the sense of Congress that the Administrator of the Environmental Protection Agency should use authority provided under the Clean Air Act (42 U.S.C. 7401 et seq.) [42 U.S.C.A. § 7401 et seq.] to require greater use of ethanol as motor fuel."

**Modification or Rescission of Rules, Regulations, Orders, Determinations, Contracts, Certifications, Authorizations, Delegations, and Other Actions**

All rules, regulations, orders, determinations, contracts, certifications, authorizations, delegations, or other actions duly issued, made, or taken by or pursuant to Act July 14, 1955, the Clean Air Act, as in effect immediately prior to the date of enactment of Pub.L. 95–95 [Aug. 7, 1977] to continue in full force and effect until modified or rescinded in accordance with Act July 14, 1955, as amended by Pub.L. 95–95 [this chapter], see section 406(b) of Pub.L. 95–95, set out as an Effective Date of 1977 Acts note under section 7401 of this title.

## § 7546. Repealed. Pub.L. 101–549, Title II, § 230(10), Nov. 15, 1990, 104 Stat. 2529

### HISTORICAL AND STATUTORY NOTES

Section, Act July 14, 1955, c. 360, Title II, § 212, as added Dec. 31, 1970, Pub.L. 91–604, § 10(c), 84 Stat. 1700, and amended Dec. 31, 1970, Pub.L. 91–605, § 202(a), 84 Stat. 1739; Apr. 9, 1973, Pub.L. 93–15, § 1(b), 87 Stat. 11; June 22, 1974, Pub.L. 93–319, § 13(b), 88 Stat. 265, related to low-emission vehicles.

A prior section 212 of Act July 14, 1955, was renumbered section 213 by Pub.L. 91–604, renumbered section 214 by Pub.L. 93–319, and renumbered section 216 by Pub.L. 95–95, and is classified to section 7550 of this title.

**Effective Date of Repeal**

Repeal of section effective Nov. 15, 1990, except as otherwise provided, see section 711(b) of Pub.L. 101–549, set out as an Effective Date of 1977 Acts note under section 7401 of this title.

## § 7547. Nonroad engines and vehicles

[CAA § 213]

**(a) Emissions standards**

(1) The Administrator shall conduct a study of emissions from nonroad engines and nonroad vehicles (other than locomotives or engines used in locomotives) to determine if such emissions cause, or significantly contribute to, air pollution which may reasonably be anticipated to endanger public health or welfare. Such study shall be completed within 12 months of November 15, 1990.

(2) After notice and opportunity for public hearing, the Administrator shall determine within 12 months after completion of the study under paragraph (1), based upon the results of such study, whether emissions of carbon monoxide, oxides of nitrogen, and volatile organic compounds from new and existing nonroad engines or nonroad vehicles (other than locomotives or engines used in locomotives) are significant contributors to ozone or carbon monoxide concentrations in more than 1 area which has failed to attain the national ambient air quality standards for ozone or carbon monoxide. Such determination shall be included in the regulations under paragraph (3).

(3) If the Administrator makes an affirmative determination under paragraph (2) the Administrator shall, within 12 months after completion of the study under paragraph (1), promulgate (and from time to time revise) regulations containing standards applicable to emissions from those classes or categories of new nonroad engines and new nonroad vehicles (other than locomotives or engines used in locomotives) which in the Administrator's judgment cause, or contribute to, such air pollution. Such standards shall achieve the greatest degree of emission reduction achievable through the application of technology which the Administrator determines will be available for the engines or vehicles to which such standards apply, giving appropriate consideration to the cost of applying such technology within the period of time available to manufacturers and to noise, energy, and safety factors associated with the application of such technology. In determining what degree of reduction will be available, the Administrator shall first consider standards equivalent in stringency to standards for comparable motor vehicles or engines (if any) regulated under section 7521 of this title, taking into account the technological feasibility, costs, safety, noise, and energy factors associated with achieving, as appropriate, standards of such stringency and lead time. The regulations shall apply to the useful life of the engines or vehicles (as determined by the Administrator).

(4) If the Administrator determines that any emissions not referred to in paragraph (2) from new nonroad engines or vehicles significantly contribute to air pollution which may reasonably be anticipated to endanger public health or welfare, the Administrator may promulgate (and from time to time revise) such regulations as the Administrator deems appropriate containing standards applicable to emissions from those classes or categories of new nonroad engines and new nonroad vehicles (other than locomotives or engines used in locomotives) which in the Administrator's judgment cause, or contribute to, such air pollution, taking into account costs, noise, safety, and energy factors associated with the application of technology which the Administrator determines will be available for the engines and vehicles to which such standards apply. The regulations shall apply to the useful life of the engines or vehicles (as determined by the Administrator).

(5) Within 5 years after November 15, 1990, the Administrator shall promulgate regulations containing standards applicable to emissions from new locomotives and new engines used in locomotives. Such

standards shall achieve the greatest degree of emission reduction achievable through the application of technology which the Administrator determines will be available for the locomotives or engines to which such standards apply, giving appropriate consideration to the cost of applying such technology within the period of time available to manufacturers and to noise, energy, and safety factors associated with the application of such technology.

**(b) Effective date**

Standards under this section shall take effect at the earliest possible date considering the lead time necessary to permit the development and application of the requisite technology, giving appropriate consideration to the cost of compliance within such period and energy and safety.

**(c) Safe controls**

Effective with respect to new engines or vehicles to which standards under this section apply, no emission control device, system, or element of design shall be used in such a new nonroad engine or new nonroad vehicle for purposes of complying with such standards if such device, system, or element of design will cause or contribute to an unreasonable risk to public health, welfare, or safety in its operation or function. In determining whether an unreasonable risk exists, the Administrator shall consider factors including those described in section 7521(a)(4)(B) of this title.

**(d) Enforcement**

The standards under this section shall be subject to sections 7525, 7541, 7542, and 7543 of this title, with such modifications of the applicable regulations implementing such sections as the Administrator deems appropriate, and shall be enforced in the same manner as standards prescribed under section 7521 of this title. The Administrator shall revise or promulgate regulations as may be necessary to determine compliance with, and enforce, standards in effect under this section.

(July 14, 1955, c. 360, Title II, § 213, as added June 22, 1974, Pub.L. 93–319, § 10, 88 Stat. 261, and amended Nov. 15, 1990, Pub.L. 101–549, Title II, § 222(a), 104 Stat. 2500.)

## HISTORICAL AND STATUTORY NOTES

**Codifications**

Section was formerly classified to section 1857f–6f of this title.

**Effective and Applicability Provisions**

1990 Acts

Amendment by Pub.L. 101–549 effective Nov. 15, 1990, except as otherwise provided, see section 711(b) of Pub.L. 101–549, set out as a note under section 7401 of this title.

**Change of Name**

The Committee on Public Works and the Committee on Commerce of the Senate were abolished and replaced by the Committee on Environment and Public Works and the Committee on Commerce, Science, and Transportation of the Senate, respectively, effective Feb. 11, 1977. See Rule XXV of the Standing Rules of the Senate, as amended by Senate Resolution 4 (popularly cited as the "Committee System Reorganization Amendments of 1977"), approved Feb. 4, 1977.

**Savings Provisions**

Suits, actions or proceedings commenced under this chapter as in effect prior to Nov. 15, 1990, not to abate by reason of the taking effect of amendments by Pub.L. 101–549, except as otherwise provided for, see section 711(a) of Pub.L. 101–549, set out as a note under section 7401 of this title.

**Prior Provisions**

A prior section 213 of Act July 14, 1955, was renumbered section 214 by Pub.L. 93–319 and renumbered section 216 by Pub.L. 95–95, and is classified to section 7550 of this title.

**Regulations Relating to Standards to Reduce Emissions**

Pub.L. 108–199, Div. G., Title IV, § 428(b), Jan. 23, 2004, 118 Stat. 418, provided that: "Not later than December 1, 2004, the Administrator of the Environmental Protection Agency shall propose regulations under the Clean Air Act [Act July 14, 1955, c. 360, 69 Stat. 322; see Tables for classification] that shall contain standards to reduce emissions from new nonroad spark-ignition engines smaller than 50 horsepower. Not later than December 31, 2005, the Administrator shall publish in the Federal Register final regulations containing such standards."

**Federal Energy Administrator**

The "Federal Energy Administrator", for purposes of this chapter, to mean the Administrator of the Federal Energy Administration established by Pub.L. 93–275 May 7, 1974, 88 Stat. 97 [section 761 et seq. of Title 15, Commerce and Trade], but with the term to mean any officer of the United States designated as such by the President until the Federal Energy Administration takes office and after it ceases to exist, see section 798(a) of Title 15, Commerce and Trade.

The Federal Energy Administration was terminated and functions vested by law in the Administrator thereof were transferred to the Secretary of Energy (unless otherwise specifically provided) by sections 7151(a) and 7293 of this title.

## § 7548. Study of particulate emissions from motor vehicles

[CAA § 214]

**(a) Study and analysis**

(1) The Administrator shall conduct a study concerning the effects on health and welfare of particulate emissions from motor vehicles or motor vehicle engines to which section 7521 of this title applies. Such study shall characterize and quantify such emissions and analyze the relationship of such emissions to various fuels and fuel additives.

(2) The study shall also include an analysis of particulate emissions from mobile sources which are not related to engine emissions (including, but not limited to tire debris, and asbestos from brake lining).

**(b) Report to Congress**

The Administrator shall report to the Congress the findings and results of the study conducted under subsection (a) of this section not later than two years after August 7, 1977. Such report shall also include recommendations for standards or methods to regulate particulate emissions described in paragraph (2) of subsection (a) of this section.

(July 14, 1955, c. 360, Title II, § 214, as added Aug. 7, 1977, Pub.L. 95–95, Title II, § 224(d), 91 Stat. 767.)

### HISTORICAL AND STATUTORY NOTES

**Effective and Applicability Provisions**

1977 Acts

Section effective Aug. 7, 1977, except as otherwise expressly provided, see section 406(d) of Pub.L. 95–95, set out as a note under section 7401 of this title.

**Prior Provisions**

A prior section 214 of Act July 14, 1955, was renumbered section 216 by Pub.L. 95–95, and is classified to section 7550 of this title.

**Study on Suspended Particulate Matter**

Section 403(a) of Pub.L. 95–95 provided that not later than 18 months after Aug. 7, 1977, the Administrator of the Environmental Protection Agency, in cooperation with the National Academy of Sciences, study and report to Congress on the relationship between the size, weight, and chemical composition of suspended particulate matter and the nature and degree of the endangerment to public health or welfare presented by such particulate matter and the availability of technology for controlling such particulate matter.

## § 7549. High altitude performance adjustments

[CAA § 215]

**(a) Instruction of the manufacturer**

(1) Any action taken with respect to any element of design installed on or in a motor vehicle or motor vehicle engine in compliance with regulations under this subchapter (including any alteration or adjustment of such element), shall be treated as not in violation of section 7522(a) of this title if such action is performed in accordance with high altitude adjustment instructions provided by the manufacturer under subsection (b) of this section and approved by the Administrator.

(2) If the Administrator finds that adjustments or modifications made pursuant to instructions of the manufacturer under paragraph (1) will not insure emission control performance with respect to each standard under section 7521 of this title at least equivalent to that which would result if no such adjustments or modifications were made, he shall disapprove such instructions. Such finding shall be based upon minimum engineering evaluations consistent with good engineering practice.

**(b) Regulations**

(1) Instructions respecting each class or category of vehicles or engines to which this title applies providing for such vehicle and engine adjustments and modifications as may be necessary to insure emission control performance at different altitudes shall be submitted by the manufacturer to the Administrator pursuant to regulations promulgated by the Administrator.

(2) Any knowing violation by a manufacturer of requirements of the Administrator under paragraph (1) shall be treated as a violation by such manufacturer of section 7522(a)(3) of this title for purposes of the penalties contained in section 7524 of this title.

(3) Such instructions shall provide, in addition to other adjustments, for adjustments for vehicles moving from high altitude areas to low altitude areas after the initial registration of such vehicles.

**(c) Manufacturer parts**

No instructions under this section respecting adjustments or modifications may require the use of any manufacturer parts (as defined in section 7522(a) of this title) unless the manufacturer demonstrates to the satisfaction of the Administrator that the use of such manufacturer parts is necessary to insure emission control performance.

**(d) State inspection and maintenance programs**

Before January 1, 1981 the authority provided by this section shall be available in any high altitude State (as determined under regulations of the Administrator under regulations promulgated before August 7, 1977) but after December 31, 1980, such authority shall be available only in any such State in which an inspection and maintenance program for the testing of motor vehicle emissions has been instituted for the portions of the State where any national ambient air quality standard for auto-related pollutants has not been attained.

**(e) High altitude testing**

(1) The Administrator shall promptly establish at least one testing center (in addition to the testing centers existing on November 15, 1990) located at a site that represents high altitude conditions, to ascertain in a reasonable manner whether, when in actual use throughout their useful life (as determined under section 7521(d) of this title), each class or category of vehicle and engines to which regulations under section 7521 of this title apply conforms to the emissions

standards established by such regulations. For purposes of this subsection, the term "high altitude conditions" refers to high altitude as defined in regulations of the Administrator in effect as of November 15, 1990.

(2) The Administrator, in cooperation with the Secretary of Energy and the Administrator of the Federal Transit Administration, and such other agencies as the Administrator deems appropriate, shall establish a research and technology assessment center to provide for the development and evaluation of less-polluting heavy-duty engines and fuels for use in buses, heavy-duty trucks, and non-road engines and vehicles, which shall be located at a high-altitude site that represents high-altitude conditions. In establishing and funding such a center, the Administrator shall give preference to proposals which provide for local cost-sharing of facilities and recovery of costs of operation through utilization of such facility for the purposes of this section.

(3) The Administrator shall designate at least one center at high-altitude conditions to provide research on after-market emission components, dual-fueled vehicles and conversion kits, the effects of tampering on emissions equipment, testing of alternate fuels and conversion kits, and the development of curricula, training courses, and materials to maximize the effectiveness of inspection and maintenance programs as they relate to promoting effective control of vehicle emissions at high-altitude elevations. Preference shall be given to existing vehicle emissions testing and research centers that have established reputations for vehicle emissions research and development and training, and that possess in-house Federal Test Procedure capacity.

(July 14, 1955, c. 360, Title II, § 215, as added Aug. 7, 1977, Pub.L. 95–95, Title II, § 211(b), 91 Stat. 757, and amended Nov. 16, 1977, Pub.L. 95–190, § 14(a)(75), 91 Stat. 1404; Nov. 15, 1990, Pub.L. 101–549, Title II, § 224, 104 Stat. 2503; Dec. 18, 1991, Pub.L. 102–240, Title III, § 3004(b), 105 Stat. 2088.)

## HISTORICAL AND STATUTORY NOTES

**Codifications**

In subsec. (d), "August 7, 1977" was substituted for "the date of enactment of this Act" to reflect the probable intent of Congress that such date of enactment meant the date of enactment of Pub.L. 95–95.

**Effective and Applicability Provisions**

1990 Acts

Amendment by Pub.L. 101–549 effective Nov. 15, 1990, except as otherwise provided, see section 711(b) of Pub.L. 101–549, set out as a note under section 7401 of this title.

1977 Acts

Section effective Aug. 7, 1977, except as otherwise expressly provided, see section 406(d) of Pub.L. 95–95, set out as a note under section 7401 of this title.

**Change of Name**

Any reference in a law, map, regulation, document, paper, or other record of the United States to the Urban Mass Transportation Administration deemed a reference to the Federal Transit Administration, see section 3004(b) of Pub.L. 102–240, set out as a note under section 107 of Title 49, Transportation.

**Savings Provisions**

Suits, actions or proceedings commenced under this chapter as in effect prior to Nov. 15, 1990, not to abate by reason of the taking effect of amendments by Pub.L. 101–549, except as otherwise provided for, see section 711(a) of Pub.L. 101–549, set out as a note under section 7401 of this title.

## § 7550. Definitions

**[CAA § 216]**

As used in this part—

(1) The term "manufacturer" as used in sections 7521, 7522, 7525, 7541, and 7542 of this title means any person engaged in the manufacturing or assembling of new motor vehicles, new motor vehicle engines, new nonroad vehicles or new nonroad engines, or importing such vehicles or engines for resale, or who acts for and is under the control of any such person in connection with the distribution of new motor vehicles, new motor vehicle engines, new nonroad vehicles or new nonroad engines, but shall not include any dealer with respect to new motor vehicles, new motor vehicle engines, new nonroad vehicles or new nonroad engines received by him in commerce.

(2) The term "motor vehicle" means any self-propelled vehicle designed for transporting persons or property on a street or highway.

(3) Except with respect to vehicles or engines imported or offered for importation, the term "new motor vehicle" means a motor vehicle the equitable or legal title to which has never been transferred to an ultimate purchaser; and the term "new motor vehicle engine" means an engine in a new motor vehicle or a motor vehicle engine the equitable or legal title to which has never been transferred to the ultimate purchaser; and with respect to imported vehicles or engines, such terms mean a motor vehicle and engine, respectively, manufactured after the effective date of a regulation issued under section 7521 of this title which is applicable to such vehicle or engine (or which would be applicable to such vehicle or engine had it been manufactured for importation into the United States).

(4) The term "dealer" means any person who is engaged in the sale or the distribution of new motor vehicles or new motor vehicle engines to the ultimate purchaser.

(5) The term "ultimate purchaser" means, with respect to any new motor vehicle or new motor

vehicle engine, the first person who in good faith purchases such new motor vehicle or new engine for purposes other than resale.

(6) The term "commerce" means (A) commerce between any place in any State and any place outside thereof; and (B) commerce wholly within the District of Columbia.

**(7) Vehicle curb weight, gross vehicle weight rating, light-duty truck, light-duty vehicle, and loaded vehicle weight**

The terms "vehicle curb weight", "gross vehicle weight rating" (GVWR), "light-duty truck" (LDT), light-duty vehicle,[1] and "loaded vehicle weight" (LVW) have the meaning provided in regulations promulgated by the Administrator and in effect as of November 15, 1990. The abbreviations in parentheses corresponding to any term referred to in this paragraph shall have the same meaning as the corresponding term.

**(8) Test weight**

The term "test weight" and the abbreviation "tw" mean the vehicle curb weight added to the gross vehicle weight rating (gvwr) and divided by 2.

**(9) Motor vehicle or engine part manufacturer**

The term "motor vehicle or engine part manufacturer" as used in sections 7541 and 7542 of this title means any person engaged in the manufacturing, assembling or rebuilding of any device, system, part, component or element of design which is installed in or on motor vehicles or motor vehicle engines.

**(10) Nonroad engine**

The term "nonroad engine" means an internal combustion engine (including the fuel system) that is not used in a motor vehicle or a vehicle used solely for competition, or that is not subject to standards promulgated under section 7411 of this title or section 7521 of this title.

**(11) Nonroad vehicle**

The term "nonroad vehicle" means a vehicle that is powered by a nonroad engine and that is not a motor vehicle or a vehicle used solely for competition.

(July 14, 1955, c. 360, Title II, § 216, formerly § 208, as added Oct. 20, 1965, Pub.L. 89–272, Title I, § 101(8), 79 Stat. 994, renumbered § 212, and amended Nov. 21, 1967, Pub.L. 90–148, § 2, 81 Stat. 503, renumbered § 213, and amended Dec. 31, 1970, Pub.L. 91–604, §§ 8(a), 10(d), 11(a)(2)(A), 84 Stat. 1694, 1703, 1705, renumbered § 214, June 22, 1974, Pub.L. 93–319, § 10, 88 Stat. 261, renumbered § 216, Aug. 7, 1977, Pub.L. 95–95, Title II, § 224(d), 91 Stat. 767; Nov. 15, 1990, Pub.L. 101–549, Title II, § 223, 104 Stat. 2503.)

[1] So in original. Probably should be set off by quotation marks.

### HISTORICAL AND STATUTORY NOTES

**Codifications**

Section was formerly classified to section 1857f–7 of this title.

**Effective and Applicability Provisions**

1990 Acts

Amendment by Pub.L. 101–549 effective Nov. 15, 1990, except as otherwise provided, see section 711(b) of Pub.L. 101–549, set out as a note under section 7401 of this title.

**Savings Provisions**

Suits, actions or proceedings commenced under this chapter as in effect prior to Nov. 15, 1990, not to abate by reason of the taking effect of amendments by Pub.L. 101–549, except as otherwise provided for, see section 711(a) of Pub.L. 101–549, set out as a note under section 7401 of this title.

## § 7551. Omitted

### HISTORICAL AND STATUTORY NOTES

**Codifications**

Section, Pub.L. 95–95, Title II, § 203, Aug. 7, 1977, 91 Stat. 754; Pub.L. 97–375, Title I, § 106(a), Dec. 21, 1982, 96 Stat. 1820, which required the Administrator of the Environmental Protection Agency to report to Congress respecting the motor vehicle fuel consumption associated with the standards applicable for the immediately preceding model year, terminated, effective May 15, 2000, pursuant to Pub.L. 104–66, § 3003, as amended, set out as a note under 31 U.S.C.A. § 1113. See, also, the 5th item on page 165 of House Document No. 103–7.

Section was enacted as part of the Clean Air Act Amendments of 1977, and not as part of the Clean Air Act, which comprises this chapter.

## § 7552. Motor vehicle compliance program fees

[CAA § 217]

**(a) Fee collection**

Consistent with section 9701 of Title 31, the Administrator may promulgate (and from time to time revise) regulations establishing fees to recover all reasonable costs to the Administrator associated with—

(1) new vehicle or engine certification under section 7525(a) of this title or part C of this subchapter,

(2) new vehicle or engine compliance monitoring and testing under section 7525(b) of this title or part C of this subchapter, and

(3) in-use vehicle or engine compliance monitoring and testing under section 7541(c) of this title or part C of this subchapter.

The Administrator may establish for all foreign and domestic manufacturers a fee schedule based on such factors as the Administrator finds appropriate and equitable and nondiscriminatory, including the number of vehicles or engines produced under a certificate of conformity. In the case of heavy-duty engine and vehicle manufacturers, such fees shall not exceed a reasonable amount to recover an appropriate portion of such reasonable costs.

**(b) Special Treasury fund**

Any fees collected under this section shall be deposited in a special fund in the United States Treasury for licensing and other services which thereafter shall be available for appropriation, to remain available until expended, to carry out the Agency's activities for which the fees were collected.

**(c) Limitation on fund use**

Moneys in the special fund referred to in subsection (b) of this section shall not be used until after the first fiscal year commencing after the first July 1 when fees are paid into the fund.

**(d) Administrator's testing authority**

Nothing in this subsection shall be construed to limit the Administrator's authority to require manufacturer or confirmatory testing as provided in this part.

(July 14, 1955, c. 360, Title II, § 217, as added Nov. 15, 1990, Pub.L. 101–549, Title II, § 225, 104 Stat. 2504.)

### HISTORICAL AND STATUTORY NOTES

**Effective and Applicability Provisions**

1990 Acts

Section effective Nov. 15, 1990, except as otherwise provided, see section 711(b) of Pub.L. 101–549, set out as a note under section 7401 of this title.

**Savings Provisions**

Suits, actions or proceedings commenced under this chapter as in effect prior to Nov. 15, 1990, not to abate by reason of the taking effect of amendments by Pub.L. 101–549, except as otherwise provided for, see section 711(a) of Pub.L. 101–549, set out as a note under section 7401 of this title.

## § 7553. Prohibition on production of engines requiring leaded gasoline

[CAA § 218]

The Administrator shall promulgate regulations applicable to motor vehicle engines and nonroad engines manufactured after model year 1992 that prohibit the manufacture, sale, or introduction into commerce of any engine that requires leaded gasoline.

(July 14, 1955, c. 360, Title II, § 218, as added Nov. 15, 1990, Pub.L. 101–549, Title II, § 226, 104 Stat. 2505.)

### HISTORICAL AND STATUTORY NOTES

**Effective and Applicability Provisions**

1990 Acts

Section effective Nov. 15, 1990, except as otherwise provided, see section 711(b) of Pub.L. 101–549, set out as a note under section 7401 of this title.

**Savings Provisions**

Suits, actions or proceedings commenced under this chapter as in effect prior to Nov. 15, 1990, not to abate by reason of the taking effect of amendments by Pub.L. 101–549, except as otherwise provided for, see section 711(a) of Pub.L. 101–549, set out as a note under section 7401 of this title.

## § 7554. Urban bus standards

[CAA § 219]

**(a) Standards for model years after 1993**

Not later than January 1, 1992, the Administrator shall promulgate regulations under section 7521(a) of this title applicable to urban buses for the model year 1994 and thereafter. Such standards shall be based on the best technology that can reasonably be anticipated to be available at the time such measures are to be implemented, taking costs, safety, energy, lead time, and other relevant factors into account. Such regulations shall require that such urban buses comply with the provisions of subsection (b) of this section (and subsection (c) of this subsection,[1] if applicable) in addition to compliance with the standards applicable under section 7521(a) of this title for heavy-duty vehicles of the same type and model year.

**(b) PM standard**

**(1) 50 percent reduction**

The standards under section 7521(a) of this title applicable to urban buses shall require that, effective for the model year 1994 and thereafter, emissions of particulate matter (PM) from urban buses shall not exceed 50 percent of the emissions of particulate matter (PM) allowed under the emission standard applicable under section 7521(a) of this title as of November 15, 1990, for particulate matter (PM) in the case of heavy-duty diesel vehicles and engines manufactured in the model year 1994.

**(2) Revised reduction**

The Administrator shall increase the level of emissions of particulate matter allowed under the standard referred to in paragraph (1) if the Administrator determines that the 50 percent reduction referred to in paragraph (1) is not technologically achievable, taking into account durability, costs, lead time, safety, and other relevant factors. The Administrator may not increase such level of emissions above 70 percent of the emissions of particulate matter (PM) allowed under the emission standard applicable under section 7521(a) of this title as of November 15, 1990, for particulate matter (PM) in the case of heavy-duty diesel vehicles and engines manufactured in the model year 1994.

**(3) Determination as part of rule**

As part of the rulemaking under subsection (a) of this section, the Administrator shall make a determination as to whether the 50 percent reduction referred to in paragraph (1) is technologically achievable, taking into account durability, costs, lead time, safety, and other relevant factors.

**(c) Low-polluting fuel requirement**

**(1) Annual testing**

Beginning with model year 1994 buses, the Administrator shall conduct annual tests of a representative sample of operating urban buses subject to the particulate matter (PM) standard applicable pursuant to subsection (b) of this section to determine whether such buses comply with such standard in use over their full useful life.

**(2) Promulgation of additional low-polluting fuel requirement**

(A) If the Administrator determines, based on the testing under paragraph (1), that urban buses subject to the particulate matter (PM) standard applicable pursuant to subsection (b) of this section do not comply with such standard in use over their full useful life, he shall revise the standards applicable to such buses to require (in addition to compliance with the PM standard applicable pursuant to subsection (b) of this section) that all new urban buses purchased or placed into service by owners or operators of urban buses in all metropolitan statistical areas or consolidated metropolitan statistical areas with a 1980 population of 750,000 or more shall be capable of operating, and shall be exclusively operated, on low-polluting fuels. The Administrator shall establish the pass-fail rate for purposes of testing under this subparagraph.

(B) The Administrator shall promulgate a schedule phasing in any low-polluting fuel requirement established pursuant to this paragraph to an increasing percentage of new urban buses purchased or placed into service in each of the first 5 model years commencing 3 years after the determination under subparagraph (A). Under such schedule 100 percent of new urban buses placed into service in the fifth model year commencing 3 years after the determination under subparagraph (A) shall comply with the low-polluting fuel requirement established pursuant to this paragraph.

(C) The Administrator may extend the requirements of this paragraph to metropolitan statistical areas or consolidated metropolitan statistical areas with a 1980 population of less than 750,000, if the Administrator determines that a significant benefit to public health could be expected to result from such extension.

**(d) Retrofit requirements**

Not later than 12 months after November 15, 1990, the Administrator shall promulgate regulations under section 7521(a) of this title requiring that urban buses which—

(1) are operating in areas referred to in subparagraph (A) of subsection (c)(2) of this section (or subparagraph (C) of subsection (c)(2) of this section if the Administrator has taken action under that subparagraph);

(2) were not subject to standards in effect under the regulations under subsection (a) of this section; and

(3) have their engines replaced or rebuilt after January 1, 1995,

shall comply with an emissions standard or emissions control technology requirement established by the Administrator in such regulations. Such emissions standard or emissions control technology requirement shall reflect the best retrofit technology and maintenance practices reasonably achievable.

**(e) Procedures for administration and enforcement**

The Administrator shall establish, within 18 months after November 15, 1990, and in accordance with section 7525(h) of this title, procedures for the administration and enforcement of standards for buses subject to standards under this section, testing procedures, sampling protocols, in-use compliance requirements, and criteria governing evaluation of buses. Procedures for testing (including, but not limited to, certification testing) shall reflect actual operating conditions.

**(f) Definitions**

For purposes of this section—

**(1) Urban bus**

The term "urban bus" has the meaning provided under regulations of the Administrator promulgated under section 7521(a) of this title.

**(2) Low-polluting fuel**

The term "low-polluting fuel" means methanol, ethanol, propane, or natural gas, or any comparably low-polluting fuel. In determining whether a fuel is comparably low-polluting, the Administrator shall consider both the level of emissions of air pollutants from vehicles using the fuel and the contribution of such emissions to ambient levels of air pollutants. For purposes of this paragraph, the term "methanol" includes any fuel which contains at least 85 percent methanol unless the Administrator increases such percentage as he deems appropriate to protect public health and welfare.

(July 14, 1955, c. 360, Title II, § 219, as added Nov. 15, 1990, Pub.L. 101–549, Title II, § 227[(a)], 104 Stat. 2505.)

[1] So in original. Probably should be "section,".

HISTORICAL AND STATUTORY NOTES

**Effective and Applicability Provisions**

1990 Acts

Section effective Nov. 15, 1990, except as otherwise provided, see section 711(b) of Pub.L. 101–549, set out as a note under section 7401 of this title.

**Savings Provisions**

Suits, actions or proceedings commenced under this chapter as in effect prior to Nov. 15, 1990, not to abate by reason of the taking effect of amendments by Pub.L. 101–549, except as otherwise provided for, see section 711(a) of Pub.L. 101–549, set out as a note under section 7401 of this title.

PART B—AIRCRAFT EMISSION STANDARDS

## § 7571. Establishment of standards

[CAA § 231]

### (a) Study; proposed standards; hearings; issuance of regulations

(1) Within 90 days after December 31, 1970, the Administrator shall commence a study and investigation of emissions of air pollutants from aircraft in order to determine—

(A) the extent to which such emissions affect air quality in air quality control regions throughout the United States, and

(B) the technological feasibility of controlling such emissions.

(2)(A) The Administrator shall, from time to time, issue proposed emission standards applicable to the emission of any air pollutant from any class or classes of aircraft engines which in his judgment causes, or contributes to, air pollution which may reasonably be anticipated to endanger public health or welfare.

(B)(i) The Administrator shall consult with the Administrator of the Federal Aviation Administration on aircraft engine emission standards.

(ii) The Administrator shall not change the aircraft engine emission standards if such change would significantly increase noise and adversely affect safety.

(3) The Administrator shall hold public hearings with respect to such proposed standards. Such hearings shall, to the extent practicable, be held in air quality control regions which are most seriously affected by aircraft emissions. Within 90 days after the issuance of such proposed regulations, he shall issue such regulations with such modifications as he deems appropriate. Such regulations may be revised from time to time.

### (b) Effective date of regulations

Any regulation prescribed under this section (and any revision thereof) shall take effect after such period as the Administrator finds necessary (after consultation with the Secretary of Transportation) to permit the development and application of the requisite technology, giving appropriate consideration to the cost of compliance within such period.

### (c) Regulations which create hazards to aircraft safety

Any regulations in effect under this section on August 7, 1977, or proposed or promulgated thereafter, or amendments thereto, with respect to aircraft shall not apply if disapproved by the President, after notice and opportunity for public hearing, on the basis of a finding by the Secretary of Transportation that any such regulation would create a hazard to aircraft safety. Any such finding shall include a reasonably specific statement of the basis upon which the finding was made.

(July 14, 1955, c. 360, Title II, § 231, as added Dec. 31, 1970, Pub.L. 91–604, § 11(a)(1), 84 Stat. 1703, and amended Aug. 7, 1977, Pub.L. 95–95, Title II, § 225, Title IV, § 401(f), 91 Stat. 769, 791; Oct. 9, 1996, Pub.L. 104–264, Title IV, § 406(b), 110 Stat. 3257.)

HISTORICAL AND STATUTORY NOTES

**Codifications**

Section was formerly classified to section 1857f–9 of this title.

**Effective and Applicability Provisions**

1977 Acts

Amendment by Pub.L. 95–95 effective Aug. 7, 1977, except as otherwise expressly provided, see section 406(d) of Pub.L. 95–95, set out as a note under section 7401 of this title.

**Applicability of Pub.L. 104–264**

Except as otherwise specifically provided, Pub.L. 104–264 and the amendments made by Pub.L. 104–264 applicable only to fiscal years beginning after Sept. 30, 1996, and not to be construed as affecting funds made available for a fiscal year ending before Oct. 1, 1996, see section 3 of Pub.L. 104–264, set out as a note under section 106 of Title 49, Transportation.

**Modification or Rescission of Rules, Regulations, Orders, Determinations, Contracts, Certifications, Authorizations, Delegations, and Other Actions**

All rules, regulations, orders, determinations, contracts, certifications, authorizations, delegations, or other actions duly issued, made, or taken by or pursuant to Act July 14, 1955, the Clean Air Act, as in effect immediately prior to the date of enactment of Pub.L. 95–95 [Aug. 7, 1977] to continue in full force and effect until modified or rescinded in accordance with Act July 14, 1955, as amended by Pub.L. 95–95 [this chapter], see section 406(b) of Pub.L. 95–95, set out as an Effective Date of 1977 Acts note under section 7401 of this title.

**Study And Investigation Of Uninstalled Aircraft Engines**

Pub.L. 101–549, Title II, § 233, Nov. 15, 1990, 104 Stat. 2529, provided that:

"(a) **Study.**—The Administrator of the Environmental Protection Agency and the Secretary of Transportation, in consultation with the Secretary of Defense, shall commence a study and investigation of the testing of uninstalled aircraft engines in enclosed test cells that shall address at a minimum the following issues and such other issues as they shall deem appropriate—

"(1) whether technologies exist to control some or all emissions of oxides of nitrogen from test cells;

"(2) the effectiveness of such technologies;

"(3) the cost of implementing such technologies;

"(4) whether such technologies affect the safety, design, structure, operation, or performance of aircraft engines;

"(5) whether such technologies impair the effectiveness and accuracy of aircraft engine safety design, and performance tests conducted in test cells; and

"(6) the impact of not controlling such oxides of nitrogen in the applicable nonattainment areas and on other sources, stationary and mobile, on oxides of nitrogen in such areas.

"**(b) Report, authority to regulate.**—Not later than 24 months after enactment of the Clean Air Act Amendments of 1990 [probably means the date of enactment of the Clean Air Act Amendments of 1990, Pub.L. 101–549, which was approved Nov. 15, 1990], the Administrator of the Environmental Protection Agency and the Secretary of Transportation shall submit to Congress a report of the study conducted under this section. Following the completion of such study, any of the States may adopt or enforce any standard for emissions of oxides of nitrogen from test cells only after issuing a public notice stating whether such standards are in accordance with the findings of the study."

## § 7572. Enforcement of standards

**[CAA § 232]**

### (a) Regulations to insure compliance with standards

The Secretary of Transportation, after consultation with the Administrator, shall prescribe regulations to insure compliance with all standards prescribed under section 7571 of this title by the Administrator. The regulations of the Secretary of Transportation shall include provisions making such standards applicable in the issuance, amendment, modification, suspension, or revocation of any certificate authorized by part A of subtitle VII of Title 49 or the Department of Transportation Act. Such Secretary shall insure that all necessary inspections are accomplished, and,[1] may execute any power or duty vested in him by any other provision of law in the execution of all powers and duties vested in him under this section.

### (b) Notice and appeal rights

In any action to amend, modify, suspend, or revoke a certificate in which violation of an emission standard prescribed under section 7571 of this title or of a regulation prescribed under subsection (a) of this section is at issue, the certificate holder shall have the same notice and appeal rights as are prescribed for such holders in the part A of subtitle VII of Title 49 or the Department of Transportation Act, except that in any appeal to the National Transportation Safety Board, the Board may amend, modify, or revoke the order of the Secretary of Transportation only if it finds no violation of such standard or regulation and that such amendment, modification, or revocation is consistent with safety in air transportation.

(July 14, 1955, c. 360, Title II, § 232, as added Dec. 31, 1970, Pub.L. 91–604, § 11(a)(1), 84 Stat. 1704.)

[1] So in original. The comma probably should not appear.

#### HISTORICAL AND STATUTORY NOTES

**References in Text**

The Department of Transportation Act, referred to in subsecs. (a) and (b), is Pub.L. 89–670, Oct. 15, 1966, 80 Stat. 931, as amended, which was classified principally to sections 1651 to 1660 of former Title 49, Transportation. The Act was repealed and the provisions thereof reenacted in Title 49, by Pub.L. 103–272, July 5, 1994, 108 Stat. 745. The Act was also repealed by Pub.L. 104–287, § 7(5), Oct. 11, 1996, 110 Stat. 3400. For Disposition of section of former Title 49, see Table at the beginning of Title 49.

The Federal Aviation Act of 1958, referred to in subsec. (b), was Pub.L. 85–726, Aug. 23, 1958, 72 Stat. 731. For classification see note relating to 'Federal Aviation Act', set out under this section.

**Codifications**

Section was formerly classified to section 1857f–10 of this title.

In subsecs. (a) and (b), "part A of subtitle VII of Title 49" substituted for "the Federal Aviation Act [49 App. U.S.C.A. § 1301 et seq.]" and "the Federal Aviation Act of 1958 [49 App. U.S.C.A. § 1301 et seq.]" on authority of Pub.L. 103–272, § 6(b), July 5, 1994, 108 Stat. 1378, the first section of which enacted subtitles II, III, and V to X of Title 49.

## § 7573. State standards and controls

**[CAA § 233]**

No State or political subdivision thereof may adopt or attempt to enforce any standard respecting emissions of any air pollutant from any aircraft or engine thereof unless such standard is identical to a standard applicable to such aircraft under this part.

(July 14, 1955, c. 360, Title II, § 233, as added Dec. 31, 1970, Pub.L. 91–604, § 11(a)(1), 84 Stat. 1704.)

#### HISTORICAL AND STATUTORY NOTES

**Codifications**

Section was formerly classified to section 1857f–11 of this title.

## § 7574. Definitions

**[CAA § 234]**

Terms used in this part (other than Administrator) shall have the same meaning as such terms have under section 40102(a) of Title 49.

(July 14, 1955, c. 360, Title II, § 234, as added Dec. 31, 1970, Pub.L. 91–604, § 11(a)(1), 84 Stat. 1705.)

HISTORICAL AND STATUTORY NOTES

**Codifications**

Section was formerly classified to section 1857f–12 of this title.

In text, "section 40102(a) of Title 49" substituted for "section 101 of the Federal Aviation Act of 1958" on authority of Pub.L. 103–272, § 6(b), July 5, 1994, 108 Stat. 1378, the first section of which enacted subtitles II, III, and V to X of Title 49.

PART C—CLEAN FUEL VEHICLES

## § 7581. Definitions

[CAA § 241]

For purposes of this part—

**(1) Terms defined in part A**

The definitions applicable to part A under section 7550 of this title shall also apply for purposes of this part.

**(2) Clean alternative fuel**

The term "clean alternative fuel" means any fuel (including methanol, ethanol, or other alcohols (including any mixture thereof containing 85 percent or more by volume of such alcohol with gasoline or other fuels), reformulated gasoline, diesel, natural gas, liquefied petroleum gas, and hydrogen) or power source (including electricity) used in a clean-fuel vehicle that complies with the standards and requirements applicable to such vehicle under this subchapter when using such fuel or power source. In the case of any flexible fuel vehicle or dual fuel vehicle, the term "clean alternative fuel" means only a fuel with respect to which such vehicle was certified as a clean-fuel vehicle meeting the standards applicable to clean-fuel vehicles under section 7583(d)(2) of this title when operating on clean alternative fuel (or any CARB standards which replaces such standards pursuant to section 7583(e) of this title).

**(3) NMOG**

The term nonmethane organic gas ("NMOG") means the sum of nonoxygenated and oxygenated hydrocarbons contained in a gas sample, including, at a minimum, all oxygenated organic gases containing 5 or fewer carbon atoms (i.e., aldehydes, ketones, alcohols, ethers, etc.), and all known alkanes, alkenes, alkynes, and aromatics containing 12 or fewer carbon atoms. To demonstrate compliance with a NMOG standard, NMOG emissions shall be measured in accordance with the "California Non–Methane Organic Gas Test Procedures". In the case of vehicles using fuels other than base gasoline, the level of NMOG emissions shall be adjusted based on the reactivity of the emissions relative to vehicles using base gasoline.

**(4) Base gasoline**

The term "base gasoline" means gasoline which meets the following specifications:

| Specifications of Base Gasoline Used as Basis for Reactivity Readjustment: | |
|---|---|
| API gravity | 57.8 |
| Sulfur, ppm | 317 |
| Color | Purple |
| Benzene, vol. % | 1.35 |
| Reid vapor pressure | 8.7 |
| Drivability | 1195 |
| Antiknock index | 87.3 |
| Distillation, D–86° F | |
| IBP | 92 |
| 10% | 126 |
| 50% | 219 |
| 90% | 327 |
| EP | 414 |
| Hydrocarbon Type, Vol. % FIA: | |
| Aromatics | 30.9 |
| Olefins | 8.2 |
| Saturates | 60.9 |

The Administrator shall modify the definitions of NMOG, base gasoline, and the methods for making reactivity adjustments, to conform to the definitions and method used in California under the Low–Emission Vehicle and Clean Fuel Regulations of the California Air Resources Board, so long as the California definitions are, in the aggregate, at least as protective of public health and welfare as the definitions in this section.

**(5) Covered fleet**

The term "covered fleet" means 10 or more motor vehicles which are owned or operated by a single person. In determining the number of vehicles owned or operated by a single person for purposes of this paragraph, all motor vehicles owned or operated, leased or otherwise controlled by such person, by any person who controls such person, by any person controlled by such person, and by any person under common control with such person shall be treated as owned by such person. The term "covered fleet" shall not include motor vehicles held for lease or rental to the general public, motor vehicles held for sale by motor vehicle dealers (including demonstration vehicles), motor vehicles used for motor vehicle manufacturer product evaluations or tests, law enforcement and other emergency vehicles, or nonroad vehicles (including farm and construction vehicles).

**(6) Covered fleet vehicle**

The term "covered fleet vehicle" means only a motor vehicle which is—

(i) in a vehicle class for which standards are applicable under this part; and

(ii) in a covered fleet which is centrally fueled (or capable of being centrally fueled).

No vehicle which under normal operations is garaged at a personal residence at night shall be considered to be a vehicle which is capable of being centrally fueled within the meaning of this paragraph.

**(7) Clean-fuel vehicle**

The term "clean-fuel vehicle" means a vehicle in a class or category of vehicles which has been certified to meet for any model year the clean-fuel vehicle standards applicable under this part for that model year to clean-fuel vehicles in that class or category.

(July 14, 1955, c. 360, Title II, § 241, as added Nov. 15, 1990, Pub.L. 101–549, Title II, § 229(a), 104 Stat. 2511.)

### HISTORICAL AND STATUTORY NOTES

**Effective and Applicability Provisions**

1990 Acts

Section effective Nov. 15, 1990, except as otherwise provided, see section 711(b) of Pub.L. 101–549, set out as a note under section 7401 of this title.

**Savings Provisions**

Suits, actions or proceedings commenced under this chapter as in effect prior to Nov. 15, 1990, not to abate by reason of the taking effect of amendments by Pub.L. 101–549, except as otherwise provided for, see section 711(a) of Pub.L. 101–549, set out as a note under section 7401 of this title.

## § 7582. Requirements applicable to clean-fuel vehicles

[CAA § 242]

**(a) Promulgation of standards**

Not later than 24 months after November 15, 1990, the Administrator shall promulgate regulations under this part containing clean-fuel vehicle standards for the clean-fuel vehicles specified in this part.

**(b) Other requirements**

Clean-fuel vehicles of up to 8,500 gvwr subject to standards set forth in this part shall comply with all motor vehicle requirements of this subchapter (such as requirements relating to on-board diagnostics, evaporative emissions, etc.) which are applicable to conventional gasoline-fueled vehicles of the same category and model year, except as provided in section 7584 of this title with respect to administration and enforcement, and except to the extent that any such requirement is in conflict with the provisions of this part. Clean-fuel vehicles of 8,500 gvwr or greater subject to standards set forth in this part shall comply with all requirements of this subchapter which are applicable in the case of conventional gasoline-fueled or diesel fueled vehicles of the same category and model year, except as provided in section 7584 of this title with respect to administration and enforcement, and except to the extent that any such requirement is in conflict with the provisions of this part.

**(c) In-use useful life and testing**

(1) In the case of light-duty vehicles and light-duty trucks up to 6,000 lbs gvwr, the useful life for purposes of determining in-use compliance with the standards under section 7583 of this title shall be—

(A) a period of 5 years or 50,000 miles (or the equivalent) whichever first occurs, in the case of standards applicable for purposes of certification at 50,000 miles; and

(B) a period of 10 years or 100,000 miles (or the equivalent) whichever first occurs, in the case of standards applicable for purposes of certification at 100,000 miles, except that in-use testing shall not be done for a period beyond 7 years or 75,000 miles (or the equivalent) whichever first occurs.

(2) In the case of light-duty trucks of more than 6,000 lbs gvwr, the useful life for purposes of determining in-use compliance with the standards under section 7583 of this title shall be—

(A) a period of 5 years or 50,000 miles (or the equivalent) whichever first occurs in the case of standards applicable for purposes of certification at 50,000 miles; and

(B) a period of 11 years or 120,000 miles (or the equivalent) whichever first occurs in the case of standards applicable for purposes of certification at 120,000 miles, except that in-use testing shall not be done for a period beyond 7 years or 90,000 miles (or the equivalent) whichever first occurs.

(July 14, 1955, c. 360, Title II, § 242, as added Nov. 15, 1990, Pub.L. 101–549, Title II, § 229(a), 104 Stat. 2513.)

### HISTORICAL AND STATUTORY NOTES

**Effective and Applicability Provisions**

1990 Acts

Section effective Nov. 15, 1990, except as otherwise provided, see section 711(b) of Pub.L. 101–549, set out as a note under section 7401 of this title.

**Savings Provisions**

Suits, actions or proceedings commenced under this chapter as in effect prior to Nov. 15, 1990, not to abate by reason of the taking effect of amendments by Pub.L. 101–549, except as otherwise provided for, see section 711(a) of Pub.L. 101–549, set out as a note under section 7401 of this title.

## § 7583. Standards for light-duty clean-fuel vehicles

[CAA § 243]

### (a) Exhaust standards for light-duty vehicles and certain light-duty trucks

The standards set forth in this subsection shall apply in the case of clean-fuel vehicles which are light-duty trucks of up to 6,000 lbs. gross vehicle weight rating (gvwr) (but not including light-duty trucks of more than 3,750 lbs. loaded vehicle weight (lvw)) or light-duty vehicles:

#### (1) Phase I

Beginning with model year 1996, for the air pollutants specified in the following table, the clean-fuel vehicle standards under this section shall provide that vehicle exhaust emissions shall not exceed the levels specified in the following table:

PHASE I CLEAN FUEL VEHICLE EMISSION STANDARDS FOR LIGHT-DUTY TRUCKS OF UP TO 3,750 LBS. LVW AND UP TO 6,000 LBS. GVWR AND LIGHT-DUTY VEHICLES

| Pollutant | NMOG | CO | $NO_x$ | PM | HCHO (formaldehyde) |
|---|---|---|---|---|---|
| 50,000 mile standard............. | 0.125 | 3.4 | 0.4 | .... | 0.015 |
| 100,000 mile standard........... | 0.156 | 4.2 | 0.6 | 0.08* | 0.018 |

Standards are expressed in grams per mile (gpm).
* Standards for particulates (PM) shall apply only to diesel-fueled vehicles.
In the case of the 50,000 mile standards and the 100,000 mile standards, for purposes of certification, the applicable useful life shall be 50,000 miles or 100,000 miles, respectively.

#### (2) Phase II

Beginning with model year 2001, for air pollutants specified in the following table, the clean-fuel vehicle standards under this section shall provide that vehicle exhaust emissions shall not exceed the levels specified in the following table.

PHASE II CLEAN FUEL VEHICLE EMISSION STANDARDS FOR LIGHT-DUTY TRUCKS OF UP TO 3,750 LBS. LVW AND UP TO 6,000 LBS. GVWR AND LIGHT-DUTY VEHICLES

| Pollutant | NMOG | CO | $NO_x$ | PM* | HCHO (formaldehyde) |
|---|---|---|---|---|---|
| 50,000 mile standard............. | 0.075 | 3.4 | 0.2 | .... | 0.015 |
| 100,000 mile standard........... | 0.090 | 4.2 | 0.3 | 0.08 | 0.018 |

Standards are expressed in grams per mile (gpm).
* Standards for particulates (PM) shall apply only to diesel-fueled vehicles.
In the case of the 50,000 mile standards and the 100,000 mile standards, for purposes of certification, the applicable useful life shall be 50,000 miles or 100,000 miles, respectively.

### (b) Exhaust standards for light-duty trucks of more than 3,750 lbs. LVW and up to 5,750 lbs. LVW and up to 6,000 lbs. GVWR

The standards set forth in this paragraph shall apply in the case of clean-fuel vehicles which are light-duty trucks of more than 3,750 lbs. loaded vehicle weight (lvw) but not more than 5,750 lbs. lvw and not more than 6,000 lbs. gross weight rating (GVWR):

#### (1) Phase I

Beginning with model year 1996, for the air pollutants specified in the following table, the clean-fuel vehicle standards under this section shall provide that vehicle exhaust emissions shall not exceed the levels specified in the following table.

PHASE I CLEAN FUEL VEHICLE EMISSION STANDARDS FOR LIGHT-DUTY TRUCKS OF MORE THAN 3,750 LBS. AND UP TO 5,750 LBS. LVW AND UP TO 6,000 LBS. GVWR

| Pollutant | NMOG | CO | $NO_x$ | PM* | HCHO (formaldehyde) |
|---|---|---|---|---|---|
| 50,000 mile standard............. | 0.160 | 4.4 | 0.7 | .... | 0.018 |
| 100,000 mile standard........... | 0.200 | 5.5 | 0.9 | 0.08 | 0.023 |

Standards are expressed in grams per mile (gpm).
* Standards for particulates (PM) shall apply only to diesel-fueled vehicles.
In the case of the 50,000 mile standards and the 100,000 mile standards, for purposes of certification, the applicable useful life shall be 50,000 miles or 100,000 miles, respectively.

(2) **Phase II**

Beginning with model year 2001, for the air pollutants specified in the following table, the clean-fuel vehicle standards under this section shall provide that vehicle exhaust emissions shall not exceed the levels specified in the following table.

PHASE II CLEAN FUEL VEHICLE EMISSION STANDARDS FOR LIGHT-DUTY TRUCKS OF MORE THAN 3,750 LBS. LVW AND UP TO 5,750 LBS. LVW AND UP TO 6,000 LBS. GVWR

| Pollutant | NMOG | CO | $NO_x$ | PM* | HCHO (formaldehyde) |
|---|---|---|---|---|---|
| 50,000 mile standard | 0.100 | 4.4 | 0.4 | .... | 0.018 |
| 100,000 mile standard | 0.130 | 5.5 | 0.5 | 0.08 | 0.023 |

Standards are expressed in grams per mile (gpm).
* Standards for particulates (PM) shall apply only to diesel-fueled vehicles.
In the case of the 50,000 mile standards and the 100,000 mile standards, for purposes of certification, the applicable useful life shall be 50,000 miles or 100,000 miles, respectively.

(c) **Exhaust standards for light-duty trucks greater than 6,000 lbs. GVWR**

The standards set forth in this subsection shall apply in the case of clean-fuel vehicles which are light-duty trucks of more than 6,000 lbs. gross weight rating (GVWR) and less than or equal to 8,500 lbs. GVWR, beginning with model year 1998. For the air pollutants specified in the following table, the clean-fuel vehicle standards under this section shall provide that vehicle exhaust emissions of vehicles within the test weight categories specified in the following table shall not exceed the levels specified in such table.

CLEAN FUEL VEHICLE EMISSION STANDARDS FOR LIGHT DUTY TRUCKS GREATER THAN 6,000 LBS. GVWR

Test Weight Category: Up to 3,750 lbs. tw

| Pollutant | NMOG | CO | $NO_x$ | PM* | HCHO (formaldehyde) |
|---|---|---|---|---|---|
| 50,000 mile standard | 0.125 | 3.4 | 0.4** | .... | 0.015 |
| 120,000 mile standard | 0.180 | 5.0 | 0.6 | 0.08 | 0.022 |

Test Weight Category: Above 3,750 but not above 5,750 lbs. tw

| Pollutant | NMOG | CO | $NO_x$ | PM* | HCHO (formaldehyde) |
|---|---|---|---|---|---|
| 50,000 mile standard | 0.160 | 4.4 | 0.7** | .... | 0.018 |
| 120,000 mile standard | 0.230 | 6.4 | 1.0 | 0.10 | 0.027 |

Test Weight Category: Above 5,750 tw but not above 8,500 lbs. gvwr

| Pollutant | NMOG | CO | $NO_x$ | PM* | HCHO (formaldehyde) |
|---|---|---|---|---|---|
| 50,000 mile standard | 0.195 | 5.0 | 1.1** | .... | 0.022 |
| 120,000 mile standard | 0.280 | 7.3 | 1.5 | 0.12 | 0.032 |

Standards are expressed in grams per mile (gpm).
* Standards for particulates (PM) shall apply only to diesel-fueled vehicles.
** Standard not applicable to diesel-fueled vehicles.
For the 50,000 mile standards and the 120,000 mile standards set forth in the table, the applicable useful life for purposes of certification shall be 50,000 miles or 120,000 miles, respectively.

(d) **Flexible and dual-fuel vehicles**

(1) **In general**

The Administrator shall establish standards and requirements under this section for the model year 1996 and thereafter for vehicles weighing not more than 8,500 lbs. gvwr which are capable of operating on more than one fuel. Such standards shall require that such vehicles meet the exhaust standards applicable under subsection [1] (a), (b), and (c) of this section for CO, $NO_x$, and HCHO, and if appropriate, PM for single-fuel vehicles of the same vehicle category and model year.

(2) **Exhaust NMOG standard for operation on clean alternative fuel**

In addition to standards for the pollutants referred to in paragraph (1), the standards established under paragraph (1) shall require that vehicle exhaust emissions of NMOG not exceed the levels (expressed in grams per mile) specified in the tables below when the vehicle is operated on the clean alternative fuel for which such vehicle is certified:

NMOG Standards for Flexible– and Dual–Fueled Vehicles When Operating on Clean Alternative Fuel

Light-duty Trucks up to 6,000 lbs. GVWR and Light-duty vehicles

| Vehicle Type | Column A (50,000 mi.) Standard (gpm) | Column B (100,000 mi.) Standard (gpm) |
|---|---|---|
| Beginning MY 1996: | | |
| LDT's (0–3,750 lbs. LVW) and light-duty vehicles | 0.125 | 0.156 |
| LDT's (3,751–5,750 lbs. LVW) | 0.160 | 0.20 |
| Beginning MY 2001: | | |
| LDT's (0–3,750 lbs. LVW) and light-duty vehicles | 0.075 | 0.090 |
| LDT's (3,751–5,750 lbs. LVW) | 0.100 | 0.130 |

For standards under column A, for purposes of certification under section 7525 of this title, the applicable useful life shall be 50,000 miles.

For standards under column B, for purposes of certification under section 7525 of this title, the applicable useful life shall be 100,000 miles.

Light-duty Trucks More than 6,000 lbs. GVWR

| Vehicle Type | Column A (50,000 mi.) Standard | Column B (120,000 mi.) Standard |
|---|---|---|
| Beginning MY 1998: | | |
| LDT's (0–3,750 lbs. TW) | 0.125 | 0.180 |
| LDT's (3,751–5,750 lbs. TW) | 0.160 | 0.230 |
| LDT's (above 5,750 lbs. TW) | 0.195 | 0.280 |

For standards under column A, for purposes of certification under section 7525 of this title, the applicable useful life shall be 50,000 miles.

For standards under column B, for purposes of certification under section 7525 of this title, the applicable useful life shall be 120,000 miles.

**(3) NMOG standard for operation on conventional fuel**

In addition to the standards referred to in paragraph (1), the standards established under paragraph (1) shall require that vehicle exhaust emissions of NMOG not exceed the levels (expressed in grams per mile) specified in the tables below:

NMOG Standards for Flexible– and Dual–Fueled Vehicles When Operating on Conventional Fuel

Light-duty Trucks of up to 6,000 lbs. GVWR and Light-duty vehicles

| Vehicle Type | Column A (50,000 mi.) Standard (gpm) | Column B (100,000 mi.) Standard (gpm) |
|---|---|---|
| Beginning MY 1996: | | |
| LDT's (0–3,750 lbs. LVW) and light-duty vehicles | 0.25 | 0.31 |
| LDT's (3,751–5,750 lbs. LVW) | 0.32 | 0.40 |
| Beginning MY 2001: | | |
| LDT's (0–3,750 lbs. LVW) and light-duty vehicles | 0.125 | 0.156 |
| LDT's (3,751–5,750 lbs. LVW) | 0.160 | 0.200 |

For standards under column A, for purposes of certification under section 7525 of this title, the applicable useful life shall be 50,000 miles.

For standards under column B, for purposes of certification under section 7525 of this title, the applicable useful life shall be 100,000 miles.

Light-duty Trucks of up to 6,000 lbs. GVWR

| Vehicle Type | Column A (50,000 mi.) Standard | Column B (120,000 mi.) Standard |
|---|---|---|
| Beginning MY 1998: | | |
| LDT's (0–3,750 lbs. TW) | 0.25 | 0.36 |
| LDT's (3,751–5,750 lbs. TW) | 0.32 | 0.46 |
| LDT's (above 5,750 lbs. TW) | 0.39 | 0.56 |

For standards under column A, for purposes of certification under section 7525 of this title, the applicable useful life shall be 50,000 miles.

For standards under column B, for purposes of certification under section 7525 of this title, the applicable useful life shall be 120,000 miles.

**(e) Replacement by CARB standards**

**(1) Single set of CARB standards**

If the State of California promulgates regulations establishing and implementing a single set of standards applicable in California pursuant to a waiver approved under section 7543 of this title to any category of vehicles referred to in subsection (a), (b), (c), or (d) of this section and such set of standards is, in the aggregate, at least as protective of public health and welfare as the otherwise applicable standards set forth in section 7582 of this title and subsection (a), (b), (c), or (d) of this section, such set of California standards shall apply to clean-fuel vehicles in such category in lieu of the standards otherwise applicable under section 7582 of this title and subsection (a), (b), (c), or (d) of this section, as the case may be.

**(2) Multiple sets of CARB standards**

If the State of California promulgates regulations establishing and implementing several different sets of standards applicable in California pursuant to a waiver approved under section 7543 of this title to any category of vehicles referred to in subsection (a), (b), (c), or (d) of this section and each of such sets of California standards is, in the aggregate, at least as protective of public health and welfare as the otherwise applicable standards set forth in section 7582 of this title and subsection (a), (b), (c), or (d) of this section, such standards shall be treated as "qualifying California standards" for purposes of this paragraph. Where more than one set of qualifying standards are established and administered by the State of California, the least stringent set of qualifying California standards shall apply to the clean-fuel vehicles concerned in lieu of the standards otherwise applicable to such vehicles under section 7582 of this title and this section.

**(f) Less stringent CARB standards**

If the Low–Emission Vehicle and Clean Fuels Regulations of the California Air Resources Board applicable to any category of vehicles referred to in subsection (a), (b), (c), or (d) of this section are modified after November 15, 1990, to provide an emissions standard which is less stringent than the otherwise applicable standard set forth in subsection (a), (b), (c), or (d) of this section, or if any effective date contained in such regulations is delayed, such modified standards or such delay (or both, as the case may be) shall apply, for an interim period, in lieu of the standard or effective date otherwise applicable under subsection (a), (b), (c), or (d) of this section to any vehicles covered by such modified standard or delayed effective date. The interim period shall be a period of not more than 2 model years from the effective date otherwise applicable under subsection (a), (b), (c), or (d) of this section. After such interim period, the otherwise applicable standard set forth in subsection (a), (b), (c), or (d) of this section shall take effect with respect to such vehicles (unless subsequently replaced under subsection (e) of this section).

**(g) Not applicable to heavy-duty vehicles**

Notwithstanding any provision of the Low–Emission Vehicle and Clean Fuels Regulations of the California Air Resources Board nothing in this section shall apply to heavy-duty engines in vehicles of more than 8,500 lbs. GVWR.

(July 14, 1955, c. 360, Title II, § 243, as added Nov. 15, 1990, Pub.L. 101–549, Title II, § 229(a), 104 Stat. 2514.)

[1] So in original. Probably should be "subsections".

### HISTORICAL AND STATUTORY NOTES

**Effective and Applicability Provisions**

1990 Acts

Section effective Nov. 15, 1990, except as otherwise provided, see section 711(b) of Pub.L. 101–549, set out as a note under section 7401 of this title.

**Savings Provisions**

Suits, actions or proceedings commenced under this chapter as in effect prior to Nov. 15, 1990, not to abate by reason of the taking effect of amendments by Pub.L. 101–549, except as otherwise provided for, see section 711(a) of Pub.L. 101–549, set out as a note under section 7401 of this title.

## § 7584. Administration and enforcement as per California standards

[CAA § 244]

Where the numerical clean-fuel vehicle standards applicable under this part to vehicles of not more than 8,500 lbs. GVWR are the same as numerical emission standards applicable in California under the Low–Emission Vehicle and Clean Fuels Regulations of the California Air Resources Board ("CARB"), such standards shall be administered and enforced by the Administrator—

**(1)** in the same manner and with the same flexibility as the State of California administers and enforces corresponding standards applicable under the Low–Emission Vehicle and Clean Fuels Regulations of the California Air Resources Board ("CARB"); and

**(2)** subject to the same requirements, and utilizing the same interpretations and policy judgments, as are applicable in the case of such CARB standards, including, but not limited to, requirements regarding certification, production-line testing, and in-use compliance,

unless the Administrator determines (in promulgating the rules establishing the clean fuel vehicle program under this section) that any such administration and enforcement would not meet the criteria for a waiver under section 7543 of this title. Nothing in this section shall apply in the case of standards under section 7585 of this title for heavy-duty vehicles.

(July 14, 1955, c. 360, Title II, § 244, as added Nov. 15, 1990, Pub.L. 101–549, Title II, § 229(a), 104 Stat. 2519.)

### HISTORICAL AND STATUTORY NOTES

**Effective and Applicability Provisions**

1990 Acts

Section effective Nov. 15, 1990, except as otherwise provided, see section 711(b) of Pub.L. 101–549, set out as a note under section 7401 of this title.

**Savings Provisions**

Suits, actions or proceedings commenced under this chapter as in effect prior to Nov. 15, 1990, not to abate by reason of the taking effect of amendments by Pub.L. 101–549, except as otherwise provided for, see section 711(a) of Pub.L. 101–549, set out as a note under section 7401 of this title.

## § 7585. Standards for heavy-duty clean-fuel vehicles (GVWR above 8,500 up to 26,000 lbs.)

[CAA § 245]

**(a) Model years after 1997; combined $NO_x$ and NMHC standard**

For classes or categories of heavy-duty vehicles or engines manufactured for the model year 1998 or thereafter and having a GVWR greater than 8,500 lbs. and up to 26,000 lbs. GVWR, the standards under this part for clean-fuel vehicles shall require that combined emissions of oxides of nitrogen ($NO_x$) and nonmethane hydrocarbons (NMHC) shall not exceed 3.15 grams per brake horsepower hour (equivalent to 50 percent of the combined emission standards applicable under section 7521 of this title for such air pollutants in the case of a conventional model year 1994 heavy-duty diesel-fueled vehicle or engine). No standard shall be promulgated as provided in this section for any heavy-duty vehicle of more than 26,000 lbs. GVWR.

**(b) Revised standards that are less stringent**

**(1)** The Administrator may promulgate a revised less stringent standard for the vehicles or engines referred to in subsection (a) of this section if the Administrator determines that the 50 percent reduction required under subsection (a) of this section is not technologically feasible for clean diesel-fueled vehicles and engines, taking into account durability, costs, lead time, safety, and other relevant factors. To provide adequate lead time the Administrator shall make a determination with regard to the technological feasibility of such 50 percent reduction before December 31, 1993.

(2) Any person may at any time petition the Administrator to make a determination under paragraph (1). The Administrator shall act on such a petition within 6 months after the petition is filed.

(3) Any revised less stringent standards promulgated as provided in this subsection shall require at least a 30 percent reduction in lieu of the 50 percent reduction referred to in paragraph (1).

(July 14, 1955, c. 360, Title II, § 245, as added Nov. 15, 1990, Pub.L. 101–549, Title II, § 229(a), 104 Stat. 2519.)

### HISTORICAL AND STATUTORY NOTES

**Effective and Applicability Provisions**

1990 Acts

Section effective Nov. 15, 1990, except as otherwise provided, see section 711(b) of Pub.L. 101–549, set out as a note under section 7401 of this title.

**Savings Provisions**

Suits, actions or proceedings commenced under this chapter as in effect prior to Nov. 15, 1990, not to abate by reason of the taking effect of amendments by Pub.L. 101–549, except as otherwise provided for, see section 711(a) of Pub.L. 101–549, set out as a note under section 7401 of this title.

## § 7586. Centrally fueled fleets

**[CAA § 246]**

### (a) Fleet program required for certain nonattainment areas

#### (1) SIP revision

Each State in which there is located all or part of a covered area (as defined in paragraph (2)) shall submit, within 42 months after November 15, 1990, a State implementation plan revision under section 7410 of this title and part D of subchapter I of this chapter to establish a clean-fuel vehicle program for fleets under this section.

#### (2) Covered areas

For purposes of this subsection, each of the following shall be a "covered area":

##### (A) Ozone nonattainment areas

Any ozone nonattainment area with a 1980 population of 250,000 or more classified under subpart 2 of part D of subchapter I of this chapter as Serious, Severe, or Extreme based on data for the calendar years 1987, 1988, and 1989. In determining the ozone nonattainment areas to be treated as covered areas pursuant to this subparagraph, the Administrator shall use the most recent interpretation methodology issued by the Administrator prior to November 15, 1990.

##### (B) Carbon monoxide nonattainment areas

Any carbon monoxide nonattainment area with a 1980 population of 250,000 or more and a carbon monoxide design value at or above 16.0 parts per million based on data for calendar years 1988 and 1989 (as calculated according to the most recent interpretation methodology issued prior to November 15, 1990, by the United States Environmental Protection Agency), excluding those carbon monoxide nonattainment areas in which mobile sources do not contribute significantly to carbon monoxide exceedances.

#### (3) Plan revisions for reclassified areas

In the case of ozone nonattainment areas reclassified as Serious, Severe, or Extreme under part D of subchapter I of this chapter with a 1980 population of 250,000 or more, the State shall submit a plan revision meeting the requirements of this subsection within 1 year after reclassification. Such plan revision shall implement the requirements applicable under this subsection at the time of reclassification and thereafter, except that the Administrator may adjust for a limited period the deadlines for compliance where compliance with such deadlines would be infeasible.

#### (4) Consultation; consideration of factors

Each State required to submit an implementation plan revision under this subsection shall develop such revision in consultation with fleet operators, vehicle manufacturers, fuel producers and distributors, motor vehicle fuel, and other interested parties, taking into consideration operational range, specialty uses, vehicle and fuel availability, costs, safety, resale values of vehicles and equipment and other relevant factors.

### (b) Phase-in of requirements

The plan revision required under this section shall contain provisions requiring that at least a specified percentage of all new covered fleet vehicles in model year 1998 and thereafter purchased by each covered fleet operator in each covered area shall be clean-fuel vehicles and shall use clean alternative fuels when operating in the covered area. For the applicable model years (MY) specified in the following table and thereafter, the specified percentage shall be as provided in the table for the vehicle types set forth in the table:

Clean Fuel Vehicle Phase–In Requirements for Fleets

| Vehicle Type | MY1998 | MY1999 | MY2000 |
|---|---|---|---|
| Light-duty trucks up to 6,000 lbs. GVWR and light-duty vehicles | 30% | 50% | 70% |
| Heavy-duty trucks above 8,500 lbs. GVWR | 50% | 50% | 50% |

The term MY refers to model year.

**(c) Accelerated standard for light-duty trucks up to 6,000 lbs. GVWR and light-duty vehicles**

Notwithstanding the model years for which clean-fuel vehicle standards are applicable as provided in section 7583 of this title, for purposes of this section, light duty [1] trucks of up to 6,000 lbs. GVWR and light-duty vehicles manufactured in model years 1998 through model year 2000 shall be treated as clean-fuel vehicles only if such vehicles comply with the standards applicable under section 7583 of this title for vehicles in the same class for the model year 2001. The requirements of subsection (b) of this section shall take effect on the earlier of the following:

(1) The first model year after model year 1997 in which new light-duty trucks up to 6,000 lbs. GVWR and light-duty vehicles which comply with the model year 2001 standards under section 7583 of this title are offered for sale in California.

(2) Model year 2001.

Whenever the effective date of subsection (b) of this section is delayed pursuant to paragraph (1) of this subsection, the phase-in schedule under subsection (b) of this section shall be modified to commence with the model year referred to in paragraph (1) in lieu of model year 1998.

**(d) Choice of vehicles and fuel**

The plan revision under this subsection shall provide that the choice of clean-fuel vehicles and clean alternative fuels shall be made by the covered fleet operator subject to the requirements of this subsection.

**(e) Availability of clean alternative fuel**

The plan revision shall require fuel providers to make clean alternative fuel available to covered fleet operators at locations at which covered fleet vehicles are centrally fueled.

**(f) Credits**

**(1) Issuance of credits**

The State plan revision required under this section shall provide for the issuance by the State of appropriate credits to a fleet operator for any of the following (or any combination thereof):

(A) The purchase of more clean-fuel vehicles than required under this section.

(B) The purchase of clean fuel [2] vehicles which meet more stringent standards established by the Administrator pursuant to paragraph (4).

(C) The purchase of vehicles in categories which are not covered by this section but which meet standards established for such vehicles under paragraph (4).

**(2) Use of credits; limitations based on weight classes**

**(A) Use of credits**

Credits under this subsection may be used by the person holding such credits to demonstrate compliance with this section or may be traded or sold for use by any other person to demonstrate compliance with other requirements applicable under this section in the same nonattainment area. Credits obtained at any time may be held or banked for use at any later time, and when so used, such credits shall maintain the same value as if used at an earlier date.

**(B) Limitations based on weight classes**

Credits issued with respect to the purchase of vehicles of up to 8,500 lbs. GVWR may not be used to demonstrate compliance by any person with the requirements applicable under this subsection to vehicles of more than 8,500 lbs. GVWR. Credits issued with respect to the purchase of vehicles of more than 8,500 lbs. GVWR may not be used to demonstrate compliance by any person with the requirements applicable under this subsection to vehicles weighing up to 8,500 lbs. GVWR.

**(C) Weighting**

Credits issued for purchase of a clean fuel [2] vehicle under this subsection shall be adjusted with appropriate weighting to reflect the level of emission reduction achieved by the vehicle.

**(3) Regulations and administration**

Within 12 months after November 15, 1990, the Administrator shall promulgate regulations for such credit program. The State shall administer the credit program established under this subsection.

(4) **Standards for issuing credits for cleaner vehicles**

Solely for purposes of issuing credits under paragraph (1)(B), the Administrator shall establish under this paragraph standards for Ultra–Low Emission Vehicles ("ULEV"s) and Zero Emissions Vehicles ("ZEV"s) which shall be more stringent than those otherwise applicable to clean-fuel vehicles under this part. The Administrator shall certify clean fuel [2] vehicles as complying with such more stringent standards, and administer and enforce such more stringent standards, in the same manner as in the case of the otherwise applicable clean-fuel vehicle standards established under this section. The standards established by the Administrator under this paragraph for vehicles under 8,500 lbs. GVWR or greater shall conform as closely as possible to standards which are established by the State of California for ULEV and ZEV vehicles in the same class. For vehicles of 8,500 lbs. GVWR or more, the Administrator shall promulgate comparable standards for purposes of this subsection.

(5) **Early fleet credits**

The State plan revision shall provide credits under this subsection to fleet operators that purchase vehicles certified to meet clean-fuel vehicle standards under this part during any period after approval of the plan revision and prior to the effective date of the fleet program under this section.

(g) **Availability to public**

At any facility owned or operated by a department, agency, or instrumentality of the United States where vehicles subject to this subsection are supplied with clean alternative fuel, such fuel shall be offered for sale to the public for use in other vehicles during reasonable business times and subject to national security concerns, unless such fuel is commercially available for vehicles in the vicinity of such Federal facilities.

(h) **Transportation control measures**

The Administrator shall by rule, within 1 year after November 15, 1990, ensure that certain transportation control measures including time-of-day or day-of-week restrictions, and other similar measures that restrict vehicle usage, do not apply to any clean-fuel vehicle that meets the requirements of this section. This subsection shall apply notwithstanding subchapter I of this chapter.

(July 14, 1955, c. 360, Title II, § 246, as added Nov. 15, 1990, Pub.L. 101–549, Title II, § 229(a), 104 Stat. 2520.)

[1] So in original. Probably should be "light-duty".

[2] So in original. Probably should be "clean-fuel".

**HISTORICAL AND STATUTORY NOTES**

**Effective and Applicability Provisions**

1990 Acts

Section effective Nov. 15, 1990, except as otherwise provided, see section 711(b) of Pub.L. 101–549, set out as a note under section 7401 of this title.

**Savings Provisions**

Suits, actions or proceedings commenced under this chapter as in effect prior to Nov. 15, 1990, not to abate by reason of the taking effect of amendments by Pub.L. 101–549, except as otherwise provided for, see section 711(a) of Pub.L. 101–549, set out as a note under section 7401 of this title.

## § 7587. Vehicle conversions

[CAA § 247]

(a) **Conversion of existing and new conventional vehicles to clean-fuel vehicles**

The requirements of section 7586 of this title may be met through the conversion of existing or new gasoline or diesel-powered vehicles to clean-fuel vehicles which comply with the applicable requirements of that section. For purposes of such provisions the conversion of a vehicle to clean fuel [1] vehicle shall be treated as the purchase of a clean fuel [1] vehicle. Nothing in this part shall be construed to provide that any covered fleet operator subject to fleet vehicle purchase requirements under section 7586 of this title shall be required to convert existing or new gasoline or diesel-powered vehicles to clean-fuel vehicles or to purchase converted vehicles.

(b) **Regulations**

The Administrator shall, within 24 months after November 15, 1990, consistent with the requirements of this subchapter applicable to new vehicles, promulgate regulations governing conversions of conventional vehicles to clean-fuel vehicles. Such regulations shall establish criteria for such conversions which will ensure that a converted vehicle will comply with the standards applicable under this part to clean-fuel vehicles. Such regulations shall provide for the application to such conversions of the same provisions of this subchapter (including provisions relating to administration enforcement) as are applicable to standards under section [2] 7582, 7583, 7584, and 7585 of this title, except that in the case of conversions the Administrator may modify the applicable regulations implementing such provisions as the Administrator deems necessary to implement this part.

(c) **Enforcement**

Any person who converts conventional vehicles to clean fuel [1] vehicles pursuant to subsection (b) of this section shall be considered a manufacturer for purposes of sections 7525 and 7541 of this title and related enforcement provisions. Nothing in the preceding sentence shall require a person who performs such conversions to warrant any part or operation of a vehicle other than as required under this part. Nothing in this paragraph shall limit the applicability of any other warranty to unrelated parts or operations.

**(d) Tampering**

The conversion from a vehicle capable of operating on gasoline or diesel fuel only to a clean-fuel vehicle shall not be considered a violation of section 7522(a)(3) of this title if such conversion complies with the regulations promulgated under subsection (b) of this section.

**(e) Safety**

The Secretary of Transportation shall, if necessary, promulgate rules under applicable motor vehicle laws regarding the safety of vehicles converted from existing and new vehicles to clean-fuel vehicles.

(July 14, 1955, c. 360, Title II, § 247, as added Nov. 15, 1990, Pub.L. 101–549, Title II, § 229(a), 104 Stat. 2523.)

[1] So in original. Probably should be "clean-fuel".

[2] So in original. Probably should be "sections".

### HISTORICAL AND STATUTORY NOTES

**Effective and Applicability Provisions**

1990 Acts

Section effective Nov. 15, 1990, except as otherwise provided, see section 711(b) of Pub.L. 101–549, set out as a note under section 7401 of this title.

**Savings Provisions**

Suits, actions or proceedings commenced under this chapter as in effect prior to Nov. 15, 1990, not to abate by reason of the taking effect of amendments by Pub.L. 101–549, except as otherwise provided for, see section 711(a) of Pub.L. 101–549, set out as a note under section 7401 of this title.

## § 7588. Federal agency fleets

[CAA § 248]

**(a) Additional provisions applicable**

The provisions of this section shall apply, in addition to the other provisions of this part, in the case of covered fleet vehicles owned or operated by an agency, department, or instrumentality of the United States, except as otherwise provided in subsection (e) of this section.

**(b) Cost of vehicles to Federal agency**

Notwithstanding the provisions of sections 601 to 611 of Title 40, the Administrator of General Services shall not include the incremental costs of clean-fuel vehicles in the amount to be reimbursed by Federal agencies if the Administrator of General Services determines that appropriations provided pursuant to this paragraph are sufficient to provide for the incremental cost of such vehicles over the cost of comparable conventional vehicles.

**(c) Limitations on appropriations**

Funds appropriated pursuant to the authorization under this paragraph shall be applicable only—

(1) to the portion of the cost of acquisition, maintenance and operation of vehicles acquired under this subparagraph which exceeds the cost of acquisition, maintenance and operation of comparable conventional vehicles;

(2) to the portion of the costs of fuel storage and dispensing equipment attributable to such vehicles which exceeds the costs for such purposes required for conventional vehicles; and

(3) to the portion of the costs of acquisition of clean-fuel vehicles which represents a reduction in revenue from the disposal of such vehicles as compared to revenue resulting from the disposal of comparable conventional vehicles.

**(d) Vehicle costs**

The incremental cost of vehicles acquired under this part over the cost of comparable conventional vehicles shall not be applied to any calculation with respect to a limitation under law on the maximum cost of individual vehicles which may be required by the United States.

**(e) Exemptions**

The requirements of this part shall not apply to vehicles with respect to which the Secretary of Defense has certified to the Administrator that an exemption is needed based on national security consideration.

**(f) Acquisition requirement**

Federal agencies, to the extent practicable, shall obtain clean-fuel vehicles from original equipment manufacturers.

**(g) Authorization of appropriations**

There are authorized to be appropriated such sums as may be required to carry out the provisions of this section: *Provided,* That such sums as are appropriated for the Administrator of General Services pursuant to the authorization under this section shall be added to the General Supply Fund established in sections 313 and 321 of Title 40.

(July 14, 1955, c. 360, Title II, § 248, as added Nov. 15, 1990, Pub.L. 101–549, Title II, § 229(a), 104 Stat. 2524.)

### HISTORICAL AND STATUTORY NOTES

**Codifications**

In subsec. (b), "sections 601 to 611 of Title 40" substituted for "section 491 of Title 40", which originally read "the provisions of section 211 of the Federal Property and Administrative Services Act of 1949", on authority of Pub.L. 107–217, § 5(c), Aug. 21, 2002, 116 Stat. 1301, which is set out as a note preceding 40 U.S.C.A. § 101. Pub.L. 107–217, § 1, enacted Title 40 into positive law. Section 211 of the Federal

Property and Administrative Services Act of 1949, June 30, 1949, c. 288, Title II, § 211, as added Sept. 5, 1950, c. 849, § 5(c), 64 Stat. 580, as amended, was classified to former 40 U.S.C.A. § 472, prior to being repealed by Pub.L. 107–217, § 6(b), Aug. 21, 2002, 116 Stat. 1313, and its substance, defining the term "excess property", reenacted as 40 U.S.C.A. § 102(3).

In subsec. (g), "sections 313 and 321 of Title 40" substituted for "section 756 of Title 40", which originally read "section 109 of the Federal Property and Administrative Services Act of 1949", on authority of Pub.L. 107–217, § 5(c), Aug. 21, 2002, 116 Stat. 1301, which is set out as a note preceding 40 U.S.C.A. § 101. Pub.L. 107–217, § 1, enacted Title 40 into positive law. Section 109 of the Federal Property and Administrative Services Act of 1949 is Act June 30, 1949, c. 288, Title I, § 109, 63 Stat. 382, as amended, which was classified to former 40 U.S.C.A. § 756 prior to being repealed by Pub.L. 107–217, § 6(b), Aug. 21, 2002, 116 Stat. 1313, and its substance, defining the term "excess property", reenacted as 40 U.S.C.A. §§ 313 and 321.

**Effective and Applicability Provisions**

1990 Acts

Section effective Nov. 15, 1990, except as otherwise provided, see section 711(b) of Pub.L. 101–549, set out as a note under section 7401 of this title.

**Savings Provisions**

Suits, actions or proceedings commenced under this chapter as in effect prior to Nov. 15, 1990, not to abate by reason of the taking effect of amendments by Pub.L. 101–549, except as otherwise provided for, see section 711(a) of Pub.L. 101–549, set out as a note under section 7401 of this title.

## § 7589. California pilot test program

[CAA § 249]

### (a) Establishment

The Administrator shall establish a pilot program in the State of California to demonstrate the effectiveness of clean-fuel vehicles in controlling air pollution in ozone nonattainment areas.

### (b) Applicability

The provisions of this section shall only apply to light-duty trucks and light-duty vehicles, and such provisions shall apply only in the State of California, except as provided in subsection (f) of this section.

### (c) Program requirements

Not later than 24 months after November 15, 1990, the Administrator shall promulgate regulations establishing requirements under this section applicable in the State of California. The regulations shall provide the following:

#### (1) Clean-fuel vehicles

Clean-fuel vehicles shall be produced, sold, and distributed (in accordance with normal business practices and applicable franchise agreements) to ultimate purchasers in California (including owners of covered fleets referred to in section 7586 of this title) in numbers that meet or exceed the following schedule:

| Model Years | Number of Clean–Fuel Vehicles |
|---|---|
| 1996, 1997, 1998 | 150,000 vehicles |
| 1999 and thereafter | 300,000 vehicles |

#### (2) Clean alternative fuels

(A) Within 2 years after November 15, 1990, the State of California shall submit a revision of the applicable implementation plan under part D of subchapter I of this chapter and section 7410 of this title containing a clean fuel plan that requires that clean alternative fuels on which the clean-fuel vehicles required under this paragraph can operate shall be produced and distributed by fuel suppliers and made available in California. At a minimum, sufficient clean alternative fuels shall be produced, distributed and made available to assure that all clean-fuel vehicles required under this section can operate, to the maximum extent practicable, exclusively on such fuels in California. The State shall require that clean alternative fuels be made available and offered for sale at an adequate number of locations with sufficient geographic distribution to ensure convenient refueling with clean alternative fuels, considering the number of, and type of, such vehicles sold and the geographic distribution of such vehicles within the State. The State shall determine the clean alternative fuels to be produced, distributed, and made available based on motor vehicle manufacturers' projections of future sales of such vehicles and consultations with the affected local governments and fuel suppliers.

(B) The State may by regulation grant persons subject to the requirements prescribed under this paragraph an appropriate amount of credits for exceeding such requirements, and any person granted credits may transfer some or all of the credits for use by one or more persons in demonstrating compliance with such requirements. The State may make the credits available for use after consideration of enforceability, environmental, and economic factors and upon such terms and conditions as the State finds appropriate.

(C) The State may also by regulation establish specifications for any clean alternative fuel produced and made available under this paragraph as the State finds necessary to reduce or eliminate an unreasonable risk to public health, welfare, or safety associated with its use or to ensure acceptable vehicle maintenance and performance characteristics.

(D) If a retail gasoline dispensing facility would have to remove or replace one or more motor vehicle fuel underground storage tanks and accompanying piping in order to comply with the provisions of this section, and it had removed and replaced such tank or tanks and accompanying piping in order to comply with subtitle I of the Solid Waste Disposal Act [42 U.S.C.A. § 6901 et seq.] prior to November 15, 1990, it shall not be required to comply with this subsection until a period of 7 years has passed from the date of the removal and replacement of such tank or tanks.

(E) Nothing in this section authorizes any State other than California to adopt provisions regarding clean alternative fuels.

(F) If the State of California fails to adopt a clean fuel program that meets the requirements of this paragraph, the Administrator shall, within 4 years after November 15, 1990, establish a clean fuel program for the State of California under this paragraph and section 7410(c) of this title that meets the requirements of this paragraph.

**(d) Credits for motor vehicle manufacturers**

(1) The Administrator may (by regulation) grant a motor vehicle manufacturer an appropriate amount of credits toward fulfillment of such manufacturer's share of the requirements of subsection (c)(1) of this section for any of the following (or any combination thereof):

(A) The sale of more clean-fuel vehicles than required under subsection (c)(1) of this section.

(B) The sale of clean fuel[1] vehicles which meet standards established by the Administrator as provided in paragraph (3) which are more stringent than the clean-fuel vehicle standards otherwise applicable to such clean-fuel vehicle. A manufacturer granted credits under this paragraph may transfer some or all of the credits for use by one or more other manufacturers in demonstrating compliance with the requirements prescribed under this paragraph. The Administrator may make the credits available for use after consideration of enforceability, environmental, and economic factors and upon such terms and conditions as he finds appropriate. The Administrator shall grant credits in accordance with this paragraph, notwithstanding any requirements of State law or any credits granted with respect to the same vehicles under any State law, rule, or regulation.

(2) Regulations and administration

The Administrator shall administer the credit program established under this subsection. Within 12 months after November 15, 1990, the Administrator shall promulgate regulations for such credit program.

(3) Standards for issuing credits for cleaner vehicles

The more stringent standards and other requirements (including requirements relating to the weighting of credits) established by the Administrator for purposes of the credit program under section 7585(e)[2] of this title (relating to credits for clean fuel[1] vehicles in the fleets program) shall also apply for purposes of the credit program under this paragraph.

**(e) Program evaluation**

(1) Not later than June 30, 1994 and again in connection with the report under paragraph (2), the Administrator shall provide a report to the Congress on the status of the California Air Resources Board Low-Emissions Vehicles and Clean Fuels Program. Such report shall examine the capability, from a technological standpoint, of motor vehicle manufacturers and motor vehicle fuel suppliers to comply with the requirements of such program and with the requirements of the California Pilot Program under this section.

(2) Not later than June 30, 1998, the Administrator shall complete and submit a report to Congress on the effectiveness of the California pilot program under this section. The report shall evaluate the level of emission reductions achieved under the program, the costs of the program, the advantages and disadvantages of extending the program to other nonattainment areas, and desirability of continuing or expanding the program in California.

(3) The program under this section cannot be extended or terminated by the Administrator except by Act of Congress enacted after November 15, 1990. Section 7507 of this title does not apply to the program under this section.

**(f) Voluntary opt-in for other States**

**(1) EPA regulations**

Not later than 2 years after November 15, 1990, the Administrator shall promulgate regulations establishing a voluntary opt-in program under this subsection pursuant to which—

(A) clean-fuel vehicles which are required to be produced, sold, and distributed in the State of California under this section, and

(B) clean alternative fuels required to be produced and distributed under this section by fuel suppliers and made available in California[3]

may also be sold and used in other States which submit plan revisions under paragraph (2).

**(2) Plan revisions**

Any State in which there is located all or part of an ozone nonattainment area classified under subpart D of subchapter I of this chapter as Serious, Severe, or Extreme may submit a revision of the applicable implementation plan under part D of subchapter I of this chapter and section 7410 of this title to provide incentives for the sale or use in such an area or State of clean-fuel vehicles which are required to be produced, sold, and distributed in the State of California, and for the use in such an area or State of clean alternative fuels required to be produced and distributed by fuel suppliers and made available in California. Such plan provisions shall not take effect until 1 year after the State has provided notice of such provisions to motor vehicle manufacturers and to fuel suppliers.

**(3) Incentives**

The incentives referred to in paragraph (2) may include any or all of the following:

(A) A State registration fee on new motor vehicles registered in the State which are not clean-fuel vehicles in the amount of at least 1 percent of the cost of the vehicle. The proceeds of such fee shall be used to provide financial incentives to purchasers of clean-fuel vehicles and to vehicle dealers who sell high volumes or high percentages of clean-fuel vehicles and to defray the administrative costs of the incentive program.

(B) Provisions to exempt clean-fuel vehicles from high occupancy vehicle or trip reduction requirements.

(C) Provisions to provide preference in the use of existing parking spaces for clean-fuel vehicles.

The incentives under this paragraph shall not apply in the case of covered fleet vehicles.

**(4) No sales or production mandate**

The regulations and plan revisions under paragraphs (1) and (2) shall not include any production or sales mandate for clean-fuel vehicles or clean alternative fuels. Such regulations and plan revisions shall also provide that vehicle manufacturers and fuel suppliers may not be subject to penalties or sanctions for failing to produce or sell clean-fuel vehicles or clean alternative fuels.

(July 14, 1955, c. 360, Title II, § 249, as added Nov. 15, 1990, Pub.L. 101–549, Title II, § 229(a), 104 Stat. 2525.)

[1] So in original. Probably should be "clean-fuel".

[2] So in original. Probably should be "section 7586(f)".

[3] So in original. Probably should be followed by a comma.

## HISTORICAL AND STATUTORY NOTES

**References in Text**

The Solid Waste Disposal Act, referred to in subsec. (c)(2)(D), is title II of Pub.L. 89–272, Oct. 20, 1965, 79 Stat. 997, as amended generally by Pub.L. 94–580, § 2, Oct. 21, 1976, 90 Stat. 2795, which is classified generally to chapter 82 (section 6901 et seq.) of this title. For complete classification of this Act to the Code, see Short Title of 1965 Acts note set out under section 6901 of this title and Tables.

November 15, 1990 referred to in subsec. (e)(3), was in the original "the date of the Clean Air Act Amendments of 1990", which was translated as meaning the date of enactment of Pub.L. 101–549, which enacted this section, to reflect the probable intent of Congress.

**Effective and Applicability Provisions**

1990 Acts

Section effective Nov. 15, 1990, except as otherwise provided, see section 711(b) of Pub.L. 101–549, set out as a note under section 7401 of this title.

**Savings Provisions**

Suits, actions or proceedings commenced under this chapter as in effect prior to Nov. 15, 1990, not to abate by reason of the taking effect of amendments by Pub.L. 101–549, except as otherwise provided for, see section 711(a) of Pub.L. 101–549, set out as a note under section 7401 of this title.

## § 7590. General provisions

**[CAA § 250]**

**(a) State refueling facilities**

If any State adopts enforceable provisions in an implementation plan applicable to a nonattainment area which provides that existing State refueling facilities will be made available to the public for the purchase of clean alternative fuels or that State-operated refueling facilities for such fuels will be constructed and operated by the State and made available to the public at reasonable times, taking into consideration safety, costs, and other relevant factors, in approving such plan under section 7410 of this title and part D [1], the Administrator may credit a State with the emission reductions for purposes of part D [1] attributable to such actions.

**(b) No production mandate**

The Administrator shall have no authority under this part to mandate the production of clean-fuel vehicles except as provided in the California pilot test program or to specify as applicable the models, lines, or types of, or marketing or price practices, policies, or strategies for, vehicles subject to this part. Nothing in this part shall be construed to give the Administrator authority to mandate marketing or pricing practices, policies, or strategies for fuels.

**(c) Tank and fuel system safety**

The Secretary of Transportation shall, in accordance with chapter 301 of Title 49, promulgate applicable regulations regarding the safety and use of fuel storage cylinders and fuel systems, including appropriate testing and retesting, in conversions of motor vehicles.

**(d) Consultation with Department of Energy and Department of Transportation**

The Administrator shall coordinate with the Secretaries of the Department of Energy and the Department of Transportation in carrying out the Administrator's duties under this part.

(July 14, 1955, c. 360, Title II, § 250, as added Nov. 15, 1990, Pub.L. 101–549, Title II, § 229(a), 104 Stat. 2528.)

[1] So in original. Probably should be "part D of subchapter I of this chapter".

### HISTORICAL AND STATUTORY NOTES

**Codifications**

In subsec. (c), "chapter 301 of Title 49" substituted for "the National Motor Vehicle Traffic Safety Act of 1966 [15 U.S.C.A. § 1381 et seq.]", meaning "the National Traffic and Motor Vehicle Safety Act of 1966 [15 U.S.C.A. § 1381 et seq.]", on authority of Pub.L. 103–272, § 6(b), July 5, 1994, 108 Stat. 1378, the first section of which enacted subtitles II, III, and V to X of Title 49.

**Effective and Applicability Provisions**

1990 Acts

Section effective Nov. 15, 1990, except as otherwise provided, see section 711(b) of Pub.L. 101–549, set out as a note under section 7401 of this title.

**Savings Provisions**

Suits, actions or proceedings commenced under this chapter as in effect prior to Nov. 15, 1990, not to abate by reason of the taking effect of amendments by Pub.L. 101–549, except as otherwise provided for, see section 711(a) of Pub.L. 101–549, set out as a note under section 7401 of this title.

## SUBCHAPTER III—GENERAL PROVISIONS

## § 7601. Administration

[CAA § 301]

**(a) Regulations; delegation of powers and duties; regional officers and employees**

(1) The Administrator is authorized to prescribe such regulations as are necessary to carry out his functions under this chapter. The Administrator may delegate to any officer or employee of the Environmental Protection Agency such of his powers and duties under this chapter, except the making of regulations subject to section 7607(d) of this title, as he may deem necessary or expedient.

(2) Not later than one year after August 7, 1977, the Administrator shall promulgate regulations establishing general applicable procedures and policies for regional officers and employees (including the Regional Administrator) to follow in carrying out a delegation under paragraph (1), if any. Such regulations shall be designed—

(A) to assure fairness and uniformity in the criteria, procedures, and policies applied by the various regions in implementing and enforcing the chapter;

(B) to assure at least an adequate quality audit of each State's performance and adherence to the requirements of this chapter in implementing and enforcing the chapter, particularly in the review of new sources and in enforcement of the chapter; and

(C) to provide a mechanism for identifying and standardizing inconsistent or varying criteria, procedures, and policies being employed by such officers and employees in implementing and enforcing the chapter.

**(b) Detail of Environmental Protection Agency personnel to air pollution control agencies**

Upon the request of an air pollution control agency, personnel of the Environmental Protection Agency may be detailed to such agency for the purpose of carrying out the provisions of this chapter.

**(c) Payments under grants; installments; advances or reimbursements**

Payments under grants made under this chapter may be made in installments, and in advance or by way of reimbursement, as may be determined by the Administrator.

**(d) Tribal authority**

(1) Subject to the provisions of paragraph (2), the Administrator—

(A) is authorized to treat Indian tribes as States under this chapter, except for purposes of the requirement that makes available for application by each State no less than one-half of 1 percent of annual appropriations under section 7405 of this title; and

(B) may provide any such Indian tribe grant and contract assistance to carry out functions provided by this chapter.

(2) The Administrator shall promulgate regulations within 18 months after November 15, 1990, specifying those provisions of this chapter for which it is appropriate to treat Indian tribes as States. Such treatment shall be authorized only if—

(A) the Indian tribe has a governing body carrying out substantial governmental duties and powers;

(B) the functions to be exercised by the Indian tribe pertain to the management and protection of air resources within the exterior boundaries of the reservation or other areas within the tribe's jurisdiction; and

(C) the Indian tribe is reasonably expected to be capable, in the judgment of the Administrator, of carrying out the functions to be exercised in a manner consistent with the terms and purposes of this chapter and all applicable regulations.

(3) The Administrator may promulgate regulations which establish the elements of tribal implementation plans and procedures for approval or disapproval of tribal implementation plans and portions thereof.

(4) In any case in which the Administrator determines that the treatment of Indian tribes as identical to States is inappropriate or administratively infeasible, the Administrator may provide, by regulation, other means by which the Administrator will directly administer such provisions so as to achieve the appropriate purpose.

(5) Until such time as the Administrator promulgates regulations pursuant to this subsection, the Administrator may continue to provide financial assistance to eligible Indian tribes under section 7405 of this title.

(July 14, 1955, c. 360, Title III, § 301, formerly § 8, as added Dec. 17, 1963, Pub.L. 88–206, § 1, 77 Stat. 400, renumbered Oct. 20, 1965, Pub.L. 89–272, Title I, § 101(4), 79 Stat. 992, and amended Nov. 21, 1967, Pub.L. 90–148, § 2, 81 Stat. 504; Dec. 31, 1970, Pub.L. 91–604, §§ 3(b)(2), 15(c)(2), 84 Stat. 1677, 1713; Aug. 7, 1977, Pub.L. 95–95, Title III, § 305(e), 91 Stat. 776; Nov. 15, 1990, Pub.L. 101–549, Title I, §§ 107(d), 108(i), 104 Stat. 2464, 2467.)

## HISTORICAL AND STATUTORY NOTES

### Codifications

Section was formerly classified to section 1857g of this title.

### Effective and Applicability Provisions

1990 Acts

Amendment by Pub.L. 101–549 effective Nov. 15, 1990, except as otherwise provided, see section 711(b) of Pub.L. 101–549, set out as a note under section 7401 of this title.

1977 Acts

Amendment by Pub.L. 95–95 effective Aug. 7, 1977, except as otherwise expressly provided, see section 406(d) of Pub.L. 95–95, set out as a note under section 7401 of this title.

### Savings Provisions

Suits, actions or proceedings commenced under this chapter as in effect prior to Nov. 15, 1990, not to abate by reason of the taking effect of amendments by Pub.L. 101–549, except as otherwise provided for, see section 711(a) of Pub.L. 101–549, set out as a note under section 7401 of this title.

### Prior Provisions

A prior section 8 of Act July 14, 1955, c. 360, as added Sept. 22, 1959, Pub.L. 86–365, § 2, 73 Stat. 646, which was classified to a prior section 1857g of this title prior to the general amendment of this chapter by Pub.L. 88–206, provided for cooperative effort.

### Disadvantaged Business Concerns; Use of Quotas Prohibited

Pub.L. 101–549, Title X, §§ 1001, 1002, Nov. 15, 1990, 104 Stat. 2708, provided that:

**"Sec. 1001. Disadvantaged business concerns.**

"(a) **In general.**—In providing for any research relating to the requirements of the amendments made by the Clean Air Act Amendments of 1990 [Pub.L. 101–549, Nov. 15, 1990, 104 Stat. 2399, for distribution which Act to the Code, see Tables] which uses funds of the Environmental Protection Agency, the Administrator of the Environmental Protection Agency shall, to the extent practicable, require that not less than 10 percent of total Federal funding for such research will be made available to disadvantaged business concerns.

"(b) **Definition.**—

"(1)(A) For purposes of subsection (a), the term 'disadvantaged business concern' means a concern—

"(i) which is at least 51 percent owned by one or more socially and economically disadvantaged individuals or, in the case of a publicly traded company, at least 51 percent of the stock of which is owned by one or more socially and economically disadvantaged individuals; and

"(ii) the management and daily business operations of which are controlled by such individuals.

"(B)(i) A for-profit business concern is presumed to be a disadvantaged business concern for purposes of subsection (a) if it is at least 51 percent owned by, or in the case of a concern which is a publicly traded company at least 51 percent of the stock of the company is owned by, one or more individuals who are members of the following groups:

"(I) Black Americans.

"(II) Hispanic Americans.

"(III) Native Americans.

"(IV) Asian Americans.

"(V) Women.

"(VI) Disabled Americans.

"(ii) The presumption established by clause (i) may be rebutted with respect to a particular business concern if it is reasonably established that the individual or individuals referred to in that clause with respect to that business concern are not experiencing impediments to establishing or developing such concern as a result of the individual's identification as a member of a group specified in that clause.

"(C) The following institutions are presumed to be disadvantaged business concerns for purposes of subsection (a):

"(i) Historically black colleges and universities, and colleges and universities having a student body in which 40 percent of the students are Hispanic.

"(ii) Minority institutions (as that term is defined by the Secretary of Education pursuant to the General Education Provision Act (20 U.S.C. 1221 et seq.) [section 1221 et seq. of Title 20], Education).

"(iii) Private and voluntary organizations controlled by individuals who are socially and economically disadvantaged.

"(D) A joint venture may be considered to be a disadvantaged business concern under subsection (a), notwithstanding the size of such joint venture, if—

"(i) a party to the joint venture is a disadvantaged business concern; and

"(ii) that party owns at least 51 percent of the joint venture.

A person who is not an economically disadvantaged individual or a disadvantaged business concern, as a party to a joint venture, may not be a party to more than 2 awarded contracts in a fiscal year solely by reason of this subparagraph.

"(E) Nothing in this paragraph shall prohibit any member of a racial or ethnic group that is not listed in subparagraph (B)(i) from establishing that they have been impeded in establishing or developing a business concern as a result of racial or ethnic discrimination.

"Sec. 1002. Use of quotas prohibited. Nothing in this title [Title X of Pub.L. 101–594, Nov. 15, 1990, 104 Stat. 2708, enacting this note] shall permit or require the use of quotas or a requirement that has the effect of a quota in determining eligibility under section 1001."

**Modification or Rescission of Rules, Regulations, Orders, Determinations, Contracts, Certifications, Authorizations, Delegations and Other Actions**

All rules, regulations, orders, determinations, contracts, certifications, authorizations, delegations, or other actions duly issued, made, or taken by or pursuant to Act July 14, 1955, the Clean Air Act, as in effect immediately prior to the date of enactment of Pub.L. 95–95 [Aug. 7, 1977] to continue in full force and effect until modified or rescinded in accordance with Act July 14, 1955, as amended by Pub.L. 95–95 [this chapter], see section 406(b) of Pub.L. 95–95, set out as an Effective Date of 1977 Acts note under section 7401 of this title.

## § 7602. Definitions

**[CAA § 302]**

When used in this chapter—

**(a)** The term "Administrator" means the Administrator of the Environmental Protection Agency.

**(b)** The term "air pollution control agency" means any of the following:

(1) A single State agency designated by the Governor of that State as the official State air pollution control agency for purposes of this chapter.

(2) An agency established by two or more States and having substantial powers or duties pertaining to the prevention and control of air pollution.

(3) A city, county, or other local government health authority, or, in the case of any city, county, or other local government in which there is an agency other than the health authority charged with responsibility for enforcing ordinances or laws relating to the prevention and control of air pollution, such other agency.

(4) An agency of two or more municipalities located in the same State or in different States and having substantial powers or duties pertaining to the prevention and control of air pollution.

(5) An agency of an Indian tribe.

**(c)** The term "interstate air pollution control agency" means—

(1) an air pollution control agency established by two or more States, or

(2) an air pollution control agency of two or more municipalities located in different States.

**(d)** The term "State" means a State, the District of Columbia, the Commonwealth of Puerto Rico, the Virgin Islands, Guam, and American Samoa and includes the Commonwealth of the Northern Mariana Islands.

**(e)** The term "person" includes an individual, corporation, partnership, association, State, municipality, political subdivision of a State, and any agency, department, or instrumentality of the United States and any officer, agent, or employee thereof.

**(f)** The term "municipality" means a city, town, borough, county, parish, district, or other public body created by or pursuant to State law.

**(g)** The term "air pollutant" means any air pollution agent or combination of such agents, including any physical, chemical, biological, radioactive (including source material, special nuclear material, and byproduct material) substance or matter which is emitted into or otherwise enters the ambient air. Such term includes any precursors to the formation of any air pollutant, to the extent the Administrator has identified such precursor or precursors for the particular purpose for which the term "air pollutant" is used.

**(h)** All language referring to effects on welfare includes, but is not limited to, effects on soils, water, crops, vegetation, manmade materials, animals, wildlife, weather, visibility, and climate, damage to and deterioration of property, and hazards to transportation, as well as effects on economic values and on personal comfort and well-being, whether caused by transformation, conversion, or combination with other air pollutants.

**(i)** The term "Federal land manager" means, with respect to any lands in the United States, the Secretary of the department with authority over such lands.

**(j)** Except as otherwise expressly provided, the terms "major stationary source" and "major emitting facility" mean any stationary facility or source of air pollutants which directly emits, or has the potential to emit, one hundred tons per year or more of any air pollutant (including any major emitting facility or source of fugitive emissions of any such pollutant, as determined by rule by the Administrator).

**(k)** The terms "emission limitation" and "emission standard" mean a requirement established by the State or the Administrator which limits the quantity, rate, or concentration of emissions of air pollutants on a continuous basis, including any requirement relating to the operation or maintenance of a source to assure continuous emission reduction, and any design, equipment, work practice or operational standard promulgated under this chapter..[1]

**(*l*)** The term "standard of performance" means a requirement of continuous emission reduction, including any requirement relating to the operation or maintenance of a source to assure continuous emission reduction.

**(m)** The term "means of emission limitation" means a system of continuous emission reduction (including the use of specific technology or fuels with specified pollution characteristics).

**(n)** The term "primary standard attainment date" means the date specified in the applicable implementation plan for the attainment of a national primary ambient air quality standard for any air pollutant.

**(*o*)** The term "delayed compliance order" means an order issued by the State or by the Administrator to an existing stationary source, postponing the date required under an applicable implementation plan for compliance by such source with any requirement of such plan.

**(p)** The term "schedule and timetable of compliance" means a schedule of required measures including an enforceable sequence of actions or operations leading to compliance with an emission limitation, other limitation, prohibition, or standard.

**(q)** For purposes of this chapter, the term "applicable implementation plan" means the portion (or portions) of the implementation plan, or most recent revision thereof, which has been approved under section 7410 of this title, or promulgated under section 7410(c) of this title, or promulgated or approved pursuant to regulations promulgated under section 7601(d) of this title and which implements the relevant requirements of this chapter.

**(r) Indian tribe.**—The term "Indian tribe" means any Indian tribe, band, nation, or other organized group or community, including any Alaska Native village, which is Federally recognized as eligible for the special programs and services provided by the United States to Indians because of their status as Indians.

**(s) VOC.**—The term "VOC" means volatile organic compound, as defined by the Administrator.

**(t) PM–10.**—The term "PM–10" means particulate matter with an aerodynamic diameter less than or equal to a nominal ten micrometers, as measured by such method as the Administrator may determine.

**(u) NAAQS and CTG.**—The term "NAAQS" means national ambient air quality standard. The term "CTG" means a Control Technique Guideline published by the Administrator under section 7408 of this title.

**(v) $NO_x$.**—The term "$NO_x$" means oxides of nitrogen.

**(w) CO.**—The term "CO" means carbon monoxide.

**(x) Small source.**—The term "small source" means a source that emits less than 100 tons of regulated pollutants per year, or any class of persons that the Administrator determines, through regulation, generally lack technical ability or knowledge regarding control of air pollution.

**(y) Federal implementation plan.**—The term "Federal implementation plan" means a plan (or portion thereof) promulgated by the Administrator to fill all or a portion of a gap or otherwise correct all or a portion of an inadequacy in a State implementation plan, and which includes enforceable emission limitations or other control measures, means or techniques (including economic incentives, such as marketable permits or auctions of emissions allowances), and provides for attainment of the relevant national ambient air quality standard.

**(z) Stationary source.**—The term "stationary source" means generally any source of an air pollutant except those emissions resulting directly from an internal combustion engine for transportation purposes or from a nonroad engine or nonroad vehicle as defined in section 7550 of this title.

(July 14, 1955, c. 360, Title III, § 302, formerly § 9, as added Dec. 17, 1963, Pub.L. 88–206, § 1, 77 Stat. 400, renumbered Oct. 20, 1965, Pub.L. 89–272, Title I, § 101(4), 79 Stat. 992, and amended Nov. 21, 1967, Pub.L. 90–148, § 2, 81 Stat. 504; Dec. 31, 1970, Pub.L. 91–604, § 15(a)(1), (c)(1), 84 Stat. 1710, 1713; Aug. 7, 1977, Pub.L. 95–95, Title II, § 218(c), Title III, § 301, 91 Stat. 761, 769; Nov. 16, 1977, Pub.L. 95–190, § 14(a)(76), 91 Stat. 1404; Nov. 15, 1990, Pub.L. 101–549, Title I, §§ 101(d)(4), 107(a), (b), 108(j), 109(b), Title III, § 302(e), Title VII, § 709, 104 Stat. 2409, 2464, 2468, 2470, 2574, 2684.)

[1] So in original.

## HISTORICAL AND STATUTORY NOTES

### Codifications

Section was formerly classified to section 1857h of this title.

### Effective and Applicability Provisions

1990 Acts

Amendment by Pub.L. 101–549 effective Nov. 15, 1990, except as otherwise provided, see section 711(b) of Pub.L. 101–549, set out as a note under section 7401 of this title.

1977 Acts

Amendment by Pub.L. 95–95 effective Aug. 7, 1977, except as otherwise expressly provided, see section 406(d) of Pub.L. 95–95, set out as a note under section 7401 of this title.

### Savings Provisions

Suits, actions or proceedings commenced under this chapter as in effect prior to Nov. 15, 1990, not to abate by reason of the taking effect of amendments by Pub.L. 101–549, except as otherwise provided for, see section 711(a) of Pub.L. 101–549, set out as a note under section 7401 of this title.

**Prior Provisions**

Provisions similar to subsecs. (b) and (d) of this section were contained in a prior section 1857e, Act July 14, 1955, c. 360, § 6, 69 Stat. 323, prior to the general amendment of this chapter by Pub.L. 88–206.

## § 7603. Emergency powers

**[CAA § 303]**

Notwithstanding any other provision of this chapter, the Administrator, upon receipt of evidence that a pollution source or combination of sources (including moving sources) is presenting an imminent and substantial endangerment to public health or welfare, or the environment, may bring suit on behalf of the United States in the appropriate United States district court to immediately restrain any person causing or contributing to the alleged pollution to stop the emission of air pollutants causing or contributing to such pollution or to take such other action as may be necessary. If it is not practicable to assure prompt protection of public health or welfare or the environment by commencement of such a civil action, the Administrator may issue such orders as may be necessary to protect public health or welfare or the environment. Prior to taking any action under this section, the Administrator shall consult with appropriate State and local authorities and attempt to confirm the accuracy of the information on which the action proposed to be taken is based. Any order issued by the Administrator under this section shall be effective upon issuance and shall remain in effect for a period of not more than 60 days, unless the Administrator brings an action pursuant to the first sentence of this section before the expiration of that period. Whenever the Administrator brings such an action within the 60-day period, such order shall remain in effect for an additional 14 days or for such longer period as may be authorized by the court in which such action is brought.

(July 14, 1955, c. 360, Title III, § 303, as added Dec. 31, 1970, Pub.L. 91–604, § 12(a), 84 Stat. 1705, and amended Aug. 7, 1977, Pub.L. 95–95, Title III, § 302(a), 91 Stat. 770; Nov. 15, 1990, Pub.L. 101–549, Title VII, § 704, 104 Stat. 2681.)

### HISTORICAL AND STATUTORY NOTES

**Codifications**

Section was formerly classified to section 1857h–1 of this title.

**Effective and Applicability Provisions**

1990 Acts

Amendment by Pub.L. 101–549 effective Nov. 15, 1990, except as otherwise provided, see section 711(b) of Pub.L. 101–549, set out as a note under section 7401 of this title.

1977 Acts

Amendment by Pub.L. 95–95 effective Aug. 7, 1977, except as otherwise expressly provided, see section 406(d) of Pub.L. 95–95, set out as a note under section 7401 of this title.

**Savings Provisions**

Suits, actions or proceedings commenced under this chapter as in effect prior to Nov. 15, 1990, not to abate by reason of the taking effect of amendments by Pub.L. 101–549, except as otherwise provided for, see section 711(a) of Pub.L. 101–549, set out as a note under section 7401 of this title.

**Prior Provisions**

A prior section 303 of Act July 14, 1955, was renumbered section 310 by Pub.L. 91–604, and is set out as section 7610 of this title.

**Modification or Rescission of Rules, Regulations, Orders, Determinations, Contracts, Certifications, Authorizations, Delegations, and Other Actions**

All rules, regulations, orders, determinations, contracts, certifications, authorizations, delegations, or other actions duly issued, made, or taken by or pursuant to Act July 14, 1955, the Clean Air Act, as in effect immediately prior to the date of enactment of Pub.L. 95–95 [Aug. 7, 1977] to continue in full force and effect until modified or rescinded in accordance with Act July 14, 1955, as amended by Pub.L. 95–95 [this chapter], see section 406(b) of Pub.L. 95–95, set out as an Effective Date of 1977 Acts note under section 7401 of this title.

**Pending Actions and Proceedings**

Suits, actions, and other proceedings lawfully commenced by or against the Administrator or any other officer or employee of the United States in his official capacity or in relation to the discharge of his official duties under Act July 14, 1955, the Clean Air Act, as in effect immediately prior to the enactment of Pub.L. 95–95 [Aug. 7, 1977], not to abate by reason of the taking effect of Pub.L. 95–95, see section 406(a) of Pub.L. 95–95, set out as an Effective Date of 1977 Acts note under section 7401 of this title.

## § 7604. Citizen suits

**[CAA § 304]**

**(a) Authority to bring civil action; jurisdiction**

Except as provided in subsection (b) of this section, any person may commence a civil action on his own behalf—

(1) against any person (including (i) the United States, and (ii) any other governmental instrumentality or agency to the extent permitted by the Eleventh Amendment to the Constitution) who is alleged to have violated (if there is evidence that the alleged violation has been repeated) or to be in violation of (A) an emission standard or limitation under this chapter or (B) an order issued by the Administrator or a State with respect to such a standard or limitation,

(2) against the Administrator where there is alleged a failure of the Administrator to perform any act or duty under this chapter which is not discretionary with the Administrator, or

(3) against any person who proposes to construct or constructs any new or modified major emitting

facility without a permit required under part C of subchapter I of this chapter (relating to significant deterioration of air quality) or part D of subchapter I of this chapter (relating to nonattainment) or who is alleged to have violated (if there is evidence that the alleged violation has been repeated) or to be in violation of any condition of such permit.

The district courts shall have jurisdiction, without regard to the amount in controversy or the citizenship of the parties, to enforce such an emission standard or limitation, or such an order, or to order the Administrator to perform such act or duty, as the case may be, and to apply any appropriate civil penalties (except for actions under paragraph (2)). The district courts of the United States shall have jurisdiction to compel (consistent with paragraph (2) of this subsection) agency action unreasonably delayed, except that an action to compel agency action referred to in section 7607(b) of this title which is unreasonably delayed may only be filed in a United States District Court within the circuit in which such action would be reviewable under section 7607(b) of this title. In any such action for unreasonable delay, notice to the entities referred to in subsection (b)(1)(A) of this section shall be provided 180 days before commencing such action.

**(b) Notice**

No action may be commenced—

(1) under subsection (a)(1) of this section—

(A) prior to 60 days after the plaintiff has given notice of the violation (i) to the Administrator, (ii) to the State in which the violation occurs, and (iii) to any alleged violator of the standard, limitation, or order, or

(B) if the Administrator or State has commenced and is diligently prosecuting a civil action in a court of the United States or a State to require compliance with the standard, limitation, or order, but in any such action in a court of the United States any person may intervene as a matter of right.

(2) under subsection (a)(2) of this section prior to 60 days after the plaintiff has given notice of such action to the Administrator,

except that such action may be brought immediately after such notification in the case of an action under this section respecting a violation of section 7412(i)(3)(A) or (f)(4) of this title or an order issued by the Administrator pursuant to section 7413(a) of this title. Notice under this subsection shall be given in such manner as the Administrator shall prescribe by regulation.

**(c) Venue; intervention by Administrator; service of complaint; consent judgment**

(1) Any action respecting a violation by a stationary source of an emission standard or limitation or an order respecting such standard or limitation may be brought only in the judicial district in which such source is located.

(2) In any action under this section, the Administrator, if not a party, may intervene as a matter of right at any time in the proceeding. A judgment in an action under this section to which the United States is not a party shall not, however, have any binding effect upon the United States.

(3) Whenever any action is brought under this section the plaintiff shall serve a copy of the complaint on the Attorney General of the United States and on the Administrator. No consent judgment shall be entered in an action brought under this section in which the United States is not a party prior to 45 days following the receipt of a copy of the proposed consent judgment by the Attorney General and the Administrator during which time the Government may submit its comments on the proposed consent judgment to the court and parties or may intervene as a matter of right.

**(d) Award of costs; security**

The court, in issuing any final order in any action brought pursuant to subsection (a) of this section, may award costs of litigation (including reasonable attorney and expert witness fees) to any party, whenever the court determines such award is appropriate. The court may, if a temporary restraining order or preliminary injunction is sought, require the filing of a bond or equivalent security in accordance with the Federal Rules of Civil Procedure.

**(e) Nonrestriction of other rights**

Nothing in this section shall restrict any right which any person (or class of persons) may have under any statute or common law to seek enforcement of any emission standard or limitation or to seek any other relief (including relief against the Administrator or a State agency). Nothing in this section or in any other law of the United States shall be construed to prohibit, exclude, or restrict any State, local, or interstate authority from—

(1) bringing any enforcement action or obtaining any judicial remedy or sanction in any State or local court, or

(2) bringing any administrative enforcement action or obtaining any administrative remedy or sanction in any State or local administrative agency, department or instrumentality,

against the United States, any department, agency, or instrumentality thereof, or any officer, agent, or employee thereof under State or local law respecting control and abatement of air pollution. For provisions requiring compliance by the United States, departments, agencies, instrumentalities, officers, agents, and employees in the same manner as nongovernmental entities, see section 7418 of this title.

**(f) "Emission standard or limitation under this chapter" defined**

For purposes of this section, the term "emission standard or limitation under this chapter" means—

(1) a schedule or timetable of compliance, emission limitation, standard of performance or emission standard,

(2) a control or prohibition respecting a motor vehicle fuel or fuel additive, or [1]

(3) any condition or requirement of a permit under part C of subchapter I of this chapter (relating to significant deterioration of air quality) or part D of subchapter I of this chapter (relating to nonattainment),,[2] section 7419 of this title (relating to primary nonferrous smelter orders), any condition or requirement under an applicable implementation plan relating to transportation control measures, air quality maintenance plans, vehicle inspection and maintenance programs or vapor recovery requirements, section 7545(e) and (f) of this title (relating to fuels and fuel additives), section 7491 of this title (relating to visibility protection), any condition or requirement under subchapter VI of this chapter (relating to ozone protection), or any requirement under section 7411 or 7412 of this title (without regard to whether such requirement is expressed as an emission standard or otherwise);[3] or

(4) any other standard, limitation, or schedule established under any permit issued pursuant to subchapter V of this chapter or under any applicable State implementation plan approved by the Administrator, any permit term or condition, and any requirement to obtain a permit as a condition of operations.[4]

which is in effect under this chapter (including a requirement applicable by reason of section 7418 of this title) or under an applicable implementation plan.

**(g) Penalty fund**

(1) Penalties received under subsection (a) of this section shall be deposited in a special fund in the United States Treasury for licensing and other services. Amounts in such fund are authorized to be appropriated and shall remain available until expended, for use by the Administrator to finance air compliance and enforcement activities. The Administrator shall annually report to the Congress about the sums deposited into the fund, the sources thereof, and the actual and proposed uses thereof.

(2) Notwithstanding paragraph (1) the court in any action under this subsection to apply civil penalties shall have discretion to order that such civil penalties, in lieu of being deposited in the fund referred to in paragraph (1), be used in beneficial mitigation projects which are consistent with this chapter and enhance the public health or the environment. The court shall obtain the view of the Administrator in exercising such discretion and selecting any such projects. The amount of any such payment in any such action shall not exceed $100,000.

(July 14, 1955, c. 360, Title III, § 304, as added Dec. 31, 1970, Pub.L. 91–604, § 12(a), 84 Stat. 1706, and amended Aug. 7, 1977, Pub.L. 95–95, Title III, § 303(a)–(c), 91 Stat. 771, 772; Nov. 16, 1977, Pub.L. 95–190, § 14(a)(77), (78), 91 Stat. 1404; Nov. 15, 1990, Pub.L. 101–549, Title III, § 302(f), Title VII, § 707(a)–(g), 104 Stat. 2574, 2682, 2683.)

[1] So in original. The word "or" probably should not appear.
[2] So in original.
[3] So in original. The semicolon probably should be comma.
[4] So in original. The period probably should be a comma.

## HISTORICAL AND STATUTORY NOTES

**References in Text**

The Federal Rules of Civil Procedure, referred to in subsec. (d), are set out in Title 28, Judiciary and Judicial Procedure.

**Codifications**

Section was formerly classified to section 1857h–2 of this title.

**Effective and Applicability Provisions**

1990 Acts

Amendment by section 302(f) of Pub.L. 101–549 effective Nov. 15, 1990, except as otherwise provided, see section 711(b) of Pub.L. 101–549, set out as a note under section 7401 of this title.

Section 707(g) of Pub.L. 101–549 provided in part that: "The amendment made by this subsection [amending this section] shall take effect with respect to actions brought after the date 2 years after the enactment of the Clean Air Act Amendments of 1990 [Nov. 15, 1990]."

1977 Acts

Amendment by Pub.L. 95–95 effective Aug. 7, 1977, except as otherwise expressly provided, see section 406(d) of Pub.L. 95–95, set out as a note under section 7401 of this title.

**Savings Provisions**

Suits, actions or proceedings commenced under this chapter as in effect prior to Nov. 15, 1990, not to abate by reason of the taking effect of amendments by Pub.L. 101–549, except as otherwise provided for, see section 711(a) of Pub.L. 101–549, set out as a note under section 7401 of this title.

**Prior Provisions**

A prior section 304 of Act July 14, 1955, was renumbered section 311 by Pub.L. 91–604, and is set out as section 7611 of this title.

**Modification or Rescission of Rules, Regulations, Orders, Determinations, Contracts, Certifications, Authorizations, Delegations, and Other Actions**

All rules, regulations, orders, determinations, contracts, certifications, authorizations, delegations, or other actions duly issued, made, or taken by or pursuant to Act July 14,

1955, the Clean Air Act, as in effect immediately prior to the date of enactment of Pub.L. 95–95 [Aug. 7, 1977] to continue in full force and effect until modified or rescinded in accordance with Act July 14, 1955, as amended by Pub.L. 95–95 [this chapter], see section 406(b) of Pub.L. 95–95, set out as an Effective Date of 1977 Acts note under section 7401 of this title.

**Pending Actions and Proceedings**

Suits, actions, and other proceedings lawfully commenced by or against the Administrator or any other officer or employee of the United States in his official capacity or in relation to the discharge of his official duties under Act July 14, 1955, the Clean Air Act, as in effect immediately prior to the enactment of Pub.L. 95–95 [Aug. 7, 1977], not to abate by reason of the taking effect of Pub.L. 95–95, see section 406(a) of Pub.L. 95–95, set out as an Effective Date of 1977 Acts note under section 7401 of this title.

## § 7605. Representation in litigation

[CAA § 305]

### (a) Attorney General; attorneys appointed by Administrator

The Administrator shall request the Attorney General to appear and represent him in any civil action instituted under this chapter to which the Administrator is a party. Unless the Attorney General notifies the Administrator that he will appear in such action, within a reasonable time, attorneys appointed by the Administrator shall appear and represent him.

### (b) Memorandum of understanding regarding legal representation

In the event the Attorney General agrees to appear and represent the Administrator in any such action, such representation shall be conducted in accordance with, and shall include participation by, attorneys appointed by the Administrator to the extent authorized by, the memorandum of understanding between the Department of Justice and the Environmental Protection Agency, dated June 13, 1977, respecting representation of the agency by the department in civil litigation.

(July 14, 1955, c. 360, Title III, § 305, as added Dec. 31, 1970, Pub.L. 91–604, § 12(a), 84 Stat. 1707, and amended Aug. 7, 1977, Pub.L. 95–95, Title III, § 304(a), 91 Stat. 772.)

### HISTORICAL AND STATUTORY NOTES

**Codifications**

Section was formerly classified to section 1857h–3 of this title.

**Effective and Applicability Provisions**

1977 Acts

Amendment by Pub.L. 95–95 effective Aug. 7, 1977, except as otherwise expressly provided, see section 406(d) of Pub.L. 95–95, set out as a note under section 7401 of this title.

**Prior Provisions**

A prior section 305 of Act July 14, 1955, was renumbered section 312 by Pub.L. 91–604, and is set out as section 7612 of this title.

Another prior section 305 of act July 14, 1955, ch. 360, title III, formerly § 12, as added Dec. 17, 1963, Pub.L. 88–206, § 1, 77 Stat. 401, was renumbered section 305 by Pub.L. 89–272, renumbered section 308 by Pub.L. 90–148, and renumbered section 315 by Pub.L. 91–604, and is classified to section 7615 of this title.

**Modification or Rescission of Rules, Regulations, Orders, Determinations, Contracts, Certifications, Authorizations, Delegations, and Other Actions**

All rules, regulations, orders, determinations, contracts, certifications, authorizations, delegations, or other actions duly issued, made, or taken by or pursuant to Act July 14, 1955, the Clean Air Act, as in effect immediately prior to the date of enactment of Pub.L. 95–95 [Aug. 7, 1977] to continue in full force and effect until modified or rescinded in accordance with Act July 14, 1955, as amended by Pub.L. 95–95 [this chapter], see section 406(b) of Pub.L. 95–95, set out as an Effective Date of 1977 Acts note under section 7401 of this title.

**Pending Actions and Proceedings**

Suits, actions, and other proceedings lawfully commenced by or against the Administrator or any other officer or employee of the United States in his official capacity or in relation to the discharge of his official duties under Act July 14, 1955, the Clean Air Act, as in effect immediately prior to the enactment of Pub.L. 95–95 [Aug. 7, 1977], not to abate by reason of the taking effect of Pub.L. 95–95, see section 406(a) of Pub.L. 95–95, set out as an Effective Date of 1977 Acts note under section 7401 of this title.

## § 7606. Federal procurement

[CAA § 306]

### (a) Contracts with violators prohibited

No Federal agency may enter into any contract with any person who is convicted of any offense under section 7413(c) of this title for the procurement of goods, materials, and services to perform such contract at any facility at which the violation which gave rise to such conviction occurred if such facility is owned, leased, or supervised by such person. The prohibition in the preceding sentence shall continue until the Administrator certifies that the condition giving rise to such a conviction has been corrected. For convictions arising under section 7413(c)(2) of this title, the condition giving rise to the conviction also shall be considered to include any substantive violation of this chapter associated with the violation of 7413(c)(2) of this title. The Administrator may extend this prohibition to other facilities owned or operated by the convicted person.

### (b) Notification procedures

The Administrator shall establish procedures to provide all Federal agencies with the notification necessary for the purposes of subsection (a) of this section.

**(c) Federal agency contracts**

In order to implement the purposes and policy of this chapter to protect and enhance the quality of the Nation's air, the President shall, not more than 180 days after December 31, 1970, cause to be issued an order (1) requiring each Federal agency authorized to enter into contracts and each Federal agency which is empowered to extend Federal assistance by way of grant, loan, or contract to effectuate the purpose and policy of this chapter in such contracting or assistance activities, and (2) setting forth procedures, sanctions, penalties, and such other provisions, as the President determines necessary to carry out such requirement.

**(d) Exemptions; notification to Congress**

The President may exempt any contract, loan, or grant from all or part of the provisions of this section where he determines such exemption is necessary in the paramount interest of the United States and he shall notify the Congress of such exemption.

**(e) omitted**

(July 14, 1955, c. 360, Title III, § 306, as added Dec. 31, 1970, Pub.L. 91–604, § 12(a), 84 Stat. 1707, and amended Nov. 15, 1990, Pub.L. 101–549, Title VII, § 705, 104 Stat. 2682.)

### HISTORICAL AND STATUTORY NOTES

**Codifications**

Section was formerly classified to section 1857h–4 of this title.

Subsec. (e) of this section, which required the President to annually report to Congress on measures taken toward implementing the purpose and intent of this section, terminated, effective May 15, 2000, pursuant to section 3003 of Pub.L. 104–66, as amended, set out as a note under 31 U.S.C.A. § 1113. See, also, the 14th item on page 20 of House Document No. 103–7.

**Effective and Applicability Provisions**

1990 Acts

Amendment by Pub.L. 101–549 effective Nov. 15, 1990, except as otherwise provided, see section 711(b) of Pub.L. 101–549, set out as a note under section 7401 of this title.

**Savings Provisions**

Suits, actions or proceedings commenced under this chapter as in effect prior to Nov. 15, 1990, not to abate by reason of the taking effect of amendments by Pub.L. 101–549, except as otherwise provided for, see section 711(a) of Pub.L. 101–549, set out as a note under section 7401 of this title.

**Prior Provisions**

A prior § 306 of Act July 14, 1955, c. 360, Title III, as added Nov. 21, 1967, Pub.L. 90–148, § 2, 81 Stat. 506, was renumbered section 313 by Pub.L. 91–604, and is classified to former section 7613 of this title.

Another prior section 306 of Act July 14, 1955, c. 360, Title III, formerly § 13, as added Dec. 17, 1963, Pub.L. 88–206, § 1, 77 Stat. 401, renumbered § 306, Oct. 20, 1965, Pub.L. 89–272, Title I, § 101(4), 79 Stat. 992, renumbered § 309, Nov. 21, 1967, Pub.L. 90–148, § 2, 81 Stat. 506, renumbered § 316, Dec. 31, 1970, Pub.L. 91–604, § 12(a), 84 Stat. 1705, which related to appropriations, was classified to prior section 1857*l* of this title and was repealed by section 306 of Pub.L. 95–95. See section 7626 of this title.

**Federal Acquisition Regulation: Contractor Certification or Contract Clause for Acquisition of Commercial Items**

Pub.L. 103–355, Title VIII, § 8301(g), Oct. 13, 1994, 108 Stat. 3397, provided that: "The Federal Acquisition Regulation may not contain a requirement for a certification by a contractor under a contract for the acquisition of commercial items, or a requirement that such a contract include a contract clause, in order to implement a prohibition or requirement of section 306 of the Clean Air Act (42 U.S.C. 7606) [this section] or a prohibition or requirement issued in the implementation of that section [this section], since there is nothing in such section 306 [this section] that requires such a certification or contract clause."

## § 7607. Administrative proceedings and judicial review

**[CAA § 307]**

**(a) Administrative subpenas; confidentiality; witnesses**

In connection with any determination under section 7410(f) of this title, or for purposes of obtaining information under section 7521(b)(4) or 7545(c)(3) of this title, any investigation, monitoring, reporting requirement, entry, compliance inspection, or administrative enforcement proceeding under the [1] chapter (including but not limited to section 7413, section 7414, section 7420, section 7429, section 7477, section 7524, section 7525, section 7542, section 7603, or section 7606 of this title),,[2] the Administrator may issue subpenas for the attendance and testimony of witnesses and the production of relevant papers, books, and documents, and he may administer oaths. Except for emission data, upon a showing satisfactory to the Administrator by such owner or operator that such papers, books, documents, or information or particular part thereof, if made public, would divulge trade secrets or secret processes of such owner or operator, the Administrator shall consider such record, report, or information or particular portion thereof confidential in accordance with the purposes of section 1905 of Title 18, except that such paper, book, document, or information may be disclosed to other officers, employees, or authorized representatives of the United States concerned with carrying out this chapter, to persons carrying out the National Academy of Sciences' study and investigation provided for in section 7521(c) of this title, or when relevant in any proceeding under this chapter. Witnesses summoned shall be paid the same fees and mileage that are paid witnesses in the courts of the

United States. In case of contumacy or refusal to obey a subpena served upon any person under this subparagraph, the district court of the United States for any district in which such person is found or resides or transacts business, upon application by the United States and after notice to such person, shall have jurisdiction to issue an order requiring such person to appear and give testimony before the Administrator to appear and produce papers, books, and documents before the Administrator, or both, and any failure to obey such order of the court may be punished by such court as a contempt thereof.

**(b) Judicial review**

**(1)** A petition for review of action of the Administrator in promulgating any national primary or secondary ambient air quality standard, any emission standard or requirement under section 7412 of this title, any standard of performance or requirement under section 7411 of this title, any standard under section 7521 of this title (other than a standard required to be prescribed under section 7521(b)(1) of this title), any determination under section 7521(b)(5) of this title, any control or prohibition under section 7545 of this title, any standard under section 7571 of this title, any rule issued under section 7413, 7419, or under section 7420 of this title, or any other nationally applicable regulations promulgated, or final action taken, by the Administrator under this chapter may be filed only in the United States Court of Appeals for the District of Columbia. A petition for review of the Administrator's action in approving or promulgating any implementation plan under section 7410 of this title or section 7411(d) of this title, any order under section 7411(j) of this title, under section 7412 of this title,,[2] under section 7419 of this title, or under section 7420 of this title, or his action under section 1857c–10(c)(2)(A), (B), or (C) of this title (as in effect before August 7, 1977) or under regulations thereunder, or revising regulations for enhanced monitoring and compliance certification programs under section 7414(a)(3) of this title, or any other final action of the Administrator under this chapter (including any denial or disapproval by the Administrator under subchapter I of this chapter) which is locally or regionally applicable may be filed only in the United States Court of Appeals for the appropriate circuit. Notwithstanding the preceding sentence a petition for review of any action referred to in such sentence may be filed only in the United States Court of Appeals for the District of Columbia if such action is based on a determination of nationwide scope or effect and if in taking such action the Administrator finds and publishes that such action is based on such a determination. Any petition for review under this subsection shall be filed within sixty days from the date notice of such promulgation, approval, or action appears in the Federal Register, except that if such petition is based solely on grounds arising after such sixtieth day, then any petition for review under this subsection shall be filed within sixty days after such grounds arise. The filing of a petition for reconsideration by the Administrator of any otherwise final rule or action shall not affect the finality of such rule or action for purposes of judicial review nor extend the time within which a petition for judicial review of such rule or action under this section may be filed, and shall not postpone the effectiveness of such rule or action.

**(2)** Action of the Administrator with respect to which review could have been obtained under paragraph (1) shall not be subject to judicial review in civil or criminal proceedings for enforcement. Where a final decision by the Administrator defers performance of any nondiscretionary statutory action to a later time, any person may challenge the deferral pursuant to paragraph (1).

**(c) Additional evidence**

In any judicial proceeding in which review is sought of a determination under this chapter required to be made on the record after notice and opportunity for hearing, if any party applies to the court for leave to adduce additional evidence, and shows to the satisfaction of the court that such additional evidence is material and that there were reasonable grounds for the failure to adduce such evidence in the proceeding before the Administrator, the court may order such additional evidence (and evidence in rebuttal thereof) to be taken before the Administrator, in such manner and upon such terms and conditions as to[3] the court may deem proper. The Administrator may modify his findings as to the facts, or make new findings, by reason of the additional evidence so taken and he shall file such modified or new findings, and his recommendation, if any, for the modification or setting aside of his original determination, with the return of such additional evidence.

**(d) Rulemaking**

**(1)** This subsection applies to—

**(A)** the promulgation or revision of any national ambient air quality standard under section 7409 of this title,

**(B)** the promulgation or revision of an implementation plan by the Administrator under section 7410(c) of this title,

**(C)** the promulgation or revision of any standard of performance under section 7411 of this title, or emission standard or limitation under section 7412(d) of this title, any standard under section 7412(f) of this title, or any regulation under section 7412(g)(1)(D) and (F) of this title, or any regulation under section 7412(m) or (n) of this title,

(D) the promulgation of any requirement for solid waste combustion under section 7429 of this title,

(E) the promulgation or revision of any regulation pertaining to any fuel or fuel additive under section 7545 of this title,

(F) the promulgation or revision of any aircraft emission standard under section 7571 of this title,

(G) the promulgation or revision of any regulation under subchapter IV–A of this chapter (relating to control of acid deposition),

(H) promulgation or revision of regulations pertaining to primary nonferrous smelter orders under section 7419 of this title (but not including the granting or denying of any such order),

(I) promulgation or revision of regulations under subchapter VI of this chapter (relating to stratosphere and ozone protection),

(J) promulgation or revision of regulations under part C of subchapter I of this chapter (relating to prevention of significant deterioration of air quality and protection of visibility),

(K) promulgation or revision of regulations under section 7521 of this title and test procedures for new motor vehicles or engines under section 7525 of this title, and the revision of a standard under section 7521(a)(3) of this title,

(L) promulgation or revision of regulations for noncompliance penalties under section 7420 of this title,

(M) promulgation or revision of any regulations promulgated under section 7541 of this title (relating to warranties and compliance by vehicles in actual use),

(N) action of the Administrator under section 7426 of this title (relating to interstate pollution abatement),

(O) the promulgation or revision of any regulation pertaining to consumer and commercial products under section 7511b(e) of this title,

(P) the promulgation or revision of any regulation pertaining to field citations under section 7413(d)(3) of this title,

(Q) the promulgation or revision of any regulation pertaining to urban buses or the clean-fuel vehicle, clean-fuel fleet, and clean fuel programs under part C of subchapter II of this chapter,

(R) the promulgation or revision of any regulation pertaining to nonroad engines or nonroad vehicles under section 7547 of this title,

(S) the promulgation or revision of any regulation relating to motor vehicle compliance program fees under section 7552 of this title,

(T) the promulgation or revision of any regulation under subchapter IV–A of this chapter (relating to acid deposition),

(U) the promulgation or revision of any regulation under section 7511b(f) of this title pertaining to marine vessels, and

(V) such other actions as the Administrator may determine.

The provisions of section 553 through 557 and section 706 of Title 5 shall not, except as expressly provided in this subsection, apply to actions to which this subsection applies. This subsection shall not apply in the case of any rule or circumstance referred to in subparagraphs (A) or (B) of subsection 553(b) of Title 5.

(2) Not later than the date of proposal of any action to which this subsection applies, the Administrator shall establish a rulemaking docket for such action (hereinafter in this subsection referred to as a "rule"). Whenever a rule applies only within a particular State, a second (identical) docket shall be simultaneously established in the appropriate regional office of the Environmental Protection Agency.

(3) In the case of any rule to which this subsection applies, notice of proposed rulemaking shall be published in the Federal Register, as provided under section 553(b) of Title 5, shall be accompanied by a statement of its basis and purpose and shall specify the period available for public comment (hereinafter referred to as the "comment period"). The notice of proposed rulemaking shall also state the docket number, the location or locations of the docket, and the times it will be open to public inspection. The statement of basis and purpose shall include a summary of—

(A) the factual data on which the proposed rule is based;

(B) the methodology used in obtaining the data and in analyzing the data; and

(C) the major legal interpretations and policy considerations underlying the proposed rule.

The statement shall also set forth or summarize and provide a reference to any pertinent findings, recommendations, and comments by the Scientific Review Committee established under section 7409(d) of this title and the National Academy of Sciences, and, if the proposal differs in any important respect from any of these recommendations, an explanation of the reasons for such differences. All data, information, and documents referred to in this paragraph on which the proposed rule relies shall be included in the docket on the date of publication of the proposed rule.

(4)(A) The rulemaking docket required under paragraph (2) shall be open for inspection by the public at reasonable times specified in the notice of proposed rulemaking. Any person may copy documents contained in the docket. The Administrator shall provide copying facilities which may be used at the expense of the person seeking copies, but the Administrator may waive or reduce such expenses in such instances as the public interest requires. Any person may request copies by mail if the person pays the expenses, including personnel costs to do the copying.

**(B)(i)** Promptly upon receipt by the agency, all written comments and documentary information on the proposed rule received from any person for inclusion in the docket during the comment period shall be placed in the docket. The transcript of public hearings, if any, on the proposed rule shall also be included in the docket promptly upon receipt from the person who transcribed such hearings. All documents which become available after the proposed rule has been published and which the Administrator determines are of central relevance to the rulemaking shall be placed in the docket as soon as possible after their availability.

**(ii)** The drafts of proposed rules submitted by the Administrator to the Office of Management and Budget for any interagency review process prior to proposal of any such rule, all documents accompanying such drafts, and all written comments thereon by other agencies and all written responses to such written comments by the Administrator shall be placed in the docket no later than the date of proposal of the rule. The drafts of the final rule submitted for such review process prior to promulgation and all such written comments thereon, all documents accompanying such drafts, and written responses thereto shall be placed in the docket no later than the date of promulgation.

**(5)** In promulgating a rule to which this subsection applies (i) the Administrator shall allow any person to submit written comments, data, or documentary information; (ii) the Administrator shall give interested persons an opportunity for the oral presentation of data, views, or arguments, in addition to an opportunity to make written submissions; (iii) a transcript shall be kept of any oral presentation; and (iv) the Administrator shall keep the record of such proceeding open for thirty days after completion of the proceeding to provide an opportunity for submission of rebuttal and supplementary information.

**(6)(A)** The promulgated rule shall be accompanied by (i) a statement of basis and purpose like that referred to in paragraph (3) with respect to a proposed rule and (ii) an explanation of the reasons for any major changes in the promulgated rule from the proposed rule.

**(B)** The promulgated rule shall also be accompanied by a response to each of the significant comments, criticisms, and new data submitted in written or oral presentations during the comment period.

**(C)** The promulgated rule may not be based (in part or whole) on any information or data which has not been placed in the docket as of the date of such promulgation.

**(7)(A)** The record for judicial review shall consist exclusively of the material referred to in paragraph (3), clause (i) of paragraph (4)(B), and subparagraphs (A) and (B) of paragraph (6).

**(B)** Only an objection to a rule or procedure which was raised with reasonable specificity during the period for public comment (including any public hearing) may be raised during judicial review. If the person raising an objection can demonstrate to the Administrator that it was impracticable to raise such objection within such time or if the grounds for such objection arose after the period for public comment (but within the time specified for judicial review) and if such objection is of central relevance to the outcome of the rule, the Administrator shall convene a proceeding for reconsideration of the rule and provide the same procedural rights as would have been afforded had the information been available at the time the rule was proposed. If the Administrator refuses to convene such a proceeding, such person may seek review of such refusal in the United States court of appeals for the appropriate circuit (as provided in subsection (b) of this section). Such reconsideration shall not postpone the effectiveness of the rule. The effectiveness of the rule may be stayed during such reconsideration, however, by the Administrator or the court for a period not to exceed three months.

**(8)** The sole forum for challenging procedural determinations made by the Administrator under this subsection shall be in the United States court of appeals for the appropriate circuit (as provided in subsection (b) of this section) at the time of the substantive review of the rule. No interlocutory appeals shall be permitted with respect to such procedural determinations. In reviewing alleged procedural errors, the court may invalidate the rule only if the errors were so serious and related to matters of such central relevance to the rule that there is a substantial likelihood that the rule would have been significantly changed if such errors had not been made.

**(9)** In the case of review of any action of the Administrator to which this subsection applies, the court may reverse any such action found to be—

**(A)** arbitrary, capricious, an abuse of discretion, or otherwise not in accordance with law;

**(B)** contrary to constitutional right, power, privilege, or immunity;

**(C)** in excess of statutory jurisdiction, authority, or limitations, or short of statutory right; or

(D) without observance of procedure required by law, if (i) such failure to observe such procedure is arbitrary or capricious, (ii) the requirement of paragraph (7)(B) has been met, and (iii) the condition of the last sentence of paragraph (8) is met.

(10) Each statutory deadline for promulgation of rules to which this subsection applies which requires promulgation less than six months after date of proposal may be extended to not more than six months after date of proposal by the Administrator upon a determination that such extension is necessary to afford the public, and the agency, adequate opportunity to carry out the purposes of this subsection.

(11) The requirements of this subsection shall take effect with respect to any rule the proposal of which occurs after ninety days after August 7, 1977.

**(e) Other methods of judicial review not authorized**

Nothing in this chapter shall be construed to authorize judicial review of regulations or orders of the Administrator under this chapter, except as provided in this section.

**(f) Costs**

In any judicial proceeding under this section, the court may award costs of litigation (including reasonable attorney and expert witness fees) whenever it determines that such award is appropriate.

**(g) Stay, injunction, or similar relief in proceedings relating to noncompliance penalties**

In any action respecting the promulgation of regulations under section 7420 of this title or the administration or enforcement of section 7420 of this title no court shall grant any stay, injunctive, or similar relief before final judgment by such court in such action.

**(h) Public participation**

It is the intent of Congress that, consistent with the policy of subchapter II of chapter 5 of Title 5, the Administrator in promulgating any regulation under this chapter, including a regulation subject to a deadline, shall ensure a reasonable period for public participation of at least 30 days, except as otherwise expressly provided in section [4] 7407(d), 7502(a), 7511(a) and (b), and 7512(a) and (b) of this title.

(July 14, 1955, c. 360, Title III, § 307, as added Dec. 31, 1970, Pub.L. 91–604, § 12(a), 84 Stat. 1707, and amended Nov. 18, 1971, Pub.L. 92–157, Title III, § 302(a), 85 Stat. 464; June 22, 1974, Pub.L. 93–319, § 6(c), 88 Stat. 259; Aug. 7, 1977, Pub.L. 95–95, Title III, §§ 303(d), 305(a), (c), (f)–(h), 91 Stat. 772, 776, 777; Nov. 16, 1977, Pub.L. 95–190, § 14(a)(79), (80), 91 Stat. 1404; Nov. 15, 1990, Pub.L. 101–549, Title I, §§ 108(p), 110(5), Title III, § 302(g), (h), Title VII, §§ 702(c), 703, 706, 707(h), 710(b), 104 Stat. 2469, 2470, 2574, 2681–2684.)

[1] So in original. Probably should be "this".

[2] So in original.

[3] So in original. The word "to" probably should not appear.

[4] So in original. Probably should be "sections".

## HISTORICAL AND STATUTORY NOTES

**References in Text**

Section 7521(b)(5) of this title, referred to in subsec. (b)(1), was repealed by Pub.L. 101–549, Title II, § 203(3), Nov. 15, 1990, 104 Stat. 2529.

Section 1857c–10(c)(2)(A), (B), or (C) of this title (as in effect before August 7, 1977), referred to in subsec. (b)(1), was in the original "section 119(c)(2)(A), (B), or (C) (as in effect before the date of enactment of the Clean Air Act Amendments of 1977)", meaning section 119 of Act July 14, 1955, c. 360, Title I, as added June 22, 1974, Pub.L. 93–319, § 3, 88 Stat. 248, (which was classified to section 1857c–10 of this title) as in effect prior to the enactment of Pub.L. 95–95, Aug. 7, 1977, 91 Stat. 691, effective Aug. 7, 1977. Section 112(b)(1) of Pub.L. 95–95 repealed section 119 of Act July 14, 1955, c. 360, Title I, as added by Pub.L. 93–319, and provided that all references to such section 119 in any subsequent enactment which supersedes Pub.L. 93–319 shall be construed to refer to section 113(d) of the Clean Air Act and to paragraph (5) thereof in particular which is classified to subsec. (d)(5) of section 7413 of this title. Section 7413(d) of this title was subsequently amended generally by Pub.L. 101–549, Title VII, § 701, Nov. 15, 1990, 104 Stat. 2672, and, as so amended, no longer relates to final compliance orders. Section 117(b) of Pub.L. 95–95 added a new section 119 of Act July 14, 1955, which is classified to section 7419 of this title.

Part C of subchapter I of this chapter, referred to in subsec. (d)(1)(J), was in the original "subtitle C of Title I", and was translated as reading "part C of Title I" to reflect the probable intent of Congress, because Title I does not contain subtitles.

**Codifications**

Section was formerly classified to section 1857h–5 of this title.

In subsec. (h), "subchapter II of chapter 5 of Title 5" was substituted for "the Administrative Procedures Act" on authority of Pub.L. 89–554, § 7(b), Sept. 6, 1966, 80 Stat. 631, the first section of which enacted Title 5, Government Organization and Employees.

**Effective and Applicability Provisions**

1990 Acts

Amendment by Pub.L. 101–549 effective Nov. 15, 1990, except as otherwise provided, see section 711(b) of Pub.L. 101–549, set out as a note under section 7401 of this title.

1977 Acts

Amendment by Pub.L. 95–95 effective Aug. 7, 1977, except as otherwise expressly provided, see section 406(d) of Pub.L. 95–95, set out as a note under section 7401 of this title.

**Savings Provisions**

Suits, actions or proceedings commenced under this chapter as in effect prior to Nov. 15, 1990, not to abate by reason of the taking effect of amendments by Pub.L. 101–549, except as otherwise provided for, see section 711(a) of Pub.L. 101–549, set out as a note under section 7401 of this title.

**Prior Provisions**

A prior section 307 of Act July 14, 1955, c. 360, Title III, as added Nov. 21, 1967, Pub.L. 90–148, § 2, 81 Stat. 506, renumbered section 314, Dec. 31, 1970, Pub.L. 91–604, § 12(a), 84 Stat. 1705, which related to labor standards, is set out as section 7614 of this title.

Another prior section 307 of act July 14, 1955, c. 360, Title III, formerly § 14, as added Dec. 17, 1963, Pub.L. 88–206, § 1, 77 Stat. 401, was renumbered section 307 by Pub.L. 89–272, renumbered section 310 by Pub.L. 90–148, and renumbered section 317 by Pub.L. 91–604, and is set out as a Short Title of 1963 Acts note under section 7401 of this title.

**Modification or Rescission of Rules, Regulations, Orders, Determinations Contracts, Certifications, Authorizations, Delegations, and Other Actions**

All rules, regulations, orders, determinations, contracts, certifications, authorizations, delegations, or other actions duly issued, made, or taken by or pursuant to Act July 14, 1955, the Clean Air Act, as in effect immediately prior to the date of enactment of Pub.L. 95–95 [Aug. 7, 1977] to continue in full force and effect until modified or rescinded in accordance with Act July 14, 1955, as amended by Pub.L. 95–95 [this chapter], see section 406(b) of Pub.L. 95–95, set out as an Effective Date of 1977 Acts note under section 7401 of this title.

**Pending Actions and Proceedings**

Suits, actions, and other proceedings lawfully commenced by or against the Administrator or any other officer or employee of the United States in his official capacity or in relation to the discharge of his official duties under Act July 14, 1955, the Clean Air Act, as in effect immediately prior to the enactment of Pub.L. 95–95 [Aug. 7, 1977], not to abate by reason of the taking effect of Pub.L. 95–95, see section 406(a) of Pub.L. 95–95, set out as an Effective Date of 1977 Acts note under section 7401 of this title.

**Termination of Advisory Committees**

Advisory Committees established after Jan. 5, 1973, to terminate not later than the expiration of the two-year period beginning on the date of their establishment, unless, in the case of a committee established by the President or an officer of the Federal Government, such committee is renewed by appropriate action prior to the expiration of such two-year period, or in the case of a committee established by the Congress, its duration is otherwise provided for by law, see section 14 of Pub.L. 92–463, Oct. 6, 1972, 86 Stat. 776, set out in Appendix 2 to Title 5, Government Organization and Employees.

## § 7608. Mandatory licensing

**[CAA § 308]**

Whenever the Attorney General determines, upon application of the Administrator—

(1) that—

(A) in the implementation of the requirements of section 7411, 7412, or 7521 of this title, a right under any United States letters patent, which is being used or intended for public or commercial use and not otherwise reasonably available, is necessary to enable any person required to comply with such limitation to so comply, and

(B) there are no reasonable alternative methods to accomplish such purpose, and

(2) that the unavailability of such right may result in a substantial lessening of competition or tendency to create a monopoly in any line of commerce in any section of the country,

the Attorney General may so certify to a district court of the United States, which may issue an order requiring the person who owns such patent to license it on such reasonable terms and conditions as the court, after hearing, may determine. Such certification may be made to the district court for the district in which the person owning the patent resides, does business, or is found.

(July 14, 1955, c. 360, Title III, § 308, as added Dec. 31, 1970, Pub.L. 91–604, § 12(a), 84 Stat. 1708.)

### HISTORICAL AND STATUTORY NOTES

**Codifications**

Section was formerly classified to section 1857h–6 of this title.

**Prior Provisions**

A prior section 308 of Act July 14, 1955, c. 360, Title III, formerly § 12, as added Dec. 17, 1963, Pub.L. 88–206, § 1, 77 Stat. 401, renumbered § 305, Oct. 20, 1965, Pub.L. 89–272, Title I, § 101(4), 79 Stat. 992, renumbered § 308, Nov. 21, 1967, Pub.L. 90–148, § 2, 81 Stat. 506, renumbered § 315, Dec. 31, 1970, Pub.L. 91–604, § 12(a), 84 Stat. 1705, which related to separability of provisions, is set out as section 7615 of this title.

**Modification or Rescission of Rules, Regulations, Orders, Determinations, Contracts, Certifications, Authorizations, Delegations, and Other Actions**

All rules, regulations, orders, determinations, contracts, certifications, authorizations, delegations, or other actions duly issued, made, or taken by or pursuant to Act July 14, 1955, the Clean Air Act, as in effect immediately prior to the date of enactment of Pub.L. 95–95 [Aug. 7, 1977] to continue in full force and effect until modified or rescinded in accordance with Act July 14, 1955, as amended by Pub.L. 95–95 [this chapter], see section 406(b) of Pub.L. 95–95, set out as an Effective Date of 1977 Acts note under section 7401 of this title.

## § 7609. Policy review

**[CAA § 309]**

### (a) Environmental impact

The Administrator shall review and comment in writing on the environmental impact of any matter relating to duties and responsibilities granted pursuant to this chapter or other provisions of the authority of the Administrator, contained in any (1) legislation proposed by any Federal department or agency, (2) newly authorized Federal projects for construction and any major Federal agency action (other than a project for construction) to which section 4332(2)(C) of this title applies, and (3) proposed regulations published by any department or agency of the Federal Government. Such written comment shall be made public at the conclusion of any such review.

**(b) Unsatisfactory legislation, action, or regulation**

In the event the Administrator determines that any such legislation, action, or regulation is unsatisfactory from the standpoint of public health or welfare or environmental quality, he shall publish his determination and the matter shall be referred to the Council on Environmental Quality.

(July 14, 1955, c. 360, Title III, § 309, as added Dec. 31, 1970, Pub.L. 91–604, § 12(a), 84 Stat. 1709.)

### HISTORICAL AND STATUTORY NOTES

**Codifications**

Section was formerly classified to section 1857h–7 of this title.

**Prior Provisions**

A prior section 309 of Act July 14, 1955, c. 360, Title III, formerly § 13, as added Dec. 17, 1963, Pub.L. 88–206, § 1, 77 Stat. 401, renumbered § 306, Oct. 20, 1965, Pub.L. 89–272, Title I, § 101(4), 79 Stat. 992, renumbered § 309, Nov. 21, 1967, Pub.L. 90–148, § 2, 81 Stat. 506, renumbered § 316, Dec. 31, 1970, Pub.L. 91–604, § 12(a), 84 Stat. 1705, which related to appropriations, was classified to section 1857l of this title and was repealed by section 306 of Pub.L. 95–95. Similar appropriation provisions are now classified to section 7626 of this title.

**Modification or Rescission of Rules, Regulations, Orders, Determinations, Contracts, Certifications, Authorizations, Delegations, and Other Actions**

All rules, regulations, orders, determinations, contracts, certifications, authorizations, delegations, or other actions duly issued, made, or taken by or pursuant to Act July 14, 1955, the Clean Air Act, as in effect immediately prior to the date of enactment of Pub.L. 95–95 [Aug. 7, 1977] to continue in full force and effect until modified or rescinded in accordance with Act July 14, 1955, as amended by Pub.L. 95–95 [this chapter], see section 406(b) of Pub.L. 95–95, set out as an Effective Date of 1977 Acts note under section 7401 of this title.

## § 7610. Other authority

[CAA § 310]

**(a) Authority and responsibilities under other laws not affected**

Except as provided in subsection (b) of this section, this chapter shall not be construed as superseding or limiting the authorities and responsibilities, under any other provision of law, of the Administrator or any other Federal officer, department, or agency.

**(b) Nonduplication of appropriations**

No appropriation shall be authorized or made under section 241, 243, or 246 of this title for any fiscal year after the fiscal year ending June 30, 1964, for any purpose for which appropriations may be made under authority of this chapter.

(July 14, 1955, c. 360, Title III, § 310, formerly § 10, as added Dec. 17, 1963, Pub.L. 88–206, § 1, 77 Stat. 401; renumbered § 303, Oct. 20, 1965, Pub.L. 89–272, Title I, § 101(4), 79 Stat. 992; Nov. 21, 1967, Pub.L. 90–148, § 2, 81 Stat. 505; and renumbered § 310 and amended Dec. 31, 1970, Pub.L. 91–604, §§ 12(a), 15(c)(2), 84 Stat. 1705, 1713.)

### HISTORICAL AND STATUTORY NOTES

**Codifications**

Section was formerly classified to section 1857i of this title.

**Prior Provisions**

A prior section 310 of Act July 14, 1955, c. 360, Title III, formerly § 14, as added Dec. 17, 1963, Pub.L. 88–206, § 1, 77 Stat. 401, renumbered § 307, Oct. 20, 1965, Pub.L. 89–272, Title I, § 101(4), 79 Stat. 992, renumbered § 310, Nov. 21, 1967, Pub.L. 90–148, § 2, 81 Stat. 506, renumbered § 317, Dec. 31, 1970, Pub.L. 91–604, § 12(a), 84 Stat. 1705, is set out as a Short Title of 1963 Acts note under section 7401 of this title.

Provisions similar to those contained in subsec. (a) of this section were contained in a prior section 1857f of this title, Act July 14, 1955, c. 360, § 7, 69 Stat. 323, prior to the general amendment of this chapter by Pub.L. 88–206.

**Modification or Rescission of Rules, Regulations, Orders, Determinations, Contracts, Certifications, Authorizations, Delegations, and Other Actions**

All rules, regulations, orders, determinations, contracts, certifications, authorizations, delegations, or other actions duly issued, made, or taken by or pursuant to Act July 14, 1955, the Clean Air Act, as in effect immediately prior to the date of enactment of Pub.L. 95–95 [Aug. 7, 1977] to continue in full force and effect until modified or rescinded in accordance with Act July 14, 1955, as amended by Pub.L. 95–95 [this chapter], see section 406(b) of Pub.L. 95–95, set out as an Effective Date of 1977 Acts note under section 7401 of this title.

## § 7611. Records and audit

[CAA § 311]

**(a) Recipients of assistance to keep prescribed records**

Each recipient of assistance under this chapter shall keep such records as the Administrator shall prescribe, including records which fully disclose the amount and disposition by such recipient of the proceeds of such assistance, the total cost of the project or undertaking in connection with which such assistance is given or used, and the amount of that portion of the cost of the project or undertaking supplied by other sources, and such other records as will facilitate an effective audit.

**(b) Audits**

The Administrator and the Comptroller General of the United States, or any of their duly authorized representatives, shall have access for the purpose of audit and examinations to any books, documents, papers, and records of the recipients that are pertinent to the grants received under this chapter.

(July 14, 1955, c. 360, Title III, § 311, formerly § 11, as added Dec. 17, 1963, Pub.L. 88–206, § 1, 77 Stat. 401; renumbered § 304, Oct. 20, 1965, Pub.L. 89–272, Title I, § 101(4), 79 Stat. 992; Nov. 21, 1967, Pub.L. 90–148, § 2, 81 Stat. 505; renumbered § 311, and amended Dec. 31, 1970, Pub.L. 91–604, §§ 12(a), 15(c)(2), 84 Stat. 1705, 1713.)

### HISTORICAL AND STATUTORY NOTES

**Codifications**

Section was formerly classified to section 1857j of this title.

**Modification or Rescission of Rules, Regulations, Orders, Determinations, Contracts, Certifications, Authorizations, Delegations, and Other Actions**

All rules, regulations, orders, determinations, contracts, certifications, authorizations, delegations, or other actions duly issued, made, or taken by or pursuant to Act July 14, 1955, the Clean Air Act, as in effect immediately prior to the date of enactment of Pub.L. 95–95 [Aug. 7, 1977] to continue in full force and effect until modified or rescinded in accordance with Act July 14, 1955, as amended by Pub.L. 95–95 [this chapter], see section 406(b) of Pub.L. 95–95, set out as an Effective Date of 1977 Acts note under section 7401 of this title.

## § 7612. Economic impact analyses

**[CAA § 312]**

**(a) Cost-benefit analysis**

The Administrator, in consultation with the Secretary of Commerce, the Secretary of Labor, and the Council on Clean Air Compliance Analysis (as established under subsection (f) of this section), shall conduct a comprehensive analysis of the impact of this chapter on the public health, economy, and environment of the United States. In performing such analysis, the Administrator should consider the costs, benefits and other effects associated with compliance with each standard issued for—

(1) a criteria air pollutant subject to a standard issued under section 7409 of this title;

(2) a hazardous air pollutant listed under section 7412 of this title, including any technology-based standard and any risk-based standard for such pollutant;

(3) emissions from mobile sources regulated under subchapter II of this chapter;

(4) a limitation under this chapter for emissions of sulfur dioxide or nitrogen oxides;

(5) a limitation under subchapter VI of this chapter on the production of any ozone-depleting substance; and

(6) any other section of this chapter.

**(b) Benefits**

In describing the benefits of a standard described in subsection (a) of this section, the Administrator shall consider all of the economic, public health, and environmental benefits of efforts to comply with such standard. In any case where numerical values are assigned to such benefits, a default assumption of zero value shall not be assigned to such benefits unless supported by specific data. The Administrator shall assess how benefits are measured in order to assure that damage to human health and the environment is more accurately measured and taken into account.

**(c) Costs**

In describing the costs of a standard described in subsection (a) of this section, the Administrator shall consider the effects of such standard on employment, productivity, cost of living, economic growth, and the overall economy of the United States.

**(d) Initial report**

Not later than 12 months after November 15, 1990, the Administrator, in consultation with the Secretary of Commerce, the Secretary of Labor, and the Council on Clean Air Compliance Analysis, shall submit a report to the Congress that summarizes the results of the analysis described in subsection (a) of this section, which reports—

(1) all costs incurred previous to November 15, 1990, in the effort to comply with such standards; and

(2) all benefits that have accrued to the United States as a result of such costs.

**(e) omitted**

**(f) Appointment of Advisory Council on Clean Air Compliance Analysis**

Not later than 6 months after November 15, 1990, the Administrator, in consultation with the Secretary of Commerce and the Secretary of Labor, shall appoint an Advisory Council on Clean Air Compliance Analysis of not less than nine members (hereafter in this section referred to as the "Council"). In appointing such members, the Administrator shall appoint recognized experts in the fields of the health and environmental effects of air pollution, economic analysis, environmental sciences, and such other fields that the Administrator determines to be appropriate.

**(g) Duties of Advisory Council**

The Council shall—

(1) review the data to be used for any analysis required under this section and make recommendations to the Administrator on the use of such data;

(2) review the methodology used to analyze such data and make recommendations to the Administrator on the use of such methodology; and

(3) prior to the issuance of a report required under subsection (d) or (e) of this section, review the findings of such report, and make recommendations to the Administrator concerning the validity and utility of such findings.

(July 14, 1955, c. 360, Title III, § 312, formerly § 305, as added Nov. 21, 1967, Pub.L. 90–148, § 2, 81 Stat. 505; renumbered § 312 and amended Dec. 31, 1970, Pub.L. 91–604, §§ 12(a), 15(c)(2), 84 Stat. 1705, 1713; Aug. 7, 1977, Pub.L. 95–95, Title II, § 224(c), 91 Stat. 767; Nov. 15, 1990, Pub.L. 101–549, Title VIII, § 812(a), 104 Stat. 2691.)

## HISTORICAL AND STATUTORY NOTES

### Codifications

Section was formerly classified to section 1857j–1 of this title.

Subsec. (e) of this section, which required the Administrator, in consultation with the Secretary of Commerce, the Secretary of Labor, and the Council on Clean Air Compliance Analysis, to submit a report to Congress that updates the report issued pursuant to subsec. (d) of this section, and which, in addition, makes projections into the future regarding expected costs, benefits, and other effects of compliance with standards pursuant to this chapter as listed in subsec. (a) of this section, terminated, effective May 15, 2000, pursuant to section 3003 of Pub.L. 104–66, as amended, set out as a note under 31 U.S.C.A. § 1113. See, also, the 4th item on page 163 of House Document No. 103–7.

### Effective and Applicability Provisions

1990 Acts

Amendment by Pub.L. 101–549 effective Nov. 15, 1990, except as otherwise provided, see section 711(b) of Pub.L. 101–549, set out as a note under section 7401 of this title.

1977 Acts

Amendment by Pub.L. 95–95 effective Aug. 7, 1977, except as otherwise expressly provided, see section 406(d) of Pub.L. 95–95, set out as a note under section 7401 of this title.

### Savings Provisions

Suits, actions or proceedings commenced under this chapter as in effect prior to Nov. 15, 1990, not to abate by reason of the taking effect of amendments by Pub.L. 101–549, except as otherwise provided for, see section 711(a) of Pub.L. 101–549, set out as a note under section 7401 of this title.

### Equivalent Air Quality Controls Among Trading Nations

Section 811 of Pub.L. 101–549 provided that:

"**(a) Findings.**—The Congress finds that—

"(1) all nations have the responsibility to adopt and enforce effective air quality standards and requirements and the United States, in enacting this Act [Pub.L. 101–549, Nov. 15, 1990, 104 Stat. 2399, popularly known as the Clean Air Act Amendments of 1990, for distribution of which to the Code, see Tables], is carrying out its responsibility in this regard;

"(2) as a result of complying with this Act, businesses in the United States will make significant capital investments and incur incremental costs in implementing control technology standards;

"(3) such compliance may impair the competitiveness of certain United States jobs, production, processes, and products if foreign goods are produced under less costly environmental standards and requirements than are United States goods; and

"(4) mechanisms should be sought through which the United States and its trading partners can agree to eliminate or reduce competitive disadvantages.

"**(b) Action by the President.**—

"**(1) In general.**—Within 18 months after the date of the enactment of the Clean Air Act Amendments of 1990 [Nov. 15, 1990], the President shall submit to the Congress a report—

"(A) identifying and evaluating the economic effects of—

"(i) the significant air quality standards and controls required under this Act, [Pub.L. 101–549, Nov. 15, 1990, 104 Stat. 2399, popularly known as the Clean Air Act Amendments of 1990, for distribution of which to the Code, see Tables] and

"(ii) the differences between the significant standards and controls required under this Act and similar standards and controls adopted and enforced by the major trading partners of the United States,

on the international competitiveness of United States manufacturers; and

"(B) containing a strategy for addressing such economic effects through trade consultations and negotiations.

"**(2) Additional reporting requirements.**—(A) The evaluation required under paragraph (1)(A) shall examine the extent to which the significant air quality standards and controls required under this Act [Pub.L. 101–549, Nov. 15, 1990, 104 Stat. 2399, popularly known as the Clean Air Act Amendments of 1990, for distribution of which to the Code, see Tables] are comparable to existing internationally-agreed norms.

"(B) The strategy required to be developed under paragraph (1)(B) shall include recommended options (such as the harmonization of standards and trade adjustment measures) for reducing or eliminating competitive disadvantages caused by differences in standards and controls between the United States and each of its major trading partners.

"**(3) Public comment.**—Interested parties shall be given an opportunity to submit comments regarding the evaluations and strategy required in the report under paragraph (1). The President shall take any such comment into account in preparing the report.

"**(4) Interim report.**—Within 9 months after the date of the enactment of the Clean Air Act Amendments of 1990 [Nov. 15, 1990], the President shall submit to the Congress an interim report on the progress being made in complying with paragraph (1)."

### GAO Reports on Costs and Benefits

Section 812(b) of Pub.L. 101–549 which directed the Comptroller General of the General Accounting Office, commencing on the second year after Nov. 15, 1990, and annually thereafter, in consultation with other agencies, to report to Congress on pollution control strategies and employment effects of the Clean Air Act Amendments of 1990 [Pub.L. 101–549, for classification of which to the Code, see Tables], was repealed by Pub.L. 104–316, Title I, §§ 101(e), 122(r), Oct. 19, 1996, 110 Stat. 3827, 3838.

**Termination of Advisory Councils**

Advisory councils established after Jan. 5, 1973, to terminate not later than the expiration of the 2–year period beginning on the date of their establishment, unless, in the case of a council established by the President or an officer of the Federal Government, such council is renewed by appropriate action prior to the expiration of such 2–year period, or in the case of a council established by Congress, its duration is otherwise provided by law. See sections 3(2) and 14 of Pub.L. 92–463, Oct. 6, 1972, 86 Stat. 770, 776, set out in Appendix 2 to Title 5, Government Organization and Employees.

## § 7613. Repealed. Pub.L. 101–549, Title VIII, § 803, Nov. 15, 1990, 104 Stat. 2689

### HISTORICAL AND STATUTORY NOTES

Section, Act July 14, 1955, c. 360, Title III, § 313, formerly § 306, as added Nov. 21, 1967, Pub.L. 90–148, § 2, 81 Stat. 506; renumbered § 313 and amended Dec. 31, 1970, Pub.L. 91–604, §§ 12(a), 15(c)(2), 84 Stat. 1705, 1713; Aug. 7, 1977, Pub.L. 95–95, Title III, § 302(b), 91 Stat. 771, required annual report to Congress on progress of programs under this chapter.

**Effective Date of Repeal**

Repeal of section effective Nov. 15, 1990, except as otherwise provided, see section 711(b) of Pub.L. 101–549, set out as a note under section 7401 of this title.

**Savings Provisions**

Suits, actions or proceedings commenced under this chapter as in effect prior to Nov. 15, 1990, not to abate by reason of the taking effect of amendments by Pub.L. 101–549, except as otherwise provided for, see section 711(a) of Pub.L. 101–549, set out as a note under section 7401 of this title.

## § 7614. Labor standards

[CAA § 314]

The Administrator shall take such action as may be necessary to insure that all laborers and mechanics employed by contractors or subcontractors on projects assisted under this chapter shall be paid wages at rates not less than those prevailing for the same type of work on similar construction in the locality as determined by the Secretary of Labor, in accordance with the Act of March 3, 1931, as amended, known as sections 3141 to 3144, 3146, 3147 of Title 40. The Secretary of Labor shall have, with respect to the labor standards specified in this subsection, the authority and functions set forth in Reorganization Plan Numbered 14 of 1950 (15 F.R. 3176; 64 Stat. 1267) and section 3145 of Title 40.

(July 14, 1955, c. 360, Title III, § 314, formerly § 307, as added Nov. 21, 1967, Pub.L. 90–148, § 2, 81 Stat. 506; renumbered § 314 and amended Dec. 31, 1970, Pub.L. 91–604, §§ 12(a), 15(c)(2), 84 Stat. 1705, 1713.)

### HISTORICAL AND STATUTORY NOTES

**References in Text**

Reorganization Plan Numbered 14 of 1950, referred to in text, is set out in Appendix 1 to Title 5, Government Organization and Employees.

**Codifications**

Section was formerly classified to section 1857j–3 of this title.

In text, "sections 3141 to 3144, 3146, 3147 of Title 40" substituted for "the Act of March 3, 1931, as amended, known as the Davis–Bacon Act (46 Stat. 1494; 40 U.S.C. 276a—276a–5)" on authority of Pub.L. 107–217, § 5(c), Aug. 21, 2002, 116 Stat. 1301, which is set out as a note preceding 40 U.S.C.A. § 101. Pub.L. 107–217, § 1, enacted Title 40 into positive law. The Davis–Bacon Act is Act Mar. 3, 1931, c. 411, 46 Stat. 1494, which was classified to former 40 U.S.C.A. §§ 276a, 276a–1 to 276a–6, prior to being repealed by Pub.L. 107–217, § 6(b), Aug. 21, 2002, 116 Stat. 1308, and its substance reenacted as 40 U.S.C.A. §§ 3141 to 3144, 3146, 3147.

In text, "section 3145 of Title 40" substituted for "section 276c of Title 40", which originally read "section 2 of the Act of June 13, 1934 (48 Stat. 948; 40 U.S.C. 276c)", on authority of Pub.L. 107–217, § 5(c), Aug. 21, 2002, 116 Stat. 1301, which is set out as a note preceding 40 U.S.C.A. § 101. Pub.L. 107–217, § 1, enacted Title 40 into positive law. Section 2 of the Act of June 13, 1934, as amended, is Act June 13, 1934, c. 482, § 2, 48 Stat. 948, which was classified to former 40 U.S.C.A. § 276c prior to being repealed by Pub.L. 107–217, § 6(b), Aug. 21, 2002, 116 Stat. 1309, and its substance reenacted as 40 U.S.C.A. § 3145.

## § 7615. Separability

[CAA § 315]

If any provision of this chapter, or the application of any provision of this chapter to any person or circumstance, is held invalid, the application of such provision to other persons or circumstances, and the remainder of this chapter shall not be affected thereby.

(July 14, 1955, c. 360, Title III, § 315, formerly § 12, as added Dec. 17, 1963, Pub.L. 88–206, § 1, 77 Stat. 401; renumbered § 305, Oct. 20, 1965, Pub.L. 89–272, Title I, § 101(4), 79 Stat. 992; renumbered § 308 and amended, Nov. 21, 1967, Pub.L. 90–148, § 2, 81 Stat. 506; renumbered § 315, Dec. 31, 1970, Pub.L. 91–604, § 12(a), 84 Stat. 1705.)

### HISTORICAL AND STATUTORY NOTES

**Codifications**

Section was formerly classified to section 1857k of this title.

## § 7616. Sewage treatment grants

[CAA § 316]

**(a) Construction**

No grant which the Administrator is authorized to make to any applicant for construction of sewage treatment works in any area in any State may be withheld, conditioned, or restricted by the Administrator on the basis of any requirement of this chapter except as provided in subsection (b) of this section.

**(b) Withholding, conditioning, or restriction of construction grants**

The Administrator may withhold, condition, or restrict the making of any grant for construction referred to in subsection (a) of this section only if he determines that—

(1) such treatment works will not comply with applicable standards under section 7411 or 7412 of this title,

(2) the State does not have in effect, or is not carrying out, a State implementation plan approved by the Administrator which expressly quantifies and provides for the increase in emissions of each air pollutant (from stationary and mobile sources in any area to which either part C or part D of subchapter I of this chapter applies for such pollutant) which increase may reasonably be anticipated to result directly or indirectly from the new sewage treatment capacity which would be created by such construction.

(3) the construction of such treatment works would create new sewage treatment capacity which—

(A) may reasonably be anticipated to cause or contribute to, directly or indirectly, an increase in emissions of any air pollutant in excess of the increase provided for under the provisions referred to in paragraph (2) for any such area, or

(B) would otherwise not be in conformity with the applicable implementation plan, or

(4) such increase in emissions would interfere with, or be inconsistent with, the applicable implementation plan for any other State.

In the case of construction of a treatment works which would result, directly or indirectly, in an increase in emissions of any air pollutant from stationary and mobile sources in an area to which part D of subchapter I of this chapter applies, the quantification of emissions referred to in paragraph (2) shall include the emissions of any such pollutant resulting directly or indirectly from areawide and nonmajor stationary source growth (mobile and stationary) for each such area.

**(c) National Environmental Policy Act**

Nothing in this section shall be construed to amend or alter any provision of the National Environmental Policy Act [42 U.S.C.A. § 4321 et seq.] or to affect any determination as to whether or not the requirements of such Act have been met in the case of the construction of any sewage treatment works.

(July 14, 1955, c. 360, Title III, § 316, as added Aug. 7, 1977, Pub.L. 95–95, Title III, § 306, 91 Stat. 777.)

### HISTORICAL AND STATUTORY NOTES

**References in Text**

The National Environmental Policy Act, referred to in subsec. (c), probably means the National Environmental Policy Act of 1969, Pub.L. 91–190, Jan. 1, 1970, 83 Stat. 852, as amended, which is classified generally to chapter 55 (section 4321 et seq.) of this title. For complete classification of this Act to the Code, see Short Title of 1970 Acts note set out under section 4321 of this title and Tables.

**Effective and Applicability Provisions**

1977 Acts

Section effective Aug. 7, 1977, except as otherwise expressly provided, see section 406(d) of Pub.L. 95–95, set out as a note under section 7401 of this title.

**Prior Provisions**

A prior section 316 of Act July 14, 1955, c. 360, Title III, formerly § 13, as added Dec. 17, 1963, Pub.L. 88–206, § 1, 77 Stat. 401; renumbered § 306 and amended Oct. 20, 1965, Pub.L. 89–272, Title I, § 101(4), (6), (7), 79 Stat. 992; Oct. 15, 1966, Pub.L. 89–675, § 2(a), 80 Stat. 954, renumbered § 309 and amended Nov. 21, 1967, Pub.L. 90–148, § 2, 81 Stat. 506; renumbered § 316 and amended Dec. 31, 1970, Pub.L. 91–604, §§ 12(a), 13(b), 84 Stat. 1705, 1709; Apr. 9, 1973, Pub.L. 93–15, § 1(c), 87 Stat. 11; June 22, 1974, Pub.L. 93–319, § 13(c), 88 Stat. 265, which authorized appropriations for air pollution control, was repealed by section 306 of Pub.L. 95–95. See section 7626 of this title.

## § 7617. Economic impact assessment

**[CAA § 317]**

**(a) Notice of proposed rulemaking; substantial revisions**

This section applies to action of the Administrator in promulgating or revising—

(1) any new source standard of performance under section 7411 of this title,

(2) any regulation under section 7411(d) of this title,

(3) any regulation under part B of subchapter I of this chapter (relating to ozone and stratosphere protection),

(4) any regulation under part C of subchapter I of this chapter (relating to prevention of significant deterioration of air quality),

(5) any regulation establishing emission standards under section 7521 of this title and any other regulation promulgated under that section,

(6) any regulation controlling or prohibiting any fuel or fuel additive under section 7545(c) of this title, and

(7) any aircraft emission standard under section 7571 of this title.

Nothing in this section shall apply to any standard or regulation described in paragraphs (1) through (7) of this subsection unless the notice of proposed rulemaking in connection with such standard or regulation is published in the Federal Register after the date ninety days after August 7, 1977. In the case of revisions of such standards or regulations, this section shall apply only to revisions which the Administrator determines to be substantial revisions.

**(b) Preparation of assessment by Administrator**

Before publication of notice of proposed rulemaking with respect to any standard or regulation to which this section applies, the Administrator shall prepare an economic impact assessment respecting such standard or regulation. Such assessment shall be included in the docket required under section 7607(d)(2) of this title and shall be available to the public as provided in section 7607(d)(4) of this title. Notice of proposed rulemaking shall include notice of such availability together with an explanation of the extent and manner in which the Administrator has considered the analysis contained in such economic impact assessment in proposing the action. The Administrator shall also provide such an explanation in his notice of promulgation of any regulation or standard referred to in subsection (a) of this section. Each such explanation shall be part of the statements of basis and purpose required under sections 7607(d)(3) and 7607(d)(6) of this title.

**(c) Analysis**

Subject to subsection (d) of this section, the assessment required under this section with respect to any standard or regulation shall contain an analysis of—

(1) the costs of compliance with any such standard or regulation, including extent to which the costs of compliance will vary depending on (A) the effective date of the standard or regulation, and (B) the development of less expensive, more efficient means or methods of compliance with the standard or regulation;

(2) the potential inflationary or recessionary effects of the standard or regulation;

(3) the effects on competition of the standard or regulation with respect to small business;

(4) the effects of the standard or regulation on consumer costs; and

(5) the effects of the standard or regulation on energy use.

Nothing in this section shall be construed to provide that the analysis of the factors specified in this subsection affects or alters the factors which the Administrator is required to consider in taking any action referred to in subsection (a) of this section.

**(d) Extensiveness of assessment**

The assessment required under this section shall be as extensive as practicable, in the judgment of the Administrator taking into account the time and resources available to the Environmental Protection Agency and other duties and authorities which the Administrator is required to carry out under this chapter.

**(e) Limitations on construction of section**

Nothing in this section shall be construed—

(1) to alter the basis on which a standard or regulation is promulgated under this chapter;

(2) to preclude the Administrator from carrying out his responsibility under this chapter to protect public health and welfare; or

(3) to authorize or require any judicial review of any such standard or regulation, or any stay or injunction of the proposal, promulgation, or effectiveness of such standard or regulation on the basis of failure to comply with this section.

**(f) Citizen suits**

The requirements imposed on the Administrator under this section shall be treated as nondiscretionary duties for purposes of section 7604(a)(2) of this title, relating to citizen suits. The sole method for enforcement of the Administrator's duty under this section shall be by bringing a citizen suit under such section 7604(a)(2) for a court order to compel the Administrator to perform such duty. Violation of any such order shall subject the Administrator to penalties for contempt of court.

**(g) Costs**

In the case of any provision of this chapter in which costs are expressly required to be taken into account, the adequacy or inadequacy of any assessment required under this section may be taken into consideration, but shall not be treated for purposes of judicial review of any such provision as conclusive with respect to compliance or noncompliance with the requirement of such provision to take cost into account.

(July 14, 1955, c. 360, Title III, § 317, as added Aug. 7, 1977, Pub.L. 95–95, Title III, § 307, 91 Stat. 778, and amended Nov. 9, 1978, Pub.L. 95–623, § 13(d), 92 Stat. 3458.)

## HISTORICAL AND STATUTORY NOTES

**References in Text**

Part B of subchapter I of this chapter, referred to in subsec. (a)(3), was repealed by Pub.L. 101–549, Title VI, § 601, Nov. 15, 1990, 104 Stat. 2648. See subchapter VI (section 7671 et seq.) of this chapter.

**Codifications**

Another section 317 of Act July 14, 1955, is set out as a Short Title of 1955 Acts note under section 7401 of this title.

**Effective and Applicability Provisions**

1977 Acts

Section effective Aug. 7, 1977, except as otherwise expressly provided, see section 406(d) of Pub.L. 95–95, set out as a note under section 7401 of this title.

## § 7618. Repealed. Pub.L. 101–549, Title I, § 108(q), Nov. 15, 1990, 104 Stat. 2469

### HISTORICAL AND STATUTORY NOTES

Section, Act July 14, 1955, c. 360, Title III, § 318, as added Aug. 7, 1977, Pub.L. 95–95, Title III, § 308, 91 Stat. 780, related to financial disclosure and conflicts of interest.

**Effective Date of Repeal**

Repeal of section effective Nov. 15, 1990, except as otherwise provided, see section 711(b) of Pub.L. 101–549, set out as a note under section 7401 of this title.

**Savings Provisions**

Suits, actions or proceedings commenced under this chapter as in effect prior to Nov. 15, 1990, not to abate by reason of the taking effect of amendments by Pub.L. 101–549, except as otherwise provided for, see section 711(a) of Pub.L. 101–549, set out as a note under section 7401 of this title.

## § 7619. Air quality monitoring

**[CAA § 319]**

Not later than one year after August 7, 1977, and after notice and opportunity for public hearing, the Administrator shall promulgate regulations establishing an air quality monitoring system throughout the United States which—

(1) utilizes uniform air quality monitoring criteria and methodology and measures such air quality according to a uniform air quality index,

(2) provides for air quality monitoring stations in major urban areas and other appropriate areas throughout the United States to provide monitoring such as will supplement (but not duplicate) air quality monitoring carried out by the States required under any applicable implementation plan,

(3) provides for daily analysis and reporting of air quality based upon such uniform air quality index, and

(4) provides for recordkeeping with respect to such monitoring data and for periodic analysis and reporting to the general public by the Administrator with respect to air quality based upon such data.

The operation of such air quality monitoring system may be carried out by the Administrator or by such other departments, agencies, or entities of the Federal Government (including the National Weather Service) as the President may deem appropriate. Any air quality monitoring system required under any applicable implementation plan under section 7410 of this title shall, as soon as practicable following promulgation of regulations under this section, utilize the standard criteria and methodology, and measure air quality according to the standard index, established under such regulations.

(July 14, 1955, c. 360, Title III, § 319, as added Aug. 7, 1977, Pub.L. 95–95, Title III, § 309, 91 Stat. 781.)

### HISTORICAL AND STATUTORY NOTES

**Effective and Applicability Provisions**

1977 Acts

Section effective Aug. 7, 1977, except as otherwise expressly provided, see section 406(d) of Pub.L. 95–95, set out as a note under section 7401 of this title.

## § 7620. Standardized air quality modeling

**[CAA § 320]**

**(a) Conferences**

Not later than six months after August 7, 1977, and at least every three years thereafter, the Administrator shall conduct a conference on air quality modeling. In conducting such conference, special attention shall be given to appropriate modeling necessary for carrying out part C of subchapter I of this chapter (relating to prevention of significant deterioration of air quality).

**(b) Conferees**

The conference conducted under this section shall provide for participation by the National Academy of Sciences, representatives of State and local air pollution control agencies, and appropriate Federal agencies, including the National Science Foundation;[1] the National Oceanic and Atmospheric Administration, and the National Institute of Standards and Technology.

**(c) Comments; transcripts**

Interested persons shall be permitted to submit written comments and a verbatim transcript of the conference proceedings shall be maintained.

**(d) Promulgation and revision of regulations relating to air quality modeling**

The comments submitted and the transcript maintained pursuant to subsection (c) of this section shall be included in the docket required to be established for purposes of promulgating or revising any regulation relating to air quality modeling under part C of subchapter I of this chapter.

(July 14, 1955, c. 360, Title III, § 320, as added Aug. 7, 1977, Pub.L. 95–95, Title III, § 310, 91 Stat. 782, and amended Aug. 23, 1988, Pub.L. 100–418, Title V, § 5115(c), 102 Stat. 1433.)

[1] So in original. Probably should be a comma.

### HISTORICAL AND STATUTORY NOTES

**Effective and Applicability Provisions**

1977 Acts

Section effective Aug. 7, 1977, except as otherwise expressly provided, see section 406(d) of Pub.L. 95–95, set out as a note under section 7401 of this title.

## § 7621. Employment effects

**[CAA § 321]**

### (a) Continuous evaluation of potential loss or shifts of employment

The Administrator shall conduct continuing evaluations of potential loss or shifts of employment which may result from the administration or enforcement of the provision of this chapter and applicable implementation plans, including where appropriate, investigating threatened plant closures or reductions in employment allegedly resulting from such administration or enforcement.

### (b) Request for investigation; hearings; record; report

Any employee, or any representative of such employee, who is discharged or laid off, threatened with discharge or layoff, or whose employment is otherwise adversely affected or threatened to be adversely affected because of the alleged results of any requirement imposed or proposed to be imposed under this chapter, including any requirement applicable to Federal facilities and any requirement imposed by a State or political subdivision thereof, may request the Administrator to conduct a full investigation of the matter. Any such request shall be reduced to writing, shall set forth with reasonable particularity the grounds for the request, and shall be signed by the employee, or representative of such employee, making the request. The Administrator shall thereupon investigate the matter and, at the request of any party, shall hold public hearings on not less than five days' notice. At such hearings, the Administrator shall require the parties, including the employer involved, to present information relating to the actual or potential effect of such requirements on employment and the detailed reasons or justification therefor. If the Administrator determines that there are no reasonable grounds for conducting a public hearing he shall notify (in writing) the party requesting such hearing of such a determination and the reasons therefor. If the Administrator does convene such a hearing, the hearing shall be on the record. Upon receiving the report of such investigation, the Administrator shall make findings of fact as to the effect of such requirements on employment and on the alleged actual or potential discharge, layoff, or other adverse effect on employment, and shall make such recommendations as he deems appropriate. Such report, findings, and recommendations shall be available to the public.

### (c) Subpenas; confidential information; witnesses; penalty

In connection with any investigation or public hearing conducted under subsection (b) of this section or as authorized in section 7419 of this title (relating to primary nonferrous smelter orders), the Administrator may issue subpenas for the attendance and testimony of witnesses and the production of relevant papers, books and documents, and he may administer oaths. Except for emission data, upon a showing satisfactory to the Administrator by such owner or operator that such papers, books, documents, or information or particular part thereof, if made public, would divulge trade secrets or secret processes of such owner, or operator, the Administrator shall consider such record, report, or information or particular portion thereof confidential in accordance with the purposes of section 1905 of Title 18, except that such paper, book, document, or information may be disclosed to other officers, employees, or authorized representatives of the United States concerned with carrying out this chapter, or when relevant in any proceeding under this chapter. Witnesses summoned shall be paid the same fees and mileage that are paid witnesses in the courts of the United States. In cases of contumacy or refusal to obey a subpena served upon any person under this subparagraph, the district court of the United States for any district in which such person is found or resides or transacts business, upon application by the United States and after notice to such person, shall have jurisdiction to issue an order requiring such person to appear and give testimony before the Administrator, to appear and produce papers, books, and documents before the Administrator, or both, and any failure to obey such order of the court may be punished by such court as a contempt thereof.

### (d) Limitations on construction of section

Nothing in this section shall be construed to require or authorize the Administrator, the States, or political subdivisions thereof, to modify or withdraw any requirement imposed or proposed to be imposed under this chapter.

(July 14, 1955, c. 360, Title III, § 321, as added Aug. 7, 1977, Pub.L. 95–95, Title III, § 311, 91 Stat. 782.)

### HISTORICAL AND STATUTORY NOTES

**Effective and Applicability Provisions**

1977 Acts

Section effective Aug. 7, 1977, except as otherwise expressly provided, see section 406(d) of Pub.L. 95–95, set out as a note under section 7401 of this title.

**Study of Potential Dislocation of Employees**

Section 403(e) of Pub.L. 95–95 provided that the Secretary of Labor, in consultation with the Administrator, conduct a study of potential dislocation of employees due to implementation of laws administered by the Administrator and that the Secretary submit to Congress the results of the study not more than one year after Aug. 7, 1977.

## § 7622. Employee protection

[CAA § 322]

### (a) Discharge or discrimination prohibited

No employer may discharge any employee or otherwise discriminate against any employee with respect to his compensation, terms, conditions, or privileges of employment because the employee (or any person acting pursuant to a request of the employee)—

(1) commenced, caused to be commenced, or is about to commence or cause to be commenced a proceeding under this chapter or a proceeding for the administration or enforcement of any requirement imposed under this chapter or under any applicable implementation plan,

(2) testified or is about to testify in any such proceeding, or

(3) assisted or participated or is about to assist or participate in any manner in such a proceeding or in any other action to carry out the purposes of this chapter.

### (b) Complaint charging unlawful discharge or discrimination; investigation; order

(1) Any employee who believes that he has been discharged or otherwise discriminated against by any person in violation of subsection (a) of this section may, within thirty days after such violation occurs, file (or have any person file on his behalf) a complaint with the Secretary of Labor (hereinafter in this subsection referred to as the "Secretary") alleging such discharge or discrimination. Upon receipt of such a complaint, the Secretary shall notify the person named in the complaint of the filing of the complaint.

(2)(A) Upon receipt of a complaint filed under paragraph (1), the Secretary shall conduct an investigation of the violation alleged in the complaint. Within thirty days of the receipt of such complaint, the Secretary shall complete such investigation and shall notify in writing the complainant (and any person acting in his behalf) and the person alleged to have committed such violation of the results of the investigation conducted pursuant to this subparagraph. Within ninety days of the receipt of such complaint the Secretary shall, unless the proceeding on the complaint is terminated by the Secretary on the basis of a settlement entered into by the Secretary and the person alleged to have committed such violation, issue an order either providing the relief prescribed by subparagraph (B) or denying the complaint. An order of the Secretary shall be made on the record after notice and opportunity for public hearing. The Secretary may not enter into a settlement terminating a proceeding on a complaint without the participation and consent of the complainant.

(B) If, in response to a complaint filed under paragraph (1), the Secretary determines that a violation of subsection (a) of this section has occurred, the Secretary shall order the person who committed such violation to (i) take affirmative action to abate the violation, and (ii) reinstate the complainant to his former position together with the compensation (including back pay), terms, conditions, and privileges of his employment, and the Secretary may order such person to provide compensatory damages to the complainant. If an order is issued under this paragraph, the Secretary, at the request of the complainant, shall assess against the person against whom the order is issued a sum equal to the aggregate amount of all costs and expenses (including attorneys' and expert witness fees) reasonably incurred, as determined by the Secretary, by the complainant for, or in connection with, the bringing of the complaint upon which the order was issued.

### (c) Review

(1) Any person adversely affected or aggrieved by an order issued under subsection (b) of this section may obtain review of the order in the United States court of appeals for the circuit in which the violation, with respect to which the order was issued, allegedly occurred. The petition for review must be filed within sixty days from the issuance of the Secretary's order. Review shall conform to chapter 7 of Title 5. The commencement of proceedings under this subparagraph shall not, unless ordered by the court, operate as a stay of the Secretary's order.

(2) An order of the Secretary with respect to which review could have been obtained under paragraph (1) shall not be subject to judicial review in any criminal or other civil proceeding.

### (d) Enforcement of order by Secretary

Whenever a person has failed to comply with an order issued under subsection (b)(2) of this section, the Secretary may file a civil action in the United States district court for the district in which the violation was found to occur to enforce such order. In actions brought under this subsection, the district courts shall have jurisdiction to grant all appropriate relief including, but not limited to, injunctive relief, compensatory, and exemplary damages.

### (e) Enforcement of order by person on whose behalf order was issued

(1) Any person on whose behalf an order was issued under paragraph (2) of subsection (b) of this section may commence a civil action against the person to whom such order was issued to require compliance with such order. The appropriate United States district court shall have jurisdiction, without regard to

the amount in controversy or the citizenship of the parties, to enforce such order.

(2) The court, in issuing any final order under this subsection, may award costs of litigation (including reasonable attorney and expert witness fees) to any party whenever the court determines such award is appropriate.

**(f) Mandamus**

Any nondiscretionary duty imposed by this section shall be enforceable in a mandamus proceeding brought under section 1361 of Title 28.

**(g) Deliberate violation by employee**

Subsection (a) of this section shall not apply with respect to any employee who, acting without direction from his employer (or the employer's agent), deliberately causes a violation of any requirement of this chapter.

(July 14, 1955, c. 360, Title III, § 322, as added Aug. 7, 1977, Pub.L. 95–95, Title III, § 312, 91 Stat. 783.)

### HISTORICAL AND STATUTORY NOTES

**Effective and Applicability Provisions**

1977 Acts

Section effective Aug. 7, 1977, except as otherwise expressly provided, see section 406(d) of Pub.L. 95–95, set out as a note under section 7401 of this title.

## § 7623. Repealed. Pub.L. 96–300, § 1(c), July 2, 1980, 94 Stat. 831

### HISTORICAL AND STATUTORY NOTES

Section, Act July 14, 1955, c. 360, Title III, § 323, as added Aug. 7, 1977, Pub.L. 95–95, Title III, § 313, 91 Stat. 785, and amended Nov. 16, 1977, Pub.L. 95–190, § 14(a)(81), 91 Stat. 1404; S.Res. 4, Feb. 4, 1977; H.Res. 549, Mar. 25, 1980; July 2, 1980, Pub.L. 96–300, § 1(a), 94 Stat. 831, established a National Commission on Air Quality, prescribed numerous subjects for study and report to Congress, enumerated specific questions for study and investigation, required specific identification of loss or irretrievable commitment of resources, and provided for appointment and confirmation of its membership, cooperation of Federal executive agencies, submission of a National Academy of Sciences study to Congress, compensation and travel expenses, termination of Commission, appointment and compensation of staff, and public participation.

**Effective Date of Repeal**

Section 1(c) of Pub.L. 96–300 provided that this section is repealed on the date on which the National Commission on Air Quality ceases to exist pursuant to provisions of former subsec. (g) of this section, which provided that not later than Mar. 1, 1981, a report be submitted containing the results of all Commission studies and investigations and that the Commission cease to exist on Mar. 1, 1981, if the report is not submitted on Mar. 1, 1981, or the Commission would cease to exist on such date, but not later than May 1, 1981, as determined and ordered by the Commission if the report is submitted on Mar. 1, 1981.

## § 7624. Cost of vapor recovery equipment

[CAA § 323]

**(a) Costs to be borne by owner of retail outlet**

The regulations under this chapter applicable to vapor recovery with respect to mobile source fuels at retail outlets of such fuels shall provide that the cost of procurement and installation of such vapor recovery shall be borne by the owner of such outlet (as determined under such regulations). Except as provided in subsection (b) of this section, such regulations shall provide that no lease of a retail outlet by the owner thereof which is entered into or renewed after August 7, 1977, may provide for a payment by the lessee of the cost of procurement and installation of vapor recovery equipment. Such regulations shall also provide that the cost of procurement and installation of vapor recovery equipment may be recovered by the owner of such outlet by means of price increases in the cost of any product sold by such owner, notwithstanding any provision of law.

**(b) Payment by lessee**

The regulations of the Administrator referred to in subsection (a) of this section shall permit a lease of a retail outlet to provide for payment by the lessee of the cost of procurement and installation of vapor recovery equipment over a reasonable period (as determined in accordance with such regulations), if the owner of such outlet does not sell, trade in, or otherwise dispense any product at wholesale or retail at such outlet.

(July 14, 1955, c. 360, Title III, § 323, formerly § 324, as added Aug. 7, 1977, Pub.L. 95–95, Title III, § 314(a), 91 Stat. 788, and amended Nov. 16, 1977, Pub.L. 95–190, § 14(a)(82), 91 Stat. 1404; renumbered § 323 and amended July 2, 1980, Pub.L. 96–300, § 1(b), (c), 94 Stat. 831.)

### HISTORICAL AND STATUTORY NOTES

**Effective and Applicability Provisions**

1977 Acts

Section effective Aug. 7, 1977, except as otherwise expressly provided, see section 406(d) of Pub.L. 95–95, set out as a note under section 7401 of this title.

**Prior Provisions**

A prior section 323 of Act July 14, 1955, was classified to section 7623 of this title and was repealed by Pub.L. 96–300, § 1(c), July 2, 1980, 94 Stat. 831.

## § 7625. Vapor recovery for small business marketers of petroleum products

[CAA § 324]

**(a) Marketers of gasoline**

The regulations under this chapter applicable to vapor recovery from fueling of motor vehicles at retail outlets of gasoline shall not apply to any outlet owned by an independent small business marketer of gasoline having monthly sales of less than 50,000 gallons. In the case of any other outlet owned by an independent small business marketer, such regulations shall provide, with respect to independent small business marketers of gasoline, for a three-year phase-in period for the installation of such vapor recovery equipment at such outlets under which such marketers shall have—

(1) 33 percent of such outlets in compliance at the end of the first year during which such regulations apply to such marketers,

(2) 66 percent at the end of such second year, and

(3) 100 percent at the end of the third year.

**(b) State requirements**

Nothing in subsection (a) of this section shall be construed to prohibit any State from adopting or enforcing, with respect to independent small business marketers of gasoline having monthly sales of less than 50,000 gallons, any vapor recovery requirements for mobile source fuels at retail outlets. Any vapor recovery requirement which is adopted by a State and submitted to the Administrator as part of its implementation plan may be approved and enforced by the Administrator as part of the applicable implementation plan for that State.

**(c) Refiners**

For purposes of this section, an independent small business marketer of gasoline is a person engaged in the marketing of gasoline who would be required to pay for procurement and installation of vapor recovery equipment under section 7624 of this title or under regulations of the Administrator, unless such person—

(1)(A) is a refiner, or

(B) controls, is controlled by, or is under common control with, a refiner,

(C) is otherwise directly or indirectly affiliated (as determined under the regulations of the Administrator) with a refiner or with a person who controls, is controlled by, or is under a common control with a refiner (unless the sole affiliation referred to herein is by means of a supply contract or an agreement or contract to use a trademark, trade name, service mark, or other identifying symbol or name owned by such refiner or any such person), or

(2) receives less than 50 percent of his annual income from refining or marketing of gasoline.

For the purpose of this section, the term "refiner" shall not include any refiner whose total refinery capacity (including the refinery capacity of any person who controls, is controlled by, or is under common control with, such refiner) does not exceed 65,000 barrels per day. For purposes of this section, "control" of a corporation means ownership of more than 50 percent of its stock.

(July 14, 1955, c. 360, Title III, § 324, formerly § 325, as added Aug. 7, 1977, Pub.L. 95–95, Title III, § 314(b), 91 Stat. 789, and renumbered § 324, July 2, 1980, Pub.L. 96–300, § 1(c), 94 Stat. 831.)

### HISTORICAL AND STATUTORY NOTES

**Effective and Applicability Provisions**

1977 Acts

Section effective Aug. 7, 1977, except as otherwise expressly provided, see section 406(d) of Pub.L. 95–95, set out as a note under section 7401 of this title.

**Prior Provisions**

A prior section 324 of Act July 14, 1955, was renumbered section 323 by Pub.L. 96–300, and is classified to section 7624 of this title.

## § 7625–1. Exemptions for certain territories

**[CAA § 325]**

**(a) In general**

(1) Upon petition by the governor [1] of Guam, American Samoa, the Virgin Islands, or the Commonwealth of the Northern Mariana Islands, the Administrator is authorized to exempt any person or source or class of persons or sources in such territory from any requirement under this chapter other than section 7412 of this title or any requirement under section 7410 of this title or part D of subchapter I of this chapter necessary to attain or maintain a national primary ambient air quality standard. Such exemption may be granted if the Administrator finds that compliance with such requirement is not feasible or is unreasonable due to unique geographical, meteorological, or economic factors of such territory, or such other local factors as the Administrator deems significant. Any such petition shall be considered in accordance with section 7607(d) of this title and any exemption under this subsection shall be considered final action by the Administrator for the purposes of section 7607(b) of this title.

(2) The Administrator shall promptly notify the Committees on Energy and Commerce and on Natural Resources of the House of Representatives and the Committees on Environment and Public Works and on Energy and Natural Resources of the Senate upon receipt of any petition under this subsection and of the approval or rejection of such petition and the basis for such action.

**(b) Power plant operating within Guam as of December 8, 1983**

Notwithstanding any other provision of this chapter, any fossil fuel fired steam electric power plant operating within Guam as of December 8, 1983, is hereby exempted from:

(1) any requirement of the new source performance standards relating to sulfur dioxide promulgated under section 7411 of this title as of December 8, 1983; and

(2) any regulation relating to sulfur dioxide standards or limitations contained in a State implementation plan approved under section 7410 of this title as of December 8, 1983: *Provided,* That such exemption shall expire eighteen months after December 8, 1983, unless the Administrator determines that such plant is making all emissions reductions practicable to prevent exceedances of the national ambient air quality standards for sulfur dioxide.

(July 14, 1955, c. 360, Title III, § 325, as added Dec. 8, 1983, Pub.L. 98–213, § 11, 97 Stat. 1461, and amended Nov. 15, 1990, Pub.L. 101–549, Title VIII, § 806, 104 Stat. 2689; Nov. 2, 1994, Pub.L. 103–437, § 15(s), 108 Stat. 4594.)

[1] So in original. Probably should be capitalized.

### HISTORICAL AND STATUTORY NOTES

**Effective and Applicability Provisions**

1990 Acts

Amendment by Pub.L. 101–549 effective Nov. 15, 1990, except as otherwise provided, see section 711(b) of Pub.L. 101–549, set out as a note under section 7401 of this title.

**Change of Name**

Any reference in any provision of law enacted before Jan. 4, 1995, to the Committee on Energy and Commerce of the House of Representatives treated as referring to the Committee on Commerce of the House of Representatives, except that any reference in any provision of law enacted before Jan. 4, 1995, to the Committee on Energy and Commerce of the House of Representatives treated as referring to the Committee on Agriculture of the House of Representatives, in the case of a provision of law relating to inspection of seafood or seafood products, the Committee on Banking and Financial Services of the House of Representatives, in the case of a provision of law relating to bank capital markets activities generally or to depository institution securities activities generally, and the Committee on Transportation and Infrastructure of the House of Representatives, in the case of a provision of law relating to railroads, railway labor, or railroad retirement and unemployment (except revenue measures related thereto), see section 1(a)(4) and (c)(1) of Pub.L. 104–14, set out as a note preceding section 21 of Title 2, The Congress.

Any reference in any provision of law enacted before Jan. 4, 1995, to the Committee on Natural Resources of the House of Representatives treated as referring to the Committee on Resources of the House of Representatives, see section 1(a)(8) of Pub.L. 104–14, set out as a note preceding section 21 of Title 2, The Congress.

**Prior Provisions**

A prior section 325 of Act July 14, 1955, was renumbered section 326 by Pub.L. 98–213 and is classified to section 7625a of this title.

Another prior section 325 of Act July 14, 1955, was renumbered section 324 by Pub.L. 96–300 and is classified to section 7625 of this title.

## § 7625a. Statutory construction

**[CAA § 326]**

The parenthetical cross references in any provision of this chapter to other provisions of the chapter, or other provisions of law, where the words "relating to" or "pertaining to" are used, are made only for convenience, and shall be given no legal effect.

(July 14, 1955, c. 360, Title III, § 326, as added Nov. 16, 1977, Pub.L. 95–190, § 14(a)(84), 91 Stat. 1404, and renumbered § 325, July 2, 1980, Pub.L. 96–300, § 1(c), 94 Stat. 831; renumbered § 326, Dec. 8, 1983, Pub.L. 98–213, § 11, 97 Stat. 1461.)

### HISTORICAL AND STATUTORY NOTES

**Prior Provisions**

A prior section 326 of Act July 14, 1955, was renumbered section 327 by Pub.L. 98–213 and is classified to section 7626 of this title.

## § 7626. Authorization of appropriations

**[CAA § 327]**

**(a) In general**

There are authorized to be appropriated to carry out this chapter such sums as may be necessary for the 7 fiscal years commencing after November 15, 1990.

**(b) Grants for planning**

There are authorized to be appropriated (1) not more than $50,000,000 to carry out section 7505 of this title beginning in fiscal year 1991, to be available until expended, to develop plan revisions required by subpart 2, 3, or 4 of part D of subchapter I of this chapter, and (2) not more than $15,000,000 for each of the 7 fiscal years commencing after November 15, 1990, to make grants to the States to prepare implementation plans as required by subpart 2, 3, or 4 of part D of subchapter I of this chapter.

(July 14, 1955, c. 360, Title III, § 327, formerly § 325, as added Aug. 7, 1977, Pub.L. 95–95, Title III, § 315, 91 Stat. 790, renumbered § 327 and amended Nov. 16, 1977, Pub.L. 95–190, § 14(a)(83), 91 Stat. 1404; renumbered § 326, July 2, 1980, Pub.L. 96–300, § 1(c), 94 Stat. 831; renumbered § 327, Dec. 8, 1983, Pub.L. 98–213, § 11, 97 Stat. 1461; Nov. 15, 1990, Pub.L. 101–549, Title VIII, § 822, 104 Stat. 2699.)

### HISTORICAL AND STATUTORY NOTES

**Effective and Applicability Provisions**

1990 Acts

Amendment by Pub.L. 101–549 effective Nov. 15, 1990, except as otherwise provided, see section 711(b) of Pub.L. 101–549, set out as a note under section 7401 of this title.

1977 Acts

Section effective Aug. 7, 1977, except as otherwise expressly provided, see section 406(d) of Pub.L. 95–95, set out as a note under section 7401 of this title.

**Savings Provisions**

Suits, actions or proceedings commenced under this chapter as in effect prior to Nov. 15, 1990, not to abate by reason of the taking effect of amendments by Pub.L. 101–549, except as otherwise provided for, see section 711(a) of Pub.L. 101–549, set out as a note under section 7401 of this title.

**Prior Provisions**

Provisions similar to those comprising this section were contained in section 1857l of this title, Act July 14, 1955, c. 360, Title III, § 316, formerly § 13, as added Dec. 17, 1963, Pub.L. 88–206, § 1, 77 Stat. 401; renumbered § 306 and amended Oct. 20, 1965, Pub.L. 89–272, Title I, § 101(4), (6), (7), 79 Stat. 992; Oct. 15, 1966, Pub.L. 89–675, § 2(a), 80 Stat. 954; renumbered § 309 and amended Nov. 21, 1967, Pub.L. 90–148, § 2, 81 Stat. 506; renumbered § 316 and amended Dec. 31, 1970, Pub.L. 91–604, §§ 12(a), 13(b), 84 Stat. 1705, 1709; Apr. 9, 1973, Pub.L. 93–15, § 1(c), 87 Stat. 11; June 22, 1974, Pub.L. 93–319, § 13(c), 88 Stat. 265, prior to its repeal by section 306 of Pub.L. 95–95.

## § 7627. Air pollution from Outer Continental Shelf activities

[CAA § 328]

### (a) Applicable requirements for certain areas

#### (1) In general

Not later than 12 months after November 15, 1990, following consultation with the Secretary of the Interior and the Commandant of the United States Coast Guard, the Administrator, by rule, shall establish requirements to control air pollution from Outer Continental Shelf sources located offshore of the States along the Pacific, Arctic and Atlantic Coasts, and along the United States Gulf Coast off the State of Florida eastward of longitude 87 degrees and 30 minutes ("OCS sources") to attain and maintain Federal and State ambient air quality standards and to comply with the provisions of part C of subchapter I of this chapter. For such sources located within 25 miles of the seaward boundary of such States, such requirements shall be the same as would be applicable if the source were located in the corresponding onshore area, and shall include, but not be limited to, State and local requirements for emission controls, emission limitations, offsets, permitting, monitoring, testing, and reporting. New OCS sources shall comply with such requirements on the date of promulgation and existing OCS sources shall comply on the date 24 months thereafter. The Administrator shall update such requirements as necessary to maintain consistency with onshore regulations. The authority of this subsection shall supersede section 5(a)(8) of the Outer Continental Shelf Lands Act [43 U.S.C.A. § 1334(a)(8) ] but shall not repeal or modify any other Federal, State, or local authorities with respect to air quality. Each requirement established under this section shall be treated, for purposes of sections 7413, 7414, 7416, 7420, and 7604 of this title, as a standard under section 7411 of this title and a violation of any such requirement shall be considered a violation of section 7411(e) of this title.

#### (2) Exemptions

The Administrator may exempt an OCS source from a specific requirement in effect under regulations under this subsection if the Administrator finds that compliance with a pollution control technology requirement is technically infeasible or will cause an unreasonable threat to health and safety. The Administrator shall make written findings explaining the basis of any exemption issued pursuant to this subsection and shall impose another requirement equal to or as close in stringency to the original requirement as possible. The Administrator shall ensure that any increase in emissions due to the granting of an exemption is offset by reductions in actual emissions, not otherwise required by this chapter, from the same source or other sources in the area or in the corresponding onshore area. The Administrator shall establish procedures to provide for public notice and comment on exemptions proposed pursuant to this subsection.

#### (3) State procedures

Each State adjacent to an OCS source included under this subsection may promulgate and submit to the Administrator regulations for implementing and enforcing the requirements of this subsection. If the Administrator finds that the State regulations are adequate, the Administrator shall delegate to that State any authority the Administrator has under this chapter to implement and enforce such requirements. Nothing in this subsection shall prohibit the Administrator from enforcing any requirement of this section.

#### (4) Definitions

For purposes of subsections (a) and (b) of this section—

##### (A) Outer Continental Shelf

The term "Outer Continental Shelf" has the meaning provided by section 2 of the Outer Continental Shelf Lands Act (43 U.S.C. 1331).

##### (B) Corresponding onshore area

The term "corresponding onshore area" means, with respect to any OCS source, the onshore attainment or nonattainment area that is closest to the source, unless the Administrator determines that another area with more stringent requirements with respect to the control and abatement of air pollution may reasonably be expected to be affected by such emissions. Such determination shall be based on the potential for air pollutants from the OCS source to reach the other onshore area and the potential of such air pollutants to affect the efforts of the other onshore area to attain or maintain any Federal or State ambient air quality standard or to comply with the provisions of part C of subchapter I of this chapter.

**(C) Outer Continental Shelf source**

The terms "Outer Continental Shelf source" and "OCS source" include any equipment, activity, or facility which—

(i) emits or has the potential to emit any air pollutant,

(ii) is regulated or authorized under the Outer Continental Shelf Lands Act [43 U.S.C.A. § 1331 et seq.], and

(iii) is located on the Outer Continental Shelf or in or on waters above the Outer Continental Shelf.

Such activities include, but are not limited to, platform and drill ship exploration, construction, development, production, processing, and transportation. For purposes of this subsection, emissions from any vessel servicing or associated with an OCS source, including emissions while at the OCS source or en route to or from the OCS source within 25 miles of the OCS source, shall be considered direct emissions from the OCS source.

**(D) New and existing OCS sources**

The term "new OCS source" means an OCS source which is a new source within the meaning of section 7411(a) of this title. The term "existing OCS source" means any OCS source other than a new OCS source.

**(b) Requirements for other offshore areas**

For portions of the United States Gulf Coast Outer Continental Shelf that are adjacent to the States not covered by subsection (a) of this section which are Texas, Louisiana, Mississippi, and Alabama, the Secretary shall consult with the Administrator to assure coordination of air pollution control regulation for Outer Continental Shelf emissions and emissions in adjacent onshore areas. Concurrently with this obligation, the Secretary shall complete within 3 years of November 15, 1990, a research study examining the impacts of emissions from Outer Continental Shelf activities in such areas that fail to meet the national ambient air quality standards for either ozone or nitrogen dioxide. Based on the results of this study, the Secretary shall consult with the Administrator and determine if any additional actions are necessary. There are authorized to be appropriated such sums as may be necessary to provide funding for the study required under this section.

**(c) Coastal waters**

(1) The study report of section 7412(n)[1] of this title shall apply to the coastal waters of the United States to the same extent and in the same manner as such requirements apply to the Great Lakes, the Chesapeake Bay, and their tributary waters.

(2) The regulatory requirements of section 7412(n)[1] of this title shall apply to the coastal waters of the States which are subject to subsection (a) of this section, to the same extent and in the same manner as such requirements apply to the Great Lakes, the Chesapeake Bay, and their tributary waters.

(July 14, 1955, c. 360, Title III, § 328, as added Nov. 15, 1990, Pub.L. 101–549, Title VIII, § 801, 104 Stat. 2685.)

[1] So in original. Probably should be section "7412(m)".

**HISTORICAL AND STATUTORY NOTES**

**References in Text**

The Outer Continental Shelf Lands Act, referred to in subsecs. (a)(1), (a)(4)(A) and (a)(4)(C)(ii), is Act Aug. 7, 1953, c. 345, 67 Stat. 462, as amended, which is classified generally to subchapter III (section 1331 et seq.) of chapter 29 of Title 43, Public Lands. Section 5(a)(8) of such Act, referred to in subsec. (a)(1), is classified to section 1334(a)(8) of Title 43. Section 2 of such Act, referred to in subsec. (a)(4)(A), is classified to section 1331 of Title 43. For complete classification of this Act to the Code, see Short Title note set out under section 1301 of Title 43 and Tables.

**Effective and Applicability Provisions**

1990 Acts

Section effective Nov. 15, 1990, except as otherwise provided, see section 711(b) of Pub.L. 101–549, set out as a note under section 7401 of this title.

## SUBCHAPTER IV—NOISE POLLUTION

**HISTORICAL AND STATUTORY NOTES**

**Codifications**

Another Title IV was enacted by Pub.L. 101–549, Title IV, § 401, Nov. 15, 1990, 104 Stat. 2584, as added to Act July 14, 1955, c. 360, and is set out as subchapter IV–A (sections 7651 to 7651*o*) of this chapter.

### § 7641. Noise abatement

**[CAA § 402]**

**(a) Office of Noise Abatement and Control**

The Administrator shall establish within the Environmental Protection Agency an Office of Noise Abatement and Control, and shall carry out through such Office a full and complete investigation and study of noise and its effect on the public health and welfare in order to (1) identify and classify causes and sources of noise, and (2) determine—

(A) effects at various levels;

(B) projected growth of noise levels in urban areas through the year 2000;

(C) the psychological and physiological effect on humans;

(D) effects of sporadic extreme noise (such as jet noise near airports) as compared with constant noise;

(E) effect on wildlife and property (including values);

(F) effect of sonic booms on property (including values); and

(G) such other matters as may be of interest in the public welfare.

**(b) Investigation techniques; report and recommendations**

In conducting such investigation, the Administrator shall hold public hearings, conduct research, experiments, demonstrations, and studies. The Administrator shall report the results of such investigation and study, together with his recommendations for legislation or other action, to the President and the Congress not later than one year after December 31, 1970.

**(c) Abatement of noise from Federal activities**

In any case where any Federal department or agency is carrying out or sponsoring any activity resulting in noise which the Administrator determines amounts to a public nuisance or is otherwise objectionable, such department or agency shall consult with the Administrator to determine possible means of abating such noise.

(July 14, 1955, c. 360, Title IV, § 402, as added Dec. 31, 1970, Pub.L. 91–604, § 14, 84 Stat. 1709.)

**HISTORICAL AND STATUTORY NOTES**

**Codifications**

Another section 402 of Act July 14, 1955, as added by Pub.L. 101–549, Title IV, § 401, Nov. 15, 1990, 104 Stat. 2585, is classified to section 7651a of this title.

Section was formerly classified to section 1858 of this title.

**Short Title**

1955 Acts

For provisions authorizing the citation of Title IV of Act July 14, 1955 [this subchapter], as the "Noise Pollution and Abatement Act of 1970", see section 401 of Act July 14, 1955, as added by Pub.L. 91–604, set out as a Short Title of 1970 Amendments note under section 7401 of this title.

## § 7642. Authorization of appropriations

**[CAA § 403]**

There is authorized to be appropriated such amount, not to exceed $30,000,000, as may be necessary for the purposes of this subchapter.

(July 14, 1955, c. 360, Title IV, § 403, as added Dec. 31, 1970, Pub.L. 91–604, § 14, 84 Stat. 1710.)

**HISTORICAL AND STATUTORY NOTES**

**Codifications**

There are two sections 403 of Act July 14, 1955, c. 360, Title IV, as amended. Section 403, as added Pub.L. 91–604, is classified as this section. Section 403, as added Pub.L. 101–549, is classified as section 7651b of this title.

Section was formerly classified to section 1858a of this title.

# SUBCHAPTER IV–A—ACID DEPOSITION CONTROL

**HISTORICAL AND STATUTORY NOTES**

**Codifications**

Another Title IV was enacted by Pub.L. 91–604, § 14, Dec. 31, 1970, 84 Stat. 1709, as added to Act July 14, 1955, c. 360, and is set out as subchapter IV (sections 7641, 7642) of this chapter.

## § 7651. Findings and purposes

**[CAA § 401]**

**(a) Findings**

The Congress finds that—

(1) the presence of acidic compounds and their precursors in the atmosphere and in deposition from the atmosphere represents a threat to natural resources, ecosystems, materials, visibility, and public health;

(2) the principal sources of the acidic compounds and their precursors in the atmosphere are emissions of sulfur and nitrogen oxides from the combustion of fossil fuels;

(3) the problem of acid deposition is of national and international significance;

(4) strategies and technologies for the control of precursors to acid deposition exist now that are economically feasible, and improved methods are expected to become increasingly available over the next decade;

(5) current and future generations of Americans will be adversely affected by delaying measures to remedy the problem;

(6) reduction of total atmospheric loading of sulfur dioxide and nitrogen oxides will enhance protection of the public health and welfare and the environment; and

(7) control measures to reduce precursor emissions from steam-electric generating units should be initiated without delay.

**(b) Purposes**

The purpose of this subchapter is to reduce the adverse effects of acid deposition through reductions in annual emissions of sulfur dioxide of ten million tons from 1980 emission levels, and, in combination with other provisions of this chapter, of nitrogen oxides emissions of approximately two million tons from 1980 emission levels, in the forty-eight contiguous States and the District of Columbia. It is the intent of this subchapter to effectuate such reductions by requiring compliance by affected sources with prescribed emission limitations by specified deadlines, which limitations may be met through alternative methods of compliance provided by an emission allocation and transfer system. It is also the purpose of this subchapter to encourage energy conservation, use of renewable and clean alternative technologies, and pollution prevention as a long-range strategy, consistent with the provisions of this subchapter, for reducing air pollution and other adverse impacts of energy production and use.

(July 14, 1955, c. 360, Title IV, § 401, as added Nov. 15, 1990, Pub.L. 101–549, Title IV, § 401, 104 Stat. 2584.)

## HISTORICAL AND STATUTORY NOTES

### Codifications

Another section 401 of Act July 14, 1955, as added by Pub.L. 91–604, § 14, Dec. 31, 1970, 84 Stat. 1709, is set out as a Short Title note under section 7401 of this title.

### Effective and Applicability Provisions

1990 Acts

Section effective Nov. 15, 1990, except as otherwise provided, see section 711(b) of Pub.L. 101–549, set out as a note under section 7401 of this title.

### Savings Provisions

Suits, actions or proceedings commenced under this chapter as in effect prior to Nov. 15, 1990, not to abate by reason of the taking effect of amendments by Pub.L. 101–549, except as otherwise provided for, see section 711(a) of Pub.L. 101–549, set out as a note under section 7401 of this title.

### Acid Deposition Standards

Section 404 of Pub.L. 101–549 provided that: "Not later than 36 months after the date of enactment of this Act [Nov. 15, 1990], the Administrator of the Environmental Protection Agency shall transmit to the Committee on Environment and Public Works of the Senate and the Committee on Energy and Commerce of the House of Representatives a report on the feasibility and effectiveness of an acid deposition standard or standards to protect sensitive and critically sensitive aquatic and terrestrial resources. The study required by this section shall include, but not be limited to, consideration of the following matters:

"(1) identification of the sensitive and critically sensitive aquatic and terrestrial resources in the United States and Canada which may be affected by the deposition of acidic compounds;

"(2) description of the nature and numerical value of a deposition standard or standards that would be sufficient to protect such resources;

"(3) description of the use of such standard or standards in other Nations or by any of the several States in acid deposition control programs;

"(4) description of the measures that would need to be taken to integrate such standard or standards with the control program required by Title IV of the Clean Air Act [this subchapter];

"(5) description of the state of knowledge with respect to source-receptor relationships necessary to develop a control program on such standard or standards and the additional research that is on-going or would be needed to make such a control program feasible; and

"(6) description of the impediments to implementation of such control program and the cost-effectiveness of deposition standards compared to other control strategies including ambient air quality standards, new source performance standards and the requirements of title IV of the Clean Air Act [this subchapter]."

[Any reference in any provision of law enacted before Jan. 4, 1995, to the Committee on Energy and Commerce of the House of Representatives treated as referring to the Committee on Commerce of the House of Representatives, except that any reference in any provision of law enacted before Jan. 4, 1995, to the Committee on Energy and Commerce of the House of Representatives treated as referring to the Committee on Agriculture of the House of Representatives, in the case of a provision of law relating to inspection of seafood or seafood products, the Committee on Banking and Financial Services of the House of Representatives, in the case of a provision of law relating to bank capital markets activities generally or to depository institution securities activities generally, and the Committee on Transportation and Infrastructure of the House of Representatives, in the case of a provision of law relating to railroads, railway labor, or railroad retirement and unemployment (except revenue measures related thereto), see section 1(a)(4) and (c)(1) of Pub.L. 104–14, set out as a note preceding section 21 of Title 2, The Congress.]

### Industrial $SO_2$ Emissions

Pub.L. 101–549, Title IV, § 406, Nov. 15, 1990, 104 Stat. 2632, provided that:

"(a) **Report.**—Not later than January 1, 1995 and every 5 years thereafter, the Administrator of the Environmental Protection Agency shall transmit to the Congress a report containing an inventory of national annual sulfur dioxide emissions from industrial sources (as defined in Title IV of the Act [this subchapter]), including units subject to section 405(g)(6) of the Clean Air Act [subsec. (g)(6) of section 7651d of this title], for all years for which data are available, as well as the likely trend in such emissions over the following twenty-year period. The reports shall also contain estimates of the actual emission reduction in each year resulting from promulgation of the diesel fuel desulfurization regulations under section 214 [section 7548 of this title].

"(b) **5.60 Million ton cap.**—Whenever the inventory required by this section indicates that sulfur dioxide emissions from industrial sources, including units subject to section 405(g)(5) of the Clean Air Act [subsec. (g)(5) of section 7651d of this title], may reasonably be expected to reach levels greater than 5.60 million tons per year, the Administrator of the Environmental Protection Agency shall take such actions under the Clean Air Act [this chapter] as may be appropriate to ensure that such emissions do not exceed 5.60 million tons per year. Such actions may include the promulgation of new and revised standards of performance for new sources, including units subject to section 405(g)(5) of the Clean Air Act, under section 111(b) of the Clean Air Act [section 7411(b) of this title], as well as promulgation of standards of performance for existing sources, including units subject to section 405(g)(5) of the Clean Air Act, under authority of this section. For an existing source regulated under this section [this note], 'standard of performance' means a standard which the Administrator determines is applicable to that source and which reflects the degree of emission reduction achievable through the application of the best system of continuous emission reduction which (taking into consideration the cost of achieving such emission reduction, and any nonair quality health and environmental impact and energy requirements) the Administrator determines has been adequately demonstrated for that category of sources.

"(c) **Election.**—Regulations promulgated under section 405(b) of the Clean Air Act [subsec. (b) of section 7651d of this title] shall not prohibit a source from electing to become an affected unit under section 410 of the Clean Air Act [section 7651i of this title]."

**Monitoring of Acid Rain Program in Canada**

Section 408 of Pub.L. 101–549 provided that:

"(a) **Reports to Congress.**—The Administrator of the Environmental Protection Agency, in consultation with the Secretary of State, the Secretary of Energy, and other persons the Administrator deems appropriate, shall prepare and submit a report to Congress on January 1, 1994, January 1, 1999, and January 1, 2005.

"(b) **Contents.**—The report to Congress shall analyze the current emission levels of sulfur dioxide and nitrogen oxides in each of the provinces participating in Canada's acid rain control program, the amount of emission reductions of sulfur dioxide and oxides of nitrogen achieved by each province, the methods utilized by each province in making those reductions, the costs to each province and the employment impacts in each province of making and maintaining those reductions.

"(c) **Compliance.**—Beginning on January 1, 1999, the reports shall also assess the degree to which each province is complying with its stated emissions cap."

**Sense of Congress on Emission Reductions Costs**

Section 407 of Pub.L. 101–549 provided that: "It is the sense of the Congress that the Clean Air Act Amendments of 1990 [Pub.L. 101–549, Nov. 15, 1990, 104 Stat. 2399, see Tables for classification], through the allowance program, allocates the costs of achieving the required reductions in emissions of sulfur dioxide and oxides of nitrogen among sources in the United States. Broad based taxes and emissions fees that would provide for payment of the costs of achieving required emissions reductions by any party or parties other than the sources required to achieve the reductions are undesirable."

## § 7651a. Definitions

**[CAA § 402]**

As used in this subchapter:

(1) The term "affected source" means a source that includes one or more affected units.

(2) The term "affected unit" means a unit that is subject to emission reduction requirements or limitations under this subchapter.

(3) The term "allowance" means an authorization, allocated to an affected unit by the Administrator under this subchapter, to emit, during or after a specified calendar year, one ton of sulfur dioxide.

(4) The term "baseline" means the annual quantity of fossil fuel consumed by an affected unit, measured in millions of British Thermal Units ("mmBtu's"), calculated as follows:

(A) For each utility unit that was in commercial operation prior to January 1, 1985, the baseline shall be the annual average quantity of mmBtu's consumed in fuel during calendar years 1985, 1986, and 1987, as recorded by the Department of Energy pursuant to Form 767. For any utility unit for which such form was not filed, the baseline shall be the level specified for such unit in the 1985 National Acid Precipitation Assessment Program (NAPAP) Emissions Inventory, Version 2, National Utility Reference File (NURF) or in a corrected data base as established by the Administrator pursuant to paragraph (3). For nonutility units, the baseline is the NAPAP Emissions Inventory, Version 2. The Administrator, in the Administrator's sole discretion, may exclude periods during which a unit is shutdown for a continuous period of four calendar months or longer, and make appropriate adjustments under this paragraph. Upon petition of the owner or operator of any unit, the Administrator may make appropriate baseline adjustments for accidents that caused prolonged outages.

(B) For any other nonutility unit that is not included in the NAPAP Emissions Inventory, Version 2, or a corrected data base as established by the Administrator pursuant to paragraph (3), the baseline shall be the annual average quantity, in mmBtu consumed in fuel by that unit, as calculated pursuant to a method which the administrator shall prescribe by regulation to be promulgated not later than eighteen months after November 15, 1990.

(C) The Administrator shall, upon application or on his own motion, by December 31, 1991, supplement data needed in support of this subchapter and correct any factual errors in data from which affected Phase II units' baselines or actual 1985 emission rates have been calculated. Corrected data shall be used for purposes of issuing allowances under the [1] subchapter. Such corrections shall not be subject to judicial review, nor shall the failure of the Administrator to correct an alleged factual error in such reports be subject to judicial review.

(5) The term "capacity factor" means the ratio between the actual electric output from a unit and the potential electric output from that unit.

(6) The term "compliance plan" means, for purposes of the requirements of this subchapter, either—

(A) a statement that the source will comply with all applicable requirements under this subchapter, or

(B) where applicable, a schedule and description of the method or methods for compliance and certification by the owner or operator that the source is in compliance with the requirements of this subchapter.

(7) The term "continuous emission monitoring system" (CEMS) means the equipment as required by section 7651k of this title, used to sample, analyze, measure, and provide on a continuous basis a permanent record of emissions and flow (expressed in pounds per million British thermal units (lbs/mmBtu), pounds per hour (lbs/hr) or such other form as the Administrator may prescribe by regulations under section 7651k of this title).

(8) The term "existing unit" means a unit (including units subject to section 7411 of this title) that commenced commercial operation before November 15, 1990. Any unit that commenced commercial operation before November 15, 1990, which is modified, reconstructed, or repowered after November 15, 1990, shall continue to be an existing unit for the purposes of this subchapter. For the purposes of this subchapter, existing units shall not include simple combustion turbines, or units which serve a generator with a nameplate capacity of 25MWe or less.

(9) The term "generator" means a device that produces electricity and which is reported as a generating unit pursuant to Department of Energy Form 860.

(10) The term "new unit" means a unit that commences commercial operation on or after November 15, 1990.

(11) The term "permitting authority" means the Administrator, or the State or local air pollution control agency, with an approved permitting program under part B of title III of the Act.

(12) The term "repowering" means replacement of an existing coal-fired boiler with one of the following clean coal technologies: atmospheric or pressurized fluidized bed combustion, integrated gasification combined cycle, magnetohydrodynamics, direct and indirect coal-fired turbines, integrated gasification fuel cells, or as determined by the Administrator, in consultation with the Secretary of Energy, a derivative of one or more of these technologies, and any other technology capable of controlling multiple combustion emissions simultaneously with improved boiler or generation efficiency and with significantly greater waste reduction relative to the performance of technology in widespread commercial use as of November 15, 1990. Notwithstanding the provisions of section 7651h(a) of this title, for the purpose of this subchapter, the term "repowering" shall also include any oil and/or gas-fired unit which has been awarded clean coal technology demonstration funding as of January 1, 1991, by the Department of Energy.

(13) The term "reserve" means any bank of allowances established by the Administrator under this subchapter.

(14) The term "State" means one of the 48 contiguous States and the District of Columbia.

(15) The term "unit" means a fossil fuel-fired combustion device.

(16) The term "actual 1985 emission rate", for electric utility units means the annual sulfur dioxide or nitrogen oxides emission rate in pounds per million Btu as reported in the NAPAP Emissions Inventory, Version 2, National Utility Reference File. For nonutility units, the term "actual 1985 emission rate" means the annual sulfur dioxide or nitrogen oxides emission rate in pounds per million Btu as reported in the NAPAP Emission Inventory, Version 2.

(17)(A) The term "utility unit" means—

(i) a unit that serves a generator in any State that produces electricity for sale, or

(ii) a unit that, during 1985, served a generator in any State that produced electricity for sale.

(B) Notwithstanding subparagraph (A), a unit described in subparagraph (A) that—

(i) was in commercial operation during 1985, but

(ii) did not, during 1985, serve a generator in any State that produced electricity for sale shall not be a utility unit for purposes of this subchapter.

(C) A unit that cogenerates steam and electricity is not a "utility unit" for purposes of this subchapter unless the unit is constructed for the purpose of supplying, or commences construction after November 15, 1990, and supplies, more than one-third of its potential electric output capacity and more than 25 megawatts electrical output to any utility power distribution system for sale.

(18) The term "allowable 1985 emissions rate" means a federally enforceable emissions limitation for sulfur dioxide or oxides of nitrogen, applicable to the unit in 1985 or the limitation applicable in such other subsequent year as determined by the Administrator if such a limitation for 1985 does not exist.

Where the emissions limitation for a unit is not expressed in pounds of emissions per million Btu, or the averaging period of that emissions limitation is not expressed on an annual basis, the Administrator shall calculate the annual equivalent of that emissions limitation in pounds per million Btu to establish the allowable 1985 emissions rate.

**(19)** The term "qualifying phase I technology" means a technological system of continuous emission reduction which achieves a 90 percent reduction in emissions of sulfur dioxide from the emissions that would have resulted from the use of fuels which were not subject to treatment prior to combustion.

**(20)** The term "alternative method of compliance" means a method of compliance in accordance with one or more of the following authorities:

**(A)** a substitution plan submitted and approved in accordance with subsections [2] 7651c(b) and (c) of this title;

**(B)** a Phase I extension plan approved by the Administrator under section 7651c(d) of this title, using qualifying phase I technology as determined by the Administrator in accordance with that section; or

**(C)** repowering with a qualifying clean coal technology under section 7651h of this title.

**(21)** The term "commenced" as applied to construction of any new electric utility unit means that an owner or operator has undertaken a continuous program of construction or that an owner or operator has entered into a contractual obligation to undertake and complete, within a reasonable time, a continuous program of construction.

**(22)** The term "commenced commercial operation" means to have begun to generate electricity for sale.

**(23)** The term "construction" means fabrication, erection, or installation of an affected unit.

**(24)** The term "industrial source" means a unit that does not serve a generator that produces electricity, a "nonutility unit" as defined in this section, or a process source as defined in section 7651i(e) [3] of this title.

**(25)** The term "nonutility unit" means a unit other than a utility unit.

**(26)** The term "designated representative" means a responsible person or official authorized by the owner or operator of a unit to represent the owner or operator in matters pertaining to the holding, transfer, or disposition of allowances allocated to a unit, and the submission of and compliance with permits, permit applications, and compliance plans for the unit.

**(27)** The term "life-of-the-unit, firm power contractual arrangement" means a unit participation power sales agreement under which a utility or industrial customer reserves, or is entitled to receive, a specified amount or percentage of capacity and associated energy generated by a specified generating unit (or units) and pays its proportional amount of such unit's total costs, pursuant to a contract either—

**(A)** for the life of the unit;

**(B)** for a cumulative term of no less than 30 years, including contracts that permit an election for early termination; or

**(C)** for a period equal to or greater than 25 years or 70 percent of the economic useful life of the unit determined as of the time the unit was built, with option rights to purchase or re-lease some portion of the capacity and associated energy generated by the unit (or units) at the end of the period.

**(28)** The term "basic Phase II allowance allocations" means:

**(A)** For calendar years 2000 through 2009 inclusive, allocations of allowances made by the Administrator pursuant to section 7651b of this title and subsections (b)(1), (3), and (4); (c)(1), (2), (3), and (5); (d)(1), (2), (4), and (5); (e); (f); (g)(1), (2), (3), (4), and (5); (h)(1); (i) and (j) of section 7651d of this title.

**(B)** For each calendar year beginning in 2010, allocations of allowances made by the Administrator pursuant to section 7651b of this title and subsections (b)(1), (3), and (4); (c)(1), (2), (3), and (5); (d)(1), (2), (4) and (5); (e); (f); (g)(1), (2), (3), (4), and (5); (h)(1) and (3); (i) and (j) of section 7651d of this title.

**(29)** The term "Phase II bonus allowance allocations" means, for calendar year 2000 through 2009, inclusive, and only for such years, allocations made by the Administrator pursuant to section 7651b of this title, subsections (a)(2), (b)(2), (c)(4), (d)(3) (except as otherwise provided therein), and (h)(2) of section 7651d of this title, and section 7651e of this title.

(July 14, 1955, c. 360, Title IV, § 402, as added Nov. 15, 1990, Pub.L. 101–549, Title IV, § 401, 104 Stat. 2585.)

[1] So in original. Probably should be "this".

[2] So in original. Probably should be "section".

[3] So in original. Probably should be section "7651i(d)".

## HISTORICAL AND STATUTORY NOTES

**References in Text**

Part B of Title III of the Act, referred to in par. (11), means Title III of the Clean Air Act, Act July 14, 1955, c. 360, as added. Title III is classified to subchapter III of this chapter, but Title III does not contain parts. For provisions of the Clean Air Act relating to permits, see subchapter V (section 7661 et seq.) of this chapter.

**Codifications**

Another section 402 of Act July 14, 1955, as added by Pub.L. 91–604, § 14, Dec. 31, 1970, 84 Stat. 1709, is classified to section 7641 of this title.

**Effective and Applicability Provisions**

1990 Acts

Section effective Nov. 15, 1990, except as otherwise provided, see section 711(b) of Pub.L. 101–549, set out as a note under section 7401 of this title.

**Savings Provisions**

Suits, actions or proceedings commenced under this chapter as in effect prior to Nov. 15, 1990, not to abate by reason of the taking effect of amendments by Pub.L. 101–549, except as otherwise provided for, see section 711(a) of Pub.L. 101–549, set out as a note under section 7401 of this title.

## § 7651b. Sulfur dioxide allowance program for existing and new units

[CAA § 403]

### (a) Allocations of annual allowances for existing and new units

(1) For the emission limitation programs under this subchapter, the Administrator shall allocate annual allowances for the unit, to be held or distributed by the designated representative of the owner or operator of each affected unit at an affected source in accordance with this subchapter, in an amount equal to the annual tonnage emission limitation calculated under section 7651c, 7651d, 7651e, 7651h, or 7651i of this title except as otherwise specifically provided elsewhere in this subchapter. Except as provided in sections 7651d(a)(2), 7651d(a)(3), 7651h and 7651i of this title, beginning January 1, 2000, the Administrator shall not allocate annual allowances to emit sulfur dioxide pursuant to section 7651d of this title in such an amount as would result in total annual emissions of sulfur dioxide from utility units in excess of 8.90 million tons except that the Administrator shall not take into account unused allowances carried forward by owners and operators of affected units or by other persons holding such allowances, following the year for which they were allocated. If necessary to meeting the restrictions imposed in the preceding sentence, the Administrator shall reduce, pro rata, the basic Phase II allowance allocations for each unit subject to the requirements of section 7651d of this title. Subject to the provisions of section 7651*o* of this title, the Administrator shall allocate allowances for each affected unit at an affected source annually, as provided in paragraphs (2) and (3) [1] and section 7651g of this title. Except as provided in sections 7651h and 7651i of this title, the removal of an existing affected unit or source from commercial operation at any time after November 15, 1990 (whether before or after January 1, 1995, or January 1, 2000) shall not terminate or otherwise affect the allocation of allowances pursuant to section 7651c or 7651d of this title to which the unit is entitled. Allowances shall be allocated by the Administrator without cost to the recipient, except for allowances sold by the Administrator pursuant to section 7651*o* of this title. Not later than December 31, 1991, the Administrator shall publish a proposed list of the basic Phase II allowance allocations, the Phase II bonus allowance allocations and, if applicable, allocations pursuant to section 7651d(a)(3) of this title for each unit subject to the emissions limitation requirements of section 7651d of this title for the year 2000 and the year 2010. After notice and opportunity for public comment, but not later than December 31, 1992, the Administrator shall publish a final list of such allocations, subject to the provisions of section 7651d(a)(2) of this title. Any owner or operator of an existing unit subject to the requirements of section 7651d(b) or (c) of this title who is considering applying for an extension of the emission limitation requirement compliance deadline for that unit from January 1, 2000, until not later than December 31, 2000, pursuant to section 7651h of this title, shall notify the Administrator no later than March 31, 1991. Such notification shall be used as the basis for estimating the basic Phase II allowances under this subsection. Prior to June 1, 1998, the Administrator shall publish a revised final statement of allowance allocations, subject to the provisions of section 7651d(a)(2) of this title and taking into account the effect of any compliance date extensions granted pursuant to section 7651h of this title on such allocations. Any person who may make an election concerning the amount of allowances to be allocated to a unit or units shall make such election and so inform the Administrator not later than March 31, 1991, in the case of an election under section 7651d of this title (or June 30, 1991, in the case of an election under section 7651e of this title). If such person fails to make such election, the Administrator shall set forth for each unit owned or operated by such person, the amount of allowances reflecting the election that would, in the judgment of the Administrator, provide the greatest benefit for the owner or operator of the unit. If such person is a Governor who may make an election under section 7651e of this title and the Governor fails to make an election, the Administrator shall set forth for each unit in the State the amount of allowances reflecting the election that would, in the judgment of the Administrator, provide the greatest benefit for units in the State.

### (b) Allowance transfer system

Allowances allocated under this subchapter may be transferred among designated representatives of the owners or operators of affected sources under this subchapter and any other person who holds such allowances, as provided by the allowance system regulations to be promulgated by the Administrator not later than eighteen months after November 15, 1990.

Such regulations shall establish the allowance system prescribed under this section, including, but not limited to, requirements for the allocation, transfer, and use of allowances under this subchapter. Such regulations shall prohibit the use of any allowance prior to the calendar year for which the allowance was allocated, and shall provide, consistent with the purposes of this subchapter, for the identification of unused allowances, and for such unused allowances to be carried forward and added to allowances allocated in subsequent years, including allowances allocated to units subject to Phase I requirements (as described in section 7651c of this title) which are applied to emissions limitations requirements in Phase II (as described in section 7651d of this title). Transfers of allowances shall not be effective until written certification of the transfer, signed by a responsible official of each party to the transfer, is received and recorded by the Administrator. Such regulations shall permit the transfer of allowances prior to the issuance of such allowances. Recorded pre-allocation transfers shall be deducted by the Administrator from the number of allowances which would otherwise be allocated to the transferor, and added to those allowances allocated to the transferee. Pre-allocation transfers shall not affect the prohibition contained in this subsection against the use of allowances prior to the year for which they are allocated.

**(c) Interpollutant trading**

Not later than January 1, 1994, the Administrator shall furnish to the Congress a study evaluating the environmental and economic consequences of amending this subchapter to permit trading sulfur dioxide allowances for nitrogen oxides allowances.

**(d) Allowance tracking system**

(1) The Administrator shall promulgate, not later than 18 months after November 15, 1990, a system for issuing, recording, and tracking allowances, which shall specify all necessary procedures and requirements for an orderly and competitive functioning of the allowance system. All allowance allocations and transfers shall, upon recordation by the Administrator, be deemed a part of each unit's permit requirements pursuant to section 7651g of this title, without any further permit review and revision.

(2) In order to insure electric reliability, such regulations shall not prohibit or affect temporary increases and decreases in emissions within utility systems, power pools, or utilities entering into allowance pool agreements, that result from their operations, including emergencies and central dispatch, and such temporary emissions increases and decreases shall not require transfer of allowances among units nor shall it require recordation. The owners or operators of such units shall act through a designated representative. Notwithstanding the preceding sentence, the total tonnage of emissions in any calendar year (calculated at the end thereof) from all units in such a utility system, power pool, or allowance pool agreements shall not exceed the total allowances for such units for the calendar year concerned.

**(e) New utility units**

After January 1, 2000, it shall be unlawful for a new utility unit to emit an annual tonnage of sulfur dioxide in excess of the number of allowances to emit held for the unit by the unit's owner or operator. Such new utility units shall not be eligible for an allocation of sulfur dioxide allowances under subsection (a)(1) of this section, unless the unit is subject to the provisions of subsection (g)(2) or (3) of section 7651d of this title. New utility units may obtain allowances from any person, in accordance with this subchapter. The owner or operator of any new utility unit in violation of this subsection shall be liable for fulfilling the obligations specified in section 7651j of this title.

**(f) Nature of allowances**

An allowance allocated under this subchapter is a limited authorization to emit sulfur dioxide in accordance with the provisions of this subchapter. Such allowance does not constitute a property right. Nothing in this subchapter or in any other provision of law shall be construed to limit the authority of the United States to terminate or limit such authorization. Nothing in this section relating to allowances shall be construed as affecting the application of, or compliance with, any other provision of this chapter to an affected unit or source, including the provisions related to applicable National Ambient Air Quality Standards and State implementation plans. Nothing in this section shall be construed as requiring a change of any kind in any State law regulating electric utility rates and charges or affecting any State law regarding such State regulation or as limiting State regulation (including any prudency review) under such a State law. Nothing in this section shall be construed as modifying the Federal Power Act [16 U.S.C.A. § 791a et seq.] or as affecting the authority of the Federal Energy Regulatory Commission under that Act. Nothing in this subchapter shall be construed to interfere with or impair any program for competitive bidding for power supply in a State in which such program is established. Allowances, once allocated to a person by the Administrator, may be received, held, and temporarily or permanently transferred in accordance with this subchapter and the regulations of the Administrator without regard to whether or not a permit is in effect under subchapter V of this chapter or section 7651g of this title with respect to the unit for which such allowance was originally allocated and recorded. Each permit under this subchapter and each permit issued under subchapter V of this chapter for any affected unit shall provide that the affected unit may not emit an annual tonnage of sulfur dioxide in excess of the allowances held for that unit.

**(g) Prohibition**

It shall be unlawful for any person to hold, use, or transfer any allowance allocated under this subchapter, except in accordance with regulations promulgated by the Administrator. It shall be unlawful for any affected unit to emit sulfur dioxide in excess of the number of allowances held for that unit for that year by the owner or operator of the unit. Upon the allocation of allowances under this subchapter, the prohibition contained in the preceding sentence shall supersede any other emission limitation applicable under this subchapter to the units for which such allowances are allocated. Allowances may not be used prior to the calendar year for which they are allocated. Nothing in this section or in the allowance system regulations shall relieve the Administrator of the Administrator's permitting, monitoring and enforcement obligations under this chapter, nor relieve affected sources of their requirements and liabilities under this chapter.

**(h) Competitive bidding for power supply**

Nothing in this subchapter shall be construed to interfere with or impair any program for competitive bidding for power supply in a State in which such program is established.

**(i) Applicability of antitrust laws**

(1) Nothing in this section affects—

(A) the applicability of the antitrust laws to the transfer, use, or sale of allowances, or

(B) the authority of the Federal Energy Regulatory Commission under any provision of law respecting unfair methods of competition or anticompetitive acts or practices.

(2) As used in this section, "antitrust laws" means those Acts set forth in section 12 of Title 15.

**(j) Public Utility Holding Company Act**

The acquisition or disposition of allowances pursuant to this subchapter including the issuance of securities or the undertaking of any other financing transaction in connection with such allowances shall not be subject to the provisions of the Public Utility Holding Company Act of 1935 [15 U.S.C.A. § 79 et seq.].

(July 14, 1955, c. 360, Title IV, § 403, as added Nov. 15, 1990, Pub.L. 101–549, Title IV, § 401, 104 Stat. 2589.)

1 So in original. No pars. (2) and (3) have been enacted.

## HISTORICAL AND STATUTORY NOTES

**References in Text**

The Federal Power Act, referred to in subsec. (f), is Act June 10, 1920, c. 285, 41 Stat. 1063, as amended, which is classified generally to chapter 12 (section 791a et seq.) of Title 16, Conservation. For complete classification of this Act to the Code, see section 791a of Title 16 and Tables.

The Public Utility Holding Company Act of 1935, referred to in subsec. (j), is Act Aug. 26, 1935, c. 687, Title I, 49 Stat. 838, as amended, which is classified generally to chapter 2C (section 79 et seq.) of Title 15, Commerce and Trade. For complete classification of this Act to the Code, see section 79 of Title 15 and Tables.

**Codifications**

Another section 403 of Act July 14, 1955, as added by Pub.L. 91–604, § 14, Dec. 31, 1970, 84 Stat. 1710, is classified to section 7642 of this title.

**Effective Date**

1990 Acts

Section effective Nov. 15, 1990, except as otherwise provided, see section 711(b) of Pub.L. 101–549, set out as a note under section 7401 of this title.

**Savings Provisions**

Suits, actions or proceedings commenced under this chapter as in effect prior to Nov. 15, 1990, not to abate by reason of the taking effect of amendments by Pub.L. 101–549, except as otherwise provided for, see section 711(a) of Pub.L. 101–549, set out as a note under section 7401 of this title.

**Fossil Fuel Use**

Section 402 of Pub.L. 101–549 provided that:

"**(a) Contracts for hydroelectric energy.**—Any person who, after the date of the enactment of the Clean Air Act Amendments of 1990 [Nov. 15, 1990], enters into a contract under which such person receives hydroelectric energy in return for the provision of electric energy by such person shall use allowances held by such person as necessary to satisfy such person's obligations under such contract.

"**(b) Federal Power Marketing Administration.**—A Federal Power Marketing Administration shall not be subject to the provisions and requirements of this title [this subchapter] with respect to electric energy generated by hydroelectric facilities and marketed by such Power Marketing Administration. Any person who sells or provides electric energy to a Federal Power Marketing Administration shall comply with the provisions and requirements of this title [this subchapter]."

## § 7651c. Phase I sulfur dioxide requirements

**[CAA § 404]**

**(a) Emission limitations**

(1) After January 1, 1995, each source that includes one or more affected units listed in table A is an affected source under this section. After January 1, 1995, it shall be unlawful for any affected unit (other than an eligible phase I unit under subsection (d)(2) of this section) to emit sulfur dioxide in excess of the tonnage limitation stated as a total number of allowances in table A for phase I, unless (A) the emissions reduction requirements applicable to such unit have been achieved pursuant to subsection (b) or (d) of this section, or (B) the owner or operator of such unit

holds allowances to emit not less than the unit's total annual emissions, except that, after January 1, 2000, the emissions limitations established in this section shall be superseded by those established in section 7651d of this title. The owner or operator of any unit in violation of this section shall be fully liable for such violation including, but not limited to, liability for fulfilling the obligations specified in section 7651j of this title.

(2) Not later than December 31, 1991, the Administrator shall determine the total tonnage of reductions in the emissions of sulfur dioxide from all utility units in calendar year 1995 that will occur as a result of compliance with the emissions limitation requirements of this section, and shall establish a reserve of allowances equal in amount to the number of tons determined thereby not to exceed a total of 3.50 million tons. In making such a determination, the Administrator shall compute for each unit subject to the emissions limitation requirements of this section the difference between:

(A) the product of its baseline multiplied by the lesser of each unit's allowable 1985 emissions rate and its actual 1985 emissions rate, divided by 2,000, and

(B) the product of each unit's baseline multiplied by 2.50 lbs/mmBtu divided by 2,000,

and sum the computations. The Administrator shall adjust the foregoing calculation to reflect projected calendar year 1995 utilization of the units subject to the emissions limitations of this subchapter that the Administrator finds would have occurred in the absence of the imposition of such requirements. Pursuant to subsection (d) of this section, the Administrator shall allocate allowances from the reserve established hereinunder until the earlier of such time as all such allowances in the reserve are allocated or December 31, 1999.

(3) In addition to allowances allocated pursuant to paragraph (1), in each calendar year beginning in 1995 and ending in 1999, inclusive, the Administrator shall allocate for each unit on Table A that is located in the States of Illinois, Indiana, or Ohio (other than units at Kyger Creek, Clifty Creek and Joppa Steam), allowances in an amount equal to 200,000 multiplied by the unit's pro rata share of the total number of allowances allocated for all units on Table A in the 3 States (other than units at Kyger Creek, Clifty Creek, and Joppa Steam) pursuant to paragraph (1). Such allowances shall be excluded from the calculation of the reserve under paragraph (2).

**(b) Substitutions**

The owner or operator of an affected unit under subsection (a) of this section may include in its section 7651g of this title permit application and proposed compliance plan a proposal to reassign, in whole or in part, the affected unit's sulfur dioxide reduction requirements to any other unit(s) under the control of such owner or operator. Such proposal shall specify—

(1) the designation of the substitute unit or units to which any part of the reduction obligations of subsection (a) of this section shall be required, in addition to, or in lieu of, any original affected units designated under such subsection;

(2) the original affected unit's baseline, the actual and allowable 1985 emissions rate for sulfur dioxide, and the authorized annual allowance allocation stated in table A;

(3) calculation of the annual average tonnage for calendar years 1985, 1986, and 1987, emitted by the substitute unit or units, based on the baseline for each unit, as defined in section 7651a(d) [1] of this title, multiplied by the lesser of the unit's actual or allowable 1985 emissions rate;

(4) the emissions rates and tonnage limitations that would be applicable to the original and substitute affected units under the substitution proposal;

(5) documentation, to the satisfaction of the Administrator, that the reassigned tonnage limits will, in total, achieve the same or greater emissions reduction than would have been achieved by the original affected unit and the substitute unit or units without such substitution; and

(6) such other information as the Administrator may require.

**(c) Administrator's action on substitution proposals**

(1) The Administrator shall take final action on such substitution proposal in accordance with section 7651g(c) of this title if the substitution proposal fulfills the requirements of this subsection. The Administrator may approve a substitution proposal in whole or in part and with such modifications or conditions as may be consistent with the orderly functioning of the allowance system and which will ensure the emissions reductions contemplated by this subchapter. If a proposal does not meet the requirements of subsection (b) of this section, the Administrator shall disapprove it. The owner or operator of a unit listed in table A shall not substitute another unit or units without the prior approval of the Administrator.

(2) Upon approval of a substitution proposal, each substitute unit, and each source with such unit, shall be deemed affected under this subchapter, and the Administrator shall issue a permit to the original and substitute affected source and unit in accordance with the approved substitution plan and section 7651g of this title. The Administrator shall allocate allowances for the original and substitute affected units in accor-

dance with the approved substitution proposal pursuant to section 7651b of this title. It shall be unlawful for any source or unit that is allocated allowances pursuant to this section to emit sulfur dioxide in excess of the emissions limitation provided for in the approved substitution permit and plan unless the owner or operator of each unit governed by the permit and approved substitution plan holds allowances to emit not less than the units total annual emissions. The owner or operator of any original or substitute affected unit operated in violation of this subsection shall be fully liable for such violation, including liability for fulfilling the obligations specified in section 7651j of this title. If a substitution proposal is disapproved, the Administrator shall allocate allowances to the original affected unit or units in accordance with subsection (a) of this section.

**(d) Eligible phase I extension units**

(1) The owner or operator of any affected unit subject to an emissions limitation requirement under this section may petition the Administrator in its permit application under section 7651g of this title for an extension of 2 years of the deadline for meeting such requirement, provided that the owner or operator of any such unit holds allowances to emit not less than the unit's total annual emissions for each of the 2 years of the period of extension. To qualify for such an extension, the affected unit must either employ a qualifying phase I technology, or transfer its phase I emissions reduction obligation to a unit employing a qualifying phase I technology. Such transfer shall be accomplished in accordance with a compliance plan, submitted and approved under section 7651g of this title, that shall govern operations at all units included in the transfer, and that specifies the emissions reduction requirements imposed pursuant to this subchapter.

(2) Such extension proposal shall—

(A) specify the unit or units proposed for designation as an eligible phase I extension unit;

(B) provide a copy of an executed contract, which may be contingent upon the Administrator approving the proposal, for the design engineering, and construction of the qualifying phase I technology for the extension unit, or for the unit or units to which the extension unit's emission reduction obligation is to be transferred;

(C) specify the unit's or units' baseline, actual 1985 emissions rate, allowable 1985 emissions rate, and projected utilization for calendar years 1995 through 1999;

(D) require CEMS on both the eligible phase I extension unit or units and the transfer unit or units beginning no later than January 1, 1995; and

(E) specify the emission limitation and number of allowances expected to be necessary for annual operation after the qualifying phase I technology has been installed.

(3) The Administrator shall review and take final action on each extension proposal in order of receipt, consistent with section 7651g of this title, and for an approved proposal shall designate the unit or units as an eligible phase I extension unit. The Administrator may approve an extension proposal in whole or in part, and with such modifications or conditions as may be necessary, consistent with the orderly functioning of the allowance system, and to ensure the emissions reductions contemplated by the [2] subchapter.

(4) In order to determine the number of proposals eligible for allocations from the reserve under subsection (a)(2) of this section and the number of allowances remaining available after each proposal is acted upon, the Administrator shall reduce the total number of allowances remaining available in the reserve by the number of allowances calculated according to subparagraphs (A), (B) and (C) until either no allowances remain available in the reserve for further allocation or all approved proposals have been acted upon. If no allowances remain available in the reserve for further allocation before all proposals have been acted upon by the Administrator, any pending proposals shall be disapproved. The Administrator shall calculate allowances equal to—

(A) the difference between the lesser of the average annual emissions in calendar years 1988 and 1989 or the projected emissions tonnage for calendar year 1995 of each eligible phase I extension unit, as designated under paragraph (3), and the product of the unit's baseline multiplied by an emission rate of 2.50 lbs/mmBtu, divided by 2,000;

(B) the difference between the lesser of the average annual emissions in calendar years 1988 and 1989 or the projected emissions tonnage for calendar year 1996 of each eligible phase I extension unit, as designated under paragraph (3), and the product of the unit's baseline multiplied by an emission rate of 2.50 lbs/mmBtu, divided by 2,000; and

(C) the amount by which (i) the product of each unit's baseline multiplied by an emission rate of 1.20 lbs/mmBtu, divided by 2,000, exceeds (ii) the tonnage level specified under subparagraph (E) of paragraph (2) of this subsection multiplied by a factor of 3.

(5) Each eligible Phase I extension unit shall receive allowances determined under subsection (a)(1) or (c) of this section. In addition, for calendar year 1995, the Administrator shall allocate to each eligible Phase I extension unit, from the allowance reserve created pursuant to subsection (a)(2) of this section, allowances equal to the difference between the lesser of the

average annual emissions in calendar years 1988 and 1989 or its projected emissions tonnage for calendar year 1995 and the product of the unit's baseline multiplied by an emission rate of 2.50 lbs/mmBtu, divided by 2,000. In calendar year 1996, the Administrator shall allocate for each eligible unit, from the allowance reserve created pursuant to subsection (a)(2) of this section, allowances equal to the difference between the lesser of the average annual emissions in calendar years 1988 and 1989 or its projected emissions tonnage for calendar year 1996 and the product of the unit's baseline multiplied by an emission rate of 2.50 lbs/mmBtu, divided by 2,000. It shall be unlawful for any source or unit subject to an approved extension plan under this subsection to emit sulfur dioxide in excess of the emissions limitations provided for in the permit and approved extension plan, unless the owner or operator of each unit governed by the permit and approved plan holds allowances to emit not less than the unit's total annual emissions.

(6) In addition to allowances specified in paragraph (5), the Administrator shall allocate for each eligible Phase I extension unit employing qualifying Phase I technology, for calendar years 1997, 1998, and 1999, additional allowances, from any remaining allowances in the reserve created pursuant to subsection (a)(2) of this section, following the reduction in the reserve provided for in paragraph (4), not to exceed the amount by which (A) the product of each eligible unit's baseline times an emission rate of 1.20 lbs/mmBtu, divided by 2,000, exceeds (B) the tonnage level specified under subparagraph (E) of paragraph (2) of this subsection.

(7) After January 1, 1997, in addition to any liability under this chapter, including under section 7651j of this title, if any eligible phase I extension unit employing qualifying phase I technology or any transfer unit under this subsection emits sulfur dioxide in excess of the annual tonnage limitation specified in the extension plan, as approved in paragraph (3) of this subsection, the Administrator shall, in the calendar year following such excess, deduct allowances equal to the amount of such excess from such unit's annual allowance allocation.

**(e) Allocation of allowances**

(1) In the case of a unit that receives authorization from the Governor of the State in which such unit is located to make reductions in the emissions of sulfur dioxide prior to calendar year 1995 and that is part of a utility system that meets the following requirements: (A) the total coal-fired generation within the utility system as a percentage of total system generation decreased by more than 20 percent between January 1, 1980, and December 31, 1985; and (B) the weighted capacity factor of all coal-fired units within the utility system averaged over the period from January 1, 1985, through December 31, 1987, was below 50 percent, the Administrator shall allocate allowances under this paragraph for the unit pursuant to this subsection. The Administrator shall allocate allowances for a unit that is an affected unit pursuant to section 7651d of this title (but is not also an affected unit under this section) and part of a utility system that includes 1 or more affected units under section 7651d of this title for reductions in the emissions of sulfur dioxide made during the period 1995–1999 if the unit meets the requirements of this subsection and the requirements of the preceding sentence, except that for the purposes of applying this subsection to any such unit, the prior year concerned as specified below, shall be any year after January 1, 1995 but prior to January 1, 2000.

(2) In the case of an affected unit under this section described in subparagraph (A), the allowances allocated under this subsection for early reductions in any prior year may not exceed the amount which (A) the product of the unit's baseline multiplied by the unit's 1985 actual sulfur dioxide emission rate (in lbs. per mmBtu), divided by 2,000, exceeds (B) the allowances specified for such unit in Table A. In the case of an affected unit under section 7651d of this title described in subparagraph (A), the allowances awarded under this subsection for early reductions in any prior year may not exceed the amount by which (i) the product of the quantity of fossil fuel consumed by the unit (in mmBtu) in the prior year multiplied by the lesser of 2.50 or the most stringent emission rate (in lbs. per mmBtu) applicable to the unit under the applicable implementation plan, divided by 2,000, exceeds (ii) the unit's actual tonnage of sulfur dioxide emission for the prior year concerned. Allowances allocated under this subsection for units referred to in subparagraph (A) may be allocated only for emission reductions achieved as a result of physical changes or changes in the method of operation made after November 15, 1990, including changes in the type or quality of fossil fuel consumed.

(3) In no event shall the provisions of this paragraph be interpreted as an event of force majeur or a commercial impracticability [3] or in any other way as a basis for excused nonperformance by a utility system under a coal sales contract in effect before November 15, 1990.

TABLE A. AFFECTED SOURCES AND UNITS IN PHASE I AND THEIR SULFUR DIOXIDE ALLOWANCES (TONS)

| State | Plant Name | Generator | Phase I Allowances |
|---|---|---|---|
| Alabama | Colbert | 1 | 13,570 |
| | | 2 | 15,310 |
| | | 3 | 15,400 |
| | | 4 | 15,410 |
| | | 5 | 37,180 |
| | E.C. Gaston | 1 | 18,100 |
| | | 2 | 18,540 |
| | | 3 | 18,310 |

| State | Plant Name | Generator | Phase I Allowances |
|---|---|---|---|
| | | 4 | 19,280 |
| | | 5 | 59,840 |
| Florida | Big Bend | 1 | 28,410 |
| | | 2 | 27,100 |
| | | 3 | 26,740 |
| | Crist | 6 | 19,200 |
| | | 7 | 31,680 |
| Georgia | Bowen | 1 | 56,320 |
| | | 2 | 54,770 |
| | | 3 | 71,750 |
| | | 4 | 71,740 |
| | Hammond | 1 | 8,780 |
| | | 2 | 9,220 |
| | | 3 | 8,910 |
| | | 4 | 37,640 |
| | J. McDonough | 1 | 19,910 |
| | | 2 | 20,600 |
| | Wansley | 1 | 70,770 |
| | | 2 | 65,430 |
| | Yates | 1 | 7,210 |
| | | 2 | 7,040 |
| | | 3 | 6,950 |
| | | 4 | 8,910 |
| | | 5 | 9,410 |
| | | 6 | 24,760 |
| | | 7 | 21,480 |
| Illinois | Baldwin | 1 | 42,010 |
| | | 2 | 44,420 |
| | | 3 | 42,550 |
| | Coffeen | 1 | 11,790 |
| | | 2 | 35,670 |
| | Grand Tower | 4 | 5,910 |
| | Hennepin | 2 | 18,410 |
| | Joppa Steam | 1 | 12,590 |
| | | 2 | 10,770 |
| | | 3 | 12,270 |
| | | 4 | 11,360 |
| | | 5 | 11,420 |
| | | 6 | 10,620 |
| | Kincaid | 1 | 31,530 |
| | | 2 | 33,810 |
| | Meredosia | 3 | 13,890 |
| | Vermilion | 2 | 8,880 |
| Indiana | Bailly | 7 | 11,180 |
| | | 8 | 15,630 |
| | Breed | 1 | 18,500 |
| | Cayuga | 1 | 33,370 |
| | | 2 | 34,130 |
| | Clifty Creek | 1 | 20,150 |
| | | 2 | 19,810 |
| | | 3 | 20,410 |
| | | 4 | 20,080 |
| | | 5 | 19,360 |
| | | 6 | 20,380 |
| | E.W. Stout | 5 | 3,880 |
| | | 6 | 4,770 |
| | | 7 | 23,610 |
| | F.B. Culley | 2 | 4,290 |
| | | 3 | 16,970 |
| | F.E. Ratts | 1 | 8,330 |
| | | 2 | 8,480 |
| | Gibson | 1 | 40,400 |
| | | 2 | 41,010 |
| | | 3 | 41,080 |
| | | 4 | 40,320 |
| | H.T. Pritchard | 6 | 5,770 |
| | Michigan City | 12 | 23,310 |
| | Petersburg | 1 | 16,430 |
| | | 2 | 32,380 |
| | R. Gallagher | 1 | 6,490 |
| | | 2 | 7,280 |
| | | 3 | 6,530 |
| | | 4 | 7,650 |
| | Tanners Creek | 4 | 24,820 |
| | Wabash River | 1 | 4,000 |
| | | 2 | 2,860 |
| | | 3 | 3,750 |
| | | 5 | 3,670 |
| | | 6 | 12,280 |
| | Warrick | 4 | 26,980 |
| Iowa | Burlington | 1 | 10,710 |
| | Des Moines | 7 | 2,320 |
| | George Neal | 1 | 1,290 |
| | M.L. Kapp | 2 | 13,800 |
| | Prairie Creek | 4 | 8,180 |
| | Riverside | 5 | 3,990 |
| Kansas | Quindaro | 2 | 4,220 |
| Kentucky | Coleman | 1 | 11,250 |
| | | 2 | 12,840 |
| | | 3 | 12,340 |
| | Cooper | 1 | 7,450 |
| | | 2 | 15,320 |
| | E.W. Brown | 1 | 7,110 |
| | | 2 | 10,910 |
| | | 3 | 26,100 |
| | Elmer Smith | 1 | 6,520 |
| | | 2 | 14,410 |
| | Ghent | 1 | 28,410 |
| | Green River | 4 | 7,820 |
| | H.L. Spurlock | 1 | 22,780 |
| | Henderson II | 1 | 13,340 |
| | | 2 | 12,310 |
| | Paradise | 3 | 59,170 |
| | Shawnee | 10 | 10,170 |
| Maryland | Chalk Point | 1 | 21,910 |
| | | 2 | 24,330 |
| | C.P. Crane | 1 | 10,330 |
| | | 2 | 9,230 |
| | Morgantown | 1 | 35,260 |
| | | 2 | 38,480 |
| Michigan | J.H. Campbell | 1 | 19,280 |
| | | 2 | 23,060 |
| Minnesota | High Bridge | 6 | 4,270 |
| Mississippi | Jack Watson | 4 | 17,910 |
| | | 5 | 36,700 |
| Missouri | Asbury | 1 | 16,190 |
| | James River | 5 | 4,850 |
| | Labadie | 1 | 40,110 |
| | | 2 | 37,710 |
| | | 3 | 40,310 |
| | | 4 | 35,940 |
| | Montrose | 1 | 7,390 |
| | | 2 | 8,200 |
| | | 3 | 10,090 |
| | New Madrid | 1 | 28,240 |
| | | 2 | 32,480 |
| | Sibley | 3 | 15,580 |
| | Sioux | 1 | 22,570 |
| | | 2 | 23,690 |
| | Thomas Hill | 1 | 10,250 |
| | | 2 | 19,390 |
| New Hampshire | Merrimack | 1 | 10,190 |
| | | 2 | 22,000 |
| New Jersey | B.L. England | 1 | 9,060 |
| | | 2 | 11,720 |
| New York | Dunkirk | 3 | 12,600 |
| | | 4 | 14,060 |
| | Greenidge | 4 | 7,540 |

| State | Plant Name | Generator | Phase I Allowances |
|---|---|---|---|
| | Milliken | 1 | 11,170 |
| | | 2 | 12,410 |
| | Northport | 1 | 19,810 |
| | | 2 | 24,110 |
| | | 3 | 26,480 |
| | Port Jefferson | 3 | 10,470 |
| | | 4 | 12,330 |
| Ohio | Ashtabula | 5 | 16,740 |
| | Avon Lake | 8 | 11,650 |
| | | 9 | 30,480 |
| | Cardinal | 1 | 34,270 |
| | | 2 | 38,320 |
| | Conesville | 1 | 4,210 |
| | | 2 | 4,890 |
| | | 3 | 5,500 |
| | | 4 | 48,770 |
| | Eastlake | 1 | 7,800 |
| | | 2 | 8,640 |
| | | 3 | 10,020 |
| | | 4 | 14,510 |
| | | 5 | 34,070 |
| | Edgewater | 4 | 5,050 |
| | Gen. J.M. Gavin | 1 | 79,080 |
| | | 2 | 80,560 |
| | Kyger Creek | 1 | 19,280 |
| | | 2 | 18,560 |
| | | 3 | 17,910 |
| | | 4 | 18,710 |
| | | 5 | 18,740 |
| | Miami Fort | 5 | 760 |
| | | 6 | 11,380 |
| | | 7 | 38,510 |
| | Muskingum River | 1 | 14,880 |
| | | 2 | 14,170 |
| | | 3 | 13,950 |
| | | 4 | 11,780 |
| | | 5 | 40,470 |
| | Niles | 1 | 6,940 |
| | | 2 | 9,100 |
| | Picway | 5 | 4,930 |
| | R.E. Burger | 3 | 6,150 |
| | | 4 | 10,780 |
| | | 5 | 12,430 |
| | W.H. Sammis | 5 | 24,170 |
| | | 6 | 39,930 |
| | | 7 | 43,220 |
| | W.C. Beckjord | 5 | 8,950 |
| | | 6 | 23,020 |
| Pennsylvania | Armstrong | 1 | 14,410 |
| | | 2 | 15,430 |
| | Brunner Island | 1 | 27,760 |
| | | 2 | 31,100 |
| | | 3 | 53,820 |
| | Cheswick | 1 | 39,170 |
| | Conemaugh | 1 | 59,790 |
| | | 2 | 66,450 |
| | Hatfield's Ferry | 1 | 37,830 |
| | | 2 | 37,320 |
| | | 3 | 40,270 |
| | Martins Creek | 1 | 12,660 |
| | | 2 | 12,820 |
| | Portland | 1 | 5,940 |
| | | 2 | 10,230 |
| | Shawville | 1 | 10,320 |
| | | 2 | 10,320 |
| | | 3 | 14,220 |
| | | 4 | 14,070 |
| | Sunbury | 3 | 8,760 |
| | | 4 | 11,450 |
| Tennessee | Allen | 1 | 15,320 |
| | | 2 | 16,770 |
| | | 3 | 15,670 |
| | Cumberland | 1 | 86,700 |
| | | 2 | 94,840 |
| | Gallatin | 1 | 17,870 |
| | | 2 | 17,310 |
| | | 3 | 20,020 |
| | | 4 | 21,260 |
| | Johnsonville | 1 | 7,790 |
| | | 2 | 8,040 |
| | | 3 | 8,410 |
| | | 4 | 7,990 |
| | | 5 | 8,240 |
| | | 6 | 7,890 |
| | | 7 | 8,980 |
| | | 8 | 8,700 |
| | | 9 | 7,080 |
| | | 10 | 7,550 |
| West Virginia | Albright | 3 | 12,000 |
| | Fort Martin | 1 | 41,590 |
| | | 2 | 41,200 |
| | Harrison | 1 | 48,620 |
| | | 2 | 46,150 |
| | | 3 | 41,500 |
| | Kammer | 1 | 18,740 |
| | | 2 | 19,460 |
| | | 3 | 17,390 |
| | Mitchell | 1 | 43,980 |
| | | 2 | 45,510 |
| | Mount Storm | 1 | 43,720 |
| | | 2 | 35,580 |
| | | 3 | 42,430 |
| Wisconsin | Edgewater | 4 | 24,750 |
| | La Crosse/Genoa | 3 | 22,700 |
| | Nelson Dewey | 1 | 6,010 |
| | | 2 | 6,680 |
| | N. Oak Creek | 1 | 5,220 |
| | | 2 | 5,140 |
| | | 3 | 5,370 |
| | | 4 | 6,320 |
| | Pulliam | 8 | 7,510 |
| | S. Oak Creek | 5 | 9,670 |
| | | 6 | 12,040 |
| | | 7 | 16,180 |
| | | 8 | 15,790 |

**(f) Energy conservation and renewable energy**

**(1) Definitions**

As used in this subsection:

**(A) Qualified energy conservation measure**

The term "qualified energy conservation measure" means a cost effective measure, as identified by the Administrator in consultation with the Secretary of Energy, that increases the efficiency of the use of electricity provided by an electric utility to its customers.

**(B) Qualified renewable energy**

The term "qualified renewable energy" means energy derived from biomass, solar, geothermal, or wind as identified by the Administrator in consultation with the Secretary of Energy.

**(C) Electric utility**

The term "electric utility" means any person, State agency, or Federal agency, which sells electric energy.

**(2) Allowances for emissions avoided through energy conservation and renewable energy**

**(A) In general**

The regulations under paragraph (4) of this subsection shall provide that for each ton of sulfur dioxide emissions avoided by an electric utility, during the applicable period, through the use of qualified energy conservation measures or qualified renewable energy, the Administrator shall allocate a single allowance to such electric utility, on a first-come-first-served basis from the Conservation and Renewable Energy Reserve established under subsection (g) of this section, up to a total of 300,000 allowances for allocation from such Reserve.

**(B) Requirements for issuance**

The Administrator shall allocate allowances to an electric utility under this subsection only if all of the following requirements are met:

(i) Such electric utility is paying for the qualified energy conservation measures or qualified renewable energy directly or through purchase from another person.

(ii) The emissions of sulfur dioxide avoided through the use of qualified energy conservation measures or qualified renewable energy are quantified in accordance with regulations promulgated by the Administrator under this subsection.

(iii)(I) Such electric utility has adopted and is implementing a least cost energy conservation and electric power plan which evaluates a range of resources, including new power supplies, energy conservation, and renewable energy resources, in order to meet expected future demand at the lowest system cost.

(II) The qualified energy conservation measures or qualified renewable energy, or both, are consistent with that plan.

(III) Electric utilities subject to the jurisdiction of a State regulatory authority must have such plan approved by such authority. For electric utilities not subject to the jurisdiction of a State regulatory authority such plan shall be approved by the entity with rate-making authority for such utility.

(iv) In the case of qualified energy conservation measures undertaken by a State regulated electric utility, the Secretary of Energy certifies that the State regulatory authority with jurisdiction over the electric rates of such electric utility has established rates and charges which ensure that the net income of such electric utility after implementation of specific cost effective energy conservation measures is at least as high as such net income would have been if the energy conservation measures had not been implemented. Upon the date of any such certification by the Secretary of Energy, all allowances which, but for this paragraph, would have been allocated under subparagraph (A) before such date, shall be allocated to the electric utility. This clause is not a requirement for qualified renewable energy.

(v) Such utility or any subsidiary of the utility's holding company owns or operates at least one affected unit.

**(C) Period of applicability**

Allowances under this subsection shall be allocated only with respect to kilowatt hours of electric energy saved by qualified energy conservation measures or generated by qualified renewable energy after January 1, 1992 and before the earlier of (i) December 31, 2000, or (ii) the date on which any electric utility steam generating unit owned or operated by the electric utility to which the allowances are allocated becomes subject to this subchapter (including those sources that elect to become affected by this subchapter, pursuant to section 7651i of this title).

**(D) Determination of avoided emissions**

**(i) Application**

In order to receive allowances under this subsection, an electric utility shall make an application which—

(I) designates the qualified energy conservation measures implemented and the qualified renewable energy sources used for purposes of avoiding emissions,[4]

(II) calculates, in accordance with subparagraphs (F) and (G), the number of tons of emissions avoided by reason of the implementation of such measures or the use of such renewable energy sources; and

(III) demonstrates that the requirements of subparagraph (B) have been met.

Such application for allowances by a State-regulated electric utility shall require approval by the State regulatory authority with jurisdiction over such electric utility. The authority shall review the application for accuracy and compliance with this subsection and the rules under this subsection. Electric utilities whose retail rates are not subject to the jurisdiction of a State regulatory authority shall apply directly to the Administrator for such approval.

**(E) Avoided emissions from qualified energy conservation measures**

For the purposes of this subsection, the emission tonnage deemed avoided by reason of the implementation of qualified energy conservation measures for any calendar year shall be a tonnage equal to the product of multiplying—

(i) the kilowatt hours that would otherwise have been supplied by the utility during such year in the absence of such qualified energy conservation measures, by

(ii) 0.004,

and dividing by 2,000.

**(F) Avoided emissions from the use of qualified renewable energy**

The emissions tonnage deemed avoided by reason of the use of qualified renewable energy by an electric utility for any calendar year shall be a tonnage equal to the product of multiplying—

(i) the actual kilowatt hours generated by, or purchased from, qualified renewable energy, by

(ii) 0.004,

and dividing by 2,000.

**(G) Prohibitions**

(i) No allowances shall be allocated under this subsection for the implementation of programs that are exclusively informational or educational in nature.

(ii) No allowances shall be allocated for energy conservation measures or renewable energy that were operational before January 1, 1992.

**(3) Savings provision**

Nothing in this subsection precludes a State or State regulatory authority from providing additional incentives to utilities to encourage investment in demand-side resources.

**(4) Regulations**

Not later than 18 months after November 15, 1990, and in conjunction with the regulations required to be promulgated under subsections (b) and (c) of this section, the Administrator shall, in consultation with the Secretary of Energy, promulgate regulations under this subsection. Such regulations shall list energy conservation measures and renewable energy sources which may be treated as qualified energy conservation measures and qualified renewable energy for purposes of this subsection. Allowances shall only be allocated if all requirements of this subsection and the rules promulgated to implement this subsection are complied with. The Administrator shall review the determinations of each State regulatory authority under this subsection to encourage consistency from electric utility to electric utility and from State to State in accordance with the Administrator's rules. The Administrator shall publish the findings of this review no less than annually.

**(g) Conservation and Renewable Energy Reserve**

The Administrator shall establish a Conservation and Renewable Energy Reserve under this subsection. Beginning on January 1, 1995, the Administrator may allocate from the Conservation and Renewable Energy Reserve an amount equal to a total of 300,000 allowances for emissions of sulfur dioxide pursuant to section 7651b of this title. In order to provide 300,000 allowances for such reserve, in each year beginning in calendar year 2000 and until calendar year 2009, inclusive, the Administrator shall reduce each unit's basic Phase II allowance allocation on the basis of its pro rata share of 30,000 allowances. If allowances remain in the reserve after January 2, 2010, the Administrator shall allocate such allowances for affected units under section 7651d of this title on a pro rata basis. For purposes of this subsection, for any unit subject to the emissions limitation requirements of section 7651d of this title, the term "pro rata basis" refers to the ratio which the reductions made in such unit's allowances in order to establish the reserve under this subsection bears to the total of such reductions for all such units.

**(h) Alternative allowance allocation for units in certain utility systems with optional baseline**

**(1) Optional baseline for units in certain systems**

In the case of a unit subject to the emissions limitation requirements of this section which (as of November 15, 1990)—

(A) has an emission rate below 1.0 lbs/mmBtu,

(B) has decreased its sulfur dioxide emissions rate by 60 percent or greater since 1980, and

(C) is part of a utility system which has a weighted average sulfur dioxide emissions rate for all fossil fueled-fired units below 1.0 lbs/mmBtu,

at the election of the owner or operator of such unit, the unit's baseline may be calculated (i) as provided under section 7651a(d)[1] of this title, or (ii) by utilizing the unit's average annual fuel consumption at a 60 percent capacity factor. Such election shall be made no later than March 1, 1991.

**(2) Allowance allocation**

Whenever a unit referred to in paragraph (1) elects to calculate its baseline as provided in clause (ii) of paragraph (1), the Administrator shall allocate allowances for the unit pursuant to section 7651b(a)(1) of this title, this section, and section 7651d of this title (as basic Phase II allowance allocations) in an amount equal to the baseline selected multiplied by the lower of the average annual emission rate for such unit in 1989, or 1.0 lbs./mmBtu. Such allowance allocation shall be in lieu of any allocation of allowances under this section and section 7651d of this title.

(July 14, 1955, c. 360, Title IV, § 404, as added Nov. 15, 1990, Pub.L. 101–549, Title IV, § 401, 104 Stat. 2592.)

[1] So in original. Probably should be section "7651a(4)".

[2] So in original. Probably should be "this".

[3] So in original. Probably should be "impracticability".

[4] So in original. The comma probably should be a "semicolon".

### HISTORICAL AND STATUTORY NOTES

**Effective and Applicability Provisions**

1990 Acts

Section effective Nov. 15, 1990, except as otherwise provided, see section 711(b) of Pub.L. 101–549, set out as a note under section 7401 of this title.

**Savings Provisions**

Suits, actions or proceedings commenced under this chapter as in effect prior to Nov. 15, 1990, not to abate by reason of the taking effect of amendments by Pub.L. 101–549, except as otherwise provided for, see section 711(a) of Pub.L. 101–549, set out as a note under section 7401 of this title.

## § 7651d. Phase II sulfur dioxide requirements

[CAA § 405]

### (a) Applicability

(1) After January 1, 2000, each existing utility unit as provided below is subject to the limitations or requirements of this section. Each utility unit subject to an annual sulfur dioxide tonnage emission limitation under this section is an affected unit under this subchapter. Each source that includes one or more affected units is an affected source. In the case of an existing unit that was not in operation during calendar year 1985, the emission rate for a calendar year after 1985, as determined by the Administrator, shall be used in lieu of the 1985 rate. The owner or operator of any unit operated in violation of this section shall be fully liable under this chapter for fulfilling the obligations specified in section 7651j of this title.

(2) In addition to basic Phase II allowance allocations, in each year beginning in calendar year 2000 and ending in calendar year 2009, inclusive, the Administrator shall allocate up to 530,000 Phase II bonus allowances pursuant to subsections (b)(2), (c)(4), (d)(3)(A) and (B), and (h)(2) of this section and section 7651e of this title. Not later than June 1, 1998, the Administrator shall calculate, for each unit granted an extension pursuant to section 7651h of this title the difference between (A) the number of allowances allocated for the unit in calendar year 2000, and (B) the product of the unit's baseline multiplied by 1.20 lbs/mmBtu, divided by 2000, and sum the computations. In each year, beginning in calendar year 2000 and ending in calendar year 2009, inclusive, the Administrator shall deduct from each unit's basic Phase II allowance allocation its pro rata share of 10 percent of the sum calculated pursuant to the preceding sentence.

(3) In addition to basic Phase II allowance allocations and Phase II bonus allowance allocations, beginning January 1, 2000, the Administrator shall allocate for each unit listed on Table A in section 7651c of this title (other than units at Kyger Creek, Clifty Creek, and Joppa Steam) and located in the States of Illinois, Indiana, Ohio, Georgia, Alabama, Missouri, Pennsylvania, West Virginia, Kentucky, or Tennessee allowances in an amount equal to 50,000 multiplied by the unit's pro rata share of the total number of basic allowances allocated for all units listed on Table A (other than units at Kyger Creek, Clifty Creek, and Joppa Steam). Allowances allocated pursuant to this paragraph shall not be subject to the 8,900,000 ton limitation in section 7651b(a) of this title.

### (b) Units equal to, or above, 75 MWe and 1.20 lbs/mmBtu

(1) Except as otherwise provided in paragraph (3), after January 1, 2000, it shall be unlawful for any existing utility unit that serves a generator with nameplate capacity equal to, or greater, than 75 MWe and an actual 1985 emission rate equal to or greater than 1.20 lbs/mmBtu to exceed an annual sulfur dioxide tonnage emission limitation equal to the product of the unit's baseline multiplied by an emission rate equal to 1.20 lbs/mmBtu, divided by 2,000, unless the owner or operator of such unit holds allowances to emit not less than the unit's total annual emissions.

(2) In addition to allowances allocated pursuant to paragraph (1) and section 7651b(a)(1) of this title as basic Phase II allowance allocations, beginning January 1, 2000, and for each calendar year thereafter until and including 2009, the Administrator shall allocate annually for each unit subject to the emissions limitation requirements of paragraph (1) with an actual 1985 emissions rate greater than 1.20 lbs/mmBtu and less than 2.50 lbs/mmBtu and a baseline capacity factor of less than 60 percent, allowances from the reserve created pursuant to subsection (a)(2) of this section in an amount equal to 1.20 lbs/mmBtu multiplied by 50 percent of the difference, on a Btu basis, between the unit's baseline and the unit's fuel consumption at a 60 percent capacity factor.

(3) After January 1, 2000, it shall be unlawful for any existing utility unit with an actual 1985 emissions rate equal to or greater than 1.20 lbs/mmBtu whose annual average fuel consumption during 1985, 1986, and 1987 on a Btu basis exceeded 90 percent in the form of lignite coal which is located in a State in which, as of July 1, 1989, no county or portion of a county was designated nonattainment under section

7407 of this title for any pollutant subject to the requirements of section 7409 of this title to exceed an annual sulfur dioxide tonnage limitation equal to the product of the unit's baseline multiplied by the lesser of the unit's actual 1985 emissions rate or its allowable 1985 emissions rate, divided by 2,000, unless the owner or operator of such unit holds allowances to emit not less than the unit's total annual emissions.

(4) After January 1, 2000, the Administrator shall allocate annually for each unit, subject to the emissions limitation requirements of paragraph (1), which is located in a State with an installed electrical generating capacity of more than 30,000,000 kw in 1988 and for which was issued a prohibition order or a proposed prohibition order (from burning oil), which unit subsequently converted to coal between January 1, 1980 and December 31, 1985, allowances equal to the difference between (A) the product of the unit's annual fuel consumption, on a Btu basis, at a 65 percent capacity factor multiplied by the lesser of its actual or allowable emissions rate during the first full calendar year after conversion, divided by 2,000, and (B) the number of allowances allocated for the unit pursuant to paragraph (1): *Provided,* That the number of allowances allocated pursuant to this paragraph shall not exceed an annual total of five thousand. If necessary to meeting the restriction imposed in the preceding sentence the Administrator shall reduce, pro rata, the annual allowances allocated for each unit under this paragraph.

**(c) Coal or oil-fired units below 75 MWe and above 1.20 lbs/mmBtu**

(1) Except as otherwise provided in paragraph (3), after January 1, 2000, it shall be unlawful for a coal or oil-fired existing utility unit that serves a generator with nameplate capacity of less than 75 MWe and an actual 1985 emission rate equal to, or greater than, 1.20 lbs/mmBtu and which is a unit owned by a utility operating company whose aggregate nameplate fossil fuel steam-electric capacity is, as of December 31, 1989, equal to, or greater than, 250 MWe to exceed an annual sulfur dioxide emissions limitation equal to the product of the unit's baseline multiplied by an emission rate equal to 1.20 lbs/mmBtu, divided by 2,000, unless the owner or operator of such unit holds allowances to emit not less than the unit's total annual emissions.

(2) After January 1, 2000, it shall be unlawful for a coal or oil-fired existing utility unit that serves a generator with nameplate capacity of less than 75 MWe and an actual 1985 emission rate equal to, or greater than, 1.20 lbs/mmBtu (excluding units subject to section 7411 of this title or to a federally enforceable emissions limitation for sulfur dioxide equivalent to an annual rate of less than 1.20 lbs/mmBtu) and which is a unit owned by a utility operating company whose aggregate nameplate fossil fuel steam-electric capacity is, as of December 31, 1989, less than 250 MWe, to exceed an annual sulfur dioxide tonnage emissions limitation equal to the product of the unit's baseline multiplied by the lesser of its actual 1985 emissions rate or its allowable 1985 emissions rate, divided by 2,000, unless the owner or operator of such unit holds allowances to emit not less than the unit's total annual emissions.

(3) After January 1, 2000, it shall be unlawful for any existing utility unit with a nameplate capacity below 75 MWe and an actual 1985 emissions rate equal to, or greater than, 1.20 lbs/mmBtu which became operational on or before December 31, 1965, which is owned by a utility operating company with, as of December 31, 1989, a total fossil fuel steam-electric generating capacity greater than 250 MWe, and less than 450 MWe which serves fewer than 78,000 electrical customers as of November 15, 1990, to exceed an annual sulfur dioxide emissions tonnage limitation equal to the product of its baseline multiplied by the lesser of its actual or allowable 1985 emission rate, divided by 2,000, unless the owner or operator holds allowances to emit not less than the units [1] total annual emissions. After January 1, 2010, it shall be unlawful for each unit subject to the emissions limitation requirements of this paragraph to exceed an annual emissions tonnage limitation equal to the product of its baseline multiplied by an emissions rate of 1.20 lbs/mmBtu, divided by 2,000, unless the owner or operator holds allowances to emit not less than the unit's total annual emissions.

(4) In addition to allowances allocated pursuant to paragraph (1) and section 7651b(a)(1) of this title as basic Phase II allowance allocations, beginning January 1, 2000, and for each calendar year thereafter until and including 2009, inclusive, the Administrator shall allocate annually for each unit subject to the emissions limitation requirements of paragraph (1) with an actual 1985 emissions rate equal to, or greater than, 1.20 lbs/mmBtu and less than 2.50 lbs/mmBtu and a baseline capacity factor of less than 60 percent, allowances from the reserve created pursuant to subsection (a)(2) of this section in an amount equal to 1.20 lbs/mmBtu multiplied by 50 percent of the difference, on a Btu basis, between the unit's baseline and the unit's fuel consumption at a 60 percent capacity factor.

(5) After January 1, 2000, it shall be unlawful for any existing utility unit with a nameplate capacity below 75 MWe and an actual 1985 emissions rate equal to, or greater than, 1.20 lbs/mmBtu which is part of an electric utility system which, as of November 15, 1990, (A) has at least 20 percent of its fossil-fuel capacity controlled by flue gas desulfurization devices, (B) has more than 10 percent of its fossil-fuel capacity consisting of coal-fired units of less than 75 MWe, and (C) has large units (greater than 400 MWe)

all of which have difficult or very difficult FGD Retrofit Cost Factors (according to the Emissions and the FGD Retrofit Feasibility at the 200 Top Emitting Generating Stations, prepared for the United States Environmental Protection Agency on January 10, 1986) to exceed an annual sulfur dioxide emissions tonnage limitation equal to the product of its baseline multiplied by an emissions rate of 2.5 lbs/mmBtu, divided by 2,000, unless the owner or operator holds allowances to emit not less than the unit's total annual emissions. After January 1, 2010, it shall be unlawful for each unit subject to the emissions limitation requirements of this paragraph to exceed an annual emissions tonnage limitation equal to the product of its baseline multiplied by an emissions rate of 1.20 lbs/mmBtu, divided by 2,000, unless the owner or operator holds for use allowances to emit not less than the unit's total annual emissions.

**(d) Coal-fired units below 1.20 lbs/mmBtu**

(1) After January 1, 2000, it shall be unlawful for any existing coal-fired utility unit the lesser of whose actual or allowable 1985 sulfur dioxide emissions rate is less than 0.60 lbs/mmBtu to exceed an annual sulfur dioxide tonnage emission limitation equal to the product of the unit's baseline multiplied by (A) the lesser of 0.60 lbs/mmBtu or the unit's allowable 1985 emissions rate, and (B) a numerical factor of 120 percent, divided by 2,000, unless the owner or operator of such unit holds allowances to emit not less than the unit's total annual emissions.

(2) After January 1, 2000, it shall be unlawful for any existing coal-fired utility unit the lesser of whose actual or allowable 1985 sulfur dioxide emissions rate is equal to, or greater than, 0.60 lbs/mmBtu and less than 1.20 lbs/mmBtu to exceed an annual sulfur dioxide tonnage emissions limitation equal to the product of the unit's baseline multiplied by (A) the lesser of its actual 1985 emissions rate or its allowable 1985 emissions rate, and (B) a numerical factor of 120 percent, divided by 2,000, unless the owner or operator of such unit holds allowances to emit not less than the unit's total annual emissions.

(3)(A) In addition to allowances allocated pursuant to paragraph (1) and section 7651b(a)(1) of this title as basic Phase II allowance allocations, at the election of the designated representative of the operating company, beginning January 1, 2000, and for each calendar year thereafter until and including 2009, the Administrator shall allocate annually for each unit subject to the emissions limitation requirements of paragraph (1) allowances from the reserve created pursuant to subsection (a)(2) of this section in an amount equal to the amount by which (i) the product of the lesser of 0.60 lbs/mmBtu or the unit's allowable 1985 emissions rate multiplied by the unit's baseline adjusted to reflect operation at a 60 percent capacity factor, divided by 2,000, exceeds (ii) the number of allowances allocated for the unit pursuant to paragraph (1) and section 7651b(a)(1) of this title as basic Phase II allowance allocations.

(B) In addition to allowances allocated pursuant to paragraph (2) and section 7651b(a)(1) of this title as basic Phase II allowance allocations, at the election of the designated representative of the operating company, beginning January 1, 2000, and for each calendar year thereafter until and including 2009, the Administrator shall allocate annually for each unit subject to the emissions limitation requirements of paragraph (2) allowances from the reserve created pursuant to subsection (a)(2) of this section in an amount equal to the amount by which (i) the product of the lesser of the unit's actual 1985 emissions rate or its allowable 1985 emissions rate multiplied by the unit's baseline adjusted to reflect operation at a 60 percent capacity factor, divided by 2,000, exceeds (ii) the number of allowances allocated for the unit pursuant to paragraph (2) and section 7651b(a)(1) of this title as basic Phase II allowance allocations.

(C) An operating company with units subject to the emissions limitation requirements of this subsection may elect the allocation of allowances as provided under subparagraphs (A) and (B). Such election shall apply to the annual allowance allocation for each and every unit in the operating company subject to the emissions limitation requirements of this subsection. The Administrator shall allocate allowances pursuant to subparagraphs (A) and (B) only in accordance with this subparagraph.

(4) Notwithstanding any other provision of this section, at the election of the owner or operator, after January 1, 2000, the Administrator shall allocate in lieu of allocation, pursuant to paragraph (1), (2), (3), (5), or (6), allowances for a unit subject to the emissions limitation requirements of this subsection which commenced commercial operation on or after January 1, 1981 and before December 31, 1985, which was subject to, and in compliance with, section 7411 of this title in an amount equal to the unit's annual fuel consumption, on a Btu basis, at a 65 percent capacity factor multiplied by the unit's allowable 1985 emissions rate, divided by 2,000.

(5) For the purposes of this section, in the case of an oil- and gas-fired unit which has been awarded a clean coal technology demonstration grant as of January 1, 1991, by the United States Department of Energy, beginning January 1, 2000, the Administrator shall allocate for the unit allowances in an amount equal to the unit's baseline multiplied by 1.20 lbs/mmBtu, divided by 2,000.

**(e) Oil and gas-fired units equal to or greater than 0.60 lbs/mmBtu and less than 1.20 lbs/mmBtu**

After January 1, 2000, it shall be unlawful for any existing oil and gas-fired utility unit the lesser of whose actual or allowable 1985 sulfur dioxide emission rate is equal to, or greater than, 0.60 lbs/mmBtu, but less than 1.20 lbs/mmBtu to exceed an annual sulfur dioxide tonnage limitation equal to the product of the unit's baseline multiplied by (A) the lesser of the unit's allowable 1985 emissions rate or its actual 1985 emissions rate and (B) a numerical factor of 120 percent divided by 2,000, unless the owner or operator of such unit holds allowances to emit not less than the unit's total annual emissions.

**(f) Oil and gas-fired units less than 0.60 lbs/mmBtu**

(1) After January 1, 2000, it shall be unlawful for any oil and gas-fired existing utility unit the lesser of whose actual or allowable 1985 emission rate is less than 0.60 lbs/mmBtu and whose average annual fuel consumption during the period 1980 through 1989 on a Btu basis was 90 percent or less in the form of natural gas to exceed an annual sulfur dioxide tonnage emissions limitation equal to the product of the unit's baseline multiplied by (A) the lesser of 0.60 lbs/mmBtu or the unit's allowable 1985 emissions, and (B) a numerical factor of 120 percent, divided by 2,000, unless the owner or operator of such unit holds allowances to emit not less than the unit's total annual emissions.

(2) In addition to allowances allocated pursuant to paragraph (1) as basic Phase II allowance allocations and section 7651b(a)(1) of this title, beginning January 1, 2000, the Administrator shall, in the case of any unit operated by a utility that furnishes electricity, electric energy, steam, and natural gas within an area consisting of a city and 1 contiguous county, and in the case of any unit owned by a State authority, the output of which unit is furnished within that same area consisting of a city and 1 contiguous county, the Administrator shall allocate for each unit in the utility its pro rata share of 7,000 allowances and for each unit in the State authority its pro rata share of 2,000 allowances.

**(g) Units that commence operation between 1986 and December 31, 1995**

(1) After January 1, 2000, it shall be unlawful for any utility unit that has commenced commercial operation on or after January 1, 1986, but not later than September 30, 1990 to exceed an annual tonnage emission limitation equal to the product of the unit's annual fuel consumption, on a Btu basis, at a 65 percent capacity factor multiplied by the unit's allowable 1985 sulfur dioxide emission rate (converted, if necessary, to pounds per mmBtu), divided by 2,000 unless the owner or operator of such unit holds allowances to emit not less than the unit's total annual emissions.

(2) After January 1, 2000, the Administrator shall allocate allowances pursuant to section 7651b of this title to each unit which is listed in table B of this paragraph in an annual amount equal to the amount specified in table B.

TABLE B

| Unit | Allowances |
|---|---|
| Brandon Shores | 8,907 |
| Miller 4 | 9,197 |
| TNP One 2 | 4,000 |
| Zimmer 1 | 18,458 |
| Spruce 1 | 7,647 |
| Clover 1 | 2,796 |
| Clover 2 | 2,796 |
| Twin Oak 2 | 1,760 |
| Twin Oak 1 | 9,158 |
| Cross 1 | 6,401 |
| Malakoff 1 | 1,759 |

Notwithstanding any other paragraph of this subsection, for units subject to this paragraph, the Administrator shall not allocate allowances pursuant to any other paragraph of this subsection, Provided [2] that the owner or operator of a unit listed on Table B may elect an allocation of allowances under another paragraph of this subsection in lieu of an allocation under this paragraph.

(3) Beginning January 1, 2000, the Administrator shall allocate to the owner or operator of any utility unit that commences commercial operation, or has commenced commercial operation, on or after October 1, 1990, but not later than December 31, 1992 allowances in an amount equal to the product of the unit's annual fuel consumption, on a Btu basis, at a 65 percent capacity factor multiplied by the lesser of 0.30 lbs/mmBtu or the unit's allowable sulfur dioxide emission rate (converted, if necessary, to pounds per mmBtu), divided by 2,000.

(4) Beginning January 1, 2000, the Administrator shall allocate to the owner or operator of any utility unit that has commenced construction before December 31, 1990 and that commences commercial operation between January 1, 1993 and December 31, 1995, allowances in an amount equal to the product of the unit's annual fuel consumption, on a Btu basis, at a 65 percent capacity factor multiplied by the lesser of 0.30 lbs/mmBtu or the unit's allowable sulfur dioxide emission rate (converted, if necessary, to pounds per mmBtu), divided by 2,000.

(5) After January 1, 2000, it shall be unlawful for any existing utility unit that has completed conversion from predominantly gas fired existing operation to coal fired operation between January 1, 1985 and December 31, 1987, for which there has been allocated a proposed or final prohibition order pursuant to section 301(b) of the Powerplant and Industrial Fuel Use Act of 1978 (42 U.S.C. 8301 et seq., repealed

1987) to exceed an annual sulfur dioxide tonnage emissions limitation equal to the product of the unit's annual fuel consumption, on a Btu basis, at a 65 percent capacity factor multiplied by the lesser of 1.20 lbs/mmBtu or the unit's allowable 1987 sulfur dioxide emissions rate, divided by 2,000, unless the owner or operator of such unit has obtained allowances equal to its actual emissions.

**(6)(A)** [3] Unless the Administrator has approved a designation of such facility under section 7651i of this title, the provisions of this subchapter shall not apply to a "qualifying small power production facility" or "qualifying cogeneration facility" (within the meaning of section 796(17)(C) or 796(18)(B) of Title 16) or to a "new independent power production facility" as defined in section 7651*o* of this title except that clause (iii) [4] of such definition in section 7651*o* of this title shall not apply for purposes of this paragraph if, as of November 15, 1990,

**(i)** an applicable power sales agreement has been executed;

**(ii)** the facility is the subject of a State regulatory authority order requiring an electric utility to enter into a power sales agreement with, purchase capacity from, or (for purposes of establishing terms and conditions of the electric utility's purchase of power) enter into arbitration concerning, the facility;

**(iii)** an electric utility has issued a letter of intent or similar instrument committing to purchase power from the facility at a previously offered or lower price and a power sales agreement is executed within a reasonable period of time; or

**(iv)** the facility has been selected as a winning bidder in a utility competitive bid solicitation.

### (h) Oil and gas-fired units less than 10 percent oil consumed

**(1)** After January 1, 2000, it shall be unlawful for any oil- and gas-fired utility unit whose average annual fuel consumption during the period 1980 through 1989 on a Btu basis exceeded 90 percent in the form of natural gas to exceed an annual sulfur dioxide tonnage limitation equal to the product of the unit's baseline multiplied by the unit's actual 1985 emissions rate divided by 2,000 unless the owner or operator of such unit holds allowances to emit not less than the unit's total annual emissions.

**(2)** In addition to allowances allocated pursuant to paragraph (1) and section 7651b(a)(1) of this title as basic Phase II allowance allocations, beginning January 1, 2000, and for each calendar year thereafter until and including 2009, the Administrator shall allocate annually for each unit subject to the emissions limitation requirements of paragraph (1) allowances from the reserve created pursuant to subsection (a)(2) of this section in an amount equal to the unit's baseline multiplied by 0.050 lbs/mmBtu, divided by 2,000.

**(3)** In addition to allowances allocated pursuant to paragraph (1) and section 7651b(a)(1) of this title, beginning January 1, 2010, the Administrator shall allocate annually for each unit subject to the emissions limitation requirements of paragraph (1) allowances in an amount equal to the unit's baseline multiplied by 0.050 lbs/mmBtu, divided by 2,000.

### (i) Units in high growth States

**(1)** In addition to allowances allocated pursuant to this section and section 7651b(a)(1) of this title as basic Phase II allowance allocations, beginning January 1, 2000, the Administrator shall allocate annually allowances for each unit, subject to an emissions limitation requirement under this section, and located in a State that—

**(A)** has experienced a growth in population in excess of 25 percent between 1980 and 1988 according to State Population and Household Estimates, With Age, Sex, and Components of Change: 1981–1988 allocated by the United States Department of Commerce, and

**(B)** had an installed electrical generating capacity of more than 30,000,000 kw in 1988,

in an amount equal to the difference between (A) the number of allowances that would be allocated for the unit pursuant to the emissions limitation requirements of this section applicable to the unit adjusted to reflect the unit's annual average fuel consumption on a Btu basis of any three consecutive calendar years between 1980 and 1989 (inclusive) as elected by the owner or operator and (B) the number of allowances allocated for the unit pursuant to the emissions limitation requirements of this section: *Provided,* That the number of allowances allocated pursuant to this subsection shall not exceed an annual total of 40,000. If necessary to meeting the 40,000 allowance restriction imposed under this subsection the Administrator shall reduce, pro rata, the additional annual allowances allocated to each unit under this subsection.

**(2)** Beginning January 1, 2000, in addition to allowances allocated pursuant to this section and section 7651b(a)(1) of this title as basic Phase II allowance allocations, the Administrator shall allocate annually for each unit subject to the emissions limitation requirements of subsection (b)(1) of this section, (A) the lesser of whose actual or allowable 1980 emissions rate has declined by 50 percent or more as of November 15, 1990, (B) whose actual emissions rate is less than 1.2 lbs/mmBtu as of January 1, 2000, (C) which commenced operation after January 1, 1970, (D) which is owned by a utility company whose combined commercial and industrial kilowatt-hour sales have increased by more than 20 percent between calendar year 1980 and November 15, 1990, and (E) whose company-wide fossil-fuel sulfur dioxide emissions rate has declined 40 per centum or more from 1980 to 1988, allowances in an amount equal to the difference between (i) the number of allowances that would be allocated for the unit pursuant to the emissions limitation requirements of subsection (b)(1) of this section adjusted to reflect the unit's annual average fuel consumption on a Btu basis for any three consecutive years between 1980 and 1989 (inclusive) as elected by the owner or operator and (ii) the number of allowances allocated for the unit pursuant to the emissions limitation requirements of subsection (b)(1) of this section: *Provided,* That the number of allowances allocated pursuant to this paragraph shall not exceed an annual total of 5,000. If necessary to meeting the 5,000–allowance restriction imposed in the last clause of the preceding sentence the Administrator shall reduce, pro rata, the additional allowances allocated to each unit pursuant to this paragraph.

### (j) Certain municipally owned power plants

Beginning January 1, 2000, in addition to allowances allocated pursuant to this section and section 7651b(a)(1) of this title as basic Phase II allowance allocations, the Administrator shall allocate annually for each existing municipally owned oil and gas-fired utility unit with nameplate capacity equal to, or less than, 40 MWe, the lesser of whose actual or allowable 1985 sulfur dioxide emission rate is less than 1.20 lbs/mmBtu, allowances in an amount equal to the product of the unit's annual fuel consumption on a Btu basis at a 60 percent capacity factor multiplied by the lesser of its allowable 1985 emission rate or its actual 1985 emission rate, divided by 2,000.

(July 14, 1955, c. 360, Title IV, § 405, as added Nov. 15, 1990, Pub.L. 101–549, Title IV, § 401, 104 Stat. 2605.)

1 So in original. Probably should be "unit's".

2 So in original. Probably should not be capitalized.

3 So in original. No subpar. (B) has been enacted.

4 So in original. Probably means clause "(C)".

## HISTORICAL AND STATUTORY NOTES

**References in Text**

Section 301(b) of the Powerplant and Industrial Fuel Use Act of 1978, referred to in subsec. (g)(5), is section 301(b) of Pub.L. 95–620, which is classified to section 8341(b) of this title. A prior section 301(b) of Pub.L. 95–620, Title III, Nov. 9, 1978, 92 Stat. 3305 which was formerly classified to section 8341(b) of this title, was repealed by Pub.L. 97–35, Title X, § 1021(a), Aug. 13, 1981, 95 Stat. 614.

**Effective and Applicability Provisions**

1990 Acts

Section effective Nov. 15, 1990, except as otherwise provided, see section 711(b) of Pub.L. 101–549, set out as a note under section 7401 of this title.

**Savings Provisions**

Suits, actions or proceedings commenced under this chapter as in effect prior to Nov. 15, 1990, not to abate by reason of the taking effect of amendments by Pub.L. 101–549, except as otherwise provided for, see section 711(a) of Pub.L. 101–549, set out as a note under section 7401 of this title.

## § 7651e. Allowances for States with emissions rates at or below 0.80 lbs/mmBtu

**[CAA § 406]**

### (a) Election of Governor

In addition to basic Phase II allowance allocations, upon the election of the Governor of any State, with a 1985 state-wide annual sulfur dioxide emissions rate equal to or less than, 0.80 lbs/mmBtu, averaged over all fossil fuel-fired utility steam generating units, beginning January 1, 2000, and for each calendar year thereafter until and including 2009, the Administrator shall allocate, in lieu of other Phase II bonus allowance allocations, allowances from the reserve created pursuant to section 7651d(a)(2) of this title to all such units in the State in an amount equal to 125,000 multiplied by the unit's pro rata share of electricity generated in calendar year 1985 at fossil fuel-fired utility steam units in all States eligible for the election.

### (b) Notification of Administrator

Pursuant to section 7651b(a)(1) of this title, each Governor of a State eligible to make an election under paragraph[1] (a) shall notify the Administrator of such election. In the event that the Governor of any such State fails to notify the Administrator of the Governor's elections, the Administrator shall allocate allowances pursuant to section 7651d of this title.

### (c) Allowances after January 1, 2010

After January 1, 2010, the Administrator shall allocate allowances to units subject to the provisions of this section pursuant to section 7651d of this title.

(July 14, 1955, c. 360, Title IV, § 406, as added Nov. 15, 1990, Pub.L. 101–549, Title IV, § 401, 104 Stat. 2613.)

1 So in original. Probably should be "subsection".

## HISTORICAL AND STATUTORY NOTES

**Effective and Applicability Provisions**

1990 Acts

Section effective Nov. 15, 1990, except as otherwise provided, see section 711(b) of Pub.L. 101–549, set out as a note under section 7401 of this title.

**Savings Provisions**

Suits, actions or proceedings commenced under this chapter as in effect prior to Nov. 15, 1990, not to abate by reason of the taking effect of amendments by Pub.L. 101–549, except as otherwise provided for, see section 711(a) of Pub.L. 101–549, set out as a note under section 7401 of this title.

## § 7651f. Nitrogen oxides emission reduction program

[CAA § 407]

### (a) Applicability

On the date that a coal-fired utility unit becomes an affected unit pursuant to sections 7651c, 7651d,[1] 7651h of this title, or on the date a unit subject to the provisions of section 7651c(d) or 7651h(b) of this title, must meet the $SO_2$ reduction requirements, each such unit shall become an affected unit for purposes of this section and shall be subject to the emission limitations for nitrogen oxides set forth herein.

### (b) Emission limitations

(1) Not later than eighteen months after November 15, 1990, the Administrator shall by regulation establish annual allowable emission limitations for nitrogen oxides for the types of utility boilers listed below, which limitations shall not exceed the rates listed below: *Provided,* That the Administrator may set a rate higher than that listed for any type of utility boiler if the Administrator finds that the maximum listed rate for that boiler type cannot be achieved using low $NO_x$ burner technology. The maximum allowable emission rates are as follows:

(A) for tangentially fired boilers, 0.45 lb/mmBtu;

(B) for dry bottom wall-fired boilers (other than units applying cell burner technology), 0.50 lb/mmBtu.

After January 1, 1995, it shall be unlawful for any unit that is an affected unit on that date and is of the type listed in this paragraph to emit nitrogen oxides in excess of the emission rates set by the Administrator pursuant to this paragraph.

(2) Not later than January 1, 1997, the Administrator shall, by regulation, establish allowable emission limitations on a lb/mmBtu, annual average basis, for nitrogen oxides for the following types of utility boilers:

(A) wet bottom wall-fired boilers;

(B) cyclones;

(C) units applying cell burner technology;

(D) all other types of utility boilers.

The Administrator shall base such rates on the degree of reduction achievable through the retrofit application of the best system of continuous emission reduction, taking into account available technology, costs and energy and environmental impacts; and which is comparable to the costs of nitrogen oxides controls set pursuant to subsection (b)(1) of this section. Not later than January 1, 1997, the Administrator may revise the applicable emission limitations for tangentially fired and dry bottom, wall-fired boilers (other than cell burners) to be more stringent if the Administrator determines that more effective low $NO_x$ burner technology is available: *Provided,* That, no unit that is an affected unit pursuant to section 7651c of this title and that is subject to the requirements of subsection (b)(1) of this section, shall be subject to the revised emission limitations, if any.

### (c) Revised performance standards

(1) Not later than January 1, 1993, the Administrator shall propose revised standards of performance to section 7411 of this title for nitrogen oxides emissions from fossil-fuel fired steam generating units, including both electric utility and nonutility units. Not later than January 1, 1994, the Administrator shall promulgate such revised standards of performance. Such revised standards of performance shall reflect improvements in methods for the reduction of emissions of oxides of nitrogen.

### (d) Alternative emission limitations

The permitting authority shall, upon request of an owner or operator of a unit subject to this section, authorize an emission limitation less stringent than the applicable limitation established under subsection (b)(1) or (b)(2) of this section upon a determination that—

(1) a unit subject to subsection (b)(1) of this section cannot meet the applicable limitation using low $NO_x$ burner technology; or

(2) a unit subject to subsection (b)(2) of this section cannot meet the applicable rate using the technology on which the Administrator based the applicable emission limitation.

The permitting authority shall base such determination upon a showing satisfactory to the permitting authority, in accordance with regulations established by the Administrator not later than eighteen months after November 15, 1990, that the owner or operator—

(1) has properly installed appropriate control equipment designed to meet the applicable emission rate;

(2) has properly operated such equipment for a period of fifteen months (or such other period of time as the Administrator determines through the regulations), and provides operating and monitoring data for such period demonstrating that the unit cannot meet the applicable emission rate; and

(3) has specified an emission rate that such unit can meet on an annual average basis.

The permitting authority shall issue an operating permit for the unit in question, in accordance with section 7651g of this title and part B of title III—

(i) that permits the unit during the demonstration period referred to in subparagraph (2) above, to emit at a rate in excess of the applicable emission rate;

(ii) at the conclusion of the demonstration period to revise the operating permit to reflect the alternative emission rate demonstrated in paragraphs (2) and (3) above.

Units subject to subsection (b)(1) of this section for which an alternative emission limitation is established shall not be required to install any additional control technology beyond low $NO_x$ burners. Nothing in this section shall preclude an owner or operator from installing and operating an alternative $NO_x$ control technology capable of achieving the applicable emission limitation. If the owner or operator of a unit subject to the emissions limitation requirements of subsection (b)(1) of this section demonstrates to the satisfaction of the Administrator that the technology necessary to meet such requirements is not in adequate supply to enable its installation and operation at the unit, consistent with system reliability, by January 1, 1995, then the Administrator shall extend the deadline for compliance for the unit by a period of 15 months. Any owner or operator may petition the Administrator to make a determination under the previous sentence. The Administrator shall grant or deny such petition within 3 months of submittal.

**(e) Emissions averaging**

In lieu of complying with the applicable emission limitations under subsection (b)(1), (2), or (d) of this section, the owner or operator of two or more units subject to one or more of the applicable emission limitations set pursuant to these sections, may petition the permitting authority for alternative contemporaneous annual emission limitations for such units that ensure that (1) the actual annual emission rate in pounds of nitrogen oxides per million Btu averaged over the units in question is a rate that is less than or equal to (2) the Btu-weighted average annual emission rate for the same units if they had been operated, during the same period of time, in compliance with limitations set in accordance with the applicable emission rates set pursuant to subsections (b)(1) and (2) of this section.

If the permitting authority determines, in accordance with regulations issued by the Administrator not later than eighteen months after November 15, 1990;[2] that the conditions in the paragraph above can be met, the permitting authority shall issue operating permits for such units, in accordance with section 7651g of this title and part B of title III, that allow alternative contemporaneous annual emission limitations. Such emission limitations shall only remain in effect while both units continue operation under the conditions specified in their respective operating permits.

(July 14, 1955, c. 360, Title IV, § 407, as added Nov. 15, 1990, Pub.L. 101–549, Title IV, § 401, 104 Stat. 2613.)

1 So in original. Probably should be followed by "or".

2 So in original. The semicolon probably should be a comma.

### HISTORICAL AND STATUTORY NOTES

**References in Text**

Part B of Title III, referred to in subsecs. (d) and (e), means Title III of the Clean Air Act, Act July 14, 1955, c. 360, as added, which is classified to subchapter III of this chapter, but Title III does not contain parts. For provisions of the Clean Air Act relating to permits, see subchapter V (section 7661 et seq.) of this chapter.

**Effective and Applicability Provisions**

1990 Acts

Section effective Nov. 15, 1990, except as otherwise provided, see section 711(b) of Pub.L. 101–549, set out as a note under section 7401 of this title.

**Savings Provisions**

Suits, actions or proceedings commenced under this chapter as in effect prior to Nov. 15, 1990, not to abate by reason of the taking effect of amendments by Pub.L. 101–549, except as otherwise provided for, see section 711(a) of Pub.L. 101–549, set out as a note under section 7401 of this title.

## § 7651g. Permits and compliance plans

**[CAA § 408]**

**(a) Permit program**

The provisions of this subchapter shall be implemented, subject to section 7651b of this title, by permits issued to units subject to this subchapter (and enforced) in accordance with the provisions of subchapter V of this chapter, as modified by this subchapter. Any such permit issued by the Administrator, or by a State with an approved permit program, shall prohibit—

(1) annual emissions of sulfur dioxide in excess of the number of allowances to emit sulfur dioxide the owner or operator, or the designated representative of the owners or operators, of the unit hold for the unit,

(2) exceedances of applicable emissions rates,

(3) the use of any allowance prior to the year for which it was allocated, and

(4) contravention of any other provision of the permit.

Permits issued to implement this subchapter shall be issued for a period of 5 years, notwithstanding subchapter V of this chapter. No permit shall be issued that is inconsistent with the requirements of this subchapter, and subchapter V of this chapter as applicable.

**(b) Compliance plan**

Each initial permit application shall be accompanied by a compliance plan for the source to comply with its requirements under this subchapter. Where an affected source consists of more than one affected unit, such plan shall cover all such units, and for purposes of section 7661a(c) of this title, such source shall be considered a "facility". Nothing in this section regarding compliance plans or in subchapter V of this chapter shall be construed as affecting allowances. Except as provided under subsection (c)(1)(B) of this section, submission of a statement by the owner or operator, or the designated representative of the owners and operators, of a unit subject to the emissions limitation requirements of sections 7651c, 7651d, and 7651f of this title, that the unit will meet the applicable emissions limitation requirements of such sections in a timely manner or that, in the case of the emissions limitation requirements of sections 7651c and 7651d of this title, the owners and operators will hold allowances to emit not less than the total annual emissions of the unit, shall be deemed to meet the proposed and approved compliance planning requirements of this section and subchapter V of this chapter, except that, for any unit that will meet the requirements of this subchapter by means of an alternative method of compliance authorized under section 7651c(b), (c), (d), or (f) of this title [1] section 7651f(d) or (e) of this title, section 7651h of this title and section 7651i of this title, the proposed and approved compliance plan, permit application and permit shall include, pursuant to regulations promulgated by the Administrator, for each alternative method of compliance a comprehensive description of the schedule and means by which the unit will rely on one or more alternative methods of compliance in the manner and time authorized under this subchapter. Recordation by the Administrator of transfers of allowances shall amend automatically all applicable proposed or approved permit applications, compliance plans and permits. The Administrator may also require—

(1) for a source, a demonstration of attainment of national ambient air quality standards, and

(2) from the owner or operator of two or more affected sources, an integrated compliance plan providing an overall plan for achieving compliance at the affected sources.

**(c) First phase permits**

The Administrator shall issue permits to affected sources under sections 7651c and 7651f of this title.

**(1) Permit application and compliance plan**

(A) Not later than 27 months after November 15, 1990, the designated representative of the owners or operators, or the owner and operator, of each affected source under sections 7651c and 7651f of this title shall submit a permit application and compliance plan for that source in accordance with regulations issued by the Administrator under paragraph (3). The permit application and the compliance plan shall be binding on the owner or operator or the designated representative of owners and operators for purposes of this subchapter and section 7651a(a) [2] of this title, and shall be enforceable in lieu of a permit until a permit is issued by the Administrator for the source.

(B) In the case of a compliance plan for an affected source under sections 7651c and 7651f of this title for which the owner or operator proposes to meet the requirements of that section by reducing utilization of the unit as compared with its baseline or by shutting down the unit, the owner or operator shall include in the proposed compliance plan a specification of the unit or units that will provide electrical generation to compensate for the reduced output at the affected source, or a demonstration that such reduced utilization will be accomplished through energy conservation or improved unit efficiency. The unit to be used for such compensating generation, which is not otherwise an affected unit under sections 7651c and 7651f of this title, shall be deemed an affected unit under section 7651c of this title, subject to all of the requirements for such units under this subchapter, except that allowances shall be allocated to such compensating unit in the amount of an annual limitation equal to the product of the unit's baseline multiplied by the lesser of the unit's actual 1985 emissions rate or its allowable 1985 emissions rate, divided by 2,000.

**(2) EPA action on compliance plans**

The Administrator shall review each proposed compliance plan to determine whether it satisfies the requirements of this subchapter, and shall approve or disapprove such plan within 6 months after receipt of a complete submission. If a plan is disapproved, it may be resubmitted for approval with such changes as the Administrator shall require consistent with the requirements of this subchapter and within such period as the Administrator prescribes as part of such disapproval.

**(3) Regulations; issuance of permits**

Not later than 18 months after November 15, 1990, the Administrator shall promulgate regulations, in accordance with subchapter V of this chapter, to implement a Federal permit program to issue permits for affected sources under this subchapter. Following promulgation, the Administrator shall issue a permit to implement the requirements of section 7651c of this title and the allowances provided under section 7651b of this title to the owner or operator of each affected source under section 7651c of this title. Such a permit shall supersede any permit application and compliance plan submitted under paragraph (1).

**(4) Fees**

During the years 1995 through 1999 inclusive, no fee shall be required to be paid under section 7661a(b)(3) of this title or under section 7410(a)(2)(L) of this title with respect to emissions from any unit which is an affected unit under section 7651c of this title.

**(d) Second phase permits**

(1) To provide for permits for (A) new electric utility steam generating units required under section 7651b(e) of this title to have allowances, (B) affected units or sources under section 7651d of this title, and (C) existing units subject to nitrogen oxide emission reductions under section 7651f of this title, each State in which one or more such units or sources are located shall submit in accordance with subchapter V of this chapter, a permit program for approval as provided by that subchapter. Upon approval of such program, for the units or sources subject to such approved program the Administrator shall suspend the issuance of permits as provided in subchapter V of this chapter.

(2) The owner or operator or the designated representative of each affected source under section 7651d of this title shall submit a permit application and compliance plan for that source to the permitting authority, not later than January 1, 1996.

(3) Not later than December 31, 1997, each State with an approved permit program shall issue permits to the owner or operator, or the designated representative of the owners and operators, of affected sources under section 7651d of this title that satisfy the requirements of subchapter V of this chapter and this subchapter and that submitted to such State a permit application and compliance plan pursuant to paragraph (2). In the case of a State without an approved permit program by July 1, 1996, the Administrator shall, not later than January 1, 1998, issue a permit to the owner or operator or the designated representative of each such affected source. In the case of affected sources for which applications and plans are timely received under paragraph (2), the permit application and the compliance plan, including amendments thereto, shall be binding on the owner or operator or the designated representative of the owners or operators and shall be enforceable as a permit for purposes of this subchapter and subchapter V of this chapter until a permit is issued by the permitting authority for the affected source. The provisions of section 558(c) of Title 5 (relating to renewals) shall apply to permits issued by a permitting authority under this subchapter and subchapter V of this chapter.

(4) The permit issued in accordance with this subsection for an affected source shall provide that the affected units at the affected source may not emit an annual tonnage of sulfur dioxide in excess of the number of allowances to emit sulfur dioxide the owner or operator or designated representative hold for the unit.

**(e) New units**

The owner or operator of each source that includes a new electric utility steam generating unit shall submit a permit application and compliance plan to the permitting authority not later than 24 months before the later of (1) January 1, 2000, or (2) the date on which the unit commences operation. The permitting authority shall issue a permit to the owner or operator, or the designated representative thereof, of the unit that satisfies the requirements of subchapter V of this chapter and this subchapter.

**(f) Units subject to certain other limits**

The owner or operator, or designated representative thereof, of any unit subject to an emission rate requirement under section 7651f of this title shall submit a permit application and compliance plan for such unit to the permitting authority, not later than January 1, 1998. The permitting authority shall issue a permit to the owner or operator that satisfies the requirements of subchapter V of this chapter and this subchapter, including any appropriate monitoring and reporting requirements.

**(g) Amendment of application and compliance plan**

At any time after the submission of an application and compliance plan under this section, the applicant may submit a revised application and compliance plan, in accordance with the requirements of this section. In considering any permit application and compliance plan under this subchapter, the permitting authority shall ensure coordination with the applicable electric ratemaking authority, in the case of regulated utilities, and with unregulated public utilities.

**(h) Prohibition**

(1) It shall be unlawful for an owner or operator, or designated representative, required to submit a permit application or compliance plan under this subchapter to fail to submit such application or plan in accordance with the deadlines specified in this section or to otherwise fail to comply with regulations implementing this section.

(2) It shall be unlawful for any person to operate any source subject to this subchapter except in compliance with the terms and requirements of a permit application and compliance plan (including amendments thereto) or permit issued by the Administrator

or a State with an approved permit program. For purposes of this subsection, compliance, as provided in section 7661c(f) of this title, with a permit issued under subchapter V of this chapter which complies with this subchapter for sources subject to this subchapter shall be deemed compliance with this subsection as well as section 7661a(a) of this title.

(3) In order to ensure reliability of electric power, nothing in this subchapter or subchapter V of this chapter shall be construed as requiring termination of operations of an electric utility steam generating unit for failure to have an approved permit or compliance plan, except that any such unit may be subject to the applicable enforcement provisions of section 7413 of this title.

### (i) Multiple owners

No permit shall be issued under this section to an affected unit until the designated representative of the owners or operators has filed a certificate of representation with regard to matters under this subchapter, including the holding and distribution of allowances and the proceeds of transactions involving allowances. Where there are multiple holders of a legal or equitable title to, or a leasehold interest in, such a unit, or where a utility or industrial customer purchases power from an affected unit (or units) under life-of-the-unit, firm power contractual arrangements, the certificate shall state (1) that allowances and the proceeds of transactions involving allowances will be deemed to be held or distributed in proportion to each holder's legal, equitable, leasehold, or contractual reservation or entitlement, or (2) if such multiple holders have expressly provided for a different distribution of allowances by contract, that allowances and the proceeds of transactions involving allowances will be deemed to be held or distributed in accordance with the contract. A passive lessor, or a person who has an equitable interest through such lessor, whose rental payments are not based, either directly or indirectly, upon the revenues or income from the affected unit shall not be deemed to be a holder of a legal, equitable, leasehold, or contractual interest for the purpose of holding or distributing allowances as provided in this subsection, during either the term of such leasehold or thereafter, unless expressly provided for in the leasehold agreement. Except as otherwise provided in this subsection, where all legal or equitable title to or interest in an affected unit is held by a single person, the certification shall state that all allowances received by the unit are deemed to be held for that person.

(July 14, 1955, c. 360, Title IV, § 408, as added Nov. 15, 1990, Pub.L. 101–549, Title IV, § 401, 104 Stat. 2616.)

1 So in original. Probably should be followed by a comma.

2 So in original. Section 7651a of this title does not contain subsections.

#### HISTORICAL AND STATUTORY NOTES

**Effective and Applicability Provisions**

1990 Acts

Section effective Nov. 15, 1990, except as otherwise provided, see section 711(b) of Pub.L. 101–549, set out as a note under section 7401 of this title.

**Savings Provisions**

Suits, actions or proceedings commenced under this chapter as in effect prior to Nov. 15, 1990, not to abate by reason of the taking effect of amendments by Pub.L. 101–549, except as otherwise provided for, see section 711(a) of Pub.L. 101–549, set out as a note under section 7401 of this title.

## § 7651h. Repowered sources

[CAA § 409]

### (a) Availability

Not later than December 31, 1997, the owner or operator of an existing unit subject to the emissions limitation requirements of section 7651d(b) and (c) of this title may demonstrate to the permitting authority that one or more units will be repowered with a qualifying clean coal technology to comply with the requirements under section 7651d of this title. The owner or operator shall, as part of any such demonstration, provide, not later than January 1, 2000, satisfactory documentation of a preliminary design and engineering effort for such repowering and an executed and binding contract for the majority of the equipment to repower such unit and such other information as the Administrator may require by regulation. The replacement of an existing utility unit with a new utility unit using a repowering technology referred to in section 7651a(2) [1] of this title which is located at a different site, shall be treated as repowering of the existing unit for purposes of this subchapter, if—

(1) the replacement unit is designated by the owner or operator to replace such existing unit, and

(2) the existing unit is retired from service on or before the date on which the designated replacement unit enters commercial operation.

### (b) Extension

(1) An owner or operator satisfying the requirements of subsection (a) of this section shall be granted an extension of the emission limitation requirement compliance date for that unit from January 1, 2000, to December 31, 2003. The extension shall be specified in the permit issued to the source under section 7651g of this title, together with any compliance schedule and other requirements necessary to meet second phase requirements by the extended date. Any unit that is granted an extension under this section shall not be eligible for a waiver under section 7411(j) of this title, and shall continue to be subject to requirements under this subchapter as if it were a unit subject to section 7651d of this title.

(2) If (A) the owner or operator of an existing unit has been granted an extension under paragraph (1) in order to repower such unit with a clean coal unit, and (B) such owner or operator demonstrates to the satisfaction of the Administrator that the repowering technology to be utilized by such unit has been properly constructed and tested on such unit, but nevertheless has been unable to achieve the emission reduction limitations and is economically or technologically infeasible, such existing unit may be retrofitted or repowered with equipment or facilities utilizing another clean coal technology or other available control technology.

**(c) Allowances**

(1) For the period of the extension under this section, the Administrator shall allocate to the owner or operator of the affected unit, annual allowances for sulfur dioxide equal to the affected unit's baseline multiplied by the lesser of the unit's federally approved State Implementation Plan emissions limitation or its actual emission rate for 1995 in lieu of any other allocation. Such allowances may not be transferred or used by any other source to meet emission requirements under this subchapter. The source owner or operator shall notify the Administrator sixty days in advance of the date on which the affected unit for which the extension has been granted is to be removed from operation to install the repowering technology.

(2) Effective on that date, the unit shall be subject to the requirements of section 7651d of this title. Allowances for the year in which the unit is removed from operation to install the repowering technology shall be calculated as the product of the unit's baseline multiplied by 1.20 lbs/mmBtu, divided by 2,000, and prorated accordingly, and are transferable.

(3) Allowances for such existing utility units for calendar years after the year the repowering is complete shall be calculated as the product of the existing unit's baseline multiplied by 1.20 lbs/mmBtu, divided by 2,000.

(4) Notwithstanding the provisions of section 7651b(a) and (e) of this title, allowances shall be allocated under this section for a designated replacement unit which replaces an existing unit (as provided in the last sentence of subsection (a) of this section) in lieu of any further allocations of allowances for the existing unit.

(5) For the purpose of meeting the aggregate emissions limitation requirement set forth in section 7651b(a)(1) of this title, the units with an extension under this subsection shall be treated in each calendar year during the extension period as holding allowances allocated under paragraph (3).

**(d) Control requirements**

Any unit qualifying for an extension under this section that does not increase actual hourly emissions for any pollutant regulated under the [2] chapter shall not be subject to any standard of performance under section 7411 of this title. Notwithstanding the provisions of this subsection, no new unit (1) designated as a replacement for an existing unit, (2) qualifying for the extension under subsection (b) of this section, and (3) located at a different site than the existing unit shall receive an exemption from the requirements imposed under section 7411 of this title.

**(e) Expedited permitting**

State permitting authorities and, where applicable, the Administrator, are encouraged to give expedited consideration to permit applications under parts C and D of subchapter I of this chapter for any source qualifying for an extension under this section.

**(f) Prohibition**

It shall be unlawful for the owner or operator of a repowered source to fail to comply with the requirement of this section, or any regulations of permit requirements to implement this section, including the prohibition against emitting sulfur dioxide in excess of allowances held.

(July 14, 1955, c. 360, Title IV, § 409, as added Nov. 15, 1990, Pub.L. 101–549, Title IV, § 401, 104 Stat. 2619.)

[1] So in original. Probably should be "section 7651a(12)".
[2] So in original. Probably should be "this".

## HISTORICAL AND STATUTORY NOTES

**Effective and Applicability Provisions**

1990 Acts

Section effective Nov. 15, 1990, except as otherwise provided, see section 711(b) of Pub.L. 101–549, set out as a note under section 7401 of this title.

**Savings Provisions**

Suits, actions or proceedings commenced under this chapter as in effect prior to Nov. 15, 1990, not to abate by reason of the taking effect of amendments by Pub.L. 101–549, except as otherwise provided for, see section 711(a) of Pub.L. 101–549, set out as a note under section 7401 of this title.

## § 7651i. Election for additional sources

[CAA § 410]

**(a) Applicability**

The owner or operator of any unit that is not, nor will become, an affected unit under section 7651b(e), 7651c, or 7651d of this title, or that is a process source under subsection (d) of this section, that emits sulfur dioxide, may elect to designate that unit or source to become an affected unit and to receive allowances under this subchapter. An election shall be submitted to the Administrator for approval, along with a permit application and proposed compliance plan in accordance with section 7651g of this title. The Administrator shall approve a designation that meets the requirements of this section, and such designated unit, or source, shall be allocated allowances, and be an affected unit for purposes of this subchapter.

**(b) Establishment of baseline**

The baseline for a unit designated under this section shall be established by the Administrator by regulation, based on fuel consumption and operating data for the unit for calendar years 1985, 1986, and 1987, or if such data is not available, the Administrator may prescribe a baseline based on alternative representative data.

**(c) Emission limitations**

Annual emissions limitations for sulfur dioxide shall be equal to the product of the baseline multiplied by the lesser of the unit's 1985 actual or allowable emission rate in lbs/mmBtu, or, if the unit did not operate in 1985, by the lesser of the unit's actual or allowable emission rate for a calendar year after 1985 (as determined by the Administrator), divided by 2,000.

**(d) Process sources**

Not later than 18 months after November 15, 1990, the Administrator shall establish a program under which the owner or operator of a process source that emits sulfur dioxide may elect to designate that source as an affected unit for the purpose of receiving allowances under this subchapter. The Administrator shall, by regulation, define the sources that may be designated; specify the emissions limitation; specify the operating, emission baseline, and other data requirements; prescribe CEMS or other monitoring requirements; and promulgate permit, reporting, and any other requirements necessary to implement such a program.

**(e) Allowances and permits**

The Administrator shall issue allowances to an affected unit under this section in an amount equal to the emissions limitation calculated under subsection (c) or (d) of this section, in accordance with section 7651b of this title. Such allowance may be used in accordance with, and shall be subject to, the provisions of section 7651b of this title. Affected sources under this section shall be subject to the requirements of sections 7651b, 7651g, 7651j, 7651k, 7651l, and 7651m of this title.

**(f) Limitation**

Any unit designated under this section shall not transfer or bank allowances produced as a result of reduced utilization or shutdown, except that, such allowances may be transferred or carried forward for use in subsequent years to the extent that the reduced utilization or shutdown results from the replacement of thermal energy from the unit designated under this section, with thermal energy generated by any other unit or units subject to the requirements of this subchapter, and the designated unit's allowances are transferred or carried forward for use at such other replacement unit or units. In no case may the Administrator allocate to a source designated under this section allowances in an amount greater than the emissions resulting from operation of the source in full compliance with the requirements of this chapter. No such allowances shall authorize operation of a unit in violation of any other requirements of this chapter.

**(g) Implementation**

The Administrator shall issue regulations to implement this section not later than eighteen months after November 15, 1990.

**(h) Small diesel refineries**

The Administrator shall issue allowances to owners or operators of small diesel refineries who produce diesel fuel after October 1, 1993, meeting the requirements of subsection [1] 7545(i) of this title.

**(1) Allowance period**

Allowances may be allocated under this subsection only for the period from October 1, 1993, through December 31, 1999.

**(2) Allowance determination**

The number of allowances allocated pursuant to this paragraph shall equal the annual number of pounds of sulfur dioxide reduction attributable to desulfurization by a small refinery divided by 2,000. For the purposes of this calculation, the concentration of sulfur removed from diesel fuel shall be the difference between 0.274 percent (by weight) and 0.050 percent (by weight).

**(3) Refinery eligibility**

As used in this subsection, the term "small refinery" shall mean a refinery or portion of a refinery—

(A) which, as of November 15, 1990, has bona fide crude oil throughput of less than 18,250,000 barrels per year, as reported to the Department of Energy, and

(B) which, as of November 15, 1990, is owned or controlled by a refiner with a total combined bona fide crude oil throughput of less than 50,187,500 barrels per year, as reported to the Department of Energy.

**(4) Limitation per refinery**

The maximum number of allowances that can be annually allocated to a small refinery pursuant to this subsection is one thousand and five hundred.

(5) **Limitation on total**

In any given year, the total number of allowances allocated pursuant to this subsection shall not exceed thirty-five thousand.

(6) **Required certification**

The Administrator shall not allocate any allowances pursuant to this subsection unless the owner or operator of a small diesel refinery shall have certified, at a time and in a manner prescribed by the Administrator, that all motor diesel fuel produced by the refinery for which allowances are claimed, including motor diesel fuel for off-highway use, shall have met the requirements of subsection [1] 7545(i) of this title.

(July 14, 1955, c. 360, Title IV, § 410, as added Nov. 15, 1990, Pub.L. 101–549, Title IV, § 401, 104 Stat. 2621.)

[1] So in original. Probably should be "section".

HISTORICAL AND STATUTORY NOTES

**Effective and Applicability Provisions**

1990 Acts

Section effective Nov. 15, 1990, except as otherwise provided, see section 711(b) of Pub.L. 101–549, set out as a note under section 7401 of this title.

**Savings Provisions**

Suits, actions or proceedings commenced under this chapter as in effect prior to Nov. 15, 1990, not to abate by reason of the taking effect of amendments by Pub.L. 101–549, except as otherwise provided for, see section 711(a) of Pub.L. 101–549, set out as a note under section 7401 of this title.

## § 7651j. Excess emissions penalty

[CAA § 411]

(a) **Excess emissions penalty**

The owner or operator of any unit or process source subject to the requirements of sections [1] 7651b, 7651c, 7651d, 7651e, 7651f or 7651h of this title, or designated under section 7651i of this title, that emits sulfur dioxide or nitrogen oxides for any calendar year in excess of the unit's emissions limitation requirement or, in the case of sulfur dioxide, of the allowances the owner or operator holds for use for the unit for that calendar year shall be liable for the payment of an excess emissions penalty, except where such emissions were authorized pursuant to section 7410(f) of this title. That penalty shall be calculated on the basis of the number of tons emitted in excess of the unit's emissions limitation requirement or, in the case of sulfur dioxide, of the allowances the operator holds for use for the unit for that year, multiplied by $2,000. Any such penalty shall be due and payable without demand to the Administrator as provided in regulations to be issued by the Administrator by no later than eighteen months after November 15, 1990. Any such payment shall be deposited in the United States Treasury pursuant to the Miscellaneous Receipts Act. Any penalty due and payable under this section shall not diminish the liability of the unit's owner or operator for any fine, penalty or assessment against the unit for the same violation under any other section of this chapter.

(b) **Excess emissions offset**

The owner or operator of any affected source that emits sulfur dioxide during any calendar year in excess of the unit's emissions limitation requirement or of the allowances held for the unit for the calendar year, shall be liable to offset the excess emissions by an equal tonnage amount in the following calendar year, or such longer period as the Administrator may prescribe. The owner or operator of the source shall, within sixty days after the end of the year in which the excess emissions occured [2], submit to the Administrator, and to the State in which the source is located, a proposed plan to achieve the required offsets. Upon approval of the proposed plan by the Administrator, as submitted, modified or conditioned, the plan shall be deemed at a condition of the operating permit for the unit without further review or revision of the permit. The Administrator shall also deduct allowances equal to the excess tonnage from those allocated for the source for the calendar year, or succeeding years during which offsets are required, following the year in which the excess emissions occurred.

(c) **Penalty adjustment**

The Administrator shall, by regulation, adjust the penalty specified in subsection (a) of this section for inflation, based on the Consumer Price Index, on November 15, 1990, and annually thereafter.

(d) **Prohibition**

It shall be unlawful for the owner or operator of any source liable for a penalty and offset under this section to fail (1) to pay the penalty under subsection (a) of this section, (2) to provide, and thereafter comply with, a compliance plan as required by subsection (b) of this section, or (3) to offset excess emissions as required by subsection (b) of this section.

(e) **Savings provision**

Nothing in this subchapter shall limit or otherwise affect the application of section 7413, 7414, 7420, or 7604 of this title except as otherwise explicitly provided in this subchapter.

(July 14, 1955, c. 360, Title IV, § 411, as added Nov. 15, 1990, Pub.L. 101–549, Title IV, § 401, 104 Stat. 2623.)

[1] So in original. Probably should be "section".

[2] So in original. Probably should be "occurred".

### HISTORICAL AND STATUTORY NOTES

**References in Text**

The Miscellaneous Receipts Act, referred to in subsec. (a), is not a recognized popular name for an act. For provisions relating to deposit of monies, see section 3302 of Title 31, Money and Finance.

**Effective and Applicability Provisions**

1990 Acts

Section effective Nov. 15, 1990, except as otherwise provided, see section 711(b) of Pub.L. 101–549, set out as a note under section 7401 of this title.

**Savings Provisions**

Suits, actions or proceedings commenced under this chapter as in effect prior to Nov. 15, 1990, not to abate by reason of the taking effect of amendments by Pub.L. 101–549, except as otherwise provided for, see section 711(a) of Pub.L. 101–549, set out as a note under section 7401 of this title.

## § 7651k. Monitoring, reporting, and recordkeeping requirements

[CAA § 412]

**(a) Applicability**

The owner and operator of any source subject to this subchapter shall be required to install and operate CEMS on each affected unit at the source, and to quality assure the data for sulfur dioxide, nitrogen oxides, opacity and volumetric flow at each such unit. The Administrator shall, by regulations issued not later than eighteen months after November 15, 1990, specify the requirements for CEMS, for any alternative monitoring system that is demonstrated as providing information with the same precision, reliability, accessibility, and timeliness as that provided by CEMS, and for recordkeeping and reporting of information from such systems. Such regulations may include limitations or the use of alternative compliance methods by units equipped with an alternative monitoring system as may be necessary to preserve the orderly functioning of the allowance system, and which will ensure the emissions reductions contemplated by this subchapter. Where 2 or more units utilize a single stack, a separate CEMS shall not be required for each unit, and for such units the regulations shall require that the owner or operator collect sufficient information to permit reliable compliance determinations for each such unit.

**(b) First phase requirements**

Not later than thirty-six months after November 15, 1990, the owner or operator of each affected unit under section 7651c of this title, including, but not limited to, units that become affected units pursuant to subsections (b) and (c) of this section and eligible units under subsection (d) of this section, shall install and operate CEMS, quality assure the data, and keep records and reports in accordance with the regulations issued under subsection (a) of this section.

**(c) Second phase requirements**

Not later than January 1, 1995, the owner or operator of each affected unit that has not previously met the requirements of subsections (a) and (b) of this section shall install and operate CEMS, quality assure the data, and keep records and reports in accordance with the regulations issued under subsection (a) of this section. Upon commencement of commercial operation of each new utility unit, the unit shall comply with the requirements of subsection (a) of this section.

**(d) Unavailability of emissions data**

If CEMS data or data from an alternative monitoring system approved by the Administrator under subsection (a) of this section is not available for any affected unit during any period of a calendar year in which such data is required under this subchapter, and the owner or operator cannot provide information, satisfactory to the Administrator, on emissions during that period, the Administrator shall deem the unit to be operating in an uncontrolled manner during the entire period for which the data was not available and shall, by regulation which shall be issued not later than eighteen months after November 15, 1990, prescribe means to calculate emissions for that period. The owner or operator shall be liable for excess emissions fees and offsets under section 7651j of this title in accordance with such regulations. Any fee due and payable under this subsection shall not diminish the liability of the unit's owner or operator for any fine, penalty, fee or assessment against the unit for the same violation under any other section of this chapter.

**(e) Prohibition**

It shall be unlawful for the owner or operator of any source subject to this subchapter to operate a source without complying with the requirements of this section, and any regulations implementing this section.

(July 14, 1955, c. 360, Title IV, § 412, as added Nov. 15, 1990, Pub.L. 101–549, Title IV, § 401, 104 Stat. 2624.)

### HISTORICAL AND STATUTORY NOTES

**Effective and Applicability Provisions**

1990 Acts

Section effective Nov. 15, 1990, except as otherwise provided, see section 711(b) of Pub.L. 101–549, set out as a note under section 7401 of this title.

**Savings Provisions**

Suits, actions or proceedings commenced under this chapter as in effect prior to Nov. 15, 1990, not to abate by reason of the taking effect of amendments by Pub.L. 101–549, except as otherwise provided for, see section 711(a) of Pub.L. 101–549, set out as a note under section 7401 of this title.

**Information Gathering on Greenhouse Gases Contributing to Global Climate Change**

Section 821 of Pub.L. 101–549 provided that:

"(a) **Monitoring.**—The Administrator of the Environmental Protection Agency shall promulgate regulations within 18 months after the enactment of the Clean Air Act Amendments of 1990 [Nov. 15, 1990] to require that all affected sources subject to Title V of the Clean Air Act [probably means Title IV of the Clean Air Act as added by Pub.L. 101–549, which is classified to section 7651 et seq. of this title] shall also monitor carbon dioxide emissions according to the same timetable as in section 511(b) and (c) [probably means section 412(b) and (c) of the Clean Air Act, which is classified to section 7651k(b) and (c) of this title]. The regulations shall require that such data be reported to the Administrator. The provisions of section 511(e) of Title V of the Clean Air Act [probably means section 412(e) of Title IV of the Clean Air Act, which is classified to section 7651k(e) of this title] shall apply for purposes of this section in the same manner and to the same extent as such provision applies to the monitoring and data referred to in section 511 [probably means section 412 of the Clean Air Act, which is classified to section 7651k of this title].

"(b) **Public availability of carbon dioxide information.**—For each unit required to monitor and provide carbon dioxide data under subsection (a), the Administrator shall compute the unit's aggregate annual total carbon dioxide emissions, incorporate such data into a computer data base, and make such aggregate annual data available to the public."

## § 7651*l*. General compliance with other provisions

[CAA § 413]

Except as expressly provided, compliance with the requirements of this subchapter shall not exempt or exclude the owner or operator of any source subject to this subchapter from compliance with any other applicable requirements of this chapter.

(July 14, 1955, c. 360, Title IV, § 413, as added Nov. 15, 1990, Pub.L. 101–549, Title IV, § 401, 104 Stat. 2625.)

### HISTORICAL AND STATUTORY NOTES

**Effective and Applicability Provisions**

1990 Acts

Section effective Nov. 15, 1990, except as otherwise provided, see section 711(b) of Pub.L. 101–549, set out as a note under section 7401 of this title.

**Savings Provisions**

Suits, actions or proceedings commenced under this chapter as in effect prior to Nov. 15, 1990, not to abate by reason of the taking effect of amendments by Pub.L. 101–549, except as otherwise provided for, see section 711(a) of Pub.L. 101–549, set out as a note under section 7401 of this title.

## § 7651m. Enforcement

[CAA § 414]

It shall be unlawful for any person subject to this subchapter to violate any prohibition of, requirement of, or regulation promulgated pursuant to this subchapter shall be a violation of this chapter. In addition to the other requirements and prohibitions provided for in this subchapter, the operation of any affected unit to emit sulfur dioxide in excess of allowances held for such unit shall be deemed a violation, with each ton emitted in excess of allowances held constituting a separate violation.

(July 14, 1955, c. 360, Title IV, § 414, as added Nov. 15, 1990, Pub.L. 101–549, Title IV, § 401, 104 Stat. 2625.)

### HISTORICAL AND STATUTORY NOTES

**Effective and Applicability Provisions**

1990 Acts

Section effective Nov. 15, 1990, except as otherwise provided, see section 711(b) of Pub.L. 101–549, set out as a note under section 7401 of this title.

**Savings Provisions**

Suits, actions or proceedings commenced under this chapter as in effect prior to Nov. 15, 1990, not to abate by reason of the taking effect of amendments by Pub.L. 101–549, except as otherwise provided for, see section 711(a) of Pub.L. 101–549, set out as a note under section 7401 of this title.

## § 7651n. Clean coal technology regulatory incentives

[CAA § 415]

**(a) "Clean coal technology" defined**

For purposes of this section, "clean coal technology" means any technology, including technologies applied at the precombustion, combustion, or post combustion stage, at a new or existing facility which will achieve significant reductions in air emissions of sulfur dioxide or oxides of nitrogen associated with the utilization of coal in the generation of electricity, process steam, or industrial products, which is not in widespread use as of November 15, 1990.

**(b) Revised regulations for clean coal technology demonstrations**

**(1) Applicability**

This subsection applies to physical or operational changes to existing facilities for the sole purpose of installation, operation, cessation, or removal of a temporary or permanent clean coal technology demonstration project. For the purposes of this section, a clean coal technology demonstration project shall mean a project using funds appropriated under the heading "Department of Energy—Clean Coal Technology", up to a total amount of $2,500,000,000 for commercial demonstration of clean coal technology, or similar projects funded through appropriations for the Environmental Protection Agency. The Federal contribution for a qualifying project shall be at least 20 percent of the total cost of the demonstration project.

**(2) Temporary projects**

Installation, operation, cessation, or removal of a temporary clean coal technology demonstration project that is operated for a period of five years or less, and which complies with the State implementation plans for the State in which the project is located and other requirements necessary to attain and maintain the national ambient air quality standards during and after the project is terminated, shall not subject such facility to the requirements of section 7411 of this title or part C or D of subchapter I of this chapter.

**(3) Permanent projects**

For permanent clean coal technology demonstration projects that constitute repowering as defined in section 7651a(1) [1] of this title, any qualifying project shall not be subject to standards of performance under section 7411 of this title or to the review and permitting requirements of part C for any pollutant the potential emissions of which will not increase as a result of the demonstration project.

**(4) EPA regulations**

Not later than 12 months after November 15, 1990, the Administrator shall promulgate regulations or interpretive rulings to revise requirements under section 7411 of this title and parts C and D, as appropriate, to facilitate projects consistent in [2] this subsection. With respect to parts C and D, such regulations or rulings shall apply to all areas in which EPA is the permitting authority. In those instances in which the State is the permitting authority under part C or D, any State may adopt and submit to the Administrator for approval revisions to its implementation plan to apply the regulations or rulings promulgated under this subsection.

**(c) Exemption for reactivation of very clean units**

Physical changes or changes in the method of operation associated with the commencement of commercial operations by a coal-fired utility unit after a period of discontinued operation shall not subject the unit to the requirements of section 7411 of this title or part C of the Act where the unit (1) has not been in operation for the two-year period prior to the enactment of the Clean Air Act Amendments of 1990 [November 15, 1990], and the emissions from such unit continue to be carried in the permitting authority's emissions inventory at the time of enactment, (2) was equipped prior to shut-down with a continuous system of emissions control that achieves a removal efficiency for sulfur dioxide of no less than 85 percent and a removal efficiency for particulates of no less than 98 percent, (3) is equipped with low-$NO_x$ burners prior to the time of commencement, and (4) is otherwise in compliance with the requirements of this chapter.

(July 14, 1955, c. 360, Title IV, § 415, as added Nov. 15, 1990, Pub.L. 101–549, Title IV, § 401, 104 Stat. 2625.)

[1] So in original. Probably should be section "7651a(12)".

[2] So in original. Probably should be "with".

### HISTORICAL AND STATUTORY NOTES

**References in Text**

Parts C and D and part C of the Act, referred to in subsecs. (b)(3), (4) and (c), probably mean parts C and D of subchapter I of this chapter.

**Effective and Applicability Provisions**

1990 Acts

Section effective Nov. 15, 1990, except as otherwise provided, see section 711(b) of Pub.L. 101–549, set out as a note under section 7401 of this title.

**Savings Provisions**

Suits, actions or proceedings commenced under this chapter as in effect prior to Nov. 15, 1990, not to abate by reason of the taking effect of amendments by Pub.L. 101–549, except as otherwise provided for, see section 711(a) of Pub.L. 101–549, set out as a note under section 7401 of this title.

## § 7651o. Contingency guarantee, auctions, reserve

**[CAA § 416]**

**(a) Definitions**

For purposes of this section—

(1) The term "independent power producer" means any person who owns or operates, in whole or in part, one or more new independent power production facilities.

(2) The term "new independent power production facility" means a facility that—

(A) is used for the generation of electric energy, 80 percent or more of which is sold at wholesale;

(B) is nonrecourse project-financed (as such term is defined by the Secretary of Energy within 3 months of November 15, 1990);

(C) does not generate electric energy sold to any affiliate (as defined in section 79b(a)(11) of Title 15) of the facility's owner or operator unless the owner or operator of the facility demonstrates that it cannot obtain allowances from the affiliate; and

(D) is a new unit required to hold allowances under this subchapter.

(3) The term "required allowances" means the allowances required to operate such unit for so much of the unit's useful life as occurs after January 1, 2000.

**(b) Special reserve of allowances**

Within 36 months after November 15, 1990, the Administrator shall promulgate regulations establishing a Special Allowance Reserve containing allowances to be sold under this section. For purposes of establishing the Special Allowance Reserve, the Administrator shall withhold—

(1) 2.8 percent of the allocation of allowances for each year from 1995 through 1999 inclusive; and

(2) 2.8 percent of the basic Phase II allowance allocation of allowances for each year beginning in the year 2000

which would (but for this subsection) be issued for each affected unit at an affected source. The Administrator shall record such withholding for purposes of transferring the proceeds of the allowance sales under this subsection. The allowances so withheld shall be deposited in the Reserve under this section.

**(c) Direct sale at $1,500 per ton**

**(1) Subaccount for direct sales**

In accordance with regulations under this section, the Administrator shall establish a Direct Sale Subaccount in the Special Allowance Reserve established under this section. The Direct Sale Subaccount shall contain allowances in the amount of 50,000 tons per year for each year beginning in the year 2000.

**(2) Sales**

Allowances in the subaccount shall be offered for direct sale to any person at the times and in the amounts specified in table 1 at a price of $1,500 per allowance, adjusted by the Consumer Price Index in the same manner as provided in paragraph (3). Requests to purchase allowances from the Direct Sale Subaccount established under paragraph (1) shall be approved in the order of receipt until no allowances remain in such subaccount, except that an opportunity to purchase such allowances shall be provided to the independent power producers referred to in this subsection before such allowances are offered to any other person. Each applicant shall be required to pay 50 percent of the total purchase price of the allowances within 6 months after the approval of the request to purchase. The remainder shall be paid on or before the transfer of the allowances.

TABLE 1—NUMBER OF ALLOWANCES AVAILABLE FOR SALE AT $1,500 PER TON

| Year of Sale | Spot Sale (same year) | Advance Sale |
|---|---|---|
| 1993–1999 | ....... | 25,000 |
| 2000 and after | 25,000 | 25,000 |

Allowances sold in the spot sale in any year are allowances which may only be used in that year (unless banked for use in a later year). Allowances sold in the advance sale in any year are allowances which may only be used in the 7th year after the year in which they are first offered for sale (unless banked for use in a later year).

**(3) Entitlement to written guarantee**

Any independent power producer that submits an application to the Administrator establishing that such independent power producer—

(A) proposes to construct a new independent power production facility for which allowances are required under this subchapter;

(B) will apply for financing to construct such facility after January 1, 1990, and before the date of the first auction under this section;

(C) has submitted to each owner or operator of an affected unit listed in table A (in section 7651c of this title) a written offer to purchase the required allowances for $750 per ton; and

(D) has not received (within 180 days after submitting offers to purchase under subparagraph (C)) an acceptance of the offer to purchase the required allowances,

shall, within 30 days after submission of such application, be entitled to receive the Administrator's written guarantee (subject to the eligibility requirements set forth in paragraph (4)) that such required allowances will be made available for purchase from the Direct Sale Subaccount established under this subsection and at a guaranteed price. The guaranteed price at which such allowances shall be made available for purchase shall be $1,500 per ton, adjusted by the percentage, if any, by which the Consumer Price Index (as determined under section 7661a(b)(3)(B)(v) of this title) for the year in which the allowance is purchased exceeds the Consumer Price Index for the calendar year 1990.

**(4) Eligibility requirements**

The guarantee issued by the Administrator under paragraph (3) shall be subject to a demonstration by the independent power producer, satisfactory to the Administrator, that—

(A) the independent power producer has—

(i) made good faith efforts to purchase the required allowances from the owners or operators of affected units to which allowances will be allocated, including efforts to purchase at annual auctions under this section, and from industrial sources that have elected to become affected units pursuant to section 7651i of this title; and

(ii) such bids and efforts were unsuccessful in obtaining the required allowances; and

(B) the independent power producer will continue to make good faith efforts to purchase the required allowances from the owners or operators of affected units and from industrial sources.

(5) **Issuance of guaranteed allowances from Direct Sale Subaccount under this section**

From the allowances available in the Direct Sale Subaccount established under this subsection, upon payment of the guaranteed price, the Administrator shall issue to any person exercising the right to purchase allowances pursuant to a guarantee under this subsection the allowances covered by such guarantee. Persons to which guarantees under this subsection have been issued shall have the opportunity to purchase allowances pursuant to such guarantee from such subaccount before the allowances in such reserve are offered for sale to any other person.

(6) **Proceeds**

Notwithstanding section 3302 of Title 31 or any other provision of law, the Administrator shall require that the proceeds of any sale under this subsection be transferred, within 90 days after the sale, without charge, on a pro rata basis to the owners or operators of the affected units from whom the allowances were withheld under subsection (b) of this section and that any unsold allowances be transferred to the Subaccount for Auction Sales established under subsection (d) of this section. No proceeds of any sale under this subsection shall be held by any officer or employee of the United States or treated for any purpose as revenue to the United States or to the Administrator.

(7) **Termination of subaccount**

If the Administrator determines that, during any period of 2 consecutive calendar years, less than 20 percent of the allowances available in the subaccount for direct sales established under this subsection have been purchased under this paragraph, the Administrator shall terminate the subaccount and transfer such allowances to the Auction Subaccount under subsection (d) of this section.

(d) **Auction sales**

(1) **Subaccount for auctions**

The Administrator shall establish an Auction Subaccount in the Special Reserve established under this section. The Auction Subaccount shall contain allowances to be sold at auction under this section in the amount of 150,000 tons per year for each year from 1995 through 1999, inclusive and 250,000 tons per year for each year beginning in the calendar year 2000.

(2) **Annual auctions**

Commencing in 1993 and in each year thereafter, the Administrator shall conduct auctions at which the allowances referred to in paragraph (1) shall be offered for sale in accordance with regulations promulgated by the Administrator, in consultation with the Secretary of the Treasury, within 12 months of November 15, 1990. The allowances referred to in paragraph (1) shall be offered for sale at auction in the amounts specified in table 2. The auction shall be open to any person. A person wishing to bid for such allowances shall submit (by a date set by the Administrator) to the Administrator (on a sealed bid schedule provided by the Administrator) offers to purchase specified numbers of allowances at specified prices. Such regulations shall specify that the auctioned allowances shall be allocated and sold on the basis of bid price, starting with the highest-priced bid and continuing until all allowances for sale at such auction have been allocated. The regulations shall not permit that a minimum price be set for the purchase of withheld allowances. Allowances purchased at the auction may be used for any purpose and at any time after the auction, subject to the provisions of this subchapter.

TABLE 2—NUMBER OF ALLOWANCES AVAILABLE FOR AUCTION

| Year of Sale | Spot Auction (same year) | Advance Auction |
|---|---|---|
| 1993 | 50,000* | 100,000 |
| 1994 | 50,000* | 100,000 |
| 1995 | 50,000* | 100,000 |
| 1996 | 150,000 | 100,000 |
| 1997 | 150,000 | 100,000 |
| 1998 | 150,000 | 100,000 |
| 1999 | 150,000 | 100,000 |
| 2000 and after | 100,000 | 100,000 |

Allowances sold in the spot sale in any year are allowances which may only be used in that year (unless banked for use in a later year), except as otherwise noted. Allowances sold in the advance auction in any year are allowances which may only be used in the 7th year after the year in which they are first offered for sale (unless banked for use in a later year).
* Available for use only in 1995 (unless banked for use in a later year).

(3) **Proceeds**

(A) Notwithstanding section 3302 of Title 31 or any other provision of law, within 90 days of receipt, the Administrator shall transfer the proceeds from the auction under this section, on a pro rata basis, to the owners or operators of the affected units at an affected source from whom allowances were withheld under subsection (b) of this section. No funds transferred from a purchaser to a seller of allowances under this paragraph shall be held by any officer or employee of the United States or treated for any purpose as revenue to the United States or the Administrator.

(B) At the end of each year, any allowances offered for sale but not sold at the auction shall be returned without charge, on a pro rata basis, to the owner or operator of the affected units from whose allocation the allowances were withheld.

**(4) Additional auction participants**

Any person holding allowances or to whom allowances are allocated by the Administrator may submit those allowances to the Administrator to be offered for sale at auction under this subsection. The proceeds of any such sale shall be transferred at the time of sale by the purchaser to the person submitting such allowances for sale. The holder of allowances offered for sale under this paragraph may specify a minimum sale price. Any person may purchase allowances offered for auction under this paragraph. Such allowances shall be allocated and sold to purchasers on the basis of bid price after the auction under paragraph (2) is complete. No funds transferred from a purchaser to a seller of allowances under this paragraph shall be held by any officer or employee of the United States or treated for any purpose as revenue to the United States or the Administrator.

**(5) Recording by EPA**

The Administrator shall record and publicly report the nature, prices and results of each auction under this subsection, including the prices of successful bids, and shall record the transfers of allowances as a result of each auction in accordance with the requirements of this section. The transfer of allowances at such auction shall be recorded in accordance with the regulations promulgated by the Administrator under this subchapter.

**(e) Changes in sales, auctions, and withholding**

Pursuant to rulemaking after public notice and comment the Administrator may at any time after the year 1998 (in the case of advance sales or advance auctions) and 2005 (in the case of spot sales or spot auctions) decrease the number of allowances withheld and sold under this section.

**(f) Termination of auctions**

The Administrator may terminate the withholding of allowances and the auction sales under this section if the Administrator determines that, during any period of 3 consecutive calendar years after 2002, less than 20 percent of the allowances available in the auction subaccount have been purchased. Pursuant to regulations under this section, the Administrator may by delegation or contract provide for the conduct of sales or auctions under the Administrator's supervision by other departments or agencies of the United States Government or by nongovernmental agencies, groups, or organizations.

(July 14, 1955, c. 360, Title IV, § 416, as added Nov. 15, 1990, Pub.L. 101–549, Title IV, § 401, 104 Stat. 2626.)

### HISTORICAL AND STATUTORY NOTES

**Effective and Applicability Provisions**

1990 Acts

Section effective Nov. 15, 1990, except as otherwise provided, see section 711(b) of Pub.L. 101–549, set out as a note under section 7401 of this title.

**Savings Provisions**

Suits, actions or proceedings commenced under this chapter as in effect prior to Nov. 15, 1990, not to abate by reason of the taking effect of amendments by Pub.L. 101–549, except as otherwise provided for, see section 711(a) of Pub.L. 101–549, set out as a note under section 7401 of this title.

## SUBCHAPTER V—PERMITS

## § 7661. Definitions

[CAA § 501]

As used in this subchapter—

**(1) Affected source**

The term "affected source" shall have the meaning given such term in subchapter IV–A of this chapter.

**(2) Major source**

The term "major source" means any stationary source (or any group of stationary sources located within a contiguous area and under common control) that is either of the following:

(A) A major source as defined in section 7412 of this title.

(B) A major stationary source as defined in section 7602 of this title or part D of subchapter I of this chapter.

**(3) Schedule of compliance**

The term "schedule of compliance" means a schedule of remedial measures, including an enforceable sequence of actions or operations, leading to compliance with an applicable implementation plan, emission standard, emission limitation, or emission prohibition.

**(4) Permitting authority**

The term "permitting authority" means the Administrator or the air pollution control agency authorized by the Administrator to carry out a permit program under this subchapter.

(July 14, 1955, c. 360, Title V, § 501, as added Nov. 15, 1990, Pub.L. 101–549, Title V, § 501, 104 Stat. 2635.)

HISTORICAL AND STATUTORY NOTES

**Effective and Applicability Provisions**

1990 Acts

Section effective Nov. 15, 1990, except as otherwise provided, see section 711(b) of Pub.L. 101–549, set out as a note under section 7401 of this title.

**Savings Provisions**

Suits, actions or proceedings commenced under this chapter as in effect prior to Nov. 15, 1990, not to abate by reason of the taking effect of amendments by Pub.L. 101–549, except as otherwise provided for, see section 711(a) of Pub.L. 101–549, set out as a note under section 7401 of this title.

## § 7661a. Permit programs

[CAA § 502]

### (a) Violations

After the effective date of any permit program approved or promulgated under this subchapter, it shall be unlawful for any person to violate any requirement of a permit issued under this subchapter, or to operate an affected source (as provided in subchapter IV–A of this chapter), a major source, any other source (including an area source) subject to standards or regulations under section 7411 or 7412 of this title, any other source required to have a permit under parts [1] C or D of subchapter I of this chapter, or any other stationary source in a category designated (in whole or in part) by regulations promulgated by the Administrator (after notice and public comment) which shall include a finding setting forth the basis for such designation, except in compliance with a permit issued by a permitting authority under this subchapter. (Nothing in this subsection shall be construed to alter the applicable requirements of this chapter that a permit be obtained before construction or modification.) The Administrator may, in the Administrator's discretion and consistent with the applicable provisions of this chapter, promulgate regulations to exempt one or more source categories (in whole or in part) from the requirements of this subsection if the Administrator finds that compliance with such requirements is impracticable, infeasible, or unnecessarily burdensome on such categories, except that the Administrator may not exempt any major source from such requirements.

### (b) Regulations

The Administrator shall promulgate within 12 months after November 15, 1990, regulations establishing the minimum elements of a permit program to be administered by any air pollution control agency. These elements shall include each of the following:

(1) Requirements for permit applications, including a standard application form and criteria for determining in a timely fashion the completeness of applications.

(2) Monitoring and reporting requirements.

(3)(A) A requirement under State or local law or interstate compact that the owner or operator of all sources subject to the requirement to obtain a permit under this subchapter pay an annual fee, or the equivalent over some other period, sufficient to cover all reasonable (direct and indirect) costs required to develop and administer the permit program requirements of this subchapter, including section 7661f of this title, including the reasonable costs of—

(i) reviewing and acting upon any application for such a permit,

(ii) if the owner or operator receives a permit for such source, whether before or after November 15, 1990, implementing and enforcing the terms and conditions of any such permit (not including any court costs or other costs associated with any enforcement action),

(iii) emissions and ambient monitoring,

(iv) preparing generally applicable regulations, or guidance,

(v) modeling, analyses, and demonstrations, and

(vi) preparing inventories and tracking emissions.

(B) The total amount of fees collected by the permitting authority shall conform to the following requirements:

(i) The Administrator shall not approve a program as meeting the requirements of this paragraph unless the State demonstrates that, except as otherwise provided in subparagraphs (ii) through (v) of this subparagraph, the program will result in the collection, in the aggregate, from all sources subject to subparagraph (A), of an amount not less than $25 per ton of each regulated pollutant, or such other amount as the Administrator may determine adequately reflects the reasonable costs of the permit program.

(ii) As used in this subparagraph, the term "regulated pollutant" shall mean (I) a volatile organic compound; (II) each pollutant regulated under section 7411 or 7412 of this title; and (III) each pollutant for which a national primary ambient air quality standard has been promulgated (except that carbon monoxide shall be excluded from this reference).

(iii) In determining the amount under clause (i), the permitting authority is not required to include any amount of regulated pollutant emitted by any source in excess of 4,000 tons per year of that regulated pollutant.

(iv) The requirements of clause (i) shall not apply if the permitting authority demonstrates that collecting an amount less than the amount specified under clause (i) will meet the requirements of subparagraph (A).

(v) The fee calculated under clause (i) shall be increased (consistent with the need to cover the reasonable costs authorized by subparagraph (A)) in each year beginning after 1990, by the percentage, if any, by which the Consumer Price Index for the most recent calendar year ending before the beginning of such year exceeds the Consumer Price Index for the calendar year 1989. For purposes of this clause—

(I) the Consumer Price Index for any calendar year is the average of the Consumer Price Index for all-urban consumers published by the Department of Labor, as of the close of the 12–month period ending on August 31 of each calendar year, and

(II) the revision of the Consumer Price Index which is most consistent with the Consumer Price Index for calendar year 1989 shall be used.

(C)(i) If the Administrator determines, under subsection (d) of this section, that the fee provisions of the operating permit program do not meet the requirements of this paragraph, or if the Administrator makes a determination, under subsection (i) of this section, that the permitting authority is not adequately administering or enforcing an approved fee program, the Administrator may, in addition to taking any other action authorized under this subchapter, collect reasonable fees from the sources identified under subparagraph (A). Such fees shall be designed solely to cover the Administrator's costs of administering the provisions of the permit program promulgated by the Administrator.

(ii) Any source that fails to pay fees lawfully imposed by the Administrator under this subparagraph shall pay a penalty of 50 percent of the fee amount, plus interest on the fee amount computed in accordance with section 6621(a)(2) of Title 26 (relating to computation of interest on underpayment of Federal taxes).

(iii) Any fees, penalties, and interest collected under this subparagraph shall be deposited in a special fund in the United States Treasury for licensing and other services, which thereafter shall be available for appropriation, to remain available until expended, subject to appropriation, to carry out the Agency's activities for which the fees were collected. Any fee required to be collected by a State, local, or interstate agency under this subsection shall be utilized solely to cover all reasonable (direct and indirect) costs required to support the permit program as set forth in subparagraph (A).

(4) Requirements for adequate personnel and funding to administer the program.

(5) A requirement that the permitting authority have adequate authority to:

(A) issue permits and assure compliance by all sources required to have a permit under this subchapter with each applicable standard, regulation or requirement under this chapter;

(B) issue permits for a fixed term, not to exceed 5 years;

(C) assure that upon issuance or renewal permits incorporate emission limitations and other requirements in an applicable implementation plan;

(D) terminate, modify, or revoke and reissue permits for cause;

(E) enforce permits, permit fee requirements, and the requirement to obtain a permit, including authority to recover civil penalties in a maximum amount of not less than $10,000 per day for each violation, and provide appropriate criminal penalties; and

(F) assure that no permit will be issued if the Administrator objects to its issuance in a timely manner under this subchapter.

(6) Adequate, streamlined, and reasonable procedures for expeditiously determining when applications are complete, for processing such applications, for public notice, including offering an opportunity for public comment and a hearing, and for expeditious review of permit actions, including applications, renewals, or revisions, and including an opportunity for judicial review in State court of the final permit action by the applicant, any person who participated in the public comment process, and any other person who could obtain judicial review of that action under applicable law.

(7) To ensure against unreasonable delay by the permitting authority, adequate authority and procedures to provide that a failure of such permitting authority to act on a permit application or permit renewal application (in accordance with the time periods specified in section 7661b of this title or, as appropriate, subchapter IV–A of this chapter) shall be treated as a final permit action solely for purposes of obtaining judicial review in State court of an action brought by any person referred to in paragraph (6) to require that action be taken by the permitting authority on such application without additional delay.

(8) Authority, and reasonable procedures consistent with the need for expeditious action by the permitting authority on permit applications and related matters, to make available to the public any permit application, compliance plan, permit, and monitoring or compliance report under section 7661b(e) of this title, subject to the provisions of section 7414(c) of this title.

(9) A requirement that the permitting authority, in the case of permits with a term of 3 or more years for major sources, shall require revisions to the permit to incorporate applicable standards and regulations promulgated under this chapter after the issuance of such permit. Such revisions shall occur as expeditiously as practicable and consistent with the procedures established under paragraph (6) but not later than 18 months after the promulgation of such standards and regulations. No such revision shall be required if the effective date of the standards or regulations is a date after the expiration of the permit term. Such permit revision shall be treated as a permit renewal if it complies with the requirements of this subchapter regarding renewals.

(10) Provisions to allow changes within a permitted facility (or one operating pursuant to section 7661b(d) of this title) without requiring a permit revision, if the changes are not modifications under any provision of subchapter I of this chapter and the changes do not exceed the emissions allowable under the permit (whether expressed therein as a rate of emissions or in terms of total emissions:[2] *Provided*, That the facility provides the Administrator and the permitting authority with written notification in advance of the proposed changes which shall be a minimum of 7 days, unless the permitting authority provides in its regulations a different timeframe for emergencies.

**(c) Single permit**

A single permit may be issued for a facility with multiple sources.

**(d) Submission and approval**

(1) Not later than 3 years after November 15, 1990, the Governor of each State shall develop and submit to the Administrator a permit program under State or local law or under an interstate compact meeting the requirements of this subchapter. In addition, the Governor shall submit a legal opinion from the attorney general (or the attorney for those State air pollution control agencies that have independent legal counsel), or from the chief legal officer of an interstate agency, that the laws of the State, locality, or the interstate compact provide adequate authority to carry out the program. Not later than 1 year after receiving a program, and after notice and opportunity for public comment, the Administrator shall approve or disapprove such program, in whole or in part. The Administrator may approve a program to the extent that the program meets the requirements of this chapter, including the regulations issued under subsection (b) of this section. If the program is disapproved, in whole or in part, the Administrator shall notify the Governor of any revisions or modifications necessary to obtain approval. The Governor shall revise and resubmit the program for review under this section within 180 days after receiving notification.

(2)(A) If the Governor does not submit a program as required under paragraph (1) or if the Administrator disapproves a program submitted by the Governor under paragraph (1), in whole or in part, the Administrator may, prior to the expiration of the 18–month period referred to in subparagraph (B), in the Administrator's discretion, apply any of the sanctions specified in section 7509(b) of this title.

(B) If the Governor does not submit a program as required under paragraph (1), or if the Administrator disapproves any such program submitted by the Governor under paragraph (1), in whole or in part, 18 months after the date required for such submittal or the date of such disapproval, as the case may be, the Administrator shall apply sanctions under section 7509(b) of this title in the same manner and subject to the same deadlines and other conditions as are applicable in the case of a determination, disapproval, or finding under section 7509(a) of this title.

(C) The sanctions under section 7509(b)(2) of this title shall not apply pursuant to this paragraph in any area unless the failure to submit or the disapproval referred to in subparagraph (A) or (B) relates to an air pollutant for which such area has been designated a nonattainment area (as defined in part D of subchapter I of this chapter).

(3) If a program meeting the requirements of this subchapter has not been approved in whole for any State, the Administrator shall, 2 years after the date required for submission of such a program under paragraph (1), promulgate, administer, and enforce a program under this subchapter for that State.

**(e) Suspension**

The Administrator shall suspend the issuance of permits promptly upon publication of notice of approval of a permit program under this section, but may, in such notice, retain jurisdiction over permits that have been federally issued, but for which the administrative or judicial review process is not complete. The Administrator shall continue to administer and enforce federally issued permits under this subchapter until they are replaced by a permit issued by a permitting program. Nothing in this subsection should be construed to limit the Administrator's ability to enforce permits issued by a State.

**(f) Prohibition**

No partial permit program shall be approved unless, at a minimum, it applies, and ensures compliance with, this subchapter and each of the following:

(1) All requirements established under subchapter IV–A of this chapter applicable to "affected sources".

(2) All requirements established under section 7412 of this title applicable to "major sources", "area sources," and "new sources".

(3) All requirements of subchapter I of this chapter (other than section 7412 of this title) applicable to sources required to have a permit under this subchapter.

Approval of a partial program shall not relieve the State of its obligation to submit a complete program, nor from the application of any sanctions under this chapter for failure to submit an approvable permit program.

**(g) Interim approval**

If a program (including a partial permit program) submitted under this subchapter substantially meets the requirements of this subchapter, but is not fully approvable, the Administrator may by rule grant the program interim approval. In the notice of final rulemaking, the Administrator shall specify the changes that must be made before the program can receive full approval. An interim approval under this subsection shall expire on a date set by the Administrator not later than 2 years after such approval, and may not be renewed. For the period of any such interim approval, the provisions of subsection (d)(2) of this section, and the obligation of the Administrator to promulgate a program under this subchapter for the State pursuant to subsection (d)(3) of this section, shall be suspended. Such provisions and such obligation of the Administrator shall apply after the expiration of such interim approval.

**(h) Effective date**

The effective date of a permit program, or partial or interim program, approved under this subchapter, shall be the effective date of approval by the Administrator. The effective date of a permit program, or partial permit program, promulgated by the Administrator shall be the date of promulgation.

**(i) Administration and enforcement**

(1) Whenever the Administrator makes a determination that a permitting authority is not adequately administering and enforcing a program, or portion thereof, in accordance with the requirements of this subchapter, the Administrator shall provide notice to the State and may, prior to the expiration of the 18–month period referred to in paragraph (2), in the Administrator's discretion, apply any of the sanctions specified in section 7509(b) of this title.

(2) Whenever the Administrator makes a determination that a permitting authority is not adequately administering and enforcing a program, or portion thereof, in accordance with the requirements of this subchapter, 18 months after the date of the notice under paragraph (1), the Administrator shall apply the sanctions under section 7509(b) of this title in the same manner and subject to the same deadlines and other conditions as are applicable in the case of a determination, disapproval, or finding under section 7509(a) of this title.

(3) The sanctions under section 7509(b)(2) of this title shall not apply pursuant to this subsection in any area unless the failure to adequately enforce and administer the program relates to an air pollutant for which such area has been designated a nonattainment area.

(4) Whenever the Administrator has made a finding under paragraph (1) with respect to any State, unless the State has corrected such deficiency within 18 months after the date of such finding, the Administrator shall, 2 years after the date of such finding, promulgate, administer, and enforce a program under this subchapter for that State. Nothing in this paragraph shall be construed to affect the validity of a program which has been approved under this subchapter or the authority of any permitting authority acting under such program until such time as such program is promulgated by the Administrator under this paragraph.

(July 14, 1955, c. 360, Title V, § 502, as added Nov. 15, 1990, Pub.L. 101–549, Title V, § 501, 104 Stat. 2635.)

[1] So in original. Probably should be "part".

[2] So in original. A closing parenthesis probably should precede the colon.

## HISTORICAL AND STATUTORY NOTES

**Effective and Applicability Provisions**

1990 Acts

Section effective Nov. 15, 1990, except as otherwise provided, see section 711(b) of Pub.L. 101–549, set out as a note under section 7401 of this title.

**Savings Provisions**

Suits, actions or proceedings commenced under this chapter as in effect prior to Nov. 15, 1990, not to abate by reason of the taking effect of amendments by Pub.L. 101–549, except as otherwise provided for, see section 711(a) of Pub.L. 101–549, set out as a note under section 7401 of this title.

## § 7661b. Permit applications

**[CAA § 503]**

**(a) Applicable date**

Any source specified in section 7661a(a) of this title shall become subject to a permit program, and required to have a permit, on the later of the following dates—

(1) the effective date of a permit program or partial or interim permit program applicable to the source; or

(2) the date such source becomes subject to section 7661a(a) of this title.

**(b) Compliance plan**

(1) The regulations required by section 7661a(b) of this title shall include a requirement that the applicant submit with the permit application a compliance plan describing how the source will comply with all applicable requirements under this chapter. The compliance plan shall include a schedule of compliance, and a schedule under which the permittee will submit progress reports to the permitting authority no less frequently than every 6 months.

(2) The regulations shall further require the permittee to periodically (but no less frequently than annually) certify that the facility is in compliance with any applicable requirements of the permit, and to promptly report any deviations from permit requirements to the permitting authority.

**(c) Deadline**

Any person required to have a permit shall, not later than 12 months after the date on which the source becomes subject to a permit program approved or promulgated under this subchapter, or such earlier date as the permitting authority may establish, submit to the permitting authority a compliance plan and an application for a permit signed by a responsible official, who shall certify the accuracy of the information submitted. The permitting authority shall approve or disapprove a completed application (consistent with the procedures established under this subchapter for consideration of such applications), and shall issue or deny the permit, within 18 months after the date of receipt thereof, except that the permitting authority shall establish a phased schedule for acting on permit applications submitted within the first full year after the effective date of a permit program (or a partial or interim program). Any such schedule shall assure that at least one-third of such permits will be acted on by such authority annually over a period of not to exceed 3 years after such effective date. Such authority shall establish reasonable procedures to prioritize such approval or disapproval actions in the case of applications for construction or modification under the applicable requirements of this chapter.

**(d) Timely and complete applications**

Except for sources required to have a permit before construction or modification under the applicable requirements of this chapter, if an applicant has submitted a timely and complete application for a permit required by this subchapter (including renewals), but final action has not been taken on such application, the source's failure to have a permit shall not be a violation of this chapter, unless the delay in final action was due to the failure of the applicant timely to submit information required or requested to process the application. No source required to have a permit under this subchapter shall be in violation of section 7661a(a) of this title before the date on which the source is required to submit an application under subsection (c) of this section.

**(e) Copies; availability**

A copy of each permit application, compliance plan (including the schedule of compliance), emissions or compliance monitoring report, certification, and each permit issued under this subchapter, shall be available to the public. If an applicant or permittee is required to submit information entitled to protection from disclosure under section 7414(c) of this title, the applicant or permittee may submit such information separately. The requirements of section 7414(c) of this title shall apply to such information. The contents of a permit shall not be entitled to protection under section 7414(c) of this title.

(July 14, 1955, c. 360, Title V, § 503, as added Nov. 15, 1990, Pub.L. 101–549, Title V, § 501, 104 Stat. 2641.)

### HISTORICAL AND STATUTORY NOTES

**Effective and Applicability Provisions**

1990 Acts

Section effective Nov. 15, 1990, except as otherwise provided, see section 711(b) of Pub.L. 101–549, set out as a note under section 7401 of this title.

**Savings Provisions**

Suits, actions or proceedings commenced under this chapter as in effect prior to Nov. 15, 1990, not to abate by reason of the taking effect of amendments by Pub.L. 101–549, except as otherwise provided for, see section 711(a) of Pub.L. 101–549, set out as a note under section 7401 of this title.

## § 7661c. Permit requirements and conditions

**[CAA § 504]**

**(a) Conditions**

Each permit issued under this subchapter shall include enforceable emission limitations and standards, a schedule of compliance, a requirement that the permittee submit to the permitting authority, no less often than every 6 months, the results of any required monitoring, and such other conditions as are necessary to assure compliance with applicable requirements of this chapter, including the requirements of the applicable implementation plan.

**(b) Monitoring and analysis**

The Administrator may by rule prescribe procedures and methods for determining compliance and for monitoring and analysis of pollutants regulated under this chapter, but continuous emissions monitoring need not be required if alternative methods are available that provide sufficiently reliable and timely information for determining compliance. Nothing in this subsection shall be construed to affect any continuous emissions monitoring requirement of subchapter

IV–A of this chapter, or where required elsewhere in this chapter.

**(c) Inspection, entry, monitoring, certification, and reporting**

Each permit issued under this subchapter shall set forth inspection, entry, monitoring, compliance certification, and reporting requirements to assure compliance with the permit terms and conditions. Such monitoring and reporting requirements shall conform to any applicable regulation under subsection (b) of this section. Any report required to be submitted by a permit issued to a corporation under this subchapter shall be signed by a responsible corporate official, who shall certify its accuracy.

**(d) General permits**

The permitting authority may, after notice and opportunity for public hearing, issue a general permit covering numerous similar sources. Any general permit shall comply with all requirements applicable to permits under this subchapter. No source covered by a general permit shall thereby be relieved from the obligation to file an application under section 7661b of this title.

**(e) Temporary sources**

The permitting authority may issue a single permit authorizing emissions from similar operations at multiple temporary locations. No such permit shall be issued unless it includes conditions that will assure compliance with all the requirements of this chapter at all authorized locations, including, but not limited to, ambient standards and compliance with any applicable increment or visibility requirements under part C of subchapter I of this chapter. Any such permit shall in addition require the owner or operator to notify the permitting authority in advance of each change in location. The permitting authority may require a separate permit fee for operations at each location.

**(f) Permit shield**

Compliance with a permit issued in accordance with this subchapter shall be deemed compliance with section 7661a of this title. Except as otherwise provided by the Administrator by rule, the permit may also provide that compliance with the permit shall be deemed compliance with other applicable provisions of this chapter that relate to the permittee if—

(1) the permit includes the applicable requirements of such provisions, or

(2) the permitting authority in acting on the permit application makes a determination relating to the permittee that such other provisions (which shall be referred to in such determination) are not applicable and the permit includes the determination or a concise summary thereof.

Nothing in the preceding sentence shall alter or affect the provisions of section 7603 of this title, including the authority of the Administrator under that section.

(July 14, 1955, c. 360, Title V, § 504, as added Nov. 15, 1990, Pub.L. 101–549, Title V, § 501, 104 Stat. 2642.)

**HISTORICAL AND STATUTORY NOTES**

**Effective and Applicability Provisions**

1990 Acts

Section effective Nov. 15, 1990, except as otherwise provided, see section 711(b) of Pub.L. 101–549, set out as a note under section 7401 of this title.

**Savings Provisions**

Suits, actions or proceedings commenced under this chapter as in effect prior to Nov. 15, 1990, not to abate by reason of the taking effect of amendments by Pub.L. 101–549, except as otherwise provided for, see section 711(a) of Pub.L. 101–549, set out as a note under section 7401 of this title.

## § 7661d. Notification to Administrator and contiguous States

**[CAA § 505]**

**(a) Transmission and notice**

(1) Each permitting authority—

(A) shall transmit to the Administrator a copy of each permit application (and any application for a permit modification or renewal) or such portion thereof, including any compliance plan, as the Administrator may require to effectively review the application and otherwise to carry out the Administrator's responsibilities under this chapter, and

(B) shall provide to the Administrator a copy of each permit proposed to be issued and issued as a final permit.

(2) The permitting authority shall notify all States—

(A) whose air quality may be affected and that are contiguous to the State in which the emission originates, or

(B) that are within 50 miles of the source,

of each permit application or proposed permit forwarded to the Administrator under this section, and shall provide an opportunity for such States to submit written recommendations respecting the issuance of the permit and its terms and conditions. If any part of those recommendations are not accepted by the permitting authority, such authority shall notify the State submitting the recommendations and the Administrator in writing of its failure to accept those recommendations and the reasons therefor.

**(b) Objection by EPA**

(1) If any permit contains provisions that are determined by the Administrator as not in compliance with the applicable requirements of this chapter, including

the requirements of an applicable implementation plan, the Administrator shall, in accordance with this subsection, object to its issuance. The permitting authority shall respond in writing if the Administrator (A) within 45 days after receiving a copy of the proposed permit under subsection (a)(1) of this section, or (B) within 45 days after receiving notification under subsection (a)(2) of this section, objects in writing to its issuance as not in compliance with such requirements. With the objection, the Administrator shall provide a statement of the reasons for the objection. A copy of the objection and statement shall be provided to the applicant.

(2) If the Administrator does not object in writing to the issuance of a permit pursuant to paragraph (1), any person may petition the Administrator within 60 days after the expiration of the 45–day review period specified in paragraph (1) to take such action. A copy of such petition shall be provided to the permitting authority and the applicant by the petitioner. The petition shall be based only on objections to the permit that were raised with reasonable specificity during the public comment period provided by the permitting agency (unless the petitioner demonstrates in the petition to the Administrator that it was impracticable to raise such objections within such period or unless the grounds for such objection arose after such period). The petition shall identify all such objections. If the permit has been issued by the permitting agency, such petition shall not postpone the effectiveness of the permit. The Administrator shall grant or deny such petition within 60 days after the petition is filed. The Administrator shall issue an objection within such period if the petitioner demonstrates to the Administrator that the permit is not in compliance with the requirements of this chapter, including the requirements of the applicable implementation plan. Any denial of such petition shall be subject to judicial review under section 7607 of this title. The Administrator shall include in regulations under this subchapter provisions to implement this paragraph. The Administrator may not delegate the requirements of this paragraph.

(3) Upon receipt of an objection by the Administrator under this subsection, the permitting authority may not issue the permit unless it is revised and issued in accordance with subsection (c) of this section. If the permitting authority has issued a permit prior to receipt of an objection by the Administrator under paragraph (2) of this subsection, the Administrator shall modify, terminate, or revoke such permit and the permitting authority may thereafter only issue a revised permit in accordance with subsection (c) of this section.

**(c) Issuance or denial**

If the permitting authority fails, within 90 days after the date of an objection under subsection (b) of this section, to submit a permit revised to meet the objection, the Administrator shall issue or deny the permit in accordance with the requirements of this subchapter. No objection shall be subject to judicial review until the Administrator takes final action to issue or deny a permit under this subsection.

**(d) Waiver of notification requirements**

(1) The Administrator may waive the requirements of subsections (a) and (b) of this section at the time of approval of a permit program under this subchapter for any category (including any class, type, or size within such category) of sources covered by the program other than major sources.

(2) The Administrator may, by regulation, establish categories of sources (including any class, type, or size within such category) to which the requirements of subsections (a) and (b) of this section shall not apply. The preceding sentence shall not apply to major sources.

(3) The Administrator may exclude from any waiver under this subsection notification under subsection (a)(2) of this section. Any waiver granted under this subsection may be revoked or modified by the Administrator by rule.

**(e) Refusal of permitting authority to terminate, modify, or revoke and reissue**

If the Administrator finds that cause exists to terminate, modify, or revoke and reissue a permit under this subchapter, the Administrator shall notify the permitting authority and the source of the Administrator's finding. The permitting authority shall, within 90 days after receipt of such notification, forward to the Administrator under this section a proposed determination of termination, modification, or revocation and reissuance, as appropriate. The Administrator may extend such 90 day period for an additional 90 days if the Administrator finds that a new or revised permit application is necessary, or that the permitting authority must require the permittee to submit additional information. The Administrator may review such proposed determination under the provisions of subsections (a) and (b) of this section. If the permitting authority fails to submit the required proposed determination, or if the Administrator objects and the permitting authority fails to resolve the objection within 90 days, the Administrator may, after notice and in accordance with fair and reasonable procedures, terminate, modify, or revoke and reissue the permit.

(July 14, 1955, c. 360, Title V, § 505, as added Nov. 15, 1990, Pub.L. 101–549, Title V, § 501, 104 Stat. 2643.)

HISTORICAL AND STATUTORY NOTES

**Effective and Applicability Provisions**

1990 Acts

Section effective Nov. 15, 1990, except as otherwise provided, see section 711(b) of Pub.L. 101–549, set out as a note under section 7401 of this title.

**Savings Provisions**

Suits, actions or proceedings commenced under this chapter as in effect prior to Nov. 15, 1990, not to abate by reason of the taking effect of amendments by Pub.L. 101–549, except as otherwise provided for, see section 711(a) of Pub.L. 101–549, set out as a note under section 7401 of this title.

## § 7661e. Other authorities

[CAA § 506]

### (a) In general

Nothing in this subchapter shall prevent a State, or interstate permitting authority, from establishing additional permitting requirements not inconsistent with this chapter.

### (b) Permits implementing acid rain provisions

The provisions of this subchapter, including provisions regarding schedules for submission and approval or disapproval of permit applications, shall apply to permits implementing the requirements of subchapter IV–A of this chapter except as modified by that subchapter.

(July 14, 1955, c. 360, Title V, § 506, as added Nov. 15, 1990, Pub.L. 101–549, Title V, § 501, 104 Stat. 2645.)

HISTORICAL AND STATUTORY NOTES

**Effective and Applicability Provisions**

1990 Acts

Section effective Nov. 15, 1990, except as otherwise provided, see section 711(b) of Pub.L. 101–549, set out as a note under section 7401 of this title.

**Savings Provisions**

Suits, actions or proceedings commenced under this chapter as in effect prior to Nov. 15, 1990, not to abate by reason of the taking effect of amendments by Pub.L. 101–549, except as otherwise provided for, see section 711(a) of Pub.L. 101–549, set out as a note under section 7401 of this title.

## § 7661f. Small business stationary source technical and environmental compliance assistance program

[CAA § 507]

### (a) Plan revisions

Consistent with sections 7410 and 7412 of this title, each State shall, after reasonable notice and public hearings, adopt and submit to the Administrator as part of the State implementation plan for such State or as a revision to such State implementation plan under section 7410 of this title, plans for establishing a small business stationary source technical and environmental compliance assistance program. Such submission shall be made within 24 months after November 15, 1990. The Administrator shall approve such program if it includes each of the following:

(1) Adequate mechanisms for developing, collecting, and coordinating information concerning compliance methods and technologies for small business stationary sources, and programs to encourage lawful cooperation among such sources and other persons to further compliance with this chapter.

(2) Adequate mechanisms for assisting small business stationary sources with pollution prevention and accidental release detection and prevention, including providing information concerning alternative technologies, process changes, products, and methods of operation that help reduce air pollution.

(3) A designated State office within the relevant State agency to serve as ombudsman for small business stationary sources in connection with the implementation of this chapter.

(4) A compliance assistance program for small business stationary sources which assists small business stationary sources in determining applicable requirements and in receiving permits under this chapter in a timely and efficient manner.

(5) Adequate mechanisms to assure that small business stationary sources receive notice of their rights under this chapter in such manner and form as to assure reasonably adequate time for such sources to evaluate compliance methods and any relevant or applicable proposed or final regulation or standard issued under this chapter.

(6) Adequate mechanisms for informing small business stationary sources of their obligations under this chapter, including mechanisms for referring such sources to qualified auditors or, at the option of the State, for providing audits of the operations of such sources to determine compliance with this chapter.

(7) Procedures for consideration of requests from a small business stationary source for modification of—

(A) any work practice or technological method of compliance, or

(B) the schedule of milestones for implementing such work practice or method of compliance preceding any applicable compliance date,

based on the technological and financial capability of any such small business stationary source. No such modification may be granted unless it is in compliance with the applicable requirements of this chapter, including the requirements of the applicable implementation plan. Where such applicable requirements are set forth in Federal regulations, only modifications authorized in such regulations may be allowed.

**(b) Program**

The Administrator shall establish within 9 months after November 15, 1990, a small business stationary source technical and environmental compliance assistance program. Such program shall—

(1) assist the States in the development of the program required under subsection (a) of this section (relating to assistance for small business stationary sources);

(2) issue guidance for the use of the States in the implementation of these programs that includes alternative control technologies and pollution prevention methods applicable to small business stationary sources; and

(3) provide for implementation of the program provisions required under subsection (a)(4) of this section in any State that fails to submit such a program under that subsection.

**(c) Eligibility**

(1) Except as provided in paragraphs (2) and (3), for purposes of this section, the term "small business stationary source" means a stationary source that—

(A) is owned or operated by a person that employs 100 or fewer individuals,[1]

(B) is a small business concern as defined in the Small Business Act [15 U.S.C.A. § 631 et seq.];

(C) is not a major stationary source;

(D) does not emit 50 tons or more per year of any regulated pollutant; and

(E) emits less than 75 tons per year of all regulated pollutants.

(2) Upon petition by a source, the State may, after notice and opportunity for public comment, include as a small business stationary source for purposes of this section any stationary source which does not meet the criteria of subparagraphs[2] (C), (D), or (E) of paragraph (1) but which does not emit more than 100 tons per year of all regulated pollutants.

(3)(A) The Administrator, in consultation with the Administrator of the Small Business Administration and after providing notice and opportunity for public comment, may exclude from the small business stationary source definition under this section any category or subcategory of sources that the Administrator determines to have sufficient technical and financial capabilities to meet the requirements of this chapter without the application of this subsection.

(B) The State, in consultation with the Administrator and the Administrator of the Small Business Administration and after providing notice and opportunity for public hearing, may exclude from the small business stationary source definition under this section any category or subcategory of sources that the State determines to have sufficient technical and financial capabilities to meet the requirements of this chapter without the application of this subsection.

**(d) Monitoring**

The Administrator shall direct the Agency's Office of Small and Disadvantaged Business Utilization through the Small Business Ombudsman (hereinafter in this section referred to as the "Ombudsman") to monitor the small business stationary source technical and environmental compliance assistance program under this section. In carrying out such monitoring activities, the Ombudsman shall—

(1) render advisory opinions on the overall effectiveness of the Small Business Stationary Source Technical and Environmental Compliance Assistance Program, difficulties encountered, and degree and severity of enforcement;

(2) make periodic reports to the Congress on the compliance of the Small Business Stationary Source Technical and Environmental Compliance Assistance Program with the requirements of the Paperwork Reduction Act, the Regulatory Flexibility Act [5 U.S.C.A. § 601 et seq.], and the Equal Access to Justice Act;

(3) review information to be issued by the Small Business Stationary Source Technical and Environmental Compliance Assistance Program for small business stationary sources to ensure that the information is understandable by the layperson; and

(4) have the Small Business Stationary Source Technical and Environmental Compliance Assistance Program serve as the secretariat for the development and dissemination of such reports and advisory opinions.

**(e) Compliance Advisory Panel**

(1) There shall be created a Compliance Advisory Panel (hereinafter referred to as the "Panel") on the State level of not less than 7 individuals. This Panel shall—

(A) render advisory opinions concerning the effectiveness of the small business stationary source technical and environmental compliance assistance program, difficulties encountered, and degree and severity of enforcement;

(B) make periodic reports to the Administrator concerning the compliance of the State Small Business Stationary Source Technical and Environmental Compliance Assistance Program with the requirements of the Paperwork Reduction Act, the Regulatory Flexibility Act [5 U.S.C.A. § 601 et seq.], and the Equal Access to Justice Act;

(C) review information for small business stationary sources to assure such information is understandable by the layperson; and

(D) have the Small Business Stationary Source Technical and Environmental Compliance Assistance Program serve as the secretariat for the development and dissemination of such reports and advisory opinions.

(2) The Panel shall consist of—

(A) 2 members, who are not owners, or representatives of owners, of small business stationary sources, selected by the Governor to represent the general public;

(B) 2 members selected by the State legislature who are owners, or who represent owners, of small business stationary sources (1 member each by the majority and minority leadership of the lower house, or in the case of a unicameral State legislature, 2 members each shall be selected by the majority leadership and the minority leadership, respectively, of such legislature, and subparagraph (C) shall not apply);

(C) 2 members selected by the State legislature who are owners, or who represent owners, of small business stationary sources (1 member each by the majority and minority leadership of the upper house, or the equivalent State entity); and

(D) 1 member selected by the head of the department or agency of the State responsible for air pollution permit programs to represent that agency.

**(f) Fees**

The State (or the Administrator) may reduce any fee required under this chapter to take into account the financial resources of small business stationary sources.

**(g) Continuous emission monitors**

In developing regulations and CTGs under this chapter that contain continuous emission monitoring requirements, the Administrator, consistent with the requirements of this chapter, before applying such requirements to small business stationary sources, shall consider the necessity and appropriateness of such requirements for such sources. Nothing in this subsection shall affect the applicability of subchapter IV–A of this chapter provisions relating to continuous emissions monitoring.

**(h) Control technique guidelines**

The Administrator shall consider, consistent with the requirements of this chapter, the size, type, and technical capabilities of small business stationary sources (and sources which are eligible under subsection (c)(2) of this section to be treated as small business stationary sources) in developing CTGs applicable to such sources under this chapter.

(July 14, 1955, c. 360, Title V, § 507, as added Nov. 15, 1990, Pub.L. 101–549, Title V, § 501, 104 Stat. 2645.)

[1] So in original. The comma probably should be a semicolon.

[2] So in original. Probably should be "subparagraph".

## HISTORICAL AND STATUTORY NOTES

**References in Text**

The Small Business Act, referred to in subsec. (c)(1)(B), is Pub.L. 85–536, July 18, 1958, 72 Stat. 384, as amended, which is classified generally to chapter 14A (section 631 et seq.) of Title 15, Commerce and Trade. For complete classification of this Act to the Code, see Short Title note set out under section 631 of Title 15 and Tables.

The Paperwork Reduction Act, referred to in subsecs. (d)(2) and (e)(1)(B), probably means the Paperwork Reduction Act of 1980, Pub.L. 96–511, Dec. 11, 1980, 94 Stat. 2812, as amended, which is classified principally to chapter 35 (section 3501 et seq.) of Title 44, Public Printing and Documents. For complete classification of this Act to the Code, see Short Title of 1980 Amendments note set out under section 101 of Title 44 and Tables.

The Regulatory Flexibility Act, referred to in subsecs. (d)(2) and (e)(1)(B), is Pub.L. 96–354, Sept. 19, 1980, 94 Stat. 1164, which is classified generally to chapter 6 (section 601 et seq.) of Title 5, Government Organization and Employees. For complete classification of this Act to the Code, see Short Title note set out under section 601 of Title 5 and Tables.

The Equal Access to Justice Act, referred to in subsecs. (d)(2) and (e)(1)(B), is Title II of Pub.L. 96–481, Oct. 21, 1980, 94 Stat. 2325. For complete classification of this Act to the Code, see Short Title note set out under section 504 of Title 5 and Tables.

**Effective and Applicability Provisions**

1990 Acts

Section effective Nov. 15, 1990, except as otherwise provided, see section 711(b) of Pub.L. 101–549, set out as a note under section 7401 of this title.

**Savings Provisions**

Suits, actions or proceedings commenced under this chapter as in effect prior to Nov. 15, 1990, not to abate by reason of the taking effect of amendments by Pub.L. 101–549, except as otherwise provided for, see section 711(a) of Pub.L. 101–549, set out as a note under section 7401 of this title.

# SUBCHAPTER VI—STRATOSPHERIC OZONE PROTECTION

## § 7671. Definitions

**[CAA § 601]**

As used in this subchapter—

**(1) Appliance**

The term "appliance" means any device which contains and uses a class I or class II substance as a refrigerant and which is used for household or commercial purposes, including any air conditioner, refrigerator, chiller, or freezer.

**(2) Baseline year**

The term "baseline year" means—

**(A)** the calendar year 1986, in the case of any class I substance listed in Group I or II under section 7671a(a) of this title,

**(B)** the calendar year 1989, in the case of any class I substance listed in Group III, IV, or V under section 7671a(a) of this title, and

**(C)** a representative calendar year selected by the Administrator, in the case of—

**(i)** any substance added to the list of class I substances after the publication of the initial list under section 7671a(a) of this title, and

**(ii)** any class II substance.

**(3) Class I substance**

The term "class I substance" means each of the substances listed as provided in section 7671a(a) of this title.

**(4) Class II substance**

The term "class II substance" means each of the substances listed as provided in section 7671a(b) of this title.

**(5) Commissioner**

The term "Commissioner" means the Commissioner of the Food and Drug Administration.

**(6) Consumption**

The term "consumption" means, with respect to any substance, the amount of that substance produced in the United States, plus the amount imported, minus the amount exported to Parties to the Montreal Protocol. Such term shall be construed in a manner consistent with the Montreal Protocol.

**(7) Import**

The term "import" means to land on, bring into, or introduce into, or attempt to land on, bring into, or introduce into, any place subject to the jurisdiction of the United States, whether or not such landing, bringing, or introduction constitutes an importation within the meaning of the customs laws of the United States.

**(8) Medical device**

The term "medical device" means any device (as defined in the Federal Food, Drug, and Cosmetic Act (21 U.S.C. 321)), diagnostic product, drug (as defined in the Federal Food, Drug, and Cosmetic Act), and drug delivery system—

**(A)** if such device, product, drug, or drug delivery system utilizes a class I or class II substance for which no safe and effective alternative has been developed, and where necessary, approved by the Commissioner; and

**(B)** if such device, product, drug, or drug delivery system, has, after notice and opportunity for public comment, been approved and determined to be essential by the Commissioner in consultation with the Administrator.

**(9) Montreal Protocol**

The terms "Montreal Protocol" and "the Protocol" mean the Montreal Protocol on Substances that Deplete the Ozone Layer, a protocol to the Vienna Convention for the Protection of the Ozone Layer, including adjustments adopted by Parties thereto and amendments that have entered into force.

**(10) Ozone-depletion potential**

The term "ozone-depletion potential" means a factor established by the Administrator to reflect the ozone-depletion potential of a substance, on a mass per kilogram basis, as compared to chlorofluorocarbon–11 (CFC–11). Such factor shall be based upon the substance's atmospheric lifetime, the molecular weight of bromine and chlorine, and the substance's ability to be photolytically disassociated, and upon other factors determined to be an accurate measure of relative ozone-depletion potential.

**(11) Produce, produced, and production**

The terms "produce", "produced", and "production", refer to the manufacture of a substance from any raw material or feedstock chemical, but such terms do not include—

**(A)** the manufacture of a substance that is used and entirely consumed (except for trace quantities) in the manufacture of other chemicals, or

**(B)** the reuse or recycling of a substance.

(July 14, 1955, c. 360, Title VI, § 601, as added Nov. 15, 1990, Pub.L. 101–549, Title VI, § 602(a), 104 Stat. 2649.)

### HISTORICAL AND STATUTORY NOTES

**References in Text**

The customs laws of the United States, referred to in par. (7), are classified generally to Title 19, Customs Duties.

The Federal Food, Drug, and Cosmetic Act, referred to in par. (8), is Act June 25, 1938, c. 675, 52 Stat. 1040, as amended, which is classified generally to chapter 9 (section 301 et seq.) of Title 21, Food and Drugs. For complete classification of this Act to the Code, see section 301 of Title 21 and Tables.

**Effective and Applicability Provisions**

1990 Acts

Section effective Nov. 15, 1990, except as otherwise provided, see section 711(b) of Pub.L. 101–549, set out as a note under section 7401 of this title.

**Savings Provisions**

Suits, actions or proceedings commenced under this chapter as in effect prior to Nov. 15, 1990, not to abate by reason of the taking effect of amendments by Pub.L. 101–549, except as otherwise provided for, see section 711(a) of Pub.L. 101–549, set out as a note under section 7401 of this title.

## § 7671a. Listing of class I and class II substances

[CAA § 602]

### (a) List of class I substances

Within 60 days after November 15, 1990, the Administrator shall publish an initial list of class I substances, which list shall contain the following substances:

Group I
chlorofluorocarbon–11 (CFC–11)
chlorofluorocarbon–12 (CFC–12)
chlorofluorocarbon–113 (CFC–113)
chlorofluorocarbon–114 (CFC–114)
chlorofluorocarbon–115 (CFC–115)
Group II
halon–1211
halon–1301
halon–2402
Group III
chlorofluorocarbon–13 (CFC–13)
chlorofluorocarbon–111 (CFC–111)
chlorofluorocarbon–112 (CFC–112)
chlorofluorocarbon–211 (CFC–211)
chlorofluorocarbon–212 (CFC–212)
chlorofluorocarbon–213 (CFC–213)
chlorofluorocarbon–214 (CFC–214)
chlorofluorocarbon–215 (CFC–215)
chlorofluorocarbon–216 (CFC–216)
chlorofluorocarbon–217 (CFC–217)
Group IV
carbon tetrachloride
Group V
methyl chloroform

The initial list under this subsection shall also include the isomers of the substances listed above, other than 1,1,2–trichloroethane (an isomer of methyl chloroform). Pursuant to subsection (c) of this section, the Administrator shall add to the list of class I substances any other substance that the Administrator finds causes or contributes significantly to harmful effects on the stratospheric ozone layer. The Administrator shall, pursuant to subsection (c) of this section, add to such list all substances that the Administrator determines have an ozone depletion potential of 0.2 or greater.

### (b) List of class II substances

Simultaneously with publication of the initial list of class I substances, the Administrator shall publish an initial list of class II substances, which shall contain the following substances:

hydrochlorofluorocarbon–21 (HCFC–21)
hydrochlorofluorocarbon–22 (HCFC–22)
hydrochlorofluorocarbon–31 (HCFC–31)
hydrochlorofluorocarbon–121 (HCFC–121)
hydrochlorofluorocarbon–122 (HCFC–122)
hydrochlorofluorocarbon–123 (HCFC–123)
hydrochlorofluorocarbon–124 (HCFC–124)
hydrochlorofluorocarbon–131 (HCFC–131)
hydrochlorofluorocarbon–132 (HCFC–132)
hydrochlorofluorocarbon–133 (HCFC–133)
hydrochlorofluorocarbon–141 (HCFC–141)
hydrochlorofluorocarbon–142 (HCFC–142)
hydrochlorofluorocarbon–221 (HCFC–221)
hydrochlorofluorocarbon–222 (HCFC–222)
hydrochlorofluorocarbon–223 (HCFC–223)
hydrochlorofluorocarbon–224 (HCFC–224)
hydrochlorofluorocarbon–225 (HCFC–225)
hydrochlorofluorocarbon–226 (HCFC–226)
hydrochlorofluorocarbon–231 (HCFC–231)
hydrochlorofluorocarbon–232 (HCFC–232)
hydrochlorofluorocarbon–233 (HCFC–233)
hydrochlorofluorocarbon–234 (HCFC–234)
hydrochlorofluorocarbon–235 (HCFC–235)
hydrochlorofluorocarbon–241 (HCFC–241)
hydrochlorofluorocarbon–242 (HCFC–242)
hydrochlorofluorocarbon–243 (HCFC–243)
hydrochlorofluorocarbon–244 (HCFC–244)
hydrochlorofluorocarbon–251 (HCFC–251)
hydrochlorofluorocarbon–252 (HCFC–252)
hydrochlorofluorocarbon–253 (HCFC–253)
hydrochlorofluorocarbon–261 (HCFC–261)
hydrochlorofluorocarbon–262 (HCFC–262)
hydrochlorofluorocarbon–271 (HCFC–271)

The initial list under this subsection shall also include the isomers of the substances listed above. Pursuant to subsection (c) of this section, the Administrator shall add to the list of class II substances any other substance that the Administrator finds is known or may reasonably be anticipated to cause or contribute to harmful effects on the stratospheric ozone layer.

**(c) Additions to the lists**

(1) The Administrator may add, by rule, in accordance with the criteria set forth in subsection (a) or (b) of this section, as the case may be, any substance to the list of class I or class II substances under subsection (a) or (b) of this section. For purposes of exchanges under section 7661f [1] of this title, whenever a substance is added to the list of class I substances the Administrator shall, to the extent consistent with the Montreal Protocol, assign such substance to existing Group I, II, III, IV, or V or place such substance in a new Group.

(2) Periodically, but not less frequently than every 3 years after November 15, 1990, the Administrator shall list, by rule, as additional class I or class II substances those substances which the Administrator finds meet the criteria of subsection (a) or (b) of this section, as the case may be.

(3) At any time, any person may petition the Administrator to add a substance to the list of class I or class II substances. Pursuant to the criteria set forth in subsection (a) or (b) of this section as the case may be, within 180 days after receiving such a petition, the Administrator shall either propose to add the substance to such list or publish an explanation of the petition denial. In any case where the Administrator proposes to add a substance to such list, the Administrator shall add, by rule, (or make a final determination not to add) such substance to such list within 1 year after receiving such petition. Any petition under this paragraph shall include a showing by the petitioner that there are data on the substance adequate to support the petition. If the Administrator determines that information on the substance is not sufficient to make a determination under this paragraph, the Administrator shall use any authority available to the Administrator, under any law administered by the Administrator, to acquire such information.

(4) Only a class II substance which is added to the list of class I substances may be removed from the list of class II substances. No substance referred to in subsection (a) of this section, including methyl chloroform, may be removed from the list of class I substances.

**(d) New listed substances**

In the case of any substance added to the list of class I or class II substances after publication of the initial list of such substances under this section, the Administrator may extend any schedule or compliance deadline contained in section 7671c or 7671d of this title to a later date than specified in such sections if such schedule or deadline is unattainable, considering when such substance is added to the list. No extension under this subsection may extend the date for termination of production of any class I substance to a date more than 7 years after January 1 of the year after the year in which the substance is added to the list of class I substances. No extension under this subsection may extend the date for termination of production of any class II substance to a date more than 10 years after January 1 of the year after the year in which the substance is added to the list of class II substances.

**(e) Ozone-depletion and global warming potential**

Simultaneously with publication of the lists under this section and simultaneously with any addition to either of such lists, the Administrator shall assign to each listed substance a numerical value representing the substance's ozone-depletion potential. In addition, the Administrator shall publish the chlorine and bromine loading potential and the atmospheric lifetime of each listed substance. One year after November 15, 1990 (one year after the addition of a substance to either of such lists in the case of a substance added after the publication of the initial lists of such substances), and after notice and opportunity for public comment, the Administrator shall publish the global warming potential of each listed substance. The preceding sentence shall not be construed to be the basis of any additional regulation under this chapter. In the case of the substances referred to in table 1, the ozone-depletion potential shall be as specified in table 1, unless the Administrator adjusts the substance's ozone-depletion potential based on criteria referred to in section 7671(10) of this title:

Table 1

| Substance | Ozone-depletion potential |
|---|---|
| chlorofluorocarbon–11 (CFC–11) | 1.0 |
| chlorofluorocarbon–12 (CFC–12) | 1.0 |
| chlorofluorocarbon–13 (CFC–13) | 1.0 |
| chlorofluorocarbon–111 (CFC–111) | 1.0 |
| chlorofluorocarbon–112 (CFC–112) | 1.0 |
| chlorofluorocarbon–113 (CFC–113) | 0.8 |
| chlorofluorocarbon–114 (CFC–114) | 1.0 |
| chlorofluorocarbon–115 (CFC–115) | 0.6 |
| chlorofluorocarbon–211 (CFC–211) | 1.0 |
| chlorofluorocarbon–212 (CFC–212) | 1.0 |
| chlorofluorocarbon–213 (CFC–213) | 1.0 |
| chlorofluorocarbon–214 (CFC–214) | 1.0 |
| chlorofluorocarbon–215 (CFC–215) | 1.0 |
| chlorofluorocarbon–216 (CFC–216) | 1.0 |
| chlorofluorocarbon–217 (CFC–217) | 1.0 |
| halon–1211 | 3.0 |
| halon–1301 | 10.0 |
| halon–2402 | 6.0 |
| carbon tetrachloride | 1.1 |
| methyl chloroform | 0.1 |
| hydrochlorofluorocarbon–22 (HCFC–22) | 0.05 |
| hydrochlorofluorocarbon–123 (HCFC–123) | 0.02 |

| Substance | Ozone-depletion potential |
|---|---|
| hydrochlorofluorocarbon–124 (HCFC–124) | 0.02 |
| hydrochlorofluorocarbon–141(b) (HCFC–141(b)) | 0.1 |
| hydrochlorofluorocarbon–142(b) (HCFC–142(b)) | 0.06 |

Where the ozone-depletion potential of a substance is specified in the Montreal Protocol, the ozone-depletion potential specified for that substance under this section shall be consistent with the Montreal Protocol.

(July 14, 1955, c. 360, Title VI, § 602, as added Nov. 15, 1990, Pub.L. 101–549, Title VI, § 602(a), 104 Stat. 2650.)

1 So in original. Probably should be section "7671f".

### HISTORICAL AND STATUTORY NOTES

**Effective and Applicability Provisions**

1990 Acts

Section effective Nov. 15, 1990, except as otherwise provided, see section 711(b) of Pub.L. 101–549, set out as a note under section 7401 of this title.

**Savings Provisions**

Suits, actions or proceedings commenced under this chapter as in effect prior to Nov. 15, 1990, not to abate by reason of the taking effect of amendments by Pub.L. 101–549, except as otherwise provided for, see section 711(a) of Pub.L. 101–549, set out as a note under section 7401 of this title.

## § 7671b. Monitoring and reporting requirements

[CAA § 603]

**(a) Regulations**

Within 270 days after November 15, 1990, the Administrator shall amend the regulations of the Administrator in effect on such date regarding monitoring and reporting of class I and class II substances. Such amendments shall conform to the requirements of this section. The amended regulations shall include requirements with respect to the time and manner of monitoring and reporting as required under this section.

**(b) Production, import, and export level reports**

On a quarterly basis, or such other basis (not less than annually) as determined by the Administrator, each person who produced, imported, or exported a class I or class II substance shall file a report with the Administrator setting forth the amount of the substance that such person produced, imported, and exported during the preceding reporting period. Each such report shall be signed and attested by a responsible officer. No such report shall be required from a person after April 1 of the calendar year after such person permanently ceases production, importation, and exportation of the substance and so notifies the Administrator in writing.

**(c) Baseline reports for class I substances**

Unless such information has previously been reported to the Administrator, on the date on which the first report under subsection (b) of this section is required to be filed, each person who produced, imported, or exported a class I substance (other than a substance added to the list of class I substances after the publication of the initial list of such substances under this section) shall file a report with the Administrator setting forth the amount of such substance that such person produced, imported, and exported during the baseline year. In the case of a substance added to the list of class I substances after publication of the initial list of such substances under this section, the regulations shall require that each person who produced, imported, or exported such substance shall file a report with the Administrator within 180 days after the date on which such substance is added to the list, setting forth the amount of the substance that such person produced, imported, and exported in the baseline year.

**(d) Monitoring and reports to Congress**

(1) The Administrator shall monitor and, not less often than every 3 years following November 15, 1990, submit a report to Congress on the production, use and consumption of class I and class II substances. Such report shall include data on domestic production, use and consumption, and an estimate of worldwide production, use and consumption of such substances. Not less frequently than every 6 years the Administrator shall report to Congress on the environmental and economic effects of any stratospheric ozone depletion.

(2) The Administrators of the National Aeronautics and Space Administration and the National Oceanic and Atmospheric Administration shall monitor, and not less often than every 3 years following November 15, 1990, submit a report to Congress on the current average tropospheric concentration of chlorine and bromine and on the level of stratospheric ozone depletion. Such reports shall include updated projections of—

(A) peak chlorine loading;

(B) the rate at which the atmospheric abundance of chlorine is projected to decrease after the year 2000; and

(C) the date by which the atmospheric abundance of chlorine is projected to return to a level of two parts per billion.

Such updated projections shall be made on the basis of current international and domestic controls on substances covered by this subchapter as well as on the basis of such controls supplemented by a year 2000 global phase out of all halocarbon emissions (the base case). It is the purpose of the Congress through the provisions of this section to monitor closely the production and consumption of class II substances to assure that the production and consumption of such substances will not:

(i) increase significantly the peak chlorine loading that is projected to occur under the base case established for purposes of this section;

(ii) reduce significantly the rate at which the atmospheric abundance of chlorine is projected to decrease under the base case; or

(iii) delay the date by which the average atmospheric concentration of chlorine is projected under the base case to return to a level of two parts per billion.

**(e) Technology status report in 2015**

The Administrator shall review, on a periodic basis, the progress being made in the development of alternative systems or products necessary to manufacture and operate appliances without class II substances. If the Administrator finds, after notice and opportunity for public comment, that as a result of technological development problems, the development of such alternative systems or products will not occur within the time necessary to provide for the manufacture of such equipment without such substances prior to the applicable deadlines under section 7671d of this title, the Administrator shall, not later than January 1, 2015, so inform the Congress.

**(f) Emergency report**

If, in consultation with the Administrators of the National Aeronautics and Space Administration and the National Oceanic and Atmospheric Administration, and after notice and opportunity for public comment, the Administrator determines that the global production, consumption, and use of class II substances are projected to contribute to an atmospheric chlorine loading in excess of the base case projections by more than 5/10ths parts per billion, the Administrator shall so inform the Congress immediately. The determination referred to in the preceding sentence shall be based on the monitoring under subsection (d) of this section and updated not less often than every 3 years.

(July 14, 1955, c. 360, Title VI, § 603, as added Nov. 15, 1990, Pub.L. 101–549, Title VI, § 602(a), 104 Stat. 2653.)

## HISTORICAL AND STATUTORY NOTES

**Effective and Applicability Provisions**

1990 Acts

Section effective Nov. 15, 1990, except as otherwise provided, see section 711(b) of Pub.L. 101–549, set out as a note under section 7401 of this title.

**Savings Provisions**

Suits, actions or proceedings commenced under this chapter as in effect prior to Nov. 15, 1990, not to abate by reason of the taking effect of amendments by Pub.L. 101–549, except as otherwise provided for, see section 711(a) of Pub.L. 101–549, set out as a note under section 7401 of this title.

**Methane Studies**

Section 603 of Pub.L. 101–549 provided that:

"**(a) Economically justified actions.**—Not later than 2 years after enactment of this Act [Nov. 15, 1990], the Administrator shall prepare and submit a report to the Congress that identifies activities, substances, processes, or combinations thereof that could reduce methane emissions and that are economically and technologically justified with and without consideration of environmental benefit.

"**(b) Domestic methane source inventory and control.**—Not later than 2 years after the enactment of this Act [Nov. 15, 1990], the Administrator, in consultation and coordination with the Secretary of Energy and the Secretary of Agriculture, shall prepare and submit to the Congress reports on each of the following:

"(1) Methane emissions associated with natural gas extraction, transportation, distribution, storage, and use. Such report shall include an inventory of methane emissions associated with such activities within the United States. Such emissions include, but are not limited to, accidental and intentional releases from natural gas and oil wells, pipelines, processing facilities, and gas burners. The report shall also include an inventory of methane generation with such activities.

"(2) Methane emissions associated with coal extraction, transportation, distribution, storage, and use. Such report shall include an inventory of methane emissions associated with such activities within the United States. Such emissions include, but are not limited to, accidental and intentional releases from mining shafts, degasification wells, gas recovery wells and equipment, and from the processing and use of coal. The report shall also include an inventory of methane generation with such activities.

"(3) Methane emissions associated with management of solid waste. Such report shall include an inventory of methane emissions associated with all forms of waste management in the United States, including storage, treatment, and disposal.

"(4) Methane emissions associated with agriculture. Such report shall include an inventory of methane emissions associated with rice and livestock production in the United States.

"(5) Methane emissions associated with biomass burning. Such report shall include an inventory of methane emissions associated with the intentional burning of agricultural wastes, wood, grasslands, and forests.

"(6) Other methane emissions associated with human activities. Such report shall identify and inventory other domestic sources of methane emissions that are deemed by the Administrator and other such agencies to be significant.

"**(c) International studies.**—

"**(1) Methane emissions.**—Not later than 2 years after the enactment of this Act [Nov. 15, 1990], the Administrator shall prepare and submit to the Congress a report on methane emissions from countries other than the United States. Such report shall include inventories of methane emissions associated with the activities listed in subsection (b).

"(2) **Preventing increases in methane concentrations.**—Not later than 2 years after the enactment of this Act [Nov. 15, 1990], the Administrator shall prepare and submit to the Congress a report that analyzes the potential for preventing an increase in atmospheric concentrations of methane from activities and sources in other countries. Such report shall identify and evaluate the technical options for reducing methane emission from each of the activities listed in subsection (b), as well as other activities or sources that are deemed by the Administrator in consultation with other relevant Federal agencies and departments to be significant and shall include an evaluation of costs. The report shall identify the emissions reductions that would need to be achieved to prevent increasing atmospheric concentrations of methane. The report shall also identify technology transfer programs that could promote methane emissions reductions in lesser developed countries.

**"(d) Natural sources.**—Not later than 2 years after the enactment of this Act [Nov. 15, 1990], the Administrator shall prepare and submit to the Congress a report on—

"(1) methane emissions from biogenic sources such as (A) tropical, temperate, and subarctic forests, (B) tundra, and (C) freshwater and saltwater wetlands; and

"(2) the changes in methane emissions from biogenic sources that may occur as a result of potential increases in temperatures and atmospheric concentrations of carbon dioxide.

**"(e) Study of measures to limit growth in methane concentrations.**—Not later than 2 years after the completion of the studies in subsections (b), (c), and (d), the Administrator shall prepare and submit to the Congress a report that presents options outlining measures that could be implemented to stop or reduce the growth in atmospheric concentrations of methane from sources within the United States referred to in paragraphs (1) through (6) of subsection (b). This study shall identify and evaluate the technical options for reducing methane emissions from each of the activities listed in subsection (b), as well as other activities or sources deemed by such agencies to be significant, and shall include an evaluation of costs, technology, safety, energy, and other factors. The study shall be based on the other studies under this section. The study shall also identify programs of the United States and international lending agencies that could be used to induce lesser developed countries to undertake measures that will reduce methane emissions and the resource needs of such programs.

**"(f) Information gathering.**—In carrying out the studies under this section, the provisions and requirements of section 114 of the Clean Air Act [section 7414 of this title] shall be available for purposes of obtaining information to carry out such studies.

**"(g) Consultation and coordination.**—In preparing the studies under this section the Administrator shall consult and coordinate with the Secretary of Energy, the Administrators of the National Aeronautics and Space Administration and the National Oceanic and Atmospheric Administration, and the heads of other relevant Federal agencies and departments. In the case of the studies under subsections (a), (b), and (e), such consultation and coordination shall include the Secretary of Agriculture."

## § 7671c. Phase-out of production and consumption of class I substances

**[CAA § 604]**

### (a) Production phase-out

Effective on January 1 of each year specified in Table 2, it shall be unlawful for any person to produce any class I substance in an annual quantity greater than the relevant percentage specified in Table 2. The percentages in Table 2 refer to a maximum allowable production as a percentage of the quantity of the substance produced by the person concerned in the baseline year.

Table 2

| Date | Carbon tetrachloride | Methyl chloroform | Other class I substances |
|---|---|---|---|
| 1991 | 100% | 100% | 85% |
| 1992 | 90% | 100% | 80% |
| 1993 | 80% | 90% | 75% |
| 1994 | 70% | 85% | 65% |
| 1995 | 15% | 70% | 50% |
| 1996 | 15% | 50% | 40% |
| 1997 | 15% | 50% | 15% |
| 1998 | 15% | 50% | 15% |
| 1999 | 15% | 50% | 15% |
| 2000 | | 20% | — |
| 2001 | | 20% | — |

### (b) Termination of production of class I substances

Effective January 1, 2000 (January 1, 2002 in the case of methyl chloroform), it shall be unlawful for any person to produce any amount of a class I substance.

### (c) Regulations regarding production and consumption of class I substances

The Administrator shall promulgate regulations within 10 months after November 15, 1990, phasing out the production of class I substances in accordance with this section and other applicable provisions of this subchapter. The Administrator shall also promulgate regulations to insure that the consumption of class I substances in the United States is phased out and terminated in accordance with the same schedule (subject to the same exceptions and other provisions) as is applicable to the phase-out and termination of production of class I substances under this subchapter.

### (d) Exceptions for essential uses of methyl chloroform, medical devices, and aviation safety

#### (1) Essential uses of methyl chloroform

Notwithstanding the termination of production required by subsection (b) of this section, during the period beginning on January 1, 2002, and ending on January 1, 2005, the Administrator, after notice and opportunity for public comment, may, to the extent such action is consistent with the Montreal Protocol, authorize the production of limited quantities of methyl chloroform solely for use in essential applications (such as nondestructive testing for metal fatigue and corrosion of existing airplane engines and airplane parts susceptible to metal fatigue) for which no safe and effective substitute is available. Notwithstanding this paragraph, the authority to produce methyl chloroform for use in medical devices shall be provided in accordance with paragraph (2).

**(2) Medical devices**

Notwithstanding the termination of production required by subsection (b) of this section, the Administrator, after notice and opportunity for public comment, shall, to the extent such action is consistent with the Montreal Protocol, authorize the production of limited quantities of class I substances solely for use in medical devices if such authorization is determined by the Commissioner, in consultation with the Administrator, to be necessary for use in medical devices.

**(3) Aviation safety**

(A) Notwithstanding the termination of production required by subsection (b) of this section, the Administrator, after notice and opportunity for public comment, may, to the extent such action is consistent with the Montreal Protocol, authorize the production of limited quantities of halon–1211 (bromochlorodifluoromethane), halon–1301 (bromotrifluoromethane), and halon–2402 (dibromotetrafluoroethane) solely for purposes of aviation safety if the Administrator of the Federal Aviation Administration, in consultation with the Administrator, determines that no safe and effective substitute has been developed and that such authorization is necessary for aviation safety purposes.

(B) The Administrator of the Federal Aviation Administration shall, in consultation with the Administrator, examine whether safe and effective substitutes for methyl chloroform or alternative techniques will be available for nondestructive testing for metal fatigue and corrosion of existing airplane engines and airplane parts susceptible to metal fatigue and whether an exception for such uses of methyl chloroform under this paragraph will be necessary for purposes of airline safety after January 1, 2005 and provide a report to Congress in 1998.

**(4) Cap on certain exceptions**

Under no circumstances may the authority set forth in paragraphs (1), (2), and (3) of subsection (d) of this section be applied to authorize any person to produce a class I substance in annual quantities greater than 10 percent of that produced by such person during the baseline year.

**(5) Sanitation and food protection**

To the extent consistent with the Montreal Protocol's quarantine and pre-shipment provisions, the Administrator shall exempt the production, importation, and consumption of methyl bromide to fumigate commodities entering or leaving the United States or any State (or political subdivision thereof) for purposes of compliance with Animal and Plant Health Inspection Service requirements or with any international, Federal, State, or local sanitation or food protection standard.

**(6) Critical uses**

To the extent consistent with the Montreal Protocol, the Administrator, after notice and the opportunity for public comment, and after consultation with other departments or instrumentalities of the Federal Government having regulatory authority related to methyl bromide, including the Secretary of Agriculture, may exempt the production, importation, and consumption of methyl bromide for critical uses.

**(e) Developing countries**

**(1) Exception**

Notwithstanding the phase-out and termination of production required under subsections (a) and (b) of this section, the Administrator, after notice and opportunity for public comment, may, consistent with the Montreal Protocol, authorize the production of limited quantities of a class I substance in excess of the amounts otherwise allowable under subsection (a) or (b) of this section, or both, solely for export to, and use in, developing countries that are Parties to the Montreal Protocol and are operating under article 5 of such Protocol. Any production authorized under this paragraph shall be solely for purposes of satisfying the basic domestic needs of such countries.

**(2) Cap on exception**

(A) Under no circumstances may the authority set forth in paragraph (1) be applied to authorize any person to produce a class I substance in any year for which a production percentage is specified in Table 2 of subsection (a) of this section in an annual quantity greater than the specified percentage, plus an amount equal to 10 percent of the amount produced by such person in the baseline year.

(B) Under no circumstances may the authority set forth in paragraph (1) be applied to authorize any person to produce a class I substance in the applicable termination year referred to in subsection (b) of this section, or in any year thereafter, in an annual quantity greater than 15 percent of the baseline quantity of such substance produced by such person.

(C) An exception authorized under this subsection shall terminate no later than January 1, 2010 (2012 in the case of methyl chloroform).

**(3) Methyl bromide**

Notwithstanding the phaseout and termination of production of methyl bromide pursuant to subsection (h) of this section, the Administrator may, consistent with the Montreal Protocol, authorize the production of limited quantities of methyl bromide, solely for use in developing countries that are Parties to the Copenhagen Amendments to the Montreal Protocol.

**(f) National security**

The President may, to the extent such action is consistent with the Montreal Protocol, issue such orders regarding production and use of CFC–114 (chlorofluorocarbon–114), halon–1211, halon–1301, and halon–2402, at any specified site or facility or on any vessel as may be necessary to protect the national security interests of the United States if the President finds that adequate substitutes are not available and that the production and use of such substance are necessary to protect such national security interest. Such orders may include, where necessary to protect such interests, an exemption from any prohibition or requirement contained in this subchapter. The President shall notify the Congress within 30 days of the issuance of an order under this paragraph providing for any such exemption. Such notification shall include a statement of the reasons for the granting of the exemption. An exemption under this paragraph shall be for a specified period which may not exceed one year. Additional exemptions may be granted, each upon the President's issuance of a new order under this paragraph. Each such additional exemption shall be for a specified period which may not exceed one year. No exemption shall be granted under this paragraph due to lack of appropriation unless the President shall have specifically requested such appropriation as a part of the budgetary process and the Congress shall have failed to make available such requested appropriation.

**(g) Fire suppression and explosion prevention**

(1) Notwithstanding the production phase-out set forth in subsection (a) of this section, the Administrator, after notice and opportunity for public comment, may, to the extent such action is consistent with the Montreal Protocol, authorize the production of limited quantities of halon–1211, halon–1301, and halon–2402 in excess of the amount otherwise permitted pursuant to the schedule under subsection (a) of this section solely for purposes of fire suppression or explosion prevention if the Administrator, in consultation with the Administrator of the United States Fire Administration, determines that no safe and effective substitute has been developed and that such authorization is necessary for fire suppression or explosion prevention purposes. The Administrator shall not authorize production under this paragraph for purposes of fire safety or explosion prevention training or testing of fire suppression or explosion prevention equipment. In no event shall the Administrator grant an exception under this paragraph that permits production after December 31, 1999.

(2) The Administrator shall periodically monitor and assess the status of efforts to obtain substitutes for the substances referred to in paragraph (1) for purposes of fire suppression or explosion prevention and the probability of such substitutes being available by December 31, 1999. The Administrator, as part of such assessment, shall consider any relevant assessments under the Montreal Protocol and the actions of the Parties pursuant to Article 2B of the Montreal Protocol in identifying essential uses and in permitting a level of production or consumption that is necessary to satisfy such uses for which no adequate alternatives are available after December 31, 1999. The Administrator shall report to Congress the results of such assessment in 1994 and again in 1998.

(3) Notwithstanding the termination of production set forth in subsection (b) of this section, the Administrator, after notice and opportunity for public comment, may, to the extent consistent with the Montreal Protocol, authorize the production of limited quantities of halon–1211, halon–1301, and halon–2402 in the period after December 31, 1999, and before December 31, 2004, solely for purposes of fire suppression or explosion prevention in association with domestic production of crude oil and natural gas energy supplies on the North Slope of Alaska, if the Administrator, in consultation with the Administrator of the United States Fire Administration, determines that no safe and effective substitute has been developed and that such authorization is necessary for fire suppression and explosion prevention purposes. The Administrator shall not authorize production under the paragraph for purposes of fire safety or explosion prevention training or testing of fire suppression or explosion prevention equipment. In no event shall the Administrator authorize under this paragraph any person to produce any such halon in an amount greater than 3 percent of that produced by such person during the baseline year.

**(h) Methyl bromide**

Notwithstanding subsections (b) and (d) of this section, the Administrator shall not terminate production of methyl bromide prior to January 1, 2005. The Administrator shall promulgate rules for reductions in, and terminate the production, importation, and consumption of, methyl bromide under a schedule that is in accordance with, but not more stringent than, the phaseout schedule of the Montreal Protocol Treaty as in effect on October 21, 1998.

(July 14, 1955, c. 360, Title VI, § 604, as added Nov. 15, 1990, Pub.L. 101–549, Title VI, § 602(a), 104 Stat. 2655, and amended Oct. 21, 1998, Pub.L. 105–277, § 101(a) [Title VII, § 764], 112 Stat. 2681–36.)

### HISTORICAL AND STATUTORY NOTES

**Effective and Applicability Provisions**

1990 Acts

Section effective Nov. 15, 1990, except as otherwise provided, see section 711(b) of Pub.L. 101–549, set out as a note under section 7401 of this title.

**Savings Provisions**

Suits, actions or proceedings commenced under this chapter as in effect prior to Nov. 15, 1990, not to abate by reason of the taking effect of amendments by Pub.L. 101–549, except as otherwise provided for, see section 711(a) of Pub.L. 101–549, set out as a note under section 7401 of this title.

## § 7671d. Phase-out of production and consumption of class II substances

**[CAA § 605]**

**(a) Restriction of use of class II substances**

Effective January 1, 2015, it shall be unlawful for any person to introduce into interstate commerce or use any class II substance unless such substance—

(1) has been used, recovered, and recycled;

(2) is used and entirely consumed (except for trace quantities) in the production of other chemicals; or

(3) is used as a refrigerant in appliances manufactured prior to January 1, 2020.

As used in this subsection, the term "refrigerant" means any class II substance used for heat transfer in a refrigerating system.

**(b) Production phase-out**

(1) Effective January 1, 2015, it shall be unlawful for any person to produce any class II substance in an annual quantity greater than the quantity of such substance produced by such person during the baseline year.

(2) Effective January 1, 2030, it shall be unlawful for any person to produce any class II substance.

**(c) Regulations regarding production and consumption of class II substances**

By December 31, 1999, the Administrator shall promulgate regulations phasing out the production, and restricting the use, of class II substances in accordance with this section, subject to any acceleration of the phase-out of production under section 7671e of this title. The Administrator shall also promulgate regulations to insure that the consumption of class II substances in the United States is phased out and terminated in accordance with the same schedule (subject to the same exceptions and other provisions) as is applicable to the phase-out and termination of production of class II substances under this subchapter.

**(d) Exceptions**

**(1) Medical devices**

**(A) In general**

Notwithstanding the termination of production required under subsection (b)(2) of this section and the restriction on use referred to in subsection (a) of this section, the Administrator, after notice and opportunity for public comment, shall, to the extent such action is consistent with the Montreal Protocol, authorize the production and use of limited quantities of class II substances solely for purposes of use in medical devices if such authorization is determined by the Commissioner, in consultation with the Administrator, to be necessary for use in medical devices.

**(B) Cap on exception**

Under no circumstances may the authority set forth in subparagraph (A) be applied to authorize any person to produce a class II substance in annual quantities greater than 10 percent of that produced by such person during the baseline year.

**(2) Developing countries**

**(A) In general**

Notwithstanding the provisions of subsection (a) or (b) of this section, the Administrator, after notice and opportunity for public comment, may authorize the production of limited quantities of a class II substance in excess of the quantities otherwise permitted under such provisions solely for export to and use in developing countries that are Parties to the Montreal Protocol, as determined by the Administrator. Any production authorized under this subsection shall be solely for purposes of satisfying the basic domestic needs of such countries.

**(B) Cap on exception**

(i) Under no circumstances may the authority set forth in subparagraph (A) be applied to authorize any person to produce a class II substance in any year following the effective date of subsection (b)(1) of this section and before the year 2030 in annual quantities greater than 110 percent of the quantity of such substance produced by such person during the baseline year.

**(ii)** Under no circumstances may the authority set forth in subparagraph (A) be applied to authorize any person to produce a class II substance in the year 2030, or any year thereafter, in an annual quantity greater than 15 percent of the quantity of such substance produced by such person during the baseline year.

**(iii)** Each exception authorized under this paragraph shall terminate no later than January 1, 2040.

(July 14, 1955, c. 360, Title VI, § 605, as added Nov. 15, 1990, Pub.L. 101–549, Title VI, § 602(a), 104 Stat. 2658.)

**HISTORICAL AND STATUTORY NOTES**

**Effective and Applicability Provisions**

1990 Acts

Section effective Nov. 15, 1990, except as otherwise provided, see section 711(b) of Pub.L. 101–549, set out as a note under section 7401 of this title.

**Savings Provisions**

Suits, actions or proceedings commenced under this chapter as in effect prior to Nov. 15, 1990, not to abate by reason of the taking effect of amendments by Pub.L. 101–549, except as otherwise provided for, see section 711(a) of Pub.L. 101–549, set out as a note under section 7401 of this title.

## § 7671e. Accelerated schedule

**[CAA § 606]**

**(a) In general**

The Administrator shall promulgate regulations, after notice and opportunity for public comment, which establish a schedule for phasing out the production and consumption of class I and class II substances (or use of class II substances) that is more stringent than set forth in section 7671c or 7671d of this title, or both, if—

(1) based on an assessment of credible current scientific information (including any assessment under the Montreal Protocol) regarding harmful effects on the stratospheric ozone layer associated with a class I or class II substance, the Administrator determines that such more stringent schedule may be necessary to protect human health and the environment against such effects,

(2) based on the availability of substitutes for listed substances, the Administrator determines that such more stringent schedule is practicable, taking into account technological achievability, safety, and other relevant factors, or

(3) the Montreal Protocol is modified to include a schedule to control or reduce production, consumption, or use of any substance more rapidly than the applicable schedule under this subchapter.

In making any determination under paragraphs (1) and (2), the Administrator shall consider the status of the period remaining under the applicable schedule under this subchapter.

**(b) Petition**

Any person may petition the Administrator to promulgate regulations under this section. The Administrator shall grant or deny the petition within 180 days after receipt of any such petition. If the Administrator denies the petition, the Administrator shall publish an explanation of why the petition was denied. If the Administrator grants such petition, such final regulations shall be promulgated within 1 year. Any petition under this subsection shall include a showing by the petitioner that there are data adequate to support the petition. If the Administrator determines that information is not sufficient to make a determination under this subsection, the Administrator shall use any authority available to the Administrator, under any law administered by the Administrator, to acquire such information.

(July 14, 1955, c. 360, Title VI, § 606, as added Nov. 15, 1990, Pub.L. 101–549, Title VI, § 602(a), 104 Stat. 2660.)

**HISTORICAL AND STATUTORY NOTES**

**Effective and Applicability Provisions**

1990 Acts

Section effective Nov. 15, 1990, except as otherwise provided, see section 711(b) of Pub.L. 101–549, set out as a note under section 7401 of this title.

**Savings Provisions**

Suits, actions or proceedings commenced under this chapter as in effect prior to Nov. 15, 1990, not to abate by reason of the taking effect of amendments by Pub.L. 101–549, except as otherwise provided for, see section 711(a) of Pub.L. 101–549, set out as a note under section 7401 of this title.

## § 7671f. Exchange authority

**[CAA § 607]**

**(a) Transfers**

The Administrator shall, within 10 months after November 15, 1990, promulgate rules under this subchapter providing for the issuance of allowances for the production of class I and II substances in accordance with the requirements of this subchapter and governing the transfer of such allowances. Such rules shall insure that the transactions under the authority of this section will result in greater total reductions in the production in each year of class I and class II substances than would occur in that year in the absence of such transactions.

**(b) Interpollutant transfers**

(1) The rules under this section shall permit a production allowance for a substance for any year to be transferred for a production allowance for another

substance for the same year on an ozone depletion weighted basis.

(2) Allowances for substances in each group of class I substances (as listed pursuant to section 7671a of this title) may only be transferred for allowances for other substances in the same Group.

(3) The Administrator shall, as appropriate, establish groups of class II substances for trading purposes and assign class II substances to such groups. In the case of class II substances, allowances may only be transferred for allowances for other class II substances that are in the same Group.

**(c) Trades with other persons**

The rules under this section shall permit 2 or more persons to transfer production allowances (including interpollutant transfers which meet the requirements of subsections (a) and (b) of this section) if the transferor of such allowances will be subject, under such rules, to an enforceable and quantifiable reduction in annual production which—

(1) exceeds the reduction otherwise applicable to the transferor under this subchapter,

(2) exceeds the production allowances transferred to the transferee, and

(3) would not have occurred in the absence of such transaction.

**(d) Consumption**

The rules under this section shall also provide for the issuance of consumption allowances in accordance with the requirements of this subchapter and for the trading of such allowances in the same manner as is applicable under this section to the trading of production allowances under this section.

(July 14, 1955, c. 360, Title VI, § 607, as added Nov. 15, 1990, Pub.L. 101–549, Title VI, § 602(a), 104 Stat. 2660.)

### HISTORICAL AND STATUTORY NOTES

**Effective and Applicability Provisions**

1990 Acts

Section effective Nov. 15, 1990, except as otherwise provided, see section 711(b) of Pub.L. 101–549, set out as a note under section 7401 of this title.

**Savings Provisions**

Suits, actions or proceedings commenced under this chapter as in effect prior to Nov. 15, 1990, not to abate by reason of the taking effect of amendments by Pub.L. 101–549, except as otherwise provided for, see section 711(a) of Pub.L. 101–549, set out as a note under section 7401 of this title.

## § 7671g. National recycling and emission reduction program

[CAA § 608]

**(a) In general**

(1) The Administrator shall, by not later than January 1, 1992, promulgate regulations establishing standards and requirements regarding the use and disposal of class I substances during the service, repair, or disposal of appliances and industrial process refrigeration. Such standards and requirements shall become effective not later than July 1, 1992.

(2) The Administrator shall, within 4 years after November 15, 1990, promulgate regulations establishing standards and requirements regarding use and disposal of class I and II substances not covered by paragraph (1), including the use and disposal of class II substances during service, repair, or disposal of appliances and industrial process refrigeration. Such standards and requirements shall become effective not later than 12 months after promulgation of the regulations.

(3) The regulations under this subsection shall include requirements that—

(A) reduce the use and emission of such substances to the lowest achievable level, and

(B) maximize the recapture and recycling of such substances.

Such regulations may include requirements to use alternative substances (including substances which are not class I or class II substances) or to minimize use of class I or class II substances, or to promote the use of safe alternatives pursuant to section 7671k of this title or any combination of the foregoing.

**(b) Safe disposal**

The regulations under subsection (a) of this section shall establish standards and requirements for the safe disposal of class I and II substances. Such regulations shall include each of the following—

(1) Requirements that class I or class II substances contained in bulk in appliances, machines or other goods shall be removed from each such appliance, machine or other good prior to the disposal of such items or their delivery for recycling.

(2) Requirements that any appliance, machine or other good containing a class I or class II substance in bulk shall not be manufactured, sold, or distributed in interstate commerce or offered for sale or distribution in interstate commerce unless it is equipped with a servicing aperture or an equally effective design feature which will facilitate the recapture of such substance during service and repair or disposal of such item.

(3) Requirements that any product in which a class I or class II substance is incorporated so as to constitute an inherent element of such product shall be disposed of in a manner that reduces, to the maximum extent practicable, the release of such substance into the environment. If the Administra-

tor determines that the application of this paragraph to any product would result in producing only insignificant environmental benefits, the Administrator shall include in such regulations an exception for such product.

**(c) Prohibitions**

(1) Effective July 1, 1992, it shall be unlawful for any person, in the course of maintaining, servicing, repairing, or disposing of an appliance or industrial process refrigeration, to knowingly vent or otherwise knowingly release or dispose of any class I or class II substance used as a refrigerant in such appliance (or industrial process refrigeration) in a manner which permits such substance to enter the environment. De minimis releases associated with good faith attempts to recapture and recycle or safely dispose of any such substance shall not be subject to the prohibition set forth in the preceding sentence.

(2) Effective 5 years after November 15, 1990, paragraph (1) shall also apply to the venting, release, or disposal of any substitute substance for a class I or class II substance by any person maintaining, servicing, repairing, or disposing of an appliance or industrial process refrigeration which contains and uses as a refrigerant any such substance, unless the Administrator determines that venting, releasing, or disposing of such substance does not pose a threat to the environment. For purposes of this paragraph, the term "appliance" includes any device which contains and uses as a refrigerant a substitute substance and which is used for household or commercial purposes, including any air conditioner, refrigerator, chiller, or freezer.

(July 14, 1955, c. 360, Title VI, § 608, as added Nov. 15, 1990, Pub.L. 101–549, Title VI, § 602(a), 104 Stat. 2661.)

### HISTORICAL AND STATUTORY NOTES

**Effective and Applicability Provisions**

1990 Acts

Section effective Nov. 15, 1990, except as otherwise provided, see section 711(b) of Pub.L. 101–549, set out as a note under section 7401 of this title.

**Savings Provisions**

Suits, actions or proceedings commenced under this chapter as in effect prior to Nov. 15, 1990, not to abate by reason of the taking effect of amendments by Pub.L. 101–549, except as otherwise provided for, see section 711(a) of Pub.L. 101–549, set out as a note under section 7401 of this title.

## § 7671h. Servicing of motor vehicle air conditioners

[CAA § 609]

**(a) Regulations**

Within 1 year after November 15, 1990, the Administrator shall promulgate regulations in accordance with this section establishing standards and requirements regarding the servicing of motor vehicle air conditioners.

**(b) Definitions**

As used in this section—

(1) The term "refrigerant" means any class I or class II substance used in a motor vehicle air conditioner. Effective 5 years after November 15, 1990, the term "refrigerant" shall also include any substitute substance.

(2)(A) The term "approved refrigerant recycling equipment" means equipment certified by the Administrator (or an independent standards testing organization approved by the Administrator) to meet the standards established by the Administrator and applicable to equipment for the extraction and reclamation of refrigerant from motor vehicle air conditioners. Such standards shall, at a minimum, be at least as stringent as the standards of the Society of Automotive Engineers in effect as of November 15, 1990, and applicable to such equipment (SAE standard J–1990).

(B) Equipment purchased before the proposal of regulations under this section shall be considered certified if it is substantially identical to equipment certified as provided in subparagraph (A).

(3) The term "properly using" means, with respect to approved refrigerant recycling equipment, using such equipment in conformity with standards established by the Administrator and applicable to the use of such equipment. Such standards shall, at a minimum, be at least as stringent as the standards of the Society of Automotive Engineers in effect as of November 15, 1990, and applicable to the use of such equipment (SAE standard J–1989).

(4) The term "properly trained and certified" means training and certification in the proper use of approved refrigerant recycling equipment for motor vehicle air conditioners in conformity with standards established by the Administrator and applicable to the performance of service on motor vehicle air conditioners. Such standards shall, at a minimum, be at least as stringent as specified, as of November 15, 1990, in SAE standard J–1989 under the certification program of the National Institute for Automotive Service Excellence (ASE) or under a similar program such as the training and certification program of the Mobile Air Conditioning Society (MACS).

**(c) Servicing motor vehicle air conditioners**

Effective January 1, 1992, no person repairing or servicing motor vehicles for consideration may perform any service on a motor vehicle air conditioner involving the refrigerant for such air conditioner without properly using approved refrigerant recycling equipment and no such person may perform such service unless such person has been properly trained and certified. The requirements of the previous sentence shall not apply until January 1, 1993 in the case of a person repairing or servicing motor vehicles for consideration at an entity which performed service on fewer than 100 motor vehicle air conditioners during calendar year 1990 and if such person so certifies, pursuant to subsection (d)(2) of this section, to the Administrator by January 1, 1992.

**(d) Certification**

(1) Effective 2 years after November 15, 1990, each person performing service on motor vehicle air conditioners for consideration shall certify to the Administrator either—

(A) that such person has acquired, and is properly using, approved refrigerant recycling equipment in service on motor vehicle air conditioners involving refrigerant and that each individual authorized by such person to perform such service is properly trained and certified; or

(B) that such person is performing such service at an entity which serviced fewer than 100 motor vehicle air conditioners in 1991.

(2) Effective January 1, 1993, each person who certified under paragraph (1)(B) shall submit a certification under paragraph (1)(A).

(3) Each certification under this subsection shall contain the name and address of the person certifying under this subsection and the serial number of each unit of approved recycling equipment acquired by such person and shall be signed and attested by the owner or another responsible officer. Certifications under paragraph (1)(A) may be made by submitting the required information to the Administrator on a standard form provided by the manufacturer of certified refrigerant recycling equipment.

**(e) Small containers of class I or class II substances**

Effective 2 years after November 15, 1990, it shall be unlawful for any person to sell or distribute, or offer for sale or distribution, in interstate commerce to any person (other than a person performing service for consideration on motor vehicle air-conditioning systems in compliance with this section) any class I or class II substance that is suitable for use as a refrigerant in a motor vehicle air-conditioning system and that is in a container which contains less than 20 pounds of such refrigerant.

(July 14, 1955, c. 360, Title VI, § 609, as added Nov. 15, 1990, Pub.L. 101–549, Title VI, § 602(a), 104 Stat. 2662.)

**HISTORICAL AND STATUTORY NOTES**

**Effective and Applicability Provisions**

1990 Acts

Section effective Nov. 15, 1990, except as otherwise provided, see section 711(b) of Pub.L. 101–549, set out as a note under section 7401 of this title.

**Savings Provisions**

Suits, actions or proceedings commenced under this chapter as in effect prior to Nov. 15, 1990, not to abate by reason of the taking effect of amendments by Pub.L. 101–549, except as otherwise provided for, see section 711(a) of Pub.L. 101–549, set out as a note under section 7401 of this title.

## § 7671i. Nonessential products containing chlorofluorocarbons

**[CAA § 610]**

**(a) Regulations**

The Administrator shall promulgate regulations to carry out the requirements of this section within 1 year after November 15, 1990.

**(b) Nonessential products**

The regulations under this section shall identify nonessential products that release class I substances into the environment (including any release occurring during manufacture, use, storage, or disposal) and prohibit any person from selling or distributing any such product, or offering any such product for sale or distribution, in interstate commerce. At a minimum, such prohibition shall apply to—

(1) chlorofluorocarbon-propelled plastic party streamers and noise horns,

(2) chlorofluorocarbon-containing cleaning fluids for noncommercial electronic and photographic equipment, and

(3) other consumer products that are determined by the Administrator—

(A) to release class I substances into the environment (including any release occurring during manufacture, use, storage, or disposal), and

(B) to be nonessential.

In determining whether a product is nonessential, the Administrator shall consider the purpose or intended use of the product, the technological availability of substitutes for such product and for such class I substance, safety, health, and other relevant factors.

**(c) Effective date**

Effective 24 months after November 15, 1990, it shall be unlawful for any person to sell or distribute, or offer for sale or distribution, in interstate commerce any nonessential product to which regulations under subsection (a) of this section implementing subsection (b) of this section are applicable.

**(d) Other products**

(1) Effective January 1, 1994, it shall be unlawful for any person to sell or distribute, or offer for sale or distribution, in interstate commerce—

(A) any aerosol product or other pressurized dispenser which contains a class II substance; or

(B) any plastic foam product which contains, or is manufactured with, a class II substance.

(2) The Administrator is authorized to grant exceptions from the prohibition under subparagraph (A) of paragraph (1) where—

(A) the use of the aerosol product or pressurized dispenser is determined by the Administrator to be essential as a result of flammability or worker safety concerns, and

(B) the only available alternative to use of a class II substance is use of a class I substance which legally could be substituted for such class II substance.

(3) Subparagraph (B) of paragraph (1) shall not apply to—

(A) a foam insulation product, or

(B) an integral skin, rigid, or semi-rigid foam utilized to provide for motor vehicle safety in accordance with Federal Motor Vehicle Safety Standards where no adequate substitute substance (other than a class I or class II substance) is practicable for effectively meeting such Standards.

**(e) Medical devices**

Nothing in this section shall apply to any medical device as defined in section 7671(8) of this title.

(July 14, 1955, c. 360, Title VI, § 610, as added Nov. 15, 1990, Pub.L. 101–549, Title VI, § 602(a), 104 Stat. 2664.)

**HISTORICAL AND STATUTORY NOTES**

**Effective and Applicability Provisions**

1990 Acts

Section effective Nov. 15, 1990, except as otherwise provided, see section 711(b) of Pub.L. 101–549, set out as a note under section 7401 of this title.

**Savings Provisions**

Suits, actions or proceedings commenced under this chapter as in effect prior to Nov. 15, 1990, not to abate by reason of the taking effect of amendments by Pub.L. 101–549, except as otherwise provided for, see section 711(a) of Pub.L. 101–549, set out as a note under section 7401 of this title.

## § 7671j. Labeling

**[CAA § 611]**

**(a) Regulations**

The Administrator shall promulgate regulations to implement the labeling requirements of this section within 18 months after November 15, 1990, after notice and opportunity for public comment.

**(b) Containers containing class I or class II substances and products containing class I substances**

Effective 30 months after November 15, 1990, no container in which a class I or class II substance is stored or transported, and no product containing a class I substance, shall be introduced into interstate commerce unless it bears a clearly legible and conspicuous label stating:

"Warning: Contains [insert name of substance], a substance which harms public health and environment by destroying ozone in the upper atmosphere".

**(c) Products containing class II substances**

(1) After 30 months after November 15, 1990, and before January 1, 2015, no product containing a class II substance shall be introduced into interstate commerce unless it bears the label referred to in subsection (b) of this section if the Administrator determines, after notice and opportunity for public comment, that there are substitute products or manufacturing processes (A) that do not rely on the use of such class II substance, (B) that reduce the overall risk to human health and the environment, and (C) that are currently or potentially available.

(2) Effective January 1, 2015, the requirements of subsection (b) of this section shall apply to all products containing a class II substance.

**(d) Products manufactured with class I and class II substances**

(1) In the case of a class II substance, after 30 months after November 15, 1990, and before January 1, 2015, if the Administrator, after notice and opportunity for public comment, makes the determination referred to in subsection (c) of this section with respect to a product manufactured with a process that uses such class II substance, no such product shall be introduced into interstate commerce unless it bears a clearly legible and conspicuous label stating:

"Warning: Manufactured with [insert name of substance], a substance which harms public health and environment by destroying ozone in the upper atmosphere" [1]

(2) In the case of a class I substance, effective 30 months after November 15, 1990, and before January 1, 2015, the labeling requirements of this subsection shall apply to all products manufactured with a process that uses such class I substance unless the Administrator determines that there are no substitute products or manufacturing processes that (A) do not rely on the use of such class I substance, (B) reduce the overall risk to human health and the environment, and (C) are currently or potentially available.

**(e) Petitions**

(1) Any person may, at any time after 18 months after November 15, 1990, petition the Administrator to apply the requirements of this section to a product

containing a class II substance or a product manufactured with a class I or II substance which is not otherwise subject to such requirements. Within 180 days after receiving such petition, the Administrator shall, pursuant to the criteria set forth in subsection (c) of this section, either propose to apply the requirements of this section to such product or publish an explanation of the petition denial. If the Administrator proposes to apply such requirements to such product, the Administrator shall, by rule, render a final determination pursuant to such criteria within 1 year after receiving such petition.

(2) Any petition under this paragaph[2] shall include a showing by the petitioner that there are data on the product adequate to support the petition.

(3) If the Administrator determines that information on the product is not sufficient to make the required determination the Administrator shall use any authority available to the Administrator under any law administered by the Administrator to acquire such information.

(4) In the case of a product determined by the Administrator, upon petition or on the Administrator's own motion, to be subject to the requirements of this section, the Administrator shall establish an effective date for such requirements. The effective date shall be 1 year after such determination or 30 months after November 15, 1990, whichever is later.

(5) Effective January 1, 2015, the labeling requirements of this subsection[3] shall apply to all products manufactured with a process that uses a class I or class II substance.

**(f) Relationship to other law**

(1) The labeling requirements of this section shall not constitute, in whole or part, a defense to liability or a cause for reduction in damages in any suit, whether civil or criminal, brought under any law, whether Federal or State, other than a suit for failure to comply with the labeling requirements of this section.

(2) No other approval of such label by the Administrator under any other law administered by the Administrator shall be required with respect to the labeling requirements of this section.

(July 14, 1955, c. 360, Title VI, § 611, as added Nov. 15, 1990, Pub.L. 101–549, Title VI, § 602(a), 104 Stat. 2665.)

1 So in original. Probably should be followed by a period.

2 So in original. Probably should be "paragraph".

3 So in original. Probably should be "section".

## HISTORICAL AND STATUTORY NOTES

**Effective and Applicability Provisions**

1990 Acts

Section effective Nov. 15, 1990, except as otherwise provided, see section 711(b) of Pub.L. 101–549, set out as a note under section 7401 of this title.

**Savings Provisions**

Suits, actions or proceedings commenced under this chapter as in effect prior to Nov. 15, 1990, not to abate by reason of the taking effect of amendments by Pub.L. 101–549, except as otherwise provided for, see section 711(a) of Pub.L. 101–549, set out as a note under section 7401 of this title.

## § 7671k. Safe alternatives policy

**[CAA § 612]**

**(a) Policy**

To the maximum extent practicable, class I and class II substances shall be replaced by chemicals, product substitutes, or alternative manufacturing processes that reduce overall risks to human health and the environment.

**(b) Reviews and reports**

The Administrator shall—

(1) in consultation and coordination with interested members of the public and the heads of relevant Federal agencies and departments, recommend Federal research programs and other activities to assist in identifying alternatives to the use of class I and class II substances as refrigerants, solvents, fire retardants, foam blowing agents, and other commercial applications and in achieving a transition to such alternatives, and, where appropriate, seek to maximize the use of Federal research facilities and resources to assist users of class I and class II substances in identifying and developing alternatives to the use of such substances as refrigerants, solvents, fire retardants, foam blowing agents, and other commercial applications;

(2) examine in consultation and coordination with the Secretary of Defense and the heads of other relevant Federal agencies and departments, including the General Services Administration, Federal procurement practices with respect to class I and class II substances and recommend measures to promote the transition by the Federal Government, as expeditiously as possible, to the use of safe substitutes;

(3) specify initiatives, including appropriate intergovernmental, international, and commercial information and technology transfers, to promote the development and use of safe substitutes for class I and class II substances, including alternative chemicals, product substitutes, and alternative manufacturing processes; and

(4) maintain a public clearinghouse of alternative chemicals, product substitutes, and alternative manufacturing processes that are available for products

and manufacturing processes which use class I and class II substances.

**(c) Alternatives for class I or II substances**

Within 2 years after November 15, 1990, the Administrator shall promulgate rules under this section providing that it shall be unlawful to replace any class I or class II substance with any substitute substance which the Administrator determines may present adverse effects to human health or the environment, where the Administrator has identified an alternative to such replacement that—

(1) reduces the overall risk to human health and the environment; and

(2) is currently or potentially available.

The Administrator shall publish a list of (A) the substitutes prohibited under this subsection for specific uses and (B) the safe alternatives identified under this subsection for specific uses.

**(d) Right to petition**

Any person may petition the Administrator to add a substance to the lists under subsection (c) of this section or to remove a substance from either of such lists. The Administrator shall grant or deny the petition within 90 days after receipt of any such petition. If the Administrator denies the petition, the Administrator shall publish an explanation of why the petition was denied. If the Administrator grants such petition the Administrator shall publish such revised list within 6 months thereafter. Any petition under this subsection shall include a showing by the petitioner that there are data on the substance adequate to support the petition. If the Administrator determines that information on the substance is not sufficient to make a determination under this subsection, the Administrator shall use any authority available to the Administrator, under any law administered by the Administrator, to acquire such information.

**(e) Studies and notification**

The Administrator shall require any person who produces a chemical substitute for a class I substance to provide the Administrator with such person's unpublished health and safety studies on such substitute and require producers to notify the Administrator not less than 90 days before new or existing chemicals are introduced into interstate commerce for significant new uses as substitutes for a class I substance. This subsection shall be subject to section 7414(c) of this title.

(July 14, 1955, c. 360, Title VI, § 612, as added Nov. 15, 1990, Pub.L. 101–549, Title VI, § 602(a), 104 Stat. 2667.)

### HISTORICAL AND STATUTORY NOTES

**Effective and Applicability Provisions**

1990 Acts

Section effective Nov. 15, 1990, except as otherwise provided, see section 711(b) of Pub.L. 101–549, set out as a note under section 7401 of this title.

**Savings Provisions**

Suits, actions or proceedings commenced under this chapter as in effect prior to Nov. 15, 1990, not to abate by reason of the taking effect of amendments by Pub.L. 101–549, except as otherwise provided for, see section 711(a) of Pub.L. 101–549, set out as a note under section 7401 of this title.

## § 7671*l*. Federal procurement

**[CAA § 613]**

Not later than 18 months after November 15, 1990, the Administrator, in consultation with the Administrator of the General Services Administration and the Secretary of Defense, shall promulgate regulations requiring each department, agency, and instrumentality of the United States to conform its procurement regulations to the policies and requirements of this subchapter and to maximize the substitution of safe alternatives identified under section 7671k of this title for class I and class II substances. Not later than 30 months after November 15, 1990, each department, agency, and instrumentality of the United States shall so conform its procurement regulations and certify to the President that its regulations have been modified in accordance with this section.

(July 14, 1955, c. 360, Title VI, § 613, as added Nov. 15, 1990, Pub.L. 101–549, Title VI, § 602(a), 104 Stat. 2668.)

### HISTORICAL AND STATUTORY NOTES

**Effective and Applicability Provisions**

1990 Acts

Section effective Nov. 15, 1990, except as otherwise provided, see section 711(b) of Pub.L. 101–549, set out as a note under section 7401 of this title.

**Savings Provisions**

Suits, actions or proceedings commenced under this chapter as in effect prior to Nov. 15, 1990, not to abate by reason of the taking effect of amendments by Pub.L. 101–549, except as otherwise provided for, see section 711(a) of Pub.L. 101–549, set out as a note under section 7401 of this title.

## § 7671m. Relationship to other laws

**[CAA § 614]**

**(a) State laws**

Notwithstanding section 7416 of this title, during the 2–year period beginning on November 15, 1990, no State or local government may enforce any requirement concerning the design of any new or recalled appliance for the purpose of protecting the stratospheric ozone layer.

**(b) Montreal Protocol**

This subchapter as added by the Clean Air Act Amendments of 1990 shall be construed, interpreted, and applied as a supplement to the terms and conditions of the Montreal Protocol, as provided in Article 2, paragraph 11 thereof, and shall not be construed, interpreted, or applied to abrogate the responsibilities or obligations of the United States to implement fully the provisions of the Montreal Protocol. In the case of conflict between any provision of this subchapter and any provision of the Montreal Protocol, the more stringent provision shall govern. Nothing in this subchapter shall be construed, interpreted, or applied to affect the authority or responsibility of the Administrator to implement Article 4 of the Montreal Protocol with other appropriate agencies.

**(c) Technology export and overseas investment**

Upon November 15, 1990, the President shall—

(1) prohibit the export of technologies used to produce a class I substance;

(2) prohibit direct or indirect investments by any person in facilities designed to produce a class I or class II substance in nations that are not parties to the Montreal Protocol; and

(3) direct that no agency of the government provide bilateral or multilateral subsidies, aids, credits, guarantees, or insurance programs, for the purpose of producing any class I substance.

(July 14, 1955, c. 360, Title VI, § 614, as added Nov. 15, 1990, Pub.L. 101–549, Title VI, § 602(a), 104 Stat. 2668.)

### HISTORICAL AND STATUTORY NOTES

**References in Text**

The Clean Air Act Amendments of 1990, referred to in subsec. (b), probably means Pub.L. 101–549, Nov. 15, 1990, 104 Stat. 2399. For complete classification of this Act to the Code, see Short Title of 1990 Amendments note set out under section 7401 of this title and Tables.

**Effective and Applicability Provisions**

1990 Acts

Section effective Nov. 15, 1990, except as otherwise provided, see section 711(b) of Pub.L. 101–549, set out as a note under section 7401 of this title.

**Savings Provisions**

Suits, actions or proceedings commenced under this chapter as in effect prior to Nov. 15, 1990, not to abate by reason of the taking effect of amendments by Pub.L. 101–549, except as otherwise provided for, see section 711(a) of Pub.L. 101–549, set out as a note under section 7401 of this title.

## § 7671n. Authority of Administrator

[CAA § 615]

If, in the Administrator's judgment, any substance, practice, process, or activity may reasonably be anticipated to affect the stratosphere, especially ozone in the stratosphere, and such effect may reasonably be anticipated to endanger public health or welfare, the Administrator shall promptly promulgate regulations respecting the control of such substance, practice, process, or activity, and shall submit notice of the proposal and promulgation of such regulation to the Congress.

(July 14, 1955, c. 360, Title VI, § 615, as added Nov. 15, 1990, Pub.L. 101–549, Title VI, § 602(a), 104 Stat. 2669.)

### HISTORICAL AND STATUTORY NOTES

**Effective and Applicability Provisions**

1990 Acts

Section effective Nov. 15, 1990, except as otherwise provided, see section 711(b) of Pub.L. 101–549, set out as a note under section 7401 of this title.

**Savings Provisions**

Suits, actions or proceedings commenced under this chapter as in effect prior to Nov. 15, 1990, not to abate by reason of the taking effect of amendments by Pub.L. 101–549, except as otherwise provided for, see section 711(a) of Pub.L. 101–549, set out as a note under section 7401 of this title.

## § 7671o. Transfers among Parties to Montreal Protocol

[CAA § 616]

**(a) In general**

Consistent with the Montreal Protocol, the United States may engage in transfers with other Parties to the Protocol under the following conditions:

(1) The United States may transfer production allowances to another Party if, at the time of such transfer, the Administrator establishes revised production limits for the United States such that the aggregate national United States production permitted under the revised production limits equals the lesser of (A) the maximum production level permitted for the substance or substances concerned in the transfer year under the Protocol minus the production allowances transferred, (B) the maximum production level permitted for the substance or substances concerned in the transfer year under applicable domestic law minus the production allowances transferred, or (C) the average of the actual national production level of the substance or substances concerned for the 3 years prior to the transfer minus the production allowances transferred.

(2) The United States may acquire production allowances from another Party if, at the time of such transfer, the Administrator finds that the other Party has revised its domestic production limits in the same manner as provided with respect to transfers by the United States in this subsection.

**(b) Effect of transfers on production limits**

The Administrator is authorized to reduce the production limits established under this chapter as required as a prerequisite to transfers under paragraph (1) of subsection (a) of this section or to increase production limits established under this chapter to reflect production allowances acquired under a transfer under paragraph (2) of subsection (a) of this section.

### (c) Regulations

The Administrator shall promulgate, within 2 years after November 15, 1990, regulations to implement this section.

### (d) "Applicable domestic law" defined

In the case of the United States, the term "applicable domestic law" means this chapter.

(July 14, 1955, c. 360, Title VI, § 616, as added Nov. 15, 1990, Pub.L. 101–549, Title VI, § 602(a), 104 Stat. 2669.)

#### HISTORICAL AND STATUTORY NOTES

**Effective and Applicability Provisions**

1990 Acts

Section effective Nov. 15, 1990, except as otherwise provided, see section 711(b) of Pub.L. 101–549, set out as a note under section 7401 of this title.

**Savings Provisions**

Suits, actions or proceedings commenced under this chapter as in effect prior to Nov. 15, 1990, not to abate by reason of the taking effect of amendments by Pub.L. 101–549, except as otherwise provided for, see section 711(a) of Pub.L. 101–549, set out as a note under section 7401 of this title.

## § 7671p. International cooperation

**[CAA § 617]**

### (a) In general

The President shall undertake to enter into international agreements to foster cooperative research which complements studies and research authorized by this subchapter, and to develop standards and regulations which protect the stratosphere consistent with regulations applicable within the United States. For these purposes the President through the Secretary of State and the Assistant Secretary of State for Oceans and International Environmental and Scientific Affairs, shall negotiate multilateral treaties, conventions, resolutions, or other agreements, and formulate, present, or support proposals at the United Nations and other appropriate international forums and shall report to the Congress periodically on efforts to arrive at such agreements.

### (b) Assistance to developing countries

The Administrator, in consultation with the Secretary of State, shall support global participation in the Montreal Protocol by providing technical and financial assistance to developing countries that are Parties to the Montreal Protocol and operating under article 5 of the Protocol. There are authorized to be appropriated not more than $30,000,000 to carry out this section in fiscal years 1991, 1992 and 1993 and such sums as may be necessary in fiscal years 1994 and 1995. If China and India become Parties to the Montreal Protocol, there are authorized to be appropriated not more than an additional $30,000,000 to carry out this section in fiscal years 1991, 1992, and 1993.

(July 14, 1955, c. 360, Title VI, § 617, as added Nov. 15, 1990, Pub.L. 101–549, Title VI, § 602(a), 104 Stat. 2669.)

#### HISTORICAL AND STATUTORY NOTES

**Effective and Applicability Provisions**

1990 Acts

Section effective effect Nov. 15, 1990, except as otherwise provided, see section 711(b) of Pub.L. 101–549, set out as a note under section 7401 of this title.

**Savings Provisions**

Suits, actions or proceedings commenced under this chapter as in effect prior to Nov. 15, 1990, not to abate by reason of the taking effect of amendments by Pub.L. 101–549, except as otherwise provided for, see section 711(a) of Pub.L. 101–549, set out as a note under section 7401 of this title.

## § 7671q. Miscellaneous provisions

**[CAA § 618]**

For purposes of section 7416 of this title, requirements concerning the areas addressed by this subchapter for the protection of the stratosphere against ozone layer depletion shall be treated as requirements for the control and abatement of air pollution. For purposes of section 7418 of this title, the requirements of this subchapter and corresponding State, interstate, and local requirements, administrative authority, and process, and sanctions respecting the protection of the stratospheric ozone layer shall be treated as requirements for the control and abatement of air pollution within the meaning of section 7418 of this title.

(July 14, 1955, c. 360, Title VI, § 618, as added Nov. 15, 1990, Pub.L. 101–549, Title VI, § 602(a), 104 Stat. 2670.)

#### HISTORICAL AND STATUTORY NOTES

**Effective and Applicability Provisions**

1990 Acts

Section effective Nov. 15, 1990, except as otherwise provided, see section 711(b) of Pub.L. 101–549, set out as a note under section 7401 of this title.

**Savings Provisions**

Suits, actions or proceedings commenced under this chapter as in effect prior to Nov. 15, 1990, not to abate by reason of the taking effect of amendments by Pub.L. 101–549, except as otherwise provided for, see section 711(a) of Pub.L. 101–549, set out as a note under section 7401 of this title.

## §§ 7671r to 7700. Reserved

# ACID PRECIPITATION PROGRAM AND CARBON DIOXIDE STUDY

## ACID PRECIPITATION ACT OF 1980 [APA § ——]

**(42 U.S.C.A. §§ 8901 to 8912)**

## CHAPTER 97—ACID PRECIPITATION PROGRAM AND CARBON DIOXIDE STUDY

SUBCHAPTER I—ACID PRECIPITATION



SUBCHAPTER II—CARBON DIOXIDE



### SUBCHAPTER I—ACID PRECIPITATION

### § 8901. Introductory provisions [APA § 702]

**(a) Congressional statement of findings and purpose**

The Congress finds and declares that acid precipitation resulting from other than natural sources—

(1) could contribute to the increasing pollution of natural and man-made water systems;

(2) could adversely affect agricultural and forest crops;

(3) could adversely affect fish and wildlife and natural ecosystems generally;

(4) could contribute to corrosion of metals, wood, paint, and masonry used in construction and ornamentation of buildings and public monuments;

(5) could adversely affect public health and welfare; and

(6) could affect areas distant from sources and thus involve issues of national and international policy.

**(b) Congressional declaration of purpose**

The Congress declares that it is the purpose of this subchapter—

(1) to identify the causes and sources of acid precipitation;

(2) to evaluate the environmental, social, and economic effects of acid precipitation; and

(3) based on the results of the research program established by this subchapter and to the extent consistent with existing law, to take action to the extent necessary and practicable (A) to limit or eliminate the identified emissions which are sources of acid precipitation, and (B) to remedy or otherwise ameliorate the harmful effects which may result from acid precipitation.

**(c) "Acid precipitation" defined**

For purposes of this subchapter the term "acid precipitation" means the wet or dry deposition from the atmosphere of acid chemical compounds.

(Pub.L. 96–294, Title VII, § 702, June 30, 1980, 94 Stat. 770.)

**HISTORICAL AND STATUTORY NOTES**

**Short Title**

1980 Acts

Section 701 of Pub.L. 96–294 provided that: "This title [enacting this chapter] may be cited as the 'Acid Precipitation Act of 1980'."

### § 8902. Comprehensive ten-year program [APA § 703]

**(a) Implementation by Acid Precipitation Task Force; membership, etc., of Task Force**

There is hereby established a comprehensive ten-year program to carry out the provisions of this subchapter; and to implement this program there shall be formed an Acid Precipitation Task Force (hereafter in this subchapter referred to as the "Task Force"), of which the Secretary of Agriculture, the Administrator of the Environmental Protection Agency, and the Administrator of the National Oceanic and Atmospheric Administration shall be joint chairmen. The remaining membership of the Task Force shall consist of—

(1) one representative each from the Department of the Interior, the Department of Health and Human Services, the Department of Commerce, the

Department of Energy, the Department of State, the National Aeronautics and Space Administration, the Council on Environmental Quality, the National Science Foundation, and the Tennessee Valley Authority;

(2) the director of the Argonne National Laboratory, the director of the Brookhaven National Laboratory, the director of the Oak Ridge National Laboratory, and the director of the Pacific Northwest National Laboratory; and

(3) four additional members to be appointed by the President.

**(b) Research management consortium; membership, responsibilities, etc.**

The four National Laboratories (referred to in subsection (a)(2) of this section) shall constitute a research management consortium having the responsibilities described in section 8903(b)(13) of this title as well as the general responsibilities required by their representation on the Task Force. In carrying out these responsibilities the consortium shall report to, and act pursuant to direction from, the joint chairmen of the Task Force.

**(c) Director of research program**

The Administrator of the National Oceanic and Atmospheric Administration shall serve as the director of the research program established by this subchapter.

(Pub.L. 96–294, Title VII, § 703, June 30, 1980, 94 Stat. 771.)

## § 8903. Comprehensive research plan

[APA § 704]

**(a) Preparation by Task Force for ten-year program; purposes**

The Task Force shall prepare a comprehensive research plan for the ten-year program (hereafter in this subchapter referred to as the "comprehensive plan"), setting forth a coordinated program (1) to identify the causes and effects of acid precipitation and (2) to identify actions to limit or ameliorate the harmful effects of acid precipitation.

**(b) Scope**

The comprehensive plan shall include programs for—

(1) identifying the sources of atmospheric emissions contributing to acid precipitation;

(2) establishing and operating a nationwide long-term monitoring network to detect and measure levels of acid precipitation;

(3) research in atmospheric physics and chemistry to facilitate understanding of the processes by which atmospheric emissions are transformed into acid precipitation;

(4) development and application of atmospheric transport models to enable prediction of long-range transport of substances causing acid precipitation;

(5) defining geographic areas of impact through deposition monitoring, identification of sensitive areas, and identification of areas at risk;

(6) broadening of impact data bases through collection of existing data on water and soil chemistry and through temporal trend analysis;

(7) development of dose-response functions with respect to soils, soil organisms, aquatic and amphibious organisms, crop plants, and forest plants;

(8) establishing and carrying out system studies with respect to plant physiology, aquatic ecosystems, soil chemistry systems, soil microbial systems, and forest ecosystems;

(9) economic assessments of (A) the environmental impacts caused by acid precipitation on crops, forests, fisheries, and recreational and aesthetic resources and structures, and (B) alternative technologies to remedy or otherwise ameliorate the harmful effects which may result from acid precipitation;

(10) documenting all current Federal activities related to research on acid precipitation and ensuring that such activities are coordinated in ways that prevent needless duplication and waste of financial and technical resources;

(11) effecting cooperation in acid precipitation research and development programs, ongoing and planned, with the affected and contributing States and with other sovereign nations having a commonality of interest;

(12) subject to subsection (f)(1) of this section, management by the Task Force of financial resources committed to Federal acid precipitation research and development;

(13) subject to subsection (f)(2) of this section, management of the technical aspects of Federal acid precipitation research and development programs, including but not limited to (A) the planning and management of research and development programs and projects, (B) the selection of contractors and grantees to carry out such programs and projects, and (C) the establishment of peer review procedures to assure the quality of research and development programs and their products; and

(14) analyzing the information available regarding acid precipitation in order to formulate and present periodic recommendations to the Congress and the appropriate agencies about actions to be taken by these bodies to alleviate acid precipitation and its effects.

**(c) Procedures applicable**

The comprehensive plan—

(1) shall be submitted in draft form to the Congress, and for public review, within six months after June 30, 1980;

(2) shall be available for public comment for a period of sixty days after its submission in draft form under paragraph (1);

(3) shall be submitted in final form, incorporating such needed revisions as arise from comments received during the review period, to the President and the Congress within forty-five days after the close of the period allowed for comments on the draft comprehensive plan under paragraph (2); and

(4) shall constitute the basis on which requests for authorizations and appropriations are to be made for the nine fiscal years following the fiscal year in which the comprehensive plan is submitted in final form under paragraph (3).

**(d) Convening of Task Force**

The Task Force shall convene as necessary, but no less than twice during each fiscal year of the ten-year period covered by the comprehensive plan.

**(e) Submission of annual report to President and Congress by Task Force**

The Task Force shall submit to the President and the Congress by January 15 of each year an annual report which shall detail the progress of the research program under this subchapter and which shall contain such recommendations as are developed under subsection (b)(14) of this section.

**(f) Applicability of other statutory provisions to Task Force or plan**

(1) Subsection (b)(12) of this section shall not be construed as modifying, or as authorizing the Task Force or the comprehensive plan to modify, any provision of an appropriation Act (or any other provision of law relating to the use of appropriated funds) which specifies (A) the department or agency to which funds are appropriated, or (B) the obligations of such department or agency with respect to the use of such funds.

(2) Subsection (b)(13) of this section shall not be construed as modifying, or as authorizing the Task Force or the comprehensive plan to modify, any provision of law (relating to or involving a department or agency) which specifies (A) procurement practices for the selection, award, or management of contracts or grants by such department or agency, or (B) program activities, limitations, obligations, or responsibilities of such department or agency.

(Pub.L. 96–294, Title VII, § 704, June 30, 1980, 94 Stat. 771.)

## § 8904. Implementation of comprehensive plan; new or existing regulatory authorities, etc., not granted or modified

**[APA § 705]**

**(a)** The comprehensive plan shall be carried out during the nine fiscal years following the fiscal year in which the comprehensive plan is submitted in its final form under section 8903(c)(3) of this title; and—

(1) shall be carried out in accord with, and meet the program objectives specified in, paragraphs (1) through (11) of section 8903(b) of this title;

(2) shall be managed in accord with paragraphs (12) through (14) of such section; and

(3) shall be funded by annual appropriations, subject to annual authorizations which shall be made for each fiscal year of the program (as provided in section 8905 of this title) after the submission of the Task Force progress report which under section 8903(e) of this title is required to be submitted by January 15 of the calendar year in which such fiscal year begins.

**(b)** Nothing in this subchapter shall be deemed to grant any new regulatory authority or to limit, expand, or otherwise modify any regulatory authority under existing law, or to establish new criteria, standards, or requirements for regulation under existing law.

(Pub.L. 96–294, Title VII, § 705, June 30, 1980, 94 Stat. 773.)

## § 8905. Authorization of appropriations

**[APA § 706]**

**(a)** For the purpose of establishing the Task Force and developing the comprehensive plan under section 8903 of this title there is authorized to be appropriated to the National Oceanic and Atmospheric Administration for fiscal year 1981 the sum of $5,000,000 to remain available until expended.

**(b)** Authorizations of appropriations for the nine fiscal years following the fiscal year in which the comprehensive plan is submitted in final form under section 8903(c)(3) of this title, for purposes of carrying out the comprehensive ten-year program established by section 8902(a) of this title and implementing the comprehensive plan under sections 8903 and 8904 of this title, shall be provided on an annual basis in authorization Acts hereafter enacted; but the total sum of dollars authorized for such purposes for such nine fiscal years shall not exceed $45,000,000 except as may be specifically provided by reference to this paragraph in the authorization Acts involved.

(Pub.L. 96–294, Title VII, § 706, June 30, 1980, 94 Stat. 773.)

### § 8906. Updated data base on acid content in precipitation; new monitoring site not required

**(a) Maintenance and availability to interested parties**

(1) The National Weather Service of the National Oceanic and Atmospheric Administration shall maintain an updated data base describing the acid content in precipitation in the United States, using information from Federal acid precipitation monitoring sites.

(2) Such data shall be available to interested parties by Weather Service Forecast Offices in the National Weather Service, or through such other facilities or means as the Assistant Administrator for Weather Services, National Oceanic and Atmospheric Administration, shall direct, for those areas of the United States where and at such time as such information is presently available, within 120 days after November 17, 1988.

(3) Where other Federal agencies collect such data in the course of carrying out their statutory missions, the heads of those agencies and the Administrator of the National Oceanic and Atmospheric Administration shall arrange for the transfer of such data to the National Weather Service.

**(b) Construction of section as not requiring new monitoring sites**

Nothing in this section shall be construed to require any Federal agency to establish any new acid precipitation monitoring site.

(Pub.L. 100–685, Title IV, § 414, Nov. 17, 1988, 102 Stat. 4101.)

**HISTORICAL AND STATUTORY NOTES**

**Codifications**

Section was enacted as part of the National Aeronautics and Space Administration Authorization Act, Fiscal Year 1989, Pub.L. 100–685, and not as part of Title VII of Pub.L. 96–294, the Acid Precipitation Act of 1980, which comprises this chapter.

## SUBCHAPTER II—CARBON DIOXIDE

### § 8911. Comprehensive study of projected impact on atmospheric levels of fossil fuel combustion, etc.

[APA § 711]

**(a) Implementing agreement between Director of Office of Science and Technology and National Academy of Sciences; contents; conduct; status report by President respecting negotiations of Office**

(1) The Director of the Office of Science and Technology Policy shall enter into an agreement with the National Academy of Sciences to carry out a comprehensive study of the projected impact, on the level of carbon dioxide in the atmosphere, of fossil fuel combustion, coal-conversion and related synthetic fuels activities authorized in this Act, and other sources. Such study should also include an assessment of the economic, physical, climatic, and social effects of such impacts. In conducting such study the Office and the Academy are encouraged to work with domestic and foreign governmental and non-governmental entities, and international entities, so as to develop an international, worldwide assessment of the problems involved and to suggest such original research on any aspect of such problems as the Academy deems necessary.

(2) The President shall report to the Congress within six months after June 30, 1980, regarding the status of the Office's negotiations to implement the study required under this section.

**(b) Final report by Office and Academy; contents; prior clearance or review of work of Academy; recommendations**

A report including the major findings and recommendations resulting from the study required under this section shall be submitted to the Congress by the Office and the Academy not later than three years after June 30, 1980. The Academy contribution to such report shall not be subject to any prior clearance or review, nor shall any prior clearance or conditions be imposed on the Academy as part of the agreement made by the Office with the Academy under this section. Such report shall in any event include recommendations regarding—

(1) how a long-term program of domestic and international research, monitoring, modeling, and assessment of the causes and effects of varying levels of atmospheric carbon dioxide should be structured, including comments by the Office on the interagency requirements of such a program and comments by the Secretary of State on the international agreements required to carry out such a program;

(2) how the United States can best play a role in the development of such a long-term program on an international basis;

(3) what domestic resources should be made available to such a program;

(4) how the ongoing United States Government carbon dioxide assessment program should be modified so as to be of increased utility in providing information and recommendations of the highest possible value to government policy makers; and

(5) the need for periodic reports to the Congress in conjunction with any long-term program the Of-

fice and the Academy may recommend under this section.

**(c) Information from other Federal agencies and departments**

The Secretary of Energy, the Secretary of Commerce, the Administrator of the Environmental Protection Agency, and the Director of the National Science Foundation shall furnish to the Office or the Academy upon request any information which the Office or the Academy determines to be necessary for purposes of conducting the study required by this section.

**(d) Separate assessment by Office of interagency implementation requirements**

The Office shall provide a separate assessment of the interagency requirements to implement a comprehensive program of the type described in the third sentence of subsection (b) of this section.

(Pub.L. 96–294, Title VII, § 711, June 30, 1980, 94 Stat. 774.)

### HISTORICAL AND STATUTORY NOTES

**References in Text**

This Act, referred to in subsec. (a), is Pub.L. 96–294, June 30, 1980, 94 Stat. 611, as amended, known as the Energy Security Act. For complete distribution of such Act to this Code, see Short Title of 1980 Acts note set out under section 8801 of this title and Tables.

## § 8912. Authorization of appropriations

[APA § 712]

For the expenses of carrying out the carbon dioxide study authorized by section 8911 of this title (as determined by the Office of Science and Technology Policy) there are authorized to be appropriated such sums, not exceeding $3,000,000 in the aggregate, as may be necessary. At least 80 percent of any amounts appropriated pursuant to the preceding sentence shall be provided to the National Academy of Sciences.

(Pub.L. 96–294, Title VII, § 712, June 30, 1980, 94 Stat. 775.)

# COMPREHENSIVE ENVIRONMENTAL RESPONSE, COMPENSATION AND LIABILITY ACT

## COMPREHENSIVE ENVIRONMENTAL RESPONSE, COMPENSATION, AND LIABILITY ACT OF 1980 [CERCLA § ____]

**(42 U.S.C.A. §§ 9601 to 9675)**

## CHAPTER 103—COMPREHENSIVE ENVIRONMENTAL RESPONSE, COMPENSATION, AND LIABILITY

SUBCHAPTER I—HAZARDOUS SUBSTANCES RELEASES, LIABILITY, COMPENSATION



SUBCHAPTER II—HAZARDOUS SUBSTANCE RESPONSE REVENUE

PART A—HAZARDOUS SUBSTANCE RESPONSE TRUST FUND



PART B—POST-CLOSURE LIABILITY TRUST FUND



SUBCHAPTER III—MISCELLANEOUS PROVISIONS



SUBCHAPTER IV—POLLUTION INSURANCE



## SUBCHAPTER I—HAZARDOUS SUBSTANCES RELEASES, LIABILITY, COMPENSATION

### § 9601. Definitions

**[CERCLA § 101]**

For purpose of this subchapter—

(1) The term "act of God" means an unanticipated grave natural disaster or other natural phenomenon of an exceptional, inevitable, and irresistible character, the effects of which could not have been prevented or avoided by the exercise of due care or foresight.

(2) The term "Administrator" means the Administrator of the United States Environmental Protection Agency.

(3) The term "barrel" means forty-two United States gallons at sixty degrees Fahrenheit.

(4) The term "claim" means a demand in writing for a sum certain.

(5) The term "claimant" means any person who presents a claim for compensation under this chapter.

(6) The term "damages" means damages for injury or loss of natural resources as set forth in section 9607(a) or 9611(b) of this title.

(7) The term "drinking water supply" means any raw or finished water source that is or may be used by a public water system (as defined in the Safe Drinking Water Act [42 U.S.C.A. § 300f et seq.] ) or as drinking water by one or more individuals.

(8) The term "environment" means (A) the navigable waters, the waters of the contiguous zone, and the ocean waters of which the natural resources are under the exclusive management authority of the United States under the Magnuson-Stevens Fishery Conservation and Management Act [16 U.S.C.A. § 1801 et seq.], and (B) any other surface water, ground water, drinking water supply, land surface or subsurface strata, or ambient air within the United States or under the jurisdiction of the United States

(9) The term "facility" means (A) any building, structure, installation, equipment, pipe or pipeline (including any pipe into a sewer or publicly owned treatment works), well, pit, pond, lagoon, impoundment, ditch, landfill, storage container, motor vehicle, rolling stock, or aircraft, or (B) any site or area where a hazardous substance has been deposited, stored, disposed of, or placed, or otherwise come to be located; but does not include any consumer product in consumer use or any vessel.

(10) The term "federally permitted release" means (A) discharges in compliance with a permit under section 1342 of Title 33, (B) discharges resulting from circumstances identified and reviewed and made part of the public record with respect to a permit issued or modified under section 1342 of Title 33 and subject to a condition of such permit, (C) continuous or anticipated intermittent discharges from a point source, identified in a permit or permit application under section 1342 of Title 33, which are caused by events occurring within the scope of relevant operating or treatment systems, (D) discharges in compliance with a legally enforceable permit under section 1344 of Title 33, (E) releases in compliance with a legally enforceable final permit issued pursuant to section 3005(a) through (d) of the Solid Waste Disposal Act [42 U.S.C.A. § 6925(a) to (d) ] from a hazardous waste treatment, storage, or disposal facility when such permit specifically identifies the hazardous substances and makes such substances subject to a standard of practice, control procedure or bioassay limitation or condition, or other control on the hazardous substances in such releases, (F) any release in compliance with a legally enforceable permit issued under section 1412 of Title 33 of[1] section 1413 of Title 33, (G) any injection of fluids authorized under Federal underground injection control programs or State programs submitted for Federal approval (and not disapproved by the Administrator of the Environmental Protection Agency) pursuant to part C of the Safe Drinking Water Act [42 U.S.C.A. § 300h et seq.], (H) any emission into the air subject to a permit or control regulation under section 111 [42 U.S.C.A. § 7411], section 112 [42 U.S.C.A. § 7412], Title I part C [42 U.S.C.A. § 7470 et seq.], Title I part D [42 U.S.C.A. § 7501 et seq.], or State implementation plans submitted in accordance with section 110 of the Clean Air Act [42 U.S.C.A. § 7410] (and not disapproved by the Administrator of the Environmental Protection Agency), including any schedule or waiver granted, promulgated, or approved under these sections, (I) any injection of fluids or other materials authorized under applicable State law (i) for the purpose of stimulating or treating wells for the production of crude oil, natural gas, or water, (ii) for the purpose of secondary, tertiary, or other enhanced recovery of crude oil or natural gas, or (iii) which are brought to the surface in conjunction with the production of crude oil or natural gas and which are reinjected, (J) the introduction of any pollutant into a publicly owned treatment works when such pollutant is specified in and in compliance with applicable pretreatment standards of section 1317(b) or (c) of Title 33 and enforceable requirements in a pretreatment program submitted by a State or municipality for Federal approval under section 1342 of Title 33, and (K) any release of source, special nuclear, or byproduct material, as those terms are defined in the Atomic Energy Act of 1954 [42 U.S.C.A. § 2011 et seq.], in compliance with a legally enforceable license, permit, regulation, or order issued pursuant to the Atomic Energy Act of 1954.

(11) The term "Fund" or "Trust Fund" means the Hazardous Substance Superfund established by section 9507 of Title 26.

(12) The term "ground water" means water in a saturated zone or stratum beneath the surface of land or water.

(13) The term "guarantor" means any person, other than the owner or operator, who provides evidence of financial responsibility for an owner or operator under this chapter.

(14) The term "hazardous substance" means (A) any substance designated pursuant to section

1321(b)(2)(A) of Title 33, (B) any element, compound, mixture, solution, or substance designated pursuant to section 9602 of this title, (C) any hazardous waste having the characteristics identified under or listed pursuant to section 3001 of the Solid Waste Disposal Act [42 U.S.C.A. § 6921] (but not including any waste the regulation of which under the Solid Waste Disposal Act [42 U.S.C.A. § 6901 et seq.] has been suspended by Act of Congress), (D) any toxic pollutant listed under section 1317(a) of Title 33, (E) any hazardous air pollutant listed under section 112 of the Clean Air Act [42 U.S.C.A. § 7412], and (F) any imminently hazardous chemical substance or mixture with respect to which the Administrator has taken action pursuant to section 2606 of Title 15. The term does not include petroleum, including crude oil or any fraction thereof which is not otherwise specifically listed or designated as a hazardous substance under subparagraphs (A) through (F) of this paragraph, and the term does not include natural gas, natural gas liquids, liquefied natural gas, or synthetic gas usable for fuel (or mixtures of natural gas and such synthetic gas).

**(15)** The term "navigable waters" or "navigable waters of the United States" means the waters of the United States, including the territorial seas.

**(16)** The term "natural resources" means land, fish, wildlife, biota, air, water, ground water, drinking water supplies, and other such resources belonging to, managed by, held in trust by, appertaining to, or otherwise controlled by the United States (including the resources of the fishery conservation zone established by the Magnuson-Stevens Fishery Conservation and Management Act [16 U.S.C.A. § 1801 et seq.] ) any State or local government, any foreign government, any Indian tribe, or, if such resources are subject to a trust restriction on alienation, any member of an Indian tribe.

**(17)** The term "offshore facility" means any facility of any kind located in, on, or under, any of the navigable waters of the United States, and any facility of any kind which is subject to the jurisdiction of the United States and is located in, on, or under any other waters, other than a vessel or a public vessel.

**(18)** The term "onshore facility" means any facility (including, but not limited to, motor vehicles and rolling stock) of any kind located in, on, or under, any land or nonnavigable waters within the United States.

**(19)** The term "otherwise subject to the jurisdiction of the United States" means subject to the jurisdiction of the United States by virtue of United States citizenship, United States vessel documentation or numbering, or as provided by international agreement to which the United States is a party.

**(20)(A)** The term "owner or operator" means (i) in the case of a vessel, any person owning, operating, or chartering by demise, such vessel, (ii) in the case of an onshore facility or an offshore facility, any person owning or operating such facility, and (iii) in the case of any facility, title or control of which was conveyed due to bankruptcy, foreclosure, tax delinquency, abandonment, or similar means to a unit of State or local government, any person who owned, operated, or otherwise controlled activities at such facility immediately beforehand. Such term does not include a person, who, without participating in the management of a vessel or facility, holds indicia of ownership primarily to protect his security interest in the vessel or facility.

**(B)** In the case of a hazardous substance which has been accepted for transportation by a common or contract carrier and except as provided in section 9607(a)(3) or (4) of this title, (i) the term "owner or operator" shall mean such common carrier or other bona fide for hire carrier acting as an independent contractor during such transportation, (ii) the shipper of such hazardous substance shall not be considered to have caused or contributed to any release during such transportation which resulted solely from circumstances or conditions beyond his control.

**(C)** In the case of a hazardous substance which has been delivered by a common or contract carrier to a disposal or treatment facility and except as provided in section 9607(a)(3) or (4) of this title, (i) the term "owner or operator" shall not include such common or contract carrier, and (ii) such common or contract carrier shall not be considered to have caused or contributed to any release at such disposal or treatment facility resulting from circumstances or conditions beyond its control.

**(D)** The term "owner or operator" does not include a unit of State or local government which acquired ownership or control involuntarily through bankruptcy, tax delinquency, abandonment, or other circumstances in which the government involuntarily acquires title by virtue of its function as sovereign. The exclusion provided under this paragraph shall not apply to any State or local government which has caused or contributed to the release or threatened release of a hazardous substance from the facility, and such a State or local government shall be subject to the provisions of this chapter in the same manner and to the same extent, both procedurally and substantively, as any nongovernmental entity, including liability under section 9607 of this title.

**(E)** Exclusion of lenders not participants in management

**(i) Indicia of ownership to protect security**

The term "owner or operator" does not include a person that is a lender that, without participating in the management of a vessel or facility, holds indicia of ownership primarily to protect the security interest of the person in the vessel or facility.

**(ii) Foreclosure**

The term "owner or operator" does not include a person that is a lender that did not participate in management of a vessel or facility prior to foreclosure, notwithstanding that the person—

**(I)** forecloses on the vessel or facility; and

**(II)** after foreclosure, sells, re-leases (in the case of a lease finance transaction), or liquidates the vessel or facility, maintains business activities, winds up operations, undertakes a response action under section 9607(d)(1) of this title or under the direction of an on-scene coordinator appointed under the National Contingency Plan, with respect to the vessel or facility, or takes any other measure to preserve, protect, or prepare the vessel or facility prior to sale or disposition,

if the person seeks to sell, re-lease (in the case of a lease finance transaction), or otherwise divest the person of the vessel or facility at the earliest practicable, commercially reasonable time, on commercially reasonable terms, taking into account market conditions and legal and regulatory requirements.

**(F)** Participation in management

For purposes of subparagraph (E)—

**(i)** the term "participate in management"—

**(I)** means actually participating in the management or operational affairs of a vessel or facility; and

**(II)** does not include merely having the capacity to influence, or the unexercised right to control, vessel or facility operations;

**(ii)** a person that is a lender and that holds indicia of ownership primarily to protect a security interest in a vessel or facility shall be considered to participate in management only if, while the borrower is still in possession of the vessel or facility encumbered by the security interest, the person—

**(I)** exercises decisionmaking control over the environmental compliance related to the vessel or facility, such that the person has undertaken responsibility for the hazardous substance handling or disposal practices related to the vessel or facility; or

**(II)** exercises control at a level comparable to that of a manager of the vessel or facility, such that the person has assumed or manifested responsibility—

**(aa)** for the overall management of the vessel or facility encompassing day-to-day decisionmaking with respect to environmental compliance; or

**(bb)** over all or substantially all of the operational functions (as distinguished from financial or administrative functions) of the vessel or facility other than the function of environmental compliance;

**(iii)** the term "participate in management" does not include performing an act or failing to act prior to the time at which a security interest is created in a vessel or facility; and

**(iv)** the term "participate in management" does not include—

**(I)** holding a security interest or abandoning or releasing a security interest;

**(II)** including in the terms of an extension of credit, or in a contract or security agreement relating to the extension, a covenant, warranty, or other term or condition that relates to environmental compliance;

**(III)** monitoring or enforcing the terms and conditions of the extension of credit or security interest;

**(IV)** monitoring or undertaking 1 or more inspections of the vessel or facility;

**(V)** requiring a response action or other lawful means of addressing the release or threatened release of a hazardous substance in connection with the vessel or facility prior to, during, or on the expiration of the term of the extension of credit;

**(VI)** providing financial or other advice or counseling in an effort to mitigate, prevent, or cure default or diminution in the value of the vessel or facility;

**(VII)** restructuring, renegotiating, or otherwise agreeing to alter the terms and conditions of the extension of credit or security interest, exercising forbearance;

**(VIII)** exercising other remedies that may be available under applicable law for the breach of a term or condition of the extension of credit or security agreement; or

**(IX)** conducting a response action under section 9607(d) of this title or under the direction of an on-scene coordinator appointed under the National Contingency Plan, if the actions do not rise to the level of participating in management (within the meaning of clauses (i) and (ii)).

(G) Other terms

As used in this chapter:

**(i) Extension of credit**

The term "extension of credit" includes a lease finance transaction—

(I) in which the lessor does not initially select the leased vessel or facility and does not during the lease term control the daily operations or maintenance of the vessel or facility; or

(II) that conforms with regulations issued by the appropriate Federal banking agency or the appropriate State bank supervisor (as those terms are defined in section 1813 of Title 12[2] or with regulations issued by the National Credit Union Administration Board, as appropriate.

**(ii) Financial or administrative function**

The term "financial or administrative function" includes a function such as that of a credit manager, accounts payable officer, accounts receivable officer, personnel manager, comptroller, or chief financial officer, or a similar function.

**(iii) Foreclosure; foreclose**

The terms "foreclosure" and "foreclose" mean, respectively, acquiring, and to acquire, a vessel or facility through—

(I)(aa) purchase at sale under a judgment or decree, power of sale, or nonjudicial foreclosure sale;

(bb) a deed in lieu of foreclosure, or similar conveyance from a trustee; or

(cc) repossession,

if the vessel or facility was security for an extension of credit previously contracted;

(II) conveyance pursuant to an extension of credit previously contracted, including the termination of a lease agreement; or

(III) any other formal or informal manner by which the person acquires, for subsequent disposition, title to or possession of a vessel or facility in order to protect the security interest of the person.

**(iv) Lender**

The term "lender" means—

(I) an insured depository institution (as defined in section 1813 of Title 12);

(II) an insured credit union (as defined in section 1752 of Title 12);

(III) a bank or association chartered under the Farm Credit Act of 1971 (12 U.S.C. 2001 et seq.);

(IV) a leasing or trust company that is an affiliate of an insured depository institution;

(V) any person (including a successor or assignee of any such person) that makes a bona fide extension of credit to or takes or acquires a security interest from a nonaffiliated person;

(VI) the Federal National Mortgage Association, the Federal Home Loan Mortgage Corporation, the Federal Agricultural Mortgage Corporation, or any other entity that in a bona fide manner buys or sells loans or interests in loans;

(VII) a person that insures or guarantees against a default in the repayment of an extension of credit, or acts as a surety with respect to an extension of credit, to a nonaffiliated person; and

(VIII) a person that provides title insurance and that acquires a vessel or facility as a result of assignment or conveyance in the course of underwriting claims and claims settlement.

**(v) Operational function**

The term "operational function" includes a function such as that of a facility or plant manager, operations manager, chief operating officer, or chief executive officer.

**(vi) Security interest**

The term "security interest" includes a right under a mortgage, deed of trust, assignment, judgment lien, pledge, security agreement, factoring agreement, or lease and any other right accruing to a person to secure the repayment of money, the performance of a duty, or any other obligation by a nonaffiliated person.

(21) The term "person" means an individual, firm, corporation, association, partnership, consortium, joint venture, commercial entity, United States Government, State, municipality, commission, political subdivision of a State, or any interstate body.

(22) The term "release" means any spilling, leaking, pumping, pouring, emitting, emptying, discharging, injecting, escaping, leaching, dumping, or disposing into the environment (including the aban-

donment or discarding of barrels, containers, and other closed receptacles containing any hazardous substance or pollutant or contaminant), but excludes (A) any release which results in exposure to persons solely within a workplace, with respect to a claim which such persons may assert against the employer of such persons, (B) emissions from the engine exhaust of a motor vehicle, rolling stock, aircraft, vessel, or pipeline pumping station engine, (C) release of source, byproduct, or special nuclear material from a nuclear incident, as those terms are defined in the Atomic Energy Act of 1954 [42 U.S.C.A. § 2011 et seq.], if such release is subject to requirements with respect to financial protection established by the Nuclear Regulatory Commission under section 170 of such Act [42 U.S.C.A. § 2210], or, for the purposes of section 9604 of this title or any other response action, any release of source byproduct, or special nuclear material from any processing site designated under section 7912(a)(1) or 7942(a) of this title, and (D) the normal application of fertilizer.

(23) The terms "remove" or "removal" means [3] the cleanup or removal of released hazardous substances from the environment, such actions as may be necessary taken in the event of the threat of release of hazardous substances into the environment, such actions as may be necessary to monitor, assess, and evaluate the release or threat of release of hazardous substances, the disposal of removed material, or the taking of such other actions as may be necessary to prevent, minimize, or mitigate damage to the public health or welfare or to the environment, which may otherwise result from a release or threat of release. The term includes, in addition, without being limited to, security fencing or other measures to limit access, provision of alternative water supplies, temporary evacuation and housing of threatened individuals not otherwise provided for, action taken under section 9604(b) of this title, and any emergency assistance which may be provided under the Disaster Relief and Emergency Assistance Act [42 U.S.C.A. § 5121 et seq.].

(24) The terms "remedy" or "remedial action" means [3] those actions consistent with permanent remedy taken instead of or in addition to removal actions in the event of a release or threatened release of a hazardous substance into the environment, to prevent or minimize the release of hazardous substances so that they do not migrate to cause substantial danger to present or future public health or welfare or the environment. The term includes, but is not limited to, such actions at the location of the release as storage, confinement, perimeter protection using dikes, trenches, or ditches, clay cover, neutralization, cleanup of released hazardous substances and associated contaminated materials, recycling or reuse, diversion, destruction, segregation of reactive wastes, dredging or excavations, repair or replacement of leaking containers, collection of leachate and runoff, onsite treatment or incineration, provision of alternative water supplies, and any monitoring reasonably required to assure that such actions protect the public health and welfare and the environment. The term includes the costs of permanent relocation of residents and businesses and community facilities where the President determines that, alone or in combination with other measures, such relocation is more cost-effective than and environmentally preferable to the transportation, storage, treatment, destruction, or secure disposition offsite of hazardous substances, or may otherwise be necessary to protect the public health or welfare; the term includes offsite transport and offsite storage, treatment, destruction, or secure disposition of hazardous substances and associated contaminated materials.

(25) The terms "respond" or "response" means [3] remove, removal, remedy, and remedial action;,[4] all such terms (including the terms "removal" and "remedial action") include enforcement activities related thereto.

(26) The terms "transport" or "transportation" means [3] the movement of a hazardous substance by any mode, including a hazardous liquid pipeline facility (as defined in section 60101(a) of Title 49), and in the case of a hazardous substance which has been accepted for transportation by a common or contract carrier, the term "transport" or "transportation" shall include any stoppage in transit which is temporary, incidental to the transportation movement, and at the ordinary operating convenience of a common or contract carrier, and any such stoppage shall be considered as a continuity of movement and not as the storage of a hazardous substance.

(27) The terms "United States" and "State" include the several States of the United States, the District of Columbia, the Commonwealth of Puerto Rico, Guam, American Samoa, the United States Virgin Islands, the Commonwealth of the Northern Marianas, and any other territory or possession over which the United States has jurisdiction.

(28) The term "vessel" means every description of watercraft or other artificial contrivance used, or capable of being used, as a means of transportation on water.

(29) The terms "disposal", "hazardous waste", and "treatment" shall have the meaning provided in section 1004 of the Solid Waste Disposal Act [42 U.S.C.A. § 6903].

(30) The terms "territorial sea" and "contiguous zone" shall have the meaning provided in section 1362 of Title 33.

(31) The term "national contingency plan" means the national contingency plan published under section 1321(c) of Title 33 or revised pursuant to section 9605 of this title.

(32) The terms "liable" or "liability" under this subchapter shall be construed to be the standard of liability which obtains under section 1321 of Title 33.

(33) The term "pollutant or contaminant" shall include, but not be limited to, any element, substance, compound, or mixture, including disease-causing agents, which after release into the environment and upon exposure, ingestion, inhalation, or assimilation into any organism, either directly from the environment or indirectly by ingestion through food chains, will or may reasonably be anticipated to cause death, disease, behavioral abnormalities, cancer, genetic mutation, physiological malfunctions (including malfunctions in reproduction) or physical deformations, in such organisms or their offspring; except that the term "pollutant or contaminant" shall not include petroleum, including crude oil or any fraction thereof which is not otherwise specifically listed or designated as a hazardous substance under subparagraphs (A) through (F) of paragraph (14) and shall not include natural gas, liquefied natural gas, or synthetic gas of pipeline quality (or mixtures of natural gas and such synthetic gas).

(34) The term "alternative water supplies" includes, but is not limited to, drinking water and household water supplies.

(35)(A) The term "contractual relationship", for the purpose of section 9607(b)(3) of this title, includes, but is not limited to, land contracts, deeds, easements, leases, or other instruments transferring title or possession, unless the real property on which the facility concerned is located was acquired by the defendant after the disposal or placement of the hazardous substance on, in, or at the facility, and one or more of the circumstances described in clause (i), (ii), or (iii) is also established by the defendant by a preponderance of the evidence:

(i) At the time the defendant acquired the facility the defendant did not know and had no reason to know that any hazardous substance which is the subject of the release or threatened release was disposed of on, in, or at the facility.

(ii) The defendant is a government entity which acquired the facility by escheat, or through any other involuntary transfer or acquisition, or through the exercise of eminent domain authority by purchase or condemnation.

(iii) The defendant acquired the facility by inheritance or bequest.

In addition to establishing the foregoing, the defendant must establish that the defendant has satisfied the requirements of section 9607(b)(3)(a) and (b) of this title, provides full cooperation, assistance, and facility access to the persons that are authorized to conduct response actions at the facility (including the cooperation and access necessary for the installation, integrity, operation, and maintenance of any complete or partial response action at the facility), is in compliance with any land use restrictions established or relied on in connection with the response action at a facility, and does not impede the effectiveness or integrity of any institutional control employed at the facility in connection with a response action.

(B) **Reason to know**

(i) **All appropriate inquiries**

To establish that the defendant had no reason to know of the matter described in subparagraph (A)(i), the defendant must demonstrate to a court that—

(I) on or before the date on which the defendant acquired the facility, the defendant carried out all appropriate inquiries, as provided in clauses (ii) and (iv), into the previous ownership and uses of the facility in accordance with generally accepted good commercial and customary standards and practices; and

(II) the defendant took reasonable steps to—

(aa) stop any continuing release;

(bb) prevent any threatened future release; and

(cc) prevent or limit any human, environmental, or natural resource exposure to any previously released hazardous substance.

(ii) **Standards and practices**

Not later than 2 years after January 11, 2002, the Administrator shall by regulation establish standards and practices for the purpose of satisfying the requirement to carry out all appropriate inquiries under clause (i).

(iii) **Criteria**

In promulgating regulations that establish the standards and practices referred to in clause (ii), the Administrator shall include each of the following:

(I) The results of an inquiry by an environmental professional.

(II) Interviews with past and present owners, operators, and occupants of the facility for the purpose of gathering information regarding the potential for contamination at the facility.

**(III)** Reviews of historical sources, such as chain of title documents, aerial photographs, building department records, and land use records, to determine previous uses and occupancies of the real property since the property was first developed.

**(IV)** Searches for recorded environmental cleanup liens against the facility that are filed under Federal, State, or local law.

**(V)** Reviews of Federal, State, and local government records, waste disposal records, underground storage tank records, and hazardous waste handling, generation, treatment, disposal, and spill records, concerning contamination at or near the facility.

**(VI)** Visual inspections of the facility and of adjoining properties.

**(VII)** Specialized knowledge or experience on the part of the defendant.

**(VIII)** The relationship of the purchase price to the value of the property, if the property was not contaminated.

**(IX)** Commonly known or reasonably ascertainable information about the property.

**(X)** The degree of obviousness of the presence or likely presence of contamination at the property, and the ability to detect the contamination by appropriate investigation.

**(iv) Interim standards and practices**

**(I) Property purchased before May 31, 1997**

With respect to property purchased before May 31, 1997, in making a determination with respect to a defendant described in clause (i), a court shall take into account—

**(aa)** any specialized knowledge or experience on the part of the defendant;

**(bb)** the relationship of the purchase price to the value of the property, if the property was not contaminated;

**(cc)** commonly known or reasonably ascertainable information about the property;

**(dd)** the obviousness of the presence or likely presence of contamination at the property; and

**(ee)** the ability of the defendant to detect the contamination by appropriate inspection.

**(II) Property purchased on or after May 31, 1997**

With respect to property purchased on or after May 31, 1997, and until the Administrator promulgates the regulations described in clause (ii), the procedures of the American Society for Testing and Materials, including the document known as 'Standard E1527–97', entitled 'Standard Practice for Environmental Site Assessment: Phase 1 Environmental Site Assessment Process', shall satisfy the requirements in clause (i).

**(v) Site inspection and title search**

In the case of property for residential use or other similar use purchased by a nongovernmental or noncommercial entity, a facility inspection and title search that reveal no basis for further investigation shall be considered to satisfy the requirements of this subparagraph.

**(C)** Nothing in this paragraph or in section 9607(b)(3) of this title shall diminish the liability of any previous owner or operator of such facility who would otherwise be liable under this chapter. Notwithstanding this paragraph, if the defendant obtained actual knowledge of the release or threatened release of a hazardous substance at such facility when the defendant owned the real property and then subsequently transferred ownership of the property to another person without disclosing such knowledge, such defendant shall be treated as liable under section 9607(a)(1) of this title and no defense under section 9607(b)(3) of this title shall be available to such defendant.

**(D)** Nothing in this paragraph shall affect the liability under this chapter of a defendant who, by any act or omission, caused or contributed to the release or threatened release of a hazardous substance which is the subject of the action relating to the facility.

**(36)** The term "Indian tribe" means any Indian tribe, band, nation, or other organized group or community, including any Alaska Native village but not including any Alaska Native regional or village corporation, which is recognized as eligible for the special programs and services provided by the United States to Indians because of their status as Indians.

**(37)(A)** The term "service station dealer" means any person—

**(i)** who owns or operates a motor vehicle service station, filling station, garage, or similar retail establishment engaged in the business of selling, repairing, or servicing motor vehicles, where a significant percentage of the gross revenue of the establishment is derived from the fueling, repairing, or servicing of motor vehicles, and

(ii) who accepts for collection, accumulation, and delivery to an oil recycling facility, recycled oil that (I) has been removed from the engine of a light duty motor vehicle or household appliances by the owner of such vehicle or appliances, and (II) is presented, by such owner, to such person for collection, accumulation, and delivery to an oil recycling facility.

**(B)** For purposes of section 9614(c) of this title, the term "service station dealer" shall, notwithstanding the provisions of subparagraph (A), include any government agency that establishes a facility solely for the purpose of accepting recycled oil that satisfies the criteria set forth in subclauses (I) and (II) of subparagraph (A)(ii), and, with respect to recycled oil that satisfies the criteria set forth in subclauses (I) and (II), owners or operators of refuse collection services who are compelled by State law to collect, accumulate, and deliver such oil to an oil recycling facility.

**(C)** The President shall promulgate regulations regarding the determination of what constitutes a significant percentage of the gross revenues of an establishment for purposes of this paragraph.

(38) The term "incineration vessel" means any vessel which carries hazardous substances for the purpose of incineration of such substances, so long as such substances or residues of such substances are on board.

**(39) Brownfield site**

**(A) In general**

The term "brownfield site" means real property, the expansion, redevelopment, or reuse of which may be complicated by the presence or potential presence of a hazardous substance, pollutant, or contaminant.

**(B) Exclusions**

The term "brownfield site" does not include—

**(i)** a facility that is the subject of a planned or ongoing removal action under this subchapter;

**(ii)** a facility that is listed on the National Priorities List or is proposed for listing;

**(iii)** a facility that is the subject of a unilateral administrative order, a court order, an administrative order on consent or judicial consent decree that has been issued to or entered into by the parties under this chapter;

**(iv)** a facility that is the subject of a unilateral administrative order, a court order, an administrative order on consent or judicial consent decree that has been issued to or entered into by the parties, or a facility to which a permit has been issued by the United States or an authorized State under the Solid Waste Disposal Act (42 U.S.C. 6901 et seq.), the Federal Water Pollution Control Act (33 U.S.C. 1321), the Toxic Substances Control Act (15 U.S.C. 2601 et seq.), or the Safe Drinking Water Act (42 U.S.C. 300f et seq.);

**(v)** a facility that—

**(I)** is subject to corrective action under section 3004(u) or 3008(h) of the Solid Waste Disposal Act (42 U.S.C. 6924(u), 6928(h)); and

**(II)** to which a corrective action permit or order has been issued or modified to require the implementation of corrective measures;

**(vi)** a land disposal unit with respect to which—

**(I)** a closure notification under subtitle C of the Solid Waste Disposal Act (42 U.S.C. 6921 et seq.) has been submitted; and

**(II)** closure requirements have been specified in a closure plan or permit;

**(vii)** a facility that is subject to the jurisdiction, custody, or control of a department, agency, or instrumentality of the United States, except for land held in trust by the United States for an Indian tribe;

**(viii)** a portion of a facility—

**(I)** at which there has been a release of polychlorinated biphenyls; and

**(II)** that is subject to remediation under the Toxic Substances Control Act (15 U.S.C. 2601 et seq.); or

**(ix)** a portion of a facility, for which portion, assistance for response activity has been obtained under subtitle I of the Solid Waste Disposal Act (42 U.S.C. 6991 et seq.) from the Leaking Underground Storage Tank Trust Fund established under section 9508 of Title 26.

**(C) Site-by-site determinations**

Notwithstanding subparagraph (B) and on a site-by-site basis, the President may authorize financial assistance under section 9604(k) of this title to an eligible entity at a site included in clause (i), (iv), (v), (vi), (viii), or (ix) of subparagraph (B) if the President finds that financial assistance will protect human health and the environment, and either promote economic development or enable the creation of, preservation of, or addition to parks, greenways, undeveloped property, other recreational property, or other property used for nonprofit purposes.

(D) **Additional areas**

For the purposes of section 9604(k) of this title, the term "brownfield site" includes a site that—

(i) meets the definition of "brownfield site" under subparagraphs (A) through (C); and

(ii)(I) is contaminated by a controlled substance (as defined in section 802 of Title 21);

(II)(aa) is contaminated by petroleum or a petroleum product excluded from the definition of "hazardous substance" under this section; and

(bb) is a site determined by the Administrator or the State, as appropriate, to be—

(AA) of relatively low risk, as compared with other petroleum-only sites in the State; and

(BB) a site for which there is no viable responsible party and which will be assessed, investigated, or cleaned up by a person that is not potentially liable for cleaning up the site; and

(cc) is not subject to any order issued under section 6991b(h) of this title; or

(III) is mine-scarred land.

(40) **Bona fide prospective purchaser**

The term "bona fide prospective purchaser" means a person (or a tenant of a person) that acquires ownership of a facility after the date of the enactment of this paragraph and that establishes each of the following by a preponderance of the evidence:

(A) **Disposal prior to acquisition**

All disposal of hazardous substances at the facility occurred before the person acquired the facility.

(B) **Inquiries**

(i) **In general**

The person made all appropriate inquiries into the previous ownership and uses of the facility in accordance with generally accepted good commercial and customary standards and practices in accordance with clauses (ii) and (iii).

(ii) **Standards and practices**

The standards and practices referred to in clauses (ii) and (iv) of paragraph (35)(B) of this section shall be considered to satisfy the requirements of this subparagraph.

(iii) **Residential use**

In the case of property in residential or other similar use at the time of purchase by a nongovernmental or noncommercial entity, a facility inspection and title search that reveal no basis for further investigation shall be considered to satisfy the requirements of this subparagraph.

(C) **Notices**

The person provides all legally required notices with respect to the discovery or release of any hazardous substances at the facility.

(D) **Care**

The person exercises appropriate care with respect to hazardous substances found at the facility by taking reasonable steps to—

(i) stop any continuing release;

(ii) prevent any threatened future release; and

(iii) prevent or limit human, environmental, or natural resource exposure to any previously released hazardous substance.

(E) **Cooperation, assistance, and access**

The person provides full cooperation, assistance, and access to persons that are authorized to conduct response actions or natural resource restoration at a vessel or facility (including the cooperation and access necessary for the installation, integrity, operation, and maintenance of any complete or partial response actions or natural resource restoration at the vessel or facility).

(F) **Institutional control**

The person—

(i) is in compliance with any land use restrictions established or relied on in connection with the response action at a vessel or facility; and

(ii) does not impede the effectiveness or integrity of any institutional control employed at the vessel or facility in connection with a response action.

(G) **Requests; subpoenas**

The person complies with any request for information or administrative subpoena issued by the President under this chapter.

(H) **No affiliation**

The person is not—

(i) potentially liable, or affiliated with any other person that is potentially liable, for response costs at a facility through—

(I) any direct or indirect familial relationship; or

(II) any contractual, corporate, or financial relationship (other than a contractual, corporate, or financial relationship that is created by the instruments by which title to the facility is conveyed or financed or by a contract for the sale of goods or services); or

(ii) the result of a reorganization of a business entity that was potentially liable.

**(41) Eligible response site**

**(A) In general**

The term "eligible response site" means a site that meets the definition of a brownfield site in subparagraphs (A) and (B) of paragraph (39) of this section, as modified by subparagraphs (B) and (C) of this paragraph.

**(B) Inclusions**

The term "eligible response site" includes—

(i) notwithstanding paragraph (39)(B)(ix) of this section, a portion of a facility, for which portion assistance for response activity has been obtained under subtitle I of the Solid Waste Disposal Act (42 U.S.C. 6991 et seq.) from the Leaking Underground Storage Tank Trust Fund established under section 9508 of Title 26; or

(ii) a site for which, notwithstanding the exclusions provided in subparagraph (C) or paragraph (39)(B) of this section, the President determines, on a site-by-site basis and after consultation with the State, that limitations on enforcement under section 9628 of this title at sites specified in clause (iv), (v), (vi) or (viii) of paragraph (39)(B) of this section would be appropriate and will—

(I) protect human health and the environment; and

(II) promote economic development or facilitate the creation of, preservation of, or addition to a park, a greenway, undeveloped property, recreational property, or other property used for nonprofit purposes.

**(C) Exclusions**

The term "eligible response site" does not include—

(i) a facility for which the President—

(I) conducts or has conducted a preliminary assessment or site inspection; and

(II) after consultation with the State, determines or has determined that the site obtains a preliminary score sufficient for possible listing on the National Priorities List, or that the site otherwise qualifies for listing on the National Priorities List; unless the President has made a determination that no further Federal action will be taken; or

(ii) facilities that the President determines warrant particular consideration as identified by regulation, such as sites posing a threat to a sole-source drinking water aquifer or a sensitive ecosystem.

(Pub.L. 96–510, Title I, § 101, Dec. 11, 1980, 94 Stat. 2767; Pub.L. 96–561, Title II, § 238(b), Dec. 22, 1980, 94 Stat. 3300; Pub.L. 99–499, Title I, §§ 101, 114(b), 127(a), Title V, § 517(c)(2), Oct. 17, 1986, 100 Stat. 1615, 1652, 1692, 1774; Pub.L. 100–707, Title I, § 109(v), Nov. 23, 1988, 102 Stat. 4710; Pub.L. 103–429, § 7(e)(1), Oct. 31, 1994, 108 Stat. 4390; Pub.L. 104–208, Div. A, Title I, § 101(a) [Title II, § 211(b)], Title II, § 2502(b), Sept. 30, 1996, 110 Stat. 3009–41, 3009–464; Pub.L. 104–287, § 6(j)(1), Oct. 11, 1996, 110 Stat. 3400; Pub.L. 106–74, Title IV, § 427, Oct. 20, 1999, 113 Stat. 1095; Pub.L. 107–118, Title II, §§ 211(a), 222(a), 223, 231(a), Jan. 11, 2002, 115 Stat. 2360, 2370, 2372, 2375.)

1 So in original. Probably should be "or".

2 So in original. Probably should be followed by a closing parenthesis.

3 So in original. Probably should be "mean".

4 So in original.

## HISTORICAL AND STATUTORY NOTES

**References in Text**

"This subchapter", referred to in text, originally read "this title", meaning Title I of Pub.L. 96–510, Dec. 11, 1980, 94 Stat. 2767, as amended, known as the Comprehensive Environmental Response, Compensation, and Liability Act of 1980, which is principally classified to this subchapter [42 U.S.C.A. § 9601 et seq.]. See Tables for complete classification.

This chapter, referred to in pars. (5), (13), (20)(D), (G), (35)(C), (D), (39)(B)(iii), and (40)(G), originally read "this Act", meaning Pub.L. 96–510, Dec. 11, 1980, 94 Stat. 2767, as amended, known as the Comprehensive Environmental Response, Compensation, and Liability Act of 1980, which is classified principally to this chapter [42 U.S.C.A. § 9601 et seq.]; See Tables for complete classification.

The Safe Drinking Water Act, referred to in pars. (7), (10), and (39)(B)(iv) is Pub.L. 93–523, Dec. 16, 1974, 88 Stat. 1660, as amended, which is classified principally to subchapter XII of chapter 6A of this title [42 U.S.C.A. § 300f et seq.]. Part C of the Safe Drinking Water Act is classified generally to part C of subchapter XII of chapter 6A of this title [42 U.S.C.A. § 300h et seq.]. See Tables for complete classification.

The Magnuson-Stevens Fishery Conservation and Management Act, referred to in pars. (8) and (16), is Pub.L. 94–265, Apr. 13, 1976, 90 Stat. 331, as amended, which is classified principally to chapter 38 (section 1801 et seq.) of Title 16, Conservation. The fishery conservation zone established by this Act, referred to in par. (16) was established by section 101 of this Act (16 U.S.C. 1811), which as amended generally by Pub.L. 99–659, title I, § 101(b), Nov. 14, 1986, 100 Stat. 3706, relating to U.S. sovereign rights and fishery management authority over fish within the exclusive economic zone as defined in section 1802 of Title 16. For complete classification of this Act to the Code, see Short Title note set out under section 1801 of Title 16 and Tables.

The Clean Air Act, referred to in par. (10), is Act July 14, 1955, c. 360, as amended generally by Pub.L. 88–206, Dec. 17, 1963, 77 Stat. 392, and later by Pub.L. 95–95, Aug. 7, 1977, 91 Stat. 685. The Clean Air Act was originally classified to chapter 15B (section 1857 et seq.) of this title. On enactment of Pub.L. 95–95, the Act was reclassified to chapter 85 (section 7401 et seq.) of this title. Parts C and D of Title I of the Clean Air Act are classified generally to parts C (section 7470 et seq.) and D (section 7501 et seq.), respectively, of subchapter I of chapter 85 of this title. For complete classification of this Act to the Code, see Short Title of 1955 Acts note set out under section 7401 of this title and Tables.

The Atomic Energy Act of 1954, referred to in pars. (10) and (22), is Act Aug. 30, 1954, c. 1073, § 1, 68 Stat. 919, as amended, which is classified generally to chapter 23 (section 2011 et seq.) of this title. For complete classification of this Act to the Code, see Short Title of 1954 Acts note set out under section 2011 of this title and Tables.

The Solid Waste Disposal Act, referred to in par. (14) and (39)(B)(iv), (v)(I), (vi)(I), and (ix), is Title II of Pub.L. 89–272, Oct. 20, 1965, 79 Stat. 997, as amended generally by Pub.L. 94–580, § 2, Oct. 21, 1976, 90 Stat. 2795, which is classified principally to chapter 82 [42 U.S.C.A. § 6901 et seq.] of this title. See Tables for complete classification.

The Farm Credit Act of 1971, referred to in par. (20)(G)(iv)(III), is Pub.L. 92–181, Dec. 10, 1971, 85 Stat. 583, as amended, which is classified generally to chapter 23 (section 2001 et seq.) of Title 12, Banks and Banking. For complete classification of this Act to the Code, see Short Title note set out under section 2001 of Title 12 and Tables.

The Disaster Relief and Emergency Assistance Act, referred to in par. (23), is Pub.L. 93–288, May 22, 1974, 88 Stat. 143, as amended, which is classified principally to chapter 68 (section 5121 et seq.) of this title. For complete classification of this Act to the Code, see Short Title of 1974 Acts note set out under section 5121 of this title and Tables.

Section 1321(c) of Title 33, referred to in par. (31), was amended generally by Pub.L. 101–380, Title IV, § 4201(a), Aug. 18, 1990, 104 Stat. 523, and no longer contains provisions directing the publishing of a National Contingency Plan. However, such provisions are contained in section 1321(d) of Title 33, Navigation and Navigable Waters.

The Federal Water Pollution Control Act, referred to in par. (39)(B)(iv), is Act June 30, 1948, c. 758, as amended generally by Pub.L. 92–500, § 2, Oct. 18, 1972, 86 Stat. 816, also known as the Clean Water Act, which is classified principally to chapter 26 of Title 33 [33 U.S.C.A. § 1251 et seq.]. See Tables for complete classification.

The Toxic Substances Control Act, referred to in par. (39)(B)(iv), (viii)(II), is Pub.L. 94–469, Oct. 11, 1976, 90 Stat. 2003, as amended, which is classified principally to chapter 53 of Title 15 [15 U.S.C.A. § 2601 et seq.]. See Tables for complete classification.

The date of the enactment of this paragraph, referred to in par. (40), probably means Jan. 11, 2002, the approval date of Pub.L. 107–118, 115 Stat. 118, which enacted par. (40) of this section.

Subtitle I of the Solid Waste Disposal Act, referred to in par. (41)(B)(i), is subtitle I of Title II of Pub.L. 89–272, Oct. 20, 1965, 79 Stat. 997, as amended generally by Pub.L. 94–580, § 2, Oct. 21, 1976, 90 Stat. 2795, which is classified principally to subchapter IX of chapter 82 of this title [42 U.S.C.A. § 6991 et seq.].

### Codifications

The amendment to par. (20)(D) by Pub.L. 106–74, Title IV, § 427, Oct. 20, 1999, 113 Stat. 1096, purporting to insert "through seizure or otherwise in connection with law enforcement activity" before "involuntary" the first place it appears, was incapable of execution. The word "involuntary" does not appear in subpar. (D).

Reference in the original text of par. (39)(D)(ii)(II)(aa) of this section to "under section 101" has been translated in the codified text as "under this section" to reflect the probable intent of Congress.

### Effective Dates

1996 Acts

Amendment by section 101(a) of Title I [Title II, § 211(b)] of Div. A of Pub.L. 104–208 effective 15 days after Oct. 11, 1996, see section 101(a) of Title I [Title II, § 211(b)] of Div. A of Pub.L. 104–208, set out as a note under section 1801 of Title 16, Conservation.

Amendment by section 2502 of Div. A of Title II of Pub.L. 104–208 applicable with respect to claims not finally adjudicated as of Sept. 30, 1996, see section 2505 of Div. A of Title II of Pub.L. 104–208, set out as a note under section 6991b of this title.

1986 Acts

Section 4 of Pub.L. 99–499 provided that: "Except as otherwise specified in section 121(b) of this Act [set out as a note under section 9621 of this title] or in any other provision of Titles I, II, III, and IV of this Act [see Tables for classification], the amendments made by Titles I through IV of this Act [enacting subchapter IV of this chapter and sections 9616 to 9626, 9658 to 9660, and 9661 of this title and sections 2701 to 2707 and 2810 of Title 10, Armed Forces, amending sections 6926, 6928, 6991 to 6991d, 6991g, 9601 to 9609, 9611 to 9614, 9651, 9656, and 9657 of this title and section 1416 of Title 33, Navigation and Navigable Waters, repealing section 9631 of this title, and renumbering former section 2701 of Title 10 as section 2721 of Title 10] shall take effect on the enactment of this Act [Oct. 17, 1986]."

Amendment by section 517(c)(2) of Pub.L. 99–499 effective Jan. 1, 1987, see section 517(e) of Pub.L. 99–499, set out as a note under section 9507 of Title 26, Internal Revenue Code.

1980 Acts

Amendment by Pub.L. 96–561 effective 15 days after Dec. 22, 1980, see section 238 of Pub.L. 96–561, set out as a Short Title of 1980 Amendments note under section 1801 of Title 16, Conservation.

### Transfer of Functions

For transfer of certain functions from the Nuclear Regulatory Commission to the Chairman thereof, see Reorg. Plan No. 1 of 1980, 45 F.R. 40561, 94 Stat. 3585, set out as a note under section 5841 of this title.

**Delegation of Functions**

Functions vested in the President by par. (24) of this section, subject to section 2(a) to (f) of Ex. Ord. No. 12580, delegated, with authority to redelegate, to the Administrator of the Environmental Protection Agency, see sections 2(g), 11(g) of Ex. Ord. No. 12580, Jan. 23, 1987, 52 F.R. 2923, set out as a note under section 9615 of this title.

Functions vested in the President by par. (37) of this section delegated to the Administrator of the Environmental Protection Agency, see section 11(a) of Ex. Ord. No. 12580, Jan. 23, 1987, 52 F.R. 2923, set out as a note under section 9615 of this title.

**Short Title**

2002 Amendments

Pub.L. 107–118, § 1, Jan. 11, 2002, 115 Stat. 2356, provided that: "This Act [enacting 42 U.S.C.A. § 9628, amending this section, 42 U.S.C.A. § 9604, 42 U.S.C.A. § 9605, 42 U.S.C.A. § 9607, and 42 U.S.C.A. § 9622, and enacting provisions set out as notes under this section and 42 U.S.C.A. § 9607] may be cited as the 'Small Business Liability Relief and Brownfields Revitalization Act'."

Pub.L. 107–118, Title I, § 101, Jan. 11, 2002, 115 Stat. 2356, provided that: "This title [Pub.L. 107–118, Title I, § 101 et seq., Jan. 11, 2002, 115 Stat. 2356, amending 42 U.S.C.A. § 9607(*o*), (p), and 42 U.S.C.A. § 9622(g)(7) to (12), and enacting provisions set out as a note under 42 U.S.C.A. § 9607] may be cited as the 'Small Business Liability Protection Act'."

Pub.L. 107–118, Title II, § 201, Jan. 11, 2002, 115 Stat. 2360, provided that: "This title [Pub.L. 107–118, Title II, § 201 et seq., Jan. 11, 2002, 115 Stat. 2360, enacting 42 U.S.C.A. § 9628, and amending pars. (35)(A) and (B) and (39) to (41) of this section, 42 U.S.C.A. § 9604(k), 42 U.S.C.A. § 9605(h), and 42 U.S.C.A. § 9607(q) and (r)] may be cited as the 'Brownfields Revitalization and Environmental Restoration Act of 2001'."

1996 Amendments

Pub.L. 104–208, Div. A, Title II, § 2501, Sept. 30, 1996, 110 Stat. 3009–462, provided that: "This [Pub.L. 104–208, Div. A, Title II, Subtitle E, § 2501 et seq., Sept. 30, 1996, 110 Stat. 3009–462, amending this section and sections 6991b and 9607 of this title and enacting provisions set out as a note under section 6991b of this title] subtitle may be cited as the 'Asset Conservation, Lender Liability, and Deposit Insurance Protection Act of 1996'."

1992 Amendments

Pub.L. 102–426, § 1, Oct. 19, 1992, 106 Stat. 2174, provided that: "This Act [amending section 9620 of this title and enacting provisions set out as a note under section 9620 of this title] may be cited as the 'Community Environmental Response Facilitation Act'."

1986 Amendments

Section 1 of Pub.L. 99–499 provided that: "This Act [enacting subchapter IV of this chapter and sections 9616 to 9626, 9658 to 9662, 11001 to 11005, 11021 to 11023, and 11041 to 11050 of this title, sections 2701 to 2707 and 2810 of Title 10, Armed Forces, and sections 59A, 4671, 4672, 9507, and 9508 of Title 26, Internal Revenue Code, amending sections 6926, 6928, 6991 to 6991d, 6991g, 9601 to 9609, 9611 to 9614, 9631, 9651, 9656, and 9657 of this title, sections 26, 164, 275, 936, 1561, 4041, 4042, 4081, 4221, 4611, 4612, 4661, 4662, 6416, 6420, 6421, 6425, 6427, 6655, 9502, 9503, and 9506 of Title 26, former section 6154 of Title 26, and section 1416 of Title 33, Navigation and Navigable Waters, renumbering former section 2701 of Title 10 as section 2721 of Title 10, repealing sections 9631 to 9633, 9641, and 9653 of this title and sections 4681 and 4682 of Title 26, and enacting provisions set out as notes under sections 6921, 6991b, 7401, 9601, 9620, 9621, 9658, 9660, 9661, and 11001 of this title, section 2703 of Title 10, sections 1, 26, 4041, 4611, 4661, 4671, 4681, 9507, and 9508 of Title 26, and section 655 of Title 29, Labor] may be cited as the 'Superfund Amendments and Reauthorization Act of 1986'."

1980 Acts

Section 1 of Pub.L. 96–510 provided: "That this Act [enacting this chapter, section 6911a of this title, and sections 4611, 4612, 4661, 4662, 4681, and former section 4682 of Title 26, Internal Revenue Code, amending section 6911 of this title, section 1364 of Title 33, Navigation and Navigable Waters, and section 11901 of Title 49, Transportation, and enacting provisions set out as notes under section 6911 of this title and sections 1 and 4611 of Title 26] may be cited as the 'Comprehensive Environmental Response, Compensation, and Liability Act of 1980'." The Act is also known as CERCLA.

**Definitions**

Section 2 of Pub.L. 99–499 provided that: "As used in this Act [see Short Title of 1986 Amendments note set out under this section]—

"(1) **CERCLA.**—The term 'CERCLA' means the Comprehensive Environmental Response, Compensation, and Liability Act of 1980 (42 U.S.C. 9601 et seq.).

"(2) **Administrator.**—The term 'Administrator' means the Administrator of the Environmental Protection Agency."

**Territorial Sea Of United States**

For extension of territorial sea of United States, see Proc. No. 5928, set out as a note under section 1331 of Title 43, Public Lands.

## § 9602. Designation of additional hazardous substances and establishment of reportable released quantities; regulations

**[CERCLA § 102]**

**(a)** The Administrator shall promulgate and revise as may be appropriate, regulations designating as hazardous substances, in addition to those referred to in section 9601(14) of this title, such elements, compounds, mixtures, solutions, and substances which, when released into the environment may present substantial danger to the public health or welfare or the environment, and shall promulgate regulations establishing that quantity of any hazardous substance the release of which shall be reported pursuant to section 9603 of this title. The Administrator may determine that one single quantity shall be the reportable quantity for any hazardous substance, regardless of the medium into which the hazardous substance is released. For all hazardous substances for which proposed regulations establishing reportable quantities were published in the Federal Register under this subsection on or before March 1, 1986, the Administrator shall promulgate under this subsection final regulations establishing reportable quantities not later than December 31, 1986. For all hazardous substances for which proposed regulations establishing reportable quantities were not published in the Federal Register under this subsection on or before March 1, 1986, the Administrator shall publish under this subsection proposed regulations establishing reportable quantities not later than December 31, 1986, and promulgate final regulations under this subsection establishing reportable quantities not later than April 30, 1988.

(b) Unless and until superseded by regulations establishing a reportable quantity under subsection (a) of this section for any hazardous substance as defined in section 9601(14) of this title, (1) a quantity of one pound, or (2) for those hazardous substances for which reportable quantities have been established pursuant to section 1321(b)(4) of Title 33, such reportable quantity, shall be deemed that quantity, the release of which requires notification pursuant to section 9603(a) or (b) of this title.

(Pub.L. 96–510, Title I, § 102, Dec. 11, 1980, 94 Stat. 2772; Pub.L. 99–499, Title I, § 102, Oct. 17, 1986, 100 Stat. 1617.)

### HISTORICAL AND STATUTORY NOTES

**Effective Dates**

1986 Acts

Amendment by Pub.L. 99–499 effective Oct. 17, 1986, see section 4 of Pub.L. 99–499, set out as a note under section 9601 of this title.

## § 9603. Notification requirements respecting released substances

### [CERCLA § 103]

**(a) Notice to National Response Center upon release from vessel or offshore or onshore facility by person in charge; conveyance of notice by Center**

Any person in charge of a vessel or an offshore or an onshore facility shall, as soon as he has knowledge of any release (other than a federally permitted release) of a hazardous substance from such vessel or facility in quantities equal to or greater than those determined pursuant to section 9602 of this title, immediately notify the National Response Center established under the Clean Water Act [33 U.S.C.A. § 1251 et seq.] of such release. The National Response Center shall convey the notification expeditiously to all appropriate Government agencies, including the Governor of any affected State.

**(b) Penalties for failure to notify; use of notice or information pursuant to notice in criminal case**

Any person—

(1) in charge of a vessel from which a hazardous substance is released, other than a federally permitted release, into or upon the navigable waters of the United States, adjoining shorelines, or into or upon the waters of the contiguous zone, or

(2) in charge of a vessel from which a hazardous substance is released, other than a federally permitted release, which may affect natural resources belonging to, appertaining to, or under the exclusive management authority of the United States (including resources under the Magnuson-Stevens Fishery Conservation and Management Act [16 U.S.C.A. § 1801 et seq.]), and who is otherwise subject to the jurisdiction of the United States at the time of the release, or

(3) in charge of a facility from which a hazardous substance is released, other than a federally permitted release,

in a quantity equal to or greater than that determined pursuant to section 9602 of this title who fails to notify immediately the appropriate agency of the United States Government as soon as he has knowledge of such release or who submits in such a notification any information which he knows to be false or misleading shall, upon conviction, be fined in accordance with the applicable provisions of Title 18 or imprisoned for not more than 3 years (or not more than 5 years in the case of a second or subsequent conviction), or both. Notification received pursuant to this subsection or information obtained by the exploitation of such notification shall not be used against any such person in any criminal case, except a prosecution for perjury or for giving a false statement.

**(c) Notice to Administrator of EPA of existence of storage, etc., facility by owner or operator; exception; time, manner, and form of notice; penalties for failure to notify; use of notice or information pursuant to notice in criminal case**

Within one hundred and eighty days after December 11, 1980, any person who owns or operates or who at the time of disposal owned or operated, or who accepted hazardous substances for transport and selected, a facility at which hazardous substances (as defined in section 9601(14)(C) of this title) are or have been stored, treated, or disposed of shall, unless such facility has a permit issued under, or has been accorded interim status under, subtitle C of the Solid Waste Disposal Act [42 U.S.C.A. § 6921 et seq.], notify the Administrator of the Environmental Protection Agency of the existence of such facility, specifying the amount and type of any hazardous substance to be found there, and any known, suspected, or likely releases of such substances from such facility. The Administrator may prescribe in greater detail the manner and form of the notice and the information included. The Administrator shall notify the affected State agency, or any department designated by the Governor to receive such notice, of the existence of such facility. Any person who knowingly fails to notify the Administrator of the existence of any such facility shall, upon conviction, be fined not more than $10,000, or imprisoned for not more than one year, or both. In addition, any such person who knowingly fails to provide the notice required by this subsection shall not be entitled to any limitation of liability or to any defenses to liability set out in section 9607 of this title: *Provided, however*, That notification under this subsection is not required for any facility which would be reportable hereunder solely as a result of any stoppage in transit which is temporary, incidental to the transportation movement, or at the ordinary operating convenience of a common or contract carrier, and such stoppage shall be considered as a continuity of movement and not as the storage of a hazardous substance. Notification received pursuant to this subsection or information obtained by the exploitation of such notification shall not be used against any such person in any criminal case, except a prosecution for perjury or for giving a false statement.

**(d) Recordkeeping requirements; promulgation of rules and regulations by Administrator of EPA; penalties for violations; waiver of retention requirements**

(1) The Administrator of the Environmental Protection Agency is authorized to promulgate rules and regulations specifying, with respect to—

(A) the location, title, or condition of a facility, and

(B) the identity, characteristics, quantity, origin, or condition (including containerization and previous treatment) of any hazardous substances contained or deposited in a facility;

the records which shall be retained by any person required to provide the notification of a facility set out in subsection (c) of this section. Such specification shall be in accordance with the provisions of this subsection.

(2) Beginning with December 11, 1980, for fifty years thereafter or for fifty years after the date of establishment of a record (whichever is later), or at any such earlier time as a waiver if obtained under paragraph (3) of this subsection, it shall be unlawful for any such person knowingly to destroy, mutilate, erase, dispose of, conceal, or otherwise render unavailable or unreadable or falsify any records identified in paragraph (1) of this subsection. Any person who violates this paragraph shall, upon conviction, be fined in accordance with the applicable provisions of Title 18 or imprisoned for not more than 3 years (or not more than 5 years in the case of a second or subsequent conviction), or both.

(3) At any time prior to the date which occurs fifty years after December 11, 1980, any person identified under paragraph (1) of this subsection may apply to the Administrator of the Environmental Protection Agency for a waiver of the provisions of the first sentence of paragraph (2) of this subsection. The Administrator is authorized to grant such waiver if, in his discretion, such waiver would not unreasonably interfere with the attainment of the purposes and provisions of this chapter. The Administrator shall promulgate rules and regulations regarding such a waiver so as to inform parties of the proper application procedure and conditions for approval of such a waiver.

(4) Notwithstanding the provisions of this subsection, the Administrator of the Environmental Protection Agency may in his discretion require any such person to retain any record identified pursuant to paragraph (1) of this subsection for such a time period in excess of the period specified in paragraph (2) of this subsection as the Administrator determines to be necessary to protect the public health or welfare.

**(e) Applicability to registered pesticide product**

This section shall not apply to the application of a pesticide product registered under the Federal Insecticide, Fungicide, and Rodenticide Act [7 U.S.C.A. § 136 et seq.] or to the handling and storage of such a pesticide product by an agricultural producer.

**(f) Exemptions from notice and penalty provisions for substances reported under other Federal law or is in continuous release, etc.**

No notification shall be required under subsection (a) or (b) of this section for any release of a hazardous substance—

(1) which is required to be reported (or specifically exempted from a requirement for reporting) under subtitle C of the Solid Waste Disposal Act [42 U.S.C.A. § 6921 et seq.] or regulations thereunder and which has been reported to the National Response Center, or

(2) which is a continuous release, stable in quantity and rate, and is—

(A) from a facility for which notification has been given under subsection (c) of this section, or

(B) a release of which notification has been given under subsections (a) and (b) of this section for a period sufficient to establish the continuity, quantity, and regularity of such release:

*Provided*, That notification in accordance with subsections (a) and (b) of this paragraph shall be given for releases subject to this paragraph annually, or at such time as there is any statistically significant increase in the quantity of any hazardous substance or constituent thereof released, above that previously reported or occurring.

(Pub.L. 96–510, Title I, § 103, Dec. 11, 1980, 94 Stat. 2772; Pub.L. 96–561, Title II, § 238(b), Dec. 22, 1980, 94 Stat. 3300; Pub.L. 99–499, Title I, §§ 103, 109(a)(1), (2), Oct. 17, 1986, 100 Stat. 1617, 1632, 1633; Pub.L. 104–208, Title I, § 101(a) [Title II, § 211(b)], Sept. 30, 1996, 110 Stat. 3009–41.)

### HISTORICAL AND STATUTORY NOTES

**References in Text**

The Clean Water Act, referred to in subsec. (a), is Act June 30, 1948, c. 758, as amended generally by Pub.L. 92–500, § 2, Oct. 18, 1972, 86 Stat. 816, also known as the Federal Water Pollution Control Act, which is classified generally to chapter 26 (section 1251 et seq.) of Title 33, Navigation and Navigable Waters. For complete classification of this Act to the Code, see Short Title note set out under section 1251 of Title 33 and Tables.

The Magnuson-Stevens Fishery Conservation and Management Act, referred to in subsec. (b)(2), is Pub.L. 94–265, Apr. 13, 1976, 90 Stat. 331, as amended, which is classified principally to chapter 38 (section 1801 et seq.) of Title 16, Conservation. For complete classification of this Act to the Code, see Short Title note set out under section 1801 of Title 16 and Tables.

The Solid Waste Disposal Act, referred to in subsecs. (c) and (f)(1), is Title II of Pub.L. 89–272, Oct. 20, 1965, 79 Stat. 997, as amended generally by Pub.L. 94–580, § 2, Oct. 21, 1976, 90 Stat. 2795. Subtitle C of the Solid Waste Disposal Act is classified generally to subchapter III (section 6921 et seq.) of chapter 82 of this title. For complete classification of this Act to the Code, see Short Title of 1965 Acts note set out under section 6901 of this title and Tables.

The Federal Insecticide, Fungicide, and Rodenticide Act, referred to in subsec. (e), is Act June 25, 1947, c. 125, as amended generally by Pub.L. 92–516, Oct. 21, 1972, 86 Stat. 973, which is classified generally to subchapter II (section 136 et seq.) of chapter 6 of Title 7, Agriculture. For complete classification of this Act to the Code, see Short Title note set out under section 136 of Title 7 and Tables.

**Effective Dates**

1996 Acts

Amendment by section 101(a) of Title I [Title II, § 211(b)] of Div. A of Pub.L. 104–208 effective 15 days after Oct. 11, 1996, see section 101(a) of Title I [Title II, § 211(b)] of Div. A of Pub.L. 104–208, set out as a note under section 1801 of Title 16, Conservation.

1986 Acts

Amendment by Pub.L. 99–499 effective Oct. 17, 1986, see section 4 of Pub.L. 99–499, set out as a note under section 9601 of this title.

1980 Acts

Amendment by Pub.L. 96–561 effective 15 days after Dec. 22, 1980, see section 238 of Pub.L. 96–561, set out as a Short Title of 1980 Amendments note under section 1801 of Title 16, Conservation.

## § 9604. Response authorities

**[CERCLA § 104]**

**(a) Removal and other remedial action by President; applicability of national contingency plan; response by potentially responsible parties; public health threats; limitations on response; exception**

(1) Whenever (A) any hazardous substance is released or there is a substantial threat of such a release into the environment, or (B) there is a release or substantial threat of release into the environment of any pollutant or contaminant which may present an imminent and substantial danger to the public health or welfare, the President is authorized to act, consistent with the national contingency plan, to remove or arrange for the removal of, and provide for remedial action relating to such hazardous substance, pollutant, or contaminant at any time (including its removal from any contaminated natural resource), or take any other response measure consistent with the national contingency plan which the President deems necessary to protect the public health or welfare or the environment. When the President determines that such action will be done properly and promptly by the owner or operator of the facility or vessel or by any other responsible party, the President may allow such person to carry out the action, conduct the remedial investigation, or conduct the feasibility study in accordance with section 9622 of this title. No remedial investigation or feasibility study (RI/FS) shall be authorized except on a determination by the President that the party is qualified to conduct the RI/FS and only if the President contracts with or arranges for a qualified person to assist the President in overseeing and reviewing the conduct of such RI/FS and if the responsible party agrees to reimburse the Fund for any cost incurred by the President under, or in connection with, the oversight contract or arrangement. In no event shall a potentially responsible party be subject to a lesser standard of liability, receive preferential treatment, or in any other way, whether direct or indirect, benefit from any such arrangements as a response action contractor, or as a person hired or retained by such a response action contractor, with respect to the release or facility in question. The President shall give primary attention to those releases which the President deems may present a public health threat.

**(2) Removal action**

Any removal action undertaken by the President under this subsection (or by any other person referred to in section 9622 of this title) should, to the extent the President deems practicable, contribute to the efficient performance of any long term remedial action with respect to the release or threatened release concerned.

(3) **Limitations on response**

The President shall not provide for a removal or remedial action under this section in response to a release or threat of release—

(A) of a naturally occurring substance in its unaltered form, or altered solely through naturally occurring processes or phenomena, from a location where it is naturally found;

(B) from products which are part of the structure of, and result in exposure within, residential buildings or business or community structures; or

(C) into public or private drinking water supplies due to deterioration of the system through ordinary use.

(4) **Exception to limitations**

Notwithstanding paragraph (3) of this subsection, to the extent authorized by this section, the President may respond to any release or threat of release if in the President's discretion, it constitutes a public health or environmental emergency and no other person with the authority and capability to respond to the emergency will do so in a timely manner.

**(b) Investigations, monitoring, coordination, etc., by President**

(1) **Information; studies and investigations**

Whenever the President is authorized to act pursuant to subsection (a) of this section, or whenever the President has reason to believe that a release has occurred or is about to occur, or that illness, disease, or complaints thereof may be attributable to exposure to a hazardous substance, pollutant, or contaminant and that a release may have occurred or be occurring, he may undertake such investigations, monitoring, surveys, testing, and other information gathering as he may deem necessary or appropriate to identify the existence and extent of the release or threat thereof, the source and nature of the hazardous substances, pollutants or contaminants involved, and the extent of danger to the public health or welfare or to the environment. In addition, the President may undertake such planning, legal, fiscal, economic, engineering, architectural, and other studies or investigations as he may deem necessary or appropriate to plan and direct response actions, to recover the costs thereof, and to enforce the provisions of this chapter.

(2) **Coordination of investigations**

The President shall promptly notify the appropriate Federal and State natural resource trustees of potential damages to natural resources resulting from releases under investigation pursuant to this section and shall seek to coordinate the assessments, investigations, and planning under this section with such Federal and State trustees.

**(c) Criteria for continuance of obligations from Fund over specified amount for response actions; consultation by President with affected States; contracts or cooperative agreements by States with President prior to remedial actions; cost-sharing agreements; selection by President of remedial actions; State credits: granting of credit, expenses before listing or agreement, response actions between 1978 and 1980, State expenses after December 11, 1980, in excess of 10 percent of costs, item-by-item approval, use of credits; operation and maintenance; limitation on source of funds for O & M; recontracting; siting**

(1) Unless (A) the President finds that (i) continued response actions are immediately required to prevent, limit, or mitigate an emergency, (ii) there is an immediate risk to public health or welfare or the environment, and (iii) such assistance will not otherwise be provided on a timely basis, or (B) the President has determined the appropriate remedial actions pursuant to paragraph (2) of this subsection and the State or States in which the source of the release is located have complied with the requirements of paragraph (3) of this subsection, or (C) continued response action is otherwise appropriate and consistent with the remedial action to be taken [1] obligations from the Fund, other than those authorized by subsection (b) of this section, shall not continue after $2,000,000 has been obligated for response actions or 12 months has elapsed from the date of initial response to a release or threatened release of hazardous substances.

(2) The President shall consult with the affected State or States before determining any appropriate remedial action to be taken pursuant to the authority granted under subsection (a) of this section.

(3) The President shall not provide any remedial actions pursuant to this section unless the State in which the release occurs first enters into a contract or cooperative agreement with the President providing assurances deemed adequate by the President that (A) the State will assure all future maintenance of the removal and remedial actions provided for the expected life of such actions as determined by the President; (B) the State will assure the availability of a hazardous waste disposal facility acceptable to the President and in compliance with the requirements of subtitle C of the Solid Waste Disposal Act [42 U.S.C.A. § 6921 et seq.] for any necessary offsite storage, destruction, treatment, or secure disposition of the hazardous substances; and (C) the State will pay or assure payment of (i) 10 per centum of the costs of the remedial action,

including all future maintenance, or (ii) 50 percent (or such greater amount as the President may determine appropriate, taking into account the degree of responsibility of the State or political subdivision for the release) of any sums expended in response to a release at a facility, that was operated by the State or a political subdivision thereof, either directly or through a contractual relationship or otherwise, at the time of any disposal of hazardous substances therein. For the purpose of clause (ii) of this subparagraph, the term "facility" does not include navigable waters or the beds underlying those waters. In the case of remedial action to be taken on land or water held by an Indian tribe, held by the United States in trust for Indians, held by a member of an Indian tribe (if such land or water is subject to a trust restriction on alienation), or otherwise within the borders of an Indian reservation, the requirements of this paragraph for assurances regarding future maintenance and cost-sharing shall not apply, and the President shall provide the assurance required by this paragraph regarding the availability of a hazardous waste disposal facility.

**(4) Selection of remedial action**

The President shall select remedial actions to carry out this section in accordance with section 9621 of this title (relating to cleanup standards).

**(5) State credits**

**(A) Granting of credit**

The President shall grant a State a credit against the share of the costs, for which it is responsible under paragraph (3) with respect to a facility listed on the National Priorities List under the National Contingency Plan, for amounts expended by a State for remedial action at such facility pursuant to a contract or cooperative agreement with the President. The credit under this paragraph shall be limited to those State expenses which the President determines to be reasonable, documented, direct out-of-pocket expenditures of non-Federal funds.

**(B) Expenses before listing or agreement**

The credit under this paragraph shall include expenses for remedial action at a facility incurred before the listing of the facility on the National Priorities List or before a contract or cooperative agreement is entered into under subsection (d) of this section for the facility if—

(i) after such expenses are incurred the facility is listed on such list and a contract or cooperative agreement is entered into for the facility, and

(ii) the President determines that such expenses would have been credited to the State under subparagraph (A) had the expenditures been made after listing of the facility on such list and after the date on which such contract or cooperative agreement is entered into.

**(C) Response actions between 1978 and 1980**

The credit under this paragraph shall include funds expended or obligated by the State or a political subdivision thereof after January 1, 1978, and before December 11, 1980, for cost-eligible response actions and claims for damages compensable under section 9611 of this title.

**(D) State expenses after December 11, 1980, in excess of 10 percent of costs**

The credit under this paragraph shall include 90 percent of State expenses incurred at a facility owned, but not operated, by such State or by a political subdivision thereof. Such credit applies only to expenses incurred pursuant to a contract or cooperative agreement under subsection (d) of this section and only to expenses incurred after December 11, 1980, but before October 17, 1986.

**(E) Item-by-item approval**

In the case of expenditures made after October 17, 1986, the President may require prior approval of each item of expenditure as a condition of granting a credit under this paragraph.

**(F) Use of credits**

Credits granted under this paragraph for funds expended with respect to a facility may be used by the State to reduce all or part of the share of costs otherwise required to be paid by the State under paragraph (3) in connection with remedial actions at such facility. If the amount of funds for which credit is allowed under this paragraph exceeds such share of costs for such facility, the State may use the amount of such excess to reduce all or part of the share of such costs at other facilities in that State. A credit shall not entitle the State to any direct payment.

**(6) Operation and maintenance**

For the purposes of paragraph (3) of this subsection, in the case of ground or surface water contamination, completed remedial action includes the completion of treatment or other measures, whether taken onsite or offsite, necessary to restore ground and surface water quality to a level that assures protection of human health and the environment. With respect to such measures, the operation of such measures for a period of up to 10 years after the construction or installation and commencement of operation shall be considered remedial action. Activities required to maintain the effectiveness of such measures following such period or the completion of remedial action, whichever is earlier, shall be considered operation or maintenance.

(7) **Limitation on source of funds for O&M**

During any period after the availability of funds received by the Hazardous Substance Superfund established under subchapter A of chapter 98 of Title 26 from tax revenues or appropriations from general revenues, the Federal share of the payment of the cost of operation or maintenance pursuant to paragraph (3)(C)(i) or paragraph (6) of this subsection (relating to operation and maintenance) shall be from funds received by the Hazardous Substance Superfund from amounts recovered on behalf of such fund under this chapter.

(8) **Recontracting**

The President is authorized to undertake or continue whatever interim remedial actions the President determines to be appropriate to reduce risks to public health or the environment where the performance of a complete remedial action requires recontracting because of the discovery of sources, types, or quantities of hazardous substances not known at the time of entry into the original contract. The total cost of interim actions undertaken at a facility pursuant to this paragraph shall not exceed $2,000,000.

(9) **Siting**

Effective 3 years after October 17, 1986, the President shall not provide any remedial actions pursuant to this section unless the State in which the release occurs first enters into a contract or cooperative agreement with the President providing assurances deemed adequate by the President that the State will assure the availability of hazardous waste treatment or disposal facilities which—

(A) have adequate capacity for the destruction, treatment, or secure disposition of all hazardous wastes that are reasonably expected to be generated within the State during the 20-year period following the date of such contract or cooperative agreement and to be disposed of, treated, or destroyed,

(B) are within the State or outside the State in accordance with an interstate agreement or regional agreement or authority,

(C) are acceptable to the President, and

(D) are in compliance with the requirements of subtitle C of the Solid Waste Disposal Act [42 U.S.C.A. § 6921 et seq.]

**(d) Contracts or cooperative agreements by President with States or political subdivisions or Indian tribes; State applications, terms and conditions; reimbursements; cost-sharing provisions; enforcement requirements and procedures**

(1) **Cooperative agreements**

(A) **State applications**

A State or political subdivision thereof or Indian tribe may apply to the President to carry out actions authorized in this section. If the President determines that the State or political subdivision or Indian tribe has the capability to carry out any or all of such actions in accordance with the criteria and priorities established pursuant to section 9605(a)(8) of this title and to carry out related enforcement actions, the President may enter into a contract or cooperative agreement with the State or political subdivision or Indian tribe to carry out such actions. The President shall make a determination regarding such an application within 90 days after the President receives the application.

(B) **Terms and conditions**

A contract or cooperative agreement under this paragraph shall be subject to such terms and conditions as the President may prescribe. The contract or cooperative agreement may cover a specific facility or specific facilities.

(C) **Reimbursements**

Any State which expended funds during the period beginning September 30, 1985, and ending on October 17, 1986, for response actions at any site included on the National Priorities List and subject to a cooperative agreement under this chapter shall be reimbursed for the share of costs of such actions for which the Federal Government is responsible under this chapter.

(2) If the President enters into a cost-sharing agreement pursuant to subsection (c) of this section or a contract or cooperative agreement pursuant to this subsection, and the State or political subdivision thereof fails to comply with any requirements of the contract, the President may, after providing sixty days notice, seek in the appropriate Federal district court to enforce the contract or to recover any funds advanced or any costs incurred because of the breach of the contract by the State or political subdivision.

(3) Where a State or a political subdivision thereof is acting in behalf of the President, the President is authorized to provide technical and legal assistance in the administration and enforcement of any contract or subcontract in connection with response actions assisted under this subchapter, and to intervene in any civil action involving the enforcement of such contract or subcontract.

(4) Where two or more noncontiguous facilities are reasonably related on the basis of geography, or on the basis of the threat, or potential threat to the public health or welfare or the environment, the President may, in his discretion, treat these related facilities as one for purposes of this section.

(e) **Information gathering and access**

(1) **Action authorized**

Any officer, employee, or representative of the President, duly designated by the President, is authorized to take action under paragraph (2), (3), or (4) (or any combination thereof) at a vessel, facility, establishment, place, property, or location or, in the case of paragraph (3) or (4), at any vessel, facility, establishment, place, property, or location which is adjacent to the vessel, facility, establishment, place, property, or location referred to in such paragraph (3) or (4). Any duly designated officer, employee, or representative of a State or political subdivision under a contract or cooperative agreement under subsection (d)(1) of this section is also authorized to take such action. The authority of paragraphs (3) and (4) may be exercised only if there is a reasonable basis to believe there may be a release or threat of release of a hazardous substance or pollutant or contaminant. The authority of this subsection may be exercised only for the purposes of determining the need for response, or choosing or taking any response action under this subchapter, or otherwise enforcing the provisions of this subchapter.

(2) **Access to information**

Any officer, employee, or representative described in paragraph (1) may require any person who has or may have information relevant to any of the following to furnish, upon reasonable notice, information or documents relating to such matter:

(A) The identification, nature, and quantity of materials which have been or are generated, treated, stored, or disposed of at a vessel or facility or transported to a vessel or facility.

(B) The nature or extent of a release or threatened release of a hazardous substance or pollutant or contaminant at or from a vessel or facility.

(C) Information relating to the ability of a person to pay for or to perform a cleanup.

In addition, upon reasonable notice, such person either (i) shall grant any such officer, employee, or representative access at all reasonable times to any vessel, facility, establishment, place, property, or location to inspect and copy all documents or records relating to such matters or (ii) shall copy and furnish to the officer, employee, or representative all such documents or records, at the option and expense of such person.

(3) **Entry**

Any officer, employee, or representative described in paragraph (1) is authorized to enter at reasonable times any of the following:

(A) Any vessel, facility, establishment, or other place or property where any hazardous substance or pollutant or contaminant may be or has been generated, stored, treated, disposed of, or transported from.

(B) Any vessel, facility, establishment, or other place or property from which or to which a hazardous substance or pollutant or contaminant has been or may have been released.

(C) Any vessel, facility, establishment, or other place or property where such release is or may be threatened.

(D) Any vessel, facility, establishment, or other place or property where entry is needed to determine the need for response or the appropriate response or to effectuate a response action under this subchapter.

(4) **Inspection and samples**

(A) **Authority**

Any officer, employee or representative described in paragraph (1) is authorized to inspect and obtain samples from any vessel, facility, establishment, or other place or property referred to in paragraph (3) or from any location of any suspected hazardous substance or pollutant or contaminant. Any such officer, employee, or representative is authorized to inspect and obtain samples of any containers or labeling for suspected hazardous substances or pollutants or contaminants. Each such inspection shall be completed with reasonable promptness.

(B) **Samples**

If the officer, employee, or representative obtains any samples, before leaving the premises he shall give to the owner, operator, tenant, or other person in charge of the place from which the samples were obtained a receipt describing the sample obtained and, if requested, a portion of each such sample. A copy of the results of any analysis made of such samples shall be furnished promptly to the owner, operator, tenant, or other person in charge, if such person can be located.

(5) **Compliance orders**

(A) **Issuance**

If consent is not granted regarding any request made by an officer, employee, or representative under paragraph (2), (3), or (4), the President may issue an order directing compliance with the request. The order may be issued after such notice and opportunity for consultation as is reasonably appropriate under the circumstances.

(B) **Compliance**

The President may ask the Attorney General to commence a civil action to compel compliance with a request or order referred to in subparagraph (A). Where there is a reasonable basis to believe there may be a release or threat of a release of a hazardous substance or pollutant or contaminant, the court shall take the following actions:

**(i)** In the case of interference with entry or inspection, the court shall enjoin such interference or direct compliance with orders to prohibit interference with entry or inspection unless under the circumstances of the case the demand for entry or inspection is arbitrary and capricious, an abuse of discretion, or otherwise not in accordance with law.

**(ii)** In the case of information or document requests or orders, the court shall enjoin interference with such information or document requests or orders or direct compliance with the requests or orders to provide such information or documents unless under the circumstances of the case the demand for information or documents is arbitrary and capricious, an abuse of discretion, or otherwise not in accordance with law.

The court may assess a civil penalty not to exceed $25,000 for each day of noncompliance against any person who unreasonably fails to comply with the provisions of paragraph (2), (3), or (4) or an order issued pursuant to subparagraph (A) of this paragraph.

**(6) Other authority**

Nothing in this subsection shall preclude the President from securing access or obtaining information in any other lawful manner.

**(7) Confidentiality of information**

**(A)** Any records, reports, or information obtained from any person under this section (including records, reports, or information obtained by representatives of the President) shall be available to the public, except that upon a showing satisfactory to the President (or the State, as the case may be) by any person that records, reports, or information, or particular part thereof (other than health or safety effects data), to which the President (or the State, as the case may be) or any officer, employee, or representative has access under this section if made public would divulge information entitled to protection under section 1905 of Title 18, such information or particular portion thereof shall be considered confidential in accordance with the purposes of that section, except that such record, report, document or information may be disclosed to other officers, employees, or authorized representatives of the United States concerned with carrying out this chapter, or when relevant in any proceeding under this chapter.

**(B)** Any person not subject to the provisions of section 1905 of Title 18 who knowingly and willfully divulges or discloses any information entitled to protection under this subsection shall, upon conviction, be subject to a fine of not more than $5,000 or to imprisonment not to exceed one year, or both.

**(C)** In submitting data under this chapter, a person required to provide such data may (i) designate the data which such person believes is entitled to protection under this subsection and (ii) submit such designated data separately from other data submitted under this chapter. A designation under this paragraph shall be made in writing and in such manner as the President may prescribe by regulation.

**(D)** Notwithstanding any limitation contained in this section or any other provision of law, all information reported to or otherwise obtained by the President (or any representative of the President) under this chapter shall be made available, upon written request of any duly authorized committee of the Congress, to such committee.

**(E)** No person required to provide information under this chapter may claim that the information is entitled to protection under this paragraph unless such person shows each of the following:

**(i)** Such person has not disclosed the information to any other person, other than a member of a local emergency planning committee established under title III of the Amendments and Reauthorization Act of 1986 [42 U.S.C.A. § 11001 et seq.], an officer or employee of the United States or a State or local government, an employee of such person, or a person who is bound by a confidentiality agreement, and such person has taken reasonable measures to protect the confidentiality of such information and intends to continue to take such measures.

**(ii)** The information is not required to be disclosed, or otherwise made available, to the public under any other Federal or State law.

**(iii)** Disclosure of the information is likely to cause substantial harm to the competitive position of such person.

**(iv)** The specific chemical identity, if sought to be protected, is not readily discoverable through reverse engineering.

**(F)** The following information with respect to any hazardous substance at the facility or vessel shall not be entitled to protection under this paragraph:

**(i)** The trade name, common name, or generic class or category of the hazardous substance.

**(ii)** The physical properties of the substance, including its boiling point, melting point, flash point, specific gravity, vapor density, solubility in water, and vapor pressure at 20 degrees celsius.

(iii) The hazards to health and the environment posed by the substance, including physical hazards (such as explosion) and potential acute and chronic health hazards.

(iv) The potential routes of human exposure to the substance at the facility, establishment, place, or property being investigated, entered, or inspected under this subsection.

(v) The location of disposal of any waste stream.

(vi) Any monitoring data or analysis of monitoring data pertaining to disposal activities.

(vii) Any hydrogeologic or geologic data.

(viii) Any groundwater monitoring data.

**(f) Contracts for response actions; compliance with Federal health and safety standards**

In awarding contracts to any person engaged in response actions, the President or the State, in any case where it is awarding contracts pursuant to a contract entered into under subsection (d) of this section, shall require compliance with Federal health and safety standards established under section 9651(f) of this title by contractors and subcontractors as a condition of such contracts.

**(g) Rates for wages and labor standards applicable to covered work**

(1) All laborers and mechanics employed by contractors or subcontractors in the performance of construction, repair, or alteration work funded in whole or in part under this section shall be paid wages at rates not less than those prevailing on projects of a character similar in the locality as determined by the Secretary of Labor in accordance with sections 3141 to 3144, 3146, 3147 of Title 40. The President shall not approve any such funding without first obtaining adequate assurance that required labor standards will be maintained upon the construction work.

(2) The Secretary of Labor shall have, with respect to the labor standards specified in paragraph (1), the authority and functions set forth in Reorganization Plan Numbered 14 of 1950 (15 F.R. 3176; 64 Stat. 1267) and section 3145 of Title 40.

**(h) Emergency procurement powers; exercise by President**

Notwithstanding any other provision of law, subject to the provisions of section 9611 of this title, the President may authorize the use of such emergency procurement powers as he deems necessary to effect the purpose of this chapter. Upon determination that such procedures are necessary, the President shall promulgate regulations prescribing the circumstances under which such authority shall be used and the procedures governing the use of such authority.

**(i) Agency for Toxic Substances and Disease Registry; establishment, functions, etc.**

(1) There is hereby established within the Public Health Service an agency, to be known as the Agency for Toxic Substances and Disease Registry, which shall report directly to the Surgeon General of the United States. The Administrator of said Agency shall, with the cooperation of the Administrator of the Environmental Protection Agency, the Commissioner of the Food and Drug Administration, the Directors of the National Institute of Medicine, National Institute of Environmental Health Sciences, National Institute of Occupational Safety and Health, Centers for Disease Control and Prevention, the Administrator of the Occupational Safety and Health Administration, the Administrator of the Social Security Administration, the Secretary of Transportation, and appropriate State and local health officials, effectuate and implement the health related authorities of this chapter. In addition, said Administrator shall—

(A) in cooperation with the States, establish and maintain a national registry of serious diseases and illnesses and a national registry of persons exposed to toxic substances;

(B) establish and maintain inventory of literature, research, and studies on the health effects of toxic substances;

(C) in cooperation with the States, and other agencies of the Federal Government, establish and maintain a complete listing of areas closed to the public or otherwise restricted in use because of toxic substance contamination;

(D) in cases of public health emergencies caused or believed to be caused by exposure to toxic substances, provide medical care and testing to exposed individuals, including but not limited to tissue sampling, chromosomal testing where appropriate, epidemiological studies, or any other assistance appropriate under the circumstances; and

(E) either independently or as part of other health status survey, conduct periodic survey and screening programs to determine relationships between exposure to toxic substances and illness. In cases of public health emergencies, exposed persons shall be eligible for admission to hospitals and other facilities and services operated or provided by the Public Health Service.

(2)(A) Within 6 months after October 17, 1986, the Administrator of the Agency for Toxic Substances and Disease Registry (ATSDR) and the Administrator of the Environmental Protection Agency (EPA) shall prepare a list, in order of priority, of at least 100 hazardous substances which are most commonly found at facilities on the National Priorities List and which, in their sole discretion, they determine are posing the most significant potential threat to human health due to their known or suspected toxicity to humans and the potential for human exposure to such substances at facilities on the National Priorities List or at facilities to which a response to a release or a threatened release under this section is under consideration.

(B) Within 24 months after October 17, 1986, the Administrator of ATSDR and the Administrator of EPA shall revise the list prepared under subparagraph (A). Such revision shall include, in order of priority, the addition of 100 or more such hazardous substances. In each of the 3 consecutive 12-month periods that follow, the Administrator of ATSDR and the Administrator of EPA shall revise, in the same manner as provided in the 2 preceding sentences, such list to include not fewer than 25 additional hazardous substances per revision. The Administrator of ATSDR and the Administrator of EPA shall not less often than once every year thereafter revise such list to include additional hazardous substances in accordance with the criteria in subparagraph (A).

(3) Based on all available information, including information maintained under paragraph (1)(B) and data developed and collected on the health effects of hazardous substances under this paragraph, the Administrator of ATSDR shall prepare toxicological profiles of each of the substances listed pursuant to paragraph (2). The toxicological profiles shall be prepared in accordance with guidelines developed by the Administrator of ATSDR and the Administrator of EPA. Such profiles shall include, but not be limited to each of the following:

(A) An examination, summary, and interpretation of available toxicological information and epidemiologic evaluations on a hazardous substance in order to ascertain the levels of significant human exposure for the substance and the associated acute, subacute, and chronic health effects.

(B) A determination of whether adequate information on the health effects of each substance is available or in the process of development to determine levels of exposure which present a significant risk to human health of acute, subacute, and chronic health effects.

(C) Where appropriate, an identification of toxicological testing needed to identify the types or levels of exposure that may present significant risk of adverse health effects in humans.

Any toxicological profile or revision thereof shall reflect the Administrator of ATSDR's assessment of all relevant toxicological testing which has been peer reviewed. The profiles required to be prepared under this paragraph for those hazardous substances listed under subparagraph (A) of paragraph (2) shall be completed, at a rate of no fewer than 25 per year, within 4 years after October 17, 1986. A profile required on a substance listed pursuant to subparagraph (B) of paragraph (2) shall be completed within 3 years after addition to the list. The profiles prepared under this paragraph shall be of those substances highest on the list of priorities under paragraph (2) for which profiles have not previously been prepared. Profiles required under this paragraph shall be revised and republished as necessary, but no less often than once every 3 years. Such profiles shall be provided to the States and made available to other interested parties.

(4) The Administrator of the ATSDR shall provide consultations upon request on health issues relating to exposure to hazardous or toxic substances, on the basis of available information, to the Administrator of EPA, State officials, and local officials. Such consultations to individuals may be provided by States under cooperative agreements established under this chapter.

(5)(A) For each hazardous substance listed pursuant to paragraph (2), the Administrator of ATSDR (in consultation with the Administrator of EPA and other agencies and programs of the Public Health Service) shall assess whether adequate information on the health effects of such substance is available. For any such substance for which adequate information is not available (or under development), the Administrator of ATSDR, in cooperation with the Director of the National Toxicology Program, shall assure the initiation of a program of research designed to determine the health effects (and techniques for development of methods to determine such health effects) of such substance. Where feasible, such program shall seek to develop methods to determine the health effects of such substance in combination with other substances with which it is commonly found. Before assuring the initiation of such program, the Administrator of ATSDR shall consider recommendations of the Interagency Testing Committee established under section 4(e) of the Toxic Substances Control Act [15 U.S.C.A. § 2603(e)] on the types of research that should be done. Such program shall include, to the extent necessary to supplement existing information, but shall not be limited to—

(i) laboratory and other studies to determine short, intermediate, and long-term health effects;

(ii) laboratory and other studies to determine organ-specific, site-specific, and system-specific acute and chronic toxicity;

(iii) laboratory and other studies to determine the manner in which such substances are metabolized or to otherwise develop an understanding of the biokinetics of such substances; and

(iv) where there is a possibility of obtaining human data, the collection of such information.

**(B)** In assessing the need to perform laboratory and other studies, as required by subparagraph (A), the Administrator of ATSDR shall consider—

**(i)** the availability and quality of existing test data concerning the substance on the suspected health effect in question;

**(ii)** the extent to which testing already in progress will, in a timely fashion, provide data that will be adequate to support the preparation of toxicological profiles as required by paragraph (3); and

**(iii)** such other scientific and technical factors as the Administrator of ATSDR may determine are necessary for the effective implementation of this subsection.

**(C)** In the development and implementation of any research program under this paragraph, the Administrator of ATSDR and the Administrator of EPA shall coordinate such research program implemented under this paragraph with the National Toxicology Program and with programs of toxicological testing established under the Toxic Substances Control Act [15 U.S.C.A. § 2601 et seq.] and the Federal Insecticide, Fungicide and Rodenticide Act [7 U.S.C.A. § 136 et seq.]. The purpose of such coordination shall be to avoid duplication of effort and to assure that the hazardous substances listed pursuant to this subsection are tested thoroughly at the earliest practicable date. Where appropriate, consistent with such purpose, a research program under this paragraph may be carried out using such programs of toxicological testing.

**(D)** It is the sense of the Congress that the costs of research programs under this paragraph be borne by the manufacturers and processors of the hazardous substance in question, as required in programs of toxicological testing under the Toxic Substances Control Act [15 U.S.C.A. § 2601 et seq.]. Within 1 year after October 17, 1986, the Administrator of EPA shall promulgate regulations which provide, where appropriate, for payment of such costs by manufacturers and processors under the Toxic Substances Control Act, and registrants under the Federal Insecticide, Fungicide, and Rodenticide Act [7 U.S.C.A. § 136 et seq.], and recovery of such costs from responsible parties under this chapter.

**(6)(A)** The Administrator of ATSDR shall perform a health assessment for each facility on the National Priorities List established under section 9605 of this title. Such health assessment shall be completed not later than December 10, 1988, for each facility proposed for inclusion on such list prior to October 17, 1986, or not later than one year after the date of proposal for inclusion on such list for each facility proposed for inclusion on such list after October 17, 1986.

**(B)** The Administrator of ATSDR may perform health assessments for releases or facilities where individual persons or licensed physicians provide information that individuals have been exposed to a hazardous substance, for which the probable source of such exposure is a release. In addition to other methods (formal or informal) of providing such information, such individual persons or licensed physicians may submit a petition to the Administrator of ATSDR providing such information and requesting a health assessment. If such a petition is submitted and the Administrator of ATSDR does not initiate a health assessment, the Administrator of ATSDR shall provide a written explanation of why a health assessment is not appropriate.

**(C)** In determining the priority in which to conduct health assessments under this subsection, the Administrator of ATSDR, in consultation with the Administrator of EPA, shall give priority to those facilities at which there is documented evidence of the release of hazardous substances, at which the potential risk to human health appears highest, and for which in the judgment of the Administrator of ATSDR existing health assessment data are inadequate to assess the potential risk to human health as provided in subparagraph (F). In determining the priorities for conducting health assessments under this subsection, the Administrator of ATSDR shall consider the National Priorities List schedules and the needs of the Environmental Protection Agency and other Federal agencies pursuant to schedules for remedial investigation and feasibility studies.

**(D)** Where a health assessment is done at a site on the National Priorities List, the Administrator of ATSDR shall complete such assessment promptly and, to the maximum extent practicable, before the completion of the remedial investigation and feasibility study at the facility concerned.

**(E)** Any State or political subdivision carrying out a health assessment for a facility shall report the results of the assessment to the Administrator of ATSDR and the Administrator of EPA and shall include recommendations with respect to further activities which need to be carried out under this section. The Administrator of ATSDR shall state such recommendation in any report on the results of any assessment carried out directly by the Administrator of ATSDR for such facility and shall issue periodic reports which include the results of all the assessments carried out under this subsection.

**(F)** For the purposes of this subsection and section 9611(c)(4) of this title, the term "health assessments" shall include preliminary assessments of the potential risk to human health posed by individual sites and facilities, based on such factors as the nature and extent of contamination, the existence of potential pathways of human exposure (including ground or surface water contamination, air emissions, and food chain contamination), the size and potential susceptibility of the community within the likely pathways of exposure, the comparison of expected human exposure levels to the short-term and long-term health effects associated with identified hazardous substances and any available recommended exposure or tolerance limits for such hazardous substances, and the comparison of existing morbidity and mortality data on diseases that may be associated with the observed levels of exposure. The Administrator of ATSDR shall use appropriate data, risk assessments, risk evaluations and studies available from the Administrator of EPA.

**(G)** The purpose of health assessments under this subsection shall be to assist in determining whether actions under paragraph (11) of this subsection should be taken to reduce human exposure to hazardous substances from a facility and whether additional information on human exposure and associated health risks is needed and should be acquired by conducting epidemiological studies under paragraph (7), establishing a registry under paragraph (8), establishing a health surveillance program under paragraph (9), or through other means. In using the results of health assessments for determining additional actions to be taken under this section, the Administrator of ATSDR may consider additional information on the risks to the potentially affected population from all sources of such hazardous substances including known point or nonpoint sources other than those from the facility in question.

**(H)** At the completion of each health assessment, the Administrator of ATSDR shall provide the Administrator of EPA and each affected State with the results of such assessment, together with any recommendations for further actions under this subsection or otherwise under this chapter. In addition, if the health assessment indicates that the release or threatened release concerned may pose a serious threat to human health or the environment, the Administrator of ATSDR shall so notify the Administrator of EPA who shall promptly evaluate such release or threatened release in accordance with the hazard ranking system referred to in section 9605(a)(8)(A) of this title to determine whether the site shall be placed on the National Priorities List or, if the site is already on the list, the Administrator of ATSDR may recommend to the Administrator of EPA that the site be accorded a higher priority.

**(7)(A)** Whenever in the judgment of the Administrator of ATSDR it is appropriate on the basis of the results of a health assessment, the Administrator of ATSDR shall conduct a pilot study of health effects for selected groups of exposed individuals in order to determine the desirability of conducting full scale epidemiological or other health studies of the entire exposed population.

**(B)** Whenever in the judgment of the Administrator of ATSDR it is appropriate on the basis of the results of such pilot study or other study or health assessment, the Administrator of ATSDR shall conduct such full scale epidemiological or other health studies as may be necessary to determine the health effects on the population exposed to hazardous substances from a release or threatened release. If a significant excess of disease in a population is identified, the letter of transmittal of such study shall include an assessment of other risk factors, other than a release, that may, in the judgment of the peer review group, be associated with such disease, if such risk factors were not taken into account in the design or conduct of the study.

**(8)** In any case in which the results of a health assessment indicate a potential significant risk to human health, the Administrator of ATSDR shall consider whether the establishment of a registry of exposed persons would contribute to accomplishing the purposes of this subsection, taking into account circumstances bearing on the usefulness of such a registry, including the seriousness or unique character of identified diseases or the likelihood of population migration from the affected area.

**(9)** Where the Administrator of ATSDR has determined that there is a significant increased risk of adverse health effects in humans from exposure to hazardous substances based on the results of a health assessment conducted under paragraph (6), an epidemiologic study conducted under paragraph (7), or an exposure registry that has been established under paragraph (8), and the Administrator of ATSDR has determined that such exposure is the result of a release from a facility, the Administrator of ATSDR shall initiate a health surveillance program for such population. This program shall include but not be limited to—

**(A)** periodic medical testing where appropriate of population subgroups to screen for diseases for which the population or subgroup is at significant increased risk; and

**(B)** a mechanism to refer for treatment those individuals within such population who are screened positive for such diseases.

**(10)** Two years after October 17, 1986, and every 2 years thereafter, the Administrator of ATSDR shall prepare and submit to the Administrator of EPA and to the Congress a report on the results of the activities of ATSDR regarding—

**(A)** health assessments and pilot health effects studies conducted;

**(B)** epidemiologic studies conducted;

**(C)** hazardous substances which have been listed under paragraph (2), toxicological profiles which have been developed, and toxicologic testing which has been conducted or which is being conducted under this subsection;

**(D)** registries established under paragraph (8); and

**(E)** an overall assessment, based on the results of activities conducted by the Administrator of ATSDR, of the linkage between human exposure to individual or combinations of hazardous substances due to releases from facilities covered by this chapter or the Solid Waste Disposal Act [42 U.S.C.A. § 6901 et seq.] and any increased incidence or prevalence of adverse health effects in humans.

**(11)** If a health assessment or other study carried out under this subsection contains a finding that the exposure concerned presents a significant risk to human health, the President shall take such steps as may be necessary to reduce such exposure and eliminate or substantially mitigate the significant risk to human health. Such steps may include the use of any authority under this chapter, including, but not limited to—

**(A)** provision of alternative water supplies, and

**(B)** permanent or temporary relocation of individuals.

In any case in which information is insufficient, in the judgment of the Administrator of ATSDR or the President to determine a significant human exposure level with respect to a hazardous substance, the President may take such steps as may be necessary to reduce the exposure of any person to such hazardous substance to such level as the President deems necessary to protect human health.

**(12)** In any case which is the subject of a petition, a health assessment or study, or a research program under this subsection, nothing in this subsection shall be construed to delay or otherwise affect or impair the authority of the President, the Administrator of ATSDR, or the Administrator of EPA to exercise any authority vested in the President, the Administrator of ATSDR or the Administrator of EPA under any other provision of law (including, but not limited to, the imminent hazard authority of section 7003 of the Solid Waste Disposal Act [42 U.S.C.A. § 6973]) or the response and abatement authorities of this chapter.

**(13)** All studies and results of research conducted under this subsection (other than health assessments) shall be reported or adopted only after appropriate peer review. Such peer review shall be completed, to the maximum extent practicable, within a period of 60 days. In the case of research conducted under the National Toxicology Program, such peer review may be conducted by the Board of Scientific Counselors. In the case of other research, such peer review shall be conducted by panels consisting of no less than three nor more than seven members, who shall be disinterested scientific experts selected for such purpose by the Administrator of ATSDR or the Administrator of EPA, as appropriate, on the basis of their reputation for scientific objectivity and the lack of institutional ties with any person involved in the conduct of the study or research under review. Support services for such panels shall be provided by the Agency for Toxic Substances and Disease Registry, or by the Environmental Protection Agency, as appropriate.

**(14)** In the implementation of this subsection and other health-related authorities of this chapter, the Administrator of ATSDR shall assemble, develop as necessary, and distribute to the States, and upon request to medical colleges, physicians, and other health professionals, appropriate educational materials (including short courses) on the medical surveillance, screening, and methods of diagnosis and treatment of injury or disease related to exposure to hazardous substances (giving priority to those listed in paragraph (2)), through such means as the Administrator of ATSDR deems appropriate.

**(15)** The activities of the Administrator of ATSDR described in this subsection and section 9611(c)(4) of this title shall be carried out by the Administrator of ATSDR, either directly or through cooperative agreements with States (or political subdivisions thereof) which the Administrator of ATSDR determines are capable of carrying out such activities. Such activities shall include provision of consultations on health information, the conduct of health assessments, including those required under section 3019(b) of the Solid Waste Disposal Act [42 U.S.C.A. § 6939a(b) ], health studies, registries, and health surveillance.

**(16)** The President shall provide adequate personnel for ATSDR, which shall not be fewer than 100 employees. For purposes of determining the number of employees under this subsection, an employee employed by ATSDR on a part-time career employment basis shall be counted as a fraction which is determined by dividing 40 hours into the average number of hours of such employee's regularly scheduled workweek.

**(17)** In accordance with section 9620 of this title (relating to Federal facilities), the Administrator of ATSDR shall have the same authorities under this section with respect to facilities owned or operated by a department, agency, or instrumentality of the United States as the Administrator of ATSDR has with respect to any nongovernmental entity.

**(18)** If the Administrator of ATSDR determines that it is appropriate for purposes of this section to treat a pollutant or contaminant as a hazardous substance, such pollutant or contaminant shall be treated as a hazardous substance for such purpose.

(j) **Acquisition of property**

(1) **Authority**

The President is authorized to acquire, by purchase, lease, condemnation, donation, or otherwise, any real property or any interest in real property that the President in his discretion determines is needed to conduct a remedial action under this chapter. There shall be no cause of action to compel the President to acquire any interest in real property under this chapter.

(2) **State assurance**

The President may use the authority of paragraph (1) for a remedial action only if, before an interest in real estate is acquired under this subsection, the State in which the interest to be acquired is located assures the President, through a contract or cooperative agreement or otherwise, that the State will accept transfer of the interest following completion of the remedial action.

(3) **Exemption**

No Federal, State, or local government agency shall be liable under this chapter solely as a result of acquiring an interest in real estate under this subsection.

(k) **Brownfields revitalization funding**

(1) **Definition of eligible entity**

In this subsection, the term "eligible entity" means—

(A) a general purpose unit of local government;

(B) a land clearance authority or other quasi-governmental entity that operates under the supervision and control of or as an agent of a general purpose unit of local government;

(C) a government entity created by a State legislature;

(D) a regional council or group of general purpose units of local government;

(E) a redevelopment agency that is chartered or otherwise sanctioned by a State;

(F) a State;

(G) an Indian Tribe other than in Alaska; or

(H) an Alaska Native Regional Corporation and an Alaska Native Village Corporation as those terms are defined in the Alaska Native Claims Settlement Act (43 U.S.C. 1601 and following) and the Metlakatla Indian community.

(2) **Brownfield site characterization and assessment grant program**

(A) **Establishment of program**

The Administrator shall establish a program to—

(i) provide grants to inventory, characterize, assess, and conduct planning related to brownfield sites under subparagraph (B); and

(ii) perform targeted site assessments at brownfield sites.

(B) **Assistance for site characterization and assessment**

(i) **In general**

On approval of an application made by an eligible entity, the Administrator may make a grant to the eligible entity to be used for programs to inventory, characterize, assess, and conduct planning related to one or more brownfield sites.

(ii) **Site characterization and assessment**

A site characterization and assessment carried out with the use of a grant under clause (i) shall be performed in accordance with section 9601(35)(B) of this title.

(3) **Grants and loans for brownfield remediation**

(A) **Grants provided by the President**

Subject to paragraphs (4) and (5), the President shall establish a program to provide grants to—

(i) eligible entities, to be used for capitalization of revolving loan funds; and

(ii) eligible entities or nonprofit organizations, where warranted, as determined by the President based on considerations under subparagraph (C), to be used directly for remediation of one or more brownfield sites owned by the entity or organization that receives the grant and in amounts not to exceed $200,000 for each site to be remediated.

(B) **Loans and grants provided by eligible entities**

An eligible entity that receives a grant under subparagraph (A)(i) shall use the grant funds to provide assistance for the remediation of brownfield sites in the form of—

(i) one or more loans to an eligible entity, a site owner, a site developer, or another person; or

(ii) one or more grants to an eligible entity or other nonprofit organization, where warranted, as determined by the eligible entity that is providing the assistance, based on considerations under subparagraph (C), to remediate sites owned by the eligible entity or nonprofit organization that receives the grant.

**(C) Considerations**

In determining whether a grant under subparagraph (A)(ii) or (B)(ii) is warranted, the President or the eligible entity, as the case may be, shall take into consideration—

**(i)** the extent to which a grant will facilitate the creation of, preservation of, or addition to a park, a greenway, undeveloped property, recreational property, or other property used for nonprofit purposes;

**(ii)** the extent to which a grant will meet the needs of a community that has an inability to draw on other sources of funding for environmental remediation and subsequent redevelopment of the area in which a brownfield site is located because of the small population or low income of the community;

**(iii)** the extent to which a grant will facilitate the use or reuse of existing infrastructure;

**(iv)** the benefit of promoting the long-term availability of funds from a revolving loan fund for brownfield remediation; and

**(v)** such other similar factors as the Administrator considers appropriate to consider for the purposes of this subsection.

**(D) Transition**

Revolving loan funds that have been established before the date of the enactment of this subsection may be used in accordance with this paragraph.

**(4) General provisions**

**(A) Maximum grant amount**

**(i) Brownfield site characterization and assessment**

**(I) In general**

A grant under paragraph (2) may be awarded to an eligible entity on a community-wide or site-by-site basis, and shall not exceed, for any individual brownfield site covered by the grant, $200,000.

**(II) Waiver**

The Administrator may waive the $200,000 limitation under subclause (I) to permit the brownfield site to receive a grant of not to exceed $350,000, based on the anticipated level of contamination, size, or status of ownership of the site.

**(ii) Brownfield remediation**

A grant under paragraph (3)(A)(i) may be awarded to an eligible entity on a community-wide or site-by-site basis, not to exceed $1,000,000 per eligible entity. The Administrator may make an additional grant to an eligible entity described in the previous sentence for any year after the year for which the initial grant is made, taking into consideration—

**(I)** the number of sites and number of communities that are addressed by the revolving loan fund;

**(II)** the demand for funding by eligible entities that have not previously received a grant under this subsection;

**(III)** the demonstrated ability of the eligible entity to use the revolving loan fund to enhance remediation and provide funds on a continuing basis; and

**(IV)** such other similar factors as the Administrator considers appropriate to carry out this subsection.

**(B) Prohibition**

**(i) In general**

No part of a grant or loan under this subsection may be used for the payment of—

**(I)** a penalty or fine;

**(II)** a Federal cost-share requirement;

**(III)** an administrative cost;

**(IV)** a response cost at a brownfield site for which the recipient of the grant or loan is potentially liable under section 9607 of this title; or

**(V)** a cost of compliance with any Federal law (including a Federal law specified in section 9601(39)(B) of this title), excluding the cost of compliance with laws applicable to the cleanup.

**(ii) Exclusions**

For the purposes of clause (i)(III), the term 'administrative cost' does not include the cost of—

**(I)** investigation and identification of the extent of contamination;

**(II)** design and performance of a response action; or

**(III)** monitoring of a natural resource.

**(C) Assistance for development of local government site remediation programs**

A local government that receives a grant under this subsection may use not to exceed 10 percent of the grant funds to develop and implement a brownfields program that may include—

**(i)** monitoring the health of populations exposed to one or more hazardous substances from a brownfield site; and

(ii) monitoring and enforcement of any institutional control used to prevent human exposure to any hazardous substance from a brownfield site.

**(D) Insurance**

A recipient of a grant or loan awarded under paragraph (2) or (3) that performs a characterization, assessment, or remediation of a brownfield site may use a portion of the grant or loan to purchase insurance for the characterization, assessment, or remediation of that site.

**(5) Grant applications**

**(A) Submission**

**(i) In general**

**(I) Application**

An eligible entity may submit to the Administrator, through a regional office of the Environmental Protection Agency and in such form as the Administrator may require, an application for a grant under this subsection for one or more brownfield sites (including information on the criteria used by the Administrator to rank applications under subparagraph (C), to the extent that the information is available).

**(II) NCP requirements**

The Administrator may include in any requirement for submission of an application under subclause (I) a requirement of the National Contingency Plan only to the extent that the requirement is relevant and appropriate to the program under this subsection.

**(ii) Coordination**

The Administrator shall coordinate with other Federal agencies to assist in making eligible entities aware of other available Federal resources.

**(iii) Guidance**

The Administrator shall publish guidance to assist eligible entities in applying for grants under this subsection.

**(B) Approval**

The Administrator shall—

(i) at least annually, complete a review of applications for grants that are received from eligible entities under this subsection; and

(ii) award grants under this subsection to eligible entities that the Administrator determines have the highest rankings under the ranking criteria established under subparagraph (C).

**(C) Ranking criteria**

The Administrator shall establish a system for ranking grant applications received under this paragraph that includes the following criteria:

(i) The extent to which a grant will stimulate the availability of other funds for environmental assessment or remediation, and subsequent reuse, of an area in which one or more brownfield sites are located.

(ii) The potential of the proposed project or the development plan for an area in which one or more brownfield sites are located to stimulate economic development of the area on completion of the cleanup.

(iii) The extent to which a grant would address or facilitate the identification and reduction of threats to human health and the environment, including threats in areas in which there is a greater-than-normal incidence of diseases or conditions (including cancer, asthma, or birth defects) that may be associated with exposure to hazardous substances, pollutants, or contaminants.

(iv) The extent to which a grant would facilitate the use or reuse of existing infrastructure.

(v) The extent to which a grant would facilitate the creation of, preservation of, or addition to a park, a greenway, undeveloped property, recreational property, or other property used for nonprofit purposes.

(vi) The extent to which a grant would meet the needs of a community that has an inability to draw on other sources of funding for environmental remediation and subsequent redevelopment of the area in which a brownfield site is located because of the small population or low income of the community.

(vii) The extent to which the applicant is eligible for funding from other sources.

(viii) The extent to which a grant will further the fair distribution of funding between urban and nonurban areas.

(ix) The extent to which the grant provides for involvement of the local community in the process of making decisions relating to cleanup and future use of a brownfield site.

(x) The extent to which a grant would address or facilitate the identification and reduction of threats to the health or welfare of children, pregnant women, minority or low-income communities, or other sensitive populations.

(6) **Implementation of brownfields programs**

(A) **Establishment of program**

The Administrator may provide, or fund eligible entities or nonprofit organizations to provide, training, research, and technical assistance to individuals and organizations, as appropriate, to facilitate the inventory of brownfield sites, site assessments, remediation of brownfield sites, community involvement, or site preparation.

(B) **Funding restrictions**

The total Federal funds to be expended by the Administrator under this paragraph shall not exceed 15 percent of the total amount appropriated to carry out this subsection in any fiscal year.

(7) **Audits**

(A) **In general**

The Inspector General of the Environmental Protection Agency shall conduct such reviews or audits of grants and loans under this subsection as the Inspector General considers necessary to carry out this subsection.

(B) **Procedure**

An audit under this subparagraph shall be conducted in accordance with the auditing procedures of the General Accounting Office, including chapter 75 of Title 31, United States Code.

(C) **Violations**

If the Administrator determines that a person that receives a grant or loan under this subsection has violated or is in violation of a condition of the grant, loan, or applicable Federal law, the Administrator may—

(i) terminate the grant or loan;

(ii) require the person to repay any funds received; and

(iii) seek any other legal remedies available to the Administrator.

(D) **Report to Congress**

Not later than 3 years after the date of the enactment of this subsection, the Inspector General of the Environmental Protection Agency shall submit to Congress a report that provides a description of the management of the program (including a description of the allocation of funds under this subsection).

(8) **Leveraging**

An eligible entity that receives a grant under this subsection may use the grant funds for a portion of a project at a brownfield site for which funding is received from other sources if the grant funds are used only for the purposes described in paragraph (2) or (3).

(9) **Agreements**

Each grant or loan made under this subsection shall—

(A) include a requirement of the National Contingency Plan only to the extent that the requirement is relevant and appropriate to the program under this subsection, as determined by the Administrator; and

(B) be subject to an agreement that—

(i) requires the recipient to—

(I) comply with all applicable Federal and State laws; and

(II) ensure that the cleanup protects human health and the environment;

(ii) requires that the recipient use the grant or loan exclusively for purposes specified in paragraph (2) or (3), as applicable;

(iii) in the case of an application by an eligible entity under paragraph (3)(A), requires the eligible entity to pay a matching share (which may be in the form of a contribution of labor, material, or services) of at least 20 percent, from non-Federal sources of funding, unless the Administrator determines that the matching share would place an undue hardship on the eligible entity; and

(iv) contains such other terms and conditions as the Administrator determines to be necessary to carry out this subsection.

(10) **Facility other than brownfield site**

The fact that a facility may not be a brownfield site within the meaning of section 9601(39)(A) of this title has no effect on the eligibility of the facility for assistance under any other provision of Federal law.

(11) **Effect on Federal laws**

Nothing in this subsection affects any liability or response authority under any Federal law, including—

(A) this chapter (including the last sentence of section 9601(14) of this title);

(B) the Solid Waste Disposal Act (42 U.S.C. 6901 et seq.);

(C) the Federal Water Pollution Control Act (33 U.S.C. 1251 et seq.);

(D) the Toxic Substances Control Act (15 U.S.C. 2601 et seq.); and

(E) the Safe Drinking Water Act (42 U.S.C. 300f et seq.).

**(12) Funding**

**(A) Authorization of appropriations**

There is authorized to be appropriated to carry out this subsection $200,000,000 for each of fiscal years 2002 through 2006.

**(B) Use of certain funds**

Of the amount made available under subparagraph (A), $50,000,000, or, if the amount made available is less than $200,000,000, 25 percent of the amount made available, shall be used for site characterization, assessment, and remediation of facilities described in section 9601(39)(D)(ii)(II) of this title.

(Pub.L. 96–510, Title I, § 104, Dec. 11, 1980, 94 Stat. 2774; Pub.L. 99–499, Title I, §§ 104, 110, Title II, § 207(b), Oct. 17, 1986, 100 Stat. 1617, 1636, 1705; Pub.L. 99–514, § 2, Oct. 22, 1986, 100 Stat. 2095; Pub.L. 102–531, Title III, § 312(h), Oct. 27, 1992, 106 Stat. 3506; Pub.L. 107–118, Title II, § 211(b), Jan. 11, 2002, 115 Stat. 2362.)

1 So in original. Probably should be followed by a comma.

## HISTORICAL AND STATUTORY NOTES

**References in Text**

"This chapter", referred to in text, originally read "this Act", meaning Pub.L. 96–510, Dec. 11, 1980, 94 Stat. 2767, as amended, known as the Comprehensive Environmental Response, Compensation, and Liability Act of 1980, which is classified principally to this chapter [42 U.S.C.A. § 9601 et seq.]; see Tables for complete classification.

The Solid Waste Disposal Act, referred to in subsecs. (c)(3), (9)(D), (i)(10)(E), and (k)(11)(B), is Title II of Pub.L. 89–272, Oct. 20, 1965, 79 Stat. 997, as amended generally by Pub.L. 94–580, § 2, Oct. 21, 1976, 90 Stat. 2795, which is classified principally to chapter 82 of this title [42 U.S.C.A. § 6901 et seq.]. Subtitle C of the Solid Waste Disposal Act is classified generally to subchapter III (section 6921 et seq.) of chapter 82 of this title. See Tables for complete classification.

Title III of the Amendments and Reauthorization Act of 1986, referred to in subsec. (e)(7)(E)(i), probably means Title III (section 300 et seq.) of the Superfund Amendments and Reauthorization Act of 1986, Pub.L. 99–499, Oct. 17, 1986, 100 Stat. 1728, known as the Emergency Planning and Community Right-To-Know Act of 1986, which is classified generally to chapter 116 (section 11001 et seq.) of this title. For complete classification of the Emergency Planning and Community Right-To-Know Act of 1986 to the Code, see Short Title of 1986 Acts note set out under section 11001 of this title and Tables.

Reorganization Plan Numbered 14 of 1950, referred to in subsec. (g)(2), is set out in Appendix 1 to Title 5, Government Organization and Employees.

The Toxic Substances Control Act, referred to in subsecs. (i)(5)(C), (D) and (k)(11)(D), is Pub.L. 94–469, Oct. 11, 1976, 90 Stat. 2003, as amended, which is classified principally to chapter 53 of Title 15 [15 U.S.C.A. § 2601 et seq.]. See Tables for complete classification.

The Federal Insecticide, Fungicide, and Rodenticide Act, referred to in subsec. (i)(5)(C), (D), is Act June 25, 1947, c. 125, as amended generally by Pub.L. 92–516, Oct. 21, 1972, 86 Stat. 973, which is classified generally to subchapter II (section 136 et seq.) of chapter 6 of Title 7, Agriculture. For complete classification of this Act to the Code, see Short Title note set out under section 136 of Title 7 and Tables.

The Alaska Native Claims Settlement Act, referred to in subsec. (k)(1)(H), is Pub.L. 92–203, Dec. 18, 1971, 85 Stat. 688, as amended, which is classified principally to chapter 33 of Title 43 [43 U.S.C.A. § 1601 et seq.]. See Tables for complete classification.

The date of the enactment of this subsection, referred to in subsec. (k)(3)(D) and (7)(D), probably means Jan. 11, 2002, the approval date of Pub.L. 107–118, 115 Stat. 2362, which enacted subsec. (k) of this section.

Chapter 75 of Title 31, referred to in subsec. (k)(7)(B), is classified to 31 U.S.C.A. § 7501 et seq.

The Federal Water Pollution Control Act, referred to in subsec. (k)(11)(C), is Act June 30, 1948, c. 758, as amended generally by Pub.L. 92–500, § 2, Oct. 18, 1972, 86 Stat. 816, also known as the Clean Water Act, which is classified principally to chapter 26 of Title 33 [33 U.S.C.A. § 1251 et seq.]. See Tables for complete classification.

The Safe Drinking Water Act, referred to in subsec. (k)(11)(E), is Pub.L. 93–523, Dec. 16, 1974, 88 Stat. 1660, as amended, which is classified principally to subchapter XII of chapter 6A of this title [42 U.S.C.A. § 300f et seq.]. Part C of the Safe Drinking Water Act is classified generally to part C of subchapter XII of chapter 6A of this title [42 U.S.C.A. § 300h et seq.]. See Tables for complete classification.

**Codifications**

In subsec. (g)(1), "sections 3141 to 3144, 3146, 3147 of Title 40" substituted for "the Davis–Bacon Act [40 U.S.C. 276a et seq.]" on authority of Pub.L. 107–217, § 5(c), Aug. 21, 2002, 116 Stat. 1301, which is set out as a note preceding 40 U.S.C.A. § 101. Pub.L. 107–217, § 1, enacted Title 40 into positive law. The Davis–Bacon Act is Act Mar. 3, 1931, c. 411, 46 Stat. 1494, which was classified to former 40 U.S.C.A. §§ 276a, 276a–1 to 276a–6, prior to being repealed by Pub.L. 107–217, § 6(b), Aug. 21, 2002, 116 Stat. 1308, and its substance reenacted as 40 U.S.C.A. §§ 3141 to 3144, 3146, 3147.

In subsec. (g)(2), "section 3145 of Title 40" substituted for "section 276c of Title 40", on authority of Pub.L. 107–217, § 5(c), Aug. 21, 2002, 116 Stat. 1301, which is set out as a note preceding 40 U.S.C.A. § 101. Pub.L. 107–217, § 1, enacted Title 40 into positive law. Former 40 U.S.C.A. § 276c was Act June 13, 1934, c. 482, § 2, 48 Stat. 948, prior to being repealed by Pub.L. 107–217, § 6(b), Aug. 21, 2002, 116 Stat. 1309, and its substance reenacted as 40 U.S.C.A. § 3145.

**Effective Dates**

1986 Acts

Amendment by Pub.L. 99–499 effective Oct. 17, 1986, see section 4 of Pub.L. 99–499, set out as a note under section 9601 of this title.

**Delegation of Functions**

Functions of the President under the first sentence of subsec. (b)(1) of this section, relating to "illness, disease, or complaints thereof", delegated to the Secretary of Health and Human Services (with authority to redelegate), who shall, in accord with subsec. (i) of this section, perform those functions through the Public Health Service, see sections 2(a) and 11(g) of Ex. Ord. No. 12580, Jan. 23, 1987, 52 F.R. 2923, set out as a note under section 9615 of this title.

Functions vested in the President by subsec. (e)(7)(C) of this section, relating to the promulgation of regulations and guidelines, delegated to the Administrator of the Environmental Protection Agency, to be exercised in consultation with the National Response Team, see section 2(b) of Ex. Ord. No. 12580, Jan. 23, 1987, 52 F.R. 2923, set out as a note under section 9615 of this title.

Functions vested in the President by subsec. (a) of this section, to the extent they require permanent relocation of residents, businesses, and community facilities or temporary evacuation and housing of threatened individuals not otherwise provided for, delegated to the Director of the Federal Emergency Management Agency, with authority to redelegate, see sections 2(c)(1), 11(g) of Ex. Ord. No. 12580, Jan. 23, 1987, 52 F.R. 2923, set out as a note under section 9615 of this title. Functions vested in the President by sections 9617(a), (c) and section 9619 of this title, to the extent such authority is needed to carry out the delegation of functions by section 2(c)(1) of Ex. Ord. No. 12580 (and subject to delegation of certain rulemaking authority to the Administrator of the Environmental Protection Agency), delegated to the Director, with authority to redelegate, see sections 2(b), (c)(2), 11(g) of Ex. Ord. No. 12580.

Functions vested in the President by subsecs. (a), (b) and (c)(4) this section delegated, with authority to redelegate, (and subject to section 2(a), (b) and (e) of Ex. Ord. No. 12580) to the Secretaries of Defense and Energy, with respect to releases or threatened releases where either the release is on or the sole source of the release is from any facility or vessel under the jurisdiction, custody or control of their departments, respectively, including vessels bare-boat chartered and operated, with such functions to be exercised consistent with the requirements of section 9620 of this title, see sections 2(d), 11(g) of Ex. Ord. No. 12580, Jan. 23, 1987, 52 F.R. 2923, set out as a note under section 9615 of this title.

Functions vested in the President by subsecs. (a), (b) and (c)(4) of this section, subject to section 2(a) to (d) of Ex. Ord. No. 12580, delegated, with authority to redelegate, to the heads of Executive departments and agencies, with respect to remedial actions for releases or threatened releases which are not on the National Priorities List and removal actions other than emergencies, where either the release is on or the sole source of the release is from any facility or vessel under the jurisdiction, custody or control of those departments and agencies, including vessels bare-boat chartered and operated with the Administrator of the Environmental Protection Agency to define the term "emergency", solely for the purposes of section 2(e) of Ex. Ord. No. 12580, either by regulation or by a memorandum of understanding with the head of an Executive department or agency, see sections 2(e)(1), 11(g) of Ex. Ord. No. 12580, Jan. 23, 1987, 52 F.R. 2923, set out as a note under section 9615 of this title.

Functions vested in the President by subsec. (b)(2) of this section, subject to section 2(b) to (d) of Ex. Ord. No. 12580, delegated, with authority to redelegate, to the heads of Executive departments and agencies, with respect to releases or threatened releases where either the release is on or the sole source of the release is from any facility or vessel under the jurisdiction, custody or control of those departments and agencies, including vessels bare-boat chartered and operated, see sections 2(e)(2), 11(g) of Ex. Ord. No. 12580, Jan. 23, 1987, 52 F.R. 2923, set out as a note under section 9615 of this title.

Functions vested in the President by subsecs. (a), (b) and (c)(4) of this section, subject to section 2(a) to (e) of Ex. Ord. No. 12580, delegated, with authority to redelegate, to the Secretary of the Department in which the Coast Guard is operating ("the Coast Guard"), with respect to any release or threatened release involving the coastal zone, Great Lakes waters, ports, and harbors, see sections 2(f), 11(g) of Ex. Ord. No. 12580, Jan. 23, 1987, 52 F.R. 2923, set out as a note under section 9615 of this title.

Functions vested in the President by subsec. (a), (b), (c)(4) and (c)(9) of this section, subject to section 2(a) to (f) of Ex. Ord. No. 12580, delegated, with authority to redelegate, to the Administrator of the Environmental Protection Agency, see sections 2(g), 11(g) of Ex. Ord. No. 12580, Jan. 23, 1987, 52 F.R. 2923, set out as a note under section 9615 of this title.

Functions vested in the President by subsec. (c)(3) of this section delegated to the Administrator of the Environmental Protection Agency, with authority to redelegate, with respect to providing assurances for Indian tribes, with such functions to be exercised in consultation with the Secretary of the Interior, see sections 2(h), 11(g) of Ex. Ord. No. 12580, Jan. 23, 1987, 52 F.R. 2923, set out as a note under section 9615 of this title.

Functions vested in the President by subsecs. (c) and (d) of this section, subject to section 2(d) to (h) of Ex. Ord. No. 12580, delegated, with authority to redelegate, to the Coast Guard, the Secretary of Health and Human Services, the Director of the Federal Emergency Management Agency, and the Administrator of the Environmental Protection Agency in order to carry out the functions delegated to them by section 2 of Ex. Ord. No. 12580, see sections 2(i), 11(g) of Ex. Ord. No. 12580, Jan. 23, 1987, 52 F.R. 2923, set out as a note under section 9615 of this title.

Functions vested in the President by subsec. (e)(5)(A) of this section delegated, with authority to redelegate, to the heads of Executive departments and agencies, with respect to releases or threatened releases where either the release is on or the sole source of the release is from any facility or vessel under the jurisdiction, custody or control of those departments and agencies, with such functions to be exercised with the concurrence of the Attorney General, see sections 2(j)(1), 11(g) of Ex. Ord. No. 12580, Jan. 23, 1987, 52 F.R. 2923, set out as a note under section 9615 of this title.

Functions vested in the President by subsec. (e) of this section, delegated, (subject to delegations by section 2(b), (j)(1) of Ex. Ord. No. 12580, and with authority to redelegate) to the heads of Executive departments and agencies in order to carry out their functions under Ex. Ord. No. 12580 or this chapter, see sections 2(j)(2), 11(g) of Ex. Ord. No. 12580, Jan. 23, 1987, 52 F.R. 2923, set out as a note under section 9615 of this title.

Functions vested in the President by subsecs. (f), (g), (h), (i)(11), and (j) of this section delegated, with authority to redelegate, to the heads of Executive departments and agencies in order to carry out the functions delegated to them by section 2 of Ex. Ord. No. 12580, with exercise of authority under subsec. (h) of this section subject to the approval of the Administrator of the Office of Federal Procurement

Policy, see sections 2(k), 11(g) of Ex. Ord. No. 12580, Jan. 23, 1987, 52 F.R. 2923, set out as a note under section 9615 of this title.

Authority under subsec. (e)(5)(A) of this section to seek information, entry, inspection, samples, or response actions from Executive departments and agencies to be exercised only with the concurrence of the Attorney General, notwithstanding any other provisions of Ex. Ord. No. 12580, see section 4(e) of Ex. Ord. No. 12580, Jan. 23, 1987, 52 F.R. 2923, set out as a note under section 9615 of this title.

**Coordination of Titles I to IV of Pub.L. 99–499**

Any provision of Titles I to IV of Pub.L. 99–499, imposing any tax, premium, or fee; establishing any trust fund; or authorizing expenditures from any trust fund, to have no force or effect, see section 531 of Pub.L. 99–499, set out as a note under section 1 of Title 26, Internal Revenue Code.

## § 9605. National contingency plan

### [CERCLA § 105]

**(a) Revision and republication**

Within one hundred and eighty days after December 11, 1980, the President shall, after notice and opportunity for public comments, revise and republish the national contingency plan for the removal of oil and hazardous substances, originally prepared and published pursuant to section 1321 of Title 33, to reflect and effectuate the responsibilities and powers created by this chapter, in addition to those matters specified in section 1321(c)(2) of Title 33. Such revision shall include a section of the plan to be known as the national hazardous substance response plan which shall establish procedures and standards for responding to releases of hazardous substances, pollutants, and contaminants, which shall include at a minimum:

(1) methods for discovering and investigating facilities at which hazardous substances have been disposed of or otherwise come to be located;

(2) methods for evaluating, including analyses of relative cost, and remedying any releases or threats of releases from facilities which pose substantial danger to the public health or the environment;

(3) methods and criteria for determining the appropriate extent of removal, remedy, and other measures authorized by this chapter;

(4) appropriate roles and responsibilities for the Federal, State, and local governments and for interstate and nongovernmental entities in effectuating the plan;

(5) provision for identification, procurement, maintenance, and storage of response equipment and supplies;

(6) a method for and assignment of responsibility for reporting the existence of such facilities which may be located on federally owned or controlled properties and any releases of hazardous substances from such facilities;

(7) means of assuring that remedial action measures are cost-effective over the period of potential exposure to the hazardous substances or contaminated materials;

(8)(A) criteria for determining priorities among releases or threatened releases throughout the United States for the purpose of taking remedial action and, to the extent practicable taking into account the potential urgency of such action, for the purpose of taking removal action. Criteria and priorities under this paragraph shall be based upon relative risk or danger to public health or welfare or the environment, in the judgment of the President, taking into account to the extent possible the population at risk, the hazard potential of the hazardous substances at such facilities, the potential for contamination of drinking water supplies, the potential for direct human contact, the potential for destruction of sensitive ecosystems, the damage to natural resources which may affect the human food chain and which is associated with any release or threatened release, the contamination or potential contamination of the ambient air which is associated with the release or threatened release, State preparedness to assume State costs and responsibilities, and other appropriate factors;

(B) based upon the criteria set forth in subparagraph (A) of this paragraph, the President shall list as part of the plan national priorities among the known releases or threatened releases throughout the United States and shall revise the list no less often than annually. Within one year after December 11, 1980, and annually thereafter, each State shall establish and submit for consideration by the President priorities for remedial action among known releases and potential releases in that State based upon the criteria set forth in subparagraph (A) of this paragraph. In assembling or revising the national list, the President shall consider any priorities established by the States. To the extent practicable, the highest priority facilities shall be designated individually and shall be referred to as the "top priority among known response targets", and, to the extent practicable, shall include among the one hundred highest priority facilities one such facility from each State which shall be the facility designated by the State as presenting the greatest danger to public health or welfare or the environment among the known facilities in such State. A State shall be allowed to designate its highest priority facility only once. Other priority facilities or incidents may be listed singly or grouped for response priority purposes;

(**9**) specified roles for private organizations and entities in preparation for response and in responding to releases of hazardous substances, including identification of appropriate qualifications and capacity therefor and including consideration of minority firms in accordance with subsection (f) of this section; and

(**10**) standards and testing procedures by which alternative or innovative treatment technologies can be determined to be appropriate for utilization in response actions authorized by this chapter.

The plan shall specify procedures, techniques, materials, equipment, and methods to be employed in identifying, removing, or remedying releases of hazardous substances comparable to those required under section 1321(c)(2)(F) and (G) and (j)(1) of Title 33. Following publication of the revised national contingency plan, the response to and actions to minimize damage from hazardous substances releases shall, to the greatest extent possible, be in accordance with the provisions of the plan. The President may, from time to time, revise and republish the national contingency plan.

**(b) Revision of plan**

Not later than 18 months after the enactment of the Superfund Amendments and Reauthorization Act of 1986 [October 17, 1986], the President shall revise the National Contingency Plan to reflect the requirements of such amendments. The portion of such Plan known as "the National Hazardous Substance Response Plan" shall be revised to provide procedures and standards for remedial actions undertaken pursuant to this chapter which are consistent with amendments made by the Superfund Amendments and Reauthorization Act of 1986 relating to the selection of remedial action.

**(c) Hazard ranking system**

**(1) Revision**

Not later than 18 months after October 17, 1986, and after publication of notice and opportunity for submission of comments in accordance with section 553 of Title 5, the President shall by rule promulgate amendments to the hazard ranking system in effect on September 1, 1984. Such amendments shall assure, to the maximum extent feasible, that the hazard ranking system accurately assesses the relative degree of risk to human health and the environment posed by sites and facilities subject to review. The President shall establish an effective date for the amended hazard ranking system which is not later than 24 months after October 17, 1986. Such amended hazard ranking system shall be applied to any site or facility to be newly listed on the National Priorities List after the effective date established by the President. Until such effective date of the regulations, the hazard ranking system in effect on September 1, 1984, shall continue in full force and effect.

**(2) Health assessment of water contamination risks**

In carrying out this subsection, the President shall ensure that the human health risks associated with the contamination or potential contamination (either directly or as a result of the runoff of any hazardous substance or pollutant or contaminant from sites or facilities) of surface water are appropriately assessed where such surface water is, or can be, used for recreation or potable water consumption. In making the assessment required pursuant to the preceding sentence, the President shall take into account the potential migration of any hazardous substance or pollutant or contaminant through such surface water to downstream sources of drinking water.

**(3) Reevaluation not required**

The President shall not be required to reevaluate, after October 17, 1986, the hazard ranking of any facility which was evaluated in accordance with the criteria under this section before the effective date of the amendments to the hazard ranking system under this subsection and which was assigned a national priority under the National Contingency Plan.

**(4) New information**

Nothing in paragraph (3) shall preclude the President from taking new information into account in undertaking response actions under this chapter.

**(d) Petition for assessment of release**

Any person who is, or may be, affected by a release or threatened release of a hazardous substance or pollutant or contaminant, may petition the President to conduct a preliminary assessment of the hazards to public health and the environment which are associated with such release or threatened release. If the President has not previously conducted a preliminary assessment of such release, the President shall, within 12 months after the receipt of any such petition, complete such assessment or provide an explanation of why the assessment is not appropriate. If the preliminary assessment indicates that the release or threatened release concerned may pose a threat to human health or the environment, the President shall promptly evaluate such release or threatened release in accordance with the hazard ranking system referred to in paragraph (8)(A) of subsection (a) of this section to determine the national priority of such release or threatened release.

**(e) Releases from earlier sites**

Whenever there has been, after January 1, 1985, a significant release of hazardous substances or pollutants or contaminants from a site which is listed by the President as a "Site Cleaned Up To Date" on the National Priorities List (revised edition, December 1984) the site shall be restored to the National Priorities List, without application of the hazard ranking system.

**(f) Minority contractors**

In awarding contracts under this chapter, the President shall consider the availability of qualified minority firms. The President shall describe, as part of any annual report submitted to the Congress under this chapter, the participation of minority firms in contracts carried out under this chapter. Such report shall contain a brief description of the contracts which have been awarded to minority firms under this chapter and of the efforts made by the President to encourage the participation of such firms in programs carried out under this chapter.

**(g) Special study wastes**

**(1) Application**

This subsection applies to facilities—

**(A)** which as of October 17, 1986, were not included on, or proposed for inclusion on, the National Priorities List; and

**(B)** at which special study wastes described in paragraph (2), (3)(A)(ii) or (3)(A)(iii) of section 6921(b) of this title are present in significant quantities, including any such facility from which there has been a release of a special study waste.

**(2) Considerations in adding facilities to NPL**

Pending revision of the hazard ranking system under subsection (c) of this section, the President shall consider each of the following factors in adding facilities covered by this section to the National Priorities List:

**(A)** The extent to which hazard ranking system score for the facility is affected by the presence of any special study waste at, or any release from, such facility.

**(B)** Available information as to the quantity, toxicity, and concentration of hazardous substances that are constituents of any special study waste at, or released from such facility, the extent of or potential for release of such hazardous constituents, the exposure or potential exposure to human population and the environment, and the degree of hazard to human health or the environment posed by the release of such hazardous constituents at such facility. This subparagraph refers only to available information on actual concentrations of hazardous substances and not on the total quantity of special study waste at such facility.

**(3) Savings provisions**

Nothing in this subsection shall be construed to limit the authority of the President to remove any facility which as of October 17, 1986, is included on the National Priorities List from such List, or not to list any facility which as of such date is proposed for inclusion on such list.

**(4) Information gathering and analysis**

Nothing in this chapter shall be construed to preclude the expenditure of monies from the Fund for gathering and analysis of information which will enable the President to consider the specific factors required by paragraph (2).

**(h) NPL deferral**

**(1) Deferral to State voluntary cleanups**

At the request of a State and subject to paragraphs (2) and (3), the President generally shall defer final listing of an eligible response site on the National Priorities List if the President determines that—

**(A)** the State, or another party under an agreement with or order from the State, is conducting a response action at the eligible response site—

**(i)** in compliance with a State program that specifically governs response actions for the protection of public health and the environment; and

**(ii)** that will provide long-term protection of human health and the environment; or

**(B)** the State is actively pursuing an agreement to perform a response action described in subparagraph (A) at the site with a person that the State has reason to believe is capable of conducting a response action that meets the requirements of subparagraph (A).

**(2) Progress toward cleanup**

If, after the last day of the 1-year period beginning on the date on which the President proposes to list an eligible response site on the National Priorities List, the President determines that the State or other party is not making reasonable progress toward completing a response action at the eligible response site, the President may list the eligible response site on the National Priorities List.

**(3) Cleanup agreements**

With respect to an eligible response site under paragraph (1)(B), if, after the last day of the 1-year period beginning on the date on which the President proposes to list the eligible response site on the National Priorities List, an agreement described in paragraph (1)(B) has not been reached, the President may defer the listing of the eligible response site on the National Priorities List for an additional period of not to exceed 180 days if the President determines deferring the listing would be appropriate based on—

**(A)** the complexity of the site;

**(B)** substantial progress made in negotiations; and

**(C)** other appropriate factors, as determined by the President.

**(4) Exceptions**

The President may decline to defer, or elect to discontinue a deferral of, a listing of an eligible response site on the National Priorities List if the President determines that—

**(A)** deferral would not be appropriate because the State, as an owner or operator or a significant contributor of hazardous substances to the facility, is a potentially responsible party;

**(B)** the criteria under the National Contingency Plan for issuance of a health advisory have been met; or

**(C)** the conditions in paragraphs (1) through (3), as applicable, are no longer being met.

(Pub.L. 96–510, Title I, § 105, Dec. 11, 1980, 94 Stat. 2779; Pub.L. 99–499, Title I, § 105, Oct. 17, 1986, 100 Stat. 1625; Pub.L. 107–118, Title II, § 232, Jan. 11, 2002, 115 Stat. 2379.)

### HISTORICAL AND STATUTORY NOTES

**References in Text**

Section 1321(c)(2) of Title 33, referred to in subsec. (a), was amended generally by Pub.L. 101–380. Title IV, § 4201(a), Aug. 18, 1990, 104 Stat. 523. Prior to general amendment, subsec. (c)(2) related to preparation of a National Contingency Plan. Provisions relating to a National Contingency Plan are contained in section 1321(d) of Title 33, Navigation and Navigable Waters.

Such amendments and the amendments made by the Superfund Amendments and Reauthorization Act of 1986, referred to in subsec. (b), are the amendments made by Pub.L. 99–499, Oct. 17, 1986, 100 Stat. 1613. For complete classification of this Act to the Code, see Short Title of 1986 Amendments note set out under section 9601 of this title and Tables.

**Effective Dates**

1986 Acts

Amendment by Pub.L. 99–499 effective Oct. 17, 1986, see section 4 of Pub.L. 99–499, set out as a note under section 9601 of this title.

**Delegation of Functions**

Responsibility for the revision of the National Contingency Plan, and all other functions vested in the President by subsecs. (a), (b), (c) and (g) of this section, delegated to the Administrator of the Environmental Protection Agency, see section 1(b)(1) of Ex. Ord. No. 12580, Jan. 23, 1987, 52 F.R. 2923, set out as a note under section 9615 of this title.

Functions vested in the President by subsec. (d) of this section delegated, with authority to redelegate, to the Administrator of the Environmental Protection Agency, except that functions vested in the President by the first two sentences thereof (relating to petitions for preliminary assessments of releases or threatened releases of hazardous substances or pollutants or contaminants) delegated, with authority to redelegate, to the heads of Executive departments and agencies with respect to facilities under the jurisdiction, custody or control of those departments and agencies, see sections 3, 11(g) of Ex. Ord. No. 12580, Jan. 23, 1987, 52 F.R. 2923, set out as a note under section 9615 of this title.

Functions vested in the President by subsec. (f) of this section, relating to reporting on minority participation in contracts, delegated to the Administrator of the Environmental Protection Agency, see section 11(b)(1) of Ex. Ord. No. 12580, Jan. 23, 1987, 52 F.R. 2923, set out as a note under section 9615 of this title.

Functions vested in the President by subsec. (f) of this section delegated, subject to section 11(b)(1) of Ex. Ord. No. 12580, to the heads of Executive departments and agencies in order to carry out the functions delegated to them by Ex. Ord. No. 12580, with each Executive department and agency to provide to the Administrator of the Environmental Protection Agency any requested information on minority contracting for inclusion in the annual report under subsec. (f), see section 11(b)(2) of Ex. Ord. No. 12580, Jan. 23, 1987, 52 F.R. 2923, set out as a note under section 9615 of this title.

## § 9606. Abatement actions

**[CERCLA § 106]**

**(a) Maintenance, jurisdiction, etc.**

In addition to any other action taken by a State or local government, when the President determines that there may be an imminent and substantial endangerment to the public health or welfare or the environment because of an actual or threatened release of a hazardous substance from a facility, he may require the Attorney General of the United States to secure such relief as may be necessary to abate such danger or threat, and the district court of the United States in the district in which the threat occurs shall have jurisdiction to grant such relief as the public interest and the equities of the case may require. The President may also, after notice to the affected State, take other action under this section including, but not limited to, issuing such orders as may be necessary to protect public health and welfare and the environment.

**(b) Fines; reimbursement**

**(1)** Any person who, without sufficient cause, willfully violates, or fails or refuses to comply with, any order of the President under subsection (a) of this section may, in an action brought in the appropriate United States district court to enforce such order, be fined not more than $25,000 for each day in which such violation occurs or such failure to comply continues.

(2)(A) Any person who receives and complies with the terms of any order issued under subsection (a) of this section may, within 60 days after completion of the required action, petition the President for reimbursement from the Fund for the reasonable costs of such action, plus interest. Any interest payable under this paragraph shall accrue on the amounts expended from the date of expenditure at the same rate as specified for interest on investments of the Hazardous Substance Superfund established under subchapter A of chapter 98 of Title 26.

(B) If the President refuses to grant all or part of a petition made under this paragraph, the petitioner may within 30 days of receipt of such refusal file an action against the President in the appropriate United States district court seeking reimbursement from the Fund.

(C) Except as provided in subparagraph (D), to obtain reimbursement, the petitioner shall establish by a preponderance of the evidence that it is not liable for response costs under section 9607(a) of this title and that costs for which it seeks reimbursement are reasonable in light of the action required by the relevant order.

(D) A petitioner who is liable for response costs under section 9607(a) of this title may also recover its reasonable costs of response to the extent that it can demonstrate, on the administrative record, that the President's decision in selecting the response action ordered was arbitrary and capricious or was otherwise not in accordance with law. Reimbursement awarded under this subparagraph shall include all reasonable response costs incurred by the petitioner pursuant to the portions of the order found to be arbitrary and capricious or otherwise not in accordance with law.

(E) Reimbursement awarded by a court under subparagraph (C) or (D) may include appropriate costs, fees, and other expenses in accordance with subsections (a) and (d) of section 2412 of Title 28.

**(c) Guidelines for using imminent hazard, enforcement, and emergency response authorities; promulgation by Administrator of EPA, scope, etc.**

Within one hundred and eighty days after December 11, 1980, the Administrator of the Environmental Protection Agency shall, after consultation with the Attorney General, establish and publish guidelines for using the imminent hazard, enforcement, and emergency response authorities of this section and other existing statutes administered by the Administrator of the Environmental Protection Agency to effectuate the responsibilities and powers created by this chapter. Such guidelines shall to the extent practicable be consistent with the national hazardous substance response plan, and shall include, at a minimum, the assignment of responsibility for coordinating response actions with the issuance of administrative orders, enforcement of standards and permits, the gathering of information, and other imminent hazard and emergency powers authorized by (1) sections 1321(c)(2), 1318, 1319, and 1364(a) of Title 33, (2) sections 6927, 6928, 6934, and 6973 of this title, (3) sections 300j–4 and 300i of this title, (4) sections 7413, 7414, and 7603 of this title, and (5) section 2606 of Title 15.

(Pub.L. 96–510, Title I, § 106, Dec. 11, 1980, 94 Stat. 2780; Pub.L. 99–499, Title I, §§ 106, 109(b), Oct. 17, 1986, 100 Stat. 1628, 1633; Pub.L. 99–514, § 2, Oct. 22, 1986, 100 Stat. 2095.)

## HISTORICAL AND STATUTORY NOTES

### References in Text

Section 1321(c)(2) of Title 33, referred to in subsec. (c), was amended generally by Pub.L. 101–380, Title IV, § 4201(a), Aug. 18, 1990, 104 Stat. 523. Prior to general amendment, subsec. (c)(2) related to preparation of a National Contingency Plan. Provisions relating to a National Contingency Plan are contained in section 1321(d) of Title 33, Navigation and Navigable Waters.

### Effective Dates

1986 Acts

Amendment by Pub.L. 99–499 effective Oct. 17, 1986, see section 4 of Pub.L. 99–499, set out as a note under section 9601 of this title.

### Delegation of Functions

Functions vested in the President by subsec. (a) of this section delegated, subject to section 4(a), (b)(1) of Ex. Ord. No. 12580, and with authority to redelegate, to the Coast Guard with respect to any release or threatened release involving the coastal zone, Great Lakes waters, ports, and harbors, see sections 4(c)(1), 11(g) of Ex. Ord. No. 12580, Jan. 23, 1987, 52 F.R. 2923, set out as a note under section 9615 of this title.

Functions vested in the President by this section delegated, subject to section 4(a), (b)(1) and (c)(1) of Ex. Ord. No. 12580, and with authority to redelegate, to the Administrator of the Environmental Protection Agency, see sections 4(d)(1), 11(g) of Ex. Ord. No. 12580, Jan. 23, 1987, 52 F.R. 2923, set out as a note under section 9615 of this title.

Authority under subsec. (a) of this section to seek information, entry, inspection, samples, or response actions from Executive departments and agencies to be exercised only with the concurrence of the Attorney General, notwithstanding any other provisions of Ex. Ord. No. 12580, see section 4(e) of Ex. Ord. No. 12580, Jan. 23, 1987, 52 F.R. 2923, set out as a note under section 9615 of this title.

Functions vested in the President by subsec. (a) of this section delegated, subject to section 4(a), (b)(1), of Ex. Ord. No. 12580, to the Secretary of the Interior, the Secretary of Commerce, the Secretary of Agriculture, the Secretary of Defense, and the Secretary of Energy, to be exercised only with the concurrence of the Coast Guard, with respect to any release or threatened release in the coastal zone, Great Lakes waters, ports, and harbors, affecting (1) natural resources under their trusteeship, or (2) a vessel or facility subject to their custody, jurisdiction, or control, and with other exceptions and stipulations, see section 4(c)(3) of Ex.

Ord. No. 12580, Jan. 23, 1987, 52 F.R. 2923, as amended, set out as a note under section 9615 of this title.

Functions vested in the President by subsec. (a) of this section delegated, subject to section 4(a), (b),and (c)(1) of Ex. Ord. No. 12580, to the Secretary of the Interior, the Secretary of Commerce, the Secretary of Agriculture, the Secretary of Defense, and the Department of Energy, to be exercised only with the concurrence of the Administrator, with respect to any release or threatened release affecting (1) natural resources under their trusteeship, or (2) a vessel or facility subject to their custody, jurisdiction, or control, and with other exceptions and stipulations, see section 4(d)(3) of Ex. Ord. No. 12580, Jan. 23, 1987, 52 F.R. 2923, as amended, set out as a note under section 9615 of this title.

**Coordination of Titles I to IV of Pub.L. 99–499**

Any provision of Titles I to IV of Pub.L. 99–499, imposing any tax, premium, or fee; establishing any trust fund; or authorizing expenditures from any trust fund, to have no force or effect, see section 531 of Pub.L. 99–499, set out as a note under section 1 of Title 26, Internal Revenue Code.

## § 9607. Liability

### [CERCLA § 107]

### (a) Covered persons; scope; recoverable costs and damages; interest rate; "comparable maturity" date

Notwithstanding any other provision or rule of law, and subject only to the defenses set forth in subsection (b) of this section—

(1) the owner and operator of a vessel or a facility,

(2) any person who at the time of disposal of any hazardous substance owned or operated any facility at which such hazardous substances were disposed of,

(3) any person who by contract, agreement, or otherwise arranged for disposal or treatment, or arranged with a transporter for transport for disposal or treatment, of hazardous substances owned or possessed by such person, by any other party or entity, at any facility or incineration vessel owned or operated by another party or entity and containing such hazardous substances, and

(4) any person who accepts or accepted any hazardous substances for transport to disposal or treatment facilities, incineration vessels or sites selected by such person, from which there is a release, or a threatened release which causes the incurrence of response costs, of a hazardous substance, shall be liable for—

(A) all costs of removal or remedial action incurred by the United States Government or a State or an Indian tribe not inconsistent with the national contingency plan;

(B) any other necessary costs of response incurred by any other person consistent with the national contingency plan;

(C) damages for injury to, destruction of, or loss of natural resources, including the reasonable costs of assessing such injury, destruction, or loss resulting from such a release; and

(D) the costs of any health assessment or health effects study carried out under section 9604(i) of this title.

The amounts recoverable in an action under this section shall include interest on the amounts recoverable under subparagraphs (A) through (D). Such interest shall accrue from the later of (i) the date payment of a specified amount is demanded in writing, or (ii) the date of the expenditure concerned. The rate of interest on the outstanding unpaid balance of the amounts recoverable under this section shall be the same rate as is specified for interest on investments of the Hazardous Substance Superfund established under subchapter A of chapter 98 of Title 26. For purposes of applying such amendments to interest under this subsection, the term "comparable maturity" shall be determined with reference to the date on which interest accruing under this subsection commences.

### (b) Defenses

There shall be no liability under subsection (a) of this section for a person otherwise liable who can establish by a preponderance of the evidence that the release or threat of release of a hazardous substance and the damages resulting therefrom were caused solely by—

(1) an act of God;

(2) an act of war;

(3) an act or omission of a third party other than an employee or agent of the defendant, or than one whose act or omission occurs in connection with a contractual relationship, existing directly or indirectly, with the defendant (except where the sole contractual arrangement arises from a published tariff and acceptance for carriage by a common carrier by rail), if the defendant establishes by a preponderance of the evidence that (a) he exercised due care with respect to the hazardous substance concerned, taking into consideration the characteristics of such hazardous substance, in light of all relevant facts and circumstances, and (b) he took precautions against foreseeable acts or omissions of any such third party and the consequences that could foreseeably result from such acts or omissions; or

(4) any combination of the foregoing paragraphs.

### (c) Determination of amounts

(1) Except as provided in paragraph (2) of this subsection, the liability under this section of an owner or operator or other responsible person for each release of a hazardous substance or incident involving release of a hazardous substance shall not exceed—

(A) for any vessel, other than an incineration vessel, which carries any hazardous substance as cargo or residue, $300 per gross ton, or $5,000,000, whichever is greater;

(B) for any other vessel, other than an incineration vessel, $300 per gross ton, or $500,000, whichever is greater;

(C) for any motor vehicle, aircraft, hazardous liquid pipeline facility (as defined in section 60101(a) of Title 49), or rolling stock, $50,000,000 or such lesser amount as the President shall establish by regulation, but in no event less than $5,000,000 (or, for releases of hazardous substances as defined in section 9601(14)(A) of this title into the navigable waters, $8,000,000). Such regulations shall take into account the size, type, location, storage, and handling capacity and other matters relating to the likelihood of release in each such class and to the economic impact of such limits on each such class; or

(D) for any incineration vessel or any facility other than those specified in subparagraph (C) of this paragraph, the total of all costs of response plus $50,000,000 for any damages under this subchapter.

(2) Notwithstanding the limitations in paragraph (1) of this subsection, the liability of an owner or operator or other responsible person under this section shall be the full and total costs of response and damages, if (A)(i) the release or threat of release of a hazardous substance was the result of willful misconduct or willful negligence within the privity or knowledge of such person, or (ii) the primary cause of the release was a violation (within the privity or knowledge of such person) of applicable safety, construction, or operating standards or regulations; or (B) such person fails or refuses to provide all reasonable cooperation and assistance requested by a responsible public official in connection with response activities under the national contingency plan with respect to regulated carriers subject to the provisions of Title 49 or vessels subject to the provisions of Title 33, 46, or 46 Appendix, subparagraph (A)(ii) of this paragraph shall be deemed to refer to Federal standards or regulations.

(3) If any person who is liable for a release or threat of release of a hazardous substance fails without sufficient cause to properly provide removal or remedial action upon order of the President pursuant to section 9604 or 9606 of this title, such person may be liable to the United States for punitive damages in an amount at least equal to, and not more than three times, the amount of any costs incurred by the Fund as a result of such failure to take proper action. The President is authorized to commence a civil action against any such person to recover the punitive damages, which shall be in addition to any costs recovered from such person pursuant to section 9612(c) of this title. Any moneys received by the United States pursuant to this subsection shall be deposited in the Fund.

**(d) Rendering care or advice**

**(1) In general**

Except as provided in paragraph (2), no person shall be liable under this subchapter for costs or damages as a result of actions taken or omitted in the course of rendering care, assistance, or advice in accordance with the National Contingency Plan ("NCP") or at the direction of an onscene coordinator appointed under such plan, with respect to an incident creating a danger to public health or welfare or the environment as a result of any releases of a hazardous substance or the threat thereof. This paragraph shall not preclude liability for costs or damages as the result of negligence on the part of such person.

**(2) State and local governments**

No State or local government shall be liable under this subchapter for costs or damages as a result of actions taken in response to an emergency created by the release or threatened release of a hazardous substance generated by or from a facility owned by another person. This paragraph shall not preclude liability for costs or damages as a result of gross negligence or intentional misconduct by the State or local government. For the purpose of the preceding sentence, reckless, willful, or wanton misconduct shall constitute gross negligence.

**(3) Savings provision**

This subsection shall not alter the liability of any person covered by the provisions of paragraph (1), (2), (3), or (4) of subsection (a) of this section with respect to the release or threatened release concerned.

**(e) Indemnification, hold harmless, etc., agreements or conveyances; subrogation rights**

(1) No indemnification, hold harmless, or similar agreement or conveyance shall be effective to transfer from the owner or operator of any vessel or facility or from any person who may be liable for a release or threat of release under this section, to any other person the liability imposed under this section. Nothing in this subsection shall bar any agreement to insure, hold harmless, or indemnify a party to such agreement for any liability under this section.

(2) Nothing in this subchapter, including the provisions of paragraph (1) of this subsection, shall bar a cause of action that an owner or operator or any other person subject to liability under this section, or a guarantor, has or would have, by reason of subrogation or otherwise against any person.

**(f) Natural resources liability; designation of public trustees of natural resources**

**(1) Natural resources liability**

In the case of an injury to, destruction of, or loss of natural resources under subparagraph (C) of subsection (a) of this section liability shall be to the United States Government and to any State for natural resources within the State or belonging to, managed by, controlled by, or appertaining to such State and to any Indian tribe for natural resources belonging to, managed by, controlled by, or appertaining to such tribe, or held in trust for the benefit of such tribe, or belonging to a member of such tribe if such resources are subject to a trust restriction on alienation: *Provided, however,* That no liability to the United States or State or Indian tribe shall be imposed under subparagraph (C) of subsection (a) of this section, where the party sought to be charged has demonstrated that the damages to natural resources complained of were specifically identified as an irreversible and irretrievable commitment of natural resources in an environmental impact statement, or other comparable environment analysis, and the decision to grant a permit or license authorizes such commitment of natural resources, and the facility or project was otherwise operating within the terms of its permit or license, so long as, in the case of damages to an Indian tribe occurring pursuant to a Federal permit or license, the issuance of that permit or license was not inconsistent with the fiduciary duty of the United States with respect to such Indian tribe. The President, or the authorized representative of any State, shall act on behalf of the public as trustee of such natural resources to recover for such damages. Sums recovered by the United States Government as trustee under this subsection shall be retained by the trustee, without further appropriation, for use only to restore, replace, or acquire the equivalent of such natural resources. Sums recovered by a State as trustee under this subsection shall be available for use only to restore, replace, or acquire the equivalent of such natural resources by the State. The measure of damages in any action under subparagraph (C) of subsection (a) of this section shall not be limited by the sums which can be used to restore or replace such resources. There shall be no double recovery under this chapter for natural resource damages, including the costs of damage assessment or restoration, rehabilitation, or acquisition for the same release and natural resource. There shall be no recovery under the authority of subparagraph (C) of subsection (a) of this section where such damages and the release of a hazardous substance from which such damages resulted have occurred wholly before December 11, 1980.

**(2) Designation of Federal and State officials**

**(A) Federal**

The President shall designate in the National Contingency Plan published under section 9605 of this title the Federal officials who shall act on behalf of the public as trustees for natural resources under this chapter and section 1321 of Title 33. Such officials shall assess damages for injury to, destruction of, or loss of natural resources for purposes of this chapter and such section 1321 of Title 33 for those resources under their trusteeship and may, upon request of and reimbursement from a State and at the Federal officials' discretion, assess damages for those natural resources under the State's trusteeship.

**(B) State**

The Governor of each State shall designate State officials who may act on behalf of the public as trustees for natural resources under this chapter and section 1321 of Title 33 and shall notify the President of such designations. Such State officials shall assess damages to natural resources for the purposes of this chapter and such section 1321 of Title 33 for those natural resources under their trusteeship.

**(C) Rebuttable presumption**

Any determination or assessment of damages to natural resources for the purposes of this chapter and section 1321 of Title 33 made by a Federal or State trustee in accordance with the regulations promulgated under section 9651(c) of this title shall have the force and effect of a rebuttable presumption on behalf of the trustee in any administrative or judicial proceeding under this chapter or section 1321 of Title 33.

**(g) Federal agencies**

For provisions relating to Federal agencies, see section 9620 of this title.

**(h) Owner or operator of vessel**

The owner or operator of a vessel shall be liable in accordance with this section, under maritime tort law, and as provided under section 9614 of this title notwithstanding any provision of the Act of March 3, 1851 (46 U.S.C. 183ff) [46 App. U.S.C.A. §§ 182, 183, 184 to 188] or the absence of any physical damage to the proprietary interest of the claimant.

**(i) Application of a registered pesticide product**

No person (including the United States or any State or Indian tribe) may recover under the authority of this section for any response costs or damages resulting from the application of a pesticide product registered under the Federal Insecticide, Fungicide, and Rodenticide Act [7 U.S.C.A. § 136 et seq.]. Nothing in this paragraph shall affect or modify in any way the obligations or liability of any person under any other provision of State or Federal law, including common law, for damages, injury, or loss resulting from a release of any hazardous substance or for removal or remedial action or the costs of removal or remedial action of such hazardous substance.

**(j) Obligations or liability pursuant to federally permitted release**

Recovery by any person (including the United States or any State or Indian tribe) for response costs or damages resulting from a federally permitted release shall be pursuant to existing law in lieu of this section. Nothing in this paragraph shall affect or modify in any way the obligations or liability of any person under any other provision of State or Federal law, including common law, for damages, injury, or loss resulting from a release of any hazardous substance or for removal or remedial action or the costs of removal or remedial action of such hazardous substance. In addition, costs of response incurred by the Federal Government in connection with a discharge specified in section 9601(10)(B) or (C) of this title shall be recoverable in an action brought under section 1319(b) of Title 33.

**(k) Transfer to, and assumption by, Post-Closure Liability Fund of liability of owner or operator of hazardous waste disposal facility in receipt of permit under applicable solid waste disposal law; time, criteria applicable, procedures, etc.; monitoring costs; reports**

**(1)** The liability established by this section or any other law for the owner or operator of a hazardous waste disposal facility which has received a permit under subtitle C of the Solid Waste Disposal Act [42 U.S.C.A. § 6921 et seq.], shall be transferred to and assumed by the Post-closure Liability Fund established by section 9641 of this title when—

**(A)** such facility and the owner and operator thereof has complied with the requirements of subtitle C of the Solid Waste Disposal Act [42 U.S.C.A. § 6921 et seq.] and regulations issued thereunder, which may affect the performance of such facility after closure; and

**(B)** such facility has been closed in accordance with such regulations and the conditions of such permit, and such facility and the surrounding area have been monitored as required by such regulations and permit conditions for a period not to exceed five years after closure to demonstrate that there is no substantial likelihood that any migration offsite or release from confinement of any hazardous substance or other risk to public health or welfare will occur.

**(2)** Such transfer of liability shall be effective ninety days after the owner or operator of such facility notifies the Administrator of the Environmental Protection Agency (and the State where it has an authorized program under section 3006(b) of the Solid Waste Disposal Act [42 U.S.C.A. § 6926(b) ] ) that the conditions imposed by this subsection have been satisfied. If within such ninety-day period the Administrator of the Environmental Protection Agency or such State determines that any such facility has not complied with all the conditions imposed by this subsection or that insufficient information has been provided to demonstrate such compliance, the Administrator or such State shall so notify the owner and operator of such facility and the administrator of the Fund established by section 9641 of this title, and the owner and operator of such facility shall continue to be liable with respect to such facility under this section and other law until such time as the Administrator and such State determines that such facility has complied with all conditions imposed by this subsection. A determination by the Administrator or such State that a facility has not complied with all conditions imposed by this subsection or that insufficient information has been supplied to demonstrate compliance, shall be a final administrative action for purposes of judicial review. A request for additional information shall state in specific terms the data required.

**(3)** In addition to the assumption of liability of owners and operators under paragraph (1) of this subsection, the Post-closure Liability Fund established by section 9641 of this title may be used to pay costs of monitoring and care and maintenance of a site incurred by other persons after the period of monitoring required by regulations under subtitle C of the Solid Waste Disposal Act [42 U.S.C.A. § 6921 et seq.] for hazardous waste disposal facilities meeting the conditions of paragraph (1) of this subsection.

**(4)(A)** Not later than one year after December 11, 1980, the Secretary of the Treasury shall conduct a study and shall submit a report thereon to the Congress on the feasibility of establishing or qualifying an optional system of private insurance for postclosure financial responsibility for hazardous waste disposal facilities to which this subsection applies. Such study shall include a specification of adequate and realistic minimum standards to assure that any such privately placed insurance will carry out the purposes of this subsection in a reliable, enforceable, and practical manner. Such a study shall include an examination of the public and private incentives, programs, and actions necessary to make privately placed insurance a practical and effective option to the financing system for the Post-closure Liability Fund provided in subchapter II of this chapter.

**(B)** Not later than eighteen months after December 11, 1980, and after a public hearing, the President shall by rule determine whether or not it is feasible to establish or qualify an optional system of private insurance for postclosure financial responsibility for hazardous waste disposal facilities to which this subsection applies. If the President determines the establishment or qualification of such a system would be infeasible, he shall promptly publish an explanation of the reasons for such a determination. If the President determines the establishment or qualification of such a system would be feasible, he shall promptly publish notice of such determination. Not later than six months after an affirmative determination under the preceding sentence and after a public hearing, the President shall by rule promulgate adequate and realistic minimum standards which must be met by any such privately placed insurance, taking into account the purposes of this chapter and this subsection. Such rules shall also specify reasonably expeditious procedures by which privately placed insurance plans can qualify as meeting such minimum standards.

**(C)** In the event any privately placed insurance plan qualifies under subparagraph (B), any person enrolled in, and complying with the terms of, such plan shall be excluded from the provisions of paragraphs (1), (2), and (3) of this subsection and exempt from the requirements to pay any tax or fee to the Post-closure Liability Fund under subchapter II of this chapter.

**(D)** The President may issue such rules and take such other actions as are necessary to effectuate the purposes of this paragraph.

**(5) Suspension of liability transfer**

Notwithstanding paragraphs (1), (2), (3), and (4) of this subsection and subsection (j) of section 9611 of this title, no liability shall be transferred to or assumed by the Post-Closure Liability Trust Fund established by section 9641 of this title prior to completion of the study required under paragraph (6) of this subsection, transmission of a report of such study to both Houses of Congress, and authorization of such a transfer or assumption by Act of Congress following receipt of such study and report.

**(6) Study of options for post-closure program**

**(A) Study**

The Comptroller General shall conduct a study of options for a program for the management of the liabilities associated with hazardous waste treatment, storage, and disposal sites after their closure which complements the policies set forth in the Hazardous and Solid Waste Amendments of 1984 and assures the protection of human health and the environment.

**(B) Program elements**

The program referred to in subparagraph (A) shall be designed to assure each of the following:

**(i)** Incentives are created and maintained for the safe management and disposal of hazardous wastes so as to assure protection of human health and the environment.

**(ii)** Members of the public will have reasonable confidence that hazardous wastes will be managed and disposed of safely and that resources will be available to address any problems that may arise and to cover costs of long-term monitoring, care, and maintenance of such sites.

**(iii)** Persons who are or seek to become owners and operators of hazardous waste disposal facilities will be able to manage their potential future liabilities and to attract the investment capital necessary to build, operate, and close such facilities in a manner which assures protection of human health and the environment.

**(C) Assessments**

The study under this paragraph shall include assessments of treatment, storage, and disposal facilities which have been or are likely to be issued a permit under section 3005 of the Solid Waste Disposal Act [42 U.S.C.A. § 6925] and the likelihood of future insolvency on the part of owners and operators of such facilities. Separate assessments shall be made for different classes of facilities and for different classes of land disposal facilities and shall include but not be limited to—

**(i)** the current and future financial capabilities of facility owners and operators;

**(ii)** the current and future costs associated with facilities, including the costs of routine monitoring and maintenance, compliance monitoring, corrective action, natural resource damages, and liability for damages to third parties; and

**(iii)** the availability of mechanisms by which owners and operators of such facilities can assure that current and future costs, including post-closure costs, will be financed.

**(D) Procedures**

In carrying out the responsibilities of this paragraph, the Comptroller General shall consult with the Administrator, the Secretary of Commerce, the Secretary of the Treasury, and the heads of other appropriate Federal agencies.

**(E) Consideration of options**

In conducting the study under this paragraph, the Comptroller General shall consider various mechanisms and combinations of mechanisms to complement the policies set forth in the Hazardous and Solid Waste Amendments of 1984 to serve the purposes set forth in subparagraph (B) and to assure that the current and future costs associated with hazardous waste facilities, including post-closure costs, will be adequately financed and, to the greatest extent possible, borne by the owners and operators of such facilities. Mechanisms to be considered include, but are not limited to—

**(i)** revisions to closure, post-closure, and financial responsibility requirements under subtitles C and I of the Solid Waste Disposal Act [42 U.S.C.A. §§ 6921 et seq. and 6991 et seq.];

**(ii)** voluntary risk pooling by owners and operators;

**(iii)** legislation to require risk pooling by owners and operators;

**(iv)** modification of the Post-Closure Liability Trust Fund previously established by section 9641 of this title, and the conditions for transfer of liability under this subsection, including limiting the transfer of some or all liability under this subsection only in the case of insolvency of owners and operators;

**(v)** private insurance;

**(vi)** insurance provided by the Federal Government;

**(vii)** coinsurance, reinsurance, or pooled-risk insurance, whether provided by the private sector or provided or assisted by the Federal Government; and

**(viii)** creation of a new program to be administered by a new or existing Federal agency or by a federally chartered corporation.

**(F) Recommendations**

The Comptroller General shall consider options for funding any program under this section and shall, to the extent necessary, make recommendations to the appropriate committees of Congress for additional authority to implement such program.

**(*l*) Federal lien**

**(1) In general**

All costs and damages for which a person is liable to the United States under subsection (a) of this section (other than the owner or operator of a vessel under paragraph (1) of subsection (a) of this section) shall constitute a lien in favor of the United States upon all real property and rights to such property which—

**(A)** belong to such person; and

**(B)** are subject to or affected by a removal or remedial action.

**(2) Duration**

The lien imposed by this subsection shall arise at the later of the following:

**(A)** The time costs are first incurred by the United States with respect to a response action under this chapter.

**(B)** The time that the person referred to in paragraph (1) is provided (by certified or registered mail) written notice of potential liability.

Such lien shall continue until the liability for the costs (or a judgment against the person arising out of such liability) is satisfied or becomes unenforceable through operation of the statute of limitations provided in section 9613 of this title.

**(3) Notice and validity**

The lien imposed by this subsection shall be subject to the rights of any purchaser, holder of a security interest, or judgment lien creditor whose interest is perfected under applicable State law before notice of the lien has been filed in the appropriate office within the State (or county or other governmental subdivision), as designated by State law, in which the real property subject to the lien is located. Any such purchaser, holder of a security interest, or judgment lien creditor shall be afforded the same protections against the lien imposed by this subsection as are afforded under State law against a judgment lien which arises out of an unsecured obligation and which arises as of the time of the filing of the notice of the lien imposed by this subsection. If the State has not by law designated one office for the receipt of such notices of liens, the notice shall be filed in the office of the clerk of the United States district court for the district in which the real property is located. For purposes of this subsection, the terms "purchaser" and "security interest" shall have the definitions provided under section 6323(h) of Title 26.

**(4) Action in rem**

The costs constituting the lien may be recovered in an action in rem in the United States district court for the district in which the removal or remedial action is occurring or has occurred. Nothing in this subsection shall affect the right of the United States to bring an action against any person to recover all costs and damages for which such person is liable under subsection (a) of this section.

**(m) Maritime lien**

All costs and damages for which the owner or operator of a vessel is liable under subsection (a)(1) of this section with respect to a release or threatened release from such vessel shall constitute a maritime lien in favor of the United States on such vessel. Such costs may be recovered in an action in rem in the district court of the United States for the district in which the vessel may be found. Nothing in this subsection shall affect the right of the United States to bring an action against the owner or operator of such vessel in any court of competent jurisdiction to recover such costs.

**(n) Liability of fiduciaries**

**(1) In general**

The liability of a fiduciary under any provision of this chapter for the release or threatened release of a hazardous substance at, from, or in connection with a vessel or facility held in a fiduciary capacity shall not exceed the assets held in the fiduciary capacity.

**(2) Exclusion**

Paragraph (1) does not apply to the extent that a person is liable under this chapter independently of the person's ownership of a vessel or facility as a fiduciary or actions taken in a fiduciary capacity.

**(3) Limitation**

Paragraphs (1) and (4) do not limit the liability pertaining to a release or threatened release of a hazardous substance if negligence of a fiduciary causes or contributes to the release or threatened release.

**(4) Safe harbor**

A fiduciary shall not be liable in its personal capacity under this chapter for—

(A) undertaking or directing another person to undertake a response action under subsection (d)(1) of this section or under the direction of an on scene coordinator designated under the National Contingency Plan;

(B) undertaking or directing another person to undertake any other lawful means of addressing a hazardous substance in connection with the vessel or facility;

(C) terminating the fiduciary relationship;

(D) including in the terms of the fiduciary agreement a covenant, warranty, or other term or condition that relates to compliance with an environmental law, or monitoring, modifying or enforcing the term or condition;

(E) monitoring or undertaking 1 or more inspections of the vessel or facility;

(F) providing financial or other advice or counseling to other parties to the fiduciary relationship, including the settlor or beneficiary;

(G) restructuring, renegotiating, or otherwise altering the terms and conditions of the fiduciary relationship;

(H) administering, as a fiduciary, a vessel or facility that was contaminated before the fiduciary relationship began; or

(I) declining to take any of the actions described in subparagraphs (B) through (H).

**(5) Definitions**

As used in this chapter:

**(A) Fiduciary**

The term "fiduciary"—

(i) means a person acting for the benefit of another party as a bona fide—

(I) trustee;

(II) executor;

(III) administrator;

(IV) custodian;

(V) guardian of estates or guardian ad litem;

(VI) receiver;

(VII) conservator;

(VIII) committee of estates of incapacitated persons;

(IX) personal representative;

(X) trustee (including a successor to a trustee) under an indenture agreement, trust agreement, lease, or similar financing agreement, for debt securities, certificates of interest or certificates of participation in debt securities, or other forms of indebtedness as to which the trustee is not, in the capacity of trustee, the lender; or

(XI) representative in any other capacity that the Administrator, after providing public notice, determines to be similar to the capacities described in subclauses (I) through (X); and

(ii) does not include—

(I) a person that is acting as a fiduciary with respect to a trust or other fiduciary estate that was organized for the primary purpose of, or is engaged in, actively carrying on a trade or business for profit, unless the trust or other fiduciary estate was created as part of, or to facilitate, 1 or more estate plans or because of the incapacity of a natural person; or

(II) a person that acquires ownership or control of a vessel or facility with the objective purpose of avoiding liability of the person or of any other person.

**(B) Fiduciary capacity**

The term "fiduciary capacity" means the capacity of a person in holding title to a vessel or facility, or otherwise having control of or an interest in the vessel or facility, pursuant to the exercise of the responsibilities of the person as a fiduciary.

**(6) Savings clause**

Nothing in this subsection—

**(A)** affects the rights or immunities or other defenses that are available under this chapter or other law that is applicable to a person subject to this subsection; or

**(B)** creates any liability for a person or a private right of action against a fiduciary or any other person.

**(7) No effect on certain persons**

Nothing in this subsection applies to a person if the person—

**(A)(i)** acts in a capacity other than that of a fiduciary or in a beneficiary capacity; and

**(ii)** in that capacity, directly or indirectly benefits from a trust or fiduciary relationship; or

**(B)(i)** is a beneficiary and a fiduciary with respect to the same fiduciary estate; and

**(ii)** as a fiduciary, receives benefits that exceed customary or reasonable compensation, and incidental benefits, permitted under other applicable law.

**(8) Limitation**

This subsection does not preclude a claim under this chapter against—

**(A)** the assets of the estate or trust administered by the fiduciary; or

**(B)** a nonemployee agent or independent contractor retained by a fiduciary.

**(*o*) De micromis exemption**

**(1) In general**

Except as provided in paragraph (2), a person shall not be liable, with respect to response costs at a facility on the National Priorities List, under this chapter if liability is based solely on paragraph (3) or (4) of subsection (a), and the person, except as provided in paragraph (4) of this subsection, can demonstrate that—

**(A)** the total amount of the material containing hazardous substances that the person arranged for disposal or treatment of, arranged with a transporter for transport for disposal or treatment of, or accepted for transport for disposal or treatment, at the facility was less than 110 gallons of liquid materials or less than 200 pounds of solid materials (or such greater or lesser amounts as the Administrator may determine by regulation); and

**(B)** all or part of the disposal, treatment, or transport concerned occurred before April 1, 2001.

**(2) Exceptions**

Paragraph (1) shall not apply in a case in which—

**(A)** the President determines that—

**(i)** the materials containing hazardous substances referred to in paragraph (1) have contributed significantly or could contribute significantly, either individually or in the aggregate, to the cost of the response action or natural resource restoration with respect to the facility; or

**(ii)** the person has failed to comply with an information request or administrative subpoena issued by the President under this chapter or has impeded or is impeding, through action or inaction, the performance of a response action or natural resource restoration with respect to the facility; or

**(B)** a person has been convicted of a criminal violation for the conduct to which the exemption would apply, and that conviction has not been vitiated on appeal or otherwise.

**(3) No judicial review**

A determination by the President under paragraph (2)(A) shall not be subject to judicial review.

**(4) NonGovernmental third-party contribution actions**

In the case of a contribution action, with respect to response costs at a facility on the National Priorities List, brought by a party, other than a Federal, State, or local government, under this chapter, the burden of proof shall be on the party bringing the action to demonstrate that the conditions described in paragraph (1)(A) and (B) of this subsection are not met.

**(p) Municipal solid waste exemption**

**(1) In general**

Except as provided in paragraph (2) of this subsection, a person shall not be liable, with respect to response costs at a facility on the National Priorities List, under paragraph (3) of subsection (a) of this section for municipal solid waste disposed of at a facility if the person, except as provided in paragraph (5) of this subsection, can demonstrate that the person is—

**(A)** an owner, operator, or lessee of residential property from which all of the person's municipal solid waste was generated with respect to the facility;

**(B)** a business entity (including a parent, subsidiary, or affiliate of the entity) that, during its 3 taxable years preceding the date of transmittal of written notification from the President of its potential liability under this section, employed on average not more than 100 full-time individuals, or the equivalent thereof, and that is a small business concern (within the meaning of the Small Business Act (15 U.S.C. 631 et seq.)) from which was generated all of the municipal solid waste attributable to the entity with respect to the facility; or

**(C)** an organization described in section 501(c)(3) of Title 26 and exempt from tax under section 501(a) of Title 26 that, during its taxable year preceding the date of transmittal of written notification from the President of its potential liability under this section, employed not more than 100 paid individuals at the location from which was generated all of the municipal solid waste attributable to the organization with respect to the facility.

For purposes of this subsection, the term "affiliate" has the meaning of that term provided in the definition of "small business concern" in regulations promulgated by the Small Business Administration in accordance with the Small Business Act (15 U.S.C. 631 et seq.).

**(2) Exception**

Paragraph (1) shall not apply in a case in which the President determines that—

**(A)** the municipal solid waste referred to in paragraph (1) has contributed significantly or could contribute significantly, either individually or in the aggregate, to the cost of the response action or natural resource restoration with respect to the facility;

**(B)** the person has failed to comply with an information request or administrative subpoena issued by the President under this chapter; or

**(C)** the person has impeded or is impeding, through action or inaction, the performance of a response action or natural resource restoration with respect to the facility.

**(3) No judicial review**

A determination by the President under paragraph (2) shall not be subject to judicial review.

**(4) Definition of municipal solid waste**

**(A) In general**

For purposes of this subsection, the term "municipal solid waste" means waste material—

**(i)** generated by a household (including a single or multifamily residence); and

**(ii)** generated by a commercial, industrial, or institutional entity, to the extent that the waste material—

**(I)** is essentially the same as waste normally generated by a household;

**(II)** is collected and disposed of with other municipal solid waste as part of normal municipal solid waste collection services; and

**(III)** contains a relative quantity of hazardous substances no greater than the relative quantity of hazardous substances contained in waste material generated by a typical single-family household.

**(B) Examples**

Examples of municipal solid waste under subparagraph (A) include food and yard waste, paper, clothing, appliances, consumer product packaging, disposable diapers, office supplies, cosmetics, glass and metal food containers, elementary or secondary school science laboratory waste, and household hazardous waste.

**(C) Exclusions**

The term "municipal solid waste" does not include—

**(i)** combustion ash generated by resource recovery facilities or municipal incinerators; or

**(ii)** waste material from manufacturing or processing operations (including pollution control operations) that is not essentially the same as waste normally generated by households.

**(5) Burden of proof**

In the case of an action, with respect to response costs at a facility on the National Priorities List, brought under this section or section 9613 of this title by—

**(A)** a party, other than a Federal, State, or local government, with respect to municipal solid waste disposed of on or after April 1, 2001; or

**(B)** any party with respect to municipal solid waste disposed of before April 1, 2001, the burden of proof shall be on the party bringing the action to demonstrate that the conditions described in paragraphs (1) and (4) for exemption for entities and organizations described in paragraph (1)(B) and (C) are not met.

**(6) Certain actions not permitted**

No contribution action may be brought by a party, other than a Federal, State, or local government, under this chapter with respect to circumstances described in paragraph (1)(A).

**(7) Costs and fees**

A nongovernmental entity that commences, after the date of the enactment of this subsection, a contribution action under this chapter shall be liable to the defendant for all reasonable costs of defending the action, including all reasonable attorney's fees and expert witness fees, if the defendant is not liable for contribution based on an exemption under this subsection or subsection (*o*) of this section.

**(q) Contiguous properties**

**(1) Not considered to be an owner or operator**

**(A) In general**

A person that owns real property that is contiguous to or otherwise similarly situated with respect to, and that is or may be contaminated by a release or threatened release of a hazardous substance from, real property that is not owned by that person shall not be considered to be an owner or operator of a vessel or facility under paragraph (1) or (2) of subsection (a) solely by reason of the contamination if—

(i) the person did not cause, contribute, or consent to the release or threatened release;

(ii) the person is not—

(I) potentially liable, or affiliated with any other person that is potentially liable, for response costs at a facility through any direct or indirect familial relationship or any contractual, corporate, or financial relationship (other than a contractual, corporate, or financial relationship that is created by a contract for the sale of goods or services); or

(II) the result of a reorganization of a business entity that was potentially liable;

(iii) the person takes reasonable steps to—

(I) stop any continuing release;

(II) prevent any threatened future release; and

(III) prevent or limit human, environmental, or natural resource exposure to any hazardous substance released on or from property owned by that person;

(iv) the person provides full cooperation, assistance, and access to persons that are authorized to conduct response actions or natural resource restoration at the vessel or facility from which there has been a release or threatened release (including the cooperation and access necessary for the installation, integrity, operation, and maintenance of any complete or partial response action or natural resource restoration at the vessel or facility);

(v) the person—

(I) is in compliance with any land use restrictions established or relied on in connection with the response action at the facility; and

(II) does not impede the effectiveness or integrity of any institutional control employed in connection with a response action;

(vi) the person is in compliance with any request for information or administrative subpoena issued by the President under this chapter;

(vii) the person provides all legally required notices with respect to the discovery or release of any hazardous substances at the facility; and

**(viii) At the time at which the person acquired the property, the person**

(I) conducted all appropriate inquiry within the meaning of section 9601(35)(B) of this title with respect to the property; and

(II) did not know or have reason to know that the property was or could be contaminated by a release or threatened release of one or more hazardous substances from other real property not owned or operated by the person.

**(B) Demonstration**

To qualify as a person described in subparagraph (A), a person must establish by a preponderance of the evidence that the conditions in clauses (i) through (viii) of subparagraph (A) have been met.

**(C) Bona fide prospective purchaser**

Any person that does not qualify as a person described in this paragraph because the person had, or had reason to have, knowledge specified in subparagraph (A)(viii) at the time of acquisition of the real property may qualify as a bona fide prospective purchaser under section 9601(40) of this title if the person is otherwise described in that section.

**(D) Ground water**

With respect to a hazardous substance from one or more sources that are not on the property of a person that is a contiguous property owner that enters ground water beneath the property of the person solely as a result of subsurface migration in an aquifer, subparagraph (A)(iii) shall not require the person to conduct ground water investigations or to install ground water remediation systems, except in accordance with the policy of the Environmental Protection Agency concerning owners of property containing contaminated aquifers, dated May 24, 1995.

**(2) Effect of law**

With respect to a person described in this subsection, nothing in this subsection—

(A) limits any defense to liability that may be available to the person under any other provision of law; or

(B) imposes liability on the person that is not otherwise imposed by subsection (a) of this section.

**(3) Assurances**

The Administrator may—

(A) issue an assurance that no enforcement action under this chapter will be initiated against a person described in paragraph (1); and

(B) grant a person described in paragraph (1) protection against a cost recovery or contribution action under section 9613(f) of this title.

**(r) Prospective purchaser and windfall lien**

**(1) Limitation on liability**

Notwithstanding subsection (a)(1) of this section, a bona fide prospective purchaser whose potential liability for a release or threatened release is based solely on the purchaser's being considered to be an owner or operator of a facility shall not be liable as long as the bona fide prospective purchaser does not impede the performance of a response action or natural resource restoration.

**(2) Lien**

If there are unrecovered response costs incurred by the United States at a facility for which an owner of the facility is not liable by reason of paragraph (1), and if each of the conditions described in paragraph (3) is met, the United States shall have a lien on the facility, or may by agreement with the owner, obtain from the owner a lien on any other property or other assurance of payment satisfactory to the Administrator, for the unrecovered response costs.

**(3) Conditions**

The conditions referred to in paragraph (2) are the following:

**(A) Response action**

A response action for which there are unrecovered costs of the United States is carried out at the facility.

**(B) Fair market value**

The response action increases the fair market value of the facility above the fair market value of the facility that existed before the response action was initiated.

**(4) Amount; duration**

A lien under paragraph (2)—

(A) shall be in an amount not to exceed the increase in fair market value of the property attributable to the response action at the time of a sale or other disposition of the property;

(B) shall arise at the time at which costs are first incurred by the United States with respect to a response action at the facility;

(C) shall be subject to the requirements of subsection (*l*)(3); and

(D) shall continue until the earlier of—

(i) satisfaction of the lien by sale or other means; or

(ii) notwithstanding any statute of limitations under section 9613 of this tile, recovery of all response costs incurred at the facility.

(Pub.L. 96–510, Title I, § 107, Dec. 11, 1980, 94 Stat. 2781; Pub.L. 99–499, Title I, §§ 107(a) to (d)(2), (e), (f), 127(b), (e), Title II, §§ 201, 207(c), Oct. 17, 1986, 100 Stat. 1628 to 1630, 1692, 1693, 1705; Pub.L. 99–514, § 2, Oct. 22, 1986, 100 Stat. 2095; Pub.L. 103–429, § 7(e)(2), Oct. 31, 1994, 108 Stat. 4390; Pub.L. 104–208, Div. A, Title II, § 2502(a), Sept. 30, 1996, 110 Stat. 3009–462; Pub.L. 104–287, § 6(j)(2), Oct. 11, 1996, 110 Stat. 3400; Pub.L. 107–118, Title I, § 102(a), Title II, §§ 221, 222(b), Jan. 11, 2002, 115 Stat. 2356, 2368, 2371.)

## HISTORICAL AND STATUTORY NOTES

**References in Text**

This chapter, referred to in text, originally read "this Act", meaning Pub.L. 96–510, Dec. 11, 1980, 94 Stat. 2767, as amended, known as the Comprehensive Environmental Response, Compensation, and Liability Act of 1980, which is classified principally to this chapter [42 U.S.C.A. § 9601 et seq.]; see Tables for complete classification.

Such amendments, referred to in subsec. (a) closing par., probably means the amendments made by Pub.L. 99–499, Oct. 17, 1986, 100 Stat. 1613, known as the "Superfund Amendments and Reauthorization Act of 1986". For complete classification of that Act to the Code, see Short Title of 1986 Amendments note set out under section 9601 of this title and Tables.

Act of March 3, 1851 (46 U.S.C. 183ff), referred to in subsec. (h), is Act Mar. 3, 1851, c. 43, 9 Stat. 635, which was incorporated into the Revised Statutes as R.S. sections 4282 to 4287 and 4289, and is classified to sections 182, 183, and 184 to 188 of Title 46, Appendix, Shipping.

The Federal Insecticide, Fungicide, and Rodenticide Act, referred to in subsec. (i), is Act June 25, 1947, c. 125, as amended generally by Pub.L. 92–516, Oct. 21, 1972, 86 Stat. 973, which is classified generally to subchapter II (section 136 et seq.) of chapter 6 of Title 7, Agriculture. For complete classification of this Act to the Code, see Short Title note set out under section 136 of Title 7 and Tables.

The Solid Waste Disposal Act, referred to in subsec. (k)(1), (3), (6)(E)(i), is Title II of Pub.L. 89–272, Oct. 20, 1965, 79 Stat. 997, as amended generally by Pub.L. 94–580, § 2, Oct. 21, 1976, 90 Stat. 2795. Subtitle C of the Solid Waste Disposal Act is classified generally to subchapter III (section 6921 et seq.) of chapter 82 of this title. Subtitle I of that Act is classified generally to subchapter IX (section 6991 et seq.) of chapter 82 of this title. For complete classification of this Act to the Code, see Short Title of 1965 Acts note set out under section 6901 of this title and Tables.

Section 9641 of this title, referred to in subsec. (k)(1) to (3), (5), (6)(E)(iv), was repealed by Pub.L. 99–499, Title V, § 514(b), Oct. 17, 1986, 100 Stat. 1767.

Subchapter II of this chapter, referred to in subsec. (k)(4)(A) and (C), was in the original, "Title II of this Act", meaning Title II of Pub.L. 96–510, Dec. 11, 1980, 94 Stat. 2796, known as the Hazardous Substance Response Revenue Act of 1980, which enacted subchapter II of this chapter and sections 4611, 4612, 4661, 4662, and former sections 4681, and 4682 of Title 26, Internal Revenue Code. Sections 221 to 223 and 232 of Pub.L. 96–510, which were classified to sections 9631 to 9633 and 9641 of this title, comprising subchapter II of this chapter, were repealed by Pub.L. 99–499, Title V, §§ 514(b), 517(c)(1), Oct. 17, 1986, 100 Stat. 1767, 1774. For complete classification of Title II to the Code, see Short Title of 1980 Amendments note set out under section 1 of Title 26 and Tables.

The Hazardous and Solid Waste Amendments of 1984, referred to in subsec. (k)(6)(A), (E), is Pub.L. 98–616, Nov. 8, 1984, 98 Stat. 3221. For complete classification of this Act to the Code, see Short Title of 1984 Amendments note set out under section 6901 of this title.

The Small Business Act, referred to in subsec. (p)(1), is Pub.L. 85–536, July 18, 1958, 72 Stat. 384, as amended, which is classified generally to chapter 14A of Title 15 [42 U.S.C.A. § 631 et seq.] see Tables for complete classification.

The date of the enactment of this subsection, referred to in subsec. (p)(7), probably means Jan. 11, 2002, the approval date of Pub.L. 107–118, 115 Stat. 2356, which enacted subsec. (p) of this section.

### Codifications

Reference in the original text of subsec. (p)(5) of this section to "section 107 or 113" has been translated in the codified text as "this section or section 9613 of this title" to reflect the probable intent of Congress.

### Effective and Applicability Provisions

1996 Acts

Amendment by section 2502 of Title II of Div. A of Pub.L. 104–208 applicable with respect to claims not finally adjudicated as of Sept. 30, 1996, see section 2505 of Title II of Div. A of Pub.L. 104–208, set out as a note under section 6991b of this title.

1986 Acts

Amendment by Pub.L. 99–499 effective Oct. 17, 1986, see section 4 of Pub.L. 99–499, set out as a note under section 9601 of this title.

### Delegation of Functions

Functions vested in the President by subsec. (c)(1)(C) of this section delegated to the Secretary of Transportation, see section 5(a) of Ex. Ord. No. 12580, Jan. 23, 1987, 52 F.R. 2923, set out as a note under section 9615 of this title.

Functions vested in the President by subsec. (c)(3) of this section delegated, with authority to redelegate, to the Coast Guard with respect to any release or threatened release involving the coastal zone, Great Lakes waters, ports, and harbors, see sections 5(b), 11(g) of Ex. Ord. No. 12580, Jan. 23, 1987, 52 F.R. 2923, set out as a note under section 9615 of this title.

Functions vested in the President by subsec. (c)(3) of this section delegated, subject to section 5(b) of Ex. Ord. No. 12580, and with authority to redelegate, to the Administrator of the Environmental Protection Agency, see sections 5(c), 11(g) of Ex. Ord. No. 12580, Jan. 23, 1987, 52 F.R. 2923, set out as a note under section 9615 of this title.

Functions vested in the President by subsec. (f)(1) of this section delegated to each of the Federal trustees for natural resources designated in the National Contingency Plan for resources under their trusteeship, see section 5(d) of Ex. Ord. No. 12580, Jan. 23, 1987, 52 F.R. 2923, set out as a note under section 9615 of this title.

Functions vested in the President by subsec. (f)(2)(B) of this section, to receive notification of the state natural resource trustee designations, delegated to the Administrator of the Environmental Protection Agency, see section 5(e) of Ex. Ord. No. 12580, Jan. 23, 1987, 52 F.R. 2923, set out as a note under section 9615 of this title.

Functions vested in the President by subsec. (k)(4)(B) of this section delegated to the Secretary of the Treasury, with the Administrator of the Environmental Protection Agency to provide the Secretary with such technical information and assistance as the Administrator may have available, see section 7(a) of Ex. Ord. No. 12580, Jan. 23, 1987, 52 F.R. 2923, set out as a note under section 9615 of this title.

### Coordination of Titles I to IV of Pub.L. 99–499

Any provision of Titles I to IV of Pub.L. 99–499, imposing any tax, premium, or fee; establishing any trust fund; or authorizing expenditures from any trust fund, to have no force or effect, see section 531 of Pub.L. 99–499, set out as a note under section 1 of Title 26, Internal Revenue Code.

### Effect on Concluded Actions

Pub.L. 107–118, Title I, § 103, Jan. 11, 2002, 115 Stat. 2360, provided that: "The amendments made by this title [Pub.L. 107–118, Title I, § 101 et seq., Jan. 11, 2002, 115 Stat. 2356, enacting provisions set out as a note under 42 U.S.C.A. § 9601 and amending subsecs. (*o*) and (p) of this section and 42 U.S.C.A. § 9622(g)(7) to (12)] shall not apply to or in any way affect any settlement lodged in, or judgment issued by, a United States District Court, or any administrative settlement or order entered into or issued by the United States or any State, before the date of the enactment of this Act [Jan. 11, 2002]."

### Recovery of Costs

Pub.L. 104–303, Title II, § 209, Oct. 12, 1996, 110 Stat. 3681, provided that: "Amounts recovered under section 107 of the Comprehensive Environmental Response, Compensation, and Liability Act of 1980 (42 U.S.C. 9607) [this section] for any response action taken by the Secretary in support of the civil works program of the Department of the Army and any other amounts recovered by the Secretary from a contractor, insurer, surety, or other person to reimburse the Department of the Army for any expenditure for environmental response activities in support of the Army civil works program shall be credited to the appropriate trust fund account from which the cost of such response action has been paid or will be charged."

## § 9608. Financial responsibility

**[CERCLA § 108]**

### (a) Establishment and maintenance by owner or operator of vessel; amount; failure to obtain certification of compliance

(1) The owner or operator of each vessel (except a nonself-propelled barge that does not carry hazardous substances as cargo) over three hundred gross tons that uses any port or place in the United States or the navigable waters or any offshore facility, shall establish and maintain, in accordance with regulations promulgated by the President, evidence of financial responsibility of $300 per gross ton (or for a vessel carrying hazardous substances as cargo, or $5,000,000, whichever is greater) to cover the liability prescribed under paragraph (1) of section 9607(a) of this title. Financial responsibility may be established by any one, or any combination, of the following: insurance, guarantee, surety bond, or qualification as a self-insurer. Any bond filed shall be issued by a bonding company authorized to do business in the United States. In cases where an owner or operator owns, operates, or charters more than one vessel subject to this subsection, evidence of financial responsibility need be established only to meet the maximum liability applicable to the largest of such vessels.

(2) The Secretary of the Treasury shall withhold or revoke the clearance required by section 91 of Title 46, Appendix, of any vessel subject to this subsection that does not have certification furnished by the President that the financial responsibility provisions of paragraph (1) of this subsection have been complied with.

(3) The Secretary of Transportation, in accordance with regulations issued by him, shall (A) deny entry to any port or place in the United States or navigable waters to, and (B) detain at the port or place in the United States from which it is about to depart for any other port or place in the United States, any vessel subject to this subsection that, upon request, does not produce certification furnished by the President that the financial responsibility provisions of paragraph (1) of this subsection have been complied with.

(4) In addition to the financial responsibility provisions of paragraph (1) of this subsection, the President shall require additional evidence of financial responsibility for incineration vessels in such amounts, and to cover such liabilities recognized by law, as the President deems appropriate, taking into account the potential risks posed by incineration and transport for incineration, and any other factors deemed relevant.

**(b) Establishment and maintenance by owner or operator of production, etc., facilities; amount; adjustment; consolidated form of responsibility; coverage of motor carriers**

(1) Beginning not earlier than five years after December 11, 1980, the President shall promulgate requirements (for facilities in addition to those under subtitle C of the Solid Waste Disposal Act [42 U.S.C.A. § 6921 et seq.] and other Federal law) that classes of facilities establish and maintain evidence of financial responsibility consistent with the degree and duration of risk associated with the production, transportation, treatment, storage, or disposal of hazardous substances. Not later than three years after December 11, 1980, the President shall identify those classes for which requirements will be first developed and publish notice of such identification in the Federal Register. Priority in the development of such requirements shall be accorded to those classes of facilities, owners, and operators which the President determines present the highest level of risk of injury.

(2) The level of financial responsibility shall be initially established, and, when necessary, adjusted to protect against the level of risk which the President in his discretion believes is appropriate based on the payment experience of the Fund, commercial insurers, courts settlements and judgments, and voluntary claims satisfaction. To the maximum extent practicable, the President shall cooperate with and seek the advice of the commercial insurance industry in developing financial responsibility requirements. Financial responsibility may be established by any one, or any combination, of the following: insurance, guarantee, surety bond, letter of credit, or qualification as a self-insurer. In promulgating requirements under this section, the President is authorized to specify policy or other contractual terms, conditions, or defenses which are necessary, or which are unacceptable, in establishing such evidence of financial responsibility in order to effectuate the purposes of this chapter.

(3) Regulations promulgated under this subsection shall incrementally impose financial responsibility requirements as quickly as can reasonably be achieved but in no event more than 4 years after the date of promulgation. Where possible, the level of financial responsibility which the President believes appropriate as a final requirement shall be achieved through incremental, annual increases in the requirements.

(4) Where a facility is owned or operated by more than one person, evidence of financial responsibility covering the facility may be established and maintained by one of the owners or operators, or, in consolidated form, by or on behalf of two or more owners or operators. When evidence of financial responsibility is established in a consolidated form, the proportional share of each participant shall be shown. The evidence shall be accompanied by a statement authorizing the applicant to act for and in behalf of each participant in submitting and maintaining the evidence of financial responsibility.

(5) The requirements for evidence of financial responsibility for motor carriers covered by this chapter shall be determined under section 31139 of title 49.

**(c) Direct action**

**(1) Releases from vessels**

In the case of a release or threatened release from a vessel, any claim authorized by section 9607 or 9611 of this title may be asserted directly against any guarantor providing evidence of financial responsibility for such vessel under subsection (a) of this section. In defending such a claim, the guarantor may invoke all rights and defenses which would be available to the owner or operator under this subchapter. The guarantor may also invoke the defense that the incident was caused by the willful misconduct of the owner or operator, but the guarantor may not invoke any other defense that the guarantor might have been entitled to invoke in a proceeding brought by the owner or operator against him.

**(2) Releases from facilities**

In the case of a release or threatened release from a facility, any claim authorized by section 9607 or 9611 of this title may be asserted directly against any guarantor providing evidence of financial responsibility for such facility under subsection (b) of this section, if the person liable under section 9607 of this title is in bankruptcy, reorganization, or arrangement pursuant to the Federal Bankruptcy Code, or if, with reasonable diligence, jurisdiction in the Federal courts cannot be obtained over a person liable under section 9607 of this title who is likely to be solvent at the time of judgment. In the case of any action pursuant to this paragraph, the guarantor shall be entitled to invoke all rights and defenses which would have been available to the person liable under section 9607 of this title if any action had been brought against such person by the claimant and all rights and defenses which would have been available to the guarantor if an action had been brought against the guarantor by such person.

**(d) Limitation of guarantor liability**

**(1) Total liability**

The total liability of any guarantor in a direct action suit brought under this section shall be limited to the aggregate amount of the monetary limits of the policy of insurance, guarantee, surety bond, letter of credit, or similar instrument obtained from the guarantor by the person subject to liability under section 9607 of this title for the purpose of satisfying the requirement for evidence of financial responsibility.

**(2) Other liability**

Nothing in this subsection shall be construed to limit any other State or Federal statutory, contractual, or common law liability of a guarantor, including, but not limited to, the liability of such guarantor for bad faith either in negotiating or in failing to negotiate the settlement of any claim. Nothing in this subsection shall be construed, interpreted, or applied to diminish the liability of any person under section 9607 of this title or other applicable law.

(Pub.L. 96–510, Title I, § 108, Dec. 11, 1980, 94 Stat. 2785; Pub.L. 99–499, Title I, §§ 108, 127(c), Oct. 17, 1986, 100 Stat. 1631, 1692.)

## HISTORICAL AND STATUTORY NOTES

**References in Text**

The Solid Waste Disposal Act, referred to in subsec. (b)(1), is Title II of Pub.L. 89–272, Oct. 20, 1965, 79 Stat. 997, as amended generally by Pub.L. 94–580, § 2, Oct. 21, 1976, 90 Stat. 2795. Subtitle C of the Solid Waste Disposal Act is classified generally to subchapter III (section 6921 et seq.) of chapter 82 of this title. For complete classification of this Act to the Code, see Short Title note set out under section 6901 of this title and Tables.

The Federal Bankruptcy Code, referred to in subsec. (c)(2), probably means a reference to Title 11, Bankruptcy.

**Codifications**

In subsec. (b)(5), "section 31139 of title 49" was substituted for "section 30 of the Motor Carrier Act of 1980, Pub. Law 96–296" on authority of Pub.L. 103–272, § 6(b), July 5, 1994, 108 Stat. 1378, the first section of which enacted subtitles II, III, and V to X of Title 49.

**Effective Dates**

1986 Acts

Amendment by Pub.L. 99–499 effective Oct. 17, 1986, see section 4 of Pub.L. 99–499, set out as a note under section 9601 of this title.

**Delegation of Functions**

Functions vested in the President by subsec. (a)(1) of this section delegated to the Coast Guard, see section 7(b)(1) of Ex. Ord. No. 12580, Jan. 23, 1987, 52 F.R. 2923, set out as a note under section 9615 of this title.

Functions vested in the President by provisions of section 9609 of this title relating to violations of subsec. (a)(1) of this section delegated, subject to section 4(a) of Ex. Ord. No. 12580, to the Coast Guard, see section 7(b)(2) of Ex. Ord. No. 12580, Jan. 23, 1987, 52 F.R. 2923, set out as a note under section 9615 of this title.

Functions vested in the President by subsec. (b) of this section delegated to the Secretary of Transportation with respect to all transportation related facilities, including any pipeline, motor vehicle, rolling stock, or aircraft, see section 7(c)(1) of Ex. Ord. No. 12580, Jan. 23, 1987, 52 F.R. 2923, set out as a note under section 9615 of this title.

Functions vested in the President by provisions of section 9609 of this title relating to violations of subsec. (a)(3) of this section delegated, subject to section 4(a) of Ex. Ord. No. 12580, to the Secretary of Transportation, see section 7(c)(2) of Ex. Ord. No. 12580, Jan. 23, 1987, 52 F.R. 2923, set out as a note under section 9615 of this title.

Functions vested in the President by provisions of section 9609 of this title relating to violations of subsec. (b) of this section delegated, subject to section 4(a) of Ex. Ord. No. 12580, to the Secretary of Transportation with respect to all transportation related facilities, including any pipeline, motor vehicle, rolling stock, or aircraft, see section 7(c)(3) of Ex.

Ord. No. 12580, Jan. 23, 1987, 52 F.R. 2923, set out as a note under section 9615 of this title.

Functions vested in the President by provisions of section 9609 of this title relating to violations of subsecs. (a)(4) and (b) of this section delegated, subject to sections 4(a) and 7(c)(3) of Ex. Ord. No. 12580, to the Administrator of the Environmental Protection Agency, see section 7(d)(2) of Ex. Ord. No. 12580, Jan. 23, 1987, 52 F.R. 2923, set out as a note under section 9615 of this title.

Functions vested in the President by subsecs. (a)(4) and (b) of this section delegated, subject to section 7(c)(1) of Ex. Ord. No. 12580, to the Administrator of the Environmental Protection Agency, see section 7(d)(1) of Ex. Ord. No. 12580, Jan. 23, 1987, 52 F.R. 2923, set out as a note under section 9615 of this title.

## § 9609. Civil penalties and awards

### [CERCLA § 109]

### (a) Class I administrative penalty

#### (1) Violations

A civil penalty of not more than $25,000 per violation may be assessed by the President in the case of any of the following—

**(A)** A violation of the requirements of section 9603(a) or (b) of this title (relating to notice).

**(B)** A violation of the requirements of section 9603(d)(2) of this title (relating to destruction of records, etc.).

**(C)** A violation of the requirements of section 9608 of this title (relating to financial responsibility, etc.), the regulations issued under section 9608 of this title, or with any denial or detention order under section 9608 of this title.

**(D)** A violation of an order under section 9622(d)(3) of this title (relating to settlement agreements for action under section 9604(b) of this title).

**(E)** Any failure or refusal referred to in section 9622(*l*) of this title (relating to violations of administrative orders, consent decrees, or agreements under section 9620 of this title).

#### (2) Notice and hearings

No civil penalty may be assessed under this subsection unless the person accused of the violation is given notice and opportunity for a hearing with respect to the violation.

#### (3) Determining amount

In determining the amount of any penalty assessed pursuant to this subsection, the President shall take into account the nature, circumstances, extent and gravity of the violation or violations and, with respect to the violator, ability to pay, any prior history of such violations, the degree of culpability, economic benefit or savings (if any) resulting from the violation, and such other matters as justice may require.

#### (4) Review

Any person against whom a civil penalty is assessed under this subsection may obtain review thereof in the appropriate district court of the United States by filing a notice of appeal in such court within 30 days from the date of such order and by simultaneously sending a copy of such notice by certified mail to the President. The President shall promptly file in such court a certified copy of the record upon which such violation was found or such penalty imposed. If any person fails to pay an assessment of a civil penalty after it has become a final and unappealable order or after the appropriate court has entered final judgment in favor of the United States, the President may request the Attorney General of the United States to institute a civil action in an appropriate district court of the United States to collect the penalty, and such court shall have jurisdiction to hear and decide any such action. In hearing such action, the court shall have authority to review the violation and the assessment of the civil penalty on the record.

#### (5) Subpoenas

The President may issue subpoenas for the attendance and testimony of witnesses and the production of relevant papers, books, or documents in connection with hearings under this subsection. In case of contumacy or refusal to obey a subpoena issued pursuant to this paragraph and served upon any person, the district court of the United States for any district in which such person is found, resides, or transacts business, upon application by the United States and after notice to such person, shall have jurisdiction to issue an order requiring such person to appear and give testimony before the administrative law judge or to appear and produce documents before the administrative law judge, or both, and any failure to obey such order of the court may be punished by such court as a contempt thereof.

### (b) Class II administrative penalty

A civil penalty of not more than $25,000 per day for each day during which the violation continues may be assessed by the President in the case of any of the following—

**(1)** A violation of the notice requirements of section 9603(a) or (b) of this title.

**(2)** A violation of section 9603(d)(2) of this title (relating to destruction of records, etc.).

**(3)** A violation of the requirements of section 9608 of this title (relating to financial responsibility, etc.), the regulations issued under section 9608 of this title, or with any denial or detention order under section 9608 of this title.

(4) A violation of an order under section 9622(d)(3) of this title (relating to settlement agreements for action under section 9604(b) of this title).

(5) Any failure or refusal referred to in section 9622(*l*) of this title (relating to violations of administrative orders, consent decrees, or agreements under section 9620 of this title).

In the case of a second or subsequent violation the amount of such penalty may be not more than $75,000 for each day during which the violation continues. Any civil penalty under this subsection shall be assessed and collected in the same manner, and subject to the same provisions, as in the case of civil penalties assessed and collected after notice and opportunity for hearing on the record in accordance with section 554 of Title 5. In any proceeding for the assessment of a civil penalty under this subsection the President may issue subpoenas for the attendance and testimony of witnesses and the production of relevant papers, books, and documents and may promulgate rules for discovery procedures. Any person who requested a hearing with respect to a civil penalty under this subsection and who is aggrieved by an order assessing the civil penalty may file a petition for judicial review of such order with the United States Court of Appeals for the District of Columbia Circuit or for any other circuit in which such person resides or transacts business. Such a petition may only be filed within the 30-day period beginning on the date the order making such assessment was issued.

**(c) Judicial assessment**

The President may bring an action in the United States district court for the appropriate district to assess and collect a penalty of not more than $25,000 per day for each day during which the violation (or failure or refusal) continues in the case of any of the following—

(1) A violation of the notice requirements of section 9603(a) or (b) of this title.

(2) A violation of section 9603(d)(2) of this title (relating to destruction of records, etc.).

(3) A violation of the requirements of section 9608 of this title (relating to financial responsibility, etc.), the regulations issued under section 9608 of this title, or with any denial or detention order under section 9608 of this title.

(4) A violation of an order under section 9622(d)(3) of this title (relating to settlement agreements for action under section 9604(b) of this title).

(5) Any failure or refusal referred to in section 9622(*l*) of this title (relating to violations of administrative orders, consent decrees, or agreements under section 9620 of this title).

In the case of a second or subsequent violation (or failure or refusal), the amount of such penalty may be not more than $75,000 for each day during which the violation (or failure or refusal) continues. For additional provisions providing for judicial assessment of civil penalties for failure to comply with a request or order under section 9604(e) of this title (relating to information gathering and access authorities), see section 9604(e) of this title.

**(d) Awards**

The President may pay an award of up to $10,000 to any individual who provides information leading to the arrest and conviction of any person for a violation subject to a criminal penalty under this chapter, including any violation of section 9603 of this title and any other violation referred to in this section. The President shall, by regulation, prescribe criteria for such an award and may pay any award under this subsection from the Fund, as provided in section 9611 of this title.

**(e) Procurement procedures**

Notwithstanding any other provision of law, any executive agency may use competitive procedures or procedures other than competitive procedures to procure the services of experts for use in preparing or prosecuting a civil or criminal action under this chapter, whether or not the expert is expected to testify at trial. The executive agency need not provide any written justification for the use of procedures other than competitive procedures when procuring such expert services under this chapter and need not furnish for publication in the Commerce Business Daily or otherwise any notice of solicitation or synopsis with respect to such procurement.

**(f) Savings clause**

Action taken by the President pursuant to this section shall not affect or limit the President's authority to enforce any provisions of this chapter.

(Pub.L. 96–510, Title I, § 109, Dec. 11, 1980, 94 Stat. 2787; Pub.L. 99–499, Title I, § 109(c), Oct. 17, 1986, 100 Stat. 1633.)

## HISTORICAL AND STATUTORY NOTES

**Effective Dates**

1986 Acts

Amendment by Pub.L. 99–499 effective Oct. 17, 1986, see section 4 of Pub.L. 99–499, set out as a note under section 9601 of this title.

**Delegation of Functions**

Functions vested in the President by subsec. (d) of this section, relating to development of regulations and guidelines, delegated to the Administrator of the Environmental Protection Agency, to be exercised in consultation with the Attorney General, see section 4(a) of Ex. Ord. No. 12580, Jan. 23, 1987, 52 F.R. 2923, set out as a note under section 9615 of this title.

Functions vested in the President by provisions of this section relating to violations of section 9622 of this title delegated, subject to section 4(a) of Ex. Ord. No. 12580, and with authority to redelegate, to the heads of Executive departments and agencies, with respect to releases or threatened releases not on the National Priorities List, where either the release is on or the sole source of the release is from any facility under the jurisdiction, custody or control of those Executive departments and agencies, with such functions to be exercised only with the concurrence of the Attorney General see sections 4(b)(2), 11(g) of Ex. Ord. No. 12580, Jan. 23, 1987, 52 F.R. 2923, set out as a note under section 9615 of this title.

Functions vested in the President by provisions of this section relating to violations of sections 9603(a) and (b) and 9622 of this title delegated, subject to section 4(a), (b)(2) of Ex. Ord. No. 12580, and with authority to redelegate, to the Coast Guard with respect to any release or threatened release involving the coastal zone, Great Lakes waters, ports, and harbors, see sections 4(c)(2), 11(g) of Ex. Ord. No. 12580, Jan. 23, 1987, 52 F.R. 2923, set out as a note under section 9615 of this title.

Functions vested in the President by provisions of this section relating to violations of sections 9603 and 9622 of this title delegated, subject to section 4(a), (b)(2), (c)(2) of Ex. Ord. No. 12580, and with authority to redelegate, to the Administrator of the Environmental Protection Agency, see sections 4(d)(2), 11(g) of Ex. Ord. No. 12580, Jan. 23, 1987, 52 F.R. 2923, set out as a note under section 9615 of this title.

Functions vested in the President by provisions of this section relating to violations of section 9608(a)(1) of this title delegated, subject to section 4(a) of Ex. Ord. No. 12580, to the Coast Guard, see section 7(b)(2) of Ex. Ord. No. 12580, Jan. 23, 1987, 52 F.R. 2923, set out as a note under section 9615 of this title.

Functions vested in the President by provisions of this section relating to violations of section 9608(a)(3) of this title delegated, subject to section 4(a) of Ex. Ord. No. 12580, to the Secretary of Transportation, see section 7(c)(2) of Ex. Ord. No. 12580, Jan. 23, 1987, 52 F.R. 2923, set out as a note under section 9615 of this title.

Functions vested in the President by provisions of this section relating to violations of section 9608(b) of this title delegated, subject to section 4(a) of Ex. Ord. No. 12580, to the Secretary of Transportation with respect to all transportation related facilities, including any pipeline, motor vehicle, rolling stock, or aircraft, see section 7(c)(3) of Ex. Ord. No. 12580, Jan. 23, 1987, 52 F.R. 2923, set out as a note under section 9615 of this title.

Functions vested in the President by provisions of this section relating to violations of section 9608(a)(4) and (b) of this title delegated, subject to sections 4(a) and 7(c)(3) of Ex. Ord. No. 12580, to the Administrator of the Environmental Protection Agency, see section 7(d)(2) of Ex. Ord. No. 12580, Jan. 23, 1987, 52 F.R. 2923, set out as a note under section 9615 of this title.

**Coordination of Titles I to IV of Pub.L. 99–499**

Any provision of Titles I to IV of Pub.L. 99–499, imposing any tax, premium, or fee; establishing any trust fund; or authorizing expenditures from any trust fund, to have no force or effect, see section 531 of Pub.L. 99–499, set out as a note under section 1 of Title 26, Internal Revenue Code.

## § 9610. Employee protection

### [CERCLA § 110]

#### (a) Activities of employee subject to protection

No person shall fire or in any other way discriminate against, or cause to be fired or discriminated against, any employee or any authorized representative of employees by reason of the fact that such employee or representative has provided information to a State or to the Federal Government, filed, instituted, or caused to be filed or instituted any proceeding under this chapter, or has testified or is about to testify in any proceeding resulting from the administration or enforcement of the provisions of this chapter.

#### (b) Administrative grievance procedure in cases of alleged violations

Any employee or a representative of employees who believes that he has been fired or otherwise discriminated against by any person in violation of subsection (a) of this section may, within thirty days after such alleged violation occurs, apply to the Secretary of Labor for a review of such firing or alleged discrimination. A copy of the application shall be sent to such person, who shall be the respondent. Upon receipt of such application, the Secretary of Labor shall cause such investigation to be made as he deems appropriate. Such investigation shall provide an opportunity for a public hearing at the request of any party to such review to enable the parties to present information relating to such alleged violation. The parties shall be given written notice of the time and place of the hearing at least five days prior to the hearing. Any such hearing shall be of record and shall be subject to section 554 of Title 5. Upon receiving the report of such investigation, the Secretary of Labor shall make findings of fact. If he finds that such violation did occur, he shall issue a decision, incorporating an order therein and his findings, requiring the party committing such violation to take such affirmative action to abate the violation as the Secretary of Labor deems appropriate, including, but not limited to, the rehiring or reinstatement of the employee or representative of employees to his former position with compensation. If he finds that there was no such violation, he shall issue an order denying the application. Such order issued by the Secretary of Labor under this subparagraph shall be subject to judicial review in the same manner as orders and decisions are subject to judicial review under this chapter.

#### (c) Assessment of costs and expenses against violator subsequent to issuance of order of abatement

Whenever an order is issued under this section to abate such violation, at the request of the applicant a sum equal to the aggregate amount of all costs and expenses (including the attorney's fees) determined by the Secretary of Labor to have been reasonably incurred by the applicant for, or in connection with, the institution and prosecution of such proceedings, shall be assessed against the person committing such violation.

**(d) Defenses**

This section shall have no application to any employee who acting without discretion from his employer (or his agent) deliberately violates any requirement of this chapter.

**(e) Presidential evaluations of potential loss of shifts of employment resulting from administration or enforcement of provisions; investigations; procedures applicable, etc.**

The President shall conduct continuing evaluations of potential loss of shifts of employment which may result from the administration or enforcement of the provisions of this chapter, including, where appropriate, investigating threatened plant closures or reductions in employment allegedly resulting from such administration or enforcement. Any employee who is discharged, or laid off, threatened with discharge or layoff, or otherwise discriminated against by any person because of the alleged results of such administration or enforcement, or any representative of such employee, may request the President to conduct a full investigation of the matter and, at the request of any party, shall hold public hearings, require the parties, including the employer involved, to present information relating to the actual or potential effect of such administration or enforcement on employment and any alleged discharge, layoff, or other discrimination, and the detailed reasons or justification therefore.[1] Any such hearing shall be of record and shall be subject to section 554 of Title 5. Upon receiving the report of such investigation, the President shall make findings of fact as to the effect of such administration or enforcement on employment and on the alleged discharge, layoff, or discrimination and shall make such recommendations as he deems appropriate. Such report, findings, and recommendations shall be available to the public. Nothing in this subsection shall be construed to require or authorize the President or any State to modify or withdraw any action, standard, limitation, or any other requirement of this chapter.

(Pub.L. 96–510, Title I, § 110, Dec. 11, 1980, 94 Stat. 2787.)

[1] So in original.

## HISTORICAL AND STATUTORY NOTES

**Delegation of Functions**

Functions vested in the President by subsec. (e) of this section delegated to the Administrator of the Environmental Protection Agency, see section 8(a) of Ex. Ord. No. 12580, Jan. 23, 1987, 52 F.R. 2923, set out as a note under section 9615 of this title.

## § 9611. Uses of Fund

**[CERCLA § 111]**

**(a) In general**

For the purposes specified in this section there is authorized to be appropriated from the Hazardous Substance Superfund established under subchapter A of chapter 98 of Title 26 not more than $8,500,000,000 for the 5-year period beginning on October 17, 1986, and not more than $5,100,000,000 for the period commencing October 1, 1991, and ending September 30, 1994, and such sums shall remain available until expended. The preceding sentence constitutes a specific authorization for the funds appropriated under title II of Public Law 99–160 (relating to payment to the Hazardous Substances Trust Fund). The President shall use the money in the Fund for the following purposes:

(1) Payment of governmental response costs incurred pursuant to section 9604 of this title, including costs incurred pursuant to the Intervention on the High Seas Act [33 U.S.C.A. § 1471 et seq.].

(2) Payment of any claim for necessary response costs incurred by any other person as a result of carrying out the national contingency plan established under section 1321(c) of Title 33 and amended by section 9605 of this title: *Provided, however,* That such costs must be approved under said plan and certified by the responsible Federal official.

(3) Payment of any claim authorized by subsection (b) of this section and finally decided pursuant to section 9612 of this title, including those costs set out in subsection 9612(c)(3) of this title.

(4) Payment of costs specified under subsection (c) of this section.

**(5) Grants for technical assistance**

The cost of grants under section 9617(e) of this title (relating to public participation grants for technical assistance).

**(6) Lead contaminated soil**

Payment of not to exceed $15,000,000 for the costs of a pilot program for removal, decontamination, or other action with respect to lead-contaminated soil in one to three different metropolitan areas.

The President shall not pay for any administrative costs or expenses out of the Fund unless such costs and expenses are reasonably necessary for and incidental to the implementation of this subchapter.

**(b) Additional authorized purposes**

**(1) In general**

Claims asserted and compensable but unsatisfied under provisions of section 1321 of Title 33, which are modified by section 304 of this Act may be asserted against the Fund under this subchapter; and other claims resulting from a release or threat of release of a hazardous substance from a vessel or a facility may be asserted against the Fund under this subchapter for injury to, or destruction or loss of, natural resources, including cost for damage assessment: *Provided, however,* That any such claim may be asserted only by the President, as trustee, for natural resources over which the United States has sovereign rights, or natural resources within the territory or the fishery conservation zone of the United States to the extent they are managed or protected by the United States, or by any State for natural resources within the boundary of that State belonging to, managed by, controlled by, or appertaining to the State, or by any Indian tribe or by the United States acting on behalf of any Indian tribe for natural resources belonging to, managed by, controlled by, or appertaining to such tribe, or held in trust for the benefit of such tribe, or belonging to a member of such tribe if such resources are subject to a trust restriction on alienation.

**(2) Limitation on payment of natural resource claims**

**(A) General requirements**

No natural resource claim may be paid from the Fund unless the President determines that the claimant has exhausted all administrative and judicial remedies to recover the amount of such claim from persons who may be liable under section 9607 of this title.

**(B) Definition**

As used in this paragraph, the term "natural resource claim" means any claim for injury to, or destruction or loss of, natural resources. The term does not include any claim for the costs of natural resource damage assessment.

**(c) Peripheral matters and limitations**

Uses of the Fund under subsection (a) of this section include—

(1) The costs of assessing both short-term and long-term injury to, destruction of, or loss of any natural resources resulting from a release of a hazardous substance.

(2) The costs of Federal or State or Indian tribe efforts in the restoration, rehabilitation, or replacement or acquiring the equivalent of any natural resources injured, destroyed, or lost as a result of a release of a hazardous substance.

(3) Subject to such amounts as are provided in appropriation Acts, the costs of a program to identify, investigate, and take enforcement and abatement action against releases of hazardous substances.

(4) Any costs incurred in accordance with subsection (m) of this section (relating to ATSDR) and section 9604(i) of this title, including the costs of epidemiologic and laboratory studies, health assessments, preparation of toxicologic profiles, development and maintenance of a registry of persons exposed to hazardous substances to allow long-term health effect studies, and diagnostic services not otherwise available to determine whether persons in populations exposed to hazardous substances in connection with a release or a suspected release are suffering from long-latency diseases.

(5) Subject to such amounts as are provided in appropriation Acts, the costs of providing equipment and similar overhead, related to the purposes of this chapter and section 1321 of Title 33, and needed to supplement equipment and services available through contractors or other non-Federal entities, and of establishing and maintaining damage assessment capability, for any Federal agency involved in strike forces, emergency task forces, or other response teams under the national contingency plan.

(6) Subject to such amounts as are provided in appropriation Acts, the costs of a program to protect the health and safety of employees involved in response to hazardous substance releases. Such program shall be developed jointly by the Environmental Protection Agency, the Occupational Safety and Health Administration, and the National Institute for Occupational Safety and Health and shall include, but not be limited to, measures for identifying and assessing hazards to which persons engaged in removal, remedy, or other response to hazardous substances may be exposed, methods to protect workers from such hazards, and necessary regulatory and enforcement measures to assure adequate protection of such employees.

**(7) Evaluation costs under petition provisions of section 9605(d)**

Costs incurred by the President in evaluating facilities pursuant to petitions under section 9605(d) of this title (relating to petitions for assessment of release).

**(8) Contract costs under section 9604(a)(1)**

The costs of contracts or arrangements entered into under section 9604(a)(1) of this title to oversee and review the conduct of remedial investigations and feasibility studies undertaken by persons other than the President and the costs of appropriate Federal and State oversight of remedial activities at

National Priorities List sites resulting from consent orders or settlement agreements.

**(9) Acquisition costs under section 9604(j)**

The costs incurred by the President in acquiring real estate or interests in real estate under section 9604(j) of this title (relating to acquisition of property).

**(10) Research, development, and demonstration costs under section 9660**

The cost of carrying out section 9660 of this title (relating to research, development, and demonstration), except that the amounts available for such purposes shall not exceed the amounts specified in subsection (n) of this section.

**(11) Local government reimbursement**

Reimbursements to local governments under section 9623 of this title, except that during the 8-fiscal year period beginning October 1, 1986, not more than 0.1 percent of the total amount appropriated from the Fund may be used for such reimbursements.

**(12) Worker training and education grants**

The costs of grants under section 9660a of this title for training and education of workers to the extent that such costs do not exceed $20,000,000 for each of the fiscal years 1987, 1988, 1989, 1990, 1991, 1992, 1993, and 1994.

**(13) Awards under section 9609**

The costs of any awards granted under section 9609(d) of this title.

**(14) Lead poisoning study**

The cost of carrying out the study under subsection (f) of section 118 of the Superfund Amendments and Reauthorization Act of 1986 (relating to lead poisoning in children).

**(d) Additional limitations**

(1) No money in the Fund may be used under subsection (c)(1) and (2) of this section, nor for the payment of any claim under subsection (b) of this section, where the injury, destruction, or loss of natural resources and the release of a hazardous substance from which such damages resulted have occurred wholly before December 11, 1980.

(2) No money in the Fund may be used for the payment of any claim under subsection (b) of this section where such expenses are associated with injury or loss resulting from long-term exposure to ambient concentrations of air pollutants from multiple or diffuse sources.

**(e) Funding requirements respecting moneys in Fund; limitation on certain claims; Fund use outside Federal property boundaries**

(1) Claims against or presented to the Fund shall not be valid or paid in excess of the total money in the Fund at any one time. Such claims become valid only when additional money is collected, appropriated, or otherwise added to the Fund. Should the total claims outstanding at any time exceed the current balance of the Fund, the President shall pay such claims, to the extent authorized under this section, in full in the order in which they were finally determined.

(2) In any fiscal year, 85 percent of the money credited to the Fund under subchapter II of this chapter shall be available only for the purposes specified in paragraphs (1), (2), and (4) of subsection (a) of this section. No money in the Fund may be used for the payment of any claim under subsection (a)(3) or subsection (b) of this section in any fiscal year for which the President determines that all of the Fund is needed for response to threats to public health from releases or threatened releases of hazardous substances.

(3) No money in the Fund shall be available for remedial action, other than actions specified in subsection (c) of this section, with respect to federally owned facilities; except that money in the Fund shall be available for the provision of alternative water supplies (including the reimbursement of costs incurred by a municipality) in any case involving groundwater contamination outside the boundaries of a federally owned facility in which the federally owned facility is not the only potentially responsible party.

(4) Paragraphs (1) and (4) of subsection (a) of this section shall in the aggregate be subject to such amounts as are provided in appropriation Acts.

**(f) Obligation of moneys by Federal officials; obligation of moneys or settlement of claims by State officials or Indian tribe**

The President is authorized to promulgate regulations designating one or more Federal officials who may obligate money in the Fund in accordance with this section or portions thereof. The President is also authorized to delegate authority to obligate money in the Fund or to settle claims to officials of a State or Indian tribe operating under a contract or cooperative agreement with the Federal Government pursuant to section 9604(d) of this title.

**(g) Notice to potential injured parties by owner and operator of vessel or facility causing release of substance; rules and regulations**

The President shall provide for the promulgation of rules and regulations with respect to the notice to be provided to potential injured parties by an owner and operator of any vessel, or facility from which a hazardous substance has been released. Such rules and regulations shall consider the scope and form of the notice which would be appropriate to carry out the purposes of this subchapter. Upon promulgation of such rules and regulations, the owner and operator of any vessel or facility from which a hazardous substance has been released shall provide notice in accordance with such rules and regulations. With respect to releases from public vessels, the President shall provide such notification as is appropriate to potential injured parties. Until the promulgation of such rules and regulations, the owner and operator of any vessel or facility from which a hazardous substance has been released shall provide reasonable notice to potential injured parties by publication in local newspapers serving the affected area.

**(h) Repealed. Pub.L. 99–499, Title I, § 111(c)(2), Oct. 17, 1986, 100 Stat. 1643**

**(i) Restoration, etc., of natural resources**

Except in a situation requiring action to avoid an irreversible loss of natural resources or to prevent or reduce any continuing danger to natural resources or similar need for emergency action, funds may not be used under this chapter for the restoration, rehabilitation, or replacement or acquisition of the equivalent of any natural resources until a plan for the use of such funds for such purposes has been developed and adopted by affected Federal agencies and the Governor or Governors of any State having sustained damage to natural resources within its borders, belonging to, managed by or appertaining to such State, and by the governing body of any Indian tribe having sustained damage to natural resources belonging to, managed by, controlled by, or appertaining to such tribe, or held in trust for the benefit of such tribe, or belonging to a member of such tribe if such resources are subject to a trust restriction on alienation, after adequate public notice and opportunity for hearing and consideration of all public comment.

**(j) Use of Post-closure Liability Fund**

The President shall use the money in the Post-closure Liability Fund for any of the purposes specified in subsection (a) of this section with respect to a hazardous waste disposal facility for which liability has transferred to such fund under section 9607(k) of this title, and, in addition, for payment of any claim or appropriate request for costs of response, damages, or other compensation for injury or loss under section 9607 of this title or any other State or Federal law, resulting from a release of a hazardous substance from such a facility.

**(k) Inspector General**

In each fiscal year, the Inspector General of each department, agency, or instrumentality of the United States which is carrying out any authority of this chapter shall conduct an annual audit of all payments, obligations, reimbursements, or other uses of the Fund in the prior fiscal year, to assure that the Fund is being properly administered and that claims are being appropriately and expeditiously considered. The audit shall include an examination of a sample of agreements with States (in accordance with the provisions of the Single Audit Act [31 U.S.C.A. § 7501 et seq.]) carrying out response actions under this subchapter and an examination of remedial investigations and feasibility studies prepared for remedial actions. The Inspector General shall submit to the Congress an annual report regarding the audit report required under this subsection. The report shall contain such recommendations as the Inspector General deems appropriate. Each department, agency, or instrumentality of the United States shall cooperate with its inspector general in carrying out this subsection.

**(*l*) Foreign claimants**

To the extent that the provisions of this chapter permit, a foreign claimant may assert a claim to the same extent that a United States claimant may assert a claim if—

(1) the release of a hazardous substance occurred (A) in the navigable waters or (B) in or on the territorial sea or adjacent shoreline of a foreign country of which the claimant is a resident;

(2) the claimant is not otherwise compensated for his loss;

(3) the hazardous substance was released from a facility or from a vessel located adjacent to or within the navigable waters or was discharged in connection with activities conducted under the Outer Continental Shelf Lands Act, as amended (43 U.S.C. 1331 et seq.) or the Deepwater Port Act of 1974, as amended (33 U.S.C. 1501 et seq.); and

(4) recovery is authorized by a treaty or an executive agreement between the United States and foreign country involved, or if the Secretary of State, in consultation with the Attorney General and other appropriate officials, certifies that such country provides a comparable remedy for United States claimants.

**(m) Agency for Toxic Substances and Disease Registry**

There shall be directly available to the Agency for Toxic Substances and Disease Registry to be used for the purpose of carrying out activities described in subsection (c)(4) of this section and section 9604(i) of this title not less than $50,000,000 per fiscal year for each of fiscal years 1987 and 1988, not less than $55,000,000 for fiscal year 1989, and not less than $60,000,000 per fiscal year for each of fiscal years 1990, 1991, 1992, 1993, and 1994. Any funds so made available which are not obligated by the end of the fiscal year in which made available shall be returned to the Fund.

**(n) Limitations on research, development, and demonstration program**

**(1) Section 9660(b)**

For each of the fiscal years 1987, 1988, 1989, 1990, 1991, 1992, 1993, and 1994, not more than $20,000,000 of the amounts available in the Fund may be used for the purposes of carrying out the applied research, development, and demonstration program for alternative or innovative technologies and training program authorized under section 9660(b) of this title (relating to research, development, and demonstration) other than basic research. Such amounts shall remain available until expended.

**(2) Section 9660(a)**

From the amounts available in the Fund, not more than the following amounts may be used for the purposes of section 9660(a) of this title (relating to hazardous substance research, demonstration, and training activities):

(A) For the fiscal year 1987, $3,000,000.

(B) For the fiscal year 1988, $10,000,000.

(C) For the fiscal year 1989, $20,000,000.

(D) For the fiscal year 1990, $30,000,000.

(E) For each of the fiscal years 1991, 1992, 1993, and 1994, $35,000,000.

No more than 10 percent of such amounts shall be used for training under section 9660(a) of this title in any fiscal year.

**(3) Section 9660(d)**

For each of the fiscal years 1987, 1988, 1989, 1990, 1991, 1992, 1993, and 1994, not more than $5,000,000 of the amounts available in the Fund may be used for the purposes of section 9660(d) of this title (relating to university hazardous substance research centers).

**(*o*) Notification procedures for limitations on certain payments**

Not later than 90 days after October 17, 1986, the President shall develop and implement procedures to adequately notify, as soon as practicable after a site is included on the National Priorities List, concerned local and State officials and other concerned persons of the limitations, set forth in subsection (a)(2) of this section, on the payment of claims for necessary response costs incurred with respect to such site.

**(p) General revenue share of Superfund**

**(1) In general**

The following sums are authorized to be appropriated, out of any money in the Treasury not otherwise appropriated, to the Hazardous Substance Superfund:

(A) For fiscal year 1987, $212,500,000.

(B) For fiscal year 1988, $212,500,000.

(C) For fiscal year 1989, $212,500,000.

(D) For fiscal year 1990, $212,500,000.

(E) For fiscal year 1991, $212,500,000.

(F) For fiscal year 1992, $212,500,000.

(G) For fiscal year 1993, $212,500,000.

(H) For fiscal year 1994, $212,500,000.

In addition there is authorized to be appropriated to the Hazardous Substance Superfund for each fiscal year an amount equal to so much of the aggregate amount authorized to be appropriated under this subsection (and paragraph (2) of section 9631(b) of this title) as has not been appropriated before the beginning of the fiscal year involved.

**(2) Computation**

The amounts authorized to be appropriated under paragraph (1) of this subsection in a given fiscal year shall be available only to the extent that such amount exceeds the amount determined by the Secretary under section 9507(b)(2) of Title 26 for the prior fiscal year.

(Pub.L. 96–510, Title I, § 111, Dec. 11, 1980, 94 Stat. 2788; Pub.L. 99–499, Title I, § 111, Title II, § 207(d), Oct. 17, 1986, 100 Stat. 1642, 1706; Pub.L. 101–144, Title III, Nov. 9, 1989, 103 Stat. 857; Pub.L. 101–508, Title VI, § 6301, Nov. 5, 1990, 104 Stat. 1388–319.)

## HISTORICAL AND STATUTORY NOTES

**References in Text**

Title II of Public Law 99–160, relating to payments to the Hazardous Substances Trust Fund, referred to in subsec. (a) in provisions preceding par. (1), probably means Pub.L. 99–160, Title II, § 201, Nov. 25, 1985, 99 Stat. 914, which in relevant part related to the Hazardous Substance Response Trust Fund. Provisions relating to that Fund were not classified to the Code.

The Intervention on the High Seas Act, referred to in subsec. (a)(1), is Pub.L. 93–248, Feb. 5, 1974, 88 Stat. 8, as amended, which is classified generally to chapter 28 (section 1471 et seq.) of Title 33, Navigation and Navigable Waters. For complete classification of this Act to the Code, see Short Title note set out under section 1471 of Title 33 and Tables.

Section 1321(c) of Title 33, referred to in subsec. (a)(2), was amended generally by Pub.L. 101–380, Title IV, § 4201(a), Aug. 18, 1990, 104 Stat. 523, and no longer contains provisions establishing a National Contingency Plan. However, such provisions are contained in section 1321(d) of Title 33, Navigation and Navigable Waters.

Section 304 of this Act, referred to in subsec. (b), is section 304 of Pub.L. 96–510, Title III, Dec. 11, 1980, 94 Stat. 2809, which enacted section 9654 of this title and amended section 1364 of Title 33.

Fishery conservation zone, referred to in subsec. (b), probably means the fishery conservation zone established by section 1811 of Title 16, Conservation, which as amended generally by Pub.L. 99–659, Title I, § 101(b), Nov. 14, 1986, 100 Stat. 3706, relates to United States sovereign rights and fishery management authority over fish within the exclusive economic zone as defined in section 1802 of Title 16.

Subsection (f) of section 118 of the Superfund Amendments and Reauthorization Act of 1986, referred to in subsec.

(c)(14), is section 118(f) of Pub.L. 99–499, Title I, Oct. 17, 1986, 100 Stat. 1657, which is not classified to the Code.

Subchapter II of this chapter, referred to in subsec. (e)(2), was in the original, "Title II of this Act", meaning Title II of Pub.L. 96–510, Dec. 11, 1980, 94 Stat. 2796, known as the Hazardous Substance Response Revenue Act of 1980, which enacted subchapter II of this chapter and sections 4611, 4612, 4661, 4662, and former sections 4681, and 4682 of Title 26, Internal Revenue Code. Sections 221 to 223 and 232 of Pub.L. 96–510, which were classified to sections 9631 to 9633 and 9641 of this title, comprising subchapter II of this chapter, were repealed by Pub.L. 99–499, Title V, §§ 514(b), 517(c)(1), Oct. 17, 1986, 100 Stat. 1767, 1774. For complete classification of Title II to the Code, see Short Title of 1980 Amendments note set out under section 1 of Title 26 and Tables.

The Single Audit Act, referred to in subsec. (k), probably means Pub.L. 98–502, Oct. 19, 1984, 98 Stat. 2327, known as the Single Audit Act of 1984, which is classified to chapter 75 (section 7501 et seq.) of Title 31, Money and Finance. For complete classification of this Act to the Code, see Short Title note set out under section 7501 of Title 31 and Tables.

The Outer Continental Shelf Lands Act, as amended, referred to in subsec. (*l*)(3), is Act Aug. 7, 1953, c. 345, 67 Stat. 462, as amended, which is classified generally to subchapter III (section 1331 et seq.) of chapter 29 of Title 43, Public Lands. For complete classification of this Act to the Code, see Short Title note set out under section 1301 of Title 43 and Tables.

The Deepwater Port Act of 1974, as amended, referred to in subsec. (*l*)(3), is Pub.L. 93–627, Jan. 3, 1975, 88 Stat. 2126, as amended, which is classified generally to chapter 29 (section 1501 et seq.) of Title 33, Navigation and Navigable Waters. For complete classification of this Act to the Code, see Short Title note set out under section 1501 of Title 33 and Tables.

Section 9631(b) of this title, referred to in subsec. (p)(1), was repealed by Pub.L. 99–499, Title V, § 517(c)(1), Oct. 17, 1986, 100 Stat. 1774.

**Effective Dates**

1986 Acts

Amendment by Pub.L. 99–499 effective Oct. 17, 1986, see section 4 of Pub.L. 99–499, set out as a note under section 9601 of this title.

**Delegation of Functions**

Functions vested in the President by subsec. (g) of this section delegated to the Secretaries of Defense and Energy with respect to releases from facilities or vessels under the jurisdiction, custody or control of their departments, respectively, including vessels bare-boat chartered and operated, see section 8(b) of Ex. Ord. No. 12580, Jan. 23, 1987, 52 F.R. 2923, set out as a note under section 9615 of this title.

Functions vested in the President by subsec. (g) of this section delegated, subject to section 8(b) of Ex. Ord. No. 12580, and with authority to redelegate, to the Administrator of the Environmental Protection Agency, see sections 8(c), 11(g) of Ex. Ord. No. 12580, Jan. 23, 1987, 52 F.R. 2923, set out as a note under section 9615 of this title.

Functions vested in the President by subsec. (a) of this section delegated, subject to the provisions of section 9 of Ex. Ord. No. 12580, Jan. 23, 1987, 52 F.R. 2923, and other applicable provisions of Ex. Ord. No. 12580, see section 9(a) of Ex. Ord. No. 12580, set out as a note under section 9615 of this title.

The Administrator of the Environmental Protection Agency and each department and agency head to whom funds are provided pursuant to section 9 of Ex. Ord. No. 12580, with respect to funds provided to them, authorized in accordance with subsec. (f) of this section to designate Federal officials who may obligate such funds, see section 9(d) of Ex. Ord. No. 12580, Jan. 23, 1987, 52 F.R. 2923, set out as a note under section 9615 of this title.

Functions vested in the President by section 9612 of this title delegated to the Administrator of the Environmental Protection Agency for all claims presented pursuant to this section, see section 9(e) of Ex. Ord. No. 12580, Jan. 23, 1987, 52 F.R. 2923, set out as a note under section 9615 of this title.

Functions vested in the President by subsec. (*o*) of this section delegated to the Administrator of the Environmental Protection Agency, see section 9(f) of Ex. Ord. No. 12580, Jan. 23, 1987, 52 F.R. 2923, set out as a note under section 9615 of this title.

**Coordination of Titles I to IV of Pub.L. 99–499**

Any provision of Titles I to IV of Pub.L. 99–499, imposing any tax, premium, or fee; establishing any trust fund; or authorizing expenditures from any trust fund, shall have no force or effect. See section 531 of Pub.L. 99–499, set out as a note under section 1 of Title 26, Internal Revenue Code.

**Designation of Federal Trustees for National Resources**

For designation by the President of the Secretaries of Defense, Interior, Agriculture, and Commerce, as among those to be designated in the national contingency plan as Federal trustees for natural resources, see section 1(d) of Ex. Ord. No. 12316, Aug. 14, 1981, 46 F.R. 42237, which was set out as a note under section 9615 of this title, prior to its repeal by section 11(h) of Ex. Ord. No. 12580, Jan. 23, 1987, 52 FR. 2923.

## § 9612. Claims procedure

### [CERCLA § 112]

### (a) Claims against Fund for response costs

No claim may be asserted against the Fund pursuant to section 9611(a) of this title unless such claim is presented in the first instance to the owner, operator, or guarantor of the vessel or facility from which a hazardous substance has been released, if known to the claimant, and to any other person known to the claimant who may be liable under section 9607 of this title. In any case where the claim has not been satisfied within 60 days of presentation in accordance with this subsection, the claimant may present the claim to the Fund for payment. No claim against the Fund may be approved or certified during the pendency of an action by the claimant in court to recover costs which are the subject of the claim.

### (b) Forms and procedures applicable

**(1) Prescribing forms and procedures**

The President shall prescribe appropriate forms and procedures for claims filed hereunder, which shall include a provision requiring the claimant to make a sworn verification of the claim to the best of his knowledge. Any person who knowingly gives or causes to be given any false information as a part of any such claim shall, upon conviction, be fined in accordance with the applicable provisions of Title 18 or imprisoned for not more than 3 years (or not more than 5 years in the case of a second or subsequent conviction), or both.

**(2) Payment or request for hearing**

The President may, if satisfied that the information developed during the processing of the claim warrants it, make and pay an award of the claim, except that no claim may be awarded to the extent that a judicial judgment has been made on the costs that are the subject of the claim. If the President declines to pay all or part of the claim, the claimant may, within 30 days after receiving notice of the President's decision, request an administrative hearing.

**(3) Burden of proof**

In any proceeding under this subsection, the claimant shall bear the burden of proving his claim.

**(4) Decisions**

All administrative decisions made hereunder shall be in writing, with notification to all appropriate parties, and shall be rendered within 90 days of submission of a claim to an administrative law judge, unless all the parties to the claim agree in writing to an extension or unless the President, in his discretion, extends the time limit for a period not to exceed sixty days.

**(5) Finality and appeal**

All administrative decisions hereunder shall be final, and any party to the proceeding may appeal a decision within 30 days of notification of the award or decision. Any such appeal shall be made to the Federal district court for the district where the release or threat of release took place. In any such appeal, the decision shall be considered binding and conclusive, and shall not be overturned except for arbitrary or capricious abuse of discretion.

**(6) Payment**

Within 20 days after the expiration of the appeal period for any administrative decision concerning an award, or within 20 days after the final judicial determination of any appeal taken pursuant to this subsection, the President shall pay any such award from the Fund. The President shall determine the method, terms, and time of payment.

**(c) Subrogation rights; actions maintainable**

(1) Payment of any claim by the Fund under this section shall be subject to the United States Government acquiring by subrogation the rights of the claimant to recover those costs of removal or damages for which it has compensated the claimant from the person responsible or liable for such release.

(2) Any person, including the Fund, who pays compensation pursuant to this chapter to any claimant for damages or costs resulting from a release of a hazardous substance shall be subrogated to all rights, claims, and causes of action for such damages and costs of removal that the claimant has under this chapter or any other law.

(3) Upon request of the President, the Attorney General shall commence an action on behalf of the Fund to recover any compensation paid by the Fund to any claimant pursuant to this subchapter, and, without regard to any limitation of liability, all interest, administrative and adjudicative costs, and attorney's fees incurred by the Fund by reason of the claim. Such an action may be commenced against any owner, operator, or guarantor, or against any other person who is liable, pursuant to any law, to the compensated claimant or to the Fund, for the damages or costs for which compensation was paid.

**(d) Statute of limitations**

**(1) Claims for recovery of costs**

No claim may be presented under this section for recovery of the costs referred to in section 9607(a) of this title after the date 6 years after the date of completion of all response action.

**(2) Claims for recovery of damages**

No claim may be presented under this section for recovery of the damages referred to in section 9607(a) of this title unless the claim is presented within 3 years after the later of the following:

(A) The date of the discovery of the loss and its connection with the release in question.

(B) The date on which final regulations are promulgated under section 9651(c) of this title.

**(3) Minors and incompetents**

The time limitations contained herein shall not begin to run—

(A) against a minor until the earlier of the date when such minor reaches 18 years of age or the date on which a legal representative is duly appointed for the minor, or

(B) against an incompetent person until the earlier of the date on which such person's incompetency ends or the date on which a legal representative is duly appointed for such incompetent person.

**(e) Other statutory or common law claims not waived, etc.**

Regardless of any State statutory or common law to the contrary, no person who asserts a claim against the Fund pursuant to this subchapter shall be deemed or held to have waived any other claim not covered or assertable against the Fund under this subchapter arising from the same incident, transaction, or set of circumstances, nor to have split a cause of action. Further, no person asserting a claim against the Fund pursuant to this subchapter shall as a result of any determination of a question of fact or law made in connection with that claim be deemed or held to be collaterally estopped from raising such question in connection with any other claim not covered or assertable against the Fund under this subchapter arising from the same incident, transaction, or set of circumstances.

**(f) Double recovery prohibited**

Where the President has paid out of the Fund for any response costs or any costs specified under section 9611(c)(1) or (2) of this title, no other claim may be paid out of the Fund for the same costs.

(Pub.L. 96–510, Title I, § 112, Dec. 11, 1980, 94 Stat. 2792; Pub.L. 99–499, Title I, §§ 109(a)(3), 112, Oct. 17, 1986, 100 Stat. 1633, 1646.)

### HISTORICAL AND STATUTORY NOTES

**Effective Dates**

1986 Acts

Amendment by Pub.L. 99–499 effective Oct. 17, 1986, see section 4 of Pub.L. 99–499, set out as a note under section 9601 of this title.

**Delegation of Functions**

Representation of any government agency pursuant to or under Ex. Ord. No. 12580 in any judicial proceeding to be by or through the Attorney General, with the conduct and control of all litigation arising under the provisions of this chapter to be the responsibility of the Attorney General, see section 6(a) of Ex. Ord. No. 12580, Jan. 23, 1987, 52 F.R. 2923, set out as a note under section 9615 of this title.

Authority under the provisions of this chapter to require the Attorney General to commence litigation retained by the President, notwithstanding any other provision of Ex. Ord. No. 12580, see section 6(b) of Ex. Ord. No. 12580, Jan. 23, 1987, 52 F.R. 2923, set out as a note under section 9615 of this title.

Functions vested in the President by this section delegated to the Administrator of the Environmental Protection Agency for all claims presented pursuant to section 9611 of this title, see section 9(e) of Ex. Ord. No. 12580, Jan. 23, 1987, 52 F.R. 2923, set out as a note under section 9615 of this title.

**Coordination of Titles I to IV of Pub.L. 99–499**

Any provision of Titles I to IV of Pub.L. 99–499, imposing any tax, premium, or fee; establishing any trust fund; or authorizing expenditures from any trust fund, shall have no force or effect. See section 531 of Pub.L. 99–499, set out as a note under section 1 of Title 26, Internal Revenue Code.

## § 9613. Civil proceedings

**[CERCLA § 113]**

**(a) Review of regulations in Circuit Court of Appeals of the United States for the District of Columbia**

Review of any regulation promulgated under this chapter may be had upon application by any interested person only in the Circuit Court of Appeals of the United States for the District of Columbia. Any such application shall be made within ninety days from the date of promulgation of such regulations. Any matter with respect to which review could have been obtained under this subsection shall not be subject to judicial review in any civil or criminal proceeding for enforcement or to obtain damages or recovery of response costs.

**(b) Jurisdiction; venue**

Except as provided in subsections (a) and (h) of this section, the United States district courts shall have exclusive original jurisdiction over all controversies arising under this chapter, without regard to the citizenship of the parties or the amount in controversy. Venue shall lie in any district in which the release or damages occurred, or in which the defendant resides, may be found, or has his principal office. For the purposes of this section, the Fund shall reside in the District of Columbia.

**(c) Controversies or other matters resulting from tax collection or tax regulation review**

The provisions of subsections (a) and (b) of this section shall not apply to any controversy or other matter resulting from the assessment of collection of any tax, as provided by subchapter II of this chapter, or to the review of any regulation promulgated under Title 26.

**(d) Litigation commenced prior to December 11, 1980**

No provision of this chapter shall be deemed or held to moot any litigation concerning any release of any hazardous substance, or any damages associated therewith, commenced prior to December 11, 1980.

**(e) Nationwide service of process**

In any action by the United States under this chapter, process may be served in any district where the defendant is found, resides, transacts business, or has appointed an agent for the service of process.

**(f) Contribution**

**(1) Contribution**

Any person may seek contribution from any other person who is liable or potentially liable under section 9607(a) of this title, during or following any civil action under section 9606 of this title or under section 9607(a) of this title. Such claims shall be brought in accordance with this section and the Federal Rules of Civil Procedure, and shall be governed by Federal law. In resolving contribution claims, the court may allocate response costs among liable parties using such equitable factors as the court determines are appropriate. Nothing in this subsection shall diminish the right of any person to bring an action for contribution in the absence of a civil action under section 9606 of this title or section 9607 of this title.

**(2) Settlement**

A person who has resolved its liability to the United States or a State in an administrative or judicially approved settlement shall not be liable for claims for contribution regarding matters addressed in the settlement. Such settlement does not discharge any of the other potentially liable persons unless its terms so provide, but it reduces the potential liability of the others by the amount of the settlement.

**(3) Persons not party to settlement**

**(A)** If the United States or a State has obtained less than complete relief from a person who has resolved its liability to the United States or the State in an administrative or judicially approved settlement, the United States or the State may bring an action against any person who has not so resolved its liability.

**(B)** A person who has resolved its liability to the United States or a State for some or all of a response action or for some or all of the costs of such action in an administrative or judicially approved settlement may seek contribution from any person who is not party to a settlement referred to in paragraph (2).

**(C)** In any action under this paragraph, the rights of any person who has resolved its liability to the United States or a State shall be subordinate to the rights of the United States or the State. Any contribution action brought under this paragraph shall be governed by Federal law.

**(g) Period in which action may be brought**

**(1) Actions for natural resource damages**

Except as provided in paragraphs (3) and (4), no action may be commenced for damages (as defined in section 9601(6) of this title) under this chapter, unless that action is commenced within 3 years after the later of the following:

**(A)** The date of the discovery of the loss and its connection with the release in question.

**(B)** The date on which regulations are promulgated under section 9651(c) of this title.

With respect to any facility listed on the National Priorities List (NPL), any Federal facility identified under section 9620 of this title (relating to Federal facilities), or any vessel or facility at which a remedial action under this chapter is otherwise scheduled, an action for damages under this chapter must be commenced within 3 years after the completion of the remedial action (excluding operation and maintenance activities) in lieu of the dates referred to in subparagraph (A) or (B). In no event may an action for damages under this chapter with respect to such a vessel or facility be commenced (i) prior to 60 days after the Federal or State natural resource trustee provides to the President and the potentially responsible party a notice of intent to file suit, or (ii) before selection of the remedial action if the President is diligently proceeding with a remedial investigation and feasibility study under section 9604(b) of this title or section 9620 of this title (relating to Federal facilities). The limitation in the preceding sentence on commencing an action before giving notice or before selection of the remedial action does not apply to actions filed on or before October 17, 1986.

**(2) Actions for recovery of costs**

An initial action for recovery of the costs referred to in section 9607 of this title must be commenced—

**(A)** for a removal action, within 3 years after completion of the removal action, except that such cost recovery action must be brought within 6 years after a determination to grant a waiver under section 9604(c)(1)(C) of this title for continued response action; and

**(B)** for a remedial action, within 6 years after initiation of physical on-site construction of the remedial action, except that, if the remedial action is initiated within 3 years after the completion of the removal action, costs incurred in the removal action may be recovered in the cost recovery action brought under this subparagraph.

In any such action described in this subsection, the court shall enter a declaratory judgment on liability for response costs or damages that will be binding on any subsequent action or actions to recover further response costs or damages. A subsequent action or actions under section 9607 of this title for further response costs at the vessel or facility may be maintained at any time during the response action, but must be commenced no later than 3 years after the date of completion of all response action. Except as otherwise provided in this paragraph, an action may be commenced under section 9607 of this title for recovery of costs at any time after such costs have been incurred.

**(3) Contribution**

No action for contribution for any response costs or damages may be commenced more than 3 years after—

(A) the date of judgment in any action under this chapter for recovery of such costs or damages, or

(B) the date of an administrative order under section 9622(g) of this title (relating to de minimis settlements) or 9622(h) of this title (relating to cost recovery settlements) or entry of a judicially approved settlement with respect to such costs or damages.

**(4) Subrogation**

No action based on rights subrogated pursuant to this section by reason of payment of a claim may be commenced under this subchapter more than 3 years after the date of payment of such claim.

**(5) Actions to recover indemnification payments**

Notwithstanding any other provision of this subsection, where a payment pursuant to an indemnification agreement with a response action contractor is made under section 9619 of this title, an action under section 9607 of this title for recovery of such indemnification payment from a potentially responsible party may be brought at any time before the expiration of 3 years from the date on which such payment is made.

**(6) Minors and incompetents**

The time limitations contained herein shall not begin to run—

(A) against a minor until the earlier of the date when such minor reaches 18 years of age or the date on which a legal representative is duly appointed for such minor, or

(B) against an incompetent person until the earlier of the date on which such incompetent's incompetency ends or the date on which a legal representative is duly appointed for such incompetent.

**(h) Timing of review**

No Federal court shall have jurisdiction under Federal law other than under section 1332 of Title 28 (relating to diversity of citizenship jurisdiction) or under State law which is applicable or relevant and appropriate under section 9621 of this title (relating to cleanup standards) to review any challenges to removal or remedial action selected under section 9604 of this title, or to review any order issued under section 9606(a) of this title, in any action except one of the following:

(1) An action under section 9607 of this title to recover response costs or damages or for contribution.

(2) An action to enforce an order issued under section 9606(a) of this title or to recover a penalty for violation of such order.

(3) An action for reimbursement under section 9606(b)(2) of this title.

(4) An action under section 9659 of this title (relating to citizens suits) alleging that the removal or remedial action taken under section 9604 of this title or secured under section 9606 of this title was in violation of any requirement of this chapter. Such an action may not be brought with regard to a removal where a remedial action is to be undertaken at the site.

(5) An action under section 9606 of this title in which the United States has moved to compel a remedial action.

**(i) Intervention**

In any action commenced under this chapter or under the Solid Waste Disposal Act [42 U.S.C.A. § 6901 et seq.] in a court of the United States, any person may intervene as a matter of right when such person claims an interest relating to the subject of the action and is so situated that the disposition of the action may, as a practical matter, impair or impede the person's ability to protect that interest, unless the President or the State shows that the person's interest is adequately represented by existing parties.

**(j) Judicial review**

**(1) Limitation**

In any judicial action under this chapter, judicial review of any issues concerning the adequacy of any response action taken or ordered by the President shall be limited to the administrative record. Otherwise applicable principles of administrative law shall govern whether any supplemental materials may be considered by the court.

**(2) Standard**

In considering objections raised in any judicial action under this chapter, the court shall uphold the President's decision in selecting the response action unless the objecting party can demonstrate, on the administrative record, that the decision was arbitrary and capricious or otherwise not in accordance with law.

**(3) Remedy**

If the court finds that the selection of the response action was arbitrary and capricious or otherwise not in accordance with law, the court shall award (A) only the response costs or damages that are not inconsistent with the national contingency plan, and (B) such other relief as is consistent with the National Contingency Plan.

**(4) Procedural errors**

In reviewing alleged procedural errors, the court may disallow costs or damages only if the errors were so serious and related to matters of such central relevance to the action that the action would have been significantly changed had such errors not been made.

**(k) Administrative record and participation procedures**

**(1) Administrative record**

The President shall establish an administrative record upon which the President shall base the selection of a response action. The administrative record shall be available to the public at or near the facility at issue. The President also may place duplicates of the administrative record at any other location.

**(2) Participation procedures**

**(A) Removal action**

The President shall promulgate regulations in accordance with chapter 5 of Title 5 establishing procedures for the appropriate participation of interested persons in the development of the administrative record on which the President will base the selection of removal actions and on which judicial review of removal actions will be based.

**(B) Remedial action**

The President shall provide for the participation of interested persons, including potentially responsible parties, in the development of the administrative record on which the President will base the selection of remedial actions and on which judicial review of remedial actions will be based. The procedures developed under this subparagraph shall include, at a minimum, each of the following:

(i) Notice to potentially affected persons and the public, which shall be accompanied by a brief analysis of the plan and alternative plans that were considered.

(ii) A reasonable opportunity to comment and provide information regarding the plan.

(iii) An opportunity for a public meeting in the affected area, in accordance with section 9617(a)(2) of this title (relating to public participation).

(iv) A response to each of the significant comments, criticisms, and new data submitted in written or oral presentations.

(v) A statement of the basis and purpose of the selected action.

For purposes of this subparagraph, the administrative record shall include all items developed and received under this subparagraph and all items described in the second sentence of section 9617(d) of this title. The President shall promulgate regulations in accordance with chapter 5 of Title 5 to carry out the requirements of this subparagraph.

**(C) Interim record**

Until such regulations under subparagraphs (A) and (B) are promulgated, the administrative record shall consist of all items developed and received pursuant to current procedures for selection of the response action, including procedures for the participation of interested parties and the public. The development of an administrative record and the selection of response action under this chapter shall not include an adjudicatory hearing.

**(D) Potentially responsible parties**

The President shall make reasonable efforts to identify and notify potentially responsible parties as early as possible before selection of a response action. Nothing in this paragraph shall be construed to be a defense to liability.

**(*l*) Notice of actions**

Whenever any action is brought under this chapter in a court of the United States by a plaintiff other than the United States, the plaintiff shall provide a copy of the complaint to the Attorney General of the United States and to the Administrator of the Environmental Protection Agency.

(Pub.L. 96–510, Title I, § 113, Dec. 11, 1980, 94 Stat. 2795; Pub.L. 99–499, Title I, § 113, Oct. 17, 1986, 100 Stat. 1647; Pub.L. 99–514, § 2, Oct. 22, 1986, 100 Stat. 2095.)

## HISTORICAL AND STATUTORY NOTES

**References in Text**

Subchapter II of this chapter, referred to in subsec. (c), was in the original, "Title II of this Act", meaning Title II of Pub.L. 96–510, Dec. 11, 1980, 94 Stat. 2796, known as the Hazardous Substance Response Revenue Act of 1980, which enacted subchapter II of this chapter and sections 4611, 4612, 4661, 4662, and former sections 4681 and 4682 of Title 26, Internal Revenue Code. Sections 221 to 223 and 232 of Pub.L. 96–510, which were classified to sections 9631 to 9633 and 9641 of this title, comprising subchapter II of this chapter, were repealed by Pub.L. 99–499, Title V, §§ 514(b), 517(c)(1), Oct. 17, 1986, 100 Stat. 1767, 1774. For complete classification of Title II to the Code, see Short Title of 1980

Amendments note set out under section 1 of Title 26 and Tables.

The Federal Rules of Civil Procedure, referred to in subsec. (f)(1), are set out in the Appendix to Title 28, Judiciary and Judicial Procedure.

The Solid Waste Disposal Act, referred to in subsec. (i), is Title II of Pub.L. 89–272, Oct. 20, 1965, 79 Stat. 997, as amended generally by Pub.L. 94–580, § 2, Oct. 21, 1976, 90 Stat. 2795, which is classified generally to chapter 82 (section 6901 et seq.) of this Title. For complete classification of this Act to the Code, see Short Title of 1965 Acts note set out under section 6901 of this title and Tables.

**Effective Dates**

1986 Acts

Amendment by Pub.L. 99–499 effective Oct. 17, 1986, see section 4 of Pub.L. 99–499, set out as a note under section 9601 of this title.

**Delegation of Functions**

Functions vested in the President by subsec. (k)(2) of this section, relating to the promulgation of regulations and guidelines, delegated to the Administrator of the Environmental Protection Agency, to be exercised in consultation with the National Response Team, see section 2(b) of Ex. Ord. No. 12580, Jan. 23, 1987, 52 F.R. 2923, set out as a note under section 9615 of this title.

Functions vested in the President by subsec. (k) of this section delegated, with authority to redelegate, (and subject to section 2(a), (b) and (c) of Ex. Ord. No. 12580) to the Secretaries of Defense and Energy, with respect to releases or threatened releases where either the release is on or the sole source of the release is from any facility or vessel under the jurisdiction, custody or control of their departments, respectively, including vessels bare-boat chartered and operated, with such functions to be exercised consistent with the requirements of section 9620 of this title, see sections 2(d), 11(g) of Ex. Ord. No. 12580, Jan. 23, 1987, 52 F.R. 2923, set out as a note under section 9615 of this title.

Functions vested in the President by subsec. (k) of this section, subject to section 2(b) to (d) of Ex. Ord. No. 12580, delegated, with authority to redelegate, to the heads of Executive departments and agencies, with respect to releases or threatened releases where either the release is on or the sole source of the release is from any facility or vessel under the jurisdiction, custody or control of those departments and agencies, including vessels bare-boat chartered and operated, see sections 2(e)(2), 11(g) of Ex. Ord. No. 12580, Jan. 23, 1987, 52 F.R. 2923, set out as a note under section 9615 of this title.

Functions vested in the President by subsec. (k) of this section, subject to section 2(a) to (e) of Ex. Ord. No. 12580, delegated, with authority to redelegate, to the Secretary of the Department in which the Coast Guard is operating ("the Coast Guard"), with respect to any release or threatened release involving the coastal zone, Great Lakes waters, ports, and harbors, see sections 2(f), 11(g) of Ex. Ord. No. 12580, Jan. 23, 1987, 52 F.R. 2923, set out as a note under section 9615 of this title.

Functions vested in the President by subsec. (k) of this section, subject to section 2(a) to (f) of Ex. Ord. No. 12580, delegated, with authority to redelegate, to the Administrator of the Environmental Protection Agency, see sections 2(g), 11(g) of Ex. Ord. No. 12580, Jan. 23, 1987, 52 F.R. 2923, set out as a note under section 9615 of this title.

Representation of any government agency pursuant to or under Ex. Ord. No. 12580 in any judicial proceeding to be by or through the Attorney General, with the conduct and control of all litigation arising under the provisions of this chapter to be the responsibility of the Attorney General, see section 6(a) of Ex. Ord. No. 12580, Jan. 23, 1987, 52 F.R. 2923, set out as a note under section 9615 of this title.

Functions vested in the President by subsec. (g) of this section, to receive notification of a natural resource trustee's intent to file suit, delegated to the heads of Executive departments and agencies with respect to response actions for which they have been delegated authority under section 2 of Ex. Ord. No. 12580, with the Administrator of the Environmental Protection Agency to promulgate procedural regulations for providing such notification, see section 6(c) of Ex. Ord. No. 12580, Jan. 23, 1987, 52 F.R. 2923, set out as a note under section 9615 of this title.

## § 9614. Relationship to other law

**[CERCLA § 114]**

### (a) Additional State liability or requirements with respect to release of substances within State

Nothing in this chapter shall be construed or interpreted as preempting any State from imposing any additional liability or requirements with respect to the release of hazardous substances within such State.

### (b) Recovery under other State or Federal law of compensation for removal costs or damages, or payment of claims

Any person who receives compensation for removal costs or damages or claims pursuant to this chapter shall be precluded from recovering compensation for the same removal costs or damages or claims pursuant to any other State or Federal law. Any person who receives compensation for removal costs or damages or claims pursuant to any other Federal or State law shall be precluded from receiving compensation for the same removal costs or damages or claims as provided in this chapter.

### (c) Recycled oil

**(1) Service station dealers, etc.**

No person (including the United States or any State) may recover, under the authority of subsection (a)(3) or (a)(4) of section 9607 of this title, from a service station dealer for any response costs or damages resulting from a release or threatened release of recycled oil, or use the authority of section 9606 of this title against a service station dealer other than a person described in subsection (a)(1) or (a)(2) of section 9607 of this title, if such recycled oil—

(A) is not mixed with any other hazardous substance, and

(B) is stored, treated, transported, or otherwise managed in compliance with regulations or standards promulgated pursuant to section 3014 of the Solid Waste Disposal Act [42 U.S.C.A. § 6935] and other applicable authorities.

Nothing in this paragraph shall affect or modify in any way the obligations or liability of any person under any other provision of State or Federal law, including common law, for damages, injury, or loss resulting from a release or threatened release of any hazardous substance or for removal or remedial action or the costs of removal or remedial action.

**(2) Presumption**

Solely for the purposes of this subsection, a service station dealer may presume that a small quantity of used oil is not mixed with other hazardous substances if it—

(A) has been removed from the engine of a light duty motor vehicle or household appliances by the owner of such vehicle or appliances, and

(B) is presented, by such owner, to the dealer for collection, accumulation, and delivery to an oil recycling facility.

**(3) Definition**

For purposes of this subsection, the terms "used oil" and "recycled oil" have the same meanings as set forth in sections 1004(36) and 1004(37) of the Solid Waste Disposal Act [42 U.S.C.A. § 6903(36), (37)] and regulations promulgated pursuant to that Act [42 U.S.C.A. § 6901 et seq.].

**(4) Effective date**

The effective date of paragraphs (1) and (2) of this subsection shall be the effective date of regulations or standards promulgated under section 3014 of the Solid Waste Disposal Act [42 U.S.C.A. § 6935] that include, among other provisions, a requirement to conduct corrective action to respond to any releases of recycled oil under subtitle C or subtitle I of such Act [42 U.S.C.A. § 6921 et seq. or § 6991 et seq.].

**(d) Financial responsibility of owner or operator of vessel or facility under State or local law, rule, or regulation**

Except as provided in this subchapter, no owner or operator of a vessel or facility who establishes and maintains evidence of financial responsibility in accordance with this subchapter shall be required under any State or local law, rule, or regulation to establish or maintain any other evidence of financial responsibility in connection with liability for the release of a hazardous substance from such vessel or facility. Evidence of compliance with the financial responsibility requirements of this subchapter shall be accepted by a State in lieu of any other requirement of financial responsibility imposed by such State in connection with liability for the release of a hazardous substance from such vessel or facility.

(Pub.L. 96–510, Title I, § 114, Dec. 11, 1980, 94 Stat. 2795; Pub.L. 99–499, Title I, § 114(a), Oct. 17, 1986, 100 Stat. 1652.)

### HISTORICAL AND STATUTORY NOTES

**References in Text**

The Solid Waste Disposal Act and that Act, referred to in subsec. (c)(3), (4), is Title II of Pub.L. 89–272, Oct. 20, 1965, 79 Stat. 997, as amended generally by Pub.L. 94–580, § 2, Oct. 21, 1976, 90 Stat. 2795, which is classified generally to chapter 82 (section 6901 et seq.) of this Title. Subtitle C of the Solid Waste Disposal Act is classified generally to subchapter III (section 6921 et seq.) of chapter 82 of this title. Subtitle I of that Act is classified generally to subchapter IX (section 6991 et seq.) of that chapter. For complete classification of this Act to the Code, see Short Title of 1965 Acts note set out under section 6901 of this title and Tables.

**Effective Dates**

1986 Acts

Amendment by Pub.L. 99–499 effective Oct. 17, 1986, see section 4 of Pub.L. 99–499, set out as a note under section 9601 of this title.

## § 9615. Presidential delegation and assignment of duties or powers and promulgation of regulations

**[CERCLA § 115]**

The President is authorized to delegate and assign any duties or powers imposed upon or assigned to him and to promulgate any regulations necessary to carry out the provisions of this subchapter.

(Pub.L. 96–510, Title I, § 115, Dec. 11, 1980, 94 Stat. 2796.)

## § 9616. Schedules

**[CERCLA § 116]**

**(a) Assessment and listing of facilities**

It shall be a goal of this chapter that, to the maximum extent practicable—

(1) not later than January 1, 1988, the President shall complete preliminary assessments of all facilities that are contained (as of October 17, 1986) on the Comprehensive Environmental Response, Compensation, and Liability Information System (CERCLIS) including in each assessment a statement as to whether a site inspection is necessary and by whom it should be carried out; and

(2) not later than January 1, 1989, the President shall assure the completion of site inspections at all facilities for which the President has stated a site inspection is necessary pursuant to paragraph (1).

**(b) Evaluation**

Within 4 years after October 17, 1986, each facility listed (as of October 17, 1986) in the CERCLIS shall be evaluated if the President determines that such evaluation is warranted on the basis of a site inspection or preliminary assessment. The evaluation shall be in accordance with the criteria established in section 9605 of this title under the National Contingency Plan for determining priorities among release for inclusion on the National Priorities List. In the case of a facility listed in the CERCLIS after October 17, 1986, the facility shall be evaluated within 4 years after the date of such listing if the President determines that such evaluation is warranted on the basis of a site inspection or preliminary assessment.

**(c) Explanations**

If any of the goals established by subsection (a) or (b) of this section are not achieved, the President shall publish an explanation of why such action could not be completed by the specified date.

**(d) Commencement of RI/FS**

The President shall assure that remedial investigations and feasibility studies (RI/FS) are commenced for facilities listed on the National Priorities List, in addition to those commenced prior to October 17, 1986, in accordance with the following schedule:

(1) not fewer than 275 by the date 36 months after October 17, 1986, and

(2) if the requirement of paragraph (1) is not met, not fewer than an additional 175 by the date 4 years after October 17, 1986, an additional 200 by the date 5 years after October 17, 1986, and a total of 650 by the date 5 years after October 17, 1986.

**(e) Commencement of remedial action**

The President shall assure that substantial and continuous physical on-site remedial action commences at facilities on the National Priorities List, in addition to those facilities on which remedial action has commenced prior to October 17, 1986, at a rate not fewer than:

(1) 175 facilities during the first 36-month period after October 17, 1986; and

(2) 200 additional facilities during the following 24 months after such 36-month period.

(Pub.L. 96–510, Title I, § 116, as added Pub.L. 99–499, Title I, § 116, Oct. 17, 1986, 100 Stat. 1653.)

### HISTORICAL AND STATUTORY NOTES

**Effective Dates**

1986 Acts

Section effective Oct. 17, 1986, see section 4 of Pub.L. 99–499, set out as a note under section 9601 of this title.

**Delegation of Functions**

Functions vested in the President by this section delegated, with authority to redelegate, to the Administrator of the Environmental Protection Agency, except that functions vested in the President by subsec. (a) of this section delegated, with authority to redelegate, to the heads of Executive departments and agencies with respect to facilities under the jurisdiction, custody or control of those departments and agencies, see sections 3, 11(g) of Ex. Ord. No. 12580, Jan. 23, 1987, 52 F.R. 2923, set out as a note under section 9615 of this title.

## § 9617. Public participation

**[CERCLA § 117]**

**(a) Proposed plan**

Before adoption of any plan for remedial action to be undertaken by the President, by a State, or by any other person, under section 9604, 9606, 9620, or 9622 of this title, the President or State, as appropriate, shall take both of the following actions:

(1) Publish a notice and brief analysis of the proposed plan and make such plan available to the public.

(2) Provide a reasonable opportunity for submission of written and oral comments and an opportunity for a public meeting at or near the facility at issue regarding the proposed plan and regarding any proposed findings under section 9621(d)(4) of this title (relating to cleanup standards). The President or the State shall keep a transcript of the meeting and make such transcript available to the public.

The notice and analysis published under paragraph (1) shall include sufficient information as may be necessary to provide a reasonable explanation of the proposed plan and alternative proposals considered.

**(b) Final plan**

Notice of the final remedial action plan adopted shall be published and the plan shall be made available to the public before commencement of any remedial action. Such final plan shall be accompanied by a discussion of any significant changes (and the reasons for such changes) in the proposed plan and a response to each of the significant comments, criticisms, and new data submitted in written or oral presentations under subsection (a) of this section.

**(c) Explanation of differences**

After adoption of a final remedial action plan—

(1) if any remedial action is taken,

(2) if any enforcement action under section 9606 of this title is taken, or

(3) if any settlement or consent decree under section 9606 of this title or section 9622 of this title is entered into,

and if such action, settlement, or decree differs in any significant respects from the final plan, the President or the State shall publish an explanation of the significant differences and the reasons such changes were made.

**(d) Publication**

For the purposes of this section, publication shall include, at a minimum, publication in a major local newspaper of general circulation. In addition, each item developed, received, published, or made available to the public under this section shall be available for public inspection and copying at or near the facility at issue.

**(e) Grants for technical assistance**

**(1) Authority**

Subject to such amounts as are provided in appropriations Acts and in accordance with rules promulgated by the President, the President may make grants available to any group of individuals which may be affected by a release or threatened release at any facility which is listed on the National Priorities List under the National Contingency Plan. Such grants may be used to obtain technical assistance in interpreting information with regard to the nature of the hazard, remedial investigation and feasibility study, record of decision, remedial design, selection and construction of remedial action, operation and maintenance, or removal action at such facility.

**(2) Amount**

The amount of any grant under this subsection may not exceed $50,000 for a single grant recipient. The President may waive the $50,000 limitation in any case where such waiver is necessary to carry out the purposes of this subsection. Each grant recipient shall be required, as a condition of the grant, to contribute at least 20 percent of the total of costs of the technical assistance for which such grant is made. The President may waive the 20 percent contribution requirement if the grant recipient demonstrates financial need and such waiver is necessary to facilitate public participation in the selection of remedial action at the facility. Not more than one grant may be made under this subsection with respect to a single facility, but the grant may be renewed to facilitate public participation at all stages of remedial action.

(Pub.L. 96–510, Title I, § 117, as added Pub.L. 99–499, Title I, § 117, Oct. 17, 1986, 100 Stat. 1654.)

### HISTORICAL AND STATUTORY NOTES

**Effective Dates**

1986 Acts

Section effective Oct. 17, 1986, see section 4 of Pub.L. 99–499, set out as a note under section 9601 of this title.

**Delegation of Functions**

Functions vested in the President by subsecs. (a) and (c) of this section delegated, with authority to redelegate, to the Director of the Federal Emergency Management Agency, to the extent such authority is needed to carry out certain other functions delegated to the Director by section 2(c)(1) of Ex. Ord. No. 12580, and subject to certain rulemaking authority of the Administrator of the Environmental Protection Agency, see sections 2(b), (c)(2), 11(g) of Ex. Ord. No. 12580, Jan. 23, 1987, 52 F.R. 2923, set out as a note under section 9615 of this title.

Functions vested in the President by subsecs. (a) and (c) of this section delegated, with authority to redelegate, (and subject to section 2(a), (b) and (c) of Ex. Ord. No. 12580) to the Secretaries of Defense and Energy, with respect to releases or threatened releases where either the release is on or the sole source of the release is from any facility or vessel under the jurisdiction, custody or control of their departments, respectively, including vessels bare-boat chartered and operated, with such functions to be exercised consistent with the requirements of section 9620 of this title, see sections 2(d), 11(g) of Ex. Ord. No. 12580, Jan. 23, 1987, 52 F.R. 2923, set out as a note under section 9615 of this title.

Functions vested in the President by subsecs. (a) and (c) of this section, subject to section 2(b) to (d) of Ex. Ord. No. 12580, delegated, with authority to redelegate, to the heads of Executive departments and agencies, with respect to releases or threatened releases where either the release is on or the sole source of the release is from any facility or vessel under the jurisdiction, custody or control of those departments and agencies, including vessels bare-boat chartered and operated, see sections 2(e)(2), 11(g) of Ex. Ord. No. 12580, Jan. 23, 1987, 52 F.R. 2923, set out as a note under section 9615 of this title.

Functions vested in the President by subsecs. (a) and (c) of this section, subject to section 2(a) to (e) of Ex. Ord. No. 12580, delegated, with authority to redelegate, to the Secretary of the Department in which the Coast Guard is operating ("the Coast Guard"), with respect to any release or threatened release involving the coastal zone, Great Lakes waters, ports, and harbors, see sections 2(f), 11(g) of Ex. Ord. No. 12580, Jan. 23, 1987, 52 F.R. 2923, set out as a note under section 9615 of this title.

Functions vested in the President by subsecs. (a) and (c) of this section, subject to section 2(a) to (f) of Ex. Ord. No. 12580, delegated, with authority to redelegate, to the Administrator of the Environmental Protection Agency, see sections 2(g), 11(g) of Ex. Ord. No. 12580, Jan. 23, 1987, 52 F.R. 2923, set out as a note under section 9615 of this title.

Functions vested in the President by subsec. (e) of this section delegated to the Administrator of Environmental Protection Agency, to be exercised in consultation with the Attorney General, see section 9(g) of Ex. Ord. No. 12580, Jan. 23, 1987, 52 F.R. 2923, set out as a note under section 9615 of this title.

## § 9618. High priority for drinking water supplies

**[CERCLA § 118]**

For purposes of taking action under section 9604 or 9606 of this title and listing facilities on the National

Priorities List, the President shall give a high priority to facilities where the release of hazardous substances or pollutants or contaminants has resulted in the closing of drinking water wells or has contaminated a principal drinking water supply.

(Pub.L. 96–510, Title I, § 118, as added Pub.L. 99–499, Title I, § 118(a), Oct. 17, 1986, 100 Stat. 1655.)

### HISTORICAL AND STATUTORY NOTES

**Effective Dates**

1986 Acts

Section effective Oct. 17, 1986, see section 4 of Pub.L. 99–499, set out as a note under section 9601 of this title.

## § 9619. Response action contractors

[CERCLA § 119]

**(a) Liability of response action contractors**

**(1) Response action contractors**

A person who is a response action contractor with respect to any release or threatened release of a hazardous substance or pollutant or contaminant from a vessel or facility shall not be liable under this subchapter or under any other Federal law to any person for injuries, costs, damages, expenses, or other liability (including but not limited to claims for indemnification or contribution and claims by third parties for death, personal injury, illness or loss of or damage to property or economic loss) which results from such release or threatened release.

**(2) Negligence, etc.**

Paragraph (1) shall not apply in the case of a release that is caused by conduct of the response action contractor which is negligent, grossly negligent, or which constitutes intentional misconduct.

**(3) Effect on warranties; employer liability**

Nothing in this subsection shall affect the liability of any person under any warranty under Federal, State, or common law. Nothing in this subsection shall affect the liability of an employer who is a response action contractor to any employee of such employer under any provision of law, including any provision of any law relating to worker's compensation.

**(4) Governmental employees**

A state employee or an employee of a political subdivision who provides services relating to response action while acting within the scope of his authority as a governmental employee shall have the same exemption from liability (subject to the other provisions of this section) as is provided to the response action contractor under this section.

**(b) Savings provisions**

**(1) Liability of other persons**

The defense provided by section 9607(b)(3) of this title shall not be available to any potentially responsible party with respect to any costs or damages caused by any act or omission of a response action contractor. Except as provided in subsection (a)(4) of this section and the preceding sentence, nothing in this section shall affect the liability under this chapter or under any other Federal or State law of any person, other than a response action contractor.

**(2) Burden of plaintiff**

Nothing in this section shall affect the plaintiff's burden of establishing liability under this subchapter.

**(c) Indemnification**

**(1) In general**

The President may agree to hold harmless and indemnify any response action contractor meeting the requirements of this subsection against any liability (including the expenses of litigation or settlement) for negligence arising out of the contractor's performance in carrying out response action activities under this subchapter, unless such liability was caused by conduct of the contractor which was grossly negligent or which constituted intentional misconduct.

**(2) Applicability**

This subsection shall apply only with respect to a response action carried out under written agreement with—

(A) the President;

(B) any Federal agency;

(C) a State or political subdivision which has entered into a contract or cooperative agreement in accordance with section 9604(d)(1) of this title; or

(D) any potentially responsible party carrying out any agreement under section 9622 of this title (relating to settlements) or section 9606 of this title (relating to abatement).

**(3) Source of funding**

This subsection shall not be subject to section 1301 or 1341 of Title 31 or section 11 of Title 41 or to section 9662 of this title. For purposes of section 9611 of this title, amounts expended pursuant to this subsection for indemnification of any response action contractor (except with respect to federally owned or operated facilities) shall be considered governmental response costs incurred pursuant to section 9604 of this title. If sufficient funds are unavailable in the Hazardous Substance Superfund established under subchapter A of chapter 98 of Title 26 to make payments pursuant to such indemnification or if the Fund is repealed, there are authorized to be appropriated such amounts as may be necessary to make such payments.

**(4) Requirements**

An indemnification agreement may be provided under this subsection only if the President determines that each of the following requirements are met:

**(A)** The liability covered by the indemnification agreement exceeds or is not covered by insurance available, at a fair and reasonable price, to the contractor at the time the contractor enters into the contract to provide response action, and adequate insurance to cover such liability is not generally available at the time the response action contract is entered into.

**(B)** The response action contractor has made diligent efforts to obtain insurance coverage from non-Federal sources to cover such liability.

**(C)** In the case of a response action contract covering more than one facility, the response action contractor agrees to continue to make such diligent efforts each time the contractor begins work under the contract at a new facility.

**(5) Limitations**

**(A) Liability covered**

Indemnification under this subsection shall apply only to response action contractor liability which results from a release of any hazardous substance or pollutant or contaminant if such release arises out of response action activities.

**(B) Deductibles and limits**

An indemnification agreement under this subsection shall include deductibles and shall place limits on the amount of indemnification to be made available.

**(C) Contracts with potentially responsible parties**

**(i) Decision to indemnify**

In deciding whether to enter into an indemnification agreement with a response action contractor carrying out a written contract or agreement with any potentially responsible party, the President shall determine an amount which the potentially responsible party is able to indemnify the contractor. The President may enter into such an indemnification agreement only if the President determines that such amount of indemnification is inadequate to cover any reasonable potential liability of the contractor arising out of the contractor's negligence in performing the contract or agreement with such party. The President shall make the determinations in the preceding sentences (with respect to the amount and the adequacy of the amount) taking into account the total net assets and resources of potentially responsible parties with respect to the facility at the time of such determinations.

**(ii) Conditions**

The President may pay a claim under an indemnification agreement referred to in clause (i) for the amount determined under clause (i) only if the contractor has exhausted all administrative, judicial, and common law claims for indemnification against all potentially responsible parties participating in the clean-up of the facility with respect to the liability of the contractor arising out of the contractor's negligence in performing the contract or agreement with such party. Such indemnification agreement shall require such contractor to pay any deductible established under subparagraph (B) before the contractor may recover any amount from the potentially responsible party or under the indemnification agreement.

**(D) RCRA facilities**

No owner or operator of a facility regulated under the Solid Waste Disposal Act [42 U.S.C.A. § 6901 et seq.] may be indemnified under this subsection with respect to such facility.

**(E) Persons retained or hired**

A person retained or hired by a person described in subsection (e)(2)(B) of this section shall be eligible for indemnification under this subsection only if the President specifically approves of the retaining or hiring of such person.

**(6) Cost recovery**

For purposes of section 9607 of this title, amounts expended pursuant to this subsection for indemnification of any person who is a response action contractor with respect to any release or threatened release shall be considered a cost of response incurred by the United States Government with respect to such release.

**(7) Regulations**

The President shall promulgate regulations for carrying out the provisions of this subsection. Before promulgation of the regulations, the President shall develop guidelines to carry out this section. Development of such guidelines shall include reasonable opportunity for public comment.

**(8) Study**

The Comptroller General shall conduct a study in the fiscal year ending September 30, 1989, on the application of this subsection, including whether indemnification agreements under this subsection are being used, the number of claims that have been filed under such agreements, and the need for this subsection. The Comptroller General shall report the findings of the study to Congress no later than September 30, 1989.

**(d) Exception**

The exemption provided under subsection (a) of this section and the authority of the President to offer indemnification under subsection (c) of this section shall not apply to any person covered by the provisions of paragraph (1), (2), (3), or (4) of section 9607(a) of this title with respect to the release or threatened release concerned if such person would be covered by such provisions even if such person had not carried out any actions referred to in subsection (e) of this section.

**(e) Definitions**

For purposes of this section—

**(1) Response action contract**

The term "response action contract" means any written contract or agreement entered into by a response action contractor (as defined in paragraph (2)(A) of this subsection) with—

(A) the President;

(B) any Federal agency;

(C) a State or political subdivision which has entered into a contract or cooperative agreement in accordance with section 9604(d)(1) of this title; or

(D) any potentially responsible party carrying out an agreement under section 9606 or 9622 of this title;

to provide any remedial action under this chapter at a facility listed on the National Priorities List, or any removal under this chapter, with respect to any release or threatened release of a hazardous substance or pollutant or contaminant from the facility or to provide any evaluation, planning, engineering, surveying and mapping, design, construction, equipment, or any ancillary services thereto for such facility.

**(2) Response action contractor**

The term "response action contractor" means—

(A) any—

(i) person who enters into a response action contract with respect to any release or threatened release of a hazardous substance or pollutant or contaminant from a facility and is carrying out such contract; and [1]

(ii) person, public or nonprofit private entity, conducting a field demonstration pursuant to section 9660(b) of this title; and

(iii) Recipients [2] of grants (including subgrantees) under section 9660a of this title for the training and education of workers who are or may be engaged in activities related to hazardous waste removal, containment, or emergency response under this chapter; and

(B) any person who is retained or hired by a person described in subparagraph (A) to provide any services relating to a response action; and

(C) any surety who after October 16, 1990, provides a bid, performance or payment bond to a response action contractor, and begins activities to meet its obligations under such bond, but only in connection with such activities or obligations.

**(3) Insurance**

The term "insurance" means liability insurance which is fair and reasonably priced, as determined by the President, and which is made available at the time the contractor enters into the response action contract to provide response action.

**(f) Competition**

Response action contractors and subcontractors for program management, construction management, architectural and engineering, surveying and mapping, and related services shall be selected in accordance with title IX of the Federal Property and Administrative Services Act of 1949 [40 U.S.C.A. § 541 et seq.]. The Federal selection procedures shall apply to appropriate contracts negotiated by all Federal governmental agencies involved in carrying out this chapter. Such procedures shall be followed by response action contractors and subcontractors.

**(g) Surety bonds**

(1) If under sections 3131 to 3133 of Title 40, surety bonds are required for any direct Federal procurement of any response action contract and are not waived pursuant to sections 3134 of Title 40, they shall be issued in accordance with such Act of August 24, 1935.

(2) If under applicable Federal law surety bonds are required for any direct Federal procurement of any response action contract, no right of action shall accrue on the performance bond issued on such response action contract to or for the use of any person other than the obligee named in the bond.

(3) If under applicable Federal law surety bonds are required for any direct Federal procurement of any response action contract, unless otherwise provided for by the procuring agency in the bond, in the event of a default, the surety's liability on a performance bond shall be only for the cost of completion of the contract work in accordance with the plans and

specifications less the balance of funds remaining to be paid under the contract, up to the penal sum of the bond. The surety shall in no event be liable on bonds to indemnify or compensate the obligee for loss or liability arising from personal injury or property damage whether or not caused by a breach of the bonded contract.

(4) Nothing in this subsection shall be construed as preempting, limiting, superseding, affecting, applying to, or modifying any State laws, regulations, requirements, rules, practices or procedures. Nothing in this subsection shall be construed as affecting, applying to, modifying, limiting, superseding, or preempting any rights, authorities, liabilities, demands, actions, causes of action, losses, judgments, claims, statutes of limitation, or obligations under Federal or State law, which do not arise on or under the bond.

(5) This subsection shall not apply to bonds executed before October 17, 1990.

(Pub.L. 96–510, Title I, § 119, as added Pub.L. 99–499, Title I, § 119, Oct. 17, 1986, 100 Stat. 1662, and amended Pub.L. 99–514, § 2, Oct. 22, 1986, 100 Stat. 2095; Pub.L. 100–202, § 101(f) [Title II, § 201], Dec. 22, 1987, 101 Stat. 1329–187, 1329–198; Pub.L. 101–584, § 1, Nov. 15, 1990, 104 Stat. 2872; Pub.L. 102–484, Div. A, Title III, § 331(a), Oct. 23, 1992, 106 Stat. 2373; Pub.L. 105–276, Title III, Oct. 21, 1998, 112 Stat. 2497.)

1 So in original. The word "and" probably should not appear.

2 So in original. Probably should not be capitalized.

## HISTORICAL AND STATUTORY NOTES

### References in Text

The Solid Waste Disposal Act, referred to in subsec. (c)(5)(D), is Title II of Pub.L. 89–272, Oct. 20, 1965, 79 Stat. 997, as amended generally by Pub.L. 94–580, § 2, Oct. 21, 1976, 90 Stat. 2795, which is classified generally to chapter 82 (section 6901 et seq.) of this title. For complete classification of this Act to the Code, see Short Title of 1965 Acts note set out under section 6901 of this title and Tables.

Section 9660a of this title, referred to in subsec. (e)(2)(A)(iii), was in the original "section 126", probably meaning section 126 of Pub.L. 99–499, Title I, Oct. 17, 1986, 100 Stat. 1690. Subsecs. (a) to (f) of section 126, which relate to worker protection standards, are set out as a note under section 655 of Title 29, Labor. Subsec. (g) of section 126, which relates to grants for training and education of workers who are or may be engaged in activities related to hazardous waste removal, etc., is classified to section 9660a of this title.

The Federal Property and Administrative Services Act of 1949, referred to in subsec. (f), is Act June 30, 1949, c. 288, 63 Stat. 377, as amended. Title IX of the Federal Property and Administrative Services Act of 1949 is classified generally to subchapter VI (section 541 et seq.) of chapter 10 of Title 40, Public Buildings, Property, and Works. For complete classification of this Act to the Code, see Short Title note set out under section 471 of Title 40 and Tables.

Act of April 29, 1941, referred to in subsec. (g)(1), is Act Apr. 29, 1941, c. 81, § 1, 55 Stat. 147 and § 2 as added Oct. 21, 1970, Pub.L. 91–469, § 39, 84 Stat. 1036, which enacted section 270e and 270f of Title 40, Public Buildings, Property, and Works. For complete classification of this Act to the Code, see Tables.

### Codifications

In subsec. (g)(1), "sections 3131 to 3133 of Title 40" substituted for "the Act of August 24, 1935 (40 U.S.C. 270a—270d), commonly referred to as the 'Miller Act' " on authority of Pub.L. 107–217, § 5(c), Aug. 21, 2002, 116 Stat. 1301, which is set out as a note preceding 40 U.S.C.A. § 101. Pub.L. 107–217, § 1, enacted Title 40 into positive law. The Miller Act is Aug. 24, 1935, c. 642, 49 Stat. 793, which was classified to former 40 U.S.C.A. §§ 270, 270a, 270b to 270d, 270d–1 prior to being repealed by Pub.L. 107–217, § 6(b), Aug. 21, 2002, 116 Stat. 1309, and its substance reenacted as 40 U.S.C.A. §§ 3131 to 3133.

In subsec. (g)(1), "sections 3134 of Title 40" substituted for "the Act of April 29, 1941 (40 U.S.C. 270e—270f)", on authority of Pub.L. 107–217, § 5(c), Aug. 21, 2002, 116 Stat. 1301, which is set out as a note preceding 40 U.S.C.A. § 101. Pub.L. 107–217, § 1, enacted Title 40 into positive law. Act Apr. 29, 1941, c. 81, 55 Stat. 147, as amended, was classified to former 40 U.S.C.A. §§ 270e and 270f prior to being repealed by Pub.L. 107–217, § 6(b), Aug. 21, 2002, 116 Stat. 1311, and its substance reenacted as 40 U.S.C.A. § 3134.

### Effective Dates

1986 Acts

Section effective Oct. 17, 1986, see section 4 of Pub.L. 99–499, set out as a note under section 9601 of this title.

### Delegation of Functions

Functions vested in the President by subsec. (c)(7) of this section, relating to the promulgation of regulations and guidelines, delegated to the Administrator of the Environmental Protection Agency, to be exercised in consultation with the National Response Team, see section 2(b) of Ex. Ord. No. 12580, Jan. 23, 1987, 52 F.R. 2923, set out as a note under section 9615 of this title.

Functions vested in the President by this section delegated, with authority to redelegate, to the Director of the Federal Emergency Management Agency, to the extent such authority is needed to carry out certain other functions delegated to the Director by section 2(c)(1) of Ex. Ord. No. 12580, and subject to certain rulemaking authority of the Administrator of the Environmental Protection Agency, see sections 2(b), (c)(2), 11(g) of Ex. Ord. No. 12580, Jan. 23, 1987, 52 F.R. 2923, set out as a note under section 9615 of this title.

Functions vested in the President by this section delegated, with authority to redelegate, (and subject to section 2(a), (b) and (c) of Ex. Ord. No. 12580) to the Secretaries of Defense and Energy, with respect to releases or threatened releases where either the release is on or the sole source of the release is from any facility or vessel under the jurisdiction, custody or control of their departments, respectively, including vessels bare-boat chartered and operated, with such functions to be exercised consistent with the requirements of section 9620 of this title, see sections 2(d), 11(g) of Ex. Ord. No. 12580, Jan. 23, 1987, 52 F.R. 2923, set out as a note under section 9615 of this title.

Functions vested in the President by this section, subject to section 2(b) to (d) of Ex. Ord. No. 12580, delegated, with authority to redelegate, to the heads of Executive departments and agencies, with respect to releases or threatened releases where either the release is on or the sole source of the release is from any facility or vessel under the jurisdiction, custody or control of those departments and agencies, including vessels bare-boat chartered and operated, see sections 2(e)(2), 11(g) of Ex. Ord. No. 12580, Jan. 23, 1987, 52 F.R. 2923, set out as a note under section 9615 of this title.

Functions vested in the President by this section, subject to section 2(a) to (e) of Ex. Ord. No. 12580, delegated, with authority to redelegate, to the Secretary of the Department in which the Coast Guard is operating ("the Coast Guard"), with respect to any release or threatened release involving the coastal zone, Great Lakes waters, ports, and harbors, see sections 2(f), 11(g) of Ex. Ord. No. 12580, Jan. 23, 1987, 52 F.R. 2923, set out as a note under section 9615 of this title.

Functions vested in the President by this section, subject to section 2(a) to (f) of Ex. Ord. No. 12580, delegated, with authority to redelegate, to the Administrator of the Environmental Protection Agency, retroactive to the date of enactment of Pub.L. 99–499, which was approved Oct. 17, 1986, see sections 2(g), 11(g) of Ex. Ord. No. 12580, Jan. 23, 1987, 52 F.R. 2923, set out as a note under section 9615 of this title.

**Coordination of Titles I to IV of Pub.L. 99–499**

Any provision of Titles I to IV of Pub.L. 99–499, imposing any tax, premium, or fee; establishing any trust fund; or authorizing expenditures from any trust fund, to have no force or effect, see section 531 of Pub.L. 99–499, set out as a note under section 1 of Title 26, Internal Revenue Code.

## § 9620. Federal facilities

**[CERCLA § 120]**

### (a) Application of chapter to Federal Government

#### (1) In general

Each department, agency, and instrumentality of the United States (including the executive, legislative, and judicial branches of government) shall be subject to, and comply with, this chapter in the same manner and to the same extent, both procedurally and substantively, as any nongovernmental entity, including liability under section 9607 of this title. Nothing in this section shall be construed to affect the liability of any person or entity under sections 9606 and 9607 of this title.

#### (2) Application of requirements to Federal facilities

All guidelines, rules, regulations, and criteria which are applicable to preliminary assessments carried out under this chapter for facilities at which hazardous substances are located, applicable to evaluations of such facilities under the National Contingency Plan, applicable to inclusion on the National Priorities List, or applicable to remedial actions at such facilities shall also be applicable to facilities which are owned or operated by a department, agency, or instrumentality of the United States in the same manner and to the extent as such guidelines, rules, regulations, and criteria are applicable to other facilities. No department, agency, or instrumentality of the United States may adopt or utilize any such guidelines, rules, regulations, or criteria which are inconsistent with the guidelines, rules, regulations, and criteria established by the Administrator under this chapter.

#### (3) Exceptions

This subsection shall not apply to the extent otherwise provided in this section with respect to applicable time periods. This subsection shall also not apply to any requirements relating to bonding, insurance, or financial responsibility. Nothing in this chapter shall be construed to require a State to comply with section 9604(c)(3) of this title in the case of a facility which is owned or operated by any department, agency, or instrumentality of the United States.

#### (4) State laws

State laws concerning removal and remedial action, including State laws regarding enforcement, shall apply to removal and remedial action at facilities owned or operated by a department, agency, or instrumentality of the United States or facilities that are the subject of a deferral under subsection (h)(3)(C) of this section when such facilities are not included on the National Priorities List. The preceding sentence shall not apply to the extent a State law would apply any standard or requirement to such facilities which is more stringent than the standards and requirements applicable to facilities which are not owned or operated by any such department, agency, or instrumentality.

### (b) Notice

Each department, agency, and instrumentality of the United States shall add to the inventory of Federal agency hazardous waste facilities required to be submitted under section 3016 of the Solid Waste Disposal Act [42 U.S.C.A. § 6937] (in addition to the information required under section 3016(a)(3) of such Act [42 U.S.C.A. § 6937(a)(3) ]) information on contamination from each facility owned or operated by the department, agency, or instrumentality if such contamination affects contiguous or adjacent property owned by the department, agency, or instrumentality or by any other person, including a description of the monitoring data obtained.

### (c) Federal Agency Hazardous Waste Compliance Docket

The Administrator shall establish a special Federal Agency Hazardous Waste Compliance Docket (hereinafter in this section referred to as the "docket") which shall contain each of the following:

(1) All information submitted under section 3016 of the Solid Waste Disposal Act [42 U.S.C.A.

§ 6937] and subsection (b) of this section regarding any Federal facility and notice of each subsequent action taken under this chapter with respect to the facility.

(2) Information submitted by each department, agency, or instrumentality of the United States under section 3005 or 3010 of such Act [42 U.S.C.A. § 6925 or 6930].

(3) Information submitted by the department, agency, or instrumentality under section 9603 of this title.

The docket shall be available for public inspection at reasonable times. Six months after establishment of the docket and every 6 months thereafter, the Administrator shall publish in the Federal Register a list of the Federal facilities which have been included in the docket during the immediately preceding 6–month period. Such publication shall also indicate where in the appropriate regional office of the Environmental Protection Agency additional information may be obtained with respect to any facility on the docket. The Administrator shall establish a program to provide information to the public with respect to facilities which are included in the docket under this subsection.

**(d) Assessment and evaluation**

**(1) In general**

The Administrator shall take steps to assure that a preliminary assessment is conducted for each facility on the docket. Following such preliminary assessment, the Administrator shall, where appropriate—

(A) evaluate such facilities in accordance with the criteria established in accordance with section 9605 of this title under the National Contingency Plan for determining priorities among releases; and

(B) include such facilities on the National Priorities List maintained under such plan if the facility meets such criteria.

**(2) Application of criteria**

**(A) In general**

Subject to subparagraph (B), the criteria referred to in paragraph (1) shall be applied in the same manner as the criteria are applied to facilities that are owned or operated by persons other than the United States.

**(B) Response under other law**

It shall be an appropriate factor to be taken into consideration for the purposes of section 9605(a)(8)(A) of this title that the head of the department, agency, or instrumentality that owns or operates a facility has arranged with the Administrator or appropriate State authorities to respond appropriately, under authority of a law other than this chapter, to a release or threatened release of a hazardous substance.

**(3) Completion**

Evaluation and listing under this subsection shall be completed in accordance with a reasonable schedule established by the Administrator.

**(e) Required action by department**

**(1) RI/FS**

Not later than 6 months after the inclusion of any facility on the National Priorities List, the department, agency, or instrumentality which owns or operates such facility shall, in consultation with the Administrator and appropriate State authorities, commence a remedial investigation and feasibility study for such facility. In the case of any facility which is listed on such list before October 17, 1986, the department, agency, or instrumentality which owns or operates such facility shall, in consultation with the Administrator and appropriate State authorities, commence such an investigation and study for such facility within one year after October 17, 1986. The Administrator and appropriate State authorities shall publish a timetable and deadlines for expeditious completion of such investigation and study.

**(2) Commencement of remedial action; interagency agreement**

The Administrator shall review the results of each investigation and study conducted as provided in paragraph (1). Within 180 days thereafter, the head of the department, agency, or instrumentality concerned shall enter into an interagency agreement with the Administrator for the expeditious completion by such department, agency, or instrumentality of all necessary remedial action at such facility. Substantial continuous physical onsite remedial action shall be commenced at each facility not later than 15 months after completion of the investigation and study. All such interagency agreements, including review of alternative remedial action plans and selection of remedial action, shall comply with the public participation requirements of section 9617 of this title.

**(3) Completion of remedial actions**

Remedial actions at facilities subject to interagency agreements under this section shall be completed as expeditiously as practicable. Each agency shall include in its annual budget submissions to the Congress a review of alternative agency funding which could be used to provide for the costs of remedial action. The budget submission shall also include a statement of the hazard posed by the facility to human health, welfare, and the environment and identify the specific consequences of failure to begin and complete remedial action.

**(4) Contents of agreement**

Each interagency agreement under this subsection shall include, but shall not be limited to, each of the following:

(A) A review of alternative remedial actions and selection of a remedial action by the head of the relevant department, agency, or instrumentality and the Administrator or, if unable to reach agreement on selection of a remedial action, selection by the Administrator.

(B) A schedule for the completion of each such remedial action.

(C) Arrangements for long-term operation and maintenance of the facility.

**(5) Annual report**

Each department, agency, or instrumentality responsible for compliance with this section shall furnish an annual report to the Congress concerning its progress in implementing the requirements of this section. Such reports shall include, but shall not be limited to, each of the following items:

(A) A report on the progress in reaching interagency agreements under this section.

(B) The specific cost estimates and budgetary proposals involved in each interagency agreement.

(C) A brief summary of the public comments regarding each proposed interagency agreement.

(D) A description of the instances in which no agreement was reached.

(E) A report on progress in conducting investigations and studies under paragraph (1).

(F) A report on progress in conducting remedial actions.

(G) A report on progress in conducting remedial action at facilities which are not listed on the National Priorities List.

With respect to instances in which no agreement was reached within the required time period, the department, agency, or instrumentality filing the report under this paragraph shall include in such report an explanation of the reasons why no agreement was reached. The annual report required by this paragraph shall also contain a detailed description on a State-by-State basis of the status of each facility subject to this section, including a description of the hazard presented by each facility, plans and schedules for initiating and completing response action, enforcement status (where appropriate), and an explanation of any postponements or failure to complete response action. Such reports shall also be submitted to the affected States.

**(6) Settlements with other parties**

If the Administrator, in consultation with the head of the relevant department, agency, or instrumentality of the United States, determines that remedial investigations and feasibility studies or remedial action will be done properly at the Federal facility by another potentially responsible party within the deadlines provided in paragraphs (1), (2), and (3) of this subsection, the Administrator may enter into an agreement with such party under section 9622 of this title (relating to settlements). Following approval by the Attorney General of any such agreement relating to a remedial action, the agreement shall be entered in the appropriate United States district court as a consent decree under section 9606 of this title.

**(f) State and local participation**

The Administrator and each department, agency, or instrumentality responsible for compliance with this section shall afford to relevant State and local officials the opportunity to participate in the planning and selection of the remedial action, including but not limited to the review of all applicable data as it becomes available and the development of studies, reports, and action plans. In the case of State officials, the opportunity to participate shall be provided in accordance with section 9621 of this title.

**(g) Transfer of authorities**

Except for authorities which are delegated by the Administrator to an officer or employee of the Environmental Protection Agency, no authority vested in the Administrator under this section may be transferred, by executive order of the President or otherwise, to any other officer or employee of the United States or to any other person.

**(h) Property transferred by Federal agencies**

**(1) Notice**

After the last day of the 6–month period beginning on the effective date of regulations under paragraph (2) of this subsection, whenever any department, agency, or instrumentality of the United States enters into any contract for the sale or other transfer of real property which is owned by the United States and on which any hazardous substance was stored for one year or more, known to have been released, or disposed of, the head of such department, agency, or instrumentality shall include in such contract notice of the type and quantity of such hazardous substance and notice of the time at which such storage, release, or disposal took place, to the extent such information is available on the basis of a complete search of agency files.

**(2) Form of notice; regulations**

Notice under this subsection shall be provided in such form and manner as may be provided in regulations promulgated by the Administrator. As promptly as practicable after October 17, 1986, but not later than 18 months after October 17, 1986, and after consultation with the Administrator of the General Services Administration, the Administrator shall promulgate regulations regarding the notice required to be provided under this subsection.

**(3) Contents of certain deeds**

**(A) In general**

After the last day of the 6–month period beginning on the effective date of regulations under paragraph (2) of this subsection, in the case of any real property owned by the United States on which any hazardous substance was stored for one year or more, known to have been released, or disposed of, each deed entered into for the transfer of such property by the United States to any other person or entity shall contain—

(i) to the extent such information is available on the basis of a complete search of agency files—

(I) a notice of the type and quantity of such hazardous substances,

(II) notice of the time at which such storage, release, or disposal took place, and

(III) a description of the remedial action taken, if any;

(ii) a covenant warranting that—

(I) all remedial action necessary to protect human health and the environment with respect to any such substance remaining on the property has been taken before the date of such transfer, and

(II) any additional remedial action found to be necessary after the date of such transfer shall be conducted by the United States; and

(iii) a clause granting the United States access to the property in any case in which remedial action or corrective action is found to be necessary after the date of such transfer.

**(B) Covenant requirements**

For purposes of subparagraphs (A)(ii)(I) and (C)(iii), all remedial action described in such subparagraph has been taken if the construction and installation of an approved remedial design has been completed, and the remedy has been demonstrated to the Administrator to be operating properly and successfully. The carrying out of long-term pumping and treating, or operation and maintenance, after the remedy has been demonstrated to the Administrator to be operating properly and successfully does not preclude the transfer of the property.

The requirements of subparagraph (A)(ii) shall not apply in any case in which the person or entity to whom the real property is transferred is a potentially responsible party with respect to such property. The requirements of subparagraph (A)(ii) shall not apply in any case in which the transfer of the property occurs or has occurred by means of a lease, without regard to whether the lessee has agreed to purchase the property or whether the duration of the lease is longer than 55 years. In the case of a lease entered into after September 30, 1995, with respect to real property located at an installation approved for closure or realignment under a base closure law, the agency leasing the property, in consultation with the Administrator, shall determine before leasing the property that the property is suitable for lease, that the uses contemplated for the lease are consistent with protection of human health and the environment, and that there are adequate assurances that the United States will take all remedial action referred to in subparagraph (A)(ii) that has not been taken on the date of the lease.

**(C) Deferral**

**(i) In general**

The Administrator, with the concurrence of the Governor of the State in which the facility is located (in the case of real property at a Federal facility that is listed on the National Priorities List), or the Governor of the State in which the facility is located (in the case of real property at a Federal facility not listed on the National Priorities List) may defer the requirement of subparagraph (A)(ii)(I) with respect to the property if the Administrator or the Governor, as the case may be, determines that the property is suitable for transfer, based on a finding that—

(I) the property is suitable for transfer for the use intended by the transferee, and the intended use is consistent with protection of human health and the environment;

(II) the deed or other agreement proposed to govern the transfer between the United States and the transferee of the property contains the assurances set forth in clause (ii);

(III) the Federal agency requesting deferral has provided notice, by publication in a newspaper of general circulation in the vicinity of the property, of the proposed transfer and of the opportunity for the public to submit, within a period of not less than 30 days after the date of the notice, written comments on the suitability of the property for transfer; and

**(IV)** the deferral and the transfer of the property will not substantially delay any necessary response action at the property.

**(ii) Response action assurances**

With regard to a release or threatened release of a hazardous substance for which a Federal agency is potentially responsible under this section, the deed or other agreement proposed to govern the transfer shall contain assurances that—

**(I)** provide for any necessary restrictions on the use of the property to ensure the protection of human health and the environment;

**(II)** provide that there will be restrictions on use necessary to ensure that required remedial investigations, response action, and oversight activities will not be disrupted;

**(III)** provide that all necessary response action will be taken and identify the schedules for investigation and completion of all necessary response action as approved by the appropriate regulatory agency; and

**(IV)** provide that the Federal agency responsible for the property subject to transfer will submit a budget request to the Director of the Office of Management and Budget that adequately addresses schedules for investigation and completion of all necessary response action, subject to congressional authorizations and appropriations.

**(iii) Warranty**

When all response action necessary to protect human health and the environment with respect to any substance remaining on the property on the date of transfer has been taken, the United States shall execute and deliver to the transferee an appropriate document containing a warranty that all such response action has been taken, and the making of the warranty shall be considered to satisfy the requirement of subparagraph (A)(ii)(I).

**(iv) Federal responsibility**

A deferral under this subparagraph shall not increase, diminish, or affect in any manner any rights or obligations of a Federal agency (including any rights or obligations under sections 9606, 9607 of this title, and this section existing prior to transfer) with respect to a property transferred under this subparagraph.

**(4) Identification of uncontaminated property**

**(A)** In the case of real property to which this paragraph applies (as set forth in subparagraph (E)), the head of the department, agency, or instrumentality of the United States with jurisdiction over the property shall identify the real property on which no hazardous substances and no petroleum products or their derivatives were known to have been released or disposed of. Such identification shall be based on an investigation of the real property to determine or discover the obviousness of the presence or likely presence of a release or threatened release of any hazardous substance or any petroleum product or its derivatives, including aviation fuel and motor oil, on the real property. The identification shall consist, at a minimum, of a review of each of the following sources of information concerning the current and previous uses of the real property:

**(i)** A detailed search of Federal Government records pertaining to the property.

**(ii)** Recorded chain of title documents regarding the real property.

**(iii)** Aerial photographs that may reflect prior uses of the real property and that are reasonably obtainable through State or local government agencies.

**(iv)** A visual inspection of the real property and any buildings, structures, equipment, pipe, pipeline, or other improvements on the real property, and a visual inspection of properties immediately adjacent to the real property.

**(v)** A physical inspection of property adjacent to the real property, to the extent permitted by owners or operators of such property.

**(vi)** Reasonably obtainable Federal, State, and local government records of each adjacent facility where there has been a release of any hazardous substance or any petroleum product or its derivatives, including aviation fuel and motor oil, and which is likely to cause or contribute to a release or threatened release of any hazardous substance or any petroleum product or its derivatives, including aviation fuel and motor oil, on the real property.

**(vii)** Interviews with current or former employees involved in operations on the real property.

Such identification shall also be based on sampling, if appropriate under the circumstances. The results of the identification shall be provided immediately to the Administrator and State and local government officials and made available to the public.

(B) The identification required under subparagraph (A) is not complete until concurrence in the results of the identification is obtained, in the case of real property that is part of a facility on the National Priorities List, from the Administrator, or, in the case of real property that is not part of a facility on the National Priorities List, from the appropriate State official. In the case of a concurrence which is required from a State official, the concurrence is deemed to be obtained if, within 90 days after receiving a request for the concurrence, the State official has not acted (by either concurring or declining to concur) on the request for concurrence.

(C)(i) Except as provided in clauses (ii), (iii), and (iv), the identification and concurrence required under subparagraphs (A) and (B), respectively, shall be made at least 6 months before the termination of operations on the real property.

(ii) In the case of real property described in subparagraph (E)(i)(II) on which operations have been closed or realigned or scheduled for closure or realignment pursuant to a base closure law described in subparagraph (E)(ii)(I) or (E)(ii)(II) by October 19, 1992, the identification and concurrence required under subparagraphs (A) and (B), respectively, shall be made not later than 18 months after October 19, 1992.

(iii) In the case of real property described in subparagraph (E)(i)(II) on which operations are closed or realigned or become scheduled for closure or realignment pursuant to the base closure law described in subparagraph (E)(ii)(II) after October 19, 1992, the identification and concurrence required under subparagraphs (A) and (B), respectively, shall be made not later than 18 months after the date by which a joint resolution disapproving the closure or realignment of the real property under section 2904(b) of such base closure law must be enacted, and such a joint resolution has not been enacted.

(iv) In the case of real property described in subparagraphs (E)(i)(II) on which operations are closed or realigned pursuant to a base closure law described in subparagraph (E)(ii)(III) or (E)(ii)(IV), the identification and concurrence required under subparagraphs (A) and (B), respectively, shall be made not later than 18 months after the date on which the real property is selected for closure or realignment pursuant to such a base closure law.

(D) In the case of the sale or other transfer of any parcel of real property identified under subparagraph (A), the deed entered into for the sale or transfer of such property by the United States to any other person or entity shall contain—

(i) a covenant warranting that any response action or corrective action found to be necessary after the date of such sale or transfer shall be conducted by the United States; and

(ii) a clause granting the United States access to the property in any case in which a response action or corrective action is found to be necessary after such date at such property, or such access is necessary to carry out a response action or corrective action on adjoining property.

(E)(i) This paragraph applies to—

(I) real property owned by the United States and on which the United States plans to terminate Federal Government operations, other than real property described in subclause (II); and

(II) real property that is or has been used as a military installation and on which the United States plans to close or realign military operations pursuant to a base closure law.

(ii) For purposes of this paragraph, the term "base closure law" includes the following:

(I) Title II of the Defense Authorization Amendments and Base Closure and Realignment Act (Public Law 100–526; 10 U.S.C. 2687 note).

(II) The Defense Base Closure and Realignment Act of 1990 (part A of title XXIX of Public Law 101–510; 10 U.S.C. 2687 note).

(III) Section 2687 of Title 10.

(IV) Any provision of law authorizing the closure or realignment of a military installation enacted on or after October 19, 1992.

(F) Nothing in this paragraph shall affect, preclude, or otherwise impair the termination of Federal Government operations on real property owned by the United States.

**(5) Notification of States regarding certain leases**

In the case of real property owned by the United States, on which any hazardous substance or any petroleum product or its derivatives (including aviation fuel and motor oil) was stored for one year or more, known to have been released, or disposed of, and on which the United States plans to terminate Federal Government operations, the head of the department, agency, or instrumentality of the United States with jurisdiction over the property shall notify the State in which the property is located of any lease entered into by the United States that will encumber the property beyond the date of termination of operations on the property. Such notification shall be made before entering into the lease and shall include the length of the lease, the name of person to whom the property is leased, and a description of the uses that will be allowed under the lease of the property and buildings and other structures on the property.

### (i) Obligations under Solid Waste Disposal Act

Nothing in this section shall affect or impair the obligation of any department, agency, or instrumentality of the United States to comply with any requirement of the Solid Waste Disposal Act [42 U.S.C.A. § 6901 et seq.] (including corrective action requirements).

**(j) National security**

**(1) Site specific Presidential orders**

The President may issue such orders regarding response actions at any specified site or facility of the Department of Energy or the Department of Defense as may be necessary to protect the national security interests of the United States at that site or facility. Such orders may include, where necessary to protect such interests, an exemption from any requirement contained in this subchapter or under title III of the Superfund Amendments and Reauthorization Act of 1986 [42 U.S.C.A. § 11001 et seq.] with respect to the site or facility concerned. The President shall notify the Congress within 30 days of the issuance of an order under this paragraph providing for any such exemption. Such notification shall include a statement of the reasons for the granting of the exemption. An exemption under this paragraph shall be for a specified period which may not exceed one year. Additional exemptions may be granted, each upon the President's issuance of a new order under this paragraph for the site or facility concerned. Each such additional exemption shall be for a specified period which may not exceed one year. It is the intention of the Congress that whenever an exemption is issued under this paragraph the response action shall proceed as expeditiously as practicable. The Congress shall be notified periodically of the progress of any response action with respect to which an exemption has been issued under this paragraph. No exemption shall be granted under this paragraph due to lack of appropriation unless the President shall have specifically requested such appropriation as a part of the budgetary process and the Congress shall have failed to make available such requested appropriation.

**(2) Classified information**

Notwithstanding any other provision of law, all requirements of the Atomic Energy Act [42 U.S.C.A. § 2011 et seq.] and all Executive orders concerning the handling of restricted data and national security information, including "need to know" requirements, shall be applicable to any grant of access to classified information under the provisions of this chapter or under title III of the Superfund Amendments and Reauthorization Act of 1986 [42 U.S.C.A. § 11001 et seq.].

(Pub.L. 96–510, Title I, § 120, as added Pub.L. 99–499, Title I, § 120(a), Oct. 17, 1986, 100 Stat. 1666, and amended Pub.L. 102–426, §§ 3, 4, 5, Oct. 19, 1992, 106 Stat. 2175 to 2177; Pub.L. 104–106, Div. B, Title XXVIII, § 2834, Feb. 10, 1996, 110 Stat. 559; Pub.L. 104–201, Div. A, Title III, §§ 330, 331, 334, Sept. 23, 1996, 110 Stat. 2484, 2486.)

## HISTORICAL AND STATUTORY NOTES

**References in Text**

This chapter, referred to in subsecs. (a)(1) to (3), (c)(1), (d)(2)(B), and (j)(2), was in the original, "this Act", meaning Pub.L. 96–510, Dec. 11, 1980, 94 Stat. 2767, as amended, known as the Comprehensive Environmental Response, Compensation, and Liability Act of 1980. For complete classification of this Act to the Code, see Short Title of 1980 Acts note set out under section 9601 of this title and Tables.

Section 2904(b) of such base closure law, referred to in subsec. (h)(4)(C)(iii), is Pub.L. 101–510, Div. B, Title XXIX, § 2904(b), Nov. 5, 1990, 104 Stat. 1812, as amended, which is set out as a note under section 2687 of Title 10, Armed Forces.

Title II of the Defense Authorization Amendments and Base Closure and Realignment Act, referred to in subsec. (h)(4)(E)(ii)(I), is Pub.L. 100–526, Title II, Oct. 24, 1988, 102 Stat. 2627, as amended, which is set out as a note under section 2687 of Title 10, Armed Forces.

The Defense Base Closure and Realignment Act of 1990, referred to in subsec. (h)(4)(E)(ii)(II), is Pub. L. 101–510, Part A, Title XXIX, §§ 2901 to 2910, Nov. 5, 1990, 104 Stat. 1808, as amended, which is set out as a note under section 2687 of Title 10, Armed Forces.

The Solid Waste Disposal Act, referred to in subsec. (i), is Title II of Pub.L. 89–272, Oct. 20, 1965, 79 Stat. 997, as amended generally by Pub.L. 94–580, § 2, Oct. 21, 1976, 90 Stat. 2795, which is classified generally to chapter 82 (section 6901 et seq.) of this title. For complete classification of this Act to the Code, see Short Title of 1965 Acts note set out under section 6901 of this title and Tables.

Title III of the Superfund Amendments and Reauthorization Act of 1986, referred to in subsec. (j), is Title III (section 300 et seq.) of Pub.L. 99–499, Oct. 17, 1986, 100 Stat. 1728, known as the Emergency Planning and Community Right-To-Know Act of 1986, which is classified principally to chapter 116 (section 11001 et seq.) of this title. For complete classification of the Emergency Planning and Community Right-To-Know Act of 1986 to the Code, see Short Title of 1986 Acts note set out under section 11001 of this title and Tables.

The Atomic Energy Act, referred to in subsec. (j)(2), probably means the Atomic Energy Act of 1954, Act Aug. 30, 1954, c. 1073, § 1, 68 Stat. 919, as amended, which is classified principally to chapter 23 (section 2011 et seq.) of this title. For complete classification of this Act to the Code, see Short Title of 1954 Acts note set out under section 2011 of this title and Tables.

**Congressional Findings**

Section 2 of Pub.L. 102–426 provided that: "The Congress finds the following:

"(1) The closure of certain Federal facilities is having adverse effects on the economies of local communities by eliminating jobs associated with such facilities, and delay in remediation of environmental contamination of real property at such facilities is preventing transfer and private development of such property.

"(2) Each department, agency, or instrumentality of the United States, in cooperation with local communities, should expeditiously identify real property that offers the greatest opportunity for reuse and redevelopment on each facility under the jurisdiction of the department, agency, or instrumentality where operations are terminating.

"(3) Remedial actions, including remedial investigations and feasibility studies, and corrective actions at such Federal facilities should be expedited in a manner to facilitate environmental protection and the sale or transfer of such excess real property for the purpose of mitigating adverse economic effects on the surrounding community.

"(4) Each department, agency, or instrumentality of the United States, in accordance with applicable law, should make available without delay such excess real property.

"(5) In the case of any real property owned by the United States and transferred to another person, the United States Government should remain responsible for conducting any remedial action or corrective action necessary to protect human health and the environment with respect to any hazardous substance or petroleum product or its derivatives, including aviation fuel and motor oil, that was present on such real property at the time of transfer."

**Identification of Uncontaminated Property at Installations to be Closed**

Pub.L. 103–160, Div. B, Title XXIX, § 2910, Nov. 30, 1993, 107 Stat. 1924, provided that: "The identification by the Secretary of Defense required under section 120(h)(4)(A) of the Comprehensive Environmental Response, Compensation, and Liability Act of 1980 (42 U.S.C. 9620(h)(4)(A)) [subsec. (h)(4)(A) of this section], and the concurrence required under section 120(h)(4)(B) of such Act [subsec. (h)(4)(B) of this section], shall be made not later than the earlier of—

"(1) the date that is 9 months after the date of the submittal, if any, to the transition coordinator for the installation concerned of a specific use proposed for all or a portion of the real property of the installation; or

"(2) the date specified in section 120(h)(4)(C)(iii) of such Act [subsec. (h)(4)(C)(iii) of this section]."

**Limited Grandfather Provision**

Section 120(b) of Pub.L. 99–499 provided that: "Section 120 of CERCLA [this section] shall not apply to any response action or remedial action for which a plan is under development by the Department of Energy on the date of enactment of this Act [Oct. 17, 1986] with respect to facilities—

"(1) owned or operated by the United States and subject to the jurisdiction of such Department;

"(2) located in St. Charles and St. Louis counties, Missouri, or the city of St. Louis, Missouri, and

"(3) published in the National Priorities List.

In preparing such plans, the Secretary of Energy shall consult with the Administrator of the Environmental Protection Agency."

## § 9621. Cleanup standards

### [CERCLA § 121]

### (a) Selection of remedial action

The President shall select appropriate remedial actions determined to be necessary to be carried out under section 9604 of this title or secured under section 9606 of this title which are in accordance with this section and, to the extent practicable, the national contingency plan, and which provide for cost-effective response. In evaluating the cost effectiveness of proposed alternative remedial actions, the President shall take into account the total short- and long-term costs of such actions, including the costs of operation and maintenance for the entire period during which such activities will be required.

### (b) General rules

(1) Remedial actions in which treatment which permanently and significantly reduces the volume, toxicity or mobility of the hazardous substances, pollutants, and contaminants is a principal element, are to be preferred over remedial actions not involving such treatment. The offsite transport and disposal of hazardous substances or contaminated materials without such treatment should be the least favored alternative remedial action where practicable treatment technologies are available. The President shall conduct an assessment of permanent solutions and alternative treatment technologies or resource recovery technologies that, in whole or in part, will result in a permanent and significant decrease in the toxicity, mobility, or volume of the hazardous substance, pollutant, or contaminant. In making such assessment, the President shall specifically address the long-term effectiveness of various alternatives. In assessing alternative remedial actions, the President shall, at a minimum, take into account:

(A) the long-term uncertainties associated with land disposal;

(B) the goals, objectives, and requirements of the Solid Waste Disposal Act [42 U.S.C.A. § 6901 et seq.];

(C) the persistence, toxicity, mobility, and propensity to bioaccumulate of such hazardous substances and their constituents;

(D) short- and long-term potential for adverse health effects from human exposure;

(E) long-term maintenance costs;

(F) the potential for future remedial action costs if the alternative remedial action in question were to fail; and

(G) the potential threat to human health and the environment associated with excavation, transportation, and redisposal, or containment.

The President shall select a remedial action that is protective of human health and the environment, that is cost effective, and that utilizes permanent solutions and alternative treatment technologies or resource recovery technologies to the maximum extent practicable. If the President selects a remedial action not appropriate for a preference under this subsection, the President shall publish an explanation as to why a remedial action involving such reductions was not selected.

(2) The President may select an alternative remedial action meeting the objectives of this subsection whether or not such action has been achieved in practice at any other facility or site that has similar characteristics. In making such a selection, the President may take into account the degree of support for such remedial action by parties interested in such site.

**(c) Review**

If the President selects a remedial action that results in any hazardous substances, pollutants, or contaminants remaining at the site, the President shall review such remedial action no less often than each 5 years after the initiation of such remedial action to assure that human health and the environment are being protected by the remedial action being implemented. In addition, if upon such review it is the judgment of the President that action is appropriate at such site in accordance with section 9604 or 9606 of this title, the President shall take or require such action. The President shall report to the Congress a list of facilities for which such review is required, the results of all such reviews, and any actions taken as a result of such reviews.

**(d) Degree of cleanup**

**(1)** Remedial actions selected under this section or otherwise required or agreed to by the President under this chapter shall attain a degree of cleanup of hazardous substances, pollutants, and contaminants released into the environment and of control of further release at a minimum which assures protection of human health and the environment. Such remedial actions shall be relevant and appropriate under the circumstances presented by the release or threatened release of such substance, pollutant, or contaminant.

**(2)(A)** With respect to any hazardous substance, pollutant or contaminant that will remain onsite, if—

**(i)** any standard, requirement, criteria, or limitation under any Federal environmental law, including, but not limited to, the Toxic Substances Control Act [15 U.S.C.A. § 2601 et seq.], the Safe Drinking Water Act [42 U.S.C.A. § 300f et seq.], the Clean Air Act [42 U.S.C.A. § 7401 et seq.], the Clean Water Act [33 U.S.C.A. § 1251 et seq.], the Marine Protection, Research and Sanctuaries Act [16 U.S.C.A. § 1431 et seq., § 1447 et seq., 33 U.S.C.A. § 1401 et seq., § 2801 et seq.], or the Solid Waste Disposal Act [42 U.S.C.A. § 6901 et seq.]; or

**(ii)** any promulgated standard, requirement, criteria, or limitation under a State environmental or facility siting law that is more stringent than any Federal standard, requirement, criteria, or limitation, including each such State standard, requirement, criteria, or limitation contained in a program approved, authorized or delegated by the Administrator under a statute cited in subparagraph (A), and that has been identified to the President by the State in a timely manner,

is legally applicable to the hazardous substance or pollutant or contaminant concerned or is relevant and appropriate under the circumstances of the release or threatened release of such hazardous substance or pollutant or contaminant, the remedial action selected under section 9604 of this title or secured under section 9606 of this title shall require, at the completion of the remedial action, a level or standard of control for such hazardous substance or pollutant or contaminant which at least attains such legally applicable or relevant and appropriate standard, requirement, criteria, or limitation. Such remedial action shall require a level or standard of control which at least attains Maximum Contaminant Level Goals established under the Safe Drinking Water Act [42 U.S.C.A. § 300f et seq.] and water quality criteria established under section 304 or 303 of the Clean Water Act [33 U.S.C.A. § 1314 or 1313], where such goals or criteria are relevant and appropriate under the circumstances of the release or threatened release.

**(B)(i)** In determining whether or not any water quality criteria under the Clean Water Act [33 U.S.C.A. § 1251 et seq.] is relevant and appropriate under the circumstances of the release or threatened release, the President shall consider the designated or potential use of the surface or groundwater, the environmental media affected, the purposes for which such criteria were developed, and the latest information available.

**(ii)** For the purposes of this section, a process for establishing alternate concentration limits to those otherwise applicable for hazardous constituents in groundwater under subparagraph (A) may not be used to establish applicable standards under this paragraph if the process assumes a point of human exposure beyond the boundary of the facility, as defined at the conclusion of the remedial investigation and feasibility study, except where—

**(I)** there are known and projected points of entry of such groundwater into surface water; and

**(II)** on the basis of measurements or projections, there is or will be no statistically significant increase of such constituents from such groundwater in such surface water at the point of entry or at any point where there is reason to believe accumulation of constituents may occur downstream; and

**(III)** the remedial action includes enforceable measures that will preclude human exposure to the contaminated groundwater at any point between the facility boundary and all known and projected points of entry of such groundwater into surface water

then the assumed point of human exposure may be at such known and projected points of entry.

**(C)(i)** Clause (ii) of this subparagraph shall be applicable only in cases where, due to the President's selection, in compliance with subsection (b)(1) of this section, of a proposed remedial action which does not permanently and significantly reduce the volume, toxicity, or mobility of hazardous substances, pollutants, or contaminants, the proposed disposition of waste generated by or associated with the remedial action selected by the President is land disposal in a State referred to in clause (ii).

**(ii)** Except as provided in clauses (iii) and (iv), a State standard, requirement, criteria, or limitation (including any State siting standard or requirement) which could effectively result in the statewide prohibition of land disposal of hazardous substances, pollutants, or contaminants shall not apply.

**(iii)** Any State standard, requirement, criteria, or limitation referred to in clause (ii) shall apply where each of the following conditions is met:

**(I)** The State standard, requirement, criteria, or limitation is of general applicability and was adopted by formal means.

**(II)** The State standard, requirement, criteria, or limitation was adopted on the basis of hydrologic, geologic, or other relevant considerations and was not adopted for the purpose of precluding onsite remedial actions or other land disposal for reasons unrelated to protection of human health and the environment.

**(III)** The State arranges for, and assures payment of the incremental costs of utilizing, a facility for disposition of the hazardous substances, pollutants, or contaminants concerned.

**(iv)** Where the remedial action selected by the President does not conform to a State standard and the State has initiated a law suit against the Environmental Protection Agency prior to May 1, 1986, to seek to have the remedial action conform to such standard, the President shall conform the remedial action to the State standard. The State shall assure the availability of an offsite facility for such remedial action.

**(3)** In the case of any removal or remedial action involving the transfer of any hazardous substance or pollutant or contaminant offsite, such hazardous substance or pollutant or contaminant shall only be transferred to a facility which is operating in compliance with section 3004 and 3005 of the Solid Waste Disposal Act [42 U.S.C.A. §§ 6924 and 6925] (or, where applicable, in compliance with the Toxic Substances Control Act [15 U.S.C.A. § 2601 et seq.] or other applicable Federal law) and all applicable State requirements. Such substance or pollutant or contaminant may be transferred to a land disposal facility only if the President determines that both of the following requirements are met:

**(A)** The unit to which the hazardous substance or pollutant or contaminant is transferred is not releasing any hazardous waste, or constituent thereof, into the groundwater or surface water or soil.

**(B)** All such releases from other units at the facility are being controlled by a corrective action program approved by the Administrator under subtitle C of the Solid Waste Disposal Act [42 U.S.C.A. § 6921 et seq.].

The President shall notify the owner or operator of such facility of determinations under this paragraph.

**(4)** The President may select a remedial action meeting the requirements of paragraph (1) that does not attain a level or standard of control at least equivalent to a legally applicable or relevant and appropriate standard, requirement, criteria, or limitation as required by paragraph (2) (including subparagraph (B) thereof), if the President finds that—

**(A)** the remedial action selected is only part of a total remedial action that will attain such level or standard of control when completed;

**(B)** compliance with such requirement at that facility will result in greater risk to human health and the environment than alternative options;

**(C)** compliance with such requirements is technically impracticable from an engineering perspective;

**(D)** the remedial action selected will attain a standard of performance that is equivalent to that required under the otherwise applicable standard, requirement, criteria, or limitation, through use of another method or approach;

**(E)** with respect to a State standard, requirement, criteria, or limitation, the State has not consistently applied (or demonstrated the intention to consistently apply) the standard, requirement, criteria, or limitation in similar circumstances at other remedial actions within the State; or

**(F)** in the case of a remedial action to be undertaken solely under section 9604 of this title using the Fund, selection of a remedial action that attains such level or standard of control will not provide a balance between the need for protection of public health and welfare and the environment at the facility under consideration, and the availability of amounts from the Fund to respond to other sites which present or may present a threat to public health or welfare or the environment, taking into consideration the relative immediacy of such threats.

The President shall publish such findings, together with an explanation and appropriate documentation.

**(e) Permits and enforcement**

**(1)** No Federal, State, or local permit shall be required for the portion of any removal or remedial action conducted entirely onsite, where such remedial action is selected and carried out in compliance with this section.

**(2)** A State may enforce any Federal or State standard, requirement, criteria, or limitation to which the remedial action is required to conform under this chapter in the United States district court for the district in which the facility is located. Any consent decree shall require the parties to attempt expeditiously to resolve disagreements concerning implementation of the remedial action informally with the appropriate Federal and State agencies. Where the parties agree, the consent decree may provide for administrative enforcement. Each consent decree shall also contain stipulated penalties for violations of the decree in an amount not to exceed $25,000 per day, which may be enforced by either the President or the State. Such stipulated penalties shall not be construed to impair or affect the authority of the court to order compliance with the specific terms of any such decree.

**(f) State involvement**

**(1)** The President shall promulgate regulations providing for substantial and meaningful involvement by each State in initiation, development, and selection of remedial actions to be undertaken in that State. The regulations, at a minimum, shall include each of the following:

**(A)** State involvement in decisions whether to perform a preliminary assessment and site inspection.

**(B)** Allocation of responsibility for hazard ranking system scoring.

**(C)** State concurrence in deleting sites from the National Priorities List.

**(D)** State participation in the long-term planning process for all remedial sites within the State.

**(E)** A reasonable opportunity for States to review and comment on each of the following:

**(i)** The remedial investigation and feasibility study and all data and technical documents leading to its issuance.

**(ii)** The planned remedial action identified in the remedial investigation and feasibility study.

**(iii)** The engineering design following selection of the final remedial action.

**(iv)** Other technical data and reports relating to implementation of the remedy.

**(v)** Any proposed finding or decision by the President to exercise the authority of subsection (d)(4) of this section.

**(F)** Notice to the State of negotiations with potentially responsible parties regarding the scope of any response action at a facility in the State and an opportunity to participate in such negotiations and, subject to paragraph (2), be a party to any settlement.

**(G)** Notice to the State and an opportunity to comment on the President's proposed plan for remedial action as well as on alternative plans under consideration. The President's proposed decision regarding the selection of remedial action shall be accompanied by a response to the comments submitted by the State, including an explanation regarding any decision under subsection (d)(4) of this section on compliance with promulgated State standards. A copy of such response shall also be provided to the State.

**(H)** Prompt notice and explanation of each proposed action to the State in which the facility is located.

Prior to the promulgation of such regulations, the President shall provide notice to the State of negotiations with potentially responsible parties regarding the scope of any response action at a facility in the State, and such State may participate in such negotiations and, subject to paragraph (2), any settlements.

**(2)(A)** This paragraph shall apply to remedial actions secured under section 9606 of this title. At least 30 days prior to the entering of any consent decree, if the President proposes to select a remedial action that does not attain a legally applicable or relevant and appropriate standard, requirement, criteria, or limitation, under the authority of subsection (d)(4) of this section, the President shall provide an opportunity for the State to concur or not concur in such selection. If the State concurs, the State may become a signatory to the consent decree.

**(B)** If the State does not concur in such selection, and the State desires to have the remedial action conform to such standard, requirement, criteria, or limitation, the State shall intervene in the action under section 9606 of this title before entry of the consent decree, to seek to have the remedial action so conform. Such intervention shall be a matter of right. The remedial action shall conform to such standard, requirement, criteria, or limitation if the State establishes, on the administrative record, that the finding of the President was not supported by substantial evidence. If the court determines that the remedial action shall conform to such standard, requirement, criteria, or limitation, the remedial action shall be so modified and the State may become a signatory to the decree. If the court determines that the remedial action need not conform to such standard, requirement, criteria, or limitation, and the State pays or assures the payment of the additional costs attributable to meeting such standard, requirement, criteria, or limitation, the remedial action shall be so modified and the State shall become a signatory to the decree.

**(C)** The President may conclude settlement negotiations with potentially responsible parties without State concurrence.

**(3)(A)** This paragraph shall apply to remedial actions at facilities owned or operated by a department, agency, or instrumentality of the United States. At least 30 days prior to the publication of the President's final remedial action plan, if the President proposes to select a remedial action that does not attain a legally applicable or relevant and appropriate standard, requirement, criteria, or limitation, under the authority of subsection (d)(4) of this section, the President shall provide an opportunity for the State to concur or not concur in such selection. If the State concurs, or does not act within 30 days, the remedial action may proceed.

**(B)** If the State does not concur in such selection as provided in subparagraph (A), and desires to have the remedial action conform to such standard, requirement, criteria, or limitation, the State may maintain an action as follows:

**(i)** If the President has notified the State of selection of such a remedial action, the State may bring an action within 30 days of such notification for the sole purpose of determining whether the finding of the President is supported by substantial evidence. Such action shall be brought in the United States district court for the district in which the facility is located.

**(ii)** If the State establishes, on the administrative record, that the President's finding is not supported by substantial evidence, the remedial action shall be modified to conform to such standard, requirement, criteria, or limitation.

**(iii)** If the State fails to establish that the President's finding was not supported by substantial evidence and if the State pays, within 60 days of judgment, the additional costs attributable to meeting such standard, requirement, criteria, or limitation, the remedial action shall be selected to meet such standard, requirement, criteria, or limitation. If the State fails to pay within 60 days, the remedial action selected by the President shall proceed through completion.

**(C)** Nothing in this section precludes, and the court shall not enjoin, the Federal agency from taking any remedial action unrelated to or not inconsistent with such standard, requirement, criteria, or limitation.

(Pub.L. 96–510, Title I, § 121, as added Pub.L. 99–499, Title I, § 121(a), Oct. 17, 1986, 100 Stat. 1672.)

## HISTORICAL AND STATUTORY NOTES

### References in Text

The Solid Waste Disposal Act, referred to in subsecs. (b)(1)(B), (d)(2)(A)(i), is Title II of Pub.L. 89–272, Oct. 20, 1965, 79 Stat. 997, as amended generally by Pub.L. 94–580, § 2, Oct. 21, 1976, 90 Stat. 2795, which is classified generally to chapter 82 (section 6901 et seq.) of this title. Subtitle C of the Solid Waste Disposal Act, referred to in subsec. (d)(3)(B), is classified generally to subchapter III (section 6921 et seq.) of chapter 82 of this title. For complete classification of this Act to the Code, see Short Title of 1965 Acts note set out under section 6901 of this title and Tables.

The Toxic Substances Control Act, referred to in subsec. (d)(2)(A)(i), (3), is Pub.L. 94–469, Oct. 11, 1976, 90 Stat. 2003, as amended, which is classified generally to chapter 53 (section 2601 et seq.) of Title 15, Commerce and Trade. For complete classification of this Act to the Code, see Short Title note set out under section 2601 of Title 15 and Tables.

The Safe Drinking Water Act, referred to in subsec. (d)(2)(A)(i), is Pub.L. 93–523, Dec. 16, 1974, 88 Stat. 1660, as amended, which is classified principally to subchapter XII (section 300f et seq.) of chapter 6A of this title. For complete classification of this Act to the Code, see Short Title of 1974 Amendments note set out under section 201 of this title and Tables.

The Clean Air Act, referred to in subsec. (d)(2)(A)(i), is Act July 14, 1955, c. 360, as amended generally by Pub.L. 88–206, Dec. 17, 1963, 77 Stat. 392, and later by Pub.L. 95–95, Aug. 7, 1977, 91 Stat. 685. The Clean Air Act was originally classified to chapter 15B (section 1857 et seq.) of this title. On enactment of Pub.L. 95–95, the Act was reclassified to chapter 85 (section 7401 et seq.) of this title. For complete classification of this Act to the Code, see Short Title of 1955 Acts note set out under section 7401 of this title and Tables.

The Clean Water Act, referred to in subsec. (d)(2)(A)(i), (B)(i), is Act June 30, 1948, c. 758, as amended generally by Pub.L. 92–500, § 2, Oct. 18, 1972, 86 Stat. 816, also known as the Federal Water Pollution Control Act, which is classified generally to chapter 26 (section 1251 et seq.) of Title 33, Navigation and Navigable Waters. For complete classification of this Act to the Code, see Short Title note set out under section 1251 of Title 33 and Tables.

The Marine Protection, Research and Sanctuaries Act, referred to in subsec. (d)(2)(A)(i), probably means the Marine Protection, Research and Sanctuaries Act of 1972, Pub.L. 92–532, Oct. 23, 1972, 86 Stat. 1052, as amended, which enacted chapters 32 (section 1431 et seq.) and 32A (section 1447 et seq.) of Title 16, Conservation, and chapters 27 (section 1401 et seq.) and 41 (section 2801 et seq.) of Title 33, Navigation and Navigable Waters. For complete classification of this Act to the Code, see Short Title note set out under section 1401 of Title 33 and Tables.

### Effective Dates

1986 Acts

Section 121(b) of Pub.L. 99–499 provided that: "With respect to section 121 of CERCLA [this section], as added by this section—

"(1) The requirements of section 121 of CERCLA shall not apply to any remedial action for which the Record of Decision (hereinafter in this section referred to as the 'ROD') was signed, or the consent decree was lodged, before date of enactment [Oct. 17, 1986].

"(2) If the ROD was signed, or the consent decree lodged, within the 30–day period immediately following enactment of the Act [Oct. 17, 1986], the Administrator shall certify in writing that the portion of the remedial action covered by the ROD or consent decree complies to the maximum extent practicable with section 121 of CERCLA.

Any ROD signed before enactment of this Act [Oct. 17, 1986] and reopened after enactment of this Act to modify or supplement the selection of remedy shall be subject to the requirements of section 121 of CERCLA [this section]."

**Delegation of Functions**

Functions vested in the President by subsec. (f)(1) of this section, relating to the promulgation of regulations and guidelines, delegated to the Administrator of the Environmental Protection Agency, to be exercised in consultation with the National Response Team, see section 2(b) of Ex. Ord. No. 12580, Jan. 23, 1987, 52 F.R. 2923, set out as a note under section 9615 of this title.

Functions vested in the President by this section delegated, with authority to redelegate, (and subject to section 2(a), (b) and (c) of Ex. Ord. No. 12580) to the Secretaries of Defense and Energy, with respect to releases or threatened releases where either the release is on or the sole source of the release is from any facility or vessel under the jurisdiction, custody or control of their departments, respectively, including vessels bare-boat chartered and operated, with such functions to be exercised consistent with the requirements of section 9620 of this title, see sections 2(d), 11(g) of Ex. Ord. No. 12580, Jan. 23, 1987, 52 F.R. 2923, set out as a note under section 9615 of this title.

Functions vested in the President by this section, subject to section 2(a) to (d) of Ex. Ord. No. 12580, delegated, with authority to redelegate, to the heads of Executive departments and agencies, with respect to remedial actions for releases or threatened releases which are not on the National Priorities List and removal actions other than emergencies, where either the release is on or the sole source of the release is from any facility or vessel under the jurisdiction, custody or control of those departments and agencies, including vessels bare-boat chartered and operated with the Administrator of the Environmental Protection Agency to define the term "emergency", solely for the purposes of section 2(e) of Ex. Ord. No. 12580, either by regulation or by a memorandum of understanding with the head of an Executive department or agency, see sections 2(e)(1), 11(g) of Ex. Ord. No. 12580, Jan. 23, 1987, 52 F.R. 2923, set out as a note under section 9615 of this title.

Functions vested in the President by this section, subject to section 2(a) to (e) of Ex. Ord. No. 12580, delegated, with authority to redelegate, to the Secretary of the Department in which the Coast Guard is operating ("the Coast Guard"), with respect to any release or threatened release involving the coastal zone, Great Lakes waters, ports, and harbors, see sections 2(f), 11(g) of Ex. Ord. No. 12580, Jan. 23, 1987, 52 F.R. 2923, set out as a note under section 9615 of this title.

Functions vested in the President by this section, subject to section 2(a) to (f) of Ex. Ord. No. 12580, delegated, with authority to redelegate, to the Administrator of the Environmental Protection Agency, see sections 2(g), 11(g) of Ex. Ord. No. 12580, Jan. 23, 1987, 52 F.R. 2923, set out as a note under section 9615 of this title.

## § 9622. Settlements

### [CERCLA § 122]

**(a) Authority to enter into agreements**

The President, in his discretion, may enter into an agreement with any person (including the owner or operator of the facility from which a release or substantial threat of release emanates, or any other potentially responsible person), to perform any response action (including any action described in section 9604(b) of this title) if the President determines that such action will be done properly by such person. Whenever practicable and in the public interest, as determined by the President, the President shall act to facilitate agreements under this section that are in the public interest and consistent with the National Contingency Plan in order to expedite effective remedial actions and minimize litigation. If the President decides not to use the procedures in this section, the President shall notify in writing potentially responsible parties at the facility of such decision and the reasons why use of the procedures is inappropriate. A decision of the President to use or not to use the procedures in this section is not subject to judicial review.

**(b) Agreements with potentially responsible parties**

**(1) Mixed funding**

An agreement under this section may provide that the President will reimburse the parties to the agreement from the Fund, with interest, for certain costs of actions under the agreement that the parties have agreed to perform but which the President has agreed to finance. In any case in which the President provides such reimbursement, the President shall make all reasonable efforts to recover the amount of such reimbursement under section 9607 of this title or under other relevant authorities.

**(2) Reviewability**

The President's decisions regarding the availability of fund financing under this subsection shall not be subject to judicial review under subsection (d) of this section.

**(3) Retention of funds**

If, as part of any agreement, the President will be carrying out any action and the parties will be paying amounts to the President, the President may, notwithstanding any other provision of law, retain and use such amounts for purposes of carrying out the agreement.

(4) **Future obligation of Fund**

In the case of a completed remedial action pursuant to an agreement described in paragraph (1), the Fund shall be subject to an obligation for subsequent remedial actions at the same facility but only to the extent that such subsequent actions are necessary by reason of the failure of the original remedial action. Such obligation shall be in a proportion equal to, but not exceeding, the proportion contributed by the Fund for the original remedial action. The Fund's obligation for such future remedial action may be met through Fund expenditures or through payment, following settlement or enforcement action, by parties who were not signatories to the original agreement.

(c) **Effect of agreement**

(1) **Liability**

Whenever the President has entered into an agreement under this section, the liability to the United States under this chapter of each party to the agreement, including any future liability to the United States, arising from the release or threatened release that is the subject of the agreement shall be limited as provided in the agreement pursuant to a covenant not to sue in accordance with subsection (f) of this section. A covenant not to sue may provide that future liability to the United States of a settling potentially responsible party under the agreement may be limited to the same proportion as that established in the original settlement agreement. Nothing in this section shall limit or otherwise affect the authority of any court to review in the consent decree process under subsection (d) of this section any covenant not to sue contained in an agreement under this section. In determining the extent to which the liability of parties to an agreement shall be limited pursuant to a covenant not to sue, the President shall be guided by the principle that a more complete covenant not to sue shall be provided for a more permanent remedy undertaken by such parties.

(2) **Actions against other persons**

If an agreement has been entered into under this section, the President may take any action under section 9606 of this title against any person who is not a party to the agreement, once the period for submitting a proposal under subsection (e)(2)(B) of this section has expired. Nothing in this section shall be construed to affect either of the following:

(A) The liability of any person under section 9606 or 9607 of this title with respect to any costs or damages which are not included in the agreement.

(B) The authority of the President to maintain an action under this chapter against any person who is not a party to the agreement.

(d) **Enforcement**

(1) **Cleanup agreements**

(A) **Consent decree**

Whenever the President enters into an agreement under this section with any potentially responsible party with respect to remedial action under section 9606 of this title, following approval of the agreement by the Attorney General, except as otherwise provided in the case of certain administrative settlements referred to in subsection (g) of this section, the agreement shall be entered in the appropriate United States district court as a consent decree. The President need not make any finding regarding an imminent and substantial endangerment to the public health or the environment in connection with any such agreement or consent decree.

(B) **Effect**

The entry of any consent decree under this subsection shall not be construed to be an acknowledgment by the parties that the release or threatened release concerned constitutes an imminent and substantial endangerment to the public health or welfare or the environment. Except as otherwise provided in the Federal Rules of Evidence, the participation by any party in the process under this section shall not be considered an admission of liability for any purpose, and the fact of such participation shall not be admissible in any judicial or administrative proceeding, including a subsequent proceeding under this section.

(C) **Structure**

The President may fashion a consent decree so that the entering of such decree and compliance with such decree or with any determination or agreement made pursuant to this section shall not be considered an admission of liability for any purpose.

(2) **Public participation**

(A) **Filing of proposed judgment**

At least 30 days before a final judgment is entered under paragraph (1), the proposed judgment shall be filed with the court.

(B) **Opportunity for comment**

The Attorney General shall provide an opportunity to persons who are not named as parties to the action to comment on the proposed judgment before its entry by the court as a final judgment. The Attorney General shall consider, and file with the court, any written comments, views, or allegations relating to the proposed judgment. The

Attorney General may withdraw or withhold its consent to the proposed judgment if the comments, views, and allegations concerning the judgment disclose facts or considerations which indicate that the proposed judgment is inappropriate, improper, or inadequate.

**(3) 9604(b) agreements**

Whenever the President enters into an agreement under this section with any potentially responsible party with respect to action under section 9604(b) of this title, the President shall issue an order or enter into a decree setting forth the obligations of such party. The United States district court for the district in which the release or threatened release occurs may enforce such order or decree.

**(e) Special notice procedures**

**(1) Notice**

Whenever the President determines that a period of negotiation under this subsection would facilitate an agreement with potentially responsible parties for taking response action (including any action described in section 9604(b) of this title) and would expedite remedial action, the President shall so notify all such parties and shall provide them with information concerning each of the following:

(A) The names and addresses of potentially responsible parties (including owners and operators and other persons referred to in section 9607(a) of this title), to the extent such information is available.

(B) To the extent such information is available, the volume and nature of substances contributed by each potentially responsible party identified at the facility.

(C) A ranking by volume of the substances at the facility, to the extent such information is available.

The President shall make the information referred to in this paragraph available in advance of notice under this paragraph upon the request of a potentially responsible party in accordance with procedures provided by the President. The provisions of subsection (e) of section 9604 of this title regarding protection of confidential information apply to information provided under this paragraph. Disclosure of information generated by the President under this section to persons other than the Congress, or any duly authorized Committee thereof, is subject to other privileges or protections provided by law, including (but not limited to) those applicable to attorney work product. Nothing contained in this paragraph or in other provisions of this chapter shall be construed, interpreted, or applied to diminish the required disclosure of information under other provisions of this or other Federal or State laws.

**(2) Negotiation**

**(A) Moratorium**

Except as provided in this subsection, the President may not commence action under section 9604(a) of this title or take any action under section 9606 of this title for 120 days after providing notice and information under this subsection with respect to such action. Except as provided in this subsection, the President may not commence a remedial investigation and feasibility study under section 9604(b) of this title for 90 days after providing notice and information under this subsection with respect to such action. The President may commence any additional studies or investigations authorized under section 9604(b) of this title, including remedial design, during the negotiation period.

**(B) Proposals**

Persons receiving notice and information under paragraph (1) of this subsection with respect to action under section 9606 of this title shall have 60 days from the date of receipt of such notice to make a proposal to the President for undertaking or financing the action under section 9606 of this title. Persons receiving notice and information under paragraph (1) of this subsection with respect to action under section 9604(b) of this title shall have 60 days from the date of receipt of such notice to make a proposal to the President for undertaking or financing the action under section 9604(b) of this title.

**(C) Additional parties**

If an additional potentially responsible party is identified during the negotiation period or after an agreement has been entered into under this subsection concerning a release or threatened release, the President may bring the additional party into the negotiation or enter into a separate agreement with such party.

**(3) Preliminary allocation of responsibility**

**(A) In general**

The President shall develop guidelines for preparing nonbinding preliminary allocations of responsibility. In developing these guidelines the President may include such factors as the President considers relevant, such as: volume, toxicity, mobility, strength of evidence, ability to pay, litigative risks, public interest considerations, precedential value, and inequities and aggravating factors. When it would expedite settlements under this section and remedial action, the President may, after completion of the remedial investigation and feasibility study, provide a nonbinding preliminary allocation of responsibility which allocates percentages of the total cost of response among potentially responsible parties at the facility.

(B) Collection of information

To collect information necessary or appropriate for performing the allocation under subparagraph (A) or for otherwise implementing this section, the President may by subpoena require the attendance and testimony of witnesses and the production of reports, papers, documents, answers to questions, and other information that the President deems necessary. Witnesses shall be paid the same fees and mileage that are paid witnesses in the courts of the United States. In the event of contumacy or failure or refusal of any person to obey any such subpoena, any district court of the United States in which venue is proper shall have jurisdiction to order any such person to comply with such subpoena. Any failure to obey such an order of the court is punishable by the court as a contempt thereof.

(C) Effect

The nonbinding preliminary allocation of responsibility shall not be admissible as evidence in any proceeding, and no court shall have jurisdiction to review the nonbinding preliminary allocation of responsibility. The nonbinding preliminary allocation of responsibility shall not constitute an apportionment or other statement on the divisibility of harm or causation.

(D) Costs

The costs incurred by the President in producing the nonbinding preliminary allocation of responsibility shall be reimbursed by the potentially responsible parties whose offer is accepted by the President. Where an offer under this section is not accepted, such costs shall be considered costs of response.

(E) Decision to reject offer

Where the President, in his discretion, has provided a nonbinding preliminary allocation of responsibility and the potentially responsible parties have made a substantial offer providing for response to the President which he rejects, the reasons for the rejection shall be provided in a written explanation. The President's decision to reject such an offer shall not be subject to judicial review.

(4) Failure to propose

If the President determines that a good faith proposal for undertaking or financing action under section 9606 of this title has not been submitted within 60 days of the provision of notice pursuant to this subsection, the President may thereafter commence action under section 9604(a) of this title or take an action against any person under section 9606 of this title. If the President determines that a good faith proposal for undertaking or financing action under section 9604(b) of this title has not been submitted within 60 days after the provision of notice pursuant to this subsection, the President may thereafter commence action under section 9604(b) of this title.

(5) Significant threats

Nothing in this subsection shall limit the President's authority to undertake response or enforcement action regarding a significant threat to public health or the environment within the negotiation period established by this subsection.

(6) Inconsistent response action

When either the President, or a potentially responsible party pursuant to an administrative order or consent decree under this chapter, has initiated a remedial investigation and feasibility study for a particular facility under this chapter, no potentially responsible party may undertake any remedial action at the facility unless such remedial action has been authorized by the President.

(f) Covenant not to sue

(1) Discretionary covenants

The President may, in his discretion, provide any person with a covenant not to sue concerning any liability to the United States under this chapter, including future liability, resulting from a release or threatened release of a hazardous substance addressed by a remedial action, whether that action is onsite or offsite, if each of the following conditions is met:

(A) The covenant not to sue is in the public interest.

(B) The covenant not to sue would expedite response action consistent with the National Contingency Plan under section 9605 of this title.

(C) The person is in full compliance with a consent decree under section 9606 of this title (including a consent decree entered into in accordance with this section) for response to the release or threatened release concerned.

(D) The response action has been approved by the President.

(2) Special covenants not to sue

In the case of any person to whom the President is authorized under paragraph (1) of this subsection to provide a covenant not to sue, for the portion of remedial action—

(A) which involves the transport and secure disposition offsite of hazardous substances in a facility meeting the requirements of sections 6924(c), (d), (e), (f), (g), (m), (*o*), (p), (u), and (v) and 6925(c) of this title, where the President has rejected a proposed remedial action that is consistent with the National Contingency Plan that does not include such offsite disposition and has thereafter required offsite disposition; or

(B) which involves the treatment of hazardous substances so as to destroy, eliminate, or permanently immobilize the hazardous constituents of such substances, such that, in the judgment of the President, the substances no longer present any current or currently foreseeable future significant risk to public health, welfare or the environment, no byproduct of the treatment or destruction process presents any significant hazard to public health, welfare or the environment, and all byproducts are themselves treated, destroyed, or contained in a manner which assures that such byproducts do not present any current or currently foreseeable future significant risk to public health, welfare or the environment,

the President shall provide such person with a covenant not to sue with respect to future liability to the United States under this chapter for a future release or threatened release of hazardous substances from such facility, and a person provided such covenant not to sue shall not be liable to the United States under section 9606 or 9607 of this title with respect to such release or threatened release at a future time.

#### (3) Requirement that remedial action be completed

A covenant not to sue concerning future liability to the United States shall not take effect until the President certifies that remedial action has been completed in accordance with the requirements of this chapter at the facility that is the subject of such covenant.

#### (4) Factors

In assessing the appropriateness of a covenant not to sue under paragraph (1) and any condition to be included in a covenant not to sue under paragraph (1) or (2), the President shall consider whether the covenant or condition is in the public interest on the basis of such factors as the following:

(A) The effectiveness and reliability of the remedy, in light of the other alternative remedies considered for the facility concerned.

(B) The nature of the risks remaining at the facility.

(C) The extent to which performance standards are included in the order or decree.

(D) The extent to which the response action provides a complete remedy for the facility, including a reduction in the hazardous nature of the substances at the facility.

(E) The extent to which the technology used in the response action is demonstrated to be effective.

(F) Whether the Fund or other sources of funding would be available for any additional remedial actions that might eventually be necessary at the facility.

(G) Whether the remedial action will be carried out, in whole or in significant part, by the responsible parties themselves.

#### (5) Satisfactory performance

Any covenant not to sue under this subsection shall be subject to the satisfactory performance by such party of its obligations under the agreement concerned.

#### (6) Additional condition for future liability

(A) Except for the portion of the remedial action which is subject to a covenant not to sue under paragraph (2) or under subsection (g) of this section (relating to de minimis settlements), a covenant not to sue a person concerning future liability to the United States shall include an exception to the covenant that allows the President to sue such person concerning future liability resulting from the release or threatened release that is the subject of the covenant where such liability arises out of conditions which are unknown at the time the President certifies under paragraph (3) that remedial action has been completed at the facility concerned.

(B) In extraordinary circumstances, the President may determine, after assessment of relevant factors such as those referred to in paragraph (4) and volume, toxicity, mobility, strength of evidence, ability to pay, litigative risks, public interest considerations, precedential value, and inequities and aggravating factors, not to include the exception referred to in subparagraph (A) if other terms, conditions, or requirements of the agreement containing the covenant not to sue are sufficient to provide all reasonable assurances that public health and the environment will be protected from any future releases at or from the facility.

(C) The President is authorized to include any provisions allowing future enforcement action under section 9606 or 9607 of this title that in the discretion of the President are necessary and appropriate to assure protection of public health, welfare, and the environment.

### (g) De minimis settlements

**(1) Expedited final settlement**

Whenever practicable and in the public interest, as determined by the President, the President shall as promptly as possible reach a final settlement with a potentially responsible party in an administrative or civil action under section 9606 or 9607 of this title if such settlement involves only a minor portion of the response costs at the facility concerned and, in the judgment of the President, the conditions in either of the following subparagraph (A) or (B) are met:

**(A)** Both of the following are minimal in comparison to other hazardous substances at the facility:

**(i)** The amount of the hazardous substances contributed by that party to the facility.

**(ii)** The toxic or other hazardous effects of the substances contributed by that party to the facility.

**(B)** The potentially responsible party—

**(i)** is the owner of the real property on or in which the facility is located;

**(ii)** did not conduct or permit the generation, transportation, storage, treatment, or disposal of any hazardous substance at the facility; and

**(iii)** did not contribute to the release or threat of release of a hazardous substance at the facility through any action or omission.

This subparagraph (B) does not apply if the potentially responsible party purchased the real property with actual or constructive knowledge that the property was used for the generation, transportation, storage, treatment, or disposal of any hazardous substance.

**(2) Covenant not to sue**

The President may provide a covenant not to sue with respect to the facility concerned to any party who has entered into a settlement under this subsection unless such a covenant would be inconsistent with the public interest as determined under subsection (f) of this section.

**(3) Expedited agreement**

The President shall reach any such settlement or grant any such covenant not to sue as soon as possible after the President has available the information necessary to reach such a settlement or grant such a covenant.

**(4) Consent decree or administrative order**

A settlement under this subsection shall be entered as a consent decree or embodied in an administrative order setting forth the terms of the settlement. In the case of any facility where the total response costs exceed $500,000 (excluding interest), if the settlement is embodied as an administrative order, the order may be issued only with the prior written approval of the Attorney General. If the Attorney General or his designee has not approved or disapproved the order within 30 days of this referral, the order shall be deemed to be approved unless the Attorney General and the Administrator have agreed to extend the time. The district court for the district in which the release or threatened release occurs may enforce any such administrative order.

**(5) Effect of agreement**

A party who has resolved its liability to the United States under this subsection shall not be liable for claims for contribution regarding matters addressed in the settlement. Such settlement does not discharge any of the other potentially responsible parties unless its terms so provide, but it reduces the potential liability of the others by the amount of the settlement.

**(6) Settlements with other potentially responsible parties**

Nothing in this subsection shall be construed to affect the authority of the President to reach settlements with other potentially responsible parties under this chapter.

**(7) Reduction in settlement amount based on limited ability to pay**

**(A) In general**

The condition for settlement under this paragraph is that the potentially responsible party is a person who demonstrates to the President an inability or a limited ability to pay response costs.

**(B) Considerations**

In determining whether or not a demonstration is made under subparagraph (A) by a person, the President shall take into consideration the ability of the person to pay response costs and still maintain its basic business operations, including consideration of the overall financial condition of the person and demonstrable constraints on the ability of the person to raise revenues.

**(C) Information**

A person requesting settlement under this paragraph shall promptly provide the President with all relevant information needed to determine the ability of the person to pay response costs.

**(D) Alternative payment methods**

If the President determines that a person is unable to pay its total settlement amount at the time of settlement, the President shall consider such alternative payment methods as may be necessary or appropriate.

(8) Additional conditions for expedited settlements

(A) Waiver of claims

The President shall require, as a condition for settlement under this subsection, that a potentially responsible party waive all of the claims (including a claim for contribution under this chapter) that the party may have against other potentially responsible parties for response costs incurred with respect to the facility, unless the President determines that requiring a waiver would be unjust.

(B) Failure to comply

The President may decline to offer a settlement to a potentially responsible party under this subsection if the President determines that the potentially responsible party has failed to comply with any request for access or information or an administrative subpoena issued by the President under this chapter or has impeded or is impeding, through action or inaction, the performance of a response action with respect to the facility.

(C) Responsibility to provide information and access

A potentially responsible party that enters into a settlement under this subsection shall not be relieved of the responsibility to provide any information or access requested in accordance with subsection (e)(3)(B) of this section or section 9604(e) of this title.

(9) Basis of determination

If the President determines that a potentially responsible party is not eligible for settlement under this subsection, the President shall provide the reasons for the determination in writing to the potentially responsible party that requested a settlement under this subsection.

(10) Notification

As soon as practicable after receipt of sufficient information to make a determination, the President shall notify any person that the President determines is eligible under paragraph (1) of the person's eligibility for an expedited settlement.

(11) No judicial review

A determination by the President under paragraph (7), (8), (9), or (10) shall not be subject to judicial review.

(12) Notice of settlement

After a settlement under this subsection becomes final with respect to a facility, the President shall promptly notify potentially responsible parties at the facility that have not resolved their liability to the United States of the settlement.

(h) Cost recovery settlement authority

(1) Authority to settle

The head of any department or agency with authority to undertake a response action under this chapter pursuant to the national contingency plan may consider, compromise, and settle a claim under section 9607 of this title for costs incurred by the United States Government if the claim has not been referred to the Department of Justice for further action. In the case of any facility where the total response costs exceed $500,000 (excluding interest), any claim referred to in the preceding sentence may be compromised and settled only with the prior written approval of the Attorney General.

(2) Use of arbitration

Arbitration in accordance with regulations promulgated under this subsection may be used as a method of settling claims of the United States where the total response costs for the facility concerned do not exceed $500,000 (excluding interest). After consultation with the Attorney General, the department or agency head may establish and publish regulations for the use of arbitration or settlement under this subsection.

(3) Recovery of claims

If any person fails to pay a claim that has been settled under this subsection, the department or agency head shall request the Attorney General to bring a civil action in an appropriate district court to recover the amount of such claim, plus costs, attorneys' fees, and interest from the date of the settlement. In such an action, the terms of the settlement shall not be subject to review.

(4) Claims for contribution

A person who has resolved its liability to the United States under this subsection shall not be liable for claims for contribution regarding matters addressed in the settlement. Such settlement shall not discharge any of the other potentially liable persons unless its terms so provide, but it reduces the potential liability of the others by the amount of the settlement.

(i) Settlement procedures

(1) Publication in Federal Register

At least 30 days before any settlement (including any settlement arrived at through arbitration) may become final under subsection (h) of this section, or under subsection (g) of this section in the case of a settlement embodied in an administrative order, the head of the department or agency which has jurisdiction over the proposed settlement shall publish in the Federal Register notice of the proposed settlement. The notice shall identify the facility concerned and the parties to the proposed settlement.

**(2) Comment period**

For a 30-day period beginning on the date of publication of notice under paragraph (1) of a proposed settlement, the head of the department or agency which has jurisdiction over the proposed settlement shall provide an opportunity for persons who are not parties to the proposed settlement to file written comments relating to the proposed settlement.

**(3) Consideration of comments**

The head of the department or agency shall consider any comments filed under paragraph (2) in determining whether or not to consent to the proposed settlement and may withdraw or withhold consent to the proposed settlement if such comments disclose facts or considerations which indicate the proposed settlement is inappropriate, improper, or inadequate.

**(j) Natural resources**

**(1) Notification of trustee**

Where a release or threatened release of any hazardous substance that is the subject of negotiations under this section may have resulted in damages to natural resources under the trusteeship of the United States, the President shall notify the Federal natural resource trustee of the negotiations and shall encourage the participation of such trustee in the negotiations.

**(2) Covenant not to sue**

An agreement under this section may contain a covenant not to sue under section 9607(a)(4)(C) of this title for damages to natural resources under the trusteeship of the United States resulting from the release or threatened release of hazardous substances that is the subject of the agreement, but only if the Federal natural resource trustee has agreed in writing to such covenant. The Federal natural resource trustee may agree to such covenant if the potentially responsible party agrees to undertake appropriate actions necessary to protect and restore the natural resources damaged by such release or threatened release of hazardous substances.

**(k) Section not applicable to vessels**

The provisions of this section shall not apply to releases from a vessel.

**(*l*) Civil penalties**

A potentially responsible party which is a party to an administrative order or consent decree entered pursuant to an agreement under this section or section 9620 of this title (relating to Federal facilities) or which is a party to an agreement under section 9620 of this title and which fails or refuses to comply with any term or condition of the order, decree or agreement shall be subject to a civil penalty in accordance with section 9609 of this title.

**(m) Applicability of general principles of law**

In the case of consent decrees and other settlements under this section (including covenants not to sue), no provision of this chapter shall be construed to preclude or otherwise affect the applicability of general principles of law regarding the setting aside or modification of consent decrees or other settlements.

(Pub.L. 96–510, Title I, § 122, as added Pub.L. 99–499, Title I, § 122(a), Oct. 17, 1986, 100 Stat. 1678, and amended Pub.L. 107–118, Title I, § 102(b), Jan. 11, 2002, 115 Stat. 2359.)

## HISTORICAL AND STATUTORY NOTES

**References in Text**

The Federal Rules of Evidence, referred to in subsec. (d)(1)(B), are set out in the Appendix to Title 28, Judiciary and Judicial Procedure.

"This chapter", referred to in text, originally read "this Act", meaning Pub.L. 96–510, Dec. 11, 1980, 94 Stat. 2767, as amended, known as the Comprehensive Environmental Response, Compensation, and Liability Act of 1980, which is classified principally to this chapter [42 U.S.C.A. § 9601 et seq.]; see Tables for complete classification.

**Effective and Applicability Provisions**

1986 Acts

Section effective Oct. 17, 1986, see section 4 of Pub.L. 99–499, set out as a note under section 9601 of this title.

**Effect on Concluded Actions**

Amendments made by Pub.L. 107–118, Title I, § 101 et seq., Jan. 11, 2002, 115 Stat. 2356 to subsec. (g)(7) to (12) of this section not applicable to and shall not in any way affect any settlement lodged in, or judgment issued by, a United States District Court, or any administrative settlement or order entered into or issued by the United States or any State, before Jan. 11, 20002, see Pub.L. 107–118, Title I, § 103, Jan. 11, 2002, 115 Stat. 2360, set out as a note under 42 U.S.C.A. § 9607.

**Delegation of Functions**

Functions vested in the President by subsec. (e)(3)(A) of this section, relating to development of regulations and guidelines, delegated to the Administrator of the Environmental Protection Agency, to be exercised in consultation with the Attorney General, see section 4(a) of Ex. Ord. No. 12580, Jan. 23, 1987, 52 F.R. 2923, set out as a note under section 9615 of this title.

Functions vested in the President by this section, except for subsec. (b)(1), and subject to the delegation of functions by section 4(a) of Ex. Ord. No. 12580 (delegating functions vested in the President by subsec. (e)(3)(A) of this section), delegated, with authority to redelegate, to the heads of Executive departments and agencies, with respect to releases or threatened releases not on the National Priorities List where either the release is on or the sole source of the release is from any facility under the jurisdiction, custody or control of those Executive departments and agencies, with such functions to be exercised only with the concurrence of the Attorney General, see sections 4(b)(1) and 11(g) of Ex. Ord. No. 12580, Jan. 23, 1987, 52 F.R. 2923, set out as a note under section 9615 of this title.

For delegation of functions vested in the President by provisions of section 9609 of this title relating to violations of this section, with authority to redelegate, see sections 4(b)(2), (c)(2), (d)(2), and 11(g) of Ex. Ord. No. 12580, Jan. 23, 1987, 52 F.R. 2923, set out as a note under section 9615 of this title.

Functions vested in the President by this section delegated, subject to section 4(a), (b)(1) of Ex. Ord. No. 12580, and with authority to redelegate, to the Coast Guard with respect to any release or threatened release involving the coastal zone, Great Lakes waters, ports, and harbors, see sections 4(c)(1), 11(g) of Ex. Ord. No. 12580, Jan. 23, 1987, 52 F.R. 2923, set out as a note under section 9615 of this title.

Functions vested in the President by this section delegated, subject to section 4(a), (b)(1) and (c)(1) of Ex. Ord. No. 12580, and with authority to redelegate, to the Administrator of the Environmental Protection Agency, see sections 4(d)(1), 11(g) of Ex. Ord. No. 12580, Jan. 23, 1987, 52 F.R. 2923, set out as a note under section 9615 of this title.

Functions vested in the President by this section, except subsec. (b)(1), delegated, subject to section 4(a), (b)(1), of Ex. Ord. No. 12580, to the Secretary of the Interior, the Secretary of Commerce, the Secretary of Agriculture, the Secretary of Defense, and the Secretary of Energy, to be exercised only with the concurrence of the Coast Guard, with respect to any release or threatened release in the coastal zone, Great Lakes waters, ports, and harbors, affecting (1) natural resources under their trusteeship, or (2) a vessel or facility subject to their custody, jurisdiction, or control, and with other exceptions and stipulations, see section 4(c)(3) of Ex. Ord. No. 12580, Jan. 23, 1987, 52 F.R. 2923, as amended, set out as a note under section 9615 of this title.

Functions vested in the President by this section, except subsec. (b)(1), delegated, subject to section 4(a), (b),and (c)(1) of Ex. Ord. No. 12580, to the Secretary of the Interior, the Secretary of Commerce, the Secretary of Agriculture, the Secretary of Defense, and the Department of Energy, to be exercised only with the concurrence of the Administrator, with respect to any release or threatened release affecting (1) natural resources under their trusteeship, or (2) a vessel or facility subject to their custody, jurisdiction, or control, and with other exceptions and stipulations, see section 4(d)(3) of Ex. Ord. No. 12580, Jan. 23, 1987, 52 F.R. 2923, as amended, set out as a note under section 9615 of this title.

#### Coordination of Titles I to IV of Pub.L. 99–499

Any provision of Titles I to IV of Pub.L. 99–499, imposing any tax, premium, or fee; establishing any trust fund; or authorizing expenditures from any trust fund, to have no force or effect, see section 531 of Pub.L. 99–499, set out as a note under section 1 of Title 26, Internal Revenue Code.

## § 9623. Reimbursement to local governments

### [CERCLA § 123]

### (a) Application

Any general purpose unit of local government for a political subdivision which is affected by a release or threatened release at any facility may apply to the President for reimbursement under this section.

### (b) Reimbursement

#### (1) Temporary emergency measures

The President is authorized to reimburse local community authorities for expenses incurred (before or after October 17, 1986) in carrying out temporary emergency measures necessary to prevent or mitigate injury to human health or the environment associated with the release or threatened release of any hazardous substance or pollutant or contaminant. Such measures may include, where appropriate, security fencing to limit access, response to fires and explosions, and other measures which require immediate response at the local level.

#### (2) Local funds not supplanted

Reimbursement under this section shall not supplant local funds normally provided for response.

### (c) Amount

The amount of any reimbursement to any local authority under subsection (b)(1) of this section may not exceed $25,000 for a single response. The reimbursement under this section with respect to a single facility shall be limited to the units of local government having jurisdiction over the political subdivision in which the facility is located.

### (d) Procedure

Reimbursements authorized pursuant to this section shall be in accordance with rules promulgated by the Administrator within one year after October 17, 1986.

(Pub.L. 96–510, Title I, § 123, as added Pub.L. 99–499, Title I, § 123(a), Oct. 17, 1986, 100 Stat. 1688.)

### HISTORICAL AND STATUTORY NOTES

#### Effective Dates

1986 Acts

Section effective Oct. 17, 1986, see section 4 of Pub.L. 99–499, set out as a note under section 9601 of this title.

#### Delegation of Functions

Functions vested in the President by this section delegated to the Administrator of the Environmental Protection Agency, see section 9(h) of Ex. Ord. No. 12580, Jan. 23, 1987, 52 F.R. 2923, set out as a note under section 9615 of this title.

## § 9624. Methane recovery

[CERCLA § 124]

### (a) In general

In the case of a facility at which equipment for the recovery or processing (including recirculation of condensate) of methane has been installed, for purposes of this chapter:

(1) The owner or operator of such equipment shall not be considered an "owner or operator", as defined in section 9601(20) of this title, with respect to such facility.

(2) The owner or operator of such equipment shall not be considered to have arranged for disposal or treatment of any hazardous substance at such facility pursuant to section 9607 of this title.

(3) The owner or operator of such equipment shall not be subject to any action under section 9606 of this title with respect to such facility.

### (b) Exceptions

Subsection (a) of this section does not apply with respect to a release or threatened release of a hazardous substance from a facility described in subsection (a) of this section if either of the following circumstances exist:

(1) The release or threatened release was primarily caused by activities of the owner or operator of the equipment described in subsection (a) of this section.

(2) The owner or operator of such equipment would be covered by paragraph (1), (2), (3), or (4) of subsection (a) of section 9607 of this title with respect to such release or threatened release if he were not the owner or operator of such equipment.

In the case of any release or threatened release referred to in paragraph (1), the owner or operator of the equipment described in subsection (a) of this section shall be liable under this chapter only for costs or damages primarily caused by the activities of such owner or operator.

(Pub.L. 96–510, Title I, § 124, as added Pub.L. 99–499, Title I, § 124(a), Oct. 17, 1986, 100 Stat. 1688.)

#### HISTORICAL AND STATUTORY NOTES

**Effective Dates**

1986 Acts

Section effective Oct. 17, 1986, see section 4 of Pub.L. 99–499, set out as a note under section 9601 of this title.

## § 9625. Section 6921(b)(3)(A)(i) waste

[CERCLA § 125]

### (a) Revision of hazard ranking system

This section shall apply only to facilities which are not included or proposed for inclusion on the National Priorities List and which contain substantial volumes of waste described in section 6921(b)(3)(A)(i) of this title. As expeditiously as practicable, the President shall revise the hazard ranking system in effect under the National Contingency Plan with respect to such facilities in a manner which assures appropriate consideration of each of the following site-specific characteristics of such facilities:

(1) The quantity, toxicity, and concentrations of hazardous constituents which are present in such waste and a comparison thereof with other wastes.

(2) The extent of, and potential for, release of such hazardous constituents into the environment.

(3) The degree of risk to human health and the environment posed by such constituents.

### (b) Inclusion prohibited

Until the hazard ranking system is revised as required by this section, the President may not include on the National Priorities List any facility which contains substantial volumes of waste described in section 6921(b)(3)(A)(i) of this title on the basis of an evaluation made principally on the volume of such waste and not on the concentrations of the hazardous constituents of such waste. Nothing in this section shall be construed to affect the President's authority to include any such facility on the National Priorities List based on the presence of other substances at such facility or to exercise any other authority of this chapter with respect to such other substances.

(Pub.L. 96–510, Title I, § 125, as added Pub.L. 99–499, Title I, § 125, Oct. 17, 1986, 100 Stat. 1689.)

#### HISTORICAL AND STATUTORY NOTES

**Effective Date**

1986 Acts

Section effective Oct. 17, 1986, see section 4 of Pub.L. 99–499, set out as a note under section 9601 of this title.

**Delegation of Functions**

Responsibility for the revision of the National Contingency Plan, and all other functions vested in the President by this section, delegated to the Administrator of the Environmental Protection Agency, see section 1(b)(1) of Ex. Ord. No. 12580, Jan. 23, 1987, 52 F.R. 2923, set out as a note under section 9615 of this title.

## § 9626. Indian tribes

[CERCLA § 126]

### (a) Treatment generally

The governing body of an Indian tribe shall be afforded substantially the same treatment as a State with respect to the provisions of section 9603(a) of this title (regarding notification of releases), section 9604(c)(2) of this title (regarding consultation on remedial actions), section 9604(e) of this title (regarding access to information), section 9604(i) of this title (regarding health authorities) and section 9605 of this title (regarding roles and responsibilities under the national contingency plan and submittal of priorities for remedial action, but not including the provision regarding the inclusion of at least one facility per State on the National Priorities List).

**(b) Community relocation**

Should the President determine that proper remedial action is the permanent relocation of tribal members away from a contaminated site because it is cost effective and necessary to protect their health and welfare, such finding must be concurred in by the affected tribal government before relocation shall occur. The President, in cooperation with the Secretary of the Interior, shall also assure that all benefits of the relocation program are provided to the affected tribe and that alternative land of equivalent value is available and satisfactory to the tribe. Any lands acquired for relocation of tribal members shall be held in trust by the United States for the benefit of the tribe.

**(c) Study**

The President shall conduct a survey, in consultation with the Indian tribes, to determine the extent of hazardous waste sites on Indian lands. Such survey shall be included within a report which shall make recommendations on the program needs of tribes under this chapter, with particular emphasis on how tribal participation in the administration of such programs can be maximized. Such report shall be submitted to Congress along with the President's budget request for fiscal year 1988.

**(d) Limitation**

Notwithstanding any other provision of this chapter, no action under this chapter by an Indian tribe shall be barred until the later of the following:

(1) The applicable period of limitations has expired.

(2) 2 years after the United States, in its capacity as trustee for the tribe, gives written notice to the governing body of the tribe that it will not present a claim or commence an action on behalf of the tribe or fails to present a claim or commence an action within the time limitations specified in this chapter.

(Pub.L. 96–510, Title I, § 126, as added Pub.L. 99–499, Title II, § 207(e), Oct. 17, 1986, 100 Stat. 1706.)

## HISTORICAL AND STATUTORY NOTES

**Effective Dates**

1986 Acts

Section effective Oct. 17, 1986, see section 4 of Pub.L. 99–499, set out as a note under section 9601 of this title.

**Delegation of Functions**

Functions vested in the President by the second sentence of subsec. (b) of this section, to the extent they require permanent relocation of residents, businesses, and community facilities or temporary evacuation and housing of threatened individuals not otherwise provided for, delegated to the Director of the Federal Emergency Management Agency, with authority to redelegate, see sections 2(c)(1), 11(g) of Ex. Ord. No. 12580, Jan. 23, 1987, 52 F.R. 2923, set out as a note under section 9615 of this title. Functions vested in the President by sections 9617(a), (c) and section 9619 of this title, to the extent such authority is needed to carry out the delegation of functions by section 2(c)(1) of Ex. Ord. No. 12580 (and subject to delegation of certain rulemaking authority to the Administrator of the Environmental Protection Agency), delegated to the Director, with authority to redelegate, see sections 2(b), (c)(2), 11(g) of Ex. Ord. No. 12580.

Functions vested in the President by subsec. (b) of this section, subject to section 2(a) to (f) of Ex. Ord. No. 12580, delegated, with authority to redelegate, to the Administrator of the Environmental Protection Agency, see sections 2(g), 11(g) of Ex. Ord. No. 12580, Jan. 23, 1987, 52 F.R. 2923, set out as a note under section 9615 of this title.

Functions vested in the President by subsec. (c) of this section delegated to the Administrator of the Environmental Protection Agency, to be exercised in consultation with the Secretary of the Interior, see section 11(c) of Ex. Ord. No. 12580, Jan. 23, 1987, 52 F.R. 2923, set out as a note under section 9615 of this title.

# § 9627. Recycling transactions

**[CERCLA § 127]**

**(a) Liability clarification**

(1) As provided in subsections (b), (c), (d), and (e) of this section, a person who arranged for recycling of recyclable material shall not be liable under sections 9607(a)(3) and 9607(a)(4) of this title with respect to such material.

(2) A determination whether or not any person shall be liable under section 9607(a)(3) of this title or section 9607(a)(4) of this title for any material that is not a recyclable material as that term is used in subsections (b) and (c), (d), or (e) of this section shall be made, without regard to subsections [1] (b), (c), (d), or (e) of this section.

**(b) Recyclable material defined**

For purposes of this section, the term "recyclable material" means scrap paper, scrap plastic, scrap glass, scrap textiles, scrap rubber (other than whole tires), scrap metal, or spent lead-acid, spent nickel-cadmium, and other spent batteries, as well as minor amounts of material incident to or adhering to the scrap material as a result of its normal and customary use prior to becoming scrap; except that such term shall not include—

(1) shipping containers of a capacity from 30 liters to 3,000 liters, whether intact or not, having any hazardous substance (but not metal bits and

pieces or hazardous substance that form an integral part of the container) contained in or adhering thereto; or

(2) any item of material that contained polychlorinated biphenyls at a concentration in excess of 50 parts per million or any new standard promulgated pursuant to applicable Federal laws.

**(c) Transactions involving scrap paper, plastic, glass, textiles, or rubber**

Transactions involving scrap paper, scrap plastic, scrap glass, scrap textiles, or scrap rubber (other than whole tires) shall be deemed to be arranging for recycling if the person who arranged for the transaction (by selling recyclable material or otherwise arranging for the recycling of recyclable material) can demonstrate by a preponderance of the evidence that all of the following criteria were met at the time of the transaction:

(1) The recyclable material met a commercial specification grade.

(2) A market existed for the recyclable material.

(3) A substantial portion of the recyclable material was made available for use as feedstock for the manufacture of a new saleable product.

(4) The recyclable material could have been a replacement or substitute for a virgin raw material, or the product to be made from the recyclable material could have been a replacement or substitute for a product made, in whole or in part, from a virgin raw material.

(5) For transactions occurring 90 days or more after November 29, 1999, the person exercised reasonable care to determine that the facility where the recyclable material was handled, processed, reclaimed, or otherwise managed by another person (hereinafter in this section referred to as a "consuming facility") was in compliance with substantive (not procedural or administrative) provisions of any Federal, State, or local environmental law or regulation, or compliance order or decree issued pursuant thereto, applicable to the handling, processing, reclamation, storage, or other management activities associated with recyclable material.

(6) For purposes of this subsection, "reasonable care" shall be determined using criteria that include (but are not limited to)—

(A) the price paid in the recycling transaction;

(B) the ability of the person to detect the nature of the consuming facility's operations concerning its handling, processing, reclamation, or other management activities associated with recyclable material; and

(C) the result of inquiries made to the appropriate Federal, State, or local environmental agency (or agencies) regarding the consuming facility's past and current compliance with substantive (not procedural or administrative) provisions of any Federal, State, or local environmental law or regulation, or compliance order or decree issued pursuant thereto, applicable to the handling, processing, reclamation, storage, or other management activities associated with the recyclable material. For the purposes of this paragraph, a requirement to obtain a permit applicable to the handling, processing, reclamation, or other management activity associated with the recyclable materials shall be deemed to be a substantive provision.

**(d) Transactions involving scrap metal**

(1) Transactions involving scrap metal shall be deemed to be arranging for recycling if the person who arranged for the transaction (by selling recyclable material or otherwise arranging for the recycling of recyclable material) can demonstrate by a preponderance of the evidence that at the time of the transaction—

(A) the person met the criteria set forth in subsection (c) of this section with respect to the scrap metal;

(B) the person was in compliance with any applicable regulations or standards regarding the storage, transport, management, or other activities associated with the recycling of scrap metal that the Administrator promulgates under the Solid Waste Disposal Act [42 U.S.C.A. § 6901 et seq.] subsequent to November 29, 1999, and with regard to transactions occurring after the effective date of such regulations or standards; and

(C) the person did not melt the scrap metal prior to the transaction.

(2) For purposes of paragraph (1)(C), melting of scrap metal does not include the thermal separation of 2 or more materials due to differences in their melting points (referred to as "sweating").

(3) For purposes of this subsection, the term "scrap metal" means bits and pieces of metal parts (e.g., bars, turnings, rods, sheets, wire) or metal pieces that may be combined together with bolts or soldering (e.g., radiators, scrap automobiles, railroad box cars), which when worn or superfluous can be recycled, except for scrap metals that the Administrator excludes from this definition by regulation.

**(e) Transactions involving batteries**

Transactions involving spent lead-acid batteries, spent nickel-cadmium batteries, or other spent batteries shall be deemed to be arranging for recycling if the person who arranged for the transaction (by selling recyclable material or otherwise arranging for the recycling of recyclable material) can demonstrate by a preponderance of the evidence that at the time of the transaction—

(1) the person met the criteria set forth in subsection (c) of this section with respect to the spent lead-acid batteries, spent nickel-cadmium batteries, or other spent batteries, but the person did not recover the valuable components of such batteries; and

(2)(A) with respect to transactions involving lead-acid batteries, the person was in compliance with applicable Federal environmental regulations or standards, and any amendments thereto, regarding the storage, transport, management, or other activities associated with the recycling of spent lead-acid batteries;

(B) with respect to transactions involving nickel-cadmium batteries, Federal environmental regulations or standards are in effect regarding the storage, transport, management, or other activities associated with the recycling of spent nickel-cadmium batteries, and the person was in compliance with applicable regulations or standards or any amendments thereto; or

(C) with respect to transactions involving other spent batteries, Federal environmental regulations or standards are in effect regarding the storage, transport, management, or other activities associated with the recycling of such batteries, and the person was in compliance with applicable regulations or standards or any amendments thereto.

**(f) Exclusions**

(1) The exemptions set forth in subsections (c), (d), and (e) of this section shall not apply if—

(A) the person had an objectively reasonable basis to believe at the time of the recycling transaction—

(i) that the recyclable material would not be recycled;

(ii) that the recyclable material would be burned as fuel, or for energy recovery or incineration; or

(iii) for transactions occurring before 90 days after November 29, 1999, that the consuming facility was not in compliance with a substantive (not procedural or administrative) provision of any Federal, State, or local environmental law or regulation, or compliance order or decree issued pursuant thereto, applicable to the handling, processing, reclamation, or other management activities associated with the recyclable material;

(B) the person had reason to believe that hazardous substances had been added to the recyclable material for purposes other than processing for recycling; or

(C) the person failed to exercise reasonable care with respect to the management and handling of the recyclable material (including adhering to customary industry practices current at the time of the recycling transaction designed to minimize, through source control, contamination of the recyclable material by hazardous substances).

(2) For purposes of this subsection, an objectively reasonable basis for belief shall be determined using criteria that include (but are not limited to) the size of the person's business, customary industry practices (including customary industry practices current at the time of the recycling transaction designed to minimize, through source control, contamination of the recyclable material by hazardous substances), the price paid in the recycling transaction, and the ability of the person to detect the nature of the consuming facility's operations concerning its handling, processing, reclamation, or other management activities associated with the recyclable material.

(3) For purposes of this subsection, a requirement to obtain a permit applicable to the handling, processing, reclamation, or other management activities associated with recyclable material shall be deemed to be a substantive provision.

**(g) Effect on other liability**

Nothing in this section shall be deemed to affect the liability of a person under paragraph (1) or (2) of section 9607(a) of this title.

**(h) Regulations**

The Administrator has the authority, under section 9615 of this title, to promulgate additional regulations concerning this section.

**(i) Effect on pending or concluded actions**

The exemptions provided in this section shall not affect any concluded judicial or administrative action or any pending judicial action initiated by the United States prior to November 29, 1999.

**(j) Liability for attorney's fees for certain actions**

Any person who commences an action in contribution against a person who is not liable by operation of this section shall be liable to that person for all reasonable costs of defending that action, including all reasonable attorney's and expert witness fees.

**(k) Relationship to liability under other laws**

Nothing in this section shall affect—

(1) liability under any other Federal, State, or local statute or regulation promulgated pursuant to any such statute, including any requirements promulgated by the Administrator under the Solid Waste Disposal Act [42 U.S.C.A. § 6901 et seq.]; or

(2) the ability of the Administrator to promulgate regulations under any other statute, including the Solid Waste Disposal Act.

(*l*) **Limitation on statutory construction**

Nothing in this section shall be construed to—

(1) affect any defenses or liabilities of any person to whom subsection (a)(1) of this section does not apply; or

(2) create any presumption of liability against any person to whom subsection (a)(1) of this section does not apply.

(Pub.L. 96–510, Title I, § 127, as added Pub.L. 106–113, Div. B, § 1000(a)(9) [Title VI, § 6001(b)(1)], Nov. 29, 1999, 113 Stat. 1536, 1501A–599.)

1 So in original. Probably should be "subsection".

### HISTORICAL AND STATUTORY NOTES

**References in Text**

November 29, 1999, referred to in subsecs. (c)(5), (f)(1)(A), in the original read "the date of enactment of this section" and "the date of the enactment of this section", respectively, meaning the date of approval of Pub.L. 106–113, 113 Stat. 1501, which in Div. B, § 1000(a)(9), enacted into law S. 1948, which, among other changes, enacted this section.

Subsequent to the enactment of this section, referred to in subsec. (d)(1)(B), means after Nov. 29, 1999, which is the date of approval of Pub.L. 106–113, Div. B, § 1000(a)(9) [S. 1948], which, among other changes, enacted this section.

Prior to enactment of this section, referred to in subsec. (i), means prior to Nov. 29, 1999, which is the date of approval of Pub.L. 106–113, Div. B, § 1000(a)(9) [S. 1948], which, among other changes, enacted this section.

**Superfund Recycling Equity**

Pub.L. 106–113, Div. B, § 1000(a)(9) [Title VI, § 6001(a)], Nov. 29, 1999, 113 Stat. 1536, 1501A–599, provided that: "The purposes of this section [enacting this section and this note] are—

"(1) to promote the reuse and recycling of scrap material in furtherance of the goals of waste minimization and natural resource conservation while protecting human health and the environment;

"(2) to create greater equity in the statutory treatment of recycled versus virgin materials; and

"(3) to remove the disincentives and impediments to recycling created as an unintended consequence of the 1980 Superfund liability provisions [probably refers to the Comprehensive Environmental Response, Compensation, and Liability Act of 1980 [42 U.S.C.A. § 9601 et seq.], which is classified to this chapter]."

## § 9628. State response programs

[CERCLA § 128]

(a) **Assistance to States**

(1) **In general**

(A) **States**

The Administrator may award a grant to a State or Indian tribe that—

(i) has a response program that includes each of the elements, or is taking reasonable steps to include each of the elements, listed in paragraph (2); or

(ii) is a party to a memorandum of agreement with the Administrator for voluntary response programs.

(B) **Use of grants by States**

(i) **In general**

A State or Indian tribe may use a grant under this subsection to establish or enhance the response program of the State or Indian tribe.

(ii) **Additional uses**

In addition to the uses under clause (i), a State or Indian tribe may use a grant under this subsection to—

(I) capitalize a revolving loan fund for brownfield remediation under section 9604(k)(3) of this title; or

(II) purchase insurance or develop a risk sharing pool, an indemnity pool, or insurance mechanism to provide financing for response actions under a State response program.

(2) **Elements**

The elements of a State or Indian tribe response program referred to in paragraph (1)(A)(i) are the following:

(A) Timely survey and inventory of brownfield sites in the State.

(B) Oversight and enforcement authorities or other mechanisms, and resources, that are adequate to ensure that—

(i) a response action will—

(I) protect human health and the environment; and

(II) be conducted in accordance with applicable Federal and State law; and

(ii) if the person conducting the response action fails to complete the necessary response activities, including operation and maintenance or long-term monitoring activities, the necessary response activities are completed.

(C) Mechanisms and resources to provide meaningful opportunities for public participation, including—

(i) public access to documents that the State, Indian tribe, or party conducting the cleanup is relying on or developing in making cleanup decisions or conducting site activities;

(ii) prior notice and opportunity for comment on proposed cleanup plans and site activities; and

(iii) a mechanism by which—

(I) a person that is or may be affected by a release or threatened release of a hazardous substance, pollutant, or contaminant at a brownfield site located in the community in which the person works or resides may request the conduct of a site assessment; and

(II) an appropriate State official shall consider and appropriately respond to a request under subclause (I).

(D) Mechanisms for approval of a cleanup plan, and a requirement for verification by and certification or similar documentation from the State, an Indian tribe, or a licensed site professional to the person conducting a response action indicating that the response is complete.

**(3) Funding**

There is authorized to be appropriated to carry out this subsection $50,000,000 for each of fiscal years 2002 through 2006.

**(b) Enforcement in cases of a release subject to State program**

**(1) Enforcement**

**(A) In general**

Except as provided in subparagraph (B) and subject to subparagraph (C), in the case of an eligible response site at which—

(i) there is a release or threatened release of a hazardous substance, pollutant, or contaminant; and

(ii) a person is conducting or has completed a response action regarding the specific release that is addressed by the response action that is in compliance with the State program that specifically governs response actions for the protection of public health and the environment,

the President may not use authority under this chapter to take an administrative or judicial enforcement action under section 9606(a) of this title or to take a judicial enforcement action to recover response costs under section 9607(a) of this title against the person regarding the specific release that is addressed by the response action.

**(B) Exceptions**

The President may bring an administrative or judicial enforcement action under this chapter during or after completion of a response action described in subparagraph (A) with respect to a release or threatened release at an eligible response site described in that subparagraph if—

(i) the State requests that the President provide assistance in the performance of a response action;

(ii) the Administrator determines that contamination has migrated or will migrate across a State line, resulting in the need for further response action to protect human health or the environment, or the President determines that contamination has migrated or is likely to migrate onto property subject to the jurisdiction, custody, or control of a department, agency, or instrumentality of the United States and may impact the authorized purposes of the Federal property;

(iii) after taking into consideration the response activities already taken, the Administrator determines that—

(I) a release or threatened release may present an imminent and substantial endangerment to public health or welfare or the environment; and

(II) additional response actions are likely to be necessary to address, prevent, limit, or mitigate the release or threatened release; or

(iv) the Administrator, after consultation with the State, determines that information, that on the earlier of the date on which cleanup was approved or completed, was not known by the State, as recorded in documents prepared or relied on in selecting or conducting the cleanup, has been discovered regarding the contamination or conditions at a facility such that the contamination or conditions at the facility present a threat requiring further remediation to protect public health or welfare or the environment. Consultation with the State shall not limit the ability of the Administrator to make this determination.

**(C) Public record**

The limitations on the authority of the President under subparagraph (A) apply only at sites in States that maintain, update not less than annually, and make available to the public a record of sites, by name and location, at which response actions have been completed in the previous year and are planned to be addressed under the State program that specifically governs response actions for the protection of public health and the environment in the upcoming year. The public record shall identify whether or not the site, on completion of the response action, will be suitable for unrestricted use and, if not, shall identify the institutional controls relied on in the remedy. Each State and tribe receiving financial assistance under subsection (a) of this section shall maintain and make available to the public a record of sites as provided in this paragraph.

(D) **Epa notification**

(i) **In general**

In the case of an eligible response site at which there is a release or threatened release of a hazardous substance, pollutant, or contaminant and for which the Administrator intends to carry out an action that may be barred under subparagraph (A), the Administrator shall—

(I) notify the State of the action the Administrator intends to take; and

(II)(aa) wait 48 hours for a reply from the State under clause (ii); or

(bb) if the State fails to reply to the notification or if the Administrator makes a determination under clause (iii), take immediate action under that clause.

(ii) **State reply**

Not later than 48 hours after a State receives notice from the Administrator under clause (i), the State shall notify the Administrator if—

(I) the release at the eligible response site is or has been subject to a cleanup conducted under a State program; and

(II) the State is planning to abate the release or threatened release, any actions that are planned.

(iii) **Immediate Federal action**

The Administrator may take action immediately after giving notification under clause (i) without waiting for a State reply under clause (ii) if the Administrator determines that one or more exceptions under subparagraph (B) are met.

(E) **Report to Congress**

Not later than 90 days after the date of initiation of any enforcement action by the President under clause (ii), (iii), or (iv) of subparagraph (B), the President shall submit to Congress a report describing the basis for the enforcement action, including specific references to the facts demonstrating that enforcement action is permitted under subparagraph (B).

(2) **Savings provision**

(A) **Costs incurred prior to limitations**

Nothing in paragraph (1) precludes the President from seeking to recover costs incurred prior to the date of the enactment of this section or during a period in which the limitations of paragraph (1)(A) were not applicable.

(B) **Effect on agreements between States and EPA**

Nothing in paragraph (1)—

(i) modifies or otherwise affects a memorandum of agreement, memorandum of understanding, or any similar agreement relating to this chapter between a State agency or an Indian tribe and the Administrator that is in effect on or before the date of the enactment of this section (which agreement shall remain in effect, subject to the terms of the agreement); or

(ii) limits the discretionary authority of the President to enter into or modify an agreement with a State, an Indian tribe, or any other person relating to the implementation by the President of statutory authorities.

(3) **Effective date**

This subsection applies only to response actions conducted after February 15, 2001.

(c) **Effect on Federal laws**

Nothing in this section affects any liability or response authority under any Federal law, including—

(1) this chapter, except as provided in subsection (b) of this section;

(2) the Solid Waste Disposal Act (42 U.S.C. 6901 et seq.);

(3) the Federal Water Pollution Control Act (33 U.S.C. 1251 et seq.);

(4) the Toxic Substances Control Act (15 U.S.C. 2601 et seq.); and

(5) the Safe Drinking Water Act (42 U.S.C. 300f et seq.).

(Pub.L. 96–510, Title I, § 128, as added Pub.L. 107–118, Title II, § 231(b), Jan. 11, 2002, 115 Stat. 2375.)

## HISTORICAL AND STATUTORY NOTES

**References in Text**

"This chapter", referred to in subsecs. (b)(1)(A), (B) and (2)(B)(i), and (c)(1) originally read "this Act", meaning Pub.L. 96–510, Dec. 11, 1980, 94 Stat. 2767, as amended, known as the Comprehensive Environmental Response, Compensation, and Liability Act of 1980, which is classified principally to this chapter [42 U.S.C.A. § 9601 et seq.]; see Tables for complete classification.

The date of the enactment of this section, referred to in subsec. (b)(2)(A), probably means Jan. 11, 2002, the approval date of Pub.L. 107–118, 115 Stat. 2375, which enacted this section.

The Solid Waste Disposal Act, referred to in subsec. (c)(2), is Title II of Pub.L. 89–272, Oct. 20, 1965, 79 Stat. 997, as amended generally by Pub.L. 94–580, § 2, Oct. 21, 1976, 90 Stat. 2795, which is classified principally to chapter 82 of this title [42 U.S.C.A. § 6901 et seq.]. See Tables for complete classification.

The Federal Water Pollution Control Act, referred to in subsec. (c)(3), is Act June 30, 1948, c. 758, as amended generally by Pub.L. 92–500, § 2, Oct. 18, 1972, 86 Stat. 816, also known as the Clean Water Act, which is classified principally to chapter 26 of Title 33 [33 U.S.C.A. § 1251 et seq.]. See Tables for complete classification.

The Toxic Substances Control Act, referred to in subsec. (c)(4), is Pub.L. 94–469, Oct. 11, 1976, 90 Stat. 2003, as amended, which is classified principally to chapter 53 of Title 15 [15 U.S.C.A. § 2601 et seq.]. See Tables for complete classification.

The Safe Drinking Water Act, referred to in subsec. (c)(5), is Pub.L. 93–523, Dec. 16, 1974, 88 Stat. 1660, as amended, which is classified principally to subchapter XII of chapter 6A of this title [42 U.S.C.A. § 300f et seq.]. See Tables for complete classification.

## SUBCHAPTER II—HAZARDOUS SUBSTANCE RESPONSE REVENUE

### PART A—HAZARDOUS SUBSTANCE RESPONSE TRUST FUND

### §§ 9631 to 9633. Repealed. Pub.L. 99–499, Title V, § 517(c)(1), Oct. 17, 1986, 100 Stat. 1774

#### HISTORICAL AND STATUTORY NOTES

Section 9631, Pub.L. 96–510, Title II, § 221, Dec. 11, 1980, 94 Stat. 2801; Pub.L. 99–499, Title II, § 204, Oct. 17, 1986, 100 Stat. 1696, provided for establishment of a "Hazardous Substances Superfund", so redesignated by Pub.L. 99–499, § 204. See section 9507 of Title 26, Internal Revenue Code.

Section 9632, Pub.L. 96–510, Title II, § 222, Dec. 11, 1980, 94 Stat. 2802, limited liability of United States to amount in Trust Fund.

Section 9633, Pub.L. 96–510, Title II, § 223, Dec. 11, 1980, 94 Stat. 2802, prescribed administrative provisions.

**Effective Date of Repeal**

Sections repealed effective Jan. 1, 1987, see section 517(e) of Pub.L. 99–499, set out as an Effective Dates of 1986 Acts note under section 9507 of Title 26, Internal Revenue Code.

### PART B—POST-CLOSURE LIABILITY TRUST FUND

### § 9641. Repealed. Pub.L. 99–499, Title V, § 514(b), Oct. 17, 1986, 100 Stat. 1767

#### HISTORICAL AND STATUTORY NOTES

Section, Pub.L. 96–510, Title II, § 232, Dec. 11, 1980, 94 Stat. 2804, provided for establishment of a "Post-closure Liability Trust Fund" in the Treasury of the United States.

**Effective Date of Repeal**

Section repealed effective Oct. 1, 1983, with proviso that if refund or credit of any overpayment of tax resulting from application of this section be barred by any law or rule of law, refund or credit of such overpayment shall be made or allowed if claim therefor is filed before the date one year after Oct. 17, 1986, see section 514(c) of Pub.L. 99–499.

## SUBCHAPTER III—MISCELLANEOUS PROVISIONS

### § 9651. Reports and studies

**[CERCLA § 301]**

**(a) Implementation experiences; identification and disposal of waste**

(1) The President shall submit to the Congress, within four years after December 11, 1980, a comprehensive report on experience with the implementation of this chapter including, but not limited to—

(A) the extent to which the chapter and Fund are effective in enabling Government to respond to and mitigate the effects of releases of hazardous substances;

(B) a summary of past receipts and disbursements from the Fund;

(C) a projection of any future funding needs remaining after the expiration of authority to collect taxes, and of the threat to public health, welfare, and the environment posed by the projected releases which create any such needs;

(D) the record and experience of the Fund in recovering Fund disbursements from liable parties;

(E) the record of State participation in the system of response, liability, and compensation established by this chapter;

(F) the impact of the taxes imposed by subchapter II of this chapter on the Nation's balance of trade with other countries;

(G) an assessment of the feasibility and desirability of a schedule of taxes which would take into account one or more of the following: the likelihood of a release of a hazardous substance, the degree of hazard and risk of harm to public health, welfare, and the environment resulting from any such release, incentives to proper handling, recycling, incineration, and neutralization of hazardous wastes, and disincentives to improper or illegal handling or disposal of hazardous materials, administrative and reporting burdens on Government and industry, and the extent to which the tax burden falls on the substances and parties which create the problems addressed by this chapter. In preparing the report, the President shall consult with appropriate Federal, State, and local agencies, affected industries and claimants, and such other interested parties as he may find useful. Based upon the analyses and consultation required by this subsection, the President shall also include in the report any recommendations for legislative changes he may deem necessary for the better effectuation of the purposes of this chapter, including but not limited to recommendations concerning authorization levels, taxes, State participation, liability and liability limits, and financial responsibility provisions for the Response Trust Fund and the Post-closure Liability Trust Fund;

(H) an exemption from or an increase in the substances or the amount of taxes imposed by section 4661 of Title 26 for copper, lead, and zinc oxide, and for feedstocks when used in the manufacture and production of fertilizers, based upon the expenditure experience of the Response Trust Fund;

(I) the economic impact of taxing coal-derived substances and recycled metals.

(2) The Administrator of the Environmental Protection Agency (in consultation with the Secretary of the Treasury) shall submit to the Congress (i) within four years after December 11, 1980, a report identifying additional wastes designated by rule as hazardous after the effective date of this chapter and pursuant to section 3001 of the Solid Waste Disposal Act [42 U.S.C.A. § 6921] and recommendations on appropriate tax rates for such wastes for the Post-closure Liability Trust Fund. The report shall, in addition, recommend a tax rate, considering the quantity and potential danger to human health and the environment posed by the disposal of any wastes which the Administrator, pursuant to subsection 3001(b)(2)(B) and subsection 3001(b)(3)(A) of the Solid Waste Disposal Act of 1980 [42 U.S.C.A. §§ 6921(b)(2)(B) and 6921(b)(3)(A)], has determined should be subject to regulation under subtitle C of such Act [42 U.S.C.A. § 6921 et seq.], (ii) within three years after December 11, 1980, a report on the necessity for and the adequacy of the revenue raised, in relation to estimated future requirements, of the Post-closure Liability Trust Fund.

**(b) Private insurance protection**

The President shall conduct a study to determine (1) whether adequate private insurance protection is available on reasonable terms and conditions to the owners and operators of vessels and facilities subject to liability under section 9607 of this title, and (2) whether the market for such insurance is sufficiently competitive to assure purchasers of features such as a reasonable range of deductibles, coinsurance provisions, and exclusions. The President shall submit the results of his study, together with his recommendations, within two years of December 11, 1980, and shall submit an interim report on his study within one year of December 11, 1980.

**(c) Regulations respecting assessment of damages to natural resources**

(1) The President, acting through Federal officials designated by the National Contingency Plan published under section 9605 of this title, shall study and, not later than two years after December 11, 1980, shall promulgate regulations for the assessment of damages for injury to, destruction of, or loss of natural resources resulting from a release of oil or a hazardous substance for the purposes of this chapter and section 1321(f)(4) and (5) of Title 33. Notwithstanding the failure of the President to promulgate the regulations required under this subsection on the required date, the President shall promulgate such regulations not later than 6 months after October 17, 1986.

(2) Such regulations shall specify (A) standard procedures for simplified assessments requiring minimal field observation, including establishing measures of damages based on units of discharge or release or units of affected area, and (B) alternative protocols for conducting assessments in individual cases to determine the type and extent of short- and long-term injury, destruction, or loss. Such regulations shall identify the best available procedures to determine such damages, including both direct and indirect injury, destruction, or loss and shall take into consideration factors including, but not limited to, replacement value, use value, and ability of the ecosystem or resource to recover.

(3) Such regulations shall be reviewed and revised as appropriate every two years.

**(d) Issues, alternatives, and policy considerations involving selection of locations for waste treatment, storage, and disposal facilities**

The Administrator of the Environmental Protection Agency shall, in consultation with other Federal agencies and appropriate representatives of State and local governments and nongovernmental agencies, conduct a study and report to the Congress within two years of December 11, 1980, on the issues, alternatives, and policy considerations involved in the selection of locations for hazardous waste treatment, storage, and disposal facilities. This study shall include—

(A) an assessment of current and projected treatment, storage, and disposal capacity needs and shortfalls for hazardous waste by management category on a State-by-State basis;

(B) an evaluation of the appropriateness of a regional approach to siting and designing hazardous waste management facilities and the identification of hazardous waste management regions, interstate or intrastate, or both, with similar hazardous waste management needs;

(C) solicitation and analysis of proposals for the construction and operation of hazardous waste management facilities by nongovernmental entities, except that no proposal solicited under terms of this subsection shall be analyzed if it involves cost to the United States Government or fails to comply with the requirements of subtitle C of the Solid Waste Disposal Act [42 U.S.C.A. § 6921 et seq.] and other applicable provisions of law;

(D) recommendations on the appropriate balance between public and private sector involvement in the siting, design, and operation of new hazardous waste management facilities;

(E) documentation of the major reasons for public opposition to new hazardous waste management facilities; and

(F) an evaluation of the various options for overcoming obstacles to siting new facilities, including needed legislation for implementing the most suitable option or options.

**(e) Adequacy of existing common law and statutory remedies**

(1) In order to determine the adequacy of existing common law and statutory remedies in providing legal redress for harm to man and the environment caused by the release of hazardous substances into the environment, there shall be submitted to the Congress a study within twelve months of December 11, 1980.

(2) This study shall be conducted with the assistance of the American Bar Association, the American Law Institute, the Association of American Trial Lawyers, and the National Association of State Attorneys General with the President of each entity selecting three members from each organization to conduct the study. The study chairman and one reporter shall be elected from among the twelve members of the study group.

(3) As part of their review of the adequacy of existing common law and statutory remedies, the study group shall evaluate the following:

(A) the nature, adequacy, and availability of existing remedies under present law in compensating for harm to man from the release of hazardous substances;

(B) the nature of barriers to recovery (particularly with respect to burdens of going forward and of proof and relevancy) and the role such barriers play in the legal system;

(C) the scope of the evidentiary burdens placed on the plaintiff in proving harm from the release of hazardous substances, particularly in light of the scientific uncertainty over causation with respect to—

(i) carcinogens, mutagens, and teratogens, and

(ii) the human health effects of exposure to low doses of hazardous substances over long periods of time;

(D) the nature and adequacy of existing remedies under present law in providing compensation for damages to natural resources from the release of hazardous substances;

(E) the scope of liability under existing law and the consequences, particularly with respect to obtaining insurance, of any changes in such liability;

(F) barriers to recovery posed by existing statutes of limitations.

(4) The report shall be submitted to the Congress with appropriate recommendations. Such recommendations shall explicitly address—

(A) the need for revisions in existing statutory or common law, and

(B) whether such revisions should take the form of Federal statutes or the development of a model code which is recommended for adoption by the States.

(5) The Fund shall pay administrative expenses incurred for the study. No expenses shall be available to pay compensation, except expenses on a per diem basis for the one reporter, but in no case shall the total expenses of the study exceed $300,000.

**(f) Modification of national contingency plan**

The President, acting through the Administrator of the Environmental Protection Agency, the Secretary of Transportation, the Administrator of the Occupational Safety and Health Administration, and the Director of the National Institute for Occupational Safety and Health shall study and, not later than two years after December 11, 1980, shall modify the national contingency plan to provide for the protection of the health and safety of employees involved in response actions.

**(g) Insurability study**

**(1) Study by Comptroller General**

The Comptroller General of the United States, in consultation with the persons described in paragraph (2), shall undertake a study to determine the insurability, and effects on the standard of care, of the liability of each of the following:

(A) Persons who generate hazardous substances: liability for costs and damages under this chapter.

(B) Persons who own or operate facilities: liability for costs and damages under this chapter.

(C) Persons liable for injury to persons or property caused by the release of hazardous substances into the environment.

**(2) Consultation**

In conducting the study under this subsection, the Comptroller General shall consult with the following:

(A) Representatives of the Administrator.

(B) Representatives of persons described in subparagraphs (A) through (C) of the preceding paragraph.

(C) Representatives (i) of groups or organizations comprised generally of persons adversely affected by releases or threatened releases of hazardous substances and (ii) of groups organized for protecting the interests of consumers.

(D) Representatives of property and casualty insurers.

(E) Representatives of reinsurers.

(F) Persons responsible for the regulation of insurance at the State level.

**(3) Items evaluated**

The study under this section shall include, among other matters, an evaluation of the following:

(A) Current economic conditions in, and the future outlook for, the commercial market for insurance and reinsurance.

(B) Current trends in statutory and common law remedies.

(C) The impact of possible changes in traditional standards of liability, proof, evidence, and damages on existing statutory and common law remedies.

(D) The effect of the standard of liability and extent of the persons upon whom it is imposed under this chapter on the protection of human health and the environment and on the availability, underwriting, and pricing of insurance coverage.

(E) Current trends, if any, in the judicial interpretation and construction of applicable insurance contracts, together with the degree to which amendments in the language of such contracts and the description of the risks assumed, could affect such trends.

(F) The frequency and severity of a representative sample of claims closed during the calendar year immediately preceding October 17, 1986.

(G) Impediments to the acquisition of insurance or other means of obtaining liability coverage other than those referred to in the preceding subparagraphs.

(H) The effects of the standards of liability and financial responsibility requirements imposed pursuant to this chapter on the cost of, and incentives for, developing and demonstrating alternative and innovative treatment technologies, as well as waste generation minimization.

**(4) Submission**

The Comptroller General shall submit a report on the results of the study to Congress with appropriate recommendations within 12 months after October 17, 1986.

**(h) Omitted**

(Pub.L. 96–510, Title III, § 301, Dec. 11, 1980, 94 Stat. 2805; Pub.L. 99–499, Title I, § 107(d)(3), Title II, §§ 208, 212, Oct. 17, 1986, 100 Stat. 1630, 1707, 1726; Pub.L. 99–514, § 2, Oct. 22, 1986, 100 Stat. 2095.

## HISTORICAL AND STATUTORY NOTES

**References in Text**

This chapter, referred to in subsecs. (a)(1)(A), (E), (G), (c)(1), (g)(1)(A), (B), (3)(D), (H), and (h)(1)(G), (3), was in the original "this Act", meaning Pub.L. 96–510, Dec. 11, 1980, 94 Stat. 2767, as amended, known as the Comprehensive Environmental Response, Compensation, and Liability Act of 1980, which enacted this chapter, section 6911a of this title, and sections 4611, 4612, 4661, and 4662 and former sections 4681 and 4682 of Title 26, Internal Revenue Code, amended section 6911 of this title, section 1364 of Title 33, Navigation and Navigable Waters, and section 11901 of Title 49, Transportation, and enacted provisions set out as notes under section 6911 of this title and sections 1 and 4611 of Title 26. For complete classification of this Act to the Code, see Short Title of 1980 Acts note set out under section 9601 of this title and Tables.

Subchapter II of this chapter, referred to in subsec. (a)(1)(F), was in the original, "Title II of this Act", meaning Title II of Pub.L. 96–510, Dec. 11, 1980, 94 Stat. 2796, known as the Hazardous Substance Response Revenue Act of 1980, which enacted subchapter II of this chapter and sections 4611, 4612, 4661, 4662 and former sections 4681 and 4682 of Title 26, Internal Revenue Code. Sections 221 to 223 and 232 of Pub.L. 96–510, which were classified to sections 9631 to 9633 and 9641 of this title, comprising subchapter II of this chapter, were repealed by Pub.L. 99–499, Title V, §§ 514(6), 517(c)(1), Oct. 17, 1986, 100 Stat. 1767, 1774. For complete classification of Title II to the Code, see Short Title of 1980 Amendments note set out under section 1 of Title 26 and Tables.

For effective date of this chapter, referred to in subsec. (a)(2), see section 9652 of this title.

Subsection 3001(b)(2)(B) and subsection 3001(b)(3)(A) of the Solid Waste Disposal Act of 1980, referred to in subsec. (a)(2), probably mean section 3001(b)(2)(B) and (3)(A) of the Solid Waste Disposal Act, as amended by the Solid Waste Disposal Act Amendments of 1980, which enacted section 6921(b)(2)(B) and (3)(A) of this title.

The Solid Waste Disposal Act, referred to in subsecs. (a)(2) and (d)(C), is Title II of Pub.L. 89–272, Oct. 20, 1965, 79 Stat. 997, as amended generally by Pub.L. 94–580, § 2, Oct. 21, 1976, 90 Stat. 2795. Subtitle C of the Solid Waste Disposal Act is classified generally to subchapter III (section 6921 et seq.) of chapter 82 of this title. For complete classification of this Act to the Code, see Short Title of 1965 Acts note set out under section 6901 of this title and Tables.

The Inspector General Act of 1978, referred to in subsec. (h)(2), is Pub.L. 95–452, Oct. 12, 1978, 92 Stat. 1101, as amended, which is set out as Appendix 3 to Title 5, Government Organization and Employees.

**Codifications**

Subsec. (h) of this section, which required the Administrator of the Environmental Protection Agency to submit an annual report to Congress of such Agency on the progress achieved in implementing this chapter during the preceding fiscal year, required the Inspector General of the Agency to review the report for reasonableness and accuracy and submit to Congress, as a part of that report, a report on the results of the review, and required the appropriate authorizing committees of Congress, after receiving those reports, to conduct oversight hearings to ensure that this chapter is being implemented according to the purposes of this chapter and congressional intent in enacting this chapter, terminated, effective May 15, 2000, pursuant to section 3003 of Pub.L. 104–66, as amended, set out as a note under 31 U.S.C.A. § 1113 and the 5th item on page 164 of House Document No. 103–7.

**Effective Dates**

1986 Acts

Amendment by Pub.L. 99–499 effective Oct. 17, 1986, see section 4 of Pub.L. 99–499, set out as a note under section 9601 of this title.

**Delegation of Functions**

Responsibility for the revision of the National Contingency Plan, and all other functions vested in the President by subsec. (f) of this section, delegated to the Administrator of the Environmental Protection Agency, see section 1(b)(1) of Ex. Ord. No. 12580, Jan. 23, 1987, 52 F.R. 2923, set out as a note under section 9615 of this title.

Functions vested in the President by subsec. (c) of this section delegated to the Secretary of the Interior, see section 11(d) of Ex. Ord. No. 12580, Jan. 23, 1987, 52 F.R. 2923, set out as a note under section 9615 of this title.

## § 9652. Effective dates; savings provisions

**[CERCLA § 302]**

**(a)** Unless otherwise provided, all provisions of this chapter shall be effective on December 11, 1980.

**(b)** Any regulation issued pursuant to any provisions of section 1321 of Title 33 which is repealed or superseded by this chapter and which is in effect on the date immediately preceding the effective date of this chapter shall be deemed to be a regulation issued pursuant to the authority of this chapter and shall remain in full force and effect unless or until superseded by new regulations issued thereunder.

**(c)** Any regulation—

**(1)** respecting financial responsibility,

**(2)** issued pursuant to any provision of law repealed or superseded by this chapter, and

**(3)** in effect on the date immediately preceding the effective date of this chapter shall be deemed to be a regulation issued pursuant to the authority of this chapter and shall remain in full force and effect unless or until superseded by new regulations issued thereunder.

**(d)** Nothing in this chapter shall affect or modify in any way the obligations or liabilities of any person under other Federal or State law, including common law, with respect to releases of hazardous substances or other pollutants or contaminants. The provisions of this chapter shall not be considered, interpreted, or construed in any way as reflecting a determination, in part or whole, of policy regarding the inapplicability of strict liability, or strict liability doctrines, to activities relating to hazardous substances, pollutants, or contaminants or other such activities.

(Pub.L. 96–510, Title III, § 302, Dec. 11, 1980, 94 Stat. 2808.)

## § 9653. Repealed. Pub.L. 99–499, Title V, § 511(b), Oct. 17, 1986, 100 Stat. 1761

### HISTORICAL AND STATUTORY NOTES

Section, Pub. L. 96–510, Title III, § 303, Dec. 11, 1980, 94 Stat. 2808, provided for termination of authority to collect taxes under this chapter.

**Effective Date of Repeal**

Section repealed effective Jan. 1, 1987, see section 511(c) of Pub.L. 99–499, set out as an Effective Dates of 1986 Acts note under section 4611 of Title 26, Internal Revenue Code.

## § 9654. Applicability of Federal water pollution control funding, etc., provisions

**[CERCLA § 304]**

**(a)** Omitted

**(b)** One-half of the unobligated balance remaining before December 11, 1980, under subsection (k) of section 1321 of Title 33 and all sums appropriated under section 1364(b) of Title 33 shall be transferred to the Fund established under subchapter II of this chapter.

**(c)** In any case in which any provision of section 1321 of Title 33 is determined to be in conflict with any provisions of this chapter, the provisions of this chapter shall apply.

(Pub.L. 96–510, Title III, § 304, Dec. 11, 1980, 94 Stat. 2809.)

### HISTORICAL AND STATUTORY NOTES

**References in Text**

Subsection (k) of section 1321 of Title 33, referred to in subsec. (b), was repealed by Pub.L. 101–380, Title II, § 2002(b)(2), Aug. 18, 1990, 104 Stat. 507.

Section 1364(b) of Title 33, referred to in subsec. (b), was repealed by Pub.L. 96–510, Title III, § 304(a), Dec. 11, 1980, 94 Stat. 2809.

Subchapter II of this chapter, referred to in subsec. (b), was in the original, "Title II of this Act", meaning Title II of Pub.L. 96–510, Dec. 11, 1980, 94 Stat. 2796, known as the Hazardous Substance Response Revenue Act of 1980, which enacted subchapter II of this chapter and sections 4611, 4612, 4661, 4662 and former sections 4681 and 4682 of Title 26, Internal Revenue Code. Sections 221 to 223 and 232 of Pub.L. 96–510, which were classified to sections 9631 to 9633 and 9641 of this title, comprising subchapter II of this chapter, were repealed by Pub.L. 99–499, Title V, §§ 514(b), 517(c)(1), Oct. 17, 1986, 100 Stat. 1767, 1774. For complete classification of Title II to the Code, see Short Title of 1980 Amendments note set out under section 1 of Title 26 and Tables.

**Codifications**

Subsec. (a) of this section repealed section 1364(b) of Title 33, Navigation and Navigable Waters.

## § 9655. Legislative veto of rule or regulation

**[CERCLA § 305]**

### (a) Transmission to Congress upon promulgation or repromulgation of rule or regulation; disapproval procedures

Notwithstanding any other provision of law, simultaneously with promulgation or repromulgation of any rule or regulation under authority of subchapter I of this chapter, the head of the department, agency, or instrumentality promulgating such rule or regulation shall transmit a copy thereof to the Secretary of the Senate and the Clerk of the House of Representatives. Except as provided in subsection (b) of this section, the rule or regulation shall not become effective, if—

(1) within ninety calendar days of continuous session of Congress after the date of promulgation, both Houses of Congress adopt a concurrent resolution, the matter after the resolving clause of which is as follows: "That Congress disapproves the rule or regulation promulgated by the _____ dealing with the matter of _____, which rule or regulation was transmitted to Congress on _____.", the blank spaces therein being appropriately filled; or

(2) within sixty calendar days of continuous session of Congress after the date of promulgation, one House of Congress adopts such a concurrent resolution and transmits such resolution to the other House, and such resolution is not disapproved by such other House within thirty calendar days of continuous session of Congress after such transmittal.

### (b) Approval; effective dates

If, at the end of sixty calendar days of continuous session of Congress after the date of promulgation of a rule or regulation, no committee of either House of Congress has reported or been discharged from further consideration of a concurrent resolution disapproving the rule or regulation and neither House has adopted such a resolution, the rule or regulation may go into effect immediately. If, within such sixty calendar days, such a committee has reported or been discharged from further consideration of such a resolution, or either House has adopted such a resolution, the rule or regulation may go into effect not sooner than ninety calendar days of continuous session of Congress after such rule is prescribed unless disapproved as provided in subsection (a) of this section.

### (c) Sessions of Congress as applicable

For purposes of subsections (a) and (b) of this section—

(1) continuity of session is broken only by an adjournment of Congress sine die; and

(2) the days on which either House is not in session because of an adjournment of more than three days to a day certain are excluded in the computation of thirty, sixty, and ninety calendar days of continuous session of Congress.

### (d) Congressional inaction on, or rejection of, resolution of disapproval

Congressional inaction on, or rejection of, a resolution of disapproval shall not be deemed an expression of approval of such rule or regulation.

(Pub.L. 96–510, Title III, § 305, Dec. 11, 1980, 94 Stat. 2809.)

#### HISTORICAL AND STATUTORY NOTES

**Transfer of Functions**

Any reference in any provision of law enacted before Jan. 4, 1995, to a function, duty, or authority of the Clerk of the House of Representatives treated as referring, with respect to that function, duty, or authority, to the officer of the House of Representatives exercising that function, duty, or authority, as determined by the Committee on House Oversight of the House of Representatives, see section 2(l) of Pub.L. 104–14, set out as a note preceding section 21 of Title 2, The Congress.

## § 9656. Transportation of hazardous substances; listing as hazardous material; liability for release

**[CERCLA § 306]**

(a) Each hazardous substance which is listed or designated as provided in section 9601(14) of this title shall, within 30 days after October 17, 1986, or at the time of such listing or designation, whichever is later, be listed and regulated as a hazardous material under chapter 51 of Title 49.

(b) A common or contract carrier shall be liable under other law in lieu of section 9607 of this title for damages or remedial action resulting from the release of a hazardous substance during the course of transportation which commenced prior to the effective date of the listing and regulation of such substance as a hazardous material under chapter 51 of Title 49, or for substances listed pursuant to subsection (a) of this section, prior to the effective date of such listing: *Provided, however,* That this subsection shall not apply where such a carrier can demonstrate that he did not have actual knowledge of the identity or nature of the substance released.

(Pub.L. 96–510, Title III, § 306(a), (b), Dec. 11, 1980, 94 Stat. 2810; Pub.L. 99–499, Title II, § 202, Oct. 17, 1986, 100 Stat. 1695.)

#### HISTORICAL AND STATUTORY NOTES

**References in Text**

Chapter 51 of Title 49, referred to in text, is 49 U.S.C.A. § 5101 et seq.

**Effective Dates**

1986 Acts

Amendment by Pub.L. 99–499 effective Oct. 17, 1986, see section 4 of Pub.L. 99–499, set out as a note under section 9601 of this title.

## § 9657. Separability; contribution

[CERCLA § 308]

If any provision of this chapter, or the application of any provision of this chapter to any person or circumstance, is held invalid, the application of such provision to other persons or circumstances and the remainder of this chapter shall not be affected thereby. If an administrative settlement under section 9622 of this title has the effect of limiting any person's right to obtain contribution from any party to such settlement, and if the effect of such limitation would constitute a taking without just compensation in violation of the fifth amendment of the Constitution of the United States, such person shall not be entitled, under other laws of the United States, to recover compensation from the United States for such taking, but in any such case, such limitation on the right to obtain contribution shall be treated as having no force and effect.

(Pub.L. 96–510, Title III, § 308, Dec. 11, 1980, 94 Stat. 2811; Pub.L. 99–499, Title I, § 122(b), Oct. 17, 1986, 100 Stat. 1688.)

### HISTORICAL AND STATUTORY NOTES

**References in Text**

This chapter, referred to in text, was in the original, "this Act", meaning Pub.L. 96–510, Dec. 11, 1980, 94 Stat. 2767, as amended, known as the Comprehensive Environmental Response, Compensation, and Liability Act of 1980, which enacted this chapter, 6911a of this title, and sections 4611, 4612, 4661, 4662 and former sections 4681 and 4682 of Title 26, Internal Revenue Code, amended 6911 of this title, 1364 of Title 33, Navigation and Navigable Waters, and 11901 of Title 49, Transportation, and enacted provisions set out as notes under section 6911 of this title and sections 1 and 4611 of Title 26. For complete classification of this Act to the Code, see Short Title of 1980 Acts note set out under section 9601 of this title and Tables.

**Effective Dates**

1986 Acts

Amendment by Pub.L. 99–499 effective Oct. 17, 1986, see section 4 of Pub.L. 99–499, set out as a note under section 9601 of this title.

## § 9658. Actions under State law for damages from exposure to hazardous substances

[CERCLA § 309]

**(a) State statutes of limitations for hazardous substance cases**

**(1) Exception to State statutes**

In the case of any action brought under State law for personal injury, or property damages, which are caused or contributed to by exposure to any hazardous substance, or pollutant or contaminant, released into the environment from a facility, if the applicable limitations period for such action (as specified in the State statute of limitations or under common law) provides a commencement date which is earlier than the federally required commencement date, such period shall commence at the federally required commencement date in lieu of the date specified in such State statute.

**(2) State law generally applicable**

Except as provided in paragraph (1), the statute of limitations established under State law shall apply in all actions brought under State law for personal injury, or property damages, which are caused or contributed to by exposure to any hazardous substance, or pollutant or contaminant, released into the environment from a facility.

**(3) Actions under section 9607**

Nothing in this section shall apply with respect to any cause of action brought under section 9607 of this title.

**(b) Definitions**

As used in this section—

**(1) Subchapter I terms**

The terms used in this section shall have the same meaning as when used in subchapter I of this chapter.

**(2) Applicable limitations period**

The term "applicable limitations period" means the period specified in a statute of limitations during which a civil action referred to in subsection (a)(1) of this section may be brought.

**(3) Commencement date**

The term "commencement date" means the date specified in a statute of limitations as the beginning of the applicable limitations period.

**(4) Federally required commencement date**

**(A) In general**

Except as provided in subparagraph (B), the term "federally required commencement date" means the date the plaintiff knew (or reasonably should have known) that the personal injury or property damages referred to in subsection (a)(1) of this section were caused or contributed to by the hazardous substance or pollutant or contaminant concerned.

**(B) Special rules**

In the case of a minor or incompetent plaintiff, the term "federally required commencement date" means the later of the date referred to in subparagraph (A) or the following:

(i) In the case of a minor, the date on which the minor reaches the age of majority, as determined by State law, or has a legal representative appointed.

(ii) In the case of an incompetent individual, the date on which such individual becomes competent or has had a legal representative appointed.

(Pub.L. 96–510, Title III, § 309, as added Pub.L. 99–499, Title II, § 203(a), Oct. 17, 1986, 100 Stat. 1695.)

### HISTORICAL AND STATUTORY NOTES

**Effective Dates**

1986 Acts

Section 203(b) of Pub.L. 99–499 provided that: "The amendment made by subsection (a) of this section [enacting this section] shall take effect with respect to actions brought after December 11, 1980."

## § 9659. Citizens suits

### [CERCLA § 310]

**(a) Authority to bring civil actions**

Except as provided in subsections (d) and (e) of this section and in section 9613(h) of this title (relating to timing of judicial review), any person may commence a civil action on his own behalf—

(1) against any person (including the United States and any other governmental instrumentality or agency, to the extent permitted by the eleventh amendment to the Constitution) who is alleged to be in violation of any standard, regulation, condition, requirement, or order which has become effective pursuant to this chapter (including any provision of an agreement under section 9620 of this title, relating to Federal facilities); or

(2) against the President or any other officer of the United States (including the Administrator of the Environmental Protection Agency and the Administrator of the ATSDR) where there is alleged a failure of the President or of such other officer to perform any act or duty under this chapter, including an act or duty under section 9620 of this title (relating to Federal facilities), which is not discretionary with the President or such other officer.

Paragraph (2) shall not apply to any act or duty under the provisions of section 9660 of this title (relating to research, development, and demonstration).

**(b) Venue**

**(1) Actions under subsection (a)(1)**

Any action under subsection (a)(1) of this section shall be brought in the district court for the district in which the alleged violation occurred.

**(2) Actions under subsection (a)(2)**

Any action brought under subsection (a)(2) of this section may be brought in the United States District Court for the District of Columbia.

**(c) Relief**

The district court shall have jurisdiction in actions brought under subsection (a)(1) of this section to enforce the standard, regulation, condition, requirement, or order concerned (including any provision of an agreement under section 9620 of this title), to order such action as may be necessary to correct the violation, and to impose any civil penalty provided for the violation. The district court shall have jurisdiction in actions brought under subsection (a)(2) of this section to order the President or other officer to perform the act or duty concerned.

**(d) Rules applicable to subsection (a)(1) actions**

**(1) Notice**

No action may be commenced under subsection (a)(1) of this section before 60 days after the plaintiff has given notice of the violation to each of the following:

(A) The President.

(B) The State in which the alleged violation occurs.

(C) Any alleged violator of the standard, regulation, condition, requirement, or order concerned (including any provision of an agreement under section 9620 of this title).

Notice under this paragraph shall be given in such manner as the President shall prescribe by regulation.

**(2) Diligent prosecution**

No action may be commenced under paragraph (1) of subsection (a) of this section if the President has commenced and is diligently prosecuting an action under this chapter, or under the Solid Waste Disposal Act [42 U.S.C.A. § 6901 et seq.] to require compliance with the standard, regulation, condition, requirement, or order concerned (including any provision of an agreement under section 9620 of this title).

**(e) Rules applicable to subsection (a)(2) actions**

No action may be commenced under paragraph (2) of subsection (a) of this section before the 60th day following the date on which the plaintiff gives notice to the Administrator or other department, agency, or instrumentality that the plaintiff will commence such action. Notice under this subsection shall be given in such manner as the President shall prescribe by regulation.

**(f) Costs**

The court, in issuing any final order in any action brought pursuant to this section, may award costs of litigation (including reasonable attorney and expert witness fees) to the prevailing or the substantially prevailing party whenever the court determines such an award is appropriate. The court may, if a temporary restraining order or preliminary injunction is sought, require the filing of a bond or equivalent security in accordance with the Federal Rules of Civil Procedure.

**(g) Intervention**

In any action under this section, the United States or the State, or both, if not a party may intervene as a matter of right. For other provisions regarding intervention, see section 9613 of this title.

**(h) Other rights**

This chapter does not affect or otherwise impair the rights of any person under Federal, State, or common law, except with respect to the timing of review as provided in section 9613(h) of this title or as otherwise provided in section 9658 of this title (relating to actions under State law).

**(i) Definitions**

The terms used in this section shall have the same meanings as when used in subchapter I of this chapter.

(Pub.L. 96–510, Title III, § 310, as added Pub.L. 99–499, Title II, § 206, Oct. 17, 1986, 100 Stat. 1703.)

### HISTORICAL AND STATUTORY NOTES

**References in Text**

The Solid Waste Disposal Act, referred to in subsec. (d)(2), is Title II of Pub.L. 89–272, Oct. 20, 1965, 79 Stat. 997, as amended generally by Pub.L. 94–580, § 2, Oct. 21, 1976, 90 Stat. 2795, which is classified generally to chapter 82 (section 6901 et seq.) of this title. For complete classification of this Act to the Code, see Short Title of 1965 Acts note set out under section 6901 of this title and Tables.

The Federal Rules of Civil Procedure, referred to in subsec. (f), are set out in Title 28, Judiciary and Judicial Procedure.

**Effective Dates**

1986 Acts

Section effective Oct. 17, 1986, see section 4 of Pub.L. 99–499, set out as a note under section 9601 of this title.

**Delegation of Functions**

Functions vested in the President by subsecs. (d) and (e) of this section, relating to the promulgation of regulations, delegated to the Administrator of the Environmental Protection Agency, see section 6(d) of Ex. Ord. No. 12580, Jan. 23, 1987, 52 F.R. 2923, set out as a note under section 9615 of this title.

## § 9660. Research, development, and demonstration

[CERCLA § 311]

**(a) Hazardous substance research and training**

**(1) Authorities of Secretary**

The Secretary of Health and Human Services (hereinafter in this subsection referred to as the Secretary), in consultation with the Administrator, shall establish and support a basic research and training program (through grants, cooperative agreements, and contracts) consisting of the following:

**(A)** Basic research (including epidemiologic and ecologic studies) which may include each of the following:

**(i)** Advanced techniques for the detection, assessment, and evaluation of the effects on human health of hazardous substances.

**(ii)** Methods to assess the risks to human health presented by hazardous substances.

**(iii)** Methods and technologies to detect hazardous substances in the environment and basic biological, chemical, and physical methods to reduce the amount and toxicity of hazardous substances.

**(B)** Training, which may include each of the following:

**(i)** Short courses and continuing education for State and local health and environment agency personnel and other personnel engaged in the handling of hazardous substances, in the management of facilities at which hazardous substances are located, and in the evaluation of the hazards to human health presented by such facilities.

**(ii)** Graduate or advanced training in environmental and occupational health and safety and in the public health and engineering aspects of hazardous waste control.

**(iii)** Graduate training in the geosciences, including hydrogeology, geological engineering, geophysics, geochemistry, and related fields necessary to meet professional personnel needs in the public and private sectors and to effectuate the purposes of this chapter.

**(2) Director of NIEHS**

The Director of the National Institute for Environmental Health Sciences shall cooperate fully with the relevant Federal agencies referred to in subparagraph (A) of paragraph (5) in carrying out the purposes of this section.

**(3) Recipients of grants, etc.**

A grant, cooperative agreement, or contract may be made or entered into under paragraph (1) with an accredited institution of higher education. The institution may carry out the research or training under the grant, cooperative agreement, or contract through contracts, including contracts with any of the following:

(A) Generators of hazardous wastes.

(B) Persons involved in the detection, assessment, evaluation, and treatment of hazardous substances.

(C) Owners and operators of facilities at which hazardous substances are located.

(D) State and local governments.

**(4) Procedures**

In making grants and entering into cooperative agreements and contracts under this subsection, the Secretary shall act through the Director of the National Institute for Environmental Health Sciences. In considering the allocation of funds for training purposes, the Director shall ensure that at least one grant, cooperative agreement, or contract shall be awarded for training described in each of clauses (i), (ii), and (iii) of paragraph (1)(B). Where applicable, the Director may choose to operate training activities in cooperation with the Director of the National Institute for Occupational Safety and Health. The procedures applicable to grants and contracts under title IV of the Public Health Service Act [42 U.S.C.A. § 281 et seq.] shall be followed under this subsection.

**(5) Advisory council**

To assist in the implementation of this subsection and to aid in the coordination of research and demonstration and training activities funded from the Fund under this section, the Secretary shall appoint an advisory council (hereinafter in this subsection referred to as the "Advisory Council") which shall consist of representatives of the following:

(A) The relevant Federal agencies.

(B) The chemical industry.

(C) The toxic waste management industry.

(D) Institutions of higher education.

(E) State and local health and environmental agencies.

(F) The general public.

**(6) Planning**

Within nine months after October 17, 1986, the Secretary, acting through the Director of the National Institute for Environmental Health Sciences, shall issue a plan for the implementation of paragraph (1). The plan shall include priorities for actions under paragraph (1) and include research and training relevant to scientific and technological issues resulting from site specific hazardous substance response experience. The Secretary shall, to the maximum extent practicable, take appropriate steps to coordinate program activities under this plan with the activities of other Federal agencies in order to avoid duplication of effort. The plan shall be consistent with the need for the development of new technologies for meeting the goals of response actions in accordance with the provisions of this chapter. The Advisory Council shall be provided an opportunity to review and comment on the plan and priorities and assist appropriate coordination among the relevant Federal agencies referred to in subparagraph (A) of paragraph (5).

**(b) Alternative or innovative treatment technology research and demonstration program**

**(1) Establishment**

The Administrator is authorized and directed to carry out a program of research, evaluation, testing, development, and demonstration of alternative or innovative treatment technologies (hereinafter in this subsection referred to as the "program") which may be utilized in response actions to achieve more permanent protection of human health and welfare and the environment.

**(2) Administration**

The program shall be administered by the Administrator, acting through an office of technology demonstration and shall be coordinated with programs carried out by the Office of Solid Waste and Emergency Response and the Office of Research and Development.

**(3) Contracts and grants**

In carrying out the program, the Administrator is authorized to enter into contracts and cooperative agreements with, and make grants to, persons, public entities, and nonprofit private entities which are exempt from tax under section 501(c)(3) of Title 26. The Administrator shall, to the maximum extent possible, enter into appropriate cost sharing arrangements under this subsection.

**(4) Use of sites**

In carrying out the program, the Administrator may arrange for the use of sites at which a response may be undertaken under section 9604 of this title for the purposes of carrying out research, testing, evaluation, development, and demonstration projects. Each such project shall be carried out under such terms and conditions as the Administrator shall require to assure the protection of human health and the environment and to assure adequate control by the Administrator of the research, testing, evaluation, development, and demonstration activities at the site.

**(5) Demonstration assistance**

**(A) Program components**

The demonstration assistance program shall include the following:

(i) The publication of a solicitation and the evaluation of applications for demonstration projects utilizing alternative or innovative technologies.

(ii) The selection of sites which are suitable for the testing and evaluation of innovative technologies.

(iii) The development of detailed plans for innovative technology demonstration projects.

(iv) The supervision of such demonstration projects and the providing of quality assurance for data obtained.

(v) The evaluation of the results of alternative innovative technology demonstration projects and the determination of whether or not the technologies used are effective and feasible.

**(B) Solicitation**

Within 90 days after October 17, 1986, and no less often than once every 12 months thereafter, the Administrator shall publish a solicitation for innovative or alternative technologies at a stage of development suitable for full-scale demonstrations at sites at which a response action may be undertaken under section 9604 of this title. The purpose of any such project shall be to demonstrate the use of an alternative or innovative treatment technology with respect to hazardous substances or pollutants or contaminants which are located at the site or which are to be removed from the site. The solicitation notice shall prescribe information to be included in the application, including technical and economic data derived from the applicant's own research and development efforts, and other information sufficient to permit the Administrator to assess the technology's potential and the types of remedial action to which it may be applicable.

**(C) Applications**

Any person and any public or private nonprofit entity may submit an application to the Administrator in response to the solicitation. The application shall contain a proposed demonstration plan setting forth how and when the project is to be carried out and such other information as the Administrator may require.

**(D) Project selection**

In selecting technologies to be demonstrated, the Administrator shall fully review the applications submitted and shall consider at least the criteria specified in paragraph (7). The Administrator shall select or refuse to select a project for demonstration under this subsection within 90 days of receiving the completed application for such project. In the case of a refusal to select the project, the Administrator shall notify the applicant within such 90-day period of the reasons for his refusal.

**(E) Site selection**

The Administrator shall propose 10 sites at which a response may be undertaken under section 9604 of this title to be the location of any demonstration project under this subsection within 60 days after the close of the public comment period. After an opportunity for notice and public comment, the Administrator shall select such sites and projects. In selecting any such site, the Administrator shall take into account the applicant's technical data and preferences either for onsite operation or for utilizing the site as a source of hazardous substances or pollutants or contaminants to be treated offsite.

**(F) Demonstration plan**

Within 60 days after the selection of the site under this paragraph to be the location of a demonstration project, the Administrator shall establish a final demonstration plan for the project, based upon the demonstration plan contained in the application for the project. Such plan shall clearly set forth how and when the demonstration project will be carried out.

**(G) Supervision and testing**

Each demonstration project under this subsection shall be performed by the applicant, or by a person satisfactory to the applicant, under the supervision of the Administrator. The Administrator shall enter into a written agreement with each applicant granting the Administrator the responsibility and authority for testing procedures, quality control, monitoring, and other measurements necessary to determine and evaluate the results of the demonstration project. The Administrator may pay the costs of testing, monitoring, quality control, and other measurements required by the Administrator to determine and evaluate the results of the demonstration project, and the limitations established by subparagraph (J) shall not apply to such costs.

**(H) Project completion**

Each demonstration project under this subsection shall be completed within such time as is established in the demonstration plan.

**(I) Extensions**

The Administrator may extend any deadline established under this paragraph by mutual agreement with the applicant concerned.

(J) **Funding restrictions**

The Administrator shall not provide any Federal assistance for any part of a full-scale field demonstration project under this subsection to any applicant unless such applicant can demonstrate that it cannot obtain appropriate private financing on reasonable terms and conditions sufficient to carry out such demonstration project without such Federal assistance. The total Federal funds for any full-scale field demonstration project under this subsection shall not exceed 50 percent of the total cost of such project estimated at the time of the award of such assistance. The Administrator shall not expend more than $10,000,000 for assistance under the program in any fiscal year and shall not expend more than $3,000,000 for any single project.

(6) **Field demonstrations**

In carrying out the program, the Administrator shall initiate or cause to be initiated at least 10 field demonstration projects of alternative or innovative treatment technologies at sites at which a response may be undertaken under section 9604 of this title, in fiscal year 1987 and each of the succeeding three fiscal years. If the Administrator determines that 10 field demonstration projects under this subsection cannot be initiated consistent with the criteria set forth in paragraph (7) in any of such fiscal years, the Administrator shall transmit to the appropriate committees of Congress a report explaining the reasons for his inability to conduct such demonstration projects.

(7) **Criteria**

In selecting technologies to be demonstrated under this subsection, the Administrator shall, consistent with the protection of human health and the environment, consider each of the following criteria:

(A) The potential for contributing to solutions to those waste problems which pose the greatest threat to human health, which cannot be adequately controlled under present technologies, or which otherwise pose significant management difficulties.

(B) The availability of technologies which have been sufficiently developed for field demonstration and which are likely to be cost-effective and reliable.

(C) The availability and suitability of sites for demonstrating such technologies, taking into account the physical, biological, chemical, and geological characteristics of the sites, the extent and type of contamination found at the site, and the capability to conduct demonstration projects in such a manner as to assure the protection of human health and the environment.

(D) The likelihood that the data to be generated from the demonstration project at the site will be applicable to other sites.

(8) **Technology transfer**

In carrying out the program, the Administrator shall conduct a technology transfer program including the development, collection, evaluation, coordination, and dissemination of information relating to the utilization of alternative or innovative treatment technologies for response actions. The Administrator shall establish and maintain a central reference library for such information. The information maintained by the Administrator shall be made available to the public, subject to the provisions of section 552 of Title 5 and section 1905 of Title 18, and to other Government agencies in a manner that will facilitate its dissemination; except, that upon a showing satisfactory to the Administrator by any person that any information or portion thereof obtained under this subsection by the Administrator directly or indirectly from such person, would, if made public, divulge—

(A) trade secrets; or

(B) other proprietary information of such person,

the Administrator shall not disclose such information and disclosure thereof shall be punishable under section 1905 of Title 18. This subsection is not authority to withhold information from Congress or any committee of Congress upon the request of the chairman of such committee.

(9) **Training**

The Administrator is authorized and directed to carry out, through the Office of Technology Demonstration, a program of training and an evaluation of training needs for each of the following:

(A) Training in the procedures for the handling and removal of hazardous substances for employees who handle hazardous substances.

(B) Training in the management of facilities at which hazardous substances are located and in the evaluation of the hazards to human health presented by such facilities for State and local health and environment agency personnel.

(10) **Definition**

For purposes of this subsection, the term "alternative or innovative treatment technologies" means those technologies, including proprietary or patented methods, which permanently alter the composition of hazardous waste through chemical, biological, or physical means so as to significantly reduce the toxicity, mobility, or volume (or any combination thereof) of the hazardous waste or contaminated materials being treated. The term also includes technologies that characterize or assess the extent of contamination, the chemical and physical character of the contaminants, and the stresses imposed by the contaminants on complex ecosystems at sites.

**(c) Hazardous substance research**

The Administrator may conduct and support, through grants, cooperative agreements, and contracts, research with respect to the detection, assessment, and evaluation of the effects on and risks to human health of hazardous substances and detection of hazardous substances in the environment. The Administrator shall coordinate such research with the Secretary of Health and Human Services, acting through the advisory council established under this section, in order to avoid duplication of effort.

**(d) University hazardous substance research centers**

**(1) Grant program**

The Administrator shall make grants to institutions of higher learning to establish and operate not fewer than 5 hazardous substance research centers in the United States. In carrying out the program under this subsection, the Administrator should seek to have established and operated 10 hazardous substance research centers in the United States.

**(2) Responsibilities of centers**

The responsibilities of each hazardous substance research center established under this subsection shall include, but not be limited to, the conduct of research and training relating to the manufacture, use, transportation, disposal, and management of hazardous substances and publication and dissemination of the results of such research.

**(3) Applications**

Any institution of higher learning interested in receiving a grant under this subsection shall submit to the Administrator an application in such form and containing such information as the Administrator may require by regulation.

**(4) Selection criteria**

The Administrator shall select recipients of grants under this subsection on the basis of the following criteria:

(A) The hazardous substance research center shall be located in a State which is representative of the needs of the region in which such State is located for improved hazardous waste management.

(B) The grant recipient shall be located in an area which has experienced problems with hazardous substance management.

(C) There is available to the grant recipient for carrying out this subsection demonstrated research resources.

(D) The capability of the grant recipient to provide leadership in making national and regional contributions to the solution of both long-range and immediate hazardous substance management problems.

(E) The grant recipient shall make a commitment to support ongoing hazardous substance research programs with budgeted institutional funds of at least $100,000 per year.

(F) The grant recipient shall have an interdisciplinary staff with demonstrated expertise in hazardous substance management and research.

(G) The grant recipient shall have a demonstrated ability to disseminate results of hazardous substance research and educational programs through an interdisciplinary continuing education program.

(H) The projects which the grant recipient proposes to carry out under the grant are necessary and appropriate.

**(5) Maintenance of effort**

No grant may be made under this subsection in any fiscal year unless the recipient of such grant enters into such agreements with the Administrator as the Administrator may require to ensure that such recipient will maintain its aggregate expenditures from all other sources for establishing and operating a regional hazardous substance research center and related research activities at or above the average level of such expenditures in its 2 fiscal years preceding October 17, 1986.

**(6) Federal share**

The Federal share of a grant under this subsection shall not exceed 80 percent of the costs of establishing and operating the regional hazardous substance research center and related research activities carried out by the grant recipient.

**(7) Limitation on use of funds**

No funds made available to carry out this subsection shall be used for acquisition of real property (including buildings) or construction of any building.

**(8) Administration through the Office of the Administrator**

Administrative responsibility for carrying out this subsection shall be in the Office of the Administrator.

**(9) Equitable distribution of funds**

The Administrator shall allocate funds made available to carry out this subsection equitably among the regions of the United States.

(10) **Technology transfer activities**

Not less than five percent of the funds made available to carry out this subsection for any fiscal year shall be available to carry out technology transfer activities.

**(e) Report to Congress**

At the time of the submission of the annual budget request to Congress, the Administrator shall submit to the appropriate committees of the House of Representatives and the Senate and to the advisory council established under subsection (a) of this section, a report on the progress of the research, development, and demonstration program authorized by subsection (b) of this section, including an evaluation of each demonstration project completed in the preceding fiscal year, findings with respect to the efficacy of such demonstrated technologies in achieving permanent and significant reductions in risk from hazardous wastes, the costs of such demonstration projects, and the potential applicability of, and projected costs for, such technologies at other hazardous substance sites.

**(f) Saving provision**

Nothing in this section shall be construed to affect the provisions of the Solid Waste Disposal Act [42 U.S.C.A. § 6901 et seq.].

**(g) Small business participation**

The Administrator shall ensure, to the maximum extent practicable, an adequate opportunity for small business participation in the program established by subsection (b) of this section.

(Pub.L. 96–510, Title III, § 311, as added Pub.L. 99–499, Title II, § 209(b), Oct. 17, 1986, 100 Stat. 1708, and amended Pub.L. 99–514, § 2, Oct. 22, 1986, 100 Stat. 2095.)

## HISTORICAL AND STATUTORY NOTES

**References in Text**

The Public Health Service Act, referred to in subsec. (a)(4), is Act July 1, 1944, c. 373, 58 Stat. 682, as amended, which is classified generally to chapter 6A (section 201 et seq.) of this title. Title IV of that Act is classified generally to subchapter III (section 281 et seq.) of chapter 6A of this title. For complete classification of this Act to the Code, see Short Title of 1944 Acts note set out under section 201 of this title and Tables.

The Solid Waste Disposal Act, referred to in subsec. (f), is Title II of Pub.L. 89–272, Oct. 20, 1965, 79 Stat. 997, as amended generally by Pub.L. 94–580, § 2, Oct. 21, 1976, 90 Stat. 2795, which is classified generally to chapter 82 (section 6901 et seq.) of this title. For complete classification of this Act to the Code, see Short Title of 1965 Acts note set out under section 6901 of this title and Tables.

**Effective Dates**

1986 Acts

Section effective Oct. 17, 1986, see section 4 of Pub.L. 99–499, set out as a note under section 9601 of this title.

**Congressional Statement of Purpose**

Section 209(a) of Pub.L. 99–499 provided that: "The purposes of this section [enacting this section] are as follows:

"(1) To establish a comprehensive and coordinated Federal program of research, development, demonstration, and training for the purpose of promoting the development of alternative and innovative treatment technologies that can be used in response actions under the CERCLA program, to provide incentives for the development and use of such technologies, and to improve the scientific capability to assess, detect and evaluate the effects on and risks to human health from hazardous substances.

"(2) To establish a basic university research and education program within the Department of Health and Human Services and a research, demonstration, and training program within the Environmental Protection Agency.

"(3) To reserve certain funds from the Hazardous Substance Trust Fund to support a basic research program within the Department of Health and Human Services, and an applied and developmental research program within the Environmental Protection Agency.

"(4) To enhance the Environmental Protection Agency's internal research capabilities related to CERCLA activities, including site assessment and technology evaluation.

"(5) To provide incentives for the development of alternative and innovative treatment technologies in a manner that supplements or coordinates with, but does not compete with or duplicate, private sector development of such technologies."

**Gulf Coast Hazardous Substance Research, Development, and Demonstration Center**

Section 118(*l*) of Pub.L. 99–499 provided that:

"(1) **Establishment of hazardous substance research, development, and demonstration center.**—The Administrator shall establish a hazardous substance research, development, and demonstration center (hereinafter in this subsection referred to as the 'Center') for the purpose of conducting research to aid in more effective hazardous substance response and waste management throughout the Gulf Coast.

"(2) **Purposes of the Center.**—The Center shall carry out a program of research, evaluation, testing, development, and demonstration of alternative or innovative technologies which may be utilized in response actions or in normal handling of hazardous wastes to achieve better protection of human health and the environment.

"(3) **Operation of Center.—(A)** For purposes of operating the Center, the Administrator is authorized to enter into contracts and cooperative agreements with, and make grants to, a university related institute involved with the improvement of waste management. Such institute shall be located in Jefferson County, Texas.

"(B) The Center shall be authorized to make grants, accept contributions, and enter into agreements with universities located in the States of Texas, Louisiana, Mississippi, Alabama, and Florida in order to carry out the purposes of the Center.

"(4) **Authorization of appropriations.**—There are authorized to be appropriated to the Administrator for purposes of carrying out this subsection for fiscal years beginning after September 30, 1986, not more than $5,000,000."

**Pacific Northwest Hazardous Substance Research, Development, and Demonstration Center**

Section 118(*o*) of Pub.L. 99–499 provided that:

"(1) **Establishment.**—The Administrator shall establish a hazardous substance research, development, and demonstration center (hereinafter in this subsection referred to as the 'Center') for the purpose of conducting research to aid in more effective hazardous substance response in the Pacific Northwest.

"(2) **Purposes of Center.**—The Center shall carry out a program of research, evaluation, testing, development, and demonstration of alternative or innovative technologies which may be utilized in response actions to achieve more permanent protection of human health and welfare and the environment.

"(3) **Operation of Center.**—

"(A) **Nonprofit entity.**—For the purposes of operating the Center, the Administrator is authorized to enter into contracts and cooperative agreements with, and make grants to, a nonprofit private entity as defined in section 201(i) of Public Law 96–517 [probably means section 201(i) of Title 35, Patents, which was enacted by section 6(a) of Pub.L. 96–517, Dec. 12, 1980, 94 Stat. 3020] which entity shall agree to provide the basic technical and management personnel. Such nonprofit private entity shall also agree to provide at least two permanent research facilities, one of which shall be located in Benton County, Washington, and one of which shall be located in Clallam County, Washington.

"(B) **Authorities.**—The Center shall be authorized to make grants, accept contributions, and enter into agreements with universities located in the States of Washington, Oregon, Idaho, and Montana in order to carry out the purposes of the Center.

"(4) **Hazardous waste research at the Hanford site.**—

"(A) **Interagency Agreements.**—The Administrator and the Secretary of Energy are authorized to enter into interagency agreements with one another for the purpose of providing for research, evaluation, testing, development, and demonstration into alternative or innovative technologies to characterize and assess the nature and extent of hazardous waste (including radioactive mixed waste) contamination at the Hanford site, in the State of Washington.

"(B) **Funding.**—There is authorized to be appropriated to the Secretary of Energy for purposes of carrying out this paragraph for fiscal years beginning after September 30, 1986, not more than $5,000,000. All sums appropriated under this subparagraph shall be provided to the Administrator by the Secretary of Energy, pursuant to the interagency agreement entered into under subparagraph (A), for the purpose of the Administrator entering into contracts and cooperative agreements with, and making grants to, the Center in order to carry out the research, evaluation, testing, development, and demonstration described in paragraph (1).

"(5) **Authorization of appropriations.**—There is authorized to be appropriated to the Administrator for purposes of carrying out this subsection (other than paragraph (4)) for fiscal years beginning after September 30, 1986, not more than $5,000,000."

**Termination of Advisory Councils**

Advisory councils established after Jan. 5, 1973, to terminate not later than the expiration of the 2–year period beginning on the date of their establishment, unless, in the case of a council established by the President or an officer of the Federal Government, such council is renewed by appropriate action prior to the expiration of such 2–year period, or in the case of a council established by the Congress, its duration is otherwise provided by law. See sections 3(2) and 14 of Pub.L. 92–463, Oct. 6, 1972, 86 Stat. 770, 776, set out in Appendix 2 to Title 5, Government Organization and Employees.

## § 9660a. Grant program

### (1) Grant purposes

Grants for the training and education of workers who are or may be engaged in activities related to hazardous waste removal or containment or emergency response may be made under this section.

### (2) Administration

Grants under this section shall be administered by the National Institute of Environmental Health Sciences.

### (3) Grant recipients

Grants shall be awarded to nonprofit organizations which demonstrate experience in implementing and operating worker health and safety training and education programs and demonstrate the ability to reach and involve in training programs target populations of workers who are or will be engaged in hazardous waste removal or containment or emergency response operations.

(Pub.L. 99–499, Title I, § 126(g), Oct. 17, 1986, 100 Stat. 1692.)

### HISTORICAL AND STATUTORY NOTES

**Codifications**

Section was enacted as a part of the Superfund Amendments and Reauthorization Act of 1986, and not as a part of the Comprehensive Environmental Response, Compensation, and Liability Act of 1980, which is classified to this chapter.

## § 9661. Love Canal property acquisition

### [CERCLA § 312]

### (a) Acquisition of property in Emergency Declaration Area

The Administrator of the Environmental Protection Agency (hereinafter referred to as the "Administrator") may make grants not to exceed $2,500,000 to the State of New York (or to any duly constituted public agency or authority thereof) for purposes of acquisition of private property in the Love Canal Emergency Declaration Area. Such acquisition shall include (but shall not be limited to) all private property within the Emergency Declaration Area, including non-owner occupied residential properties, commercial, industrial, public, religious, non-profit, and vacant properties.

**(b) Procedures for acquisition**

No property shall be acquired pursuant to this section unless the property owner voluntarily agrees to such acquisition. Compensation for any property acquired pursuant to this section shall be based upon the fair market value of the property as it existed prior to the emergency declaration. Valuation procedures for property acquired with funds provided under this section shall be in accordance with those set forth in the agreement entered into between the New York State Disaster Preparedness Commission and the Love Canal Revitalization Agency on October 9, 1980.

**(c) State ownership**

The Administrator shall not provide any funds under this section for the acquisition of any properties pursuant to this section unless a public agency or authority of the State of New York first enters into a cooperative agreement with the Administrator providing assurances deemed adequate by the Administrator that the State or an agency created under the laws of the State shall take title to the properties to be so acquired.

**(d) Maintenance of property**

The Administrator shall enter into a cooperative agreement with an appropriate public agency or authority of the State of New York under which the Administrator shall maintain or arrange for the maintenance of all properties within the Emergency Declaration Area that have been acquired by any public agency or authority of the State. Ninety (90) percent of the costs of such maintenance shall be paid by the Administrator. The remaining portion of such costs shall be paid by the State (unless a credit is available under section 9604(c) of this title). The Administrator is authorized, in his discretion, to provide technical assistance to any public agency or authority of the State of New York in order to implement the recommendations of the habitability and land-use study in order to put the land within the Emergency Declaration Area to its best use.

**(e) Habitability and land use study**

The Administrator shall conduct or cause to be conducted a habitability and land-use study. The study shall—

(1) assess the risks associated with inhabiting of the Love Canal Emergency Declaration Area;

(2) compare the level of hazardous waste contamination in that Area to that present in other comparable communities; and

(3) assess the potential uses of the land within the Emergency Declaration Area, including but not limited to residential, industrial, commercial and recreational, and the risks associated with such potential uses.

The Administrator shall publish the findings of such study and shall work with the State of New York to develop recommendations based upon the results of such study.

**(f) Funding**

For purposes of section 9611 of this title [and 9631(c) of this title], the expenditures authorized by this section shall be treated as a cost specified in section 9611(c) of this title.

**(g) Response**

The provisions of this section shall not affect the implementation of other response actions within the Emergency Declaration Area that the Administrator has determined (before October 17, 1986) to be necessary to protect the public health or welfare or the environment.

**(h) Definitions**

For purposes of this section:

**(1) Emergency Declaration Area**

The terms "Emergency Declaration Area" and "Love Canal Emergency Declaration Area" mean the Emergency Declaration Area as defined in section 950, paragraph (2) of the General Municipal Law of the State of New York, Chapter 259, Laws of 1980, as in effect on October 17, 1986.

**(2) Private property**

As used in subsection (a) of this section, the term "private property" means all property which is not owned by a department, agency, or instrumentality of—

(A) the United States, or

(B) the State of New York (or any public agency or authority thereof).

(Pub.L. 96–510, Title III, § 312, as added Pub.L. 99–499, Title II, § 213(b), Oct. 17, 1986, 100 Stat. 1727.)

## HISTORICAL AND STATUTORY NOTES

**References in Text**

Section 9631 of this title, referred to in subsec. (f), was repealed by Pub.L. 99–499, Title V, § 517(c)(1), Oct. 17, 1986, 100 Stat. 1774.

**Effective Dates**

1986 Acts

Section effective Oct. 17, 1986, see section 4 of Pub.L. 99–499, set out as a note under section 9601 of this title.

**Coordination of Titles I to IV of Pub.L. 99–499**

Any provision of Titles I to IV of Pub.L. 99–499, imposing any tax, premium, or fee; establishing any trust fund; or authorizing expenditures from any trust fund, to have no force or effect, see section 531 of Pub.L. 99–499, set out as a note under section 1 of Title 26, Internal Revenue Code.

**Love Canal Property Acquisition; Congressional Findings**

Section 213(a) of Pub.L. 99–499 provided that:

"(1) The area known as Love Canal located in the city of Niagara Falls and the town of Wheatfield, New York, was the first toxic waste site to receive national attention. As a result of that attention Congress investigated the problems associated with toxic waste sites and enacted CERCLA [this chapter] to deal with these problems.

"(2) Because Love Canal came to the Nation's attention prior to the passage of CERCLA and because the fund under CERCLA was not available to compensate for all of the hardships endured by the citizens in the area, Congress has determined that special provisions are required. These provisions do not affect the lawfulness, implementation, or selection of any other response actions at Love Canal or at any other facilities."

## § 9662. Limitation on contract and borrowing authority

Any authority provided by this Act, including any amendment made by this Act, to enter into contracts to obligate the United States or to incur indebtedness for the repayment of which the United States is liable shall be effective only to such extent or in such amounts as are provided in appropriation Acts.

(Pub.L. 99–499, § 3, Oct. 17, 1986, 100 Stat. 1614.)

### HISTORICAL AND STATUTORY NOTES

**References in Text**

This Act, referred to in text, is Pub.L. 99–499, Oct. 17, 1986, 100 Stat. 1613, as amended, known as the Superfund Amendments and Reauthorization Act of 1986. For complete classification of this Act to the Code, see Short Title of 1986 Amendments note set out under section 9601 of this title and Tables.

**Codifications**

Section was enacted as part of the Superfund Amendments and Reauthorization Act of 1986, and not as part of the Comprehensive Environmental Response, Compensation, and Liability Act of 1980, which comprises this chapter.

**Effective Dates**

1986 Acts

Section effective Oct. 17, 1986, see section 4 of Pub.L. 99–499, set out as a note under section 9601 of this title.

# SUBCHAPTER IV—POLLUTION INSURANCE

## § 9671. Definitions

### [CERCLA § 401]

As used in this subchapter—

**(1) Insurance**

The term "insurance" means primary insurance, excess insurance, reinsurance, surplus lines insurance, and any other arrangement for shifting and distributing risk which is determined to be insurance under applicable State or Federal law.

**(2) Pollution liability**

The term "pollution liability" means liability for injuries arising from the release of hazardous substances or pollutants or contaminants.

**(3) Risk retention group**

The term "risk retention group" means any corporation or other limited liability association taxable as a corporation, or as an insurance company, formed under the laws of any State—

(A) whose primary activity consists of assuming and spreading all, or any portion, of the pollution liability of its group members;

(B) which is organized for the primary purpose of conducting the activity described under subparagraph (A);

(C) which is chartered or licensed as an insurance company and authorized to engage in the business of insurance under the laws of any State; and

(D) which does not exclude any person from membership in the group solely to provide for members of such a group a competitive advantage over such a person.

**(4) Purchasing group**

The term "purchasing group" means any group of persons which has as one of its purposes the purchase of pollution liability insurance on a group basis.

**(5) State**

The term "State" means any State of the United States, the District of Columbia, the Commonwealth of Puerto Rico, Guam, American Samoa, the Virgin Islands, the Commonwealth of the Northern Marianas, and any other territory or possession over which the United States has jurisdiction.

(Pub.L. 96–510, Title IV, § 401, as added Pub.L. 99–499, Title II, § 210(a), formerly § 210, Oct. 17, 1986, 100 Stat. 1716, as renumbered Pub.L. 99–563, § 11(c)(1), Oct. 27, 1986, 100 Stat. 3177.)

### HISTORICAL AND STATUTORY NOTES

**Effective Dates**

1986 Acts

Section effective Oct. 17, 1986, see section 4 of Pub.L. 99–499, set out as a note under section 9601 of this title.

**State Powers and Authorities under Risk Retention Amendments of 1986**

Section 210(b) of Pub.L. 99–499, as added Pub.L. 99–563, § 11(c)(1), Oct. 27, 1986, 100 Stat. 3177, effective Oct. 27, 1986, pursuant to Pub.L. 99–563, § 11(a), provided that: "For purposes of subsection (a) of this section [enacting this subchapter], the powers and authorities of States addressed by the Risk Retention Amendments of 1986 [for classification to the Code, see Short Title of 1986 Amendment note under section 3901 of Title 15, Commerce and Trade] are in addition to those of this Act [see Short Title of 1986 Amendments note set out under 9601 of this title]."

## § 9672. State laws; scope of subchapter

**[CERCLA § 402]**

### (a) State laws

Nothing in this subchapter shall be construed to affect either the tort law or the law governing the interpretation of insurance contracts of any State. The definitions of pollution liability and pollution liability insurance under any State law shall not be applied for the purposes of this subchapter, including recognition or qualification of risk retention groups or purchasing groups.

### (b) Scope of subchapter

The authority to offer or to provide insurance under this subchapter shall be limited to coverage of pollution liability risks and this subchapter does not authorize a risk retention group or purchasing group to provide coverage of any other line of insurance.

(Pub.L. 96–510, Title IV, § 402, as added Pub.L. 99–499, Title II, § 210(a), formerly § 210, Oct. 17, 1986, 100 Stat. 1716, as renumbered Pub.L. 99–563, § 11(c)(1), Oct. 27, 1986, 100 Stat. 3177.)

### HISTORICAL AND STATUTORY NOTES

**Effective Dates**

1986 Acts

Section effective Oct. 17, 1986, see section 4 of Pub.L. 99–499, set out as a note under section 9601 of this title.

## § 9673. Risk retention groups

**[CERCLA § 403]**

### (a) Exemption

Except as provided in this section, a risk retention group shall be exempt from the following:

(1) A State law, rule, or order which makes unlawful, or regulates, directly or indirectly, the operation of a risk retention group.

(2) A State law, rule, or order which requires or permits a risk retention group to participate in any insurance insolvency guaranty association to which an insurer licensed in the State is required to belong.

(3) A State law, rule, or order which requires any insurance policy issued to a risk retention group or any member of the group to be countersigned by an insurance agent or broker residing in the State.

(4) A State law, rule, or order which otherwise discriminates against a risk retention group or any of its members.

### (b) Exceptions

#### (1) State laws generally applicable

Nothing in subsection (a) of this section shall be construed to affect the applicability of State laws generally applicable to persons or corporations. The State in which a risk retention group is chartered may regulate the formation and operation of the group.

#### (2) State regulations not subject to exemption

Subsection (a) of this section shall not apply to any State law which requires a risk retention group to do any of the following:

**(A)** Comply with the unfair claim settlement practices law of the State.

**(B)** Pay, on a nondiscriminatory basis, applicable premium and other taxes which are levied on admitted insurers and surplus line insurers, brokers, or policyholders under the laws of the State.

**(C)** Participate, on a nondiscriminatory basis, in any mechanism established or authorized under the law of the State for the equitable apportionment among insurers of pollution liability insurance losses and expenses incurred on policies written through such mechanism.

**(D)** Submit to the appropriate authority reports and other information required of licensed insurers under the laws of a State relating solely to pollution liability insurance losses and expenses.

**(E)** Register with and designate the State insurance commissioner as its agent solely for the purpose of receiving service of legal documents or process.

**(F)** Furnish, upon request, such commissioner a copy of any financial report submitted by the risk retention group to the commissioner of the chartering or licensing jurisdiction.

**(G)** Submit to an examination by the State insurance commissioner in any State in which the group is doing business to determine the group's financial condition, if—

**(i)** the commissioner has reason to believe the risk retention group is in a financially impaired condition; and

**(ii)** the commissioner of the jurisdiction in which the group is chartered has not begun or has refused to initiate an examination of the group.

(H) Comply with a lawful order issued in a delinquency proceeding commenced by the State insurance commissioner if the commissioner of the jurisdiction in which the group is chartered has failed to initiate such a proceeding after notice of a finding of financial impairment under subparagraph (G).

**(c) Application of exemptions**

The exemptions specified in subsection (a) of this section apply to—

(1) pollution liability insurance coverage provided by a risk retention group for—

(A) such group; or

(B) any person who is a member of such group;

(2) the sale of pollution liability insurance coverage for a risk retention group; and

(3) the provision of insurance related services or management services for a risk retention group or any member of such a group.

**(d) Agents or brokers**

A State may require that a person acting, or offering to act, as an agent or broker for a risk retention group obtain a license from that State, except that a State may not impose any qualification or requirement which discriminates against a nonresident agent or broker.

(Pub.L. 96–510, Title IV, § 403, as added Pub.L. 99–499, Title II, § 210(a), formerly § 210, Oct. 17, 1986, 100 Stat. 1717, as renumbered Pub.L. 99–563, § 11(c)(1), Oct. 27, 1986, 100 Stat. 3177.)

### HISTORICAL AND STATUTORY NOTES

**Effective Dates**

1986 Acts

Section effective Oct. 17, 1986, see section 4 of Pub.L. 99–499, set out as a note under section 9601 of this title.

## § 9674. Purchasing groups

[CERCLA § 404]

**(a) Exemption**

Except as provided in this section, a purchasing group is exempt from the following:

(1) A State law, rule, or order which prohibits the establishment of a purchasing group.

(2) A State law, rule, or order which makes it unlawful for an insurer to provide or offer to provide insurance on a basis providing, to a purchasing group or its member, advantages, based on their loss and expense experience, not afforded to other persons with respect to rates, policy forms, coverages, or other matters.

(3) A State law, rule, or order which prohibits a purchasing group or its members from purchasing insurance on the group basis described in paragraph (2) of this subsection.

(4) A State law, rule, or order which prohibits a purchasing group from obtaining insurance on a group basis because the group has not been in existence for a minimum period of time or because any member has not belonged to the group for a minimum period of time.

(5) A State law, rule, or order which requires that a purchasing group must have a minimum number of members, common ownership or affiliation, or a certain legal form.

(6) A State law, rule, or order which requires that a certain percentage of a purchasing group must obtain insurance on a group basis.

(7) A State law, rule, or order which requires that any insurance policy issued to a purchasing group or any members of the group be countersigned by an insurance agent or broker residing in that State.

(8) A State law, rule, or order which otherwise discriminate [1] against a purchasing group or any of its members.

**(b) Application of exemptions**

The exemptions specified in subsection (a) of this section apply to the following:

(1) Pollution liability insurance, and comprehensive general liability insurance which includes this coverage, provided to—

(A) a purchasing group; or

(B) any person who is a member of a purchasing group.

(2) The sale of any one of the following to a purchasing group or a member of the group:

(A) Pollution liability insurance and comprehensive general liability coverage.

(B) Insurance related services.

(C) Management services.

**(c) Agents or brokers**

A State may require that a person acting, or offering to act, as an agent or broker for a purchasing group obtain a license from that State, except that a State may not impose any qualification or requirement which discriminates against a nonresident agent or broker.

(Pub.L. 96–510, Title IV, § 404, as added Pub.L. 99–499, Title II, § 210(a), formerly § 210, Oct. 17, 1986, 100 Stat. 1718, as renumbered Pub.L. 99–563, § 11(c)(1), Oct. 27, 1986, 100 Stat. 3177.)

[1] So in original. Probably should be "discriminates".

### HISTORICAL AND STATUTORY NOTES

**Effective Dates**

1986 Acts

Section effective Oct. 17, 1986, see section 4 of Pub.L. 99–499, set out as a note under section 9601 of this title.

## § 9675. Applicability of securities laws

[CERCLA § 405]

### (a) Ownership interests

The ownership interests of members of a risk retention group shall be considered to be—

(1) exempted securities for purposes of section 77e of Title 15 and for purposes of section 78*l* of Title 15; and

(2) securities for purposes of the provisions of section 77q of Title 15 and the provisions of section 78j of Title 15.

### (b) Investment Company Act

A risk retention group shall not be considered to be an investment company for purposes of the Investment Company Act of 1940 (15 U.S.C. 80a–1 et seq.).

### (c) Blue sky law

The ownership interests of members in a risk retention group shall not be considered securities for purposes of any State blue sky law.

(Pub.L. 96–510, Title IV, § 405, as added Pub.L. 99–499, Title II, § 210(a), formerly § 210, Oct. 17, 1986, 100 Stat. 1719, as renumbered Pub.L. 99–563, § 11(c)(1), Oct. 27, 1986, 100 Stat. 3177.)

### HISTORICAL AND STATUTORY NOTES

**References in Text**

The Investment Company Act of 1940, referred to in subsec. (b), is Title I of Act Aug. 22, 1940, c. 686, 54 Stat. 789, as amended, which is classified principally to subchapter I (section 80a–1 et seq.) of chapter 2D of Title 15, Commerce and Trade. For complete classification of this Act to the Code, see section 80a–51 of Title 15 and Tables.

**Effective Dates**

1986 Acts

Section effective Oct. 17, 1986, see section 4 of Pub.L. 99–499, set out as a note under section 9601 of this title.

# NUCLEAR WASTE POLICY

## NUCLEAR WASTE POLICY ACT OF 1982 [NWPA § _____]

**(42 U.S.C.A. §§ 10101 to 10270)**

## CHAPTER 108—NUCLEAR WASTE POLICY

**Related Provisions**

*See, also, Uranium Mill Tailings Radiation Control, 42 U.S.C.A. § 7901 et seq., ante.*

## § 10101. Definitions

[NWPA § 2]

For purposes of this chapter:

(1) The term "Administrator" means the Administrator of the Environmental Protection Agency.

(2) The term "affected Indian tribe" means any Indian tribe—

(A) within whose reservation boundaries a monitored retrievable storage facility, test and evaluation facility, or a repository for high-level radioactive waste or spent fuel is proposed to be located;

(B) whose federally defined possessory or usage rights to other lands outside of the reservation's boundaries arising out of congressionally ratified treaties may be substantially and adversely affected by the locating of such a facility: *Provided,* That the Secretary of the Interior finds, upon the petition of the appropriate governmental officials of the tribe, that such effects are both substantial and adverse to the tribe;[1]

(3) The term "atomic energy defense activity" means any activity of the Secretary performed in whole or in part in carrying out any of the following functions:

(A) naval reactors development;

(B) weapons activities including defense inertial confinement fusion;

(C) verification and control technology;

(D) defense nuclear materials production;

(E) defense nuclear waste and materials byproducts management;

(F) defense nuclear materials security and safeguards and security investigations; and

(G) defense research and development.

(4) The term "candidate site" means an area, within a geologic and hydrologic system, that is recommended by the Secretary under section 10132 of this title for site characterization, approved by the President under section 10132 of this title for site characterization, or undergoing site characterization under section 10133 of this title.

(5) The term "civilian nuclear activity" means any atomic energy activity other than an atomic energy defense activity.

(6) The term "civilian nuclear power reactor" means a civilian nuclear powerplant required to be licensed under section 2133 or 2134(b) of this title.

(7) The term "Commission" means the Nuclear Regulatory Commission.

(8) The term "Department" means the Department of Energy.

(9) The term "disposal" means the emplacement in a repository of high-level radioactive waste, spent

nuclear fuel, or other highly radioactive material with no foreseeable intent of recovery, whether or not such emplacement permits the recovery of such waste.

(10) The terms "disposal package" and "package" mean the primary container that holds, and is in contact with, solidified high-level radioactive waste, spent nuclear fuel, or other radioactive materials, and any overpacks that are emplaced at a repository.

(11) The term "engineered barriers" means man-made components of a disposal system designed to prevent the release of radionuclides into the geologic medium involved. Such term includes the high-level radioactive waste form, high-level radioactive waste canisters, and other materials placed over and around such canisters.

(12) The term "high-level radioactive waste" means—

(A) the highly radioactive material resulting from the reprocessing of spent nuclear fuel, including liquid waste produced directly in reprocessing and any solid material derived from such liquid waste that contains fission products in sufficient concentrations; and

(B) other highly radioactive material that the Commission, consistent with existing law, determines by rule requires permanent isolation.

(13) The term "Federal agency" means any Executive agency, as defined in section 105 of Title 5.

(14) The term "Governor" means the chief executive officer of a State.

(15) The term "Indian tribe" means any Indian tribe, band, nation, or other organized group or community of Indians recognized as eligible for the services provided to Indians by the Secretary of the Interior because of their status as Indians, including any Alaska Native village, as defined in section 3(c) of the Alaska Native Claims Settlement Act (43 U.S.C. 1602(c) ).

(16) The term "low-level radioactive waste" means radioactive material that—

(A) is not high-level radioactive waste, spent nuclear fuel, transuranic waste, or by-product material as defined in section 2014(e)(2) of this title; and

(B) the Commission, consistent with existing law, classifies as low-level radioactive waste.

(17) The term "Office" means the Office of Civilian Radioactive Waste Management established in section 10224 of this title.

(18) The term "repository" means any system licensed by the Commission that is intended to be used for, or may be used for, the permanent deep geologic disposal of high-level radioactive waste and spent nuclear fuel, whether or not such system is designed to permit the recovery, for a limited period during initial operation, of any materials placed in such system. Such term includes both surface and subsurface areas at which high-level radioactive waste and spent nuclear fuel handling activities are conducted.

(19) The term "reservation" means—

(A) any Indian reservation or dependent Indian community referred to in clause (a) or (b) of section 1151 of Title 18; or

(B) any land selected by an Alaska Native village or regional corporation under the provisions of the Alaska Native Claims Settlement Act (43 U.S.C. 1601 et seq.).

(20) The term "Secretary" means the Secretary of Energy.

(21) The term "site characterization" means—

(A) siting research activities with respect to a test and evaluation facility at a candidate site; and

(B) activities, whether in the laboratory or in the field, undertaken to establish the geologic condition and the ranges of the parameters of a candidate site relevant to the location of a repository, including borings, surface excavations, excavations of exploratory shafts, limited subsurface lateral excavations and borings, and in situ testing needed to evaluate the suitability of a candidate site for the location of a repository, but not including preliminary borings and geophysical testing needed to assess whether site characterization should be undertaken.

(22) The term "siting research" means activities, including borings, surface excavations, shaft excavations, subsurface lateral excavations and borings, and in situ testing, to determine the suitability of a site for a test and evaluation facility.

(23) The term "spent nuclear fuel" means fuel that has been withdrawn from a nuclear reactor following irradiation, the constituent elements of which have not been separated by reprocessing.

(24) The term "State" means each of the several States, the District of Columbia, the Commonwealth of Puerto Rico, the Virgin Islands, Guam, American Samoa, the Northern Mariana Islands, the Trust Territory of the Pacific Islands, and any other territory or possession of the United States.

(25) The term "storage" means retention of high-level radioactive waste, spent nuclear fuel, or transuranic waste with the intent to recover such waste or fuel for subsequent use, processing, or disposal.

(26) The term "Storage Fund" means the Interim Storage Fund established in section 10156(c) of this title.

(27) The term "test and evaluation facility" means an at-depth, prototypic, underground cavity with subsurface lateral excavations extending from a central shaft that is used for research and development purposes, including the development of data and experience for the safe handling and disposal of solidified high-level radioactive waste, transuranic waste, or spent nuclear fuel.

(28) The term "unit of general local government" means any borough, city, county, parish, town, township, village, or other general purpose political subdivision of a State.

(29) The term "Waste Fund" means the Nuclear Waste Fund established in section 10222(c) of this title.

(30) The term "Yucca Mountain site" means the candidate site in the State of Nevada recommended by the Secretary to the President under section 10132(b)(1)(B) of this title on May 27, 1986.

(31) The term "affected unit of local government" means the unit of local government with jurisdiction over the site of a repository or a monitored retrievable storage facility. Such term may, at the discretion of the Secretary, include units of local government that are contiguous with such unit.

(32) The term "Negotiator" means the Nuclear Waste Negotiator.

(33) As used in subchapter IV of this chapter, the term "Office" means the Office of the Nuclear Waste Negotiator established under subchapter IV of this chapter.

(34) The term "monitored retrievable storage facility" means the storage facility described in section 10161(b)(1) of this title.

(Pub.L. 97–425, § 2, Jan. 7, 1983, 96 Stat. 2202; Pub.L. 100–202, § 101(d) [Title III, § 300], Dec. 22, 1987, 101 Stat. 1329–104, 1329–121; Pub.L. 100–203, Title V, § 5002, Dec. 22, 1987, 101 Stat. 1330–227.)

[1] So in original. The semicolon probably should be a period.

## HISTORICAL AND STATUTORY NOTES

### References in Text

Section 10224 of this title, referred to in par. (17), was in the original a reference to section 305 of Pub.L. 97–425, which is classified to section 10225 of this title, and was translated as section 10224 of this title as the probable intent of Congress, in view of the Office of Civilian Radioactive Waste Management being established by section 10224 of this title.

The Alaska Native Claims Settlement Act, referred to in par. (19)(B), is Pub.L. 92–203, Dec. 18, 1971, 85 Stat. 688, as amended, which is classified generally to chapter 33 (section 1601 et seq.) of Title 43, Public Lands. Section 3 of the Alaska Native Claims Settlement Act, referred to in par. (15), is classified to section 1602 of Title 43. For complete classification of this Act to the Code, see Short Title note set out under section 1601 of Title 43 and Tables.

Section 10156(c) of this title, referred to in par. (26), was in the original a reference to section 137(c) of Pub.L. 97–425, which is classified to section 10157(c) of this title, and has been translated as section 10156(c) of this title as the probable intent of Congress, in view of the Interim Storage Fund being established by section 10156(c) of this title.

### Short Title

1987 Amendments

Section 101(d) [Title III] of Pub.L. 100–202 and section 5001 of Pub.L. 100–203 provided that: "This subtitle [enacting sections 10162, 10163, 10164, 10165, 10166, 10167, 10168, 10169, 10172, 10172a, 10173, 10173a, 10173b, 10173c, 10174, 10174a, 10175, 10204, 10241, 10242, 10243, 10244, 10245, 10246, 10247, 10248, 10249, 10250, 10251, 10261, 10262, 10263, 10264, 10265, 10266, 10267, 10268, 10269, and 10270 of this title, amending sections 10101, 10132, 10133, 10134, 10136, 10137 and 10138 of this title and enacting provisions set out as a note under section 5841 of this title] may be cited as the Nuclear Waste Policy Amendments Act of 1987'."

1983 Acts

Section 1 of Pub.L. 97–425 provided that: "This Act [enacting this chapter] may be cited as the 'Nuclear Waste Policy Act of 1982'."

### Nuclear Waste Management Plan; Report

Pub.L. 102–486, Title VIII, § 803, Oct. 24, 1992, 106 Stat. 2923, provided that:

"(a) **Preparation and submission of report.**—The Secretary of Energy, in consultation with the Nuclear Regulatory Commission and the Environmental Protection Agency, shall prepare and submit to the Congress a report on whether current programs and plans for management of nuclear waste as mandated by the Nuclear Waste Policy Act of 1982 (42 U.S.C. 10101 et seq.) [this chapter] are adequate for management of any additional volumes or categories of nuclear waste that might be generated by any new nuclear power plants that might be constructed and licensed after the date of the enactment of this Act [Oct. 24, 1992]. The Secretary shall prepare the report for submission to the President and the Congress within 1 year after the date of the enactment of this Act [Oct. 24, 1992]. The report shall examine any new relevant issues related to management of spent nuclear fuel and high-level radioactive waste that might be raised by the addition of new nuclear-generated electric capacity, including anticipated increased volumes of spent nuclear fuel or high-level radioactive waste, any need for additional interim storage capacity prior to final disposal, transportation of additional volumes of waste, and any need for additional repositories for deep geologic disposal.

"(b) **Opportunity for public comment.**—In preparation of the report required under subsection (a), the Secretary of Energy shall offer members of the public an opportunity to provide information and comment and shall solicit the views of the Nuclear Regulatory Commission, the Environmental Protection Agency, and other interested parties.

"(c) **Authorization of appropriations.**—There are authorized to be appropriated such sums as may be necessary to carry out this section [this note]."

## § 10102. Separability

[NWPA § 3]

If any provision of this chapter, or the application of such provision to any person or circumstance, is held invalid, the remainder of this chapter, or the application of such provision to persons or circumstances other than those as to which it is held invalid, shall not be affected thereby.

(Pub.L. 97–425, § 3, Jan. 7, 1983, 96 Stat. 2205.)

## § 10103. Territories and possessions

[NWPA § 4]

Nothing in this chapter shall be deemed to repeal, modify, or amend the provisions of section 1491 of Title 48.

(Pub.L. 97–425, § 4, Jan. 7, 1983, 96 Stat. 2205.)

## § 10104. Ocean disposal

[NWPA § 5]

Nothing in this chapter shall be deemed to affect the Marine Protection, Research, and Sanctuaries Act of 1972 (33 U.S.C. 1401 et seq.).

(Pub.L. 97–425, § 5, Jan. 7, 1983, 96 Stat. 2205.)

### HISTORICAL AND STATUTORY NOTES

**References in Text**

The Marine Protection, Research and Sanctuaries Act of 1972, referred to in text, is Pub.L. 92–532, Oct. 23, 1972, 86 Stat. 1052, as amended, which enacted chapters 32 (section 1431 et seq.) and 32A (section 1447 et seq.) of Title 16, Conservation and chapters 27 (section 1401 et seq.) and 41 (section 2801 et seq.) of Title 33, Navigation and Navigable Waters. For complete classification of this Act to the Code, see Short Title note set out under section 1401 of Title 33 and Tables.

## § 10105. Limitation on spending authority

[NWPA § 6]

The authority under this chapter to incur indebtedness, or enter into contracts, obligating amounts to be expended by the Federal Government shall be effective for any fiscal year only to such extent or in such amounts as are provided in advance by appropriation Acts.

(Pub.L. 97–425, § 6, Jan. 7, 1983, 96 Stat. 2205.)

## § 10106. Protection of classified national security information

[NWPA § 7]

Nothing in this chapter shall require the release or disclosure to any person or to the Commission of any classified national security information.

(Pub.L. 97–425, § 7, Jan. 7, 1983, 96 Stat. 2205.)

## § 10107. Applicability to atomic energy defense activities

[NWPA § 8]

**(a) Atomic energy defense activities**

Subject to the provisions of subsection (c) of this section, the provisions of this chapter shall not apply with respect to any atomic energy defense activity or to any facility used in connection with any such activity.

**(b) Evaluation by President**

(1) Not later than 2 years after January 7, 1983, the President shall evaluate the use of disposal capacity at one or more repositories to be developed under part A of subchapter I of this chapter for the disposal of high-level radioactive waste resulting from atomic energy defense activities. Such evaluation shall take into consideration factors relating to cost efficiency, health and safety, regulation, transportation, public acceptability, and national security.

(2) Unless the President finds, after conducting the evaluation required in paragraph (1), that the development of a repository for the disposal of high-level radioactive waste resulting from atomic energy defense activities only is required, taking into account all of the factors described in such subsection, the Secretary shall proceed promptly with arrangement for the use of one or more of the repositories to be developed under part A of subchapter I of this chapter for the disposal of such waste. Such arrangements shall include the allocation of costs of developing, constructing, and operating this repository or repositories. The costs resulting from permanent disposal of high-level radioactive waste from atomic energy defense activities shall be paid by the Federal Government, into the special account established under section 10222 of this title.

(3) Any repository for the disposal of high-level radioactive waste resulting from atomic energy defense activities only shall (A) be subject to licensing under section 5842 of this title; and (B) comply with all requirements of the Commission for the siting, development, construction, and operation of a repository.

**(c) Applicability to certain repositories**

The provisions of this chapter shall apply with respect to any repository not used exclusively for the disposal of high-level radioactive waste or spent nuclear fuel resulting from atomic energy defense activities, research and development activities of the Secretary, or both.

(Pub.L. 97–425, § 8, Jan. 7, 1983, 96 Stat. 2205.)

## § 10108. Applicability to transportation

[NWPA § 9]

Nothing in this chapter shall be construed to affect Federal, State, or local laws pertaining to the transportation of spent nuclear fuel or high-level radioactive waste.

(Pub.L. 97–425, § 9, Jan. 7, 1983, 96 Stat. 2206.)

# SUBCHAPTER I—DISPOSAL AND STORAGE OF HIGH-LEVEL RADIOACTIVE WASTE, SPENT NUCLEAR FUEL, AND LOW-LEVEL RADIOACTIVE WASTE

## § 10121. State and affected Indian tribe participation in development of proposed repositories for defense waste

[NWPA § 101]

### (a) Notification to States and affected Indian tribes

Notwithstanding the provisions of section 10107 of this title, upon any decision by the Secretary or the President to develop a repository for the disposal of high-level radioactive waste or spent nuclear fuel resulting exclusively from atomic energy defense activities, research and development activities of the Secretary, or both, and before proceeding with any site-specific investigations with respect to such repository, the Secretary shall notify the Governor and legislature of the State in which such repository is proposed to be located, or the governing body of the affected Indian tribe on whose reservation such repository is proposed to be located, as the case may be, of such decision.

### (b) Participation of States and affected Indian tribes

Following the receipt of any notification under subsection (a) of this section, the State or Indian tribe involved shall be entitled, with respect to the proposed repository involved, to rights of participation and consultation identical to those provided in sections 10135 through 10138 of this title, except that any financial assistance authorized to be provided to such State or affected Indian tribe under section 10136(c) or 10138(b) of this title shall be made from amounts appropriated to the Secretary for purposes of carrying out this section.

(Pub.L. 97–425, Title I, § 101, Jan. 7, 1983, 96 Stat. 2206.)

# PART A—REPOSITORIES FOR DISPOSAL OF HIGH-LEVEL RADIOACTIVE WASTE AND SPENT NUCLEAR FUEL

## § 10131. Findings and purposes

[NWPA § 111]

(a) The Congress finds that—

(1) radioactive waste creates potential risks and requires safe and environmentally acceptable methods of disposal;

(2) a national problem has been created by the accumulation of (A) spent nuclear fuel from nuclear reactors; and (B) radioactive waste from (i) reprocessing of spent nuclear fuel; (ii) activities related to medical research, diagnosis, and treatment; and (iii) other sources;

(3) Federal efforts during the past 30 years to devise a permanent solution to the problems of civilian radioactive waste disposal have not been adequate;

(4) while the Federal Government has the responsibility to provide for the permanent disposal of high-level radioactive waste and such spent nuclear fuel as may be disposed of in order to protect the public health and safety and the environment, the costs of such disposal should be the responsibility of the generators and owners of such waste and spent fuel;

(5) the generators and owners of high-level radioactive waste and spent nuclear fuel have the primary responsibility to provide for, and the responsibility to pay the costs of, the interim storage of such waste and spent fuel until such waste and spent fuel is accepted by the Secretary of Energy in accordance with the provisions of this chapter;

(6) State and public participation in the planning and development of repositories is essential in order to promote public confidence in the safety of disposal of such waste and spent fuel; and

(7) high-level radioactive waste and spent nuclear fuel have become major subjects of public concern, and appropriate precautions must be taken to ensure that such waste and spent fuel do not adversely affect the public health and safety and the environment for this or future generations.

(b) The purposes of this part are—

(1) to establish a schedule for the siting, construction, and operation of repositories that will provide a reasonable assurance that the public and the environment will be adequately protected from the hazards posed by high-level radioactive waste and such spent nuclear fuel as may be disposed of in a repository;

(2) to establish the Federal responsibility, and a definite Federal policy, for the disposal of such waste and spent fuel;

(3) to define the relationship between the Federal Government and the State governments with respect to the disposal of such waste and spent fuel; and

(4) to establish a Nuclear Waste Fund, composed of payments made by the generators and owners of such waste and spent fuel, that will ensure that the costs of carrying out activities relating to the disposal of such waste and spent fuel will be borne by the persons responsible for generating such waste and spent fuel.

(Pub.L. 97–425, Title I, § 111, Jan. 7, 1983, 96 Stat. 2207.)

## § 10132. Recommendation of candidate sites for site characterization

[NWPA § 112]

### (a) Guidelines

Not later than 180 days after January 7, 1983, the Secretary, following consultation with the Council on Environmental Quality, the Administrator of the Environmental Protection Agency, the Director of the United States Geological Survey, and interested Governors, and the concurrence of the Commission shall issue general guidelines for the recommendation of sites for repositories. Such guidelines shall specify detailed geologic considerations that shall be primary criteria for the selection of sites in various geologic media. Such guidelines shall specify factors that qualify or disqualify any site from development as a repository, including factors pertaining to the location of valuable natural resources, hydrology, geophysics, seismic activity, and atomic energy defense activities, proximity to water supplies, proximity to populations, the effect upon the rights of users of water, and proximity to components of the National Park System, the National Wildlife Refuge System, the National Wild and Scenic Rivers System, the National Wilderness Preservation System, or National Forest Lands. Such guidelines shall take into consideration the proximity to sites where high-level radioactive waste and spent nuclear fuel is generated or temporarily stored and the transportation and safety factors involved in moving such waste to a repository. Such guidelines shall specify population factors that will disqualify any site from development as a repository if any surface facility of such repository would be located (1) in a highly populated area; or (2) adjacent to an area 1 mile by 1 mile having a population of not less than 1,000 individuals. Such guidelines also shall require the Secretary to consider the cost and impact of transporting to the repository site the solidified high-level radioactive waste and spent fuel to be disposed of in the repository and the advantages of regional distribution in the siting of repositories. Such guidelines shall require the Secretary to consider the various geologic media in which sites for repositories may be located and, to the extent practicable, to recommend sites in different geologic media. The Secretary shall use guidelines established under this subsection in considering candidate sites for recommendation under subsection (b) of this section. The Secretary may revise such guidelines from time to time, consistent with the provisions of this subsection.

### (b) Recommendation by Secretary to President

(1)(A) Following the issuance of guidelines under subsection (a) of this section and consultation with the Governors of affected States, the Secretary shall nominate at least 5 sites that he determines suitable for site characterization for selection of the first repository site.

(B) Subsequent to such nomination, the Secretary shall recommend to the President 3 of the nominated sites not later than January 1, 1985 for characterization as candidate sites.

(C) Such recommendations under subparagraph (B) shall be consistent with the provisions of section 10225 of this title.

(D) Each nomination of a site under this subsection shall be accompanied by an environmental assessment, which shall include a detailed statement of the basis for such recommendation and of the probable impacts of the site characterization activities planned for such site, and a discussion of alternative activities relating to site characterization that may be undertaken to avoid such impacts. Such environmental assessment shall include—

(i) an evaluation by the Secretary as to whether such site is suitable for site characterization under the guidelines established under subsection (a) of this section;

(ii) an evaluation by the Secretary as to whether such site is suitable for development as a repository under each such guideline that does not require site characterization as a prerequisite for application of such guideline;

(iii) an evaluation by the Secretary of the effects of the site characterization activities at such site on the public health and safety and the environment;

(iv) a reasonable comparative evaluation by the Secretary of such site with other sites and locations that have been considered;

(v) a description of the decision process by which such site was recommended; and

(vi) an assessment of the regional and local impacts of locating the proposed repository at such site.

(E) (i) [1] The issuance of any environmental assessment under this paragraph shall be considered to be a final agency action subject to judicial review in accordance with the provisions of chapter 7 of Title 5 and section 10139 of this title. Such judicial review shall be limited to the sufficiency of such environmental assessment with respect to the items described in clauses (i) through (vi) of subparagraph (E).

(F) Each environmental assessment prepared under this paragraph shall be made available to the public.

(G) Before nominating a site, the Secretary shall notify the Governor and legislature of the State in which such site is located, or the governing body of the affected Indian tribe where such site is located, as the case may be, of such nomination and the basis for such nomination.

(2) Before nominating any site the Secretary shall hold public hearings in the vicinity of such site to inform the residents of the area in which such site is located of the proposed nomination of such site and to receive their comments. At such hearings, the Secretary shall also solicit and receive any recommendations of such residents with respect to issues that should be addressed in the environmental assessment described in paragraph (1) and the site characterization plan described in section 10133(b)(1) of this title.

(3) In evaluating the sites nominated under this section prior to any decision to recommend a site as a candidate site, the Secretary shall use available geophysical, geologic, geochemical and hydrologic, and other information and shall not conduct any preliminary borings or excavations at a site unless (i) such preliminary boring or excavation activities were in progress on January 7, 1983, or (ii) the Secretary certifies that such available information from other sources, in the absence of preliminary borings or excavations, will not be adequate to satisfy applicable requirements of this chapter or any other law: *Provided*, That preliminary borings or excavations under this section shall not exceed a diameter of 6 inches.

### (c) Presidential review of recommended candidate sites

(1) The President shall review each candidate site recommendation made by the Secretary under subsection (b) of this section. Not later than 60 days after the submission by the Secretary of a recommendation of a candidate site, the President, in his discretion, may either approve or disapprove such candidate site, and shall transmit any such decision to the Secretary and to either the Governor and legislature of the State in which such candidate site is located, or the governing body of the affected Indian tribe where such candidate site is located, as the case may be. If, during such 60-day period, the President fails to approve or disapprove such candidate site, or fails to invoke his authority under paragraph (2) to delay his decision, such candidate site shall be considered to be approved, and the Secretary shall notify such Governor and legislature, or governing body of the affected Indian tribe, of the approval of such candidate site by reason of the inaction of the President.

(2) The President may delay for not more than 6 months his decision under paragraph (1) to approve or disapprove a candidate site, upon determining that the information provided with the recommendation of the Secretary is insufficient to permit a decision within the 60-day period referred to in paragraph (1). The President may invoke his authority under this paragraph by submitting written notice to the Congress, within such 60-day period, of his intent to invoke such authority. If the President invokes such authority, but fails to approve or disapprove the candidate site involved by the end of such 6-month period, such candidate site shall be considered to be approved, and the Secretary shall notify such Governor and legislature, or governing body of the affected Indian tribe, of the approval of such candidate site by reason of the inaction of the President.

### (d) Preliminary activities

Except as otherwise provided in this section, each activity of the President or the Secretary under this section shall be considered to be a preliminary decisionmaking activity. No such activity shall require the preparation of an environmental impact statement under section 102(2)(C) of the National Environmental Policy Act of 1969 (42 U.S.C. 4332(2)(C)), or to require any environmental review under subparagraph (E) or (F) of section 102(2) of such Act.

(Pub.L. 97–425, Title I, § 112, Jan. 7, 1983, 96 Stat. 2208; Pub.L. 100–202, § 101(d) [Title III, § 300], Dec. 22, 1987, 101 Stat. 1329–104, 1329–121; Pub.L. 100–203, Title V, § 5011(b) to (d), Dec. 22, 1987, 101 Stat. 1330–228; Pub.L. 102–154, Title I, Nov. 13, 1991, 105 Stat. 1000.)

[1] So in original. There is no cl. (ii).

## HISTORICAL AND STATUTORY NOTES

**References in Text**

The National Environmental Policy Act of 1969, referred to in subsec. (d), is Pub.L. 91–190, Jan. 1, 1970, 83 Stat. 852, as amended, which is classified generally to chapter 55 (section 4321 et seq.) of this title. For complete classification of this Act to the Code, see Short Title of 1970 Acts note set out under section 4321 of this title and Tables.

**Change of Name**

"United States Geological Survey" substituted for "Geological Survey" in subsec. (a) pursuant to provision of Title I of Pub.L. 102–154, set out as a Change of Name note under section 31 of Title 43, Public Lands.

## LETTER OF PRESIDENT

**May 28, 1986, 51 F.R. 19531**

DELEGATION OF NOTIFICATION FUNCTIONS TO SECRETARY OF ENERGY

You are hereby authorized to perform the notification function vested in the President pursuant to Section 112(c)(1) of the Nuclear Waste Policy Act of 1982, 42 U.S.C. § 10132(c)(1) [subsec. (c)(1) of this section].

This document shall be published in the Federal Register.

Sincerely,

RONALD REAGAN

THE WHITE HOUSE,
Washington, May 28, 1986.

## § 10133. Site characterization

[NWPA § 113]

### (a) In general

The Secretary shall carry out, in accordance with the provisions of this section, appropriate site characterization activities at the Yucca Mountain site. The Secretary shall consider fully the comments received under subsection (b)(2) of this section and section 10132(b)(2) of this title and shall, to the maximum extent practicable and in consultation with the Governor of the State of Nevada, conduct site characterization activities in a manner that minimizes any significant adverse environmental impacts identified in such comments or in the environmental assessment submitted under subsection (b)(1) of this section.

### (b) Commission and States

(1) Before proceeding to sink shafts at the Yucca Mountain site, the Secretary shall submit for such candidate site to the Commission and to the Governor or legislature of the State of Nevada, for their review and comment—

(A) a general plan for site characterization activities to be conducted at such candidate site, which plan shall include—

(i) a description of such candidate site;

(ii) a description of such site characterization activities, including the following: the extent of planned excavations, plans for any onsite testing with radioactive or nonradioactive material, plans for any investigation activities that may affect the capability of such candidate site to isolate high-level radioactive waste and spent nuclear fuel, and plans to control any adverse, safety-related impacts from such site characterization activities;

(iii) plans for the decontamination and decommissioning of such candidate site, and for the mitigation of any significant adverse environmental impacts caused by site characterization activities if it is determined unsuitable for application for a construction authorization for a repository;

(iv) criteria to be used to determine the suitability of such candidate site for the location of a repository, developed pursuant to section 10132(a) of this title; and

(v) any other information required by the Commission;

(B) a description of the possible form or packaging for the high-level radioactive waste and spent nuclear fuel to be emplaced in such repository, a description, to the extent practicable, of the relationship between such waste form or packaging and the geologic medium of such site, and a description of the activities being conducted by the Secretary with respect to such possible waste form or packaging or such relationship; and

(C) a conceptual repository design that takes into account likely site-specific requirements.

(2) Before proceeding to sink shafts at the Yucca Mountain site, the Secretary shall (A) make available to the public the site characterization plan described in paragraph (1); and (B) hold public hearings in the vicinity of such candidate site to inform the residents of the area in which such candidate site is located of such plan, and to receive their comments.

(3) During the conduct of site characterization activities at the Yucca Mountain site, the Secretary shall report not less than once every 6 months to the Commission and to the Governor and legislature of the State of Nevada, on the nature and extent of such activities and the information developed from such activities.

### (c) Restrictions

(1) The Secretary may conduct at the Yucca Mountain site only such site characterization activities as the Secretary considers necessary to provide the data required for evaluation of the suitability of such site for an application to be submitted to the Commission for a construction authorization for a repository at such site, and for compliance with the National Environmental Policy Act of 1969 (42 U.S.C. 4321 et seq.).

(2) In conducting site characterization activities—

(A) the Secretary may not use any radioactive material at a site unless the Commission concurs that such use is necessary to provide data for the preparation of the required environmental reports and an application for a construction authorization for a repository at such site; and

(B) if any radioactive material is used at a site—

(i) the Secretary shall use the minimum quantity necessary to determine the suitability of such site for a repository, but in no event more than the curie equivalent of 10 metric tons of spent nuclear fuel; and

(ii) such radioactive material shall be fully retrievable.

(3) If the Secretary at any time determines the Yucca Mountain site to be unsuitable for development as a repository, the Secretary shall—

(A) terminate all site characterization activities at such site;

(B) notify the Congress, the Governor and legislature of Nevada of such termination and the reasons for such termination;

(C) remove any high-level radioactive waste, spent nuclear fuel, or other radioactive materials at or in such site as promptly as practicable;

(D) take reasonable and necessary steps to reclaim the site and to mitigate any significant adverse environmental impacts caused by site characterization activities at such site;

(E) suspend all future benefits payments under part F of this subchapter with respect to such site; and

(F) report to Congress not later than 6 months after such determination the Secretary's recommendations for further action to assure the safe, permanent disposal of spent nuclear fuel and high-level radioactive waste, including the need for new legislative authority.

**(d) Preliminary activities**

Each activity of the Secretary under this section that is in compliance with the provisions of subsection (c) of this section shall be considered a preliminary decisionmaking activity. No such activity shall require the preparation of an environmental impact statement under section 102(2)(C) of the National Environmental Policy Act of 1969 (42 U.S.C. 4332(2)(C)), or to[1] require any environmental review under subparagraph (E) or (F) of section 102(2) of such Act.

(Pub.L. 97–425, Title I, § 113, Jan. 7, 1983, 96 Stat. 2211; Pub.L. 100–202, § 101(d) [Title III, § 300], Dec. 22, 1987, 101 Stat. 1329–104, 1329–121; Pub.L. 100–203, Title V, § 5011(e) to (g), Dec. 22, 1987, 101 Stat. 1330–228.)

[1] So in original. The word "to" probably should not appear.

### HISTORICAL AND STATUTORY NOTES

**References in Text**

The National Environmental Policy Act of 1969, referred to in subsec. (c)(1), is Pub.L. 91–190, Jan. 1, 1970, 83 Stat. 852, as amended, which is classified generally to chapter 55 (section 4321 et seq.) of this title. For complete classification of this Act to the Code, see Short Title of 1970 Acts note set out under section 4321 of this title and Tables.

## § 10134. Site approval and construction authorization

### [NWPA § 114]

**(a) Hearings and Presidential recommendation**

(1) The Secretary shall hold public hearings in the vicinity of the Yucca Mountain site, for the purposes of informing the residents of the area of such consideration and receiving their comments regarding the possible recommendation of such site. If, upon completion of such hearings and completion of site characterization activities at the Yucca Mountain site, under section 10133 of this title, the Secretary decides to recommend approval of such site to the President, the Secretary shall notify the Governor and legislature of the State of Nevada, of such decision. No sooner than the expiration of the 30–day period following such notification, the Secretary shall submit to the President a recommendation that the President approve such site for the development of a repository. Any such recommendation by the Secretary shall be based on the record of information developed by the Secretary under section 10133 of this title and this section, including the information described in subparagraph (A) through subparagraph (G). Together with any recommendation of a site under this paragraph, the Secretary shall make available to the public, and submit to the President, a comprehensive statement of the basis of such recommendation, including the following:

(A) a description of the proposed repository, including preliminary engineering specifications for the facility;

(B) a description of the waste form or packaging proposed for use at such repository, and an explanation of the relationship between such waste form or packaging and the geologic medium of such site;

(C) a discussion of data, obtained in site characterization activities, relating to the safety of such site;

(D) a final environmental impact statement prepared for the Yucca Mountain site pursuant to subsection (f) of this section and the National Environmental Policy Act of 1969 (42 U.S.C. 4321 et seq.), together with comments made concerning such environmental impact statement by the Secretary of the Interior, the Council on Environmental Quality, the Administrator, and the Commission, except that the Secretary shall not be required in any such environmental impact statement to consider the need for a repository, the alternatives to geological disposal, or alternative sites to the Yucca Mountain site;

(E) preliminary comments of the Commission concerning the extent to which the at-depth site characterization analysis and the waste form proposal for such site seem to be sufficient for inclusion in any application to be submitted by the Secretary for licensing of such site as a repository;

(F) the views and comments of the Governor and legislature of any State, or the governing body of any affected Indian tribe, as determined by the Secretary, together with the response of the Secretary to such views;

(G) such other information as the Secretary considers appropriate; and

(H) any impact report submitted under section 10136(c)(2)(B) of this title by the State of Nevada.

(2)(A) If, after recommendation by the Secretary, the President considers the Yucca Mountain site qualified for application for a construction authorization for a repository, the President shall submit a recommendation of such site to Congress.

**(B)** The President shall submit with such recommendation a copy of the statement for such site prepared by the Secretary under paragraph (1).

**(3)(A)** The President may not recommend the approval of the Yucca Mountain site unless the Secretary has recommended to the President under paragraph (1) approval of such site and has submitted to the President a statement for such site as required under such paragraph.

**(B)** No recommendation of a site by the President under this subsection shall require the preparation of an environmental impact statement under section 102(2)(C) of the National Environmental Policy Act of 1969 (42 U.S.C. 4332(2)(C)), or to [1] require any environmental review under subparagraph (E) or (F) of section 102(2) of such Act [42 U.S.C.A. § 4332(2)(E) or (F)].

**(b) Submission of application**

If the President recommends to the Congress the Yucca Mountain site under subsection (a) of this section and the site designation is permitted to take effect under section 10135 of this title, the Secretary shall submit to the Commission an application for a construction authorization for a repository at such site not later than 90 days after the date on which the recommendation of the site designation is effective under such section and shall provide to the Governor and legislature of the State of Nevada a copy of such application.

**(c) Status report on application**

Not later than 1 year after the date on which an application for a construction authorization is submitted under subsection (b) of this section, and annually thereafter until the date on which such authorization is granted, the Commission shall submit a report to the Congress describing the proceedings undertaken through the date of such report with regard to such application, including a description of—

(1) any major unresolved safety issues, and the explanation of the Secretary with respect to design and operation plans for resolving such issues;

(2) any matters of contention regarding such application; and

(3) any Commission actions regarding the granting or denial of such authorization.

**(d) Commission action**

The Commission shall consider an application for a construction authorization for all or part of a repository in accordance with the laws applicable to such applications, except that the Commission shall issue a final decision approving or disapproving the issuance of a construction authorization not later than the expiration of 3 years after the date of the submission of such application, except that the Commission may extend such deadline by not more than 12 months if, not less than 30 days before such deadline, the Commission complies with the reporting requirements established in subsection (e)(2) of this section. The Commission decision approving the first such application shall prohibit the emplacement in the first repository of a quantity of spent fuel containing in excess of 70,000 metric tons of heavy metal or a quantity of solidified high-level radioactive waste resulting from the reprocessing of such a quantity of spent fuel until such time as a second repository is in operation. In the event that a monitored retrievable storage facility, approved pursuant to part C of this subchapter, shall be located, or is planned to be located, within 50 miles of the first repository, then the Commission decision approving the first such application shall prohibit the emplacement of a quantity of spent fuel containing in excess of 70,000 metric tons of heavy metal or a quantity of solidified high-level radioactive waste resulting from the reprocessing of spent fuel in both the repository and monitored retrievable storage facility until such time as a second repository is in operation.

**(e) Project decision schedule**

**(1)** The Secretary shall prepare and update, as appropriate, in cooperation with all affected Federal agencies, a project decision schedule that portrays the optimum way to attain the operation of the repository, within the time periods specified in this part. Such schedule shall include a description of objectives and a sequence of deadlines for all Federal agencies required to take action, including an identification of the activities in which a delay in the start, or completion, of such activities will cause a delay in beginning repository operation.

**(2)** Any Federal agency that determines that it cannot comply with any deadline in the project decision schedule, or fails to so comply, shall submit to the Secretary and to the Congress a written report explaining the reason for its failure or expected failure to meet such deadline, the reason why such agency could not reach an agreement with the Secretary, the estimated time for completion of the activity or activities involved, the associated effect on its other deadlines in the project decision schedule, and any recommendations it may have or actions it intends to take regarding any improvements in its operation or organization, or changes to its statutory directives or authority, so that it will be able to mitigate the delay involved. The Secretary, within 30 days after receiving any such report, shall file with the Congress his response to such report, including the reasons why the

Secretary could not amend the project decision schedule to accommodate the Federal agency involved.

**(f) Environmental impact statement**

(1) Any recommendation made by the Secretary under this section shall be considered a major Federal action significantly affecting the quality of the human environment for purposes of the National Environmental Policy Act of 1969 (42 U.S.C. 4321 et seq.). A final environmental impact statement prepared by the Secretary under such Act shall accompany any recommendation to the President to approve a site for a repository.

(2) With respect to the requirements imposed by the National Environmental Policy Act of 1969 (42 U.S.C. 4321 et seq.), compliance with the procedures and requirements of this chapter shall be deemed adequate consideration of the need for a repository, the time of the initial availability of a repository, and all alternatives to the isolation of high-level radioactive waste and spent nuclear fuel in a repository.

(3) For purposes of complying with the requirements of the National Environmental Policy Act of 1969 (42 U.S.C. 4321 et seq.) and this section, the Secretary need not consider alternate sites to the Yucca Mountain site for the repository to be developed under this part.

(4) Any environmental impact statement prepared in connection with a repository proposed to be constructed by the Secretary under this part shall, to the extent practicable, be adopted by the Commission in connection with the issuance by the Commission of a construction authorization and license for such repository. To the extent such statement is adopted by the Commission, such adoption shall be deemed to also satisfy the responsibilities of the Commission under the National Environmental Policy Act of 1969 (42 U.S.C. 4321 et seq.) and no further consideration shall be required, except that nothing in this subsection shall affect any independent responsibilities of the Commission to protect the public health and safety under the Atomic Energy Act of 1954 (42 U.S.C. 2011 et seq.).

(5) Nothing in this chapter shall be construed to amend or otherwise detract from the licensing requirements of the Nuclear Regulatory Commission established in title II of the Energy Reorganization Act of 1974 (42 U.S.C. 5841 et seq.).

(6) In any such statement prepared with respect to the repository to be constructed under this part, the Nuclear Regulatory Commission need not consider the need for a repository, the time of initial availability of a repository, alternate sites to the Yucca Mountain site, or nongeologic alternatives to such site.

(Pub.L. 97–425, Title I, § 114, Jan. 7, 1983, 96 Stat. 2213; Pub.L. 100–202, § 101(d) [Title III, § 300], Dec. 22, 1987, 101 Stat. 1329–104, 1329–121; Pub.L. 100–203, Title V, § 5011(h) to (*l*), Dec. 22, 1987, 101 Stat. 1330–229, 1330–230.)

[1] So in original. The word "to" probably should not appear.

## HISTORICAL AND STATUTORY NOTES

**References in Text**

The National Environmental Policy Act of 1969 and such Act, referred to in subsecs. (a)(1)(D) and (f), is Pub.L. 91–190, Jan. 1, 1970, 83 Stat. 852, as amended, which is classified generally to chapter 55 (section 4321 et seq.) of this title. For complete classification of this Act to the Code, see Short Title of 1970 Acts note set out under section 4321 of this title and Tables.

The Atomic Energy Act of 1954, referred to in subsec. (f)(4), is Act Aug. 30, 1954, c. 1073, 68 Stat. 919, as amended, which is classified generally to chapter 23 (section 2011 et seq.) of this title. For complete classification of this Act to the Code, see Short Title of 1954 Acts note set out under section 2011 of this title and Tables.

The Energy Reorganization Act of 1974, referred to in subsec. (f)(5), is Pub.L. 93–438, Oct. 11, 1974, 88 Stat. 1233, as amended. Title II of the Energy Reorganization Act of 1974 is classified generally to subchapter II (section 5841 et seq.) of chapter 73 of this title. For complete classification of this Act to the Code, see Short Title of 1974 Acts note set out under section 5801 of this title and Tables.

**Viability Assessment of Yucca Mountain Site**

Pub.L. 104–206, Title III, Sept. 30, 1996, 110 Stat. 2995, provided in part: "That no later than September 30, 1998, the Secretary shall provide to the President and to the Congress a viability assessment of the Yucca Mountain site. The viability assessment shall include:

"(1) the preliminary design concept for the critical elements for the repository and waste package;

"(2) a total system performance assessment, based upon the design concept and the scientific data and analysis available by September 30, 1998, describing the probable behavior of the repository in the Yucca Mountain geological setting relative to the overall system performance standards;

"(3) a plan and cost estimate for the remaining work required to complete a license application; and

"(4) an estimate of the costs to construct and operate the repository in accordance with the design concept."

# § 10135. Review of repository site selection [NWPA § 115]

**(a) "Resolution of repository siting approval" defined**

For purposes of this section, the term "resolution of repository siting approval" means a joint resolution of the Congress, the matter after the resolving clause of which is as follows: "That there hereby is approved the site at ..... for a repository, with respect to which a notice of disapproval was submitted by ..... on .....". The first blank space in such resolution shall be filled with the name of the geographic location of the proposed site of the repository to which such resolution pertains; the second blank space in such resolution shall be filled with the designation of the State Governor and legislature or Indian tribe governing body submitting the notice of disapproval to which such resolution pertains; and the last blank space in such resolution shall be filled with the date of such submission.

(b) **State or Indian tribe petitions**

The designation of a site as suitable for application for a construction authorization for a repository shall be effective at the end of the 60-day period beginning on the date that the President recommends such site to the Congress under section 10134 of this title, unless the Governor and legislature of the State in which such site is located, or the governing body of an Indian tribe on whose reservation such site is located, as the case may be, has submitted to the Congress a notice of disapproval under section 10136 or 10138 of this title. If any such notice of disapproval has been submitted, the designation of such site shall not be effective except as provided under subsection (c) of this section.

(c) **Congressional review of petitions**

If any notice of disapproval of a repository site designation has been submitted to the Congress under section 10136 or 10138 of this title after a recommendation for approval of such site is made by the President under section 10134 of this title, such site shall be disapproved unless, during the first period of 90 calendar days of continuous session of the Congress after the date of the receipt by the Congress of such notice of disapproval, the Congress passes a resolution of repository siting approval in accordance with this subsection approving such site, and such resolution thereafter becomes law.

(d) **Procedures applicable to Senate**

(1) The provisions of this subsection are enacted by the Congress—

(A) as an exercise of the rulemaking power of the Senate, and as such they are deemed a part of the rules of the Senate, but applicable only with respect to the procedure to be followed in the Senate in the case of resolutions of repository siting approval, and such provisions supersede other rules of the Senate only to the extent that they are inconsistent with such other rules; and

(B) with full recognition of the constitutional right of the Senate to change the rules (so far as relating to the procedure of the Senate) at any time, in the same manner and to the same extent as in the case of any other rule of the Senate.

(2)(A) Not later than the first day of session following the day on which any notice of disapproval of a repository site selection is submitted to the Congress under section 10136 or 10138 of this title, a resolution of repository siting approval shall be introduced (by request) in the Senate by the chairman of the committee to which such notice of disapproval is referred, or by a Member or Members of the Senate designated by such chairman.

(B) Upon introduction, a resolution of repository siting approval shall be referred to the appropriate committee or committees of the Senate by the President of the Senate, and all such resolutions with respect to the same repository site shall be referred to the same committee or committees. Upon the expiration of 60 calendar days of continuous session after the introduction of the first resolution of repository siting approval with respect to any site, each committee to which such resolution was referred shall make its recommendations to the Senate.

(3) If any committee to which is referred a resolution of siting approval introduced under paragraph (2)(A), or, in the absence of such a resolution, any other resolution of siting approval introduced with respect to the site involved, has not reported such resolution at the end of 60 days of continuous session of Congress after introduction of such resolution, such committee shall be deemed to be discharged from further consideration of such resolution, and such resolution shall be placed on the appropriate calendar of the Senate.

(4)(A) When each committee to which a resolution of siting approval has been referred has reported, or has been deemed to be discharged from further consideration of, a resolution described in paragraph (3), it shall at any time thereafter be in order (even though a previous motion to the same effect has been disagreed to) for any Member of the Senate to move to proceed to the consideration of such resolution. Such motion shall be highly privileged and shall not be debatable. Such motion shall not be subject to amendment, to a motion to postpone, or to a motion to proceed to the consideration of other business. A motion to reconsider the vote by which such motion is agreed to or disagreed to shall not be in order. If a motion to proceed to the consideration of such resolution is agreed to, such resolution shall remain the unfinished business of the Senate until disposed of.

(B) Debate on a resolution of siting approval, and on all debatable motions and appeals in connection with such resolution, shall be limited to not more than 10 hours, which shall be divided equally between Members favoring and Members opposing such resolution. A motion further to limit debate shall be in order and shall not be debatable. Such motion shall not be subject to amendment, to a motion to postpone, or to a motion to proceed to the consideration of other business, and a motion to recommit such resolution shall not be in order. A motion to reconsider the vote by which such resolution is agreed to or disagreed to shall not be in order.

(C) Immediately following the conclusion of the debate on a resolution of siting approval, and a single quorum call at the conclusion of such debate if requested in accordance with the rules of the Senate, the vote on final approval of such resolution shall occur.

(D) Appeals from the decisions of the Chair relating to the application of the rules of the Senate to the procedure relating to a resolution of siting approval shall be decided without debate.

(5) If the Senate receives from the House a resolution of repository siting approval with respect to any site, then the following procedure shall apply:

(A) The resolution of the House with respect to such site shall not be referred to a committee.

(B) With respect to the resolution of the Senate with respect to such site—

(i) the procedure with respect to that or other resolutions of the Senate with respect to such site shall be the same as if no resolution from the House with respect to such site had been received; but

(ii) on any vote on final passage of a resolution of the Senate with respect to such site, a resolution from the House with respect to such site where the text is identical shall be automatically substituted for the resolution of the Senate.

**(e) Procedures applicable to House of Representatives**

(1) The provisions of this section are enacted by the Congress—

(A) as an exercise of the rulemaking power of the House of Representatives, and as such they are deemed a part of the rules of the House, but applicable only with respect to the procedure to be followed in the House in the case of resolutions of repository siting approval, and such provisions supersede other rules of the House only to the extent that they are inconsistent with such other rules; and

(B) with full recognition of the constitutional right of the House to change the rules (so far as relating to the procedure of the House) at any time, in the same manner and to the same extent as in the case of any other rule of the House.

(2) Resolutions of repository siting approval shall upon introduction, be immediately referred by the Speaker of the House to the appropriate committee or committees of the House. Any such resolution received from the Senate shall be held at the Speaker's table.

(3) Upon the expiration of 60 days of continuous session after the introduction of the first resolution of repository siting approval with respect to any site, each committee to which such resolution was referred shall be discharged from further consideration of such resolution, and such resolution shall be referred to the appropriate calendar, unless such resolution or an identical resolution was previously reported by each committee to which it was referred.

(4) It shall be in order for the Speaker to recognize a Member favoring a resolution to call up a resolution of repository siting approval after it has been on the appropriate calendar for 5 legislative days. When any such resolution is called up, the House shall proceed to its immediate consideration and the Speaker shall recognize the Member calling up such resolution and a Member opposed to such resolution for 2 hours of debate in the House, to be equally divided and controlled by such Members. When such time has expired, the previous question shall be considered as ordered on the resolution to adoption without intervening motion. No amendment to any such resolution shall be in order, nor shall it be in order to move to reconsider the vote by which such resolution is agreed to or disagreed to.

(5) If the House receives from the Senate a resolution of repository siting approval with respect to any site, then the following procedure shall apply:

(A) The resolution of the Senate with respect to such site shall not be referred to a committee.

(B) With respect to the resolution of the House with respect to such site—

(i) the procedure with respect to that or other resolutions of the House with respect to such site shall be the same as if no resolution from the Senate with respect to such site had been received; but

(ii) on any vote on final passage of a resolution of the House with respect to such site, a resolution from the Senate with respect to such site where the text is identical shall be automatically substituted for the resolution of the House.

**(f) Computation of days**

For purposes of this section—

(1) continuity of session of Congress is broken only by an adjournment sine die; and

(2) the days on which either House is not in session because of an adjournment of more than 3 days to a day certain are excluded in the computation of the 90-day period referred to in subsection (c) of this section and the 60-day period referred to in subsections (d) and (e) of this section.

**(g) Information provided to Congress**

In considering any notice of disapproval submitted to the Congress under section 10136 or 10138 of this title, the Congress may obtain any comments of the Commission with respect to such notice of disapproval. The provision of such comments by the Commission shall not be construed as binding the Commission with respect to any licensing or authorization action concerning the repository involved.

(Pub.L. 97–425, Title I, § 115, Jan. 7, 1983, 96 Stat. 2217.)

**HISTORICAL AND STATUTORY NOTES**

**Yucca Mountain Repository**

Pub.L. 107–200, July 23, 2002, 116 Stat. 735, which was entitled "Joint Resolution Approving the site at Yucca Mountain, Nevada, for the development of a repository for the disposal of high-level radioactive waste and spent nuclear fuel, pursuant to the Nuclear Waste Policy Act of 1982", provided: "That there hereby is approved the site at Yucca Mountain, Nevada, for a repository, with respect to which a notice of disapproval was submitted by the Governor of the State of Nevada on April 8, 2002."

## § 10136. Participation of States

[NWPA § 116]

**(a) Notification of States and affected tribes**

The Secretary shall identify the States with one or more potentially acceptable sites for a repository within 90 days after January 7, 1983. Within 90 days of such identification, the Secretary shall notify the Governor, the State legislature, and the tribal council of any affected Indian tribe in any State of the potentially acceptable sites within such State. For the purposes of this subchapter, the term "potentially acceptable site" means any site at which, after geologic studies and field mapping but before detailed geologic data gathering, the Department undertakes preliminary drilling and geophysical testing for the definition of site location.

**(b) State participation in repository siting decisions**

(1) Unless otherwise provided by State law, the Governor or legislature of each State shall have authority to submit a notice of disapproval to the Congress under paragraph (2). In any case in which State law provides for submission of any such notice of disapproval by any other person or entity, any reference in this part to the Governor or legislature of such State shall be considered to refer instead to such other person or entity.

(2) Upon the submission by the President to the Congress of a recommendation of a site for a repository, the Governor or legislature of the State in which such site is located may disapprove the site designation and submit to the Congress a notice of disapproval. Such Governor or legislature may submit such a notice of disapproval to the Congress not later than the 60 days after the date that the President recommends such site to the Congress under section 10134 of this title. A notice of disapproval shall be considered to be submitted to the Congress on the date of the transmittal of such notice of disapproval to the Speaker of the House and the President pro tempore of the Senate. Such notice of disapproval shall be accompanied by a statement of reasons explaining why such Governor or legislature disapproved the recommended repository site involved.

(3) The authority of the Governor or legislature of each State under this subsection shall not be applicable with respect to any site located on a reservation.

**(c) Financial assistance**

(1)(A) The Secretary shall make grants to the State of Nevada and any affected unit of local government for the purpose of participating in activities required by this section and section 10137 of this title or authorized by written agreement entered into pursuant to section 10137(c) of this title. Any salary or travel expense that would ordinarily be incurred by such State or affected unit of local government, may not be considered eligible for funding under this paragraph.

(B) The Secretary shall make grants to the State of Nevada and any affected unit of local government for purposes of enabling such State or affected unit of local government—

(i) to review activities taken under this part with respect to the Yucca Mountain site for purposes of determining any potential economic, social, public health and safety, and environmental impacts of a repository on such State, or affected unit of local government and its residents;

(ii) to develop a request for impact assistance under paragraph (2);

(iii) to engage in any monitoring, testing, or evaluation activities with respect to site characterization programs with regard to such site;

(iv) to provide information to Nevada residents regarding any activities of such State, the Secretary, or the Commission with respect to such site; and

(v) to request information from, and make comments and recommendations to, the Secretary regarding any activities taken under this part with respect to such site.

(C) Any salary or travel expense that would ordinarily be incurred by the State of Nevada or any affected unit of local government may not be considered eligible for funding under this paragraph.

(2)(A)(i) The Secretary shall provide financial and technical assistance to the State of Nevada, and any affected unit of local government requesting such assistance.

(ii) Such assistance shall be designed to mitigate the impact on such State or affected unit of local government of the development of such repository and the characterization of such site.

(iii) Such assistance to such State or affected unit of local government of such State shall commence upon the initiation of site characterization activities.

(B) The State of Nevada and any affected unit of local government may request assistance under this subsection by preparing and submitting to the Secretary a report on the economic, social, public health and safety, and environmental impacts that are likely to result from site characterization activities at the Yucca Mountain site. Such report shall be submitted to the Secretary after the Secretary has submitted to the State a general plan for site characterization activities under section 10133(b) of this title.

(C) As soon as practicable after the Secretary has submitted such site characterization plan, the Secretary shall seek to enter into a binding agreement with the State of Nevada setting forth—

(i) the amount of assistance to be provided under this subsection to such State or affected unit of local government; and

(ii) the procedures to be followed in providing such assistance.

(3)(A) In addition to financial assistance provided under paragraphs (1) and (2), the Secretary shall grant to the State of Nevada and any affected unit of local government an amount each fiscal year equal to the amount such State or affected unit of local government, respectively, would receive if authorized to tax site characterization activities at such site, and the development and operation of such repository, as such State or affected unit of local government taxes the non-Federal real property and industrial activities occurring within such State or affected unit of local government.

(B) Such grants shall continue until such time as all such activities, development, and operation are terminated at such site.

(4)(A) The State of Nevada or any affected unit of local government may not receive any grant under paragraph (1) after the expiration of the 1-year period following—

(i) the date on which the Secretary notifies the Governor and legislature of the State of Nevada of the termination of site characterization activities at the site in such State;

(ii) the date on which the Yucca Mountain site is disapproved under section 10135 of this title; or

(iii) the date on which the Commission disapproves an application for a construction authorization for a repository at such site;

whichever occurs first.

(B) The State of Nevada or any affected unit of local government may not receive any further assistance under paragraph (2) with respect to a site if repository construction activities or site characterization activities at such site are terminated by the Secretary or if such activities are permanently enjoined by any court.

(C) At the end of the 2-year period beginning on the effective date of any license to receive and possess for a repository in a State, no Federal funds, shall be made available to such State or affected unit of local government under paragraph (1) or (2), except for—

(i) such funds as may be necessary to support activities related to any other repository located in, or proposed to be located in, such State, and for which a license to receive and possess has not been in effect for more than 1 year;

(ii) such funds as may be necessary to support State activities pursuant to agreements or contracts for impact assistance entered into, under paragraph (2), by such State with the Secretary during such 2-year period; and

(iii) such funds as may be provided under an agreement entered into under subchapter IV of this chapter.

(5) Financial assistance authorized in this subsection shall be made out of amounts held in the Waste Fund.

(6) No State, other than the State of Nevada, may receive financial assistance under this subsection after December 22, 1987.

### (d) Additional notification and consultation

Whenever the Secretary is required under any provision of this chapter to notify or consult with the governing body of an affected Indian tribe where a site is located, the Secretary shall also notify or consult with, as the case may be, the Governor of the State in which such reservation is located.

(Pub.L. 97–425, Title I, § 116, Jan. 7, 1983, 96 Stat. 2220; Pub.L. 100–202, § 101(d) [Title III, § 300], Dec. 22, 1987, 101 Stat. 1329–104, 1329–121; Pub.L. 100–203, Title V, § 5032(a), Dec. 22, 1987, 101 Stat. 1330–241.)

## § 10137. Consultation with States and affected Indian tribes

[NWPA § 117]

### (a) Provision of information

(1) The Secretary, the Commission, and other agencies involved in the construction, operation, or regulation of any aspect of a repository in a State shall provide to the Governor and legislature of such State, and to the governing body of any affected Indian tribe, timely and complete information regarding determinations or plans made with respect to the site characterization siting, development, design, licensing, construction, operation, regulation, or decommissioning of such repository.

(2) Upon written request for such information by the Governor or legislature of such State, or by the governing body of any affected Indian tribe, as the case may be, the Secretary shall provide a written response to such request within 30 days of the receipt of such request. Such response shall provide the information requested or, in the alternative, the reasons why the information cannot be so provided. If the Secretary fails to so respond within such 30 days, the Governor or legislature of such State, or the governing body of any affected Indian tribe, as the case may be, may transmit a formal written objection to such failure to respond to the President. If the President or Secretary fails to respond to such written request within 30 days of the receipt by the President of such formal written objection, the Secretary shall immediately suspend all activities in such State authorized by this part, and shall not renew such activities until the Governor or legislature of such State, or the governing body of any affected Indian tribe, as the case may be, has received the written response to such written request required by this subsection.

**(b) Consultation and cooperation**

In performing any study of an area within a State for the purpose of determining the suitability of such area for a repository pursuant to section 10132(c) of this title, and in subsequently developing and loading [1] any repository within such State, the Secretary shall consult and cooperate with the Governor and legislature of such State and the governing body of any affected Indian tribe in an effort to resolve the concerns of such State and any affected Indian tribe regarding the public health and safety, environmental, and economic impacts of any such repository. In carrying out his duties under this part, the Secretary shall take such concerns into account to the maximum extent feasible and as specified in written agreements entered into under subsection (c) of this section.

**(c) Written agreement**

Not later than 60 days after (1) the approval of a site for site characterization for such a repository under section 10132(c) of this title, or (2) the written request of the State or Indian tribe in any affected State notified under section 10136(a) of this title to the Secretary, whichever,[2] first occurs, the Secretary shall seek to enter into a binding written agreement, and shall begin negotiations, with such State and, where appropriate, to enter into a separate binding agreement with the governing body of any affected Indian tribe, setting forth (but not limited to) the procedures under which the requirements of subsections (a) and (b) of this section, and the provisions of such written agreement, shall be carried out. Any such written agreement shall not affect the authority of the Commission under existing law. Each such written agreement shall, to the maximum extent feasible, be completed not later than 6 months after such notification. Such written agreement shall specify procedures—

(1) by which such State or governing body of an affected Indian tribe, as the case may be, may study, determine, comment on, and make recommendations with regard to the possible public health and safety, environmental, social, and economic impacts of any such repository;

(2) by which the Secretary shall consider and respond to comments and recommendations made by such State or governing body of an affected Indian tribe, including the period in which the Secretary shall so respond;

(3) by which the Secretary and such State or governing body of an affected Indian tribe may review or modify the agreement periodically;

(4) by which such State or governing body of an affected Indian tribe is to submit an impact report and request for impact assistance under section 10136(c) of this title or section 10138(b) of this title, as the case may be;

(5) by which the Secretary shall assist such State, and the units of general local government in the vicinity of the repository site, in resolving the offsite concerns of such State and units of general local government, including, but not limited to, questions of State liability arising from accidents, necessary road upgrading and access to the site, ongoing emergency preparedness and emergency response, monitoring of transportation of high-level radioactive waste and spent nuclear fuel through such State, conduct of baseline health studies of inhabitants in neighboring communities near the repository site and reasonable periodic monitoring thereafter, and monitoring of the repository site upon any decommissioning and decontamination;

(6) by which the Secretary shall consult and cooperate with such State on a regular, ongoing basis and provide for an orderly process and timely schedule for State review and evaluation, including identification in the agreement of key events, milestones, and decision points in the activities of the Secretary at the potential repository site;

(7) by which the Secretary shall notify such State prior to the transportation of any high-level radioactive waste and spent nuclear fuel into such State for disposal at the repository site;

(8) by which such State may conduct reasonable independent monitoring and testing of activities on the repository site, except that such monitoring and testing shall not unreasonably interfere with or delay onsite activities;

(9) for sharing, in accordance with applicable law, of all technical and licensing information, the utilization of available expertise, the facilitating of permit

procedures, joint project review, and the formulation of joint surveillance and monitoring arrangements to carry out applicable Federal and State laws;

(10) for public notification of the procedures specified under the preceding paragraphs; and

(11) for resolving objections of a State and affected Indian tribes at any stage of the planning, siting, development, construction, operation, or closure of such a facility within such State through negotiation, arbitration, or other appropriate mechanisms.

**(d) On-site representative**

The Secretary shall offer to any State, Indian tribe or unit of local government within whose jurisdiction a site for a repository or monitored retrievable storage facility is located under this subchapter an opportunity to designate a representative to conduct on-site oversight activities at such site. Reasonable expenses of such representatives shall be paid out of the Waste Fund.

(Pub.L. 97–425, Title I, § 117, Jan. 7, 1983, 96 Stat. 2222; Pub.L. 100–202, § 101(d) [Title III, § 300], Dec. 22, 1987, 101 Stat. 1329–104, 1329–121; Pub.L. 100–203, Title V, § 5011(m), Dec. 22, 1987, 101 Stat. 1330–231; Pub.L. 104–66, Title I, § 1051(i), Dec. 21, 1995, 109 Stat. 716.)

[1] So in original. Probably should be "locating".

[2] So in original. The comma probably should not appear.

## § 10138. Participation of Indian tribes

[NWPA § 118]

**(a) Participation of Indian tribes in repository siting decisions**

Upon the submission by the President to the Congress of a recommendation of a site for a repository located on the reservation of an affected Indian tribe, the governing body of such Indian tribe may disapprove the site designation and submit to the Congress a notice of disapproval. The governing body of such Indian tribe may submit such a notice of disapproval to the Congress not later than the 60 days after the date that the President recommends such site to the Congress under section 10134 of this title. A notice of disapproval shall be considered to be submitted to the Congress on the date of the transmittal of such notice of disapproval to the Speaker of the House and the President pro tempore of the Senate. Such notice of disapproval shall be accompanied by a statement of reasons explaining why the governing body of such Indian tribe disapproved the recommended repository site involved.

**(b) Financial assistance**

(1) The Secretary shall make grants to each affected tribe notified under section 10136(a) of this title for the purpose of participating in activities required by section 10137 of this title or authorized by written agreement entered into pursuant to section 10137(c) of this title. Any salary or travel expense that would ordinarily be incurred by such tribe, may not be considered eligible for funding under this paragraph.

(2)(A) The Secretary shall make grants to each affected Indian tribe where a candidate site for a repository is approved under section 10132(c) of this title. Such grants may be made to each such Indian tribe only for purposes of enabling such Indian tribe—

(i) to review activities taken under this part with respect to such site for purposes of determining any potential economic, social, public health and safety, and environmental impacts of such repository on the reservation and its residents;

(ii) to develop a request for impact assistance under paragraph (2);

(iii) to engage in any monitoring, testing, or evaluation activities with respect to site characterization programs with regard to such site;

(iv) to provide information to the residents of its reservation regarding any activities of such Indian tribe, the Secretary, or the Commission with respect to such site; and

(v) to request information from, and make comments and recommendations to, the Secretary regarding any activities taken under this part with respect to such site.

(B) The amount of funds provided to any affected Indian tribe under this paragraph in any fiscal year may not exceed 100 percent of the costs incurred by such Indian tribe with respect to the activities described in clauses (i) through (v) of subparagraph (A). Any salary or travel expense that would ordinarily be incurred by such Indian tribe may not be considered eligible for funding under this paragraph.

(3)(A) The Secretary shall provide financial and technical assistance to any affected Indian tribe requesting such assistance and where there is a site with respect to which the Commission has authorized construction of a repository. Such assistance shall be designed to mitigate the impact on such Indian tribe of the development of such repository. Such assistance to such Indian tribe shall commence within 6 months following the granting by the Commission of a construction authorization for such repository and following the initiation of construction activities at such site.

(B) Any affected Indian tribe desiring assistance under this paragraph shall prepare and submit to the Secretary a report on any economic, social, public health and safety, and environmental impacts that are likely as a result of the development of a repository at a site on the reservation of such Indian tribe. Such report shall be submitted to the Secretary following the completion of site characterization activities at such site and before the recommendation of such site to the President by the Secretary for application for a construction authorization for a repository. As soon as practicable following the granting of a construction authorization for such repository, the Secretary shall seek to enter into a binding agreement with the Indian tribe involved setting forth the amount of assistance to be provided to such Indian tribe under this paragraph and the procedures to be followed in providing such assistance.

(4) The Secretary shall grant to each affected Indian tribe where a site for a repository is approved under section 10132(c) of this title an amount each fiscal year equal to the amount such Indian tribe would receive were it authorized to tax site characterization activities at such site, and the development and operation of such repository, as such Indian tribe taxes the other commercial activities occurring on such reservation. Such grants shall continue until such time as all such activities, development, and operation are terminated at such site.

(5)[1] An affected Indian tribe may not receive any grant under paragraph (1) after the expiration of the 1-year period following—

(i) the date on which the Secretary notifies such Indian tribe of the termination of site characterization activities at the candidate site involved on the reservation of such Indian tribe;

(ii) the date on which such site is disapproved under section 10135 of this title;

(iii) the date on which the Commission disapproves an application for a construction authorization for a repository at such site;[2]

(iv) December 22, 1987;

whichever occurs first, unless there is another candidate site on the reservation of such Indian tribe that is approved under section 10132(c) of this title and with respect to which the actions described in clauses (i), (ii), and (iii) have not been taken.

(B) An affected Indian tribe may not receive any further assistance under paragraph (2) with respect to a site if repository construction activities at such site are terminated by the Secretary or if such activities are permanently enjoined by any court.

(C) At the end of the 2-year period beginning on the effective date of any license to receive and possess for a repository at a site on the reservation of an affected Indian tribe, no Federal funds shall be made available under paragraph (1) or (2) to such Indian tribe, except for—

(i) such funds as may be necessary to support activities of such Indian tribe related to any other repository where a license to receive and possess has not been in effect for more than 1 year; and

(ii) such funds as may be necessary to support activities of such Indian tribe pursuant to agreements or contracts for impact assistance entered into, under paragraph (2), by such Indian tribe with the Secretary during such 2-year period.

(6) Financial assistance authorized in this subsection shall be made out of amounts held in the Nuclear Waste Fund established in section 10222 of this title.

(Pub.L. 97–425, Title I, § 118, Jan. 7, 1983, 96 Stat. 2225; Pub.L. 100–202, § 101(d) [Title III, § 300], Dec. 22, 1987, 101 Stat. 1329–104, 1329–121; Pub.L. 100–203, Title V, § 5033, Dec. 22, 1987, 101 Stat. 1330–243.)

[1] So in original. Probably should be designated as subpar. (A).

[2] So in original. Probably should be followed by "or".

## § 10139. Judicial review of agency actions

**[NWPA § 119]**

### (a) Jurisdiction of United States courts of appeals

(1) Except for review in the Supreme Court of the United States, the United States courts of appeals shall have original and exclusive jurisdiction over any civil action—

(A) for review of any final decision or action of the Secretary, the President, or the Commission under this part;

(B) alleging the failure of the Secretary, the President, or the Commission to make any decision, or take any action, required under this part;

(C) challenging the constitutionality of any decision made, or action taken, under any provision of this part;

(D) for review of any environmental impact statement prepared pursuant to the National Environmental Policy Act of 1969 (42 U.S.C. 4321 et seq.) with respect to any action under this part, or as required under section 10155(c)(1) of this title, or alleging a failure to prepare such statement with respect to any such action;

(E) for review of any environmental assessment prepared under section 10132(b)(1) or 10155(c)(2) of this title; or

(F) for review of any research and development activity under subchapter II of this chapter.

(2) The venue of any proceeding under this section shall be in the judicial circuit in which the petitioner involved resides or has its principal office, or in the United States Court of Appeals for the District of Columbia.

### (c)[1] Deadline for commencing action

A civil action for judicial review described under subsection (a)(1) of this section may be brought not later than the 180th day after the date of the decision or action or failure to act involved, as the case may be, except that if a party shows that he did not know of the decision or action complained of (or of the failure to act), and that a reasonable person acting under the circumstances would not have known, such party may bring a civil action not later than the 180th day after the date such party acquired actual or constructive knowledge of such decision, action, or failure to act.

(Pub.L. 97-425, Title I, § 119, Jan. 7, 1983, 96 Stat. 2227.)

[1] So in original. Section enacted without a subsec. (b).

### HISTORICAL AND STATUTORY NOTES

**References in Text**

The National Environmental Policy Act of 1969, referred to in subsec. (a)(1)(D), is Pub.L. 91-190, Jan. 1, 1970, 83 Stat. 852, as amended, which is classified generally to chapter 55 (section 4321 et seq.) of this title. For complete classification of this Act to the Code, see Short Title of 1970 Acts note set out under section 4321 of this title and Tables.

## § 10140. Expedited authorizations

[NWPA § 120]

**(a) Issuance of authorizations**

(1) To the extent that the taking of any action related to the site characterization of a site or the construction or initial operation of a repository under this part requires a certificate, right-of-way, permit, lease, or other authorization from a Federal agency or officer, such agency or officer shall issue or grant any such authorization at the earliest practicable date, to the extent permitted by the applicable provisions of law administered by such agency or officer. All actions of a Federal agency or officer with respect to consideration of applications or requests for the issuance or grant of any such authorization shall be expedited, and any such application or request shall take precedence over any similar applications or requests not related to such repositories.

(2) The provisions of paragraph (1) shall not apply to any certificate, right-of-way, permit, lease, or other authorization issued or granted by, or requested from, the Commission.

**(b) Terms of authorizations**

Any authorization issued or granted pursuant to subsection (a) of this section shall include such terms and conditions as may be required by law, and may include terms and conditions permitted by law.

(Pub.L. 97-425, Title I, § 120, Jan. 7, 1983, 96 Stat. 2227.)

## § 10141. Certain standards and criteria

[NWPA § 121]

**(a) Environmental Protection Agency standards**

Not later than 1 year after January 7, 1983, the Administrator, pursuant to authority under other provisions of law, shall, by rule, promulgate generally applicable standards for protection of the general environment from offsite releases from radioactive material in repositories.

**(b) Commission requirements and criteria**

(1)(A) Not later than January 1, 1984, the Commission, pursuant to authority under other provisions of law, shall, by rule, promulgate technical requirements and criteria that it will apply, under the Atomic Energy Act of 1954 (42 U.S.C. 2011 et seq.) and the Energy Reorganization Act of 1974 (42 U.S.C. 5801 et seq.), in approving or disapproving—

(i) applications for authorization to construct repositories;

(ii) applications for licenses to receive and possess spent nuclear fuel and high-level radioactive waste in such repositories; and

(iii) applications for authorization for closure and decommissioning of such repositories.

(B) Such criteria shall provide for the use of a system of multiple barriers in the design of the repository and shall include such restrictions on the retrievability of the solidified high-level radioactive waste and spent fuel emplaced in the repository as the Commission deems appropriate.

(C) Such requirements and criteria shall not be inconsistent with any comparable standards promulgated by the Administrator under subsection (a) of this section.

(2) For purposes of this chapter, nothing in this section shall be construed to prohibit the Commission from promulgating requirements and criteria under paragraph (1) before the Administrator promulgates standards under subsection (a) of this section. If the Administrator promulgates standards under subsection (a) of this section after requirements and criteria are promulgated by the Commission under paragraph (1), such requirements and criteria shall be revised by the Commission if necessary to comply with paragraph (1)(C).

**(c) Environmental impact statement**

The promulgation of standards or criteria in accordance with the provisions of this section shall not require the preparation of an environmental impact statement under section 102(2)(C) of the National Environmental Policy Act of 1969 (42 U.S.C. 4332(2)(C)), or to require any environmental review under subparagraph (E) or (F) of section 102(2) of such Act.

(Pub.L. 97-425, Title I, § 121, Jan. 7, 1983, 96 Stat. 2228.)

### HISTORICAL AND STATUTORY NOTES

**References in Text**

The Atomic Energy Act of 1954, referred to in subsec. (b)(1)(A), is Act Aug. 30, 1954, c. 1073, 68 Stat. 919, as amended, which is classified generally to chapter 23 (section

2011 et seq.) of this title. For complete classification of this Act to the Code, see Short Title of 1954 Acts note set out under section 2011 of this title and Tables.

The Energy Reorganization Act of 1974, referred to in subsec. (b)(1)(A), is Pub.L. 93–438, Oct. 11, 1974, 88 Stat. 1233, as amended, which is classified principally to chapter 73 (section 5801 et seq.) of this title. For complete classification of this Act to the Code, see Short Title of 1974 Acts note set out under section 5801 of this title and Tables.

The National Environmental Policy Act of 1969, referred to in subsec. (c), is Pub.L. 91–190, Jan. 1, 1970, 83 Stat. 852, as amended, which is classified generally to chapter 55 (section 4321 et seq.) of this title. Section 102 of such Act is classified to section 4332 of this title. For complete classification of this Act to the Code, see Short Title of 1970 Acts note set out under section 4321 of this title and Tables.

**Nuclear Waste Storage and Disposal at Yucca Mountain Site**

Pub.L. 102–486, Title VIII, § 801, Oct. 24, 1992, 106 Stat. 2921, provided that:

"**(a) Environmental Protection Agency standards.**—

"**(1) Promulgation.**—Notwithstanding the provisions of section 121(a) of the Nuclear Waste Policy Act of 1982 (42 U.S.C. 10141(a) [subsec. (a) of this section]), section 161 b. of the Atomic Energy Act of 1954 (42 U.S.C. 2201(b) [section 2201(b) of this title]), and any other authority of the Administrator of the Environmental Protection Agency to set generally applicable standards for the Yucca Mountain site, the Administrator shall, based upon and consistent with the findings and recommendations of the National Academy of Sciences, promulgate, by rule, public health and safety standards for protection of the public from releases from radioactive materials stored or disposed of in the repository at the Yucca Mountain site. Such standards shall prescribe the maximum annual effective dose equivalent to individual members of the public from releases to the accessible environment from radioactive materials stored or disposed of in the repository. The standards shall be promulgated not later than 1 year after the Administrator receives the findings and recommendations of the National Academy of Sciences under paragraph (2) and shall be the only such standards applicable to the Yucca Mountain site.

"**(2) Study by National Academy of Sciences.**—Within 90 days after the date of the enactment of this Act [Oct. 24, 1992], the Administrator shall contract with the National Academy of Sciences to conduct a study to provide, by not later than December 31, 1993, findings and recommendations on reasonable standards for protection of the public health and safety, including—

"**(A)** whether a health-based standard based upon doses to individual members of the public from releases to the accessible environment (as that term is defined in the regulations contained in subpart B of part 191 of title 40, Code of Federal Regulations, as in effect on November 18, 1985) will provide a reasonable standard for protection of the health and safety of the general public;

"**(B)** whether it is reasonable to assume that a system for post-closure oversight of the repository can be developed, based upon active institutional controls, that will prevent an unreasonable risk of breaching the repository's engineered or geologic barriers or increasing the exposure of individual members of the public to radiation beyond allowable limits; and

"**(C)** whether it is possible to make scientifically supportable predictions of the probability that the repository's engineered or geologic barriers will be breached as a result of human intrusion over a period of 10,000 years.

"**(3) Applicability.**—The provisions of this section [this note] shall apply to the Yucca Mountain site, rather than any other authority of the Administrator to set generally applicable standards for radiation protection.

"**(b) Nuclear Regulatory Commission requirements and criteria.**—

"**(1) Modifications.**—Not later than 1 year after the Administrator promulgates standards under subsection (a), the Nuclear Regulatory Commission shall, by rule, modify its technical requirements and criteria under section 121(b) of the Nuclear Waste Policy Act of 1982 (42 U.S.C. 10141(b) [subsec. (b) of this section]), as necessary, to be consistent with the Administrator's standards promulgated under subsection (a).

"**(2) Required assumptions.**—The Commission's requirements and criteria shall assume, to the extent consistent with the findings and recommendations of the National Academy of Sciences, that, following repository closure, the inclusion of engineered barriers and the Secretary's post-closure oversight of the Yucca Mountain site, in accordance with subsection (c), shall be sufficient to—

"**(A)** prevent any activity at the site that poses an unreasonable risk of breaching the repository's engineered or geologic barriers; and

"**(B)** prevent any increase in the exposure of individual members of the public to radiation beyond allowable limits.

"**(c) Post-closure oversight.**—Following repository closure, the Secretary of Energy shall continue to oversee the Yucca Mountain site to prevent any activity at the site that poses an unreasonable risk of—

"(1) breaching the repository's engineered or geologic barriers; or

"(2) increasing the exposure of individual members of the public to radiation beyond allowable limits."

## § 10142. Disposal of spent nuclear fuel

**[NWPA § 122]**

Notwithstanding any other provision of this part, any repository constructed on a site approved under this part shall be designed and constructed to permit the retrieval of any spent nuclear fuel placed in such repository, during an appropriate period of operation of the facility, for any reason pertaining to the public health and safety, or the environment, or for the purpose of permitting the recovery of the economically valuable contents of such spent fuel. The Secretary shall specify the appropriate period of retrievability with respect to any repository at the time of design of such repository, and such aspect of such repository shall be subject to approval or disapproval by the Commission as part of the construction authorization process under subsections (b) through (d) of section 10134 of this title.

(Pub.L. 97–425, Title I, § 122, Jan. 7, 1983, 96 Stat. 2228.)

## § 10143. Title to material

**[NWPA § 123]**

Delivery, and acceptance by the Secretary, of any high-level radioactive waste or spent nuclear fuel for a repository constructed under this part shall constitute a transfer to the Secretary of title to such waste or spent fuel.

(Pub.L. 97–425, Title I, § 123, Jan. 7, 1983, 96 Stat. 2229.)

## § 10144. Consideration of effect of acquisition of water rights

**[NWPA § 124]**

The Secretary shall give full consideration to whether the development, construction, and operation of a repository may require any purchase or other acquisition of water rights that will have a significant adverse effect on the present or future development of the area in which such repository is located. The Secretary shall mitigate any such adverse effects to the maximum extent practicable.

(Pub.L. 97–425, Title I, § 124, Jan. 7, 1983, 96 Stat. 2229.)

## § 10145. Termination of certain provisions

**[NWPA § 125]**

Sections 10139 and 10140 of this title shall cease to have effect at such time as a repository developed under this part is licensed to receive and possess high-level radioactive waste and spent nuclear fuel.

(Pub.L. 97–425, Title I, § 125, Jan. 7, 1983, 96 Stat. 2229.)

### Part B—Interim Storage Program

## § 10151. Findings and purposes

**[NWPA § 131]**

**(a)** The Congress finds that—

**(1)** the persons owning and operating civilian nuclear power reactors have the primary responsibility for providing interim storage of spent nuclear fuel from such reactors, by maximizing, to the extent practical, the effective use of existing storage facilities at the site of each civilian nuclear power reactor, and by adding new onsite storage capacity in a timely manner where practical;

**(2)** the Federal Government has the responsibility to encourage and expedite the effective use of existing storage facilities and the addition of needed new storage capacity at the site of each civilian nuclear power reactor; and

**(3)** the Federal Government has the responsibility to provide, in accordance with the provisions of this part, not more than 1,900 metric tons of capacity for interim storage of spent nuclear fuel for civilian nuclear power reactors that cannot reasonably provide adequate storage capacity at the sites of such reactors when needed to assure the continued, orderly operation of such reactors.

**(b)** The purposes of this part are—

**(1)** to provide for the utilization of available spent nuclear fuel pools at the site of each civilian nuclear power reactor to the extent practical and the addition of new spent nuclear fuel storage capacity where practical at the site of such reactor; and

**(2)** to provide, in accordance with the provisions of this part, for the establishment of a federally owned and operated system for the interim storage of spent nuclear fuel at one or more facilities owned by the Federal Government with not more than 1,900 metric tons of capacity to prevent disruptions in the orderly operation of any civilian nuclear power reactor that cannot reasonably provide adequate spent nuclear fuel storage capacity at the site of such reactor when needed.

(Pub.L. 97–425, Title I, § 131, Jan. 7, 1983, 96 Stat. 2229.)

## § 10152. Available capacity for interim storage of spent nuclear fuel

**[NWPA § 132]**

The Secretary, the Commission, and other authorized Federal officials shall each take such actions as such official considers necessary to encourage and expedite the effective use of available storage, and necessary additional storage, at the site of each civilian nuclear power reactor consistent with—

**(1)** the protection of the public health and safety, and the environment;

**(2)** economic considerations;

**(3)** continued operation of such reactor;

**(4)** any applicable provisions of law; and

**(5)** the views of the population surrounding such reactor.

(Pub.L. 97–425, Title I, § 132, Jan. 7, 1983, 96 Stat. 2230.)

## § 10153. Interim at—reactor storage

**[NWPA § 133]**

The Commission shall, by rule, establish procedures for the licensing of any technology approved by the Commission under section 10198(a) of this title for use at the site of any civilian nuclear power reactor. The establishment of such procedures shall not preclude the licensing, under any applicable procedures or rules of the Commission in effect prior to such establishment, of any technology for the storage of civilian spent nuclear fuel at the site of any civilian nuclear power reactor.

(Pub.L. 97–425, Title I, § 133, Jan. 7, 1983, 96 Stat. 2230.)

### HISTORICAL AND STATUTORY NOTES

**References in Text**

Section 10198(a) of this title, referred to in text, was in the original a reference to section 219(a) of Pub.L. 97–425, which is classified to section 10199(a) of this title, and has been translated as section 10198(a) of this title as the probable intent of Congress, in view of the subject matter of section 10198(a), which relates to development of technologies for storage of spent nuclear fuel, and the subject matter of section 10199(a), which relates to payments to States and Indian tribes.

## § 10154. Licensing of facility expansions and transshipments

[NWPA § 134]

**(a) Oral argument**

In any Commission hearing under section 189 of the Atomic Energy Act of 1954 (42 U.S.C. 2239) on an application for a license, or for an amendment to an existing license, filed after January 7, 1983, to expand the spent nuclear fuel storage capacity at the site of a civilian nuclear power reactor, through the use of high-density fuel storage racks, fuel rod compaction, the transshipment of spent nuclear fuel to another civilian nuclear power reactor within the same utility system, the construction of additional spent nuclear fuel pool capacity or dry storage capacity, or by other means, the Commission shall, at the request of any party, provide an opportunity for oral argument with respect to any matter which the Commission determines to be in controversy among the parties. The oral argument shall be preceded by such discovery procedures as the rules of the Commission shall provide. The Commission shall require each party, including the Commission staff, to submit in written form, at the time of the oral argument, a summary of the facts, data, and arguments upon which such party proposes to rely that are known at such time to such party. Only facts and data in the form of sworn testimony or written submission may be relied upon by the parties during oral argument. Of the materials that may be submitted by the parties during oral argument, the Commission shall only consider those facts and data that are submitted in the form of sworn testimony or written submission.

**(b) Adjudicatory hearing**

(1) At the conclusion of any oral argument under subsection (a) of this section, the Commission shall designate any disputed question of fact, together with any remaining questions of law, for resolution in an adjudicatory hearing only if it determines that—

(A) there is a genuine and substantial dispute of fact which can only be resolved with sufficient accuracy by the introduction of evidence in an adjudicatory hearing; and

(B) the decision of the Commission is likely to depend in whole or in part on the resolution of such dispute.

(2) In making a determination under this subsection, the Commission—

(A) shall designate in writing the specific facts that are in genuine and substantial dispute, the reason why the decision of the agency is likely to depend on the resolution of such facts, and the reason why an adjudicatory hearing is likely to resolve the dispute; and

(B) shall not consider—

(i) any issue relating to the design, construction, or operation of any civilian nuclear power reactor already licensed to operate at such site, or any civilian nuclear power reactor for which a construction permit has been granted at such site, unless the Commission determines that any such issue substantially affects the design, construction, or operation of the facility or activity for which such license application, authorization, or amendment is being considered; or

(ii) any siting or design issue fully considered and decided by the Commission in connection with the issuance of a construction permit or operating license for a civilian nuclear power reactor at such site, unless (I) such issue results from any revision of siting or design criteria by the Commission following such decision; and (II) the Commission determines that such issue substantially affects the design, construction, or operation of the facility or activity for which such license application, authorization, or amendment is being considered.

(3) The provisions of paragraph (2)(B) shall apply only with respect to licenses, authorizations, or amendments to licenses or authorizations, applied for under the Atomic Energy Act of 1954 (42 U.S.C. 2011 et seq.) before December 31, 2005.

(4) The provisions of this section shall not apply to the first application for a license or license amendment received by the Commission to expand onsite spent fuel storage capacity by the use of a new technology not previously approved for use at any nuclear powerplant by the Commission.

**(c) Judicial review**

No court shall hold unlawful or set aside a decision of the Commission in any proceeding described in subsection (a) of this section because of a failure by the Commission to use a particular procedure pursuant to this section unless—

(1) an objection to the procedure used was presented to the Commission in a timely fashion or there are extraordinary circumstances that excuse the failure to present a timely objection; and

(2) the court finds that such failure has precluded a fair consideration and informed resolution of a significant issue of the proceeding taken as a whole.

(Pub.L. 97–425, Title I, § 134, Jan. 7, 1983, 96 Stat. 2230.)

### HISTORICAL AND STATUTORY NOTES

**References in Text**

The Atomic Energy Act of 1954, referred to in subsec. (b)(3), is Act Aug. 30, 1954, c. 1073, 68 Stat. 919, as amended, which is classified generally to chapter 23 (section 2011 et seq.) of this title. Section 189 of the Atomic Energy Act of 1954, referred to in subsec. (a), is classified to section 2239 of this title. For complete classification of this Act to the Code, see Short Title of 1954 Acts note set out under section 2011 of this title and Tables.

## § 10155. Storage of spent nuclear fuel

[NWPA § 135]

**(a) Storage capacity**

(1) Subject to section 10107 of this title, the Secretary shall provide, in accordance with paragraph (5), not more than 1,900 metric tons of capacity for the storage of spent nuclear fuel from civilian nuclear power reactors. Such storage capacity shall be provided through any one or more of the following methods, used in any combination determined by the Secretary to be appropriate:

(A) use of available capacity at one or more facilities owned by the Federal Government on January 7, 1983, including the modification and expansion of any such facilities, if the Commission determines that such use will adequately protect the public health and safety, except that such use shall not—

(i) render such facilities subject to licensing under the Atomic Energy Act of 1954 (42 U.S.C. 2011 et seq.) or the Energy Reorganization Act of 1974 (42 U.S.C. 5801 et seq.); or

(ii) except as provided in subsection (c) of this section require the preparation of an environmental impact statement under section 102(2)(C) of the National Environmental Policy Act of 1969 (42 U.S.C. 4332(2)(C)), such facility is already being used, or has previously been used, for such storage or for any similar purpose.

(B) acquisition of any modular or mobile spent nuclear fuel storage equipment, including spent nuclear fuel storage casks, and provision of such equipment, to any person generating or holding title to spent nuclear fuel, at the site of any civilian nuclear power reactor operated by such person or at any site owned by the Federal Government on January 7, 1983;

(C) construction of storage capacity at any site of a civilian nuclear power reactor.

(2) Storage capacity authorized by paragraph (1) shall not be provided at any Federal or non-Federal site within which there is a candidate site for a repository. The restriction in the preceding sentence shall only apply until such time as the Secretary decides that such candidate site is no longer a candidate site under consideration for development as a repository.

(3) In selecting methods of providing storage capacity under paragraph (1), the Secretary shall consider the timeliness of the availability of each such method and shall seek to minimize the transportation of spent nuclear fuel, the public health and safety impacts, and the costs of providing such storage capacity.

(4) In providing storage capacity through any method described in paragraph (1), the Secretary shall comply with any applicable requirements for licensing or authorization of such method, except as provided in paragraph (1)(A)(i).

(5) The Secretary shall ensure that storage capacity is made available under paragraph (1) when needed, as determined on the basis of the storage needs specified in contracts entered into under section 10156(a) of this title, and shall accept upon request any spent nuclear fuel as covered under such contracts.

(6) For purposes of paragraph (1)(A), the term "facility" means any building or structure.

**(b) Contracts**

(1) Subject to the capacity limitation established in subsections (a)(1) and (d) of this section, the Secretary shall offer to enter into, and may enter into, contracts under section 10156(a) of this title with any person generating or owning spent nuclear fuel for purposes of providing storage capacity for such spent fuel under this section only if the Commission determines that—

(A) adequate storage capacity to ensure the continued orderly operation of the civilian nuclear power reactor at which such spent nuclear fuel is generated cannot reasonably be provided by the person owning and operating such reactor at such site, or at the site of any other civilian nuclear power reactor operated by such person, and such capacity cannot be made available in a timely manner through any method described in subparagraph (B); and

(B) such person is diligently pursuing licensed alternatives to the use of Federal storage capacity for the storage of spent nuclear fuel expected to be generated by such person in the future, including—

(i) expansion of storage facilities at the site of any civilian nuclear power reactor operated by such person;

(ii) construction of new or additional storage facilities at the site of any civilian nuclear power reactor operated by such person;

(iii) acquisition of modular or mobile spent nuclear fuel storage equipment, including spent nuclear fuel storage casks, for use at the site of any civilian nuclear power reactor operated by such person; and

(iv) transshipment to another civilian nuclear power reactor owned by such person.

(2) In making the determination described in paragraph (1)(A), the Commission shall ensure maintenance of a full core reserve storage capability at the site of the civilian nuclear power reactor involved unless the Commission determines that maintenance of such capability is not necessary for the continued orderly operation of such reactor.

(3) The Commission shall complete the determinations required in paragraph (1) with respect to any request for storage capacity not later than 6 months after receipt of such request by the Commission.

**(c) Environmental review**

(1) The provision of 300 or more metric tons of storage capacity at any one Federal site under subsection (a)(1)(A) of this section shall be considered to be a major Federal action requiring preparation of an environmental impact statement under section 102(2)(C) of the National Environmental Policy Act of 1969 (42 U.S.C. 4332(2)(C)).

(2)(A) The Secretary shall prepare, and make available to the public, an environmental assessment of the probable impacts of any provision of less than 300 metric tons of storage capacity at any one Federal site under subsection (a)(1)(A) of this section that requires the modification or expansion of any facility at the site, and a discussion of alternative activities that may be undertaken to avoid such impacts. Such environmental assessment shall include—

(i) an estimate of the amount of storage capacity to be made available at such site;

(ii) an evaluation as to whether the facilities to be used at such site are suitable for the provision of such storage capacity;

(iii) a description of activities planned by the Secretary with respect to the modification or expansion of the facilities to be used at such site;

(iv) an evaluation of the effects of the provision of such storage capacity at such site on the public health and safety, and the environment;

(v) a reasonable comparative evaluation of current information with respect to such site and facilities and other sites and facilities available for the provision of such storage capacity;

(vi) a description of any other sites and facilities that have been considered by the Secretary for the provision of such storage capacity; and

(vii) an assessment of the regional and local impacts of providing such storage capacity at such site, including the impacts on transportation.

(B) The issuance of any environmental assessment under this paragraph shall be considered to be a final agency action subject to judicial review in accordance with the provisions of chapter 7 of Title 5. Such judicial review shall be limited to the sufficiency of such assessment with respect to the items described in clauses (i) through (vii) of subparagraph (A).

(3) Judicial review of any environmental impact statement or environmental assessment prepared pursuant to this subsection shall be conducted in accordance with the provisions of section 10139 of this title.

**(d) Review of sites and State participation**

(1) In carrying out the provisions of this part with regard to any interim storage of spent fuel from civilian nuclear power reactors which the Secretary is authorized by this section to provide, the Secretary shall, as soon as practicable, notify, in writing, the Governor and the State legislature of any State and the Tribal Council of any affected Indian tribe in such State in which is located a potentially acceptable site or facility for such interim storage of spent fuel of his intention to investigate that site or facility.

(2) During the course of investigation of such site or facility, the Secretary shall keep the Governor, State legislature, and affected Tribal Council currently informed of the progress of the work, and results of the investigation. At the time of selection by the Secretary of any site or existing facility, but prior to undertaking any site-specific work or alterations, the Secretary shall promptly notify the Governor, the legislature, and any affected Tribal Council in writing of such selection, and subject to the provisions of paragraph (6) of this subsection, shall promptly enter into negotiations with such State and affected Tribal Council to establish a cooperative agreement under which such State and Council shall have the right to participate in a process of consultation and cooperation, based on public health and safety and environmental concerns, in all stages of the planning, development, modification, expansion, operation, and closure of storage capacity at a site or facility within such State for the interim storage of spent fuel from civilian nuclear power reactors. Public participation in the negotiation of such an agreement shall be provided for and encouraged by the Secretary, the State,

and the affected Tribal Council. The Secretary, in cooperation with the States and Indian tribes, shall develop and publish minimum guidelines for public participation in such negotiations, but the adequacy of such guidelines or any failure to comply with such guidelines shall not be a basis for judicial review.

(3) The cooperative agreement shall include, but need not be limited to, the sharing in accordance with applicable law of all technical and licensing information, the utilization of available expertise, the facilitating of permitting procedures, joint project review, and the formulation of joint surveillance and monitoring arrangements to carry out applicable Federal and State laws. The cooperative agreement also shall include a detailed plan or schedule of milestones, decision points and opportunities for State or eligible Tribal Council review and objection. Such cooperative agreement shall provide procedures for negotiating and resolving objections of the State and affected Tribal Council in any stage of planning, development, modification, expansion, operation, or closure of storage capacity at a site or facility within such State. The terms of any cooperative agreement shall not affect the authority of the Nuclear Regulatory Commission under existing law.

(4) For the purpose of this subsection, "process of consultation and cooperation" means a methodology by which the Secretary (A) keeps the State and eligible Tribal Council fully and currently informed about the aspects of the project related to any potential impact on the public health and safety and environment; (B) solicits, receives, and evaluates concerns and objections of such State and Council with regard to such aspects of the project on an ongoing basis; and (C) works diligently and cooperatively to resolve, through arbitration or other appropriate mechanisms, such concerns and objections. The process of consultation and cooperation shall not include the grant of a right to any State or Tribal Council to exercise an absolute veto of any aspect of the planning, development, modification, expansion, or operation of the project.

(5) The Secretary and the State and affected Tribal Council shall seek to conclude the agreement required by paragraph (2) as soon as practicable, but not later than 180 days following the date of notification of the selection under paragraph (2). The Secretary shall periodically report to the Congress thereafter on the status of the agreements approved under paragraph (3). Any report to the Congress on the status of negotiations of such agreement by the Secretary shall be accompanied by comments solicited by the Secretary from the State and eligible Tribal Council.

(6)(A) Upon deciding to provide an aggregate of 300 or more metric tons of storage capacity under subsection (a)(1) of this section at any one site, the Secretary shall notify the Governor and legislature of the State where such site is located, or the governing body of the Indian tribe in whose reservation such site is located, as the case may be, of such decision. During the 60-day period following receipt of notification by the Secretary of his decision to provide an aggregate of 300 or more metric tons of storage capacity at any one site, the Governor or legislature of the State in which such site is located, or the governing body of the affected Indian tribe where such site is located, as the case may be, may disapprove the provision of 300 or more metric tons of storage capacity at the site involved and submit to the Congress a notice of such disapproval. A notice of disapproval shall be considered to be submitted to the Congress on the date of the transmittal of such notice of disapproval to the Speaker of the House and the President pro tempore of the Senate. Such notice of disapproval shall be accompanied by a statement of reasons explaining why the provision of such storage capacity at such site was disapproved by such Governor or legislature or the governing body of such Indian tribe.

(B) Unless otherwise provided by State law, the Governor or legislature of each State shall have authority to submit a notice of disapproval to the Congress under subparagraph (A). In any case in which State law provides for submission of any such notice of disapproval by any other person or entity, any reference in this part to the Governor or legislature of such State shall be considered to refer instead to such other person or entity.

(C) The authority of the Governor and legislature of each State under this paragraph shall not be applicable with respect to any site located on a reservation.

(D) If any notice of disapproval is submitted to the Congress under subparagraph (A), the proposed provision of 300 or more metric tons of storage capacity at the site involved shall be disapproved unless, during the first period of 90 calendar days of continuous session of the Congress following the date of the receipt by the Congress of such notice of disapproval, the Congress passes a resolution approving such proposed provision of storage capacity in accordance with the procedures established in this paragraph and subsections (d) through (f) of section 10135 of this title and such resolution thereafter becomes law. For purposes of this paragraph, the term "resolution" means a joint resolution of either House of the Congress, the matter after the resolving clause of which is as follows: "That there hereby is approved the provision of 300 or more metric tons of spent nuclear fuel storage capacity at the site located at _____, with respect to which a notice of disapproval was submitted by _____ on _____.". The first blank space in such resolution shall be filled with the geographic location of the site involved; the second blank space in such resolution shall be filled with the designation of the

State Governor and legislature or affected Indian tribe governing body submitting the notice of disapproval involved; and the last blank space in such resolution shall be filled with the date of submission of such notice of disapproval.

(E) For purposes of the consideration of any resolution described in subparagraph (D), each reference in subsections (d) and (e) of section 10135 of this title to a resolution of repository siting approval shall be considered to refer to the resolution described in such subparagraph.

(7) As used in this section, the term "affected Tribal Council" means the governing body of any Indian tribe within whose reservation boundaries there is located a potentially acceptable site for interim storage capacity of spent nuclear fuel from civilian nuclear power reactors, or within whose boundaries a site for such capacity is selected by the Secretary, or whose federally defined possessory or usage rights to other lands outside of the reservation's boundaries arising out of congressionally ratified treaties, as determined by the Secretary of the Interior pursuant to a petition filed with him by the appropriate governmental officials of such tribe, may be substantially and adversely affected by the establishment of any such storage capacity.

**(e) Limitations**

Any spent nuclear fuel stored under this section shall be removed from the storage site or facility involved as soon as practicable, but in any event not later than 3 years following the date on which a repository or monitored retrievable storage facility developed under this chapter is available for disposal of such spent nuclear fuel.

**(f) Report**

The Secretary shall annually prepare and submit to the Congress a report on any plans of the Secretary for providing storage capacity under this section. Such report shall include a description of the specific manner of providing such storage selected by the Secretary, if any. The Secretary shall prepare and submit the first such report not later than 1 year after January 7, 1983.

**(g) Criteria for determining adequacy of available storage capacity**

Not later than 90 days after January 7, 1983, the Commission pursuant to section 553 of the Administrative Procedures Act [5 U.S.C.A. § 553], shall propose, by rule, procedures and criteria for making the determination required by subsection (b) of this section that a person owning and operating a civilian nuclear power reactor cannot reasonably provide adequate spent nuclear fuel storage capacity at the civilian nuclear power reactor site when needed to ensure the continued orderly operation of such reactor. Such criteria shall ensure the maintenance of a full core reserve storage capability at the site of such reactor unless the Commission determines that maintenance of such capability is not necessary for the continued orderly operation of such reactor. Such criteria shall identify the feasibility of reasonably providing such adequate spent nuclear fuel storage capacity, taking into account economic, technical, regulatory, and public health and safety factors, through the use of high-density fuel storage racks, fuel rod compaction, transshipment of spent nuclear fuel to another civilian nuclear power reactor within the same utility system, construction of additional spent nuclear fuel pool capacity, or such other technologies as may be approved by the Commission.

**(h) Application**

Notwithstanding any other provision of law, nothing in this chapter shall be construed to encourage, authorize, or require the private or Federal use, purchase, lease, or other acquisition of any storage facility located away from the site of any civilian nuclear power reactor and not owned by the Federal Government on January 7, 1983.

**(i) Coordination with research and development program**

To the extent available, and consistent with the provisions of this section, the Secretary shall provide spent nuclear fuel for the research and development program authorized in section 10198 of this title from spent nuclear fuel received by the Secretary for storage under this section. Such spent nuclear fuel shall not be subject to the provisions of subsection (e) of this section.

(Pub.L. 97–425, Title I, § 135, Jan. 7, 1983, 96 Stat. 2232.)

### HISTORICAL AND STATUTORY NOTES

**References in Text**

The Atomic Energy Act of 1954, referred to in subsec. (a)(1)(A)(i), is Act Aug. 30, 1954, c. 1073, 68 Stat. 919, as amended, which is classified generally to chapter 23 (section 2011 et seq.) of this title. For complete classification of this Act to the Code, see Short Title of 1954 Acts note set out under section 2011 of this title and Tables.

The Energy Reorganization Act of 1974, referred to in subsec. (a)(1)(A)(i), is Pub.L. 93–438, Oct. 11, 1974, 88 Stat. 1233, as amended, which is classified principally to chapter 73 (section 5801 et seq.) of this title. For complete classification of this Act to the Code, see Short Title of 1974 Acts note set out under section 5801 of this title and Tables.

The National Environmental Policy Act of 1969, referred to in subsecs. (a)(1)(A)(ii) and (c)(1), is Pub.L. 91–190, Jan. 1, 1970, 83 Stat. 852, as amended, which is classified generally to chapter 55 (section 4321 et seq.) of this title. Section 102 of such Act is classified to section 4332 of this title. For complete classification of this Act to the Code, see Short Title of 1970 Acts note set out under section 4321 of this title and Tables.

The Administrative Procedure Act, referred to in subsec. (g), was repealed by Pub.L. 89–554, § 8(a), Sept. 6, 1966, 80 Stat. 632, and reenacted by the first section thereof principally in subchapter II (section 551 et seq.) of chapter 5, and chapter 7 (section 701 et seq.) of Title 5, Government Organization and Employees.

Section 10198 of this title, referred to in subsec. (i), was in the original a reference to section 217 of Pub.L. 97–425, which is classified to section 10197 of this title, and has been translated as section 10198 of this title as the probable intent of Congress in view of section 10198(c)(2), which directs the Secretary to provide spent nuclear fuel for the research and development program authorized by section 10198(c) of this title from spent nuclear fuel received by the Secretary for storage under section 10155 of this title.

## § 10156. Interim Storage Fund

**[NWPA § 136]**

### (a) Contracts

(1) During the period following January 7, 1983, but not later than January 1, 1990, the Secretary is authorized to enter into contracts with persons who generate or own spent nuclear fuel resulting from civilian nuclear activities for the storage of such spent nuclear fuel in any storage capacity provided under this part: *Provided, however,* That the Secretary shall not enter into contracts for spent nuclear fuel in amounts in excess of the available storage capacity specified in section 10155(a) of this title. Those contracts shall provide that the Federal Government will (1) take title at the civilian nuclear power reactor site, to such amounts of spent nuclear fuel from the civilian nuclear power reactor as the Commission determines cannot be stored onsite, (2) transport the spent nuclear fuel to a federally owned and operated interim away-from-reactor storage facility, and (3) store such fuel in the facility pending further processing, storage, or disposal. Each such contract shall (A) provide for payment to the Secretary of fees determined in accordance with the provisions of this section; and (B) specify the amount of storage capacity to be provided for the person involved.

(2) The Secretary shall undertake a study and, not later than 180 days after January 7, 1983, submit to the Congress a report, establishing payment charges that shall be calculated on an annual basis, commencing on or before January 1, 1984. Such payment charges and the calculation thereof shall be published in the Federal Register, and shall become effective not less than 30 days after publication. Each payment charge published in the Federal Register under this paragraph shall remain effective for a period of 12 months from the effective date as the charge for the cost of the interim storage of any spent nuclear fuel. The report of the Secretary shall specify the method and manner of collection (including the rates and manner of payment) and any legislative recommendations determined by the Secretary to be appropriate.

(3) Fees for storage under this part shall be established on a nondiscriminatory basis. The fees to be paid by each person entering into a contract with the Secretary under this subsection shall be based upon an estimate of the pro rata costs of storage and related activities under this part with respect to such person, including the acquisition, construction, operation, and maintenance of any facilities under this part.

(4) The Secretary shall establish in writing criteria setting forth the terms and conditions under which such storage services shall be made available.

(5) Except as provided in section 10157 of this title, nothing in this chapter or any other Act requires the Secretary, in carrying out the responsibilities of this section, to obtain a license or permit to possess or own spent nuclear fuel.

### (b) Limitation

No spent nuclear fuel generated or owned by any department of the United States referred to in section 101 or 102 of Title 5 may be stored by the Secretary in any storage capacity provided under this part unless such department transfers to the Secretary, for deposit in the Interim Storage Fund, amounts equivalent to the fees that would be paid to the Secretary under the contracts referred to in this section if such spent nuclear fuel were generated by any other person.

### (c) Establishment of Interim Storage Fund

There hereby is established in the Treasury of the United States a separate fund, to be known as the Interim Storage Fund. The Storage Fund shall consist of—

(1) all receipts, proceeds, and recoveries realized by the Secretary under subsections (a), (b), and (e) of this section, which shall be deposited in the Storage Fund immediately upon their realization;

(2) any appropriations made by the Congress to the Storage Fund; and

(3) any unexpended balances available on January 7, 1983, for functions or activities necessary or incident to the interim storage of civilian spent nuclear fuel, which shall automatically be transferred to the Storage Fund on such date.

### (d) Use of Storage Fund

The Secretary may make expenditures from the Storage Fund, subject to subsection (e) of this section, for any purpose necessary or appropriate to the conduct of the functions and activities of the Secretary, or the provision or anticipated provision of services, under this part, including—

(1) the identification, development, licensing, construction, operation, decommissioning, and post-decommissioning maintenance and monitoring of any interim storage facility provided under this part;

(2) the administrative cost of the interim storage program;

(3) the costs associated with acquisition, design, modification, replacement, operation, and construction of facilities at an interim storage site, consistent with the restrictions in section 10155 of this title;

(4) the cost of transportation of spent nuclear fuel; and

(5) impact assistance as described in subsection (e) of this section.

**(e) Impact assistance**

(1) Beginning the first fiscal year which commences after January 7, 1983, the Secretary shall make annual impact assistance payments to a State or appropriate unit of local government, or both, in order to mitigate social or economic impacts occasioned by the establishment and subsequent operation of any interim storage capacity within the jurisdicational [1] boundaries of such government or governments and authorized under this part: *Provided, however,* That such impact assistance payments shall not exceed (A) ten per centum of the costs incurred in paragraphs (1) and (2), or (B) $15 per kilogram of spent fuel, whichever is less;

(2) Payments made available to States and units of local government pursuant to this section shall be—

(A) allocated in a fair and equitable manner with a priority to those States or units of local government suffering the most severe impacts; and

(B) utilized by States or units of local governments only for (i) planning, (ii) construction and maintenance of public services, (iii) provision of public services related to the providing of such interim storage authorized under this subchapter, and (iv) compensation for loss of taxable property equivalent to that if the storage had been provided under private ownership.

(3) Such payments shall be subject to such terms and conditions as the Secretary determines necessary to ensure that the purposes of this subsection shall be achieved. The Secretary shall issue such regulations as may be necessary to carry out the provisions of this subsection.

(4) Payments under this subsection shall be made available solely from the fees determined under subsection (a) of this section.

(5) The Secretary is authorized to consult with States and appropriate units of local government in advance of commencement of establishment of storage capacity authorized under this part in an effort to determine the level of the payment such government would be eligible to receive pursuant to this subsection.

(6) As used in this subsection, the term "unit of local government" means a county, parish, township, municipality, and shall include a borough existing in the State of Alaska on January 7, 1983, and any other unit of government below the State level which is a unit of general government as determined by the Secretary.

**(f) Administration of Storage Fund**

(1) The Secretary of the Treasury shall hold the Storage Fund and, after consultation with the Secretary, annually report to the Congress on the financial condition and operations of the Storage Fund during the preceding fiscal year.

(2) The Secretary shall submit the budget of the Storage Fund to the Office of Management and Budget triennially along with the budget of the Department of Energy submitted at such time in accordance with chapter 11 of Title 31. The budget of the Storage Fund shall consist of estimates made by the Secretary of expenditures from the Storage Fund and other relevant financial matters for the succeeding 3 fiscal years, and shall be included in the Budget of the United States Government. The Secretary may make expenditures from the Storage Fund, subject to appropriations which shall remain available until expended. Appropriations shall be subject to triennial authorization.

(3) If the Secretary determines that the Storage Fund contains at any time amounts in excess of current needs, the Secretary may request the Secretary of the Treasury to invest such amounts, or any portion of such amounts as the Secretary determines to be appropriate, in obligations of the United States—

(A) having maturities determined by the Secretary of the Treasury to be appropriate to the needs of the Storage Fund; and

(B) bearing interest at rates determined to be appropriate by the Secretary of the Treasury, taking into consideration the current average market yield on outstanding marketable obligations of the United States with remaining periods to maturity comparable to the maturities of such investments, except that the interest rate on such investments shall not exceed the average interest rate applicable to existing borrowings.

(4) Receipts, proceeds, and recoveries realized by the Secretary under this section, and expenditures of amounts from the Storage Fund, shall be exempt from annual apportionment under the provisions of subchapter II of chapter 15 of Title 31.

(5) If at any time the moneys available in the Storage Fund are insufficient to enable the Secretary to discharge his responsibilities under this part, the Secretary shall issue to the Secretary of the Treasury obligations in such forms and denominations, bearing such maturities, and subject to such terms and conditions as may be agreed to by the Secretary and the Secretary of the Treasury. The total of such obligations shall not exceed amounts provided in appropriation Acts. Redemption of such obligations shall be made by the Secretary from moneys available in the Storage Fund. Such obligations shall bear interest at a rate determined by the Secretary of the Treasury, which shall be not less than a rate determined by taking into consideration the average market yield on outstanding marketable obligations of the United States of comparable maturities during the month preceding the issuance of the obligations under this paragraph. The Secretary of the Treasury shall purchase any issued obligations, and for such purpose the Secretary of the Treasury is authorized to use as a public debt transaction the proceeds from the sale of any securities issued under chapter 31 of Title 31, and the purposes for which securities may be issued under such Act are extended to include any purchase of such obligations. The Secretary of the Treasury may at any time sell any of the obligations acquired by him under this paragraph. All redemptions, purchases, and sales by the Secretary of the Treasury of obligations under this paragraph shall be treated as public debt transactions of the United States.

(6) Any appropriations made available to the Storage Fund for any purpose described in subsection (d) of this section shall be repaid into the general fund of the Treasury, together with interest from the date of availability of the appropriations until the date of repayment. Such interest shall be paid on the cumulative amount of appropriations available to the Storage Fund, less the average undisbursed cash balance in the Storage Fund account during the fiscal year involved. The rate of such interest shall be determined by the Secretary of the Treasury taking into consideration the average market yield during the month preceding each fiscal year on outstanding marketable obligations of the United States of comparable maturity. Interest payments may be deferred with the approval of the Secretary of the Treasury, but any interest payments so deferred shall themselves bear interest.

(Pub.L. 97–425, Title I, § 136, Jan. 7, 1983, 96 Stat. 2237.)

[1] So in original. Probably should be "jurisdictional".

### HISTORICAL AND STATUTORY NOTES

**References in Text**

Such Act, referred to in subsec. (f)(5), probably means chapter 31 of Title 31, 31 U.S.C.A. § 3101 et seq.

## § 10157. Transportation

[NWPA § 137]

(a)(1) [1] Transportation of spent nuclear fuel under section 10156(a) of this title shall be subject to licensing and regulation by the Commission and by the Secretary of Transportation as provided for transportation of commercial spent nuclear fuel under existing law.

(2) The Secretary, in providing for the transportation of spent nuclear fuel under this chapter, shall utilize by contract private industry to the fullest extent possible in each aspect of such transportation. The Secretary shall use direct Federal services for such transportation only upon a determination of the Secretary of Transportation, in consultation with the Secretary, that private industry is unable or unwilling to provide such transportation services at reasonable cost.

(Pub.L. 97–425, Title I, § 137, Jan. 7, 1983, 96 Stat. 2241.)

[1] So in original. No subsec. (b) was enacted.

### PART C—MONITORED RETRIEVABLE STORAGE

## § 10161. Monitored retrievable storage

[NWPA § 141]

**(a) Findings**

The Congress finds that—

(1) long-term storage of high-level radioactive waste or spent nuclear fuel in monitored retrievable storage facilities is an option for providing safe and reliable management of such waste or spent fuel;

(2) the executive branch and the Congress should proceed as expeditiously as possible to consider fully a proposal for construction of one or more monitored retrievable storage facilities to provide such long-term storage;

(3) the Federal Government has the responsibility to ensure that site-specific designs for such facilities are available as provided in this section;

(4) the generators and owners of the high-level radioactive waste and spent nuclear fuel to be stored in such facilities have the responsibility to pay the costs of the long-term storage of such waste and spent fuel; and

(5) disposal of high-level radioactive waste and spent nuclear fuel in a repository developed under this chapter should proceed regardless of any construction of a monitored retrievable storage facility pursuant to this section.

**(b) Submission of proposal by Secretary**

(1) On or before June 1, 1985, the Secretary shall complete a detailed study of the need for and feasibility of, and shall submit to the Congress a proposal for,

the construction of one or more monitored retrievable storage facilities for high-level radioactive waste and spent nuclear fuel. Each such facility shall be designed—

(A) to accommodate spent nuclear fuel and high-level radioactive waste resulting from civilian nuclear activities;

(B) to permit continuous monitoring, management, and maintenance of such spent fuel and waste for the foreseeable future;

(C) to provide for the ready retrieval of such spent fuel and waste for further processing or disposal; and

(D) to safely store such spent fuel and waste as long as may be necessary by maintaining such facility through appropriate means, including any required replacement of such facility.

(2) Such proposal shall include—

(A) the establishment of a Federal program for the siting, development, construction, and operation of facilities capable of safely storing high-level radioactive waste and spent nuclear fuel, which facilities are to be licensed by the Commission;

(B) a plan for the funding of the construction and operation of such facilities, which plan shall provide that the costs of such activities shall be borne by the generators and owners of the high-level radioactive waste and spent nuclear fuel to be stored in such facilities;

(C) site-specific designs, specifications, and cost estimates sufficient to (i) solicit bids for the construction of the first such facility; (ii) support congressional authorization of the construction of such facility; and (iii) enable completion and operation of such facility as soon as practicable following congressional authorization of such facility; and

(D) a plan for integrating facilities constructed pursuant to this section with other storage and disposal facilities authorized in this chapter.

(3) In formulating such proposal, the Secretary shall consult with the Commission and the Administrator, and shall submit their comments on such proposal to the Congress at the time such proposal is submitted.

(4) The proposal shall include, for the first such facility, at least 3 alternative sites and at least 5 alternative combinations of such proposed sites and facility designs consistent with the criteria of paragraph (1). The Secretary shall recommend the combination among the alternatives that the Secretary deems preferable. The environmental assessment under subsection (c) of this section shall include a full analysis of the relative advantages and disadvantages of all 5 such alternative combinations of proposed sites and proposed facility designs.

**(c) Environmental impact statements**

(1) Preparation and submission to the Congress of the proposal required in this section shall not require the preparation of an environmental impact statement under section 102(2)(C) of the National Environmental Policy Act of 1969 (42 U.S.C. 4332(2)(C)). The Secretary shall prepare, in accordance with regulations issued by the Secretary implementing such Act [42 U.S.C.A. § 4321 et seq.], an environmental assessment with respect to such proposal. Such environmental assessment shall be based upon available information regarding alternative technologies for the storage of spent nuclear fuel and high-level radioactive waste. The Secretary shall submit such environmental assessment to the Congress at the time such proposal is submitted.

(2) If the Congress by law, after review of the proposal submitted by the Secretary under subsection (b) of this section, specifically authorizes construction of a monitored retrievable storage facility, the requirements of the National Environmental Policy Act of 1969 (42 U.S.C. 4321 et seq.) shall apply with respect to construction of such facility, except that any environmental impact statement prepared with respect to such facility shall not be required to consider the need for such facility or any alternative to the design criteria for such facility set forth in subsection (b)(1) of this section.

**(d) Licensing**

Any facility authorized pursuant to this section shall be subject to licensing under section 5842(3) of this title. In reviewing the application filed by the Secretary for licensing of the first such facility, the Commission may not consider the need for such facility or any alternative to the design criteria for such facility set forth in subsection (b)(1) of this section.

**(e) Clarification**

Nothing in this section limits the consideration of alternative facility designs consistent with the criteria of subsection (b)(1) of this section in any environmental impact statement, or in any licensing procedure of the Commission, with respect to any monitored, retrievable facility authorized pursuant to this section.

**(f) Impact assistance**

(1) Upon receipt by the Secretary of congressional authorization to construct a facility described in subsection (b) of this section, the Secretary shall commence making annual impact aid payments to appropriate units of general local government in order to mitigate any social or economic impacts resulting from the construction and subsequent operation of any such

facility within the jurisdictional boundaries of any such unit.

(2) Payments made available to units of general local government under this subsection shall be—

(A) allocated in a fair and equitable manner, with priority given to units of general local government determined by the Secretary to be most severely affected; and

(B) utilized by units of general local government only for planning, construction, maintenance, and provision of public services related to the siting of such facility.

(3) Such payments shall be subject to such terms and conditions as the Secretary determines are necessary to ensure achievement of the purposes of this subsection. The Secretary shall issue such regulations as may be necessary to carry out the provisions of this subsection.

(4) Such payments shall be made available entirely from funds held in the Nuclear Waste Fund established in section 10222(c) of this title and shall be available only to the extent provided in advance in appropriation Acts.

(5) The Secretary may consult with appropriate units of general local government in advance of commencement of construction of any such facility in an effort to determine the level of payments each such unit is eligible to receive under this subsection.

**(g) Limitation**

No monitored retrievable storage facility developed pursuant to this section may be constructed in any State in which there is located any site approved for site characterization under section 10132 of this title. The restriction in the preceding sentence shall only apply until such time as the Secretary decides that such candidate site is no longer a candidate site under consideration for development as a repository. Such restriction shall continue to apply to any site selected for construction as a repository.

**(h) Participation of States and Indian tribes**

Any facility authorized pursuant to this section shall be subject to the provisions of sections 10135, 10136(a), 10136(b), 10136(d), 10137, and 10138 of this title. For purposes of carrying out the provisions of this subsection, any reference in sections 10135 through 10138 of this title to a repository shall be considered to refer to a monitored retrievable storage facility.

(Pub.L. 97–425, Title I, § 141, Jan. 7, 1983, 96 Stat. 2241.)

### HISTORICAL AND STATUTORY NOTES

**References in Text**

The National Environmental Policy Act of 1969 and such Act, referred to in subsec. (c), is Pub.L. 91–190, Jan. 1, 1970, 83 Stat. 852, as amended, which is classified generally to chapter 55 (section 4321 et seq.) of this title. Section 102 of such Act is classified to section 4332 of this title. For complete classification of this Act to the Code, see Short Title of 1970 Acts note set out under section 4321 of this title and Tables.

## § 10162. Authorization of monitored retrievable storage

**[NWPA § 142]**

**(a) Nullification of Oak Ridge siting proposal**

The proposal of the Secretary (EC–1022, 100th Congress) to locate a monitored retrievable storage facility at a site on the Clinch River in the Roane County portion of Oak Ridge, Tennessee, with alternative sites on the Oak Ridge Reservation of the Department of Energy and on the former site of a proposed nuclear powerplant in Hartsville, Tennessee, is annulled and revoked. In carrying out the provisions of sections 10164 and 10165 of this title, the Secretary shall make no presumption or preference to such sites by reason of their previous selection.

**(b) Authorization**

The Secretary is authorized to site, construct, and operate one monitored retrievable storage facility subject to the conditions described in sections 10163 through 10169 of this title.

(Pub.L. 97–425, Title I, § 142, as added Pub.L. 100–202, § 101(d), [Title III, § 300], Dec. 22, 1987, 101 Stat. 1329–104, 1329–121, and Pub.L. 100–203, Title V, § 5021, Dec. 22, 1987, 101 Stat. 1330–232.)

### HISTORICAL AND STATUTORY NOTES

**Codifications**

Pub.L. 100–202 and Pub.L. 100–203 added identical sections.

## § 10163. Monitored Retrievable Storage Commission

**[NWPA § 143]**

**(a) [1] Establishment**

(1)(A) There is established a Monitored Retrievable Storage Review Commission (hereinafter in this section referred to as the "MRS Commission"), that shall consist of 3 members who shall be appointed by and serve at the pleasure of the President pro tempore of the Senate and the Speaker of the House of Representatives.

(B) Members of the MRS Commission shall be appointed not later than 30 days after December 22, 1987, from among persons who as a result of training, experience and attainments are exceptionally well qualified to evaluate the need for a monitored retrievable storage facility as a part of the Nation's nuclear waste management system.

(C) The MRS Commission shall prepare a report on the need for a monitored retrievable storage facility as a part of a national nuclear waste management system that achieves the purposes of this chapter. In preparing the report under this subparagraph, the MRS Commission shall—

(i) review the status and adequacy of the Secretary's evaluation of the systems advantages and disadvantages of bringing such a facility into the national nuclear waste disposal system;

(ii) obtain comment and available data on monitored retrievable storage from affected parties, including States containing potentially acceptable sites;

(iii) evaluate the utility of a monitored retrievable storage facility from a technical perspective; and

(iv) make a recommendation to Congress as to whether such a facility should be included in the national nuclear waste management system in order to achieve the purposes of this chapter, including meeting needs for packaging and handling of spent nuclear fuel, improving the flexibility of the repository development schedule, and providing temporary storage of spent nuclear fuel accepted for disposal.

(2) In preparing the report and making its recommendation under paragraph (1) the MRS Commission shall compare such a facility to the alternative of at-reactor storage of spent nuclear fuel prior to disposal of such fuel in a repository under this chapter. Such comparison shall take into consideration the impact on—

(A) repository design and construction;

(B) waste package design, fabrication and standardization;

(C) waste preparation;

(D) waste transportation systems;

(E) the reliability of the national system for the disposal of radioactive waste;

(F) the ability of the Secretary to fulfill contractual commitments of the Department under this chapter to accept spent nuclear fuel for disposal; and

(G) economic factors, including the impact on the costs likely to be imposed on ratepayers of the Nation's electric utilities for temporary at-reactor storage of spent nuclear fuel prior to final disposal in a repository, as well as the costs likely to be imposed on ratepayers of the Nation's electric utilities in building and operating such a facility.

(3) The report under this subsection, together with the recommendation of the MRS Commission, shall be transmitted to Congress on November 1, 1989.

(4)(A)(i) Each member of the MRS Commission shall be paid at the rate provided for level III of the Executive Schedule for each day (including travel time) such member is engaged in the work of the MRS Commission, and shall receive travel expenses, including per diem in lieu of subsistence in the same manner as is permitted under sections 5702 and 5703 of Title 5.

(ii) The MRS Commission may appoint and fix compensation, not to exceed the rate of basic pay payable for GS–18 of the General Schedule, for such staff as may be necessary to carry out its functions.

(B)(i) The MRS Commission may hold hearings, sit and act at such times and places, take such testimony and receive such evidence as the MRS Commission considers appropriate. Any member of the MRS Commission may administer oaths or affirmations to witnesses appearing before the MRS Commission.

(ii) The MRS Commission may request any Executive agency, including the Department, to furnish such assistance or information, including records, data, files, or documents, as the Commission considers necessary to carry out its functions. Unless prohibited by law, such agency shall promptly furnish such assistance or information.

(iii) To the extent permitted by law, the Administrator of the General Services Administration shall, upon request of the MRS Commission, provide the MRS Commission with necessary administrative services, facilities, and support on a reimbursable basis.

(iv) The MRS Commission may procure temporary and intermittent services from experts and consultants to the same extent as is authorized by section 3109(b) of Title 5 at rates and under such rules as the MRS Commission considers reasonable.

(C) The MRS Commission shall cease to exist 60 days after the submission to Congress of the report required under this subsection.

(Pub.L. 97–425, Title I, § 143, as added Pub.L. 100–202, § 101(d) [Title III, § 300], Dec. 22, 1987, 101 Stat. 1329–104, 1329–121, and Pub.L. 100–203, Title V, § 5021, Dec. 22, 1987, 101 Stat. 1330–232; Pub.L. 100–507, § 2, Oct. 18, 1988, 102 Stat. 2541.)

[1] So in original. No subsec. (b) has been enacted.

## HISTORICAL AND STATUTORY NOTES

### Reference in Text

Level III of the Executive Schedule referred to in subsec. (a)(4)(A)(i), is set out in section 5314 of Title 5, Government Organization and Employees.

The General Schedule, referred to in subsec. (a)(4)(A)(ii), is set out under section 5332 of Title 5.

### Codifications

Pub.L. 100–202 and Pub.L. 100–203 added identical sections.

**References in Other Laws to GS-16, 17 or 18 Pay Rates**

Reference in laws to the rates of pay under the General Schedule, to be considered references to rates payable under specified sections of Title 5, Government Organization and Employees, see section 529 [Title I, § 101(c)(1)] of Pub. L. 101–509, set out in a note under section 5376 of Title 5.

## § 10164. Survey

[NWPA § 144]

After the MRS Commission submits its report to the Congress under section 10163 of this title, the Secretary may conduct a survey and evaluation of potentially suitable sites for a monitored retrievable storage facility. In conducting such survey and evaluation, the Secretary shall consider the extent to which siting a monitored retrievable storage facility at each site surveyed would—

(1) enhance the reliability and flexibility of the system for the disposal of spent nuclear fuel and high-level radioactive waste established under this chapter;

(2) minimize the impacts of transportation and handling of such fuel and waste;

(3) provide for public confidence in the ability of such system to safely dispose of the fuel and waste;

(4) impose minimal adverse effects on the local community and the local environment;

(5) provide a high probability that the facility will meet applicable environmental, health, and safety requirements in a timely fashion;

(6) provide such other benefits to the system for the disposal of spent nuclear fuel and high-level radioactive waste as the Secretary deems appropriate; and

(7) unduly burden a State in which significant volumes of high-level radioactive waste resulting from atomic energy defense activities are stored.

(Pub.L. 97–425, Title I, § 144, as added Pub.L. 100–202, § 101(d), [Title III, § 300], Dec. 22, 1987, 101 Stat. 1329–104, 1329–121, and amended Pub.L. 100–203, Title V, § 5021, Dec. 22, 1987, 101 Stat. 1330–234.)

### HISTORICAL AND STATUTORY NOTES

**Codifications**

Pub.L. 100–202 and Pub.L. 100–203 added identical sections.

## § 10165. Site selection

[NWPA § 145]

### (a) In general

The Secretary may select the site evaluated under section 10164 of this title that the Secretary determines on the basis of available information to be the most suitable for a monitored retrievable storage facility that is an integral part of the system for the disposal of spent nuclear fuel and high-level radioactive waste established under this chapter.

### (b) Limitation

The Secretary may not select a site under subsection (a) of this section until the Secretary recommends to the President the approval of a site for development as a repository under section 10134(a) of this title.

### (c) Site specific activities

The Secretary may conduct such site specific activities at each site surveyed under section 10164 of this title as he determines may be necessary to support an application to the Commission for a license to construct a monitored retrievable storage facility at such site.

### (d) Environmental assessment

Site specific activities and selection of a site under this section shall not require the preparation of an environmental impact statement under section 102(2)(C) of the National Environmental Policy Act of 1969 (42 U.S.C. 4332(2)(C)). The Secretary shall prepare an environmental assessment with respect to such selection in accordance with regulations issued by the Secretary implementing such Act [42 U.S.C.A. § 4321 et seq.]. Such environmental assessment shall be based upon available information regarding alternative technologies for the storage of spent nuclear fuel and high-level radioactive waste. The Secretary shall submit such environmental assessment to the Congress at the time such site is selected.

### (e) Notification before selection

(1) At least 6 months before selecting a site under subsection (a) of this section, the Secretary shall notify the Governor and legislature of the State in which such site is located, or the governing body of the affected Indian tribe where such site is located, as the case may be, of such potential selection and the basis for such selection.

(2) Before selecting any site under subsection (a) of this section, the Secretary shall hold at least one public hearing in the vicinity of such site to solicit any recommendations of interested parties with respect to issues raised by the selection of such site.

### (f) Notification of selection

The Secretary shall promptly notify Congress and the appropriate State or Indian tribe of the selection under subsection (a) of this section.

### (g) Limitation

No monitored retrievable storage facility authorized pursuant to section 10162(b) of this title may be constructed in the State of Nevada.

(Pub.L. 97–425, Title I, § 145, as added Pub.L. 100–202, § 101(d), [Title III, § 300], Dec. 22, 1987, 101 Stat. 1329–104, 1329–121, and Pub.L. 100–203, Title V, § 5021, Dec. 22, 1987, 101 Stat. 1330–234.)

### HISTORICAL AND STATUTORY NOTES

**References in Text**

The National Environmental Policy Act of 1969 and such Act, referred to in subsec. (d), is Pub.L. 91–190, Jan. 1, 1970, 83 Stat. 852, as amended, which is classified generally to chapter 55 (section 4321 et seq.) of this title. For complete classification of this Act to the Code, see Short Title of 1970 Acts note set out under section 4321 of this title and Tables.

**Codifications**

Pub.L. 100–202 and Pub.L. 100–203 added identical sections.

## § 10166. Notice of disapproval

[NWPA § 146]

**(a) In general**

The selection of a site under section 10165 of this title shall be effective at the end of the period of 60 calendar days beginning on the date of notification under such subsection, unless the governing body of the Indian tribe on whose reservation such site is located, or, if the site is not on a reservation, the Governor and the legislature of the State in which the site is located, has submitted to Congress a notice of disapproval with respect to such site. If any such notice of disapproval has been submitted under this subsection, the selection of the site under section 10165 of this title shall not be effective except as provided under section 10135(c) of this title.

**(b) References**

For purposes of carrying out the provisions of this subsection, references in section 10135(c) of this title to a repository shall be considered to refer to a monitored retrievable storage facility and references to a notice of disapproval of a repository site designation under section 10136(b) or 10138(a) of this title shall be considered to refer to a notice of disapproval under this section.

(Pub.L. 97–425, Title I, § 146, as added Pub.L. 100–202, § 101(d), [Title III, § 300], Dec. 22, 1987, 101 Stat. 1329–104, 1329–121, and Pub.L. 100–203, Title V, § 5021, Dec. 22, 1987, 101 Stat. 1330–235.)

### HISTORICAL AND STATUTORY NOTES

**Codifications**

Pub.L. 100–202 and Pub.L. 100–203 added identical sections.

## § 10167. Benefits agreement

[NWPA § 147]

Once selection of a site for a monitored retrievable storage facility is made by the Secretary under section 10165 of this title, the Indian tribe on whose reservation the site is located, or, in the case that the site is not located on a reservation, the State in which the site is located, shall be eligible to enter into a benefits agreement with the Secretary under section 10173 of this title.

(Pub.L. 97–425, Title I, § 147, as added Pub.L. 100–202, § 101(d), [Title III, § 300], Dec. 22, 1987, 101 Stat. 1329–104, 1329–121, and Pub.L. 100–203, Title V, § 5021, Dec. 22, 1987, 101 Stat. 1330–235.)

### HISTORICAL AND STATUTORY NOTES

**Codifications**

Pub.L. 100–202 and Pub.L. 100–203 added identical sections.

## § 10168. Construction authorization

[NWPA § 148]

**(a) Environmental impact statement**

(1) Once the selection of a site is effective under section 10166 of this title, the requirements of the National Environmental Policy Act of 1969 (42 U.S.C. 4321 et seq.) shall apply with respect to construction of a monitored retrievable storage facility, except that any environmental impact statement prepared with respect to such facility shall not be required to consider the need for such facility or any alternative to the design criteria for such facility set forth in section 10161(b)(1) of this title.

(2) Nothing in this section shall be construed to limit the consideration of alternative facility designs consistent with the criteria described in section 10161(b)(1) of this title in any environmental impact statement, or in any licensing procedure of the Commission, with respect to any monitored retrievable storage facility authorized under section 10162(b) of this title.

**(b) Application for construction license**

Once the selection of a site for a monitored retrievable storage facility is effective under section 10166 of this title, the Secretary may submit an application to the Commission for a license to construct such a facility as part of an integrated nuclear waste management system and in accordance with the provisions of this section and applicable agreements under this chapter affecting such facility.

**(c) Licensing**

Any monitored retrievable storage facility authorized pursuant to section 10162(b) of this title shall be subject to licensing under section 5842(3) of this title.

In reviewing the application filed by the Secretary for licensing of such facility, the Commission may not consider the need for such facility or any alternative to the design criteria for such facility set forth in section 10161(b)(1) of this title.

**(d) Licensing conditions**

Any license issued by the Commission for a monitored retrievable storage facility under this section shall provide that—

(1) construction of such facility may not begin until the Commission has issued a license for the construction of a repository under section 10135(d) of this title;

(2) construction of such facility or acceptance of spent nuclear fuel or high-level radioactive waste shall be prohibited during such time as the repository license is revoked by the Commission or construction of the repository ceases;

(3) the quantity of spent nuclear fuel or high-level radioactive waste at the site of such facility at any one time may not exceed 10,000 metric tons of heavy metal until a repository under this chapter first accepts spent nuclear fuel or solidified high-level radioactive waste; and

(4) the quantity of spent nuclear fuel or high-level radioactive waste at the site of such facility at any one time may not exceed 15,000 metric tons of heavy metal.

(Pub.L. 97–425, Title I, § 148, as added Pub.L. 100–202, § 101(d), [Title III, § 300], Dec. 22, 1987, 101 Stat. 1329–104, 1329–121, and Pub.L. 100–203, Title V, § 5021, Dec. 22, 1987, 101 Stat. 1330–235.)

### HISTORICAL AND STATUTORY NOTES

**References in Text**

The National Environmental Policy Act of 1969, referred to in subsec. (a)(1), is Pub.L. 91–190, Jan. 1, 1970, 83 Stat. 852, as amended, which is classified generally to chapter 55 (section 4321 et seq.) of this title. For complete classification of this Act to the Code, see Short Title of 1970 Acts note set out under section 4321 of this title and Tables.

**Codifications**

Pub.L. 100–202 and Pub.L. 100–203 added identical sections.

## § 10169. Financial assistance

[NWPA § 149]

The provisions of section 10136(c) or 10138(b) of this title with respect to grants, technical assistance, and other financial assistance shall apply to the State, to affected Indian tribes and to affected units of local government in the case of a monitored retrievable storage facility in the same manner as for a repository.

(Pub.L. 97–425, Title I, § 149, as added Pub.L. 100–202, § 101(d), [Title III, § 300], Dec. 22, 1987, 101 Stat. 1329–104, 1329–121, and Pub.L. 100–203, Title V, § 5021, Dec. 22, 1987, 101 Stat. 1330–236.)

### HISTORICAL AND STATUTORY NOTES

**Codifications**

Pub.L. 100–202 and Pub.L. 100–203 added identical sections.

### PART D—LOW-LEVEL RADIOACTIVE WASTE

## § 10171. Financial arrangements for low-level radioactive waste site closure

[NWPA § 151]

**(a) Financial arrangements**

(1) The Commission shall establish by rule, regulation, or order, after public notice, and in accordance with section 2231 of this title, such standards and instructions as the Commission may deem necessary or desirable to ensure in the case of each license for the disposal of low-level radioactive waste that an adequate bond, surety, or other financial arrangement (as determined by the Commission) will be provided by a licensee to permit completion of all requirements established by the Commission for the decontamination, decommissioning, site closure, and reclamation of sites, structures, and equipment used in conjunction with such low-level radioactive waste. Such financial arrangements shall be provided and approved by the Commission, or, in the case of sites within the boundaries of any agreement State under section 2021 of this title, by the appropriate State or State entity, prior to issuance of licenses for low-level radioactive waste disposal or, in the case of licenses in effect on January 7, 1983, prior to termination of such licenses.

(2) If the Commission determines that any long-term maintenance or monitoring, or both, will be necessary at a site described in paragraph (1), the Commission shall ensure before termination of the license involved that the licensee has made available such bonding, surety, or other financial arrangements as may be necessary to ensure that any necessary long-term maintenance or monitoring needed for such site will be carried out by the person having title and custody for such site following license termination.

**(b) Title and custody**

(1) The Secretary shall have authority to assume title and custody of low-level radioactive waste and the land on which such waste is disposed of, upon request of the owner of such waste and land and following termination of the license issued by the Commission for such disposal, if the Commission determines that—

(A) the requirements of the Commission for site closure, decommissioning, and decontamination have been met by the licensee involved and that such licensee is in compliance with the provisions of subsection (a) of this section;

(B) such title and custody will be transferred to the Secretary without cost to the Federal Government; and

(C) Federal ownership and management of such site is necessary or desirable in order to protect the public health and safety, and the environment.

(2) If the Secretary assumes title and custody of any such waste and land under this subsection, the Secretary shall maintain such waste and land in a manner that will protect the public health and safety, and the environment.

**(c) Special sites**

If the low-level radioactive waste involved is the result of a licensed activity to recover zirconium, hafnium, and rare earths from source material, the Secretary, upon request of the owner of the site involved, shall assume title and custody of such waste and the land on which it is disposed when such site has been decontaminated and stabilized in accordance with the requirements established by the Commission and when such owner has made adequate financial arrangements approved by the Commission for the long-term maintenance and monitoring of such site.

(Pub.L. 97–425, Title I, § 151, Jan. 7, 1983, 96 Stat. 2244.)

PART E—REDIRECTION OF THE NUCLEAR WASTE PROGRAM

## § 10172. Selection of Yucca Mountain site

[NWPA § 160]

**(a) In general**

(1) The Secretary shall provide for an orderly phase-out of site specific activities at all candidate sites other than the Yucca Mountain site.

(2) The Secretary shall terminate all site specific activities (other than reclamation activities) at all candidate sites, other than the Yucca Mountain site, within 90 days after December 22, 1987.

**(b) Eligibility to enter into benefits agreement**

Effective on December 22, 1987, the State of Nevada shall be eligible to enter into a benefits agreement with the Secretary under section 10173 of this title.

(Pub.L. 97–425, Title I, § 160, as added Pub.L. 100–202, § 101(d), [Title III, § 300], Dec. 22, 1987, 101 Stat. 1329–104, 1329–121, and Pub.L. 100–203, Title V, § 5011(a), Dec. 22, 1987, 101 Stat. 1330–227.)

HISTORICAL AND STATUTORY NOTES

**Codifications**

Pub.L. 100–202 and Pub.L. 100–203 added identical sections.

## § 10172a. Siting a second repository

[NWPA § 161]

**(a) Congressional action required**

The Secretary may not conduct site-specific activities with respect to a second repository unless Congress has specifically authorized and appropriated funds for such activities.

**(b) Report**

The Secretary shall report to the President and to Congress on or after January 1, 2007, but not later than January 1, 2010, on the need for a second repository.

**(c) Termination of granite research**

Not later than 6 months after December 22, 1987, the Secretary shall phase out in an orderly manner funding for all research programs in existence on December 22, 1987, designed to evaluate the suitability of crystalline rock as a potential repository host medium.

**(d) Additional siting criteria**

In the event that the Secretary at any time after December 22, 1987, considers any sites in crystalline rock for characterization or selection as a repository, the Secretary shall consider (as a supplement to the siting guidelines under section 10132 of this title) such potentially disqualifying factors as—

(1) seasonal increases in population;

(2) proximity to public drinking water supplies, including those of metropolitan areas; and

(3) the impact that characterization or siting decisions would have on lands owned or placed in trust by the United States for Indian tribes.

(Pub.L. 97–425, Title I, § 161, as added Pub.L. 100–202, § 101(d), [Title III, § 300], Dec. 22, 1987, 101 Stat. 1329–104, 1329–121, and Pub.L. 100–203, Title V, § 5012, Dec. 22, 1987, 101 Stat. 1330–231.)

HISTORICAL AND STATUTORY NOTES

**Codifications**

Pub.L. 100–202 and Pub.L. 100–203 added identical sections.

PART F—BENEFITS

## § 10173. Benefits agreements

[NWPA § 170]

**(a) In general**

(1) The Secretary may enter into a benefits agreement with the State of Nevada concerning a repository or with a State or an Indian tribe concerning a monitored retrievable storage facility for the acceptance of high-level radioactive waste or spent nuclear fuel in that State or on the reservation of that tribe, as appropriate.

(2) The State or Indian tribe may enter into such an agreement only if the State Attorney General or the appropriate governing authority of the Indian tribe or the Secretary of the Interior, in the absence of an appropriate governing authority, as appropriate, certifies to the satisfaction of the Secretary that the laws of the State or Indian tribe provide adequate authority for that entity to enter into the benefits agreement.

(3) Any benefits agreement with a State under this section shall be negotiated in consultation with affected units of local government in such State.

(4) Benefits and payments under this part may be made available only in accordance with a benefits agreement under this section.

**(b) Amendment**

A benefits agreement entered into under subsection (a) of this section may be amended only by the mutual consent of the parties to the agreement and terminated only in accordance with section 10173c of this title.

**(c) Agreement with Nevada**

The Secretary shall offer to enter into a benefits agreement with the Governor of Nevada. Any benefits agreement with a State under this subsection shall be negotiated in consultation with any affected units of local government in such State.

**(d) Monitored retrievable storage**

The Secretary shall offer to enter into a benefits agreement relating to a monitored retrievable storage facility with the governing body of the Indian tribe on whose reservation the site for such facility is located, or, if the site is not located on a reservation, with the Governor of the State in which the site is located and in consultation with affected units of local government in such State.

**(e) Limitation**

Only one benefits agreement for a repository and only one benefits agreement for a monitored retrievable storage facility may be in effect at any one time.

**(f) Judicial review**

Decisions of the Secretary under this section are not subject to judicial review.

(Pub.L. 97–425, Title I, § 170, as added Pub.L. 100–202, § 101(d), [Title III, § 300], Dec. 22, 1987, 101 Stat. 1329–104, 1329–121, and amended Pub.L. 100–203, Title V, § 5031, Dec. 22, 1987, 101 Stat. 1330–237.)

**HISTORICAL AND STATUTORY NOTES**

**Codifications**

Pub.L. 100–202 and Pub.L. 100–203 added identical sections.

## § 10173a. Content of agreements

**[NWPA § 171]**

**(a) In general**

(1) In addition to the benefits to which a State, an affected unit of local government or Indian tribe is entitled under this subchapter, the Secretary shall make payments to a State or Indian tribe that is a party to a benefits agreement under section 10173 of this title in accordance with the following schedule:

BENEFITS SCHEDULE
(amounts in $ millions)

| Event | MRS | Repository |
|---|---|---|
| (A) Annual payments prior to first spent fuel receipt.... | 5 | 10 |
| (B) Upon first spent fuel receipt | 10 | 20 |
| (C) Annual payments after first spent fuel receipt until closure of the facility ....... | 10 | 20 |

(2) For purposes of this section, the term—

(A) "MRS" means a monitored retrievable storage facility,

(B) "spent fuel" means high-level radioactive waste or spent nuclear fuel, and

(C) "first spent fuel receipt" does not include receipt of spent fuel or high-level radioactive waste for purposes of testing or operational demonstration.

(3) Annual payments prior to first spent fuel receipt under paragraph (1)(A) shall be made on the date of execution of the benefits agreement and thereafter on the anniversary date of such execution. Annual payments after the first spent fuel receipt until closure of the facility under paragraph (1)(C) shall be made on the anniversary date of such first spent fuel receipt.

(4) If the first spent fuel payment under paragraph (1)(B) is made within six months after the last annual payment prior to the receipt of spent fuel under paragraph (1)(A), such first spent fuel payment under paragraph (1)(B) shall be reduced by an amount equal to one-twelfth of such annual payment under paragraph (1)(A) for each full month less than six that has not elapsed since the last annual payment under paragraph (1)(A).

(5) Notwithstanding paragraph (1), (2), or (3), no payment under this section may be made before January 1, 1989, and any payment due under this subchapter before January 1, 1989, shall be made on or after such date.

(6) Except as provided in paragraph (7), the Secretary may not restrict the purposes for which the payments under this section may be used.

(7)(A) Any State receiving a payment under this section shall transfer an amount equal to not less than one-third of the amount of such payment to affected units of local government of such State.

(B) A plan for this transfer and appropriate allocation of such portion among such governments shall be included in the benefits agreement under section 10173 of this title covering such payments.

(C) In the event of a dispute concerning such plan, the Secretary shall resolve such dispute, consistent with this chapter and applicable State law.

**(b) Contents**

A benefits agreement under section 10173 of this title shall provide that—

(1) a Review Panel be established in accordance with section 10173b of this title;

(2) the State or Indian tribe that is party to such agreement waive its rights under this subchapter to disapprove the recommendation of a site for a repository;

(3) the parties to the agreement shall share with one another information relevant to the licensing process for the repository or monitored retrievable storage facility, as it becomes available;

(4) the State or Indian tribe that is party to such agreement participate in the design of the repository or monitored retrievable storage facility and in the preparation of documents required under law or regulation governing the effects of the facility on the public health and safety; and

(5) the State or Indian tribe waive its rights, if any, to impact assistance under sections 10136(c)(1)(B)(ii), 10136(c)(2), 10138(b)(2)(A)(ii), and 10138(b)(3) of this title.

**(c) Payments by Secretary**

The Secretary shall make payments to the States or affected Indian tribes under a benefits agreement under this section from the Waste Fund. The signature of the Secretary on a valid benefits agreement under section 10173 of this title shall constitute a commitment by the United States to make payments in accordance with such agreement.

(Pub.L. 97–425, Title I, § 171, as added Pub.L. 100–202, § 101(d), [Title III, § 300], Dec. 22, 1987, 101 Stat. 1329–104, 1329–121, and Pub.L. 100–203, Title V, § 5031, Dec. 22, 1987, 101 Stat. 1330–237.)

### HISTORICAL AND STATUTORY NOTES

**Codifications**

Pub.L. 100–202 and Pub.L. 100–203 added identical sections.

## § 10173b. Review Panel

**[NWPA § 172]**

**(a) In general**

The Review Panel required to be established by section 10173a(b)(1) of this title shall consist of a Chairman selected by the Secretary in consultation with the Governor of the State or governing body of the Indian tribe, as appropriate, that is party to such agreement and 6 other members as follows:

(1) 2 members selected by the Governor of such State or governing body of such Indian tribe;

(2) 2 members selected by units of local government affected by the repository or monitored retrievable storage facility;

(3) 1 member to represent persons making payments into the Waste Fund, to be selected by the Secretary; and

(4) 1 member to represent other public interests, to be selected by the Secretary.

**(b) Terms**

(1) The members of the Review Panel shall serve for terms of 4 years each.

(2) Members of the Review Panel who are not full-time employees of the Federal Government, shall receive a per diem compensation for each day spent conducting work of the Review Panel, including their necessary travel or other expenses while engaged in the work of the Review Panel.

(3) Expenses of the Panel shall be paid by the Secretary from the Waste Fund.

**(c) Duties**

The Review Panel shall—

(1) advise the Secretary on matters relating to the proposed repository or monitored retrievable storage facility, including issues relating to design, construction, operation, and decommissioning of the facility;

(2) evaluate performance of the repository or monitored retrievable storage facility, as it considers appropriate;

(3) recommend corrective actions to the Secretary;

(4) assist in the presentation of State or affected Indian tribe and local perspectives to the Secretary; and

(5) participate in the planning for and the review of preoperational data on environmental, demographic, and socioeconomic conditions of the site and the local community.

**(d) Information**

The Secretary shall promptly[1] make available promptly[1] any information in the Secretary's possession requested by the Panel or its Chairman.

**(e) Federal Advisory Committee Act**

The requirements of the Federal Advisory Committee Act shall not apply to a Review Panel established under this subchapter.

(Pub.L. 97–425, Title I, § 172, as added Pub.L. 100–202, § 101(d), [Title III, § 300], Dec. 22, 1987, 101 Stat. 1329–104, 1329–121, and Pub.L. 100–203, Title V, § 5031, Dec. 22, 1987, 101 Stat. 1330–239.)

[1] So in original.

### HISTORICAL AND STATUTORY NOTES

**References in Text**

The Federal Advisory Committee Act, referred to in subsec. (e), is Pub.L. 92–463, Oct. 6, 1972, 86 Stat. 770, as amended, which is set out as Appendix 2 to Title 5, Government Organization and Employees.

**Codifications**

Pub.L. 100–202 and Pub.L. 100–203 added identical sections.

## § 10173c. Termination

[NWPA § 173]

**(a) In general**

The Secretary may terminate a benefits agreement under this subchapter if—

(1) the site under consideration is disqualified for its failure to comply with guidelines and technical requirements established by the Secretary in accordance with this chapter; or

(2) the Secretary determines that the Commission cannot license the facility within a reasonable time.

**(b) Termination by State or Indian tribe**

A State or Indian tribe may terminate a benefits agreement under this subchapter only if the Secretary disqualifies the site under consideration for its failure to comply with technical requirements established by the Secretary in accordance with this chapter or the Secretary determines that the Commission cannot license the facility within a reasonable time.

**(c) Decisions of Secretary**

Decisions of the Secretary under this section shall be in writing, shall be available to Congress and the public, and are not subject to judicial review.

(Pub.L. 97–425, Title I, § 173, as added Pub.L. 100–202, § 101(d), [Title III, § 300], Dec. 22, 1987, 101 Stat. 1329–104, 1329–121, and Pub.L. 100–203, Title V, § 5031, Dec. 22, 1987, 101 Stat. 1330–240.)

### HISTORICAL AND STATUTORY NOTES

**Codifications**

Pub.L. 100–202 and Pub.L. 100–203 added identical sections.

PART G—OTHER BENEFITS

## § 10174. Consideration in siting facilities

[NWPA § 174]

The Secretary, in siting Federal research projects, shall give special consideration to proposals from States where a repository is located.

(Pub.L. 97–425, Title I, § 174, as added Pub.L. 100–202, § 101(d), [Title III, § 300], Dec. 22, 1987, 101 Stat. 1329–104, 1329–121, and Pub.L. 100–203, Title V, § 5031, Dec. 22, 1987, 101 Stat. 1330–240.)

### HISTORICAL AND STATUTORY NOTES

**Codifications**

Pub.L. 100–202 and Pub.L. 100–203 added identical sections.

## § 10174a. Report

[NWPA § 175]

**(a) In general**

Within one year of December 22, 1987, the Secretary shall report to Congress on the potential impacts of locating a repository at the Yucca Mountain site, including the recommendations of the Secretary for mitigation of such impacts and a statement of which impacts should be dealt with by the Federal Government, which should be dealt with by the State with State resources, including the benefits payments under section 10173a of this title, and which should be a joint Federal-State responsibility. The report under this subsection shall include the analysis of the Secretary of the authorities available to mitigate these impacts and the appropriate sources of funds for such mitigation.

**(b) Impacts to be considered**

Potential impacts to be addressed in the report under this[1] subsection (a) of this section shall include impacts on—

(1) education, including facilities and personnel for elementary and secondary schools, community colleges, vocational and technical schools and universities;

(2) public health, including the facilities and personnel for treatment and distribution of water, the treatment of sewage, the control of pests and the disposal of solid waste;

(3) law enforcement, including facilities and personnel for the courts, police and sheriff's depart-

ments, district attorneys and public defenders and prisons;

(4) fire protection, including personnel, the construction of fire stations, and the acquisition of equipment;

(5) medical care, including emergency services and hospitals;

(6) cultural and recreational needs, including facilities and personnel for libraries and museums and the acquisition and expansion of parks;

(7) distribution of public lands to allow for the timely expansion of existing, or creation of new, communities and the construction of necessary residential and commercial facilities;

(8) vocational training and employment services;

(9) social services, including public assistance programs, vocational and physical rehabilitation programs, mental health services, and programs relating to the abuse of alcohol and controlled substances;

(10) transportation, including any roads, terminals, airports, bridges, or railways associated with the facility and the repair and maintenance of roads, terminals, airports, bridges, or railways damaged as a result of the construction, operation, and closure of the facility;

(11) equipment and training for State and local personnel in the management of accidents involving high-level radioactive waste;

(12) availability of energy;

(13) tourism and economic development, including the potential loss of revenue and future economic growth; and

(14) other needs of the State and local governments that would not have arisen but for the characterization of the site and the construction, operation, and eventual closure of the repository facility.

(Pub.L. 97–425, Title I, § 175, as added Pub.L. 100–202, § 101(d), [Title III, § 300], Dec. 22, 1987, 101 Stat. 1329–104, 1329–121, and Pub.L. 100–203, Title V, § 5031, Dec. 22, 1987, 101 Stat. 1330–240.)

[1] So in original. The word "this" probably should not appear.

### HISTORICAL AND STATUTORY NOTES

**Codifications**

Pub.L. 100–202 and Pub.L. 100–203 added identical sections.

## PART H—TRANSPORTATION

## § 10175. Transportation

**[NWPA § 180]**

**(a) Packaging**

No spent nuclear fuel or high-level radioactive waste may be transported by or for the Secretary under part A of this subchapter or under part C of this subchapter except in packages that have been certified for such purpose by the Commission.

**(b) Advance notification**

The Secretary shall abide by regulations of the Commission regarding advance notification of State and local governments prior to transportation of spent nuclear fuel or high-level radioactive waste under part A of this subchapter or under part C of this subchapter.

**(c) Training for public safety officials**

The Secretary shall provide technical assistance and funds to States for training for public safety officials of appropriate units of local government and Indian tribes through whose jurisdiction the Secretary plans to transport spent nuclear fuel or high-level radioactive waste under part A of this subchapter or under part C of this subchapter. Training shall cover procedures required for safe routine transportation of these materials, as well as procedures for dealing with emergency response situations. The Waste Fund shall be the source of funds for work carried out under this subsection.

(Pub.L. 97–425, Title I, § 180, as added Pub.L. 100–202, § 101(d), [Title III, § 300], Dec. 22, 1987, 101 Stat. 1329–104, 1329–121, and Pub.L. 100–203, Title V, § 5061, Dec. 22, 1987, 101 Stat. 1330–251.)

### HISTORICAL AND STATUTORY NOTES

**Codifications**

Pub.L. 100–202 and Pub.L. 100–203 added identical sections.

# SUBCHAPTER II—RESEARCH, DEVELOPMENT, AND DEMONSTRATION REGARDING DISPOSAL OF HIGH-LEVEL RADIOACTIVE WASTE AND SPENT NUCLEAR FUEL

## § 10191. Purpose

**[NWPA § 211]**

It is the purpose of this subchapter—

(1) to provide direction to the Secretary with respect to the disposal of high-level radioactive waste and spent nuclear fuel;

(2) to authorize the Secretary, pursuant to this subchapter—

(A) to provide for the construction, operation, and maintenance of a deep geologic test and evaluation facility; and

(B) to provide for a focused and integrated high-level radioactive waste and spent nuclear fuel research and development program, including the development of a test and evaluation facility to carry out research and provide an integrated demonstration of the technology for deep geologic disposal of high-level radioactive waste, and the development of the facilities to demonstrate dry storage of spent nuclear fuel; and

(3) to provide for an improved cooperative role between the Federal Government and States, affected Indian tribes, and units of general local government in the siting of a test and evaluation facility.

(Pub.L. 97–425, Title II, § 211, Jan. 7, 1983, 96 Stat. 2245.)

## § 10192. Applicability

[NWPA § 212]

The provisions of this subchapter are subject to section 10107 of this title and shall not apply to facilities that are used for the disposal of high-level radioactive waste, low-level radioactive waste, transuranic waste, or spent nuclear fuel resulting from atomic energy defense activities.

(Pub.L. 97–425, Title II, § 212, Jan. 7, 1983, 96 Stat. 2245.)

## § 10193. Identification of sites

[NWPA § 213]

**(a) Guidelines**

Not later than 6 months after January 7, 1983 and notwithstanding the failure of other agencies to promulgate standards pursuant to applicable law, the Secretary, in consultation with the Commission, the Director of the United States Geological Survey, the Administrator, the Council on Environmental Quality, and such other Federal agencies as the Secretary considers appropriate, is authorized to issue, pursuant to section 553 of Title 5, general guidelines for the selection of a site for a test and evaluation facility. Under such guidelines the Secretary shall specify factors that qualify or disqualify a site for development as a test and evaluation facility, including factors pertaining to the location of valuable natural resources, hydrogeophysics, seismic activity, and atomic energy defense activities, proximity to water supplies, proximity to populations, the effect upon the rights of users of water, and proximity to components of the National Park System, the National Wildlife Refuge System, the National Wild and Scenic Rivers System, the National Wilderness Preservation System, or National Forest Lands. Such guidelines shall require the Secretary to consider the various geologic media in which the site for a test and evaluation facility may be located and, to the extent practicable, to identify sites in different geologic media. The Secretary shall use guidelines established under this subsection in considering and selecting sites under this subchapter.

**(b) Site identification by Secretary**

(1) Not later than 1 year after January 7, 1983, and following promulgation of guidelines under subsection (a) of this section, the Secretary is authorized to identify 3 or more sites, at least 2 of which shall be in different geologic media in the continental United States, and at least 1 of which shall be in media other than salt. Subject to Commission requirements, the Secretary shall give preference to sites for the test and evaluation facility in media possessing geochemical characteristics that retard aqueous transport of radionuclides. In order to provide a greater possible protection of public health and safety as operating experience is gained at the test and evaluation facility, and with the exception of the primary areas under review by the Secretary on January 7, 1983, for the location of a test and evaluation facility or repository, all sites identified under this subsection shall be more than 15 statute miles from towns having a population of greater than 1,000 persons as determined by the most recent census unless such sites contain high-level radioactive waste prior to identification under this subchapter. Each identification of a site shall be supported by an environmental assessment, which shall include a detailed statement of the basis for such identification and of the probable impacts of the siting research activities planned for such site, and a discussion of alternative activities relating to siting research that may be undertaken to avoid such impacts. Such environmental assessment shall include—

(A) an evaluation by the Secretary as to whether such site is suitable for siting research under the guidelines established under subsection (a) of this section;

(B) an evaluation by the Secretary of the effects of the siting research activities at such site on the public health and safety and the environment;

(C) a reasonable comparative evaluation by the Secretary of such site with other sites and locations that have been considered;

(D) a description of the decision process by which such site was recommended; and

(E) an assessment of the regional and local impacts of locating the proposed test and evaluation facility at such site.

(2) When the Secretary identifies a site, the Secretary shall as soon as possible notify the Governor of the State in which such site is located, or the governing body of the affected Indian tribe where such site is located, of such identification and the basis of such identification. Additional sites for the location of the test and evaluation facility authorized in section 10222(d) of this title may be identified after such 1 year period, following the same procedure as if such sites had been identified within such period.

(Pub.L. 97–425, Title II, § 213, Jan. 7, 1983, 96 Stat. 2245; Pub.L. 102–154, Title I, Nov. 13, 1991, 105 Stat. 1000; Pub.L. 102–285, § 10(a), May 18, 1992, 106 Stat. 171.)

### HISTORICAL AND STATUTORY NOTES

**Change of Name**

Pub.L. 102–285, § 10(a), May 18, 1992, 106 Stat. 171, redesignated the Geological Survey and provided that on and after May 18, 1992, it shall be known as the United States Geological Survey. An earlier statute [Pub.L. 102–154, Title I, Nov. 13, 1991, 105 Stat. 1000] had provided for the identical change of name effective on and after Nov. 13, 1991. See note under section 31 of Title 43, Public Lands.

## § 10194. Siting research and related activities

**[NWPA § 214]**

### (a) In general

Not later than 30 months after the date on which the Secretary completes the identification of sites under section 10193 of this title, the Secretary is authorized to complete sufficient evaluation of 3 sites to select a site for expanded siting research activities and for other activities under section 10198 of this title. The Secretary is authorized to conduct such preconstruction activities relative to such site selection for the test and evaluation facility as he deems appropriate. Additional sites for the location of the test and evaluation facility authorized in section 10222(d) of this title may be evaluated after such 30-month period, following the same procedures as if such sites were to be evaluated within such period.

### (b) Public meetings and environmental assessment

Not later than 6 months after the date on which the Secretary completes the identification of sites under section 10193 of this title, and before beginning siting research activities, the Secretary shall hold at least 1 public meeting in the vicinity of each site to inform the residents of the area of the activities to be conducted at such site and to receive their views.

### (c) Restrictions

Except as provided in section 10198 of this title with respect to a test and evaluation facility, in conducting siting research activities pursuant to subsection (a) of this section—

(1) the Secretary shall use the minimum quantity of high-level radioactive waste or other radioactive materials, if any, necessary to achieve the test or research objectives;

(2) the Secretary shall ensure that any radioactive material used or placed on a site shall be fully retrievable; and

(3) upon termination of siting research activities at a site for any reason, the Secretary shall remove any radioactive material at or in the site as promptly as practicable.

### (d) Title to material

The Secretary may take title, in the name of the Federal Government, to the high-level radioactive waste, spent nuclear fuel, or other radioactive material emplaced in a test and evaluation facility. If the Secretary takes title to any such material, the Secretary shall enter into the appropriate financial arrangements described in subsection (a) or (b) of section 10222 of this title for the disposal of such material.

(Pub.L. 97–425, Title II, § 214, Jan. 7, 1983, 96 Stat. 2247.)

## § 10195. Test and evaluation facility siting review and reports

**[NWPA § 215]**

### (a) Consultation and cooperation

The Governor of a State, or the governing body of an affected Indian tribe, notified of a site identification under section 10193 of this title shall have the right to participate in a process of consultation and cooperation as soon as the site involved has been identified pursuant to such section and throughout the life of the test and evaluation facility. For purposes of this section, the term "process of consultation and cooperation" means a methodology—

(1) by which the Secretary—

(A) keeps the Governor or governing body involved fully and currently informed about any potential economic or public health and safety impacts in all stages of the siting, development, construction, and operation of a test and evaluation facility;

(B) solicits, receives, and evaluates concerns and objections of such Governor or governing body with regard to such test and evaluation facility on an ongoing basis; and

(C) works diligently and cooperatively to resolve such concerns and objections; and

(2) by which the State or affected Indian tribe involved can exercise reasonable independent monitoring and testing of onsite activities related to all stages of the siting, development, construction and operation of the test and evaluation facility, except that any such monitoring and testing shall not unreasonably interfere with onsite activities.

### (b) Written agreements

The Secretary shall enter into written agreements with the Governor of the State in which an identified site is located or with the governing body of any affected Indian tribe where an identified site is located in order to expedite the consultation and cooperation process. Any such written agreement shall specify—

(1) procedures by which such Governor or governing body may study, determine, comment on, and make recommendations with regard to the possible health, safety, and economic impacts of the test and evaluation facility;

(2) procedures by which the Secretary shall consider and respond to comments and recommenda-

tions made by such Governor or governing body, including the period in which the Secretary shall so respond;

(3) the documents the Department is to submit to such Governor or governing body, the timing for such submissions, the timing for such Governor or governing body to identify public health and safety concerns and the process to be followed to try to eliminate those concerns;

(4) procedures by which the Secretary and either such Governor or governing body may review or modify the agreement periodically; and

(5) procedures for public notification of the procedures specified under subparagraphs (A) through (D).

**(c) Limitation**

Except as specifically provided in this section, nothing in this subchapter is intended to grant any State or affected Indian tribe any authority with respect to the siting, development, or loading of the test and evaluation facility.

(Pub.L. 97–425, Title II, § 215, Jan. 7, 1983, 96 Stat. 2247.)

## § 10196. Federal agency actions

**[NWPA § 216]**

**(a) Cooperation and coordination**

Federal agencies shall assist the Secretary by cooperating and coordinating with the Secretary in the preparation of any necessary reports under this subchapter and the mission plan under section 10221 of this title.

**(b) Environmental review**

(1) No action of the Secretary or any other Federal agency required by this subchapter or section 10221 of this title with respect to a test and evaluation facility to be taken prior to the initiation of onsite construction of a test and evaluation facility shall require the preparation of an environmental impact statement under section 102(2)(C) of the Environmental Policy Act of 1969 (42 U.S.C. 4332(2)(C) ), or to require the preparation of environmental reports, except as otherwise specifically provided for in this subchapter.

(2) The Secretary and the heads of all other Federal agencies shall, to the maximum extent possible, avoid duplication of efforts in the preparation of reports under the National Environmental Policy Act of 1969 (42 U.S.C. 4321 et seq.).

(Pub.L. 97–425, Title II, § 216, Jan. 7, 1983, 96 Stat. 2248.)

### HISTORICAL AND STATUTORY NOTES

**References in Text**

The National Environmental Policy Act of 1969, referred to in subsec. (b), is Pub.L. 91–190, Jan. 1, 1970, 83 Stat. 852, as amended, which is classified generally to chapter 55 (section 4321 et seq.) of this title. Section 102 of such Act is classified to section 4332 of this title. For complete classification of this Act to the Code, see Short Title of 1970 Acts note set out under section 4321 of this title and Tables.

## § 10197. Research and development on disposal of high-level radioactive waste

**[NWPA § 217]**

**(a) Purpose**

Not later than 64 months after January 7, 1983, the Secretary is authorized to, to the extent practicable, begin at a site evaluated under section 10194 of this title, as part of and as an extension of siting research activities of such site under such section, the mining and construction of a test and evaluation facility. Prior to the mining and construction of such facility, the Secretary shall prepare an environmental assessment. The purpose of such facility shall be—

(1) to supplement and focus the repository site characterization process;

(2) to provide the conditions under which known technological components can be integrated to demonstrate a functioning repository-like system;

(3) to provide a means of identifying, evaluating, and resolving potential repository licensing issues that could not be resolved during the siting research program conducted under section 10192 of this title;

(4) to validate, under actual conditions, the scientific models used in the design of a repository;

(5) to refine the design and engineering of repository components and systems and to confirm the predicted behavior of such components and systems;

(6) to supplement the siting data, the generic and specific geological characteristics developed under section 10194 of this title relating to isolating disposal materials in the physical environment of a repository;

(7) to evaluate the design concepts for packaging, handling, and emplacement of high-level radioactive waste and spent nuclear fuel at the design rate; and

(8) to establish operating capability without exposing workers to excessive radiation.

**(b) Design**

The Secretary shall design each test and evaluation facility—

(1) to be capable of receiving not more than 100 full-sized canisters of solidified high-level radioactive waste (which canisters shall not exceed an aggregate weight of 100 metric tons), except that spent nuclear fuel may be used instead of such waste if such waste cannot be obtained under reasonable conditions;

(2) to permit full retrieval of solidified high-level radioactive waste, or other radioactive material used by the Secretary for testing, upon completion of the technology demonstration activities; and

(3) based upon the principle that the high-level radioactive waste, spent nuclear fuel, or other radioactive material involved shall be isolated from the biosphere in such a way that the initial isolation is provided by engineered barriers functioning as a system with the geologic environment.

**(c) Operation**

(1) Not later than 88 months after January 7, 1983, the Secretary shall begin an in situ testing program at the test and evaluation facility in accordance with the mission plan developed under section 10221 of this title, for purposes of—

(A) conducting in situ tests of bore hole sealing, geologic media fracture sealing, and room closure to establish the techniques and performance for isolation of high-level radioactive waste, spent nuclear fuel, or other radioactive materials from the biosphere;

(B) conducting in situ tests with radioactive sources and materials to evaluate and improve reliable models for radionuclide migration, absorption, and containment within the engineered barriers and geologic media involved, if the Secretary finds there is reasonable assurance that such radioactive sources and materials will not threaten the use of such site as a repository;

(C) conducting in situ tests to evaluate and improve models for ground water or brine flow through fractured geologic media;

(D) conducting in situ tests under conditions representing the real time and the accelerated time behavior of the engineered barriers within the geologic environment involved;

(E) conducting in situ tests to evaluate the effects of heat and pressure on the geologic media involved, on the hydrology of the surrounding area, and on the integrity of the disposal packages;

(F) conducting in situ tests under both normal and abnormal repository conditions to establish safe design limits for disposal packages and to determine the effects of the gross release of radionuclides into surroundings, and the effects of various credible failure modes, including—

(i) seismic events leading to the coupling of aquifers through the test and evaluation facility;

(ii) thermal pulses significantly greater than the maximum calculated; and

(iii) human intrusion creating a direct pathway to the biosphere; and

(G) conducting such other research and development activities as the Secretary considers appropriate, including such activities necessary to obtain the use of high-level radioactive waste, spent nuclear fuel, or other radioactive materials (such as any highly radioactive material from the Three Mile Island nuclear powerplant or from the West Valley Demonstration Project) for test and evaluation purposes, if such other activities are reasonably necessary to support the repository program and if there is reasonable assurance that the radioactive sources involved will not threaten the use of such site as a repository.

(2) The in situ testing authorized in this subsection shall be designed to ensure that the suitability of the site involved for licensing by the Commission as a repository will not be adversely affected.

**(d) Use of existing Department facilities**

During the conducting of siting research activities under section 10194 of this title and for such period thereafter as the Secretary considers appropriate, the Secretary shall use Department facilities owned by the Federal Government on January 7, 1983, for the conducting of generically applicable tests regarding packaging, handling, and emplacement technology for solidified high-level radioactive waste and spent nuclear fuel from civilian nuclear activities.

**(e) Engineered barriers**

The system of engineered barriers and selected geology used in a test and evaluation facility shall have a design life at least as long as that which the Commission requires by regulations issued under this chapter, or under the Atomic Energy Act of 1954 (42 U.S.C. 2011 et seq.), for repositories.

**(f) Role of Commission**

(1)(A) Not later than 1 year after January 7, 1983, the Secretary and the Commission shall reach a written understanding establishing the procedures for review, consultation, and coordination in the planning, construction, and operation of the test and evaluation facility under this section. Such understanding shall establish a schedule, consistent with the deadlines set forth in this subchapter, for submission by the Secretary of, and review by the Commission of and necessary action on—

(i) the mission plan prepared under section 10221 of this title; and

(ii) such reports and other information as the Commission may reasonably require to evaluate any health and safety impacts of the test and evaluation facility.

(B) Such understanding shall also establish the conditions under which the Commission may have access to the test and evaluation facility for the purpose of assessing any public health and safety concerns that it may have. No shafts may be excavated for the test and evaluation until the Secretary and the Commission enter into such understanding.

(2) Subject to section 10225 of this title, the test and evaluation facility, and the facilities authorized in this section, shall be constructed and operated as research, development, and demonstration facilities, and shall not be subject to licensing under section 5842 of this title.

(3)(A) The Commission shall carry out a continuing analysis of the activities undertaken under this section to evaluate the adequacy of the consideration of public health and safety issues.

(B) The Commission shall report to the President, the Secretary, and the Congress as the Commission considers appropriate with respect to the conduct of activities under this section.

**(g) Environmental review**

The Secretary shall prepare an environmental impact statement under section 102(2)(C) of the National Environmental Policy Act of 1969 (42 U.S.C.A. § 4332(2)(C)) prior to conducting tests with radioactive materials at the test and evaluation facility. Such environmental impact statement shall incorporate, to the extent practicable, the environmental assessment prepared under subsection (a) of this section. Nothing in this subsection may be construed to limit siting research activities conducted under section 10194 of this title. This subsection shall apply only to activities performed exclusively for a test and evaluation facility.

**(h) Limitations**

(1) If the test and evaluation facility is not located at the site of a repository, the Secretary shall obtain the concurrence of the Commission with respect to the decontamination and decommissioning of such facility.

(2) If the test and evaluation facility is not located at a candidate site or repository site, the Secretary shall conduct only the portion of the in situ testing program required in subsection (c) of this section determined by the Secretary to be useful in carrying out the purposes of this chapter.

(3) The operation of the test and evaluation facility shall terminate not later than—

(A) 5 years after the date on which the initial repository begins operation; or

(B) at such time as the Secretary determines that the continued operation of a test and evaluation facility is not necessary for research, development, and demonstration purposes;

whichever occurs sooner.

(4) Notwithstanding any other provisions of this subsection, as soon as practicable following any determination by the Secretary, with the concurrence of the Commission, that the test and evaluation facility is unsuitable for continued operation, the Secretary shall take such actions as are necessary to remove from such site any radioactive material placed on such site as a result of testing and evaluation activities conducted under this section. Such requirement may be waived if the Secretary, with the concurrence of the Commission, finds that short-term testing and evaluation activities using radioactive material will not endanger the public health and safety.

(Pub.L. 97–425, Title II, § 217, Jan. 7, 1983, 96 Stat. 2249.)

### HISTORICAL AND STATUTORY NOTES

**References in Text**

The Atomic Energy Act of 1954, referred to in subsec. (e), is Act Aug. 30, 1954, c. 1073, 68 Stat. 919, as amended, which is classified principally to chapter 23 (section 2011 et seq.) of this title. For complete classification of this Act to the Code, see Short Title of 1954 Acts note set out under section 2011 of this title and Tables.

This subchapter, referred to in subsec. (f)(1)(A), was in the original "this subtitle", and was translated as this subchapter to reflect the probable intent of Congress because Title II of Pub.L. 97–425, which enacted this subchapter, does not contain subtitles.

## § 10198. Research and development on spent nuclear fuel

**[NWPA § 218]**

**(a) Demonstration and cooperative programs**

The Secretary shall establish a demonstration program, in cooperation with the private sector, for the dry storage of spent nuclear fuel at civilian nuclear power reactor sites, with the objective of establishing one or more technologies that the Commission may, by rule, approve for use at the sites of civilian nuclear power reactors without, to the maximum extent practicable, the need for additional site-specific approvals by the Commission. Not later than 1 year after January 7, 1983, the Secretary shall select at least 1, but not more than 3, sites evaluated under section 10194 of this title at such power reactors. In selecting such site or sites, the Secretary shall give preference to civilian nuclear power reactors that will soon have a shortage of interim storage capacity for spent nuclear fuel. Subject to reaching agreement as provided in subsection (b) of this section, the Secretary shall undertake activities to assist such power reactors with demonstration projects at such sites, which may use one of the following types of alternate storage technologies: spent nuclear fuel storage casks, caissons, or silos. The Secretary shall also undertake a cooperative program with civilian nuclear power reactors to encourage the development of the technology for spent nuclear fuel rod consolidation in existing power reactor water storage basins.

**(b) Cooperative agreements**

To carry out the programs described in subsection (a) of this section, the Secretary shall enter into a cooperative agreement with each utility involved that specifies, at a minimum, that—

(1) such utility shall select the alternate storage technique to be used, make the land and spent nuclear fuel available for the dry storage demonstration, submit and provide site-specific documentation for a license application to the Commission, obtain a license relating to the facility involved, construct such facility, operate such facility after licensing, pay the costs required to construct such facility, and pay all costs associated with the operation and maintenance of such facility;

(2) the Secretary shall provide, on a cost-sharing basis, consultative and technical assistance, including design support and generic licensing documentation, to assist such utility in obtaining the construction authorization and appropriate license from the Commission; and

(3) the Secretary shall provide generic research and development of alternative spent nuclear fuel storage techniques to enhance utility-provided, at-reactor storage capabilities, if authorized in any other provision of this chapter or in any other provision of law.

**(c) Dry storage research and development**

(1) The consultative and technical assistance referred to in subsection (b)(2) of this section may include, but shall not be limited to, the establishment of a research and development program for the dry storage of not more than 300 metric tons of spent nuclear fuel at facilities owned by the Federal Government on January 7, 1983. The purpose of such program shall be to collect necessary data to assist the utilities involved in the licensing process.

(2) To the extent available, and consistent with the provisions of section 10155 of this title, the Secretary shall provide spent nuclear fuel for the research and development program authorized in this subsection from spent nuclear fuel received by the Secretary for storage under section 10155 of this title. Such spent nuclear fuel shall not be subject to the provisions of section 10155(e) of this title.

**(d) Funding**

The total contribution from the Secretary from Federal funds and the use of Federal facilities or services shall not exceed 25 percent of the total costs of the demonstration program authorized in subsection (a) of this section, as estimated by the Secretary. All remaining costs of such program shall be paid by the utilities involved or shall be provided by the Secretary from the Interim Storage Fund established in section 10156 of this title.

**(e) Relation to spent nuclear fuel storage program**

The spent nuclear fuel storage program authorized in section 10155 of this title shall not be construed to authorize the use of research development or demonstration facilities owned by the Department unless—

(1) a period of 30 calendar days (not including any day in which either House of Congress is not in session because of adjournment of more than 3 calendar days to a day certain) has passed after the Secretary has transmitted to the Committee on Science, Space, and Technology of the House of Representatives and the Committee on Energy and Natural Resources of the Senate a written report containing a full and complete statement concerning (A) the facility involved; (B) any necessary modifications; (C) the cost thereof; and (D) the impact on the authorized research and development program; or

(2) each such committee, before the expiration of such period, has transmitted to the Secretary a written notice to the effect that such committee has no objection to the proposed use of such facility.

(Pub.L. 97–425, Title II, § 218, Jan. 7, 1983, 96 Stat. 2252; Pub.L. 103–437, § 15(c)(10), Nov. 2, 1994, 108 Stat. 4592.)

### HISTORICAL AND STATUTORY NOTES

**Change of Name**

Any reference in any provision of law enacted before Jan. 4, 1995, to the Committee on Science, Space, and Technology of the House of Representatives treated as referring to the Committee on Science of the House of Representatives, see section 1(a)(10) of Pub.L. 104–14, set out as a note preceding section 21 of Title 2, The Congress.

## § 10199. Payments to States and Indian tribes

**[NWPA § 219]**

**(a) Payments**

Subject to subsection (b) of this section, the Secretary shall make payments to each State or affected Indian tribe that has entered into an agreement pursuant to section 10195 of this title. The Secretary shall pay an amount equal to 100 percent of the expenses incurred by such State or Indian tribe in engaging in any monitoring, testing, evaluation, or other consultation and cooperation activity under section 10195 of this title with respect to any site. The amount paid by the Secretary under this paragraph shall not exceed $3,000,000 per year from the date on which the site involved was identified to the date on which the decontamination and decommission of the facility is complete pursuant to section 10197(h) of this title. Any such payment may only be made to a State in which a potential site for a test and evaluation facility has been identified under section 10193 of this title, or to an affected Indian tribe where the potential site has been identified under such section.

(b) Limitation

The Secretary shall make any payment to a State under subsection (a) of this section only if such State agrees to provide, to each unit of general local government within the jurisdictional boundaries of which the potential site or effectively selected site involved is located, at least one-tenth of the payments made by the Secretary to such State under such subsection. A State or affected Indian tribe receiving any payment under subsection (a) of this section shall otherwise have discretion to use such payment for whatever purpose it deems necessary, including the State or tribal activities pursuant to agreements entered into in accordance with section 10195 of this title. Annual payments shall be prorated on a 365-day basis to the specified dates.

(Pub.L. 97–425, Title II, § 219, Jan. 7, 1983, 96 Stat. 2253.)

## § 10200. Study of research and development needs for monitored retrievable storage proposal

[NWPA § 220]

Not later than 6 months after January 7, 1983, the Secretary shall submit to the Congress a report describing the research and development activities the Secretary considers necessary to develop the proposal required in section 10161(b) of this title with respect to a monitored retrievable storage facility.

(Pub.L. 97–425, Title II, § 220, Jan. 7, 1983, 96 Stat. 2254.)

## § 10201. Judicial review

[NWPA § 221]

Judicial review of research and development activities under this subchapter shall be in accordance with the provisions of section 10139 of this title.

(Pub.L. 97–425, Title II, § 221, Jan. 7, 1983, 96 Stat. 2254.)

## § 10202. Research on alternatives for permanent disposal of high-level radioactive waste

[NWPA § 222]

The Secretary shall continue and accelerate a program of research, development, and investigation of alternative means and technologies for the permanent disposal of high-level radioactive waste from civilian nuclear activities and Federal research and development activities except that funding shall be made from amounts appropriated to the Secretary for purposes of carrying out this section. Such program shall include examination of various waste disposal options.

(Pub.L. 97–425, Title II, § 222, Jan. 7, 1983, 96 Stat. 2254.)

## § 10203. Technical assistance to non-nuclear weapon states in field of spent fuel storage and disposal

[NWPA § 223]

(a) Statement of policy

It shall be the policy of the United States to cooperate with and provide technical assistance to non-nuclear weapon states in the field of spent fuel storage and disposal.

(b) Publication of joint notice; update

(1) Within 90 days of January 7, 1983, the Secretary and the Commission shall publish a joint notice in the Federal Register stating that the United States is prepared to cooperate with and provide technical assistance to non-nuclear weapon states in the fields of at-reactor spent fuel storage; away-from-reactor spent fuel storage; monitored, retrievable spent fuel storage; geologic disposal of spent fuel; and the health, safety, and environmental regulation of such activities. The notice shall summarize the resources that can be made available for international cooperation and assistance in these fields through existing programs of the Department and the Commission, including the availability of: (i) data from past or ongoing research and development projects; (ii) consultations with expert Department or Commission personnel or contractors; and (iii) liaison with private business entities and organizations working in these fields.

(2) The joint notice described in the preceding subparagraph shall be updated and reissued annually for 5 succeeding years.

(c) Notification to non-nuclear weapon states; expressions of interest

Following publication of the annual joint notice referred to in paragraph (2), the Secretary of State shall inform the governments of non-nuclear weapon states and, as feasible, the organizations operating nuclear powerplants in such states, that the United States is prepared to cooperate with and provide technical assistance to non-nuclear weapon states in the fields of spent fuel storage and disposal, as set forth in the joint notice. The Secretary of State shall also solicit expressions of interest from non-nuclear weapon state governments and non-nuclear weapon state nuclear power reactor operators concerning their participation in expanded United States cooperation and technical assistance programs in these fields. The Secretary of State shall transmit any such expressions of interest to the Department and the Commission.

(d) Funding requests

With his budget presentation materials for the Department and the Commission for fiscal years 1984 through 1989, the President shall include funding requests for an expanded program of cooperation and technical assistance with non-nuclear weapon states in the fields of spent fuel storage and disposal as appropriate in light of expressions of interest in such cooperation and assistance on the part of non-nuclear weapon state governments and non-nuclear weapon state nuclear power reactor operators.

**(e) "Non-nuclear weapon state" defined**

For the purposes of this subsection,[1] the term "non-nuclear weapon state" shall have the same meaning as that set forth in article IX of the Treaty on the Non-Proliferation of Nuclear Weapons (21 U.S.C. 438[2]).

**(f) Unauthorized actions**

Nothing in this subsection[1] shall authorize the Department or the Commission to take any action not authorized under existing law.

(Pub.L. 97–425, Title II, § 223, Jan. 7, 1983, 96 Stat. 2254.)

[1] So in original. Probably should be "section".

[2] So in original. Probably should be "21 UST 438".

### HISTORICAL AND STATUTORY NOTES

**References in Text**

The Treaty on the Non-Proliferation of Nuclear Weapons, referred to in subsec. (e), is set out in 21 UST 483; TIAS 6839.

## § 10204. Subseabed disposal

[NWPA § 224]

**(a) Repealed. Pub.L. 104–66, Title I, § 1051(d), Dec. 21, 1995, 109 Stat. 716**

**(b) Office of Subseabed Disposal Research**

(1) There is hereby established an Office of Subseabed Disposal Research within the Office of Science of the Department of Energy. The Office shall be headed by the Director, who shall be a member of the Senior Executive Service appointed by the Director of the Office of Science, and compensated at a rate determined by applicable law.

(2) The Director of the Office of Subseabed Disposal Research shall be responsible for carrying out research, development, and demonstration activities on all aspects of subseabed disposal of high-level radioactive waste and spent nuclear fuel, subject to the general supervision of the Secretary. The Director of the Office shall be directly responsible to the Director of the Office of Science, and the first such Director shall be appointed within 30 days of December 22, 1987.

(3) In carrying out his responsibilities under this chapter, the Secretary may make grants to, or enter into contracts with, the Subseabed Consortium described in subsection (d) of this section, and other persons.

(4)(A) Within 60 days of December 22, 1987, the Secretary shall establish a university-based Subseabed Consortium involving leading oceanographic universities and institutions, national laboratories, and other organizations to investigate the technical and institutional feasibility of subseabed disposal.

(B) The Subseabed Consortium shall develop a research plan and budget to achieve the following objectives by 1995:

(i) demonstrate the capacity to identify and characterize potential subseabed disposal sites;

(ii) develop conceptual designs for a subseabed disposal system, including estimated costs and institutional requirements; and

(iii) identify and assess the potential impacts of subseabed disposal on the human and marine environment.

(C) In 1990, and again in 1995, the Subseabed Consortium shall report to Congress on the progress being made in achieving the objectives of paragraph (2).

(5) Repealed. Pub.L. 104–66, Title I, § 1051(d), Dec. 21, 1995, 109 Stat. 716

(Pub.L. 97–425, Title II, § 224, as added Pub.L. 100–202, § 101(d) [Title III], Dec. 22, 1987, 101 Stat. 1329–104, 1329–121, and Pub.L. 100–203, Title V, § 5063, Dec. 22, 1987, 101 Stat. 1330–253, and amended Pub.L. 104–66, Title I, § 1051(d), Dec. 21, 1995, 109 Stat. 716; Pub.L. 105–245, Title III, § 309(b)(2)(E), Oct. 7, 1998, 112 Stat. 1853.)

### HISTORICAL AND STATUTORY NOTES

**Codifications**

This section was enacted by both Pub.L. 100–202 and Pub.L. 100–203. The enactment by Pub.L. 100–202 was achieved under the following provision of section 101(d) [Title III] of Pub.L. 100–202: "Subtitle A of Title V, Nuclear Waste Policy Amendments Act of 1987, contained in H.R. 3545, Omnibus Budget Reconciliation Act of 1987 as agreed to and reported by the Committee on Conference on H.R. 3545 is included herein and shall be effective as if it has been enacted into law." H.R. 3545 was enacted into law as Pub.L. 100–203.

# SUBCHAPTER III—OTHER PROVISIONS RELATING TO RADIOACTIVE WASTE

## § 10221. Mission plan

[NWPA § 301]

**(a) Contents of mission plan**

The Secretary shall prepare a comprehensive report, to be known as the mission plan, which shall provide an informational basis sufficient to permit informed decisions to be made in carrying out the repository program and the research, development, and demonstration programs required under this chapter. The mission plan shall include—

(1) an identification of the primary scientific, engineering, and technical information, including any necessary demonstration of engineering or systems integration, with respect to the siting and construction of a test and evaluation facility and repositories;

(2) an identification of any information described in paragraph (1) that is not available because of any unresolved scientific, engineering, or technical questions, or undemonstrated engineering or systems integration, a schedule including specific major milestones for the research, development, and technology demonstration program required under this chapter and any additional activities to be undertaken to provide such information, a schedule for the activities necessary to achieve important programmatic milestones, and an estimate of the costs required to carry out such research, development, and demonstration programs;

(3) an evaluation of financial, political, legal, or institutional problems that may impede the implementation of this chapter, the plans of the Secretary to resolve such problems, and recommendations for any necessary legislation to resolve such problems;

(4) any comments of the Secretary with respect to the purpose and program of the test and evaluation facility;

(5) a discussion of the significant results of research and development programs conducted and the implications for each of the different geologic media under consideration for the siting of repositories, and, on the basis of such information, a comparison of the advantages and disadvantages associated with the use of such media for repository sites;

(6) the guidelines issued under section 10132(a) of this title;

(7) a description of known sites at which site characterization activities should be undertaken, a description of such siting characterization activities, including the extent of planned excavations, plans for onsite testing with radioactive or nonradioactive material, plans for any investigations activities which may affect the capability of any such site to isolate high-level radioactive waste or spent nuclear fuel, plans to control any adverse, safety-related impacts from such site characterization activities, and plans for the decontamination and decommissioning of such site if it is determined unsuitable for licensing as a repository;

(8) an identification of the process for solidifying high-level radioactive waste or packaging spent nuclear fuel, including a summary and analysis of the data to support the selection of the solidification process and packaging techniques, an analysis of the requirements for the number of solidification packaging facilities needed, a description of the state of the art for the materials proposed to be used in packaging such waste or spent fuel and the availability of such materials including impacts on strategic supplies and any requirements for new or reactivated facilities to produce any such materials needed, and a description of a plan, and the schedule for implementing such plan, for an aggressive research and development program to provide when needed a high-integrity disposal package at a reasonable price;

(9) an estimate of (A) the total repository capacity required to safely accommodate the disposal of all high-level radioactive waste and spent nuclear fuel expected to be generated through December 31, 2020, in the event that no commercial reprocessing of spent nuclear fuel occurs, as well as the repository capacity that will be required if such reprocessing does occur; (B) the number and type of repositories required to be constructed to provide such disposal capacity; (C) a schedule for the construction of such repositories; and (D) an estimate of the period during which each repository listed in such schedule will be accepting high-level radioactive waste or spent nuclear fuel for disposal;

(10) an estimate, on an annual basis, of the costs required (A) to construct and operate the repositories anticipated to be needed under paragraph (9) based on each of the assumptions referred to in such paragraph; (B) to construct and operate a test and evaluation facility, or any other facilities, other than repositories described in subparagraph (A), determined to be necessary; and (C) to carry out any other activities under this chapter; and

(11) an identification of the possible adverse economic and other impacts to the State or Indian tribe involved that may arise from the development of a test and evaluation facility or repository at a site.

**(b) Submission of mission plan**

(1) Not later than 15 months after January 7, 1983, the Secretary shall submit a draft mission plan to the States, the affected Indian tribes, the Commission, and other Government agencies as the Secretary deems appropriate for their comments.

(2) In preparing any comments on the mission plan, such agencies shall specify with precision any objections that they may have. Upon submission of the mission plan to such agencies, the Secretary shall publish a notice in the Federal Register of the submission of the mission plan and of its availability for public inspection, and, upon receipt of any comments of such agencies respecting the mission plan, the Secretary shall publish a notice in the Federal Regis-

ter of the receipt of comments and of the availability of the comments for public inspection. If the Secretary does not revise the mission plan to meet objections specified in such comments, the Secretary shall publish in the Federal Register a detailed statement for not so revising the mission plan.

(3) The Secretary, after reviewing any other comments made by such agencies and revising the mission plan to the extent that the Secretary may consider to be appropriate, shall submit the mission plan to the appropriate committees of the Congress not later than 17 months after January 7, 1983. The mission plan shall be used by the Secretary at the end of the first period of 30 calendar days (not including any day on which either House of Congress is not in session because of adjournment of more than 3 calendar days to a day certain) following receipt of the mission plan by the Congress.

(Pub.L. 97–425, Title III, § 301, Jan. 7, 1983, 96 Stat. 2255.)

## § 10222. Nuclear Waste Fund

[NWPA § 302]

### (a) Contracts

(1) In the performance of his functions under this chapter, the Secretary is authorized to enter into contracts with any person who generates or holds title to high-level radioactive waste, or spent nuclear fuel, of domestic origin for the acceptance of title, subsequent transportation, and disposal of such waste or spent fuel. Such contracts shall provide for payment to the Secretary of fees pursuant to paragraphs (2) and (3) sufficient to offset expenditures described in subsection (d) of this section.

(2) For electricity generated by a civilian nuclear power reactor and sold on or after the date 90 days after January 7, 1983, the fee under paragraph (1) shall be equal to 1.0 mil per kilowatt-hour.

(3) For spent nuclear fuel, or solidified high-level radioactive waste derived from spent nuclear fuel, which fuel was used to generate electricity in a civilian nuclear power reactor prior to the application of the fee under paragraph (2) to such reactor, the Secretary shall, not later than 90 days after January 7, 1983, establish a 1 time fee per kilogram of heavy metal in spent nuclear fuel, or in solidified high-level radioactive waste. Such fee shall be in an amount equivalent to an average charge of 1.0 mil per kilowatt-hour for electricity generated by such spent nuclear fuel, or such solidified high-level waste derived therefrom, to be collected from any person delivering such spent nuclear fuel or high-level waste, pursuant to section 10143 of this title, to the Federal Government. Such fee shall be paid to the Treasury of the United States and shall be deposited in the separate fund established by subsection (c) of this section. In paying such a fee, the person delivering spent fuel, or solidified high-level radioactive wastes derived therefrom, to the Federal Government shall have no further financial obligation to the Federal Government for the long-term storage and permanent disposal of such spent fuel, or the solidified high-level radioactive waste derived therefrom.

(4) Not later than 180 days after January 7, 1983, the Secretary shall establish procedures for the collection and payment of the fees established by paragraph (2) and paragraph (3). The Secretary shall annually review the amount of the fees established by paragraphs (2) and (3) above to evaluate whether collection of the fee will provide sufficient revenues to offset the costs as defined in subsection (d) of this section. In the event the Secretary determines that either insufficient or excess revenues are being collected, in order to recover the costs incurred by the Federal Government that are specified in subsection (d) of this section, the Secretary shall propose an adjustment to the fee to insure full cost recovery. The Secretary shall immediately transmit this proposal for such an adjustment to Congress. The adjusted fee proposed by the Secretary shall be effective after a period of 90 days of continuous session have elapsed following the receipt of such transmittal unless during such 90-day period either House of Congress adopts a resolution disapproving the Secretary's proposed adjustment in accordance with the procedures set forth for congressional review of an energy action under section 6421 of this title.

(5) Contracts entered into under this section shall provide that—

(A) following commencement of operation of a repository, the Secretary shall take title to the high-level radioactive waste or spent nuclear fuel involved as expeditiously as practicable upon the request of the generator or owner of such waste or spent fuel; and

(B) in return for the payment of fees established by this section, the Secretary, beginning not later than January 31, 1998, will dispose of the high-level radioactive waste or spent nuclear fuel involved as provided in this subchapter.

(6) The Secretary shall establish in writing criteria setting forth the terms and conditions under which such disposal services shall be made available.

### (b) Advance contracting requirement

(1)(A) The Commission shall not issue or renew a license to any person to use a utilization or production facility under the authority of section 2133 or 2134 of this title unless—

(i) such person has entered into a contract with the Secretary under this section; or

(ii) the Secretary affirms in writing that such person is actively and in good faith negotiating with the Secretary for a contract under this section.

(B) The Commission, as it deems necessary or appropriate, may require as a precondition to the issuance or renewal of a license under section 2133 or 2134 of this title that the applicant for such license shall have entered into an agreement with the Secretary for the disposal of high-level radioactive waste and spent nuclear fuel that may result from the use of such license.

(2) Except as provided in paragraph (1), no spent nuclear fuel or high-level radioactive waste generated or owned by any person (other than a department of the United States referred to in section 101 or 102 of Title 5) may be disposed of by the Secretary in any repository constructed under this chapter unless the generator or owner of such spent fuel or waste has entered into a contract with the Secretary under this section by not later than—

(A) June 30, 1983; or

(B) the date on which such generator or owner commences generation of, or takes title to, such spent fuel or waste;

whichever occurs later.

(3) The rights and duties of a party to a contract entered into under this section may be assignable with transfer of title to the spent nuclear fuel or high-level radioactive waste involved.

(4) No high-level radioactive waste or spent nuclear fuel generated or owned by any department of the United States referred to in section 101 or 102 of Title 5 may be disposed of by the Secretary in any repository constructed under this chapter unless such department transfers to the Secretary, for deposit in the Nuclear Waste Fund, amounts equivalent to the fees that would be paid to the Secretary under the contracts referred to in this section if such waste or spent fuel were generated by any other person.

**(c) Establishment of Nuclear Waste Fund**

There hereby is established in the Treasury of the United States a separate fund, to be known as the Nuclear Waste Fund. The Waste Fund shall consist of—

(1) all receipts, proceeds, and recoveries realized by the Secretary under subsections (a), (b), and (e) of this section, which shall be deposited in the Waste Fund immediately upon their realization;

(2) any appropriations made by the Congress to the Waste Fund; and

(3) any unexpended balances available on January 7, 1983, for functions or activities necessary or incident to the disposal of civilian high-level radioactive waste or civilian spent nuclear fuel, which shall automatically be transferred to the Waste Fund on such date.

**(d) Use of Waste Fund**

The Secretary may make expenditures from the Waste Fund, subject to subsection (e) of this section, only for purposes of radioactive waste disposal activities under subchapters I and II of this chapter, including—

(1) the identification, development, licensing, construction, operation, decommissioning, and post-decommissioning maintenance and monitoring of any repository, monitored,[1] retrievable storage facility[2] or test and evaluation facility constructed under this chapter;

(2) the conducting of nongeneric research, development, and demonstration activities under this chapter;

(3) the administrative cost of the radioactive waste disposal program;

(4) any costs that may be incurred by the Secretary in connection with the transportation, treating, or packaging of spent nuclear fuel or high-level radioactive waste to be disposed of in a repository, to be stored in a monitored,[1] retrievable storage site[2] or to be used in a test and evaluation facility;

(5) the costs associated with acquisition, design, modification, replacement, operation, and construction of facilities at a repository site, a monitored,[1] retrievable storage site[2] or a test and evaluation facility site and necessary or incident to such repository, monitored,[1] retrievable storage facility[2] or test and evaluation facility; and

(6) the provision of assistance to States, units of general local government, and Indian tribes under sections 10136, 10138, and 10199 of this title.

No amount may be expended by the Secretary under this subchapter for the construction or expansion of any facility unless such construction or expansion is expressly authorized by this or subsequent legislation. The Secretary hereby is authorized to construct one repository and one test and evaluation facility.

**(e) Administration of Waste Fund**

(1) The Secretary of the Treasury shall hold the Waste Fund and, after consultation with the Secretary, annually report to the Congress on the financial condition and operations of the Waste Fund during the preceding fiscal year.

(2) The Secretary shall submit the budget of the Waste Fund to the Office of Management and Budget triennially along with the budget of the Department of Energy submitted at such time in accordance with chapter 11 of Title 31. The budget of the Waste Fund shall consist of the estimates made by the Secretary of expenditures from the Waste Fund and other relevant

financial matters for the succeeding 3 fiscal years, and shall be included in the Budget of the United States Government. The Secretary may make expenditures from the Waste Fund, subject to appropriations which shall remain available until expended. Appropriations shall be subject to triennial authorization.

(3) If the Secretary determines that the Waste Fund contains at any time amounts in excess of current needs, the Secretary may request the Secretary of the Treasury to invest such amounts, or any portion of such amounts as the Secretary determines to be appropriate, in obligations of the United States—

(A) having maturities determined by the Secretary of the Treasury to be appropriate to the needs of the Waste Fund; and

(B) bearing interest at rates determined to be appropriate by the Secretary of the Treasury, taking into consideration the current average market yield on outstanding marketable obligations of the United States with remaining periods to maturity comparable to the maturities of such investments, except that the interest rate on such investments shall not exceed the average interest rate applicable to existing borrowings.

(4) Receipts, proceeds, and recoveries realized by the Secretary under this section, and expenditures of amounts from the Waste Fund, shall be exempt from annual apportionment under the provisions of subchapter II of chapter 15 of Title 31.

(5) If at any time the moneys available in the Waste Fund are insufficient to enable the Secretary to discharge his responsibilities under this subchapter, the Secretary shall issue to the Secretary of the Treasury obligations in such forms and denominations, bearing such maturities, and subject to such terms and conditions as may be agreed to by the Secretary and the Secretary of the Treasury. The total of such obligations shall not exceed amounts provided in appropriation Acts. Redemption of such obligations shall be made by the Secretary from moneys available in the Waste Fund. Such obligations shall bear interest at a rate determined by the Secretary of the Treasury, which shall be not less than a rate determined by taking into consideration the average market yield on outstanding marketable obligations of the United States of comparable maturities during the month preceding the issuance of the obligations under this paragraph. The Secretary of the Treasury shall purchase any issued obligations, and for such purpose the Secretary of the Treasury is authorized to use as a public debt transaction the proceeds from the sale of any securities issued under chapter 31 of Title 31, and the purposes for which securities may be issued under such Act are extended to include any purchase of such obligations. The Secretary of the Treasury may at any time sell any of the obligations acquired by him under this paragraph. All redemptions, purchases, and sales by the Secretary of the Treasury of obligations under this paragraph shall be treated as public debt transactions of the United States.

(6) Any appropriations made available to the Waste Fund for any purpose described in subsection (d) of this section shall be repaid into the general fund of the Treasury, together with interest from the date of availability of the appropriations until the date of repayment. Such interest shall be paid on the cumulative amount of appropriations available to the Waste Fund, less the average undisbursed cash balance in the Waste Fund account during the fiscal year involved. The rate of such interest shall be determined by the Secretary of the Treasury taking into consideration the average market yield during the month preceding each fiscal year on outstanding marketable obligations of the United States of comparable maturity. Interest payments may be deferred with the approval of the Secretary of the Treasury, but any interest payments so deferred shall themselves bear interest.

(Pub.L. 97–425, Title III, § 302, Jan. 7, 1983, 96 Stat. 2257.)

[1] So in original. The comma probably should not appear.

[2] So in original. Probably should be followed by a comma.

### HISTORICAL AND STATUTORY NOTES

**References in Text**

Subsection (c) of this section, referred to in subsec. (a)(3), was in the original "subsection (c) 126(b)" and was translated as subsection (c) of this section as the probable intent of Congress in view of the establishment of the Nuclear Waste Fund by subsec. (c) of this section and the absence of a section 126 in Pub.L. 97–425.

This subchapter, referred to in subsecs. (a)(5)(B), (d), and (e)(5), was in the original "this subtitle", and was translated as this subchapter to reflect the probable intent of Congress because Title III of Pub.L. 97–425, which enacted this subchapter, does not contain subtitles.

Such Act, referred to in subsec. (e)(5), probably means chapter 31 of Title 31, Money and Finance.

## § 10223. Alternative means of financing

**[NWPA § 303]**

The Secretary shall undertake a study with respect to alternative approaches to managing the construction and operation of all civilian radioactive waste management facilities, including the feasibility of establishing a private corporation for such purposes. In conducting such study, the Secretary shall consult with the Director of the Office of Management and Budget, the Chairman of the Commission, and such other Federal agency representatives as may be appropriate. Such study shall be completed, and a report containing the results of such study shall be submitted to the Congress, within 1 year after January 7, 1983.

(Pub.L. 97–425, Title III, § 303, Jan. 7, 1983, 96 Stat. 2261.)

## § 10224. Office of Civilian Radioactive Waste Management

**[NWPA § 304]**

**(a) Establishment**

There hereby is established within the Department of Energy an Office of Civilian Radioactive Waste Management. The Office shall be headed by a Director, who shall be appointed by the President, by and with the advice and consent of the Senate, and who shall be compensated at the rate payable for level IV of the Executive Schedule under section 5315 of Title 5.

**(b) Functions of Director**

The Director of the Office shall be responsible for carrying out the functions of the Secretary under this chapter, subject to the general supervision of the Secretary. The Director of the Office shall be directly responsible to the Secretary.

**(c) Annual report to Congress**

The Director of the Office shall annually prepare and submit to the Congress a comprehensive report on the activities and expenditures of the Office.

**(d) Audit by GAO**

If requested by either House of the Congress (or any committee thereof) or if considered necessary by the Comptroller General, the General Accounting Office shall conduct an audit of the Office, in accord with such regulations as the Comptroller General may prescribe. The Comptroller General shall have access to such books, records, accounts, and other materials of the Office as the Comptroller General determines to be necessary for the preparation of such audit. The Comptroller General shall submit a report on the results of each audit conducted under this section.

(Pub.L. 97–425, Title III, § 304, Jan. 7, 1983, 96 Stat. 2261; Pub.L. 104–66, Title I, § 1052(*l*), Dec. 21, 1995, 109 Stat. 719.)

## § 10225. Location of test and evaluation facility

**[NWPA § 305]**

**(a) Report to Congress**

Not later than 1 year after January 7, 1983, the Secretary shall transmit to the Congress a report setting forth whether the Secretary plans to locate the test and evaluation facility at the site of a repository.

**(b) Procedures**

(1) If the test and evaluation facility is to be located at any candidate site or repository site (A) site selection and development of such facility shall be conducted in accordance with the procedures and requirements established in subchapter I of this chapter with respect to the site selection and development of repositories; and (B) the Secretary may not commence construction of any surface facility for such test and evaluation facility prior to issuance by the Commission of a construction authorization for a repository at the site involved.

(2) No test and evaluation facility may be converted into a repository unless site selection and development of such facility was conducted in accordance with the procedures and requirements established in subchapter I of this chapter with respect to the site selection and development of respositories.[1]

(3) The Secretary may not commence construction of a test and evaluation facility at a candidate site or site recommended as the location for a repository prior to the date on which the designation of such site is effective under section 10135 of this title.

(Pub.L. 97–425, Title III, § 305, Jan. 7, 1983, 96 Stat. 2262.)

[1] So in original. Probably should be "repositories."

## § 10226. Nuclear Regulatory Commission training authorization

**[NWPA § 306]**

The Nuclear Regulatory Commission is authorized and directed to promulgate regulations, or other appropriate Commission regulatory guidance, for the training and qualifications of civilian nuclear powerplant operators, supervisors, technicians and other appropriate operating personnel. Such regulations or guidance shall establish simulator training requirements for applicants for civilian nuclear powerplant operator licenses and for operator requalification programs; requirements governing NRC administration of requalification examinations; requirements for operating tests at civilian nuclear powerplant simulators, and instructional requirements for civilian nuclear powerplant licensee personnel training programs. Such regulations or other regulatory guidance shall be promulgated by the Commission within the 12-month period following January 7, 1983, and the Commission within the 12-month period following January 7, 1983, shall submit a report to Congress setting forth the actions the Commission has taken with respect to fulfilling its obligations under this section.

(Pub.L. 97–425, Title III, § 306, Jan. 7, 1983, 96 Stat. 2262.)

# SUBCHAPTER IV—NUCLEAR WASTE NEGOTIATOR

## § 10241. "State" defined

**[NWPA § 401]**

For purposes of this subchapter, the term "State" means each of the several States and the District of Columbia.

(Pub.L. 97–425, Title IV, § 401, as added Pub.L. 100–202, § 101(d) [Title III], Dec. 22, 1987, 101 Stat. 1329–104, 1329–121, and Pub.L. 100–203, Title V, § 5041, Dec. 22, 1987, 101 Stat. 1330–243; Pub.L. 102–486, Title VIII, § 802(b), Oct. 24, 1992, 106 Stat. 2923.)

HISTORICAL AND STATUTORY NOTES

**Codifications**

This section was enacted by both Pub.L. 100–202 and Pub.L. 100–203. The enactment by Pub.L. 100–202 was achieved under the following provision of section 101(d) [Title III] of Pub.L. 100–202: "Subtitle A of Title V, Nuclear Waste Policy Amendments Act of 1987, contained in H.R. 3545, Omnibus Budget Reconciliation Act of 1987 as agreed to and reported by the Committee on Conference on H.R. 3545 is included herein and shall be effective as if it has been enacted into law." H.R. 3545 was enacted into law as Pub.L. 100–203.

## § 10242. Office of Nuclear Waste Negotiator

[NWPA § 402]

### (a) Establishment

There is established the Office of the Nuclear Waste Negotiator that shall be an independent establishment in the executive branch.

### (b) Nuclear Waste Negotiator

(1) The Office shall be headed by a Nuclear Waste Negotiator who shall be appointed by the President, by and with the advice and consent of the Senate. The Negotiator shall hold office at the pleasure of the President, and shall be compensated at the rate provided for level III of the Executive Schedule in section 5314 of Title 5.

(2) The Negotiator shall attempt to find a State or Indian tribe willing to host a repository or monitored retrievable storage facility at a technically qualified site on reasonable terms and shall negotiate with any State or Indian tribe which expresses an interest in hosting a repository or monitored retrievable storage facility.

(Pub.L. 97–425, Title IV, § 402, as added Pub.L. 100–202, § 101(d) [Title III], Dec. 22, 1987, 101 Stat. 1329–104, 1329–121, and Pub.L. 100–203, Title V, § 5041, Dec. 22, 1987, 101 Stat. 1330–243; Pub.L. 100–507, § 1, Oct. 18, 1988, 102 Stat. 2541.)

HISTORICAL AND STATUTORY NOTES

**Codifications**

This section was enacted by both Pub.L. 100–202 and Pub.L. 100–203. The enactment by Pub.L. 100–202 was achieved under the following provision of section 101(d) [Title III] of Pub.L. 100–202: "Subtitle A of Title V, Nuclear Waste Policy Amendments Act of 1987, contained in H.R. 3545, Omnibus Budget Reconciliation Act of 1987 as agreed to and reported by the Committee on Conference on H.R. 3545 is included herein and shall be effective as if it has been enacted into law." H.R. 3545 was enacted into law as Pub.L. 100–203.

## § 10243. Duties of Negotiator

[NWPA § 403]

### (a) Negotiations with potential hosts

(1) The Negotiator shall—

(A) seek to enter into negotiations on behalf of the United States, with—

(i) the Governor of any State in which a potential site is located; and

(ii) the governing body of any Indian tribe on whose reservation a potential site is located; and

(B) attempt to reach a proposed agreement between the United States and any such State or Indian tribe specifying the terms and conditions under which such State or tribe would agree to host a repository or monitored retrievable storage facility within such State or reservation.

(2) In any case in which State law authorizes any person or entity other than the Governor to negotiate a proposed agreement under this section on behalf of the State, any reference in this subchapter to the Governor shall be considered to refer instead to such other person or entity.

### (b) Consultation with affected States, subdivisions of States, and tribes

In addition to entering into negotiations under subsection (a) of this section, the Negotiator shall consult with any State, affected unit of local government, or any Indian tribe that the Negotiator determines may be affected by the siting of a repository or monitored retrievable storage facility and may include in any proposed agreement such terms and conditions relating to the interest of such States, affected units of local government, or Indian tribes as the Negotiator determines to be reasonable and appropriate.

### (c) Consultation with other Federal agencies

The Negotiator may solicit and consider the comments of the Secretary, the Nuclear Regulatory Commission, or any other Federal agency on the suitability of any potential site for site characterization. Nothing in this subsection shall be construed to require the Secretary, the Nuclear Regulatory Commission, or any other Federal agency to make a finding that any such site is suitable for site characterization.

### (d) Proposed agreement

(1) The Negotiator shall submit to the Congress any proposed agreement between the United States and a State or Indian tribe negotiated under subsection (a) of this section and an environmental assessment prepared under section 10244(a) of this title for the site concerned.

(2) Any such proposed agreement shall contain such terms and conditions (including such financial and institutional arrangements) as the Negotiator and the host State or Indian tribe determine to be reasonable and appropriate and shall contain such provisions as are necessary to preserve any right to participation or compensation of such State, affected unit of local

government, or Indian tribe under sections 10136(c), 10137, and 10138(b) of this title.

(3)(A) No proposed agreement entered into under this section shall have legal effect unless enacted into Federal law.

(B) A State or Indian tribe shall enter into an agreement under this section in accordance with the laws of such State or tribe. Nothing in this section may be construed to prohibit the disapproval of a proposed agreement between a State and the United States under this section by a referendum or an act of the legislature of such State.

(4) Notwithstanding any proposed agreement under this section, the Secretary may construct a repository or monitored retrievable storage facility at a site agreed to under this subchapter only if authorized by the Nuclear Regulatory Commission in accordance with the Atomic Energy Act of 1954 [42 U.S.C.A. § 2011 et seq.], Title II of the Energy Reorganization Act of 1982 (42 U.S.C. 5841 et seq.) and any other law applicable to authorization of such construction.

(Pub.L. 97–425, Title IV, § 403, as added Pub.L. 100–202, § 101(d) [Title III], Dec. 22, 1987, 101 Stat. 1329–104, 1329–121, and Pub.L. 100–203, Title V, § 5041, Dec. 22, 1987, 101 Stat. 1330–244.)

### HISTORICAL AND STATUTORY NOTES

**References in Text**

The Atomic Energy Act of 1954, referred to in subsec. (d)(4), is Act Aug. 30, 1954, c. 1073, 68 Stat. 919, as amended, which is classified principally to chapter 23 (section 2011 et seq.) of this title. For complete classification of this Act to the Code, see Short Title of 1954 Acts note set out under section 2011 of this title and Tables.

The Energy Reorganization Act of 1982, referred to in subsec. (d)(4), probably means the Energy Reorganization Act of 1974, Pub.L. 93–438, Oct. 11, 1974, 88 Stat. 1233, as amended. Title II of the Energy Reorganization Act of 1974 is classified generally to subchapter II (Section 5841 et seq.) of chapter 73 of this title. For complete classification of this Act to the Code, see Short Title of 1974 Acts note set out under section 5801 of this title and Tables.

**Codifications**

This section was enacted by both Pub.L. 100–202 and Pub.L. 100–203. The enactment by Pub.L. 100–202 was achieved under the following provision of section 101(d) [Title III] of Pub.L. 100–202: "Subtitle A of Title V, Nuclear Waste Policy Amendments Act of 1987, contained in H.R. 3545, Omnibus Budget Reconciliation Act of 1987 as agreed to and reported by the Committee on Conference on H.R. 3545 is included herein and shall be effective as if it has been enacted into law." H.R. 3545 was enacted into law as Pub.L. 100–203.

## § 10244. Environmental assessment of sites

[NWPA § 404]

**(a) In general**

Upon the request of the Negotiator, the Secretary shall prepare an environmental assessment of any site that is the subject of negotiations under section 10243(a) of this title.

**(b) Contents**

(1) Each environmental assessment prepared for a repository site shall include a detailed statement of the probable impacts of characterizing such site and the construction and operation of a repository at such site.

(2) Each environmental assessment prepared for a monitored retrievable storage facility site shall include a detailed statement of the probable impacts of construction and operation of such a facility at such site.

**(c) Judicial review**

The issuance of an environmental assessment under subsection (a) of this section shall be considered to be a final agency action subject to judicial review in accordance with the provisions of chapter 7 of Title 5 and section 10139 of this title.

**(d) Public hearings**

(1) In preparing an environmental assessment for any repository or monitored retrievable storage facility site, the Secretary shall hold public hearings in the vicinity of such site to inform the residents of the area in which such site is located that such site is being considered and to receive their comments.

(2) At such hearings, the Secretary shall solicit and receive any recommendations of such residents with respect to issues that should be addressed in the environmental assessment required under subsection (a) of this section and the site characterization plan described in section 10133(b)(1) of this title.

**(e) Public availability**

Each environmental assessment prepared under subsection (a) of this section shall be made available to the public.

**(f) Evaluation of sites**

(1) In preparing an environmental assessment under subsection (a) of this section, the Secretary shall use available geophysical, geologic, geochemical and hydrologic, and other information and shall not conduct any preliminary borings or excavations at any site that is the subject of such assessment unless—

(A) such preliminary boring or excavation activities were in progress on or before December 22, 1987; or

(B) the Secretary certifies that, in the absence of preliminary borings or excavations, adequate information will not be available to satisfy the requirements of this chapter or any other law.

(2) No preliminary boring or excavation conducted under this section shall exceed a diameter of 40 inches.

(Pub.L. 97–425, Title IV, § 404, as added Pub.L. 100–202, § 101(d) [Title III], Dec. 22, 1987, 101 Stat. 1329–104, 1329–121, and Pub.L. 100–203, Title V, § 5041, Dec. 22, 1987, 101 Stat. 1330–245.)

### HISTORICAL AND STATUTORY NOTES

**Codifications**

This section was enacted by both Pub.L. 100–202 and Pub.L. 100–203. The enactment by Pub.L. 100–202 was achieved under the following provision of section 101(d) [Title III] of Pub.L. 100–202: "Subtitle A of Title V, Nuclear Waste Policy Amendments Act of 1987, contained in H.R. 3545, Omnibus Budget Reconciliation Act of 1987 as agreed to and reported by the Committee on Conference on H.R. 3545 is included herein and shall be effective as if it has been enacted into law." H.R. 3545 was enacted into law as Pub.L.100–203.

## § 10245. Site characterization; licensing

**[NWPA § 405]**

### (a) Site characterization

Upon enactment of legislation to implement an agreement to site a repository negotiated under section 10243(a) of this title, the Secretary shall conduct appropriate site characterization activities for the site that is the subject of such agreement subject to the conditions and terms of such agreement. Any such site characterization activities shall be conducted in accordance with section 10133 of this title, except that references in such section to the Yucca Mountain site and the State of Nevada shall be deemed to refer to the site that is the subject of the agreement and the State or Indian tribe entering into the agreement.

### (b) Licensing

(1) Upon the completion of site characterization activities carried out under subsection (a) of this section, the Secretary shall submit to the Nuclear Regulatory Commission an application for construction authorization for a repository at such site.

(2) The Nuclear Regulatory Commission shall consider an application for a construction authorization for a repository or monitored retrievable storage facility in accordance with the laws applicable to such applications, except that the Nuclear Regulatory Commission shall issue a final decision approving or disapproving the issuance of a construction authorization not later than 3 years after the date of the submission of such application.

(Pub.L. 97–425, Title IV, § 405, as added Pub.L. 100–202, § 101(d) [Title III], Dec. 22, 1987, 101 Stat. 1329–104, 1329–121, and Pub.L. 100–203, Title V, § 5041, Dec. 22, 1987, 101 Stat. 1330–246.)

### HISTORICAL AND STATUTORY NOTES

**Codifications**

This section was enacted by both Pub.L. 100–202 and Pub.L. 100–203. The enactment by Pub.L. 100–202 was achieved under the following provision of section 101(d) [Title III] of Pub.L. 100–202: "Subtitle A of title V, Nuclear Waste Policy Amendments Act of 1987, contained in H.R. 3545, Omnibus Budget Reconciliation Act of 1987 as agreed to and reported by the Committee on Conference on H.R. 3545 is included herein and shall be effective as if it has been enacted into law." H.R. 3545 was enacted into law as Pub.L. 100–203.

## § 10246. Monitored retrievable storage

**[NWPA § 406]**

### (a) Construction and operation

Upon enactment of legislation to implement an agreement negotiated under section 10243(a) of this title to site a monitored retrievable storage facility, the Secretary shall construct and operate such facility as part of an integrated nuclear waste management system in accordance with the terms and conditions of such agreement.

### (b) Financial assistance

The Secretary may make grants to any State, Indian tribe, or affected unit of local government to assess the feasibility of siting a monitored retrievable storage facility under this section at a site under the jurisdiction of such State, tribe, or affected unit of local government.

(Pub.L. 97–425, Title IV, § 406, as added Pub.L. 100–202, § 101(d) [Title III], Dec. 22, 1987, 101 Stat. 1329–104, 1329–121, and Pub.L. 100–203, Title V, § 5041, Dec. 22, 1987, 101 Stat. 1330–246.)

### HISTORICAL AND STATUTORY NOTES

**Codifications**

This section was enacted by both Pub.L. 100–202 and Pub.L. 100–203. The enactment by Pub.L. 100–202 was achieved under the following provision of section 101(d) [Title III] of Pub.L. 100–202: "Subtitle A of Title V, Nuclear Waste Policy Amendments Act of 1987, contained in H.R. 3545, Omnibus Budget Reconciliation Act of 1987 as agreed to and reported by the Committee on Conference on H.R. 3545 is included herein and shall be effective as if it has been enacted into law." H.R. 3545 was enacted into law as Pub.L. 100–203.

## § 10247. Environmental impact statement

**[NWPA § 407]**

### (a) In general

Issuance of a construction authorization for a repository or monitored retrievable storage facility under section 10245(b) of this title shall be considered a major Federal action significantly affecting the quality of the human environment for purposes of the National Environmental Policy Act of 1969 (42 U.S.C. 4321 et seq.).

**(b) Preparation**

A final environmental impact statement shall be prepared by the Secretary under such Act and shall accompany any application to the Nuclear Regulatory Commission for a construction authorization.

**(c) Adoption**

**(1)** Any such environmental impact statement shall, to the extent practicable, be adopted by the Nuclear Regulatory Commission, in accordance with section 1506.3 of title 40, Code of Federal Regulations, in connection with the issuance by the Nuclear Regulatory Commission of a construction authorization and license for such repository or monitored retrievable storage facility.

**(2)(A)** In any such statement prepared with respect to a repository to be constructed under this subchapter at the Yucca Mountain site, the Nuclear Regulatory Commission need not consider the need for a repository, the time of initial availability of a repository, alternate sites to the Yucca Mountain site, or nongeologic alternatives to such site.

**(B)** In any such statement prepared with respect to a repository to be constructed under this subchapter at a site other than the Yucca Mountain site, the Nuclear Regulatory Commission need not consider the need for a repository, the time of initial availability of a repository, or nongeologic alternatives to such site but shall consider the Yucca Mountain site as an alternate to such site in the preparation of such statement.

(Pub.L. 97–425, Title IV, § 407, as added Pub.L. 100–202, § 101(d) [Title III], Dec. 22, 1987, 101 Stat. 1329–104, 1329–121, and Pub.L. 100–203, Title V, § 5041, Dec. 22, 1987, 101 Stat. 1330–246.)

### HISTORICAL AND STATUTORY NOTES

**References in Text**

The National Environmental Policy Act of 1969 and such Act, respectively, referred to in subsecs. (a) and (b), is Pub.L. 91–190, Jan. 1, 1970, 83 Stat. 852, as amended, which is classified generally to chapter 55 (section 4321 et seq.) of this title. For complete classification of this Act to the Code, see Short Title of 1970 Acts note set out under section 4321 of this title and Tables.

**Codifications**

This section was enacted by both Pub.L. 100–202 and Pub.L. 100–203. The enactment by Pub.L. 100–202 was achieved under the following provision of section 101(d) [Title III] of Pub.L. 100–202: "Subtitle A of Title V, Nuclear Waste Policy Amendments Act of 1987, contained in H.R. 3545, Omnibus Budget Reconciliation Act of 1987 as agreed to and reported by the Committee on Conference on H.R. 3545 is included herein and shall be effective as if it has been enacted into law." H.R. 3545 was enacted into law as Pub.L. 100–203.

## § 10248. Administrative powers of Negotiator

**[NWPA § 408]**

In carrying out his functions under this subchapter, the Negotiator may—

**(1)** appoint such officers and employees as he determines to be necessary and prescribe their duties;

**(2)** obtain services as authorized by section 3109 of Title 5, at rates not to exceed the rate prescribed for grade GS–18 of the General Schedule by section 5332 of Title 5;

**(3)** promulgate such rules and regulations as may be necessary to carry out such functions;

**(4)** utilize the services, personnel, and facilities of other Federal agencies (subject to the consent of the head of any such agency);

**(5)** for purposes of performing administrative functions under this subchapter, and to the extent funds are appropriated, enter into and perform such contracts, leases, cooperative agreements, or other transactions as may be necessary and on such terms as the Negotiator determines to be appropriate, with any agency or instrumentality of the United States, or with any public or private person or entity;

**(6)** accept voluntary and uncompensated services, notwithstanding the provisions of section 1342 of Title 31;

**(7)** adopt an official seal, which shall be judicially noticed;

**(8)** use the United States mails in the same manner and under the same conditions as other departments and agencies of the United States;

**(9)** hold such hearings as are necessary to determine the views of interested parties and the general public; and

**(10)** appoint advisory committees under the Federal Advisory Committee Act (5 U.S.C. App.).

(Pub.L. 97–425, Title IV, § 408, as added Pub.L. 100–202, § 101(d) [Title III], Dec. 22, 1987, 101 Stat. 1329–104, 1329–121, and Pub.L. 100–203, Title V, § 5041, Dec. 22, 1987, 101 Stat. 1330–247.)

### HISTORICAL AND STATUTORY NOTES

**References in Text**

The Federal Advisory Committee Act, referred to in par. (10), is Pub.L. 92–463, Oct. 6, 1972, 86 Stat. 770, as amended, which is set out in Appendix 2 to Title 5, Government Organization and Employees.

**Codifications**

This section was enacted by both Pub.L. 100–202 and Pub.L. 100–203. The enactment by Pub.L. 100–202 was achieved under the following provision of section 101(d) [Title III] of Pub.L. 100–202: "Subtitle A of title V, Nuclear Waste Policy Amendments Act of 1987, contained in H.R. 3545, Omnibus Budget Reconciliation Act of 1987 as agreed to and reported by the Committee on Conference on H.R. 3545 is included herein and shall be effective as if it has been enacted into law." H.R. 3545 was enacted into law as Pub.L. 100–203.

**References in Other Laws to GS–16, 17, or 18 Pay Rates**

References in laws to the rates of pay for GS–16, 17, or 18, or to maximum rates of pay under the General Schedule, to be considered references to rates payable under specified sections of Title 5, Government Organization and Employees, see section 529 [Title I, § 101(c)(1) ] of Pub.L. 101–509, set out in a note under section 5376 of Title 5.

## § 10249. Cooperation of other departments and agencies

**[NWPA § 409]**

Each department, agency, and instrumentality of the United States, including any independent agency, may furnish the Negotiator such information as he determines to be necessary to carry out his functions under this subchapter.

(Pub.L. 97–425, Title IV, § 409, as added Pub.L. 100–202, § 101(d) [Title III], Dec. 22, 1987, 101 Stat. 1329–104, 1329–121, and Pub.L. 100–203, Title V, § 5041, Dec. 22, 1987, 101 Stat. 1330–247.)

### HISTORICAL AND STATUTORY NOTES

**Codifications**

This section was enacted by both Pub.L. 100–202 and Pub.L. 100–203. The enactment by Pub.L. 100–202 was achieved under the following provision of section 101(d) [Title III] of Pub.L. 100–202: "Subtitle A of title V, Nuclear Waste Policy Amendments Act of 1987, contained in H.R. 3545, Omnibus Budget Reconciliation Act of 1987 as agreed to and reported by the Committee on Conference on H.R. 3545 is included herein and shall be effective as if it has been enacted into law." H.R. 3545 was enacted into law as Pub.L. 100–203.

## § 10250. Termination of Office

**[NWPA § 410]**

The Office shall cease to exist not later than 30 days after the date 7 years after December 22, 1987.

(Pub.L. 97–425, Title IV, § 410, as added Pub.L. 100–202, § 101(d) [Title III], Dec. 22, 1987, 101 Stat. 1329–104, 1329–121, and amended Pub.L. 100–203, Title V, § 5041, Dec. 22, 1987, 101 Stat. 1330–247; Pub.L. 102–486, Title VIII, § 802(a), Oct. 24, 1992, 106 Stat. 2923.)

### HISTORICAL AND STATUTORY NOTES

**Codifications**

This section was enacted by both Pub.L. 100–202 and Pub.L. 100–203. The enactment by Pub.L. 100–202 was achieved under the following provision of section 101(d) [Title III] of Pub.L. 100–202: "Subtitle A of Title V, Nuclear Waste Policy Amendments Act of 1987, contained in H.R. 3545, Omnibus Budget Reconciliation Act of 1987 as agreed to and reported by the Committee on Conference on H.R. 3545 is included herein and shall be effective as if it has been enacted into law." H.R. 3545 was enacted into law as Pub.L. 100–203.

## § 10251. Authorization of appropriations

**[NWPA § 411]**

Notwithstanding subsection (d) of section 10222 of this title, and subject to subsection (e) of such section, there are authorized to be appropriated for expenditures from amounts in the Waste Fund established in subsection (c) of such section, such sums as may be necessary to carry out the provisions of this subchapter.

(Pub.L. 97–425, Title IV, § 411, as added Pub.L. 100–202, § 101(d) [Title III], Dec. 22, 1987, 101 Stat. 1329–104, 1329–121, and Pub.L. 100–203, Title V, § 5041, Dec. 22, 1987, 101 Stat. 1330–248.)

### HISTORICAL AND STATUTORY NOTES

**Codifications**

This section was enacted by both Pub.L. 100–202 and Pub.L. 100–203. The enactment by Pub.L. 100–202 was achieved under the following provision of section 101(d) [Title III] of Pub.L. 100–202: "Subtitle A of Title V, Nuclear Waste Policy Amendments Act of 1987, contained in H.R. 3545, Omnibus Budget Reconciliation Act of 1987 as agreed to and reported by the Committee on Conference on H.R. 3545 is included herein and shall be effective as if it has been enacted into law." H.R. 3545 was enacted into law as Pub.L. 100–203.

# SUBCHAPTER V—NUCLEAR WASTE TECHNICAL REVIEW BOARD

## § 10261. Definitions

**[NWPA § 501]**

As used in this subchapter:

(1) The term "Chairman" means the Chairman of the Nuclear Waste Technical Review Board.

(2) The term "Board" means the Nuclear Waste Technical Review Board established under section 10262 of this title.

(Pub.L. 97–425, Title V, § 501, as added Pub.L. 100–202, § 101(d) [Title III], Dec. 22, 1987, 101 Stat. 1329–104, 1329–121, and Pub.L. 100–203, Title V, § 5051, Dec. 22, 1987, 101 Stat. 1330–248.)

### HISTORICAL AND STATUTORY NOTES

**Codifications**

This section was enacted by both Pub.L. 100–202 and Pub.L. 100–203. The enactment by Pub.L. 100–202 was achieved under the following provision of section 101(d) [Title III] of Pub.L. 100–202: "Subtitle A of Title V, Nuclear Waste

Policy Amendments Act of 1987, contained in H.R. 3545, Omnibus Budget Reconciliation Act of 1987 as agreed to and reported by the Committee on Conference on H.R. 3545 is included herein and shall be effective as if it has been enacted into law." H.R. 3545 was enacted into law as Pub.L. 100–203.

## § 10262. Nuclear Waste Technical Review Board

**[NWPA § 502]**

**(a) Establishment**

There is established a Nuclear Waste Technical Review Board that shall be an independent establishment within the executive branch.

**(b) Members**

**(1)** The Board shall consist of 11 members who shall be appointed by the President not later than 90 days after December 22, 1987, from among persons nominated by the National Academy of Sciences in accordance with paragraph (3).

**(2)** The President shall designate a member of the Board to serve as chairman.

**(3)(A)** The National Academy of Sciences shall, not later than 90 days after December 22, 1987, nominate not less than 22 persons for appointment to the Board from among persons who meet the qualifications described in subparagraph (C).

**(B)** The National Academy of Sciences shall nominate not less than 2 persons to fill any vacancy on the Board from among persons who meet the qualifications described in subparagraph (C).

**(C)(i)** Each person nominated for appointment to the Board shall be—

**(I)** eminent in a field of science or engineering, including environmental sciences; and

**(II)** selected solely on the basis of established records of distinguished service.

**(ii)** The membership of the Board shall be representative of the broad range of scientific and engineering disciplines related to activities under this subchapter.

**(iii)** No person shall be nominated for appointment to the Board who is an employee of—

**(I)** the Department of Energy;

**(II)** a national laboratory under contract with the Department of Energy; or

**(III)** an entity performing high-level radioactive waste or spent nuclear fuel activities under contract with the Department of Energy.

**(4)** Any vacancy on the Board shall be filled by the nomination and appointment process described in paragraphs (1) and (3).

**(5)** Members of the Board shall be appointed for terms of 4 years, each such term to commence 120 days after December 22, 1987, except that of the 11 members first appointed to the Board, 5 shall serve for 2 years and 6 shall serve for 4 years, to be designated by the President at the time of appointment.

(Pub.L. 97–425, Title V, § 502, as added Pub.L. 100–202, § 101(d) [Title III], Dec. 22, 1987, 101 Stat. 1329–104, 1329–121, and Pub.L. 100–203, Title V, § 5051, Dec. 22, 1987, 101 Stat. 1330–248.)

### HISTORICAL AND STATUTORY NOTES

**Codifications**

This section was enacted by both Pub.L. 100–202 and Pub.L. 100–203. The enactment by Pub.L. 100–202 was achieved under the following provision of section 101(d) [Title III] of Pub.L. 100–202: "Subtitle A of Title V, Nuclear Waste Policy Amendments Act of 1987, contained in H.R. 3545, Omnibus Budget Reconciliation Act of 1987 as agreed to and reported by the Committee on Conference on H.R. 3545 is included herein and shall be effective as if it has been enacted into law." H.R. 3545 was enacted into law as Pub.L. 100–203.

**Continued Board Service After Expiration of Term**

Pub.L. 104–46, Title V, § 503, Nov. 13, 1995, 109 Stat. 419, provided that: "Without fiscal year limitation and notwithstanding section 502(b)(5) of the Nuclear Waste Policy Act, as amended [subsec. (b)(2) of this section], or any other provision of law, a member of the Nuclear Waste Technical Review Board whose term has expired may continue to serve as a member of the Board until such member's successor has taken office."

## § 10263. Functions

**[NWPA § 503]**

The Board shall evaluate the technical and scientific validity of activities undertaken by the Secretary after December 22, 1987, including—

**(1)** site characterization activities; and

**(2)** activities relating to the packaging or transportation of high-level radioactive waste or spent nuclear fuel.

(Pub.L. 97–425, Title V, § 503, as added Pub.L. 100–202, § 101(d) [Title III], Dec. 22, 1987, 101 Stat. 1329–104, 1329–121, and Pub.L. 100–203, Title V, § 5051, Dec. 22, 1987, 101 Stat. 1330–249.)

### HISTORICAL AND STATUTORY NOTES

**Codifications**

This section was enacted by both Pub.L. 100–202 and Pub.L. 100–203. The enactment by Pub.L. 100–202 was achieved under the following provision of section 101(d) [Title III] of Pub.L. 100–202: "Subtitle A of Title V, Nuclear Waste Policy Amendments Act of 1987, contained in H.R. 3545, Omnibus Budget Reconciliation Act of 1987 as agreed to and reported by the Committee on Conference on H.R. 3545 is included herein and shall be effective as if it has been enacted into law." H.R. 3545 was enacted into law as Pub.L. 100–203.

## § 10264. Investigatory powers

[NWPA § 504]

### (a) Hearings

Upon request of the Chairman or a majority of the members of the Board, the Board may hold such hearings, sit and act at such times and places, take such testimony, and receive such evidence, as the Board considers appropriate. Any member of the Board may administer oaths or affirmations to witnesses appearing before the Board.

### (b) Production of documents

(1) Upon the request of the Chairman or a majority of the members of the Board, and subject to existing law, the Secretary (or any contractor of the Secretary) shall provide the Board with such records, files, papers, data, or information as may be necessary to respond to any inquiry of the Board under this subchapter.

(2) Subject to existing law, information obtainable under paragraph (1) shall not be limited to final work products of the Secretary, but shall include drafts of such products and documentation of work in progress.

(Pub.L. 97–425, Title V, § 504, as added Pub.L. 100–202, § 101(d) [Title III], Dec. 22, 1987, 101 Stat. 1329–104, 1329–121, and Pub.L. 100–203, Title V, § 5051, Dec. 22, 1987, 101 Stat. 1330–249.)

### HISTORICAL AND STATUTORY NOTES

**Codifications**

This section was enacted by both Pub.L. 100–202 and Pub.L. 100–203. The enactment by Pub.L. 100–202 was achieved under the following provision of section 101(d) [Title III] of Pub.L. 100–202: "Subtitle A of Title V, Nuclear Waste Policy Amendments Act of 1987, contained in H.R. 3545, Omnibus Budget Reconciliation Act of 1987 as agreed to and reported by the Committee on Conference on H.R. 3545 is included herein and shall be effective as if it has been enacted into law." H.R. 3545 was enacted into law as Pub.L. 100–203.

## § 10265. Compensation of members

[NWPA § 505]

### (a) In general

Each member of the Board shall be paid at the rate of pay payable for level III of the Executive Schedule for each day (including travel time) such member is engaged in the work of the Board.

### (b) Travel expenses

Each member of the Board may receive travel expenses, including per diem in lieu of subsistence, in the same manner as is permitted under sections 5702 and 5703 of Title 5.

(Pub.L. 97–425, Title V, § 505, as added Pub.L. 100–202, § 101(d) [Title III], Dec. 22, 1987, 101 Stat. 1329–104, 1329–121, and Pub.L. 100–203, Title V, § 5051, Dec. 22, 1987, 101 Stat. 1330–249.)

### HISTORICAL AND STATUTORY NOTES

**References in Text**

Level III of the Executive Schedule, referred to in subsec. (a), is set out in section 5314 of Title 5, Government Organization and Employees.

**Codifications**

This section was enacted by both Pub.L. 100–202 and Pub.L. 100–203. The enactment by Pub.L. 100–202 was achieved under the following provision of section 101(d) [Title III] of Pub.L. 100–202: "Subtitle A of Title V, Nuclear Waste Policy Amendments Act of 1987, contained in H.R. 3545, Omnibus Budget Reconciliation Act of 1987 as agreed to and reported by the Committee on Conference on H.R. 3545 is included herein and shall be effective as if it has been enacted into law." H.R. 3545 was enacted into law as Pub.L. 100–203.

## § 10266. Staff

[NWPA § 506]

### (a) Clerical staff

(1) Subject to paragraph (2), the Chairman may appoint and fix the compensation of such clerical staff as may be necessary to discharge the responsibilities of the Board.

(2) Clerical staff shall be appointed subject to the provisions of Title 5 governing appointments in the competitive service, and shall be paid in accordance with the provisions of chapter 51 and subchapter III of chapter 53 of such title relating to classification and General Schedule pay rates.

### (b) Professional staff

(1) Subject to paragraphs (2) and (3), the Chairman may appoint and fix the compensation of such professional staff as may be necessary to discharge the responsibilities of the Board.

(2) Not more than 10 professional staff members may be appointed under this subsection.

(3) Professional staff members may be appointed without regard to the provisions of Title 5 governing appointments in the competitive service, and may be paid without regard to the provisions of chapter 51 and subchapter III of chapter 53 of such title relating to classification and General Schedule pay rates, except that no individual so appointed may receive pay in excess of the annual rate of basic pay payable for GS–18 of the General Schedule.

(Pub.L. 97–425, Title V, § 506, as added Pub.L. 100–202, § 101(d) [Title III], Dec. 22, 1987, 101 Stat. 1329–104, 1329–121, and amended Pub.L. 100–203, Title V, § 5051, Dec. 22, 1987, 101 Stat. 1330–249.)

HISTORICAL AND STATUTORY NOTES

**References in Text**

The provisions of Title 5 governing appointments in the competitive service, referred to in subsecs. (a)(2) and (b)(3), are classified generally to section 3301 et seq. of Title 5, Government Organization and Employees.

The General Schedule, referred to in subsec. (b)(3), is set out under section 5332 of Title 5.

**Codifications**

This section was enacted by both Pub.L. 100–202 and Pub.L. 100–203. The enactment by Pub.L. 100–202 was achieved under the following provision of section 101(d) [Title III] of Pub.L. 100–202: "Subtitle A of Title V, Nuclear Waste Policy Amendments Act of 1987, contained in H.R. 3545, Omnibus Budget Reconciliation Act of 1987 as agreed to and reported by the Committee on Conference on H.R. 3545 is included herein and shall be effective as if it has been enacted into law." H.R. 3545 was enacted into law as Pub.L. 100–203.

**References in Other Laws to GS–16, 17, or 18 Pay Rates**

References in laws to the rates of pay for GS–16, 17, or 18, or to maximum rates of pay under the General Schedule, to be considered references to rates payable under specified sections of Title 5, Government Organization and Employees, see section 529 [Title I § 101(c)(1) ] of Pub.L. 101–509, set out in a note under section 5376 of Title 5.

## § 10267. Support services

[NWPA § 507]

### (a) General services

To the extent permitted by law and requested by the Chairman, the Administrator of General Services shall provide the Board with necessary administrative services, facilities, and support on a reimbursable basis.

### (b) Accounting, research, and technology assessment services

The Comptroller General, the Librarian of Congress, and the Director of the Office of Technology Assessment shall, to the extent permitted by law and subject to the availability of funds, provide the Board with such facilities, support, funds and services, including staff, as may be necessary for the effective performance of the functions of the Board.

### (c) Additional support

Upon the request of the Chairman, the Board may secure directly from the head of any department or agency of the United States information necessary to enable it to carry out this subchapter.

### (d) Mails

The Board may use the United States mails in the same manner and under the same conditions as other departments and agencies of the United States.

### (e) Experts and consultants

Subject to such rules as may be prescribed by the Board, the Chairman may procure temporary and intermittent services under section 3109(b) of Title 5, but at rates for individuals not to exceed the daily equivalent of the maximum annual rate of basic pay payable for GS–18 of the General Schedule.

(Pub.L. 97–425, Title V, § 507, as added Pub.L. 100–202, § 101(d) [Title III], Dec. 22, 1987, 101 Stat. 1329–104, 1329–121, and Pub.L. 100–203, Title V, § 5051, Dec. 22, 1987, 101 Stat. 1330–250.)

HISTORICAL AND STATUTORY NOTES

**References in Text**

The General Schedule, referred to in subsec. (e), is set out under section 5332 of Title 5, Government Organization and Employees.

**Codifications**

This section was enacted by both Pub.L. 100–202 and Pub.L. 100–203. The enactment by Pub.L. 100–202 was achieved under the following provision of section 101(d) [Title III] of Pub.L. 100–202: "Subtitle A of Title V, Nuclear Waste Policy Amendments Act of 1987, contained in H.R. 3545, Omnibus Budget Reconciliation Act of 1987 as agreed to and reported by the Committee on Conference on H.R. 3545 is included herein and shall be effective as if it has been enacted into law." H.R. 3545 was enacted into law as Pub.L. 100–203.

**References in Other Laws to GS–16, 17, or 18 Pay Rates**

References in laws to the rates of pay for GS–16, 17, or 18, or to maximum rates of pay under the General Schedule, to be considered references to rates payable under specified sections of Title 5, Government Organization and Employees, see section 529 [Title I, § 101(c)(1) ] of Pub.L. 101–509, set out in a note under section 5376 of Title 5.

## § 10268. Report

[NWPA § 508]

The Board shall report not less than 2 times per year to Congress and the Secretary its findings, conclusions, and recommendations. The first such report shall be submitted not later than 12 months after December 22, 1987.

(Pub.L. 97–425, Title V, § 508, as added Pub.L. 100–202, § 101(d) [Title III], Dec. 22, 1987, 101 Stat. 1329–104, 1329–121, and Pub.L. 100–203, Title V, § 5051, Dec. 22, 1987, 101 Stat. 1330–250.)

HISTORICAL AND STATUTORY NOTES

**Codifications**

This section was enacted by both Pub.L. 100–202 and Pub.L. 100–203. The enactment by Pub.L. 100–202 was achieved under the following provision of section 101(d) [Title III] of Pub.L. 100–202: "Subtitle A of Title V, Nuclear Waste Policy Amendments Act of 1987, contained in H.R. 3545, Omnibus Budget Reconciliation Act of 1987 as agreed to and reported by the Committee on Conference on H.R. 3545 is included herein and shall be effective as if it has been enacted into law." H.R. 3545 was enacted into law as Pub.L. 100–203.

## § 10269. Authorization of appropriations

**[NWPA § 509]**

Notwithstanding subsection (d) of section 10222 of this title, and subject to subsection (e) of such section, there are authorized to be appropriated for expenditures from amounts in the Waste Fund established in subsection (c) of such section such sums as may be necessary to carry out the provisions of this subchapter.

(Pub.L. 97–425, Title V, § 509, as added Pub.L. 100–202, § 101(d) [Title III], Dec. 22, 1987, 101 Stat. 1329–104, 1329–121, and Pub.L. 100–203, Title V, § 5051, Dec. 22, 1987, 101 Stat. 1330–251.)

### HISTORICAL AND STATUTORY NOTES

**Codifications**

This section was enacted by both Pub.L. 100–202 and Pub.L. 100–203. The enactment by Pub.L. 100–202 was achieved under the following provision of section 101(d) [Title III] of Pub.L. 100–202: "Subtitle A of Title V, Nuclear Waste Policy Amendments Act of 1987, contained in H.R. 3545, Omnibus Budget Reconciliation Act of 1987 as agreed to and reported by the Committee on Conference on H.R. 3545 is included herein and shall be effective as if it has been enacted into law." H.R. 3545 was enacted into law as Pub.L. 100–203.

## § 10270. Termination of Board

**[NWPA § 510]**

The Board shall cease to exist not later than 1 year after the date on which the Secretary begins disposal of high-level radioactive waste or spent nuclear fuel in a repository.

(Pub.L. 97–425, Title V, § 510, as added Pub.L. 100–202, § 101(d) [Title III], Dec. 22, 1987, 101 Stat. 1329–104, 1329–121, and Pub.L. 100–203, Title V, § 5051, Dec. 22, 1987, 101 Stat. 1330–251.)

### HISTORICAL AND STATUTORY NOTES

**Codifications**

This section was enacted by both Pub.L. 100–202 and Pub.L. 100–203. The enactment by Pub.L. 100–202 was achieved under the following provision of section 101(d) [Title III] of Pub.L. 100–202: "Subtitle A of Title V, Nuclear Waste Policy Amendments Act of 1987, contained in H.R. 3545, Omnibus Budget Reconciliation Act of 1987 as agreed to and reported by the Committee on Conference on H.R. 3545 is included herein and shall be effective as if it has been enacted into law." H.R. 3545 was enacted into law as Pub.L. 100–203.

# EMERGENCY PLANNING AND COMMUNITY RIGHT-TO-KNOW

## EMERGENCY PLANNING AND COMMUNITY RIGHT-TO-KNOW ACT OF 1986 [EPCRTKA § ____]

**(42 U.S.C.A. §§ 11001 to 11050)**

## CHAPTER 116—EMERGENCY PLANNING AND COMMUNITY RIGHT-TO-KNOW

SUBCHAPTER I—EMERGENCY PLANNING AND NOTIFICATION



### SUBCHAPTER I—EMERGENCY PLANNING AND NOTIFICATION

### § 11001. Establishment of State commissions, planning districts, and local committees

**[EPCRTKA § 301]**

#### (a) Establishment of State emergency response commissions

Not later than six months after October 17, 1986, the Governor of each State shall appoint a State emergency response commission. The Governor may designate as the State emergency response commission one or more existing emergency response organizations that are State-sponsored or appointed. The Governor shall, to the extent practicable, appoint persons to the State emergency response commission who have technical expertise in the emergency response field. The State emergency response commission shall appoint local emergency planning committees under subsection (c) of this section and shall supervise and coordinate the activities of such committees. The State emergency response commission shall establish procedures for receiving and processing requests from the public for information under section 11044 of this title, including tier II information under section 11022 of this title. Such procedures shall include the designation of an official to serve as coordinator for information. If the Governor of any State does not designate a State emergency response commission within such period, the Governor shall operate as the State emergency response commission until the Governor makes such designation.

#### (b) Establishment of emergency planning districts

Not later than nine months after October 17, 1986, the State emergency response commission shall designate emergency planning districts in order to facilitate preparation and implementation of emergency plans. Where appropriate, the State emergency response commission may designate existing political subdivisions or multijurisdictional planning organizations as such districts. In emergency planning areas that involve more than one State, the State emergency response commissions of all potentially affected States may designate emergency planning districts and local emergency planning committees by agreement. In making such designation, the State emergency response commission shall indicate which facilities subject to the requirements of this subchapter are within such emergency planning district.

#### (c) Establishment of local emergency planning committees

Not later than 30 days after designation of emergency planning districts or 10 months after October 17, 1986, whichever is earlier, the State emergency response commission shall appoint members of a local emergency planning committee for each emergency planning district. Each committee shall include, at a minimum, representatives from each of the following groups or organizations: elected State and local officials; law enforcement, civil defense, firefighting, first aid, health, local environmental, hospital, and transportation personnel; broadcast and print media; community groups; and owners and operators of facilities subject to the requirements of this subchapter. Such committee shall appoint a chairperson and shall establish rules by which the committee shall function. Such rules shall include provisions for public notification of committee activities, public meetings to discuss the emergency plan, public comments, response to such comments by the committee, and distribution of the emergency plan. The local emergency planning committee shall establish procedures for receiving and processing requests from the public for information under section 11044 of this title, including tier II information under section 11022 of this title. Such procedures shall include the designation of an official to serve as coordinator for information.

**(d) Revisions**

A State emergency response commission may revise its designations and appointments under subsections (b) and (c) of this section as it deems appropriate. Interested persons may petition the State emergency response commission to modify the membership of a local emergency planning committee.

(Pub.L. 99–499, Title III, § 301, Oct. 17, 1986, 100 Stat. 1729.)

### HISTORICAL AND STATUTORY NOTES

**Effective and Applicability Provisions**

1986 Acts

Section effective Oct. 17, 1986, see section 4 of Pub. L. 99–499, set out as a note under section 9601 of this title.

**Short Title**

1986 Acts

Section 300(a) of Title III of Pub.L. 99–499 provided that: "This title [enacting this chapter] may be cited as the 'Emergency Planning and Community Right-To-Know Act of 1986'."

## § 11002. Substances and facilities covered and notification

**[EPCRTKA § 302]**

**(a) Substances covered**

**(1) In general**

A substance is subject to the requirements of this subchapter if the substance is on the list published under paragraph (2).

**(2) List of extremely hazardous substances**

Within 30 days after October 17, 1986, the Administrator shall publish a list of extremely hazardous substances. The list shall be the same as the list of substances published in November 1985 by the Administrator in Appendix A of the "Chemical Emergency Preparedness Program Interim Guidance".

**(3) Thresholds**

(A) At the time the list referred to in paragraph (2) is published the Administrator shall—

(i) publish an interim final regulation establishing a threshold planning quantity for each substance on the list, taking into account the criteria described in paragraph (4), and

(ii) initiate a rulemaking in order to publish final regulations establishing a threshold planning quantity for each substance on the list.

(B) The threshold planning quantities may, at the Administrator's discretion, be based on classes of chemicals or categories of facilities.

(C) If the Administrator fails to publish an interim final regulation establishing a threshold planning quantity for a substance within 30 days after October 17, 1986, the threshold planning quantity for the substance shall be 2 pounds until such time as the Administrator publishes regulations establishing a threshold for the substance.

**(4) Revisions**

The Administrator may revise the list and thresholds under paragraphs (2) and (3) from time to time. Any revisions to the list shall take into account the toxicity, reactivity, volatility, dispersability, combustability, or flammability of a substance. For purposes of the preceding sentence, the term "toxicity" shall include any short- or long-term health effect which may result from a short-term exposure to the substance.

**(b) Facilities covered**

(1) Except as provided in section 11004 of this title, a facility is subject to the requirements of this subchapter if a substance on the list referred to in subsection (a) of this section is present at the facility in an amount in excess of the threshold planning quantity established for such substance.

(2) For purposes of emergency planning, a Governor or a State emergency response commission may designate additional facilities which shall be subject to the requirements of this subchapter, if such designation is made after public notice and opportunity for

comment. The Governor or State emergency response commission shall notify the facility concerned of any facility designation under this paragraph.

**(c) Emergency planning notification**

Not later than seven months after October 17, 1986, the owner or operator of each facility subject to the requirements of this subchapter by reason of subsection (b)(1) of this section shall notify the State emergency response commission for the State in which such facility is located that such facility is subject to the requirements of this subchapter. Thereafter, if a substance on the list of extremely hazardous substances referred to in subsection (a) of this section first becomes present at such facility in excess of the threshold planning quantity established for such substance, or if there is a revision of such list and the facility has present a substance on the revised list in excess of the threshold planning quantity established for such substance, the owner or operator of the facility shall notify the State emergency response commission and the local emergency planning committee within 60 days after such acquisition or revision that such facility is subject to the requirements of this subchapter.

**(d) Notification of Administrator**

The State emergency response commission shall notify the Administrator of facilities subject to the requirements of this subchapter by notifying the Administrator of—

(1) each notification received from a facility under subsection (c) of this section, and

(2) each facility designated by the Governor or State emergency response commission under subsection (b)(2) of this section.

(Pub.L. 99–499, Title III, § 302, Oct. 17, 1986, 100 Stat. 1730.)

### HISTORICAL AND STATUTORY NOTES

**Effective and Applicability Provisions**

1986 Acts

Section effective Oct. 17, 1986, see section 4 of Pub.L. 99–499, set out as a note under section 9601 of this title.

## § 11003. Comprehensive emergency response plans

**[EPCRTKA § 303]**

**(a) Plan required**

Each local emergency planning committee shall complete preparation of an emergency plan in accordance with this section not later than two years after October 17, 1986. The committee shall review such plan once a year, or more frequently as changed circumstances in the community or at any facility may require.

**(b) Resources**

Each local emergency planning committee shall evaluate the need for resources necessary to develop, implement, and exercise the emergency plan, and shall make recommendations with respect to additional resources that may be required and the means for providing such additional resources.

**(c) Plan provisions**

Each emergency plan shall include (but is not limited to) each of the following:

(1) Identification of facilities subject to the requirements of this subchapter that are within the emergency planning district, identification of routes likely to be used for the transportation of substances on the list of extremely hazardous substances referred to in section 11002(a) of this title, and identification of additional facilities contributing or subjected to additional risk due to their proximity to facilities subject to the requirements of this subchapter, such as hospitals or natural gas facilities.

(2) Methods and procedures to be followed by facility owners and operators and local emergency and medical personnel to respond to any release of such substances.

(3) Designation of a community emergency coordinator and facility emergency coordinators, who shall make determinations necessary to implement the plan.

(4) Procedures providing reliable, effective, and timely notification by the facility emergency coordinators and the community emergency coordinator to persons designated in the emergency plan, and to the public, that a release has occurred (consistent with the emergency notification requirements of section 11004 of this title).

(5) Methods for determining the occurrence of a release, and the area or population likely to be affected by such release.

(6) A description of emergency equipment and facilities in the community and at each facility in the community subject to the requirements of this subchapter, and an identification of the persons responsible for such equipment and facilities.

(7) Evacuation plans, including provisions for a precautionary evacuation and alternative traffic routes.

(8) Training programs, including schedules for training of local emergency response and medical personnel.

(9) Methods and schedules for exercising the emergency plan.

**(d) Providing of information**

For each facility subject to the requirements of this subchapter:

(1) Within 30 days after establishment of a local emergency planning committee for the emergency planning district in which such facility is located, or within 11 months after October 17, 1986, whichever is earlier, the owner or operator of the facility shall notify the emergency planning committee (or the Governor if there is no committee) of a facility representative who will participate in the emergency planning process as a facility emergency coordinator.

(2) The owner or operator of the facility shall promptly inform the emergency planning committee of any relevant changes occurring at such facility as such changes occur or are expected to occur.

(3) Upon request from the emergency planning committee, the owner or operator of the facility shall promptly provide information to such committee necessary for developing and implementing the emergency plan.

**(e) Review by State emergency response commission**

After completion of an emergency plan under subsection (a) of this section for an emergency planning district, the local emergency planning committee shall submit a copy of the plan to the State emergency response commission of each State in which such district is located. The commission shall review the plan and make recommendations to the committee on revisions of the plan that may be necessary to ensure coordination of such plan with emergency response plans of other emergency planning districts. To the maximum extent practicable, such review shall not delay implementation of such plan.

**(f) Guidance documents**

The national response team, as established pursuant to the National Contingency Plan as established under section 9605 of this title, shall publish guidance documents for preparation and implementation of emergency plans. Such documents shall be published not later than five months after October 17, 1986.

**(g) Review of plans by regional response teams**

The regional response teams, as established pursuant to the National Contingency Plan as established under section 9605 of this title, may review and comment upon an emergency plan or other issues related to preparation, implementation, or exercise of such a plan upon request of a local emergency planning committee. Such review shall not delay implementation of the plan.

(Pub.L. 99–499, Title III, § 303, Oct. 17, 1986, 100 Stat. 1731.)

**HISTORICAL AND STATUTORY NOTES**

**Effective and Applicability Provisions**

1986 Acts

Section effective Oct. 17, 1986, see section 4 of Pub. L. 99–499, set out as a note under section 9601 of this title.

## § 11004. Emergency notification

**[EPCRTKA § 304]**

**(a) Types of releases**

**(1) 11002(a) substance which requires CERCLA notice**

If a release of an extremely hazardous substance referred to in section 11002(a) of this title occurs from a facility at which a hazardous chemical is produced, used, or stored, and such release requires a notification under section 103(a) of the Comprehensive Environmental Response, Compensation, and Liability Act of 1980 [42 U.S.C.A. § 9603(a)] (hereafter in this section referred to as "CERCLA") (42 U.S.C. 9601 et seq.), the owner or operator of the facility shall immediately provide notice as described in subsection (b) of this section.

**(2) Other 11002(a) substance**

If a release of an extremely hazardous substance referred to in section 11002(a) of this title occurs from a facility at which a hazardous chemical is produced, used, or stored, and such release is not subject to the notification requirements under section 103(a) of CERCLA [42 U.S.C.A. § 9603(a) ], the owner or operator of the facility shall immediately provide notice as described in subsection (b) of this section, but only if the release—

(A) is not a federally permitted release as defined in section 101(10) of CERCLA [42 U.S.C.A. § 9601(10) ],

(B) is in an amount in excess of a quantity which the Administrator has determined (by regulation) requires notice, and

(C) occurs in a manner which would require notification under section 103(a) of CERCLA [42 U.S.C.A. § 9603(a)].

Unless and until superseded by regulations establishing a quantity for an extremely hazardous substance described in this paragraph, a quantity of 1 pound shall be deemed that quantity the release of which requires notice as described in subsection (b) of this section.

**(3) Non-11002(a) substance which requires CERCLA notice**

If a release of a substance which is not on the list referred to in section 11002(a) of this title occurs at a facility at which a hazardous chemical is produced, used, or stored, and such release requires notification under section 103(a) of CERCLA [42 U.S.C.A.

§ 9603(a)], the owner or operator shall provide notice as follows:

(A) If the substance is one for which a reportable quantity has been established under section 102(a) of CERCLA [42 U.S.C.A. § 9602(a)], the owner or operator shall provide notice as described in subsection (b) of this section.

(B) If the substance is one for which a reportable quantity has not been established under section 102(a) of CERCLA [42 U.S.C.A. § 9602(a)]—

(i) Until April 30, 1988, the owner or operator shall provide, for releases of one pound or more of the substance, the same notice to the community emergency coordinator for the local emergency planning committee, at the same time and in the same form, as notice is provided to the National Response Center under section 103(a) of CERCLA [42 U.S.C.A. § 9603(a)].

(ii) On and after April 30, 1988, the owner or operator shall provide, for releases of one pound or more of the substance, the notice as described in subsection (b) of this section.

**(4) Exempted releases**

This section does not apply to any release which results in exposure to persons solely within the site or sites on which a facility is located.

**(b) Notification**

**(1) Recipients of notice**

Notice required under subsection (a) of this section shall be given immediately after the release by the owner or operator of a facility (by such means as telephone, radio, or in person) to the community emergency coordinator for the local emergency planning committees, if established pursuant to section 11001(c) of this title, for any area likely to be affected by the release and to the State emergency planning commission of any State likely to be affected by the release. With respect to transportation of a substance subject to the requirements of this section, or storage incident to such transportation, the notice requirements of this section with respect to a release shall be satisfied by dialing 911 or, in the absence of a 911 emergency telephone number, calling the operator.

**(2) Contents**

Notice required under subsection (a) of this section shall include each of the following (to the extent known at the time of the notice and so long as no delay in responding to the emergency results):

(A) The chemical name or identity of any substance involved in the release.

(B) An indication of whether the substance is on the list referred to in section 11002(a) of this title.

(C) An estimate of the quantity of any such substance that was released into the environment.

(D) The time and duration of the release.

(E) The medium or media into which the release occurred.

(F) Any known or anticipated acute or chronic health risks associated with the emergency and, where appropriate, advice regarding medical attention necessary for exposed individuals.

(G) Proper precautions to take as a result of the release, including evacuation (unless such information is readily available to the community emergency coordinator pursuant to the emergency plan).

(H) The name and telephone number of the person or persons to be contacted for further information.

**(c) Followup emergency notice**

As soon as practicable after a release which requires notice under subsection (a) of this section, such owner or operator shall provide a written followup emergency notice (or notices, as more information becomes available) setting forth and updating the information required under subsection (b) of this section, and including additional information with respect to—

(1) actions taken to respond to and contain the release,

(2) any known or anticipated acute or chronic health risks associated with the release, and

(3) where appropriate, advice regarding medical attention necessary for exposed individuals.

**(d) Transportation exemption not applicable**

The exemption provided in section 11047 of this title (relating to transportation) does not apply to this section.

(Pub.L. 99–499, Title III, § 304, Oct. 17, 1986, 100 Stat. 1733.)

## HISTORICAL AND STATUTORY NOTES

**References in Text**

The Comprehensive Environmental Response, Compensation, and Liability Act of 1980, and CERCLA, referred to in subsec. (a)(1), is Pub.L. 96–510, Dec. 11, 1980, 94 Stat. 2767, as amended, which is classified principally to chapter 103 (section 9601 et seq.) of this title. For complete classification of this Act to the Code, see Short Title of 1980 Acts note set out under section 9601 of this title and Tables.

**Effective and Applicability Provisions**

1986 Acts

Section effective Oct. 17, 1986, see section 4 of Pub. L. 99–499, set out as a note under section 9601 of this title.

## § 11005. Emergency training and review of emergency systems

[EPCRTKA § 305]

(a) Emergency training

(1) Programs

Officials of the United States Government carrying out existing Federal programs for emergency training are authorized to specifically provide training and education programs for Federal, State, and local personnel in hazard mitigation, emergency preparedness, fire prevention and control, disaster response, long-term disaster recovery, national security, technological and natural hazards, and emergency processes. Such programs shall provide special emphasis for such training and education with respect to hazardous chemicals.

(2) State and local program support

There is authorized to be appropriated to the Federal Emergency Management Agency for each of the fiscal years 1987, 1988, 1989, and 1990, $5,000,000 for making grants to support programs of State and local governments, and to support university-sponsored programs, which are designed to improve emergency planning, preparedness, mitigation, response, and recovery capabilities. Such programs shall provide special emphasis with respect to emergencies associated with hazardous chemicals. Such grants may not exceed 80 percent of the cost of any such program. The remaining 20 percent of such costs shall be funded from non-Federal sources.

(3) Other programs

Nothing in this section shall affect the availability of appropriations to the Federal Emergency Management Agency for any programs carried out by such agency other than the programs referred to in paragraph (2).

(b) Review of emergency systems

(1) Review

The Administrator shall initiate, not later than 30 days after October 17, 1986, a review of emergency systems for monitoring, detecting, and preventing releases of extremely hazardous substances at representative domestic facilities that produce, use, or store extremely hazardous substances. The Administrator may select representative extremely hazardous substances from the substances on the list referred to in section 11002(a) of this title, for the purposes of this review. The Administrator shall report interim findings to the Congress not later than seven months after October 17, 1986, and issue a final report of findings and recommendations to the Congress not later than 18 months after October 17, 1986. Such report shall be prepared in consultation with the States and appropriate Federal agencies.

(2) Report

The report required by this subsection shall include the Administrator's findings regarding each of the following:

(A) The status of current technological capabilities to (i) monitor, detect, and prevent, in a timely manner, significant releases of extremely hazardous substances, (ii) determine the magnitude and direction of the hazard posed by each release, (iii) identify specific substances, (iv) provide data on the specific chemical composition of such releases, and (v) determine the relative concentrations of the constituent substances.

(B) The status of public emergency alert devices or systems for providing timely and effective public warning of an accidental release of extremely hazardous substances into the environment, including releases into the atmosphere, surface water, or groundwater from facilities that produce, store, or use significant quantities of such extremely hazardous substances.

(C) The technical and economic feasibility of establishing, maintaining, and operating perimeter alert systems for detecting releases of such extremely hazardous substances into the atmosphere, surface water, or groundwater, at facilities that manufacture, use, or store significant quantities of such substances.

(3) Recommendations

The report required by this subsection shall also include the Administrator's recommendations for—

(A) initiatives to support the development of new or improved technologies or systems that would facilitate the timely monitoring, detection, and prevention of releases of extremely hazardous substances, and

(B) improving devices or systems for effectively alerting the public in a timely manner, in the event of an accidental release of such extremely hazardous substances.

(Pub.L. 99–499, Title III, § 305, Oct. 17, 1986, 100 Stat. 1735.)

### HISTORICAL AND STATUTORY NOTES

**Effective and Applicability Provisions**

1986 Acts

Section effective Oct. 17, 1986, see section 4 of Pub.L. 99–499, set out as a note under section 9601 of this title.

## SUBCHAPTER II—REPORTING REQUIREMENTS

## § 11021. Material safety data sheets

[EPCRTKA § 311]

(a) Basic requirement

**(1) Submission of MSDS or list**

The owner or operator of any facility which is required to prepare or have available a material safety data sheet for a hazardous chemical under the Occupational Safety and Health Act of 1970 [29 U.S.C.A. § 651 et seq.] and regulations promulgated under that Act shall submit a material safety data sheet for each such chemical, or a list of such chemicals as described in paragraph (2), to each of the following:

(A) The appropriate local emergency planning committee.

(B) The State emergency response commission.

(C) The fire department with jurisdiction over the facility.

**(2) Contents of list**

(A) The list of chemicals referred to in paragraph (1) shall include each of the following:

(i) A list of the hazardous chemicals for which a material safety data sheet is required under the Occupational Safety and Health Act of 1970 [29 U.S.C.A. § 651 et seq.] and regulations promulgated under that Act, grouped in categories of health and physical hazards as set forth under such Act and regulations promulgated under such Act, or in such other categories as the Administrator may prescribe under subparagraph (B).

(ii) The chemical name or the common name of each such chemical as provided on the material safety data sheet.

(iii) Any hazardous component of each such chemical as provided on the material safety data sheet.

(B) For purposes of the list under this paragraph, the Administrator may modify the categories of health and physical hazards as set forth under the Occupational Safety and Health Act of 1970 [29 U.S.C.A. § 651 et seq.] and regulations promulgated under that Act by requiring information to be reported in terms of groups of hazardous chemicals which present similar hazards in an emergency.

**(3) Treatment of mixtures**

An owner or operator may meet the requirements of this section with respect to a hazardous chemical which is a mixture by doing one of the following:

(A) Submitting a material safety data sheet for, or identifying on a list, each element or compound in the mixture which is a hazardous chemical. If more than one mixture has the same element or compound, only one material safety data sheet, or one listing, of the element or compound is necessary.

(B) Submitting a material safety data sheet for, or identifying on a list, the mixture itself.

**(b) Thresholds**

The Administrator may establish threshold quantities for hazardous chemicals below which no facility shall be subject to the provisions of this section. The threshold quantities may, in the Administrator's discretion, be based on classes of chemicals or categories of facilities.

**(c) Availability of MSDS on request**

**(1) To local emergency planning committee**

If an owner or operator of a facility submits a list of chemicals under subsection (a)(1) of this section, the owner or operator, upon request by the local emergency planning committee, shall submit the material safety data sheet for any chemical on the list to such committee.

**(2) To public**

A local emergency planning committee, upon request by any person, shall make available a material safety data sheet to the person in accordance with section 11044 of this title. If the local emergency planning committee does not have the requested material safety data sheet, the committee shall request the sheet from the facility owner or operator and then make the sheet available to the person in accordance with section 11044 of this title.

**(d) Initial submission and updating**

(1) The initial material safety data sheet or list required under this section with respect to a hazardous chemical shall be provided before the later of—

(A) 12 months after October 17, 1986, or

(B) 3 months after the owner or operator of a facility is required to prepare or have available a material safety data sheet for the chemical under the Occupational Safety and Health Act of 1970 [29 U.S.C.A. § 651 et seq.] and regulations promulgated under that Act.

(2) Within 3 months following discovery by an owner or operator of significant new information concerning an aspect of a hazardous chemical for which a material safety data sheet was previously submitted to the local emergency planning committee under subsection (a) of this section, a revised sheet shall be provided to such person.

**(e) "Hazardous chemical" defined**

For purposes of this section, the term "hazardous chemical" has the meaning given such term by section 1910.1200(c) of title 29 of the Code of Federal Regulations, except that such term does not include the following:

(1) Any food, food additive, color additive, drug, or cosmetic regulated by the Food and Drug Administration.

(2) Any substance present as a solid in any manufactured item to the extent exposure to the substance does not occur under normal conditions of use.

(3) Any substance to the extent it is used for personal, family, or household purposes, or is present in the same form and concentration as a product packaged for distribution and use by the general public.

(4) Any substance to the extent it is used in a research laboratory or a hospital or other medical facility under the direct supervision of a technically qualified individual.

(5) Any substance to the extent it is used in routine agricultural operations or is a fertilizer held for sale by a retailer to the ultimate customer.

(Pub.L. 99–499, Title III, § 311, Oct. 17, 1986, 100 Stat. 1736.)

### HISTORICAL AND STATUTORY NOTES

**References in Text**

The Occupational Safety and Health Act of 1970, referred to in subsecs. (a)(1), (2)(A)(i), (B), (d)(1)(B), is Pub.L. 91–596, Dec. 29, 1970, 84 Stat. 1590, as amended, which is classified principally to chapter 15 (section 651 et seq.) of Title 29, Labor. For complete classification of this Act to the Code, see Short Title note set out under section 651 of Title 29 and Tables.

**Effective and Applicability Provisions**

1986 Acts

Section effective Oct. 17, 1986, see section 4 of Pub.L. 99–499, set out as a note under section 9601 of this title.

## § 11022. Emergency and hazardous chemical inventory forms

### [EPCRTKA § 312]

**(a) Basic requirement**

(1) The owner or operator of any facility which is required to prepare or have available a material safety data sheet for a hazardous chemical under the Occupational Safety and Health Act of 1970 [29 U.S.C.A. § 651 et seq.] and regulations promulgated under that Act shall prepare and submit an emergency and hazardous chemical inventory form (hereafter in this chapter referred to as an "inventory form") to each of the following:

(A) The appropriate local emergency planning committee.

(B) The State emergency response commission.

(C) The fire department with jurisdiction over the facility.

(2) The inventory form containing tier I information (as described in subsection (d)(1) of this section) shall be submitted on or before March 1, 1988, and annually thereafter on March 1, and shall contain data with respect to the preceding calendar year. The preceding sentence does not apply if an owner or operator provides, by the same deadline and with respect to the same calendar year, tier II information (as described in subsection (d)(2) of this section) to the recipients described in paragraph (1).

(3) An owner or operator may meet the requirements of this section with respect to a hazardous chemical which is a mixture by doing one of the following:

(A) Providing information on the inventory form on each element or compound in the mixture which is a hazardous chemical. If more than one mixture has the same element or compound, only one listing on the inventory form for the element or compound at the facility is necessary.

(B) Providing information on the inventory form on the mixture itself.

**(b) Thresholds**

The Administrator may establish threshold quantities for hazardous chemicals covered by this section below which no facility shall be subject to the provisions of this section. The threshold quantities may, in the Administrator's discretion, be based on classes of chemicals or categories of facilities.

**(c) Hazardous chemicals covered**

A hazardous chemical subject to the requirements of this section is any hazardous chemical for which a material safety data sheet or a listing is required under section 11021 of this title.

**(d) Contents of form**

**(1) Tier I information**

**(A) Aggregate information by category**

An inventory form shall provide the information described in subparagraph (B) in aggregate terms for hazardous chemicals in categories of health and physical hazards as set forth under the Occupational Safety and Health Act of 1970 [29 U.S.C.A. § 651 et seq.] and regulations promulgated under that Act.

**(B) Required information**

The information referred to in subparagraph (A) is the following:

(i) An estimate (in ranges) of the maximum amount of hazardous chemicals in each category present at the facility at any time during the preceding calendar year.

(ii) An estimate (in ranges) of the average daily amount of hazardous chemicals in each category present at the facility during the preceding calendar year.

(iii) The general location of hazardous chemicals in each category.

**(C) Modifications**

For purposes of reporting information under this paragraph, the Administrator may—

(i) modify the categories of health and physical hazards as set forth under the Occupational Safety and Health Act of 1970 [29 U.S.C.A. § 651 et seq.] and regulations promulgated under that Act by requiring information to be reported in terms of groups of hazardous chemicals which present similar hazards in an emergency, or

(ii) require reporting on individual hazardous chemicals of special concern to emergency response personnel.

**(2) Tier II information**

An inventory form shall provide the following additional information for each hazardous chemical present at the facility, but only upon request and in accordance with subsection (e) of this section:

(A) The chemical name or the common name of the chemical as provided on the material safety data sheet.

(B) An estimate (in ranges) of the maximum amount of the hazardous chemical present at the facility at any time during the preceding calendar year.

(C) An estimate (in ranges) of the average daily amount of the hazardous chemical present at the facility during the preceding calendar year.

(D) A brief description of the manner of storage of the hazardous chemical.

(E) The location at the facility of the hazardous chemical.

(F) An indication of whether the owner elects to withhold location information of a specific hazardous chemical from disclosure to the public under section 11044 of this title.

**(e) Availability of tier II information**

**(1) Availability to State commissions, local committees, and fire departments**

Upon request by a State emergency planning commission, a local emergency planning committee, or a fire department with jurisdiction over the facility, the owner or operator of a facility shall provide tier II information, as described in subsection (d) of this section, to the person making the request. Any such request shall be with respect to a specific facility.

**(2) Availability to other State and local officials**

A State or local official acting in his or her official capacity may have access to tier II information by submitting a request to the State emergency response commission or the local emergency planning committee. Upon receipt of a request for tier II information, the State commission or local committee shall, pursuant to paragraph (1), request the facility owner or operator for the tier II information and make available such information to the official.

**(3) Availability to public**

**(A) In general**

Any person may request a State emergency response commission or local emergency planning committee for tier II information relating to the preceding calendar year with respect to a facility. Any such request shall be in writing and shall be with respect to a specific facility.

**(B) Automatic provision of information to public**

Any tier II information which a State emergency response commission or local emergency planning committee has in its possession shall be made available to a person making a request under this paragraph in accordance with section 11044 of this title. If the State emergency response commission or local emergency planning committee does not have the tier II information in its possession, upon a request for tier II information the State emergency response commission or local emergency planning committee shall, pursuant to paragraph (1), request the facility owner or operator for tier II information with respect to a hazardous chemical which a facility has stored in an amount in excess of 10,000 pounds present at the facility at any time during the preceding calendar year and make such information available in accordance with section 11044 of this title to the person making the request.

**(C) Discretionary provision of information to public**

In the case of tier II information which is not in the possession of a State emergency response commission or local emergency planning committee and which is with respect to a hazardous chemical which a facility has stored in an amount less than 10,000 pounds present at the facility at any time during the preceding calendar year, a request from a person must include the general need for the information. The State emergency response commission or local emergency planning committee may, pursuant to paragraph (1), request the facility owner or operator for the tier II information on behalf of the person making the request. Upon receipt of any information requested on behalf of such person, the State emergency response commission or local emergency planning committee shall make the information available in accordance with section 11044 of this title to the person.

(D) **Response in 45 days**

A State emergency response commission or local emergency planning committee shall respond to a request for tier II information under this paragraph no later than 45 days after the date of receipt of the request.

**(f) Fire department access**

Upon request to an owner or operator of a facility which files an inventory form under this section by the fire department with jurisdiction over the facility, the owner or operator of the facility shall allow the fire department to conduct an on-site inspection of the facility and shall provide to the fire department specific location information on hazardous chemicals at the facility.

**(g) Format of forms**

The Administrator shall publish a uniform format for inventory forms within three months after October 17, 1986. If the Administrator does not publish such forms, owners and operators of facilities subject to the requirements of this section shall provide the information required under this section by letter.

(Pub.L. 99–499, Title III, § 312, Oct. 17, 1986, 100 Stat. 1738.)

### HISTORICAL AND STATUTORY NOTES

**References in Text**

The Occupational Safety and Health Act of 1970, referred to in subsecs. (a)(1) and (d)(1)(A), (C)(i) is Pub.L. 91–596, Dec. 29, 1970, 84 Stat. 1590, as amended, which is classified principally to chapter 15 (section 651 et seq.) of Title 29, Labor. For complete classification of this Act to the Code, see Short Title note set out under section 651 of Title 29 and Tables.

**Effective and Applicability Provisions**

1986 Acts

Section effective Oct. 17, 1986, see section 4 of Pub.L. 99–499, set out as a note under section 9601 of this title.

## § 11023. Toxic chemical release forms

**[EPCRTKA § 313]**

**(a) Basic requirement**

The owner or operator of a facility subject to the requirements of this section shall complete a toxic chemical release form as published under subsection (g) of this section for each toxic chemical listed under subsection (c) of this section that was manufactured, processed, or otherwise used in quantities exceeding the toxic chemical threshold quantity established by subsection (f) of this section during the preceding calendar year at such facility. Such form shall be submitted to the Administrator and to an official or officials of the State designated by the Governor on or before July 1, 1988, and annually thereafter on July 1 and shall contain data reflecting releases during the preceding calendar year.

**(b) Covered owners and operators of facilities**

**(1) In general**

**(A)** The requirements of this section shall apply to owners and operators of facilities that have 10 or more full-time employees and that are in Standard Industrial Classification Codes 20 through 39 (as in effect on July 1, 1985) and that manufactured, processed, or otherwise used a toxic chemical listed under subsection (c) of this section in excess of the quantity of that toxic chemical established under subsection (f) of this section during the calendar year for which a release form is required under this section.

**(B)** The Administrator may add or delete Standard Industrial Classification Codes for purposes of subparagraph (A), but only to the extent necessary to provide that each Standard Industrial Code to which this section applies is relevant to the purposes of this section.

**(C)** For purposes of this section—

(i) The term "manufacture" means to produce, prepare, import, or compound a toxic chemical.

(ii) The term "process" means the preparation of a toxic chemical, after its manufacture, for distribution in commerce—

(I) in the same form or physical state as, or in a different form or physical state from, that in which it was received by the person so preparing such chemical, or

(II) as part of an article containing the toxic chemical.

**(2) Discretionary application to additional facilities**

The Administrator, on his own motion or at the request of a Governor of a State (with regard to facilities located in that State), may apply the requirements of this section to the owners and operators of any particular facility that manufactures, processes, or otherwise uses a toxic chemical listed under subsection (c) of this section if the Administrator determines that such action is warranted on the basis of toxicity of the toxic chemical, proximity to other facilities that release the toxic chemical or to population centers, the history of releases of such chemical at such facility, or such other factors as the Administrator deems appropriate.

**(c) Toxic chemicals covered**

The toxic chemicals subject to the requirements of this section are those chemicals on the list in Committee Print Number 99–169 of the Senate Committee on Environment and Public Works, titled "Toxic Chemicals Subject to Section 313 of the Emergency Planning and Community Right-To-Know Act of 1986" [42 U.S.C.A. § 11023] (including any revised version of the list as may be made pursuant to subsection (d) or (e) of this section).

**(d) Revisions by Administrator**

**(1) In general**

The Administrator may by rule add or delete a chemical from the list described in subsection (c) of this section at any time.

**(2) Additions**

A chemical may be added if the Administrator determines, in his judgment, that there is sufficient evidence to establish any one of the following:

**(A)** The chemical is known to cause or can reasonably be anticipated to cause significant adverse acute human health effects at concentration levels that are reasonably likely to exist beyond facility site boundaries as a result of continuous, or frequently recurring, releases.

**(B)** The chemical is known to cause or can reasonably be anticipated to cause in humans—

**(i)** cancer or teratogenic effects, or

**(ii)** serious or irreversible—

**(I)** reproductive dysfunctions,

**(II)** neurological disorders,

**(III)** heritable genetic mutations, or

**(IV)** other chronic health effects.

**(C)** The chemical is known to cause or can reasonably be anticipated to cause, because of—

**(i)** its toxicity,

**(ii)** its toxicity and persistence in the environment, or

**(iii)** its toxicity and tendency to bioaccumulate in the environment,

a significant adverse effect on the environment of sufficient seriousness, in the judgment of the Administrator, to warrant reporting under this section. The number of chemicals included on the list described in subsection (c) of this section on the basis of the preceding sentence may constitute in the aggregate no more than 25 percent of the total number of chemicals on the list.

A determination under this paragraph shall be based on generally accepted scientific principles or laboratory tests, or appropriately designed and conducted epidemiological or other population studies, available to the Administrator.

**(3) Deletions**

A chemical may be deleted if the Administrator determines there is not sufficient evidence to establish any of the criteria described in paragraph (2).

**(4) Effective date**

Any revision made on or after January 1 and before December 1 of any calendar year shall take effect beginning with the next calendar year. Any revision made on or after December 1 of any calendar year and before January 1 of the next calendar year shall take effect beginning with the calendar year following such next calendar year.

**(e) Petitions**

**(1) In general**

Any person may petition the Administrator to add or delete a chemical from the list described in subsection (c) of this section on the basis of the criteria in subparagraph (A) or (B) of subsection (d)(2) of this section. Within 180 days after receipt of a petition, the Administrator shall take one of the following actions:

**(A)** Initiate a rulemaking to add or delete the chemical to the list, in accordance with subsection (d)(2) or (d)(3) of this section.

**(B)** Publish an explanation of why the petition is denied.

**(2) Governor petitions**

A State Governor may petition the Administrator to add or delete a chemical from the list described in subsection (c) of this section on the basis of the criteria in subparagraph (A), (B), or (C) of subsection (d)(2) of this section. In the case of such a petition from a State Governor to delete a chemical, the petition shall be treated in the same manner as a petition received under paragraph (1) to delete a chemical. In the case of such a petition from a State Governor to add a chemical, the chemical will be added to the list within 180 days after receipt of the petition, unless the Administrator—

**(A)** initiates a rulemaking to add the chemical to the list, in accordance with subsection (d)(2) of this section, or

**(B)** publishes an explanation of why the Administrator believes the petition does not meet the requirements of subsection (d)(2) of this section for adding a chemical to the list.

**(f) Threshold for reporting**

**(1) Toxic chemical threshold amount**

The threshold amounts for purposes of reporting toxic chemicals under this section are as follows:

**(A)** With respect to a toxic chemical used at a facility, 10,000 pounds of the toxic chemical per year.

**(B)** With respect to a toxic chemical manufactured or processed at a facility—

**(i)** For the toxic chemical release form required to be submitted under this section on or before July 1, 1988, 75,000 pounds of the toxic chemical per year.

(ii) For the form required to be submitted on or before July 1, 1989, 50,000 pounds of the toxic chemical per year.

(iii) For the form required to be submitted on or before July 1, 1990, and for each form thereafter, 25,000 pounds of the toxic chemical per year.

**(2) Revisions**

The Administrator may establish a threshold amount for a toxic chemical different from the amount established by paragraph (1). Such revised threshold shall obtain reporting on a substantial majority of total releases of the chemical at all facilities subject to the requirements of this section. The amounts established under this paragraph may, at the Administrator's discretion, be based on classes of chemicals or categories of facilities.

**(g) Form**

**(1) Information required**

Not later than June 1, 1987, the Administrator shall publish a uniform toxic chemical release form for facilities covered by this section. If the Administrator does not publish such a form, owners and operators of facilities subject to the requirements of this section shall provide the information required under this subsection by letter postmarked on or before the date on which the form is due. Such form shall—

(A) provide for the name and location of, and principal business activities at, the facility;

(B) include an appropriate certification, signed by a senior official with management responsibility for the person or persons completing the report, regarding the accuracy and completeness of the report; and

(C) provide for submission of each of the following items of information for each listed toxic chemical known to be present at the facility:

(i) Whether the toxic chemical at the facility is manufactured, processed, or otherwise used, and the general category or categories of use of the chemical.

(ii) An estimate of the maximum amounts (in ranges) of the toxic chemical present at the facility at any time during the preceding calendar year.

(iii) For each wastestream, the waste treatment or disposal methods employed, and an estimate of the treatment efficiency typically achieved by such methods for that wastestream.

(iv) The annual quantity of the toxic chemical entering each environmental medium.

**(2) Use of available data**

In order to provide the information required under this section, the owner or operator of a facility may use readily available data (including monitoring data) collected pursuant to other provisions of law, or, where such data are not readily available, reasonable estimates of the amounts involved. Nothing in this section requires the monitoring or measurement of the quantities, concentration, or frequency of any toxic chemical released into the environment beyond that monitoring and measurement required under other provisions of law or regulation. In order to assure consistency, the Administrator shall require that data be expressed in common units.

**(h) Use of release form**

The release forms required under this section are intended to provide information to the Federal, State, and local governments and the public, including citizens of communities surrounding covered facilities. The release form shall be available, consistent with section 11044(a) of this title, to inform persons about releases of toxic chemicals to the environment; to assist governmental agencies, researchers, and other persons in the conduct of research and data gathering; to aid in the development of appropriate regulations, guidelines, and standards; and for other similar purposes.

**(i) Modifications in reporting frequency**

**(1) In general**

The Administrator may modify the frequency of submitting a report under this section, but the Administrator may not modify the frequency to be any more often than annually. A modification may apply, either nationally or in a specific geographic area, to the following:

(A) All toxic chemical release forms required under this section.

(B) A class of toxic chemicals or a category of facilities.

(C) A specific toxic chemical.

(D) A specific facility.

**(2) Requirements**

A modification may be made under paragraph (1) only if the Administrator—

(A) makes a finding that the modification is consistent with the provisions of subsection (h) of this section, based on—

(i) experience from previously submitted toxic chemical release forms, and

(ii) determinations made under paragraph (3), and

(B) the finding is made by a rulemaking in accordance with section 553 of Title 5.

(3) **Determinations**

The Administrator shall make the following determinations with respect to a proposed modification before making a modification under paragraph (1):

(A) The extent to which information relating to the proposed modification provided on the toxic chemical release forms has been used by the Administrator or other agencies of the Federal Government, States, local governments, health professionals, and the public.

(B) The extent to which the information is (i) readily available to potential users from other sources, such as State reporting programs, and (ii) provided to the Administrator under another Federal law or through a State program.

(C) The extent to which the modification would impose additional and unreasonable burdens on facilities subject to the reporting requirements under this section.

(4) **5-year review**

Any modification made under this subsection shall be reviewed at least once every 5 years. Such review shall examine the modification and ensure that the requirements of paragraphs (2) and (3) still justify continuation of the modification. Any change to a modification reviewed under this paragraph shall be made in accordance with this subsection.

(5) **Notification to Congress**

The Administrator shall notify Congress of an intention to initiate a rulemaking for a modification under this subsection. After such notification, the Administrator shall delay initiation of the rulemaking for at least 12 months, but no more than 24 months, after the date of such notification.

(6) **Judicial review**

In any judicial review of a rulemaking which establishes a modification under this subsection, a court may hold unlawful and set aside agency action, findings, and conclusions found to be unsupported by substantial evidence.

(7) **Applicability**

A modification under this subsection may apply to a calendar year or other reporting period beginning no earlier than January 1, 1993.

(8) **Effective date**

Any modification made on or after January 1 and before December 1 of any calendar year shall take effect beginning with the next calendar year. Any modification made on or after December 1 of any calendar year and before January 1 of the next calendar year shall take effect beginning with the calendar year following such next calendar year.

(j) **EPA management of data**

The Administrator shall establish and maintain in a computer data base a national toxic chemical inventory based on data submitted to the Administrator under this section. The Administrator shall make these data accessible by computer telecommunication and other means to any person on a cost reimbursable basis.

(k) **Report**

Not later than June 30, 1991, the Comptroller General, in consultation with the Administrator and appropriate officials in the States, shall submit to the Congress a report including each of the following:

(1) A description of the steps taken by the Administrator and the States to implement the requirements of this section, including steps taken to make information collected under this section available to and accessible by the public.

(2) A description of the extent to which the information collected under this section has been used by the Environmental Protection Agency, other Federal agencies, the States, and the public, and the purposes for which the information has been used.

(3) An identification and evaluation of options for modifications to the requirements of this section for the purpose of making information collected under this section more useful.

(*l*) **Mass balance study**

(1) **In general**

The Administrator shall arrange for a mass balance study to be carried out by the National Academy of Sciences using mass balance information collected by the Administrator under paragraph (3). The Administrator shall submit to Congress a report on such study no later than 5 years after October 17, 1986.

(2) **Purposes**

The purposes of the study are as follows:

(A) To assess the value of mass balance analysis in determining the accuracy of information on toxic chemical releases.

(B) To assess the value of obtaining mass balance information, or portions thereof, to determine the waste reduction efficiency of different facilities, or categories of facilities, including the effectiveness of toxic chemical regulations promulgated under laws other than this chapter.

(C) To assess the utility of such information for evaluating toxic chemical management practices at facilities, or categories of facilities, covered by this section.

(D) To determine the implications of mass balance information collection on a national scale similar to the mass balance information collection carried out by the Administrator under paragraph (3), including implications of the use of such collection as part of a national annual quantity toxic chemical release program.

**(3) Information collection**

(A) The Administrator shall acquire available mass balance information from States which currently conduct (or during the 5 years after October 17, 1986, initiate) a mass balance-oriented annual quantity toxic chemical release program. If information from such States provides an inadequate representation of industry classes and categories to carry out the purposes of the study, the Administrator also may acquire mass balance information necessary for the study from a representative number of facilities in other States.

(B) Any information acquired under this section shall be available to the public, except that upon a showing satisfactory to the Administrator by any person that the information (or a particular part thereof) to which the Administrator or any officer, employee, or representative has access under this section if made public would divulge information entitled to protection under section 1905 of Title 18, such information or part shall be considered confidential in accordance with the purposes of that section, except that such information or part may be disclosed to other officers, employees, or authorized representatives of the United States concerned with carrying out this section.

(C) The Administrator may promulgate regulations prescribing procedures for collecting mass balance information under this paragraph.

(D) For purposes of collecting mass balance information under subparagraph (A), the Administrator may require the submission of information by a State or facility.

**(4) Mass balance definition**

For purposes of this subsection, the term "mass balance" means an accumulation of the annual quantities of chemicals transported to a facility, produced at a facility, consumed at a facility, used at a facility, accumulated at a facility, released from a facility, and transported from a facility as a waste or as a commercial product or byproduct or component of a commercial product or byproduct.

(Pub.L. 99–499, Title III, § 313, Oct. 17, 1986, 100 Stat. 1741.)

**HISTORICAL AND STATUTORY NOTES**

**Effective and Applicability Provisions**

1986 Acts

Section effective Oct. 17, 1986, see section 4 of Pub.L. 99–499, set out as a note under section 9601 of this title.

## SUBCHAPTER III—GENERAL PROVISIONS

### § 11041. Relationship to other law

**[EPCRTKA § 321]**

**(a) In general**

Nothing in this chapter shall—

(1) preempt any State or local law,

(2) except as provided in subsection (b) of this section, otherwise affect any State or local law or the authority of any State or local government to adopt or enforce any State or local law, or

(3) affect or modify in any way the obligations or liabilities of any person under other Federal law.

**(b) Effect on MSDS requirements**

Any State or local law enacted after August 1, 1985, which requires the submission of a material safety data sheet from facility owners or operators shall require that the data sheet be identical in content and format to the data sheet required under subsection (a) of section 11021 of this title. In addition, a State or locality may require the submission of information which is supplemental to the information required on the data sheet (including information on the location and quantity of hazardous chemicals present at the facility), through additional sheets attached to the data sheet or such other means as the State or locality considers appropriate.

(Pub.L. 99–499, Title III, § 321, Oct. 17, 1986, 100 Stat. 1747.)

**HISTORICAL AND STATUTORY NOTES**

**Effective and Applicability Provisions**

1986 Acts

Section effective Oct. 17, 1986, see section 4 of Pub.L. 99–499, set out as a note under section 9601 of this title.

### § 11042. Trade secrets

**[EPCRTKA § 322]**

**(a) Authority to withhold information**

**(1) General authority**

(A) With regard to a hazardous chemical, an extremely hazardous substance, or a toxic chemical, any person required under section 11003(d)(2), 11003(d)(3), 11021, 11022, or 11023 of this title to submit information to any other person may withhold from such submittal the specific chemical identity (including the chemical name and other specific identification), as defined in regulations prescribed by the Administrator under subsection (c) of this section, if the person complies with paragraph (2).

**(B)** Any person withholding the specific chemical identity shall, in the place on the submittal where the chemical identity would normally be included, include the generic class or category of the hazardous chemical, extremely hazardous substance, or toxic chemical (as the case may be).

**(2) Requirements**

**(A)** A person is entitled to withhold information under paragraph (1) if such person—

**(i)** claims that such information is a trade secret, on the basis of the factors enumerated in subsection (b) of this section,

**(ii)** includes in the submittal referred to in paragraph (1) an explanation of the reasons why such information is claimed to be a trade secret, based on the factors enumerated in subsection (b) of this section, including a specific description of why such factors apply, and

**(iii)** submits to the Administrator a copy of such submittal, and the information withheld from such submittal.

**(B)** In submitting to the Administrator the information required by subparagraph (A)(iii), a person withholding information under this subsection may—

**(i)** designate, in writing and in such manner as the Administrator may prescribe by regulation, the information which such person believes is entitled to be withheld under paragraph (1), and

**(ii)** submit such designated information separately from other information submitted under this subsection.

**(3) Limitation**

The authority under this subsection to withhold information shall not apply to information which the Administrator has determined, in accordance with subsection (c) of this section, is not a trade secret.

**(b) Trade secret factors**

No person required to provide information under this chapter may claim that the information is entitled to protection as a trade secret under subsection (a) of this section unless such person shows each of the following:

**(1)** Such person has not disclosed the information to any other person, other than a member of a local emergency planning committee, an officer or employee of the United States or a State or local government, an employee of such person, or a person who is bound by a confidentiality agreement, and such person has taken reasonable measures to protect the confidentiality of such information and intends to continue to take such measures.

**(2)** The information is not required to be disclosed, or otherwise made available, to the public under any other Federal or State law.

**(3)** Disclosure of the information is likely to cause substantial harm to the competitive position of such person.

**(4)** The chemical identity is not readily discoverable through reverse engineering.

**(c) Trade secret regulations**

As soon as practicable after October 17, 1986, the Administrator shall prescribe regulations to implement this section. With respect to subsection (b)(4) of this section, such regulations shall be equivalent to comparable provisions in the Occupational Safety and Health Administration Hazard Communication Standard (29 C.F.R. 1910.1200) and any revisions of such standard prescribed by the Secretary of Labor in accordance with the final ruling of the courts of the United States in United Steelworkers of America, AFL-CIO-CLC v. Thorne G. Auchter.

**(d) Petition for review**

**(1) In general**

Any person may petition the Administrator for the disclosure of the specific chemical identity of a hazardous chemical, an extremely hazardous substance, or a toxic chemical which is claimed as a trade secret under this section. The Administrator may, in the absence of a petition under this paragraph, initiate a determination, to be carried out in accordance with this subsection, as to whether information withheld constitutes a trade secret.

**(2) Initial review**

Within 30 days after the date of receipt of a petition under paragraph (1) (or upon the Administrator's initiative), the Administrator shall review the explanation filed by a trade secret claimant under subsection (a)(2) of this section and determine whether the explanation presents assertions which, if true, are sufficient to support a finding that the specific chemical identity is a trade secret.

**(3) Finding of sufficient assertions**

**(A)** If the Administrator determines pursuant to paragraph (2) that the explanation presents sufficient assertions to support a finding that the specific chemical identity is a trade secret, the Administrator shall notify the trade secret claimant that he has 30 days to supplement the explanation with detailed information to support the assertions.

**(B)** If the Administrator determines, after receipt of any supplemental supporting detailed information under subparagraph (A), that the assertions in the explanation are true and that the specific chemical identity is a trade secret, the Administrator shall so notify the petitioner and the petitioner may seek judicial review of the determination.

(C) If the Administrator determines, after receipt of any supplemental supporting detailed information under subparagraph (A), that the assertions in the explanation are not true and that the specific chemical identity is not a trade secret, the Administrator shall notify the trade secret claimant that the Administrator intends to release the specific chemical identity. The trade secret claimant has 30 days in which he may appeal the Administrator's determination under this subparagraph to the Administrator. If the Administrator does not reverse his determination under this subparagraph in such an appeal by the trade secret claimant, the trade secret claimaint[1] may seek judicial review of the determination.

**(4) Finding of insufficient assertions**

(A) If the Administrator determines pursuant to paragraph (2) that the explanation presents insufficient assertions to support a finding that the specific chemical identity is a trade secret, the Administrator shall notify the trade secret claimant that he has 30 days to appeal the determination to the Administrator, or, upon a showing of good cause, amend the original explanation by providing supplementary assertions to support the trade secret claim.

(B) If the Administrator does not reverse his determination under subparagraph (A) after an appeal or an examination of any supplementary assertions under subparagraph (A), the Administrator shall so notify the trade secret claimant and the trade secret claimant may seek judicial review of the determination.

(C) If the Administrator reverses his determination under subparagraph (A) after an appeal or an examination of any supplementary assertions under subparagraph (A), the procedures under paragraph (3) of this subsection apply.

**(e) Exception for information provided to health professionals**

Nothing in this section, or regulations adopted pursuant to this section, shall authorize any person to withhold information which is required to be provided to a health professional, a doctor, or a nurse in accordance with section 11043 of this title.

**(f) Providing information to Administrator; availability to public**

Any information submitted to the Administrator under subsection (a)(2) of this section or subsection (d)(3) of this section (except a specific chemical identity) shall be available to the public, except that upon a showing satisfactory to the Administrator by any person that the information (or a particular part thereof) to which the Administrator has access under this section if made public would divulge information entitled to protection under section 1905 of Title 18, such information or part shall be considered confidential in accordance with the purposes of that section, except that such information or part may be disclosed to other officers, employees, or authorized representatives of the United States concerned with carrying out this chapter.

**(g) Information provided to State**

Upon request by a State, acting through the Governor of the State, the Administrator shall provide to the State any information obtained under subsection (a)(2) of this section and subsection (d)(3) of this section.

**(h) Information on adverse effects**

(1) In any case in which the identity of a hazardous chemical or an extremely hazardous substance is claimed as a trade secret, the Governor or State emergency response commission established under section 11001 of this title shall identify the adverse health effects associated with the hazardous chemical or extremely hazardous substance and shall assure that such information is provided to any person requesting information about such hazardous chemical or extremely hazardous substance.

(2) In any case in which the identity of a toxic chemical is claimed as a trade secret, the Administrator shall identify the adverse health and environmental effects associated with the toxic chemical and shall assure that such information is included in the computer database required by section 11023(j) of this title and is provided to any person requesting information about such toxic chemical.

**(i) Information provided to Congress**

Notwithstanding any limitatio[2] contained in this section or any other provision of law, all information reported to or otherwise obtained by the Administrator (or any representative of the Administrator) under this chapter shall be made available to a duly authorized committee of the Congress upon written request by such a committee.

(Pub.L. 99–499, Title III, § 322, Oct. 17, 1986, 100 Stat. 1747.)

[1] So in original. Probably should be "claimant".

[2] So in original. Probably should be "limitation".

## HISTORICAL AND STATUTORY NOTES

**Effective and Applicability Provisions**

1986 Acts

Section effective Oct. 17, 1986, see section 4 of Pub.L. 99–499, set out as a note under section 9601 of this title.

## § 11043. Provision of information to health professionals, doctors, and nurses [EPCRTKA § 323]

### (a) Diagnosis or treatment by health professional

An owner or operator of a facility which is subject to the requirements of section 11021, 11022, or 11023 of this title shall provide the specific chemical identity, if known, of a hazardous chemical, extremely hazardous substance, or a toxic chemical to any health professional who requests such information in writing if the health professional provides a written statement of need under this subsection and a written confidentiality agreement under subsection (d) of this section. The written statement of need shall be a statement that the health professional has a reasonable basis to suspect that—

(1) the information is needed for purposes of diagnosis or treatment of an individual,

(2) the individual or individuals being diagnosed or treated have been exposed to the chemical concerned, and

(3) knowledge of the specific chemical identity of such chemical will assist in diagnosis or treatment.

Following such a written request, the owner or operator to whom such request is made shall promptly provide the requested information to the health professional. The authority to withhold the specific chemical identity of a chemical under section 11042 of this title when such information is a trade secret shall not apply to information required to be provided under this subsection, subject to the provisions of subsection (d) of this section.

### (b) Medical emergency

An owner or operator of a facility which is subject to the requirements of section 11021, 11022, or 11023 of this title shall provide a copy of a material safety data sheet, an inventory form, or a toxic chemical release form, including the specific chemical identity, if known, of a hazardous chemical, extremely hazardous substance, or a toxic chemical, to any treating physician or nurse who requests such information if such physician or nurse determines that—

(1) a medical emergency exists,

(2) the specific chemical identity of the chemical concerned is necessary for or will assist in emergency or first-aid diagnosis or treatment, and

(3) the individual or individuals being diagnosed or treated have been exposed to the chemical concerned.

Immediately following such a request, the owner or operator to whom such request is made shall provide the requested information to the physician or nurse. The authority to withhold the specific chemical identity of a chemical from a material safety data sheet, an inventory form, or a toxic chemical release form under section 11042 of this title when such information is a trade secret shall not apply to information required to be provided to a treating physician or nurse under this subsection. No written confidentiality agreement or statement of need shall be required as a precondition of such disclosure, but the owner or operator disclosing such information may require a written confidentiality agreement in accordance with subsection (d) of this section and a statement setting forth the items listed in paragraphs (1) through (3) as soon as circumstances permit.

### (c) Preventive measures by local health professionals

#### (1) Provision of information

An owner or operator of a facility subject to the requirements of section 11021, 11022, or 11023 of this title shall provide the specific chemical identity, if known, of a hazardous chemical, an extremely hazardous substance, or a toxic chemical to any health professional (such as a physician, toxicologist, or epidemiologist)—

(A) who is a local government employee or a person under contract with the local government, and

(B) who requests such information in writing and provides a written statement of need under paragraph (2) and a written confidentiality agreement under subsection (d) of this section.

Following such a written request, the owner or operator to whom such request is made shall promptly provide the requested information to the local health professional. The authority to withhold the specific chemical identity of a chemical under section 11042 of this title when such information is a trade secret shall not apply to information required to be provided under this subsection, subject to the provisions of subsection (d) of this section.

#### (2) Written statement of need

The written statement of need shall be a statement that describes with reasonable detail one or more of the following health needs for the information:

(A) To assess exposure of persons living in a local community to the hazards of the chemical concerned.

(B) To conduct or assess sampling to determine exposure levels of various population groups.

(C) To conduct periodic medical surveillance of exposed population groups.

(D) To provide medical treatment to exposed individuals or population groups.

(E) To conduct studies to determine the health effects of exposure.

(F) To conduct studies to aid in the identification of a chemical that may reasonably be anticipated to cause an observed health effect.

**(d) Confidentiality agreement**

Any person obtaining information under subsection (a) or (c) of this section shall, in accordance with such subsection (a) or (c) of this section, be required to agree in a written confidentiality agreement that he will not use the information for any purpose other than the health needs asserted in the statement of need, except as may otherwise be authorized by the terms of the agreement or by the person providing such information. Nothing in this subsection shall preclude the parties to a confidentiality agreement from pursuing any remedies to the extent permitted by law.

**(e) Regulations**

As soon as practicable after October 17, 1986, the Administrator shall promulgate regulations describing criteria and parameters for the statement of need under subsection [1] (a) and (c) of this section and the confidentiality agreement under subsection (d) of this section.

(Pub.L. 99–499, Title III, § 323, Oct. 17, 1986, 100 Stat. 1750.)

[1] So in original. Probably should be "subsections".

HISTORICAL AND STATUTORY NOTES

**Effective and Applicability Provisions**

1986 Acts

Section effective Oct. 17, 1986, see section 4 of Pub.L. 99–499, set out as a note under section 9601 of this title.

## § 11044. Public availability of plans, data sheets, forms, and followup notices [EPCRTKA § 324]

**(a) Availability to public**

Each emergency response plan, material safety data sheet, list described in section 11021(a)(2) of this title, inventory form, toxic chemical release form, and followup emergency notice shall be made available to the general public, consistent with section 11042 of this title, during normal working hours at the location or locations designated by the Administrator, Governor, State emergency response commission, or local emergency planning committee, as appropriate. Upon request by an owner or operator of a facility subject to the requirements of section 11022 of this title, the State emergency response commission and the appropriate local emergency planning committee shall withhold from disclosure under this section the location of any specific chemical required by section 11022(d)(2) of this title to be contained in an inventory form as tier II information.

**(b) Notice of public availability**

Each local emergency planning committee shall annually publish a notice in local newspapers that the emergency response plan, material safety data sheets, and inventory forms have been submitted under this section. The notice shall state that followup emergency notices may subsequently be issued. Such notice shall announce that members of the public who wish to review any such plan, sheet, form, or followup notice may do so at the location designated under subsection (a) of this section.

(Pub.L. 99–499, Title III, § 324, Oct. 17, 1986, 100 Stat. 1752.)

HISTORICAL AND STATUTORY NOTES

**Effective and Applicability Provisions**

1986 Acts

Section effective Oct. 17, 1986, see section 4 of Pub.L. 99–499, set out as a note under section 9601 of this title.

## § 11045. Enforcement

[EPCRTKA § 325]

**(a) Civil penalties for emergency planning**

The Administrator may order a facility owner or operator (except an owner or operator of a facility designated under section 11002(b)(2) of this title) to comply with section 11002(c) of this title and section 11003(d) of this title. The United States district court for the district in which the facility is located shall have jurisdiction to enforce the order, and any person who violates or fails to obey such an order shall be liable to the United States for a civil penalty of not more than $25,000 for each day in which such violation occurs or such failure to comply continues.

**(b) Civil, administrative, and criminal penalties for emergency notification**

**(1) Class I administrative penalty**

(A) A civil penalty of not more than $25,000 per violation may be assessed by the Administrator in the case of a violation of the requirements of section 11004 of this title.

(B) No civil penalty may be assessed under this subsection unless the person accused of the violation is given notice and opportunity for a hearing with respect to the violation.

(C) In determining the amount of any penalty assessed pursuant to this subsection, the Administrator shall take into account the nature, circumstances, extent and gravity of the violation or violations and, with respect to the violator, ability to pay, any prior history of such violations, the degree of culpability, economic benefit or savings (if any) resulting from the violation, and such other matters as justice may require.

(2) **Class II administrative penalty**

A civil penalty of not more than $25,000 per day for each day during which the violation continues may be assessed by the Administrator in the case of a violation of the requirements of section 11004 of this title. In the case of a second or subsequent violation the amount of such penalty may be not more than $75,000 for each day during which the violation continues. Any civil penalty under this subsection shall be assessed and collected in the same manner, and subject to the same provisions, as in the case of civil penalties assessed and collected under section 2615 of Title 15. In any proceeding for the assessment of a civil penalty under this subsection the Administrator may issue subpoenas for the attendance and testimony of witnesses and the production of relevant papers, books, and documents and may promulgate rules for discovery procedures.

(3) **Judicial assessment**

The Administrator may bring an action in the United States District[1] court for the appropriate district to assess and collect a penalty of not more than $25,000 per day for each day during which the violation continues in the case of a violation of the requirements of section 11004 of this title. In the case of a second or subsequent violation, the amount of such penalty may be not more than $75,000 for each day during which the violation continues.

(4) **Criminal penalties**

Any person who knowingly and willfully fails to provide notice in accordance with section 11004 of this title shall, upon conviction, be fined not more than $25,000 or imprisoned for not more than two years, or both (or in the case of a second or subsequent conviction, shall be fined not more than $50,000 or imprisoned for not more than five years, or both).

**(c) Civil and administrative penalties for reporting requirements**

(1) Any person (other than a governmental entity) who violates any requirement of section 11022 or 11023 of this title shall be liable to the United States for a civil penalty in an amount not to exceed $25,000 for each such violation.

(2) Any person (other than a governmental entity) who violates any requirement of section 11021 or 11043(b) of this title, and any person who fails to furnish to the Administrator information required under section 11042(a)(2) of this title shall be liable to the United States for a civil penalty in an amount not to exceed $10,000 for each such violation.

(3) Each day a violation described in paragraph (1) or (2) continues shall, for purposes of this subsection, constitute a separate violation.

(4) The Administrator may assess any civil penalty for which a person is liable under this subsection by administrative order or may bring an action to assess and collect the penalty in the United States district court for the district in which the person from whom the penalty is sought resides or in which such person's principal place of business is located.

**(d) Civil, administrative, and criminal penalties with respect to trade secrets**

(1) **Civil and administrative penalty for frivolous claims**

If the Administrator determines—

(A) (i) under section 11042(d)(4) of this title that an explanation submitted by a trade secret claimant presents insufficient assertions to support a finding that a specific chemical identity is a trade secret, or (ii) after receiving supplemental supporting detailed information under section 11042(d)(3)(A) of this title, that the specific chemical identity is not a trade secret; and

(B) that the trade secret claim is frivolous,

the trade secret claimant is liable for a penalty of $25,000 per claim. The Administrator may assess the penalty by administrative order or may bring an action in the appropriate district court of the United States to assess and collect the penalty.

(2) **Criminal penalty for disclosure of trade secret information**

Any person who knowingly and willfully divulges or discloses any information entitled to protection under section 11042 of this title shall, upon conviction, be subject to a fine of not more than $20,000 or to imprisonment not to exceed one year, or both.

**(e) Special enforcement provisions for section 11043**

Whenever any facility owner or operator required to provide information under section 11043 of this title to a health professional who has requested such information fails or refuses to provide such information in accordance with such section, such health professional may bring an action in the appropriate United States district court to require such facility owner or operator to provide the information. Such court shall have jurisdiction to issue such orders and take such other action as may be necessary to enforce the requirements of section 11043 of this title.

**(f) Procedures for administrative penalties**

(1) Any person against whom a civil penalty is assessed under this section may obtain review thereof in the appropriate district court of the United States by filing a notice of appeal in such court within 30

days after the date of such order and by simultaneously sending a copy of such notice by certified mail to the Administrator. The Administrator shall promptly file in such court a certified copy of the record upon which such violation was found or such penalty imposed. If any person fails to pay an assessment of a civil penalty after it has become a final and unappealable order or after the appropriate court has entered final judgment in favor of the United States, the Administrator may request the Attorney General of the United States to institute a civil action in an appropriate district court of the United States to collect the penalty, and such court shall have jurisdiction to hear and decide any such action. In hearing such action, the court shall have authority to review the violation and the assessment of the civil penalty on the record.

(2) The Administrator may issue subpoenas for the attendance and testimony of witnesses and the production of relevant papers, books, or documents in connection with hearings under this section. In case of contumacy or refusal to obey a subpoena issued pursuant to this paragraph and served upon any person, the district court of the United States for any district in which such person is found, resides, or transacts business, upon application by the United States and after notice to such person, shall have jurisdiction to issue an order requiring such person to appear and give testimony before the administrative law judge or to appear and produce documents before the administrative law judge, or both, and any failure to obey such order of the court may be punished by such court as a contempt thereof.

(Pub.L. 99–499, Title III, § 325, Oct. 17, 1986, 100 Stat. 1753.)

1 So in original. Probably should be "district".

### HISTORICAL AND STATUTORY NOTES

**Effective and Applicability Provisions**

1986 Acts

Section effective Oct. 17, 1986, see section 4 of Pub.L. 99–499, set out as a note under section 9601 of this title.

## § 11046. Civil actions

### [EPCRTKA § 326]

**(a) Authority to bring civil actions**

**(1) Citizen suits**

Except as provided in subsection (e) of this section, any person may commence a civil action on his own behalf against the following:

**(A)** An owner or operator of a facility for failure to do any of the following:

**(i)** Submit a followup emergency notice under section 11004(c) of this title.

**(ii)** Submit a material safety data sheet or a list under section 11021(a) of this title.

**(iii)** Complete and submit an inventory form under section 11022(a) of this title containing tier I information as described in section 11022(d)(1) of this title unless such requirement does not apply by reason of the second sentence of section 11022(a)(2) of this title.

**(iv)** Complete and submit a toxic chemical release form under section 11023(a) of this title.

**(B)** The Administrator for failure to do any of the following:

**(i)** Publish inventory forms under section 11022(g) of this title.

**(ii)** Respond to a petition to add or delete a chemical under section 11023(e)(1) of this title within 180 days after receipt of the petition.

**(iii)** Publish a toxic chemical release form under 11023(g) [1] of this title.

**(iv)** Establish a computer database in accordance with section 11023(j) of this title.

**(v)** Promulgate trade secret regulations under section 11042(c) of this title.

**(vi)** Render a decision in response to a petition under section 11042(d) of this title within 9 months after receipt of the petition.

**(C)** The Administrator, a State Governor, or a State emergency response commission, for failure to provide a mechanism for public availability of information in accordance with section 11044(a) of this title.

**(D)** A State Governor or a State emergency response commission for failure to respond to a request for tier II information under section 11022(e)(3) of this title within 120 days after the date of receipt of the request.

**(2) State or local suits**

**(A)** Any State or local government may commence a civil action against an owner or operator of a facility for failure to do any of the following:

**(i)** Provide notification to the emergency response commission in the State under section 11002(c) of this title.

**(ii)** Submit a material safety data sheet or a list under section 11021(a) of this title.

**(iii)** Make available information requested under section 11021(c) of this title.

**(iv)** Complete and submit an inventory form under section 11022(a) of this title containing tier I information unless such requirement does not apply by reason of the second sentence of section 11022(a)(2) of this title..[2]

**(B)** Any State emergency response commission or local emergency planning committee may commence a civil action against an owner or operator of a facility for failure to provide information under section 11003(d) of this title or for failure to submit tier II information under section 11022(e)(1) of this title.

(C) Any State may commence a civil action against the Administrator for failure to provide information to the State under section 11042(g) of this title.

**(b) Venue**

(1) Any action under subsection (a) of this section against an owner or operator of a facility shall be brought in the district court for the district in which the alleged violation occurred.

(2) Any action under subsection (a) of this section against the Administrator may be brought in the United States District Court for the District of Columbia.

**(c) Relief**

The district court shall have jurisdiction in actions brought under subsection (a) of this section against an owner or operator of a facility to enforce the requirement concerned and to impose any civil penalty provided for violation of that requirement. The district court shall have jurisdiction in actions brought under subsection (a) of this section against the Administrator to order the Administrator to perform the act or duty concerned.

**(d) Notice**

(1) No action may be commenced under subsection (a)(1)(A) of this section prior to 60 days after the plaintiff has given notice of the alleged violation to the Administrator, the State in which the alleged violation occurs, and the alleged violator. Notice under this paragraph shall be given in such manner as the Administrator shall prescribe by regulation.

(2) No action may be commenced under subsection (a)(1)(B) or (a)(1)(C) of this section prior to 60 days after the date on which the plaintiff gives notice to the Administrator, State Governor, or State emergency response commission (as the case may be) that the plaintiff will commence the action. Notice under this paragraph shall be given in such manner as the Administrator shall prescribe by regulation.

**(e) Limitation**

No action may be commenced under subsection (a) of this section against an owner or operator of a facility if the Administrator has commenced and is diligently pursuing an administrative order or civil action to enforce the requirement concerned or to impose a civil penalty under this Act with respect to the violation of the requirement.

**(f) Costs**

The court, in issuing any final order in any action brought pursuant to this section, may award costs of litigation (including reasonable attorney and expert witness fees) to the prevailing or the substantially prevailing party whenever the court determines such an award is appropriate. The court may, if a temporary restraining order or preliminary injunction is sought, require the filing of a bond or equivalent security in accordance with the Federal Rules of Civil Procedure.

**(g) Other rights**

Nothing in this section shall restrict or expand any right which any person (or class of persons) may have under any Federal or State statute or common law to seek enforcement of any requirement or to seek any other relief (including relief against the Administrator or a State agency).

**(h) Intervention**

**(1) By the United States**

In any action under this section the United States or the State, or both, if not a party, may intervene as a matter of right.

**(2) By persons**

In any action under this section, any person may intervene as a matter of right when such person has a direct interest which is or may be adversely affected by the action and the disposition of the action may, as a practical matter, impair or impede the person's ability to protect that interest unless the Administrator or the State shows that the person's interest is adequately represented by existing parties in the action.

(Pub.L. 99–499, Title III, § 326, Oct. 17, 1986, 100 Stat. 1755.)

[1] So in original. Probably should be preceded by "section".
[2] So in original.

### HISTORICAL AND STATUTORY NOTES

**References in Text**

This Act, referred to in subsec. (e), is Pub.L. 99–499, Oct. 17, 1986, 100 Stat. 1613, as amended, known as the Superfund Amendments and Reauthorization Act of 1986. For complete classification of this Act to the Code, see Short Title of 1986 Amendments note set out under section 9601 of this title and Tables.

The Federal Rules of Civil Procedure, referred to in subsec. (f), are set out in Title 28, Judiciary and Judicial Procedure.

**Effective and Applicability Provisions**

1986 Acts

Section effective Oct. 17, 1986, see section 4 of Pub.L. 99–499, set out as a note under section 9601 of this title.

## § 11047. Exemption

**[EPCRTKA § 327]**

Except as provided in section 11004 of this title, this chapter does not apply to the transportation, including the storage incident to such transportation, of any substance or chemical subject to the requirements of this chapter, including the transportation and distribution of natural gas.

(Pub.L. 99–499, Title III, § 327, Oct. 17, 1986, 100 Stat. 1757.)

### HISTORICAL AND STATUTORY NOTES

**Effective and Applicability Provisions**

1986 Acts

Section effective Oct. 17, 1986, see section 4 of Pub.L. 99–499, set out as a note under section 9601 of this title.

## § 11048. Regulations

### [EPCRTKA § 328]

The Administrator may prescribe such regulations as may be necessary to carry out this chapter.

(Pub.L. 99–499, Title III, § 328, Oct. 17, 1986, 100 Stat. 1757.)

### HISTORICAL AND STATUTORY NOTES

**Effective and Applicability Provisions**

1986 Acts

Section effective Oct. 17, 1986, see section 4 of Pub.L. 99–499, set out as a note under section 9601 of this title.

## § 11049. Definitions

### [EPCRTKA § 329]

For purposes of this chapter—

**(1) Administrator**

The term "Administrator" means the Administrator of the Environmental Protection Agency.

**(2) Environment**

The term "environment" includes water, air, and land and the interrelationship which exists among and between water, air, and land and all living things.

**(3) Extremely hazardous substance**

The term "extremely hazardous substance" means a substance on the list described in section 11002(a)(2) of this title.

**(4) Facility**

The term "facility" means all buildings, equipment, structures, and other stationary items which are located on a single site or on contiguous or adjacent sites and which are owned or operated by the same person (or by any person which controls, is controlled by, or under common control with, such person). For purposes of section 11004 of this title, the term includes motor vehicles, rolling stock, and aircraft.

**(5) Hazardous chemical**

The term "hazardous chemical" has the meaning given such term by section 11021(e) of this title.

**(6) Material safety data sheet**

The term "material safety data sheet" means the sheet required to be developed under section 1910.1200(g) of Title 29 of the Code of Federal Regulations, as that section may be amended from time to time.

**(7) Person**

The term "person" means any individual, trust, firm, joint stock company, corporation (including a government corporation), partnership, association, State, municipality, commission, political subdivision of a State, or interstate body.

**(8) Release**

The term "release" means any spilling, leaking, pumping, pouring, emitting, emptying, discharging, injecting, escaping, leaching, dumping, or disposing into the environment (including the abandonment or discarding of barrels, containers, and other closed receptacles) of any hazardous chemical, extremely hazardous substance, or toxic chemical.

**(9) State**

The term "State" means any State of the United States, the District of Columbia, the Commonwealth of Puerto Rico, Guam, American Samoa, the United States Virgin Islands, the Northern Mariana Islands, and any other territory or possession over which the United States has jurisdiction.

**(10) Toxic chemical**

The term "toxic chemical" means a substance on the list described in section 11023(c) of this title.

(Pub.L. 99–499, Title III, § 329, Oct. 17, 1986, 100 Stat. 1757.)

### HISTORICAL AND STATUTORY NOTES

**Effective and Applicability Provisions**

1986 Acts

Section effective Oct. 17, 1986, see section 4 of Pub.L. 99–499, set out as a note under section 9601 of this title.

## § 11050. Authorization of appropriations

### [EPCRTKA § 330]

There are authorized to be appropriated for fiscal years beginning after September 30, 1986, such sums as may be necessary to carry out this chapter.

(Pub.L. 99–499, Title III, § 330, Oct. 17, 1986, 100 Stat. 1758.)

HISTORICAL AND STATUTORY NOTES

Effective and Applicability Provisions

1986 Acts

Section effective Oct. 17, 1986, see section 4 of Pub.L. 99–499, set out as a note under section 9601 of this title.

# POLLUTION PREVENTION

## POLLUTION PREVENTION ACT OF 1990 [PPA § ____]

**(42 U.S.C.A. §§ 13101 to 13109)**

## CHAPTER 133—POLLUTION PREVENTION

Sec.



### § 13101. Findings and policy

**[PPA § 6602]**

**(a) Findings**

The Congress finds that:

(1) The United States of America annually produces millions of tons of pollution and spends tens of billions of dollars per year controlling this pollution.

(2) There are significant opportunities for industry to reduce or prevent pollution at the source through cost-effective changes in production, operation, and raw materials use. Such changes offer industry substantial savings in reduced raw material, pollution control, and liability costs as well as help protect the environment and reduce risks to worker health and safety.

(3) The opportunities for source reduction are often not realized because existing regulations, and the industrial resources they require for compliance, focus upon treatment and disposal, rather than source reduction; existing regulations do not emphasize multi-media management of pollution; and businesses need information and technical assistance to overcome institutional barriers to the adoption of source reduction practices.

(4) Source reduction is fundamentally different and more desirable than waste management and pollution control. The Environmental Protection Agency needs to address the historical lack of attention to source reduction.

(5) As a first step in preventing pollution through source reduction, the Environmental Protection Agency must establish a source reduction program which collects and disseminates information, provides financial assistance to States, and implements the other activities provided for in this chapter.

**(b) Policy**

The Congress hereby declares it to be the national policy of the United States that pollution should be prevented or reduced at the source whenever feasible; pollution that cannot be prevented should be recycled in an environmentally safe manner, whenever feasible; pollution that cannot be prevented or recycled should be treated in an environmentally safe manner whenever feasible; and disposal or other release into the environment should be employed only as a last resort and should be conducted in an environmentally safe manner.

(Pub.L. 101–508, Title VI, § 6602, Nov. 5, 1990, 104 Stat. 1388–321.)

#### HISTORICAL AND STATUTORY NOTES

**References in Text**

This chapter, referred to in subsec. (a)(5), was in the original "this subtitle", meaning subtitle F (sections 6501, 6601 to 6610) of Title VI of Pub.L. 101–508, which is classified generally to this chapter. For complete classification of subtitle F to the Code, see Short Title of 1990 Acts note set out under this section and Tables.

**Short Title**

1990 Acts

Section 6601 of Pub.L. 101–508 provided that: This subtitle [subtitle F (sections 6501, 6601 to 6610) of Title VI of Pub.L. 101–508, enacting this chapter and section 4370c of this title] may be cited as the 'Pollution Prevention Act of 1990'."

**Federal Compliance with Right-to-Know Laws and Pollution Prevention Requirements**

For provisions requiring that all necessary actions be taken for the prevention of pollution with respect to the activities and facilities of each Federal agency, and for ensuring each such agency's compliance with pollution prevention and emergency planning and community right-to-know provisions established pursuant to all implementing regulations issued pursuant to chapters 116 [section 11001 et seq.] and 133 [section 13101 et seq.] of this title, and additional provisions for implementation, agency coordination, compliance, exemptions, etc., see Ex. Ord. No. 12856, Aug. 3, 1993, 58 F.R. 41981, set out as a note under section 11001 of this title.

## § 13102. Definitions

[PPA § 6603]

For purposes of this chapter—

(1) The term "Administrator" means the Administrator of the Environmental Protection Agency.

(2) The term "Agency" means the Environmental Protection Agency.

(3) The term "toxic chemical" means any substance on the list described in section 11023(c) of this title.

(4) The term "release" has the same meaning as provided by section 11049(8) of this title.

(5)(A) The term "source reduction" means any practice which—

(i) reduces the amount of any hazardous substance, pollutant, or contaminant entering any waste stream or otherwise released into the environment (including fugitive emissions) prior to recycling, treatment, or disposal; and

(ii) reduces the hazards to public health and the environment associated with the release of such substances, pollutants, or contaminants.

The term includes equipment or technology modifications, process or procedure modifications, reformulation or redesign of products, substitution of raw materials, and improvements in housekeeping, maintenance, training, or inventory control.

(B) The term "source reduction" does not include any practice which alters the physical, chemical, or biological characteristics or the volume of a hazardous substance, pollutant, or contaminant through a process or activity which itself is not integral to and necessary for the production of a product or the providing of a service.

(6) The term "multi-media" means water, air, and land.

(7) The term "SIC codes" refers to the 2-digit code numbers used for classification of economic activity in the Standard Industrial Classification Manual.

(Pub.L. 101–508, Title VI, § 6603, Nov. 5, 1990, 104 Stat. 1388–321.)

## § 13103. EPA activities

[PPA § 6604]

### (a) Authorities

The Administrator shall establish in the Agency an office to carry out the functions of the Administrator under this chapter. The office shall be independent of the Agency's single-medium program offices but shall have the authority to review and advise such offices on their activities to promote a multi-media approach to source reduction. The office shall be under the direction of such officer of the Agency as the Administrator shall designate.

### (b) Functions

The Administrator shall develop and implement a strategy to promote source reduction. As part of the strategy, the Administrator shall—

(1) establish standard methods of measurement of source reduction;

(2) ensure that the Agency considers the effect of its existing and proposed programs on source reduction efforts and shall review regulations of the Agency prior and subsequent to their proposal to determine their effect on source reduction;

(3) coordinate source reduction activities in each Agency Office [1] and coordinate with appropriate offices to promote source reduction practices in other Federal agencies, and generic research and development on techniques and processes which have broad applicability;

(4) develop improved methods of coordinating, streamlining and assuring public access to data collected under Federal environmental statutes;

(5) facilitate the adoption of source reduction techniques by businesses. This strategy shall include the use of the Source Reduction Clearinghouse and State matching grants provided in this chapter to foster the exchange of information regarding source reduction techniques, the dissemination of such information to businesses, and the provision of technical assistance to businesses. The strategy shall also consider the capabilities of various businesses to make use of source reduction techniques;

(6) identify, where appropriate, measurable goals which reflect the policy of this chapter, the tasks necessary to achieve the goals, dates at which the principal tasks are to be accomplished, required resources, organizational responsibilities, and the means by which progress in meeting the goals will be measured;

(8) [2] establish an advisory panel of technical experts comprised of representatives from industry, the States, and public interest groups, to advise the Administrator on ways to improve collection and dissemination of data;

(9) establish a training program on source reduction opportunities, including workshops and guidance documents, for State and Federal permit issuance, enforcement, and inspection officials working within all agency program offices.[3]

(10) identify and make recommendations to Congress to eliminate barriers to source reduction including the use of incentives and disincentives;

(11) identify opportunities to use Federal procurement to encourage source reduction;

(12) develop, test and disseminate model source reduction auditing procedures designed to highlight source reduction opportunities; and

(13) establish an annual award program to recognize a company or companies which operate outstanding or innovative source reduction programs.

(Pub.L. 101–508, Title VI, § 6604, Nov. 5, 1990, 104 Stat. 1388–322.)

[1] So in original. Probably should not be capitalized.

[2] So in original. Subsec. (b) enacted without a paragraph (7).

[3] So in original. The period probably should be a semicolon.

## § 13104. Grants to States for State technical assistance programs

[PPA § 6605]

### (a) General authority

The Administrator shall make matching grants to States for programs to promote the use of source reduction techniques by businesses.

### (b) Criteria

When evaluating the requests for grants under this section, the Administrator shall consider, among other things, whether the proposed State program would accomplish the following:

(1) Make specific technical assistance available to businesses seeking information about source reduction opportunities, including funding for experts to provide onsite technical advice to business [1] seeking assistance and to assist in the development of source reduction plans.

(2) Target assistance to businesses for whom lack of information is an impediment to source reduction.

(3) Provide training in source reduction techniques. Such training may be provided through local engineering schools or any other appropriate means.

### (c) Matching funds

Federal funds used in any State program under this section shall provide no more than 50 per centum of the funds made available to a State in each year of that State's participation in the program.

### (d) Effectiveness

The Administrator shall establish appropriate means for measuring the effectiveness of the State grants made under this section in promoting the use of source reduction techniques by businesses.

### (e) Information

States receiving grants under this section shall make information generated under the grants available to the Administrator.

(Pub.L. 101–508, Title VI, § 6605, Nov. 5, 1990, 104 Stat. 1388–323.)

[1] So in original. Probably should be "businesses".

## § 13105. Source Reduction Clearinghouse

[PPA § 6606]

### (a) Authority

The Administrator shall establish a Source Reduction Clearinghouse to compile information including a computer data base which contains information on management, technical, and operational approaches to source reduction. The Administrator shall use the clearinghouse to—

(1) serve as a center for source reduction technology transfer;

(2) mount active outreach and education programs by the States to further the adoption of source reduction technologies; and

(3) collect and compile information reported by States receiving grants under section 13104 of this title on the operation and success of State source reduction programs.

### (b) Public availability

The Administrator shall make available to the public such information on source reduction as is gathered pursuant to this chapter and such other pertinent information and analysis regarding source reduction as may be available to the Administrator. The data base shall permit entry and retrieval of information to any person.

(Pub.L. 101–508, Title VI, § 6606, Nov. 5, 1990, 104 Stat. 1388–324.)

## § 13106. Source reduction and recycling data collection

[PPA § 6607]

### (a) Reporting requirements

Each owner or operator of a facility required to file an annual toxic chemical release form under section 11023 of this title for any toxic chemical shall include with each such annual filing a toxic chemical source reduction and recycling report for the preceeding [1] calendar year. The toxic chemical source reduction and recycling report shall cover each toxic chemical required to be reported in the annual toxic chemical release form filed by the owner or operator under section 11023(c) of this title. This section shall take effect with the annual report filed under section 11023 of this title for the first full calendar year beginning after November 5, 1990.

### (b) Items included in report

The toxic chemical source reduction and recycling report required under subsection (a) of this section shall set forth each of the following on a facility-by-facility basis for each toxic chemical:

(1) The quantity of the chemical entering any waste stream (or otherwise released into the environment) prior to recycling, treatment, or disposal during the calendar year for which the report is filed and the percentage change from the previous year. The quantity reported shall not include any amount reported under paragraph (7). When actual measurements of the quantity of a toxic chemical entering the waste streams are not readily available, reasonable estimates should be made based on best engineering judgment.

(2) The amount of the chemical from the facility which is recycled (at the facility or elsewhere) during such calendar year, the percentage change from the previous year, and the process of recycling used.

(3) The source reduction practices used with respect to that chemical during such year at the facility. Such practices shall be reported in accordance with the following categories unless the Administrator finds other categories to be more appropriate:

(A) Equipment, technology, process, or procedure modifications.

(B) Reformulation or redesign of products.

(C) Substitution of raw materials.

(D) Improvement in management, training, inventory control, materials handling, or other general operational phases of industrial facilities.

(4) The amount expected to be reported under paragraph[2] (1) and (2) for the two calendar years immediately following the calendar year for which the report is filed. Such amount shall be expressed as a percentage change from the amount reported in paragraphs (1) and (2).

(5) A ratio of production in the reporting year to production in the previous year. The ratio should be calculated to most closely reflect all activities involving the toxic chemical. In specific industrial classifications subject to this section, where a feedstock or some variable other than production is the primary influence on waste characteristics or volumes, the report may provide an index based on that primary variable for each toxic chemical. The Administrator is encouraged to develop production indexes to accommodate individual industries for use on a voluntary basis.

(6) The techniques which were used to identify source reduction opportunities. Techniques listed should include, but are not limited to, employee recommendations, external and internal audits, participative team management, and material balance audits. Each type of source reduction listed under paragraph (3) should be associated with the techniques or multiples of techniques used to identify the source reduction technique.

(7) The amount of any toxic chemical released into the environment which resulted from a catastrophic event, remedial action, or other one-time event, and is not associated with production processes during the reporting year.

(8) The amount of the chemical from the facility which is treated (at the facility or elsewhere) during such calendar year and the percentage change from the previous year. For the first year of reporting under this subsection, comparison with the previous year is required only to the extent such information is available.

**(c) SARA provisions**

The provisions of sections 11042, 11045(c), and 11046 of this title shall apply to the reporting requirements of this section in the same manner as to the reports required under section 11023 of this title. The Administrator may modify the form required for purposes of reporting information under section 11023 of this title to the extent he deems necessary to include the additional information required under this section.

**(d) Additional optional information**

Any person filing a report under this section for any year may include with the report additional information regarding source reduction, recycling, and other pollution control techniques in earlier years.

**(e) Availability of data**

Subject to section 11042 of this title, the Administrator shall make data collected under this section publicly available in the same manner as the data collected under section 11023 of this title.

(Pub.L. 101–508, Title VI, § 6607, Nov. 5, 1990, 104 Stat. 1388–324.)

1 So in original. Probably should be "preceding".

2 So in original. Probably should be "paragraphs".

### HISTORICAL AND STATUTORY NOTES

**References in Text**

SARA, referred to in the heading of subsec. (c), means the Superfund Amendments and Reauthorization Act of 1986, Pub.L. 99–499, Oct. 17, 1986, 100 Stat. 1613, as amended. For complete classification of this Act to the Code, see Short Title of 1986 Amendments note set out under section 9601 of this title.

## § 13107. EPA report

[PPA § 6608]

**(a) Biennial reports**

The Administrator shall provide Congress with a report within eighteen months after November 5,

1990, and biennially thereafter, containing a detailed description of the actions taken to implement the strategy to promote source reduction developed under section 13103(b) of this title and of the results of such actions. The report shall include an assessment of the effectiveness of the clearinghouse and grant program established under this chapter in promoting the goals of the strategy, and shall evaluate data gaps and data duplication with respect to data collected under Federal environmental statutes.

**(b) Subsequent reports**

Each biennial report submitted under subsection (a) of this section after the first report shall contain each of the following:

(1) An analysis of the data collected under section 13106 of this title on an industry-by-industry basis for not less than five SIC codes or other categories as the Administrator deems appropriate. The analysis shall begin with those SIC codes or other categories of facilities which generate the largest quantities of toxic chemical waste. The analysis shall include an evaluation of trends in source reduction by industry, firm size, production, or other useful means. Each such subsequent report shall cover five SIC codes or other categories which were not covered in a prior report until all SIC codes or other categories have been covered.

(2) An analysis of the usefulness and validity of the data collected under section 13106 of this title for measuring trends in source reduction and the adoption of source reduction by business.

(3) Identification of regulatory and nonregulatory barriers to source reduction, and of opportunities for using existing regulatory programs, and incentives and disincentives to promote and assist source reduction.

(4) Identification of industries and pollutants that require priority assistance in multi-media source reduction [1]

(5) Recommendations as to incentives needed to encourage investment and research and development in source reduction.

(6) Identification of opportunities and development of priorities for research and development in source reduction methods and techniques.

(7) An evaluation of the cost and technical feasibility, by industry and processes, of source reduction opportunities and current activities and an identification of any industries for which there are significant barriers to source reduction with an analysis of the basis of this identification.

(8) An evaluation of methods of coordinating, streamlining, and improving public access to data collected under Federal environmental statutes.

(9) An evaluation of data gaps and data duplication with respect to data collected under Federal environmental statutes.

In the report following the first biennial report provided for under this subsection, paragraphs (3) through (9) may be included at the discretion of the Administrator.

(Pub.L. 101–508, Title VI, § 6608, Nov. 5, 1990, 104 Stat. 1388–326.)

[1] So in original. Probably should be followed by a period.

### HISTORICAL AND STATUTORY NOTES

**References in Text**

Section 13103(b) of this title, referred to in subsec. (a), was in the original "section 4(b)" and was translated as reading "section 6604(b)", meaning section 6604(b) of Pub.L. 101–508, because Pub.L. 101–508 has no section 4 but section 6604(b) of Pub.L. 101–508 relates to development of a strategy to promote source reduction.

**Codifications**

Reference in the original text of subsec. (a) of this section to "section 4(b)" has been translated in the codified text as "section 13103(b) of this title" to reflect the probable intent of Congress.

## § 13108. Savings provisions

**[PPA § 6609]**

(a) Nothing in this chapter shall be construed to modify or interfere with the implementation of title III of the Superfund Amendments and Reauthorization Act of 1986 [42 U.S.C.A. § 11001 et seq.].

(b) Nothing contained in this chapter shall be construed, interpreted or applied to supplant, displace, preempt or otherwise diminish the responsibilities and liabilities under other State or Federal law, whether statutory or common.

(Pub.L. 101–508, Title VI, § 6609, Nov. 5, 1990, 104 Stat. 1388–327.)

### HISTORICAL AND STATUTORY NOTES

**References in Text**

Title III of the Superfund Amendments and Reauthorization Act of 1986, referred to in subsec. (a), is Title III (section 300 et seq.) of Pub.L. 99–499, Oct. 17, 1986, 100 Stat. 1728, known as the Emergency Planning and Community Right–To–Know Act of 1986, which is classified principally to chapter 116 (section 11001 et seq.) of this title. For complete classification of the Emergency Planning and Community Right–To–Know Act of 1986 to the Code, see Short Title of 1986 Acts note set out under section 11001 of this title and Tables.

## § 13109. Authorization of appropriations

**[PPA § 6610]**

There is authorized to be appropriated to the Administrator $8,000,000 for each of the fiscal years 1991, 1992 and 1993 for functions carried out under this chapter (other than State Grants [1]), and $8,000,000 for each of the fiscal years 1991, 1992, and

1993, for grant programs to States issued pursuant to section 13104 of this title.

(Pub.L. 101–508, Title VI, § 6610, Nov. 5, 1990, 104 Stat. 1388–327.)

[1] So in original. Probably should not be capitalized.

# TITLE 43
# PUBLIC LANDS

## DISPOSAL OF PUBLIC LANDS

## RECREATION AND PUBLIC PURPOSES ACT [RPPA § 3]

**(43 U.S.C.A. § 869–2)**

## CHAPTER 20—RESERVATIONS AND GRANTS TO STATES FOR PUBLIC PURPOSES



### § 869. Disposal of lands for public or recreational purposes

**(a) Application; conditions; classification; restoration if not applied for**

The Secretary of the Interior upon application filed by a duly qualified applicant under section 869–1 of this title may, in the manner prescribed by sections 869 to 869–4 of this title, dispose of any public lands to a State, Territory, county, municipality, or other State, Territorial, or Federal instrumentality or political subdivision for any public purposes, or to a nonprofit corporation or nonprofit association for any recreational or any public purpose consistent with its articles of incorporation or other creating authority. Before the land may be disposed of under sections 869 to 869–4 of this title it must be shown to the satisfaction of the Secretary that the land is to be used for an established or definitely proposed project, that the land involved is not of national significance nor more than is reasonably necessary for the proposed use, and that for proposals of over 640 acres comprehensive land use plans and zoning regulations applicable to the area in which the public lands to be disposed of are located have been adopted by the appropriate State or local authority. The Secretary shall provide an opportunity for participation by affected citizens in disposals under sections 869 to 869–4 of this title, including public hearings or meetings where he deems it appropriate to provide public comments, and shall hold at least one public meeting on any proposed disposal of more than six hundred forty acres under sections 869 to 869–4 of this title. The Secretary may classify public lands in Alaska for disposition under sections 869 to 869–4 of this title. Lands so classified may not be appropriated under any other public land law unless the Secretary revises such classification or authorizes the disposition of an interest in the lands under other applicable law. If, within eighteen months following such classification, no application has been filed for the purpose for which the lands have been so classified, then the Secretary shall restore such lands to appropriation under the applicable public land laws.

**(b) Acreage limitations**

Conveyances made in any one calendar year shall be limited as follows:

(i) For recreational purposes:

(A) To any State or the State park agency or any other agency having jurisdiction over the State park system of such State designated by the Governor of that State as its sole representative for acceptance of lands under this provision, hereinafter referred to as the State, or to any political subdivision of such State, six thousand four hundred acres, and such additional acreage as may be needed for small roadside parks and rest sites of not more than ten acres each.

(B) To any nonprofit corporation or nonprofit association, six hundred and forty acres.

(C) No more than twenty-five thousand six hundred acres may be conveyed for recreational purposes under sections 869 to 869–4 of this title in any one State per calendar year. Should any State or political subdivision, however, fail to secure, in any one year, six thousand four hundred acres, not counting lands for small roadside parks and rest sites, conveyances may be made thereafter if pursuant to an application on file with the Secretary of the Interior on or before the last day of said year and to the extent that the conveyance would not have exceeded the limitations of said year.

**(ii)** For public purposes other than recreation:

**(A)** To any State or agency or instrumentality thereof, for any one program, six hundred and forty acres.

**(B)** To any political subdivision of a State, six hundred and forty acres.

**(C)** To any nonprofit corporation or nonprofit association, six hundred and forty acres.

**(c) Lands withdrawn in aid of functions of a department, agency, State, etc.; lands excepted from disposal**

Where the lands have been withdrawn in aid of a function of a Federal department or agency other than the Department of the Interior, or of a State, Territory, county, municipality, water district, or other local governmental subdivision or agency, the Secretary of the Interior may make disposals under sections 869 to 869–4 of this title only with the consent of such Federal department or agency, or of such State, Territory, or local governmental unit. Nothing in sections 869 to 869–4 of this title shall be construed to apply to lands in any national forest, national park, or national monument, or national wildlife refuge, or to any Indian lands or lands set aside or held for the use or benefit of Indians, including lands over which jurisdiction has been transferred to the Department of the Interior by Executive order for the use of Indians, or, except insofar as sections 869 to 869–4 of this title apply to leases of land to States and counties and to State and Federal instrumentalities and political subdivisions and to municipal corporations, to the revested Oregon and California Railroad grant lands and the reconveyed Coos Bay Wagon Road grant lands in the State of Oregon. Nor shall any disposition be made under sections 869 to 869–4 of this title for any use authorized under any other law, except for a use authorized under sections 682a to 682e of this title.

(June 14, 1926, c. 578, § 1, 44 Stat. 741; June 4, 1954, c. 263, 68 Stat. 173; June 23, 1959, Pub.L. 86–66, § 2, 73 Stat. 110; Sept. 21, 1959, Pub.L. 86–292, § 1, 73 Stat. 571; Sept. 13, 1960, Pub.L. 86–755, 74 Stat. 899; Oct. 21, 1976, Pub.L. 94–579, Title II, § 212(a), (b), 90 Stat. 2759.)

### HISTORICAL AND STATUTORY NOTES

**References in Text**

Sections 682a to 682e of this title, referred to in subsec. (c), were repealed by Pub.L. 94–579, Title VII, § 702, Oct. 21, 1976, 90 Stat. 2787.

**Effective and Applicability Provisions**

1960 Acts

Pub.L. 86–755 provided in part that the amendment of subsec. (b)(i)(A) shall be effective Sept. 21, 1959.

**Savings Provisions**

Amendment by Pub.L. 94–579 not to be construed as terminating any valid lease, permit, patent, etc., existing on Oct. 21, 1976, see section 701 of Pub.L. 94–579, set out as a note under section 1701 of this title.

**Short Title**

1988 Amendments

Pub.L. 100–648, § 1, Nov. 10, 1988, 102 Stat. 3813, provided that: "This Act [amending section 869–2 of this title, and enacting provisions set out as notes under section 869–2 of this title] may be cited as the 'Recreation and Public Purposes Amendment Act of 1988'."

1926 Acts

Act June 14, 1926, c. 578, 44 Stat. 741, which enacted sections 869 to 869–4 of this title, is popularly known as the "Recreation and Public Purposes Act".

## § 869–1. Sale or lease to State or nonprofit organization; reservation of mineral deposits; termination of lease for nonuse

The Secretary of the Interior may after due consideration as to the power value of the land, whether or not withdrawn therefor, (a) sell such land to the State, Territory, county, or other State, Territorial, or Federal instrumentality or political subdivision in which the lands are situated, or to a nearby municipal corporation in the same State or Territory, for the purpose for which the land has been classified, and conveyances of such land for historic-monument purposes or recreational purposes under this section shall be made without monetary consideration, while conveyances for any other purpose under this section shall be made at a price to be fixed by the Secretary of the Interior through appraisal or otherwise, after taking into consideration the purpose for which the lands are to be used, (b) lease such land to the State, Territory, county, or other State, Territorial, or Federal instrumentality or political subdivision in which the lands are situated, or to a nearby municipal corporation in the same State or Territory, for the purpose for which the land has been classified, at a reasonable annual rental, except that leases of such lands for recreational purposes shall be made without monetary consideration, for a period up to twenty-five years, and, at the discretion of the Secretary, with a privilege of renewal for a like period, (c) sell such land to a nonprofit corporation or nonprofit association, for the purpose for which the land has been classified, at a price to be fixed by the Secretary of the Interior through appraisal, after taking into consideration the purpose for which the lands are to be used, or (d) lease such land to a nonprofit corporation or nonprofit association at a reasonable annual rental, for a period up to twenty years, and, at the discretion of the Secretary, with a privilege of renewal for a like period. Each patent or lease so issued shall contain a reservation to the United States of all mineral deposits in the lands conveyed or leased and of the right to mine and remove the same, under applicable laws and regulations to be established by the Secretary. Each lease shall contain a provision for its termination upon a finding by the Secretary that the land has not been used by the lessee for the purpose specified in the lease for such period, not over five years, as may be specified in the lease, or that such land or any part thereof is being devoted to another use.

(June 14, 1926, c. 578, § 2, as added June 4, 1954, c. 263, 68 Stat. 174, and amended June 20, 1966, Pub.L. 89–457, § 1, 80 Stat. 210; Oct. 21, 1976, Pub.L. 94–579, Title II, § 212(c), (d), 90 Stat. 2760.)

### HISTORICAL AND STATUTORY NOTES

**Savings Provisions**

Amendment by Pub.L. 94–579 not to be construed as terminating any valid lease, permit, patent, etc., existing on Oct. 21, 1976, see section 701 of Pub.L. 94–579, set out as a note under section 1701 of this title.

**Prior Provisions**

Provisions similar to those comprising this section were formerly contained in section 869 of this title. See 1954 Amendment note set out under that section. Those prior provisions did not require, as in this section, the Secretary of the Interior to take into account the possible power value of the lands, whether withdrawn therefor, or not, before authorizing any disposal of them under section 869 of this title; did not provide, as in this section, for the sale or lease of those lands to Federal instrumentalities, to Territories and to political subdivisions other than States, counties, and municipalities, and to nonprofit corporations and associations; and did not provide, as in this section, that conveyances of that land for historic-monument purposes should be made without monetary consideration. See section 869 of this title.

**Period of Leases**

Section 2 of Pub.L. 89–457 provided that: "Upon application by a lessee holding a lease under the Recreation and Public Purposes Act [sections 869 to 869–4 of this title] the Secretary of the Interior may enter into a new lease for a term not to exceed twenty-five years from the date of the new lease."

## § 869–2. Conditions of transfer by grantee; solid waste disposal

[RPPA § 3]

**(a) Conditions of transfer by grantee**

Title to lands conveyed by the Government under sections 869 to 869–4 of this title may not be transferred by the grantee or its successor except, with the consent of the Secretary of the Interior, to a transferee which would be a qualified grantee under section 869–1(a) or 869–1(c) of this title and subject to the acreage limitation contained in section 869(b) of this title. A grantee or its successor may not change the use specified in the conveyance to another or additional use except, with the consent of the Secretary, to a use for which such grantee or its successor could obtain a conveyance under sections 869 to 869–4 of this title. If at any time after the lands are conveyed by the Government, the grantee or its successor attempts to transfer title to or control over these lands to another or the lands are devoted to a use other than that for which the lands were conveyed, without the consent of the Secretary, title to the lands shall revert to the United States.

**(b) New disposal sites**

(1) Notwithstanding the provisions of subsection (a) of this section, if the Secretary receives an application for conveyance of land under sections 869 to 869–4 of this title for the express purpose of solid waste disposal or for another purpose which the Secretary finds may include the disposal, placement, or release of any hazardous substance, the Secretary may convey such land subject only to the provisions of this subsection.

(2) Prior to issuance of any conveyance of land under this subsection the Secretary shall investigate the land covered by an application for such conveyance to determine whether or not any hazardous substance is present on such land. Such investigation shall include a review of any available records as to the use of such land and all appropriate analysis of the soil, water and air associated with such land. No land shall be conveyed under this subsection if such investigation indicates that any hazardous substance is present on such land.

(3) No application for conveyance under this subsection shall be acted on by the Secretary until the applicant has furnished evidence, satisfactory to the Secretary, that a copy of the application and information concerning the proposed use of the land covered by the application has been provided to the Environmental Protection Agency and to all other State and Federal agencies with responsibility for enforcement of State and Federal laws applicable to lands used for the disposal, placement, or release of solid waste or any hazardous substance.

(4) No application for conveyance under this subsection shall be acted on by the Secretary until the applicant has given a warranty that use of the land covered by the application will be consistent with all applicable State and Federal laws, including laws dealing with the disposal, placement, or release of hazardous substances, and that the applicant will hold the United States harmless from any liability that may arise out of any violation of any such law.

(5) A conveyance under this subsection shall be made to the extent that the applicant has demonstrated to the Secretary that the land covered by an application meets all applicable State and local requirements and is appropriate in character and reasonable in acreage in order to meet an existing or reasonably anticipated need for solid waste disposal or

for another proposed use that the Secretary finds may include the disposal, placement, or release of any hazardous substance.

(6) A conveyance under this subsection shall be subject to the following conditions:

(A) Except as otherwise provided in subparagraphs (B) and (D) of this paragraph, the document of conveyance shall provide that the lands conveyed under this subsection shall revert to the United States, unless substantially all of the lands have been used, on or before the date five years after the date of conveyance, for the purpose or purposes specified in the application, or for other use or uses authorized under subsection (a) of this section with the consent of the Secretary.

(B) In the event that at any time after such conveyance any portion of such lands has not been used for the purpose or purposes specified in the application, and the party to whom such lands were conveyed by the Secretary shall transfer ownership of such unused portion to any other party, the party to whom such lands were conveyed by the Secretary shall be liable to pay the Secretary, on behalf of the United States, the fair market value of such transferred portion as of the date of such transfer, including the value of any improvements thereon. Subject to appropriations, all amounts received by the Secretary under this subparagraph shall be retained by the Secretary and used for the management of public lands and shall remain available until expended.

(C) Pricing for conveyances of land under this subsection shall be in accordance with the provisions of section 869–1 of this title, except that no compensation shall be required for the inclusion of only the limited reverter specified in this paragraph.

(D) Each patent issued under this subsection shall specify that no portion of the lands covered by such patent shall under any circumstances revert to the United States if such portion has been used for solid waste disposal or for any other purpose that the Secretary finds may result in the disposal, placement, or release of any hazardous substance.

(7) For purposes of this section the term "hazardous substance" has the same meaning as such term has when used in the Comprehensive Environmental Response, Compensation, and Liability Act (42 U.S.C. 9601 et seq.).

**(c) Existing disposal sites**

(1) Upon the application or with the concurrence of any party to whom the Secretary, prior to November 10, 1988, conveyed land under sections 869 to 869–4 of this title, the Secretary may renounce the reversionary interests of the United States in such land, or portion thereof, if the Secretary finds that such land, or portion thereof, has been used for solid waste disposal or for any other purpose which the Secretary finds may result in the disposal, placement, or release of any hazardous substance, and the Secretary may rescind any portion of any patent or other instrument of conveyance inconsistent with such renunciation. After such renunciation, affected lands shall not under any circumstances revert to the United States by the operation of law, and shall cease to be subject to the provisions of subsection (a) of this section.

(2) Upon the application or with the concurrence of a party to whom the Secretary, prior to November 10, 1988, leased lands pursuant to sections 869 to 869–4 of this title, the Secretary may convey in fee the lands covered by such lease or any portion thereof which have been used for solid waste disposal or for any other purpose that the Secretary finds may result in the disposal, placement, or release of any hazardous substance. Notwithstanding any other provision of sections 869 to 869–4 of this title, a patent issued pursuant to this paragraph shall not contain a reverter provision and the lands covered by such patent shall not under any circumstances revert to the United States by operation of law after the issuance of such patent and shall not be subject to the provisions of subsection (a) of this section.

(June 14, 1926, c. 578, § 3, as added June 4, 1954, c. 263, 68 Stat. 175, and amended Sept. 21, 1959, Pub.L. 86–292, § 2, 73 Stat. 571; Nov. 10, 1988, Pub.L. 100–648, § 2, 102 Stat. 3813.)

## HISTORICAL AND STATUTORY NOTES

### References in Text

The Comprehensive Environmental Response, Compensation, and Liability Act, referred to in subsec. (b), is Pub.L. 96–510, Dec. 11, 1980, 94 Stat. 2767, as amended, which is classified principally to chapter 103 (section 9601 et seq.) of Title 42, The Public Health and Welfare. For complete classification of this Act to the Code, see Short Title note set out under section 9601 of Title 42 and Tables.

### Savings Provisions

Section 3 of Pub.L. 100–648 provided that: "Nothing in this Act or the amendments made thereby [amending this section and enacting provisions set out as notes under this section] shall be construed to affect the applicability and operation of the Comprehensive Environmental Response, Compensation, and Liability Act (42 U.S.C. 9601 et seq.) as amended, and the Resource Conservation and Recovery Act of 1976 (42 U.S.C. 6901 et seq.), as amended."

### Prior Provisions

Prior provisions on the subject of reverter were formerly contained in section 869 of this title. See 1954 Amendment note set out under that section. Those prior provisions permanently restricted the lands conveyed to a single use, and did not provide, as in this section, for transfer by the original grantee or its successor.

**Congressional Review of Conveyance of Land or Renunciation of Reversionary Interests**

Section 4 of Pub.L. 100-648 provided that:

"(a) The Secretary shall not make any conveyance of land or renunciation of reversionary interests under this Act [amending this section and enacting provisions set out as notes under this section] until he has published in the Federal Register regulations implementing this Act and until sixty days (not counting days on which the House of Representatives or the Senate has adjourned for more than three days) after these regulations have been submitted to the Committee on Energy and Natural Resources of the Senate and the Committee on Interior and Insular Affairs [now Committee on Natural Resources] of the House of Representatives.

"(b) During the first three years after enactment of this Act [November 10, 1988] the Secretary shall not make any conveyance of land or renunciation of reversionary interests under this Act until thirty days (not counting days on which the House of Representatives or the Senate has adjourned for more than three days) after notice of intention to do so has been submitted to the Committee on Energy and Natural Resources of the Senate and the Committee on Interior and Insular Affairs [now Committee on Natural Resources] of the House of Representatives."

[Any reference in any provision of law enacted before Jan. 4, 1995, to the Committee on Natural Resources of the House of Representatives treated as referring to the Committee on Resources of the House of Representatives, see section 1(a)(8) of Pub.L. 104-14, set out as a note preceding section 21 of Title 2, The Congress.]

## § 869-3. Authority for transfers; applicability of section 869-2 to prior patents; termination of restrictions

The Secretary may authorize transfers of title or changes in use in accordance with the provisions of section 869-2 of this title with respect to any patent heretofore issued under any Act upon application by a patentee qualified to obtain a conveyance under section 869-1(a) or 869-1(c) of this title. If the Secretary, pursuant to such an application, authorizes such transfer or use, all reverter provisions and other limitations on transfer or use, under sections 869 to 869-4 of this title or any other Act affecting the lands involved, shall cease to be in effect twenty-five years after the Secretary authorizes the transfer or use for a changed or additional purpose under the provisions of this section.

(June 14, 1926, c. 578, § 4, as added June 4, 1954, c. 263, 68 Stat. 175.)

## § 869-4. Disposition of moneys received from or on account of revested Oregon and California Railroad grant lands or reconveyed Coos Bay Wagon Road grant lands

All moneys received from or on account of any revested Oregon and California Railroad grant lands or reconveyed Coos Bay Wagon Road grant lands under sections 869 to 869-4 of this title shall be deposited respectively in the Oregon and California land-grant fund and the Coos Bay Wagon Road grant fund, and shall be applied in the manner prescribed respectively by section 1181f of this title, and by the Act of May 24, 1939 (53 Stat. 753).

(June 14, 1926, c. 578, § 6, as added June 23, 1959, Pub.L. 86-66, § 3, 73 Stat. 111.)

### HISTORICAL AND STATUTORY NOTES

**References in Text**

The Act of May 24, 1939, referred to in the text, is Act May 24, 1939, c. 144, 53 Stat. 753, which is not classified to the Code.

# FEDERAL LAND POLICY AND MANAGEMENT

## FEDERAL LAND POLICY AND MANAGEMENT ACT OF 1976 [FLPMA § ____]

**(43 U.S.C.A. §§ 1701 to 1785)**

## CHAPTER 35—FEDERAL LAND POLICY AND MANAGEMENT

SUBCHAPTER I—GENERAL PROVISIONS

**Sec.**

1701. Congressional declaration of policy.
1702. Definitions.

SUBCHAPTER II—LAND USE PLANNING AND LAND ACQUISITION AND DISPOSITION

1711. Continuing inventory and identification of public lands; preparation and maintenance.
1712. Land use plans.
1713. Sales of public land tracts.
1714. Withdrawals of lands.
1715. Acquisitions of public lands and access over non-Federal lands to National Forest System units.
1716. Exchanges of public lands or interests therein within the National Forest System.
1717. Qualifications of conveyees.
1718. Documents of conveyance; terms, covenants, etc.
1719. Mineral interests; reservation and conveyance requirements and procedures.
1720. Coordination by Secretary of the Interior with State and local governments.
1721. Conveyances of public lands to States, local governments, etc.
1722. Sale of public lands subject to unintentional trespass.
1723. Temporary revocation authority.

SUBCHAPTER III—ADMINISTRATION

1731. Bureau of Land Management.
1732. Management of use, occupancy, and development of public lands.
1733. Enforcement authority.
1734. Fees, charges, and commissions.
1734a. Availability of excess fees.
1735. Forfeitures and deposits.
1736. Working capital fund.
1736a. Revolving fund derived from disposal of salvage timber.
1737. Implementation provisions.
1738. Contracts for surveys and resource protection; renewals; funding requirements.
1739. Advisory councils.
1740. Rules and regulations.
1741. Annual reports.
1742. Search, rescue, and protection forces; emergency situations authorizing hiring.

**Sec.**

SUBCHAPTER III—ADMINISTRATION—Cont'd

1743. Disclosure of financial interests by officers or employees.
1744. Recordation of mining claims.
1745. Disclaimer of interest in lands.
1746. Correction of conveyance documents.
1747. Loans to States and political subdivisions; purposes; amounts; allocation; terms and conditions; interest rate; security; limitations; forebearance for benefit of borrowers; recordkeeping requirements; discrimination prohibited; deposit of receipts.
1748. Funding requirements.

SUBCHAPTER IV—RANGE MANAGEMENT

1751. Grazing fees; feasibility study; contents; submission of report; annual distribution and use of range betterment funds; nature of distributions.
1752. Grazing leases and permits.
1753. Grazing advisory boards.

SUBCHAPTER V—RIGHTS-OF-WAY

1761. Grant, issue, or renewal of rights-of-way.
1762. Roads.
1763. Right-of-way corridors; criteria and procedures applicable for designation.
1764. General requirements.
1765. Terms and conditions.
1766. Suspension or termination; grounds; procedures applicable.
1767. Rights-of-way for Federal departments and agencies.
1768. Conveyance of lands covered by right-of-way; terms and conditions.
1769. Existing right-of-way or right-of-use unaffected; exceptions; rights-of-way for railroad and appurtenant communication facilities; applicability of existing terms and conditions.
1770. Applicability of provisions to other Federal laws.
1771. Coordination of applications.

SUBCHAPTER VI—DESIGNATED MANAGEMENT AREAS

1781. California Desert Conservation Area.
1782. Bureau of Land Management Wilderness Study.
1783. Yaquina Head Outstanding Natural Area.

**Related Provisions**

*See, also, Coastal Zone Management, 16 U.S.C.A. § 1451 et seq., ante; Rural Environmental Conservation Program, 16 U.S.C.A. § 1501 et seq., ante; and Soil and Water Resources, 16 U.S.C.A. § 2001 et seq., ante.*

## SUBCHAPTER I—GENERAL PROVISIONS

### § 1701. Congressional declaration of policy [FLPMA § 102]

(a) The Congress declares that it is the policy of the United States that—

(1) the public lands be retained in Federal ownership, unless as a result of the land use planning procedure provided for in this Act, it is determined that disposal of a particular parcel will serve the national interest;

(2) the national interest will be best realized if the public lands and their resources are periodically and systematically inventoried and their present and future use is projected through a land use planning process coordinated with other Federal and State planning efforts;

(3) public lands not previously designated for any specific use and all existing classifications of public lands that were effected by executive action or statute before October 21, 1976, be reviewed in accordance with the provisions of this Act;

(4) the Congress exercise its constitutional authority to withdraw or otherwise designate or dedicate Federal lands for specified purposes and that Congress delineate the extent to which the Executive may withdraw lands without legislative action;

(5) in administering public land statutes and exercising discretionary authority granted by them, the Secretary be required to establish comprehensive rules and regulations after considering the views of the general public; and to structure adjudication procedures to assure adequate third party participation, objective administrative review of initial decisions, and expeditious decisionmaking;

(6) judicial review of public land adjudication decisions be provided by law;

(7) goals and objectives be established by law as guidelines for public land use planning, and that management be on the basis of multiple use and sustained yield unless otherwise specified by law;

(8) the public lands be managed in a manner that will protect the quality of scientific, scenic, historical, ecological, environmental, air and atmospheric, water resource, and archeological values; that, where appropriate, will preserve and protect certain public lands in their natural condition; that will provide food and habitat for fish and wildlife and domestic animals; and that will provide for outdoor recreation and human occupancy and use;

(9) the United States receive fair market value of the use of the public lands and their resources unless otherwise provided for by statute;

(10) uniform procedures for any disposal of public land, acquisition of non-Federal land for public purposes, and the exchange of such lands be established by statute, requiring each disposal, acquisition, and exchange to be consistent with the prescribed mission of the department or agency involved, and reserving to the Congress review of disposals in excess of a specified acreage;

(11) regulations and plans for the protection of public land areas of critical environmental concern be promptly developed;

(12) the public lands be managed in a manner which recognizes the Nation's need for domestic sources of minerals, food, timber, and fiber from the public lands including implementation of the Mining and Minerals Policy Act of 1970 (84 Stat. 1876, 30 U.S.C. 21a) as it pertains to the public lands; and

(13) the Federal Government should, on a basis equitable to both the Federal and local taxpayer, provide for payments to compensate States and local governments for burdens created as a result of the immunity of Federal lands from State and local taxation.

(b) The policies of this Act shall become effective only as specific statutory authority for their implementation is enacted by this Act or by subsequent legislation and shall then be construed as supplemental to and not in derogation of the purposes for which public lands are administered under other provisions of law.

(Pub.L. 94–579, Title I, § 102, Oct. 21, 1976, 90 Stat. 2744.)

#### HISTORICAL AND STATUTORY NOTES

**References in Text**

This Act, referred to in subsecs. (a)(1), (3) and (b), is Pub.L. 94–579, Oct. 21, 1976, 90 Stat. 2743, as amended, known as the Federal Land Policy and Management Act of 1976. For complete classification of this Act to the Code, see Tables.

The Mining and Minerals Policy Act of 1970, referred to in subsec. (a)(12) is Pub. L. 91–631, Dec. 31, 1970, 84 Stat. 1876, which is classified to section 21a of Title 30, Mineral Lands and Mining.

**Savings Provisions**

Section 701 of Pub.L. 94–579 provided that:

"(a) Nothing in this Act [see Short Title note under this section], or in any amendment made by this Act, shall be construed as terminating any valid lease, permit, patent, right-of-way, or other land use right or authorization existing on the date of approval of this Act [Oct. 21, 1976].

"(b) Notwithstanding any provision of this Act, in the event of conflict with or inconsistency between this Act and the Acts of August 28, 1937 (50 Stat. 874; 43 U.S.C. 1181a–1181j), and May 24, 1939 (53 Stat. 753), insofar as they relate to management of timber resources, and disposition of revenues from lands and resources, the latter Acts shall prevail.

"(c) All withdrawals, reservations, classifications, and designations in effect as of the date of approval of this Act [Oct. 21, 1976] shall remain in full force and effect until modified under the provisions of this Act or other applicable law.

"(d) Nothing in this Act, or in any amendments made by this Act, shall be construed as permitting any person to place, or allow to be placed, spent oil shale, overburden, or byproducts from the recovery of other minerals found with oil shale, on any Federal land other than Federal land which has been leased for the recovery of shale oil under the Act of February 25, 1920 (41 Stat. 437, as amended; 30 U.S.C. 181 et seq.).

"(e) Nothing in this Act shall be construed as modifying, revoking, or changing any provision of the Alaska Native Claims Settlement Act (85 Stat. 688, as amended; 43 U.S.C. 1601 et seq.).

"(f) Nothing in this Act shall be deemed to repeal any existing law by implication.

"(g) Nothing in this Act shall be construed as limiting or restricting the power and authority of the United States or—

"(1) as affecting in any way any law governing appropriation or use of, or Federal right to, water on public lands;

"(2) as expanding or diminishing Federal or State jurisdiction, responsibility, interests, or rights in water resources development or control;

"(3) as displacing, superseding, limiting, or modifying any interstate compact or the jurisdiction or responsibility of any legally established joint or common agency of two or more States or of two or more States and the Federal Government;

"(4) as superseding, modifying, or repealing, except as specifically set forth in this Act, existing laws applicable to the various Federal agencies which are authorized to develop or participate in the development of water resources or to exercise licensing or regulatory functions in relation thereto;

"(5) as modifying the terms of any interstate compact;

"(6) as a limitation upon any State criminal statute or upon the police power of the respective States, or as derogating the authority of a local police officer in the performance of his duties, or as depriving any State or political subdivision thereof of any right it may have to exercise civil and criminal jurisdiction on the national resource lands; or as amending, limiting, or infringing the existing laws providing grants of lands to the States.

"(h) All actions by the Secretary concerned under this Act shall be subject to valid existing rights.

"(i) The adequacy of reports required by this Act to be submitted to the Congress or its committees shall not be subject to judicial review.

"(j) Nothing in this Act shall be construed as affecting the distribution of livestock grazing revenues to local governments under the Granger–Thye Act (64 Stat. 85, 16 U.S.C. 580h), under the Act of May 23, 1908 (35 Stat. 260, as amended; 16 U.S.C. 500), under the Act of March 4, 1913 (37 Stat. 843, as amended; 16 U.S.C. 501), and under the Act of June 20, 1910 (36 Stat. 557)."

**Severability of Provisions**

Section 707 of Pub.L. 94–579 provided that: "If any provision of this Act [see Short Title note set out above] or the application thereof is held invalid, the remainder of the Act and the application thereof shall not be affected thereby."

**Short Title**

1988 Amendments

Pub.L. 100–409, § 1, Aug. 20, 1988, 102 Stat. 1086, provided that: "This Act [enacting section 1723 of this title, amending section 1716 of this title and sections 505a, 505b, and 521b of Title 16, Conservation, and enacting provisions set out as notes under sections 751 and 1716 of this title] may be cited as the 'Federal Land Exchange Facilitation Act of 1988'."

1976 Acts

Section 101 of Pub.L. 94–579 provided that: "This Act [enacting this chapter and amending and repealing numerous other laws, which for complete distribution, see Tables Volume] may be cited as the 'Federal Land Policy and Management Act of 1976'."

**Pilot Test of Agency-wide Joint Permitting and Leasing Programs**

Pub.L. 106–291, Title III, § 330, Oct. 11, 2000, 114 Stat. 996, provided that: "In fiscal years 2001 through 2005, the Secretaries of the Interior and Agriculture may pilot test agency-wide joint permitting and leasing programs, subject to annual review of Congress, and promulgate special rules as needed to test the feasibility of issuing unified permits, applications, and leases. The Secretaries of the Interior and Agriculture may make reciprocal delegations of their respective authorities, duties and responsibilities in support of the 'Service First' initiative agency-wide to promote customer service and efficiency. Nothing herein shall alter, expand or limit the applicability of any public law or regulation to lands administered by the Bureau of Land Management or the Forest Service."

**Existing Rights-of-Way**

Section 706(b) of Pub.L. 94–579 provided that: "Nothing in section 706(a) [see Tables for classification], except as it pertains to rights-of-way, may be construed as affecting the authority of the Secretary of Agriculture under the Act of June 4, 1897 (30 Stat. 35, as amended, 16 U.S.C. 551); the Act of July 22, 1937 (50 Stat. 525, as amended, 7 U.S.C. 1010–1212); or the Act of September 3, 1954 (68 Stat. 1146, 43 U.S.C. 931c)."

## § 1702. Definitions
[FLPMA § 103]

Without altering in any way the meaning of the following terms as used in any other statute, whether or not such statute is referred to in, or amended by, this Act, as used in this Act—

(a) The term "areas of critical environmental concern" means areas within the public lands where special management attention is required (when such areas are developed or used or where no development is required) to protect and prevent irreparable damage to important historic, cultural, or scenic values, fish and wildlife resources or other natural systems or processes, or to protect life and safety from natural hazards.

(b) The term "holder" means any State or local governmental entity, individual, partnership, corporation, association, or other business entity receiving or using a right-of-way under subchapter V of this chapter.

(c) The term "multiple use" means the management of the public lands and their various resource values so that they are utilized in the combination that will best meet the present and future needs of the American people; making the most judicious use of the land for some or all of these resources or related services over areas large enough to provide sufficient latitude for periodic adjustments in use to conform to changing needs and conditions; the use of some land for less than all of the resources; a combination of balanced and diverse resource uses that takes into account the long-term needs of future generations for renewable and nonrenewable resources, including, but not limited to, recreation, range, timber, minerals, watershed, wildlife and fish, and natural scenic, scientific and historical values; and harmonious and coordinated management of the various resources without permanent impairment of the productivity of the land and the quality of the environment with consideration being given to the relative values of the resources and not necessarily to the combination of uses that will give the greatest economic return or the greatest unit output.

(d) The term "public involvement" means the opportunity for participation by affected citizens in rulemaking, decisionmaking, and planning with respect to the public lands, including public meetings or hearings held at locations near the affected lands, or advisory mechanisms, or such other procedures as may be necessary to provide public comment in a particular instance.

(e) The term "public lands" means any land and interest in land owned by the United States within the several States and administered by the Secretary of the Interior through the Bureau of Land Management, without regard to how the United States acquired ownership, except—

(1) lands located on the Outer Continental Shelf; and

(2) lands held for the benefit of Indians, Aleuts, and Eskimos.

(f) The term "right-of-way" includes an easement, lease, permit, or license to occupy, use, or traverse public lands granted for the purpose listed in subchapter V of this chapter.

(g) The term "Secretary", unless specifically designated otherwise, means the Secretary of the Interior.

(h) The term "sustained yield" means the achievement and maintenance in perpetuity of a high-level annual or regular periodic output of the various renewable resources of the public lands consistent with multiple use.

(i) The term "wilderness" as used in section 1782 of this title shall have the same meaning as it does in section 1131(c) of Title 16.

(j) The term "withdrawal" means withholding an area of Federal land from settlement, sale, location, or entry, under some or all of the general land laws, for the purpose of limiting activities under those laws in order to maintain other public values in the area or reserving the area for a particular public purpose or program; or transferring jurisdiction over an area of Federal land, other than "property" governed by the Federal Property and Administrative Services Act, as amended from one department, bureau or agency to another department, bureau or agency.

(k) An "allotment management plan" means a document prepared in consultation with the lessees or permittees involved, which applies to livestock operations on the public lands or on lands within National Forests in the eleven contiguous Western States and which:

(1) prescribes the manner in, and extent to, which livestock operations will be conducted in order to meet the multiple-use, sustained-yield, economic and other needs and objectives as determined for the lands by the Secretary concerned; and

(2) describes the type, location, ownership, and general specifications for the range improvements to be installed and maintained on the lands to meet the livestock grazing and other objectives of land management; and

(3) contains such other provisions relating to livestock grazing and other objectives found by the Secretary concerned to be consistent with the provisions of this Act and other applicable law.

(*l*) The term "principal or major uses" includes, and is limited to, domestic livestock grazing, fish and wildlife development and utilization, mineral exploration and production, rights-of-way, outdoor recreation, and timber production.

**(m)** The term "department" means a unit of the executive branch of the Federal Government which is headed by a member of the President's Cabinet and the term "agency" means a unit of the executive branch of the Federal Government which is not under the jurisdiction of a head of a department.

**(n)** The term "Bureau[1] means the Bureau of Land Management.

**(*o*)** The term "eleven contiguous Western States" means the States of Arizona, California, Colorado, Idaho, Montana, Nevada, New Mexico, Oregon, Utah, Washington, and Wyoming.

**(p)** The term "grazing permit and lease" means any document authorizing use of public lands or lands in National Forests in the eleven contiguous western States for the purpose of grazing domestic livestock.

(Pub.L. 94–579, Title I, § 103, Oct. 21, 1976, 90 Stat. 2745.)

1 So in original. Probably should have a close quote.

### HISTORICAL AND STATUTORY NOTES

**References in Text**

This Act, referred to in the opening par. and in subsec. (k), is Pub.L. 94–579, Oct. 21, 1976, 90 Stat. 2743, as amended, known as the Federal Land Policy and Management Act of 1976. For complete classification of this Act to the Code, see Tables.

The general land laws, referred to in subsec. (j), are classified generally to this title.

The Federal Property and Administrative Services Act of 1949, referred to in subsec. (j), is Act June 30, 1949, c. 288, 63 Stat. 377, as amended, Title III of which is currently classified to subchapter IV of chapter 4 of Title 41, 41 U.S.C.A. § 251 et seq., and the remainder of which was formerly classified to chapter 10 of former Title 40, 40 U.S.C.A. § 471 et seq., prior to being repealed by Pub.L. 107–217, § 6(b), Aug. 21, 2002, 116 Stat. 1313; see now generally chapter 1 of Title 40, 40 U.S.C.A. § 101 et seq.

## SUBCHAPTER II—LAND USE PLANNING AND LAND ACQUISITION AND DISPOSITION

## § 1711. Continuing inventory and identification of public lands; preparation and maintenance

### [FLPMA § 201]

**(a)** The Secretary shall prepare and maintain on a continuing basis an inventory of all public lands and their resource and other values (including, but not limited to, outdoor recreation and scenic values), giving priority to areas of critical environmental concern. This inventory shall be kept current so as to reflect changes in conditions and to identify new and emerging resource and other values. The preparation and maintenance of such inventory or the identification of such areas shall not, of itself, change or prevent change of the management or use of public lands.

**(b)** As funds and manpower are made available, the Secretary shall ascertain the boundaries of the public lands; provide means of public identification thereof including, where appropriate, signs and maps; and provide State and local governments with data from the inventory for the purpose of planning and regulating the uses of non-Federal lands in proximity of such public lands.

(Pub.L. 94–579, Title II, § 201, Oct. 21, 1976, 90 Stat. 2747.)

## § 1712. Land use plans

### [FLPMA § 202]

**(a) Development, maintenance, and revision by Secretary**

The Secretary shall, with public involvement and consistent with the terms and conditions of this Act, develop, maintain, and, when appropriate, revise land use plans which provide by tracts or areas for the use of the public lands. Land use plans shall be developed for the public lands regardless of whether such lands previously have been classified, withdrawn, set aside, or otherwise designated for one or more uses.

**(b) Coordination of plans for National Forest System lands with Indian land use planning and management programs for purposes of development and revision**

In the development and revision of land use plans, the Secretary of Agriculture shall coordinate land use plans for lands in the National Forest System with the land use planning and management programs of and for Indian tribes by, among other things, considering the policies of approved tribal land resource management programs.

**(c) Criteria for development and revision**

In the development and revision of land use plans, the Secretary shall—

(1) use and observe the principles of multiple use and sustained yield set forth in this and other applicable law;

(2) use a systematic interdisciplinary approach to achieve integrated consideration of physical, biological, economic, and other sciences;

(3) give priority to the designation and protection of areas of critical environmental concern;

(4) rely, to the extent it is available, on the inventory of the public lands, their resources, and other values;

(5) consider present and potential uses of the public lands;

(6) consider the relative scarcity of the values involved and the availability of alternative means

(including recycling) and sites for realization of those values;

(7) weigh long-term benefits to the public against short-term benefits;

(8) provide for compliance with applicable pollution control laws, including State and Federal air, water, noise, or other pollution standards or implementation plans; and

(9) to the extent consistent with the laws governing the administration of the public lands, coordinate the land use inventory, planning, and management activities of or for such lands with the land use planning and management programs of other Federal departments and agencies and of the States and local governments within which the lands are located, including, but not limited to, the statewide outdoor recreation plans developed under the Act of September 3, 1964 (78 Stat. 897), as amended [16 U.S.C.A. § 460*l*–4 et seq.], and of or for Indian tribes by, among other things, considering the policies of approved State and tribal land resource management programs. In implementing this directive, the Secretary shall, to the extent he finds practical, keep apprised of State, local, and tribal land use plans; assure that consideration is given to those State, local, and tribal plans that are germane in the development of land use plans for public lands; assist in resolving, to the extent practical, inconsistencies between Federal and non-Federal Government plans, and shall provide for meaningful public involvement of State and local government officials, both elected and appointed, in the development of land use programs, land use regulations, and land use decisions for public lands, including early public notice of proposed decisions which may have a significant impact on non-Federal lands. Such officials in each State are authorized to furnish advice to the Secretary with respect to the development and revision of land use plans, land use guidelines, land use rules, and land use regulations for the public lands within such State and with respect to such other land use matters as may be referred to them by him. Land use plans of the Secretary under this section shall be consistent with State and local plans to the maximum extent he finds consistent with Federal law and the purposes of this Act.

**(d) Review and inclusion of classified public lands; review of existing land use plans; modification and termination of classifications**

Any classification of public lands or any land use plan in effect on October 21, 1976, is subject to review in the land use planning process conducted under this section, and all public lands, regardless of classification, are subject to inclusion in any land use plan developed pursuant to this section. The Secretary may modify or terminate any such classification consistent with such land use plans.

**(e) Management decisions for implementation of developed or revised plans**

The Secretary may issue management decisions to implement land use plans developed or revised under this section in accordance with the following:

(1) Such decisions, including but not limited to exclusions (that is, total elimination) of one or more of the principal or major uses made by a management decision shall remain subject to reconsideration, modification, and termination through revision by the Secretary or his delegate, under the provisions of this section, of the land use plan involved.

(2) Any management decision or action pursuant to a management decision that excludes (that is, totally eliminates) one or more of the principal or major uses for two or more years with respect to a tract of land of one hundred thousand acres or more shall be reported by the Secretary to the House of Representatives and the Senate. If within ninety days from the giving of such notice (exclusive of days on which either House has adjourned for more than three consecutive days), the Congress adopts a concurrent resolution of nonapproval of the management decision or action, then the management decision or action shall be promptly terminated by the Secretary. If the committee to which a resolution has been referred during the said ninety day period, has not reported it at the end of thirty calendar days after its referral, it shall be in order to either discharge the committee from further consideration of such resolution or to discharge the committee from consideration of any other resolution with respect to the management decision or action. A motion to discharge may be made only by an individual favoring the resolution, shall be highly privileged (except that it may not be made after the committee has reported such a resolution), and debate thereon shall be limited to not more than one hour, to be divided equally between those favoring and those opposing the resolution. An amendment to the motion shall not be in order, and it shall not be in order to move to reconsider the vote by which the motion was agreed to or disagreed to. If the motion to discharge is agreed to or disagreed to, the motion may not be made with respect to any other resolution with respect to the same management decision or action. When the committee has reprinted, or has been discharged from further consideration of a resolution, it shall at any time thereafter be in order (even though a previous motion to the same effect has been disagreed to) to move to proceed to the consideration of the resolution. The motion shall be highly privileged and shall not be debatable. An amendment to the motion shall not

be in order, and it shall not be in order to move to reconsider the vote by which the motion was agreed to or disagreed to.

(3) Withdrawals made pursuant to section 1714 of this title may be used in carrying out management decisions, but public lands shall be removed from or restored to the operation of the Mining Law of 1872, as amended (R.S. 2318–2352; 30 U.S.C. 21 et seq.) or transferred to another department, bureau, or agency only by withdrawal action pursuant to section 1714 of this title or other action pursuant to applicable law: *Provided,* That nothing in this section shall prevent a wholly owned Government corporation from acquiring and holding rights as a citizen under the Mining Law of 1872.

**(f) Procedures applicable to formulation of plans and programs for public land management**

The Secretary shall allow an opportunity for public involvement and by regulation shall establish procedures, including public hearings where appropriate, to give Federal, State, and local governments and the public, adequate notice and opportunity to comment upon and participate in the formulation of plans and programs relating to the management of the public lands.

(Pub.L. 94–579, Title II, § 202, Oct. 21, 1976, 90 Stat. 2747.)

### HISTORICAL AND STATUTORY NOTES

**References in Text**

This Act, referred to in subsecs. (a) and (c)(9), is Pub.L. 94–579, Oct. 21, 1976, 90 Stat. 2743, as amended, known as the Federal Land Policy and Management Act of 1976. For complete classification of this Act to the Code, see Tables.

The Act of September 3, 1964 (78 Stat. 897), as amended, referred to in subsec. (c)(9), is Pub.L. 88–578, Sept. 3, 1964, 78 Stat. 897, as amended, known as the Land and Water Conservation Fund Act of 1965, which is classified generally to part B (section 460*l*–4 et seq.) of subchapter LXIX of chapter 1 of Title 16, Conservation. For complete classification of this Act to the Code, see Short Title note set out under section 460*l*–4 of Title 16 and Tables volume.

The Mining Law of 1872, as amended, referred to in subsec. (e)(3), is Act May 10, 1872, c. 152, 17 Stat. 91, as amended, which was incorporated into the Revised Statutes of 1878 as R.S. §§ 2319 to 2328, 2331, 2333 to 2337, and 2344, which are classified to sections 22 to 24, 26 to 28, 29, 30, 33 to 35, 37, 39 to 42, and 47 of Title 30, Mineral Lands and Mining. For complete classification of R.S. §§ 2318–2352, see Tables volume.

## § 1713. Sales of public land tracts

### [FLPMA § 203]

**(a) Criteria for disposal; excepted lands**

A tract of the public lands (except land in units of the National Wilderness Preservation System, National Wild and Scenic Rivers Systems, and National System of Trails) may be sold under this Act where, as a result of land use planning required under section 1712 of this title, the Secretary determines that the sale of such tract meets the following disposal criteria:

(1) such tract because of its location or other characteristics is difficult and uneconomic to manage as part of the public lands, and is not suitable for management by another Federal department or agency; or

(2) such tract was acquired for a specific purpose and the tract is no longer required for that or any other Federal purpose; or

(3) disposal of such tract will serve important public objectives, including but not limited to, expansion of communities and economic development, which cannot be achieved prudently or feasibly on land other than public land and which outweigh other public objectives and values, including, but not limited to, recreation and scenic values, which would be served by maintaining such tract in Federal ownership.

**(b) Conveyance of land of agricultural value and desert in character**

Where the Secretary determines that land to be conveyed under clause (3) of subsection (a) of this section is of agricultural value and is desert in character, such land shall be conveyed either under the sale authority of this section or in accordance with other existing law.

**(c) Congressional approval procedures applicable to tracts in excess of two thousand five hundred acres**

Where a tract of the public lands in excess of two thousand five hundred acres has been designated for sale, such sale may be made only after the end of the ninety days (not counting days on which the House of Representatives or the Senate has adjourned for more than three consecutive days) beginning on the day the Secretary has submitted notice of such designation to the Senate and the House of Representatives, and then only if the Congress has not adopted a concurrent resolution stating that such House does not approve of such designation. If the committee to which a resolution has been referred during the said ninety day period, has not reported it at the end of thirty calendar days after its referral, it shall be in order to either discharge the committee from further consideration of such resolution or to discharge the committee from consideration of any other resolution with respect to the designation. A motion to discharge may be made only by an individual favoring the resolution, shall be highly privileged (except that it may not be made after the committee has reported such a resolution), and debate thereon shall be limited to not more than one hour, to be divided equally between those favoring and those opposing the resolution. An amendment to the motion shall not be in order, and it shall not be in order to move to reconsider the vote by which the motion was agreed to or disagreed to. If the motion to discharge is agreed to or disagreed to, the motion may not be made with respect to any other resolution with respect to the same designation. When the committee has reprinted, or has been discharged from further consideration of a resolution, it shall at any time thereafter be in order (even though a previous motion to the same effect has been disagreed to) to move to proceed to the consideration of the resolution. The motion shall be highly privileged and shall not be debatable. An amendment to the motion shall not be in order, and it shall not be in order to move to reconsider the vote by which the motion was agreed to or disagreed to.

**(d) Sale price**

Sales of public lands shall be made at a price not less than their fair market value as determined by the Secretary.

**(e) Maximum size of tracts**

The Secretary shall determine and establish the size of tracts of public lands to be sold on the basis of the land use capabilities and development requirements of the lands; and, where any such tract which is judged by the Secretary to be chiefly valuable for agriculture is sold, its size shall be no larger than necessary to support a family-sized farm.

**(f) Competitive bidding requirements**

Sales of public lands under this section shall be conducted under competitive bidding procedures to be established by the Secretary. However, where the Secretary determines it necessary and proper in order (1) to assure equitable distribution among purchasers of lands, or (2) to recognize equitable considerations or public policies, including but not limited to, a preference to users, he may sell those lands with modified competitive bidding or without competitive bidding. In recognizing public policies, the Secretary shall give consideration to the following potential purchasers:

(1) the State in which the land is located;

(2) the local government entities in such State which are in the vicinity of the land;

(3) adjoining landowners;

(4) individuals; and

(5) any other person.

**(g) Acceptance or rejection of offers to purchase**

The Secretary shall accept or reject, in writing, any offer to purchase made through competitive bidding at his invitation no later than thirty days after the receipt of such offer or, in the case of a tract in excess of two thousand five hundred acres, at the end of thirty days after the end of the ninety-day period provided in subsection (c) of this section, whichever is later, unless the offeror waives his right to a decision within such thirty-day period. Prior to the expiration of such periods the Secretary may refuse to accept any offer or may withdraw any land or interest in land from sale under this section when he determines that consummation of the sale would not be consistent with this Act or other applicable law.

(Pub.L. 94–579, Title II, § 203, Oct. 21, 1976, 90 Stat. 2750.)

**Unconstitutionality of Legislative Veto Provisions**

*The provisions of former section 1254(c)(2) of Title 8, Aliens and Nationality, which authorized a House of Congress, by resolution, to invalidate an action of the Executive Branch, were declared unconstitutional in Immigration and Naturalization Service v. Chadha, 1983, 103 S.Ct. 2764, 462 U.S. 919, 77 L.Ed.2d 317. See similar provisions in subsec. (c) of this section.*

**HISTORICAL AND STATUTORY NOTES**

**References in Text**

This Act, referred to in subsecs. (a) and (g), is Pub.L. 94–579, Oct. 21, 1976, 90 Stat. 2743, as amended, known as the Federal Land Policy and Management Act of 1976. For complete classification of this Act to the Code, see Tables.

## § 1714. Withdrawals of lands

**[FLPMA § 204]**

**(a) Authorization and limitation; delegation of authority**

On and after the effective date of this Act the Secretary is authorized to make, modify, extend, or revoke withdrawals but only in accordance with the provisions and limitations of this section. The Secretary may delegate this withdrawal authority only to individuals in the Office of the Secretary who have been appointed by the President, by and with the advice and consent of the Senate.

**(b) Application and procedures applicable subsequent to submission of application**

(1) Within thirty days of receipt of an application for withdrawal, and whenever he proposes a withdrawal on his own motion, the Secretary shall publish a notice in the Federal Register stating that the application has been submitted for filing or the proposal has been made and the extent to which the land is to be segregated while the application is being considered by the Secretary. Upon publication of such notice the land shall be segregated from the operation of the public land laws to the extent specified in the notice. The segregative effect of the application shall terminate upon (a) rejection of the application by the Secretary, (b) withdrawal of lands

by the Secretary, or (c) the expiration of two years from the date of the notice.

(2) The publication provisions of this subsection are not applicable to withdrawals under subsection (e) hereof.

**(c) Congressional approval procedures applicable to withdrawals aggregating five thousand acres or more**

(1) On and after October 21, 1976, a withdrawal aggregating five thousand acres or more may be made (or such a withdrawal or any other withdrawal involving in the aggregate five thousand acres or more which terminates after such date of approval may be extended) only for a period of not more than twenty years by the Secretary on his own motion or upon request by a department or agency head. The Secretary shall notify both Houses of Congress of such a withdrawal no later than its effective date and the withdrawal shall terminate and become ineffective at the end of ninety days (not counting days on which the Senate or the House of Representatives has adjourned for more than three consecutive days) beginning on the day notice of such withdrawal has been submitted to the Senate and the House of Representatives, if the Congress has adopted a concurrent resolution stating that such House does not approve the withdrawal. If the committee to which a resolution has been referred during the said ninety day period, has not reported it at the end of thirty calendar days after its referral, it shall be in order to either discharge the committee from further consideration of such resolution or to discharge the committee from consideration of any other resolution with respect to the Presidential recommendation. A motion to discharge may be made only by an individual favoring the resolution, shall be highly privileged (except that it may not be made after the committee has reported such a resolution), and debate thereon shall be limited to not more than one hour, to be divided equally between those favoring and those opposing the resolution. An amendment to the motion shall not be in order, and it shall not be in order to move to reconsider the vote by which the motion was agreed to or disagreed to. If the motion to discharge is agreed to or disagreed to, the motion may not be made with respect to any other resolution with respect to the same Presidential recommendation. When the committee has reprinted, or has been discharged from further consideration of a resolution, it shall at any time thereafter be in order (even though a previous motion to the same effect has been disagreed to) to move to proceed to the consideration of the resolution. The motion shall be highly privileged and shall not be debatable. An amendment to the motion shall not be in order, and it shall not be in order to move to reconsider the vote by which the motion was agreed to or disagreed to.

(2) With the notices required by subsection (c)(1) of this section and within three months after filing the notice under subsection (e) of this section, the Secretary shall furnish to the committees—

(1) a clear explanation of the proposed use of the land involved which led to the withdrawal;

(2) an inventory and evaluation of the current natural resource uses and values of the site and adjacent public and nonpublic land and how it appears they will be affected by the proposed use, including particularly aspects of use that might cause degradation of the environment, and also the economic impact of the change in use on individuals, local communities, and the Nation;

(3) an identification of present users of the land involved, and how they will be affected by the proposed use;

(4) an analysis of the manner in which existing and potential resource uses are incompatible with or in conflict with the proposed use, together with a statement of the provisions to be made for continuation or termination of existing uses, including an economic analysis of such continuation or termination;

(5) an analysis of the manner in which such lands will be used in relation to the specific requirements for the proposed use;

(6) a statement as to whether any suitable alternative sites are available (including cost estimates) for the proposed use or for uses such a withdrawal would displace;

(7) a statement of the consultation which has been or will be had with other Federal departments and agencies, with regional, State, and local government bodies, and with other appropriate individuals and groups;

(8) a statement indicating the effect of the proposed uses, if any, on State and local government interests and the regional economy;

(9) a statement of the expected length of time needed for the withdrawal;

(10) the time and place of hearings and of other public involvement concerning such withdrawal;

(11) the place where the records on the withdrawal can be examined by interested parties; and

(12) a report prepared by a qualified mining engineer, engineering geologist, or geologist which shall include but not be limited to information on: general geology, known mineral deposits, past and present mineral production, mining claims, mineral leases, evaluation of future mineral potential, present and potential market demands.

**(d) Withdrawals aggregating less than five thousand acres; procedure applicable**

A withdrawal aggregating less than five thousand acres may be made under this subsection by the Secretary on his own motion or upon request by a department or an agency head—

(1) for such period of time as he deems desirable for a resource use; or

(2) for a period of not more than twenty years for any other use, including but not limited to use for administrative sites, location of facilities, and other proprietary purposes; or

(3) for a period of not more than five years to preserve such tract for a specific use then under consideration by the Congress.

**(e) Emergency withdrawals; procedure applicable; duration**

When the Secretary determines, or when the Committee on Natural Resources of the House of Representatives or the Committee on Energy and Natural Resources of the Senate notifies the Secretary, that an emergency situation exists and that extraordinary measures must be taken to preserve values that would otherwise be lost, the Secretary notwithstanding the provisions of subsections (c)(1) and (d) of this section, shall immediately make a withdrawal and file notice of such emergency withdrawal with both of those Committees. Such emergency withdrawal shall be effective when made but shall last only for a period not to exceed three years and may not be extended except under the provisions of subsection (c)(1) or (d), whichever is applicable, and (b)(1) of this section. The information required in subsection (c)(2) of this subsection shall be furnished the committees within three months after filing such notice.

**(f) Review of existing withdrawals and extensions; procedure applicable to extensions; duration**

All withdrawals and extensions thereof, whether made prior to or after October 21, 1976, having a specific period shall be reviewed by the Secretary toward the end of the withdrawal period and may be extended or further extended only upon compliance with the provisions of subsection (c)(1) or (d) of this section, whichever is applicable, and only if the Secretary determines that the purpose for which the withdrawal was first made requires the extension, and then only for a period no longer than the length of the original withdrawal period. The Secretary shall report on such review and extensions to the Committee on Natural Resources of the House of Representatives and the Committee on Energy and Natural Resources of the Senate.

**(g) Processing and adjudication of existing applications**

All applications for withdrawal pending on October 21, 1976 shall be processed and adjudicated to conclusion within fifteen years of October 21, 1976, in accordance with the provisions of this section. The segregative effect of any application not so processed shall terminate on that date.

**(h) Public hearing required for new withdrawals**

All new withdrawals made by the Secretary under this section (except an emergency withdrawal made under subsection (e) of this section) shall be promulgated after an opportunity for a public hearing.

**(i) Consent for withdrawal of lands under administration of department or agency other than Department of the Interior**

In the case of lands under the administration of any department or agency other than the Department of the Interior, the Secretary shall make, modify, and revoke withdrawals only with the consent of the head of the department or agency concerned, except when the provisions of subsection (e) of this section apply.

**(j) Applicability of other Federal laws withdrawing lands as limiting authority**

The Secretary shall not make, modify, or revoke any withdrawal created by Act of Congress; make a withdrawal which can be made only by Act of Congress; modify or revoke any withdrawal creating national monuments under the Act of June 8, 1906 (34 Stat. 225; 16 U.S.C. 431–433); or modify, or revoke any withdrawal which added lands to the National Wildlife Refuge System prior to October 21, 1976, or which thereafter adds lands to that System under the terms of this Act. Nothing in this Act is intended to modify or change any provision of the Act of February 27, 1976 (90 Stat. 199; 16 U.S.C. 668dd(a)).

**(k) Authorization of appropriations for processing applications**

There is hereby authorized to be appropriated the sum of $10,000,000 for the purpose of processing withdrawal applications pending on the effective date of this Act, to be available until expended.

**(*l*) Review of existing withdrawals in certain States; procedure applicable for determination of future status of lands; authorization of appropriations**

(1) The Secretary shall, within fifteen years of October 21, 1976, review withdrawals existing on October 21, 1976, in the States of Arizona, California, Colorado, Idaho, Montana, Nevada, New Mexico, Oregon, Utah, Washington, and Wyoming of (1) all Federal lands other than withdrawals of the public lands administered by the Bureau of Land Management and of lands which, on October 21, 1976, were part of Indian reservations and other Indian holdings, the National Forest System, the National Park System, the National Wildlife Refuge System, other lands administered

by the Fish and Wildlife Service or the Secretary through the Fish and Wildlife Service, the National Wild and Scenic Rivers System, and the National System of Trails; and (2) all public lands administered by the Bureau of Land Management and of lands in the National Forest System (except those in wilderness areas, and those areas formally identified as primitive or natural areas or designated as national recreation areas) which closed the lands to appropriation under the Mining Law of 1872 (17 Stat. 91, as amended; 30 U.S.C. 22 et seq.) or to leasing under the Mineral Leasing Act of 1920 (41 Stat. 437, as amended; 30 U.S.C. 181 et seq.).

(2) In the review required by paragraph (1) of this subsection, the Secretary shall determine whether, and for how long, the continuation of the existing withdrawal of the lands would be, in his judgment, consistent with the statutory objectives of the programs for which the lands were dedicated and of the other relevant programs. The Secretary shall report his recommendations to the President, together with statements of concurrence or nonconcurrence submitted by the heads of the departments or agencies which administer the lands. The President shall transmit this report to the President of the Senate and the Speaker of the House of Representatives, together with his recommendations for action by the Secretary, or for legislation. The Secretary may act to terminate withdrawals other than those made by Act of the Congress in accordance with the recommendations of the President unless before the end of ninety days (not counting days on which the Senate and the House of Representatives has adjourned for more than three consecutive days) beginning on the day the report of the President has been submitted to the Senate and the House of Representatives the Congress has adopted a concurrent resolution indicating otherwise. If the committee to which a resolution has been referred during the said ninety day period, has not reported it at the end of thirty calendar days after its referral, it shall be in order to either discharge the committee from further consideration of such resolution or to discharge the committee from consideration of any other resolution with respect to the Presidential recommendation. A motion to discharge may be made only by an individual favoring the resolution, shall be highly privileged (except that it may not be made after the committee has reported such a resolution), and debate thereon shall be limited to not more than one hour, to be divided equally between those favoring and those opposing the resolution. An amendment to the motion shall not be in order, and it shall not be in order to move to reconsider the vote by which the motion was agreed to or disagreed to. If the motion to discharge is agreed to or disagreed to, the motion may not be made with respect to any other resolution with respect to the same Presidential recommendation. When the committee has reprinted, or has been discharged from further consideration of a resolution, it shall at any time thereafter be in order (even though a previous motion to the same effect has been disagreed to) to move to proceed to the consideration of the resolution. The motion shall be highly privileged and shall not be debatable. An amendment to the motion shall not be in order, and it shall not be in order to move to reconsider the vote by which the motion was agreed to or disagreed to.

(3) There are hereby authorized to be appropriated not more than $10,000,000 for the purpose of paragraph (1) of this subsection to be available until expended to the Secretary and to the heads of other departments and agencies which will be involved.

(Pub.L. 94–579, Title II, § 204, Oct. 21, 1976, 90 Stat. 2751; Pub.L. 103–437, § 16(d)(1), Nov. 2, 1994, 108 Stat. 4594.)

## HISTORICAL AND STATUTORY NOTES

### References in Text

On and after the effective date of this Act, referred to in subsecs. (a) and (k), probably means on and after the date of enactment of Pub.L. 94–579, which was approved Oct. 21, 1976.

The Act of June 8, 1906, referred to in subsec. (j), is Act June 8, 1906, c. 3060, 34 Stat. 225, popularly known as the Antiquities Act of 1906, which is classified generally to sections 431, 432, and 433 of Title 16, Conservation. For complete classification of this Act to the Code, see Short Title note set out under section 431 of Title 16 and Tables volume.

The Act of February 27, 1976 (90 Stat. 199; 16 U.S.C. 668dd(a)), referred to in subsec. (j), is Pub.L. 94–223, Feb. 27, 1976, 90 Stat. 199, which amended section 668dd of Title 16, Conservation. For complete classification of this Act to the Code, see Tables volume.

This Act, referred to in subsec. (j), is Pub.L. 94–579, Oct. 21, 1976, 90 Stat. 2743, as amended, known as the Federal Land Policy and Management Act of 1976. For complete classification of this Act to the Code, see Tables volume.

The Mining Law of 1872 (17 Stat. 91, as amended; 30 U.S.C. 22 et seq.), referred to in subsec. (*l*)(1), is Act May 10, 1972, c. 152, 17 Stat. 91, as amended, which was incorporated into the Revised Statutes of 1878 as R.S. §§ 2319 to 2328, 2331, 2333 to 2337, and 2344, which are classified to sections 22 to 24, 26 to 28, 29, 30, 33 to 35, 37, 39 to 42, and 47 of Title 30, Mineral Lands and Mining. For complete classification of such Revised Statutes sections to the Code, see Tables volume.

The Mineral Leasing Act of 1920 (41 Stat. 437, as amended; 30 U.S.C. 181 et seq.), referred to in subsec. (*l*)(1), is Act Feb. 25, 1920, c. 85, 41 Stat. 437, as amended, which is classified principally to chapter 3A (section 181 et seq.) of Title 30, Mineral Lands and Mining. For complete classification of this Act to the Code, see Short Title note set out under section 181 of Title 30 and Tables volume.

### Change of Name

Any reference in any provision of law enacted before Jan. 4, 1995, to the Committee on Natural Resources of the House of Representatives treated as referring to the Committee on

Resources of the House of Representatives, see section 1(a)(8) of Pub.L. 104–14, set out as a note preceding section 21 of Title 2, The Congress.

The Committee on Interior and Insular Affairs of the Senate, referred to in subsecs. (e) and (f), was abolished and replaced by the Committee on Energy and Natural Resources of the Senate, effective Feb. 11, 1977. See Rule XXV of the Standing Rules of the Senate, as amended by Senate Resolution 4 (popularly cited as the "Committee System Reorganization Amendments of 1977"), approved Feb. 4, 1977.

## § 1715. Acquisitions of public lands and access over non-Federal lands to National Forest System units

**[FLPMA § 205]**

### (a) Authorization and limitations on authority of Secretary of the Interior and Secretary of Agriculture

Notwithstanding any other provisions of law, the Secretary, with respect to the public lands and the Secretary of Agriculture, with respect to the acquisition of access over non-Federal lands to units of the National Forest System, are authorized to acquire pursuant to this Act by purchase, exchange, donation, or eminent domain, lands or interests therein: *Provided*, That with respect to the public lands, the Secretary may exercise the power of eminent domain only if necessary to secure access to public lands, and then only if the lands so acquired are confined to as narrow a corridor as is necessary to serve such purpose. Nothing in this subsection shall be construed as expanding or limiting the authority of the Secretary of Agriculture to acquire land by eminent domain within the boundaries of units of the National Forest System.

### (b) Conformity to departmental policies and land-use plan of acquisitions

Acquisitions pursuant to this section shall be consistent with the mission of the department involved and with applicable departmental land-use plans.

### (c) Status of lands and interests in lands upon acquisition by Secretary of the Interior; transfers to Secretary of Agriculture of lands and interests in lands acquired within National Forest System boundaries

Except as provided in subsection (e) of this section, lands and interests in lands acquired by the Secretary pursuant to this section or section 1716 of this title shall, upon acceptance of title, become public lands, and, for the administration of public land laws not repealed by this Act, shall remain public lands. If such acquired lands or interests in lands are located within the exterior boundaries of a grazing district established pursuant to section 315 of this title, they shall become a part of that district. Lands and interests in lands acquired pursuant to this section which are within boundaries of the National Forest System may be transferred to the Secretary of Agriculture and shall then become National Forest System lands and subject to all the laws, rules, and regulations applicable thereto.

### (d) Status of lands and interests in lands upon acquisition by Secretary of Agriculture

Lands and interests in lands acquired by the Secretary of Agriculture pursuant to this section shall, upon acceptance of title, become National Forest System lands subject to all the laws, rules, and regulations applicable thereto.

### (e) Status and administration of lands acquired in exchange for lands revested in or reconveyed to United States

Lands acquired by the Secretary pursuant to this section or section 1716 of this title in exchange for lands which were revested in the United States pursuant to the provisions of the Act of June 9, 1916 (39 Stat. 218) or reconveyed to the United States pursuant to the provisions of the Act of February 26, 1919 (40 Stat. 1179), shall be considered for all purposes to have the same status as, and shall be administered in accordance with the same provisions of law applicable to, the revested or reconveyed lands exchanged for the lands acquired by the Secretary.

(Pub.L. 94–579, Title II, § 205, Oct. 21, 1976, 90 Stat. 2755; Pub.L. 99–632, § 5, Nov. 7, 1986, 100 Stat. 3521.)

**HISTORICAL AND STATUTORY NOTES**

**References in Text**

This Act, referred to in subsecs. (a) and (c), is Pub.L. 94–579, Oct. 21, 1976, 90 Stat. 2743, as amended, known as the Federal Land Policy and Management Act of 1976. For complete classification of this Act to the Code, see Tables.

The public land laws, referred to in subsec. (c), are classified generally to this title.

The Act of June 9, 1916 (39 Stat. 218), referred to in subsec. (e), was not classified to the Code.

The Act of February 26, 1919 (40 Stat. 1179), referred to in subsec. (e), probably means Act Feb. 26, 1919, c. 47, 40 Stat. 1179, which was not classified to the Code.

## § 1716. Exchanges of public lands or interests therein within the National Forest System

**[FLPMA § 206]**

### (a) Authorization and limitations on authority of Secretary of the Interior and Secretary of Agriculture

A tract of public land or interests therein may be disposed of by exchange by the Secretary under this Act and a tract of land or interests therein within the National Forest System may be disposed of by exchange by the Secretary of Agriculture under applicable law where the Secretary concerned determines that the public interest will be well served by making that exchange: *Provided*, That when considering public interest the Secretary concerned shall give full consideration to better Federal land management and the needs of State and local people, including needs for lands for the economy, community expansion, recreation areas, food, fiber, minerals, and fish and wildlife and the Secretary concerned finds that the values and the objectives which Federal lands or interests to be conveyed may serve if retained in Federal ownership are not more than the values of the non-Federal lands or interests and the public objectives they could serve if acquired.

**(b) Implementation requirements; cash equalization waiver**

In exercising the exchange authority granted by subsection (a) of this section or by section 1715(a) of this title, the Secretary concerned may accept title to any non-Federal land or interests therein in exchange for such land, or interests therein which he finds proper for transfer out of Federal ownership and which are located in the same State as the non-Federal land or interest to be acquired. For the purposes of this subsection, unsurveyed school sections which, upon survey by the Secretary, would become State lands, shall be considered as "non-Federal lands". The values of the lands exchanged by the Secretary under this Act and by the Secretary of Agriculture under applicable law relating to lands within the National Forest System either shall be equal, or if they are not equal, the values shall be equalized by the payment of money to the grantor or to the Secretary concerned as the circumstances require so long as payment does not exceed 25 per centum of the total value of the lands or interests transferred out of Federal ownership. The Secretary concerned and the other party or parties involved in the exchange may mutually agree to waive the requirement for the payment of money to equalize values where the Secretary concerned determines that the exchange will be expedited thereby and that the public interest will be better served by such a waiver of cash equalization payments and where the amount to be waived is no more than 3 per centum of the value of the lands being transferred out of Federal ownership or $15,000, whichever is less, except that the Secretary of Agriculture shall not agree to waive any such requirement for payment of money to the United States. The Secretary concerned shall try to reduce the amount of the payment of money to as small an amount as possible.

**(c) Status of lands acquired upon exchange by Secretary of the Interior**

Lands acquired by the Secretary by exchange under this section which are within the boundaries of any unit of the National Forest System, National Park System, National Wildlife Refuge System, National Wild and Scenic Rivers System, National Trails System, National Wilderness Preservation System, or any other system established by Act of Congress, or the boundaries of the California Desert Conservation Area, or the boundaries of any national conservation area or national recreation area established by Act of Congress, upon acceptance of title by the United States shall immediately be reserved for and become a part of the unit or area within which they are located, without further action by the Secretary, and shall thereafter be managed in accordance with all laws, rules, and regulations applicable to such unit or area.

**(d) Appraisal of land; submission to arbitrator; determination to proceed or withdraw from exchange; use of other valuation process; suspension of deadlines**

(1) No later than ninety days after entering into an agreement to initiate an exchange of land or interests therein pursuant to this Act or other applicable law, the Secretary concerned and other party or parties involved in the exchange shall arrange for appraisal (to be completed within a time frame and under such terms as are negotiated by the parties) of the lands or interests therein involved in the exchange in accordance with subsection (f) of this section.

(2) If within one hundred and eighty days after the submission of an appraisal or appraisals for review and approval by the Secretary concerned, the Secretary concerned and the other party or parties involved cannot agree to accept the findings of an appraisal or appraisals, the appraisal or appraisals shall be submitted to an arbitrator appointed by the Secretary from a list of arbitrators submitted to him by the American Arbitration Association for arbitration to be conducted in accordance with the real estate valuation arbitration rules of the American Arbitration Association. Such arbitration shall be binding for a period of not to exceed two years on the Secretary concerned and the other party or parties involved in the exchange insofar as concerns the value of the lands which were the subject of the appraisal or appraisals.

(3) Within thirty days after the completion of the arbitration, the Secretary concerned and the other party or parties involved in the exchange shall determine whether to proceed with the exchange, modify the exchange to reflect the findings of the arbitration or any other factors, or to withdraw from the exchange. A decision to withdraw from the exchange may be made by either the Secretary concerned or the other party or parties involved.

(4) Instead of submitting the appraisal to an arbitrator, as provided in paragraph (2) of this section, the Secretary concerned and the other party or parties involved in an exchange may mutually agree to em-

ploy a process of bargaining or some other process to determine the values of the properties involved in the exchange.

(5) The Secretary concerned and the other party or parties involved in an exchange may mutually agree to suspend or modify any of the deadlines contained in this subsection.

**(e) Simultaneous issue of patents or titles**

Unless mutually agreed otherwise by the Secretary concerned and the other party or parties involved in an exchange pursuant to this Act or other applicable law, all patents or titles to be issued for land or interests therein to be acquired by the Federal Government and lands or interest therein to be transferred out of Federal ownership shall be issued simultaneously after the Secretary concerned has taken any necessary steps to assure that the United States will receive acceptable title.

**(f) New rules and regulations; appraisal rules and regulations; "costs and other responsibilities or requirements" defined**

(1) Within one year after August 20, 1988, the Secretaries of the Interior and Agriculture shall promulgate new and comprehensive rules and regulations governing exchanges of land and interests therein pursuant to this Act and other applicable law. Such rules and regulations shall fully reflect the changes in law made by subsections (d) through (i) of this section and shall include provisions pertaining to appraisals of lands and interests therein involved in such exchanges.

(2) The provisions of the rules and regulations issued pursuant to paragraph (1) of this subsection governing appraisals shall reflect nationally recognized appraisal standards, including, to the extent appropriate, the Uniform Appraisal Standards for Federal Land Acquisitions: *Provided, however,* That the provisions of such rules and regulations shall—

(A) ensure that the same nationally approved appraisal standards are used in appraising lands or interest therein being acquired by the Federal Government and appraising lands or interests therein being transferred out of Federal ownership; and

(B) with respect to costs or other responsibilities or requirements associated with land exchanges—

(i) recognize that the parties involved in an exchange may mutually agree that one party (or parties) will assume, without compensation, all or part of certain costs or other responsibilities or requirements ordinarily borne by the other party or parties; and

(ii) also permit the Secretary concerned, where such Secretary determines it is in the public interest and it is in the best interest of consummating an exchange pursuant to this Act or other applicable law, and upon mutual agreement of the parties, to make adjustments to the relative values involved in an exchange transaction in order to compensate a party or parties to the exchange for assuming costs or other responsibilities or requirements which would ordinarily be borne by the other party or parties.

As used in this subparagraph, the term "costs or other responsibilities or requirements" shall include, but not be limited to, costs or other requirements associated with land surveys and appraisals, mineral examinations, title searches, archeological surveys and salvage, removal of encumbrances, arbitration pursuant to subsection (d) of this section, curing deficiencies preventing highest and best use, and other costs to comply with laws, regulations and policies applicable to exchange transactions, or which are necessary to bring the Federal or non-Federal lands or interests involved in the exchange to their highest and best use for the appraisal and exchange purposes. Prior to making any adjustments pursuant to this subparagraph, the Secretary concerned shall be satisfied that the amount of such adjustment is reasonable and accurately reflects the approximate value of any costs or services provided or any responsibilities or requirements assumed.

**(g) Exchanges to proceed under existing laws and regulations pending new rules and regulations**

Until such time as new and comprehensive rules and regulations governing exchange of land and interests therein are promulgated pursuant to subsection (f) of this section, land exchanges may proceed in accordance with existing laws and regulations, and nothing in the Act shall be construed to require any delay in, or otherwise hinder, the processing and consummation of land exchanges pending the promulgation of such new and comprehensive rules and regulations. Where the Secretary concerned and the party or parties involved in an exchange have agreed to initiate an exchange of land or interests therein prior to the day of enactment of such subsections, subsections (d) through (i) of this section shall not apply to such exchanges unless the Secretary concerned and the party or parties involved in the exchange mutually agree otherwise.

**(h) Exchange of lands or interests of approximately equal value; conditions; "approximately equal value" defined**

(1) Notwithstanding the provisions of this Act and other applicable laws which require that exchanges of land or interests therein be for equal value, where the Secretary concerned determines it is in the public interest and that the consummation of a particular

exchange will be expedited thereby, the Secretary concerned may exchange lands or interests therein which are of approximately equal value in cases where—

(A) the combined value of the lands or interests therein to be transferred from Federal ownership by the Secretary concerned in such exchange is not more than $150,000; and

(B) the Secretary concerned finds in accordance with the regulations to be promulgated pursuant to subsection (f) of this section that a determination of approximately equal value can be made without formal appraisals, as based on a statement of value made by a qualified appraiser and approved by an authorized officer; and

(C) the definition of and procedure for determining "approximately equal value" has been set forth in regulations by the Secretary concerned and the Secretary concerned documents how such determination was made in the case of the particular exchange involved.

(2) As used in this subsection, the term "approximately equal value" shall have the same meaning with respect to lands managed by the Secretary of Agriculture as it does in the Act of January 22, 1983 (commonly known as the "Small Tracts Act").

### (i) Segregation from appropriation under mining and public land laws

(1) Upon receipt of an offer to exchange lands or interests in lands pursuant to this Act or other applicable laws, at the request of the head of the department or agency having jurisdiction over the lands involved, the Secretary of the Interior may temporarily segregate the Federal lands under consideration for exchange from appropriation under the mining laws. Such temporary segregation may only be made for a period of not to exceed five years. Upon a decision not to proceed with the exchange or upon deletion of any particular parcel from the exchange offer, the Federal lands involved or deleted shall be promptly restored to their former status under the mining laws. Any segregation pursuant to this paragraph shall be subject to valid existing rights as of the date of such segregation.

(2) All non-Federal lands which are acquired by the United States through exchange pursuant to this Act or pursuant to other law applicable to lands managed by the Secretary of Agriculture shall be automatically segregated from appropriation under the public land law, including the mining laws, for ninety days after acceptance of title by the United States. Such segregation shall be subject to valid existing rights as of the date of such acceptance of title. At the end of such ninety day period, such segregation shall end and such lands shall be open to operation of the public land laws and to entry, location, and patent under the mining laws except to the extent otherwise provided by this Act or other applicable law, or appropriate actions pursuant thereto.

(Pub.L. 94–579, Title II, § 206, Oct. 21, 1976, 90 Stat. 2756; Pub.L. 100–409, §§ 3, 9, Aug. 20, 1988, 102 Stat. 1087, 1092.)

## HISTORICAL AND STATUTORY NOTES

**References in Text**

This Act, referred to in subsecs. (a), (b), (d)(1), (e), (f)(1), (2)(B)(ii), (g), (h)(1), and (i), is Pub.L. 94–579, Oct. 21, 1976, 90 Stat. 2743, as amended, known as the Federal Land Policy and Management Act of 1976. For complete classification of this Act to the Code, see Tables.

Act of January 22, 1983 (commonly known as the "Small Tracts Act)", referred to in subsec. (h)(2), is Pub.L. 97–465, Jan. 12, 1983, 96 Stat. 2535, which enacted sections 521c to 521i of Title 16, Conservation, and amended section 484a of Title 16. For complete classification of this Act to the Code, see Tables.

The mining laws, referred to in subsec. (i), are classified generally to Title 30, Mineral Lands and Mining.

The public land laws, referred to in subsec. (i)(1), are classified generally to this title.

**Congressional Statement of Findings and Purposes**

Section 2 of Pub.L. 100–409 provided that:

"(a) **Findings.**—The Congress finds and declares that—

"(1) land exchanges are a very important tool for Federal and State land managers and private landowners to consolidate Federal, State, and private holdings of land or interests in land for purposes of more efficient management and to secure important objectives including the protection of fish and wildlife habitat and aesthetic values; the enhancement of recreation opportunities; the consolidation of mineral and timber holdings for more logical and efficient development; the expansion of communities; the promotion of multiple-use values; and fulfillment of public needs;

"(2) needs for land ownership adjustments and consolidation consistently outpace available funding for land purchases by the Federal Government and thereby make land exchanges an increasingly important method of land acquisition and consolidation for both Federal and State land managers and private landowners;

"(3) the Federal Land Policy and Management Act of 1976 [Pub.L. 94–579, see Short Title note set out under section 1701 of this title] and other laws provide a basic framework and authority for land exchanges involving lands under the jurisdiction of the Secretary of the Interior and the Secretary of Agriculture; and

"(4) such existing laws are in need of certain revisions to streamline and facilitate land exchange procedures and expedite exchanges.

"(b) **Purposes.**—The purposes of this Act [see Short Title of 1988 Amendment note set out under section 1701 of this title] are:

"(1) to facilitate and expedite land exchanges pursuant to the Federal Land Policy and Management Act of 1976 and other laws applicable to exchanges involving lands managed by the Departments of the Interior and Agriculture by—

"(A) providing more uniform rules and regulations pertaining to land appraisals which reflect nationally recognized appraisal standards; and

"(B) establishing procedures and guidelines for the resolution of appraisal disputes.

"(2) to provide sufficient resources to the Secretaries of the Interior and Agriculture to ensure that land exchange activities can proceed consistent with the public interest; and

"(3) to require a study and report concerning improvements in the handling of certain information related to Federal and other lands."

**Land Exchange Funding Authorization**

Section 4 of Pub.L. 100–409 provided that: "In order to ensure that there are increased funds and personnel available to the Secretaries of the Interior and Agriculture to consider, process, and consummate land exchanges pursuant to the Federal Land Policy and Management Act of 1976 [Pub.L. 94–579, see Short Title note set out under section 1701 of this title] and other applicable law, there are hereby authorized to be appropriated for fiscal years 1989 through 1998 an annual amount not to exceed $4,000,000 which shall be used jointly or divided among the Secretaries as they determine appropriate for the consideration, processing, and consummation of land exchanges pursuant to the Federal Land Policy and Management Act of 1976, as amended, and other applicable law. Such moneys are expressly intended by Congress to be in addition to, and not offset against, moneys otherwise annually requested by the Secretaries, and appropriated by Congress for land exchange purposes."

**Savings Provisions; Severability of Provisions**

Section 5 of Pub.L. 100–409 provided that: "Nothing in this Act [see Short Title of 1988 Amendment note set out section 1701 of this title] shall be construed as amending the Alaska Native Claims Settlement Act (Public Law 92–203, as amended) [section 1601 et seq. of this title] or the Alaska National Interest Lands Conservation Act (Public Law 96–487, as amended) [Pub.L. 96–487, Dec. 2, 1980, 94 Stat. 2371, see Short Title note set out under section 3101 of Title 16, Conservation] or as enlarging or diminishing the authority with regard to exchanges conferred upon either the Secretary of the Interior or the Secretary of Agriculture by either such Acts. If any provision of this Act or the application thereof is held invalid, the remainder of the Act and the application thereof shall not be affected thereby. Nothing in this Act shall be construed to change the discretionary nature of land exchanges or to prohibit the Secretary concerned or any other party or parties involved in a land exchange from withdrawing from the exchange at any time, unless the Secretary concerned and the other party or parties specifically commit otherwise by written agreement."

## § 1717. Qualifications of conveyees

[FLPMA § 207]

No tract of land may be disposed of under this Act, whether by sale, exchange, or donation, to any person who is not a citizen of the United States, or in the case of a corporation, is not subject to the laws of any State or of the United States.

(Pub.L. 94–579, Title II, § 207, Oct. 21, 1976, 90 Stat. 2757.)

### HISTORICAL AND STATUTORY NOTES

**References in Text**

This Act, referred to in text, is Pub.L. 94–579, Oct. 21, 1976, 90 Stat. 2743, as amended, known as the Federal Land Policy and Management Act of 1976. For complete classification of this Act to the Code, see Tables.

## § 1718. Documents of conveyance; terms, covenants, etc.

[FLPMA § 208]

The Secretary shall issue all patents or other documents of conveyance after any disposal authorized by this Act. The Secretary shall insert in any such patent or other document of conveyance he issues, except in the case of land exchanges, for which the provisions of subsection[1] 1716(b) of this title shall apply, such terms, covenants, conditions, and reservations as he deems necessary to insure proper land use and protection of the public interest: *Provided*, That a conveyance of lands by the Secretary, subject to such terms, covenants, conditions, and reservations, shall not exempt the grantee from compliance with applicable Federal or State law or State land use plans: *Provided further*, That the Secretary shall not make conveyances of public lands containing terms and conditions which would, at the time of the conveyance, constitute a violation of any law or regulation pursuant to State and local land use plans, or programs.

(Pub.L. 94–579, Title II, § 208, Oct. 21, 1976, 90 Stat. 2757.)

[1] So in original. Probably should be "section".

### HISTORICAL AND STATUTORY NOTES

**References in Text**

This Act, referred to in text, is Pub.L. 94–579, Oct. 21, 1976, 90 Stat. 2743, as amended, known as the Federal Land Policy and Management Act of 1976. For complete classification of this Act to the Code, see Tables.

## § 1719. Mineral interests; reservation and conveyance requirements and procedures

[FLPMA § 209]

(a) All conveyances of title issued by the Secretary, except those involving land exchanges provided for in section 1716 of this title, shall reserve to the United States all minerals in the lands, together with the right to prospect for, mine, and remove the minerals under applicable law and such regulations as the Secretary may prescribe, except that if the Secretary makes the findings specified in subsection (b) of this section, the minerals may then be conveyed together with the surface to the prospective surface owner as provided in subsection (b) of this section.

(b)(1) The Secretary, after consultation with the appropriate department or agency head, may convey mineral interests owned by the United States where the surface is or will be in non-Federal ownership, regardless of which Federal entity may have administered the surface, if he finds (1) that there are no known mineral values in the land, or (2) that the reservation of the mineral rights in the United States is interfering with or precluding appropriate nonmineral development of the land and that such development is a more beneficial use of the land than mineral development.

(2) Conveyance of mineral interests pursuant to this section shall be made only to the existing or proposed record owner of the surface, upon payment of administrative costs and the fair market value of the interests being conveyed.

(3) Before considering an application for conveyance of mineral interests pursuant to this section—

(i) the Secretary shall require the deposit by the applicant of a sum of money which he deems sufficient to cover administrative costs including, but not limited to, costs of conducting an exploratory program to determine the character of the mineral deposits in the land, evaluating the data obtained under the exploratory program to determine the fair market value of the mineral interests to be conveyed, and preparing and issuing the documents of conveyance: *Provided*, That, if the administrative costs exceed the deposit, the applicant shall pay the outstanding amount; and, if the deposit exceeds the administrative costs, the applicant shall be given a credit for or refund of the excess; or

(ii) the applicant, with the consent of the Secretary, shall have conducted, and submitted to the Secretary the results of, such an exploratory program, in accordance with standards promulgated by the Secretary.

(4) Moneys paid to the Secretary for administrative costs pursuant to this subsection shall be paid to the agency which rendered the service and deposited to the appropriation then current.

(Pub.L. 94–579, Title II, § 209, Oct. 21, 1976, 90 Stat. 2757.)

## § 1720. Coordination by Secretary of the Interior with State and local governments

**[FLPMA § 210]**

At least sixty days prior to offering for sale or otherwise conveying public lands under this Act, the Secretary shall notify the Governor of the State within which such lands are located and the head of the governing body of any political subdivision of the State having zoning or other land use regulatory jurisdiction in the geographical area within which such lands are located, in order to afford the appropriate body the opportunity to zone or otherwise regulate, or change or amend existing zoning or other regulations concerning the use of such lands prior to such conveyance. The Secretary shall also promptly notify such public officials of the issuance of the patent or other document of conveyance for such lands.

(Pub.L. 94–579, Title II, § 210, Oct. 21, 1976, 90 Stat. 2758.)

### HISTORICAL AND STATUTORY NOTES

**References in Text**

This Act, referred to in text, is Pub.L. 94–579, Oct. 21, 1976, 90 Stat. 2743, as amended, known as the Federal Land Policy and Management Act of 1976. For complete classification of this Act to the Code, see Tables.

## § 1721. Conveyances of public lands to States, local governments, etc.

**[FLPMA § 211]**

### (a) Unsurveyed islands; authorization and limitations on authority

The Secretary is authorized to convey to States or their political subdivisions under the Recreation and Public Purposes Act (44 Stat. 741 as amended; 43 U.S.C. 869 et seq.), as amended, but without regard to the acreage limitations contained therein, unsurveyed islands determined by the Secretary to be public lands of the United States. The conveyance of any such island may be made without survey: *Provided, however*, That such island may be surveyed at the request of the applicant State or its political subdivision if such State or subdivision donates money or services to the Secretary for such survey, the Secretary accepts such money or services, and such services are conducted pursuant to criteria established by the Director of the Bureau of Land Management. Any such island so surveyed shall not be conveyed without approval of such survey by the Secretary prior to the conveyance.

### (b) Omitted lands; authorization and limitations on authority

(1) The Secretary is authorized to convey to States and their political subdivisions under the Recreation and Public Purposes Act [43 U.S.C.A. §§ 869 to 869–4], but without regard to the acreage limitations contained therein, lands other than islands determined by him after survey to be public lands of the United States erroneously or fraudulently omitted from the original surveys (hereinafter referred to as "omitted lands"). Any such conveyance shall not be made without a survey: *Provided,* That the prospective recipient may donate money or services to the Secretary for the surveying necessary prior to conveyance if the Secretary accepts such money or services, such services are conducted pursuant to criteria established by the Director of the Bureau of Land Management,

and such survey is approved by the Secretary prior to the conveyance.

(2) The Secretary is authorized to convey to the occupant of any omitted lands which, after survey, are found to have been occupied and developed for a five-year period prior to January 1, 1975, if the Secretary determines that such conveyance is in the public interest and will serve objectives which outweigh all public objectives and values which would be served by retaining such lands in Federal ownership. Conveyance under this subparagraph shall be made at not less than the fair market value of the land, as determined by the Secretary, and upon payment in addition of administrative costs, including the cost of making the survey, the cost of appraisal, and the cost of making the conveyance.

**(c) Conformity with land use plans and programs and coordination with State and local governments of conveyances**

(1) No conveyance shall be made pursuant to this section until the relevant State government, local government, and areawide planning agency designated pursuant to section 204 of the Demonstration Cities and Metropolitan Development Act of 1966 (80 Stat. 1255, 1262) [42 U.S.C.A. § 3334] and/or section 6506 of Title 31 have notified the Secretary as to the consistency of such conveyance with applicable State and local government land use plans and programs.

(2) The provisions of section 1720 of this title shall be applicable to all conveyances under this section.

**(d) Applicability of other statutory requirements for authorized use of conveyed lands**

The final sentence of section 1(c) of the Recreation and Public Purposes Act [43 U.S.C.A. § 869(c) ] shall not be applicable to conveyances under this section.

**(e) Limitations on uses of conveyed lands**

No conveyance pursuant to this section shall be used as the basis for determining the baseline between Federal and State ownership, the boundary of any State for purposes of determining the extent of a State's submerged lands or the line of demarcation of Federal jurisdiction, or any similar or related purpose.

**(f) Applicability to lands within National Forest System, National Park System, National Wildlife Refuge System, and National Wild and Scenic Rivers System**

The provisions of this section shall not apply to any lands within the National Forest System, defined in the Act of August 17, 1974 (88 Stat. 476; 16 U.S.C. 1601), the National Park System, the National Wildlife Refuge System, and the National Wild and Scenic Rivers System.

**(g) Applicability to other statutory provisions authorizing sale of specific omitted lands**

Nothing in this section shall supersede the provisions of the Act of December 22, 1928 (45 Stat. 1069; 43 U.S.C. 1068), as amended, and the Act of May 31, 1962 (76 Stat. 89), or any other Act authorizing the sale of specific omitted lands.

(Pub.L. 94–579, Title II, § 211, Oct. 21, 1976, 90 Stat. 2758.)

### HISTORICAL AND STATUTORY NOTES

**References in Text**

The Recreation and Public Purposes Act, referred to in subsecs. (a) and (b)(1), is Act June 14, 1926, c. 578, 44 Stat. 741, as amended, which is classified to sections 869 to 869–4 of this title. For complete classification of this Act to the Code, see Short Title note set out under section 869 of this title and Tables.

The Act of August 17, 1974 (88 Stat. 476; 16 U.S.C. 1601), referred to in subsec. (f), is Pub.L. 93–378, Aug. 17, 1974, 88 Stat. 476, as amended, known as the Forest and Rangelands Renewable Resources Planning Act of 1974, which is classified generally to subchapter I (section 1600 et seq.) chapter 36 of Title 16, Conservation. The provisions of such Act defining the lands within the National Forest System are set out in section 1609 of Title 16. For complete classification of this Act to the Code, see Short Title note set out under section 1600 of Title 16 and Tables volume.

The Act of December 22, 1928 (45 Stat. 1069; 43 U.S.C. 1068), as amended, referred to in subsec. (g), is Act Dec. 22, 1928, c. 47, 45 Stat. 1069, as amended, which is classified generally to chapter 25A (section 1068 et seq.) of this title. For complete classification of this Act to the Code, see Tables volume.

The Act of May 31, 1962, referred to in subsec. (g), is Pub.L. 87–469, May 31, 1962, 76 Stat. 89, which is not classified to the Code.

**Codifications**

In subsec. (c)(1), "section 6506 of Title 31" was substituted for "Title IV of the Intergovernmental Cooperation Act of 1968 (82 Stat. 1098, 1103–4) [42 U.S.C.A. § 4231 et seq.]" on authority of Pub.L. 97–258, § 4(b), Sept. 13, 1982, 96 Stat. 1067, the first section of which enacted Title 31, Money and Finance.

## § 1722. Sale of public lands subject to unintentional trespass

[FLPMA § 212]

**(a) Preference right of contiguous landowners; offering price**

Notwithstanding the provisions of the Act of September 26, 1968 (82 Stat. 870; 43 U.S.C. 1431–1435), hereinafter called the "1968 Act", with respect to applications under the 1968 Act which were pending before the Secretary as of the effective date of this subsection and which he approves for sale under the criteria prescribed by the 1968 Act, he shall give the right of first refusal to those having a preference right under section 2 of the 1968 Act [43 U.S.C.A. § 1432].

The Secretary shall offer such lands to such preference right holders at their fair market value (exclusive of any values added to the land by such holders and their predecessors in interest) as determined by the Secretary as of September 26, 1973.

**(b) Procedures applicable**

Within three years after October 21, 1976, the Secretary shall notify the filers of applications subject to paragraph (a) of this section whether he will offer them the lands applied for and at what price; that is, their fair market value as of September 26, 1973, excluding any value added to the lands by the applicants or their predecessors in interest. He will also notify the President of the Senate and the Speaker of the House of Representatives of the lands which he has determined not to sell pursuant to paragraph (a) of this section and the reasons therefor. With respect to such lands which the Secretary determined not to sell, he shall take no other action to convey those lands or interests in them before the end of ninety days (not counting days on which the House of Representatives or the Senate has adjourned for more than three consecutive days) beginning on the date the Secretary has submitted such notice to the Senate and House of Representatives. If, during that ninety-day period, the Congress adopts a concurrent resolution stating the length of time such suspension of action should continue, he shall continue such suspension for the specified time period. If the committee to which a resolution has been referred during the said ninety-day period, has not reported it at the end of thirty calendar days after its referral, it shall be in order to either discharge the committee from further consideration of such resolution or to discharge the committee from consideration of any other resolution with respect to the suspension of action. A motion to discharge may be made only by an individual favoring the resolution, shall be highly privileged (except that it may not be made after the committee has reported such a resolution), and debate thereon shall be limited to not more than one hour, to be divided equally between those favoring and those opposing the resolution. An amendment to the motion shall not be in order, and it shall not be in order to move to reconsider the vote by which the motion was agreed to or disagreed to. If the motion to discharge is agreed to or disagreed to, the motion may not be made with respect to any other resolution with respect to the same suspension of action. When the committee has reprinted, or has been discharged from further consideration of a resolution, it shall at any time thereafter be in order (even though a previous motion to the same effect has been disagreed to) to move to proceed to the consideration of the resolution. The motion shall be highly privileged and shall not be debatable. An amendment to the motion shall not be in order, and it shall not be in order to move to reconsider the vote by which the motion was agreed to or disagreed to.

**(c) Time for processing of applications and sales**

Within five years after October 21, 1976, the Secretary shall complete the processing of all applications filed under the 1968 Act and hold sales covering all lands which he has determined to sell thereunder.

(Pub.L. 94–579, Title II, § 214, Oct. 21, 1976, 90 Stat. 2760.)

### HISTORICAL AND STATUTORY NOTES

**References in Text**

The Act of Sept. 26, 1968, referred to in subsec. (a), is Pub.L. 90–516, Sept. 26, 1968, 82 Stat. 870, which was classified generally to subchapter VII (section 1431 et seq.) of chapter 30 of this title, and was omitted from the Code pursuant to section 1435 of this title, which provided that the authority granted by that subchapter was to expire three years from September 26, 1968, with certain exceptions. For complete classification of this Act to the Code prior to omission, see Tables.

The effective date of this subsection, referred to in subsec. (a), probably means the date of the enactment of such subsection (a) by Pub.L. 94–579, which was approved Oct. 21, 1976.

## § 1723. Temporary revocation authority

**[FLPMA § 215]**

**(a) Exchange involved**

When the sole impediment to consummation of an exchange of lands or interests therein (hereinafter referred to as an exchange) determined to be in the public interest, is the inability of the Secretary of the Interior to revoke, modify, or terminate part or all of a withdrawal or classification because of the order (or subsequent modification or continuance thereof) of the United States District Court for the District of Columbia dated February 10, 1986, in Civil Action No. 85–2238 (National Wildlife Federation v. Robert E. Burford, et al.), the Secretary of the Interior is hereby authorized, notwithstanding such order (or subsequent modification or continuance thereof), to use the authority contained herein, in lieu of other authority provided in this Act including section 1714 of this title, to revoke, modify, or terminate in whole or in part, withdrawals or classifications to the extent deemed necessary by the Secretary to enable the United States to transfer land or interests therein out of Federal ownership pursuant to an exchange.

**(b) Requirements**

The authority specified in subsection (a) of this section may be exercised only in cases where—

(1) a particular exchange is proposed to be carried out pursuant to this Act, as amended, or other applicable law authorizing such an exchange;

(2) the proposed exchange has been prepared in compliance with all laws applicable to such exchange;

(3) the head of each Federal agency managing the lands proposed for such transfer has submitted to the Secretary of the Interior a statement of concurrence with the proposed revocation, modification, or termination;

(4) at least sixty days have elapsed since the Secretary of the Interior has published in the Federal Register a notice of the proposed revocation, modification, or termination; and

(5) at least sixty days have elapsed since the Secretary of the Interior has transmitted to the Committee on Natural Resources of the House of Representatives and the Committee on Energy and Natural Resources of the United States Senate a report which includes—

(A) a justification for the necessity of exercising such authority in order to complete an exchange;

(B) an explanation of the reasons why the continuation of the withdrawal or a classification or portion thereof proposed for revocation, modification, or termination is no longer necessary for the purposes of the statutory or other program or programs for which the withdrawal or classification was made or other relevant programs;

(C) assurances that all relevant documents concerning the proposed exchange or purchase for which such authority is proposed to be exercised (including documents related to compliance with the National Environmental Policy Act of 1969 [42 U.S.C.A. § 4321 et seq.] and all other applicable provisions of law) are available for public inspection in the office of the Secretary concerned located nearest to the lands proposed for transfer out of Federal ownership in furtherance of such exchange and that the relevant portions of such documents are also available in the offices of the Secretary concerned in Washington, District of Columbia; and

(D) an explanation of the effect of the revocation, modification, or termination of a withdrawal or classification or portion thereof and the transfer of lands out of Federal ownership pursuant to the particular proposed exchange, on the objectives of the land management plan which is applicable at the time of such transfer to the land to be transferred out of Federal ownership.

**(c) Limitations**

(1) Nothing in this section shall be construed as affirming or denying any of the allegations made by any party in the civil action specified in subsection (a) of this section, or as constituting an expression of congressional opinion with respect to the merits of any allegation, contention, or argument made or issue raised by any party in such action, or as expanding or diminishing the jurisdiction of the United States District Court for the District of Columbia.

(2) Except as specifically provided in this section, nothing in this section shall be construed as modifying, terminating, revoking, or otherwise affecting any provision of law applicable to land exchanges, withdrawals, or classifications.

(3) The availability or exercise of the authority granted in subsection (a) of this section may not be considered by the Secretary of the Interior in making a determination pursuant to this Act or other applicable law as to whether or not any proposed exchange is in the public interest.

**(d) Termination**

The authority specified in subsection (a) of this section shall expire either (1) on December 31, 1990, or (2) when the Court order (or subsequent modification or continuation thereof) specified in subsection (a) of this section is no longer in effect, whichever occurs first.

(Pub.L. 94–579, Title II, § 215, as added Pub.L. 100–409, § 10, Aug. 20, 1988, 102 Stat. 1092, and amended Pub.L. 103–437, § 16(d)(2), Nov. 2, 1994, 108 Stat. 4595.)

## HISTORICAL AND STATUTORY NOTES

**References in Text**

This Act, referred to in subsecs. (a), (b)(1), and (c)(3), is Pub.L. 94–579, Oct. 21, 1976, 90 Stat. 2743, as amended, known as the Federal Land Policy and Management Act of 1976. For complete classification of this Act to the Code, see Tables.

The National Environmental Policy Act of 1969, referred to in subsec. (b)(5)(C), is Pub.L. 91–190, Jan. 1, 1970, 83 Stat. 852, as amended, which is classified generally to chapter 55 (section 4321 et seq.) of Title 42, The Public Health and Welfare. For complete classification of this Act to the Code, see Short Title note set out under section 4321 of Title 42 and Tables.

**Change of Name**

Any reference in any provision of law enacted before Jan. 4, 1995, to the Committee on Natural Resources of the House of Representatives treated as referring to the Committee on Resources of the House of Representatives, see section 1(a)(8) of Pub.L. 104–14, set out as a note preceding section 21 of Title 2, The Congress.

**Savings Provisions; Severability of Provisions**

Nothing in Pub.L. 100–409 construed as amending the Alaska Native Claims Settlement Act, Pub.L. 92–203, or the Alaska National Interest Lands Conservation Act, Pub.L. 96–487, as enlarging or diminishing the authority with regard to exchanges conferred upon either the Secretary of the Interior or the Secretary of Agriculture by either such Acts, or as changing the discretionary nature of land exchanges or prohibiting the Secretary concerned or any other party or parties involved in a land exchange from withdrawing from the exchange at any time, unless the Secretary concerned and the other party or parties specifically commit otherwise by written agreement, with any provision of Pub.L. 100–409 or the application thereof being held invalid not affecting the remainder of Pub.L. 100–409 and the application thereof, see section 5 of Pub.L. 100–409, set out as a note under section 1716 of this title.

## SUBCHAPTER III—ADMINISTRATION

### § 1731. Bureau of Land Management

**[FLPMA § 301]**

**(a) Director; appointment, qualifications, functions, and duties**

The Bureau of Land Management established by Reorganization Plan Numbered 3, of 1946 shall have as its head a Director. Appointments to the position of Director shall hereafter be made by the President, by and with the advice and consent of the Senate. The Director of the Bureau shall have a broad background and substantial experience in public land and natural resource management. He shall carry out such functions and shall perform such duties as the Secretary may prescribe with respect to the management of lands and resources under his jurisdiction according to the applicable provisions of this Act and any other applicable law.

**(b) Statutory transfer of functions, powers and duties relating to administration of laws**

Subject to the discretion granted to him by Reorganization Plan Numbered 3 of 1950, the Secretary shall carry out through the Bureau all functions, powers, and duties vested in him and relating to the administration of laws which, on October 21, 1976, were carried out by him through the Bureau of Land Management established by section 403 of Reorganization Plan Numbered 3 of 1946. The Bureau shall administer such laws according to the provisions thereof existing as of October 21, 1976, as modified by the provisions of this Act or by subsequent law.

**(c) Associate Director, Assistant Directors, and other employees; appointment and compensation**

In addition to the Director, there shall be an Associate Director of the Bureau and so many Assistant Directors, and other employees, as may be necessary, who shall be appointed by the Secretary subject to the provisions of Title 5 governing appointments in the competitive service, and shall be paid in accordance with the provisions of chapter 51 and subchapter 3[1] of chapter 53 of such title relating to classification and General Schedule pay rates.

**(d) Existing regulations relating to administration of laws**

Nothing in this section shall affect any regulation of the Secretary with respect to the administration of laws administered by him through the Bureau on October 21, 1976.

(Pub.L. 94–579, Title III, § 301, Oct. 21, 1976, 90 Stat. 2762.)

[1] So in original. Probably should be subchapter "III".

#### HISTORICAL AND STATUTORY NOTES

**References in Text**

The provision of Reorg. Plan No. 3 of 1946 establishing the Bureau of Land Management, referred to in subsec. (a), is section 403 of such Reorg. Plan. Section 403 of Reorg. Plan No. 3 of 1946, also referred to in subsec. (b), is set out as a note under section 1 of this title.

This Act, referred to in subsecs. (a) and (b), is Pub.L. 94–579, Oct. 21, 1976, 90 Stat. 2743, as amended, known as the Federal Land Policy and Management Act of 1976. For complete classification of this Act to the Code, see Tables volume.

Reorg. Plan No. 3 of 1950, referred to in subsec. (b), is set out under section 1451 of this title.

The provisions of Title 5, governing appointments in the competitive service, referred to in subsec. (c), are classified to section 3301 et seq. of Title 5, Government Organization and Employees.

The General Schedule, referred to in subsec. (c), is set out under section 5332 of Title 5.

**Use of Appropriated Funds For Protection of Lands and Surveys of Federal Lands in Alaska**

Pub.L. 102–381, Title I, Oct. 5, 1992, 106 Stat. 1378, provided in part: "That appropriations herein made, in fiscal year 1993 and thereafter, may be expended for surveys of Federal lands and on a reimbursable basis for surveys of Federal lands and for protection of lands for the State of Alaska[.]".

### § 1732. Management of use, occupancy, and development of public lands

**[FLPMA § 302]**

**(a) Multiple use and sustained yield requirements applicable; exception**

The Secretary shall manage the public lands under principles of multiple use and sustained yield, in accordance with the land use plans developed by him under section 1712 of this title when they are available, except that where a tract of such public land has been dedicated to specific uses according to any other provisions of law it shall be managed in accordance with such law.

**(b) Easements, permits, etc., for utilization through habitation, cultivation, and development of small trade or manufacturing concerns; applicable statutory requirements**

In managing the public lands, the Secretary shall, subject to this Act and other applicable law and under such terms and conditions as are consistent with such law, regulate, through easements, permits, leases, licenses, published rules, or other instruments as the Secretary deems appropriate, the use, occupancy, and development of the public lands, including, but not limited to, long-term leases to permit individuals to utilize public lands for habitation, cultivation, and the development of small trade or manufacturing concerns: *Provided*, That unless otherwise provided for by law, the Secretary may permit Federal departments and agencies to use, occupy, and develop public lands only through rights-of-way under section 1767 of this title, withdrawals under section 1714 of this title, and, where the proposed use and development are similar or closely related to the programs of the Secretary for the public lands involved, cooperative agreements under section 1737(b) of this title: *Provided further*, That nothing in this Act shall be construed as authorizing the Secretary concerned to require Federal permits to hunt and fish on public lands or on lands in the National Forest System and adjacent waters or as enlarging or diminishing the responsibility and authority of the States for management of fish and resident wildlife. However, the Secretary concerned may designate areas of public land and of lands in the National Forest System where, and establish periods when, no hunting or fishing will be permitted for reasons of public safety, administration, or compliance with provisions of applicable law. Except in emergencies, any regulations of the Secretary concerned relating to hunting and fishing pursuant to this section shall be put into effect only after consultation with the appropriate State fish and game department. Nothing in this Act shall modify or change any provision of Federal law relating to migratory birds or to endangered or threatened species. Except as provided in section 1744, section 1782, and subsection (f) of section 1781 of this title and in the last sentence of this paragraph, no provision of this section or any other section of this Act shall in any way amend the Mining Law of 1872 or impair the rights of any locators or claims under that Act, including, but not limited to, rights of ingress and egress. In managing the public lands the Secretary shall, by regulation or otherwise, take any action necessary to prevent unnecessary or undue degradation of the lands.

**(c) Revocation or suspension provision in instrument authorizing use, occupancy or development; violation of provision; procedure applicable**

The Secretary shall insert in any instrument providing for the use, occupancy, or development of the public lands a provision authorizing revocation or suspension, after notice and hearing, of such instrument upon a final administrative finding of a violation of any term or condition of the instrument, including, but not limited to, terms and conditions requiring compliance with regulations under Acts applicable to the public lands and compliance with applicable State or Federal air or water quality standard or implementation plan: *Provided*, That such violation occurred on public lands covered by such instrument and occurred in connection with the exercise of rights and privileges granted by it: *Provided further*, That the Secretary shall terminate any such suspension no later than the date upon which he determines the cause of said violation has been rectified: *Provided further*, That the Secretary may order an immediate temporary suspension prior to a hearing or final administrative finding if he determines that such a suspension is necessary to protect health or safety or the environment: *Provided further*, That, where other applicable law contains specific provisions for suspension, revocation, or cancellation of a permit, license, or other authorization to use, occupy, or develop the public lands, the specific provisions of such law shall prevail.

**(d) Authorization to utilize certain public lands in Alaska for military purposes**

(1) The Secretary of the Interior, after consultation with the Governor of Alaska, may issue to the Secretary of Defense or to the Secretary of a military department within the Department of Defense or to the Commandant of the Coast Guard a nonrenewable general authorization to utilize public lands in Alaska (other than within a conservation system unit or the Steese National Conservation Area or the White Mountains National Recreation Area) for purposes of military maneuvering, military training, or equipment testing not involving artillery firing, aerial or other gunnery, or other use of live ammunition or ordnance.

(2) Use of public lands pursuant to a general authorization under this subsection shall be limited to areas where such use would not be inconsistent with the plans prepared pursuant to section 1712 of this title. Each such use shall be subject to a requirement that the using department shall be responsible for any necessary cleanup and decontamination of the lands used, and to such other terms and conditions (including but not limited to restrictions on use of off-road or all-terrain vehicles) as the Secretary of the Interior may require to—

**(A)** minimize adverse impacts on the natural, environmental, scientific, cultural, and other resources and values (including fish and wildlife habitat) of the public lands involved; and

**(B)** minimize the period and method of such use and the interference with or restrictions on other uses of the public lands involved.

**(3)(A)** A general authorization issued pursuant to this subsection shall not be for a term of more than three years and shall be revoked in whole or in part, as the Secretary of the Interior finds necessary, prior to the end of such term upon a determination by the Secretary of the Interior that there has been a failure to comply with its terms and conditions or that activities pursuant to such an authorization have had or might have a significant adverse impact on the resources or values of the affected lands.

(B) Each specific use of a particular area of public lands pursuant to a general authorization under this subsection shall be subject to specific authorization by the Secretary and to appropriate terms and conditions, including such as are described in paragraph (2) of this subsection.

(4) Issuance of a general authorization pursuant to this subsection shall be subject to the provisions of section 1712(f) of this title, section 3120 of Title 16, and all other applicable provisions of law. The Secretary of a military department (or the commandant of the Coast Guard) requesting such authorization shall reimburse the Secretary of the Interior for the costs of implementing this paragraph. An authorization pursuant to this subsection shall not authorize the construction of permanent structures or facilities on the public lands.

(5) To the extent that public safety may require closure to public use of any portion of the public lands covered by an authorization issued pursuant to this subsection, the Secretary of the military department concerned or the Commandant of the Coast Guard shall take appropriate steps to notify the public concerning such closure and to provide appropriate warnings of risks to public safety.

(6) For purposes of this subsection, the term "conservation system unit" has the same meaning as specified in section 3102 of Title 16.

(Pub.L. 94–579, Title III, § 302, Oct. 21, 1976, 90 Stat. 2762; Pub.L. 100–586, Nov. 3, 1988, 102 Stat. 2980.)

### HISTORICAL AND STATUTORY NOTES

**References in Text**

This Act, referred to in subsec. (b), is Pub.L. 94–579, Oct. 21, 1976, 90 Stat. 2743, as amended, known as the Federal Land Policy and Management Act of 1976. For complete classification of this Act to the Code, see Tables.

The Mining Law of 1872, referred to in subsec. (b), is Act May 10, 1872, c. 152, 17 Stat. 91, which was incorporated into the Revised Statutes of 1878 as R.S. §§ 2319 to 2328, 2331, 2333 to 2337, and 2344, which are classified to sections 22 to 24, 26 to 28, 29, 30, 33 to 35, 37, 39 to 42, and 47 of Title 30, Mineral Lands and Mining. For complete classification of such Revised Statutes sections to the Code, see Tables volume.

**Transfer of Functions**

Enforcement functions of Secretary or other official in Department of Interior related to compliance with land use permits for temporary use of public lands and other associated land uses, issued under sections 1732, 1761, and 1763 to 1771 of this title, with respect preconstruction, construction, and initial operation of transportation systems for Canadian and Alaskan natural gas were transferred to the Federal Inspector, Office of Federal Inspector for the Alaska Natural Gas Transportation System, until the first anniversary of date of initial operation of the Alaska Natural Gas Transportation System, see Reorg. Plan No. 1 of 1979, §§ 102(e), 203(a), 44 F.R. 33663, 33666, 93 Stat. 1373, 1376, effective July 1, 1979, set out in Appendix 1 to Title 5, Government Organization and Employees.

## § 1733. Enforcement authority

**[FLPMA § 303]**

### (a) Regulations for implementation of management, use, and protection requirements; violations; criminal penalties

The Secretary shall issue regulations necessary to implement the provisions of this Act with respect to the management, use, and protection of the public lands, including the property located thereon. Any person who knowingly and willfully violates any such regulation which is lawfully issued pursuant to this Act shall be fined no more than $1,000 or imprisoned no more than twelve months, or both. Any person charged with a violation of such regulation may be tried and sentenced by any United States magistrate judge designated for that purpose by the court by which he was appointed, in the same manner and subject to the same conditions and limitations as provided for in section 3401 of Title 18.

### (b) Civil actions by Attorney General for violations of regulations; nature of relief; jurisdiction

At the request of the Secretary, the Attorney General may institute a civil action in any United States district court for an injunction or other appropriate order to prevent any person from utilizing public lands in violation of regulations issued by the Secretary under this Act.

### (c) Contracts for enforcement of Federal laws and regulations by local law enforcement officials; procedure applicable; contract requirements and implementation

(1) When the Secretary determines that assistance is necessary in enforcing Federal laws and regulations relating to the public lands or their resources he shall offer a contract to appropriate local officials having law enforcement authority within their respective jurisdictions with the view of achieving maximum feasible reliance upon local law enforcement officials in enforcing such laws and regulations. The Secretary shall negotiate on reasonable terms with such officials who have authority to enter into such contracts to enforce such Federal laws and regulations. In the performance of their duties under such contracts such officials and their agents are authorized to carry firearms; execute and serve any warrant or other process issued by a court or officer of competent jurisdiction; make arrests without warrant or process

for a misdemeanor he has reasonable grounds to believe is being committed in his presence or view, or for a felony if he has reasonable grounds to believe that the person to be arrested has committed or is committing such felony; search without warrant or process any person, place, or conveyance according to any Federal law or rule of law; and seize without warrant or process any evidentiary item as provided by Federal law. The Secretary shall provide such law enforcement training as he deems necessary in order to carry out the contracted for responsibilities. While exercising the powers and authorities provided by such contract pursuant to this section, such law enforcement officials and their agents shall have all the immunities of Federal law enforcement officials.

(2) The Secretary may authorize Federal personnel or appropriate local officials to carry out his law enforcement responsibilities with respect to the public lands and their resources. Such designated personnel shall receive the training and have the responsibilities and authority provided for in paragraph (1) of this subsection.

**(d) Cooperation with regulatory and law enforcement officials of any State or political subdivision in enforcement of laws or ordinances**

In connection with the administration and regulation of the use and occupancy of the public lands, the Secretary is authorized to cooperate with the regulatory and law enforcement officials of any State or political subdivision thereof in the enforcement of the laws or ordinances of such State or subdivision. Such cooperation may include reimbursement to a State or its subdivision for expenditures incurred by it in connection with activities which assist in the administration and regulation of use and occupancy of the public lands.

**(e) Uniformed desert ranger force in California Desert Conservation Area; establishment; enforcement of Federal laws and regulations**

Nothing in this section shall prevent the Secretary from promptly establishing a uniformed desert ranger force in the California Desert Conservation Area established pursuant to section 1781 of this title for the purpose of enforcing Federal laws and regulations relating to the public lands and resources managed by him in such area. The officers and members of such ranger force shall have the same responsibilities and authority as provided for in paragraph (1) of subsection (c) of this section.

**(f) Applicability of other Federal enforcement provisions**

Nothing in this Act shall be construed as reducing or limiting the enforcement authority vested in the Secretary by any other statute.

**(g) Unlawful activities**

The use, occupancy, or development of any portion of the public lands contrary to any regulation of the Secretary or other responsible authority, or contrary to any order issued pursuant to any such regulation, is unlawful and prohibited.

(Pub.L. 94–579, Title III, § 303, Oct. 21, 1976, 90 Stat. 2763; Pub.L. 101–650, Title III, § 321, Dec. 1, 1990, 104 Stat. 5117.)

### HISTORICAL AND STATUTORY NOTES

**References in Text**

This Act, referred to in subsecs. (a), (b), and (f), is Pub.L. 94–579, Oct. 21, 1976, 90 Stat. 2743, as amended, known as the Federal Land Policy and Management Act of 1976. For complete classification of this Act to the Code, see Tables.

**Modification of Regulations Relating to Mining Operations on Public Lands; Posting of Reclamation Bond for All Operations Involving Significant Surface Disturbance**

Pub.L. 99–500, Title I, § 101(h) [Title I, § 100], Oct. 18, 1986, 100 Stat. 1783–243; Pub.L. 99–591, Title I, § 101(h) [Title I, § 100], Oct. 30, 1986, 100 Stat. 3341–243, provided: "That regulations pertaining to mining operations on public lands conducted under the Mining Law of 1872 (30 U.S.C. 22, et seq.) [30 U.S.C.A. §§ 22 to 24, 26 to 28, 29, 30, 33 to 35, 37, 39 to 42, 47] and sections 302, 303, and 603 of the Federal Land Policy and Management Act of 1976 (43 U.S.C. 1732, 1733, and 1782) [sections 1732, 1733, and 1782 of this title] shall be modified to include a requirement for the posting of reclamation bonds by operators for all operations which involve significant surface disturbance, (a) at the discretion of the authorized officer for operators who have a record of compliance with pertinent regulations concerning mining on public lands, and (b) on a mandatory basis only for operators with a history of noncompliance with the aforesaid regulations: *Provided further,* That surety bonds, third party surety bonds, or irrevocable letters of credits shall qualify as bond instruments: *Provided further,* That evidence of an equivalent bond posted with a State agency shall be accepted in lieu of a separate bond: *Provided further,* That the amount of such bonds shall be sufficient to cover the costs of reclamation as estimated by the Bureau of Land Management."

**Change of Name**

United States magistrate appointed under section 631 of Title 28, Judiciary and Judicial Procedure, to be known as United States magistrate judge after Dec. 1, 1990, with any reference to United States magistrate or magistrate in Title 28, in any other Federal statute, etc., deemed a reference to United States magistrate judge appointed under section 631 of Title 28, see section 321 of Pub.L. 101–650, set out as a note under section 631 of Title 28.

## § 1734. Fees, charges, and commissions [FLPMA § 304]

**(a) Authority to establish and modify**

Notwithstanding any other provision of law, the Secretary may establish reasonable filing and service fees and reasonable charges, and commissions with respect to applications and other documents relating to the public lands and may change and abolish such fees, charges, and commissions.

**(b) Deposits for payments to reimburse reasonable costs of United States**

The Secretary is authorized to require a deposit of any payments intended to reimburse the United States for reasonable costs with respect to applications and other documents relating to such lands. The moneys received for reasonable costs under this subsection shall be deposited with the Treasury in a special account and are hereby authorized to be appropriated and made available until expended. As used in this section "reasonable costs" include, but are not limited to, the costs of special studies; environmental impact statements; monitoring construction, operation, maintenance, and termination of any authorized facility; or other special activities. In determining whether costs are reasonable under this section, the Secretary may take into consideration actual costs (exclusive of management overhead), the monetary value of the rights or privileges sought by the applicant, the efficiency to the government processing involved, that portion of the cost incurred for the benefit of the general public interest rather than for the exclusive benefit of the applicant, the public service provided, and other factors relevant to determining the reasonableness of the costs.

**(c) Refunds**

In any case where it shall appear to the satisfaction of the Secretary that any person has made a payment under any statute relating to the sale, lease, use, or other disposition of public lands which is not required or is in excess of the amount required by applicable law and the regulations issued by the Secretary, the Secretary, upon application or otherwise, may cause a refund to be made from applicable funds.

(Pub.L. 94–579, Title III, § 304, Oct. 21, 1976, 90 Stat. 2765.)

### HISTORICAL AND STATUTORY NOTES

**Filing Fees for Applications for Non-competitive Oil and Gas Leases; Study and Report of Rental Charges on Oil and Gas Leases**

Pub.L. 97–35, Title XIV, § 1401(d), Aug. 13, 1981, 95 Stat. 748, provided that:

"(1) Notwithstanding any other provision of law, effective October 1, 1981, all applications for noncompetitive oil and gas leases shall be accompanied by a filing fee of not less than $25 for each such application: *Provided*, That any increase in the filing fee above $25 shall be established by regulation and subject to the provisions of the Act of August 31, 1951 (65 Stat. 290) [probably means Title V of that Act which was classified to section 483a of former Title 31, Money and Finance and was repealed and reenacted as section 9701 of Title 31 by Pub.L. 97–258] the Act of October 20, 1976 (90 Stat. 2765) [probably should be Oct. 21, 1976, meaning this chapter] but not limited to actual costs. Such fees shall be retained as a service charge even though the application or offer may be rejected or withdrawn in whole or in part.

"(2) The Secretary of the Interior is hereby directed to conduct a study and report to Congress within one year of the date of enactment of this Act [Aug. 13, 1981], regarding the current annual rental charges on all noncompetitive oil and gas leases to investigate the feasibility and effect of raising such rentals."

## § 1734a. Availability of excess fees

In fiscal year 1997 and thereafter, all fees, excluding mining claim fees, in excess of the fiscal year 1996 collections established by the Secretary of the Interior under the authority of section 1734 of this title for processing, recording, or documenting authorizations to use public lands or public land natural resources (including cultural, historical, and mineral) and for providing specific services to public land users, and which are not presently being covered into any Bureau of Land Management appropriation accounts, and not otherwise dedicated by law for a specific distribution, shall be made immediately available for program operations in this account and remain available until expended.

(Pub.L. 104–208, Div. A, Title I, § 101(d) [Title I], Sept. 30, 1996, 110 Stat. 3009–182.)

### HISTORICAL AND STATUTORY NOTES

**Codifications**

Section was enacted as part of the Department of the Interior and Related Agencies Appropriations Act, 1997, and not as part of the Federal Land Policy and Management Act of 1976, Pub.L. 94–579, which comprises this chapter.

## § 1735. Forfeitures and deposits

**[FLPMA § 305]**

**(a) Credit to separate account in Treasury; appropriation and availability**

Any moneys received by the United States as a result of the forfeiture of a bond or other security by a resource developer or purchaser or permittee who does not fulfill the requirements of his contract or permit or does not comply with the regulations of the Secretary; or as a result of a compromise or settlement of any claim whether sounding in tort or in contract involving present or potential damage to the public lands shall be credited to a separate account in the Treasury and are hereby authorized to be appropriated and made available, until expended as the Secretary may direct, to cover the cost to the United States of any improvement, protection, or rehabilitation work on those public lands which has been rendered necessary by the action which has led to the forfeiture, compromise, or settlement.

**(b) Expenditure of moneys collected administering Oregon and California Railroad and Coos Bay Wagon Road Grant lands**

Any moneys collected under this Act in connection with lands administered under the Act of August 28, 1937 (50 Stat. 874; 43 U.S.C. 1181a–1181j), shall be expended for the benefit of such land only.

**(c) Refunds**

If any portion of a deposit or amount forfeited under this Act is found by the Secretary to be in excess of the cost of doing the work authorized under this Act, the Secretary, upon application or otherwise, may cause a refund of the amount in excess to be made from applicable funds.

(Pub.L. 94–579, Title III, § 305, Oct. 21, 1976, 90 Stat. 2765.)

**HISTORICAL AND STATUTORY NOTES**

**References in Text**

This Act, referred to in subsecs. (b) and (c), is Pub.L. 94–579, Oct. 21, 1976, 90 Stat. 2743, as amended, known as the Federal Land Policy and Management Act of 1976. For complete classification of this Act to the Code, see Tables.

The Act of Aug. 28, 1937 (50 Stat. 874; 43 U.S.C. 1181a–1181j), referred to in subsec. (b), is Act Aug. 28, 1937, c. 876, 50 Stat. 874, as amended, which enacted sections 1181a to 1181f of this title. Sections 1181f–1 to 1181f–4, included within the parenthetical reference to sections 1181a to 1181j, were enacted by Act May 24, 1939, c. 144, 53 Stat. 753. Sections 1181g to 1181j, also included within the parenthetical reference to sections 1181a to 1181j, were enacted by Act June 24, 1954, c. 357, 68 Stat. 270. For complete classification of these Acts to the Code, see Tables.

**Availability of Moneys for Improvement, Protection, or Rehabilitation of Public Lands Damaged by Unauthorized Persons**

Pub.L. 108–108, Title I, Nov. 10, 2003, 117 Stat. 1244, provided in part: "That notwithstanding any provision to the contrary of section 305(a) of Public Law 94–579 (43 U.S.C. 1735(a) [subsec. (a) of this section]), any moneys that have been or will be received pursuant to that section, whether as a result of forfeiture, compromise, or settlement, if not appropriate for refund pursuant to section 305(c) of that Act (43 U.S.C. 1735(c) [subsec. (c) of this section]), shall be available and may be expended under the authority of this Act [Department of the Interior and Related Agencies Appropriations Act, 2004, Pub.L. 108–108, Nov. 10, 2003, 117 Stat. 1241; see Tables for complete classification] by the Secretary to improve, protect, or rehabilitate any public lands administered through the Bureau of Land Management which have been damaged by the action of a resource developer, purchaser, permittee, or any unauthorized person, without regard to whether all moneys collected from each such action are used on the exact lands damaged which led to the action: Provided further, That any such moneys that are in excess of amounts needed to repair damage to the exact land for which funds were collected may be used to repair other damaged public lands."

Similar provisions were contained in the following prior Appropriations Acts:

Pub.L. 108–7, Div. F, Title I, Feb. 20, 2003, 117 Stat. 219.

Pub.L. 107–63, Title I, Nov. 5, 2001, 115 Stat. 418.

Pub.L. 106–291, Title I, Oct. 11, 2000, 114 Stat. 925.

Pub.L. 106–113, Div. B, § 1000(a)(3) [Title I], Nov. 29, 1999, 113 Stat. 1535, 1501A–138.

Pub.L. 105–277, Div. A, § 101(e) [Title I], Oct. 21, 1998, 112 Stat. 2681–234.

Pub.L. 105–83, Title I, Nov. 14, 1997, 111 Stat. 1545.

Pub.L. 104–208, Div. A, Title I, § 101(d) [Title I], Sept. 30, 1996, 110 Stat. 3009–184.

Pub.L. 104–134, Title I, § 101(c) [Title I], Apr. 26, 1996, 110 Stat. 1321–158; renumbered Title I, Pub.L. 104–140, § 1(a), May 2, 1996, 110 Stat. 1327.

Pub.L. 103–332, Title I, Sept. 30, 1994, 108 Stat. 2501.

Pub.L. 103–138, Title I, Nov. 11, 1993, 107 Stat. 1381.

Pub.L. 102–381, Title I, Oct. 5, 1992, 106 Stat. 1377.

Pub.L. 102–154, Title I, Nov. 13, 1991, 105 Stat. 992.

Pub.L. 101–512, Title I, Nov. 5, 1990, 104 Stat. 1917.

Pub.L. 101–121, Title I, Oct. 23, 1989, 103 Stat. 703.

Pub.L. 100–446, Title I, Sept. 27, 1988, 102 Stat. 1776.

Pub.L. 100–202, § 101(g) [Title I], Dec. 22, 1987, 101 Stat. 1329–215.

## § 1736. Working capital fund

**[FLPMA § 306]**

**(a) Establishment; availability of fund**

There is hereby established a working capital fund for the management of the public lands. This fund shall be available without fiscal year limitation for expenses necessary for furnishing, in accordance with the Federal Property and Administrative Services Act of 1949 (63 Stat. 377, as amended), and regulations promulgated thereunder, supplies and equipment services in support of Bureau programs, including but not limited to, the purchase or construction of storage facilities, equipment yards, and related improvements and the purchase, lease, or rent of motor vehicles, aircraft, heavy equipment, and fire control and other resource management equipment within the limitations set forth in appropriations made to the Secretary for the Bureau.

**(b) Initial funding; subsequent transfers**

The initial capital of the fund shall consist of appropriations made for that purpose together with the fair and reasonable value at the fund's inception of the inventories, equipment, receivables, and other assets, less the liabilities, transferred to the fund. The Secretary is authorized to make such subsequent transfers to the fund as he deems appropriate in connection with the functions to be carried on through the fund.

**(c) Payments credited to fund; amount; advancement or reimbursement**

The fund shall be credited with payments from appropriations, and funds of the Bureau, other agencies of the Department of the Interior, other Federal agencies, and other sources, as authorized by law, at rates approximately equal to the cost of furnishing the facilities, supplies, equipment, and services (including depreciation and accrued annual leave). Such payments may be made in advance in connection with firm orders, or by way of reimbursement.

**(d) Authorization of appropriations**

There is hereby authorized to be appropriated a sum not to exceed $3,000,000 as initial capital of the working capital fund.

(Pub.L. 94–579, Title III, § 306, Oct. 21, 1976, 90 Stat. 2766.)

### HISTORICAL AND STATUTORY NOTES

**References in Text**

The Federal Property and Administrative Services Act of 1949, referred to in subsec. (a), is Act June 30, 1949, c. 288, 63 Stat. 377, as amended, Title III of which is currently classified to subchapter IV of chapter 4 of Title 41, 41 U.S.C.A. § 251 et seq., and the remainder of which was formerly classified to chapter 10 of former Title 40, 40 U.S.C.A. § 471 et seq., prior to being repealed by Pub.L. 107–217, § 6(b), Aug. 21, 2002, 116 Stat. 1313; see now generally chapter 1 of Title 40, 40 U.S.C.A. § 101 et seq.

## § 1736a. Revolving fund derived from disposal of salvage timber

There is hereby established in the Treasury of the United States a special fund to be derived on and after October 5, 1992, from the Federal share of moneys received from the disposal of salvage timber prepared for sale from the lands under the jurisdiction of the Bureau of Land Management, Department of the Interior. The money in this fund shall be immediately available to the Bureau of Land Management without further appropriation, for the purposes of planning and preparing salvage timber for disposal, the administration of salvage timber sales, and subsequent site preparation and reforestation.

(Pub.L. 102–381, Title I, Oct. 5, 1992, 106 Stat. 1376.)

### HISTORICAL AND STATUTORY NOTES

**References in Text**

Reference in text to funds "derived hereafter" probably means funds derived after Oct. 5, 1992, the date of approval of Pub.L. 102–381.

**Codifications**

Section was enacted as part of the Department of the Interior and Related Agencies Appropriations Act, 1993, and not as part of the Federal Land Policy and Management Act of 1976, which comprises this chapter.

**Distribution of Receipts**

Title I of Pub.L. 102–381 provided in part that: "Nothing in this provision [this section] shall alter the formulas currently in existence by law for the distribution of receipts for the applicable lands and timber resources."

## § 1737. Implementation provisions [FLPMA § 307]

**(a) Investigations, studies, and experiments**

The Secretary may conduct investigations, studies, and experiments, on his own initiative or in cooperation with others, involving the management, protection, development, acquisition, and conveying of the public lands.

**(b) Contracts and cooperative agreements**

Subject to the provisions of applicable law, the Secretary may enter into contracts and cooperative agreements involving the management, protection, development, and sale of public lands.

**(c) Contributions and donations of money, services, and property**

The Secretary may accept contributions or donations of money, services, and property, real, personal, or mixed, for the management, protection, development, acquisition, and conveying of the public lands, including the acquisition of rights-of-way for such purposes. He may accept contributions for cadastral surveying performed on federally controlled or intermingled lands. Moneys received hereunder shall be credited to a separate account in the Treasury and are hereby authorized to be appropriated and made available until expended, as the Secretary may direct, for payment of expenses incident to the function toward the administration of which the contributions were made and for refunds to depositors of amounts contributed by them in specific instances where contributions are in excess of their share of the cost.

**(d) Recruitment of volunteers**

The Secretary may recruit, without regard to the civil service classification laws, rules, or regulations, the services of individuals contributed without compensation as volunteers for aiding in or facilitating the activities administered by the Secretary through the Bureau of Land Management.

**(e) Restrictions on activities of volunteers**

In accepting such services of individuals as volunteers, the Secretary—

(1) shall not permit the use of volunteers in hazardous duty or law enforcement work, or in policymaking processes or to displace any employee; and

(2) may provide for services or costs incidental to the utilization of volunteers, including transportation, supplies, lodging, subsistence, recruiting, training, and supervision.

**(f) Federal employment status of volunteers**

Volunteers shall not be deemed employees of the United States except for the purposes of—

(1) the tort claims provisions of Title 28;

(2) subchapter 1 [1] of chapter 81 of Title 5; and

(3) claims relating to damage to, or loss of, personal property of a volunteer incident to volunteer service, in which case the provisions of section 3721 of Title 31 shall apply.

**(g) Authorization of appropriations**

Effective with fiscal years beginning after September 30, 1984, there are authorized to be appropriated such sums as may be necessary to carry out the provisions of subsection (d) of this section, but not more than $250,000 may be appropriated for any one fiscal year.

(Pub.L. 94–579, Title III, § 307, Oct. 21, 1976, 90 Stat. 2766; Pub.L. 98–540, § 2, Oct. 24, 1984, 98 Stat. 2718; Pub.L. 101–286, Title II, § 204(c), May 9, 1990, 104 Stat. 175.)

[1] So in original. Probably should be subchapter "I".

### HISTORICAL AND STATUTORY NOTES

**References in Text**

The civil service classification laws, referred to in subsec. (d), probably should refer to civil service and classification laws. The civil service laws are set forth in Title 5, Government Organization and Employees. See, particularly, section 3301 et seq. of Title 5. The classification laws are set forth in chapter 51 and subchapter III of chapter 53 of Title 5.

The tort claims provisions of Title 28, referred to in subsec. (f), are the provisions of the Federal Tort Claims Act, which is classified generally to section 1346(b) and to chapter 171 (§ 2671 et seq.) of Title 28, Judiciary and Judicial Procedure.

## § 1738. Contracts for surveys and resource protection; renewals; funding requirements

**[FLPMA § 308]**

(a) The Secretary is authorized to enter into contracts for the use of aircraft, and for supplies and services, prior to the passage of an appropriation therefor, for airborne cadastral survey and resource protection operations of the Bureau. He may renew such contracts annually, not more than twice, without additional competition. Such contracts shall obligate funds for the fiscal years in which the costs are incurred.

(b) Each such contract shall provide that the obligation of the United States for the ensuing fiscal years is contingent upon the passage of an applicable appropriation, and that no payment shall be made under the contract for the ensuing fiscal years until such appropriation becomes available for expenditure.

(Pub.L. 94–579, Title III, § 308, Oct. 21, 1976, 90 Stat. 2767.)

## § 1739. Advisory councils

**[FLPMA § 309]**

**(a) Establishment; membership; operation**

The Secretary shall establish advisory councils of not less than ten and not more than fifteen members appointed by him from among persons who are representative of the various major citizens' interests concerning the problems relating to land use planning or the management of the public lands located within the area for which an advisory council is established. At least one member of each council shall be an elected official of general purpose government serving the people of such area. To the extent practicable there shall be no overlap or duplication of such councils. Appointments shall be made in accordance with rules prescribed by the Secretary. The establishment and operation of an advisory council established under this section shall conform to the requirements of the Federal Advisory Committee Act (86 Stat. 770).

**(b) Meetings**

Notwithstanding the provisions of subsection (a) of this section, each advisory council established by the Secretary under this section shall meet at least once a year with such meetings being called by the Secretary.

**(c) Travel and per diem payments**

Members of advisory councils shall serve without pay, except travel and per diem will be paid each member for meetings called by the Secretary.

**(d) Functions**

An advisory council may furnish advice to the Secretary with respect to the land use planning, classification, retention, management, and disposal of the public lands within the area for which the advisory council is established and such other matters as may be referred to it by the Secretary.

**(e) Public participation; procedures applicable**

In exercising his authorities under this Act, the Secretary, by regulation, shall establish procedures, including public hearings where appropriate, to give the Federal, State, and local governments and the public adequate notice and an opportunity to comment upon the formulation of standards and criteria for, and to participate in, the preparation and execution of plans and programs for, and the management of, the public lands.

(Pub.L. 94–579, Title III, § 309, Oct. 21, 1976, 90 Stat. 2767; Pub.L. 95–514, § 13, Oct. 25, 1978, 92 Stat. 1808.)

### HISTORICAL AND STATUTORY NOTES

**References in Text**

The Federal Advisory Committee Act (86 Stat. 770), referred to in subsec. (a), is Pub.L. 92–463, Oct. 6, 1972, 86

Stat. 770, as amended, and is set out in Appendix 2 to Title 5, Government Organization and Employees.

This Act, referred to in subsec. (e), is Pub.L. 94–579, Oct. 21, 1976, 90 Stat. 2743, as amended, known as the Federal Land Policy and Management Act of 1976. For complete classification of this Act to the Code, see Tables volume.

**Termination of Advisory Councils**

Advisory councils established after Jan. 5, 1973, to terminate not later than the expiration of the two-year period beginning on the date of their establishment, unless, in the case of a council established by the President or an officer of the Federal Government, such council is renewed by appropriate action prior to the expiration of such two-year period, or in the case of a council established by the Congress, its duration is otherwise provided for by law, see sections 3(2) and 14 of Pub.L. 92–463, Oct. 6, 1972, 86 Stat. 770, 776, set out in Appendix 2 to Title 5, Government Organization and Employees.

## § 1740. Rules and regulations

**[FLPMA § 310]**

The Secretary, with respect to the public lands, shall promulgate rules and regulations to carry out the purposes of this Act and of other laws applicable to the public lands, and the Secretary of Agriculture, with respect to lands within the National Forest System, shall promulgate rules and regulations to carry out the purposes of this Act. The promulgation of such rules and regulations shall be governed by the provisions of chapter 5 of Title 5, without regard to section 553(a)(2). Prior to the promulgation of such rules and regulations, such lands shall be administered under existing rules and regulations concerning such lands to the extent practical.

(Pub.L. 94–579, Title III, § 310, Oct. 21, 1976, 90 Stat. 2767.)

### HISTORICAL AND STATUTORY NOTES

**References in Text**

This Act, referred to in text is Pub.L. 94–579, Oct. 21, 1976, 90 Stat. 2743, as amended, known as the Federal Land Policy and Management Act of 1976. For complete classification of this Act to the Code, see Tables.

## § 1741. Annual reports

**[FLPMA § 311]**

**(a) Purpose; time for submission**

For the purpose of providing information that will aid Congress in carrying out its oversight responsibilities for public lands programs and for other purposes, the Secretary shall prepare a report in accordance with subsections (b) and (c) of this section and submit it to the Congress no later than one hundred and twenty days after the end of each fiscal year beginning with the report for fiscal year 1979.

**(b) Format**

A list of programs and specific information to be included in the report as well as the format of the report shall be developed by the Secretary after consulting with the Committee on Natural Resources of the House of Representatives and the Committee on Energy and Natural Resources of the Senate and shall be provided to the committees prior to the end of the second quarter of each fiscal year.

**(c) Contents**

The report shall include, but not be limited to, program identification information, program evaluation information, and program budgetary information for the preceding current and succeeding fiscal years.

(Pub.L. 94–579, Title III, § 311, Oct. 21, 1976, 90 Stat. 2768; Pub.L. 103–437, § 16(d)(3), Nov. 2, 1994, 108 Stat. 4595.)

### HISTORICAL AND STATUTORY NOTES

**Change of Name**

Any reference in any provision of law enacted before Jan. 4, 1995, to the Committee on Natural Resources of the House of Representatives treated as referring to the Committee on Resources of the House of Representatives, see section 1(a)(8) of Pub.L. 104–14, set out as a note preceding section 21 of Title 2, The Congress.

The Committee on Interior and Insular Affairs of the Senate, referred to in subsec. (b), was abolished and replaced by the Committee on Energy and Natural Resources of the Senate, effective Feb. 11, 1977. See Rule XXV of the Standing Rules of the Senate, as amended by Senate Resolution 4 (popularly cited as the "Committee System Reorganization Amendments of 1977"), approved Feb. 4, 1977.

## § 1742. Search, rescue, and protection forces; emergency situations authorizing hiring

**[FLPMA § 312]**

Where in his judgment sufficient search, rescue, and protection forces are not otherwise available, the Secretary is authorized in cases of emergency to incur such expenses as may be necessary (a) in searching for and rescuing, or in cooperating in the search for and rescue of, persons lost on the public lands, (b) in protecting or rescuing, or in cooperating in the protection and rescue of, persons or animals endangered by an act of God, and (c) in transporting deceased persons or persons seriously ill or injured to the nearest place where interested parties or local authorities are located.

(Pub.L. 94–579, Title III, § 312, Oct. 21, 1976, 90 Stat. 2768.)

## § 1743. Disclosure of financial interests by officers or employees

**[FLPMA § 313]**

**(a) Annual written statement; availability to public**

Each officer or employee of the Secretary and the Bureau who—

(1) performs any function or duty under this Act; and

(2) has any known financial interest in any person who (A) applies for or receives any permit, lease, or right-of-way under, or (B) applies for or acquires any land or interests therein under, or (C) is otherwise subject to the provisions of, this Act,

shall, beginning on February 1, 1977, annually file with the Secretary a written statement concerning all such interests held by such officer or employee during the preceding calendar year. Such statement shall be available to the public.

**(b) Implementation of requirements**

The Secretary shall—

(1) act within ninety days after October 21, 1976—

(A) to define the term "known financial interests" for the purposes of subsection (a) of this section; and

(B) to establish the methods by which the requirement to file written statements specified in subsection (a) of this section will be monitored and enforced, including appropriate provisions for the filing by such officers and employees of such statements and the review by the Secretary of such statements; and

(2) report to the Congress on June 1 of each calendar year with respect to such disclosures and the actions taken in regard thereto during the preceding calendar year.

**(c) Exempted personnel**

In the rules prescribed in subsection (b) of this section, the Secretary may identify specific positions within the Department of the Interior which are of a nonregulatory or nonpolicymaking nature and provide that officers or employees occupying such positions shall be exempt from the requirements of this section.

**(d) Violations; criminal penalties**

Any officer or employee who is subject to, and knowingly violates, this section, shall be fined not more than $2,500 or imprisoned not more than one year, or both.

(Pub.L. 94–579, Title III, § 313, Oct. 21, 1976, 90 Stat. 2768.)

### HISTORICAL AND STATUTORY NOTES

**References in Text**

This Act, referred to in subsec. (a)(1), (2), is Pub.L. 94–579, Oct. 21, 1976, 90 Stat. 2743, as amended, known as the Federal Land Policy and Management Act of 1976. For complete classification of this Act to the Code, see Tables.

## § 1744. Recordation of mining claims

**[FLPMA § 314]**

**(a) Filing requirements**

The owner of an unpatented lode or placer mining claim located prior to October 21, 1976, shall, within the three-year period following October 21, 1976 and prior to December 31 of each year thereafter, file the instruments required by paragraphs (1) and (2) of this subsection. The owner of an unpatented lode or placer mining claim located after October 21, 1976 shall, prior to December 31 of each year following the calendar year in which the said claim was located, file the instruments required by paragraphs (1) and (2) of this subsection:

(1) File for record in the office where the location notice or certificate is recorded either a notice of intention to hold the mining claim (including but not limited to such notices as are provided by law to be filed when there has been a suspension or deferment of annual assessment work), an affidavit of assessment work performed thereon, on a detailed report provided by section 28–1 of Title 30, relating thereto.

(2) File in the office of the Bureau designated by the Secretary a copy of the official record of the instrument filed or recorded pursuant to paragraph (1) of this subsection, including a description of the location of the mining claim sufficient to locate the claimed lands on the ground.

**(b) Additional filing requirements**

The owner of an unpatented lode or placer mining claim or mill or tunnel site located prior to October 21, 1976 shall, within the three-year period following October 21, 1976, file in the office of the Bureau designated by the Secretary a copy of the official record of the notice of location or certificate of location, including a description of the location of the mining claim or mill or tunnel site sufficient to locate the claimed lands on the ground. The owner of an unpatented lode or placer mining claim or mill or tunnel site located after October 21, 1976 shall, within ninety days after the date of location of such claim, file in the office of the Bureau designated by the Secretary a copy of the official record of the notice of location or certificate of location, including a description of the location of the mining claim or mill or tunnel site sufficient to locate the claimed lands on the ground.

**(c) Failure to file as constituting abandonment; defective or untimely filing**

The failure to file such instruments as required by subsections (a) and (b) of this section shall be deemed conclusively to constitute an abandonment of the mining claim or mill or tunnel site by the owner; but it shall not be considered a failure to file if the instrument is defective or not timely filed for record under other Federal laws permitting filing or recording thereof, or if the instrument is filed for record by or on behalf of some but not all of the owners of the mining claim or mill or tunnel site.

**(d) Validity of claims, waiver of assessment, etc., as unaffected**

Such recordation or application by itself shall not render valid any claim which would not be otherwise valid under applicable law. Nothing in this section shall be construed as a waiver of the assessment and other requirements of such law.

(Pub.L. 94–579, Title III, § 314, Oct. 21, 1976, 90 Stat. 2769.)

## § 1745. Disclaimer of interest in lands

**[FLPMA § 315]**

**(a) Issuance of recordable document; criteria**

After consulting with any affected Federal agency, the Secretary is authorized to issue a document of disclaimer of interest or interests in any lands in any form suitable for recordation, where the disclaimer will help remove a cloud on the title of such lands and where he determines (1) a record interest of the United States in lands has terminated by operation of law or is otherwise invalid; or (2) the lands lying between the meander line shown on a plat of survey approved by the Bureau or its predecessors and the actual shoreline of a body of water are not lands of the United States; or (3) accreted, relicted, or avulsed lands are not lands of the United States.

**(b) Procedures applicable**

No document or disclaimer shall be issued pursuant to this section unless the applicant therefor has filed with the Secretary an application in writing and notice of such application setting forth the grounds supporting such application has been published in the Federal Register at least ninety days preceding the issuance of such disclaimer and until the applicant therefor has paid to the Secretary the administrative costs of issuing the disclaimer as determined by the Secretary. All receipts shall be deposited to the then-current appropriation from which expended.

**(c) Construction as quit-claim deed from United States**

Issuance of a document of disclaimer by the Secretary pursuant to the provisions of this section and regulations promulgated hereunder shall have the same effect as a quit-claim deed from the United States.

(Pub.L. 94–579, Title III, § 315, Oct. 21, 1976, 90 Stat. 2770.)

## § 1746. Correction of conveyance documents

**[FLPMA § 316]**

The Secretary may correct patents or documents of conveyance issued pursuant to section 1718 of this title or to other Acts relating to the disposal of public lands where necessary in order to eliminate errors. In addition, the Secretary may make corrections of errors in any documents of conveyance which have heretofore been issued by the Federal Government to dispose of public lands. Any corrections authorized by this section which affect the boundaries of, or jurisdiction over, land administered by another Federal agency shall be made only after consultation with, and the approval of, the head of such other agency.

(Pub.L. 94–579, Title III, § 316, Oct. 21, 1976, 90 Stat. 2770; Pub.L. 108–7, Div. F, Title IV, § 411(e), Feb. 20, 2003, 117 Stat. 291.)

### HISTORICAL AND STATUTORY NOTES

**Effective and Applicability Provisions**

2003 Acts

Amendment by Pub.L. 108–7, Div. F, § 411(e), effective February 20, 2003, see Pub.L. 108–7, Div. F, Title IV, § 415, set out as a note under 16 U.S.C.A. § 539m.

## § 1747. Loans to States and political subdivisions; purposes; amounts; allocation; terms and conditions; interest rate; security; limitations; forebearance for benefit of borrowers; recordkeeping requirements; discrimination prohibited; deposit of receipts

**[FLPMA § 317]**

(1) The Secretary is authorized to make loans to States and their political subdivisions in order to relieve social or economic impacts occasioned by the development of minerals leased in such States pursuant to the Act of February 25, 1920, as amended [30 U.S.C.A. § 181 et seq.]. Such loans shall be confined to the uses specified for the 50 per centum of mineral leasing revenues to be received by such States and subdivisions pursuant to section 35 of such Act [30 U.S.C.A. § 191].

(2) The total amount of loans outstanding pursuant to this section for any State and political subdivisions thereof in any year shall be not more than the anticipated mineral leasing revenues to be received by that State pursuant to section 35 of the Act of February 25, 1920, as amended [30 U.S.C.A. § 191], for the ten years following.

(3) The Secretary, after consultation with the Governors of the affected States, shall allocate such loans among the States and their political subdivisions in a fair and equitable manner, giving priority to those States and subdivisions suffering the most severe impacts.

(4) Loans made pursuant to this section shall be subject to such terms and conditions as the Secretary determines necessary to assure the achievement of the

purpose of this section. The Secretary shall promulgate such regulations as may be necessary to carry out the provisions of this section no later than three months after August 20, 1978.

(5) Loans made pursuant to this section shall bear interest equivalent to the lowest interest rate paid on an issue of at least $1,000,000 of tax exempt bonds of such State or any agency thereof within the preceding calendar year.

(6) Any loan made pursuant to this section shall be secured only by a pledge of the revenues received by the State or the political subdivision thereof pursuant to section 35 of the Act of February 25, 1920, as amended [30 U.S.C.A. § 191], and shall not constitute an obligation upon the general property or taxing authority of such unit of government.

(7) Notwithstanding any other provision of law, loans made pursuant to this section may be used for the non-Federal share of the aggregate cost of any project or program otherwise funded by the Federal Government which requires a non-Federal share for such project or program and which provides planning or public facilities otherwise eligible for assistance under this section.

(8) Nothing in this section shall be construed to preclude any forebearance[1] for the benefit of the borrower including loan restructuring, which may be determined by the Secretary as justified by the failure of anticipated mineral development or related revenues to materialize as expected when the loan was made pursuant to this section.

(9) Recipients of loans made pursuant to this section shall keep such records as the Secretary shall prescribe by regulation, including records which fully disclose the disposition of the proceeds of such assistance and such other records as the Secretary may require to facilitate an effective audit. The Secretary and the Comptroller General of the United States or their duly authorized representatives shall have access, for the purpose of audit, to such records.

(10) No person in the United States shall, on the grounds of race, color, religion, national origin, or sex be excluded from participation in, be denied the benefits of, or be subjected to discrimination under, any program or activity funded in whole or part with funds made available under this section.

(11) All amounts collected in connection with loans made pursuant to this section, including interest payments or repayments of principal on loans, fees, and other moneys, derived in connection with this section, shall be deposited in the Treasury as miscellaneous receipts.

(Pub.L. 94–579, Title III, § 317(c), Oct. 21, 1976, 90 Stat. 2771; Pub.L. 95–352, § 1(f), Aug. 20, 1978, 92 Stat. 515.)

[1] So in original.

### HISTORICAL AND STATUTORY NOTES

**References in Text**

The Act of February 25, 1920, as amended, referred to in par. (1), is Act Feb. 25, 1920, c. 85, 41 Stat. 437, as amended, popularly known as the Mineral Leasing Act of 1920, which is classified principally to chapter 3A (section 181 et seq.) of Title 30, Mineral Lands and Mining. For complete classification of this Act to the Code, see Short Title note set out under section 181 of Title 30 and Tables.

**Codifications**

Section is comprised of subsec. (c) of section 317 of Pub.L. 94–579. Subsecs. (a) and (b) of section 317 of Pub.L. 94–579 are classified to section 191 of Title 30, Mineral Lands and Mining, and a note set out under that section; respectively.

## § 1748. Funding requirements

**[FLPMA § 318]**

**(a) Authorization of appropriations**

There are authorized to be appropriated such sums as are necessary to carry out the purposes and provisions of this Act, but no amounts shall be appropriated to carry out after October 1, 2002, any program, function, or activity of the Bureau under this or any other Act unless such sums are specifically authorized to be appropriated as of October 21, 1976 or are authorized to be appropriated in accordance with the provisions of subsection (b) of this section.

**(b) Procedure applicable for authorization of appropriations**

Consistent with section 1110 of Title 31, beginning May 15, 1977, and not later than May 15 of each second even numbered year thereafter, the Secretary shall submit to the Speaker of the House of Representatives and the President of the Senate a request for the authorization of appropriations for all programs, functions, and activities of the Bureau to be carried out during the four-fiscal-year period beginning on October 1 of the calendar year following the calendar year in which such request is submitted. The Secretary shall include in his request, in addition to the information contained in his budget request and justification statement to the Office of Management and Budget, the funding levels which he determines can be efficiently and effectively utilized in the execution of his responsibilities for each such program, function, or activity, notwithstanding any budget guidelines or limitations imposed by any official or agency of the executive branch.

**(c) Distribution of receipts from Bureau from disposal of lands, etc.**

Nothing in this section shall apply to the distribution of receipts of the Bureau from the disposal of lands, natural resources, and interests in lands in accordance with applicable law, nor to the use of contributed funds, private deposits for public survey work, and townsite trusteeships, nor to fund allocations from other Federal agencies, reimbursements from both Federal and non-Federal sources, and funds expended for emergency firefighting and rehabilitation.

**(d) Purchase of certain public lands from Land and Water Conservation Fund**

In exercising the authority to acquire by purchase granted by section 1715(a) of this title, the Secretary may use the Land and Water Conservation Fund to purchase lands which are necessary for proper management of public lands which are primarily of value for outdoor recreation purposes.

(Pub.L. 94–579, Title III, § 318, Oct. 21, 1976, 90 Stat. 2771; Pub.L. 104–333, Div. I, Title III, § 310, Nov. 12, 1996, 110 Stat. 4139.)

### HISTORICAL AND STATUTORY NOTES

**References in Text**

This Act, referred to in subsec. (a), is Pub.L. 94–579, Oct. 21, 1976, 90 Stat. 2743, as amended, known as the Federal Land Policy and Management Act of 1976. For complete classification of this Act to the Code, see Tables.

**Codifications**

In subsec. (b), "section 1110 of Title 31" was substituted for "section 607 of the Congressional Budget Act of 1974 [31 U.S.C.A. § 11c]" on authority of Pub.L. 97–258, § 4(b), Sept. 13, 1982, 96 Stat. 1067, the first section of which enacted Title 31, Money and Finance.

## SUBCHAPTER IV—RANGE MANAGEMENT

### § 1751. Grazing fees; feasibility study; contents; submission of report; annual distribution and use of range betterment funds; nature of distributions

**[FLPMA § 401]**

**(a)** The Secretary of Agriculture and the Secretary of the Interior shall jointly cause to be conducted a study to determine the value of grazing on the lands under their jurisdiction in the eleven Western States with a view to establishing a fee to be charged for domestic livestock grazing on such lands which is equitable to the United States and to the holders of grazing permits and leases on such lands. In making such study, the Secretaries shall take into consideration the costs of production normally associated with domestic livestock grazing in the eleven Western States, differences in forage values, and such other factors as may relate to the reasonableness of such fees. The Secretaries shall report the result of such study to the Congress not later than one year from and after October 21, 1976, together with recommendations to implement a reasonable grazing fee schedule based upon such study. If the report required herein has not been submitted to the Congress within one year after October 21, 1976, the grazing fee charge then in effect shall not be altered and shall remain the same until such report has been submitted to the Congress. Neither Secretary shall increase the grazing fee in the 1977 grazing year.

**(b)(1)** Congress finds that a substantial amount of the Federal range lands is deteriorating in quality, and that installation of additional range improvements could arrest much of the continuing deterioration and could lead to substantial betterment of forage conditions with resulting benefits to wildlife, watershed protection, and livestock production. Congress therefore directs that 50 per centum or $10,000,000 per annum, whichever is greater of all moneys received by the United States as fees for grazing domestic livestock on public lands (other than from ceded Indian lands) under the Taylor Grazing Act (48 Stat. 1269; 43 U.S.C. 315 et seq.) and the Act of August 28, 1937 (50 Stat. 874; 43 U.S.C. 1181d), and on lands in National Forests in the sixteen contiguous Western States under the provisions of this section shall be credited to a separate account in the Treasury, one-half of which is authorized to be appropriated and made available for use in the district, region, or national forest from which such moneys were derived, as the respective Secretary may direct after consultation with district, regional, or national forest user representatives, for the purpose of on-the-ground range rehabilitation, protection, and improvements on such lands, and the remaining one-half shall be used for on-the-ground range rehabilitation, protection, and improvements as the Secretary concerned directs. Any funds so appropriated shall be in addition to any other appropriations made to the respective Secretary for planning and administration of the range betterment program and for other range management. Such rehabilitation, protection, and improvements shall include all forms of range land betterment including, but not limited to, seeding and reseeding, fence construction, weed control, water development, and fish and wildlife habitat enhancement as the respective Secretary may direct after consultation with user representatives. The annual distribution and use of range betterment funds authorized by this paragraph shall not be considered a major Federal action requiring a detailed statement pursuant to section 4332(c) of Title 42.

(2) All distributions of moneys made under subsection (b)(1) of this section shall be in addition to distributions made under section 10 of the Taylor Grazing Act [43 U.S.C.A. § 315i] and shall not apply to distribution of moneys made under section 11 of that Act [43 U.S.C.A. § 315j]. The remaining moneys received by the United States as fees for grazing domestic livestock on the public lands shall be deposited in the Treasury as miscellaneous receipts.

(Pub.L. 94–579, Title IV, § 401(a), (b)(1), (2), Oct. 21, 1976, 90 Stat. 2772; Pub.L. 95–514, § 6(b), Oct. 25, 1978, 92 Stat. 1806.)

HISTORICAL AND STATUTORY NOTES

**References in Text**

The Taylor Grazing Act (48 Stat. 1269; 43 U.S.C. 315 et seq.), referred to in subsec. (b), is Act June 28, 1934, c. 865, 48 Stat. 1269, as amended, which is classified principally to subchapter I (section 315 et seq.) of chapter 8A of this title. For complete classification of this Act to the Code, see Short Title note set out under section 315 of this title and Tables.

The Act of August 28, 1937, referred to in subsec. (b)(2), is Act Aug. 28, 1937, c. 876, 50 Stat. 874, as amended, which is classified to sections 1181a to 1181f of this title. For complete classification of this Act to the Code, see Tables volume.

Codifications

Subsec. (b)(2) of this section is comprised of the second and third sentences of section 401(b)(2) of Pub.L. 94–579. The first sentence of such section 401(b)(2) amended section 315i(b) of this title.

**Moratorium on Increase of Grazing Fee for 1978 Grazing Year**

Pub.L. 95–321, July 21, 1978, 92 Stat. 394, in order to allow the Congress sufficient time to analyze the report and recommendations of the Secretaries of Interior and Agriculture under subsec. (a) of this section and to take appropriate action, provided that the 1978 grazing year fee was not to be raised by the Secretary of the Interior for the grazing of livestock on public lands nor by the Secretary of Agriculture for such grazing on lands under the jurisdiction of the Forest Service.

## § 1752. Grazing leases and permits

**[FLPMA § 402]**

### (a) Terms and conditions

Except as provided in subsection (b) of this section, permits and leases for domestic livestock grazing on public lands issued by the Secretary under the Act of June 28, 1934 (48 Stat. 1269, as amended; 43 U.S.C. 315 et seq.) or the Act of August 28, 1937 (50 Stat. 874, as amended; 43 U.S.C. 1181a–1181j), or by the Secretary of Agriculture, with respect to lands within National Forests in the sixteen contiguous Western States, shall be for a term of ten years subject to such terms and conditions the Secretary concerned deems appropriate and consistent with the governing law, including, but not limited to, the authority of the Secretary concerned to cancel, suspend, or modify a grazing permit or lease, in whole or in part, pursuant to the terms and conditions thereof, or to cancel or suspend a grazing permit or lease for any violation of a grazing regulation or of any term or condition of such grazing permit or lease.

### (b) Terms of lesser duration

Permits or leases may be issued by the Secretary concerned for a period shorter than ten years where the Secretary concerned determines that—

(1) the land is pending disposal; or

(2) the land will be devoted to a public purpose prior to the end of ten years; or

(3) it will be in the best interest of sound land management to specify a shorter term: *Provided*, That the absence from an allotment management plan of details the Secretary concerned would like to include but which are undeveloped shall not be the basis for establishing a term shorter than ten years: *Provided further*, That the absence of completed land use plans or court ordered environmental statements shall not be the sole basis for establishing a term shorter than ten years unless the Secretary determines on a case-by-case basis that the information to be contained in such land use plan or court ordered environmental impact statement is necessary to determine whether a shorter term should be established for any of the reasons set forth in items (1) through (3) of this subsection.

### (c) First priority for renewal of expiring permit or lease

So long as (1) the lands for which the permit or lease is issued remain available for domestic livestock grazing in accordance with land use plans prepared pursuant to section 1712 of this title or section 1604 of Title 16, (2) the permittee or lessee is in compliance with the rules and regulations issued and the terms and conditions in the permit or lease specified by the Secretary concerned, and (3) the permittee or lessee accepts the terms and conditions to be included by the Secretary concerned in the new permit or lease, the holder of the expiring permit or lease shall be given first priority for receipt of the new permit or lease.

### (d) Allotment management plan requirements

All permits and leases for domestic livestock grazing issued pursuant to this section may incorporate an allotment management plan developed by the Secretary concerned. However, nothing in this subsection shall be construed to supersede any requirement for completion of court ordered environmental impact statements prior to development and incorporation of allotment management plans. If the Secretary concerned elects to develop an allotment management plan for a given area, he shall do so in careful and considered consultation, cooperation and coordination with the lessees, permittees, and landowners involved, the district grazing advisory boards established pursuant to section 1753 of this title, and any State or States having lands within the area to be covered by such allotment management plan. Allotment management plans shall be tailored to the specific range condition of the area to be covered by such plan, and shall be reviewed on a periodic basis to determine whether they have been effective in improving the range condition of the lands involved or whether such lands can be better managed under the provisions of subsection (e) of this section. The Secretary concerned may revise or terminate such plans or develop new plans from time to time after such review and careful and considered consultation, cooperation and coordination with the parties involved. As used in this subsection, the terms "court ordered environmental impact statement" and "range condition" shall be defined as in the "Public Rangelands Improvement Act of 1978 [43 U.S.C.A. § 1901 et seq.]".

**(e) Omission of allotment management plan requirements and incorporation of appropriate terms and conditions; reexamination of range conditions**

In all cases where the Secretary concerned has not completed an allotment management plan or determines that an allotment management plan is not necessary for management of livestock operations and will not be prepared, the Secretary concerned shall incorporate in grazing permits and leases such terms and conditions as he deems appropriate for management of the permitted or leased lands pursuant to applicable law. The Secretary concerned shall also specify therein the numbers of animals to be grazed and the seasons of use and that he may reexamine the condition of the range at any time and, if he finds on reexamination that the condition of the range requires adjustment in the amount or other aspect of grazing use, that the permittee or lessee shall adjust his use to the extent the Secretary concerned deems necessary. Such readjustment shall be put into full force and effect on the date specified by the Secretary concerned.

**(f) Allotment management plan applicability to non-Federal lands; appeal rights**

Allotment management plans shall not refer to livestock operations or range improvements on non-Federal lands except where the non-Federal lands are intermingled with, or, with the consent of the permittee or lessee involved, associated with, the Federal lands subject to the plan. The Secretary concerned under appropriate regulations shall grant to lessees and permittees the right of appeal from decisions which specify the terms and conditions of allotment management plans. The preceding sentence of this subsection shall not be construed as limiting any other right of appeal from decisions of such officials.

**(g) Cancellation of permit or lease; determination of reasonable compensation; notice**

Whenever a permit or lease for grazing domestic livestock is canceled in whole or in part, in order to devote the lands covered by the permit or lease to another public purpose, including disposal, the permittee or lessee shall receive from the United States a reasonable compensation for the adjusted value, to be determined by the Secretary concerned, of his interest in authorized permanent improvements placed or constructed by the permittee or lessee on lands covered by such permit or lease, but not to exceed the fair market value of the terminated portion of the permittee's or lessee's interest therein. Except in cases of emergency, no permit or lease shall be canceled under this subsection without two years' prior notification.

**(h) Applicability of provisions to rights, etc., in or to public lands or lands in National Forests**

Nothing in this Act shall be construed as modifying in any way law existing on October 21, 1976, with respect to the creation of right, title, interest or estate in or to public lands or lands in National Forests by issuance of grazing permits and leases.

(Pub.L. 94–579, Title IV, § 402, Oct. 21, 1976, 90 Stat. 2773; Pub.L. 95–514, §§ 7, 8, Oct. 25, 1978, 92 Stat. 1807.)

## HISTORICAL AND STATUTORY NOTES

**References in Text**

The Act of June 28, 1934, referred to in subsec. (a) is Act June 28, 1934, c. 865, 48 Stat. 1269, as amended, known as the Taylor Grazing Act, which is classified principally to subchapter I (section 315 et seq.) of chapter 8A of this title. For complete classification of this Act to the Code, see Short Title note set out under section 315 of this title and Tables.

The Act of Aug. 28, 1937 (50 Stat. 874; 43 U.S.C. 1181a–1181j), referred to in subsec. (a), is Act Aug. 28, 1937, c. 876, 50 Stat. 874, as amended, which enacted sections 1181a to 1181f of this title. Sections 1181f–1 to 1181f–4, included within the parenthetical reference to sections 1181a to 1181j, were enacted by Act May 24, 1939, c. 144, 53 Stat. 753. Sections 1181g to 1181j, also included within the parenthetical reference to sections 1181a to 1181j, were enacted by Act June 24, 1954, c. 357, 68 Stat. 270. For complete classification of these Acts to the Code, see Tables volume.

The Public Rangelands Improvement Act of 1978, referred to in subsec. (d), is Pub.L. 95–514, Oct. 25, 1978, 92 Stat. 1803, which is classified principally to chapter 37 (section 1901 et seq.) of this title. For complete classification of this Act to the Code, see Short Title note set out under section 1901 of this title and Tables volume.

This Act, referred to in subsecs. (h), is Pub.L. 94–579, Oct. 21, 1976, 90 Stat. 2743, as amended, known as the Federal Land Policy and Management Act of 1976. For complete classification of this Act to the Code, see Tables volume.

**Reports to Congress on Grazing Permits**

Pub.L. 108–108, Title III, § 325, Nov. 10, 2003, 117 Stat. 1307, provided in part: "That beginning in November 2004, and every year thereafter, the Secretaries of the Interior and Agriculture shall report to Congress the extent to which they are completing analysis required under applicable laws prior to the expiration of grazing permits, and beginning in May 2004, and every two years thereafter, the Secretaries shall provide Congress recommendations for legislative provisions necessary to ensure all permit renewals are completed in a timely manner. The legislative recommendations provided shall be consistent with the funding levels requested in the Secretaries' budget proposals."

**Reductions in Grazing Allotments on Public Rangelands**

Pub.L. 102–381, Title I, Oct. 5, 1992, 106 Stat. 1378, provided in part: "That an appeal of any reductions in grazing allotments on public rangelands must be taken within thirty days after receipt of a final grazing allotment decision. Reductions of up to 10 per centum in grazing allotments shall become effective when so designated by the Secretary of the Interior. Upon appeal any proposed reduction in excess of 10 per centum shall be suspended pending final action on the appeal, which shall be completed within two years after the appeal is filed[.]".

Similar provisions were contained in the following prior Appropriations Acts:

Pub.L. 102–154, Title I, Nov. 13, 1991, 105 Stat. 993.

Pub.L. 101–512, Title I, Nov. 5, 1990, 104 Stat. 1917.

Pub.L. 101–121, Title I, Oct. 23, 1989, 103 Stat. 704.

Pub.L. 100–446, Title I, Sept. 27, 1988, 102 Stat. 1776.

Pub.L. 100–202, § 101(g) [Title I], Dec. 22, 1987, 101 Stat. 1329 216.

Pub.L. 99–591, Title I, § 101(h) [Title I, § 100], Oct. 30, 1986, 100 Stat. 3341–245.

Pub.L. 99–500, Title I, § 101(h) [Title I, § 100], Oct. 18, 1986, 100 Stat. 1783.

Pub.L. 99–190, § 101(d) [Title I, § 100], Dec. 19, 1985, 99 Stat. 1226.

Pub.L. 98–473, Title I, § 101(c), Oct. 12, 1984, 98 Stat. 1840.

Pub.L. 98–146, Title I, § 100, Nov. 4, 1983, 97 Stat. 921.

Pub.L. 97–394, Title I, § 1, Dec. 30, 1982, 96 Stat. 1968.

Pub.L. 97–100, Title I, § 100, Dec. 23, 1981, 95 Stat. 1393.

Pub.L. 96–514, Title I, § 100, Dec. 12, 1980, 94 Stat. 2959.

Pub.L. 96–126, Title I, § 100, Nov. 27, 1979, 93 Stat. 956.

## § 1753. Grazing advisory boards

### [FLPMA § 403]

**(a) Establishment; maintenance**

For each Bureau district office and National Forest headquarters office in the sixteen contiguous Western States having jurisdiction over more than five hundred thousand acres of lands subject to commercial livestock grazing (hereinafter in this section referred to as "office"), the Secretary and the Secretary of Agriculture, upon the petition of a simple majority of the livestock lessees and permittees under the jurisdiction of such office, shall establish and maintain at least one grazing advisory board of not more than fifteen advisers.

**(b) Functions**

The function of grazing advisory boards established pursuant to this section shall be to offer advice and make recommendations to the head of the office involved concerning the development of allotment management plans and the utilization of range-betterment funds.

**(c) Appointment and terms of members**

The number of advisers on each board and the number of years an adviser may serve shall be determined by the Secretary concerned in his discretion. Each board shall consist of livestock representatives who shall be lessees or permittees in the area administered by the office concerned and shall be chosen by the lessees and permittees in the area through an election prescribed by the Secretary concerned.

**(d) Meetings**

Each grazing advisory board shall meet at least once annually.

**(e) Federal Advisory Committee Act applicability**

Except as may be otherwise provided by this section, the provisions of the Federal Advisory Committee Act (86 Stat. 770) shall apply to grazing advisory boards.

**(f) Expiration date**

The provisions of this section shall expire December 31, 1985.

(Pub.L. 94–579, Title IV, § 403, Oct. 21, 1976, 90 Stat. 2775; Pub.L. 95–514, § 10, Oct. 25, 1978, 92 Stat. 1808.)

### HISTORICAL AND STATUTORY NOTES

**References in Text**

The Federal Advisory Committee Act, referred to in subsec. (e), is Pub.L. 92–463, Oct. 6, 1972, 86 Stat. 770, as amended, and is set out in Appendix 2 to Title 5, Government Organization and Employees.

## SUBCHAPTER V—RIGHTS-OF-WAY

## § 1761. Grant, issue, or renewal of rights-of-way

### [FLPMA § 501]

**(a) Authorized purposes**

The Secretary, with respect to the public lands (including public lands, as defined in section 1702(e) of this title, which are reserved from entry pursuant to section 24 of the Federal Power Act (16 U.S.C. 818)) and, the Secretary of Agriculture, with respect to lands within the National Forest System (except in each case land designated as wilderness), are authorized to grant, issue, or renew rights-of-way over, upon, under, or through such lands for—

(1) reservoirs, canals, ditches, flumes, laterals, pipes, pipelines, tunnels, and other facilities and systems for the impoundment, storage, transportation, or distribution of water;

(2) pipelines and other systems for the transportation or distribution of liquids and gases, other than water and other than oil, natural gas, synthetic liquid or gaseous fuels, or any refined product pro-

duced therefrom, and for storage and terminal facilities in connection therewith;

(3) pipelines, slurry and emulsion systems, and conveyor belts for transportation and distribution of solid materials, and facilities for the storage of such materials in connection therewith;

(4) systems for generation, transmission, and distribution of electric energy, except that the applicant shall also comply with all applicable requirements of the Federal Energy Regulatory Commission under the Federal Power Act, including part 1[1] thereof (41 Stat. 1063, 16 U.S.C. 791a–825r).;[2]

(5) systems for transmission or reception of radio, television, telephone, telegraph, and other electronic signals, and other means of communication;

(6) roads, trails, highways, railroads, canals, tunnels, tramways, airways, livestock driveways, or other means of transportation except where such facilities are constructed and maintained in connection with commercial recreation facilities on lands in the National Forest System; or

(7) such other necessary transportation or other systems or facilities which are in the public interest and which require rights-of-way over, upon, under, or through such lands.

**(b) Procedures applicable; administration**

(1) The Secretary concerned shall require, prior to granting, issuing, or renewing a right-of-way, that the applicant submit and disclose those plans, contracts, agreements, or other information reasonably related to the use, or intended use, of the right-of-way, including its effect on competition, which he deems necessary to a determination, in accordance with the provisions of this Act, as to whether a right-of-way shall be granted, issued, or renewed and the terms and conditions which should be included in the right-of-way.

(2) If the applicant is a partnership, corporation, association, or other business entity, the Secretary concerned, prior to granting a right-to-way[3] pursuant to this subchapter, shall require the applicant to disclose the identity of the participants in the entity, when he deems it necessary to a determination, in accordance with the provisions of this subchapter, as to whether a right-of-way shall be granted, issued, or renewed and the terms and conditions which should be included in the right-of-way. Such disclosures shall include, where applicable: (A) the name and address of each partner; (B) the name and address of each shareholder owning 3 per centum or more of the shares, together with the number and percentage of any class of voting shares of the entity which such shareholder is authorized to vote; and (C) the name and address of each affiliate of the entity together with, in the case of an affiliate controlled by the entity, the number of shares and the percentage of any class of voting stock of that affiliate owned, directly or indirectly, by that entity, and, in the case of an affiliate which controls that entity, the number of shares and the percentage of any class of voting stock of that entity owned, directly or indirectly, by the affiliate.

(3) The Secretary of Agriculture shall have the authority to administer all rights-of-way granted or issued under authority of previous Acts with respect to lands under the jurisdiction of the Secretary of Agriculture, including rights-of-way granted or issued pursuant to authority given to the Secretary of the Interior by such previous Acts.

**(c) Permanent easement for water systems; issuance, preconditions, etc.**

(1) Upon receipt of a written application pursuant to paragraph (2) of this subsection from an applicant meeting the requirements of this subsection, the Secretary of Agriculture shall issue a permanent easement, without a requirement for reimbursement, for a water system as described in subsection (a)(1) of this section, traversing Federal lands within the National Forest System ("National Forest Lands"), constructed and in operation or placed into operation prior to October 21, 1976, if—

(A) the traversed National Forest lands are in a State where the appropriation doctrine governs the ownership of water rights;

(B) at the time of submission of the application the water system is used solely for agricultural irrigation or livestock watering purposes;

(C) the use served by the water system is not located solely on Federal lands;

(D) the originally constructed facilities comprising such system have been in substantially continuous operation without abandonment;

(E) the applicant has a valid existing right, established under applicable State law, for water to be conveyed by the water system;

(F) a recordable survey and other information concerning the location and characteristics of the system as necessary for proper management of National Forest lands is provided to the Secretary of Agriculture by the applicant for the easement; and

(G) the applicant submits such application on or before December 31, 1996.

(2)(A) Nothing in this subsection shall be construed as affecting any grants made by any previous Act. To the extent any such previous grant of right-of-way is a valid existing right, it shall remain in full force and effect unless an owner thereof notifies the Secretary of Agriculture that such owner elects to have a water system on such right-of-way governed by the provisions of this subsection and submits a written application for issuance of an easement pursuant to this subsection, in which case upon the issuance of an easement pursuant to this subsection such previous grant shall be deemed to have been relinquished and shall terminate.

**(B)** Easements issued under the authority of this subsection shall be fully transferable with all existing conditions and without the imposition of fees or new conditions or stipulations at the time of transfer. The holder shall notify the Secretary of Agriculture within sixty days of any address change of the holder or change in ownership of the facilities.

**(C)** Easements issued under the authority of this subsection shall include all changes or modifications to the original facilities in existence as of October 21, 1976, the date of enactment of this Act.

**(D)** Any future extension or enlargement of facilities after October 21, 1976, shall require the issuance of a separate authorization, not authorized under this subsection.

(3)(A) Except as otherwise provided in this subsection, the Secretary of Agriculture may terminate or suspend an easement issued pursuant to this subsection in accordance with the procedural and other provisions of section 1766 of this title. An easement issued pursuant to this subsection shall terminate if the water system for which such easement was issued is used for any purpose other than agricultural irrigation or livestock watering use. For purposes of subparagraph (D) of paragraph (1) of this subsection, non-use of a water system for agricultural irrigation or livestock watering purposes for any continuous five-year period shall constitute a rebuttable presumption of abandonment of the facilities comprising such system.

**(B)** Nothing in this subsection shall be deemed to be an assertion by the United States of any right or claim with regard to the reservation, acquisition, or use of water. Nothing in this subsection shall be deemed to confer on the Secretary of Agriculture any power or authority to regulate or control in any manner the appropriation, diversion, or use of water for any purpose (nor to diminish any such power or authority of such Secretary under applicable law) or to require the conveyance or transfer to the United States of any right or claim to the appropriation, diversion, or use of water.

**(C)** Except as otherwise provided in this subsection, all rights-of-way issued pursuant to this subsection are subject to all conditions and requirements of this Act.

**(D)** In the event a right-of-way issued pursuant to this subsection is allowed to deteriorate to the point of threatening persons or property and the holder of the right-of-way, after consultation with the Secretary of Agriculture, refuses to perform the repair and maintenance necessary to remove the threat to persons or property, the Secretary shall have the right to undertake such repair and maintenance on the right-of-way and to assess the holder for the costs of such repair and maintenance, regardless of whether the Secretary had required the holder to furnish a bond or other security pursuant to subsection (i) of this section.

**(d) Rights–of–way on certain Federal lands**

With respect to any project or portion thereof that was licensed pursuant to, or granted an exemption from, part I of the Federal Power Act [16 U.S.C.A. §§ 791a et seq.] which is located on lands subject to a reservation under section 24 of the Federal Power Act [16 U.S.C.A. § 818] and which did not receive a permit, right-of-way or other approval under this section prior to October 24, 1992, no such permit, right-of-way, or other approval shall be required for continued operation, including continued operation pursuant to section 15 of the Federal Power Act [16 U.S.C.A. § 808], of such project unless the Commission determines that such project involves the use of any additional public lands or National Forest lands not subject to such reservation.

(Pub.L. 94–579, Title V, § 501, Oct. 21, 1976, 90 Stat. 2776; Pub.L. 99–545, § 1(b), (c), Oct. 27, 1986, 100 Stat. 3047, 3048; Pub.L. 102–486, Title XXIV, § 2401, Oct. 24, 1992, 106 Stat. 3096.)

[1] So in original. Probably should be "part I".

[2] So in original. The period preceding the semicolon probably should not appear.

[3] So in original. Probably should be "right-of-way".

## HISTORICAL AND STATUTORY NOTES

**References in Text**

The Federal Power Act, referred to in text, is Act June 10, 1920, c. 285, 41 Stat. 1063, as amended. Part I of the Federal Power Act is classified generally to subchapter I (section 791a et seq.) of chapter 12 of Title 16, Conservation. For complete classification of this Act to the Code, see section 791a of Title 16 and Tables.

This Act, referred to in subsec. (b)(1), is Pub.L. 94–579, Oct. 21, 1976, 90 Stat. 2743, as amended, known as the Federal Land Policy and Management Act of 1976. For complete classification of this Act to the Code, see Tables.

**Transfer of Functions**

The Federal Power Commission was terminated and its functions, personnel, property, funds, etc., were transferred to the Secretary of Energy (except for certain functions which were transferred to the Federal Energy Regulatory Commission) by sections 7151(b), 7171(a), 7172(a), 7291, and 7293 of Title 42, The Public Health and Welfare.

Enforcement functions of the Secretary or other official in Department of Agriculture, insofar as they involve lands and programs under jurisdiction of that Department, related to compliance with land use permits for other associated land uses issued under sections 1761, and 1763 to 1771 of this title, and such functions of Secretary or other official in Department of Interior related to compliance with land use permits for temporary use of public lands and other associated land uses, issued under sections 1732, 1761, and 1763 to 1771 of this title, with respect to pre-construction, construction, and initial operation of transportation systems for Canadian and Alaskan natural gas were transferred to the Federal Inspector, Office of Federal Inspector for the Alaska Natural Gas Transportation System, until the first anniversary of date of initial operation of the Alaska Natural Gas Transportation System, see Reorg. Plan No. 1 of 1979, §§ 102(e), (f), 203(a), 44 F.R. 33663, 33666, 93 Stat. 1373, 1376, effective July 1, 1979, set out in Appendix 1 to Title 5, Government Organization and Employees.

## § 1762. Roads

**[FLPMA § 502]**

### (a) Authority to acquire, construct, and maintain; financing arrangements

The Secretary, with respect to the public lands, is authorized to provide for the acquisition, construction, and maintenance of roads within and near the public lands in locations and according to specifications which will permit maximum economy in harvesting timber from such lands tributary to such roads and at the same time meet the requirements for protection, development, and management of such lands for utilization of the other resources thereof. Financing of such roads may be accomplished (1) by the Secretary utilizing appropriated funds, (2) by requirements on purchasers of timber and other products from the public lands, including provisions for amortization of road costs in contracts, (3) by cooperative financing with other public agencies and with private agencies or persons, or (4) by a combination of these methods: *Provided*, That, where roads of a higher standard than that needed in the harvesting and removal of the timber and other products covered by the particular sale are to be constructed, the purchaser of timber and other products from public lands shall not, except when the provisions of the second proviso of this subsection apply, be required to bear that part of the costs necessary to meet such higher standard, and the Secretary is authorized to make such arrangements to this end as may be appropriate: *Provided further*, That when timber is offered with the condition that the purchaser thereof will build a road or roads in accordance with standards specified in the offer, the purchaser of the timber will be responsible for paying the full costs of construction of such roads.

### (b) Recordation of copies of affected instruments

Copies of all instruments affecting permanent interests in land executed pursuant to this section shall be recorded in each county where the lands are located.

### (c) Maintenance or reconstruction of facilities by users

The Secretary may require the user or users of a road, trail, land, or other facility administered by him through the Bureau, including purchasers of Government timber and other products, to maintain such facilities in a satisfactory condition commensurate with the particular use requirements of each. Such maintenance to be borne by each user shall be proportionate to total use. The Secretary may also require the user or users of such a facility to reconstruct the same when such reconstruction is determined to be necessary to accommodate such use. If such maintenance or reconstruction cannot be so provided or if the Secretary determines that maintenance or reconstruction by a user would not be practical, then the Secretary may require that sufficient funds be deposited by the user to provide his portion of such total maintenance or reconstruction. Deposits made to cover the maintenance or reconstruction of roads are hereby made available until expended to cover the cost to the United States of accomplishing the purposes for which deposited: *Provided*, That deposits received for work on adjacent and overlapping areas may be combined when it is the most practicable and efficient manner of performing the work, and cost thereof may be determined by estimates: *And provided further*, That unexpended balances upon accomplishment of the purpose for which deposited shall be transferred to miscellaneous receipts or refunded.

### (d) Fund for user fees for delayed payment to grantor

Whenever the agreement under which the United States has obtained for the use of, or in connection with, the public lands a right-of-way or easement for a road or an existing road or the right to use an existing road provides for delayed payments to the Government's grantor, any fees or other collections received by the Secretary for the use of the road may be placed in a fund to be available for making payments to the grantor.

(Pub.L. 94–579, Title V, § 502, Oct. 21, 1976, 90 Stat. 2777.)

## § 1763. Right-of-way corridors; criteria and procedures applicable for designation

**[FLPMA § 503]**

In order to minimize adverse environmental impacts and the proliferation of separate rights-of-way, the utilization of rights-of-way in common shall be required to the extent practical, and each right-of-way or permit shall reserve to the Secretary concerned the right to grant additional rights-of-way or permits for compatible uses on or adjacent to rights-of-way granted pursuant to this Act. In designating right-of-way corridors and in determining whether to require that rights-of-way be confined to them, the Secretary concerned shall take into consideration national and State land use policies, environmental quality, economic efficiency, national security, safety, and good engineering and technological practices. The Secretary concerned shall issue regulations containing the criteria and procedures he will use in designating such corridors. Any existing transportation and utility corridors may be designated as transportation and utility corridors pursuant to this subsection without further review.

(Pub.L. 94–579, Title V, § 503, Oct. 21, 1976, 90 Stat. 2778.)

### HISTORICAL AND STATUTORY NOTES

**References in Text**

This Act, referred to in text, is Pub.L. 94–579, Oct. 21, 1976, 90 Stat. 2743, as amended, known as the Federal Land Policy and Management Act of 1976. For complete classification of this Act to the Code, see Tables.

**Transfer of Functions**

Enforcement functions of Secretary or other official in Department of Agriculture, insofar as they involve lands and programs under jurisdiction of that Department, related to compliance with land use permits for other associated land uses issued under sections 1761, and 1763 to 1771 of this title, and such functions of Secretary or other official in Department of Interior related to compliance with land use permits for temporary use of public lands and other associated land uses, issued under sections 1732, 1761, and 1763 to 1771 of this title, with respect to pre-construction, construction, and initial operation of transportation systems for Canadian and Alaskan natural gas were transferred to the Federal Inspector, Office of Federal Inspector for Alaska Natural Gas Transportation System, until the first anniversary of date of initial operation of the Alaska Natural Gas Transportation System, see Reorg. Plan No. 1 of 1979, §§ 102(e), (f), 203(a), 44 F.R. 33663, 33666, 93 Stat. 1373, 1376, effective July 1, 1979, set out in Appendix 1 to Title 5, Government Organization and Employees.

## § 1764. General requirements

[FLPMA § 504]

**(a) Boundary specifications; criteria; temporary use of additional lands**

The Secretary concerned shall specify the boundaries of each right-of-way as precisely as is practical. Each right-of-way shall be limited to the ground which the Secretary concerned determines (1) will be occupied by facilities which constitute the project for which the right-of-way is granted, issued, or renewed, (2) to be necessary for the operation or maintenance of the project, (3) to be necessary to protect the public safety, and (4) will do no unnecessary damage to the environment. The Secretary concerned may authorize the temporary use of such additional lands as he determines to be reasonably necessary for the construction, operation, maintenance, or termination of the project or a portion thereof, or for access thereto.

**(b) Terms and conditions of right-of-way or permit**

Each right-of-way or permit granted, issued, or renewed pursuant to this section shall be limited to a reasonable term in light of all circumstances concerning the project. In determining the duration of a right-of-way the Secretary concerned shall, among other things, take into consideration the cost of the facility, its useful life, and any public purpose it serves. The right-of-way shall specify whether it is or is not renewable and the terms and conditions applicable to the renewal.

**(c) Applicability of regulations or stipulations**

Rights-of-way shall be granted, issued, or renewed pursuant to this subchapter under such regulations or stipulations, consistent with the provisions of this subchapter or any other applicable law, and shall also be subject to such terms and conditions as the Secretary concerned may prescribe regarding extent, duration, survey, location, construction, maintenance, transfer or assignment, and termination.

**(d) Submission of plan of construction, operation, and rehabilitation by new project applicants; plan requirements**

The Secretary concerned prior to granting or issuing a right-of-way pursuant to this subchapter for a new project which may have a significant impact on the environment, shall require the applicant to submit a plan of construction, operation, and rehabilitation for such right-of-way which shall comply with stipulations or with regulations issued by that Secretary, including the terms and conditions required under section 1765 of this title.

**(e) Regulatory requirements for terms and conditions; revision and applicability of regulations**

The Secretary concerned shall issue regulations with respect to the terms and conditions that will be included in rights-of-way pursuant to section 1765 of this title. Such regulations shall be regularly revised as needed. Such regulations shall be applicable to every right-of-way granted or issued pursuant to this subchapter and to any subsequent renewal thereof, and may be applicable to rights-of-way not granted or issued, but renewed pursuant to this subchapter.

**(f) Removal or use of mineral and vegetative materials**

Mineral and vegetative materials, including timber, within or without a right-of-way, may be used or disposed of in connection with construction or other purposes only if authorization to remove or use such materials has been obtained pursuant to applicable laws or for emergency repair work necessary for those rights-of-way authorized under section 1761(c) of this title.

**(g) Rental payments; amount, waiver, etc.**

The holder of a right-of-way shall pay in advance the fair market value thereof, as determined by the Secretary granting, issuing, or renewing such right-of-way. The Secretary concerned may require either annual payment or a payment covering more than one year at a time except that private individuals may make at their option either annual payments or payments covering more than one year if the annual fee is greater than one hundred dollars. The Secretary concerned may waive rentals where a right-of-way is granted, issued or renewed in consideration of a right-of-way conveyed to the United States in connection with a cooperative cost share program between the United States and the holder. The Secretary concerned may, by regulation or prior to promulgation of such regulations, as a condition of a right-of-way, require an applicant for or holder of a right-of-way to reimburse the United States for all reasonable administrative and other costs incurred in processing an application for such right-of-way and in inspection and monitoring of construction, operation, and termination of the facility pursuant to such right-of-way: *Provided, however,* That the Secretary concerned need not secure reimbursement in any situation where there is in existence a cooperative cost share right-of-way program between the United States and the holder of a right-of-way. Rights-of-way may be granted, issued, or renewed to a Federal, State, or local government or any agency or instrumentality thereof, to nonprofit associations or nonprofit corporations which are not themselves controlled or owned by profitmaking corporations or business enterprises, or to a holder where he provides without or at reduced charges a valuable benefit to the public or to the programs of the Secretary concerned, or to a holder in connection with the authorized use or occupancy of Federal land for which the United States is already receiving compensation for such lesser charge, including free use as the Secretary concerned finds equitable and in the public interest. Such rights-of-way issued at less than fair market value are not assignable except with the approval of the Secretary issuing the right-of-way. The moneys received for reimbursement of reasonable costs shall be deposited with the Treasury in a special account and are hereby authorized to be appropriated and made available until expended. Rights-of-way shall be granted, issued, or renewed, without rental fees, for electric or telephone facilities eligible for financing pursuant to the Rural Electrification Act of 1936, as amended [7 U.S.C.A. § 901 et seq.], determined without regard to any application requirement under that Act, or any extensions from such facilities: *Provided,* That nothing in this sentence shall be construed to affect the authority of the Secretary granting, issuing, or renewing the right-of-way to require reimbursement of reasonable administrative and other costs pursuant to the second sentence of this subsection.

**(h) Liability for damage or injury incurred by United States for use and occupancy of rights-of-way; indemnification of United States; no-fault liability; amount of damages**

(1) The Secretary concerned shall promulgate regulations specifying the extent to which holders of rights-of-way under this subchapter shall be liable to the United States for damage or injury incurred by the United States caused by the use and occupancy of the rights-of-way. The regulations shall also specify the extent to which such holders shall indemnify or hold harmless the United States for liabilities, damages, or claims caused by their use and occupancy of the rights-of-way.

(2) Any regulation or stipulation imposing liability without fault shall include a maximum limitation on damages commensurate with the foreseeable risks or hazards presented. Any liability for damage or injury in excess of this amount shall be determined by ordinary rules of negligence.

**(i) Bond or security requirements**

Where he deems it appropriate, the Secretary concerned may require a holder of a right-of-way to furnish a bond, or other security, satisfactory to him to secure all or any of the obligations imposed by the terms and conditions of the right-of-way or by any rule or regulation of the Secretary concerned.

**(j) Criteria for grant, issue, or renewal of right-of-way**

The Secretary concerned shall grant, issue, or renew a right-of-way under this subchapter only when he is satisfied that the applicant has the technical and financial capability to construct the project for which the right-of-way is requested, and in accord with the requirements of this subchapter.

(Pub.L. 94–579, Title V, § 504, Oct. 21, 1976, 90 Stat. 2778; Pub.L. 98–300, May 25, 1984, 98 Stat. 215; Pub.L. 99–545, § 2, Oct. 27, 1986, 100 Stat. 3048; Pub.L. 104–333, Div. I, Title X, § 1032(a), Nov. 12, 1996, 110 Stat. 4239.)

## HISTORICAL AND STATUTORY NOTES

**References in Text**

The Rural Electrification Act of 1936, as amended, referred to in subsec. (g), is Act May 20, 1936, c. 432, 49 Stat. 1363, as amended, which is classified generally to chapter 31 (section 901 et seq.) of Title 7, Agriculture. For complete classification of this Act to the Code, see section 901 of Title 7 and Tables.

**Effective and Applicability Provisions**

1996 Acts

Section 1032(b) of Title X of Div. I of Pub.L. 104–333 provided that: "The amendment made by subsection (a) [amending subsec. (g) of this section] shall apply with respect to rights-of-way leases held on or after the date of enactment of this Act [Nov. 12, 1996].

**Transfer of Functions**

See note set out under section 1763 of this title.

## § 1765. Terms and conditions

**[FLPMA § 505]**

Each right-of-way shall contain—

**(a)** terms and conditions which will (i) carry out the purposes of this Act and rules and regulations issued thereunder; (ii) minimize damage to scenic and esthetic values and fish and wildlife habitat and otherwise protect the environment; (iii) require compliance with applicable air and water quality standards established by or pursuant to applicable Federal or State law; and (iv) require compliance with State standards for public health and safety, environmental protection, and siting, construction, operation, and maintenance of or for rights-of-way for similar purposes if those standards are more stringent than applicable Federal standards; and

**(b)** such terms and conditions as the Secretary concerned deems necessary to (i) protect Federal property and economic interests; (ii) manage efficiently the lands which are subject to the right-of-way or adjacent thereto and protect the other lawful users of the lands adjacent to or traversed by such right-of-way; (iii) protect lives and property; (iv) protect the interests of individuals living in the general area traversed by the right-of-way who rely on the fish, wildlife, and other biotic resources of the area for subsistence purposes; (v) require location of the right-of-way along a route that will cause least damage to the environment, taking into consideration feasibility and other relevant factors; and (vi) otherwise protect the public interest in the lands traversed by the right-of-way or adjacent thereto.

(Pub.L. 94–579, Title V, § 505, Oct. 21, 1976, 90 Stat. 2780.)

### HISTORICAL AND STATUTORY NOTES

**References in Text**

This Act, referred to in par. (a), is Pub.L. 94–579, Oct. 21, 1976, 90 Stat. 2743, as amended, known as the Federal Land Policy and Management Act of 1976. For complete classification of this Act to the Code, see Tables.

**Transfer of Functions**

See note set out under section 1763 of this title.

## § 1766. Suspension or termination; grounds; procedures applicable

**[FLPMA § 506]**

Abandonment of a right-of-way or noncompliance with any provision of this subchapter condition of the right-of-way, or applicable rule or regulation of the Secretary concerned may be grounds for suspension or termination of the right-of-way if, after due notice to the holder of the right-of-way and, and[1] with respect to easements, an appropriate administrative proceeding pursuant to section 554 of Title 5, the Secretary concerned determines that any such ground exists and that suspension or termination is justified. No administrative proceeding shall be required where the right-of-way by its terms provides that it terminates on the occurrence of a fixed or agreed-upon condition, event, or time. If the Secretary concerned determines that an immediate temporary suspension of activities within a right-of-way for violation of its terms and conditions is necessary to protect public health or safety or the environment, he may abate such activities prior to an administrative proceeding. Prior to commencing any proceeding to suspend or terminate a right-of-way the Secretary concerned shall give written notice to the holder of the grounds for such action and shall give the holder a reasonable time to resume use of the right-of-way or to comply with this subchapter condition, rule, or regulation as the case may be. Failure of the holder of the right-of-way to use the right-of-way for the purpose for which it was granted, issued, or renewed, for any continuous five-year period, shall constitute a rebuttable presumption of abandonment of the right-of-way except that where the failure of the holder to use the right-of-way for the purpose for which it was granted, issued, or renewed for any continuous five-year period is due to circumstances not within the holder's control, the Secretary concerned is not required to commence proceedings to suspend or terminate the right-of-way.

(Pub.L. 94–579, Title V, § 506, Oct. 21, 1976, 90 Stat. 2780.)

[1] So in original.

### HISTORICAL AND STATUTORY NOTES

**Transfer of Functions**

See note under section 1763 of this title.

## § 1767. Rights-of-way for Federal departments and agencies

**[FLPMA § 507]**

**(a)** The Secretary concerned may provide under applicable provisions of this subchapter for the use of any department or agency of the United States a right-of-way over, upon, under or through the land administered by him, subject to such terms and conditions as he may impose.

**(b)** Where a right-of-way has been reserved for the use of any department or agency of the United States, the Secretary shall take no action to terminate, or otherwise limit, that use without the consent of the head of such department or agency.

(Pub.L. 94–579, Title V, § 507, Oct. 21, 1976, 90 Stat. 2781.)

HISTORICAL AND STATUTORY NOTES

**Transfer of Functions**

See note set out under section 1763 of this title.

## § 1768. Conveyance of lands covered by right-of-way; terms and conditions

**[FLPMA § 508]**

If under applicable law the Secretary concerned decides to transfer out of Federal ownership any lands covered in whole or in part by a right-of-way, including a right-of-way granted under the Act of November 16, 1973 (87 Stat. 576; 30 U.S.C. 185), the lands may be conveyed subject to the right-of-way; however, if the Secretary concerned determines that retention of Federal control over the right-of-way is necessary to assure that the purposes of this subchapter will be carried out, the terms and conditions of the right-of-way complied with, or the lands protected, he shall (a) reserve to the United States that portion of the lands which lies within the boundaries of the right-of-way, or (b) convey the lands, including that portion within the boundaries of the right-of-way, subject to the right-of-way and reserving to the United States the right to enforce all or any of the terms and conditions of the right-of-way, including the right to renew it or extend it upon its termination and to collect rents.

(Pub.L. 94–579, Title V, § 508, Oct. 21, 1976, 90 Stat. 2781.)

HISTORICAL AND STATUTORY NOTES

**References in Text**

The Act of November 16, 1973, referred to in text, is Pub.L. 93–153, Nov. 16, 1973, 87 Stat. 576. For complete classification of this Act to the Code, see Tables.

**Transfer of Functions**

See note set out under section 1763 of this title.

## § 1769. Existing right-of-way or right-of-use unaffected; exceptions; rights-of-way for railroad and appurtenant communication facilities; applicability of existing terms and conditions

**[FLPMA § 509]**

**(a)** Nothing in this subchapter shall have the effect of terminating any right-of-way or right-of-use heretofore issued, granted, or permitted. However, with the consent of the holder thereof, the Secretary concerned may cancel such a right-of-way or right-of-use and in its stead issue a right-of-way pursuant to the provisions of this subchapter.

**(b)** When the Secretary concerned issues a right-of-way under this subchapter for a railroad and appurtenant communication facilities in connection with a realinement [1] of a railroad on lands under his jurisdiction by virtue of a right-of-way granted by the United States, he may, when he considers it to be in the public interest and the lands involved are not within an incorporated community and are of approximately equal value, notwithstanding the provisions of this subchapter, provide in the new right-of-way the same terms and conditions as applied to the portion of the existing right-of-way relinquished to the United States with respect to the payment of annual rental, duration of the right-of-way, and the nature of the interest in lands granted. The Secretary concerned or his delegate shall take final action upon all applications for the grant, issue, or renewal of rights-of-way under subsection (b) of this section no later than six months after receipt from the applicant of all information required from the applicant by this subchapter.

(Pub.L. 94–579, Title V, § 509, Oct. 21, 1976, 90 Stat. 2781.)

[1] So in original. Probably should be "realignment".

HISTORICAL AND STATUTORY NOTES

**Transfer of Functions**

See note set out under section 1763 of this title.

## § 1770. Applicability of provisions to other Federal laws

**[FLPMA § 510]**

### (a) Right-of-way

Effective on and after October 21, 1976, no right-of-way for the purposes listed in this subchapter shall be granted, issued, or renewed over, upon, under, or through such lands except under and subject to the provisions, limitations, and conditions of this subchapter: *Provided*, That nothing in this subchapter shall be construed as affecting or modifying the provisions of sections 532 to 538 of Title 16 and in the event of conflict with, or inconsistency between, this subchapter and sections 532 to 538 of Title 16, the latter shall prevail: *Provided further*, That nothing in this Act should be construed as making it mandatory that, with respect to forest roads, the Secretary of Agriculture limit rights-of-way grants or their term of years or require disclosure pursuant to section 1761(b) of this title or impose any other condition contemplated by this Act that is contrary to present practices of that Secretary under sections 532 to 538 of Title 16. Any pending application for a right-of-way under any other law on the effective date of this section shall be considered as an application under this subchapter. The Secretary concerned may require the applicant to submit any additional information he deems necessary to comply with the requirements of this subchapter.

### (b) Highway use

Nothing in this subchapter shall be construed to preclude the use of lands covered by this subchapter for highway purposes pursuant to sections 107 and 317 of Title 23.

### (c) Application of antitrust laws

(1) Nothing in this subchapter shall be construed as exempting any holder of a right-of-way issued under this subchapter from any provision of the antitrust laws of the United States.

(2) For the purposes of this subsection, the term "antitrust laws" includes the Act of July 2, 1890 (26 Stat.[1] 15 U.S.C. 1 et seq.); the Act of October 15, 1914 (38 Stat. 730, 15 U.S.C. 12 et seq.); the Federal Trade Commission Act (38 Stat. 717; 15 U.S.C. 41 et seq.); and sections 73 and 74 of the Act of August 27, 1894 [15 U.S.C.A. §§ 8, 9].

(Pub.L. 94–579, Title V, § 510, Oct. 21, 1976, 90 Stat. 2782.)

[1] So in original. Probably should be "26 Stat. 209,".

### HISTORICAL AND STATUTORY NOTES

**References in Text**

This Act, referred to in subsec. (a), is Pub.L. 94–579, Oct. 21, 1976, 90 Stat. 2743, as amended, known as the Federal Land Policy and Management Act of 1976. For complete classification of this Act to the Code, see Tables.

The effective date of this section, referred to in subsec. (a), probably means the date of enactment of this section by Pub.L. 94–579, which was approved Oct. 21, 1976.

Act of July 2, 1890, referred to in subsec. (c)(2), is Act July 2, 1890, c. 647, 26 Stat. 209, as amended, known as the Sherman Act, which is classified to sections 1 to 7 of Title 15, Commerce and Trade. For complete classification of this Act to the Code, see Short Title note set out under section 1 of Title 15 and Tables volume.

Act of October 15, 1914, referred to in subsec. (c)(2), is Act Oct. 15, 1914, c. 323, 38 Stat. 730, as amended, known as the Clayton Act, which is classified generally to sections 12, 13, 14 to 19, 20, 21, and 22 to 27 of Title 15, Commerce and Trade, and sections 52 and 53 of Title 29, Labor. For further details and complete classification of this Act to the Code, see References in Text note set out under section 12 of Title 15 and Tables volume.

The Federal Trade Commission Act, referred to in subsec. (c)(2), is Act Sept. 26, 1914, c. 311, 38 Stat. 717, as amended, which is classified generally to subchapter I (section 41 et seq.) of chapter 2 of Title 15, Commerce and Trade. For complete classification of this Act to the Code, see section 58 of Title 15 and Tables volume.

Sections 73 and 74 of the Act of August 27, 1894, referred to in subsec. (c), are sections 73 and 74 of Act Aug. 27, 1894, c. 349, 28 Stat. 570, which are classified to sections 8 and 9 of Title 15, Commerce and Trade.

**Transfer of Functions**

See note set out under section 1763 of this title.

## § 1771. Coordination of applications

### [FLPMA § 511]

Applicants before Federal departments and agencies other than the Department of the Interior or Agriculture seeking a license, certificate, or other authority for a project which involve a right-of-way over, upon, under, or through public land or National Forest System lands must simultaneously apply to the Secretary concerned for the appropriate authority to use public lands or National Forest System lands and submit to the Secretary concerned all information furnished to the other Federal department or agency.

(Pub.L. 94–579, Title V, § 511, Oct. 21, 1976, 90 Stat. 2782.)

### HISTORICAL AND STATUTORY NOTES

**Transfer of Functions**

See note set out under section 1763 of this title.

## SUBCHAPTER VI—DESIGNATED MANAGEMENT AREAS

## § 1781. California Desert Conservation Area

### [FLPMA § 601]

**(a) Congressional findings**

The Congress finds that—

(1) the California desert contains historical, scenic, archeological, environmental, biological, cultural, scientific, educational, recreational, and economic resources that are uniquely located adjacent to an area of large population;

(2) the California desert environment is a total ecosystem that is extremely fragile, easily scarred, and slowly healed;

(3) the California desert environment and its resources, including certain rare and endangered species of wildlife, plants, and fishes, and numerous archeological and historic sites, are seriously threatened by air pollution, inadequate Federal management authority, and pressures of increased use, particularly recreational use, which are certain to intensify because of the rapidly growing population of southern California;

(4) the use of all California desert resources can and should be provided for in a multiple use and sustained yield management plant[1] to conserve these resources for future generations, and to provide present and future use and enjoyment, particularly outdoor recreation uses, including the use, where appropriate, of off-road recreational vehicles;

(5) the Secretary has initiated a comprehensive planning process and established an interim management program for the public lands in the California desert; and

(6) to insure further study of the relationship of man and the California desert environment, preserve the unique and irreplaceable resources, including archeological values, and conserve the use of the economic resources of the California desert, the public must be provided more opportunity to participate in such planning and management, and additional management authority must be provided to the Secretary to facilitate effective implementation of such planning and management.

**(b) Statement of purpose**

It is the purpose of this section to provide for the immediate and future protection and administration of the public lands in the California desert within the framework of a program of multiple use and sustained yield, and the maintenance of environmental quality.

**(c) Description of Area**

(1) For the purpose of this section, the term "California desert" means the area generally depicted on a map entitled "California Desert Conservation Area—Proposed" dated April 1974, and described as provided in subsection (c)(2) of this section.

(2) As soon as practicable after October 21, 1976, the Secretary shall file a revised map and a legal description of the California Desert Conservation Area with the Committees on Interior and Insular Affairs of the United States Senate and the House of Representatives, and such map and description shall have the same force and effect as if included in this Act. Correction of clerical and typographical errors in such legal description and a map may be made by the Secretary. To the extent practicable, the Secretary shall make such legal description and map available to the public promptly upon request.

**(d) Preparation and implementation of comprehensive long-range plan for management, use, etc.**

The Secretary, in accordance with section 1712 of this title, shall prepare and implement a comprehensive, long-range plan for the management, use, development, and protection of the public lands within the California Desert Conservation Area. Such plan shall take into account the principles of multiple use and sustained yield in providing for resource use and development, including, but not limited to, maintenance of environmental quality, rights-of-way, and mineral development. Such plan shall be completed and implementation thereof initiated on or before September 30, 1980.

**(e) Interim program for management, use, etc.**

During the period beginning on October 21, 1976, and ending on the effective date of implementation of the comprehensive, long-range plan, the Secretary shall execute an interim program to manage, use, and protect the public lands, and their resources now in danger of destruction, in the California Desert Conservation Area, to provide for the public use of such lands in an orderly and reasonable manner such as through the development of campgrounds and visitor centers, and to provide for a uniformed desert ranger force.

**(f) Applicability of mining laws**

Subject to valid existing rights, nothing in this Act shall affect the applicability of the United States mining laws on the public lands within the California Desert Conservation Area, except that all mining claims located on public lands within the California Desert Conservation Area shall be subject to such reasonable regulations as the Secretary may prescribe to effectuate the purposes of this section. Any patent issued on any such mining claim shall recite this limitation and continue to be subject to such regulations. Such regulations shall provide for such measures as may be reasonable to protect the scenic, scientific, and environmental values of the public lands of the California Desert Conservation Area against undue impairment, and to assure against pollution of the streams and waters within the California Desert Conservation Area.

**(g) Advisory Committee; establishment; functions**

(1) The Secretary, within sixty days after October 21, 1976, shall establish a California Desert Conservation Area Advisory Committee (hereinafter referred to as "advisory committee") in accordance with the provisions of section 1739 of this title.

(2) It shall be the function of the advisory committee to advise the Secretary with respect to the preparation and implementation of the comprehensive, long-range plan required under subsection (d) of this section.

**(h) Management of lands under jurisdiction of Secretary of Agriculture and Secretary of Defense**

The Secretary of Agriculture and the Secretary of Defense shall manage lands within their respective jurisdictions located in or adjacent to the California Desert Conservation Area, in accordance with the laws relating to such lands and wherever practicable, in a manner consonant with the purpose of this section. The Secretary, the Secretary of Agriculture, and the Secretary of Defense are authorized and directed to consult among themselves and take cooperative actions to carry out the provisions of this subsection, including a program of law enforcement in accordance with applicable authorities to protect the archeological and other values of the California Desert Conservation Area and adjacent lands.

**(i) Omitted**

**(j) Authorization of appropriations**

There are authorized to be appropriated for fiscal years 1977 through 1981 not to exceed $40,000,000 for the purpose of this section, such amount to remain available until expended.

(Pub.L. 94–579, Title VI, § 601, Oct. 21, 1976, 90 Stat. 2782.)

[1] So in original. Probably should be "plan".

## HISTORICAL AND STATUTORY NOTES

**References in Text**

This Act, referred to in subsecs. (c)(2) and (f), is Pub.L. 94–579, Oct. 21, 1976, 90 Stat. 2743, as amended, known as the Federal Land Policy and Management Act of 1976. For complete classification of this Act to the Code, see Tables.

The United States mining laws, referred to in subsec. (f), are classified generally to Title 30, Mineral Lands and Mining.

**Codifications**

Subsec. (i) of this section, which required the Secretary to report annually to Congress on the progress in, and any problems concerning, the implementation of this section, terminated, effective May 15, 2000, pursuant to section 3003 of Pub.L. 104–66, as amended, set out as a note under section 1113 of Title 31, Money and Finance. See, also, the last item on page 107 of House Document No. 103097.

**Change of Name**

Committee on Interior and Insular Affairs of the House of Representatives changed to Committee on Natural Resources of the House of Representatives on Jan. 5, 1993, by House Resolution No. 5, One Hundred Third Congress.

Any reference in any provision of law enacted before Jan. 4, 1995, to the Committee on Natural Resources of the House of Representatives treated as referring to the Committee on Resources of the House of Representatives, see section 1(a)(8) of Pub.L. 104–14, set out as a note preceding section 21 of Title 2, The Congress.

The Committee on Interior and Insular Affairs of the Senate, referred to in subsec. (c)(2), was abolished and replaced by the Committee on Energy and Natural Resources of the Senate, effective Feb. 11, 1977. See Rule XXV of the Standing Rules of the Senate, as amended by Senate Resolution 4 (popularly cited as the "Committee System Reorganization Amendments of 1977"), approved Feb. 4, 1977.

**Desert Lily Sanctuary**

Pub.L. 103–433, Title I, § 107, Oct. 31, 1994, 108 Stat. 4483, provided that:

"**(a) Designation.**—There is hereby established the Desert Lily Sanctuary within the California Desert Conservation Area, California, of the Bureau of Land Management, comprising approximately two thousand forty acres, as generally depicted on a map entitled 'Desert Lily Sanctuary', dated February 1986. The Secretary shall administer the area to provide maximum protection to the desert lily.

"**(b) Withdrawal.**—Subject to valid existing rights, all Federal lands within the Desert Lily Sanctuary are hereby withdrawn from all forms of entry, appropriation, or disposal under the public land laws; from location, entry, and patent under the United States mining laws; and from disposition under all laws pertaining to mineral and geothermal leasing, and mineral materials, and all amendments thereto."

**Dinosaur Trackway Area of Critical Environmental Concern**

Pub.L. 103–433, Title I, § 108, Oct. 31, 1994, 108 Stat. 4483, provided that:

"**(a) Designation.**—There is hereby established the Dinosaur Trackway Area of Critical Environmental Concern within the California Desert Conservation Area, of the Bureau of Land Management, comprising approximately five hundred and ninety acres as generally depicted on a map entitled 'Dinosaur Trackway Area of Critical Environmental Concern', dated July 1993. The Secretary shall administer the area to preserve the paleontological resources within the area.

"**(b) Withdrawal.**—Subject to valid existing rights, the Federal lands within and adjacent to the Dinosaur Trackway Area of Critical Environmental Concern, as generally depicted on a map entitled 'Dinosaur Trackway Mineral Withdrawal Area', dated July 1993, are hereby withdrawn from all forms of entry, appropriation, or disposal under the public land laws; from location, entry, and patent under the United States mining laws; and from disposition under all laws pertaining to mineral and geothermal leasing, and mineral materials, and all amendments thereto."

## § 1782. Bureau of Land Management Wilderness Study

**[FLPMA § 603]**

### (a) Lands subject to review and designation as wilderness

Within fifteen years after October 21, 1976, the Secretary shall review those roadless areas of five thousand acres or more and roadless islands of the public lands, identified during the inventory required by section 1711(a) of this title as having wilderness characteristics described in the Wilderness Act of September 3, 1964 (78 Stat. 890; 16 U.S.C. 1131 et seq.) and shall from time to time report to the President his recommendation as to the suitability or nonsuitability of each such area or island for preservation as wilderness: *Provided,* That prior to any recommendations for the designation of an area as wilderness the Secretary shall cause mineral surveys to be conducted by the United States Geological Survey and the United States Bureau of Mines to determine the mineral values, if any, that may be present in such areas: *Provided further,* That the Secretary shall report to the President by July 1, 1980, his recommendations on those areas which the Secretary has prior to November 1, 1975, formally identified as natural or primitive areas. The review required by this subsection shall be conducted in accordance with the procedure specified in section 3(d) of the Wilderness Act [16 U.S.C.A. § 1132(d)].

### (b) Presidential recommendation for designation as wilderness

The President shall advise the President of the Senate and the Speaker of the House of Representatives of his recommendations with respect to designation as wilderness of each such area, together with a map thereof and a definition of its boundaries. Such advice by the President shall be given within two years of the receipt of each report from the Secretary. A recommendation of the President for designation as wilderness shall become effective only if so provided by an Act of Congress.

**(c) Status of lands during period of review and determination**

During the period of review of such areas and until Congress has determined otherwise, the Secretary shall continue to manage such lands according to his authority under this Act and other applicable law in a manner so as not to impair the suitability of such areas for preservation as wilderness, subject, however, to the continuation of existing mining and grazing uses and mineral leasing in the manner and degree in which the same was being conducted on October 21, 1976: *Provided*, That, in managing the public lands the Secretary shall by regulation or otherwise take any action required to prevent unnecessary or undue degradation of the lands and their resources or to afford environmental protection. Unless previously withdrawn from appropriation under the mining laws, such lands shall continue to be subject to such appropriation during the period of review unless withdrawn by the Secretary under the procedures of section 1714 of this title for reasons other than preservation of their wilderness character. Once an area has been designated for preservation as wilderness, the provisions of the Wilderness Act [16 U.S.C.A. § 1131 et seq.] which apply to national forest wilderness areas shall apply with respect to the administration and use of such designated area, including mineral surveys required by section 4(d)(2) of the Wilderness Act [16 U.S.C.A. § 1133(d)(2)], and mineral development, access, exchange of lands, and ingress and egress for mining claimants and occupants.

(Pub.L. 94–579, Title VI, § 603, Oct. 21, 1976, 90 Stat. 2785; Pub.L. 102–154, Title I, Nov. 13, 1991, 105 Stat. 1000; Pub.L. 102–285, § 10, May 18, 1992, 106 Stat. 171.)

### HISTORICAL AND STATUTORY NOTES

**References in Text**

The Wilderness Act of September 3, 1964, referred to in subsecs. (a) and (c), is Pub.L. 88–577, Sept. 3, 1964, 78 Stat. 890, as amended, which is classified generally to chapter 23 (section 1131 et seq.) of Title 16, Conservation. For complete classification of this Act to the Code, see Short Title note set out under section 1131 of Title 16 and Tables.

This Act, referred to in subsec. (c), is Pub.L. 94–579, Oct. 21, 1976, 90 Stat. 2743, as amended, known as the Federal Land Policy and Management Act of 1976. For complete classification of this Act to the Code, see Tables volume.

The mining laws, referred to in subsec. (c), are classified generally to Title 30, Mineral Lands and Mining.

**Change of Name**

Pub.L. 102–285, § 10(a), May 18, 1992, 106 Stat. 171, redesignated the Geological Survey and provided that on and after May 18, 1992, it shall be known as the United States Geological Survey. An earlier statute [Pub.L. 102–154, Title I, Nov. 13, 1991, 105 Stat. 1000] had provided for the identical change of name effective on and after Nov. 13, 1991. See note under section 31 of Title 43, Public Lands.

Pub.L. 102–285, §10(b), May 18, 1992, 106 Stat. 172, provided that, on and after May 18, 1992, the Bureau of Mines is redesignated and shall thereafter be known as the United States Bureau of Mines. See note under section 1 of Title 30, Mineral Lands and Mining.

**Transfer of Functions**

Pub.L. 104–134, Title I, § 101(c)[Title I], Apr. 26, 1996, 110 Stat. 1321–165; renumbered Title I Pub.L. 104–140, § 1(a), May 2, 1996, 110 Stat. 1327, provided in part: "That the authority granted to the United States Bureau of Mines to conduct mineral surveys and to determine mineral values by section 603 of Public Law 94–579 [enacting this section] is hereby transferred to, and vested in, the Director of the United States Geological Survey."

## § 1783. Yaquina Head Outstanding Natural Area

**(a) Establishment**

In order to protect the unique scenic, scientific, educational, and recreational values of certain lands in and around Yaquina Head, in Lincoln County, Oregon, there is hereby established, subject to valid existing rights, the Yaquina Head Outstanding Natural Area (hereinafter referred to as the "area"). The boundaries of the area are those shown on the map entitled "Yaquina Head Area", dated July 1979, which shall be on file and available for public inspection in the Office of the Director, Bureau of Land Management, United States Department of the Interior, and the State Office of the Bureau of Land Management in the State of Oregon.

**(b) Administration by Secretary of the Interior; management plan; quarrying permits**

(1) The Secretary of the Interior (hereinafter referred to as the "Secretary") shall administer the Yaquina Head Outstanding Natural Area in accordance with the laws and regulations applicable to the public lands as defined in section 103(e) of the Federal Land Policy and Management Act of 1976, as amended (43 U.S.C. 1702) [43 U.S.C.A. § 1702(e)], in such a manner as will best provide for—

(A) the conservation and development of the scenic, natural, and historic values of the area;

(B) the continued use of the area for purposes of education, scientific study, and public recreation which do not substantially impair the purposes for which the area is established; and

(C) protection of the wildlife habitat of the area.

(2) The Secretary shall develop a management plan for the area which accomplishes the purposes and is consistent with the provisions of this section. This plan shall be developed in accordance with the provisions of section 202 of the Federal Land Policy and

Management Act of 1976, as amended (43 U.S.C. 1712).

(3) Notwithstanding any other provision of this section, the Secretary is authorized to issue permits or to contract for the quarrying of materials from the area in accordance with the management plan for the area on condition that the lands be reclaimed and restored to the satisfaction of the Secretary. Such authorization to quarry shall require payment of fair market value for the materials to be quarried, as established by the Secretary, and shall also include any terms and conditions which the Secretary determines necessary to protect the values of such quarry lands for purposes of this section.

### (c) Revocation of 1866 reservation of lands for lighthouse purposes; restoration to public lands status

The reservation of lands for lighthouse purposes made by Executive order of June 8, 1866, of certain lands totaling approximately 18.1 acres, as depicted on the map referred to in subsection (a) of this section, is hereby revoked. The lands referred to in subsection (a) of this section are hereby restored to the status of public lands as defined in section 103(e) of the Federal Land Policy and Management Act of 1976, as amended (43 U.S.C. 1702) [43 U.S.C.A. § 1702(e)], and shall be administered in accordance with the management plan for the area developed pursuant to subsection (b) of this section, except that such lands are hereby withdrawn from settlement, sale, location, or entry, under the public land laws, including the mining laws (30 U.S.C., ch. 2), leasing under the mineral leasing laws (30 U.S.C. 181 et seq.), and disposals under the Materials Act of July 31, 1947, as amended (30 U.S.C. 601, 602) [30 U.S.C.A. § 601 et seq.].

### (d) Acquisition of lands not already in Federal ownership

The Secretary shall, as soon as possible but in no event later than twenty-four months following March 5, 1980, acquire by purchase, exchange, donation, or condemnation all or any part of the lands and waters and interests in lands and waters within the area referred to in subsection (a) of this section which are not in Federal ownership except that State land shall not be acquired by purchase or condemnation. Any lands or interests acquired by the Secretary pursuant to this section shall become public lands as defined in the Federal Land Policy and Management Act of 1976, as amended [43 U.S.C.A. § 1701 et seq.]. Upon acquisition by the United States, such lands are automatically withdrawn under the provisions of subsection (c) of this section except that lands affected by quarrying operations in the area shall be subject to disposals under the Materials Act of July 31, 1947, as amended (30 U.S.C. 601, 602) [30 U.S.C.A. § 601 et seq.]. Any lands acquired pursuant to this subsection shall be administered in accordance with the management plan for the area developed pursuant to subsection (b) of this section.

### (e) Wind energy research

The Secretary is authorized to conduct a study relating to the use of lands in the area for purposes of wind energy research. If the Secretary determines after such study that the conduct of wind energy research activity will not substantially impair the values of the lands in the area for purposes of this section, the Secretary is further authorized to issue permits for the use of such lands as a site for installation and field testing of an experimental wind turbine generating system. Any permit issued pursuant to this subsection shall contain such terms and conditions as the Secretary determines necessary to protect the values of such lands for purposes of this section.

### (f) Reclamation and restoration of lands affected by quarrying operations

The Secretary shall develop and administer, in addition to any requirements imposed pursuant to subsection (b)(3) of this section, a program for the reclamation and restoration of all lands affected by quarrying operations in the area acquired pursuant to subsection (d) of this section. All revenues received by the United States in connection with quarrying operations authorized by subsection (b)(3) of this section shall be deposited in a separate fund account which shall be established by the Secretary of the Treasury. Such revenues are hereby authorized to be appropriated to the Secretary as needed for reclamation and restoration of any lands acquired pursuant to subsection (d) of this section. After completion of such reclamation and restoration to the satisfaction of the Secretary, any unexpended revenues in such fund shall be returned to the general fund of the United States Treasury.

### (g) Authorization of appropriations

There are hereby authorized to be appropriated in addition to that authorized by subsection (f) of this section, such sums as may be necessary to carry out the provisions of this section.

(Pub.L. 96–199, Title I, § 119, Mar. 5, 1980, 94 Stat. 71.)

## HISTORICAL AND STATUTORY NOTES

**References in Text**

The public land laws, referred to in subsec. (c), are classified generally to this title.

The mining laws, referred to in subsec. (c), are classified generally to Title 30, Mineral Lands and Mining.

Mineral leasing laws, referred to in subsec. (c), have been defined in sections 351, 505, 530, and 541e of Title 30 to mean Acts Oct. 20, 1914, c. 330, 38 Stat. 741; Feb. 25, 1920, c. 85, 41 Stat. 437; Apr. 17, 1926, c. 158, 44 Stat. 301; and Feb. 7,

1927, c. 66, 44 Stat. 1057. The Act of Oct. 20, 1914, was repealed by Pub.L. 86–252, § 1, Sept. 9, 1959, 73 Stat. 490. The Act of Feb. 25, 1920, is popularly known as the Mineral Lands Leasing Act and is classified principally to chapter 3A (section 181 et seq.) of Title 30. The Act of Apr. 17, 1926, is classified generally to subchapter VIII (section 271 et seq.) of chapter 3A of Title 30. The Act of Feb. 7, 1927, is classified principally to subchapter IX (section 281 et seq.) of chapter 3A of Title 30. For complete classification of these Acts to the Code, see Tables volume.

The Materials Act of July 31, 1947, as amended (30 U.S.C. 601, 602), referred to in subsecs. (c) and (d), is Act July 31, 1947, c. 406, 61 Stat. 681, as amended, which is classified generally to subchapter I (section 601 et seq.) of chapter 15 of Title 30. For complete classification of this Act to the Code, see Short Title note set out under section 601 of Title 30 and Tables volume.

The Federal Land Policy and Management Act of 1976, as amended, referred to in subsec. (d), is Pub.L. 94–579, Oct. 21, 1976, 90 Stat. 2743, as amended, which is classified principally to chapter 35 (section 1701 et seq.) of this title. For complete classification of this Act to the Code, see Short Title note set out under section 1701 of this title and Tables volume.

**Codifications**

Section was not enacted as part of the Federal Land Policy and Management Act of 1976 which enacted this chapter.

## § 1784. Lands in Alaska; designation as wilderness; management by Bureau of Land Management pending Congressional action

Notwithstanding any other provision of law, section 1782 of this title shall not apply to any lands in Alaska. However, in carrying out his duties under sections 1711 and 1712 of this title and other applicable laws, the Secretary may identify areas in Alaska which he determines are suitable as wilderness and may, from time to time, make recommendations to the Congress for inclusion of any such areas in the National Wilderness Preservation System, pursuant to the provisions of the Wilderness Act [16 U.S.C.A. § 1131 et seq.]. In the absence of congressional action relating to any such recommendation of the Secretary, the Bureau of Land Management shall manage all such areas which are within its jurisdiction in accordance with the applicable land use plans and applicable provisions of law.

(Pub.L. 96–487, Title XIII, § 1320, Dec. 2, 1980, 94 Stat. 2487.)

### HISTORICAL AND STATUTORY NOTES

**References in Text**

The Wilderness Act, referred to in text, is Pub.L. 88–577, Sept. 3, 1964, 78 Stat. 890, as amended, which is classified generally to chapter 23 (§ 1131 et seq.) of Title 16, Conservation. For complete classification of this Act to the Code, see Short Title note set out under section 1131 of Title 16 and Tables.

**Codifications**

Section was enacted as part of the Alaska National Interest Lands Conservation Act and not as part of the Federal Land Policy and Management Act of 1976, which comprises this chapter.

**Kenai Natives Association Land Exchange**

Pub.L. 104–333, Div. I, Title III, § 311, Nov. 12, 1996, 110 Stat. 4139; Pub.L. 106–176, Title I, § 105, Mar. 10, 2000, 114 Stat. 25, provided that:

"(a) **Short title.**—This section [this note] may be cited as the 'Kenai Natives Association Equity Act Amendments of 1996'.

"(b) **Findings and purpose.**—

"(1) **Findings.**—The Congress finds the following:

"(A) The United States Fish and Wildlife Service and Kenai Natives Association, Inc., have agreed to transfers of certain land rights, in and near the Kenai National Wildlife Refuge, negotiated as directed by Public Law 102–458 [Pub.L. 102–458, Oct. 23, 1996, 106 Stat. 2267].

"(B) The lands to be acquired by the Service are within the area impacted by the Exxon Valdez oil spill of 1989, and these lands included important habitat for various species of fish and wildlife for which significant injury resulting from the spill has been documented through the EVOS Trustee Council restoration process. This analysis has indicated that these lands generally have value for the restoration of such injured natural resources as pink salmon, dolly varden, bald eagles, river otters, and cultural and archaeological resources. This analysis has also indicated that these lands generally have high value for the restoration of injured species that rely on these natural resources, including wilderness quality, recreation, tourism, and subsistence.

"(C) Restoration of the injured species will benefit from acquisition and the prevention of disturbances which may adversely affect their recovery.

"(D) It is in the public interest to complete the conveyances provided for in this section.

"(2) **Purpose.**—The purpose of this section is to authorize and direct the Secretary, at the election of KNA, to complete the conveyances provided for in this section.

"(c) **Definitions.**—For purposes of this section, the term—

"(1) 'ANCSA' means the Alaska Native Claims Settlement Act of 1971 (43 U.S.C. 1601 et seq.) [Pub.L. 92–203, Dec. 18, 1971, 85 Stat. 688, as amended; for distribution of which to the Code, see Short Title note set out under section 1601 of this title and Tables];

"(2) 'ANILCA' means the Alaska National Interest Lands Conservation Act (Public Law 96–487; 94 Stat. 2371 et seq.) [Pub.L. 96–487, Dec. 2, 1980, 94 Stat. 2371, as amended; for distribution of which to the Code, see Short Title note set out under section 3101 of Title 16, Conservation, and Tables];

"(3) 'conservation system unit' has the same meaning as in section 102(4) of ANILCA (16 U.S.C. 3102(4)) [section 3102(4) of Title 16];

"(4) 'CIRI' means the Cook Inlet Region, Inc., a Native Regional Corporation incorporated in the State of Alaska pursuant to the terms of ANCSA;

"(5) 'EVOS' means the Exxon Valdez oil spill;

"(6) 'KNA' means the Kenai Natives Association, Inc., an urban corporation incorporated in the State of Alaska pursuant to the terms of ANCSA;

"(7) 'lands' means any lands, waters, or interests therein;

"(8) 'Refuge' means the Kenai National Wildlife Refuge;

"(9) 'Secretary' means the Secretary of the Interior;

"(10) 'Service' means the United States Fish and Wildlife Service; and

"(11) 'Terms and Conditions' means the Terms and Conditions for Land Consolidation and Management in the Cook Inlet Area, as clarified on August 31, 1976, ratified by section 12 of Public Law 94–204 (43 U.S.C. 1611 note) [Pub.L. 94–204, § 12, Jan. 2, 1976, 89 Stat. 1150, as amended, set out as a note under section 1611 of this title].

"(d) **Acquisition of lands.**—

"(1) **Offer to KNA.**—

"(A) **In general.**—Subject to the availability of the funds identified in paragraph (2)(C), no later than 90 days after the date of enactment of this section [Nov. 12, 1996], the Secretary shall offer to convey to KNA the interests in land and rights set forth in paragraph (2)(B), subject to valid existing rights, in return for the conveyance by KNA to the United States of the interests in land or relinquishment of ANCSA selections set forth in paragraph (2)(A). Payment for the lands conveyed to the United States by KNA is contingent upon KNA's acceptance of the entire conveyance outlined herein.

"(B) **Limitation.**—The Secretary may not convey any lands or make payment to KNA under this section unless title to the lands to be conveyed by KNA under this section has been found by the United States to be sufficient in accordance with the provisions of section 355 of the Revised Statutes (40 U.S.C. 255) [see now 40 U.S.C.A. §§ 3111, 3112].

"(2) **Acquisition lands.**—

"(A) **Lands to be conveyed to the United States.**—The lands to be conveyed by KNA to the United States, or the valid selection rights under ANCSA to be relinquished, all situated within the boundary of the Refuge, are the following:

"(i) The conveyance of approximately 803 acres located along and on islands within the Kenai River, known as the Stephanka Tract.

"(ii) The conveyance of approximately 1,243 acres located along the Moose River, known as the Moose River Patented Lands Tract.

"(iii) The relinquishment of KNA's selection known as the Moose River Selected Tract, containing approximately 753 acres located along the Moose River.

"(iv) The relinquishment of KNA's remaining ANCSA entitlement of approximately 454 acres.

"(v) The relinquishment of all KNA's remaining overselections. Upon completion of all relinquishments outlined above, all KNA's entitlement shall be deemed to be extinguished and the completion of this acquisition will satisfy all of KNA's ANCSA entitlement.

"(vi) The conveyance of an access easement providing the United States and its assigns access across KNA's surface estate in the SW¼ of section 21, T. 6 N., R. 9 W., Seward Meridian, Alaska.

"(vii) The conveyance of approximately 100 acres within the Beaver Creek Patented Tract, which is contiguous to lands being retained by the United States contiguous to the Beaver Creek Patented Tract, in exchange for 280 acres of Service lands currently situated within the Beaver Creek Selected Tract.

"(B) **Lands to be conveyed to KNA.**—The rights provided or lands to be conveyed by the United States to KNA, are the following:

"(i) The surface and subsurface estate to approximately 5 acres, subject to reservations of easements for existing roads and utilities, located within the city of Kenai, Alaska, identified as United States Survey 1435, withdrawn by Executive Order 2943 and known as the old Fish and Wildlife Service Headquarters site.

"(ii) The remaining subsurface estate held by the United States to approximately 13,651 acres, including portions of the Beaver Creek Patented Tract, the Beaver Creek Selected Tract, and portions of the Swanson River Road West Tract and the Swanson River Road East Tract, where the surface was previously or will be conveyed to KNA pursuant to this Act [this note] but excluding the SW¼ of section 21, T. 6 N., R. 9 W., Seward Meridian, Alaska, which will be retained by the United States. The conveyance of these subsurface interests will be subject to the rights of CIRI to the coal, oil, gas, and to all rights CIRI, its successors, and assigns would have under paragraph 1(B) of the Terms and Conditions, including the right to sand and gravel, to construct facilities, to have rights-of-way, and to otherwise develop it subsurface interests.

"(iii)(I) The nonexclusive right to use sand and gravel which is reasonably necessary for on-site development without compensation or permit on those portions of the Swanson River Road East Tract, comprising approximately 1,738.04 acres; where the entire subsurface of the land is presently owned by the United States. The United States shall retain the ownership of all other sand and gravel located within the subsurface and KNA shall not sell or dispose of such sand and gravel.

"(II) The right to excavate within the subsurface estate as reasonably necessary for structures, utilities, transportation systems, and other development of the surface estate.

"(iv) The nonexclusive right to excavate within the subsurface estate as reasonably necessary for structures, utilities, transportation systems, and other development of the surface estate on the SW¼, section 21, T. 6 N., R. 9 W., Seward Meridian, Alaska, where the entire subsurface of the land is owned by the United States and which public lands shall continue to be withdrawn from mining following their removal from the Refuge boundary under paragraph (3)(A)(ii). The United States shall retain the ownership of all other sand and gravel located within the subsurface of this parcel.

"(v) The surface estate of approximately 280 acres known as the Beaver Creek Selected Tract. This tract shall be conveyed to KNA in exchange for lands conveyed to the United States as described in paragraph (2)(A)(ii).

"(C) **Payment.**—The United States shall make a total cash payment to KNA for the above-described lands of

$4,443,000, contingent upon the appropriate approvals of the Federal or State of Alaska EVOS Trustees (or both) necessary for any expenditure of the EVOS settlement funds.

"**(D) National Register of Historic Places.**—Upon completion of the acquisition authorized in paragraph (1), the Secretary shall, at no cost to KNA, in coordination with KNA, promptly undertake to nominate the Stephanka Tract to the National Register of Historic Places, in recognition of the archaeological artifacts from the original Dena'ina Settlement. If the Department of the Interior establishes a historical, cultural, or archaeological interpretive site, KNA shall have the exclusive right to operate a Dena'ina interpretive site on the Stephanka Tract under the regulations and policies of the department. If KNA declines to operate such a site, the department may do so under its existing authorities. Prior to the department undertaking any archaeological activities whatsoever on the Stephanka Tract, KNA shall be consulted.

"(3) **[Omitted.** Amended provisions set out as a note under section 668dd of Title 16]

"(e) **[Omitted.** Amended provisions set out as a note under section 1132 of Title 16]

"**(f) Designation of Lake Todatonten Special Management Area.**—

"**(1) Purpose.**—To balance the potential effects on fish, wildlife, and habitat of the removal of KNA lands from the Refuge System, the Secretary is hereby directed to withdraw, subject to valid existing rights, from location, entry, and patent under the mining laws and to create as a special management unit for the protection of fish, wildlife, and habitat, certain unappropriated and unreserved public lands, totaling approximately 37,000 acres adjacent to the west boundary of the Kanuti National Wildlife Refuge to be known as the 'Lake Todatonten Special Management Area', as depicted on the map entitled 'Proposed: Lake Todatonten Special Management Area', dated June 13, 1996, and to be managed by the Bureau of Land Management.

"**(2) Management.**—

"**(A)** Such designation is subject to all valid existing rights as well as the subsistence preferences provided under title VIII of ANILCA [subchapter II (section 3111 et seq.) of chapter 51 of Title 16]. Any lands conveyed to the State of Alaska shall be removed from the Lake Todatonten Special Management Area.

"**(B)** The Secretary may permit any additional uses of the area, or grant easements, only to the extent that such use, including leasing under the mineral leasing laws, is determined to not detract from nor materially interfere with the purposes for which the Special Management Area is established.

"**(C)(i)** The BLM shall establish the Lake Todatonten Special Management Area Committee. The membership of the Committee shall consist of 11 members as follows:

"**(I)** Two residents each from the villages of Alatna, Allakaket, Hughes, and Tanana.

"**(II)** One representative from each of Doyon Corporation, the Tanana Chiefs Conference, and the State of Alaska.

"**(ii)** Members of the Committee shall serve without pay.

"**(iii)** The BLM shall hold meetings of the Lake Todatonten Special Management Area Committee at least once per year to discuss management issues within the Special Management Area. The BLM shall not allow any new type of activity in the Special Management Area without first conferring with the Committee in a timely manner.

"**(3) Access.**—The Secretary shall allow the following:

"**(A)** Private access for any purpose, including economic development, to lands within the boundaries of the Special Management Area which are owned by third parties or are held in trust by the Secretary for third parties pursuant to the Alaska Native Allotment Act (25 U.S.C. 336) [probably means section 336 of Title 25, Indians]. Such rights may be subject to restrictions issued by the BLM to protect subsistence uses of the Special Management Area.

"**(B)** Existing public access across the Special Management Area. Section 1110(a) of ANILCA [section 3170(a) of Title 16] shall apply to the Special Management Area.

"**(4) Secretarial order and maps.**—The Secretary shall file with the Committee on Resources of the House of Representatives and the Committee on Energy and Natural Resources and the Committee on Environment and Public Works of the Senate, the Secretarial Order and maps setting forth the boundaries of the Area within 90 days of the completion of the acquisition authorized by this section [this note]. Once established, this Order may only be amended or revoked by Act of Congress.

"**(5) Authorization of appropriations.**—There are authorized to be appropriated such sums as may be necessary to carry out the purposes of this section [this note]."

## § 1785. Fossil Forest Research Natural Area

### (a) Establishment

To conserve and protect natural values and to provide scientific knowledge, education, and interpretation for the benefit of future generations, there is established the Fossil Forest Research Natural Area (referred to in this section as the "Area"), consisting of the approximately 2,770 acres in the Farmington District of the Bureau of Land Management, New Mexico, as generally depicted on a map entitled "Fossil Forest", dated June 1983.

### (b) Map and legal description

#### (1) In general

As soon as practicable after November 12, 1996, the Secretary of the Interior shall file a map and legal description of the Area with the Committee on Energy and Natural Resources of the Senate and the Committee on Resources of the House of Representatives.

**(2) Force and effect**

The map and legal description described in paragraph (1) shall have the same force and effect as if included in this Act.

**(3) Technical corrections**

The Secretary of the Interior may correct clerical, typographical, and cartographical errors in the map and legal description subsequent to filing the map pursuant to paragraph (1).

**(4) Public inspection**

The map and legal description shall be on file and available for public inspection in the Office of the Director of the Bureau of Land Management, Department of the Interior.

**(c) Management**

**(1) In general**

The Secretary of the Interior, acting through the Director of the Bureau of Land Management, shall manage the Area—

**(A)** to protect the resources within the Area; and

**(B)** in accordance with this Act, the Federal Land Policy and Management Act of 1976 (43 U.S.C. 1701 et seq.), and other applicable provisions of law.

**(2) Mining**

**(A) Withdrawal**

Subject to valid existing rights, the lands within the Area are withdrawn from all forms of appropriation under the mining laws and from disposition under all laws pertaining to mineral leasing, geothermal leasing, and mineral material sales.

**(B) Coal preference rights**

The Secretary of the Interior is authorized to issue coal leases in New Mexico in exchange for any preference right coal lease application within the Area. Such exchanges shall be made in accordance with applicable existing laws and regulations relating to coal leases after a determination has been made by the Secretary that the applicant is entitled to a preference right lease and that the exchange is in the public interest.

**(C) Oil and gas leases**

Operations on oil and gas leases issued prior to November 12, 1996, shall be subject to the applicable provisions of Group 3100 of title 43, Code of Federal Regulations (including section 3162.5–1), and such other terms, stipulations, and conditions as the Secretary of the Interior considers necessary to avoid significant disturbance of the land surface or impairment of the natural, educational, and scientific research values of the Area in existence on November 12, 1996.

**(3) Grazing**

Livestock grazing on lands within the Area may not be permitted.

**(d) Inventory**

Not later than 3 full fiscal years after November 12, 1996, the Secretary of the Interior, acting through the Director of the Bureau of Land Management, shall develop a baseline inventory of all categories of fossil resources within the Area. After the inventory is developed, the Secretary shall conduct monitoring surveys at intervals specified in the management plan developed for the Area in accordance with subsection (e) of this section.

**(e) Management plan**

**(1) In general**

Not later than 5 years after November 12, 1996, the Secretary of the Interior shall develop and submit to the Committee on Energy and Natural Resources of the Senate and the Committee on Resources of the House of Representatives a management plan that describes the appropriate use of the Area consistent with this subsection.

**(2) Contents**

The management plan shall include—

**(A)** a plan for the implementation of a continuing cooperative program with other agencies and groups for—

**(i)** laboratory and field interpretation; and

**(ii)** public education about the resources and values of the Area (including vertebrate fossils);

**(B)** provisions for vehicle management that are consistent with the purpose of the Area and that provide for the use of vehicles to the minimum extent necessary to accomplish an individual scientific project;

**(C)** procedures for the excavation and collection of fossil remains, including botanical fossils, and the use of motorized and mechanical equipment to the minimum extent necessary to accomplish an individual scientific project; and

**(D)** mitigation and reclamation standards for activities that disturb the surface to the detriment of scenic and environmental values.

(Pub.L. 98–603, Title I, § 103, Oct. 30, 1984, 98 Stat. 3156; Pub.L. 104–333, Div. I, Title X, § 1022(e), Nov. 12, 1996, 110 Stat. 4213; Pub.L. 106–176, Title I, § 124, Mar. 10, 2000, 114 Stat. 30.)

## HISTORICAL AND STATUTORY NOTES

**References in Text**

November 12, 1996, referred to in subsecs. (b)(1), (c)(2)(C), (d), and (e)(1), was in the original "the date of enactment of this paragraph", "date of enactment of this subsection" and "the date of enactment of this Act", respectively. Such phrases were translated as Nov. 12, 1996, the date of approval of Pub.L. 104–333, section 1022(e) of which amended this section generally, as the probable intent of Congress.

This Act, referred to in subsecs. (b)(2) and (c)(1)(B), is the San Juan Basin Wilderness Protection Act of 1984, Pub.L. 98–603, Oct. 30, 1984, 98 Stat. 3155, as amended. See Tables for complete classification.

The Federal Land Policy and Management Act of 1976, referred to in subsec. (c)(1)(B), is Pub.L. 94–579, Oct. 21, 1976, 90 Stat. 2743, as amended, which is classified principally to chapter 35 (§ 1701 et seq.) of this title. For complete classification of this Act to the Code, see Short Title note set out under section 1701 of this title and Tables.

Mining laws, referred to in subsec. (c)(2)(A), are classified generally to Title 30, Mineral Lands and Mining.

Mineral leasing laws, referred to in subsec. (c)(2)(A), have been defined in sections 351, 505, 530, and 541e of Title 30, Mineral Lands and Mining, to mean Acts Oct. 20, 1914, c. 330, 38 Stat. 741; Feb. 25, 1920, c. 85, 41 Stat. 437; Apr. 17, 1926, c. 158, 44 Stat. 301; and Feb. 7, 1927, c. 66, 44 Stat. 1057. The Act of Oct. 20, 1914, was repealed by Pub.L. 86–252, § 1, Sept. 9, 1959, 73 Stat. 490. The Act of Feb. 25, 1920, is known as the Mineral Leasing Act and is classified generally to chapter 3A (section 181 et seq.) of Title 30. The Act of Apr. 17, 1926, is classified generally to subchapter VIII (section 271 et seq.) of chapter 3A of Title 30. The Act of Feb. 7, 1927, is classified principally to subchapter IX (section 281 et seq.) of chapter 3A of Title 30. For complete classification of these Acts to the Code, see Tables.

Geothermal leasing laws, referred to in subsec. (c)(2)(A), are classified principally to chapter 23 (section 1001 et seq.) of Title 30, Mineral Lands and Mining.

**Codifications**

Section was enacted as part of the San Juan Basin Wilderness Protection Act of 1984, and not as part of the Federal Land Policy and Management Act of 1976, which comprises this chapter.

Amendments by Pub.L. 106–176, Title I, § 124, Mar. 10, 2000, 114 Stat. 30, were executed to this section as the probable intent of Congress, despite directory language referencing section 178 of this title; directory language correctly referred to laws which enacted and amended this section.

# OUTER CONTINENTAL SHELF RESOURCE MANAGEMENT

## OUTER CONTINENTAL SHELF LANDS ACT AMENDMENTS OF 1978 [OCSLAA § ———]

**(43 U.S.C.A. §§ 1801 to 1866)**

## CHAPTER 36—OUTER CONTINENTAL SHELF RESOURCE MANAGEMENT



**Related Provisions**

*See, also, Soil and Water Resources, 16 U.S.C.A. § 2001 et seq., ante.*

## § 1801. Congressional findings

**[OCSLAA § 101]**

The Congress finds and declares that—

(1) the demand for energy in the United States is increasing and will continue to increase for the foreseeable future;

(2) domestic production of oil and gas has declined in recent years;

(3) the United States has become increasingly dependent upon imports of oil from foreign nations to meet domestic energy demand;

(4) increasing reliance on imported oil is not inevitable, but is rather subject to significant reduction by increasing the development of domestic sources of energy supply;

(5) consumption of natural gas in the United States has greatly exceeded additions to domestic reserves in recent years;

(6) technology is or can be made available which will allow significantly increased domestic production of oil and gas without undue harm or damage to the environment;

(7) the Outer Continental Shelf contains significant quantities of oil and natural gas and is a vital national resource reserve which must be carefully managed so as to realize fair value, to preserve and maintain competition, and to reflect the public interest;

(8) there presently exists a variety of technological, economic, environmental, administrative, and legal problems which tend to retard the development of the oil and natural gas reserves of the Outer Continental Shelf;

(9) environmental and safety regulations relating to activities on the Outer Continental Shelf should be reviewed in light of current technology and information;

(10) the development, processing, and distribution of the oil and gas resources of the Outer Continental Shelf, and the siting of related energy facilities, may cause adverse impacts on various States and local governments;

(11) policies, plans, and programs developed by States and local governments in response to activities on the Outer Continental Shelf cannot anticipate and ameliorate such adverse impacts unless such States, working in close cooperation with affected local governments, are provided with timely access to information regarding activities on the Outer Continental Shelf and an opportunity to re-

view and comment on decisions relating to such activities;

(12) funds must be made available to pay for the prompt removal of any oil spilled or discharged as a result of activities on the Outer Continental Shelf and for any damages to public or private interests caused by such spills or discharges;

(13) because of the possible conflicts between exploitation of the oil and gas resources in the Outer Continental Shelf and other uses of the marine environment, including fish and shellfish growth and recovery, and recreational activity, the Federal Government must assume responsibility for the minimization or elimination of any conflict associated with such exploitation;

(14) the oil and gas resources of the Outer Continental Shelf are limited, nonrenewable resources which must be developed in a manner which takes into consideration the Nation's long-range energy needs and also assures adequate protection of the renewable resources of the Outer Continental Shelf which are a continuing and increasingly important source of food and protein to the Nation and the world; and

(15) funds must be made available to pay for damage to commercial fishing vessels and gear resulting from activities involving oil and gas exploration, development, and production on the Outer Continental Shelf.

(Pub.L. 95–372, Title I, § 101, Sept. 18, 1978, 92 Stat. 630.)

### HISTORICAL AND STATUTORY NOTES

**Short Title**

1988 Amendments

Pub.L. 100–610, Title I, § 1, Nov. 5, 1988, 102 Stat. 3176, provided that: "This Act [probably means 'title', which amended section 1815 of this title] may be cited as the 'Outer Continental Shelf Operations Indemnification Clarification Act of 1988'."

1978 Acts

Section 1 of Pub.L. 95–372 provided: "That this Act [enacting this chapter, sections 1344 to 1356 of this title, and section 237 of Title 30, Mineral Lands and Mining, amending sections 1456, 1456a, and 1464 of Title 16, Conservation, sections 1331, 1332, 1333, 1334, 1337 1340, and 1343 of this title, and section 6213 of Title 42, The Public Health and Welfare, and enacting provisions set out as notes under sections 1348 and 1811 of this title] may be cited as the 'Outer Continental Shelf Lands Act Amendments of 1978'."

## § 1802. Congressional declaration of purposes

**[OCSLAA § 102]**

The purposes of this chapter are to—

(1) establish policies and procedures for managing the oil and natural gas resources of the Outer Continental Shelf which are intended to result in expedited exploration and development of the Outer Continental Shelf in order to achieve national economic and energy policy goals, assure national security, reduce dependence on foreign sources, and maintain a favorable balance of payments in world trade;

(2) preserve, protect, and develop oil and natural gas resources in the Outer Continental Shelf in a manner which is consistent with the need (A) to make such resources available to meet the Nation's energy needs as rapidly as possible, (B) to balance orderly energy resource development with protection of the human, marine, and coastal environments, (C) to insure the public a fair and equitable return on the resources of the Outer Continental Shelf, and (D) to preserve and maintain free enterprise competition;

(3) encourage development of new and improved technology for energy resource production which will eliminate or minimize risk of damage to the human, marine, and coastal environments;

(4) provide States, and through States, local governments, which are impacted by Outer Continental Shelf oil and gas exploration, development, and production with comprehensive assistance in order to anticipate and plan for such impact, and thereby to assure adequate protection of the human environment;

(5) assure that States, and through States, local governments, have timely access to information regarding activities on the Outer Continental Shelf, and opportunity to review and comment on decisions relating to such activities, in order to anticipate, ameliorate, and plan for the impacts of such activities;

(6) assure that States, and through States, local governments, which are directly affected by exploration, development, and production of oil and natural gas are provided an opportunity to participate in policy and planning decisions relating to management of the resources of the Outer Continental Shelf;

(7) minimize or eliminate conflicts between the exploration, development, and production of oil and natural gas, and the recovery of other resources such as fish and shellfish;

(8) establish an oilspill liability fund to pay for the prompt removal of any oil spilled or discharged as a result of activities on the Outer Continental Shelf and for any damages to public or private interests caused by such spills or discharges;

(9) insure that the extent of oil and natural gas resources of the Outer Continental Shelf is assessed at the earliest practicable time; and

(10) establish a fishermen's contingency fund to pay for damages to commercial fishing vessels and gear due to Outer Continental Shelf activities.

(Pub.L. 95–372, Title I, § 102, Sept. 18, 1978, 92 Stat. 631.)

#### HISTORICAL AND STATUTORY NOTES

**References in Text**

This chapter, referred to in opening provision, in the original read "this Act", meaning Pub.L. 95–372, Sept. 18, 1978, 92 Stat. 629, known as the Outer Continental Shelf Lands Act Amendments of 1978, which enacted this chapter, sections 1344 to 1356 of this title, and section 237 of Title 30, Mineral Lands and Mining, amended sections 1331 to 1334, 1337, 1340, and 1343 of this title, sections 1456, 1456a, and 1464 of Title 16, Conservation, and section 6213 of Title 42, The Public Health and Welfare, and enacted provisions set out as notes under sections 1348 and 1811 of this title. For complete classification of this Act to the Code, see Short Title note set out under section 1801 of this title and Tables.

## SUBCHAPTER I—OFFSHORE OIL SPILL POLLUTION FUND [REPEALED]

### § 1811. Repealed. Pub.L. 101–380, Title II, § 2004, Aug. 18, 1990, 104 Stat. 507

#### HISTORICAL AND STATUTORY NOTES

Section, Pub.L. 95–372, Title III, § 301, Sept. 18, 1978, 92 Stat. 670, defined the terms used in the provisions governing the operation of the Offshore Oil Pollution Compensation Fund. See section 9509 of Title 26, Internal Revenue Code.

Section 315 of Pub.L. 95–372, which had been set out as a note under former section 1811 and had set the effective dates for the sections of this subchapter, was repealed by Pub.L. 101–380, Title II, § 2004, Aug. 18, 1990, 104 Stat. 507.

### § 1812. Repealed. Pub.L. 101–380, Title II, § 2004, Aug. 18, 1990, 104 Stat. 507

#### HISTORICAL AND STATUTORY NOTES

Section, Pub.L. 95–372, Title III, § 302, Sept. 18, 1978, 92 Stat. 672; Pub.L. 101–239, Title IX, § 9001(a), Dec. 19, 1989, 103 Stat. 2470, established the Offshore Oil Pollution Compensation Fund. See section 9509 of Title 26, Internal Revenue Code.

**Disposition of Amounts Remaining in Offshore Oil Pollution Compensation Fund**

Amounts remaining in the Offshore Oil Pollution Compensation Fund established under this section to be deposited in the Oil Spill Liability Trust Fund established under section 9509 of Title 26, Internal Revenue Code, with the Fund to assume all liability incurred by the Offshore Oil Pollution Compensation Fund, see section 2004 of Pub.L. 101–380, set out as a note under section 9509 of Title 26.

### §§ 1813 to 1824. Repealed. Pub.L. 101–380, Title II, § 2004, Aug. 18, 1990, 104 Stat. 507

#### HISTORICAL AND STATUTORY NOTES

Section 1813, Pub.L. 95–372, Title III, § 303, Sept. 18, 1978, 92 Stat. 674, provided for the asserting of claims for economic loss from oil pollution.

Section 1814, Pub.L. 95–372, Title III, § 304, Sept. 18, 1978, 92 Stat. 675, set the scope of the liability of owners and operators of vessels and offshore facilities.

Section 1815, Pub.L. 95–372, Title III, § 305, Sept. 18, 1978, 92 Stat. 677; Pub.L. 100–610, Title I, §§ 2, 3, Nov. 8, 1988, 102 Stat. 3176, required owners and operators of offshore facilities and vessels using offshore facilities to provide evidence of financial responsibility to cover liability for oil pollution.

Section 1816, Pub.L. 95–372, Title III, § 306, Sept. 18, 1978, 92 Stat. 678, provided for the notification, designation, and advertisement of incidents involving vessels or offshore facilities.

Section 1817, Pub.L. 95–372, Title III, § 307, Sept. 18, 1978, 92 Stat. 679, related to the presentment of claims to owners, operators, or guarantors, or to the Offshore Oil Pollution Compensation Fund.

Section 1818, Pub.L. 95–372, Title III, § 308, Sept. 18, 1978, 92 Stat. 682, provided for the subrogation of any person or governmental entity which pays compensation for an economic loss to all rights, claims, and causes of action which the claimant had under this subchapter.

Section 1819, Pub.L. 95–372, Title III, § 309, Sept. 18, 1978, 92 Stat. 683, provided for the jurisdiction and venue of controversies arising under this subchapter.

Section 1820, Pub.L. 95–372, Title III, § 310, Sept. 18, 1978, 92 Stat. 684, outlined the relationship of this subchapter to other State or Federal laws.

Section 1821, Pub.L. 95–372, Title III, § 311, Sept. 18, 1978, 92 Stat. 684, prohibited the harmful discharge of oil from any offshore facility or vessel.

Section 1822, Pub.L. 95–372, Title III, § 312, Sept. 18, 1978, 92 Stat. 684, set the civil and criminal penalties for violations of the provisions of this subchapter.

Section 1823, Pub.L. 95–372, Title III, § 313, Sept. 18, 1978, 92 Stat. 685, authorized appropriations for the administration of this subchapter.

Section 1824, Pub.L. 95–372, Title III, § 314, Sept. 18, 1978, 92 Stat. 685, directed the Secretary to submit a report annually to Congress on the operation of this subchapter.

## SUBCHAPTER II—FISHERMEN'S CONTINGENCY FUND

### § 1841. Definitions

**[OCSLAA § 401]**

As used in this subchapter, the term—

(1) "area affected by Outer Continental Shelf activities" means any geographic area:

(A) which is under oil or gas lease on the Outer Continental Shelf;

(B) where Outer Continental Shelf exploration, development or production activities have been permitted, except geophysical activities;

(C) where pipeline rights-of-way have been granted; or

(D) otherwise impacted by such activities including but not limited to expired lease areas, relinquished rights-of-way and easements, Outer Continental Shelf supply vessel routes, or other areas as determined by the Secretary;

(2) "citizen of the United States" means any person who is a United States citizen by law, birth, or naturalization, any State, any agency of a State or a group of States, or any corporation, partnership, or association organized under the laws of any State which has as its president or other chief executive officer and as its chairman of the board of directors, or holder of a similar office, a person who is a United States citizen by law, birth, or naturalization, and which has at least 75 per centum of the interest of[1] therein owned by citizens of the United States. Seventy-five per centum of the interest in the corporation shall not be deemed to be owned by citizens of the United States—

(A) if the title to 75 per centum of its stock is not vested in such citizens free from any trust or fiduciary obligation in favor of any person not a citizen of the United States;

(B) if 75 per centum of the voting power in such corporation is not vested in citizens of the United States;

(C) if through any contract or understanding it is so arranged that more than 25 per centum of the voting power may be exercised, directly or indirectly, in behalf of any person who is not a citizen of the United States; or

(D) if by any other means whatsoever control of any interest in the corporation in excess of 25 per centum is conferred upon or permitted to be exercised by any person who is not a citizen of the United States;

(3) "commercial fisherman" means any citizen of the United States who owns, operates, or derives income from being employed on a commercial fishing vessel;

(4) "commercial fishing vessel" means any vessel, boat, ship, or other craft which is (A) documented under the laws of the United States or, if under five net tons, registered under the laws of any State, and (B) used for, equipped to be used for, or of a type which is normally used for commercial purposes for the catching, taking, or harvesting of fish or the aiding or assisting of any activity related to the catching, taking, or harvesting of fish, including, but not limited to, preparation, supply, storage, refrigeration, transportation, or processing;

(5) "fish" means finfish, mollusks, crustaceans, and all other forms of marine animal and plant life other than marine mammals, birds, and highly migratory species;

(6) "fishing gear" means (A) any commercial fishing vessel, and (B) any equipment of such vessel, whether or not attached to such a vessel;

(7) "Fund" means the Fishermen's Contingency Fund established under section 1842 of this title; and

(8) "Secretary" means the Secretary of Commerce or the designee of such Secretary.

(Pub.L. 95–372, Title IV, § 401, Sept. 18, 1978, 92 Stat. 685; Pub. L. 97–212, §§ 1, 8, June 30, 1982, 96 Stat. 143, 147.)

[1] So in original. The "of" is probably unnecessary.

### HISTORICAL AND STATUTORY NOTES

**Effective and Applicability Provisions**

1982 Acts

Section 9 of Pub. L. 97–212 provided that:

"(a) Except as provided for in subsection (b), the amendments made by this Act [amending sections 1841 to 1845 of this title, repealing section 1847 of this title, enacting a provision set out as a note under section 1823 of Title 16, Conservation, and amending a provision set out as a note under section 1823 of Title 16] shall apply with respect to claims for damages that are filed, on or after the date of the enactment of this Act [June 30, 1982], with the Secretary of Commerce under section 405(a) of the Outer Continental Shelf Lands Act Amendments of 1978 [section 1845(a) of this title].

"(b)(1) Any commercial fisherman who filed a claim with the Secretary of Commerce for compensation under title IV of such amendments of 1978 [this subchapter] before the date of the enactment of this Act [June 30, 1982] may, if no decision on such claim was rendered under section 405(d) of such title IV [section 1845(d) of this title] before such date of enactment [June 30, 1982], refile such claim with the Secretary if the claimant notifies the Secretary in writing within thirty days after notification under paragraph (2) of his eligibility to refile the claim that he intends to so refile. If timely notification of intent to refile is made under the preceding sentence, any action pending with respect to the original claim shall be suspended pending the refiling of the claim under paragraph (2) and, if such refiling is timely made, such action shall be vacated.

"(2) The Secretary shall notify each claimant eligible to refile a claim under paragraph (1) of such eligibility within 10 days after the date of enactment of this Act [June 30, 1982].

"(3) A claim for which notification on intent to refile was timely made under paragraph (1) must be refiled with the Secretary within the thirty-day period after the date on which the regulations promulgated to implement the amendments made by this Act become final or action shall be resumed with respect to such claim without regard to the amendments made by this Act.

"(4) The amendments made by this Act shall apply with respect to any claim that is refiled on a timely basis under paragraph (3)."

## § 1842. Fishermen's Contingency Fund

[OCSLAA § 402]

**(a) Establishment; availability; source of deposits; limitation on amount; interest-bearing accounts; litigation**

(1) There is established in the Treasury of the United States a Fishermen's Contingency Fund. The Fund shall be available to the Secretary without fiscal year limitations as a revolving fund for the purpose of making payments pursuant to this section. The Fund shall consist of—

(A) revenues received from investments made under paragraph (3);

(B) amounts collected under subsection (b) of this section; and

(C) amounts recovered by the Secretary under section 1845(h)(2) of this title.

The total amount in the Fund that is collected under subsection (b) of this section may at no time exceed $2,000,000; and the total amount in the Fund which is attributable to revenue received under paragraph (3) or recovered by the Secretary under section 1845(h)(2) of this title shall be expended prior to amounts collected under subsection (b) of this section. Not more than 8 percent of the total amount in the Fund may be expended in any fiscal year for paying the administrative and personnel expenses referred to in paragraph (2)(A).

(2) The Fund shall be available, as provided for in appropriation Acts solely for the payment of—

(A) the personnel and administrative expenses incurred in carrying out this subchapter;

(B) any claim, in accordance with procedures established under this section, for damages that are compensable under this subchapter; and

(C) attorney and other fees awarded under section 1845(e) of this title with respect to any such claim.

(3) Sums in the Fund that are not currently needed for the purposes of the Fund shall be kept on deposit in appropriate interest-bearing accounts that shall be established by the Secretary of the Treasury or invested in obligations of, or guaranteed by, the United States. Any revenue accruing from such deposits and investments shall be deposited into the Fund.

(4) The Fund may sue and be sued in its own name. All litigation by or against the Fund shall be referred to the Attorney General.

**(b) Payments by each holder of lease, permit, easement, or right-of-way**

(1) Except as provided in paragraph (2), each holder of a lease that is issued or maintained under the Outer Continental Shelf Lands Act [43 U.S.C.A. § 1331 et seq.] and each holder of an exploration permit, or an easement or right-of-way for the construction of a pipeline in any area of the Outer Continental Shelf, shall pay an amount specified by the Secretary. The Secretary of the Interior shall collect such amount and deposit it into the Fund. In any calendar year, no holder of a lease, permit, easement, or right-of-way shall be required to pay an amount in excess of $5,000 per lease, permit, easement, or right-of-way.

(2) Payments may not be required under paragraph (1) by the Secretary of the Interior with respect to geological permits and geophysical permits, other than prelease exploratory drilling permits issued under section 11 of the Outer Continental Shelf Lands Act (43 U.S.C. 1340).

(Pub.L. 95–372, Title IV, § 402, Sept. 18, 1978, 92 Stat. 686; Pub. L. 97–212, § 2, June 30, 1982, 96 Stat. 143.)

### HISTORICAL AND STATUTORY NOTES

**References in Text**

The Outer Continental Shelf Lands Act, referred to in subsec. (b)(1), is Act Aug. 7, 1953, c. 345, 67 Stat. 462, as amended, which is classified generally to subchapter III (§ 1331 et seq.) of chapter 29 of this title. For complete classification of this Act to the Code, see Short Title note set out under section 1331 of this title and Tables.

**Effective and Applicability Provisions**

1982 Acts

Amendment by Pub. L. 97–212 applicable with respect to claims for damages that are filed, on, or after June 30, 1982, with the Secretary of Commerce under section 1845(a) of this title, with provision for the refiling of previously filed claims under certain circumstances, see section 9 of Pub. L. 97–212, set out as a note under section 1841 of this title.

## § 1843. Duties and powers of Secretary

[OCSLAA § 403]

**(a) Prescription and amendment of regulations respecting settlement of claims; identification classification of potential hazards to commercial fishing**

In carrying out the provisions of this subchapter, the Secretary shall—

(1) prescribe, and from time to time amend, regulations for the filing, processing, and fair and expeditious settlement of claims pursuant to this subchapter, including a time limitation of not less than 90 days on the filing of such claims (except that, notwithstanding any other provision of law, final regulations implementing the 1981 amendments to this subchapter shall be published in the Federal Register within 120 days after the date of the enactment of such amendments); and

(2) identify and classify all potential hazards to commercial fishing caused by Outer Continental Shelf oil and gas exploration, development, and production activities, including all obstructions on the bottom, throughout the water column, and on the surface.

**(b) Establishment of regulations respecting color coding, stamping, or labeling of equipment, tools, etc., used on Outer Continental Shelf**

The Secretary of the Interior shall establish regulations requiring all materials, equipment, tools, containers, and all other items used on the Outer Continental Shelf to be properly color coded, stamped, or labeled, wherever practicable, with the owner's identification prior to actual use.

**(c) Disbursement of payments to compensate commercial fishermen; restrictions**

**(1)** Payments shall be disbursed by the Secretary from the Fund to compensate commercial fishermen for actual and consequential damages, including resulting economic loss, due to damages to, or loss of, fishing gear by materials, equipment, tools, containers, or other items associated with Outer Continental Shelf oil and gas exploration, development, or production activities. The compensation payable under this section for resulting economic loss shall be an amount equal to 50 per centum of such loss. For purposes of this subsection, the term "resulting economic loss" means the gross income, as estimated by the Secretary, that a commercial fisherman who is eligible for compensation under this section will lose by reason of not being able to engage in fishing, or having to reduce his fishing effort, during the period before the damaged or lost fishing gear concerned is repaired or replaced and available for use.

**(2)** Notwithstanding the provisions of paragraph (1) of this subsection, no payment may be made by the Secretary from the Fund—

**(A)** to the extent that damages were caused by the negligence or fault of the commercial fisherman making the claim;

**(B)** if the damage set forth in the claim was sustained prior to September 18, 1978;

**(C)** in the case of a claim for damage to, or loss of, fishing gear, in an amount in excess of the replacement value of the fishing gear with respect to which the claim is filed; and

**(D)** for any portion of the damages claimed with respect to which the claimant has received, or will receive, compensation from insurance.

(Pub.L. 95–372, Title IV, § 403, Sept. 18, 1978, 92 Stat. 687; Pub.L. 96–561, Title II, § 240(b)(2), Dec. 22, 1980, 94 Stat. 3301; Pub. L. 97–212, §§ 3, 7, June 30, 1982, 96 Stat. 144, 147; Pub.L. 98–498, Title IV, § 420(1), (2), Oct. 19, 1984, 98 Stat. 2309.)

### HISTORICAL AND STATUTORY NOTES

**References in Text**

The 1981 amendments to this subchapter, referred to in subsec. (a)(1), probably means the amendments made to this subchapter in 1982 by Pub.L. 97–212, which amended sections 1841 to 1845 of this title, repealed section 1847 of this title, and enacted a provision set out as a note under section 1841 of this title. Pub.L. 97–212 also enacted a provision set out as a note under section 1823 of Title 16, Conservation, and amended a provision set out as a note under section 1823 of Title 16.

The date of enactment of such amendments, referred to in subsec. (a)(1), probably means the date of enactment of Pub.L. 97–212, which was approved June 30, 1982.

**Effective and Applicability Provisions**

1978 Acts

Amendment by Pub. L. 97–212 applicable with respect to claims for damages that are filed, on, or after June 30, 1982, with the Secretary of Commerce under section 1845(a) of this title, with provision for the refiling of previously filed claims under certain circumstances, see section 9 of Pub. L. 97–212, set out as a note under section 1841 of this title.

## § 1844. Burden of proof

**[OCSLAA § 404]**

With respect to any claim for damages filed under this subchapter, there shall be a presumption that such damages were due to activities related to oil and gas exploration, development, or production if the claimant establishes that—

**(1)** the commercial fishing vessel was being used for fishing and was located in an area affected by Outer Continental Shelf activities;

**(2)** a report on the location of the material, equipment, tool, container, or other item which caused such damages and the nature of such damages was made within fifteen days after the date on which the vessel first returns to a port after discovering such damages;

**(3)** there was no record on the latest nautical charts or Notice to Mariners in effect at least 15 days prior to the date such damages were sustained that such material, equipment, tool, container, or other item existed where such damages occurred, except that in the case of damages caused by a pipeline, the presumption established by this section shall obtain whether or not there was any such record of the pipeline on the damage date; and

**(4)** there was no proper surface marker or lighted buoy which was attached or closely anchored to such material, equipment, tool, container, or other item.

(Pub.L. 95–372, Title IV, § 404, Sept. 18, 1978, 92 Stat. 688; Pub. L. 97–212, § 4, June 30, 1982, 96 Stat. 145.)

### HISTORICAL AND STATUTORY NOTES

**Effective and Applicability Provisions**

1982 Acts

Amendment by Pub. L. 97–212 applicable with respect to claims for damages that are filed, on, or after June 30, 1982, with the Secretary of Commerce under section 1845(a) of this title, with provision for the refiling of previously filed claims under certain circumstances, see section 9 of Pub. L. 97–212, set out as a note under section 1841 of this title.

## § 1845. Claims procedure

[OCSLAA § 405]

**(a) Filing requirement; time to file**

Any commercial fisherman suffering damages compensable under this subchapter may file a claim for compensation with the Secretary under subsection (d)(1) of this section.

**(b) Transmittal of copy of claim to Secretary of the Interior; reference to Secretary**

Upon receipt of any claim under this section, the Secretary shall transmit a copy of the claim to the Secretary of the Interior and shall take such further action regarding the claim that is required under subsection (d) of this section.

**(c) Notification to persons engaged in activities associated with Outer Continental Shelf energy activities; response of persons notified; submittal of evidence**

The Secretary of the Interior shall make reasonable efforts to notify all persons known to have engaged in activities associated with Outer Continental Shelf energy activity in the vicinity. Each such person shall promptly notify the Secretary and the Secretary of the Interior as to whether he admits or denies responsibility for the damages claimed. Any such person, including lessees or permittees or their contractors or subcontractors, may submit evidence at any proceeding conducted with respect to such claim.

**(d) Acceptance of claim by Secretary; time to render decision; review of initial determination**

(1) The Secretary shall, under regulations prescribed pursuant to section 1843(a) of this title, specify the time, form and manner in which claims must be filed.

(2) The Secretary may not accept any claim that does not meet the filing requirements specified under paragraph (1), and shall give a claimant whose claim is not accepted written notice of the reasons for nonacceptance. Such written notice must be given to the claimant within 30 days after the date on which the claim was filed and if the claimant does not refile an acceptable claim within 30 days after the date of such written notice, the claimant is not eligible for compensation under this subchapter for the damages concerned; except that the Secretary—

(A) shall in any case involving a good faith effort by the claimant to meet such filing requirements, or

(B) may in any case involving extenuating circumstances, accept a claim that does not meet the 30-day refiling requirement.

(3)(A) The Secretary shall make an initial determination with respect to the claim within 60 days after the day on which the claim is accepted for filing. Within 30 days after the day on which the Secretary issues an initial determination on a claim, the claimant, or any other interested person who submitted evidence relating to the initial determination, may petition the Secretary for a review of that determination.

(B) If a petition for the review of an initial determination is not filed with the Secretary within the 30-day period provided under subparagraph (A), the initial determination shall thereafter be treated as a final determination by the Secretary on the claim involved.

(C) If a petition for review of an initial determination is timely filed under subparagraph (A), the Secretary shall allow the petitioner 30 days after the day on which the petition is received to submit written or oral evidence relating to the initial determination. The Secretary shall then undertake such review and, on the basis of such review, issue a final determination no later than the 60th day after the day on which the Secretary received the petition for review of an initial determination.

**(e) Claim preparation fees; attorney's fees**

If the decision of the Secretary under subsection (d) of this section is in favor of the commercial fisherman filing the claim, the Secretary, as a part of the amount awarded, shall include reasonable claim preparation fees and reasonable attorney's fees, if any, incurred by the claimant in pursuing the claim.

**(f) Powers of Secretary**

(1) For purposes of any proceeding conducted pursuant to this section, the Secretary shall have the power to administer oaths and subpena the attendance or testimony of witnesses and the production of books, records, and other evidence relative or pertinent to the issues being presented for determination.

(2) In any proceeding conducted pursuant to this section with respect to a claim for damages resulting from activities on any area of the Outer Continental Shelf, the Secretary shall consider evidence of obstructions in such area which have been identified pursuant to the survey conducted under section 1847 of this title.

**(g) Place of proceeding**

Any proceeding conducted with respect to an initial determination on a claim under subsection (d)(3)(A) of this section shall be conducted within such United States judicial district as may be mutually agreeable to the claimant and the Secretary or, if no agreement can be reached, within the United States judicial district in which the home port of the claimant is located.

**(h) Certification and disbursement of award; subrogation of rights; payment of costs of proceedings**

(1) The amount awarded in an initial determination by the Secretary under subsection (d) of this section shall be immediately disbursed, subject to the limitations of this section, by the Secretary if the claimant—

(A) states in writing that he will not petition for review of the initial determination; and

(B) enters into an agreement with the Secretary to repay to the Secretary all or any part of the amount of the award if, after review under subsection (d)(3)(C) of this section or, if applicable, after judicial review, the amount of the award, or any part thereof, is not sustained.

(2) Upon payment of a claim by the Secretary pursuant to this subsection, the Secretary shall acquire by subrogation all rights of the claimant against any person found to be responsible for the damages with respect to which such claim was made. Any moneys recovered by the Secretary through subrogation shall be deposited into the Fund.

(3) Any person who denies responsibility for damages with respect to which a claim is made and who is subquently[1] found to be responsible for such damages, and any commercial fisherman who files a claim for damages and who is subsequently found to be responsible for such damages, shall pay the costs of the proceedings under this section with respect to such claim.

**(i) Judicial review**

Any claimant or other person who suffers a legal wrong or who is adversely affected or aggrieved by a final determination of the Secretary under subsection (d) of this section, may, no later than 30 days after such determination is made, seek judicial review of the determination in the United States district court for such United States judicial district as may be mutually agreeable to the parties concerned or, if no agreement can be reached, in the United States district court for the United States judicial district in which is located the home port of the claimant.

(Pub.L. 95–372, Title IV, § 405, Sept. 18, 1978, 92 Stat. 688; Pub.L. 97–212, § 5, June 30, 1982, 96 Stat. 145; Pub.L. 98–498, Title IV, § 420(3), (4), Oct. 19, 1984, 98 Stat. 2309, 2310.)

[1] So in original. Probably should be "subsequently".

### HISTORICAL AND STATUTORY NOTES

**References in Text**

Section 1847 of this title, referred to in subsec. (f)(2), was repealed by Pub. L. 97–212, § 6(a), June 30, 1982, 96 Stat. 147.

**Effective and Applicability Provisions**

1982 Acts

Amendment by Pub. L. 97–212 applicable with respect to claims for damages that are filed, on, or after June 30, 1982, with the Secretary of Commerce under section 1845(a) of this title, with provision for the refiling of previously filed claims under certain circumstances, see section 9 of Pub. L. 97–212, set out as a note under section 1841 of this title.

**Compensation for Certain Fishing Vessel and Gear Damage; Application**

Authority to owners or operators of fishing vessels and commercial fishermen failing to make application for compensation within the time limitations of this section or section 1980 of Title 22 to make application for compensation within the 60-day period beginning on Dec. 22, 1980, see section 240(a), (b)(1) of Pub.L. 96–561, Title II, Dec. 22, 1980, 94 Stat. 3300, set out as a note under section 1980 of Title 22, Foreign Relations and Intercourse.

## § 1846. Repealed. Pub.L. 104–66, Title I, § 1021(f), Dec. 21, 1995, 109 Stat. 713

### HISTORICAL AND STATUTORY NOTES

Section, Pub.L. 95–372, Title IV, § 406, Sept. 18, 1978, 92 Stat. 689, required Secretary to submit annual reports to Congress setting forth Fishermen's Contingency Fund damage descriptions and compensation amounts and, in the first annual report, evaluate the feasibility of fine or penalty impositions.

## § 1847. Repealed. Pub. L. 97–212, § 6(a), June 30, 1982, 96 Stat. 147

### HISTORICAL AND STATUTORY NOTES

Section, Pub.L. 95–372, Title IV, § 407, Sept. 18, 1978, 92 Stat. 690, related to survey of obstructions on Outer Continental Shelf and the development of charts for commercial fishermen.

**Effective Date of Repeal**

Repeal effective June 30, 1982 and applicable with respect to claims for damages that are filed, on, or after such date, with the Secretary of Commerce under section 1845(a) of this title, see section 9(a) of Pub. L. 97–212, set out as a note under section 1841.

# SUBCHAPTER III—MISCELLANEOUS PROVISIONS

## § 1861. Repealed. Pub.L. 99–367, § 2(b), July 31, 1986, 100 Stat. 774

### HISTORICAL AND STATUTORY NOTES

Section, Pub.L. 95–372, Title VI, § 601, Sept. 18, 1978, 92 Stat. 693, which required the Secretary of the Interior, within six months of Sept. 18, 1978, and in his annual report thereafter, to report to the Comptroller General on shut-in and flaring oil and gas wells and required the Comptroller General, within six months after receipt of the report, to review and evaluate the methodology used by the Secretary in allowing wells to be shut-in or flare natural gas and submit his findings and recommendations to Congress, was repealed by Pub.L. 99–367, § 2(b), July 31, 1986, 100 Stat. 774.

## § 1862. Natural gas distribution

**[OCSLAA § 603]**

### (a) Expanded participation by local distribution companies in acquisition of leases and development of natural gas resources

The purpose of this section is to encourage expanded participation by local distribution companies in acquisition of leases and development of natural gas resources on the Outer Continental Shelf by facilitating the transportation in interstate commerce of natural gas, which is produced from a lease located on the Outer Continental Shelf and owned, in whole or in part, by a local distribution company, from such lease to the service area of such local distribution company.

### (b) Application and issuance of certificates of public convenience and necessity for transportation of natural gas

The Federal Energy Regulatory Commission shall, after opportunity for presentation of written and oral views, promulgate and publish in the Federal Register a statement of Commission policy which carries out the purpose of this section and sets forth the standards under which the Commission will consider applications for, and, as appropriate, issue certificates of public convenience and necessity, pursuant to section 717f of Title 15, for the transportation in interstate commerce of natural gas, which is produced from a lease located on the Outer Continental Shelf and owned, in whole or in part, by a local distribution company, from such lease to the service area of such local distribution company. Such statement of policy shall specify the criteria, limitations, or requirements the Commission will apply in determing—[1]

(1) whether the application of any local distribution company qualifies for consideration under the statement of policy; and

(2) whether the public convenience and necessity will be served by the issuance of the requested certificate of transportation.

Such statement of policy shall also set forth the terms or limitations on which the Commission may condition, pursuant to section 717f of Title 15, the issuance of a certificate of transportation under such statement of policy. To the maximum extent practicable, such statement shall be promulgated and published within one year after September 18, 1978.

### (c) Definitions

For purposes of this section, the term—

(1) "local distribution company" means any person—

(A) engaged in the distribution of natural gas at retail, including any subsidiary or affiliate thereof engaged in the exploration and production of natural gas; and

(B) regulated, or operated as a public utility, by a State or local government or agency thereof;

(2) "interstate commerce" shall have the same meaning as such term has under section 717a(7) of Title 15; and

(3) "Commission" means the Federal Energy Regulatory Commission.

(Pub.L. 95–372, Title VI, § 603, Sept. 18, 1978, 92 Stat. 694.)

[1] So in original. Probably should be "determining—".

## § 1863. Unlawful employment practices; regulations

**[OCSLAA § 604]**

Each agency or department given responsibility for the promulgation or enforcement of regulations under this chapter or the Outer Continental Shelf Lands Act [43 U.S.C.A. § 1331 et seq.] shall take such affirmative action as deemed necessary to prohibit all unlawful employment practices and to assure that no person shall, on the grounds of race, creed, color, national origin, or sex, be excluded from receiving or participating in any activity, sale, or employment, conducted pursuant to the provisions of this chapter or the Outer Continental Shelf Lands Act. The agency or department shall promulgate such rules as it deems necessary to carry out the purposes of this section, and any rules promulgated under this section, whether through agency and department provisions or rules, shall be similar to those established and in effect under Title VI and Title VII of the Civil Rights Act of 1964 [42 U.S.C.A. §§ 2000d et seq., 2000e et seq.].

(Pub.L. 95–372, Title VI, § 604, Sept. 18, 1978, 92 Stat. 695.)

### HISTORICAL AND STATUTORY NOTES

**References in Text**

This chapter, referred to in text, in the original read "this Act", meaning Pub. L. 95–372, Sept. 18, 1978, 92 Stat. 629, known as the Outer Continental Shelf Lands Act Amendments of 1978, which enacted this chapter, sections 1344 to 1356 of this title, and section 237 of Title 30, Mineral Lands and Mining, amended sections 1331 to 1334, 1337, 1340, and 1343 of this title, sections 1456, 1456a, and 1464 of Title 16, Conservation, and section 6213 of Title 42, The Public Health and Welfare, and enacted provisions set out as notes under sections 1348 and 1811 of this title. For complete classification of this Act to the Code, see Short Title note set out under section 1801 of this title and Tables.

The Outer Continental Shelf Lands Act, referred to in text, is Act Aug. 7, 1953, c. 345, 67 Stat. 462, as amended, which is classified generally to subchapter III (section 1331 et seq.) of chapter 29 of this title. For complete classification of this Act to the Code, see Short Title note set out under section 1331 of this title and Tables volume.

The Civil Rights Act of 1964, referred to in text, is Pub.L. 88–352, July 2, 1964, 78 Stat. 252, as amended. Title VI and VII of the Civil Rights Act of 1964 are classified generally to subchapters V (section 2000d et seq.) and VI (section 2000e et seq.) of chapter 21 of Title 42, The Public Health and Welfare. For complete classification of this Act to the Code, see Short Title note set out under section 2000a of Title 42 and Tables volume.

## § 1864. Disclosure of financial interests by officers and employees of Department of the Interior

[OCSLAA § 605]

### (a) Annual written statement

Each officer or employee of the Department of the Interior who—

(1) performs any function or duty under this chapter or the Outer Continental Shelf Lands Act [43 U.S.C.A. § 1331 et seq.], as amended by this Act; and

(2) has any known financial interest in any person who (A) applies for or receives any permit or lease under, or (B) is otherwise subject to the provisions of this chapter or the Outer Continental Shelf Lands Act [43 U.S.C.A. § 1331 et seq.],

shall, beginning on February 1, 1979, annually file with the Secretary of the Interior a written statement concerning all such interests held by such officer or employee during the preceeding[1] calendar year. Such statement shall be available to the public.

### (b) "Known financial interest" defined; enforcement; report to Congress

The Secretary of the Interior shall—

(1) within ninety days after September 18, 1978—

(A) define the term "known financial interest" for purposes of subsection (a) of this section; and

(B) establish the methods by which the requirement to file written statements specified in subsection (a) of this section will be monitored and enforced, including appropriate provisions for the filing by such officers and employees of such statements and the review by the Secretary of such statements; and

(2) report to the Congress on June 1 of each calendar year with respect to such disclosures and the actions taken in regard thereto during the preceding calendar year.

### (c) Officers and employees in nonregulatory or nonpolicymaking positions

In the rules prescribed in subsection (b) of this section, the Secretary may identify specific positions within the Department of the Interior which are of a nonregulatory or nonpolicymaking nature and provide that officers or employees occupying such positions shall be exempt from the requirements of this section.

### (d) Penalties

Any officer or employee who is subject to, and knowingly violates, this section shall be fined not more than $2,500 or imprisoned not more than one year, or both.

(Pub.L. 95–372, Title VI, § 605, Sept. 18, 1978, 92 Stat. 695.)

[1] So in original. Probably should be "preceding".

### HISTORICAL AND STATUTORY NOTES

**References in Text**

This chapter, referred to in subsec. (a)(1) and (2), in the original read "this Act", meaning Pub. L. 95–372, Sept. 18, 1978, 92 Stat. 629, known as the Outer Continental Shelf Lands Act Amendments of 1978, which enacted this chapter, sections 1344 to 1356 of this title, and section 237 of Title 30, Mineral Lands and Mining, amended sections 1331 to 1334, 1337, 1340, and 1343 of this title, sections 1456, 1456a, and 1464 of Title 16, Conservation, and section 6213 of Title 42, The Public Health and Welfare, and enacted provisions set out as notes under sections 1348 and 1811 of this title. For complete classification of this Act to the Code, see Short Title note set out under section 1801 of this title and Tables.

This Act, referred to in subsec. (a)(1), is Pub. L. 95–372, Sept. 18, 1978, 92 Stat. 629. See note above.

The Outer Continental Shelf Lands Act, referred to in subsec. (a)(1) and (2), is Act Aug. 7, 1953, c. 345, 67 Stat. 462, as amended, which is classified generally to subchapter III (section 1331 et seq.) of chapter 29 of this title. For complete classification of this Act to the Code, see Short Title note set out under section 1331 of this title and Tables volume.

## § 1865. Investigation of reserves of oil and gas in Outer Continental Shelf

[OCSLAA § 606]

The Secretary of the Interior shall conduct a continuing investigation to determine an estimate of the total discovered crude oil and natural gas reserves by fields (including proved and indicated reserves) and undiscovered crude oil and natural gas resources (including hypothetical and speculative resources) of the Outer Continental Shelf.

The Secretary of the Interior shall provide a biennial report to Congress on June 30 of every odd numbered year on the results of such investigation.

(Pub.L. 95–372, Title VI, § 606, as added Pub.L. 99–367, § 2(c), July 31, 1986, 100 Stat. 774.)

HISTORICAL AND STATUTORY NOTES

**Prior Provisions**

A prior section 1865, Pub.L. 95–372, Title VI, § 606, Sept. 18, 1978, 92 Stat. 696, which required the Secretary of the Interior to conduct a continuing investigation of reserves of oil and gas in the Outer Continental Shelf, specified items to be included in the investigation, provided for initial and subsequent reports to Congress, and required consultation with the Federal Trade Commission and information be made available to the Federal Trade Commission, was repealed by Pub.L. 99–367, § 2(c), July 31, 1986, 100 Stat. 774.

## § 1866. Relationship to existing law

[OCSLAA § 608]

**(a)** Except as otherwise expressly provided in this chapter, nothing in this chapter shall be construed to amend, modify, or repeal any provision of the Coastal Zone Management Act of 1972 [16 U.S.C.A. § 1451 et seq.], the National Environmental Policy Act of 1969 [42 U.S.C.A. § 4321 et seq.], the Mining and Mineral Policy Act of 1970 [30 U.S.C.A. § 21a], or any other Act.

**(b)** Nothing in this chapter or any amendment made by this Act to the Outer Continental Shelf Lands Act (43 U.S.C. 1331 et seq.) or any other Act shall be construed to affect or modify the provisions of the Department of Energy Organization Act (42 U.S.C. 7101 et seq.) which provide for the transferring and vesting of functions to and in the Secretary of Energy or any component of the Department of Energy.

(Pub.L. 95–372, Title VI, § 608, Sept. 18, 1978, 92 Stat. 698.)

HISTORICAL AND STATUTORY NOTES

**References in Text**

This chapter, referred to in text, in the original read "this Act", meaning Pub. L. 95–372, Sept. 18, 1978, 92 Stat. 629, known as the Outer Continental Shelf Lands Act Amendments of 1978, which enacted this chapter, sections 1344 to 1356 of this title, and section 237 of Title 30, Mineral Lands and Mining, amended sections 1331 to 1334, 1337, 1340, and 1343 of this title, sections 1456, 1456a, and 1464 of Title 16, Conservation, and section 6213 of Title 42, The Public Health and Welfare, and enacted provisions set out as notes under sections 1348 and 1811 of this title. For complete classification of this Act to the Code, see Short Title note set out under section 1801 of this title and Tables.

The Coastal Zone Management Act of 1972, referred to in subsec. (a), is Title III of Pub. L. 89–454 as added by Pub. L. 92–583, Oct. 27, 1972, 86 Stat. 1280, which is classified generally to chapter 33 (section 1451 et seq.) of Title 16, Conservation. For complete classification of this Act to the Code, see Short Title note set out under section 1451 of Title 16 and Tables volume.

The National Environmental Policy Act of 1969, referred to in subsec. (a), is Pub. L. 91–190, Jan. 1, 1970, 83 Stat. 852, as amended, which is classified generally to chapter 55 (section 4321 et seq.) of Title 42, The Public Health and Welfare. For complete classification of this Act to the Code, see Short Title note set out under 4321 of Title 42 and Tables volume.

The Mining and Mineral Policy Act of 1970, referred to in subsec. (a), is Pub. L. 91–631, Dec. 31, 1970, 84 Stat. 1876, which is classified to section 21a of Title 30, Mineral Lands and Mining.

This Act, referred to in subsec. (b), is Pub. L. 95–372, Sept. 18, 1978, 92 Stat. 629. See note above.

The Outer Continental Shelf Lands Act, referred to in subsec. (b), is Act Aug. 7, 1953, c. 345, 67 Stat. 462, as amended, which is classified generally to subchapter III (section 1331 et seq.) of chapter 29 of this title. For complete classification of this Act to the Code, see Short Title note set out under section 1331 of this title and Tables volume.

The Department of Energy Organization Act, referred to in subsec. (b), is Pub. L. 95–91, Aug. 4, 1977, 91 Stat. 565, which is classified principally to chapter 84 (section 7101 et seq.) of Title 42, The Public Health and Welfare. For complete classification of this Act to the Code, see Short Title note set out under section 7101 of Title 42 and Tables volume.

*

# TITLE 46
# SHIPPING

## CARRIAGE OF LIQUID BULK DANGEROUS CARGOES

## OIL POLLUTION ACT OF 1990 [OPA § 4115(a)]

**(46 U.S.C.A. § 3703a)**

## CHAPTER 37—CARRIAGE OF LIQUID BULK DANGEROUS CARGOES



### § 3703a. Tank vessel construction standards [OPA § 4115(a)]

(a) Except as otherwise provided in this section, a vessel to which this chapter applies shall be equipped with a double hull—

(1) if it is constructed or adapted to carry, or carries, oil in bulk as cargo or cargo residue; and

(2) when operating on the waters subject to the jurisdiction of the United States, including the Exclusive Economic Zone.

(b) This section does not apply to—

(1) a vessel used only to respond to a discharge of oil or a hazardous substance;

(2) a vessel of less than 5,000 gross tons as measured under section 14502 of this title, or an alternate tonnage measured under section 14302 of this title as prescribed by the Secretary under section 14104 of this title equipped with a double containment system determined by the Secretary to be as effective as a double hull for the prevention of a discharge of oil;

(3) before January 1, 2015—

(A) a vessel unloading oil in bulk at a deepwater port licensed under the Deepwater Port Act of 1974 (33 U.S.C. 1501 et seq.); or

(B) a delivering vessel that is offloading in lightering activities—

(i) within a lightering zone established under section 3715(b)(5) of this title; and

(ii) more than 60 miles from the baseline from which the territorial sea of the United States is measured;

(4) a vessel documented under chapter 121 of this title that was equipped with a double hull before August 12, 1992;

(5) a barge of less than 1,500 gross tons (as measured under chapter 145 of this title) carrying refined petroleum product in bulk as cargo in or adjacent to waters of the Bering Sea, Chukchi Sea, and Arctic Ocean and waters tributary thereto and in the waters of the Aleutian Islands and the Alaskan Peninsula west of 155 degrees west longitude; or

(6) a vessel in the National Defense Reserve Fleet pursuant to section 11 of the Merchant Ship Sales Act of 1946 (50 App. U.S.C. 1744).

(c)(1) In this subsection, the age of a vessel is determined from the later of the date on which the vessel—

(A) is delivered after original construction;

(B) is delivered after completion of a major conversion; or

(C) had its appraised salvage value determined by the Coast Guard and is qualified for documentation under section 4136 of the Revised Statutes of the United States (46 App. U.S.C. 14).

(2) A vessel of less than 5,000 gross tons as measured under section 14502 of this title, or an alternate tonnage measured under section 14302 of this title as prescribed by the Secretary under section 14104 of this title for which a building contract or contract for major conversion was placed before June 30, 1990, and that is delivered under that contract before January 1, 1994, and a vessel of less than 5,000 gross tons as measured under section 14502 of this title, or an alternate tonnage measured under section 14302 of this title as prescribed by the Secretary under section 14104 of this title that had its appraised salvage value determined by the Coast Guard before June 30, 1990, and that qualifies for documentation under section 4136 of the Revised Statutes of the United States (46 App. U.S.C. 14) before January 1, 1994, may not operate in the navigable waters or the Exclusive Economic Zone of the United States after January 1,

2015, unless the vessel is equipped with a double hull or with a double containment system determined by the Secretary to be as effective as a double hull for the prevention of a discharge of oil.

(3) A vessel for which a building contract or contract for major conversion was placed before June 30, 1990, and that is delivered under that contract before January 1, 1994, and a vessel that had its appraised salvage value determined by the Coast Guard before June 30, 1990, and that qualifies for documentation under section 4136 of the Revised Statutes of the United States (46 App. U.S.C. 14) before January 1, 1994, may not operate in the navigable waters or Exclusive Economic Zone of the United States unless equipped with a double hull—

**(A)** in the case of a vessel of at least 5,000 gross tons but less than 15,000 gross tons as measured under section 14502 of this title, or an alternate tonnage measured under section 14302 of this title as prescribed by the Secretary under section 14104 of this title—

**(i)** after January 1, 1995, if the vessel is 40 years old or older and has a single hull, or is 45 years old or older and has a double bottom or double sides;

**(ii)** after January 1, 1996, if the vessel is 39 years old or older and has a single hull, or is 44 years old or older and has a double bottom or double sides;

**(iii)** after January 1, 1997, if the vessel is 38 years old or older and has a single hull, or is 43 years old or older and has a double bottom or double sides;

**(iv)** after January 1, 1998, if the vessel is 37 years old or older and has a single hull, or is 42 years old or older and has a double bottom or double sides;

**(v)** after January 1, 1999, if the vessel is 36 years old or older and has a single hull, or is 41 years old or older and has a double bottom or double sides;

**(vi)** after January 1, 2000, if the vessel is 35 years old or older and has a single hull, or is 40 years old or older and has a double bottom or double sides; and

**(vii)** after January 1, 2005, if the vessel is 25 years old or older and has a single hull, or is 30 years old or older and has a double bottom or double sides;

**(B)** in the case of a vessel of at least 15,000 gross tons but less than 30,000 gross tons as measured under section 14502 of this title, or an alternate tonnage measured under section 14302 of this title as prescribed by the Secretary under section 14104 of this title—

**(i)** after January 1, 1995, if the vessel is 40 years old or older and has a single hull, or is 45 years old or older and has a double bottom or double sides;

**(ii)** after January 1, 1996, if the vessel is 38 years old or older and has a single hull, or is 43 years old or older and has a double bottom or double sides;

**(iii)** after January 1, 1997, if the vessel is 36 years old or older and has a single hull, or is 41 years old or older and has a double bottom or double sides;

**(iv)** after January 1, 1998, if the vessel is 34 years old or older and has a single hull, or is 39 years old or older and has a double bottom or double sides;

**(v)** after January 1, 1999, if the vessel is 32 years old or older and has a single hull, or 37 years old or older and has a double bottom or double sides;

**(vi)** after January 1, 2000, if the vessel is 30 years old or older and has a single hull, or is 35 years old or older and has a double bottom or double sides;

**(vii)** after January 1, 2001, if the vessel is 29 years old or older and has a single hull, or is 34 years old or older and has a double bottom or double sides;

**(viii)** after January 1, 2002, if the vessel is 28 years old or older and has a single hull, or is 33 years old or older and has a double bottom or double sides;

**(ix)** after January 1, 2003, if the vessel is 27 years old or older and has a single hull, or is 32 years old or older and has a double bottom or double sides;

**(x)** after January 1, 2004, if the vessel is 26 years old or older and has a single hull, or is 31 years old or older and has a double bottom or double sides; and

**(xi)** after January 1, 2005, if the vessel is 25 years old or older and has a single hull, or is 30 years old or older and has a double bottom or double sides; and

**(C)** in the case of a vessel of at least 30,000 gross tons as measured under section 14502 of this title, or an alternate tonnage measured under section 14302 of this title as prescribed by the Secretary under section 14104 of this title—

**(i)** after January 1, 1995, if the vessel is 28 years old or older and has a single hull, or 33 years old or older and has a double bottom or double sides;

**(ii)** after January 1, 1996, if the vessel is 27 years old or older and has a single hull, or is 32 years old or older and has a double bottom or double sides;

**(iii)** after January 1, 1997, if the vessel is 26 years old or older and has a single hull, or is 31 years old or older and has a double bottom or double sides;

**(iv)** after January 1, 1998, if the vessel is 25 years old or older and has a single hull, or is 30 years old or older and has a double bottom or double sides;

**(v)** after January 1, 1999, if the vessel is 24 years old or older and has a single hull, or 29 years old or older and has a double bottom or double sides; and

**(vi)** after January 1, 2000, if the vessel is 23 years old or older and has a single hull, or is 28 years old or older and has a double bottom or double sides.

(4) Except as provided in subsection (b) of this section—

**(A)** a vessel that has a single hull may not operate after January 1, 2010; and

**(B)** a vessel that has a double bottom or double sides may not operate after January 1, 2015.

**(d)** The operation of barges described in subsection (b)(5) outside waters described in that subsection shall be on any conditions as the Secretary may require.

**(e)(1)** For the purposes of this section and except as otherwise provided in paragraphs (2) and (3) of this subsection, the gross tonnage of a vessel shall be the gross tonnage that would have been recognized by the Secretary on July 1, 1997, as the tonnage measured under section 14502 of this title, or as an alternate tonnage measured under section 14302 of this title as prescribed by the Secretary under section 14104 of this title.

**(2)(A)** The Secretary may waive the application of paragraph (1) to a tank vessel if—

**(i)** the owner of the tank vessel applies to the Secretary for the waiver before January 1, 1998;

**(ii)** the Secretary determines that—

**(I)** the owner of the tank vessel has entered into a binding agreement to alter the tank vessel in a shipyard in the United States to reduce the gross tonnage of the tank vessel by converting a portion of the cargo tanks of the tank vessel into protectively located segregated ballast tanks; and

**(II)** that conversion will result in a significant reduction in the risk of a discharge of oil;

**(iii)** at least 60 days before the date of the issuance of the waiver, the Secretary—

**(I)** publishes notice that the Secretary has received the application and made the determinations required by clause (ii), including a description of the agreement entered into pursuant to clause (ii)(I); and

**(II)** provides an opportunity for submission of comments regarding the application; and

**(iv)** the alterations referred to in clause (ii)(I) are completed before the later of—

**(I)** the date by which the first special survey of the tank vessel is required to be completed after the date of the enactment of the National Defense Authorization Act for Fiscal Year 1998; or

**(II)** July 1, 1999.

**(B)** A waiver under subparagraph (A) shall not be effective after the expiration of the 3-year period beginning on the first date on which the tank vessel would have been prohibited by subsection (c) from operating if the alterations referred to in subparagraph (A)(ii)(I) were not made.

(3) This subsection does not apply to a tank vessel that, before July 1, 1997, had undergone, or was the subject of a contract for, alterations that reduce the gross tonnage of the tank vessel, as shown by reliable evidence acceptable to the Secretary.

(Added Pub.L. 101–380, Title IV, § 4115(a), Aug. 18, 1990, 104 Stat. 517, and amended Pub.L. 104–324, Title VII, § 715, Title XI, § 1103, Oct. 19, 1996, 110 Stat. 3937, 3966; Pub.L. 105–85, Div. C, Title XXXVI, § 3606, Nov. 18, 1997, 111 Stat. 2077.)

## HISTORICAL AND STATUTORY NOTES

### References in Text

The Deepwater Port Act of 1974, referred to in subsec. (b)(3)(A), is Pub.L. 93–627, Jan. 3, 1975, 88 Stat. 2126, as amended, which is classified generally to chapter 29 (section 1501 et seq.) of Title 33, Navigation and Navigable Waters. For complete classification of this Act to the Code, see Short Title note set out under § 1501 of Title 33 and Tables.

Section 11 of the Merchant Ship Sales Act of 1946, referred to in subsec. (b)(6), is section 11 of Act Mar. 8, 1946, c. 82, 60 Stat. 49, which is classified to section 1744 of the Appendix to Title 50, War and National Defense.

Section 4136 of the Revised Statutes of the United States (46 U.S.C. 14), referred to in subsec. (c)(1)(C), is classified to section 14 of the Appendix to this title.

The date of the enactment of the National Defense Authorization Act for Fiscal Year 1998, referred to in subsec. (e)(2)(A)(iv)(I), is Nov. 18, 1997, the date of enactment of Pub.L. 105–85.

### Tank Vessels Over 5,000 Gross Tons to Comply Until Jan. 1, 2015 with Environmentally Protective Structural and Operational Requirements

Section 4115(b) of Pub.L. 101–380 provided that: "The Secretary shall, within 12 months after the date of the enactment of this Act [Aug. 18, 1990], complete a rulemaking proceeding and issue a final rule to require that tank vessels over 5,000 gross tons affected by section 3703a of title 46, United States Code [this section], as added by this section, comply until January 1, 2015, with structural and operational requirements that the Secretary determines will provide as substantial protection to the environment as is economically and technologically feasible:[.]"

**Study on Other Structural and Operational Tank Vessel Requirements; Impact on Marine Environment; Assessment and Review; Reports to Congress**

Section 4115(e) of Pub.L. 101–380, as amended Pub.L. 105–383, Title IV, § 423, Nov. 13, 1998, 112 Stat. 3440, provided that:

"(1) **Other requirements.**—Not later than 6 months after the date of enactment of this Act [Aug. 18, 1990], the Secretary shall determine, based on recommendations from the National Academy of Sciences or other qualified organizations, whether other structural and operational tank vessel requirements will provide protection to the marine environment equal to or greater than that provided by double hulls, and shall report to the Congress that determination and recommendations for legislative action.

"(2) **Review and assessment.**—The Secretary shall—

"(A) periodically review recommendations from the National Academy of Sciences and other qualified organizations on methods for further increasing the environmental and operational safety of tank vessels;

"(B) not later than 5 years after the date of enactment of this Act [Aug. 18, 1990], assess the impact of this section on the safety of the marine environment and the economic viability and operational makeup of the maritime oil transportation industry; and

"(C) report the results of the review and assessment to the Congress with recommendations for legislative or other action.

"(3)(A) The Secretary of Transportation shall coordinate with the Marine Board of the National Research Council to conduct the necessary research and development of a rationally based equivalency assessment approach, which accounts for the overall environmental performance of alternative tank vessel designs. Notwithstanding the Coast Guard opinion of the application of sections 101 and 311 of the Clean Water Act (33 U.S.C. 1251 and 1321), the intent of this study is to establish an equivalency evaluation procedure that maintains a high standard of environmental protection, while encouraging innovative ship design. The study shall include:

"(i) development of a generalized cost spill data base, which includes all relevant costs such as clean-up costs and environmental impact costs as a function of spill size;

"(ii) refinement of the probability density functions used to establish the extent of vessel damage, based on the latest available historical damage statistics, and current research on the crash worthiness of tank vessel structures;

"(iii) development of a rationally based approach for calculating an environmental index, to assess overall outflow performance due to collisions and groundings; and

"(iv) application of the proposed index to double hull tank vessels and alternative designs currently under consideration.

"(B) A Marine Board committee shall be established not later that 2 months after the date of the enactment of the Coast Guard Authorization Act of 1998 [Nov. 13, 1998]. The Secretary of Transportation shall submit to the Committee on Commerce, Science, and Transportation of the Senate and the Committee on Transportation and Infrastructure in the House of Representatives a report on the results of the study not later than 12 months after the date of the enactment of the Coast Guard Authorization Act of 1998 [Nov. 13, 1998].

"(C) Of the amounts authorized by section 1012(a)(5)(A) of this Act [33 U.S.C.A. § 2712], $500,000 is authorized to carry out the activities under subparagraphs (A) and (B) of this paragraph."

# DOCUMENTATION OF VESSELS

## CHAPTER 121—DOCUMENTATION OF VESSELS



[1] So in original. Two sections 12123 were enacted.

### § 12106. Coastwise endorsements

(a) A certificate of documentation may be endorsed with a coastwise endorsement for a vessel that—

(1) is eligible for documentation;

(2)(A) was built in the United States; or

(B) if not built in the United States, was captured in war by citizens of the United States and lawfully condemned as prize, was adjudged to be forfeited for a breach of the laws of the United States, or qualified for documentation under section 4136 of the Revised Statutes (46 App. U.S.C. 14); and

(3) otherwise qualifies under laws of the United States to be employed in the coastwise trade.

(b) Subject to the laws of the United States regulating the coastwise trade, only a vessel for which a certificate of documentation with a coastwise endorsement is issued may be employed in the coastwise trade.

(c) A coastwise endorsement to engage in the coastwise trade of fisheries products between places in Guam, American Samoa, and the Northern Mariana Islands may be issued for a vessel that—

(1) is less than 200 gross tons as measured under section 14502 of this title, or an alternate tonnage measured under section 14302 of this title as prescribed by the Secretary under section 14104 of this title;

(2) was not built in the United States;

(3) is eligible for documentation; and

(4) otherwise qualifies under the laws of the United States to be employed in the coastwide[1] trade.

(d)(1) A vessel may be issued a certificate of documentation with a coastwise endorsement if—

(A) the vessel is owned by a not-for-profit oil spill response cooperative or by members of such a cooperative who dedicate the vessel to use by the cooperative;

(B) the vessel is at least 50 percent owned by persons or entities described in section 12102(a) of this title;

(C) the vessel otherwise qualifies under section 12106 to be employed in the coastwise trade; and

(D) use of the vessel is restricted to—

(i) the deployment of equipment, supplies, and personnel to recover, contain, or transport oil discharged into the navigable waters of the United States, or within the Exclusive Economic Zone, or

(ii) for training exercises to prepare to respond to such a discharge.

(2) For purposes of the first proviso of section 27 of the Merchant Marine Act, 1920, section 2 of the Shipping Act of 1916, and section 12102(a) of this title, a vessel meeting the criteria of this subsection shall be considered to be owned exclusively by citizens of the United States.

(e)(1) A certificate of documentation for a vessel may be endorsed with a coastwise endorsement if—

(A) the vessel is eligible for documentation;

(B) the person that owns the vessel, a parent entity of that person, or a subsidiary of a parent entity of that person, is primarily engaged in leasing or other financing transactions;

(C) the vessel is under a demise charter to a person that certifies to the Secretary that the person is a citizen of the United States for engaging in the coastwise trade under section 2 of the Shipping Act, 1916;

(D) the demise charter is for a period of at least 3 years or a shorter period as may be prescribed by the Secretary; and

(E) the vessel is otherwise eligible for documentation under this section.

(2) The demise charter and any amendments to that charter shall be filed with the certificate required by this subsection, or within 10 days following the filing of an amendment to the charter, and such charter and amendments shall be made available to the public.

(3) Upon termination by a demise charterer required under paragraph (1)(C), the coastwise endorsement of the vessel may, in the sole discretion of the Secretary, be continued after the termination for default of the demise charter for a period not to exceed 6 months on such terms and conditions as the Secretary may prescribe.

(4) For purposes of section 2 of the Shipping Act, 1916, and section 12102(a) of this title, a vessel meet-

ing the criteria of this subsection is deemed to be owned exclusively by citizens of the United States.
(Pub.L. 98–89, Aug. 26, 1983, 97 Stat. 586; Pub.L. 98–454, Title III, § 301(b), Oct. 5, 1984, 98 Stat. 1734; Pub.L. 100–239, § 6(a)(2), (3), Jan. 11, 1988, 101 Stat. 1781; Pub.L. 101–225, Title III, § 301(a)(6), Dec. 12, 1989, 103 Stat. 1921; Pub.L. 101–380, Title IV, § 4205, Aug. 18, 1990, 104 Stat. 533; Pub.L. 104–324, Title VII, § 743, Title XI, § 1113(d), Oct. 19, 1996, 110 Stat. 3942, 3971.)

[1] So in original. Probably should be "coastwise".

### HISTORICAL AND STATUTORY NOTES

**References in Text**

Section 27 of the Merchant Marine Act, 1920, referred to in subsec. (d)(2), is classified to section 883 of the Appendix to this title.

Section 2 of the Shipping Act of 1916, referred to in subsecs. (d)(2) and (e)(1)(C), (4), is classified to sections 802 and 803, respectively, of the Appendix to this title.

**Effective and Applicability Provisions**

1989 Acts

Amendment by Pub.L. 101–225 effective Dec. 12, 1989, see section 309 of Pub.L. 101–225, set out as a note under section 12101 of this title.

**Repeal of Sunset**

Pub.L. 107–295, Title II, § 207(c)(1), Nov. 25, 2002, 116 Stat. 2097, provided that: "Section 505 of the Coast Guard Authorization Act of 1998 (46 U.S.C. 12106 note) [formerly set out in a note under this section] is repealed. The repeal of section 505 shall have no effect on the validity of any certificate or endorsement issued under section 502 of that Act [set out in a note under this section]."

**Administrative Process for Jones Act Waivers**

Pub.L. 105–383, Title V, §§ 501 to 505, Nov. 13, 1998, 112 Stat. 3445, as amended Pub.L. 107–295, Title II, § 207(c), Nov. 25, 2002, 116 Stat. 2097, provided that:

**"Sec. 501. Findings.**

"The Congress finds that—

"(1) current coastwise trade laws provide no administrative authority to waive the United-States-built requirement of those laws for the limited carriage of passengers for hire on vessels built or rebuilt outside the United States;

"(2) requests for such waivers require the enactment of legislation by the Congress;

"(3) each Congress routinely approves numerous such requests for waiver and rarely rejects any such request; and

"(4) the review and approval of such waiver requests is a ministerial function which properly should be executed by an administrative agency with appropriate expertise.

**"Sec. 502. Administrative Waiver of Coastwise Trade Laws.**

"Notwithstanding sections 12106 and 12108 of title 46, United States Code, section 8 of the Act of June 19, 1886 (46 U.S.C. App. 289), and section 27 of the Merchant Marine Act, 1920 (46 U.S.C. App. 883), the Secretary of Transportation may issue a certificate of documentation with appropriate endorsement for employment in the coastwise trade as a small passenger vessel or an uninspected passenger vessel for an eligible vessel authorized to carry no more than 12 passengers for hire if the Secretary, after notice and an opportunity for public comment, determines that the employment of the vessel in the coastwise trade will not adversely affect—

"(1) United States vessel builders; or

"(2) the coastwise trade business of any person who employs vessels built in the United States in that business.

**Sec. 503. Revocation.**

"(a) **Revocation for fraud.**—The Secretary shall revoke a certificate or an endorsement issued under section 502 [of this note], after notice and an opportunity for a hearing, if the Secretary determines that the certificate or endorsement was obtained by fraud.

"(b) **Application with criminal penalties.**—Nothing in this section affects—

"(1) the criminal prohibition on fraud and false statements provided by section 1001 of title 18, United States Code; or

"(2) any other authority of the Secretary to revoke a certificate or endorsement issued under section 502 of this Act [this note].

**"Sec. 504. Definitions.**

"In this title [this note]:

"(1) **Secretary.**—The term 'Secretary' means the Secretary of Transportation.

"(2) **Eligible vessel.**—The term 'eligible vessel' means a vessel that—

"(A) was not built in the United States and is at least 3 years of age; or

"(B) if rebuilt, was rebuilt outside the United States at least 3 years before the certification requested under section 502 [of this note], if granted, would take effect.

"(3) **Small passenger vessel; uninspected passenger vessel; passenger for hire.**—The terms 'small passenger vessel', 'uninspected passenger vessel', and 'passenger for hire' have the meaning given such terms by section 2101 of title 46, United States Code.

**"Sec. 505. [Repealed. Pub.L. 107–295, Title II, § 207(c)(1), Nov. 25, 2002, 116 Stat. 2097.]"**

**Study and Report on Financing Methods**

Section 1113(f) of Pub.L. 104–324 provided that:

"(1) **Study.**—The Secretary of Transportation shall conduct a study of the methods for leasing, demise chartering, and financing of vessels operating in the coastal trades of other countries and whether the laws of other countries provide reciprocity for United States banks, leasing companies, or other financial institutions with respect to the rights granted under the amendment made by subsection (d) [enacting subsec. (e) of this section]. The study shall develop recommendations whether additional laws requiring reciprocity should be considered for non-United States banks, leasing companies, or other financial institutions.

"(2) **Report.**—The Secretary shall submit to the Congress a report 1 year after the date of enactment of this Act [Oct. 19, 1996] of the results of the study required under paragraph (1), including recommendations developed in the study."

**Application of Weight Limitations to Northern Mariana Islands**

Section 303 of Pub.L. 98–454 provided that: "The weight limitations contained in subsections (b) and (c) of section 301 above [enacting subsec. (c) of this section and section 12108(c) of this title] shall not apply to the Northern Mariana Islands until the termination of the Trusteeship Agreement for the Trust Territory of the Pacific Islands (61 Stat. 3301)."

*

# TITLE 46 APPENDIX
# SHIPPING

## FEDERAL SHIP MORTGAGE INSURANCE

## MERCHANT MARINE ACT OF 1936 [MMA § 1104B]

**(46 U.S.C.A. App. § 1274a)**

## CHAPTER 27—MERCHANT MARINE ACT, 1936

### § 1274a. Authorization of Secretary to guarantee obligations arising from statutorily mandated change in standards for the operation of vessels

**[MMA § 1104B]**

#### (a) Purpose of obligations; principal and interest

Notwithstanding the provisions of this subchapter, except as provided in subsection (d) of this section, the Secretary, upon the terms the Secretary may prescribe, may guarantee or make a commitment to guarantee, payment of the principal of and interest on an obligation which aids in financing and refinancing, including reimbursement to an obligor for expenditures previously made, of a contract for construction or reconstruction of a vessel or vessels which are designed and to be employed for commercial use in the coastwise or intercoastal trade or in foreign trade as defined in section 1244 of this Appendix if—

(1) the construction or reconstruction by an applicant is made necessary to replace vessels the continued operation of which is denied by virtue of the imposition of a statutorily mandated change in standards for the operation of vessels, and where, as a matter of law, the applicant would otherwise be denied the right to continue operating vessels in the trades in which the applicant operated prior to the taking effect of the statutory or regulatory change;

(2) the applicant is presently engaged in transporting cargoes in vessels of the type and class that will be constructed or reconstructed under this section, and agrees to employ vessels constructed or reconstructed under this section as replacements only for vessels made obsolete by changes in operating standards imposed by statute;

(3) the capacity of the vessels to be constructed or reconstructed under this subchapter will not increase the cargo carrying capacity of the vessels being replaced;

(4) the Secretary has not made a determination that the market demand for the vessel over its useful life will diminish so as to make the granting of the guarantee fiduciarily imprudent; and

(5) the Secretary has considered the provisions of section 1274(d)(1)(A)(iii), (iv), and (v) of this Appendix.

#### (b) Limitations on length and amount of guaranteed obligations; useful life of vessel

For the purposes of this section—

(1) the maximum term for obligations guaranteed under this program may not exceed 25 years;

(2) obligations guaranteed may not exceed 87½ percent of the actual cost or depreciated actual cost to the applicant for the construction or reconstruction of the vessel; and

(3) reconstruction cost obligations may not be guaranteed unless the vessel after reconstruction will have a useful life of at least 15 years.

The Secretary may not by rule, regulation, or procedure establish any percentage within the 87½ percent or less limitation in paragraph (2) that is, or is intended to be, applied uniformly to all guarantees or commitments to guarantee made under this section.

#### (c) Security against default; fees; Vessel Replacement Guarantee Fund

(1) The Secretary shall by rule require that the applicant provide adequate security against default. The Secretary may, in addition to any fees assessed under section 1274(e) of this Appendix, establish a Vessel Replacement Guarantee Fund into which shall be paid by obligors under this section—

(A) annual fees which may be an additional amount on the loan guarantee fee in section 1274(e) of this Appendix not to exceed an additional 1 percent; or

(B) fees based on the amount of the obligation versus the percentage of the obligor's fleet being replaced by vessels constructed or reconstructed under this section.

(2) The Vessel Replacement Guarantee Fund shall be a subaccount in the Federal Ship Financing Fund, and shall—

(A) be the depository for all moneys received by the Secretary under sections 1271 to 1276 and 1279 of this Appendix with respect to guarantee or commitments to guarantee made under this section;

(B) not include investigation fees payable under section 1274(f) of this Appendix which shall be paid to the Federal Ship Financing Fund; and

(C) be the depository, whenever there shall be outstanding any notes or obligations issued by the Secretary under section 1275(d) of this Appendix with respect to the Vessel Replacement Guarantee Fund, for all moneys received by the Secretary under sections 1271 to 1276 and 1279 of this Appendix from applicants under this section.

**(d) Additional requirements**

The program created by this section shall, in addition to the requirements of this section, be subject to the provisions of sections 1271 to 1273; 1274(b)(1), (4), (5), (6); 1274(e), 1274(f); 1274(h); and 1275, 1276 and 1279 of this Appendix; except that the Federal Ship Financing Fund is not liable for any guarantees or commitments to guarantee issued under this section.

(June 29, 1936, c. 858, Title XI, § 1104B, as added Pub.L. 101–380, Title IV, § 4115(f)(2), Aug. 18, 1990, 104 Stat. 521, and amended Nov. 4, 1992, Pub.L. 102–587, Title VI, § 6204, 106 Stat. 5094; Nov. 30, 1993, Pub.L. 103–160, Div. A, Title XIII, § 1356(4), 107 Stat. 1814; Oct. 8, 1996, Pub.L. 104–239, § 11(2), 110 Stat. 3134.)

### HISTORICAL AND STATUTORY NOTES

**References in Text**

Sections 1276 and 1279 of this Appendix, referred to in subsecs. (c)(2)(A), (C), and (d), were repealed by Pub.L. 101–225, Title III, § 307(7), Dec. 12, 1989, 103 Stat. 1925.

**Codifications**

Amendment to subsec. (b)(2) by section 6204 of Pub.L. 102–587, which in the original directed substitution for "73 percent" was executed by substituting for "75 percent", as the probable intent of Congress, since "75 percent" and not "73 percent" appeared in text.

# TITLE 49
# TRANSPORTATION

## ABATEMENT OF AVIATION NOISE

**(49 U.S.C.A. §§ 47501 to 47510)**

## CHAPTER 475—NOISE



**Related Provisions**

*See, also, Noise Control, 42 U.S.C.A. § 4901 et seq., ante.*

## SUBCHAPTER I—NOISE ABATEMENT

### § 47501. Definitions

In this subchapter—

(1) "airport" means a public-use airport as defined in section 47102 of this title.

(2) "airport operator" means—

(A) for an airport serving air carriers that have certificates from the Secretary of Transportation, any person holding an airport operating certificate issued under section 44706 of this title; and

(B) for any other airport, the person operating the airport.

(Added Pub.L. 103–272, § 1(e), July 5, 1994, 108 Stat. 1284.)

**HISTORICAL AND STATUTORY NOTES**

**Airport Noise Study**

Pub.L. 106–181, Title VII, § 745, Apr. 5, 2000, 114 Stat. 178, as amended Pub.L. 106–528, § 7(a), Nov. 22, 2000, 114 Stat. 2521, provided that:

"**(a) In general.**— The Secretary shall enter into an agreement with the National Academy of Sciences to conduct a study on airport noise in the United States.

"**(b) Contents of study.**— In conducting the study, the National Academy of Sciences shall examine—

"(1) the threshold of noise at which health begins to be affected;

"(2) the effectiveness of noise abatement programs at airports located in the United States;

"(3) the impacts of aircraft noise on communities, including schools; and

"(4) the noise assessment practices of the Federal Aviation Administration and whether such practices fairly and accurately reflect the burden of noise on communities.

"**(c) Report.**— Not later than 18 months after the date of the agreement entered into under subsection (a), the National Academy of Sciences shall transmit to the Secretary a report on the results of the study. Upon receipt of the report, the Secretary shall transmit a copy of the report to the appropriate committees of Congress.

"**(d) Authorization of appropriations.**— There is authorized to be appropriated such sums as may be necessary to carry out this section."

[Amendment by Pub.L. 106–181 applicable only to fiscal years beginning after September 30, 1999, see section 3 of Pub.L. 106–181, set out as a note under section 106 of this title.]

[Amendment by Pub.L. 106–528, effective 30 days after November 22, 2000, see Pub.L. 106–528, § 9, set out as a note under section 106 of this title.]

**Nonmilitary Helicopter Noise**

Pub.L. 106–181, Title VII, § 747, Apr. 5, 2000, 114 Stat. 179, provided that:

"**(a) In general.**—The Secretary shall conduct a study—

"(1) on the effects of nonmilitary helicopter noise on individuals in densely populated areas in the continental United States; and

"(2) to develop recommendations for the reduction of the effects of nonmilitary helicopter noise.

"**(b) Focus.**—In conducting the study, the Secretary shall focus on air traffic control procedures to address helicopter noise problems and shall take into account the needs of law enforcement.

"**(c) Consideration of views.**—In conducting the study, the Secretary shall consider the views of representatives of the helicopter industry and organizations with an interest in reducing nonmilitary helicopter noise.

"(d) **Report.**—Not later than 1 year after the date of the enactment of this Act [Apr. 5, 2000], the Secretary shall transmit to Congress a report on the results of the study conducted under this section."

[Amendment by Pub.L. 106–181 applicable only to fiscal years beginning after September 30, 1999, see section 3 of Pub.L. 106–181, set out as a note under section 106 of this title.]

## § 47502. Noise measurement and exposure systems and identifying land use compatible with noise exposure

After consultation with the Administrator of the Environmental Protection Agency and United States Government, State, and interstate agencies that the Secretary of Transportation considers appropriate, the Secretary shall by regulation—

(1) establish a single system of measuring noise that—

(A) has a highly reliable relationship between projected noise exposure and surveyed reactions of individuals to noise; and

(B) is applied uniformly in measuring noise at airports and the surrounding area;

(2) establish a single system for determining the exposure of individuals to noise resulting from airport operations, including noise intensity, duration, frequency, and time of occurrence; and

(3) identify land uses normally compatible with various exposures of individuals to noise.

(Added Pub.L. 103–272, § 1(e), July 5, 1994, 108 Stat. 1284.)

## § 47503. Noise exposure maps

**(a) Submission and preparation.**—An airport operator may submit to the Secretary of Transportation a noise exposure map showing the noncompatible uses in each area of the map on the date the map is submitted, a description of estimated aircraft operations during a forecast period that is at least 5 years in the future, and how those operations will affect the map. The map shall—

(1) be prepared in consultation with public agencies and planning authorities in the area surrounding the airport; and

(2) comply with regulations prescribed under section 47502 of this title.

**(b) Revised maps.**—If, in an area surrounding an airport, a change in the operation of the airport would establish a substantial new noncompatible use, or would significantly reduce noise over existing noncompatible uses, that is not reflected in either the existing conditions map or forecast map currently on file with the Federal Aviation Administration, the airport operator shall submit a revised noise exposure map to the Secretary showing the new noncompatible use or noise reduction.

(Added Pub.L. 103–272, § 1(e), July 5, 1994, 108 Stat. 1284, and amended Pub.L. 108–176, Title III, § 324, Dec. 12, 2003, 117 Stat. 2542.)

### HISTORICAL AND STATUTORY NOTES

**Effective and Applicability Provisions**

2003 Acts

Except as otherwise provided, amendments by Pub.L. 108–176 applicable to fiscal years beginning after Sept. 30, 2003, see Pub.L. 108–176, § 3, set out as a note under 49 U.S.C.A. § 106.

**Noise Disclosure**

Pub.L. 108–176, Title III, § 322, Dec. 12, 2003, 117 Stat. 2540, provided that:

"**(a) Noise disclosure system implementation study.**—The Administrator of the Federal Aviation Administration shall conduct a study to determine the feasibility of developing a program under which prospective home buyers of property located in the vicinity of an airport could be notified of information derived from noise exposure maps that may affect the use and enjoyment of the property. The study shall assess the scope, administration, usefulness, and burdensomeness of any such program, the costs and benefits of such a program, and whether participation in such a program should be voluntary or mandatory.

"**(b) Public availability of noise exposure maps.**—The Administrator shall make noise exposure and land use information from noise exposure maps available to the public via the Internet on its website in an appropriate format.

"**(c) Noise exposure map.**—In this section, the term 'noise exposure map' means a noise exposure map prepared under section 47503 of title 49, United States Code [49 U.S.C.A. § 47503]."

[Except as otherwise provided, amendments by Pub.L. 108–176 applicable to fiscal years beginning after Sept. 30, 2003, see Pub.L. 108–176, § 3, set out as a note under 49 U.S.C.A. § 106.]

## § 47504. Noise compatibility programs

**(a) Submissions.—**(1) An airport operator that submitted a noise exposure map and related information under section 47503(a) of this title may submit a noise compatibility program to the Secretary of Transportation after—

(A) consulting with public agencies and planning authorities in the area surrounding the airport, United States Government officials having local responsibility for the airport, and air carriers using the airport; and

(B) notice and an opportunity for a public hearing.

(2) A program submitted under paragraph (1) of this subsection shall state the measures the operator has taken or proposes to take to reduce existing noncompatible uses and prevent introducing additional

noncompatible uses in the area covered by the map. The measures may include—

(A) establishing a preferential runway system;

(B) restricting the use of the airport by a type or class of aircraft because of the noise characteristics of the aircraft;

(C) constructing barriers and acoustical shielding and soundproofing public buildings;

(D) using flight procedures to control the operation of aircraft to reduce exposure of individuals to noise in the area surrounding the airport; and

(E) acquiring land, air rights, easements, development rights, and other interests to ensure that the property will be used in ways compatible with airport operations.

(b) **Approvals.**—(1) The Secretary shall approve or disapprove a program submitted under subsection (a) of this section (except as the program is related to flight procedures referred to in subsection (a)(2)(D) of this section) not later than 180 days after receiving it. The Secretary shall approve the program (except as the program is related to flight procedures referred to in subsection (a)(2)(D)) if the program—

(A) does not place an unreasonable burden on interstate or foreign commerce;

(B) is reasonably consistent with achieving the goal of reducing noncompatible uses and preventing the introduction of additional noncompatible uses; and

(C) provides for necessary revisions because of a revised map submitted under section 47503(b) of this title.

(2) A program (except as the program is related to flight procedures referred to in subsection (a)(2)(D) of this section) is deemed to be approved if the Secretary does not act within the 180-day period.

(3) The Secretary shall submit any part of a program related to flight procedures referred to in subsection (a)(2)(D) of this section to the Administrator of the Federal Aviation Administration. The Administrator shall approve or disapprove that part of the program.

(4) The Secretary shall not approve in fiscal years 2004 through 2007 a program submitted under subsection (a) if the program requires the expenditure of funds made available under section 48103 for mitigation of aircraft noise less than 65 DNL.

(c) **Grants.**—(1) The Secretary may incur obligations to make grants from amounts available under section 48103 of this title to carry out a project under a part of a noise compatibility program approved under subsection (b) of this section. A grant may be made to—

(A) an airport operator submitting the program; and

(B) a unit of local government in the area surrounding the airport, if the Secretary decides the unit is able to carry out the project.

(2) **Soundproofing and acquisition of certain residential buildings and properties.**—The Secretary may incur obligations to make grants from amounts made available under section 48103 of this title—

(A) for projects to soundproof residential buildings—

(i) if the airport operator received approval for a grant for a project to soundproof residential buildings pursuant to section 301(d)(4)(B) of the Airport and Airway Safety and Capacity Expansion Act of 1987;

(ii) if the airport operator submits updated noise exposure contours, as required by the Secretary; and

(iii) if the Secretary determines that the proposed projects are compatible with the purposes of this chapter;

(B) to an airport operator and unit of local government referred to in paragraph (1)(A) or (1)(B) of this subsection to soundproof residential buildings located on residential properties, and to acquire residential properties, at which noise levels are not compatible with normal operations of an airport—

(i) if the airport operator amended an existing local aircraft noise regulation during calendar year 1993 to increase the maximum permitted noise levels for scheduled air carrier aircraft as a direct result of implementation of revised aircraft noise departure procedures mandated for aircraft safety purposes by the Administrator of the Federal Aviation Administration for standardized application at airports served by scheduled air carriers;

(ii) if the airport operator submits updated noise exposure contours, as required by the Secretary; and

(iii) if the Secretary determines that the proposed projects are compatible with the purposes of this chapter;

(C) to an airport operator and unit of local government referred to in paragraph (1)(A) or (1)(B) of this subsection to carry out any part of a program developed before February 18, 1980, or before implementing regulations were prescribed, if the Secretary decides the program is substantially consistent with reducing existing noncompatible uses and preventing the introduction of additional noncompatible uses and the purposes of this chapter will be furthered by promptly carrying out the program;

(D) to an airport operator and unit of local government referred to in paragraph (1)(A) or (1)(B) of this subsection to soundproof a building in the noise impact area surrounding the airport that is used primarily for educational or medical purposes and that the Secretary decides is adversely affected by airport noise; and

**(E)** to an airport operator of a congested airport (as defined in section 47175) and a unit of local government referred to in paragraph (1)(B) of this subsection to carry out a project to mitigate noise in the area surrounding the airport if the project is included as a commitment in a record of decision of the Federal Aviation Administration for an airport capacity enhancement project (as defined in section 47175) even if that airport has not met the requirements of part 150 of title 14, Code of Federal Regulations.

**(3)** An airport operator may agree to make a grant made under paragraph (1)(A) of this subsection available to a public agency in the area surrounding the airport if the Secretary decides the agency is able to carry out the project.

**(4)** The Government's share of a project for which a grant is made under this subsection is the greater of—

**(A)** 80 percent of the cost of the project; or

**(B)** the Government's share that would apply if the amounts available for the project were made available under subchapter I of chapter 471 of this title for a project at the airport.

**(5)** The provisions of subchapter I of chapter 471 of this title related to grants apply to a grant made under this chapter, except—

**(A)** section 47109(a) and (b) of this title; and

**(B)** any provision that the Secretary decides is inconsistent with, or unnecessary to carry out, this chapter.

**(6) Aircraft noise primarily caused by military aircraft.**—The Secretary may make a grant under this subsection for a project even if the purpose of the project is to mitigate the effect of noise primarily caused by military aircraft at an airport.

**(d) Government relief from liability.**—The Government is not liable for damages from aviation noise because of action taken under this section.

(Added Pub.L. 103–272, § 1(e), July 5, 1994, 108 Stat. 1285, and amended Pub.L. 103–305, Title I, § 119, Aug. 23, 1994, 108 Stat. 1580; Pub.L. 103–429, § 6(71), Oct. 31, 1994, 108 Stat. 4387; Pub.L. 106–181, Title I, § 154, Apr. 5, 2000, 114 Stat. 88; Pub.L. 108–176, Title I, § 189, Title III, § 306, Dec. 12, 2003, 117 Stat. 2519, 2539.)

## HISTORICAL AND STATUTORY NOTES

**References in Text**

Section 301(d)(4)(B) of the Airport and Airway Safety and Capacity Expansion Act of 1987, referred to in subsec. (c)(2)(A)(i), is section 301(d)(4)(B) of Pub.L. 100–223, which was set out as a note under section 2104 of former Title 49, Transportation, prior to repeal by Pub.L. 103–272, § 7(b), July 5, 1994, 108 Stat. 1379.

Part 150 of title 14, Code of Federal Regulations, referred to in subsec. (c)(2)(E), is 14 C.F.R. § 150.1 et seq.

**Effective and Applicability Provisions**

2003 Acts

Except as otherwise provided, amendments by Pub.L. 108–176 applicable to fiscal years beginning after Sept. 30, 2003, see Pub.L. 108–176, § 3, set out as a note under 49 U.S.C.A. § 106.

2000 Acts

Amendment by Pub.L. 106–181 applicable only to fiscal years beginning after September 30, 1999, see section 3 of Pub.L. 106–181, set out as a note under section 106 of this title.

## § 47505. Airport noise compatibility planning grants

**(a) General authority.**—The Secretary of Transportation may make a grant to a sponsor of an airport to develop, for planning purposes, information necessary to prepare and submit—

**(1)** a noise exposure map and related information under section 47503 of this title, including the cost of obtaining the information; or

**(2)** a noise compatibility program under section 47504 of this title.

**(b) Availability of amounts and Government's share of costs.**—A grant under subsection (a) of this section may be made from amounts available under section 48103 of this title. The United States Government's share of the grant is the percent for which a project for airport development at an airport would be eligible under section 47109(a) and (b) of this title.

(Added Pub.L. 103–272, § 1(e), July 5, 1994, 108 Stat. 1286.)

## § 47506. Limitations on recovering damages for noise

**(a) General limitations.**—A person acquiring an interest in property after February 18, 1980, in an area surrounding an airport for which a noise exposure map has been submitted under section 47503 of this title and having actual or constructive knowledge of the existence of the map may recover damages for noise attributable to the airport only if, in addition to any other elements for recovery of damages, the person shows that—

**(1)** after acquiring the interest, there was a significant—

**(A)** change in the type or frequency of aircraft operations at the airport;

**(B)** change in the airport layout;

**(C)** change in flight patterns; or

**(D)** increase in nighttime operations; and

(2) the damages resulted from the change or increase.

**(b) Constructive knowledge.**—Constructive knowledge of the existence of a map under subsection (a) of this section shall be imputed, at a minimum, to a person if—

(1) before the person acquired the interest, notice of the existence of the map was published at least 3 times in a newspaper of general circulation in the county in which the property is located; or

(2) the person is given a copy of the map when acquiring the interest.

(Added Pub.L. 103–272, § 1(e), July 5, 1994, 108 Stat. 1286.)

## § 47507. Nonadmissibility of noise exposure map and related information as evidence

No part of a noise exposure map or related information described in section 47503 of this title that is submitted to, or prepared by, the Secretary of Transportation and no part of a list of land uses the Secretary identifies as normally compatible with various exposures of individuals to noise may be admitted into evidence or used for any other purpose in a civil action asking for relief for noise resulting from the operation of an airport.

(Added Pub.L. 103–272, § 1(e), July 5, 1994, 108 Stat. 1287.)

## § 47508. Noise standards for air carriers and foreign air carriers providing foreign air transportation

**(a) General requirements.**—The Secretary of Transportation shall require each air carrier and foreign air carrier providing foreign air transportation to comply with noise standards—

(1) the Secretary prescribed for new subsonic aircraft in regulations of the Secretary in effect on January 1, 1977; or

(2) of the International Civil Aviation Organization that are substantially compatible with standards of the Secretary for new subsonic aircraft in regulations of the Secretary at parts 36 and 91 of title 14, Code of Federal Regulations, prescribed between January 2, 1977, and January 1, 1982.

**(b) Compliance at phased rate.**—The Secretary shall require each air carrier and foreign air carrier providing foreign air transportation to comply with the noise standards at a phased rate similar to the rate for aircraft registered in the United States.

**(c) Nondiscrimination.**—The requirement for air carriers providing foreign air transportation may not be more stringent than the requirement for foreign air carriers.

(Added Pub.L. 103–272, § 1(e), July 5, 1994, 108 Stat. 1287.)

### HISTORICAL AND STATUTORY NOTES

**Implementation of Chapter 4 Noise Standards**

Pub.L. 108–176, Title III, § 325, Dec. 12, 2003, 117 Stat. 2542, provided that; "Not later than April 1, 2005, the Secretary of Transportation shall issue final regulations to implement Chapter 4 noise standards, consistent with the recommendations adopted by the International Civil Aviation Organization."

Except as otherwise provided, amendments by Pub.L. 108–176 applicable to fiscal years beginning after Sept. 30, 2003, see Pub.L. 108–176, § 3, set out as a note under 49 U.S.C.A. § 106.

**Standards for Aircraft and Aircraft Engines to Reduce Noise Levels**

Pub.L. 106–181, Title VII, § 726, Apr. 5, 2000, 114 Stat. 167, provided that:

"**(a) Development of new standards.**—The Secretary shall continue to work to develop through the International Civil Aviation Organization new performance standards for aircraft and aircraft engines that will lead to a further reduction in aircraft noise levels.

"**(b) Goals to be considered in developing new standards.**—In negotiating standards under subsection (a), the Secretary shall give high priority to developing standards that—

"(1) are performance based and can be achieved by use of a full range of certifiable noise reduction technologies;

"(2) protect the useful economic value of existing Stage 3 aircraft in the United States fleet;

"(3) ensure that United States air carriers and aircraft engine and hushkit manufacturers are not competitively disadvantaged;

"(4) use dynamic economic modeling capable of determining impacts on all aircraft in service in the United States fleet; and

"(5) continue the use of a balanced approach to address aircraft environmental issues, taking into account aircraft technology, land use planning, economic feasibility, and airspace operational improvements.

"**(c) Annual report.**—Not later than July 1, 2000, and annually thereafter, the Secretary shall transmit to Congress a report regarding the application of new standards or technologies to reduce aircraft noise levels."

[Enactment of this note by Pub.L. 106–181 applicable only to fiscal years beginning after September 30, 1999, see section 3 of Pub.L. 106–181, set out as a note under section 106 of this title.]

**Aircraft Noise Research Program**

Pub.L. 102–581, Title III, § 304, Oct. 31, 1992, 106 Stat. 4896, provided that:

"**(a) Establishment.**—The Administrator of the Federal Aviation Administration and the Administrator of the National Aeronautics and Space Administration shall jointly conduct a research program to develop new technologies for quieter subsonic jet aircraft engines and airframes.

"**(b) Goal.**—The goal of the research program established by subsection (a) is to develop by the year 2000 technologies for subsonic jet aircraft engines and airframes which would permit a subsonic jet aircraft to operate at reduced noise levels.

"(c) **Participation.**—In carrying out the program established by subsection (a), the Administrator of the Federal Aviation Administration and the Administrator of the National Aeronautics and Space Administration shall encourage the participation of representatives of the aviation industry and academia.

"(d) **Report to Congress.**—The Administrator of the Federal Aviation Administration and the Administrator of the National Aeronautics and Space Administration shall jointly submit to Congress, on an annual basis during the term of the program established by subsection (a), a report on the progress being made under the program toward meeting the goal described in subsection (b)."

## § 47509. Research program on quiet aircraft technology for propeller and rotor driven aircraft

(a) **Establishment.**—The Administrator of the Federal Aviation Administration and the Administrator of the National Aeronautics and Space Administration shall conduct a study to identify technologies for noise reduction of propeller driven aircraft and rotorcraft.

(b) **Goal.**—The goal of the study conducted under subsection (a) is to determine the status of research and development now underway in the area of quiet technology for propeller driven aircraft and rotorcraft, including technology that is cost beneficial, and to determine whether a research program to supplement existing research activities is necessary.

(c) **Participation.**—In conducting the study required under subsection (a), the Administrator of the Federal Aviation Administration and the Administrator of the National Aeronautics and Space Administration shall encourage the participation of the Department of Defense, the Department of the Interior, the airtour industry, the aviation industry, academia and other appropriate groups.

(d) **Report.**—Not less than 280 days after August 23, 1994, the Administrator of the Federal Aviation Administration and the Administrator of the National Aeronautics and Space Administration shall transmit to Congress a report on the results of the study required under subsection (a).

(e) **Research and development program.**—If the Administrator of the Federal Aviation Administration and the Administrator of the National Aeronautics and Space Administration determine that additional research and development is necessary and would substantially contribute to the development of quiet aircraft technology, then the agencies shall conduct an appropriate research program in consultation with the entities listed in subsection (c) to develop safe, effective, and economical noise reduction technology (including technology that can be applied to existing propeller driven aircraft and rotorcraft) that would result in aircraft that operate at substantially reduced levels of noise to reduce the impact of such aircraft and rotorcraft on the resources of national parks and other areas.

(Added Pub.L. 103–305, Title III, § 308(a), Aug. 23, 1994, 108 Stat. 1593, and amended Pub.L. 104–287, § 5(86), Oct. 11, 1996, 110 Stat. 3398.)

## § 47510. Tradeoff allowance

Notwithstanding another law or a regulation prescribed or order issued under that law, the tradeoff provisions contained in appendix C of part 36 of title 14, Code of Federal Regulations, apply in deciding whether an aircraft complies with subpart I of part 91 of title 14.

(Added Pub.L. 103–429, § 6(72)(A), Oct. 31, 1994, 108 Stat. 4387.)

# FEDERAL ENVIRONMENTAL LAWS INDEX

**References are to U.S. Code Sections**

# INDEX

# INDEX

INDEX

†